ENCYCLOPÆDIA
BRITANNICA

MACROPÆDIA

The Encyclopædia Britannica
is published with the editorial advice
of the faculties of the University of Chicago;
a committee of persons holding
academic appointments at the universities
of Oxford, Cambridge, London, and Edinburgh;
a committee at the University of Toronto;
and committees drawn from members of the faculties
of the University of Tokyo
and the Australian National University.

THE UNIVERSITY OF CHICAGO

"Let knowledge grow from more to more
and thus be human life enriched."

The New Encyclopædia Britannica

in 30 Volumes

MACROPÆDIA
Volume 3

Knowledge in Depth

FOUNDED 1768
15 TH EDITION

Encyclopædia Britannica, Inc.
William Benton, Publisher, 1943–1973
Helen Hemingway Benton, Publisher, 1973–1974

Chicago
Auckland/Geneva/London/Manila/Paris/Rome
Seoul/Sydney/Tokyo/Toronto

First Edition	1768-1771
Second Edition	1777-1784
Third Edition	1788-1797
Supplement	1801
Fourth Edition	1801-1809
Fifth Edition	1815
Sixth Edition	1820-1823
Supplement	1815-1824
Seventh Edition	1830-1842
Eighth Edition	1852-1860
Ninth Edition	1875-1889
Tenth Edition	1902-1903

Printed in U.S.A.

Library of Congress Catalog Card Number: 82-84048
International Standard Book Number: 0-85229-413-1

Bolivia

Bolivia is a landlocked republic in central South America with an area of 424,165 square miles (1,098,581 square kilometres) and a population that in the early 1970s numbered about 5,000,000. The country has been landlocked since it lost its Pacific coast territory to Chile toward the end of the 19th century. It is bordered to the north and east by Brazil, to the southeast by Paraguay, to the south by Argentina, and to the southwest and west by Chile and Peru. Its constitutional capital is the city of Sucre (population about 70,000), where the Supreme Court is established, but the de facto capital is the city of La Paz (population more than 850,000), where the executive and legislative branches function.

Bolivia is also widely known by the name of República del Altiplano (Republic of the High Plateau) because the most developed and densely populated part of its territory is situated on a plateau between the two branches of the Andes mountain range. The country itself was once a part of the ancient Inca empire and later formed part of the Spanish viceroyalty of Peru. Spanish, though spoken by less than half of the population, remains the official language; in religion, the overwhelming majority of the people are Roman Catholic. Bolivia is still an underdeveloped country whose economic life is based principally upon the production of raw materials, notably tin. (For associated physical features see ANDES MOUNTAIN RANGES; GRAN CHACO; and TITICACA, LAKE; for historical aspects, see BOLIVIA, HISTORY OF.) (V.A.U.)

THE LANDSCAPE

Relief. Although three-fifths of Bolivia's area consists of vast low plains, the western part is one of the highest inhabited areas in the world and constitutes Bolivia's heartland. The Andes there attain the greatest breadth and are divided into two great parallel ranges—the Cordillera Oriental to the east and the Cordillera Real to the west—enclosing a plateau the surface of which lies only a few thousand feet below the summits of the mountains themselves. Between these ranges lies the monotonous, bleak Altiplano (High Plateau), bordered to the west by the Cordillera Occidental. The plateau is a relatively flat-floored depression about 500 miles long and 80 miles wide, lying at elevations of between 12,000 and 12,500 feet. The floor of this great depression, mostly composed of water-laid deposits from the bordering mountains and appearing quite level, slopes gently southward. Its evenness is broken by occasional hills and ridges. The margins of the basin are marked by numerous interlocking alluvial fans (accumulations of debris that have spread out in the shape of a fan), which have built up an almost continuous plain of fairly gentle grade lying at the foot of the mountains.

The Altiplano

The northern and eastern sections of the country, called the Oriente (meaning east), cover three-fifths of Bolivia. They are composed of low alluvial plains, great swamps, flooded bottomlands, and gently undulating forest regions. In the extreme south is the Bolivian Chaco, which forms part of the Gran Chaco; it is a fairly level and low area that varies strikingly with the seasons of rain. It is a veritable swamp during the rainy season and a hot semidesert during the remaining eight or nine months of the year. Northward from the Chaco, but still a portion of the Oriente, is the Santa Cruz area. It is generally level, with a downward slope to the north. Drainage is not the problem there that it is in the Chaco, because several small north-flowing streams interlace the area. The northernmost segment of the Oriente is the Upper Beni, a low, wet plain covered in large part by heavy tropical rain forest. Much of it is subject to heavy inundation during the rainy season—November to May inclusive.

Extremely high mountains (some exceeding 21,000 feet) rise northeast of the Titicaca Basin, which lies in the northwest and also extends into Peru; the descent from these mountains to the eastern plains is extremely precipitous. This rainy and heavily forested belt of rugged terrain (deep valleys and gorges separated by high ridges), known as the Yungas, is situated on the northeast slope of the Cordillera Oriental and extends southward as far as a line drawn from Santa Cruz to Cochabamba. The Yungas, a distinct natural division, is the southern part of an unbroken region that extends along the eastern Andes of Colombia, Ecuador, Peru, and Bolivia as far south as Santa Cruz.

Drainage. The rivers belong to three distinct systems—the Amazon system in the northeast, the Río de la Plata system in the extreme southeast, and the Lake Titicaca system in the west. The eastern lowlands of Bolivia have many lakes, most of them little known.

The great swampy plains along the Beni and Mamoré rivers, which are headwaters of the Amazon, contain several lakes and lagoons, some of them large, such as Lago Rogoaguado.

In the vicinity of the Río Paraguay, which is connected to the La Plata Basin and runs parallel to part of Bolivia's eastern border without entering national territory (though touching a small segment of the frontier in the extreme southeast), there are several lakes, partly produced by obstructed outlets, such as Bahía Negra, Laguna Cáceres, Laguna Mandioré, Laguna Gaiba, and Laguna Uberaba. North of these are the great Zarayes swamps. This region, like that in the northeast, is subject to inundations during the summer.

The third drainage system is that of the great central plateau. One of the most elevated of all inland basins, it consists of Lake Titicaca near the north end; the Río Desaguadero to the southeast, its outlet; Lago de Poopó, into which the Río Desaguadero flows; the Salar de Coipasa (Salt Lake or Marsh of Coipasa) to the southwest of Lago de Poopó (connected with Poopó by the Río Lacajahuira, the small outlet of the latter); and the great Salar de Uyuni, independent of the rest of the system but receiving the waters of an extensive, though very arid area at the south end. Into this system enter many short streams from the neighbouring heights. Having no outlet to the sea, the water of this extensive basin is wholly absorbed by the dry soil and by excessive evaporation.

Lakes Titicaca and Poopó

Lake Titicaca itself is the highest large navigable lake in the world. Situated on the Bolivian–Peruvian border at an elevation of 12,500 feet (3,810 metres), it is about 120 miles long and 50 miles wide; many islands dot its surface. Lago de Poopó is quite different in character from Lake Titicaca. Occupying a very shallow depression in the plateau, only a few feet below the general level of the surrounding land, it is nowhere more than 15 feet deep at its normal level. When its waters are low, it covers an area of 977 square miles; the surrounding land is so flat, however, that at high water the lake reaches sometimes almost to Oruro to the north, fully 30 miles from the low-water shore. The Río Lacajahuira, the only visible outlet of Lago de Poopó, moves underneath the sand and empties into the Salar de Coipasa, which, at high water, covers about the same area as Lago de

MAP INDEX

Political subdivisions
Chuquisaca......20·00s 64·20w
Cochabamba....17·30s 65·40w
El Beni..........14·00s 65·30w
La Paz...........15·30s 68·00w
Oruro............18·40s 67·30w
Pando............11·20s 67·40w
Potosí............20·40s 67·00w
Santa Cruz......17·30s 61·30w
Tarija............21·30s 64·00w

Cities and towns
Achacachi.......16·03s 68·43w
Aiquile...........18·10s 65·10w
Amarete
(Charazani).....15·14s 68·58w
Andamarca......18·49s 67·31w
Añez.............17·19s 63·43w
Antequera.......18·29s 66·53w
Anzaldo..........17·50s 65·55w
Apolo.............14·43s 68·31w
Arampampa.....17·55s 66·04w
Arani.............17·34s 65·46w
Arque............17·48s 66·23w
Atocha...........20·56s 66·14w
Ayacucho.......17·51s 63·20w
Ayoayo..........17·05s 68·00w
Azurduy.........19·59s 64·29w
Baures...........13·35s 63·35w
Bella Flor........11·09s 67·49w
Betanzos........19·34s 65·27w
Boyuibe.........20·25s 63·17w
Buena Vista.....17·27s 63·40w
Cabezas.........18·46s 63·24w
Cachuela
Esperanza......10·32s 65·38w
Caiza............20·02s 65·40w
Calamarca.......16·55s 68·09w
Calcha...........21·06s 67·31w
Camargo.........20·39s 65·13w
Camiri............20·03s 63·31w
Campamento
Chimoré........16·42s 64·49w
Capinota.........17·43s 66·14w
Caquiaviri.......17·03s 68·38w
Caracollo........17·39s 67·10w
Caranavi.........15·46s 67·36w
Carandaiti.......20·45s 63·04w
Caraparí.........21·49s 63·46w
Cataricahua.....18·14s 66·49w
Cerdas...........20·48s 66·29w
Chaguaya.......21·49s 64·50w
Challapata.......18·54s 66·47w
Chaqui...........19·36s 65·32w
Charagua........19·48s 63·13w
Charaña.........17·36s 69·28w
Charazani, see
Amarete
Chayanta........18·27s 66·30w
Chimore, see
Campamento
Chimoré
Chulumani.......16·24s 67·31w
Chuma...........15·24s 68·56w
Cliza.............17·36s 65·56w
Cobija............11·02s 68·44w
Cochabamba....17·24s 66·09w
Cohoni...........16·44s 67·51w
Colcapirhua.....17·25s 66·15w
Colquechaca...18·40s 66·01w
Colquencha......17·00s 68·17w
Colquiri..........17·25s 67·08w
Comarapa.......17·54s 64·29w
Concepción.....11·29s 66·42w
Coripata.........16·18s 67·36w
Corocoro........17·12s 68·29w
Coroico..........16·10s 67·44w
Corque...........18·21s 67·42w
Cosapa..........18·11s 68·40w
Cotagaita.......20·50s 65·41w
Cotoca...........17·49s 63·03w
Cuevo...........20·27s 63·32w
Culpina..........20·50s 64·58w
Curahuara......17·40s 68·02w
Desaguadero....16·34s 69·02w
El Carmen.......18·49s 58·33w
El Cerro.........17·31s 61·34w
El Palmar........21·54s 63·39w
Entre Ríos.......21·32s 64·12w
Eucaliptus, see
Tomás Barrón
Exaltación.......13·16s 65·15w
General
Saavedra.......17·15s 63·10w
Guadalupe.......18·33s 64·05w
Guanay..........15·28s 67·52w
Guaqui...........16·35s 68·51w
Guayaramerín
(Puerto Sucre)..10·48s 65·23w
Gutiérrez........19·25s 63·34w
Huacaraje........13·33s 63·45w
Huachacalla.....18·45s 68·17w
Huanchaca......20·20s 66·39w
Huanuni.........18·16s 66·51w
Huari............19·00s 66·48w
Huarina..........16·12s 68·38w
Ichoca...........17·12s 67·17w
Independencia...17·07s 66·53w
Ipitá.............19·20s 63·32w
Irupana..........16·28s 67·28w
Itapaya..........17·34s 66·21w
Ivo...............20·27s 63·26w
Ixiamas..........13·45s 68·09w
La Estrella.......16·30s 63·45w
La Guardia.......17·54s 63·20w
Lagunillas.......19·38s 63·43w
La Paz...........16·30s 68·09w
Las Piedras......11·06s 66·10w
Llallagua........18·25s 66·38w
Llanquera.......18·06s 67·47w
Llica.............19·52s 68·16w
Loreto...........15·13s 64·40w
Los Chacos......14·33s 62·11w
Luribay..........17·06s 67·39w
Macha...........18·49s 66·05w
Machacamarca..18·10s 67·02w
Magdalena.......13·20s 64·08w
Manoa............9·40s 65·27w
Mapiri............15·15s 68·10w
Mizque...........17·56s 65·19w
Mocomoco.......15·22s 68·59w
Monteagudo.....19·49s 63·59w
Monte Cristo.....14·43s 61·14w
Montero..........17·20s 63·15w
Moraya...........21·45s 65·32w
Morococala......18·10s 66·44w
Ocurí............18·50s 65·50w
Oruro............17·59s 67·09w
Padcaya.........21·52s 64·48w
Padilla..........19·19s 64·20w
Palca............16·34s 67·59w
Pampa Grande...18·05s 64·06w
Panacachi.......18·23s 66·21w
Pasorapa........18·16s 64·37w
Patacamaya.....17·14s 67·55w
Pazña...........18·36s 66·55w
Pelechuco.......14·48s 69·04w
Perotó...........14·50s 64·31w
Perseverancia...14·44s 62·48w
Pocoata.........18·41s 66·11w
Pocona..........17·39s 65·24w
Pojo.............17·45s 64·49w
Poopó...........18·23s 66·59w
Porco............19·50s 65·59w
Poroma..........18·29s 65·30w
Portachuelo.....17·21s 63·24w
Postrevalle.......18·29s 63·51w
Potosí............19·35s 65·45w
Presto...........18·55s 64·56w
Pucará..........18·43s 64·11w
Pucarani........16·23s 68·30w
Puerto Acosta...15·32s 69·15w
Puerto Alegre...13·53s 61·36w
Puerto Heath....12·30s 68·40w
Puerto Rico......11·05s 67·38w
Puerto Siles.....12·48s 65·05w
Puerto Suárez...18·57s 57·51w
Puerto Sucre, see
Guayaramerín
Pulacayo.........20·25s 66·41w
Puna.............19·46s 65·28w
Punata...........17·32s 65·50w
Quetena.........22·10s 67·25w
Quiabaya........15·37s 68·46w
Quillacas........19·14s 66·58w
Quillacollo.......17·26s 66·17w
Quime............17·02s 67·15w
Ravelo...........18·48s 65·32w
Reyes............14·19s 67·23w
Riberalta.........10·59s 66·06w
Río Mulatos......19·42s 66·47w
Roboré...........18·20s 59·45w
Rurrenabaque....14·28s 67·34w
Sabaya...........19·01s 68·23w
Sacaca...........18·05s 66·25w
Sajama...........18·07s 69·00w
Salinas de Garci
Mendoza........19·38s 67·43w
Samaipata.......18·09s 63·52w
Sanandita.......21·40s 63·35w
San Benito.......17·31s 65·55w
San Borja........14·49s 66·51w
San Buena
Ventura.........14·28s 67·35w
San Ignacio......14.53s 65·36w
San Ignacio......16·23s 60·59w
San Javier........14·34s 64·42w
San Javier........16·20s 62·38w
San Joaquín.....13·04s 64·49w
San José de
Chíquitos.......17·51s 60·47w
San José de
Chupiamonas...14·13s 68·05w
San Juan del
Piray............20·16s 64·09w
San Lorenzo.....21·26s 64·47w
San Lucas.......20·06s 65·07w
San Miguel......16·42s 61·01w
San Pedro.......14·20s 64·50w
San Pedro de
Buena Vista...18·13s 65·59w
San Ramón......13·17s 64·43w
Santa Ana.......13·45s 65·35w
Santa Ana.......15·31s 67·30w
Santa Ana.......18·43s 58·44w
Santa Cruz......17·48s 63·10w
Santa Rosa......14·10s 66·53w
Santa Rosa......10·36s 67·25w
Santa Rosa......17·07s 63·35w
Santa Rosa de la
Roca............16·04s 61·32w
Santa Rosa del
Palmar.........16·54s 62·24w
Santiago.........18·19s 59·34w
Santiago de
Machaca.......17·05s 69·16w
Santo Corazón...17·59s 58·51w
Sena.............11·32s 67·11w
Sicasica.........17·22s 67·45w
Sopachuy........19·29s 64·31w
Sorata...........15·47s 68·40w
Sotomayor.......19·18s 65·03w
Sucre............19·02s 65·17w
Tacacoma.......15·35s 68·43w
Tapacarí.........17·31s 66·36w
Taperas..........17·45s 6·23w
Tarabuco.........19·10s 64·57w
Tarata...........17·37s 66·01w
Tarija............21·31s 64·45w
Tiahuanaco......16·33s 68·42w
Tinguipaya......19·11s 65·51w
Tiraque..........17·25s 65·43w
Todos Santos....16·48s 65·08w
Toledo...........18·10s 67·25w
Tomás Barrón
(Eucaliptus)....17·35s 67·31w
Tomave..........20·06s 66·35w
Torotoro.........18·07s 65·46w
Totora...........17·42s 65·09w
Totora...........17·49s 68·07w
Totora Palca.....19·55s 65·26w
Trigal............18·17s 64·08w
Trinidad.........14·47s 64·47w
Tumupasa.......14·09s 67·55w
Tupiza...........21·27s 65·43w
Uncia............18·27s 66·37w
Uyuni............20·28s 66·50w
Vaca Guzmán...19·54s 63·48w
Vallegrande.....18·29s 64·06w
Viacha...........16·39s 68·18w
Villa Abecia.....21·00s 65·23w
Villa Bella.......10·23s 65·24w
Villa Eufronio
Viscarra........17·59s 65·36w
Villa Martín.....20·46s 67·47w
Villa Montes.....21·15s 63·30w
Villa Rivero......17·37s 65·48w
Villa Serrano....19·06s 64·22w
Villa Tunari......16·55s 65·25w
Vitichi...........20·13s 65·29w
Warnes..........17·30s 63·10w
Yaco.............17·09s 67·24w
Yacuiba.........22·02s 63·45w
Yamparáez......19·10s 65·10w
Yanacachi.......16·23s 67·43w
Yata.............13·20s 66·35w
Yotala...........19·10s 65·17w
Yotaú...........16·03s 63·03w
Zudañez.........19·06s 64·44w

Physical features and points of interest
Abuná, *river*.....9·41s 65·23w
Acre, *river*.......11·00s 68·45w
Aguaragüe,
Cordillera de,
mountains......21·30s 63·40w
Altamachi, *river*..16·08s 66·50w
Altiplano, *upland*.18·00s 68·00w
Andes,
mountains......18·30s 67·30w
Apere, *river*......13·44s 65·18w
Bala, Cerros de,
mountains......14·20s 67·50w
Beni, *river*.......10·23s 65·24w
Benicito, *river*....11·32s 65·47w
Bermejo, *river*....22·53s 64·21w
Blanco, *river*......12·30s 64·18w
Boopi, *river*......15·41s 67·15w
Bravo, Cerro,
mountain.......17·40s 64·35w
Cáceres, Laguna,
lake............18·56s 57·48w
Camblaya, *river*..20·57s 64·45w
Caine, *river*......18·23s 65·21w
Camata, *river*....15·09s 68·26w
Central,
Cordillera,
mountains......18·30s 64·55w
Chacaltaya,
Nevado,
mountain.......16·20s 68·08w
Challviri, Salar
de, *salt flat*....22·32s 67·34w
Chaparé, *river*...15·58s 64·42w
Chichas,
Cordillera de,
mountains......20·30s 66·30w
Chiquitos, Llanos
de, *plain*.......18·00s 61·30w
Chochis, Cerro,
mountain.......18·10s 59·53w
Choro, *river*......16·25s 64·35w
Chorolque, Cerro,
mountain.......20·56s 66·01w
Cirque, Cerro,
mountain.......17·22s 69·22w
Coipasa, Lago de,
lake............19·12s 68·07w
Coipasa, Salar
de, *salt flat*.....19·26s 68·09w
Concepción,
Laguna, *lake*....17·29s 61·25w
Cotacajes, *river*..16·00s 67·01w
Cotagaita, *river*..21·01s 65·23w
Cololo, Nevado,
mountain.......14·53s 69·06w
Cuevas, Cerro,
mountain.......22·00s 65·12w
Desaguadero,
river............18·24s 67·05w
Emero, *river*......13·19s 67·17w
Gaiba, Laguna,
lake............17·45s 57·43w
Grande, *river*.....15·51s 64·39w
Grande de Lipez,
river............20·47s 67·14w
Gran Pampa
Salada, *plain*....20·35s 67·15w
High Plateau,
see Altiplano
Huachi, Lago,
lake............14·11s 63·30w
Huanchaca,
Serrania de,
mountains......14·30s 60·39w
Huatunas,
Laguna, *lakes*...13·06s 66·15w
Huayna Potosí,
Nevado,
mountain.......16·16s 68·11w
Ichilo, *river*......15·57s 64·42w
Illampu, Nevado,
mountain.......15·50s 68·34w
Illimani, Nevado,
mountain.......16·39s 67·48w
Isiboro, *river*.....15·28s 65·05w
Iténez, *river*......11·55s 65·04w
Itonamas, *river*...12·28s 64·24w
Ivón, *river*........11·06s 66·08w
Izozog, Bañados
de, *marsh*.......18·48s 62·10w
Lacajahuira,
river............19·21s 67·54w
La Cal, *river*......17·27s 58·15w
La Fortuna, Rio
de, *river*.........16·36s 58·46w
La Paz, Rio de,
river............16·27s 67·19w
Lauca, *river*......19·09s 68·10w
Lipez, Cordillera
de, *mountains*...21·40s 66·35w
Los Arroyos,
Lago de, *lake*...12·38s 65·00w
Machupo, *river*...12·34s 64·25w
Madeira, *river*.....9·41s 65·23w
Madidi, *river*......12·32s 66·52w
Madre de Dios,
river............10·59s 66·08w
Mamoré, *river*....10·23s 65·53w
Mandioré,
Laguna, *lake*....18·08s 57·33w
Manupari, *river*..11·50s 67·16w
Manuripi, *river*...11·06s 67·36w
Mapiri, *river*......9·52s 66·21w
Matos, *river*......14·07s 65·25w
Mauri, *river*......17·18s 68·41w
Moxos, Llanos de,
plain............15·00s 65·00w
Negra, Bahia,
marsh...........20·00s 58·00w
Negra, Serranía,
mountains......13·45s 60·58w
Negro, *river*......14·11s 63·07w
Nuevo Mundo,
Cerro, *mountain*.21·55s 66·53w
Occidental,
Cordillera,
mountains......19·20s 68·40w
Olca, Volcán,
volcano.........20·57s 68·30w
Ollague, Volcán,
volcano.........21·18s 68·12w
Oriental,
Cordillera,
mountains......17·30s 64·30w
Ortón, *river*......10·50s 66·04w
Pacahuaras,
river............10·04s 65·46w
Paila, *river*.......16·02s 64·12w
Palometillas,
river............16·36s 64·18w
Paraguá, *river*...13·34s 61·53w
Parapetí, *river*...18·58s 62·21w
Pilaya, *river*......20·55s 64·04w
Pilcomayo, *river*..22·17s 62·40w
Piray, *river*.......16·32s 63·45w
Poopó, Lago,
lake............18·45s 67·07w

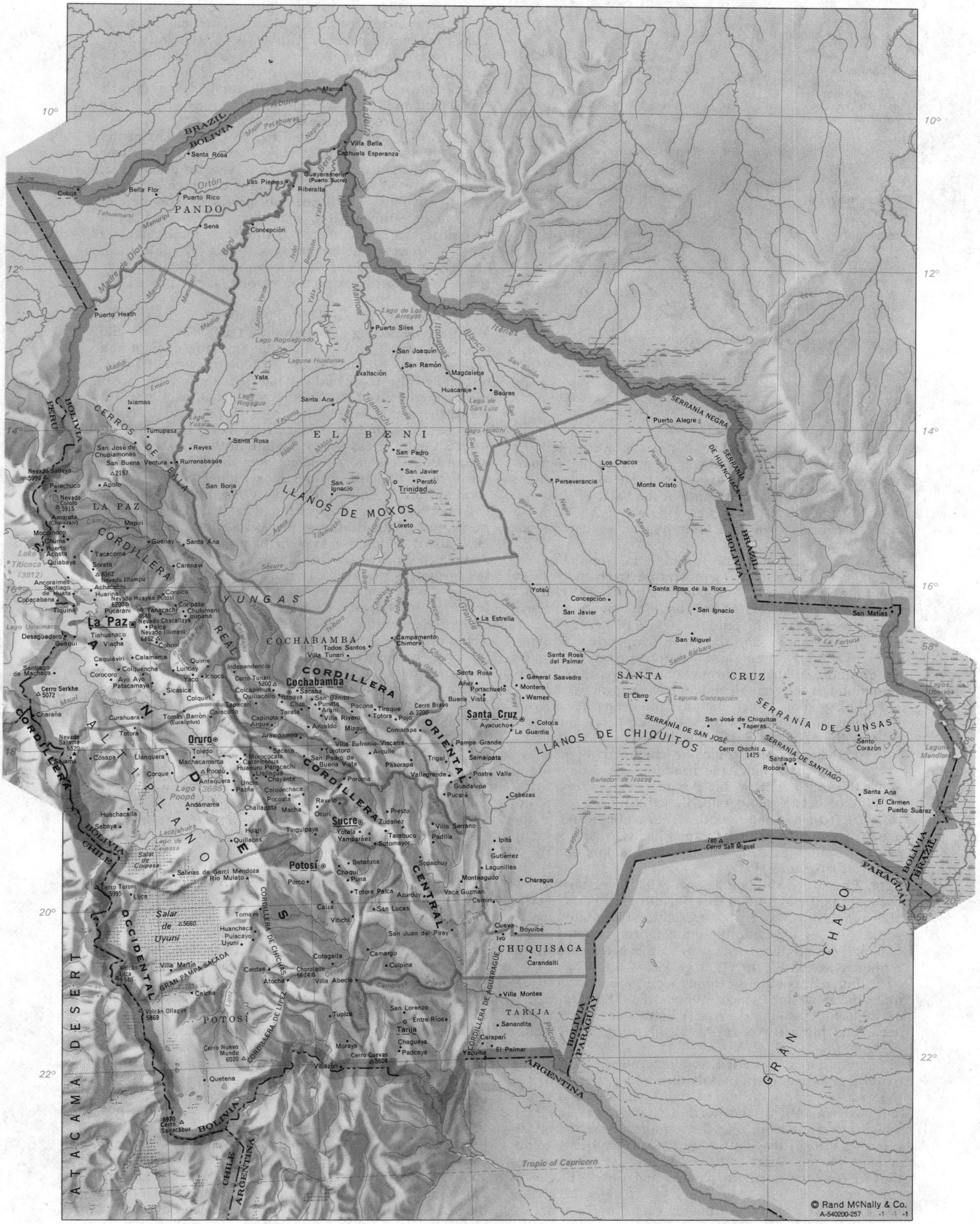

BOLIVIA Size of symbol indicates relative size of town

Elevations in metres

0 50 100 200 300 km

0 50 100 200 mi

BOLIVIA—

MAP INDEX (continued)

Puna, see Altiplano
Rápulo, *river*.....13·43s 65·32w
Real, Cordillera, *mountains*......17·00s 67·10w
Rogagua, Lago, *lake*.............13·43s 66·54w
Rogoaguado, Lago, *lake*.......12·52s 65·43w
Sairecábur, Cerro, *mountain*.......22·43s 67·54w
Sajama, Nevado, *mountain*.......18·06s 68·54w
Salluyo, Nevado, *mountain*.......14·38s 69·14w
San Joaquín, *river*............13·08s 63·41w
San José, Serranía de, *hills*............17·25s 60·49w
San Juan, *river*...21·02s 65·19w
San Luis, Lago de, *lake*.........13·45s 64·00w
San Martín, *river*.13·08s 63·43w
San Miguel, *river*............13·52s 63·56w
San Miguel, *river*............19·15s 59·45w
San Simón, *river*.13·13s 63·31w
Santa Bárbara, *river*............16·58s 61·39w
Santiago, Serranía de, *mountains*......18·25s 59·25w
Sécure, *river*.....15·10s 64·52w
Serkhe, Cerro, *mountain*.......17·22s 69·22w
Sunsas, Serranía de, *mountains*...17·57s 59·35w
Tahuamanu, *river*............11·06s 67·36w
Tijamuchi, *river*..14·10s 64·58w
Titicaca, Lake....15·50s 69·20w
Toroni, Cerro, *mountain*.......19·43s 68·41w
Tucavaca, *river*..18·37s 58·59w
Tuichi, *river*.....14·36s 67·35w
Tunari, Cerro, *mountain*.......17·18s 66·22w
Turvo, *river*......14·47s 61·03w
Uberaba, Laguna, *lake*.............17·30s 57·50w
Uyuni, Salar de, *salt flat*.........20·20s 67·42w
Verde, Arroyo, *river*............11·25s 66·20w
Xipamanu, *river*..10·43s 67·50w
Yacuma, *river*....13·38s 65·23w
Yapacani, *river*...16·00s 64·25w
Yata, *river*.......10·29s 65·26w
Yungas, *physical region*...........16·20s 66·45w
Yura, *river*.......20·22s 65·45w
Yusala, Lago, *lake*.............14·05s 67·12w

Poopó at low water; it usually consists, however, only of wide, marshy, salt-encrusted wastes, with a small permanent body of water in the lowest part. There is no outlet. The Salar de Uyuni, to the south of the Salar de Coipasa, is similar but much larger. Covering about 3,500 square miles, it consists of a great, totally arid, windswept salt flat.

Climate. Bolivia lies wholly within the tropics but possesses every gradation of temperature from that of the equatorial lowlands to Arctic cold. The Yungas climatic zone comprises all the lowlands and the mountain valleys up to an elevation of approximately 6,000 feet. The atmosphere is humid, and the mean temperature is about 77° F (25° C), with no great departures from this figure; the rainfall, occurring throughout the year, is heavy, amounting to between 30 and 50 inches or more.

The valley zone, which includes the deep valleys lying at heights of from 6,000 to 9,500 feet, has a warm climate with moderate variations in temperature and no cold weather; it is semitropical in character.

The zone that includes the heads of the deep valleys, above the valley zone, with elevations ranging from 9,500 to 11,000 feet, is temperate, though subject to an occasional frost in winter. Both in the valleys and in the heads of the deep valleys there is likely to be a scarcity of rain, though there is usually an abundant supply of water for irrigation.

The Puna (or Altiplano) zone, which lies mostly between 11,000 and 14,000 feet, includes the great central plateau. Always cool, it varies little from summer to winter, except for rainfall; summer brings rain, but occasional snow falls in winter. The mean temperature is estimated at 50° F (10° C) at La Paz.

The Puna Brava zone extends from about 13,000 feet up to the snow line, which is about 18,000 feet, and covers a bleak inhospitable territory, inhabited only by shepherds and miners. Above this is an Arctic zone within the tropics.

Precipitation is as varied as temperature. East of the Cordillera Oriental, rains fall throughout the year. On the west side of this cordillera, the elevated plateaus have a limited rainfall in the north (23 inches at La Paz), which occurs only during the summer months and diminishes toward the south until the surface becomes absolutely barren. Brief and furious thunderstorms sometimes sweep the northern plateau and Lake Titicaca in summer. (G.McC.McB./Ed.)

Vegetation. On the Altiplano, where the amount of rainfall is relatively small, vegetation is scarce. In the higher valleys (at mean altitudes of about 8,500 feet) the typical vegetation consists of small trees and bushes, such as the molle (pepper tree), the chanar (a thorny shrub with sweet edible berries), and the pacae (a leguminous tree used as shade for coffee plants). The heights of the Yunga region are covered with great forests; among the trees represented are green pine, black walnut, aliso (a shrublike tree), laurel, cedar, *tarco* (a shade tree producing masses of yellow-white flowers), *saúco* (which yields fruit used to make medicinal syrups), and quina (an evergreen tree yielding quinine).

Tree species

The tropical area constituted by the great plains of the east is divided into the Amazon and La Plata River Basins, which are separated by a vast forested area, densely covered with tall trees, many of which are valuable hardwoods. The principal species of commercial value include rubber, Brazil nut, and two types of South American mahogany; there are altogether more than 100 types of trees suited to the wood industry, while there are at least 14 kinds of palm trees, many of which have fruits suited to the extraction of oils, as well as 11 varieties of resinous trees.

The plains of the La Plata Basin are characterized by low brush consisting of such resinous plants as quebracho (the bark of which is used for tanning and dyeing) and *palo santo* (a shrublike tree with blue or purple flowers, also called the soap bush), while the lower lying areas are covered with *mistol* (a bush that produces a nutritive seed); the algarrobo (carob) tree, which has a beanlike pod, is also found. In some areas there are forests of very tall palm trees. The vegetation of the Amazon Basin within Bolivia is more tropical than that of the La Plata Basin, having taller trees and thicker jungles. (V.A.U.)

Animal life. Animal life closely resembles that in the neighbouring areas of Argentina, Brazil, and Peru. In the rain forest of the northeast there is a wide range of species, all of which are kept in balance by competition. Among the snakes are the anaconda, the water boa, and the bushmaster (a kind of viper); caymans (members of the crocodile family) are common, as are lizards. The forest, with its constantly saturated warm air, provides a favourable habitat for salamanders, frogs, and toads. There are large numbers of birds, among which are fruit pigeons, parakeets, toucans, hornbills, and touracos (brightly coloured birds with helmet-like crests). Seen high in the sky, gliding in search of carrion, are king and black vultures. Conspicuous among mammals are the sloth, monkey, jaguar (largest of the American cats), ocelot, opossum, tapir, capybara (so-called water pig, largest of the rodents), peccary, armadillo, and anteater. Insects are particularly abundant because there is no winter and they can breed throughout the year. Among those of the greatest concern to man are mosquitoes, flies, leaf-cutting ants, and termites.

In the grasslands and scrub forest to the south of the rain forest are found jaguar, puma, and deer (among the mammals), the cayman, and some snakes (including the bushmaster and the fer-de-lance, which is a large kind of viper). Conspicuous among the birds are the rhea (a large flightless South American ostrich), a species of large stork, and the common vulture. Waterfowl are abundant, and there are myriad forms of insect life. Since much of the country is swampy for an extended period, mosquitoes of all kinds are present in enormous numbers. Flies, gnats, and ants are also abundant and are a major source of discomfort to man.

In the flat valley bottoms, where the thick tropical forest occurs, mammals are more abundant on the lower slopes and in the valleys than higher up. Here are found deer, armadillo, various opossums, the spectacled bear, peccary, jaguar, capybara, and the tayra—a huge weasel, described as ugly and vicious.

The animals of the highlands are most distinctive, differing markedly from the animals of the adjacent rain forest. On the Puna the most striking animals are the guanaco (a wild ruminant, of which the llama and the alpaca are believed to be the domesticated varieties) and the vicuña (which is related to the guanaco but smaller, yielding a soft, delicate wool). These animals live at altitudes of between about 8,200 and 18,000 feet. Highland rodents include the chinchilla (a small animal with soft, silvery-gray fur), viscacha (a burrowing rodent), mara (a long-legged, long-eared rodent), and cavy, or guinea pig; the cavy inhabits the more deserted parts of the Altiplano.

Bird life

Bird life is abundant in the highlands, particularly on Lakes Poopó and Titicaca, and includes geese, ducks, grebes, coots, cormorants, and gulls. In the swamps there are curlews, plovers, and snipes. The condor (a large New World vulture, which is the largest flying bird in the Western Hemisphere) roosts and breeds at heights between 10,000 and 16,000 feet but descends to sea level in search of food on the west side of the Andes, but not to low altitudes on the east side of the mountains. Insect life is largely absent above 10,000 feet.

Among domesticated animals indigenous to Bolivia are the llama, alpaca, cavy, and muscovy duck. The llama is the beast of burden in the bleak and barren wastes of the Puna but is seldom to be seen below heights of 7,500 feet; in addition to being a beast of burden, it also yields meat, wool, leather, tallow, hair, and fuel (dung). The alpaca is best adapted to high altitudes and thrives in the wet, marshy ground at high elevations; it is not a pack animal but is reared for wool. The cavy is raised by almost every Indian family in the highlands as a source of meat and as a pet, from 5 to 15 being kept in the average household. The muscovy duck is raised for food and is the only bird that has been domesticated in the central Andes.

Traditional regions. The three principal regions are the Altiplano, the Valleys (Valles, or Montañas), and the Oriente.

The Altiplano, which comprises about one-seventh of the total land area of Bolivia, is high, windswept, bleak, cold, and barren. Strangely enough, this hostile region, one of the highest inhabited areas on Earth, is Bolivia's most densely populated region; about 55 percent of the total population lives there. In this region are located most of the important cities, including La Paz and Oruro, many of the small towns, and most of the mines. The most important crop is the potato, which is dehydrated and frozen to form *chuño*, which keeps indefinitely. Other crops include barley, *quinoa* (a widely-used grain, grown at very high elevations), broad beans, wheat, alfalfa, and *oca* (an edible tuber). These crops are rotated in a three-year cycle, after which a plot of land is not cultivated but is pastured by llamas, alpaca, and sheep for about 12 years. Unfortunately, the Altiplano does not produce enough food for its population, and much has to be imported.

Farming is still largely of the subsistence type, and most of the farm work is performed by Indians. Until the early 1950s, most of the land was held in the form of large estates, most of which dated back to the days of the Spanish conquistadores; the rest of the land was held communally by the Indians. In 1952 the large estates were broken up and plots of land given to the Indians to be paid for within 25 years. As a result, the number of landowners in Bolivia increased 16 times over. By the mid-1960s, however, there was much confusion, and the land of the once productive large estates had become little more than kitchen gardens for the new owners.

The Altiplano is a difficult land for raising crops and most livestock, and fuel for cooking or for comfort is scarce. Clothing and blankets are made from the wool of sheep and llamas. Most Indians chew coca, primarily because it numbs their senses to the cold and deadens the appetite. A cud of dried coca leaves bulges from the cheek of almost every Altiplano Indian. Life is an endless struggle to wrest from a stubborn nature enough food, fuel, and wool to live by. The Altiplano has been Indian for centuries and promises to remain so. Centuries of bitter experience have taught the Indians to have as little as possible to do with white men if they are to protect their tiny plots of land or their harvests.

The Valles, or Montañas, consists of a complex area of deep valleys and high mountain spurs. The most important part of the region is the Yungas. Because of poor transport facilities, the area must produce such subsistence crops as ají (a widely used chili pepper), alfalfa, barley, cacao, coffee, corn, rice, yuca (cassava, or manioc), wheat, and fruits. Such cash crops as coca, sugarcane, and coffee, which have high value per unit of weight or bulk and thus can pay the costly transportation to the Altiplano, are raised wherever climatic conditions permit. Only by exploiting the Indian, however, is it possible to make a profit on these crops. Most important of the three is coca, which is restricted to the lower Yungas, north and east of La Paz, where it is grown by Indians on terraces of steep slopes of valley walls. Since coca is one of the principal items of family expenditure in the highlands, coca production provides the principal source of cash income in the Yungas, which has become Bolivia's richest subregion. The Yungas is one of the most densely populated areas in the country; it is reported to have 30 percent of the total population and about 40 percent of all the country's cultivated land.

The Oriente

The Oriente is the largest, least productive, and most sparsely populated region; it contains probably less than 15 percent of Bolivia's population. Comprising the vast semicircular territory to the north and east of the Valles, it is also probably the least known area. There is sufficient diversity to justify division into subregions: the northern rain forest; the humid subtropical central zone (comprising the northern and southern parts, respectively, of the departments of Santa Cruz and El Beni); and the semi-arid Chaco. Through the centuries this region has been effectively separated from the Yungas and the Altiplano by poor communications.

The Oriente is thus an enormous region, the central portion of which is believed to have promising possibilities for crops and cattle. It is handicapped by poor transport facilities, though they have improved with the completion of the Cochabamba to Santa Cruz highway; arteries connecting with this highway were completed by 1956. Cut off by the mountain barrier, except for this highway, the low-lying Oriente has had little to do with the rest of Bolivia. Its few agricultural and livestock products have trickled into Brazil and Argentina rather than to the Altiplano.

Urban settlements. The city of La Paz including metropolitan area (population estimated at 850,000 in 1971) is the largest and most important of Bolivia. It can be considered a highland city, though a great part of it is in a large canyon, 3,000 feet deep, produced by glacier erosion. The canyon is now drained by the Río Choqueyapu, one of the sources of the Río Beni, which is in turn one of the great tributaries of the Amazonic system. This city has spectacular mountain scenery. It is unique in that one part of it is at an altitude of 13,500 feet and the other at 10,500 feet. This difference of about 3,000 feet between the areas of the city results in peculiar differences in temperature, vegetation, and economic and social activities. The industrial and lower income areas of the city are in the heights, while the residential areas are at the lower levels.

The other cities of the Altiplano—Oruro (with a population of about 95,000), Potosí (64,000), Uyuni (15,000), Tupiza (17,000), and others of lesser importance—are generally connected with the mining industry. The aspect they present is influenced by the scenery of the steppes (extensive treeless plains) and the activities of the mines. Potosí merits special attention as the oldest large city of Bolivia. It was established in 1545 on the slopes of the mountain of Potosí, which was the richest silver mine found by the Spaniards. Potosí had nearly 200,000 inhabitants at the beginning of the 17th century, when it was the largest city in the Americas. It is one of the few cities of America to retain its architectural personality through the years: the large government and religious buildings of the silver mining era remain almost intact.

The most important cities in the valleys are: Cochabamba (180,000), Sucre (70,000), and Tarija (28,000). All of these cities are surrounded by fruit orchards and dairying country. Life is pleasant because of the mildness of the climate, and the inhabitants are inclined to the pursuit of literature; the most important writers and men of politics in the history of Bolivia have been born in these regions.

The most important of the cities of the eastern plains is Santa Cruz. In 1950 this city had a population of 40,000; by the early 1970s, with the growth of several industries and the opening of the road to the west, its population had risen to 135,000 inhabitants.

PEOPLE AND POPULATION

The three ethnic groups

Ethnic and linguistic groups. The population of Bolivia consists of three groups—the Indians, the mestizos (of mixed Indian and Spanish descent), and the descendants of the Spaniards. After four centuries of intermixing it is, however, virtually impossible to measure accurately the percentage of each.

The Indians are the descendants of the Aymaras, Quechua, and forest tribes, the great majority being farmers, mine workers, or factory and construction workers. About 90 percent of this group speak Spanish, but for traditional and cultural reasons the Indian languages, especially Aymara and Quechua, are still widely used.

The mestizos have traditionally devoted themselves to handicrafts, trades, or small business in the cities. Since the initiation of the great social reforms in 1952, a considerable proportion of this group has had access to schools, colleges, and universities; in the early 1970s, about 60 percent of those graduated in the liberal professions in Bolivian universities, a great percentage of whom are women, belong to this group.

Among the descendants of the Spaniards, the Indian element is less apparent, and the outward characteristics of the Spaniards are predominant. Traditionally, this group has formed the local aristocracy. Since the 1940s this group has increasingly intermarried with the mestizos. The division between these groups is rapidly becoming less defined, and total integration is foreseeable. Attached to this group are recent European immigrants, who occupy a lesser position; families and last names are of particular importance, as in Spanish tradition.

Religious groups. The Roman Catholic religion has the adherence of more than 90 percent of the population. Its hierarchy consists of one primate cardinalship, two archbishoprics, and five bishoprics.

The churches and cathedrals, most of which were built during colonial times, constitute a national architectural treasure. They are generally in the extravagantly ornamented baroque style, although some are in Renaissance (*e.g.*, the cathedral of La Paz) or in later styles.

Pre-Columbian religious revivals

In the Indian communities of the Altiplano, some of the characteristics of pantheistic pre-Columbian religion have survived. Its deities were the sun god Pachacama and his spouse Pachamama, the earth goddess. The Catholic religion has been forced through the centuries to accept some of these practices by assimilating them into the cult of these communities.

Protestant denominations that are active include the Methodist Episcopal church, the Baptists, and the Jehovah's Witnesses. The congregations of these denominations, plus Christian non-Catholic immigrants, make up approximately 10 percent of the total population. Other religions, such as Judaism and Islām, claim the adherence of small groups. Freedom of religion is guaranteed by the Constitution. The comparatively few atheists and agnostics are found principally in university circles and among labour leaders.

Since the 1940s the Catholic church, reflecting the new social dynamism of the church, has ventured from an almost exclusively ceremonial role into the fields of social aid and guidance.

Demography. In 1971 the total population of Bolivia was just under 5,000,000. The index of population growth was 2.6 percent; yet, paradoxically, Bolivia remained almost stationary in its population. The primary reason for this was the great volume of emigration, especially of the working population, to the labour markets of neighbouring countries. In Argentina, for example, it is estimated that there are more than 600,000 Bolivian immigrants. Most of them were hired for temporary work in the sugarcane fields, but many later moved to Buenos Aires and its outskirts. Professional unemployment constitutes a serious problem in Bolivia. It is conservatively estimated that there are at least 100,000 Bolivians, more than half of whom are university graduates, in the United States. A factor in this trend is said to be that nationalization and centralization of industry have resulted in an undue emphasis on political influence rather than professional efficiency.

Bolivia, Area and Population

	area		population	
	sq mi	sq km	1950 census*	1971 estimate
Departments (*departamentos*)				
Chuquisaca	19,984	51,524	282,980	474,000
Cochabamba	21,479	55,631	490,475	822,000
El Beni	82,458	213,564	119,770	200,900
La Paz	51,732	133,985	948,446	1,590,000
Oruro	20,690	53,588	210,260	352,600
Pando	24,644	63,827	19,804	33,200
Potosí	45,644	118,218	534,399	896,000
Santa Cruz	143,098	370,621	286,145	479,800
Tarija	14,526	37,623	126,752	212,600
Total Bolivia	424,165	1,098,581	3,019,031	5,062,500†

*Figures adjusted to account for an estimated 8.4 percent underenumeration; population actually enumerated was 2,704,165.
†Figures do not add to total given because of rounding.
Source: Official government figures.

Traditionally, the great majority of the population has been concentrated in the Altiplano and in the high valleys, mainly because of the conjunction of a healthy climate with exploitable natural resources. Health programs, launched in cooperation with the United States, have nearly eradicated diseases such as malaria, yellow fever, bubonic plague, and yaws, that once afflicted the lowlands, and the construction of roads has made access easier. In consequence, these regions, in the 1950s and 1960s, experienced a migratory influx.

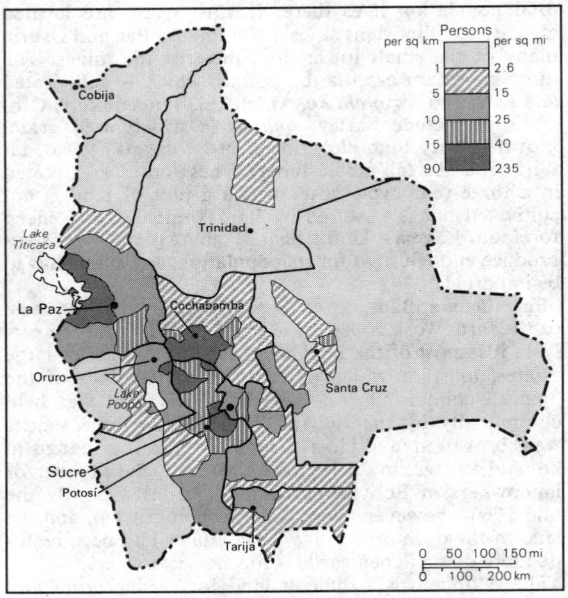

Population density of Bolivia.

THE NATIONAL ECONOMY

Economic trends

Until the 1940s, the economy of Bolivia was based mainly upon the production of minerals for export and the meagre consumption of goods by a population that remained separated from the outside world, not only by the high mountains but also by cultural barriers. The rural workers, who made up 80 percent of the population, were both culturally and economically isolated from the rest of the world. They made their own houses with local mud bricks and thatched roofs, their own clothing with sheep or alpaca wool; and they cultivated their own foods, including corn, potatoes, and *quinoa.* Contact with urban centres was negligible, resulting mainly from obligations imposed by landlords.

The export of minerals was used to finance life in the

cities, which required the importation of foodstuffs, furniture, construction materials, textiles, and clothing. Taxes on mineral exports and imports of consumer goods served to pay governmental expenses. Thus, the country lived within its limited horizons, without expectations of economic progress, except from occasional windfalls that might result from exceptionally good market conditions for minerals.

By the early 1970s, this situation had begun to change fundamentally. While minerals still represented over 80 percent of all exports, they no longer represented the decisive economic factor, for the population had become less dependent upon export earnings. An accelerated production of domestic foodstuffs had begun, internal commercial activity had increased tenfold within a quarter of a century, and the consumer indexes for the majority of the population had increased. Rural inhabitants had begun to consume such articles as beef, sugar, shortening, and textiles; to these were also added such totally new articles as transistor radios and bicycles.

Minerals. The strategic importance of Bolivian minerals, especially tin, and of Bolivia's oil and natural-gas reserves, in the very heart of South America, have remained unaltered. Bolivia remains the only secure source of tin in the Western Hemisphere, a factor of immense importance in the event of a worldwide conflict. Such strategic considerations also apply to the oil and natural-gas deposits in the area of Santa Cruz.

In 1971, minerals produced included tin, lead, zinc, copper, antimony, tungsten, bismuth, gold, and silver.

The oil industry

Oil prospecting first began in 1927, when the Standard Oil Company (New Jersey) located some oil fields with relatively low yields in southeastern Bolivia. From 1937 to 1956, oil production was the responsibility of a Bolivian state agency, but, after that, United States companies continued prospecting, and the Gulf Oil Corporation located oil fields near the city of Santa Cruz. In 1969, when the production of Gulf Oil Corporation amounted to 40,000 barrels daily, the Bolivian government cancelled the Gulf Oil Corporation concessions and made the state agency, Yacimientos Petrolíferos Fiscales Bolivianos (YPFB), responsible for production. This action affected the external credit of Bolivia, so that the government experienced temporary difficulty in selling the exportable surplus of oil on the international market. Oil production, which amounted to about 8,800,000 barrels in 1970, rose to 13,200,000 barrels in 1971.

Agricultural resources. Bolivia's most significant agricultural resources consist of its cattle-raising areas and its great forests. Livestock includes cattle, horses, mules, asses, sheep, pigs, goats, llamas, and alpacas.

About 43 percent of the total surface area of the country, amounting to about 180,000 square miles, is covered by natural tropical and subtropical forests, with excellent species of hardwoods. Limited means of access and long distances to the nearest seaports have, however, delayed the development of these riches.

Power resources. There has been a considerable increase in the production of electricity, although consumption is still relatively low. The installed capacity of thermal power, for example, rose from about 17,000 kilowatts (kw) in 1940 to 95,000 kilowatts in 1970, while hydroelectric capacity rose from 31,000 kilowatts in 1940 to 172,000 kilowatts in 1970.

The great differences in altitude between the snow-capped peaks, which rise to 21,000 feet, and the plains, which are nearly at sea level, offer a great potential for the future development of hydroelectric power. Two projects are worthy of notice for the future development not only of Bolivia but also of South America. The first is concerned with the utilization of the waters of Lake Titicaca, which constitutes the highest reservoir in the world with a potential not yet calculated. Because the lake is jointly owned by Peru and Bolivia, the project would have to be jointly financed and implemented. The second project concerns the construction of a dam on the Río Beni, which has a volume of water comparable to that of the Nile. Near the eastern plains, the river passes through a narrow canyon with walls of solid rock, a scant 600 feet apart, rising to about 2,000 feet. The projected dam would form a lake nearly as large as Lake Titicaca, with possibilities for transportation, fishing, and settlement. The power output of this dam would, it is calculated, be similar to that of the Aswān Dam in Egypt. These two projects, if realized, would exert a decisive influence upon the industrialization of Bolivia, Peru, northern Chile, and western Brazil.

Trade and industrial production. More than 80 percent of Bolivia's exports are minerals. In the early 1970s the balance of payments was consistently favourable. The economic situation of the country was not flourishing, however, because of the lack of internal savings and the scarcity of foreign investment. The state agencies, which have taken over most of the means of production, function with permanent deficits because of a mushrooming bureaucracy and poor individual production. Private enterprise has been restricted to small industry and to medium and small-sized mining operations. In manufacturing, the principal private activities are concerned with textiles and drinks; food production is scattered among many small farmers or small primary industries. Sugar production, for the most part, is in the hands of the state.

The state corporations

There are four principal state corporations, all of which were operating at a deficit in the early 1970s. The Corporación Minera de Bolivia (Bolivian Mining Corporation) is responsible for the administration of the large mines nationalized in 1952; Yacimientos Petrolíferos Fiscales Bolivianos (Bolivian National Oilfields) is concerned with the production and exportation of oil and natural gas; the Empresa Nacional de Ferrocarriles (National Railroad Corporation) operates with a government subsidy; Lloyd Aéreo Boliviano, the national airline, is mostly state-controlled.

In general, it appeared that the policy of nationalization and state control of industry resulted in losses.

Transportation. Because of its landlocked situation, Bolivia depends on railroads, highways, and airlines for both internal and external transportation. River navigation is still not developed, partly because the navigable rivers are in the least populated areas, and partly because of geographic problems posed by the other rivers into which they flow.

Bolivia is connected with foreign seaports on the Atlantic and the Pacific by five railways, which have a total length of 2,310 miles. These railways are: La Paz to Arica (Chile); La Paz to Antofagasta (Chile); La Paz to Buenos Aires via La Quiaca (Argentina); Santa Cruz to Buenos Aires via Yacuiba, in southern Bolivia; and Santa Cruz to São Paulo (Brazil) on the Atlantic coast via Corumbá, in southeast Brazil.

The railways to the Atlantic ports are used for the export of agricultural products, and the Pacific railways are used mainly for the export of minerals. Road construction intensified during the late 1960s and early 1970s, with credits being advanced by the United States. In the early 1970s there were about 16,000 miles of roads of which about 600 miles were paved first-class highways; 7,200 miles were crushed stone, 1,600 miles graded earth, and the rest unimproved. The most important paved highways are from La Paz to Oruro, from Cochabamba to Santa Cruz, from Santa Cruz to the north, and from Cochabamba to Chimoré. Studies are being made for the construction of highways toward Chilean and Peruvian seaports.

A permanent bus service runs to Peru over the La Paz–Desaguadero–Puno roads. Throughout Bolivia, bus lines connect the principal cities.

Air transport

Internal air transport is primarily in the hands of a mixed corporation—Lloyd Aéreo Boliviano—of which 74 percent is owned by the state and the rest by private individuals. This airline connects the principal Bolivian cities with international airports in Buenos Aires, Santiago (Chile), Lima (Peru), and São Paulo (Brazil). In its domestic service, it operates regular flights to most Bolivian cities. Airport administration is in the hands of AASANA (the National Council of Aeronautics), a fiscal entity that operates about 30 airports.

The geographic situation of Bolivia poses particularly

difficult transportation problems. The double Andes mountain range, which has only a few mountain passes lower than 15,000 feet, has made road and railway construction particularly expensive. Thus, while mountain roads offer incomparable scenic views for tourists, they also present the difficulties and dangers that attend winding roads, while steep inclines preclude accelerated travel.

ADMINISTRATION AND SOCIAL CONDITIONS

The structure of government. *The constitutional framework.* The executive, legislative, and judicial branches of government are theoretically independent. Since the founding of the Republic in 1825, Bolivia has had a republican and unitary system of government. The central government appoints lesser political authorities, such as the prefects, who govern the nine departments; the subprefects, who govern the provinces into which the departments are divided; and the corregidores, who are the highest authorities in still smaller units called cantons.

According to the constitution, the central government must be elected every four years by popular elections, in which a president and vice president are chosen. The president appoints a 16-member ministerial cabinet; these ministers are heads of the executive branches of government.

The legislative branch consists of a Chamber of Deputies, with approximately 102 members, and a Senate, with a total of 27 (three senators per department). Deputies remain in office four years and senators for six.

The constitution can be changed only by two legislatures, and then only if the second one has been returned after an election in which the issue of the constitutional amendment forms part of the electoral platform. Laws must be sanctioned by the legislative branch and promulgated by the president, who has the power of veto, which can be overridden by a two-thirds majority vote in the legislature. The existing tradition of violent changes of government in Latin America has, however, frequently resulted in these constitutional norms being set aside. Most of the time the country has been governed by de facto regimes headed by members of the armed forces. Between 1900 and 1971 there were 28 presidents, of whom only 14 were elected by popular vote in accordance with the constitution. In addition, during the administration of the de facto regimes, the legislature is not convened, and the central government assumes its functions, promulgating decrees that have the force of law. In the same way, these governments frequently declare judicial offices to be vacant and name new judges to the Supreme Court, which in turn makes appointments to the lesser judicial posts.

The administrative process has generally been inspired by the presidential mode of government in the United States, with certain Anglo-French parliamentary overtones. A vote of no confidence, if approved, can result in the automatic resignation of a Cabinet or of an individual minister.

Constitutionally, municipal governments should be organized through the election of mayors and municipal counsellors. The last municipal elections were, however, held in 1928; since then, centralist tendencies have prevailed, and the central government appoints the mayors.

The electoral system

The political process. Until 1956, only a small minority of the inhabitants of the Republic voted in general elections. Women were not allowed to vote, and literacy requirements disenfranchised more than 70 percent of the men. There were also property and income restrictions, which further diminished the numbers of the electorate. Thus, out of a population of about 5,000,000, a president could be elected with only 80,000 votes. In 1956, however, an electoral reform law eliminated sex and literacy requirements, establishing the voting age at 21 years for men, and 19 for women; as a result, 1,400,000 voters participated in the 1956 elections.

A political party of substantial influence in the early 1970s was the Movimiento Nacionalista Revolucionario, which governed the country from 1952 to 1964. Its program, based on three fundamental points—a universal vote, agrarian reform, and the nationalization of the mines—gained unprecedented popular support. The personal ambitions of its principal leaders, however, resulted in schisms that its adversaries in the armed forces were able to exploit, and the party was ousted from office in 1964.

Another important party has been Falange Socialista Boliviana, a group inspired by the Falangista Party of Spain. The influence of this party reached its peak when totalitarian movements controlled most of central Europe, but—like similar parties throughout South America—it changed direction after the defeat of the Axis forces in World War II. It then took the name Partido Social Cristiano (Christian Social Party).

The parties of the extreme left have become aggressive as a result of the influence of Castroism (the doctrines of Fidel Castro of Cuba) in South America. These parties have had difficulty, however, in following a central authority and are divided into such factions as Moscovite Communists, Maoists, Trotskyites, Castroites, etc. As a result of the opportunities given them by two leftist military governments—that of Alfredo Ovando Candía from 1969 to 1970 and that of Juan José Torres from 1970 to 1971—these groups became active in the Bolivian universities and labour unions. Bolivia seemed capable of becoming one of the first South American countries to have a Communist government until the armed forces ousted the Torres government. A nationalist government was organized in 1971 under the presidency of Col. Hugo Banzer Suárez, with the cooperation of a segment of the Movimiento Nacionalista Revolucionario and the Falange Socialista Boliviana.

The armed forces. The armed forces, in order of importance, consist of the forces of the land army, the air force, and the naval force. There is a commander general for the three combined forces, as well as a commander for each. Since 1904, there has been a one-year military obligation for all male Bolivians who reach the age of 19. The standing army numbers about 20,000 men, and the air force—organized with United States assistance—is a small one. The Bolivian navy is small; it operates on the navigable rivers, as well as on Lake Titicaca, to prevent smuggling and to assist river transport.

Education, health and welfare. Civil education is divided in three categories—elementary, secondary, and university. Most education is state-supported, but private institutions are not forbidden. The Catholic, Protestant, and Jewish churches are active in primary and secondary education. One of the country's eight universities is Catholic. The Bureau of Indian and Rural Education maintains regional schools for teaching trades and crafts. The national illiteracy rate is estimated to be about 60 percent.

Health services

There are three kinds of health services—those supported by the state through the Ministry of Health, those provided by the social security system for its affiliates, and private clinics. In general, the medical services and the hospitals in the cities are adequate. This is not so in rural areas, however; both doctors and nurses are lacking. Nationally, there is approximately one doctor to care for every 2,700 people. The most serious health problems confronting the country are malnutrition, tuberculosis, prenatal and birth attention, and the tropical diseases that break out regularly in the warmer areas.

Cultural life and institutions. Bolivian culture consists of a combination of Indian culture with the Mediterranean cultures brought by the Spaniards. On religious feast days, for example, pagan pre-Columbian rites are still practiced, and the Indians express themselves through dances and songs that blend the two cultures. In such festivities, some symbolic dress presents the Indian interpretation of European attitudes: the dance of the *palla-palla* or *loco palla-palla* caricatures the European invaders; the dance of the *waka-tokoris* satirizes bullfights; and the *morenada* mocks white men, who are represented leading imported African slaves. Indian musical instruments are used to accompany these dances. In the music itself, the mixture of cultures is also evident, since many of the tunes are based on Spanish dances. The more commonly used instruments are: *el sicu* (pan pipes), and *la tarka*, *la kena*, and *el pinquillo* (vertical flutes). Percussion instruments of various sizes are used. The costumes, highly embroidered and colourful, imitate the dress of the pre-Columbian natives or the dress of 16th-century Spaniards.

Daily dress in the rural regions of Bolivia still reflects the Spanish colonial influence. The men wear short jackets and wide trousers, and the women wear wide pleated skirts and colourful shawls. The hats the women wear vary according to the different regions.

Since the 1940s, Indian culture has experienced a blossoming. Previously, Indians attempted to imitate Europeans, in custom as well as in dress. By the early 1970s, however, Indian values had been re-established; Indian music rose to a higher standard, painters abandoned the imitation of European fashions, and some of the characteristics of Indian culture re-emerged in the general life-style.

Cultural institutions

The National Academy of Fine Arts in La Paz offers courses in music, painting, sculpture, and ceramics. There are two galleries of pictorial arts, and a permanent collection in the National Museum of Art. Jewelry in silver and gold, with pre-Columbian decorations and styles, has been made since colonial times. The local markets offer a profusion of colourful handicrafts and fine woodcarvings.

In the city of Potosí the building of the Mint (Casa de Moneda), erected in the 17th century, has been restored, and its great halls are used to house a collection of fine colonial paintings. Various old temples have been restored, and folk festivals are held periodically. The most important is the one held in Oruro during the carnival holidays; many Indian music and dance groups compete, providing a magnificent display of costumes and decorations. In La Paz there is the National Symphony Orchestra, and at the University of San Andres (also known as the University of La Paz) a choral group specializes in Indian musical themes.

There are five newspapers published daily in La Paz—three in the morning and two in the evening—and there are 17 radio stations and one television channel. In the other large cities there are also local newspapers, and each department capital has at least three radio stations. Some radio stations broadcast in Quechua or Aymara. There is an Academy of the Aymara Language in La Paz; its avowed purpose is the preservation of the purity of this language.

Prospects for the future. Bolivia faces serious problems that hinder its progress. Among them are its lack of access to the ocean and its difficult terrain. It nevertheless constitutes one of the world's reserves: it is capable of supporting a larger population because the extent of its arable lands is great and the density of its population very low. The areas of land without adequate rainfall for human habitation are relatively small, and the energy sources, mineral reserves, and biological possibilities are promising. The fundamental human problem lies in the difficulty of establishing a form of government and social structure stable enough to permit the development of potential resources.

The migratory currents from other continents, which have had so much influence elsewhere in the Americas, have had a minimal influence in Bolivia. The great majority of the population are still either of Indian or of mixed Indian and Spanish blood.

In Bolivia, a great desire to emerge from backwardness can be perceived; in this desire, however, the political tendencies of the modern world play a dramatic role. In the universities, many lean toward the adoption of Socialist methods as a solution to Bolivia's problems, but many of those in the professions and many technicians are inclined toward free enterprise and private initiative. The result of this difference has been a division in a national community that—perhaps more than any other—needs common objectives in order to overcome its enormous problems.

BIBLIOGRAPHY. ALCIDES ARGUEDAS, *Historia General de Bolivia (El Proceso de la Nacionalidad) 1809–1921* (1922, reprinted 1967); JOSE MARIA CAMACHO, *Compendio de la Historia de Bolivia*, 13th ed. (1945); ROBERT BARTON, *A Short History of the Republic of Bolivia*, 2nd ed. (1968); CHARLES ARNADE, *The Emergence of the Republic of Bolivia* (1957), are the best studies of the history of Bolivia. The rather negative approach of Arguedas is contested in CARLOS MONTENEGRO, *Nacionalismo y Coloniaje*, 2nd ed. (1943, reprinted 1967). FEDERICO E. AHLFELD, *Geografía de Bolivia* (1969) and *General Considerations Concerning the Possibilities of Discovery of Mineral Deposits in Bolivia* (UN, 1951), are studies on geological and physical aspects; further studies are GOVER BORJA BERRIOS and ARMANDO GONZALES CARDOZO, *Geografía Agrícola de Bolivia* (1971); ENRIQUE OBLITAS POBLETE, *Plantas medicinales de Bolivia* (1969); and JORGE PANDO GUTIERREZ, *Bolivia y el Mundo: Geografía Económica*, 2 vol. (1947), dealing with biological and economic resources.

People and population: GEORGES ROUMA, *Les Indiens Quitchouas et Aymaras des hauts plateaux de la Bolivie* (1913), a description of the rural population; ARTURO VILELA DEL VILLAR, *Bolivia: Visión de Conjunto* (1942); and MIGUEL BONIFAZ, *Bolivia: Frustración y Destino* (1965), are works of reference.

National economy: See the publications of various national ministries for analysis and statistical information on the economy, production, energy resources, population, roads, and education.

Administration, social conditions, political parties, and armed forces: For background, see ROBERT J. ALEXANDER, *The Bolivian National Revolution* (1958); AUGUSTO CESPEDES, *El Dictador Suicida: 40 Años de Historia de Bolivia* (1956) and *El Presidente Colgado: Historia Boliviana* (1966). ROBERTO QUEREJAZU CALVO, *Masamaclay* (1965), is the best book on the Chaco War between Bolivia and Paraguay; MANUEL FRONTAURA ARGANDONA, *El Litoral de Bolivia* (1968), describes the landlocked condition of the country and its influence on its social and economic situation.

Cultural life and institutions: H.S. BELLAMY, *Built Before the Flood: The Problem of the Tiahuanaco Ruins* (1943); ARTHUR POSNANSKY, *Tiahuanacu: The Cradle of American Man*, 4 vol. in 2 (1945–57); SIR CLEMENS MARKHAM, *The Incas of Peru* (1910); LOUIS BAUDIN, *L'Empire socialiste des Incas* (1928); ERLAND NORDENSKIOELD, *Investigaciones Arqueológicas en la Región Fronteriza de Perú y Bolivia*, trans. by CARLOS PONCE SANGINES and STIG RYDEN (1953), works containing information on the foundations of the Aymara and Quechua cultures that have influenced the shaping of modern Bolivia. ENRIQUE FINOT, *Spanish Colonial Culture in Upper Peru* (1935); JOSE and TERESA GISBERT DE MESA, "El Estilo Mestizo en la Arquitectura Virreinal Boliviana," *Revista de Arte y Letras "Khana,"* vol. 4, no. 7 and 8 (1955) and *Holguin y la Pintura Altoperuana del Virreinato* (1956); GUSTAVO ADOLFO OTERO, *La Vida Social del Coloniaje (Esquema de la Historia del Alto Perú, hoy Bolivia, de los Siglos XVI, XVII y XVIII)* (1942; Eng. trans., *Life in the Spanish Colonies, with Particular Reference to Upper Peru, now Bolivia*, 1955); LEWIS U. HANKE, *The Imperial City of Potosí* (1956), provide information on the influence of Spanish colonization.

(V.A.U.)

Bolivia, History of

Pre-Columbian civilizations

Bolivian society traces its origins to the advanced pre-Columbian civilizations of South America. The high Bolivian plateau known as the *altiplano* was already densely populated several centuries before the Spanish conquest in the 16th century.

The Bolivia region, to 1825. From the 7th century, the Tiahuanaco empire, the first of the great Andean empires to extend over both the Peruvian coast and highlands, had its centre in the *altiplano* region. By the 11th century it had reached its apogee and was replaced by more simple regional states.

In the centuries that followed the collapse of Tiahuanaco, the Bolivian highland region maintained its dense populations and technological civilizations with irrigation agriculture. By the 15th century the region was mostly controlled by some 12 nations of Aymara-speaking Indians. Competitors to the Quechuan-speaking nation at Cuzco in what is now Peru, these Aymara tribes fought with the latter for control of the central Andean highland region. Though the Aymara nations were eventually dominated by Cuzco, they nevertheless remained the most important non-Quechuan group within the expanding Incan empire; because of their importance they were the only conquered coastal or highland peoples able to retain their language and cultural identity to such an extent that their Aymara language survived the Spanish conquest. But the Aymara were forced to accept a large body of Quechuan-speaking immigrants within their midst as part of a deliberate Incan policy of colonization. It was this early pattern of colonization and nonassimilation that gave Bolivia its current linguistic and cultural identity (the two major Indian languages in Bolivia today are Quechua, spoken by over a third, and Aymara, spoken by a fourth of the population).

Part of the Spanish Empire

The southern Andean valleys and central plateau of Bolivia, with their dense Indian populations, became a core population area within the Spanish empire after the conquest. To the wealth represented by Indian labour there was added the mineral wealth from newly discovered silver deposits of Potosí (1545)—the largest silver mines then known in the Western world. The arid, high altitude mines of Potosí, along with others discovered near the town of Oruro (founded in 1606), were supplied with food and other basic necessities by such supportive towns as Chuquisaca (founded in 1538), La Paz (1548), and Cochabamba (1571). From the 16th to well into the 18th centuries, this southern Andean area, known then as Charcas, or Upper Peru, was one of the wealthiest and most densely populated centres of Spain's American empire. Its mines were supplied with forced drafts (*mita*) of Indian labourers from all over the Andes; and by the middle of the 17th century, its central mining city of Potosí was the largest city in the Americas, with a population estimated at 150,000. But by the last quarter of the 18th century this famous mining zone was in decay. The exhaustion of the richest and most accessible veins, the poverty of the miners and their ignorance of advanced technology, and the absorption of colonial capital into the thriving international commerce of the late 18th century all contributed to its decline. Though a reduced Potosí continued to be Upper Peru's most important economic centre, the intellectual and political centre of the area was Chuquisaca (also known in the colonial period as Charcas and La Plata and, since independence, as Sucre). With its academies and University, Chuquisaca was the major educational centre for the entire Rio de la Plata region, it also served as the seat of Upper Peru's government, which was known from its foundation in 1559 as the Audiencia of Charcas. The Audiencia was first placed under the Viceroyalty of Peru at Lima; but in 1776 it was finally shifted to a new viceroyalty established at Buenos Aires.

Independence movement

In 1809 revolts first at Chuquisaca and then at La Paz gave rise to the Wars of Independence in South America. But, despite several invasions by patriot armies and constant guerilla warfare, Upper Peru was the last major area in South America to be freed from Spanish rule. It was only with Antonio José de Sucre's victory over the Spanish armies in Lower Peru (1824) that Upper Peru's elite groups finally supported a full independence movement. Though the South American liberator Simón Bolívar was pressing for multiregional confederations, he permitted an Upper Peruvian congress to declare itself an independent republic on Aug. 6, 1825.

Bolivia from 1825 to c. 1930. In recognition of Bolívar's support, the leaders of the congress named the new republic Bolivia after the liberator and invited Sucre, his chief aide, to be the first president.

Foundation and early national history. But the new republic was not as viable as its leaders fervently hoped it would be. It was economically retarded, despite the legendary colonial wealth and prominence of the region. The late-18th-century mining decline had given way to severe depression as a result of the Independence wars. Between 1803 and 1825 silver production at Potosí declined by over 80 percent; and by the time of the first national census in 1846, the republic listed more than 10,000 abandoned mines.

Incapable of exporting its silver at the levels of colonial production, Bolivia rapidly lost its previously advanced economic standing within Spanish America. Already by the end of the colonial period, such marginal areas as the Rio de la Plata and Chile were forging ahead on the basis of meat and cereal production. Bolivia, on the other hand, was a net importer of basic foods, even those exclusively consumed by its Indian population. And none of its mineral resources was of sufficient value to overcome the high transportation costs involved in getting the minerals to the coast. The Bolivian republic, with little trade to tax and with few resources to export beyond its very modest precious metals production, was forced to rely on direct taxation of its Indian peasant masses, who made up over two-thirds of the estimated 1,100,000 population in 1825. Until well into the last quarter of the 19th century, this regressive Indian taxation was the largest source of national government revenue. With the more progressive South American states relying almost exclusively on import and export taxes of a constantly expanding international commerce, the Bolivian state rapidly lost its prominent position within the continent and became known as one of the most backward of the new republics.

Economic decline and political stagnation

This economic decline was mirrored by political stagnation. Bolivia emerged initially with a series of military strongmen (caudillos), among whom was Marshal Andrés de Santa Cruz, president from 1829 to 1839. Temporarily reorganizing the war-torn Bolivian economy and state finances, Santa Cruz in the 1830s was able to unite Bolivia with Peru, through the successful overthrow of the Lima regime of Gen. Agustín Gamarra, into a government known as the Confederation (1836–39). But Chilean military intervention destroyed the Confederation attempt; Bolivia quickly turned in upon itself and thenceforth abandoned all attempts at international expansion.

Bolivia's efforts for the next half-century were primarily to integrate its far-flung regions into a coherent relationship between the core of the republic, the *altiplano*, and the eastern Andean valleys. This attempt was doomed to failure, however, because Bolivia lacked the population and resources to exploit either its Amazonian or its Pacific frontiers. Despite the enormous wealth in nitrates and guano available on the Bolivian Pacific coast, the nation was incapable of exploiting them even with the help of foreign capital. What little capital was available within Bolivia's upper class was totally committed to *altiplano* mining. It was Peruvians, Chileans, North Americans, and Englishmen who exploited these resources. Between the Chilean War of the Confederation (1838–39) and the outbreak of the Pacific War (1879), Chile constantly and successfully expanded its claims, both by diplomatic pressure and, finally, by war, against Bolivian sovereignty in the enormous Bolivian Pacific coastal territories.

War with Chile

Loss of the coastal region. The War of the Pacific (1879–84) had its origins in heavy Anglo-Chilean investments in Bolivia, beginning in the 1840s with those in the guano deposits on Bolivia's Atacama coastal province. With the discovery of nitrate deposits in the 1860s, Chilean aggressive expansion along the coast increased even further. By a series of treaties Chile expanded its territorial claims and obtained commercial concessions within Bolivian territory. As a response to this pressure, Bolivia signed an alliance treaty with Peru in 1873; but this did not intimidate the Chileans. When the Bolivian government attempted to increase taxation on Chilean nitrate companies working in Bolivia, Chile unilaterally invaded Bolivian territory in 1879 and forced a war with both Bolivia and Peru. In May 1880, at the Battle of Tacna, Chile defeated a combined Bolivian–Peruvian army, ending effective Bolivian resistance. Rather than attack the Andean core of Bolivia, the Chileans ignored Bolivia for the rest of the war and proceeded on a massive invasion of Peru, which resulted in their eventual capture of Lima.

The fall of the Pacific littoral to Chile may, in many ways, have been a blessing for Bolivia. The War of the Pacific marked a major turning point in national history. From the fall of the Confederation to the War of the Pacific, Bolivia had gone through one of the worst periods of caudillo rule in all Latin America during the 19th century. The decades of the 1860s and 1870s, however, were those in which Andean silver mining had revived under the impact of new capital inputs from Chile and Great Britain. By the time of the War of the Pacific, international market conditions for silver and the introduction of new technology and capital had greatly revived the national mining industry. The War of the Pacific enabled the new mining entrepreneurs to capture political control of the nation and to break the hold of the by then discredited barracks officers on national political life.

Formation of Liberal and Conservative parties. Starting in 1880, under the presidency (1880–84) of Narciso Campero, Bolivia moved into an era of civilian governments with the national upper class dividing into Liberal and Conservative parties, which then proceeded to share power. This intraclass political party system finally brought Bolivia the stability it needed for economic development. Though the parties split on personality and anticlerical issues, they were identical in their desire to promote economic growth. From 1880 to 1899 the nation was ruled by the Conservatives, whose principal function was to encourage the mining industry through the development of an international rail network.

Era of civilian government

It was thus an economically expanding nation that the Liberals inherited when they seized power from the Conservatives in the so-called Federal Revolution of 1899. Supposedly fought over the permanent placing of national institutions in the cities of Sucre or La Paz, the federal revolt was primarily a power struggle between the Conservative and Liberal parties. Unfortunately for the Conservatives, their strength was too closely tied to the traditional Chuquisaca elite, much of which was coterminous with the silver-mining class. The Liberals, however, had the bulk of their strength in La Paz, which by this period was three times the size of Sucre and had the largest urban concentration (some 72,000 persons) in the national population, which was estimated at 1,700,000 persons in 1900.

Increase in tin mining. The Liberal victory was also closely associated with a basic shift in the mining economy. As the world silver market began to collapse in the 1880s and early 1890s, a major shift to tin mining began on the Bolivian *altiplano.* Found in association with silver, tin did not become an important product until the end of the 19th century, when demand suddenly soared in all the major industrialized countries. Thus by 1900 tin had completely superseded silver as Bolivia's primary export, accounting for over 50 percent of national exports.

The shift to tin mining not only occurred at the same time as the Liberal revolt and was closely associated with the new party but it also brought about a basic change within the capitalist class in Bolivia. Whereas the silver mining elite had been almost exclusively Bolivian, the new tin miners were far more cosmopolitan, including, in the early years, foreigners of all nationalities as well as some new Bolivian entrepreneurs. Tin mining itself absorbed far more capital and produced far more wealth than had the old silver-mining industry, and the new companies that emerged became complex international ventures directed by professional managers.

Given this new economic complexity and the political stability already achieved by the Conservatives and perpetuated by the Liberals, the tin-mining elite found it profitable to withdraw from direct involvement in national political life. Whereas Bolivian presidents under Conservative rule in the 19th century had either been silver magnates themselves (Gregorio Pacheco, 1884–88; Aniceto Arce, 1888–92), or closely associated with such magnates as partners or representatives (Mariano Baptista, 1892–96; Severo Fernández Alonso, 1896–99), the Liberals and subsequent 20th-century presidents were largely outside the mining elite. No tin magnate actively participated in leadership positions within the political system. Rather, they came to rely on a more effective system of pressure group politics.

Liberal rule (1899–1920). The primary task of the Liberal politicians, who ruled Bolivia from 1899 to 1920 under the leadership of Ismael Montes (twice president: in 1904–08 and 1913–17), was to settle Bolivia's chronic border problems and to continue and expand the communications network initiated by the Conservatives. A definitive peace treaty was signed with Chile (1904), accepting the loss of all Bolivia's former coastal territories. Also, the Acre problem was resolved: this involved an unsuccessful attempt by the central government to crush an autonomist rebellion (1889–1903) in the rubber boom territory of Acre on the Brazilian border. Brazil's covert support of the rebels and the defeat of Bolivian forces finally convinced the Liberals to sell the territory to Brazil in the Treaty of Petrópolis (1903). As a result of the financial indemnities provided by both treaties, Bolivia was able to finance a great railroad construction era—by 1920 most of the major cities were tied together by rails and La Paz was connected to the two Chilean Pacific ports of Antofagasta and Arica; new lines had begun or had been built to Lake Titicaca and thus the Peruvian border, and to Tarija and the Argentine frontier.

Railroad-building era

The period of Liberal rule was also the most calm in Bolivian political history. Dominated by the figure of Montes, the Liberal Party easily destroyed the federalists, who had supported the party during the revolution, and Liberal success led to the total collapse of the Conservative Party. Not until 1914 was an effective two party system again established, when many of the political "outs," along with a large number of new and younger elements, finally organized the Republican Party. Like its predecessors, the Republican Party was a white, upper and middle class grouping, with a fundamental belief in liberal and positivist ideologies.

The Republican Party. The abrasive quality of the strong-willed Montes and the disintegration of the ruling Liberal Party finally permitted the Republicans to stage a successful coup d'etat, in 1920, and become the ruling party. Upon achieving political power, however, the new party immediately split into two warring sections based on a conflict of personalities and led by two Montes-style politicians—Juan Bautista Saavedra, a La Paz lawyer who captured control of the Republican Party and was national president from 1930–34, and Daniel Salamanca, a Cochabamba landowner who took his following into a separate party, the so-called Partido Republicano Genuino (or Genuine Republican Party). The rivalry between these two men became the dominant theme in Bolivian politics for the next decade, until the Salamanca forces captured the presidency.

Below the surface of this political battle of personalities, the national economy in the 1920s was undergoing serious change. The early years of the decade had witnessed a brilliant post-World War I recovery of the Bolivian tin-mining industry, which led to the achievement by 1929 of its highest production figures. This enormous output occurred, however, in a period of steady price decline (a trend that continued long after the Great Depression of the 1930s). By 1930 the international tin market was in a serious crisis, and Bolivian production suffered. The year 1930 marked the end of major new capital investment in tin mining; thereafter the industry in Bolivia would become an ever higher cost producer of lower grade ores for the international market.

Bolivia since 1930. The installation of Salamanca in the presidency after the revolt of 1930 seemingly involved little change in traditional Bolivian government. But the Great Depression cut brutally into national income and forced the closing of a large part of the vital mining industry. Salamanca was thus forced to take new measures. Attempting a policy of inflation and money manipulation, he ran into bitter hostility from the Liberal Party, his key partner in the 1930 overthrow of the regular Republican Party. The opposition of these two forces in the central government led to a tense political climate, the result of which was to force Salamanca to accept a Liberal veto over internal economic decisions. He refused, however, to permit the Liberals to join his cabinet; rather, he sought to overcome Liberal congressional control and to destroy growing strike movements by turning national attention to other themes. Salamanca had the traditional recourse to patriotism and foreign war open to him in a long-standing border conflict with Paraguay.

Already in the mid-1920s, Bolivia and Paraguay both had begun a major program of fort construction in the largely uninhabited and poorly demarcated Chaco Boreal territory, on the southeastern Bolivian frontier. At the height of the Depression, Salamanca had advocated an even heavier armament and fortification program and had contracted for major European loans. In June 1932 a border incident developed between the two states, and Salamanca deliberately provoked a full-scale Bolivian reprisal, which inevitably led into open war between the two nations.

Conflict with Paraguay

The Chaco War (1932–35). The Chaco War was a long and costly disaster for Bolivia. In the three years of bitter fighting on its southeastern frontiers, Bolivia lost 100,000 men dead, wounded, deserted, or captured; it also lost far more territory than Paraguay had claimed even in its most extreme prewar demands. The fact that Bolivia had entered the war with a better equipped and supposedly far better trained army only aggravated the sense of frustration among the younger literate veterans—the so-called Chaco generation—at the total failure of Bolivian arms. Charging that the traditional politicians and the international oil companies had led Bolivia into its disastrous war, the returning veterans set up rival Socialist and radical parties and challenged the traditional political system.

Return to military rule. The initial result of this challenge was the overthrow of the civilian government and the first advent of military rule in Bolivia since 1880. In 1936 the younger army officers seized the government, and under two leaders, Col. David Toro in 1936–37 and Maj. Germán Busch in 1937–39, they tried to reform Bolivian society. Little was accomplished during this so-called era of military socialism except for the confiscation of the Standard Oil Company holdings, the creation of an important labour code, and the writing in 1938 of an advanced; socially oriented constitution.

Rise of new political groups. Beginning in the 1940s, civilian dissident groups finally began to organize themselves into powerful national opposition parties. The two most important of these were the middle class and initially fascist-oriented Movimiento Nacionalista Revolucionario (MNR) and the Marxist and largely pro-Russian Partido de la Izquierda Revolucionaria (PIR). Both groups established important factions in the national congress of 1940–44. In 1943 the civilian president Gen. Enrique Peñaranda was overthrown by a secret military group, Razón de Patria (Radepa), which allied itself with the MNR and tried to create a new-style government. Under Col. Gualberto Villaroel (1943–46) little was accomplished, except for an initial political mobilization of the Indian peasants by the MNR. Opposed as fascist-oriented by the right and left, the Villaroel government was overthrown in 1946, in a bloody revolution in which Villaroel was hanged before the presidential palace by revolutionary crowds.

Political chaos

During the next six years the PIR tried to rule in alliance with many of the older, traditional parties. But this effort failed, and the PIR was eventually dissolved and replaced in early 1950 by the more radical Bolivian Communist Party. The Conservative parties proved unable to control the situation; and after the MNR won a plurality victory in the presidential elections of 1951, the military intervened directly and formed a military junta government. As for the MNR, its disaster under Villaroel led it to disassociate itself from its fascist wing and to seek an alliance with a small Trotskyite party, which had important mine-union support. The resulting alliance brought the labour leader Juan Lechín into the MNR. After several unsuccessful revolts, each more violent than the preceding one, the MNR, in several days of fighting, finally overthrew the military regime in April 1952. During this struggle, workers, civilians, and peasants were armed and the army was almost totally destroyed.

The Bolivian National Revolution (1952). Thus in April 1952 began the so-called Bolivian National Revolution, which became one of Latin America's most important social revolutions. The MNR and its mine-worker and peasant supporters were pledged to a fundamental attack on the tin-mining industry and its allied political supporters. In October 1952 the three biggest tin-mine companies were nationalized. In August 1953 came one of the most far-reaching land-reform decrees ever enacted in the Western Hemisphere. Universal suffrage was granted with the abolition of literacy requirements. Not only were Indians granted land, freed from servile labour obligations, and given the vote, but they were also given large supplies of arms. From that point on, the Indian peasants of Bolivia became a powerful, if largely passive, political force, upon which all subsequent governments based their strength.

Social reforms

Post-1952 regimes. The most important leader of the MNR, Víctor Paz Estenssoro, was president of Bolivia in 1952–56 and instituted the most revolutionary part of the party's program. In 1956 he was replaced by the more conservative Hernando Siles Zuazo, whose primary concern was to stop an inflation that had followed the 1952 revolution. That inflation had in many ways completed the revolutionary process by virtually destroying the older middle class supporters of the MNR. With massive financial support from the United States, the inflation was stopped; but most of the advanced social programs of the revolution were suspended as well. The government ended worker co-administration of the nationalized mine companies and cut back on expanded social services and other such measures. It also invited U.S. petroleum companies back into Bolivia for the first time since 1937, when Standard Oil of Bolivia had been confiscated by the Toro government.

The return of Paz Estenssoro to the presidency in 1960 did not bring a new movement toward social reform. Rather, the consolidation achieved by Siles Zuazo was further developed, with the power of the army being revived under U.S. support. The attempt of Paz Estenssoro to renew his presidential term for another four years, in 1964, led to the splintering and temporary destruction of the MNR and to the overthrow of his government by the military.

With the support of many conservative elements and the peasant masses, the vice president, Gen. René Barrientos, seized the government and proceeded to dissolve most of the organized labour opposition. From 1964 until his death in 1969, Barrientos continued with the process of conservative economic reform and political retrenchment, with a deliberate attempt to demobilize all popular groups except the peasants, who had risen to some power as a result of the National Revolution. It was during Barrientos' period in office that a poorly organized antigovernment campaign, led by the Argentinian-born revolutionary Ernesto (Che) Guevara, was destroyed in 1967, largely because of its failure to mobilize the peasants.

The Barrientos regime

The death of Barrientos brought the vice president, Luis Adolfo Siles Salinas, into office; he was forcibly replaced in mid-1969 by Gen. Alfredo Ovando Candía, who in turn was forced out of office, after he had nationalized Gulf Oil Company holdings, by the more radical Gen. Juan José Torres in October 1970. Of the several military regimes that governed between 1964 and 1979, that led by Torres was the most radical; for a time the Torres government replaced Congress with a workers' soviet. In 1971, Torres was replaced by Col. Hugo Banzer Suárez, and the most repressive regime of the period came to power. During the next seven years, the labour movement was suppressed, the mines were occupied by troops, all civil rights were suspended, and the peasant syndicates were prohibited. Nevertheless, this was also an era of unprecedented growth in the Bolivian economy, fuelled by the sudden increase in world mineral prices and the completion of some of the basic changes in the social and economic infrastructure begun with the Revolution of 1952. These long-term economic changes involved the relative decline of the importance of tin and the emergence of commercial agricultural exports for the first time in republican history. It was also a period of extraordinarily rapid increase in the national population, which between 1950 and 1976 achieved an annual net growth rate of 2.1 percent. Finally, the Banzer regime was unique in contemporary Bolivian affairs because it provided the new commercial agricultural interests of the Santa Cruz region with national representation.

In 1978, the old MNR re-emerged and a complex set of

new political parties and movements developed. In the national elections of 1978 and 1979, these new groups gained wide support and the electorate showed an even balance between conservative and radical positions. Moreover, peasants for the first time no longer voted in block, but were as equally divided as the urban populace.

These democratic changes were fragile, however. The results of the elections of July 9, 1978, were voided in the wake of charges of mismanagement and fraud. Banzer Suárez resigned on July 21 under threat of a coup led by Gen. Juan Pereda Asbún, the government's presidential candidate in the voided elections. Pereda Asbún was overthrown in November and was replaced by a three-man military junta. An attempt was made to return to constitutional democracy with the elections of July 1, 1979. None of the three presidential candidates—Paz Estenssoro, Siles Zuazo, or Banzer Suárez—gained a majority, however. Walter Guevara Arze, then president-elect of the Senate, was chosen as interim president until elections could be held in 1980. He was deposed on November 1 by Col. Alberto Natusch Busch, who held power until November 16, when Lydia Gueiler Tejada was chosen by military, political, and union leaders to serve for one year as Bolivia's first woman president.

BIBLIOGRAPHY. The standard work on the independence wars in Bolivia is C.W. ARNADE, *The Emergence of the Republic of Bolivia* (1957); for the history of the 19th and 20th centuries, see H.S. KLEIN, *Parties and Political Change in Bolivia, 1880–1952* (1969); and for the developments of the 1952 revolution, the latest and most complete work is J.W. MALLOY, *Bolivia: The Uncompleted Revolution* (1970). All three works have extensive bibliographies in all relevant languages. For a broad survey of the economic, social, and political condition of Bolivia in the last two decades, see J.W. MALLOY and R. THORNE (eds.), *Bolivia Since the Revolution* (1971).

(H.S.K.)

Bombay

Bombay, the capital of Mahārāshtra state, India, is the country's financial and commercial centre and the principal port on the Arabian Sea. It is the seventh largest city in the world, with an estimated population in 1978 of more than 7,000,000. It is also one of the most densely populated cities, its inhabitants crowded within an area of 233 square miles (603 square kilometres). Located on a site of ancient settlement, the city took its name from the local goddess Mumba—a form of Pārvatī, the consort of Śiva (Shiva), one of the principal gods of Hinduism—whose temple stood in the southeast of contemporary Bombay.

Long the centre of India's cotton-textile industry, its manufactures are now well diversified and its commercial and financial institutions strong and vigorous. Bombay suffers, however, from the chronic ills of most large, expanding industrial cities—air and water pollution, slums, and overcrowding. Confined by its island location, Bombay seems ready to burst at its seams. A regional planning board, the City Industrial Development Corporation (CIDCO), is developing a new urban centre or "twin city" on the mainland opposite Bombay, taking advantage of the Thāna Creek Bridge built in the early 1970s, to relieve congestion in Bombay. With an area of 140 square miles (350 square kilometres) including Panvel, and stretching down to Uran, almost opposite Bombay's Gateway of India, the twin city to be completed by 1991 will be an autonomous economic and cultural urban centre, with a population of 2,000,000 and its own industries, schools, university, airport, and rapid transit system. A second bridge linking the twin city at Uran to Bombay across the creek is planned. Simultaneously, a second port at Nava-Sheva is being built. CIDCO is also planning to convert 450 square miles of marshland in the Bāndra-Kurla area into a business-cum-downtown complex, relieving congestion in South Bombay.

History. The Kolis, an aboriginal tribe of fishermen, were the earliest known inhabitants, though Paleolithic stone implements found at Kandivli, in Greater Bombay, indicate human occupation during the Stone Age. Known as Heptanesia to the ancient Greek astronomer and geographer Ptolemy, the area was a centre of maritime trade with Persia and Egypt in 1000 BC. It was part of Aśoka's empire in the 3rd century BC and was ruled in the 6th to 8th centuries AD by the Cālukyas, who left their mark on Elephanta Island (Ghārāpuri). The Walkeswar temple at Malabar Point was probably built during the rule of Śilāhāra chiefs from the Konkan Coast (9th–13th centuries). Under the Yadāvas of Devagiri (1187–1312) the settlement of Mahikavati (Māhīm) on Bombay Island was founded in response to raids by the Khālji dynasty of Hindustān in 1294. Descendants of these settlers are found in contemporary Bombay, and most of the place-names on the island date from this era. In 1348 Bombay was conquered by invading Muslim forces and became part of the kingdom of Gujarāt.

In 1507 a Portuguese attempt to conquer Māhīm failed. Twenty-seven years later, Sultan Bahādur Shāh, the ruler of Gujarāt, ceded the islands to the Portuguese who divided them into manors and fiefs and gave them to individuals or religious orders in return for military service or rent.

The British period

The British and Dutch partially sacked the islands and burned portions of the city in 1626, though they failed to establish control. In 1661 the island was ceded to Britain under the terms of the marriage treaty between the English king Charles II and Catherine of Braganza, sister of the King of Portugal; it was not until 1664 that formal possession was taken in the name of the British crown. In 1668 the crown ceded Bombay to the British East India Company, and the company headquarters were shifted to the island four years later. The company settled problems of land revenue, established law courts, strengthened defenses, and secured the freedom of trade and worship to all. The population increased to 50,000, and the modern city was founded.

The city grew steadily during the 18th century, and services and communications to mainland India and Europe were extended. In 1857 the first spinning-and-weaving mill was established, and by 1860 Bombay had become the great cotton market of western and central India. The United States Civil War from 1861 to 1865 and its resultant cutoff of cotton supplies to Britain caused a great trade boom in which financial empires sprouted. When the commercial delirium was at its height, the Civil War ended; the price of cotton fell, and the bubble burst. The city's commercial stability suffered no lasting damage, however, and much construction was carried out in the late 1800s.

Authenticated News

Downtown Bombay, with the Municipal Corporation of Greater Bombay at left.

	Major streets
	Other streets
	Railroads
	Old City (Fort)
■	Points of interest
	Parks

0   ¼   ½ mi
0   ¼   ½   ¾ km

Arabian Sea

PAREL

LOVEGROVE RD.
HAINES RD.
DELISLE RD.
ARTHUR RD.
KALACHOWKI RD.
PAREL TANK RD.

Vallabhbhai Patel Stadium
Mahalakshmi Race Track
Hājī 'Alī Tomb
Mahālakshmī Temple

HAJI 'ALI PARK

JACOB CIRCLE

Cotton Green Station
COTTON GREEN
HAJI BUNDER RD.

SUPARI BAUG RD.
REAY RD.
VICTORIA GARDENS
Victoria and Albert Museum
ZOO

Bunders

CLERK RD.
Willingdon Sports Club
GOLF COURSE
Railway
Western
DR. ANANDRAO NAIR RD.
RIPON RD.
Textile Mill
BYCULLA
GARDENS RD.
PARK RD.

Parsi Hospital
GARDENS
Cumballa Hill
PEDDER RD.
TARDEO RD.
Central Station
BELLASIS RD.
FALKLAND RD.
GRANT RD.
DUNCAN RD.

Grant Medical College
J. J. Hospital
MAZAGAON
Naoroji Hill
Wadi Bunder Goods Yard

VICTORIA RD.
MAZAGAON RD.

Bombay Harbour

TARDEO

Parsi Sanitorium
Towers of Silence
PHEROZSHAH META GARDENS (HANGING GARDENS)
KAMALA NEHRU PARK
NEPEAN SEA RD.
RIDGE RD.
WALKESHWAR RD.
Malabar Hill

GIRGAUM
SARDAR PATEL (SANDHURST) RD.
CHOWPATI
THAKURDWAR RD.
BHULESWAR
Mumbadevi Temple
DADABHAI NAOROJI (HORNBY) RD.
Bhendi Bazaar
Zakarīya Mosque
Crawford Market
CARNAC RD.
KALBA DEVI RD.
St. George Hospital
FRERE RD.
Central Railway

Prince's Dock
Victoria Dock
Cross Island

Walkeswar Temple
Jain Temple
Aquarium
MARINE DRIVE
QUEENS RD.
SPORTS CLUBS
All-India Radio
Municipal Corporation of Greater Bombay
Victoria Terminus
AZAD MAIDAN
St. George Hospital

Back Bay

Government House
Malabar Point
LLOYD RECREATION AREA
Churchgate Station
CROSS MAIDAN
General Post Office
FORT
Customs House
Alexandra Dock
Ferry

Brabourne Stadium
Cricket Club of India
University of Bombay
Old Secretariat
HORNIMAN CIRCLE
Mint
Ft. George
Flora Fountain

6
8
5
7
3 4
2

Nirmal Bldg.
Sachivalaya
Life Insurance Corporation of India
Council Hall
1 Gateway of India
Taj Mahal Hotel
Government Dockyard

Tata Institute of Fundamental Research
Afghan (St. John's) Church

COLĀBA
COLABA RD.
COLABA CAUSEWAY

Oyster Rock

Observatory
Lighthouse
Colāba Point

1	Brabha Atomic Research Centre
2	Institute of Science
3	Jehangir Art Gallery
4	Prince of Wales Museum of Western India
5	Reserve Bank of India
6	State Bank of India
7	Stock Exchange
8	Town Hall

	Major roads
	Other roads
	Railroads
	City limits
	Ferries
■	Points of interest
	Swamps
	Salt flats
	Greenbelts
	Built-up areas

0   2½   5 mi
0   2½   5   7½ km

Kandivli
MALAD
Kanheri Caves
PAHADI
Tulsi Lake
Vehār Lake
Thana
Kalwa
Salsette Island
MULAND
ANDHERI
Juhu Beach
Indian Institute of Technology
Powai Lake
Santa Cruz Internat. Airport
327 m
SANTA CRUZ
BĀNDRA
KURLA
GHATKOPAR
Pisarve
Arabian Sea
Māhīm Bay
SION
MĀHIM
Mithi R.
Mahul R.
303 m
Taloje
Kāgadī Creek
Belapurpāda
SEWRI
Haffkine Institute
MAHUL
Panvel
Panvel Creek
Elephanta Island
Bombay
Butcher Island
Sheva
Mora
Uran
Bombay Harbour
Back Bay
Colāba Point
Phuturnkhal Creek
538 m

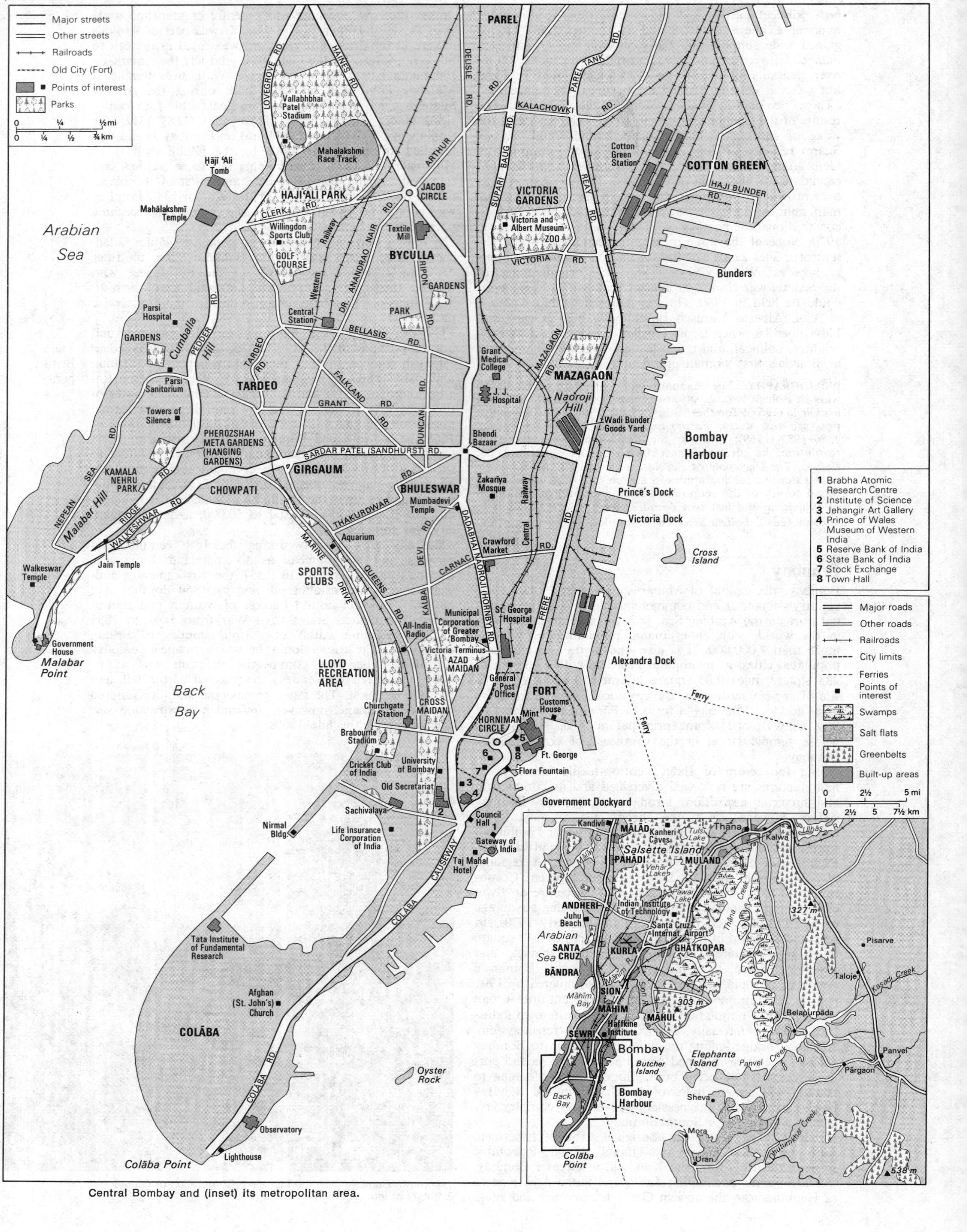

Central Bombay and (inset) its metropolitan area.

Urban expansion

With the opening of the Suez Canal in 1869, Bombay prospered, and its population, slums, and insanitary conditions steadily multiplied. Plague broke out in 1896, and a City Improvement Trust was set up to open new localities and erect dwellings for the artisan classes. An ambitious scheme for the construction of a seawall to enclose an area of 1,300 acres was proposed in 1918 but not completed until the completion of Marine Drive from Colāba Point to Malabar Point—the first two-way highway of its kind in India—after World War II. In the postwar years the development of residential quarters in suburban areas was begun, and the administration of Bombay city through a municipal corporation was extended to the suburbs of Greater Bombay. The former capital of Bombay Presidency and Bombay state, it was made the capital of Mahārāshtra state in 1960.

The contemporary city. *The city site.* Bombay occupies a group of isles lying off the Konkan Coast that are united by causeways and breakwaters. Known as Bombay Island, the site is joined on the north with the larger island of Salsette, which is connected with the mainland to the east.

Trapezoid-shaped Bombay Island consists of a low-lying plain, one-fourth of which lies below sea level; the plain is flanked on the east and west by two parallel ridges of low hills. Colāba Point, the headland formed on the extreme south by the longer of these ridges, protects Bombay Harbour on its eastern side from the open sea. The western ridge terminates at Malabar Hill, 180 feet (55 metres) above sea level and the highest point in Bombay. Between the two ridges lies the shallow expanse of Back Bay. On a slightly raised strip of land between the head of Back Bay and the harbour is the Fort, the original nucleus around which the city grew; it is now chiefly occupied by public and commercial offices. From Back Bay, land slopes westward to the central plain. To the north and east, reclamation schemes have shut out the sea and partly redeemed the foreshore for commerce. The extreme north of the island is occupied by a large salt marsh.

The old city covered about 26 square miles from Colāba in the south to Māhīm and Sion in the north. In 1950 Bombay expanded northward with the inclusion of Salsette Island, and by 1957 a number of suburban municipal boroughs—including Bāndra, Kurla, Andheri, Juhu, Ghātkopar, Mālād, and Muland—and some villages of Thāna were incorporated into Greater Bombay, with an area of 169 square miles (434 square kilometres). The metropolitan area has continued to expand and by 1971 had an area of 239 square miles. By the early 1970s, a bridge across Thāna Creek, linking the island with the mainland, had been built, and it was planned to build a "twin city" on the mainland to relieve congestion on the island.

The environment. The natural beauty of Bombay is unsurpassed by that of any city in the region. The entrance into Bombay Harbour from the sea discloses a magnificent panorama framed by the mountains of the Western Ghāts on the mainland. The wide harbour, studded with islands and dotted with the white sails of innumerable native craft, affords secure shelter to ships, particularly when storms lash the coast.

Bombay Harbour

The climate of Bombay is hot and humid. There are roughly four seasons. Cold weather prevails in December and January, and hot weather from March to May. The rainy season, brought by the southwest monsoon winds, lasts from June to September, and the post-monsoon season, when the weather is again hot, lasts through October and November. Mean monthly temperatures vary from 91° F (33° C) in May to 67° F (19° C) in January. Annual rainfall is 71 inches, with an average of 24 inches falling in July alone.

Typical trees include coconut palms, mango trees, and tamarinds, as well as banyan trees. In the past Salsette Island was the haunt of wild animals, including tigers, leopards, jackals, and deer, but these are now extinct. Animal life now consists of cows, oxen, sheep, goats, and other domestic species. Birdlife includes vultures, pigeons, cranes, and ducks.

The older part of the city is much built up, but more affluent areas, such as Malabar Hill, contain some greenery; there are also a few open playgrounds and parks. Burgeoning urbanization has created slums in sections of the city. An alarming rate of air and water pollution has been caused by the smokestacks of the many factories still crowding the city, the growing volume of auto traffic, and the nearby oil refineries.

The financial district is located in the south of the city (around the old Ft. Bombay). Further south (around Colāba) and to the west along Marine Drive and on Malabar Hill are residential areas. To the north of the Fort area is the principal business district, which gradually merges into a commercial–residential area. Most of the older factories are in this area. Still further north are residential areas, and beyond them are the new industrial areas as well as some shantytown districts.

Transport and communications. Bombay is connected by road to the north, east, and south of India. The city itself has a good system of paved roads, and expressways run along the island connecting it to the mainland on the north at Thāna. Bombay is the railhead for the Western and Central railway systems, and trains run from it to all parts of India. The Santa Cruz International Airport on Salsette Island offers extensive domestic services; it is an important point of entry served by many foreign airlines. The city is also India's major western port. Although the ports at Kandla to the north and Goa and Cochin to the south have grown, most of India's international trade still moves through Bombay.

Inside Bombay, the city is literally bursting at its seams. The main public-transportation facility consists of two suburban electric-train systems owned and run by the Western and Central railways (part of the government-owned Indian Railways system), which daily bring in hundreds of thousands of commuters. There is also a municipally owned and run bus fleet and a dwindling number of trams (trolley cars). The growing number of private automobiles and taxis choke the city's streets and create traffic jams during rush hours.

Satellite communications

Bombay is the main international communications outlet. It is linked to the satellite communications system through a ground station at Arvi, near Pune (Poona), to the southeast and through underground cables from Pune to the national headquarters of the Overseas Communications Service. Bombay is also served by domestic and international telex and radio-telephone facilities.

The population. Bombay's growth since the 1940s has been steady if not phenomenal. At the turn of the 20th century, its population was 85,000; by 1941 it had doubled to 1,695,000, and in 1961 it had grown to 4,152,000. The 1971 census showed a decennial growth rate of 43.75, compared to the all-India average of 24.66. The city's birth rate is much lower than that of the nation because of family-planning schemes, and the higher growth rate is entirely attributable to the influx of people in search of employment.

The city has one of the highest population densities in the world, with an average of 35,317 persons per square mile in Greater Bombay. In the older parts of the city, the density is about 116,000 persons per square mile, or 181 persons per acre; there are 1,800 to 2,000 persons per acre (4,400 to 4,900 persons per hectare) in areas such as Girgaum, Bhendi Bazaar, and Bhuleswar.

The city is truly cosmopolitan and has representatives of almost every religion and region of the world. Almost half of the population is Hindu; there are also important communities of Muslims, Christians, Buddhists, Jains, Sikhs, Zoroastrians, and Jews.

Almost every Indian language and many foreign languages are spoken. Marathi is the dominant Indian language, followed by Gujarati and Hindi. Others include Bengali; Afghan, Kabuli, and Pashto; Arabic; Chinese; English; Goanese; Kacchi; Kanarese; Konkani; Marwari; Nepali; Oriya; Parsi; Punjabi; Rajasthani; Sindhi; Tamil; Telugu; Tulu; and Urdu.

Housing. Housing is crowded and scarce and is largely comprised of privately owned apartment buildings. Public housing has been built by the government either directly or through the municipality and by private co-operatives with public funds. Workers' housing is also financed by employers and the government. The city is so overcrowded that town planners want to stop the further influx of population by prohibiting the addition of industrial and commercial establishments in the city, by creating a twin city across the bay, and even by forcibly removing some of the establishments and their employees.

Bombay's architecture is a mixture of florid Gothic styles, characteristic of the 18th and 19th centuries, and contemporary designs. The older administrative and commercial buildings are intermingled with skyscrapers and four- or five-story concrete block buildings.

The economy. Bombay is the economic hub and commercial and financial centre of India. Its economic composition in some respects demonstrates India's peculiar acceptance of the nuclear and cow-dung ages. The city contains the Indian Atomic Energy Commission's establishment, including nuclear reactors and plutonium separators, while in many areas primitive sources of fuel and energy are still in use.

Manufacturing. The cotton textile industry, on which the city's 19th-century prosperity was founded, is still of importance. Other establishments are concerned with general engineering, printing, and the production of automobiles, chemicals and paints, fertilizers, food products, silk and artificial fibres, oils and soaps, metals, and plastics. In 1968 there were about 4,500 factories that employed about 540,000 workers.

Commerce. Bombay houses the headquarters of the Reserve Bank of India and the nation's leading banking institution, the State Bank of India. The offices of the Life Insurance Corporation of India, the Bombay Mint, Air India (in the Nirmal Building) and a number of private commercial houses are also located in the city.

The Bombay Stock Exchange

The Bombay Stock Exchange is the country's leading stock and share market and is considered the financial barometer of the country. It occupied a pivotal position before and just after independence in 1947, but its importance has been reduced with the growing diversification of India's economic life, the spread of industries and entrepreneurs around the country, and the national government's economic policies, which give the state a primary role.

Administration and social conditions. *Government.* As the capital of Mahārāshtra state, the city is an integral political division of the state government, the headquarters of which are called the Sachivalaya. The state administers the police force and has administrative control over certain of the city's departmental institutions. The central government controls communications such as the post-and-telegraph system, the railways, the port, and the airport. Bombay is also the headquarters of India's western fleet and the base for the Indian flagship.

The Municipal Corporation

The government of the city is vested in the fully autonomous Municipal Corporation of Greater Bombay. Its legislative body has 131 members elected on adult franchise once every four years and functions through its various standing committees. The chief executive, who is appointed every three years by the state government, is the municipal commissioner. The mayor is annually elected by the corporation; he presides over its meetings and enjoys the highest honour in the city, though he has no real power.

Services. The manifold functions of the corporation include the provision or maintenance of medical relief, education, water supply, fire services, markets, gardens, and engineering projects such as drainage development and the improvement of roads and street lighting.

The municipal corporation operates the bus transport system inside the city and the supply of electricity as public utilities. Electric energy is obtained from a grid system supplied by state, government, and privately owned agencies and is then distributed throughout the city. The water supply, also maintained by the municipality, comes from Tulsī and Vehār lakes on Salsette Island. Pawai Lake, originally harnessed for water supply, has proved unsatisfactory because its water is not potable.

Health services

The city has more than 100 hospitals, including those run by the federal, state, or corporation governments and those that are privately run with the aid of state funds. There are also several private clinics and nursing homes, and the state operates an Ayurvedic (an indigenous system of medicine) hospital. A number of institutions specialize in the treatment of tuberculosis and cancer, and the maternity clinics and child-welfare centres run by the state and the corporation are combined with family-planning centres. Bombay is also the site of the Haffkine Institute, a bacteriological-research centre specializing in tropical diseases.

The state-run police force, more than 18,000 strong, is headed by the commissioner of police, who is responsible for the maintenance of law and order in Greater Bombay. He exercises powers and performs functions in matters such as strength, recruitment, promotion, uniforms, and arms. He is assisted by a number of deputy commissioners of police and other officers.

Education. Bombay has a high literacy rate of 64 percent, compared to the national rate of 29 percent. Primary education is free and compulsory; it is the responsibility of the municipal corporation. Secondary education is provided by public and private schools supervised by the state government. There are also public and private polytechnic institutes and institutions offering diploma courses in mechanical and chemical engineering. The central government's Indian Institute of Technology is also located in the city. The University of Bombay, established in 1857, has 70 affiliated colleges and 16 postgraduate departments and in 1970 had almost 96,000 students. Nine colleges in Goa are also affiliated to the university.

Cultural life. Bombay's cultural life reflects its polyglot population. The city has a number of museums, libraries, literary and other cultural institutions, art galleries, and theatres. Perhaps no other city in India can boast of such a high degree of cultural and entertainment facilities. Bombay is the stronghold of the Indian cinema industry and has several open-air theatres. Throughout the year Western and Indian music concerts and festivals and Indian dance shows are performed. The Prince of Wales Museum of Western India, housed in a building of Indo-Saracenic architecture, contains three main sections of art, archaeology, and natural history. Nearby is the Jehangir Art Gallery, Bombay's first permanent art gallery and centre of cultural and educational activities.

Publishing and broadcasting

Bombay is an important centre for the Indian printing industry and has a vigorous press. The city boasts of five morning and two afternoon English dailies and two Hindi, five Gujarati, ten Marathi, one Sindhi, and nine Urdu dailies. There are also several biweeklies and weeklies. The regional stations of All-India Radio are centred in Bombay, and television services for the city were provided in 1972.

Borivli National Park, in the north of Greater Bombay, is a pleasant holiday resort located near the Kanheri Caves, site of an ancient Buddhist university; the more than 100 caves contain gigantic Buddhist sculptures dating from the 2nd to 9th centuries AD. There are several public gardens including the Victoria Gardens, which house Bombay's zoo in the city proper, the Baptista Garden located on a water reservoir in Mazagaon, and the Hanging Gardens, the Kamala Nehru Park, and the Sloping Park—all on Malabar Hill.

Brabourne Stadium has a seating capacity of 35,000 and is the scene of cricket, football (soccer), and hockey matches. Athletic and cycling track events are held at the Vallabhbhai Patel Stadium. Juhu Beach is the most fashionable area for bathing and swimming.

BIBLIOGRAPHY. *The Imperial Gazetteer of India*, vol. 8 (1908); and STEPHEN MEREDYTH EDWARDES, *The Gazetteer of Bombay City and Island*, 3 vol. (1909–10), provide a wealth of detail on Bombay's history up to British times. The *Maharashtra State Gazetteer*, pt. 1–3, published by the Mahārāshtra State Government (1960–68) and its companion volume for Bombay district bring the city's history up to date and give a contemporary, rather than an imperial, view of the city. B.K. BOMAN-BEHRAM, *The Decline of Bombay* (1969); and JAL BULSARA, *Patterns of Social Life in Metropolitan*

Areas, with Particular Reference to Greater Bombay (1970), include perspectives on current urban problems. See also the Mahārāshtra Government Administration reports for various departments.

(C.Ra.)

Bonaventure, Saint

St. Bonaventure, Christian theologian, minister general of the Franciscan Order, and cardinal bishop of Albano, was renowned in his own day as a master of the spiritual life. He is now proclaimed a doctor of the Roman Catholic Church with the special title Seraphic Doctor, denoting the sublimity of his wisdom. For restoring the Franciscans to their original ideal of evangelical perfection, he is honoured as the second founder of their order.

St. Bonaventure, detail of a fresco by Benozzo Gozzoli (1420–1497). In the Church of S. Francesco, Montefalco, Italy.
Alinari

Education and academic career

Named John, he was born about 1217 at Bagnoregio (near Viterbo, Italy), a son of John of Fidanza, a physician, and Maria of Ritella. He fell ill while a boy and, according to his own words, was saved from death by the intercession of St. Francis of Assisi. Entering the University of Paris in 1235, he received the master of arts degree in 1243 and then joined the Franciscan Order, which named him Bonaventure in 1244. He studied theology in the Franciscan school at Paris from 1243 to 1248. His masters, especially Alexander of Hales, recognized in him a student with a keen memory and unusual intelligence; pursuing his studies with a lofty devotion, he reflected with a growing love on every truth he perceived. He was also under the tutelege of John of La Rochelle. After their deaths (1245) he studied further under Eudes Rigauld and William of Meliton. He was later probably influenced by the Dominican Guerric of Saint-Quentin.

By turning the pursuit of truth into a form of divine worship, he integrated his study of theology with the Franciscan mode of the mendicant life. In 1248, he began to teach the Bible; from 1251 to 1253 he lectured on the *Sentences*, a medieval theology textbook by Peter Lombard, an Italian theologian of the 12th century, and became a master of theology in 1254, when he assumed control of the Franciscan school in Paris. He taught there until 1257, producing many works, notably commentaries on the Bible and the *Sentences* and the *Breviloquium* (Summary), which presented a summary of his theology. These works showed his deep understanding of Scripture, the Fathers of the early church, principally St. Augustine, the great Western theologian, and a wide knowledge of the philosophers, particularly Aristotle.

Bonaventure was particularly noted in his day as a man with the rare ability to reconcile diverse traditions in theology and philosophy. He united different doctrines in a synthesis containing his personal conception of truth as a road to the love of God. In 1256, he defended the Franciscan ideal of the Christian life against William of Saint-Amour, a university teacher who accused the mendicants—friars who wandered about and begged for a living—of defaming the Gospel by their practice of poverty and who wanted to prevent the Franciscans and their fellow mendicants, the Dominicans, from attaining teaching positions. Bonaventure's defense of the Franciscans and his personal probity as a member of his religious order led to his election as minister general of the Franciscans on February 2, 1257.

Career as a monastic leader

Founded by St. Francis according to strict views about poverty, the Franciscan Order was at that time undergoing internal discord. One group, the Spirituals, disrupted the order by a rigorous view of poverty; another, the Relaxati, disturbed it by a laxity of life. Bonaventure used his authority so prudently that, placating the first group and reproving the second, he preserved the unity of the order and reformed it in the spirit of St. Francis. The work of restoration and reconciliation owed its success to Bonaventure's tireless visits, despite delicate health, to each province of the order and to his own personal realization of the Franciscan ideal. In his travels, he preached the Gospel constantly and so elegantly that he was recognized everywhere as a most eloquent preacher. As a theologian, he based the revival of the order on his conception of the spiritual life, which he expounded in mystical treatises manifesting his Franciscan experience of contemplation as a perfection of the Christian life. His *Journey of the Mind to God* (1259) was a masterpiece showing the way by which man as a creature ought to love and contemplate God through Christ after the example of St. Francis. Revered by his order, Bonaventure recodified its constitutions (1260), wrote for it a new *Life of St. Francis of Assisi* (1263), and protected it (1269) from an assault by Gerard of Abbeville, a teacher of theology at Paris, who renewed the charge of William of Saint-Amour. He also protected the church during the period 1267–73 by upholding the truth of Christian faith while denouncing the errors of unorthodox masters at Paris who contradicted revelation in their philosophy.

Bonaventure's wisdom and ability to reconcile opposing views moved Pope Gregory X to name him cardinal bishop of Albano, Italy, in May 1273, though Bonaventure earlier had declined to accept appointment to the see of York, England, from Pope Clement IV in 1265. Gregory consecrated him in November at Lyons, where he resigned as minister general in May 1274. At the second Council of Lyons he was the leading figure in the reform of the church, reconciling the secular (parish) clergy with the mendicant orders. He also had a part in restoring the Greek Church to union with Rome. He died at the council on July 15, 1274. His death was viewed as the loss of a wise and holy man, full of compassion and virtue, captivating with love all who knew him. He was buried the same day in a Franciscan church with the Pope in attendance. The respect and love that was held for Bonaventure is exemplified in the formal announcement of the council: "At the funeral there was much sorrow and tears; for the Lord has given him this grace, that all who saw him were filled with an immense love for him." His exemplary life as a Franciscan and the continual influence of his doctrine on the life and devotion of the Western Church won for him a declaration of sanctity by Pope Sixtus IV on April 14, 1482, and the designation Doctor of the Church by Sixtus V on March 14, 1587. Thereafter, St. Bonaventure was regarded as a truly great theologian, a Franciscan of fervent devotion, and a prominent leader of his time.

Modern scholars consider him to have been one of the foremost men of his age, an intrepid defender of human and divine truth, and an outstanding exponent of a mystical and Christian wisdom.

BIBLIOGRAPHY. The critical edition of Bonaventure's works is *Opera omnia*, 10 vol. (Quaracchi; 1882–1902). Translations of his works by JOSE DE VINCK are "The Journey of the Mind to God," in vol. 1 of *The Works of Bonaventure* (1960); and vol. 2, *Breviloquium* (1963). Studies of his doctrine and life (with bibliographies) are J.G. BOUGEROL, *Introduction à l'étude de Saint Bonaventure* (1961; Eng. trans., 1964); and I.C. BRADY, "Bonaventure, St.," in *New Catholic Encyclopedia*, vol. 2, pp. 658–664 (1967).

(J.F.Q.)

Bone

Bone is a rigid body tissue consisting of cells embedded in an abundant, hard intercellular material. The two principal components of this material, collagen and calcium phosphate, distinguish bone from such other hard tissues as chitin, enamel, and shell.

The functions of bone include (1) structural support for the mechanical action of soft tissues, such as contraction of muscles, expansion of lungs; (2) protection of soft parts, as by the brain case; (3) provision of a protective site for specialized tissues such as the blood-forming system (bone marrow); and (4) a mineral reservoir or sink, whereby endocrine systems regulate the level of calcium and phosphate in the circulating body fluids.

EVOLUTIONARY ORIGIN AND SIGNIFICANCE

Bone is found only in vertebrates, and, among modern vertebrates, only in bony fish and higher classes. Although fossil ancestors of the elasmobranchs and cyclostomes had armoured headcases, serving largely a protective function, which appear to have been true bone, modern cyclostomes have only an endoskeleton, or inner skeleton, of noncalcified cartilage, and elasmobranchs, a skeleton of calcified cartilage. Although a rigid endoskeleton performs obvious body supportive functions for land-living vertebrates, it is doubtful that bone offered any such mechanical advantage to the teleost (bony fish) in which it first appeared, for in a supporting aquatic environment, great structural rigidity is not essential for maintaining body configuration. The sharks and rays are superb examples of mechanical engineering efficiency, and their perseverance from the Devonian attests to the suitability of their nonbony endoskeleton.

Bone and homeostasis

In modern vertebrates true bone is found only in animals also capable of controlling the osmotic and ionic composition of their internal fluid environment.

Marine invertebrates exhibit interstitial fluid compositions essentially the same as that of the surrounding sea water. Early signs of regulability are seen in cyclostomes and elasmobranchs, but only at or above the level of true-bone fishes does the composition of the internal body fluids become constant. The mechanisms involved in this regulation are many and complex and include both the kidney and the gills. Fresh and marine waters provide abundant calcium, but only traces of phosphate, and, because relatively high levels of phosphate are characteristic of the body fluids of higher vertebrates, it seems likely that a large, readily available internal phosphate reservoir would confer significant independence of external environment on bony vertebrates. With the emergence of terrestrial forms, the availability of calcium regulation became equally significant. Along with the kidney and the various component glands of the endocrine system, bone has contributed to development of internal fluid homeostasis—the maintenance of an equilibrium with respect to its chemical composition. This was a necessary step for emergence of land-living vertebrates. Moreover, out of the buoyancy of water, structural rigidity of bone afforded the characteristic mechanical advantages of the modern vertebrate skeleton.

THE STRUCTURE OF BONE

Chemical composition. Depending upon species, age, and type of bone, the bone cells represent 1–15 percent of the volume of bone, but in mature bone in most higher animals usually they represent 1–5 percent. The nonliving intercellular material consists of an organic component, collagen (a fibrous protein arranged in long strands or bundles similar in structure and organization to the collagen of ligaments, tendons, and skin), with small amounts of proteinpolysaccharides, mucopolysaccharides chemically bound to protein and dispersed within and around the collagen fibre bundles, and an inorganic mineral component in the form of innumerable rod-shaped crystals with diameters on the order of 50 Å and lengths from 200 to 2,000 Å. These crystals are arranged parallel with the long axes of collagen bundles and many actually lie in voids within the bundles themselves. Organic material comprises 50 percent of the volume and 30 percent of the dry weight of the intercellular composite, and mineral the remainder. The major minerals are calcium and phosphate, present in proportions ranging from 1.4:1 to 2.1:1. When first deposited, mineral is crystallographically amorphous but with maturation becomes typical of the apatite minerals, the major component being hydroxyapatite, $Ca_{10}(PO_4)_6(OH)_2$. Carbonate is also present, in amounts varying from 4 percent of bone ash in fish and 8 percent in most mammals to more than 13 percent in the turtle, and occurs in two distinct phases, calcium carbonate and a carbonate apatite. Except for that associated with its cellular elements, there is little free water in adult mammalian bone (approximately 8 percent of total volume). As a result, diffusion from surfaces into the interior of the intercellular substance occurs at the slow rates more typical of diffusion from surfaces of solids than within liquids.

Physical properties. The structural role of the skeleton depends on the hardness, strength, and rigidity of bone. The mineral crystals are responsible for hardness, rigidity, and the great compressive strength of bone, but they share with other crystalline materials a great weakness in tension, arising from the tendency for stress to concentrate about defects and for these defects to propagate. On the other hand, the collagen fibrils of bone possess high elasticity, little compressive strength, and considerable intrinsic tensile strength. The tensile strength of bone depends, however, not on collagen alone but on the intimate association of mineral with collagen, which confers on bone many of the general properties exhibited by two-phase materials such as fibre glass and bamboo. In such materials the dispersion of a rigid but brittle material in a matrix of quite different elasticity prevents the propagation of stress failure through the brittle material and hence allows a closer approach to the theoretical limiting strength of single crystals.

Hardness, rigidity, and compressive and tensile strength

The fine structure of bone has thus far frustrated attempts to determine the true strength of the mineral-matrix composite at the "unit" structural level. Compact bone specimens have been found to have tensile strength in the range of 10,000–20,000 pounds per square inch (psi), and compressive strengths in the range of 20,000–30,000 psi. These values are of the same general order as for aluminum or mild steel, but bone has an advantage over such materials in that it is considerably lighter. The great strength of bone exists principally along its long axis and hence roughly parallel both to the collagen fibre axis and to the long axis of the mineral crystals.

Elasticity of bone

Although apparently stiff, bones exhibit a considerable degree of elasticity, which is important to the skeleton's ability to withstand impact. Estimates of modulus of elasticity of bone samples are of the order of 6,000 to 10,000 psi, a value very much less than steel, for example, indicating much greater elasticity of bone. Perfect elasticity exists with loads up to 30 to 40 percent of breaking strength; above this, creep occurs, presumably along natural defects within the bony structure. The modulus of elasticity in bone is strikingly dependent upon the rate at which loads are applied, bones being stiffer during rapid deformation than during slow; this behaviour suggests an element of viscous flow during deformation.

As might be anticipated from consideration of the two-phase composition of bone, variation in the mineral-collagen ratio leads to change in physical properties: less mineral tends ultimately to greater flexibility, and more mineral to increased brittleness. Optimal ratios, as reflected in maximal tensile strength, are observed at an ash content of approximately 66 percent, a value that is characteristic of the weight-bearing bones of mammals.

Bone morphology. Grossly, bone tissue is organized into a variety of shapes and configurations adapted to the function of the bone concerned: broad, flat plates, such as scapula, as anchors for large muscle masses, or hollow, thick-walled tubes, such as femur, radius, ulna, for supporting weight or for use as a lever arm (see SKELETAL

SYSTEM, HUMAN). These different types of bone are distinguished more by their external shape than by their basic structure.

In all bones the basic bone has an exterior layer, termed cortex, that is smooth, dense, continuous, and of varying thickness. In its interior, bony tissue is arranged in a network of intersecting plates and spicules, varying in amount in different bones, enclosing spaces filled with blood vessels and marrow. This honeycombed bone is termed cancellous, and the plates and spicules trabeculae. In mature bone, trabeculae are arranged in an orderly pattern that provides continuous units of bony tissue aligned parallel with the lines of major compressive or tensile force. Trabeculae thus provide a complex series of cross-braced interior struts so arranged as to give maximal rigidity with minimal material.

Bones such as vertebrae, subject to primarily compressive or tensile forces, usually have thin cortices and provide necessary structural rigidity through trabeculae; whereas bones such as the femur, subject to prominent bending, shear, or torsional forces, usually have thick cortices, a tubular configuration, and a continuous cavity running through their centres (medullary cavity). The cortical material of tubular bones is termed compact bone and differs in a number of fine structural details from cancellous bone.

Long bones, distinctive of the body's extremities, exhibit a number of gross structural features in common. The central region of the bone (diaphysis) is the most clearly tubular. At one or commonly both ends the diaphysis flares outward and assumes a predominantly cancellous internal structure. This region (metaphysis) functions to transfer loads from weight-bearing joint surfaces to the diaphysis. Finally, at the end of a long bone is a region known as an epiphysis, which exhibits a cancellous internal structure and which comprises the bony substructure of the joint surface. Prior to full skeletal maturity the epiphysis is separated from the metaphysis by a cartilaginous plate, the growth plate or physis; in bones with complex articulations (such as the humerus at its lower end) or bones with multiple protuberances (such as the femur at its upper end) there may be several separate epiphyses, each with its growth plate.

Four types of cells in bone

Microscopically, bone consists of hard, apparently homogeneous intercellular material, within or upon which can be found four characteristic cell types: osteoblast, osteocyte, osteoclast, and undifferentiated bone mesenchymal cells. The osteoblast is responsible for the synthesis and deposition on bone surfaces of the protein matrix of new intercellular material. The osteocyte is an osteoblast that has been trapped within intercellular material, residing in a cavity (lacuna) and communicating with other osteocytes as well as with free bone surfaces by means of extensive filamentous protoplasmic extensions that occupy long, meandering channels (canaliculi) through the bone substance. With the exception of certain higher orders of modern fish, all bone, including primitive vertebrate fossil bone, exhibits an osteocytic structure. Osteoclasts are usually large, multinucleated cells that, working from bone surfaces, resorb bone by direct chemical and enzymatic attack. Undifferentiated mesenchymal cells of the bone reside in the loose connective tissue between trabeculae, along vascular channels, and in the condensed fibrous tissue covering the outside of the bone (periosteum); they give rise under appropriate stimuli to either osteoblasts or osteoclasts.

Depending on how the protein fibrils and osteocytes of bone are arranged, bone is of two major types: woven, in which collagen bundles and the long axes of the osteocytes are randomly oriented, and lamellar, in which both the fibrils and osteocytes are aligned in clear layers. In lamellar bone the layers alternate every few microns, and the primary direction of the fibrils shifts approximately 90°. In compact bone of many mammalian species lamellar bone is further organized into units known as osteons, or haversian systems, which consist of concentric cylindrical lamellar elements several millimetres long and 0.2–0.3 millimetre in diameter. Osteons exhibit a gently spiral course oriented along the axis of the bone. In their centre is a canal (haversian canal) containing one or more small blood vessels, and at their outer margins is a boundary layer known as a "cement line," which serves both as a means of fixation for new bone deposited on an old surface and as a diffusion barrier. Osteocytic processes do not penetrate the cement line, and hence these barriers constitute the outer envelope of a nutritional unit, osteocytes on opposite sides of a cement line deriving their nutrition from different vascular channels. Cement lines are found in all types of bone, as well as in osteons, and in general they indicate lines at which new bone was deposited on an old surface.

Vascular supply and circulation. In a typical long bone, blood is supplied by three separate systems: nutrient artery, periosteal vessels, and epiphyseal vessels. The diaphysis and metaphysis are nourished primarily by the nutrient artery, which passes through the cortex into the medullary cavity and then ramifies outward through haversian and Volkmann's canals to supply the cortex. Extensive vessels in the periosteum, the membrane surrounding the bone, supply the superficial layers of the cortex and connect with the nutrient-artery system. In the event of obstruction of the nutrient artery, periosteal vessels are capable of meeting the needs of both systems. The epiphyses are supplied by a separate system that consists of a ring of arteries entering the bone along a circular band between the growth plate and the joint capsule. In the adult these vessels become connected to the other two systems at the metaphyseal-epiphyseal junction, but while the growth plate is open there is no such connection, and the epiphyseal vessels are the sole source of nutrition for the growing cartilage; hence they are essential for skeletal growth.

Drainage of blood is by a system of veins that runs parallel with the arterial supply and by veins leaving the cortical periosteum through muscle insertions. Muscle contraction milks blood outward, giving rise to a centrifugal pattern of flow from the axial nutrient artery through the cortex and out through muscle attachments.

PHYSIOLOGY AND BIOCHEMISTRY OF BONE

Remodelling, growth, and development. *Bone resorption and renewal.* Whereas renewal in tissues such as muscle occurs largely at a molecular level, renewal of bone occurs at a tissue level and is similar to the remodelling of buildings in that local removal (resorption) of old bone must precede new bone deposition. Remodelling is most vigorous during the years of active growth, when deposition predominates over resorption. Thereafter remodelling gradually declines, in man until about age 35, after which its rate remains unchanged or increases slightly. From the fourth decade on resorption exceeds formation, resulting in a 5–10 percent loss in bone mass per decade, equivalent to a daily loss of 15–30 milligrams of calcium.

Except for the addition of the ossification mechanisms within cartilage, growth and development involve exactly the same type of remodelling as that in the adult skeleton. Both require continuous, probably irreversible differentiation of osteoclasts and osteoblasts from the undifferentiated bone mesenchyme. Life span of osteoclasts is from a few hours to at most a few days, that of osteoblasts a few days to at most a few weeks.

Bone resorption

Resorption is produced by clusters of osteoclasts that either erode free bone surfaces or form "cutting cones" that tunnel through compact bone and create the cylindrical cavities that may be subsequently filled by osteons. Osteoclastic cells secrete enzymes and hydrogen ions onto the bone surface, dissolving the mineral and digesting the matrix at virtually the same moment. The process is associated with locally augmented blood flow and with a greater surface acidity than elsewhere in bone, despite the fact that the process of dissolving apatite consumes hydrogen ions. Resorption is usually a much more rapid process than formation. Osteoclastic cutting cones have been observed to advance at rates up to 500 microns per day.

Bone formation

Bone is formed on previously resorbed surfaces by deposition of a protein matrix material (osteoid) and its subsequent mineralization. Osteoblasts elaborate matrix as a continuous membrane covering the surface on which they are working at a linear rate that varies with both age and species, but which in large adult mammals is on the order of 1.0 micron per day. The unmineralized matrix constitutes an osteoid seam or border, averaging 6 to 10 microns in thickness during active bone formation. The biochemical and physical sequence of events that prepare matrix for mineralization includes intracellular biosynthesis of collagen by osteoblasts, extrusion of collagen extracellularly in soluble form, maturation or polymerization of collagen into an array of fibrils (in random orientation in rapidly deposited bone, in a highly ordered, regular pattern in slowly formed lamellar bone), binding of calcium to collagen fibrils, and formation of protein-mucopolysaccharide complexes. Mineralization itself depends upon establishment of crystal nuclei within the matrix; this process requires five to ten days and is under the control of the osteoblast, but its exact chemistry is obscure. A suitable nucleating configuration is somehow established, and once nuclei reach a critical size further mineralization proceeds spontaneously in the presence of usual body fluid calcium and phosphorus concentrations. Other collagenous tissues, such as dermis, tendon, and ligament, do not normally calcify, even though bathed by the same body fluids as bone. Although extracellular fluid is a highly supersaturated solution with respect to hydroxylapatite, calcium and phosphorus will not spontaneously precipitate in this crystalline form at physiological pH, so that one and the same fluid is indefinitely stable in non-bone-forming regions, yet richly supports mineralization in the presence of suitable crystal nuclei. Mineral movement into new bone is initially rapid and in compact cortical bone is known to reach approximately 70 percent of full mineralization within a few hours after matrix nucleation. This mineral deposition involves replacement of the water that occupied half of the original matrix volume. As water content falls, further mineral diffusion is impeded; and the final mineralization occurs progressively more slowly over a period of many weeks. In normal adult man new bone formation takes up about 400 milligrams of calcium per day, an amount approximately equal to that in the circulating blood.

Osteocyte function

Osteocytes, once thought of as resting cells, are now recognized to be metabolically active and to possess, at least in latent form, the ability to resorb and reform bone on their lacunar walls. Although osteocytes constitute only a small fraction of total bone volume, they are so arranged within bone, and the network of their protoplasmic extensions is so extensive that there is essentially no volume of bony material situated more than a fraction of a micron from a cell or its processes. Of the more than 1,200 square metres of anatomic surface within the skeleton of an adult man, about 99 percent is accounted for by the lacunar and canalicular surfaces. Resorption and deposition on this surface serve both to regulate plasma-calcium concentration and to renew bony material. This renewal may be particularly important because all composite materials change in their physical properties with time. It is not known whether bone properties change sufficiently to have biologic consequence, but to the extent that such change does occur, renewal around osteocytes would provide for the physical maintenance of bone structural material.

Growth and development of bone

Types of bone formation. Bone is formed in the embryo in two general ways. For most bones the general shape is first laid down as a cartilage model, which is then progressively replaced by bone (endochondral bone formation). A few bones (such as clavicle and calvarium) develop within a condensed region of fibrous tissue without a cartilaginous intermediate (membrane bone formation). In long bones a collar of spongy membrane bone is first laid down in the fibrous tissues surrounding the cartilaginous model of the shaft. At the same time the cartilage deep to this collar begins to degenerate and calcify. The bone is then penetrated by blood vessels, which grow into the degenerating model and remove the calcified cartilage enclosed within the collar. Vascular invasion proceeds toward both ends of the model in parallel with continued extension of the bony collar. This leaves a structure consisting of two cartilaginous epiphyses at the ends of a hollow, bony shaft.

Growth from this point on is accomplished in two ways. Radial growth occurs by deposition of new bone on the periosteal surface and roughly equivalent resorption at the endosteal surface. Longitudinal growth involves replacement of cartilage by bone from the shaft side of the growth plate, at a rate closely matched to the production of new cartilage by the plate itself. The growth plate consists of highly ordered rows of cartilage cells; the row farthest removed from the bony shaft is a basal or germinal layer; it is responsible for cell replication and cartilage growth. The complex sequence of longitudinal growth consists of cartilage cell degeneration farthest from the germinal layer, calcification of cartilage in that area, deposition over it of a thin layer of true bone (primary spongiosa), and, finally, osteoclastic resorption to extend the medullary cavity in parallel with longitudinal growth and to reshape the contour of the shaft.

Cartilage growth, degeneration, calcification, and ultimate replacement by bone is responsible for most growth in length in vertebrates. It first begins in the embryo and continues until full skeletal maturity, when in most species the growth plates fuse and disappear.

From *Journal of Bone and Joint Surgery* (1952)

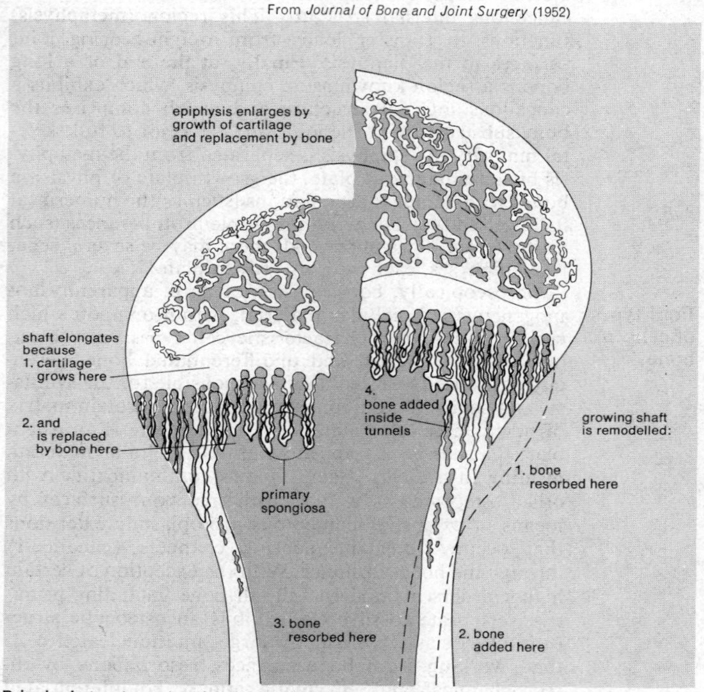

Principal structures involved in (left) growth and (right) remodelling of a typical long bone.

The appearance of epiphyseal ossification centres and their ultimate fusion, both of which can be detected by ordinary X-rays, normally follows an orderly and predictable sequence that is of great value in the evaluation of disorders of growth and development. Because of the complicated interaction of several tissue elements in the process of endochondral ossification, the metaphyseal region of bones is the seat of, or prominently reflects, many nutritional or metabolic disturbances of growth. Examples of disorders involving this growth mechanism include rickets and achondroplastic dwarfism (see BONE DISEASES AND INJURIES).

Physiology of bone. *Calcium and phosphate equilibrium.* As important as the structural properties of bone is the role bone plays in the maintenance of the ionic composition of the blood and interstitial fluids of the body. All vertebrates possessing true bone exhibit body-fluid calcium-ion concentrations of approximately 50 milligrams per litre (1.25 millimoles) and phosphorus concentrations in the range of 30–100 milligrams per litre (1–3 millimoles). These levels, particularly those of calcium, are extremely important for the maintenance of normal neuromuscular function, interneuronal transmission, cell membrane integrity and permeability, and blood coagulation. The rigid constancy with which calcium levels are maintained, both in the individual and throughout all the higher vertebrate classes, attests to the biological importance of such regulation. Approximately 99 percent of total body calcium and 85 percent of total body phosphorus reside in the mineral deposits of bone, and thus bone is quantitatively in a position to mediate adjustments in concentration of these two ions in the circulating body fluids. Such adjustments are provided by two hormonal control loops (control systems with feedbacks) and by at least two locally acting mechanisms. The hormonal loops involve parathyroid hormone (PTH) and calcitonin (CT) and are concerned exclusively with regulation of calcium-ion concentration.

Calcium and phosphate homeostasis

PTH acts to elevate the ionized calcium level in body fluids and CT (from the ultimobranchial body or C cells of the thyroid) to depress it, and the secretion of each hormone is sensitively controlled by the level of calcium ion in the circulating blood, PTH secretion being inversely related and CT secretion being directly related to calcium ion concentration. At normal calcium concentrations there is a low level of secretion of both hormones.

PTH acts on at least two nonbony effector organs (kidney and intestine) as well as on bone, whereas CT appears to act primarily on bone. The skeletal effects of these hormones are exerted predominantly on the resorptive process. PTH stimulates mesenchymal proliferation and osteoclast induction and accelerates the osteolytic activity of osteocytes. The principal long-term effect of the hormone is a considerable increase in the number of osteoclasts with correspondingly increased resorption. Vitamin D is required for the osseous effects of PTH, and in pharmacological quantities stimulates both osteocytic and osteoclastic resorption in the absence of PTH. Finally, PTH produces acute inhibition of osteoblast function, thus decreasing calcium deposition in new bone in periods of total body-calcium need.

With respect to action on organs other than bone, PTH enhances gastrointestinal absorption of calcium from the diet and, by increasing calcium reabsorption from the fluid within the renal (kidney) tubules, reduces renal excretory losses of calcium. The intestinal effect, like that on bone, requires vitamin D for its expression. Finally, PTH, by interfering with renal tubular phosphate reabsorption, also enhances the renal excretion of phosphate. This mechanism, which serves to lower the level of phosphates in the bloodstream, is significant because high phosphate levels inhibit and low levels enhance osteoclastic resorption. Thus phosphate concentration itself directly modulates the calcium-mediated effects of both parathyroid hormone and the many other agencies that influence bone resorption. Calcium ion itself has similar effects on the osteoclastic process, high levels inhibiting and low levels enhancing the effect of systemically acting agents such as PTH. These local effects constitute the only recognizable control of phosphate, but the PTH loop appears to be the more important regulatory process in calcium-ion homeostasis. At extremely low levels both calcium and phosphate become rate-limiting at the mineralization site as well, reducing both deposition of mineral and osteoblast function.

Calcitonin, acting to offset elevations in calcium ion level, works primarily to inhibit bone resorption, whether by osteoclasts or by osteocytes. It does not appear to have significant effects on tissues other than bone. Calcitonin differs further from PTH in its much more rapid action (minutes as opposed to hours) and in its short duration of action. Its primary function seems to be to offset acute elevations in plasma calcium during feeding.

Physiological and mechanical controls. In the language of control mechanics, remodelling depends upon two control loops with negative feedback: a homeostatic loop involving the effects of PTH and CT on resorption and a mechanical loop that brings about changes in skeletal mass and arrangement to meet changing structural needs. The PTH-CT loop is basically a systemic process, and the mechanical loop is local; the two loops do interact significantly at the level of the cells that act as intermediaries in both processes. A large number of other factors, including minerals in the diet, hormonal balance, disease, and aging, have important effects on the skeleton that interact with the control system.

The controls exerted by mechanical forces, recognized for over a century, have been formulated as Wolff's law: "Every change in the function of a bone is followed by certain definite changes in its internal architecture and its external conformation." Of the many theories proposed to explain how mechanical forces communicate with the cells responsible for bone formation and resorption, the most appealing has been postulation of induced local electrical fields that mediate this information exchange. Many crystalline or semicrystalline materials, including both bone collagen and its associated mineral, exhibit piezoelectric properties. Deformation of macroscopic units of bone by mechanical force produces a charge in the millivolt range and current flow on the order of 10^{-15} ampere; both voltage and current flow are proportional to the applied force. Regions under tension act as anode and compressed regions as cathode. Currents of this magnitude are capable of aligning collagen fibrils as they aggregate from the solution phase and are known also to alter the cell-based development of regeneration buds in amphibia. The negative-feedback characteristic of this mechanism lies in the fact that bone accumulates about the cathodal region of this system, hence reducing the electrical effects produced by an applied force. The mechanisms by which the bone mesenchyme responds to mechanical stimuli (whether or not mediated by electrical signals) are uncertain. In general, heavy usage leads to heavy bone, and disuse, as in immobilization associated with injury or severe disease, results in decrease in bone mass and increased excretion of calcium, phosphorus, and nitrogen. The cellular response, however, is discouragingly complex. In broad outline it appears that the local expression of decreased stress is an increase in bone resorption coupled variably with a smaller and secondary increase in bone formation, whereas increased stress appears to be accompanied by a decrease in bone resorption coupled also with a smaller and probably secondary increase in bone formation. The decrease in resorption represents a decreased sensitivity to systemic stimuli, such as PTH, and reflects an interaction between hormonal and physical forces at the cellular level. PTH is the major determinant of all remodelling, structural as well as homeostatic; mechanical forces are the major determinant of where that remodelling occurs.

Controls exerted by mechanical forces

One of the most arresting features of skeletal remodelling is the tendency for rates of bone resorption and bone formation to change in the same direction. Three mechanisms for this coupling can be identified. The first is homeostatic and rises from the mineral demand created by formation of crystal nuclei in the bone matrix. Unless the calcium demands of increased bone formation can be met from some other source (such as increased diet calcium), they will inevitably lead to increased PTH secretion and bone resorption. Since the level of PTH is a principal determinant of bone resorption, it follows that high levels of formation tend to produce high levels of resorption (and vice versa). A second mechanism is the mechanical force-piezoelectric system discussed earlier. Local bone resorption, by reducing structural volume, concentrates applied forces in the remaining bone; this leads to increased strain and presumably increases the stimulus for local bone repair. A third mechanism is inferred from the observation in adult animals that the induction of specialized bony cells from the mesenchyme proceeds in a predetermined sequence: first osteoclasts and then osteoblasts, so that even on free surfaces resorption usually precedes formation. The ultimate basis of this cellular coupling is not known.

Because of the paramount influences that parathyroid hormone and calcitonin have on bone, their effects have been described in detail in the discussions of calcium and phosphate homeostasis and control of skeletal remodelling.

Estrogens

Hormonal influences. The most striking effects of estrogens are seen in birds, in which during the part of the cycle prior to egg formation a marked increase in osteoblastic activity occurs along the inside surfaces of the long bones, and the medullary cavities become filled with spongy bone. As the egg is formed, this spongy bone is rapidly resorbed, plasma calcium rises dramatically, and calcium is deposited in the shell. In mammals studied prior to skeletal maturity, administration of estrogens produces an accelerated appearance of ossification centres, a slowing in growth of cartilage and bone, and fusion of the epiphyses; the result is an adult skeleton smaller than normal. In older mammals estrogens in certain dosages and schedules of administration may inhibit trabecular bone resorption, and in some species prolonged administration of estrogen may lead to increased bone porosity. In postmenopausal women administration of estrogen suppresses bone resorption and produces a transient decrease in serum calcium and phosphorus and in renal reabsorption of phosphorus, as well as positive calcium balance, effects which help to stabilize the total skeletal bone mass.

The effects described are for estrogens as a general class of steroid hormone, and no attempt has been made to differentiate between the actions of natural estrogenic hormones and the many synthetic varieties now in wide use to suppress ovulation. Extremely few studies have been conducted to determine the effects of the latter on bone.

Effects of progesterone, testosterone, adrenal corticosteroids, thyroid hormone

Very little is known of the effects of progesterone on bone beyond studies in young guinea pigs suggesting slight inhibition of the activity of such hormones as estrogens, which speed skeletal development.

In mammals, including humans, just prior to sexual maturity, the growth spurt occurring in males is attributable principally to the growth-promoting action of the male sex hormone testosterone. When administered, testosterone and related steroids stimulate linear growth for a limited period; ultimately, however, particularly if they are given in large doses, they suppress bone growth as the result of hastened skeletal development and premature epiphyseal closure. Studies have indicated that testosterone derivatives administered to adult mammals suppress the turnover and resorption of bone and increase the retention of nitrogen, phosphorus, and calcium.

The influence of the adrenal corticosteroid hormones on bone is varied, but the principal result is slowing of growth in the young and decrease in bone mass in the adult. In Cushing's syndrome, in which there is abnormally high secretion of corticosteroids, bone loss to the point of fractures often occurs. Cortisol in high concentration suppresses protein and mucopolysaccharide synthesis, with inhibition of bone matrix formation and of incorporation of nucleosides into bone cells.

Lack of the internal secretion of the thyroid gland results in retardation of skeletal growth and development. Action of this hormone to facilitate growth and skeletal maturation is probably indirect, through its general effects on cell metabolism. Thyroid hormone in excess leads in the young to premature appearance of ossification centres and closure of the epiphyses, and in the adult to increased bone-cell metabolism. Commonly in the hyperthyroid adult bone resorption predominates over increased bone formation with resultant loss of bone mass.

The anterior lobe of the pituitary gland secretes a hormone essential for growth and development of the skeleton. This effect of the hormone is indirect and mediated by "sulfation factor," a substance produced in the liver in response to stimulation by the growth hormone. The extent to which growth hormone is involved in skeletal remodelling in the adult is not known, but excessive elaboration of the hormone after maturity leads to distorted enlargement of all bones in the condition known as acromegaly. Excessive elaboration of growth hormone prior to epiphyseal closure leads to gigantism. Studies of the administration of growth hormone to man have indicated marked species specificity; growth in hypopituitary dwarfs is stimulated only by human or primate growth hormone. The principal metabolic effects in man of the hormone are retention of nitrogen and increased turnover of calcium, resulting in increases both in intestinal calcium absorption and in urinary calcium excretion.

Effects of growth hormone and of insulin

Insulin participates in the regulation of bone growth; it may enhance or even be necessary for the effect of growth hormone on bone. Insulin has been found to stimulate growth and epiphyseal widening in rats whose pituitaries have been removed and to promote chondroitin sulfate synthesis in cartilage and bone and the transport of amino acids and nucleosides into bone.

Nutritional influences. The most significant nutritional influence on bone is the availability of calcium. The close relationship between bone and calcium is indicated by the principal processes of calcium metabolism. Bone contains 99 percent of the calcium in the body and can behave as an adequate buffer for maintenance of a constant level of freely moving calcium in soft tissues, extracellular fluid, and blood. The free-calcium concentration in this pool must be kept within fairly narrow limits (50–65 milligrams per litre of extracellular fluid) to maintain the constant internal milieu necessary for neuromuscular irritability, blood clotting, muscle contractility, and cardiac function. Calcium leaves the pool by way of bone formation, by such routes as the urine, feces, and sweat, and periodically by way of lactation and transplacental movement. Calcium enters the pool by the mechanism of bone resorption and by absorption from dietary calcium in the upper intestinal tract.

The significance with respect to bone of adequate availability of calcium to animal or man is that the mechanical strength of bone is proportional to its mineral content. All of the other components of bone, organic and inorganic, are, of course, also essential for bone integrity, but the importance of availability of structural materials is most easily illustrated by consideration of calcium balance (dietary intake versus excretory output). If intake of calcium is limited, maintenance of normal levels of extracellular and soft tissue calcium in the face of mandatory daily losses from this pool by various excretory routes requires that calcium be mined from its storage depot, bone. Abundant mineral intake, then, tends to preserve bone mass, and an increase of positivity of calcium balance has been shown to suppress resorption of bone.

The Recommended Dietary Allowances of the Food and Nutrition Board, National Academy of Sciences–National Research Council (1968) for calcium daily are 800 milligrams for adults and 1.0 to 1.4 grams for adolescents and pregnant and lactating women. The usual daily intake of this element, however, ranges between 500 and 800 milligrams, about 150–250 milligrams from green vegetables and the remainder usually from milk and milk products. Daily urinary excretion of calcium is normally from 50 to 150 or 200 milligrams (the upper limit of normal being uncertain), varying sharply with intake at very low levels but rising only very gradually with increasing intake above 300 to 400 milligrams. Fecal excretion of calcium is much larger than urinary, most of the calcium in the feces being unabsorbed dietary calcium. A man's losses from the skin and in the sweat range from less than 30 milligrams per day to as high as 200 milligrams per day during active sweating. Calcium absorption varies considerably depending on previous and current levels of intake and type of diet. At intakes of 400 milligrams per day, absorption averages 32 percent; at 1,000 milligrams per day, 21 percent.

The other principal mineral constituent of bone, phosphorus, is abundantly available in both milk and in other protein-rich foods, and its daily recommended allowance is the same as for calcium. A prolonged dietary deficiency of phosphate and an extreme deficiency of calcium will result in mineral-poor bone, known as rickets or osteomalacia. The skeleton serves as a storage reservoir for two other cations of considerable physiologic importance, magnesium and sodium. Magnesium ion has a calcium-like effect on parathyroid hormone secretion, and magnesium deficiency has a number of the same effects as calcium deficiency.

Fluoride, an element of proven value and safety in prevention of dental caries when provided in drinking water at concentrations of one part per million, is absorbed into bone lattice structure as well as into enamel and produces a larger crystal more resistant to resorption. Amounts ten or more times that normally taken in fluoridated drinking water have been noted to cause abnormalities of bone collagen synthesis. Extremely large dosages produce in man the more dense but irregularly structured and brittle bone of fluorosis.

Vitamins; proteins

The function of vitamin A remains to be clarified, but it is apparently necessary for proliferation of cartilage and bone growth. Without vitamin A, bone remodelling is also impaired and bones develop in abnormal shapes. Excessive amounts of the vitamin result in thinning of cortical bone and fracture.

Ascorbic acid, or vitamin C, is essential for intracellular formation of collagen and for hydroxylation of proline. In scurvy, a vitamin C deficiency disease, the collagen matrix of bone is either partially or completely unable to calcify (see discussion above on formation of bone).

Vitamin D has several complex physiologic actions that affect the metabolism of bone. The oldest known effect is facilitation of intestinal absorption of calcium and, indirectly, of phosphate. The second target of vitamin D action is the renal tubule. In the child who has rickets administration of the vitamin restores the impaired tubular reabsorption of phosphorus to normal; in the person whose secretion of parathyroid hormone is subnormal, however, the vitamin in large doses has a parathyroid hormone-like effect and reduces the elevated serum phosphorus by suppression of the renal tubular reabsorption of phosphorus. The third site of vitamin D action is the bone cells, in which the vitamin increases citrate production by conversion from pyruvate; the way in which this action is related to the effect of the vitamin on mobilization of bone mineral is at present uncertain. Also at the cellular level both parathyroid hormone and vitamin D stimulate release of calcium from mitochondria, but the hormone cannot do so in the absence of vitamin D, further evidence of the closely coordinated relationship of these important factors. Recent research has shown that to exert its physiologic effects, vitamin D must be converted to 25-hydroxycholecalciferol in the liver and this compound further in the kidney to 1,25-dihydroxycholecalciferol.

Other nutritional factors include protein, which as an essential component of the matrix of bone must be provided by a combination of dietary intake and conversion from other tissues. Changes in acid-base balance also have an influence on the skeleton—acidosis in various clinical disorders and ingestion of acid salts being accompanied by mineral loss.

BIBLIOGRAPHY. F.C. MCLEAN and M.R. URIST, *Bone: Fundamentals of the Physiology of Skeletal Tissue*, 3rd ed. (1968), a comprehensive survey, with excellent bibliography, of bone structure and metabolic function; G.H. BOURNE (ed.), *Biochemistry and Physiology of Bone* (1956); and H.M. FROST (ed.), *Bone Biodynamics* (1964), two works containing a series of authoritative essays, with bibliographies, on topics of chemistry, structure, function, and disease; W.H. HARRIS and R.P. HEANEY, *Skeletal Renewal and Metabolic Bone Disease* (1970), a review of skeletal remodelling processes, with special emphasis on their control mechanisms and on methods of measuring remodelling in the living skeleton; K. RODAHL, J.T. NICHOLSON, and E.M. BROWN (eds.), *Bone as a Tissue* (1960), a series of essays and reviews on various topics of bone structure, physiology, and disease; C.L. COMAR and F. BRONNER (eds.), *Mineral Metabolism*, vol. 1B, 2A, and 3 (1960–69), exhaustive and definitive reviews of the chemistry and metabolism of the principal mineral components of bone.

(R.P.He./G.D.W.)

Bone Diseases and Injuries

Bone diseases and injuries are major causes of disease of the locomotor system, the complex of structures and processes that enable the body to move. Traditionally these conditions belong in the category of orthopedic surgery, but they are often associated with problems of other surgical and medical specialties, notably pediatrics, neurology, and rheumatology.

Physical injury, causing fracture, dominates over other diseases causing locomotor system abnormality. No sharp distinction can be drawn, however, between physical injury and other disease in this respect. Fracture is but one of several common causes of hip disease; and bone disease is a common cause of fracture.

The nature of locomotor disease changes with age. In children, problems related to development and to the nervous system dominate; in young adults, rheumatoid arthritis, back problems, and traffic accident injuries are particularly significant; and, in the aged, metabolic abnormalities of bone, cartilage, and vessels cause fracture, joint disease, and deficient circulation. Moreover, congenital abnormalities frequently do not make their effects known until middle age. Fracture problems also change with age. Fractures in children are usually benign; in young adults they are often associated with severe injury to the soft tissues; and in the aged, fracture is often a symptom of systemic, life-threatening disease.

Bone diseases and injuries were formerly regarded as conditions that were more mechanical than metabolic, more static than dynamic. An improved understanding of the dual mechanical and chemical function of bone has permitted a more integrated biological view of bone disease and injuries.

THE STRUCTURE, FUNCTION, AND METABOLISM OF BONE

The characteristic hardness and elasticity of bones are due to the two-part arrangement of the components of the bone tissue: an organic matrix encrusted with inorganic mineral. The organic fraction is chiefly collagen, a fibrous protein that is also a chief component of cartilage, tendons, and skin. Bone collagen is organized as fibrils—minute fibres—which are also found in attached tendons, fascia (sheaths of connective tissue), and muscles. The main components of bone mineral are calcium, phosphate, and carbonate; a part of it is present in crystal form as hydroxyapatite, closely packed in and between the collagen fibrils. The skeleton contains 1,000–1,500 grams of calcium; *i.e.*, more than 99 percent of the total amount of calcium in the body. Bone cells are of three types that differ in both microscopic appearance and function: osteocytes for maintenance, osteoblasts for formation, and osteoclasts for destruction (resorption) of bone. The cells are interconnected by cellular processes and distributed so that the maximal distance between matrix and the closest cell is one-hundredth of a millimetre, and between a cell and the closest blood capillary, one-fifth of a millimetre.

Functions of bone

The skeleton has two functions, one mechanical and one chemical. The mechanical function of the skeleton is to fight gravity and inertia by providing leverage and support for locomotion and to give protection to sensitive structures such as the brain, spinal cord, heart, lungs, and abdominal organs. The chemical function of the skeleton is associated with the need for the cell membranes of the body to be exposed at all times to a precisely regulated concentration of ionized calcium; the bone tissue provides a store of calcium for deposition or withdrawal as need may be.

The mechanical and the chemical functions of the skeleton are closely interrelated in the sense that they share mechanisms for formation and resorption of bone tissues and yet control these metabolic processes in different ways. Mechanical demands trigger the formation of bone tissue in areas of stress, and resorption occurs in areas where stress is minimal; an electric signal seems to mediate the response of the bone cells to stress. The chemical function of the bone tissue is regulated by the parathyroid glands, which secrete parathyroid hormone in response to low levels of ionized calcium in the blood and stop secretion when the calcium reaches high levels. The parathyroid hormone in turn raises the blood level of calcium by resorption of bone tissue; in addition to its effect on bone, it promotes absorption of calcium from the gut and restricts loss of calcium through the kidney. The cellular activity of the bone tissue is thus controlled by two partly synergistic and partly antagonistic processes. The two processes are further interrelated by the fact that vitamin D promotes both resorption and formation of bone and that the bone effect of parathyroid hormone is decreased in the absence of vitamin D. The vitamin promotes the mechanical function of bone by resorption of inadequate or superfluous tissue, returning calcium and phosphate to the blood for mineralization at new building sites. The action of vitamin D is clearly important both for remodelling associated with growth and, in the adult, for continued remodelling of the bone tissue that permits adaptation to structural demand and rejuvenation of aged structures.

The average life-span of bone tissue relative to that of other tissues is long; in adult life it is some ten years, in adolescence about two years, and in the newborn infant less than one year. But these average values are misleading inasmuch as the cancellous (spongy) bone in the vertebrae and pelvis and in the long bones close to joints is renewed five to ten times faster than the solid (cortical) bone in the shafts of the long bones. Also, both in cancellous and in cortical bone, only a small part of the tissue is being renewed at any one time.

The demand on the metabolic processes and its regulators described here is illustrated by the fact that new bone mineralization in an adult uses 400–600 milligrams of calcium daily, an amount greater than the total calcium content of the entire blood volume. Furthermore, the rates of formation and resorption are capable of being increased 10- to 100-fold when the mechanical or chemical function of the bone is challenged by disease.

PRINCIPAL TYPES OF DISEASES AND INJURIES

Effects of inactivity and hyperactivity

Abnormal stress on bone. Inactivity has a profound effect on the bone tissue, probably because the mechanical stimulus to bone formation is decreased.

In congenital dislocation of the hip, the socket part of the joint, the acetabulum, has lost the mechanical stimulus to normal growth and development because the ball part of the joint, the head of the femur, does not rest in the joint. The acetabulum and a large part of the pelvis develop poorly or not at all, whereas the femoral head, if it makes contact higher up on the pelvis, may stimulate development of a new joint structure. In the same way, nerve injury during the period of childhood growth results in markedly retarded growth and development. Poliomyelitis affecting the lower extremity in children results in short, thin bones with sometimes severe leg-length discrepancy. In adults, an extremity affected by nerve injury gradually develops osteopenia (a reduced amount of bone tissue), so that it fractures easily. In the elderly, bed rest is regarded as a cause of increased osteopenia with vertebral fractures. The loss of bone tissue and of calcium from the skeleton in space flight has been reported; the resultant high level of calcium in the urine may perhaps make kidney stones a hazard in prolonged weightlessness.

The skeleton is capable of considerable hypertrophy (increased development) when needed. The ballet dancer's big toe, for example, hypertrophies remarkably because of its subjection to abnormal mechanical demands. The bone tissue's capacity for remodelling in response to mechanical demand is retained even in the aged. In osteoarthritis the weight distribution across the knee or hip joints is uneven because of degeneration of the joint cartilage; the bone beneath the cartilage hypertrophies on the compression side of the joint and atrophies on the extension side.

Metabolic bone disease. The normal function of bone requires an adequate supply to the tissue of amino acids (building blocks for proteins) for synthesis of collagen, the chief component for the organic matrix; of calcium and phosphate for mineralization of the organic matrix; and of many more organic compounds and mineral elements. In addition, growth, repair, and remodelling of the bone tissue require a precisely regulated supply of hormones, vitamins, and enzymes. Skeletal disease when it is due to inadequacies in the supply or action of the above essentials, associated with abnormalities outside the skeleton, is termed "metabolic." Examples of such abnormalities are dietary deficiency and gastrointestinal, liver, kidney, and hormonal diseases. In addition, the most important of all bone diseases, osteoporosis (age-related loss of bone with tendency to fractures) is traditionally included among the metabolic conditions even though its cause is not known; it may or may not be associated with one or more of the above abnormalities.

Osteopenia and osteosclerosis

Changes in bone tissue due to metabolic abnormalities are classified with regard to the amount and composition of the bone tissue. When the amount of bone is lower or higher than normal, the conditions are termed, respectively, osteopenia and osteosclerosis. These terms do not imply any specific disease but serve simply to describe the amount of bone. Osteopenia is common both locally and generally throughout the skeleton. Localized osteopenia is evident in X-rays of tumours or infections of bone, in osteonecrosis (death of bony tissue), often in fracture, and in conditions of diminished mechanical demand. Osteopenia may thus be associated both with atrophy from disuse and with active remodelling of bone; it occurs when bone resorption has outstripped formation, regardless of the absolute rates of these processes. Generalized osteopenia occurs in osteomalacia, osteoporosis, and osteogenesis imperfecta. Osteosclerosis occurs locally in osteoarthritis, osteonecrosis, and osteomyelitis; it represents an attempt at structural strengthening by thickening of bony trabeculae, but its X-ray appearance may be confused with that of dead bone (sequestra in osteomyelitis), retaining its density while adjacent normal bone has become osteopenic. Widespread, but hardly ever truly generalized, osteosclerosis occurs in marble bone disease and in Paget's disease. Except in the latter condition, however, osteopenia and osteosclerosis are not associated with detectable biochemical abnormalities. (The diseases mentioned are characterized below.)

When the normal composition of bone tissue is altered by deficient mineralization of the organic matrix, the condition is called rickets if in children and osteomalacia if in adults. The mineralization deficiency is due in part to a lower than normal calcium–phosphate ion product in the body fluids. In rickets the bones become tender, soft, and deformed; X-rays show characteristic abnormalities at the growth zones, especially evident at the wrist, knee, and ankle joints. In osteomalacia, bone tenderness and pain accompany the slow development of spontaneous, often symmetric fractures characteristically present in the pelvis and the thigh bones; these breaks are thus in the category of fatigue fractures rather than traumatic in origin. The X-ray appearance of osteomalacia is rather normal until visible fracture has developed. Biochemical abnormalities, usually present in rickets and osteomalacia, are increased blood concentration of the enzyme alkaline phosphatase, believed to be important for bone formation or resorption, and decreased blood concentrations of calcium, or phosphate, or both; the calcium concentration may occasionally fall to levels so low that muscle and nerve function are impaired (tetany). Examination of the bone tissue in the microscope reveals the deficient mineralization of the organic matrix. The entire skeleton is affected in both rickets and osteomalacia, even though abnormalities are more evident in certain regions; *i.e.*, growth centres in children and areas of maximal mechanical load in adults.

Insufficient protein, caloric, and vitamin intake interferes with bone formation during growth and remodelling, directly because of an inadequate supply for matrix formation and indirectly because of a deficient production of crucial hormones and enzymes. The effect in the young is stunted growth and in adults is osteopenia, the condition seen during World War II in concentration camp inmates (hunger osteopathy).

Effect of dietary abnormalities

Deficient intake of calcium or phosphate or both, unassociated with vitamin D deficiency, causes a compensatory action of parathyroid hormone whereby the mineral is mobilized from the skeleton with eventual development of osteopenia. Deficient calcium intake (milk) and excessive phosphate intake (meat) causes osteopenia, fractures, and loss of teeth in dogs, cats, and other animals by excessive compensatory parathyroid hormone action. Whether this mechanism could at least contribute to osteoporosis and loss of teeth in old age is being debated.

Excessive intake of fluoride, many times higher than that commonly used for the prevention of dental decay, may cause asymptomatic sclerosis of the skeleton (fluorosis); in the Punjab region of India the fluoride intake is extremely high, and bone changes are associated with severe joint and nerve disease.

Insufficient intake of vitamin D is one of many ways in which rickets may develop. The condition, once universally prevalent, is now rare in countries that ensure adequate supply of vitamin D in fortified milk and healthy living habits including adequate exposure to sunshine.

Malabsorption of calcium and vitamin D may be caused by disease of the digestive tract, surgical removal of part of the stomach or intestine, or disease of the pancreas or the liver ducts. The condition causes a mixture of osteopenia and osteomalacia and requires high intake of calcium and vitamin D.

Most hormones have some effect on the bone tissue, but only two play important roles in bone disease: parathyroid and corticosteroid hormones.

Parathyroid hormone is concerned with the maintenance of calcium concentration at the cell membranes. It functions by increasing the passage of calcium through the lining of the intestine, by increasing the resorption of bone tissue, and by increasing the reabsorption of calcium in the renal tubuli. Overactive parathyroid hormone causes osteopenia by excessive resorption of bone; in extreme cases spontaneous fractures may occur. Excessive secretion of parathyroid hormone may be due to a tumour of the parathyroid glands or may be secondary to dietary deficiency or malabsorption of calcium and vitamin D; overactivity of the parathyroid glands is also an integral element in renal osteodystrophy (see below).

Adrenal corticosteroid hormone is associated with skeletal abnormalities, osteopenia, and osteonecrosis. Osteopenia develops because increased levels of corticosteroids, caused by disease (pituitary or adrenal tumour) or by long-term medication (*e.g.*, for asthma), depress the rate of formation of bone tissue. Osteonecrosis is associated with even short-term intake of large doses of high corticosteroid medication; for example, to prevent rejection of a transplanted kidney.

The interrelation between bone and kidney disease is becoming increasingly important as use of the artificial kidney (dialysis) and transplantation have dramatically reduced the incidence of death and illness for chronic kidney failure.

Effects of kidney disease

The effects of kidney disease on bone reflect the role of the kidney in maintaining calcium and phosphate balance, mediated by parathyroid hormone. The two main units of the kidney, the tubules and the glomerulus, are associated with two groups of bone diseases: the former with a low level of phosphate in the blood (hypophosphatemia) and the latter with renal osteodystrophy (see below), both characterized by rickets and osteomalacia. In addition, kidney transplantation is associated with overactivity of the parathyroid glands and osteonecrosis.

Reabsorption of phosphate by the kidney tubules is deficient in a hereditary disorder, familial hypophosphatemia; the phosphate leak causes low concentration of blood phosphate (hypophosphatemia) and, in turn, deficient mineralization of bone tissue, rickets in children and osteomalacia in adults. Since rickets due to vitamin D deficiency has been greatly reduced, familial hypophosphatemia is the most common cause of rickets in Europe and the United States. Until recently this condition was called vitamin-D-resistant rickets, because treatment with the vitamin failed to correct the biochemical and skeletal abnormalities. Better understanding of the basic deficiency has led to more satisfactory treatment with high oral doses of phosphate. Advanced forms of the disease still result in stunted growth and skeletal deformity, often necessitating repeated operative correction. More complex tubular reabsorption defects are the cause of bicarbonate, amino acid, and glucose losses in addition to loss of phosphate; the resulting disease is so severe that the bony abnormalities usually become less important.

Renal glomerular disease with high levels of urea in the blood—uremia—is associated with a complex skeletal abnormality, renal osteodystrophy. The condition leads to severe rickets or osteomalacia associated with compensatory secondary hyperparathyroidism. In children, stunted growth may be the first symptom that leads to detection of the kidney disease; the skeletal abnormality cannot be ascribed solely to an abnormal mineral balance but is probably due also to an adverse effect of uremia on protein metabolism. Growth may resume after successful kidney transplantation, and gross deformity of the extremities may be corrected surgically. Chronic uremia in adults, even when treated by use of the artificial kidney, causes osteoporosis and deposition of calcium apatite in arterial walls and tendon sheaths, probably associated with hyperparathyroidism.

Kidney transplantation is occasionally followed by hyperparathyroidism and osteonecrosis. The overactivity of the parathyroids is ascribed to the fact that prior to correction of the kidney disease, the glands have had to function at an abnormally high level for such a long time that the mechanisms for shutting them off have become deficient. The cause of osteonecrosis after kidney transplantation is at least partly the high doses of corticosteroid treatment used to prevent rejection of the transplant. Osteonecrosis of the hip or knee joints may cause residual disability after succesful kidney transplantation.

Osteoporosis

Generalized osteopenia without evidence of osteomalacia is termed osteoporosis. It may be secondary to metabolic abnormalities discussed above or may be without known cause. Osteoporosis from unknown cause is by far the most common bone disease; it probably occurs in all aged individuals and may sometimes become evident as early as age 30–40. The spine is particularly affected.

Diagnosis of less severe stages of osteoporosis is complicated by the fact that the condition is not associated with measurable chemical abnormalities or with observable tissue abnormality other than a decrease in bone mass. It is generally believed that the common fractures in old age, those of the hip, knee, and wrist, are due to osteoporosis. Unlike the vertebral fractures in osteoporosis, these fractures of the limbs hardly ever occur spontaneously—without a distinct accident—and, unlike fracture in osteomalacia, they are never preceded by bone pain or tenderness. In fact, whereas the diminished quantity of bone tissue, the characteristic feature of osteoporosis, is clearly implicated in the diminished resistance of the bones to fracture, there may also be a change in the quality of the bone tissue.

In women the condition is usually more severe and starts earlier than in men. For this reason osteoporosis is sometimes termed "postmenopausal," to imply that it is caused by a change in the hormonal pattern, and hormonal substitution therapy is sometimes used. So far, hormonal therapy in osteoporosis has not been shown to have any significant effect on the bone disease. Other medical therapy used in osteoporosis includes the administration of fluorides (because of their effect in dental decay and because they are known to cause osteosclerosis in high dosage) and diets high in vitamin D and calcium (because of the possibility that osteoporosis may be due to hyperparathyroidism secondary to nutritional deficiencies or malabsorption in the aged). Except for the occurrence of extremity fractures, the outlook in osteoporosis is on the whole good. In the majority of even severe cases the progress of osteopenia eventually ceases, and pain subsides with healing of vertebral fractures. Perhaps the bone structure eventually reaches another biomechanical equilibrium with adequate response to stress; for this reason active muscle exercises are advocated both as prevention and as therapy in osteoporosis.

Paget's disease of bone, increasingly common after middle age, is characterized by widespread areas of osteosclerosis. The sclerotic regions have a high rate of bone metabolism; when the legs are affected deformities gradually develop. Pain in Paget's disease may be due to fatigue fracture or development of a malignant tumour (osteosarcoma). The cause of Paget's disease is unknown.

Deficient blood supply to bone. The cells of the bone tissue die if deprived of arterial blood supply for more than a few hours. The condition is called necrosis of bone or osteonecrosis.

Causes and course of osteonecrosis

Osteonecrosis may be caused by injury to blood vessels, associated with dislocation or fracture of bone; by blood clots or gas bubbles in the blood vessels; by invasion of foreign tissue; and by metabolic disease (as in alcoholism).

Osteonecrosis may involve the shaft (diaphysis) or the ends (epiphyses) of the long bones. Sometimes the bone marrow of the diaphysis is primarily involved, and in osteomyelitis it is usually the compact (cortical) bone of the shaft that undergoes necrosis. For mechanical reasons, and because there is a poorer blood supply to cortical bone than to the cancellous bone of the epiphyses, the course of events following osteonecrosis differs in the two types of bone. When cortical bone is involved, the dead bone may prevent healing of osteomyelitis by mechanical irritation. When the cancellous bone of the epiphyses is involved, the lesion is invaded by blood vessels from adjacent bone, and a vigorous repair process ensues, characterized by removal of dead, and the formation of new, bone. The lesion may heal with reconstitution of both structural and mechanical properties, or the process of rebuilding may weaken the bone structure so that it collapses from the mechanical forces across the joint. In these circumstances the joint cartilage is damaged, and osteoarthritis eventually develops. It is for this reason that treatment of osteonecrosis in the early stage consists of protecting the joint from weight bearing; the condition is most often encountered in the hip and the knee.

Whereas it has long been recognized that osteonecrosis may occur in association with fracture or dislocation, it only recently has been recognized that the condition may often develop spontaneously or in association with the use of corticosteroid hormone (*e.g.*, in treatment of hepatitis—liver inflammation—or to prevent rejection of a kidney transplant) and in pancreatic disease. In these conditions the immediate cause of impaired blood supply is not clear; current speculation involves abnormal fat metabolism.

Ionizing radiation injury to bone. Bone tissue and the metaphyseal growth cartilage (the cartilage, between the end of the bone and the shaft, that later becomes bone) may be injured during the course of X-ray treatment of tumours. The risk is well recognized but can not always be avoided. The most common radiation injury to bone is fracture of the neck of the thigh bone (the femur) following radiation treatment of cancer of the uterus or the bladder. There is pain in the bone before this type of fracture can be seen by X-ray; the fracture usually heals without displacement. In children, the X-ray treatment of certain kidney tumours may cause growth abnormalities of the spine with development of lateral curvature (scoliosis); and radium treatment of hemangioma (a tumour made up of blood vessels) of the knee region may cause growth retardation in parts of the metaphyseal cartilages with knock-knee or bowleg deformity. X-ray treatment of certain premalignant bone tumours may make them fully malignant. Intense radiation may cause osteonecrosis, sometimes associated with secondary osteomyelitis. This latter condition was common in dial painters who had ingested radium by licking the brush.

The diagnostic use of radioactive substances or of X-ray techniques is not associated with measurable effects on bone tissue. Higher doses of bone-seeking radioactive substances are currently tried for selective radiation treatment of cancer.

Infectious diseases of bone. Infection of bone tissue by micro-organisms is termed osteomyelitis. Micro-organisms may gain access to bone either by spreading with the bloodstream from an infectious lesion elsewhere in the body (hematogenous osteomyelitis) or through a skin wound, accidental or surgical.

Causes and incidence of osteomyelitis

The incidence of hematogenous osteomyelitis reflects the fact that the body is more susceptible to invasion by micro-organisms when nutrition and hygiene are poor. Thus, hematogenous osteomyelitis is common in South America, Asia, and Africa, but in the developed countries the incidence has declined sharply during the last 50 years. In these latter countries hematogenous osteomyelitis is often associated with slum conditions or systemic disease; for example, infection of the genito-urinary tract in the elderly or blood-clotting abnormalities in children (sickle-cell anemia). On the other hand, high-energy fractures, notably motor or missile accidents, and extensive surgery, associated with the direct introduction of micro-organisms into bone, are increasingly common causes of osteomyelitis all over the world.

Osteomyelitis is commonly caused by pus-forming (pyogenic) micro-organisms, usually *Staphylococcus aureus* or *Mycobacterium tuberculosis*. Pyogenic osteomyelitis occurs both by direct routes and by hematogenous spread from an infection of the skin, urogenital tract, lung, or upper respiratory tract. Tuberculosis of the bone is always hematogenous in origin, usually disseminated from lesions in the lungs or the kidneys.

Goran C.H. Bauer

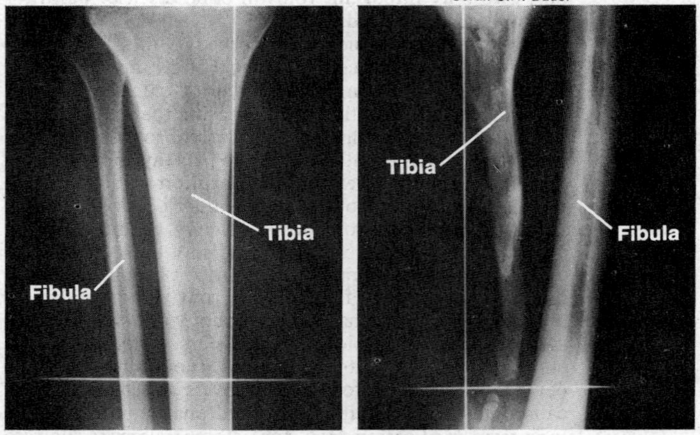

Figure 1: Defect of tibia, caused by septic osteomyelitis in childhood, with compensatory thickening of the fibula (right). The normal bones are shown at left.

Hematogenous osteomyelitis is more common in children than in adults. In children it is usually located in the growing end of the long bones; at the hip, for example, or just above or below the knee. In adults, hematogenous osteomyelitis is commonly located in the vertebrae of the spine (tuberculous or septic spondylitis). Osteomyelitis caused by direct invasion of micro-organisms often complicates open fractures—for example, of the shaft of the tibia—and operations for fracture or for degenerative joint disease—for example, at the hip joint. The risk of introduction of micro-organisms into wounds, either at or after an operation (hospital infections), can be minimized by careful precautions in the operating room and during the dressing of wounds and by the isolation of infected patients.

Osteomyelitis is associated with the cardinal symptoms of inflammation: complaints of illness, fever, local redness, swelling, warmth, pain, and tenderness. In the early stages the X-ray appearance may be normal; later, signs of destruction and repair of bone ensue. Untreated, the condition may cause extensive destruction of bone, blocking of the nutrient blood vessels with death of bone tissue, extension to an adjacent joint with development of arthritis, and eventually a break through the skin with the evacuation of pus. The acute condition has now become chronic. It may heal, but the future course usually is marked by occasional flare-ups, with evacuation of pus and small pieces of dead bone (sequestra) through a persistent communication from skin to bone (a chronic sinus).

The treatment of osteomyelitis is primarily aimed at killing micro-organisms with antibiotics and, in later stages, getting rid of pus and sequestra by surgery.

Contributing factors in fractures

Fractures. A fracture occurs when the bone tissue is subjected to tensile, compressive, or shear forces in excess of its strength. Both the strength of the bone tissue and the nature of the forces acting on bone change from infancy to old age, both normally and as a result of disease. Therefore, the incidence and type of fractures change dramatically with age. The three factors, age, disease, and force, are all involved in the causation of most fractures.

As compared to children and the elderly, the bone tissue in young adults has high resistance to mechanical deformation. Fractures of cortical bone in adults require tremendous forces, such as those encountered in motor accidents, and are therefore often associated with severe skin injuries and other lesions of soft tissue. Bones in children are springy and resilient, like a freshly cut sapling, and the membrane enclosing the bones—the periosteum—is thick. Angular deformation of long bones in children therefore often results in incomplete or "greenstick" fractures. In the elderly the bone tissue becomes more brittle, especially the cancellous bone in vertebrae and in shoulder, wrist, hip, and knee joints; the majority of fractures in the elderly involve these regions.

Children are often exposed to injury because of their lively behaviour and lack of experience. Their bodies are small and light, however, and the forces acting on the skeleton usually are caused by only a fall at ground level. Fractures in children are therefore rarely severely displaced or associated with severe soft tissue injury; the only common exception to this rule is a certain type of elbow fracture. By contrast, in age groups 20–50 years, especially among males, fractures are often caused by direct, high-energy forces sustained in motor vehicles, factories, construction sites, and the like. These forces often have an explosive effect on bone and soft tissues and may cause severely displaced open fractures. Finally, in the aged, fracture is usually caused by mild forces acting on brittle bone. Such fractures are rarely associated with soft tissue injury and often involve cancellous rather than cortical bone.

Many diseases decrease the strength of the bone tissue, either throughout the skeleton or locally, and some expose the body to increased mechanical forces. The most important generalized condition is osteoporosis, which is prevalent in women over 50 and dominates in fractures in old age. Less common causes of decreased bone strength are osteogenesis imperfecta (a hereditary disease in which fragility of bone is associated with deafness and other manifestations), long term corticosteroid treatment, and osteomalacia. Common causes of locally decreased bone strength are injury of peripheral nerves and tumour. Hemiplegia (paralysis of one side of the body) and blindness increase the risk of accidents that may produce fracture in the aged.

Diagnosis and classification of fracture

The existence of a fracture is often deduced from a history of injury and observation of swelling, tenderness, faulty alignment, the sound that the broken ends make, loss of function, and associated injuries. Precise diagnosis is made by X-ray examination.

Most fractures occur without skin injury. These are called closed fractures. The skin wound in open fractures is caused either by severe direct violence or by a sharp bone fragment that pierces the skin from within. Because of the nature of the forces involved, open fracture of the diaphysis is usually transverse, whereas closed fractures, often caused by a twisting injury, are more often spiral-shaped. In fracture through diaphyseal cortical bone, the fragments are usually displaced by muscle action, while fractures of a cancellous bone (as in the vertebrae), more often cause compression. Diaphyseal fractures are therefore usually unstable in contrast to compression fractures, which are stable. Fracture of cancellous bone associated with dislocation of joints may result in severe instability, however. Tear fractures are associated with sudden, violent muscle pull and are usually markedly displaced. Disruption of the growth cartilage in children may cause the epiphysis to slide and form an angle (a condition called epiphyseolysis).

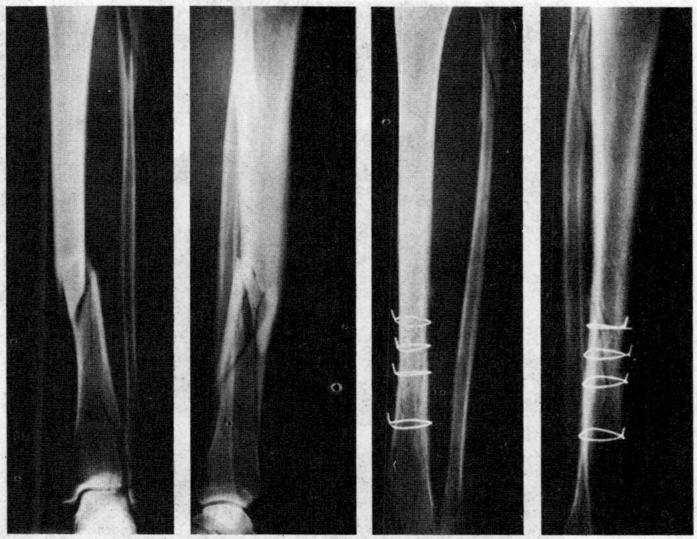

Figure 2: (Left) Front and (centre left) lateral projections of a fractured tibia and fibula. (Centre right and right) Corresponding projections following reduction of the dislocation and immobilization with the aid of four steel wires encircling the tibia. By reducing the fracture of the tibia the less important fracture of the fibula is also reduced and immobilized. Additional immobilization is accomplished with the aid of a groin-to-toe plaster cast.
Goran C.H. Bauer

Fracture sometimes develops slowly rather than suddenly. These fatigue, or stress, fractures occur either because the bone tissue is exposed to forces that overwhelm its capacity for structural adaptation or because there is pre-existing disease. Examples of the former are fracture of the thigh bone and fracture of the bones of the foot (march fracture) in soldiers during their initial months of physical training. Bone diseases associated with fatigue fracture are osteomalacia, Paget's disease, and radiation injury to bone. Fatigue fracture usually produces pain even before bony abnormality can be seen in the X-rays.

Except in missile injury, in which the forces act with explosive suddenness, vessels and nerves usually escape injury because of their elasticity and resilience. For anatomic reasons, however, nerve injury may occur in fracture-dislocation of the hip and in fracture of the long bone of the upper arm (the humerus) through the diaphysis in adults and just above the elbow in children; the latter fracture is associated with compression of the accompanying artery. Fracture and dislocation of the vertebrae caused by motor accidents or other severe forces may be associated with spinal cord injury. This injury is particularly common in young adults. Certain fractures injure the nutrient blood vessels of the bone tissue with osteonecrosis as a result.

The bone tissue has a rich supply of blood vessels that rupture when there is fracture. The resultant bleeding causes swelling at the site of fracture (fracture hematoma) and later discoloration of the skin. Occasionally the bleeding is so severe (two to three litres in fracture of the thigh) that the circulating blood volume is significantly diminished and shock ensues.

The nerve endings of the periosteum are distended by the bleeding caused by fracture, and motion or pressure at the fracture site is painful.

Healing of fracture

A fracture starts to heal at the very moment that it occurs. The fracture hematoma is invaded by cellular ele-

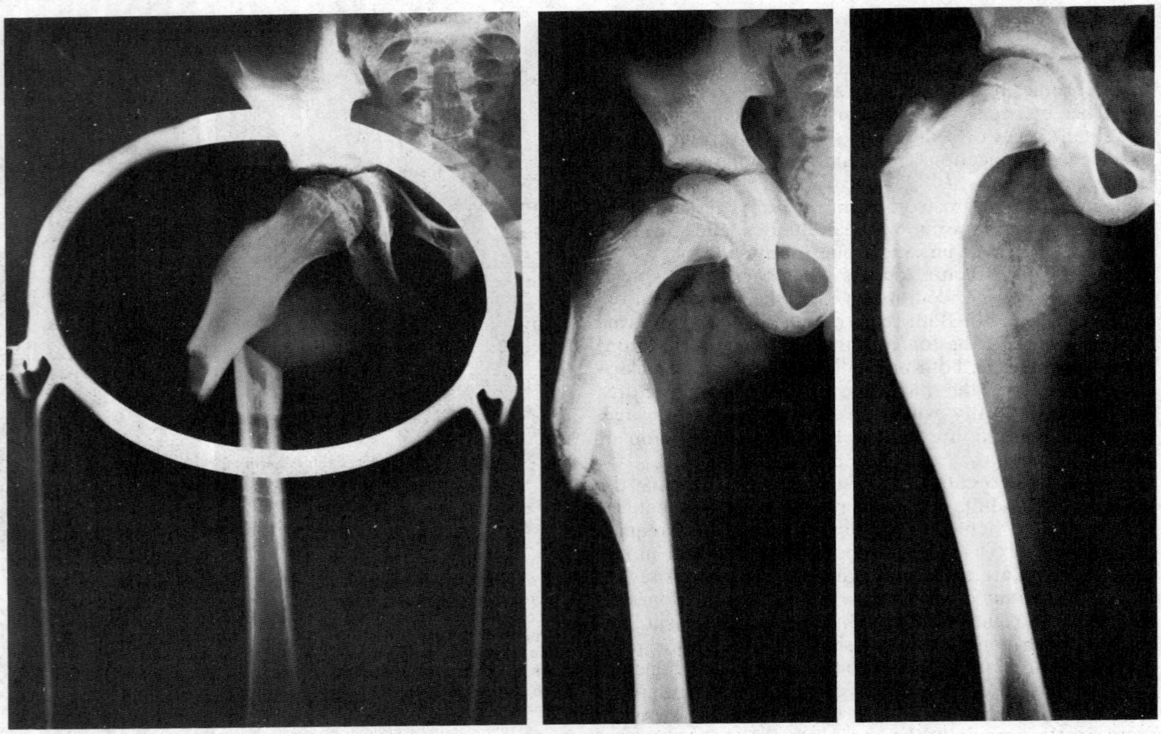

Figure 3: *Fracture of the shaft of the femur sustained by a seven-year-old boy after falling from a tree.*
(Left) Considerable angulation; transport splint visible in radiograph. (Centre) After four months the fracture has healed, with shortening and a reduction in angulation. (Right) By three years the malalignment was disappearing because of the remodelling of the bone tissue. Seven years later both the malalignment and the shortening had disappeared completely.
Goran C.H. Bauer

ments; these form organic matrix and mineral into bone (callus) that bridges the fracture. Formation of callus is faster in children than in adults and in cancellous bone than in cortical bone. Fracture of the thigh, which may heal in four to six weeks in a toddler, may require as many months in an adult. Similarly, fracture of the cancellous bone of the upper end of the humerus usually requires one-third or less of the time required for healing of a fracture of the cortical shaft of the same bone. Bridging of the fracture is hindered by separation and motion of the bone fragments, poor blood supply, and infection. After the fracture has healed, the region is remodelled by resorption and formation of bone so as to accommodate the microstructure of the bone tissue to precise mechanical demands. This remodelling also is most effective in children; a fracture of the humerus sustained during birth may heal in right-angle deformity and yet, in a few months, the normal anatomy will have been restored. In adults, on the other hand, gross deformity may exceed the remodelling capacity.

The most severe and most common cause of deficient healing is infection, osteomyelitis, associated with open fractures, which permit direct access for disease-causing organisms. The condition is prevented by treatment of open fractures with antibiotics and closure of the skin. A fracture may also unite slowly or not at all because of deficient blood supply to one or more of the bone fragments, separation of the fragments by distention or interposition of a tendon or ligament, or excessive motion at the fracture site.

The guiding principle in treatment of fractures is restoration of normal length and alignment when necessary and avoidance of motion between the fracture fragments.

Some fractures, notably compression fractures of cancellous bone (spine, upper end of humerus), are inherently stable (remain in normal alignment) and require temporary immobilization by bed rest or a sling only because of pain. Most fractures are stable in acceptable position only after reduction of dislocation and immobilization by fixation, externally by traction or plaster or internally by introduction of metallic screws, plates, nail, or wire (internal fixation).

Nonunion results in a false joint—pseudarthrosis—characterized by pain and motion at the fracture site. Healing may be achieved by immobilization with or without internal fixation and by transplantation of bone to bridge the defect.

Fracture may cause permanent deformity by residual angulation or by shortening because of overlap of cortical bone fragments, compression of cancellous bone, or, in children, arrest of metaphyseal cartilage growth.

Osteoarthritis is a late complication of fracture at a joint when the joint cartilage surfaces are disturbed and the joint is unstable. Abnormal weight distribution because of an abnormal angle of the diaphysis rarely causes osteoarthritis.

Bone tumour. Bone tumour is either primary or, more commonly, secondary (metastatic) to malignant conditions elsewhere.

Primary tumours, more common in children than in adults, are classified as malignant or benign; intermediary forms exist, however, and benign bone tumour may present therapeutic problems because of its location. Primary bone tumours are characterized by their origin in the skeletal tissue elements; for example, bone tissue tumours (the malignant osteogenic sarcoma and the benign osteoma), cartilage tumours (the malignant chondrosarcoma and the benign chondroma), bone marrow tumours (the malignant myeloma and the benign eosinophilic granuloma). Metastatic tumours are malignant by definition and are characterized by their site of origin, commonly cancer of the breast, prostate, lung, and kidney.

Symptoms of bone tumour

Common symptoms of bone tumour are pain, swelling, and fracture that is spontaneous or is caused by only trivial forces. Most bone tumours cause abnormalities observable in X-rays; defects in the bone tissue can be seen or bone that has formed in reaction to the tumour or, in some types of tumour, the tumours themselves, which consist of bone. Some bone tumours cause biochemical abnormalities detectable by examination of blood samples: myeloma (production of characteristic protein, a globulin), metastatic cancer of the prostate (production of the enzyme acid phosphatase). The ultimate identification of bone tumour rests on examination of tissue samples.

Benign tumours may be excised and the defect filled with a bone transplant if necessary for structural support. Malignant tumours may be treated by ionizing radiation, by chemical agents, or by surgical operation. Treatment of metastatic bone tumour is aimed at suppression of pain and prevention or repair of imminent or frank fracture by external support or, occasionally, by internal fixation. Treatment of malignant primary bone tumour is aimed at destruction of the tumour either by segmental resection of the involved region or by amputation.

Congenital bone diseases. Many important diseases of the locomotor system are congenital in the sense that they become evident at or soon after birth. This does not imply that they all are genetically determined or heritable. On the contrary, the majority are certainly or probably caused by factors operating during pregnancy, delivery, or early infancy.

Developmental abnormalities

Developmental abnormalities may affect isolated or multiple regions of the skeleton, or they may involve a specific tissue system; the latter are often heritable. Examples of isolated abnormalities are partial or total absence of the collarbone, radius (the long bone on the thumb side of the lower arm), and the thigh bone; congenital false joint in the shin bone (tibia); and absence of a middle segment of a limb (phocomelia; see below). Treatment of these conditions is difficult, often requiring advanced transplantation or orthopedic devices and sometimes necessitating amputation in childhood. Multiple abnormalities are represented by polyostotic fibrous dysplasia, in which affected bone is replaced by connective-tissue matrix of obscure origin. The condition may cause multiple deformities that require surgical correction. Heritable disorders of the skeleton include osteogenesis imperfecta, the Hurler and Marfan syndromes (see below), and several disorders of epiphyseal and metaphyseal growth centres. Osteogenesis imperfecta is characterized by thin bones that fracture spontaneously or from only minimal forces; the tendency to fracture usually decreases with age. The condition also typically involves the skin, which is thin and translucent; the sclerae, which are of slate blue colour; and progressive deafness. Osteogenesis imperfecta is a heritable disease, possibly a deficiency in synthesis of the collagen molecule. The Marfan syndrome is an inherited disorder of the skeleton, the aorta, and the eye. The extremities are long and thin, and the ligaments are lax, producing "loose-jointedness." The basic abnormality may be in the elastic or collagen molecules. The Hurler syndrome was previously thought to be a clinical entity but is now known to be only one of several heritable connective tissue disorders, all characterized by abnormal mucopolysaccharide metabolism. In the prototype condition dwarfism and multiple diaphyseal deformities are conspicuous. Other varieties of this group have primarily epiphyseal abnormalities. Heritable metaphyseal dysplasias, causing bone deformities near the joints, exist in several forms. The primary defect lies in the growth zone of the long bones. One of these conditions (hypophosphatasia) results from a deficiency in the enzyme alkaline phosphatase and is one of the few hereditary generalized disorders of the bony skeleton in which an enzyme defect has been identified. Multiple defects in the growth zones of the skeleton are distinct from familial hypophosphatemia, a condition characterized by low phosphate levels in the blood; it affects the kidney primarily and the skeleton only secondarily. Hemophilia, finally, is a generalized heritable condition that affects the locomotor system only secondarily by bleeding in bones and joints.

Intrauterine and birth injuries

Intrauterine injuries of the locomotor system are dramatically exemplified by the thalidomide catastrophe: children born of some women who received this drug during the initial three months of pregnancy had severe extremity defects (phocomelia). Most intrauterine injuries are probably not caused by drugs, however, but perhaps by viral, hormonal, or mechanical factors. Intrauterine amputations, clubfeet, and congenital dislocation of the hip probably belong to this group.

Birth injuries with fracture of the collarbone or humerus occur because of mechanical difficulties during delivery. These fractures heal extremely fast.

THERAPEUTIC AND CORRECTIVE MEASURES

Diagnosis of locomotor abnormalities is at present generally easier than choice of therapy. Pertinent structures are available for clinical and X-ray examination, and diagnostic categories based on chemical analysis are few in number. By contrast, an individual condition may offer an amazing number of therapeutic alternatives. It is not unusual, for example, that in osteoarthritis a choice has to be made, first, between nonsurgical (conservative) and surgical treatment and, second, between elimination of motion by immobilization of the joint (arthrodesis) and enhancement of motion by creation of an artificial joint (arthroplasty).

Traction counteracts muscle pull on the skeleton and is used to reduce and stabilize fractures and to prevent muscle shortening. Traction is applied by ropes and pulleys fastened to the skin by adhesive tape or directly to the skeleton with the aid of metal pins drilled into bone through the skin.

Internal fixation (osteosynthesis) of bone is aimed at restoration of continuity and stability during healing of a fracture, arthrodesis, or osteotomy (see below). For this purpose a variety of metal screws, pins, plates, and wires have been developed. The metal used is either stainless steel or a chromium–cobalt–molybdenum alloy that resists the corrosive action of the body fluids.

Arthroplasty, aimed at restoration of normal joint motion, is usually performed because of pain and restricted motion—for example, in rheumatoid arthritis of the elbow or the hip—but occasionally to restrict mobility—for example, in recurrent dislocation of the shoulder. Structural support and smooth gliding surfaces can be obtained by insertion of metallic devices; in the hip, for example, both the ball and the socket of the joint can be replaced. Osteotomy is aimed at correction of bony or articular deformity by cutting through bone and letting the fracture heal in the desired position, usually with the aid of internal fixation.

Arthrodesis is aimed at elimination of motion in a joint (fusion) in order to eliminate pain in osteoarthritis and rheumatoid arthritis, stabilize a joint that is either unstable or lacks useful muscle power, and remove an infectious lesion in arthritis. The operation involves removal of joint cartilage and immobilization; a bone transplant is sometimes used for more rapid restoration of continuity.

Bone resection implies surgical removal of bone and is performed either in the course of an arthroplasty or independently. The operation is performed in certain fractures—for example, of the knee cap in crush fracture—and for removal of tumour.

Epiphysiodesis (the fixing of the epiphysis to the bone shaft) is aimed at temporary or permanent cessation of growth in a metaphyseal cartilage. The operation is performed at the knee for compensation of growth in the other leg—for example, because of poliomyelitis—or in one of the other growth cartilages in the same knee—for example, because of injury.

Tendon transfer is aimed at changing the mechanical effect of the corresponding muscle. The operation is performed to restore function lost by paralysis and to correct an abnormality in the motion of a joint.

Transplantation of bone

Transplantation of bone is aimed at stimulation of bone formation and giving structural support until a defect has been bridged by new bone. If the bone cells of the transplant survive, they can continue to form bone and can stimulate adjacent tissue to formation of bone. Without survival, the transplant may function as a scaffold for invasion by tissue from adjacent bone, guided by the microstructure of the dead transplant. Cell-rich cancellous bone stimulates bone formation more effectively than does cortical bone, which gives better structural support.

The fundamental problems in transplantation of bone, as with other tissues, are cell death because of deficient blood supply and a tendency toward rejection. The smaller the transplant, the better are the possibilities that blood vessels will reach the cells in time; this is why many small chips are used for stimulation of bone formation. Another possibility is to transplant bone in continuity with attached vessels in order to preserve the blood supply of the transplant. The immunologic problem is usually circumvented by use of bone from the individual himself (autotransplantation). In children sufficient bone for autotransplantation is often not available; bone from another individual will then be used. An attempt to modify the immunologic reaction to such a transplant is usually made by radiation and by storage in a deep freeze (bone bank).

Common indications for transplantation of bone are nonunion of a fracture, a bone cyst, arthrodesis, and structural defects in cancellous bone caused by compression fracture—for example, the heel bone.

Amputation is performed for four reasons: arterial disease, gross injury, tumour, and developmental abnormality, all more common in the legs than in the arms. Arterial disease, arteriosclerosis ("hardening of the arteries"), often associated with diabetes, is common in the aged. Gross injury to nerves, vessels, and soft tissues and primary tumours of bone or other connective tissue usually involve relatively young individuals. Developmental abnormalities—for example, congenital false joint in the tibia or abnormal development of the thigh bone—may occasion amputation in childhood.

BIBLIOGRAPHY. R.B. SALTER, *Textbook of Disorders and Injuries of the Musculoskeletal System* (1970), a comprehensive modern text dealing with all aspects of orthopedics, rheumatology, metabolic bone disease, rehabilitation, and fractures as they relate to joint diseases, including bibliographies in each subsection; W.J.W. SHARRARD, *Paediatric Orthopaedics and Fractures* (1971), a comprehensive textbook written by a specialist in neurologic and developmental abnormalities in children; E.E. AEGERTER and J.A. KIRKPATRICK, JR., *Orthopaedic Diseases: Physiology, Pathology, Radiology*, 3rd ed. (1968), the standard text on bone pathology, particularly tumour pathology; L. LICHTENSTEIN, *Diseases of Bones and Joints* (1970), a modern text on nontumorous diseases; A.H. CRENSHAW (ed.), *Campbell's Operative Orthopaedics*, 5th ed, 2 vol. (1971), the standard text on bone and joint surgery.

(G.C.H.B.)

Bonhoeffer, Dietrich

Dietrich Bonhoeffer, one of the most influential Protestant theologians of the mid-20th century, derives his stature and influence from both his thought and his life. He is important for his cogent and vivid insistence on the role of Christianity in the modern secularized world; for his role in the ecumenical movement, striving not only for the unity of Christians but also for peace among nations; and for his militant resistance to the Nazi rulers of his German homeland (to the point of conspiring to assassinate Hitler), culminating in his own imprisonment and execution. This final dramatic episode not only bore witness to his uncompromising ideals and made his thought far more widely known than it might otherwise have been but it fostered the expression of his most novel and radical theological concepts in the posthumously published *Letters and Papers from Prison*.

Born in Breslau on February 4, 1906, Bonhoeffer grew up amid the academic circles of the University of Berlin, where his father, Karl Bonhoeffer, was professor of psychiatry and neurology. From 1923 to 1927 he studied theology at the universities of Tübingen and Berlin. At Berlin he was influenced by the historical theologians Adolf von Harnack, Reinhold Seeberg, and Karl Holl, but also was strongly attracted by the new "theology of revelation" being propounded elsewhere by Karl Barth. His concern to relate himself critically to Barth is seen in his doctoral thesis, *Sanctorum Communio* (1930; *The Communion of Saints*, 1963), in which he tried to com-

Bonhoeffer, 1939.
By courtesy of Eberhard Bethge

bine a sociological and a theological understanding of the church, and in *Akt und Sein* (1931; *Act and Being*, 1962), in which he traces the influence of transcendental philosophy and ontology, Kantian and post-Kantian theories of knowledge and of being, on Protestant and Catholic theologies.

After serving in 1928–29 as assistant pastor of a German-speaking congregation in Barcelona, he spent a year as an exchange student at Union Theological Seminary in New York. On his return to Germany in 1931 he took up an appointment as lecturer in systematic theology at the University of Berlin. From the first days of the Nazi accession to power in 1933 he was involved in protests against the regime, especially its anti-Semitism, and despite another 18-month absence when he served as pastor of two small German congregations in London (1933–35), Bonhoeffer became a leading spokesman for the Confessing Church, the centre of German Protestant resistance to the Nazi regime. In 1935 he was appointed to organize and head a new seminary for the Confessing Church at Finkenwald (Pomerania), which continued in disguised form until 1940, despite its proscription by the political authorities in 1937. Here he introduced the practices of prayer, private confession, and common discipline described in his book *Gemeinsames Leben* (1939; *Life Together*, 1954). From this period also dates *Nachfolge* (1937; *The Cost of Discipleship*, 1948, rev. ed., 1959), a study of the Sermon on the Mount in which he attacked the "cheap grace" being marketed in Protestant (especially Lutheran) churches—*i.e.*, an unlimited offer of forgiveness, which in fact served as a cover for ethical laxity. It was in this rigorous and even ascetic guise (to which his later theme of "Christian worldliness" provides a contrast if not a contradiction) that Bonhoeffer first became widely known. His views on international affairs at this time were close to pacifism.

Opponent of the Nazis

After attending the ecumenical conference at Cambridge in 1931, Bonhoeffer was appointed a European youth secretary of the World Alliance for Promoting International Friendship through the Churches, and he remained an active participant in ecumenical affairs despite the increasingly nationalistic mood in Germany. In his efforts to interpret to Christians elsewhere the significance of the German Church struggle, he found a sympathetic advocate in G.K.A. Bell, bishop of Chichester, England. Bonhoeffer's own involvement took an increasingly political character after 1938, when his brother-in-law, the jurist Hans von Dohnanyi, introduced him to the group seeking Hitler's overthrow. In 1939 he considered taking refuge in the United States but returned after only two weeks in New York, writing to his sponsor, the theologian Reinhold Niebuhr that "I will have no right to participate in the reconstruction of Christian life in Germany after the war if I do not share the trials of this time with my people." Despite the restrictions imposed on him, Bonhoeffer was able to continue his work for the resistance movement under cover of employment in the Military Intelligence Department, which in fact was a centre of the resistance. In May 1942, he flew to Sweden to convey to the British government, through Bishop Bell, the conspirators' proposals for a negotiated peace; these hopes were thwarted, however, by the Allies' "unconditional surrender" policy. Bonhoeffer was arrested on April 5, 1943, and imprisoned in Berlin. Following the failure of the attempt on Hitler's life on July 20, 1944, the discovery of documents linking Bonhoeffer directly with the conspiracy led to his further interrogation and eventual execution at Flössenberg (Bavaria) on April 9, 1945. Bonhoeffer never married, his engagement having been announced just before his imprisonment.

Ethical and religious thought

During the years 1940–43 Bonhoeffer worked intermittently on a volume on Christian ethics but completed only fragments, which were published posthumously (*Ethik*, 1949; Eng. trans., *Ethics*, 1955). Abjuring all "thinking in terms of two spheres,"—*i.e.*, any dualistic separation of the church and the world, nature and grace, the sacred and the profane—he called for a unitive, concrete ethic founded on Christology (doctrines about the person and work of Christ), an ethic in which labour, marriage, and government are to be viewed dynamically as divinely imposed tasks or functions ("mandates") rather than orders of creation. Bonhoeffer welcomed the rapprochement of Christianity and humanism in the face of modern tyrannies and urged a recovery of the concept of "the natural" in Protestant thought. The prison writings, published in 1951 (German title *Widerstand und Ergebung*; Eng. trans. *Letters and Papers from Prison*, 1955, rev. ed., 1964), are of interest both for the remarkable richness of cultural and spiritual life that they display and for the theological themes developed especially in the letters to Bonhoeffer's friend and later editor and biographer, Eberhard Bethge. Reviewing the history of secularization in the West since the Renaissance, Bonhoeffer asked whether man's increasing ability to cope with his problems without the hypothesis of God may not indicate the obsolescence of the "religious premise" upon which Christianity has hitherto been based. Rather than looking for gaps in human knowledge or accenting human weaknesses as a basis for apologetics, he asserted that the church ought to affirm man's maturity in a "world come of age." The stripping off of "religion," in the sense of otherworldliness and preoccupation with personal salvation, Bonhoeffer suggested, will in fact free Christianity for its authentic this-worldliness in accordance with its Judaic roots. The church should give up its inherited privileges in order to free Christians to "share in God's sufferings in the world" in imitation of Jesus, "the man for others." These ideas have subsequently been influential in movements for the reform of church and ministry; in the "Honest to God" debate initiated by John A.T. Robinson, the bishop of Woolwich, England; in efforts to propound a "secular Christianity" or "the secular meaning of the Gospel"; in the "death of God" controversy of the 1960s; and, from a different perspective, in the articulation of a "theology of hope."

The chief works by Bonhoeffer in addition to those already mentioned are *Creation and Fall: A Theological Interpretation of Genesis 1–3* (1933; Eng. trans. 1959) and the collected shorter writings, *Gesammelte Schriften* (5 vol., 2nd ed., 1965–69), selections from which have been published in English translation under the titles *No Rusty Swords* (1965), *Christ the Center* (1966; British title *Christology*), and *The Way to Freedom* (1966).

BIBLIOGRAPHY. The definitive biography is EBERHARD BETHGE, *Dietrich Bonhoeffer* (1967; Eng. trans., 1970). See also WOLF-DIETER ZIMMERMANN and R.G. SMITH (eds.), *I Knew Dietrich Bonhoeffer* (1966), reminiscences by friends and associates. Symposia dealing with Bonhoeffer's thought are: M.E. MARTY (ed.), *The Place of Bonhoeffer* (1962); R.G. SMITH (ed.), *World Come of Age* (1967); PETER VORKINK (ed.), *Bonhoeffer in a World Come of Age* (1968); and EBERHARD BETHGE (ed.), *Die mündige Welt*, 5 vol. (1955–69). Other major studies include: J.D. GODSEY, *The Theology of Dietrich Bonhoeffer* (1960); J.A. PHILLIPS, *Christ for Us in the Theology of Dietrich Bonhoeffer* (1967; British title, *The Form of Christ in the World*, 1967); WILLIAM KUHNS, *In Pursuit of Dietrich Bonhoeffer* (1967); and J.W. WOELFEL, *Bonhoeffer's Theology: Classical and Revolutionary* (1970).

(F.S.)

Boniface, Saint

The most important figure in the Christianization of Germany, St. Boniface is often called the Apostle of Germany, because his work there in the 8th century is comparable to that of Peter in Rome and of Paul among the Gentiles. A great organizer, a reformer and leader of men, Boniface set the church in Germany on a firm course of undeviating piety and irreproachable conduct. In his letters and in the writings of his contemporaries, he appears as a man of purpose and dedication, an innovator with a powerful though willful personality.

By courtesy of the Staatsbibliothek Bamberg

St. Boniface baptizing converts into the German Church; detail from a manuscript from Fulda Abbey, 10th–11th century. In the Staatsbibliothek Bamberg (MS. Lit. 1).

Boniface, originally called Wynfrid or Wynfrith, was born *c.* 675 of a noble family of Wessex, England. He received an excellent education in the Benedictine abbeys of Adescancastre (Exeter) and Nhutscelle (Nursling, between Winchester and Southampton) and became a Benedictine monk, being ordained priest at about the age of 30. From 716 to 722 he made two attempts to evangelize the Frisian Saxons on the Continent but was balked by their king, Radbod. On his return to England he learned that his abbot had died and that he had been elected in his stead—an honour he declined in favour of a second attempt at a missionary career. In 718 he accompanied a group of Anglo-Saxon pilgrims to Rome, where Pope Gregory II entrusted him with a mission to the pagans east of the Rhine, asking him only to use the Roman formula for Baptism, rather than the Celtic, and to consult with Rome on major problems arising from his work. Gregory II changed Wynfrid's name to Boniface. In the meantime, Radbod had died (719), and Boniface returned to Frisia to assist his countryman Bishop Willibrord in his missionary activities. In 722 he went to Hesse, where he established the first of many Benedictine monasteries as a means of consolidating his work.

So great was his success that he was called to Rome, where Gregory consecrated him a missionary bishop. The Pope also provided him with a collection of canons (ecclesiastical regulations) and letters of recommendation to such important personages as Charles Martel, master of the Frankish kingdom, whose protection was essential to Boniface's success. It was the pagan awe of Martel's name that allowed Boniface to destroy the sacred oak of the Germanic god Thor at Geismar.

For ten years (725–735) Boniface was active in Thuringia, converting pagans and renewing the faith of Christians who had been converted earlier by Irish missionaries, whose haphazard methods of evangelization were henceforth to be the bane of Boniface's life. He met opposition, he said, "from ambitious and free-living clerics" whom he pursued relentlessly, even when they appealed to the popes. On a later occasion, Pope Zachary was forced to moderate the zeal of Boniface, who requested not only excommunication but also solitary confinement for two "heretical" missionaries, Adelbert and Clement the Irishman—sentences that the Pope avoided imposing by deliberate delay. Boniface's handling of missionaries whose methods he deplored sheds light on his personality and temperament; he turned immediately to Rome; he expected prompt and ruthless action; and he seems at times to have been excessively severe in his judgments.

Role as reformer and organizer of the church

Boniface's career was assisted in a unique and moving way by his brother and sister Benedictines from England. They supported him by gifts and encouraged him by their faithful love, expressed in letters that were delightful in their openness and humanity. Their final expression of love for him was to cast their lots with him in Germany, where they formed the nucleus of four monasteries that served as centres of civilized Christian life.

Ordered by Pope Gregory III (731–741) to organize the church in Bavaria, Boniface initially established four bishoprics there. His work had far-reaching political repercussions, for his Christianization of Bavaria paved the way for the ultimate incorporation of the country into the Carolingian Empire. After 740 he added another see in Bavaria and also created three in central Germany. Aided by his new suffragan bishops—for such they were, in fact, though his appointment as archbishop of Mainz came later (751)—Boniface undertook the reform of the Frankish clergy and, wherever possible, of Irish missionaries. Between 740 and 745, five synods were convened for this purpose. In 747 a reforming council was held for the entire Frankish kingdom with the wholehearted collaboration of Carloman and Pepin, the sons and heirs of Charles Martel. Though Charles had protected Boniface, he had, at the same time, given church land to his magnates and used the discipline of the church as a means of taming recalcitrant Germanic tribes. Carloman and Pepin, on the other hand, made the decisions of the council of 747 binding in Frankish law.

Martyrdom

Boniface's life ended in martyrdom at the hands of a band of pagan Frisians, who killed him as he was reading the Scriptures to Christian neophytes on Pentecost Sunday (June 5, 754). Boniface had asked to be buried at Fulda, the monastery he had entrusted (744) to his Bavarian disciple Sturmi. There his body rests in a magnificent baroque sarcophagus.

Organizer, educator, and reformer, Boniface profoundly influenced the course of intellectual, political, and ecclesiastical history in Germany and France throughout the Middle Ages. He unified the missionary movement by bringing it under the control of Rome. Through his monasteries, which furnished bishops and teachers for many generations, he significantly improved the quality of life in the Frankish kingdom.

BIBLIOGRAPHY. G.F. BROWNE, *Boniface of Crediton and His Companions* (1910); E.S. DUCKETT, *Anglo Saxon Saints and Scholars*, pp. 337–455 (1947), a popular account based on excellent scholarship; E. EMERTON, *Letters of St. Boniface* (1940), a translation of letters to and from St. Boniface; A. ERDLE and H. BUTTERWEGGE (eds.), *Bonifatius, Wanderer Christi* (1954); G.W. GREENAWAY, *Saint Boniface* (1955); S. HILPISCH and C.M. AHERNE, *New Catholic Encyclopedia*, vol. 2, pp. 665–668 (1967), contains an excellent bibliography; E. KYLIE (ed. and trans.), *The English Correspondence of Saint Boniface* (1924, reprinted 1966); W. LEVISON, *England and the Continent in the Eighth Century*, pp. 70–93 (1946), gives insight into the impact of England on the Continent; *Die Gedichte*, in *Monumenta Germaniae Historica Poetae*, 1:3–23, the critical edition of the poems; J.B. RUSSELL, "Saint Boniface and the Eccentrics," *Church History*, 33: 235–247 (1964), gives new insight into Boniface's reaction to Irish missionaries; WILLIBALD, *The Life of Saint Boniface* (Eng. trans. 1916).

(C.M.A.)

Boniface VIII, Pope

Boniface VIII, who was pope from 1294 to 1303, engaged in a fierce struggle over the extent of papal authority with the powerful monarchies of the emerging nations of the West, especially the French monarchy. His stubborn claims to full temporal and spiritual power were certainly no more extravagant than those of his predecessors, but the new forces of nationalism were no longer willing to accept these well-established claims. The conflict culminated in a brutal attack on the person of Boniface VIII, perpetrated by the emissary of King Philip IV of France. Only six years after Boniface's death, the seat of the papacy was moved to Avignon, France, where it remained for 68 years, reaching a low ebb in its international prestige.

Anderson—Alinari

Boniface VIII; fresco by Giotto, c. 1300. In the church of S. Giovanni in Laterano, Rome.

Early life and election to the papacy

Benedict Caetani was born in Anagni, near Rome, probably between 1235 and 1240, of an old and influential Roman family. He studied law in Bologna and then for many years held increasingly important functions in the papal government. Martin IV made him cardinal-deacon of St. Nicholas in Carcere Tulliano in 1281; under Nicholas IV he became cardinal-priest of St. Martin in Montibus in 1291. As papal legate to a church council in Paris from 1290 to 1291, he succeeded in delaying the outbreak of renewed war between France and England and in bringing about peace between France and Aragon. It was Cardinal Benedict Caetani who confirmed the unhappy pope Celestine V in his wish to resign and then, after he had succeeded him as Boniface VIII, found it advisable to intern the old man in the castle of Fumone, where he soon died. Although Celestine died of natural causes, the death was open to suspicion and incriminating aspersions by Boniface's enemies. Among those who carried on the propaganda and opposition against Boniface were many of the Franciscan "Spirituals" (members of the order founded by St. Francis of Assisi who followed a literal observance of his rule of poverty), including the poet Iacopone da Todi, some of whose poems were written during his imprisonment by Boniface.

The two principal international conflicts that existed from the beginning of Boniface's pontificate were that between France and England concerning Guyenne and Flanders, and that between the kingdoms of Naples and Aragon concerning the island of Sicily, which, after much provocation, had broken away from the Neapolitan king, disregarding papal feudal overlordship. Boniface finally, though unwillingly, accepted the independence of the island kingdom under Frederick of Aragon. His attempts to stop hostilities between Edward I of England and Philip IV of France, however, became enmeshed with another important problem, the increasing tendency of these warring monarchs to tax the clergy without obtaining papal consent. Although the desire of the late-medieval rulers to tax the wealth of their clergy has been defended and can perhaps be understood, the practice was unquestionably contrary to the canon law (ecclesiastical law) of the time. That Boniface refused to look on inactively while the struggle between France and England, which he was trying to terminate, was being financed at the cost and to the prejudice of the church and the papacy is not surprising. In 1296 he issued the bull *Clericis Laicos*, which forbade under the sanction of automatic excommunication any imposition of taxes on the clergy without express license by the pope. This bull had some effect in England, chiefly because of its support by the archbishop of Canterbury, Robert Winchelsey; but in France there was no strong defender of papal prerogative against the concerted action of the king and his civil lawyers. Philip IV countered or even forestalled the publication of *Clericis Laicos* with an order forbidding all export of money and valuables from France and with the expulsion of foreign merchants.

Conflicts with Philip IV of France

Although Philip's measures were a serious threat to papal revenues, they alone probably would not have forced Boniface to the far-reaching concessions that he had to grant the French king within the year, concessions that almost amounted to revocation of *Clericis Laicos*. The necessity of coming to terms was primarily the result of an insurrection against Boniface by a section of the Colonna family, a powerful antipapal Roman family that included two cardinals, culminating in the armed robbery of a large amount of papal treasure in May 1297. A year of military action against the Colonna followed, which ended with their unconditional surrender. They were absolved from excommunication but were not reinstated in their offices and possessions; they therefore rebelled again and fled; some of them went to Philip, with whom they had conspired, perhaps, even before the issue of *Clericis Laicos*.

Boniface's first conflict with the French king was followed by an apparent reconciliation, which was emphasized by the Pope's canonization of Philip's holy ancestor Louis IX. A second conflict, which broke out in 1301 around the trumped-up charges against a southern French bishop Bernard Saisset of Pamiers and his summary trial and imprisonment, proved to be irreconcilable. Now the King threatened and meant to destroy one of the most fundamental gains that the papacy had made and maintained in the great struggles of the last two centuries: papal, rather than secular, control of the clergy. The Pope could not compromise here, and in the bull *Ausculta Fili* ("Listen Son") he sharply rebuked Philip and demanded amends, especially the release of the Bishop, who had appealed to Rome. Instead, the King's chancellor, Pierre Flotte, was allowed to circulate a distorted extract of the bull and thus to prepare public opinion for the great assembly of the estates-general (the legislative body of France) in April 1302, in which nobles and burghers enthusiastically, and the clergy reluctantly, supported the King.

Boniface, nevertheless, appears to have had good reason to hope for a favourable termination of the conflict, because Philip's army was shortly afterward disastrously defeated by a league of Flemish townspeople and because the German king and prospective emperor Albert I of Habsburg, was ready to give up his French alliance if the Pope would recognize the contested legitimacy of his rule. This recognition was granted early in 1303 in terms that exalted the ideal and traditional, though rarely realized, harmonious relationship between the papacy and the Holy Roman Empire. This empire now was said by the Pope to possess—under ultimate papal supremacy—an overlordship over all other kingdoms, including France. In November 1302 Boniface had issued an even more fundamental declaration concerning the position of the papacy in the Christian world, the bull *Unam Sanctam* ("One Holy"), which has become the most widely known of all papal documents of the Middle Ages because of its allegedly radical and extreme formulation of the content of the papal office. The bull as a whole is indeed a strong but not a novel invocation of the supremacy of the spiritual over the temporal power. Nevertheless, the old Gelasian doctrine that both powers are distinct and both are from God is clearly stated, and in the final dogmatic sentence the Pope speaks not of the temporal power but of the human creature as the object of the papal plenitude of power, submission to which is said to be necessary for salvation.

Meanwhile in France, Philip IV's councillor Guillaume de Nogaret had taken Flotte's place as the leader of an actively antipapal royal policy. Philip was supported in this policy by other enemies of the Pope, including the legate whom Boniface had dispatched to France in these critical months and who betrayed his master, the French cardinal Jean Lemoine (Johannes Monachus). Many unjustified accusations against Boniface, ranging from unlawful entry into the papal office to heresy, were raised against him at a secret meeting of the King and his advisers held in the Louvre at Paris; these accusations were to be taken up and elaborated upon later during the posthumous trial against the Pope pursued by Philip IV. Shortly after the Louvre meeting, at which Nogaret had demanded the condemnation of the Pope by a general council of the church, Nogaret went to Italy to stir up, if possible, rebellion against the Pope. He was unsuccessful in this attempt, but when he learned that Boniface was about to publish a new bull announcing Philip's excommunication, Nogaret, with the assistance of Sciarra Colonna—a popular member of the powerful family—and with the connivance of some of the cardinals, decided to capture the Pope at Anagni, where the Pope was spending the summer. In this he succeeded through the momentary complicity of the local leaders of the city of Anagni, who, however, after two days changed their minds, rescued the Pope, and thus frustrated whatever further plans Nogaret may have had. During these two days Boniface, whom Sciarra Colonna would have killed but for Nogaret's wish to drag the Pope before a council, was probably physically ill-treated. He bore everything with great courage and patience. Boniface returned to Rome physically and mentally broken and died soon after, on October 11, 1303.

Boniface's capture

Among the lasting achievements of Boniface VIII's turbulent pontificate were the publication of the third part of the *Corpus Juris Canonici* (*Corpus of Canon Law*), the so-called *Liber Sextus* ("Sixth Book"), and the institution of the Jubilee of 1300, the first Holy Year. The event was commemorated in a painting by Giotto, a fragment of which still survives in the basilica of San Giovanni in Laterano. Boniface VIII was a figure of some importance in the revival of the arts in the age of Dante and Giotto. His sepulchre came from the workshop of Arnolfo di Cambio; his tomb with his reclining statue is in the Vatican grottoes. Of the numerous memorial statues erected in his honour by himself or others—and later used by his enemies to brand him as an idolater—several still survive. They are visual evidence for the fact, known also from other sources, that Boniface VIII extended the height of the papal tiara and increased the number of crowns that circle the tiara from one to two and perhaps to three, which is their number in modern times.

Assessment

The violent attack on Boniface VIII marks the first open rejection of papal spiritual dominance by the rising national monarchies of the West and, above all, by France. Boniface's assertions of papal plenitude of power did not go beyond those of his predecessors in the 13th century. They were in fact more moderate than, for instance, those of Innocent IV and were in any case well within the range of the opinions gradually elaborated in the schools of theology and canon law in the period between the age of Gregory VII, the great 11th-century reformer, and that of Boniface. Boniface's failure was not caused by any novelty of his views or claims but by changed circumstances, by his inability or unwillingness to gauge their significance adequately, and, last but not least, by his own character: conscious of his superior intellect and at the same time tormented by illness, he was impulsive to the point of imprudence and short-tempered to the point of uncharitableness. It was his exaggerated harshness against the Colonna—whose hatred for the Caetani Pope was largely the result of conflicting interests of the two families—as well as his shortsighted underestimation of the ruthlessness of Philip IV of France and his helpers that led to the coalition of these two disparate forces and to the Pope's downfall. Boniface VIII's personal failings, however, can in no way exculpate Philip IV the Fair and his ministers, who used forgery, defamation, intimidation, and finally violence against the Pope.

BIBLIOGRAPHY. An excellent work and the only full-scale biography in English is T.S.R. BOASE, *Boniface VIII* (1933). The following studies are concerned specifically with Boniface's quarrel with the French king Philip IV: A.F.J.P.M. DE LEVIS-MIREPOIX, *Le Conflit entre la Papauté et le roi de France, 7 Septembre 1303* (1969); J. RIVIERE, *Le Problème de l'église et de l'état au temps de Philippe le Bel* (1926); and C.T. WOOD, *Philip the Fair and Boniface VIII* (1967). Boniface's correspondence and promulgations may be studied in *Les Registres de Boniface VIII*, ed. by G.A.L. DIGARD *et al.*, 4 vol. (1884–1939).

(G.B.L.)

Bonn

Formerly a peaceful cluster of pleasant townships and villages situated on the banks of the Rhine about 15 miles south of Cologne, present-day Bonn was suddenly plunged into a new role of government administration and high politics when it was chosen as the provisional capital of the German Federal Republic in 1949. The home of more than 300,000 people by the early 1970s, Bonn has become the 18th Federal German city in order of size, a position attained in 1969 when the old city of Bonn was amalgamated with the towns of Bad Godesberg and Beuel and several minor parishes. These communities had already been developing into an extensive, built-up urban region during previous decades. The accelerated development of the metropolitan region since 1949 and its integration into the new municipality in 1969 underline the political fact that Bonn is now regarded as the actual capital of the German Federal Republic. As any other capital of a major nation, Bonn has felt the impact of its growing federal administration and its associated institutions. Bonn is also a major and expanding university centre; and as Beethoven's birthplace, it is a town particularly devoted to the promotion of the musical arts.

History. The oldest settlement known by the name of Bonn was a prehistoric river crossing discovered by Roman legionaries in the 1st century BC. The settlement itself probably disappeared soon afterward, but its name was continued in Castra Bonnensia, the fortress the Romans founded about the middle of the 1st century AD and occupied until the 5th. In the centuries that followed the breakup of the Roman Empire, Castra Bonnensia survived as a civilian settlement; and its walls, still intact, enclosed the 9th-century Bonnburg of the Franks.

Roman fortress of Castra Bonnensia

The medieval city, however, did not grow up on the site of the Roman camp but farther away on the Roman burial ground, which, from the 3rd century onward, was a Christian centre and was known later as the Villa Basilica. In the 9th century the Villa Basilica began to take over some of the functions of Bonnburg, until by the 11th century it was firmly established as the leading settlement of the region. As a monastic sanctuary the Villa Basilica was a settlement of clergy served by laymen. Craftsmen, merchants, and other groups, attracted by the expanding town, settled beside it in an emergent Oppidum Bonnense. In the 13th century, both settlements were surrounded by a wall extensive enough to meet the city's spatial needs for centuries to come.

Although Bonn did not expand from the 13th to the 19th century, it did grow in importance, becoming the capital of the Electorate and Archbishopric of Cologne, and then a sovereign state in its own right. This era ended abruptly in 1794, when the French Revolutionary forces occupied the city. Deprived of its function as a capital and reduced to poverty by the Napoleonic Wars, Bonn was annexed to Prussia in 1815. Although the founding of the university in 1818 marked a turning point in the city's history, there was little further development until the second half of the 19th century when the city became fashionable as one of Germany's residential towns. In 1914 the prosperous residential areas to the south and west of the city, enlarged by the incorporation of several villages, accommodated some 200 millionaires. It was their wealth, not industrial or commercial activity, that made the city prosperous. With the disappearance of its wealthy residents after World War I, Bonn again suffered losses from which it had not recovered when it was severely hit by the air raids of World War II. The raids destroyed 19 percent of its buildings and damaged 70 percent. The development of the city since the war is primarily the result of its having been chosen as the provisional capital of West Germany in 1949.

The contemporary city. *Layout and boundaries.* As the city owes its present boundaries and conglomerate makeup to the Bonn Act of 1969, it does not possess a dominant single centre but many centres and subcentres. The heart of the old city of Bonn with its narrow streets and those of the former towns of Bad Godesberg and Beuel form the major centres of the new city, but their influence is very much diminished by the incorporation of some 30 former villages, each with a centre of its own, into Bonn. It is this historical polycentricity that makes Bonn appear to be very much smaller than most cities of its population. The conurbation of Bonn is embedded in a landscape the most important elements of which are the lowlands of the Lower Rhine, Rheinische Schiefergebirge (the Rhine Slate Mountains), and the Rhine River itself. Near the river, the lowlands extend far to the south, while farther from the river the mountains range far to the north. The Rhine flows northwest through both of these regions, which drop toward the river in a series of terraces.

The surrounding landscape

The city has spread along both banks of the river, where multiple railway lines, busy trunk roads, and the intervening built-up areas intersect the city from north to south, causing considerable hindrance to intercity communications.

Population. Since the 1950s both the population increase in Bonn and the mobility of population have exceeded those of any other German city except Munich. In 1969 the number of persons moving out of Bonn (26,803) had risen slightly above that of those moving in (26,496), and the mobility rate (178 migrants per 1,000 inhabitants) is high. These and other demographic facts were in sharp contrast with the national average. Other contrasts include: the high and still-growing proportion of female inhabitants (1,117 per 1,000 male), the high and growing rate of salaried employees (554 per 1,000 persons employed), and the low and declining number of manual workers (320 per 1,000 persons employed). All of those trends reflected the function of Bonn as a capital, whereas the high rate of single-person households (400 per 1,000) was influenced by the fact that Bonn is the seat of a large university. The above figures apply to the city as a whole. Within the city itself, there are differences corresponding to its polycentric structure. The centres of older areas, in contrast with the newer surrounding ones, have a smaller percentage of children, a higher percentage of old people, and a smaller average household. It is the functioning of Bonn as a capital and as a university town that largely determines its demographic structure and particularly its changes.

Economic life. Those responsible for economic development in the late 19th century did their utmost to keep large industries out to preserve the city's attractions as a residential town for the rich. As a result, Bonn has remained a poorly industrialized city. By far the most important employers are the service industries, including the many organizations associated with Bonn's function as a capital, for they employ more than half the working forces. Next are commercial enterprises employing 25,000 persons, or 15.8 percent of the total. Manufacturing employs 23,400 persons in 1,050 plants, or 14.8 percent of the total. A large number and wide range of products supply small and dispersed markets. Typical products are laboratory equipment, switchgear, organs, and flags. The trades are, by West German standards, rather over-

Principal employers

represented, employing some 20,500 persons, or about 13 percent of the total, mainly in the building industry. Produce, supplied mainly by the neighbouring villages, is auctioned in the market in Bonn, which remains a major German centre for the distribution of fruits and vegetables, sold mainly to the Ruhr district.

Bonn has a large civic debt. Politically motivated reluctance to invest in the "provisional" capital ended only in 1970, when the federal government agreed to compensate the city for services rendered; but such payments were thought unlikely to solve the financial problems of a city where economic imbalance prevails and is growing.

Political and governmental institutions. The Bundestag and the Bundesrat (legislative bodies), the *Bundespräsident* (head of state), and the *Bundeskanzler* (head of government) all are found in Bonn. These and other central institutions are located in the south of the old city, in an area that has become the geographical centre. It is here that the government is concentrating the many administrative offices that had previously been dispersed. More than 100 nations are represented in Bonn by embassies or missions, which have put nearly all the former manor houses and 19th-century villas to new use as residences, legations, and consulates. The number of people with diplomatic status exceeds 6,000. Bonn accommodates many regional institutions, such as the offices of the Archaeological Survey, the Geodetic Survey, the Road Survey of North Rhine-Westphalia, the Rhenish Chamber of Agriculture, the Chamber of Industry and Commerce, the Labour Office, and the local and regional courts of justice.

Services and transportation. The city's services are unevenly distributed. Their highest concentration, particularly of the health services, is to be found in old Bonn, which provides 5,099 of the total 5,643 hospital beds. The fact that most of the beds are predominantly occupied by nonresidents emphasizes the function of Bonn as a services centre. There are 27 homes for some 1,500 elderly and disabled, 98 kindergartens for about 6,000 children, and special institutions for the mentally handicapped and 6,000 or so others in need of public assistance.

Water, gas, and electricity are mainly supplied by the municipality, which also provides most local and much regional transport. The number of transit passengers, however, is declining, while private transport is increasing. National and international travel facilities, provided mainly by the Federal Railways and by Cologne Airport, are well developed. The autobahn (expressway) and the four federal roads passing through Bonn attract much of the long-distance traffic, however.

Cultural life. As Beethoven's birthplace, Bonn is particularly devoted to the promotion of the musical arts. It maintains a municipal orchestra and arranges numerous national and international concerts. Many concerts and vocal recitals also are performed by local philharmonic and musical societies. The Beethovenhalle, a modern concert hall, is the centre of Bonn's musical life.

Apart from the spacious municipal theatre (drama, opera, operetta, musicals, and ballet), there are several private theatres renowned for their avant-garde productions. Other important institutions are the Rheinische Landesmuseum (Rhine Provincial Museum; archaeology), the Museum Alexander Koenig (zoology), and well-known city and university art galleries as well as private collections.

Historic churches and palaces

Prominent among surviving historic buildings are the cathedral, a Romanesque basilica (11th–13th century) surmounted by five towers of which the central (315 feet, or 96 metres high) is a landmark in the Rhine Valley, and the old village churches of Muffendorf (10th century), Vilich (11th century), and Schwarz Rheindorf (12th century). The former Kurfürstliche Residenz (Electoral Palace, later university) and the Poppelsdorf Palace, with its botanical gardens, along with the city's beautiful avenues and parks are reminders of the electoral and archiepiscopal capital. The parks, though limited in area, have a high recreational value, since they adjoin some of the densely populated parts of the city. More extensive recreational areas are the forests of Venusberg, Kreuzberg, Kottenforst, and Ennert on the southern and western fringes of the city. Beyond the city, the mountain country of the Westerwald and the Eifel are within easy reach.

BIBLIOGRAPHY. J. NIESSEN, *Geschichte der Stadt Bonn*, vol. 1 (1956); and E. ENNEN, *Geschichte der Stadt Bonn*, vol. 2 (1962), an extensive, scholarly, yet readable history of the city—the standard work on the subject; E. ENNEN and D. HOROLDT, *Kleine Geschichte der Stadt Bonn* (1967), a brief, more general, history of the city, with an appendix containing more than 100 illustrations and photographs; *Bonner Geschichtsblätter*, an annual publication of the Bonn History Society that includes learned articles, mainly on history—occasionally also on the geography and related subjects of the city and its region; A. PHILIPPSON, *Die Stadt Bonn: Ihre Lage und räumliche Entwicklung* (1947), a definitive descriptive

Elisabeth Niggemeyer—Bavaria-Verlag

The Rheinische Friedrich-Wilhelms-Universität Bonn (University of Bonn).

geography of the city, its layout and spatial development; *Bonner Zahlen: Statistische Berichte der Stadt Bonn* (quarterly), a valuable statistical reference; W. KULS *et al.*, *Eine Karte der Bevölkerungsverteilung in der Stadt Bonn* (1971), a methodological and critical study of the distribution of the population within the old city of Bonn; P. CLEMEN, *Die Kunstdenkmäler der Stadt und des Kreises Bonn* (1905), an account of the historic monuments of the city and the region of Bonn that is still a classic work of reference; KARL BAEDEKER, *Cologne and Bonn, with Environs* (1961), a handbook for travellers, now somewhat dated.

(G.H.P.A.)

Bonnard, Pierre

Assimilating the lessons of Impressionism, Pierre Bonnard evolved an art style that, though traditional in many aspects, looked ahead to some of the most daring experiments of Modernism. He moved far during his career; his dissolution of form in favour of passages of emotive colour made him a pioneer of abstraction, yet he never forgot that the basis of his art was in nature. His determination to capture the nuances of colour, tone, and light made him one of the most subtle yet brilliant colorists and masters of light of his age.

Private collection, Europe

Bonnard, self-portrait, oil on canvas, 1938. In a private collection. 58.42 cm × 66.68 cm.

Bonnard was born on October 3, 1867, at Fontenay-aux-Roses, near Paris. After taking his baccalaureate, in which he distinguished himself in classics, Bonnard studied law at the insistence of his father, and for a short time in 1888 he worked in a government office. In the meantime he attended the École des Beaux-Arts, but, failing to win the Prix de Rome (a prize to study at the French Academy in Rome), he transferred to the Académie Julian, where he came into contact with some of the major figures of the new artistic generation—Maurice Denis, Ker-Xavier Roussel, Paul Sérusier, Édouard Vuillard, and Félix Vallotton. In 1890, after a year's military service, he shared a studio in Montmartre with Denis and Vuillard. Later they were joined by the theatrical producer Aurélien-Marie Lugné-Poe, with whom Bonnard collaborated on productions for the Théâtre de l'Oeuvre, in Paris. At this time he became influenced by Japanese prints, which had earlier attracted the Impressionists.

Member of the Nabis

During the 1890s Bonnard became one of the leading members of the Nabis, a group of artists who specialized in painting intimate domestic scenes as well as decorative curvilinear compositions akin to those produced by painters of the contemporary Art Nouveau movement. Bonnard's pictures of charming interiors lighted by oil lamps, nudes on voluptuous beds, and Montmartre scenes made him a recorder of France's *Belle Époque*. It was typical of his humour and taste for urban life at the time that he illustrated *Petites scènes familières* and *Petit solfège illustré* (1893), written by his brother-in-law Claude Terrasse, and executed the lithograph series *Quelques aspects de la vie de Paris* ("Aspects of the Life of Paris"), which was issued by the famous art dealer Ambroise Vollard in 1895. He also contributed illustrations to the celebrated avant-garde review *La Revue blanche*. A new phase in book illustration was inaugurated with Bonnard's decoration of the pages in Paul Verlaine's book of Symbolist poetry, *Parallèlement*, published by Vollard in 1900. He undertook the illustration of other books during the 1900s.

His ability as a large-scale decorator is sometimes overlooked, in view of his more quiet, domestic paintings in the Intimist style. But around 1906 he painted "Pleasure, Study, Play, and the Voyage," a series of four decorations made to resemble tapestries, for the salon of Misia Natanson, the wife of one of the editors of *La Revue blanche*. These pictures show that he was an heir to the French grand tradition of pictorial design that may be traced to Charles Le Brun, the director of all artistic activity under Louis XIV, and François Boucher, the most fashionable painter in the mid-18th century.

By about 1908 Bonnard's Intimist period had concluded. A picture such as "Nude Against the Light" (1908; Musée Royaux des Beaux-Arts de Belgique, Brussels) was painted not only on a bigger scale but also with broader and more coloristic effects. Because of his increasing interest in landscape painting, he had begun painting scenes in northern France. In 1910, however, he discovered the south of France, and from then onward he became the magical painter of this region. The Mediterranean was considered by many of the period to be a source of French civilization. Bonnard was eager to emphasize the connections between his art and France's classical heritage. This was evident in the pose of certain of his figures, which hark back to ancient Hellenistic sculpture. He was also enamoured of the coloristic tradition of the 16th-century Venetian school. "The Abduction of Europa" (1919; Toledo Museum of Art, Ohio), for example, is in a direct line of descent from the work of Titian.

Landscape painting

The subjects of Bonnard's pictures are simple, but the means by which he rendered such familiar themes as a table laden with fruit or a sun-drenched landscape show that he was one of the most subtle masters of his day; he was particularly fascinated with tricks of perspective, as the Postimpressionist painter Paul Cézanne had been. In "The Dining Room," for example, he employed different levels of perspective and varied the transitions of tone, from warm to cool.

By about 1915 Bonnard realized that he had tended to sacrifice form for colour, so from that point until the late 1920s he painted nudes that reflect a new concern for structure without losing their strong colour values. In the 1920s he undertook a series of paintings on one of his most famous themes—a nude in a bath. From the end of the 1920s onward, the subject matter of his pictures hardly varied—still lifes, searching self-portraits, seascapes at Saint-Tropez on the Riviera, and views of his garden at Le Cannet, near Cannes, where he had moved in 1925 after marrying his model and companion of 30 years, Maria Boursin. These are paintings intense with colour.

Subject matter of later works

The chronological order of Bonnard's paintings is difficult to determine, for he would make sketches in pencil or colour and then use them as the basis for several pictures on which he would work simultaneously. When working in the studio, he would rely on his memory of the subject and constantly retouch the surface, building up a mosaic of colours. It is impossible, therefore, to give more than approximate dates for many of his works.

In 1944 Bonnard illustrated a group of early letters, which were published in facsimile under the appropriate title of *Correspondances. Formes et couleurs.* He died on January 23, 1947, at Le Cannet.

MAJOR WORKS

PAINTINGS: "The Croquet Game" (1892; private collection, Paris); "Street Scene with Two Dogs" (1895; private collection, Mexico City); "The Bridge at Chatou" (*c.* 1896; private collection, New York); "Interior" (1898; Norton Simon Collection, Los Angeles); "Place Blanche" (*c.* 1902; private collection, Los Angeles); "Girl in a Straw Hat" (1903; Milwaukee Art Center); "Repas des bêtes" (*c.* 1906; private collection, New York); "Regatta" (1908–12; Carnegie Institute, Pittsburgh); "The Dining Room" (1913; Minneapolis Institute of Arts, Minnesota); "Woman with Basket of Fruit" (1915–18; Baltimore Museum of Art); "The Brothers Jean and Gaston Bernheim" (1920; Musée d'Art Moderne de la Ville de Paris); "Interior with Woman in Wicker Chair" (1920; Nationalmuseum, Stockholm); "Still Life" (*c.* 1924; Art Gallery of Toronto); "The Table" (1925; Tate Gallery, London); "The Palm" (1926; Phillips Collection, Washington, D.C.); "The Road to Nantes" (*c.* 1930; Cleveland Museum of Art); "The Breakfast Room" (*c.* 1930–31; Museum of Modern Art, New York); "Bowl of Fruit" (*c.* 1933; Philadelphia Museum of Art); "Dining Room on the Garden" (*c.* 1933; Solomon R. Guggenheim Museum, New York); "Nude Before a Mirror" (1933; Galleria Internazionale d'Arte Moderna, Venice); "Table Before Window" (1943; private collection, New York); "Flowering Almond Tree" (1946; Musée d'Art Moderne de la Ville de Paris).

LITHOGRAPHS: "Child with Lamp" (1896); "The Laundry Girl" (1896); "Boating" (*c.* 1897); "Place Clichy" (*c.* 1923); *Quelques aspects de la vie de Paris* (1895); also illustrations for *La Revue blanche* (1891–1903).

BIBLIOGRAPHY. JEAN and HENRI DAUBERVILLE, *Bonnard: Catalogue raisonné de l'oeuvre peint*, vol. 1, 1888–1905 (1966), vol. 2, *1906–1919* (1968), consists of a detailed catalog of the artist's work and is still in progress. CHARLES TERRASSE, *Bonnard* (1927), in French; and THADEE NATANSON, *Le Bonnard que je propose*, 1867–1947 (1951), contain much firsthand information about the artist by writers who knew him. JOHN REWALD, *Pierre Bonnard* (1948), is a valuable account of the artist's development with notes on his technique. ANTOINE TERRASSE, *Bonnard* (1964; Eng. trans., 1964) and *Pierre Bonnard* (1967), in French; and ANDRE FERMIGIER, *Pierre Bonnard* (1969; Eng. trans., 1971), are two modern studies with fresh information and good plates. CLAUDE ROGER-MARX, *Bonnard, lithographe* (1952), is an illustrated catalog of the artist's lithographs. *Bonnard and His Environment*, Museum of Modern Art, New York (1964); and *Pierre Bonnard, 1867–1947*, Royal Academy of Arts, London, 2nd ed. (1966), are two important exhibition catalogs.

(D.Su.)

Bookkeeping

Bookkeeping is the recording branch of accounting (see ACCOUNTING, PRINCIPLES OF). Accounting is the art of recording, classifying, and summarizing transactions of an enterprise and interpreting the results thereof. To make a distinction between bookkeeping and accounting is difficult. Accounting includes bookkeeping but is a broader subject; an accountant, for example, designs the system of records used by the bookkeeper. The bookkeeper accumulates the figures; the accountant summarizes and interprets these figures.

Information provided by bookkeeping

Essentially bookkeeping provides two kinds of information: (1) the current value, or equity, of an enterprise and (2) the change in value—profit or loss—taking place in the enterprise over a given period of time. Management officials, investors, and credit grantors all require such information: management in order to interpret the results of operations, to control costs, to budget for the future, and to make financial policy decisions; investors in order to interpret the results of business operations and make decisions about buying, holding, and selling securities; and credit grantors in order to analyze the financial statements of an enterprise in deciding whether or not to grant a loan.

History. Traces of financial and numerical records can be found for nearly every civilization with a commercial background. Records of commercial contracts have been found in the ruins of Babylon, and accounts for both farms and estates were kept in ancient Greece and Rome. The double-entry method of bookkeeping (see below) began with the development of the commercial republics of Italy. The first double-entry books known to exist date from the year 1340 in Genoa. Because they were in excellent double-entry form, it is assumed that the system must have been in general use long before that time. Double-entry bookkeeping also was used by the members of the Hanseatic League (an association of north German towns and groups of merchants active from the late 13th through the 15th centuries); by the banking houses of the Medici family of Florence in the 15th century and the Fugger family of Germany in the 16th century; and by the great trading companies, such as the East India companies, chartered by the governments of England, France, and Holland in the 17th century; it also was used by the monasteries, the papacy, and individual merchants and adventurers in the early days of capitalism.

Instruction manuals for bookkeeping were developed during the 15th century in various Italian cities, a notable example being *Summa de arithmetica geometria proportioni et proportionalità* (1494), by a monk, Lucas (Luca) Pacioli. The thoroughness of Pacioli's volume, with its extended discussion of debit and credit, establishes him as a pioneer in double-entry bookkeeping. Many books of instruction based on Pacioli's material appeared in Germany, England, and Holland during the 16th and 17th centuries with technical modifications to suit the needs of international trading operations. In 1586 Don Pietra, a Benedictine monk, made a significant contribution by stressing the fact that a business enterprise was a separate economic entity, distinct from its owner or owners.

In the late 18th and early 19th centuries, the Industrial Revolution provided an important stimulus to accounting and bookkeeping. The rise of manufacturing, trading, shipping, and subsidiary services made accurate financial records a necessity. The history of bookkeeping, in fact, closely reflects the history of commerce, industry, and government. In the second half of the 20th century, for example, the vast expansion of industrial and commercial activity required more sophisticated decision-making processes, which in turn required more sophistication in the selection, classification, and presentation of information, increasingly with the aid of computers. Taxation and government regulation became more important and resulted in increased demand for information; business firms had to have available information to support their income tax, payroll tax, sales tax, and other tax reports. Governmental agencies and educational and other nonprofit institutions also grew in size, and the demand for bookkeeping for their own operations increased.

The increasing complexity of bookkeeping

The advent of the computer changed the complexion of the bookkeeping process for many firms, particularly those firms that were able to lease or own computers. But in all firms, large and small, the process of recording transactions continued to benefit through greater mechanization. There was a rapid expansion in the use of electronic tabulating and calculating machines of all sizes. These machines were used for information-processing tasks such as payroll accounting and preparing analyses of sales. They were further used to provide the informational inputs in the decision-making process of modern managers.

Bookkeeping processes. Although bookkeeping procedures can be extremely complex, basically there are two types of books used in the bookkeeping process—journals and ledgers. A journal contains the daily transactions (sales, purchases, and so on), and the ledger contains the record of individual accounts. The daily records from the journals are entered in the ledgers.

Journalizing. Cash slips, check books, stock cards, deposit slips, time cards, sales slips, sales invoices, credit memos, and purchase invoices are some of the original documents with which the bookkeeper is concerned. These transactions are analyzed and entered in a journal. The journal is the book used to make the first record of a transaction. There are many different forms of journals. One journal may be designed to take care of only one kind of transaction—cash receipts or sales on account, for example. In a small business all transactions may be entered in one journal.

Posting in the ledger. The process of transferring journal entries to the accounts in the ledger is known as posting. Entries are made in accounts in terms of debits and credits. A debit signifies an entry in one side of a ledger account. A credit, on the other hand, signifies an entry in the other side of a ledger account. The debits recorded in the ledger for each entry in the journal are always equal in amount to the credits for that entry. Thus, if no errors are made in posting, the total of all debit amounts in the ledger equals the total of all credit amounts in the ledger. The "trial balance" is a method of testing the accuracy of posting by proving the equality of the debits and the credits in the ledger.

Preparation of the financial statements. The management of a firm is interested in determining whether its operations have resulted in a profit or loss. They are also interested in the financial condition of the firm. Each month, as a general rule, an income statement and a balance sheet are prepared from the trial balance. The purpose of the income statement or profit-and-loss statement is to present an analysis of the changes that have taken place in the ownership equity as a result of the operations of the period. The balance sheet shows the financial condition of a company at a particular date in terms of assets, liabilities, and the ownership equity.

Double-entry recording process. The financial condition of an enterprise at any point in time can therefore be expressed in the form of an equation that expresses the relationship between assets, liabilities, and the ownership equity. This equation is important, for it is the basis for the double-entry recording process. The assets of any enterprise minus its liabilities must equal the ownership equity. That is, if the claims of outsiders other than the owners (liabilities) are subtracted from the things of value owned by the enterprise (assets), the result will be the value of the ownership equity. The basic equation is $A - L = P$, in which A stands for assets, L for liabilities, and P for the proprietorship or ownership equity.

Double-entry equation

No matter how complex the transactions of an enterprise, this equation always stays in balance. The financial condition of a going concern is always changing as cash is collected, bills are paid, and merchandise is purchased. These transactions must be analyzed in terms of their effect on the assets, liabilities, and proprietorship.

Because there are only two ways in which an item (a quantity of merchandise, for instance) can change—increase or decrease—accounts are set up so that increases are placed on one side of the account and decreases are placed on the other side. For example, purchase of merchandise for $2,500 cash would result in an increase in an asset merchandise for $2,500 and a decrease in an asset cash of $2,500. In other words, for every transaction, more than one item is affected; and complete recording of the effects of any transaction means that such a double entry is made in the ledger accounts.

BIBLIOGRAPHY. L.L. VANCE and R. TAUSSIG, *Accounting Principles and Control*, rev. ed. (1966); and H.A. FINNEY and H.E. MILLER, *Principles of Accounting*, 6th ed. (1963), are both introductory accounting texts that contain the best statements of accounting and bookkeeping principles and concepts. L.D. BOYNTON *et al.* (eds.), *Twentieth Century Bookkeeping and Accounting*, 23rd ed. (1967), has long been a standard bookkeeping text. For information on electronic processing and automation, see H. ANTON and W.S. BOUTELL, *Fortran and Business Data Processing* (1968); and G. WOHL and H. JAUCH, *The Computer: An Accounting Tool* (1965).

Boole, George

George Boole, English mathematician and logician, helped to establish modern symbolic logic. As a pioneer of the algebra of logic, now known as Boolean algebra, his ideas have been applied successfully in the design of computer circuits.

Early life

Born on November 2, 1815, at Lincoln, England, the son of a tradesman, he was given his first lessons in mathematics by his father, who also taught him to make optical instruments. Aside from his father's help and a few years at local schools, however, Boole was self-taught in mathematics. When his father's business declined, George had to work to support the family. From the age of 16 he taught in village schools in West Riding, Yorkshire, and opened his own school in Lincoln when he was 20. During scant leisure time he read mathematics journals in the Mechanics Institute, founded about that time for science education. There he wrestled with the *Principia* of the 17th-century English physicist and mathematician Isaac Newton, the *Mécanique céleste* of Pierre-Simon Laplace, and the *Mécanique analytique* of Joseph-Louis Lagrange, both 18th- and early-19th-century French mathematicians, and began to solve advanced problems in algebra.

Boole, engraving by an unknown artist.

By courtesy of the trustees of the British Museum; photograph, J.R. Freeman & Co. Ltd.

Boole submitted a stream of original papers to the new *Cambridge Mathematical Journal*, beginning in 1839 with his "Researches on the Theory of Analytical Transformations." These papers were on differential equations and the algebraic problem of linear transformation, emphasizing the concept of invariance. In 1844 he discussed how methods of algebra and calculus may be combined in an important paper in the *Philosophical Transactions of the Royal Society*. The same year he was awarded a medal by the Royal Society for his contributions to analysis (*i.e.*, using algebra and calculus to deal with the infinitely large and the infinitely small). Boole soon saw that his algebra could also be applied in logic.

Developing novel ideas on logical method, and confident in the symbolic reasoning he had derived from his mathematical investigations, he published in 1847 a pamphlet, "Mathematical Analysis of Logic," in which he argued persuasively that logic should be allied with mathematics, not philosophy. He won the admiration of the English logician, Augustus De Morgan, who published *Formal Logic* the same year. On the basis of his publications, Boole in 1849 was appointed professor of mathematics at Queen's College, County Cork, even though he had no university degree.

In 1854 he published *An Investigation into the Laws of Thought, on Which Are Founded the Mathematical Theories of Logic and Probabilities*, which he regarded as a mature statement of his ideas. The next year he married Mary Everest, niece of Sir George Everest, for whom the mountain is named. The Booles had five daughters.

One of the first Englishmen to write on logic, Boole pointed out the analogy between the algebraic symbols and those that can represent logical forms and syllogisms, showing how the symbols of quantity can be separated from those of operation. With Boole in 1847 and 1854 began the algebra of logic, or what is now called Boolean algebra (see ALGEBRAIC STRUCTURES: *Boolean algebra*). It is basically two-valued in that it involves a subdivision of objects into separate classes, each with a given property. Different classes can then be treated as to the presence or absence of the same property.

Boolean algebra

Boole's original and remarkable general symbolic method of logical inference, fully stated in *Laws of Thought* (1854), enables one, given any propositions involving any number of terms, to draw conclusions, by the symbolic treatment of the premises, that are logically contained in the premises. He also attempted a general method in probabilities, which would make it possible from the given probabilities of any system of events to determine the consequent probability of any other event logically connected with the given events. In 1857 he was elected a Fellow of the Royal Society.

The influential *Treatise on Differential Equations* appeared in 1859 and was followed the next year by its sequel, *Treatise on the Calculus of Finite Differences.*

Used as texts for many years, these works embody an elaboration of Boole's more important discoveries.

Boole's abstruse reasoning led to applications of which he never dreamed: telephone switching and electronic computers use binary digits, which allow a series of dual alternative routines in the mathematical sequence of instructions to these devices. A lung ailment led to his death on December 8, 1864, in Ballintemple, County Cork.

BIBLIOGRAPHY. For details about Boole's life and contributions to logic, see WILLIAM KNEALE, "Boole and the Revival of Logic," *Mind*, 57:149–175 (1948), with bibliography; see also "Boole" by T.A.A. BROADBENT in the *Dictionary of Scientific Biography*, vol. 2 (1970); and E.T. BELL, *Men of Mathematics* (1937, reprinted 1961).

Booth, Edwin

Edwin Booth was a renowned American tragedian of the 19th century, best remembered as one of the greatest of all performers of Shakespeare's *Hamlet,* and as the innocent brother of John Wilkes Booth, assassin of Pres. Abraham Lincoln.

Edwin Thomas Booth was born November 13, 1833, near Belair, Maryland. At 13 he became companion and chaperon to his eccentric father, the actor Junius Brutus Booth (born in London, 1796), who in 1821 moved to the United States, where he achieved popularity second only to that of the American actor Edwin Forrest.

Travelling with his father, whom he endeavoured to keep sane and sober, Edwin absorbed the rudiments of acting in the bombastic style then fashionable. He made his stage debut at the Boston Museum on September 10, 1849, in the part of Tressel to his father's Richard III in an adaptation of Shakespeare's play. Two years later in New York City, when his father refused to act one night, Edwin replaced him as Richard III, giving an imitative but creditable performance.

Early career

In 1852 Edwin accompanied his father to California, and, after his father's death that year, continued acting, barnstorming through the California mining towns, and, in 1854–55, touring Australia and the Sandwich Islands (now Hawaii). His first important appearances as a star were in Boston and New York City in 1857. Younger playgoers flocked to see him, and in 1860, in a series of brilliant performances in New York, he challenged and overcame the dramatic supremacy of the veteran Forrest.

Booth had not yet, however, overcome the unruly temperament inherited from his father. His acting was occasionally fuddled by drink. In 1860 he married the actress Mary Devlin, by whom he had one daughter. It was the double shock of Mary's death in 1863 and his failure to be at her side because he was too drunk to respond to the summons of friends that henceforth made him abstemious.

Booth, photograph by Bradley and Rulofson.
By courtesy of the Theatre Collection, the New York Public Library at Lincoln Center, Astor, Lenox and Tilden Foundations

In 1864 Edwin Booth became comanager of the Winter Garden Theatre in New York. There, he and his brothers, Junius Brutus and John Wilkes, appeared together for the only time on November 25, 1864, playing Brutus, Cassius, and Mark Antony, respectively, in Shakespeare's *Julius Caesar.* From November 26, 1864, to March 22, 1865, Edwin played Hamlet for 100 consecutive nights. Thereafter, he was identified with the part, for which his looks, voice, and bearing suited him. He was slight and dark, with a musical, sympathetic voice and a natural air of reserve. His acting style, quieter than his father's had been, became increasingly sensitive and subdued.

The assassination of President Lincoln by John Wilkes Booth on April 14, 1865, was a blow from which Edwin's spirit never recovered, causing his withdrawal from the stage until January, 1866, when he reappeared at the Winter Garden as Hamlet and received an ovation.

In 1869 Booth married the actress Mary McVicker, whose nervous instability made the marriage unhappy. In the same year he opened his own theatre in New York City. His Shakespearean and other productions were beautifully mounted, but his lack of business acumen ultimately cost him his theatre and left him bankrupt at 40. By hard work he recouped his losses, acting from then on under the management of others.

European acclaim

Booth first acted in London in 1861. When he revisited England in 1880, his appearances at London's Princess Theatre were near failures until Henry Irving, star and manager of the much superior Lyceum Theatre, invited him to costar at the Lyceum in what proved a memorable engagement, the two actors alternating as Othello and Iago. In 1882, the year after his wife's death, Booth again played England and the next year toured Germany, where the acclaim given his Hamlet, Iago, and King Lear (considered, after Hamlet, his finest roles) made the German engagement the peak of his career. At home, his financial affairs improved permanently when, in 1886, he formed a business and acting partnership with the American actor-manager Lawrence Barrett.

In 1888 Booth founded a club, the Players, in New York City, that was intended as a gathering place for actors and eminent men in other professions. He lived at the club in his last years. His farewell stage appearance was as Hamlet, in 1891 at the Academy of Music in Brooklyn.

Booth died on June 7, 1893, long freed from the excesses of his youth and dissociated in the public mind from the dishonour of his brother's crime. To his own and later generations, the nobility of his mature character, his splendid achievement in his art, and his zeal to raise both the moral and social standing of his fellow actors combined to make him one of the great figures of the American stage.

BIBLIOGRAPHY. ELEANOR RUGGLES, *Prince of Players* (1953), is the most recent and comprehensive biography. Earlier biographies are: RICHARD LOCKRIDGE, *Darling of Misfortune* (1932), especially interesting for details of Booth's business misadventures; CHARLES TOWNSEND COPELAND, *Edwin Booth* (1901), an admirably concise profile; and WILLIAM WINTER, *Life and Art of Edwin Booth* (1893), a standard and valuable study by a contemporary. An exhaustive work by STANLEY KIMMEL, *The Mad Booths of Maryland* (1940), examines the entire Booth clan. Family information and reminiscences by Booth's sister and daughter, respectively, are in ASIA BOOTH CLARKE, *The Elder and the Younger Booth* (1882); and EDWINA BOOTH GROSSMAN, *Edwin Booth: Recollections* (1894). KATHERINE GOODALE, *Behind the Scenes with Edwin Booth* (1931), is a touching reminiscence of the aging actor by a young coworker. OTIS SKINNER, *The Last Tragedian* (1939), presents a sensitive selection of Booth's letters, together with Skinner's vivid memories of him.

(E.Ru.)

Borden, Sir Robert Laird

The eighth prime minister of Canada (1911–20) and leader of the Conservative Party (1901–20), Robert Laird Borden, by insisting on separate Canadian membership in the League of Nations, played a decisive role in the transformation of Canada's status from colony to nation. His Conservative administration confronted unprecedented administrative, financial, and political challenges during the years of World War I, and when, despite the voluntary recruitment of half a million Canadians for overseas service, conscription was required to maintain the Canadian forces at full strength, he initiated the formation of a coalition government. The electoral success of the Unionist forces in the election of 1917 ensured a continuation of Borden's policies of total commitment to the war effort and an international role for Canada—but at the price of antagonizing the French-Canadian population, who were unrepresented in the government and opposed to its policies.

National Film Board of Canada

Borden.

Robert Laird Borden was born on June 26, 1854, in Grand Pré, Nova Scotia. He cut short his formal education before his 15th year, when he accepted the post of assistant master of the private school he was attending. His teaching career ended in 1874, when he became articled to a Halifax law firm. Admitted to the bar of Nova Scotia in 1878, he rose to a commanding position in legal circles, and after his marriage to Laura Bond (1889) he founded a law firm that subsequently acquired one of the largest practices in the Maritime Provinces. His friendship with Sir Charles Hibbert Tupper, son of one of the original "Fathers of Confederation," led him to accept the conservative nomination for Halifax in 1896. Borden's entry into politics coincided with the victory of the Liberal Party under the leadership of Sir Wilfrid Laurier. Though he remained an obscure backbench opposition member during his first term, Borden was invited by the caucus upon his re-election in 1900 to assume temporarily the leadership of the party. He accepted the post, and, despite repeated intrigues against his leadership and his own professions of distaste for it, he occupied it until 1911, when the Liberal decision to accept a reciprocal-trade agreement with the United States led to Laurier's defeat.

Anglo-Canadian relations

As prime minister, Borden's major interest was Anglo-Canadian relations. He had long argued for the establishment of a Canadian voice in imperial policy. His prewar naval policy, which involved a grant of $35,000,000 to Britain for the construction of three battleships, was a mixture of opportunism and wishful thinking about the extension of Canada's influence in the councils of empire. During the first two years of war Borden frequently referred to the necessity of Canadian participation in British decisions, but it was not until the British prime minister David Lloyd George created the Imperial War Cabinet (IWC) in 1917 that Borden was given a chance to express Canada's point of view. At the meetings of the IWC in London and its subsequent sessions in Paris during the negotiation of the Treaty of Versailles, Borden supported the Fourteen Points of United States president Woodrow Wilson and argued that Canada's interests demanded the closest possible alliance between the British Empire and the United States. (Borden saw nothing incompatible between insisting on the right to participate in shaping imperial policy and Canada's independent membership of the League of Nations. He seemed to envisage the empire-commonwealth as an alliance in which smaller members might have to defer to the interests of the great power—but after a process of continuous consultation.)

Borden's "imperial" preoccupations may partially account for his first administration's poor performance in domestic affairs. He dealt indecisively with his controversial minister of militia, Sam Hughes, whom he did not remove from office until the end of 1916. As charges of incompetence, patronage, and war profiteering were levelled against Borden's government, public confidence in him decreased. His decision, however, to form a coalition government in order to implement conscription gave him the opportunity of reconstructing his Cabinet and of surrounding himself with a group of able colleagues. With Arthur Meighen, his eventual successor as prime minister, to manage the House of Commons and two liberals, Newton Rowell and Alexander K. Maclean, in charge of key Cabinet committees, Borden was free to concentrate on the larger questions under discussion in London and Paris. He supported the policy of Allied intervention in the Russian Civil War, in which he was anxious to have Canadian troops participate. Public opinion forced the return of a 3,000-man expeditionary force from Vladivostok, which Borden had hoped would establish a Canadian presence leading eventually to trade concessions. His policy of arresting the leaders of the Winnipeg General Strike (1919) and of charging them under a revised definition of sedition that was rushed through Parliament in the form of an amendment to the criminal code won him the enmity of labour. He resigned from office in July 1920.

Formation of coalition government

In retirement he attended the Washington Naval Disarmament Conference (1921) as Canada's delegate and wrote *Canadian Constitutional Studies* (1922) and *Canada in the Commonwealth* (1929). He also published his *Memoirs* (1938) under the editorship of his nephew, Henry Borden. He died on June 10, 1937.

BIBLIOGRAPHY. For a brief biographical sketch, see CRAIG BROWN, "Sir Robert Borden, the Great War and Anglo-Canadian Relations," in JOHN MOIR (ed.), *Character and Circumstance* (1970). An official biography also by Brown, the first volume of which will cover the years to 1914, will be published soon. HAROLD A. WILSON, *The Imperial Policy of Sir Robert Borden* (1966), is a recent examination of Borden's quest for a voice in British foreign and imperial policy.

(J.T.C.)

Borges, Jorge Luis

Since 1961, when he and Samuel Beckett shared the prestigious international award the Formentor Prize, the Argentine writer Jorge Luis Borges has seen his tales and poems increasingly acclaimed as classics of 20th-century world literature. Prior to that time, Borges was little known, even in his native Buenos Aires, except to other writers, many of whom regarded him merely as a craftsman of ingenious techniques and tricks. Now, the nightmare world of his "fictions," which are often compared to the stories of Franz Kafka, are praised for concentrating common language into its most enduring form. Through his work more than that of any other contemporary, Latin-American literature emerges from the academic realm into that of generally educated readers throughout the Western world.

Borges was born on August 24, 1899, in Buenos Aires and was raised in the shabby suburb of Palermo, the setting of some of his works. His family, which had been notable in Argentine history, included British ancestry, and he learned English before Spanish. The first books he read—from the library of his father, a man of wide-ranging intellect who taught at an English school—included *Huckleberry Finn*, the novels of H.G. Wells, *The Thousand and One Nights*, and *Don Quixote*, all in English. Under the constant stimulus and example of his father, the young Borges from his earliest years realized that he was destined for a literary career.

Borges.
By courtesy of Wellesley College, Wellesley, Massachusetts

In 1914, on the eve of World War I, Borges was taken by his family to Geneva, Switzerland, where he learned French and German and received his B.A. from the Collège de Genève. Leaving there in 1919, the family spent a year in Majorca and a year in Spain, where Borges joined the young writers of the Ultraist movement, a group that rebelled against what it considered the decadence of the established writers of the "generation of '98."

Return to Buenos Aires

Returning to Buenos Aires in 1921, Borges rediscovered his native city and began to sing of its beauty in poems that imaginatively reconstructed its past and present. His first published book was a volume of poems, *Fervor de Buenos Aires* (1923). He is also credited with establishing the Ultraist movement in South America, though he later repudiated it. This period of his career, which included the authorship of several volumes of essays and poems and the founding of three literary journals, ended with a biography, *Evaristo Carriego* (1930).

During his next phase, Borges gradually overcame his shyness in creating pure fiction. At first he preferred to retell the lives of more or less infamous men, as in the sketches of his *Historia universal de la infamia*. To earn his living, in 1938 he took a major post at a Buenos Aires library named for one of his ancestors. He remained there for nine unhappy years.

In 1938, the year his father died, Borges suffered a severe head wound, and subsequent blood poisoning, which left him near death, bereft of speech, and fearing for his sanity. This experience appears to have freed in him the deepest forces of creation. In the next eight years he produced his best fantastic stories, those later collected in the series of *Ficciones* and the volume titled *The Aleph and Other Stories, 1933–69*. During this time, he and another writer, Adolfo Bioy Casares, jointly wrote detective stories under the pseudonym H. Bustos Domecq (combining ancestral names of the two writers' families), which were published in 1942 as *Seis problemas para don Isidro Parodi* ("Six Problems for Don Isidro Parodi"). The works of this period revealed for the first time Borges' entire dreamworld, an ironical or paradoxical version of the real one, with its own language and systems of symbols.

When the dictatorship of Juan Perón came to power in 1946, Borges was dismissed from his library position for having expressed support of the Allies in World War II. With the help of friends, he earned his way by lecturing, editing, and writing. A 1952 collection of essays, *Other Inquisitions, 1937–1952* revealed him at his analytical best.

When Perón was deposed in 1955, Borges became director of the national library, an honorific position, and also professor of English and American literature at the University of Buenos Aires.

Blindness

By this time, Borges suffered from total blindness, a hereditary affliction that had also attacked his father and had progressively diminished his own eyesight from the 1920s onward. It had forced him to abandon the writing of long texts and to begin dictating to his mother or to secretaries or friends.

The works that date from this late period, such as *Dreamtigers* and *The Book of Imaginary Beings*, almost erase the distinctions between the genres of prose and poetry. A later collection of stories, *El informe de Brodie* (1970; "Doctor Brodie's Report"), comprises tales of revenge, murder, and horror—allegories combining the simplicity of a folk storyteller with the complex vision of a man who has explored the labyrinths of his own being to its core.

MAJOR WORKS

POEMS: *Fervor de Buenos Aires* (1923); *Luna de enfrente* (1925); *Cuaderno San Martín* (1929); *Poemas* (1943); *Poemas 1923–1953* (1954); *Poemas* (1958); *Obra poética, 1923–1966* (1966; vol. 6 of Borges' *Obras completas*).

PROSE (ESSAYS): *Inquisiciones* (1925), miscellaneous essays; *El tamaño de mi esperanza* (1926), collected essays; *El idioma de los Argentinos* (1928), essays, one of which was revised and included in *El lenguaje de Buenos Aires* (1963); *Discusión* (1932); *Historia de la eternidad* (1936); *Aspectos de la literatura gauchesca* (1950); *El "Martín Fierro"* (1953), *Otras inquisiciones, 1937–1952* (1952; *Other Inquisitions, 1937–1952*, 1964); *Crónicas de Bustos Domecq* (1967), on aesthetics. (SHORT STORIES AND PARABLES): *Historia universal de la infamia* (1935), translations, adaptations, original stories, and parables; *El jardín de senderos que se bifurcan* (1942), collected stories; *Ficciones 1935–1944* (1944; several later series, 6th enl. ed., 1966), stories; *El Aleph* (1949; *The Aleph and Other Stories, 1933–69*, ed. and trans. by Norman Thomas di Giovanni in collaboration with the author, 1970), collected stories; *La muerte y la brújula* (1951), collected stories; *El hacedor* (1960; *Dreamtigers*, 1964), collected stories, parables, and poems; *El libro de los seres imaginarios* (1967; *The Book of Imaginary Beings*, written by Borges with Margarita Guerrero, rev. and trans. by Norman Thomas di Giovanni in collaboration with the author, 1969). (BIOGRAPHY): *Evaristo Carriego* (1930). (ANTHOLOGIES): Chosen by Borges from his own published and unpublished writings *Antologia personal* (1961), stories, essays, and poems; trans. in *A Personal Anthology*, ed. by A. Kerrigan (1967). Other Eng. trans. in *Labyrinths: Selected Stories and Other Writings of J.L. Borges*, ed. and trans. by D.A. Yates and J.E. Irby (1962; rev. ed. 1970); *Fictions*, selections from the series of *Ficciones*, ed. and trans. by A. Kerrigan (1968).

BIBLIOGRAPHY. ANA MARIA BARRENECHEA, *La expresión de la irrealidad en la obra de Jorge Luis Borges* (1957; Eng. trans., *Borges, the Labyrinth Maker*, 1965), the best critical study, with bibliography; RONALD CHRIST, *The Narrow Act: Borges' Art of Allusion* (1969), a very perceptive analysis of one of Borges' key methods of creation; MARTIN S. STABB, *Jorge Luis Borges* (1970), a superficial over-all presentation; EMIR RODRIGUEZ MONEGAL, *Borgès par lui-même* (1970), a critical introduction, with iconography.

(E.R.-M.)

Borgia, Cesare

Cesare Borgia was the son of Alexander VI, the most notorious and controversial of the Renaissance popes. His career was a classic example of how the popes of the 15th century made use of their families in attempting to recover the power and prestige lost by the papacy during the Great Schism (1378–1417, when two or more claimants fought over the papal throne). Cesare helped his father in preserving the independence of the papacy during the French invasions of Italy after 1494 and in re-establishing his control within the Papal States of central Italy. For this purpose he was made duke of the Romagna and captain general of the armies of the church; at the same time he shared with his father that glow of infamous notoriety that was to become associated with the name of Borgia.

Cesare was cited by his contemporary Machiavelli as an example of the new "Prince," and it is perhaps for this characterization by the famous Renaissance political theorist that he is best known.

Youth and education. Born 1475/1476, probably in Rome, he was the son of his father's most famous mistress, Vannozza Catanei. His father, at that time Cardinal

Borgia, oil painting by an unknown artist. In the Uffizi, Florence.
Alinari

Rodrigo Borgia, was vice chancellor of the church and had had three earlier children by other mistresses. Cesare was, however, the oldest of the four children born to Vannozza and Rodrigo (the others being Juan, Lucrezia, and Jofre) and was Rodrigo's second son. As was customary for second sons he was educated for a career in the church and in 1480 was dispensed from the slur of illegitimacy by Pope Sixtus IV so that he might hold ecclesiastical offices.

Although he was born in Italy and spent most of his life there, Cesare's family and cultural background was almost entirely Spanish. His elder half brother, Pedro Luis, was duke of Gandía, and all of his early benefices were in Spain. At the age of seven Cesare was made an apostolic protonotary and canon of the Cathedral of Valencia.

His early tutors were Paolo Pompilio and Giovanni Vera, both Catalans, and he was recognized as being exceptionally brilliant, as well as being, according to at least one observer, "the handsomest man in Italy." In 1489 he went to the University of Perugia to study law and then passed on to the University of Pisa, where he studied under the famous jurist Filippo Decio and gained a degree in canon and civil law. In 1491 he became bishop of Pamplona, and in 1492, after the accession of his father to the papal throne, he was made archbishop of Valencia.

Archbishop

Rise to power. The election of his father as pope in 1492 changed the fortunes of Cesare Borgia. Besides becoming an archbishop, he was also made a cardinal in 1493, with the titular Church of Sta. Maria Nova; he was now one of his father's principal advisers. It was already clear, however, that he did not have a true religious vocation; he was better known at the papal court for his hunting parties, his amorous liaisons, and his magnificent clothes than for the meticulous observance of his ecclesiastical duties.

On the death of Pedro Luis in 1488 the title of duke of Gandía had by-passed him and gone to his younger brother Juan, and it was he who was made commander of the papal army in 1496 for the first of Alexander's campaigns against his rebellious nobility, the Orsini. Cesare was reputed to have been extremely jealous of his brother, and when Juan was mysteriously murdered in 1497 the rumour gradually spread that Cesare was the culprit. There is, however, no evidence that Cesare murdered his brother (who had many other enemies) beyond the fact that he was certainly capable of murder, as he subsequently proved.

After the death of Juan, Cesare's martial and political leanings and his father's need for a trustworthy secular lieutenant coincided, and in 1498 Cesare gave up his cardinalate. Plans were laid for an important dynastic marriage for him, and, after an abortive attempt to win the hand of Carlotta, daughter of the King of Naples, he travelled to France to marry Charlotte d'Albret, sister of the King of Navarre. At the same time he received from Louis XII, the French king, the title of duke of Valentinois, and from this title he derived his nickname—Il Valentino.

The French marriage of Cesare ensured for him and his father French assistance in their plans to re-establish control in the Papal States and, if possible, to carve out a permanent Borgia state in Italy for Cesare. In 1499 Cesare, as captain general of the papal army, assisted by a large contingent of French troops, began a systematic occupation of the cities of Romagna and the Marches, which had largely fallen under the control of semi-independent papal vicars.

Papal campaigns

The campaign of 1499 saw the conquest of Imola and Forlì; that of 1500–01 brought Rimini, Pesaro, and Faenza into Cesare's hands; finally, in 1502, he captured Urbino, Camerino, and Senigallia. It was in this last campaign that Machiavelli, as one of the Florentine ambassadors attached to Cesare's camp, was able to observe at first hand the methods of the man who was to figure so largely in his later writings.

The activities of Alexander and Cesare, although they conformed very much to a pattern established by earlier 15th-century popes, aroused immense opposition within the Papal States and from the other Italian states. The propaganda war waged against them was vitriolic and lastingly effective. Cesare was portrayed as a monster of lust and cruelty who had gained an unnatural ascendancy over his father after having supposedly killed his favourite son, Juan. It seems likely, however, that the two Borgias worked very much in harmony; Alexander was by far the more astute politician, and Cesare the more ruthless man of action. Ambitious and arrogant, he was determined to establish himself as an Italian prince before his father died and left him deprived of the political and financial support of the Papacy. *Aut Caesar, aut nihil* ("Either Caesar or Nothing") was the motto he adopted to indicate the single-mindedness of his purpose. A number of political assassinations have been attributed to him, but the crime of which he was most clearly the author was the murder in August 1500 of his brother-in-law Alfonso, duke of Bisceglie, the second husband of Lucrezia. It seems likely that this was an act of personal vengeance rather than a politically motivated assassination, but it contributed greatly to the fear and loathing in which Cesare was held.

The best example of Cesare's methods was his third Romagna campaign (1502–03). He opened with a lightning march on unsuspecting Urbino, which surrendered without a shot being fired. He then turned on Camerino, which was also quickly subdued. At this stage his leading commanders, fearing his power, turned against him in the so-called Magione conspiracy. Cesare, stripped of most of his troops, was forced to fight defensively in the Romagna. With lavish use of papal funds, however, he managed to rebuild his army while at the same time working on the diplomatic front to break up the league of the conspirators. Having succeeded in breaking it up, he arranged a rendezvous for reconciliation with some of the conspirators at Senigallia and, having isolated them from their troops, he then arrested and executed them (December 1502).

Magione conspiracy

Cesare, with a powerful army he could trust, now seemed to be at the zenith of his fortunes. It is probable that he was planning an attack on Tuscany, which would have provided him with the independent state he craved, when his father died on August 18, 1502. He himself was also ill at the time, and this circumstance, together with the subsequent election of a bitter enemy of the Borgias, Giuliano della Rovere, as Pope Julius II, lessened his already slim chances of survival. Julius refused to confirm Cesare as duke of the Romagna or captain general of the church and demanded the restoration of the Romagna cities. Cesare was arrested, won a brief respite by agreeing to surrender his cities, and fled to Naples only to be arrested once more by Gonsalvo di Córdoba, the Spanish viceroy, who refused to join him in a league against the Pope. Cesare was then taken to Spain and imprisoned,

Arrest and fall from power

first in the castle of Chinchilla near Valencia, and then at Medina del Campo, from whence he escaped in 1506. Unable to see any immediate prospect of returning to Italy, he took service with his brother-in-law, the king of Navarre, and was killed in 1507 in a skirmish with Navarrese rebels outside Viana. He was buried in the Church of Sta. Maria in Viana.

Assessment. Cesare Borgia was a man of extraordinary contrasts. Machiavelli found that he could be at times secretive and taciturn, at others loquacious and boastful. He alternated bursts of demonic activity, when he stayed up all night receiving and dispatching messengers, with moments of unaccountable sloth, when he remained in bed refusing to see anyone. He was quick to take offense and rather remote from his immediate entourage and yet very open with his subjects in the Romagna, loving to join in local sports and to cut a dashing figure.

There can be no doubt of the impact that he made in the Italy of his own day, but this impression was largely because of the backing he received from papal money and French arms. He was undoubtedly a master of politico-military manoeuvre, and it was a combination of daring and duplicity that brought him his striking successes and made him feared all over Italy. His abilities as a soldier and an administrator, however, were never really tested. He fought no major battles in his short military career, but this was perhaps a measure of his success as a planner. He had little time for the organization of the government of his Romagna duchy, but there are indications that he had plans for centralized government and bureaucratic efficiency, which to some extent justify the claims made for him as an administrator by Machiavelli. His interests tended to be scientific and literary rather than artistic, but once again time was too short for him to emerge as an important Renaissance patron. Leonardo da Vinci was for a short time his inspector of fortresses but executed no artistic commissions for him.

Model for Machiavelli's *Prince*

Machiavelli's apparent admiration for a man who was so widely feared and abhorred has led many critics to regard his portrayal of Cesare as an idealization. This interpretation, however, is not really the case. Machiavelli was well aware of the failings and limitations of Cesare Borgia, but he saw in him some of the qualities that he considered essential for the man who aspired to be a prince. The aggressiveness, the speed and ruthlessness of planning and execution, the opportunism of Cesare all delighted Machiavelli, who saw far too little of these qualities in the Italy of his day. Machiavelli was not attempting a rounded portrait of Cesare's character and qualities, which baffled him as much as they did most of his contemporaries.

BIBLIOGRAPHY. The standard biography is still W.H. WOODWARD, *Cesare Borgia* (1913), which may be supplemented by the fuller but less balanced study by E. ALVISI, *Cesare Borgia, duca di Romagna* (1878). More recent but less useful are C.E. YRIARTE, *Cesare Borgia* (Eng. trans. 1947); and C.M.L. BEUF, *Cesare Borgia: The Machiavellian Prince* (1942). On the background of the period and the family, see L. COLLISON-MORLEY, *The Story of the Borgias* (1932); and M.E. MALLETT, *The Borgias* (1969), with the most complete bibliography.

(Mi.Ma.)

Boris I of Bulgaria

Khan Boris I of Bulgaria was one of the most remarkable rulers of medieval Bulgaria. His long reign (852–889) witnessed the conversion of the Bulgarians to Christianity; the founding of an autocephalous Bulgarian Church; and the advent of Slavonic literature and the establishment of the first centres of Slav-Bulgarian scholarship and education. Boris' active domestic and foreign diplomacy was of great importance in forming a united Bulgarian ethnical community, and it left lasting traces on Bulgaria's later development.

When Boris inherited the throne from his father, Bulgaria's territorial, military, and political potential had made it one of the largest states in Europe. Bulgaria's approximate frontiers were the Dnepr (Dnieper) in the northeast; the Carpathians in the north; the Tisa (Tisza) in the northwest; the Adriatic in the west; and the Tomorr (Tomor), Belasica, Pirin, Rhodope, and Strandzha mountains in the south. Many Slavic tribes lived within the boundaries of the state, together with the proto-Bulgarians, a tribe of Turkic origin that had settled in the Balkan Peninsula at the end of the 7th century. In view of the religious, ethnic, and language difficulties between the Slavs and Bulgars, the introduction of a common and compulsory religion for all subjects was one of the principal preconditions for the formation of a united Bulgaria. Pagan Bulgaria needed to join the "family of Christian states," but the existence of two competing centres of Christianity—Rome and Constantinople—made it difficult for Boris to make his choice. Boris originally intended to accept Roman Christianity, but an unsuccessful war with the Byzantines forced Boris to adopt the Orthodox faith of Constantinople (864). Boris (at his baptism he took the Christian name Michael), his family, and the nobles who supported his policy were baptized one night in secret by a Byzantine bishop and priests who had been sent to Pliska, the Bulgarian capital. There was serious opposition by both the nobility and the common people to Boris' attempt to enforce mass baptism. A pagan rebellion broke out, and Boris retaliated by executing 52 boyars, together with their families.

Conversion of the Bulgars

Negotiations took place between Boris and Photius, patriarch of Constantinople, on the status of the Bulgarian diocese but did not lead to the result expected by the Bulgarians. The Byzantines demanded that the Bulgarian church organization should be entirely subjected to Constantinople. Dissatisfied, Boris renewed his diplomatic contacts with the West. In 866 he sent embassies to Pope Nicholas I (858–867) and to King Ludwig of Germany. The Pope immediately responded by sending a mission to Bulgaria. The Roman clergy's stay (866–870) soon became a sore point in the acute rivalry between Rome and Constantinople. But since Pope Nicholas I and his successor, Adrian II, proved dilatory on the question of church organization in Bulgaria (they hesitated over the creation of an independent Bulgarian archbishopric), Boris again reopened negotiations with Constantinople. The Bulgarian church question was finally solved at the eighth ecumenical council in Constantinople in 869–870. Bulgaria was formally placed under the nominal ecclesiastical jurisdiction of the patriarch of Constantinople but received an independent archbishopric. The attempts of the popes to bring the Bulgarian ruler back into the Roman church by pleas and promises of concessions continued until 882 but produced no results.

Boris was quite active in inculcating the Christian faith among the Bulgarian people, in organizing the Bulgarian Church as an independent institution, and in building churches throughout the country. In 886 he gave asylum to Clement, Nahum, and Angelarius, the disciples of Cyril and Methodius, missionaries to the Slavs, who had been driven out of Moravia. With Boris' active assistance and material support, these disciples founded centres of Slavic learning at Pliska, Preslav, and Okhrid. As a result of the intensive work of the Slav scholars, the Slavic language replaced Greek in church services and in literary life and became the country's official language.

In 889 Boris I abdicated and became a monk, but he retained the right to take an active part in the government of the state. Boris' eldest son and heir, Vladimir (889–893), abandoned his father's policy and became the instrument of a pagan reaction and a leader of the opponents of Slavic letters and literature. Boris then returned to active politics. With the aid of loyal boyars and the army, Boris drove his son from the throne. Vladimir was blinded, unfitting him for rule, and was replaced by Boris' third son, who ruled as Symeon the Great (893–927). Boris afterward retired to his monastery, making generous grants to the Bulgarian Church and patronizing Slav scholarship. He died on May 2, 907, in Preslav. He was canonized by the Orthodox Church, and his feast is celebrated on May 15 (new style; May 2, old style).

Return to politics

BIBLIOGRAPHY. VASIL GJUZELEV, *Knjaz Boris Părvi* (1969), the most recent and complete study in line with the achievements of modern historiography; FRANTISEK DVORNIK, *Les Slaves, Byzance et Rome au IXe siècle* (1926), chiefly concerning the diplomacy of Boris I of Bulgaria with a view to relations between the churches of Rome and Constantinople; *The Photian Schism: History and Legend* (1948), a brilliant study in which the author gives an appreciation of the work of Boris I.

(W.T.G.)

Boron Group Elements and Their Compounds

The five elements comprising the so-called boron group are: boron (symbol B, atomic number 5), aluminum (symbol Al, atomic number 13), gallium (symbol Ga, atomic number 31), indium (symbol In, atomic number 49), and thallium (symbol Tl, atomic number 81). Constituting Group IIIa of the periodic table (see Figure 1), they are characterized as a group by having three electrons in the outermost parts of their atomic structure. Boron, the lightest of these elements, is a nonmetal but the other members of the group are silvery-white metals.

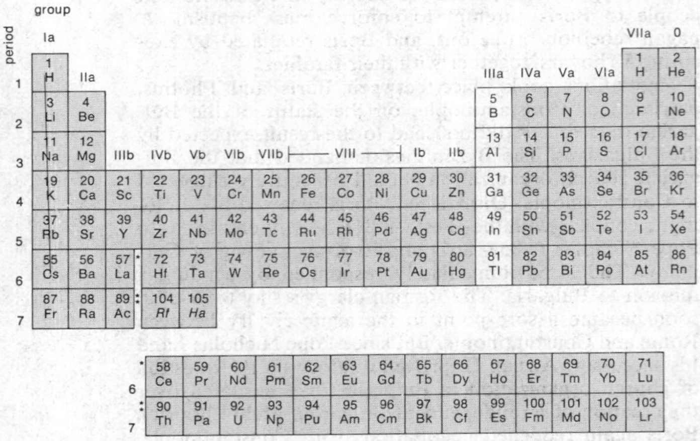

Figure 1: Boron group elements in the periodic table.

None of these elements was known in a pure state before modern chemistry isolated them. Very soon after a method had been found to produce it in commercial quantities, aluminum revolutionized industry. The other members of the group, including boron, still have little commercial value. Some of the compounds of boron and aluminum, however, are indispensable in modern technology and have been widely used in many parts of the world throughout recorded history.

History. The use of a boron compound known as borax (sodium tetraborate, $Na_2B_4O_7 \cdot 10H_2O$) can be traced back to the ancient Egyptians, who used it as a metallurgical flux (a substance that aids the heat joining or soldering of metals), in medicine, and in mummification. During the 13th century, Marco Polo introduced borax into Europe but not until the mid-19th century, when vast deposits of borates were discovered in the Mojave Desert, did borax become relatively common. The ancient Egyptians, Greeks, and Romans used a compound of aluminum known as alum (the compound potassium aluminum sulfate) in dyeing as a mordant; *i.e.*, a substance that fixes dye molecules to the fabric. Lapis lazuli, a rare, dark blue mineral (the compound sodium aluminum silicate containing sulfur), has been widely used as a semiprecious stone throughout history. The metal aluminum was first isolated early in the 19th century but it was not until a modern electrolytic process based on the use of bauxite was developed that commercial production of aluminum became economically feasible. The other elements of the boron group were first detected spectroscopically (*i.e.*, by analysis of the light emitted by or passed through substances containing the element) in the late 19th century. The existence and properties of gallium were predicted by a Russian chemist, Dmitry Ivanovich Mendeleyev, on the basis of the periodic table of the elements that he had developed; the ultimate discovery of gallium and the accuracy of his description of the properties of the then unknown element convinced scientists of the theoretical soundness of the table. Gallium is one of two metals (the other is cesium) whose melting points are low enough for them to turn to liquid when held in the hand.

Historical importance of gallium

GENERAL PROPERTIES OF THE BORON GROUP

Atomic structure. The chemical and physical properties of the elements and their compounds can be understood in terms of their atomic structures. Each of the atoms which make up the various elements in the periodic table has as its core a massive nucleus carrying positive electrical charges. The number of charges is called the atomic number of the element in question. In the periodic table, the elements are arranged in sequence according to their atomic numbers. Since atoms are neutral, every nucleus is surrounded by as many electrons (each carrying a single negative electric charge) as there are positive charges, these electrons being housed in orbitals. The electrons in orbitals closest to the nucleus are held most tightly; those in the outermost orbitals are shielded by intervening electrons and are the most loosely held by the nucleus. Depending on their energy and on rules dictated by quantum mechanics, orbitals are arranged in families, or shells, the more massive atoms having seven such shells. The total energy of each electron varies with its position in the structure, and each position is defined in terms of the number of the shell in which it occurs (the numbers proceeding outward from the nucleus), followed by one of four letters—*s*, *p*, *d*, or *f*—representing different classes of orbitals within the shells. As a result of receiving more energy an electron may move from one orbital to another, as from a 3*s* to a 3*p* orbital. The number of electrons in each orbital is customarily given as a superscript following the orbital designation; thus the notation $4s^2 4p^1$ means that the atoms of a particular element carry two *s* electrons and one *p* electron in their fourth shell. In boron, the outermost shell is 2, in aluminum it is 3, and so on.

Chemical bonding

There are three main types of chemical bonding. In one called ionic, or electrovalent, electrons are actually donated by one atom to another and the resulting ions, being oppositely charged, then associate in a crystal. In another called covalent, a pair of electrons is shared by two atoms, and the sharing is represented in terms of overlapping orbitals. In a third type of bond called metallic, valence electrons are freed to move about among the bonded atoms. Since some electrons in inner shells also participate in chemical bonds, though to a lesser extent, it is more convenient to use the concept of what is called the oxidation state for bonds in general. (Oxidation is a process of losing electrons.) The oxidation state of an element is the total number of its electrons involved in a chemical bond, without regard to the nature of the bond; most elements have more than one oxidation state; *i.e.*, they can form compounds involving more than one arrangement of their electrons. Oxidation states are depicted as roman numerals following the name of the element: boron(III), thus, is boron in oxidation-state three; B^{III} means the same thing. Another way of examining chemical properties is by measuring the energy required to eliminate an electron from an atom, called the ionization energy. The ionization energy required to remove the first electron from a neutral atom is the lowest; since the rest will then be held more tightly by the nucleus, each successive electron that is removed will require increasingly more energy. (Further explanations of general chemical behaviour may be found in detail in articles such as ATOMIC STRUCTURE; CHEMICAL REACTIONS; PERIODIC LAW.) Molecules of a compound are represented by a formula in which the symbols of the elements comprising the compound are listed with subscripts indicating the number of each atom in the molecule. Thus, $AlCl_3$ means that there are one atom of aluminum and three atoms of chlorine in a molecule of the compound aluminum trichloride.

Ionization behaviour. The Table gives a list of the electronic configurations and several ionization energies of the boron group elements. Every element in the boron group has three electrons in its outermost shell, and for each element there is a sharp jump in the amount of energy required to remove the fourth electron, reflecting the fact that this electron must be removed from an inner shell. Consequently the elements of the group will have maximum oxidation numbers of three, corresponding to loss of the first three electrons, and will form ions with three positive charges.

The apparently erratic way in which ionization energies vary among the elements of the group is due to the presence of the filled inner *d* orbitals in gallium, indium, and thallium, and the *f* orbital in thallium, which do not shield the outermost electrons from the pull of the nuclear charge as efficiently as do the inner *s* and *p* electrons. In Groups Ia and IIa, in contrast to the boron group, outer shell (always referred to as n) electrons are shielded in every case by a constant inner set of electrons, in the $(n\text{-}1)s^2(n\text{-}1)p^6$ orbitals, and the ionization energies of these Group-Ia and Group-IIa elements decrease smoothly down the group. The ionization energies of Ga, In, and Tl are thus higher than expected from their Group II counterparts because their outer electrons, being poorly shielded by the inner *d* and *f* electrons, are more strongly bound to the nucleus. This shielding effect also makes the atoms of gallium, indium, and thallium smaller than the atoms of their Group Ia and IIa neighbours by causing the outer electrons to be pulled closer toward the nucleus.

The M^{3+} state for Ga, In, and Tl will be energetically less favourable than Al^{3+} because the high ionization energies of these three elements cannot always be balanced by the crystal energies of possible reaction products. For example, of the simple, anhydrous compounds of trivalent thallium only the trifluoride, TlF_3, is ionic. For the group as a whole, therefore, the M^{3+} ionic state is the exception rather than the rule. More commonly the elements of the group form covalent bonds and achieve an oxidation state of three by promoting one electron from the *s* orbital in the outer shell (designated *ns* orbital) to an *np* orbital, the shift permitting the formation of hybrid, or combination, orbitals (of the variety designated as sp^2). Increasingly down the group there is a tendency toward the formation of M^+ ions and at thallium the monovalent state is the more stable one. The basicity (a property of metals) of the elements also increases in proceeding down the group as shown by the oxides they form: boric oxide (formula B_2O_3) is acidic, the next three oxides, of aluminum, gallium, and indium (formulas Al_2O_3, Ga_2O_3, and In_2O_3) are either acidic or basic depending on the environment (a property called amphoterism), and thallic oxide (Tl_2O_3) is wholly basic.

Basicity of oxides

The ionization energies listed in the Table suggest that the formation of salts of the M^{2+} ions might be feasible. At first glance, such appears to be the case, since gallium compounds with the formula GaX_2 (X representing chlorine, bromine, or iodine) can be made, and similar cases occur with the other metals of this group. Such compounds, however, are generally found to be of mixed valency—that is, they contain metal atoms in both the one and the three oxidation states, a condition symbolized as $M^+(M^{III}X_4)^-$. The nearest approach to M^{2+} derivatives occurs in gallium sulfide, selenide, and telluride, which are made by heating gallium with stoichiometric amounts of sulfur, selenium, and tellurium, respectively. Studies of the structure of these compounds by X-ray methods show that they contain $(Ga\text{-}Ga)^{4+}$ units arranged in a layer-like lattice; the coupling of the gallium atoms in such a manner pairs the electrons available for the bonds and thereby explains the diamagnetism of the compounds (diamagnetism is a property associated with paired electrons).

The large amount of energy required to remove three electrons from a boron atom makes the formation of salts containing the bare B^{3+} cation impossible; even water of hydration associated with such ions would be too highly deformed to be stable and hence the aquated ion $B^{3+}_{(aq)}$ is unknown. Much less energy is required to promote electrons from 2*s* orbitals into 2*p* orbitals in boron atoms with the result that boron compounds are always covalent. The boron orbitals are hybridized to either the sp^2 (when boron forms bonds with three other atoms) or the sp^3 (when boron forms bonds with four atoms) configuration (see CHEMICAL BONDING).

Some Properties of the Boron Group Elements

	boron	aluminum	gallium	indium	thallium
Atomic number	5	13	31	49	81
Atomic weight	10.811	26.9815	69.72	114.82	204.37
Colour of element	brown	silver white	gray blue	silver white	blue white
Melting point (°C)	2,100–2,200	659.7	29.75	156.4	303
Boiling point (°C)	sublimes 2,550	2,467	2,403	2,000 ± 10	1,457 ± 10
Density					
Solid (g/cm^3)	2.34 (20° C)	2.699 (20° C)	5.903 (25° C)	7.31 (20° C)	11.85 (20° C)
Liquid (g/ml)	2.34 (2,100° C)	2.382 (659.7° C)	6.095 (29.8° C)	—	11.29 (306° C)
Valence	3	3	3	3, 1	3, 1
Electronic configuration	$1s^22s^22p^1$	(Ne) $3s^23p^1$	(Ar) $3d^{10}4s^24p^1$	(Kr) $4d^{10}5s^25p^1$	(Xe) $4f^{14}5d^{10}6s^26p^1$
Isotopic abundance (terrestrial, percent)	boron-10 (18.8), boron-11 (81.2)	aluminum-27 (100)	gallium-69 (61.2), gallium-71 (38.8)	indium-113 (4.23), indium-115 (95.77)	thallium-203 (29.52), thallium-205 (70.48)
Radioactive isotopes (mass numbers)	8, 9, 12, 13	24–26, 28–30	63–68, 70, 72–76	106–112, 114, 116–124	191–202, 204, 206–210
Colour imparted to flame	green	colourless	violet	blue	green
Colour of ions in solution					
M^{3+}	—	colourless	colourless	colourless	colourless
M^+	—	—	—	—	colourless
Heat of fusion (kcal per gram atom)	5.3	2.55	1.34	0.78	1.02
Specific heat at 20° C (cal/g/°C)	0.307	0.214	0.079	0.057	0.031
Electrical resistivity (microhm-cm)	7.7×10^{11} (27° C)	2.65 (20° C)	56.8 (20° C)	9 (20° C)	18 (0° C)
Hardness (Mohs' scale)	9.5	2–2.9	1.5–2.5	1.2	1.4 (approx)
Crystal structure at 20° C	α-rhombohedral, β-rhombohedral, tetragonal	face-centred cubic	orthorhombic	face-centred tetragonal	hexagonal close-packed
Radius					
Atomic (Å)	0.80	1.18	1.25	1.50	1.71
Ionic (M^{3+}, Å)	(0.20)	0.50	0.62	0.81	0.95
Ionization energy (electron volts)					
First	8.296	5.984	6.00	5.79	6.106
Second	23.98	18.82	18.9	18.86	20.42
Third	37.92	28.44	30.70	28.0	29.8
Fourth	259.30	119.96	64.2	57.8	50
Oxidation potential at 25° C ($M \rightarrow M^{3+} + 3e^-$, volts)	—	1.67	0.52	0.34	−1.25
Electronegativity (Pauling)	2.0	1.5	1.6	1.7	1.8

Although simple M^{3+} cations are uncommon in anhydrous compounds of the boron group elements, the hydrated (combined with water) trivalent ions of aluminum, gallium, indium, and thallium are well known in water solution. Nuclear magnetic resonance studies reveal that there are six water molecules held strongly by these positive ions in solution, and their salts often can be crystallized from solution combined with six water molecules. The high charge on the central cation of such hydrates induces the ionization of protons, or hydrogen nuclei, on the coordinated water molecules and thereby leads to the formation of basic salts. This reaction is represented in the following equations:

$$M(H_2O)_n^{3+} \rightleftharpoons (HO)M(H_2O)_{n-1}^{2+} + H^+_{aq}$$
$$\rightleftharpoons (HO)_2M(H_2O)_{n-2}^{+} + 2H^+_{aq} \rightleftharpoons M(OH)_3 + 3H^+_{(aq)}$$

in which, as before, M represents an ion of one of the boron group elements; n is the number of water molecules joined to it; (HO)M represents a hydroxide group joined to the metal ion; and $H(aq)^+$ is a hydrated hydrogen ion. In these and other equations the arrows pointing in two directions indicate that the chemical reactions can proceed both ways depending on the reaction conditions. When acid is added to such aqueous solutions it depresses the hydrolytic processes by reversing the above reactions. At high acid concentrations, however, complex anions (negative ions) are sometimes formed, especially with the aqueous hydrogen halides. The following equation illustrates this: $Ga(aq)^{3+}$ + HX (conc.) $\rightarrow GaX_4^-$, X being chlorine, bromine, or iodine. Intermediate complex ions, MX^{2+} and MX_2^+ can be detected in several cases.

The electrical conductivity of solid aluminum trichloride (formula $AlCl_3$), in which each aluminum ion has three positive charges, increases rapidly as the temperature is elevated toward the melting point, at which the conductivity suddenly falls to zero. This phenomenon occurs because the aluminum and chloride ions form an ionic lattice that partially conducts electricity; but upon melting, the compound changes to the electrically nonconducting, covalent state. The explanation is that the distribution of energy in the liquid state is insufficient to compensate for the ionization energy required to separate the Al^{3+} and Cl^- ions and these then acquire covalent bonds. The liquid consists of double or dimeric molecules with the formula Al_2Cl_6, which may be represented in the following manner that shows a molecule with the position of its atoms in three dimensions; the solid lines are in the plane of the paper, the dotted lines are behind the paper, and the shaded lines indicate that they extend toward the viewer:

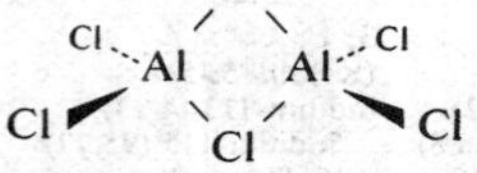

The delicate energy balance between ionic and covalent bonding for aluminum in the trivalent state can be appreciated when it is realized that whereas solid aluminum trifluoride, formula AlF_3, is ionic like the chloride, aluminum tribromide forms molecular crystals containing dimers, with the formula Al_2Br_6.

In contrast with the dimers, the single, or monomeric, trihalides of the boron group elements have trigonal planar structures. If M is the metal and X is any halogen, the arrangement of the atoms can be sketched as follows:

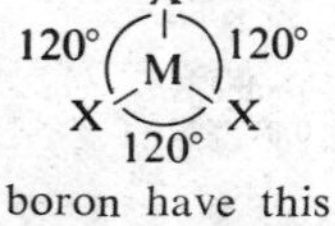

The trihalides of boron have this configuration in all phases whereas the trihalides of Al, Ga, In, and Tl become monomeric only on being heated in the gas phase. In MX_3 molecules, the central atom M has added three electrons to its own making only six electrons in the outer shell, although eight are required to achieve the desired inert-gas configuration. These halides, therefore, readily accept two more electrons from many donor molecules (*e.g.*, ethers, alcohols, amines, and phosphines) that carry unshared pairs of electrons. A typical case, the reaction of gallium tribromide with trimethylamine, is represented in the following equation:

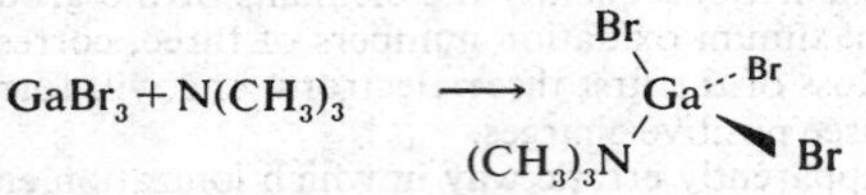

The central gallium atom is coordinated or bonded to three bromine atoms and one nitrogen atom. The electron donor also can be a halide ion, in which case the tetrahedral complex anion, MX_4^- results.

A few compounds are known in which aluminum, gallium, indium, and thallium are coordinated to five or six atoms. These compounds have structures of the following types, M again representing any boron group element, D any donor molecule, and X any halogen (again, the solid lines are bonds in the plane of the paper, the atoms so bonded lying in that plane; the dotted lines lead behind the paper; the shaded lines reach toward the viewer):

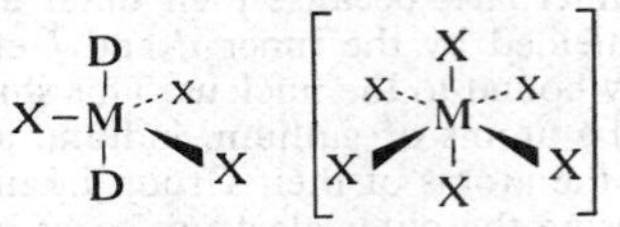

In such compounds it is possible, but by no means certain, that the central element makes use of its vacant nd orbitals (see above) to increase its valency by way of sp^3d (five-coordination) or sp^3d^2 (six-coordination) hybridization. If the concept of the participation of d orbitals in the bonding of these compounds is valid, it would account for the fact that boron, which has no available d orbitals, does not form five- and six-coordinate compounds. In many cases, however, spatial requirements also would rule out the possibility of boron increasing its covalency above four because the boron atom is so small no more than four atoms can be arranged around it.

Halides of elements

In the gas phase at high temperature all the boron group elements form diatomic halides MX, either by dissociation of the trihalides or, more commonly, by reduction of the trihalides with the free element as in the following equations for two such reactions:

$$2B + BF_3 \xrightarrow{2{,}000^\circ} 3BF$$

boron, boron trifluoride, boron monofluoride

$$2Al + AlCl_3 \xrightarrow{800^\circ-1{,}000^\circ} 3AlCl.$$

aluminum, aluminum trichloride, aluminum monochloride

Most of these monohalides, especially those of boron, aluminum, and gallium, are unstable in the solid state under normal conditions; they exist only at high temperatures as gases; all are covalently bonded, except thallium fluoride, which exists as the ion pair, Tl^+F^-.

Thallium is the only element that forms a stable ion having an $(n\text{-}1)d^{10}ns^2$ outer electronic configuration. There is, therefore, no ion to which direct comparisons with the thallium(I) ion, Tl^+, might be made.

COMPOUNDS OF THE INDIVIDUAL BORON GROUP ELEMENTS

Boron. The first three ionization energies of boron, atomic number 5, are much too high to allow the formation of compounds containing the B^{3+} ion; in all its compounds boron is covalently bonded. One of boron's $2s$ electrons is promoted to a $2p$ orbital, giving the outer electron configuration $2s^12p^2$; the s and p orbitals can then be mixed to give sp^2 and sp^3 hybrids, which allow boron to be three- and four-coordinated, respectively. The three-coordinate derivatives (*e.g.*, halides, alkyls, aryls) are planar molecules that readily form donor-acceptor complexes (called adducts) with compounds containing lone pairs of electrons; in these adducts the boron atom is four coordinated, the four groups being tetrahedrally disposed around it.

Boron is an essential trace element for the healthy growth of many plants, and typical effects of long-term boron deficiency are stunted, misshapen growth and, in root crops, heart rot and dry rot; the deficiency can be alleviated by the application of soluble borates to the soil. Gigantism of several species of plants growing in soil naturally abundant in boron has been reported. It is not yet clear what the precise role of boron in plant life is, but most researchers agree that the element is in some way essential for the normal growth and functioning of apical meristems, the growing tips of plant shoots.

Boron is unique in its group in that it forms a rather large number of compounds with hydrogen, or hydrides, called boranes, many of which have most unusual, three-dimensional structures; it also forms a series of halides with the general formula B_nX_n. These molecules are interesting because they contain closed cages of boron atoms. Examples are the boron chlorides whose formulas are B_4Cl_4, B_8Cl_8, and B_9Cl_9. Unfortunately these interesting halides, most of which are highly coloured in sharp contrast to the more typical boron derivatives, are exceedingly difficult to prepare and to handle. The substance, formula B_4Cl_4, for example, can be prepared only in milligram quantities, and complex electrical-discharge techniques are needed for its production; furthermore, it ignites spontaneously in air and is rapidly decomposed both by water and even by the grease used to lubricate the vacuum equipment employed in its preparation. Closed cages containing 12 boron atoms arranged in the form of an icosahedron (see Figure 2) also occur in the various crystalline forms of elemental boron.

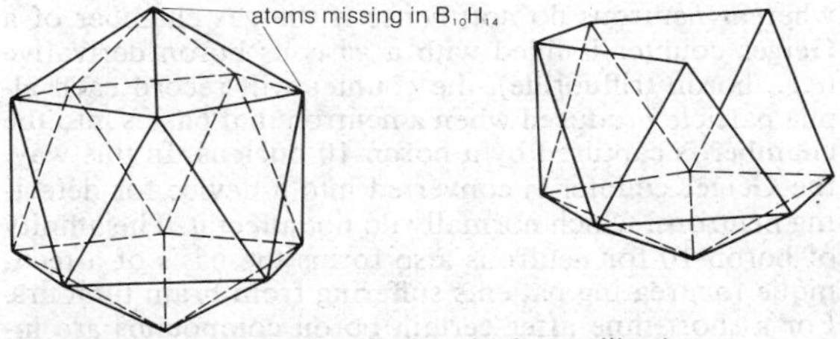

Figure 2: (Left) Icosahedron, basic unit of crystalline boron. (Right) $B_{10}H_{14}$ skeleton (see text).

Boric acid, formula H_3BO_3 or $B(OH)_3$, is obtained as a white solid by the action of sulfuric acid on a concentrated solution of borax. It is a weak acid; the addition of a sugar (*e.g.*, mannitol) to its aqueous solution increases the acidity (the tendency to give up a proton, see ACID-BASE REACTIONS AND EQUILIBRIA) and allows it to be neutralized with an alkali. The sugar forms a complex with the acid, and a hydrated proton [symbolized as $H(aq)^+$] is released into solution at the same time. These reactions are written in equations as follows:

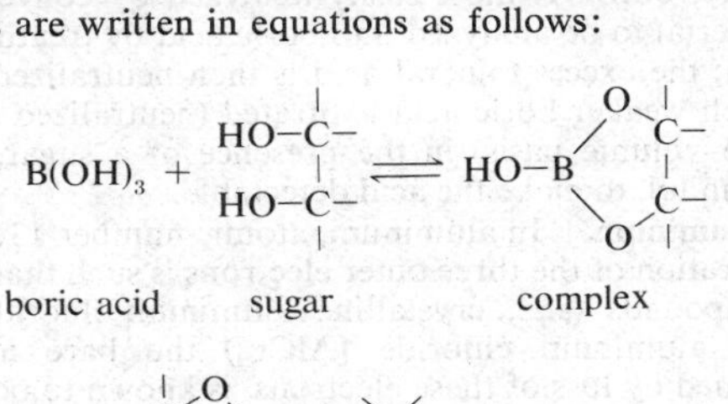

Heating solid boric acid to a red heat produces boric oxide as a hygroscopic (water-absorbing) glassy substance; the glass-forming properties of the oxide lead to its extensive use in the glass industry.

Boron reacts with all halogen elements to give monomeric, highly reactive trihalides, which readily form complexes with amines, phosphines, ethers, and halide ions. Examples of complex formation between boron trichloride and trimethylamine, as well as between boron trifluoride and fluoride ion, are shown in the following equations:

$$BCl_3 + N(CH_3)_3 \longrightarrow (CH_3)_3N \cdot BCl_3$$

$$BF_3 + F^- \longrightarrow BF_4^-$$

in which the heavy dot indicates that a bond is formed between the nitrogen and boron atoms. When boron trichloride is passed at low pressure through devices delivering an electric discharge, diboron tetrachloride, the formula written as $Cl_2B{-}BCl_2$, and tetraboron tetrachloride, formula B_4Cl_4, are formed. Diboron tetrachloride decomposes at room temperatures to give a series of monochlorides having the general formula $(BCl)_n$, in which n may be 8, 9, 10, or 11; the compounds with formulas B_8Cl_8 and B_9Cl_9 are known to contain closed cages of boron atoms.

Boranes and carboranes

Reduction of the boron trihalides with lithium aluminum hydride gives diborane, formula B_2H_6; the expected hydride, formula BH_3, does not exist under normal conditions, although it has been detected by mass spectroscopy when diborane is heated under low pressure. Diborane has a most unusual bridged structure represented in three dimensions as:

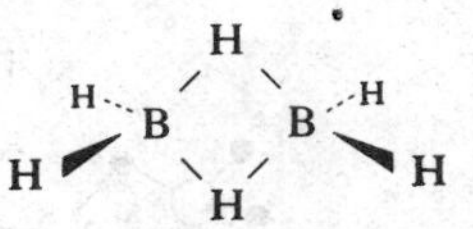

(Again, the bonds shown as solid lines lie in the plane of the paper, those shown as dotted lines extend behind the paper, and the shaded lines represent bonds that extend toward the viewer.) The B–H–B bridges are held together by unique bonds in which electrons normally associated with two atoms are instead associated with three (three-centre bonds). By a variety of techniques, including heating and the application of electrical discharges, diborane can be transformed into a number of higher boranes containing as many as ten boron atoms. (Hydrides containing more than ten boron atoms can be made starting from decaborane-14, formula $B_{10}H_{14}$.) The higher boranes derived from diborane fall into two distinct series one of which has the general formula B_nH_{n+4} and the other the formula B_nH_{n+6}. The unusual molecular structures of certain of these boranes are shown in Figure 3; the bonding in the boranes is complex and involves molecular orbitals extending over several atoms.

The boron skeleton of decaborane-14 (the number indicates the number of hydrogen atoms in the molecular formula $B_{10}H_{14}$) is closely related in shape to an icosahedron, the difference being that it lacks two atoms required to complete the cage (see Figure 2).

The two missing atoms can be added to the decaborane structure by treating the substance either with an amine adduct of BH_3, which completes the icosahedron with boron atoms, or with an acetylene, which completes the cage with carbon atoms. Equations for these reactions are:

$$B_{10}H_{14} + 2(C_2H_5)_3N \cdot BH_3 \longrightarrow [(C_2H_5)_3NH]_2^+(B_{12}H_{12})^{2-}$$

$$B_{10}H_{14} + C_2R_2 \longrightarrow B_{10}C_2H_{10}R_2 + 2H_2.$$

(a carborane)

These cage derivatives are exceptionally stable. Many other carboranes, normally containing two carbon atoms, and cage-borohydrides have been prepared. Isomers (*i.e.*, compounds with identical formulas but a different arrangement of the atoms in the molecules) of the carboranes can be prepared that differ in the relative positions of the two carbon atoms; the most stable isomers are those in which the carbon atoms are farthest apart and are bonded to the lowest possible number of neighbouring atoms. Of the $B_nH_n^{2-}$ ions, by far the most research has been carried out on the $B_{10}H_{10}^{2-}$ salts, which are prepared from decaborane-14 by reaction with amines. Two B_{10} cages can be linked together to give $B_{20}H_{18}$ ions, which are capable of existing in three isomeric forms, differing in the manner in which the cages are joined together.

The bonding in the borane- and carborane-cage compounds is complex; a large number of multicentre molecular orbitals derived from suitable combinations of boron

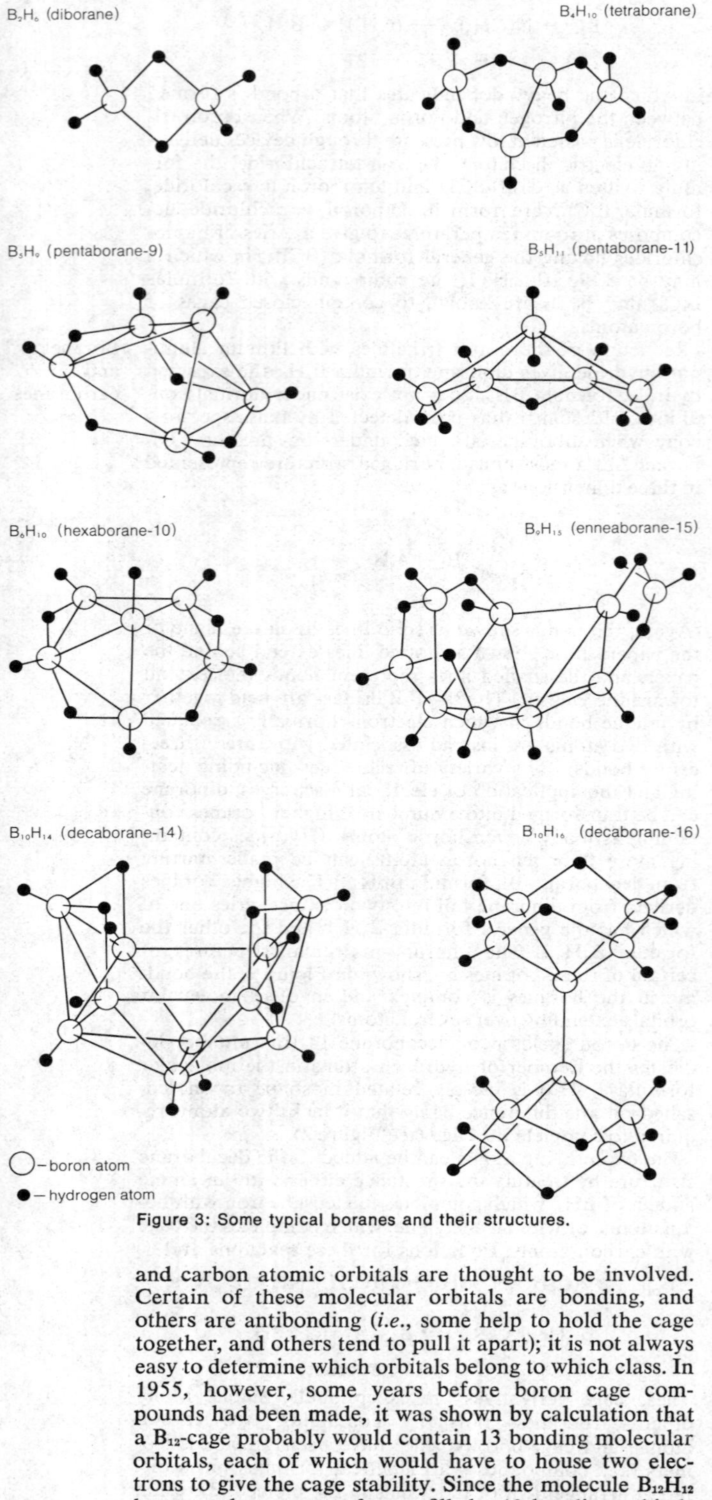

Figure 3: Some typical boranes and their structures.

and carbon atomic orbitals are thought to be involved. Certain of these molecular orbitals are bonding, and others are antibonding (*i.e.*, some help to hold the cage together, and others tend to pull it apart); it is not always easy to determine which orbitals belong to which class. In 1955, however, some years before boron cage compounds had been made, it was shown by calculation that a B_{12}-cage probably would contain 13 bonding molecular orbitals, each of which would have to house two electrons to give the cage stability. Since the molecule $B_{12}H_{12}$ has two electrons too few to fill the 13 bonding orbitals (of the 48 electrons available, 24 are used to form B–H bonds, leaving 24 to fill 12 of the 13 bonding molecular orbitals), it was predicted that $B_{12}H_{12}$ probably would be unstable, while the corresponding ion with two negative charges, $B_{12}H_{12}^{2-}$, might be stable because the two extra electrons could fill the final bonding orbital of the cage. Because of the relative positions of boron and carbon in the periodic table, a $B_{10}C_2$ cage structure would be expected to have the same electronic distribution as would a B_{12}^{2-} cage; thus all 13 bonding orbitals in a $B_{10}C_2$ icosahedral carborane should be filled, and the structure should be stable. Like considerations are thought to account for bonding in smaller-cage compounds.

A B–N bond has the same number of electrons as does a C–C bond and, as might be expected, several boron–nitrogen derivatives are physically similar to their carbon counterparts. This situation is best illustrated by boron nitride itself, which, like carbon, can exist in two allotropic (chemically identical, but physically different) forms—one of which has a layer structure resembling graphite, and the other (borazon) is extremely hard and has a diamond-like structure.

Nuclear properties of boron

Boron exists in nature as two isotopes, one of atomic mass 10 (18.8 percent) and one of atomic mass 11 (81.2 percent). Both nuclei (see NUCLEUS, ATOMIC) possess nuclear spin (rotation of the atomic nuclei); that of boron-10 has a value of 3 and that of boron-11, 3/2, the values being dictated by quantum factors. These isotopes are, therefore, of use in nuclear magnetic resonance spectroscopy; and spectrometers adapted to detecting the boron-11 nucleus are available commercially. The boron-10 and boron-11 nuclei also cause splitting in the resonances (that is, the appearance of new bands in the resonance spectra) of other nuclei (*e.g.*, those of hydrogen atoms bonded to boron). The boron-10 isotope is unique in possessing a very large capture cross section for thermal neutrons (*i.e.*, it readily absorbs neutrons of low energy). The capture of a neutron by a nucleus of this isotope results in the expulsion of an alpha particle (nucleus of a helium atom, symbolized α):

$$^{10}B + {}^{1}n \longrightarrow {}^{7}Li + {}^{4}\alpha.$$

Since the high-energy alpha particle does not travel far in normal matter, boron may be used in the fabrication of neutron shields (materials not penetrable by neutrons). In the Geiger counter, alpha particles trigger a response, whereas neutrons do not; hence if the gas chamber of a Geiger counter is filled with a gaseous boron derivative (*e.g.*, boron trifluoride), the counter will record each alpha particle produced when a neutron that passes into the chamber is captured by a boron-10 nucleus. In this way, the Geiger counter is converted into a device for detecting neutrons, which normally do not affect it. The affinity of boron-10 for neutrons also forms the basis of a technique for treating patients suffering from brain tumours. For a short time after certain boron compounds are injected into a patient with a brain tumour, the compounds collect preferentially in the tumour; irradiation of the tumour area with thermal neutrons, which cause relatively little general injury to tissue, results in the release of a tissue-damaging alpha particle in the tumour each time a boron-10 nucleus captures a neutron. In this way destruction can be limited preferentially to the tumour, leaving the normal brain tissue less affected.

Analytical chemistry of boron

The presence of boron compounds can be detected qualitatively by the green coloration they impart to the flame of an ordinary laboratory, or bunsen, burner. Quantitatively, boron is most easily analyzed by converting the material to be analyzed into boric acid by treatment with acid; the excess mineral acid is then neutralized and the much weaker boric acid is titrated (neutralized on a volume–volume basis) in the presence of a sugar, such as mannitol, to make the acid detectable.

Aluminum. In aluminum, atomic number 13, the configuration of the three outer electrons is such that in a few compounds (*e.g.*, crystalline aluminum fluoride [AlF_3] and aluminum chloride [$AlCl_3$]) the bare ion, Al^{3+}, formed by loss of these electrons, is known to occur. The energy required to form the Al^{3+} ion, however, is very high; and, in the majority of cases, it is energetically more favourable for the aluminum atom to form covalent compounds by way of sp^2 hybridization, as boron does. The Al^{3+} ion can be stabilized by hydration, and the octahedral ion $Al(H_2O)_6^{3+}$ occurs both in aqueous solution and in several salts. The alums, double salts of formula $M^{I}Al(SO_4)_2 \cdot 12H_2O$, also contain this ion; the univalent ion M can be sodium, potassium, rubidium, cesium, ammonium, or thallium, and the aluminum may be replaced by a variety of other M^{3+} ions; *e.g.*, gallium, indium, titanium, vanadium, chromium, manganese, iron, or cobalt. Although the alums were once thought to be completely isomorphous (*i.e.*, crystallographically identical), X-ray diffraction techniques show that three slight variations in structure occur, depending on the size of the univalent ion, M^+. These variations occur in such a manner that the ions pack together in the most efficient way and maximize the lattice energy of the crystal. The name aluminum (British usage is aluminium) is derived from the Latin word *alumen* used to describe potassium alum, formula $KAl(SO_4)_2 \cdot 12H_2O$.

Unlike boron, aluminum forms only a few tricoordinate derivatives except at elevated temperatures. For example, the anhydrous tribromide occurs as the dimer, formula Al_2Br_6, both in the solid and liquid states; the vapour at 400° still contains the same molecules, but on stronger heating a breaking up or dissociation of the Al_2Br_6 to the trigonal planar molecule, formula $AlBr_3$, occurs, as shown in the equation:

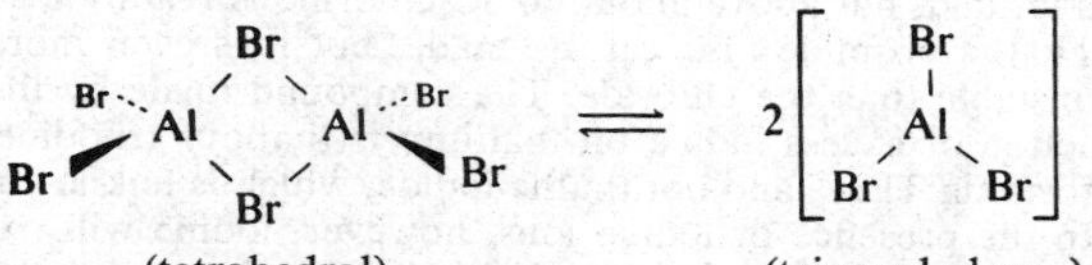

(tetrahedral) (trigonal planar)

Tricoordinate aluminum compounds are strong Lewis acids—that is, they readily accept electrons from a wide variety of donor molecules such as amines, phosphines, and ethers. In the dimer of aluminum tribromide, one bromine atom in each molecule of $AlBr_3$ acts as an electron donor to the aluminum atom in the other $AlBr_3$ molecule:

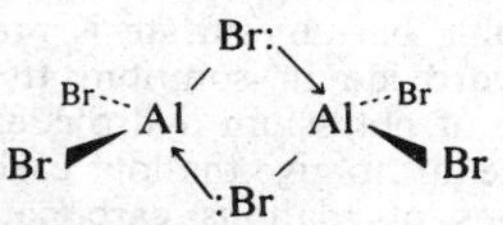

Alumina

Crystalline aluminum oxide, also called alumina, occurs naturally as corundum, which is almost as hard as diamond; impure corundum is known as emery. Transparent corundum coloured by traces of the oxides of other metals forms the following gems: sapphires, which have iron, chromium, or titanium as the impurity; rubies, which contain chromium. These gems can now be made artificially. Alumina has a very high melting point (2,050° C) and is used as a refractory (heat-resistant) material for furnaces and crucibles. The addition of alkali hydroxide to an aluminum salt gives a white precipitate of aluminum hydroxide, $Al(OH)_3$, that is soluble in acids, giving aluminum salts, and in alkalies, giving aluminates (substances containing the AlO_2^- ion). Colloidal aluminum hydroxide gives rainproof qualities to fabrics when it is deposited in the pores of the material.

All the trihalides of aluminum are known in the anhydrous state; aluminum trifluoride and aluminum trichloride form ionic crystalline lattices, whereas the bromide and iodide form molecular crystals containing the dimers, formula Al_2X_6 (X being bromine or iodine). When fused (melted), aluminum chloride changes to the covalent dimer, formula Al_2Cl_6, and the coordination number of the aluminum atom alters from six in the crystal to four in the liquid dimer, resulting in a large increase (about 40 percent) in volume when the trichloride melts. The fluoride is only slightly soluble in water, while the other halides react readily with water—for example, the chloride is hydrolyzed in a reaction that is represented by the equation:

$$AlCl_3 + 3H_2O \rightleftharpoons Al(OH)_3 + 3HCl.$$

Crystalline hydrates of the halides can be obtained from acid solutions (the presence of acid reverses equilibria of the above type and prevents hydrolysis). Complex halide anions, such as AlF_6^{3-} (found naturally in cryolite) and AlX_4^- (X being chlorine, bromine, or iodine), also are known.

Aluminum chloride reacts with lithium hydride to form lithium aluminum hydride, formula $LiAlH_4$. It is a powerful reducing agent and is widely used in organic chemistry—for example, to reduce aldehydes and ketones to primary and secondary alcohols, respectively. Aluminum hydride is unstable thermally and is readily attacked by water. With Lewis bases it forms complexes, such as $(CH_3)_3NAlH_3$; with diborane it forms a volatile borohydride, formula $Al(BH_4)_3$.

Aluminum alkyls and aryls

Grignard reagents (organomagnesium compounds) react with aluminum chloride to give either aluminum alkyls or aluminum aryls with the general formula AlR_3, the R being either an alkyl or aryl radical. The lowest members of the alkyl series are spontaneously inflammable in air and explosively decomposed by water. Unlike their boron, gallium, indium, and thallium counterparts, many aluminum alkyls and aryls are dimeric, with bridged structures which can be represented in the following manner:

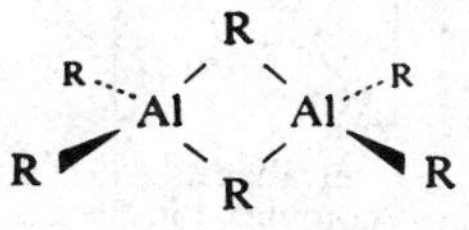

dimer of AlR_3

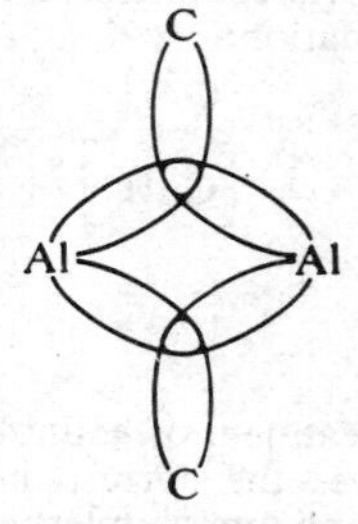

bonding in bridge

It is possible that bonding in the bridge involves three-centre molecular orbitals formed by overlap of two sp^3 orbitals from aluminum and one from carbon.

It is not clear why aluminum is the only boron group element to form dimeric organoderivatives in the solid, liquid, and gaseous phases. (Very weak associations of a different type are believed to occur in solid organoderivatives of gallium, indium, and thallium.) The aluminum alkyls are important commercially as polymerization and isomerization catalysts for olefins. Titanium tetrachloride and aluminum triethyl, for example, react to produce a catalyst that polymerizes ethylene to polyethylene at room temperature and pressure.

Aluminum can be detected in concentrations as low as one part per million using emission spectroscopy. Aluminum can be quantitatively analyzed as the oxide (formula Al_2O_3) or as a derivative of the organic nitrogen compound 8-hydroxyquinoline. The derivative has the molecular formula $Al(C_9H_6ON)_3$.

Gallium. Gallium, atomic number 31, is comparable to aluminum in its chemical properties. It does not dissolve in nitric acid because a protective film of gallium oxide is formed over the surface by the action of the acid, but the metal does dissolve in other acids to give gallium salts and it dissolves in alkalies, with evolution of hydrogen, to give gallates (compounds in which gallium appears in the anion). Of the halides, only gallium trifluoride is ionic; the others have molecular lattices containing dimeric molecules, with formula Ga_2X_6. Unlike aluminum, however, gallium forms several derivatives that contain gallium(I) oxidation state; for example, the oxide, formula Ga_2O. The sulfide (GaS), selenide (GaSe), and telluride (GaTe), made directly by combination of the elements at high temperature, are diamagnetic and contain gallium–gallium units with four positive charges, $(Ga–Ga)^{4+}$ in a layer lattice. The metal gallium is stable in dry air. On burning in air or oxygen it forms the white oxide, formula Ga_2O_3. This oxide can be reduced to the metal when heated strongly in hydrogen, and with gallium metal at 700° C it gives the lower oxide Ga_2O. The hydroxide, formula $Ga(OH)_3$, is amphoteric; *i.e.*, it reacts either as an acid or a base depending on the circumstance; it is precipitated from solutions of gallium salts by alkali hydroxides.

Gallium halides

All the anhydrous trihalides of gallium are known; of these only the fluoride is ionic. The other solid trihalides have molecular lattices containing dimer molecules, formula Ga_2X_6, which persist in the liquid and vapour states, although the proportion of dimer to monomer falls in the halogen series as one proceeds from chlorine to iodine. When gallium trichloride is heated with an equivalent amount of gallium metal, a diamagnetic solid, formula $GaCl_2$, is formed; this, however, is not a gallium(II) derivative but is an ionic, mixed-valency compound whose formula is written $Ga^+(Ga^{III}Cl_4)^-$. Aluminum can replace the gallium(III) atom, forming $Ga^+(AlCl_4)^-$, and the other halogens (except fluorine) can replace chlorine. When the trihalides are reduced with an excess of gallium the monohalides, GaX, are produced.

Gallium hydride, formula GaH_3, is polymeric, like aluminum hydride, but the gallium compound is much less stable thermally. Gallium hydride forms two types of adduct with suitable donor molecules: $GaH_3 \cdot D$ and $GaH_3 \cdot 2D$ (in which D stands for an amine or other donor molecule). When the donor is a hydride, a tetrahedral complex ion is formed according to the following equation:

$$\left[GaH_3\right] + H^- \longrightarrow \left[\begin{array}{c} H \\ H \end{array} Ga \begin{array}{c} H \\ H \end{array}\right]^-$$

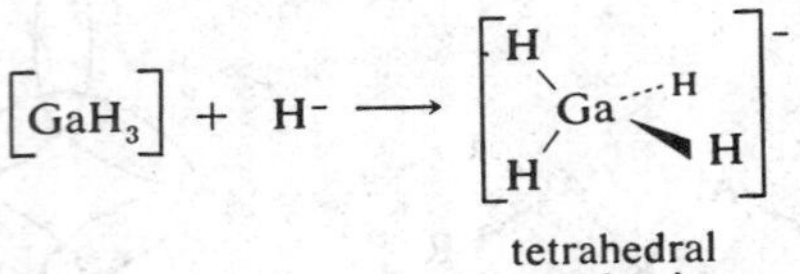

tetrahedral
complex ion

Treatment of gallium trichloride with Grignard reagents gives the corresponding alkyls and aryls; unlike their aluminum counterparts, these substances are monomeric under all conditions.

Indium. Indium, atomic number 49, is an amphoteric element; it dissolves in acids to give indium salts and it also dissolves in concentrated alkalies to give indates. All anhydrous indium(III) derivatives, except indium trifluoride, formula InF_3, are covalent. There is a marked tendency for two of the outer electrons of the indium atom (the outer $5s^2$ electrons) not to be used in bonding; this circumstance results in univalent indium compounds.

Indium burns to the yellow oxide, formula In_2O_3, when heated in air or oxygen; a better method of preparation for the oxide is to heat the hydroxide, nitrate, or sulfate. This oxide is easily reduced to the metal, and on strong heating it loses oxygen to give the monoxide In^I_2O. Indium hydroxide dissolves in both acids and alkalies.

Indium halides   Of the anhydrous trihalides, all are known, and only the fluoride (InF_3) is ionic. Although dimers (double molecules) of the chloride, bromide, and iodide exist in the solid state, their vapours are largely dissociated to the monomers, represented by the general formula in which X stands for any halogen: InX_3. Heating indium trichloride with the metal, or treating the metal with an equivalent amount of mercuric chloride, results in the formation of the mixed-valency salt, whose formula is written $In^+(In^{III}Cl_4)^-$. By reducing the indium trihalides, except the fluoride, with an excess of indium metal, solid monohalides can be obtained.

Thallium. Thallium, atomic number 81, is typical of the Group IIIa elements in having an s^2p^1 outer electron configuration. Promoting an electron from an s to a p orbital allows the element to be three or four covalent. With thallium, however, the energy required for $s \rightarrow p$ promotion is high relative to the Tl–X covalent bond energy which is regained on formation of TlX_3; hence, a trivalent derivative is not a very energetically favoured reaction product. Thallium normally forms the more stable thallium(I), or thallous, salts containing the ion Tl^+ (in which the $6s^2$ electrons remain unused); it is the only element to form a stable univalent cation with the outer electron configuration $(n-1)d^{10}ns^2$, which is, unusually enough, not an inert gas configuration. In its oxidation state three, indicated as thallium(III), or commonly called thallic, thallium resembles aluminum, although the ion Tl^{3+} appears to be too large to form alums. In the *Monovalent thallium* monovalent state, thallium(I) displays properties similar to those of both the heavier alkali metals and silver. The very close similarity in size of the thallium(I) ion, Tl^+, and the rubidium ion, Rb^+, makes many thallium(I) salts, such as the chromate, sulfate, nitrate, and halides, isomorphous (*i.e.*, have an identical crystal structure) to the corresponding rubidium salts; also the ion Tl^+ is able to replace the ion Rb^+ in the alums. Thus, thallium does

form an alum; but in doing so it replaces the M^I ion, rather than the expected metal atom M^{III}, in the formula $M^IM^{III}(SO_4)_2 \cdot 12H_2O$.

Thallic oxide, formula Tl_2O_3, which is formed when thallium is burned in oxygen, is brown in colour; on strong heating, this substance loses oxygen to form thallous oxide, formula Tl_2O.

Thallous chloride, formula TlCl, prepared by the action of dilute hydrochloric acid on thallium metal, is like silver chloride in that it is light-sensitive and becomes violet on exposure to sunlight. Unlike silver chloride, however, thallous chloride is only slightly soluble in aqueous ammonia. Chlorine oxidizes a suspension of thallous chloride in water to thallic chloride and, from the solution, colourless crystals of the hydrate, formula $TlCl_3 \cdot 4H_2O$, can be obtained. These crystals may be dehydrated, but above about 60° C chlorine is readily lost. Thallic bromide also can be made, but it is even more unstable than the chloride. The compound made by the action of excess iodine on thallium is thallous triiodide, formula $Tl^+I_3^-$, and not thallic iodide, which is unknown. In the presence of iodide ions, however, iodine will oxidize thallium metal to the thallium(III) state, giving the complex anion $(Tl^{III}I_4)^-$. Mixed-valency halides of thallium are known, for example $Tl^+(Tl^{III}Cl_4)^-$ and $Tl_3^+(Tl^{III}Cl_6)^{3-}$. Thallic salts (*e.g.*, the chloride, sulfate, and nitrate) may be made by dissolving thallic oxide in the respective acids, whereas thallous salts result when thallium metal dissolves in dilute acids.

Thallous hydroxide is a strong base, prepared by adding barium hydroxide solution to thallium(I) sulfate, whereupon the insoluble barium sulfate is precipitated, leaving thallous hydroxide in solution. Its aqueous solutions, like those of potassium hydroxide, absorb carbon dioxide from the air, to give thallous carbonate, formula Tl_2CO_3; solutions of thallous carbonate are partially hydrolyzed.

Thallium imparts a brilliant green coloration to a bunsen flame. Thallous chromate, formula Tl_2CrO_4, is best used in the quantitative analysis of thallium, after any thallic ion present in the sample has been reduced to the thallous state.

BIBLIOGRAPHY. F.A. COTTON and G. WILKINSON, *Advanced Inorganic Chemistry*, 2nd rev. ed. (1966), an excellent general text on modern inorganic chemistry in which the boron group is treated in detail; N.H. FURMAN (ed.), *Standard Methods of Chemical Analysis*, 6th ed., vol. 1 (1962), a comprehensive text on analysis with further information on the boron group; J. KANE and A.G. MASSEY, *Boron* (1972), a booklet describing the modern uses of boron and its compounds; A.G. MASSEY, *The Typical Elements* (1972), an undergraduate text on the non-transition elements.

(A.G.M.)

Borromini, Francesco

A difficult person, solitary, compulsive, at times beset by depression, Francesco Borromini offered 17th-century Europe a revolutionary style of architecture. Contemporary Baroque design adhered to the anthropometric architectural theories established during the Renaissance. These held that the human body, created in the image of God, contained the harmonic, divine proportions of the universe; that these proportions could be discovered by arithmetical measure; and that to properly relate a building to this universe, it also must be planned according to arrangements of arithmetical units. Borromini challenged these assumptions by basing his architecture on geometric configurations and subdivisions. In these visually striking plans, he developed the use of space and light as major elements of design. Moreover, his workman's knowledge of building techniques allowed him to introduce structural innovations that other architects would not have dared. Though the catalyst for a century of far-reaching developments, he ended his life in frustration and despair, one of the few known suicides in the history of art prior to the 19th century.

Youth and education. Born to Giovanni Domenico Castelli and Anastasia Garogo on September 25, 1599, in Bissone, on Lake Lugano (Lombardy) in northern

Interior of the dome of the church of S. Ivo della Sapienza, Rome, by Francesco Borromini, 1642–60.
GEKS

Italy, he was christened Francesco Castelli (a name he changed 28 years later). While still a boy, he was introduced to the craft specialities of architecture by his father, who sent him to Milan (1608 or 1614) to learn stonecutting. After several years training in the skills and technology of both architecture and sculpture, he collected a debt owed to his father and, without informing his parents, fled to Rome in 1620. There he became a draftsman and stonemason in the office of his kinsman, Carlo Maderno, who had established himself as the major practicing architect in Italy.

Training under Maderno

Celibate and irascible, Borromini dedicated himself to the discipline of architecture. Maderno quickly recognized Borromini's potential. The aging master and his young pupil worked together closely on various problems at St. Peter's, whose fundamental plan was revised by Maderno. For the Palazzo Barberini, Maderno determined a basic concept, then entrusted Borromini with the realization of specifics. A convergence of both talents produced the facade design of S. Andrea della Valle, and Borromini was permitted to undertake the lantern of the church's dome himself. Borromini's personality is apparent in these projects, though Maderno's style dominates them. This was not always the case. A facade to be attached to the late-16th-century oval church of S. Anna dei Palafrenieri was Borromini's personal project; attempting to integrate a five-bay front and two towers with the existing oval dome, it prefigured his later S. Agnese in Agone (in Piazza Navona) in its placement of plastic volumes in space. Equally significant was his transformation of Maderno's plan for S. Ignazio; through his use of pairs of free-standing columns, he suggested an articulation of space, a major characteristic of his style. Space in his structures is not merely a void but rather something corporeal, an element in itself, molded by the surrounding shell of the building. Later he would develop this concept by replacing the enclosing wall with an extensively penetrated framework, as in the Re Magi chapel.

Collaboration with Bernini

Maderno died in January 1629, three months after construction had begun at the Palazzo Barberini. The famous Gian Lorenzo Bernini was appointed architect in charge, though his architectural abilities were underdeveloped. Borromini continued in a key position, working out the specifics of Maderno's plan and collaborating successfully with Bernini. The patron, however, began to draw heavily on the advice of a third designer, Pietro da Cortona, and eventually abandoned Maderno's project for the east facade of the palace. Unable to work with Cortona and despairing of these changes, Borromini left the project in 1631. With Bernini he now dedicated himself entirely to the task of designing the Baldacchino in St. Peter's, which was conceived as a monumental canopy raised over the tomb of St. Peter, recalling the canopy that is traditionally supported over the pope when he is carried in state through the church. The enormous bronze Baldacchino was realized through the closest coordination between Borromini and Bernini; the huge, S-shaped volutes that crown four corkscrew columns represent their most important common creation. Bernini was in command of all enterprises at St. Peter's, but he paid Borromini a substantial sum from 1631 to 1633 for this work, indicating the great importance of his contribution.

An independent architect. The Baldacchino was completed in 1633. The year before, on the recommendation of Bernini and Cardinal Francesco Barberini, Borromini was awarded the office of university architect. With his new position as support, he began to seek his own patronage as an independent architect. His first independent commission represented an extraordinary challenge to tradition; it was the Roman church and monastery of S. Carlo alle Quattro Fontane, begun in 1638. No larger inside than the dimensions of a single pier at St. Peter's, the small church electrified Rome, and its reputation spread like wildfire through Europe. Borromini began by stacking together three distinct units that normally would have been employed only in separate buildings: a curious, undulating lower zone; a middle one suggesting the standard Greek-cross plan; and an oval dome, a relatively new and still little-used form. This audacious combination of precedent and novelty is integrated by complex, interweaving rhythms. Bold, illusionistic effects, achieved by calculated lighting, intensify the space. The dome appears to be floating above the interior of the church like a hallucinatory vision because its springing point and its light sources are concealed by the zone below.

Borromini established contacts with the eminent Spada family and was sponsored by Pope Innocent X for a decade, but his relations with patrons were frequently estranged and at times reached an impasse because of his intransigent, defiant attitude. Though bitterly resentful of what he felt to be a lack of just recognition, he was indifferent toward wealth and rejected the fashions of normal dress. Intractable and melancholic, his capacity for rage was legend. On one of his building sites he was infuriated to discover a man damaging some materials and had him so violently beaten that he died.

Conflict with Bernini

Given Borromini's gloomy disposition, it is not surprising that a conflict developed with the famous and popular Bernini. While they were working together, the relationship between the two artistic giants had been mutually profitable: Borromini's style was injected with a new vitality under Bernini's influence, and Bernini was strongly impressed by Borromini's novel formulations of architectural detail. Later, however, a bitter conflict arose between them. Perhaps Borromini's subordinate position at St. Peter's sufficiently rankled him to provoke his departure. He definitely felt this way later in life, claiming that Bernini had begged him not to abandon him on the work at St. Peter's and had promised to recognize his many labours with a worthy reward. Borromini felt that after he had carried out the work, Bernini drew the remunerations and rewards, never giving him anything except good words and grand promises.

Divergent characters, disparate backgrounds, and different attitudes toward life presumably provoked the antagonism. Bernini worked easily with the aristocratic and powerful; immensely successful as a sculptor and painter as well as an architect, he was outgoing, charming, and witty. Borromini, on the other hand, was a lonely, withdrawn man; he prided himself on his highly specialized training, and he resented his modest degree of recognition. Conflict between the two became public in 1645 over the decision to eliminate the towers Maderno had designed for the facade of St. Peter's. Maderno left them as substructures, and in 1636 Bernini submitted a proposal for completing them. After one was erected, however, technical deficiences halted further construction in 1641, and four years later a commission decided on its removal. Borromini emerged as Bernini's most effective and destructive critic, accusing him of incompetence.

Bernini seldom indulged in professional envy, however, but, during his Paris visit of 1665, he accused Borromini of abandoning the anthropometric basis of architecture. Because the body of Adam was modeled not only by God but also in his image and likeness, it was argued, the proportions of buildings should be derived from those of the body of man and woman. Borromini, however, based his buildings on geometric configurations in an essentially medieval manner that he probably learned in Lombardy, where medieval building procedures had been handed down from generation to generation. Borromini's approach consisted of establishing a geometric figure for a building or room, then articulating this figure by means of geometric subunits. He thus stood accused of denying the basis of good architecture. He never divorced himself completely from the anthropometric basis of design, however; he insisted, at least once, that his architecture contained human references. The concave facade of St. Philip Neri represented to him the welcoming gesture of outstretched arms: the central unit stood for the chest, the two-part wings for arm and forearm.

Basis of Borromini's design

The bizarre quality of Borromini's designs was as unsettling as his departure from anthropomorphism. Even his supporters felt uneasy with his novel creations. Presumably his license departed too far from orthodox interpretations of antiquity, which were accepted at this time as the fundamental standards of form for architecture. This seems paradoxical because he was an avid student of the ancient world: his drawings of antique fragments demonstrate a critical contact with Roman architecture, and his evocations of classical thought on the project for the Villa Pamphili at San Pancrazio are recorded with philological exactness. Nevertheless, the notion was in the air that it was possible to use and then progress beyond the achievements of antiquity, and Borromini strongly identified with this attitude. He said that he certainly would never have given himself to architecture with the idea of being merely a "copyist," and he invoked the example of Michelangelo, who said that he who follows others never goes ahead. Borromini declared antiquity and nature as his points of departure (though including the work of Michelangelo as well), but he actually spurned the regular and orthodox compositional motifs of the ancient world. Instead he turned to novel, curious, and marvelous interpretations, such as could be found in Hadrian's Villa at Tivoli, and to Roman structural achievements, such as their brickwork and their use of bevelled corners for vault supports.

Just as Borromini's attitude toward antiquity was uncommon, so too were his historical roots in medieval architecture in an era that had rejected medieval culture as corrupt. Yet his tendency toward the annulment of the wall, his use of structural ribwork to strengthen vaults, his designs derived from geometric configurations, his use of decorative motifs, and perhaps even his awareness that light can be given major compositional importance, all represent ideas stimulated by the medieval experience. Closer to his own time, Borromini investigated certain formal qualities found in both Florentine architecture of the 15th century and Mannerist architecture of the 16th century, especially that of Michelangelo, whose architecture was of decisive importance, suggesting Borromini's still more radical experiments. The manner in which space seemed to expand and contract in a number of Michelangelo's designs indicated to Borromini the dynamic potential of this medium. Responding to the past with greater freedom than his contemporaries, Borromini employed those elements that suited his purposes.

This broad selection of pedigree was complemented by his understanding of structures and materials. The artisan tradition of Lombardy stressed technical excellence, providing him with the knowledge to approach a full range of structural problems. It gave him a firm base for his technical virtuosity, which is demonstrated by a long list of achievements, including the careful balancing of his towers for the facade of St. Peter's, the supporting metal cage for a barrel vault in the Palazzo Pamphili in Piazza Navona, the precise brickwork of the Oratory of St. Philip Neri, and his inventive domes and vaults, such as those of S. Ivo della Sapienza or the Re Magi chapel. He used the building yard as an extension of his drafting table and as a place where he could experiment and improvise to generate a fruitful exchange between design and execution. At S. Carlo alle Quattro Fontane, for example, the three-dimensional curve of the arches opening to the chapel vaults, as well as other features, could not have been realized without Borromini's personal guidance of the stonecutters on the site.

His technical virtuosity

Borromini's urban sensibilities were also highly developed, as one of his unexecuted schemes demonstrates. He wished to create a dynamic setting for the facade of S. Giovanni in Laterano by means of a piazza. The street passing through this space was to be seen with 24 uniform building fronts, establishing a large scale, tightly organized arrangement of spaces. Always alert in his commissions to responsible contextual readings, he displayed a deep sensitivity to the relationship of his buildings to the surrounding urban fabric. The bell-tower facade of St. Philip Neri, for example, is composed to conclude and monumentalize the street running up to it.

Later years and influence. Even late in his life, Borromini's innovations continued to be as energetic and radical as ever. For the Re Magi chapel in the Collegio di Propaganda Fide, on which he worked until his death, he designed six pairs of colossal pilasters to define a generally rectangular space with bevelled corners.

Despair and death

In the 1660s, Borromini's fortunes tragically declined. He was increasingly frustrated by the fame and success of his rival, Bernini. His only disciple, Francesco Righi, and his most sympathetic patron, Padre Virgilio Spada, both died early in the decade. His major commission of S. Agnese in Agone, in Piazza Navona, was taken from him; work on another of his projects, S. Andrea delle Fratte, came to a halt; and his facade of St. Philip Neri was disfigured by lateral extensions. Suffering severe melancholia, he travelled to Lombardy, but when he returned to Rome his melancholy returned with him, and he spent whole weeks without ever leaving his house. He burned all of his drawings in his possession. Taken ill, his condition was made worse by hypochondriac hallucinations; when he suffered fits, it was decided that he should be denied all activity so that he might sleep. On a hot summer's night, unable to rest and forbidden to work, he arose in a fury, found a sword, and fell upon it. Though to a Catholic, suicide is a sin, Borromini recovered a lucid mind after mortally wounding himself, repented, received the last sacraments of the church, and wrote his will before he died, on August 2, 1667. At his own request, he was buried anonymously in the grave of his teacher and friend, Maderno. It has been suggested that Borromini's suicide was the result of an increasing schizophrenia and that this pathological process is reflected in his architecture, but this contention is impossible to demonstrate. His career appears to have been successful until the disillusionments of the last years.

In denying the restrictive, enclosing qualities of wall in order to treat space and light as architectonic components, Borromini confronted his architectural inheritance with its most complete and compelling challenge. Scores of designers would capitalize upon this revolutionary legacy. Borromini's works from the first had created an uproar in Rome, and his influence proved highly suggestive for design in northern Italy and in central Europe over the course of the next century. Later, as Neoclassical attitudes gained force, he was increasingly despised. Largely forgotten during most of the 19th century, Borromini's architecture has again been recognized in the 20th century as the creation of genius.

MAJOR WORKS

All works are in Rome—S. Andrea della Valle (with Maderno, *c.* 1622); Palazzo Barberini (with Bernini, 1629–31); St. Peter's (with Bernini, Baldacchino, 1631–33; facade design to 1645); Oratory of St. Philip Neri (begun 1637); S. Carlo alle Quattro Fontane (1638–41); S. Ivo della Sapienza (1642–60); Palazzo Pamphili (vault, 1645–50); Collegio di Propaganda Fide (1646–67, including the Re Magi chapel [1662–64]); S. Giovanni in Laterano (reconstruction, 1647–50); S. Agnese in Agone (continuation, begun 1652; Piazza

Navona); S. Andrea delle Fratte (exterior, 1653–65); Biblioteca Alessandrina in S. Ivo della Sapienza (1659–61).

BIBLIOGRAPHY. *Opera del Borromini . . .* (1720) and *Opus architectonicum* (1725), Borromini's discussion and engravings of S. Ivo della Sapienza and the monastery of St. Philip Neri—both reprinted in the critical edition by PAOLO PORTOGHESI, *Opera and Opus architectonicum* (1964). The Graphische Sammlung Albertina in Vienna holds more than 450 Borromini drawings.

EBERHARD HEMPEL, *Francesco Borromini* (1924), the first complete monograph (in German), still basic to any study of Borromini and his work, though outdated in some respects; PAOLO PORTOGHESI, *Borromini* (1967; Eng. trans., 1968), not distinguished by its scholarship, yet the most exhaustive monograph to date, with a thorough bibliography; HEINRICH THELEN (ed.), Francesco *Borromini: Die Handzeichnungen*, pt. 1 (1967), Borromini's drawings to 1633.

(C.F.O.)

Bose, Subhas Chandra

Described as a "patriot of patriots" by Mahatma Gandhi, Subhas Chandra Bose fought for Indian independence with courage and devotion. But his role in the Indian struggle was different from that of Gandhi himself, for Bose's most spectacular gestures were military ones.

He was born on January 23, 1897, the son of a prominent lawyer in Cuttack, Orissa Province. As a boy Subhas Chandra sought an ideal to which he could devote his life, poring over the letters and speeches of Swami Vivekananda, a Hindu saint and religious leader of the late 19th century, while hardly 15. He later enjoyed a career at the University of Calcutta, proceeding thence to Cambridge. In 1920 he passed the Indian civil service examination, but soon after he resigned to fight for his people and hurried back to India.

Influence of Gandhi and Das

The noncooperation movement had been started by Mahatma Gandhi, who had made the Indian National Congress a powerful, though nonviolent, organization. Bose was advised by Gandhi to work under C.R. Das (Indian politician, founder, and leader of the Swaraj [Self-rule] Party) in Bengal. There he became a youth educator, journalist, and commandant of the Bengal Congress volunteers. His activities led to his imprisonment in December 1921. When the Swaraj Party was formed in 1923, Bose was a devoted adherent. In 1924 he was appointed chief executive officer of the corporation of Calcutta, with Das as mayor. Bose was soon after deported to Burma, suspected of connections with secret revolutionary movements. Released in 1927, he returned to find Bengal Congress affairs in disarray after the death of Das.

Gandhi now resumed his Congress activity, and Bose was elected president of the Bengal Congress. In 1928 he was general officer commanding the Congress volunteers in the Indian National Congress session at Calcutta. His imposing figure, leading a parade of disciplined youth in military formation, gave people visions of a national militia, which accorded ill with Gandhi's philosophy. In the Congress session Bose moved a resolution demanding India's independence. He did not get a majority this time, but in the 1929 session Gandhi himself sponsored the independence resolution. It received overwhelming support. When the civil disobedience movement was started in 1930, Bose was already in detention. Released and then re-arrested, he was finally allowed to proceed to Europe after a year's detention. In enforced exile, he wrote *The Indian Struggle*, 1920–34, made a firsthand study of Europe after the Treaty of Versailles, and pleaded India's cause with European leaders. He returned from Europe in 1936, was again taken into custody, and released after a year. In 1938 he was elected president of the Indian National Congress and formed a national planning committee, as well as a policy of industrialization. This did not harmonize with Gandhian economic thought, which clung to the spinning wheel as a symbol. Bose's vindication came in 1939, when he defeated a Gandhian rival for re-election. Nonetheless, the "rebel president" felt bound to resign because of the lack of Gandhi's support. He founded the Forward Bloc, hoping to rally radical elements, but was again incarcerated in July 1940. His refusal to remain in prison at this critical period of India's history was expressed in a determination to fast to death, which frightened the British government into releasing him. Though closely watched, he escaped from his residence in disguise and reached Germany, hoping to exploit the international situation in favour of India.

Military leadership

In Germany Bose raised a body of Indian volunteers to fight against the Western powers. After the Japanese attack on Pearl Harbor and the fall of Singapore to the Japanese, he thrilled the East by arriving at Penang Island off the west coast of Malaya after about three months' hazardous passage in a German submarine. He then flew to Tokyo, planning to strengthen the independence struggle in India by obtaining Japanese aid against the British. Indian soldiers of the British Indian Army in Japanese captivity were set free to join him, and Indians from Singapore and other places in Southeast Asia also volunteered. He formed a trained army of three active divisions, each consisting of 10,000 soldiers and 20,000 volunteers. In October 1943 he proclaimed the establishment of an independent Indian government, and his Indian National Army, enjoying equal status with the Japanese Army, advanced to Rangoon and thence overland into India, reaching Kohīma and the plains of Imphāl (near the Burmese border, about 200 miles north of the Bay of Bengal). In a stubborn battle the army, lacking Japanese aerial support, was defeated and forced to retreat but for some time succeeded in maintaining its identity as the liberation army of India. Bose was unbroken in defeat and reportedly died in a Japanese hospital on August 19, 1945, after his plane had crashed in Taiwan. By his actions Bose proved that Indians in the British Indian Army could also be inspired by patriotic fervour, and by his work he influenced the conference that led to Indian independence.

BIBLIOGRAPHY. SUBHAS CHANDRA BOSE, *An Indian Pilgrim; or, Autobiography of Subhas Chandra Bose, 1897–1920* (1948); *The Indian Struggle, 1920–1934* (1935); *The Indian Struggle, 1920–1942*, compiled by the NETAJI RESEARCH BUREAU (1964), perhaps the best account of India's freedom movement up to 1942 (also gives an idea of Bose's revolutionary ardour and his troubled though affectionate relationship to Gandhi); J.S. BRIGHT (ed.), *Important Speeches and Writings of Subhas Bose* (1946), valuable source material; KITTY KURTI, *Subhas Chandra Bose As I Knew Him* (1966), and N. MOOKERJEE, *Netaji Through German Lens* (1970), emphasize his dislike of Hitler and Nazism; D.K. ROY, *Subhas As I Knew Him* (1946), a very intimate character study; SHAH NAWAZ KHAN, *My Memories of I.N.A. and Its Netaji* (1946), a detailed history of the Indian National Army; HUGH TOYE, *The Springing Tiger* (1959), a study of Bose emphasizing his reckless courage, enthusiasm, and inspiration and criticizing some traits of his character.

(N.K.S.)

Bossuet, Jacques-Bénigne

Bossuet, a prominent French churchman of the late 17th century, is known as the most celebrated of all French orators; as one of the chief theoreticians supporting the absolute monarchy of Louis XIV; and as the leading opponent of Quietism, a form of mysticism espoused by his contemporary, Archbishop Fénelon.

Jacques-Bénigne Bossuet was born of a family of magistrates on September 25, 1627, in Dijon, Burgundy. There he spent his first 15 years and was educated at the Jesuit college. Intended early for an ecclesiastical career, he was tonsured at the age of ten. In 1642 he went to study in Paris, where he remained for ten years; at the Collège de Navarre, he received a sound theological education. He was deeply impressed by the interest that was then developing among many of the clergy in renewing the ideal of the priesthood; the simple eloquence of St. Vincent de Paul, the founder of hospitals and missionary orders, in particular exerted an influence on him. At the same time, he frequented scientific and intellectual circles and was an eyewitness of the Fronde, an uprising in Paris against the absolutism of the King. In 1652 he was ordained priest and received his doctorate of divinity. Refusing a high appointment offered him at the Collège de

Bossuet, oil painting by Hyacinthe Rigaud, 1698. In the Uffizi, Florence.
Alinari—Mansell

Navarre, he chose instead to settle in Metz, where his father had obtained a canonry for him.

Canon at Metz

Though Bossuet belonged to the Metz clergy until 1669, he divided his time between Metz and Paris from 1656 to 1659, and after 1660 he left Paris hardly at all. When in Metz, he zealously performed his duties as canon. His main concerns, however, were preaching and controversy with the Protestants, and it was at Metz that he began to master these skills. His first book, the *Réfutation du catéchisme du sieur Paul Ferry*, was the result of his discussions with Paul Ferry, the minister of the Protestant reformed church at Metz. Bossuet's reputation as a preacher spread to Paris, where his "Panégyrique de l'apôtre saint Paul" (1657) and his "Sermon sur l'eminente dignité des pauvres dans l'Église" (1659), a sermon on the sublime dignity of the poor in the church, were particularly admired.

Lenten sermons and funeral orations. Bossuet's career as a great popular preacher unfolded during the next ten years in Paris. He preached the Lenten sermons of 1660 and 1661 in two famous convents there—the Minims' and the Carmelites'—and in 1662 was called to preach them before King Louis XIV. The Lenten sermons, abundant with biblical citations and paraphrases, epitomize Baroque eloquence; yet, while they exhibit the majesty and the pathos of the Baroque ideal, the exaggeration and mannerism are conspicuously absent. The content of the sermons included not only religious matters, such as a sermon on death but also political matters, such as the discourse on the duties of kings, a subject that did not endear him to the monarch. Nevertheless, he was summoned in 1669 to deliver the funeral orations that were customary after the death of an important national figure. These first "Oraisons funèbres" include panegyrics on Henrietta Maria of France, queen of England (1669), and on her daughter Henrietta Anne of England, Louis XIV's sister-in-law (1670). Masterpieces of French classical prose, the orations display dignity, balance, and slow thematic development, with emotionally charged passages but organized according to logical argumentation. From the life of the departed subject, Bossuet selected qualities and episodes from which he could draw a moral. Appealing directly to the heart, he convinced his listeners by the passion of his religious feelings, which he expressed in clear, simple rhetoric.

Role in Jansenist quarrel and Protestant controversy

Apart from his work as a preacher, Bossuet, as a doctor of divinity, felt compelled to intervene in the controversy over Jansenism, a movement in the Catholic Church emphasizing a heightened sense of original sin and the role of God's grace in salvation. Bossuet tried to steer a middle course in the quarrel caused by the Jansenist reform movement within the Catholic Church, devoting himself to his controversy with the Protestants. At one point he negotiated with Paul Ferry for a union of the churches, but the project came to nothing. In 1668 he played a decisive part in the conversion to Catholicism of the marshal Henri de Turenne, a former Calvinist, and one of Louis XIV's leading generals. The following year, Bossuet was designated bishop of Condom, a diocese in southwest France, but had to resign the see in 1670 after his appointment as tutor to the Dauphin, the King's eldest son. This post brought about his election to the Académie Française.

Bishop of Condom and tutor to the Dauphin. Thoroughly absorbed in the duties of his new office, Bossuet found time to publish a work against Protestantism, *Exposition de la doctrine de l'église catholique sur les matières de controverse* (1671). He preached only occasionally thereafter. Primarily concerned with religious and moral instruction, he also taught Latin, history, philosophy, and politics. He wrote several treatises for his pupil: the *Discours sur l'histoire universelle* (1681), on the role of divine providence in history, and the *Traité de la connaissance de Dieu et de soi-même*, discussing knowledge of God, oneself, and the concept of divine providence. His major political work, the *Politique tirée des propres paroles de l'Écriture sainte*—which uses the Bible as evidence of divine authority for the power of kings—earned Bossuet his reputation as a great theoretician of absolutism. In the *Politique*, he developed the doctrine of divine right, the theory that any government legally formed expresses the will of God, that its authority is sacred, and that any rebellion against it is criminal. But he also emphasized the dreadful responsibility of the sovereign, who was to behave as God's image, govern his subjects as a good father, and yet remain unaffected by his power. At this time, Bossuet was constantly in the entourage of the King, and he acquired an expertise both in politics and in court life that he had previously lacked. Soon he was engaged to act as Louis XIV's counsellor as well as tutor to the Dauphin. The latter, who was not a very bright pupil, profited little from his tutor's teaching, but Bossuet greatly expanded his own fund of knowledge.

Bishop of Meaux. Bossuet became, in 1681, bishop of Meaux, a post he held until his death. In this period he delivered his second series of great funeral orations, including those of Princess Anne de Gonzague (1685), the chancellor Michel Le Tellier (1686), and the Great Condé (1687). Though he kept in close touch with the Dauphin and the King, he was not primarily a court prelate; he was, rather, a devoted bishop, living mostly among his diocesans, preaching, busying himself with charitable organizations, and directing his clergy. His excursions outside the diocese were in relation to the theological controversies of his time: Gallicanism, Protestantism, and Quietism.

The Gallican controversy

In the Gallican controversy, Louis XIV maintained that the French monarch could limit papal authority in collecting revenues of vacant sees and in certain other matters, while the Ultramontanists held that the pope was supreme. To avert the schism that seemed imminent between the King and the Pope, Bossuet sought to modify the Gallican attitude without totally giving in to the Ultramontane position. An extraordinary general assembly of the French clergy was held to consider this question in 1681–82. Bossuet delivered the inaugural sermon to this body and also drew up its final statement, the *Déclaration des quatre articles* (Declaration of Four Articles), which was delivered, along with his famous inaugural sermon on the unity of the church, to the assembly of the French clergy in 1682. The articles asserted the king's independence from Rome in secular matters and proclaimed that, in matters of faith, the pope's judgment is not to be regarded as infallible without the assent of the total church. They were accepted by all parties of the assembly, and his role in this controversy remained perhaps the most significant of Bossuet's life.

Concurrently, he was engaged in the controversy with the Protestants. The campaign to limit their religious freedom culminated in 1685 in the revocation of the

Edict of Nantes by Louis XIV. The revocation, in effect, forbade French Protestants to practice their religion. Bossuet, who bore no responsibility for this decision, supported the royal policy, though he opposed persecution and endeavoured to convert the Protestants by intellectual argument. In 1688 he published a history of variations in the Protestant churches, *Histoire des variations des églises protestantes*, which was followed by information and advice to Protestants, *Avertissements aux protestants* (1689–91). He maintained an ecumenical correspondence with the great German philosopher Leibniz.

Though Bossuet had displayed moderation in the Gallican quarrel and in the controversy with the Protestants, he showed himself less tolerant in other cases. He violently attacked the theatre as immoral in *Maximes et réflexions sur la comédie* (1694). He had the books of the biblical critic Richard Simon condemned, and he assailed Simon, who was modernizing exegesis, in *Défense de la tradition et des saints pères*, a defense of the Church Fathers and of the Catholic tradition.

Quarrel with Quietism

Above all, he led an attack on the form of religious mysticism known as Quietism, which was being practiced by the archbishop of Cambrai, François Fénelon. Although not inaccessible to forms of spirituality other than his own, he was by nature very intellectual and had been nourished on theology. Thus he had been rendered unable to understand a form of mysticism that consisted of passive devotional contemplation and total abandonment to the Divine Presence of God. He wrote such harsh and unfair works against the "new mystics" as his statement on Quietism, *Instruction sur les états d'oraison* (1697), and the *Relation sur le quiétisme* (1698). After a duel of pamphlets and some unpleasant intrigue, he obtained Fénelon's condemnation in Rome in 1699. Bossuet died in Paris on April 12, 1704.

Reputation. In the centuries since his death, Bossuet's reputation has been the subject of much controversy. The only point of agreement is the excellence of his style and eloquence. From a political point of view, he was praised by nationalists and monarchists, but spurned by the liberal tradition, as espoused by Victor Hugo, for example. From a religious point of view, he was often quoted as a master of French Catholic thought, but he had, and has still, against him the Ultramontanists, Catholic progressives and modernists, and many of Fénelon's numerous admirers. His emphasis on immutability of doctrine and the perfection of the Church make him seem old-fashioned in the atmosphere of Catholicism after the second Vatican Council.

BIBLIOGRAPHY. There is no general or bibliographical work in English worth mentioning. The only important study in English is SISTER G. TERSTEGGE, *Providence As idée-maîtresse in the Works of Bossuet: Theme and Stylistic Motif* (1948; reprinted 1970). The most accessible book in French is J. CALVET, *Bossuet*, new ed. rev. by J. TRUCHET (1968), with a detailed bibliography. Scholarly works include A.G. MARTIMORT, *Le Gallicanisme de Bossuet* (1953); J. TRUCHET, *La Prédication de Bossuet*, 2 vol. (1960); T. GOYET, *L'Humanisme de Bossuet*, 2 vol. (1965); and J. LE BRUN, *La Spiritualité de Bossuet* (1972).

(J.T.)

Boston

Boston, the capital of the Commonwealth of Massachusetts in the United States, lies on Massachusetts Bay, an arm of the Atlantic Ocean. The city proper has an unusually small area for a major city, only 46 square miles (119 square kilometres), more than one-fourth of it water. In the 1980 census Boston had a population of more than 560,000, ranking 20th among U.S. cities. Its metropolitan area, which includes five counties of eastern Massachusetts, had a population of about 2,760,000 and ranked 10th in the United States.

The city's symbolic role in America

The area, the people, and the institutions within its political boundaries can only begin, however, to define the essence of Boston. As a city and as a name, Boston is a symbol of much that has gone into the development of the American consciousness. Its presence reaches far beyond its immediate environs: as the spiritual capital of the New England states, as the nation's closest link to its European heritage, as the progenitor of the American Revolution and the nation, and as the earliest centre of American culture, its influence pervaded the country for nearly three centuries. Though Boston, like New England in general, has played a lessening role in national life during much of the 20th century, it remains the focal point of what may be the most diversified and dynamic combination of educational, cultural, and medical-scientific activities in the United States. (For information on related topics, see the articles MASSACHUSETTS; UNITED STATES, HISTORY OF THE.)

THE HISTORY OF BOSTON

Settlement and growth. Boston was settled in 1630 by Puritan Englishmen of the Massachusetts Bay Company, who, for religious reasons, put the Atlantic Ocean between themselves and the Church of England. Ostensibly founded for commercial reasons, the Massachusetts Bay Company, under its governor, John Winthrop, brought its charter—which it regarded as authorization to set up a self-governing settlement in the New England wilderness—along to the New World. The new town was named for Boston in Lincolnshire, the former home of many of the immigrants.

Through necessity rather than choice, New Englanders turned to the sea for a livelihood and became shipbuilders, merchants, seamen, and fishermen because there was little else to do. The Shawmut Peninsula, upon which Boston was settled, was an ideal setting for a seaport. It was described in 1634 by William Wood in his *New England's Prospect* as "fittest for such as can Trade into England, for such commodities as the Country wants, being the chiefe place for shipping and Merchandize." With the triumph of the Puritan Party in England in 1648, people moved freely between New England and the homeland, and close ties of family and trade linked Boston and London. By the end of the 17th century, Boston's fleet of seagoing vessels was exceeded only by those of London and Bristol in the English-speaking world. Boston held its place as the largest town in British North America until the middle of the 18th century, when it fell behind the faster growing ports of Philadelphia and New York.

Political life and revolutionary activity. During its first 50 years Boston was a homogeneous, self-governing Puritan community in which the leaders of the Massachusetts Bay Company ruled as they saw fit. The three Puritan churches, established on the congregational principle, accounted for almost all the organized religion in Boston. Religious dissidents were banished, and some Quakers who persisted in returning were hanged for their pains. Although the increasing prosperity of the colonial merchants made London quite aware of Massachusetts Bay, steps to assert royal authority there were taken only near the end of Charles II's reign, in the 1680s. The company's charter was declared null and void in 1684. In 1686, with the arrival of Sir Edmund Andros as the first royal governor of the Province of Massachusetts Bay, the authority of the crown was established in Boston itself. With this change, the Church of England first came to the town, and the Puritan isolation was over. Although the Congregational clergy, particularly the voluble father–son combination of Increase and Cotton Mather, still made themselves heard, the lines of authority had altered.

Protests against British rule

Boston never proved wholly docile. When word of the "Glorious Revolution" of 1688 reached them, the citizens on April 18, 1689, dumped Andros out of office and imprisoned him. The memory of the autonomous first half-century lingered. As London endeavoured to enforce navigation laws and gain revenue from the Boston trade at the expense of the colonies, the aggrieved inhabitants indulged in what they felt to be justified resistance against unlawful authority. After passage of the Stamp Act by Parliament in 1765, disaffection grew, and the governor's house was stormed and gutted, an act that destroyed many irreplaceable records of the colony's history. The Boston Massacre of 1770, in which British troops fired on a crowd of civilian hecklers and killed several persons, and the Boston Tea Party of 1773, in which colonists disguised as Indians dumped three shiploads of tea into

Boston Harbor, were key incidents in measuring popular sentiment prior to the Revolution.

With the confrontations and exchange of shots at Lexington and Concord on April 19, 1775, the die was cast. When George Washington's army besieged the British in Boston during the following winter, normal life in the town was suspended. On March 17, 1776, impelled by Washington's artillery positioned on Dorchester Heights, British troops and officials left. They were accompanied by loyal supporters of the crown, including a number of the principal merchants. A constitution was framed in 1780, and John Hancock was elected the first governor of the Commonwealth of Massachusetts.

Adjustment to independence. New men risen from obscurity by way of political or military service or ventures at sea during the Revolution quickly filled the places left vacant by departed Loyalists. Independence gravely imperilled Boston's maritime trade, for, at the close of the Revolution, Boston merchants automatically became foreigners in the ports of the British Empire. Thus, survival depended on finding new channels of trade. The crisis was solved by sending ships to distant and hitherto unfamiliar ports. The development of the China trade and other new routes, such as those to India, raised Boston to greater prosperity than ever before.

Throughout the first half of the 19th century, maritime commerce produced substantial fortunes, which were supplemented by others achieved in mercantile and manufacturing pursuits without recourse to the sea. Bostonians from the 1810s established textile mills, first at Waltham in 1813 and then in new towns along the Merrimack River, where waterpower was plentiful. The advent of railroads in the 1830s brought these once-distant towns suddenly closer. The burgeoning of Boston's population was due not only to maritime commerce and manufacturing but also to the unanticipated arrivals of immigrants from Europe in such numbers that the city grew more than 20-fold during the 19th century. By 1822 the traditional form of government, in which a board of selectmen administered the decisions reached by vote by all citizens at an annual town meeting, had become unmanageable, and a city charter was obtained from the legislature.

The era of culture. The 19th century also saw Boston assume its focal position in the religious and educational life of the new nation. The rapid and large-scale infusion of immigrant groups and the loss of dominance by the Congregational descendants of the Puritan settlers were major factors in the change. When it was built in 1799, the Church of the Holy Cross was the only Roman Catholic church in town. In 1808 its founder, Jean-Louis Lefebvre de Cheverus, a refugee from the French Revolution, was created the first bishop of Boston, and in 1875, when the see was raised to the dignity of an archdiocese, there were 28 Catholic parishes.

Religious diversity

The religious climate of Protestant Boston also changed dramatically. The Anglican King's Chapel, whose Loyalist rector had left with the British in 1776, became Unitarian in 1787, though not until the first quarter of the 19th century did Unitarian doctrine produce permanent cleavage and splinter organizations in many Congregational churches. The creation in 1825 of the American Unitarian Association, in which William Ellery Channing took the leading part, transformed into a separate denomination what had previously been the liberal wing of Congregationalism. From "Channing Unitarianism" it was only a step to the philosophy of Transcendentalism, which affected a great part of the region's artistic output and thought for much of the century; to the abolitionist movement championed by the outspoken writer and editor William Lloyd Garrison and others; and to liberal high-mindedness in social causes, which preoccupied many 19th-century Bostonians at a time when others were simply making money with great Yankee diligence. In the second half of the century, the city was also the founding place of Christian Science by Mary Baker Eddy. It remains the site of The Mother Church and the headquarters of this faith, which grew into an international Christian denomination.

Educational and cultural institutions had a similarly rapid growth. Across the Charles River in New Towne, later Cambridge, a college had been founded in 1636 to provide the infant colony with religious scholars and ministers. Named for the Charlestown minister John Harvard, who bequeathed his library to the institution in 1638, it was the sole college in the area until the third quarter of the 19th century. Though Harvard retained the most prestigious position throughout the century, many other major institutions of higher learning were founded, and Boston became synonymous nationally with scholarship and cultural refinement. It became also the mecca for persons—from abroad or from the "less civilized" parts of the nation outside New England—who sought these qualities amid the bustling commercialism and rambunctious growth that characterized much of 19th-century America.

Financial growth. The Civil War, in which a majority of Bostonians strongly supported the Union, put an end to shipping as a major consideration in the life of Boston. Shipowners and merchants invested thenceforth in manufacturing, in railroads, and in the development of the rapidly expanding frontier. Banking and investment, with the interplay that they implied with various forms of manufacturing and of business, superseded maritime commerce as the principal occupation of Boston in the second half of the century. In the early 20th century, however, the business horizons contracted. Though large sums continued to be invested outside of New England, fewer distant companies were controlled from Boston. The city's financial capital was as strong, but the rising strength of New York and Chicago and of the developing states of the American West gradually reduced the proportion of capital that Boston could muster. Nevertheless, Boston's financial-management firms showed a skill in investment that caused them to be well-regarded in other parts of the country. This led eventually to a major growth of those Boston companies that administered mutual investment funds. Thus, the "prudent man," whether in a private trustee's office or an investment company, has survived as a Boston asset, whereas the textile mills and railroads proved less permanent. The textile industry passed into crisis in the 1920s, and the industrial cities on the Merrimack River, created by Boston investment, entered on decades of hardship. In the following years some mills went out of business entirely, while others moved to the South in search of cheaper labour and raw materials.

Problems in the early 20th century

The first half of the 20th century in Boston was a divisive and unhappy period, for, in addition to corruption in local politics, it included two world wars separated by Prohibition and the Great Depression. After World War I, the increase of automobiles led more and more Bostonians to move outside the city limits, with consequent detriment to older central residential districts. Many of the defense industries that sprang up after World War II, based on the imagination of scientists from Harvard, the Massachusetts Institute of Technology, and other centres, were located outside the city limits.

THE CONTEMPORARY CITY

The physical environment. Boston and its sheltered deepwater harbour are ringed by modest hills, from the Middlesex Fells on the north to the Blue Hills on the south.

The area of the colonial town. The hilly Shawmut Peninsula, upon which Boston was settled, originally was almost completely surrounded by water. It was connected with mainland Roxbury on the south by a narrow neck of land along the line of today's Washington Street. To the west of the neck were great reaches of mud flats and salt marshes, which were covered by tides at high water and known collectively as the Back Bay. Beyond this, the Charles River flowed down to the peninsula, further dividing it from the mainland on the north and west as it approached Boston Harbor. On the east the peninsula fronted on the harbour, and Town Cove, jutting in from the harbour, divided Boston into the North End and the South End. The centre of the colonial town was at the present Old State House (1711–47), where the only road from the mainland intersected with the principal approach from the harbour.

Original topography

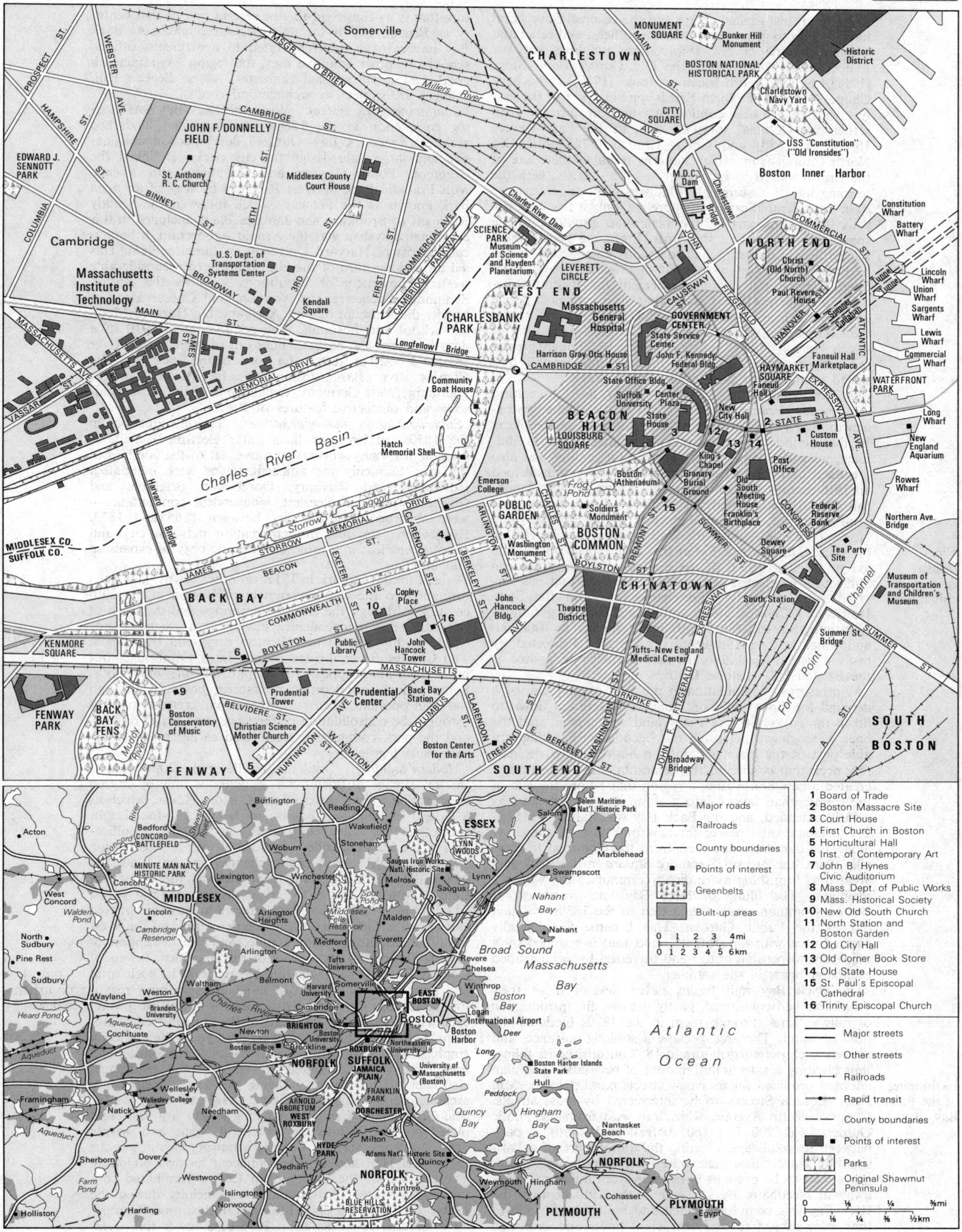

Central Boston and (inset) its metropolitan area.

Although this original centre and the colonial South End have long been given over to banks, offices, and retail and wholesale trade, a few 18th-century buildings survive: Faneuil Hall (1742–1805), the Old Corner Book Store (1711), the Old South Meeting House (1729), and King's Chapel (1750). The North End is the only part of the early town that has been continuously lived in since the 1630 settlement. Colonial survivals such as the Paul Revere House (*c.* 1680) and Christ Church (1723)—the Old North Church from which lanterns revealed the route of the British march to Lexington in 1775—coexist with the teeming life of a seemingly Mediterranean community.

The considerable extent of shoreline, only a few minutes' walk from any part of the peninsula, provided ample space for wharves and shipyards. From the beginning of the settlement, the shoreline constantly encroached on the harbour as wharves were built and marshy coves were filled. Beyond the original settlement lay Boston Common, a 45-acre (18-ha) tract that has remained public open space since its purchase by the town in 1634. Above the Common rose the Trimountain, a three-peaked hill of which Beacon Hill is the only surviving, though greatly reduced, remnant. The other hills became landfill that added to the city's area in the 19th century.

Bulfinch's designs. In the last years of the 18th century, when space became scarce, a series of major changes began to alter radically the physical lineaments of the place. In this period of expansion, the architect Charles Bulfinch, who for more than a quarter of a century was also the head of the town government, skillfully transformed an 18th-century English town into a 19th-century American city. Although many of Bulfinch's finest works have been destroyed, the central portion of the present State House (1795–98), above the Common on Beacon Hill, is his work. The construction of the State House on this site led to the conversion of the upland pastures of Beacon Hill into a handsome new residential district that has survived with relatively little change. Between the State House and Charles Street are streets, including famous Louisburg Square, filled with many houses by Bulfinch and other leading 19th-century architects. Protected by historic district legislation, the area has been designated as the Beacon Hill Historic District.

Nineteenth-century architecture

As pressures of population in the 19th century caused a demand for more and more land, hills were cut down to fill in the coves. So much new land was created that the once water-ringed peninsula has become an indistinguishable part of the mainland. Fill on both sides of the narrow neck that connected the peninsula with the mainland created a new South End, a region that before the end of the century had lapsed into a slum. The waterfront was greatly extended, and the Back Bay was dammed (1818–21) to create tidal power for new mill sites. A causeway along the dam extended west from the Common to Sewell's Point, the present Kenmore Square in the Back Bay area, thus furnishing more direct communication with the mainland. The filling of Back Bay flats just west of Boston Common created land that in the 1830s was laid out as the Public Garden. This became a splendidly planted area with an artificial pond that is spanned by a miniature suspension bridge and traversed by swan-shaped excursion boats in the summer.

The Back Bay mill basins never developed as their promoters had envisioned, partly because the introduction of railway lines through them in the 1830s hindered the flow of water. The area became a stinking nuisance, and the Massachusetts legislature in 1857 authorized its filling, thus creating a substantial amount of new land. The plan adopted provided for four new streets parallel to the Mill Dam (Beacon Street), to be intersected by cross streets. Commonwealth Avenue, which ran west from the Public Garden, was 200 feet (60 metres) wide with a park between its roadways, creating the atmosphere of a Parisian boulevard. Since there were no hills left to cut down, gravel had to be brought in by train from pits some miles away in Needham. By the end of the 19th century the Back Bay was completely filled and built up with houses that were subject to uniform height limits and setbacks. The region today presents a picture of American architecture that is as consistent for the second half of that century as Beacon Hill is for the first. Although many Back Bay houses have been converted to apartments, offices, schools, or other adaptive uses, the region has retained a good deal of its original character. As on Beacon Hill, changes are subject to architectural control.

Fashioning of the Back Bay

Continuous park system. When the Back Bay was nearing completion in the 1880s, the American landscape architect Frederick Law Olmsted developed an imaginative and large-scale design for city parks. It linked the Common, Public Garden, and Commonwealth Avenue with Franklin Park in West Roxbury by way of an open park known as the Fenway, which followed the Muddy River off to Brookline and Jamaica Plain. Included in this coordinated system was the Arnold Arboretum, a botanical outpost of Harvard University in Jamaica Plain. This led around the turn of the 20th century to a considerable western movement of institutions such as the Boston Symphony Orchestra, the New England Conservatory of Music, the Museum of Fine Arts, and the Harvard Medical School and hospitals. The completion in 1910 of a dam that kept the harbour tides out of the Charles River created a body of fresh water north of the Back Bay. The Charles River Basin, inspired by the Alster Basin in Hamburg, West Germany, remains one of the most handsome and distinctive features of Boston.

Suburbanization and annexations. The introduction, in the 1850s, of horsecar lines (later electrified) made it possible for many workers to move out of the confines of the city. Suddenly the adjacent towns were inundated. Roxbury, West Roxbury, Dorchester, Brighton, and Charlestown—once pleasant, independent communities—were absorbed into the city between 1855 and 1873. Everywhere, the line of demarcation between city and country was lost in a rapid and chaotic orgy of expansion and building.

Except for Hyde Park in 1912, no other towns have been brought into the city government of Boston in the 20th century. Although the city of Cambridge and the town of Brookline are independently governed, a casual visitor would hardly guess where Boston stops and they begin. The Charles River divides Boston from Cambridge, but both riverbanks appear to be part of one metropolis. Some regional cooperation is assured, however, through the Metropolitan District Commission, created in 1919 through the consolidation of the sewer and water districts and the park commission established earlier by the Massachusetts legislature.

Modern building. Until the middle of the 20th century, the low skyline of Boston was punctuated only by church steeples and by the tower of the Custom House, which as a federal building was not bound by the 125-foot height restriction that prevailed generally in the city. Modification of the building code, coincidental with a construction boom, brought about great changes in the 1960s, of which the first conspicuous example was the Prudential Center, with a 52-story tower on the site of train yards. The first major effort in urban renewal in Boston, initiated early in 1958, led to the wholesale demolition of the West End, the displacement of people, and the disruption of neighbourhoods to make way for the apartment towers of Charles River Park. Unfavourable reaction to such total and large-scale demolition of large areas without regard for the feelings of people led the mayor in 1960 to put an experienced lawyer at the head of the Boston Redevelopment Authority. During the next seven years the authority emphasized renewal rather than wholesale demolition and rebuilding. It endeavoured to enhance the traditional character of the city by bringing the best contemporary architecture and imaginative civic design to new projects. The Government Center, containing a new city hall completed in 1968, in addition to federal, state, and private office buildings, thereby became a harmonious neighbour to Faneuil Hall and to other adjacent historic buildings. The creation of the Government Center stimulated considerable private construction in the vicinity during the 1960s. The John Hancock Mutual Life Insurance Company completed construction in 1976 of a tower that overtopped the Prudential Tower, while the Christian Science

Controls on urban renewal

Church sponsored the reconstruction of large blocks of property near The Mother Church. Downtown waterfront renewal during the 1960s and 1970s along Atlantic Avenue and later developments on the site of the former Boston Naval Shipyard to the north have helped to open up the waterfront for commercial, residential, and recreational use and to preserve buildings of historical or architectural value. As seen from a distance, however, the profile of Boston is no longer low but is dominated by a series of towers from the waterfront to well inland.

The narrow and crowded streets of the central city are better suited for walking than driving, for Bostonians are incorrigible jaywalkers. The street markets around Faneuil Hall and in the North End are as essential a part of the city as ever, yet the terraced square of the Government Center provides a handsome setting for the new City Hall that is a welcome great open space. The second-empire exterior of the old City Hall has been preserved by adapting its interior for revenue-producing use by offices, a bank, and a restaurant.

Demography. Between 1800 and 1900 Boston changed from a relatively simple and homogeneous seaport of some 24,000 inhabitants, mainly of English extraction, to a polyglot city of more than 560,000, of whom about one-half were Irish and one-fifth were from the Canadian Maritime Provinces. After counting smaller groups of immigrants from Russia, Italy, Germany, and other European countries, as well as American-born blacks, less than 11 percent of the city's population was of traditional New England origin. The burgeoning of Boston's population in the 19th century was due to seemingly endless waves of immigrants that added not less than 23.6 percent in each decade from 1810 to 1900, while during five decades the increase was more than 40 percent. The greatest increases were 52.1 percent in the 1830s and 46.6 percent in the 1840s. Many of the new arrivals, who brought with them experience in trades and crafts, though disembarking at Boston, rapidly moved westward to the expanding frontier, where their skills were in demand. Those with only unskilled labour to offer remained in Boston, crowded into urban slums. As earlier arrivals prospered and moved elsewhere, often outside the city limits, their places were taken by more unskilled immigrants. By the middle of the century, Irish immigrants had taken over the North End, but in the last third of the century it became the centre of the first exclusively eastern European Jewish community in Boston. Today its residents are predominantly of Italian descent. Similar changes have occurred in many parts of the city.

Inundation by immigration

In the 20th century the greatly reduced immigration helped to slow the population increase from 19.6 percent in 1910 to 4.4 in 1930. The 1940 census showed a decrease of 1.3 percent. Although in 1950 there was a 4-percent increase, the trend since then has been steadily downward. Partly through migration from the South, the black population of Boston, nearly 43,000 in 1950, reached 126,000 by 1980, the majority crowded into the decaying slums of the Roxbury section.

Economic life. Banking, insurance, investment management, and other financial and business-service activities are the chief elements in the economic life of the city. The Federal Reserve Bank of the New England district is located in Boston. The chief industries are food products, clothing, printing and publishing, and the manufacture of machinery, transport equipment, and instruments. The greater part of the research-and-development activity that burgeoned after World War II is based in the metropolitan area outside the city limits. Although Boston continues as a centre of retail trade, much wholesale activity has moved outside the city. The great number of universities and hospitals make higher education and health a significant element in the economic life of Boston. Although only one-fifth of the people in the metropolitan area live in Boston, the city produces almost half of the metropolitan area's goods. A large share of the 500,000 jobs estimated to exist in Boston in the 1970s were filled by commuters from the suburban area.

Political and governmental institutions. Boston is governed by a mayor, who is elected for a four-year term, and by a city council of nine members. The government of the Commonwealth of Massachusetts is centred in the State House at the top of Beacon Hill and in other buildings, some of them constructed during the late 1960s adjacent to the Government Center. Other federal offices occupy an earlier federal building and the Custom House. Boston is the headquarters of the 1st Naval District, but the Boston Naval Shipyard was closed in 1974.

Transportation. Public transportation is maintained by the Massachusetts Bay Transportation Authority through a network of subway, elevated, and surface lines. The subway system, begun in 1897, was the first in the country, and, though it has been designated as a historic place, it still works to a useful purpose. Railroad passenger service to the metropolitan area, once excellent, has badly deteriorated through competition from private automobiles and buses. Such vehicles increasingly choke the city, especially the narrow and winding downtown streets laid out in colonial times. The Logan International Airport in East Boston is a busy centre for European as well as domestic flights.

Educational and medical facilities. Universities, colleges, and schools of every kind fill 15 pages in the classified section of the Boston telephone directory. Boston University (founded 1869), Northeastern University (1898), Suffolk University (1906), and the Boston campus of the University of Massachusetts, as well as Simmons (1899), Emmanuel (1919), and Emerson (1880) colleges, are based within the city, as are the Harvard faculties of medicine, dentistry, public health, and business administration. The rest of Harvard University, Radcliffe College (1879), and the Massachusetts Institute of Technology (1861) are just across the Charles River in Cambridge. Boston College (1863), a Jesuit institution that is a university in everything except name, is in Chestnut Hill, only a step beyond the city limits. Tufts University (1852), although based in Medford, has its medical school in Boston. Massachusetts General, the oldest of the hospitals, has been joined, among others, by the Beth Israel, Children's, Deaconess, and Brigham and Women's hospitals and the Tufts–New England Medical Center. There are few aspects of higher education or health that are not dealt with somewhere within or close to the city.

Cultural life and recreation. Boston has a rich and varied cultural life. The city has a repertory theatre group and resident ballet and opera companies; in addition, numerous road companies visit the city. Boston and its environs offer opportunities for all kinds of participatory or spectator sports including several major-league teams.

The arts. The Boston Symphony Orchestra, which was founded in 1881 and performs in Symphony Hall, is one of the foremost orchestras in the world and the chief musical attraction of Boston. The New England Conservatory of Music is nearby, as are other music schools. Chamber music abounds, as does an interest in early music encouraged by the presence of several harpsichord and other instrument makers in the region. The summer Esplanade Concerts at the Hatch Memorial Shell by the Charles River Basin are one of the few outdoor events that have thrived consistently over a long period. Most of the concerts are given by the Boston Pops Orchestra. Overall, however, the cultural life of the city depends more upon colleges, museums, libraries, and small private groups than upon a public proliferation of the performing arts.

Museums and galleries

The Museum of Fine Arts, a major world gallery incorporated in 1870, preserves and exhibits Oriental, Egyptian, and classical collections of international distinction, as well as important examples of paintings, prints, textiles, and the decorative arts. The Isabella Stewart Gardner Museum in the Fenway is rich in Italian Renaissance painting. Since its arrangement has remained unchanged since the death in 1924 of its creator, Mrs. John Lowell Gardner, in whose home the collection is housed, it is an important monument as well in the history of taste. Across the river at Harvard, there are also a fine arts museum and several museums devoted to science and natural history. The Museum of Science at Science Park, overlooking the Charles River Basin, and the Children's Mu-

Faneuil Hall Marketplace, Boston.
© Steve Solum—Bruce Coleman Inc.

seum at Museum Wharf are aimed at the instruction of the young.

Libraries. Boston is equally rich in libraries. The Boston Public Library (1854) was the first major instance in the United States of a tax-supported free library. It has been housed since 1895 in a building designed by the architectural firm of McKim, Mead, and White and is a masterpiece of 19th-century American architecture. Its interior decor, including murals by the Frenchman Pierre Puvis de Chavannes and the American John Singer Sargent, is a striking feature, in addition to its fine library collection. Much of its function is carried out through branches spread throughout the city. The Boston Athenaeum, a proprietary library founded in 1807, the Massachusetts Historical Society, the New England Historic Genealogical Society, the State Library, and the libraries of the colleges and universities provide remarkable resources, while, across the Charles, Harvard possesses one of the greatest libraries for scholarship in the world.

Sporting and sight-seeing. College crews row on the Charles River, and small boats sail on the wide basin between the Back Bay and the Cambridge shore. Little recreational use has been made of the harbour, however, for in the 19th century Boston turned its back on the sea. The Boston Redevelopment Authority has worked to reverse this trend. The downtown waterfront area contains the New England Aquarium, and a section of the Charlestown Navy Yard has been made part of the Boston National Historic Park. The fine park system designed by Olmsted has suffered from the encroachments of automobiles, save in the Arnold Arboretum in Jamaica Plain, from which they are excluded.

One of the principal forms of recreation in Boston is just looking at the city. Many thousands of visitors come annually to Boston because of its numerous historic sites and the architectural character of the city. Boston has preserved some colonial buildings and an extraordinary number of fine 19th-century structures, yet in the city and its surroundings may be seen a great variety of the works of the principal American and European architects of the second half of the 20th century. As an example, an addition to the Boston Public Library, designed by Philip Johnson with singular respect to the mass and materials of the older building, is as remarkable an example of American architecture of the 1970s as the original was in 1895.

Prospects. Though the great majority of the city's citizens may be only a few generations removed from Europe, and though the past few decades have seen great changes in the look of the city, there is a deliberate attempt to preserve the essential elements of Boston's traditional character and life. Public officials attempting to balance budgets often speak despairingly of the very high percentage of Boston's real estate that is tax-exempt because of educational use. Yet, in the second half of the 20th century, learning is the principal industry of Boston, and among the city's major resources in planning for the future are these educational institutions and their faculties, facilities, and student bodies. Since the middle of this century, many observers believe, the level of integrity and intelligence in city government has risen, with a corresponding improvement in civic life. Consequently, there is in most quarters greater hope of solving the problems of Boston than at any time in the memories of those now living.

BIBLIOGRAPHY. JUSTIN WINSOR (ed.), *The Memorial History of Boston, including Suffolk County, Massachusetts: 1630–1880,* 4 vol. (1880–81), is an excellent reference work on most aspects of Boston's history. ELIZABETH M. HERLIHY *et al., Fifty Years of Boston* (1932), is a sequel for the years 1880–1930. WALTER MUIR WHITEHILL, *Boston: A Topographical History,* 2nd ed. (1968), describes the extraordinary physical changes in the city from the settlement to the mid-1960s. HAROLD KIRKER, *The Architecture of Charles Bulfinch* (1969); WALTER H. KILHAM, *Boston after Bulfinch* (1946); and BAINBRIDGE BUNTING, *Houses of Boston's Back Bay: An Architectural History, 1840–1917* (1967), describe characteristic aspects of Boston's buildings. SAMUEL ELIOT MORISON, *The Maritime History of Massachusetts, 1783–1860* (1921; reprinted 1979); BERNARD BAILYN, *The New England Merchants in the Seventeenth Century* (1955, reissued 1979), and, with LOTTE BAILYN, *Massachusetts Shipping 1697–1714* (1959), give the essentials about Boston shipping. OSCAR HANDLIN, *Boston's Immigrants: A*

Study in Acculturation, rev. and enl. ed. (1959, reissued 1979), deals with the changes brought about by 19th-century immigration. WALTER MUIR WHITEHILL, *Boston Public Library: A Centennial History* (1956), and *Museum of Fine Arts, Boston: A Centennial History*, 2 vol. (1970), describe two pioneering institutions. MICHAEL P. CONZEN and GEORGE K. LEWIS, *Boston: A Geographical Portrait* (1976), gives an overview of the metropolitan area and of the dramatic changes in its demographies and land use. WALTER MUIR WHITEHILL, *Boston in the Age of John Fitzgerald Kennedy* (1966), briefly deals with the institutions that make modern Boston a centre of civilization. DAVID MCCORD, *About Boston* (1948, reissued 1973), is a poetic evocation of the sights and sounds of the city.

(W.M.Wh./G.K.L.)

Boswell, James

Friend and biographer of Samuel Johnson, James Boswell was revealed by the publication of his journal in the 20th century to be also one of the world's greatest diarists. His *Life of Johnson*, which has made his companionship with Johnson one of the best known in history, is generally regarded as one of the supreme achievements in biography.

By courtesy of the National Portrait Gallery, London

Boswell, oil painting from the studio of Sir Joshua Reynolds, 1786. In the National Portrait Gallery, London.

LIFE

He was born in Edinburgh on October 29, 1740. His father, Alexander Boswell, advocate and laird of Auchinleck in Ayrshire from 1749, was in 1754 raised to the bench with the judicial title of Lord Auchinleck. The Boswells were an old and well-connected family, and James was subjected to the strong pressure of family ambition. Alexander Boswell was hardheaded and undemonstrative; his wife, retiring and mystical. James, a delicate child, was coddled physically but given severe Calvinistic instruction. He grew up timid, afraid of Hell, with painfully vivid images of predestination fixed in his mind, and at the age of 12 suffered some sort of acute nervous illness.

Education

Boswell hated the select day school to which he was sent at the age of 5, and from 8 to 13 he was taught at home by tutors. From 1753 to 1758 he went through the arts course at the University of Edinburgh. An encounter with metaphysics in the logic class (1756–57) revived the terrors of his childhood and induced a serious depression. On his recovery, he threw off all outward signs of delicacy and attained apparently robust health. He was rather under average height and tended to plumpness, with very swarthy skin, black eyes, and black hair. His expression was alert and masculine and he was conspicuously good humoured. But his nervous limitation persisted, manifesting itself in recurrent periods of depression all the more painful for not being prostrating. And he never outgrew the adolescent faculty of entertaining incompatibles simultaneously.

His conduct began to give his father concern. Returning to the university in 1758 to study law, he became enthralled by the theatre and fell in love with a Roman Catholic actress. Lord Auchinleck thought it prudent to send him to the University of Glasgow, where he attended the lectures of Adam Smith. In the spring of 1760 he ran away to London and made his submission to the Roman Catholic Church. He had hitherto had no sexual experience and had entertained notions of becoming a monk. But a disreputable man of letters, Samuel Derrick, introduced him to various ladies of the town, while the Earl of Eglinton, an Ayrshire neighbour, schooled him in Deism and brought him into the company of the young Duke of York and of Laurence Sterne. Boswell discovered London and himself simultaneously. He was, he found, passionately fond of metropolitan culture, gregarious, high-spirited, sensual, and attractive to women, and London offered just the combination of gross and refined pleasures that seemed to fulfill him. In order that he might stay permanently in London, he fixed his heart on a commission in the foot guards. When Lord Auchinleck finally went to fetch him (May 1760), he found him suffering from gonorrhea, an affliction that he was to endure many times in the course of his life.

From 1760 to 1763 Boswell was in open though unhappy rebellion. He studied law at home under strict supervision and sought release from boredom in gallantry; in a waggish society called the Soaping Club; and in scribbling, his crony and literary model being a young army officer, the Honourable Andrew Erskine. His publications (mostly in verse) give no indication of conspicuous talent. During these years he deliberately fashioned the personality that he was to show the world, completing the unfinished structure of his good upbringing with a facade of boisterousness, buffoonery, and impudence. His famous vanity consisted simply in avowing what other people think but do not say. He had remarkable gifts as a mimic and at this time exercised them freely.

Boswell came of age still stubborn in his desire to enter the guards. Lord Auchinleck then agreed that if he would pass his trials in civil law, he would supplement his annuity of £100 and allow him to go to London to seek a commission through influence. Boswell passed the examination in July 1762.

Beginning of his journal

It was in anticipation of this great era in his life that he began, in the autumn, the journal that was to be the central expression of his genius. His great zest for life was not fully savoured until life was all written down, and he had a rare faculty for imaginative verbal reconstruction of his past in terms of average human perception. His journal is much more dramatic than most because he wrote up each event as though he were still living through it, with no knowledge of anything that had happened later. People in his journal talk and are given their characteristic gestures. His gifts for the imaginative reporting of conversation have never been paralleled. If he made brief notes on a conversation soon after it occurred, he could at any distance of time recall "the heads and the very words of a great part" of that conversation and construct a miniature having the vividness and economy of fiction while keeping within the bounds of historical circumstance. His power of eliciting memorable conversation was no less remarkable. He had a generousness of mind that enabled him, as he once remarked, so to tune himself to the tone of any bearable man that that man would be as free with him as with another self.

Boswell's second London visit lasted from November 1762 to August 1763. Soon after his arrival, he was informed of the birth in Scotland of a son, Charles, for whom he arranged Anglican Baptism. The mother (Peggy Doig) was probably a servant. He laid siege to a handsome actress, one Mrs. Lewis ("Louisa"), and paid for victory with an infection. He and Erskine roused Lord Auchinleck's fury by publishing a book of their own bantering letters. he met Oliver Goldsmith, the novelist, playwright, and poet, as well as John Wilkes, the politician and polemicist. And on May 16, 1763, in the back parlour of the actor and bookseller Thomas Davies, he secured an unexpected introduction to Samuel Johnson, whose works he admired and whom he had long been trying to meet. Johnson was rough with him, but Boswell kept his temper, went to call a week later, found himself

Meeting with Johnson

liked, and the great friendship was cemented. Johnson was 53 years old when they met, Boswell 22. There was condescension on both sides, Johnson deferring to Boswell's superior birth and Boswell to Johnson's superior wit and wisdom. Having become genuinely convinced that the guards scheme was not practicable, Boswell capitulated to his father and consented to become a lawyer. It was agreed that he should spend a winter studying civil law at Utrecht and should then make a modest foreign tour. Johnson, with touching kindness, made a four-day journey to see him off from Harwich.

Travels abroad

Boswell had been deeply affected by Johnson's piety and goodness and in Holland made a sincere effort to study hard and to keep out of mischief. On Christmas Day, in the ambassador's chapel at The Hague, he received communion for the first time in the Church of England. He engaged in a sparring courtship with the exquisite ironist Belle de Zuylen, who told him that she found him odd and lovable. His strict program proved stimulating for a time but palled when it had lost its novelty. He received word that his little boy had died. In the depression that ensued he had recurring nightmares of being hanged. He was discouraged to find that dissipation brought him more happiness than chastity and hard work and soon lapsed into his former promiscuity.

From Utrecht Boswell travelled to Berlin in the company of the old Jacobite Earl Marischal, friend and counsellor of Frederick the Great, but was never able to meet the King—his greatest and almost his only social defeat. Passing through Switzerland (December 1764), he secured interviews with both Rousseau and Voltaire. His approach to Rousseau was a characteristic piece of bravura. Lord Marischal had provided him with a letter, but he chose to present one of his own describing himself as a man of singular merit.

Boswell stayed nine months in Italy, devoting himself systematically to sightseeing. He established an intimacy with Wilkes (then outlawed) at Naples and travelled with Lord Mountstuart, eldest son of the Earl of Bute, the chief target of Wilkes's scurrilities. His cherished dream of high intrigue—he made blunt proposals to three countesses almost simultaneously on arriving in Turin—finally came true in Siena at the very end of his tour, when Girolama Piccolomini, wife of the chief official of the city, fell deeply and touchingly in love with him.

The most original act of his life followed when he made a six weeks' tour of the island of Corsica (autumn 1765) to interview the heroic Corsican chieftain Pasquale Paoli, then engaged in establishing his country's independence of Genoa. Paoli succumbed to his charm and became his lifelong friend. On his return to the mainland, Boswell sent off paragraphs to the newspapers, mingling facts with fantastic political speculation.

In Paris he was stunned to read in an English newspaper of his mother's death. He was disappointed not to see Rousseau, who had just left for England; but Thérèse Le Levasseur, Rousseau's mistress, accepted his offer to escort her there. During the journey he and Thérèse undoubtedly engaged in an amorous affair, but its details have been lost through family censorship of Boswell's notes.

Edinburgh law practice

Boswell was admitted to the Faculty of Advocates on July 26, 1766, and for 17 years practiced law at Edinburgh with complete regularity and a fair degree of assiduity. His cherished trips to London were by no means annual and until 1784 were always made during the vacations. He had plenty of business, though an uncomfortable amount of it consisted of causes that his father was to try. He was an able courtroom lawyer, especially in criminal cases, but in Scotland neither fortune nor fame could be won in the criminal court and an ambitious lawyer needed to give all and not part of his vacations to study. Also, Boswell hurt his reputation for professional soundness by emotional involvement in his clients' fortunes and by resorting to extralegal tactics in matters before the court.

In February 1768 Boswell published *An Account of Corsica, The Journal of a Tour to That Island; and Memoirs of Pascal Paoli* and stepped into fame. France had unmasked its intention of annexing the island, and people were greedy for information about Corsica and Paoli. Boswell's book (which was promptly translated into French, German, Italian, and Dutch) embarrassed both the French and British ministers, the French because they thought it might force British intervention, the British because they had already written Corsica off. The *Account* is a graceful ad hoc compilation; *The Journal of a Tour to That Island*, Boswell's first work exploiting his journal, is a minor masterpiece. Motives of propaganda caused him to present himself as completely naïve and to cut the tour to a mere frame for the memoirs of Paoli, but the result is still pleasing. Paoli, probably wisely, is presented in a manner reminiscent of that which Plutarch employed in his lives of great men.

Marriage

Between 1766 and 1769 Boswell amused himself with various well-hedged schemes of marriage, maintaining meantime a liaison with a young Mrs. Dodds. Their daughter Sally, like Charles, seems to have died in infancy. He ended by marrying (November 1769) the only woman he had ever wanted to marry, his first cousin, Margaret Montgomerie. Lord Auchinleck, who was deeply disappointed, for the match brought neither lands nor money, took a new wife himself on the very day of his son's wedding.

During the first few years of his marriage, Boswell was on the whole happy, hard-working, faithful to his wife, and confident of getting a seat in Parliament, a good post in the government, or at the very least a Scots judgeship. Paoli visited him in Scotland in 1771; in 1773 he was elected to The Club, the brilliant circle that Sir Joshua Reynolds had formed around Dr. Johnson; and later in the year Johnson made with him the famous tour of the Hebrides. He ultimately had five healthy and promising children. He was made an examinator of the Faculty of Advocates and one of the curators of the Advocates' Library; he served twice as master of the Canongate Kilwinning Lodge of Masons and declined nomination for the grand mastership of Scotland. But by 1776 he began to feel strong intimations of failure. A headlong entry into Ayrshire politics had ranged him in opposition to Henry Dundas, who was then emerging as a political despot in the management of the Scottish elections. His practice was not becoming more notable. He began to drink heavily to replenish his spirits, not, as formerly, to give them vent. He returned to his old traffic with women of the town when separated from his wife by distance, by her pregnancy, or by her frequent complaints. As early as 1778 it was obvious that she was critically ill with tuberculosis.

Between 1777 and 1783 he published in *The London Magazine* a series of 70 essays, significantly entitled *The Hypochondriack*, which deserve to be better known, though they do not engage his full powers. At the end of 1783, in the hope of attracting the attention of Pitt's new government, he published a pamphlet attacking the East India Bill that had been introduced by Charles James Fox, Pitt's great rival. Pitt sent a note of thanks but made no move to employ him. Boswell succeeded to Auchinleck in 1782 and managed his estate with attention and some shrewdness. But he thought he could be happy only in London and encouraged himself in the groundless notion that he could be more successful at the English than at the Scots bar.

Hebridean journal

Johnson died on Dec. 13, 1784. Boswell decided to take his time in writing the *Life* but to publish his journal of the Hebridean tour as a first installment. In the spring of 1785 he went to London to prepare the work for the press but became diverted by dinners and girls and by the writing of a frothy pamphlet against Henry Dundas' bill for diminishing the number of the lords of session. The Irish scholar and editor Edmond Malone, a fellow member of The Club but not previously a close friend, got sight of the work in progress and offered his daily assistance in preparing the remainder of the copy. Boswell's journals show little variation in literary excellence, but in matter the Hebridean journal tops all the others. It comes from the soundest and happiest period of Boswell's life, the narrative of the tour is interesting in itself, and it provides us with 101 consecutive days with Johnson. The book was a best seller, but it provoked the scornful charge of personal fatuity that has dogged Boswell's name ever since. His intelligence was not really in question. Boswell had a good mind, and his imprudences and sins were of the sort that the world usually tolerates in artists. But he deliberately defied the basic literary rule that no author who wishes respect as a man may publish his own follies without suggesting compensatory strengths of character. Boswell analyzed and recorded his own vanity and weakness with the objectivity of a historian, and in his Johnsonian scenes he ruthlessly subordinated his own personality, reporting the blows that Johnson occasionally gave him without constantly reassuring the reader that he understood the implications of what he had written.

In 1786 Boswell was called to the English bar from the Inner Temple and moved his family to London. Thereafter he had almost no legal practice. His principal business was the writing of the *Life of Johnson*, which he worked at irregularly but with anxious attention. The revision of manuscript and proofs was labyrinthine. Malone again gave him tactful support and sat with him during much of the rewriting.

Though straitened in income, he gave his children expensive educations. He visited Edinburgh only once after his emigration and then almost surreptitiously. Mrs. Boswell pined for Auchinleck and insisted on being taken there when her health grew desperate. Boswell felt that he had to be in London in order to finish the *Life* and to be at the call of the Earl of Lonsdale, who had given him unexpected encouragement and caused him to be elected recorder of Carlisle. When she died (June 4, 1789), he was not at her side; and when he tried to detach himself from Lonsdale, he was treated with shocking brutality.

Publication of the *Life*

The Life of Samuel Johnson, LL.D. was published on May 16, 1791. Contemporary criticism set the pattern of acclaim for the work and derision for its author, which was to receive consummate expression from Macaulay in his well-known essays (1831 and 1856). Boswell took intense pleasure in his literary fame but felt himself to be a failure. His later years were prevailingly unhappy. His eccentricities of manner seemed merely self-indulgent in a man of 50 or over; people were afraid to talk freely in his presence, fearing that their talk would be reported; and his habit of getting drunk and noisy at other people's tables (he was never a solitary drinker) made him a difficult guest in any case. But his five children loved him deeply, and he never lost the solicitous affection of Malone and a few other friends who recognized his worth and his need. He saw the second edition of the *Life* through the press (July 1793) and was at work on the third when he died on May 19, 1795.

ASSESSMENT

For long it was believed that Boswell's private papers had been destroyed shortly after his death, but the bulk of them were recovered in the 1920s at Malahide Castle near Dublin and sold to an American collector, Ralph H. Isham, by Boswell's great-great-grandson, Lord Talbot de Malahide. These papers, as well as others found at Malahide Castle during the 1930s, were united with another portion discovered by Professor Claude Colleer Abbott in Aberdeenshire in the home of descendants of Boswell's executor and sold to Yale University, which began a systematic program of their publication.

The *Life of Johnson* will always be regarded as Boswell's greatest achievement, although, since the publication of his papers, its unique values can be seen to be derivative. It is the stretches of Johnson's conversation that make it superior to all other biographies, and those conversations were lifted bodily from the journal, sometimes with so little change that the journal leaves served as printer's copy. The extended commercial publication of the journal, by proving his ability to compete with 20th-century authors on their own terms, has confirmed and added to Boswell's stature as artist. It also for the first time gives the general reader a properly complex portrait.

MAJOR WORKS

An Account of Corsica, the Journal of a Tour to That Island; and Memoirs of Pascal Paoli (1768); *The Hypochondriack* (1777–83); *The Journal of a Tour to the Hebrides, with Samuel Johnson, LL.D.* (1785); *The Life of Samuel Johnson, LL.D.*, 2 vol. (1791).

BIBLIOGRAPHY. F.A. POTTLE in *The Literary Career of James Boswell* (1929, reprinted 1966) and in the article on Boswell in *The New Cambridge Bibliography of English Literature*, vol. 2 (1971), provides a detailed bio-bibliography and selected list of works about Boswell. The *Private Papers of James Boswell from Malahide Castle*, ed. by GEOFFREY SCOTT and F.A. POTTLE, 18 vol. (1928–34, index 1937), is a virtual autobiography. The commercially published volumes of the Yale editions, beginning with *Boswell's London Journal, 1762–63* (1950, eight subsequent volumes published), present the journal for the general reader. Biographical studies include F.A. POTTLE, *James Boswell: The Earlier Years, 1740–69* (1966), the first biography to draw on all the recovered papers; D.B. WYNDHAM LEWIS, *The Hooded Hawk* (1946; reprinted as *James Boswell: A Short Life*, 1952), warmly pro-Boswellian; C.B. TINKER, *Young Boswell* (1922), a charming portrait; and FRANK BRADY, *Boswell's Political Career* (1965), on a neglected aspect of Boswell's life. For the history of the Boswell papers, see C. COLLEER ABBOTT, *Catalogue of Papers . . . Found at Fettercairn House* (1936); and F.A. POTTLE, "The History of the Boswell Papers," in Heinemann's limited edition of Boswell's *London Journal* (1951). For scholarly reference, L.F. POWELL's revision of G.B. HILL's edition of the *Life of Johnson*, 6 vol. (1934–60, 1964); the *Letters of James Boswell*, 2 vol., ed. by C.B. TINKER (1924); and the research series of the Yale editions (2 vol. of correspondence now published) are recommended. Critical studies (chronologically arranged) are: T.B. MACAULAY, "Essay on Boswell's Life of Johnson," *Edinburgh Review*, vol. 54 (1831) and "Samuel Johnson," *Encyclopædia Britannica*, 8th ed. (1856), brilliant but wrongheaded; THOMAS CARLYLE, "Biography" and "Boswell's Life of Johnson," in *Critical and Miscellaneous Essays* (1839), a masterly assessment of Boswell's literary virtues; GEOFFREY SCOTT, introductions to vol. 1–5 of *Private Papers* and vol. 6, *The Making of the Life of Johnson* (1928–29), a modern view of Boswell by a great stylist; SIR HAROLD NICOLSON, "The Boswell Formula, 1791," in *The Development of English Biography* (1927), Boswell shows great literary skill, his character distasteful; F.A. POTTLE, "The Power of Memory in Boswell and Scott," in *Essays on the Eighteenth Century Presented to David Nichol Smith* (1945), Boswell's memory accurate; B.H. BRONSON, "Boswell's Boswell," in his *Johnson Agonistes and Other Essays* (1946), on Boswell's consciousness of himself; F.A. POTTLE, "The Life of Boswell," *Yale Review*, 35:445–460 (1946); and "Boswell Revalued," in CARROLL CAMDEN (ed.), *Literary Views* (1964), Boswell first of all a writer, his style that of the 20th century; W.K. WIMSATT, "Boswell: The Man and the Journal," in his *Hateful Contraries* (1965), Boswell not to be liked or disliked but valued; J.N. MORRIS, *Versions of the Self* (1966), Boswell modern in his anxiety; R.W. RADER, "Literary Form in Factual Narrative: The Example of Boswell's Johnson," in *Essays in Eighteenth-Century Biography*, ed. by P.B. DAGHLIAN (1968), the *Life* organized by a coherent idea of Johnson; and F.A. POTTLE, "The Life of Johnson: Art and Authenticity," in J.L. CLIFFORD (ed.), *Twentieth Century Interpretations of Boswell's Life of Johnson* (1970), the conversations in the *Life*, the quintessence of Boswell's view of Johnson.

(F.A.Po.)

Botanical Garden

A botanical garden, or botanic garden, as it is often called, was originally a collection of living plants designed chiefly to illustrate relationships within plant groups. Today, most botanical gardens are concerned primarily with exhibiting ornamental plants, insofar as possible in a scheme that emphasizes natural relationships. Thus, the two functions are blended: eye appeal and taxonomic order. Plants that were once of medicinal value and extremely important in early botanical gardens are now chiefly of historical interest and are not particularly represented in contemporary collections. A display garden that concentrates on woody plants (shrubs and trees) is often referred to as an arboretum. It may be a collection in its own right or a part of a botanical garden.

This article deals only with public and institutional botanical gardens and arboretums (see also GARDEN AND LANDSCAPE DESIGN; GARDENING; and HORTICULTURE).

General considerations and history. A major contemporary objective of botanical gardens is to maintain extensive collections of plants, labelled with common and scientific names and regions of origin. Plant collections in such gardens vary in number from a few hundred to several thousand different kinds, depending on the land area available and the financial and scholarly resources of the institution.

As world populations become more urbanized, botanical gardens are increasingly recognized as among the important cultural resources of civilized nations. Botanical gardens offer the city dweller part of the natural environment he no longer has access to; furthermore, they offer a mental escape from population pressure and suggest new interests and hobbies having to do with the natural world.

Early botanical gardens

What can be called the roots of the botanical garden as an institution are traceable to ancient China and many of the countries bordering the Mediterranean. These actually were centres for the raising of fruit trees, vegetables, and herbs used in making the crude medicines of the time. After the discovery of printing, manuscripts on plants, which had been in existence for centuries, became more widely circulated, and these stimulated further publication of descriptive works called herbals. The herbalists and their herbals, in turn, stimulated the founding of botanical gardens. By the end of the 16th century there were five such gardens in Europe, and by the mid-20th century several hundred. The first two were in Italy, at Padua and Pisa (1545). At first, such gardens were associated with the medical schools of universities. Professors of medicine were mainly the botanists of that time, and their "physic gardens" served for the training of students as well as for growing plants to make medicines. But they served in other ways as well. Carolus Clusius, a noted botanist of the 16th century, for example, brought together an extensive collection of flowering bulbs at the botanical garden in Leiden, the Netherlands, which proved to be the beginning of the Dutch bulb industry.

In the early 1800s Jean Gesner, a Swiss physician and botanist, noted that by the end of the 18th century there were 1,600 botanical gardens in Europe. During the 18th and 19th centuries, the science of botany took form, and many of the important botanists of the period were directors of the botanical gardens of their day. Since that time, the classical botanical garden as a teaching and medicinal garden declined, to be replaced by gardens devoted mainly to plant culture and the display of ornamental plants and plant groups of special interest.

Function and purpose. The larger collections of living plants constitute a formidable resource for professional scholars; but, more importantly, they provide a rich opportunity for the general public to learn more about plants and how to grow them. Some gardens offer popular-level short courses on plants and plant cultivation each year, both for adults and for children.

Botanic gardens constitute reservoirs of valuable heritable characteristics, potentially important in the breeding of new varieties of plants. Longwood Gardens, near Kennett Square, Pennsylvania, in collaboration with the U.S. Department of Agriculture, has in recent years sent out several expeditions to collect species that have promise as breeding stock or, in some instances, are already attractive ornamental plants. Historically, England's Royal Botanic Gardens at Kew are most famous for their collecting expeditions and the distribution of economic plants to parts of the world where they could be grown most successfully. Kew is responsible for the wide popularity and spread of such plants as the rubber tree (*Hevea brasiliensis*), pineapple, banana, tea, coffee, cacao, various timbers, and cinchona (yielding quinine) and other drug producers.

Still another function of botanical gardens is the training of gardeners. Canada has long had such a program at the Niagara Falls Parks Commission's School of Horticulture. Such training programs at Kew, Edinburgh, Dublin, and the Royal Horticultural Society's garden at Wisley have produced many able gardeners for supervisory positions in many countries.

Design. Botanical gardens and arboretums differ from parks in that they are generally laid out according to the scientific relationships of their plant collections, rather than exclusively for landscape effect or for playing fields or other essentially recreational endeavours. The traditional practice in laying out a botanical garden is, for example, to gather the trees and shrubs together in an arboretum section of the garden. Oftentimes, though, trees and shrubs are used to enhance landscape effects by interspersing them throughout the garden, in their respective taxonomic groups, with herbaceous collections.

Botanical gardens, or parts of them, are sometimes planned according to the geographic origin of plants. Not infrequently the layout is based on small, special gardens within the greater garden, such as rose, iris, rock, wildflower, and Japanese landscape gardens. As to area, it may be seen in the Table that botanical gardens range in size from a few acres to as many as 2,000.

Selected Botanical Gardens

location	title	number of species and varieties	approximate area (acres)
Australia			
Melbourne	Royal Botanical Gardens and National Arboretum	20,000	88
Belgium			
Meise	National Botanic Garden	15,000	18
Canada			
Montreal, Quebec	Montreal Botanical Garden	20,000	175
Ottawa, Ontario	Dominion Botanic Garden	10,000	100
Denmark			
Copenhagen	Botanic Garden of the Royal Veterinary and Agricultural College	15,000	20
France			
Lyon	Botanic Garden	10,000	15
Germany			
Berlin-Dahlem	Botanic Garden and Museum of the University	18,000	100
Ireland			
Dublin (Glasnevin)	National Botanic Garden	25,000	47
South Africa			
Capetown (Kirstenbosch)	National Botanical Gardens of South Africa	6,200	1,365
Sweden			
Uppsala	Botanical Garden of the University	10,000	46
Switzerland			
Geneva	Botanic Garden	15,000	28
United Kingdom			
Kew, Eng.	Royal Botanic Gardens	25,000	288
Wisley, Eng.	Royal Horticultural Society Garden	10,000	198
Edinburgh, Scot.	Royal Botanic Garden	15,000	60
United States			
Berkeley, Calif.	University of California Botanical Garden	15,000	20
Brooklyn, N.Y.	Brooklyn Botanic Garden and Arboretum	12,000	50
Bronx, N.Y.	New York Botanical Garden	15,000	240
Mentor, O.	Holden Arboretum	5,000	2,200
Kennett Square, Penn.	Longwood Gardens	12,500	1,000
U.S.S.R.			
Moscow	Botanical Garden	16,000	890

Taxonomic groupings

Although the layouts mentioned above often preclude the possibility of arranging plants strictly according to their taxonomic relationships, this is still possible for certain groups. The genus *Rosa*, for example, includes a great many species and hundreds of named man-made hybrids. In addition to the genus *Rosa*, there are many other genera in the rose family (Rosaceae), with their species and innumerable cultivars. The rose family would be a typical taxonomic grouping for a botanical garden, though the tree species would be grown separately from the rose bushes. The same general principle of taxonomic groupings holds for other plant families and genera.

Usually associated with botanical gardens are the service or display greenhouses in which to propagate plants or to grow those that may not survive seasonal changes. In temperate climates, where the winters are cold, for example, tropical orchids must be greenhouse grown. The same is true of tropical ferns, bromeliads, economic plants of the tropics or near-tropics, many cacti and other succulents, African violets, and begonias. Hotbeds as well as greenhouses serve for starting seedling plants that are to be set outdoors as soon as the weather is warm enough.

A botanical garden that aspires to large plant collections must also have storage areas that provide temperature conditions favourable to certain species at particular seasons. Cold frames may serve this purpose for many kinds of plants and for the wintering over of younger plants that need a cold period but will not tolerate freezing temperatures. Houses built of lathing may also be important for the temporary storage of some species in semishade or even for the growing of certain plants that are intolerant of the hot summer sun.

Herbaria

Many gardens possess herbaria, or collections of a few to many thousands of dried plant specimens mounted on sheets of paper. The species thus mounted have been identified by experts and labelled by their proper scientific names, together with information on where they were collected, how they grew, and so on. They are filed in cases according to families and genera, always available for ready reference. Herbaria, like living plant collections, are the "dictionaries" of the plant kingdom, the reference specimens essential to the proper naming of unknown plants.

Many botanical gardens associated with universities possess extensive libraries, herbaria, and laboratory research facilities. Such gardens offer essential services for the professional plant taxonomist. Some large urban botanical gardens provide classroom and greenhouse workshop facilities for the novice gardener, and the trend for popular-level instruction is growing.

Most large botanical gardens publish technical journals and popular brochures. Books of general appeal and films are produced by some of the larger botanical gardens.

Maintenance. The prime consideration in maintaining plant collections is, of course, good plant-culture practices. Skilled lawn maintenance is particularly important for botanical gardens in cities; the discerning citizen judges a garden more by its general appearance than by the excellence of its plant collections. Tree and shrub collections require systematic pruning, and no important tree should go for more than two years without such attention. Older trees require special pruning attention and care of wounds so that decay does not set in. Spraying for control of pests and diseases is often necessary.

In the early years of botanical gardens, new kinds of plants could be secured only by sending out knowledgeable collectors on expeditions, often to distant places. They would seek out new species growing in the wild and bring back samples of the plants desired. But the nursery industry has now become so great that many smaller firms specialize in particular groups of plants; thus, numerous species and cultivars can be purchased directly from nursery firms, ready for planting. Exchanges of seeds as well as rare plants are often carried out between botanical gardens. Some gardens issue seed-exchange lists annually.

Equipment for the care of plant collections depends upon the size of the operation. Aside from a building adequate to take care of physical needs of the gardening staff and housing space for tools and equipment, attractive and efficient classroom space is essential for gardens with an educational program. A section of a greenhouse arranged for practical work by students (*i.e.*, a greenhouse classroom) is also desirable.

Staff needs

Staff needs depend upon the specific objectives of a botanical garden as well as upon the resources available, the climate, and the area to be cared for. At least one gardener should be a skilled propagator or nursery man. The head gardener, with advanced horticultural training and experience, supervises the entire operation. If the physical plant is of sufficient size, a combination of skilled craftsmen and a superintendent is required to look after all structures and oversee the cleaning, heating, and other routine services.

Professional staff needs also depend upon an institution's objectives as well as financial resources. A general botanist is essential. A taxonomist is basic for the herbarium, as is a librarian, if the book and journal collection is of any size. The taxonomist usually has supervision over the making and placing of plant labels. A plant pathologist, or specialist in plant diseases, is desirable if the plant collections are large. If a teaching program for adults and children is part of the educational pattern of the institution, at least a skeleton force of teachers or part-time instructors who come in and conduct classes is necessary. The total botanical garden program, from gardening through professional staff, is coordinated by a director, who, in turn, is responsible to a board of trustees if the garden is a private corporation. A garden that is part of a university is generally the primary responsibility of a professor of botany or horticulture and is operated as an adjunct of his particular department. Gardens that are government supported usually operate under a director and advisory group.

Some botanical gardens are independently established and financially provided for through endowments set up by wealthy persons. Gardens directly operated by government agencies are usually supported by tax monies. Private colleges and universities with botanical gardens are privately supported and often receive financial assistance by organized, dues-paying-membership groups or by endowment funds established in their behalf.

BIBLIOGRAPHY. H.R. FLETCHER, D.M. HENDERSON, and H.T. PRENTICE, *International Directory of Botanical Gardens*, 2nd ed. (1969), a list of the world's botanical gardens with vital statistics on each; E.S. HYAMS and W. MacQUITTY, *Great Botanical Gardens of the World* (1969); H. REISIGL (ed.), *The World of Flowers* (1965), a collection of articles by international botanists, with a section on botanical gardens, parks, and floral regions. Regional and national handbooks on botanical gardens are published frequently.

(G.S.A.)

Botany

Botany is the study of plants. Plants were of paramount importance to early man; he depended upon them as sources of food, shelter, clothing, medicine, ornament, tools, and magic. Today it is known that, in addition to their practical and economic values, green plants are indispensable to all life on earth: through the process of photosynthesis, plants transform energy from the sun into the chemical energy of food, which makes all life possible. A second unique and important capacity of green plants is the formation and release of oxygen as a by-product of photosynthesis. The oxygen of the atmosphere, so absolutely essential to many forms of life, represents the accumulation of over 3,500,000,000 years of photosynthesis by green plants.

Although the many steps in the process of photosynthesis have become fully understood only in recent years, even in prehistoric times man somehow recognized intuitively that some important relation existed between the sun and plants. Such recognition is suggested by the fact that, in primitive tribes and early civilizations, worship of the sun was often combined with the worship of plants.

Earliest man, like the other anthropoid mammals (*e.g.*, apes, monkeys), depended totally upon the natural resources of his environment, which, until he developed methods for hunting, consisted almost completely of plants. The behaviour of pre-Stone Age man can be inferred by studying the botany of aboriginal peoples in various parts of the world. Isolated tribal groups in South America, Africa, and New Guinea, for example, have extensive knowledge about plants and distinguish hundreds of kinds according to their utility, as edible, poisonous, or otherwise important in their culture. They have developed surprisingly sophisticated systems of nomenclature and classification, which approximate the binomial system (*i.e.*, generic and specific names) found in modern biology. The urge to recognize different kinds of plants and to give them names thus seems to be as old as the human race.

In time plants were not only collected by primitive man but also grown by him. This domestication resulted not only in the development of agriculture but also in a greater stability of human populations that had previously been nomadic. From the settling down of agricultural peoples in places where they could depend upon adequate food supplies came the first villages and the earliest civilizations.

The basis of botany

Because of the long preoccupation of man with plants, a large body of folklore, general information, and actual scientific data has accumulated, which has become the basis for the science of botany.

HISTORY

Early concepts. Theophrastus, a Greek philosopher who studied first with Plato and then became a disciple of Aristotle, is credited with founding botany. Only two of an estimated 200 botanical treatises written by him are known to science: originally written in Greek about 300 BC, they have survived in the form of Latin manuscripts, *De causis plantarum* and *De historia plantarum*. His basic concepts of morphology, classification, and the natural history of plants, accepted without question for many centuries, are now of interest primarily because of Theophrastus' independent and philosophical viewpoint.

Pedanius Dioscorides, a Greek botanist of the 1st century AD, was the most important botanical writer after Theophrastus. In his major work, an herbal in Greek, he described some 600 kinds of plants, with comments on their habit of growth and form as well as on their medicinal properties. Unlike Theophrastus, who classified plants as trees, shrubs, and herbs, Dioscorides grouped his plants under three headings: as aromatic, culinary, and medicinal. His herbal, unique in that it was the first treatment of medicinal plants to be illustrated, remained for about 15 centuries the last word on medical botany in Europe.

From the 2nd century BC to the 1st century AD, a succession of Roman writers—Cato, Varro, Virgil, and Columella—prepared Latin manuscripts on farming, gardening, and fruit growing but showed little evidence of the spirit of scientific inquiry for its own sake that was so characteristic of Theophrastus. In the 1st century AD, Pliny the Elder, though no more original than his Roman predecessors, seemed more industrious as a compiler. His *Historia naturalis*—an encyclopaedia of 37 volumes, compiled from some 2,000 works representing 146 Roman and 327 Greek authors—has 16 volumes devoted to plants. Although uncritical and containing much misinformation, this work contains much information otherwise unavailable, since most of the volumes to which he referred have been destroyed.

The significance of herbals

The printing press revolutionized the availability of all types of literature, including that of plants. In the 15th and 16th centuries, many herbals were published with the purpose of describing plants useful in medicine. Written by physicians and medically oriented botanists, the earliest herbals were based largely on the work of Dioscorides and to a lesser extent on Theophrastus, but gradually they became the product of original observation. The increasing objectivity and originality of herbals through the decades is clearly reflected in the improved quality of the woodcuts prepared to illustrate these books. Among the herbals most important for their contributions to botany are those by Otto Brunfels (published 1532–37), Hieronymus Bock (1539), Leonhard Fuchs (1542), and Valerius Cordus (published by Conrad von Gesner in 1561 after the death of Fuchs) in Germany; by Rembert Dodoens (1554, 1563), Charles de L'Ecluse (Carolus Clusius; 1601), and Matthias de L'Obel (1570, 1571) in the Netherlands; by Pierandrea Mattioli (1544) in Italy; and by William Turner (1551–62) and John Gerard (1597) in England.

In 1552 an illustrated manuscript on Mexican plants, written in Aztec, was translated into Latin by Badianus; other similar manuscripts known to have existed seem to have disappeared. Whereas herbals in China date back much further than those in Europe, they have become known only recently and so have contributed little to the progress of Western botany.

The invention of the optical lens during the 16th century and the development of the compound microscope about 1590 opened an era of rich discovery about plants; prior to that time, all observations by necessity had been made with the unaided eye. The botanists of the 17th century turned away from the earlier emphasis on medical botany and began to describe all plants, including the many new ones that were being introduced in large numbers from Asia, Africa, and America. Among the most prominent botanists of this era was Gaspard Bauhin, who for the first time developed, in a tentative way, many botanical concepts still held as valid. In 1665 Robert Hooke published, under the title *Micrographia*, the results of his microscopic observations on several plant tissues. He is remembered as the coiner of the word cell, referring to the cavities he observed in thin slices of cork; his observation that living cells contain sap and other materials too often has been forgotten. In the following decade, Nehemiah Grew and Marcello Malpighi founded plant anatomy; in 1671 they communicated the results of microscopic studies simultaneously to the Royal Society of London, and both later published major treatises.

The founding of plant anatomy

Experimental plant physiology began with the brilliant work of Stephen Hales, who published his observations on the movements of water in plants under the title *Vegetable Staticks* (1727). His conclusions on the mechanics of water transpiration in plants are still valid, as is his discovery—at the time a startling one—that air contributes something to the materials produced by plants. In 1774, Joseph Priestley showed that plants exposed to sunlight give off oxygen, and Jan Ingenhousz demonstrated, in 1779, that plants in the dark give off carbon dioxide. In 1804 Nicolas de Saussure demonstrated convincingly that plants in sunlight absorb water and carbon dioxide and increase in weight, as had been reported by Hales nearly a century earlier.

The widespread use of the microscope by plant morphologists provided a turning point in the 18th century—botany became largely a laboratory science. Until the invention of simple lenses and the compound microscope, the recognition and classification of plants were, for the most part, based on such large morphological aspects of the plant as size, shape, and external structure of leaves, roots, and stems. Such information was also supplemented by observations on more subjective qualities of plants, such as edibility and medicinal uses.

Binomial nomenclature

In 1753 Carl Linné (Carolus Linnaeus) published his master work, *Species Plantarum*, which contains careful descriptions of 6,000 species of plants from all of the parts of the world known at the time. In this work, which is still the basic reference work for modern plant taxonomy, Linnaeus established the practice of binomial nomenclature—that is, the denomination of each kind of plant by two words, the genus name and the specific name, as *Rosa canina*, the dog rose. Binomial nomenclature had been introduced much earlier by some of the herbalists, but it was not generally accepted; most botanists continued to use cumbersome formal descriptions, consisting of many words, to name a plant. Linnaeus for the first time put the contemporary knowledge of plants into an orderly system, with full acknowledgment to past authors, and produced a nomenclatural methodology so useful that it has not been greatly improved upon. Linnaeus also introduced a "sexual system" of plants, by which the numbers of flower parts—especially stamens, which produce male sex cells, and styles, which are prolongations of plant ovaries that receive pollen grains—became useful tools for easy identification of plants. This simple system, although effective, had many imperfections. Other classification systems, in which as many characters as possible were considered in order to determine the degree of relationship, were developed by other botanists; indeed, some appeared before the time of Linnaeus. The application of the concepts of Charles Darwin (on evolution) and Gregor Mendel (on genetics) to plant taxonomy has provided insights into the process of evolution and the production of new species.

Systematic botany now uses information and techniques from all the subdisciplines of botany, incorporating them into one body of knowledge. Phytogeography (the biogeography of plants), plant ecology, population genetics, and various techniques applicable to cells—cytotaxonomy and cytogenetics—have contributed greatly to the current status of systematic botany and have to some degree become part of it. More recently, phytochemistry, computerized statistics, and fine-structure morphology have been added to the activities of systematic botany.

Recent concepts. The 20th century has seen an enormous increase in the rate of growth of research in botany and the results derived therefrom. The combination of more botanists, better facilities, and new technologies, all with the benefit of experience from the past, has resulted in a series of new discoveries, new concepts, and new fields of botanical endeavour. Some important examples are mentioned below.

New and more precise information is being accumulated concerning the process of photosynthesis, especially with reference to energy-transfer mechanisms.

The discovery of phytochrome

The discovery of the pigment phytochrome, which constitutes a previously unknown light-detecting system in plants, has greatly increased knowledge of the influence of both internal and external environment on the germination of seeds and the time of flowering.

Several types of plant hormones (internal regulatory substances) have been discovered—among them auxin, gibberellin, and kinetin—whose interactions provide a new concept of the way in which the plant functions as a unit.

The discovery that plants need certain trace elements usually found in the soil has made it possible to cultivate areas lacking some essential element by adding it to the deficient soil.

The development of genetical methods for the control of plant heredity has made possible the generation of improved and enormously productive crop plants.

The development of radioactive-carbon dating of plant materials as old as 50,000 years is useful to the paleobotanist, the ecologist, the archaeologist, and especially to the climatologist, who now has a better basis on which to predict climates of future centuries.

The discovery of alga-like and bacteria-like fossils in Precambrian rocks has pushed the estimated origin of plants on earth to 3,500,000,000 years ago.

The isolation of antibiotic substances from fungi and bacteria-like organisms has provided control over many bacterial diseases and has contributed biochemical information of basic scientific importance as well.

THE SCOPE OF BOTANY

For convenience, but not on any mutually exclusive basis, several major areas or approaches are recognized commonly as disciplines of botany; these are morphology, physiology, ecology, and systematics.

The major botanical disciplines. *Morphology*. Morphology deals with the structure and form of plants and includes such subdivisions as: cytology, the study of the cell; histology, the study of tissues; anatomy, the study of the organization of tissues into the organs of the plant; reproductive morphology, the study of life cycles; and experimental morphology, or morphogenesis, the study of development.

The close relationship of plant form and function

Physiology. Physiology deals with the functions of plants. Its development as a subdiscipline has been closely interwoven with the development of other aspects of botany, especially morphology. In fact, structure and function are sometimes so closely related that it is impossible to consider one independently of the other. The study of function is indispensable for the interpretation of the incredibly diverse nature of plant structures. In other words, around the functions of the plant, structure and form have evolved. Physiology also blends imperceptibly into the fields of biochemistry and biophysics, as the research methods of these fields are used to solve problems in plant physiology.

Ecology. Ecology deals with the mutual relationships and interactions between organisms and their physical environment. The physical factors of the atmosphere, the climate, and the soil affect the physiological functions of the plant in all its manifestations, so that, to a large degree, plant ecology is a phase of plant physiology under natural and uncontrolled conditions; in fact, it has been called "outdoor physiology." Plants are intensely sensitive to the forces of the environment, and both their association into communities and their geographical distribution are determined largely by the character of climate and soil. Moreover, the pressures of the environment and of organisms upon each other are potent forces, which lead to new species and the continuing evolution of larger groups.

Systematics. Systematics deals with the identification and ranking of all plants; it includes classification and nomenclature (naming) and enables the botanist to comprehend the broad range of plant diversity and evolution.

Specialized botanical disciplines. In addition to the major subdisciplines, several specialized branches of botany have developed as a matter of custom or convenience. Among them are bacteriology, the study of bacteria; mycology, the study of fungi; algology or phycology, the study of algae; bryology, the study of mosses and liverworts; pteridology, the study of ferns and their relatives; and paleobotany, the study of fossil plants. Palynology is the study of modern and fossil pollen and spores, with particular reference to their identification; plant pathology deals with the diseases of plants; economic botany deals with plants of practical use to man; and ethnobotany covers the use of plants by aboriginal peoples, now and in the distant past.

Botany also relates to other scientific disciplines in many ways, especially to zoology, medicine, microbiology, agriculture, chemistry, forestry, and horticulture, and specialized areas of botanical information may relate closely to such humanistic fields as art, literature, history, religion, archaeology, sociology, and psychology.

Fundamentally, botany remains a pure science, including any research into the life of plants and limited only by man's technical means of satisfying his curiosity. It has often been considered an important part of a liberal education, not only because it is necessary for an understanding of agriculture, horticulture, forestry, pharmacology, and other applied arts and sciences, but also because an understanding of plant life is related to life in general.

The aesthetic influence of plants

Because man has always been dependent upon plants and surrounded by them, he has woven them into his designs, into the ornamentation of his life, even into his religious symbolism. A Persian carpet and a bedspread from a New England loom both employ conventional designs derived from the forms of flowers. Medieval painters and great masters of the Renaissance represented various revered figures surrounded by roses, lilies, violets, and other flowers, which symbolized chastity, martyrdom, humility, and other Christian attributes.

METHODOLOGY

Morphological aspects. The invention of the compound microscope provided a valuable and durable instrument for the investigation of the inner structure of plants. Early plant morphologists, especially those studying cell structure, were handicapped as much by the lack of adequate knowledge of how to prepare specimens as they were by the imperfect microscopes of the time. A revolution in the effectiveness of microscopy occurred in the second half of the 19th century with the introduction of techniques for fixing cells and for staining their component parts. Before the development of these techniques, the cell, viewed with the microscope, appeared as a minute container with a dense portion called the nucleus. The discovery that parts of the cell respond to certain stains made observation easier. The development of techniques for preparing tissues of plants for microscopic examination was continued in the 1870s and 1880s and resulted in the gradual refinement of the field of nuclear cytology, or karyology. Chromosomes were recognized as constant structures in the life cycle of cells, and the nature and meaning of meiosis, a type of cell division in which the daughter cells have half the number of chromosomes of the parent, was discovered; without this discovery, the significance of Mendel's laws of heredity might have gone unrecognized. Vital stains, dyes that can be used on living material, were first used in 1886 and have been greatly refined since then.

Improvement of the methodology of morphology has not been particularly rapid, even though satisfactory techniques for histology, anatomy, and cytology have been developed. The embedding of material in paraffin wax, the development of the rotary microtome for slicing very thin sections of tissue for microscope viewing, and the development of stain techniques are refinements of previously known methods. The invention of the phase microscope made possible the study of unfixed and unstained living material—hopefully nearer its natural state. The development of the electron microscope, however, has provided the plant morphologist with a new dimension of magnification of the structure of plant cells and tissues. The fine structure of the cell and of its components, such as mitochondria and the Golgi apparatus, have come under intensive study. Knowledge of the fine structure of plant cells has enabled investigators to determine the sites of important biochemical activities, especially those involved in the transfer of energy during photosynthesis and respiration. The scanning electron microscope, a relatively recent development, provides a three-dimensional image of surface structures at very great magnifications.

Fine structure a clue to biochemical activities

For experimental research on the morphogenesis of plants, isolated organs in their embryonic stage, clumps of cells, or even individual cells are grown. One of the most interesting techniques developed thus far permits the growing of plant tissue of higher plants as single cells; aeration and continuous agitation keep the cells suspended in the liquid culture medium.

Physiological aspects. Plant physiology and plant biochemistry are the most technical areas of botany; most major advances in physiology also reflect the development of either a new technique or the dramatic refinement of an earlier one to give a new degree of precision. Fortunately, the methodology of measurement has been vastly improved in recent decades, largely through the development of various electronic devices. The phytotron at the California Institute of Technology represents the first serious attempt to control the environment of living plants on a relatively large scale; much important information has been gained concerning the effects on plants of day length and night length and the effects on growth, flowering, and fruiting of varying night temperatures. Critical measurements of other plant functions have also been obtained.

Certain complex biochemical processes, such as photosynthesis and respiration, have been studied stepwise by immobilizing the process through the use of extreme cold or biochemical inhibitors and by analyzing the enzymatic activity of specific cell contents after spinning cells at very high speeds in a centrifuge. The pathways of energy transfer from molecule to molecule during photosynthesis and respiration have been determined by biophysical methods, especially those utilizing radioactive isotopes.

An investigation of the natural metabolic products of plants requires, in general, certain standard biochemical techniques—*e.g.*, gas and paper chromatography, electrophoresis, and various kinds of spectroscopy, including infrared, ultraviolet, and nuclear magnetic resonance. Useful information on the structure of the extremely large cellulose molecule has been provided by X-ray crystallography.

Ecological aspects. When plant ecology first emerged as a subscience of botany, it was largely descriptive; today, however, it has become a common meeting ground for all the plant sciences, as well as for other sciences. In addition, it has become much more quantitative. As a result, the tools and methods of plant ecologists are those available for measuring the intensity of the environmental factors that impinge on the plant and the reaction of the plant to these factors. The extent of the variability of many physical factors must be measured. The integration and reporting of such measurements, which cannot be regarded as constant, may therefore conceal some of the most dynamic and significant aspects of the environment and the responses of the plant to them. Because the physical environment is a complex of biological and physical components, it is measured by biophysical tools. The development of electronic measuring and recording devices has been crucial for a better understanding of the dynamics of the environment. Such devices, however, produce so much information that computer techniques must be used to reduce the data to meaningful results.

The ecologist, concerned primarily with measuring the effect of the external environment on a plant, adapts the methodology of the plant physiologist to field conditions.

The plant sociologist

The plant sociologist, on the other hand, is concerned with both the relation of different kinds of plants to each other and the nature and constitution of their association into natural communities. One widely used technique in this respect is to count the various kinds of plants within a standard area in order to determine such factors as the percentage of ground cover, dominance of species, aggressiveness, and other characteristics of the community. In general, the plant sociologist has relatively few quantitative factors to measure and must therefore take a subjective and intuitive approach, which, nevertheless, gives extremely useful results and some degree of predictability.

Some ecologists are most concerned with the inner environment of the plant and the way in which it reacts to the external environment. This approach, which is essentially physiological and biochemical, is useful for determining energy flow in ecosystems. The physiological ecologist is also concerned with evaluating the adaptations that certain plants have made toward survival in a hostile environment.

In summary, the techniques and methodology of plant ecology are as diverse and as varied as the large number of sciences that are drawn upon by ecologists. Completely new techniques, although few, are important; among them are techniques for measuring the amount of radioactive carbon-14 in plant deposits up to 50,000 years old. The most important new method in plant ecology is the rapidly growing use of computer techniques for handling vast amounts of data. Furthermore, modern digital computers can be used to simulate simple ecosystems and to analyze real ones.

Taxonomic aspects. Experimental research under controlled conditions, made possible by botanical gardens and their ranges of greenhouses and controlled environmental chambers, has become an integral part of the methodology of modern plant taxonomy.

A second major tool of the taxonomist is the herbarium, a reference collection consisting of carefully selected and dried plants attached to paper sheets of a standard size and filed in a systematic way so that they may be easily retrieved for examination. Each specimen is a reference point representing the features of one plant of a certain species; it lasts indefinitely if properly cared for, and, if the species becomes extinct in nature—as hundreds have—it remains the only record of the plant's former existence. The library is also an essential reference resource for descriptions and illustrations of plants that may not be represented in a particular herbarium.

One of the earliest methods of the taxonomist, the study of living plants in the field, has benefitted greatly by fast and easy methods of transportation; botanists may carry on fieldwork in any part of the world and make detailed studies of the exact environmental conditions under which each species grows.

New approaches in systematic botany

During the present century, many new approaches have been applied to the elucidation of problems in systematic botany. The transmission electron microscope and the scanning electron microscope have added to the knowledge of plant morphology, upon which classical taxonomy so much depends.

Refined methods for cytological and genetical studies of plants have given the taxonomist new insights into the origin of the great diversity among plants, especially the mechanisms by which new species arise and by which they then maintain their individuality in nature. From such studies have arisen further methods and also the subdisciplines of cytotaxonomy, cytogenetics, and population genetics.

Phytochemistry, or the chemistry of plants, one of the early subdivisions of organic chemistry, has been of great importance in the identification of plant substances of medicinal importance. With the development of new phytochemical methods, new information has become available for use in conjunction with plant taxonomy; thus has arisen the modern field of chemotaxonomy, or biochemical systematics. Each species tends to differ to some degree from every other species, even in the same genus, in the biochemistry of its natural metabolic products. Sometimes the difference is subtle and difficult to determine; sometimes it is obvious and easily perceptible. With new analytical techniques, a large number of individual compounds from one plant can be identified quickly and with certainty. Such information is extremely useful in adding confirmatory or supplemental evidence of an objective and quantitative nature. An interesting by-product of chemical plant taxonomy has resulted in understanding better the restriction of certain insects to specific plants.

Computer techniques have recently been applied to plant taxonomy to develop a new field, numerical taxonomy, or taximetrics, by which relationships between plant species or those within groups of species are determined quantitatively and depicted graphically. Another method measures the degree of molecular similarity of deoxyribonucleic acid (DNA) molecules in different plants. By this procedure it should be possible to determine the natural taxonomic relationships among different plants and plant groups by determining the extent of the relationship of their DNA's: closely related plants will have more similarities in their DNA's than will unrelated ones.

The use of nucleic acids in taxonomy

ECONOMIC ROLE

Botany has been a source for other arts and sciences, such as medicine and organic chemistry; it still provides the base upon which depend various applied plant sciences—agriculture, agronomy, horticulture, forestry, pharmacology, and other related fields.

In early civilizations, as among primitive peoples today, knowledge about plants, especially those of medicinal importance, lent special prestige and power to the priests, medicine men, and other practitioners who often cloaked their knowledge with magic, superstition, secrecy, religious rituals, and other manifestations of professional mystery.

Gardens have been an integral part of every civilization from early times. When contrasted with agriculture, gardening is a more specialized pursuit that lends itself to both avocation and vocation. Many centuries before written history, gardens of various kinds existed, from the Garden of Eden to the Hanging Gardens of Babylon; the forerunners of modern botanical gardens, these were devoted to ornamental plants, vegetables, culinary herbs, fruit trees, and interesting plants. See BOTANICAL GARDEN; GARDEN AND LANDSCAPE DESIGN; and GARDENING.

Agricultural products. As with many other aspects of the plant sciences, the origins of agriculture precede recorded history. Most of today's cultivated plants were domesticated in prehistoric times. In fact, it is remarkable that so few important agricultural plants have been domesticated within historical times; on the other hand, most crop plants have been greatly improved through hybridization, selection, and other technological advances in breeding. The questions of where and how plants were domesticated are obscured as much by the absence of "missing links" in the sequence from wild plants to cultivated ones as by the total lack of any written record. See DOMESTICATION, PLANT AND ANIMAL.

Food. The historical record, both written and archaeological, shows that at least 3,000 species of plants have been used as food; early man undoubtedly ate what he could of every plant he encountered. Most present knowledge of edible wild plants has been gained from aboriginal people around the world. Of the 1,000 or so species that truly have been domesticated and cultivated intensively, only about 200 have become productive enough to enter into international commerce. The rapid growth of world population has inevitably set the trend through the centuries to reduce or eliminate the cultivation of less efficient crops and to concentrate on the more productive ones. As a result, the majority of the world's population is now nourished by only 12 plant species, which include three cereals, rice, wheat, and corn (maize); two sugar plants, sugarcane and the sugar beet; three "root" crops, the potato, the sweet potato, and the cassava; two legumes, the common bean and the soybean; and two "tree" crops, the coconut and the banana. The next three most highly utilized species are the peanut, sorghum, and barley. These few crop plants stand between most men and starvation.

The ubiquity of stimulating beverages

Beverages. Early centres of civilization developed their own plant-derived stimulating beverages, both fermented and nonfermented. The stimulants found in nonalcoholic drinks include caffeine, as found in coffee, which was developed in Abyssinia and Arabia; tea, developed in Southeast Asia; guarana and maté, in Paraguay and Argentina; cola, in tropical Africa; and kat, in Arabia. Fermented alcoholic beverages also precede history; although certainly much older, wine is first recorded before 4000 BC. Mead, fermented from honey, and palm wine, as well as the fermented juice of other fruits, are also very ancient alcoholic drinks. The use of pulque, the fermented juice of *Agave*, long antedated the arrival of Europeans in the New World. Beers, made from rice in the Orient (sake), from maize in South America (chicha), and from other grains in Europe, must first be malted to change the starch into sugars, which are then fermented; despite the two-stage process, which is more difficult than that of wine making, beers are extremely ancient. Distillation was also known to the ancients: apparently cloth and sheepskins were held over boiling fermented mash to condense the alcohol, which was then wrung out of them.

Fibres. In addition to food and shelter, man needs clothing, especially in cooler climates. The inner bark of many species of trees was once beaten into a natural cloth; in fact, this technique may have antedated the weaving of plant fibres into cloth. Tapa cloth so fabricated is still used in the South Pacific, and other bark cloths persist elsewhere.

Fibres are long cells or clusters of cells that give strength to the stems, leaves, and roots of a plant. Thousands of plant species yield useful fibres and have been used locally by primitive peoples all over the world. Fibres still in use were discovered in prehistoric times and were already highly refined by the earliest historic times. Cotton is the world's chief fibre plant and one of the oldest; two different types originated in India and in the Americas. Flax has been cultivated for at least 10,000 years. It is frequently mentioned in the Bible and was cultivated in prehistoric times by the Swiss Lake Dwellers and by the Egyptians. Hemp, the fibre from *Cannabis sativa*, has been used since ancient times for the production of rope and cordage. In addition to hemp fibre, *Cannabis* contains various hallucinogenic compounds perhaps most commonly called hashish and marijuana. Other important fibres of great economic importance are jute, from which burlap is made, and ramie. Manila hemp, or abaca, is made from the leafstalks of a banana relative, *Musa textilis*. In the New World, several important fibres have been used since prehistoric times, including sisal, henequin, istle, and pita; all are from the leaves of species of *Agave* and its related genus, *Furcraea*. In tropical Africa and Asia, a strong fibre is produced from the leaves of the bowstring hemp, *Sanseverinia*. Filling fibres for pillows are furnished by kapok (the silk-cotton tree), milkweeds, and cattails. Coir, the important fibre produced from the husk of the coconut, has long been used locally for many purposes.

The importance of *Cannabis*

Lumber industry and forest products. By the early Stone Age men were already proficient in the manipulation of wood for a wide range of purposes—making small objects such as bows and arrows, making boats, and building shelters.

Civilization today depends on wood and wood products at great cost to the world's natural resources. The original forests of Europe, especially, have been severely depleted because they have long been utilized for wood, as well as being cleared for agriculture. And in the time that has elapsed since the English colonized the United States, at least half of its forests have disappeared as well.

Forest trees provide man with a number of useful products including wood, food, fibres, gums, and resins. Some aboriginal groups in tropical America, Africa, and Asia still depend entirely on the forest for all their needs and do not attempt any agriculture. The prehistoric discovery that hardwood subjected to distillation, or incomplete combustion, produces charcoal is said to be the oldest chemical process known to man. Modern technology has increased the efficiency of wood distillation as well as the number of products that can be recovered during that process; among them, in addition to charcoal, are acetic acid, acetone, methanol, or wood alcohol, wood gas, and wood tar and oils. Softwood from conifers, especially old pine stumps, is distilled to produce turpentine, rosin, pine oil, and creosote, as well as charcoal and wood gas. Many modern techniques have been developed to give wood greater strength or to enhance other properties. Several chemical processes remove lignin and other materials from wood fibres, leaving almost pure cellulose ready for manufacture into paper. Other processes utilize cellulose to manufacture fibres such as rayon, films such as cellophane, and many different types of wood and plastic products. Discovered as part of the normal process of manufacturing ("cooking") paper pulp from wood, the partial or complete hydrolysis of cellulose has assumed considerable economic importance. In northern Europe, especially in Scandinavia, wood is cooked under pressure to produce an edible, pulpy, starchlike food for cattle and other livestock. If cooked long enough, the cellulose can be converted into simple sugars, which can then be fermented by yeast to produce alcohol.

Chemical rendering of wood into cellulose

Modern forestry now has a much broader scope than it once did, when improved timber production was almost the sole aim. Today, forestry is concerned with the management of wooded lands of all types (including grasslands), not only for lumber production but also for a series of desirable but less tangible benefits, such as water yield, watershed protection, grazing, protection of wildlife, scenic values and recreation, and game and fish production.

Other products. *Essential oils.* The most important sources of perfumes, spices, and many kinds of flavourings for food and beverages are an enormous variety of essential oils produced by a vast array of plants. From earliest times, essential oils have also been used for religious offerings, for medicinal purposes, and for embalming the dead. Many plant families produce their own easily recognizable essential oils; best known are those of the pines and other conifers, the laurels, the myrtles (including *Eucalyptus*), the mints, and the citrus fruits.

Medicinal plants. The number of plants that have been used for medicinal purposes is nearly as large as the list of edible plants. Root drugs that date back to 5000 BC include aconite, colchicum, gentian, squill, and valerian. Other root drugs in use are goldenseal, ginseng, ipecac, licorice, jalap, podophyllum, rhubarb, and senega; several have their origin in the New World and were well known in aboriginal medicine. All bark drugs in common use are from the New World; they include cascara sagrada, curare, and quinine. Of drugs extracted from stems and wood, ephedrine is of Chinese origin, and guaiacum and quassia are from tropical America. Many drugs occur in leaves, which are the primary source of chemical compounds in plants; such are aloe, belladonna, cocaine, digitalis, eucalyptus, witch hazel, henbane, horehound, lobelia, pennyroyal, senna, stramonium, and wormwood. A few drugs occur in flowers, of which the best known are chamomile and hops. Many seeds and fruits that are poisonous contain ingredients that, in moderation, may be of medicinal importance; examples are croton oil, nux vomica, opium, psyllium, strychnine, strophanthus, and wormseed.

Plant poisons of medicinal value

Narcotics. Narcotics are closely related to medicinal plants in their physiological and biological effects. Most aboriginal peoples discovered some such plant that eased the cares of everyday life. These drugs were often under the control of chiefs or medicine men and were sometimes of religious importance. Examples are coca from the Andes; opium from the Orient; betel from Indonesia; cola from tropical Africa; *Cannabis* from Asia; peyote from Mexico; fly agaric (*Amanita muscaria*) from Siberia; datura from Asia; henbane from the Mediterranean area; kavakava from Oceania; and tobacco from the New World.

Insecticides. Many narcotic plants and their products, such as nicotine, have been used to control insects; in fact, the distinctions between poisonous plants, medicinal plants, narcotic plants, and insecticidal plants are uncomfortably narrow or even nonexistent. Pyrethrum, the dried powdered flower heads of certain composite plants, has the advantage of killing insects without being strongly toxic to humans and other warm-blooded animals. Rotenone, derived from derris root in Asia and from several species of *Lonchocarpus* in tropical America, has an action very similar to pyrethrum. Rotenone is also widely used as a fish poison; since it causes suffocation by inhibiting oxygen absorption, the fish killed in this way are edible.

Fuel. The two major types of fossil fuels, coal (including lignite) and petroleum (including natural gas), are both derived from plant deposits accumulated millions of years ago and transformed into their present fuel state by heat and pressure.

BOTANICAL SOCIETIES AND PUBLICATIONS

Societies and journals devoted largely, or entirely, to plant science began to emerge in the late 19th and early 20th centuries. Partly because of the vast expanse and large population of the United States and partly because of the exuberance of American science, a surfeit of botanical societies exist today in the United States; each has its own journal. Some of the more important ones are the Botanical Society of America (*American Journal of Botany*), American Society of Plant Physiologists (*Plant Physiology*), Torrey Botanical Club (*Bulletin* and *Memoirs*), American Society of Plant Taxonomists (*Brittonia*), and Society for Economic Botany (*Economic Botany*). Several important journals are published by institutions other than societies, as *Botanical Gazette* (University of Chicago) and *Botanical Review* (New York Botanical Garden).

The United Kingdom produces several publications, among which *Annals of Botany* and the *Journal of Experimental Botany* are published by Oxford University; *New Phytologist* is published commercially.

In Canada, several botanical periodicals are published by the National Research Council.

All older and well-established countries of the world have their own botanical societies and publications. In addition to the serial publications issued by societies for their members, many important contributions to botany, especially monographic works, are published in the memoirs, annals, transactions, and proceedings of national and local academies of science, by individual universities, by botanical gardens, and by other types of organizations and institutions. In addition, several major botanical journals are issued by commercial publishers. A list of some of the 8,000 major periodicals in biology published around the globe appears annually in *Biological Abstracts*, which reviews all publications in the life sciences. A compilation of all the world's botanical writings from the beginnings of botanical literature was published by the Hunt Botanical Library in 1968.

BIBLIOGRAPHY. H.S. REED, *A Short History of the Plant Sciences* (1942), an interesting and thought-provoking account with many useful insights; K.V. THIMANN, *The Plant Sciences, Now and in the Coming Decade* (1966), a thoughtful and persuasive statement, well-written and readable; J. REYNOLDS GREEN, *A History of Botany, 1860–1900* (1909, reprinted 1967), a scholarly treatment designed to supplement the classic work of JULIUS VON SACHS, *History of Botany, 1530–1860,* trans. by HENRY E.F. GARNSEY, rev. by ISAAC BAYLEY BALFOUR (1890, reprinted 1967), arranged by botanical structure and function; AGNES ARBER, *Herbals, Their Origin and Evolution: A Chapter in the History of Botany, 1470–1670,* 2nd ed. rev. (1938, reprinted 1970), a readable and authoritative work; ELLISON HAWKS and G.S. BOULGER, *Pioneers of Plant Study* (1928, reprinted 1969), an interesting account of major historical figures.

(W.C.St.)

Botswana

Botswana is a landlocked republic in southern Africa with an area of about 224,600 square miles (581,700 square kilometres) and a population of about 937,000 (1981). The greater part of the country is covered by the Kalahari desert region. It is bounded by South Africa to the southeast and south, Bophuthatswana to the south, South West Africa/Namibia to the west and north, Zambia to the north, and Zimbabwe to the northeast and east. Zambia and Zimbabwe are the only independent black states on which Botswana fronts. The actual border with Zambia along the Zambezi River, at the east end of the thin finger of South West African/Namibian territory known as the Caprivi Strip, is only several hundred yards long. The Caprivi Strip has not been established by international treaty and is a source of controversy among Botswana, Zimbabwe, and South Africa (the latter acting as trustee for South West Africa/Namibia).

Before its independence in 1966, Botswana was a British protectorate known as Bechuanaland; one of the first acts of the nation was to move the capital from Mafeking in South Africa (since 1980 Mafikeng, Bophuthatswana) to Gaborone (formerly Gaberones). The country is named after its people, the Tswana (or Batswana). The language is Tswana (Setswana or Siswana).

Botswana is a member of the United Nations, the Commonwealth, and the Organization of African Unity, and it is a signatory of the Lomé Convention. It maintains economic links with South Africa as well as diplomatic ties with black states to the north and east. Lacking adequate water and having a small population, Botswana was once primarily a stock-raising country. Large-scale mining of substantial diamond, copper, and nickel deposits and of other less important minerals began in the 1970s, diversifying and improving the economy. Programs to develop underground water sources have begun to assist agricultural production, particularly of food crops. (Associated physical features can be found under KALAHARI [DESERT]; OKAVANGO RIVER; and ZAMBEZI RIVER; for historical aspects, see SOUTHERN AFRICA, HISTORY OF.)

The landscape. *Relief and drainage.* Botswana extends from the Chobe River (which drains into the Zambezi) in the north, to the Molopo River, a tributary of the Orange River, in the south. Most of the nation's territory lies within the Kalahari, a semidesert in the west. A plateau, with an altitude of about 4,000 feet (1,200 metres), divides the country into two distinctive regions, each with its own drainage system. After forming the watershed between the Molopo just to the south and the Notwani River to the southeast, the plateau extends northward from a point about 20 miles (32 kilometres) west of Kanye, a town in the southeast, to the border of Zimbabwe in the northeast. The area to the east of the plateau is crossed by ephemeral streams that flow eastward into the Marico, Limpopo, and Notwani rivers; the western system, which once drained the tableland into the Makgadikgadi Pans, is now covered with deep sand. The plateau

The country has a mean altitude of 3,300 feet and is almost entirely flat or gently undulating, with Kalahari sands overlying Precambrian rock (from 570,000,000 to 4,600,000,000 years old). The greater part of the south has no surface drainage, and the rest of the country's drainage, except for the Limpopo and Chobe rivers on the borders, does not reach the sea.

The main drainage system is provided by the Okavango River, which, after flowing southeastward for 90 miles from the Angola border in the northwest, drains into a vast depression to form the 4,000-square-mile Okavango Swamp, as well as Lake Ngami, a 70-square-mile pan, or basin. This system seasonally drains eastward along the Boteti River to Lake Xau (Dow) near the centre of the country, and finally flows into the Makgadikgadi Pans farther east. The Molopo and Ramatlabama, which form the southern boundary, are both tiny streams.

The Kalahari is a "thirstland," rather than a true desert, being covered with grass and acacia thorn scrub; its tsama melons (a species of watermelon) help to sustain the San (Bushman) who live there. In areas where underground water is close to the surface, the Kalahari resembles parkland. The only typical desert occurs in the southwestern corner, where there are sand dunes.

Climate. Temperatures vary from temperate to subtropical. In summer (which lasts from October to March)

Wide World Photos

Village in Botswana.

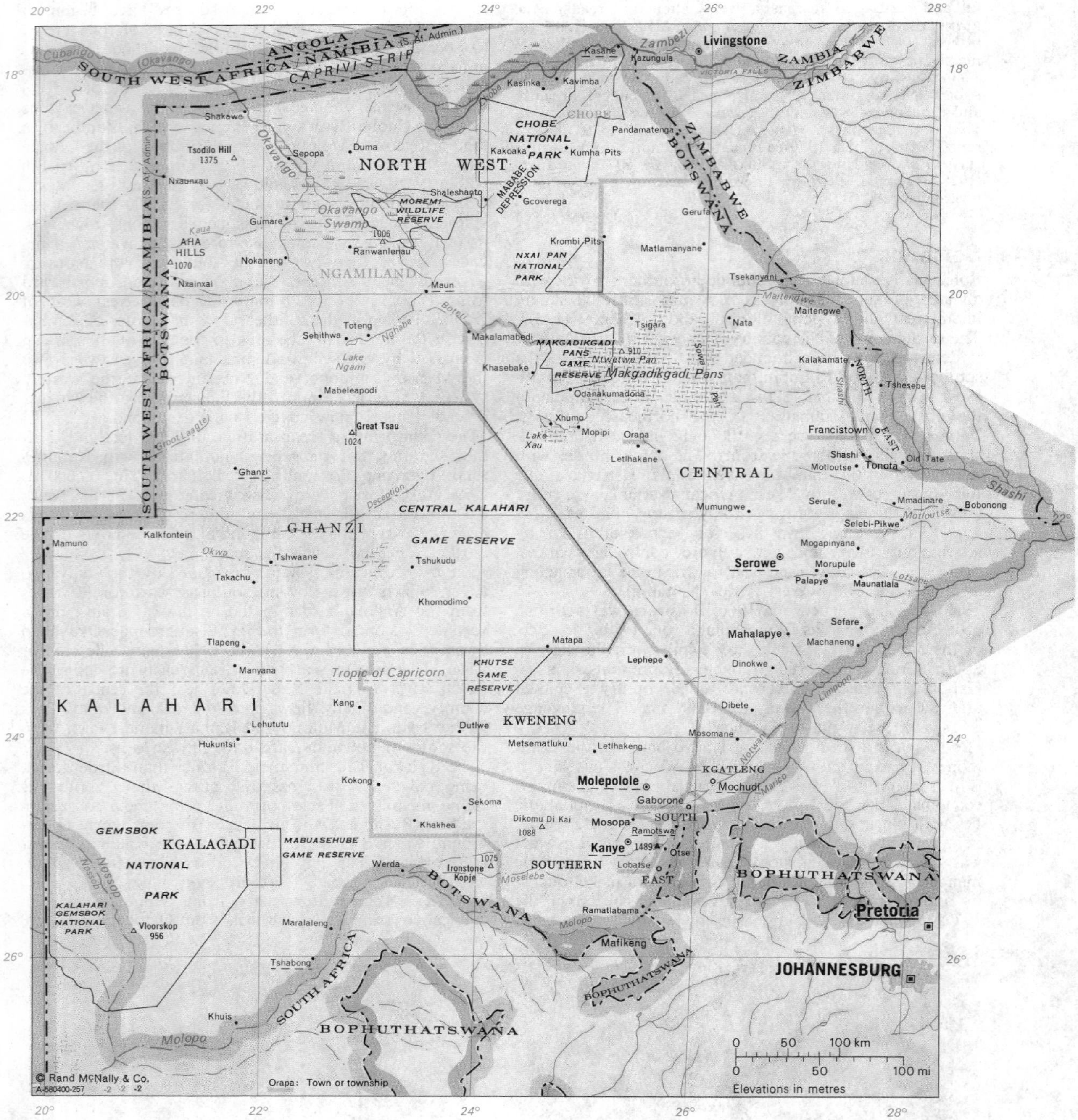

BOTSWANA

MAP INDEX

Political subdivisions

Central	21·30s	26·00e
Chobe	18·30s	25·00e
Francistown	21·11s	27·32e
Gaborone	24·45s	25·55e
Ghanzi	22·00s	23·00e
Kgalagadi	25·00s	22·00e
Kgatleng	24·28s	26·05e
Kweneng	24·00s	24·00e
Lobatse	25·11s	25·40e
Ngamiland	19·09s	22·47e
North East	21·11s	27·32e
North West	19·00s	23·00e
Orapa	21·17s	25·22e
Selebi-Pikwe	22·00s	27·50e
South East	25·00s	25·45e
Southern	24·45s	24·00e

Cities and towns

Bobonong	21·58s	28·17e
Dibete	23·45s	25·26e
Dinokwe	23·24s	26·40e
Duma	18·45s	22·46e
Dutlwe	23·55s	23·47e
Francistown	21·11s	27·32e
Gaborone	24·45s	25·55e
Gcoverega	19·08s	24·15e
Gerufa	19·17s	26·02e
Ghanzi	21·38s	21·45e
Gumare	19·21s	22·12e
Hukuntsi	24·02s	21·48e
Kakoaka	18·40s	24·22e
Kalakamate	20·39s	27·21e
Kalkfontein	22·08s	20·53e
Kang	23·41s	22·50e
Kanye	24·59s	25·19e
Kasinka	18·13s	24·22e
Kavimba	18·02s	24·38e
Kazungula	17·45s	25·20e
Khakhea	24·51s	23·20e
Khasebake	20·41s	24·29e
Khomodimo	22·46s	23·52e
Khuis	26·37s	21·45e
Kokong	24·27s	23·03e
Krombi Pits	19·30s	25·02e
Kumha Pits	18·45s	24·45e
Lehututu	23·58s	21·51e
Lephepe	23·20s	25·50e
Letlhakane	21·27s	25·30e
Letlhakeng	24·08s	25·02e
Lobatse	25·11s	25·40e
Mabeleapodi	20·58s	22·36e
Machaneng	23·10s	27·26e
Mahalapye	23·04s	26·50e
Maitengwe	20·06s	27·13e
Makalamabedi	20·19s	23·51e
Mamuno	22·16s	20·01e
Manyana	23·23s	21·44e
Maralaleng	25·47s	22·45e
Matapa	23·11s	24·39e
Matlamanyane	19·33s	25·57e
Maun	20·00s	23·25e
Maunatlala	22·32s	27·28e
Metsematluku	24·01s	24·40e
Mmadinare	21·57s	27·52e
Mochudi	24·28s	26·05e
Mogapinyana	22·19s	27·27e
Molepolole	24·25s	25·30e
Mopipi	21·07s	24·55e
Morupule	22·36s	27·05e
Mosomane	24·04s	26·15e
Mosopa	24·50s	25·31e
Motloutse	21·28s	27·24e
Mumungwe	21·59s	26·24e
Nata	20·12s	26·12e
Nokaneng	19·40s	22·16e
Nxainxai	19·50s	21·13e
Nxaunxau	18·19s	21·04e
Odanakuma-dona	20·53s	24·45e
Old Tate	21·22s	27·46e
Orapa	21·17s	25·22e
Otse	25·02s	25·45e
Palapye	22·37s	27·06e
Pandama-tenga	18·35s	25·42e
Ramatlabama	25·40s	25·30e
Ramotswa	25·50s	25·50e
Ranwanlenau	19·35s	22·47e
Sefare	23·02s	27·28e
Sehithwa	20·23s	22·45e
Sekoma	24·41s	23·50e
Selebi-Pikwe	22·00s	27·50e
Sepopa	18·13s	22·13e
Serowe	22·25s	26·44e
Shakawe	18·23s	21·50e
Shaleshanto	19·09s	23·58e
Shashe	21·20s	27·29e
Takachu	22·37s	21·58e
Tlapeng	23·15s	21·49e
Tonota	21·29s	27·29e
Toteng	20·22s	22·58e
Tsekanyani	19·52s	26·39e
Tshabong	26·03s	22·29e
Tshesebe	21·51s	27·35e
Tshukudu	22·30s	23·22e
Tshwaane	22·29s	22·03e
Tsigara	20·10s	25·18e
Werda	25·15s	23·16e
Xhumo	21·07s	24·42e

temperatures rise to 100° F (38° C); in winter (which lasts from April to September) there is frequent frost, and temperatures fall below 32° F (0° C). Hot August winds carry sand from the Kalahari across the entire country. The average annual rainfall is 18 inches (460 millimetres), representing a variation from 25 inches in the north to five inches or even less in the southwest. Most rain falls in heavy downpours between December and the end of April. Cyclical droughts, often lasting several years, are calamitous for both crops and cattle. One such drought occurred in the mid-1960s.

Vegetation. Woodland savanna (grassy parkland), in which species of acacia predominate, covers much of the country. In the northeast the most characteristic vegetation consists of mopane (African ironwood), mogonono (country almond), and mokusi (Rhodesian teak), while morukuru (*Spirostachys africanus*) frequently occurs in the central Kalahari. In the abundant grazing areas grasses include love grass, panicum, crabgrass, and bristle grass. True forest, which occurs only on the banks of the Chobe, consists mainly of mokwa (bloodwood), mokusi, and monato (Rhodesian ash).

The game reserves

Animal life. Herds of wild game teem on the plains, and the national parks and game reserves are well stocked. National parks include the Chobe, Nxai Pan, and Gemsbok; other wildlife areas are the Okavango delta and Lake Ngami, the Moremi Wildlife Reserve, and the Makgadikgadi Pans, Khutse, Mabuasehube, and Central Kalahari game reserves. Besides many species of large and small antelopes, there are lions, elephants, leopards, hippopotamuses, giraffes, buffaloes, and crocodiles. Poisonous snakes, among them the cobra and puff adder, abound; and there are many varieties of scorpions, spiders (including tarantulas), and termites. Bird life is prolific and includes ostriches, pelicans, and bustards. The principal fish, especially in the Okavango and Chobe rivers, are tilapia, tiger fish, and catfish.

The landscape under human settlement. The Tswana are divided into eight principal tribal groups, each occupying its own separate territory with its own traditional chiefs and retaining a communal ownership over its tribal lands that is inalienable. Associated with each of the dominant tribes are smaller related or formerly subject tribes. Only the nomadic San of the Kalahari, the few thousand Europeans, and some Tswana who have moved to the urban areas are not included in this traditional system. The largest tribe is the Ngwato (Bamangwato), which numbers about 250,000, comprises about one-fourth of the total population, and owns one-fifth of all the land; its territory lies in eastern Botswana. The Ngwato capital, Serowe, is spread out beneath rocky hills and is a large circular village consisting mostly of thatched huts. The next two largest tribes are the Kwena (Bakwena) and the Ngwaketse (Bangwaketse), who live in the southeast, near Gaborone; both tribes number about 80,000. The other smaller tribes are the Kgatla (Bakgatla), numbering about 35,000, the Bamalete, numbering 14,000, and the Tlokwa (Batlokwa), numbering 4,000, all of whom live in the southeast; the Rolong (Barolong), numbering about 11,000, who spill over into South Africa; and the Tawana (Batawana), numbering about 50,000, who live on the border with South West Africa/Namibia.

In the 19th century several large blocks of land were transferred from African to European ownership around Lobatse, Gaborone, and Tuli in the southeast; Ghanzi in the west; and on the banks of the Molopo River in the south. The former Tati Concession in the Francistown District (now part of the North East District), for example, gave a private company the right in 1869 to mine a potentially rich area of more than 2,000 square miles.

The Tswana way of life

Unlike most Africans, the Tswana have a tradition of living in large villages, which are, in effect, capital centres for each tribe but are often located at great distances from the grazing lands. Cattle posts provide shelters for herdsmen and watering places for cattle. Richer cattle farmers have a large number of cattle posts, which are sometimes spread out at distances of 100 miles or more from each other. The farmers' practice is to spend several days of each week at their cattle posts, returning to their central village and families for long weekends.

Each village has its subchief, headmen, and *kgotla*, or *lekhotlo*, a court and public meeting place situated near the chief's house (usually under a large tree but always beside the communal cattle enclosures, or kraals). The *kgotla* remains the centre of daily social life, at which disputes are settled in public and matters of local importance discussed. Most villages have a school, a store, and sometimes a dispensary. Villages, small or large, are always divided into wards comprising the extended family, each part of which lives within its own compound. In the larger villages each ward tries to have its own borehole for water. Water carrying still forms a large part of the daily routine of women and girls, just as cattle herding occupies the lives of boys, often conflicting with their schooling. The outlying villages are related closely to their tribal capital, which is the seat of the paramount chief and the royal *kgotla*. This system of village democracy has, to a great extent, survived the politicizing of the nation and forms an integral part of the contemporary political structure.

Cattle, land, and rain are the most important factors in the lives of the people. Because the lives of people and cattle both depend on an unpredictable climate, rain (*pula*) is of particular significance. *Pula* is the people's familiar greeting on meeting each other and is the name of the currency.

The Towns

There is considerable underemployment in Botswana, and many thousands of young people seek temporary work each year in South Africa. Outside the small tribal villages, employment within the country is mostly found in the half-dozen villages and towns along the railway line in the east—which links Botswana with South Africa and Zimbabwe—and at Selebi-Pikwe, the fast-growing centre of the copper- and nickel-mining industries. The estimated populations of these major centres in the early 1980s totalled more than 250,000. In such areas modern Tswana often free themselves from tribal constraints to form nationally integrated social and political groups.

Gaborone, the capital city, has grown at the fastest rate. During the 1970s it passed Serowe, the largest of the tribal villages, in population; by the early 1980s its population of about 60,000 was more than twice that of Serowe. Francistown, the former centre of the Tati Concession area in the northeast, is the home of most of the European population. Mochudi and Lobatse, both with about 19,000 inhabitants in 1981, have become commercial centres on the railroad line in the southeast. In 1950 Botswana was only about 1 percent urban, but by the early 1980s it had become about 20 percent urban. This rate of urbanization was unmatched by any other African nation during the period.

People and population. *Ethnic groups.* The original in-

Botswana Area and Population

	area		population	
	sq mi	sq km	1971 census	1981 census*
Districts				
Central (Ngwato)	57,039	147,730	216,000	322,000
Ghanzi	45,525	117,910	12,000	19,000
Kgalagadi	41,290	106,940	15,000	24,000
Kgatleng	3,073	7,960	31,000	42,000
Kweneng	13,857	35,890	65,000	116,000
North East	1,977	5,120	26,000	37,000
North West†				
Chobe	8,031	20,800	5,000	8,000
Ngamiland	42,135	109,130	48,000	68,000
Southern (Ngwaketse)	10,992	28,470	82,000	125,000
South East	687	1,780	20,000	31,000
Towns				
Francistown	‡	‡	19,000	31,000
Gaborone	§	§	18,000	60,000
Lobatse	§	§	12,000	19,000
Selebi-Pikwe	‖	‖	5,000	30,000
Townships				
Mahalapye	‖	‖	12,000	21,000
Orapa	‖	‖	1,000	5,000
Serowe	‖	‖	16,000	24,000
Total Botswana	224,610¶	581,730	608,000♀	937,000¶♂

*Preliminary figures. †Comprises political districts of Chobe and Ngamiland. ‡Included in area of North East District. §Included in area of South East District. ‖Included in area of Central District. ¶Figures do not add to totals given because of rounding. ♀Total includes 10,550 nomads and an estimated 23,000 people not enumerated. ♂Total includes the nine districts and four towns as separate administrative units.
Source: Official government figures.

habitants were the San (known locally as the Sarwa or Masarwa), who now number some 30,000. Only about one-sixth of the San still follow a nomadic way of life in the Kalahari, moving across the border of South West Africa/Namibia; they belong to the Naron, Auen, Kung, and Heikum groups. Those who have abandoned nomadism are mainly employed in servile positions by the dominant tribes or by the government.

The European population, mainly from South Africa, totals only a few thousand. They are farmers, traders, public officials, missionaries, and teachers. There are also a few thousand Eurafricans, who are of mixed descent, and a few hundred Asians living in Botswana.

The two official languages are Tswana and English. English is spoken only among the educated Africans or those who have worked for some time in South Africa. Afrikaans is spoken only by sections of the white community. Approximately one-third of the population is literate in Tswana and one-fourth in English.

Religious groups. The majority of people are Christians, although only a minority are active churchgoers; many are only nominal Christians in the sense that they still show some attachment to their traditional religion, which is based on ancestor worship. Less than one-third are practicing Christians. The majority of these are Anglicans, Congregationalists, Methodists, and Presbyterians; these four groups have united to worship as a single congregation. There are also smaller communities of the Dutch Reformed, African Methodist Episcopal, and Roman Catholic churches.

Demography. The country is sparsely populated, largely because of the shortage of water. Population growth averages about 3 percent per annum. Only about 10 percent of the area suitable for cultivation is actively farmed. More than 85 percent of the people are concentrated in the eastern region, which has a population density of about nine people per square mile, (three per square kilometre), compared with less than one per square mile over the rest of the country.

The national economy. Most Tswana live by raising cattle; the nation's herds were estimated at about 3,000,000 in 1980. Mining, however, overtook the beef industry in the 1970s as the basis for the country's most important exports, and the mining of diamonds became the fastest growing source of revenue. A series of national economic plans after independence have given particular attention to energy needs, mining development, beef exports, and crop production. The economy has grown rapidly, but the distribution of this increased wealth has been disproportionate; wage-earning urban dwellers and large-scale livestock farmers have benefitted most, while the rural majority has experienced little or no gain.

At independence Botswana's monetary system was linked with that of South Africa, but in 1975 the government established a national bank. The pula, a separate currency, was adopted in 1976; originally at a par with the South African rand, the pula has become independently valued.

Foreign aid. Loans and grants from foreign governments have been the basis for most of Botswana's development programs. Following independence, Great Britain was the principal source of aid, but other Western nations, particularly the United States, Canada, and the Scandinavian countries, have also assisted Botswana. As a signatory to the Lomé Convention, Botswana has received aid from the European Economic Community (EEC) countries, mainly for projects in education and transportation.

The violent confrontations in Zimbabwe, South West Africa/Namibia, and South Africa have produced severe strains on the economy of Botswana; the country has given asylum to thousands of refugees. International aid, proposed by a UN study of the situation, has helped Botswana meet the needs of the refugees and assisted in the establishment of a small self-defense force.

Mining. Diamond mines at Orapa, with a 50 percent share held by the government, began production in 1971; a second mine at nearby Letlhakane began production in 1977. By the early 1980s diamonds had become the single most important export. A major new diamond pipe was discovered at Jwaneng in the late 1970s, and mining began there in the early 1980s.

Nickel and copper

The fastest growing area of Botswana, however, has been around Selebi-Pikwe, the location of the Shashi Project, which includes nickel and copper mines and water and power projects. Nickel and copper mining, begun in 1974, was initially hampered by technical problems but has come to play an increasingly important role in the economy of the country. Prospecting for other minerals has continued, and legislation in 1977 vested all mineral rights in the state.

Agriculture. Beef and animal products are Botswana's second most important source of export revenue. South Africa and Great Britain traditionally were Botswana's principal agricultural markets. Under the Lomé Convention, however, Botswana gained preferential access to EEC markets, and during the 1970s it also began to develop beef markets in Africa. Overgrazing has continued to be a problem, but the government enacted legislation during the 1970s to strengthen its efforts at land reform. Government programs to control animal diseases have been generally effective, especially since the early 1980s, when a plant producing vaccine for foot-and-mouth disease was opened. The abattoir and processing plant at Lobatse, which was expanded and modernized following independence, is the centre of the beef industry.

Farming in Botswana is risky because of the constant threat of drought and is limited primarily to a subsistence level. Sorghum, corn (maize), and millet are the principal crops, while peanuts (groundnuts), sunflower seeds, and cotton are the main cash crops. The establishment of a national marketing board has improved crop distribution and encouraged higher crop production.

Industry. Almost all of Botswana's industries are associated with mining and agriculture, and there is virtually no manufacturing. The Botswana Development Corporation has assisted in the establishment of some industrial and commercial enterprises. Many of the smaller projects have been built in rural areas in an effort to decentralize employment.

Employment. In the early 1980s only about one-fifth of the potential labour force was formally employed as wage earners. The prospects of substantially increased employment depend largely on the increased development of the mining sector and, to a lesser degree, on the ability of the country to diversify its economy and create a wider industrial base.

Trade. The value of Botswana's exports has increased dramatically since the advent of mineral exploitation in the mid-1970s. There has also been a substantial increase in imports, however, and this has produced sizable trade deficits. Food, beverages, tobacco, manufactured goods, and fuel account for most of Botswana's imports.

Transport. During the 1970s the government began taking over the country's principal railway, which is owned and operated by The National Railways of Zimbabwe. The takeover has been slowed both by the cost of the needed equipment and by the shortage of trained personnel to operate the railroad.

A main north–south road was completed in 1980, giving Botswana an all-weather road that runs the entire length of the country. Botswana has, in addition, several thousand miles of gravel and dirt roads. Air Botswana maintains domestic service and, with other airlines, provides international connections for travellers.

Administration and social conditions. *The structure of government.* Legislative power is vested in the Parliament, which consists of the president and the National Assembly of 32 members elected by adult suffrage, four specially chosen members, and the attorney general. The president is the executive head of government; he is a member of and presides over the Cabinet, consisting of the vice president and other ministers who are members of the National Assembly. Elections for the presidency and National Assembly are held every five years. The House of Chiefs advises the government; no legislation affecting tribal affairs may be passed without reference to this house. A code of human rights is enforceable by the High Court. A nonpolitical public service commission controls all matters relating to the public service. The local government system operates through nine district councils, as well as four town councils located in Gaborone, Francistown, Selebi-Pikwe, and Lobatse.

The House of Chiefs

There are three nationalist parties, which represent more militant ideas than the ruling Botswana Democratic Party (BDP); they are the Botswana People's Party (BPP), the Botswana Independence Party (BIP), and the Botswana National Front (BNF). All four parties are national in the sense of having multitribal members; they usually attract both modern and tradition-minded supporters. The BDP, led by Sir Seretse Khama, assumed power after independence and has continued to rule the country. After Khama's death in 1980, Quett K.J. Masire, the vice president of Botswana and cofounder (with Khama) of the BDP, was elected president by the National Assembly.

Justice. The High Court, consisting of a chief justice and puisne (associate) judges, exercises jurisdiction over all criminal and civil cases. The Court of Appeals deals with matters emanating from the High Court. There are subordinate magistrates' courts and African courts with limited jurisdiction in the local administrative districts.

Education. One of the priorities of the government of Botswana has been the expansion and improvement of education at all levels. By 1980 there were more than 400 primary and 35 secondary schools, with a total enrollment of some 190,000 students. Most schools are run by the government. Advanced education is provided by teacher-training colleges and the University College of Botswana, in Gaborone. There is also a system of technical education throughout the country.

Health. Since independence the government has promoted the development of health clinics and posts throughout the country so that all citizens have access to medical treatment. There are several general hospitals. Care for mothers and children has been emphasized, and dental treatment was introduced in the 1970s.

Cultural life and institutions. The life of the majority of the people is still strongly influenced by tribal institutions and cultures; there is a rich tradition of folklore, music, and dancing. While not much vernacular literature of exceptional quality exists as yet, there are the beginnings of a modern vernacular literary tradition.

The government publishes the *Botswana Daily News* in Tswana and English, as well as a monthly journal, *Kutlwano*. A trilingual weekly is published in Mafikeng. The three nationalist parties publish their own monthly journals, *Masa* ("Dawn"; BPP), *Puo Pha* ("Straight Talk"; BNF), and *Therisanyo* ("Consultation"; BIP).

Radio Botswana, a government-owned station, broadcasts in both Tswana and English to all parts of the country. The programming includes entertainment (with an emphasis on local culture), government information services, and educational broadcasting. To promote ownership of radios, the license fee was abolished, and by the early 1980s there were some 68,000 radios in use in Botswana. Television transmitters relay programs from South Africa.

Prospects for the future. Despite Botswana's geographic and economic vulnerability, the government has pursued a remarkably independent foreign policy since independence. While increasing its links with other African governments, Botswana has promoted majority rule in Zimbabwe, South West Africa/Namibia, and South Africa. With other African leaders, President Khama carried on delicate negotiations with African nationalist guerrillas and with Western governments concerning Zimbabwe and South West Africa/Namibia. Internally, the government has continued its commitment to building a multiracial society in overt defiance of the apartheid system in neighbouring South Africa. The development of mining and subsequent strengthening of Botswana's economy has been an important factor in the independence of the country's foreign and internal policies.

BIBLIOGRAPHY

Geography: HARM J. DE BLIJ, *A Geography of Subsaharan Africa* (1964); ANTHONY SILLERY, *Africa: A Social Geography*, 2nd ed. (1972); ALAN B. MOUNTJOY and CLIFFORD EMBLETON, *Africa: A New Geographical Survey*, rev. ed. (1967); WILLIAM A. HANCE, *The Geography of Modern Africa*, 2nd ed. (1975).

Land, vegetation, and water resources: I.B. POLE-EVANS, *Report No. 2: A Reconnaissance Trip Through the Eastern Portion of the Bechuanaland Protectorate in Search of Pasture Grasses* (1930); A.J.C. MOLYNEUX, "A Contribution to the Geology of the Bechuanaland Protectorate," *Proceedings of the Rhodesia Scientific Association*, 6:73–86 (1907), and "Prospecting in Bechuanaland," *S. Afr. Min. Engng. J.*, 51:705–707 (1940); DARRELL RANDALL, *Factors of Economic Development and the Okovango Delta* (1957).

People, institutions, culture, and history: BOTSWANA SOCIETY. GABORONE, *Botswana Notes and Records* (annual); RICHARD P. STEVENS, *Historical Dictionary of the Republic of Botswana* (1975); JACK HALPERN, *South Africa's Hostages: Basutoland, Bechuanaland and Swaziland* (1965); VERNON GEORGE JOHN SHEDDICK, *The Southern Sotho* (1953); C.W. DE KIEWIET, *A History of South Africa: Social and Economic* (1941, reissued 1957); ERIC WALKER, *A History of Southern Africa*, 3rd ed. (1957, reissued 1968); RICHARD P. STEVENS, *Lesotho, Botswana and Swaziland* (1967); I. SCHAPERA, *A Handbook of Tswana Law and Custom*, 2nd ed. (1955, reprinted 1970), and *The Tswana* (1953, reissued 1968); ANTHONY SILLERY, *Botswana: A Short Political History* (1974), and *Sechele: The Story of an African Chief* (1954); TSHEKEDI KHAMA, *Bechuanaland and South Africa* (1955), and *Political Change in African Society: A Study of the Development of Representative Government* (1956).

Administration, and social, political, and constitutional affairs: ZDENEK ČERVENKA, *Republic of Botswana: A Brief Outline of Its Geographical Setting, History, Economy and Politics* (1970); COLIN LEGUM *et al.* (eds.), *Africa Contemporary Record* (annual); GREAT BRITAIN. COLONIAL OFFICE, *Annual Report on Bechuanaland* (to 1966), useful official reports reviewing all aspects of policy and development; GREAT BRITAIN. OFFICE OF COMMONWEALTH RELATIONS, *Basutoland, the Bechuanaland Protectorate and Swaziland: History of Discussions with the Union of South Africa, 1909–1939* (1952); RICHARD VENGROFF, *Botswana: Rural Development in the Shadow of Apartheid* (1977); MARY BENSON, *Tshekedi Khama* (1960), a biography.

Economy: PENELOPE HARTLAND-THUNBERG, *Botswana: An African Growth Economy* (1978); GREAT BRITAIN. HIGH COMMISSIONER FOR BASUTOLAND, THE BECHUANALAND PROTECTORATE AND SWAZILAND, *Basutoland, Bechuanaland Protectorate and Swaziland: Report of an Economic Survey Mission* (the Morse report) (1960); *National Development Plan, 1970–75* (1970); *National Development Plan, 1979–85* (1980).

(Co.L.)

Botticelli, Sandro

Living in late 15th-century Italy at a time of profound change in the course of art, Botticelli proved himself to

"The Birth of Venus," oil on canvas by Sandro Botticelli, *c.* 1485. In the Uffizi, Florence, Italy. 1.72 m × 2.79 m.
Anderson—Alinari

be a painter of individual sensibilities of the highest order—although he belonged to a slightly older generation than the creators of the High Renaissance style, he may be seen in his paintings to have been fully abreast of the currents of his day. Nonetheless, his reputation remained in eclipse for several hundred years after his death, until he was rediscovered at the end of the 19th century. At that time, in addition to an appreciation of his paintings for their exquisite linear rhythms and deep-hued colour, there evolved a highly romantic and subjective conception of their subjects. Despite the clarifications of 20th-century scholarship, much of this mysticism still remains in attempts to reach an understanding of his work. There is no doubt, however, that Botticelli was seeking in his painting to express the gods as the living and potent spirits they had been to the ancient peoples who had conceived them. To this end he sought, in ancient and contemporary authors, not a simple text to illustrate but rather a deeper understanding of Venus and her fellow Olympians as gods. He was so successful in this attempt that his "Birth of Venus" continues to express to modern viewers the very spirit of the Renaissance itself.

Early development. Reliable biographical information concerning Botticelli is, unfortunately, in short supply, a fact that is important to keep in mind, for he has been characterized variously as a painter of great erudition, as a pure aesthete who was indifferent to subject matter, as an artist imbued with Neoplatonic philosophy, and as a saintly spirit who, toward the end of his life, was profoundly affected by the theology of the reforming monk Savonarola. His very name is derived from his elder brother Giovanni, a pawnbroker who was called Il Botticello ("little barrel").

Birth and early training

Documentary evidence has established that Botticelli was born Alessandro di Mariano Filipepi in 1445 and that he was still in school in 1458 at the relatively advanced age of 13. Giorgio Vasari, a biographer of Renaissance Italian artists, reports that Botticelli's earliest training was in a goldsmith's shop, and a slender thread of evidence suggests that this may have been the shop of Apollonio di Giovanni and Marco del Buono, who are primarily known as manuscript illuminators and as painters of panels for wedding chests and furniture. Stock motifs from this shop recur in works that were produced by Botticelli and his shop, notably in the architectural frieze portraying the story of Horatius. Of Botticelli's subsequent apprenticeship to the painter Fra Filippo Lippi there is no doubt; most of Botticelli's earliest works have at one time or another carried an attribution to Lippi or his school, and in many cases the final attribution is still under debate. From Lippi, Botticelli learned a more intimately conceived version of the monumental and generalizing manner of the great innovator of Florentine painting Masaccio; the style that Botticelli learned owed much to Masaccio's handling of light and shade but was more concerned with detail and was directed to a softer sentiment. The influence of his Florentine contemporary Andrea del Verrocchio also is felt in Botticelli's earlier painting.

First commissions

By 1470 Botticelli had his own workshop. In that year he painted the "Fortitude" for the hall of the Arte di Mercanzia, a commission for which Piero Pollaiuolo, who painted six other Virtues, was primarily responsible; from this time the influence of the Pollaiuolo brothers may be seen in Botticelli's work. In 1472 Filippino Lippi (Fra Filippo's son) is mentioned as an apprentice in Botticelli's shop.

By January 1474 Botticelli had finished the "St. Sebastian," now in Berlin. From the beginning of the decade, the development of Botticelli's painting was characterized by a steady progression away from a full three-dimensional conception of a figure, lighted with softly blurred shadows, toward a conception based on low relief, bounded by continuous and rhythmic outline, the figure being lighted with bright and steady illumination. The "St. Sebastian" represents an early phase of this latter style, which is in close sympathy with the linear style of the Pollaiuoli.

Also in January 1474, Botticelli went to Pisa hoping to complete a series of frescoes begun by Benozzo Gozzoli for the Campo Santo, but he lost the commission, evidently because of dissatisfaction with an "Assumption of the Virgin" that he began for the Cappella dell'Incoronata in the Duomo, which he never finished and which was later destroyed.

The culmination of his career. "The Primavera," or "Allegory of Spring," painted about 1477, illustrates the next stage of Botticelli's development and "The Birth of Venus" (*c.* 1485) its culmination. Both were painted for the villa of Lorenzo di Pierfrancesca de' Medici at Castello; both are now in the Uffizi (Florence). The influence of the International style, a late-14th-century Gothic style in which natural details were rendered with vivid colour and realism, is a great part of the conception of "The Primavera" but is softened and subjected to Botticelli's new understanding of the art of antiquity. These three paintings—"Fortitude," "The Primavera," and "The Birth of Venus"—present Botticelli's art at its most familiar and most famous and are expressive of that quality for which it has always been primarily valued, whether characterized as "grace" as it was by Vasari in the 16th century, or described in terms of linear rhythm, as it was first by the English critic John Ruskin and later by art historians of the 20th century.

Characteristic paintings

In 1478 Botticelli painted a fresco (destroyed in 1494) of the conspirators hanged in the Pazzi uprising in 1478 in Florence. In 1480 he was commissioned by the Vespucci to paint, in competition with Ghirlandajo, the fresco of St. Augustine in the Church of the Ognissanti (where his father was buried two years later); and in 1481 he painted a fresco of the "Annunciation," which has since been detached, for the church of S. Martino della Scala.

From the summer of 1481 until the spring of 1482, Botticelli was in Rome at the invitation of Pope Sixtus IV to paint some of the papal portraits and three of the large frescoes on the wall of the Sistine Chapel, a commission in which such eminent painters as Perugino, Ghirlandajo, Cosimo Rosselli, Signorelli, Pinturricchio, and Piero di Cosimo also took part. While in Rome, he also painted a "St. Jerome" (now lost). The new understanding of ancient art that Botticelli combined with his earlier manner in "The Birth of Venus" was undoubtedly the result of this trip to Rome. In fact, his new acquaintance with the art of ancient Rome is strikingly evident in the frescoes he painted there, especially in the "Punishment of Korah" (Sistine Chapel, Vatican); in it a pedantic presentation of Roman forms and schemata (akin to Pinturricchio) is combined with harsh naturalism and monumentality. Although undoubtedly dictated by the nature and scale of the commission, these paintings are nonetheless counter to the direction his art had been taking and are among Botticelli's less happy efforts. It was not until several years after his return to Florence that he fully assimilated and most nobly expressed what he had learned in Rome with the paintings of the "Mars and Venus" and "The Birth of Venus" in 1485–86.

Botticelli returned to Florence by October 1482 with Perugino and Ghirlandajo; they were commissioned to paint, together with Piero Pollaiuolo and Biagio d'Antonio Tucci, the walls of the Sala dei Gigli in the Palazzo della Signoria, a project that was never realized. In 1483 Botticelli designed and supervised the painting of four panels for two wedding chests (cassoni) commissioned for the marriage of Giannozzo Pucci to Lucrezia Bini, and, at about the same time, he was again at work on a major fresco cycle with Perugino, Ghirlandajo, and Filippino Lippi, for Lorenzo the Magnificent's Villa della Spadaletto near Volterra.

By the end of 1484, Botticelli was at work on the "Virgin and Child with St. John the Baptist and St. John the Evangelist" for the Cappella di Agnolo de' Bardi in S. Spirito. The detached frescoes from the Tornabuoni-Lemmi Villa (now in the Louvre) were most probably painted in commemoration of the wedding of Lorenzo Tornabuoni in 1486. In 1487 he painted a tondo (circular painting), probably "The Madonna of the Pomegranate," for the Massai della Camera in the Palazzo della Signoria, and between 1488–90 he painted "The Annunciation" for the Guardi chapel in the Sta. Maria Maddalena dei Pazzi, as well as a "Coronation of the Virgin" for the Cappella di S. Eligio of the goldsmiths in the church of S. Marco.

In 1491 Botticelli served on a committee to decide upon a design for the facade of the Duomo of Florence, and in the same year he was commissioned to design the mosaic decoration for two vaults in the Cappella di S. Zenobius, which he did not complete. He and his brother Simone bought a house and some land near the gate of San Frediano in 1494. In 1495 he had an uncertain commission from Lorenzo di Pierfrancesco de' Medici to paint some things for his villa at Trebbio. In the summer of 1496 he painted a "St. Francis" in the convent of Sta. Maria di Monticelli near San Frediano, and in 1497 he was at work with some assistants on decorations for Lorenzo di Pierfrancesco's villa at Castello. He was living in Florence, in the quarter of Sta. Maria Novella, in 1498 (as is known from a tax return), and an entry in his brother's diary for 1499 indicates that Botticelli felt Savonarola's execution to have been unjust. In the same year he joined the Arte dei Medici e degli Speziali.

Late style and last years. Botticelli's late style—that is, his work of the last decade of the 15th century and the first decade of the 16th—is difficult to define, and its development is difficult to trace, in part because of the scarcity of fixed dates as points of reference. Early in the 1490s Botticelli worked to a grandeur of scale and conception that brought him, undoubtedly under the influence of new ideas being formulated in particular by Leonardo da Vinci, to the very brink of a High Renaissance style without quite passing into it.

Leonardo's influence

Although Botticelli's carefully orchestrated sequences of formal and emotional themes and responses reflect the influence of Leonardo, the latter's treatment of light and deep shadow, his sfumato, did not interest him. Particularly revealing in this respect are two paintings of the "Pietà," one in Munich (Alte Pinakothek) and the other in Milan (Museo Poldi Pezzoli). In these examples Botticelli's use of colour and light, his handling of masses, and his low-relief style much more closely anticipate the youthful manner of Michelangelo, as exemplified by his "Doni Madonna," than the manner of Leonardo. The Munich "Pietà" presents a grouping of figures and poses that is unmistakably related to the Flemish master Rogier van der Weyden's "Descent from the Cross" (Prado, Madrid) but conceived in a native Italian style, a hair-breadth away from the High Renaissance.

The extraordinary "Mystic Nativity" in London, dated to 1501, occupies a pivotal point in Botticelli's development. It shows him at work on a smaller scale, working with a richer and more deeply saturated colour scheme. His brushwork is looser, his forms more abstractly modelled, and space is conceived in a conventionalized manner, which has been described as archaic but which also, together with his new colour scheme, owes something to a renewed interest in the art of northern Europe. The painting carries an inscription in Greek, which indicates that the subject is not based on the biblical accounts of the Nativity in the Gospels but on the book of Revelations; moreover, the apocalyptic vision of St. John is recreated in the Italy of 1500.

This painting has been cited as evidence of Botticelli's involvement with Savonarola's theology (which also was apocalyptic), an argument that is fortified by the account of Botticelli's sympathy with Savonarola in his brother's diary and by Vasari's statement that he was a follower of him. The issue is not settled, however, and, while the "Mystic Nativity" is most unusual in its treatment of the subject, it also bears important iconographical parallels with the Flemish Hugo van der Goes's "Portinari Altarpiece," for example. The identification of the Madonna with the Apocalyptic Woman, moreover, is commonplace in 15th-century Italian art. Thus, the notion that Botticelli is creating a mystic style on Savonarolan example must remain suspect.

Retreat from the "grand manner"

From a point in the mid-1490s, when he seemed on the verge of achieving a style in the "grand manner," Botticelli inexplicably retreated, beginning with "The Calumny of Apelles" of *c.* 1495, continuing with "The Tragedy of Lucretia" and "The Story of Virginia Romana," the "Mystic Nativity" of 1501, the "Magdalene at the Foot of the Cross," and ending with the latest paintings known by him, the series devoted to the life of St. Zenobius, now in London, New York, and Dresden. His progression is marked by an increasing diminution of scale and the adoption of consciously old-fashioned formats modelled on northern examples and on the conventions of the cassoni painters of his youth. He uses expressively and decoratively distorted figures conceived with no regard for anatomical verisimilitude. Also evident in his later work is the more deeply saturated colour scheme, based on rainbow hues, which has already been mentioned with reference to the "Mystic Nativity." Nothing, however, quite anticipates the St. Zenobius panels. In them Botticelli painted a series of visions in which the stylistic characteristics outlined above may roughly be said to apply but with significant modifications: the settings are rendered in a way that recalls the clarity of the earlier architectural perspectives attributed to the architect Luciano Laurana, and the works are painted in purely abstract and non-naturalistic colour planes that resemble the early-15th-century paintings of Fra Angelico. Botticelli peopled these panels with figures of the most intense simplicity and emotion.

Last years

Even in the last decade of his life, facts about Botticelli are still meagre. A letter of 1502 from Francesco de' Malatesti to Isabella d'Este suggested that she commission Botticelli to complete the decoration of her *studiolo,* noting him to be an excellent painter and at the moment unoccupied. In November of the same year Botticelli was accused of sodomy, but the charges were evidently dropped. He was a member of a commission appointed in 1504 to decide where to place the "David" of Michelangelo. That his financial situation was less than prosperous during these last years is demonstrated by the fact that, between 1503 and 1505, when he settled the account, he was behind in his payment of dues to the Compagnia di San Luca, the artists' confraternity. Botticelli died on May 17, 1510, and was buried in the Church of the Ognissanti, Florence.

The evidence clearly indicates that Botticelli had a successful career, following conventional lines, which brought him important patrons and financial rewards. The slight indications of financial unsteadiness from the last decade of his life tend to support Vasari's claim that Botticelli was careless of his money. His ecclesiastical commissions included work for all the major churches of Florence and were crowned by his being summoned to Rome on a papal commission to take part in the decoration of the Sistine Chapel; his private commissions included work for the Palazzo della Signoria, the administrative centre of Florence, and for various members of the Medici family. His chief patron was Lorenzo di Pierfrancesco, for whom, in addition to the works mentioned above, he undertook an important series of illustrations for Dante's *Divina commedia.*

Posthumous reputation. Botticelli lived in a time that saw a rapid and profoundly considered change in painting. Because he was of an older generation than the great fathers of the High Renaissance style, he cuts rather a poor figure in the criticism and historical accounts of the centuries following his death, insofar as he is mentioned at all. Not until the Pre-Raphaelite artists of late-19th-century England, particularly Dante Gabriel Rossetti, were his due merits recognized and acclaimed. The critics of that day and afterward, such as John Ruskin, Walter Pater, and Bernard Berenson, wrote the pioneering accounts analyzing his style, and these still form the foundation of modern criticism.

Botticelli's restoration to fame derived, however, from an aesthetic and historical attitude that was itself of a very particular colour and bias, one based on a highly romantic conception of the Florence in which he lived. Thus, there grew up around Botticelli an aura of myth and fantasy that arose from a highly individual and subjective reading of both the subjects and formal content of his paintings. Although modern art history has since done much to dispel this aura, part of its mystery and mystification still remains.

In the 20th century a great amount of scholarly attention has been concentrated on the complex problem of Botticelli's subject matter. Scholars have sought to isolate its sources in particular poetic and philosophical texts and in the understanding of these texts by the Humanists of the Medici circle. This done, they have gone on to seek an understanding of Botticelli's art through the measurement of the system of thought expressed in these texts against their expression in the style of Botticelli's paintings.

The most brilliant example of this approach was an essay by the German art historian Aby Warburg, which, of itself, established an entire school of art history. In an attempt to understand the historical and psychological import of the linear style of Botticelli and his contemporaries, Warburg subjected the texts behind "The Primavera" and "The Birth of Venus" to close philological scrutiny and then incorporated his findings into an analysis of Renaissance formulas for expressing emotion. Subsequent studies sought the basis of Botticelli's pictures in the poetry, philosophy, and scholarship of Humanists contemporary with him.

Warburg's contribution

Although the complexities of the imagery of Botticelli's paintings with religious subject matter have been fully appreciated, if not completely understood, primary attention has been focussed upon his paintings with Classical and mythological subject matter—in particular the "Mars and Venus," "The Primavera," and "The Birth of Venus."

The precise significance of the subjects of these paintings still remains a matter of vigorous debate, but this much can be said with confidence. The approach to the subject matter of these paintings is as new and as radically conceived as any of the contemporary innovations in style. The paintings are not mere illustrations of particular texts; rather, each depends upon several texts and upon attempts to define fully the particular nature of the subject depicted. Therefore, in "The Calumny of Apelles," some elements derive from the ancient Greek satirist Lucian, some derive from Guarino Veronese's translation of Lucian, and some derive from Leon Battista Alberti's paraphrase of Lucian, and other sources may be ascertained as well. Thus, Botticelli's conception of the painting may be seen to depend upon the disciplined gathering and collation of several texts. The same is true for "The Primavera" and "The Birth of Venus," which are founded in Lucretius, Horace, Ovid, and other Classical authors severally. Even these texts alone may be insufficient to explain Botticelli's imagery: contemporary philosophical exegeses of the gods may be required in order to reach a complete understanding of his remarkably unique paintings.

MAJOR WORKS

"The Madonna of the Guides of Faenza" (*c.* 1468; Louvre, Paris); "Judith and Holofernes," 2 panels (*c.* 1469; Uffizi, Florence); "Fortitude" (1470; Uffizi); "St. Sebastian" (1474; Staatliche Museen Preussischer Kulturbesitz, Berlin); "The Adoration of the Magi" (*c.* 1475; Uffizi); "The Primavera" ("Allegory of Spring"; 1477–78; Uffizi); "Portrait of a Young Man" (National Gallery, London); "Giuliano de' Medici" (probably after 1478; National Gallery of Art, Washington, D.C.); "Madonna of the Eucharist" (Isabella Stewart Gardner Museum, Boston); Sistine Chapel frescoes (1481–82; Vatican); "The Adoration of the Magi" (1482; National Gallery of Art, Washington, D.C.); "Pallas and the Centaur" (*c.* 1485; Uffizi); "The Madonna of the Magnificat" (*c.* 1485; Uffizi); "Mars and Venus" (*c.* 1485; National Gallery, London); "The Birth of Venus" (*c.* 1485; Uffizi); "Virgin and Child with St. John the Baptist and St. John the Evangelist" (1484–85; Staatliche Museen Preussischer Kulturbesitz, Berlin); "The Madonna of the Pomegranate" (*c.* 1487; Uffizi); "The Annunciation" (1488–90; Uffizi); "Coronation of the Virgin" (1490; Uffizi); "The Calumny of Apelles" (*c.* 1495; Uffizi); "St. Augustine in His Cell" (*c.* 1495; Uffizi); "The Tragedy of Lucretia" (*c.* 1499; Isabella Stewart Gardner Museum, Boston); "The Story of Virginia Romana" (1499; Accademia Carrara, Bergamo); "Magdalene at the Foot of the Cross" (*c.* 1500; Fogg Art Museum, Cambridge, Massachusetts); "Scenes from the Life of St. Zenobius" (*c.* 1500–05, including his latest known works; Gemäldegalerie, Dresden; National Gallery, London; and Metropolitan Museum of Art, New York); "Mystic Nativity" (1501; National Gallery, London).

BIBLIOGRAPHY. The principal monographic studies are: HEINRICH ULMANN, *Sandro Botticelli* (1893), in German; HERBERT HORNE, *Alessandro Filipepi, Commonly Called Sandro Botticelli, Painter of Florence* (1908); WILHELM BODE, *Sandro Botticelli* (1921), in German; and ARGUST SCHMARSOW, *Sandro del Botticello* (1923); YUKIO YASHIRO, *Sandro Botticelli,* 2nd ed., 3 vol. (1929); ADOLFO VENTURI, *Botticelli* (1925), in Italian; JACQUES MESNIL, *Botticelli* (1938), in French; SERGIO BETTINI, *Botticelli* (1942); G.C. ARGAN, *Botticelli* (1957); ROBERTO SALVINI, *Tutta la pittura del Botticelli,* 2 vol. (1958; Eng. trans., *All the Paintings of Botticelli,* 1965); and MICHAEL LEVEY, *The Complete Paintings of Botticelli* (1969). Important studies of particular paintings include: ABY WARBURG, *Sandro Botticellis "Geburt der Venus" und Frühling* (1893), in *Gesammelte Schriften* (1932); R. FORSTER in *Jahrbuch der königlich preussischen Kunstsammlungen* (1887); EDGAR WIND in *Pagan Mysteries in the Renaissance,* rev. ed. (1967); and articles in the *Journal of the Warburg and Courtauld Institutes* by RUDOLF WITTKOWER, vol. 2 (1939), by E.H. GOMBRICH, vol. 8 (1945), and by CHARLES DEMPSEY, vol. 31 (1968). For further documentation Horne is especially valuable; see also the bibliographical references cited in the works of Salvini and Levey.

Bourbon, House of

The House of Bourbon is one of the greatest of the formerly sovereign dynasties of Europe. It provided reigning kings of France from 1589 to 1792 and from 1814 to 1830, after which another Bourbon reigned as king of the French until 1848; kings or queens of Spain from 1700 to 1808, from 1814 to 1868, and from 1874 to 1931; dukes of Parma from 1731 to 1735, from 1748 to 1802, and from 1847 to 1859; kings of Naples and of Sicily from 1734 to 1808 and of the Two Sicilies from 1816 to 1860; kings of Etruria from 1801 to 1807; and ducal sovereigns of Lucca from 1815 to 1847. The present article attempts a rapid survey of the dynasty as a whole, relying mainly on genealogical tables to display necessary details. In these tables the names and titles of sovereigns are mostly anglicized, but those of other persons are mostly given in the original form, except where princesses, having married into another country, are better known under that country's name for them. The tables also omit perforce the Bourbon bastards, whose multitude lends some colour to the popular notion that the "Bourbon nose" (larger and more prominent than the normal aquiline) betokens a "Bourbon temperament" or enormous appetite for sexual intercourse.

Origins. The House of Bourbon is a branch of the House of Capet, which constituted the so-called third race of France's kings. King Louis IX, a Capetian of the "direct line," was the ancestor of all the Bourbons through his sixth son, Robert count of Clermont (see Table 1). When the "direct line" died out in 1328, the House of Valois, genealogically senior to the Bourbons, prevented the latter from accession to the French crown until 1589. The Valois, however, established the so-called Salic Law of Succession, under which the crown passed through males according to primogeniture, not through females. On this principle, the senior Bourbon became the rightful king of France on the extinction of the legitimate male line of the Valois.

Robert of Clermont had married the heiress of the lordship of Bourbon (Bourbon-l'Archambault, in the modern *département* of Allier). This lordship was made a duchy for his son Louis I in 1327 and so gave its name to the dynasty. From this duchy, the nucleus of the future province of Bourbonnais, the elder Bourbons, mainly through marriages, expanded their territory southeastward and southward. On their western frontier, meanwhile, the countship of La Marche (acquired by Louis I in 1322 in exchange for Clermont) was held from 1327 by a junior line of Louis I's descendants, who soon added the distant countship of Vendôme to their holdings.

The first ducs de Bourbon

The title of duc de Bourbon passed in 1503 to Charles de Bourbon-Montpensier, who was to become famous as constable of France. His later treason led to the confiscation of his lands by the French crown in the year of his death, 1527. Headship of the House of Bourbon then passed to the line of La Marche-Vendôme (see again Table 1).

Table 1: The Bourbon Descent from Louis IX of France

- LOUIS IX (1214–70) king of France = Margaret of Provence
  - PHILIP III (1245–85) king of France
    - (kings of France to 1589)
  - 4 other sons
  - Robert (1256–1318) count of Clermont = Béatrix de Bourbon
    - Louis I (1279–1342) duc de Bourbon = Marie de Hainaut
      - Pierre I (1311–56) duc de Bourbon = Isabelle de Valois
        - Louis II (1337–1410) duc de Bourbon = Anne dauphine d'Auvergne
          - Jean I (c. 1381–1434) duc de Bourbon = Marie de Berry, comtesse de Montpensier
            - Charles I (1401–56) duc de Bourbon = Agnes of Burgundy
              - Jean II (1427–88) duc de Bourbon = (1) Jeanne de France; (2) Catherine d'Armagnac; (3) Jeanne de Vendôme
              - Charles II (c. 1434–88) archbishop of Lyon
              - Louis (1438–82) bishop of Liège
              - Pierre II (1439–1503) sire de Beaujeu, duc de Bourbon = Anne of France
                - Suzanne (1491–1521) = Charles de Montpensier
                - Charles (died young)
              - 7 others including Isabella (d. 1465) = Charles the Bold
            - Louis I (d. 1486) comte de Montpensier = (1) Jeanne d'Auvergne; (2) Gabrielle de La Tour d'Auvergne
              - Gilbert (1445–96) comte de Montpensier = Clara di Gonzaga
                - Louis II (1488–1501) comte de Montpensier
                - Charles (1490–1527) comte de Montpensier, duc de Bourbon = Suzanne de Bourbon
                  - 3 sons died young
                - François (d. 1515) duc de Châtellerault
                - Louise (d. 1561) = (1) André de Chauvigny; (2) Louis de La Roche-sur-Yon
                - Renée (d. 1539) = Antoine duke of Lorraine
                - Anne (died young)
          - 3 others
        - 7 daughters including 1. Blanche (1335–61) = Pedro of Castile 2. Jeanne (1338–78) = CHARLES V of France
      - 2 sons died young
      - 4 daughters, including Béatrix = John king of Bohemia
      - Jacques I (c. 1315–61) comte de La Marche = Jeanne de Châtillon-Saint-Pol
        - Pierre (d. 1362) comte de La Marche
        - Jean (1337–93) comte de La Marche = Catherine de Vendôme
          - Charlotte (d. 1434) = John II of Cyprus
          - Jacques II (1367–1438) comte de La Marche = (1) Béatrix of Navarre; (2) Joan II of Naples
            - Eléonore = Bernard d'Armagnac comte de Pardiac
          - Louis (c. 1376–1446) comte de Vendôme = (1) Blanche de Roucy; (2) Jeanne de Laval
            - Jean (1429–78) comte de Vendôme = Isabelle de Beauvau
              - François (1470–95) comte de Vendôme = Marie de Luxembourg
                - Charles (1489–1537) duc de Vendôme (1515) = Françoise d'Alençon
                  - Louis (1514–16) comte de Marle
                  - Antoine (1518–62) duc de Vendôme = Jeanne d'Albret titular queen of Navarre
                    - HENRY (1553–1610) titular king of Navarre 1572 king of France, as HENRY IV, 1589 (see Table 2) = (1) Margaret of France; (2) Marie de Médicis
                    - 2 sons died young
                    - Catherine (1558–1604) = Henry duke of Lorraine
                  - François (1519–46) seigneur d'Enghien
                  - Louis (1522–25)
                  - Charles (1523–90) cardinal de Bourbon
                  - Jean (1528–57) comte de Soissons = Marie de Saint-Pol
                  - Louis (1530–69) prince de Condé (see Table 3)
                  - 6 daughters including Marguerite (1516–89) = François duc de Nevers
                - Jacques (1490–91)
                - François (1491–1545) comte de Saint-Pol = Adrienne d'Estouteville
                  - François (1537–1546) duc d'Estouteville
                  - Marie (1539–1604) = Jean comte de Soissons
                - Louis (1493–1557) archbishop of Sens
                - Antoinette (1494–1584) = Claude de Guise
                - Louise (1495–1545) abbess of Fontevrault
              - Louis (d. c. 1520) prince de La Roche-sur-Yon = Louise de Montpensier
                - Louis (1513–82) duc de Montpensier 1539 = (1) Jacqueline de Longwy; (2) Catherine de Guise
                  - François (1543–92) duc de Montpensier = Renée d'Anjou-Mézières
                    - Henry (1573–1608) duc de Montpensier = Henriette de Joyeuse
                      - Marie (1605–27) duchesse de Montpensier = Gaston duc d'Orléans (see Table 2)
                  - Charlotte (1547–82) = William the Silent, prince of Orange
              - 6 daughters
          - Jean (d. c. 1458) seigneur de Carency (male line extinct 1515)
        - Jacques (d. 1417) seigneur de Préaux (male line extinct 1429)
    - 2 other sons
    - 3 daughters

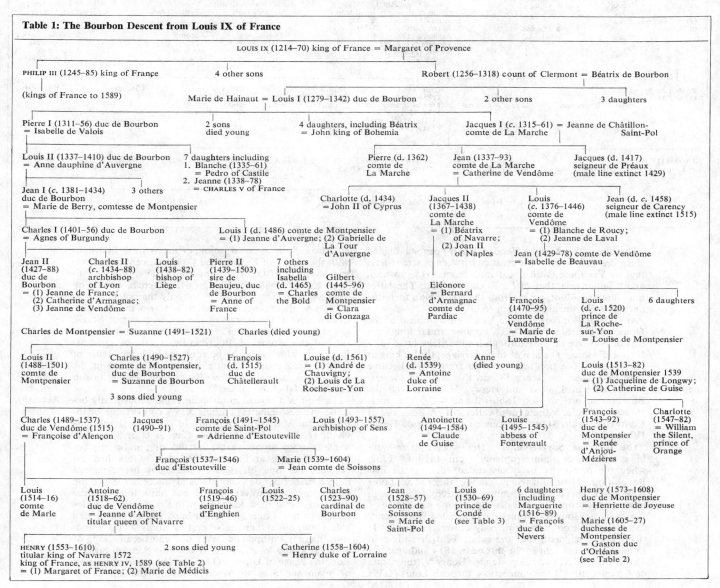

Table 2: The Bourbon Kings of France, with the House of Orléans to 1830

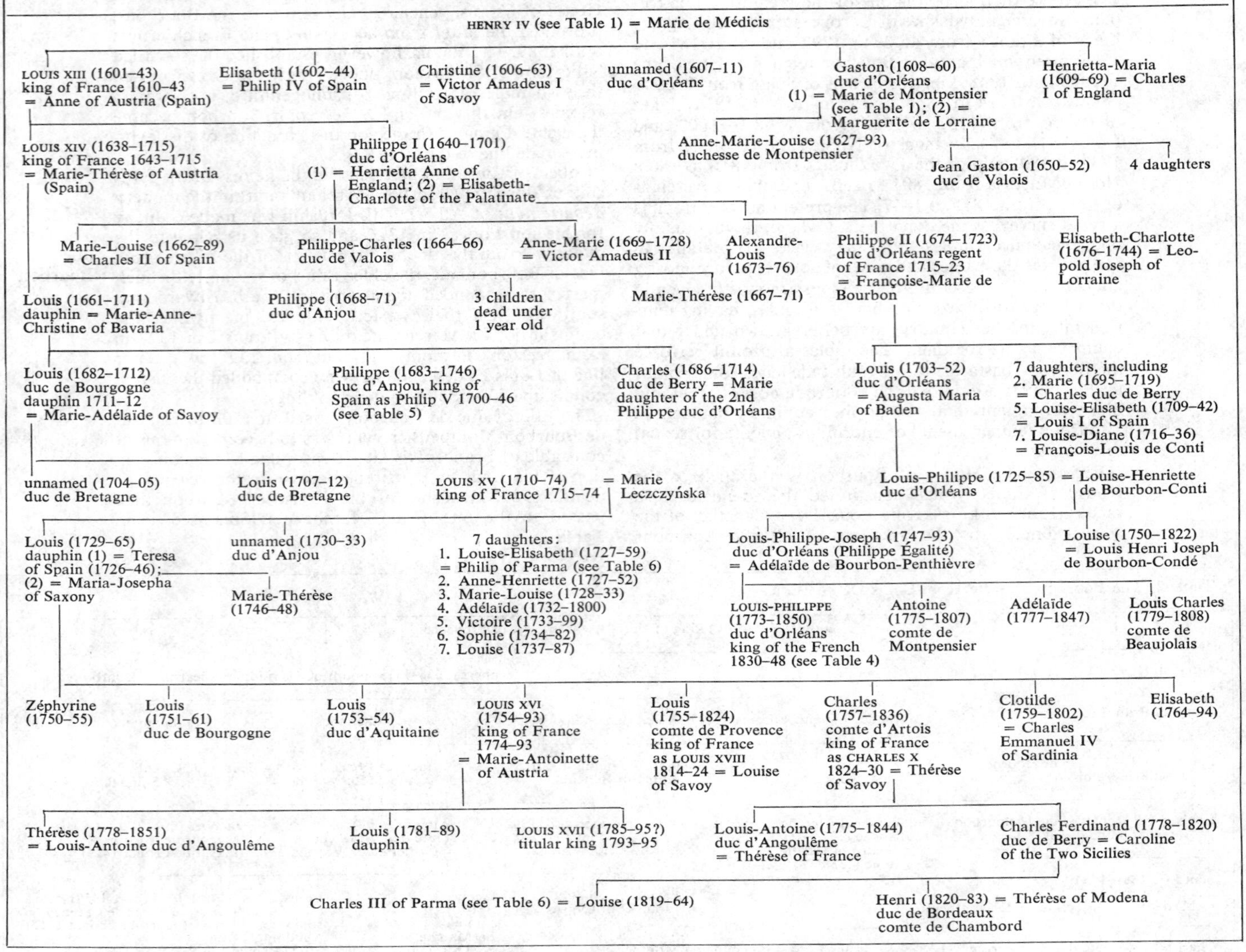

The line of La Marche-Vendôme had been subdivided since the end of the 15th century between a senior line, that of Vendôme (with ducal rank from 1515 onward), and a junior one, that of La Roche-sur-Yon. The latter line obtained Montpensier from the constable's forfeited heritage (with ducal rank from 1539).

Antoine de Bourbon, duc de Vendôme and head of the House of Bourbon from 1537, became titular king-consort of Navarre in 1555 through his marriage in 1548 to Jeanne d'Albret. The son of that marriage, titular king of Navarre in succession to his mother from 1572, became

The French kingdom

king of France, as Henry IV, on the death of the last Valois king in 1589. From Henry IV descend all the Bourbon sovereigns (see Tables 2 and 4–7). The great House of Condé, with its ramifications of Soissons and of Conti (see Table 3), was descended from one of Henry IV's uncles.

The Bourbon Sovereignties. Henry IV's heirs were kings of France uninterruptedly from 1610 to 1792, when the monarchy was "suspended" during the first Revolution. Most illustrious among them was Louis XIV (*q.v.*), who brought absolute monarchy to its zenith in western Europe. Table 2 displays (1) the senior line of Bourbon, or House of France, as descended from Henry IV, the succession running directly down to Louis XVII (who never reigned), and thereafter being resumed in Louis XVIII (brought to the throne in 1814 and again in 1815), Charles X, and the pretender Henry V (the comte de Chambord); (2) the connection, through Louis XIV's grandson Philippe duc d'Anjou, of the Spanish Bourbons with the House of France; and (3) the descent of the collateral House of Orléans from Louis XIV's brother Philippe I to Louis-Philippe king of the French. Louis-Philippe's descendants, including not only the potential pretenders to the French succession but also the Bourbon descendants of the heiress of the last emperor of Brazil, are shown in Table 4. The last-mentioned princes constituted the House of Bourbon-Brazil, or of Orléans-Braganza, which is not to be confused with the House of Borbón-Braganza, a Spanish branch originating in the Portuguese marriage of the infante Don Gabriel (a son of Charles III of Spain; see Table 5).

Accession in Spain

The Bourbon accession to Spain came about partly because the descendants of Louis XIV's consort, the Spanish infanta Marie-Thérèse, were in 1700 the closest surviving relatives of the childless Charles II of Spain (see HABSBURG, HOUSE OF; SPAIN, HISTORY OF); and partly because, although at her marriage the Infanta had renounced her Spanish rights, Charles by his testament named one of her descendants as his successor. Since the other powers, however, would not have tolerated the union of the Spanish kingdom with the French, Charles named neither Louis XIV's heir apparent nor the latter's eldest son, but rather the second of Louis XIV's grandsons, namely Philippe duc d'Anjou, who became king of Spain as Philip V. After the War of the Spanish Succession, the Peace of Utrecht (1713) left Philip in possession of Spain and Spanish America but obliged him to re-

Table 3: Condé, Conti, and Soissons

Louis I (1530–69) prince de Condé (see Table 1)
= (1) Eléonore de Roye; (2) Françoise d'Orléans-Longueville

Henry I (1552–88)
prince de Condé
= (1) Marie de Clèves-Nevers;
(2) Charlotte de La Trémoille

François (1558–1614)
prince de Conti
= (1) Jeanne de Coësme;
(2) Marguerite de Guise

Charles
(1562–94)
cardinal
de Vendôme

5 others

Charles (1566–1612)
comte de Soissons
= Anne de Montafié

2 sons died
young

Catherine
(1574–95)

Eléonore (1587–1619)
= Philip William of
Orange-Nassau

Henry II (1588–1646)
prince de Condé
= Charlotte de Montmorency

Louis (1604–41)
comte de Soissons

3 daughters:
1. Louise (1603–37)
= Henri d'Orléans
duc de Longueville;
2. Marie (1606–92)
= Thomas de Savoie
prince de Carignan;
3. Charlotte-Anne
(1608–23)

Anne-Geneviève
(1619–79) = Henri
d'Orléans duc de
Longueville

Louis II (1621–86)
duc d'Enghien till 1646,
then prince de Condé
= Claire-Clémence de Maillé-Brézé

Armand (1629–66)
prince de Conti
= Anne-Marie Martinozzi
niece of Cardinal Mazarin

Henri-Jules (1643–1709)
prince de Condé = Anne of Bavaria
daughter of Edward of the Palatinate

2 sons died
in infancy

1 son died
in infancy
1658

Louis-Armand I
(1661–85)
prince de Conti
= Marie-Anne legitimated
daughter of Louis XIV

François-Louis (1664–1709)
comte de La Marche 1677–85,
then prince de Conti
= Marie-Thérèse de
Bourbon-Condé

Henri
(1657–70)

Louis III (1668–1710)
duc de Bourbon
= Louise-Françoise
legitimated daughter of Louis XIV

2 sons died
in infancy

6 daughters
including
1. Marie-Thérèse (1666–1732)
= François-Louis de Bourbon-Conti
4. Anne-Louise-Bénédicte
(1676–1753) = Louis-Auguste duc
du Maine legitimated son of
Louis XIV
5. Marie-Anne (1678–1718)
= Louis-Joseph duc de Vendôme

Louis-Armand II
(1695–1727)
prince de Conti
= Louise-Elisabeth
de Bourbon-Condé

3 sons died
in infancy
and 3 daughters,
including
1. Marie-Anne
(1689–1720)
= Louis-Henri
duc de Bourbon

Louis-Henri
(1692–1740)
duc de Bourbon
= (1) Marie-Anne
de Bourbon-Conti;
(2) Charlotte of
Hesse-Rheinfels

2 other sons:
1. Charles (1700–60)
comte de Charolais;
2. Louis (1707–71)
comte de Clermont

6 daughters
including
2. Louise-
Elisabeth
= Louis-
Armand II
prince de Conti

Louis-François
(1717–76)
prince de Conti
= Louise-Diane
(1716–36) daughter of
the regent duc d'Orléans (see Table 2)

3 sons died
in infancy

Louise-Henriette
(1726–59)
= Louis-Philippe
(1725–85)
duc d'Orléans
(see Table 2)

Louis-Joseph (1736–1818) prince de Condé
= Godefride de Rohan-Soubise

Louis-François-Joseph (1734–1814)
prince de Conti = Maria Fortunata d'Este

Louis-Henri-Joseph (1756–1830) duc de Bourbon
= Louise d'Orléans (1750–1822; see Table 2)

Louise-Adélaïde
(1757–1824)
Benedictine nun

Louis-Antoine (1772–1804) duc d'Enghien

Table 4: The House of Orléans from 1830

LOUIS-PHILIPPE (see Table 2) = Marie-Amélie of the Two
king of the French 1830–1848 Sicilies (see Table 7)

Ferdinand
(1810–42)
duc d'Orléans
1830–42
= Helena of
Mecklenburg-
Schwerin

Louis
(1814–96)
duc de Nemours
= Victoria of
Saxe-Coburg

François
(1818–1900)
prince de
Joinville
= Francesca
of Brazil

Charles
(1820–29)
duc de
Penthièvre

Henri (1822–97)
duc d'Aumale
= Carolina daughter
of principe di Salerno
(see Table 7)

Antoine (1824–90)
duc de Montpensier
= infanta Luisa
(see Table 5)

3 daughters:
1. Louise (1812–50)
= Leopold I of the Belgians
2. Christine (1813–39)
= Frederick William of
Württemberg
3. Clementine (1817–1907)
= Augustus of Saxe-Coburg

Louis (1845–66)
prince de Condé

François (1854–72)
duc de Guise

Françoise
(1844–1925)
= duc de Chartres

Pierre
(1845–1919)
duc de Penthièvre

Fernando
(1859–73)

Antonio (1866–1930)
duca di Galliera
= infanta Eulalia
(see Table 5)

2 sons

Luis
(1867–74)

3 daughters, including
2. Isabel (1848–1919)
= comte de Paris
3. Mercedes (1860–78)
= Alfonso XII of Spain

Gaston (1842–1922) = Isabela (1846–1921)
comte d'Eu heiress of Pedro II of Brazil

Ferdinand
(1844–1910)
duc d'Alençon
= Sophia of Bavaria

Pedro
(1875–1940)
renounced
succession 1908

Luis
(1878–1920)
= Pia, daughter
of Alfonso di Caserta (see Table 7)

Antonio
(1881–1918)

1 daughter

Emmanuel (1872–1931) = Henriette of Belgium
duc de Vendôme, duc
d'Alençon

Pedro Enrique (1909–) = Maria of Bavaria

3 daughters

Charles Philippe (1905–
duc de Nemours
= Marguerite Watson

Henri comte de Paris = Isabelle (1911–)

4 others

6 sons

Louis-Philippe-Albert (1838–94) comte de Paris
= Isabel daughter of Antoine duc de Montpensier

Robert (1840–1910) duc de Chartres = Françoise de Joinville

2 daughters

Robert
(1866–83)

Henri
(1867–1901)

Jean (1874–1940) = Isabelle
duc de Guise daughter of comte
de Paris

Louis-Philippe-Robert (1869–1926)
duc d'Orléans = Maria of Austria

4 daughters

Ferdinand (1884–1924)
duc de Montpensier

Isabelle of Orléans-Braganza = Henri (1908–) comte de Paris

3 daughters

Marie-Thérèse of Württemberg = Henri (1933–) comte de Clermont

4 other sons

6 daughters

François (1961–)

Jean (1965–)

2 daughters

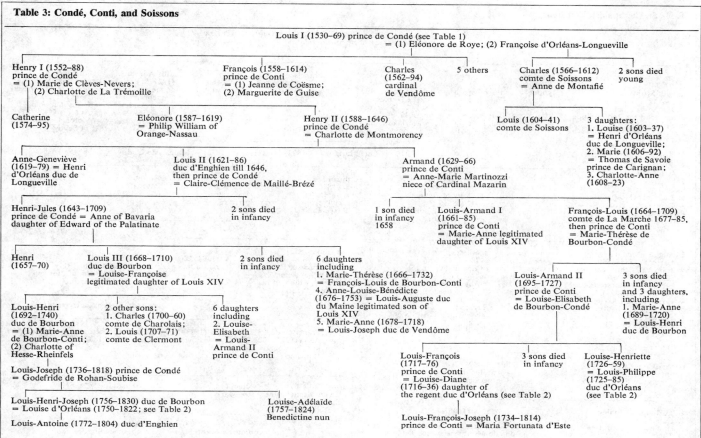

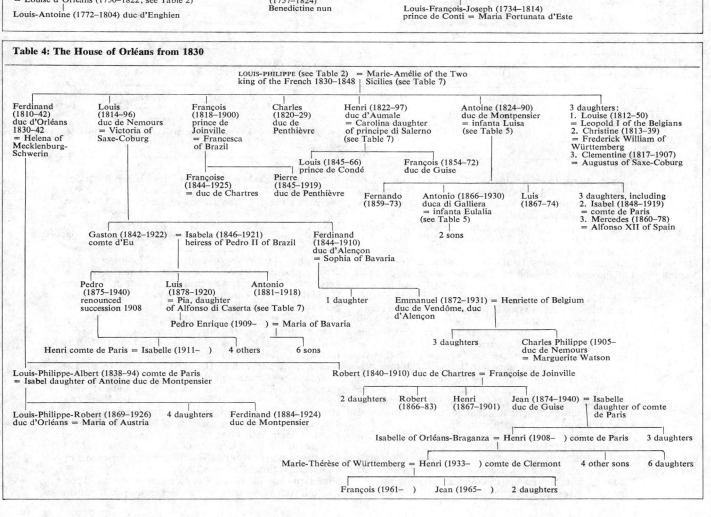

Table 5: The Spanish Bourbons

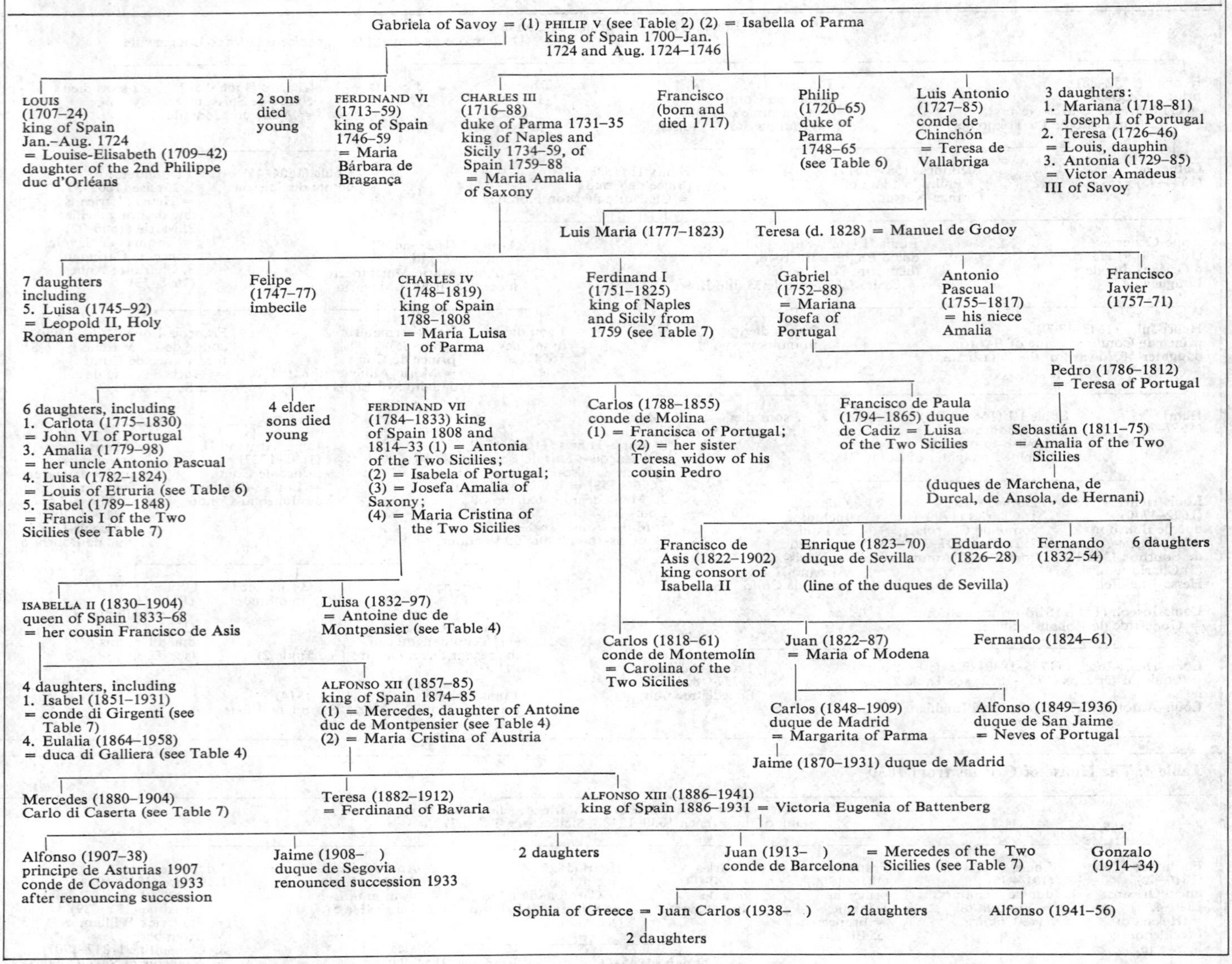

nounce any natural right that he or his descendants might have to France. Table 5 shows how the Spanish Bourbons all descend from Philip V; it also shows the origin of the branches of Parma and of Naples-Sicily.

The infante Don Carlos, the future Charles III of Spain, was the founder of the Bourbon fortunes in Italy. The eldest son of Philip V's second marriage, he became duke

Parma and Naples-Sicily

of Parma in 1731 by right of his mother, heiress of the last Farnese dukes; and in 1734, during the War of the Polish Succession, he conquered the Kingdom of Naples-Sicily (Kingdom of the Two Sicilies) for himself. Though the settlement of 1735–38 obliged him to renounce Parma in order to win international recognition as king of Naples-Sicily, Parma was eventually secured for his brother Philip (Don Felipe) under the Treaty of Aix-la-Chapelle in 1748—with the proviso, however, that he and his heirs should renounce it in the event that they succeeded to Naples-Sicily or to Spain. Finally, when Don Carlos became king of Spain as Charles III in 1759, he resigned Naples-Sicily to his third son Ferdinand on the express condition that that kingdom and Spain should never be united under one sovereign.

Table 6 shows the descendants of Philip of Parma, Table 7 those of Ferdinand I of Naples–Sicily.

Etruria and Lucca

The Kingdom of Etruria (1801–07) was a contrivance of the Napoleonic period. Devised by the French for the House of Bourbon-Parma in compensation for the impending annexation of Parma to France at a time when France still needed the goodwill of the Spanish Bourbons, it was dissolved as soon as Napoleon was ready to depose the latter. The Bourbon Duchy of Lucca (1815–47), on the other hand, was a creation of the Congress of Vienna: having assigned Parma to Napoleon's estranged consort Marie-Louise for her lifetime, the Congress had to find some alternative compensation for the still-dispossessed Bourbons. The Treaty of Paris of 1817, however, prescribed that on Marie-Louise's death Parma should revert to the Bourbons, who in 1847 renounced Lucca to the Habsburgs of Tuscany nine weeks before succeeding her (see again Table 6).

In France, the senior or "legitimate" line of the Bourbons, restored to sovereignty in France after the Napoleonic Wars, was deposed at the Revolution of 1830. The House of Orléans, which took the legitimate line's place, was in turn deposed in the Revolution of 1848. The Bourbons of Parma and of the Two Sicilies were dethroned in 1859–60, in the course of the unification of Italy under the House of Savoy. The Spanish Bourbons, after many disturbances in the 19th century, lost their sovereignty in 1931; but the Law of Succession promulgated in Spain in 1947 and General Franco's subsequent gestures in favour of Don Juan Carlos (see again Table 5 and SPAIN, HISTORY OF) gave solid grounds for expecting a Bourbon restoration in the 1970s.

Solidarity and discord. The accession of the duc d'Anjou to Spain would never have been secured without the resolute support of his grandfather, the French king; and similarly the Bourbon sovereignties in Italy owed their establishment chiefly to the Bourbon power in Spain. Dynastic harmony between France and Spain, however, was momentarily suspended in 1718–20, when France took part in the War of the Quadruple Alliance against Spain—for reasons arising in part from the internal affairs of the House of Bourbon. A series of sudden deaths in the French Royal House between 1704 and 1714 had produced a situation in which, on Louis XIV's death in 1715, no one but a five-year-old child, Louis XV, stood before Philip V of Spain in the natural line of succession of France; and Philip, though he had renounced that succession, still felt himself better entitled, as the child's uncle, to exercise the regency in France than the child's cousin twice removed, Philippe duc d'Orléans, against whom Spanish agents promoted a plot. The marriage (1722) of the Spanish king's son to a daughter of the French regent sealed the reconciliation.

In 1733 the Treaty of the Escorial pledged the French and the Spanish Bourbons to collaborate with each other notwithstanding any previous obligations. This treaty and the similarly conceived Treaty of Fontainebleau (1743) are sometimes called the "First" and the "Second Family Compact"; and the term Family Compact, or Pacte de Famille, was actually used in a third treaty, signed in Paris in 1761, during the Seven Years' War. By this last treaty France and Spain not only guaranteed one another against all enemies but also promised like protection to the Bourbon states in Italy in the event of their acceding to the compact; and no state not belonging to the House of Bourbon was to be allowed to accede.

Cooperation between French and Spanish Bourbons came to a miserable end in the French Revolutionary and Napoleonic Wars (q.v.), and the later decades of the 19th century brought new complications. A French Bourbon prince led a force into Spain in 1823 to crush the liberalism to which Ferdinand VII was succumbing; but such Bourbon solidarity could not survive two events which were to rend both the Spanish and the French houses.

First, in March 1830, Ferdinand VII of Spain announced the revocation of the Salic Law of Succession, which Philip V had introduced into Spain in 1713. This meant that the sonless Ferdinand could be succeeded not by his brother Don Carlos conde de Molina but by his elder daughter Isabella (born after the revocation); and though Ferdinand temporarily reinstated the Salic Law in September 1832, he revoked it again 13 days later. On his death in 1833 the partisans of the disappointed Don Carlos started the first of the Carlist Wars in protest against Isabella's accession (see again SPAIN, HISTORY OF).

Carlism and the House of Orléans

Secondly, in France, the July Revolution of 1830 overthrew the "legitimate" Bourbon monarchy and transferred the throne to Louis-Philippe, head of the collateral line of Orléans. Odious enough already because Louis-Philippe's father, the self-styled Philippe Égalité, had voted in 1793 for the death sentence on Louis XVI, the House of Orléans became, by the usurpation of 1830, so much more odious to the Legitimists that some of the latter, when the "legitimate" male of France died out with the comte de Chambord in 1883, declined to recognize the head of the House of Orléans as the rightful pretender to France, as indeed he now was if the renunciation of 1713 was still to be observed (see again Tables 3 and 4); instead they preferred to disregard that renunciation and so to regard a Spanish prince as their rightful king. These Legitimists were known in France as "Blancs d'Espagne" ("Spanish Whites"). Most Legitimists, however, followed the final advice of the comte de Chambord by recognizing the rights of the House of Orléans to France.

While the dispossessed Bourbons—Spanish Carlists and French Legitimists—naturally sympathized with each other, their opponents—Queen Isabella and the House of Orléans—conversely gravitated together. One result was the crisis of the "Spanish Marriages" in the 1840s. While both Queen Isabella and her sister Luisa remained unmarried, the Spanish succession was an open prospect of great interest to governments concerned with maintaining the balance of power in Europe. If both sisters had married princes of the House of Orléans, as Louis-Philippe and the sister's mother, Maria Cristina, had originally suggested, French influence over Spain would have become too strong for the liking of the British government, which proposed instead that Isabella should marry Prince Leopold of Saxe-Coburg (more intimately linked with Great Britain than with France). Then, in 1843, the French and the British came to an understanding: Isabella should marry some "neutral" prince, preferably a Spanish Bourbon cousin; and only after the birth of a child to Isabella should Luisa marry Louis-Philippe's son Antoine duc de Montpensier. Of Isabella's eligible cousins, the conte de Montemolín was disfavoured by the Spanish government as a Carlist; the next senior was the doubtfully virile Don Francisco de Asis, who was generally thought unlikely to become a father; the third was

Table 6: The Bourbons of Parma

	PHILIP (see Table 5) = Louise Elisabeth of	
	duke of Parma 1748–65 | France (see Table 2)	
Isabella (1741–63)	FERDINAND (1751–1802)	Maria Luisa (1751–1819)
= Joseph, later Holy	duke of Parma 1765–1802	= Charles IV of Spain
Roman emperor	= Maria Amalia of Austria	(see Table 5)
4 daughters, including:	LOUIS (1773–1803) = Luisa (1782–1824)	
Carolina (1770–1804)	king of Etruria / regent of Etruria	
= Maximilian of Saxony	1801–03 / 1803–07, duchess of Lucca 1815–24	
Teresa	= CHARLES (1799–1883)	Luisa (1802–57)
of Savoy	king of Etruria 1803–07	= her aunt's widower
	duke of Lucca 1824–47	Maximilian of Saxony
	duke of Parma 1847–49	
Luisa Francesca	CHARLES III (1823–54) = Louise daughter of last duc	
(1821–28)	duke of Parma 1849–54 | de Berry (see Table 2)	
Margarita	ROBERT	Alicia / Enrico
(1847–93)	(1848–1907)	(1849–1935) / (1851–1905)
= Carlos duque	duke of Parma	= Ferdinand / conte di
de Madrid	1854–59	IV of Tuscany / Bardi
(see Table 5)		

11 children by Pia of the	12 children by Antonia
Two Sicilies, including	of Braganza, including
1. Maria Luisa (1870–99)	2. Sixtus (1886–1934)
= Ferdinand of Bulgaria	3. Francis Xavier (1889–
4. Enrico (1873–1939)	5. Zita (1892–)
8. Giuseppe (1875–1950)	= Charles emperor of Austria
10. Elias (1880–1959)	6. Felix (1893–1970)
	= Charlotte of Luxembourg

Don Enrique duque de Sevilla, whose outspoken liberalism recommended him to the British government but not to the Spanish. Inadvertently, however, the British government in 1846 gave the French the impression that it was still secretly trying to press Prince Leopold on Spain, and the French reacted by arranging the Spanish marriages in a way quite contrary to British desire: Isabella and Luisa were married on the same day, Oct. 10, 1846, to Don Francisco de Asis and to Montpensier respectively. The immediate upshot was that the House of Orléans, apparently intending that Montpensier or a son of his should eventually be king of Spain, incurred the serious resentment of its former friends in Great Britain.

Isabella, who would have preferred to marry Don Enrique, spent conspicuously long periods apart from her consort and behaved indiscreetly with other men. When she bore a son in 1857, ill-wishers were able to cast doubts on his paternity. These doubts served the purposes of the extreme Carlists when the male line of Don Carlos died out in 1936, because they could argue that Isabella's male descendants were not those of Don Francisco de Asis—whose issue, under Salic Law, would have been the next male heirs. Nearly all the other Bourbon princes, however, either had already recognized Isabella's rights or were maintaining incompatible pretensions to other thrones. The Carlists therefore had to look far afield in their search for a new pretender.

Certain princes of Bourbon-Parma responded to Carlist overtures but did not at the same time renounce their Parmesan titles, which under the settlement of 1748 were

Carlism and Bourbon-Parma

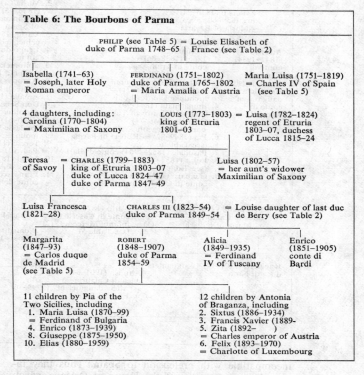

Table 7: The Bourbons of the Two Sicilies

FERDINAND I (see Table 5) = Maria Carolina of Austria
king of Naples and Sicily 1759–1808, of the Two Sicilies 1816–25

- Clementina of Austria = (1) FRANCIS I (2) = Isabel of Spain (see Table 5)
  - FRANCIS I (1777–1830), king 1825–30
  - by (1): Caroline (1798–1870) = last duc de Berry (see Table 2)
- Leopoldo (1790–1851) principe di Salerno
- 4 daughters:
  1. Theresa (1772–1807) = Francis I of Austria
  2. Cristina (1779–1849) = Charles Felix of Sardinia
  3. Marie-Amélie (1782–1866) = Louis Philippe (see Table 4)
  4. Antonia (1784–1806) = Ferdinand VII of Spain

Children of Francis I and Isabel:

- Cristina of Sardinia = (1) FERDINAND II (2) = Theresia of Austria
  - FERDINAND II (1810–59), king 1830–59
- 11 others:
  1. Luisa (1804–44) = duque de Cádiz (see Table 5)
  2. Maria Cristina (1806–78) = Ferdinand VII of Spain (see Table 5)
  3. Carlo (1811–62) principe di Capua
  4. Leopoldo (1813–60) conte di Siracusa
  5. Antonieta (1814–98) = Leopold II of Tuscany
  6. Antonio (1816–43) conte di Lecce
  7. Amalia (1818–57) = Don Sebastián (see Table 5)
  8. Carolina (1820–61) = conde de Montemolín (see Table 5)
  9. Teresa (1822–99) = Pedro II of Brazil
  10. Luigi (1824–97) conte d'Aquila
  11. Francesco (1827–92) conte di Trapani

Children of Ferdinand II:

- by (1): FRANCIS II (1836–94), king 1859–60 = Maria of Bavaria
- by (2): Alfonso (1841–1934) conte di Caserta = his cousin Antonieta daughter of conte di Trapani
- 9 others:
  1. Luigi (1838–86) conte di Trani
  2. Alberto (1839–44) conte di Castrogiovanni
  3. Annunziata (1843–71) = archduke Charles Louis
  4. Immaculata (1844–99) = Charles Salvator of Tuscany
  5. Gaetano (1846–71) conte di Girgenti
  6. Pia (1849–82) = Robert of Parma (see Table 6)
  7. Pasquale (1852–1904) conte di Bari
  8. Luisa (1855–74) = conte di Bardi (see Table 6)
  9. Gennaro (1857–67) conte di Caltagirone

Children of Alfonso, conte di Caserta:

- Ferdinando (1869–1960) duca di Calabria = Maria of Bavaria
  - Ruggiero (1901–14) duca di Noto
  - 5 daughters
- Carlo (1870–1949) conte di Caserta (1) = infanta Mercedes (see Table 5); (2) = Louise daughter of Louis-Philippe-Albert comte de Paris
  - by (1): Alfonso (1901–64) duca di Calabria = Alicia daughter of Elias of Parma
    - 2 daughters
    - Carlo (1938–) duca di Noto
  - by (1): Carlo (1908–36)
  - by (2): 3 daughters including 2. Mercedes (1910–) = conde de Barcelona (see Table 5)
- 4 other sons and 4 daughters

incompatible with pretension to Spain. Thus they incurred the displeasure of the House of Orléans, which had to respect the settlement of 1748 because its own pretension to France depended on the analogous settlement of 1713.

BIBLIOGRAPHY. For the English reader in the 20th century, an introduction is provided by SANCHE DE GRAMONT, *Epitaph for Kings* (1968). Those interested in genealogy may readily consult H. VRIGNAULT, *Généalogie de la maison de Bourbon*, 2nd ed. rev. (1957), with 12 tables; and, on the bastard branches, *Légitimés de France de la maison de Bourbon de 1594 à 1820* (1965). Vrignault's work of 1957 may be brought up to date through the successive volumes of the periodical *Genealogisches Handbuch des Adels*, series "Fürstliche Häuser," whose first article "Bourbon" appeared in 1953 (vol. 2 of the series, 3 of the collection). While the story of the French Bourbon sovereigns is too vast to be resumed collectively in any single work other than a history of France, there are helpful works in English on the Spanish Bourbons and on the Neapolitan: SIR CHARLES PETRIE, *The Spanish Royal House* (1958), supplemented by T. ARONSON on the Carlist question, *Royal Vendetta: The Crown of Spain, 1829–1965* (1966); and HAROLD ACTON, *The Bourbons of Naples, 1734–1825* (1956) and *The Last Bourbons of Naples, 1825–1861* (1961). Of the many popular and suggestive writings on the physiological aspect, the reader may first consult A. DE MARICOURT and M. DE BERTRANDFOSSE, *Les Bourbons, 1553–1830: hérédité, pathologie, amours et grandeur* (1937).

(J.R.-S.)

Bourguiba, Habib

Habib Bourguiba, the architect of Tunisia's independence, and its first president, combined great gifts of leadership with rare organizational ability to free his country from French rule. He was born, the seventh child of Ali Bourguiba, a former lieutenant in the army of the bey (ruler) of Tunisia, at al-Munastīr, a small fishing village, on August 3, 1902. Sent to Tunis at an early age, he received a good education in Arabic and in the foundations of Islām, as well as in French and in Western thought.

Between 1924 and 1927 Bourguiba studied law and po-

Stuart—Pix from Publix

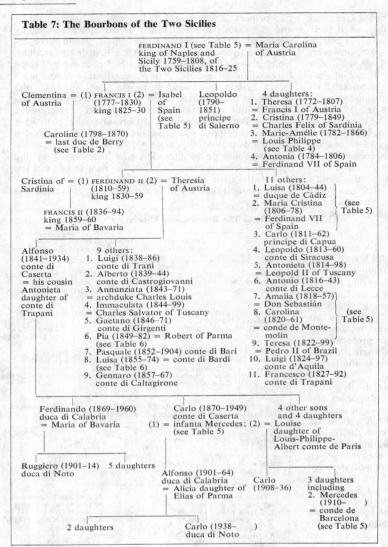

Bourguiba.

litical science at the Sorbonne, in Paris, where he established contacts with a number of French liberals and with Algerians and Moroccans who were working for the independence of their countries.

For seven years after his return to Tunis, in 1927, Bourguiba practiced law and founded, in 1932, a nationalist newspaper in French. In 1934, when it became apparent that the leading nationalist political group, the Destour (Constitution) Party, was unable to make headway in the struggle for independence, Bourguiba and his younger colleagues seceded and established the Neo-Destour Party, with Bourguiba as its secretary general. He would become its president 14 years later.

Role in the struggle for independence

From 1934 onward, Bourguiba was the central figure in the Tunisian national struggle. In his work he showed integrity, persistence, consistency, and courage. A practical man, he believed in doing things in stages, and his gradualist policy came to be known as "Bourguibism." It was he who in one word formulated the demands of the Tunisians: independence. Under him the people came to identify with the national movement that had been almost a monopoly of the urban elite. An exceptionally able organizer, Bourguiba not only established branches of the party in out-of-the-way villages, but, realizing that the French government would resort to repressive measures, he also saw to it that a new set of party executives would always fill the vacuum created by arrest or exile. Between 1934 and 1952 nine such groups succeeded one another, thus keeping the struggle alive; Bourguiba himself spent about ten years in detention during this period (1934–36, 1938–42, 1952–55).

Imprisoned in Vichy, France, at the outbreak of World War II, Bourguiba refused to throw in his lot with the Axis powers unless they declared Tunisian independence first. He was convinced that the Allies would win the war and strove to keep Tunisia neutral.

In 1945–46 and 1951 Bourguiba travelled extensively in the Middle East, the United States, the Far East, and Europe, publicizing the cause of Tunisian independence.

When, in 1952–54, the nationalists increasingly took to terrorism, the French government became seriously concerned. Repression ceased to be effective, and in 1954 the government of Pierre Mendès-France began negotiations with Bourguiba; in April 1955 he secured autonomy for his country from Edgar Faure, Mendès-France's successor. Foreign affairs and defense were reserved for France.

President of Tunisia

On March 20, 1956, Bourguiba, following his policy of gradualism, concluded, with Guy Mollet, the French premier, a treaty giving Tunisia its independence. In 1957 agreement in principle for evacuation of the French forces from Tunisia, except Bizerte, was reached. Since the abolition of the monarchy in 1957, Bourguiba has been elected three times president of Tunisia. In 1959 he gave Tunisia a constitution in which, while retaining Islām as the state religion, he abolished polygamy, controlled divorce, and would not allow the month-long fast of Ramaḍān to curtail workers' productivity.

Bearing in mind the need to economize as well as the danger from military coups, Bourguiba has kept the Tunisian army small. Tunisia's defense expenditures have never exceeded 5 percent of the budget, while education and agriculture usually receive 25 percent each and health even a little more. One of the most successful of his projects is the settlement of about 50,000 nomads in southern Tunisia, which under French rule was under military administration. He divided the country into 14 provinces under civilian administration with modern administrative laws.

Since Tunisia depends for its development on foreign aid from various sources, Bourguiba observes a policy of neutrality. Intellectually, culturally, and educationally, however, Tunisia leans toward France. Yet after independence two incidents imperilled Tunisia's close ties with that country.

In 1961, probably in response to pressures by other Arab leaders, Bourguiba asked France to evacuate Bizerte, which, according to the agreement on independence (1956), was to remain a French military and naval base. When the French did not immediately respond, he ordered an attack on their forces, which returned the fire. Over two years later Bizerte was evacuated, but at the cost of more than 1,000 Tunisian lives. The nationalization of all land still owned by French settlers in 1964 further strained relations with France. The evacuation of Bizerte caused economic loss to Tunisia by cutting off a source of revenue from France, but Bourguiba apparently gained in prestige.

For many years Bourguiba has been a controversial figure in Arab politics, primarily because he takes a courageous and independent stand against "unanimous" decisions or dictates by the Arab League, but also possibly because he cuts a figure on the international scene far bigger than in his own country.

Bourguiba believes in a moderate form of socialism, which he is trying to introduce into Tunisia. In the mid-1960s Tunisia tried a strict form of agricultural cooperatives and state control of trade and industry, but the result was disastrous and Bourguiba has gone back to his more deliberate methods. There is, however, far from unanimous agreement that Bourguiba owes his overall success, both domestically and in foreign affairs, to his gradualist approach. Some feel that his method would not work for a leader who did not possess both Bourguiba's fighting spirit and his great gifts as a negotiator, as well as an integrity that has made some of his former opponents, even such as Premiers Mendès-France and Edgar Faure, his friends and admirers.

> He achieved stability for his regime by a combination of moderation in all things and shrewdness in judging men and events. . . . he judiciously permitted private capital to operate side by side with government-run economic enterprises. He shied away from creating a military Frankenstein monster, and succeeded in obtaining economic assistance from France, the United States, West Germany, and other nations. In his dealings with his benefactors he is dignified, appreciative, and gracious; he often goes out of his way to demonstrate his deep gratitude. (Samuel Merlin in *The Search of Peace in the Middle East.*)

BIBLIOGRAPHY. Unfortunately there is not as yet a really good biography of Bourguiba, although there are a number of essays on him: FELIX GARAS, *Bourguiba et la naissance d'une nation* (1956), an attempt to explain Bourguiba's struggle and his leadership of the national movement in Tunisia to the beginning of the serious negotiations with France; JEAN LACOUTURE, *Cinq hommes et la France* (1961), a work that explains the role of Bourguiba in Tunisian national life; SAMUEL MERLIN, *The Search for Peace in the Middle East*, ch. 13–32 (1968), a penetrating study of Bourguiba's Arab policy and of his statements on Arab-Israeli relations made on his tour of the Arab East, Iran, Turkey, and Greece in 1965.

(N.A.Z.)

Bowen, Norman Levi

Norman Levi Bowen, petrologist and mineral chemist, ranks as the great pioneer investigator in the field of experimental petrology, the science that deals with the origin, history, occurrence, structure, chemical composition, and classification of rocks. His contributions in this field were unique; no one else broke so much new ground or contributed in such rich measure to the solution of fundamental problems of petrogenesis (rock origins).

Bowen was born at Kingston, Ontario, on June 21, 1887, the son of W.A. Bowen, who had emigrated to Canada from London. Educated at Queen's University, Kingston, he specialized in chemistry, mineralogy, and geology. When he won an 1851 International Exhibition Scholarship, he proceeded to the Massachusetts Institute of Technology, Cambridge. He spent 1910–11 at the Geophysical Laboratory of the Carnegie Institution of Washington, D.C., undertaking experimental studies of a mineral group (a silicate system, nepheline–anorthite), which formed part of a thesis submitted for his Ph.D. degree at the Institute in 1912. In all, Bowen spent six summers in the field during his university career (1907–12), working in Canada for the Ontario Bureau of Mines and for the Geological Survey of Canada in British Columbia along the Canadian Pacific Railway.

After completing his doctorate, Bowen returned to the Geophysical Laboratory in Washington. The nature of

Bowen.
By courtesy of Queen's University at Kingston, Ontario

the work at the laboratory enabled him to avoid having to make an outright choice between geology and chemistry. By 1915 he had executed a group of experimental studies that proved to be critically important to petrology and formed the basis of his critical review *The Later Stages of the Evolution of the Igneous Rocks* (1915), a paper of such outstanding merit that it established Bowen's position at the age of 28 as an international figure in petrology.

The United States' entry into World War I in 1917 deflected Bowen's researches into the study of optical glass, which had become a research priority, and he worked for a time in the glass plant of the Bausch and Lomb Optical Company.

After the war ended, he resigned from the Geophysical Laboratory to return briefly to Queen's University, as professor of mineralogy (1919), but after two years he returned again to the laboratory in Washington.

Work on silicate systems

There he remained for 16 years, broadening his attack on silicate systems. His researches carried great weight when he applied his experimental physicochemical data to field petrological problems. To this end he diligently visited classical localities relating to problems of igneous rocks: the Bushveld of South Africa, the alkalic lavas of East Africa, and the peridotites of Skye and the Fen area of Norway. He was perfectly suited to a lifetime of work in a research institution. Quiet and retiring in disposition, he enjoyed the sheltered environment such an institution can offer, one in which he could spend his days almost uninterruptedly on the research he loved.

In the spring of 1927, Bowen delivered a course of lectures to advanced students in geology at Princeton University, the substance of which was published in 1928 as *The Evolution of the Igneous Rocks*. In this vigorous presentation, Bowen provided a survey and a synthesis that have exerted a profound influence on petrologic thought. Later Bowen collaborated extensively with J.F. Schairer, a young and able experimenter who had joined the laboratory from Yale University. Together they worked on silicate systems containing iron oxide, beginning with ferric oxide and later ferrous oxide.

Work at the University of Chicago

Bowen made a second and more extended break from the Geophysical Laboratory when he was attracted to fill the Charles L. Hutchinson Distinguished Service Professorship of petrology at the University of Chicago, where he remained from 1937 to 1947. He rapidly developed a school of experimental petrology there and produced a succession of papers by his pupils that dealt with equilibrium studies of alkali systems Bowen himself presented a synthesis of these results in their bearing on the origin and differentiation of alkaline rocks (1945).

After World War II, Bowen was induced to return once more to the Geophysical Laboratory in 1947 to cooperate in research on mineral systems embracing volatiles, particularly water. This work culminated in studies (published in 1958), with O.F. Tuttle as a collaborator, on the granite system.

Bowen's association with the Geophysical Laboratory extended in all more than 35 years, and his long and splendid record was recognized by the award of honours from learned societies in the United States and Europe.

After his retirement in 1952, he moved to Clearwater, Florida, but a year later returned to Washington. Despite poor health, he was still active and had an office in the Geophysical Laboratory as research associate until his death on September 11, 1956.

BIBLIOGRAPHY. C.E. TILLEY, "Norman Levi Bowen," *Biogr. Mem. Fellows R. Soc.*, 3:7–22 (1957).

(C.E.T.)

Bowling

The name bowling covers a number of games of common but complex origins in which a ball is rolled down a long narrow lane with one of two general aims. One of these, in the game of bowls or lawn bowling, is to have the ball come to rest near a stationary ball called a jack; the other, in tenpins, commonly known as bowling, is to knock down more wooden pins than an opponent. One form or another of these games is probably played by more peoples of the world than any other, with the possible exception of soccer football. Tenpins, the most widely played variation, is the principal form of bowling in the United States, Canada, Japan, the Scandinavian countries, Mexico, Australia, and Central and South America. Its many variations include duckpins, candlepins, fivepins, skittles, and ninepins, and differences within the framework of each of the games. Lawn bowling, the most widely played of bowls games, in a sense is akin to curling on ice. Both are among the earliest known outdoor pastimes.

HISTORY

Origins and early history. Bowling has been connected to articles found in the tomb of an Egyptian child buried in 5200 BC. The primitive implements included nine pieces of stone, to be set up as pins, at which a stone "ball" was rolled, the ball having first to roll through an archway made of three pieces of marble. Another ancient discovery was the Polynesian game of Ula Maika, also utilizing pins and balls of stone. The stones were rolled a distance of 60 feet (18 metres), a distance which is, by coincidence, the regulation length of the modern tenpin bowling lane.

Origin of boccie

Still another ancient form of bowls was played in the Italian Alps about 2,000 years ago. It involved the underhand tossing of stones at an object, differentiating it from the rolling of the stones, and is believed to have been the origin of boccie, still a widely played game in Italy and among persons of Italian descent around the world. The Basque *quilles*, another of the ancient European games, originated as an outdoor pastime using a wooden ball, probably made from tree roots, with a slot-like grip. The player held onto the ball as he swung it against the first of nine three-foot-tall pins arranged in a large rectangular court. As that pin fell, hopefully to knock down its neighbour, the player rolled the ball toward the center of the court, trying to apply reverse spin that would send the ball ricocheting against several other pins. The pins were arranged in three rows of three each.

Bowling at pins. Bowling at pins probably originated in ancient Germany, not as a sport but as a religious ceremony. It has been conjectured that as early as the 3rd or 4th century AD, in rites held in the cloisters of churches, parishioners placed their ever-present club or *Kegel* (the implement most Germans carried for sport and, certainly, self-protection) at one end of a runway resembling today's bowling lane. The *Kegel* was said to represent the *Heide*, the "heathen." A stone was rolled at the *Heide*, and those successfully toppling it were believed to have cleansed themselves of sin. The practice, described in the chronicles of Paderborn, evidently lasted less than two centuries. But the activity persisted as a pastime and eventually was taken up by the nobility and landed gentry. Although the peasants' club evolved into pins, the association remained and even today bowlers often are referred to as "kegelers."

The passage of time brought an increase in the size of the stone rolled at pins and eventually the ball came to be made of wood. In 1300, according to German historians, in some sections of Germany a game was played with three pins; in others as many as 17 were used. Martin Luther is credited with settling on the idea that nine was the ideal number of pins. A biographer of the 16th-century cleric has written that Luther found little time for recreation, yet

> to the young people in his family and household he gladly allowed recreation and even built a bowling lane for them and occasionally visited them while they were bowling and now and then threw the first ball . . . .

There are numerous ancient references to bowling, among them an account of a great feast given the citizenry of Frankfurt in 1463, at which the venison dinner was followed by bowling. Notations on papers dating to 1325 in which "gambling on bowling" was limited to five shillings have been discovered. In 1518, the city of Breslau (now Wrocław, Poland) gave an ox to the winner of a bowling competition.

In the 15th, 16th, and 17th centuries, the game spread into the lowland countries and also into Austria and Switzerland. The playing surfaces were usually cinders or clay, specially treated and sun-baked to a hardness resembling concrete. When the lanes were covered or put into sheds, the playing surface usually was wood. The roofing over of the lanes, first done in London for lawn bowls around the year 1455, was the true beginning of modern bowling as an all-weather, around-the-clock game.

Bowling on the green. Though most of the Continent was taking to bowling at pins in the Middle Ages, there is little evidence that residents of the British Isles were changing from their historic preference for bowls or lawn bowling. Originally, the game probably consisted of two or more persons using rounded stones or pebbles. Evidence that a form of bowls was known in ancient Egypt has been cited above. Later it was developed by the Greeks and Romans. Scenes of lawn bowls have been depicted on pottery and tapestries dating to ancient times. The Romans developed the game into boccie, which they carried into Northern Europe as early as the 10th century, and the British are thought to have refined the Italian version of "tossing" the ball at the object into the one of rolling it on the lawn, or green, in the game originally called "bowles." Evidence in 13th- and 14th-century manuscripts depicts the game being played on lines similar to those employed today. One manuscript of that period, preserved in the Royal Library at Windsor, shows two players delivering one bowl each toward a small conical marker. A link with those times is provided by the Southampton Town Bowling Club, founded in 1299 and still in existence.

From the first days of the game's popularity, kings frowned upon it as likely to seduce men from archery, a pastime deemed in those days to be the chief guarantee of England's integrity and safety. In 1388 Richard II prohibited the game. Further acts in the reigns of Henry IV and Edward IV renewed the ban on the game for commoners. The sport also was criticized because of its gambling aspects. In 1511 King Henry VIII issued an edict declaring

> the game of bowles is an evil because the alleys are in operation in conjunction with saloons, or dissolute places, and bowling has ceased to be a sport, and rather a form of vicious gambling.

Though it was not rescinded until 1845, the ban was seldom observed, and that bowls continued to flourish is seen from a famous game played on "Plymouth Hoe" in 1588 by Sir Francis Drake and Sir John Hawkins, when even the news of the Spanish Armada's impending arrival was not allowed to interrupt the play. Shakespeare mentions the game in several of his plays. In *Richard II* a lady at court suggests the queen should play a game of bowls and Queen Isabella replies "Twill make me think the world is full of rubs, and that my fortune runs against the bias." It is apparent that, by that time, ladies played as well as men, and that bias (shaping or weighting the bowls so that they would swerve when rolled) had been introduced. In *The Book of Sports* (1618) James I recommended the game to his son, and the 17th-century diarist Samuel Pepys several times records meeting personalities at bowls. But more and more the game became associated with pothouses and taverns, and the excesses of drinking and gambling by the shady characters who met there caused bowls to fall into disrepute. (J.B.P.)

Development of modern lawn bowls. *Bowls in Scotland.* The game was preserved in Scotland, which took to bowls in the 16th century and where, stripped of its undesirable surroundings, it was for some time the national sport. Two main factors led to the revitalization and spread of the game. The Scots decided to formulate rules, and in 1849 a code of laws was produced, so excellently constructed that basically there has been little cause to change it ever since. The Scots also produced truly level greens, often using sea-washed turf for the purpose. Good conditions for play made the game one of scientific and strategic skill, while surpassing other pastimes in the promotion of social fellowship.

Spread of the game. Scots emigrants were responsible for the spread of the game to British Commonwealth countries, particularly Australia, New Zealand, and South Africa. It was in New South Wales and Victoria that the first bowling associations were formed in 1890. In 1892 the Scottish Bowling Association came into being. In 1903 the English Bowling Association was established. Two years later the International Bowling Board encompassing all of the associations in England and those of Scotland, Ireland, and Wales was set up. Although colonists also took the game to North America, where a park at the lower end of Broadway in New York and several small American towns still bear the name of Bowling Green, it was only in 1915 that the American Lawn Bowls Association was formed, and affiliation to the International Bowling Board was delayed until 1938. (See further under *The modern game* below.) Nevertheless, many municipalities in the U.S. maintain public bowling greens. The game is also played in parts of the Middle East and South America.

Tournaments and championships. The Irish and Welsh associations were formed in 1904, and international matches have been played between Scotland, England, Ireland, and Wales (the Home Countries) since 1903, except during the World War years. Teams of bowlers from Australia and New Zealand visited Great Britain in 1901, and from Canada in 1904. Since then teams from the British Isles, Australia, New Zealand, Canada, South Africa, and the United States have exchanged visits at regular intervals. All of them hold national championships. In the British Isles, each Home Country holds annual championships in singles, pairs, triples, and fours, qualifying for the British Isles championships, established in 1959, in which the national champions meet to decide the overall winner in each event. The popularity of competitive bowls can be measured by the fact that entries in the English National Championships in the 1970s exceeded in singles 11,000, in pairs 10,000, in triples 6,000, and in fours 4,000, involving more than 70,000 players from more than 2,500 clubs covering 34 countries. Entries in the championships continued to increase every year.

International matches

Lawn bowls was one of the sports included in the quadrennial British Commonwealth Games (inaugurated 1930). The first World Bowling Championships were held in 1966, in Sydney, Australia, with 16 national teams taking part. The second World Championships were held in 1972 in Worthing, England.

Outstanding bowlers. Bowls, highly organized for competition play, has produced outstanding bowlers.

These have included Percy Baker, for several years the supreme English bowler. An international (*i.e.*, selected to represent his nation in international play), he won the English national singles championship on four occasions and pairs, triples, and fours. He has been superseded by David J. Bryant, who won the inaugural World Championship singles and claimed gold medals in the 1962 and 1970 Commonwealth Games. He has won all the English National titles and is an indoor champion too. He was awarded the Order of the British Empire in 1969 for his services to bowls.

Glyn Bosisto dominated the Australian scene for nearly 30 years, and his achievements include four wins in the Australian singles. Norman White represented South Africa in three Commonwealth Games series, and on four occasions won the South African National singles and fours. Roy Fulton (Northern Ireland) is an international, both indoor and outdoor, who has won national titles and has also been successful in the British Isles singles and pairs. He also holds bronze medals for singles in Commonwealth Games and World Championships. Harry Reston (Scotland), an indoor and outdoor international, holds a bronze medal for the World Championships and is a triple winner of the Scottish Indoor singles.

For a list of world champions, see SPORTING RECORD in the *Ready Reference and Index*. (G.T.F.)

THE MODERN GAME

Bowls and pins in North America. There is confusion about how and when bowling at pins was carried to North America, arising from the interuse of the terms bowl, bowler, and bowling in referring both to ninepins (and tenpins) and lawn bowling. The early British settlers brought lawn bowls with them to America because that was the game they knew best. Dutch explorers under Henry Hudson, however, were said to have been just as instrumental in bringing with them some form of pin bowling, probably one called Dutch skittles and played principally outdoors. While some say bowling at pins came to America about 1650, the fact remains that many parts of Europe, even bowls-oriented England, had known a game in which pins were used for at least a century before. This was skittles, or a variation thereof, a game somewhat akin to boccie because the "ball" was tossed at the pins, rather than rolled. In the English version, the bowl or "cheese"—so called for its resemblance to a large Edam cheese—weighs between eight and 16 pounds (3.6 and 7.2 kilograms). It is hurled at the pins, which vary in height and dimension in relation to the size of the bowl, from a distance of 21 feet (6.4 metres). The nine pins are arranged in the standard diamond-shaped formation found in all ninepin games. The object in skittles is to knock down all the pins with the fewest throws.

Early pin games

Another pin game of the England of the Middle Ages was half-bowl, played with half a sphere of wood. The object was to roll the ball past a setup of 15 small conical pins and "bring it back" in a wide arc into the pins. As in skittles, one point, or "chalk," is scored for each pin knocked over. The game in each is 31 pins.

Most of the early European pin games involved rolling the ball along a wooden plank, 12 to 18 inches (30 to 46 centimetres) wide and 60 to 90 feet (18 to 27 metres) long, toward a diamond-shaped formation of nine pins. If the ball fell off the plank before reaching the pins, it was charged as a delivery against the player, but any pins knocked down were reset. The plank, or raised centre, still is used in several kinds of ninepin games in Europe and parts of the United States. For no known reason the flat-suface lane, then called an "alley bed," gained early usage in the "American" game, although when the tenth pin was added still is a mystery. It is believed tenpins was played in New York City in the 1820s; the earliest known reference to bowling at pins was made by Washington Irving in *Rip Van Winkle* (about 1818) in which he likens thunder to the sound of a ball rolling at pins.

Emergence of the tenpin game. By the mid-1830s, bowling at pins was flourishing. It was then that the same scourge that struck lawn bowling in medieval England—gambling—became the evil of the American bowling scene. The situation became so critical in Connecticut that the state legislature passed an act in 1841 banning the game. Myth has it that some quick-witted genius, to circumvent the prohibition which was popularly supposed to refer only to the ninepin diamond formation, added the tenth pin and arranged them in an equilateral triangle. Regardless of how tenpins came into being, it became so popular by mid-19th century that indoor lanes were being built throughout New York City, Syracuse, Buffalo, Cincinnati, Chicago, Milwaukee, and other cities with large German populations. Many bowling lanes were built and operated by Turnvereins—fraternal gymnastic societies—but they quickly spread to wide public usage. While gambling continued to be a problem in some areas, it was the lack of uniform playing rules and equipment specifications that stifled the development of the game as a whole. In 1875 delegates from nine bowling clubs in New York and Brooklyn organized the National Bowling Association. Some of the legislation agreed on then is still in effect in modified form, but the group lacked breadth and was followed in 1890 by a short-lived American Amateur Bowling Union.

Organization: tournaments. Disagreement continued between East and West, principally an alignment of New York state bowlers against everyone else. On September 9, 1895, the American Bowling Congress (ABC) was organized in New York City. Rules and equipment standards were developed—and adhered to—and the game as it finally was organized has remained basically unchanged, except for alterations adopted to meet the changes brought on by technological advancements such as automatic pin setters and other equipment, and the introduction of plastics, nylon, and other synthetics.

Once the ABC came into the picture, bowling began its growth. Two early technological developments helped. Pins had been set mostly by hand; machines were designed to do the job. Balls had been made of lignum vitae, a tropical wood that was almost indestructible, except that it chipped and lost its shape: suddenly all sorts of balls made of hard rubber, still the basic ingredient, appeared. As many as 16 to 24 lanes were built into one building—pin palaces they were called—and nationally known players began to emerge. In 1901 the ABC started its national tournament, drawing a turnout of 41 five-man teams to a four-day contest in Chicago. In 1953, at its Golden Jubilee tournament (three years having been lost to World War II), the ABC tournament drew an entry of 8,180 teams or upwards of 41,000 individuals.

The Women's International Bowling Congress (WIBC), organized in 1916, has conducted annual national championships since 1917. More than 48,000 women took part in the largest single tournament, the 1973 event in Las Vegas, Nevada.

The largest individual event is the Petersen Classic, for both men and women, held since 1921 for about 10 months each year in Chicago, and offering a first prize in excess of $50,000 and attracting more than 20,000 entrants, most of them men.

The Professional Bowlers Association (PBA) was organized in 1958. It quickly developed a star system and a tournament tour fashioned after that of professional golf. Helped by television, PBA members were soon playing for more than $1,000,000 in yearly prize money. Don Carter became the leading winner in the 1950s and was succeeded by Dick Weber. The Professional Women's Bowling Association (1959) began modest tournament play in the early 1960s.

Professional tours

A major influence at the structural level of the game has been the Bowling Proprietors Association of America, founded in 1932. In addition to its trade association functions, it formerly conducted a number of tournaments for both men and women. Its most notable was the All-Star tournament, a match game event that began in 1941 and continued until 1970, when it was given over to the Professional Bowlers Association, renamed the U.S. Open, and made a part of the PBA tour. The National Bowling Council, founded 1943, is made up of the manufacturers, proprietors, and membership groups. It concerns itself with national promotional campaigns and other activities requiring joint application of the industry's efforts.

League bowling. Nearly 52,000,000 persons are said to bowl at least once or twice a year in the United States. But while the thousands of occasional weekend and holiday bowlers swell the total number, the backbone of the sport continues to be its highly organized, competitive league structure. This structure is based on the members of the major bowling congresses who participate in leagues organized in cities and towns throughout North America. The American Bowling Congress has a male membership of more than 4,000,000. The Women's International Bowling Congress has reached a membership of nearly 3,500,000 women.

Most men's and women's leagues consist of eight to 12 teams. Some leagues have 40 or more teams, depending on the number of lanes in the bowling centre. Both the ABC and WIBC sanction more than 100,000 leagues each year, almost half of which are mixed.

League play in the three major membership organizations is conducted under rules laid down by the parent bodies including the handling of prize funds by the adult leagues. The latter helps illustrate the magnitude of bowling. About $150,000,000 in league prize money is disbursed at season's end. Upwards of $50,000,000 in women's league prize funds is also distributed.

Tenpins in other countries. *Europe.* As membership in the three bowling groups—ABC, WIBC, and AJBC (American Junior Bowling Congress), plus the Youth Bowling Association of the Bowling Proprietors Association of America—peaked at 8,000,000 in the mid-1960s, the leading manufacturers of equipment in the United States began to look elsewhere for markets. So did investors in other countries. Suddenly tenpins, the game that had crossed the Atlantic as a ninepin game years and years before, was on its way back to Europe. Foreseeing the development, some British bowlers asked the American Bowling Congress to lend its aid in the formation of an association. The British Ten Pin Bowling Association came into being in 1961, its equipment specifications exactly those of the ABC, its rules only slightly modified. Australia followed suit and other countries hurried to restructure their regulations as tenpin centres were built in Paris, Antwerp, Berlin, and so on. Two chains of British film makers turned many of their cinemas into bowling centres. The British alone reached a playing membership of more than 40,000 in five years.

British Ten Pin Association

Until the advent of American-style centres in the early 1960s, tenpins was little known in Europe outside Sweden. Two lanes for tenpins in a basement near the Rue de Saint-Petersburg in Paris in 1909 were an unsuccessful experiment. In the same year 12 lanes were installed for the White City Exhibition in London. The builder dismantled the lanes after the exhibition season ended, then installed ten lanes the next year (1910) in the Piccadilly area. This project was unsuccessful too, and the next "invasion" of tenpins in the British Isles came during World War II when hundreds of lanes were installed on American bases.

Japan. Japan in the 1970s has experienced the kind of bowling boom that swept the United States in the 1960s. Early in the decade there were more than 10,000 lanes in 2,800 establishments; one centre in Tokyo, the world's largest, has 504 lanes on four floors. Some centres open at 6 o'clock in the morning and operate all day and night at near capacity. The Japan Bowling Congress reports 70,000 male and 7,000 female members. Bowling also is growing in popularity in other Asian countries including Hong Kong, Thailand, Singapore, and Indonesia.

The game's growth in Sweden has been less phenomenal, though in 1909 it had the first tenpin lanes in Europe. The Federation has 21,000 members and modern tenpin centres in more than two dozen cities. Canada has the largest tenpin population outside the United States; its 50,000 male and 17,000 female players belong to the ABC and WIBC, respectively. Some other leading areas are Australia, 13,000 men, 11,000 women; Mexico, 9,000 and 2,500; Finland 9,000 and 1,000; and Venezuela, 6,500 and 1,200.

International bowling. Informal international bowling competition had been held as early as 1892, when a team of Americans played in a bowling "festival" in Hamburg, Germany. After the turn of the 20th century, teams from New York made several more trips to Germany. An international event was held in Union Hill, New Jersey, during the summer of 1900, but the use of the word "international" was only thinly justified by the appearance of some teams from Canada; the rest were Americans. A group of Americans toured Sweden in 1923 and 1929, then hosted a number of European teams in matches held in New York in 1934. The first attempt to create a tenpin bowling organization on the Continent came in 1925. The group sponsored some scattered competition and in 1936 staged a series of bowling events concurrent with the summer Olympic Games in Berlin. More than 50 Americans made the trip. It was the last international get-together of any consequence until the Fédération Internationale des Quilleurs (FIQ) came on the scene in 1951, as a reorganization of the Continental group.

The international federation

Seven European nations sent teams to the first world tournament of the FIQ in Helsinki, Finland, in 1954. Nine teams took part at Essen, Germany, in 1955, a dozen at Hälsingborg, Sweden, in 1958 and 15 at Hamburg, Germany, in 1960. The world meet moved to Mexico in 1963, when it was put on a four-year basis, and back to Malmö, Sweden, in 1967. Milwaukee, Wisconsin, was the site in 1971 with 32 nations sending teams from an organization that had grown to 48 members. Competition is held in zones—American, European, and Asian—also at four-year intervals. The headquarters of FIQ is in Zürich, Switzerland. The organization has four sections, the principal one being devoted to tenpins. The other three are "small ball" games, those using a duckpin-type ball that can be held in the palm of the hand and has no finger holes. They are schere, bohle, and asphalt, the latter an outdoor game played on an asphalt surface. All are little known or played outside of Germany, Austria, and some of the eastern European countries such as Hungary, Yugoslavia, Poland, Romania, and Czechoslovakia. FIQ competition is for nonprofessionals; and gold, silver, and bronze medals are awarded to champions and runners-up. The American style of alternating lanes after each frame is used, plus two European styles, one in which an entire game is bowled on one lane, the other in which half the game is bowled on one lane, the second half on the other.

For listing of world champions, all-time records for U.S. league and tournament play, and all-events champions, see also SPORTING RECORD in the *Ready Reference and Index.*

Other bowling games. In addition to the "small ball" games recognized by the international federation, many other variations are played regionally and locally in the countries of their origins, and many have been introduced to other countries by emigrants. These include versions of the early prototype games discussed above under the history and development of bowls and bowling—skittles and boccie, for example. The latter, controlled by the Unione Federazioni Italiane Bocce, is popular in Piedmont (where the first organization was formed in Turin, in 1898) and Liguria, and is also played in Italian communities throughout the United States and Australia and has a large following in South America. All of the variants are based on the principles either of bowls or of bowling, and use either "small ball" or regulation size equipment. (J.B.P.)

THE GAME OF BOWLS

The green and equipment. By far the most widely played form of bowls is the flat green game that, as its name implies, is played on a green, 40 to 42 yards (37 to 38 metres) square with a flat, level playing surface. The green is surrounded by a ditch approximately one foot (30 centimetres) wide, beyond which are grassed banks not less than nine inches (23 centimetres) above the level of the green. The green is divided into six rinks each 18 to 21 feet (5.5 to 6.4 metres) wide.

The bowls, or woods, are oblate spheroids that have a standard bias, produced by skilled craftsman who turn them on a lathe to make one side more convex than the other. Weighting of bowls in any way, to produce bias, is illegal. Originally, practically all bowls were made from lignum vitae, but the modern trend, especially among competition bowlers, is to play with composition bowls that are molded from a plastic compound and then turned on a lathe to produce the required bias. These appear to suit all climatic conditions, and hold a course more firmly on rougher types of turf. The maximum measurements for composition bowls are a diameter of 5⅛ inches (13 centimetres) and a weight of 3½ pounds (1.6 kilograms). The target, called the jack, is a white sphere with a diameter of 2½ inches (6.4 centimetres). Players deliver their bowls with one foot on a mat 24 inches (61 centimetres) long and 14 inches (35.6 centimetres) wide.

Composition bowls

Principles of play. To begin play for an end, one player, called the leader, places the mat and rolls the jack. It must come to rest at least 25 yards (23 metres) from the mat, and then serves as the target.

The players then deliver their woods in turn by rolling them along the turf, their primary object being to position the bowls as near as possible to the jack. The end is completed by a point or points being scored for the bowl or bowls nearer the jack than any bowl played by the opposing players. The next end is begun by a player rolling the jack back to the opposite end of the rink.

In national competitions, in singles events each player has four bowls and 21 points constitute a game; in pairs two players on-a-side each use four woods and a game is 21 ends; in triples three players on-a-side each use three woods and a game is 18 ends; and in fours four players on-a-side each use two woods and a game is 21 ends.

A team, known as a rink, consists of a number of fours, usually four or six, and the winners are the side with the highest aggregate score. Variation and interest in the game is heightened by the fact that the jack can be moved by a bowl, and is still alive if run into the ditch, within the confines of the rink. Any bowl in its original course touching the jack is termed a toucher. This is indicated by a chalk mark on the bowl and the toucher is counted live as long as it stays within the confines of the rink, including the ditch.

East Anglian bowls. A variation of the flat green game was adopted by the English Bowling Federation, which came into being in 1926. This game is played in ten counties in eastern England, and is sometimes referred to as East Anglian bowls. The essential difference is that the order of players may be altered at any stage of a game, whereas in the English Bowling Association the players must always keep the order in which they start. In the team only three players constitute a rink and usually six rinks take part. "Touchers" are not given any special consideration, and if the jack goes into the ditch the end is dead and must be replayed. Only bowls within six feet (1.8 metres) of the jack are allowed to count, and the minimum length of throw of the jack is 21 yards (19 metres).

The Crown green game. In North Wales, the Isle of Man, North Midlands, Lancashire, and part of Yorkshire, the Crown green game is very popular. Here the green is six inches to 13 inches (21 to 33 centimetres) higher in the centre and slopes away gradually to the edges of the green. Slightly smaller bowls with rather less bias are used, and, in this game, the jack is biassed. Whereas on a flat green play takes place up and down the green on a line parallel to the sides, crown green play may be in any direction. The game is essentially a singles event with each player using two bowls, and only rarely are pairs events staged.

Indoor bowls. The British outdoor season normally lasts from May to September. To pass the winter months, bowlers derived amusement and companionship by making use of any available hall with space enough to play a modified game of bowls. Most surfaces were much too short and inaccurate, and consisted of matting that could be put down and rolled up at will. Despite this, the short green game became very popular. During the last 20 years, a vast improvement has taken place. Stadiums with full-sized greens have been constructed for indoor play. An increasing number are being used in England and Scotland, and Cardiff and Belfast provide excellent facilities. These stadiums allow the game to be played under normal rules. Standard bowls are used, but the jack is heavier than the outdoor type, to reduce the number of dead ends that tended to occur when the normal outdoor jack was used. A hard, durable level bed is laid and covered with a pliable underlay over which is placed a surface of felt or jute threaded with nylon. The thickness of the underlay controls the running speed of the green. Indoor associations have been formed in the four Home Countries, and international matches, national championships, and British Isles championships are played annually. (G.T.F.)

Bowling stadiums

THE GAME OF TENPINS

Lanes and equipment. The American game of tenpins is played according to the rules and specifications of the American Bowling Congress. The game is played indoors on wooden lanes with maximum dimensions of 62 feet 10$^{11}/_{16}$ inches (19 metres) in length and 42 inches (107 centimetres) in width. The surface, coated with lacquer or plastic-type material, must be free of continuous grooves and be within 40/1,000th inch (1 millimetre) of perfect levelness. The distance from the foul line, past which the player may not slide when delivering the ball, to the centre of the spot on which the headpin stands is 60 feet (18 metres). The approach on which the player advances to the foul line has a minimum length of 15 feet (4.6 metres).

The pins are 15 inches (38 centimetres) tall and arranged in a triangle formation with the point or No. 1 pin at the head of the formation facing the bowler. The centres of the pin spots are 12 inches (30.5 centimetres) apart. The pins are made of maple, either in a single piece or laminated, and most are covered by a plastic coating. The weight ranges between three pounds two ounces and three pounds ten ounces (1.4 kilograms and 1.6 kilograms), although the maximum allowed for synthetic (nonwood) pins is three pounds six ounces (1.5 kilograms).

The ball is of nonmetallic composition, usually hard rubber, with a circumference of 27 inches (68.6 centimetres) and a weight limit of 16 pounds (7.3 kilograms). There is no minimum weight; a number of women and children use regulation-size balls weighing ten pounds (4.5 kilograms) and less in sanctioned competition.

Principles of play. A game of tenpins consists of ten frames. Two deliveries per frame are allowed, the ideal being to knock down all pins on the first (roll of the ball) for a strike. If the pins are left standing after the first delivery, the fallen or "dead" wood is removed and a second delivery permitted. If successful, a spare has been recorded. A miss also is called an error. A split can occur on the first ball when two or more pins are left standing, separated by at least one fallen pin. Stepping over the foul line is a foul and results in loss of all pins knocked down. There are depressed troughs on each side of the lane; a ball falling therein is a "gutterball" and out of play, with resulting loss of one delivery.

Both a strike and a spare count ten pins, or points. If two strikes in a row are recorded (a double), the player counts 20 pins in the first frame plus the number of pins he knocks down on his first delivery in the third frame. Should he score another strike (triple, or turkey), he will have 30 pins in his first frame. A perfect game is 300 and consists of 12 strikes in a row, two additional deliveries being permitted in the tenth or final frame. In scoring, the number of pins knocked down by the first ball in each frame is marked in the first small box on the score sheet; the number of remaining pins knocked down with the second ball, including the making of a spare, is indicated in the second small box. The score attained by each bowler for a frame is recorded in the large box.

Competition in league and tournament play includes individual, as well as teams of two, three, four, and five players; the five-player team is most prevalent. Two teams are assigned to a pair of lanes, and the players bowl in the order in which their captain lines them up on the scoresheet. The first or leadoff bowler for each team bowls on his assigned lane, followed by the second bowler, third bowler, and so on through the fifth bowler, also called the anchor. After the five bowlers on each team have completed their frame, they switch lanes for the second frame. A complete game consists of five frames bowled on each of the two lanes. Most competition is three games in league play. Tournaments range from three games for individuals to as many as 40 in marathon events. A common format is three games per player on a five-player team in the team, doubles, and singles events, the total of the nine games being the individual's total for all of the events. The listing of winners for each of the four separate events is most common in tournaments.

(J.B.P.)

BIBLIOGRAPHY

General history: AMERICAN BOWLING CONGRESS, *History of Bowling* (1959), a booklet discussing the early beginnings of bowling, the many offshoots and variations of bowls and bowling, and their evolution into widely played participation sports.

Bowls (lawn bowls): G.R. BOLSOVER, *Who's Who and Encyclopaedia of Bowls* (1959), a comprehensive book of reference on all aspects of bowls, as well as pen pictures of leading bowlers; G. BOSISTO, *Bowling Along* (1963), an Australian expert's ideas on bowling techniques that provide a racy, readable account of the methods he adopts in top tournament play; D.J. BRYANT, *Bryant on Bowls* (1966), an attractive, detailed study giving the modern approach to competitive bowling at the highest level, with a full explanation of the principles of technique and a sound theoretical analysis; H.J. DINGLEY, *Touchers and Rubs* (1893), an interesting, instructive insight into bowls at the end of the 19th century; J.W. FISHER, *New Ways to Better Bowls* (1948), a short, simplified attempt to cover the basic requirements of the game with suggestions for grip, delivery, and the shots used in play; C.M. JONES (ed.), *Winning Bowls* (1965), an interesting and accurate introduction to the main requirements of the game, followed by detailed comments on varied aspects of the game by several international bowlers, and *Bowls: How to Become a Champion* (1972); J.A. MANSON, *Complete Bowler*, 2nd ed. (1912), a lucid account of the game and its development; J.P. MONRO, *Bowls Encyclopaedia*, 2nd ed. (1953), incorporates detailed information on all aspects of the game, including the history, organization, administration, and records; J. POLLARD, *Gregory's Australian Guide to Bowls* (1962), a factual handbook with a basic instructional course for beginners, followed by a complete directory of Australian bowling clubs and concluding with the constitution laws and bylaws of Australian bowls; A. SWEENEY, *Indoor Bowls* (1966), an authoritative treatise describing the beginnings and growth of indoor bowls, with advice on the building of indoor bowling stadiums and chapters on skills for beginners, and strategies for the more experienced bowler.

Bowling (Tenpins): AMERICAN BOWLING CONGRESS, *Constitution, Specifications and Rules* (annual), the official rules of tenpins for members of the American Bowling Congress, which are also the basis for rules of federations in many other countries, includes suggested rules for the operation of bowling leagues; *Bowling Magazine* (August 1970), the 75th anniversary issue, traces the development of the organization, and *ABC Bowling Equipment Specifications* (rev. periodically), includes diagrams and cross sections of bowling lanes and pins and a more extensive explanation of the subject than is found in the ABC rule book; HERMAN WEISKOPF, *The Perfect Game: The World of Bowling* (1978), a well-illustrated history; S. CRUCHON, C. PEZZANO, and B. PLUCKHAHN, *Pins and Needlers* (1967), a book of bowling humour.

Instructions: J. HEISE, *How You Can Bowl Better Using Self-Hypnosis* (1961); CHUCK PEZZANO, *Professional Bowlers Association Guide to Better Bowling* (1974); J.J. ARCHIBALD, *Bowling for Boys and Girls* (1963); L. BELLISIMO, *The Bowler's Manual*, 4th ed. (1982); D. TAYLOR, *The Secret of Bowling Strikes* (1960); G.E. SULLIVAN (ed.), *Bowling Secrets of the Pros* (1968), and *The Complete Book of Family Bowling* (1968); D. WEBER, *Weber on Bowling* (1981); H. SMITH and S. CRUCHON, *Instant Bowling* (1965); D. CARTER, *10 Secrets of Bowling* (1958).

(J.B.P./G.T.F.)

Boxing

Boxing is the art of attack and defense with the fists in which the two contestants wear padded gloves, box bouts of from three to 15 rounds (each round normally lasting three minutes), and generally observe the code that is set forth in the Marquess of Queensberry rules (see below *The bareknuckle era*). Boxing contestants are matched in weight and ability, each trying to land hard and often with his own fists and, while doing so, attempting to avoid the blows of his opponent.

The terms pugilism and prizefighting in 20th-century usage are practically synonymous with boxing, although the first term indicates the ancient origins of the sport in its derivation from the Latin *pugil*, "a fighter with the cestus (a hand covering)," related to the Latin *pugnus*, "fist," and derived in turn from the Greek *pyx*, "with clenched fist"; while "prizefighting" emphasizes pursuit of the sport for gain. Samuel Johnson in his *Dictionary* (1755) defined a prizefighter as "one that fights publicly for a reward."

This article is intended for the general reader who may have no knowledge of boxing. Therefore, in addition to tracing its history and outlining its present status, the article is designed to help a spectator understand a match. For information on specific rules or on boxing techniques, the reader should consult the works listed in the bibliography. For lists of world professional boxing champions, see SPORTING RECORD in the *Ready Reference and Index*. See also *Olympic Games* tables in ATHLETIC GAMES AND CONTESTS.

HISTORY

Early History. Presumably people used their fists to settle arguments for many centuries before anyone thought of staging bouts for the entertainment of others. There is evidence that boxing existed by about 1500 BC in ancient Crete. Centuries before the arrival of the Greeks, boxing was practiced in the Aegean.

The descriptions of fighting in ancient Greece are not evocative of Queensberry skill. The Greeks believed in developing physical as well as mental abilities. But the young Greek male was always conscious of his possible role as a soldier or warrior, and it was with this sort of destiny in mind that he exercised. Therefore, the Greeks fought largely to prove their courage, strength, and endurance—not their agility or cleverness. They fought in the open air, bounded by spectators, with no resined surface to manoeuvre upon, and no corners or ropes to employ in their strategy. There were no rounds—the bout continued until one of the fighters admitted himself beaten.

In the early days fighters wore thongs of soft leather bound around their fists and often around two-thirds of their forearms in order to protect their hands and wrists. Beginning in the 4th century BC, harder leather was used for the thongs, with the result that they became weapons as well as protection. Late in the history of the Roman Empire, the Greeks adopted the hand covering called the cestus, which was studded with iron or brass nuggets and was used in gladiatorial battles to the death in the Roman arenas.

Ancient Olympic boxing

Although the Greeks of the classic period considered fistfighting a feature of the mythological games at Olympia, the sport was not actually introduced into the Olympic contests until the XXIII Olympiad (688 BC). Onomastos of Smyrna was one of the first Olympic victors. A sport called pancratium ("complete contest"), which combined boxing and wrestling, was introduced in the XXXIII Olympiad (648 BC). In the XLI Olympiad a boxing competition for youths was added. There were no weight divisions, and size and strength were prime qualifications for the pugilist.

The first Greek fighters were not paid; glory was the reward they sought. Later, wealthy men trained their slaves as boxers and had them perform for special entertainments. In the 1st century AD, Romans forced cestusclad slaves to bludgeon one another to death in a gruesome perversion of sport for the entertainment of crowds who thronged to arenas to see the kill. With the rise of Christianity and the concurrent decline of the Roman Empire, pugilism as entertainment apparently ceased to exist. At least, there is no record of it.

The bareknuckle era. With the rise of London as a major city came a type of encounter called a prizefight. Prizefighters were strong men from different sections of the city, whose admirers were willing to bet that they could beat one another and arranged fights to settle the issue. The fighters performed for whatever purses were agreed upon plus stakes (side bets). At first there were few tactics that were not allowed. Wrestling was permitted and it was common to fall on a foe after throwing him. It also was common practice to hit a man who was down. The fighters wore no gloves of any kind and welcomed variations upon punching because their hands could not take the punishment involved in delivering many hard punches consecutively. Nevertheless, by 1719 one man had so captured public imagination that he was acclaimed champion of England. His name was James Figg and he held the title for a span that may have been as great as 15 years, turning back during this time an Italian challenger named Tito Alberta di Carni. For years the only outstanding fighters were English. Occasionally an Irishman or American came to London to ply his trade. These invasions increased as the popularity of prizefighting (and the size of prizes offered) grew.

The first fighter greatly to aid the sport itself was Jack Broughton (1704–89), a 200-pound Englishman who won the championship of his country sometime between 1734 and 1740 (versions differ) and lost it in 1750. Broughton's reign was long enough and his character good enough to win a new respect for prizefighting. He discarded the barroom techniques, which his predecessors favoured, and relied primarily on his fists. (He did, however, like all fighters of the time, also use wrestling holds.) He brought some degree of order out of a brawling chaos not only by the way he fought but by a set of rules that so clarified the proper conditions for a bout that they governed boxing, with only minor changes, until the more detailed London Prize Ring rules superseded them in 1838. Under Broughton's rules, a round continued until a man went down; after 30 seconds of rest he had to square off a yard from his opponent or be declared beaten. Also, one could not hit an opponent who was down or grasp him below the waist.

Broughton's rules

Broughton capitalized upon his good name among sportsmen by conducting classes in "the mystery of boxing . . . that wholly British art," as he advertised it, for gentlemen at his Haymarket academy in 1747. To attract pupils, he devised "mufflers," ancestors of modern boxing gloves, with the assurance that these would be used in all bouts to protect against bruised faces and hands. This contribution alone established his importance to modern boxing. But the man who beat him inaugurated a period of dishonesty, in which one fixed bout followed another and sportsmen lost faith entirely in the sport. Prizefighting was re-established in good repute by Tom Johnson, who became champion in the 1780s and lost the title, in an unquestionably honest bout, in 1791 to Ben Brain.

The man who succeeded Brain was the first scientific fighter in the history of pugilism. He was an English Jew named Daniel Mendoza (1763–1836) who weighed only 160 pounds (a middleweight by modern standards) but beat the best and biggest fighters in England. Mendoza had good, quick footwork and a swift, straight left jab. By combining agility with the jab, he easily befuddled his lumbering opponents. After losing his title to John Jackson (1769–1845), known as "Gentleman Jackson," in 1795, Mendoza opened a school in London at which he coached young noblemen in fighting techniques.

Jackson's chief contribution in the transformation of prizefighting into boxing was to gain friends of distinction for the sport of fist fighting—people who were interested in seeing it progress and who could give it a badly needed aura of respectability.

Of the bareknuckle champions who followed, the first to assure himself sports immortality was Tom Cribb (1781–1848), who defeated two American-born former slaves, Bill Richmond (1763–1829) and Tom Molineaux (1784–1818). Richmond was the first man born in America to win acclaim in England as a first-class pugilist. Gen. Hugh Percy, who commanded some of the British troops occupying New York, discovered Richmond's talents and took him to England in 1777. Cribb beat Richmond in 90 minutes in 1805. Later, after winning the English championship, he twice beat Molineaux in his greatest performances.

In 1839, new London Prize Ring rules were first used in a championship fight in which James ("Deaf") Burke lost the English title to William Thompson ("Bendigo"). These rules (later revised in 1853) provided for a ring 24 feet square and bounded by ropes. When a fighter went down, the round ended and he was helped to his corner. Time was called after 30 seconds, and, if he could not get unaided to a mark in the centre of the ring by the end of eight additional seconds, he was declared "not up to scratch" and beaten. Kicking, gouging, butting with the head, biting, and low blows were all declared fouls. The London rules governed pugilism in England and America for over 50 years.

London Prize Ring rules

By 1860 America had produced a number of good fighters. One of them, the handsome John C. Heenan, not content with the championship of the United States, challenged English champion Tom Sayers. They met at Farnborough, Hampshire, April 17, 1860. There was a great difference in weights—195 pounds for Heenan to the Englishman's 149 pounds—but Sayers held Heenan to a 42-round draw, the last five rounds fought after a crowd entered the ring.

The Bettmann Archive

Bareknuckle championship match between John C. Heenan and Tom Sayers at Farnborough, Hampshire, April 17, 1860. Lithograph by Currier and Ives.

Although the Heenan–Sayers bout attracted a good deal of attention, the brawling that distinguished old-time pugilism continued to alienate most of the better people of England. It became apparent that if a widely popular sport was to emerge and endure it would have to be extracted from, rather than preserved in, the hurly-burly of prizefighting. When John Graham Chambers of the Amateur Athletic Club devised a new set of rules, he tried to emphasize aspects of pugilism that Daniel Mendoza had first exploited—that is, boxing technique and skill. These attributes were expected to draw a better class of patron than the old London rules.

The rules appeared in 1867 and differed from the London rules in four major respects: contestants wore padded gloves; each round consisted of three minutes of fighting followed by a minute of rest; wrestling was illegal; and any fighter who went down had to get up unaided within ten seconds—if he could not do so, he was declared knocked out and the fight was over.

Queensberry rules. John Sholto Douglas, 9th marquess of Queensberry (1844–1900), lent his name to Chambers' rules so that they would be associated with the nobility. At first professionals scorned the new code and thought its practitioners somewhat effete. But gradually, although championships among professionals continued to be decided by the London rules, more and more fighters who were quick with their hands and feet and preferred punching to wrestling learned the Queensberry style. Prominent among these was James ("Jem") Mace (1831–1910), who, though weighing only 160 pounds, won the English heavyweight title in 1861 through judicious use of a good left jab and a quick pair of feet. Having proved that he could win under the London code, he was more or less free to do as he pleased and he chose to do two things that had a vast influence on the course of boxing history. The first was to go abroad to fight. The second was to show growing interest in the Queensberry style of fighting.

It was only a matter of time before Mace arrived in America, since prizefighting was then frowned upon by the clergy and the law in England. He actually was at his best when sparring with gloves. His enthusiasm for glove fighting did much to advance the Queensberry code, for it was generally conceded that there was nothing effete about Jem Mace. Both the London and Queensberry rules were followed by a new generation of fighters in America and the time for decision between them was near.

John L. Sullivan, who claimed the world's heavyweight championship in 1882, made the move that finally aligned professional fighters on the side of the Queensberry rules. He did so not out of a desire to benefit sport but because he felt he could not afford to do otherwise.

Having won the American heavyweight title at the age of 23, Sullivan squandered remarkable speed of hands and feet on the London era, when these qualities were less appreciated than might later have been the case. Luckily, he also had great strength and a mighty punch. These latter qualities made and kept him a bareknuckle champion. Public authorities had, however, grown increasingly hostile to pugilism. In 1889, when Sullivan defended against Jake Kilrain in the last heavyweight championship bareknuckle fight to be held in America, prizefighting (London rules) was illegal in every state of the union. Subsequent to the Kilrain fight, Sullivan was arrested and plagued with legal actions that interfered with his making a living for the next year. He complained that it cost him $18,670 to settle for the Kilrain match. Therefore, when at the age of 33 Sullivan agreed to defend his title against quick, clever "Gentleman Jim" Corbett, he insisted on Queensberry rules. Sullivan lost to the epitome of Queensberry skill. Corbett in a five-year reign (1892–97) proved that a big man could be highly scientific and launched boxing on a lucrative new era.

Economic impetus. When Victorian boxers left England, they went not only to the United States but to Australia and Canada and, occasionally, to continental Europe. The reasons that professional boxing became centred in the United States were chiefly two: first, the expanding American economy made it possible for promoters to conduct bouts fairly regularly for the entertainment of factory hands, miners, lumberjacks, and other workers who flooded into the new country and demanded excitement in their off hours; second, successive waves of immigration provided husky, hungry boys who had little education and were willing to fight for quick money. Boxing became a shortcut to riches and social acceptance for those near the foot of the economic ladder.

Immigrant boxers

The famines that drove thousands of Irish to seek refuge in America furnished important raw material for the greatest era professional boxing has known. Before 1915, the Irish had become dominant in every division from heavyweight through bantamweight. Terry McGovern, "Philadelphia" Jack O'Brien, Mike ("Twin") Sullivan and his brother Jack, Packey McFarland, Jimmy Clabby, Jack Britton—these were only a few of the colourful, courageous, and highly skilled men who made a profession of boxing.

German, Scandinavian, and central European immigration, which increased after the political troubles of 1848, also contributed greatly to this golden age of boxing in the United States. Polish-American Stanley Ketchel and German-Americans Billy Papke, Frank Klaus, and Frank Mantell dominated the middleweight division 1908–13. Danish-American Battling Nelson and German-American Ad Wolgast ruled the lightweights 1908–12. Such outstanding Jewish fighters as Joe Choynski, Abe Attell, Battling Levinsky, and Harry Lewis were active before 1915, but even more outstanding Jewish fighters fought from 1915 to 1930, when Benny Leonard, Sid Terris, Lew Tendler, Al Singer, Maxie Rosenbloom, and Max Baer were in the ring.

Beginning about 1920, Italian-Americans assumed an importance in boxing. Their influence has continued great and has produced such champions as featherweight and lightweight Tony Canzoneri, heavyweight Rocky Marciano, and featherweights Johnny Dundee (nicknamed the "Scotch Wop") and Willie Pep.

Meanwhile, American Negroes also turned to boxing to fight their way to the top. Foreign-born Negroes (such as Peter Jackson, Sam Langford, Joe Walcott, and George Dixon) came to the United States to capitalize on the opportunities offered by boxing. Lightweight Joe Gans, born in Baltimore, was perhaps the cleverest boxer, pound for pound, in professional annals. He became world champion (1902–08), as did heavyweight Jack Johnson (1908–15). Prejudice against black fighters at times was great. John L. Sullivan found it convenient to "draw the colour line" in refusing to defend against Peter Jackson, and Jack Dempsey would not fight Harry Wills. But Joe Louis won complete acceptance, and his reign as heavyweight champion (1937–49) was one of the most popular in boxing history. Greatly encouraged, and further prompted by the rigours of depression years, Negroes flooded into the ring beginning in the mid-1930s to start a domination comparable to that enjoyed by the Irish prior to 1910. Among them were Henry Armstrong, who held the featherweight, lightweight, and welterweight titles simultaneously; "Sugar" Ray Robinson, welterweight and five-time middleweight champion; Archie Moore, light-heavyweight champion; and heavyweight champions Ezzard Charles, "Jersey" Joe Walcott, Floyd Patterson, Charles "Sonny" Liston, Cassius Clay (Muhammad Ali), and Joe Frazier.

The rise of black fighters to prominence

PHOTOWORLD

Jack Johnson (right) fighting Jim Jeffries at Reno, Nevada, 1910. Jeffries was beaten after 15 rounds.

Spread of boxing. In the 18th century, British boxers including Daniel Mendoza visited France, but it was not until late in the following century that a real interest in boxing developed on the Continent. In France it replaced *savate*, or *la boxe français*, which permitted kicking as well as hitting with the fists. Swiss boxer Frank Erne, who won the world lightweight title in 1899, was a leading instructor as gymnasiums and coaching schools were opened. Eight years later, Victor Breyer and Theodore Vienne opened the Wonderland Francais arena, and some of the world's best heavyweights visited France. The famous French boxer Georges Carpentier fought in every weight division from 1907 to 1926 and won the world light-heavyweight title in 1920.

In most of Asia the sport developed more slowly. In 1909 Frank Churchill formed the Olympic Club in Manila and, with American Eddie Duarte, taught boxing to the Filipinos. Previously there had been only occasional contests when British and American battleships came to ports like Manila or Hong Kong. The first boxer of note in the Philippines was Pancho Villa, who won the world flyweight title in 1923. Since then boxers from the Oriental countries have specialized in this division, winning several world titles in recent years. Japan, especially, and Thailand, which also developed a sport similar to the French *savate*, made great progress in boxing.

PHOTOWORLD

Leo Espinoza (left) of the Philippines fighting Yoshio Shirai of Japan for the world flyweight title at Tokyo, May 24, 1954. Shirai, who was titleholder from 1952–54, retained title in the match.

Development of amateur boxing. During the 19th century, boxing was a favourite sport among the gentry of Britain. In 1867 the first amateur championships took place under the Marquess of Queensberry rules, with the Marquess himself presenting cups to the winners. The rules however, came in for criticism because they forbade infighting. Boxers who, because of their shorter stature, had to work at close quarters to be effective, were cautioned, and one prominent amateur, T. Anderson, was disqualified for "fighting." Criticism became so strong that a number of influential men with a love of boxing met in London in 1880 and devised new rules. Thus the Amateur Boxing Association (ABA), the world's first amateur governing body, was formed. The following year the ABA staged its first official championships. Originally there were 12 member clubs, and the number rose to 46 by 1906. Today, there are thousands and for the ABA championships each year boxers throughout Britain must qualify on a regional basis.

In 1888 the Amateur Athletic Union (AAU) of the United States was formed, instituting its annual championships in boxing the same year. The AAU has remained the ruling body for the United States. In 1923 another amateur competition was started by the *Chicago Tribune*. Called the Golden Gloves (the name was first used in New York in 1927), it grew quickly into a national competition rivalling that of the AAU.

Golden Gloves

Amateur boxing spread rapidly to other countries and resulted in several major international competitions, taking place annually, every two years, or, as in the case of the Olympic Games, every four years. Important events are the European Championships, the British Empire and Commonwealth Championships, the Pan American Championships, and more recently the All-Africa Championships and the World Military Championships. All international matches and competitions of this nature are controlled by the Association Internationale de Boxe Amateur (AIBA), formed in 1946 with headquarters in London.

Because of their political and economic structures, the U.S.S.R. and other Communist countries do not have professional sportsmen. One notable exception was the Hungarian boxer Laszlo Papp, winner of Olympic gold medals in 1948, 1952, and 1956. Papp was permitted to turn professional at the age of 31 and won the European middleweight title in 1962, retiring undefeated some three years later to coach the Hungarian amateur team.

Although there is a record of boxing schools in Moscow at the turn of the 20th century, national championships were not instituted until 1933. The U.S.S.R. joined the AIBA in 1950 and entered the Olympic Games in 1952 to emerge, together with other Communist countries such as Poland and Hungary, as one of the strongest amateur boxing nations in the world. There are over 300,000 boxers in the U.S.S.R., which has three main sources for subsidizing sport—government allocations, trade union allocations, and dues paid by members of voluntary sports societies. No boxer has to pay for coaching or for gymnasium use, and all equipment and medical advice is free. These factors give Communist countries a distinct advantage over other countries, whose amateurs must pay for everything out of their own pockets, and the best of whom invariably turn professional, thus making team building an impossibility.

African champions

African countries advanced considerably after gaining their independence in the 1950s and 1960s, thanks mainly to former professionals Hogan Bassey of Nigeria and Roy Ankrah of Ghana, who were appointed as national coaches to their respective teams. Bassey was world featherweight champion (1957–59), and Ankrah was Empire titleholder. Africa dominated the 1970 British Commonwealth Games in Edinburgh, winning eight of eleven gold medals. In addition, six Africans were losing finalists. Uganda and Kenya joined Nigeria and Ghana among the top amateur boxing nations of the world.

Professional purses. In 1860 John C. Heenan and Tom Sayers fought for $2,500 a side and a championship belt. John L. Sullivan fought Corbett in 1892 for a $25,000 purse and a $10,000 side bet. The man who made boxing big business was George ("Tex") Rickard, the first great promoter of the sport. After staging the world's lightweight championship bout between Joe Gans and Battling Nelson to publicize the mining town of Goldfield, Nevada, in 1906, he saw that boxing as spectacle had great potential. Through clever press agentry Rickard made it fashionable to be seen at ringside at major bouts. Five of the fights he promoted for Jack Dempsey, heavyweight champion 1919–26, drew over $1,000,000 in receipts. They were two bouts against Gene Tunney (1926 and 1927) and one each against Georges Carpentier of France (1921), Luis Angel Firpo of Argentina (1923), and Jack Sharkey (1927). A natural showman and gambler, Rickard made an art of boxing publicity, playing on people's prejudices in pitting Negro against white (Gans–Nelson and Jack Johnson–Jim Jeffries), alleged slacker against war hero (Dempsey–Carpentier), and American against foreigner (Dempsey–Firpo). His fortunes were tied to Dempsey, however, and after Dempsey's retirement Rickard began to lose money and dropped from his position of prominence.

In the depression years that followed, receipts from boxing shows dwindled greatly. The financial centre of boxing remained the United States, although the bout between Primo Carnera of Italy and Paulino Uzcudun of Spain fought in 1930 in Barcelona drew more ($110,000) than all but a few U.S. bouts that year. In 1935 Mike Jacobs, who had been associated with Rickard, signed Joe Louis to a contract and thus launched a new boxing era. With Louis fighting exclusively for him, Jacobs had the best drawing card since Dempsey. In two years he was promoting for Madison Square Garden in New York. Louis fought in three bouts that grossed over $1,000,000: Max Baer (1935), Max Schmeling (1938), and Billy Conn (1946). In 1945 the receipts from a year of boxing at Madison Square Garden exceeded $2,000,000 for the first time.

Some lucrative bouts were also staged outside the United States. British light heavyweight Freddie Mills drew crowds paying $200,000 and $182,000 respectively in London bouts against Americans Gus Lesnevich and

Joey Maxim. In 1953 English Randy Turpin drew $238,-000 in London against French Charles Humez. When Thai bantamweight Chamrern Songkitrat developed into a contender for the world championship, he drew receipts of over $200,000 in 1954 Bangkok bouts against Australian Jimmy Carruthers and Frenchman Robert Cohen.

Influence of television

Beginning in the late 1940s, boxing in the United States underwent a great change brought about by televising of bouts. Attendance fell off sharply for all but the most attractive matches, as people preferred to watch televised bouts at home or in theatres. Receipts from the crowd attending became steadily of less importance. When Charles "Sonny" Liston defended his title against former champion Floyd Patterson in 1963, live gate receipts were only $247,690, but closed circuit TV and other media fees raised the total to $4,747,690, of which each fighter's share was $1,434,000.

Professional organization. World professional boxing has no single controlling body that is universally recognized. The situation started in the U.S., where two organizations were set up in 1920: the National Boxing Association, a private body, which at that time had a membership of 13 states; and the New York State Athletic Commission, a state agency. Divided control led to a situation in which competing organizations sometimes recognized different boxers as world champion at the same weight.

In Europe the ruling body was the International Boxing Union, which in 1948 became the European Boxing Union. Several attempts were made to induce all major organizations to agree to the formation of one international ruling body, but to little avail. There were always differences over voting power. In 1963, however, the World Boxing Council was formed. It includes the British and Commonwealth Boards of Control, Continental European Boxing Union, and the North American, Central American, South American, Oriental, Pan Pacific, and African Boxing federations.

The National Boxing Association changed its name to the World Boxing Association in the early 1960s and currently has control over most of the United States. Eleven states are not members of the WBA, however, and they stage most of the professional boxing events that take place in the U.S. The WBA still names its world champions, and there are still cases of two world champions at the same weight—one WBA and the other WBC.

At its 1970 annual congress, the World Boxing Council stated its aim to formulate one standard set of rules for boxing in all countries.

MODERN BOXING

Weight divisions. During the 19th and again at the beginning of the 20th century, the increasing popularity of professional boxing brought about the formation of weight divisions other than heavyweight class to obviate the handicap of a contestant having to concede excessive weight, sometimes two or three stones (28–42 lb, or 11–18 kg), to his opponent. Some divisions originated in the U.S., others in Great Britain. Title fights usually were arranged, but in many cases a boxer simply claimed a championship and held it until he was beaten. If he found he could no longer meet the required weight limit, he would simply alter the limit to suit himself. As long as he did not go to extremes, this was considered in order.

Gradually this practice ceased, the rules governing world championship bouts became more strict, and eight weight divisions came to be universally recognized with the limits as follows: flyweight (not over 112 lb), bantamweight (118 lb), featherweight (126 lb), lightweight (135 lb), welterweight (147 lb), middleweight (160 lb), light-heavyweight, or cruiserweight (175 lb), and heavyweight (any weight).

In all world and national title fights the above weight limits must be strictly observed. If a boxer is over the limit, he is normally given a short time in which to make the stipulated weight. If he still fails, the bout ceases to be regarded as a championship contest and the champion, if he was at fault, forfeits his title.

Two additional divisions, junior lightweight (130 lb) and junior welterweight (140 lb), were introduced in the U.S. in the 1920s. These still exist and world champions at these weights are recognized by some federations. Also, a junior middleweight (154 lb) division was introduced in the U.S. and a junior featherweight division in Oriental countries. The term junior in boxing has nothing to do with age. These divisions were formed for the benefit of boxers who were too heavy for one of the eight recognized divisions and too light for the next higher division.

There were seven divisions in the Olympic Games of 1904, and five in 1908. When the Games were resumed in 1920, there were eight, and the required weights were the same as for professionals. This situation continued until the European Championships of 1951, when the Association Internationale de Boxe Amateur (AIBA) instituted ten weight classes. This procedure was followed in the Olympic Games from 1952 until 1968, when yet another division was added. The AIBA weights, however, were almost entirely different from the professional weights and officially expressed in kilograms, instead of pounds. The 11 divisions now recognized in all major international amateur competitions are as follows: light-flyweight, 48 kg (105 lb 13 oz); flyweight, 51 kg (112 lb 7 oz); bantamweight, 54 kg (119 lb 1 oz); featherweight, 57 kg (125 lb 10½ oz); lightweight, 60 kg (132 lb 4½ oz); light-welterweight, 63.5 kg (140 lb); welterweight, 67 kg (147 lb 11 oz); light-middleweight, 71 kg (156 lb 8½ oz); middleweight, 75 kg (165 lb 5½ oz); light-heavyweight, 81 kg (178 lb 9 oz); and heavyweight (no limit). These divisions are also adopted in principle for the ABA Championships in Great Britain and the AAU Championships in the U.S., except that their limits are taken to the nearest pound and there are slight variations in the four divisions from featherweight to welterweight.

AIBA amateur classes recognized

Rules and equipment. Because there is no accepted world ruling body for professional boxing, each country has its own rules, and in the United States there are different rules for each state. Generally speaking, however, bouts take place in a "ring" that is 14 to 20 feet square and surrounded by three strands of ropes to stop the contestants' falling out. Professional bouts are from 4 to 15 rounds in duration, which is the usual distance for world championship contests.

In Britain the referee, who works in the ring with the boxers, is the sole adjudicator and regulates the bout. In most other countries, two judges outside the ring also keep scorecards, and a fighter must win on two of the three cards to score a decision. National championship bouts vary from 15 rounds in Great Britain to 10 in Japan and Korea. Padded gloves, ranging from six to eight ounces in weight, are worn by the boxers.

A bout ends in a knockout when a boxer is knocked down and is adjudged not ready to resume the contest at the count of "ten," whether he still be down or in the act of rising. A fight can be stopped (called a technical knockout in the United States) when a boxer is deemed by the referee to be incapable of defending himself, even though he has not been counted out; when a boxer is deemed by the referee to have sustained too serious an injury for him to continue, or to be too far behind in ability to have a chance of winning; or when a boxer himself retires. A bout may also end in a decision, when a bout goes the scheduled number of rounds and is won on points awarded by the referee and judges; in a draw, when the referee and judges agree that both boxers fought equally well; in a "no contest," when the referee deems that both men are not giving their best or are persistently infringing the rules; or in a disqualification.

Disqualification may be made by the referee for fouls such as hitting below the "belt" (an imaginary line drawn across the body from the top of the hip bone); hitting on the back of the head or neck; punching to the lower back, the region of the kidneys; hitting with the open glove, the inside or butt of the hand, or with the wrist or elbow; holding, butting with, or careless use of, the head; shouldering, wrestling, or roughing; not trying; persistently ducking below the waistline; intentionally falling without receiving a blow; failing to separate when ordered to do so, or striking or attempting to strike an opponent while separating; deliberately striking an opponent when he is falling or when he is down; or ungentlemanly conduct. A boxer is usually penalized at first by having marks deducted from his score and then disqualified if he persists in his actions. It is accepted in the United States that, since a boxer must wear a protective cup, disqualifications for low punching are quite rare, although the offending boxer would be penalized. In other nations, however, referees are often much stricter in dealing with this offense, and a low blow that is considered by the referee to have been deliberately delivered could bring immediate disqualification.

Amateur rules

The rules for conducting amateur boxing are very similar in Great Britain, the United States, and continental Europe, with the main difference being that in the United States referees manually separate the boxers; elsewhere, on the command "break," the boxers are expected to do so themselves, and also to take one step back. Bouts are normally three rounds, fought in rings 12 to 20 feet square, using eight- to 10-ounce gloves. Bending below the waist is prohibited by international rules, because it may lead to butting with the head. Voting, under international rules, is carried out entirely by three judges; the referee simply supervises the boxing. In the United States, however, the scoring is done by the referee and two judges, with each scorer awarding a maximum of 20 points for each round.

Technique. No one phase of boxing is more important than another. Boxing demands coordination of hands, feet, and brain. Good footwork is as important as being able to punch correctly, defense as important as attack. Perfect balance is essential at all times. The two generally recognized stances are "orthodox" and "southpaw." The former has the left hand and left foot forward, the latter the right hand and right foot forward. A boxer adopts the stance he finds most natural and effective. For the orthodox stance, the right heel is in a line behind the left heel, knees slightly bent, and all movements carried out on the balls of the feet. The hands are held in front of the body, with the left hand shoulder high and extended about 12 inches. The left hand is slightly higher than the right, with the left forearm held across the chest, the right fist almost touching it, and both elbows bent and resting lightly against the ribs. The right fist is held near the chin for protection, the chin tucked into the chest and the shoulders hunched.

There are three basic punches: the straight, hook, and uppercut. All others, such as the jab, swing, bolo, and cross, are modifications of these basic punches. The straight punch moves directly out from the shoulder, the back of the hand facing upwards. The hook is a short, lateral movement of arm and fist, elbow bent and wrist twisted inwards at the moment of impact. The uppercut is an upward blow delivered from the direction of the toes. The jab, a shortened version of the straight punch that reaches its target before the arm can be fully extended, is the punch most used in boxing. The swing is a long-range hook, a desperation punch that may be used when a fighter cannot reach his opponent by any other method. The bolo is an uppercut that starts from behind the body, with the arm wound up as if to throw a baseball. The cross is similar to a straight punch or a hook, and is used by boxers mainly as a follow-up to a lead from the other hand.

Changing styles. In bareknuckle fighting the accent was on the power of the punch, since bouts ended when one contestant could not continue. The hands were held in front of the body in no particular position, and footwork was nonexistent. With the advent of padded gloves and contests decided on points, boxing skill and footwork became more important. More regard was paid to defense to prevent an opponent from landing scoring punches. James J. Corbett was the first of the modern heavyweight champions to concentrate on technique. Ten years after Corbett lost the title, heavyweight champion Jack Johnson showed that he too could box as well as punch. Spectators were divided; they enjoyed watching clever boxers, but when it came to the heavyweights they looked for the "big punch." Hence the tremendous popularity of Jack Dempsey, an exciting, aggressive fighter who always sought to knock his man out. He fought from a crouch, bobbing and weaving to leave as little of himself exposed as possible. His style was later adopted by many other U.S. boxers.

Heavyweights are not expected to move quickly, but a notable exception to this was Muhammad Ali, who won the world heavyweight title in 1964, forfeited it in 1967 when he refused to be inducted into the U.S. armed forces, and regained it in 1974 and again in 1978, becoming the first heavyweight to capture the title three times. At his peak Ali was probably the fastest and the most skillful heavyweight champion of all time. He finished every early fight unmarked and had a style all his own, dancing around, arms dangling by his sides, but always in position to attack or defend at the right time. It has been alleged that Ali did not possess a heavy punch, but his record before his 1971 fight with Joe Frazier of 31 victories in 31 professional bouts, 25 being gained inside the scheduled number of rounds, suggests that he had plenty of power.

Styles remain a matter of individual choice. In Britain many still adopt a form of the traditional upright stance originated by bareknuckle fighters, but in the United States a modified Dempsey-style crouch is more prevalent.

BIBLIOGRAPHY. BOHUN LYNCH, *The Prize Ring* (1925), traces the history of boxing from the bareknuckle period to the time when gloves were substituted for bare fists; HARRY CARPENTER, *Boxing* (1975), a history of boxing from 1890 to the 1970s, focusses on the professional sport with brief sections on amateur and Olympic boxing; NAT FLEISCHER, *Black Dynamite*, 5 vol. (1938–47), is a history of blacks in boxing from 1782 to 1938, with biographies of the most important black fighters and descriptions of their greatest fights. *Heavyweight Championship*, rev. ed. (1961), by the same author, deals with all champions in this division from 1719, describing how they won their titles and how they fared in title defenses, with full statistical data for each title fight; JOHN DURANT, *The Heavyweight Champions*, 6th ed. (1976), includes the champions of the 1960s and early 1970s. RON OLVER and TIM RILEY, *Boxing* (1962), is written for the young man who wishes to take up boxing as an amateur and includes descriptions of basic blows, stance, training, diet and weight, tactics, and technique, and the special problems of the left-handed boxer. CURTIS COKES, *The Complete Book of Boxing for Fighters and Fight Fans* (1980), is an introduction to all aspects of boxing by a former welterweight champion. *The Ring Record Book and Boxing Encyclopedia* (annual) is a comprehensive work on boxing statistics; *Boxing News Annual and Record Book* (annual) is the British counterpart to the *Ring Record Book* of the United States, providing all relevant historical data and statistics.

(R.O.)

Boyle, Robert

A 17th-century natural philosopher, Robert Boyle devised many original experiments and developed a corpuscular concept of matter. He contributed much toward overthrowing the ancient Aristotelian view of nature that was based on forms and qualities, and substituting a particulate explanation in terms of matter and motion. All the intellectual interests of his day were harmonized in his twin enthusiasms, religion and experimental science. His attitude toward the study of nature in all its aspects was that such study helped to reveal the greatness of the Creator. He was a leading member of the Royal Society of London.

Early life

Boyle was born on January 25, 1627, in Lismore, County Waterford, Ireland, the 14th child of a family of wealth and influence. In 1635 he was sent to Eton College, which was in favour for the education of gentlemen's sons. He spent the years from 1639 to 1644 with a tutor on the Continent, for the most part in Switzerland, though they also toured France and Italy.

On his return to England during the Civil War, Boyle was reunited with his sister Katherine, Lady Ranelagh. Through her his circle of acquaintances was extended,

Boyle, oil painting by an unknown artist after F. Kerseboom (1632–90). In the National Portrait Gallery, London.
By courtesy of the National Portrait Gallery, London

and some of them, including Samuel Hartlib, certainly stimulated his interest in experimental work. Between 1645 and 1655, Boyle lived partly in Dorset, where he wrote moral essays, some of which appeared in 1655 in *Occasional Reflections upon Several Subjects.* One of his essays is reputed to have inspired the writing of *Gulliver's Travels* by Jonathan Swift. He spent some time in Ireland in connection with his estates, engaged in anatomical dissection. There was also a brief visit to the Low Countries in 1648.

From 1656 to 1668 he resided at Oxford, where he had the good fortune to secure the assistance of Robert Hooke, the able inventor and subsequent curator of experiments to the Royal Society, who helped him to construct an air pump. Recognizing at once its scientific possibilities, Boyle conducted pioneering experiments in which he demonstrated the physical characteristics of air and that air is necessary for combustion, respiration, and the transmission of sound. Boyle described this work in 1660 in *New Experiments Physio-Mechanicall, Touching the Spring of the Air and its Effects.* In a work appended to the second edition in 1662, he published his report of 1661 to the Royal Society on the relationship, now known as Boyle's law, that at a constant temperature the volume of a gas is inversely proportional to the pressure. In *The Sceptical Chymist,* Boyle in 1661 attacked the Aristotelian theory of the four elements (earth, air, fire, and water) and also the three principles (salt, sulfur, mercury) proposed by Paracelsus. Instead, he developed the concept of primary particles which by coalition produce corpuscles. Different substances result from the number, position, and motion of the primary matter. All natural phenomena were therefore explained not by Aristotelian elements and qualities, but by the motion and organization of primary particles. Thus, Boyle did not postulate different kinds of primary elements—the 19th-century view—but his ideas are valid within certain limits.

The air pump

Beginning in 1668, he resided with his sister Katherine in London. In this final period of his life he continued his experimental work with the help of laboratory assistants, one of whom founded a chemical manufacturing firm that had an independent existence until the early part of the 20th century.

In his experimental work he studied also the calcination of metals and proposed a means of distinguishing between acid and alkaline substances, which was the origin of the use of chemical indicators. He was also interested in trades and manufacturing processes. In an age that was not noted for its humanitarianism, Boyle not infrequently was compassionate enough to refrain from subjecting a living creature to the rigours of experiment for a second time.

Boyle acquired great renown in his lifetime, and foreigners of distinction invariably tried to visit him. Numerous poetical references were made to him, before and after his death. His many scientific and religious writings never led to acrimonious controversies. As a devout Protestant, he took a special interest in promoting the Christian religion abroad, giving money to translate and publish the New Testament into Irish and Turkish. He contributed also to the transcription, revision, and printing of an existing Irish version of the Old Testament. In 1690 he developed his theological views in *The Christian Virtuoso,* which he wrote to show that the study of nature was a central religious duty. In his view of divine providence, nature was a clocklike mechanism that had been made and set in motion by the Creator at the beginning and now functioned according to secondary laws, which could be studied by science. But the soul of man was incorporeal and nobler than the moving corpuscles of which his body was composed.

Interest in religion

During the final years of Boyle's life, he continued to take interest in the Royal Society, in the New England Company, and in his charitable activities. By his will he endowed a series of Boyle lectures, or sermons, which still continue, "for proving the Christian Religion against notorious Infidels."

Robert Boyle, who never married, died on December 31, 1691. He was buried in the church of St. Martin-in-the-Fields, Westminster, London.

BIBLIOGRAPHY. T. BIRCH (ed.), *The Works of the Honourable Robert Boyle, to Which Is Prefixed the Life of the Author,* 5 vol. (1744, reprinted 1965–66), a collection of Boyle's publications, and *The Life of the Honourable Robert Boyle* (1744), still an indispensable biographical study; J.F. FULTON, *A Bibliography of the Honourable Robert Boyle, Fellow of the Royal Society,* 2nd ed. (1961), an indispensable guide to serious study; M.B. HALL, *Robert Boyle and Seventeenth-Century Chemistry* (1968), an excellent account of the subject; R.E.W. MADDISON, "The Portraiture of the Honourable Robert Boyle, F.R.S.," *Ann. Sci.,* 15:141–214 (1959), and *The Life of the Honourable Robert Boyle* (1969), an exhaustive biographical study, which supplements Birch's *Life;* F. MASSON, *Robert Boyle* (1914), a pleasing, romantic account; L.T. MORE, *The Life and Works of the Honourable Robert Boyle* (1944); R. PILKINGTON, *Robert Boyle: Father of Chemistry* (1959), a useful general introduction to Boyle and his scientific work.

Brachiopoda

The Brachiopoda are a phylum of marine invertebrates that are covered by two valves, or shells; one valve covers the dorsal, or top, side; the other covers the ventral, or bottom, side. The valves, of unequal size, are bilaterally symmetrical; *i.e.,* the right and left sides are mirror images of one another.

Brachiopods occur in all oceans. Although no longer numerous, they were once one of the most abundant forms of life.

Brachiopods (from the Greek words meaning "arm" and "foot") are commonly known as lamp shells, because they resemble early Roman oil lamps.

Members of this phylum first appeared rather early in zoological history. It is possible, by means of fossil representatives, to survey their evolution from the Cambrian Period (about 570,000,000 years ago) to the present. Although some of the evolutionary development is revealed, it is still imperfectly understood. Other than their usefulness in dating geological periods, members of this phylum have no economic value, except as curios and museum pieces.

Earliest fossil forms

General features. *Size range and diversity of structure.* Most brachiopods are small, 2.5 centimetres (about one inch) or less in length or width; some are minute, measuring one millimetre or slightly more; some fossil forms are relative giants—about 38 centimetres (15 inches) wide. The largest modern brachiopod is about ten centimetres (four inches) in length.

Great diversity existed among brachiopods in the past; modern brachiopods, however, exhibit little variety. They are commonly tongue-shaped and oval lengthwise and in cross section. The surface may be smooth, spiny, covered with platelike structures, or ridged. Most modern brachiopods are yellowish or white, but some have red stripes or spots; others are pink, brown, or dark gray. The tongue-shaped shells (*Lingula*) are brown with dark-green splotches; rarely, they are cream yellow and green.

Distribution and abundance. Today, brachiopods, numbering about 300 species representing 75 genera, are abundant only locally. In parts of the Antarctic they outnumber all other large invertebrates. They are common in the waters around Japan, southern Australia, and New Zealand. Although rare in the Indian Ocean, some unusual types are common along the coast of South Africa. In Caribbean and West Indian waters, 12 species occur. The east and west coasts of the North Atlantic Ocean are sparsely occupied by brachiopods; the waters around the British Isles contain a few species, and a few genera live in the Mediterranean Sea. The West Coast of the United States and Hawaii have a number of brachiopod species, and the coasts of Chile and Argentina have a considerable variety, including the largest living species. Some live in the polar regions, and a few are abyssal; *i.e.*, they inhabit deep parts of the ocean.

By courtesy of the United States National Museum

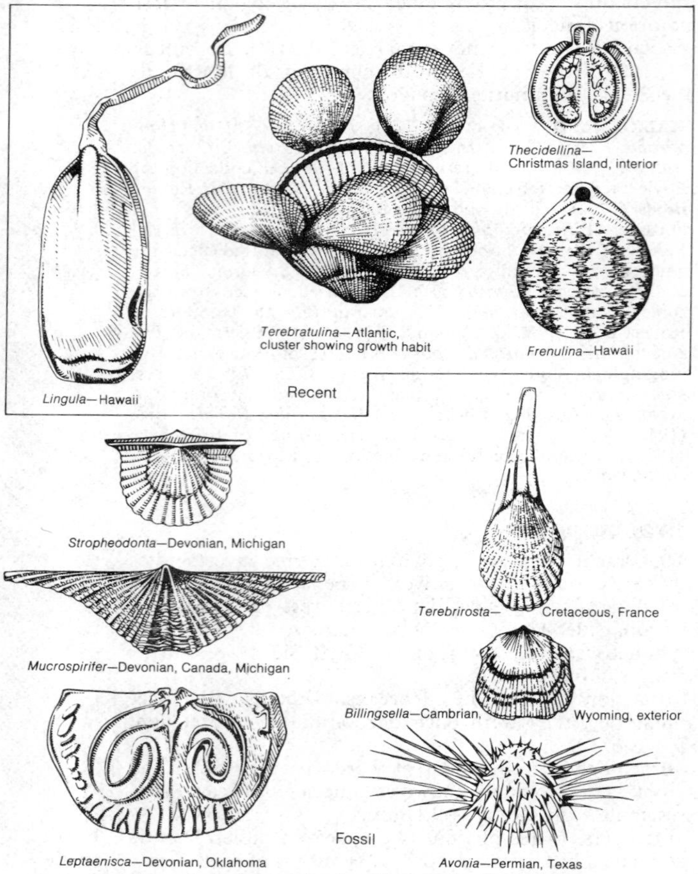

Figure 1: Representative brachiopods, fossil and living.

Natural history. *Reproduction.* Not much is known about the reproduction of brachiopods. Except in three genera, the sexes are separate. Eggs and sperm are discharged into the mantle cavity through funnel-shaped nephridia, or excretory organs, on each side of the mouth. Fertilization takes place outside the shell. In a few genera the young develop inside the female in brood pouches formed by a fold of the mantle, a soft extension of the body wall. Some fossil forms had internal cavities that may have served as brood chambers. The egg develops into a free-swimming larva that settles to the bottom. The free-swimming stage of the articulate brachiopods (whose valves articulate by means of teeth and sockets) lasts only a few days, but that of the inarticulates may last a month or six weeks. In inarticulate larvae the pedicle, a stalklike organ, develops from a so-called mantle fold along the valve margin; in articulates it develops from the caudal, or hind, region.

Articulate and inarticulate forms

Behaviour and ecology. About 60 percent of brachiopods live in shallow water (less than 100 fathoms—about 180 metres [600 feet]) on the shelf areas around the continents. More than 35 percent occupy waters deeper than 100 fathoms, and a few live in the abyss down to more than 6,000 metres (about 20,000 feet). *Lingula* lives from the tidal zone to 23 fathoms (about 42 metres [138 feet]). Most modern branchiopods anchor by the pedicle to pebbles, to the undersides of stones, or to other hard objects. They prefer quiet water and protected surroundings. *Lingula* lives in mud or sand and is attached at the bottom of its burrow.

Brachiopods feed by opening the shell and bringing in food-bearing currents by lashing of the cilia (hairlike structures) attached to the filaments of the lophophore, a horseshoe-shaped organ that filters food particles from the seawater. Cilia in lophophore grooves bring food particles, often trapped in mucus, to the mouth. Brachiopods feed on minute organisms or organic particles. Articulate brachiopods, which have a blind intestine, may depend partly on dissolved nutrients.

Shells of some articulate brachiopods have a fold, which forms a trilobed anterior that helps keep lateral, incoming food-bearing currents separated from outgoing, waste-bearing currents. When feeding, *Lingula* protrudes its anterior (front) end above the mud and arranges its setae (bristle-like structures) into three tubes. These channel the water into lateral incoming and medial, or central, outgoing currents. Some coralliform brachiopods of the Permian Period (280,000,000 to 225,000,000 years ago) are thought to have fed by rapid beating of the dorsal valve, causing a sucking in and expulsion of food-bearing water. Some ostreiform (oyster-shaped) types of the same period are believed to have fed by gentle pulsation of the dorsal valve.

Form and function. Two major groups of brachiopods are recognized, based on the presence or absence of articulation of the valves by teeth and sockets. The valves of inarticulate brachiopods are held together by muscles. *Lingula*, with its elongated, tonguelike shell, is an example of such an inarticulate. Its convex valves bulge outward at the middle and taper posteriorly, or away from the hinge. A long, fleshy pedicle protrudes between the valves at the tapered end. The pedicle of *Lingula* differs from that of most other brachiopods in being flexible and capable of movement—an aid in burrowing and in attaching the animal in its burrow. The shell interior is divided into posterior coelomic (internal-body) and anterior mantle cavities. The internal organs are located in the coelom. The digestive system consists of mouth, gullet, stomach, intestine, and anus, all surrounded by a liver, or digestive gland. A complex set of muscles opens the valves and slides them laterally, or sideways, when feeding. The mantle cavity is occupied by the lophophore. *Lingula* lives in a burrow in mud or sand with the tip of its pedicle attached in mucus at the bottom of the burrow. The contractile pedicle permits extension of the shell when feeding or retraction if the animal is startled.

The cavities within the shell

The articulate-brachiopod shell is typified by *Waltonia*, which is small (about two centimetres [¾ inch]) and red in colour, with a smooth or slightly ridged shell. This type of shell is more highly specialized than that of most inarticulate species and is composed of three layers. The outer layer, called periostracum, is made of organic substance and is seldom seen in fossils. A middle layer consists of calcium carbonate (calcite). The inner layer is composed of calcite fibres and may be punctate—*i.e.*, perforated by minute pits—or it may be pseudopunctate, with rods (taleolae) of calcite vertical to the surface. Impunctate shells have neither pits nor taleolae.

Many hinged brachiopods attach to the substrate, or surface, by a tough, fibrous pedicle; but some specialized forms are cemented to the substrate by the beak of the ventral valve. Cemented forms are commonly distorted, scalelike, or oyster shaped or resemble a cup coral. The pedicle of some brachiopods is atrophied; their shells lie loose on the sea floor.

The shell of an articulate brachiopod tapers posteriorly to a beak. The ventral valve is usually the larger. The hinge may be narrow or wide. Many hinged genera have a flat or curved shelf, called the palintrope, between the beak and the hinge line. The ventral palintrope is divided at the middle by the delthyrium, a triangular opening for the pedicle. The delthyrium may remain open or be wholly or partly closed by small plates growing from its margins. In some families the delthyrium is closed completely or partly by one plate, the pseudodeltidium, anchored to the delthyrial margins. The articulating teeth occur at the angles of the delthyrium and may or may not be supported by vertical dental plates, which may be separate or united to form a so-called spondylium. Teeth are of two types, deltidiodont and cyrtomatodont. Deltidiodont teeth grow anteriorly with the palintrope and leave a growth path along the delthyrial edge; cyrtomatodont teeth are knoblike and occur in shells without a hinge line. They grow anteriorly but are kept knoblike by posterior resorption.

Muscles, sockets, and related structures

The dorsal valve contains structures called crura that diverge from the beak. In some fossil forms the crural bases (brachiophores) bound a triangular cavity, the notothyrium, in which the diductor, or opening, muscles are attached onto the floor or to a ridge, or boss, called the cardinal process at the apex. The notothyrium may be closed by a solid plate, the chilidium. In more highly developed genera a hinge plate bearing the pedicle or dorsal adjustor muscles occurs between the crural bases. The hinge plate is said to be divided when it is incomplete but undivided when it forms a flat or concave structure. The hinge plate is often supported by a median septum, or wall. The hinge sockets are located between the inside shell wall and a socket ridge to which the hinge plate is attached. In many specialized genera the crura support calcareous loops or spires (brachidia), the inner skeleton of the lophophore. Structures corresponding in function but of different origin and with different names occur in the pedicle region of some inarticulate brachiopods.

The fleshy body of the articulate brachiopod is divided transversely by the body wall into a posterior visceral cavity filled with coelomic fluid and an anterior mantle cavity filled with seawater. The visceral cavity contains the U-shaped digestive canal, four reproductive glands, and a liver, or digestive gland, held in place by mesenteries (sheets of tissue). Extensions of the coelom into the mantle hold the eggs and sperm. The mouth leads into a saclike stomach that ends in an intestine; there is no anus. The liver surrounds the stomach. Waste is excreted through the mouth. The nervous system, which consists of two principal ganglia, or nerve centres, encircles the esophagus and sends branches to other parts of the body. One pair of excretory organs (nephridia) occurs in most brachiopods, but two pairs may be present.

The mantle cavity is lined by the thin, shell-secreting mantle that is fringed by setae at its edges. Within the mantle cavity is the lophophore, which may be a simple or complicated loop, often horseshoe-shaped. Ciliated filaments along the loop direct food-bearing currents to the mouth, which is located on the body wall between the branches of the lophophore and crura.

The shell opens by contraction of diductor muscles that extend from near the centre of the ventral valve to the process under the dorsal beak. These muscles pull the dorsal beak forward, rotating it on a line joining the hinge teeth. Contraction of the adductor muscles closes the valves; in the ventral valve these are located between the diductors. Pedicle muscles or adjustors extending from the pedicle to the hinge plate of the dorsal valve rotate the shell on the pedicle. Where the muscles are attached to the shell there are scars, which are helpful in the identification of genera.

Early evolution

Paleontology. Brachiopods were among the first animals to appear at the beginning of the Cambrian Period (570,000,000 years ago). Their evolution and distribution was wide and rapid. More than 30,000 species in more than 2,100 genera are known, and the number of described species increases yearly. Articulate and inarticulate brachiopods appeared at the same time in a relatively advanced state of development, indicating a long evolution from forms without shells, an evolution apparently lost or unrecorded in Precambrian times.

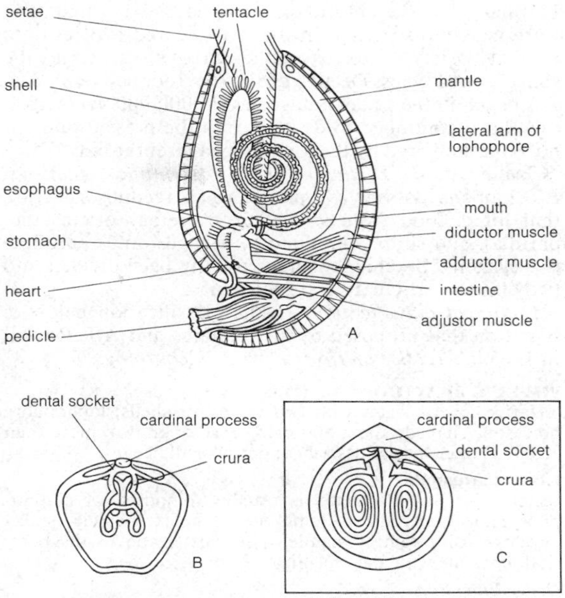

Figure 2: *Body plans of Brachiopoda.*
(A) *Magellania*, side view. (B) *Magellania*, top view of brachial valve. (C) *Atrypa*, interior view of brachial valve.
From Invertebrate Zoology by Paul A. Meglitsch. Copyright© 1967 by Oxford University Press, Inc. Reprinted by permission

The Inarticulata, the most abundant brachiopods of the Cambrian, soon gave way to the Articulata and declined greatly in number and variety toward the end of the Cambrian. They were represented in the Ordovician (500,000,000 to 430,000,000 years ago) but decreased thereafter. In the Cretaceous (136,000,000 to 65,000,000 years ago) the punctate calcareous Inarticulata proliferated, but this trend soon ended. The Inarticulata dwindled through the Cenozoic (65,000,000 years ago) to the Recent. Only nine genera are known during the Recent Epoch (last 10,000 years). Inarticulate genera represent about 6.5 percent of all brachiopod genera.

The Articulata, diverse and most numerous from Ordovician times to the present, were, in the Cambrian, represented by several specialized forms. Articulate evolution tended toward shell elaboration for bottom dwelling and perfection of feeding mechanisms from the simple looped lophophore to the elaborate lobate and spiral forms. The Orthida, the most common articulate brachiopods of the Cambrian and Ordovician, decreased in numbers after the Ordovician, and the impunctate Orthida became extinct in the Early Devonian (about 395,000,000 years ago); the punctate Orthida lingered into the Permian Period (280,000,000 to 225,000,000 years ago). The Strophomenida appeared in the Early Ordovician and increased rapidly. They were abundant and varied in the Devonian, becoming even more so by Permian times. This large order became greatly reduced at the end of the Permian Period. The Pentamerida, never prolific, flourished in the Ordovician; an evolutional burst of huge forms occurred in the Silurian (430,000,000 to 395,000,000 years ago), but after that the pentamerids decreased into the Devonian (395,000,000–345,000,000 years ago) and became extinct early in the late part of that period. The Spiriferida are conspicuous for the great elaboration of the spiral brachidium. They appeared in the Ordovician, were widely distributed into the Permian, and survived into the Jurassic, which began 190,000,000 years ago. The Rhynchonellida were abundant from mid-Ordovician throughout the Paleozoic. They survived into the Triassic (225,000,000 to 190,000,000 years ago) and had a rebirth in the Jurassic, after which they declined into the Cenozoic. They now number only 12 genera.

Development of modern dominant forms

The Terebratulida, now the dominant group, appeared in the early Devonian and rapidly expanded in the mid-Devonian to produce a number of gigantic forms; a few long-looped and short-looped genera persisted into the

Permian. The Terebratulida survived the Permian and were widely distributed in the Triassic and evolved into a great variety of forms in the Jurassic, especially the short-looped types. Decline of the short-looped terebratulids began in the Late Cretaceous (75,000,000 years ago); they have continued to dwindle into the present and are now outnumbered by the long-looped terebratulids.

Classification. *Distinguishing taxonomic features.* Brachiopods possess a lophophore (a feeding structure that filters food from seawater), excretory organs (nephridia), and simple circulatory, nervous, and reproductive systems. Brachiopods have usually been divided into two classes, Articulata and Inarticulata.

Annotated classification. The classification below is based on that proposed by A. Williams and A.J. Rowell in 1965 in *Treatise on Invertebrate Paleontology*.

PHYLUM BRACHIOPODA (lamp shells)
Marine invertebrates with two valves, or shells; lophophore horseshoe-shaped; about 300 living species known; more than 30,000 extinct species described; occur in all oceans.

Class Inarticulata
Shell does not articulate, is usually composed of chitinophosphatic material; shell muscles complex; pedicle (stalk) develops from ventral mantle, a soft extension of the body wall; intestine with anal opening.

Order Lingulida
Shell usually contains phosphate, rarely calcareous, biconvex (*i.e.*, both valves convex), beak for attachment to surface apical, or located at the tip, in both valves; fleshy pedicle emerging between the valves at the tapered end; about 51 genera; Cambrian to Recent.

Order Acrotretida
Usually circular in outline; shell either contains phosphate or is punctate calcareous; pedicle opening confined to the ventral valve; 62 genera; Early Cambrian (550,000,000 years ago) to Recent.

Order Obolellida
Mostly calcareous, biconvex, shape nearly circular to elongated; position of pedicle opening variable; dorsal valve with marginal beak; 5 genera; Early to mid-Cambrian.

Order Paterinida
Shell with phosphate, rounded or elliptical; pedicle opening partly closed by a cover called a homeodeltidium; dorsal valve similar to the ventral one but with a convex homeochilidium; 7 genera; Early Cambrian to mid-Ordovician (450,000,000 years ago).

Class Articulata
Shells articulate by means of teeth and sockets; shells always calcareous; musculature less complicated than in Inarticulata; larval pedicle develops from rear region; no outside opening from intestine.

Order Kutorginida
Calcareous, biconvex interarea (smooth surface in area between beak and hinge line) present; delthyrium (opening in the pedicle) closed by a plate, the pseudodeltidium; dorsal valve with interarea; muscle area narrow and elongated in both valves; 3 genera; Early to mid-Cambrian.

Order Orthida
Usually biconvex, wide-hinged, with interareas in both valves; teeth deltidiodont (leave a growth path along the margin of the pedicle opening); hinge structures consist of brachiophores (supporting structures), shell substance punctate or impunctate—*i.e.*, with or without pits; more than 200 genera; Early Cambrian through Permian (225,000,000 years ago).

Order Strophomenida
Teeth deltidiodont when present; ventral muscles large; shell substance pseudopunctate (with rods of calcite), rarely impunctate; more than 400 genera; Early Ordovician (490,000,000 years ago) to Early Jurassic (180,000,000 years ago).

Order Pentamerida
Biconvex, ventral valve usually with a spondylium (united dental plates); delthyrium usually open; dorsal-valve brachiophores supported by bracing plates; impunctate; nearly 100 genera; mid-Cambrian to Late Devonian (350,000,000 years ago).

Order Rhynchonellida
Narrow-hinged with functional pedicle; dorsal valve with or without a median septum; lophophore (of Recent genera) dorsally spiral and attached to crura (supporting structures); spondylia rare; nearly 300 genera; Ordovician to Recent.

Order Spiriferida
Lophophore supported by a calcareous spiral structure (brachidium); punctate or impunctate, usually biconvex; delthyrium open or closed; more than 300 genera; mid-Ordovician to Jurassic (136,000,000 years ago).

Order Terebratulida
Pedicle functional, cyrtomatodont teeth; lophophore supported wholly or in part by a calcareous loop, short or long and free or attached to a median septum; more than 300 genera; Early Devonian to Recent.

Critical appraisal. The classes Articulata and Inarticulata were first proposed by T.H. Huxley in 1869. Before 1932 they were further subdivided into four orders based on the imperfectly known larval development and formation of the shell around the pedicle opening. In 1927 a fifth order was proposed, and it was suggested that a classification be based on the pedicle development of the larvae.

The great majority of brachiopods are extinct forms whose larval development can only be conjectured. Because of this and other inadequacies, the early classification schemes have been abandoned. Eleven orders distributed in Huxley's classes have been retained in the present classification, which is still being modified. On the basis of hinge and tooth types some systematists have divided the Articulata into two subclasses, Protremata and Telotremata. The Protremata are wide-hinged forms with deltidiodont teeth. The Telotremata are narrow-hinged brachiopods with cyrtomatodont teeth.

BIBLIOGRAPHY. M.J.S. RUDWICK, *Living and Fossil Brachiopods* (1970), a modern, readable, and comprehensive account of the brachiopods; R.C. MOORE (ed.) *Treatise on Invertebrate Paleontology*, pt. H, *Brachiopoda*, 2 vol. (1965), a technical, thorough account of brachiopods and their current classification, with extensive topical bibliographies.

(G.A.C.)

Bradley, James

James Bradley was an 18th-century English astronomer noted for his accurate stellar observations that confirmed the theoretical celestial mechanics of Sir Isaac Newton. By skillfully using improved telescopes, he detected the aberration (apparent displacement of an object) of light, which was the first observational proof for the revolution of the Earth around the Sun; measured nutation, the slight change in the direction of the Earth's axis that is caused by the gravitational pull of the Moon; and cataloged positions of 3,000 stars.

By courtesy of the National Portrait Gallery, London

Bradley, oil painting after Thomas Hudson, *c.* 1742–47. In the National Portrait Gallery, London.

Born at Sherborne, Gloucestershire, in March 1693, Bradley was educated at Balliol College, Oxford, where he received the B.A. in 1714 and the M.A. in 1717. He was instructed in observational astronomy at Wanstead, Essex, by his uncle, the Rev. James Pound, clergyman and skilled amateur astronomer, who introduced him to the famous astronomer Edmond Halley.

Bradley's scientific acumen was stimulated by his membership in the Royal Society, to which he was elected a fellow in 1718 on the recommendation of Halley. Bradley took church orders and became vicar of Bridstow in 1719. The income from that position was augmented by a sinecure as an absentee rector in a parish in Pembrokeshire, Wales, which was procured for him by his friend and astronomical collaborator, Samuel Molyneux. Bradley resigned his church offices when he was appointed in 1721 to the Savilian chair of astronomy at Oxford and henceforth devoted his full time to astronomy.

Measuring the parallactic displacement of a star

After the publication of *De revolutionibus orbium coelestium* by Copernicus in 1543, it became increasingly imperative for astronomers to be able to observe and measure the parallactic displacement of a star—the change in a star's position over a six-month period—to confirm the orbital motion of the Earth around the Sun. Such information would provide the empirical evidence needed to augment the mathematical and conceptual arguments hitherto advanced for the idea that the Sun does not revolve around the Earth. In the absence of such evidence for parallax, Tycho Brahe, the 16th-century astronomer, had not been favourably disposed to Copernican theory. Ole Rømer, a Danish astronomer, measured an apparent displacement of the stars Sirius and Vega in the 17th century, but his observations were found to be erroneous. Robert Hooke, one of the founding members of the Royal Society, measured the star Gamma Draconis in a series of observations in 1669 for a similar attempt but was forced to report failure.

In 1725, using Molyneux's house as an observatory, Bradley attempted to repeat Hooke's measurements on Gamma Draconis with a telescope aimed so as to avoid any error resulting from the refraction of light. Although he failed to detect parallax because the star was too far away, Bradley made one of the two discoveries for which he is famous. He observed that Gamma Draconis shifted south in position by an astonishing 1″ of arc in three days—the wrong direction and by too large an amount to be accounted for by parallax. It is said that the explanation for this phenomenon came to Bradley as he sailed on the Thames, observing how the wind vane on the mast shifted position with the varying motion of the boat, even though the wind had not changed direction. He concluded that the apparent stellar shift was brought about by the aberration of light, which was a resultant of the velocity of light and the forward motion of the Earth in its orbit. Bradley communicated this discovery to the Royal Society in 1728, shortly after the death of Molyneux. Based upon his quantitative observations of aberration, Bradley confirmed the velocity of light to be 295,000 kilometres (183,000 miles) per second and gave a proof for the Copernican theory.

Calculation of the speed of light

Bradley's star measurements in 1727–32 also revealed what he called the "annual change of declination in some of the fixed stars," which could not be accounted for by aberration. He concluded that this was caused by the slight and uneven, nodding motion of the Earth's axis (nutation) and resulted from the changing direction of the gravitational pull of the Moon. But he withheld this announcement until he had made careful confirmatory observations during one complete set of revolutions of the Moon in its orbit. For this achievement the Royal Society of London awarded him the Copley Medal in 1748.

Members of the Royal Society in their function as "visitors and directors" of the Royal Greenwich Observatory recommended Bradley in 1742 to succeed Halley in the post of astronomer royal. (Halley, the second astronomer royal, had followed John Flamsteed, the first.) Bradley received £250 a year and the then sizable grant of £1,000 for instruments, notably an eight-foot (2.4-metre) quadrant for more precise measurements. In 1744 he married Susannah Peach, by whom he had one daughter. He held his important scientific, administrative, and consultative position at Greenwich until a few years before his death in Chalford, in his native Gloucestershire, on July 13, 1762.

The bulk of Bradley's observations was published after his death in an atmosphere of acrimony. Dispute between his heirs and the British Admiralty over the ownership of his work delayed publication until 1798–1805. The German mathematician Friedrich Bessel analyzed and organized his data, first detecting Bradley's instrumental errors, which were relatively few in number, and then computing the actual astronomical values.

Bradley was one of the first post-Newtonian observational astronomers who led the quest for precision.

BIBLIOGRAPHY. No complete biography exists. Additional information may be found in the preface to Bradley's *Miscellaneous Works and Correspondence*, ed. by S.P. RIGAUD (1832); and in the article, "James Bradley, 1693–1762: Bicentary Contributions," *Q. Jl. R. Astr. Soc.*, 4:38–61 (1963).

(G.S.H.)

Bragg, Sir Lawrence

William Lawrence Bragg, who discovered a fundamental law of physics—Bragg's law—only three years after he took up study in that field, continued a long, distinguished career in physics, especially in the X-ray analysis of crystals. He later founded three famous research schools for the study of silicates, metals and alloys, and protein crystals.

Camera Press—Pix from Publix

Sir Lawrence Bragg, 1962.

"Willie" Bragg was born in Adelaide, Australia, on March 31, 1890, the eldest child of Sir William Henry Bragg (*q.v.*). His maternal grandfather, Sir Charles Todd, was postmaster general and government astronomer of South Australia. Educated at St. Peter's College, Adelaide, and then at Adelaide University, Bragg gained high honours in mathematics at an age when most boys were still in secondary school.

In 1909 he went to England to enter Trinity College, Cambridge. He began the study of physics, which he had not studied earlier, although he had taken some chemistry. During the summer vacation of 1912, his father discussed with him a recent book on the work of the German physicist Max von Laue, who asserted that X-rays could be diffracted by passing them through crystals. Upon his return to Cambridge, young Bragg, believing that Laue's explanation was incorrect in detail, carried out a series of ingenious original experiments, as the result of which he published the Bragg equation, which tells at what angles X-rays will be most efficiently diffracted off of a crystal when the X-ray wavelength and distance between the crystal atoms are known. This equation is basic to X-ray diffraction, a process used to analyze crystal structure by studying the characteristic patterns of X-rays that deviate from their original paths because of the closely spaced atoms in the crystal. He also showed that in rock salt the two kinds of atoms, sodium and chlorine,

The Bragg equation

are arranged alternately, so that atoms of the same element never touch each other. Meanwhile, his father had designed the X-ray spectrometer, a device to make exact measurements of X-ray wavelengths. The two scientists then spent vacations using the Bragg spectrometer to determine many other atomic arrangements, including that of diamonds.

In 1914 Bragg became a fellow and lecturer in natural sciences at Trinity College. Later that year he and his father were jointly awarded the Barnard Gold Medal of the U.S. Academy of Sciences, the first of many such honours and awards. From 1915 to 1919 Bragg served in World War I as technical advisor on sound ranging (determining the distance of enemy artillery from the sound of their guns) in the map section of British army headquarters in France, and he was there when the 1915 Nobel Prize for Physics was awarded jointly to his father and himself for demonstrating the use of X-rays for revealing the structure of crystals.

After the war Bragg succeeded Ernest Rutherford as professor of physics at Victoria University of Manchester, and there he built his first research school, for the study of metals and alloys and silicates. His work on silicates transformed a chemical riddle into a system of simple and elegant architecture. In 1921 he married Alice Hopkinson, a doctor's daughter, by whom he had two sons and two daughters. His wife's charm and character greatly helped him throughout his professional career. In the same year he was elected a Fellow of the Royal Society.

From 1937 to 1938 Bragg was director of the National Physical Laboratory, but he was impatient with committee work. About this period of his life he often used to remark that he found the engagement book, the in-tray, and the list of matters requiring urgent attention to be the deadly enemies of scientific work.

So he gladly left pure administration to succeed Rutherford again, this time as Cavendish Professor of Experimental Physics at Cambridge. Here he founded a second flourishing research school to study metals and alloys, silicates, and proteins, but he was also deeply concerned that science students should have time to enjoy a full education and come to understand something of the meaning and purpose of life.

School for research in metals and minerals

In January 1954, Bragg became director of the Royal Institution, London, as his father had been before 1940. He introduced several successful innovations: year-round lectures for schoolchildren, illustrated by demonstrations requiring apparatus too large or too costly for school resources (some 20,000 children attended each year); courses for science teachers; and lectures for civil servants whose early training had not included science. Popular and successful as a lecturer, Bragg was also in great demand for radio and television appearances. At an age at which many scientists lose interest in research, he built up a third research team, some of whose members successfully tackled the structures of complex organic crystals. Bragg retired from active scientific work in 1965 and died in Ipswich on July 1, 1971.

BIBLIOGRAPHY. W.L. BRAGG, "Personal Reminiscences," in P.P. EWALD (ed.), *Fifty Years of X-Ray Diffraction*, pp. 531–539 (1962).

(K.Lo.)

Bragg, Sir William

William Henry Bragg, later Sir William Bragg, made his international reputation as a scientist with his son, William Lawrence Bragg (*q.v.*), by showing that X-rays could be used to determine the patterns of atoms and molecules in crystalline solids. They were thus the founders of the modern science of solid-state physics, the study of the atomic structure of solids, which led to the development of transistors and other solid-state devices.

W.H. Bragg was born in Cumberland in northwestern England on July 2, 1862. He came on his father's side from a family without academic traditions, mainly yeoman farmers and merchant seamen. His mother was the daughter of the local vicar. Upon her death, when he was barely seven, he went to live with two paternal uncles

Sir William Bragg.
By courtesy of the Nobelstiftelsen, Stockholm

who had set up a pharmacy and grocery shop in Market Harborough, Leicestershire. There he attended an old school re-established by one of his uncles. He did well, and in 1875 his father sent him to school at King William College, Isle of Man. At first he found it difficult to adjust himself, but he was good at his lessons and at sports and finally became head boy. During his last year, however, the school was swept by a storm of religious emotionalism. The boys were frightened by the stories of hellfire and eternal damnation, and the experience left a strong mark on Bragg. Later he wrote, "It was a terrible year . . . for many years the Bible was a repelling book, which I shrank from reading." And in a lecture *Science and Faith* at Cambridge in 1941, he said, "I am sure that I am not the only one to whom when young the literal interpretation of Biblical texts caused years of acute misery and fear." On the other hand, he attributed his clear, balanced style of writing to his early grounding in the Authorized (King James) Version of the Bible; in *The World of Sound* he wrote, "From religion comes a man's purpose; from science his power to achieve it."

In 1882 he was granted a scholarship at Trinity College, Cambridge; and two years later he obtained third place in the Mathematical Tripos (final examinations), a splendid achievement that led to his appointment, in 1885, as professor of mathematics and physics at the young University of Adelaide, South Australia. He then not only trained himself to become a good, lucid lecturer but he also apprenticed himself to a firm of instrument makers and made all the equipment he needed for practical laboratory teaching. It was this early training that enabled him, later (in 1912), after his return to England, to design the Bragg ionization spectrometer, the prototype of all modern X-ray and neutron diffractometers, with which he made the first exact measurements of X-ray wavelengths and crystal data.

Bragg ionization spectrometer

It was not until 1904, when Bragg became president of the physics section of the Australian Association for the Advancement of Science, that he began to think about original research. His subsequent work on α (alpha), β (beta), and γ (gamma) rays led the renowned British physicist Ernest Rutherford to propose him for fellowship of the Royal Society. He was elected in 1907 and within a year was offered a professorship in Leeds, England, where he developed his view that both γ rays and X-rays have particle-like properties.

In 1912 the German physicist Max von Laue announced that crystals could diffract X-rays, thus implying that X-rays must be waves like light but of much shorter wavelength. As a consequence, Bragg and his elder son, William Lawrence, who was studying physics at Cambridge, then began to apply X-rays to the study of crystal structure. These researches earned them jointly the award of the 1915 Nobel Prize for physics.

After World War I, during which he worked on anti-submarine devices, Bragg established a school of crystallographic research at University College, London; and then, upon the death of the chemist and physicist Sir James Dewar, he succeeded him as director of the Royal Institution and of the Davy Faraday Research Laboratories, London. To these institutions he attracted many young scientists whose researches he inspired and stimulated and who subsequently achieved fame. Bragg was also a popular scientific lecturer and writer. He gave "Christmas Lectures" for children, which, when published, became best sellers. With Lady Bragg, he established a salon to which famous scientists came from far and wide. He was president of the Royal Society from 1935 to 1940 and received many other honours, but, to the last, he remained simple, gentle, and humble about his own success and proud of his son's. He died in London on March 12, 1942.

BIBLIOGRAPHY. SIR LAWRENCE BRAGG and G.M. CAROE (Gwendolen Bragg), "Sir William Bragg, F.R.S. (1862–1942)," *Notes and Records of the Royal Society of London*, 17:169–182 (1962), is a brief, personal biography by his son and daughter. See also the *Obituary Notices of Fellows of the Royal Society*, 4:277–300 (1943), with a complete bibliography.

(K.Lo.)

Brahe, Tycho

The observations made by the 16th-century Danish astronomer, Tycho Brahe, were the most accurate possible before the telescope came into use. His observational work eventually helped thoughtful Europeans to accept the Copernican system and became the basis for the 17th-century reformation of astronomy.

By courtesy of Det Nationalhistoriske Museum Paa Frederiksborg, Denmark

Brahe, engraving by H. Goltzius of a drawing by an unknown artist, *c.* 1586.

Youth and education

Tycho was born on December 14, 1546, in the town of Knudstrup in Scania, Denmark. His father was a privy councillor and later governor of the castle of Hälsingborg, which controls the main waterway to the Baltic Sea. His wealthy and childless uncle abducted Tycho at a very early age and, after the initial parental shock was overcome, raised him at his castle in Tostrup, Scania, also financing the youth's education, which began with the study of law at the University of Copenhagen in 1559–62.

Several important natural events turned Tycho from law to astronomy. The first was the total eclipse of the Sun predicted for August 21, 1560. Such a prediction seemed audacious and marvellous to a 14-year-old student, but when it arrived on schedule Tycho saw and believed—the spark was lit—and, as his many later references testify, he never forgot the event. His subsequent student life was divided between his daytime lectures on jurisprudence, in response to the wishes of his uncle, and his nighttime vigil of the stars. The professor of mathematics helped him with the only printed astronomical book available, the *Almagest* of Ptolemy, the astronomer of antiquity who described the geocentric conception of the cosmos. Other teachers helped him to construct small globes, on which star positions could be plotted, and compasses and cross-staffs, with which he could estimate the angular separation of stars.

In 1562 Brahe's uncle sent him to the University of Leipzig, where he studied until 1565. Another significant event in Brahe's life occurred in August 1563, when he made his first recorded observation, a conjunction, or overlapping, of Jupiter and Saturn. Almost immediately he found that the existing almanacs and ephemerides, which record stellar and planetary positions, were grossly inaccurate. The Copernican tables were several days off in predicting this event. In his youthful enthusiasm Brahe decided to devote his life to the accumulation of accurate observations of the heavens, in order to correct the existing tables.

Between 1565 and 1570 (or 1572?) he travelled widely throughout Europe, studying at Wittenberg, Rostock, Basel, and Augsburg and acquiring mathematical and astronomical instruments, including a huge quadrant. Inheriting the estates of his father and of his uncle Jørgen, Tycho then settled in Scania in 1571 (?) and constructed a small observatory on property owned by a relative. Here occurred the third and most important astronomical event in Brahe's life. On November 11, 1572, he suddenly saw a "new star," brighter than Venus and where no star was supposed to be, in the constellation Cassiopeia. He carefully observed the new star and showed that it lay beyond the Moon and therefore was in the realm of the fixed stars. To the world at the time, this was a disquieting discovery, because the intellectual community protected itself against the uncertainties of the future by confidence in the Aristotelian doctrine of inner and continuous harmony of the whole world. This harmony was ruled by the stars, which were, hopefully, perfect and unchanging. The news that a star could change as dramatically as that described by Tycho, together with the reports of the Copernican theory that the Sun, not the Earth, was the centre of the universe, shook confidence in the immutable laws of antiquity and suggested that the chaos and imperfections of Earth were reflected in the heavens. Tycho's discovery of the new star in Cassiopeia in 1572 and his publication of his observations of it in *De nova stella* in 1573 marked his transformation from a Danish dilettante to an astronomer with a European reputation.

Discovery of the nova in Cassiopeia

By marrying a peasant's daughter, named Kirstine, in 1573, Tycho—as a nobleman's son—scandalized most of his contemporaries. He seldom mentioned her in his extensive correspondence (which still exists), and it is probable that he was interested mainly in a companion who would superintend his household without being involved in court functions and intrigues. Tycho and Kirstine had eight children, six of whom survived him.

The new star in the constellation Cassiopeia had caused Tycho to rededicate himself to astronomy; one immediate decision was to establish a large observatory for regular observations of celestial events. His plan to establish this observatory in Germany prompted King Frederick II to keep him in Denmark by granting him title in 1576 to the island of Ven (formerly Hven), in the middle of the Sound and about halfway between Copenhagen and Helsingør, together with financial support for the observatory and laboratory buildings. Tycho called the observatory Uraniborg, after Urania, the Muse of astronomy. Surrounded by scholars and visited by learned travellers from all over Europe, Tycho and his assistants collected observations and substantially corrected nearly every known astronomical record.

Tycho was an artist as well as a scientist and craftsman, and everything he undertook, or surrounded himself with, had to be innovative and beautiful. He established a printing shop to produce and bind his manuscripts in his own way; he imported Augsburg craftsmen to construct the finest astronomical instruments; he induced Italian and Dutch artists and architects to design and decorate his observatory; and he invented a pressure system to provide the then uncommon convenience of sanitary lavatory facilities. Uraniborg fulfilled the hopes of Tycho's king and friend, Frederick II, that it would become the centre of astronomical study and discovery in northern Europe.

But Frederick died in 1588 and under his son, Christian IV, Tycho's influence dwindled; most of his income was stopped, partly because of the increasing needs of the state for money. Spoiled by Frederick, however, Tycho had become both unreasonably demanding of more money and less inclined to carry out the civic duties required by his income from state lands.

Move to Prague

At odds with the three great powers—king, church, and nobility—Tycho left Ven in 1597, and, after short stays at Rostock and at Wandsbek, near Hamburg, he settled in Prague in 1599, under the patronage of Emperor Rudolf II, who also in later years supported the astronomer Johannes Kepler.

The major portion of Tycho's lifework—making and recording accurate astronomical observations—had already been done at Uraniborg. To his earlier observations, particularly his proof that the nova of 1572 was a star, he added a comprehensive study of the solar system, his proof that the orbit of the comet of 1577 lay beyond the Moon, and accurate positions of more than 777 fixed stars. He proposed a modified Copernican system in which the planets revolved around the Sun, which in turn moved around the stationary Earth. What Tycho accomplished, using only his simple instruments and practical talents, remains an outstanding accomplishment of the Renaissance.

Tycho attempted to continue his observations at Prague with the few instruments he had salvaged from Uraniborg, but the spirit was not there, and he died on October 24, 1601, leaving all his observational data to Johannes Kepler, his pupil and assistant in the final years. With these data Kepler laid the groundwork for the work of Sir Isaac Newton.

BIBLIOGRAPHY. J.A. GADE, *The Life and Times of Tycho Brahe* (1947), is the best account in English of Tycho's life and contains a fairly complete bibliography. J.L.E. DREYER, *Tycho Brahe* (1890), presents an authoritative picture of his work and his astronomical instruments, by the astronomer who also prepared his collected works for publication. Any volume on the history of scientific ideas contains some account of Tycho's work.

(O.J.E.)

Brahmaputra River

The mighty Brahmaputra River flows for 1,800 miles (2,900 kilometres) from its source in the Himalayas to its confluence with the Ganges, after which the mingled waters of the two rivers empty into the Bay of Bengal. Along its course it passes through the Tibetan Autonomous Region of China; the union territory of Arunachal Pradesh (NEFA) and the state of Assam, India; and Bangladesh. It is known to the Tibetans as the Tsangpo, to the Chinese as the Ya-lu-ts'ang-pu, to the Indians as the Brahmaputra, and to the people of Bangladesh as the Jamuna. For most of its length, the river serves as an important inland waterway; it is not, however, navigable between the mountains of Tibet and the plains of India. In its lower course, the river is both a creator and a destroyer—depositing large amounts of fertile alluvial soil but also causing disastrous and frequent floods. (For associated physical features, see BENGAL, BAY OF; GANGES RIVER; and HIMALAYAN MOUNTAIN RANGES.)

The course of the river. The river's source lies in the Chema-Yungdung Glacier, which covers the slopes of the Himalayas about 60 miles southeast of Lake Manasarowar in southwestern Tibet. The three headstreams are the Kubi, the Angsi, and the Chema-Yungdung. From its source the river runs for nearly 700 miles in a generally easterly direction between the main Himalayan range to the south and the Nien-ch'ing-t'ang-ku-la Shan (Nyenchen Tangla) to the north. Throughout its upper course the river is generally known as the Tsangpo (the Purifier); it is also known by the Chinese name Ya-lu-tsang-pu Chiang and other local Tibetan names along its course.

The river's upper course

In Tibet the Tsangpo receives a number of tributaries. The most important left-bank tributaries are the Jo-k'a tsang-pu (Raga Tsangpo), which joins the river west of Jih-k'a-tse (Zhikatze), and the La-sa Ho (Kyi Chu), which flows past the Tibetan capital of Lhasa and joins the Tsangpo at Ch'ü-shui. The Ni-yang Ho (Gyamda Chu) joins the river from the north at Tse-la (Tsela Dzong). On the right bank the Nien-ch'u Ho (Nyang) meets the river at Jih-k'a-tse.

After passing P'i (Pe) in Tibet, the river turns suddenly to the northeast and cuts a course through a succession of great, narrow gorges between the mountainous complex of Gyala Peri (23,458 feet, or 7,150 metres, in height) and Na-mu-cho-pa-erh-wa Shan (Namcha Barwa) (25,446 feet, or 7,756 metres, in height) in a series of rapids and cascades. Thereafter, the river turns south and forces its way through the eastern extremity of the Himalayas to enter the Assam Valley of northeastern India as the Dihāng River.

At the town of Sadiya, India, the Dihāng turns to the southwest and is joined by the two mountain streams of Luhit and Dibang. After the confluence, about 900 miles from the Bay of Bengal, the river is known as the Brahmaputra (the Son of Brahmā [the Creator]). In Assam the river is mighty, even in the dry season, and during the rains its banks are more than five miles apart. As the river follows its braided, 450-mile course through the valley, it receives several rapidly rushing Himalayan streams, including the Subansirī, Bhareli, Dhansiri, Manās, Chāmpamāti, Saralbhānga, and Sankosh rivers. The main tributaries from the hills and from the plateau to the south are the Burhi Dihing, the Disāng, the Dikhu, and the Kāpili.

The Brahmaputra enters the plains of Bangladesh after turning south around the Gāro Hills below Dhubri, India. After flowing past Chilmāri, Bangladesh, it is joined on its right bank by the Tīsta River, following a 150-mile course due south as the Jamuna River. (South of Gaibānda, the Old Brahmaputra leaves the left bank of the main stream and flows past Jamālpur and Mymensingh to join the Meghna River at Bhairab Bāzār.) Before its confluence with the Ganges River, the Jamuna receives the combined waters of the Baral, Atrai, and Hurāsāgar rivers on its right bank and becomes the point of departure of the large Dhaleswari River on its left bank. A distributary of the Dhaleswari, the Burhi Ganga, flows past Dacca and joins the Meghna River above Munshiganj.

The complex lower course

The Jamuna joins with the Ganges north of Goalundo Ghāt, after which, as the Padma, their combined waters flow to the southeast for a distance of about 65 miles. The Padma reaches its confluence with the Meghna River near Chāndpur and then enters the Bay of Bengal through the Meghna Estuary and lesser channels.

The natural environment. *Climate.* The climate of the Brahmaputra Valley varies from the harsh, cold, and dry conditions found in Tibet to the generally hot and humid conditions prevailing in the Assam Valley and Bangladesh. Tibetan winters are severely cold, with minimum temperatures below 32° F (0° C), while summers are mild and sunny. The river valley lies in the rain shadow of the Himalayas; there is little rain in the summer, but some snow and rain falls during the winter. In the Indian and Bangladesh part of the valley, the monsoon climate is somewhat modified; the hot season is shorter than usual, and the average temperature is 82° F (28° C). Precipitation is relatively heavy, and humidity is high throughout the year. The annual rainfall of between 70 and 150 inches falls mostly between June and early October; light rains also fall from March to May.

Vegetation and animal life. Large areas in Assam are covered with sal (valuable timber trees that yield resin) forests, and tall reed jungle grows in the swamps and depressed, water-filled areas (*jhīls*) of the immense floodplains. Around the settlements in the Assam Valley, the many fruit trees yield plantains, papayas, mangos, and jackfruit. Bamboo thickets abound everywhere.

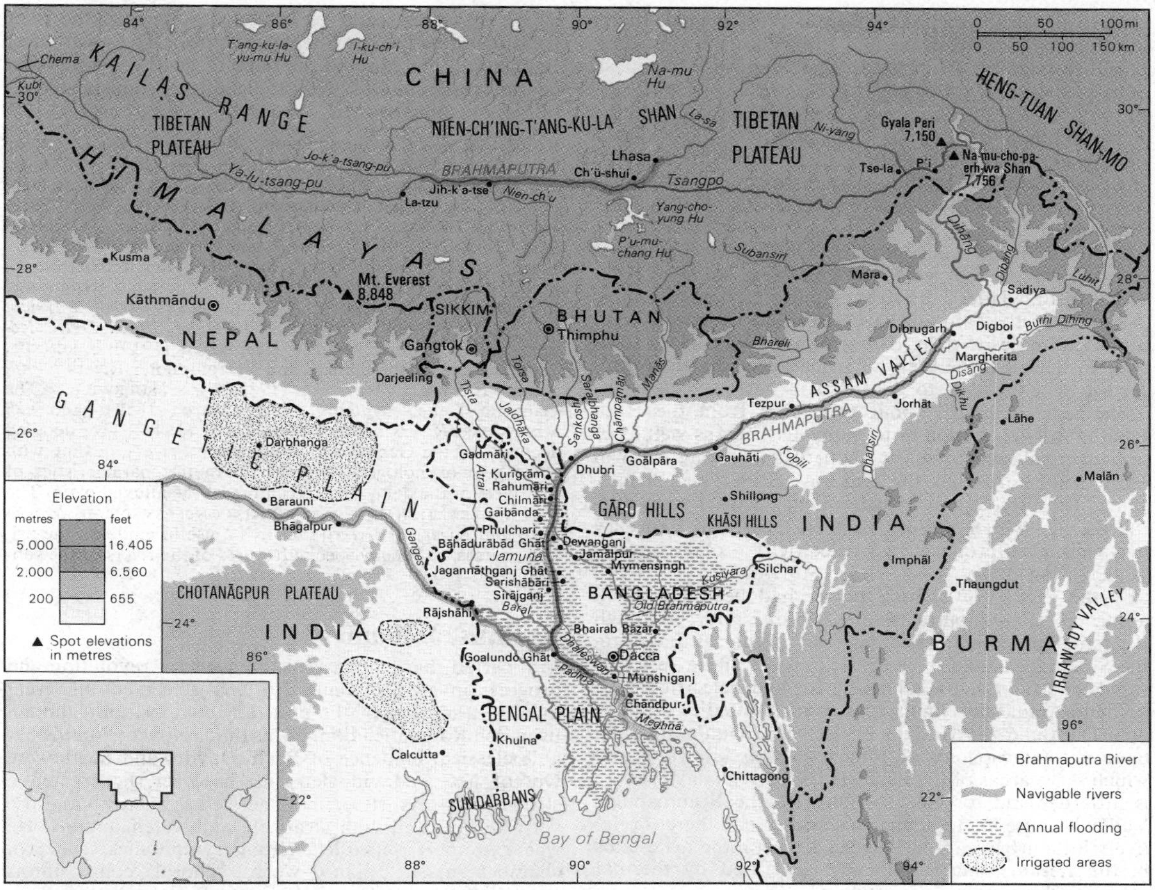

The Brahmaputra River Basin.
Flooding data from R. Rawson, *The Monsoon Lands of Asia;* irrigation data from L. Cantor, *A World Geography of Irrigation* (1970), Oliver and Boyd, Edinburgh

The most notable animal of the swamps in Assam is the one-horned rhinoceros, which has become extinct in other parts of the world. Tigers and elephants are also found. Numerous varieties of fish include the betki, pabda, ruhi, chital, and mrigal.

Hydrology. Constant changes of the river's course constitute a significant factor in the hydrology of the Brahmaputra; the most spectacular of these changes was the eastward diversion of the Tīsta River and the ensuing development of the new channel of the Jamuna, which occurred in 1787 with an exceptionally high flood in the Tīsta. The waters were suddenly diverted eastward into an old abandoned course, causing the river to join the Brahmaputra opposite Bāhādurābād Ghāt in Mymensingh District. Until the late 18th century the Brahmaputra flowed past the town of Mymensingh and joined the Meghna River near Bhairab Bāzār (the path of the present-day Old Brahmaputra Channel). At that time, the course of the Jamuna River (now the main Brahmaputra Channel) was a minor stream called the Konai-Jenai, which was probably a spill channel of the Old Brahmaputra. After being reinforced by the Tīsta flood of 1787, the Brahmaputra began to cut a new channel along the Konai-Jenai and gradually converted it after 1810 into the main stream, now known as the Jamuna.

Changes in the river's course

Along the lower courses of the Ganges and Brahmaputra and along the Meghna, the land is subjected to constant erosion and deposition of silt because of the shifts and changes in these active river courses. Vast areas are subject to large-scale inundation during the monsoon months from June to September. The oscillations of the Jamuna since 1787 have been considerable, and the river is never in exactly the same place for two successive years. Islands and sizable newly deposited lands (*chars*) in the river appear and disappear seasonally. The *chars* are valuable to the economy of Bangladesh as additional cultivable areas.

In Tibet the waters of the Brahmaputra are clear because little silt is carried downstream. As soon as the river enters the Assam Valley, however, the silt charge becomes heavy. Because of the speed and volume of water in the northern tributaries that flow down from the rain-soaked Himalayan slopes, their silt charge is much heavier than that carried by the tributaries that cross the hard rocks of the old plateau to the south. In Assam the deep channel of the Brahmaputra follows the southern bank closer than the northern bank. This tendency is reinforced by the silt-laden northern tributaries that tend to push the channel to the south.

Another important hydrographic feature of the river is its tendency to flood. The quantity of water carried by the Brahmaputra in India and Bangladesh is enormous. The Assam Valley is enclosed by hill ranges on the north, east, and south and receives over 100 inches of rainfall annually, while in the Bengal Plain heavy rainfall (70 to 100 inches) is reinforced by the huge discharge of the Tīsta, Torsa, and Jaldhāka rivers. This results in heavy annual floods and an estimated discharge during the rainy season of 500,000 cubic feet per second. The Assam earthquake of 1950 led to numerous landslides on the Himalayan slopes of the Assam Valley; the resulting enlarged discharge, combined with enormous amounts of silt, caused extraordinary floods. Between 1950 and 1970 there were heavy flood conditions every year except 1951, 1952, and 1958.

The imprint of man. *The people of the river valley.* The people living in the different sections of the Brahmaputra Valley are of diverse origin and culture. North of the Himalayan rampart, the Tibetans practice Buddhism and speak the Tibetan language. They engage in animal husbandry and cultivate the valley with irrigation water taken from the river.

The Assamese are a mixture of Mongolian–Tibetan, Aryan, and Burmese ethnic origins. Their language is akin to Bengali, which is spoken in West Bengal, India, and Bangladesh. From the late 19th century a vast number of immigrants from the Bengal Plain of Bangladesh entered the valley; they settled there to cultivate the almost empty lands, particularly the low floodplains. In the Bengal Plain itself the river flows through an area that is densely populated by the Bengali people, who cultivate the fertile valley. The hilly margins of the plain are inhabited by the hill tribes of the Garos, Khāsis, and Hajangs.

Irrigation and flood control. Flood-control schemes and the building of embankments were initiated after 1954. In Bangladesh the Brahmaputra embankment will run west of the Jamuna River from north to south for about 135 miles to help to control floods. The Tīsta Barrage Project is to be both an irrigation and a flood-protection scheme; it is to consist of a barrage across the Tīsta near Gadmāri, about two miles from the Hātibāndha railway station in Rangpur District, as well as of a main canal, which will be about 30 miles long and will drain southward into the Karatoya River near Khānsāma. The project will irrigate about 800,000 acres during the dry winter season from November to February and will also produce hydroelectricity (total capacity 10,000 kilowatts).

The Tīsta Barrage Project

By the early 1970s, little power had been harnessed along the Brahmaputra or the Assam Valley, although the estimated potential is great. The tributaries that drain the Shillong plateau have deep stretches and a series of rapids and falls that are suitable for hydroelectric development. Actual development is so far limited to the Barpani Dam and the Umiam Project near Gauhāti, which have a total capacity of almost 60,000 kilowatts and which serve areas of the Khāsi Hills in Meghalaya. There is little demand for electric power in the Brahmaputra Valley because manufacturing is limited and there is relatively little urbanization. Power needed on the tea estates in the Assam Valley is locally generated by thermal sources, which mainly use crude oil.

Navigation and transport. The river is navigable in Tibet for about 400 miles between La-tzu (Lhatse Dzong) and Lhasa. Coracles (boats made of hides and bamboo) and large ferries ply its waters at 12,000 feet above sea level. The Tsangpo is spanned in several places by suspension bridges.

Because it flows through a region of heavy rainfall in Assam and Bangladesh, the Brahmaputra is more important for inland navigation than for irrigation. The river has long formed a waterway between West Bengal and Assam. It is navigable throughout the Bengal Plain and Assam upstream to Dibrugarh, 800 miles from the sea. Besides all types of local craft, powered launches and steamers may easily ply up and down the river, carrying bulky raw materials, timber, and crude oil. After the conflict between India and Pakistan in 1965, however, heavy traffic was suspended.

The Brahmaputra remains unbridged throughout its course in the plains. Roads and railroads run along the river but never cross it; ferries carry traffic between its banks. Sadiya, Dibrugarh, Jorhāt, Tezpur, Gauhāti, Goālpāra, and Dhubri are important towns and ferry-crossing points in Assam, while Kurīgrām, Rahumāri, Chilmāri, Bāhādurābād Ghāt, Phulchari, Sarishābāri, Jagannāthganj Ghāt, Nagarbāri, Sirājganj, and Goalundo Ghāt are important crossing points in Bangladesh. The railheads are located at Bāhādurābād Ghāt, Phulchari, Jagannāthganj Ghāt, Sirājganj, and Goalundo Ghāt.

History. The upper course of the Brahmaputra was unknown until the 19th century. The explorations of the Indian surveyor Kinthup in 1884 and of J.F. Needham in Assam in 1886 established the Tsangpo as the upper course of the Brahmaputra. Various British expeditions in the first quarter of the 20th century explored the Tsangpo upstream to Jih-k'a-tse, as well as the river's mountain gorges.

Economic resources and the future. The main economic resources of the Lower Brahmaputra Valley are the tea estates, the forests, and the oil, coal, and natural gas deposits of Assam, as well as the jute of Bangladesh. These resources could be further developed if the river itself could be used for heavy transport. The creation of Bangladesh in 1971 and the hope of good economic and commercial relations with India offer promising possibilities of future growth.

BIBLIOGRAPHY. M.D.N. WADIA, *Minerals of India*, ed. by D.N. WADIA (1966); and M.S. KRISHNAN, *The Geology of India and Burma*, 4th ed. (1960), provide basic geological descriptions of the Indian subcontinent. E.H. PASCOE, "The Early History of the Indus, Brahmaputra, and Ganges," *Q. Jl. Geol. Soc. Lond.*, 75:138–157 (1919); and B. PRASAD, "The Indo-Brahm or the Siwalik River," *Rec. Geol. Surv. India*, vol. 74, pt. 4 (1939–40), deal specifically with the possible existence of the Indo-Brahm, or Siwalik, River. H.G. REAKS, *On the Physical and Hydraulic Characteristics of the Rivers of the Delta*, Report on Hooghly River and its Headwaters (1919); J. RENNEL, "An Account of the Ganges and Burrampooter Rivers," *Phil. Trans. R. Soc.*, 71:87–114 (1781); W.S. SHERWILL, "The Gangetic Delta," *Calcutta Rev.* (March 1859); and S.C. MAJUMDAR, *Rivers of the Bengal Delta* (1942), give detailed accounts of the Ganges and Brahmaputra rivers, dealing with some geomorphological aspects, hydraulic characteristics of the rivers of the delta, and the nature of the alluvial plain. The 21ST INTERNATIONAL GEOGRAPHICAL CONGRESS, DELHI, *Mountains and Rivers of India* (1968), is a useful guide on the origin, courses, and many special features of the rivers of the subcontinent.

(N.A.)

Brahms, Johannes

In a period that emphasized the need for revolution and progress in art, Johannes Brahms preserved the great musical traditions of the past. His compositions, though using the Romantic idiom of his time, show the unmistakable classical influence of Bach, Haydn, and Beethoven. Out of new and old elements, however, he created a strongly personal style, characterized by warmth and fire yet often imbued with strangely ambivalent moods. He was extremely versatile, writing symphonies, concerti, chamber music, piano works, choral compositions (among them the famous *German Requiem*), and more than 200 songs; but it is characteristic of his reticent and introverted nature that he avoided opera, although this form stood in the forefront of artistic interest during the 19th century.

By courtesy of the Osterreichische Nationalbibliothek, Vienna

Brahms, lithograph by Rudolf Fenzl, 1897.

Youth. Johannes Brahms was born on May 7, 1833, in Hamburg, Germany. His father, Johann Jakob, had run away from the village where his family kept an inn to become a musician. Eventually, he gained a modest foothold in Hamburg as a horn and double-bass player performing in various places of entertainment, in the militia, and ultimately in the opera orchestra. Brahms's mother, who was 17 years older than her husband, had from the age of 13 supported herself as a seamstress and general maid. Though poorly educated, she was a woman of great sensitivity and spiritual resources. The couple had to live in Hamburg's poorest district and exercise the utmost frugality to raise their three children on Johann's modest earnings. Yet their home was a happy one, for both drew enjoyment from the simplest pleasures. It was their aim to give their children a good education and see them rise in the world. In the case of Johannes, who at an early age displayed outstanding musical talent, it was not hard to secure a first-rate teacher. From the age of seven he was instructed by a fine German pianist, F.W. Cossel, and made such progress that within three years he could successfully take part in a chamber-music concert. An impresario tried to induce the Brahms family to travel to the United States, where the young pianist could have become rich. The temptation was great, but Cossel, aware that a concert tour at this early stage would endanger Johannes' artistic growth, pleaded against the plan. To enlist moral support, he induced Eduard Marxsen, Hamburg's most renowned music teacher, to take over the boy's education without pay, and this decided the matter.

First lessons in composition

Marxsen, a competent composer, instructed Johannes in music theory and thus laid the groundwork for Brahms's future career. He developed into an outstanding pianist but considered this an avocation since he was determined to devote himself mainly to composition. During these formative years, however, his piano playing secured the family an added, badly needed income. From the age of 13, Johannes performed in taverns, restaurants, and nightclubs, often late into the night. While contributing to household expenses, he kept some of the money for buying books, which he avidly devoured; he even copied favourite passages into special notebooks. He also worked for a music publisher, doing arrangements and supplying fashionable drawing-room compositions under a pseudonym. These activities did not seem likely to lead to a successful career.

A recital he gave in 1848 made little impression on the Hamburg public, who were used to the appearance of more glamorous virtuosos, and hardly anybody was aware of the youth's ability to compose. Convinced that he had reached a dead end, Brahms wanted to leave home and prove himself in the musical world. At the age of 20, his wish was granted when Eduard Reményi, a Hungarian violinist whom Brahms had previously accompanied in a recital, invited Brahms to join him on a concert tour. They started on April 19, 1853, a date that marked a turning point for Brahms. The venture itself was not particularly successful and ended in a quarrel, but Brahms met three musicians who were to play highly important parts in his artistic and personal life. He became a close friend of a famous violin virtuoso, Joseph Joachim, who from the outset recognized Brahms's genius. Even more important, however, was Brahms's visit at the Düsseldorf home of the composer Robert Schumann and his wife, Clara, a magnificent concert pianist. Both were deeply impressed by his works, and Schumann immediately decided to recommend their publication to his own publishers, Breitkopf and Härtel, in Leipzig. He also decided to tell the musical world of the genius he had discovered and published an article entitled "Neue Bahnen" ("New Paths") in a widely circulated periodical named *Neue Zeitschrift für Musik* ("New Magazine for Music"), which he had founded years earlier. In his essay he glowingly described the impressions received of Brahms's compositions and prophesied a splendid career for the youth "called forth to give us the highest expression of ideals in our time." The article created a sensation, though some critics were inclined to distrust so enthusiastic an encomium. But Brahms's personality quickly silenced the opposition. The remarks in a lady's diary written after the composer had performed in her salon suggested the prevailing attitude:

Encouragement from Robert Schumann

> There he sat . . ., Schumann's young Messiah . . .; his face showed the triumph of his spirit. Purity, innocence, naturalness, power, and depth—this describes his character. Schumann's prophecy tempts one perhaps to . . . be severe with him, but one forgets everything, and loves and admires him without restraint.

The young composer himself felt somewhat crushed by the great responsibility laid on him by such a forecast. He reacted by applying relentless self-criticism to the works he prepared for publication and discarded several, as he was wont to do also in later phases of his development. Finally, he entrusted Breitkopf and Härtel with the publication of his first two piano sonatas, six songs, and the *Scherzo in E Flat Minor*.

The years 1854–56 were mostly devoted to studies and creative work carried out while he was staying with Joachim at Göttingen or near the Schumanns' home in Düsseldorf. It was a time of deepest emotional turmoil for the young composer. In February 1854 Robert Schumann, tormented by a nervous disorder of increasing proportions, attempted suicide and had to be removed to an asylum. His wife, a mother of six children, with a seventh on the way, was in despair. Brahms felt he had to help in whatever way he could and stayed near Clara, supporting himself modestly through music lessons. He continued his creative work, finishing his *Trio in B Major* for piano, violin, and cello and composing piano variations on a theme by "him" (Robert Schumann) dedicated to "her" (Clara).

Brahms fell more and more under the spell of Clara, who, at the age of 35, was still a very beautiful woman. His initial reverent friendship turned into ardent love. But Clara was the loyal wife of his great friend, for whose suffering he felt the deepest compassion and whose recovery he desired with all his heart. His mental agony was described by Brahms himself when explaining the meaning of his *Piano Quartet No. 3 in C Minor* conceived at that time: "Just picture a man who is going to shoot himself and has no other choice left." Yet, when Schumann died in July 1856, Brahms and Clara did not marry. Clara probably decided that she could not burden the young genius with a wife 14 years his senior and with seven children. Brahms himself may have felt too immature and unsettled in his career to undertake such responsibilities. Most of all, he was by nature unable to accept any encroachment on his freedom. He had to go through an agonizing struggle between his love and his zest for independence until the latter won. This pattern was to repeat itself. Brahms often fell in love with beautiful girls—though never so intensely as with Clara—but ultimately he could never commit himself. The relationship with Clara gradually changed into a lifelong friendship. She was privileged to watch the growth of his mastery: she was introduced to any new work as soon as the ink was dry, and her sensitive comments meant a great deal to Brahms.

The transitional phase. In 1857 Brahms obtained his first official position when he was engaged for three months by the princely court of Detmold as pianist-in-residence and conductor of the choral society, part-time duties he performed for three years. This post provided valuable practical experience and left him enough time for his own work. Now that the emotional conflict was to some extent resolved, his productivity increased. Apart from the two delightful *Serenades* for orchestra and the colourful first *String Sextet in B Flat Major*, the turbulent *Piano Concerto No. 1 in D Minor* was completed after undergoing various changes and revisions. Brahms's main aim at that time was to gain a permanent position in his native town. He was gradually establishing contacts with leading musicians in Hamburg, and it was his hope that on the retirement of Friedrich Wilhelm Grund, conductor of the Philharmonic Concerts, the post would be offered to him. To pass the time and also to increase his standing in Hamburg by winning success in a famous music centre, Brahms left for Vienna in September 1862. The Viennese musicians showed great interest in his work, and before long he had opportunities to reveal in various concerts his mastery both as a pianist and a composer. But this eventful time was overshadowed by inner tension while he waited for the decision in Hamburg and finally by the severe disappointment when, in May 1863, the position was offered not to him but to a singer, his friend Julius Stockhausen. Under the first impact he wrote to Clara:

Completion of first piano concerto

> This is a much sadder business for me than you think. . . . As I am altogether a rather old-fashioned person, so I am

in this, that I am not a cosmopolitan, but love my native town as a mother . . . And now this hostile friend comes and ousts me . . . perhaps for ever. How rare it is for one of us to find a permanent niche and how glad I should have been to find mine in my native town! . . . One wants to be bound, and to acquire the things that make life worth living, and one dreads solitude. Work in active association with others, with live social intercourse, and family happiness . . . who is so little human that he does not long for these things?

Brahms longed at times for such security, yet as events in his life were to reveal again and again, he was fundamentally unwilling to be "bound," be it in his human relationships or in a permanent position. This great disappointment decisively contributed to a change in Brahms's personality. He grew more reserved, ironical, and even maliciously sarcastic in his utterances. It is significant that he eventually hid his sensitive features under a large beard. Brahms the artist, however, may have benefitted from Hamburg's rejection. Looking for a new home, he chose, after some years of wandering, the one place that differed decisively from Hamburg: Vienna. For the narrow provincial atmosphere of his native town he substituted that of the cosmopolitan imperial city with an abundant musical life and inhabitants more outgoing and friendly than the cool, reserved northern Germans. Under the impact of Vienna's peculiar atmosphere, his artistic personality was enriched, and this led to the peak of achievements in his work, which won him outstanding renown.

Move to Vienna

Maturity. Vienna certainly offered Brahms what Hamburg had denied him. In 1863 he accepted an invitation to take over direction of the Singakademie, a fine choral society; his concerts, distinguished by interesting programs, were appreciated by critics and audiences alike, Yet some aspects of the position, such as arguments about program policy, irked him, and after a year, he declined to continue directing the group. He showed somewhat more perseverance when, in 1872, he was appointed artistic director of the Vienna Gesellschaft der Musikfreunde (Society of Friends of Music), a venerable organization founded in 1812 that had counted Beethoven and Schubert among its members. Brahms remained with this group for three years, and in his sensitive interpretation of music from different epochs he exerted a lasting educational influence on Viennese music lovers. He was sometimes criticized for planning unvaried programs, with a serious mood predominating. This led to a jesting remark that circulated in Vienna's musical circles: "When Brahms is in extra good spirits, he sings 'The grave is my joy'." Whether as a result of this criticism or because he was impatient with routine administrative duties, Brahms resigned in 1875, greatly relieved to have regained his independence. It was the last time in his life that he held a position of this kind, although offers were received from German cities such as Cologne (three times) and Düsseldorf (twice). Nevertheless, he maintained cordial relations with the Vienna Gesellschaft, which elected him an honorary member, and proved his attachment by making the society his sole heir.

In between the two appointments in Vienna, Brahms's work flourished and some of his most significant works were composed. The year 1868 witnessed the completion of his most famous choral work, *Ein deutsches Requiem* (*A German Requiem*), which had occupied him since Schumann's death and was taken up again in 1865 when Brahms's mother died. The work, based on biblical texts selected by the composer, made a strong impact at its first performance at Bremen on Good Friday, 1868; after this, it was performed all over Germany. With the *Requiem*, which is still considered one of the most significant works of 19th-century choral music, Brahms moved into the front rank of German composers.

Completion of the *German Requiem*

Brahms was also writing successful works in a lighter vein. In 1869 he offered two volumes of *Hungarian Dances* for piano duet, brilliant arrangements of gypsy tunes he had collected in the course of the years. Their success was phenomenal, and they were played all over the world. Similarly, in 1868–69 he paid a gracious compliment to his adopted hometown by presenting his *Liebeslieder* (*Love Song*) waltzes, Opus 52, for vocal quartet and four-hand piano accompaniment—a work sparkling with humour and incorporating graceful Viennese dance tunes.

Among the songs Brahms wrote during these years are the deeply felt "Die Mainacht" ("May Night"), Opus 43, No. 2; the dreamy "Feldeinsamkeit" ("In Lonely Meadow"), Opus 86, No. 2; the humorous "Vergebliches Ständchen" ("Unavailing Serenade"), Opus 84, No. 4; and the most famous of all, "Wiegenlied" ("Lullaby"), Opus 49, No. 4, which he sent in July 1868 to his Viennese friend Bertha Faber to congratulate her on the birth of her child. Into the rocking accompaniment he wove an Austrian ländler dance Bertha had sung to him long before.

Brahms also wrote several significant chamber works in this period. He completed his powerful *Piano Quintet in F Minor;* the *String Sextet No. 2 in G Major*, quieter and more restrained in character than the first one, and, inspired by his mother's death, the *Trio for French Horn, Violin, and Piano*, a work imbued with a delicate melancholy but also with a deep feeling for the beauty of nature. A climax of stylistic perfection and artistic economy was reached with the magnificent *String Quartets in C Minor* and *A Minor*, Opus 51, soon followed by the joyful and bucolic third *Quartet in B Flat Major*, Opus 67. Brahms was moving with great deliberation along the path to purely orchestral composition. In 1873 he offered the masterly orchestral version of his *Variations on a Theme by Haydn*. After this experiment, which even the self-critical Brahms had to consider completely successful, he felt ready to embark on the completion of his *Symphony No. 1 in C Minor*, the opening movement of which he had shown Clara Schumann six years earlier. The magnificent work was completed in 1876 and first heard in the same year. Now that the composer had proved to himself his full command of the symphonic idiom, within the next year he produced his *Symphony No. 2 in D Major*. This is basically a serene and idyllic work, avoiding the heroic pathos of the *C Minor Symphony*. He let six years elapse before his *Symphony No. 3 in F Major*. In its first three movements this work, too, appears to be a comparatively calm and serene composition—until the finale, which presents a gigantic conflict of elemental forces. Again after only one year, Brahms's last symphony, *No. 4 in E Minor*, was begun. This work may well have been inspired by the ancient Greek tragedies of Sophocles that Brahms had been reading at the time. The symphony's most important movement is once more the finale. Brahms took a simple theme he found in Bach's Cantata Number 150 and developed it in a set of 31 highly intricate variations, but the technical skill displayed here is as nothing compared with the clarity of thought and the intensity of feeling.

Composition of the first symphony

Materially, too, his music proved most successful. The compositions published since the 1860s by Fritz Simrock in Bonn were widely performed and brought Brahms a sizable income. Strangely enough, the composer who had grown up in poverty treated his fortune rather carelessly. He left its management to the publisher and had no complaint when Simrock lost substantial sums through speculation on the stock market. Although Brahms spent little on himself, feeling most comfortable when leading a simple life, free of luxuries, he derived pleasure from his vast earnings when he had a chance to help others. He was generous to his family, especially to his father and to his stepmother, whom Johann Jakob had married after his wife's death. Even when his father died, Johannes continued providing for the second Mrs. Brahms and her relatives. Moreover, many young musicians secretly received financial assistance.

International renown

Gradually, Brahms's renown spread beyond Germany and Austria. Switzerland and The Netherlands showed true appreciation of his art, and Brahms's concert tours—partly in the company of Joachim—to these countries as well as to Hungary and Poland won great acclaim. Urgent invitations reached him from England, too, and in April 1876 the University of Cambridge offered him the honorary degree of doctor of music. At first Brahms was delighted, but when he found out that the degree had to be conferred on him in person, he tried to persuade the authorities to change this condition. As the university's statutes made this impossible, he declined to attend. Apparently, fear of seasickness made him reluctant to cross the English Channel; and his poor English, as well as an aversion to formal ceremonies, may also have played some part in his decision. Brahms's English admirers had to accept the composer's idiosyncrasy. To make up for the loss of the Cambridge degree, the Philharmonic Society of London awarded him their gold medal in 1877. Brahms was not, moreover, to be deprived of a doctor's title, for the University of Breslau (now Wrocław, Poland) conferred an honorary degree on him in 1879. The composer thanked the University by writing the *Academic Festival Overture* based on various German student songs, the first performance of which he conducted himself in Breslau.

Brahms's followers and detractors

By now the composer's contemporaries were keenly aware of the outstanding significance of Brahms's works. Following the example of the German conductor Hans von Bülow, they spoke of the "three great B's" (Bach, Beethoven, and Brahms), who were given the same rank of eminence. Yet, despite his honours from various quarters, there was a sizable circle of musicians who did not admit Brahms's greatness. Fervent admirers of the avant-garde composers of the day, most notably Franz Liszt and Richard Wagner, looked down on Brahms's contributions as too old-fashioned and inexpressive. Brahms himself was to some extent to blame for their hostile attitude, because as early as 1860 he had prepared, in conjunction with Joachim and two other composers, a "manifesto" expressing an unfriendly attitude toward the tenets of the progressive "Neo-German" school of composition. Brahms became, in Vienna, a good friend of Eduard Hanslick, an eminent critic and one of Wagner's most outspoken adversaries; this alone would have prompted the Wagnerites to vilify Brahms. The most vicious attacks came from the pen of Hugo Wolf, the German lied (song) composer, who during 1884–87 served as music critic of the fashionable weekly *Wiener Salonblatt* and in this position launched fierce assaults against the works of his older contemporary. Brahms was not upset by these diatribes but instead found them amusing.

With advancing age he established a certain pattern in his way of life that seemed to be beneficial for his creative work. After 1871 he lived in Vienna close to his beloved Gesellschaft der Musikfreunde in a simple three-room apartment kept up by a friendly and helpful landlady. When he went on concert tours, he conducted or performed only his own works, and so many demands reached him that he often had to decline them. In spring he loved to travel to Italy, to "bathe in beauty," as he wrote. Between 1871 and 1893 he made nine such trips, often in the company of an eminent surgeon, Theodor Billroth, himself a sensitive musician to whom Brahms dedicated his *String Quartet*, Opus 67. Another welcome companion was a Swiss poet, J.V. Widmann, who left an interesting account of these trips. Brahms prepared himself thoroughly for every journey and received lasting inspiration from Italian art. Reverberations of his first experience in Italy are noticeable in his *Piano Concerto No. 2 in B Flat Major*, which is imbued with a beautifully balanced serenity.

Travel in Italy

The summer was always spent in the country. Like Beethoven, Brahms was an outdoor person who worked best on extensive walks. He responded deeply to nature, which acted as the most powerful stimulant on his creative process; and many of his works bear the imprint of specific summer resorts. The pastoral *Second Symphony*, the romantic *Violin Concerto*, and the sparkling *Rhapsodies* for piano were written near charming Wörther See (Lake Wörther) in southern Austria, where Brahms stayed during 1877–79. The grandiose Lake Thun in Switzerland was likewise enjoyed for three summers (1886–88), and there Brahms composed the boldly conceived *Double Concerto in A Minor for Violin and Cello*, the *Cello Sonata in F Major*, the powerful *Piano Trio No. 3 in C Minor*, and the *Violin Sonata in D Minor*. The charming Austrian spa Bad Ischl, summer residence of Emperor Francis Joseph I, was another Brahms favourite. He visited it for the first time in 1880 and spent the last eight summers of his life there. It was there that he completed the radiantly joyous first *String Quintet in F Major*, Opus 88, and years later the energetic second *String Quintet in G Major*, Opus 111.

Final years. It was Brahms's intention to conclude his creative work with the second *String Quintet*, which he finished in 1890, but during the following summer he felt inspired to start on a new experiment. He began to include the clarinet in his chamber music because of his acquaintance with an outstanding clarinetist, Richard Mühlfeld, whom Brahms had heard perform some months before. With Mühlfeld in mind, Brahms wrote at Bad Ischl his *Trio for Clarinet, Cello, and Piano*, Opus 114; the great *Quintet for Clarinet and Strings*, Opus 115; and two *Sonatas for Clarinet and Piano*, Opus 120, Nos. 1 and 2. The works are perfect in structure and beautifully adapted to the potentialities of the wind instrument.

Clarinet works

In 1894 Brahms saw his lifelong wish fulfilled. Hamburg, most eager to make amends for its previous behaviour, offered him the position as conductor of its philharmonic orchestra, after having awarded to him, five years earlier, the honorary freedom of the city. At the age of 61, Brahms felt less inclined than ever before to shoulder new responsibilities, but when he refused, he could not refrain from the following remarks:

> There are not many things that I have desired so long and so ardently at the time—that is at the right time. Many years had to pass before I could reconcile myself to the thought of being forced to tread other paths. Had things gone according to my wish, I might today be celebrating my jubilee with you, while you would be, as you are today, looking for a capable younger man. May you find him soon, and may he work in your interests with the same good will, and the same modest degree of ability, and the same wholehearted zeal, as would have done yours.

On his 63rd birthday, Brahms completed his *Vier ernste Gesänge* (*Four Serious Songs*), for bass voice and piano, on texts from both the Old and the New Testament, a pessimistic work dealing with the vanity of all earthly things and welcoming death as the healer of pain and weariness. In the last song, however, the power of love is rapturously glorified in words from the First Letter of Paul to the Corinthians. The conception of this work arose from Brahms's thoughts of Clara Schumann, whose physical condition had gravely deteriorated. He was aware that he was soon to lose his dearest friend (who, in his own words, was "the most beautiful experience of his life, its greatest wealth, and its noblest content"). On May 20, 1896, Clara died, and Brahms, receiving the news in Ischl, travelled for 40 hours by train to Bonn to attend her funeral. On his return, his changed appearance alarmed his friends. He believed he was suffering from what he called a "petty bourgeois jaundice," but the doctors recognized an advanced state of an incurable liver disease. In the summer of 1896 Brahms was still able to write his *Eleven Chorale Preludes* for organ, the last of these a fantasia on "O Welt, ich muss dich lassen" ("Oh World, I Must Depart from Thee"). On April 3, 1897, he died in Vienna, mourned by music lovers all over the world. His funeral was attended by representatives from music centres in various countries, and in Hamburg the flags were flown at half-mast on all the ships in the harbour. He was buried in Vienna, the city he had adopted as his home, near the graves of Beethoven and Schubert.

Brahms is one of the few composers whose greatness was recognized in his lifetime, and it has not been questioned by later generations. The solid craftsmanship displayed in his compositions, their decided intellectual qualities, and his richly flowing, Romantic inspiration have made Brahms as much appreciated today as he was in the 19th century.

MAJOR WORKS

Orchestral music

SYMPHONIES: *No 1 in C Minor*, op. 68 (1876); *No 2 in D Major*, op. 73 (1877); *No. 3 in F Major*, op. 90 (1883); *No. 4 in E Minor*, op. 98 (1885).

CONCERTOS: (PIANO): *No. 1 in D Minor*, op. 15 (1854–58); *No. 2 in B Flat Major*, op. 83 (1881). (VIOLIN): op. 77 in D major (1878). (VIOLIN AND CELLO): *Double Concerto in A Minor*, op. 102 (1887).

OTHER ORCHESTRAL WORKS: Two overtures: *Academic Festival*, op. 80 (1880) and *Tragic*, op. 81 (1880); two serenades: *No. 1 in D Major*, op. 11 and *No. 2 in A Major*, op. 16 (1857–59); *Variations on a Theme by Haydn* (Chorale St. Antoni), op. 56a (1873); *Hungarian Dances* arranged from his own piano duets (published 1873).

Chamber music

SONATAS: Three for violin and piano: *No. 1 in G Major*, op. 78 (1879), *No. 2 in A Major*, op. 100 (1886), and *No. 3 in D Minor*, op. 108 (1886–88); two for cello and piano: *No. 1 in E Minor*, op. 38 (1862–65) and *No. 2 in F Major*, op. 99 (1886); two for clarinet and piano, op. 120 (1894), *No. 1 in F Minor* and *No. 2 in E Flat Major*.

OTHER CHAMBER WORKS: Two string sextets, two string quintets, and three string quartets, one clarinet quintet, one piano quintet; three piano quartets for violin, viola, cello, and piano; three trios for violin, cello, and piano; one trio for clarinet (or viola), cello, and piano; one trio for violin, horn (or cello or viola), and piano.

Solo Piano Music

SONATAS: *No. 1 in C Major*, op. 1 (1852–53); *No. 2 in F Sharp Minor*, op. 2 (1852); *No. 3 in F Minor*, op. 5 (1853).

VARIATIONS: Five sets, including *Variations on a Theme by Schumann*, op. 9 (1854); *Variations and Fugue on a Theme by Handel*, op. 24 (1861); *Variations on a Theme by Paganini*, op. 35 (1862–63).

OTHER SOLO PIANO WORKS: Numerous ballads, capriccios, fantasies, intermezzos, and rhapsodies, including *Four Ballads*, op. 10 (1854); two *Rhapsodies*, op. 79 (1879); op. 116, 117, 118, 119 (1891–93).

PIANO DUETS: *Variations on a Theme by Schumann*, op. 23 (1861); various waltzes, including *Liebeslieder* waltzes, op. 52a (1874) and *Neue Liebeslieder* waltzes, op. 65a (1877); four sets of *Hungarian Dances*.

MUSIC FOR TWO PIANOS: *Variations on a Theme by Haydn*, op. 56b (1873); *Sonata in F Minor*, op. 34b (1864; an arrangement of his *Piano Quintet*, op. 34).

Organ music

Two preludes and fugues; *Fugue in A Flat Minor; Chorale Prelude and Fugue in A Minor;* and *Eleven Chorale Preludes*, op. 122 (1896).

Vocal music

ACCOMPANIED CHORAL MUSIC: *Ein deutsches Requiem*, op. 45 (1857–68); various sacred and secular works for female, male, and mixed voices; some arrangements.

UNACCOMPANIED CHORAL MUSIC: 117 German folk songs for four-part chorus; various sacred songs, motets, secular part-songs, and canons for female, male, and mixed voices.

SONGS: 214 solo songs with piano, composed throughout the course of his life, published in 32 sets, including *Vier Ernste Gesänge*, op. 121 (1896).

DUETS AND QUARTETS: 25 duets, mostly for soprano, contralto, and piano; 16 quartets for soprano, contralto, tenor, and bass; *Liebeslieder* waltzes, op. 52 (1868–69), and *Neue Liebeslieder* waltzes, for piano duet and voices ad lib, op. 65 (1874); and 11 *Zigeunerlieder*, op. 103 (1887).

BIBLIOGRAPHY. JOSEPH BRAUNSTEIN (ed.), *Thematic Catalog of the Collected Works of Brahms*, enl. ed. based on the 4th ed. of Simrock's *Thematisches Verzeichnis* (1956), is a complete list of Brahms's works. The most important collection of his memorabilia may be found in the Gesellschaft der Musikfreunde (Society of Friends of Music) in Vienna, which owns autographs of the *German Requiem*, the *Double Concerto*, the *Piano Trio in C Minor*, the *Clarinet Quintet*, the *String Quintet in G Major*, and of many other works, in all more than 600 sheets. The Gesellschaft preserves the personal copies of Brahms's printed works with the composer's autograph corrections and changes; Brahms's own library is to be found there, including his collection of autographs by other composers and the large collection of letters he received from various writers and carefully preserved. The DEUTSCHE BRAHMS-GESELLSCHAFT published Brahms's correspondence (in German) in 16 vol. (1908–22). A small selection of outstanding letters addressed by Brahms to various friends may be found in the appendix to KARL GEIRINGER, *Johannes Brahms: Leben und Schaffen eines deutschen Meisters* (1935; Eng. trans., *Brahms: His Life and Work*, 2nd ed., 1947), which was written by the curator of the Gesellschaft der Musikfreunde, who has drawn extensively on the unpublished material in this collection. MAX KALBECK, *Johannes Brahms*, 4 vol. (1904–14), is the most extensive Brahms biography (in German). HANS GAL, *Johannes Brahms: Werk und Persönlichkeit* (1961; Eng. trans., *Johannes Brahms: His Work and Personality*, 1963), is a sensitive account by one of the editors of the collected edition of Brahms's compositions. EDWIN EVANS, *Historical, Descriptive and Analytical Account of the Entire Works of Johannes Brahms*, 4 vol. (1912–36, reprinted 1970), is very thorough, though somewhat pedantic.

(K.G.)

Braille

Braille, the universally accepted system of writing used by and for blind persons, consists of a code of 63 characters, each made up of one to six raised dots arranged in a six-position matrix or cell. These Braille characters are embossed in lines on paper and read by passing the fingers lightly over the manuscript. Louis Braille (1809–52), who was blinded at the age of three, invented the system in 1824 while a student at the Institution Nationale des Jeunes Aveugles (National Institute for Blind Children), Paris.

Early systems of writing for the blind. Before the invention of Braille, various forms of tangible alphabets had been devised for the use of the blind, including letters engraved in wood, cast in lead, and cut in cardboard. The Frenchman Valentin Haüy (1745–1822) was the first person to emboss paper as a means of reading for the blind. His printing of normal letters in relief led others to devise simplified versions and modifications of the alphabet that could be more readily identified by touch than facsimile letters. Most of these early systems were cumbersome to handle and difficult to learn. With one exception, they are no longer in use. The single exception is Moon type, invented in 1845 by William Moon (1818–94) of Brighton, England, which partly retains the outlines of the Roman letters and is easily learned by those who have become blind in later life. Books in this type are still in limited use by elderly people, particularly in Great Britain.

Alphabets for the blind

Braille's invention. When Louis Braille entered the school for the blind in Paris, in 1819, it had 14 books in embossed characters available for the students, but they were rarely used. In addition to the difficulty encountered by even the best readers using this system, and the slow pace at which they had to proceed, there was another disadvantage of which the young Braille and his classmates were keenly aware: there was no way for them to write using the raised lines of this system. Braille learned of a system of tangible writing using dots, invented in 1819 by Capt. Charles Barbier, a French army officer. It was called night writing and was intended for nighttime battlefield communications. In 1824, when he was only 15 years old, Braille developed a six-dot "cell" system. He used Barbier's system as a starting point and cut its 12-dot configuration in half. The system was first published in 1829; a more complete elaboration appeared in 1837.

Description of Braille. To aid in identifying the 63 different dot patterns, or characters, that are possible within the six-dot cell, Braille numbered the dot positions 1–2–3 downward on the left and 4–5–6 downward on the right. The illustration shows the formation of each cell and its simplest designated meaning. The first ten letters of the alphabet are formed with dots 1, 2, 4, and 5. When preceded by the numeric indicator diagrammed in line 6, these signs have number values. The letters *k* through *t* are formed by adding dot 3 to the signs in line 1. Five of the remaining letters of the alphabet and five very common words are formed by adding dots 3 and 6 to the signs in line 1. When dot 6 is added to the first ten letters, the letter *w* and nine common letter combinations are formed (see line 4). Punctuation marks and two additional common letter combinations are made by placing the signs in line 1 in dot positions 2, 3, 5, and 6 (line 5). Three final letter combinations, the numeric indicator, and two more punctuation marks are formed with dots 3, 4, 5, and 6 as shown in line 6. The last seven dot patterns indicated in line 7 are formed by dots 4, 5, and 6 and have no true equivalents in ordinary written language. Like the numeric indicator, these signs serve as

Braille system explained

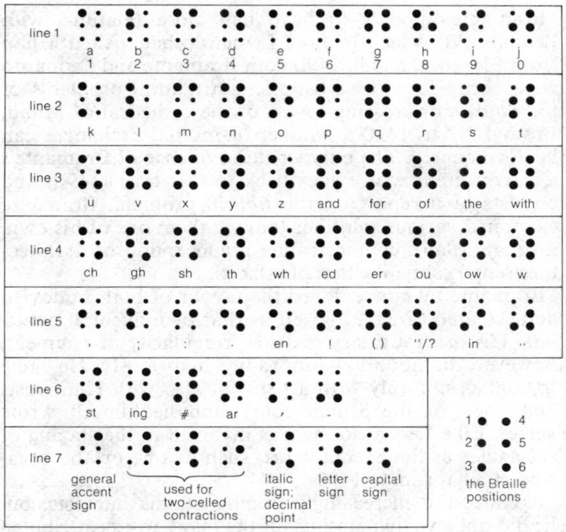

The Braille characters.

modifiers when placed before any of the other signs. Through the application of this principle, the various signs can function in multiple ways. For example, dot 5 added before the sign for the letter *d* forms the Braille contraction for "day."

Diffusion of Braille. Braille's system was immediately accepted and used by his fellow students, but wider acceptance was slow in coming. The system was not officially adopted by the school in Paris until 1854, two years after Braille's death. In the United States, in the 1860s, another dot system, known as New York point, was developed by William B. Wait at the New York Institute for the Education of the Blind. In the 1870s a modification of Braille, called American Braille, was invented by a blind teacher, Joel W. Smith of Boston. These codes were used by many of the schools for the blind in the United States until 1916, when Braille's original alphabet and a series of contractions were officially adopted. A universal Braille code for the English-speaking world, however, was not adopted until 1932, when representatives from agencies for the blind in Great Britain and the United States met in London and agreed upon a system known as Standard English Braille, grade 2. In 1957 Anglo-American experts again met in London to further improve the system.

In addition to the literary Braille code, there are other codes utilizing the Braille cell but with other meanings assigned to each configuration. The "Nemeth Code of Braille Mathematics and Scientific Notation" (1965) provides for Braille representation of the many special symbols used in advanced mathematical and technical material. There are also special Braille codes or modifications for the representation of musical notation, shorthand, and, of course, many of the more common languages of the world.

Writing with Braille

Handwritten Braille. Writing Braille by hand is accomplished by means of a device called a slate that consists of two metal plates hinged together to permit a sheet of paper to be inserted between them. Some slates have a wooden base or guide board onto which the paper is clamped. The upper of the two metal plates, the guide plate, has cell-sized windows; under each of these, in the lower plate, are six slight pits in the Braille dot pattern. A stylus is used to press the paper against the pits to form the raised dots. A person using Braille writes from right to left; when the sheet is turned over, the dots face upward and are read from left to right.

Machine-produced Braille. Braille is also produced by special machines with six keys, one for each dot in the Braille cell. The first Braille writing machine, the Hall Braille writer, was invented in 1892 by Frank H. Hall, superintendent of the Illinois School for the Blind. A modified form of this device is still in use today as are later, similar devices like the Perkins Brailler and the Lavendar Braillewriter. Braille is also produced by electric embossing machines that are similar to electric typewriters.

Multiple copies of Braille materials are made with embossed zinc plates that are used for press masters. These plates are produced by a stereograph machine invented by Hall in 1893. In the 1920s the interpoint system was developed to emboss both sides of a sheet of paper without the dots on one side opposing those on the other side. A computer program for automatically translating printed English into contracted Braille has been used to produce stereograph plates and to provide Braille feedback from a standard teletypewriter keyboard.

BIBLIOGRAPHY. *Proceedings of the International Congress on Technology and Blindness,* 4 vol. (1963), ed. by L.L. CLARK, is a collection of papers on the relationship of man and machines, sensory loss, and the use of aids and appliances, including the latest findings on Braille writing and reading. The last volume is a catalog-appendix listing appliances available from sources all over the world. *Understanding Braille* (1968), prepared by the AMERICAN FOUNDATION FOR THE BLIND, describes the workings of the Braille system and its use by blind persons. A manual for learning to read and write Braille is *Braille in Brief* (1968) by B.M. KREBS. The following publications treat the Braille notations of English and other languages: C.N. MACKENZIE, *World Braille Usage: A Survey of Efforts Towards Uniformity of Braille Notation* (1954); L.H. GOLDISH, *Braille in the United States: Its Production, Distribution and Use* (1967); JOINT UNIFORM BRAILLE COMMITTEE, *English Braille, American Edition, 1959* (1959); and NATIONAL INSTITUTE FOR THE BLIND, *Standard English Braille: Grades I and II* (1932). In *As I Saw It* (1955), R.B. IRWIN, a prominent figure in the development of the uniform Braille code, tells the story of that struggle, plus the progress in Braille embossing and the development of libraries for the blind. The original work on Braille is LOUIS BRAILLE, *Nouveau Procédé pour représenter par des points la forme même des lettres . . .* (1839); *Les doigts qui lisent* (1951; Eng. trans., *The Reading Fingers: Life of Louis Braille, 1809–1852,* 1955), by J. ROBLIN is Braille's biography.

(M.R.B.)

Bramante, Donato

Through his last works in Rome, from 1500 to 1514, Donato Bramante introduced what came to be known as the High Renaissance style in architecture, which rapidly spread throughout Italy and the rest of Europe. His works, which include the design for St. Peter's Basilica, synthesized early Renaissance ideas with the fruits of his own ceaseless experimentation. The result was a style that continued to exercise a powerful influence over architects until the end of the 18th century.

Early years and training. Donato (Donino, Donnino) Bramante was probably born at Monte Asdruvaldo (now Fermignano, near Urbino, Italy) in 1444 of a family of well-to-do peasants. In his childhood, says the 16th-century biographer and artist Giorgio Vasari, "besides reading and writing, he practiced much at the abacus." His father probably directed him toward painting.

Little is known of Bramante's life and works before 1477. He probably served as an assistant to Piero della Francesca in Urbino, which under the nobleman Federico da Montefeltro (died 1482) had become a Humanist centre of considerable importance. In 1477 Bramante was working in Bergamo as a painter of illusionistic murals of architecture. He probably derived his training not only from the works of artists active in Urbino but also from those of other artists he may have observed in his travels, such as those of Leon Battista Alberti (in Rimini and Mantua), Andrea Mantegna (in Mantua and Padua), Ercole de'Roberti (in Ferrara), and Filippo Brunelleschi (in Florence).

None of Bramante's youthful productions has survived, though some historians attribute various architectural perspectives to him. Almost all of them show some characteristics of Bramante's work, but they appear very different from each other. Before 1477, Bramante may have been primarily a planner, designer, and painter of architectural perspectives that other artists partly modified and inserted into their own paintings or carried out in construction; there are a number of later instances

Tempietto, S. Pietro In Montorio, Rome, designed by Bramante, 1502.
Anderson—Alinari

in which he is known to have furnished painters with such architectural perspectives.

Lombard period. By 1477 Bramante had left Urbino for unknown reasons and had settled in the northern Italian province of Lombardy. He worked on frescoes for the facade of the Palazzo del Podestà (later altered) in Bergamo showing classical figures of philosophers in a complex architectural setting. Vasari (though poorly informed on this period) says that Bramante, after working in various cities on "things of no great cost and little value," went to Milan "to see the cathedral." The cathedral workshop, in which Italian, German, and French craftsmen worked by turns, constituted an important centre for the exchange of knowledge, planning methods, and techniques. Moreover, Milan was a large and wealthy metropolis, the capital of a state ruled by Ludovico Sforza, called Il Moro, and Renaissance architecture was a commodity to be imported. Thus the city represented an opportunity for a young and up-to-date architect like Bramante.

Early work in Milan

The first architectural work that can be definitely attributed to Bramante is a design: a print made in 1481 by a Milanese engraver, Bernardo Prevedari, from a Bramante drawing representing a ruined temple with human figures. About the same time, Bramante was working on the church of Sta. Maria presso S. Satiro, the first structure definitely attributed to him. Along with a certain adherence to local taste, this church shows traces of the influence of Alberti, Mantegna, Brunelleschi, and the Urbino school. This last influence is particularly evident in its choir, which was painted in perspective to give an illusion of a much larger space. Perhaps from the same period (*c.* 1480–85) is Bramante's decoration of a room in Casa Panigarola in Milan (fragments in the Brera, Milan) that consists of architectural settings and the figures of men at arms rendered by means of illusionistic perspective. Similar experiments, perhaps also in the same years, seem to have been carried out by Bramante on the facades of buildings, such as Casa Fontana, later called Silvestri, in Milan.

In 1488 Bramante, along with a number of other architects, was asked by Cardinal Ascanio Sforza, brother of Ludovico Sforza and bishop of Pavia, to draw up a new plan for the cathedral of Pavia. Bramante went many times to that city during this period, and it was probably under his direction that the crypt and the lower portion of the building were executed.

Plan for the cathedral of Pavia

Bramante appears to have had close relations with Leonardo da Vinci. In 1482 Leonardo had visited Milan from Florence, and in 1490 both Bramante and Leonardo were occupied with stylistic and structural problems of the *tiburio*, or crossing tower, of the cathedral of Milan. From 1487 to 1490 a number of mutual exchanges can be documented. The only written evidence of Bramante's ideas on architecture goes back to this time (1490) and consists of a report on the *tiburio* problem. Bramante examined various solutions (among them one of his own, a square plan), demonstrating a conception of architecture remarkably like that of Alberti.

Bramante by now enjoyed the favour of both Ludovico and Ascanio Sforza, as well as that of influential courtiers. His modest salary and the irregularity of payment, however, did not allow him to live luxuriously. He came in contact not only with artists but also with Humanists and poets of the Sforza court, and he himself wrote verses. Like Leonardo, he was involved in the staging of spectacles at the Sforza court, such as one on the occasion of a baptism in 1492.

Architecture increasingly dominated his interests, but he did not give up painting. Of the many works attributed to him by various 16th-century writers, however, none seems to have been preserved. The only extant easel picture that has ever been attributed to him is the "Christ at the Column" ("Cristo alla colonna") of the Abbey of Chiaravalle (*c.* 1490, now in the Brera, Milan). A fresco in a complex architectural setting (*c.* 1490–92) in the Castello Sforzesco in Milan is probably his, with the collaboration of his pupil Il Bramantino.

Starting in 1492, Bramante was entrusted by Ludovico and Ascanio Sforza with the reconstruction of the *canonica* (rectory) of S. Ambrogio in Milan. The work was interrupted by the fall of Ludovico, and, though resumed in the 16th century, only one side of the building was executed. Though Bramante's responsibility cannot be proved, the idea for the new *tribuna* (chancel) for Sta. Maria delle Grazie probably originated with him; destined to be the burial mausoleum of the Sforzas, the *tribuna* was in an overall project of reconstruction, begun in 1492, for the entire church. Bramante also may have planned the painted decoration of the interior, but the execution and the clarification of details, particularly on the exterior, were probably done by Lombard masters.

Bramante's activities in the 1490s, before he left Milan finally for Rome, are sporadically documented. It has been conjectured that in the summer of 1492 he was in Florence studying the work of Brunelleschi, in view of the emphatic Brunelleschian character of the S. Ambrogio *canonica.* In 1493 he made a report on certain fortifications on the Swiss border for Ludovico.

His last few years in Lombardy were marked by the restless activity that characterized the remainder of his career. He was probably responsible for the designs of the piazza of Vigevano (carried out between 1492 and 1494, partly transformed in the late 17th century), of the painted architectural decoration on the arcaded facades that marked its limits, and for the designs of other structures of the Vigevano complex, as well as the painted decoration (now disappeared) for the interior of the castle of the same city. His covered passageway (*ponticella*) for the Castello Sforzesco in Milan must also be from this period, and the facade of the church of Sta. Maria Nascente ad Abbiategrasso (near Milan) dates from 1497. Between 1497 and 1498, in addition to a chapel (later altered) of S. Ambrogio in Milan, he worked on the Cistercian Monastery being erected in Milan under the auspices of Ascanio Sforza; like his work on the *canonica*, it was suspended in 1499 and is unfinished.

Endowed with an extremely receptive character, Bramante was by no means immune to the influence of other artists active in Milan. He was also influenced by his study of Lombard monuments dating from the late ancient and Carolingian periods, the memory of which was to be useful to him in Rome. Conversely, Bramante's presence (together with Leonardo's) in Milan was of fundamental importance for the later artistic developments in that city.

Influences on Bramante

Roman period. Bramante probably remained in Milan until Ludovico was forced to flee before the city was occupied by the French in September 1499. Bramante appears to have been active from the first in Rome on a variety of projects, such as a painting (now lost) at S. Giovanni in Laterano celebrating the Holy Year 1500. As under-architect of Pope Alexander VI, he probably executed the fountains in Piazza Sta. Maria in Trastevere and in St. Peter's Square (later altered) and served on several architectural councils. It is probable that in these years he had reduced his activity as a designer and was devoting himself to the study of the ancient monuments in and around Rome, even ranging as far south as Naples. In the meantime, he had come in contact with Oliviero Carafa, the wealthy and politically influential cardinal of Naples, who had a deep interest in letters, the arts, and antiquity. Carafa commissioned the first work in Rome known to be by Bramante: the monastery and cloister of Sta. Maria della Pace (finished 1504). Bramante seems to have been engaged in 1502 to begin the small church known as the Tempietto in S. Pietro in Montorio, on the site where St. Peter was said to have been crucified.

The patronage of Julius II

The election of Pope Julius II in October 1503 began a new phase in Bramante's work—the grand, or mature, manner. Almost immediately he entered the service of the new Pope, one of the greatest patrons in art history. Bramante became the interpreter, in architecture and city planning, of the pontiff's dream of re-creating the ancient empire of the Caesars (*renovatio imperii*). Bramante planned gigantic building complexes that adhered as never before to the idiom of antiquity. At the same time, the buildings often represented an unbiased, personal, and contemporary interpretation of that idiom.

Perhaps as early as 1505, Bramante designed the immense courtyard of the Belvedere, extending the nucleus of the older Vatican palaces to the north and connecting them with the pre-existing villa of Innocent VIII. Though the work was carried forward with great speed, the scale was so large that on the death of Julius II, in 1513, and of Bramante himself, in 1514, it was still far from completion. The project, which continued throughout the 16th century and later, suffered so many changes that today Bramante's concept is almost unrecognizable.

Basilica of St. Peter

Beginning in 1505, at first in competition with two other architects, Giuliano da Sangallo and Fra Giocondo, Bramante planned the new Basilica of St. Peter in Rome—his greatest work and one of the most ambitious building projects up to that date in the history of mankind. The first stone was placed on April 18, 1506 (after Bramante's first plan had been rejected by the Pope, according to a contemporary). The project's site had to be cleared first of the old, crumbling Basilica of Constantine. Bramante's part in its demolition earned him the nicknames of "Maestro Ruinante" or "Maestro Guastante"—"Master Wrecker" or "Master Breaker." At the time of his death the new construction had scarcely begun to take shape.

Named general superintendent of all papal construction, a well-paid office, Bramante was not only the Pope's principal architect and the engineer at the service of his military enterprises but also his personal friend. Concurrent with his work on the Belvedere and St. Peter's, Bramante presented Julius with a highly ambitious plan for the complete remodelling of the Vatican palaces, which was, however, set aside.

Despite the grandiose scale of the St. Peter's undertaking, Bramante continued to work on lesser projects. Between 1505 and 1509 he carried out an enlargement of the choir of the church of Sta. Maria del Popolo, some construction work in Castel Sant'Angelo, and a remodelling of the Rocca di Viterbo. In addition, in 1506, as a military engineer, he accompanied the Pope to Bologna (where the grand staircase of the Palazzo degli Anziani has been attributed to him).

City plan for Rome

About 1508, when Julius II's new city plan for Rome began to be put into effect, Bramante played an important role as architect and town planner. Within the framework of an organic plan, the Via Giulia (from the Ponte Sisto to the Vatican) was laid out with a large piazza that was to constitute a centre of activity for the city government; the Via della Lungara (from the Vatican across Trastevere to the river port installations of Ripa Grande) was begun; the Via dei Banchi, on which were erected the offices of the most important banks of the time, was widened at the entrance of the Ponte Sant'Angelo; and several streets in the old structure of the medieval city were modified. On the Via Giulia, Bramante designed a huge new Palazzo dei Tribunali (1508), incorporating the church of S. Biagio (1509, also by Bramante). The structure is notable as a model for 16th-century architecture.

Within the framework of Bramante's overall plan, the basin of the port was dug out, and a marine fortress was built at Civitavecchia. The west facade of the Vatican Palace (now the side of the S. Damaso courtyard) was also constructed according to his design, though it was later taken up and completed by Raphael. Around the year 1509, Bramante probably furnished a plan for the church of Roccaverano, whose facade anticipates certain solutions of the late-16th-century architect Andrea Palladio.

Another noteworthy design was that of the Palazzo Caprini (House of Raphael; later destroyed) in the Borgo, which became the model for many 16th-century palaces. This palazzo was later acquired by Raphael. According to Vasari, Bramante, around 1509, had designed the architectural background for the "School of Athens" by Raphael (1508–11; Vatican, Rome), and in return, Raphael represented Bramante in the fresco in the guise of Euclid.

Bramante and Raphael

After the death of Julius II, Bramante, though elderly and perhaps in declining health, remained in favour under Pope Leo X. According to a late and uncertain source, in 1513 he presented to Leo X an audacious water-control plan for the city, designed to avoid the periodic floodings of the Tiber. At the end of 1513, however, when consulted about the cathedral of Foligno (S. Feliciano), he was too ill to accept the commission. Bramante died on April 11, 1514, and was buried in St. Peter's. He was carried there, according to Vasari, "by the papal court and by all the sculptors, architects, and painters."

Personality and interests. Even though he was called unlettered (as were Leonardo, Julius II, and others), probably because he was ignorant of Latin and Greek, Bramante must have acquired considerable learning, however fragmentary. His contemporaries esteemed him not only as an architect and painter and for his knowledge of perspective but also as a poet and an amateur musician. He had an almost fanatical interest in Dante. He also wrote some 20 sonnets on amorous, humorous, and religious themes, and, though somewhat crude in style, they are full of spirit.

His theoretical writings, apart from his report on the *tiburio* of the Milan cathedral, have all been lost, but their subjects are indicative of his interests; *e.g.*, works on perspective, on the "German manner," (*i.e.*, on Gothic architecture), on fortification methods, and others.

Bramante seems to have been an extrovert. He was said to be very friendly to persons with talent, and he did much to help them. Humour, irony, a taste for intelligent jokes, and mockery of himself as well as others often appear in his sonnets. Full of faith in himself, he was an irreverent person who took pleasure in proposing paradoxical ideas. He was critical of priests and courtiers but also capable of deep religious feeling. In the treacherous atmosphere of courts, he was able to manoeuvre skillfully. He must have been highly ambitious and not overscrupulous when it came to securing an important commission. His biographers emphasize his impatience and speed in the conception and conduct of his work (Vasari calls him a "resolute, rapid, and excellent inventor"). This quality was combined with imaginative genius and an artful and lively curiosity. His insatiable thirst for experiment and for new knowledge forced him, as Bramante himself remarks in one of his sonnets, to "change himself" continually ("as time changes in a moment / my thought, its follower, changes too"). This trait of instability and inconstancy seems to have led him away from convention in his works to a multiplicity of attitudes and expressions. Perhaps these characteristics indicate a certain dissatisfaction, an inner melancholy, or a deep sense of solitude. He apparently never married or had children. In unceasing experiments in his work, he may have been seeking a remedy for his incurable restlessness.

MAJOR WORKS

Frescoes on the facade of the Palazzo del Podestà, Bergamo (1477); Sta. Maria presso S. Satiro, Milan (*c.* 1480); cathedral at Pavia (plan, crypt, etc., 1488); *tribuna* of the Sta. Maria delle Grazie, Milan (1492); *canonica* and cloisters at S. Ambrogio, Milan (1492–99); cloister, Sta. Maria della Pace, Rome (1500–04); Tempietto, S. Pietro in Montorio, Rome (1502); Belvedere courtyard, Vatican, Rome (begun *c.* 1505); plans for rebuilding St. Peter's, Rome (1505–06); Sta. Maria del Popolo, Rome (new choir, 1505–09); Palazzo dei Tribunali, Rome (never completed, 1508); House of Raphael (formerly Palazzo Caprini), Rome (*c.* 1510? destroyed).

BIBLIOGRAPHY. The most important general biographical and critical publications with extensive bibliographies on the life and work of Bramante are COSTANTINO BARONI, *Bramante* (1944), in Italian; OTTO FORSTER, *Bramante* (1956), in German; F.G. WOLFF METTERNICH, "Der Kupferstich . . .," in *Römisches Jahrbuch für Kunstgeschichte*, 11:9–108 (1967–68), for the Urbino and Milanese periods; ARNALDO BRUSCHI, *Bramante architetto* (1969); "Bramante" in the *Dizionario biografico degli Italiani*, vol. 13 (1971); F. SANGIORGI, *Bramante "hastrubaldino," documenti per una biografia bramantesca* (1970), for the problem of his birthplace and biographical dates for the Urbino period; and *Bramante tra Umanesimo e Manierismo* (1970), the catalog of the historical and critical exhibition commemorating Bramante, held in Rome, September 1970. More recent works dealing with specific aspects include PASQUALE ROTONDI, *Il palazzo ducale di Urbino*, 2 vol. (1950–51), on Bramante's early years in Urbino; JAMES S. ACKERMAN, *The cortile del Belvedere* (1954), and by the same author, various essays on particular themes and his effective critical evaluation of Bramante in *The Architecture of Michelangelo* (1961); and PETER MURRAY, "Bramante milanese: The Printings and Engravings," *Arte lombarda*, 7: 25–42 (1962); "Leonardo and Bramante," *Archit. Rev.*, 134: 346–351 (1963); and "Observations on Bramante's St. Peter's," in DOUGLAS FRASER, HOWARD HIBBARD, and MILTON J. LEWINE (eds.), *Essays in the History of Architecture* (1967), which also contains other important essays on Bramante.

(Ar.B.)

Branchiopoda

The four living orders of the invertebrate subclass Branchiopoda (class Crustacea) have few common features. The back of the head in the Notostraca, or tadpole shrimps, for example, is expanded into a broad thin plate, or carapace, that projects backward over the trunk. In the Conchostraca and Cladocera, however, the carapace is folded into two valves that enclose the trunk limbs. The Anostraca, which lack a carapace, have elongated wormlike bodies and stalked eyes; the eyes of the other three orders lack stalks. The main structural feature that links these diverse forms is the typically flattened and paddle-like trunk limbs, which are used as part of an elaborate filter-feeding mechanism.

Four living orders and one extinct order form the branchiopods. They range in size from 0.25 millimetre (0.01 inch) in *Alonella* to ten centimetres (about four inches) in *Branchinecta gigas*. Branchiopods are abundant in all types of freshwater, from temporary desert pools to great lakes. A few species are found in the sea.

Natural history. *Reproduction and life cycle.* A typical branchiopod begins its life cycle as a nauplius larva, which has a simple undivided body and three pairs of appendages: antennae, antennules (smaller antennae), and mandibles. The antennae are used for swimming. As the nauplius feeds and grows, it gradually changes into the adult form—the body becomes segmented, or jointed, and additional limbs appear. In the orders Anostraca and Notostraca, the antennae lose their swimming function, but, in the orders Conchostraca and Cladocera, they remain large and functional. One conchostracan (*Cyclestheria*) and all cladocerans except one do not hatch as nauplius larvae; rather, they develop directly in the egg and hatch as miniature adults.

Branchiopods mature rapidly. A small cladoceran can lay eggs in the warm water of a temporary desert pool when only two days old. In temperate latitudes in the summer, a cladoceran may become mature in less than a week.

The sexual arrangement in some branchiopods is that of separate males and females. Some populations of the brine shrimp, *Artemia salina*, have both sexes; others are parthenogenetic—*i.e.*, producing only females without fertilization of eggs. Some populations of *Triops cancriformis* have the sexes separate, others are hermaphroditic (*i.e.*, the individuals contain functional reproductive systems of both sexes).

Among the branchiopods, the Cladocera show the greatest variety of reproductive habits. Under favourable conditions the eggs are laid in a brood pouch between the carapace and the trunk. There they develop rapidly and, after about two days, hatch as females, which, in turn, lay eggs that give rise to more females. No males are necessary for this process. When food is scarce, or when there is a sudden temperature change, some of the eggs develop into males, and some of the females begin producing eggs that must be fertilized by sperm from the males. These fertilized eggs are remarkably resistant to unfavourable environmental conditions; even if frozen or dried, they will hatch when returned to favourable conditions. Many Cladocera go through the winter as fertilized eggs; species dwelling in temporary pools lay such eggs to survive periods of drought. Certain Arctic Cladocera produce resistant eggs that do not require fertilization. The resistant, or resting, eggs normally hatch in the following spring, giving rise to the usual miniature adult females. In *Leptodora* the resting egg hatches into a nauplius larva.

Resistance of eggs to environmental hazards

From L. Borradaile and F. Potts, *The Invertebrata*; published by Cambridge University Press

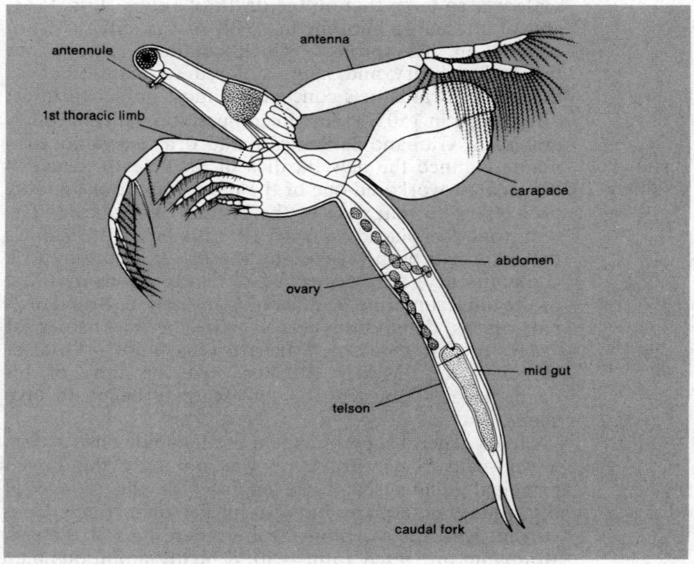

Figure 1: A female *Leptodora kindtii*, a cladoceran branchiopod.

Members of the other branchiopod orders can also produce resting eggs. Many desert-pool species produce only resting eggs. They must abbreviate their life cycles to coincide with the brief period of favourable conditions, and their eggs must be capable of remaining dry for long periods. Sometimes several years elapse before conditions are again favourable.

Ecology. Some species of *Daphnia* in temperate lakes show a remarkable seasonal change in form. In the winter the females have rounded heads, but the females of generations in late spring and summer have pointed heads. It has been demonstrated that high temperature and water turbulence favour the development of a pointed head. The most plausible explanation seems to be related to predation by fish. The feeding activity of plankton-eating fish decreases in winter and increases rapidly in the spring and summer. The fish select the large conspicuous *Daphnia*, the most conspicuous part of which is the carapace with its enclosed limbs and eggs. When the head is enlarged, the size of the carapace is reduced, so that an overall decrease in conspicuousness occurs in the summer forms. A change in form in relation to the environment also takes place in the *Artemia salina*. This species lives in very saline water, and the proportions of the body vary with the salinity of the water.

Food gathering

The trunk limbs of all branchiopods are used to gather food. Most commonly, small particles are collected from the water passing between the limbs, filters formed by setae, or fine hairs, separate the particles from the water, and an elaborate mechanism shifts food from the filters forward to the mouth. The filters, which may be very efficient, enable branchiopods to collect material as small as bacteria for food. The ability to utilize bacteria is important in the cleansing of water in reservoirs, where Cladocera are often abundant.

The notostracans *Triops* and *Lepidurus* can collect small particles, but they can also act as predators. *Triops* eats small oligochaete worms and the larvae of chironomid midges. *Lepidurus arcticus* has been observed feeding on another arctic branchiopod, the anostracan *Branchinecta paludosa*, which often lives in the same tundra pools.

Predators are also found among the Cladocera. In *Leptodora* and *Polyphemus* the carapace forms only a brood pouch and does not cover the trunk limbs. In these forms the limbs are not paddle-like but are modified and used for grasping other small Crustacea.

Locomotion. The Notostraca and Anostraca swim with their trunk limbs, which beat in a rhythm so that jets of water are forced out sideways and backward from the spaces between the limbs to drive the animal ahead. Some of the anostracans, such as *Chirocephalus*, have a complex system of flaps and muscles in the trunk limbs, and they modify the limb movement in order to hover in one position for long periods.

The Conchostraca and Cladocera swim by means of their antennae, which have two branches bearing feather-like setae that increase the effective area of the antenna. Because the Conchostraca are slow, clumsy swimmers, they are highly vulnerable to predation by fish; thus, they are most commonly found in temporary pools, where fish are absent. The Cladocera, although smaller, are much livelier swimmers. In some of the larger forms, the rate of limb movement may be one beat per second, but, in smaller forms, there may be several beats per second.

Responses to light. The most notable behavioral responses of branchiopods are in relation to light. The Anostraca are remarkable in showing a ventral light response: when light is directed from above, they turn their ventral surface toward the light. If they are artificially lit from below, and not from above, they will turn over. In the Cladocera the response to light is complex and varies with the colour of the light. In red light, *Daphnia* maintains its position in the water by a hop-and-drop type of swimming. In blue light, it swims more rapidly in a horizontal direction. These two types of swimming are related to the presence of food. When foods such as small green algae are present in the water, they absorb most of the blue light, and the light that penetrates is mainly red; remaining in one place is advantageous to *Daphnia*, and it maintains its position. In the absence of food such as green algae, more blue light is present in the water; as a result, *Daphnia* is stimulated to swim horizontally and to search a wider area. If *Daphnia* is starved and kept in red light, it eventually swims horizontally; *i.e.*, starvation blocks out the normal response to red light.

Form and function. *Structural features.* The number of trunk limbs in the branchiopods varies greatly. The Cladocera have four to six pairs; the Anostraca 11, 17, or 19 pairs; and the Conchostraca between ten and 27 pairs. Among the Notostraca there is little apparent correlation between the number of trunk segments and the number of trunk limbs. Some of the posterior segments may have three or four pairs of limbs; as a result, some notostracans have up to 71 pairs of trunk limbs.

Excretion. The excretory organ in the branchiopods is the maxillary, or shell, gland, so-called because loops of the excretory duct can be seen in the wall of the carapace. Some excretion also occurs in the wall of the gut, which transfers substances from the blood into the gut lumen, from which it passes to the outside.

Vision. The most conspicuous sense organs of the Branchiopoda are the eyes. The four living orders show notable differences in eye arrangement. The large paired eyes of Anostraca are on movable stalks; the paired eyes of Notostraca lie close together on the top of the head; in Conchostraca and Cladocera, the two eyes are joined together in the midline. The process of fusion of the eyes can be seen in the developing embryo of the cladocerans; the organs appear as small red dots that enlarge, darken, and then join together. *Polyphemus* is unique in having green eye rudiments that darken and fuse to form its large multilensed eye. All branchiopod eyes are provided with muscles and show rather rapid trembling movements, thought to be part of a scanning process that gives more information about the surroundings than could be gained with a stationary eye.

Presence of hemoglobin

Biochemistry. The branchiopods are unusual among crustaceans in possessing the pigment hemoglobin in their blood. The pigment is dissolved in the plasma rather than contained in blood cells as in man and other vertebrates. The concentration of hemoglobin in branchiopod blood varies inversely with the oxygen content of the surrounding water. When little oxygen is in the water, the blood contains a large quantity of hemoglobin and is bright red. A branchiopod whose blood contains a high concentration of hemoglobin can be made to change its blood colour from bright red to pale by transferring it to well-aerated water; the transformation requires about ten days.

From L. Borradaile and F. Potts, *The Invertebrata*; published by Cambridge University Press

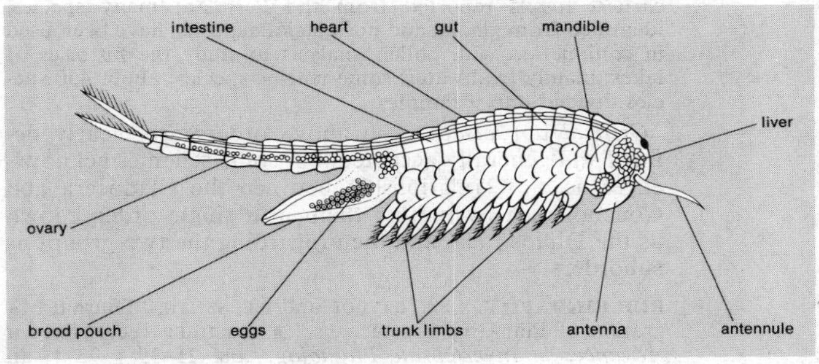

Figure 2: *Chirocephalus diaphanus*, an anostracan branchiopod.

The chemical breakdown of hemoglobin in *Daphnia* is unusual in that it does not involve bile pigments. Hemoglobin in all other animal groups breaks down into green, red, or yellow bile pigments.

Evolution and classification. *Paleontology.* The order Lipostraca is represented only by the remarkable fossil of *Lepidocaris rhyniensis* from the Devonian Period (345,000,000 to 395,000,000 years ago), which was discovered in the Old Red Sandstone of Scotland. The fragmentary remains of this minute branchiopod are so perfectly preserved that its structure is known in greater detail than is that of any other fossil crustacean. Many other forms probably failed to leave any fossil record because of their small size and delicate structure.

Distinguishing taxonomic features. Branchiopods are free-living forms, the most primitive members of the phylum Crustacea. They have compound eyes and usually a protective plate, or carapace. There are many body segments and four or more pairs of trunk limbs that are usually lobed, broad, and fringed on the inner side. The mouthparts are small and simple, and the nervous system is primitive. Most species occur in freshwater.

Annotated classification. The group indicated by a dagger (†) is extinct and known only from fossils.

SUBCLASS BRANCHIOPODA

Four distinct living types, 1 extinct; distinguishing features include form of trunk limbs and carapace; more than 800 species.

†Order Lipostraca

Includes only the fossil *Lepidocaris rhyniensis,* about 3 millimetres (0.12 inch) long; no carapace; 11 pairs of trunk limbs, 1 pair of large branched antennae resembling those of the Cladocera and probably used in swimming; the 1st maxillae (head appendages) of the male were enlarged as claspers, probably to hold the female during mating; eggs carried in a pouch behind the last pair of trunk limbs.

Order Anostraca

Elongated forms, with paired stalked eyes, no carapace; eggs carried in pouch behind the last pair of trunk limbs; up to 19 pairs of trunk limbs; antennae in the male modified as claspers for holding the female during mating, some species in family Thamnocephalidae having elaborate branched outgrowths from head; freshwater and inland saline waters.

Order Notostraca

Large horseshoe-shaped carapace extending back over trunk, up to 71 pairs of trunk limbs; antennae reduced or absent; 1st trunk limb elongated, functions as a tactile organ; eggs carried in pouch on the 11th pair of trunk limbs; 2 genera, *Triops* and *Lepidurus;* fossils known from the Permian Period (280,000,000 to 225,000,000 years ago), 1 living species, *Triops cancriformis,* known from the Triassic Period (225,000,000 to 190,000,000 years ago); freshwater habitat.

Order Conchostraca

Large carapace with 2 valves enclosing head and trunk (except in *Lynceus,* where head is free); up to 32 pairs of trunk limbs, antennae large, used in swimming; eggs carried between trunk and carapace; 1st trunk limb of the male modified to clasp carapace of female during mating; among earliest fossil Crustacea, known from the Cambrian Period (570,000,000 to 500,000,000 years ago); about 200 species divided into 5 families; freshwater habitat.

Order Cladocera

Carapace with 2 valves not enclosing head; the number of trunk limbs reduced to 4, 5, or 6 pairs; eggs carried between trunk and carapace; antennae large, used in swimming; males often with hooks on 1st trunk limbs for coupling with females; earliest fossils reported from the Permian; many species, identified from glacial and postglacial deposits, have been used in conjunction with pollen analysis to study the histories of lakes; mainly freshwater; some marine species; about 430 species divided into 9 families.

Critical appraisal. The above orders are clearly defined and generally accepted, but some schemes acknowledge the close relationship between the Cladocera and Conchostraca by uniting them in a single order known as the Diplostraca, and then regarding the two groups as suborders.

BIBLIOGRAPHY. E.R. BAYLOR and F.E. SMITH, "Diurnal Migration of Plankton Crustaceans," B.T. SCHEER (ed.), *Recent Advances in Invertebrate Physiology,* pp. 21–35 (1957), an excellent analysis of the reactions of *Daphnia* to light; K. BERG, "Cyclic Reproduction, Sex Determination and Depression in the Cladocera," *Biol. Rev.,* 9:139–174 (1934); H.G. CANNON "On the Feeding Mechanism of the Branchiopoda," *Phil. Trans. R. Soc.,* Series B, 222:267–352 (1933), a classical, beautifully illustrated account; A. KAESTNER, *Lehrbuch der Speziellen Zoologie,* 2nd ed. (1965; Eng. trans., *Invertebrate Zoology,* vol. 2, 1968), a detailed textbook dealing with all groups of Crustacea; F. LINDER, "Contributions to the Morphology and the Taxonomy of the Branchiopoda Anostraca, *Zool. Bidr. Upps.,* 20:103–302 (1941), a technical revision with descriptions of new species; A.R. LONGHURST, "A Review of the Notostraca," *Bull. Br. Mus. Nat. Hist.,* 3:1–57 (1955), a thorough revision of the systematics of the Notostraca, and the standard work on the subject.

(J.Gre.)

Brancusi, Constantin

A Romanian who lived the greater part of his life in France, Constantin Brancusi occupies a primary place in the history of modern sculpture because of his influence on artists who were trying to free themselves from representation of the subject. Historically, the evolution of his work paralleled that of sculpture, from figurative to abstract, as he gradually developed forms that were very close to pure abstraction, although always linked in some way with the human or animal figures that had served as their model. His work, extending throughout the first half of the 20th century, was marked by the use of perfectly polished surfaces and by the search for an ever more rigorous synthesis of form.

Wayne Miller—Magnum

Brancusi, 1955.

Early life and works. Constantin Brancusi (properly pronounced brahn koosh′) was born on February 21, 1876, in Hobiţa, a small hamlet belonging to the village of Pestisani, in the Oltenia region, between plain and mountain. His parents, Nicolas and Maria Brancusi, were poor countryfolk, and, like other village children of that time, Constantin did not go to school. From the age of seven he worked as a herdsman, first watching the family flock, then working for other countrypeople in the Carpathian Mountains. It was then that the young shepherd learned to carve wood by fashioning tools and implements. This popular art had always been very widespread in the Romanian countryside, not only for making spoons, bedposts, or cheese presses, all of which were ornamented with carvings, but also for making the facades of homes. The style of these ornaments would influence several of Brancusi's works. And he himself maintained in his tastes, his carriage, and his way of life the mark of his country origins: simplicity, good sense, love of nature, and a side to his character that was at once both childlike and crafty.

He was no older than nine when he went to Tîrgu Jiu, a town near Pestisani, to look for work. First he worked for a dyer; two years later he went into the service of a grocer in Slatina; and then he became a domestic in a public house in Craiova, Oltenia's chief town, where he remained for several years. His taste for working in wood, however, did not abandon him. On one occasion he even undertook the construction of a violin from an orange crate. Later he would become a violinist and he would always remember his country's popular melodies. On another occasion he carved a lily. Such apparently small feats attracted the attention of an industrialist, who, in 1894, entered him in the Craiova School of Arts and Crafts, where Brancusi was particularly interested in woodwork. He had to learn how to read and write on his own.

In 1896, at the age of 20, he began to travel for the first time: he went to Vienna on the Danube and hired himself out as a woodworker to earn money for his stay. Nevertheless, since his ambition was to be a sculptor, in 1898 he entered the contest for admission to the Bucharest School of Fine Arts and was admitted. Although he was far more attracted to the work of the "independents" than to that of the academicians at his school, he nevertheless studied modelling and anatomy seriously. Among the sculptures of his school period, an "Anatomical Model" ("Ecorché," 1902) was bought by the school and served it a long time for the teaching of anatomy. In 1903 he received his first commission, a bust of Gen. Carol Davila, a founder of medical pedagogy in Romania.

Academic training and early sculptures

In that same year, on return from his military service, Brancusi's interest was aroused by the fame of Auguste Rodin, which reached from Paris even to Bucharest. Rodin's audacious conceptions inspired the enthusiasm of the avant-garde and the indignation of the academicians. Brancusi became curious about what was going on beyond the boundaries of his country. First he went to Munich, where he stayed until the spring of 1904, and then he decided to go to Paris, a costly trip for one of modest means. He made the greater part of the trip on foot, with his pack on his back, and still had to sell his watch to pay for a boat crossing on Lake Constance. He arrived in Paris in July.

Brancusi entered the École des Beaux-Arts, and there he again entered an academician's workshop, that of Antonin Mercié (died 1916), who derived his work from Florentine Renaissance statuary. Brancusi worked with him for two years, but in order to earn a living he was, in succession, a dishwasher in a restaurant at night and the cantor of the Romanian Orthodox chapel. Orders for portraits from a few compatriots also helped him through those difficult times.

In 1906 he exhibited for the first time in Paris, in the Salon (Salon de la Société Nationale des Beaux-Arts) and then at the Salon d'Automne. With a spirit that was still quite classical but showing great energy, his first works were influenced by the sinewy work of Rodin. In order to get away from that influence, Brancusi refused to enter Rodin's workshop, for, he said, "one can do nothing beneath great trees."

In 1907, charged with executing a rich landowner's funeral monument in the Buzau Cemetery in Romania, he sculptured a statue of a young girl kneeling, "The Prayer," which represented the first stage of his evolution toward simplified forms. He participated for the first time in the Tinerimea Artistica exposition, an annual exhibition of new talent, in Bucharest, and he rented a workshop in Montparnasse, in Paris. Rodin's influence appeared for one last time in 1908 in the first version of the "Sleeping Muse," a woman's face in which the features suggest an unformed block of marble. In that same year, Brancusi executed his first truly original work, "The Kiss," in which the vertical figures of two entwined adolescents form a closed volume with symmetrical lines. Here he affirmed the geometrization that was to become his trademark and that would influence the work of numerous artists, most immediately a series of sculptures executed, following his advice, by his friend Amedeo Modigliani starting in 1910.

Evolution from Rodin's influence to works in simplified forms

Mature life and works. An important work executed by Brancusi in 1910 was a new version of the "Sleeping Muse," a bronze in which the head is isolated, with all relief reduced so as to make it egg shaped. The "Sleeping Muse" was treated in this form by the artist in a dozen ways up to 1912, with variations in both plaster and bronze. The egg theme reappeared frequently in his sculpture, sometimes with a very light relief: to suggest the features of "Prometheus" in 1911; to break the curves of "The New-Born" in 1915. These tendencies finally led to the creation in 1924 of a pure marble egg shape, "The Beginning of the World," which the sculptor called "sculpture for a blind man." It may be Brancusi's most representative and most accomplished work.

Another theme occupying a privileged place in his work was that of the bird. It appears in 1912 with "Maiastra," the name of a miraculous bird in Romanian popular legends. This first version in marble, in which the bird, purified in form, is represented with its head raised in flight, was followed by 28 other versions until 1940; after 1919 "Maiastra" became the "Bird in Space"—a polished bronze, the elliptical, slender lines of which put into concrete form the very essence of rapid flight.

"Bird in Space"

In 1912 Brancusi received the first prize for sculpture of the official Bucharest Salon. In 1913, while continuing to exhibit in the Paris Salon des Indépendants, he participated in the Armory Show in New York, Chicago, and Boston with five works including "Mademoiselle Pogany," a schematized bust that would have numerous variations until 1933. Already known in the United States, Brancusi found faithful collectors there. Meanwhile, the critics maintained their attacks.

Above all, Brancusi loved carving itself, which required, he said, "a confrontation without mercy between the artist and his materials." Passionately fond of working in wood, he often created in oak or in chestnut objects that he would later treat in bronze or marble. His first sculpture in wood, "The Prodigal Son," in 1914, was very close to abstraction: a piece of rudely carved oak with the scarcely perceptible features of a person. This would be the way with a whole series of wood sculptures that are among his strangest works. He attached great importance to the base of a work and always constructed it himself, sometimes of five or six superimposed pieces, making frequent changes. He constructed his furniture with his own hands, even his bed, and most of his utensils, including his pipe.

In 1918 he sculptured in wood the first version of the "Endless Column." Created through the repetition of superimposed symmetrical elements, this column, inspired by the pillars of Romanian peasant houses, could, in fact, have been extended into the sky to infinity. It answered a need for spiritual elevation that Brancusi often expressed in his works. For, with the simple means that suited his attachment to the rustic life, he was always preoccupied with expressing a certain metaphysical relationship between man and the universe.

His contribution to the Salon of 1920, "Princess X," a portrait of an imaginary person in a curiously phallic form, created a scandal. The police intervened and forced him to retire a work that allowed for improper interpretation. In Bucharest he exhibited with the Arta Romana group. In 1922 he sculptured the first versions of "The Fish" in marble and the "Torso of a Young Man" in wood. In 1924 he returned to Romania for the first time, and in 1926 he visited the United States for an important exhibition of his works at the Brummer Gallery in New York. His shipments from France involved him in a two-year court case with U.S. customs officials, because a work in copper, "Bird in Space," was so abstract that customs refused to believe it was sculpture: Brancusi was accused of clandestinely introducing an industrial part into the United States. In 1928, he again travelled to the United States, where he had numerous buyers, and won his court case.

Court case with U.S. customs officials

Late life and works. The Maharajah of Indore went to see him in Paris in 1933 and commissioned him to create a temple that would house his sculptures. Brancusi worked several years to create this Temple of Contemplation and Deliverance, and in 1937 he went to India on the Maharajah's invitation. The latter's death, however, prevented Brancusi from realizing the project. In the meantime he had returned to New York for a new exhibit at the Brummer Gallery in 1933, and in 1934 he participated in the exhibition "20th Century Painting and Sculpture" at the Chicago Renaissance Society. He returned to Romania again in 1937 and in 1938 for the inauguration of three monumental works in a public garden in Tîrgu Jiu: a new version, 30 metres (100 feet) high and in steel, of the "Endless Column"; "Gate of the Kiss"; and "Table of Silence."

In 1939 he made his last trip to the United States to participate in the "Art in Our Time" exhibition at the Museum of Modern Art in New York. His last important work was the "Flying Turtle" in 1943. Henceforth, numerous expositions in the United States and in Europe would secure his fame. The largest was an exhibit of all of his work at the Solomon R. Guggenheim Museum in New York in 1955. By a naturalization decree dated June 13, 1952, he acquired French nationality.

Brancusi died March 16, 1957, in Paris. He left to the Musée d'Art Moderne de la Ville de Paris everything his workshop contained (more than 80 sculptures) on the condition that the workshop itself be removed to the museum and restored to its original condition. His rustic furniture and his tools can be seen there, as well as his golf clubs, even though he never played golf once in his life.

MAJOR WORKS
"General Dr. Carol Davila" (1903; bronze, Military Hospital of Bucharest); "The Prayer" ("La Prière"; 1907; bronze, Muzeul de Artă R.S.R., Bucharest); "Portrait of Nicolae Darascu" (1908; bronze, Muzeul de Artă, Bucharest); "Sleeping Muse" ("La Muse endormie"; 1908; marble, Muzeul de Artă, Bucharest; other versions in bronze—1910, 1911, 1912); "The Kiss" ("Le Baiser"; 1908; plaster, Muzeul de Artă, Craiova; another version in stone, 1910, funeral monument, Montparnasse Cemetery, Paris); "The Wisdom of the Earth" (1909, stone, Muzeul de Artă, Bucharest); "Prometheus" (1911; marble, Philadelphia Museum of Art); "Muse" (1912; marble, Solomon R. Guggenheim Museum, New York); "Maiastra" (1912; marble, Museum of Modern Art, New York); "Mlle. Pogany" (1913; marble, Philadelphia Museum of Art); "The Prodigal Son" ("Le Fils prodigue"; 1914, oak, Philadelphia Museum of Art); "The New-Born" ("Le Nouveau-né"; 1915; marble, Philadelphia Museum of Art); "Princess X" (1916; polished bronze, Philadelphia Museum of Art); "The Sorceress" (1916; wood, Solomon R. Guggenheim Museum, New York); "Golden Bird" (1919; polished bronze, Arts Club of Chicago); "Adam and Eve" (1921; wood, Solomon R. Guggenheim Museum, New York); "The Fish" ("Poisson"; 1922; marble, Philadelphia Museum of Art); "The Cock" (1924; wood, Museum of Modern Art, New York); "The Beginning of the World" ("Le Commencement du monde"; 1924; marble, Philadelphia Museum of Art); "Miracle" ("The White Seal"; 1936; marble, Solomon R. Guggenheim Museum, New York); "Endless Column" ("La Colonne sans fin"; 1937; steel, Tîrgu Jiu); "Flying Turtle" ("La Tortue volante"; 1943; marble, Solomon R. Guggenheim Museum, New York).

BIBLIOGRAPHY. CAROLA GIEDION-WELCKER (ed.), *Constantin Brancusi* (1958; Eng. trans., 1959), is the most important work on the sculptor, comprising a serious analysis of his work and numerous photographic documents. SIDNEY GEIST, *Brancusi* (1968), is also an excellent monograph. IONEL JIANOU, *Brancusi* (1963), contains a biographical study, a descriptive catalog of his work, a list of his exhibitions, and 109 reproductions. Other well-documented works include V.G. PALEOLOG, *Brancusi* (1947); DAVID LEWIS, *Constantin Brancusi* (1957); and CHRISTIAN ZERVOS, *Constantin Brancusi* (1957), in French. The first study to reveal the sculptor to the United States was "Brancusi," by EZRA POUND, in *The Little Review* (Autumn 1921), with 24 reproductions. JEAN SELZ, *Modern Sculpture: Origins and Evolution* (1963), contains an analysis of Brancusi's work, a biography, three reproductions in black and white and a plate in colour. Also of interest are ATHENA SPEAR, *Brancusi's Birds* (1969); and the prefaces to certain catalogs: PAUL MORAND, exposition at the Brummer Gallery, New York (1926); ROGER VITRAC, exposition at the Brummer Gallery, New York (1933); HANS BOLLIGER, exposition "Begründer der modernen Plastik," Zurich (1954); H.P. ROCHE and MICHEL SEUPHOR, exposition "Sept Pionniers de la sculpture moderne," Yverdon (1954); SIDNEY GEIST, expositions at the Solomon R. Guggenheim Museum, New York; the Philadelphia Museum of Art; and the Art Institute of Chicago (1969). See also the catalogs of the Brancusi exhibitions at the Arts Club of Chicago (1927); at the Solomon R. Guggenheim Museum, New York (1955); and at the Staempfli Gallery, New York (1960).

(Je.S.)

Braque, Georges

Co-launcher with Pablo Picasso of the Cubist movement in the years just preceding World War I, and thus one of the important revolutionaries in 20th-century cultural history, the French painter Georges Braque was an artist for whom "distinguished" seemed, to many contemporaries, the most appropriate adjective. During a career of 60 years he attracted attention only with his works, which are predominantly still lifes, remarkable for robust construction, subtle, low-keyed colour harmonies, and an air of integrity and reticence. Although thoroughly modern in his style, Braque has often been compared with an earlier meditator before a quiet, domestic world: the 18th-century master Jean-Baptiste Chardin.

Braque was born on May 13, 1882 (seven months after Picasso), at Argenteuil, a small community on the Seine

Braque, photograph by Arnold Newman, 1956.

near Paris and one of the centres of the Impressionist movement in the 1870s. His father and a grandfather were the owners of a prosperous house-painting firm, and both were amateur artists. In 1890 the family moved to Le Havre, which had also been, back in the time of the seascapist Eugène Boudin and the young Claude Monet, an early centre of Impressionism. The boy attended the local public school, accompanied his father on painting expeditions, and developed an interest in sports, including eventually boxing, that gave him, as an adult, the look of a professional athlete. He also learned to play the flute. At 15 he enrolled in the evening course at the Le Havre academy of fine arts. He left school at 17 for a year of apprenticeship as a house painter and interior decorator, first in Le Havre and then in Paris; during this period he picked up his solidly professional handling of materials and his knowledge of the artisan's tricks—the imitation of wood grain, for instance—frequently utilized in his Cubist pictures. After a year of military service he decided, with the help of an allowance from his family, to become an artist. Between 1902 and 1904 he studied in a Paris private academy and, very briefly, at the official École des Beaux-Arts; in his free hours he frequented the Louvre, where he admired especially Egyptian and archaic Greek works.

Early training and influences

His early paintings reveal, as might be expected from a childhood spent in Normandy, the influence of the Impressionists, in particular that of Monet and of Camille Pissarro. A little later came the revelation of the firm structures and the union of colour and tone values in the work of Paul Cézanne. But Braque can be said to have begun to find his way only in 1905, when he visited the Paris Salon d'Automne and saw the violent explosion of arbitrary colour in the room occupied by the paintings of the group nicknamed the Fauves (Wild Beasts). During the next two years he was a convinced, if rather prudent and tradition-minded, Fauvist, working for a while at Antwerp and then on the Mediterranean coast near Marseilles, at L'Estaque and La Ciotat. Representative pictures from this period are "Le Port d'Anvers," "The Port of La Ciotat," and "View from the Hôtel Mistral, L'Estaque."

In the spring of 1907 he exhibited six paintings at the Paris Salon des Indépendants and sold them all. Later that year he signed a contract with a dealer, David Henry Kahnweiler, who had recently opened a small Paris gallery destined to play an important role in the history of modern art. Kahnweiler brought around the avant-garde poet and critic Guillaume Apollinaire, who introduced Braque to Picasso in the latter's Montmartre studio. Braque was at first disconcerted by Picasso's recently painted "Demoiselles d'Avignon" (Museum of Modern Art, New York City). "Listen," he is reported to have said, "in spite of your explanations your painting looks as if you wanted to make us eat tow, or drink gasoline and spit fire." But the two artists became close friends, and within a few months they were engaged in the unprecedented process of mutual influence from which Cubism emerged.

Meeting with Picasso

It is impossible to say which of the two was the principal inventor of the revolutionary new style, for at the height of their collaboration they exchanged ideas almost daily and produced pictures so alike as to be practically indistinguishable. Picasso provided, with his proto-Cubist

"Demoiselles," the initial liberating shock. But it was Braque, largely because of his admiration for Cézanne, who provided much of the early tendency toward geometrical forms. During the summer of 1908 in southern France, he painted a series of radically innovative canvases, of which the most celebrated is "Houses at L'Estaque"; here already can be seen the slab volumes, sober colouring, and warped perspective typical of the first part of what has been called the analytical phase of Cubism. That fall he had a show at Kahnweiler's gallery and provoked from the Paris critic Louis Vauxcelles a remark about "cubes" that soon blossomed into a stylistic label.

By 1911 Braque—now teamed, as he said later, with Picasso as if they were roped alpinists—was well into the so-called hermetic part of the analytical phase of Cubism, of which "Man with a Guitar" is an example; here the colours are brown, gray, and green, the pictorial space is almost flat, viewpoints and light sources are multiplied, contours are broken, volumes are often transparent, and facets are turned into apparently illogical simultaneous views. Also in 1911, Braque stencilled letters into "The Portuguese" and thus significantly strengthened the idea, full of consequences for the future of art, that a picture was not a representation but an autonomous object. In 1912 he went further in the same direction and created what is generally considered the first *papier collé* (pasted-paper picture) by attaching three pieces of wallpaper to the drawing "Fruit Dish and Glass."

During the early part of the Cubist adventure, he had a studio in Montmartre but often worked elsewhere: in 1909 at La Roche-Guyon, on the Seine, west of Paris; in 1910 back at L'Estaque; and in 1911 at Céret, a village on the Mediterranean side of the foothills of the Pyrenees. In 1912 he married Marcelle Lapré and rented a house at Sorgues, a small town in the Rhône valley near Avignon. With the outbreak of World War I he entered the army as an infantry sergeant and served with distinction, being decorated twice in 1914 for bravery. In 1915 he suffered a serious head wound, which was followed by a trepanation, several months in the hospital, and a long period of convalescence at home at Sorgues. During this period he added to the aphorisms he had been in the habit of scribbling on the margins of drawings; and in 1917 a collection of these sayings, put together by his friend the poet Pierre Reverdy, was published in the review *Nord–Sud* as "Thoughts and Reflections on Painting." Even a brief sampling can suggest the quality, at once poetic and rational, of Braque's mind and the sort of thinking that lay behind Cubism:

Aphorisms on painting

> New means, new subjects . . . . The aim is not to *reconstitute* an anecdotal fact, but to *constitute* a pictorial fact . . . . To work from nature is to improvise . . . . The senses deform, the mind forms . . . . I love the rule that corrects emotion.

Released from further military service, the artist rejoined the Cubist movement, which by then was in what is sometimes called its synthetic phase—a not very adequate way of referring to a tendency to use more colour and to represent objects not by the previous spider web of analytical signs but by relatively large emblematic planes. In 1917–18 he painted, partly under the influence of his friend Juan Gris, a Spanish-born Cubist master whose paintings were strongly Synthetic Cubist, the geometrical, strongly coloured, nearly abstract "Woman Musician" and some still lifes in a similar manner. Rapidly, however, he moved away from austere geometry toward forms softened by looser drawing and freer brushwork; an example of the change is the 1919 "Still Life with Playing Cards." From this point onward his style ceased to evolve in the methodical way it had during the successive phases of Cubism; it became a series of personal variations on the stylistic heritage of the eventful years before World War I.

International acclaim and prosperity

By now he was a prosperous, established modern master, much in the favour of the well-to-do, up-to-date members of postwar French society. Working again much of the time in Paris, he transferred his studio from Montmartre to Montparnasse in 1922 and three years later moved into a new Left Bank house designed for him by a modern-minded architect, Auguste Perret. In 1923 and again in 1925 he had commissions from Sergey Diaghilev, the great ballet impresario, for the design of stage sets. In 1930 he acquired a country residence at Varengeville, a group of hamlets on the Normandy coast near Dieppe. His painting during these years is most easily classified, because of its stylistic variety, on the basis of subject matter. From 1922 to around 1926 he did a series of *canéphores*, pagan-looking women carrying fruit. Overlapping with this group in time is the series of *cheminées*, fireplace mantelpieces laden with fruit and perhaps a guitar. By 1928 he was doing a series of *guéridons*, pedestal tables holding the material previously assigned to mantelpieces.

In 1931 he undertook a new medium of expression: incised, white drawings, reminiscent of ancient Greek pottery designs, executed on plaster plaques painted black. Later in the 1930s he began a series of figure paintings; first-rate examples are "Le Duo" and "The Painter and His Model." In 1937 he won the Carnegie Prize with "The Yellow Tablecloth." During World War II he produced a collection of small, generally flat, very decorative pieces of sculpture, in a style recalling again ancient Greece and on vaguely mythological themes. After the war he resumed his practice of doing a number of paintings on a single subject: first came a series of billiard tables, then one of studio interiors, and then one of birds—large, lumbering creatures that seem charged with some forgotten archaic symbolic meaning.

During the last years of his life Braque was honoured with important retrospective exhibitions throughout the world. In December 1961 he became the first living artist to have his works exhibited in the Louvre. He died in Paris on August 31, 1963.

MAJOR WORKS

"Le Port d'Anvers" (1906; National Gallery of Canada, Ottawa); "L'Estaque, l'embarcadère" (1906; Musée National d'Art Moderne, Paris); "The Port of La Ciotat" (1907; John Hay Whitney Collection, New York); "View from the Hôtel Mistral, L'Estaque" (1907; Werner E. Joster Collection, New York City); "Houses at L'Estaque" (1908; Hermann Rupf Collection, Bern, Switz.); "Piano and Lute" (1910; Solomon R. Guggenheim Museum, New York); "Violin and Jug" (1910; Kunstmuseum, Basel); "Man with a Guitar" (1911; Museum of Modern Art, New York); "The Portuguese" (1911; Kunstmuseum, Basel); "Fruit Dish and Glass" (1912; Douglas Cooper Collection, France); "Composition à l'as de trèfle" (*c.* 1912–13; Musée National d'Art Moderne, Paris); "Jeune Fille a la Guitare" (1913; Musée National d'Art Moderne, Paris); "The Musician's Table" (1913; Kunstmuseum, Basel); "Music" (1914; Phillips Collection, Washington, D.C.); "The Woman Musician" (1917–18; Kunstmuseum, Basel); "Musical Forms" ("Guitar and Clarinet," 1918; Philadelphia Museum of Art); "Café bar" (1919; Kunstmuseum, Basel); "Still Life with Playing Cards" (1919; Rijksmuseum Kröller-Müller, Otterlo, The Netherlands); "The Mantelpiece" (1922; Richard K. Weil Collection, St. Louis, Missouri); "Nude Woman with Basket of Fruit" (1926; National Gallery of Art, Washington, D.C.); "Black Rose" (1927; Burton Tremaine Collection, Meriden, Connecticut); "Still Life: The Table" (1928; National Gallery of Art, Washington, D.C.); "Lemons and Napkin Ring" (1928; Phillips Collection, Washington, D.C.); "Boats on the Beach, Dieppe" (1929; Willy Schniewind Collection, Neviges); "Still Life: Le Jour" (1929; National Gallery of Art, Washington, D.C.); "The Round Table" (1929; Phillips Collection, Washington, D.C.); "The Bathers" (1931; Walter P. Chrysler, Jr. Collection, New York); "Still Life" (1934; Kunstmuseum, Basel); "The Yellow Tablecloth" (1935; Samuel A. Marx Collection, Chicago) "Still Life with a Mandolin" (1935; Louis Bergman Collection, New York); "Woman with Hat" (1937; Jacqueline Delubac Collection, Paris); "Le Duo" (1937; Musée National d'Art Moderne, Paris); "The Studio" (1939; private collection, U.S.); "The Painter and His Model" (1939; Walter P. Chrysler, Jr. Collection, New York City); "La Table de cuisine au gril" (1942; Gustav Zumsteg Collection, Zürich); "Le Tapis vert" (1943; Musée National d'Art Moderne, Paris); "Le Billard" (1945; Musée National d'Art Moderne, Paris); "The Studio, VI" (1950; Aimé Maeght Collection, Paris); "The Shower" (1952; Phillips Collection, Washington, D.C.); "Seascape" (1953; private collection, Paris); "The Black Birds" (1957; Aimé Maeght Collection, Paris).

BIBLIOGRAPHY. Standard biographies are JOHN RUSSELL, *Georges Braque* (1959); and JEAN LEYMARIE, *Braque* (1961), although written before the painter died. EDWIN B. MULLINS,

The Art of Georges Braque (British title, *Braque;* 1969), provides a basic introduction to the subject. Good analyses of the work are DOUGLAS COOPER, *Georges Braque: Paintings, 1909–1947* (1948); and H.R. HOPE, *Georges Braque* (1949). The best study of the period of Braque's collaboration with Picasso is in JOHN GOLDING, *Cubism: A History and an Analysis, 1907–1914* (1959).

(R.McMu.)

Brasília

In 1957 Brasília was no more than an architect's dream on a drawing board, a city that was to be raised in the middle of a virtual wilderness. In 1960, however, it was inaugurated as the newest capital in Latin America, and by 1970 almost 550,000 Brazilians and foreigners crowded the federal district and over 272,000 inhabitants lived in the as yet unfinished city. Its master plan, drawn by the urban designer Lúcio Costa, and its major buildings, designed by the world-famous Brazilian architect Oscar Niemeyer, had no need to accommodate within themselves remnants of the past or to work around its errors. The city stood as a symbol for Brazilians of the national will to overcome chronic economic and social problems by bringing together the resources of the country's vast untapped interior and the large coastal populations living on the boundaries of poverty. As the city went forward toward its completion in the 1970s, it remained one of the rare opportunities in world history for an orderly total-city design in terms of physical layout, architecture, and human habitation. (For additional details, see the related articles BRAZIL; SOUTH AMERICA.)

Municipal planning

Environment. Brasília and its eight satellite towns are located in the federal district of 2,245 square miles (5,814 square kilometres) carved out of Goiás state on the cen-

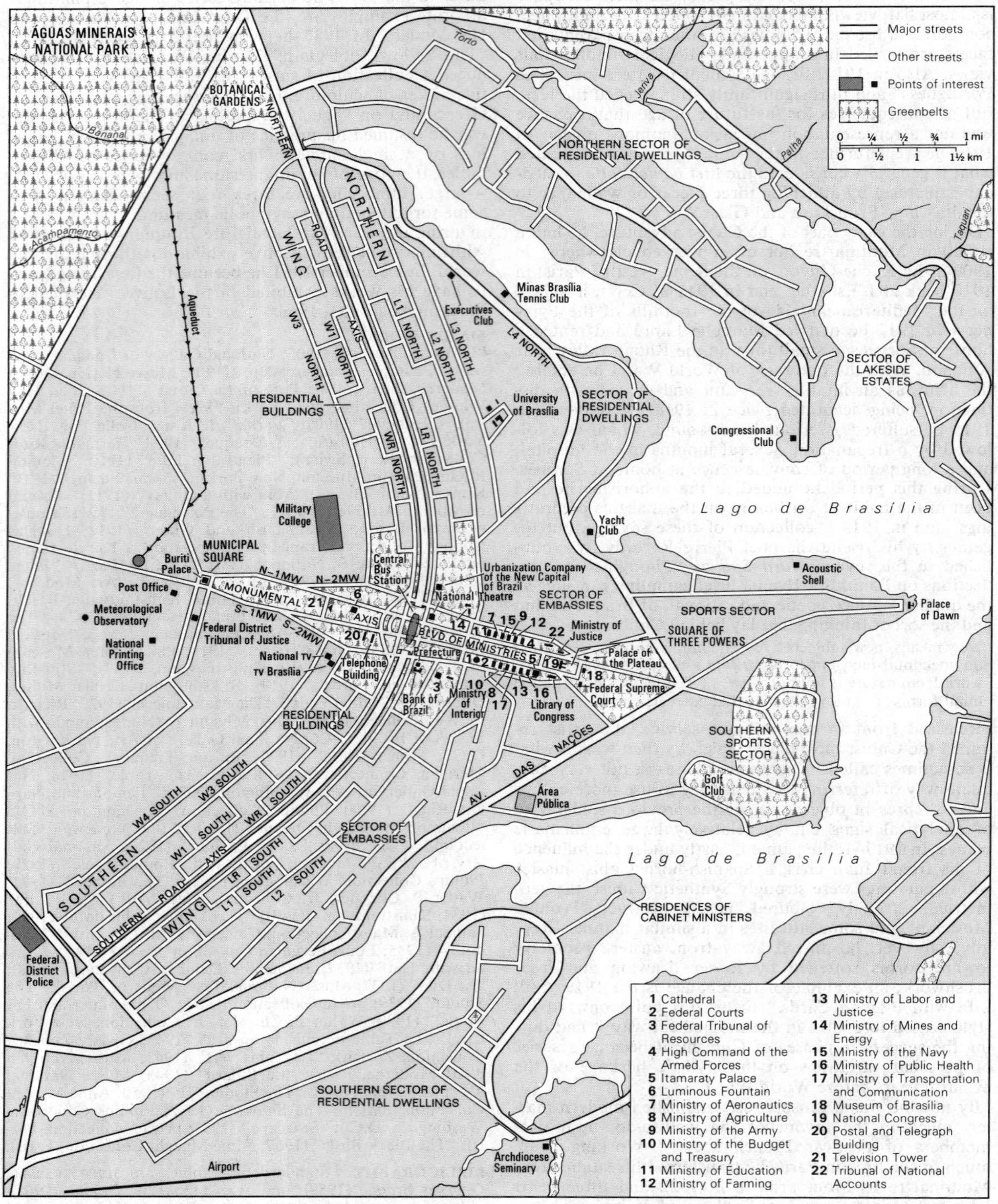

The city of Brasília.

Government buildings in Brasília, Brazil's federal capital. "Goddess of Justice" (foreground), with the National Congress Building (centre) and legislative office buildings (right).
Per Olle Stackman—Tiofoto

tral plateau of Brazil at an altitude of about 3,500 feet (1,100 metres). The region was formerly one of mining and cattle raising. The climate is dry and mild with a dry season from March to October and average minimum and maximum temperatures of about 57° F (14° C) and 81° F (27° C), respectively.

History. The idea of a capital city located in the interior had been proposed in 1789, was reiterated in 1822 when Brazil gained its independence from Portugal and was embodied in the constitution of 1891. Eight years of surveying and testing in the interior preceded the selection of Brasília's present site in 1956 and the beginning of work under Pres. Juscelino Kubitschek de Oliveira. In April 1960 the central Square of Three Powers was dedicated and the federal government began its move from Rio de Janeiro. In 1962 the University of Brasília began academic activities, one of its main objectives being to provide scientific and cultural assistance to the city and government. In accordance with a governmental decree all foreign embassies were to begin operations in Brasília starting in September 1972.

Physical layout. An artificial lake surrounds much of the city and separates it from the suburban towns to the north. The cross-shaped plan of the central city is emphasized by the North–South Axis, Brasília's main transportation artery, and the East–West, or Monumental Axis, lined by the federal and civic buildings. At the west end of the Monumental Axis are municipal buildings, while at the east end, around the Square of Three Powers, stand the executive, judicial, and legislative buildings. The National Congress Building comprises dome and saucer forms atop a huge concrete platform and central twin administration towers. The cathedral is considered by many to be Niemeyer's finest achievement.

Design

Transportation and utilities. Highways and air routes link Brasília with the rest of Brazil, and there is regular national and international air service. A network of roads connects central Brasília, and its suburbs and bus services are extensive—both necessitated by the great distances within the district. The water supplies are treated in two modern plants, and 60 percent of the garbage is transformed into fertilizer. The city is entirely electrified, and telephone service is widespread.

The people and conditions of life. Brasília's approximately 200,000 inhabitants include both foreigners and Brazilians, many of whom came from economically impoverished areas in the east to take part in the city's building. Both low-cost and luxury housing were built by the government in the central city area. In the suburbs private building has been augmented by federal support for low-cost units.

Economic life. The major roles of construction and of food and related services in Brasília's economy are natural in view of the city's growth and its status as a governmental, rather than an industrial, centre. Industries connected with construction and furnishing are booming, as are publishing and printing. Many nationwide companies and associations are headquartered there, as are the legations of foreign governments. The average per capita income is high, accounting for the rapid development of local commerce and banking.

Economic boom

Local government. The governor of the federal district, who is appointed by the Brazilian president and confirmed by the Senate, is the chief administrative officer in charge of numerous secretaries responsible for public works, welfare, education, law enforcement, and the like. The Senate acts as the legislative branch of local government. Monies and courts are under control of the federal district. A regional administrator appointed by the governor provides decentralized government for the satellite communities.

Education. The educational council of the federal district administers a diversified school system from kindergarten through high school, with broad extracurricular programs in physical training and the arts. Business and technical skills are also taught at the higher levels. School placements and enrollments were carefully planned in the early stages. The federally founded University of Brasília is divided into a number of separate institutes and faculties with their own departments. The buildings, between North–South Axis and the lake, were still under construction in the 1970s. It was hoped that the university would play a leading role in the nation's development.

Health and safety. Six municipal hospitals supplement a broad system of preventive medicine, health care under a federal social security system, clinics, outlying health centres, and private and religious hospitals. Fire and police services are extensive and modern, the latter connected with both the territorial government and the federal Ministry of Justice.

Cultural life and recreation. The university is central to much of Brasília's cultural life. The Cultural Foundation of the federal district sponsors many national meetings in the arts and letters, and several foreign information centres are available. The two auditoriums in the National Theatre (Teatro Nacional) have more than 1,700 seats for dramatic, symphonic, and operatic works as well as modern staging facilities. Historical institutions include the Museum of Brasília, with a historical record of Brasília's creation, and the Institute of History. The university library is open to the public, and other libraries are being developed throughout the area.

The newspaper *Correio Brasiliense* supplements other dailies from Rio de Janeiro and São Paulo. Numerous publications and magazines originate in the governmental departments. Television and radio stations present local programs and material transmitted from coastal cities.

An early lack of recreation facilities has been overcome in Brasília by numerous cinemas and night clubs and a proliferation of sporting grounds in the city and suburbs. The city has more swimming pools than any other Brazilian city. A zoological park and forest reserves are under development, and boating and fishing are popular on the lake and the numerous nearby rivers.

BIBLIOGRAPHY. R.M. FRONTINI, "The Achievement of Brasília," in *Optima* (1968), a quarterly publication of the Anglo-American Corporation and of De Beers and Chartered Consolidated Groups of Companies, is a full account with illustrations. See also WILLY STAUBLI, *Brasília* (1966), a well-illustrated general account of the city; MARCEL GAUTHEROT, *Brasília* (1966), a brief description (in English, German, and French) and itinerary with excellent colour photographs; ANDRE MALRAUX, *Brasília, la capitale de l'espoir* (1959), a historical and literary account (in French, Spanish, and German) suggested by the author's visit, as French minister of culture, to the city shortly before its dedication; OSCAR NIEMEYER, *Minha Experiēncia em Brasília* (1961), a well-illustrated account by the city's architect; and DAVID G. EPSTEIN, *Brasília, Plan and Reality* (1973), an urban development study. GREGORIO ZOLKO and ALFREDO WIESENTHAL (eds.), *Brasília: História, Urbanismo, Arquitetura, Construção,* 2nd ed. (1960), provides a complete historical survey in Portuguese and English of the creation of Brasília as capital.

(C.B.D.)

Braun, Wernher von

Braun, 1962.
By courtesy of NASA; photograph, © Fabian Bachrach

Wernher von Braun, rocket engineer and proponent of space exploration, conducted some of the first rocket experiments in Germany and contributed substantially to the coordination of personnel and technology in the successful effort of the United States to land a man on the moon. He played a leading role in the development of all aspects of rocketry.

Early years

Braun was born in Wirsitz, Germany, now Wyrzysk, Poland, on March 23, 1912. One of three boys, he had an older brother, Sigismund, and a younger one, Magnus. Both his parents came from prosperous, aristocratic families. His father, Baron Magnus von Braun, was a cabinet member of the Weimar Republic and later minister of agriculture and a banker. His mother, the former Emmy von Quistorp, encouraged young Wernher's curiosity by giving him a telescope upon his confirmation in the Lutheran Church. Braun's early interest in astronomy and the realm of space never left him.

In the spring of 1920, his family moved to the seat of government in Berlin. He did not do well in school, particularly in physics and mathematics. A turning point in his life occurred in 1925 when he acquired a copy of *Die Rakete zu den Planetenräumen* ("The Rocket into Interplanetary Space") by a rocket pioneer, Hermann Oberth. Frustrated by his inability to understand the mathematics, he applied himself at school until he led his class.

In the spring of 1930, while enrolled in the Berlin Institute of Technology, Braun joined the German Society for Space Travel. In his spare time he assisted Oberth in liquid-fuelled rocket motor tests. At about this time he took gliding lessons and eventually obtained his pilot's license in powered aircraft. In 1932 he was graduated from the Technical Institute (B.S. in mechanical engineering) and entered the University of Berlin.

By the fall of 1932 the rocket society was experiencing grave financial difficulties. At that time Capt. Walter Dornberger (later major general) was in charge of solid-fuel rocket research and development in the Ordnance Department of Germany's 100,000-man Reichswehr. He recognized the military potential of liquid-fuelled rockets and the ability of Braun. Dornberger arranged a research grant from the Ordnance Department for Braun, who then did research at a small development station that was set up adjacent to Dornberger's existing solid-fuel rocket test facility at the Kummersdorf Army Proving Grounds near Berlin. Two years later Braun received a Ph.D. in physics from the University of Berlin. His thesis, which, for reasons of military security, bore the nondescript title "About Combustion Tests," contained the theoretical investigation and developmental experiments on 300- and 660-pound-thrust rocket engines.

Early rocket tests

By December 1934 Braun's group, which then included one additional engineer and three mechanics, had successfully launched two rockets which rose vertically to more than 1.5 miles (2.4 kilometres). But by this time there was no longer a German rocket society; rocket tests had been forbidden by decree, and the only way open to such research was through the military forces. Fifteen years later, Braun pointed out in a paper, "Weltraumfahrt—eine Aufgabe für die internationale wissenschaftliche Zusammenarbeit" ("Space Flight—a Program for International Scientific Research"), that the rocket motor was like the ancient Roman god, Janus, depicted as having two faces pointing in opposite directions. The rocket could be used for peaceful purposes in the exploration of space, or it could be used for war. Just as with the airplane, the actual use was controlled by the sponsor of the development, not by the inventor or engineer who designed the equipment.

Since the test grounds near Berlin had become too small, a large military development facility was erected at the village of Peenemünde in northwest Germany on the Baltic Sea, with Dornberger as the military commander and Braun as the technical director. Liquid-fuelled rocket aircraft and jet-assisted takeoffs were successfully demonstrated, and the long-range ballistic missile A-4 and the supersonic anti-aircraft missile Wasserfall were developed. The A-4 was designated by the Propaganda Ministry as V-2, meaning Vengeance Weapon 2. By 1944 the level of technology of rockets and missiles at Peenemünde was many years ahead of that in any other country.

Braun always recognized the value of the work of the U.S. rocket pioneer Robert H. Goddard. "Until 1936," said Braun, "Goddard was ahead of us all." At the end of World War II, Braun, his younger brother (Magnus), Dornberger, and the entire rocket development team surrendered to U.S. troops. Within a few months Braun and about 100 key members of his group were at the U.S. Army Ordnance Corps test site at White Sands, New Mexico, where they tested, assembled, and supervised the launching of captured V-2s for high-altitude research purposes. Developmental studies were made of advanced ramjet and rocket missiles. Moving to Huntsville, Alabama, in 1952, he became technical director (later chief) of the U.S. Army ballistic-weapon program. Under his leadership, the Redstone, Jupiter-C, Juno, and Pershing missiles were developed. In 1955 he became a U.S. citizen, and, characteristically, accepted citizenship wholeheartedly. During the 1950s Braun became a national and international focal point for promotion of space flight. He was the author and coauthor of popular articles and books and made addresses on the subject. Confident, persuasive, and eloquent, he was criticized by some scientists and missile men as a dreamer, wishful thinker, and salesman. Some of this criticism was founded on professional jealousy, lack of imagination, and remnants of wartime emotion. At the end of the war the United States had entered the field of guided missiles with practically no previous experience. The technical competence of Braun's group was outstanding. "After all," he said, "If we are good, it's because we've had 15 more years of experience in making mistakes and learning from them!"

In 1954 a secret army–navy project to launch an Earth satellite, Project Orbiter, was thwarted. The situation was changed by the launching of Sputnik 1 by the Soviet Union on October 4, 1957, followed by Sputnik 2 on November 3. Given leave to proceed on November 8, Braun and his army group launched the first U.S. satellite, Explorer 1, on January 31, 1958.

Work with NASA

After the National Aeronautics and Space Administration (NASA) was formed to carry out the U.S. space program, Braun and his organization were transferred from the army to that agency. As director of the NASA George C. Marshall Space Flight Center in Huntsville, Braun led the development of the large launch vehicles Saturn I, IB, and V. The engineering success of each of the Saturn class of space boosters, which contain millions of individual parts, has not yet been equalled in rocket history. Each has been launched successfully and on time and has met safe performance requirements.

In March 1970 Braun was transferred to NASA headquarters in Washington as deputy associate administrator for planning. He resigned from the agency in 1972 to become vice president for engineering at Fairchild Industries Inc., an aerospace company. In 1975 he founded the National Space Institute, a private organization whose objective was to gain public support and understanding of space activities.

Physically active, Braun enjoyed skin diving, sailing, and the outdoors; he also had an airline transport pilot's rating. In 1947 he married his cousin, Maria Louise von Quistorp, and he was devoted to her and to their two daughters, Iris and Margrit, and son, Peter Constantine. He held strong religious beliefs in the existence of God and the order of the universe. He justified his involvement in the development of the German V-2 rocket with a credo that in times of war a man has to stand up for his country, regardless of whether or not he agrees with the policy it is pursuing. Despite the fact that during World War II he fully dedicated himself to the development of the long-range rocket as a weapon, he was arrested by the Gestapo and accused of having space flight really in mind.

In 1971 he said,

> Science, by itself, has no moral dimension. The drug which cures when taken in small doses may kill when taken in excess. The knife in the hands of a skillful surgeon may save a life but it will kill when thrust just a few inches deeper. The nuclear energies that produce cheap electrical power when harnessed in a reactor may kill when abruptly released in a bomb. Thus it does not make sense to ask a scientist whether his drug . . . or knife or his nuclear energy is "good" or "bad" for mankind.

Braun, who believed that it is in the nature of humans to be curious and to explore, pointed out that social problems existed in the times of Columbus and other explorers and that it would have been as foolish then as now to have ceased exploration until all social ills were eliminated. Rather, he insisted that, quite apart from the new understanding of nature obtainable from space research, satellites increasingly will be necessary tools in the management of world resources.

Braun received numerous high awards from U.S. government agencies and professional societies in the United States and abroad. He died of cancer on June 16, 1977, in Alexandria, Virginia.

BIBLIOGRAPHY

Books by Braun: Das Marsprojekt (1952; Eng. trans., *The Mars Project,* 1953), a technical treatise, written in 1952, on an expedition of 10 spacecraft with 70 men to Mars (a brilliant tour de force); *Space Frontier,* rev. ed. (1971), an easily understandable discussion of the fundamental principles of rocketry and space flight.

Books by Braun and others: Across the Space Frontier (1952), *Conquest of the Moon* (1953), and *Exploration of Mars* (1956), a series of three popular books describing concepts for the exploration of space (beautifully illustrated by CHESLEY BONESTELL); *First Men to the Moon* (1960), an early popular work for young people; *History of Rocketry and Space Travel,* rev. ed. (1969), an excellent history and reference work, profusely illustrated; *Moon* (1970), a beautiful tribute to the Apollo 11 lunar landing, including a history of man's study of the Moon (lavishly illustrated).

Biographies: ERIK BERGAUST, *Reaching for the Stars* (1960), a definitive and authoritative biography; HEATHER M. DAVID, *Wernher von Braun* (1967), and JOHN C. GOODRUM, *Wernher von Braun: Space Pioneer* (1969), two popular biographies written for young people.

(F.C.D.III)

Brazil

Brazil (Brasil) is a federal republic that occupies nearly half the continent of South America. Its population in 1980 was estimated at more than 119,000,000. Among the nations of the world, it is exceeded in area only by the Soviet Union, China, Canada, and the United States. It has an area of 3,286,487 square miles (8,511,965 square kilometres) and extends for almost 2,700 miles (4,300 kilometres) from north to south and about the same distance from east to west. Its territory touches that of all the other South American countries except Chile and Ecuador; the greater part of the Amazon River Basin lies within northern Brazil. The republic is bounded to the north by Venezuela, Guyana, Suriname, and French Guiana; east by the Atlantic Ocean; south by Uruguay; southwest by Argentina and Paraguay; west by Bolivia and Peru; and northwest by Colombia.

In many ways Brazil stands in strong contrast to the other countries of the Western Hemisphere. Brazil is made up of the former colonies of Portugal in South America; unlike the Spanish colonies, which became separate countries, the Portuguese colonies became united into one huge country. The language of Brazil is Portuguese. Since 1960 the federal capital has been Brasília, replacing Rio de Janeiro. Since 1964 military officers have controlled the government. (For articles on associated subjects, see BRASÍLIA; RIO DE JANEIRO; SÃO PAULO; and articles on the component states of the Brazilian federation. For physical features, see AMAZON RAIN FOREST; AMAZON RIVER; IGUAÇU FALLS; PARAGUAY RIVER; PARANÁ RIVER; and SÃO FRANCISCO RIVER. For historical aspects, see BRAZIL, HISTORY OF.)

The landscape

THE NATURAL ENVIRONMENT

Relief. The greater part of the area of Brazil consists of hilly uplands, plateaus, and low mountains. Very little of the national territory can be described as plain. The largest area of plain is in the Upper Amazon Basin, and Brazil shares with Bolivia a part of the basin of the Up-

BRAZIL Size of symbol indicates relative size of town

Elevations in metres

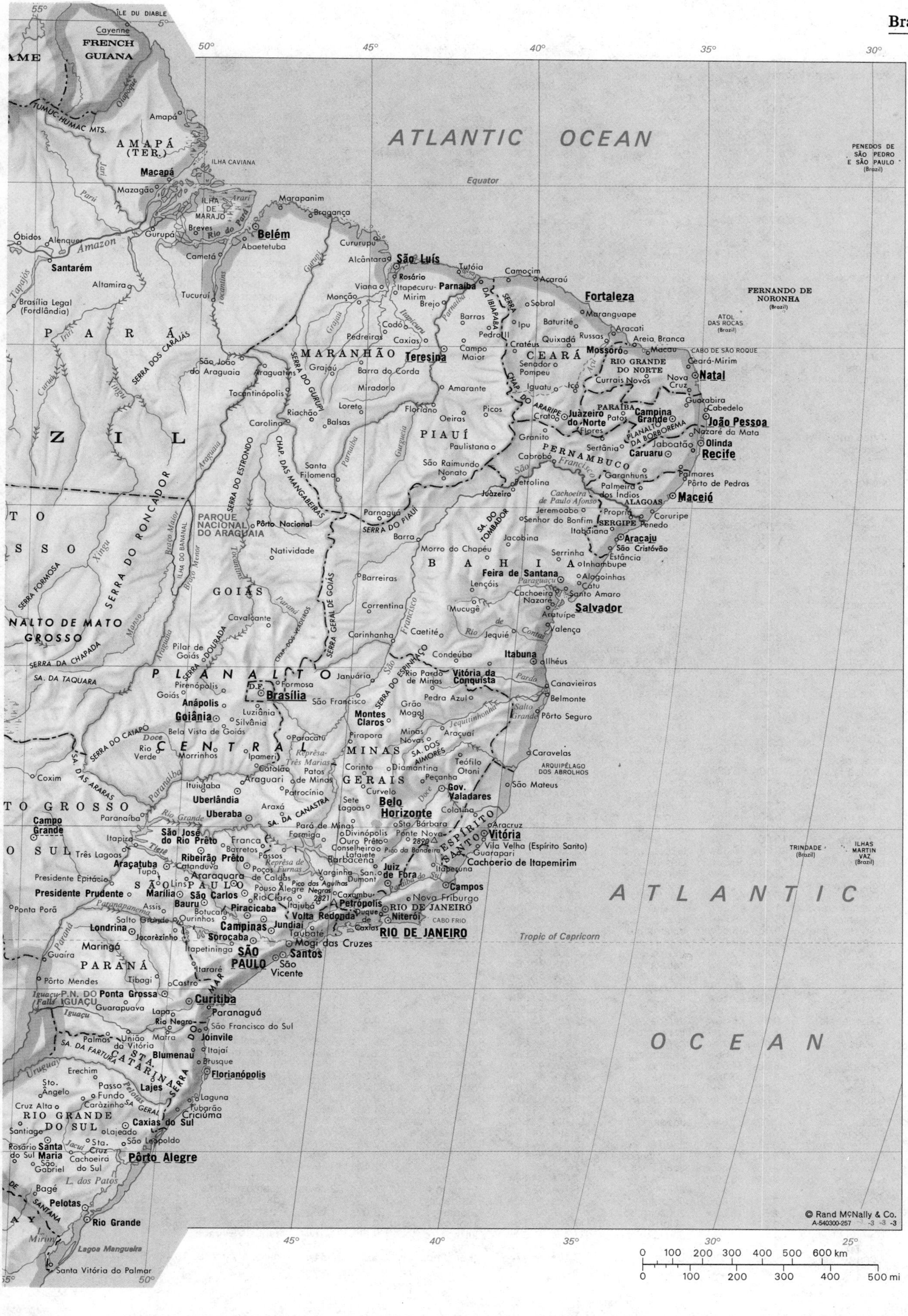
ATLANTIC OCEAN
Equator
Tropic of Capricorn
ATLANTIC
OCEAN
FRENCH GUIANA
Cayenne
ÎLE DU DIABLE
TUMUC-HUMAC MTS.
AMAPÁ (TER.)
Amapá
Macapá
Mazagão
ILHA CAVIANA
ILHA DE MARAJÓ
Marapanim
Bragança
Belém
Abaetetuba
Breves
Rio do Pará
Gurupá
Cametá
Óbidos
Alenquer
Amazon
Santarém
Altamira
Tucuruí
Brasília Legal (Fordlândia)
P A R Á
SERRA DOS CARAJÁS
São João do Araguaia
Araguatins
Tocantinópolis
Carolina
Riachão
Balsas
Loreto
Cururupu
Alcântara
São Luís
Rosário
Itapecuru-Mirim
Viana
Monção
Brejo
Codó
Caxias
Pedreiras
Grajaú
Barra do Corda
Mirador
MARANHÃO
SERRA DO GURUPI
Tutóia
Parnaíba
Camocim
Acaraú
SERRA DA IBIAPABA
Sobral
Ipu
Barras
Pedro II
Teresina
Campo Maior
Crateús
Fortaleza
Maranguape
Baturité
Quixadá
Russas
Aracati
Areia Branca
Macau
Mossoró
CEARÁ
Senador Pompeu
Iguatu
Icó
RIO GRANDE DO NORTE
Currais Novos
Nova Cruz
Natal
Ceará-Mirim
CABO DE SÃO ROQUE
Amarante
Floriano
Oeiras
Picos
PIAUÍ
Paulistana
São Raimundo Nonato
CHAP. DO ARARIPE
Crato
Juàzeiro do Norte
Flores
PARAÍBA
Patos
Campina Grande
PLANALTO DA BORBOREMA
Guarabira
Cabedelo
João Pessoa
Nazaré da Mata
Granito
Cabrobó
PERNAMBUCO
Sertânia
Caruaru
Jaboatão
Olinda
Recife
Garanhuns
Palmares
Pôrto de Pedras
Palmeira dos Índios
ALAGOAS
Maceió
Petrolina
Juàzeiro
Cachoeira de Paulo Afonso
Jeremoabo
Senhor do Bonfim
Propriá
SERGIPE
Penedo
Coruripe
Itabaiana
Aracaju
São Cristóvão
Estância
SA. DO TOMBADOR
Jacobina
Serrinha
Inhambupe
Alagoinhas
Catu
Santo Amaro
Salvador
Feira de Santana
Cachoeira
Nazaré
Aratuípe
Valença
Lençóis
Mucugê
BAHIA
Rio de Contas
Jequié
Itabuna
Ilhéus
Canavieiras
Belmonte
Pôrto Seguro
Caravelas
ARQUIPÉLAGO DOS ABROLHOS
Morro do Chapéu
Barra
Parnaguá
SERRA DO PIAUÍ
CHAP. DAS MANGABEIRAS
Santa Filomena
Barreiras
Correntina
Carinhanha
Caetité
Condeúba
Vitória da Conquista
Rio Pardo de Minas
Januária
São Francisco
SERRA GERAL DE GOIÁS
CHAP. DOS VEADEIROS
SERRA DO ESPINHAÇO
PARQUE NACIONAL DO ARAGUAIA
Pôrto Nacional
Natividade
GOIÁS
Cavalcante
ILHA DO BANANAL
SERRA DO ESTRONDO
SERRA DO RONCADOR
ZIL
MATO GROSSO
SERRA FORMOSA
PLANALTO DE MATO GROSSO
SERRA DA CHAPADA
SA. DA TAQUARA
Pilar de Goiás
SERRA DOURADA
PLANALTO CENTRAL
Pirenópolis
Goiás
Anápolis
Goiânia
Bela Vista de Goiás
D.F.
Formosa
Brasília
Luziânia
Silvânia
SERRA DO CAIAPÓ
Rio Verde
Morrinhos
Ipameri
Catalão
Paracatu
Coxim
SA. DAS ARARAS
Ituiutaba
Uberlândia
Uberaba
Araguari
Patrocínio
Araxá
SA. DA CANASTRA
Paranaíba
Montes Claros
Grão Mogol
Pedra Azul
Jequitinhonha
Pirapora
Minas Novas
Araçuaí
SA. DOS AIMORÉS
MINAS GERAIS
Represa Três Marias
Patos de Minas
Corinto
Diamantina
Teófilo Otoni
Peçanha
Curvelo
Sete Lagoas
Belo Horizonte
Gov. Valadares
São Mateus
Colatina
Sta. Bárbara
ESPÍRITO SANTO
Aracruz
Vitória
Vila Velha (Espírito Santo)
Guarapari
Cachoerio de Itapemirim
Itapemirim
Campos
Pará de Minas
Formiga
Divinópolis
Ouro Prêto
Ponte Nova
Pico da Bandeira 2890
Conselheiro Lafaiete
Barbacena
Juiz de Fora
São João del Rei
Campo Grande
Itapira
São José do Rio Prêto
Franca
Barretos
Passos
Represa de Furnas
Ribeirão Prêto
Araçatuba
Três Lagoas
Catanduva
Tupã
Araraquara
Poços de Caldas
Varginha
Presidente Epitácio
Presidente Prudente
Marília
São Carlos
Lins
SÃO PAULO
Bauru
Pouso Alegre
Pico das Agulhas Negras 2821
Itajubá
Caxambu
Petrópolis
Nova Friburgo
RIO DE JANEIRO
Niterói
CABO FRIO
Volta Redonda
Duque de Caxias
Ponta Porã
Assis
Botucatu
Piracicaba
Rio Claro
Ourinhos
Salto Grande
Campinas
Jundiaí
Taubaté
Londrina
Jacarèzinho
Sorocaba
Mogi das Cruzes
Santos
São Vicente
Itapetininga
Maringá
Guaíra
PARANÁ
Tibagi
Itararé
Pôrto Mendes
Castro
SERRA DO MAR
Iguaçu Falls
P.N. DO IGUAÇU
Ponta Grossa
Guarapuava
Curitiba
Paranaguá
Lapa
Rio Negro
São Francisco do Sul
Palmas
União da Vitória
Mafra
Joinvile
SA. DA FARTURA
STA. CATARINA
Blumenau
Itajaí
Brusque
Florianópolis
Erechim
Passo Fundo
Lajes
Laguna
Tubarão
Criciúma
Sto. Ângelo
Cruz Alta
Carazinho
SERRA GERAL
RIO GRANDE DO SUL
Santiago
Lajeado
Caxias do Sul
São Leopoldo
Rosário do Sul
Santa Maria
Sta. Cruz
São Gabriel
Cachoeira do Sul
Pôrto Alegre
L. dos Patos
Bagé
Pelotas
Rio Grande
Lagoa Mangueira
Mirim
Santa Vitória do Palmar
Uruguay
PENEDOS DE SÃO PEDRO E SÃO PAULO (Brazil)
FERNANDO DE NORONHA (Brazil)
ATOL DAS ROCAS (Brazil)
TRINDADE (Brazil)
ILHAS MARTIN VAZ (Brazil)
© Rand McNally & Co.
A-540300-257
0 100 200 300 400 500 600 km
0 100 200 300 400 500 mi

MAP INDEX

Political subdivisions

Acre	9.00s	70.00w
Alagoas	9.00s	36.00w
Amapá	1.00n	52.00w
Amazonas	5.00s	63.00w
Bahia	12.00s	42.00w
Ceará	5.00s	40.00w
Distrito Federal	15.45s	47.45w
Expírito Santo	19.30s	40.30w
Goiás	12.00s	48.00w
Maranhão	5.00s	45.00w
Mato Grosso	16.00s	56.00w
Mato Grosso do Sul	20.00s	55.00w
Minas Gerais	18.00s	44.00w
Pará	4.00s	53.00w
Paraíba	7.15s	36.30w
Paraná	24.00s	51.00w
Pernambuco	8.00s	37.00w
Piauí	7.00s	43.00w
Rio de Janeiro	22.00s	42.30w
Rio Grande do Norte	5.45s	36.00w
Rio Grande do Sul	30.00s	54.00w
Rondônia	11.00s	63.00w
Roraima	1.00n	61.00w
Santa Catarina	27.00s	50.00w
São Paulo	22.00s	49.00w
Sergipe	10.30s	37.30w

Cities and towns

Abaetetuba	1.42s	48.54w
Acaraú	2.53s	40.07w
Alagoinhas	12.07s	38.26w
Alcântara	2.24s	44.24w
Alegrete	29.46s	55.46w
Alenquer	1.56s	54.46w
Altamira	3.12s	52.12w
Amapá	2.03n	50.48w
Amarante	6.14s	42.50w
Amolar	18.01s	57.30w
Anápolis	16.20s	48.58w
Aquidauana	20.28s	55.48w
Aracaju	10.55s	37.04w
Aracati	4.34s	37.46w
Araçatuba	21.12s	50.25w
Aracruz	19.49s	40.16w
Araçuaí	16.52s	42.04w
Araguari	18.38s	48.11w
Araguatins	5.38s	48.07w
Araraquara	21.47s	48.10w
Aratuípe	13.05s	39.00w
Araxá	19.35s	46.55w
Areia Branca	22.44s	43.25w
Assis	22.40s	50.25w
Bagé	31.20s	54.06w
Bahia, see Salvador		
Balsas	7.31s	46.02w
Barão de Melgaço	16.13s	55.58w
Barbacena	21.14s	43.46w
Barcelos	0.58s	62.57w
Barra	11.05s	43.10w
Barra do Corda	5.30s	45.15w
Barras	4.15s	42.18w
Barreiras	12.08s	45.00w
Barretos	20.33s	48.33w
Baturité	4.20s	38.53w
Bauru	22.19s	49.04w
Bela Vista de Goiás	16.58s	48.57w
Belém (Pará)	1.27s	48.29w
Belmonte	15.51s	38.54w
Belo Horizonte	19.55s	43.56w
Blumenau	26.56s	49.03w
Boa Vista	2.49n	60.41w
Borba	4.24s	59.35w
Botucatu	22.52s	48.26w
Bragança	1.03s	46.46w
Brasília	15.47s	47.55w
Brasília Legal (Fordlândia)	3.49s	55.36w
Brejo	3.41s	42.47w
Breves	1.40s	50.29w
Brusque	27.06s	48.56w
Cabedelo	6.58s	34.50w
Cabrobó	8.31s	39.19w
Cáceres	16.04s	57.41w
Cachoeira	12.36s	38.58w
Cachoeira do Sul	30.02s	52.54w
Cachoeiro de Itapemirim	20.51s	41.06w
Caetité	14.04s	42.29w
Cametá	2.15s	49.30w
Camoçim	2.54s	40.50w
Campina Grande	7.13s	35.53w
Campinas	22.54s	47.05w
Campo Grande	20.27s	54.37w
Campo Maior	4.49s	42.10w
Campos	21.45s	41.18w
Canavieiras	15.39s	38.57w
Caravelas	17.45s	39.15w
Caràzinho	28.18s	52.48w
Carinhanha	14.18s	43.47w
Carolina	7.20s	47.28w
Caruaru	8.17s	35.58w
Castro	24.47s	50.00w
Catalão	18.10s	47.57w
Catanduva	21.08s	48.58w
Catu	12.21s	38.23w
Cavalcante	13.48s	47.30w
Caxambu	21.59s	44.56w
Caxias	4.50s	43.21w
Caxias do Sul	29.10s	51.11w
Ceará, see Fortaleza		
Ceará-Mirim	5.38s	35.26w
Coari	4.05s	63.08w
Codajás	3.50s	62.05w
Codó	4.29s	43.53w
Colatina	19.32s	40.37w
Condeúba	14.53s	41.59w
Conselheiro Lafaiete	20.40s	43.48w
Corinto	18.21s	44.27w
Correntina	13.20s	44.39w
Corumbá	19.01s	57.39w
Coruripe	10.08s	36.10w
Coxim	18.30s	54.45w
Cratéus	5.10s	40.40w
Crato	7.14s	39.23w
Criciúma	28.40s	49.23w
Cruz Alta	28.39s	53.36w
Cruzeiro do Sul	7.38s	72.36w
Cuiabá	15.35s	56.05w
Curitiba	25.25s	49.15w
Currais Novos	6.15s	36.31w
Cururupu	1.50s	44.52w
Curvelo	18.45s	44.25w
Diamantina	18.15s	43.36w
Diamantino	14.25s	56.27w
Divinópolis	20.09s	44.54w
Duque de Caxias	22.47s	43.18w
Eirunepé	6.40s	69.52w
Erechim	27.38s	52.17w
Espirito Santo, see Vila Velha		
Estância	11.16s	37.26w
Faro	2.11s	56.44w
Feira de Santana	12.15s	38.57w
Flores	7.51s	37.59w
Floriano	6.47s	43.01w
Florianópolis	27.35s	48.34w
Fonte Boa	2.32s	66.01w
Fordlândia, see Brasília Legal		
Formiga	20.27s	45.25w
Formosa	15.32s	47.20w
Fortaleza (Ceará)	3.43s	38.30w
Franca	20.32s	47.24w
Garanhuns	8.54s	36.29w
Goiânia	16.40s	49.16w
Goiás	15.56s	50.08w
Governador Valadares	18.51s	41.56w
Grajaú	5.49s	46.08w
Granito	7.43s	39.36w
Grão Mogol	16.34s	42.54w
Guaíra	24.04s	54.15w
Guajará-Mirim	10.48s	65.22w
Guarabira	6.51s	35.29w
Guarapari	20.40s	40.30w
Guarapuava	25.23s	51.27w
Gurupá	1.25s	51.39w
Humaitá	7.31s	63.02w
Içana	0.21n	67.19w
Icó	6.24s	38.51w
Iguatu	6.22s	39.18w
Ilhéus	14.49s	39.02w
Inhambupe	11.47s	38.21w
Ipameri	17.43s	49.09w
Ipu	4.20s	40.42w
Itabaiana	10.41s	37.26w
Itabuna	14.48s	39.16w
Itacoatiara	3.08s	58.25w
Itaituba	4.17s	55.59w
Itajaí	26.53s	48.39w
Itajubá	22.26s	45.27w
Itapecuru-Mirim	3.24s	44.20w
Itaperuna	21.12s	41.54w
Itapetininga	23.36s	48.03w
Itapira	22.26s	46.50w
Itararé	24.07s	49.20w
Ituiutaba	18.58s	49.28w
Jaboatão	8.07s	35.01w
Jacarèzinho	23.09s	49.59w
Jacobina	11.11s	40.31w
Januária	15.29s	44.22w
Jequié	13.51s	40.05w
Jeremoabo	10.04s	38.21w
João Pessoa (Paraíba)	7.07s	34.52w
Joinvile	26.18s	48.50w
Juàzeiro	9.25s	40.30w
Juàzeiro do Norte	7.12s	39.20w
Juiz de Fora	21.45s	43.20w
Jundiaí	23.11s	46.52w
Lábrea	7.16s	64.47w
Lafaiete, see Conselheiro Lafaiete		
Laguna	28.29s	48.47w
Lajeado	29.27s	51.58w
Lajes	27.48s	50.19w
Lapa	25.45s	49.42w
Lençóis	12.34s	41.23w
Lins	21.40s	49.45w
Londrina	23.18s	51.09w
Loreto	7.05s	45.09w
Luziânia	16.15s	47.56w
Macapá	0.02n	51.03w
Macau	5.07s	36.38w
Maceió	9.40s	35.43w
Mafra	26.07s	49.49w
Manaus	3.08s	60.01w
Manicoré	5.49s	61.17w
Maranguape	3.53s	38.40w
Maranhão, see São Luís		
Marapanim	0.42s	47.42w
Marília	22.13s	49.56w
Maringá	23.25s	51.55w
Mato Grosso	15.00s	59.57w
Maués	3.24s	57.42w
Mazagão	0.07s	51.17w
Minas Novas	17.15s	42.36w
Mirador	6.22s	44.22w
Mogi das Cruzes	23.31s	46.11w
Monção	3.30s	45.15w
Montes Claros	16.43s	43.52w
Morrinhos	17.44s	49.07w
Morro do Chapéu	11.33s	41.09w
Mossoró	5.11s	37.20w
Moura	1.27s	61.38w
Mucugê	13.00s	41.23w
Natal	5.47s	35.13w
Natividade	11.43s	47.47w
Nazaré	13.02s	39.00w
Nazaré da Mata	7.44s	35.14w
Nioaque	21.08s	55.48w
Niterói	22.53s	43.07w
Nova Cruz	6.28s	35.26w
Nova Friburgo	22.16s	42.32w
Óbidos	1.55s	55.31w
Oeiras	7.01s	42.08w
Olinda	8.01s	34.51w
Ourinhos	22.59s.	49.52w
Ouro Prêto	20.54s	43.30w
Palmares	8.41s	35.36w
Palmas	26.30s	52.00w
Palmeira dos Indios	9.25s	36.37w
Pará, see Belém		
Paracatu	17.13s	46.52w
Pará de Minas	19.51s	44.37w
Paraíba, see João Pessoa		
Paranaguá	25.31s	48.30w
Paranaíba	19.40s	51.11w
Parintins	2.36s	56.44w
Parnaguá	10.13s	44.38w
Parnaíba	2.54s	41.47w
Passo Fundo	28.15s	52.24w
Passos	20.43s	46.37w
Patos	7.01s	37.16w
Patos de Minas	18.35s	46.32w
Patrocínio	18.57s	46.59w
Paulistana	8.09s	41.09w
Peçanha	18.33s	42.34w
Pedra Azul	16.01s	41.16w
Pedreiras	4.30s	44.35w
Pedro II	4.25s	41.28w
Pelotas	31.46s	52.20w
Penedo	10.17s	36.36w
Pernambuco, see Recife		
Petrolina	9.24s	40.30w
Petrópolis	22.31s	43.10w
Picos	7.05s	41.28w
Pilar de Goiás	14.41s	49.27w
Piracicaba	22.43s	47.38w
Pirapora	17.21s	44.56w
Pirenópolis	15.51s	48.57w
Poços de Caldas	21.48s	46.34w
Ponta Grossa	25.05s	50.09w
Ponta Porã	22.32s	55.43w
Ponte Nova	20.24s	42.54w
Pôrto Acre	9.34s	67.31w
Pôrto Alegre	30.04s	51.11w
Pôrto de Pedras	9.10s	35.17w
Pôrto Mendes	24.30s	54.20w
Pôrto Murtinho	21.42s	57.52w
Pôrto Nacional	10.42s	48.25w
Pôrto Seguro	16.26s	39.05w
Pôrto Velho	8.46s	63.54w
Pouso Alegre	22.13s	45.56w
Presidente Epitácio	21.46s	52.06w
Presidente Prudente	22.07s	51.22w
Propriá	10.13s	36.51w
Quixadá	4.58s	39.01w
Recife (Pernambuco)	8.03s	34.54w
Riachão	7.22s	46.37w
Ribeirão Prêto	21.10s	47.48w
Rio Branco	9.58s	67.48w
Rio Claro	22.24s	47.33w
Rio de Janeiro	22.54s	43.15w
Rio Grande	32.02s	52.05w
Rio Negro	26.06s	49.48w
Rio Pardo de Minas	15.37s	42.33w
Rio Verde	17.43s	50.56w
Rosário	2.57s	44.14w
Rosário Oeste	14.50s	56.25w
Rosário do Sul	30.15s	54.55w
Russas	4.56s	37.58w
Salto Grande	22.54s	49.59w
Salvador	12.59s	38.31w
Santa Bárbara	19.56s	43.24w
Santa Cruz	29.43s	52.26w
Santa Filomena	9.07s	45.56w
Santa Maria	29.41s	53.48w
Santana do Livramento	30.53s	55.31w
Santarém	2.26s	54.42w
Santa Vitória do Palmar	33.31s	53.21w
Santiago	29.11s	54.53w
Santo Amaro	12.32s	38.43w
Santo Ângelo	28.18s	54.16w
Santos	23.57s	46.20w
Santos Dumont	21.28s	43.34w
São Borja	28.39s	56.00w
São Carlos	22.01s	47.54w
São Cristóvão	11.01s	37.12w
São Francisco	15.57s	44.52w
São Francisco do Sul	26.14s	48.39w
São Gabriel	30.20s	54.19w
São Gabriel da Cachoeria	0.08s	67.05w
São João do Araguaia	5.23s	48.46w
São José do Rio Prêto	20.48s	49.23w
São Leopoldo	29.46s	51.09w
São Luís (Maranhão)	2.31s	44.16w
São Mateus	18.44s	39.51w
São Paulo	23.32s	46.37w
São Paulo de Olivença	3.27s	68.48w
São Raimundo Nonato	9.01s	42.42w
São Vicente	23.58s	46.23w
Senador Pompeu	5.35s	39.22w
Senhor do Bonfim	10.27s	40.11w
Serrinha	11.39s	39.00w
Sertânia	8.05s	37.16w
Sete Lagoas	19.27s	44.14w
Silvânia	16.42s	48.38w
Sobral	3.42s	40.21w
Sorocaba	23.29s	47.27w
Taubaté	23.02s	45.33w
Tefé	3.22s	64.42w
Teófilo Otoni	17.51s	41.30w
Teresina	5.05s	42.49w
Tibagi	24.30s	50.24w
Tocantinópolis	6.20s	47.25w
Três Lagoas	20.48s	51.43w
Tubarão	28.30s	49.01w
Tucuruí	3.42s	49.27w
Tupã	21.56s	50.30w
Tutóia	2.45s	42.16w
Uberaba	19.45s	47.55w
Uberlândia	18.56s	48.18w
União da Vitória	26.13s	51.05w
Uruguaiana	29.45s	57.05w
Valença	13.22s	39.05w
Varginha	21.33s	45.26w
Viana	3.13s	45.00w
Vila Velha (Espirito Santo)	20.20s	40.17w
Vitória	20.19s	40.21w
Vitória da Conquista	14.51s	40.51w
Volta Redonda	22.32s	44.07w

Physical features and points of interest

Abrolhos, Arquipélago dos, *islands*	18.00s	38.40w
Abuná, *river*	9.41s	65.23w
Acaraí Mountains	1.50n	57.40w
Acre, *river*	8.45s	67.22w
Agulhas Negras, Pico das, *peak*	22.23s	44.38w
Aimorés, Serra dos, *mountains*	19.00s	41.00w
Amambai, Serra de, *mountains*	21.00s	57.00w
Amazon, *river*	0.05s	50.00w
Araguaia, *river*	5.21s	48.41w
Araguaia, Parque Nacional do, *national park*	10.45s	50.15w

MAP INDEX (continued)

Araras, Serra das, *hills*	25.10s	52.00w
Arari, *lake*	0.37s	49.07w
Araripe, Chapada do, *upland*	7.20s	40.00w
Arinos, *river*	10.25s	58.20w
Aripuanã, *river*	5.07s	60.24w
Atlantic Ocean	2.00n	40.00w
Bananal Ilha do, *Island*	11.30s	50.15w
Bandeira, Pico da, *peak*	20.26s	41.47w
Borborema, Planalto da, *plateau*	7.00s	37.00w
Braço Maior, *river*	9.50s	50.12w
Braço Menor, *river*	9.50s	50.12w
Branco, *river*	1.24s	61.51w
Brazilian Highlands, see Central, Planalto		
Canastra, Serra da, *mountains*	20.00s	46.20w
Carajás Serra dos, *mountains*	6.00s	51.20w
Caiapó, Serra do, *mountains*	17.00s	52.00w
Canumã, *river*	3.55s	59.10w
Caviana, Ilha, *island*	0.10n	50.10w
Central, Planalto (Brazilian Highlands)	18.00s	47.00w
Chapada, Serra da, *upland*	15.25s	55.45w
Contas, Rio de, *river*	14.00s	38.30w
Curuá, *river*	5.23s	54.22w
Curupira, Serra, *mountains*	1.25n	64.30w
Doce, *river*	18.28s	51.05w
Dourada, Serra, *upland*	13.10s	48.45w
Espinhaço, Serra do, *mountains*	17.30s	43.30w
Estrondo, Serra do, *upland*	9.00s	48.45w
Fartura, Serra da, *hills*	26.21s	52.52w
Fernando de Noronha, *islands*	3.51s	32.25w
Formosa, Serra, *upland*	12.00s	55.00w
Frio, Cabo, *cape*	22.53s	42.00w
Furnas, Reprêsa de, *reservoir*	20.45s	46.00w
Geral, Serra, *escarpment*	26.30s	50.30w
Geral de Goiás, Serra, *escarpment*	13.00s	46.15w
Grajaú, *river*	3.41s	44.48w
Grande, Rio, *river*	20.06s	51.04w
Grande, Salto, *waterfalls*	16.00s	39.58w
Great Escarpment, see Mar, Serra do		
Guaporé, *river*	11.55s	65.04w
Gurgueia, *river*	6.50s	43.24w
Gurupi, *river*	1.13s	46.06w
Gurupi, Serra do, *upland*	5.00s	47.30w
Ibiapaba, serra da, *mountain*	4.00s	41.00w
Içá, *river*	3.07s	67.58w
Iguaçu, *river*	25.36s	54.36w
Iguaçu, Parque Nacional do, *national park*	25.20s	53.45w
Iguaçu Falls, *waterfalls*	25.41s	54.26w
Iriri, *river*	3.52s	52.37w
Itapicuru, *river*	2.52s	44.12w
Jacui, *river*	30.00s	52.00w
Japurá, *river*	3.08s	64.46w
Jari, *river*	5.07s	62.21w
Javari, *river*	4.21s	70.02w
Jequitinhonha, *river*	15.51s	38.53w
Jiparaná, *river*	8.03s	62.52w
Juruena, *river*	7.20s	58.03w
Jutaí, *river*	2.43s	66.57w
Madeira, *river*	3.30s	57.00w
Mangabeiras, Chapada das, *hills*	10.00s	46.30w
Mangueira, Lagoa, *lagoon*	33.06s	52.48w
Manso, *river*	14.42s	56.16w
Mar, Serra do (Great Escarpment)	25.00s	48.00w
Marajó, Ilha de, *island*	1.00s	49.30w
Martin Vas, Ilhas, *islands*	20.30s	28.15w
Mato Grosso, Planalto de, *plateau*	15.30s	56.00w
Mirim, Lagoa, *lagoon*	32.45s	52.50w
Neblina, Pico da, *peak*	0.45n	65.59w
Negro, Rio, *river*	3.08s	59.55w
Nhamundá, *river*	2.12s	56.41w
Norte, Serra do, *upland*	11.20s	59.00w
Oiapoque, *river*	4.08n	51.40w
Pacaás Novos, Serra dos, *mountains*	10.45s	64.15w
Pakaraima Mountains	5.30n	60.40w
Pará, Rio do, *river*	1.40s	49.15w
Paraguaçu, *river*	12.45s	38.54w
Paraguai, *river*	22.06s	58.02w
Paraíba do Sul, *river*	21.37s	41.03w
Paraná, *river*	25.36s	54.36w
Paranaíba, *river*	20.06s	51.04w
Paranapanema, *river*	22.40s	53.09w
Pardo, *river*	15.39s	38.57w
Parecis, Serra dos, *mountains*	13.00s	60.00w
Parima, Serra, *mountains*	3.00n	64.20w
Parnaíba, *river*	3.00s	41.50w
Parú, *river*	1.33s	52.38w
Patos, Lagoa dos, *lagoon*	31.06s	51.15w
Paulo Afonso, Cachoeira de, *waterfalls*	9.24s	38.13w
Pelotas, *river*	27.28s	51.55w
Piaui, Serra do, *hills*	9.25s	43.00w
Purus, *river*	3.42s	61.28w
Rocas, Atol das, *atoll*	3.52s	33.59w
Roncador, Serra do, *upland*	12.00s	52.00w
Roosevelt, *river*	7.35s	60.20w
Roraima, Mount, *mountain*	5.12n	60.44w
Santana, Coxilha de, *mountains*	30.50s	55.35w
São Francisco, *river*	10.30s	36.24w
São Manuel, *river*	7.21s	58.03w
São Pedro e São Paulo, Penedos do, *rocks*	0.56n	29.22w
São Roque, Cabo de, *cape*	5.29s	35.16w
Selvas, *forest*	5.00s	68.00w
Tapajós, *river*	2.24s	54.41w
Taquari, *river*	19.15s	57.17w
Taquara, Serra da, *ridge*	22.12s	43.53w
Tietê, *river*	20.40s	51.35w
Tocantins, *river*	1.45s	49.10w
Tombador, Serra do, *ridge*	11.05s	44.40w
Tombador, Serra do, *upland*	12.00s	57.40w
Três Marias, Reprêsa, *reservoir*	18.12s	45.15w
Trindade, *island*	20.31s	29.19w
Tumuc-Humuc Mountains	2.20n	55.00w
Tupinambarana, Ilha, *island*	3.30s	58.00w
Uruguay, *river*	30.12s	57.36w
Veadeiros, Chapada dos, *upland*	14.05s	47.28w
Xingu, *river*	1.30s	51.53w

per Paraguay River. There is no extensive coastal plain. The Guiana Highlands north of the Amazon and the Brazilian Highlands south of the Amazon are similar in geology and surface features. Underlying them are some of the oldest geological formations on Earth. Constituting what has been described as the Brazilian complex, these consist of ancient rocks, which are igneous (solidified from the molten state) and metamorphic (formed by heat and pressure); they date from the early part of the Precambrian Era (from 4,600,000,000 to 570,000,000 years ago). The rocks are granites, gneisses (coarse-grained rocks in which alternate bands of granular minerals and schistose minerals are found), and metamorphic schists (medium- or coarse-grained rocks containing micaceous minerals) that are folded and faulted and cut in many places by veins of pegmatite (a coarsely crystalline granite containing much silica), in which are found gold, diamonds, and a variety of semiprecious stones. The ancient crystalline rocks weather rapidly under the rainy conditions of the tropics, forming convex slopes, rounded hilltops, and narrow valleys.

Rocks of the Brazilian complex

More resistant than these Early Precambrian rocks are Late Precambrian formations, consisting of phyllites (clayey metamorphic rocks, intermediate in grade between slates and schists), quartzites, and limestones. Where these formations occur, they include massive mountains that stand rounded and low above the general level of the Early Precambrian rocks. The Serra do Espinhaço and Serra Geral running northward from central Minas Gerais into Bahia are made up of Late Precambrian rocks, as also is the Pico da Bandeira, one of Brazil's highest peaks (9,482 feet, or 2,890 metres), located near the border of Minas Gerais and Espírito Santo. These rocks contain the chief occurrences of iron ore, gold, and manganese.

A large part of the Brazilian and Guiana highlands consists of tabular landforms. There the Brazilian complex is covered by sedimentary rocks of the Paleozoic Era (from 570,000,000 to 225,000,000 years ago). The Permian beds of southern Brazil contain seams of low-grade coal and the remains of plants, some of which belong to the *Glossopteris* genus. In some of the Permian formations, also, there are traces of ancient glaciation. When the limestones are exposed, as in the Middle São Francisco Valley, karst landforms (in which the limestone rock forms an irregular topography, honeycombed with sink holes and tunnels) are developed.

Overlying the Paleozoic rocks, especially in São Paulo and the southern states, there are soft, reddish sandstones of Triassic age interbedded with sheets and flows of diabase lava. The diabase is very resistant, and wherever it occurs it holds up prominent cuestas (gently sloping surfaces, terminated on one side by a steep slope) and mesas (flat-topped plateaus), and the rivers are frequently interrupted by falls and rapids.

The great waterfalls (Salto das Sete Quedas, or Guairá Falls) of the Paraná River and the Iguaçu Falls on the Rio Iguaçu are formed where the rivers pour over the edge of the diabase. One of the world's largest lava plateaus, the Paraná Plateau, is located in southern Brazil.

Still more recent rocks of the Cretaceous Period (from 136,000,000 to 65,000,000 years ago) and the Tertiary Period (from 65,000,000 to 2,500,000 years ago) occur along parts of the Brazilian coast, especially in the Northeast. These sedimentary strata create mesa-like forms, called *tabuleiros* (low plateaus), along the coast.

From the vicinity of Salvador a sedimentary basin filled with Tertiary strata extends northward across the Lower São Francisco.

Brazilian and Guiana highlands

The Brazilian and Guiana highlands are made up of an intricate pattern of hilly upland, low mountain, and tabular uplands. Each surface form reflects its underlying geological structure. The hilly upland, associated with Early Precambrian rocks, stands at a general elevation of about 2,600 feet above sea level. The low mountains on the Late Precambrian formations stand about 1,000 feet higher, with a few peaks that are just under 10,000 feet. The highest tabular uplands, such as Mount Roraima (9,094 feet), are also just under 10,000 feet, but the general elevation of the plateaus is between 3,000 and 4,000 feet.

The remarkable similarity of the landforms of southern Africa and Brazil has frequently been commented upon. The various levels, such as the conspicuous summit level at about 2,600 feet, are the result of successive cycles of erosion. The oldest cycle, now preserved on a few of the highest summits, was probably developed in the Cretaceous Period—so that these highest surfaces have been exposed to erosion for a very long period of time. As the rock material was stripped off during each cycle of erosion, the land rose higher because of the effect of isostatic compensation (an equilibrium condition in which such elevated masses as continents and mountains are compensated by a mass deficiency in the crust beneath them). Each rise of the land initiated a new cycle, which cut back into the older and higher lands, thus creating a landscape that looks much like a relief model when the layers have been put together but before the edges have been smoothed over.

The Great Escarpment. The eastern margin of the Brazilian Highlands descends abruptly to the sea. In some places the descent is over a series of steps; but in back of Rio de Janeiro, Santos, and Paranaguá, there are places where the descent from about 2,600 feet to sea level is accomplished in one steep slope. Whether there is one slope, or a series of steps, the eastern edge of the highland is sharply marked all the way from Salvador to Pôrto Alegre. This feature is called the Great Escarpment. In back of Santos it was given the name Serra do Mar, although incorrectly described as a mountain (*serra*). According to some, the Great Escarpment is not a fault scarp but rather a monoclinal flexure (a fold in which strata dip in one direction). The same erosion levels that stand at different elevations in the interior are warped down below sea level along the eastern margin of the highlands. From Cabo Frio (Cape Frio) southward the Great Escarpment is unbroken by rivers; but north of Cabo Frio a succession of rivers have cut back across the escarpment, from the Rio Paraíba in the south to the Rio Paraguaçu in the north, west of Salvador. The Rio Doce, which reaches the sea north of Vitória, provides a relatively easy route back into the highlands from the sea.

The coast. Although there is no true coastal plain along the Brazilian coast, there is a zone of varying width in which there are sandbars and lagoons. There are many miles of white, sandy beaches, and many places where there are sand dunes. The largest zone of sandbars and lagoons is in the south, where two large lakes are separated from the ocean by bars—the Lagoa dos Patos and Lagoa Mirim. But the bar and lagoon coast is interrupted in a few places where the rocky slopes of the Great Escarpment plunge directly into the ocean, as they do east of Santos. The coast, 4,603 miles (7,408 kilometres) in length, has several very fine, deep harbours. Most famous are the Baía de Guanabara, on which Rio de Janeiro and Niterói are situated, and the Baía de Todos os Santos (All Saints Bay) on which Salvador is located. But there are also many smaller harbours from São Francisco in the south to São Luís in the north. Especially important among these smaller harbours are Paranaguá, Vitória, Ilhéus, and Recife. The Amazon itself is drowned at its mouth, providing deep water for ocean-going ships as far inland as Manaus, and for ships drawing 14 feet of water as far as Iquitos in eastern Peru.

The three major river systems

Drainage and soils. The Brazilian Highlands are drained by three major river systems. In the north is the great Amazon River, with its succession of great tributaries, such as the Tocantins–Araguaia, the Xingu, the Tapajós, and the Madeira on the southern side, and the Rio Negro on the northern side. The headwaters of the Amazon collect the water from the Andes all the way from Bolivia to Colombia. The Amazon lowland has the peculiarity of being widest along the eastern base of the Andes. It becomes narrower toward the east, until, east of Manaus, only a narrow ribbon of floodplain separates the Guiana Highlands to the north from the Brazilian Highlands to the south. At Óbidos the floodplain is less than a mile wide. The floodplain opens up again as it approaches the Atlantic. The main river, as noted above, is navigable all the way into eastern Peru. But the tributaries are all interrupted by falls and rapids where they descend from the Brazilian Highlands.

The second of the great river systems of Brazil is that of the Paraguay–Paraná–Plata. From southwestern Minas Gerais southward, the highlands are drained into the Paraná. The water that falls at the crest of the Great Escarpment overlooking the Atlantic Ocean in back of Santos flows westward and then southward, eventually reaching the sea through the Río de la Plata, near Buenos Aires. The two southernmost states are drained through the Uruguay River (Portuguese Rio Uruguai; Spanish Río Uruguay) also to the Plata. None of these rivers in Brazil is navigable except for short stretches.

The third of Brazil's great river systems is that of the São Francisco River, the largest river wholly within Brazil and a river for which many Brazilians have an almost mystical feeling. The São Francisco, like the Paraná and the Tocantins, rises in the Brazilian Highlands in western Minas Gerais and southern Goiás, inland from Rio de Janeiro. A place on the high country, about 4,000 feet above sea level, where the three great rivers have their origin, was selected as the site for Brasília, the new capital. The São Francisco flows for over 1,000 miles northward into the state of Bahia and the border of Pernambuco before it turns eastward to the ocean. The great river is navigable for shallow-draft riverboats between Pirapora in Minas Gerais north of Belo Horizonte and Juàzeiro in Bahia. Below Juàzeiro the river current becomes swifter as it approaches the Cachoeira de Paulo Afonso (Waterfalls of Paulo Afonso), 279 feet high, where the water plunges into a deep trench. Only the last 172 miles of the lower river are navigable for ocean ships. The Brazilian government has built a hydroelectric plant at Paulo Afonso.

The smaller rivers

There are also a number of smaller rivers that drain more directly to the Atlantic, and, because they pass through the most densely populated part of Brazil, they are of great importance. In the state of Piauí, the Rio Parnaíba flows northward to the ocean and is navigable for hundreds of miles for river barges. South of the Rio Paraguaçu, which drains into the Baía de Todos os Santos, there are several short streams descending from the Serra do Espinhaço across the Great Escarpment to the coast. Among these are the Rio de Contas, the Rio Jequitinhonha and the Rio Doce—the latter by far the most important. The Rio Paraíba rises in São Paulo state and starts flowing toward the west. A little east of São Paulo city the river turns completely around and flows eastward parallel to the coast. In its middle course it meanders across a wide floodplain used now for the production of rice. It then plunges on eastward through a narrow gorge, finally to emerge on its delta near Campos. The headwaters of the Rio Paraíba, which flow toward the west, were formerly a part of the Rio Tietê, a tributary of the Paraná, but were captured by the Paraíba. In the far south, in the state of Rio Grande do Sul, the Rio Jacuí drains eastward past Pôrto Alegre into the Lagoa dos Patos (Lagoon of Patos). The water of both Lagoa Mirim and Lagoa dos Patos enters the sea through an opening in the bar near the port of Rio Grande do Sul. The Jacuí together with the Lagoa dos Patos is the inland river system of Brazil that carries the largest tonnage of goods, partly because of coal shipments to Pôrto Alegre.

The soil of Brazil's southern plateau is famous as a producer of coffee; known as *terra roxa*, because of its dark-purple colour, it results from the weathering of the plateau's diabase. The northeastern coastal strip is characterized by a rich clay soil, but in the immediate hinterland the soil is poor.

Climate. The climate of Brazil contains no extremes of temperature or rainfall. Contrary to popular opinion, the temperatures of the equatorial regions are not excessively high. The average annual temperatures in the Amazon Basin are between 77° and 79° F (25° and 26° C), with ranges between warmest and coldest months of about 4.7° F (2.6° C). Temperatures as high as 100° F (about 38° C) have never been experienced in the Amazon, nor are there temperatures below 50° F (10° C). In the Northeast of Brazil temperatures of more than 100° do occur during the dry season each year, but this is the hottest part of the country. At Rio de Janeiro the average temperature of the warmest month is 80° F (27° C). The average of the coldest month in Rio de Janeiro is about

71° F (22° C). The temperatures on the highlands are several degrees lower than those of the coast, with frosts occurring every winter as far as the southern border of São Paulo state. Frosts also occur at sea level in southern Rio Grande do Sul.

Rainfall patterns

Most of Brazil receives moderate rainfall. Very heavy rains are received in the Upper Amazon and near its mouth; and along the sea-facing slope of the Great Escarpment in São Paulo state. Moisture deficiency is encountered in the Northeast, and in this region there is a record of recurring droughts that cause great distress for the inhabitants. Over most of Brazil the rainfall is between 40 and 60 inches (1,000 to 1,500 millimetres). In the Amazon the rainy season is from January to June, but there is also rainfall during the rest of the year. In most of the country the rains come in summer (*verão*) from December to April, and the winters (*inverno*) are dry.

Vegetation and animal life. *Vegetation.* The various conditions of the climate together with those of soil and drainage are reflected in the cover of vegetation. Seven major kinds of vegetation are found in Brazil. In the Amazon Basin and in those places along the Atlantic coast where the rainfall is very heavy, there is a tropical rain forest, or *selva*, composed of broadleaf evergreen trees growing luxuriantly. The *selva* is made up of a great many different species—as many as 3,000 in a square mile. The trees have tall, straight trunks, and the branches are interlaced overhead, with foliage so thick that little light reaches the ground below. The soil under the *selva* is deeply leached, and when the forest is cleared the land quickly loses its capacity to produce shallow-rooted crops.

Where the rainfall is slightly less and the dry season is really dry, there is a semideciduous forest, composed of broadleaf trees most of which are evergreen but a few of which lose their leaves in the dry season. The trees are smaller than in the *selva*, and the land is easier to clear. This type of forest extends in a narrow band from near Natal southward to Pôrto Alegre. It covers a wide area in southern Minas Gerais and in São Paulo state. This kind of land supported Brazilian agriculture during the 400 years of Portuguese settlement, but because of the lack of soil conservation techniques it is now largely destroyed.

In the dry area of the Northeast, inland from the semideciduous forest, there is a scrubby thorn woodland, or *caatinga*, consisting of gnarled low broadleaf trees that lose their leaves in the dry periods. The land is of little value except for the grazing of goats.

The *campo cerrado*

The greater part of the interior of Brazil, south of the forest of the Amazon Basin and west of the semideciduous forest, is covered with a woodland savanna known as *campo cerrado*. This is a mixture of scrubby deciduous woodland and savanna (grassy parkland). There are patches of pure savanna (*campo limpo*), probably produced by repeated burning of the grass, and patches of uninterrupted woodland (*cerradão*). Where rivers have cut back into the upland surface, the valleys are often covered with semideciduous forest. Without fertilizers, attempts to use the *campo cerrado* for the growing of crops have not been successful, nor is this vegetation good for cattle grazing. The soils are very poor, and the grass is lacking in essential minerals.

In the floodplain of the Upper Paraguay River, the area that is covered annually with floodwaters is covered with a mixture of wet savanna and palms—known as *pantanal*. In the dry season the savanna can be used for the grazing of cattle.

In the southern part of Brazil two vegetation types reflect the recurrence of frosts. Where the land is covered with grass, the *campo cerrado* gives way to a tall-grass prairie with little clumps of trees on the hillsides where water emerges in springs at the valley heads. These open prairies extend southward from the vicinity of Sorocaba in São Paulo state through Rio Grande do Sul into Uruguay. These prairies have long been used by the Portuguese for pasture land. There has been some effort to use these lands for wheat, but with uncertain results.

Where the land is covered with forest, recurring frosts limit the southward extension of the semideciduous forest. This tropical type of forest is replaced by an *Araucaria*, or Paraná-pine, forest, consisting of evergreen needle-leaved trees, which are taller and thus form an "upper story," and broadleaf deciduous trees, which do not grow so high and form a "lower story"; among the lower trees is the tree (*Ilex paraguariensis*) that is used to produce Paraguay tea known as maté. The Paraná pine is not a producer of high-grade lumber, but the better stands are used for this purpose. A paper mill makes use of this pine in the state of Santa Catarina.

The part of Brazil that has been used most completely for agriculture is the semideciduous forest, and this forest, also, has furnished most of the cabinet woods for which Brazil is famous. A serious problem has arisen as this forest has been largely destroyed, partly through burning to clear the land and partly through charring wood for charcoal, which is used both for cooking throughout Brazil and in some of the steel plants for fuel. It is uncertain whether any of the other kinds of land in Brazil can be developed for agriculture. Many Brazilian political leaders are urging the advance of farmers onto the *campo cerrado*.

Animal life. Brazil has no large game animals of the type found in the savannas and forests of Africa. Several species of the cat family (including the jaguar) are found, as well as sloths, anteaters, tapir, and armadillos. Among the members of the monkey family in Brazil, about 50 species of broad-nosed monkeys are found in the Amazon region. There is also a large variety of snakes and rodents. Many kinds of birds are to be seen, a large number of which are multicoloured; there are several kinds of parrot. In the waters of the Amazon River, the manatee (an aquatic mammal) is encountered; there are many kinds of river fish. Gigantic leeches also occur, and there is a great variety of insects.

THE LANDSCAPE UNDER HUMAN SETTLEMENT

The six major regions

The vast national territory of Brazil may be divided into six major regions. These are the North, the Northeast, the Southeast, São Paulo, the South, and the Central-West. While these regions are shown on the map as states or groups of states, in most cases the more accurate construction of regional boundaries would cut across state territories, but for census purposes whole states are placed in one or another region.

The North. The largest of Brazil's regions includes the world's most extensive area of tropical rain forest, or *selva*, and the central part of the Amazon Basin. There are low-lying alluvial lands around the embayed mouth of the great river and in a narrow ribbon along the floodplain. But most of the surface of the North consists of low plateaus, or low, rolling hills. Very little of the area is subject to floods, for the floodplain of the Amazon in the vicinity of Óbidos is scarcely a mile wide, and the tributary rivers occupy narrow valleys and descend to the main stream over falls and rapids. The rain forest, consisting of enormous trees with boughs interlaced overhead and with little undergrowth, covers most of the North. The dense tangle of vegetation, sometimes described as "steaming jungle," exists only in old clearings or along the river banks. The soil, except on the floodplains, has been so deeply leached during long exposure to heavy rainfall that it has little sustained fertility for shallow-rooted crops.

Developmental problems of the North

The main problem in the economic development of the North is the lack of inhabitants. A million rice-growing farmers working the floodplain as is done in East Asia might make this region highly productive; but the few thousand Brazilians and foreign immigrants, limiting their agriculture to the high ground away from the river where soils are poor, are lost in the great forest. At one time this was the world's only source of natural rubber. Rubber workers went along the rivers and into the forest to look for rubber trees growing wild. The rubber boom ended in 1910, when rubber was produced more cheaply on plantations in Southeast Asia. Attempts by the Ford industries to plant rubber in the Amazon failed not because of climate or health or agronomical problems but because there were not enough workers in the whole basin to clear land and plant enough trees. In the late 1950s there was a new speculative boom of planting along the Lower Amazon where Japanese settlers were raising jute and black pepper. The manganese deposits in Amapá were being rapidly developed. But most of the region remained unexploited. A new pioneer zone was appearing in the early 1970s along an east–west highway being built westward from Belém.

The Northeast. There are two contrasted parts of the Northeast. Along the east coast there is a belt of dependable rainfall, supporting a strip of forest running northward from Bahia as far as Natal. The rest of the region is one of recurring calamities of flood or drought, which, in this densely populated area, cause widespread suffering. The rainy belt was originally occupied by a semideciduous tropical forest not so dense as the *selva*. Most of this forest has been cleared away for crops or pastures. The other part of the region is covered with a thorny deciduous scrub woodland known as *caatinga*. The western part of Maranhão is covered with *selva* and resembles the North; and the southern part of Bahia, south of Salvador, resembles the Southeast. Bahia and Sergipe have been included in the Northeast, being typical of this region; only the southern part of Bahia really fits the geographical characteristics of the Southeast.

The sugar-growing tradition

The Northeast was the first part of Brazil to achieve great wealth. In the 16th century the Portuguese established the world's first large-scale sugarcane plantations with imported African slave labour in the forested areas of Pernambuco and Bahia. This part of the Northeast still produces sugar, largely, but not exclusively, for the Brazilian domestic market. In Rio Grande do Norte large areas are used to grow cotton. The chief profits are made from the sale of cottonseed cake to the cattlemen. In the State of Paraíba there is a boom area of sisal planting; and in Pernambuco there are coffee plantations. In the State of Bahia, west of the sugarcane plantations, there is a tobacco-growing area. The greater part of the Northeast, however, is used for a shifting cultivation of food crops and for the pasture of animals. Cattle can only be raised where the rainfall is adequate; the dry interior is mostly used for goats. In Maranhão there is an area where the babassu palm (a source of oil) grows wild; and Ceará is the world's chief source of carnauba wax, derived from the leaves of a palm.

Politically, the states of the Northeast often cooperate to decide national issues in their favour. The region has a sense of unity, based on long history and cultural tradition, far stronger than any other Brazilian region.

The Southeast. This is a region of complex terrain. Immediately in back of the swampy lowlands along the coast, the Great Escarpment rises like a wall, breached in only a few places by rivers. From the top of the Great Escarpment, 2,600 to 2,800 feet above sea level, the land rises in a series of steps to the top of the Serra do Espinhaço, between 6,000 and 6,500 feet above sea level. Most of the Southeast receives abundant rainfall, but toward the interior the rains are concentrated in a rainy season from October to April. The slopes of the Great Escarpment and the uplands to the east of the Serra do Espinhaço were originally covered with a tropical semideciduous forest, most of which has now been cleared. Western Minas Gerais is within the area of the *campo cerrado* characteristic of the Central-West.

Settlement of the Southeast

The settlement of the Southeast took place largely between 1700 and 1800. Gold was discovered in the stream gravels in 1698 and diamonds soon after. Rio de Janeiro was selected as the outlet of the mining region and made its start as a great city when a road was built to Ouro Prêto in 1701. But gold mining declined about 1800, and the 19th century was one of decline. Sugarcane and coffee were planted and remained productive for a time. The major use of the land in this region remains the grazing of cattle on planted pastures. The shifting of the cultivation of such food crops (maize [corn], rice, beans) to ever-changing areas has resulted in the widespread destruction of the forest. In the 20th century the Southeast has again become an important mining region. Now iron and manganese are of major significance. Iron ore is mined at Lafaiete for use in the steel plant at Volta Redonda in the Paraíba Valley. Other ore bodies are used to supply the large charcoal-burning steel plants in and around the Serra do Espinhaço. Just north of Vitória is a new port for the shipment of iron ore, chiefly to Japan. Manganese and limestone are also supplied from this region; and other minerals include semiprecious stones, industrial diamonds, and quartz crystals. Rio de Janeiro is second only to São Paulo in manufacturing industry, and in southern Minas Gerais and Rio de Janeiro states there are many industrial towns, such as Juiz de Fora.

São Paulo. Although administratively a part of the Southeast, São Paulo is identified as a separate region because of its outstanding economic development. It was formerly classified as part of the South, to which it bears many physiographic similarities. Immediately in back of Santos the Great Escarpment stands like a wall, rising to 2,600 feet. Transportation up or down this steep slope has always been a problem. In 1867 a British company completed a cable railroad to connect São Paulo with its port, and until 1946 this railroad had a monopoly of all shipments in or out. In the 1950s a four-lane highway was built for motor vehicles. The escarpment, too, is used for Latin America's largest single hydroelectric installation at Cubatão. The greater part of the interior of the state is a hilly upland, covered with semideciduous forest or woodland savanna.

During the gold period of the 18th century, São Paulo was a frontier. The cities of Sorocaba and Campinas were on the margin between settled country and the wilderness. São Paulo as a geographical region was created during the coffee period from 1850 to 1930. The rise of São Paulo city as an industrial centre came after 1930, and only in 1954, at its 400th anniversary, did São Paulo declare itself larger than Rio de Janeiro. Coffee is produced in the interior and also sugarcane, cotton, oranges, and cattle. São Paulo leads Brazil in the production of almost everything except cacao (from Bahia), tobacco (from Bahia and Rio Grande do Sul), and minerals.

The South. The surface features of this region in many ways resemble those of São Paulo. The Great Escarpment continues southward as far as Pôrto Alegre. Along the southern border of São Paulo is the northern limit of occasional winter frosts, marking the southern limit of such tropical products as coffee. The forest in the South consists of a mixture of pine and deciduous broadleaf trees; but a large part of the area, especially of Rio Grande do Sul, is a tall-grass prairie.

Colonization of the South

The Portuguese gave scant attention to this part of Brazil. Finding no source of wealth in the forested areas, they left this part of the South to the Indians. They settled on the prairies and raised cattle and mules to supply the miners of the Southeast. Starting in 1822 in Rio Grande do Sul and in 1850 in Santa Catarina, German colonists were settled in the previously unoccupied forests. Later came colonists from Italy, Poland, and other European countries. The South is today very largely populated by the descendants of these European colonists. Lacking the speculative profits from sugarcane or coffee, the South has developed a less spectacular kind of agricultural economy, producing pork and lard, rice, cattle and sheep, and manufactured products based on these raw materials. Rio Grande do Sul supplies a quarter of the rice needed in São Paulo and the Southeast and a large part of the *carne seca*, or "dried beef." From the Paraná pine forests come timber, charcoal, and *yerba maté* (or Paraguay tea). The Italian settlements in Rio Grande do Sul produce most of Brazil's wines. And in both Santa Catarina and Rio Grande do Sul there are coal mines. Pôrto Alegre is a rapidly growing industrial city.

The Central-West. This region includes a vast area of the Planalto Central, or Central Plateau, an old erosion surface standing now about 3,300 feet above sea level. Into this old erosion surface the numerous streams are in the process of extending their valleys. Where the valleys have been cut into the high surface, the land is hilly and the streams torrential; but the high country along the drainage divides is conspicuously level. The old erosion surface has probably been exposed to the work of the weather since the Cretaceous Period, during which time the soils have been deeply leached. The undissected part of this surface is covered with a woodland savanna, or *campo cerrado;* where the stream valleys have been cut below this surface, however, the valleys are filled with semideciduous forest. The annual rainfall is about 40 inches but is concentrated in the rainy season from October to April. In the dry season the woodlands lose most of their leaves, and the savanna grasses turn brown.

Although the Central-West has been crossed over in search for gold or other sources of wealth, it has been sparsely settled. The campo cerrado has never been easily occupied by farmers or cattlemen. (P.E.J.)

People and population

Brazil has the largest population of any Latin-American state and equals the combined population of the next three most populous—Mexico, Argentina, and Colombia—and is equal to about half of the entire population of South America. Though its population has increased very rapidly (10,000,000 in 1872, 42,000,000 in 1940, and 119,000,000 in 1980), its mean density remains low, amounting to 36 per square mile (14 per square kilometre). It is, moreover, spread very unequally over the territory. In contrast to the vast emptiness of the interior, there are great concentrations of people on the Atlantic coast. Although Brazil was formed by numerous ethnic groups that are diverse, unequal, and often antagonistic, it has become a homogeneous community, due to the intermingling over a long period of Indians, whites, and blacks, and due to the almost general adoption of the Portuguese language and of the Roman Catholic religion.

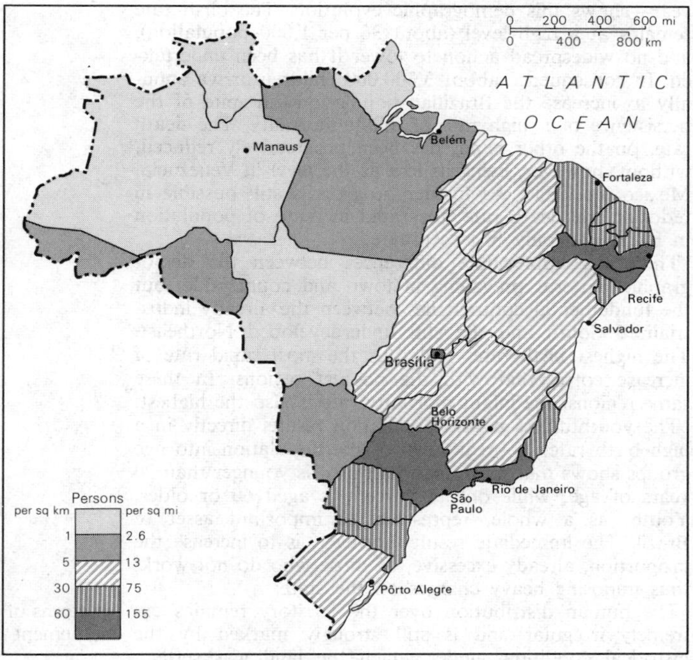

Population density of Brazil.

GROUPS HISTORICALLY ASSOCIATED WITH THE CONTEMPORARY COUNTRY

The indigenous peoples. When, after the discovery of Brazil by the 16th-century navigator Pedro Álvares Cabral, the Portuguese penetrated into the country, they did not find the elaborate Indian civilizations that the Spaniards found in Mexico or in the Andes. With the exception of some more developed tribes—settled along the Lower Amazon and on the Ilha de Marajó—they found only widely scattered tribes of nomads. These tribes practiced food gathering, hunting, and fishing and cultivated manioc and sweet potatoes on patches of ground cleared by burning. The most numerous of these tribes belonged to the Tupí-Guaraní groups.

As long as the Portuguese limited their activities to barter, their relationship with the Indians remained peaceful. But it changed quickly the moment the colonizers decided to use the indigenous population either as soldiers in battles against their French and Dutch competitors or as manual workers—first for the exploitation of Brazilwood and afterward for the cultivation of cane sugar. Incapable of submitting to the economic and social constraints of the plantation system, the Indians died or fled. They buried themselves in the interior and took refuge in the most distant and inaccessible areas—in the forest regions between the rivers of the Amazon Basin or in the savannas of the Mato Grosso. They did not, however, find themselves completely sheltered there, for, from the 16th to the 18th century, the Portuguese organized to hunt down Indians. The first form of penetration toward the west and the north were the *bandeiras* ("raids"), launched from São Paulo or the northeastern towns, to seize manual workers. These raids contributed to the decimation of the Indian tribes, either by massacre or by simple contact between whites and Indians, since the Indians were very sensitive to European diseases (influenza, measles, smallpox) and had little resistance to alcohol. Although there is no precise data available about the Indian population at the time of the conquest, it is certain that Portuguese colonization resulted in the disappearance of various tribes and in the general diminution in their numbers, which dropped from some millions in the 16th century to approximately 245,000 by 1979.

The flight to the interior

The black slaves. Due to the partial failure to enslave the Indians and because of the increasing need for slaves, the Portuguese turned, as early as 1538, toward new sources of manual labour. The slave trade, between the 16th and the 19th century, brought 3,000,000 to 4,000,000 Africans to Brazil. The principal groups imported came from West Africa (Dahomeyan and Yoruba) and from Angola. It was often a question of poor peasants selling themselves voluntarily in times of famine; others were captured by trick or violence. But Brazil also received small but complete black communities, sold as prisoners of war by victorious native chiefs. Unlike the Indians, the Africans gave good results as labourers. Most who worked on the plantations or in the sugar mills, notably those from Angola and elsewhere, were good farmers; others were employed in domestic service. Some, however, refused to be confined by the large plantation system and fled into the interior. These *quilombolas* ("fugitive blacks"), taught the Indians their agricultural technique.

During the 16th and 17th centuries, the majority of blacks went to the Northeast, from Bahia to Maranhão, and were employed in the sugarcane plantations. From the 18th century onward, when the mining of gold and diamonds began, they went to Minas Gerais. After the abolition of slavery in 1888, many blacks left the regions where they had worked as slaves, either for other agricultural regions—such as the cocoa region of Bahia—or, more frequently, for the towns. The black population then became dispersed to all parts of Brazil, although its status remained very unequal.

Historic distribution of the black population

The Europeans. European elements constitute the majority of the Brazilian population, a result of the steady influx of the Portuguese to all regions. For three centuries Lusitanian (*i.e.,* Portuguese) immigrants were practically the only Europeans to enter Brazil, and no limitation has ever been placed on their coming. They were found in all classes of society and were anxious to obtain wealth quickly in the plantations or in commerce. They largely contributed to the creation of the Brazilian community, of which they form the root and foundation.

It was only after the proclamation of independence in 1822 that immigrants of diverse origins were added to the Portuguese. The immigrant influx grew steadily, reaching a peak at the end of the 19th century. Since the end of World War II Brazil has received only a few tens of thousands of immigrants each year. Since the beginning of the 19th century an estimated 5,000,000 people have settled in Brazil. The Portuguese always formed the majority of these arrivals. They were followed by the Italians, particularly numerous in the state of São Paulo, where they represented a third of all immigrants and where the coffee planters employed them as agricultural workers. Other Italians became small landowners in the Rio Grande do Sul or shopkeepers in the southern towns. The Germans were asked by the Brazilian authorities to pacify, populate, and farm the southern states. They have cleared and developed the plateaus of Santa Catarina and of Rio Grande do Sul, where they are grouped into "colonies" of small landowners. They have also contributed to the development of commercial and industrial activities at Pôrto Alegre. Among other immigrants were the Syrians and Lebanese, who specialized in commercial activities; Asians (Japanese), who entered São Paulo state and the north of Paraná mainly between 1928 and 1935; and eastern Europeans.

The contemporary ethnic mix. The different ethnic groups have progressively melded together due to a repeated intermixing over a long period. At a very early stage the Portuguese mixed with the Indians, as well as with the Africans. Ethnic elements that have remained unmixed are now rare. The official statistics, which report about 60 percent white, 30 percent of mixed origin, and 10 percent black, therefore have little significance. First, the estimate is subjective; in a predominantly white society, it is normal that, in a census, people should have a tendency to declare themselves white. Second, the terminology covers extremely varied realities—thus the same term, mixed blood, designates an Indian of mixed blood in Amazonas, while it would mean a mulatto in Bahia.

It is more important to note the unequal distribution of ethnic groups according to regions. Blacks are more numerous in Bahia, Rio de Janeiro, Maranhão, and Minas Gerais. They form, in certain sectors of these states, more than half the total population. The south, on the contrary, which has acquired almost all recent immigrants, is predominantly white (85 percent), and few blacks are seen outside the towns. The areas controlled by Indians are always restricted to the most remote parts of Amazonas.

Because of the progressive disappearance of the Indians and the reduction in the black population, the Brazilian population has become increasingly white. Most blacks belong to the less favoured sectors of society, and their conditions of life are inferior to those of the whites. Mortality, and especially infant mortality, therefore strikes them harder. Thus the "whitening" process, begun by the mixing of blood and accentuated by immigration, is continued by the demographic process, linked with economic and social structures.

The influence of language and religion on the population

The Brazilian population has succeeded in preserving its unity in spite of the heterogeneity of the elements that constitute it. This result has been achieved by imposing the Portuguese language and the Roman Catholic religion on Brazilian society. With the exception of some Indian tribes and a few groups of immigrants, the majority of Brazilians understand and speak a Portuguese that has been somewhat transformed and enriched, notably under African influences. In the same way, nearly all Brazilians profess the Roman Catholic religion; this makes Brazil the largest Roman Catholic nation in the world. Roman Catholicism ceased to be the official religion after the proclamation of the republic in 1889, and since then the close links that existed between church and state have been loosened. The predominance of Latins among the immigrants of the 19th and 20th centuries, however, has allowed the supremacy of the Roman Catholic religion to be maintained.

Religious cults

Neither the Indians nor the Africans, however, have completely abandoned their worships and their beliefs, although evangelization of the former has been attempted, and Baptism has been imposed on the latter. Thus the Yoruba have preserved their ancestral religion; the Dahomeyan cult of Voodoo has survived; fetish societies remained. A mixture of the gods of Europe, Africa, and America, moreover, has given birth to "strange cults, with crucifix and Latin words, with drums and Bantu chants, with totems and Indian dancers." In their turn, the immigrants have brought new religions: German and Anglo-Saxon Protestantism, eastern European Catholic Orthodoxy, the Maronite Catholicism of the Syrians, the Buddhism and Shintō of the Japanese, and Islām. These concern only small groups, however, mainly in the towns. The Protestant minorities, which, it must be stressed, are growing, and the Spiritualists (as the adherents of the "strange cults" are called) together make up about 8,000,000 members.

The assimilation of the different groups seems to have been achieved. The Germans and the Japanese who had, up to World War II, resisted integration, no longer pose a separatist problem, since the laws of 1934 have limited their entrance, and the government has made great efforts to spread the Portuguese language in their communities. The most serious question remains that of the integration of the Indians. Neither the efforts of the Jesuits, undertaken since the beginning of colonization, nor the action of the Service for the Protection of the Indians, established in 1911, have succeeded in integrating this group into the Brazilian community. Some tribes, certainly, are more or less integrated. Others, however, continue to live away from the population centres and on the edge of a contemporary civilization from which they expect nothing, except to have to flee before the advance of pioneers or of a new road through the Amazonian forest.

DEMOGRAPHIC TRENDS

The Brazilian population is characterized by rapid growth, by its youth, by diverse distribution, and by mobility. The strong and continued increase in the number of Brazilians has tended to accelerate since the 1950s. Within a century, the population has grown tenfold. After the first census the population doubled within 33 years (1872–1905); it doubled a second time, again in 33 years (1905–38), and doubled once more in 27 years (1938–65). The natural high rate of increase—about 2.8 percent a year—shows this demographic evolution. The birth rate remains at a high level (about 36 per 1,000 population), and no widespread action to lower it has been undertaken. In consequence about 3,300,000 children arrive annually to increase the Brazilian population—in spite of the persistence of a high rate of infant mortality. The death rate, on the other hand, has been progressively reduced, without, however, being as low as the level in Venezuela, Mexico, or Chile. As further progress is still possible in reducing the death rate, the rapid increase of population in Brazil can only be accentuated.

There are appreciable differences between the demographic patterns prevailing in town and countryside, but the fundamental contrast lies between the already industrialized South and the still underdeveloped Northeast. The highest birth rates and thus the most rapid rate of increase correspond with the poorest regions. In these same regions, the infant mortality rate is also the highest.

The youthfulness of the population results directly in a high birth rate. A breakdown of the population into age groups shows that more than half of it is younger than 20 years of age, while only 5 percent is aged 60 or older. Youth, as a whole, represents an important asset of Brazil. The immediate result, however, is to increase the proportion, already excessive, of those who do not work, thus imposing heavy charges on the state.

Patterns of settlement

The human distribution over the territory remains extremely irregular and is still strongly marked by the historical conditions under which the land was settled. The Atlantic states (from Maranhão to Rio Grande do Sul, including the Minas Gerais) were the first to be developed; they only cover 35 percent of the area, but contain 90 percent of the population of Brazil. The interior, on the contrary, not yet developed, only has 10 percent of the population on 65 percent of the area (Amazonas and the Central-West region). The same contrasts are found within individual states. In Pernambuco, as in the other states of the Northeast, a coastal belt to a depth of 60 to 90 miles comprises the sugar plantations of the Mata and the transitional zone of the Agreste and contains four-fifths of the population, while the vast *sertão* ("wasteland") has only a limited and scattered number of people. In Minas Gerais, the districts of the southeast often have

Brazil, Area and Population

	area		population	
	sq mi	sq km	1970 census	1980 census*
Regions *(regiões)*				
Central-West (Centro-Oeste)				
Federal district	2,245	5,814	537,000	1,177,000
States *(estados)*				
Goiás	247,913	642,092	2,939,000	3,865,000
Mato Grosso	340,156	881,001	1,597,000	1,141,000
Mato Grosso do Sul	135,347	350,548	—	1,369,000
North (Norte)				
States				
Acre	58,915	152,589	215,000	302,000
Amazonas†	604,036	1,564,445	955,000	1,430,000
Pará†	481,872	1,248,042	2,167,000	3,411,000
Rondônia	93,840	243,044	111,000	493,000
Territories *(territorios)*				
Amapá	54,161	140,276	114,000	176,000
Roraima	88,844	230,104	41,000	79,000
Northeast (Nordeste)				
States				
Alagoas	10,707	27,731	1,588,000	1,988,000
Bahia	216,613	561,026	7,493,000	9,471,000
Ceará‡	57,149	148,016	4,362,000	5,294,000
Maranhão	126,898	328,663	2,993,000	4,003,000
Paraíba	21,765	56,372	2,383,000	2,773,000
Pernambuco	37,946	98,281	5,161,000	6,145,000
Piauí‡	96,886	250,934	1,681,000	2,140,000
Rio Grande do Norte	20,469	53,015	1,550,000	1,900,000
Sergipe	8,492	21,994	901,000	1,142,000
Territory				
Fernando de Noronha§	10	26	1,000	1,000
South (Sul)				
States				
Paraná	77,048	199,554	6,930,000	7,630,000
Rio Grande do Sul	108,952	282,184	6,665,000	7,776,000
Santa Catarina	37,060	95,985	2,902,000	3,629,000
Southeast (Sudeste)				
States				
Espírito Santo‖	17,605	45,597	1,599,000	2,024,000
Minas Gerais	226,708	587,172	11,487,000	13,383,000
Rio de Janeiro	17,092	44,268	8,994,000	11,298,000
São Paulo	95,714	247,898	17,772,000	25,023,000
Total Brazil	3,286,488¶	8,511,965	93,139,000	119,062,000¶

*Preliminary figures. †Excludes an area of 1,035 sq mi (2,680 sq km) to be demarcated between the states of Amazonas and Pará. ‡Excludes an area of 1,009 sq mi (2,614 sq km) to be demarcated between the states of Piauí and Ceará. §Includes the areas of Atol das Rocas and Penedos de São Pedro and São Paulo. ‖Includes the areas of Ilhas Trindade and Martin Vas. ¶Figures do not add to total given because of rounding.
Sources: IBGE, *Anuário Estatístico do Brasil* (1980), the Organization of American States, and official government figures.

more than 20 inhabitants per square mile; those of the Northwest have almost always fewer than 5 to the square mile. Even the state of São Paulo, relatively densely settled at the time of the expansion of the coffee plantations, has strong concentrations of people next to empty regions. In the Rio Grande do Sul, the southern Campanha—land of the gauchos (cowboys or herdsmen)—has a much lower population density than the cultivated plateaus of the North. Finally, the zone of high density only covers a strip along the Atlantic coast, narrow to the north, wider to the south, together with a few isolated enclaves lost in the middle of the interior desert.

This distribution is not, however, permanently fixed. The movements of residents are transforming it, little by little, to the benefit of the regions of the South and the Central-West region. These migrations have resulted from the advance of pioneers in the west of the states of São Paulo, Paraná, and Santa Catarina, and in the south of the states of Mato Grosso and Goiás. Other migrations were caused by the creation of the federal capital of Brasília, and still others by the building of great interior roads. Thus the Central-West region has the strongest percentage of population growth in Brazil: from 1950 to 1980 the population of Goiás grew by more than 200 percent. But it is the South and São Paulo that benefit the most from substantial influxes. It is the richest, the best equipped, the most industrialized, and the most vital region of Brazil; it receives at the same time the greater part of the flow of international immigration, as well as that of domestic immigration. Foreigners, who constitute only 2 percent of the population of Brazil, represent 7.5 percent of the population of the state of São Paulo. This group is principally composed of Mediterranean elements (Portuguese, Spaniards, Italians, Lebanese), together with Japanese, Americans from the United States, and Germans. The technicians and skilled workers among them hold a much more important place than they did in the 19th century. The domestic movement of population, however, does not follow the same social pattern, and misery and hunger remain. The domestic migrations are, in effect, motivated primarily by the lowering of rural income, affecting above all the northeastern states and Minas Gerais; they are also due to the persistence of an archaic agrarian structure and to an increase in demographic densities. Bahia and Minas Gerais have the largest contingents of migrants. Whole families of miserable *sertanejos* ("inhabitants of the wasteland"), and also farmers from the Mata and the Agreste areas, flee toward the towns, the population of which is thus swelled by a mass of unqualified, underemployed people with a very low standard of living. São Paulo, Rio de Janeiro, Brasília, and the pioneer towns receive immigrants from all parts of the country. The other towns attract primarily the rural populations of their regions. But, if in the South the urban industrial jobs justify the rural exodus, in the other parts of the country, urbanization is not accompanied by new professional opportunities. In the old littoral capitals of the Northeast, in particular, the population has grown at a high rate, without any relation to urban or regional economic growth. The immigrants only occasionally find work and crowd together in nondescript and pitiable dwellings, similar to those of shantytowns. Approximately two-fifths of the population of Recife live in *mocambos* (shantytowns), the poorest of the Brazilian *favelas* ("slums").

Urban growth

Migration is responsible for two-thirds of urban growth. In 1940 the urban population constituted only 30 percent of the total population. In the early 1970s urban population slightly exceeded rural population, and by the early 1980s urban population constituted two-thirds of the total population. Brazil has 25 municipalities of more than 250,000 residents, which constitute more than half of the total urban population. São Paulo, which had only 31,000 residents in 1872, in the early 1980s had more than 8,000,000. Rio de Janeiro had passed a peak of 5,000,000. Eight other cities had a population of more than 1,000,000—Belo Horizonte (which had only 13,000 in 1900), Salvador, Fortaleza, Recife, Brasília, Pôrto Alegre, Nova Iguaçu, and Curitiba. But apart from these very large cities and since 1940, medium and small centres have also shown spectacular increase. These include cities that act as gateways to the *sertão*, like Campina Grande; crossroads cities such as Governador Valadares; pioneer cities like Londrina; or cities that are situated in the middle of rich agricultural zones, like Presidente Prudente; industrial cities like Santo André, São Bernardo do Campo, São José dos Campos, or Campinas; and, lastly, tourist cities, like Petrópolis.

A strong movement, therefore, carries Brazilians toward the cities and accelerates the mixing process, placing regional groups, which for a long time have not known each other, in contact again. It also induces—notably among the poorest people—a consciousness of regional economic imbalances and of excessive social inequalities.

If the present rate of growth continues—and there appears to be no prospect of it slackening—Brazil, in the year 2000, will have a population of more than 200,000,000. It will by then have become one of the great demographic world powers. Will this growth be accompanied by a territorial redistribution ending in a more harmonious and more balanced reapportionment? Will it be accompanied by an economic development sufficiently wide and sufficiently speedy not only to give work to all new citizens but also to ameliorate the standard of living of the whole community? Such are the two fundamental questions that emerge from an examination of the demographic situation. Brazil has succeeded in giving to racial, linguistic, and religious groups, differing greatly from each other, the consciousness of belonging to the same nation. The nation still has the task of removing the spatial and social imbalances and of harmonizing demographic as well as economic growth.

(M.Ml.)

The national economy

A COMPARATIVE VIEW OF THE COUNTRY'S REGIONAL AND WORLDWIDE STANDING

The sheer extent of Brazil's primary resources places its economy, despite its lack of development, among the world's leading producers of a number of important commodities. In 1980, for example, it was the world's leading producer of coffee, sugar, and bananas; second in cocoa and soy beans; third in tobacco, corn, and edible beans; fourth in cattle; and fifth in cotton, asbestos, and manganese. It is the largest rice producer outside Asia. It is also important for what it has not yet fully exploited—about one-half of the world's total high-grade iron-ore deposits, its vast hydroelectric potential, its hardwood forests, and some 2,100,000,000 acres (850,000,000 hectares) of soil, most of which could be fertile given adequate water and fertilizer. As its manufacturing sector develops, Brazil also has taken a significant place among the world's industrial producers. It is the leading manufacturer of vehicles, merchant vessels, crude steel, and cement in Latin America, and the city of São Paulo is the largest industrial centre in the region.

Economic growth

Mainly as the result of industrial development, Brazil's economy recorded real growth of about 8 percent during the early 1980s, which placed it among the fastest expanding economies in the world. Gross domestic product (GDP) per person in São Paulo, where most industry is concentrated, reached some U.S. $1,100 in the late 1970s—about the average for Latin America. The national average, however, was U.S. $775, because large areas of the country are developing at a much slower rate from a much less developed base. The GDP per person in the Northeast, for example, was about U.S. $360 in the late 1970s—comparable to South and Southeast Asian levels.

The Brazilian economy is also renowned for a negative achievement—a phenomenal rate of inflation, which accelerated to an annual rate of 100 percent in 1964 but was reduced to about 25 percent in the late 1960s. During the early 1980s, however, inflation rose again to more than 120 percent, chiefly because of the increased cost of imported oil and shortages in the agricultural sector.

THE EXTENT AND DISTRIBUTION OF RESOURCES

Mineral resources. Brazil is known to contain extremely rich mineral deposits, although the country's resources have yet to be comprehensively surveyed. The country's known iron-ore reserves, at 65,000,000,000 tons, are second only to those of the Soviet Union. About 48,000,000,000 tons, or three-quarters of these reserves, are located in what is known as the Iron Quadrilateral Zone of Minas Gerais, and the remainder is located in Mato Grosso do Sul. Known manganese-ore deposits are estimated at 152,500,000 tons—more than two-thirds in Mato Grosso and the remainder in Amapá and Minas Gerais. Low-quality coal resources of 3,200,000,000 tons are located in Rio Grande do Sul and Santa Catarina, but only about a third of this—found in the latter state—is suitable for processing to produce metallurgical coal for steel manufacture. About 300,000 tons of thorium (a radioactive metallic element), almost a third of the world's known deposits, exist in the form of continental deposits and monazite (phosphate of the cerium metals—the most abundant elements of the rare-earth group—and of thorium) sands. In addition, the country is thought to have substantial reserves of tungsten (an element used for hardening steel), rock crystal, salt, nickel, tin, lead, bauxite, graphite, chrome, steatite (soapstone), zirconium (a strong ductile, metallic element with many industrial uses), silver, gold, and diamonds.

Oil and natural gas

Brazil has extensive oil and natural-gas reserves. In 1980 Brazilian oil reserves were estimated at about 1,340,000,000 barrels, of which about three-fourths were located in the Recôncavo (Bahia) and one-fourth in the Alagoas–Sergipe area. Natural-gas reserves, located mainly in Bahia, were estimated at 1,589,000,000,000 cubic feet (45,000,000,000 cubic metres).

A peculiar feature of Brazil's mineral resources is that they tend to be located far from their internal market. Thus there are no natural-gas deposits in the industrialized Southeast, while the coal that could conveniently be used in steel manufacture is located in the South.

Biological resources. Nearly two-thirds of the country is under forest, providing about one-seventh of the world's total forest area. Hardwoods predominate in the Amazon and Atlantic coastal zone, and Paraná pine in the South. The timber stand was estimated by the United Nations Food and Agriculture Organization (FAO) in 1963 at 2,800,000,000,000 cubic feet. Exploitation of the Amazon rain forest, however, has been hampered by the inadequacy of transport facilities and by the large variety of species of vegetation, estimated at an average of 40 per acre (100 per hectare).

By the late 1970s almost 512,000,000 acres, or a fourth of Brazil, was under agriculture. Of this area, 4 percent was under permanent crops, 16 percent was used for cultivation, and 80 percent was meadows and pastures. About one-half of the total cultivated area was in the South and São Paulo regions, another one-third in the Northeast, and about one-sixth in the Southeast, excluding São Paulo. The FAO estimates that as much as 80 percent of Brazil is suitable for some type of agriculture.

Livestock

Brazil has one of the largest livestock populations in the world, with about 217,000,000 head recorded in 1980. Cattle numbered 93,000,000 in the same year. Although pure-breed cattle are reared in the temperate regions of the South and Southeast, most cattle are of the zebu (humped Asiatic ox) variety; the Brazilian Highlands—Minas Gerais, Mato Grosso, and Goiás—account for almost half of all cattle raised. The raising of hogs is important in Paraná, Minas Gerais, and Rio Grande do Sul, while the latter two states are the most important producers of horses. More than half of all sheep are raised in Rio Grande do Sul.

With a coastline of more than 4,600 miles, Brazil has access to substantial fishing grounds. Activity is concentrated in the Northeast (Pará and Maranhão) and in the South (Rio Grande do Sul and Santa Catarina), but this resource is underdeveloped. Only one-tenth of the total fishing boats registered were motorized in the late 1970s.

Hydroelectric resources. With one of the most extensive river systems in the world and with plentiful rainfall in all of the country except the Northeast, Brazil has one of the four largest hydroelectric potentials in the world. It is estimated at 150,000,000 kilowatts, although much of this capacity cannot readily be developed because of its remoteness—for example, the 44,000,000-kilowatt estimated capacity for the state of Amazonas. By the early 1980s installed generating capacity was concentrated in the Southeast and the South, which consume more than three-quarters of all power produced in Brazil.

From 1950 to 1980 there was a rapid expansion in total power capacity, mainly through hydroelectric development. The capacity rose from 2,000,000 kilowatts in the early 1950s to 24,000,000 kilowatts by the late 1970s; about four-fifths is provided by hydroelectric power. The government has given high priority to harnessing the country's substantial hydroelectric resources, as the scope for expansion in thermal capacity is limited by the poor quality of Brazilian coal and the inadequacy of crude-oil supplies to meet refining demand. Brazil's first nuclear reactor, Angra I, began operation in early 1982 in Rio de Janeiro; the Angra Dos Reis nuclear power complex, comprising eight other reactors, was under construction.

SOURCES OF NATIONAL INCOME

Agriculture, forestry, and fishing. Agriculture is the most important single sector of the economy, accounting for about 11 percent of the GDP and almost half of all exports. It provided employment for some 15,500,000 people in 1960—more than half the active labour force. By the early 1980s, however, it represented only about a third of the total force. Agriculture, forestry, and fishing have lagged behind the expansion of the rest of the economy. In general, the increase in agricultural production has been the reflection not of greater labour productivity through the use of machinery nor of higher plant yield through improved seeds or fertilizer but of the increase in the area under crops—from 75,000,000 acres in 1960 to 132,000,000 in 1970 and 153,000,000 acres in 1980. Much of this expansion has been in the states of Maranhão (in the Northeast) and Paraná (in the South), in the form of small farms of less than 25 acres, while cultivation on large farms, of 2,500 acres or more, has taken place in Acre, Roraima, and Amapá (in the North).

The agricultural sector

The agricultural sector is still very backward. Despite the high acidity of soils throughout most of Brazil, the country is one of the lowest users of fertilizer per crop acre in the world. Fertilizer consumption per acre of arable land increased fivefold between 1968 and 1978, but it was still only half of the world average. More than half of all fertilizer use is concentrated in São Paulo state. The use of human labour is still dominant; less than 10 percent of all farms use electric or mechanized energy sources. Labour productivity is thus very low, and one rural worker is estimated to produce enough for five residents—compared with a ratio of one to 30 in the United States. The more advanced techniques (fertilizer, power, and machinery) tend to be concentrated in the São Paulo–Paraná–Minas Gerais triangle, which provides the bulk of the country's agricultural production. The states of São Paulo, Paraná, Santa Catarina, and Rio Grande do Sul account for more than half of all the agricultural land, three-quarters of all buildings, and nearly half of all the equipment used in Brazil's farming sector.

During the mid-1970s the average farm size was 160 acres. About 10 percent of the farms, occupying three-fourths of the total crop area, were more than 250 acres in size, and more than half of the farms, occupying one-twentieth of the total crop area, were less than 10 acres in size. Farm size as well as farming techniques vary greatly among the different regions of Brazil. In the densely populated North, Northeast, and South, more than half of the farms are small single-family units, producing chiefly beans, rice, and corn, while in the sparsely populated Southeast and Central-West, large farms with mechanized commercial crop operations and extensive cattle ranches predominate. The disparity in farm productivity is acute, as 90 percent of the tractor and fertilizer use is concentrated in the central and southern regions.

Major crops

Coffee is the most important crop and accounted for one-eighth of all export earnings in 1980; its cultivation employs about 1,000,000 people. Output, however, has fallen steadily—from 4,400,000 tons in 1959 to 1,996,000 in 1980—largely as the result of government policies encouraging crop diversification; prices paid to coffee producers are held down and the destruction of plantings subsidized. The area planted to coffee therefore declined from 10,600,000 acres in 1959 to 5,475,000 acres in 1980, and the introduction of higher yield strains has been insufficient to balance the consequent production decline.

The next most important agricultural exports, sugar and soybeans, have expanded production as the area cultivated more than doubled between 1950 and 1980, with their area increasing to 6,530,000 and 21,660,000 acres, respectively. Sugarcane production reached 163,600,000 tons in 1980, compared with 53,500,000 tons in 1959, and that of soybeans increased from 271,000 tons to 16,700,000 tons. Sugar has benefited from the extension of cultivation in the fertile São Paulo area, while planting in the Northeast has declined. In the 1970s the output of cocoa, the fourth ranking export crop, fluctuated at a level of about 270,000 tons a year, to which it was held by low levels of technology and by tree aging. Production of cotton, the fifth most important export crop, rose from 1,400,000 tons in 1959 to 1,673,000 tons in 1980. Production of dry edible beans rose during the same period—from 1,500,000 tons in 1959 to 2,177,000 tons in 1980—as the area cultivated expanded by about half, to 11,000,000 acres.

Spectacular expansion has been recorded in the production of rice and corn, essentially for the domestic market and achieved mainly through colonization in Mato Grosso and Goiás. Output of rice rose from 4,100,000 tons in 1959 to 10,740,000 tons in 1980, and the area cultivated increased from 6,700,000 to 15,340,000 acres. Corn production rose from 7,800,000 tons in 1959 to 22,500,000 tons in 1980, and the area cultivated expanded from 6,200,000 to 28,300,000 acres. Brazil is nearly self-sufficient in basic foodstuffs; in value, rice and corn ranked first and second in the country's agriculture in 1970.

About a third of total agricultural income is derived from livestock, whose contribution to the domestic food supply has expanded appreciably. Total output rose by about a fifth in the 1960s—the most significant feature being the rapid rise in milk production, from 1,300,000,000 gallons (4,900,000,000 litres) in 1960 to 2,171,000,000 gallons in 1980. No clear distinction, however, is made between beef and dairy cattle, and the return from beef-cattle raising is poor; the slaughter rate is about 11 percent a year, and carcasses on an average weigh a fifth less than in the United States.

Fish output doubled in the 1970s, reaching almost 945,000 tons in 1980. Productivity, however, is low—about one ton per fisherman per year.

Forest resources

Much of the country's forest resources remain untapped, as about three-fourths of them are inaccessible; moreover, only about 75 percent of the accessible area is in commercial production. This sector, however, is expanding, with roundwood output of 241,000,000 cubic yards (184,000,000 cubic metres) in 1979, and saw logs about 9,800,000 tons. While most hardwood is consumed locally, with much being used as fuel, pinewood is used for export. Wood and wood products ranked 12th among all of Brazil's exports in 1979.

With few exceptions, agricultural and forestry production suffers from inadequate capital investment. Savings tend to be attracted to the higher yields offered by industry, and—in time of inflation—real estate; therefore investment in agriculture has generally taken the form of increasing the area of land under cultivation instead of investing in the technology needed to increase productivity. Farm income cannot expand significantly nor can rural areas provide a wider basis for industrial development until agriculture uses improved technology.

Mining and quarrying. Although the country's mineral resources are still largely undeveloped, and mining provides employment for less than 2 percent of the labour force, mining output more than quadrupled in the 1970s, as the result of rising demand from domestic industry and a firm export market. Iron ore, mined chiefly in Minas Gerais, is the most important single metallic mineral product; production rose from 9,300,000 tons in 1960 to 106,000,000 in 1980. About three-fourths of output is exported. The second ranking is manganese, output of which rose from 1,000,000 tons in 1960 to 2,200,000 in 1980—about three-fourths for export. About 80 percent of the ore is produced in Amapá. Other minerals produced in large quantities include bauxite, apatite (a mineral used in the manufacture of phosphate fertilizers), dolomite (for building stone), lead, magnesite (magnesium carbonate, used in manufacturing), tin, chromite, and asbestos. Production of raw coal rose from 2,300,000 tons in 1960 to 8,300,000 in 1980; the coal, however, is of limited significance because of its poor quality.

Manufacturing. Manufacturing has been the most dynamic sector of the economy since World War II, with an average annual growth of nearly 10 percent from 1947 to 1961; during the same time industrial employment rose by about a quarter. Development took the form primarily of import substitution, which was encouraged by protective tariffs, tax concessions, and a multiple exchange rate that reduced the cost of foreign capital equipment. The 1960s were marked by widely fluctuating trends: the immediate scope for import substitution was exhausted, the phenomenal rate of inflation discouraged investment in production, and the austerity program of 1964 to 1966 reduced the home market. From 1962 to 1966 output of the manufacturing and mining sectors rose by only 3 percent a year. In the late 1960s, as domestic demand recovered and export production was stimulated, annual industrial expansion strengthened to about 10 percent, and during the 1970s manufacturing was the strong point of the economy. In 1980 it was estimated to represent about one-third of the country's GDP—just exceeding the contributions of agriculture, forestry, and fishing, as well as commerce and finance. It was, however, less important as a source of employment, providing jobs for only about a sixth of the labour force. It also displayed, in exaggerated form, the unevenness of distribution characteristic of the Brazilian economy. More than four-fifths of the country's industrial output comes from the São Paulo area, which employs only half the total industrial labour force.

In the 1960s there was rapid growth in four crucial sectors—iron and steel, vehicles, ships, and petroleum products. By the early 1970s Brazil was self-sufficient in steel ingots, after output rose from 1,800,000 tons in 1960 to 5,400,000 tons in 1970 and 13,000,000 tons in 1980. By the late 1970s there were about 45 steel companies producing about 17,000,000 tons of crude steel annually. Shipbuilding also has been a growth sector. Brazil's merchant fleet is the largest in Latin America. The petroleum-refining industry has also expanded rapidly, with output up from 64,000,000 barrels in 1960 to 402,000,000 barrels in 1979. Much more spectacular growth has been recorded by the Brazilian motor-vehicle industry, whose output rose from about 31,000 units in 1957 (its first year of large-scale operation) to nearly 420,000 in 1970 and to 550,000 in 1979. Brazil is the leading vehicle manufacturer in Latin America and the fifth largest in the world. Other major industries are textiles (accounting for nearly a fifth of all employment in manufacturing), tobacco (Brazil is among the top 10 cigarette producers in the world), cement, and chemicals (particularly caustic soda, soda ash, and nitrate and phosphate fertilizer).

The motor vehicle industry

Energy. Total energy production by the late 1970s was 31,000,000 tons (coal equivalent), of which electricity accounted for 44 percent, liquid fuels (domestic and imported) about 40 percent, solids (coal) 11 percent, and natural gas almost 5 percent. Production of electricity rose nearly threefold during the 1970s, reaching 127,000,000,000 kilowatt-hours in 1980. Crude-oil production more than doubled and reached about 66,400,000 barrels by 1980—about 17 percent of the domestic demand. The production of natural gas expanded rapidly; it was 101,850,000,000 cubic feet in 1980, compared with about 15,000,000,000 cubic feet annually in the early 1970s.

The government's energy program is designed to reduce Brazil's dependence on imported oil and to develop oil and coal reserves. Under a national program (Proálcool), approximately 150,000 barrels of oil per day is expected to be substituted by the mid-1980s by the use of distilled alcohol from sugarcane. By 1981 about 6 percent of all cars ran completely on alcohol, and the World Bank had approved a loan of U.S. $250,000,000 to help finance the construction of some 250 distilleries.

Financial services. The banking and financial structure is based on the banking reform introduced in 1965. The functions of a central bank—the issue of currency and overall control of banking operations—were then vested in the Central Bank of Brazil. The National Monetary Council, a technically independent body headed by the Minister of Finance, formulates the monetary policies to be implemented by the Central Bank, while the Bank of Brazil (which the Central Bank replaced in 1965) is the main instrument of government credit policy. The Bank of Brazil remains by far the largest bank in the country, operating more than 1,100 agencies, several of which are located in Latin-American and European countries.

Banking institutions

The financial system also includes private and state commercial banks, development banks, private investment banks, savings banks, and the National Housing Bank (BNH), as well as specialized operations such as the Industrial Finance Fund, insurance companies, and real-estate finance companies. The National Bank for Economic Development (BNDE) channels official funds to development projects (chiefly utilities, basic industries, and agriculture) in the form of loan guarantees and equity investment. The commercial banks operate mainly in the field of short-term finance, typically (for working capital) in loans of under 90 days. They are not allowed to accept savings accounts, and more than 90 percent of deposits are sight. The high rate of inflation has stimulated rapid expansion by the banks, and since 1970 the Central Bank has tried to reduce their numbers, mainly through mergers.

Commercial banking is dominated by the public sector. The federally owned Bank of Brazil and the commercial banks owned by the state account for more than half of the deposits of the banking system, while long-term financing comes from official institutions, especially the BNDE and the BNH, although private investment banks have grown in importance. There are about 40 such banks, chiefly providing medium-term loans (one to two years) at free-market rates and funding their operations by selling acceptances and certificates of deposit on the open market. Among its other roles, the Bank of Brazil acts as an agricultural bank and extends medium- and long-term export credits.

Capital financing institutions in Brazil are inadequate to meet medium- and long-term funding requirements, and much long-term investment must be financed by short-term domestic and foreign borrowing. The government's financial intermediaries (BNDE and BNH) remain the main sources of long-term finance, and private institutions are as yet lesser sources; institutional investors (such as life-insurance companies or pension funds) are of little significance. The private capital market deals largely in equity shares. There is, consequently, a critical need for some form of fixed-yield, long-term securities (with correction for inflation) to stimulate financing of private investment.

The most important of the numerous stock exchanges in Brazil are those of São Paulo and of Rio de Janeiro. Both expanded rapidly after 1967, and about 500 and 200 stocks were actively traded, respectively, during the early 1980s. Most of the buying was for speculative purposes (capital gains are not taxed), and much of the increase in activity was due to the operations of more than 100 mutual funds. There are commodity exchanges at Pôrto Alegre, Vitória, Recife, Santos, and São Paulo. Many observers believe that the Brazilian stock exchange as a whole should be more strictly regulated and should have more underwriting support.

Correction for inflation is an important feature of financial life. Since 1964 this has been applied to business assets, government bonds, mortgages, urban rents, and *letras de cambio* (the most common short-term instrument for private finance) to counteract the distorting effects of inflation. Despite the easing in the rate of inflation in the late 1960s and early 1970s, effective interest rates remained high because of the rising demand for credit in a restimulated economy.

Foreign trade. The contribution of exports to the national income is not high—about 10 percent—but is significant in view of the country's need to import capital equipment and raw materials, including crude oil.

Exports

After virtual stagnation in the 1950s, export earnings expanded 116 percent during the 1960s and 560 percent during the 1970s. Although coffee remained the major single export, the near-stagnation of its output brought about a decline of its relative importance, from 36 percent in 1970 to 12.3 percent by 1980. Other traditional agricultural exports—cotton, cocoa, and soybeans—on the whole have kept pace with the overall expansion. Sales of iron ore have been strong, rising 170 percent during the 1970s. The second traditional mineral export, manganese, has declined to less than 0.5 percent of all export earnings. Among agricultural products, meat, which accounted for almost 3 percent of exports in 1970, dropped to 1.5 percent in 1980. The most significant trend in the 1970s, however, was probably the rapid expansion in nontraditional exports. The share of manufactured goods in trade rose from one-fifth of the total exports in 1970 to about one-half in 1980.

The export recovery dates from the 1964 revolution, when the government adopted export promotion as a fundamental policy objective. It ended the system of license allocation that favoured the domestic market at the expense of exports and gave tax incentives to export manufacture. It also established, in 1968, a flexible exchange rate resulting in a continuous devaluation of the cruzeiro.

Imports have shown similar upward movement, although they fluctuated widely as a result of the austerity program introduced in 1964 and of frequent devaluations. On the whole, however, their growth slightly exceeded the overall growth of national income, since they reflected very closely the pace of industrial development. Thus machinery and vehicles accounted for about one-fifth of all imports in 1980, while oil and derivatives—the most important single import—accounted for 43 percent. At the beginning of the 1980s foreign trade was not balanced, with imports showing more dynamic growth.

The pattern of Brazilian trade has undergone important changes. While the United States remains by far the most important single market for Brazilian exports, taking 17 percent of all shipments in 1980, it was superseded in that year by the European Economic Community (EEC, or Common Market), which bought 27 percent. Another regional grouping with a strong demand for Brazilian goods is the Latin American Integration Association (LAIA), successor of the Latin American Free Trade Association (1961–80). Brazilian sales within LAIA were U.S. $1,230,000,000 in 1980, or 15 percent of all exports; they have benefited particularly from the tariff reductions negotiated in 1968, which affected a large number of relatively sophisticated manufactured goods. On the import side, the dominant position of the United States has also been challenged by the EEC, whose respective shares of imports in 1980 were 18 and 15 percent.

MANAGEMENT OF THE ECONOMY

The private and public sectors and the role of government. A central element in all government policy since 1964 has been the reduction in the role of the government in the national economy. The aim is to achieve this by reversing the trend toward the nationalization of certain industries, by cutting down the budget deficit, and by stimulating the private sector, specifically through providing incentives to investment. Nevertheless, through direct participation in certain sectors and through its own infrastructure investment program, the government's share of total fixed capital formation is expected to match that of the private sector.

Development planning

Three agencies coordinate development planning at the federal, state, and substate levels—the Ministry for Planning and Economic Coordination, the Consultative Council on Planning (CONSPLAN), and the Ministry of the Interior—but their role is seen as supplementary to that of the free market. Thus, while development programs incorporate growth targets for sectors of private industry, it is assumed that these will be achieved as a voluntary response to fiscal incentives offered by the government.

These are offered for four purposes: the establishment and expansion of industries important to national economic development; the development of agriculture, forestry, and fishing; the curbing of inflation; and the stimulation of backward regions (the Northeast, administered by Superintendency for Development of the Northeast [SUDENE], and the North, administered by Superintendency for Development of Amazonia [SUDAM]). The incentives take the form of exemptions from specific taxes (such as import duties and the tax on industrial goods) and rebates on income tax, up to a 50 percent limit, provided the rebate is reinvested in approved projects. Agriculture incentives also take the form of minimum commodity prices, credits, and subsidies for fertilizer use.

There are few restrictions on private enterprise, with the exception of the crude-oil industry. Mining, hydroelectric development, and certain sectors of communications and transport are reserved for Brazilian citizens and companies organized in accordance with Brazilian legislation.

Only one sphere of productive activity is reserved to the government—the prospecting and exploration of oil deposits, the refining of crude oil, and the coastal and pipeline transportation of petroleum and its products by coastal shipping. This monopoly has been operated, since 1953, by Petrobrás—a mixed corporation in which the federal government has a majority holding. Petrobrás also has a monopoly of oil imports; their transportation is carried out by the National Fleet of Petroleum Tankers (FRONAPE), a state company affiliated to Petrobrás. A subsidiary, Petroquisa, may associate with private capital in petrochemical developments.

The government also participates in certain public utilities. The Federal Railway Network, RFFSA, operates about half of the railway companies active in Brazil, while the Merchant Marine Commission (CMM) is responsible for the supervision of all maritime shipping (and shipbuilding) and of the five government companies operating in this field. The government participates in the electricity-generating industry through Electrobrás, a corporation established in 1961 and owned by the federal government. One of the largest enterprises in Latin America, Electrobrás operates about a fifth of the country's capacity, acts as financing agency for all electric utilities, and is responsible for the planning of national power development.

Taxation. A major cause of the economic crisis of 1963 to 1964 was the massive budget deficit, financed by inflationary borrowing from the Bank of Brazil. The government subsequently succeeded in reducing the deficit by holding down the rate of growth in public spending and by a very substantial increase in government revenues.

The tax structure

The present system of taxation was introduced in 1965 and incorporated in the 1967 constitution. The federal government is empowered to decree taxes on imports, exports (when prices rise above 5 percent over a base price set by the Central Bank), rural land, incomes (a withholding tax on salaries was introduced), industrial goods, financial operations, transport and communication services, and the production, import, distribution, and consumption of fuels, lubricants, electricity, and minerals. A proportion of the yield of these taxes is then allocated to the states and municipalities; the states levy taxes on merchandise transactions (rates are set by the federal government) and on the transfer of real estate, and the municipalities tax urban real estate.

The most important indirect taxes are the federal industrial goods tax, which by the late 1970s amounted to about one-fifth of the value added in various stages of production, and the merchandise-transaction tax of the states, varying from 15 to 18 percent of value added. Exemption from a large proportion of these taxes is offered under the government's incentive program for manufactured exports. Direct taxes are levied at the rate of between 3 and 50 percent on personal income and 30 percent on company profits; a reduced rate operates for public utilities, certain professional services, and firms adhering to the price-control program.

The total government revenues amounted to some 10 percent of the GDP in the late 1970s, the lowest among Latin-American countries. Steps have been taken to reduce the tax burden: the industrial goods tax and the merchandise-transaction tax were both reduced by 0.5 percent each year. Credits against income tax were allowed for contributions to the literacy campaign. In addition, the Workers Participation Fund, inaugurated in 1971, required companies to direct tax credits as well as an amount equal to a fixed proportion of gross sales to the Social Integration Program. The program then aimed to redistribute income to wage earners and to channel low-cost credit to small enterprises.

Trade unions and employer associations. In 1971 there were more than 5,900 rural and urban labour unions and employers' associations in Brazil. Labour courts and labour conciliation boards have exclusive jurisdiction over labour disputes. The power of the unions has been greatly reduced since 1964. In 1978 a decree-law was published that prohibited strikes in public services and activities that are considered essential. Strikes are legal only after they have been approved by a general assembly of the union involved, with at least 10 days' notice of the meeting and with at least a two-thirds vote in favour of the strike, taken in a secret ballot. Written notice of the union's demands and of its intention to strike if settlement is not reached within five days must then be given to the employer or employers' association. The five-day period is reduced to three days when the strike is caused by nonpayment of wages or when the employers fail to comply with a labour-court decision.

Contemporary economic policies. The revolution of 1964 was economic as well as political. The new regime immediately attacked the runaway inflation by reducing the budget deficit, increasing government tax revenues, and reducing expenditure. Spending restraint mainly took the form of eliminating wheat and petroleum import subsidies, raising railway, shipping and postal rates, and holding down pay increases. At the same time the amortization of the treasury debt, from 1965 on, far exceeded new borrowings by the government, which by the early 1970s had come to rely, for deficit financing, on securities rather than loans from the banking system.

Wage controls

The second major instrument of economic stabilization was the stringent control of wage increases. In 1964 a formula was implemented for increases in the legal minimum wage; a minimum one-year period was set between adjustments. In 1970 new minimum wage rates were established for three years, with no adjustment allowed. As a corollary to wage control, the government attempted—not very successfully—to operate price controls by setting maximum prices for certain foodstuffs and by offering tax incentives to companies to hold down price increases.

The emphasis in the 1964 to 1967 period was on stabilization—at the cost of economic growth, which averaged less than 1 percent a year during this period. Since 1967 the government has pursued a policy of encouraging growth. Export manufacturing has benefited from tax incentives and from the introduction in 1968 of the system by which the cruzeiro is devalued by small amounts. Special incentives also have been given to investment in agriculture and in the backward regions. The development plan for 1969 to 1973 aimed for an increase of more than half in the value of tax rebates in the Northeast and about three-fourths in the North. Location of the new capital of Brasília in Goiás, in the Brazilian Highlands, fitted in with the policy of integrating backward areas of the country.

One of the government's priority aims has continued to be the improvement of the payments position—first by boosting exports and second by attracting foreign public and private capital (the latter through imposing a minimum of controls). By 1980 total foreign investment in Brazil reached to U.S. $18,000,000,000. In fact, the capital inflow was the major cause of the rapid rise in the country's reserves. Brazil was the largest recipient of new lending commitments by the World Bank in the 1970s. The government intended to convert many of its substantial foreign obligations to medium- or long-term credits.

At the end of the 1960s there were some signs of a slight modification in government economic policies. The 1969–73 development plan continued the expansionary policies introduced in 1967. The plan specified increases in the GDP, investment, industrial production, and exports—but more attention was paid to sectors that are not immediately productive in accounting terms, such as roads, houses, and schools. Promotion policies in the Northeast were modified in the 1970s, with the maximum tax rebate on investment in the region reduced from 50 to 35 percent in 1971. This was because the rebate system had encouraged capital investment at the expense of projects employing many people, which would be of more value in a densely populated area. Road construction was designed to open up some 23,000 square miles for development. At the same time, the government appeared to have decided to ease the tax burden somewhat.

Problems and prospects. In the early 1980s short-term prospects for the Brazilian economy were good. The country received a rising inflow of medium- and long-term capital from abroad that reached about $1,000,000,000 a year in the mid-1970s. While import demand would continue high, as the widening in local production was offset by the easing of some import restraints and the capital equipment needs of expanding industry, export prospects were also very good. World demand for iron ore expanded, and the flexible exchange rate increased the competitiveness of Brazilian manufactured goods; LAIA also was expected to provide a market for commodities that were less competitive on international markets. Given overall buoyancy in world trade, Brazil's exports were expected to maintain an 18 percent growth rate in the 1980s. With the government operating its incentives for private sector investment and not seeking to restrict the expansion of credit, the prospect was that investment in the economy would expand, and a high rate of growth—9 to 10 percent—would be achieved by the late 1980s.

There were several problems, however, in Brazil's economy. Although export prospects were generally good, the share of coffee in total exports declined steadily during the 1970s as the result of the government's export diversification policy. The two-year International Coffee Agreement negotiated in late 1980 brought about the distribution of quotas based on historical market shares. The largest allotment went to Brazil, thereby providing a measure of stability in world markets for the period. While the inflow of foreign capital was essential to the achievement of the country's investment targets, the external debt reached U.S. $53,847,000,000 by 1980, which made the burden of debt service substantial. Internally, industry was approaching a crossroads. Its growth since 1967 had mainly taken the form of the use of idle capacity—both plant and manpower—in response to increased domestic and export demand. The shift within the agricultural sector to nontraditional and minor crops was accelerated to raise rural income enough to provide Brazilian manufacturing with a mass market to make its goods competitive. The level of investment spending was not sufficient to generate the overall economic growth forecast. The scope for further fiscal restraint was limited, and its impact could be only marginal. The government's target of a maximum rate of growth of 10 percent a year would be difficult to achieve when the currency was constantly being devalued.

External debt

But the single most serious problem was that of the discrepancy between the Southeast and the South, which both had reached an intermediate stage of economic development and had a GDP of about U.S. $930 per person in 1980, and the remainder of the country, which still had a backward economy, with GDP per person at the level of U.S. $450. Despite incentives and greater government participation in the Northeast and North, their economic growth was not expected to exceed the overall national rate and might well lag behind, widening the gap even further. Despite an ambitious road construction program, development of many potentially rich areas would continue to be hampered by their inaccessibility, yet, with a growth in the labour force of near 1,700,000 people a year, it was essential that Brazil should exploit its basic resources effectively.

Although Brazil has reduced its dependence on imported oil and trade deficits were expected to be largely eliminated by the 1980s, several problems persisted. Unemployment is high, inflation is close to record levels, the country is vulnerable to further oil price increases, and international trade and financial transactions are likely to remain in deficit for several years. If the government's tight fiscal and monetary policies are effective, however, Brazil is expected to resume the rapid economic expansion it sustained throughout most of the 1960s and 1970s.

(E.I.U.)

TRANSPORTATION AND COMMUNICATIONS

Road networks. One of Brazil's major problems of economic development is its inadequate transportation. Part of the lack of good inland transportation can be laid to the difficulty of traversing the Great Escarpment; but a part also is the result of a scarcity of domestic capital. The deficiency of other means of transportation has given considerable stimulation to highway construction. This development was accompanied by a substantial increase in the number of motor vehicles in use; there were 9,000,000 by 1979. Highway construction is financed with the help of a gasoline tax.

State of the roads

The Brasília–Behém highway was completed in the 1960s, opening up a large area of the country for development. Since then, several interior roads have been constructed. The São Paulo–Santos highway, built at a cost of U.S. $350,000,000, was completed in the 1970s. The Transamazônica highway, more than 3,000 miles long, connects the Atlantic coast near Recife with the Peruvian border, south of the Amazon River. The Northern Perimeter Road, under construction since 1973, is expected to stretch for more than 2,000 miles along the northern side of the Amazon. These paved, all-weather routes, however, are not typical of Brazil's road system—861,000 miles in 1980—of which less than 10 percent is paved. The bulk consists of unpaved dirt roads, many of which are in disrepair. Because of these conditions, the operating costs of the trucking (road haulage) industry are very high.

Railways. The large area of Brazil is served by a railroad network that declined from a peak of 24,000 miles in 1960 to less than 19,000 miles by the late 1970s. This trackage is distributed among some 40 lines, many of which are inadequately interconnected. There are more than three gauges. With only a few exceptions the lines are poorly built, badly maintained, and inefficiently operated. Routes often are tortuous, with many curves and steep grades. Much of the equipment is old and poorly maintained. Traffic density, while light in the Northeast, is very high in the South. The bulk of the railroads, with more than 80 percent of the trackage, are owned by the federal government. The rest are owned by states, private companies, and mixed state and private organizations. To cope with the growth of urban traffic, mass-transit systems were under construction in Rio de Janeiro and São Paulo in the early 1980s.

Shipping. Because of the growth of road transport, coastwise shipping is no longer as important as it was prior to 1960, when it was the only means of communication for many regions. The total volume of freight carried amounts to 80,000,000 tons per year. The two government-owned shipping companies, Lloyd Brasileiro and Rio Doce Valley Transportation Company, handle about 90 percent of all shipping operations.

The hub of the coastwide shipping is Rio de Janeiro. Except for the Amazon, which is open to ships of all nations, Brazilian coastal commerce is restricted to Brazilian-owned ships, but numerous foreign shipping lines connect Brazil with the rest of the world. A number of port facilities have been modernized and expanded, and single-purpose terminals have been constructed to handle specific goods. Recife's sugar-loading terminal, for example, can handle 100 tons of sugar per hour.

The extensive Brazilian river system has a total navigability of about 27,000 miles. The inland waterways, especially the Amazon, São Francisco, and Jacuí rivers, provide important communication and shipping routes.

Air transport. Commercial aviation came to the fore during the 1940s and 1950s. The lack of alternative facilities has led to the use of airplanes as carriers of some bulk commodities, including certain minerals. There are more than 1,000 airports in Brazil, but only a small number have paved runways or are large enough for four-engine planes.

Telecommunications. There are radiotelephone connections between Rio de Janeiro, São Paulo, and Brasília and the major cities of North America, South America, and Europe. Submarine cables also link Brazil with countries of the Northern Hemisphere.

(H.W.S.)

Administration, social conditions, and cultural life

THE STRUCTURE OF GOVERNMENT

The constitutional context. Brazil is a federal republic divided into 23 states, three territories, and one federal district; the states and territories are subdivided into municipalities. The municipalities are autonomous politico-administrative units created by the states, on condition that they have a minimum of population and their own fiscal resources. The municipalities are governed by mayors (*prefeitos*) and municipal councillors. Since 1964 the mayors have been named by the president. The municipal councillors are elected officials, whose number is proportionate to the strength of the electorate.

The federal district, Brasília, is the capital of the union. Its *prefeito* is named by the president with the approval of the Senate.

The states are ruled by autonomous laws and constitutions within the framework of the principles defined by the federal constitution. The union can intervene in the internal affairs of the states, in cases foreseen by the federal constitution. Each state has a governor and a legislative assembly. Before 1966 governors were elected by direct vote with secret ballots. Due to the reforms adopted by the military regime in 1966, however, they are now chosen indirectly by an electoral college, formed by members of the state assemblies and representatives of the municipal chambers. There is one representative from each municipal chamber and one deputy for every 200,000 population in each municipality.

The constitution

A new constitution was promulgated on October 7, 1969, two years after the previous one. It was the seventh constitution since the country's independence in 1822. As the fundamental law, the constitution defines the rights of the citizen and the functions of the executive, legislative, and judiciary powers. After the military takeover of 1964, however, two new instruments were created—institutional acts and complementary acts. These acts were promulgated by the executive, who is the sole arbiter of their use. The most important of these acts was Institutional Act No. 5, issued in December 1968. It gave dictatorial powers to the executive, such as the power to legislate or to suspend the political rights of any citizen, including congressional representatives or members of the judiciary. A political reform sponsored by the executive in October 1978 directed the suspension of such acts after January 1, 1979, but it incorporated into the constitution some of the political devices that these acts had introduced, thereby strengthening the powers of the executive with respect to the Congress and internal security.

According to the constitution, legislative power is exercised by the National Congress, composed of the Chamber of Deputies and the Senate. Congress meets every year, in two sessions of four months each. The constitution gives Congress the power to rule in all matters that come under the jurisdiction of the union, particularly those related to the political or administrative organization of the union and to fiscal policies. Congress also has the power to rule on international treaties concluded by the executive, to authorize the president to declare war, and to approve or disapprove federal intervention in the states. Projects approved by Congress can be totally or partially vetoed by the executive. Congress has 45 days to overrule a veto by a two-thirds majority vote.

The Chamber of Deputies is composed of representatives of the states and territories, elected every four years by direct universal suffrage and secret ballot. The number of deputies is in proportion to the population of each state, but no state can be represented in the chamber by more than 55 or by fewer than five deputies. Each territory, however, can only elect two deputies. The total number of deputies is limited to a maximum of 420.

The Senate is formed by representatives of the states (three from each state) for a term of eight years. The Senate is renewed every four years: the first time by a third of its members and the second time by the other two-thirds. Until 1977 senators were elected by the electorate of each state in a straight majority poll. Due to the political reform of that year, however, one-third of the Senate is now chosen indirectly, by the same electoral college that chooses state governors.

Executive power

Executive power is exercised by the president, who is assisted by ministers of state. From 1945 to 1964 the president was elected for a five-year term by direct universal suffrage and secret ballot. Since 1964 the president and the vice president have been elected indirectly, first by the National Congress, and later by an electoral college that is formed of members of Congress and representatives of state assemblies. Each assembly nominates three of its members and one deputy for every 1,000,000 residents, to represent it in the electoral college. The reform adopted in 1978 extended the mandate of the president to six years.

The executive has wide powers, particularly in economic and foreign policy, finances, and internal security. Congress, for example, must approve or reject the executive's federal budget as a whole, without having the right to amend it or increase the level of expenditure. The executive also can decide that any of its projects submitted to the legislative branch shall be discussed and voted upon by Congress in a maximum of 45 days. If Congress is un-

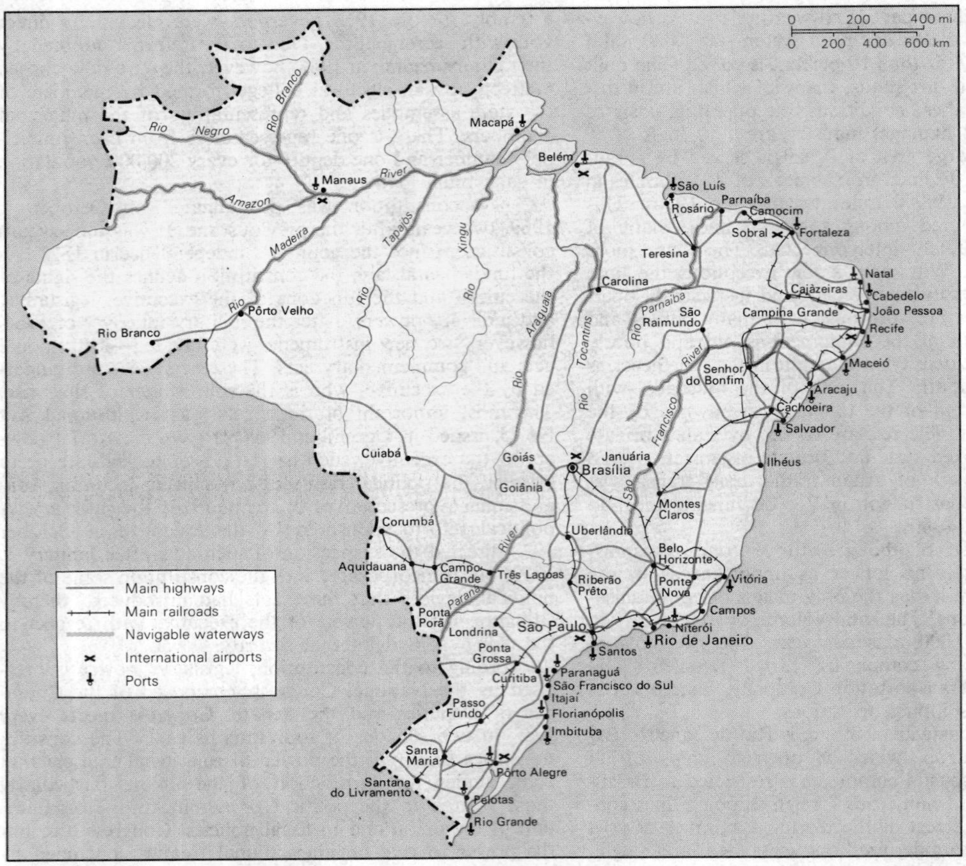

Principal transport routes of Brazil.

able to vote on it within this period, the project is considered approved, a procedure that gives the executive wide room for manoeuvring.

Judiciary power

The judiciary power is made up of several institutions. The Federal Supreme Tribunal is composed of 11 members named by the president with approval of the Senate. It alone decides on litigations between foreign states and the different entities of the union, as well as on differences between the political or administrative divisions of the union. The tribunal also deals with either the demands or "mandates of safeguards" against acts of the highest authorities of the republic (the president, Congress, and judiciary), and decides on demands of habeas corpus already judged at a lower level. It also pronounces on the constitutionality of laws and decrees, and it judges common-law crimes by the president, ministers of state, members of Congress, or magistrates of higher courts. The political reforms of 1978 gave the tribunal the power to hear and decide matters related to the suspension of political rights of any citizen, including congressmen, upon the executive's request.

The National Council of Judicature, created in 1977, is composed of seven judges chosen by the Federal Supreme Tribunal from among its members. It hears cases against any member of the judiciary and determines their suspension (temporary or permanent).

The Tribunal of Appeals instructs and judges the lawsuits under revision in criminal matters and rules on appeals in cases already judged by federal judges. It also judges common-law suits against federal judges. This tribunal is composed of 27 members, nominated for life by the president. Fifteen of them are recommended by the tribunal itself, and 12 are recommended by the Senate.

Each state or territory, as well as the federal district, constitutes a judiciary section. The federal judges there instruct and judge in the first instance certain cases of "mandate of safeguards," certain political crimes, crimes committed against the labour organization or crimes committed on the occasion of strikes, and cases related to public organizations.

Military tribunals and judges have the power to prosecute and judge members of the armed forces for crimes defined by the law; they may also prosecute civilians implicated in crimes against national security. The military judiciary is composed of the Superior Military Tribunal (composed of 15 members nominated for life by the president, on the recommendation of the Senate), and tribunals and judges of inferior rank.

Electoral tribunals and judges are responsible for the registration of political parties and the control of their finances. They also fix the date of elections and prosecute and make judgments on any electoral crimes committed.

Labour tribunals and their judges mediate in individual or collective conflicts between management and workers.

The political process. From the fall of the Vargas dictatorship (1945) to the military takeover (1964), Brazil's political life was formally organized along the lines of the classic democratic–pluralist model. Political institutions, however, were always under constant stress, due in part to the very rapid changes in economic and social structures. Representation of interests was limited to the higher echelons of society, and the political process was chronically unstable. From the early 1950s to the mid-1960s, for example, Brazilians had elected five presidents. Under political pressure, one of them (Getúlio Vargas) committed suicide, and another (Jânio Quadros) resigned after one year in power. Two others (João Café Filho and João Goulart) were overthrown by political opposition allied to factions of the army. Notwithstanding this pattern of instability, political participation was relatively high until the military's establishment of an authoritarian regime in 1964. By the late 1970s demands for an end to the military regime and a return to democratic rule increased.

The electorate. According to the constitution, voting in political elections is mandatory for all citizens over the age of 18 who are literate and have not been deprived of their political rights. The electorate has increased—about 42 percent of the population voted in 1980, as compared with 32 percent in 1970. Since 1964, however, the president, state governors, and (after 1977) one-third of the

Senate are not elected by direct suffrage. Civilian political participation through elections was also greatly reduced after 1977 because of a government decree that restricted political propaganda over radio and television. The discouraging effects of such a decree on electoral participation was evident by the relatively high proportion (20 percent on the average) of blank and void voting papers during the 1978 legislative elections.

Political parties. The Brazilian political parties, which were to mark the political life of the country until 1964, were born in 1945. Familiarity with the most important of these former political parties greatly aids in understanding the developments that led to the political situation of the 1970s.

The former political parties

The Democratic Social Party (Partido Social Democrático; PSD), with conservative tendencies, was founded with the support of the majority of the state governors and based its strength on the rural sectors. Until the 1962 elections the PSD had a majority in Congress. The PSD had a stabilizing influence and by its conciliatory attitude contributed to a resolution of the periodic crises that threatened the former regime. The PSD was dissolved in 1965, and the majority of its members passed to the new governmental party, the National Renewal Alliance (Aliança Renovadora Nacional; Arena).

The National Democratic Union (União Democrática Nacional; UDN) gathered together the majority of Brazilians who were opposed to the dictatorship that characterized the Estado Novo (New State) regime of 1937–45. It was the party most representative of the urban middle classes, but it also drew some strength from the rural areas. It defended economic liberalism and democratic liberties and sought to combat corruption in public administration. Once the second most important political party of Brazil, from 1962 onward it lost membership to the Brazilian Labor Party (Partido Trabalhista Brasileiro; PTB). After its suppression in 1965, its members were divided between the governmental party, Arena, and the party in opposition, the Democratic National Movement (Movimento Democrático Brasileiro; MDB).

The PTB, founded in 1945, was a party of the urban masses and of the "populist" movement. After 1962 it became Brazil's second political party. One of its tendencies was a slight movement to the left, and it campaigned for agrarian reform, nationalization of foreign enterprises, and the extension of the right to vote to illiterates and soldiers. After 1964 the principal leaders of the PTB were deprived of their political rights, while other members of the party mostly went to swell the ranks of the new opposition party, the MDB.

In addition to these large parties, there were 10 small parties active in the Brazilian political system before 1964. Among the more important of these were the Democratic Christian Party (Partido Democrata Cristão; PDC) and the Social Progressive Party (Partido Social Progressista; PSP). After 1947 the Brazilian Communist Party (Partido Comunista Brasileiro; PCB) had no legal existence and so assumed a semiclandestine or clandestine character, finally being split by multiple divisions. Some of its members have made common cause with the student-supported extraparliamentary opposition groups.

In the 1978 elections the opposition MDB won the majority of votes, but, because Brazilian law prohibits the control of Congress by an opposition party, the pro-government Arena held 231 of the 420 seats in the lower house and 42 of the 67 Senate seats.

In November 1979 a bill was passed that disbanded the Arena and MDB in favour of the formation of new parties. This arrangement replaced the bipartisan regime that was established in 1965. New parties receive legal recognition if they have the support of 10 percent of the votes in Congress and that of six senators. By the early 1980s several parties had been organized.

In 1980 the Social Democratic Party (Partido Democrático Social; PDS) was the ruling government party. The opposition parties were the Democratic Labour Party (Partido Democrático Trabalhista; PDT), the Brazil Democratic Movement Party (Partido do Movemento Democrático Brasileiro; PMDB), the Popular Party (Partido Popular; PP), and the National Labour Party (Partido Trabalhista Nacional; PTN). All Communist parties remained outlawed.

Organized labour

Participation of the citizen. In addition to voting, citizens also participate in the political process through organized labour. According to a 1942 law trade unions are placed under the control of the Ministry of Labour and Social Security, strikes are forbidden, and labour tribunals are entrusted with the task of resolving conflicts between management and labour. Union dues are compulsory and are fixed by the administration. The use of the financial resources of the trade unions is under the control of the Ministry of Labour and Social Security.

Although prohibited, a number of strikes erupted between 1950 and 1964. During this period, the formation of the General Confederation of Labor (Confederacão Geral do Trabalho; CGT) was effected, despite the law, with the tacit agreement of the authorities. The CGT was later dissolved by the military revolutionary government, which assumed control of labour organizations and applied the law forbidding strikes. Strikes nevertheless occurred in São Paulo and Belo Horizonte in 1968 and in the late 1970s.

De facto political developments. Prior to 1964, the military's role in the political process always followed a pattern of brief interventions in order to restore the equilibrium among political forces or to avoid disruption of the political system. In April 1964, however, with the overthrow of the constitutional government of President Goulart, it was the armed forces, as an institution, that assumed power for an unlimited period of time. Through the faction known as Grupo da Sorbonne—so named because its members belonged to a nucleus of officers formed at the Superior War Academy, and hence considered as the "intellectuals" of the army—the armed forces instituted an authoritarian regime dedicated to the ideology of "national security and economic development," a concept that the group had developed at the academy in the late 1950s.

After stripping more than 2,000 citizens—military officers, civil servants, political and union leaders, and intellectuals—of their political rights immediately after the coup, the high command of the armed forces nominated Marshal Castelo Branco as president. He was confirmed by the Congress and announced his intention of restoring democratic rule "at the right time." He held the elections of the governors on the appointed date in 1965, but the victory of a few candidates who were opposed to the new regime led the president, under pressure from other military leaders, to modify his intentions. A new period of severity opened with the proclamation of Institutional Act No. 2, which dissolved the political parties, restricted freedom of the press, applied political sanctions, and annulled the mandates of six federal deputies.

In 1967 the presidency was transferred from Marshal Castelo Branco to his War Minister, Marshal Costa e Silva, who announced his wish to make "the revolution more human." The former governor of Guanabara, Carlos Lacerda, attempted a regrouping of the opposition, and sought the support of three ex-presidents, all of whom had been deprived of their political rights. This resulted in the formation of the "enlarged front," the *frente ampla*, which demanded a return to direct elections, the restoration of public liberties, moderate economic nationalism, and economic development. Student street demonstrations took place, supported by some of the clergy and some heterogeneous elements of the population. At first tolerated, these demonstrations were later repressed by the army. The *frente ampla* was banned, and Lacerda was stripped of his political rights.

In December 1968 the Chamber of Deputies refused to suspend the parliamentary immunity of a deputy accused of having insulted the armed forces during a speech in Congress, as demanded by the military. Institutional Act No. 5 was issued immediately, giving full powers to the president and suspending Congress for an indefinite period. The press was censored, and hundreds of citizens lost their political rights, as political repression grew more violent.

In mid-1969 the extraparliamentary opposition adopted urban guerrilla tactics for the first time in Brazil. The kidnapping of the U.S. ambassador (September 1969) was the first and the most spectacular of such guerrilla tactics. The ministers of the three armed forces then formed a junta, assumed power, promulgated the new constitution, and initiated a period of violent repression that lasted for more than four years. Congress was reopened in 1970 in order to elect Gen. Emílio Garrastazú Médici, chosen by the junta, as president of Brazil for a four-year term. The guerrilla groups had been totally suppressed by the end of 1973.

Despite this phase of unrestrained political violence, the country's economy, under strong state intervention and backed by important flows of foreign capital, began a cycle of dramatic growth known as the "Brazilian miracle." This recovery, which lasted until the oil crisis of the mid-1970s, served in many ways to conceal the extent of political opposition to the regime.

In 1974 the presidency was transferred from General Médici to Gen. Ernesto Geisel. The new president announced a program of "gradual liberalization" of the government. The repression was partially curbed, cases of torture of political prisoners were investigated, and the president began to limit the influence of military groups in politics by centralizing power in his office. Also in 1974, elections—the freest since 1964—were held for Congress. The opposition party, MDB, made important gains throughout the country, although the government party, Arena, maintained its majority in both houses of Congress. Following these results, the government adopted contradictory policies. On one hand, the government gave signs of political liberalization, such as the suspension of censorship of the press. On the other hand, Congress was put in recess in April 1977, after denying approval for a government project for reform of the judiciary. Subsequently, the executive issued a new set of laws restricting political and electoral activity.

In January 1978 General Geisel announced that his successor in the presidency would be Gen. João Baptista de Figueiredo. For the first time since 1964 there were signs of dissent among the military. A retired army general, Euler Bentes Monteiro, announced his candidacy for the presidency, under the auspices of the MDB, with a three-point program: (1) political amnesty, (2) immediate suppression of all repressive legislation, and (3) the calling of a constituent assembly within two years following his election. The presence of an alternative military candidate, backed by the opposition, increased the level of political competition and participation. On October 15, 1978, General de Figueiredo was confirmed by the electoral college as president for a six-year term, beginning March 15, 1979.

The administrative structure. The administrative structure of the federal government is composed of 17 ministries divided into six sectors: the political sector (ministries of Justice and Foreign Affairs); the planning sector (Secretariat of Planning); the economic sector (ministries of Finance, Agriculture, Industry and Commerce, Mines and Energy); the infrastructure sector (ministries of Interior, Transport, and Communications); the social sector (ministries of Education, Labour, Social Security, and Health); and the military sector (ministries of the Army, Navy, and Air Force). The ministers of state, in addition to the head of the Joint Chiefs of Staff and the head of the Intelligence Bureau (Servico Nacional de Informacoes), comprise the National Security Council, which is chaired by the president.

Literacy

Education. In 1980 only about one-fourth of the population over 15 years of age was illiterate. By 1979 the primary school system comprised 187,000 units, some 42,000 units more than in 1970; about 23,000,000 children were enrolled in primary schools and 3,200,000 students in secondary schools, an increase of 100 percent since 1971. There were some 65 universities and 700 institutions of higher education throughout the country.

Welfare and health. The social security service set up in 1923 was slow and irregular in its expansion until the early 1960s. During the 1970s the financial resources were considerably increased, and in 1976 about 2,900,000 people received benefits, an increase of 72 percent since 1972. Social security also was extended to cover workers in rural areas. In 1978 the social service administrative structure was replaced by the National System of Social Insurance and Assistance.

Public health

Malnutrition and endemic diseases have been a permanent problem in Brazil. National programs to eradicate malaria have been established. The task of improving health conditions is difficult, however, because of problems inherent in the environment, the isolation of rural populations, and the poverty of the common diet of the population.

In 1978 there were 4.1 hospital beds per 1,000 population, an increase of 17 percent since 1973. Although the number of doctors increased during the 1970s (7 per 10,000, compared with 4.4 per 10,000 in 1968), medical assistance is far from satisfactory. In 1981 the government introduced a federally administered health and welfare program, Prevsaúde, under which health services would be doubled by 1987. The scope of Prevsaúde is limited, however, as 90 percent of Brazil's 15,000 health establishments are operated by the private medical sector.

Housing. The National Housing Bank (Banco Nacional da Habitação; BNH) was created in 1967 with a program for building 200,000 houses in 10 years. The bank, which operates with medium- and long-term mortgages, later revised its programs, which were hampered by chronic inflation. To avoid a loss of capital by the BNH, the interest charges on the loans have been readjusted in keeping with the rate of inflation. Consequently, only wealthier people have been able to continue to make applications to the bank. The delicate problem of the *favelas* and the *mocambos* in Rio de Janeiro, Recife, Belo Horizonte, and other large cities remains unresolved.

Social conditions. Social conditions and income distribution vary considerably according to region and social stratum. The São Paulo and South regions, with 35 percent of the Brazilian population, had more than half of the GDP in 1960, while the North and Northeast regions, with 30 percent of the population, had less than 16 percent. By the mid-1970s these disparities had widened, as concentration of income by social class gradually increased. The lower half of all wage earners in Brazil receive only 14 percent of the national revenue, while the 5 percent at the top of the social pyramid receive 36 percent. During the late 1970s minimum-wage earners spent at least half of their salaries on food. The government has said that this squeeze on lower income groups is necessary to raise exports.

(L.Ms.)

CULTURAL LIFE AND INSTITUTIONS

The cultural milieu. The cultures of the Indians, the Africans, and the Portuguese have together formed the modern Brazilian way of life. By far the most dominant of these cultures is that of the Portuguese, from whom Brazilians acquired their language, their religion, and most of their traditional customs. Throughout Brazil, the Portuguese were able to establish a remarkably homogeneous pattern of living.

Brazilians share a common set of traditions, either inherited from Portugal or formed in the New World during their own history as a nation. Among the important popular festivals is St. John's Eve, or the Festa de São João (June 23), during which families and friends gather around bonfires to roast yams, set off fireworks, play with paper balloons, and sing. This is a Roman Catholic festival, which is also celebrated in Portugal. Brazilians also celebrate their national Independence Day (September 7) in memory of their separation from Portugal, and other patriotic holidays.

Although the Portuguese were able to impose their way of life on the Indians, blacks, and mixed population, the influence of the aborigines and Africans is still apparent in the rural areas. Throughout the country, Brazilian farmers use a rather wasteful type of aboriginal shifting (slash-and-burn) agriculture, and they plant manioc (cassava) and other crops that were cultivated by the Indians.

Tupi, the language that was spoken by most of the Indians along the Brazilian coast, was adapted as early as the 16th century by missionaries for teaching the catechism and came to be called the *lingua geral* ("general language"). For a time, this language was spoken widely throughout the interior of northern Brazil by Indians, mestizos, Portuguese, and blacks. From this language come many of the names of plants, animals, and places in Brazilian Portuguese. Some of these terms of Tupi origin have come to be used in English, such as tapioca (a by-product of the manioc tuber) and cashew (*acajú* in Tupi). The Indian contribution to Brazilian culture is most apparent in the Amazon Basin, where many Indian customs and beliefs have been retained by the rubber collectors and isolated farmers.

African cultural influence

African influence on the Brazilian way of life is strongest in the old plantation region north along the coast from Rio de Janeiro. Particularly in Salvador, the capital of Bahia state, there are traditional dishes of African origin, such as *vatapá*—made of rice flour, coconut oil, fish and shrimps, red peppers, and many condiments—and *acarajé*, a bean cake fried in coconut oil. In most northern coastal cities there are macumba religious cults of African origin, called *umbanda* in Rio de Janeiro and *candomblé* in Bahia, which are analogous to the voodoo, or vodun, of Haiti. These cults worship West African deities as well as Roman Catholic saints. African influence is also apparent in Brazilian popular music, especially in the highly rhythmic sambas.

Because of the great environmental variation over this large country, there are marked regional differences in Brazilian culture. The extreme southern state of Rio Grande do Sul is known for the gauchos, the cowboys of the Pampas. The southern states of Rio Grande do Sul, Paraná, and Santa Catarina are known for their colonies of European farmers. The people of the progressive city of São Paulo have the reputation of being the energetic "yankees" of Brazil. Rio de Janeiro is known for the cosmopolitan charm of its people, spoken of as *cariocas*, and for the gaiety of its pre-Lenten carnival. The northeastern semidesert is characterized by another type of cowboy, the vaquero, who dresses in leather for protection against the thorny bushes of the region. The Amazon Basin has the lonely seringueiro, the gatherer of wild rubber from the tropical forest. The coffee plantations of São Paulo and Paranã states, the cocoa plantations in southern Bahia state, and the sugar plantations of the Northeast coast also provide distinctive settings for regional variations in the Brazilian way of life.

The state of the arts. Brazil's varied racial and cultural past and striking regional differences are reflected in art, literature, and music. Without doubt the outstanding artist of the 18th century was the crippled mulatto architect and sculptor Antônio Francisco Lisboa, who was known simply as Aleijadinho (Little Cripple). His famous carvings in soapstone may be seen in the 18th-century churches of Minas Gerais state.

The artistic and musical heritage

Brazil's most famous modern artist, Cándido Portinari, was the son of Italian immigrants; regional scenes are the subject of many of his paintings. The internationally famous contemporary composer Heitor Villa-Lobos incorporated folk music from the Brazilian blacks and Indians into his compositions. The new school of contemporary Brazilian architecture, which stresses open terraces and large windows that are shuttered against the sun, has become famous throughout the world.

In the field of literature, the mixed racial and cultural heritage of Brazil is also strong. The poetic, imaginative novels of Joaquim Maria Machado de Assis won international acclaim during the late 19th century. In the 20th century a series of outstanding writers have appeared whose works concern regional subjects. A modern Brazilian classic is *Casa-Grande e Senzala* (translated into English as *The Masters and the Slaves*) by Gilberto Freyre; it is a masterly social history of the Brazilian slave system of the Northeast and the fusion of Indian, black, and Portuguese social patterns into the national culture. Jorge Amado has written in *Terras do Sem Fim* (translated as *The Violent Land*) of the frontier days of the early 20th century in the cocoa-growing region of Bahia; and, in *Jubiabá*, of a heroic black character from the slums of Bahia.

Cultural institutions. Among the many modern universities and scientific institutions is the Instituto Butantan, in São Paulo, and the Instituto Oswaldo Cruz in Rio de Janeiro, famous for its scientific work in tropical disease.

Modern mass media have expanded rapidly in recent years. Television was introduced in 1950 in São Paulo. By 1980 there were more than 90 television stations in the larger cities, with an estimated 18,000,000 television receiving sets. The Brazilian television system is connected with the rest of the world by satellite. Brazilians also have become a more sports-loving people. Thousands crowd the beautiful beaches, and hundreds of thousands attend the soccer matches for which a stadium seating 200,000 was constructed in Rio de Janeiro.

(C.W.W./T.L.S.)

Prospects for the future

The armed forces have been the final arbiters of the political process in Brazil since the end of World War II, and they seem likely to retain that function indefinitely. Sharing similar points of view with the urban middle-income groups that have come to prominence, the military officers are convinced that Brazil is destined to become a world power and that it is the duty of the armed services to work toward that end by providing efficient, nationwide administration. This attitude is reinforced by their long-standing low regard for professional politicians. Between 1945 and 1964 no single political party was able to elect a president of Brazil or a majority in Congress, a situation that encouraged political irresponsibility. In these circumstances, and always at the behest of civilian political elements, the armed forces intervened on four occasions to protect national institutions against the effects of what they considered to be civilian incompetence.

Since the revolution of March 31, 1964, in contrast to their earlier practice, military leaders have retained direct command of the government and have carried out a major revision of the political system, progressively enhancing the authority of the national executive at the expense of state governors, state and national legislatures, political parties, and the Brazilian electorate. Through rigorous fiscal austerity, revision of the tax structure, promotion of private enterprise, and heavy investment of public funds in the economic infrastructure, the post-1964 regimes have reversed the downward economic trend to give Brazil one of the highest rates of economic growth in the world. Ambitious highway-building and colonization programs in the interior of the country and more modest support of education and social welfare are designed to hasten the effective occupation and development of the national territory and the modernization of Brazilian society. Sustained economic growth and widespread public apathy in political matters will probably continue to be the norm in Brazil. The military may be expected to remain at the centre of the political stage until it feels that its "revolutionary" policies are irreversible by a successor regime.

(R.E.P.)

BIBLIOGRAPHY

The Land and people: AMERICAN UNIVERSITY, *Area Handbook for Brazil*, 3rd. ed. (1975), a broad overview of history, geography, and culture; FERNANDO BASTOS DE AVILA, *Immigration in Latin America* (1964), a text on the influx of foreigners and their influence in society and economy; EUCLYDES DA CUNHA, *Rebellion in the Backlands* (1944), a fine work on the attempts by settlers to conquer northeastern Brazil; FUNDAÇÃO INSTITUTO BRASILEIRO DE GEOGRAFIA E ESTATÍSTICA (IBGE), *Geografia do Brasil*, 5 vol. (1977), the most comprehensive description, arranged according to the standard regions of Brazil, and *Indicatores Sociais* (1979), a statistical overview; MARVIN HARRIS, *Town and Country in Brazil* (1956, reprinted 1969), a good account of Brazilian population settlement; INTERNATIONAL GEOGRAPHICAL UNION, *Excursion Guidebooks* (1–9, 1956), valuable guidebooks covering the regions of Brazil; PRESTON E. JAMES, *Latin America*, 4th ed. (1969), a standard text including coverage of Brazil; WILLIAM F. JENKS (ed.), *Handbook of South American Geology* (1956), covers the natural features of Latin America; PIERRE MONBEIG, *Ensaios de*

Geografia Humana Brasileira (1940), a collection of essays on Brazil's human geography; DONALD PIERSON, *Negroes in Brazil* (1942, reprinted 1967), a good account of the history and sociology of this group; ROLLIE E. POPPINO, *Brazil: The Land and People* (1968), an excellent, historically oriented introduction to Brazil; T. LYNN SMITH, *Brazil: People and Institutions*, 4th ed. (1972), a sociologist's view of the regions, agriculture, land settlements, and sociopolitical institutions; JULIAN H. STEWARD (ed.), *Handbook of South American Indians*, 7 vol. (1946–59), an indispensable reference work.

The Economy: LUELLA N. DAMBAUGH, *The Coffee Frontier in Brazil* (1959), a monograph on one aspect of the Brazilian economy; G.-A. FIECHTER, *Brazil Since 1964: Modernization Under a Military Regime* (1975), an analysis of Brazil's economic development during a decade of military control; GILBERTO FREYRE, *Brazil: An Interpretation* (1945), a sociologist's view of development; IBGE, *Recursos Naturais do Brasil*, 3rd ed. (1980), an extensive discussion of the major physical and biological resources; T. LYNN SMITH and ALEXANDER MARCHANT (eds.), *Brazil: Portrait of Half a Continent* (1951), a collection of noted works covering sociological and economic aspects; STANLEY J. STEIN, *The Brazilian Cotton Manufacture* (1957), on the textile industry from 1850 to 1950; KEMPTON E. WEBB, *The Geography of Food Supply in Central Minas Gerais* (1959), a basic regional study; GEORGE WYTHE, *Brazil: An Expanding Economy* (1949, reprinted 1968), a comprehensive study, emphasizing industrialization.

Transportation: IBGE, *Anuário Estatístico do Brasil* (annual), contains the most contemporary statistical data; ALAN ABOUCHAR, *Diagnostic of the Transport Situation in Brazil* (1967), a technical economic analysis; WORLD BANK, *Telecommunication* (Sector Working Paper, November 1971), includes basic data for Brazil.

Administration, social conditions, and cultural life: FERNANDO DE AZEVEDO, *A Cultura Brasileira* (1943; Eng. trans., *Brazilian Culture*, 1950), a lavish book covering many aspects of Brazilian culture; JOHN J. JOHNSON, *Political Change in Latin America* (1958), a major synthesis on South American politics; MANOEL B. LOURENCO, *La Educación en el Brasil* (1950; Eng. trans., *Education in Brazil*, 1951), a general account; SAMUEL PUTNAM, *Marvelous Journey: A Survey of Four Centuries of Brazilian Writing* (1948), a standard text; H. JON ROSENBAUM (comp.), *Contemporary Brazil: Issues in Economic and Political Development* (1972), a discussion of new directions in Brazilian government policies of national integration and economic development; JOHN V.D. SAUNDERS (ed.), *Modern Brazil: New Patterns and Development* (1971), essays by 13 specialists, five Brazilians, on population, society, the economy, and the arts; RONALD M. SCHNEIDER, *The Political System of Brazil: Emergence of a "Modernizing" Authoritarian Regime, 1964–1970* (1971), an analysis of the social origins, political views, and continuing policy objectives of Brazil's military leadership; T. LYNN SMITH (*op. cit.*), a vast compilation on major social aspects; CHARLES WAGLEY, *An Introduction to Brazil*, rev. ed. (1971), a penetrating and sympathetic interpretation of Brazilian society, its values and aspirations.

Brazil, History of

This article covers the history of Brazil, with emphasis on the national period, and consists of the following sections:

Brazil to 1889
- Colonial period
- The independence of Brazil
- The Brazilian Empire (1822–89)

Brazil since 1889
- The early republican period
- Return to representative government
- Military intervention
- Social and political changes after 1945

BRAZIL TO 1889

The discovery and early settlement of Brazil appear in the larger perspective of history as episodes in the great movement of Portuguese colonial expansion to the east. Vasco da Gama's discovery in 1498 of an all-water route to the East Indies and Spice Islands by way of the Cape of Good Hope led the Portuguese crown to dispatch to India an imposing armada under command of Pedro Álvares Cabral. To avoid the calms off the Gulf of Guinea, Cabral bore so far to the west that on April 22, 1500, the mainland of South America was sighted; the region was promptly claimed by Portugal, as it lay well within the zone assigned to Portugal by the Treaty of Tordesillas (1494).

Colonial period. The coast of Brazil had been touched in January 1500 by the Spanish navigator Vicente Yáñez Pinzón, but the Spanish crown made no effort to follow up the discovery. Cabral called the territory Vera Cruz (True Cross), but it was renamed Santa Cruz (Holy Cross) by King Manuel. These names, however, were abandoned in favour of Brazil, which probably was derived from the valuable red dyewood (*pau-brasil*) that abounded in coastal areas.

During the colonial period Brazil was expanded beyond the line of Tordesillas (a vertical line that was drawn 370 leagues west of the Cape Verde Islands) westward to the slopes of the Andes and northward and southward to the Amazon and the Río de la Plata. In the north the movement was led by missionaries, who established missions along the Amazon in the 17th century. In the northeast cattlemen from the sugar zones of Pernambuco and Bahia pushed inland into the present area of Piauí, Maranhão, and Goiás in search of new pastures. The brunt of the "march to the west," however, was borne by the Paulistas, the settlers of São Paulo who organized great expeditions into the interior, known as *bandeiras*, to capture Indian slaves and to find gold and precious stones. Some of these expeditions, involving entire families, lasted for years.

During the 17th century, Paulistas explored the area of Mato Grosso and attacked the Indian missions of Misiones and southern Brazil, generally meeting resistance from the Indians and their Jesuit protectors; only along the Río de la Plata, in modern Uruguay, did the Spanish settlers eventually push the Paulistas back. The treaties of Madrid (1750), El Pardo (1761), and San Ildefonso (1777) with Spain gave some legality to Portuguese claims, including the conquests of the *bandeiras*.

An important factor in the unification of the people of Brazil was the heritage of Portugal; the Portuguese language formed a common bond between plantation residents, cattlemen, miners, slaves (both Indian and black), slave hunters, and city dwellers from the Amazon to the Río de la Plata and distinguished them from their Spanish-speaking counterparts elsewhere in South America. Although Tupí-Guaraní continued to serve as a sort of lingua franca throughout much of the interior of the colony, Portuguese remained the official and the common language.

The expanded, patriarchal family structure, also derived from Portugal, was nearly uniform throughout Brazil, and power was exercised by the heads of those families controlling the land, slaves, cattle, and, later, mines that produced the wealth of the colony. Brazilian society and the economy were rurally based. The population was divided unevenly between those who possessed landed wealth and prestige and those who were dependent upon them. No great cities grew up during the colonial period. Moreover, contact with Portugal was maintained in all parts of Brazil, and there was little trade or other regular contact between Brazil and neighbouring Spanish colonies. These common factors proved far stronger than did regional variants when Brazilian unity was under severe stress in the second quarter of the 19th century. (See also LATIN AMERICA AND THE CARIBBEAN, COLONIAL.)

The independence of Brazil. In 1789 the first rebellion against Portuguese authority was instigated by José Joaquim da Silva Xavier, who was known as Tiradentes (Tooth Puller) because of his occasional practice of extracting teeth. The uprising was put down, and Tiradentes was executed.

Despite its isolation, Brazil could not escape the effects of the revolutionary and Napoleonic epoch in Europe. In 1807 Napoleon resolved upon the invasion and conquest of Portugal, a traditional British ally, largely to tighten the European blockade of Great Britain. The Portuguese prince regent Dom John, afterward King John VI, decided to take refuge in Brazil, the only time a colony ever served as the seat of government for its mother country. He sailed from the Tagus on November 29, 1807, under the protection of the British fleet. Accompanied by the royal family and a horde of nobles and functionaries, he arrived at Rio de Janeiro on March 7, 1808. Arrival of Dom John in 1808

The colonists, convinced that a new era had dawned for

Brazil, welcomed their sovereign. The Prince Regent promptly decreed a number of reforms that radically altered the status of the colony. These included practical recognition of Brazil's position as seat of the Portuguese Empire and its new requirements in view of the war in Europe. The old Portuguese commercial monopoly was abolished and Brazilian harbours were opened to the commerce of all friendly nations. British trade with Brazil immediately took on important proportions, and a number of British trading companies established offices in the colony.

A ministry with four portfolios and a council of state were installed in Rio de Janeiro, and a supreme court of justice, a court of exchequer and royal treasury, the royal mint, the Bank of Brazil, and the royal printing office were established. A royal library, a military academy, and medical and law schools were founded. Industries were encouraged, foreign scholars and artists were welcomed, and immigrants from northern Europe were brought in at government expense. The changed status of Brazil was reflected in the decree of December 16, 1815, by which the Portuguese dominions were designated the United Kingdom of Portugal, Brazil, and the Algarves, thus making Brazil coequal with Portugal. In 1816 the queen, Maria I, died, and the Prince Regent became king.

Although John VI enjoyed a certain degree of personal popularity, his corrupt and extravagant government aroused much opposition, which was increased by the fermentation of liberal ideas produced by the French Revolution. In Pernambuco a revolt broke out in 1817 and was put down with difficulty after a republic had been formed that lasted for 90 days. After the departure of the French, Portugal had been governed by an arbitrary and tyrannical regency. A revolution in 1820 swept aside the regency, and the Cortes, which had not met for more than a century, was summoned to draw up a constitution.

The regency of Dom Pedro

The presence of John VI in Portugal was imperative if the revolutionary movement was to be kept in hand. On April 22, 1821, he appointed his son Dom Pedro regent, and two days later he set sail for Lisbon. Meanwhile, antagonisms between the Portuguese and Brazilians were becoming increasingly bitter, republican propaganda was active, and Dom Pedro had to face the responsibility of a separation of Brazil from Portugal as a result of the shortsighted policy of the Cortes at Lisbon. The majority of this assembly favoured the restoration of Brazil to its former status of colonial dependence. Without waiting for the Brazilian deputies, they proceeded to undo most of the reforms introduced into Brazil by John VI. Fearful that Dom Pedro might head a movement for independence, the Cortes ordered the prince to return to Europe.

Supported by the majority of Brazilians, Dom Pedro defied the Cortes by his refusal to return to Lisbon. In January 1822 he formed a ministry in which the chief portfolio was held by the distinguished Paulista, José Bonifácio de Andrada e Silva. On June 3 Dom Pedro convoked a legislative and constituent assembly. On September 7, on the plain of Ipiranga, near the city of São Paulo, he solemnly proclaimed the independence of Brazil, and on December 1, 1822, he was crowned the nation's emperor.

The strong Portuguese garrisons were forced to return to Europe. Before the end of 1823 independence had become an accomplished fact. The United States was first to recognize the new government, on May 26, 1824. Portuguese recognition was secured in 1825. The early resumption of formal relations with Portugal was due in large part to the influence and good offices of the British government.

The first years of independence

The Brazilian Empire (1822–89). The first years of independence were difficult. The nation was without experience in self-government, and the Emperor was inclined to be despotic and arbitrary. When the constituent assembly proved unmanageable, Pedro I dissolved it in 1823 and sent the radical Andrada e Silva and his two brothers into exile. Fortunately, however, he came to realize that the days of absolutism were past; a new and liberal constitution, drawn up by the Council of State, was submitted to the municipal councils of the provinces and sworn to by the Emperor on March 25, 1824. Pedro's remaining years saw a growing estrangement between the monarch and his subjects. Parliamentary government was little to his liking, and the opposition generally commanded a majority in the chamber of deputies. Brazil became involved in a disastrous war with Argentina resulting in the loss of the Provincia Cisplatina (the present republic of Uruguay). Finally, Pedro formally abdicated on April 7, 1831, in favour of the heir apparent, Dom Pedro de Alacântara, then only five years of age.

The regency (1831–40). The next decade proved the most agitated period in Brazilian history. From 1831 to 1835 a triple regency tried in vain to end civil war in the provinces and lawlessness and insubordination in the army. In 1834 the constitution was amended to grant a measure of decentralization to the provinces, through the creation of provincial assemblies with considerable local power, and to provide for a sole regent to be elected for four years. For this office in 1835 a priest, Diogo António Feijó, was chosen. For two years he struggled against disintegration, but he was forced to resign in 1837 and was succeeded by Pedro de Araújo Lima. As the end of the decade approached, sentiment began to crystallize in favour of a declaration of majority of the young Dom Pedro. The Brazilians, impatient with the regency, hoped to find in the Emperor a symbol to which the entire nation might rally. On July 23, 1840, both houses of parliament passed a declaration that Pedro de Alcântara had attained his majority.

Pedro II. The reign of Pedro II, lasting practically a half century, constitutes perhaps the most interesting and fruitful epoch in Brazilian history. The prestige and progress of the nation were due largely to the enlightened statesmanship of its ruler. Pedro cared little for the trappings of royalty. Though not without personal distinction he was always simple, modest, and democratic. He possessed an insatiable intellectual curiosity and was never more happy than when conversing with scholars. He was generous and magnanimous to a fault. One of his favourite occupations was inspecting schools. He was wont to declare, "If I were not emperor I should like to be a school teacher." Yet this kindly, genial, and scholarly ruler took his prerogatives and duties as sovereign with great seriousness, and in all matters of first importance he was the final arbiter. According to the moderative power granted to the executive under the constitution of 1824, the Emperor had the right to dissolve the Chamber of Deputies, to select the members of the life senate from triple lists submitted by the province, and to appoint and dismiss ministers of state. That parliamentary life in Brazil was pitched upon a high plane, that the highest officials in the state generally left office poorer than when they entered it, that the machinery of government functioned smoothly year after year was due in large measure to the vigilance of the Emperor.

Prestige and progress under Pedro II

Pedro's government maintained an active interest in the affairs of the Plata republics, especially of Uruguay, which it sought to control through indirect measures. Brazil aided in the overthrow of the Argentine dictator Juan Manuel de Rosas in 1852. In 1864 Brazil intervened in Uruguayan internal affairs and brought about war with Paraguay. In alliance with Argentina and Uruguay, Brazil successfully waged the costly and bloody Paraguayan War of 1864–70, eventually overthrowing the Paraguayan dictator Francisco Solano López. The empire's relations with the United States and with Europe were generally cordial. Pedro personally did much to cement these international friendships, visiting Europe in 1871, 1876, and 1888 and going to the United States in 1876.

Slavery

The empire's major social and economic problems were related to slave-based plantation agriculture. Real political power remained with large rural landholders, who formed the core of the social and economic elite of Brazil. Industrialization was still economically insignificant, and, with the decline of gold mining, agriculture was unrivalled as the source of Brazil's wealth. Cotton, and increasingly coffee, cultivated by slave labour, competed with sugar as the leading export crop. The rural landholders were largely insulated from the antislavery current of the times. Although manumission was common, and the number of freedmen and their descendants far surpassed the number of slaves in Brazil, the slave owners as a group resisted pressures for the complete abolition of slavery. Partly as a result of pressure from Great Britain, Brazil had agreed to abolish the slave trade in 1831, but it was not until 1853 that slave traffic completely ceased. Agitation to abolish slavery as such began in the 1860s. Pedro was opposed to slavery, but he had to reckon with the slave owners. In 1871 a bill for gradual emancipation was passed by Parliament. The importance of this act lay in the provision that, henceforth, all children born of slave mothers should be free. But this concession did not satisfy many of the abolitionists, who, led by a young lawyer and writer, Joaquim Nabuco de Araújo, demanded immediate and complete abolition. Nabuco's book *O Abolicionismo* (1883) endeavoured to prove that slavery was poisoning the very life of the nation. In 1884 Ceará and Amazonas freed their slaves; in 1885 all slaves over 60 years of age were liberated. Finally, complete emancipation without compensation to the owners was decreed by the Princess Regent in the absence of the Emperor on May 13, 1888. About 700,000 slaves were freed.

The collapse of the empire. Under Pedro II's wise guidance Brazil had made very real progress. His rule witnessed a growth in population from 4,000,000 to 14,000,000, a fourteenfold increase in public revenues, and a tenfold increase in the value of the products of the Empire. Railroad mileage in 1889 exceeded 5,000 miles (8,000 kilometres); that year more than 100,000 immigrants came to Brazil. Yet there were grave causes of dissatisfaction. Propaganda in favour of a republic, launched in 1871, had gained many recruits. The great landowners, who had lost their slaves without compensation, withdrew their support from the monarchy. The clergy had been antagonized by the punishment of several recalcitrant bishops. Isabel, the heiress to the throne, and her husband, the Conde d'Eu, were unpopular. Most serious, important elements in the army, which had become a political force after 1870, turned against the Emperor, largely because Pedro insisted that they stay out of politics. A conspiracy was hatched by these disgruntled military elements, and on November 15, 1889, a revolt of part of the army was the signal for the collapse of the empire. Pedro formally abdicated and, with his family, was banished to Europe.

BRAZIL SINCE 1889

Military autocracy

The early republican period. During the next 14 months Brazil was ruled by a military autocracy in which Marshal Deodoro da Fonseca, as chief of the provisional government, was virtually supreme. Decisions of great importance were reached. Church and state were separated, civil marriage was introduced, and a constituent assembly was summoned, which adopted in 1891 a constitution that was modelled closely on that of the United States.

The presidencies. As president, Deodoro da Fonseca employed the same dictatorial methods that he had followed as head of the provisional regime. On November 3, 1891, he forcibly dissolved Congress and proclaimed himself dictator. But opposition was so widespread that on November 23 he resigned in favour of the vice president, Marshal Floriano Peixoto. But Peixoto differed little in his methods from his predecessor. Of the meaning of constitutionalism in the strict sense, he had scant understanding. Growing opposition finally culminated in 1893 in a naval revolt and military uprising that lasted until the following year and were put down only with the greatest difficulty.

The advent of a civilian as president was hailed with undisguised relief. Prudente de Morais, who assumed office in 1894, was a distinguished lawyer of São Paulo and a republican of long standing. Though his intentions were excellent and his ability and honesty unquestioned, his ad-

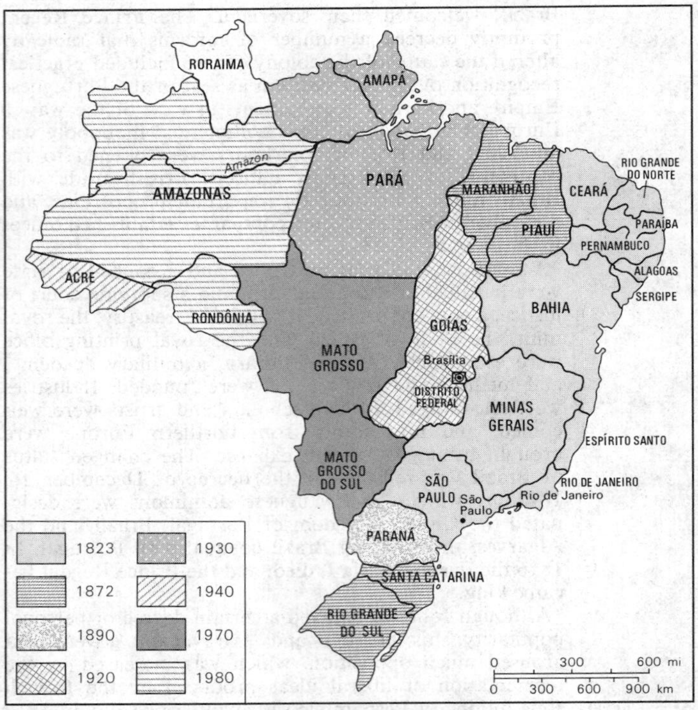

Growth of population in Brazil: dates by which the states had achieved a population density of more than two persons per square mile.

Adapted from A.C. Wilgus, *Latin America in Maps* (1943); Barnes and Noble, Inc.

ministration was rendered largely sterile through the opposition of the disgruntled military elements and the necessity of putting down a rebellion in the hinterland of Bahia. His successor, Manuel Ferraz de Campos Sales (served 1898–1902), former president of the State of São Paulo, is chiefly remembered for his striking success in saving Brazil from the financial collapse threatened by the orgy of extravagance, inflated currency, and speculation that had followed the overthrow of the monarchy. While still president-elect, Campos Sales in 1898 negotiated through the Rothschilds a funding loan of £10,000,000, interest on which was to be suspended for three years and amortization payments for 10. Because of the able and economical administration of Campos Sales and the marvelous recuperative power of the country, the credit and finances of Brazil were again placed on a sound foundation. Francisco de Paula Rodrigues Alves (served 1902–06), likewise a Paulista, is generally regarded as Brazil's ablest civilian president. During his term of office the capital was transformed into one of the world's most beautiful cities. Under the direction of the distinguished physician and scientist Oswaldo Cruz, Rio de Janeiro was completely freed from yellow fever. Some of Brazil's most thorny boundary controversies were settled during the presidencies of Campos Sales and Rodrigues Alves by the able minister of foreign affairs, José Maria da Silva Paranhos, barão do Rio Branco.

The development of Rio de Janeiro

Pres. Afonso Pena (served 1906–09) took an important step toward the stabilization of the exchange through the creation of the so-called Caixa de Conversão, or Bank of Conversion, whose function was to redeem inconvertible paper currency by the issue of convertible notes secured through the deposit of gold. This project had to be abandoned on the outbreak of World War I. Pena died in 1909 and was succeeded by the vice president, Nilo Peçanha. In the campaign of 1910 the official candidate, Marshal Hermes da Fonseca, nephew of Deodoro da Fonseca, was opposed by Rui Barbosa, a noted lawyer and publicist. Though the conviction was general that Barbosa had received a majority of the votes cast, the official machine easily secured the election of Hermes da Fonseca, during whose administration (1910–14) the high standards set by the first three civilian executives were largely abandoned.

World War I and its aftermath. A change for the better came with the election of Wenceslau Brás (served 1914–18), a former governor of Minas Gerais. His administration was closely associated with Brazil's reaction to and participation in World War I. The sympathies of most Brazilians inclined toward the Allies. On April 11, 1917, Brazil broke off relations with Germany following the torpedoing of the steamer "Paraná" off France. On June 1 Brazil revoked its decree of neutrality in the war as a mark of continental solidarity and friendship with the United States. On October 26, following the sinking of more Brazilian ships, Brazil declared war on Germany. Brazil's participation in the war was confined to the dispatch of a part of its fleet to European waters and the sending of a medical mission and a number of aviators to the Western Front. Its chief contribution was the placing of its food supplies and other resources unreservedly at the disposal of the Allies. Brazil participated in the peace conference and was given a temporary seat on the Council of the League of Nations.

Postwar boom and bust

In the election of 1918 a precedent was established by the re-election of Rodrigues Alves. He was too ill to accept office, however, and died on January 18, 1919. In April, Epitácio Pessoa, a lawyer of note and head of the Brazilian delegation at the Versailles conference, was elected. His presidency, coinciding with a wave of postwar prosperity, was an era of reckless expenditure accompanied by an immense increase in both the internal and foreign debt. Large sums were absorbed by the Brazilian centenary exposition, which was celebrated in 1922. The presidency of Artur Bernardes (served 1922–26) was beset with difficulties. The collapse of the boom found Brazil in financial extremities, and the new executive endeavoured to carry out a policy of strict economy: governmental expenses were cut down, costly public works were postponed, and new sources of revenue, such as the income tax, were created. The success of this program of retrenchment and reform was compromised by a dangerous flareup of militarism. In the closing weeks of Pessoa's administration a military group made a desperate but fruitless attempt to prevent Bernardes' inauguration. Another revolt was launched in July 1924 at São Paulo city. This, too, was suppressed, but only after heavy loss of life and much property damage. In 1926 Washington Luís, minister of justice in the two preceding administrations, was elected president without a contest.

The shift from empire to republic produced little immediate change in Brazil's basic political or social institutions. Under the constitution of 1891, state and municipal governments were granted somewhat greater freedom from central control, with a consequent increase in the power of local bosses. But no significant new elements were added to the political spectrum, and the bulk of the population remained outside the political process. Rural landholders, particularly in the States of São Paulo and Minas Gerais, adjusted to the loss of slave labour and retained their pre-eminence. In São Paulo massive immigration from the Mediterranean area before World War I provided a new source of rural labour for the expanding coffee industry. By the late 19th century, coffee had become the outstanding export crop and source of government revenue. Diversification of agriculture and the expansion and diversification of the mining industry provided economic stimulus in Minas Gerais. The old areas of Bahia and Pernambuco gradually declined in political significance and were eventually replaced by the increasingly important state of Rio Grande do Sul, but the latter did not challenge the political hegemony of the central states until 1930. Thus, economic and political power was concentrated in São Paulo and Minas Gerais during the first four decades of the republic, and national policies usually reflected the interests of those states.

Political role of the military

The principal new factor was the political role of the military. After 1889 the armed forces asserted their claim as guarantors of the constitutional process and served usually as a check upon the civilian administrations. The military also provided the leadership of occasional protest movements. The first stirrings of social unrest and vaguely expressed demands for a modification of the institutional patterns of the republic were voiced by young military officers, the *tenentes*, in the mid-1920s; the movement they headed culminated in the revolution of 1930, which marked the end of the so-called old republic and the beginning of a new era.

The Vargas era. When the administration-sponsored presidential candidate was officially declared winner in the 1930 election, a revolt broke out. This successful rebellion was led by Getúlio Vargas, governor of the state of Rio Grande do Sul, who was to remain central in Brazilian national life until his suicide in 1954.

Vargas held office as chief executive on two occasions, 1930–45 and 1951–54. Early in the first of these periods, the country's difficulties were essentially economic, accentuated by a policy of subsidizing coffee production, and the tremendous powers of the states served as steady irritants to the country. In 1934 a new constitution gave the central government greater powers. Three years later, President Vargas suddenly seized practically absolute power and set up still another constitution, under which he continued as president. The new administration, known as the Estado Nôvo (New State), so concentrated power in Vargas' hands that he was able to suppress all manifestations of popular will. Vargas stripped Brazil of most of the trappings through which it might eventually hope to become a democracy. On the other hand, considerable social legislation was enacted, with positive benefits to the labouring man.

Vargas' policy concentrated upon curtailment of states' rights, emphasis on nationalism, and the transfer of the locus of power from the country to the city. The states were increasingly subordinated to the central government, politically, economically, and socially. The ruinous coffee policies of the past were discarded, manufacturing was advanced, and the diversification of agriculture was encouraged.

After the outbreak of World War II in 1939, Vargas' government supported inter-American solidarity; on August 22, 1942, it declared war against Germany and Italy. Besides participating in the defense of the South Atlantic against Axis submarines, Brazil sent an expeditionary force to Italy in July 1944 that distinguished itself in several battles. Brazil also allowed the United States to use certain Brazilian naval and air bases during the war. A number of agreements were signed between the two governments for the economic development and production of Brazilian raw materials.

Return to representative government. On October 29, 1945, Vargas was overthrown in a bloodless revolution. When it appeared that the President intended to continue indefinitely in power, a group of high army officers forced him to resign, transferring the government to Chief Justice José Linhares on an interim basis.

Overthrow of Vargas

Dutra and Vargas. On December 2, 1945, Gen. Eurico Gaspar Dutra, the former war minister and a loyal friend of Vargas, was elected to a five-year term as president. In September 1946 a constituent assembly at Rio de Janeiro adopted a new constitution, which confirmed and strengthened the civil and personal liberties and the multiparty system of representative democracy that had taken effect after the overthrow of Vargas. As was customary in Brazilian constitutions, it recognized the armed forces as permanent national institutions and the guarantors of constitutional powers.

Dutra showed a sincere determination to govern the country in harmony with the measures of the new constitution. He outlawed the Communist Party as an undemocratic, foreign-based organization in May 1947 but did not otherwise interfere with the free play of political expression or political party activities. Major accomplishments of the Dutra administration included the Paulo Afonso Dam on the São Francisco River, to provide electric power to northeastern Brazil, and the opening of an all-weather highway linking that region with the industrial zones of Minas Gerais and São Paulo.

The general elections of 1950 resulted in a substantial victory for Vargas. While he failed to secure a clear majority in the four-way race, he polled 1,500,000 more votes than the runner-up and nearly as many as the combined total for the three rival candidates. Accordingly, despite serious reservations by the military leaders who had deposed him in 1945, he was installed in the presidency once more on January 31, 1951. During his second period in power, Vargas was unable to dominate the political forces of the country or to exploit social and economic trends to his advantage; he endeavoured to abide by the constitution of 1946 and was criticized in some quarters for weak leadership. Lacking a firm majority in the Congress, he could neither enact his own program nor resist the contradictory pressures of his supporters and opponents. The most serious continuing problem was economic. Brazilians were agreed upon the need for more rapid industrial development and measures to ameliorate the effects of gradual monetary inflation, which persisted as government expenditures consistently outran revenues. Vargas maintained a precarious balance between the advocates of greater state intervention in the economy and those who insisted upon a favourable climate for domestic and foreign private investment. The situation was complicated by the simultaneous emotional, antiforeign campaign to nationalize the natural resources of the country. The campaign culminated in the creation of the national petroleum corporation, Petrobrás, in 1953.

For three years Vargas' popularity largely protected him from attack by political adversaries, who directed their criticism against members of his administration. João Goulart, Vargas' young protégé and vice president of the Brazilian Labour Party (PTB), who became minister of labour in 1953, was accused of using his office to transform organized labour into a political machine loyal to Vargas. His sponsorship of a decree doubling the minimum wage, thus strengthening labour–administration ties and contributing to the inflationary spiral, led to his dismissal in 1954. A series of crises followed, climaxed on August 5, 1954, by the murder of an air force officer and the attempted assassination of opposition newspaper editor Carlos Lacerda. Investigation revealed that the assassins had been hired by the President's personal guard. The exposure of widespread corruption within the administration caused a wave of revulsion against the former dictator. A group of army officers presented Vargas with a demand for his resignation; Vargas complied on August 24, 1954, and later that day committed suicide.

Vargas' suicide

Kubitschek's administration. Vice president João Café Filho served out the remainder of Vargas' term. His Cabinet included military leaders who had been instrumental in removing Vargas and civilian moderates who generally favoured political democracy, limited social change, and an orthodox approach to economic ills. Marshal Teixeira Lott, a highly respected professional soldier not identified with any political group, was made war minister. Much of the Café Filho administration was occupied by preparations for the presidential election of October 3, 1955. After the failure of attempts to find a single candidate around whom all major political parties might rally, three strong candidates for the presidency emerged: former Minas Gerais state governor Juscelino Kubitschek de Oliveira, popularly regarded as Vargas' political heir; former São Paulo state governor Ademar de Barros, with broad backing from financial and commercial groups; and Marshal Juárez Távora, considered as the representative of conservative military and civilian groups. In the 1955 election Kubitschek was the victor with slightly more than one third of the total vote, Távora ran a close second, and Barros was a somewhat more distant third; in the separate vice-presidential election, João Goulart won with a large plurality. The election was widely interpreted as a popular vindication of the Vargas position. The illegal but active Communist Party, which had thrown its unsolicited support to Kubitschek, claimed to have provided his margin of victory. Rumours of a Café Filho administration plot to use unconstitutional means to prevent the inauguration of Kubitschek and Goulart were not proved, but the conservative press—which regarded Kubitschek as a dangerous radical—added to the tension. President Café Filho suffered a mild heart attack and on November 8, 1955, transferred power temporarily to his constitutional successor, Carlos Luz, speaker of the Chamber of Deputies. The following day Luz indicated that he would dismiss Marshal Lott to resolve a conflict of authority between the executive and the war minister. This was interpreted by Kubitschek's backers as the signal for a coup d'etat by anti-Kubitschek forces. On November 11, 1955, War Minister Lott and Marshal Odílio Denys, commander of army troops in Rio de Janeiro, staged a "countercoup" to guarantee Kubitschek's inauguration. Luz was deposed, his constitutional successor, Sen. Nereu de Oliveira Ramos, was installed as interim president under a state of siege, and Lott remained as war minister and the strongest figure in the government. Kubitschek and Goulart took office as scheduled and without incident on January 31, 1956.

Spread of nationalism

During his term of office Kubitschek encouraged the widespread spirit of nationalism, appealing to the popular demand for economic development and to the belief that Brazil was destined to become a great power among the nations of the world. Kubitschek felt that the national government should play a vital role in economic areas unattractive to private capital; thus, his administration undertook ambitious developmental programs for the construction of interregional highways and vast hydroelectric power projects, the expansion of iron, steel, petroleum, and coal production, and assistance to the rapidly growing private industrial sector. Perhaps his outstanding accomplishment was the construction of Brasília on an inland plateau 580 miles (930 kilometres) northwest of Rio de Janeiro. Although not yet completed, Brasília was dedicated as the official capital of Brazil on April 21, 1960. The purpose of Brasília was to focus the attention of Brazilians on the interior of the country and to hasten settlement of the region and the development of its largely untapped resources. The new capital was denounced by residents of Rio de Janeiro, but Brazilians elsewhere generally regarded it as a symbol of the nation's future greatness. In inter-American relations, the Kubitschek administration proposed the adoption of Operation Pan America, a cooperative program for the economic development of Latin America, which foreshadowed the Alliance for Progress.

The great material progress during the Kubitschek period was achieved at a high cost in terms of inflation and repeated foreign borrowing. The cost of living and the volume of currency in circulation tripled between 1956 and 1961, while Brazil's large foreign debt nearly doubled. The gross national product rose to unprecedented levels, but living standards for much of the population remained stationary or actually declined. At the same time, indications of large-scale graft and favouritism in public office disturbed even the normally tolerant Brazilian electorate.

Quadros and Goulart. This situation was debated in the electoral campaign of 1960. Again there were three candidates for the presidency: Marshal Teixeira Lott who had served as Kubitschek's war minister for more than four years; Jânio Quadros, the unorthodox former governor of São Paulo and at that time congressman from the State of Paraná; and Adhemar de Barros, then mayor of the city of São Paulo. It was soon clearly a race between Lott and Quadros. Lott received official backing and campaigned on the Kubitschek record. Quadros, who was not a regular member of any political party was supported by the largest conservative party, the National Democratic Union (UDN), and a heterogeneous grouping of lesser political factions. With a new broom as his symbol, Quadros caught the public's imagination as the candidate of the common man. He promised a scrupulously honest administration, curbs on inflation, effective economic development, dignity for the individual, and an aggressively "independent" foreign policy. Goulart was once more a candidate for the vice-presidency. At the polls on October 3, 1960, Quadros won election with a plurality of 48 percent of the popular vote. He received more than 5,600,000 votes, the largest number ever cast for a presidential candidate in Brazil.

Goulart, a political enemy of Quadros, won a narrow victory in the vice presidential race, polling slightly more than 4,000,000 votes. Quadros and Goulart were inaugurated on January 31, 1961.

Control by anti-Vargas groups

The election of Quadros was hailed as a revolution by ballot. For the first time in three decades, anti-Vargas political groups controlled the presidency. Quadros took office in an atmosphere of popular expectation, but almost immediately he encountered resistance from the Congress, where parties loyal to the Vargas tradition still commanded a large majority. Quadros' arbitrary and autocratic manner, which soon alienated many of his former adherents, further reduced the possibility of enacting a meaningful reform program or effective measures to retard inflation. In foreign affairs Quadros was more successful; his foreign policy, which was applauded by ultranationalists and deplored by moderates, seemed designed to move Brazil toward neutralist nations and away from the traditional ties with the United States. He opposed any inter-American action to censure the Castro regime in Cuba and initiated proceedings to resume or establish diplomatic and commercial relations with the Soviet Union and its European satellites. On August 25, 1961, after less than seven months in office, Quadros resigned unexpectedly, alleging that "terrible forces" had deterred him. The congress promptly installed Pascoal Ranieri Mazzilli, speaker of the Chamber of Deputies, as temporary president. Vice president João Goulart, the constitutional successor, was then en route home from a state visit to China.

Succession crisis

Brazil stood at the brink of civil war. Many military commanders and conservatives regarded Goulart as too radical to be entrusted with the nation's highest office, while the great majority of civilian political leaders upheld his constitutional right to the presidency. War Minister Odílio Denys now emerged as the chief spokesman of the anti-Goulart forces, demanding that the Congress declare the office of vice president vacant and hold new elections. The Congress refused. In southern Brazil the commanders of the powerful army and air force units defied orders from the capital and sided with Goulart. Goulart arrived in Pôrto Alegre, insisting that he was already president of Brazil. Faced with the imminent prospect of armed conflict, the Congress and the anti-Goulart group in the military agreed upon a compromise solution: that Goulart be allowed to take office, but only as a figurehead. On September 2, 1961, the parliamentary system of government was adopted by constitutional amendment; most presidential powers were transferred to the newly created post of prime minister. Provision was made for a national plebiscite on the parliamentary experiment before the end of the presidential term. Goulart accepted these conditions and was formally confirmed as president on September 7, 1961.

Once the immediate crisis of the presidential succession was settled, the political parties resumed debate on pressing national issues but postponed significant legislation pending the outcome of congressional elections in October 1962. When these failed to indicate a clear mandate for or against the administration's reform proposals, the opponents of parliamentarianism, led by Goulart, demanded a quick return to presidential rule. On January 6, 1963, a national plebiscite by a margin of more than five to one gave Goulart full presidential powers. Goulart was unable to secure majority support for his legislative program, however, and repeated Cabinet changes and new plans for economic and social development did nothing to restrict inflation and soaring living costs, which reached alarming proportions under Goulart. During the two and one-half years of his administration, there was a tenfold drop in the dollar value of the currency, the cost of living tripled, and the growth of the gross national product, which had been rising by 6 to 7 percent yearly, was brought to a complete halt.

Military intervention. As the situation grew more desperate, cooperation between the regime and its critics became more difficult. The administration identified itself increasingly with the ultranationalistic left, while most of the military officer corps sympathized with the moderate and conservative opposition. Goulart surrounded himself with left-wing advisers. He sought to neutralize the armed forces by frequent command changes and by developing a personal following among noncommissioned officers and enlisted personnel. After failing to obtain authorization for a state of siege, which would have enhanced his powers, Goulart appealed directly to the people for support. At a mass rally in Rio de Janeiro in March 1964, he instituted a controversial agrarian reform and nationalized certain privately owned oil refineries. Many military officers and opposition political leaders had already become convinced that Goulart was seeking to establish a dictatorship of the left. During 1963 active plotting began among separate civilian and military groups in different parts of the country. Gov. José de Magalhães Pinto of Minas Gerais state and Marshal Humberto de Alencar Castelo Branco, chief of staff of the army, emerged as the chief coordinators of the conspiracy. An attempt was made to find a formula to prevent a coup d'etat by the President and still permit him to complete his term in office. At the same time, plans were made to overthrow the regime if necessary. The administration's refusal to suppress a strike by naval enlisted men in late March 1964 was regarded by the opposition as intolerable, for military authority and discipline were considered the last check on Goulart's alleged ambitions. On March 31, 1964, Magalhães Pinto proclaimed a revolution against the government by the civil and military forces in Minas Gerais; the following day he was joined by the political leaders of the States of São Paulo and Guanabara and by the armed forces throughout most of Brazil. On April 2 Goulart fled into exile and two days later he reached Uruguay. The Congress declared his office vacant and designated Mazzilli as interim president until a successor could be chosen to serve out the remainder of term.

Opposition to Goulart

Castelo Branco's administration. With the fall of Goulart, real power passed to the leaders of the revolution, who instituted sweeping political changes. The revolutionary commanders set out to restore economic and financial order, to eliminate what the generals claimed was "Communist infiltration," and to purge corrupt and subversive elements. At the same time they desired to retain a modified form of representative government. On April 9, 1964, these goals were combined in the First Institutional Act, a modification of the 1946 constitution. The executive was granted temporary authority to cancel the mandates of elected officials, to dismiss public servants, and to revoke for ten years the political rights of those found guilty of subversion or misuse of public funds.

The First Institutional Act

During the six months these provisions were in effect, thousands were arrested, and hundreds of persons—including union and government officials and former presidents Goulart, Quadros, and Kubitschek—were deprived of political rights. The Congress was retained as a legislative body with power to debate and amend but not reject proposals submitted to it by the executive. On April 11, 1964, Castelo Branco was elected president by the Congress. José Maria Alkmin, finance minister under Kubitschek, was chosen as vice president. On July 22 the Congress extended the terms of Castelo Branco and Alkmin to March 15, 1967.

Castelo Branco's extended term was regarded by the revolutionaries as a transition period during which sweeping political and economic reforms should be enacted before the nation could again be entrusted to a popularly elected government. It was generally agreed by the new leaders that such alleged shortcomings of the political process as the multiplicity of small, regional, and personalist parties, opportunistic electoral coalitions, and the separate election of president and vice president must be corrected, but they were divided over the best means to attain these ends. The President's determination to achieve reform by legislation, while permitting normal political activities and full freedom of expression by critics of the regime, was challenged by civilian and military extremists who called for dissolution of Congress, abolition of political parties, and suspension of all partisan activities until the revolutionary regime had enough time to consolidate its power.

The test came in October 1965, when gubernatorial elections were held in 11 states and opposition candidates were elected by substantial majorities in the key states of Minas Gerais and Guanabara. The extremists interpreted the results as a great setback for the revolutionary government. Accusing Castelo Branco of not pressing the revolutionary reform program with enough vigour, they blamed him for the defeat of their candidates and demanded that he annul the two elections. When he refused to comply with their demands, they plotted a coup d'etat. At this point, Marshal Artur da Costa e Silva, the minister of war, intervened and persuaded the dissident leaders to keep the peace in return for Castelo Branco's promise to take stronger measures to enact the revolution's reform program.

Emergency measures

On October 27, 1965, Castelo Branco signed the Second Institutional Act, which suspended all existing political parties, restored the president's emergency powers for the remainder of his term, and set October 3, 1966, as the date for new presidential elections. An artificial two-party system was imposed upon the country. The new political parties were the Aliança Renovadora Nacional (or National Renewal Alliance, called Arena), sponsored by the government, and an opposition party, the Movimento Democrático Brasileiro (or Brazilian Democratic Movement; MDB). A third party was theoretically possible, but as a practical matter all active political factions were required to function within those two parties. Arena soon attracted a heterogeneous grouping of pro-administration elements, while the MDB came to be composed largely of former followers of Goulart and of politicians who had broken with the revolutionary regime. Neither party enjoyed strong grass-roots support. Because the president was elected by the Arena-dominated Congress, the MDB refused to nominate candidates. The administration candidates, Costa e Silva and Pedro Aleixo, the minister of education, were elected.

Castelo Branco in December 1966 called an extraordinary session of Congress to approve a new constitution drafted by a government-appointed commission. The new document, promulgated on January 24, 1967, incorporated much of the revolutionary reform program and confirmed the expansion of the power of the executive and of the central government. Important changes included the indirect election of the president and vice president from a single ticket; reduction of the presidential term from five to four years; the use of military courts to judge civilians charged with violation of national security laws; the granting of authority to the president to issue emergency decrees without consulting Congress; and denial to the Congress of the right to delay action on legislation requested by the executive.

Constitution of 1967

The Castelo Branco administration engaged in unprecedented economic planning in order to contain inflation and to revive the flagging economy. It employed emergency powers to limit and regulate sources of credit, to restructure the tax system and collection procedures, and to impose wage and salary controls. These measures affected all sectors of society but bore most heavily on urban labour and white-collar workers, whose real income was held below the rising cost of living. The adverse effects were partially offset by tax incentives to encourage increased industrial and agricultural productivity. At the same time the government poured substantial investments into electric power and transportation to provide for continued orderly economic development. Although the administration did not achieve all of its goals, Brazil's credit rating abroad was firmly re-established, the annual rise in living costs fell from 86 percent in 1964 to 41 percent in 1966, and the increase in the gross national product rose significantly. With the exception of labour, every major sector of the Brazilian economy was on the upswing when Castelo Branco left office.

Administrations of Costa e Silva, Médici, and Geisel. Costa e Silva promised to humanize the revolution, and it was widely expected that he would soon relax the more severe political and economic policies. Yet he did not depart markedly from the course set by his predecessor. His administration rejected petitions for a general amnesty, resisted all proposals to amend the new constitution to restore direct elections, quashed attempts to form a second opposition party, and forcefully suppressed student disturbances. More serious political opposition, however, was muted in part by the government's achievements in the economic field.

Growing opposition

The political situation deteriorated rapidly late in 1968. Faced with a resurgence of public and congressional criticism, Costa e Silva, under strong pressure from the armed forces, seized emergency powers. The Fifth Institutional Act issued on December 13 suspended all legislative bodies indefinitely, authorized the executive to rule by decree, and provided the legal basis for a new purge of outstanding political critics.

When in August 1969 Costa e Silva suffered a paralytic stroke, the government was taken over by the three armed forces ministers, who held power till October when the government selected Gen. Emílio Garrastazú Médici as the new president. Elections for federal and state senators and deputies and municipal officials in November 1970 showed a clear victory for Médici and the Arena party. Disturbances continued, however, through 1970 and 1971, kidnapping of foreign consular and diplomatic officials being added to the arsenal of the dissidents.

Médici in 1971 presented the First National Development Plan, which was aimed at 8 to 10 percent annual economic growth and per capita income of at least $500 (U.S.) per year (in 1972 it was estimated to be $400). Development of the Northeast and the Amazon area, especially by means of a program of road construction and one of redistribution of land, was also planned.

In August 1973 a bill creating the electoral college that from 1974 onward would elect the president and vice president became law. In September the national convention of the Arena party selected as its candidates for president and vice president, respectively, Gen. Ernesto Geisel, a chief executive of the government-owned petroleum company, Petrobrás, and Gen. Adalberto Pereira dos Santos. They were duly elected by the electoral college on January 15, 1974.

The 10th anniversary of the revolution was celebrated by lifting the prohibition on political activities of 106 leaders of the former regime, among them Kubitschek, Quadros, and Goulart. The Fifth Institutional Act, however, remained in force. A surprising victory for the MDB in the congressional elections in November 1974, in which the opposition gained 20 seats in the Senate, was not repeated in the municipal elections of November 1976.

In April 1977 President Geisel dismissed Congress when it failed to pass judicial reforms that he had requested. Under the emergency powers of the Fifth Institutional Act, Geisel then issued decrees instituting those reforms and other electoral and constitutional changes. Among these were provisions for the indirect election of state governors and one-third of the federal senators and the increase of the presidential term to six years. The number of members of the Chamber of Deputies was to be based on the total population of the states instead of on the number of registered voters, and constitutional amendment could be effected by an absolute majority of Congress rather than the two-thirds vote of two successive sessions formerly required.

Brazil's phenomenal rate of economic growth in these years—the gross national product of 1973 was nearly double that of 1964—was halted by the petroleum crisis of 1973–74. Because the country imported 70 to 80 percent of its oil, the trade deficit had risen to $6,000,000,000 by the end of 1976 and inflation had reached an annual rate of 45 percent. A stringent program to reduce government spending and imports and to increase exports was introduced in 1977.

Social and political changes after 1945. In certain respects, the phase of Brazilian political history that began with the overthrow of the Estado Novo and the election of a president and Congress responsible to the electorate ended with the revolution of 1964. The latter event dispelled any lingering doubts that the armed forces were the strongest political organization in Brazil. The ease with which military leaders assumed and retained power clearly revealed the failure of the postwar political parties to develop into cohesive national bodies capable of winning the respect and allegiance of the voting public and of resolving the critical problems of economic development and social justice. Charges made by the right-wing opposition of the ineffectiveness of populist civilian administrations in the early 1960s paved the way for the retreat after 1964 to paternalistic rule by a narrow elite.

Yet, in a deeper sense, fundamental economic and social trends encouraged by the Vargas regime after 1930 were only slightly modified by the representative governments after 1945 or by the revolutionary governments after 1964. The fact that the political forces that had just regained freedom of expression in 1945 were unanimously agreed upon the need for a new national charter dramatically illustrated their awareness that a return to the pre-1930 status quo was impossible. While the constitution of 1946 borrowed heavily from that of 1891 in certain exterior forms, a comparison of the two charters reveals the nature and extent of the socio-economic transformation that Brazil experienced after 1930. The constitution of 1891, despite its positivist trappings, was essentially a 19th-century liberal document that stressed the rights of the individual and of state governments as opposed to the national administration. The constitution of 1946 largely reaffirmed Vargas' concentration of power in the central government and acknowledged the federal responsibility for maintaining and fostering economic development and social welfare programs. These trends were accelerated under the military rulers in the new national charter of 1967.

Rural and urban developments. The changes that began in 1930 reflect basic socio-economic developments, such as population growth and an increase in urbanization and in participation in the political process, which gave new dimensions and added complexity to Brazilian politics. In 1930 Brazil had a population of about 33,500,000, of whom at least three-fourths were rural and illiterate, hence could not vote. By 1945 the population had risen to about 46,000,000; two-thirds of these were rural and largely outside the political arena. In 1964 the population surpassed 80,000,000 and was divided equally between rural and urban inhabitants; the proportion of literates was also about 50 percent, but at least half of these were under voting age. By the time of the election of 1974, the population had reached almost 105,000,000, of which 56 percent was urban. Attendance at the polls rose to 80 percent of the total of 36,000,000 registered voters. It appeared certain that the bulk of the voters enfranchised after 1930 belonged to the urban working class and government bureaucracy.

Urban proletariat

With the formation of government-directed trade unions in the 1930s, a politically conscious urban proletariat developed. This did not, however, signify the emergence of a true labour-based political movement or an authentic labour party. Leadership of this new political force was contested by the traditional elite, principally landowners and large merchants, and by a new middle class composed of industrial, commercial, and professional persons who had gained elite status. The governments after 1964 continued to control labour organizations in an effort to gain labour support while discouraging the formation of a potentially dissident labour movement.

Before 1966 the new middle class, which had not yet acquired a strong enough sense of class consciousness to regard itself as a distinct social element, did not seek a unified political expression. Rather, it vied with the traditional ruling groups for control of existing political organizations. Members of both groups were found in the leadership of virtually every party for two decades after 1945, although urban-oriented parties grew consistently at the expense of more traditional, rural-based parties. By and large the middle class endorsed the revolution of 1964, but many of its political spokesmen later broke with the revolutionary regime, and middle class political leaders were found in each of the new political parties created in 1965.

Extension of the franchise to illiterates would greatly enlarge the size of the electorate and increase the influence of the lower class on Brazilian politics. It would also enhance the political power of rural society at the expense of the city dwellers. But even though about 59 percent of the rural population was still unable to read and write in the early 1970s and was therefore still denied the vote, the political consciousness of the peasantry had been awakened. Through illegal peasant leagues, founded in the late 1950s, and legitimate rural unions, which were authorized in 1962, many peasants were able for the first time to make their needs known to the political leaders. Before the revolution of 1964, the Communists, a few clergymen, and members of nearly all legal parties were competing for the allegiance of the rural masses, appealing to their demands for social justice and higher standards of living. Although most peasant organizations were abolished and many agitators were jailed or exiled after 1964, limited measures were enacted by the federal government to assuage rural unrest. The peasantry remains potentially the most powerful political force in Brazil.

Rural political power

The church. After 1964 the Roman Catholic Church in Brazil, as one of the few effective institutions organized nationwide, was drawn into the partial political vacuum caused by the purge of populist civilian leaders and the abolition of established political parties. Several bishops led the secular and regular clergy in denouncing the government's apparent indifference to the vast inequities in Brazilian society. Clerics also served as champions of the right of dissent, and by the late 1960s the church had become a rallying point for political opposition.

Influence of the armed forces

The armed forces. The armed forces, final arbiters of the political process in Brazil, were neither blind nor indifferent to the objectives of the new groups that entered the political scene after 1945. The traditional alliance of the military forces and conservative rural landholders had long since been replaced by an informal similarity of views between military officers and urban middle class sectors. The armed services consistently defended centralized government, rapid industrialization, and the development of an efficient, organized labour force. They were quick, however, to resent the exploitation of organized labour by political leftists as a counterweight to the political influence of the military officers. Between 1945 and 1964 no single political party was able to elect a president or a majority in Congress. Because this situation encouraged political irresponsibility, the armed forces, always at the behest of civilian political elements, intervened on four occasions to protect national institutions against what they considered to be civilian incompetence. Beginning in 1964, military leaders initiated a major revision of the political system, which, in their view, would make it impossible for men who placed partisan before national interest to come to power.

BIBLIOGRAPHY. E. BRADFORD BURNS (ed.), *A Documentary History of Brazil* (1966), excerpts from historical documents from between 1595 and 1964, translated into English—an indispensable work because of the original information it gives; JOSE HONORIO RODRIGUES, *Aspirações Nacionais,* 4th rev. ed. (1970; Eng. trans., *The Brazilians: Their Character and Aspirations,* 1967), a synthesis and interpretation of principal facets of the Brazilian character and of the objectives of the nation; CAIO PRADO, JR., *Formação do Brasil Contemporâneo,* 7th ed. (1963; Eng. trans., *The Colonial Background of Modern Brazil,* 1967), a masterpiece of interpretation of the colonial period; ALAN K. MANCHESTER, *British Preëminence in Brazil, Its Rise and Decline* (1933; reprinted 1964), a study of relations between Great Britain and Brazil, with emphasis on the British influence in Brazil; C.H. HARING, *Empire in Brazil: A New World Experiment with Monarchy* (1958; reprinted 1968), a good introductory book to the imperial period in Brazilian history; JOSE MARIA BELLO, *História da República,* 5th ed. (1964; Eng. trans., *A History of Modern Brazil, 1889–1964,* with a new concluding chapter by ROLLIE E. POPPINO, 1966), a basic work in English dealing with the history of republican Brazil; HENRY W. SPIEGEL, *The Brazilian Economy: Chronic Inflation and Sporadic Industrialization* (1949), an analysis of Brazil's economic problems, with emphasis on the contradictions that plague its structure; THOMAS E. SKIDMORE, *Politics in Brazil, 1930–1964* (1967), the best available study of Brazilian politics for this period.

Brecht, Bertolt

Twentieth-century German poet, playwright, and theatrical reformer, Bertolt Brecht expressed in his work the moral and political dilemmas of a mass society in which man is isolated and helpless. In turn influenced by the symbolist poetry of Paul Verlaine and Arthur Rimbaud, the expressionism of playwrights such as August Strindberg and Frank Wedekind, and the terminology of Marxism, in the end he arrived, like most great writers, at a language that was his alone: simple, precise, and blunt—a language that made him one of the masters of modern German.

Ullstein Bilderdienst

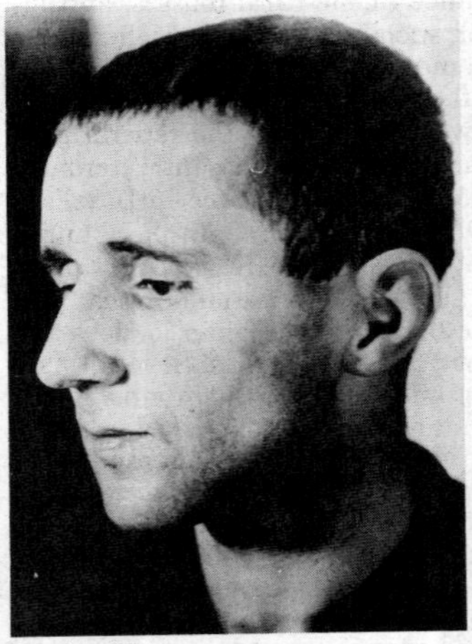

Brecht, 1931.

Eugen Berthold Friedrich Brecht (who later changed his name to Bertolt) was born on Feb. 10, 1898, at Augsburg, Bavaria, where his father was managing director of a paper mill. Both sides of his family were of peasant stock; his father was a Roman Catholic, his mother a Lutheran. Brecht himself was raised as a Lutheran and always acknowledged the influence of Luther's earthy and direct Bible translation on his own writing style.

After graduating from secondary school in Augsburg, Brecht entered the University of Munich in the fall of 1917 as a medical student. But from the first he showed a greater interest in literature and drama; he had already published poems in an Augsburg newspaper. When he was called for military service in the last year of World War I, the fact that he had studied medicine kept him from being sent to the front; he was inducted into the medical corps and through his father's influence was assigned to the military hospital of his home town. Although in later life he tended to exaggerate the horrors which he had witnessed in the military hospital (he had worked in the venereal disease clinic), there can be no doubt that his experiences in the military service made him a lifelong pacifist and determined his later political outlook.

Early career. In his early years Brecht was the centre of a circle of devoted followers, among them the painter and designer Caspar Neher, who was to remain Brecht's close collaborator to the end of his life. Brecht wrote, composed, and sang his songs and ballads to these friends, and he read them his early plays. In 1918 he completed his first play, *Baal*, a wild and powerful effusion on the life of a young poet, so drunk with life that he abandons all social convention and becomes a vagabond and murderer.

After the collapse of the Kaiser's Germany, Brecht returned to Munich, but devoted less and less time to his university studies, and more and more to the theatre; for a time he acted as drama critic for the left-wing Augsburg newspaper *Der Volkswille*. In 1919 Brecht submitted his second play, *Spartakus* (later renamed *Drums in the Night*) to Lion Feuchtwanger, then the literary adviser of one of the Munich theatres, the Kammerspiele, and later famous as a novelist. Feuchtwanger, who was also to become a lifelong friend of Brecht's, instantly recognized the great merits of the play, which, when it was performed on Sept. 29, 1922, brought the young playwright immediate recognition and the award of the coveted Kleist-Preis, a literary prize for the most promising young dramatist of the year. Having achieved his first decisive success Brecht, in November of that year, married the actress Marianne Zoff.

Pre-Marxist phase

Drums in the Night, a play about a German soldier who returns from World War I, finds his fiancée pregnant by another man but nevertheless elects a comfortable life by her side rather than joining the communist revolutionary uprising of the Spartakists in January 1919, was followed first by the equally cynical and disillusioned *In the Jungle of the Cities* (first performed at Munich in March 1923) and then by Brecht's own production of his adaptation—in collaboration with Feuchtwanger—of Christopher Marlowe's *Life of Edward II* at the Munich Kammerspiele in 1924. In 1924 Brecht moved to Berlin, Germany's political and theatrical capital. There he worked for a time as a dramaturg (a play reader and editorial assistant) in Max Reinhardt's Deutsches Theatre and again became the centre of a circle of left-wing artists and intellectuals. In 1928—having been granted a divorce from his first wife—he married the actress Helene Weigel.

The main impulse of Brecht's art is a violently antibourgeois attitude that reflects his generation's deep disappointment in the civilization that had come crashing down at the end of World War I. Among Brecht's friends were members of the Dadaist group that aimed at destroying what they condemned as the false standards of bourgeois art through derision and iconoclastic satire. Brecht's own antibourgeois attitude took the form of a cynical anarchism that found its most perfect expression in the poems of *Hauspostille* ("Domestic Breviary"; translated by Eric Bentley under the title *Manual of Piety*) which appeared in 1927; these are the poems of a young man who feels threatened by the irrational violence of nature, sex, aggression, and death, and yearns for a cynical detachment from these primordial forces. It was first through his discovery of Marxism and second through his commitment to the political discipline of a cause that promised a solution to the ills of mankind as based on an assertedly scientific analysis of history, that Brecht mastered the threat of anarchic nihilism. The man who taught him the elements of Marxism in the late nineteen twenties was Karl Korsch, an eminent Marxist theoretician who had been a Communist member of the Reichstag but had been expelled from the German Communist Party in 1926.

Marxist influence

The mature playwright. The transition from the wild exuberance, as exemplified in *Baal*, of his pre-Marxist phase (dominated by the influence of such writers as the French symbolist poets Paul Verlaine and Arthur Rimbaud, the English novelist Rudyard Kipling, and the German dramatists Georg Büchner and Frank Wedekind) to the severely controlled Marxist writings of the early nineteen thirties is marked by plays like *A Man's a Man* (first performed at Darmstadt in September 1926), *The Threepenny Opera* (which in its premiere at the Schiffbauerdamm Theatre in Berlin on Aug. 31, 1928, gave Brecht his first great popular success—though much of the success was due to Kurt Weill's music), and the opera *Rise and Fall of the City of Mahagonny* (music by Kurt Weill; first performed at Leipzig on March 9, 1930).

Didactic plays

In these plays the forces of chaos, sex, greed, and violence are already seen from the point of view of a personality who identifies them with the cruelty and selfishness of capitalism. In a series of *Lehrstücke* (didactic plays) and *Schulopern* (didactic operas) Brecht began to preach the Marxist gospel of self-discipline and self-denial in the interests of mankind in a new style of austerity and compression. The exuberant images of his earlier writing made way for the terse statement of the Marxist's "scientific fact." Foremost among the didactic plays are *The Flight of the Lindberghs* and the *Didactic Play of Baden on Consent* (in which consent stands for self-discipline even up to the point of agreeing to one's own annihilation) which received their first performances in 1929; *He who says Yes* and *He who says No* (both variants of a Japanese No play, also concerned with the problem of suicide for the common good), *The Exception and the Rule* and *The Measures Taken* (all dating from 1930). *The Measures Taken* (*Die Massnahme*) a dramatic cantata—with music by Hans Eisler—is one of Brecht's masterpieces. It deals with a young Communist revolutionary in China who breaks party discipline and then asks to be liquidated so that the struggle he endangered can be continued.

These short didactic pieces were followed by two full-length plays of a severely didactic nature. The first, performed on Jan. 12, 1932, was *The Mother*, an adaptation of Maksim Gorky's novel of the same name. The second, *St. Joan of the Stockyards*, was an attempt to analyze the causes of the great depression through an account of meat speculation in the Chicago stock market. Owing to the political situation in Germany the play could not get a stage performance but was broadcast in a shortened version on April 11, 1932.

When Hitler came to power on January 30, 1933, it was clear that Brecht could not remain in Germany. A long period of exile began. Brecht first went to Denmark where he acquired a house near the town of Svendborg on the island of Fyn. In the first years after the Nazi rise to power, when Brecht was mainly occupied by the day-to-day struggle against Hitler, his work was primarily propagandistic, so much so that some of it remained largely ephemeral; *e.g.*, the play *The Roundheads and the Peakheads*, a satire on racism; *Fears and Miseries of the Third Reich*, a sequence of short scenes on life in Hitler's Germany; and *Señora Carrar's Rifle*, a play on the Spanish Civil War.

The great plays. After the occupation of Austria in March 1938, when it became clear to Brecht that war was inevitable and that nothing he could do could alter the course of events, he reverted to work that reflected his deeper personal and philosophical concerns. Thus began the fourth and most creative phase of his life; it produced plays that combine the exuberance of his youthful phase with the severe ideological discipline of his didactic period and fused these elements in a series of deeply felt poetic parables. Foremost among the plays of this period are: *The Life of Galileo*, which deals with the responsibilities of a man of genius in a hostile world; *The Good Woman of Setzuan*, a parable on the question whether it is possible to be a good human being in a society based on greed; *Mother Courage and her Children*, a bold canvas of the Thirty Years' War that shows that even simple people are responsible for war's brutalities if they contribute, in however small a way, to the war's conduct.

Poetic parables

As the Second World War approached, Brecht no longer felt safe in Denmark, and in April 1939 he moved to Sweden. A year later he was again on the move, this time to Finland, where he wrote a play with a Finnish setting, *Mr. Puntila and his Servant Matti*, another parable on the impossibility of combining human kindness with efficiency as a capitalist, and *The Resistible Rise of Arturo Ui*, the story of Hitler transferred to a setting among Chicago gangsters.

Brecht was determined to escape the horrors of war in Europe. It is notable that he, the committed Marxist sympathizer, and onetime co-editor of a German literary review published in Moscow from 1936 to 1939, did not even consider settling in the Soviet Union. Instead, after receiving his U.S. visa in Helsinki in May 1941 he travelled to the United States by crossing the entire Soviet Union and taking a ship from Vladivostok only a few days before the German invasion of Russia.

Brecht in the U.S. In the United States Brecht lived at Santa Monica, California, but visited New York several times for extended periods. He tried to work for the Hollywood film industry but sold only one script, *Hangmen Also Die*, which Fritz Lang directed in 1942. Yet it was in the United States that he completed his last great play, *The Caucasian Chalk Circle*, another bold treatment of the problem of goodness and the difficulties of achieving justice in a wicked world.

In Hollywood Brecht met the British actor Charles Laughton and worked with him on an English version of his *Galileo* which, Laughton realized, contained an ideal part for him. Laughton opened as Galileo in Los Angeles in July 1947; a Broadway production was due to open at the end of that year. It seemed that Brecht was at last to find fame and recognition in the United States. But on October 30, 1947 he appeared under subpoena as a witness before the House of Representatives' Committee on Un-American Activities, which was investigating Communist sympathizers in the Hollywood movie community. Brecht parried the inept questioning of the committee's investigators with such brilliant evasiveness that he was congratulated on being a cooperative witness. But the experience proved so distasteful to him that the following day he left for Europe.

Berliner Ensemble. With his usual caution he did not hurry to return to Germany, but settled first in Switzerland to explore the possibilities of finding a theatre where he could put into practice his theories about staging his plays. He was much attracted by Austria, as a German-speaking area from which he could visit both West and East Germany; at one time it looked as though he might be offered the post of artistic director of the Salzburg Festival, and he applied for Austrian citizenship. In October 1948 he was invited to East Berlin to produce his play *Mother Courage*. After the play opened, with immense success, on Jan. 11, 1949, Brecht returned to Zürich and continued to press for his Austrian citizenship; but when he was offered the chance to have his own company of actors, the Berliner Ensemble, in East Berlin, he finally decided to settle there instead. On Nov. 12, 1949, the Berliner Ensemble officially opened with *Puntila*. Yet even then, Brecht, who wanted freedom to travel wherever he wanted to go, persisted in seeking Austrian nationality, which was granted him in April 1950. He also vested the copyright of his plays with a West German publisher, thus retaining a measure of freedom from East German censorship and keeping his Western earnings in the West.

In East Berlin Brecht at last had an opportunity of testing his theories about the stage by producing the great plays he had written in the years of exile. His theory of drama is contained in *A Little Organum for the Theatre*, which he had completed in Zürich in 1948.

Theory of drama

The essence of his theory of drama is the idea that a truly Marxist drama must avoid the Aristotelian premise that the audience should be made to believe that what they are witnessing is happening here and now. For he saw that if the audience really felt that the emotions of heroes of the past—Oedipus, or Lear, or Hamlet—could equally have been their own reactions, then the Marxist idea that human nature is not constant but a result of changing historical conditions would automatically be invalidated. Brecht therefore argued that the theatre should not seek to make its audience believe in the presence of the characters on the stage—should not make it identify with them, but should rather follow the method of the epic poet's art, which is to make the audience realize that what it sees on the stage is merely an account of past events that it should watch with critical detachment. Hence, the "epic" (narrative, nondramatic) theatre is based on detachment, on the *Verfremdungs-Effekt* (distancing effect), achieved through a number of devices that remind the spectator that he is being presented with a demonstration of human behaviour in a scientific spirit rather than with an illusion of reality, in short, that the theatre is only a theatre and not the world itself.

In East Berlin Brecht, the Bohemian rebel of the Berlin of the 1920s, became the grand old man of the East German Communist régime. Under his direction, the Berliner Ensemble won worldwide acclaim and toured eastern and western Europe. But Brecht also had his share of difficulties with the Ulbricht régime. In 1951 the opera *The Trial of Lucullus* (based on a radio play by Brecht dating from 1940, with music by Paul Dessau) had to be withdrawn after a few performances because the government objected to its pacifism. In 1954 the Berliner Ensemble moved into its own theatre building, the old

Schiffbauerdamm theatre, where *The Threepenny Opera* had had its triumphant opening in 1928. In May 1955 Brecht went to Moscow to receive the Stalin Peace Prize. On Aug. 14, 1956, shortly before the Berliner Ensemble made its debut in London, Brecht died of a heart attack.

Assessment. Although his attempts to create a truly Marxist aesthetics of the drama are open to criticism, his importance as a playwright and, above all, as a poet, is beyond question. His later poetry, which expresses his melancholy disillusionment with the ideals of his youth, is, in its terseness and simplicity, among the greatest German verse of this or any other epoch. In his great plays Brecht's refusal to let his political commitment override his vision of the world produces a depth of insight and a richness of character rare in modern drama. Brecht's example illustrates the problem and the paradox of the committed writer: his commitment to Marxism gave him a strong motivation to write and a firm viewpoint from which he could survey the world; but at the same time his integrity as a poet prevented him from departing from the truth of characterization, the true dramatist's impartiality when dealing with his characters. Thus Brecht's later plays, though conceived as lessons in Marxism, transcend his intention and emerge as great drama.

MAJOR WORKS

THEATRICAL WORKS: *Baal* (published 1922, performed 1923; Eng. trans., 1970); *Trommeln in der Nacht* (performed 1922, published 1923); *Im Dickicht der Städte* (performed 1923, later revised, published 1927; trans. as *In the Swamp*, 1961; *In the Jungle of Cities*, 1970); (with Lion Feuchtwanger), *Leben Eduards des Zweiten von England* (1924, adapted from Marlowe's *Edward II; Edward II*, 1961; *The Reign of Edward the Second of England*, 1971); *Mann ist Mann* (performed 1926, later revised with music by Kurt Weill; 1st version published 1927, 2nd version published 1938; *A Man's a Man*, 1961; *Man is Man*, 1966; *Man Equals Man*, 1971), to which is attached the one-act farcical interlude or entr'acte, *Das Elefantenkalb* (*The Baby Elephant*, 1956; *The Elephant Baby*, 1971); *Die Dreigroschenoper*, a ballad opera based on John Gay's *The Beggar's Opera* (1728), with music by Kurt Weill (performed 1928, published 1929; later revised, *The Threepenny Opera*, 1955); *Aufstieg und Fall der Stadt Mahagonny*, opera with music by Kurt Weill (performed and published 1930; several later versions *Rise and Fall of the City of Mahagonny*, 1956; *Rise and Fall of the Town Mahagonny*, 1971, based on *Mahagonny* (trans. as *The Little Mahagonny*, 1957), a *Singspiel* (performed 1927, published posthumously 1965); *Die heilige Johanna der Schlachthöfe* (performed 1932, published 1933, later revised with music by Paul Dessau; *St. Joan of the Stockyards*, 1962); *Der Jasager* and *Der Neinsager*, two school operas intended to be performed together, based on Arthur Waley's Eng. trans. of the Japanese Nō play, *Taniko*, with music by Kurt Weill (*He Says Yes* and *He Says No*, 1960; *He Who Says Yes* and *He Who Says No*, 1971); *Die Massnahme*, a *Lehrstück*, or didactic piece, with music by Hanns Eisler (performed 1930, published 1931; trans. as *The Punitive Measures*, 1956; as *The Measures Taken*, 1959; and *The Expedient*, 1971); *Die Ausnahme und die Regel*, short *Lehrstück* for schools (published 1937, performed with music by Paul Dessau, 1947; trans. as *The Rule and the Exception*, 1939); *Die Mutter* (1932); *Lehrstück* based on Gorky's novel, with music by Hanns Eisler; *Die Rundköpfe und die Spitzköpfe*, with music by Hanns Eisler (first professionally performed in a Danish version, 1936, published 1938; *Round Heads and Pointed Heads*, 1958; *Round Heads, Peak Heads*, 1971); *Die sieben Todsünden der Kleinbürger* (1933), libretto for ballet with choreography by George Balanchine, based on 10 poems by Brecht with music by Kurt Weill, also known as *Die sieben Todsünden* and as *Anna-Anna* (trans. by Chester Kallmann and W.H. Auden, *The Seven Deadly Sins of the Petty Bourgeoisie*, 1959); *Furcht und Elend des dritten Reich* (performed 1937, partially published Moscow 1941, fuller version New York 1945, revised version Berlin 1948), consisting of 24 (or 32) short scenes linked by poem, with music by Hanns Eisler (1st version trans. as *The Private Life of the Master Race* (1944; revised version trans. as *Fear and Misery of the Third Reich*, 1970); *Die Gewehre der Frau Carrar*, one-act play based on J.M. Synge's *Riders to the Sea* (1904; first performed London 1937, *Señora Carrar's Rifles*, 1938); *Leben des Galilei*, with music by Hanns Eisler (1st version performed 1943, 2nd version written in English by Brecht and Charles Laughton and performed as *Galileo*, New York 1947; revised version performed and published in German 1955, *The Life of Galileo*, 1960); *Mutter Courage und ihre Kinder*, based on Grimmelshausen's *Die Landstörtzerin Courasche* (1669), with music by Paul Dessau (performed Zürich 1941, published 1949; *Mother Courage and Her Children: A Chronicle Play of the Thirty Years' War*, 1948; *Mother Courage and her Children*, 1962); *Das Verhör des Lukullus* (broadcast 1940, 1st version published Moscow 1940, expanded version with music by Roger Sessions performed London 1947, published London 1955; *The Trial of Lucullus*, 1960), the basis of the opera *Die Verurteilung des Lukullus*, with music by Paul Dessau (performed 1951); *Der gute Mensch von Sezuan*, parable play with music by Paul Dessau (performed 1943, published 1956, several revised versions; trans. as *The Good Woman of Setzwan*, 1961; *The Good Person of Szechwan*, 1962); *Herr Puntila und sein Knecht Matti*, a *Volksstück*, or "folk play," 12 short scenes linked by the "Puntila-Song," with music by Paul Dessau (performed 1948, published 1956; trans. as *Mr. Puntila and His Hired Man Matti*, 1954; *Herr Puntila and his Man Matti*, 1962); *Der aufhaltsame Aufstieg des Arturo Ui*, parable play (performed 1958 by the Staatstheater, Stuttgart; published posthumously 1957; *The Resistible Rise of Arturo Ui*, 1965; *Arturo Ui*, 1968); (with Lion Feuchtwanger), *Die Gesichte der Simone Machard*, with incidental music by Hanns Eisler (performed and published posthumously 1957); *Schweyk im zweiten Weltkrieg*, based on Jaroslav Hašek's novel *The Good Soldier Schweik* (pub. in Czech, 1920–23), with music by Hanns Eisler (performed 1956, published posthumously 1959; *Schweyk in the Second World War*, 1963); *Der kaukasische Kreidekreis*, parable play with music by Paul Dessau (first performed in English as *The Caucasian Chalk Circle*, Northfield, Minnesota 1948; published Berlin 1949, later revised, performed in German 1955; published 1956, Eng. trans. of revised versions 1960 and 1963); *Die Antigone des Sophokles*, based on Hölderlin's translation 1804 (performed 1948, published 1949; later revised as *Antigone*, 1956); *Die Tage der Commune*, unfinished, performed with music by Hanns Eisler (published posthumously 1957; *The Days of the Commune*, 1962); *Der Salzburger Totentanz*, unfinished morality play (published posthumously 1959). (ADAPTATIONS AND TRANSLATIONS): *Der Hofmeister* (performed 1950, published 1954), from Lenz's comedy of the same name, 1774; *Coriolan* (published posthumously 1959), from Shakespeare's *Coriolanus; Pauken und Trompeten* (performed 1956, published posthumously 1964), from George Farquhar's *The Recruiting Officer*, 1706; with songs added by Brecht and music by Rudolf Wagner-Régeny.

POETICAL WORKS: *Hauspostille* (1927, revised 1951, poems written 1913–26 and first collected in *Taschenpostille*, privately printed, 1926; Eng. trans. in Eric Bentley's bilingual ed., *Die Hauspostille: A Manual of Piety*, 1966); "Die drei Soldaten," narrative poems for children, published in Brecht's *Versuche #6* (1932); *Lieder, Gedichte, Chöre*, Paris (1934), songs from plays, etc., with settings by Hanns Eisler; *Svendborger Gedichte* (1939), poems written in exile in Denmark; *Gedichte im Exil. Buckower Elegien* (published posthumously 1964), poems written in exile in Denmark and Finland; *Hundert Gedichte, 1918–50* (1952); *Bertolt Brechts Gedichte und Lieder* (1956), a posthumous collection by Peter Suhrkamp; *Letzte Gedichte*, Brecht's last poems (written 1953–56, published 1957). Many of Brecht's poems were first published posthumously in *Gedichte*, 9 vol. (1960–65); Eng. trans. of 50 poems with German text in H.R. Hays (ed. and trans.), *Selected Poems of Bertolt Brecht* (1959).

PROSE (NARRATIVE): *Der Dreigroschenroman* (1934), novel with songs; trans. by Desmond Vesey and Christopher Isherwood as *A Penny for the Poor* (1937, retitled *The Threepenny Novel*, 1956). (TALES, NOVELLEN, AND SKETCHES): *Geschichten vom Herrn Keuner* (1930 and 1958), aphoristic anecdotes; *Kalendergeschichten* (1948), short stories, Keuner anecdotes, with some narrative poems; *Tales from the Calendar* (1961); *Die Geschäfte des Herrn Julius Caesar. Romanfragment* (published posthumously 1957), unfinished historical novel in diary form. Many of Brecht's short stories and sketches were first published posthumously in *Prosa*, 5 vol. (1965–67). (WRITINGS ON THE THEATRE AND AESTHETICS): (Some of these works were first published in periodicals and newspapers, and first collected or published after Brecht's death. Prefaces, Notes, to his own works and Productions collected in *Schriften zum Theater*, 7 vol. (1964–67). Accounts of Productions containing early drafts, scenarios, and photographs: *Antigonemodell 1948* (1949), the first of Brecht's "modellbücher" of productions; *Die Geuehre der Frau Carrar* (1952); *Aufbau einer Rolle: Galilei* (1956); *Couragemodell 1949* (1958).

(OTHER PROSE): *Flüchtlingesprāche* (published posthumously 1962), autobiographical and philosophical dialogues written in exile 1940–41; *Me-ti: Buch der Wendungen* (written 1934–51, unrevised), Brecht's unfinished philosophical, political, and ethical "breviary."

BIBLIOGRAPHY. A complete bibliography of Brecht's writings published up to the time of his death by WALTER

NUBEL may be found in the Second Special Brecht Number of the East German periodical *Sinn und Form* (1957); a concise summary of Brecht literature is contained in *Bertolt-Brecht-Bibliographie* by KLAUS-DIETRICH PETERSEN (1968). Brecht's voluminous literary remains are held in the Bertolt Brecht Archiv in East Berlin. The first volume of a catalog of these works, *Bertolt Brecht Archiv: Bestandsverzeichnis des literarischen Nachlasses* (1969), is devoted to Brecht's dramatic work. Collected works in the original German are available in an edition in 8 thin-paper or 20 paperback volumes: *Gesammelte Werke* (1967). This edition, however, is far from complete and the principles according to which it was edited are open to doubt. A major collected edition of Brecht's works in English, under the joint editorship of JOHN WILLETT and RALPH MANHEIM started publication with the first volume of *Collected Plays* (1970). ERIC BENTLEY has edited *Seven Plays by Bertolt Brecht* (1961), a series of paperback volumes of Brecht's plays, and has translated the poetry collection, *Hauspostille* (1927; *Manual of Piety*, 1966). A good selection of Brecht's theoretical writings is *Brecht on Theatre*, trans. by JOHN WILLETT (1964).

Critical and biographical works available in English include: JOHN WILLETT, *The Theatre of Bertolt Brecht* (1959); MARTIN ESSLIN, *Brecht: A Choice of Evils* (1959; revised edition under the title, *Brecht: The Man and His Work*, 1971); and FREDERIC EWEN, *Bertolt Brecht: His Life, His Art and His Times* (1967, 1970). MAX SPALTER, *Brecht's Tradition* (1967), analyzes the chief influences on Brecht in German literature. (M.J.E.)

Bremen

Bremen, situated on the Weser some 43 miles (70 kilometres) from the North Sea, is one of the largest ports of West Germany and one of the more dynamic of that nation's cities. It is also one of the major industrial cities of northern Europe. Together with the port of Bremerhaven, situated 37 miles (59 kilometres) to the north, it forms the *Land*, or state, of Bremen, smallest of the ten *Länder* of the Federal Republic of Germany but of vital economic significance. This article describes both the *Land* and the city that dominates it.

The earliest settlement (called *Breme* or *Bremum*) on the right bank of the river was favoured by an advantageous position at the junction of important early trading routes from the Rhine River to the Elbe and from the North Sea to southern Germany. In 787 Charlemagne, the Western (Holy Roman) emperor, established the diocese of Bremen (to become an archbishopric in 845), which became the base for missionary activity covering the whole of northern Europe. The market rights—including customs and coinage—that were conferred on Bremen in 965 brought increased mercantile activity, and the young city soon became one of the commanding religious and economic centres of north Germany, especially after entering the Hanseatic League—an economic and political association of the rising urban mercantile class—in 1358. The imperial free city, as Bremen became known, occupying a strongly fortified position on either side of the Weser, defended its independence in the Thirty Years' War (1618–48) and later repelled both Swedish and Hanoverian aggression. As an autonomous republic—the oldest in Germany—it joined the German Confederation in 1815 and the reconstituted German Empire in 1871. It attained increasing economic importance as a leader in international trade and world shipping by entering the German customs union (Zollverein) in 1888, through expanding its port facilities, and by developing manufacturing industry.

Medieval heritage

The city of the early 1970s is an interesting amalgam of medieval and modern architecture. The outstanding features in the Altstadt, or Old Town, in the restored heart of the city, are the famous marketplace with its 11th-century cathedral; the Gothic Town Hall with its Renaissance facade; the statue of Roland (1404), symbolizing market rights and imperial jurisdiction; a picturesque row of old, gabled houses; and the modern-style Parliament. Districts heavily bombed in World War II (69 percent of the houses were destroyed) have since been rebuilt, allowing for growing traffic and extensive public parks. About three miles from the city centre, the modern satellite town of Neue Vahr, built between 1957 and 1962, accommodates 40,000 people and is one of a ring of peripheral settlements that have coalesced with the expanding and dynamic city.

The site. Located at the first ford above the river estuary, the Old Town grew on a sand dune, sited above flood level on the Weser spillway, the glacially widened river channel. The windblown sand accummulated, in the postglacial period, up to a height of 45 feet (15 metres) above the flat marshes and moors of the Bremer Becken (lowlands). Because of the effect of North Sea tides and of the high subterranean water level, 71 miles of dikes, associated with a complicated drainage system, play an important role in the Bremen urban area. The dune—25 miles long and two miles wide—has thus decisively influenced the northward and southward expansion of the city. The territorial possessions of the city also included large sections of the swampy, cultivated lowlands and stretches along the Weser, which became associated with the rise of further smaller settlements. The gradual incorporation of these rural communities—which had always had close economic relations with Bremen—started in 1849 and in 1945 brought the administrative area of the city of Bremen to its contemporary size of approximately 125 square miles (324 square kilometres).

The people. With a total population that passed 600,000 in the late 1960s, Bremen ranks among the 10 largest cities in the Federal Republic of Germany. A small town of only 30,000 inhabitants a century and a half ago, its subsequent growth, closely linked with its economic development, occasioned a population rise that reached 162,000 by 1880 and 264,000 in 1920. By the end of World War II, the population of the war-torn city had dropped from 424,000 (1939) to 362,000, but it rose sharply with the extensive postwar reconstruction. By the early 1970s, Bremen population was characterized by an annual birthrate of less than 2%. This, together with an insignificant inward migration rate, made it one of the more demographically stable German cities. The age structure of the population shows that some 21% are under 15, 66% in the age group from 15 to 65, and 13% over 65. As might be expected in an industrial city nearly half of the 15 to 65 age group are employed (66% of the men and 34% of the women). Living as they are in the heart of the strongly Protestant north of Germany, some 83% of Bremen citizens are members of the Protestant Church, with only 10% adhering to the Roman Catholic faith.

Economic life. In the early 1970s, the economic life of the *Land* continued to reflect the historic interconnection of shipping, foreign trade, and industry. The port facilities of Bremen and Bremerhaven, which, administratively and economically, form one unit, incorporate free-port status, whereby imported goods can be handled and stored without time limits and without customs formalities. The turnover of goods in the two ports—some 16% of the national total—reached an annual total of 20,000,000 tons by the close of the 1960s, more than half of which were imported. Bremerhaven handles about a quarter of the total tonnage, just over half of which is mixed cargo, the remainder being composed of such bulk goods as grain, coal, ore, and oil. The merchant fleet of Bremen—whose number rose sharply after the foundation of the Norddeutscher Lloyd Shipping Company in 1857—consisted, by the early 1970s, of over 370 seagoing vessels (totalling 1,370,000 gross registered tonnage) and 30 barges (totalling almost 200,000 gross registered tonnage). The port of Bremerhaven was the home of the largest German fishing fleet, consisting of more than 85 trawlers of about 80,000 gross registered tonnage.

Traditional port function of the city

In Hanseatic times, Bremen's importance rested almost entirely on its character as a trading centre and as a seaport for handling raw materials and foodstuffs. Grain from the Baltic countries, for example, was sent to western Europe via the city, and, in return, wine, salt, and, later, colonial products—notably cotton, for which it was the European marketing centre—passed through it. Since the end of the 18th century, the port has handled, in increasing quantities, grain (14% of the total West German imports by 1970), timber (19%), coffee (36%), tobacco (40%), wool (65%), and cotton (67%). These items are manufactured on a large scale by local firms, which are among the biggest of their kind in the country.

Originally, the city's entire industrial potential—except for food industries—depended upon the shipyards and their supporting firms. By means of industrial enterprises founded after 1900, the Bremen economy increasingly became more diversified, supplying the internal market and ensuring sufficient freight for outward-sailing ships. Steel for the city's shipbuilding industry—the seven major companies of which comprised more than 20 percent of the national shipyard capacity by the 1970s—derives from local steelworks, the output of which exceeds 2,000,000 tons annually. In addition, machine-building industries specialize in engines and equipment for ships and trucks and machinery for growth industries. The aircraft industry comprises more than one-third of the total German capacity. Production in the electrical industry ranges from industrial equipment to radio and television sets and modern electronic materials. By the early 1970s, about 700 industrial firms in the region employed 85,000 workers, with capital goods industries accounting for half of the workers, the food industry 21%, consumer goods industries 16%, and raw materials industries 13%.

Diversification

Political and governmental institutions. Bremen *Land*, the overall administrative unit, has a total area of 156 square miles (404 square kilometres), and the population exceeded three-quarters of a million by 1970. The city of Bremerhaven, which covers 31 square miles (80 square kilometres) and had a population of about 150,000 by the early 1970s, was founded as an outer port for Bremen because of the silting up of the lower Weser: it joined the Bremen *Land* in 1947.

A new constitution, adopted in the same year, placed the legislative power in the City Council (Bürgerschaft). The council appoints the executive body (Senate), which is composed of a president (Bürgermeister) and nine senators. Bremen entered the 1970s dominated by a left-centre coalition of Social Democrats (holding 50 council seats) and Free Democrats (ten seats). The right-centre Christian Democrats held 32 council seats; and others, eight seats. The council—which has 80 members from Bremen and 20 from Bremerhaven—and the Senate are elected every four years. The *Land* has three seats in the Upper House of the Federal Council (Bundesrat).

Services. In the early 1970s, more than 45 percent of all Bremen employees worked in commerce, transport, and various services. Bremen is the home of several banks, insurance companies, a stock exchange, and cotton- and tobacco-marketing centres. The importance of its overseas connections is illustrated by the presence of consulates of 30 countries. Warehouses, stores, and specialist shops also cater for people from the surrounding rural area, while imports and exports are dealt with by numerous shipping companies and agents. The railways are an important factor in the transportation of piece (cloth) goods, carrying 60 percent of the total, as other links between the port and its hinterland were slow to develop. Quick electric passenger trains and motorways link modern Bremen with the country's major cities; and, apart from direct flights to London and Amsterdam, Bremen airport is connected with many inland airports, handling more than a quarter of a million passengers annually by the 1970s.

Transportation links

The city has about 150 primary and secondary schools, 18 vocational schools, 14 academies, a number of technical schools—among which are a school of engineering, and a merchant marine school—and a teacher's training college. A university was under construction by the early 1970s. Bremen has a radio and television transmitting station, and three daily and two weekly newspapers are published.

Cultural life and recreation. Four theatres, 11 libraries and archives, and 19 museums and galleries contributed to the rich cultural life of Bremen in the early 1970s. Most of these facilities were concentrated in the pleasant surroundings of the old town, especially in the Schnoorviertel, a district that was restored to its original 16th- and 17th-century appearance in the post-World War II reconstruction. In keeping with the worldwide connections of the city, international congresses are often held in Bremen, which offers about 100 hotels, several conference halls, and a congress hall seating 10,000 people. As in many German industrial cities, there are extensive sports grounds, associated with 240 or more clubs. Parks, located all over the city, offer a relaxing contrast to the often hectic pace of economic activities. The best known are the Bürgerpark, with its famous rhododendron gardens, and the former ramparts, which were demolished in 1802 and which now form promenades surrounding the Old Town.

BIBLIOGRAPHY. G.O.A. BESSELL, *Bremen: Geschichte einer deutschen Stadt*, 3rd ed. (1955), a general review of the history of the city; FREIE HANSESTADT, *Bremen: Werden, Vergehen und Wiederaufbau* (1947), an atlas of views and maps of the city (1567–1945), with descriptive text; BREMEN, SENATOR FUR WIRTSCHAFT UND AUSSENHANDEL, *Bremen/Bremerhaven: Industrie am Strom* (1969), a discussion of the individual branches of industry and their development within the Bremen economy, *Die Wirtschaftsstruktur Bremens*, 2nd ed. (1969), a general review of the Bremen economy; G. DEISSMANN (ed.), *Wachsende Städte an der Unterweser*, 2nd ed. (1965), a general review of the economy of the cities of Bremen and Bremerhaven and their individual development, with valuable statistics and maps of the ports; *Zuhause in Bremen* (1970), a guide through Bremen with particular reference to cultural life and recreation, with detailed statistics and an extensive bibliography.

(M.O.W.F.)

Brethren

The Brethren (Church of the Brethren, Brethren Church, National Fellowship of Brethren Churches, Old German Baptist Brethren), with a total adult membership of 266,000, trace their origin to Germany in 1708. In that year five men and three women covenanted to form a brotherhood following the commandments of Jesus Christ as revealed in the New Testament. Their course was shaped by three influences—the Protestant faith in which they had been raised, a reform movement known as Pietism, and Anabaptist teachings from the Radical Reformation of the 16th century.

The first Brethren were known in Europe as New Baptists (to distinguish them from the Mennonites, the direct descendants of the Anabaptists, whom they resembled in many ways) or as Schwarzenau Baptists (because of their place of origin). In North America they were commonly called Dunkers, Dunkards, or Tunkers, a reference to their distinctive practice of baptism by a threefold forward immersion. In 1836 they took the name Fraternity of German Baptists, which was replaced in 1871 by German Baptist Brethren.

Following a three-way split in the early 1880s a conservative wing called itself the Old German Baptist Brethren to emphasize the conviction that it was holding to the earlier beliefs. The liberal party chose to be called the Brethren Church. The middle-of-the-road majority continued as the German Baptist Brethren until 1908 when the title Church of the Brethren was officially adopted. In 1939 the Brethren Church divided into the Brethren Church (Ashland, Ohio) and the National Fellowship of Brethren Churches (Grace Brethren).

The Brethren are considered one of the three historic "peace churches," along with the Religious Society of Friends (Quakers) and Mennonites, because of a continuing (but not unanimous) adherence to the principle of conscientious objection to all wars.

History. In late-17-century Germany a reform movement led by Philipp Jakob Spener (1635–1705) and August Hermann Francke (1663–1727) attempted to restore religious vitality to Lutheran church life. Better education of theological students, more active congregations, more inspiring sermons, more piety in daily life earned for the movement the name Pietism. Most pietists remained within the church as a renewal element, but some were forced outside. Of the latter, many were driven from their homes because of their radical and

Pietism

separatist concerns, and some found asylum in Wittgenstein. The kindly disposed count, Henrich Albrecht, located them in the village Schwarzenau, on the river Eder. Subsequent differences in religious belief among those gathered at Schwarzenau caused some to become disheartened by the disunity and to return to German Lutheran or Reformed churches; others became religiously indifferent.

One small group led by Alexander Mack (1679–1735) determined to "establish a covenant of a good conscience with God, to accept all ordinances of Jesus Christ as an easy yoke, and thus follow their Lord Jesus . . . until a blessed end." They sought baptism from the German Mennonites but could not come to full agreement with them on church practices. The Brethren then decided to proceed with baptism themselves. They chose one of their number by lot to baptize Mack, who then baptized his baptizer and the remaining six.

These first Brethren developed great zeal for their cause and won converts in Wittgenstein and in other sections of Germany and Switzerland. The largest congregation after Schwarzenau was organized in the Marienborn area near Büdingen, Germany. In 1715 the Marienborn congregation was forced to leave because of a change in the religious policy of the local government. The members moved to Krefeld on the Lower Rhine, where they soon came into conflict with the authorities because of their proselyting. Several were sentenced to long terms of imprisonment. Added to this pressure was internal disagreement, which facilitated the decision of the majority of the congregation to move from Krefeld to Pennsylvania in 1719.

In the meantime, August, a brother of Henrich Albrecht, who was intolerant of the Schwarzenau Brethren, assumed co-regency. This, plus the low productivity of the land in Wittgenstein, caused them to leave. In 1720 the group under Mack's leadership migrated to West Friesland. In 1729 they joined the earlier migrants in America. Others left Europe in the 1730s with the result that no organized congregation of Brethren was left on the Continent after 1750, other than a group in Denmark that claims it can trace its origin to the Schwarzenau Brethren.

The American settlements

From the initial stronghold in Germantown, north of Philadelphia, the Brethren settled in the surrounding areas of Pennsylvania and New Jersey. Some moved into Maryland and the Southern colonies. By 1770 the Brethren had 1,500 adult members with a total following of about 5,000 in 28 congregations along the Atlantic seaboard.

An interesting offshoot of the colonial Brethren was the Ephrata Community in Lancaster County, Pennsylvania, a Protestant monastic establishment directed by Johann Conrad Beissel (1690–1768). At one time a minister of the Brethren congregation at Conestoga, Pennsylvania, Beissel broke with the Brethren and took with him a large number of the members. Ephrata became widely known for its cultural accomplishments, especially in choral singing and manuscript illustrating.

The most influential family connected with the 18th-century Brethren was that of Christopher Sower (Sauer; 1695–1758), the noted Germantown printer. Although the first Sower was a Separatist in his religious views, he shared many convictions with the Brethren. His namesake, Christopher Sower II (1721–1784), continued his father's business and became a Brethren elder. The Sower Press was famed for its three editions of the German Bible (1743, 1763, 1776). The Eliot Indian Bible of New England was the only previous biblical publication in the Colonies.

As followers of the doctrine of absolute nonresistance and therefore opposed to military service, the Brethren were put in a difficult position by the outbreak of the American Revolution. Some of them tended toward loyalism, because they were grateful to the British crown for freedoms enjoyed in America. There were scattered instances of mob violence and deprivation of Brethren property by action of the American revolutionary government. The shock that the Brethren suffered at this time may well have been a cause of their isolation and withdrawn character in the 19th century.

Westward movement in America

The Brethren joined in the general push westward following the Revolution and were the first settlers in some sections of Ohio, Indiana, and Illinois and other prairie states. Almost all Brethren were agriculturalists, and they sought good limestone soil to establish their fertile farms. They tended to settle in groups, often migrating as colonies to new locations. The first Brethren reached the Pacific coast by 1850. When the transcontinental railroads were completed, more Brethren moved west, settling in the Dakotas, the Pacific Northwest, and California.

Although the Brethren avoided schism during the Civil War (unlike most American denominations), the cultural changes of the latter half of the 19th century shattered their unity. A younger and progressive element pressed for the adoption of new methods and practices such as other American churches used. These included Sunday schools, revival services, institutions of higher learning, salaried pastors, foreign missions, and a free religious press. As the Brethren emerged from rural cultural isolation, which had been enhanced by their rural life and Germanic speech, such practices seemed essential to a vocal minority in the brotherhood. The periodicals of Henry Kurtz (1796–1874) and James Quinter (1816–1888), although moderate in their reform wishes, were influential in creating these demands.

Proposals such as these alarmed the conservative leadership, which insisted that the status quo be preserved. This "Old Order" group left the church when they saw they could not prevent the innovations. In 1881 they formed the Old German Baptist Brethren. Shortly thereafter the liberal wing, led by Henry Holsinger (1833–1905), was expelled for insubordination to church rulings. He and his followers organized the Brethren Church in 1883. Each of the factions numbered around 4,000.

These schisms left deep wounds in the brotherhood but, nevertheless, freed the main body from its previous paralysis. With both extremes gone, energies could be turned outward. The late 19th century was one of great activity in the areas of education, publication, foreign missions, and church extension. By 1900 the membership of the Brethren had reached 75,000. These developments and those coming later were effected in such a way as to preserve further unity, except for a minor split in 1928 of the Dunkard Brethren. At issue was a conference decision in 1911 that upheld the practice of using a plain style in dress, but most congregations had abandoned church discipline on this point, other than the Dunkard Brethren. During the 19th century the Brethren had uniformly worn the plain style of dress similar to the Amish, with beards and broad-brimmed hats for the men and aprons and bonnets for the women. This garb now has almost entirely disappeared, except for the Old German Baptist Brethren and in some parts of eastern Pennsylvania for the Church of the Brethren.

Beliefs and practices. Brethren beliefs and practices are historically rooted in the central Christian statements of faith as expressed by Protestantism, such as the centrality of Scriptures and the priesthood of all believers. Although they have ordained ministers, the Brethren have generally held the view that all Christians are ordained to the ministry through baptism, with some set apart for special functions. For many years Brethren had a "free ministry" in which ministers supported themselves by other jobs during the week, without formal theological study. Today seminary education is expected and usually completed before ordination (except among the Old Orders), although there are alternate methods of private study for the purpose of ordination. Brethren have avoided dogmatism in theological matters, and in fact there are extensive differences among Brethren in doctrinal belief. The Brethren are noncreedal; that is, they do not require adherence to the historic Christian creeds. They state that they have no creed but the New Testament.

Church rites are usually called ordinances (commandments of the Lord) rather than sacraments. These include baptism by trine (threefold) immersion of those old enough to confess their faith; the love feast, which is a semi-annual re-enactment of the Upper Room (Last Supper) experience of Christ and his disciples (John 13), consisting of an examination service, feetwashing, a fellowship meal, and the bread and cup as a memorial to Christ; anointing for bodily and spiritual health (James 5); and the laying on of hands in the ordination of the clergy and the commissioning of church workers. Traditionally, they have used affirmation in legal procedures rather than swearing oaths.

Church government is a combination of congregational and presbyterial patterns. Local churches have great independence but the Annual Conference has final authority over "procedure, program, polity, and discipline." In practice most congregations follow the decisions of the annual meeting, which is composed of congregational delegates, plus a Standing Committee of delegates from the several geographical districts into which the denomination is divided. A General Board of 25 persons administers the program of the church through an employed staff. The Brethren Church and the Grace Brethren are strongly congregational in polity, with a minimum of denominational machinery. Separate boards administer home and foreign missions, publications, and denominational institutions. The Old German Baptist Brethren, on the other hand, follow strictly the decisions of their annual conferences.

Social concerns

None of the above three groups is very active on social issues, unlike the Church of the Brethren, which has an extensive program of social concern. In 1941 the Brethren Service Commission was organized to work in the areas of peace and social service. It developed its program on a worldwide scale especially after World War II, when annual budgets of goods and services exceeded $1,000,000. Brethren were involved in other agencies, such as Church World Service and Christian Rural Overseas Program and initiated the Heifer Project, Inc., to send livestock to refugees and other needy people. The International Christian Youth Exchange, an ecumenical agency, was begun by Brethren initiative; and the Brethren helped to start International Voluntary Services, the forerunner of the Peace Corps.

All branches of the Brethren have been active in sponsoring missionaries with the exception of the Old German Baptist Brethren. Major areas of concentration have been India, China, South America, Europe, and Africa. The Brethren Church cooperates with the Church of the Brethren in supporting the fast-growing mission work in Nigeria.

Present state of Brethren communities. The Church of the Brethren numbers about 215,000 in 1,120 congregations, principally in the U.S. Congregations in Canada, India, Nigeria, and Ecuador have joined or were joining united churches in their nations. The general offices of the Brethren are in Elgin, Illinois, with suboffices in Washington, D.C., and New Windsor, Maryland. The denominational journal is *Messenger;* an independent quarterly, *Brethren Life and Thought,* carries articles of scholarship and opinion. The Church of the Brethren is affiliated in the U.S. with six liberal arts colleges, two hospitals, and numerous homes for the aging. It sponsors one graduate school of theology, Bethany Theological Seminary in Oak Brook, Illinois.

The Brethren Church has some 17,000 members in 120 congregations. Its boards have offices in Ashland, Ohio, the site of Ashland College and Seminary. The official periodical is the *Brethren Evangelist;* the seminary issues annually the *Ashland Theological Bulletin.* Grace Brethren offices are in Winona Lake, Indiana, the home of Grace College and Theological Seminary. The *Grace Journal* is published by the seminary three times yearly. The denominational periodical is the *Brethren Missionary Herald.* Membership of the Grace Brethren is about 29,500 members in about 200 congregations. The Old German Baptist Brethren number about 4,000 in 54 congregations. They publish the *Vindicator.* The Church of the Brethren joined the Federal Council of Churches (later National Council of Churches of Christ in the U.S.A.) in 1941 and the World Council of Churches in 1948. The Brethren Church cooperates with the National Association of Evangelicals. The other two groups remain independent.

BIBLIOGRAPHY

Source books: D.F. DURNBAUGH (comp.), *European Origins of the Brethren* (1958), and *The Brethren in Colonial America* (1967).

Church of the Brethren: M.G. BRUMBAUGH, *A History of the German Baptist Brethren in Europe and America* (1899), a pioneer history; D.F. DURNBAUGH (ed.), *The Church of the Brethren: Past and Present* (1971); F.E. MALLOTT, *Studies in Brethren History* (1954), standard history; R.E. SAPPINGTON, *Brethren Social Policy, 1908–1958* (1961), monograph based on documents.

Brethren Church: A.T. RONK, *History of the Brethren Church* (1968).

Grace Brethren: H.A. KENT, *250 Years Conquering Frontiers* (1958), a popular history.

Old German Baptist Brethren: J.M. KIMMEL, *Chronicles of the Brethren* (1951), basic historical source for the Old Orders.

(D.F.D.)

Brewing

Brewing is the process of producing alcoholic beverages from starchy raw materials by steeping in water; boiling, usually with hops; and fermenting. In some countries beer is legally defined, as in Germany, where the standard ingredients, apart from water, are germinated barley, hops, and yeast.

HISTORY

Beer. Most of the beverages made from cereals over the past 8,000 years, especially those produced from malted barley, would now be considered "beers." According to Egyptian legend, Osiris, the god of agriculture, taught humans to prepare beer; besides Egypt, there were brewing operations in Babylon and Ur. Originally, barley was buried in pots to effect germination; the resulting malt, mixed with water, was allowed to ferment by the action of airborne yeasts. The addition of hops dates from between the 10th and 7th centuries BC. There are ancient references to millet beers in China and Japan, and the similar South African Kaffir beer is a traditional beverage of the Congo. Brewing probably reached Western culture from Egypt via Greece, where Pliny mentions the practice, including the use of hops. Brewing readily took hold in areas of northern and western Europe where grape culture for winemaking was impractical. According to Pliny, beer was known in Mediterranean countries before viticulture became popular. There are frequent references (*e.g.,* by Tacitus) early in the Christian Era to malt beverages consumed by Germanic and Nordic tribes, as well as by the Saxons and Celts, and even to the establishment of *tabernae,* or "taverns." Most of the common English terms used in modern brewing are of Anglo-Saxon or North European origin, including malt, mash, wash, wort, ale, and beer.

Britain's Domesday Book records 43 *cerevisiarii* ("breweries"). Medieval monasteries improved brewing techniques; and Trappist beer is still made in Belgium. "Home" brewing became important in Great Britain from about the 12th century AD, closely followed, with the growth of towns, by simple commercial operations with brewing and selling in the same establishment. Later, breweries ceased to be the point of sale and were usually centrally located to facilitate distribution in the town or city. Growth was slow until the Industrial Revolution made the large commercial brewery possible. The modern practice of national and international beer distribution is mainly a 20th-century development, although such terms as "India Pale Ale," referring to beer cargoes carried by shipping traders returning to Eastern markets, recall its earlier beginnings.

Other brewed beverages. Although beer usually implies a beverage of Western civilization, other cultures employ procedures similar to brewing—often without systematized technology. Sake, the Japanese rice beverage, and the Mexican pulque, made from the agave plant, are produced by brewing methods, although the resulting beverage is sometimes considered closer to wines or spirits; pulque, for instance, becomes mescal on distillation. African beverages related to Western beers are *khadi* (Botswana), brewed from honey and wild berries, and two beverages made with sorghum, *burukutu* (Nigeria) and, probably best known, Kaffir beer (South Africa). The last two are essentially fermented extracts of malted sorghum seeds, widely used in Africa with the addition, especially in Nigeria, of *gari*, a starchy cassava preparation. The relatively crude extracts, or worts, are usually fermented directly, producing beers thick with undegraded starchy products. *Saccharomyces cerevisiae* is considered the main fermentative organism, though lactic organisms also play some part.

Distinctions in terminology

Such terms as ale, lager, stout, and porter are commonly applied to commercially produced beers, but in modern practice there are no strict definitions of these terms. "Beer" and "ale" are now almost interchangeable in English-speaking communities; the same is true of "beer" and "lager" in many European countries. "Beer" originally denoted a relatively weak beverage for regular consumption, with "ale" referring to a stronger liquor, presumably comparable to modern strong ale. Originally, hops were used only in ale preparation, and beers were brewed unhopped. Beers, ales, and lagers now usually have an alcohol content of about 3.5 percent by weight, and strong ales may contain 11–12 percent. "Near beer," rarely brewed commercially except in Belgium, has a maximum alcoholic content of 2 percent. Although lager often implies a beverage light both in colour and alcohol content, the word itself refers only to the method of brewing and particularly to the traditional long period of cold storage or "lagering." Commercial lagers, in fact, include some dark beverages of relatively high alcohol content.

Stout is brewed by methods similar to those employed in the modern brewing of ale, except that a proportion of roasted barley or malt is included with the normal malt and other ingredients before mashing to give the final beverage its dark colour. "Porter," a term now practically obsolete, apparently referred to a brew intermediate between ale and stout and is said to derive its name from the demand by market porters for a blend of ale and beer ("half-and-half"), later met by brewing an unblended ("entire") beer of appropriate strength, coloured by means of roasted cereal. "Cooper" refers to a mixture of stout and porter.

Both ales and lagers are described in a number of ways, often based on their individual characteristics, such as "brown ale," "mild," "bitter," and "stingo." Audit ale was a strong drink brewed to mark audit days in a number of colleges of ancient foundation. Pilsener (pale), Munich (dark), and the Scandinavian "Easter brews" reflect some of the many variants on the lager side.

Other beverages have been termed beers, including "spruce beer," a fermented, sugary solution flavoured with an extract of spruce leaves; "mum," a beer treated with fir bark and various herbs; "bragget," consisting of fermented honey and ale; "mulled ale," heated and flavoured with spices; and "lambswool," a beverage similar to mulled ale, containing roasted apples.

In modern practice, hops are used alone to give beer bitterness and aroma not provided by the cereals themselves nor by fermentation products. A variety of herbs and other materials were formerly added specifically to impart bitterness, including gentian, camomile, and quassia. Catechu resin may have been used more for its preservative value than its flavour, and the others probably produced a harsh bitterness rather than functioning as satisfactory substitutes for hops. Ferrous sulfate conferred a grating, harsh flavour, and was apparently used mainly to improve foam character. Many countries now prohibit use of these materials, and they were probably never used in organized industrial operations.

THE BREWING PROCESS

Most commercial brewing includes four stages: malting, mashing, wort boiling, and fermentation.

Malting. Cereal, usually barley, is converted into malt form, from which an extract is obtained for fermentation. Untreated barley produces an inferior wort (extract); grain steeped in water and germinated under controlled conditions develops a complex of enzymes, facilitating production of a satisfactory wort.

The steeping stage normally lasts for 40 to 80 hours under controlled conditions of temperature (usually 13°–15° C; 55°–59° F) and oxygenation. Alkalinity is sometimes controlled by the use of limewater. The grain, with water content ranging from 12 to 14 percent depending upon storage conditions, is allowed to take up further moisture to a level of 35–45 percent, depending upon the procedure to be used for the later part of the malting process.

Grain is sometimes dormant, exhibiting some unwillingness to germinate. Dormancy exhibits two phases. The first, common in all barleys, is evident for a few weeks immediately after harvesting, disappearing spontaneously during storage. Some barleys, especially those grown in maritime climates, retain a second type of dormancy, or "water sensitivity," and benefit from steeping to a low moisture content level, with more water being added after an air-rest period.

Germination

In traditional malting, steeped grain is spread on floors after draining. It is piled in thick heaps, or "couches," to initiate germination and, after about 24 hours, is spread more thinly, either by hand or mechanical raking, to moderate the temperature, which is maintained by the maltster at 15°–25° C (59°–77° F), depending on the nature of the malt being produced. The later stage formerly lasted ten or more days, but modern management of water uptake and other factors often reduces the germination period to five days.

In modern operations, the malting floors, which required considerable space for the spreading of grain, have been replaced by mechanical devices allowing greater grain depths. Germination is achieved in compartments, such as the Saladin box, or in drums and is controlled by mechanically turning the contents of the boxes or by rotating the drums on an inclined axis while aerating the grain with streams of humidified air. Malted wheat, rye, and oats are occasionally used in small quantities to improve the worts and, in the case of wheat, for the brewing of special beers. Various malting systems have been devised that control growth by allowing the respiratory carbon dioxide to accumulate; by exact control of the temperatures of successive steeps; by carrying out the combined steeping and germination steps in a single vessel; and by continuous means whereby the barley, placed on moving belts and treated by water sprays, is washed, steeped, and germinated.

Malting takes advantage of enzymes produced by the young plant. Starch-splitting enzymes, mainly α- and β-amylase, break down the residual starch of the malt, and of any unmalted grain mixed with it, to largely fermentable sugars. Proteolytic and other enzymes, such as ribonuclease, phosphatase and β-gluconase also help make the wort a suitable nutrient for the yeast, by providing for nucleoside and phosphate formation and by breaking down gums and thus avoiding difficulties that may arise from high viscosity. Production of a satisfactory level of enzymes formerly required considerable growth of rootlets and respiration, so that a given amount of barley gave only 90 percent or less of its dry content as malt, the rootlets being rubbed off and removed when the malt was dried. This "malting loss" has been reduced by more modern methods. Malting technique has been further improved by the use of minute amounts of gibberellic acid, a microbial product having plant hormone properties, used in the steeping water or as a spray during germination to accelerate malting. It appears identical with a material secreted by the barley embryo and is believed to trigger normal malting.

In most major beer-producing countries, barleys are es-

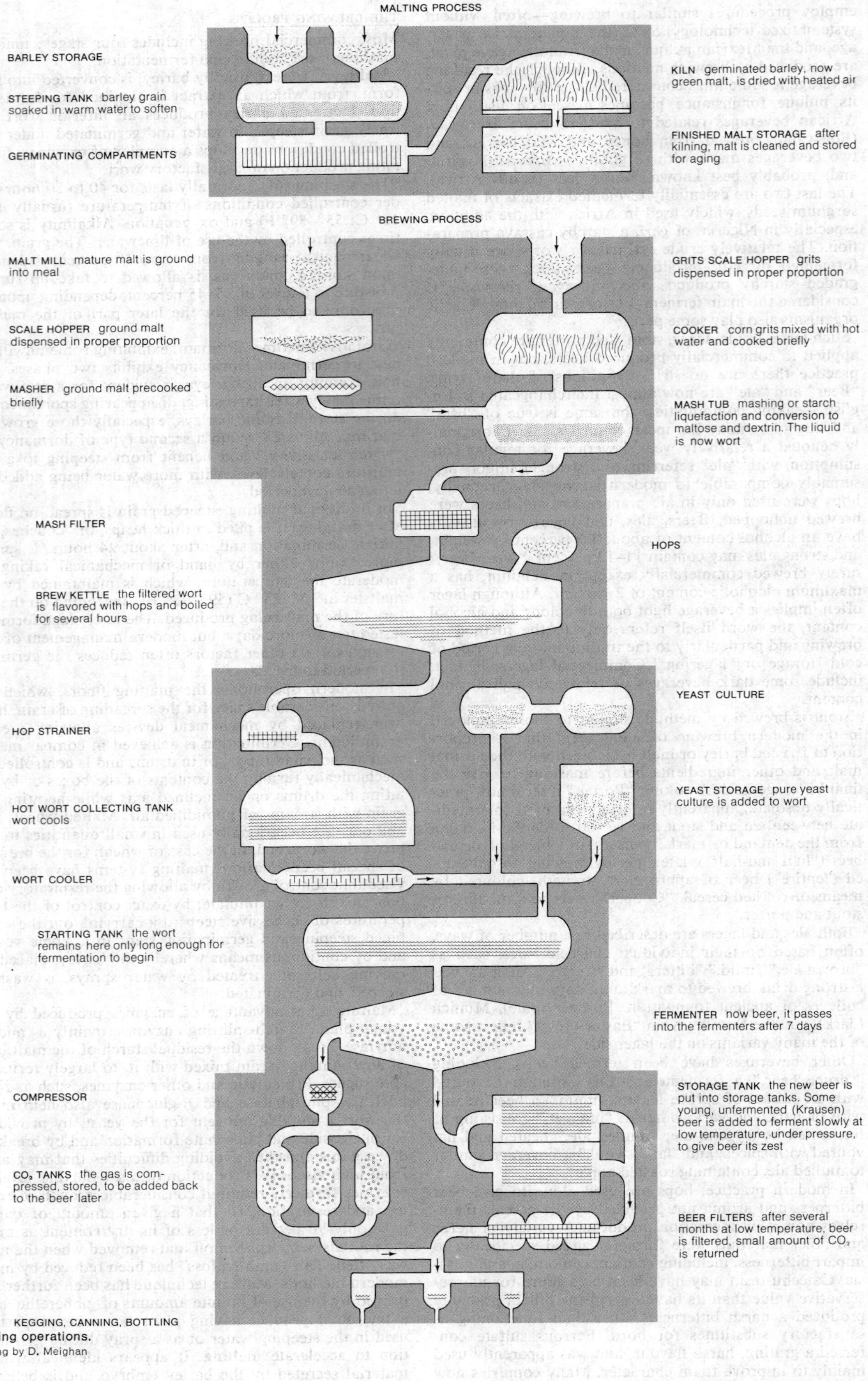

Brewing operations.
Drawing by D. Meighan

pecially selected for malting, and constant efforts are made to improve quality. Selection is based on agricultural, economic, and technical factors, such as agricultural yield and response to varying climatic conditions, and the amount of starch and eventually useful carbohydrate that can be extracted from the malt. Barleys of relatively high nitrogen content, while valuable as animal feedstuffs, are less desirable for malting; barleys of unusually low nitrogen content sometimes fail to yield malts of sufficiently high enzyme content and may produce worts deficient in nitrogenous yeast nutrients. Barleys containing 1.5–1.8 percent of nitrogen are usually preferred.

Most malts, termed "green" and containing about 45 percent of water after germination, are dried and given additional heat treatment, or "curing," before use. Controlled drafts of hot air, formerly from open fires but now mostly from oil-fired installations, are forced through the malt held in "kilns" on perforated floors. Designed for economical operation, kilns turn the malt so that the rootlets are rubbed off and also provide adequate hot-air distribution. Kilning consists of: (1) a phase of drying to about 10 percent of moisture at not more than 45–50° C and (2) a curing stage at 100° C or higher, depending on the purpose of the malt, when its moisture content is reduced to about 5 percent or, as in ale brewing, to about 2 percent. The remaining rootlets ("culms" or "kaulms") are removed by screening and polishing. Chemically, kilning results in: (1) a loss of about 30–60 percent of the enzymatic activity of the green malt, as well as arresting further enzyme activity in the malt itself, and (2) the development of a controllable degree of colour believed mainly due to formation of melanoidins, by the interaction of amino acids or similar compounds with sugars, and the formation of typical "malty" flavour and odour.

Kilning

Mashing. Physically, malt resembles the original barley but is friable and has a biscuity flavour. In brewing, the malt is ground in roller mills to provide a suitable mixture of husks, flour, and grits, then mixed with two to four parts of hot water, depending upon the procedure used. The hot water (or "liquor") usually contains, either originally or as a result of pretreatment, large amounts of calcium and frequently magnesium salts. Temperature is carefully controlled by simple operating steps. The whole process is carried out either in a single vessel (infusion mashing) at 63–68° C (145–155° F) as in ale brewing, or in an arrangement in decoction mashing for lager brewing. In this method, when the mash reaches around 45° C (113° F), a portion is withdrawn to a "mash kettle," boiled, and then added back to the main mash. By replication of this step the main mashing temperature of 62° C (144° F) is attained, usually followed by a final period at 70–75° C (158°–167° F).

As much as 50 percent of the mash grist may be composed of unmalted cereals such as rice, maize, wheat flour, barley grain, ground barley, or prepared forms of barley flakes, which sometimes need gelatinization before mixing with the main mash. Carefully chosen in relation to wort composition, these unmalted cereals improve the quality of the final beer, including foam character (head retention) and capacity to remain clear and free from off-flavours during storage (shelf life).

Preparing the wort

When mashing is complete, the aqueous solution, or wort, is separated from the spent grains by filtration, either in the mashing vessel itself through a slotted bottom plate or in a second vessel called a lauter tub. Wort collection is completed by freeing the spent grain from adherent wort by "sparging" with hot liquor. Many time-consuming variations in traditional methods add at least several hours to the process. The process is now commonly shortened by the adoption of shorter "stand-times," by the use of shallow depths of grain during filtration and by other means, allowing up to 12 mashes to be carried in a 24 hour period. Modern, fully continuous processes allow continuous brewery operation. There is also a trend toward preparing worts with extraneous enzymes of mold or bacterial origin, or with acid, which may be made elsewhere, then stored and transported to the brewery as wort syrups.

Mashing is largely a chemical process in which the malt enzymes act to convert the starch to a mixture of soluble carbohydrates. Ninety-seven percent or more of the starch is extracted; the wort for an average type of beer consists of perhaps a 10 percent solution of carbohydrates, about three-fourths of the carbohydrate material being fermentable sugar. It also contains about 0.08 percent of nitrogen, important in managing both the fermentation and final beer quality. The spent grains, or "brewers" grains, are useful as a nitrogenous addition to cattle feed.

Wort boiling. The wort is next boiled with hops for up to 2½ hours in large "kettles," formerly directly fired but now usually operated by oil firing. The amount and variety of the hops may vary from 200 to 700 grams per hectolitre (0.27 to 0.9 ounces per gallon), according to the beer. Boiling regulates composition and sterilizes the final wort so that some protein coagulates, removing a proportion of tannin, and the wort acquires the desired bitterness from the uptake of hop resins.

In addition to technical improvements of kettle design and greater understanding of the effects of boiling at various rates, degrees of evaporation, and boiling under pressure with varying access to air, extensive work has been done on the selection of hop varieties and their relative value. This is often linked with their agricultural characteristics and susceptibility to wilt and other plant diseases.

The role of hops

The hop, usually *Humulus lupulus*, is a perennial plant whose dried cones are used in brewing. More than 200,000,000 pounds are produced annually. A small proportion is used in "dry hopping," in which the beer at a late stage is kept in contact with hop cones for several days. Hops of especially agreeable aroma are selected, since their main purpose is to impart a small amount of the essential oil of hops to the beer. The oil, an exceedingly complex mixture, is sometimes added directly to the beer. The main role of the hops, however, is to impart an agreeable bitterness, effected chiefly through the "α-acids," a family of chemical compounds, the humulones, making up 5–10 percent of the whole cones and about one-third of the total resin content of the hops. The ultimate bitterness is not due directly to humulones but mostly to "isohumulones" derived from the α-acids during boiling. For some time, the isohumulones have been known to add the desirable constituents of hops to wort as an extract; and, more recently, the isohumulones usually have been added in the form of "isomerized extracts" at a suitable point, sometimes after fermentation.

When hop cones are used, they are eventually removed, traditionally on a "hop back" in which the debris forms its own filter bed. Spent hops, compounded with ferrous sulfate and other mineral salts, are a by-product of brewing, providing an artificial horticultural fertilizer.

Fermentation. Bittered wort, after any necessary storage at a high or a low temperature to inhibit infection, is brought to a selected temperature and transferred into large open or closed vessels for fermentation. The wort is "pitched" with a selected yeast used in varying forms of moisture content from "liquid" to "pressed," usually 250–400 grams of pressed yeast per hectolitre. Top fermentations are usually carried out using selected strains of *Saccharomyces cerevisiae*, botanically identical with bakers' yeast. Ales and stouts are usually fermented at 15°–20° C, formerly from four to six days but now shortened by modern methods to as little as one day. Much of the yeast, multiplying severalfold, rises to the surface (top fermentation) as the main part of the fermentation takes place. When the reaction has moderated, the yeast is separated either by running off the beer or by skimming or centrifuging the yeast. The brewer usually does this before fermentation is completed to allow for secondary fermentation or maturation in a separate vessel. In the case of cask beers, the small residual fermentation gives the natural "condition" of the beer. Most bottled beers are chilled, filtered, and carbonated, often with the carbon dioxide produced earlier in fermentation. They may also be pasteurized and in some countries are sterilized by addition of specific inhibitory materials.

Lagers are fermented (bottom fermentation) 10 to 12 days at a lower starting temperature (6° to 8° C), using selected strains of *Saccharomyces carlsbergensis*, and are matured at 0° C, sometimes for several months. During fermentation, yeast is carried temporarily to the surface ("krausen") but most eventually flocculates, and the beer is run off into the conditioning vessel. The lager, or storage, cellar gives its name (derived from the German *lagern*, meaning "to store") to lagers in general.

Chemically, fermentation involves the conversion of glucose into ethyl alcohol, carbon dioxide, and water. Average beers contain around 3.5 percent of ethanol, but some contain up to 12 percent. During fermentation the specific gravity falls, average figures being from 1.045 to 1.012. The specific gravity never falls to one or less, as might theoretically seem possible, since unfermented carbohydrate always remains and nitrogen compounds also make a contribution. The strength of a beer, however, is usually quoted by reference to the original gravity. The glucose is not usually present in the wort but is formed by enzymatic action of the yeast on maltose and maltotriose, leaving 25 percent or more of the carbohydrates of the wort as unfermentable.

Both ales and lagers are sometimes produced by continuous fermentation, especially in New Zealand. The object of the commercial brewer is not merely to produce a solution of alcohol but to brew a generally agreeable beverage. His choice of yeast is based on the objective of producing beers with agreeable nuances of flavour and aroma, due in part to minor fermentation products (fusel oils; see below), and an avoidance of such undesirable minor products as acetaldehyde, diacetyl, and any excess of volatile sulfur compounds. In addition, he must ensure consistency of such qualities as colour, clarity, and foam character.

Importance of colour and flavour

Colour and flavour are distinctive features of beers. The basic pale-yellow colour results from the combination of malt with other cereals, and much of the colour results from the malt kilning. High kilning temperature usually produces deep colour in the final beer, the colour of the malt and wort being used to control the final beer colour. The incorporation of highly roasted barley or malt leads to very dark beers of the stout type. Light kilning alone is often insufficient to achieve the requisite degree of colour together with the appropriate composition of the derived wort to produce a desired degree of fermentation. In such circumstances the natural pale colour of the beer is usually darkened by the addition of caramel. Colour in beer results from the presence of melanoidins, substances formed by interaction of the carbohydrates present in malts and worts with amino compounds as typified by the α-amino acids also present in the same brewing materials. Some formation of melanoidins occurs on boiling wort; and even a very pale sweet wort, derived from unkilned malt, acquires considerable colour when boiled.

The characteristic flavour and aroma of malt is not identifiable in the final beer, since most of the aroma is removed during the boiling process. Malt "quality," although often partly reflected by malt flavour and aroma, mainly resides in the detailed composition of the wort, influencing formation of minor fermentation products contributing to the character of the final beer. These products are mainly "fusel oils" consisting of a mixture of compounds including normal propanol, isobutanol, 2- and 3-methylbutanols, ethyl, isobutyl, and isoamylacetates. The amounts of fusel oil in most beers range from about 50 to 150 parts per million. The varying nuances of flavour in beers result from both the amounts of fusel oil and the proportions of the individual components. The taste response to the latter is variable and is dependent on the other flavourful components present. The many delicate nuances of flavour are not formed by single compounds but by mixtures that, because they are still incompletely defined, cannot presently be controlled by instrumentation but only by subjective means such as taste testing.

ECONOMIC ASPECTS

Approximately 13,000,000,000 imperial gallons of beer are produced annually throughout the world. The three largest producing countries are the United States, West Germany, and Great Britain, with 3,200,000,000; 1,700,000,000; and 1,200,000,000 gallons, respectively. Annual per capita consumption ranges from little more than two imperial gallons in Italy and Argentina up to 28.4 gallons in Czechoslovakia. (An imperial gallon is four litres, or about 1.2 U.S. gallons.) The rates for the United States and Great Britain are 13.9 and 20.5 gallons, respectively. Beer drinking is increasing and fiscally encouraged in many countries, probably seeming sociologically less undesirable than spirit drinking. Apart from Denmark and Holland, the proportion of beer export to beer production is comparatively small though increasing. National distribution, however, has become more common than the earlier practice of local distribution.

In some areas of large geographic extent, such as the United States, distribution of beer concentrates intended for reconstitution has grown as an alternative to the more costly distribution of the beer itself or the duplication of a main brewery in a distant area. Such concentrates, usually 20–25 percent of the original beer volume, are obtainable either by limited distillation or by freezing the beer and separating the ice crystals from the concentrate. With the addition of both water and carbon dioxide, these concentrates are reconstituted into a beverage like the original beer.

BIBLIOGRAPHY. A.H. BURGESS, *Hops* (1964), a major book on hop cultivation and the historical, scientific, and technical aspects of the use of hops in beer brewing; A.H. COOK (ed.), *Barley and Malt* (1962), a series of authoritative essays on such subjects as the botany and diseases of barley, breeding and identification of barley varieties, and the technical and scientific aspects of the malting process and malt, *Chemistry and Biology of Yeasts* (1958), a systematic account of the classification, ecology, life history, and genetics of yeast in general; J. DE CLERCK, *A Textbook of Brewing*, 2 vol., trans. by K. BARTON-WRIGHT (1957–58), a discussion of technical brewing practice throughout the world and analytical procedures for the examination of brewing materials and beers; M. HOFFMAN, *5000 Jahre Bier* (1956), a largely historical account of the development of brewing techniques, notable for its insight into the role of beer and brewing in ancient civilizations; P. MATHIAS, *The Brewing Industry in England, 1700–1830* (1959), an extensive account of the rise of brewing as an organized industry and the development of major British breweries now of international repute; H.A. MONCKTON, *A History of English Ale and Beer* (1966), a highly entertaining, informative, and essentially nontechnical volume on such matters as the development of brewing from Roman times through monastery and home brewing to the present-day industry; I.A. PREECE, *Biochemistry of Brewing* (1954), a scientific as distinct from technical account of the chemistry of the raw materials and processes of malting and brewing; F. SCHOELLHORN, *Bibliographie des Brauwesens* (1928), lists of technical references to Latin literature from the 15th century onwards, to about 1750 German sources, and to similar scientific papers written in the English, French, Swedish, Danish, Czech, Russian, Dutch, Norwegian, Italian, and Hungarian languages.

(A.H.C.)

Brick and Tile Production

The brick, first produced in a sun-dried form at least 6,000 years ago, and the forerunner of a wide range of clay building products used today, is a small building unit in the form of a rectangular block, formed from clay or shale or mixtures and burned (fired) in a kiln, or oven, to produce strength, hardness, and heat resistance. The original concept of ancient brickmakers was that the unit should not be larger than what one man could easily handle; today, brick size varies from country to country, and every nation's brickmaking industry produces a range of sizes that may run into the hundreds. The majority of bricks for most construction purposes have dimensions of approximately 2¼ × 3¾ × 8 inches (5.5 × 9.5 × 20 centimetres).

Structural clay tile, also called terra-cotta, is a larger building unit, containing many hollow spaces (cells), and is used mainly as backup for brick facing or for plastered partitions.

Structural clay-facing tile is often glazed for use as an exposed finish. Wall and floor tile is a thin material of fired clay with a natural or glazed finish. Quarry tile is a dense pressed fired-clay product for floors, patios, and industrial installations in which a high resistance to abrasion or acids is required.

Firebrick is used in incinerators, boilers, industrial and home furnaces, and fireplaces. Sewer pipe is fired and glazed for use in sewage-disposal systems, industrial-waste systems, and general drainage. Drain tile is porous, round, sometimes perforated and is used mainly for agricultural drainage. Roofing tile is made in the form of half-round (Spanish tile) and various flat tiles made to resemble slate or cedar shakes; it is used extensively in the Mediterranean countries.

There are also many products made from cement and aggregates that substitute for, and generally perform the same functions as, the clay products listed above.

Data on the quantity of brick and tile produced throughout the world is not available. The United States Bureau of Commerce has fairly accurate data indicating that approximately 6,500,000,000 bricks are produced annually (1970s). Other data indicate that England produces about as many bricks per year as the United States, and it is probable that the large countries of western Europe produce as many bricks as the United States. Australia is high in per capita production. Many countries having hot and dry climates (including the southwest United States) still produce sun-dried bricks.

HISTORY

Mud brick (dried in the sun) was one of the first building materials. It is conceivable that on the Nile, Euphrates, or Tigris rivers, following floods, the deposited mud or silt cracked and formed cakes that could be shaped into crude building units to build huts for protection from the weather. In the ancient city of Ur, in Mesopotamia (Iraq), the first true arch of sun-baked brick was made about 4000 BC. The arch itself has not survived, but a description of it includes the first known reference to mortars other than mud. A bitumen slime was used to bind the bricks together.

Burned brick, no doubt, had already been produced simply by containing a fire with mud bricks. In Ur the potters discovered the principle of the closed kiln, in which heat could be controlled. The ziggurat at Ur is an example of early monumental brickwork perhaps built of sun-dried brick; the steps had to be replaced after 2,500 years (about 1500 BC) by burned brick.

As civilization spread eastward and westward from the Middle East, so did the manufacture and use of brick. The Great Wall of China (210 BC) was built of both burned and sun-dried bricks. Early examples of brickwork in Rome were the reconstruction of the Pantheon (AD 123) with an unprecedented brick and concrete dome, 142 feet (43 metres) in diameter and height, and the Baths of Hadrian, where pillars of terra-cotta were used to support floors heated by roaring fires.

Enamelling or glazing of brick and tile was known to the Babylonians and Assyrians as early as 600 BC, again stemming from the potter's art. The great mosques of Jerusalem (Dome of the Rock), Isfahan, and Teheran are excellent examples of glazed tile used as mosaics. Some of the blues found in these glazes cannot be reproduced by present manufacturing processes.

Western Europe probably exploited brick as a building and architectural unit more than any other area in the world. It was particularly important in combatting the disastrous fires that chronically affected medieval cities. After the Great Fire of 1666, London changed from being a city of wood and became one of brick, solely to gain protection from fire.

Bricks and brick construction were taken to the New World by the earliest European settlers. The Coptic descendants of the ancient Egyptians on the upper Nile called their technique of making mud brick *tōbe*. The Arabs transmitted the name to the Spaniards, who, in turn, brought the art of adobe brickmaking to the southern portion of North America. In the north the Dutch West India Company built the first brick building on Manhattan Island in 1633.

MANUFACTURING

Basically, the process of making brick has not changed since the first fired bricks were produced some thousands of years ago. The steps used then are used today, but with refinements. The various phases of manufacture are as follows: securing the clay, preparation, mixing and forming, drying, firing, and cooling.

Clays used today are more varied than those used by the first brickmakers. Digging, mining, and various methods of grinding enable the modern manufacturer to utilize many raw materials.

Clays used in brickmaking represent a wide range of materials that include varying percentages of silica and alumina. They may be grouped in three classes: first, surface clays found near or on the surface of the earth, typically in river bottoms; second, shales, clays subjected to high geologic pressures and varying in hardness from a slate to a form of partially decomposed rock; and third, fireclays, found deeper under the surface and requiring mining. Fireclays have a more uniform chemical composition than surface clays or shale. Classes of clays used

Securing (winning) the clay. Surface clays are typically recovered by means of power shovels, bulldozers with scraper blades, and dragline operations. Shales are recovered by blasting and power shovels. Fireclays are mined by conventional techniques.

Preparation. Raw clays are often blended to obtain a more uniform consistency. In many cases the material is ground to reduce large rocks or clumps of clay to usable size and is placed in storage sheds. As additional material is stored, samples are blended from a whole cross section of the storage pile. The material is then transferred to secondary grinders and screens (if necessary) to secure the optimum particle size for mixing with water. In certain processes (*e.g.*, soft-mud), the clay is transferred directly to the mixing area, eliminating all grinding, screening, and blending.

Mixing and forming. All clays must be mixed with water to form the finished product. The amount of water added will depend on the nature of the clays and their plasticity. This water is removed during drying and firing, which causes shrinkage of the units; to compensate for this shrinkage the molds are made larger than the desired finished products. Three basic processes are used in the forming and mixing phase. In the stiff-mud process, the clay is mixed with water to render it plastic, after which it is forced through a die that extrudes a column of clay like the toothpaste squeezed from a tube. The column gives two dimensions of the unit being manufactured; it is cut to give the third dimension. All structural clay tile is made by this process, as is a great percentage of brick. In the older method of forming bricks, the soft-mud process, much more water is used, and the mix is placed in wooden molds to form the size unit desired. To keep the clay from sticking, the molds are lubricated with sand or water; after they are filled, excess clay is struck from the top of the mold. It is from this process that the terms wood-mold, sand-struck, or water-struck brick were derived. Clays with very low plasticity are used in the dry press process. A minimum of water is added, the material is placed in steel molds, and pressures up to 1,500 pounds per square inch are applied.

Drying. After the bricks are formed, they must be dried to remove as much free water as possible (they could literally explode if subjected to fire without drying). Drying, apart from sun drying, is done in drier kilns with controlled temperature, draft, and humidity.

Firing and cooling. Bricks are fired and cooled in a kiln, an oven-type chamber capable of producing temperatures of 1,600° to over 2,000° F (870° to 1,100° C), depending on the type of raw material. There are two general types of kilns, periodic and continuous.

The earliest type of kiln, the scove, is merely a pile of dried bricks with tunnels at the bottom allowing heat from fires to pass through and upward in the pile of bricks. The walls and top are plastered with a mixture of sand, clay, and water to retain the heat; at the top the bricks are placed close together and vented for circulation to pull the heat up through the brick. The clamp kiln is an improvement over the scove kiln in that the exterior walls are permanent, with openings at the bottom to permit firing of the tunnels.

A further refinement of the scove kiln, round or rectangular in form, is designated as updraft or downdraft, indicating the direction of heat flow. In these kilns the walls and crown are permanent and there are firing ports around the exterior.

In so-called periodic kilns, the bricks are placed with sufficient air space to allow the heat from the fires to reach all surfaces. They are placed directly from the drier, and heat is gradually increased until the optimum firing temperature is reached. When they are sufficiently fired, the heat is reduced, and they are allowed to cool gradually before removal from the kiln.

Series of kilns

The periodic kiln was improved in efficiency by placing several kilns in line with connecting passages. The first chamber is fired first and the excess heat passed to the next chamber to start heating. Successively, the various chambers are brought to optimum firing and cooling temperatures, until all bricks have been fired and cooled. This arrangement is known as the moving fire zone. In the more modern fixed fire zone, dried bricks are placed on cars carrying as many as 3,000 or more bricks; the cars are started at the cool end of a long tunnel kiln and moved slowly forward through gradually increasing temperatures until they reach the firing zone, pass and emerge through decreasing heat zones until cooled.

Automation. Since the development of the tunnel, kiln brickmakers have sought to increase automation in their plants. Handling of the finished product has been automated to the point that bricks emerging from the kiln are now automatically stacked in packages of approximately 500, strapped with metal bands, and stored, shipped, and delivered by mechanical equipment.

In some plants bricks are taken from the cutter machine, placed in the drier or on drier cars by mechanical means, placed on kiln cars by mechanical fingers, removed from the kiln cars mechanically, stacked, strapped, and prepared for shipment without being touched by hand.

COLOURS AND TEXTURES

Colour of clay products may be natural or applied.

Natural colours. These depend on the type of clay used in the production processes. They range from whites through grays, buffs, light to dark reds, and into the purple range. Fireclays are associated with the lighter colours such as the grays and buffs. Ordinary clays and shales are associated with the red ranges. By regulating the oxidizing conditions in the kiln, browns, purples, and blacks can be obtained. The process is known as flashing, and in general the change of colour of the bricks is only on the surface, the body of the unit retaining its natural colour. Some metals, such as manganese, are mixed with the clays to develop special colours.

Applied colours. Colours are applied to many brick products, particularly structural glazed tile, wall and floor tile, and brick. Ceramic glazes are applied to units before or after the firing and cooling stage. If after, the units must be refired. These glazes provide almost all of the basic colours plus some special colours used for "accent" in the design of a wall. The glazes become an integral part of the face of the units since they are burned to the same degree of heat as the units. Finishes and colours other than ceramic glazes are applied to the units either fired or unfired and are surface coatings that conceal the natural colour of the burned unit. In some countries a demand for old brick has led to application of mixtures of cement or lime and sand and many other combinations to give brick an aged appearance.

Types of finishes

Texture. The texture of clay products is directly associated with the manufacturing processes. The soft-mud process produces either a sand- or water-struck finish in a non-uniform texture, which gives the brick (only bricks are made under this process) the appearance of handmade or antique brick. The dry-press process, using steel molds, gives a smooth texture only. This process is seldom used in modern-day brick production but is used in the manufacture of quarry tile as well as floor and wall tile. The stiff-mud process offers the most possibilities for texturing brick. As the prepared clay is extruded through the die, the pressure produces a smooth surface similar to that of concrete when smoothed with a steel trowel. This surface is called the die skin; its removal and further treatment produce other textures.

In wire cutting, a wire placed in front of the column of clay as it comes from the die removes the die skin, creating a semi-rough surface.

In sand finishing, sand is applied to the column of clay by various means to give a very even surface of sand, which is fired into the unit. The desired texture is similar to a wood-mold brick except that the unit is much more uniform in size and in finish. Colour also may be changed by the type of sand used.

Scored finishing is used mostly on tile where the surface of the tile is grooved to give a better bond between the unit and plaster. This is also true of a roughened or combed finish produced by wire brushing or scratching.

Roughened finishing is used when the die skin is removed by various means. In one method, the material cut in removing the die skin may be rolled back into the face of the unit.

Other finishes are applied by rollers on the column to give certain effects such as bark, log, or emblems. Terracotta for architectural decoration is both machine extruded and handmade (molded or pressed). It is distinguished from other clay products by the generally larger size of the units. It may be hand carved and used mostly in murals as bas-relief. Both natural and glazed finishes are produced.

USES OF BRICK

By far the largest use of brick products is, as it always has been, in building construction. Many significant changes have taken place in building with brick.

Building construction. It may be roughly accurate to say that about 65 percent of all the brick in the world goes into dwellings, and 35 percent goes into commercial, industrial, and institutional buildings. Construction techniques change yearly and from country to country, but basically most brick and tile are used in walls, with lesser use in roofs and floors.

Walls may be classified in three general categories, load-bearing, non-load-bearing, and veneer. A load-bearing wall supports the loads of a structure, such as floors, equipment, furniture, and people. At one time, buildings were constructed with very thick brick walls carrying all floor and other loads. Design of these walls was not based on engineering data but only on well-intentioned but unscientific building codes. As buildings grew taller, the building code requirements for thickness of a brick wall became economically prohibitive. The last truly high-rise, load-bearing brick structure built under older codes was the Monadnock Building in Chicago (1889–91), 16 stories tall with the brick walls 6 feet (2 metres) thick at the base, tapering to 12 inches (30 centimetres) at the top story. The arrival of structural steel on the building scene put a temporary end to the brick bearing-wall skyscraper, but research in the 20th century has led to a resurgence. Thinner walls can be designed for high-rise buildings and built safely at a reasonable cost. Apartment buildings in Switzerland, Germany, Denmark, England, and other countries have risen 15 or more stories supported by brick bearing walls no more than 12 inches (30 centimetres) thick. The use of reinforced brickwork (a combination of brick, reinforcing steel, mortar, and cement grout) permits even thinner walls; a 17-story building designed to resist earthquake shocks uses only 11-inch walls.

Types of bearing walls

Bearing walls may be classified into five general groups: (1) brick, including brick tied together with cross brick (headers) or with metal ties; (2) composite walls of brick and tile tied together with headers or metal ties; (3) cavity walls, in which the inner and outer wythes (tiers) of units are tied together with metal ties but separated by an air space usually two or more inches in width; (4) reinforced walls, similar to cavity walls except that steel is placed in the cavity and the cavity filled with a soupy mortar (grout); (5) single unit walls, using a unit of necessary thickness to meet design requirements.

Non-load-bearing walls carry only their own weight and may be any one of the types discussed under load-bearing walls. This type of wall is used to close in a steel or concrete frame building. It is usually carried by supports, normally steel shelf angles at each floor, and is called a panel wall. When the wall is supported at the base only, it is called a curtain wall.

Veneer walls are similar to non-load-bearing walls in that they carry no weight except their own. The brick or tile is fastened to a backing, but it does not exert a common action with the backing. Perhaps the most common use is brick veneer on wood frame dwellings. Other examples are architectural terra-cotta and thin ceramic veneer on monumental buildings.

Tile roofs are popular in the Mediterranean area and in the Low Countries of western Europe. In Italy, craftsmen have developed an art of using relatively thin tile to form self-supporting arches. Tile roofs in many other areas, particularly on residences, have been used extensively in the past, but economic considerations limit their use now; in addition to the cost of the tile is the cost of roof framing to support the heavier weight of the tile.

Miscellaneous uses in building construction include retaining walls, brick floors, patios, and walks. Most of these uses are decorative as well as utilitarian. The retaining wall of reinforced brick provides an economical means of restraining earth movement and at the same time maintains a continuity of architectural effect, particularly if the adjoining structure is built of brick.

Brick floors, patios, and walks utilize the physical properties of brick, such as resistance to abrasion and to the elements. Paving brick, per se, is practically nonexistent, except for replacement where roads and streets were brick paved long ago. Industrial floor brick, however, supplies many industries whose manufacturing and handling processes require floors that resist acids and provide a high degree of resistance to abrasion. Brick floors and patios, besides providing a long-lasting, low-maintenance material, offer the designer a medium for developing architectural effects in both colours and patterns.

Clay drainage products. Sewer pipe plays an important part in the world's ecology. An almost impervious material because of its firing, denseness, and glazing, it can carry highly corrosive waste materials that few other products can handle economically.

Drain tile performs a service that ensures a higher yield in farm production of food throughout the world. Many farming areas are plagued with too much water at the wrong times. Drain tile reduces the water level during these times, thereby allowing the root growth of plants to penetrate deeper into the soil, which, in turn, permits them later to resist hot dry weather.

Art in clay products. The walls of ancient Babylon were decorated work, and brick has served decorative and artistic purposes ever since. Terra-cotta, molded, formed, and glazed, has been used for years in murals. Many architects use patterns of brickwork to relieve the monotony of a large expanse of plain wall, while others deliberately use the starkness of large plain walls to emphasize form.

MANUFACTURING NONCLAY BRICK AND TILE

Following the introduction of portland cement in the 19th century, a growing number of products have appeared which resemble clay products in size and intended use. In some countries the production of them, if reduced to brick equivalents, exceeds that of clay products. A brief review of these products, the material used, and the manufacturing processes may serve to suggest the interrelation between these and clay products.

Concrete block is a large unit, usually 8 inches high, 16 inches long, and of various thicknesses, made from a mixture of cement and an aggregate, which may be cinders, limestone, or expanded clay or shale (burned in a rotary kiln). The mixture of cement, aggregate, and a minimum of water is placed in steel molds and vibrated to compact the mixture. The formed units are removed from the molds and cured either in air, steam, or under autoclaving processes (steam under pressure).

Concrete brick is a mixture of cement and aggregate, usually sand, formed in molds and cured. Certain mineral colours are added to produce a concrete brick resembling clay. Concrete pipe is made of cement and aggregate and cured as above. Used as a substitute for clay sewer pipe, it does not have as much resistance to the corrosive action of certain acids. Concrete drain tile and concrete roofing tile are produced similarly.

Sand–lime brick is a product that uses lime instead of cement. It is usually a white brick made of lime and selected sands, cast in molds and cured. Production is limited, with greater use in the United States and Germany.

BIBLIOGRAPHY. H.C. PLUMMER, *Brick and Tile Engineering*, 2nd ed. (1962), a comprehensive technical publication on brick manufacturing, sizes, design, and uses, including a bibliography of intensive investigation into the behaviour of clay products in structural systems; B. FOERSTER (ed.), *Man and Masonry* (1960), pictorial presentation of masonry structures, new and old, as related to the environment of man; *Technical Notes*, a monthly publication of the Structural Clay Products Institute, McLean, Virginia, on all phases of brick and tile production and use, previous issues are updated as research reveals new data; E.A. SPEISER and H.M. HERBERT, "Ancient Mesopotamia," *Nat. Geogr. Mag.*, 99:41–105 (1951), excellent coverage of the ancient use of brick, with references to brickmaking; S.E. JONES, "When in Rome," *ibid.*, 137:741–789 (1970), an illustrated history of masonry, including construction during Hadrian's reign and the brick dome on the Pantheon.

(J.A.Le.)

Bridge

Bridge is the name applied to the modern card game of Contract Bridge and also to the earlier games of Auction Bridge and Bridge Whist. All are derived from the old English game of Whist and retain its essential features: four players participate, two against two in partnership; play is with a 52-card pack, divided into four suits—spades, hearts, diamonds, and clubs; each suit has 13 cards, ranking from the ace, king, queen, jack, ten, down to the two; the cards are dealt face downward one at a time, clockwise; when play begins, the object is to win tricks, consisting of a card from each player in rotation; players must, if able, contribute a card of the suit led, and the trick is won by the highest card; before play begins a suit may be designated the trump suit, in which case any card in it beats any card of the other suits.

Essential features of the Bridge games

Such are the elements of Whist, Bridge Whist, Auction Bridge, and Contract Bridge, which, from the early 18th century, have reigned in turn as the most intellectually stimulating of the card games. Successive improvements in other features of the games have greatly enlarged the scope for inferential reasoning, psychological stratagems, and partnership cooperation. In Whist the trump suit was settled arbitrarily by turning up a card; in Bridge Whist it was selected by the dealer or his partner; in Auction Bridge there was competition (bidding) for the right to choose trumps; and in Contract Bridge a side must try to judge the exact number of tricks it can take and bid accordingly. These and other developments have given rise to a very elaborate technique for skillful bidding and play.

Contract Bridge takes longer to learn than other card games but is by far the most fascinating and shows no sign of losing its appeal. By the 1970s it was played by 80,000,000 men and women in every part of the world. There were more than 5,500 clubs in North America alone, many national governing bodies and continent-wide leagues, and a World Bridge Federation whose Olympiads and annual championships were treated as seriously as other international sporting contests. More than 5,000 books on the game had been published, those still in print selling an estimated 1,000,000 copies annually, and there were at least 60 periodicals. The majority of newspapers in the Western world carried Bridge articles, and the International Bridge Press Association had well over 200 members.

The first part of this article is a historical survey describing Whist and its development into Bridge Whist, Auction Bridge, and Contract Bridge. The second part describes the laws and strategy of Contract Bridge. A bibliography is provided for the reader who seeks instruction in this game.

The Whist and Bridge family is of English origin, having evolved gradually from several other games, principally Triumph, a name that became corrupted to Trump. Triumph was also known as English Ruff and Honours and was based on the concept of one card being able to beat another, with a particular suit predominating. It is referred to in a sermon preached by Hugh Latimer at Cambridge in 1529 and in Shakespeare's *Anthony and Cleopatra*.

WHIST

Origin. The name Whist, or Whisk, appears to have originated in the early 17th century. Whisk, as a game, is referred to in a poem (1621) by John Taylor, while Charles Cotton's *Compleat Gamester* (1674) devotes a section to it and says, "Ruff and Honours, [alias slamm] and Whist are games so commonly known in England in all parts thereof, that every child almost of eight years old hath a competent knowledg [sic] in that recreation." At first Whist was a game for the lower orders and also a rural accomplishment, but early in the 18th century it was taken up by gentlemen who frequented London's coffee houses. In 1742 the first book wholly devoted to it, Edmond Hoyle's *Short Treatise on Whist*, was published and was a best seller. The game then became extremely popular in the fashionable world, spreading quickly to Europe and America and remaining for one and a half centuries the king of card games.

Duplicate Whist, in which the same hands were played at two tables and the results compared, was played in London in 1857 under the direction of Henry Jones, who, under the pseudonym Cavendish, became the leading writer on the game. The duplicate principle (see below) became popular, and contests were held, resulting in the formation of the American Whist League in 1891.

Essential features. The two players facing each other are partners against the other two. The cards are dealt singly, and the last is turned up to determine the trump suit. The player at the left of the dealer leads by playing any one of his cards face upward on the table, and each player in turn, clockwise, contributes a card of the same suit if he can; if he cannot, he may play any card, including a trump. The four cards played constitute a trick, which is gathered up by the side that played the highest card of the suit led or the highest trump. The winner of a trick leads to the next, and play continues until every card has been played. The side winning the most tricks scores a point for each odd trick (*i.e.*, each trick over six).

Strategy. Best results are achieved by winning tricks with the lowest sufficient card and by capturing high cards played by the opponents whenever possible. The players try to gauge the whereabouts of the unplayed cards and, by collaborating with their partners, to win tricks, not only with high cards and trumps but with low cards that become winners when all of the higher cards in the suit have been played.

Signalling conventions

The development of an optimum strategy is difficult, for each player's hand is known only to himself, and information can be exchanged only by signalling; *i.e.*, playing one's cards in a sequence that, by convention, conveys a message. An example, proposed by Lord Henry Bentinck in 1834, is the "echo" or "peter" in a suit other than the trump suit—the play of an unnecessarily high spot card followed by a lower card in the same suit—asking partner to lead trump. Signalling became highly developed, and in 1883 Nicholas B. Trist proposed a complex schedule of opening leads that was enthusiastically adopted on both sides of the Atlantic.

With all hands concealed, however, even the greatest players could employ only the most elementary strategies. Hoyle and his successors, including William Payne (*Maxims*, 1773), Thomas Mathews (*Advice to the Young Whist Player*, 1804), James Clay, Guillaume Deschapelles (according to his contemporaries the finest of all Whist players), and finally Cavendish, concluded that it was expedient to assume that the best strategy, in most cases, was simply to lead first from one's longest and strongest suit in an attempt to establish it.

The widespread employment of this strategy led to a most valuable device, known as the rule of 11 and widely used in modern Bridge. It was published by Robert F. Foster in 1890 and was based on the mathematical fact that when a player leads the fourth highest card of a long suit, the number of higher cards held in the other three hands can be found by subtracting from 11 the number of the card led.

As signals became more and more elaborate, Whist became a ritual, and players were ready to turn to the new game, Bridge, which allowed more scope for reason. Whist still has a following in Great Britain and in certain areas of North America, but the status it enjoyed under Cavendish has vanished.

Variations. *Solo Whist.* Solo Whist differs from Whist in that, as in Bridge, each player in turn is entitled to make a call; *i.e.*, announce his willingness to attempt to take a certain number of tricks. The name Solo derives from the fact that, as a result of the calling, the subsequent play usually takes the form of one against three. The range of calls is limited and includes two, *misère*, in which the caller undertakes to win no trick against the combined efforts of the other players to make him take one, and *misère ouvert* (open *misère*), in which he undertakes to take no tricks even though he exposes his hand. The game is popular in Britain, where some devotees display a flair for card play equal to that of an expert Bridge player.

Boston Whist. This is said to have been invented by naval officers during the siege of Boston by the British and the terms great misery and little misery to have been derived from islands thus called in Marblehead harbour, where the French fleet lay for a time. William Tudor, in his *Letters on the Eastern States* (1820), wrote, however, that "A game of cards was invented in Versailles and was called in honour of the town, Boston. . . . It is composed partly of whist and partly of quadrille, though partaking mostly of the former." Boston, and a variation called Boston de Fontainbleu, was played for high stakes in Europe and to a lesser extent in the U.S. until the mid-19th century, when it declined. It was probably the precursor of Solo Whist and resembles it in that there are no partners, but it has many more calls: a player may bid to make any number of tricks from 5 to 13 with his own trump suit and may also bid to lose 12 or 13 tricks. Also, a suit is arbitrarily designated the first preference suit and any call in it beats a similar call in the second preference suit, which in turn beats either of the two remaining suits. After the hand the stakes are settled according to whether or not the player made his call.

Bidding to take or lose tricks

Boston and Solo are of significance in the development of card games since, like Contract Bridge, they employ the idea of a competitive auction in which players estimate how many tricks they can take and bid accordingly.

Vint. This is a partnership game that bears a marked resemblance to both Whist and Bridge. Now obsolete, it was popular in Russia during the period when bridge was developing in the Western countries. Writing in 1897, Foster, then the world's leading authority on card games, says of Vint:

> . . . this game is by some persons thought to be the forerunner of bridge, and might be classed as one of the whist family, but . . . it is at present . . . little known outside of Russia, where it is the national game.
>
> Vint has been variously described as bridge without a Dummy, and as auction whist. It resembles bridge in the making of the trump, and whist in the manner of the play.

The principal affinity with Bridge is that each player in

turn bids to make a certain number of tricks with a suit of his own choosing. But the suits rank differently—hearts, diamonds, clubs, and spades—and, as in Whist, each player can see only his own hand. The scoring too is different, and points are gained for holding a "coronet," a sequence of three or more cards in any suit or three or four aces. A distinctive feature is that every trick taken by either side is counted when it comes to the scoring. Thus, although the bidder's side may make their contract, their opponents may conceivably win the game.

BRIDGE WHIST

Bridge Whist dethroned Whist and, by introducing an exposed dummy, made it possible for the play of the cards to provide a more testing intellectual exercise. This important innovation presumably evolved from three-hand Whist games, resorted to by inveterate players when there were only three available to play; a fourth hand was dealt as usual, but for the play of the hand it was laid out face up on the table, providing much additional and very useful information to all three players, each of whom then could see the cards held in two of the four hands. This exposed hand, called the dummy, was incorporated into the four-handed game by the expedient of making the declarer's (*i.e.*, dealer's) partner the dummy, his hand being exposed upon the opponent's lead to the first trick and played by the declarer. The new game was known first simply as Bridge, the term Bridge Whist being coined later to distinguish it from Auction Bridge.

Origin. A similar game, Khedive, had been played in Constantinople before 1870 and another version in Greece before that. Khedive was played on the French Riviera in the 1870s under the name of Biritch and was called Bridge by the 1880s. It was played at the Whist Club of New York in 1893, and in the following year Lord Brougham, playing in a Whist game at the Portland Club, apologized for failing to turn up the trump card with the excuse that he had forgotten he was not playing Bridge, "the finest card game ever introduced."

Principal innovations. The trump suit was named by the dealer or, at the dealer's option, by his partner; there was also the option of requiring that the hand be played without a trump suit (no-trump); the dealer's partner always became the dummy, and his hand, exposed when the opening lead was made, was played by the declarer. The scoring was more elaborate than at Whist, for after the dealer (or his partner) had declared the trump suits, the player on his left (or his partner) could double; *i.e.*, double the scoring values of the tricks. Calls could then be redoubled and doubled again indefinitely unless limits were placed. The first side to score 30 or more points won a game, and the first to win two games won the rubber and a 100-point bonus.

Introduction of no-trump, exposed dummy, and doubling

Popularity. The new game appealed to women as much as to men and quickly became the favourite of the fashionable world. Although in its relatively brief reign it did not reach the middle and lower classes, as Auction Bridge did later, it provided the means for fuller intellectual and social enjoyment. The exposure of the dummy gave the other three players a basis for reasoning and inference that had previously been lacking and made the play of the hand a much more cerebral activity, while the new method of determining the trump suit introduced a further element of volition. In addition, the no-trump call brought with it a whole new range of tactical problems in the development of long suits. By 1897 almost all leading Whist players had gone over to Bridge, and even Cavendish, who refused for a period to enter the Portland Club because Whist had been all but abandoned there, was converted before his death in 1899.

AUCTION BRIDGE

Bridge Whist had been in vogue for only a few years when the great change was made that produced Auction Bridge—the introduction of competitive bidding for the right to name the trump suit (or no-trump). It quickly rendered the other game obsolete.

Origin. It is not certain to whom Auction Bridge should be credited. A letter in *The Times* (London), January 16, 1905, signed by Oswald Crawfurd, describes Auction Bridge for three players, while a book by "John Doe" (F. Roe), published in Allāhābād, India, in 1899, puts forward three-hand Auction Bridge as an invention of Roe and two other members of the Indian Civil Service, when, at an isolated post, they had no "fourth" for Bridge Whist. By 1904 the best club players in England and America were turning to it, by 1907 the Portland Club had adopted the game, and by 1910 Auction Bridge was king.

Principal innovations. The trump suit, instead of being named by the dealer or his partner, was determined by competitive bidding, as a result of which any one of the four players might become declarer. Thus a player who said "One spade" was bidding to make one-odd (six tricks, comprising a "book," plus one) with spades as trumps, while a player who said "Pass" (in Britain, "No bid") was signifying a disinclination to contract to win any number of tricks. The main principles of the auction remain good for Contract Bridge: a bid must name a greater number of odd tricks than any preceding bid or must name the same number in a higher suit (no-trump ranks highest, followed by spades, hearts, diamonds, and clubs). A player may double the last preceding bid if it was made by an opponent and had not previously been doubled, and a double, similarly, may be redoubled (by the bidder or his partner). A bid may be overcalled whether doubled or not, and the auction continues until three consecutive passes occur. The highest bid possible is seven-odd. The partner of the declarer (the player winning the auction) becomes the dummy, tabling his hand face up after the opening lead is made. If the declarer's side wins fewer odd tricks than it has bid for, the opponents receive points for each undertrick, but these do not count toward game.

Competitive bidding

Popularity of Auction Bridge. By the late 1920s Auction Bridge had become the most popular card game ever known, with at least 15,000,000 followers. This may be attributed to the fact that all four players were able to compete for the right to name the trump suit and become declarer and to the challenge offered to psychology and reason. The best players began to perceive that the combination of the auction principle and the new scoring (see below) gave rise to the concept of an "optimum contract," beyond which neither side could bid without losing more points than it gained, but this was fully understood only after Auction Bridge had been superseded by Contract. External social factors, such as the rapid growth of a leisured middle class, may also have played a part in the popularity of Auction Bridge, which still has a substantial although steadily declining following.

Scoring. In Auction Bridge, unlike Contract, all odd tricks count toward game, unless they are fewer than the number bid for. With clubs as trump, each odd trick counts six; diamonds, seven; hearts, eight; spades, nine; and no-trump, ten. These values are multipled by two if the contract is doubled, by four if it is redoubled. These trick scores are entered "below the line" (referring to the Bridge score pad, which is divided horizontally by a line, with all points counting toward game scored below that line and all other points scored above it).

Trick points and honour points

As in Bridge Whist, a game is won by scoring 30 or more trick points, a rubber by winning two out of three games, but the bonus for a rubber is 250 points instead of 100 as in the older game.

If the declarer's side does not fulfill its contract, its adversaries score 50 points for each undertrick (100 if doubled, 200 if redoubled). These points go in the honour score ("above the line") and do not count toward game. Other entries in the honour score are: for holding three or more of the honours (A, K, Q, J, 10 of the trump suit or the aces at no-trump), bonuses ranging from 30 points for three trump-suit honours in one hand or shared with partner to 100 points for all five trump-suit honours in one hand or all four aces in one hand at no-trump; for making a small, or little, slam (12 tricks), 50, and a grand slam (all 13 tricks), 100. All of these scores are credited to the side earning them, regardless of who is declarer.

If the declarer fulfills a doubled contract, he receives a bonus of 50 points scored above the line, plus 50 points for each trick he wins above his contract, and 100 points in each case at a redoubled contract.

The side that scores the greater total of honour plus trick points is the winner, by the difference between the two total scores.

CONTRACT BRIDGE

As an intellectual pastime Auction Bridge was vastly superior to its forerunners, but a further great innovation remained: the principle that only the tricks contracted for could count toward game, overtricks as well as all bonuses being entered in the honour score scored above the line. With this innovation accuracy in bidding became immensely more important: the object now was to bid what could be made rather than to outbid the opposition as cheaply as possible. At the same time, a more definite target appeared in the play of the cards: the aim was to make or defeat the contract rather than simply to win as many tricks as possible.

Origin. The contract principle appears first to have become established in the French game, Plafond (literally, "ceiling"; *i.e.*, a player aimed to bid to his ceiling of tricks), which was played in Paris in 1918 and from about 1922 to 1931 was more popular than either Auction or Contract Bridge in French and Belgian clubs. Several unofficial attempts were made to introduce the same principle to Bridge, and the proposal was considered but rejected by the laws committee of the Whist Club of New York in 1917 and again in 1920.

In 1925 Harold S. Vanderbilt of New York, who had become convinced, as he later put it, that the time had come to take another step forward to perfect the successive games of the Whist family, incorporated the Plafond principle in a more deliberate way than had previously been attempted. He also proposed that slam bonuses should be awarded only when contracted for and added the intriguing new element of vulnerability, whereby a side that won a game became "vulnerable" and subject to heavier penalties for failure to make a contract. Finally, he introduced the decimal system of scoring (see below), later giving it as his opinion that this feature, by greatly increasing all trick values and bonuses, added enormously to the attraction of the new game, which he described as Contract Bridge.

In 1926 Vanderbilt tried out the game when voyaging from the Pacific Coast to New York, and back in New York he gave copies of the scoring table to some of his friends. Thanks to the combination of the Plafond principle and Vanderbilt's well-balanced scoring proposals, the game caught on immediately. Laws were proposed, and by 1928 the code issued by the Whist Club of New York had been accepted. By 1929 Contract had become the standard game on both sides of the Atlantic; the American Auction Bridge League had dropped the word Auction from its title; and Ely Culbertson, one of several then struggling for leadership in the new game, had founded the first Contract Bridge magazine, *Bridge World*.

Scoring. As mentioned above, trick values were greatly increased. A side fulfilling its contract for each odd trick scores, if trumps were clubs or diamonds, 20 points for each trick (instead of 6 or 7); if trumps were hearts or spades, 30 (instead of 8 or 9); and at no-trump, 40 for the first and 30 for each subsequent trick (instead of 10).

Higher trick values and bonuses

Such of these tricks as were included in the contract are scored below the line and count toward game. The remainder, if any, are scored above the line and do not count toward game.

If the contract was doubled, tricks scored below the line count twice the normal value, and overtricks count 100 each if not vulnerable, 200 if vulnerable. These values for overtricks are doubled if the contract was redoubled. For making either a doubled or redoubled contract a 50-point bonus is scored above the line.

Vulnerability is also a factor if declarer fails to fulfill his contract. His opponents score for each undertrick:

	undoubled	doubled	redoubled
if declarer were not vulnerable:			
First undertrick	50	100	200
Each subsequent undertrick	50	200	400
if declarer were vulnerable:			
First undertrick	100	200	400
Each subsequent undertrick	100	300	600

For bidding and making a contract of six-odd (a small slam) a bonus of 500 is scored if not vulnerable, 750 if vulnerable. For seven-odd (grand slam), the bonus is 1,000 if not vulnerable, 1,500 if vulnerable. A side bidding six and making seven scores only the small-slam bonus plus one overtrick. A side bidding seven and making only six has not fulfilled its contract, and its opponents score an undertrick penalty.

Vulnerability does not affect bonuses scored for holding honours. The ace, king, queen, jack, and ten of the trump suit are honours. One player holding four of them scores 100 above the line; for five honours or four aces at a no-trump contract his side scores 150. Fewer than four honours and honours shared with partner do not count.

When either side totals 100 or more below the line it wins a game. Both sides then begin a new game. In Rubber Bridge, the first side to win two games wins the rubber and receives a bonus of 700 if the opponents have not won a game, 500 if they have. All points scored by each side are then totalled, and the side with the higher score wins the difference.

Development of Contract Bridge. Despite its immediate popularity in club circles, Contract Bridge did not progress rapidly elsewhere until Culbertson, who possessed great organizational ability and a flair for publicity, launched a series of manoeuvres designed to publicize the game and to establish himself as its principal authority. In 1930 his team won nearly every important American tournament, and he seized the occasion to publish his *Blue Book*, a revolutionary work setting out the principles that still underlie most bidding systems. He also went to England and defeated the leading British teams, including one headed by Lt. Col. Walter Buller, who had engaged the attention of the British public with bidding methods that were directly opposed to Culbertson's.

Role of Ely Culbertson

Culbertson sealed these achievements when at the beginning of 1932 he vanquished in a match of 150 rubbers a team representing the anti-Culbertson faction led by Sidney Lenz. American newspapers called the match "The Bridge Battle of the Century," and for more than a month it was featured on their front pages. The unprecedented publicity made Contract Bridge a fad not only in North America but also in Europe and South America.

For all the promotional aspects of Culbertson's campaign, his ideas were basically sound. He saw the fallacy in the British approach, which was to open with the bid that seemed most likely to represent the best final contract. He also saw that in the new game the search for a trump suit was more rewarding than previously. Auction Bridge did not favour trump contracts unless based on strong suits, for honour bonuses were high relative to trick values, and defenders who held honours could outscore a declarer who made only eight or nine total tricks. Players therefore opened at one no-trump almost indiscriminately when lacking a strong honour combination. Culbertson recognized that it was a serious error, in Contract, to open one no-trump on hands that might develop more tricks at a trump declaration, and he therefore formulated the "approach" principle: "Whenever a hand contains a biddable suit . . . that suit and not no-trump should usually first be bid." To enable the approach principle to be more safely employed, he stipulated that certain bids were "forcing"; *i.e.*, could not properly be passed by the partner. Hence his system and those like it are termed approach-forcing systems. Another of Culbertson's achievements was a method of valuing the strength of a hand by "honour tricks," high cards or combinations of cards that could normally be expected to take tricks by force. It had long been known that, on average, just over eight tricks in each deal are won by high cards, and Culbertson's honour tricks corresponded with these. So long as the tricks won by lower cards accrued in the same proportion as those won by honour tricks, the method was accurate.

Culbertson's impact caused Contract to supersede Auction very rapidly. The game then settled down as an accepted form of social intercourse, and the next landmark did not occur until Culbertson, who had become interested in international relations, was succeeded in his position as the leading authority by Charles H. Goren, who in the late 1940s popularized an improved method of hand valuation (see below). This enabled even beginners to judge the strength of their hand and so reach reasonable contracts almost from the start instead of after a long period of study and practice. It thus removed an obstacle to the increased popularity of the game. The weight of Goren's authority as a player and writer also caused the bidding methods that he favoured to be termed Standard American.

Party Bridge, Chicago, and Duplicate. These are forms of Contract Bridge in which the method of scoring or the method of arranging partnerships used in Rubber Bridge is modified in some degree, either for social reasons or to emphasize the competitive element.

Party Bridge. This term may be used of any private Bridge game consisting of two or more tables, but it is also used in the laws of Duplicate Contract Bridge as a general term for special games of a social character and for Duplicate for home play.

Replay Duplicate enables one pair to play competitively against another. The same hands are played twice, first by one pair and then the other. The results are compared as at Duplicate (see below). The appeal of the game is limited by the fact that a retentive memory can count for more than skill. Both Pivot Bridge and Individual contests enable the players to play once with each other as partners and twice against each other as opponents. Progressive Bridge, in which partners change tables after every four deals, has enjoyed a vogue for larger gatherings not serious enough to warrant the use of the duplicate principle. A social desideratum is that pairs should consist of one member of each sex.

Chicago. In North America, especially, all forms of party Bridge lost ground in the 1960s to four-deal Bridge, called Chicago for the city in which it originated. Because it avoids long rubbers of uncertain duration, it became popular in clubs as well as for home play.

A rubber of Chicago consists of four deals. A passed-out deal does not count, and the same player deals again. On the first deal neither side is vulnerable; on the second and third deals dealer's side only is vulnerable (or, in some games, nondealer's side only); and on the fourth deal both sides are vulnerable.

A premium of 300 points is awarded for a nonvulnerable game, 500 when vulnerable. There is no further premium for winning two or more games. A part-score or scores made previously (earned for contracts worth less than game—*e.g.*, two clubs bid and made worth 40 points or one heart worth 30 points) may be combined with a part-score in the current deal to complete a game, in which case the game premium is determined by the vulnerability on the deal that completes it. A part-score made on the fourth deal receives a premium of 100 points.

Duplicate Bridge. Duplicate is the principle, developed in Whist, according to which all serious competitions (tournaments) are conducted: a hand that has been dealt and played at one table is played again at one or more other tables. The object is to reduce the element of luck and enable a direct comparison of skill to be made between players who hold identical hands.

Duplicate boards are used to keep the cards intact for replay. The board, or tray, is a rectangular container having four pockets, one for each hand (North, East, South, and West) and marked to indicate vulnerability and which hand is dealer (*i.e.*, opening bidder). After the play of a hand each player, who keeps his own cards directly in front of him, returns his original hand to the appropriate pocket of the board. The board is passed on to another table, and his table receives a new board. At the conclusion of play it is possible to compare results obtained on each deal by players who held identical cards under identical conditions. In pairs contests, the scores of each North-South pair are compared with those of all other North-South pairs; the scores of each East-West pair with those of all other East-West pairs.

Dealer and vulnerability for each board follow a schedule that is standard in most countries. North is dealer on board 1, East on board 2, and so on. The vulnerability of each 16 boards follows the mnemonic word square, ONEB, NEBO, EBON, BONE. O = neither side vulnerable; N = North-South vulnerable; E = East-West vulnerable; B = both sides vulnerable.

Each deal is scored as a separate event. To the usual trick scores and slam bonuses, 50 points are added for making a part-score. Premium for making game is as in Chicago, 300 for a nonvulnerable game, 500 if vulnerable. Honours do not count. The scores may be totalled to produce a winner, but in modern pairs Duplicate they are first converted to "match points" thus: the North-South pair with the worst score on a board receives no match points, the next pair gets one match point, and so on, each receiving one point for every score it betters and one-half point for every score it exactly equals. (To avoid fractions, scores for each deal are sometimes calculated by doubling the match point awards.) This method of scoring gives equal importance to each deal, whether a part-score or a grand slam, with far-reaching effects on the strategy of bidding and play. In a team event the points scored on each board may be converted to International Match Points in proportion to each team's margin of victory on each winning board on the basis of a scale ranging from 0–10 = 0, 20–40 = 1, and 50–80 = 2 and so on to 4,000 and up = 24.

Match points

Duplicate games require the use of a schedule for the movement of players and boards, known as a movement. The first pair movement was invented in 1892 by John T. Mitchell of Chicago for use in Whist. It is still the commonest movement today. With this movement, half of the pairs playing are assigned to North-South positions and half to East-West. The tables are numbered from one through whatever number is required. After every round (a round consists of the play of a specified number of boards, usually from two to four) North-South pairs remain seated, while all East-West pairs move to the next higher numbered table, those at the highest table going back to number 1, and each set of boards is moved to the next lower numbered table. If the number of tables is even, a relay stand is used to hold one set of boards out of play on each round, the set moving to the next lower numbered table on the next round. A game consists of all pairs playing all boards, but in tournaments with more than 13 tables in one section play is usually limited to 26 deals, two each against 13 opposing pairs. The Mitchell movement requires two independent winners, one pair for North-South and one for East-West. Other movements, permitting each pair to play against each other pair, for example, become more complex and usually require printed guides and often skilled directors to direct the movements of players and boards.

The use of the duplicate principle in Contract Bridge is very popular indeed. By emphasizing the competitive aspect it has greatly spurred the development of the game.

Tournament Bridge. This term is applied to the more serious competitions conducted according to the duplicate principle, usually under the auspices of a regional, national, or international league.

Regional and national tournaments. The first Auction Bridge tournaments were run by the American Bridge League, founded in 1927. In 1937 it amalgamated with the United States Bridge Association to form the American Contract Bridge League (ACBL), whose membership grew from 9,000 in 1940 to more than 175,000 by the late 1960s, its principal tournaments, called Nationals, attracting 5,000 or more players three times a year. Several hundred regional and sectional tournaments are held annually by local units. The ACBL is the governing body for North America, and its contributions to the development of the game include the ranking of players under a scheme, since adopted in many other countries, whereby success in tournaments is recognized by the award of master points for winning or placing high. Nearly every country in Europe and the Western Hemisphere, and many elsewhere, has its own national Bridge league, Sweden's being second in size to the ACBL. In Great Britain national championships are run by the English Bridge Union, whose membership was 10,000 early in the 1970s, and by the Northern Ireland, Scottish, and Welsh Bridge unions. County associations run their own championships, and the unions, with some overseas bodies, constitute the British Bridge League, which selects teams for European championships and world events.

Early international competition

International tournaments. The first international Contract Bridge matches were those played by Culbertson's team against three British teams in 1930. (In that year Culbertson's team played a Plafond match against leading French players including Baron Robert de Nexon, who subsequently became the first president of the World Bridge Federation.) A European Championship was held in 1932 and was won by Austria. In the two following years American teams beat Great Britain for a trophy given by Charles M. Schwab of New York, while in 1935 the first America versus Europe match took place when an American champion team, the Four Aces, beat France, the reigning European champions. In 1937 two American teams competed in the last pre-World War II European championship, which was won by Austria from a 16-team field.

International Bridge grew rapidly after World War II. In 1947 the European Bridge League was founded at Copenhagen, and European Championships, for both open and women's teams, became annual events except (beginning in 1960) in Olympic Team years. In 1950 the U.S. resumed international play by winning a three-cornered match at Bermuda against Britain and the rest of Europe. The trophy, the Bermuda Bowl, became the emblem of world Bridge supremacy, played for annually. For a time it was a two-team event between North America and the winners of the European Championship, but it became a three-cornered event in 1958 with the inclusion of the South American champions. In 1966 the winners of the Far East Bridge Championship competed for the first time; in 1971 the South Pacific zone champions joined in, making it a six-team event, including the defending champions.

In 1958 the World Bridge Federation was formed to control the Bermuda Bowl competition, also known as the World Team Championships, and to institute quadrennial Olympiad championships for open and women's teams, beginning in 1960 and replacing, in Olympic years, the Bermuda Bowl. The federation also arranged the first pair Olympiad in 1962 and at four-year intervals. For Bermuda Bowl and Olympiad winners, see SPORTING RECORD in the *Ready Reference and Index*.

LAWS OF BRIDGE

Bridge has never lacked well-drafted and comprehensive laws, although the legislative bodies have not always acted in concert. The first official laws were those for Bridge Whist, adopted by the Portland Club of London in 1895, but a different code was adopted by the Whist Club of New York in 1897. In 1909 the Portland Club published the first code for Auction Bridge (last revised in 1928), and in 1910 the Whist Club published its own Auction laws (revised in 1912, 1913, 1915, 1917, 1920, and, for the last time, 1926).

Development of the Contract Bridge laws. The first Contract Bridge laws were promulgated by the Knickerbocker Whist Club of New York in 1927 but were superseded in the same year by those issued by the Whist Club. The Portland Club issued a code in 1929. Since 1932, when representatives of the Portland and Whist clubs met and adopted the first international code, to which the Commission Française du Bridge also subscribed, the Rubber Bridge laws (though not the laws of Duplicate) have always been international, except for the single case of a 1943 American code issued unilaterally because of wartime circumstances. In 1947 three members of the Whist Club of New York were appointed to the ABCL's National Laws Commission, which became the sole American promulgating body. The laws were revised in 1948 and 1963 by the ACBL, the Portland Club, and the European Bridge League.

The first code for Duplicate was adopted by the American Bridge League in 1928 and revised in 1935 and 1943. In 1949 the first international Duplicate code was promulgated by the Portland Club, the European Bridge League, and the ACBL, remaining in force until revised in 1963. The Duplicate laws, known as the Laws of Duplicate Contract Bridge, follow the Rubber Bridge laws as closely as conditions permit, changes being made only where procedural differences in the game require them.

Principles of the laws. The laws are concerned with the procedure of the deal, auction, and play and with the imposition of appropriate penalties when an infringement has taken place. Few players find it necessary to learn them in detail, for in a friendly rubber, infringements, such as a call out of turn, are often overlooked. In clubs the published laws are always available and can be consulted if need be; disagreements, which rarely occur, are resolved by a committee of the club. In tournament Bridge a tournament director supervises the contest and applies the laws, subject to a right of appeal to a committee and thence to a national or international governing body.

The laws of Bridge are not intended to protect against intentional offences, for the integrity of everyone at the table is taken for granted. Cheating at Rubber Bridge is almost unheard of in recognized clubs, for the game does not lend itself to it: success achieved otherwise than by skillful bidding and play soon attracts attention. But cheating is not unknown at Duplicate, arising usually from the contravention of the principle that communication between partners during the auction and play periods may be effected only by means of the calls and plays themselves. Cases of purported cheating are heard by the responsible national or international governing body, which has power to suspend offenders from membership.

The laws themselves are intended to provide a remedy where a player accidentally, carelessly, or inadvertently disturbs the proper course of the game. Some of the more frequent infringements are as follows:

Common infringements

Revoke. A player who fails to follow suit when able to do so commits a revoke. The penalty varies according to whether the revoke is corrected within a certain period. For an "established" revoke the penalty may be the loss of as many as two tricks if these tricks are won subsequent to the infraction.

Exposed card. If a card is exposed otherwise than in the normal course of play, its owner may be liable to a penalty, depending on the stage reached in the bidding or play. For example, a defender who exposes a card may be obliged to leave it face up on the table and play it at the first legal opportunity.

Lead out of turn. Different penalties are provided for leads by the declarer and those by defenders and also for leading too soon and attempting to lead when it is another player's turn. The object is to redress the advantage the offender may wrongfully have gained. A lead out of turn is condoned (escapes penalty) if the next hand plays before attention is drawn to it. The same applies to a bid out of turn.

Improper remark. Should a player, by a thoughtless act or remark other than an illegal call or play, give his partner unauthorized information, that is an improper remark or gesture for which redress is provided by the laws.

Appended to the laws is a statement of proprieties covering violations of ethical conduct such as may lead to an unfair advantage and the observance of proper etiquette, the breach of which may spoil the pleasure of the game. An important propriety is that the intentional infringement of any law is a serious breach of ethics. In Rubber Bridge the laws provide no penalty for a breach of the proprieties as such, but in Duplicate the director may award an adjusted score if no adequate penalty is assessed by the laws.

The scope of the proprieties may be gathered from the fact that they specify seven types of violation of ethical conduct, one of which is "Any indication of approval or disapproval of partner's call, or of satisfaction with an opponent's call." As to conventions, the laws say that

> It is improper to use, in calling or play, any convention the meaning of which may not be understood by the opponents. Conventional calls or plays should be explained to the opponents before any player has looked at his cards. Advanced notice may be given of the intention to use certain conventions of which full explanation may be deferred until the occasion arises. The full explanation may be given only by the player whose *partner* made the conventional call or play. At any time this player must reply to an enquiry by an opponent as to the significance of a call or play that may be conventional, and should supply any information that may have been withheld.

Restrictions on use of conventions

Any sponsoring organization, club, or tournament committee or group of persons playing Contract Bridge may restrict the use of conventions in games under its jurisdiction. The view generally taken is that the use of conventions should be related to the seriousness of the occasion: at international level there are virtually no restrictions, while by 1970 the ACBL had named over 70 conventions permitted in its major tournaments. Fewer are permitted in local tournaments and fewer still in clubs where Rubber Bridge is played and where it is generally held that the unrestricted use of conventions would spoil the pleasure of the game.

CONTRACT BRIDGE BIDDING

In the course of the bidding each side estimates how many tricks it can take at its best contract. It then selects that call (or permits its opponents to play at that call) which, on a balance of probabilities, is likely to maximize its own score or minimize the opponents' score. This may involve making a bid that is expected to fail.

The strategy of bidding. Each player attempts to inform his partner as to the nature and strength of his hand, either by making one or more bids or by passing. When such information is given and received, it becomes possible to decide the best contract. Thus, if one player defines the strength and character of his hand by opening at one no-trump, his partner (the responder) may be able to determine the best contract without further exploratory bidding. Certain calls by responder would then be understood as a declaration of the intended final contract: for example, a bid that would give the partnership a game, such as three no-trump or four spades or a pass. Other calls would be understood as exploratory, indicating that the best contract was still uncertain.

Bids are selected with a regard for the realities of the scoring table: a game can be made by bidding four-odd at a major suit or three-odd at no-trump, and this provides a motive for describing those features of the hand most likely to lead to a no-trump or major-suit contract. The attempt to make game at five-odd of a minor suit is much less frequent.

More tricks may be taken if a satisfactory trump suit is present: the ideal is eight or more trumps in the combined hands, with at least four in each. Bids are therefore selected with a view to ascertaining whether such a suit is present.

Exchanging information with one's partner is not the only consideration, and bids may be made with the object of disrupting the opponents' exchanges. A recognized manoeuvre, though one employed by only a small minority of players, is the "psychic" bid: one that pretends to nonexistent values.

Thus an optimum strategy of bidding must aim to reconcile conflicting factors, and that is what is attempted by a "system": a set of principles by which partners may express any two hands. Unlike a convention, which is a partnership arrangement whereby a special meaning, not obvious on the surface, is attached to a particular bid, a system covers the entire range of constructive bidding (*i.e.*, bidding to arrive at the best contract). To use a system effectively a player has to be able to assess the strength of his hand. By far the most popular way of doing so is by means of the Goren point count (described below), and the majority of players are not aware of any other. It is, however, possible to value a hand in quite different terms: for example, a method of assessing a hand in terms of losers for play at an agreed trump suit (the losing trick count) was put forward by F. Dudley Courtenay and later revived by British and Italian experts. The idea is to add the number of cards lower than the queen (up to a maximum of three in each suit) to the number of losers revealed by the partner's bidding. The total is subtracted from 18, and the answer indicates how many odd tricks the combined hands are likely to take.

Bidding systems

The first bidding system was proposed by Harold S. Vanderbilt. A player with a strong hand opened one club: with a weak hand his partner responded one diamond, after which the bidding proceeded on the basis that the responder was known to be weak; with a stronger hand the first response would be other than one diamond, and in this case the exchanges would proceed on the basis that the responder was known to hold certain values. The Vanderbilt club also had the advantage that any opening bid other than one club was known to be limited in strength. Despite its technical excellence, the system was not widely popular, but the idea was later revived in the highly successful Italian systems (see below).

The most successful system of the first 20 years of Contract Bridge was devised by Culbertson, whose contribution to theory has already been described. Despite competition from other systems, his was paramount throughout the world until the late 1940s, when it was superseded largely because a new method of hand valuation was developed, superior to Culbertson's honour-trick method, rather than through any great improvement in the principles of bidding. The new method was put forward in 1949 by Goren, who proposed an extension of a method known since 1904 but one that reflected and measured in identical terms—point count—the power of long suits and trumps as well as high cards. It was immediately successful, and Goren's system (embracing both his method of valuation and principles of bidding) was swiftly adopted by the majority of players.

Comparison of principal systems. *Goren system.* This employs the concept of "distributional points," which are added to high-card points (one to four points for each J, Q, K, A held) to arrive at an overall valuation. The strength needed for every bid in a constructive auction is defined in these terms. Thus, the strength needed to raise an opening bid of one in a suit to three in the same suit is defined as 13 to 16 points, including distribution. (Other factors may be required; *e.g.*, for a raise from one to three, at least four trumps are needed.)

High-card and distributional points

Points are counted by adding to high-card points distributional points for a void suit (three points for an opening bid, for example, five when raising a partner's suit bid), for a holding of one card in a suit, a singleton (two points and three), and for two cards in a suit, a doubleton (one point).

In addition, opener adds a point for four aces and deducts one for an aceless hand. A player raising his partner's suit adds a point for an honour in it, unless he has already counted four or more for high-card points in the suit. A player rebidding after his partner has raised adds a point for a fifth trump and two for the sixth and subsequent cards. A point is deducted for an inadequately guarded honour, such as Q-x (queen and any one lesser card), or a singleton king, queen, or jack. A player raising his partner's suit deducts a point if he has only three trumps or if he has a 4-3-3-3 pattern.

The basis of this method of distributional valuation was devised by William Anderson of Toronto and was adopted and developed by Goren. The 4-3-2-1 count for high cards was previously publicized by Milton Work.

Point count is used not only to select single bids but also to select the level of the final contract. A total of 26 points is normally needed in a partnership's combined hands for a game at no-trump or a major suit, 33 points for a small slam, 37 points for a grand slam. Thus, when the bidding has indicated the number of points held in the combined hands, it is possible to decide at what level the deal should be played.

Other features of the Goren system are as follows: Most hands are opened with a bid of one in a "biddable" suit; *i.e.*, a suit containing five or more cards or four cards including, normally, at least four high-card points. Hands containing 14 or more points must be opened, while those containing 12 or less are usually passed. A 13-point hand may be opened if a suitably descriptive rebid (second-round bid) is available. A response in a new suit is forcing for one round, meaning that responder's partner must bid again to keep the auction open or to contribute additional information (*e.g.*, strength in another suit) to the partnership's joint effort to reach their optimum contract. An opening two-bid in a suit is forcing until the partnership reaches a bid of game or until the opponents have been doubled. Opening no-trump bids are based on a balanced hand pattern (4-3-3-3, 4-4-3-2, or 5-3-3-2) with a high point count and no doubleton weaker than Q-x.

Pre-emptive bids are used; *i.e.*, bids higher than the minimum legal level made in an attempt to obstruct the opponents. Pre-emptive openings usually indicate no more than ten points in high cards, with a seven-card or longer trump suit and the ability to win within two tricks if the contract is vulnerable or three tricks if not.

Acol system. This system is employed by the majority of British tournament players and by some elsewhere. Its name derives from a small London club where the system was developed in the 1930s by a group of young players who subsequently became famous. It was developed from the Culbertson system but has fewer forcing bids and employs in most cases the principle of bidding the full value of the hand when a trump suit has been agreed or when raising at no-trump. Holding four cards in the opener's suit, for example, and 10 to 12 points, an Acol player raises to three of that suit, a non-forcing (or "limit") bid indicating that the combined hands are likely to produce nine tricks if the opener has a minimum. (In standard American, a raise to three is forcing and indicates the ability to win more than nine tricks.) An opening two spades, two hearts, or two diamonds shows 18 to 22 points, with at least eight playing tricks (*i.e.*, tricks that a hand may reasonably be expected to take when playing at its own best trump suit). Stronger hands are opened with a conventional artificial bid of two clubs.

Bidding full value

Italian bidding systems. Italy's Squadra Azzurra (Blue Team), which held the Bermuda Bowl from 1957 to 1969, used two principal systems—the Neapolitan system and the Roman system. The Neapolitan system resembles the Vanderbilt system in that strong hands (17 points or powerful distribution) are opened with one club. Responses are by the step system to show strength and "controls"; ace counts as two controls; king as one control: one diamond—zero–five points; one heart—six or more points but fewer than three controls; one spade—three controls; one no-trump—four controls; two clubs—five; two diamonds—six; two no-trump—seven or more. The two hearts and two spades responses are reserved to show six-card suits with two honours but less than six points. Openings of one diamond, one heart, or one spade bids show limited hands.

The Roman system is more complicated, with many conventional bids. One club may show any of four types of hand, ranging from a balanced 12 to 16 points to an unbalanced strong hand similar to a standard American forcing two bid; responder cannot tell which until opener bids again. A set of conventional responses is prescribed. An opening bid of one diamond, one heart, or one spade is forcing for one round and usually shows a genuine suit. A bid in the next higher suit is the mandatory minimum response. Opening suit bids of two show specific holdings: for example, two hearts show at least five hearts and four clubs.

Other systems. Scores of systems are used, but the majority, like the British two club system, are based substantially on Culbertson's and Goren's methods. In France an idea popular with tournament players is that the opener should begin with the shorter of two biddable suits and rebid his stronger suit on the next round (the canapé principle).

The canapé, relay, transfer, and interrogator principles

In Sweden the Efos system (Economical Forcing System) makes intensive use of the "relay" principle: the responder, in many situations, does not attempt to describe his hand but makes a minimum bid in the next suit above the opener's suit, asking the opener to describe his hand further. Some European systems extend this idea, and serious tournament players in nearly every country make some use of the allied concept of the "transfer" principle, by which the responder can require his partner to make a certain bid: thus a bid of two hearts in response to one no-trump may require the opener, by arrangement, to bid two spades. Transfers have several theoretical advantages, including the more productive use of bidding space. Some theorists hold that the use of the "interrogator" principle, in which one player does all the asking and the other all the telling, may eventually predominate.

In North America some systems are designed for special effect in tournament play, such as the Roth–Stone system, which contains many original ideas and provides that an opening bid in a major suit is based on at least a five-card suit and that a one no-trump response is forcing.

Nonsystemic bidding. Some areas of bidding are nonsystemic in that they are regulated by separate conventions that can be used no matter which basic system is employed or because the practice is the same in nearly all systems, as with defensive bidding.

Conventions. Many hundreds of conventions have been proposed and a dozen or so have gained very wide acceptance. Conventions may be divided into five groups. (1) Slam conventions such as Blackwood, invented by Easley Blackwood of Indianapolis in the early 1930s: a conventional bid of four no-trump asks for aces: a response of five clubs shows no aces or four aces, five diamonds shows one ace, five hearts shows two aces, and so on. If the four no-trump bidder next bids five no-trump, his partner shows his kings according to the same schedule. (2) No-trump bidding: most conventions in this category are set in motion by the partner of a player who has opened at no-trump. They are designed to discover particular features in the opener's hand: thus, using the Stayman convention, responder bids two clubs over one no-trump to ask for a four-card major suit. (3) Suit bidding: an example is the Swiss convention, a direct bid of four of a minor in response to a major-suit opening, indicating at least the values for game and inviting opener to indicate if his hand is suitable for slam. (4) Suit openings of two: because the forcing-two opening evolved by Culbertson occurs infrequently, many systems employ a conventional two clubs for all hands that would be opened with a two bid in standard American, so freeing the opening bids of two diamonds, two hearts, and two spades for other purposes. (5) Competitive bidding: many conventions have been proposed for use in competitive auctions. Thus, the Roth–Stone system employs a double by opener's partner of an opponent's overcall as a takeout request, that is, a request that his partner make a bid. The same meaning is assigned to a "responsive double" when the partner of a player who has made a takeout double in turn doubles a pre-emptive raise of opener's bid made by his right-hand opponent. Many other bids with conventional meanings—for example, overcalls, doubles, and cue bids of the opponent's suit used to show certain two-suited hands—are also employed in defensive bidding.

Slam and no-trump conventions

Defensive bidding. This term covers all bidding by a side whose opponents have opened. Exploratory sequences have little place in defensive bidding, where players may have only a brief opportunity to show their hands. The common practice is similar in nearly all systems: a minimum overcall in a suit suggests a limited hand, no stronger than a sound opening. Playing tricks are the main consideration, and overcalls at the level of two are seldom made with less than five trumps. An immediate double of an opponent's low-level bid is a request for partner to name a suit. Occasionally an overcall may be made with the object of suggesting a good suit to lead.

Apart from the attempt to reach a makable contract, the motives for defensive bidding may extend to the discovery of a satisfactory sacrifice: a contract the bidder knows cannot be made but that, if doubled, will result in a loss smaller than the score the opponents could have made. In deciding how far to bid in competition account is taken of hidden values that do not appear on the score sheet. Thus, a side scores nothing above the line for its first game, but the game has a mathematical value since it increases the chances of winning the rubber. In the same way a part-score is worth more than the points actually entered on the pad. These values cannot be exactly computed, but it is generally reckoned that, with neither side vulnerable, to save the first game at the cost of only 300 (down two tricks doubled, not vulnerable) shows a slight profit in real terms, while to save it at the cost of 500 (down three doubled, not vulnerable, or two doubled, vulnerable) shows a slight loss. A nonvulnerable side can afford to lose 500 to save the rubber, but the vulnerable side loses slightly if it goes down 500 to stop a nonvulnerable game. With both sides vulnerable, to save a game at a cost of 500 shows a profit, for the opponents would have had 500 for rubber, plus the trick score.

Sacrifice bids

PLAY OF THE CARDS

At Rubber Bridge the declarer's first aim is to make his contract, overtricks being a minor consideration. For the defenders, the defeat of the contract is paramount. The same is not necessarily true in tournament Bridge, where the object is to outscore players holding the same cards at other tables. The principles of play described below hold good for all forms of Bridge.

The technique of card play is complex, rivalling that of Chess, but its elements have been analyzed so intensively since Contract became popular that a tournament player of average proficiency may execute, as a matter of course, plays that would have been beyond the finest players of earlier periods in the history of the game.

The declarer's strategy. When the opening lead has been made, the dummy is exposed, and the declarer plans the play of the two hands in concert. The initial approach is to count the tricks that can surely be won, as by playing a card that cannot be beaten or by leading from one hand and ruffing (playing a trump) in the other hand. If these tricks are not enough to fulfill the contract, the declarer may (1) try to win tricks with cards that are not the highest, as by leading toward a king in the hope that the ace is in the hand of the defender who has to play first, or (2) try to establish long cards, which are the cards remaining in one hand when the other three hands have been exhausted of the suit. A long card, if led, will win unless an opponent can trump it.

Sizing up the hand

The chances of success depend on how the unseen cards are distributed, and to fill in the gaps in his knowledge the declarer may make use of assumption. If his contract can be endangered only by a certain distribution of the unseen cards, he assumes that they are so distributed and endeavours to develop the play in such a way that the contract can be made in spite of that. If the contract cannot be made unless the cards are favourably distributed, the declarer assumes that the necessary distribution exists. Thus a relationship arises between the tricks required and the dangers that may prevent their being won, resulting in the formation of a tactical plan.

Declarer also makes frequent use of mathematical probabilities. As the play progresses, he also gains information that can be used as a basis for deduction: the opening lead may indicate the defender's holding in the suit; the bidding may indicate the nature of an opponent's hand, and so on.

The use of deduction is very highly developed among skillful players, who frequently determine the location of the material cards early in the hand, thereafter playing as effectively as if the opponents' hands were visible. Less proficient players can achieve a high measure of success by following well-established methods of play, such as the principle that it is usually more profitable to ruff in the hand that has fewer trumps than in the other hand.

The defender's strategy. The defenders have a harder task than the declarer, for it is more difficult to make the best of two hands when each is hidden from the other. To overcome this handicap the defenders exchange information, as was done in Whist, by means of signals and conventions. Like the declarer, they also follow certain principles of play, such as "Lead through strength and up to weakness."

Exchanging information

The exchange of messages begins with the opening lead. The leader may decide upon one of several tactical plans: against a trump contract, for example, he may simply try to take the tricks that are immediately available, while against a no-trump contract it is more common to lead from a long suit with the object of trying to establish it. In each case the suit led depends on the tactical plan, but the card led is determined by convention, with the object of indicating the leader's holding in the suit. The convention of leading the fourth best of the longest and strongest suit against no-trump and the rule of 11 have been discussed above, but if that suit is headed by A-K-J-x or better it is conventional to lead the king. Against a trump contract it is conventional to lead K from A-K-x or better, but to lead A from A-K bare. (Most treatises on Bridge include detailed tables of conventional leads: see *Bibliography* at the end of this article.)

The exchange of information continues throughout the play, based on the idea that since it is natural, if not trying to win a trick, to play the lowest card, a defender who does otherwise is conveying a message. Thus a defender who plays an unnecessarily high card when his partner leads a winner is asking for a continuation (a "come-on"); a defender who, when evidently not giving a come-on on the strength of high cards, plays high-low in a suit (an "echo") is indicating an even number of cards; a defender who echoes in trump is indicating at least three trumps. In winning or attempting to win a trick to which another player has led, it is conventional to play the lowest card in a sequence: the queen from K-Q-x (the K-Q forming the sequence) and so on.

A special manoeuvre, known as a suit-preference signal, makes it possible to request a partner to lead a suit other than the one being played. When a defender leads a suit for his partner to ruff he can, by playing an unnecessarily high card, ask his partner to lead, at his next opportunity, the higher ranking of the two remaining suits (the trump suit being excluded). The same idea can be extended to many other situations.

These and the many other signals and conventions in defenders' play (which also are covered in detail in the books in the *Bibliography*) do not violate the spirit of the game if they are known to the opponents but they do make possible more effective defense and, therefore, more exciting overall play.

BIBLIOGRAPHY

General works: R.L. FREY and A. TRUSCOTT, *The Official Encyclopedia of Bridge* (1971); C.H. GOREN, *Goren's Bridge Complete*, rev. ed. (1971); R.L. FREY, *How to Win at Contract Bridge in 10 Easy Lessons* (1961).

Bidding: A.L. ROTH and J. RUBENS, *Modern Bridge Bidding, Complete* (1968); T. REESE and A. DORMER, *The Acol System Today* (1961); B. GAROZZO, P. FORQUET, and E. MINGONI, *The Italian Blue Team Bridge Book* (1963).

Card play: C.H. GOREN, *Go with the Odds* (1969); M. MILES, *All Fifty-two Cards: How to Reconstruct the Concealed Hands at the Bridge Table* (1963); T. REESE, *The Expert Game* (1953); C.E. LOVE, *Bridge Squeezes Complete* (1959);

L.H. WATSON and S. FRY, *Play of the Hand at Bridge*, rev. ed. (1958).

Duplicate bridge: A. GRONER, *Duplicate Bridge Direction* (1967); M. MILES, *How to Win at Duplicate Bridge*, 3rd ed. (1957); T. REESE and A. DORMER, *Bridge for Tournament Players* (1968).

Laws: AMERICAN CONTRACT BRIDGE LEAGUE, *Laws of Contract Bridge* (1963), and *Laws of Duplicate Contract Bridge* (1963).

(C.H.Go.)

Bridges, Construction and History of

A bridge is a structure surmounting an obstacle such as a river, declivity, road, or railway and used as a passageway for pedestrian, motor, or rail traffic. In this article, the development of bridge design and construction is dealt with chronologically from early times. Consideration is given to the wide variety of foundations required, the superstructures of all types of bridges (*i.e.*, girder, arch, suspension, and combinations thereof), the materials used in construction and their strength and properties, advances in theory and methods of calculation, and the evolution of erection techniques. Late developments and trends are discussed. The article is divided into the following sections:

I. Early bridge building
- Primitive bridges
- Roman bridges
- Bridge developments in Asia
- Medieval and Renaissance bridges in Europe

II. Development of the modern bridge
- The covered (timber-truss) bridge
- The iron bridge
- The modern suspension bridge
- The foundation problem: compressed air
- The steel bridge
- Reinforced-concrete bridges
- Movable and pontoon spans
- 20th-century long-span bridges

III. Contemporary developments in bridge engineering
- Improved materials
- New designs
- Improvements in techniques
- Safety problems and solutions
- Future trends

I. Early bridge building

The first bridges were natural, such as the huge, pointed arch of rock that spans the Ardèche River in Ardèche *département*, France, or the rock bridge near Lexington, Virginia. The first man-made bridges were flat stones or tree trunks, laid across a stream to make a girder bridge, and festoons of creepers hung in suspension.

The three great bridge forms

Three types of bridge—beam or girder, arch, and suspension—have been known and built from the earliest times (see Figure 1). The essential difference among them is in the way they bear their own weight. The ends of beam or girder bridges simply rest on the ground, the weight thrusting straight down. Arch bridges thrust outward as well as down at the ends and are said to be in compression. The cables of suspension bridges pull inward against their anchorages and are said to be in tension. In their simplest forms, beam or girder bridges are known as simple spans; if two or more are joined together over piers, they become continuous. A more complex form, the cantilever, is based on the girder (see below). Later variations of the arch have taken the shape of the tied arch, in which a tension member is supplied, usually at deck level, to carry the horizontal component of the thrust, creating a form similar to that of a string bow. In an analogous variation of the suspension bridge, a strut is provided in the deck, between the two anchorages, to relieve them of horizontal pull. Such a bridge is called self-anchored. The three types—girder, arch, and suspension—may also be combined in a variety of ways to form a composite structure. Through the ages, materials of construction have evolved from those ready to hand, such as timber and stone, to manufactured materials, such as brick, dimension stone concrete, reinforced and precast concrete, iron, and steel.

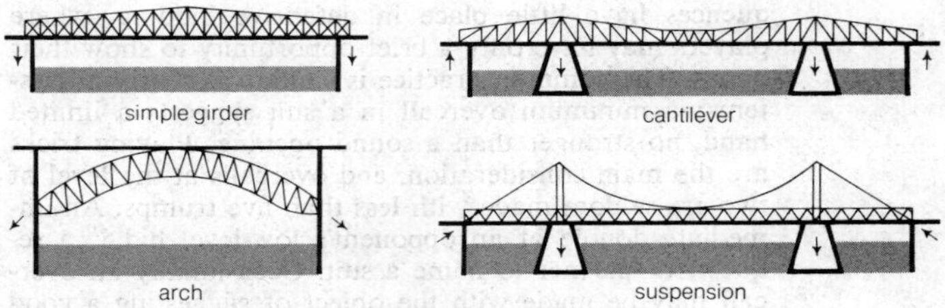

Figure 1: Principal types of bridge. Arrows indicate the forces each exerts onto or away from its foundations.

The type of bridge to be preferred at any site depends on the nature of the ground, the length of the span required, the kind of traffic anticipated, and the materials of construction available. For some of the early bridges in Persia (now Iran), where the riverbed was stony and no timber was available, a site was selected where there were outcrops of rocks across the river on which to build the piers. The resulting structures, such as the bridge over the Kārūn River at Shūshtar, were not straight but wound across from outcrop to outcrop. Alternatively, mounds of stone could be built up on the riverbed, or, if the ground was not too hard, timber piles could be driven through the water to form trestles, as in Caesar's bridge over the Rhine (55 BC).

Accounts by Herodotus and others tell of a remarkable bridge built more than 4,000 years ago across the Euphrates in the city of Babylon. It is said that the river, which is very shallow in the dry season, was diverted well above the city so that the stone bridge piers could be built in the dry riverbed. Part of the timber roadway was removable and was taken up each night as a security measure.

Another prehistoric practice is believed to have been that of human sacrifice in the foundations of bridges to appease the river gods. Surviving into Roman times, the practice helped give rise to the Faust legend and is responsible for the many Devil's bridges that are to be found.

PRIMITIVE BRIDGES

Some of the simplest uses of beams are in the "clapper" bridges of Dartmoor, Devon. The beams are actually huge, flat boulders that outcrop on the surface. In the Postbridge over the East Dart River, for example, the three 15-foot- (5-metre-) wide openings of this bridge are spanned by unchiselled slabs of granite, 6 feet (2 metres) wide, on piers of piled-up stone. Elsewhere, as in south-east Cornwall, where timber is more plentiful than stone, primitive crossings take the shape of "clam" bridges, built of tree trunks laid side by side. "Clam" and "clapper" are Anglo-Saxon words denoting, respectively, timber and stepping-stones. Clapper-type bridges are also found in Spain and were probably used in Egypt, Babylon, and China.

Ewing Galloway

Primitive grass-rope bridge over the Indus River in western Tibet.

Xerxes' pontoon over the Hellespont

A special type of beam bridge is the pontoon. The earliest account of pontoon bridges of substantial size, again by Herodotus, describes a bridge of boats built by Xerxes, king of Persia, across the Hellespont at Abydos in 481 BC. No fewer than 674 vessels were used, tied together by ropes and securely anchored. Persian armies then crossed, for the invasion of Europe, on a roadway of earth and brushwood, supported by transverse tree trunks. Then, as in modern times, pontoon bridges probably had the same disadvantages: short life, costly maintenance, and, in most locations, obstruction to navigation.

Most primitive suspension bridges were supported by three cables, two on either side acting as handrails and a third, stouter one, on which the passenger walked. Twisted lianas, creepers, oxhide thongs, bamboo, cane, or similar materials made up the cables. In construction, they were towed across the river, hauled up, and tied high on tree trunks or posts driven in the ground, beyond which they were carried again and securely anchored. Such bridges are found in India, Africa, China, and South America. Built with spans of up to 500 feet (150 metres), they sway and sag in use in a manner to alarm timid passengers.

ROMAN BRIDGES

The Romans were among the greatest bridge builders of antiquity. Their three most important contributions to the art may have been the discovery of a natural cement; the development of the cofferdam, a temporary enclosure built in the stream, within which a concrete pier foundation could be built; and their exploitation of the circular masonry arch. The cement, known as pozzolana, was made by mixing finely ground tuff (a rock formed of compacted volcanic fragments) found near the Italian town of Pozzuoli with lime, sand, and water. The Romans also made pozzolanic cement from powdered pottery fragments. The pozzolanic cements were for a long time the only cements known to resist exposure to water. Their cofferdams were made by driving timber piles to enclose the site of the pier and then pouring in concrete through the water. Alternatively, if the riverbed was very soft, they drove a double row of sheathing piles and filled in the space between with clay to make the cofferdam watertight. They could then empty the cofferdam with waterwheels, dig out the greater part of the soft ground inside it, and pour the concrete for the pier in the dry. The Sant'Angelo Bridge in Rome stands on cofferdam foundations built in the Tiber River more than 1,800 years ago. Nevertheless, the Roman underwater foundations were rarely built deep enough or given sufficient protection against scour to enable them to survive for long. Most of the Roman bridges that remain were built on solid rock.

The superstructures of many Roman bridges, such as Emperor Trajan's bridge built by Apollodorus of Damascus over the Danube in AD 104–105, was of timber on stone piers. None of the bridges of this type has survived. The fame of Roman bridge builders rests largely on their majestic masonry bridges, built on the grand scale, always with circular arches (see Figure 2), which perhaps

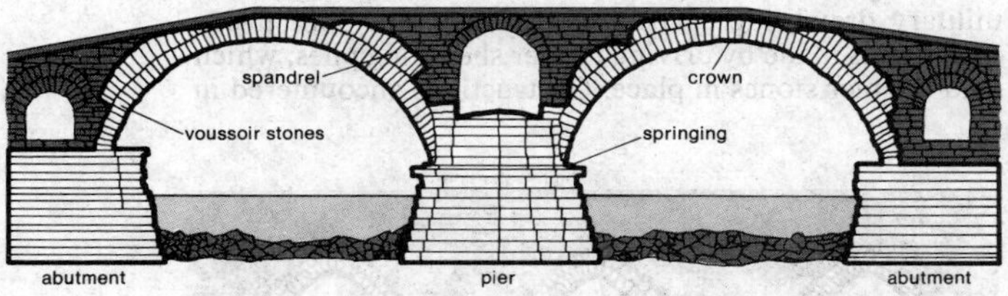

Figure 2: Roman circular arch as seen in the original Pons Fabricius, Rome, 62 BC.

Roman Alcántara bridge over the Tagus

reached the peak of achievement in a mighty bridge over the Tagus at Alcántara, Spain. Built by Caius Julius Lacer for Trajan, the tall granite piers and 98-foot- (30-metre-) wide arches that carry the roadway 170 feet (52 metres) above the river have stood for nearly 2,000 years. The huge stones forming the arch (voussoirs) weigh up to eight tons each and were so accurately shaped that no mortar was needed in the joints. The arches must have been built on temporary timber structures (falsework). The heavy arch stones were no doubt lifted by a system of pulley blocks, operated by means of a winch, probably powered by a treadmill.

Tools used by the Roman masons included saws, chisels, bevels, wedges, and trowels; their instruments for horizontal and vertical alignment included plumb bobs and levels.

Roman bridges required for a military campaign, such as that over the Danube, were usually built by legionaries and financed by the treasury; nonmilitary bridges employed forced labour and generally relied for finance on contributions by townships. Engineers and skilled workmen formed into semimilitary guilds were dispatched throughout the empire to supervise the work. By this means, engineering knowledge was spread and interchanged, and a foundation for schools in which professional standards were formulated was set down. From these fragmentary beginnings evolved the laws of the art of building drawn up by the Roman engineering authority Vitruvius in the 1st century AD in his work *De architectura*.

BRIDGE DEVELOPMENTS IN ASIA

A refinement of the beam that enables it to be used for longer spans is known as a cantilever. Primitive cantilever bridges were made wholly of timber; there are picturesque examples over the River Jhelum at Srīnagar, the capital of Kashmir. For the foundations of the river piers, piles were driven, and old boats filled with stones were sunk at the site, until a desired height above low-water level was reached. Then, on top of the piers, layers of rough-hewn logs were laid crisscross, in such a way that the logs on two adjacent piers jutted further toward each other as the height increased. The two ends of these projecting arms, or cantilevers, were then joined below roadway level by long tree trunks placed across the gap. The roadways on these bridges were usually lined with shops, and the skeleton piers were able to weather severe floods, because they offered less resistance to the flow of water than would a solid pier. Similar ancient bridges are to be found in Tibet and Scandinavia.

A stone cantilever bridge 1,100 feet (335 metres) long is said to have been built over the Dragon River in Poh Lam, Fukien Province, China. The spans, up to 70 feet (21 metres) in length, were composed of three huge stones, two of which rested on top of the pier at each end, while the third spanned the gap between them. How stones of such a size, weighing up to 200 tons, were quarried and transported in those times is not known.

Chinese stone arches

In other parts of China, where bridges had to stand in the spongy, plastic silt of the river valleys, construction developed along very different lines. Here, masonry arch bridges were built of thin, curved slabs, jointed in such a way that they could yield to considerable deformation before failure. These bridges might be described as consisting of stone chains employed in compression. The arches were originally built in the Roman semicircular forms; the bridges were high and narrow, often covered, and with stone steps at the ends. Their amazing flexibility enabled them to adapt both to the rise and fall of the silt foundations and to the weight of the traffic.

Other fine medieval bridges were built in Persia, such as the Red Bridge, which consisted of four pointed arches, on the road from Tiflis (Tbilisi) to Tabriz. Even more distinctive were bridges such as the Allah Verdi Khan and the Pul Khajoo, which were designed as cool, shaded retreats, where the traveller could find rooms for rest and refreshment after crossing the hot desert sands. The two-storied Pul Khajoo at Isfahan (1642–67) is composed of 24 pointed arches that carry an 85-foot-wide roadway, with walled passageways above it, along the top of a pierced dam. Flanked by tall, hexagonal pavilions and watchtowers, the bridge constitutes a magnificent example of engineering and architectural harmony.

In Japan are to be found small, picturesque bridges of timber arches, such as the famous Kintai-kyo (Kintai

Timber bridges.
(Left) Timber arches and stone piers of the Kintai-kyo (Kintai Bridge) spanning the Nishiki-gawa (Nishiki River) at Iwakuni, Japan. Dating from 1673, it has been rebuilt several times. (Right) Timber cantilever bridge set on piers of crossed logs in Kashmir.
(Left) Sakamoto Photo Research Laboratory, (right) Alice Schalek—Black Star

Bridge) at Iwakuni, which for centuries had its five arches rebuilt in succession, one every 5 years, so that the whole bridge was renewed every 25 years. Completely rebuilt in 1953, it now carries an automobile roadway across the Nishikigawa (Nishiki River).

MEDIEVAL AND RENAISSANCE BRIDGES IN EUROPE

After the fall of the Roman Empire, bridge building in Europe languished for some eight centuries. Its revival was marked by the spread of the ogival, or pointed arch, westward across the continent from Egypt and the Middle East, where it originated. Medieval workmanship was at first not as good as that of the Romans, and the pointed arch may have been preferred because it demanded less precision than the circular form. In the pointed arch, the tendency to sag at the crown is less dangerous, and there is less thrust on the abutments.

Medieval bridges had other functions besides carrying traffic. Chapels, shops, tollhouses, and customhouses were built on them, and they were used for fairs and tournaments. Fortified bridges, such as the Pont Valentré at Cahors, France, the bridge over the Gave de Pau at Orthez, France, or the bridge over the River Monnow at Monmouth, Monmouthshire, Wales, were defended by means of ramparts, towers with firing slits, and often a drawbridge, an original medieval invention. The upkeep of bridges was considered a pious work, for which money was obtained by alms, by endowment, or from tolls levied on both road and river traffic.

One of the most famous medieval bridges in Europe is the Pont d'Avignon over the Rhône at Avignon, France, which was begun under the direction of St. Bénézet in 1177 and completed ten years later. The bridge spanned the river by means of about 20 lofty, elliptical arches, each 100 feet (30 metres) wide. St. Bénézet, who believed that he had been divinely inspired to build the bridge, died before its completion and was buried in a chapel on one of the piers. Because of the ravages of war and damage from ice in the river, little more than the chapel at the Avignon end of the bridge, which has now become a place of pilgrimage, remains standing.

A year before the commencement of the Pont d'Avignon, Peter of Colechurch undertook a far more formidable task—the building of the Old London Bridge. This was the first stone bridge with masonry foundations to be built in a swiftly flowing river having a large tidal range. The bridge was to consist of 19 pointed arches, each with about a 24-foot (7-metre) span, built on piers 20 feet (6 metres) wide (see Figure 3). The 13th arch from the city was designed as a tollgate for merchant shipping with a military drawbridge. The foundations were built inside cofferdams made by driving timber sheathing piles, which held the pier stones in place. Obstructions encountered in

By courtesy of (bottom) the French Government Tourist Office; photograph, (top) Archivo Mas, Barcelona

Stone arch bridges.
(Top) Roman bridge over the Tagus at Alcántara, Spain, built by Caius Julius Lacer for Trajan. (Bottom) Pont Valentré at Cahors, France, a medieval fortified bridge.

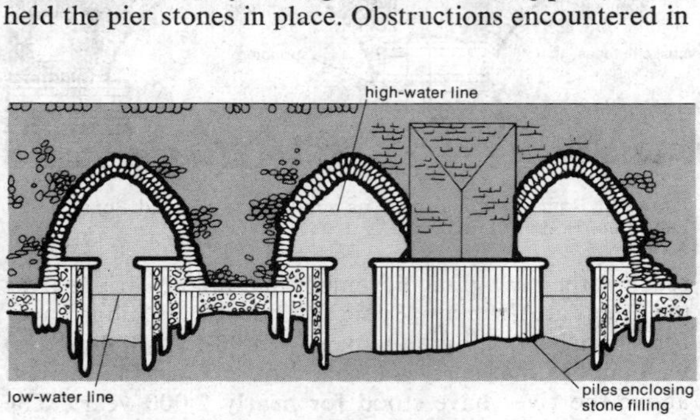

Figure 3: Pointed arches of Old London Bridge.

pile driving resulted in variations in the span of the arches of from 15 to 34 feet (5 to 10 metres). The width of the protective starlings (loose stone filling enclosed by piles at the base of each pier) was so great that the total waterway was reduced to a quarter of its original width, and the tide flowed under the narrow archways like a millrace. The bridge, nevertheless, was completed in 1209 and survived, together with its famous tunnellike street of shops and houses, for more than 600 years.

Leonardo's design for the Golden Horn

The confidence and the unbounded enterprise of the Renaissance is reflected in Leonardo da Vinci's offer in 1502 to build a masonry arch bridge with a clear span of 787 feet, over the Golden Horn at Istanbul. Leonardo's design appears to have been practical, except for the difficulty of supporting the falsework (centring), the temporary wooden supports on which the enormous arch would have been built. Less grandiose but more economically and technically feasible bridges were actually built; they included some of the most famous bridges in the world, such as the Pont Notre Dame and the Pont Neuf in Paris, the Rialto in Venice, Italy, and the Santa Trinità in Florence, Italy. Though engineers had learned much about bridge foundations since Roman times, they were still rarely able to excavate deep enough—*i.e.*, down to rock or really hard strata—but they had learned to spread the base of the pier over a wide area and to lay the foundation stones on a broad timber grillage, supported, if necessary, on piles. In the foundation of the Rialto Bridge, for example, Antonio da Ponte, the designer, had 6,000 timber piles driven under each of the two abutments and placed the masonry in such a way that the bed joints of the stones were perpendicular to the thrust of the arch. So well were these foundations built that, although they have to support in soft alluvial soil a wide arch carrying a street of shops, they stand today.

In his beautiful Santa Trinità Bridge in Florence, built 1567–69, Bartolomeo Ammanati, working on scientific principles, evolved a new type of arch. He adopted the ogival (pointed) shape, with the angle at the crown concealed and the curves of the arches starting vertically in their springings from the piers. This elliptical shape of arch, in which the rise-to-span ratio was as low as one to seven, became known as basket-handled and has been widely adopted since. Demolished by the retreating Germans in World War II, the Santa Trinità Bridge was later rebuilt exactly as it stood and, so far as possible, with the original materials, recovered from the bed of the river. An even earlier bridge in Florence, and one that was spared in World War II, was the Ponte Vecchio, ascribed to Taddeo Gaddi in the 14th century. Its three well-balanced arches, supported on peaked piers, are elliptical in shape. The narrow, gently sloping roadway is lined on both sides with tiny shops.

By the middle of the 18th century, bridge building in masonry reached its zenith. Jean-Rodolphe Perronet (1708–94), builder of some of the finest bridges of his day, developed very flat arches supported on slender piers. He served as director of the first engineering school in the world, the famous École des Ponts et Chaussées (School of Bridges and Highways), founded in 1747, and his works included the Neuilly Bridge, over the Seine, the Pont Sainte-Maxence, over the Oise, and the beautiful Pont de la Concorde, over the Seine, in Paris. In Great Britain, William Edwards built what many people consider the most beautiful arch bridge in the British Isles—the Pontypridd Bridge, over the Taff in Wales, with a lofty span of 140 feet (43 metres). In London, the young Swiss engineer Charles Labelye, entrusted with the building of the first bridge at Westminster, evolved a novel and ingenious method of sinking the foundations, employing huge timber caissons (boxes) that were filled with masonry after they had been floated into position for each pier. The twelve semicircular arches of Portland stone, rising in a graceful camber over the river, set a high standard of engineering and architectural achievement for the next generation and stood for a hundred years.

First Waterloo Bridge

Also in London, John Rennie, engaged by private enterprise in 1811, built the first Waterloo Bridge, whose level-topped masonry arches were described by Canova as "the noblest bridge in the world." It was replaced by a modern bridge in 1935–42. Rennie subsequently designed and built old Southwark Bridge (1814–19), which consisted of three cast-iron arches with spans of up to 240 feet (73 metres), and the New London Bridge of multiple masonry arches, which was completed in 1831, after his death, and subsequently widened.

II. Development of the modern bridge

In the 17th and 18th centuries, bridge building became a science. Early in this period, scientists, including Galileo, had investigated the theory of beams and framed structures, and before the end of the period bridge builders were required to work to detailed specifications.

THE COVERED (TIMBER-TRUSS) BRIDGE

The truss, a structural form based on the triangle, had long been used to support roofs when it was adapted to bridge design by the Italian Renaissance architect Andrea Palladio. In the 18th century, Swiss carpenters used it to build a covered timber bridge having spans of 193 feet (59 metres) and 171 feet (52 metres) over the Rhine at Schaffhausen, Switzerland. This feat was followed by a similar timber bridge with a 240-foot span at Reichenau, Switzerland. The barnlike covering of timber-truss bridges was necessary to protect the structural members against the weather. In North America, many outstanding timber-truss bridges were built, the first probably that over the Connecticut River at Bellows Falls, Vermont, in 1785. The so-called Colossus Bridge, with a 340-foot span over the Schuylkill River at Fairmount Park, Philadelphia, was constructed in 1812. One of the best long-span truss designs was developed by Theodore Burr, of Torrington, Connecticut, and based on a drawing by Palladio: a truss strengthened by an arch, which set a new pattern for covered bridges in the United States. Burr's McCall's Ferry Bridge (1815; on the Susquehanna River, Lancaster, Pennsylvania) had a record-breaking span of 360 feet (110 metres), and hundreds of his bridges are still in use.

THE IRON BRIDGE

It was not until late in the 18th century that iron came to be generally employed in structures, freeing bridge builders from their exclusive dependence on timber, brick, and stone. The possibilities opened up by the new material were quickly exploited, and by 1860 numerous iron arches, suspension bridges, and girders had been built. This period also witnessed the first use of compressed air in the construction of bridge foundations below water. Iron chains had been used in suspension bridges for centuries, but the world's first all-iron bridge was a semicircular arch with a 100-foot (30-metre) span, built over the Severn at Coalbrookdale, Shropshire, in 1779. It carried roadway traffic for more than 170 years. This was followed by a number of cast-iron arches designed by the gifted, self-educated Scottish engineer and road builder Thomas Telford, of which the first was the Buildwas Bridge, Shropshire, with a 130-foot (40-metre) span, and the most ambitious was a design for a high-level, 600-foot (180-metre) span (which was never built) to replace Old London Bridge.

In 1840 American patents were granted for a timber truss, in which the verticals consisted of iron ties. This was followed by numerous other trusses. The first major iron-truss bridge, with pin connections, was built in the United States in 1851, and the earliest iron-cantilever girder, which consisted of alternate cantilever and continuous spans, was built over the Main River at Hassfurt, Germany, in 1867.

Robert Stephenson's Britannia Bridge

The Britannia railway bridge (1845–50) across the Menai Strait, north Wales, was designed by Robert Stephenson and William Fairbairn. Employing the prototype of the box, or plate, girder of the kind now used throughout the world, it was originally intended to be a stiffened suspension bridge. It has four spans, each consisting of two wrought-iron tubes side by side, through which the trains run; the two spans over the water are each 459 feet (140 metres) long, and the shore spans are

230 feet (70 metres). In spite of the fact that L.-M.-H. Navier's lectures on the theory of elasticity and structures had been published some years earlier, so little was known of structural-design theory that Stephenson had to proceed empirically by testing, modifying, and retesting a series of models. Workshops were built at the site to fabricate the wrought-iron plates and sections (of the kind that had recently been produced for shipbuilding), which were raised and moved by means of overhead gantries. Rivetting was done mostly by hand but in part by hydraulic machines designed by Fairbairn. During the erection of the bridge, it was found to be possible to dispense with the suspending chains altogether, and the tubes for the spans over the water, each weighing 1,285 tons, were floated out on pontoons and raised to their final level by means of huge hydraulic jacks located on the piers. Carrying locomotives 12 times heavier than those in use when it was designed, the Britannia Bridge survived until it was severely damaged by fire in May 1970. Comprehensive reconstruction was at once undertaken with the object of reopening the bridge with the addition of a three-lane roadway above the two railway tracks.

A major early iron-bridge disaster occurred in December 1879, when the 13 high spans of the new railway bridge over the Firth of Tay, Perth, were blown down in a great gale 18 months after completion. The Edinburgh mail train was crossing the bridge at the time, and it is estimated that 75 persons lost their lives. Consisting of wrought-iron trusses 245 feet (75 metres) long, the girders that fell stood on cast-iron columns rising from piers of brick and concrete. At the time, little if anything was known of the wind pressures that should be considered in the design of bridges. There was no continuous, lateral wind bracing provided below the deck, and, in fact, the designer subsequently said that no special provision had been made for wind pressure.

The second half of the 19th century was outstanding for the advances made in the theory of design and knowledge of the strength of materials by scientists such as Karl Culmann of Germany, and James Clerk Maxwell and W.J.M. Rankine of Britain. As a result of work in basic science and mathematics, graphic methods of structural analysis were developed, and engineers were able to draw stress diagrams and influence lines; *i.e.*, curves showing, for one component part of a beam or truss, the resistance to various types of stress for all positions of a moving load.

THE MODERN SUSPENSION BRIDGE

In the design of the Menai suspension bridge (1820–26), a 580-foot (177-metre) span in north Wales, Telford used chains of wrought-iron links, all of which were tested and pinned together. The chains, laid out full length, were then towed across the waterway and hoisted into place; and the deck was suspended beneath them. The roadway was only 24 feet (7 metres) wide and, in the absence of any kind of stiffening girders or storm bracing, was highly vulnerable to damage by wind and had to be rebuilt at least twice before the whole of the bridge was reconstructed in 1940. In view of the fate of most of the early suspension bridges in both Europe and the United States, it is a credit to Telford that the Menai Bridge survived for 115 years. Another chain suspension bridge that had a long life was a span over the Danube at Budapest, Hungary. Completed in 1849, it survived for nearly 100 years, until it was destroyed in World War II.

The first engineer to employ wire cables instead of chains on suspension birdges was M. Chaley, a French engineer who not only built the bridges at Beaucaire, Chasey, and other places in the south of France but was also responsible for the Fribourg Bridge (1830–34) in Switzerland, which had a span of 870 feet, at that time the longest in the world. Each of the main cables, 1,280 feet (390 metres) long from anchorage to anchorage, was made up of 2,000 separate iron wires, which passed over the top of masonry towers, beyond which they were anchored in 58-foot-deep shafts. The bridge carried a roadway 16 feet (5 metres) wide, separated by oaken balustrades from footpaths three feet (1 metre) wide on either side, all at a height of 163 feet (50 metres) above the River Saône. Another early suspension bridge with iron-wire cables was the Bry-sur-Marne Bridge, opened to traffic in 1831 and destroyed during the war of 1870.

The multiple-span suspension bridge (*i.e.*, a bridge made up of more than three successive suspension spans without any intermediate anchorage) appeared as early as 1839 in the Dordogne River Bridge, with five equal spans of 357 feet (109 metres) each, supported on wire cables, at Cubzag, France; another was the Dnepr River Bridge (1853) at Kiev, Russia, with two spans of 226 feet (69 metres) and four spans of 400 feet (134 metres), supported by wrought-iron chains.

Early suspension failures

The weaknesses of the early suspension bridges in storms or under repeated rhythmic loads were fatal for most of them. In 1831 the Broughton suspension bridge collapsed because of oscillations set up by a body of troops marching in step. Four other bridges in the U.S. and Britain were destroyed simply by the impact of flocks of sheep or droves of cattle. The Chain Pier Bridge at Brighton, Sussex, and the Union Bridge over the Tweed at Berwick, Northumberland, were both blown down. The first railway suspension bridge, built in 1830 to carry the Stockton and Darlington Railway over the Tees, was hammered to destruction in a few years by the weight and impact of the trains. In the U.S., the Fairmount Bridge, supported by a number of small wire cables, over the Schuylkill River, was a success, but a 1,000-foot (300-metre) span over the Ohio River at Wheeling, West Virginia, survived only five years.

Credit for designing and building the first suspension bridge that was rigid enough to withstand not only wind action but also the impact of railway traffic belongs to John A. Roebling, an immigrant from Germany to the United States. In his Grand Trunk Bridge of 821-foot (250-metre) span below Niagara Falls, there were two decks, one above the other, for rail and road traffic, respectively, with a pair of stiffening trusses 18 feet (five metres) deep connecting them. In addition, the deck was braced by means of inclined wire stays overhead and others below, anchored to the sides of the gorge. For the four main cables, instead of the separate stranded or twisted ropes that had been used for cables in Europe, Roebling used parallel wrought-iron wires, spun in place, bunched together, and wrapped, a process he had patented in 1841; each cable was 10 inches (25 centimetres) overall in diameter. The bridge was completed in 1855 and survived for 42 years, although not without considerable repair work and reconstruction necessitated by the wear and tear of traffic.

The famous Brooklyn Bridge (1869–83), with a record-breaking span of 1,595 feet (486 metres), was designed by John Roebling and erected under the direction of his son, Washington. It has four cables with an overall diameter of 15.75 inches, built up of parallel steel wires. The method of cable spinning devised by Roebling was so simple and effective that it has been used in principle, although now much elaborated, for all the large suspension bridges subsequently built in the United States (see Figure 4). The wire is delivered to the site in reels, from which loops are carried over the tops of the towers to the far anchorage, where each loop is pulled off the sheave and placed around a strand shoe, by which it is anchored.

By the time of the Brooklyn Bridge, the stiffening truss had been established as an indispensable part of the suspension-bridge deck. In the Point Bridge at Pittsburgh, Pennsylvania (1877), an attempt was made to stiffen the cables instead of the deck, but this proved less effective.

THE FOUNDATION PROBLEM: COMPRESSED AIR

Up to the middle of the 19th century, cofferdams were the only means by which bridge foundations could be properly constructed below water. But, because of the limited length of the sheet piling and the difficulties caused by obstructions or by very hard or soft ground, cylinders or wells were employed and sunk either by dredging or under compressed air. The first use of pneu-

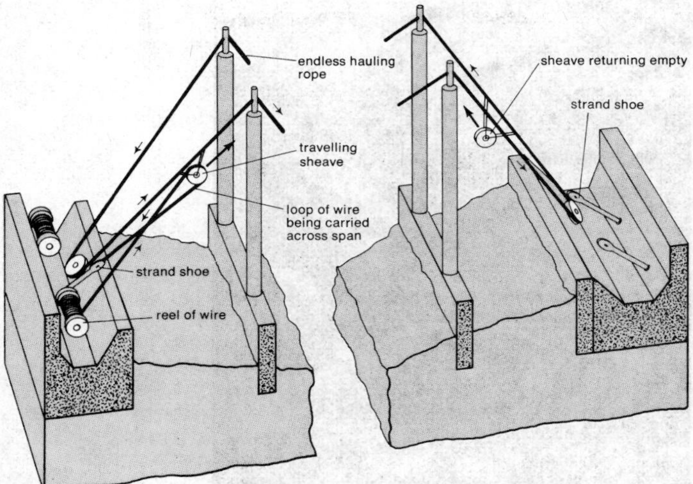

Figure 4: Method of spinning parallel wire cable on a suspension bridge.

Use of pneumatic caissons

matic caissons (Figure 5) for bridgework was on the foundations of a bridge over the Medway at Rochester, Kent, in 1851. Subsequently I.K. Brunel used this method for sinking the foundations of Chepstow Bridge, Monmouth, and, on a much greater scale, for the Royal Albert Bridge at Saltash, Cornwall (1855–59). In the latter, a wrought-iron cylinder 35 feet (11 metres) in diameter was designed for the central pier and sunk through 70 feet of water and 16 feet (5 metres) of mud to a rock bottom. Water was expelled by compressed air from the floorless working chamber at the bottom of the cylinder; workers entered the chamber through an air lock and excavated the mud and rock, causing the caisson slowly to sink until a hard stratum was reached. They then securely plugged the bottom of the foundation with concrete.

Many early tragedies in the use of compressed air were caused by men working excessively long shifts or coming out of the air lock and decompressing too quickly and

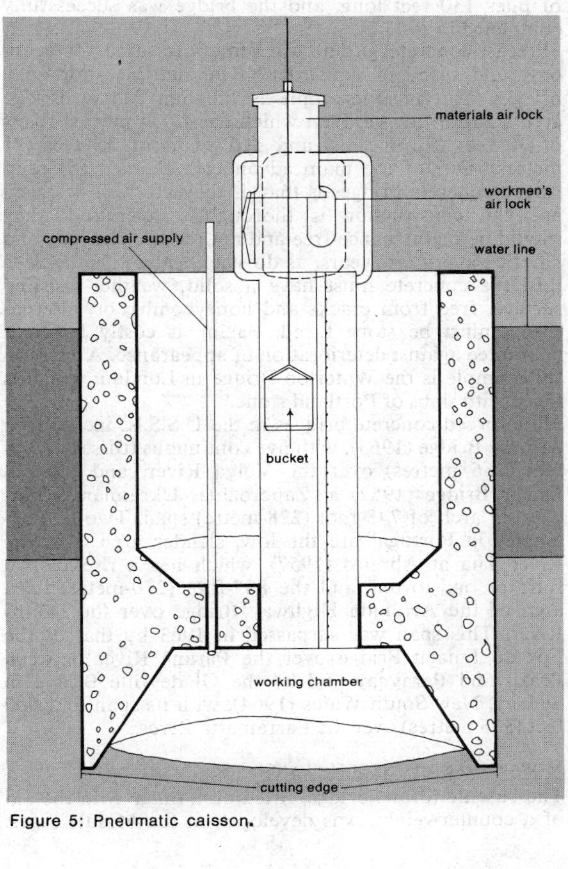

Figure 5: Pneumatic caisson.

being afflicted by caisson disease, or bends. With the limiting of the length of the working shift according to the air pressure and with slow decompression in the air lock, the incidence of caisson disease was reduced. Further investigations at the beginning of the 20th century robbed the disease of its worst terrors, except for the danger of bone necrosis, for which no cure has yet been found.

By courtesy of the National Monuments Record, London

Royal Albert Bridge over the Tamar at Saltash, Cornwall. Designer Isambard Brunel employed a wrought iron cylinder 35 feet in diameter for the central pier in this innovative design of 1855–59.

THE STEEL BRIDGE

The last 30 years of the 19th century saw the introduction of steel plates and rectangular, rolled-steel sections, which came to be mass-produced and fabricated in shops by standardized methods. This inevitably led to an enormous production of steel-truss and plate-girder bridges throughout the world and to spans of ever-increasing size. Arch and cantilever bridges were favoured for long spans in the railway era because they could withstand the impact of heavy railway traffic better than could suspension bridges.

The Eads Bridge

The first big bridge to be built of steel was the Eads Bridge built over the Mississippi River (1867–74) at St. Louis, Missouri. It was designed with three steel arches with spans of 502, 520, and 502 feet (153, 158, and 153 metres), respectively. The spans were made double-decked to carry wagon and pedestrian traffic on the upper deck and two railway tracks below. To reach bedrock, the foundations had to be excavated more than 100 feet deep, although this necessitated working under compressed air at depths greater than men had ever worked before. So little was known of the precautions needed under these conditions that, of the 600 men employed in sinking, there were 119 serious cases of bends and 14 deaths.

An innovation on this bridge that has since been widely copied was the erection of the arches by cantilevering. Arch ribs were built out in either direction from the pier and held by cables extending from a temporary wooden tower atop the pier. Halfway to the next pier (or abutment), the half-arch met and joined a half-arch similarly cantilevered out to meet it.

In 1898 an arch bridge with a span of 840 feet (256 metres) was completed below Niagara Falls; it stood for 40 years, until the ends of the steel ribs were wrecked by a huge ice jam in the river. In the same year, the first major steel bridge in France was opened, the Viaur Viaduct, which consisted of an arch 721 feet (220 metres) long, flanked by cantilever spans of 311 feet (95 metres). Seven years later the Victoria Falls Bridge, with a braced arch spanning 500 feet (152 metres), was built in Africa to carry the Cape-to-Cairo Railway, then projected by Cecil Rhodes, across the 400-foot- (122-metre-) deep gorge of the Zambezi River.

For the design of the Forth Railway Bridge between North and South Queensferry (1882–90), with two main spans of 1,710 feet (521 metres) each, in Scotland, the designer conducted an extensive series of wind-pressure tests, using gauges installed at the site, over a period of two years. As a result, he was satisfied that the pressure of 56 pounds per square foot, specified for the design by the committee set up after the Tay Bridge disaster, was "considerably in excess of anything likely to be realised," and so it proved.

The two main spans of the bridge each consist of two 680-foot (207-metre) cantilever arms, with a 350-foot (107-metre) suspended span between them. About 54,000 tons of Siemens-Martin open-hearth steel, which has a substantially higher ultimate strength than modern, commercial mild steel, was used. The biggest compression members were designed as tubular struts 12 feet (4 metres) in diameter, and all of the steelwork was fabricated in shops built for the purpose at South Queensferry. The spans were built out as balanced cantilevers from each main pier, the tubular members being erected plate by plate by means of two-ton hydraulic cranes.

The latter half of the 19th century witnessed the construction in India of a large number of multispan railway bridges more than 1,000 feet long. Their British builders learned how to utilize the simplest kind of equipment and unskilled labour; they had to study and develop the use of guide banks as a means of keeping the rivers under the bridges and preventing them from meandering; and, sinking brick wells by dredging in the sand, they built the deepest foundations ever constructed up to then, as a safeguard against undermining when the sand of the riverbeds was scoured away during the flood seasons.

In 1896 the first Vierendeel truss, in which the bracing consisted of a series of framed portals with rigid verticals and no diagonal members, was built for the Brussels Exhibition.

REINFORCED-CONCRETE BRIDGES

Engineers in the late 19th century first demonstrated the possibilities of reinforced concrete as a new structural material. Visualizing the novel forms that could be molded, with concrete resisting the compression forces and steel bars taking the tension, they designed bridges in sweeping curves. The basic element in reinforced concrete was the slab, which replaced the beams, posts, and ties associated with steelwork design. From the start, Switzerland, France, and the Scandinavian countries took the lead, and the longest and most impressive reinforced spans were built in those nations.

Robert Maillart's Pont de Chatellerault

The first notable reinforced-concrete arch, the Pont de Chatellerault (1898), was designed with a span of 172 feet (52 metres). Robert Maillart designed three-hinged arches, in which the deck and the arch rib were combined to produce closely integrated structures. The first of these was the Tavanasa Bridge, a span of 167 feet (51 metres) over the Vorderrhein, Switzerland, which was destroyed by a landslide in 1927. In these bridges, Maillart recaptured the beauty of the pointed arch of medieval times. He then developed arches of very thin reinforced-concrete slabs, typified by the Schwandbach Bridge (1924) near Schwarzenberg, Switzerland, which was curved in plan and carried a roadway across a deep ravine.

One of the biggest reinforced-concrete bridges in the United States, the Tunkhannock Creek Viaduct, Pennsylvania, was completed in 1915. Its overall length of 2,375 feet (724 metres) comprises ten semicircular arches that carry a double-track railway at a height of 240 feet (73 metres). In Great Britain, the first major reinforced-concrete structure was the Royal Tweed Bridge at Berwick. Completed in 1928, it has four arch spans varying from 167 feet (51 metres) to 361 feet (110 metres). It was followed in 1935–42 by the new Waterloo Bridge in London. Because of its slender simplicity and absence of decoration, it is frequently held to be the finest bridge over the Thames.

In France, a then record span of 430 feet (131 metres) was built in 1923 over the Seine at Saint-Pierre du Vauvray. It was surpassed seven years later by the Albert-Louppe (or Plougastel) Bridge at Brest. The latter had three arch spans of 567 feet (173 metres). The centring (supporting falsework) consisted of a timber arch 500 feet (152 metres) long and 90 feet (27 metres) high, the ends of which were tied together by cables. It was built on shore, floated out on pontoons, and secured in place for pouring each arch rib in turn.

Salginatobel Bridge near Schiers, Switzerland, a reinforced-concrete bridge designed by Robert Maillart and built 1929–30.
By courtesy of the Grisons Tourist Office, Chur, Switzerland

In Sweden, the Traneberg Bridge was built in 1934 in Stockholm. It has an arch 593 feet (181 metres) long. It was surpassed by the Esla Bridge in Spain, with a 631-foot (192-metre) span completed in 1942, but a year later Sweden regained the lead with an 866-foot (264-metre) span of the Sandö Bridge, over the Angermanälven River. In 1939, during the pouring of the rib, the wooden arch that formed the centring collapsed. Its failure was ascribed to persistent damp weather and the long loading period. New centring for the bridge had to be built in the form of huge timber trestles supported on 13 groups of piles 130 feet long, and the bridge was successfully completed in 1943.

Precast-concrete girders are sometimes used for economy and speed of construction in multiple short-span bridges. A typical example is the San Mateo Bridge across San Francisco Bay, which has 1,054 precast spans of 30 feet (9.1 metres) and 116 spans of 35 feet (11 metres). One of the main advantages claimed for reinforced-concrete bridges is that, if they are well designed and the construction is thoroughly supervised, they should be maintenance-free and not require cleaning and painting every few years, as do steel bridges. To achieve this, the concrete must have a solid, weather-resisting surface, free from cracks and honeycombs, or, alternatively, must be stone faced. Facing is costly but is a guarantee against deterioration of appearance. A successful example is the Waterloo Bridge in London, which is faced with slabs of Portland stone.

Reinforced-concrete bridges in the U.S.S.R. include the Saratov Bridge (1965), with five continuous trusses of 544 feet (166 metres) over the Volga River, and the old Dnepr Bridge (1952) at Zaporozhia, Ukrainian S.S.R., with an arch of 748-foot (228-metre) span. Two fine examples in Portugal are the low, slender arch over the River Tua at Abreiro (1957), which has a rise-to-span ratio of one to ten, and the 885-foot (270-metre) fixed arch of the Arrábida Highway Bridge over the Douro River. This span was surpassed in 1963 by that of the Foz do Iguaçu Bridge over the Paraná River between Brazil and Paraguay and by the Gladesville Bridge in Sydney, New South Wales (1964), with its span of 1,000 feet (305 metres) over the Parramatta River.

MOVABLE AND PONTOON SPANS

The bascule (draw) bridge, lifted on a hinge with the aid of a counterweight, was developed in the Middle Ages.

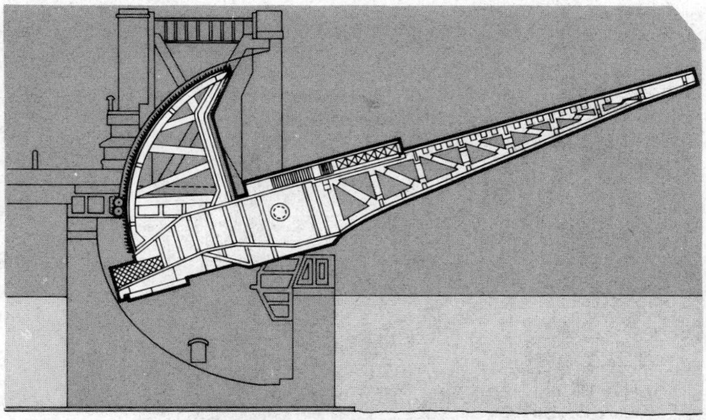

Figure 6: Sectional elevation of the bascule, Tower Bridge, London, 1886–94.
From O.E. Hovey, *Movable Bridges* (1927); John Wiley & Sons, Inc.

Old London Bridge had such a drawbridge. The first swing, or pivot, bridges appeared in London early in the 19th century. The heavy, powered bascule and the vertical-lift bridge were evolved in the latter half of the 19th century. The Tower Bridge in London (1886–94) is a double-leaf bascule that provides an opening 260 feet (76 metres) wide and is operated by hydraulic power derived from steam (see Figure 6). The biggest bascule span to date is the Sault Sainte Marie, Michigan (1941), which has an opening span of 336 feet (102 metres). A variety of bascule that requires no counterweight is the rolling lift bridge, in which the leaves roll back on tracks to open the bridge.

Notable modern bascules

In vertical-lift bridges, the span remains horizontal and is lifted by means of counterweighted cables that pass over the end towers. The Arthur Kill Bridge is of this type. Built in 1959 to link Staten Island, New York City, with New Jersey, it has a lifting span of 558 feet (170 metres).

The longest swing bridge yet built is the al Firdan Bridge over the Suez Canal, Egypt, composed of twin swing spans, pivoted on piers at either shore, 552 feet (165 metres) from turntable to turntable. Ordinary swing spans, pivoted on a central pier, cause more interference with river traffic than bascules and may obstruct valuable wharf space. Another advantage of bascules is that they can be partially opened to let small craft pass.

Table 1: Longest Span Movable Bridges

bridge	location	year completed	span (feet)
Vertical lift			
Arthur Kill*	Elizabeth, N.J.	1959	558
Cape Cod Canal*	Massachusetts	1935	544
Delair	Delair, N.J.	1960	542
Marine Parkway	New York City	1937	540
Swing span			
al Firdan	Suez Canal, U.A.R.	1965	552
Mississippi River	Fort Madison, Iowa*	1927	525†
Willamette River	Portland, Ore.*	1908	521†
Missouri River	East Omaha, Neb.	1893	520†
Bascule			
Sault Sainte Marie*	Michigan	1941	336
Erie Avenue	Lorain, Ohio	1940	333
Tennessee River	Chattanooga, Tenn.	1917	310

*Railway bridge. †Combined length, including both arms.

The longest floating spans in the world are clustered around Seattle, Washington; the longest, over the Hood Canal, measures 7,131 feet (2,139 metres). The second and third longest stretch side by side over Lake Washington, a distance of 6,560 feet (1,999 metres). Other famous floating bridges, since replaced by high-level fixed bridges, include a 3,165-foot (965-metre) curved pontoon span at Hobart, Tasmania, a pontoon bridge at Calcutta (built in 1874), and a 1,500-foot (457-metre) bridge over the Golden Horn at Istanbul. All these bridges had movable spans that could be opened to permit shipping to pass.

By courtesy of (top) U. S. Army Corps of Engineers, (bottom) Bethlehem Steel Corp.

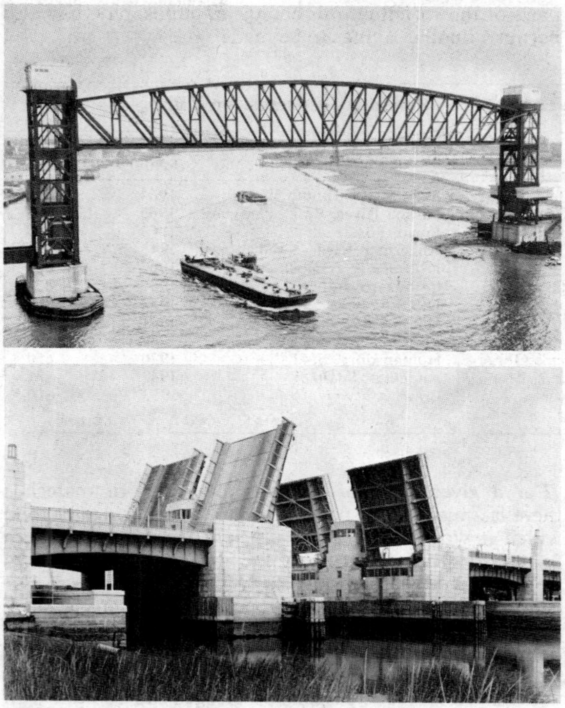

Movable bridges.
(Top) Arthur Kill Bridge completed in 1959, a vertical-lift bridge spanning the Arthur Kill River between New Jersey and New York. (Bottom) Double-leaf bascule bridges spanning the Flushing River, Long Island, New York.

20TH-CENTURY LONG-SPAN BRIDGES

Loadings and forces. The most important weights and forces to which a bridge is subject are its own weight; the weight of the traffic and its dynamic effects; natural forces set up by wind, changes in temperature, snow loads, earthquakes, etc.; and stresses arising temporarily during erection. Railway bridges must withstand not only the weight of the locomotives and rolling stock but also the impact and effects of lurching and lateral motion of the locomotive. On the highways of several countries, automotive vehicles weighing up to 200 tons are not uncommon, and new bridges must be designed to support them.

Considerable research has been carried out on wind forces, which can now be closely estimated, but wind-tunnel tests on a model are still usually carried out to assess the effects of wind forces on a long-span suspension bridge. Although no bridge could withstand an earthquake of catastrophic force, bridges in India and New Zealand are designed to resist a horizontal force equal to one-tenth and, in Japan, Italy, and the U.S.S.R., to one-fifth of the weight of the superstructure. The designs of the Golden Gate and San Francisco-Oakland Bay bridges in San Francisco, the Auckland Harbour Bridge in New Zealand, and the Howrah and Ganga bridges in India were all calculated to resist earthquake shocks, which in the past have damaged or destroyed many bridges.

Wind-tunnel tests on models

It remains for the engineer to exercise his judgment in assessing future traffic developments and deciding what combinations of loading and forces should be adopted and the factor of safety applicable in each case. Factors of safety are now considered from the point of view of "limit states," which are states in which the structure in whole or in part threatens to cease to fulfill the function for which it was designed. The field is enormous, because the effect of numerous factors, such as loading, impact, fatigue, and corrosion, must be assessed for different types of structures and materials of construction and suitable margins of safety provided for various causes of failure, such as deformation, buckling, fatigue, brittle fracture, or collapse of some element. While conferring greater uniformity of strength throughout all parts of the structure, this change in philosophy may also permit valuable savings to be made.

Table 2: Longest Span Reinforced-Concrete Arch Bridges

bridge	location	year of completion	span (feet)
Gladesville	Sydney, New South Wales	1964	1,000
Foz do Iguaçu	Paraná River, Braz.–Paraguay	1965	951
Arrábida	Porto, Port.	1963	885
Sandö	Ångerman River, Swed.	1943	866
Shibenik	Krka River, Yugos.	1967	808
Fiumarella	Catanzaro, Italy	1961	758
Old Dnepr	U.S.S.R.	1952	748
Novi Sad	Danube River, Yugos.	1961	692
Lingenau	Bregenz, Austria	1967	689
Van Staden's Gorge	Humansdorp, S.Af.	1970	650
Esla River	Andavias, Spain	1942	631
Antas River	Brazil	1953	610
Traneberg	Sweden	1934	593

For a given ratio of strength to weight of materials there is a maximum span for each type of bridge beyond which it would have an insufficient margin of strength to support the weight of traffic in addition to its own weight and other forces to which it might be subject. For cantilever bridges built with modern high-tensile steel, the maximum span would approach 2,500 feet and, for arch bridges, 3,000 feet. On account of the much higher strength-to-weight ratio of steel-wire cables as compared with structural steel, suspension bridges can be built with much longer spans. In a period of 80 years, the maximum suspension span has increased from 1,500 to 4,260 feet (457 to 1,298 metres), bearing out predictions made by Roebling in 1855.

Table 3: Chronological Record of Maximum Spans Since 1820

year of completion	bridge	location	type	span (feet)
1826	Menai	Wales	suspension	580
1834	Fribourg*	Switzerland	suspension	870
1849	Wheeling	Wheeling, W.Va.	suspension	1,010
1851	Niagara River*	Lewiston, N.Y.	suspension	1,043
1867	Cincinnati	Cincinnati, Ohio	suspension	1,057
1869	Niagara-Clifton* (1st)	Niagara Falls	suspension	1,268
1883	Brooklyn	New York City	suspension	1,595
1890	Forth†	Scotland	cantilever	1,710
1918	Quebec†	Quebec	cantilever	1,800
1929	Ambassador	Detroit	suspension	1,850
1931	George Washington	New York City	suspension	3,500
1937	Golden Gate	San Francisco	suspension	4,200
1964	Verrazano Narrows	New York City	suspension	4,260

*Not standing †Railway bridge.

Cantilever bridges. In 1904 work began on the first Quebec Bridge, which was to carry two railway tracks on a cantilever span of 1,800 feet (549 metres). The two giant cantilevers were erected without incident, and the relatively short suspended span between was developed from both sides. Suddenly the whole of the structure on the south side, some 20,000 tons of steel, collapsed, killing 75 workmen, the most costly bridge-construction disaster on record. Investigation revealed that the failure was caused by buckling of web plates in which the lacing was too weak and by certain unrivetted connections. Other grave disclosures, however, were that the specifications were inadequate, the weight of the bridge was underestimated, and the working stresses were unwarrantably high.

The Quebec cantilever disasters

For the new design, made after an exhaustive series of tests on structural members and rivetted joints, high-tensile nickel steel was used for the main trusses, and the

Quebec Bridge across the St. Lawrence River, designed by Theodore Cooper. The steel cantilever railroad bridge, spanning 1,800 feet, was completed in 1918.
By courtesy of Canadian National Railways

width of the bridge was increased from 67 to 85 feet, greatly increasing its strength. The suspended span, 640 feet (195 metres) long, was built, floated out, and attached to lifting links at the four corners of the cantilever arms. As it arose, suddenly, one of the castings at the end of a lifting link failed, and the span tilted, broke, and fell into the water, carrying 11 workmen with it. Within 12 months, a new span had been constructed and successfully lifted into place. First opened to traffic in August 1918, it has remained the longest cantilever span in the world.

Another great cantilever is the Howrah Bridge (1936–43), over the Hooghly River at Calcutta, which has a span of 1,500 feet (457 metres). An interesting innovation on the Howrah Bridge was that the high-tensile steelwork was prestressed during erection; this measure obviated secondary bending stresses that would otherwise have occurred at the rivetted connections. The span of the Howrah Bridge has since been exceeded by the Greater New Orleans Bridge (1958), in Louisiana, and the Delaware River Bridge, in Chester, Pennsylvania, due for completion in 1971.

Table 4: Longest Span Steel Cantilever Bridges

bridge	location	year of completion	span (feet)
Quebec*	Quebec	1918	1,800
Forth*	Queensferry, Scot.	1890	2 spans, each 1,710
Delaware River	Chester, Pa.	1971	1,644
Greater New Orleans	Mississippi River, La.	1958	1,575
Howrah	Calcutta	1943	1,500
San Francisco-Oakland Bay	San Francisco	1936	1,400
Baton Rouge	Mississippi River, La.	1968	1,235
Tappan Zee	Hudson River, N.Y.	1955	1,212
Longview	Columbia River, Wash.	1930	1,200
Queensboro	New York City	1909	1,182

*Railway bridge.

Arch bridges. The Sydney Harbour Bridge (1924–32), New South Wales, may be considered the world's greatest steel arch because of its immense carrying capacity and the difficulties overcome in erecting it across a deep harbour in which no temporary supports were practicable (Figure 7). With a span of 1,650 feet (503 metres), it was built to carry four interurban rail or streetcar tracks, in addition to a roadway 57 feet (17 metres) wide and two pedestrain walkways.

The two-hinged arch, flanked by granite-faced pylons, has a deck suspended at a height of 172 feet (52 metres) over the water. Most of the 38,390-ton arch is of rivetted, high-tensile silicon steel made in Britain and fabricated in shops built for the purpose in Sydney. The 11-foot-

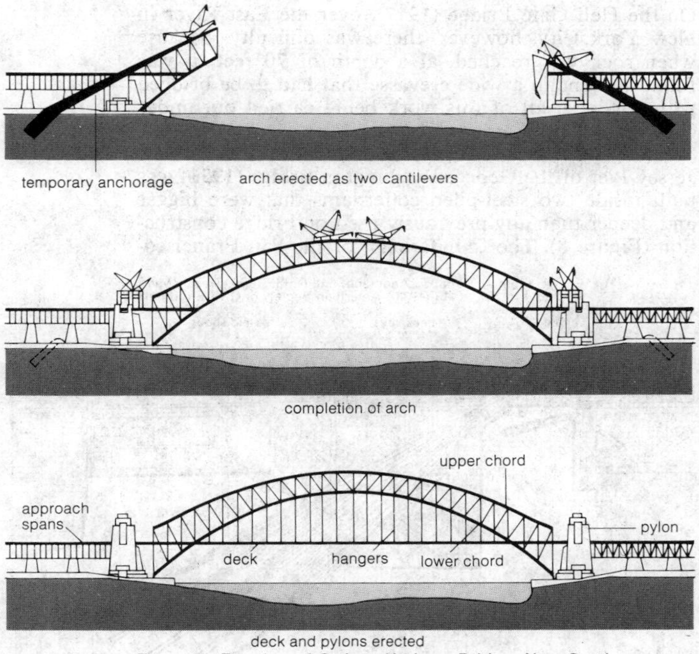

Figure 7: Erection of Sydney Harbour Bridge, New South Wales.

(3.5-metre-) wide webbed chords (top and bottom members) of the arch are the heaviest steelwork of this kind ever constructed. The two halves of the arch were built out as cantilevers, temporarily held back by wire-rope anchorages until they met and were joined in the middle. All of the steelwork was assembled by two cranes that moved out along the upper chords of the arch until it was complete and then erected the hangers and the deck as they retreated.

Another large steel arch, the Bayonne Bridge, over the Kill van Kull between Staten Island and Bayonne, New Jersey, was begun after the commencement of Sydney Harbour Bridge and completed a few months before. It was built over a waterway shallow enough to permit erection of the arch on temporary trestles. Twenty-five inches longer than the bridge at Sydney, it carries automobile and truck traffic.

Table 5: Longest Span Steel Arch Bridges

bridge	location	year of completion	span (feet)
Bayonne	New York City	1931	1,652
Sydney Harbour*	New South Wales	1932	1,650
Fremont†	Portland, Ore.	1971	1,255
Port Mann†	Vancouver, B.C.	1964	1,200
Thatcher Ferry†	Balbao, Panama	1962	1,128
Laviolette	Trois-Rivières, Que.	1967	1,100
Žďákov	Vltava River, Czech.	1967	1,083
Runcorn–Widnes	Mersey River, Eng.	1961	1,082
Birchenough	Sabi River, Rhodesia	1935	1,080
Nagasaki Sasebo	Kyushu, Japan	1955	1,042
Glen Canyon	Colorado River, Ariz.	1959	1,028
Lewiston–Queenston	Niagara River, U.S.–Canada	1962	1,000
Hell Gate*	New York City	1917	977

*Railway bridge. †Tied arch.

Suspension bridges. In the series of suspension bridges of ever-increasing span built in the United States between World Wars I and II, cables of parallel wires were invariably used. Although the ultimate strength of a given weight of wire increases as it is drawn thinner, it is found most economical to use wire of about 0.19-inch (5-millimetre) diameter, because the thicker the wire the less length there is to be spun to make up a cable of the necessary diameter.

In Canada, cables of stranded-wire ropes have been adopted, notably on the Island of Orleans Bridge at Quebec (1935) and the 1,550-foot-(472-metre-) span Lions Gate Bridge at Vancouver, British Columbia (1939). A third variant, known as "locked-coil" cables, in which the wires of each strand are specially shaped so as to form a smooth circumference, was used in the Cologne–Mulheim Bridge over the Rhine in West Germany.

In the 1,750-foot (533-metre) span of the Philadelphia–Camden Bridge (1926) on the Delaware River, cold-drawn parallel wire continued to be used in the cables, and cellular construction, in which towers were built up of a number of vertical cells, was adopted for the first time.

To increase the allowable stress in the cables, heat-treated wires were introduced in the bridge at Mount Hope, Rhode Island, and in the 1,850-foot-(564-metre-) span Ambassador Bridge over the Detroit River in Detroit, both completed in 1929. During erection of the cables, however, a number of broken wires were detected at the bends around the strand shoes at the anchorages. Investigation showed that the fine-grained, heat-treated wires could not withstand the alternating stresses to which suspension cables were subject; they had to be replaced by cold-drawn wire, which has a tough, fibrous structure and can resist such stresses.

The next advance was the George Washington Bridge (1927–31), over the Hudson River at New York City. Designed by Othmar H. Ammann, Swiss-born U.S. engineer, it has a span of 3,500 feet (1,067 metres) and two roadways, one above the other. Four cables, 36 inches in diameter, each built up of 26,474 parallel galvanized wires with an ultimate strength of 98 tons per square inch, were used. Initially, there were no stiffening trusses; only the upper roadway was built. The construction of

By courtesy of the Port of New York Authority

Cable compactor working on the George Washington Bridge over the Hudson River, New York City, during its construction in 1930.

the lower deck and of stiffening trusses between the two decks was completed in 1962. The great mass of wire in the cables (a total of 105,000 miles) prompted a higher degree of mechanization in the cable erection than had ever been achieved before.

In 1933 work began in San Francisco on two major suspension bridges, the double-decked San Francisco-Oakland Bay Bridge, designed with an overall length of nearly 5.25 miles (8.45 kilometres), and the Golden Gate Bridge, with a span of 4,200 feet (1,280 metres), across the entrance to the harbour.

The Mackinac Bridge (1954–57), with a span of 3,800 feet (1,158 metres) across the Straits of Mackinac in Michigan, was, in the early 1970s, the third longest suspension span built.

The Forth Road Bridge (1958–64) and the Severn Bridge (1961–66) in Great Britain are the first major suspension bridges outside the United States to be built with parallel wire cables spun in place. Although both exceed 3,000 feet (914 metres) in span, they are lighter in weight, more slender, and more economical in cost than any other suspension bridges of comparable size. The Forth Road Bridge, in latitude 56° N, the furthest north major bridge in the world and built in an area notorious for its high winds and storms, presented extraordinary difficulties during erection.

Verrazano Narrows Bridge

The longest single span so far built is the 4,260-foot (1,298-metre) Verrazano Narrows Bridge (1959–64), at the entrance to New York Harbor. A double-deck structure, it carries and was planned to take 12 lanes of roadway traffic. It has rivetted-steel towers 680 feet (207 metres) high, built up of square vertical cells. There are four main cables, each 36 inches (0.9 metres) in diameter and made up of a total of 142,500 miles (229,300 kilometres) of wire. On a span of this magnitude, the tops of the vertical towers are 1.6 inches further apart than the tower bases, owing to the curvature of the earth's surface, and the length of cable wire would stretch more than halfway to the moon. The total weight of steelwork in the bridge is 144,000 tons, a weight (and cost) many times greater than that of the contemporary Severn Bridge. In 1966 the Salazar Bridge was completed across the Tagus River at Lisbon, with a span of 3,323 feet (1,013 metres), the first major suspension bridge so designed that it could subsequently be double decked, if desired, to carry railway traffic.

Other recent suspension spans of between 2,000 and 3,000 feet are the Quebec Road Bridge, built alongside the existing railway crossing, and named at its opening in 1970 the Pierre Laporte Bridge; the second Delaware Memorial Bridge (1968), built alongside the first; the Angostura Bridge in Venezuela; and the Tacoma Narrows II Bridge at Puget Sound, Washington. The longest span in the U.S.S.R. is the Amu-Darja suspension bridge (1964), which has a 1,278-foot (390-metre) span, in Buhara-Ural; while the longest in Denmark is the Little Belt Bridge (1970) with a span of 1,968 feet (600 metres), designed to carry a six-lane motorway on a streamlined box deck. The towers are of reinforced concrete and the cables built up of strands of twisted wire.

Table 6: Longest Span Steel Suspension Bridges

bridge	location	year of completion	span (feet)
Verrazano Narrows	New York City	1964	4,260
Golden Gate	San Francisco	1937	4,200
Mackinac	Mackinac Straits, Mich.	1957	3,800
Bosphorus	Istanbul	1973	3,520
George Washington	New York City	1931	3,500
Salazar	Lisbon	1966	3,323
Forth Road	Queensferry, Scot.	1964	3,300
Severn	Beachley, Eng.	1966	3,240
Tacoma Narrows II	Puget Sound, Wash.	1950	2,800
Kanmon Straits	Shimonosaki, Japan	1973	2,350
Angostura	Ciudad Bolívar, Venezuela	1967	2,336
San Francisco-Oakland Bay	San Francisco	1936	2 spans, each 2,310
Bronx–Whitestone	New York City	1939	2,300
Pierre Laporte	Quebec City	1970	2,190
Delaware Memorial	Wilmington, Del.	1951	2,150
Second Delaware Memorial	Wilmington	1968	2,150

Foundation techniques. For the main piers of the Howrah Bridge in Calcutta, huge monolith foundations measuring 180 feet by 81 feet (55 by 25 metres), in plan the biggest ever sunk on land, were required. Each reinforced-concrete monolith was divided into 21 wells 20 feet square and was sunk by open excavating. The monolith on the Calcutta side was set at a depth of 103 feet (31 metres) under compressed air. This technique was applied to each well in turn, after a temporary steel air deck was fitted near the bottom of the well to form the roof of a working chamber. This method was successfully used on a number of major bridges in India and Burma and also on the huge Lower Zambezi Bridge in Mozambique.

There is rarely much difficulty with the foundations for large arch bridges, because they are usually in rock and at no great depth. For the foundations of the Sydney Harbour Bridge, it was necessary only to excavate yellow sandstone rock some 30 to 40 feet beneath each bearing. On the Hell Gate Bridge (1917), over the East River in New York City, however, there was difficulty, because when rock was reached, at a depth of 70 feet, it was found to contain a wide crevasse that had to be bridged with concrete, all of this work being carried out under compressed air.

Among suspension bridges, the foundation for the New Jersey Pier of the George Washington Bridge (1931) was built inside two steel-piled cofferdams that were bigger and deeper than any previously used on bridge construction (Figure 8). The foundations for the San Francisco-

From A. Dana, A. Anderson, and G. M. Rapp, *Transactions*, vol. 97, p 113 (1933); American Society of Civil Engineers

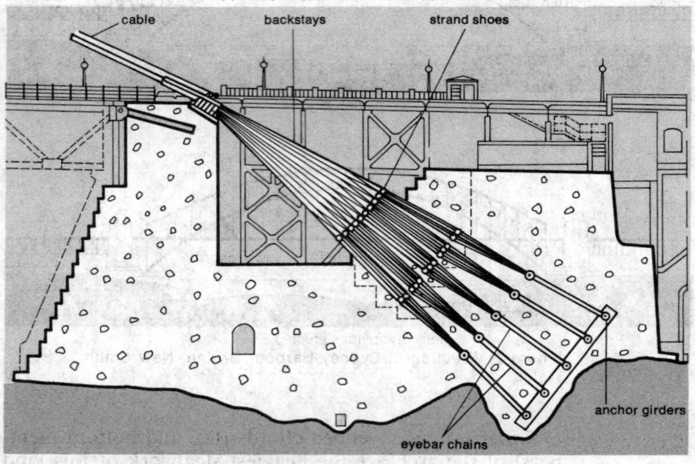

Figure 8: Cable anchorage of the George Washington Bridge, New York City.

The San Francisco-Oakland Bay Bridge

Oakland Bay Bridge, at San Francisco, presented extraordinary difficulties because caissons of unprecedented size had to be sunk through deep water and a current of 7.5 knots to a depth considerably deeper than men can work under compressed air. For the biggest caisson, at the central anchorage, connecting two suspension bridges, an entirely new technique was devised. The caisson was a honeycomb built up of 55 vertical steel cylinders, each sealed by means of a steel dome welded on top. Built on a slipway, it was launched, towed to the site, anchored, and sunk onto a sloping bottom more than 200 feet down, which had to be levelled so that the caisson could be founded on a horizontal plane. To provide buoyancy and control during the sinking, compressed air was used inside the cylinders in turn to enable muck to be grabbed out as sinking proceeded, and new steel lengths had to be welded on before the domes were replaced, as the depth increased. When rock was reached, it was broken up by dropping pointed, five-ton weights through the cylinder, after which the surface was cleaned up and levelled by divers. The middle 25 cylinders were then sealed by concrete deposited under water, followed by the sealing of the remaining 30.

Still different problems were presented by the foundation for the Golden Gate Bridge. For the south pier, located in deep water, virtually in the open sea and exposed to ocean swell, it was decided to build the foundations inside a huge elliptical cofferdam, founded on bedrock 100 feet (30 metres) below water level. The rock was first excavated some 15 feet deep all over the area; blasting was carried out by bombs of increasing size exploded in holes bored in the rock. After the cofferdam had been closed, its bottom was sealed by depositing a 65-foot depth of concrete below water. The water inside the cofferdam was then pumped out and the pier of the bridge built in the dry.

On the Verrazano Narrows Bridge in New York City, the foundations for the main piers were located in shallow water a few hundred feet off shore at the entrance to New York Harbor, where few difficulties were encountered. The site of each pier was enclosed by a rectangular cofferdam and the water inside pumped out. A reinforced-concrete monolith with a steel cutting edge, measuring 130 feet by 230 feet (40 × 70 metres) in plan and enclosing 66 circular wells 17 feet (5 metres) in diameter, was sunk by open dredging, the walls being built up to keep them above water level. The monolith on the Staten Island side was finally founded at a depth of 170 feet (52 metres).

Tacoma Narrows failure, 1940; impetus to aerodynamics. The collapse of the Tacoma Narrows Bridge, at Puget Sound, in 1940, only 4 months after its completion and after more than 50 years of immunity from suspension-bridge failure of this kind, brought the study of aerodynamic stability sharply to the fore. This bridge was by far the most flexible among its contemporaries. It had a span of 2,800 feet (853 metres) with a width of only 39 feet (12 metres), and the deck was stiffened throughout its length not by the deep open trusses formerly used but by two plate girders only 8 feet (2.4 metres) deep. Under quite moderate winds, the deck not only swayed sideways but also was subject to severe torsional (twisting) vibrations, and ultimately, in a wind of only 42 miles (70 kilometres) per hour, the vibrations became so violent that the deck was torn away and crashed into the water. Other U.S. suspension bridges had also shown undesirable aerodynamic action, and further bracing or stiffening was quickly incorporated.

Sway and torsional vibrations

A committee appointed to investigate the Tacoma failure found that the oscillations caused by wind were due to (1) natural turbulence or gusts and (2) the eddies created by the solid cross section and shed from the bridge structure. A dangerous buildup of oscillations, possibly leading to collapse, might result if the frequency of the eddies coincided with any of the natural frequencies of oscillation of the bridge. Bridge designers thereafter reverted to the use of heavy, stiff deck structures to provide torsional rigidity and also left longitudinal openings or slots along the deck, between the dual roadways and the girders, similar to the antistall slots originally used in the wings of aircraft. All these modifications were adopted for the Tacoma Narrows II Bridge, completed in 1950, in which width and rigidity were considerably increased as compared with its predecessor, and also for the Mackinac Bridge, the Forth Road Bridge, and others.

Engineers completing the final design for the Severn Bridge, however, realized that serious eddy sheddings might well be avoided on bridge decks by adopting the principles that had been used for years to avoid it in aircraft structures. The deck of the bridge was designed as a box girder, shaped like an aerofoil, and enclosed by stiffened plates at the top and bottom and inclined plates at the sides, so as to make it in a large measure streamlined. The upper surface constitutes the deck, on which the roadway is constructed, projecting platforms being provided at the sides to carry cycle tracks and footways. Extending throughout the span, the deck is only 10 feet (3 metres) deep and is suspended from the cables by inclined hangers at 60-feet (18-metre) intervals. These triangulated hangers damp out the small degree of oscillation that might otherwise occur with winds blowing slightly upwards from the horizontal.

Considerable economy is achieved not only by the saving in weight in the deck itself but also by the fact that its shallow airfoil profile reduces the wind loads on the bridge and, thus, leads to further economies in the weight of cables and towers. Moreover, the tower legs are of single-box section, so that their weight is reduced to a minimum. These innovations have undoubtedly set high standards of economy and sophistication for the future of suspension-bridge design.

Aerodynamic action may also be a source of trouble during the erection of a suspension bridge. When the north tower of the Forth Road Bridge had reached a height of over 400 feet, it began to sway alarmingly under quite light crosswinds of only 20–25 miles per hour, although in a heavy gale it moved only a few inches. The sway developed an amplitude of over 7 feet (2.1 metres) at the tower top, with a period of 4.5 seconds, and built up and died down every few minutes. This novel phenomenon was quickly checked by means of a damping device consisting of a 16-ton counterweight that was connected to the top of the tower by long steel cables and arranged so that it could slide up and down a ramp inclined at 45° to the horizontal. Any movement of the tower top of more than a few inches began to pull the counterweight up the ramp; this interrupted the rhythmic buildup of the oscillations and brought the top of the tower to rest. The steelwork of the suspended deck of this bridge was erected in two passes by four 15-ton derricks, working outward from each of the towers to the centre and then returning again. Wind-tunnel tests made on models of the deck during erection demonstrated that it was necessary to leave a longitudinal strip 20 feet wide open along the centre line of the bridge, during the first pass of the derricks, in order to maintain the aerodynamic stability of the deck, until the first pass had been completed, connecting the stiffening trusses of the deck at midspan.

III. Contemporary developments in bridge engineering

The period since World War II has been the greatest bridge-building era in the history of the world. This is due partly to postwar reconstruction and urban development but even more to the unprecedented advance of motorways. In the U.S.S.R. the seven-year plan of the 1960s called for 650 large and 2,600 medium-sized bridges, four times as many as in the previous seven-year period. In China, too, there has been a great upsurge in the construction of roads and railways, all requiring their quota of bridges. This unprecedented activity has led not only to important improvements in materials available for bridge construction but also to novel types of foundations and superstructures and new techniques of calculation, fabrication, and erection.

IMPROVED MATERIALS

Steel. Research in steelwork has concentrated on the commercial production of structural steel of high-tensile quality that is also suitable for electric-arc welding and fabrication by flame cutting. Other important qualities sought include ductility and resistance to fatigue and corrosion. New forms of connection include welding, which reduces the weight of the structure, and the use of friction-grip bolts. Steel trusses may be built of all-welded, mild or high-tensile tubular members; hollow rectangular sections up to 13 inches (33 centimetres) square and one inch (2.5 centimetres) thick, which are seamless and rolled, can be obtained. Meehanite, a form of cast iron, is increasingly used for bearings of bridges, and expansion joints may be built up of layers of rubber bonded between steel plates.

For girder bridges of span greater than 300 feet (90 metres), steel is usually the most economical material to use; for arches, the economically critical span is longer. As the length increases, low-alloy or high-tensile steel is preferable. The saving in weight on long spans is suggested by the fact that, on the Sydney Harbour Bridge, every ton of steel in the arch required 0.7 tons to support it. The new, stronger, low-alloy steels can be used at substantially higher working stresses than mild steel. Low-alloy steels cost little more to produce than mild steel but are not usually as readily available. Other, even stronger special steels have been produced, but their cost is double that of mild steel. About 3,000 tons of such a steel were used in the second Carquinez Bridge (1958), near San Francisco.

Use of low-alloy steel

Laminations in steel plates are more serious in welded than they are in rivetted work, and a system of ultrasonic tests has been evolved whereby laminations can be detected before fabrication. Light alloys such as aluminum may play a greater part in bridge building when their elasticity and cost can be reduced. They have been used to make light service spans used in the erection of bridges and also to reconstruct the decks of old bridges at reduced weight. It has not yet proved possible to produce stainless steel of structural quality, but high-tensile weathering steel is being increasingly used. When exposed to weather, this kind of steel forms a coat of oxide on the surface, which inhibits any further corrosion.

Prestressed concrete. The process of prestressing concrete, which consists of putting it into a state of compression by tensioning steel bars or wires that pass through it, was conceived at the beginning of the 20th century and came to be recognized as the most important advance to have taken place in bridge construction since reinforced concrete came into general use. The economies in material that prestressing rendered possible led to its rapid development in the period of shortages during and after World War II.

Use of precast concrete units

To obtain the full benefits of the process, concrete of high quality and strength is necessary. Rapid advances in concrete technology have resulted in its strength being doubled and its surface greatly improved since World War II. The use of precast units, often of substantial size, supported on novel systems of cantilevered and suspended centring and thereafter prestressed, have led to a marked increase in the length of simple or continuous spans, which can now be built economically up to lengths of 400 feet or more.

Quality of concrete. Concrete can be made with an ultimate compression strength of 8,000 to 12,000 pounds per square inch. This permits working stresses in the range of 2,000 to 3,000 pounds per square inch, but the upper limit must not be exceeded because, beyond it, the rate of creep (*i.e.*, nonelastic deformation resulting from stress) of the concrete increases too quickly. This improvement in quality was achieved by further refinements in the water-to-cement ratio, the grading of the aggregate (by improvements in vibrating), and by innovations such as steam curing. Because of the thinness of the wire used in prestressed work, it is essential that it should be completely protected against corrosion. The elimination of cracks in the concrete and the production of a dense, flawless surface therefore become of first importance. The compression induced in the concrete tends to eliminate cracks, and new materials for forms, such as hardboard, have enabled the surface of the concrete, whether flat or curved, to be of good texture, free from imperfections, easy to clean, and pleasing to the eye.

Systems of prestressing. During World War II, when shortages of timber for forms and steel for reinforcement precluded the use of conventional reinforced-concrete design, Eugène Freyssinet reconstructed bridges in Tunisia by designing them to be built of precast blocks subsequently assembled on site and joined together by prestressing done by threading steel wires and grouting them in. Various systems of prestressing have since been evolved, but the most usual procedures are those outlined below. For reinforcement, narrow, high-tensile-steel bars with an ultimate strength of 64 to 72 tons per square inch are used at a working stress of about 45 tons per square inch. Alternatively, cables made up of a number of parallel steel wires, with an ultimate strength of 90 to 110 tons per square inch (similar to those used in the parallel-wire cables of suspension bridges), may be used at a working stress of about 70 tons per square inch. Another development has been the use of stranded-wire ropes. There is always a loss of about 15 percent in the working stresses due to shrinkage and creep of the concrete and relaxation (reduction in stress intensity) of the steel.

Before the concrete is cast, thin-gauge, flexible sheathing is fixed permanently in position in the molds for the bars or wires to pass through. When the bars or wires have been placed in position, they are tensioned; in bars, the tension is held by screwing nuts on the ends of the bar against steel anchor plates; if wires are used, the tensioning is done by means of hydraulic jacks, after which the wires are held by wedges. Cement is then forced into the sheaths under pressure to grout in the wires or bars and prevent corrosion or slip.

The amount of prestress is usually greater than the tension stress that would otherwise be induced under full dead load and live load. The methods can be applied to concrete, whether it is poured at the site or precast. On account of the great saving in material, which amounts to at least one-third of the volume of concrete and three-quarters of the weight of reinforcement that would otherwise be used, prestressed-concrete bridges are striking in their slender proportions. They are also economical in cost, provided the necessary trained labour is available, and in favourable circumstances may be competitive with structural-steel designs for spans up to about 500 feet. Because of the very high stresses employed, skilled supervision is, of course, essential throughout the work.

NEW DESIGNS

Battle decks and composite construction. Battle decks, first used in ships but adapted for bridges after World War II, consist of decks made of flat steel plates welded together and stiffened by means of flats, angles, or some other section welded on the underside. Further economy can be achieved by making the deck act integrally with the main members of the bridge, in effect becoming the top flange of a box girder. Battle decks are economical on long spans, where their saving in weight is important. They require more maintenance than do reinforced-concrete slabs.

In composite construction, the concrete roadway slab is anchored to the steel girders and made to act in conjunction with them. This form of deck was used on an all-welded steel highway bridge with a span of 334 feet over the Moscow River in the U.S.S.R. (1956). In the 1,240-foot Cologne–Rodenkirchen Bridge over the Rhine (1954) in West Germany, the concrete deck was prestressed; it not only carries the traffic but also acts as part of the upper chord (horizontal member) of the stiffening trusses and provides lateral bracing.

On both steel and concrete decks, waterproofing and wearing surfaces have to be provided. The most satisfactory solution appears to be a coat of mastic asphalt, a mixture of asphalt with fine aggregate rolled in, which produces a dense, hard-wearing surface and gives waterproof protection for the steel beneath.

Steel-plate and box girders. The modern tendency in steel-bridge design, particularly in western Europe, is towards box girders, of rectangular or trapezoidal section, in preference to simple or continuous trusses. The destruction of nearly 5,000 bridges in West Germany in World War II gave an opportunity for the development of new designs and techniques, and the fact that steel was then in short supply stimulated the search for economy in weight. The Cologne–Deutz Bridge (1947–48), the first of the big postwar box-girder spans over the Rhine, showed the sort of major advances in appearance, span, and economy that could be made by taking full advantage of modern techniques. In the triple box girders of this bridge, web plates 25 feet (8 metres) deep over the piers and only about 0.5 inch (1.27 centimetres) thick were first employed, stiffened both horizontally and vertically. Much of the 5,760 tons of steelwork is high-tensile, and its weight is only 61 percent of the steelwork in the old bridge it replaces. Three years later, the Düsseldorf–Neuss Bridge, with its 675-foot (206-metre) span and steel battledeck, was completed. Both these bridges were erected in heavy sections of 200 to 300 tons assembled on the riverbank, floated out, and lifted by cranes that had been used to clear away the debris of the old bridges.

The Cologne-Deutz Bridge

The longest plate-girder bridge built through 1970 was that across the Sava River at Belgrade, Yugoslavia, completed in 1957, which has a span of 856 feet (261 metres) and replaces the King Alexander suspension bridge. Designed in West Germany, it consists of an inverted-U-shaped girder of high-tensile steel. The new autobahn bridge over the Wupper Valley (1959) in West Germany, with seven spans varying from 144 to 239 feet (44 to 73 metres), has a reinforced-concrete deck slab in composite construction with steel box girders of novel trapeze-shaped section and inclined webs. The basic similarity of these modern box girders to the Britannia tubular bridge first conceived more than a century before is notable. Apart from materials and details of construction, the most significant difference is that in the first the trains ran through the boxes, whereas in the modern bridges the roadway traffic flows on top.

In comparison with plated I-girders, rectangular box girders have the advantage of reducing the initial cost by providing stable compression flanges (horizontal surfaces) and torsional rigidity (resistance to twisting forces). They also conceal all the web and flange stiffeners and thus improve appearance and reduce maintenance charges. Trapezoidal sections, in which the outer web plates are inclined, may be used to limit the lower flange area to the desired amount while at the same time providing a wide flange plate for the deck, as in the 770-foot- (235-metre-) span Wye Bridge in England. While offering reduced wind resistance, these inclined webs tend to increase the cost of fabrication and erection, unless the bridges are erected in preassembled units or boxes. Preassembly has been generally adopted in the U.K., but on the Continent erection is usually done on the site, plate by plate. Thus, during the last decade, boxes with inclined webs have been favoured by British engineers (*e.g.*, the Beachley, Severn, Erskine, and White Cart bridges) but rectangular box girders have been employed on the Continent (*e.g.*, the Europa Bridge, the Fourth Danube Bridge in Vienna, Austria, the Zoo Bridge in Cologne, West Germany, and the Lehener Bridge in Salzburg, Austria). In the early 1970s, the Rio-Niterói high-level bridge over Guanabara Bay at Rio de Janeiro was the longest continuous box girder in the world.

Table 7: Longest Span Steel Plate and Box Girders

bridge	location	year of completion	span (feet)
Rio-Niterói	Rio de Janeiro, Brazil	1971	984
Sava I	Belgrade, Yugoslavia	1957	856
Zoobrücke	Cologne, West Germany	1966	850
Sava II	Belgrade, Yugoslavia	1970	820
Auckland Harbour (Widening)	Auckland, New Zealand	1969	800
Grand Duchess Charlotte	Luxembourg City, Luxembourg	1966	768
Bonn Südd	Rhine River, West Germany	1971	755
San Mateo–Hayward	San Francisco	1967	750
Cleddau	Milford Haven, Pembrokeshire	1972	700
Fourth Danube	Vienna, Austria	1970	690
Düsseldorf–Neuss	West Germany	1951	675

Steel cable-braced bridges. A further development, in which the girders are supported by groups of prestressed cables passing over the tops of towers on the main piers, was first introduced in the Strömsund Highway Bridge in Sweden (1956). This method was adopted in the Theodore Heuss Bridge (1957) over the Rhine at Düsseldorf, West Germany, which has a main span of 853 feet (260 metres). The two box girders, of shop-welded low-alloy steel, are supported by three parallel tiers of cables that were prestressed during erection. In the Severin Bridge (1959) at Cologne, there is a cable-braced span of 991 feet (302 metres) supported by three sets of cables that pass over the top of an A-shaped tower built on a pier near the east bank. The first monocable bridge was built over the Elbe at Hamburg (1961). The 564-foot (172-metre) span was braced by cables only on the longitudinal centre line of the bridge. The towers over which they pass consist of single posts with roadways on either side. Since then, many cable-braced bridges have been built, mostly in western Europe, the longest being the Duisburg–Neuenkamp Bridge, in West Germany, with a span of 1,148 feet (350 metres), completed in 1970. Monocables have only about 70 percent of the weight of dual cables, because they are less affected by asymmetric live load.

The monocable bridge at Hamburg

Steel truss bridges. In the United States and Japan, continuous trusses are favoured for spans in the 700- to 1,250-foot range (about 210 to 380 metres). The longest span, of 1,232 feet (376 metres), is that of the Astoria Bridge in Oregon, completed in 1966. As will be seen in Table 9, eight of the longest steel spans are in the U.S., the longest elsewhere being the Tenmon Bridge (1966) of 984-foot (300-metre) span at Kumamoto, Japan. Two major bridges of this type in China are the huge double-deck rail and road bridges over the Yangtze River, the first completed in 1957 at Wu-han, Hupeh Province, and

Table 8: Longest Span Steel Cable-Braced Bridges

bridge	location	year of completion	span (feet)
Duisburg–Neuenkamp	Rhine River, W.Ger.	1970	1,148
Brazo Largo	Río Paraná Guazú, Arg.	1972	1,115
Zárate	Río Paraná de las Palmas, Arg.	1972	1,115
West Gate	Melbourne, Victoria		1,102.5
Kniebrücke	Düsseldorf, W.Ger.	1969	1,050
Erskine	Glasgow, Lanarkshire	1971	1,000
Bratislava	Danube River, Czech.	1972	994
Severin	Cologne, W.Ger.	1959	991
Mannheim-Nord	Mannheim, W.Ger.	1971	951
Leverkusen	Leverkusen, W.Ger.	1965	919
Bonn-Nord	Bonn, W.Ger.	1967	919
Theodore Heuss	Düsseldorf	1957	853

the second, replacing the train ferry and opening up a long-needed north–south route, at Nanking, Kiangsu Province, in 1968. Other great multispans built in the last 40 years include the 2.25-mile- (3.62-kilometre-) long Lower Zambezi railway bridge (1934) in Mozambique; the Ava Bridge, comprising nine spans of 350 feet (107 metres) carrying railway and road over the Irrawaddy River in Burma; the mile-long Ganga Bridge (1959) at Mokameh, India; and the Brahmaputra Bridge (1962) at Amingaon-Pandu in India, both of which carry road and rail traffic.

Eastfoto

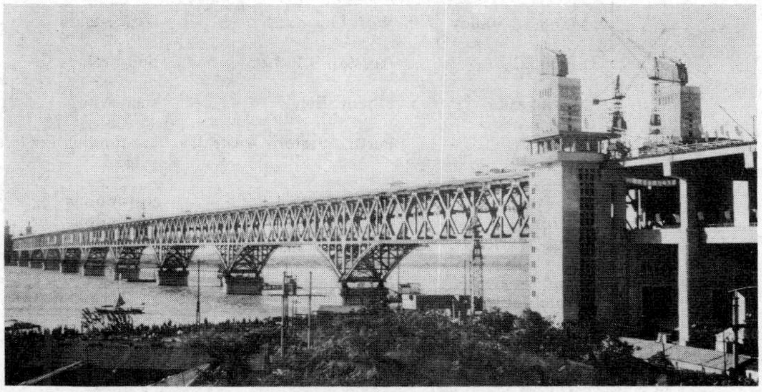

Steel truss bridge over the Yangtze River at Nanking, China. Completed in 1968, it carries rail and highway traffic.

Prestressed-concrete bridges. A wide variety of designs, including simple or continuous beams, cantilevers, arches, and girders, can be made with prestressed concrete. For spans of up to 140 feet (43 metres), simply supported beams are generally the most economical. The Vauban highway bridge (1956) in Strasbourg, France, has four simple spans of varying lengths, consisting of 8 beams of I-section, prestressed by 17 cables of 12 strands. As the span increases, continuous beams, as used in the Oléron Viaduct, France (1966), with 26 spans of 259 feet (79 metres), become economical (see Table 10). A bridge built over the Moscow River in 1957 has three continuous, prestressed-concrete spans, including a midspan of 485 feet (148 metres).

For still longer spans, cantilever bridges may be used. The 500-foot (152-metre) span of the Medway Bridge (1963) at Rochester has since been surpassed by the record 682-foot (209-metre) span of the Bendorf Bridge, completed in 1964 in Koblenz, West Germany. It is notable that the Bendorf Bridge, together with two other major cantilever bridges, the Eastern Scheldt Bridge (1965) in The Netherlands and the Öland Bridge in Sweden, were designed as twin cantilevers with no suspended spans. Work on the destruction of John Rennie's London Bridge, dating from 1831, began in 1967, and the masonry facades of the old arches were sold to a private developer and re-erected at Lake Havasu in Arizona. In 1972 London Bridge was replaced by a new prestressed concrete structure.

Concrete arch bridges are rarely prestressed to any significant extent, because an arch is normally in compres-

Table 9: Longest Span Steel Truss Bridges

bridge	location	year of completion	span (feet)
Astoria	Columbia River, Ore.	1966	1,232
Tenmon	Kumamoto, Japan	1966	984
Dubuque	Mississippi River, Iowa	1943	845
Admiral Graf Spee*	Duisburg, W.Ger.	1936	839
Braga Memorial	Somerset, Mass.	1966	830
Earl S. Clements	Morganfield, Ky.	1956	two spans, each 825
Cannelton	Ohio River, Ind.	1966	825
Kingston–Rhinecliff	Hudson River, N.Y.	1957	two spans, each 800
Sciotoville	Ohio River, Ohio	1917	two spans, each 775
Matthew E. Welsh	Mauckport, Ind.	1966	two spans, each 725

*Not standing.

Table 10: Longest Span Prestressed-Concrete Bridges Other Than Cantilevers

bridge	location	type	year of completion	span (feet)
Wadi Kuf	Cyrenaica, Libya	cable-braced	1970	983
General Rafael Urdaneta	Maracaibo, Venezuela	cable-braced	1961	5 spans, each 775
Save River	Mozambique	multiple-suspension	1970	2 spans, each 328; 3 spans, 688
Tete	Zambezi River, Mozambique	multiple-suspension	1971	2 spans, each 295; 3 spans, 590
Moscow River	U.S.S.R.	continuous	1957	2 spans, each 144; 1 span, 485
Notesund	Orust, Swed.	box-girder	1966	2 spans, each 222; 1 span, 360
Mangfall Valley	West Germany	lattice-truss	1960	2 spans, each 295; 1 span, 354
Luzhniki	Russian S.F.S.R.	tied-arch	1959	2 spans, each 147; 1 span, 354
Mariakerke	Ghent, Belg.	suspension	1960	2 spans, each 131; 1 span, 328
Narrows	Perth, Western Australia	continuous for live load	1959	2 spans, each 160; 2 spans, 230; 1 span, 320
Pont du Jour	Paris	continuous	1968	302
Oléron	Gironde, Fr.	continuous	1966	26 spans, each 259
Saint-Michel	Toulouse, Fr.	multiple-portal	1957	5 spans, each 214; 1 span, 197
Semorile Gorge	Italy	box-girder	1968	5 spans, each 161
Pontchartrain I	Louisiana	simple spans	1956	2,170 spans, each 56
Pontchartrain II	Louisiana	simple spans	1969	2,174 spans, each 56

Concrete arch bridges

sion. The Luzhniki Bridge (1959) in the U.S.S.R. is a prestressed-concrete tied arch, with spans of 147, 354, and 147 feet (45, 108, and 45 metres). Portal bridges and multiple portals simply represent an angular type of arch, so shaped that prestressing is helpful to keep the resultant thrust due to dead load and external loads within allowable limits. A fine multiple portal with sloping legs is the Saint-Michel Bridge (1957), at Toulouse, France, which has one span of 197 feet (60 metres) and five of 214 feet (65 metres) each.

Bridges of latticed construction are economical in material, but the unit costs are high; the saving in weight, however, makes it possible to achieve longer spans. The first prestressed-concrete latticed girder constructed was the Mangfall Valley Bridge (1958–60), with three spans

Table 11: Longest Span Prestressed-Concrete Cantilever Bridges

bridge	location	year of completion	span (feet)
Bendorf	Koblenz, W.Ger.	1964	2 spans, each 232; 1 span, 682
Medway	Rochester, Kent	1963	2 spans, each 312; 1 span, 500
Amakusa	Japan	1966	479
Alnö	Sweden	1964	3 spans, each 439; 1 span, 416
Oland	Kalmar Sound, Swed.	1972	6 spans, each 426
Tsing Yi Bridge	Hong Kong	1973	4 spans, each 400; 2 spans, 200
New London	London	1971	2 spans, each 260; 1 span, 340
Eastern Scheldt	Netherlands, The	1965	55 spans, each 300
Kinnaird	British Columbia	1965	3 spans, each 262; 2 spans, 238

of 295, 354, and 295 feet (90, 108, and 90 metres) over the Munich–Salzburg highway in West Germany.

The first self-anchored suspension bridges with continuous stiffening trusses were built in Belgium. These are the Merelbeke and the Mariakerke bridges near Ghent, with main spans of 185 and 328 feet (56 and 100 metres), respectively. A novel method for prestressing the girders on the Merelbeke Bridge consisted in jacking up the towers, which were independent of the deck and stiffening girders. The jacks were afterwards replaced by permanent steel castings.

A novel form of construction was adopted for the five 775-foot (236-metre) navigation spans of the 5.5-mile-long multispan bridge over the Maracaibo Lagoon in Venezuela (1958–61). These are designed as six continuous beams in prestressed concrete, supported on double trestles below and by tension cables above. The cables pass over the top of A-shaped towers on the piers and are connected near the ends of each beam. Another bridge of this type, with a span of 983 feet (300 metres), was designed to cross over the Wadi Kuf Gorge in central Cyrenaica, Libya; construction was completed in 1971. Two notable new bridges in Mozambique are multispan suspension bridges of five spans each with inclined suspenders supporting prestressed-concrete decks. The first, the longest of its type in the world, is 2,860 feet (872 metres) overall and was completed in 1970 over the Save River; the second was planned for completion a year later at Tete over the Zambezi River.

IMPROVEMENTS IN TECHNIQUES

Shop fabrication. Shop fabrication now includes the use of techniques by which steel can be flame-cut and the

Prestressed-concrete bridges.
(Left) The Moscow River Bridge at Lenin Hills, Moscow. Completed in 1957, it carries general traffic on the top level and rail cars below. (Right) The General Rafael Urdaneta Bridge, a 5.5 mile multispan bridge over the Maracaibo Lagoon, Venezuela; designed by R. Morandi and built 1958–61.
(Left) Sovfoto, (right) Julius Berger-Bauboag

edges bevelled for welding, if required; rotary jigs are used for the assembly of members, and automatic submerged-arc machines, which give complete penetration, are used for welding the seams of columns or girders. The quality of the welds can be determined by means of X- and gamma-ray photographs.

Methods of erection: steel bridges. For erection on the site, welding may be used for plate girders, but it is not usually suitable for trusses. Rivetting has been largely superseded by the use of friction-grip bolts which can be used in clearance holes and act as high-tension clamps. Pneumatic wrenches are used to tighten the bolts and calibrated torque wrenches to check their tension. The system is quicker, cleaner, more efficient, and more economical than rivetting. It was used in the erection of the Forth Road Bridge, the Mackinac and Carquinez bridges in the United States, and the Adomi Bridge (formerly Volta) in Ghana. The method employed in using these friction-grip bolts in the 805-foot (245-metre) steel arch of the Adomi Bridge represented a major advance in bridge-building technique. At the connections between the chord members in the bridge, four friction-grip bolts were used longitudinally as pretensioned ties, so arranged as to interconnect pairs of plates welded across the corners of the section. During erection of the two halves of the arch as cantilevers, therefore, the stability of the structure depended on these groups of bolts acting in tension in the connection of the upper chords.

Use of friction-grip bolts

By courtesy of Freeman, Fox & Partners and Sir William Halcrow & Partners

Adomi (formerly Volta) Bridge in Ghana, completed in 1956. This steel arch bridge utilizes high-strength friction-grip bolts at the connections between the chord members.

On box girders, the tendency in the U.K. is to prefabricate the structure in large sections (*i.e.*, full-width steel boxes that may be 60 feet [18 metres] long and weigh up to 100 tons) before erecting them in position. This saves the cost of assembling many small sections in high and exposed places under awkward weather conditions. Cantilever erection may be adopted, as on the Wye and Erskine bridges, where the boxes were rolled out along the top of the cantilever arm, lowered into position by two heavy launching arms, adjusted against the section last erected, and connected by butt welding or bolting. On the Continent, the system of "pushing out" large lengths of superstructure on rollers over the tops of the piers has been successfully used. Assembly is carried out in an erection bay behind the abutment. This system was used in Switzerland in 1968 on the Veveyse Bridge, which consists of two box girders, built on a curve and supporting a composite slab deck. The box girders of the Lao Bridge in southern Italy in the early 1970s are supported on the highest piers in the world. The three spans of the bridge, which also curves, were erected to carry the motorway over a deep ravine, the bottom of which is 800 feet (244 metres) below roadway level.

Cable-stayed bridges are usually erected as cantilevers, temporary supporting trestles being used where necessary. The cables are assembled on the towers and connected to the box girders and tensioned at the appropriate stages of erection.

Methods of erection: prestressed-concrete bridges. Prestressed-concrete bridges can be built (1) by assembly of precast units at the site; (2) by casting in place; and (3) by a combination of precasting and casting in place.

The Narrows Bridge (1959) over the Swan River at Perth, Western Australia, is a good example of a bridge built up of precast units and subsequently prestressed after assembly at the site. The world's longest precast structure was the 24-mile (39-kilometre) Pontchartrain Causeway (1956) in Louisiana, until it was surpassed by a slightly longer sister span in 1969. The first causeway consists of a series of spans 56 feet (17 metres) long and 28 feet (8.5 metres) wide, supported by beams resting on hollow prestressed-concrete piles. Each span, made up of seven beams and the roadway slab, was precast in one piece and erected by means of a floating crane. So well was the work organized that eight spans weighing 180 tons each and comprising 448 feet (137 metres) of bridge were placed each day.

The world's longest precast structure

Precasting has been widely adopted in the U.S.S.R., an outstanding example being the huge two-level bridge

(1959) over the Moscow River at Luzhniki, Russian S.F.S.R., which, with its approaches, measures 6,650 feet (2,027 metres) and carries a six-lane roadway on the upper deck and interurban railways below. The three spans, of 147, 354, and 147 feet (45, 109, and 45 metres), over the river were assembled in halves longitudinally on the shore from large, precast units, floated out on barges, and set on piers. In the U.S.S.R., standardization developed to such an extent that, by 1958, reinforced-concrete designs were automatically adopted for new railway bridges with spans of less than 50 feet (15 metres) and prestressed-concrete designs for spans of 50 to 90 feet (15 to 27 metres). Methods of pouring concrete safely in cold weather were studied.

Casting in place is more likely to be economical when there is little, if any, repetitive work; this technique was adopted for the three arches of 499, 479, and 452 feet (152, 146, and 138 metres) designed in 1953 for the new Caracas–La Guaira highway in Venezuela. In these bridges, the decks were prestressed both longitudinally and laterally, and prestressing cables were used temporarily to relieve the arch ribs during erection. Cantilevered centring was built out from each arch pier for a quarter of the span. For the middle, timber forms were built in the valley below and hoisted into place.

A combination of precast and in place construction may be economically used for continuous and cantilever bridges, the concrete ends of the span near the piers being poured in place and the central parts precast. In the 214-foot (65-metre) spans of the Casalmaggiore Bridge, over the Po in Italy, the lengths over the piers and the cantilever arms were poured in place, and the 118-foot (36-metre) suspended beams, each weighing 65 tons, were precast and erected by floating cranes. In the Mancunian Way, opened in Manchester, Lancashire, in 1967, although a high degree of standardization of precast units was achieved, it was found preferable to cast certain lengths of the overpass in place.

Pile-cylinder foundations. The most significant trend in foundation design is the tendency to support bridge piers on groups of large-diameter piles or thin-shelled cylinders, where possible, in preference to using pneumatic caissons. In the foundations of the Narrows Bridge in Perth, 180 long piles nearly three feet (one metre) in diameter were driven as hollow cylinders by means of a hammer running inside the pile and striking near its foot and were subsequently reinforced and filled with concrete. For the huge Wu-han double-deck rail and road bridge built in 1955–57 over the Yangtze River in China, a new system of colonnade foundations on large-diameter piles was designed by Soviet specialists. In the Tasman Bridge, Hobart (1965), the foundations were of boxed cylinder piles, some of which penetrated to a depth of 260 feet (79 metres). The three cylinder piles used per pier of the three-mile-long Eastern Scheldt Bridge (1965) in The Netherlands are of 14-foot (4.3-metre) diameter and up to 165 feet (50 metres) in length.

In the U.S.S.R., thin-shelled reinforced- or prestressed-concrete cylinders are sunk by electric-powered vibro pile drivers.

Use of computers. In the last decade, computers have been increasingly used for making the calculations involved in the design and erection of both steel and concrete bridges. The most laborious and detailed calculations can thus be made quickly and economically.

During the erection of the Forth Road Bridge and the Severn Bridge, computers were used to calculate the shape of the suspension cables under the changing pattern of applied loads as the deck panels were assembled. Computers can be used just as efficiently in reinforced- and prestressed-concrete work and provide a full set of calculations and detailed instructions, which entirely replace traditional drawings and details of reinforcement.

SAFETY PROBLEMS AND SOLUTIONS

During the last few years, much more attention has been paid to reducing accidents on bridges and, indeed, on all engineering structures. Most failures occur during erection, and safety can be considered under three heads: the safety of the structure during erection or demolition, the safety of construction plant, and the safety of personnel. Statutory regulations, which are continually being widened, exist in all countries to ensure the safety of structures, plant, and personnel. But, in spite of these regulations, far too many accidents still occur.

The three main safety factors

The catastrophic failure of the all-welded Duplessis Bridge at Trois-Rivières, Quebec, at a temperature of −30° F (−34° C), in February 1951, followed by that of the Kings Bridge at Melbourne, Victoria, in July 1962, were ascribed to brittle fracture from the nature of the steel used and the low temperatures prevailing at the time. The failure of three Vierendeel truss bridges in Belgium in 1938–40 and 250 all-welded Liberty ships in 1942–52 had drawn attention to the liability of steel to brittle fracture. The flange plates of the 180-foot (55-metre) plate girders of the Duplessis Bridge that failed proved to be of poor-quality steel that was abnormally notch sensitive, even at ordinary temperatures. In June 1958, two spans of the six-highway Second Narrows Bridge in Vancouver collapsed, wrecking 2,500 tons of steel and killing 18 men, during the cantilevering of the 465-foot (142-metre) anchor arm. The cause was the failure of a steel grillage supporting one of the temporary trestles, on which the stiffeners had been omitted due to an error in calculations. During the erection of the Barton High Level Bridge, England, there were two accidents in February and December 1959, in which six men were killed. The first accident was due to the failure of two inadequately designed and braced temporary trestles, and the second was due to four steel girders standing side by side overturning because they were inadequately braced together.

A most unusual accident to a completed span was the 1967 collapse of the Silver Bridge over the Ohio River at Point Pleasant, West Virginia, with a loss of 46 lives. This was a chain-suspension bridge with a span of 698 feet (213 metres), built as recently as 1928, and its failure ruled out the building of any more bridges suspended in this way in the U.S. Another accident, but without any loss of life, occurred immediately after the closure of the Fourth Danube Bridge in Vienna in November 1969. This was a three-span motorway bridge of twin box girders. A sudden fall of temperature at night resulted in failure at the closing joint; the bridge sagged three feet, and within ten seconds two more bucklings occurred several hundred feet away on either side. In this case, the margin of safety was eroded by four different factors, one of which was the sudden temperature differential.

Two tragic collapses of sophisticated designs of trapezoidal-box-girder bridges, resulting in the death of 4 men and 35 men, respectively, occurred during erection in 1970. The first of these was the Milford Haven Bridge, Pembrokeshire, in which a 196-foot (60-metre) steel cantilever collapsed in June 1970, owing to the failure of the vertical steel diaphragm over the pier from which it was being cantilevered. The second was the collapse of a 367-foot (112-metre) steel span of the West Gate high level bridge over the Lower Yarra River in Melbourne, in October 1970. Failing at the middle, the span plunged to the water, bringing down the river pier in its collapse. Failures have also occurred on concrete bridges, one of the most recent, in which two men were killed, in August 1967, being the collapse of two completed sections of the Calder Bridge, which was being built to carry the M.1. motorway over the River Calder near Wakefield, Yorkshire. Here the collapse was caused by the failure of temporary supports due to mild-steel joists being used by mistake instead of joists of high-tensile steel.

In order to combat risk of brittle fracture, high-tensile steel has now been greatly improved in strength at low temperatures. Another most complex problem under research is that of metal fatigue, to which both steel and aluminum are prone, caused by undergoing continual variations of stress that reduce ultimate strength and cause cracks or failure. Susceptibility to fatigue is increased by welding; particularly, by welds across tension members; or by an abrupt change of shape or thickness. All possible data are being obtained as to the number and

The problem of metal fatigue

nature of the stress cycles to which bridges are subject and to types of construction and the quality of steel that can withstand them.

As a result of the tragic collapse of the box-girder bridges at Milford Haven and Melbourne, the government in Great Britain has appointed a team of experts to enquire into the safety of this type of bridge, which has been described as pioneer work pushed toward the limits of the engineer's knowledge, and to examine the design and construction methods.

Accidents caused by failure of plant are too varied to detail here. They can be largely avoided by ensuring that all plant and equipment is kept in good repair and used only within its capacity, with all moving parts adequately guarded and with fail-safe devices provided as necessary. The causes of accidents to personnel are also diverse. The first necessity is to provide safe means of access and safe place of work, by means of ladders, gangways, and working platforms with guardrails, toeboards, and cradles, as necessary. Accidents to men working aloft can be prevented by means of safety harness and safety nets; safety helmets should be worn by all men on site.

FUTURE TRENDS

Great suspension spans of the future include an accepted British design for the new Bosporus Straits Bridge, with a main span of 3,520 feet (1,073 metres), on which work started in 1970, and a new bridge over the Humber in England, with a span of 4,580 feet (1,396 metres), scheduled for construction in the 1970s. Both these designs are similar to that of the Severn Bridge. There are also projects for a bridge over the Messina Straits; where major difficulties are presented by the great depth of water (400 feet [122 metres]) and the fact that the site is in a recently active earthquake area. Far more ambitious schemes have been suggested for crossings of the English Channel and the Strait of Gibraltar, but neither seems likely for many years to come.

In Japan, studies have been made for a proposed suspension bridge of 4,200-foot (1,280-metre) span across the Akashi Straits between the islands of Honshu and Shikoku, which would have to withstand typhoons, in addition to seismic shocks; and another, even longer span has been proposed for a bridge over Tokyo Bay. With materials of the weight and strength available today, engineers could theoretically build a suspension bridge to carry normal traffic, with a single span two miles long. But there would be many imponderable factors to consider in such a vast enterprise, which must be many years ahead. In the near future, it appears that the system of cable spinning may soon be simplified by pulling across strands each consisting of some hundreds of parallel wires and subsequently compacting them together, instead of simply carrying over a few loops of wire at a time by means of spinning wheels. A major economy would also be achieved in the weight and cost of the main cables if some means could be found by which to vary their cross-sectional area, so that it would conform throughout the length of the cable to the actual section required, which is much smaller at midspan. Improved methods of protection will, no doubt, also be found, as was attempted in the Newport Bridge, Rhode Island (1967), where the cables were protected by a layer of glass-reinforced resin.

In trying to foresee the materials of the future, it must be borne in mind that all normal structural materials, such as steel, aluminum, glass, and wood, have very similar elasticity-to-weight ratios. To make lighter, stiffer structures, new materials are needed, with high elasticity and low weight. At the Royal Aircraft Establishment, Farnborough, Hampshire, a method has been developed by which carbon fibres and carbon-fibre plastics have been produced with these properties. Compared with a high-tensile aircraft steel, these carbon fibres have about a quarter of the weight and more than twice the tensile strength. At present they are being developed primarily for use in the aerospace field, in chemical plants where resistance to corrosion is important, and for bearing materials and marine purposes. But it would appear that the materials to be used in long-span bridges of the future will be evolved through development along the above lines. The essential reduction in cost of such new materials can be made only through large-scale production. But in the light of the immense diversity and the amazing advances in the production of plastics, which have led to their worldwide adoption in a very few years, for thousands of applications, there seems little doubt that the economic production of greatly improved bridge materials is only a question of time.

BIBLIOGRAPHY. F. BRANGWYN and W.S. SPARROW, *A Book of Bridges* (1915), a popular treatment of early bridges; G.A. HOOL and W.S. KINNE (eds.), *Movable and Long-Span Steel Bridges* (1923), a good treatment of the beginnings of two major modern bridge types; SIR A.G. PUGSLEY, *The Theory of Suspension Bridges* (1957); O.A. KERENSKY, *Bridges: A Survey* (1959); CALIFORNIA DEPARTMENT OF PUBLIC WORKS, BRIDGE DEPARTMENT, *Manual of Bridge Design Practice* (1960); R.E. ROWE, *Concrete Bridge Design* (1962); H. SHIRLEY-SMITH, *The World's Great Bridges*, 2nd ed. (1964), designed to explain bridge history and engineering to the layman; MINISTRY OF TRANSPORT, *The Appearance of Bridges* (HMSO, 1964); E.M. YOUNG, *The Great Bridge: The Verrazano-Narrows Bridge* (1965), includes fine sketches of construction details by artist Lili Rethi; J. VIROLA, "The World's Greatest Bridges," *Civ. Engng.*, 38:52–55 (1968); Y. GUYON, "Long-Span Prestressed Concrete Bridges Constructed by the Freyssinet System," *Proc. Instn. Civ. Engrs.*, 7:110–168 (1957); SIR GILBERT ROBERTS *et al.*, "Severn Bridge," *ibid.*, 41:1–48 (1968).

(H.S.-Sm.)

Bridgman, Percy Williams

One of the pioneering physicists of the 20th century, P.W. Bridgman devoted himself for 50 years with remarkable singleness of purpose to the experimental study of materials at very high pressures. He is remembered also for his contributions to the philosophy of science.

By courtesy of the Harvard University News Service

Bridgman.

He was born in Cambridge, Massachusetts, on April 21, 1882, the son of a journalist. He entered Harvard University in 1900, taking his M.A. in 1905 and his Ph.D. in 1908. His experimental work on static high pressures was begun in 1908. It was at first confined to pressures of about 6,500 atmospheres (one atmosphere = 14.7 pounds per square inch), but he gradually extended the range to over 100,000 atmospheres and ultimately reached about 400,000 atmospheres. In this unexplored field, he had to invent much of the equipment himself. His most important invention was a special type of seal, in which the pressure in the gasket always exceeds that in the pressurized fluid, so that the closure is self-sealing; without this his work at very high pressures would not have been possible. Later he was able to make full use

Laboratory work

of the new steels and of alloys of metals with heat-resistant compounds such as carboloy (tungsten carbide cemented in cobalt). Most of this work involved measurements of the compressibilities of liquids and solids, studies of the phase changes of solids under pressure (which included the discovery of new high-pressure forms of ice), and measurements of the physical properties of solids (such as electrical resistance). As the range of pressures was extended, new and unexpected phenomena appeared; thus he discovered that the electrons in cesium undergo a rearrangement at a certain transition pressure. Although he did not himself synthesize diamonds, despite repeated attempts, his pioneer work led directly to their synthesis by scientists of the General Electric Company in 1955. Many other minerals have been synthesized by the adoption and extension of his techniques; a new school of geology, based on experimental work at high pressures and temperatures, developed from his endeavours.

He was something of an individualist. He liked to work by himself, spending long hours in the laboratory and eschewing attendance at academic committees. He published over 260 papers (only two of which listed a co-author) and 13 books. His papers are a mine of information for the experimentalist; they also reveal a masterly grasp of mathematical physics.

Bridgman's "operational" philosophy of science

During a course of lectures he gave in 1914 on advanced electrodynamics, he was struck by the obscurities and ambiguities inherent in defining scientific ideas. This led him to the "operational" approach to scientific meaning, discussed in his first philosophical book, *The Logic of Modern Physics* (1927). He defined concepts (*e.g.*, length) in terms of the operations, both physical and mental, involved in their measurement. Since all measurements are relative to the frame of reference of the observer, concepts are also relative; length, for example, is a different concept when measured terrestrially than when measured astronomically. His views had affinities with those of the Austrian positivist Ernst Mach, the American empiricists Charles Peirce and William James, and the logical positivists of the Viennese school, although he retained an individual approach. He was motivated in his logical explorations by the uncritical use of the current language in physics. He noted that the apparent precision of mathematical equations concealed a mass of crude observations and approximate verbal explanations. He wrote in *The Logic of Modern Physics:*

> In general, we mean by any concept nothing more than a set of operations; *the concept is synonymous with the corresponding set of operations*. . . . If a specific question has meaning, it must be possible to find operations by which answers may be given to it. It will be found in many cases that the operations cannot exist, and the question therefore has no meaning.

He rose steadily through the hierarchical levels of university status, becoming a full professor at Harvard in 1919, Hollis Professor in 1926, and Higgins Professor in 1950. He was awarded the Nobel Prize for Physics in 1946 for his discoveries in the domain of high-pressure physics. After retirement, he continued his scientific work until he died in Randolph, New Hampshire, on August 20, 1961. He was married and had two children.

One of Bridgman's strongest characteristics was his concern for intellectual integrity in every activity, from the laboratory experiment to the conduct of life itself. When he found himself dying of cancer, he asked his doctors to put an end to his life; when they refused, he found his own way, leaving behind a two-sentence note: "It isn't decent for Society to make a man do this thing himself. Probably this is the last day I will be able to do it myself. P.W.B."

BIBLIOGRAPHY. Bridgman's scientific papers have been published in *Collected Experimental Papers*, 7 vol. (1964). Further biographical information may be found in the *Dictionary of Scientific Biography*, vol. 2, pp. 457–461 (1970); and in *Biog. Mem. Fellows R. Soc.*, vol. 8 (1962). The latter contains a complete bibliography of his papers and books. His best known book on philosophy is *The Logic of Modern Physics* (1927, reprinted 1960).

(R.S.B.)

Bright, John

English reform politician, friend and chief lieutenant of Richard Cobden in the early Victorian campaign for free trade and internationalism, John Bright was a powerful orator on behalf of the Anti-Corn Law League (1839–46), against the Crimean War (1853–56), and in favour of parliamentary reform.

By courtesy of the Gernsheim Collection, The University of Texas at Austin

Bright, photographed by Herbert Barraud.

Bright was born at Rochdale on November 16, 1811, the eldest surviving son of Jacob Bright, a self-made cotton-mill owner. John Bright inherited bluntness of manner from his father, imaginative sensitivity from his mother. The Brights were Quakers, and John was educated at a succession of Quaker schools in the north of England, where, instead of receiving a classical education, he developed a lifelong love of the Bible and of the 17th-century English Puritan poets (especially Milton), a love often revealed in his speeches. Quaker beliefs shaped his politics, which consisted mainly of demands for an end to inequalities (social, political, or religious) between individuals and between peoples. While still in his 20s he had led a successful campaign in his native borough against the payment of compulsory taxes for the Anglican church.

Partnership with Cobden

In the same spirit he became a founder-member of the Anti-Corn Law League, which fought for lower grain prices, and by 1841 he had emerged as the chief supporting speaker to Cobden, the leader of the league. For five years, until repeal of the Corn Laws in 1846, Cobden and Bright spoke frequently together from platforms throughout the country. Cobden's speeches provided persuasive arguments; Bright concentrated upon denouncing the privileged political position of the agricultural landlords, which had enabled them to use Parliament to pass the Corn Laws. Although Cobden had taught Bright the high moral and economic case for free trade, Bright tended to speak in narrower terms on behalf of the manufacturers and mill hands, who (he insisted to the latter) shared a common interest in overturning the Corn Laws.

Bright became a member of Parliament for Durham in 1843 and for Manchester in 1847. In 1839 he had married a fellow Quaker, Elizabeth Priestman; but she died of consumption in September 1841, leaving Bright with one daughter. In later life he liked to tell an emotional story of how Cobden visited him after his bereavement and how the two friends made a compact together to crusade against the Corn Laws. Bright's old-age recollections, however, tended to be unconsciously self-inflating, sacrificing accuracy for effect. In reality, he had begun to work closely with Cobden well before his wife's death. He also deeply disliked being opposed, even by Cobden. This was an unfortunate product of his sensitive nature, and he often expressed his disappointment with a brusqueness that hurt the feelings of others.

In 1847 Bright married again; his second wife was Margaret Elizabeth Leatham, another Quaker, two of whose brothers later became Liberal members of Parliament. She, too, took an interest in politics, though Bright did little to encourage this. Certainly, he strongly disapproved discussion of "women's rights" by the females of his family. Four sons and three daughters were born to the Brights, their father adopting a typical Victorian patriarchal attitude, affectionate but dominating. As he grew older, Bright even came to look like an Old Testament patriarch, his striking appearance adding to the effect of his oratory.

During his prime in the 1850s and 1860s, Bright's speeches came to be widely reported, winning admiration even from opponents. He regarded his speaking powers as a gift from God, comparing himself on the platform to a clergyman in his pulpit. In this spirit the greatest of all his oratorical series was delivered against British involvement in the Crimean War. He variously denounced the war as un-Christian, contrary to the principles of international free trade, and harmful to British interests. "The Angel of Death," he said, "has been abroad throughout the land; you may almost hear the beating of his wings." He blamed Lord Palmerston and the aristocracy for deluding the British people; British foreign policy and the expensive network of diplomatic appointments constituted "a gigantic system of outdoor relief for the aristocracy."

Frustration at his failure to stop the war plunged Bright into a severe nervous breakdown (1856–58). His antiwar views also helped to lose him his Manchester seat in 1857; but within a few months he was elected member of Parliament for Birmingham, which he was to represent for the rest of his life. A speech-making campaign for parliamentary reform launched from Birmingham by Bright at the end of 1858 faded out within a few months, but it marked the beginning of the movement toward the great reform agitation of the mid-1860s.

Hero of the reformers

During the second half of 1866 Bright suddenly found himself the hero and chief mouthpiece of the reformers, accepted alike by those who demanded universal suffrage and those who wanted more limited reform. In terms of immediate influence this was the high point of his career. Paradoxically, his position was strengthened by the uncertainty of his own precise preference—he had always left details and close logic to Cobden, who died in 1865. But Bright was well satisfied with the household franchise introduced by the 1867 Reform Act, which extended the vote to skilled urban artisans but still excluded the town and country labourers. He was impressed by the artisans' intelligence and independence, and he recommended every man who wanted the vote to acquire these qualities. The Brights were benevolent employers, but this same faith in self-help and independence placed Bright at the head of those manufacturers who opposed factory legislation, trade unions, and social reform. This was the negative side of his belief in equality. Its positive side led him strongly to support the North against the slave-owning South during the American Civil War (1861–65) and to press both before and after the Indian Mutiny (1857) for less authoritarian British rule in India.

Government service

He entered Gladstone's Cabinet as president of the Board of Trade in 1868, but another breakdown forced his resignation in 1870. Although he served twice more in Gladstone cabinets (1873–74, 1880–82), the rest of his career was but an epilogue. His radicalism no longer seemed dangerous, allowing him during the last 20 years of his life to be widely accepted (as the economist and journalist Walter Bagehot remarked) as "a great institution." He helped to shape Gladstone's Irish land reforms of 1870 and 1881, but his pugnacious streak (always strong, even in the cause of peace) led him in 1886 to reject Gladstone's lead in proposing Irish Home Rule. Bright announced that he was not prepared to see power given to Irish nationalists who had insulted the Queen and made a mockery of parliamentary government. He died on March 27, 1889.

G.M. Trevelyan, his official biographer (1913), wrote of the "odour of sanctity" that surrounded Bright in old age. Trevelyan himself encouraged such an approach, but later historians have taken a more critical view of Bright's personality and achievement.

BIBLIOGRAPHY. G.M. TREVELYAN, *The Life of John Bright* (1913), is the official life; W. ROBERTSON, *The Life and Times of the Right Hon. John Bright* (1883), is the most voluminous of contemporary accounts. J. VINCENT, *The Formation of the Liberal Party 1857–1868* (1966), contains a penetrating analysis; D. READ, *Cobden and Bright: A Victorian Political Partnership* (1967), concentrates upon comparing the personalities and policies of the two men and also contains full primary and secondary references. Bright's *Speeches on Questions of Public Policy* (1868), his *Public Addresses* (1879), and *Public Letters* (1885), should be read for their omissions as well as their emphases.

(D.Re.)

Britain, Ancient

Apart from a few short references in the classics, knowledge of Britain before the Roman conquest (begun AD 43) is derived entirely from archaeological research. It is thus lacking in detail, for archaeology can rarely identify personalities, motives, or exact dates. All that is available is a picture of successive cultures and some knowledge of economic development. But even in Roman times, Britain lay on the periphery of the civilized world, and Roman historians, for the most part, provide for that period only a framework into which the results of archaeological research can be fitted. Britain emerged into the light of true history only after the Saxon settlements in the 5th century AD.

Until late in the Mesolithic (Middle Stone) Age, Britain formed part of the continental landmass and was easily accessible to migrating hunters. The cutting of the landbridge, *c.* 6000–5000 BC, had important effects: migration became more difficult and remained for long impossible to large numbers. Thus Britain developed insular characteristics, absorbing and adapting rather than fully participating in successive continental cultures. And within the island geography worked to a similar end; the fertile southeast was more receptive of influence from the adjacent continent than were the less accessible hill areas of the west and north. Yet in certain periods the use of sea routes brought these too within the ambit of the continent.

From the end of the Ice Age (*c.* 11,000 BC), there was a gradual amelioration of climate leading to the replacement of tundra by forest and of reindeer hunting by that of red deer and elk. Valuable light on contemporary conditions was gained by the excavation of a lakeside settlement at Star Carr, Yorkshire, which was occupied for about 20 successive winters by hunting people in the 8th millennium BC.

PRE-ROMAN BRITAIN

Neolithic Age. A major change occurred *c.* 4000 BC with the introduction of agriculture by Neolithic immigrants from the coasts of western and possibly northwestern Europe. They were pastoralists as well as tillers of the soil. Tools were commonly of flint, which toward the close of the period was won by mining, but axes of volcanic rock were also traded by prospectors exploiting distant outcrops. The dead were buried in communal graves of two main kinds: in the west, tombs were built out of stone and concealed under mounds of rubble; in the stoneless eastern areas the dead were buried under long barrows (mounds of earth), which normally contained timber structures. Other evidence of religion comes from campsites (*e.g.*, Windmill Hill, Wiltshire), which are now believed to have been centres of ritual and of seasonal tribal feasting. From them developed, late in the 3rd millennium, more clearly ceremonial ditch-enclosed earthworks known as henge monuments. Some, like Durrington Walls, Wiltshire, are of great size and enclose subsidiary timber circles. British Neolithic culture thus developed an individuality of its own.

Ritual centres

Bronze Age. Early in the 2nd millennium or perhaps even earlier, from *c.* 2300 BC, changes were introduced by the Beaker folk from the Low Countries and the middle Rhine. These people, whose round skulls differentiate them from the long-headed Neolithic people, buried their dead in individual graves, often with the drinking vessel that gives their culture its name. The earliest of them still used flint; later groups, however, brought a knowledge of metallurgy and were responsible for the exploitation of gold and copper deposits in Britain and Ireland. They may also have introduced an Indo-European language. Control of the trade routes was soon taken over by the chieftains of Wessex, whose rich graves testify to their success as middlemen. Commerce was far-flung, in one direction to Ireland and Cornwall and in the other to central Europe and the Baltic, whence amber was imported. Amber bead spacers from Wessex have been found in the shaft-graves at Mycenae in Greece. It was, perhaps, this contact which enabled the Wessex chieftains to construct the remarkable monument of shaped sarsens (large sandstones) known as Stonehenge III. Originally a late Neolithic henge, Stonehenge was uniquely transformed in Beaker times with a circle of large bluestone monoliths transported from southwest Wales.

Stonehenge

Little is known in detail of the Middle Bronze Age and the Late Bronze Age. Because of present ignorance of domestic sites, these periods are mainly defined only by technological advances and changes in tools or weapons. In general, the southeast of Britain continued in close contact with the continent and the north and west with Ireland.

From about 1200 BC there is clearer evidence for agriculture in the south; the farms consisted of circular huts in groups with small oblong fields and stock enclosures. This type of farm became standard in Britain down to and into the Roman period. From the 8th century, expansion of continental Urnfield and Hallstatt groups brought new people (mainly the Celts) to Britain; at first, perhaps, these were small prospecting groups, but soon new settlements developed. Some of the earliest hill forts in Britain were constructed in this period (*e.g.*, Beacon Hill, near Ivinghoe, of Buckinghamshire; or Finavon, Angus); though formally belonging to the Late Bronze Age, they usher in the succeeding period.

Iron Age. The introduction of knowledge of iron was in fact merely incidental: it does not signify a change of population. The centuries 700–400 BC saw a succession of small migrations; the newcomers mingled easily with existing inhabitants. Yet the greater availability of iron facilitated land clearance and the growth of population. The earliest ironsmiths made daggers of the Hallstatt type but of distinctively British form; and the settlements were also of a distinctively British type with the traditional round house, the "Celtic" system of farming with its small fields, and storage pits for grain. Thus Britain absorbed the newcomers.

Celtic field system

Conditions in the 4th century grew more disturbed. By the year 300 BC, swords were being made once more in place of daggers; hill forts grew more numerous and elaborate. Finally, from the 3rd century, a British form of La Tène Celtic art was developed to decorate warlike equipment such as scabbards, shields, and helmets, and eventually also bronze mirrors and even domestic pottery. During the 2nd century, the export of Cornish tin, noted before 300 by Pytheas of Massilia, a Greek explorer, continued; evidence of its destination is provided by the Paul (Cornwall) hoard of north Italian silver coins. In the 1st century BC this trade was in the hands of the Veneti of Brittany; their conquest (56 BC) by Julius Caesar, who destroyed their fleet, seems to have put an end to it.

By 200 Britain had fully developed its insular Celtic character. The emergence, however, of the British tribes known to Roman historians was due to a further phase of settlement, by tribesmen from Belgic Gaul. Coin finds suggest that the earliest movements of this migration began before the end of the 2nd century; the decisive settlements were made in the 1st century probably as a result of pressures in Gaul created by Germanic and Roman expansion. The result was a distinctive culture in southeast Britain (especially in Kent and north of the Thames), that represented a later phase of the continental Celtic La Tène culture. Its people used coins and the potter's wheel, cremated their dead, and their better equipment enabled them to begin the exploitation of heavier soils for agriculture.

ROMAN BRITAIN

The conquest. Caesar's description of Britain at the time of his invasions of 55 or 54 BC is the first coherent account extant, and it was his conquest of Gaul that brought the island into close contact with the Roman world. From about 20 BC it is possible to distinguish two principal powers: The Catuvellauni north of the Thames led by Tasciovanus, successor of Caesar's adversary Cassivellaunus, and, south of the river, the kingdom of the Atrebates ruled by Commius and his sons Tincommius, Eppillus, and Verica. Tasciovanus was succeeded in about AD 5 by his son Cunobelinus, who, during a long reign, established a paramount power all over the southeast, which he ruled from Camulodunum (Colchester). Beyond these kingdoms lay the Iceni in what is now Norfolk, the Coritani in the Midlands, the Dobuni (Dobunni) in the area of Gloucestershire, and the Durotriges in that of Dorset, all of whom issued coins and probably had Belgic rulers. Behind these again lay further independent tribes—the Dumnonii of Devon, the Brigantes of Yorkshire, the Silures and Ordovices in Wales. It was the Belgic and semi-Belgic tribes who later formed the civilized nucleus of the Roman province: the Belgic contribution to Roman Britain is great.

The client relationships that Caesar had established with certain British tribes were extended by Augustus. In particular, the Atrebatic kings welcomed Roman aid in their resistance to Catuvellaunian expansion. The decision of the emperor Claudius to conquer the island was the result partly of his personal ambition, partly of British aggression. Verica had been driven from his kingdom and appealed for help, and it may have been calculated that a hostile Catuvellaunian supremacy would endanger stability across the Channel. Under Aulus Plautius an army of four legions was assembled, together with a number of auxiliary regiments consisting of cavalry and infantry raised among warlike tribes subject to the empire. After delay caused by the troops' unwillingness to cross the ocean, which they then regarded as the boundary of the human world, a landing was made at Richborough, Kent, in AD 43. The British under Togodumnus and Caratacus, sons and successors of Cunobelinus, were taken by surprise and defeated. They retired to defend the Medway crossing near Rochester but were again defeated in a hard battle. The way to Camulodunum lay open, but Plautius halted at the Thames to await the arrival of the emperor, who took personal command of the closing stages of the campaign. In one short season, the main military opposition had been crushed: Togodumnus was dead and Caratacus fled to Wales. The rest of Britain was by no means united, for Belgic expansion had created tensions. Some tribes submitted, and the overrunning of the rest remained the task for the year 44. For this purpose smaller expeditionary forces were formed consisting of single legions or parts of legions with their *auxilia* (subsidiary allied troops). The best documented campaign is that of Legion II under its legate Vespasian starting from Chichester, where the Atrebatic kingdom was restored; the Isle of Wight was taken, and the hill forts of Dorset reduced. Legion IX advanced into Lincolnshire, and Legion XIV probably across the Midlands toward Leicester. Colchester was the chief base, but the fortresses of individual legions at this stage have not yet been identified.

By the year 47, when Plautius was succeeded as commanding officer by Ostorius Scapula, a frontier had been established from Exeter to the Humber based on the road known as the Fosse Way; from this fact it appears that Claudius did not plan the annexation of the whole island but only of the arable southeast. The intransigence of the

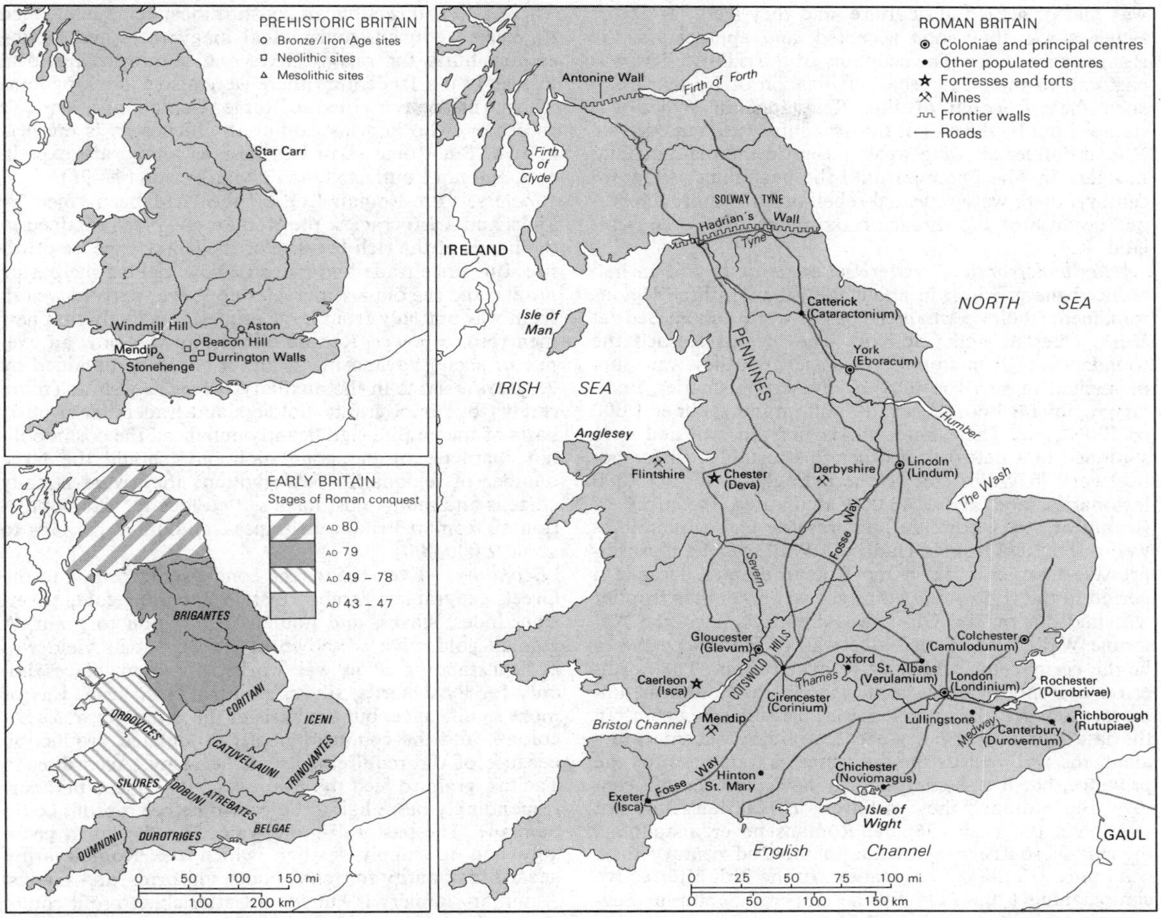

Ancient Britain.
(Left) Adapted from *The Reader's Digest Complete Atlas of the British Isles*, published by The Reader's Digest Association Ltd., London, 1965; (right) based upon the Ordnance Survey Map with the sanction of the Controller of Her Britannic Majesty's Stationery Office, Crown copyright reserved

tribes of Wales spurred on by Caratacus, however, caused Scapula to occupy the lowlands beyond the Fosse Way up to the River Severn and to move forward his forces into this area for the struggle with the Silures and Ordovices; they were strengthened by the addition of Legion XX, released for this purpose by the foundation of a veteran settlement (*colonia*) at Camulodunum in the year 49. The *colonia* would form a strategic reserve as well as setting the Britons an example of Roman urban organization and life. A provincial centre for the worship of the emperor was also established. Scapula's right flank was secured by the treaty relationship that had been established with Cartimandua, queen of the Brigantes. Hers was the largest kingdom in Britain, occupying the whole area between Derbyshire and the Tyne; unfortunately it lacked stability, nor was it united behind its queen, who lost popularity when she surrendered the British resistance leader, Caratacus, to the Romans. Nevertheless, with occasional Roman military support, Cartimandua was maintained in power down to 69 against the opposition led by her husband, Venutius, and this enabled Roman governors to concentrate on Wales.

By AD 60 much success had been achieved; Suetonius Paulinus, governor from 59 to 61, was invading the island of Anglesey, the last stronghold of independence, when a serious setback occurred: this was the rebellion of Boudicca, queen of the Iceni. This tribe had enjoyed a position of alliance and independence under its king Prasutagus; but on his death (60) the territory was forcibly annexed and outrages occurred. Boudicca was able to rally other tribes to her assistance; chief of these were the Trinovantes of Essex, who had many grievances against the settlers of Camulodunum for their arrogant seizure of lands. Roman forces were distant and scattered; and, before peace could be restored, the rebels had

Boudicca's rebellion

sacked Camulodunum, Verulamium (St. Albans), and London, the three chief centres of Romanized life in Britain. Paulinus acted harshly after his victory, but the procurator of the province, Julius Classicianus, with the revenues in mind and perhaps also because, as a Gaul by birth, he possessed a truer vision of provincial partnership with Rome, brought about his recall.

In the first 20 years of occupation, some progress had been made in spreading Roman civilization. Towns had been founded, the imperial cult had been established, and merchants were busily introducing the Britons to material benefits. It was not, however, until the Flavian Period, AD 69–96, that real advances were made in this field. With the occupation of Wales by Julius Frontinus (governor from 74 to 78) and the advance into northern Scotland by Gnaeus Julius Agricola (78–84), troops were removed from southern Britain, and self-governing *civitates,* administrative areas based for the most part on the indigenous tribes, took over local administration. This involved a large program of urbanization and also of education, which continued on into the 2nd century; Tacitus, in his biography of Agricola, emphasizes the encouragement given to it. The conquest of Wales was complete by 78, but Agricola's invasion of Scotland failed through shortage of manpower to complete the occupation of the whole island, and when the British garrison was reduced (*c.* AD 90) by a legion because of continental needs, it became evident that a frontier would have to be maintained in the north. After several experiments, the Solway–Tyne isthmus was chosen, and there the emperor Hadrian built his stone wall (*c.* 122–130).

Condition of the province. There was a marked contrast in attitude toward the Roman occupation between the lowland Britons and the inhabitants of Wales and of the hill country of the north. The economy of the former was that of settled agriculture, and they were largely of Belgic stock; they soon accepted, and appreciated, the Roman way of life. The economy of the hill dwellers was pastoral; to them the urban civilization of Rome threatened their freedom of life. Resistance in Wales was stamped out by the end of the 1st century AD, but even so, Roman influences were weak except in the plain of Glamorgan. In The Pennines until the beginning of the 3rd century, there were repeated rebellions, the more dangerous because of the threat of assistance from free Scotland.

Army and frontier. After the emperor Domitian had reduced the garrison in about the year 90, three legions remained; their permanent bases were established at York, Chester, and Caerleon. The legions formed the foundation of Roman military power, but they were supplemented in garrison duty by numerous smaller auxiliary regiments both of cavalry and infantry, either 1,000 or 500 strong. These latter garrisoned the wall and were stationed in a network of other forts established for police work in Wales and northern England. With 15,000 legionaries, and about 40,000 auxiliaries, the army of Britain was very powerful; its presence had economic as well as political results. Hadrian's Wall was the most impressive frontier-work in the Roman empire. Despite a period in the following two reigns when another frontier was laid out on the Glasgow–Edinburgh line—the Antonine Wall, built of turf—the wall of Hadrian came to be the permanent frontier of Roman Britain. The northern tribes only twice succeeded in passing it, and then at moments when the garrison was fighting elsewhere. In the late Roman period, when sea-raiding became prevalent, the wall lost its pre-eminence as a defense for the province, but it was continuously held until the 5th century. But although they withdrew to Hadrian's line not later than the year 196, the Romans never abandoned interest in southern Scotland. In the 2nd century their solution was military occupation. In the 3rd, after active campaigning (208–211) by the emperor Septimius Severus and his sons during which permanent bases were built on the east coast of Scotland, the solution adopted by the emperor Caracalla was regulation of relationship by treaties. These, perhaps supported by subsidies, were enforced by supervision of the whole Lowlands by patrols based on forts beyond the wall. During the 4th century, more and more reliance was placed on friendly native states, and patrols were withdrawn.

Hadrian's Wall

Administration. Britain was an imperial province. The governor represented the emperor, exercising supreme military as well as civil jurisdiction. As commander of three legions, he was a senior general of consular rank. From the late 1st century, he was assisted on the legal side by a *legatus juridicus.* The finances were in the hands of the provincial procurator, an independent official of equestrian status whose staff supervised imperial domains and the revenues of mines in addition to normal taxation. In the early 3rd century, Britain was divided into two provinces in order to reduce the power of its governor to rebel as Albinus had done in 196: Britannia Superior had its capital at London and a consular governor in control of two legions and a few auxiliaries; Britannia Inferior, with its capital at York, was under a praetorian governor with one legion but many more auxiliaries.

Finance and taxation

Local administration was of varied character. First came the chartered towns. By the year 98, Lincoln and Gloucester had joined Camulodunum as *coloniae*, and by 237 York had become a fourth. *Coloniae* of Roman citizens enjoyed autonomy with a constitution based on that of republican Rome, and Roman citizens had various privileges before the law. It is likely that Verulamium was chartered as a Latin *municipium* (free town); in such a town the annual magistrates were rewarded with Roman citizenship. The remainder of the provincials ranked as *peregrini* (subjects). In military districts control was in the hands of fort prefects responsible to legionary commanders; but, by the late 1st century, local self-government, as already stated, was granted to *civitates peregrinae*, whose number tended to increase with time. These also had republican constitutions, being controlled by elected councils and annual magistrates and having responsibility for raising taxes and administering local justice. In the 1st century there were also client kingdoms whose rulers were allied to Rome; Cogidubnus, Verica's successor, who had his capital at Chichester, is the best known. But Rome regarded these as temporary expedients, and none outlasted the Flavian Period (69–96).

Society. Pre-Roman Celtic tribes had been ruled by kings and aristocracies; the Roman *civitates* remained in the hands of the rich because of the heavy expense of office. But since trade and industry now yielded increasing profits, and the old aristocracies no longer derived wealth from war but only from large estates, it is likely that new men rose to power. Roman citizenship was now an avenue of social advancement, and it could be obtained by 25 years' service in the auxiliary forces as well as (more rarely) by direct grants. Soldiers and traders from other parts of the empire significantly enhanced the cosmopolitan character of the population, nor should the large number of legionaries be forgotten: they were already citizens and many must have settled locally. The population of Roman Britain at its peak amounted perhaps to about 2,000,000.

Roman citizenship

Economy. Even before the conquest, according to the Greek geographer Strabo, Britain exported gold, silver, iron, hides, slaves, and hounds in addition to grain. A Roman gold mine is known in Wales, but its yield was not outstanding. Iron was worked in many places but only for local needs; silver, obtained from lead, was of more significance, but the basis of the economy was agriculture, and the conquest greatly stimulated production because of the requirements of the army. According to Tacitus, grain to feed the troops was levied as a tax; correspondingly more had to be grown before a profit could be made. The pastoralists in Wales and the north probably had to supply leather, which the Roman army needed in quantity for tents, boots, uniforms, and shields. A military tannery is known at Catterick. A profit could, nonetheless, be won from the land because of the increasing demand from the towns, and at the same time the development of a system of large estates (villas) relieved the ancient "Celtic" farming system of the necessity of shouldering the whole burden. Small peasant farmers tended to till the lighter, less productive, easier-worked soils. Villa estates were established on heavier richer soils, sometimes on land recently won by forest clearance, itself a result of the enormous new demand for building timber from the army and the new towns and for fuel for domestic heating and for public baths. The villa owners had access to the precepts of classical farming manuals and also to the improved equipment made available by Roman technology. Their growing prosperity is vouched for by excavation: there are few villas that did not increase in size and luxury as corridors and wings were added or mosaics and bath blocks provided. At least by the 3rd century, some landowners were finding great profit in wool; Diocletian's price edict (AD 301) shows that at least two British cloth products had won an empire-wide reputation. Archaeological evidence indicates that the Cotswold district was one of the centres of this industry.

Trade in imported luxury goods ranging from wine to table wares and bronze trinkets was vastly increased as traders swarmed in behind the army to exploit new markets. The profits of developing industries went similarly at first to foreign capitalists. This is clearly seen in the exploitation of silver-lead and even in the pottery industry. The Mendip lead-field was being worked under military control as early as the year 49, but under Nero (54–68) both there and in Flintshire, and not much later also in the Derbyshire lead-field, freedmen—the representatives of Roman capital—were at work. By Vespasian's reign (69–79) organized companies (*societates*) of prospectors are attested. Roman citizens, who must in the context be freedmen, are also found organizing the pottery industry in the late 1st century. Large profits were made by continental businessmen in the first two centuries not only from such sources but also by the import on a vast scale of high-class pottery from Gaul and the Rhineland, and on a lesser scale of glass vessels, luxury metalware, and Spanish oil and wine. A large market existed among the military, and the Britons themselves provided a second. Eventually this adverse trade balance was rectified by the gradual capture of the market by British products. Much of the exceptional prosperity of 4th-century Britain must have been due to its success in retaining available profits at home.

A final important point is the role of the Roman army in the economic development of the frontier regions. The presence as consumers of large forces in northern Britain created a revolution in previous patterns of trade and civilized settlement. Cereal production was encouraged in regions where it had been unknown, and large settlements grew up in which many of the inhabitants must have been retired soldiers with an interest in the land as well as in trade and industry.

Towns. Belgic Britain had large centres of population but not towns in the Roman sense, which meant not merely streets and public buildings but also the amenities and local autonomy of a city. In Britain these had therefore to be provided if Roman civilization and normal methods of provincial administration were to be introduced. Thus an urbanizing policy existed in which the assistance of the legions, as the nearest convenient source of architects and craftsmen, played an organizing role. The earlier towns consisted of half-timbered buildings; before AD 100 only public buildings seem to have been of stone. The administrative capitals had regular street grids, a forum with basilica (public hall), public baths, and temples; a few had theatres and amphitheatres, too. With few exceptions they were undefended. Town walls were provided in the 3rd century, not so much as a precaution in unsettled times as a means of keeping operational the earthwork defenses already provided to meet a crisis at the end of the 2nd century. In size these towns grew to about 100–130 acres with populations of about 5,000; a few were twice this size. The majority of towns in Roman Britain seem to have developed out of traders' settlements in the vicinity of early garrison-forts: those that were not selected as administrative centres remained dependent on economic factors as centres of trade or manufacture or else as markets for the agricultural peasantry. They varied considerably in size. In the north, where garrisons were permanently established, quite large trading settlements grew up in their vicinity, and at least some of these would rank as towns.

Urbanization

Villas. Apart from the exceptional establishment at Fishbourne, in West Sussex, whose Italian style and luxurious fittings show that it was the palace of King Cogidubnus, the houses of Roman-British villas had simple beginnings and were of a provincial type. A few were prosperous enough in the 2nd century to afford mosaics; but the great period of villa prosperity lay in the 4th century, when many villas grew to impressive size. Their importance was economic and has already been described. Much remains to be learnt from full excavation of their subsidiary work buildings. Larger questions of tenure and organization are probably insoluble in the absence of documentary evidence, for it is dangerous to draw analogies from classical sources since conditions in Celtic Britain were very different from those of the Mediterranean world.

Religion and culture. A great variety of religious cults were to be found, for, in addition to numerous Celtic deities of local or wider significance, the gods of the classical pantheon were introduced and were often identified with their Celtic counterparts. In official circles the worship of the state gods of Rome and of the imperial cult was duly observed. In addition merchants and soldiers introduced oriental cults, among them Christianity. The latter, however, made little headway until the late 4th century, though the frescoes at Lullingstone in Kent and the mosaics at Hinton St. Mary in Dorset attest its presence among villa owners. Classical temples are sometimes found in towns, but the normal temple was of the Romano-Celtic type with a small square shrine and surrounding portico; these are found in town and country alike.

Romanization was strongest in the towns and among the upper classes, as would be expected; there is evidence that in the countryside Celtic continued to be spoken, though it was not written. Many people were bilingual: graffiti prove that even artisans wrote Latin. Evidence of the classical education of the villa owners is provided by their mosaics, which prove an aquaintance with classical mythology and even with the *Aeneid* of Virgil. Sculpture and wall painting were both novelties in Roman Britain. Statues or busts in bronze or marble were imported from Gaulish or Mediterranean workshops, but British sculptors soon learned their trade and at their best produced attractive works in a provincial idiom, very often for votive purposes. Many cruder works were also executed: their interest lies in the proof they afford that the conventions of the classical world had penetrated even to the lower classes. Mosaic floors are found in towns and villas, at first, as at Fishbourne, laid by imported craftsmen; there is evidence that by the middle of the 2nd century a local firm was at work at Colchester and Verulamium, and in the 4th century, a number of local mosaic workshops can be recognized by their styles. One of the most skilled of these was based in Cirencester.

Mosaics

Roman civilization thus took root in Britain. The resulting growth was more obvious in urban circles than among the agricultural peasants and weakest in the resistant highland zone. It was a provincial version of Roman culture, but one with recognizably British traits.

ROMAN BRITAIN AND THE SAXON CONQUEST

Britain, AD 286–410. The reforms of Diocletian ended the chaos of the 3rd century and ushered in the late imperial period. Britain, however, for a short period became a separate empire through the rebellion (286/287) of Carausius. This man had commanded against the Saxon pirates in the Channel and by his naval power was able to maintain his independence. His main achievement was to complete the new system of Saxon Shore forts around the southeastern coasts. At first he sought recognition as coemperor, but this was refused; in 293 the fall of Boulogne to Roman forces led to his murder and the accession of Allectus, who, however, fell in his turn when Constantius I invaded Britain in 296. Allectus had withdrawn troops from the north to oppose the landing, and Hadrian's Wall seems to have been attacked, for Constantius had to restore the frontier as well as to reform the administration. He divided Britain into four provinces, and in the same period, the civil power was separated from the military. Late Roman sources show three separate commands respectively under the *dux Britanniarum* (commander of the Britains), the *comes litoris Saxonici* (count of the Saxon Shore), and the *comes Britanniarum*, though the dates of their establishment are unknown and may not have been identical. The 4th century was a period of great prosperity in towns and countryside alike. Britain had escaped the invasions of the 3rd century and may have seemed a safe refuge for wealthy continentals. Its weakness lay in the fact that its defense was ultimately controlled by distant rulers rather than by local responsibility. The garrison was perhaps weakened by withdrawals for the civil war of Magnentius (350–351); at any rate in 367 there was a military disaster due to concerted sea-borne attacks from the Picts of Scotland and the Scots of Ireland. But, though the frontier and forts behind it suffered severely, there is little trace of damage to towns or villas. Count Theodosius in 369 restored the situation and strengthened the defenses of the towns with external towers designed to mount artillery. Prosperity continued, but there were ominous withdrawals of troops by Magnus Maximus in 383 and again at the end of the century by Stilicho. Thus, when in 407 Constantine III was declared emperor by the army in Britain and took further troops to Gaul, the forces remaining in the island were insufficient to provide protection against increasing Pictish and Saxon raids. The Britons appealed to the legitimate emperor, Honorius, who was unable to send assistance but authorized the cities to provide for their own defense (410). This marks the end of Roman Britain, for the central government never re-established control: but for a generation there was little other outward change.

The rise of tyrants

Britain in the 5th century. Power fell gradually into the hands of tyrants. Chief of these was Vortigern (*c.* 425), but he, unlike earlier usurpers, made no attempt to become Roman emperor, being content with power in Britain. Independence was producing separate interests. By this date Christianity had made considerable headway in the island, but the leaders followed the heretical teaching of Pelagius, himself a Briton, who had emphasized the importance of the human will over divine grace in the achievement of salvation. It has been held that the self-reliance shown in the maintenance of national independence was inspired by this philosophy. Yet there was also a powerful Catholic party anxious to reforge the links with Rome, in support of whom St. Germanus of Auxerre visited Britain in 429. It may have been partly to thwart the plans of this party that Vortigern made the mistake (*c.* 430; the "traditional" date given by Bede is between 446 and 454) of inviting Saxons to settle and garrison strategic areas of the east coast, though he certainly also had in mind the need to ward off sea-borne raids by Picts, which at this time were troublesome. Planned settlement of this sort is the best explanation for the earliest Saxon settlements found around the mouths of the east coast estuaries and also in the central-southeast region around Oxford. For a time the system worked successfully; but when, in 442, these Saxon *foederati* ("allies") rebelled and called in others of their race to help them, it was found that they had been given a stranglehold on Britain. A long period of warfare and chaos was inaugurated that was economically disastrous. It was probably this period that saw the disintegration of the majority of the villa estates; with the breakdown of markets and the escape of slaves, villas ceased to be viable and must have gradually fallen into ruin, though the land itself did not cease to be cultivated. A few villas met a violent end. The towns, under the protection of their strong defenses, at first provided refuge at any rate for the rich who could leave their lands; but by degrees decay set in as trade declined and finally the supply of food was itself threatened. In about 446 the British made a vain appeal for help to the Roman general Aetius (the "Groans of the Britons" mentioned in the *De excidio et conquestu Britanniae* of the British writer Gildas). For several decades they suffered reverses; many emigrated to Brittany. In the second half of the 5th century Ambrosius Aurelianus and the shadowy figure of Arthur began to turn the tide by the use of cavalry against the ill-armed Saxon infantry. A great victory was won at Mons Badonicus (a site not identifiable) toward 500: now it was Saxons who emigrated, and the British lived in peace all through the first half of the 6th century, as Gildas records. But in the second half the situation slowly worsened.

The Anglo-Saxons. Except in outline, the history of the settlements before 600 is hard to assess; the evidence consists partly of archaeological material difficult to date with precision, partly of place-names and early traditions, royal pedigrees, and annals later written down and of dubious accuracy. The traditions of the Kentish kingdom can be linked with what is known of federate settlement as outlined above, and it is likely that the Kingdoms of Deira in East Yorkshire, Wessex, and East Anglia originated similarly. By the late 5th century the Kingdom of Sussex had been established by conquest. The division of the settlers into Angles, Saxons, and Jutes in Bede's *Ecclesiastical History of the English People* is oversimplified to judge by archaeological evidence, and perhaps reflects the origins of kings rather than of their subjects who were of much more mixed extraction; in addition to the three sources named, Frisian and also Frankish elements can sometimes be identified.

In the later 6th century, the picture becomes clearer. By 577 Ceawlin had extended the Wessex kingdom to the Bristol Channel, though the British Kingdom of Dumnonia still held Devon and Cornwall. Slightly earlier (547), Ida had established the nucleus of the Bernician kingdom at Bamburgh from which the British states in The Pennines and southern Scotland were by degrees subdued. Under Aethelfrith soon after 600, Bernicia and Deira were united as the Kingdom of Northumbria, and by this date Lindsey (south of the Humber), Essex, Mercia, Middle Anglia, and two small kingdoms on the Welsh border are known to have emerged as states. Lindsey too may go back to a federate settlement.

On these foundations the historical kingdoms of the Anglo-Saxons were built. But British resistance was lasting in the west and north. The highland zone still exerted its age-old influence.

BIBLIOGRAPHY. S.S. FRERE, *Britannia* (1967), a full-scale history of Roman Britain with discussions of the archaeological remains; S. PIGGOTT, *Ancient Europe* (1965), a modern account of the archaeology and prehistory of Europe from the introduction of agriculture to the beginning of the Roman period; A.L.F. RIVET (ed.), *The Roman Villa in Britain* (1969), a collection of six essays describing various aspects of the Roman villas of Britain and the agricultural system and way of life they represent; A. BIRLEY, *Life in Roman Britain* (1964), a short description of the light thrown by archaeology and the ancient historians upon the government, institutions, life, and religions of Roman Britain; E. BIRLEY, *Roman Britain and the Roman Army* (1953), a collection of essays dealing with the organization of the Roman army based on the evidence of inscriptions; P.H. BLAIR, *Introduction to Anglo-Saxon England* (1956), a short history of Anglo-Saxon England from the end of the Roman period.

(S.S.F.)

Britain and Ireland, History of

This article deals with the history of Britain and Ireland in medieval and modern times, beginning with the Anglo-Saxon (Germanic) occupation of England. For the earlier history of what is now England, see the article BRITAIN, ANCIENT.

This article is divided into the following sections:

I. England to 1066

THE INVADERS AND THEIR EARLY SETTLEMENTS

Germanic tribes began to settle in Britain from about the middle of the 5th century AD. The first arrivals, according to the 6th-century British writer Gildas, were invited by a British king to defend his kingdom against the Picts and Scots. A tradition reached the historian Bede that the first settlers were from three tribes—the Angles, Saxons, and Jutes—which he locates on the Cimbric Peninsula and the coastlands of northwestern Germany, though the Jutes should perhaps be connected with the Rhineland rather than with Jutland, where Bede, by implication, puts them. Early settlements, near the coasts and the basins of navigable rivers in eastern and southern Britain, were halted about 500 by the Britons at the Battle of Mons Badonicus at an unidentified location; but a new Germanic drive began about 550, and before the century had ended the Britons had been driven west to the borders of Dumnonia (Cornwall and Devon) and to the Welsh Marches, while invaders were advancing west of the Pennines and northward into Lothian.

The distinction between the three Germanic tribes soon lost significance; certainly by the end of the 7th century men regarded themselves as "the nation of the English," though divided into several kingdoms. They were conscious of their kinship with the continental Germans and were little influenced by the civilization of the previous inhabitants (thus forming a striking contrast to the Germanic tribes that settled in Gaul); few Britons in England were above servile condition. This sense of unity was strengthened during long periods when all kingdoms south of the Humber acknowledged the overlordship (called by Bede an *imperium*) of a single ruler, known as a *bretwalda*, a word first recorded in the 9th century.

The first such overlord was Aelle of Sussex, in the late 5th century; the second was Ceawlin of Wessex, who died in 593. The third overlord, Aethelberht of Kent, held this power in 597 when the monk Augustine led a mission from Rome to Kent; Kent was the first English kingdom to be converted to Christianity. The Christian Church provided another unifying influence, overriding political divisions, although it was not until 669 that the church in England acknowledged a single head.

The social system. When Aethelberht set a code of laws down in writing, under Christian influence, the sys-

Adapted from R. Treharne and H. Fullard (eds.), *Muir's Historical Atlas: Ancient, Medieval and Modern*, 9th ed. (1965); George Philip & Son Ltd., London

Anglo-Saxon England.

tem underlying the laws was already old, in its main lines brought over from the Continent. Its strongest bond was that of kinship; every free man depended on his kindred for protection, and the social classes were distinguished by the amount of their wergild (the sum that the kindred could accept in place of vengeance if a man were killed). The normal free man was the *ceorl*, an independent peasant landowner; below him in Kent were persons with lower wergilds, who were either freedmen or, as were similar persons in Wessex, members of a subject population; above the *ceorls* were the nobles—some perhaps noble by birth but more often men who had risen by service as companions of the king—with a wergild three times that of a *ceorl* in Kent, six times that of a *ceorl* elsewhere. The tie that bound a man to his lord was as strong as that of the kindred. Both nobles and *ceorls* might possess slaves, who had no wergild and were regarded as chattels.

The rights of the king

The king had special rights—compensations for offenses committed in his presence or his home or against anyone under his protection; rights to hospitality, which later became a food rent charged on all land; and rights to various services. He rewarded his followers with grants of land, probably at first for their lifetime only; but the need to provide permanent endowment for the church brought into being a type of land free from most royal dues and that did not revert to the king. From the latter part of the 7th century such land was sometimes conferred by charter. It became common to make similar grants by charter to laymen, with power to bequeath; but three services—the building of forts and bridges and service in the army—were almost invariably excepted from the immunity. The king received fines for various crimes; but a man's guilt was established in an assembly of freemen, where the accused tried to establish his innocence by his oath—supported by oath helpers—and, if this failed, by ordeal. On matters of importance, the king normally consulted his *witan* (wise men).

There were local variations in the law. And over a period of time the law developed to meet changed circumstances. As kingdoms grew larger, for example, an official called an "ealdorman" was needed to administer part of the area, and, later, a sheriff was needed to look after the royal rights in each shire. The acceptance of Christianity made it necessary to fit the clergy into the scale of compensations and assign a value to their oaths and to fix penalties for offenses such as sacrilege, heathen practices, and breaches of the marriage law. But the basic principles were little changed.

The conversion to Christianity. Place-names containing the names of gods or other heathen elements are plentiful enough to prove the vitality of heathenism and to account for the slow progress of conversion in some areas. In Kent, the first kingdom to accept Christianity, King Wihtred's laws in 695 contained clauses against heathen worship. The conversion renewed relations with Rome and the Continent; but the full benefit of this was delayed by the conversion of much of England by the Celtic Church, which had lost contact with Rome.

Augustine's mission in 597 converted Kent; but it had only temporary success in Essex, which reverted to heathenism in 616. A mission sent from Kent under Paulinus to Northumbria that, in 627, converted King Edwin and many of his subjects in Northumbria and Lindsey received a setback in 632 when Edwin was killed and Paulinus withdrew to Kent. About 630 Archbishop Honorius of Canterbury sent a Burgundian, Felix, to convert East Anglia, and the East Anglian church thenceforth remained faithful to Canterbury. Soon after, the West Saxons were converted by Birinus, who came from Rome. Meanwhile, King Oswald began to restore Christianity in Northumbria, bringing Celtic missionaries from Iona. And it was the Celtic Church that began in 653 to spread the faith among the Middle Angles, the Mercians, and the peoples of the Severn Valley; it also won back Essex.

At first there was little friction between the Roman and Celtic missions. Oswald of Northumbria joined with Cynegils of Wessex in giving Dorchester-on-Thames as seat for Birinus' bishopric; the Irishmen Maildubh in Wessex and Fursey in East Anglia worked in areas converted by the Roman Church; and James the Deacon continued Paulinus' work in Northumbria. Later, however, differences in usage—especially in the calculation of the date of Easter—caused controversy, which was settled in favour of the Roman party at the Synod of Whitby in 664. The adherents of Celtic usage conformed or withdrew, and advocates of Roman practice became active in the north, the Midlands, and Essex. Theodore of Tarsus (arrived 669), the first archbishop to be acknowledged all over England, was active in establishing a proper diocesan system, whereas in the Celtic Church bishops tended to move freely without fixed sees and settled boundaries; he held the first synod of the English church at Hertford in 672, and this forbade a bishop to interfere in another's diocese or any priest to move into another diocese without his bishop's permission. Sussex and the Isle of Wight—the last outposts of heathenism—were converted by Bishop Wilfrid and his followers from 681 to 687 and thenceforth followed Roman usages.

The Anglo-Saxons attributed their conversion to Pope Gregory I, "the Apostle of the English," who had sent Augustine. This may seem less than fair to the Celtic mission, but modern scholars have tended to undervalue the work of the Roman Church. The Celtic Church made a great impression by its asceticism, fervour, and simplicity, and it had a lasting influence on scholarship. Yet the period of Celtic dominance was only 30 years. The decision at Whitby reunited the English to the universal church and made possible a form of organization better fitted for permanent needs than the looser system of the Celtic Church.

Early Northumbrian missionaries

The conversion of the English was hardly completed before they began to take the faith to the continental Germans. The earliest missionaries were Northumbrians who worked in Frisia. Wilfrid converted some Frisians in the winter of 677 on his way to Rome, but the permanent conversion began about 690 with the work of Willibrord, a Northumbrian missionary.

Willibrord converted Frankish Frisia and founded the see of Utrecht. He was joined by the West Saxon Wynfrith (better known as Boniface), who worked with him from 718 to 721. Boniface's main missionary work was in Thuringia and Hesse. The Pope consecrated him bishop to the Germans in 722, archbishop in 732. In addition to his success as a missionary and his founding of sees among the Germans, Boniface reorganized the church of Bavaria and helped the Frankish leaders Pippin and Carloman to reform the Frankish church, bringing it into relations with the papacy and thus profoundly affecting Frankish history. He was joined by many men and women from England, mainly from Wessex. Boniface was martyred by the heathens in northern Frisia in 754.

The "Golden Age" of Bede. Within a century of Augustine's landing, England was in the forefront of scholarship. This high standard arose from a combination of influences: that from Ireland, which had escaped the decay caused elsewhere by the barbarian invasions, and that from the Mediterranean, which reached England mainly through Archbishop Theodore and his companion, the abbot Adrian. Under Theodore and Adrian, Canterbury became a famous school, and men trained there took their learning to other parts of England. One of these was Aldhelm, who had been a pupil of Maildubh (the Irish founder of Malmesbury); under Aldhelm, Malmesbury became an influential centre of learning. Aldhelm's own works, in Latin verse and prose, reveal a familiarity with many Latin authors; his writings became popular among admirers of the ornate and artificial style he had learned from his Celtic teachers. Before long a liberal education could be had at such other West Saxon monasteries as Nursling and Wimborne.

The finest centre of scholarship was Northumbria. There Celtic and classical influences had met: missionaries brought books from Ireland, and many Englishmen went to Ireland to study. Other Northumbrians went abroad, especially to Rome; among them was Benedict Biscop. Benedict returned from Rome with Theodore (668–669) and spent some time in Canterbury, and he brought the learning acquired there to Northumbria. He founded the monasteries at Wearmouth (674) and Jarrow (682), where Bede spent his life. Benedict and Ceolfrith, abbot of Jarrow, brought books from the Continent and assembled the fine library that was available to Bede.

Bede (*c.* 672–735) is remembered as a great historian whose work has never lost its value; but he was also a theologian regarded throughout the Middle Ages as second only to the Church Fathers. Though he was outstanding, he did not work in isolation. Other Northumbrian houses—Lindisfarne, Whitby, and Ripon—produced saints' lives, and Bede was in touch with many learned men, not only in Northumbria; there are also signs of scholarly activity in London and in East Anglia.

Moreover, in this period religious poetry was composed in the diction and technique of the older vernacular, secular poetry. *Beowulf*, considered the greatest Old English poem, is sometimes assigned to this age, but the dating is uncertain. Art flourished, with a combination of native elements and of influences from Ireland and the Mediterranean. The Hiberno-Saxon (or Anglo-Irish) style of illumination was evolved, its greatest example—the Lindisfarne Gospels—also showing classical influence. Masons from Gaul and Rome built stone churches. In Northumbria stone monuments with figure sculpture and vine-scroll patterns were set up. Churches were equipped with precious objects—some from abroad, some of native manufacture (even in heathen times the English had been skilled metalworkers). Manuscripts and works of art were taken abroad to churches founded by the English missions, and these churches, in turn, became centres of production.

Visual arts and architecture

THE HEPTARCHY

The supremacy of Northumbria and the rise of Mercia. When Northumbria became eminent in scholarship, its age of political importance was over. This political dominance had begun when Aethelfrith, ruling over the united Northumbrian kingdoms of Bernicia and Deira, defeated the Dalriadic Scots at Degsastan in 603 and the Welsh at Chester in 613–616. Aethelfrith was himself defeated and killed in 616 by Edwin, the exiled heir to Deira, with the help of Raedwald of East Anglia, then overlord of the southern peoples.

Edwin continued to defeat the Welsh and became the acknowledged overlord of all England except Kent: he annexed the British kingdom of Elmet, invaded North Wales, and captured Anglesey and the Isle of Man. But he fell at Hatfield in 632 before the forces of Cadwallon, king of Gwynedd, and of Penda, a Mercian chieftain. A year later Aethelfrith's son Oswald destroyed Cadwallon and restored the kingdom of Northumbria, and he became overlord of all the lands south of the River Humber. But Mercia was becoming a serious rival; originally a small kingdom in the northwest midlands, it had absorbed the peoples of the Severn Valley, including the Hwicce, a West Saxon people annexed in 628 after a victory by Penda at Cirencester.

Penda threw off Northumbrian control when he defeated and killed Oswald in 641. He drove out Cenwalh of Wessex, who took refuge in East Anglia from 645 to 648. Penda's control of Middle Anglia, where he made his son subking in 653, brought him to the East Anglian frontier; and he invaded this kingdom three times, killing three of their kings. He was able to draw an army from a wide area, including East Anglia, when he invaded Northumbria in 654; nevertheless, he was defeated and killed by Oswiu, Oswald's successor.

For a short time Oswiu was overlord of southern England; but a Mercian revolt put Penda's son Wulfhere on the throne in 657, and he greatly extended Mercian power to the southeast and south. Wulfhere became overlord of Essex, with London, and of Surrey; he held the West Saxon lands along the middle Thames and blocked any eastward advance of the West Saxons by capturing the Isle of Wight and the mainland opposite and giving them to his godson, Aethelwalh of Sussex. Yet Wulfhere's reign ended in disaster; the Kentish monk Aedde, in his *Life of St. Wilfrid*, said Wulfhere roused all the southern peoples in an attack on Ecgfrith of Northumbria in 674 but was defeated and died soon after.

Ecgfrith took possession of Lindsey, a section of modern Lincolnshire, but he lost it to Aethelred of Mercia after the Battle of the Trent in 678. Thenceforward Northumbria was no threat to Mercian dominance; it was occupied in fighting the Picts in the north, and after Ecgfrith was slain by them in 685, his successors took little part in external affairs.

Yet Mercian power was threatened from the south. Though Aethelred invaded Kent in 676 and though part of Kent was ruled after 686 in subordination to him by a member of the royal house of Essex, Caedwalla of Wessex also obtained some power in Kent. Caedwalla had added Surrey, Sussex, and the Isle of Wight to the West Saxon kingdom and thus came near to uniting all lands south of the Thames into a single kingdom, which might have held its own against Mercia. But this kingdom was short-lived (it was left to Egbert of Wessex to make such a kingdom a reality in 825). Kent became free from foreign interference in 694, two years after the accession of Wihtred, who re-established the Kentish royal line. Sussex appears again as an independent kingdom; and Caedwalla's successor, Ine, was mainly occupied in extending his territory to the west. After Wihtred's death in 725 and Ine's abdication in 726, both Kent and Wessex had internal troubles and could not resist the Mercian kings Aethelbald and Offa.

The reigns of Aethelbald and Offa

The great age of Mercia. Aethelbald succeeded in 716 to the rule of all the midlands and to the control of Essex and London. By 731 all provinces south of the Humber were subject to him. Some of his charters use a regnal style suited to this dignity, such as "king not only of the Mercians but also of all provinces . . . of the South English" and "rex Britanniae" (a Latinization of "bretwalda"). Aethelbald held this position, with only occasional warfare, until his death, in 757—far longer than any previous holder of the *imperium*. St. Boniface praised the good order he maintained in his kingdom, though complaining of his immoral life and his encroachment on church privileges. Aethelbald was murdered by his own household, perhaps suborned by Beornred, a rival who was driven out by Offa before the end of the year.

Offa did not at once attain the powerful position that later caused Charles the Great (Charlemagne) to treat with him on equal terms; Cynewulf of Wessex recovered West Saxon lands by the middle Thames and did not submit until 779. Offa was overlord in Kent by 764, in Sussex and the district of Hastings by 771; he apparently lost his authority in Kent after the Battle of Otford in 776 but recovered it in 785. His use of an East Anglian mint shows him supreme there. He claimed greater powers than earlier overlords—subkings among the Hwicce and in Sussex dropped their royal titles and appeared as ealdormen, and he referred to a Kentish king as his thegn. The English scholar Alcuin spoke of the blood shed by Offa to secure the succession of his son, and fugitives from his kingdom sought asylum with Charles the Great. Charles treated Offa as if he were sole king of England, at least of the region south of the Humber; the only other king he acknowledged was the Northumbrian ruler. Offa seemed not to have claimed authority beyond the Humber but instead allied himself with King Aethelred of Northumbria by giving him his daughter in 794.

Offa appears on the continental scene more than had any previous English king. Charles wrote to him as "his dearest brother" and wished for a marriage between his own son Charles and Offa's daughter. Offa's refusal unless Charles let one of his daughters marry Offa's son Ecgfrith led to a three-year quarrel in which Charles closed his ports to traders from England. This and a letter about regulating trade, written when the quarrel was over, provide evidence for the importance of cross-Channel trade, which was one reason for Offa's reform of the coinage.

Imitating the action of Pepin in 755, Offa took responsibility for the coinage, and thenceforward the king's name normally appeared on coins. But the excellent quality in design and workmanship of his coins, especially those with his portrait, served an additional purpose: they had a propaganda value in bringing home the pre-eminence of the Mercian king not only to his English subjects but also on the Continent. Pope Adrian I regarded Offa with awe and respect.

Because Offa's laws are lost, little is known of his internal government, though Alcuin praises it. Offa was able to draw on immense resources to build a dike to demarcate his frontier against Wales. In the greatness of its conception and the skill of its construction, the dike forms a fitting memorial to him. It probably belongs to his later years, and it secured Mercia from sudden incursions.

The spread of missionary activities and learning

The church and scholarship in Offa's time. The missionary activities of Willibrord and Boniface were continued after their deaths by Lull, Boniface's successor at Mainz, and by the Northumbrians Willehad and Aluberht, who converted the Old Saxons. Northumbria was still pre-eminent in scholarship, and the fame of the school of York, founded by Bede's pupil Archbishop Egbert, attracted students from the Continent and from Ireland. Eventually it supplied Alcuin to take charge of the revival of learning inaugurated by Charles the Great; Alcuin's writings exercised great influence on theological, biblical, and liturgical studies, and his pupils carried on his work well into the 9th century.

Learning was not confined to Northumbria; one Latin work was produced in East Anglia, and recent attribution of manuscripts to Lichfield suggests that Mercian scholarship has been underestimated. Offa himself took an interest in education, and men from all areas corresponded with the missionaries. The Mercian schools that supplied Alfred with scholars in the 9th century may go back to this period. Vernacular poetry was composed, perhaps including *Beowulf* and the poems of Cynewulf.

A steady advance was made in the creation of parishes, and monasticism flourished and received support from Offa. A great event in ecclesiastical history was the arrival of a papal legation in 787, the first since the conversion. It drew up reforming statutes, which were accepted by the two ecclesiastical provinces, meeting separately under the presidency of Offa and Aelfwald of Northumbria. Offa used the visit to secure the consecration of his son—the first recorded coronation ceremony in England—and also to have Mercia made into a metropolitan province with its see at Lichfield. The latter was because of Offa's dislike of the Kentish archbishop of Canterbury, Jaenberht, but it would also seem fitting to him that the leading kingdom should be free from external interference in ecclesiastical affairs. This move was unpopular with the church, and in 802, when improved relations with Canterbury had been established, the archbishopric of Lichfield was abolished.

The papal legation of 787

The decline of Mercia and the rise of Wessex. Offa died in 796, and his son died a few weeks later. Cenwulf, their successor, suppressed revolts in Kent and East Anglia, but he never attained Offa's position. Cenwulf allowed Charles to intervene in Northumbria in 808 and restore Eardwulf (who had been driven from his kingdom) to the throne—a unique incident in Anglo-Saxon history. Mercian influence in Wessex was ended when Egbert became king there in 802, though there is no recorded warfare between the kingdoms for many years, during which Egbert conquered Cornwall and Cenwulf fought in Wales. But in 825 Egbert defeated Beornwulf of Mercia and then sent an army into Kent, with the result that he was accepted as king of Kent, Surrey, Sussex, and Essex. In that same year the East Angles threw off the Mercian yoke, killing Beornwulf. In 829 Egbert became ruler of Mercia and all south of the Humber, which caused the chronicler to add his name to Bede's list of kings who held the *imperium*, calling him *bretwalda*. The Northumbrians accepted Egbert without fighting. Yet he held this proud position only one year; then Wiglaf recovered the Mercian throne and ruled without subjection to Egbert.

Mercian-West Saxon alliance

By this time Danish Viking raids were a grave menace, and Aethelwulf, who succeeded his father Egbert in 839, had the wisdom to see that Mercia and Wessex must combine against the Vikings. Friendly relations between them were established by marriage alliances and by a peaceful settlement of boundaries; this paved the way for the acceptance in 886 of Alfred, king of Wessex, as lord of all the English who had not fallen under Danish rule.

THE PERIOD OF THE SCANDINAVIAN INVASIONS

Viking invasions and settlements. Small scattered Viking raids began in the last years of the 8th century; in the 9th century, large-scale plundering incursions were made in Britain and in the Frankish empire as well. Though Egbert defeated, in 838, a large Viking force that had combined with the Britons of Cornwall, and Aethelwulf won a great victory in 851 over a Viking army that had stormed Canterbury and London and put the Mercian king to flight, it was difficult to deal with an enemy that could attack anywhere on a long and undefended coastline. Destructive raids are recorded for Northumbria, East Anglia, Kent, and Wessex.

A large Danish army came to East Anglia in the autumn of 865, apparently intent on conquest. By 871, when it first attacked Wessex, it had already captured York, been bought off by Mercia, and had taken possession of East Anglia. Many battles were fought in Wessex, including a Danish defeat at Ashdown in 871, before Alfred the Great, a son of Aethelwulf, who succeeded to the throne in the course of the year, made peace; this gave him a respite until 876. Meanwhile the Danes drove out Burgred of Mercia, putting a puppet king in his place, and one division of them made a permanent settlement in Northumbria.

Alfred's defense of Wessex

Alfred was able to force the Danes to leave Wessex in 877, and they settled northeastern Mercia; but a Viking attack in the winter of 878 came near to conquering Wessex. That it did not is to be attributed to Alfred's tenacity. He retired to the Somerset marshes, and in the spring he secretly assembled an army that routed the Danes at Edington. Their king, Guthrum, accepted Christianity and took his forces to East Anglia, where they settled.

The importance of Alfred's victory cannot be exaggerated. It prevented the Danes from becoming masters of the whole of England. Wessex was never again in such danger, and from Wessex, in the next century, the Danish areas were reconquered. Alfred's capture of London in 886, and the resultant acceptance of him by all the English outside the Danish areas, was a preliminary to this reconquest. That Wessex stood when the other kingdoms had fallen must be put down to Alfred's courage and wisdom, to his defensive measures in reorganizing his army, to his building fortresses and ships, and to his diplomacy, which made the Welsh kings his allies. Renewed attacks by Viking hosts in 892–896, supported by the Danes resident in England, caused widespread damage but had no lasting success.

Alfred's government and his revival of learning. Good internal government contributed to Alfred's successful resistance to the Danes. He reorganized his finances and the services due from thegns, issued an important code of laws, and scrutinized carefully the exercise of justice. Alfred saw the Viking invasions as a punishment from God, especially because of a neglect of learning, without which men could not know and follow the will of God. He deplored the decay of Latin and enjoined its study by those destined for the church; but he also wished all young free men of adequate means to learn to read English, and he aimed at supplying men with "the books most necessary for all men to know," in their own language.

Alfred had acquired an education despite great difficulties, and he translated some books himself, with the help of scholars from Mercia, the Continent, and Wales. Among them they made available works of Bede and Orosius, Gregory and Augustine, and the *De consolatione philosophiae* of Boethius. Compilation of the Anglo-Saxon Chronicle began in his reign. The effects of Alfred's educational reforms can be glimpsed in succeeding reigns, and his works continued to be copied. Only in an attempt to revive monasticism did he achieve little, for the monastic idea had lost its appeal—in England as well as on the Continent—during the Viking Age.

THE ACHIEVEMENT OF POLITICAL UNITY

The reconquest of the Danelaw. When Alfred died in 899 his son Edward succeeded him. Edward had to deal with a rival, his cousin Aethelwold, who obtained support from the Northumbrian and East Anglian Danes; but Aethelwold and the Danish king of East Anglia fell before Edward's forces in 902. A large-scale incursion by the Danes of Northumbria ended in their crushing defeat at Tettenhall in 910. Edward completed his father's plan of building a ring of fortresses round Wessex, and his sister Aethelflaed took similar measures in Mercia. In 912 Edward was ready to begin the series of campaigns by which he relentlessly advanced into the Danelaw (Danish territory in England), securing each advance by a fortress, until he won back Essex, East Anglia, and the east-midland Danish areas. Aethelflaed moved similarly against the Danish territory of the Five Boroughs (Derby, Leicester, Nottingham, Lincoln, and Stamford). She obtained Derby and Leicester and gained a promise of submission from the Northumbrian Danes before she died in 918. Edward had by then reached Stamford, but he broke off his advance to secure his acceptance by the Mercians at Tamworth and to prevent their setting up an independent kingdom. Then he took Nottingham, and all the Danes in Mercia submitted to him.

Edward's successes in England

Meanwhile another danger had arisen: Norsemen from Ireland had been settling for some time west of the Pennines, and Northumbria was threatened by Raegnald, a Norse leader from Dublin, who made himself king at York in 919. Edward built fortresses at Thelwall and Manchester, and in 920 he received Raegnald's submission, along with that of the Scots, the Strathclyde Welsh, and all the Northumbrians. Yet Norse kings reigned at York intermittently until 954.

The Kingdom of England. Athelstan succeeded his father Edward in 924. He made terms with Raegnald's successor Sihtric and gave him his sister in marriage. When Sihtric died in 927, Athelstan took possession of Northumbria, thus becoming the first king to have direct rule of all England. He received the submission of the kings of Wales and Scotland and of the English ruler of Northumbria beyond the Tyne.

Athelstan's ascendancy over all England

Athelstan was proud of his position, calling himself "king of all Britain" on some of his coins and using in his charters flamboyant styles with the same meaning; he held great courts attended by dignitaries from all over England and by Welsh kings; he subjected the Welsh to tribute and quelled a revolt of the Britons of Cornwall. His sisters were married to continental princes—Charles the Simple, king of the Franks; Otto, son of Henry the Fowler; Hugh, duke of the Franks. Among those brought up at his court were Louis, Charles's son; Alan of Brittany, Athelstan's godson; and Hakon, son of Harald Haarfager of Norway; they all returned to win their respective inheritances with his support. He received spectacular embassies from Harald Haarfager and Duke Hugh, and he was a generous donor to continental and English churches. But Athelstan is remembered chiefly as the victor at Brunanburh, against a combine of Olaf Guthfrithson, king of Dublin; Owain of Strathclyde; and Constantine, king of the Scots, whom Athelstan had defeated in 934. They invaded England in 937, and their defeat is celebrated by a poem in the Anglo-Saxon Chronicle.

Immediately after Athelstan's death in 939, Olaf seized not only Northumbria but also the Five Boroughs. By 944 Athelstan's successor, his younger brother Edmund, had retrieved the situation, and in 945 Edmund conquered Strathclyde and gave it to Malcolm of Scotland. But Edmund's successor, Eadred, lost control of Northumbria for part of his reign to the Norse kings Eric Bloodaxe (son of Harald Haarfager) and Olaf Sihtricson. When Eric was killed in 954 Northumbria became a permanent part of the kingdom of England.

By becoming rulers of all England, the West Saxon kings had to administer regions with variant customs, governed under West Saxon, Mercian, or Danish law. In some parts of the area of Danish occupation, especially in Yorkshire and the district of the Five Boroughs, the evidence of place-names, personal names, and dialect proves a dense Danish settlement; but Danish law also prevailed in such other regions as Essex, Middlesex, and Buckinghamshire, with differences from the rest of England in procedure and in the system of fines, including much higher fines for serious crimes. There were other differences. Money was calculated in marks and ores instead of shillings in Danish areas, and arable land was divided into plowlands and oxgangs instead of hides and virgates in the northern and northeastern parts of the Danelaw; most important was the presence in some areas of a number of small landholders with a much greater degree of independence than their counterparts elsewhere where many *ceorls* had so suffered under the Danish ravages that they had bought a lord's support by sacrificing some of their independence.

Variant laws and customs within the kingdom

The kings did not try to eradicate these local peculiarities. King Edgar (reigned 959–975) expressly granted local autonomy to the Danes. But from Athelstan's time it was decreed that there was to be one coinage over all the king's dominion, and a measure of uniformity in administrative divisions was gradually achieved. Mercia became divided into shires on the pattern of those of Wessex. It is uncertain how early the smaller divisions of the shires were called "hundreds," but they now became universal (except in the northern Danelaw, where an area called a *wapentake* carried on their fiscal and jurisdictional functions); an ordinance of the mid-10th century laid down that the court in each hundred (called "hundred courts") must meet every four weeks to handle local legal matters, and Edgar enjoined that the shire courts must meet twice a year, the borough courts three times. This pattern of local government survived the Norman Conquest.

The church and the monastic revival. To those who judged the church solely by the state of its monasteries, the first half of the 10th century seemed a period of inertia. In fact, the great tasks of converting the heathen settlers, restoring ecclesiastical organization in Danish areas, and repairing the damages of the invasions elsewhere must have absorbed much energy. Even so, learning and book production were not at so low an ebb as monastic reformers claimed. Moreover, new monasteries were founded and benefactions were made to older ones, even though, by post-revival standards, none of these was leading a strict monastic life and several were held by secular priests. Alfred had failed to arouse much enthusiasm for monasticism. The movement for reform began in England about 940 and soon came under the influence of reforms in Fleury and Lorraine. King Edgar, an enthusiastic supporter, promoted the three chief reformers to important positions—Dunstan to Canterbury, Aethelwold to Winchester, and Oswald to Worcester and later to York. The secular clergy were violently ejected from Winchester and some other places; Oswald gradually replaced them with monks at Worcester. All three reformers founded new houses, including the great monasteries in the Fenlands, where older houses had perished in the Danish invasion; but Oswald had no success in Northumbria. The reformers, however, were concerned with more than monasticism—they paid great attention to other needs of their dioceses; the scholars Abbot Aelfric and Archbishop Wulfstan, trained by the reformers, directed much of their writings to improving the education and morals of the parish clergy and, through them, of the people.

Movement for monastic reform

The monastic revival resulted in a great revival of both vernacular and Latin literature, of manuscript production and illumination, and of other forms of art. It reached its zenith in the troubled years of King Ethelred II (reigned 978–1016), after a brief, though violent, reaction to monasticism following Edgar's death. In the 11th century, monasteries continued to be productive and new houses were founded; there was also a movement to impose a communal life on bodies of secular priests and to found houses of secular canons.

THE ANGLO-DANISH STATE

The Danish conquest and the reigns of the Danish kings. Ethelred succeeded as a child in 978, after the murder of his stepbrother Edward. He took the throne in an atmosphere of insecurity and distrust, which partly accounts for the incompetence and treachery rife in his reign. Viking raids began in 980 and steadily increased in intensity. They were led by formidable leaders: from 991 to 994 by Olaf Tryggvason, later king of Norway, and frequently from 994 by Sweyn, king of Denmark. Ethelred's massacre of the Danes in England on St. Brice's Day, 1002, called for vengeance by Sweyn and, from 1009 to 1012, by a famous Viking, Thorkell the Tall. In 1013 the English, worn out by continuous warfare and heavy tributes to buy off the invaders, accepted Sweyn as king. Ethelred, his wife Emma, and his younger sons sought asylum with Richard, duke of Normandy, brother of Emma. Ethelred was recalled to England after Sweyn's death in 1014; but Sweyn's son Canute (Cnut) renewed the invasions and, in spite of valiant resistance by Ethelred's son and successor, Edmund, obtained half of England after a victory at Ashingdon in October 1016 and the rest after Edmund's death that November.

Revival of Danish attacks

Canute rewarded some of his followers with English lands, and he made the Viking leader Eric of Hlathir earl of Northumbria and Thorkell the Tall earl of East Anglia. He ruthlessly got rid of some prominent Englishmen, among them Edmund's brother Edwy, but Edmund's infant sons were carried away to safety in Hungary. Yet Canute's rule was not tyrannical, and his reign was remembered as a time of good order. The Danish element in his entourage diminished; and the Englishmen, Leofric, earl of Mercia, and Godwine, earl of Wessex, became the most powerful magnates. Canute married Ethelred's widow, Emma, thus removing the danger of Norman support for her sons by Ethelred. Canute fought a successful campaign in Scotland in 1031, and Englishmen were drawn into his wars in Scandinavia, which made him lord of Norway. But at home there was peace. Probably under the influence of Archbishop Wulfstan, he became a stout supporter of the church, which in his reign had the vitality to engage in missionary work in Scandinavia. Religious as well as political motives may have caused his pilgrimage to Rome in 1027, to attend the coronation of the emperor Conrad; from the Pope, the Emperor, and the princes whom he met he obtained concessions for English pilgrims and traders going to Rome. Canute's laws, drafted by Archbishop Wulfstan, are mainly based on those of earlier kings, especially Edgar.

Already in 1018 the English and Danes had come to an agreement "according to Edgar's law." No important changes were made in the machinery of government except that small earldoms were combined to make great earldoms, which placed much power in the hands of their holders. No attempt was made to restore the English line when Canute died in 1035; he was followed by his sons Harold and Hardecanute, whose reigns were unpopular. Denmark passed to Sweyn, son of Canute's sister Estrith, in 1043. Meanwhile the Norwegians in 1035 had driven out another Sweyn, the son whom Canute had set to rule over them with his mother, Aelfgifu, and had elected Magnus.

Canute's successors

The close links with Scandinavia had benefitted English trade, but they left one awkward heritage: Hardecanute and Magnus made an agreement that if either died without a son, the survivor was to succeed to both kingdoms. Hardecanute died without a son in 1042, and he was succeeded by Ethelred's son Edward, who was known as the "Confessor" or the "Saint" because of his reputation for chastity. Magnus was prevented by trouble with Denmark from invading England as he intended in 1046; but Harold Hardraada inherited Magnus' claim to the English throne, and he came to enforce it in 1066.

The reign of Edward the Confessor and the Norman Conquest. It is easy to regard the years of Edward's rule simply as a prelude to the catastrophe of 1066, yet there are other aspects of his reign. Harrying caused by political disturbances or by incursions of the Scots or Welsh was only occasional and localized; friendly relations were usually maintained with Malcolm of Scotland, whom Earl Siward of Northumbria had supported against Macbeth in 1054; and in 1063 the victories of Harold, earl of Wessex, and his brother Tostig ended the trouble from Wales. The normal course of administration was maintained, with efficient mints, writing office, taxation system, and courts of justice. Trade was prosperous. The church contained several good and competent leaders, and bad appointments—like those of the Normans, Ulf to Dorchester and Robert to London and Canterbury, and of Stigand to Winchester—were the exception. Scholarship was not decadent, and manuscripts were produced in great number. English illumination and other forms of art were admired abroad.

The troubles of the reign came from the excessive power concentrated in the hands of the rival houses of Leofric of Mercia and Godwine of Wessex and from resentment caused by the King's introduction of Norman friends, though their influence has sometimes been exaggerated. A crisis arose in 1051 when Godwine defied the King's order to punish the men of Dover, who had resisted an attempt by Eustace of Boulogne to quarter his men on them by force. The support of Earl Leofric and Earl Siward enabled Edward to secure the outlawry of Godwine and his sons; and Duke William of Normandy paid Edward a visit during which Edward may have promised William succession to the English throne, if this Norman claim was not mere propaganda. Godwine and his sons came back the following year with a strong force, and the magnates were not prepared to engage them in civil war but forced the king to make terms. Some unpopular Normans were driven out, including Archbishop Robert, whose archbishopric was given to Stigand; this act supplied one excuse for the papal support of William's cause.

Harold succeeded his father Godwine as earl of Wessex in 1053; Tostig was made earl of Northumbria in 1055; and their younger brothers were also provided with earldoms. To settle the question of succession, negotiations were begun in 1054 to bring Edward, Edmund's son (nephew of Edward the Confessor), from Hungary; but he died in 1057, leaving a son, Edgar Aetheling, then a child, who was passed over in 1066. In about 1064 Harold of Wessex, when visiting Normandy, swore to support William's claim; only Norman versions of the incident survive and the true circumstances cannot be ascertained, but William used Harold's broken oath to help secure papal support later. In 1065 Harold had to acquiesce in the appointment of Morcar, brother of Earl Edwin of Mercia, to replace Tostig when the Northumbrians revolted against him, and thus Harold turned his brother into an enemy. King Edward when dying named Harold to succeed him, and he was universally accepted after he had overcome Northumbrian reluctance with the help of Bishop Wulfstan of Worcester.

Harold might have proved an effective ruler, but the forces against him were too strong. The papacy, without hearing the defense, gave its blessing to an invasion of a people who had always been distinguished for their loyalty to Rome, and this helped William to collect his army widely. The threat from Harold III Hardraade, who was joined by Tostig, prevented Harold from concentrating his forces in the south and took him north at a critical moment. He fought at Hastings only 24 days after the armies of Mercia and Northumbria had been put out of action by enormous losses at Fulford and only 19 days after he had defeated and killed Harold III Hardraade and Tostig at Stamford Bridge. Harold was slain at Hastings, and on Christmas Day, 1066, William of Normandy was crowned king of England. Unwise decisions and out-of-date methods of fighting may have played a part in Harold's defeat at Hastings, but it is not difficult to understand the English chronicler's view that God was angry with the English people. (D.W.)

The crowning of William

II. The Normans (1066–1154)

WILLIAM I (1066–87)

Scholars argue endlessly about the significance of the Norman Conquest: whether the results were good or bad, whether there was more continuity than change, whether feudalism existed in England before the Conquest, to what extent Anglo-Saxon institutions survived the Conquest, and so forth. No one doubts that there was change and also continuity, but on balance the argument seems to be in favour of change.

The introduction of feudalism. The major change was the subordination of England to a Norman aristocracy. William distributed estates to his followers on a piecemeal basis as the lands were conquered. Fewer than 180 great tenants in chief were given large parcels of land distributed about the country. Most of these, however, held concentrations of land in some one part of the country, where they centred their "honours," or feudal states. From these centres, usually fortified by a castle, the Norman tenants in chief conducted their administration and organized their military power. They held their land from the Conqueror in return for units of knight service; that is, in return for supplying a certain number of knights to the king's feudal army—which had no necessary relationship to the quantity or quality of land held. In the beginning of the reign, many tenants in chief maintained their quotas of knights out of their own households, but before the end of the reign they had subinfeudated portions of their lands to rear vassals. Private warfare, endemic in Normandy despite efforts of the Duke to suppress it, was, however, successfully prohibited in England. Castles could be built only with the King's license, and the only feudal army permitted was that of the King himself. As an added precaution, rear vassals were required to take an oath of fealty

Distribution of land

directly to the King. With the Conquest, England became that anomaly, a unified and centralized feudal state.

Government and justice. William professed a desire to govern England as it had been ruled by his Anglo-Saxon predecessors, and he tried to fulfill his promise. Under William the Anglo-Saxon *witenagemot*, the assemblage of the wise men of the realm, became the King's Curia Regis, an assemblage of the King's ecclesiastical and lay tenants in chief, called together in part or in full when occasion required. Three times in the year—at Christmas, Easter, and Whitsuntide—William was alleged by contemporary chroniclers to have held especially full and solemn assemblages of his court, to which were summoned all the great men of the realm and at which he wore his crown. Inevitably, because of the great number of disputes about land, the Curia Regis became a court for the administration of justice to the King's great tenants in chief. William tried to learn English in order to better his administration of justice, and he is said to have sat one Sunday "from morn to eve" to hear a plea between William de Braose and the Abbot of Fécamp.

William also tried at first to preserve Anglo-Saxon administrative organization. The central administration under Edward the Confessor had probably been quite similar to that of Normandy, except for the titles of the officers. At first, even the personnel did not change. But, by the end of William's reign, all important administrative officers were Norman, and their titles corresponded to the titles in the duchy administration. There were a steward, a butler, a chamberlain, a constable, a marshall, and, finally, a head of the royal scriptorium (or chancellor). The royal scriptorium was the source from which all writs (*i.e.*, written royal commands) were issued. At the beginning of William's reign the writs were in English, by the end of the reign in Latin.

Local government

In local government the Anglo-Saxon shire and hundred courts continued to function as units of administration and of justice but with important changes. Bishops and earls ceased to preside over the shire courts. Bishops henceforth were to have their own ecclesiastical courts. Earls exercised feudal jurisdiction in their honour courts but took as a prerequisite a third of the proceeds of the shire court. But the new earls created by the Conqueror did not wield the vast local power of their pre-Conquest counterparts.

The office of shire-reeve (or sheriff) was continued under William, as were many of the English incumbents in the early part of the reign. But soon the native sheriffs were replaced by men of the new Norman aristocracy, and the office came to resemble the office of the Norman *vicomte*, a title that also appears in English documents. Their duties remained those that they had exercised before the Conquest. Royal officers exercising the king's will, they were responsible for collecting the royal revenue, for administering local justice, and for keeping the castles that had been built to subdue and protect the country.

William made the most of the financial system that he inherited. In addition to customary dues, the revenues from justice, and the proceeds from their own estates, his predecessors had been able to levy a geld, or tax, distributed over the whole realm. This has been called the "first system of national taxation known to western Europe." William levied a geld at least four times during his reign. He was also able to levy extensive duties on trade with the Continent. Trade had been temporarily disrupted by the Conquest, but it recovered rapidly and proved to be an important source of revenue.

The Conqueror strengthened immensely the administration of justice in his new realm. He occasionally appointed justiciars to preside over local administration of justice and occasionally also sent down commissioners from the central administration. There were a number of great trials during the reign. The most famous of them was the trial at Pinnenden Heath of a case between Lanfranc, archbishop of Canterbury, and the King's half-brother, Odo, bishop of Bayeux and earl of Kent. To this trial came not only all of the Frenchmen of the shire but also a great number of Englishmen, especially those learned in the customary law. In these trials held before the king's officers, jurors were sometimes summoned to give a collective verdict under oath. It is debated among historians whether this institution of the jury was introduced by the Danish kings or was drawn from the Carolingian kings through the Normans. The important point, however, is that the jury came into common use under the Normans.

Church–state relations. The upper ranks of the clergy were Normanized and feudalized following the pattern of lay society. Bishops received their temporal estates and the symbols of spiritual office from the king. They owed service of knights in return for tenure of their temporal estates, and they were brought under firm royal control. In time, all the leading bishoprics were held by continental clergy. In 1070 Lanfranc replaced Stigand as archbishop of Canterbury. Ecclesiastical lawyer, teacher, and statesman of the church, Lanfranc was Italian in origin and had been a monk at Bec and abbot of Saint-Étienne's at Caen. Lanfranc and William understood each other and worked together to introduce discipline and order into the English church. The see of York was definitively subordinated to Canterbury, and the ecclesiastical affairs of Ireland and Scotland were brought under Lanfranc's control—this despite the fact that papal policy of the period was to bring each province directly under the control of Rome. Several church councils were held in England to legislate for the English church as similar councils did in Normandy. William refused to give homage to the pope for the realm of England, although he acknowledged papal support in winning the new realm. To further implement his headship of the English church, William laid down some general rules where disputes might arise. No pope was to be recognized in England without his decision. Without William's consent no papal letter was to be received, no ecclesiastical council was to legislate, and no baron or officer of the realm was to be excommunicated. William and Lanfranc resisted Gregory VII's claim to papal supremacy but based their resistance on English tradition. During William's reign the controversy over the right of lay rulers to invest ecclesiastics with the symbols of their spiritual offices did not affect England, as it did other parts of Latin Christendom.

William's accomplishments. In 1085 William, after "deep speech" with his assembled barons, ordered a general survey of the land, manor by manor and vill by vill. Historians have debated the purpose of this "Domesday" survey, some putting more emphasis on its usefulness for tax purposes, some emphasizing its importance as a basis for feudal rights and duties. It was probably, in fact, a multipurpose document with the main emphasis on resources for taxation. It constitutes a unique record for the time and offers rich materials for research.

The Domesday survey

One innovation of the Norman kings that caused deep resentment under William I and even more hatred under William II Rufus was the taking over of vast tracts of land for the king's forests. In some areas, whole villages were destroyed and the people driven out; elsewhere, people living in the forest areas were not necessarily removed, but drastic penalties were imposed for poaching.

William the Conqueror is presented in contemporary chronicles as a ruthless tyrant who rigorously put down rebellion and devastated vast areas, especially in his pacification of the north. He was, however, an able administrator. Perhaps his greatest contribution to England's future was the linking up of England with continental affairs. If the country had been conquered again by the Danes, it might well have remained in a kind of backwater of European development. As it happened, England was linked in economic and cultural development with France and the Mediterranean states, with a common Latin language and a common church organization.

WILLIAM II RUFUS (1087–1100) AND HENRY I (1100–35)

William II. Under William's two sons William II and Henry I strong, centralized government continued in a feudalized society. Under William II, a rebellion of

Norman barons led by the King's two half-uncles, Odo of Bayeux and Robert of Mortain, was put down with the help of the fyrd. The King promised good government, relief from taxation and from the severity of the forest laws in return for this valuable support and won a quick victory. Odo of Bayeux was banished, and William of St. Calais, bishop of Durham, was tried for treason. As an ecclesiastic he refused jurisdiction of the king's court. But Lanfranc pointed out that it was not as bishop but as lord of his temporal fiefs that he was tried. William threatened to take the case to Rome, but the matter was ultimately compromised by the permission given him to leave the the country in return for surrender of his fiefs.

The King forgot his promise and became a notoriously tyrannical ruler. His main preoccupation during his reign was the endeavour to recover Normandy and rejoin it with England. William I had given Normandy to Robert, the eldest and least able of his three sons, Robert, William, and Henry. William II preferred to use peaceful methods if possible.

After brief skirmishes in which he won from Robert the southern part of the duchy, William II joined Robert in warfare against Henry. William's plans were interrupted by a second rebellion of the Norman earls in 1095 but were furthered by Robert's decision to go on Crusade in 1096. Robert mortaged his Norman lands to William for 10,000 marks. William raised the money in England by drastic and unpopular taxation but died before he achieved his ambition. His death was the result of an "accident" in the New Forest in which he was shot through the back with an arrow. Henry, who was conveniently of the hunting party, rode posthaste to Winchester, seized the treasury, and was chosen king the next day.

Henry I. A good politician and a competent administrator, Henry I was the ablest of the Conqueror's sons. At his coronation on August 5, 1100, he issued a charter intended to win the support of the nation. In general this was a propaganda document, but it does show the extent to which feudal institutions had come to stay. Henry promised not to exploit church vacancies as his brother had done. He remitted debts due his brother as well as penalties for killing Normans due at the time of William's death. He promised a return to those practices of his Anglo-Saxon predecessors that had been superseded under his father and brother. He promised return to the laws of Edward the Confessor with only such amendments as had been made with the counsel of the barons in his father's time. The main provisions of the charter guaranteed feudal custom as it had developed in England and Normandy. Reliefs to be paid by feudal vassals to the king when they took over the estates of their fathers were to be "just and legitimate." Henry certainly did not mean this charter to be enforced literally. He did not return to the laws of Edward the Confessor nor did he afterward adhere rigorously to feudal law and custom.

Henry's coronation charter

Henry inherited from William II a quarrel with the church that became part of the Europe-wide Investiture Controversy. After Lanfranc's death, William had delayed appointing a successor, presumably for the privilege of wasting the resources of the province. After four years, during a bout of illness, he appointed Anselm of Bec, one of the greatest scholars of his time (1193). Anselm did homage for his temporalities but, in keeping with the decrees of Pope Gregory VII, refused to receive the symbols of his spiritual office from the King. Papal confirmation was complicated by the fact that there were two popes: Urban II, a reform pope in the tradition of Gregory VII, and Clement III, an antipope nominated by the Holy Roman emperor Henry IV. A church council was held to decide whether Anselm should go to Rome for confirmation. Anselm refused to accept a decision given by the King's supporters, and he finally got his pallium from a cardinal legate sent by Urban. Conflict between King and Archbishop flared up again in 1097 over what William considered to be an inadequate Canterbury contingent for the Welsh war. The upshot of this was that Anselm went into exile until William's death.

Anselm supported Henry I's bid for the throne and returned from exile at Henry's accession in 1100. But he quarrelled almost immediately with Henry over the homage for his temporal estates. After various ineffectual appeals to Rome, Anselm again went into exile. A compromise was finally arranged with the help of Ivo of Chartres in 1107. Although no authoritative text has survived of the terms of this compromise, it appears to have been agreed that the king would surrender investiture with the symbols of spiritual office in return for an agreement that the king should supervise the election and take homage for the temporalities before investiture with the spiritual symbols. The compromise, in fact, changed very little the king's power in ecclesiastical elections.

Henry continued and extended the administrative reforms of his father. He appointed a justiciar to be a kind of deputy king when he himself was occupied in Normandy. In his reign, the writ, or sealed royal letter of command, became the normal method of initiating judicial action. The Exchequer became organized as a department of government dealing with royal revenues and independent of the meetings of the Curia Regis. Justices in eyre (*i.e.*, itinerant justices) began to be sent out into the counties to inquire concerning crown pleas, the king's revenues, and other matters of interest to the king. This was a kind of extension of the procedure of the Domesday inquest, especially in its use of the jury procedure.

Henry's most spectacular success was his conquest of Normandy. His reign opened with a rebellion of Robert, newly returned from the First Crusade. Henry reissued his coronation charter, called out the shire levies to defeat the invading army, and, in two years of war, captured all the important castles in England. By Holy Week 1105, he was ready to take the offensive and began a severe onslaught on the Cotentin, the maritime province of Normandy. In September 1106 he won a decisive battle at Tinchebrai (modern Tinchebray) that gave him control of the whole of Normandy. Robert was captured and spent the remainder of his 80 years in castle dungeons. His son, William Clito, escaped and remained until his death in 1128 a thorn in Henry's flesh. Henry had won the support of the French king Philip I against Robert, but he was not so successful in winning the support of Philip's son and successor, Louis VI. A coalition of rebellious Norman barons with Louis VI, Fulk of Anjou, and the Count of Flanders temporarily kept Henry out of the county of Maine. But by 1120 Henry was everywhere successful both in diplomacy and war. He had arranged a marriage for William, his only legitimate son, to Matilda, daughter of Fulk of Anjou, and had received Fulk's homage for Maine. Pope Calixtus I, his cousin, gave him support for his control of Normandy on condition that his son William do homage to the French king.

Henry's conquest of Normandy

During the last 15 years of his reign, the most important question was the succession. William, Henry's only legitimate son, died in 1120, leaving Henry's daughter Matilda, wife of the Holy Roman emperor Henry V, as heir. When Henry V died in 1125, Matilda returned to England. Henry persuaded his barons to take an oath in her support in 1127 but did not consult them concerning her second marriage to Geoffrey Plantagenet of Anjou.

Geoffrey was 14, the Empress 25, and they took an instant dislike to one another. Geoffrey repudiated her within a year but was persuaded to take her back, just long enough for her to bear him three children. Henry spent his declining years doting on his grandchildren and died, probably of a heart attack, on December 1, 1135.

THE PERIOD OF ANARCHY (1135–54)

Matilda and Stephen. Henry's death precipitated a 20-year crisis. No one was very enthusiastic about accepting Matilda as queen, especially since her husband, Geoffrey, was tied in friendship to Henry's Norman enemies and was actually at war with Henry at the time of his death. Robert, earl of Gloucester, one of Henry's illegitimate sons, was an impressive candidate.

Then there were Henry's two nephews, Thibaut and Stephen of Blois. The matter took an unexpected turn: while Thibaut was receiving the homage of the continental vassals in Normandy, Stephen took ship for England and claimed the kingship. On December 22, having first secured the treasury at Winchester, he was crowned. The Pope confirmed him early in 1136, thus relieving the English barons of their oath to support Matilda.

Stephen's clash with King David

Stephen had shown himself quick in decision and resolute in securing the crown. But, after the first flush of victory, he seems to have expected to win support by concessions. King David of Scotland was an earl in England with respect to the honour of Huntingdon. When he heard the news of Stephen's accession, he crossed the border and took Carlisle and other northern fortresses. Stephen, surprisingly in view of his lack of feudal support, assembled an army consisting mainly of Flemish mercenaries and marched north. David was persuaded to negotiate an agreement under which Stephen surrendered Doncaster and Carlisle. King David's son was to have Huntingdon on the condition of doing homage to Stephen. To the church Stephen granted a charter forbidding simony and granting that all clerics should be tried under canon law.

Stephen's first concern in governing England seems to have been to get his own men into the main posts in central government, replacing Henry I's administrators. He increased the number of earls from seven to 16. These earls were evidently intended to exercise real power and to undermine that of the sheriffs. In the central government, power had become concentrated in the hands of Roger, bishop of Salisbury, and his family. Roger had been justiciar under Henry; his son Roger le Poer was chancellor, his nephew Nigel, bishop of Ely, was treasurer, and his nephew Alexander was bishop of Lincoln. The Beaumont earl of Leicester and his family on both sides of the Channel were jealous of this power and pressed Stephen to end it. The question was how to do so without incurring obloquy for attacking bishops of the church. An incident was planned for the Oxford meeting of the great council of magnates and prelates in June 1139. A street brawl broke out between Alan of Brittany's men and Bishop Roger's men. The King summoned the bishops before him to make satisfaction for the disturbance of the peace. They were to surrender their castles as a sign of their good faith. Nigel of Ely took refuge in Devizes Castle and prepared for a siege until the King appeared and threatened to hang the Chancellor if Nigel refused to surrender.

This whole episode constituted a turning point for Stephen. Henceforth he was in disfavour with the clergy. He had already forfeited the favour of his brother, Henry of Blois, bishop of Winchester, by failing to make him archbishop of Canterbury when the position fell open in 1137. Henry was papal legate throughout the pontificate of Innocent II and was the most influential member of the clergy in the realm.

Civil war. War for the succession in England did not begin until the landing of Matilda at Arundel in 1139, supported by her half-brother Robert of Gloucester. They established themselves in the southwest, seizing various castles. Stephen fought back in desultory fashion, besieging castles, then abandoning siege. He finally sent the Empress to Bristol under escort. The decisive year in the early part of the war was 1141, when Stephen, acting on information from the citizens of Lincoln that the castle there was lightly guarded, attempted to win it back from Ranulf of Chester and William of Roumare, his half-brother, who had seized it by strategy. Unfortunately for Stephen, Ranulf escaped and brought up troops to attack the royal army. Many of the great magnates deserted Stephen in the course of the battle. He was defeated and taken prisoner along with many lesser barons.

Matilda took advantage of the victory by going to Winchester, where, on March 3, 1141, she was received in state and then, on April 8, given the title *domina Anglorum*. Her great mistake, which ultimately turned the tide of war against her, was her treatment of the Londoners. When she demanded their allegiance and a tallage (tax) as well, they flew to arms "like a swarm of bees from a hive" and forced her to leave the city. Meanwhile, Stephen's queen had rallied the King's forces in Kent and moved into London. Stephen was exchanged for Robert of Gloucester, who had been captured at Winchester, and Stephen was again in the ascendant. He was supported by a church council and wore his crown at Westminster for the second time. Matilda's fortunes waned from this event on, although she continued to dominate the southwest. The deaths of Miles, earl of Hereford, in 1143 and of Robert, earl of Gloucester, in 1147 deprived her of two royal and able supporters. A brief and rash invasion on her behalf by her 14-year-old son, Henry, in 1147 did nothing to change the balance of forces. Henry lacked both troops and money. Early in 1148 Matilda left England for Normandy, never to return.

The revolt of London against Matilda

Her son Henry did return in 1153 and carried on a vigorous and successful campaign. This, the sudden death of his elder son, Eustace, and his precarious hold over the magnates persuaded Stephen to a compromise peace at the end of 1153. Stephen was to continue as king so long as he lived and to receive Henry's homage. In turn, Stephen was to recognize Henry as his heir. Certain of Stephen's castles were to be surrendered to castellans who took oath to turn them over to Henry at Stephen's death. The most difficult questions to be settled after the long period of "the Anarchy" were the titles to land of various members of the nobility. The general principle that was accepted was that whoever had held the titles in the time of Henry I had the best right. Clearly what was intended was that the feudal principle of succession should prevail. But this principle was not easy to enforce because so much land had changed hands during the reign of Henry I and after. In the last year of Stephen's reign many of the "adulterine castles" (those castles built during the Anarchy without royal license) were destroyed. They are said to have disappeared in 1154 like "wax before a flame," except for certain castles that Stephen continued to hold, somewhat to the distrust of his recognized heir.

The Anarchy was chiefly important in its effect on government. Henry I had left a tightly governed country in which a royally appointed bureaucracy carried on the functions of central government and supervised local government. Under Stephen this had broken down. And local offices such as that of sheriff and castellan had changed hands frequently with the change in the fortunes of war. On the other hand, it cannot be shown that the Exchequer or the regular administration of justice in the county and hundred courts had broken down. Power seems to have been fragmented and decentralized as in a typically feudal state, but order did not disappear altogether.

III. The early Plantagenets (1154–1216)

HENRY II (1154–89)

Matilda's son Henry Plantagenet, the first and greatest of three Angevin kings of England, succeeded Stephen in 1154. At age 21, he was in the prime of life and already possessed a reputation for restless energy and decisive action. He was heir to a vast feudal empire. As heir to his mother and to Stephen, he held England and Normandy; as heir to his father, he held Anjou (hence Angevin) and Touraine; as heir to his brother Geoffrey he got Brittany; as husband of Eleanor, divorced wife of Louis VII of France, he held Aquitaine, the major part of southern France. Altogether his holdings in France were far larger than those of the French king. From the beginning Henry showed himself determined to assert and maintain his rights in all these lands and to reassert in England the centralized power of his grandfather, Henry I. His success in these aims is the measure of his greatness.

Henry's reforms. After completing the destruction of the adulterine castles, Henry carried through certain changes in the military and in government administration. In 1166 he issued writs commanding his tenants in chief to disclose the number of knights they had subinfeudated on their lands in excess of their quotas of service owed to the king. Henry's intent was to demand the excess either in service or scutage (money payment in lieu of service). In principle, barons did not need feudal military vassals for private warfare because it was forbidden. The evidence is that Henry preferred scutage to service because mercenaries were more efficient than feudal contingents. In the Assize of Arms of 1181, Henry required of every free man that he have and maintain arms appropriate to his rank based on his income from land. This measure was intended to provide the basis for the maintenance of the fyrd, which could be called to repress rebellion or meet invasion. Henry, no more than his Norman predecessors, depended on a feudal army for his wars. He did, however, try to make sure that he could tap all the existing sources of men or money to constitute his army.

The Inquest of Sheriffs

A major administrative reform of his reign was the so-called Inquest of Sheriffs in 1170. Inquiries were instituted into the details of local administration. Many sheriffs were dismissed, especially those in shires in which local barons had become too great in the control of the office. Henry revived the device of his grandfather of sending out itinerant justices to check on local administration and to hold the possessory assizes (see below). Royal writs were used, as in Henry I's time, to begin actions in the royal courts.

Henry greatly expanded royal powers of justice by bringing all land held in feudal tenure under royal jurisdiction. Sometime in his reign or earlier the grand assize was introduced. In order to call a grand assize, the plaintiff went to the chancery and got a writ to the sheriff calling on him to demand the attendance of the possessor of the land that the plaintiff claimed and to call four men who would then choose 12 men to determine the case. An alternative of this writ merely called on the lord of the complainant to do justice to him or appear before the king's officers. Various other actions less formidable in character than the writ of right and the grand assize were available to parties in land disputes at this time. These were the so-called possessory assizes. They determined who had the right to immediate possession of land rather than who had the best fundamental right. The result of these measures was that no freeman could be brought to answer for his freehold save in a royal court. The acceptance of these innovations indicates that feudal land tenure and feudal jurisdiction over land tenure were already on their way out.

Struggle with Becket. Henry attempted also to restore the close relationship between church and state that had existed under the Norman kings. His first move in this direction was the appointment in 1162 of Thomas Becket as archbishop of Canterbury. Becket had served as Henry's chancellor from 1155 and had proved to be an unusually efficient royal servant as well as the King's boon companion. Henry assumed that Thomas, as archbishop, would continue in these roles. Becket disappointed him. As soon as he was appointed archbishop, Becket became a militant defender of the church against royal encroachments and a champion of Pope Gregory VII's program of ecclesiastical supremacy over the lay world. Becket recognized the need for better church discipline but thought that reform should be carried out by the church itself. The struggle between Henry and Becket reached a crisis at the Council of Clarendon in 1164, the main issue proving to be the jurisdiction over "criminous clerks" (members of the clergy who had committed crimes). The King maintained that clergy should be subject to the same penalties as laymen. After accusation in the king's court, they should be turned over to the bishop's officers, tried in ecclesiastical court, and, if found guilty, should be returned to the king's officers to be punished. Other important principles laid down at Clarendon included the following: disputes concerning the right to present to eccesiastical office were to be tried in royal courts; appeals to the papal Curia should be undertaken only with royal premission; disputes as to whether land was of lay fee or free alms should be decided in royal courts. A clause concerning ecclesiastical elections simply reiterated current custom: elections were to be free, but the king was to have the revenues during vacancy.

The Council of Clarendon

Becket accepted this document verbally and led the other bishops to accept it also, but he later refused to seal it. In expiation of his previous consent, he suspended himself from office for the sin of yielding to royal will in the matter. He applied to the Pope for absolution, and Alexander III ultimately came to his support against the Constitutions. Later in the same year, the Archbishop was charged with peculation of royal funds during his chancellorship. Becket appeared briefly at the Council of Northampton but took flight to France when he became convinced that the King intended to destroy him. Henry confiscated the revenues of the province, exiled Becket's friends, and confiscated their revenues. And, most serious of his offenses, Henry had his eldest son crowned in 1170 by the archbishop of York, rather than by the archbishop of Canterbury, as was customary. Becket, in exile, appealed to Rome and excommunicated the clergy who had taken part in the offensive ceremony. A reconciliation between Becket and Henry at the end of the same year settled none of the points at issue. But when Becket returned to England he took further measures against those clergy who had taken part in the coronation. In Normandy the enraged King, hearing the news, burst out with the fateful words that incited four of his knights to take ship for England to murder the Archbishop.

Almost overnight the martyred Thomas became a saint in the eyes of the people. Henry repudiated responsibility for the murder and reconciled himself with the church at the expense of promising to go on a crusade, to allow appeals from English courts to Rome, to restore the possessions of Canterbury, and to renounce practices of his time that were detrimental to the church. He seems to have made no formal withdrawal of the Constitutions of Clarendon. But henceforth criminous clerks were to be tried in ecclesiastical courts except for treason, breach of forest laws, or petty misdemeanours. Disputes between laymen and ecclesiastics over land or over presentation to church offices were to be tried by lay courts. Finally, Henry did penance at Canterbury, allowing the monks to scourge him.

Rebellions of Henry's sons. Henry's sons, urged on by their mother and by a coalition of his enemies, took advantage of Henry's weakness in public opinion as a result of the Becket murder and in 1173 raised a rebellion throughout his domains. The lack of cooperation among the rebels allowed Henry to defeat them one at a time. Eleanor was retired to polite imprisonment for the remainder of Henry's life. The King's sons and his baronial rebels were treated with leniency. There followed a brief period of amity between Henry and Louis of France, and the years between 1175 and 1182 marked the zenith of Henry's prestige and power. In 1183 the younger Henry again tried to organize opposition to his father, but he died in June of that year. Henry spent the last years of his life locked in combat with the new French king, Philip II Augustus, with whom his son Richard had entered into alliance.

RICHARD I (1189–99)

Henry II died in 1189, an embittered old man. He was succeeded by his son Richard I, nicknamed the Lion-Heart. Richard was mainly interested in the crusade to recover Jerusalem and in the struggle to maintain his French holdings against Philip Augustus. During his ten-year reign Richard spent only about six months in England. During his frequent absences he left a committee in charge of the realm. Inevitably one or another of the group became dominant. Chancellor William Longchamp, bishop of Ely, dominated the early part of the reign until 1191, when a rebellion of the barons forced him into exile. Walter of Coutances, archbishop of Rouen, succeeded Longchamp and took the title of justiciar. But the most important and able of Richard's ministers was Hubert Walter, archbishop of Canterbury, justiciar from 1193 to 1198, and also chancellor from 1199 to 1205. These strong ministers kept government without the King from being catastrophic. A revolt led by Richard's brother John was put down with severe measures in 1193 by Hubert Walter and Eleanor, the King's mother. An oath of allegiance was required of all freemen and the royal castles were strengthened. The fyrd was called

Richard's ministers

out, and John's supporters were outlawed or excommunicated. But when Richard returned from abroad, he forgave John and promised him the succession.

Richard was responsible for some innovations in taxation and for an attempt at military reorganization. At the beginning of his reign, a tax levied by Henry II to support his proposed crusade had to be collected. This so-called Saladin Tithe was levied on personal property rather than real estate and was collected from both clergy and laity and on spiritual as well as temporal revenues. On his return from the crusade Richard was captured by Leopold of Austria and held for a high ransom. According to the chroniclers, the 150,000 marks demanded was five times the King's annual revenue, and its collection created a financial crisis. Traditional feudal revenues were insufficient. Heavy taxes levied on towns and on demesne serfs caused protests against its incidence on the poor of London. A general levy of one-quarter of all revenue on land in 1194 was more successful. And in 1198 a carucage, or a levy on all plowlands, was tried. The ransom, though never paid in full, caused Richard's government to become highly unpopular.

Richard's capture and ransom

Richard also aroused opposition by attempting to put an army on permanent standing. He found it increasingly difficult to maintain an army consisting of feudal contingents and foreign mercenaries. Daily wages for a knight had risen from eightpence a day in Henry II's time to one shilling, and other costs rose correspondingly. The English baronage began to resist the demand that they serve abroad. In order to deal with these problems, Richard tried to set up a standing army of 300 knights who were expected to serve a whole year. This was to be accomplished by asking each holder of a knight's fee to contribute enough to pay for such an army. The barons, led by the bishops of Lincoln and Salisbury, opposed Richard's scheme, preventing the most serious threat yet conceived against the feudal organization of society.

KING JOHN (1199–1216)

Richard, killed during a seige operation in France in 1199, was succeeded by his brother John, one of the most unpopular and unfortunate of English kings. John bears the main responsibility for his misfortunes, but it is only fair to recognize that he inherited some resentments built up against his brother and father. Henry had encroached on feudal jurisdictions, and Richard had drained England of money for his crusade, his ransom, and his war in France. John inherited also claims to the large and heterogeneous Angevin empire. In England and Normandy, he was recognized as heir to Richard. Brittany, Anjou, Maine, and Touraine recognized Arthur, son of John's brother Geoffrey, as heir. Arthur's mother, Constance of Brittany, saw to it that her 12-year-old son went to do his homage to his suzerain, Philip II. John's mother, Eleanor, held Aquitaine as dowager duchess, but the province would devolve upon John at her death.

Loss of French possessions. John had nothing like the military ability or reputation of his brother, although he could sometimes win a battle in a fit of energy, only to lose his advantage in a spell of indolence. Richard's ally, the Count of Flanders, decided that John was a bad risk. John alienated some of his vassals in Aquitaine by repudiating his first wife, Isabella of Gloucester, and then carrying off the fiancée of Hugh de Lusignan, one of his vassals in Poitou. For this offense he was summoned to answer to Philip II, John's feudal overlord for his holdings in France. He refused to attend. For the disobedience his lands in France were declared forfeit. John, in a brilliant spurt of energy, marched 80 miles (130 kilometres) in 48 hours, captured young Arthur near Poitiers along with 200 Poitevins, and retired to Rouen. There, if contemporaries can be believed, he murdered Arthur in anger during a bout of drunkenness. John failed to follow up his advantage, and he let a strategic castle, the Château Gaillard, fall to the enemy in March 1204. By 1206 all that was left of the inheritance of the Norman kings was the Channel Islands.

Struggle with the papacy. John returned to England and, unlike any king since the Conquest, devoted his undivided attention to the realm for the next few years. Immediately he became involved in a conflict with Pope Innocent III over the choice of an archbishop. At Hubert Walter's death in 1205, the monks of Canterbury had resorted to a secret election in the night in order to avoid participation of the clergy of the province and the interference of the King's officers. They elected the subprior and sent him to Rome to receive the pallium from the Pope. The secret got out, and John went angrily to Canterbury to force the monks to elect John de Gray, bishop of Norwich and one of John's close confidants. He, too, was sent to Rome. Pope Innocent III could not be expected to miss so good an opportunity to demonstrate the plenitude of papal power. He quashed both elections and persuaded a delegation of Canterbury monks sent by his command to Rome to elect the learned and talented Stephen Langton, an English cardinal. John refused to receive Stephen, who retired to Pontigny, where Archbishop Thomas before him had taken refuge. John seized the revenues of Canterbury. He had already quarrelled with his half brother Geoffrey, archbishop of York, over Geoffrey's leadership in 1207 of resistance to a tax on movables. Geoffrey fled to the Continent, where he died in 1212. England was without either archbishop. In March 1208 Innocent placed England under an interdict, or ban forbidding the administration of the sacraments and certain religious rites. All but five of the 16 bishops either died or fled to the Continent. In November 1209 Innocent excommunicated John. In response, the bishops of Bath, Salisbury, and Rochester left their posts. Peter des Roches of Winchester and John de Gray of Norwich remained the sole support of John's power in the church, and John made the most of the opportunity to gather in the revenues of the vacant ecclesiastical sees.

John's excommunication

John's excommunication freed his vassals from their oaths of fealty to him. Strangely, however, there was no immediate revolt. Indeed, the interdict seems to have had some popular support, perhaps because the King, by taking over ecclesiastical property, temporarily relieved the laity of burdensome taxes. John was able to conduct highly successful expeditions to Scotland, Wales, and Ireland in the period. It was not until 1212, when John's plans for the reconquest of his former French possessions began to reach the boiling point, that rebellion flared up. Ever since the loss of Normandy, John had been busy building up a coalition of German rulers to assist him against the French king. His chief ally was Otto of Saxony, claimant to the German throne, who became the Holy Roman emperor Otto IV. Meanwhile, John issued writs to the leading towns of England, demanding contingents for war on the Continent, and he ordered an inquest of fees under which each of his tenants in chief was required to report the service due from his fiefs.

At this point the Welsh raised a revolt with the support of Philip of France, and John's troops had to be diverted to Wales. But before he could take punitive measures against the Welsh, a plan of the barons to depose him was rumoured, and Robert Fitzwalter and Eustace de Vesci fled the country to the King's enemies. John's brilliant solution of the problem of multiple threats was to effect a reconciliation with the papacy. He agreed to receive Stephen Langton as archbishop, to reinstate the clergy in exile, and to compensate the church for his depredations on revenues. In addition, without papal prompting, John resigned his kingdoms in England and Ireland and received them back as fiefs from the Pope in return for an annual contribution of 1,000 marks. He now had an able ally against his adversaries at no great cost in terms of concessions on his own part.

John now made a second attempt to set out for Poitou. This time it was the northern barons who revolted and prevented him from going. John was furious and marched north to the attack. Only Stephen Langton's persuasion finally effected a reconciliation and made possible the Poitou venture. The campaign in Poitou failed when John's painfully assembled allies were decisively defeated at Bouvines on July 27, 1214. John was forced to withdraw from France and to return home to face his disgruntled barons.

Revolt of the barons and Magna Carta. Even so, rebellion developed slowly. Stephen Langton is alleged to have read to the barons a copy of Henry I's coronation charter as early as August 14, 1214, presumably to stir them to action. It was not until the spring of the following year that the opposition to John took shape, and the so-called Unknown Charter was drawn up. It was based on Henry I's charter but reflected more recent grievances. Resistance to the King came chiefly from the northern barons who had rebelled against service in Poitou, but by the spring of 1215 many others had joined to support the protest against the scutage for Poitou and John's abuse or disregard of feudal law and custom.

On June 15, 1215, the rebellious barons met John at Runnymede on the Thames near Windsor (modern New Windsor), and, on the basis of the Articles of the Barons presented to the King, Magna Carta was drawn up. For a document hallowed in history during more than 750 years and frequently cited as a forerunner of the Declaration of Independence and the Declaration of the Rights of Man and of the Citizen, Magna Carta is a singularly undramatic document. It is thorny with problems of a feudal age that are largely untranslatable into modern idiom. Read in its historical context, the charter was a guarantee against the sort of arbitrary disregard of feudal right that the three Angevin kings had made familiar. The main importance of Magna Carta derives first from the fact that it was agreed upon between the King's party and the baronial party and therefore has the character of a contract, and second that, even though John was released by the Pope from his obligations under it, the charter was reissued under John's son and so became a part of the permanent law of the land. The King's repudiation and the barons' reluctance to fulfill their part of the agreement of June 1215 led to renewal of civil war. The barons announced their *diffidatio* and chose Louis, son of Philip Augustus, as their king. But John's death in October of 1216 brought an end to the civil war.

IV. The 13th century

The 13th century was an important formative period in the history of England. It was during that century that the concept of the community of the realm developed in sufficient strength to provide the foundation for parliamentary government. Something like the phrase had first been used formally in clause 61 of Magna Carta. The barons, in devising a method of enforcement for the provisions of the charter, had provided that if grievances occurred they should be carried to a committee of four barons among 25 who were to enforce the charter, and that if the king or his justiciar, on being duly advised of the problem, did not provide a remedy, the 25 chosen barons "with the commune of all the land" were to distrain and distress the king in every possible way until he should offer remedy.

The notion of the community of the realm

The notion that the realm was a community and that it was governed by representatives of that community perhaps got its start in the period following Magna Carta in which a council of regency ruled on behalf of a child-king not yet able to govern in his own right. The phrase community of the realm used to mean just the totality of the baronage. Yet the representative idea had made some headway. In a writ of 1237 for the collection of a tax earlier granted to the King, the earls, barons, knights, and freemen are said to have acted "for themselves and their villeins." But it is in the conflict that broke out between the King and a party among the barons in the latter part of the reign that all these terms acquire some sophistication.

HENRY III (1216–72)

Early reign. The issue on which conflict centred in Henry III's reign was whether the King should be allowed to choose his own counsellors or whether he was bound to consult his barons. The King himself pointed out that the barons denied him the right of free choice of his servants that they exercised in conducting their own affairs. Men of the 13th century realized that the kingship was different from any other feudal lordship, but it was not clear to contemporaries in what precise way it differed.

So long as Henry was under tutelage the question did not become a critical one. Henry declared himself of age in 1227, but he did not immediately take control. After the death of the regent, William Marshal, in 1219, Hubert de Burgh, the justiciar, dominated the group of officers surrounding the King. Hubert was the King's chief minister until two others among Henry's close advisers engineered his fall. A subsequent revolt of the barons led by Richard, son of William Marshal, ended in tragedy. Richard was killed in Ireland, and Henry found that he had unknowingly signed an authorization for the killing. In 1236 Henry married Eleanor of Provence and introduced her relatives as a new element in English politics.

Simon de Montfort and the Barons' War. In all the crises of his younger years, Henry showed himself to be naïve; on the one hand he was overtrustful, and on the other bitter against those who betrayed his trust. The main crisis of his reign came in 1258, when he asked for taxes to pay the 135,000 marks he had promised the Pope as the price of making his second son king of Sicily. Henry had already made himself unpopular by asking for taxes to pay the costs of expeditions to Gascony in which he showed his incompetence as a military leader and failed to gain either vassals or prestige on the Continent.

The crisis began in May 1258, when the King was persuaded to agree to the meeting of a "parliament" and to the appointment of a joint committee of the dissident barons and of his own supporters. Twelve were to be elected by each side and were to recommend the necessary measures for the reform of the kingdom. Simon de Montfort, the King's brother-in-law, was the able but fanatical leader of the opposition party.

The Provisions of Oxford

The Provisions of Oxford, which the 24 drew up by mid-June, would have made the king a constitutional monarch if they had been permanently effective. The 24 were to choose four: two on the king's side, two on the barons' side. These four were to choose a 15-member council that would supervise the king's government. There were to be three "parliaments" a year—at Michelmas, Candlemas, and the first of June—to which were to come the 15 of the king's council and 12 to be elected by the "community" (*le commun* in the original French). The community was to accept as established what the 12 should do. The office of justiciar was to be revived, and this officer was to account at the end of his term of office before the council. The treasurer and the chancellor were likewise to account before the council, and the chancellor was to seal nothing merely by the king's will but was to act by advice of the council. The households of the king and queen were to be reformed. Sheriffs were to be knights of the shire and to hold office for one year only.

The Provisions of Oxford led to two years in which the King was again under tutelage, less even than a *primus inter pares* because he was not free to choose his own councillors. A Welsh truce was arranged against the opposition of the King's party. The King's men were dismissed from their positions as castellans and banished from the country. Discussions of aid broke down because the Sicilian project fell through and the King no longer needed the money. Peace with France had been arranged in November 1258 so that Henry was free of financial necessity for war in France. In October 1259 the *communitas bacheleriae* (a group of lesser vassals of the barons) petitioned for fulfillment of the promises of the magnates and King to remedy their grievances. The results were embodied in the Provisions of Westminster, mainly reforms of the common law in the interest of the knights bachelors of England—that is, the tenants of the magnates who had imposed the Provisions of Oxford on the King.

Breakdown of the Oxford settlement

The Oxford settlement began to break down in 1260. Henry became suspicious that his eldest son, Edward, had come to some agreement with the rebels. A reconciliation was arranged, and Edward, aged 21, went off to the Continent on a jousting expedition intending eventually to settle down to deal with the problems of governing Gascony. Odo Rigaud, archbishop of Rouen, arrived in the summer of 1260 intent on reconciling Simon de Montfort and the King, and peace was temporarily restored. Then in April 1261 the Pope sent a bull absolving Henry from his oath to support the Oxford Provisions. The King, encouraged by this release, dismissed the baronial sheriffs, castellans, and other officers imposed on him by his council. Simon de Montfort returned from abroad and again raised rebellion against the King. In January 1264 Henry appealed to Louis IX of France, his fellow sovereign and his overlord with respect to his French holdings, to decide the case between him and his barons. In the Mise of Amiens, Louis released Henry from his commitments, insisting on Henry's right to appoint his own ministers. Louis incorporated a saving clause in favour of "charters, liberties, establishments, and praiseworthy customs . . . existing before the time of such provisions."

Inevitably war broke out, in April 1264. In the first phase of the war, Simon and his supporters were successful. Near Lewes, in May, Simon captured the King, the King's son Edward, and the entire leadership of the royal party. Henry was forced to agree to govern by the Charters and Provisions of Oxford, and in the King's name a "parliament" was called for June in which four knights from each shire were to assist in setting up a new form of government to control the King. Simon governed in the King's name, though still considering himself to be the King's loyal subject. Early in 1265 he called a second parliament, this time to include representative burgesses of the boroughs as well as knights of the shire. Simon's motivation was undoubtedly political, to win support from elements in the community of the realm below the baronage, especially the moneyed class in the towns. Peace negotiations with the royal party failed, despite the efforts of the papal legates, Gui and Ottobuono. But in May, young Edward escaped by collusion with his captors, and the war became Edward's war. He rallied the royal forces, particularly the Marcher earls, whom Simon had allowed to go free after Lewes, and in August he defeated Simon by turning against him his own tactics. Simon himself was killed.

Later reign. The rest of Henry's reign was spent in settling the problems created by the rebellion. Simon's supporters were deprived of their lands, and as "the Disinherited" they fought back from redoubts in forest or fens. The original of the Robin Hood legends may have been one of them. The Statute of Marlborough (1267) was the final document of the reign. It was a confirmation, restatement, and implementation of the Provisions of Westminster and of the peace terms ending the war. With it went a confirmation of the charters. The parliament that adopted it included representatives of the lower classes as well as the barons. It granted a subsidy for the crusade, and "Lord Edward" went off to war against the Muslims, not to return until two years after his father's death.

"The Disinherited"

EDWARD I (1272–1307)

Lord Edward, who became King Edward I in 1272, was in many ways the ideal medieval king. He had learned early in life, in the conflict with Earl Simon de Montfort and his followers, how to command an army and something about strategy and tactics. He was a good fighter, according to one contemporary "the best lance in the world." He had learned from his father's experience something about the mistakes a medieval king must avoid. He enjoyed both war and statecraft. He looked on kingship as good management of the king's possessions and prerogatives.

Statute law. In his reign, statute law began to take shape as a kind of supplement to the common law. Statutes remedied deficiencies in the "law and custom of the realm" either in protection of the king's rights or in remedy of grievances of his subjects. To protect his own rights, for example, there were the *quo warranto* proceedings under the Statute of Gloucester of 1278 and the Statute of Quo Warranto of 1290. Under these statutes, the king's subjects were asked by what warrant they claimed possession of royal franchises. Edward's object was not so much to recover such franchises as to discover which of them were held legitimately. It was found that over half the hundred courts were in private hands. By the Statute of Mortmain of 1279, it was provided that no more land might be given into the hands of the church without royal license. The Statute of Quia Emptores of 1290 had the effect of forbidding further subinfeudation of land. Two great statutes of Westminster, one of 1275 and one a decade later, remedied deficiencies in the common law and provided improvements in legal procedures on behalf of the king's subjects.

Edward also established an alliance between the king and the merchant class. He offered the merchants his protection in return for a grant of export duties on wool, wool-fells, and hides, payable at London and 12 other ports to royal customs officials. The tax brought in a good income—an average of £8,800 in a good year. In return for this new source of income, Edward granted royal favour to the merchants. The Statute of Acton Burnell (the name of a castle of Edward's chancellor, Robert Burnell) facilitated the collection of merchants' debts by establishing debtors' prisons. Finally, in 1303, Edward negotiated with the foreign merchants the so-called *Carta Mercatoria*, whereby he granted them freedom of trade in England in return for additional customs revenues. Despite this assured income from trade, Edward, in the critical period of the 1290s, seized the whole output of wool to support his wars in Wales or in France.

Edward's encouragement of merchants

The growth of Parliament. Edward also fostered the concept of the *communitas regni* and the practice of calling representative knights of the shire and burgesses of the borough. Of the 45 parliaments called during Edward's reign, knights and burgesses attended 17 of them. In 1295 Edward called the gathering that older historians have called the "Model Parliament," because it contained all the elements later associated with the word parliament and because the writs to the sheriffs to call knights and burgesses expressed the representative principle very clearly. They were to be summoned

The "Model Parliament"

> so that the said knights shall then and there have full and sufficient authority on behalf of themselves and the community of the county aforesaid, and the said citizens and burgesses on behalf of themselves and the respective communities of the cities and boroughs aforesaid, to do whatever in the aforesaid matters may be ordained by common counsel; and so that through default of such authority, the aforesaid business shall by no means remain unfinished.

So this parliament to Edward was representative of local communities and of the whole community of the realm.

Edward's wars. Edward aimed to be as successful in war as he was in peace, but only in relation to Wales did he succeed fully. There Llewelyn ap Gruffydd, prince of Snowdonia, had taken advantage of the Barons' War against Henry III to try to make himself ruler of all Wales. In 1277 Edward conducted a short and methodical war against Llewelyn. Using a fleet from the Cinque Ports and a paid army combined with feudal contingents from the Marcher lords, Edward won a quick victory and exacted from Llewelyn the Treaty of Conway, whereby Llewelyn agreed to take an oath of fealty, pay homage for his lands, surrender to Edward certain northern districts of Wales, hold all his other lands subject to Edward's justice, and pay a large indemnity.

David, the younger brother of Llewelyn, was responsible for the breach of the Treaty of Conway. He waged war against Edward and was joined by Llewelyn in 1282. David was captured and executed as a traitor; Llewelyn was killed in battle. The army with which Edward won his victory was a paid army rather than a feudal levy. In the peace following, North Wales was organized into counties and the whole realm was to become the appanage of Edward's son, Edward of Caernarvon, who was given the title Prince of Wales—a title borne ever since by the heir to the English throne. Edward built four great castles (Conway, Caernarvon, Criccieth, and Harlech) at strategic points in North Wales; founded merchant settlements that he colonized with English craftsmen and merchants; and revised Welsh law to bring it into conformity with the English common law. Archbishop Pecham reorganized the Welsh church and brought it more fully under the sway of Canterbury. A final revolt in 1294–95 was quickly quelled, and Wales became the *communitas Walliae*, which granted its share of subsidies in support of the king.

Edward also tried to bring Ireland into closer relationship to England and to enforce some sort of peace and order there. The outcome was the establishment of the English Pale, an area in which English law, customs, and speech were enforced, and the establishment of an Irish Parliament on the model of the English Parliament, which met in 1297 to consider Edward's demands for troops for war in France.

Attempts to secure Scotland

Edward's efforts to bring Scotland under English suzerainty met with only temporary success. Alexander III (1249–86) had married Margaret, Edward's sister. During his reign, peaceful relations prevailed, and parliaments, or assemblies of prelates and magnates, met to consider the problems of the king and the kingdom. A crisis developed only when Alexander rode off a cliff in a wild storm in 1286, leaving as his only immediate heir his three-year-old granddaughter, Margaret, the "Maid of Norway." A regency council was set up and ruled the realm until 1290, when Margaret was brought from Norway to become queen. Edward had negotiated a marriage for her with his son Edward, and all seemed auspicious for a friendly and close relation between the two kingdoms. These plans were defeated by Margaret's death in September 1290. The whole question was thrown open to challenge and conflict. Edward claimed and received the right of arbitration. There were three main candidates, all descendants of David, earl of Huntingdon, the brother of William the Lion, king of Scotland from 1165 to 1214. John de Balliol was the grandson of David's eldest daughter; Robert de Bruce was the son of David's second daughter; and John de Hastings was the grandson of David's youngest daughter. A commission consisting of one-half chosen by Bruce and one-half by Balliol designated Balliol as king. Balliol took an oath of fealty and did homage to Edward and was accepted in Scotland.

This settlement by no means ended the problem of Scotland. In 1294 the Scottish lords' committee set up a system of restraints on the king modelled on the Provisions of Oxford. In 1295 a treaty was negotiated with France that provided for the marriage of John de Balliol's son Edward to the French king's niece. The king of England then demanded the surrender of three border castles and, on John's refusal, summoned him to his court. John did not appear and war became inevitable. Edward conquered the country in five months in 1296–97. But he appointed inept agents to enforce peace in Scotland. Revolt broke out again when William Wallace, a free tenant of the Scottish king's steward, slew an English official. Wallace was eventally captured and executed. Meanwhile, Robert Bruce, grandson of the original claimant to the throne, had taken over the leadership of the rebel party. War continued into the new reign when Edward II succeeded his father in 1307.

French campaign

In his war against Philip the Fair of France, Edward I encountered opposition both in raising men and money and he achieved little success. In the last years of the reign, a peace with France was negotiated based on a double marriage agreement: Edward himself was to marry Philip's sister Margaret, and the Prince of Wales was to marry Philip's daughter Isabella. This peace freed Edward for a stronger effort against Scotland. He died on campaign in the North.

V. The 14th century

The 14th century in English history is a difficult century to characterize. At the beginning and end of the century two kings' reigns ended in tragic failure. In between there was the 50-year reign of Edward III, the most popular with his contemporaries of England's medieval kings. Certain general themes are clear. There was continuous development during the century of the importance of the Commons in Parliament. War between England and France continued intermittently throughout the century, and that part of it from 1337 on is called the Hundred Years' War. The Black Death struck in 1348–49, remained endemic, and recurred several times during the latter part of the century, bringing with it profound economic and social change.

EDWARD II (1307–27)

Edward II's reign was an almost unmitigated disaster. He inherited some of his problems from his father. The most important were a treasury deficit of £60,000 and the Scottish war. He inherited none of his father's strengths and seems to have developed his own weaknesses in rebellion against his father. Surrounded with a ruling class strongly tied to his family by blood and service, he rejected the company of his peers, seeking that of the lower orders of society. He enjoyed swimming, ditch digging, thatching, theatricals, but not swordplay or tournaments. His "dear friend" Piers Gaveston, the son of a Gascon knight, was a man of simple birth and no claim to breeding. Edward's father had exiled Gaveston in an attempt to quash the friendship. Edward, the son, recalled him and conferred on him the highest honours he had to bestow; that is, the earldom of Cornwall and marriage with Margaret de Clare, sister of the Earl of Gloucester. Edward also recalled Archbishop Winchelsey and Bishop Bek of Durham, whom his father had banished. He dismissed one of his father's most trusted servants, Walter Langton, the treasurer.

Edward's ministers

Edward II failed as king, but his reign is important for a new attempt of the barons to set up a system of checks on the king's exercise of power similar to the system set up to control his grandfather. At the beginning of the reign, in the coronation oath—which he took in French rather than Latin—he was asked, in addition to the promises extracted from his ancestors, to promise to keep such laws "as the community of your realm shall have chosen."

From the beginning of the reign the hostility of the barons toward Edward was strong. The barons came armed to the 1308 Parliament and warned the king that "homage and the oath of allegiance are stronger and bind more by reason of the crown than by reason of the person of the king" and that "if the king by chance be not guided by reason, in relation to the estate of the crown, his liege subjects are bound by the oath made to the crown to guide the king back to reason and amend the estate of the crown." To the Parliament of 1310 they again came armed and forced the king to allow the election of 21 lords ordainers, "prelates, earls and barons," to make ordinances for the betterment of the estate of the realm.

The lords ordainers

Apart from a third banishment of Gaveston and the demotion of the Frescobaldi family from control over collection of the wool customs, the main provisions of the ordinances had as their object a reduction of the king's control over his own ministers. A long list of officers, including the chancellor, the treasurer, and the justices of both benches, were to be chosen with the advice and consent of the barons in Parliament. Parliament was to meet twice a year. Consent of the baronage was also required for participation in foreign war and in the appointment of a keeper of the realm in the king's absence. Letters of the king under privy seal were to be null and void if they interfered with justice. The ordinances, like the earlier Provisions of Oxford, if they had been fully enforced, would have created a constitutional monarchy.

The middle years of Edward's reign were a period of uneasy truce between King and barons. Thomas of Lancaster, leader of the opposition, had supervised the capture and execution of Piers Gaveston in 1312. He maintained a kind of surly enforcement of the ordinances. In 1314 the King went off to Scotland with an army raised by county muster and therefore not dependent on the barons for consent. In the Battle of Bannockburn, the Scots were victorious with an army consisting of pikemen and bowmen, giving the English a lesson they did not forget in the French war. The Scottish war continued in somewhat desultory fashion until 1323, when a truce was arranged. In 1315–17 there were torrential rains that destroyed the crops. In the ensuing famine, the government could think of no better remedy than trying to enforce maximum prices of wheat without any apparatus for enforcement.

In 1321 conflict again erupted between King and the opposition barons. The King's ablest ministers, Hugh Despenser, father and son, were banished in 1321 by act of Parliament. Civil war ensued in which the King was victorious. He got his revenge against Thomas of Lancaster by executing him after a pretended trial. Popular sympathy was with Lancaster, who was spontaneously canonized, though he had been anything but saintly in his life. In 1322 at York, Parliament repealed the ordinances and got from the king a promise

The Statute of York

> that matters which are to be determined with regard to the estate of our lord the king and of his heirs or with regard to the estate of the kingdom and of the people shall be considered, granted, and established in parliament by our lord the king with the consent of the prelates, earls, and barons, and of the community of the kingdom, as has been accustomed in times past.

The meaning of this Statute of York has been much debated by historians, the main problem being whether to give to the term parliament its later meaning of lords and representatives of the community of the realm, or to give it the narrower meaning of earlier times. However it is interpreted, there was clearly some notion of limiting the king's powers.

The final period of the reign was one in which the Despensers, restored to power, carried out various administrative reforms, ably assisted by Walter Stapledon, the treasurer. The reign ended with a renewal of conflict. Isabella, the king's French wife, with the assistance of Roger Mortimer, earl of March, landed in England with a force of only 700 men and, with popular support, especially in London, overthrew the government. The Despensers were tried and hanged, and the King was imprisoned. Parliament was called in his name, Edward II was charged with breaking his coronation oath and was persuaded to abdicate in favour of his son, Edward III. After two conspiracies to release him, the King was killed and his body was exhibited publicly to avoid further attempts on his behalf.

Edward's deposition

EDWARD III (1327–77)

Outbreak of the Hundred Years' War. Edward III's long reign was relatively uneventful in terms of political and constitutional crises. He was crowned at 14 and overthrew his mother's and Mortimer's dominance when he was 17. Mortimer was tried and condemned by the Lords in Parliament. Edward's mother was retired to her estates; she later repented her sins and died a sister of the Poor Clares. Her son began his fortunate military career by winning the Battle of Halidon Hill against the Scots (1333). From then until 1337, it was just a matter of time until Edward took up war against his French overlord, Philip IV, beginning over a century of Anglo-French warfare known as the Hundred Years' War. The causes of the war were several. Friction over allegiances in Gascony had been chronic since 1294. Both sides had built *bastides*, or new fortified towns, to try to keep one another at bay. English and French seamen had long engaged in acts of piracy along the coasts. The Count of Flanders was a vassal of the French king, but the livelihood of his state depended on wool from England, as the livelihood of England did on selling the wool in Flanders. The rulership of Brittany was in dispute, and both the English and French kings had their candidates. Finally, there was the matter of the French throne itself. Edward, through his mother, was closer in blood to the last of the Capetians than was Philip of Valois. Edward did not present his claim to the French throne in dead seriousness, but he used to the full its propaganda value. The French complained that he had not done liege homage to Philip for his possessions in Gascony in accordance with the agreement of Saint-Germain-en-Laye (1331). War began in somewhat desultory fashion in 1337 (see also HUNDRED YEARS' WAR).

Edward's claim to the French throne

Domestic achievements. In the domestic history of Edward III's reign there is little of interest except for a crisis in 1341–43 over the King's finances in the conduct of the war and a critical period at the end of the reign, when Edward was in his dotage. Edward received generous grants for the war in the years from 1336 to 1340, but he found himself short in 1340 because of his grants and promises of grants to his allies. He seized the wool exports and had recourse to reckless borrowing from Italian merchants in anticipation of future parliamentary grants. In 1341 he returned from France and charged John Stratford, archbishop of Canterbury, with working against him and delaying the grant and collection of subsidies. In the Parliament of April–May 1341, various statutes were passed that were reminiscent of the kind of restraints put on earlier and less popular kings. Officers of state and the king's household were to be appointed and sworn in Parliament. Commissioners were to be sworn in Parliament to audit the king's accounts. Peers of the realm were to be arraigned and tried only before their peers in Parliament. Breaches of the charters were to be reported in Parliament and tried there. Stratford was summoned before a committee of two bishops and four earls who were to hear the charges against him, but the charges were dropped, and in 1343 the record of the case was annulled. Also in 1343, the King repudiated the statutes. Only the Commons protested, and they did not persist. The chief lesson of the crisis was that it illustrated the king's dependence on Parliament and, particularly the Commons, for supply.

Later legislation

The later legislation of Edward III's reign had to do with matters that had for some time needed remedy or were related to the social and economic crisis that followed in the wake of the Black Death. The Statute of Treasons (1352) had as its object the clear definition of great treason, that is, treason against the king involving forfeiture of land and goods, as against petty treason against a lesser lord, in which case forfeiture to the crown was not involved. The Statute of Provisors gave statutory authority to measures already in use to prevent papal provisors from usurping the right of Englishmen to present to church offices in England. The Statute of Praemunire (1353) introduced better procedures for checking appeals to the papal courts in cases involving rights of Englishmen to present candidates to church offices. These acts were accepted by the King only with reservations on his side about enforcement. Many of his ministers and clerks were clerics, and it was often to his advantage to negotiate with the pope concerning appointments. The Statute of Labourers (1351) attempted to fix wages during the labour shortage following the devastation of the Black Death. In 1362 Parliament passed an act to make English rather than French the official language of pleadings in the law courts. This measure failed because of resistance of the lawyers, who complained that they could not state their cases properly in English. In parliamentary rolls and statutes on the other hand, the English language made its way slowly, so that English ultimately became the official language.

The crises of Edward's later reign. The last ten years of Edward III's reign were a time of suppressed crisis. The king was in his dotage and, since the death of his wife, Philippa, in 1369, in the clutches of Alice Perrers, the rather unscrupulous wife of a London citizen. Edward, the Black Prince, heir to the throne, was ill and dying. Lionel, duke of Clarence, the next eldest son, died in 1368, leaving a daughter, Phillippa, as heiress. Her husband, Edmund Mortimer, would not arrive at his majority until 1373. John of Gaunt, the fourth son, was occupied with his claims to Castile, his inheritance from his second wife, Constance of Castile, whom he had married in 1371. Edmund of Langley, the fifth son, earl of Cambridge, later duke of York, was a man of no ability and had nothing to offer toward establishing good and responsible government. Thomas of Woodstock, the King's youngest son, was not yet of age. John of Gaunt was the only real leader among the King's sons, and after 1373 he was under a cloud because of an ineffectual and fruitless campaign in France. A parliament met in 1371 and dismissed William of Wykeham, the chancellor, a notorious curialist and pluralist, and demanded the ap-

The rise of John of Gaunt

pointment of laymen to state offices. This proved to be a not very practical manoeuvre. It mainly illustrates the anticlericalism of the times, a spirit already illustrated by the Statutes of Provisors and Praemunire.

No parliaments were held in 1374 or 1375, and by the time the Good Parliament of 1376 was elected there was an accumulation of grievances to be dealt with. Petitions and protests included a demand for annual parliaments, for the election of sheriffs and knights of the shire by the better people of the county, reform of local government, measures to deal with "rogues, vagabonds, and sturdy beggars," a check to the peculations of royal officers (Gaunt's following especially), reform of the navy, and improvement in the protection of the borders of the realm. As in previous crises, a committee consisting of four bishops, four earls, and four barons was set up to take the responsibility for the reforms. Then, under the leadership of the speaker, Peter de la Mare, steward in the household of the Earl of March, the Commons stumbled onto a new procedure. They impeached Alice Perrers and the royal officers who profited personally from administration of the royal finances. The Commons took the role of prosecutors before the Lords as judges.

The achievement of the Good Parliament was ephemeral. John of Gaunt soon recovered his power in the government. Peter de la Mare was jailed in Nottingham. William of Wykeham was attacked for alleged peculations as chancellor, and Alice Perrers was restored to court. The Parliament of 1377 reversed all the important acts of the Good Parliament. But Richard, son of Edward, the Black Prince, was created prince of Wales, duke of Cornwall, and earl of Chester, allaying suspicions that John of Gaunt aimed at the throne. Richard was asked to make peace between John and the citizens of London. So the reign ended in truce if not peace.

RICHARD II (1377–99)

Richard II's reign was fraught with crises—economic, social, political, and constitutional. Richard was ten years old when his grandfather died, and the first problem that had to be dealt with was the King's minority. A "continual council" was set up to "govern the king and his kingdom." John of Gaunt was still clearly the dominant figure in the royal family, but neither he nor his brothers were included in the council.

The Peasants' Revolt (1381). Immediately the matter of finances for the war in France came up. In the last Parliament of Edward III's reign, a poll tax of fourpence per head had been introduced. It had not been a great success. The 1379 Parliament introduced a graduated tax based on rank in society. This, too, was a failure, and crown jewels had to be sold to meet expenses. In 1380 the tax was set up at one shilling per head with the proviso that the rich should help the poor in paying it. This was obviously an inequitable and impractical tax, and trouble developed rapidly when the government tried to speed up its collection in the spring of 1381. By May the whole of southeast England was on the verge of rebellion. The poll tax was the immediate cause of unrest, but the deeper origins of the so-called Peasants' Revolt of 1381 go back to earlier developments, particularly to the demographic crisis caused by the Black Death in 1348 and 1349.

Imposition of the poll tax

This outbreak of bubonic and pneumonic plague had carried off from one-third to one-half of the population and had been particularly severe among the lower social levels. The result was a labour crisis. Hired labourers, being fewer, asked for higher wages and better food, and peasant tenants, also fewer, asked for better conditions of tenure when they took up land. Some landlords, in trying to come to terms with the new conditions, attempted to reassert labour services where they had been commuted. They ran into strong opposition from the peasants. An Ordinance of Labourers (1349) and a Statute of Labourers (1351) had tried to set maximum wages at the levels of the years before the Black Death, but strict enforcement was impossible. Still the friction and the frustration provided by the acts persisted, and the peasants resented the efforts to prevent them from making the most of their new opportunities. Meanwhile, popular poor preachers were spreading subversive ideas about relations among the ranks of English society. A popular slogan asked:

When Adam delved and Eve span
Who was then the gentleman?

Sharper than the attacks on the gentlemen were the attacks on the clergy. A proposal widely accepted was that all the lands held by the clergy be confiscated and distributed among the peasantry.

Government policies that added coal to the fire were the fostering of the expanding powers of the justices of the peace at the expense of local courts and manorial courts and the attempts at levying the poll tax. Attempts at levying back taxes in Essex and Kent were the immediate signal for revolt. A royal justice on a special commission in Essex was seized and forced to swear not to hold further sessions of his court. The appearance of a tax collector in Kent was the signal for revolt there. Widespread outbreaks occurred in the southeastern part of the country: attacks on landlords and their manor houses and the destruction of documentary evidence of villein status, assaults on royal officers trying to collect taxes, and attacks on lawyers because of their association with the landed classes. Attacks on religious houses were particularly severe, perhaps because they had been the most conservative among the landlords about commuting labour services.

The attack on London

Meanwhile, men of Essex and men of Kent were moving on London to attack the King's evil councillors and to demand from him redress for their grievances. In this curiously spontaneous revolt, the men of Essex and the men of Kent arrived outside London at approximately the same time. By June 11 the men of Essex were assembled outside the northeast gates of the city. The Kentishmen gathered at Blackheath on June 13 and attacked the Marshalsea Prison and Lambeth Palace, both on the south side of the Thames. The rebels were let into London by sympathizers among the citizenry and attacked the Fleetstreet Prison and the town house of John of Gaunt, duke of Lancaster. On June 14 the young King rode out to Mile End to meet the rebels and, in default of sufficient available force to turn them back, promised them charters of liberation from serfdom. Meanwhile, rebels broke into the Tower and killed Sudbury, the chancellor, Hales, the treasurer, and two other ministers of the King. On the next day, Richard met the rebels at Smithfield. The rebel leader Wat Tyler presented the rebels' demands in the presence of the royal party and his own followers drawn up in battle array. During a parley with the King's forces Tyler was attacked and fatally wounded by the Mayor of London and a follower. The young King rode forward to reassure Tyler's men, who had not clearly seen the murder, and asked them to follow him to Clerkenwell. This proved to be the turning point of the rebellion. Having exhausted their supplies and got promises regarding their grievances, the rebels began to make their way home. Disorders in the countryside continued, although retaliatory measures were taken by the government. On June 23 the King and Sir Robert Tresilian began a tour of the eastern counties and trial of the ringleaders. When challenged about his promises at Mile End, the King replied: "Villeins ye are and villeins ye shall remain." Special commissions continued to act until August 30, when the King ordered all further arrest and executions to cease. In November a Parliament confirmed the King's revocation of charters but demanded amnesty except for a few special offenders.

The results of the uprising, though not spectacular, were important. The government never again attempted to collect a poll tax. The landlord class learned to fear the peasants. The London uprising would probably not have succeeded to the extent that it did if it had not been for the support of London citizens, but the march on London was bound to fail in the end because the peasants had no practical program to present to the King, in whom they placed their entire trust for the improvement of their condition. Richard seems to have derived a rather exalted idea of his own powers and prerogatives from the appeal to him and his success in meeting the peasants at Smithfield. But the very real improvement in the position of the peasants—the abandonment of labour services and the leasing out of the demesne lands to them—seems to have occurred not so much as a consequence of the revolt as of changes in the economy that would have occurred anyhow.

John Wycliffe. Religious unrest was another subversive factor in the reign of Richard II. John Wycliffe, a priest and an Oxford scholar, began his career as a religious reformer with two treatises on divine and civil *dominium* in 1375–76. According to him, *dominium*, that is, the power of possession and of government, was a gift of God to those who were in his grace, that is, those who served him faithfully. He conceived *dominium* in feudal terms as power and possession granted in return for service, not in the hierarchical terms of contemporary feudalism. *Dominium* was exercised not mediately through kings or popes but immediately by anyone who was in God's grace. Everyone standing in God's grace has all the gifts of God. And, contrariwise, no one who is not in the grace of God has any sort of *dominium*. Priests, therefore, have no power to administer the sacraments unless they are in a state of grace. The pope himself has no power except through grace.

This doctrine brought Wycliffe into direct conflict with the church hierarchy. In the next years he was twice summoned before an assembly of bishops, first at St. Paul's (February 1377), then at Lambeth (March 1378). Both times, the trial was effectively interrupted by an outbreak of hostility between the London citizens and the retinue of John of Gaunt, Wycliffe's patron and protector. The beginnings of the Great Schism in 1378 gave Wycliffe further opportunities for attack on the papacy. And in 1379, in a treatise on the Eucharist, he espoused heresy. Christ, he said, was present in the bread and wine, not literally as the result of a miracle performed by the priest, but spiritually as the result of the faith of the believer. The miracle is God's miracle, not that of some sinful priest.

Wycliffe's denial of transubstantiation

Wycliffe was tried twice again and, after the second trial, was banished from Oxford. He retired to his parish at Lutterworth, in Leicestershire, which became the centre of the so-called Lollard movement. Two of Wycliffe's followers translated the Bible into English and others went out as missionaries in London and Leicestershire and in the West Country. Wycliffe died in 1384, but the movement continued to expand despite the loss of the founder and despite the government's attempts to destroy it.

Political struggles and Richard's deposition. Richard's reign is of great interest from the political and constitutional point of view as well as for economic and social developments. Soon after his success in putting down the peasant rebels, the King began to build up a court party. He used the signet for warranty of royal actions as against the Privy Seal and the Great Seal. He got control of the treasurership, the keepership of the Privy Seal, the subchamberlainship, the chamberlainship, and, eventually, the chancellorship itself. There was ground for thinking that these measures were in part directed against the King's uncle, John of Gaunt. But even the Londoners who hated Gaunt withdrew their support from Richard when he appointed the young and inexperienced Robert de Vere, earl of Oxford, as lieutenant of Ireland. A crisis was precipitated in 1386, when Parliament was asked for a subsidy to finance an expedition to France. Parliament demanded dismissal of the King's favourites, and the King withdrew to Eltham. Richard defied Parliament, threatened to enlist the King of France in his cause, and said that he would not dismiss so much as a scullion in his kitchen at the request of Parliament. In the end, however, he was forced by the impeachment of his ministers to agree to the appointment of a council to reform the King and the kingdom. He withdrew from London and made an appeal to the country. He also called the judges before him at Shrewsbury and asked them to pronounce the illegality of Parliament's actions. The King's appeal to the people and the judges failed, and a pitched battle at Radcot Bridge was needed to settle the matter of ascendancy. In the "Merciless Parliament" of 1388 five lords accused the King's friends of treason under a very expansive definition of the crime.

"The Merciless Parliament"

Richard was chastened. He pardoned those lords who had made the accusations and proceeded to rule with moderation for the few years until 1394, when Anne of Bohemia, his queen, died. He put down a rebellion in Ireland and was, for a time, almost popular. Then, after Anne's death, he began to implement his personal policy and to rebuild a royal party. He made a 25-year peace with France and married the seven-year-old daughter of the French king as security for the treaty. He built up a household of faithful servants, including the notorious Sir John Bussy, Sir William Bagot, and Sir Henry Green. He enlisted household troops wearing his personal badge, the white hart.

In January 1397 a Parliament met. Thomas Haxey, a clerical proctor, submitted a long bill of complaints concerning maladministration, extravagance in the royal household, and the inadequate defense of the Scottish border. Haxey was arrested and adjudged in Parliament a traitor, thus extending the definition of treason even beyond the scope adopted in the Merciless Parliament. The lords apellant, who had accused the King's friends in 1388, were taken into custody—that is, those who could be found. A second Parliament in September 1397 repealed the pardons of the lords who had accused the King's friends in 1388. Three of them were now accused. One was beheaded on Tower Hill; one was exiled; the third was secretly murdered. Parliament annulled all the acts of the Parliament of 1388, granted the customs on wool for the King's life, and delegated the powers of Parliament to a committee that was to continue to sit and finish the business after the Parliament was dissolved. After this other events followed quickly. The Duke of Norfolk and Henry, son of John of Gaunt, duke of Hereford, quarrelled, accusing each other of treason. They were both banished, the former for life and the latter for ten years. Following this, John of Gaunt, duke of Lancaster, died and Richard confiscated his estates instead of allowing his son, Henry, to return to claim them. Richard went off to Ireland seemingly secure.

Richard was unduly confident. Henry landed at Ravenspur in Yorkshire, as he said, to claim his father's estates and the hereditary stewardship. The Percys, the chief lords of the north, welcomed him and promised their aid. Popular support was far more than Henry had expected. Richard returned from Ireland to negotiate first with Archbishop Arundel at Conway, then with Henry at Flint. According to Lancastrian history, he abdicated at Flint. Other evidence is that he tried to keep his estate and his life and that Henry demanded only his father's lands and the stewardship. The historian is at a disadvantage in reconstructing events because the official records were altered and even the chroniclers were given an official version after the fact. The end was swift. A Parliament was called for September 30 in Richard's name. Before this body had fully assembled, its members, the "estates of the realm," and the *populus* of London were presented with Richard's alleged abdication and Henry's claim as legitimate descendant of Henry III and by right of conquest. Thirty-three articles of deposition were set forth against Richard, accusing him of misgovernment. The abdication and deposition were accepted, and Henry sent out writs for Parliament to meet on October 6.

Richard's deposition

Richard made a last futile appeal based on the sacred character of the power conferred on him. He was taken from the Tower and transferred to Pontefract Castle, where he either died of self-starvation or was murdered by smothering. Thus ended the last attempt of a medieval king to assert arbitrary power. Whether Richard had been motivated by an ideal of medieval monarchy or, as his accusers said, by new ideas about monarchy, he failed in the practical measures necessary to sustain his power.

VI. Lancaster and York (1399–1485)

HENRY IV (1399–1413)

Henry of Lancaster seemed to promise better rapport with his people. He was a warrior of great renown. He had travelled to Jerusalem and had fought in Prussia against infidels. He had a reputation for affability and for statesmanlike self-control. But he had won his crown with the support of "the estates of the realm." It did not matter much whether that meant Parliament or something more vague and symbolic. His parliaments, from the first, expected him to govern with the advice and consent of his council and to listen in Parliament with respect to requests for money to carry on his government. And Henry himself, in order to demonstrate his superiority to Richard, emphasized his desire to govern with council and Parliament.

The rebellions. Henry's immediate task after his acceptance as king was to put down a rebellion threatening to restore Richard. The earls of Rutland, Kent, and Huntingdon, degraded from their former dukedoms but nonetheless members of the new king's council, supported by the former bishop of Carlisle, planned an attack on the King and his son at Windsor. Warned by Rutland's confession of the details to his father, the Duke of York, Henry went up to London, successfully raised an army there, and defeated the rebels near Cirencester. This event was followed by Richard's death at Pontefract. But though Richard's body was exhibited publicly in London and elsewhere, sentiment in his favour continued to crop up until well into Henry V's reign.

Owen Glendower's rebellion

A more serious rebellion was levied by Owen Glendower in 1402. He was the descendant of Welsh princes and a man of statesmanlike abilities. He sought an alliance with the French king and received some small contingents of raiders. He captured Edmund Mortimer, uncle of another Edmund, who was the only legitimate heir to Richard. He also won the valuable support of the northern barons of England including, first and foremost, the Percys of Northumberland. They had enormous prestige in the north and were connected to most of the other baronial families. Henry defeated the coalition at Shrewsbury in July 1403, and the younger Henry Percy ("Hotspur") was killed in battle. The elder Percy was pardoned on condition of surrendering his castles.

Owen Glendower meanwhile seized castles in Wales, renewed the alliance with the elder Percy, and got the support of Richard Scrope, archbishop of York. This new alliance had to be broken up in 1405. Henry won a victory at Shipton Moor and executed Scrope in a barley field without trial and over the protests of the Archbishop of Canterbury. He then defeated the elder Percy at Bramham Moor. The traitor's head was displayed on London Bridge, and his body was quartered, pickled, and sent for public exhibition to various parts of England. The war in Wales continued for some time because Henry had not enough resources to support the garrisons in the Welsh castles. But Glendower was pushed into the mountains of North Wales, and Henry was vastly more secure after 1408, although Glendower was never captured.

Henry and Parliament. Henry's relations with his Parliaments were uneasy. The main problem, of course, was money. Henry, as duke of Lancaster, was a wealthy man, wealthier than any private landlord in England. But, as king, he had forfeited some of his income by repudiating Richard's tactics. Richard had had an annual income of over £115,000, whereas Henry had only £90,000, and his income was diminished by his gifts of royal lands and revenues to his supporters. But his needs were as great as or greater than Richard's. He was threatened by rebellion at home and war from France. He borrowed as heavily as Richard but was slower in paying back. His first Parliament began the attack on royal extravagance.

They asked that he submit to the council the grants he had made to his supporters. They also asked for resumption of lands granted since 1327. Henry agreed to be advised concerning these matters but would not agree to a general resumption. On the other hand, issue was clearly joined, and the slogan that the "king should live of his own" had been introduced.

In Henry's second Parliament (1401), the Commons fired a salvo at the beginning, asking for redress of grievances before grant of supply. The King promised to confer with the Lords but in the end turned down the proposition as "unprecedented." Nonetheless, the grant of funds in the form of tenths and fifteenths and of customs is recorded in the Parliament roll as of March 10, the last day of the session. In this Parliament also, King, Lords, and Commons cooperated in a bill that required secular officers to assist ecclesiastical authorities in wiping out the Lollard heresy.

Henry called ten Parliaments in his 13 years as king. The main issues between him and these Parliaments were the demand for the resumption of crown lands so that the king might "live of his own," the demand for supervision of grants of crown lands and of expenditure generally, and finally the organization and personnel of the king's and queen's household.

The Parliament of 1406

The critical year in Henry's relations with Parliament was 1406. The Parliament of that year, the longest of the medieval period, met for 159 days and lasted from March to December. The grant of a subsidy was discussed early in the session but was promised only on condition that grants should be expended with the advice of "Lords and officers named and elected in the present parliament for defense of the realm and safeguard of the seas," except for £6,000 to be spent "as the king wishes." A grant of tonnage and poundage for safeguard of the seas was made to the merchants, but when they asked for an advance of £4,000 to deal with immediate problems, the King's reply was "Il n'y a de quoi" ("There is no money"). The second session of the Parliament demanded nomination of the King's council in Parliament. The King agreed but in no spirit of allowing interference with his choices of men to serve on the council. It was also agreed that warrants for payments from the subsidy after the safeguard of the seas had been provided for should be endorsed and made by the advice of the council. Audit of account was agreed to on the last day of the session. The third and final session of the Parliament dealt with household matters. A subsidy was granted as had been promised at the beginning of Parliament, and the Parliament broke up for Christmas on December 22.

The later Parliaments of Henry brought up no new issues, but Henry became less active in government as he was more and more incapacitated by illness. Archbishop Arundel and Henry, the King's eldest son, conducted the government until 1411, when young Henry was dismissed because of his father's suspicions concerning his loyalty. These uneasy relations between the Prince and his father lasted for the rest of the reign and kept young Henry from taking part in a campaign in France. Henry IV died on March 20, 1413. There was no question about Prince Henry's succession despite the fact of his father's usurpation.

HENRY V (1413–22)

Henry V's brief reign is important mainly for the glorious victories in the war with France, which visited on his infant son the enormous and not so glorious burden of governing both France and England. Two rebellions troubled the security of the realm in the first two years of the reign. The first was organized by Sir John Oldcastle, a Lollard and a former confidant of the new king. Oldcastle was tried by the archbishop's court and condemned to excommunication for heresy. He was handed over to the secular authorities and imprisoned in the Tower of London. He escaped with the help of two London citizens and formulated a plot against the life of the King and his brothers to take place during the Christmas celebrations in 1413–14. Some 38 of his supporters were caught and sentenced to execution. Oldcastle himself escaped arrest until 1417. Another plot against Henry's life gathered around Richard, earl of Cambridge, a younger brother of the Duke of York. Richard had married Anne Mortimer, daughter of Roger Mortimer and sister to Edmund Mortimer, the nearest legitimate claimant to the throne by descent from Lionel, duke of Clarence, second son to Edward III. Edmund gave the plot away, and the leading conspirators were tried and executed on the eve of the King's departure for France.

Sir John Oldcastle

In general, after these early disorders, the reign was internally a peaceful one. The King appointed a council to carry on the government in his absence but kept the seals in his own hands abroad. The Parliaments of the reign granted the subsidies requested.

The Treaty of Troyes

The Treaty of Troyes marks the high point of Henry's greatest achievement; that is, his conquest of northern France. Under its terms, Henry was to marry Catherine, daughter of Charles VI. He was to be heir to the French throne, and that throne was to descend to his heirs in perpetuity. Charles VI's son, the Dauphin, was not party to the treaty, and so the war continued. Henry tried to make his possessions in France pay for their own upkeep, but he still needed money for the war. Reluctant to ask for subsidies at a time when he needed all the support he could get for the treaty, he asked for loans. That they were forthcoming as readily as they were is an indication of his popularity. Meanwhile, he contracted dysentery at the siege of Meaux on the Marne and died on August 31, 1422, just six weeks before the death of his father-in-law, Charles VI. He left as his heir a son less than a year old. There could be no immediate question of the accession of that infant to the French throne. On the other hand, no question was raised about the infant's title to the English throne even though the dynasty was of dubious legitimacy and was relatively new to tenure of the throne. Under the terms of Henry V's will a council of nine was set up in which Humphrey, duke of Gloucester and second brother to Henry V, was to be the protector and defender of the realm and the Church of England, and John Plantagenet, duke of Bedford, Henry's third brother, was to take over the rule of Normandy and of France also if the Duke of Burgundy would not accept the latter responsibility.

HENRY VI (1422–61 AND 1470–71)

Henry VI, whose long reign lasted from 1422 to 1461 with a brief revival of his power in 1470–71, was never a ruler in his own person. Until 1437 he was a child under the regency of a council of nobles dominated by his uncles of Lancaster and his Beaufort kin. When he was declared of age in 1437, John, duke of Bedford, had died, and the Beauforts were the real rulers of England. In 1445, through the initiative of the Duke of Suffolk, he married Margaret of Anjou, who with Suffolk dominated the King. Finally, in the period from 1450 to 1461, he suffered two bouts of mental illness. During these crises Richard, duke of York, ruled the kingdom as protector.

Domestic rivalries and the loss of France. In the first period of the reign, the Duke of Bedford proved to be as able a commander in the French war as his brother, Henry. He pushed the French back everywhere south of the Loire except at Orléans. Then, in 1429, Joan of Arc appeared and revitalized French resistance. Orléans was relieved, and Joan persuaded the Dauphin to go deep into Anglo-Burgundian country, to Reims (the traditional city for French coronations) to be crowned. Joan's brief career as charismatic leader of the French army ended in May 1430, when she was captured by the Burgundians and sold to the English. She was tried as a heretic and a witch by an Inquisition court and burned at the stake in May 1431. John, duke of Bedford, died in 1435, and the Congress of Arras, an effort at general peace settlement, failed. Philip of Burgundy deserted the English alliance and came to terms with Charles VII. From then on the war was one of attrition until the English had lost all their possessions save Calais.

Joan of Arc

At home there were no great political issues. The main problem was the financing of the war. The country was ruled by a council of magnates with the increasingly reluctant financial support of the Parliament. Humphrey, duke of Gloucester, and Henry Beaufort, bishop of Winchester (cardinal from 1426), were the main figures in the government. The Bishop was supported by his nephew John, duke of Somerset. He was enormously wealthy and effectively increased his wealth by lending money to the king and getting control of the customs for repayment. Gloucester was completely unscrupulous and irresponsible where his own interests were engaged.

In 1447 both the Cardinal and the Duke died, the latter under circumstances that suggested the possibility of murder by poison. The Duke of Suffolk, who had arranged the King's marriage with Margaret of Anjou, was in the ascendant. He was the leader of the so-called peace party, but his peace lasted only two years, from 1444 to 1446. Margaret proved to be a high-spirited, determined, and ambitious young woman of 16 who dominated King Henry throughout the rest of his reign and fought for her son's right long after the Lancastrian cause was lost.

Though the Duke of Suffolk was in the ascendant, he was blamed for the failure of the French peace and held accountable for rumours that Maine and Anjou had been surrendered. He was impeached in the Parliament of March 1450. The King tried to save him by exiling him for five years. But when he took ship for France, the ship "Nicholas de la Tour" waylaid him. "And thanne a knave of Yrlong smot of his hed" with six strokes of a rusty sword. Suffolk was succeeded by Edmund, duke of Somerset, as the leader of the court party.

Cade's rebellion. Less than three months later, in the southeast of England, Jack Cade, who sometimes styled himself as Mortimer, presumably to associate himself with the Yorkist claimant to the throne, led a rebellion against the government. Unlike the rising of 1381, this was not a peasant movement; Cade's followers were mainly middle class, from the rank of knight down, and their complaints were mainly about the want of governance rather than of economic repression. The rebels protested feigned indictments under forest law, failure of justice, excessive bail, those who endeavoured to teach the King that he was above the law, and rigged elections to Parliament. The remedies they proposed were political: they advocated reclamation of the King's land so that he might live off his own, the removal of his corrupt councillors, and improved methods of collecting taxes. Lord Saye and Sele, the treasurer, and Crowmer, sheriff of Kent, were singled out for special attack and were captured and executed after a military victory by Cade's forces near Sevenoaks. At the end of June the rebels brutally murdered Bishop Ayscogh of Salisbury, a friend of Suffolk. The revolt was put down in early July by troops under Lord Scales. He seized London Bridge from the rebels, and with the capture at Rochester of Cade, mortally wounded, the rebellion was over.

The beginning of the Wars of the Roses. Cade's rebellion was the signal for the beginning of the so-called Wars of the Roses—the struggle between the Lancastrian and the Yorkist descendants of Edward III for control of the crown and of local government. Richard, duke of York and heir apparent, claimed under two lines of descent. His mother was great-granddaughter of Lionel, duke of Clarence, second son of Edward III. His father was son of Edmund of Langley, duke of York, fourth son of Edward III. According to feudal principle he had a better hereditary right than anyone of the Lancastrian line. Henry VI was great-grandson to John of Gaunt, duke of Lancaster, third son of Edward III.

The Duke of York's claim to the throne

Richard returned from Ireland with 4,000 men in 1450 to assert his right to participate in the King's council and to counter the machinations of the court party, especially Edmund, duke of Somerset. Somerset was recalled from France to meet Richard's charges. In the Parliament of 1450 Richard supported a measure for rigorous reclamation of the King's grants, and Thomas Young, member of the Commons from Bristol, urged the recognition of Richard as heir apparent. Young was committed to the Tower, and Richard was not called to the council until 1453. That August the King fell into insanity. The Queen and the court party attempted to conceal this, but in March 1454 Richard was made protector; he represented himself as leader of a reform faction. Early in 1455 Henry recovered his wits. During Henry's illness, on October 13, 1454, there had been born to him a son, Edward; this changed the balance of politics because Richard of York was no longer the heir apparent.

Richard went north to gather his forces, alleging that he could not safely attend a council summoned to meet at Leicester without the support of his troops. He met the King near St. Albans and first tried to prefer his charges against Somerset. But the King would neither listen nor

Battle of St. Albans

have those whom Richard designated as traitors arrested. A brief battle followed, and York's forces, larger than the King's, won a decisive victory. As a result, a Yorkist regime was set up with York as constable of England and the Earl of Warwick, emerging as the strong support of the Yorkist cause, as captain of Calais. Somerset was killed in the battle and was succeeded in the title by his son, Henry. The King fell ill again in the autumn of 1455, and York was again protector for a brief period; the King recovered early in 1456.

Hostilities were renewed in 1459. The Yorkists were defeated at Ludford Bridge, giving the Lancastrians an opportunity to recover their influence. The latter failed to meet the challenge. Demands for money, purveyances, and commissions of array increased the burdens but not the benefits of Lancastrian rule. A brief battle at Northampton on July 10, 1460, went overwhelmingly for the Yorkists, and the King was captured. Parliament was summoned to meet at Westminster on October 7. There Richard showed unwarranted self-confidence; he put his hand on the cushion of the empty throne as if he intended to sit there. When the Archbishop asked if he wanted to see the King, Richard replied with a claim to the realm of England as heir to Richard II. The Commons and judges refused to consider a matter so high, leaving it to the Lord's decision. During the fortnight of debate, the Lancastrians had an opportunity to re-form their forces. When Richard finally met them at Wakefield (December 30) in Yorkshire, he was defeated and killed.

The death of York

The Yorkist cause would have been lost if not for Richard's son, Edward, earl of March, who defeated the Lancastrian forces at Mortimer's Cross (February 3, 1461) and marched on to an enthusiastic reception in London. The Lancastrians retreated northward. At Towton Moor on March 29, Edward won a victory that put the Lancastrians decisively to flight into Scotland. Edward was crowned king on June 28, but he dated his reign from March 4, the day the London citizens and soldiers recognized his title as king.

EDWARD IV (1461–70 AND 1471–83)

During the early years of his reign, from 1461 to 1470, Edward was chiefly concerned with putting down the opposition to his rule. He was occupied with trying to keep order and defeating Lancastrian plots against him. He was also involved with France and with Burgundy because Margaret of Anjou's chief hope of recovering Lancastrian fortunes lay in the support of the French king; but Louis XI was miserly in his aid to Margaret. Edward's main internal problem lay in his relations with Warwick, who had been his chief supporter in 1461. Richard Neville, earl of Warwick and Salisbury, called the "Kingmaker," was cousin to the King and was related to much of the English nobility. But Edward refused to let himself be dominated, particularly with respect to his marriage. When the crucial moment came in Warwick's negotiations for the French king's sister-in-law, Edward disclosed his secret marriage in 1464 to Elizabeth Woodville, a commoner. In addition, Edward conducted his own negotiations for the marriage of his sister, Margaret, to Charles the Bold of Burgundy in 1467. Warwick now allied himself with the Duke of Clarence, Edward's younger brother, basing the alliance in part on the marriage to Clarence of Warwick's daughter, Isabel; but he seemed to have no clear objective except to re-establish his authority with Edward. Ultimately, through the machinations of Louis XI, Warwick joined forces with Margaret of Anjou, deposed Edward in October 1470, and brought back Henry VI. The old king was from time to time exhibited to the London citizens in worn and unregal clothing, while Warwick conducted the government. Edward went into a brief exile in the Netherlands, but with the help of his brother-in-law, Charles, duke of Burgundy, he recovered his throne in the spring of 1471. Henry VI was put to death in the Tower, and his son was killed in battle.

Warwick, the "Kingmaker"

The second half of Edward's reign, 1471–83, was a period of relative order, peace, and security. A council with extensive judicial and military powers was set up to govern the marches of Wales on behalf of the Prince of Wales; and Edward's brother, Richard of Gloucester, ruled ably in the north, presiding over a council that became the model for the Tudor Council of the North. Edward was popular. He levied few subsidies; in fact, he called Parliament only six times during his 25-year reign, and Parliament made only four grants of direct taxes. Early in his reign Edward had agreed to acts of resumption of royal estates, and he had also invested his personal fortune in trade; he thus had a considerable personal income, which allowed him more independence of parliamentary grants than his predecessors. Nonetheless, he levied benevolences, or supposedly voluntary gifts, from his subjects. In 1475 he took an army to France, but he accepted a pension from the King of France for not fighting. This increased Edward's financial independence and enabled him to leave a sizable fortune to his son. "False, fleeting, perjured Clarence," his eldest living brother, was attainted in Parliament in 1478 for involvement in a plot to depose Edward (Louis XI had planned for Clarence to marry Mary of Burgundy, the greatest hieress in Christendom, to stir up enmity between the two brothers). Clarence died in the Tower in 1478, reportedly executed by drowning in his bath.

Edward died in 1483, at age 40, worn out, it was said, by his sexual excesses. He left two sons, Edward and Richard, to the protection of his brother Richard, duke of Gloucester, although young Edward was actually at Ludlow with Earl Rivers, his maternal grandfather. After a series of skirmishes with the Queen's party, the Duke domiciled both young princes in the Tower. The Queen took sanctuary in Westminster Abbey; her father and a brother were arrested and later killed. Young Edward's coronation was set for June 24. Meanwhile, Richard eliminated those who opposed his function as protector and defender of the realm and guardian to the young King. Eventually, even William, Lord Hastings, who had sent Richard word of Edward IV's death and had warned him against the Queen's party, was accused of treachery and summarily executed. Then on the day after the date originally set for Edward V's coronation, Lords and Commons summoned to Parliament unanimously adopted a petition requesting Richard to take over the crown and royal dignity. Richard accepted and rode to Westminster to sit on the royal throne in the King's Bench. Richard was crowned on July 6, taking the oath in English.

Accession of Richard III

RICHARD III (1483–85)

Richard was readily accepted no doubt because of his reputed ability and because people feared the insecurity of a long minority. The tide began to turn against him, however, in October 1483, when it began to be rumoured that he had murdered or connived at the murder of his nephews. Whether this was true or not mattered less than that it was thought to be true and that it obscured the King's able governance during his brief tenure of the royal estate. Legislation against benevolences and protection for English merchants and craftsmen did little to counteract his reputation as a treacherous friend and a wicked uncle; and in the summer of 1485, when Henry Tudor, Lancastrian claimant to the throne, landed at Milford Haven, Richard's supporters widely deserted him and he was defeated and killed at the Battle of Bosworth Field.

ENGLAND IN THE LATE MIDDLE AGES

Bosworth Field has traditionally been taken as the date of the end of the Middle Ages in English history. Recently, however, a strong case has been made for setting the division between medieval and modern at 1536 or 1540. Henry Tudor did not bring to England any unique concept of monarchy, nor did he bring new order and peace to the country until toward the end of his reign. Yet he was the first of a dynasty under which, in the course of a century, English society and culture took on the peculiarly national characteristics that account for England's place in the modern world.

The emergence of the English nationality

The outstanding change in late medieval England was the emergence of an English nationality, largely because of the adoption of English as the language not only of everyday speech but also of documents and literature. An attempt as early as 1362 to legislate English into use in the law courts failed because the lawyers contended that they could not accurately plead in English. But in spite of this failure, English began to creep into public documents and records, including a City of London proclamation in 1384, Henry of Lancaster's claiming of the throne in 1399, royal letters of Henry V, some parliamentary petitions, and some 15th-century chronicles. Chaucer wrote his great work in English, and 15th-century writers followed his example, even though there was as yet no standard form of the language. The printer William Caxton set up his press in 1476 to publish English works for the growing reading public.

Sir Thomas More estimated, perhaps optimistically, that in his time (the early 16th century) more than half the people of England could read. The 15th century was a great period in the foundation of song schools, English reading schools, grammar schools, and colleges. Some schools were set up as adjuncts to chantries, some by guilds or by collegiate churches. Henry VI founded Eton College in 1440 and King's College in the University of Cambridge in 1441. His wife founded Queens' College in 1448. St. Catharine's was founded in 1473. By midcentury Lincoln, All Souls, and Magdalen had all been founded at Oxford.

The academies of English law (*i.e.*, the Inns of Court) expanded their membership and systematized their teaching of the law in this period. Many gentlemen's sons became members of the inns though not necessarily lawyers; many attended to learn the rudiments of the law in order to be able to defend and extend their estates. Two lawyers—Sir John Fortescue and Sir Thomas Littleton—wrote treatises on law and government that are studied down to the present day. Fortescue, a Lancastrian supporter, wrote while in exile a book in Latin in praise of English law; later, returning to England, he wrote in English a book titled *The Governance of England*. Littleton wrote in law French a learned treatise on tenures.

Change in the economy

Basic to all social change in the 15th century was change in the economy. Though England remained a predominantly agrarian society, it had begun to manufacture woollen cloth, which by the end of the 15th century had become an important source of wealth and a major export. As early as the 13th century the woollen industry had begun moving from the guild-ridden towns to the country, where waterpower could be harnessed. This movement had by the 15th century reduced the population of many formerly prosperous towns and contributed to the growth of new villages and towns. Oxford, Winchester, and Lincoln, for example, declined; Halifax and Leeds grew at the expense of York, and the West Riding at the expense of the eastern parts of Yorkshire; Suffolk and the Cotswolds region became important in the national economy.

In England's agrarian society, towns remained intricately involved with the countryside surrounding them. Land was still the most conspicuous form of wealth, and even money gained by trade or by plunder and rich ransons in war was invested in land. But land ceased to be the main basis of feudal relationships. Money fiefs, in the form of annual stipends, increasingly took the place of landed fiefs in interconnections among the ruling classes. A great lord's power was no longer judged by the number of landed vassals who owed him service but by the number of liveried retainers he could call out to accompany him on important journeys. Contracted by indenture, a great man's retinue could be used to intimidate sheriffs or other local officers, to "labour" juries (to use prestige or force to persuade a jury to a verdict), and to assert rights of possession over land. This late medieval feudalism in England has been called bastard feudalism, because instead of acting as a substitute for public power in maintaining order it became on the part of the powerful lord a means of subverting it. When public power was weak, as it was in the latter part of Henry VI's reign, great lords implemented their rivalries in struggles for control of land and local offices.

On the lower social levels, villein labour service largely disappeared and serfdom or villeinage declined. Many serfs had taken up holdings deserted by victims of the Black Death at advantageous terms; others had escaped into the agrarian wage-labour force or taken refuge in towns. By the end of the 14th century many landlords had begun to see their best interest in letting out demesne lands formerly cultivated by villein or wage labour to tenants who would pay them a settled rent. Copyhold tenure (tenure by copy of the record of the manorial court) replaced villein tenure. In a time of falling prices, leaseholders were not necessarily better off financially than they had been as villeins, but they probably had more food. There was an active land market among peasants, some of whom managed to rise above their neighbours and began to constitute a class called yeomen. By the end of the 15th century villein status had ceased to have any importance.

Scholars disagree about what happened to the level of population in the century after the Black Death. An increase in the level of wages in a time of declining prices, extending well into the 15th century, can best be explained by a decline in population. But population figures for particular regions raise questions about this generalization. Part of the difficulty arises because there was in some areas a change in land use. Many landlords solved the problem of labour shortage and decline of food prices by converting their holdings to sheep pasture; this often involved displacement of peasant agriculturists. Some peasant cultivators also converted their lands to pasture. More land was enclosed for sheep pasture in the north, and there was a shift of population density to the southwest and southeast.

The main development in England's trade in the late Middle Ages was the increasing participation of Englishmen and the shift from trade in raw wool to trade in woollens. Edward III ruined the Italian bankers by failing to repay loans for conduct of the war. He then gave English merchants a monopoly of the wool export in return for their support. Many of these merchants were also ruined, but families like the de la Poles of Hull made lasting fortunes and eventually joined the ranks of the nobility. The Merchants of the Staple, who held a monopoly on raw wool exports, were more or less permanently established at Calais from the mid-14th century. As the cloth trade grew, a new association, the Merchant Adventurers, grew in power and wealth. Their chief export was cloth, and their chief market was the Netherlands, where they had their headquarters. In spite of xenophobia in England, which led to outbreaks in London against foreign merchants, the Italians reached their zenith of prosperity in Yorkist England, and Edward IV had to make important concessions to the Hanseatic merchants who helped him regain his throne in 1471.

Art and architecture in the 15th century

Culturally, in the 15th century monastic chronicles came to an end and the writing of history declined. Thomas Walsingham (died 1422) was the last of the St. Albans chroniclers. There were some English chronicles written by citizens of London, and two lives of Henry V, but no great work of history came until later. Neither were there great works of philosophy or theology, although Reginald Pecock wrote an English treatise against the Lollards and various other works emphasizing the rational element in the Christian faith; he was judged guilty of heresy for his pains. No great poets succeeded to Chaucer, perhaps partly because there was no standard English language in which to express thought. The influence of the Italian Renaissance scarcely affected England before 1485. The full impact of the new learning was not felt until the 16th century.

In architecture alone, England showed originality. The 15th century was a great period of building of parish churches. Especially in the areas where the woollen industry had produced wealth, large churches were built in the peculiarly English Perpendicular style. The tomb of Richard Beauchamp at Warwick and King's College Chapel in Cambridge show what heights could be reached in English architecture and sculpture in the period.

England in the 15th century presents a confused picture politically and socially, and the economy is still something of an enigma. But as more work is done to elucidate their mysteries, these "scrambling and unquiet times" seem to promise a rich period to come. (M.Has.)

VII. England under the Tudors, 1485–1603

HENRY VII (1485–1509)

When the Lancastrian Henry Tudor, earl of Richmond, seized the throne on August 22, 1485, leaving the Yorkist Richard III dead upon the field of battle, few Englishmen would have predicted that 118 years of Tudor rule had begun. Eight sovereigns had come and gone, and at least 15 major battles had been fought between rival contenders to the throne since that moment in 1399 when the divinity that "doth hedge a king" was violated and Richard II was forced to abdicate. Simple arithmetic forecast that Henry VII would last no more than a decade. Bosworth Field appeared to be nothing more than another of the erratic swings of the military pendulum in the struggle between the houses of York and Lancaster, and further evidence that the English crown had become a political football to be kicked about by overmighty magnates who captained semimercenary armies financed largely by foreign sources. What gave Henry Tudor victory in 1485 was not so much personal charisma as the fact that key noblemen deserted Richard III at the moment of his greatest need, that Thomas Stanley, 2nd Baron Stanley (later 1st earl of Derby), and his brother, Sir William, stood aside during most of the battle in order to be on the winning team, and that Louis XI of France supplied the Lancastrian forces with 1,000 mercenary troops.

The weakness of Henry's claim to the throne

The desperateness of the new monarch's gamble was equalled only by the doubtfulness of his claim. Henry VII's Plantagenet blood was tainted by bastardy, for he was descended on his mother's side from the Beaufort family, the offspring of John of Gaunt and his mistress Catherine Swynford, and though their children had been legitimized by act of Parliament, they had been specifically barred from the succession. His father's genealogy was equally suspect: Edmund Tudor, earl of Richmond, was born to Catherine of Valois, widowed queen of Henry V, by her clerk of the wardrobe, Owen Tudor; and the precise marital status of their relationship has never been established. Had quality of Plantagenet blood, not military conquest, been the essential condition of monarchy, Edward, earl of Warwick, the ten-year-old nephew of Edward IV, would have sat upon the throne. Might, not soiled right, had won out on the high ground at Bosworth Field, and Henry VII claimed his title by conquest. The new king, however, wisely sought to fortify his doubtful genealogical pretension first by parliamentary acclamation and then by royal marriage. The Parliament of November 1485 did not confer regal power on the first Tudor monarch—victory in war had already done that; but it did acknowledge Henry as "our new sovereign lord." Then on January 18, 1486, Henry of Lancaster married Elizabeth of York, the eldest daughter of Edward IV, thereby uniting "the white rose and the red" and launching England upon a century of "smooth-fac'd peace with smiling plenty and fair prosperous days."

"God's fair ordinance," which Shakespeare and later generations so clearly observed in the events of 1485–86, was not limited to military victory, parliamentary sanction, and a fruitful marriage; the hidden hand of economic, social, and intellectual change was also on Henry's side. The day was coming when the successful prince would be more praised than the heroic monarch and the solvent sovereign more admired than the pious one. Henry Tudor was probably no better or worse than the first Lancastrian, Henry IV; they both worked diligently at their royal craft and had to fight hard to keep their crowns; but the seventh Henry achieved what the fourth had not—a secure and permanent dynasty—because England in 1485 was moving into a period of unprecedented economic growth and social change.

Economy and society. Long before 1485 the kingdom had begun to recover from the demographic catastrophe of the Black Death and the agricultural depression of the late 14th century; but as the 15th century came to a close, the rate of revival increased. The population in 1400 may have dropped as low as 2,500,000; by 1500 it was back up to at least 3,000,000, and a century later it was over 4,000,000. More people meant more mouths to feed, more backs to cover, and more vanity to satisfy. In response, yeoman farmers, gentleman sheep growers, urban cloth manufacturers, and merchant adventurers produced a social and economic revolution. With extraordinary speed the export of raw wool gave way to the export of woollen cloth manufactured at home, and the wool clothier or entrepreneur was soon buying fleece from sheep raisers, transporting the wool to cottagers for spinning and weaving, paying the farmer's wife and children by the piece, and collecting the finished article for shipment to Bristol, London, and eventually Europe. By the time Henry VII seized the throne, the Merchant Adventurers, an association of London wool exporters, were controlling the London–Antwerp market, replacing in economic importance the Staplers who dealt in raw wool. By 1496 they were a chartered organization with a legal monopoly of the woollen cloth trade, and largely as a consequence of their political and international importance, Henry successfully negotiated the Intercursus Magnus, a highly favourable commercial treaty between England and the Low Countries.

Revolution in the wool industry

As landlords increased the size of their flocks to the point that ruminants outnumbered human beings three to one, and as clothiers such as John Winchcombe (better known as Jack of Newbury) grew so rich that they could afford to entertain kings, inflation injected new life into the economy. England was caught up in a vast European spiral of rising prices, declining real wages, and cheap money. Inflation was largely the result of the growing abundance of gold and silver that flooded in upon the European economy from the New World and drove down the value and purchasing power of the traditional coinage, forcing up the cost of services and supplies. Between 1500 and 1540 prices in England doubled, and they doubled again in the next generation. In 1450 the cost of wheat had been what it was in 1300; by 1550 it had tripled.

Inflation and the wool trade together created an economic and social upheaval. Land plenty, labour shortage, low rents, and high wages, which had prevailed throughout the early 15th century as a consequence of economic depression and reduced population, were replaced by land shortage, labour surplus, high rents, and declining wages. The landlord, who a century before could find neither tenants nor labourers for his land and had left his fields fallow, could now convert his meadows into sheep runs. His rents and profits soared; his need for labour declined, for one shepherd and his dog could do the work of half a dozen men who had previously tilled the same field. Slowly the medieval system of land tenure and communal farming broke down. The common land of the manor was divided up and fenced in, and the peasant farmer who held his tenure either by copy (a document recorded in the manor court) or by unwritten custom was evicted. The total extent of enclosure and eviction is difficult to assess, but between 1455 and 1607 in 34 counties 516,573 acres (208,954 hectares), or 2.76 percent of the total, were enclosed, and some 50,000 persons were forced off the land. Statistics, however, are deceptive both as to emotional impact and extent of change. The most disturbing aspect of the land revolution was not the emergence of a vagrant and unemployable labour force for whom society felt no social responsibility but an unprecedented increase in what men feared most—change. Farming techniques were transformed, the gap between rich and poor increased, the timeless quality of village life was upset, and on all levels of society old families were being replaced by new.

Enclosures

The beneficiaries of change, as always, were the most grasping, the most ruthless, and the best educated segments of the population: the landed country gentlemen and their socially inferior cousins, the merchants and lawyers. By 1500 the essential economic basis for the landed country gentleman's future political and social ascendancy was taking shape—the 15th-century knight of the shire was changing from a desperate and irresponsible land proprietor, ready to support the baronial feuding of the Wars of the Roses, into a respectable landowner desiring strong, practical government and the rule of law. The gentry did not care whether Henry VII's royal pedigree could bear close inspection; their own lineage was not above suspicion, and they were willing to serve the prince "in parliament, in council, in commission and other offices of the commonwealth."

Dynastic threats. It is no longer fashionable to call Henry VII a "new monarch," and indeed if the first Tudor had a model for reconstructing the monarchy it was the example of the great medieval kings. Newness, however, should not be totally denied Henry Tudor; his royal blood was very "new," and the extraordinary efficiency of his regime introduced a spirit into government that had rarely been present in the medieval past. It was, in fact, "newness" that governed the early policy of the reign, for the Tudor dynasty had to be secured and all those with a better or older claim to the throne liquidated. Elizabeth of York was deftly handled by marriage; the sons of Edward IV had already been removed from the list, presumably murdered by their uncle Richard III; the Earl of Warwick was promptly imprisoned; but the descendants of Edward IV's sister and daughters remained a threat to the new government. Equally dangerous was the persistent myth that the younger of the two princes murdered in the Tower had escaped his assassin and that the Earl of Warwick had escaped his jailers. The existence of pretenders acted as a catalyst for further baronial discontent and Yorkist aspirations, and in 1487 John de la Pole, a nephew of Edward IV by his sister Elizabeth, with the support of 2,000 mercenary troops paid for with Burgundian gold, landed in England to support the pretensions of Lambert Simnel, who passed himself off as the authentic Earl of Warwick. Again Henry Tudor was triumphant in war; at the Battle of Stoke, de la Pole was killed and Simnel captured and demoted to a scullery boy in the royal kitchen. Ten years later Henry had to do it all over again, this time with a handsome Flemish lad named Perkin Warbeck, who for six years was accepted in Yorkist circles in Europe as the real Richard IV, brother of the murdered Edward V. Warbeck tried to take advantage of Cornish anger against heavy royal taxation and increased government efficiency and sought to lead a Cornish army of social malcontents against the Tudor throne. It was a measure of the new vigour and popularity of the Tudor monarchy, as well as the support of the gentry, that social revolution and further dynastic war were total failures, and Warbeck found himself in the Tower along with the Earl of Warwick. In the end both men proved too dangerous to live, even in captivity, and in 1499 they were executed.

The threats of pretenders

The policy of dynastic extermination did not cease with the new century. Under Henry VIII, the Duke of Buckingham was destroyed in 1521; the Earl of Warwick's sister, the Countess of Salisbury, was beheaded in 1541 and her descendants harried out of the land; and in 1546 the poet Henry Howard, earl of Surrey, the grandson of Buckingham, was put to death. By the end of Henry VIII's reign the job had been so well done that the curse of Edward III's fecundity had been replaced by the opposite problem—the Tudor line proved to be infertile when it came to producing healthy male heirs. Henry VII sired Arthur, who died in 1502, and Henry VIII in turn produced only one legitimate son, Edward VI, who died at the age of 16, thereby ending the direct male descent.

Financial policy. It was not enough for Henry VII to secure his dynasty; he also had to re-establish the financial credit of his crown and reassert the authority of royal law. Feudal kings had traditionally lived off four sources of nonparliamentary income: rents from the royal estates, revenues from import and export taxes, fees from the administration of justice, and moneys extracted on the basis of a vassal's duty to his overlord. The first Tudor was no different from his Yorkist or medieval predecessors; he was simply more ruthless and successful in demanding every penny that was owed him. Henry's first move was to confiscate all the estates of Yorkist adherents and to restore all property over which the crown had lost control since 1455 (in some cases as far back as 1377). To these essentially statutory steps he added efficiency of rent collection. In 1485 income from crown lands had totalled £29,000; by 1509 land revenues had risen to £42,000 and the profits from the Duchy of Lancaster had jumped from £650 to £6,500. At the same time, the Tudors profited from the growing economic prosperity of the realm, and custom receipts rose from over £20,000 to an average of £40,000 by the time Henry died.

Henry's sources of revenue

The increase in custom and land revenues was applauded, for it meant fewer parliamentary subsidies and fitted the medieval formula that kings should live on their own, not parliamentary, income. But the collection of revenues from feudal sources and from the administration of justice caused great discontent and earned for Henry his reputation as a miser and extortionist. Generally, Henry demanded no more than his due as the highest feudal overlord, and a year after he became sovereign he established a commission to look into land tenure to discover who held property by knight's fee—that is, by obligation to perform military services. Occasionally he overstepped the bounds of feudal decency and abused his rights. In 1504, for instance, he levied a feudal aid (tax) to pay for the knighting of his son—who had been knighted 15 years before and had been dead for two. Henry VIII continued his father's policy of fiscal feudalism, forcing through Parliament in 1536 the Statute of Uses to prevent landowners from escaping "relief" and wardship (feudal inheritance taxes) by legal trickery and establishing the Court of Wards and Liveries in 1540 to handle the profits of feudal wardship. The howl of protest was so great that in 1540 Henry VIII had to compromise, and by the Statute of Wills a subject who held his property by knight's fee was permitted to bequeath two-thirds of his land without feudal obligation.

To fiscal feudalism Henry VII added rigorous administration of justice. As law became more effective it also became more profitable, and the policy of levying heavy fines as punishment upon those who dared break the king's peace proved to be a useful whip over the mighty magnate and a welcome addition to the King's exchequer. Even war and diplomacy were sources of revenue, and one of the major reasons why Henry VII wanted his second son, Henry, to marry his brother's widow was that the King was reluctant to return the dowry of 200,000 crowns that Ferdinand and Isabella of Spain had given for the marriage of their daughter, Catherine of Aragon. Generally Henry believed in a good neighbour policy—alliance with Spain by the marriage of Arthur and Catherine in 1501 and peace with Scotland by the marriage of his daughter Margaret to James IV in 1503—on the grounds that peace was cheap and trade profitable. In 1489, however, he was faced with the threat of the union of the Duchy of Brittany with the French crown; and England, Spain, the empire, and Burgundy went to war to stop it. Nevertheless, as soon as it became clear that nothing could prevent France from absorbing the duchy, Henry negotiated the unheroic but financially rewarding Treaty of Étaples in 1492, whereby he disclaimed all historic rights to French territory (except Calais) in return for an indemnity of £159,000. By fair means or foul, when the first Tudor died, his total nonparliamentary annual income had risen at least twofold and stood in the neighbourhood of £113,000 (some estimates are as high as £142,000). From land alone the King received £42,000, while the greatest landlord in the realm had to make do with less than £5,000; economically speaking, there were no longer any overmighty magnates.

Income from the law courts and from marriage arrangements

The administration of justice. Money could buy power, but really successful kings, be they medieval or Tudor, had to earn the respect of their subjects by enforcing and administering the law. The problem for Henry VII was not to replace an old system of government with a new—no Tudor was consciously a revolutionary—but to make the ancient system work tolerably well. He had to tame but not destroy the nobility, develop organs of administration directly under his control, and wipe out provincialism and privilege wherever they appeared. In the task of curbing the old nobility, the King was immeasurably helped by the high aristocratic death rate during the Wars of the Roses; but where war left off, policy took over. Within three years of Bosworth Field, Thomas Howard, earl of Surrey, who had fought for Richard III, was liberated from the Tower of London and his estates restored; six years later Sir William Stanley, whose betrayal of Richard had helped Henry win his crown, was executed for high treason. The former was willing to become a devoted Tudor workhorse; the latter persisted in the anachronistic code of the divine right of nobility. Commissions of Array composed of local notables were appointed by the crown for each county in order to make use of the power of the aristocracy in raising troops but to prevent them from maintaining private armies (livery) with which to intimidate justice (maintenance) or threaten the throne.

Previous monarchs had sought to enforce the laws against livery and maintenance, but the first two Tudors, though they never totally abolished such evils, built up a reasonably efficient machine for enforcing the law, based on the historic premise that the king in the midst of his council was the fountain of justice. Traditionally the royal council had heard all sorts of cases, and very rapidly its members began to specialize. The Court of Chancery had for years dealt with civil offenses, the Court of Star Chamber evolved to handle criminal cases, the Court of Requests for poor men's suits, and the Court of Admiralty to cope with piracy. The process by which the conciliar courts developed was largely accidental, and the Court of Star Chamber acquired its name from the star-painted ceiling of the room in which the councillors sat, not from the statute of 1487 that simply recognized its existence. Conciliar justice was popular because the ordinary courts where common law prevailed were slow, cumbersome, favoured the rich and mighty, and tended to break down when asked to deal with riot, maintenance, livery, perjury, and fraud. The same search for efficiency applied to matters of finance. The traditional fiscal agency of the crown, the exchequer, was burdened down with archaic procedures and restrictions, and Henry VII turned to the more intimate and flexible departments of his personal household—specifically to the treasurer of the chamber, whom he could supervise directly—as the central tax-raising, rent-collecting, and money-disbursing segment of government.

Conciliar government

The Tudors sought to enforce law in every corner of their kingdom, and step by step the blurred medieval profile of a realm shattered by semi-autonomous franchises, in which local law and custom were obeyed more than the king's law, was transformed into the clear outline of a single state filled with loyal subjects obeying the king's decrees. By 1500 royal government had been extended into the northern counties and Wales by the creation of a Council of the North and a Council for the Welsh Marches. The Welsh principalities had always been difficult to control, and it was not until 1536 that Henry VIII brought royal law directly into Wales and incorporated the 136 self-governing lordships into a greater England with five new shires.

Henry VII's achievements

If the term "new monarchy" was inappropriate in 1485, the same cannot be said for the year of Henry VII's death, for when he died in 1509, after 24 years of reign, he bequeathed to his son something quite new in English history: a safe throne, a full treasury, a solvent government, a prosperous land, and a united kingdom. Only one vital aspect of the past remained untouched, the independent Catholic Church, and it was left to the second Tudor to destroy this remaining vestige of medievalism.

HENRY VIII (1509–47)

Cardinal Wolsey. A prince of 18 inherited his father's throne, but the son of an Ipswich butcher carried on the first Tudor's administrative policies. While the young sovereign enjoyed his inheritance, Thomas Wolsey collected titles—archbishop of York in 1514, lord chancellor and cardinal legate in 1515, and papal legate for life in 1524. He exercised a degree of power never before wielded by king or minister, for as lord chancellor and cardinal legate he united in his portly person the authority of church and state. He sought to tame both the lords temporal and spiritual, administering to the nobility the "new law of the Star Chamber," protecting the rights of the underprivileged in the poor men's Court of Requests, and teaching the abbots and bishops that they were subjects as well as ecclesiastical princes. Long before Henry assumed full power over his subjects' souls as well as their bodies, his servant had marked the way. The cardinal's administration, however, was stronger on promise than performance, and for all his fine qualities and many talents he exposed himself to the accusation that he prostituted policy for pecuniary gain and personal pride. Together, the King and Cardinal plunged the kingdom into international politics and war and helped make England one of the centres of Renaissance learning and brilliance; had Henry VIII died before 1529 he would have had to share the accolades with his chief minister. The King, however, lived on for 17 crucial years, and three interrelated factors brought Wolsey's career to an end—England's weakness as an international power, Henry's "Great Matter," and the growth of heresy.

Foreign policy

Both the sovereign and his chief servant overestimated England's international position in the continental struggle between Francis I of France and the emperor Charles V. Militarily, the kingdom was of the same magnitude as the papacy—the English king had about the same revenues and could field about the same size army—and, as one contemporary noted, England with its back door constantly exposed to Scotland and with its economy dependent upon the Flanders wool trade was a mere "morsel among those choppers" of Europe. Nevertheless, Wolsey's diplomacy was based on the expectation that England could swing the balance of power either to France or to the empire and by holding that position could maintain the peace of Europe. The hollowness of the cardinal's policy was revealed in 1525 when Charles disastrously defeated and captured Francis at the Battle of Pavia. Italy was overrun with the Emperor's troops, the Pope became an imperial chaplain, all of Europe bowed before the conqueror, and England sank from being the fulcrum of continental diplomacy to the level of a second-rate power just at the moment when Henry had decided to rid himself of his wife, the 42-year-old Catherine of Aragon.

The divorce question. It is still a subject of debate whether Henry's decision to seek an annulment of his marriage and wed Anne Boleyn was a matter of state, of love, or of conscience. Quite possibly all three operated; Catherine was fat, seven years her husband's senior, incapable of bearing further children, and Anne was everything that the Queen was not—pretty, vivacious, and fruitful. Catherine had produced only one child and that was a girl, Princess Mary, and it semed ironic indeed that the first Tudor should have solved the question of the succession only to expose the kingdom to an even greater peril in the second generation: a female ruler. The need for a male heir was paramount, for the last queen of England, Matilda, in the 12th century, had been a disaster, and there was no reason to believe that another would be any better. Finally, there was the question of the King's conscience. Henry had married his brother's widow, and though the Pope had granted a dispensation, the fact of the matter remained that every male child born to Henry and Catherine had died, and it was clearly written in Leviticus: "If a man takes his brother's wife, it is impurity; he has uncovered his brother's nakedness, they shall be childless" (20:21).

Unfortunately, Henry's divorce was not destined to stand or fall upon the theological issue of whether a papal dispensation could set aside such a prohibition, for Catherine was not simply the King's wife, she was also the aunt of the emperor Charles V, the most powerful sovereign in Europe. Both Henry and his cardinal knew that the divorce would never be granted unless the Emperor's power in Italy could be overthrown by an Anglo-French military alliance and the Pope rescued from imperial domination, and for three years Wolsey worked desperately to achieve this diplomatic and military end. Caught between an all-powerful emperor and a truculent English king, Clement VII procrastinated and offered all sorts of doubtful solutions short of divorce, including the marriage of Princess Mary and the King's illegitimate son, Henry Fitzroy, duke of Richmond; the legitimizing of all children begotten of Anne Boleyn; and the suggestion that Catherine go into a nunnery so that the King could be given permission to remarry. Wolsey's purpose was to have the divorce trial held in London, but in 1529, despite the arrival of Cardinal Lorenzo Campeggio to set up the machinery for a hearing, Wolsey's plans exploded. In July the Pope ordered Campeggio to transfer the case to Rome, where a decision against the King was a foregone conclusion; and in August Francis and the Emperor made peace at the Treaty of Cambrai. Wolsey's policies were a failure, and he was dismissed from office in October 1529. He died on November 29, just in time to escape trial for treason.

The fall of Wolsey

The Reformation background. Henry now began groping for new means to achieve his purpose. At first he contemplated little more than blackmail to frighten the Pope into submission; but slowly, reluctantly, and not realizing the full consequences of his actions, he moved step by step to open defiance and a total break with Rome. Wolsey in his person and his policies had represented the past. He was the last of the great ecclesiastical statesmen who had been as much at home in the cosmopolitan world of European Christendom, with its spiritual centre in Rome, as in a provincial capital such as London. By the time of Henry's divorce, Christendom was dissolving. Not only were feudal kingdoms assuming the character of independent nation-states but the spiritual unity of Christ's seamless cloak was also being torn apart by heresy. Possibly Henry would never have won his divorce had there not existed in England men who desired a break with Rome, not because it was dynastically expedient but because they regarded the Pope as the "whore of Babylon."

The medieval church had become an anachronism out of touch with the 16th-century reality of changing economic practices, governmental structure, and social values. More and more, God was French or German or English, and his representative in Rome was having ever greater difficulty in speaking so many languages and in persuading his international flock that he was the spiritual leader of all Christians and not simply a petty Italian potentate motivated by family ambition and political aggrandizement. The church was also withering from within. Historically, it was a state within a state—an independent clerical body possessed of special rights and privileges because of the fundamental division of man into body and soul. In the eyes of many, however, the church's duties in matters spiritual had been superseded by matters temporal. Absenteeism and pluralism were rife, and by 1520 in Oxfordshire alone 58 percent of the county's 192 parish priests were absentees. Bishops and high ecclesiastics were meant to tend to the cure of souls, but in fact they were engrossed in worldly affairs. Wolsey himself, as the greatest and richest clerical statesman, seemed to epitomize the worst aspects of that worldliness and corruption. Men continued to go to church, but it was increasingly difficult, especially for the landed gentleman and the wealthy merchant, to respect the old church. A sure sign that zeal for the ancient structure was flagging was the economic decline of the monasteries: in Norfolk, Yorkshire, and Buckinghamshire the capital wealth of the religious foundations rose only 1.13 percent between 1480 and 1540, which was not enough to offset normal depreciation, let alone keep up with inflation. More and more surplus wealth was being directed into other than religious channels; in the 15th century, the wool merchant Thomas Paycocke of Coggeshall had used the proceeds of trade to found a chantry to sing masses for his soul; a century later, William Sanderson of London invested the profits of fishmongering into two small ships to carry Capt. John Davis over the top of the world in search of the Northwest Passage to Cathay.

Abuses within the church

As the old church lived on in a fossilized condition, Christians looked elsewhere for inner contentment, and all over Europe men like Martin Luther, the German monk in Saxony, and Thomas Bilney, the Cambridge scholar in England, sought spiritual meaning and relief from ritualism, worldliness, and religious apathy. Luther in his monastery and Bilney in his college turned to the Bible, and each stumbled across the knowledge that even in the midst of despair, faith in God's mercy could save sinners. The new religious ideas flowed into England largely in the form of Lutheran doctrines, but they found a receptive audience not only because there were upper-class individuals who could find no spiritual satisfaction in the old religious formulas and who were looking for exactly what Luther and Bilney had to offer but also because there existed in England a religious subculture in the form of Lollardy. Its existence was always officially denied by the established church, but the ideas of John Wycliffe (died 1384) had never been exterminated. They lived on just below the surface, and by the time of the Reformation Lollardy was once again becoming respectable. Though Henry himself was never a Protestant, and during the first 20 years of his reign was a zealous persecutor of religious nonconformity, be it Lutheran or Lollard, the King would never have been able to push through the break with Rome simply on the basis of anticlericalism or apathy within the existing church. If his headship of an independent English church was to live in "the hearts of his subjects" and not "post alone hidden in acts of parliament," he had to call upon the support of the "zely people" (Protestant zealots) who viewed the political and constitutional steps by which Henry's divorce was legalized as being the prelude to a thorough spiritual reformation.

Lollardy

The break with Rome. With Wolsey and his papal authority gone, Henry turned to the authority of the state to obtain his divorce, and the so-called Reformation Parliament that first met in November 1529 was unprecedented—it lasted seven years, enacted 137 statutes (32 of which were of vital importance), and legislated in areas that no feudal Parliament had ever dreamed of entering. "King in Parliament" became the revolutionary instrument by which the medieval church was destroyed. The first step was to intimidate the church, and in 1531 Convocation was forced under threat of praemunire (a statute prohibiting the legal and financial jurisdiction of the pope without royal consent) to grant the sovereign a gift of £119,000 and to acknowledge him supreme head of the church "as far as the law of Christ allows." Then the government struck at the papacy, threatening to cut off its revenues; the Annate's Statute of 1532 empowered Henry, if he saw fit, to abolish payment to Rome of the first year's income of all newly installed bishops. The implied threat had little effect on the Pope; and time was running out, for by December 1532 Anne Boleyn was pregnant, and on January 25, 1533, she was secretly married to Henry. If the King was to be saved from bigamy and his child born in wedlock, he had less than eight months to get rid of Catherine of Aragon. Archbishop William Warham conveniently died in August 1532, and in March 1533 a demoralized and frightened pontiff sanctioned the installation of Thomas Cranmer as primate of the English church. Cranmer was a friend of the divorce, but before he could oblige his sovereign the Queen's right of appeal from the archbishop's court to Rome had to be destroyed; and this could be done only by cutting the constitutional cords holding England to the papacy. Consequently, in April 1533 the crucial statute was enacted; the Act of Restraint of Appeals boldly decreed that "this realm of England is an empire." A month later an obliging archbishop heard the divorce case and adjudged the King's marriage to be null and void. On June 1 Anne was crowned rightful queen of England, and three months and a week later, on September 7, 1533, the royal child was born. To "the great shame and con-

Thomas Cranmer and the divorce

fusion" of astrologers, it turned out to be Elizabeth Tudor.

Henry was mortified; he had risked his soul and his crown for yet another girl, but Anne had proved her fertility and it was hoped that a male heir would shortly follow. In the meantime it was necessary to complete the break with Rome and rebuild the Church of England. By the Act of Succession of March 1534, subjects were ordered to accept the King's marriage to Anne as "undoubted, true, sincere and perfect." A second Annate's Statute severed most of the financial ties with Rome, and in November the constitutional revolution was solemnized in the Act of Supremacy, which announced that Henry Tudor was and always had been "Supreme Head of the Church of England"; not even the qualifying phrase "as far as the law of Christ allows" was retained.

The consolidation of the Reformation. The medieval tenet that church and state were separate entities with divine law standing higher than human law had been legislated out of existence; the new English Church was in effect a department of the Tudor state. The destruction of the Catholic Church led inevitably to the dissolution of the monasteries. As monastic religious fervour and economic resources began to dry up, it was easy enough for the government to build a case that monasteries were centres of vice and corruption. In the end, however, what destroyed them was neither apathy nor abuse but the fact that they were contradictions within a national church, for religious foundations by definition were international, supranational organizations that traditionally supported papal authority. Though they bowed to the royal supremacy, the government continued to view them with suspicion, arguing that they had obeyed only out of fear, and their destruction got underway early in 1536. In the name of fiscal reform and efficiency, foundations with endowments of under £200 a year (nearly 400 of them) were dissolved on the grounds that they were too small to do their job effectively. By late 1536 confiscation had become state policy, for the Pilgrimage of Grace Catholic-inspired uprising in the north seemed to be clear evidence that all monasteries were potential nests of traitors. By 1539 the foundations, both great and small, were gone, and property worth possibly £2,000,000 was nationalized and incorporated into the crown lands, thereby almost doubling the government's normal peacetime, nonparliamentary income. Had those estates remained in the possession of the crown, English history might have been very different, for the kings of England would have been able to rule without calling upon Parliament, and the constitutional authority that evolved out of the crown's fiscal dependence on Parliament would never have developed. For better or for worse, Henry and his descendants had to sell the profits of the Reformation; and by 1603 three-fourths of the monastic loot had passed into the hands of the landed gentry. The legend of a "golden shower" is false. Monastic property was never given away at bargain prices, nor was it consciously presented to the kingdom in order to win the support of the ruling elite. Instead, most of the land was sold at its fair market value to pay for Henry's wars and foreign policy. The effect, however, was crucial—the most powerful elements within Tudor society now had a vested interest in protecting their property against papal Catholicism.

The dissolution of the monasteries

The divorce, the break with Rome, and even the destruction of the monasteries went through with surprisingly little opposition. It had been foreseen that the royal supremacy might have to be enacted in blood, and the Act of Supremacy (March 1534) and the Act of Treason (December) were designed to root out and liquidate the dissent. The former was a loyalty test requiring subjects to take an oath swearing to accept not only the matrimonial results of the break with Rome but also the principles on which it stood; the latter extended the meaning of treason to include all those who did "maliciously wish, will or desire, by words or writing or by craft imagine" the King's death or slander his marriage. Sir Thomas More (who had succeeded Wolsey as lord chancellor), Bishop John Fisher (who almost alone among the episcopate had defended Catherine during her trial), and a handful of monks suffered death for their refusal to accept the concept of a national church. Even the Pilgrimage of Grace of 1536–37 was a short-lived eruption. The uprisings in Lincolnshire in October and in Yorkshire during the winter were without doubt religiously motivated, but they were also as much feudal and social rebellions as revolts in support of Rome. Peasants, landed country gentlemen, and feudal barons could unite in defense of the monasteries and the old religion, and for a moment the rebels seemed on the verge of toppling the Tudor state. The nobility were angered that they had been excluded from the King's government by men of inferior social status, and they resented the encroachment of bureaucracy into the northern shires. The gentry were concerned by rising taxes and the peasants by threatened enclosure; but the three elements had little in common outside religion, and the uprisings fell apart from within. The rebels were soon crushed and their leaders—including Robert Aske, one of the most pleasing figures of the century—brutally executed.

The acts of Supremacy and Treason

Henry's last years. Henry was so securely seated upon his throne that the French Ambassador announced that he was more an idol to be worshipped than a king to be obeyed, and the King successfully survived four more matrimonial experiments, the enmity of every major power in Europe, and an international war. On May 19, 1536, Anne Boleyn's career was terminated by the executioner's ax. She had failed in her promise to produce further children to secure the succession. The King's love had turned to hatred, but what sealed the Queen's fate was the death of her rival, Catherine of Aragon, on January 8, 1536. From that moment it was clear that should Henry again marry, whoever was his wife, the children she might bear would be legitimate in the eyes of Catholics and Protestants alike. How much policy, how much repulsion for Anne, how much attraction for Jane Seymour played in the final tragedy is beyond analysis, but 11 days after Anne's execution Henry married Jane. Sixteen months later the future Edward VI was born. The mother died as a consequence, but the father finally had what it had taken a revolution to achieve, a legitimate male heir.

Birth of Edward VI

Henry married thrice more, once for reasons of diplomacy, once for love, and once for peace and quiet. Anne of Cleves, his fourth wife, was the product of Reformation international politics. For a time in 1539 it looked as if Charles V and Francis would come to terms and unite against the schismatic King of England, and the only allies Henry possessed were the Lutheran princes of Germany. In something close to panic, he was stampeded into marriage with Anne of Cleves, but the following year, the moment the diplomatic scene changed, he dropped both his wife and the man who had engineered the marriage, his vicar general in matters spiritual, Thomas Cromwell. Anne was divorced July 12, Cromwell was executed July 28, and Henry married Catherine Howard the same day. The second Catherine did not do as well as her cousin, the first Anne; she lasted only 18 months. Catherine proved to be neither a virgin before her wedding nor a particularly faithful damsel after her marriage. With the execution of his fifth wife, Henry turned into a sick old man, and he took as his last spouse Catherine Parr, who was as much a nursemaid as a wife. During those final years, the King's interests turned to international affairs. Henry's last war (1543–46) was fought not to defend his church against resurgent European Catholicism but to renew a much older policy of military conquest in France. Though he enlarged the English Pale at Calais by seizing the small French port of Boulogne, the war had no lasting diplomatic or international effects except to assure that the monastic lands would pass into the hands of the gentry.

By the time Henry died (January 28, 1547) medievalism had nearly vanished. The crown stood at the pinnacle of its power, able to demand and receive a degree of obedience from both great and small that no feudal monarch had been able to achieve. The measure of that authority was threefold: (1) the extent to which Henry had been

The achievements of Henry VIII

able to thrust a very unpopular divorce and supremacy legislation down the throat of Parliament; (2) his success in raising unprecedented sums of money through taxation; and (3) his ability to establish a new church on the ashes of the old. It is difficult to say whether these feats were the work of the King or his chief minister, Thomas Cromwell. The will was probably Henry's, the parliamentary means his minister's, but whoever was responsible, by 1547 England was a long way along the road of Reformation. The crown had assumed the authority of the papacy without as yet fundamentally changing the old creed, but the ancient structure was severely shaken. Throughout England men were arguing that because the pontiff had been proved false, the entire Catholic creed was suspect; and the cry went up to "get rid of the poison with the author." It was not long before every aspect of Catholicism was under attack—the miracle of the mass whereby the bread and wine were converted into the body and blood of Christ, the doctrine of purgatory, the efficacy of saints and images, the concept of an ordained priesthood with miraculous powers, and the doctrine of the celibacy of the clergy. The time had come for Parliament and the supreme head to decide what constituted the "true" faith for Englishmen. Henry never worked out a consistent religious policy: the Ten Articles of 1536 and the *Bishop's Book* of the following year tended to be somewhat Lutheran in tone; the Six Articles of 1539, or the Act for Abolishing Diversity of Opinion, and the *King's Book* of 1543 were mildly Catholic. Whatever the religious colouring, Henry's ecclesiastical *via media* was based on obedience to an authoritarian old king and on subjects who were expected to live "soberly, justly and devoutly." Unfortunately for the religious, social, and political peace of the kingdom, both these conditions disappeared the moment Henry died and a nine-year-old boy sat upon the throne.

EDWARD VI (1547–53)

Seymour's protectorate

Henry was legally succeeded by his son Edward VI, but power passed to his brother-in-law, Edward Seymour, earl of Hertford, who became duke of Somerset and lord protector shortly after the new reign began. Seymour ruled *in loco parentis;* the divinity of the crown resided in the boy king, but authority was exercised by an uncle who proved himself to be more merciful than tactful, more idealistic than practical. Sweet reason and tolerance were substituted for the old King's brutal laws. The treason and heresy acts were repealed or modified, and the result came close to destroying the Tudor state. The moment idle tongues could speak with impunity, the kingdom broke into a chorus of religious and social discord. To stem religious dissent, the Lord Protector introduced the Prayer Book of 1549 and an act of uniformity to enforce it. Written by Thomas Cranmer, the Prayer Book was a literary masterpiece but a political flop, for it failed in its purpose. It sought to bring into a single Protestant fold all varieties of middle-of-the-road religious beliefs by deliberately obscuring the central issue of the exact nature of the mass—whether it was a miraculous sacrament or a commemorative service. The Prayer Book succeeded only in antagonizing Protestants and Catholics alike.

Somerset was no more successful in solving the economic and social difficulties of the reign. Rising prices, debasement of the currency, and the cost of war had produced an inflationary crisis in which prices doubled between 1547 and 1549. A false prosperity ensued in which the wool trade boomed, but so also did enclosurers with all their explosive potential. The result was social revolution. Whether Somerset deserved his title of "the good duke" is a matter of opinion. Certainly the peasants thought that he favoured the element in the House of Commons that was anxious to tax sheep raisers and curb enclosures and that section of the clergy that was lashing out at economic inequality. In the summer of 1549 the peasantry in Cornwall and Devonshire revolted against the Prayer Book in the name of the good old religious days under Henry VIII, and almost simultaneously the humble folk in Norfolk rose up against the economic and social injustices of the century. At the same time that domestic rebellion was stirring, the protector had to face a political and international crisis, and he proved himself to be neither a far-sighted statesman nor a shrewd politician. He embroiled the country in war with Scotland that soon involved France and ended in total defeat, and he earned the enmity and disrespect of the members of his own council. In the eyes of the ruling elite, he was responsible for governmental ineptitude and social and religious revolution. The result was inevitable: a palace revolution in October 1549 ensued in which Seymour was arrested and deprived of office, and two and a half years later he was executed on trumped-up charges of treason.

The fall of Seymour

The protector's successor and the man largely responsible for his fall was John Dudley, earl of Warwick, who became duke of Northumberland. The Duke was a man of action who represented most of the acquisitive aspects of the landed elements in society and who allied himself with the extreme section of the Protestant reformers. Under Northumberland, England pulled out of Scotland and in 1550 returned Boulogne to France; social order was ruthlessly re-established in the countryside, the more conservative of the Henrician bishops were imprisoned, the wealth of the church was systematically looted, and uncompromising Protestantism was officially sanctioned. The Ordinal of 1550 transformed the divinely ordained priest into a governmental appointee, the new Prayer Book of 1552 was avowedly Protestant, altars were turned into tables, clerical vestments gave way to plain surplices, and religious orthodoxy was enforced by a new and more stringent Act of Uniformity. How long a kingdom still attached to the outward trappings of Catholicism would have tolerated doctrinal radicalism and the plundering of chantry lands and episcopal revenues under Somerset and Northumberland is difficult to say, but in 1553 the ground upon which Northumberland had built his power crumbled: Edward was dying of consumption. To save himself from Catholic Mary, who was Edward's legal heir as established both by Parliament and her father's will, the Duke tried his hand at kingmaking. He persuaded Edward to declare his sister illegitimate and to bequeath his throne to Lady Jane Grey, the granddaughter of Henry VIII's sister (Mary, duchess of Suffolk), and incidentally Northumberland's daughter-in-law. The gamble failed, for when Edward died on July 6, 1533, the kingdom rallied to the daughter of Catherine of Aragon. Whatever their religious inclinations, Englishmen preferred a Tudor on the throne to a kingmaker ruling behind a puppet queen; in nine days the interlude was over, and Northumberland and his daughter-in-law were in the Tower.

Lady Jane Grey

MARY I (1553–58)

The new Catholic Queen had many fine qualities, and contemporaries announced that she was "a prince of heart and courage more than commonly is in womanhood"; but she was hopelessly outdated. She envisioned the return of a Catholic Church that had long since ceased to exist anywhere in Europe. The worldly and pliable church of pre-Reformation days had been destroyed by the fire of religious war and extremism, and both Catholic and Protestant now denied the tolerant humanistic principle that "men who live according to equity and justice shall be saved" no matter what their creed. By 1553 salvation was strictly a matter of right belief. For Mary it was a sacred obligation to return England to the Catholic fold, and it was almost as great a duty to marry Philip of Spain, her Habsburg cousin and the son of Charles V, the man who had defended her mother's marital rights. She married Philip on July 25, 1554, and six months later, after the landed elements had been assured that their monastic property would not be taken from them, Parliament repealed the Act of Supremacy, reinstated the heresy laws, and petitioned for reunion with Rome. In the end both achievements proved sterile. Her marriage was without love or children, and by associating Catholicism in the popular mind with Spanish arrogance, it triggered a rebellion that almost overthrew the Tudor throne. In January 1554, under the leadership of Sir Thomas Wyat, the peasants of Kent rose up against the Queen's Catholic and Spanish policies, and 3,000 men marched on London. The rebellion was crushed, but it revealed to Mary and her chief minister, Cardinal Reginald Pole, that the kingdom was filled with disloyal hearts who placed Protestantism and nationalism higher than their obedience to the throne.

The Smithfield martyrs

The tragedy of Mary's reign was the belief not only that the old church of her mother's day could be restored but also that it could be best served by fire and blood. Some 300 men and women were martyred in the Smithfield Fires during the last three years of her reign; compared to the Continent, the numbers were not large, but the emotional impact was great. Among the first half-dozen martyrs were the Protestant leaders Cranmer, Ridley, Latimer, and Hooper, and they were burned to strike terror into the hearts of lesser men. Their deaths, however, had the opposite effect; their bravery encouraged others to withstand the flames, and the Smithfield Fires continued to burn because nobody could think of what to do with heretics except to put them to death. The law required it, the prisons were overflowing, and the martyrs themselves offered the government no way out except to enforce the grisly laws.

Mary's reign was a study in failure. Her husband, who was ten years her junior, remained in England as little as possible; the war between France and the Habsburg Empire, into which her Spanish marriage had dragged the kingdom, was a disaster and resulted in the loss of England's last continental outpost, Calais; her subjects learned to call her "bloody," and Englishmen greeted the news of her death and the succession of her sister Elizabeth on November 17, 1558, with ringing bells and bonfires.

ELIZABETH I (1558–1603)

No one in 1558, any more than in 1485, would have predicted that despite the social discord, political floundering, and international humiliation of the past decade, the kingdom again stood on the threshold of an extraordinary reign. Elizabeth had much in common with her grandfather; in both cases their pedigrees were suspect and the political omens unfavourable, and to make matters worse the new monarch was the wrong sex. Englishmen knew that it was unholy and unnatural that "a woman should reign and have empire above men." At 25, however, Elizabeth was better prepared than most women to have empire over men. She had survived the palace revolutions of her brother's reign and the Catholicism of her sister's; she was the product of a fine Renaissance education, and she had learned the need for strong secular leadership devoid of religious bigotry. Moreover, she possessed her father's magnetism without his egotism or ruthlessness. She was also her mother's daughter, and the offspring of Anne Boleyn had no choice but to re-establish the royal supremacy and once again sever the ties with Rome.

Religious policy

Elizabeth herself would have preferred a variety of her father's Catholicism without the pope, but she needed the support of the "zely people" and had to take her religious stand well to the left of centre. Her religious settlement was based on the Protestant Prayer Book of 1552. Many of the ceremonial trappings of Catholicism, however, were retained, and the tone of the document was softened to allow the communion service to become a mass for those Catholics who were looking for a way of conforming with the new settlement. The compromise worked largely because the Queen and her advisers correctly argued that Catholics were better losers than Protestants and that the structure of the new religious establishment should be large, comfortable, and popular, with authority stemming from the royal prerogative. The ecclesiastical history of Elizabeth's reign was, in fact, a long debate with the radicals over the source of divine power—whether it was hierarchical and ultimately emanated from the crown itself or whether it was democratic and was centred in the congregation of all believers.

The Tudor ideal of government. The religious settlement was part of a larger social arrangement that was authoritarian to its core. Elizabeth was determined to be queen in fact as well as in name. She tamed the House of Commons with tact combined with firmness, and she carried on a love affair with her kingdom in which womanhood, instead of being a disadvantage, became her greatest asset. The men she appointed to help her run and stage-manage the government were *politiques* like herself: William Cecil (later Lord Burghley), her principal secretary and in 1572 her lord treasurer; Matthew Parker, her archbishop of Canterbury; and a small group of other moderate and secular men.

In setting her house in order, the Queen followed the hierarchical assumptions of her day. All creation was presumed to be a Great Chain of Being, running from the tiniest insect to the godhead itself, and the universe was seen as an organic whole in which each part played a divinely prescribed role. In politics every element was expected to obey "one head, one governor, one law" in exactly the same way as all parts of the human body obeyed the brain. The crown was divine and gave leadership, but it did not exist alone, nor could it claim a monopoly of divinity, for all parts of the body politic had been created by God. The organ that spoke for the entire kingdom was not the king alone, but "King in Parliament," and when Elizabeth sat in the midst of her Lords and Commons it was said that "every Englishman is intended to be there present from the prince to the lowest person in England." The Tudors needed no standing army in "the French fashion" because God's will and the monarch's decrees were enshrined in acts of Parliament, and this was society's greatest defense against rebellion. The controlling mind within this mystical union of crown and Parliament belonged to the Queen. The Privy Council, acting as the spokesman of royalty, planned and initiated all legislation, and Parliament was expected to turn that legislation into law.

Benevolent paternalism

Inside and outside Parliament the goal of Tudor government was benevolent paternalism in which the strong hand of authoritarianism was masked by the careful shaping of public opinion, the artistry of pomp and ceremony, and the deliberate effort to tie the ruling elite to the crown by catering to the financial and social aspirations of the landed country gentleman. Every aspect of government was intimate because it was small and rested on the support of probably no more than 5,000 key persons. The bureaucracy consisted of a handful of privy councillors at the top and at the bottom possibly 500 paid civil servants—the 15 members of the secretariat, the 265 clerks and custom officials of the treasury, a staff of 50 in the judiciary, and approximately 150 more scattered in other departments. Tudor government was not predominantly professional. Most of the work was done by unpaid amateurs: the sheriffs of the shires, the lord lieutenants of the counties, and above all the Tudor maids-of-all-work—the 1,500 or so justices of the peace.

Smallness did not mean lack of government, for the 16th-century state was conceived of as an organic totality in which the possession of land carried with it duties of leadership and service to the throne, and inferior social position bore the obligation to accept the decisions of elders and betters. The Tudors were essentially medieval in their economic and social philosophy. The usurer and capitalist were considered as dangerous to the commonweal as the overmighty magnate. The aim of government was to curb competition and regulate life so as to attain an ordered and stable society in which all could share according to status. The Statute of Apprentices of 1563 embodied this concept, for it assumed the moral obligation of all men to work, the existence of divinely ordered social distinctions, and the need for the state to define and control all occupations in terms of their utility to society.

The Elizabethan Poor Law

The same assumption operated in the famous Elizabethan Poor Law of 1601—the need to assure a minimum standard of living to all men within an organic and noncompetitive society. By 1600 poverty, unemployment, and vagrancy had become too widespread for the church to handle, and the state had to take over, instructing each parish to levy taxes to pay for poor relief, and to provide work for the able-bodied, punishment for the indolent, and charity for the sick, the aged, and the disabled. The

Tudor social ideal was to achieve a static class structure by guaranteeing a fixed labour supply, restricting social mobility, curbing economic freedom, and creating a kingdom in which subjects could fulfill their ultimate purpose in life—spiritual salvation, not material well-being.

Elizabethan society. Social reality, at least for the poor and powerless, was probably a far cry from the ideal, but for a few years Elizabethan England seemed to possess an extraordinary internal balance and external dynamism. In part the Queen herself was responsible. She demanded no windows into men's souls, and she charmed both great and small with her artistry and tact. In part, however, the Elizabethan age was a success because men had at their disposal new and exciting areas into which to channel their energy. From a kingdom that had once been known for its "sluggish security," Englishmen suddenly turned to the sea and the world that was opening up around them. The first hesitant steps had been taken under Henry VII when John Cabot in 1497 sailed in search of a Northwest Passage to China and as a consequence discovered Cape Breton Island. The search for Cathay became an economic necessity in 1550 when the wool trade collapsed and merchants had to find new markets for their cloth. In response, the Muscovy Company was established to trade with Russia, and by 1588 a hundred vessels a year were visiting the Baltic. Martin Frobisher during the 1570s made a series of voyages to northern Canada in the hope of finding gold and a shortcut to the Orient; John Hawkins encroached upon Spanish and Portuguese preserves and sailed in 1562 for Africa in quest of slaves to sell to West Indian plantation owners; and Sir Francis Drake circumnavigated the globe (December 13, 1577–September 26, 1580) in search not only of the riches of the East Indies but also of Terra Australis, the great southern continent, and new worlds to open up to English trade and colonization. Suddenly Englishmen were on the move: Sir Humphrey Gilbert and his band of settlers set forth for Newfoundland (1583); Sir Walter Raleigh organized the equally ill-fated "lost colony" at Roanoke (1587–91); John Davis in his two small ships, the "Moonshine" and the "Sunshine," reached 72° north, the farthest north any Englishman had ever been (1585–87); and the honourable East India Company was founded to organize the silk and spice trade with the Orient on a permanent basis. The outpouring was certainly inspired by the urge for riches, but it was also religious—the desire to labour in the Lord's vineyard and to found in the wilderness a new and better nation. As it was said, Englishmen went forth "to seek new worlds for gold, for praise, for glory." The same dynamism was manifest in art and culture. Elizabeth's reign was the age of Shakespeare, Marlowe, Spenser, Raleigh, Sidney, Bacon, Donne, and a host of lesser literary lights. It was also the century of stately homes, when the houses of the great were no longer fortresses to defend a man's retainers and dependents but were unprotected residences open to the sunshine. They were designed to reflect man's rational control over nature and were built by gentlemen with enormous confidence in England's future as well as their own. Even the dangers of the reign—the precariousness of Elizabeth's throne and the struggle with Catholic Spain—somehow contrived to generate a self-confidence that had been lacking under "the little Tudors."

The English explorers

Mary, Queen of Scots. The first decade of Elizabeth's reign was relatively quiet, but after 1568 three interrelated matters set the stage for the crisis of the century: the Queen's refusal to marry, the various plots to replace her with Mary of Scotland, and the religious and economic clash with Spain. Elizabeth Tudor's virginity was the cause of great international discussion, for every bachelor prince of Europe hoped to win a throne through marriage with Gloriana, and the source of even greater domestic concern, for everyone except the Queen herself was convinced that Elizabeth should marry and produce heirs. The issue was the cause of her first major confrontation with the House of Commons, which was informed that royal matrimony was not a subject for commoners to discuss. Elizabeth preferred maidenhood; it was politically safer and her most useful diplomatic weapon, but it gave poignancy to the intrigues of her cousin Mary, Queen of Scots. Mary had been an unwanted visitor-prisoner in England ever since 1568, after she had been forced to abdicate her Scottish throne in favour of her 13-month-old son, James VI. She was Henry VIII's grandniece and, in the eyes of many Catholics and a number of political malcontents, the rightful ruler of England, for Mary of Scotland was a Catholic. As the religious hysteria mounted, there was steady pressure put on Elizabeth to rid England of this dangerous threat, but the Queen delayed a final decision for almost 19 years. In the end, however, she had little choice. Jesuit priests were entering the kingdom to harden the hearts of the Queen's subjects against her, forcing the government to introduce harsher and harsher recusancy laws (the fine for failure to attend Anglican service on Sundays was raised from one shilling a week to £20 a month). Puritans were thundering for even stiffer penalties, and Mary played into the hands of her religious and political enemies by involving herself in a series of schemes to unseat her cousin. One plot helped to trigger the rebellion of the northern earls in 1569. Another, the Ridolfi plot of 1571, called for an invasion by Spanish troops stationed in the Netherlands and resulted in the execution in 1572 of the Duke of Norfolk, the ranking peer of the realm. Yet another, the Babington plot of 1586, was in fact a carefully arranged government trap to gain sufficient evidence to have Mary tried and executed for high treason.

The question of the Queen's marriage

Plots on Mary's behalf

The clash with Spain. Mary was executed on February 8, 1587; by then England had moved from cold war to open war against Spain. Philip II was the colossus of Europe and leader of resurgent Catholicism. His kingdom was strong; Spanish troops were the best in Europe, Spain itself had been carved out of territory held by the infidel and still retained its crusading zeal, and the wealth of the New World poured into the treasury at Madrid. Spanish pre-eminence was directly related to the weakness of France, which ever since the accidental death of Henry II in 1559 had been torn by factional strife and civil and religious war. In response to this diplomatic and military imbalance, English foreign policy underwent a fundamental change. By the Treaty of Blois in 1572 England gave up its historic enmity with France, accepting by implication that Spain was the greater danger. It is difficult to say at what point a showdown between Elizabeth and her former brother-in-law became unavoidable—there were so many areas of disagreement—but the two chief points were the refusal of English merchants-cum-buccaneers to recognize Philip's claims to a monopoly of trade wherever the Spanish flag flew throughout the world, and the military and financial support given by the English to Philip's rebellious and heretical subjects in the Netherlands.

The most blatant act of English poaching in Spanish imperial waters was Drake's circumnavigation of the earth, during which Spanish shipping was looted, Spanish claims to California ignored, and Spanish world dominion proved to be a paper empire. But the encounter that really poisoned Anglo-Iberian relations was the Battle of San Juan de Ulúa in September 1568. It concerned John Hawkins' third and final slaving expedition to the Caribbean. After a highly successful voyage in which he exchanged African slaves for West Indian sugar, gold, and hides in defiance of Spanish commercial regulations, Hawkins' fleet of ten vessels put in for repairs at San Juan de Ulúa on the Mexican coast. The next day the Spanish Caribbean fleet appeared, and on the Spanish commander's written statement of peaceful intentions, Hawkins made room in the crowded harbour. No sooner were the Spanish anchored than they launched a surprise attack; only Hawkins in the "Minion" and Drake in the "Judith" escaped. The English cried foul treachery, the Spanish dismissed the action as sensible tactics when dealing with pirates. Drake and Hawkins never forgot or forgave, and it was Hawkins who, as treasurer of the navy, began to build the revolutionary ships that destroyed the old-fashioned galleons of the Spanish Armada.

The harassment of Spain at sea

If the English never forgave Philip's treachery at San Juan de Ulúa, the Spanish never forgot Elizabeth's interference in the Netherlands, where Dutch Protestants were in full revolt. At first, aid had been limited to money and the harbouring of Dutch ships in English ports; but after the assassination of the Protestant leader, William of Orange, in 1584, the position of the rebels became so desperate that Elizabeth in August 1585 sent over an army of 6,000 under the command of the Earl of Leicester. Reluctantly, Philip decided on war against England as the only way of exterminating heresy and disciplining his subjects in the Netherlands. Methodically, he began to build a fleet of 130 vessels, 31,000 men, and 2,431 cannons to hold naval supremacy in the Channel long enough for the Duke of Parma's army, stationed at Dunkirk, to cross over to England. Nothing Elizabeth could do seemed to be able to stop the *Armada Catholica*. She sent Drake to Spain in April 1587 in a spectacular strike at that portion of the fleet forming at Cádiz, but it succeeded only in delaying the sailing date. That delay, however, was important, for Philip's Admiral of the Ocean Seas, the veteran Marqués de Santa Cruz, died, and the job of sailing the Armada was given to the Duque de Medina-Sidonia, who was invariably seasick and confessed that he knew more about gardening than war. What ensued was not the new commander's fault. He did the best he could in an impossible situation, for Philip's Armada was invincible in name only. It was technologically and numerically outclassed by an English fleet of close to 200. Worse, its strategic purpose was grounded on a fallacy: that Parma's troops could be conveyed to England; for the Spanish controlled no deep-water port in the Netherlands in which the Armada's great galleons and Parma's light troop-carrying barges could rendezvous. Even the deity seemed to be more English than Spanish, and in the end the fleet, buffeted by gales, was dashed to pieces as it sought to escape home via the northern route around Scotland and Ireland. Of the 130 ships that left Spain, only 76 crept home; 10 had been captured, sunk, or driven aground by English guns, 24 were sacrificed to wind and storm, and 20 others were "lost, fate unknown."

Defeat of the Armada

Internal discontent. When the Armada died during the first weeks of August 1588, the crisis of Elizabeth's reign was reached and successfully passed. The last years were an anticlimax, for the moment the international danger was surmounted, domestic strife ensued. There were moments of great heroism and success—as when Essex, Raleigh, and Howard made a second descent on Cádiz in 1596, seized the city, and burned the entire West Indian treasure fleet—but the war so gloriously begun deteriorated into a costly campaign in the Netherlands and France and an endless guerrilla action in Ireland, where Philip discovered he could do to Elizabeth what she had been doing to him in the Low Countries. Even on the high seas, the days of fabulous victories were over, for the King of Spain soon learned to defend his empire and his treasure fleets. Both Drake and Hawkins died in 1596 on the same ill-conceived expedition into Spanish Caribbean waters—symbolic proof that the good old days of buccaneering were gone forever. At home the cost of almost two decades of war (£4,000,000) raised havoc with the Queen's finances. It forced her to sell her capital (about £800,000, or roughly one-fourth of all crown lands) and increased her dependence upon parliamentary sources of income, which rose from an annual average of £35,000 to over £112,000 a year.

Elizabeth's financial difficulties were a symptom of a mounting political crisis which under her successors would destroy the entire Tudor system of government. The 1590s were years of depression—bad harvests, soaring prices, peasant unrest, high taxes, and increasing parliamentary criticism of the Queen's economic policies and political leadership. Imperceptibly, the House of Commons was becoming the instrument through which the will of the landed classes could be heard and not an obliging organ of royal control. In Tudor political theory this was a distortion of the proper function of Parliament, which was meant to beseech and petition, never to command or initiate. Three things, however, forced theory to make way for reality. First was the government's financial dependence on Commons, for the organ that paid the royal piper eventually demanded that it also call the governmental tune. Second, under the Tudors, Parliament had been summoned so often and forced to legislate on such crucial matters of church and state—legitimizing and bastardizing monarchs, breaking with Rome, proclaiming the supreme headship (governorship under Elizabeth), establishing the royal succession, and legislating in areas that no Parliament had ever dared enter before—that Commons got into the habit of being consulted. Inevitably a different constitutional question emerged: if Parliament is asked to give authority to the crown, can it also take away that authority? Finally, there was the growth of a vocal, politically conscious, and economically dominant gentry; and the increase in the size of the House of Commons reflected the activity and importance of that class. In Henry VIII's first Parliament there were 74 knights who sat for 37 shires, and 224 burgesses who represented the chartered boroughs of the kingdom. By the end of Elizabeth's reign, borough representation had been increased by 135 seats. Commons was replacing the Lords in importance because the social element it represented had become economically and politically more important than the nobility. Should the crown's leadership falter, there existed by the end of the century an organization that was quite capable of seizing the political initiative, for as one disgruntled contemporary noted: "the foot taketh upon him the part of the head and commons is become a king." Elizabeth had sense enough to avoid a showdown with Commons, and she retreated under parliamentary attack on the issue of her prerogative rights to grant monopolies regulating and licensing the economic life of the kingdom, but on the subject of her religious settlement she refused to budge.

Elizabeth and Parliament

By the last decade of the reign, Puritanism was on the increase. During the 1570s and '80s "cells" had sprung up to spread God's word and rejuvenate the land, and Puritan strength was centred in exactly that segment of society that had the economic and social means to control the realm—the gentry and merchant classes. What set a Puritan off from other Protestants was the literalness with which he held to his creed, the discipline with which he watched his soul's health, the militancy of his faith, and the sense that he was somehow apart from the rest of corrupt humanity. This disciplined spiritual elite clashed with the Queen over the purification of the church and the stamping out of the last vestiges of Catholicism. The controversy went to the root of society: was the purpose of life spiritual or political, was the role of the church to serve God or the crown? In 1576 two brothers, Paul and Peter Wentworth, led the Puritan attack in Commons, criticizing the Queen for her refusal to allow Parliament to debate religious issues. The crisis came to a head in 1586, when Puritans called for legislation to abolish the episcopacy and the Anglican Prayer Book. Elizabeth ordered the bills to be withdrawn, and when Peter Wentworth raised the issue of freedom of speech in Commons, she answered by clapping him in the Tower of London. There was emerging in England a group of religious idealists who derived their spiritual authority from a source that stood higher than the crown and who thereby violated the concept of the organic society and endangered the very existence of the Tudor paternalistic monarchy. As early as 1573 the threat had been recognized:

The growth of Puritanism

> At the beginning it was but a cap, a surplice, and a tippet [over which Puritans complained]; now, it is grown to bishops, archbishops, and cathedral churches, to the overthrow of the established order, and to the Queen's authority in causes ecclesiastical.

James I later reduced the problem to one of his usual *bon mots*—"no bishop, no king." Elizabeth's answer was less catchy but more effective; she appointed as archbishop John Whitgift, who was determined to destroy Puritanism as a politically organized sect. Whitgift was only partially successful, but the Queen was correct: the moment the international crisis was over and a premium was no longer placed on loyalty, Puritans were potential security risks.

The final years of Gloriana's life were difficult both for the theory of Tudor kingship and for Elizabeth herself. She began to lose hold over the imaginations of her subjects, and she faced the only palace revolution of her reign when her favourite, Robert Devereux, earl of Essex, sought to touch her crown. There was still fight in the old Queen, and Essex ended on the scaffold in 1601, but his angry demand could not be ignored:

> What! Cannot princes err? Cannot subjects receive wrong? Is an earthly power or authority infinite? Pardon me, pardon me, my good Lord, I can never subscribe to these principles.

When the old Queen died on March 24, 1603, it was as if the critics of her style of rule and her concept of government had been waiting patiently for her to step down. It was almost with relief that men looked forward to the problems of a new reign, a new dynasty, and a new century. (La.B.S.)

VIII. Wales to c. 1540

WALES BEFORE THE NORMAN CONQUEST

The Roman influence. The early history of Wales (Cymru, Gwalia, Cambria) is largely gleaned from what is known of the withdrawal of Roman authority from the land by the end of the 4th century AD. Wales in the Roman period had shared broadly the experience of the other parts of highland Britain, and the Welsh evidence can often be better understood by analogy with that of other areas. The Latin element in the Welsh language and some features of the literary tradition, such as the legends associated with the Roman emperor Magnus Maximus (Maxen Wledig in Welsh legend), suggest that the Celtic, and largely Brythonic, population of Wales assimilated some aspects of Roman culture and that the memory of imperial governance was cherished. Brythonic refers to one of the two major divisions of Celtic languages (*q.v.*), the other being Goidelic. The former comprises Welsh, Cornish, and Breton; the latter, Irish, Scots Gaelic, and Manx.

The extent of Roman influence on political and social organization is difficult to assess. Roman authors provide the names of some of the "tribes" that occupied parts of Wales, such as the Silures in the southeast and the Demetae in the southwest, but the precise boundaries of these "tribal" territories and their relationship to the political entities that emerged in the following centuries present problems not easily resolved. With others—tribes such as the Ordovices, located roughly in central and northwest Wales—the difficulties are even more pronounced. Archaeological evidence suggests that the civilizing influence of Rome, best exemplified in the Roman town of Caerwent, was most potent along the eastern borderland and the southeast. There is certainly a marked contrast between the Roman villas of the southeast and the enclosed homesteads of the northwest. But even in those areas in which the military aspects of imperial governance are predominant, the evidence indicates increasingly that a more general infusion of Roman culture had been at work. The question of the extent of Roman influence is complicated, however, by the effects both of late migrations into Wales and the processes by which Christianity was established in the land.

Cunedda Wledig's migration

The *Historia Brittonum* of Nennius, a compilation of historical and geographical lore dating from about AD 800, records a tradition that a certain Cunedda Wledig and his sons migrated to northwest Wales from Manaw, a small province round the head of the Firth of Forth in the land of Gododdin, one of the Brythonic kingdoms of north Britain, in order to expel the Irish who had occupied the area. The tradition, which may be authentic in its essentials, points to a movement about AD 400 by an aristocratic group drawn from an area of strong Romano-British traditions. It would seem that Cunedda brought stability to the area that was later to be known as Gwynedd and that he was the founder of its royal dynasty. His descendants were to rule as kings, the assumption of a royal estate being inferred from the inscribed stone at Llangadwaladr, Anglesey, which commemorates his 7th-century descendant Catamanus Rex (Cadfan the King). The ostensible reason for Cunedda's intervention in Wales was the presence of an Irish population, and independent evidence does indicate the existence of Goidelic features in the northwest. In southwest Wales the Irish influences were particularly marked; this was due to an immigration of Goidelic people from the land of the Deisi in southern Ireland, probably in the late 4th and 5th centuries. The royal dynasty that emerged in the southwestern kingdom of Dyfed was distinctly Irish in origin, but the adoption of some Romano-British characteristics is suggested in the inscribed stone commemorating a 6th-century ruler styled "Voteporix the Protector." Irish connections are discernible, too, in the dynasty of the inland kingdom of Brycheiniog. In the southeast, where the Roman *civitas*, or urban community, had perhaps been most firmly established, the consolidation of stable kingdoms was probably accomplished later than elsewhere. Here the territories of Glywysing and Gwent emerged to be united, though not permanently, in the 7th century and called Morgannwg. Finally, among the major divisions, an area in north-central Wales was stabilized to form the kingdom of Powys (Powis), the name being derived from the *paganses*, or country people, of the *civitas* of the Cornovii upon the Welsh borderland. It was this once large kingdom, centred at Pengwern upon the Severn, that bore the brunt of Anglo-Saxon penetration of Wales.

Early Christianity. The extent of the Romano-British inheritance is again problematical in considering the origins of the Christian Church in Wales, for direct literary and archaeological evidence is slight. Traces of Romano-British Christian influence have been detected in the southeast, the area in closest cultural contact with romanized southern Britain. But Wales as a whole was undoubtedly affected by a western reorientation of trade and cultural connections that occurred in the 5th century. Wales and Ireland participated in renewed trade with the Mediterranean and reopened traditional culture routes that had exercised a powerful influence in prehistoric times. The early Christian stone inscriptions point to the strength of the Christian influences derived from Gaul and transmitted along the western seaways. Epigraphic studies reveal, in the script and in the formulas employed upon the stones, a fusion of Gallic Christian and Celtic influences. The stones, especially numerous in southwest Wales, which bear inscriptions in the ogham script (an alphabet comprised of notches), reflect the mingling of Christian with what were essentially Goidelic influences. In its forms, the church revealed a monastic character due both to its Gallic origins and to the needs of a Celtic society that did not possess important urban centres. Major monasteries were established in Wales by the 6th century, associated with figures such as St. Illtud at Llantwit Major or St. Cadog at Llancarfan. The founding of these centres was probably followed by a secondary movement, characterized by intense activity within the church, associated particularly with the names of St. David in south Wales and St. Beuno in north Wales. An examination of the distribution of the dedications of the churches and of the evidence of place-names in which the *llan* element (signifying a sacred enclosure) is often coupled with a personal name has served to suggest the spheres of influence of the Christian missionaries, or "saints," and to illustrate the close contacts with other Celtic lands that were maintained by means of the western seaways in this creative period. During the 6th century, in fact, the characteristics of the pre-Norman church were well established. Church organization was based upon a monastic church, or *clas*, akin to a minster, with which lesser churches were associated.

Westward orientation

Relations with the Anglo-Saxons. The settlement of Anglo-Saxon peoples along the Welsh borderland separated the Brythonic people of Wales from their compatriots in the north and southwest of Britain, and the name Cymry ("compatriots"; *i.e.*, the Welsh) dates from this period. The campaign waged by Cadwallon, king of

Gwynedd, in Northumbria early in the 7th century represents a late involvement of a Welsh king in the conflict between the Brythonic kingdoms of northern Britain and the English. That conflict in the north had already provided the subject matter of the earliest poetry in the Welsh language, the work of Taliesin and Aneirin. The conflict upon the Welsh border itself is echoed in the Llywarch Hen poems, which, though probably dating from the 9th century, have their setting two centuries earlier in the contest between Powys and Mercia. The gradual colonization of the approaches to Wales by English peoples, a process marked by short dikes still visible upon the landscape, led to a final demarcation of the line of Mercian penetration with the construction in the time of King Offa (died 796) of the great linear earthwork known as Offa's Dyke.

Attempts at unity

Attempts during the next two centuries to bring the Welsh kingdoms west of the dike into a political unity proved to be only partially successful and impermanent. Rhodri Mawr ("the Great"; died 878), the king of Gwynedd who provided stern resistance to the Viking attacks, brought Powys within his dominion and then briefly extended his sway over two areas in the southwest (lying north and east of Dyfed), namely Ceredigion and Ystrad Tywi, which had previously been united to form the kingdom of Seisyllwg. The period following Rhodri's death proved to be of far-reaching significance. The outlying kingdoms of Wales—Dyfed, Brycheiniog, Glywysing, and Gwent—being subjected to pressure exerted by Rhodri's sons or by Mercia, turned to the kingdom of Wessex and by a formal commendation entered into that allegiance, ultimately expressed in homage and fealty, which each of the kings of Wales owed, individually and directly, to the English monarchy. Anarawd (died 916), a son of Rhodri, and his brothers, who shared the governance of their father's lands, subsequently submitted to Alfred (died 899) and completed the theoretical subjection of the Welsh kingdoms to the English sovereign. Rhodri's grandson, Hywel ap Cadell (Hywel Dda, "the Good"; died 950), starting from a patrimony in Seisyllwg, secured Dyfed by marriage, thereby creating the kingdom of Deheubarth. Eventually Gwynedd and Powys also came under his rule. Hywel accepted the position of a *sub-regulus*, or under-king, of the king of Wessex and seems to have endeavoured to emulate the advanced institutions of the contemporary West Saxon kingdom. Hywel's appeasement of Athelstan of Wessex (died 939) provoked a reaction expressed in the poem *Armes Prydein*, which envisages the formation of an alliance of Celtic peoples to oppose the Anglo-Saxon *mechdeyrn*, or overlord.

The conflicting impulses that were to be a feature of Welsh medieval political history were already discernible by the 10th century. Before its close, Maredudd ap Owain (died 999), a grandson of Hywel Dda, brought the northern and western kingdoms once more into a transitory unity. But his death opened a period of prolonged turmoil in which internal conflicts were complicated and intensified by Anglo-Saxon and Norse intervention. The established dynasties were challenged by men who asserted themselves within the kingdoms and exercised ephemeral supremacies. Of these, the most successful was Gruffudd ap Llywelyn (died 1063), who brought Gwynedd, then Deheubarth, and finally (though briefly) the whole of Wales under his dominion. The devastation wrought upon the English borderland, still not erased at the time of the making of Domesday Book (1086), was probably in large measure due to him. His death in 1063 meant that the most powerful ruler of independent Wales was destroyed only a few years before the coming of Norman forces to the Anglo-Welsh frontier.

Temporary unity under Gruffudd

Early Welsh society. The endeavours of the dynasties in the 9th and 10th centuries, though only partially successful with regard to the problem of Welsh unification, had important and lasting consequences. Scholarly activity such as that represented in the *Historia Brittonum* and in annals and genealogies, material relating both to north Britain and to Wales, may well reflect the attempt of the descendants of Rhodri Mawr to consolidate their position and enhance their prestige. In creative literature it is likely that the origins of some texts preserved in medieval manuscripts, including some material in triad form (triple groupings of legal, literary, historical, and other materials), may be traced back to this period. The earliest Welsh law texts, though they date from the late 12th century onward, attribute the original codification of law to Hywel Dda; and the possibility that a significant development in Welsh jurisprudence took place under the aegis of that ruler is not improbable. The presence not only of a stratum of early indigenous law but of Anglo-Saxon influences (reflected, for instance, in the use of the term *edling* for the heir to the throne) points to a conscious adoption by the Welsh kings of some Anglo-Saxon concepts and procedures. These indications accord well with others, including that of the late inscribed stones, which point to an eastward reorientation of Welsh culture in this period.

Organization of the kingdoms

The law texts, studied in association with other materials, reveal an early society ruled by kings (*brenhinoedd*) of independent kingdoms who possessed an authority, notably a recognized function in the public enforcement of legal obligations, that stood in contrast to traditional Celtic custom. The kingdoms were normally divided for purposes of royal administration into *cantrefs*. These in turn consisted of groups of *maenors* occupied by the bond or free elements of which Welsh society was composed. The bond population, which was probably larger than was at one time thought and which was concentrated in fairly compact *maenors* in lowland areas favourable to an agrarian economy, was organized on conventional manorial principles. In the economy of the upland areas the emphasis was upon a pastoral economy practiced by free communities, which were accorded more extensive *maenors*. The *maenor* organization as a whole represents a stage in the economic organization of Welsh society that was to be gradually superseded as a result of changes, quickened considerably in the 12th century, designed to ensure a more intensive exploitation of the soil. A smaller unit, the *tref*, or township, then replaced the *maenor*. In the sphere of royal administration the *cantref*, by a process probably well advanced on the eve of the first Norman invasions, was largely replaced by a small unit, the *commote*, which was to remain, under Welsh and alien lords, the basic unit of administration and jurisdiction throughout the medieval period.

WALES FROM THE 11TH TO THE 16TH CENTURY

Norman infiltration. The Norman conquest of England saw the establishment upon the Welsh border of the three earldoms of Chester, Shrewsbury, and Hereford, and from each of these strongpoints advances were made into Wales. Norman progress in southern Wales in the reign of William I (1066–87) was limited to the colonization of Gwent in the southeast. Domesday Book contains evidence suggesting that King William and Rhys ap Tewdwr, king of Deheubarth (died 1093), made a compact that recognized the Welsh ruler's authority in his own kingdom and perhaps also his influence in those other areas of southern Wales outside Deheubarth, particularly Morgannwg and Brycheiniog, that still lay outside Norman control. Meanwhile, from Chester and Shrewsbury, the Normans had penetrated more deeply into Wales, so that at Domesday, though the area colonized was limited, Norman lordship had been asserted over numerous *cantrefs* and *commotes* that had previously formed portions of the kingdoms of Gwynedd and Powys. The political situations in the northern and southern parts of the country were reversed during a period of renewed conflict in the reign (1087–1100) of William II who invaded Wales three times, unsuccessfully. The death of Rhys ap Tewdwr in 1093, opposing the Norman advance into Brycheiniog, was quickly followed by the invasion of virtually the whole of southern Wales. Advances from several bases along the Welsh border enabled Norman lords to establish the major lordships of Cardigan, Pembroke, Brecon, and Glamorgan. This advance constituted the decisive stage in the creation of the March of Wales (that portion of Wales under the author-

Creation of the March

ity of the English Crown). In each lordship of the March, the Norman lord, who was himself responsible for the conquest of the land, assumed the wide range of powers previously exercised there by the Welsh kings. These indigenous rights, enlarged and given definition during the course of the following centuries, formed the basis of the Custom of the March. This was a regality that enabled the lords to exercise extensive jurisdictional powers over the largely Welsh communities of their lordships and afforded them an extraordinary degree of autonomy in their relations with the English monarchy.

Gwynedd, Powys, and Deheubarth. The crucial years after 1093 saw also the initiation in northern Wales of a period of conflict by which the area was gradually recovered from Norman rule and the kingdoms of Gwynedd and Powys reconstituted as major political entities. Gwynedd, first under Gruffudd ap Cynan (died 1137) and then under his son Owain Gwynedd (died 1170), gained a firm governance that enabled the younger ruler, controlling a kingdom extending from the Dyfi to the Dee, to withstand foreign pressure, which was particularly severe during the reign (1154–89) of Henry II. In Powys the rule of Madog ap Maredudd (died 1160) likewise proved to be a period of stability and of expansion eastward beyond Offa's Dyke into lands that had been subjected to alien settlement in both the Anglo-Saxon and Norman periods. In southwest Wales, too, representatives of the dynasty of Deheubarth for over 30 years waged a campaign that finally enabled Rhys ap Gruffudd (died 1197), a grandson of Rhys ap Tewdwr, to win from Henry II a recognition of his position. Rhys ruled a land that was not as extensive as the ancient kingdom, for Norman control of the lordship of Pembroke and of other lordships along the southern coastline was conceded, but it nevertheless constituted a considerable dominion. The three kingdoms of Gwynedd, Powys, and Deheubarth formed by the third quarter of the 12th century a well-defined sphere of Welsh political influence (Wallia, or Pura Wallia) in contradistinction to the sphere of Norman influence (Marchia Wallie). Throughout the remainder of the period of Welsh independence there remained a memory that Wales, outside the March, had consisted historically of three kingdoms ruled from the three principal seats of Aberffraw in Gwynedd, Mathrafal in Powys, and Dinefwr in Deheubarth. The evidence, especially that of Welsh jurisprudence as revealed in texts dating from the late 12th century onward, reflects an endeavour on the part of these rulers to formulate a concept of Welsh kingship in which indigenous elements were blended with the new influences at work in the feudal monarchies. Each ruler, still known as a king (*rex*, *brenin*) but later to be styled prince (*princeps*, *tywysog*) or lord (*dominus*, *arglwydd*), governed an autonomous kingdom. The kings' relationship with the English monarchy was formalized in the homage and fealty that was done by each ruler in respect of his patrimony.

Welsh kings outside the March

The stability provided by these rulers enabled their territories to recover from the depredations suffered during the conflicts of the Norman period. There are strong indications that the kings effected changes in social organization designed to increase the resources of the royal demesne, or crown land, and to promote generally a more intensive exploitation of the agrarian resources of their territories. The rulers deployed, especially on the coastal lowlands, communities characterized by personal servitude and the obligation to provide labour services. The organization of the large bond element in the population was in some areas adjusted to provide more favourable tenurial conditions as an incentive to the colonization of marginal lands. The agrarian changes also involved the settlement upon the soil of kindred groups of freemen. Stemming from a primary settlement of a single family in a shareland, the combined effect of successive divisions—the result of partible inheritance and of the expansion of the cultivated area—produced a pattern of dispersed settlement, in contrast to the nucleated (clustered) settlement of the bond communities. The endowment of some privileged free proprietors with substantial estates facilitated the growth of a class of landowners, who, linked to the royal lineages by ties of service, supplied the Welsh rulers with the personnel of their increasingly sophisticated administration. A renewed cultural vitality is revealed in Latin scholarship and in a flowering of the literary tradition.

Ecclesiastical affairs in the Norman period

In ecclesiastical affairs, the early Norman period saw the inauguration of a process by which the *clas* organization was replaced by arrangements consonant with the practice of the reformed church. The four territorial dioceses of Bangor, St. David's, Llandaff, and St. Asaph were created, and a parochial organization was gradually established. The church structure was a creation of the Normans, and the bishops appointed to Welsh sees owed a profession of obedience to Canterbury. Even so, Bernard, bishop of St. David's in 1115–48, claimed the status of an archbishop and, in furthering his campaign, appealed to the historical legacy of an early independent Welsh church. His bid was revived at the end of the century by Giraldus Cambrensis, but more significant was the resistance of the clergy of Bangor, who, acting under the protection of Owain Gwynedd at a time of national resistance toward the end of his reign, steadfastly refused to meet the demands of Thomas Becket, archbishop of Canterbury, that the newly elected bishop should swear fealty to Canterbury. The lay powers found adherents in the Cistercian Order. Houses such as Margam and Tintern, situated in the March, had close associations with their marcher patrons. The offshoots of the Cistercian monastery of Whitland, notably Strata Florida and Aberconway, were handsomely endowed by the Welsh rulers, who in return were supported in their political endeavours.

Llywelyn ap Iorwerth. In each of the three kingdoms of Gwynedd, Powys, and Deheubarth, the death of its powerful ruler was followed by a contested succession. The resulting conflicts portended a furthering of the fractionization characteristic of Welsh political history. In Powys and Deheubarth the unity of the kingdom was never restored; but with the emergence to power in the late 12th century of Llywelyn ap Iorwerth (died 1240), a grandson of Owain Gwynedd, Gwynedd was united once more under the strong hand of a single ruler. Llywelyn's aggression against neighbouring territories incurred resistance, which King John turned to his advantage in a campaign in 1211 whereby the Prince of Gwynedd was subjected to humiliating terms. But availing himself of a general Welsh reaction to John's measures for the permanent subjugation of the country, Llywelyn directed a sustained campaign in which his former adversaries participated. Llywelyn achieved a dominant position among the princes, which, while the contest with John persisted, augured the forging of a Welsh polity by bonds of homage and fealty to himself. But though he remained a powerful influence over the other Welsh princes and thereby minimized the crown's involvement in the affairs of Wales, Llywelyn was unable to secure a formal royal recognition of the territorial and conceptual achievements of the period of conflict. Llywelyn's aspirations for a wider Welsh principality based upon the supremacy of Gwynedd then centred upon David (later David II), his son by Joan, daughter of King John. David was designated as Llywelyn's heir in preference to his elder but bastard son, Gruffudd, and the Welsh dynasty looked to the English monarchy to ensure an unchallenged succession. In the event, the crown was able to use the dissension between the two sons and the disparate ambitions of the other Welsh princes to restrict David's power to Gwynedd alone. During the war of 1244–46 David contended for a broader influence, but his promising endeavour was cut short by his early death in 1246, without heir.

In the following year his nephews Owain and Llywelyn, two of the four sons of Gruffudd, entered into a treaty obligation by which the crown decreed the partition of a truncated Gwynedd into two parts, with the prospect of further division to provide for the younger brothers. But between 1255 and 1258 Llywelyn ap Gruffudd (died 1282), one of the four brothers, asserted his supremacy first in Gwynedd and then farther afield. Helped by the preoccupation of the English crown with the baronial conflict, the Prince secured a hegemony formally acknowledged by Henry III in 1267 by the Treaty of Montgomery, when Llywelyn's style, "prince of Wales," first assumed in 1258, and his right to the homage and fealty of the Welsh lords of Wales were recognized. Llywelyn had thereby brought into being a Principality of Wales comprised of the lands that had formed the 12th-century kingdoms of Gwynedd, Powys, and Deheubarth as well as parts of the March. Historically, this meant the reversal of a situation, for which there were several centuries of precedent, whereby the increasingly fragmented territories under Welsh rule had been fiefs held directly from the king of England. The opportunity to consolidate the governance of the principality proved to be brief. Friction between Llywelyn and Edward I led in 1277 to a war in which the Prince, isolated by the withdrawal of his vassals' fealty and confronted with the great resources and superior organization of England, was forced to accept terms that restricted his power to Gwynedd west of the Conway. By 1282 a deterioration in relations between Edward and a number of Welsh princes resulted in renewed conflict, which, widespread and vigorous, became a true war of Welsh independence. Although sustained even after the death of Llywelyn in December 1282, the resistance finally collapsed in the summer of the following year.

War with Edward I

The Edwardian settlement. Edward I provided for the security of his conquests by means of a program of castle building, initiated after the war of 1277 and subsequently extended to include the great structures of Conway, Caernarfon, Harlech, and, later, Beaumaris. Each castle sheltered a borough where English colonists were settled. The king's arrangements for the governance of Llywelyn's former lands in northwest Wales were embodied in the Statute of Wales (1284). Three counties—Anglesey, Caernarfon, and Merioneth—were created and placed under the custody of a justice of North Wales. In northeast Wales a fourth county, Flint, was attached to the earldom of Chester. In southwest Wales the counties of Cardigan and Carmarthen, under the custody of the justice of West Wales, were formed out of lands over which royal power had been gradually extended by a process completed upon the failure, in 1287, of the revolt of Rhŷs ap Maredudd, the last of the princes of the dynasty of Deheubarth. Structurally, the shires that formed the Principality of Wales were similar to those of England, and certain common-law procedures were introduced into their courts, but the shires remained outside the jurisdiction of the central courts of Westminster, and they did not elect representatives to Parliament. The March of Wales was extended through the creation by royal charters, out of parts of Gwynedd and Powys, of the lordships of Denbigh, Ruthin, Bromfield and Yale, and Chirk. In his relations with two of the major barons of the older March, Gilbert de Clare of Glamorgan and Humphrey de Bohun of Brecon, Edward showed a determination to assert the sovereignty of the crown over the March and to eradicate abuses of the Custom of the March such as the claim, defiantly expressed by Gilbert, to the right to wage war in the March. But neither Edward nor his successors attempted any far-reaching changes in the organization of the March, and political fractionization persisted over the next two centuries.

Rebellion and annexation. Both the crown and the marcher lords employed in the administration of their lands Welshmen drawn from an administrative class that had been fostered by the princes themselves. Those of the principality revealed a particular loyalty to Edward II in the political crises of his reign, and their continued attachment to his cause even after his deposition created a tense situation in 1327. During the 14th century there were occasional variances, but the identity of interest established between the crown and the leading Welshmen proved durable. Even so, the community endured both the economic difficulties encountered over wide areas of Europe at this time and the specifically Welsh problems created by the fact that an important phase in the transition from early medieval social arrangements coincided with the pressures exerted by an alien and fiscally extractive administration. At the very end of the century, the deposition of Richard II, who had influential Welshmen among his partisans, released from allegiance to the monarchy a group that, associated with Owain Glyndŵr (Owen Glendower), raised a great rebellion that drew its strength from the community as a whole. In the period 1400–07 the royal government lost control of the greater part of Wales, and in some areas the insurrection remained unextinguished several years later.

The rebellion, however, quickened certain processes that were to lead ultimately to the enfranchisement provided by Tudor legislation. In northern Wales particularly, the availability of civil actions by English law led to an early but unrequited demand for English land law. After the rebellion the disabilities incurred by reason of Welsh nationality were underlined. Though often expressed in literature in militant terms and, during the years of dynastic conflict, manipulated by the protagonists of York and Lancaster, the aspirations of the community were focussed in a demand for English denizenship. First individual petitioners looked for enfranchisement and then whole communities in northern Wales secured from Henry VII, by negotiation and payment, charters conferring upon them English land law and other advantages. A realization by the crown of its inability to reverse a decline in the financial yield of its Welsh lands, an experience shared by the marcher lords, contributed to Henry VII's policy, and it may also have influenced Henry VIII's advisers in formulating the union legislation. The acts of 1536 and 1543, opening Wales to parliamentary taxation, extended to all of Wales practices already at work in the Principality of North Wales and introduced new features. The March was finally eradicated, and Wales was now divided into 13 counties. English common law was made applicable, and justice was to be administered by justices of the peace in quarter sessions and, in 12 counties (other arrangements being made for Monmouthshire), by the judges upon the four circuits of the Great Sessions. Wales was given a jurisdiction that remained separate from the Westminster courts, though each of its shires was represented at the Westminster Parliament. (J.B.Sm.)

The union of 1536

IX. Scotland to 1603

EARLY HISTORY

Evidence of human settlement in the area later known as Scotland dates from the 3rd millennium BC. The earliest people, Mesolithic (Middle Stone Age) hunters and fishermen, were to be found on the west coast, near Oban, and as far south as Kirkcudbright, where their settlements are marked by large deposits of discarded mollusk shells. There were also settlements in the Forth estuary, where, in the area of Stirling, they obtained meat from stranded whales. These were followed, early in the 2nd millennium BC by Neolithic (New Stone Age) farmers who knew the use of cereals and of cattle and sheep. They made settlements on the west coast and as far north as Shetland. Many built collective chamber tombs, that at Maeshowe in Orkney being the finest in Britain. A settlement of such people at Skara Brae in Orkney consists of a cluster of seven self-contained huts connected by covered galleries or alleys. The "Beaker folk," so called from the shape of their drinking vessels, came to east Scotland from northern Europe, probably from about 1800 BC on. They buried their dead individually and were pioneers in bronze working. The most impressive monuments of Bronze Age Scotland are the stone circles, presumably for religious ceremonies, like those at Callanish in Lewis and Brodgar in Orkney, the latter being over 300 feet (91 metres) in diameter.

From about 700 BC onward there was a distinct final period in Scottish prehistory. This period is the subject of current archaeological controversy, with somewhat less stress than in the past being placed on the importance of the introduction of iron using or on the impact of large new groups of iron-using settlers. One key development in the middle of the 1st millennium was the change from a relatively warm and dry climate to one that was cooler and wetter. Another was the appearance of hill forts, having stone ramparts with an internal frame of timber: a good example is at Abernethy near the Tay. Some of these forts have recently been dated to the 7th and 6th centuries BC, and this might suggest that they were adopted by already established tribes rather than introduced by incomers, whose presence at this early date has yet to be proved. Massive decorated bronze armlets with Celtic ornamentation, found in northeastern Scotland and dated to the period AD 50–150, suggest that chieftains from outside may have come to these tribes at this period, displaced from farther south by fresh settlers from the Continent and then by the advent of the Romans in AD 43. From 100 BC the "brochs" appeared in the extreme north of Scotland and the northern isles. These were high, round towers, that at Mousa in Shetland standing almost 50 feet (15 metres) in height. The broch dwellers may have carried on intermittent warfare with the fort builders of farther south. On the other hand, the two types of structures may not represent two wholly distinct cultures, and the two peoples may have together comprised the ancestors of the people later known as the Picts.

The "brochs"

The houses of this people were circular, sometimes standing alone, sometimes in groups of 15 or more, as at Hayhope Knowe in the Cheviot Hills on the border between modern Scotland and England. Some single steadings, set in bogs or on lakesides, are called crannogs. Corn growing was probably of minor importance in the economy; the people were pastoralists and food-gatherers. They were ruled by a warrior aristocracy whose bronze and iron parade equipment has, in a few instances, survived.

Roman penetration and the Dark Age peoples. Gnaeus Julius Agricola, the Roman governor of Britain (AD 77–84), was the first Roman general to operate extensively in Scotland. He defeated the natives at Mons Graupius, possibly in Banffshire, probably in AD 84. In the following year he was recalled, and his policy of containing the hostile tribes within the Highland zone, which he had marked by building a legionary fortress at Inchtuthil in Strathmore, was not continued. His tactics were logical, if Scotland was to be subdued, but probably required the commitment of more troops than the overall strategy of the Roman Empire could afford. The only other period that a forward policy was attempted was between about 144 and about 190, when a turf wall, the Antonine Wall (named after the emperor Antoninus Pius), was manned between the Forth and the Clyde.

The still-impressive stone structure known as Hadrian's Wall had been built between the Tyne and Solway Firth in the years 122–128, and it was to be the permanent northern frontier of Roman Britain. After a northern rising, the emperor Severus supervised the restoring of the Hadrianic line in the years 209–211, and thereafter southeast Scotland seems to have enjoyed almost a century of peace. In the 4th century there were successive raids from north of the Wall and periodic withdrawals of Roman troops to the Continent. Despite increasing use of native buffer-states in front of the Wall, the Romans found their frontier indefensible by the end of the 4th century.

At Housesteads, at about the midpoint of Hadrian's Wall, archaeologists have uncovered a market where northern natives exchanged cattle and hides for Roman products: in this way some Roman wares, and possibly more general cultural influences, found their way north, but the scale of this was probably small. Roman civilization, typified by the towns and villas, or country houses, of southern Britain, was unknown in Scotland. Thus Scotland as a whole was never dominated by the Romans, nor even strongly influenced by them.

From about AD 400 there was a long period for which written evidence is scanty. Four peoples—the Picts, the Scots, the Britons, and the Angles—were eventually to merge and thus form the kingdom of Scots.

The peoples of early Scotland

The Picts occupied Scotland north of the Forth. Their identity has been much debated, but they possessed a distinctive culture, seen particularly in their carved symbol stones. Their original language, presumably non-Indo-European, has disappeared: some Picts probably spoke a Brythonic Celtic language. Pictish unity may have been impaired by their custom of succession to the throne, which is thought to have been matrilinear.

The Scots, from Dalriada in northern Ireland, colonized the Argyll area, probably in the late 5th century. Their continuing connection with Ireland was a source of strength to them, and Scots and Irish Gaelic (Goidelic Celtic languages) did not become distinct from one another until the late Middle Ages. Scottish Dalriada soon extended its cultural as well as its military sway east and south, though one of its greatest kings, Aidan, was, in 603, defeated by the Angles at Degsastan near the later Scottish border.

The Britons, speaking a Brythonic Celtic language, colonized Scotland from farther south, probably from the first century BC onward. They lost control of southeastern Scotland to the Angles in the early 7th century AD. The British heroic poem *Gododdin* describes a stage in this process. The British kingdom of Strathclyde in southwestern Scotland remained, with its capital at Dumbarton.

The Angles were Teutonic-speaking invaders from across the North Sea. Settling from the 5th century, they had by the early 7th century created the kingdom of Northumbria, stretching from the Humber to the Forth. A decisive check to their northward advance was administered in 685 by the Picts at the Battle of Nechtansmere in Angus.

Christianity. Christianity was introduced to Scotland in late Roman times, and traditions of St. Ninian's evangelizing in the southwest have survived. He is a shadowy figure, and it is doubtful if his work extended very far north.

Christianity was firmly established throughout Scotland by the Celtic clergy, coming with the Scots settlers from Ireland, and possibly giving the Scots a decisive cultural advantage in the early unification of Scotland. The Celtic Church lacked a territorial organization of parishes and dioceses and a division between secular and regular clergy: its communities of missionary monks were ideal agents of conversion. The best known figure, possibly the greatest, is St. Columba who founded his monastery at Iona, an island of the Inner Hebrides, in 565: his life was written by Adamnan, abbot of Iona, within a century of his death. Columba is believed to have been influential in converting the Picts, and he certainly did much to support the Scots king Aidan politically.

St. Columba

St. Aidan brought the Celtic Church to Northumbria in the 630s, establishing his monastery at Lindisfarne. At the Synod of Whitby in 664 the king of Northumbria had to decide between the Celtic and the Roman styles of Christianity: he chose the latter. There had been differences over such observances as the dating of Easter, but there was no question of the Celtic monks being regarded as schismatics. The *Ecclesiastical History of the English People*, by Bede, a monk of Jarrow in Northumbria (died 735) is a first-rate source for the history of Dark Age Scotland and shows remarkable sympathy with the Celtic clergy, though Bede was a Roman monk.

In the early 8th century the church among the Picts and Scots accepted Roman usages on such questions as Easter. Nevertheless, the church in Scotland remained Celtic in many ways until the 11th century: still dominated by its communities of clergy (who were called Célidé or Culdees), it clearly corresponded well to the tribal nature of society.

The Norse influence. Viking raids on the coasts of Britain began at the end of the 8th century, Lindisfarne and Iona being pillaged in the 790s. By the mid-9th century, Norse settlement of the western and northern isles and of Caithness and Sutherland had begun: the main cause was probably overpopulation on the west coast of Norway. During the 10th century, Orkney and Shetland were ruled by Norse earls nominally subject to Norway. In 1098 Magnus II Barefoot, king of Norway, successfully asserted his authority in the northern and western isles and made an agreement with the king of Scots on their respective spheres of influence. A mid-12th-century earl of Orkney, Ragnvald, built the great cathedral at Kirkwall in honour of his martyred uncle St. Magnus.

The Norse legacy to Scotland was long lasting. In the mid-12th century there was a rising against the Norse in the west under a native leader, Somerled, who drove them from the greater part of mainland Argyll. A Norwegian expedition of 1263 under King Haakon IV failed to maintain the Norse presence in the Hebrides, and three years later they were ceded to Scotland by the Treaty of Perth. In 1468–69 the northern isles of Orkney and Shetland were pawned to Scotland as part of a marriage settlement with the crown of Denmark-Norway. A Scandinavian language, the Norn, was spoken in these Viking possessions, and some Norse linguistic influence is discernible in Shetland to the present day.

THE UNIFICATION OF THE KINGDOM

In 843 Kenneth I MacAlpin, king of Scots, also became king of the Picts and crushed resistance to his assuming the throne. Kenneth may have had a claim on the Pictish throne through the matrilinear law of succession: probably the Picts, too, had been weakened by Norse attacks. The Norse threat helped to weld together the new kingdom of Alba and to cause its heartlands to be located in eastern Scotland, the former Pictland, with Dunkeld becoming its religious capital. But within Alba it was the Scots who established a cultural and linguistic supremacy, no doubt merely confirming a tendency seen before 843.

Ascendancy of the Scots

As the English kingdom was consolidated, its kings, in the face of Norse attacks, found it useful to have an understanding with Alba. In 945 Edmund of England is said to have leased to Malcolm I of Alba the whole of Cumbria, probably an area including land on both sides of the western half of the later Anglo-Scottish border. In the late 10th century a similar arrangement seems to have been made for Lothian, the corresponding territory to the east. The Scots confirmed their hold on Lothian, from the Forth to the Tweed, when, about 1016, Malcolm II defeated a Northumbrian army at Carham. About the same time, Malcolm II placed his grandson Duncan I upon the throne of the British kingdom of Strathclyde. Duncan succeeded Malcolm in 1034 and brought Strathclyde into the kingdom of Scots. During the next two centuries the Scots kings pushed their effective power north and west—William I was successful in the north and Alexander II in the west—until mainland Scotland became one political unit. Less discernible but as important was the way the various peoples grew together, though significant linguistic and other differences remained.

According to the Celtic system of succession, known as tanistry, a king could be succeeded by any male member of the *derbfine*, a family group of four generations: members of collateral branches seem to have been preferred to descendants, and the successor, or tanist, might be named in his predecessor's lifetime. This system, in practice, led to many successions by the killing of one's predecessor. Thus Duncan I was killed by his cousin Macbeth in 1040, and Macbeth was killed by Malcolm III Canmore, Duncan I's son, in 1057. Shakespeare freely adapted the story of Macbeth, who historically seems to have been a successful king and who may have gone on pilgrimage to Rome.

Up to the 11th century the unification was the work of a Scots Gaelic-speaking dynasty, and there is place-name evidence of the penetration of Gaelic south of the Forth. But from then on, the Teutonic English speech that had come to Scotland from the kingdom of Northumbria began to attain mastery, and Gaelic began its slow retreat north and west. This is not obscured by the fact that, from the 12th century onward, Anglo-Norman was for a time the speech of the leaders of society in England and Scotland alike. By the later Middle Ages, Old English had evolved into two separate languages, Middle English and Middle Scots, the latter with the court of the Stewart (Stuart) kings of Scots as its focus. After 1603, the increasing political and cultural assimilation of Scotland to England checked the further development of Scots as a separate language.

The persistence of distinctively Celtic institutions in post-12th-century Scotland is a more complex question, as will be seen from the way in which primogeniture replaced tanistry as the system of royal succession. It can be argued, however, that a Celtic stress on the family bond in society persisted throughout the Middle Ages and beyond—and not only in the Highlands, with its clan organization of society.

The royal succession

The development of the monarchy. Malcolm III Canmore (1058–93) came to the throne by disposing of his rivals and thereafter sought, in five unsuccessful raids, to extend his kingdom into northern England. Whereas his first wife, Ingibjorg, was the daughter of a Norse earl of Orkney, his second, Margaret, came from the Saxon royal house of England. With Margaret and her sons, Scotland entered a phase of being particularly receptive to cultural influence from the south. Margaret was a great patroness of the church but without altering its organization as her sons were to do.

On the death of Malcolm III on his last English raid, sustained attempts were made to prevent the application of the southern custom of succession by primogeniture. Both Malcolm's brother and Malcolm's son by his first marriage held the throne for short periods: but it was the three sons of Malcolm and Margaret who eventually established themselves—Edgar (1097–1107), Alexander I (1107–24), and David I (1124–53). The descendants of Malcolm III's first marriage continued to trouble the ruling dynasty until the early 13th century, but the descendants of his second retained the throne. It happened that until the late 13th century, the heir to the throne by primogeniture was always the obvious candidate. It is noteworthy that in charters of about 1145, David I's son Henry (who was to die before his father) is described as *rex designatus*, very much like the tanist of the Celtic system. It is thus very hard to date precisely the acceptance of southern custom as exemplified by primogeniture.

Such was the force of Celtic reaction against southern influence that Edgar and Alexander I could be said to owe their thrones solely to English aid and were feudally subject to the English king.

David I. David I was by marriage a leading landowner in England and was well-known at the English court: he was, nevertheless, an independent monarch, making Scotland strong by drawing on English cultural and organizational influences. Under him and his successors many Anglo-Norman families came to Scotland, and their members were rewarded with lands and offices. Among the most important were the Bruces in Annandale, the de Morvilles in Ayrshire and Lauderdale, and the Fitzalans, who became hereditary High Stewards and who, as the Stewart dynasty, were to inherit the throne, in Renfrewshire. (After the 16th century the Stewart dynasty was known by its French spelling, "Stuart," the French language having no "w.") Such men were often given large estates in outlying areas to bolster the king's authority where it was weak.

Anglo-Norman settlement in Scotland

The decentralized form of government and society that resulted was one of the many variants of what is known as "feudalism," with tenants in chief holding lands, with jurisdiction over their inhabitants, from the king, in return for the performance of military and other services. An essentially new element in Scottish society was the written charter, setting out the rights and obligations involved in landholding. But the way in which the Anglo-Norman families, in their position as tenants in chief, were successfully grafted onto the existing society suggests that the Celtic and feudal social systems, although one stressed family bonds and the other legal contracts, were by no means mutually incompatible. The clan system of Highland Scotland became tinged with feudal influences, whereas Lowland Scottish feudalism retained a strong emphasis on the family.

David began to spread direct royal influence through the kingdom by the creation of the office of sheriff (*vicecomes*), a royal judge and administrator ruling an area of the kingdom from one of the royal castles. Centrally, a nucleus of government officials, such as the chancellor, the chamberlain, and the justiciar, was created by David and his successors: these officials, with other tenants in chief called to give advice, made up the royal court (Curis Regis). This body became formalized in various ways: by the mid-13th century it might meet as the king's council to discuss various types of business; and before the Wars of Independence (see below) the royal court in its capacity as the Supreme Court of Law was already being described as a Parliament. The almost total loss of all of the Scottish governmental records from before the early 14th century should not lead one to underestimate the efficiency of the Scots kings' government in this period; historians in recent years have done much to assemble the surviving royal documents from scattered sources.

From David's time onward, the burghs, or incorporated towns, were created as centres of trade and small-scale manufacture in an overwhelmingly agrarian economy. At first, all burghs probably had equal rights. Later, however, royal burghs had, by their charters, the exclusive right of overseas trade, though tenants in chief could create burghs with local trade privileges. Burghs evolved their own law to govern trading transactions, and disputes could be referred to the Court of the Four Burghs (originally Berwick, Edinburgh, Roxburgh, and Stirling). Many of the original townspeople, or burgesses, were newcomers to Scotland. At Berwick, the great trading town of the 13th century, exporting the wool of the border monasteries, Flemish merchants had their own Red Hall, which they defended to the death against English attack in 1296. Besides commercial contacts with England, there is evidence of Scottish trading with the Low Countries and with Norway in the period before the Wars of Independence.

David's reorganization of the church

The church was decisively remodelled by David I and his successors. A clear division emerged between secular and regular clergy according to the normal western European pattern. A complete system of parishes and dioceses was established. But the system of "appropriating" the revenue of parish churches to central religious institutions meant that the top-heaviness in wealth and resources of the church in Scotland was a built-in feature of its existence until the Reformation. Kings and other great men vied in setting up monasteries. Alexander I had founded houses of Augustinian canons at Scone and Inchcolm, while among David's foundations were the Cistercian houses of Melrose and Newbattle and the Augustinian houses of Cambuskenneth and Holyrood. Augustinian canons might also serve as the clergy of a cathedral, as they did at St. Andrews. Prominent foundations by the magnates included Walter Fitzalan's Cluniac house at Paisley, and Hugh de Morville's Premonstratensian house at Dryburgh. Later royal foundations included that of the Benedictine house at Arbroath, established by William I.

From the standpoint of a later age, when the monasteries had lost their spiritual force, the piety of David I especially seemed a misapplication of royal resources. But the original monasteries, with their supply of trained manpower for royal service, their hospitality, and their learning, epitomized that stability which it was royal policy to achieve.

From at least 1072, the English Church, particularly the Archbishop of York, sought some control over the Scottish Church: the Scottish Church was weakened in face of such a threat through having no metropolitan see. But, probably in 1192, the Pope by the bull *Cum Universi* declared the Scottish Church to be subject only to Rome; and in 1225 the bull *Quidam Vestrum* permitted the Scottish Church, lacking a metropolitan see, to hold provincial councils by authority of Rome. Such councils, which might have served to check abuses, were, however, seldom held.

It has been argued that the cultural developments encouraged by the church in pre-Reformation Scotland were not as great as might be expected, but this may be a false impression created because the manuscript evidence has failed to survive. The monasteries of Melrose and Holyrood had each a chronicle, and Adam of Dryburgh was an able theologian of the late 12th century. Surviving Romanesque churches show that Scotland partook of the common European architectural tradition of the time: good small examples are at Dalmeny, near Edinburgh, and at Leuchars, in Fife. Glasgow and Elgin cathedrals are noteworthy, and St. Andrews Cathedral is impressive even in its ruined state. There are also distinguished examples of castle architecture, such as Bothwell in Lanarkshire; and the castles of Argyll may reflect a distinctive mixture of influences, including Norse ones.

David's successors

Malcolm IV (1153–65) was a fairly successful king, defeating Somerled when the latter, who had been triumphant over the Scandinavians in Argyll, turned against the kingdom of Scots. Malcolm's brother, William I the Lion (1165–1214) subdued much of the north, and established royal castles there. After his capture on a raid into England, he was forced to become feudally subject to the English king by the Treaty of Falaise (1174); he was able, however, to buy back his kingdom's independence by the Quitclaim of Canterbury in 1189, though it should be emphasized that this document disposed of the Treaty of Falaise and not of the less precise claims of superiority over Scotland that English kings had put forward over the previous century. William's son, Alexander II (1214–49), subdued Argyll and was about to proceed against the Hebrides at the time of his death. His son, Alexander III (1249–86), brought these islands within the Scottish kingdom in 1266, adroitly fended off English claims to overlordship, and brought to Scotland the peace and prosperity typified by the commercial growth of Berwick. In the perspective of the subsequent Wars of Independence, it was inevitable that men should look back on his reign as a golden age.

THE WARS OF INDEPENDENCE

The "Maid of Norway"

Competition for the throne. With the death, in 1286, of Alexander III and of his young granddaughter Margaret, the "Maid of Norway," four years later, almost two centuries of relatively amicable Anglo-Scottish relations came to an end. A complete uncertainty as to the proper succession to the throne provided Edward I of England and his successors with a chance to intervene in and then to assimilate Scotland. Though the two countries were feudal monarchies of a largely similar type, the English attempt was, in practice, too tactless to have any hope of success. Besides, the struggle for independence disclosed that a marked degree of national unity had arisen among the different peoples of Scotland. The Anglo-Scottish conflict thus begun gave Scotland a basic tendency—to seek self-sufficiency and at the same time to look to continental Europe for alliances and inspiration—that persisted at least until 1560.

Before the death of the Maid of Norway, the Scottish interim government of "guardians" had agreed (by the Treaty of Birgham, 1290) that she should marry the heir of Edward I of England, though Scotland was to be preserved as a separate kingdom. After her death, 13 claimants for the Scottish crown emerged, most of them Scottish magnates. The Scots had initially no reason to suspect the motives of Edward I in undertaking to judge the various claims. It emerged, however, that Edward saw himself not as an outside arbitrator but as the feudal superior of the Scots monarch and, therefore, able to dispose of Scotland as a fief. That Edward's interpretation was disingenuous is suggested by the fact that he had not invoked the old and vague English claims to superiority over Scotland while the Maid of Norway was still alive and had made a treaty with Scotland on a basis of equality, not as a feudal superior claiming rights of wardship and marriage over the Maid.

The leading competitors, who had much to lose by antagonizing Edward, agreed to acknowledge his superior lordship over Scotland. But a different answer to his claim to lordship was given by the "community of the realm" (the important laymen and churchmen of Scotland as a group), who declined to commit whoever was to be king of Scots on this issue and thus displayed a sophisticated sense of national unity.

Bruce and Balliol

Robert Bruce and John Balliol, descendants of a younger brother of Malcolm IV and William, emerged as the leading competitors, and in 1292 Edward I named the latter as king. When Edward sought to exert his overlordship by taking law cases on appeal from Scotland and by summoning Balliol to do military service for him in France, the Scots determined to resist. In 1295 they concluded an alliance with France, and in 1296 Edward's army marched north, sacking Berwick on its way.

Edward forced the submission of Balliol and of Scotland with ease. National resistance to English government of Scotland grew slowly thereafter and was led by William Wallace, a knight's son, in the absence of a lead from the magnates: Wallace defeated the English at Stirling Bridge in 1297 but lost at Falkirk the next year. He was executed in London in 1305, having shown that heroic leadership without sufficient social status was not enough. When Robert Bruce, grandson of the competitor, rose in revolt in 1306 and had himself crowned Robert I, he supplied the focus necessary for the considerable potential of national resistance.

In several years of mixed fortunes thereafter, Robert had both the English and his opponents within Scotland to contend with. Edward I's death, in 1307, and the dissension in England under Edward II were assets that Bruce took full advantage of. He excelled as a statesman and as a military leader specializing in harrying tactics: it is ironic that he should be remembered best for the atypical set-piece battle that he incurred and won at Bannockburn in 1314. The Declaration of Arbroath of 1320 is perhaps more informative about his methods. Ostensibly a letter from the magnates of Scotland to the Pope, pledging their support for King Robert, it seems in reality to have been framed by Bernard de Linton, Robert's chancellor. In committing Robert to see the independence struggle through, it likewise committed those who set their seals to it. Some of them were waverers in the national cause, whether or not Robert had proof of this at the time, and his hand was now strengthened against them.

Robert I secured from England a recognition of Scotland's independence by the Treaty of Northampton in 1328; 1329 saw the Pope's granting to the independent kings of Scots the right to be anointed with holy oil, but it also saw the death of Bruce. By the appropriate standards of medieval kingship his success had been total; but by the nature of medieval kingship, his successor was left with the same struggle to wage all over again.

David II. Robert I's son, David II (1329–71), has perhaps received unfair treatment from historians through having been contrasted with his illustrious father. Just over five years of age at his accession, he was soon confronted with a renewal of the Anglo-Scottish war, exacerbated by the ambitions of those Scots who had been deprived of their property by Robert I or otherwise disaffected. In the 1330s Edward Balliol, pursuing the claim to the throne of his father John, overran southern Scotland. In return for English help, he gave away to England southern lands and strongpoints not recaptured fully by the Scots for a century. After the Scots defeat at Halidon Hill near Berwick in 1333, David was forced to flee to France in the following year. Berwick itself fell to the English and was never again in Scots hands except in the period 1461–82.

Battle of Halidon Hill

The Scots gradually regained the initiative, and in 1341 David was able to return to Scotland. But in 1346 David II himself was captured at the Battle of Neville's Cross near Durham. He was released in 1357 for a ransom of 100,000 merks. This ransom, if paid (and three-quarters of it eventually was), would constitute a serious burden on Scotland, and there is evidence of Parliament's using this national emergency to establish some checks on the actions of the crown. In addition, the representatives of the royal burghs, which were important as an accessible source of finance, established a continuing right to sit in Parliament with the magnates and churchmen from the 1360s on, thus constituting the third of the "Three Estates."

Complex evidence relating to these transactions has been uniformly interpreted in a way discreditable to David. Another interpretation is possible. That he collected revenues more assiduously than he made ransom payments may indicate a reasoned attempt to strengthen the crown financially; and his negotiations, especially of 1363, whereby a member of the English royal house was to succeed him on the Scottish throne, may have been a diplomatic charade. Whatever his faults, David left Scotland with both its economy and its independence intact.

The long wars with England necessarily took their toll, retarding Scotland's economy and weakening the authority of her government. The buildings that have survived from this era are inferior to earlier work, much of which, of course, suffered damage at this time. War was increasingly expensive, and taxation was increased drastically to pay David II's ransom. But again, a rosier alternative picture can be painted, suggesting that the burgesses were able to meet the increased taxation because of increased prosperity through the still-continuing trade with England.

SCOTLAND IN THE 15TH CENTURY

The early Stewart kings. David was succeeded by Robert II (1371–90), previously the high steward and son of Robert I's daughter Marjory. The next king was Robert II's son John, restyled Robert III (1390–1406). It may be that Robert II's conduct was responsible for dissension in Scotland during David II's reign, particularly during his captivity in England. At any rate, neither Robert II nor his son Robert III were strong kings and some nobles regarded both as upstarts, and the latter as of doubtful legitimacy. There thus began a long period of monarchical weakness in Scotland, accentuated by a series of royal minorities in the 15th and 16th centuries. Historians have made much of the turbulence of these times, but there were comparable periods of governmental weakness in contemporary England and France: and "bonds of manrent" and other alliances made by the magnates with each other and with their social inferiors should be seen as much as attempts to secure political stability in their own localities as threats to the overall peace of the kingdom.

Robert III's younger brother, Robert Stewart, 1st duke of Albany, more than once was given powers to rule in his brother's name, and Robert's son James may have been sent to France in 1406 in order to keep him out of Albany's clutches. But James was captured at sea by the English, and shortly afterward Robert III died. Albany (died 1420) and then his son Murdac misgoverned the realm until 1424, when James I, then 29, was ransomed.

The Douglas family was becoming particularly powerful at this time. They had been rewarded with the gift of the royal forest of Selkirk and other lands in south and southwest Scotland for loyal service to Robert I. But the growing power of the Douglases in this vital border area posed by the end of the 14th century a growing threat to the crown, no longer able to count on the direct personal loyalty of the Douglas family. At the same time the Lords of the Isles had attained a stature in the western Highlands that overtopped that of the kings of Scots.

One notable event was the founding of Scotland's first university at St. Andrews. The Wars of Independence led Scots students to go to Paris rather than to Oxford or Cambridge. But universities were the training grounds of the clergy, and when, in the period 1408–18, Scotland recognized the anti-Pope Benedict XIII after he had been abandoned by France, it became expedient for Scotland to have its own university. The bulls of foundation from Benedict XIII reached St. Andrews in 1414.

The reign of James I

James I (1406–37) was an active and able king, keen to make the crown wealthy and powerful again. Perhaps he was overimpatient to make up for time lost in his captivity, and thus he prompted the opposition to him that led to his death. New posts, those of the comptroller and treasurer, were created to gather royal revenues more efficiently. Murdac, 2nd duke of Albany, was executed in 1425, and other powerful men were overawed, even in the far north. The laws were to be revised, and in 1426 a court for civil cases was set up, presaging the later Court of Session.

Possibly to balance the power of the magnates, it was

enacted in 1426 that all tenants in chief should attend Parliament in person. More realistically, they were, from 1428, permitted to send representatives from each shire. Even this system did not operate until the late 16th century. If James had been inspired during his captivity by the English House of Commons, he was unable to transplant that institution to Scotland. The Scots Parliament, like that of many other European countries, remained throughout the medieval period the feudal court of the kings of Scots: not undergoing the distinctive development of the English Parliament, it did not differ essentially in kind from the feudal court of any great magnate. Despite, or perhaps because of, his innovative vigour, James made enemies for himself. His murder in 1437 was part of an attempt to seize the throne for Walter Stewart, earl of Atholl, but the conspirators were executed and James's young son succeeded him.

James II (1437–60) was six at the time of his accession. His minority was marked by struggles between the Crichton and Livingstone families. During this minority and that of James III, James Kennedy, bishop of St. Andrews, played a statesmanlike part in seeking to preserve peace. James II took a violent line against overmighty subjects. In 1452 he stabbed William Douglas, 8th earl of Douglas to death, and in 1455 James Douglas, 9th earl, was attainted. The main line of the Douglas family never regained its position, though a younger, or cadet, branch of the family, the earls of Angus, was important in the late 15th century. James II, like his father, thus sought manfully to reassert royal authority, and Scotland lost an able king when he was killed by the bursting of a cannon at the siege of Roxburgh Castle, one of the last Scottish strongpoints in English hands. Roxburgh was subsequently captured by the Scots. Among the cultural advances of the reign was the founding, in 1451, by Bishop William Turnbull of the University of Glasgow, Scotland's second university.

James III (1460–88), James's son, was eight years old at his accession. During his minority he was for a time the pawn of the Boyd family. The so-called Treaty of Westminster-Ardtornish of 1462 showed that John, Lord of the Isles, and the exiled Douglas were prepared to try to carve Scotland into two vassal states of England for themselves. The alliance came to nothing, but the Lords of the Isles were a threat to the territorial integrity of Scotland until their final forfeiture in 1493. On the other hand, the power vacuum left by their removal was responsible for much of the unrest in the western Highlands thereafter. It was in James III's reign that the territory of Scotland attained its fullest extent with the acquisition of Orkney and Shetland in 1468–69.

Character of James III

As James III came of age, he seems to have given grave offense to his nobles by shunning their company for that of artistic people. It has been suggested that his fine sensibility did him credit, but this is probably an anachronistic view. When it is seen what political disorder could follow from the absence of an adult male ruler in later medieval Scotland, it may be thought correspondingly important that such a ruler, when present, should have cultivated the nobles who were his natural companions and political associates and who tended to support a ruler who combined tact with good government. So serious was James's lack of authority that Berwick fell in 1482, when the nobles, led by Archibald Douglas, 5th earl of Angus, chose—rather than defend it against the English—to seize their opportunity to hang some of James's favourites. In 1488 James was murdered while fleeing from a battle against his opponents at Sauchieburn, though it seems that the death of the king was not intended, and he was succeeded without trouble by his son.

Fifteenth-century society. There is evidence of economic recovery in Scotland in this period, despite the continuing war and unrest. Castle-building and the extending of monasteries and cathedrals were widespread: work was done on the royal residences at Linlithgow and Stirling. The building of collegiate churches and of fine burgh churches is additional evidence of prosperity. Royal burghs with their share in international trade and baronial burghs with their rights in their own locality were alike flourishing. The craftsmen threatened to rival the merchants in the running of burgh affairs, but an act of 1469 gave the merchants the majority on the town councils: this allowed self-perpetuating cliques to misapply the assets of the burghs, an abuse not remedied until the 19th century. Accompanying the prosperity general in Scotland at this time was a tendency to inflation, and a debasement of the coinage added to the troubles of James III's reign.

Cultural life

From the late 14th century onward, interesting Scottish writing, both in the vernacular and in Latin, has survived. John Barbour (1316?–95) wrote a verse life of Robert I in Scots. A Latin history of Scotland was compiled by John of Fordun and continued by Walter Bower, abbot of Inchcolm, in his *Scotichronicon*. Andrew of Wyntoun wrote a history of Scotland in Scots verse.

Little is left of the corpus of medieval writings in Scottish Gaelic. But the sophistication of the west Highland stone carvings of the later Middle Ages suggests that a strong literary culture, too, was associated with the courts of the Lords of the Isles and other chiefs. The *Book of Deer*, containing the Gospels, has in its margins an 11th-century Gaelic account of Columba's foundation of the monastery of Deer in Aberdeenshire, and a series of *notitiae*, or lists of church rights, which provide clues to the nature of Celtic society. The early-16th-century *Book of the Dean of Lismore* (the seat of the Bishop of Argyll) contains over 60 Gaelic poems. From the quality of the architecture that has survived from the 15th century, one can infer the existence of paintings and other objects, such as church furnishings, that have largely disappeared. An outstandingly intricate collegiate church is that at Roslin near Edinburgh, founded by Sir William Sinclair, 3rd earl of Orkney, about 1450. There are fine burgh churches, such as St. John's in Perth and the Church of the Holy Rood in Stirling. Perhaps the outstanding piece of evidence of royal patronage of the arts is the altarpiece for James III's Trinity College Church in Edinburgh: the altarpiece is almost certainly the work of the great Flemish painter Hugo van der Goes.

The church

In the 14th century the papacy had built up its claims to appoint to the higher offices in the church and in Scotland had established a system of "provisions," or papal appointments, to vacant offices. This cut not merely across the rights of rulers who used the church to provide their loyal bureaucrats with a living and the rights of other local patrons; it also meant a drain to Rome of money in the form of the tax payable by a cleric "provided" to a vacant post by the pope. James I resisted these developments, and at the same time, in the Council of Basel (1431–49), the "conciliarists" were seeking to curb papal power in the church: a distinguished member of the Council of Basel was the Scot Thomas Livingston, one of the first St. Andrews graduates.

James also sought to revive the monastic ideal in its early purity and established a house of the strict Carthusians at Perth. A compromise between James I and the Pope was probably pending when James was murdered, and his successors tended to let the popes collect their money as long as they "provided" to church offices along lines acceptable to the monarchy. In 1487 James III was granted the concession that the Pope would delay promotions to the higher offices for eight months so that the king could propose his nominee.

St. Andrews was made the seat of an archbishopric in 1472, in itself a desirable step. But the first archbishop of St. Andrews secured the honour by supporting the papacy against the king, and there was, as a result, no welcome for it in Scotland. Glasgow also became an archbishopric in 1492.

SCOTLAND IN THE 16TH CENTURY

James IV and James V. James IV (1488–1513) was well equipped for kingship, being physically impressive, cultured, generous, and active in politics and war alike. He eliminated a potential rival by carrying out the forfeiture of the last Lord of the Isles, in 1493, and dealt severely with unrest on the English border and elsewhere. James and Bishop William Elphinstone of Aberdeen founded King's College, Scotland's third university, in Aberdeen in 1495. This was the great age of Scots poetry, and while one of the leading "makars," or poets, Robert Henryson (1430?–1506?), author of the *Testament of Cresseid*, was a burgh schoolmaster, the others were members of the court circle: Gavin Douglas (1474–1522), bishop of Dunkeld and kinsman to the earls of Angus, translated Virgil's *Aeneid* splendidly into Scots, and William Dunbar (1460?–1520), a technically brilliant poet, showed the versatility of which Scots was capable.

After initial disharmony with England, James concluded a "treaty of perpetual peace" with Henry VII in 1502 and married Margaret, Henry's daughter, in 1503. But Henry VIII of England became involved in the anti-French schemes of Pope Julius II, and in 1512 France and Scotland renewed their "auld alliance" as a counterbalance. In 1513 Henry VIII invaded France: James IV, consequently, invaded England; there he died, along with thousands of his army, in the rashly fought and calamitous Battle of Flodden.

Battle of Flodden

James's efficiency at home was thus offset by his excessive international ambitions. And both had cost money—for artillery; for a navy whose greatest ship, the "Michael," cost £30,000; for embassies. The crown granted lands in feu-ferme tenure, which gave heritable possession in return for a substantial down payment and an unchangeable annual rent thereafter. In the great European price rise of the 16th century, this policy in the long term weakened the crown.

James V (1513–42) was in his second year at his accession. The factional struggles of his minority were given shape by the division between those who adhered to Scotland's pro-French alignment, and those who were determined that the price Scotland paid at Flodden should not be repeated. John Stewart, duke of Albany, was regent until 1524, and favoured France: Archibald Douglas, 6th earl of Angus, then maintained a pro-English policy until 1528 when James began his personal rule. James now found Scotland's support in international politics being sought on all sides. In the 1530s he obtained papal financial help in establishing a College of Justice, and he concluded two successive French marriages, each bringing a substantial dowry: his second wife was Mary, daughter of the duc de Guise and mother of Mary, Queen of Scots. James's support for the papacy and France alienated some of his subjects, however, and his rule was not simply strict and financially vigorous but rather avaricious and vindictive. Lack of noble support seems to have caused the rout at Solway Moss in November 1542 of a force invading England. This, and the deaths of his infant sons, led to the death of James, probably from nervous prostration, in December, a week after the birth of his daughter Mary.

Mary and the Scottish Reformation. The church in 16th-century Scotland may not have had more ignorant or immoral priests than in previous generations, but restiveness at their shortcomings was becoming more widespread. And the power structure of the church seemed to preclude the possibility of reform without revolution. The church made a poor showing at the parish level, since by 1560 the bulk of the revenues of nearly nine parishes in every ten was appropriated to monasteries and other central institutions. The papacy, in return for receiving its share of this wealth, abandoned spiritual direction of the Scottish Church: from 1487, royal control over appointments to the higher church offices grew steadily. All this, at a time when the church's annual revenue—reckoned at £400,000 in 1560—was ten times that of the crown, readily explains the attraction of church office for unspiritual career-seeking nobles. Church lands were feued to laymen, who also became collectors of church revenues and were given abbeys as benefices. Church property, particularly monastic property, was effectively being secularized, and if Protestantism offered to the nobles and lairds of Scotland a more spiritually alive church—and one with lay participation—it probably also appealed to them as a system under which they would not have to hand back what they had grabbed.

Particular laymen were as pious as ever, endowing collegiate churches as they had once endowed monasteries, and trenchant criticism of church abuses was expressed in the play *Ane Pleasant Satyre of the Thrie Estaitis* by Sir David Lyndsay (*c.* 1490–*c.* 1555). But reform from within was probably almost impossible: Archbishop John Hamilton, for instance, a would-be reformer who gave his name to a vernacular catechism (1552), belonged to the family who had most to lose if the careerists were curbed.

Mary, Queen of Scots

Mary (1542–67) began her reign as another Stewart child ruler in the hands of factions: the pro-French party upheld the old church, while the pro-English desired reform. By the Treaties of Greenwich (1543), Mary was to marry Edward, Henry VIII's heir. Cardinal David Beaton and Mary of Guise, the queen mother, had this policy rescinded, and the murder of Beaton (1546) and English punitive raids culminating in the Scots defeat at Pinkie (1547) did not cause Scotland to love England more. France helped Scotland to expel the English but only in return for such a hold over the country that by the time of young Mary's marriage to the Dauphin in 1558 it was France that appeared to be about to absorb Scotland.

Anti-French feeling combined with Protestant preaching to bring about revolt. In 1559 the reformers took up arms to forestall Mary of Guise's action against them. Despite the preaching of John Knox and others and the plundering of the monasteries, the decisive issues were political and military: Queen Elizabeth of England sent troops to check French plans in Scotland. Mary of Guise died in June 1560, and by the Treaty of Edinburgh in July, both France and England undertook to withdraw their troops. With Scotland thus neutralized, England had the important advantage over France of relative nearness.

The Scots Parliament in August 1560 abolished papal authority and adopted a reformed Confession of Faith, but Mary, still in France, did not ratify this legislation. Still, the organization of local congregations, which had been going on for some years, continued, and the General Assembly emerged as the central legislative body for the church. In the *First Book of Discipline* (1560), John Knox and other ministers proposed for the church a striking social program, providing education and poor relief. But laymen had not despoiled the old church to enrich the new, and, as an interim settlement secured by Mary's government in 1562, the church and crown were together to share but one-third of the old church's revenue.

John Knox

Mary's husband died in 1560, and in 1561 she returned to Scotland. As a Catholic in a Protestant land and as nearest heir, by descent from Henry VII's daughter, to Elizabeth of England, she had many enemies. Her personal reign was brief and dramatic—she married her cousin Darnley (1565); their son James was born (1566); Darnley was murdered (1567); Mary married the adventurer James Hepburn, 4th earl of Bothwell; was imprisoned and forced to abdicate (1567); escaped and fled to England (1568). Her task as a ruler was hard, and the harder for her own errors of judgment, but she essayed it bravely and was a truly tragic rather than a pathetic figure.

James VI (1567–1625). James lived through the usual disrupted minority to become one of Scotland's most successful kings. In a civil war between his and his mother's followers, laird (landed proprietor) and merchant support for James may have been decisive in his eventual victory. Elizabeth detained Mary in England and assisted James Douglas, 4th earl of Morton, regent from 1572, to achieve stability in Scotland.

James's government ratified the reformed church settlement, and more permanent measures of church endowment were taken. The Concordat of Leith (1572) allowed the crown to appoint bishops with the church's approval. As in Mary's reign, the crown was intervening to prevent the wealth of the old church from being entirely laicized. And if the bishopric revenues were saved from going the same way as the monastic wealth, the crown expected a share in them for its services.

A new presbyterian party in the church, whose members wanted parity of all ministers and freedom from state control, rejected this compromise. Led by Andrew Melville, a rigid academic theorist, they demanded, in the *Second Book of Discipline* (1578), that the new church should receive all the wealth of the old, that it be run by a hierarchy of courts, not one of bishops, and that the state should leave the church alone but be prepared to take advice from it. Many historians have seen these demands, as James undoubtedly did, as an attempt to achieve full-blown theocracy. James was not strong enough for out-and-out resistance immediately, and he sometimes made concessions, as in the Golden Act of 1592, which gave parliamentary sanction to the system of presbyterian courts. But he gradually showed his determination to run the church his own way, through the agency of his bishops, who were brought into Parliament in 1600. From 1606 Melville was detained in London and later banished. By 1610 the civil and ecclesiastical status of the bishops was secure. The continued existence of church courts—kirk sessions, presbyteries, synods, and the General Assembly—show James's readiness for compromise; and he showed a wise cautiousness toward liturgical reform after encountering hostility over his Five Articles of Perth (1618), which imposed kneeling at communion, observance of holy days, confirmation, infant Baptism, and other practices.

In the 1580s James, as he became personally responsible for royal policy, faced the need to control unruly subjects at home, nobles and kirkmen alike, and to win friends abroad. He concluded a league with England in 1586, and when Elizabeth executed his mother in the following year, he acquiesced in what he could not prevent. He thus inherited his mother's claim to the English throne, and his efforts thereafter to keep in the good graces of Elizabeth and her minister William Cecil were successful. He succeeded peacefully to the English throne in 1603, though his two monarchies, despite his own personal inclinations, remained distinct from one another.

Accession to English throne

His policy was one of overall insurance: he avoided giving offense to Catholic continental rulers, and, while he dealt effectively with lawbreakers on the border and elsewhere, he showed marked leniency to his Catholic nobles, even when the discovery of letters and blank documents (the "Spanish Blanks" affair, 1592) showed that several of them were in treasonable conspiracy with a foreign power. Neither a heroic king, like James IV, nor the pedantic and cowardly buffoon depicted in Sir Walter Scott's *The Fortunes of Nigel*, James VI was a supple and able politician. His theories of Divine Right monarchy were a scholar-king's response to an age when the practice and theory of regicide were fashionable. Except perhaps at the very end of his life, James was too realistic to let his theories entirely govern his conduct.

James excelled in picking good servants from among the lairds and burgesses: they were his judges and privy councillors, and sat on the Committee of Articles, with which he dominated Parliament. After 1603 they governed Scotland smoothly in his absence. From 1587 Parliament was made more representative by the admission of shire commissioners to speak for the lairds, thus realizing the program of James I. The privy council had judicial as well as legislative and administrative functions: there were, in addition, the Court of Session for civil cases (it had evolved from the council in the early 16th century and, as the College of Justice, had been endowed with church funds in the 1530s) and justice courts for criminal cases. Local justice and administration continued, however, despite James VI's efforts, to be largely the prerogative of the landowners.

Scotland still had a subsistence economy, exporting raw materials and importing finished goods, including luxuries. But such luxury imports showed that the greater landowners and merchants were gaining in prosperity. Despite the absence of adequate endowment, the reformed church began to create a network of parish schools and there was advance in the universities: Andrew Melville brought discipline and the latest scholarship to Glasgow and St. Andrews in turn, and there were new foundations at Edinburgh (the Town's College, 1582) and Aberdeen (Marischal College, 1593).

Scotland and England were drawing closer together, as the period of continual strife between them receded in time. Though the two national churches were not identical in structure, they shared a common desire to protect and preserve the Reformation. James VI's accession to the English throne in 1603 as James I encouraged further cultural and economic assimilation. It was far from guaranteeing further political assimilation, but a century of the barely workable personal union of the crowns was continually to sharpen for the Scots the dilemma of choosing between complete union and complete separation. (J.M.S.)

X. The early Stuarts and the Commonwealth (1603–60)

THE CONDITION OF ENGLAND IN 1603

In 1603 England was a nation of some 4,000,000–4,500,000 people, mostly living in the south and east, who were divided into social classes based, as Shakespeare observed in *Troilus and Cressida* (1609), upon "degree, priority, and place." At the top of the social hierarchy was the Stuart royal family, headed by King James I (1603–25), whose hereditary claim to the English throne came from his mother, Mary, Queen of Scots. Also, as James VI of Scotland, the King represented a personal union between the two kingdoms. Advising the King were his privy councillors, men of lesser political stature than those who had served under Elizabeth and, consequently, far less successful in managing the houses of Parliament. The ablest of them was Robert Cecil, 1st earl of Salisbury, son of Elizabeth's great minister Lord Burghley. After Salisbury's death in 1612, two young men captured James's affections: Robert Carr, earl of Somerset, who fell from power after his lovely young wife caused a court scandal by poisoning her detractor, Sir Thomas Overbury; and George Villiers, who rose from a gentleman of the bedchamber to become the 1st duke of Buckingham (1623). The King's fondness for young men can be seen in his statement to the Privy Council in 1617: "I love the Earl of Buckingham more than anyone else. . . . Christ had his John, and I have my George."

Social classes

Below the royal family came some 60 hereditary members of the nobility or aristocracy, ranging in descending order from dukes, marquesses, earls, viscounts, and barons who, together with 26 nonhereditary bishops, sat in the House of Lords. The doubling of the number of lay nobles as a result of "bargain and sale" by Buckingham not only brought the monarchy into disrepute but also brought a loss of prestige to the nobility. This crisis of confidence in the nobility, aggravated by its conspicuous consumption and the slow decay of its military power, greatly weakened the effectiveness of the Lords as a mediating body between the King and the House of Commons. The decline in the prestige of the nobility had been preceded by a financial crisis among the aristocracy from about 1590 to 1610 as a result of the shrinkage of their landed wealth. A member of the nobility claimed in 1628 that the Commons, which was made up mostly of gentry, could buy up the Lords three times over. By 1640 the aristocracy had probably recovered from its financial crisis.

Below the nobility came the gentry, who numbered less than 5 percent of the population. They were technically those large landowners to whom the College of Arms had granted the right of gentility—*i.e.*, the right to bear a coat of arms—but a small number of them held nonhereditary titles (either baronetcies or knighthoods), which, like the titles of the nobility, were sold by the crown or its ministers. Nearly 1,000 knights were created in James's first year on the throne. A fairly high turnover in the ownership of land, because of the inflation of prices, resulted in some changes in the composition of the gentry: some new families rose to the top (a few becoming peers), whereas some older families either died out or declined, sometimes falling into the social category of yeomen, or chief farmers, who were only one step above the husbandmen, or petty farmers. Some members of both the gentry and the nobility engaged in careful estate management in order to meet the price squeeze, and a number of these improving landlords sought positions at court. These officeholders were part of the Court Party in the House of Commons. At the local county level, the justices of the peace—unpaid administrative officers of the crown—tended to be Country, or opposition, gentry, whereas the lords lieutenant—the unpaid military officers of the crown—frequently were Court, or government, peers. The conflict between the Court and Country parties was one of the long-range causes of the English Civil War later in the century, but it would be a mistake to assume that the difference, either at the national or local level, was as simple as an affluent rising Court Party and a poverty-stricken declining Country Party.

The economy

Although the economy of England was predominantly tied to land, there was a commercial society of financiers, manufacturers, merchants, shopkeepers, tradesmen, and artisans who lived in the cities and towns, the largest of which was London, with a population of about 250,000; Norwich, Norfolk, with 15,000, was the second largest. There were four times as many borough seats in the Commons as County seats, but the merchants comprised only a small fraction of the Commons. Many successful merchants acquired landed estates and married their daughters into the gentry and aristocracy. Conversely, the younger sons of gentry families who could not succeed to the family estate under the law of primogeniture frequently turned to trade and commerce in order to make their livings. As a result, there was a horizontal social mobility between town and country in addition to the vertical mobility within the town and country hierarchies that gave a certain vigour and freedom of opportunity to English society that tended to offset its rigid social structure.

JAMES I (1603–25)

Religious policy. When James travelled south from Edinburgh in April 1603 to take up his duties at Westminster, he was presented with the Millenary Petition (so called because it was allegedly supported by 1,000 ministers) calling for reforms of the Anglican Church.

The King, though a Calvinist in his theology, was an Erastian in church government, advocating state supremacy in ecclesiastical affairs; he responded to the Millenary Petition by calling a conference at Hampton Court in London to which he invited moderate Puritan divines and Anglican bishops. The Puritans presented their case for recasting the Thirty-Nine Articles along more Calvinist lines, for revitalizing popular preaching, and for excluding the "relics of popery" from the Anglican prayer book. The Puritans also proposed that religious questions should be settled by episcopal synods made up of a bishop and a presbytery (or a group of elders) rather than by the bishops alone. But James erroneously assumed that the Puritan proposal for a "reduced episcopacy" was in fact a proposal for a "Scottish presbytery," which, as he knew from personal experience in Scotland, tried to subordinate the state to the church. After all, it had been in reaction to this hierocratic view that the King had exhumed the medieval notion of divine-right monarchy in order to counteract the clerical demands of both Scottish Presbyterians and Roman Catholics. As James had written in his *Trew Law of Free Monarchies* (1598), "Kings are called Gods . . . because they sit upon GOD his Throne in the earth, and have the count of their administration to give unto [H]im." The King regarded any diminution of episcopal power as having the same effect, as stated in his often-quoted political aphorism: "no bishop, no king." The bishops were instrumental in getting the Convocation of the clergy to pass the Canons of 1604, which provided for the excommunication of anyone who impugned the royal supremacy, the Anglican prayer book, or the Thirty-nine Articles. Shortly afterward a group of Puritan Separatists—separatists because they no longer felt a binding tie with the Anglican Church—were forced to leave England, settling in Holland until their transatlantic crossing as Pilgrims to Plymouth Rock in 1620. Perhaps some of them were attracted by stories they had heard about an earlier English settlement at Jamestown, Virginia, in 1607. The only significant Puritan accomplishment to come out of the Hampton Court conference was the authorization for a new translation of the Bible—the King James Version used by all English-speaking Protestants until well into the 20th century. The King's experience with English Catholics was about as bad as it had been with Scottish Catholics, especially when a group of them, including Guy Fawkes, was caught in an abortive plot on November 5, 1605, to blow up the houses of Parliament. The Gunpowder Plot, which provoked Parliament to require an oath of allegiance to the King from Catholic recusants, jeopardized the Catholic cause for a number of years.

The Gunpowder Plot

James and Parliament. The first session of James's first Parliament in 1604 was primarily concerned with several questions of parliamentary privilege, which set the tone for the constitutional struggle with the crown. In a disputed parliamentary election case (*Goodwin* v. *Fortescue*), it was decided that in the future the Commons, rather than the Court of Chancery, was the proper judge of election returns. In a dispute over the parliamentary privilege of freedom from arrest, it was decided that a member of Parliament, Sir Thomas Shirley, who had been imprisoned for a private debt, should not be molested while Parliament was in session. Both of these privileges, together with that of freedom of speech (especially in matters of religion), were eloquently set forth at the end of the session by some of the members in *The Form of Apology and Satisfaction*. The *Apology* was a lecture to a foreign king on how parliamentary privileges were "our right and due inheritance," not something bestowed by the grace of the crown. Although the extremist language of the *Apology*—"the voice of the people, in the things of their knowledge, is said to be as the voice of God"—kept it from coming to a vote in the Commons and although James probably never received the intended instruction, it was a shadow of things to come.

The most important difference between the King and his parliaments arose over the question of money. James's conventional sources of revenue were several: the income from crown lands, feudal dues (especially wardship, or the right to collect income from estates left to minors), purveyance (buying at less than the market price), monopolies, and customs duties called tonnage and poundage on imported wine and exported wool. Since all of these fiscal sources were inadequate to handle the extravagance of the court, the rising costs, and the debt from the recently concluded war with Spain, the crown decided to levy impositions (additional customs duties). The legality of impositions had been upheld in 1606 in the trial of John Bate, a merchant who had refused to pay an imposition on currants. Chief Baron Thomas Fleming had ruled that impositions fell under the king's "absolute power," which, unlike his "ordinary power," could not be changed by Parliament. The new Book of Rates of 1608 increased impositions, but in the parliamentary session of 1610, when James had forbidden the members to discuss that subject, once again the Commons claimed the privilege of free speech. Salisbury's proposal in that session for a Great Contract (1610)—by which the King would give up his feudal dues and purveyance in exchange for an annual parliamentary grant of £200,000—was never completed because of the King's dissolution of Parliament. The short-lived "Addled" Parliament of 1614 was no more successful in solving the crown's financial problems. In that same year a syndicate formed by a London alderman, William Cockayne, tried to increase James's revenue by substituting the export of finished woollen cloth (with its higher duties) for the export of undyed woollen cloth previously handled by the monopoly company of the Merchant Adventurers. But the Dutch boycotted the new product,

The Great Contract

and, as a result, the woollen-cloth industry, the largest after agriculture, suffered severe dislocation, drastically reducing the King's revenue from customs.

According to Attorney General Francis Bacon, the king's judges were supposed to be "lions *under* the throne," but Chief Justice Edward Coke, who disagreed with the decision in the Bate case, thought that the judges, as interpreters of the common law, should be mediators between the prerogative of the king and the rights of Parliament. In the case of Dr. Thomas Bonham (1606), Coke stated: "when an act of Parliament is against common right and reason, or repugnant, or impossible to be performed, the common law will control it, and judge such an act to be void." American scholars in particular have regarded the "higher law background" of this case as an important precedent for the American doctrine of judicial review, whereby a supreme court may annul legislation or executive acts as contrary to a constitution. In the matter of prohibitions, whereby the common-law courts would take over proceedings in the Anglican Church courts dealing with the collection of tithes, Coke told James, much to the joy of the Puritans, that matters of property were not to be decided by "natural reason," which the king and the bishops admittedly possessed, but by "artificial reason," which only common lawyers possessed. In a dispute between the King and Parliament over the use, or abuse, of royal proclamations in 1610, Coke and his colleagues told James that the king had no prerogative except that which the law allowed him. The final showdown between James and Coke came in the case of *Commendams* (1616), when Bacon requested the 12 judges to delay their decision until the King—who said that, in cases involving the prerogative, he was a party to the suit—had spoken with them, but Coke alone, while lying prostrate before the throne, contended for the independence of the judiciary. Coke was dismissed as a judge but later joined the Country opposition in Parliament. Bacon became lord chancellor, only to be impeached by Parliament for bribery the year after he published his scientific treatise, *Novum Organum* (1620).

The Spanish marriage

Foreign policy. In matters of foreign policy, James was anxious to marry his surviving son, Charles, to the Spanish princess Donna Maria (in order to obtain a large dowry) and to become a peacemaker for Europe. But, at the same time, the German Catholic League, which Spain supported, toppled James's son-in-law, Frederick of the Palatinate, from his newly acquired kingdom of Bohemia and invaded the Upper Palatinate in what were to be the opening moves of the Thirty Years' War. Said James: "I like not to marry my son with my daughter's tears." The King reluctantly called his third Parliament in 1621 for funds to aid Frederick. The Commons continued to encroach upon the Stuart royal prerogative by criticizing the Spanish marriage and by urging a naval war with Spain, but James ordered them to desist from such "deep matters of State." At once the Commons issued the Protestation stating that foreign policy was a proper subject for the exercise of free speech in Parliament; the King, in turn, promptly tore the Protestation out of the journal of the House of Commons and dissolved Parliament. Even though the Rhenish Palatinate was occupied by Spanish troops in 1622, Prince Charles and Buckingham journeyed to Madrid the following year in an attempt to sweep the Princess off her feet. But they were so humiliated by their treatment there—Charles's leap over a wall to see the Princess was a fiasco—that they returned to England calling for war against Spain and the impeachment in Parliament of the pro-Spanish privy councillor, Sir Lionel Cranfield. At this, James told Buckingham that he was "making a rod with which you will be scourged yourself." England went to war with Spain in 1624, and negotiations were opened with France for a marriage between Charles and the French Catholic princess Henrietta Maria.

The economy. One of the results of the Thirty Years' War was a severe slump in the woollen-cloth trade in 1620, just after Cranfield had been successful in bringing about a temporary recovery following the disastrous Cockayne project. The most important cause of the slump was a devaluation of currencies in Germany and eastern Europe that made it difficult for the Merchant Adventurers and the Eastland Company to export cloth profitably. The ensuing unemployment and poverty in the West Country and Suffolk, the home of the Old Draperies, or broadcloths, together with bad harvests beginning in 1621 that sent food prices spiralling, produced the worst depression of the first half of the century. The parish register of Ashton-under-Lyne, Lancashire, indicates a possible famine condition during the bad harvest year of 1623–24, when burials were up 250 percent and births fell 43 percent from the previous year. The development of New Draperies, or worsted cloths, in East Anglia, which were sold in Spain and the semitropical climates by the Levant Company, did not offset the loss from the older markets. The King, who insisted that the regulation of economic affairs (not in any mercantile sense but as a part of his concern for public order and economic stability) was part of the royal prerogative, appointed a Commission of Trade, the precursor of the Board of Trade, to look into the whole matter. On its recommendation the Parliament of 1624 was able to get the Privy Council to loosen the grip of the Merchant Adventurers on trade to the Low Countries and Germany by allowing any merchant to join the export trade in the cheaper varieties of the Old Draperies and in the New Draperies. But Sir Edward Coke drew up a bill that prevented the granting of monopolies to individuals by the crown on the grounds that these monopolies constituted only a different form of taxation. Even though specific exemptions were made for charters of trading companies and town corporations and for patents on inventions, the Monopolies Act was a clear blow to the royal prerogative. By 1625 the stabilization of the foreign currencies permitted the cloth trade to return almost to normal, but the problem of Dutch competition remained, as was indicated by the massacre of East India Company traders in 1623 by the Dutch at Amboina in the Dutch East Indies.

Economic depression of 1620s

CHARLES I (1625–49)

Charles and Parliament. Unlike his father, Charles I (1625–49) was shy and nervous but handsome and dignified, as can be seen in portraits by Van Dyck, whom, with Rubens, he brought to England. Like James, Charles was an advocate of divine right, and, as James had warned, he was to have his "bellyfull of Parliament." Charles's immediate problem was to get Parliament to pay for the war against Spain. His first Parliament, in 1625, refused to grant him tonnage and poundage duties for life, so he dissolved this Parliament without getting any money to fight the war. From the King's rapidly dwindling resources, Buckingham was able to finance an expedition to attack the Spanish port of Cádiz. The venture failed disastrously, and Charles was again forced to turn to Parliament for funds. Charles's second Parliament, under the leadership of Sir John Eliot, demanded (as James had predicted) the impeachment of Buckingham. Charles again dissolved Parliament, still without money, because of the attack on his favourite. Instead, Charles and Buckingham resorted to the collection of forced loans and began to billet troops under martial law in private homes. Moreover, they foolishly went to war with the Catholic monarchy in France in addition to the ongoing war with Spain. The militant Puritans in Parliament were delighted with the opportunity to aid the rebelling French Calvinists (Huguenots), but Buckingham's military operations at La Rochelle in their behalf ended in failure, as at Cádiz. Five knights from the Country gentry, who were imprisoned for refusing to pay forced loans in 1627, obtained a writ of habeas corpus, but Chief Justice Nicholas Hyde ruled that their arrest, which had been at the special command of the King, was for "matters of state." In Charles's third Parliament of 1628 (the fifth Parliament in eight years), Coke, Eliot, and Sir Thomas Wentworth, somewhat incorrectly claiming the precedent of Magna Carta, drew up a petition asking the King not to levy taxes without the consent of

Parliament, not to imprison his subjects without due cause being shown, not to billet soldiers in private homes, and not to put civilians under martial law. Charles reluctantly agreed to the Petition of Right, thereby receiving the money he needed to fight Spain and France. Within a few months, however, Buckingham was dead from an assassin's knife.

The Petition of Right

In addition to the problems of finance and constitutional privilege, Charles's first three Parliaments also were greatly concerned with the growth of Arminianism within the Anglican Church. Beginning in the 17th century, many followers of the Dutch theologian Jacobus Arminius modified the Calvinist doctrine of predestination and election. The Arminians moved in the direction of free will and good works for the salvation of all men, not merely a few elect. An international synod was held at Dort (Dordrecht, in the Netherlands) in 1618–19, at which the orthodox followers of Calvin refused to alter their position. Nevertheless, several Anglican churchmen opted for Arminianism. Among them was the archdeacon of Hereford, Herefordshire, Richard Montagu, whose book *Appello Caesarem* (1625) won him a bishopric from the King. Another Arminian was William Laud, bishop of London (1628), who introduced innovations in the church service—for example, placing the communion table "altar-wise" at the east end of the chancel—and who stressed the divine right of bishops, a view that tended to erode the royal supremacy. Laud shared the anti-Calvinist theology but not the Erastianism of the Dutch Arminians, since he believed, as did many Puritans, that the king should be merely a member, not the supreme governor (a tenet to which he only paid lip service), of the church. Because these innovations in theology, liturgy, and episcopacy were so close to Roman Catholicism, the Arminians, as high churchmen, were in effect Anglo-Catholics. In an eloquent speech before the Commons in 1629, the Puritan Francis Rous called Arminianism "an Error that makes the Grace of God Lackey it after the will of man," a "Trojan Horse . . . ready to open the Gates to *Romish* Tyranny, and Spanish Monarchy." Apparently other members agreed with Rous, for the Commons passed Eliot's three resolutions against Arminianism and tonnage and poundage duties, with the Speaker held in his chair to prevent adjournment. (The King had continued to collect the duties because he believed they were not included in the Petition of Right.) In this instance, at least, the Puritan and Country opposition were united against Anglo-Catholicism and the court.

The years of personal rule. By 1629 Charles had had enough of Parliament, and for the next 11 years he conducted a policy of personal rule, sometimes with the aid of the "Thorough" policy of Laud and Wentworth, the latter having defected from the Country opposition. Thorough is the name applied to the governmental policies of these two ministers, who called for strong and efficient central government under the King. In order to cut down on his expenses, Charles terminated the wars with France (1629) and with Spain (1630), but the immediate advantages to the nation's economy from the return to peace were offset by a temporary slump in the cloth trade, especially the New Draperies of East Anglia, plus two consecutive harvest failures. The Privy Council's attempt to meet the crisis, particularly with a rigorous enforcement of the Elizabethan Poor Law, or Statute of Poor Relief (1601), was to give rise to a limited policy of state paternalism. Some paternalistic projects, such as the monopoly of pin making, were designed to inaugurate new industries, but others, such as the London Society of Soap Boilers, had the effect of an embryonic excise tax. The King attempted to raise revenue from the commercial classes by obtaining long-term loans from London financiers who managed the traditional customs revenue (though he did add some impositions), but he milked the gentry through the absurd revival of obsolete feudal dues (fines on forest lands once owned by the crown and fines on those who refused to buy knighthoods) and Ship Money. As late as 1626 writs for Ship Money, in the form of either ships or cash, had been temporarily levied on all of the commercial ports in order to raise a navy to protect commerce from pirates or to provide for the national defense. When the King, against the advice of Laud and Wentworth, extended the writs to the whole country, thereby making it a regular assessment like the future land tax, John Hampden, a Puritan gentleman from an inland county, refused to pay. In the Hampden Ship Money case (1637), Attorney General John Bankes, arguing for the King's "absolute power" as promulgated in Bate's case, stated that there was no such "King-yoking" policy requiring parliamentary consent. A bare majority of the common-law judges found Hampden guilty, a decision that alienated many Country gentry.

The "Thorough" policy

Although there was an appearance of a Catholic revival in England during the mid-1630s—Laud himself was twice offered a cardinal's hat but refused "til Rome were other than it is"—the period is better characterized as the Laudian counterreformation. With the appointment of Laud as archbishop of Canterbury (1633) and Bishop William Juxon as lord treasurer (1636), it was the highest point of clerical influence since the days of Cardinal Wolsey. As Laud said: "a bishop may preach the Gospel more publicly, and to far greater edification, in a court of judicature, or at a council table." The persecution of the Puritans now began in the Courts of High Commission and Star Chamber. When Charles reissued James's Book of Sports (1618), permitting lawful recreations on Sundays, a Puritan lawyer named William Prynne published his *Histrio-Mastix* (1633), an attack upon stage plays, mixed dancing, lewd pictures, face makeup, and long hair, among other things. An index entry listed women actors, which the Queen aspired to be, as "notorious whores." Prynne was found guilty of seditious libel in the Court of Star Chamber, a royal prerogative court made up of Laudian bishops. His sentence consisted of imprisonment for life, expulsion from the law profession, a fine of £5,000, a session in the pillory, and the hacking off of both ears (the stumps of which he could cover, ironically, only by growing long hair). In prison Prynne was joined by a Puritan clergyman, Henry Burton, and a Puritan physician, John Bastwick, and all of them busied themselves by writing vitriolic pamphlets attacking the bishops for their Arminianism. All three were brought before Star Chamber for libel and given the usual severe punishments, Prynne being specially branded on both cheeks with an *SL* (seditious libeler). From Ireland, where he was serving as lord deputy, Wentworth (now earl of Strafford) wrote to Laud: "these men do but begin with the Church, that they might have freer access to the State." Laud's harassment of the Puritans, with an assist from the depressed cloth industry in East Anglia, contributed greatly to that exodus of Puritans to New England in the 1630s that is sometimes called the Great Migration.

Persecution of Puritans

Religious reform in Scotland. With the nation at peace, trade recovering, a revenue coming into the crown, and the bishops seemingly in control of the Puritans, Charles conceivably could have carried on for some time, if not indefinitely, without calling Parliament into session. A turning point in the fortunes of the monarchy, however, was reached when the King and the Archbishop decided to bring the Scottish Presbyterian Church, or Kirk, into closer accord with the Anglican Church. Accordingly, a new prayer book was prepared by the Scottish bishops, who had been reinstituted by James I (1610). When the new liturgy was first read in Edinburgh (1637), rioting broke out against what many Scots considered popery. Large numbers of Scots drew up the National Covenant (1638), a civil compact to resist all of the innovations in worship. The General Assembly of the Scottish Kirk quickly rejected the new prayer book and the Scottish episcopacy. Faced by such defiance to the royal prerogative, Charles made his fateful decision to send an army into Scotland. The English troops, lacking money and discipline, ended the First Bishops' War (1639) without fighting by signing a truce. At the advice of Laud and Strafford, in 1640 Charles summoned his first Parliament in 11 years, with its concomitant Convocation of the clergy. Although the proposed agreement in this Short Parliament for the King to abandon Ship

The Bishops' Wars

Money in exchange for 12 subsidies fell through, Convocation did give him six benevolences (gifts of money) plus a new set of canons defining the church liturgy. The Canons of 1640 were severely criticized by the Puritans in Parliament for enshrining Arminian practices as well as requiring of all clergy and selected laymen the Etcetera Oath never to alter the Anglican hierarchy of archbishops, bishops, etc. Without having learned the obvious lesson from these events, Charles opened the Second Bishops' War (1640), but this time the Scottish Covenanters encamped on English soil with a large army, charging Charles £850 per day for its upkeep until their demands were met. The King could not tolerate such ignominy, and, since loans were not forthcoming from the London financiers, a new Parliament, the most eventful in all of English history, had to be called, this time to sit for 13 years.

The meeting of the Long Parliament. The first session of the Long Parliament met from November 1640 to September 1641 with the support of the Scottish army. The new Parliament, under the leadership of John Pym, immediately set about redressing its grievances against what it considered the arbitrary authority of the royal government. The first order of business was to release the political prisoners—including Prynne, Burton, and Bastwick—and to impeach both Laud and Strafford for treason, the latter allegedly having advised Charles that he had an army in Ireland with which he could overawe Parliament. When impeachment proceedings by Pym against Strafford looked doubtful, both Houses passed a Bill of Attainder—*i.e.*, an arbitrary political sentence of death without trial. The King, fearful for the Queen's life from a London mob, reluctantly signed the bill. Laud remained imprisoned in the Tower of London until his execution in 1645. Action was next taken to guarantee Parliament's own existence against future periods of "personal rule"; the Triennial Act stated that there should be no more than three years between Parliaments, and another act—in many ways the most significant of all—stated that the present Parliament could not be adjourned without its own consent. The constitutional revolution continued with statutes abolishing the courts of Star Chamber and High Commission and abolishing Ship Money, forest and knighthood fines, and tonnage and poundage duties, except with parliamentary consent. On the matter of religious reform, all agreed that the Canons of 1640 were invalid, but it was soon apparent that there was considerable division of thought among the Country opposition. Some radical Puritans in the Commons, such as Henry Vane the Younger, thought that the Anglican form of church government should be destroyed "root and branch"; some moderate Puritans and Low Church Anglicans, such as Edward Hyde, only wished to trim branches by removing the bishops and clergy from all secular offices. A bill containing the moderate proposal passed the Commons overwhelmingly, but it was rejected by the Lords. In the Lords the Calvinist archbishop James Ussher advocated a reduced episcopacy, as advanced at Hampton Court, conjoining episcopal and presbyterian church government. The only agreement came in a protestation by the Lords and Commons, reminiscent of the Scottish National Covenant, to defend the "*true reformed Protestant Religion . . . against all Popery and Popish innovations.*" Just before a six weeks' autumn recess, both houses voted sufficient funds to send the Scottish army back home since it was no longer useful or necessary.

Laud's fall

The outbreak of rebellion in Ireland during the autumn recess (with the attendant question as to who should control the army needed to quell it) only added to the differences about religion already existing within the Country opposition. These differences became even more apparent in November with the slim 11-vote majority given to the Grand Remonstrance, creating new royalist and parliamentary parties in place of the old parties. The Grand Remonstrance, which demanded that the King should appoint only advisors approved by Parliament and that an international synod of divines should be called to resolve the religious question, contained a long list of political and religious grievances that later became a model for Jefferson's Declaration of Independence. Had the Remonstrance not passed, Oliver Cromwell is supposed to have said that he would leave England—perhaps for Massachusetts. At Christmastime the Commons impeached, and the Lords sequestered, 12 bishops who had the audacity to claim that Parliament was "not free" after they had been jostled by a London mob while en route to the House of Lords. Charles panicked at the mob and at the Lords' about-face on the bishops; yet, in an uncharacteristically bold but ill-advised counterrevolutionary act, he attempted to arrest five members of Parliament, including Pym and Hampden, on January 4, 1642. Shortly before the King's arrival in the Commons' chamber with troops, the five members sought refuge in the City of London, the new government of which was sympathetic to them. When Charles asked where they had gone, the Speaker of the House boldly spoke: "I have neither eyes to see nor tongue to speak . . . but as this house is pleased to direct me." The Speaker's independence from the crown dates from this occasion. The King's violent breach of parliamentary privilege against arrest, as established in Shirley's case, had so backfired that he and the Queen left Westminster on January 10, he not to return for seven years and she for 18.

The Grand Remonstrance

From mid-January through mid-August, Charles and Parliament seemed to be playing out the last few scenes of a tragic drama the climax of which had already taken place. The Lords, with their numbers now decimated by royalist defections, gave their assent to the Bishops' Exclusion Bill, which prevented all clergymen from holding secular office and all bishops from sitting in the Lords. On February 5 the King reluctantly signed the bill, either to save the bishops from a worse fate or, more likely, to gain time for effective military resistance. The final break came with the passage of the Militia Ordinance without Charles's signature. From that moment until 1660 all parliamentary legislation was technically illegal. The Militia Ordinance, which seemed directed more toward Parliament's self-preservation than toward the reconquest of Ireland, gave control over the militia to lords lieutenant appointed by Parliament rather than by the king. Some members of Parliament now claimed that the person of the king should be distinguished from the office and that the office could be better administered by them. In June 1642, Parliament issued its Nineteen Propositions, terms for Charles's surrender that called for acceptance of the Militia Ordinance and a church synod, as well as approval by Parliament of the King's ministers and the education and marriage of his children. Charles of course refused, but his response, written by the moderate Lord Falkland, surprisingly set forth a "mixed" theory of government by king, Lords, and Commons. The events of the preceding year and a half had clearly shown that the Parliamentary Party had become just as arbitrary as Charles, if not more so. But on August 22 at the small county town of Nottingham, the King, in a rebel-like action, raised his military standard against Parliament. Ireland was practically forgotten for ten years.

The Militia Ordinance

THE CIVIL WAR

The causes. The various reasons that historians have given for the cause(s) of the English Civil War indicate that there is no simple explanation. Some contemporaries, such as Richard Baxter, observed that the nobility, gentry, and the "poorest of the people" followed the King, whereas tradesmen, freeholders, and the "middle sort of men" followed Parliament. Recent research, however, indicates that there were no important economic or social differences within the leadership of the two parties; about two-thirds of the nobles became royalists; almost three-fifths of the gentry became parliamentarians. The gentry of some northern and western counties, such as Yorkshire and Cheshire (agricultural areas of traditional royal power), were predominantly royalist, whereas the gentry of some eastern and southeastern counties, cloth-making areas accessible to European trade, were predominantly parliamentarian. Cities such as London, Bristol, and Norwich tended to be parliamentarian, but other cities, such as Newcastle upon Tyne and Chester had a majority of royalists. Textile areas such as East Anglia and the West Riding of Yorkshire also tended to be centres of Puritanism, partly because these areas had once been the home of the Lollard heresy, partly because of the Calvinist ethic of work (emphasizing public service but not profit-making acquisitiveness), and partly, perhaps, because of the relief provided by the Calvinist doctrine of election from the anxiety that characterized an urban and commercial milieu such as London. Although the religious issue had been divisive in the summer of 1641, the parliamentary leaders had kept it to a minimum in the debate over the Grand Remonstrance, and, with the Bishops' Exclusion Act, it temporarily lost some of its importance. Nevertheless, religion was a determining factor in the selection of sides, because the men who stayed at Westminster at the outbreak of hostilities were mostly Puritan in sympathy. The decisive issue—one that had been building up for several decades and reached its peak with the impeachment of Strafford, the Grand Remonstrance, the attempted arrest of the five members, and, above all, in the Militia Ordinance—was constitutional in nature: who should have the sovereign power in the kingdom? Only a civil war would determine the answer to that question.

Parliamentary victory. The Civil War began on August 22, 1642, when Charles, like the feudal barons of old, erected his standard before only a few hundred followers and onlookers at Nottingham, an unimportant county town. The King controlled most of the north and west of England, including Wales, and had the advantage of a well-trained cavalry led by his nephew, Prince Rupert of the Palatinate. Parliament, on the other hand, possessed London and most of the east and southeastern England and had the advantage of more regular sources of revenue and manpower. The inconclusive outcome of the Battle of Edgehill (1642) accentuated the political divisions within the Parliamentary Party. In the Commons a war group wanted the unconditional surrender of the King before negotiations; a middle group, led by Pym, wanted to negotiate only from a position of strength; a peace group wanted immediate negotiations, which shortly resulted in the Oxford Propositions, a document more conciliatory on constitutional matters than the Nineteen Propositions, although demanding ("root and branch") on religion. But Charles rejected them. Some royalist victories in the summer of 1643 forced Pym to obtain military assistance from the Scots, but the price—Scotland's revenge for Laud's imposition of the prayer book—was agreement to the Solemn League and Covenant, which called for the complete reformation of the Anglican Church "according to the Word of God [Vane's phrase] and the example of the best reformed churches," obviously meaning Scottish Presbyterianism. At long last the synod of Puritan divines called for in the Grand Remonstrance met at Westminster. The Scottish and English divines of the Westminster Assembly drew up a Calvinistic confession of faith and agreed to substitute the Scottish Directory for Public Worship for the Anglican prayer book. The adoption by Parliament of the Directory, plus the victory by an East Anglian cavalry leader, Oliver Cromwell, over Prince Rupert at Marston Moor (1644), produced the stronger Uxbridge Marston Moor
Propositions to the King in 1645, constitutional proposals similar to the Nineteen Propositions but, in addition, requiring agreement to the Solemn League and Covenant. Again Charles refused. On matters of church government and church discipline in the Assembly, the Presbyterian majority called for a compulsory national church with a hierarchy of church courts that would suspend scandalous members from the Sacrament, but a group of "dissenting brethren" called Independents advocated voluntary congregational churches, independent of any higher ecclesiastical authority, the visible saints of which covenanted together on the basis of a conversion experience. By 1645 the members of the peace group in Parliament were called the Presbyterian Party because they sometimes overlapped with that kind of Puritanism, and for a similar reason the members of the war group were called the Independent Party. The middle group tended

Adapted from R. Treharne and H. Fullard (eds.), *Muir's Historical Atlas: Ancient, Medieval and Modern*, 9th ed. (1965); George Philip & Son Ltd., London

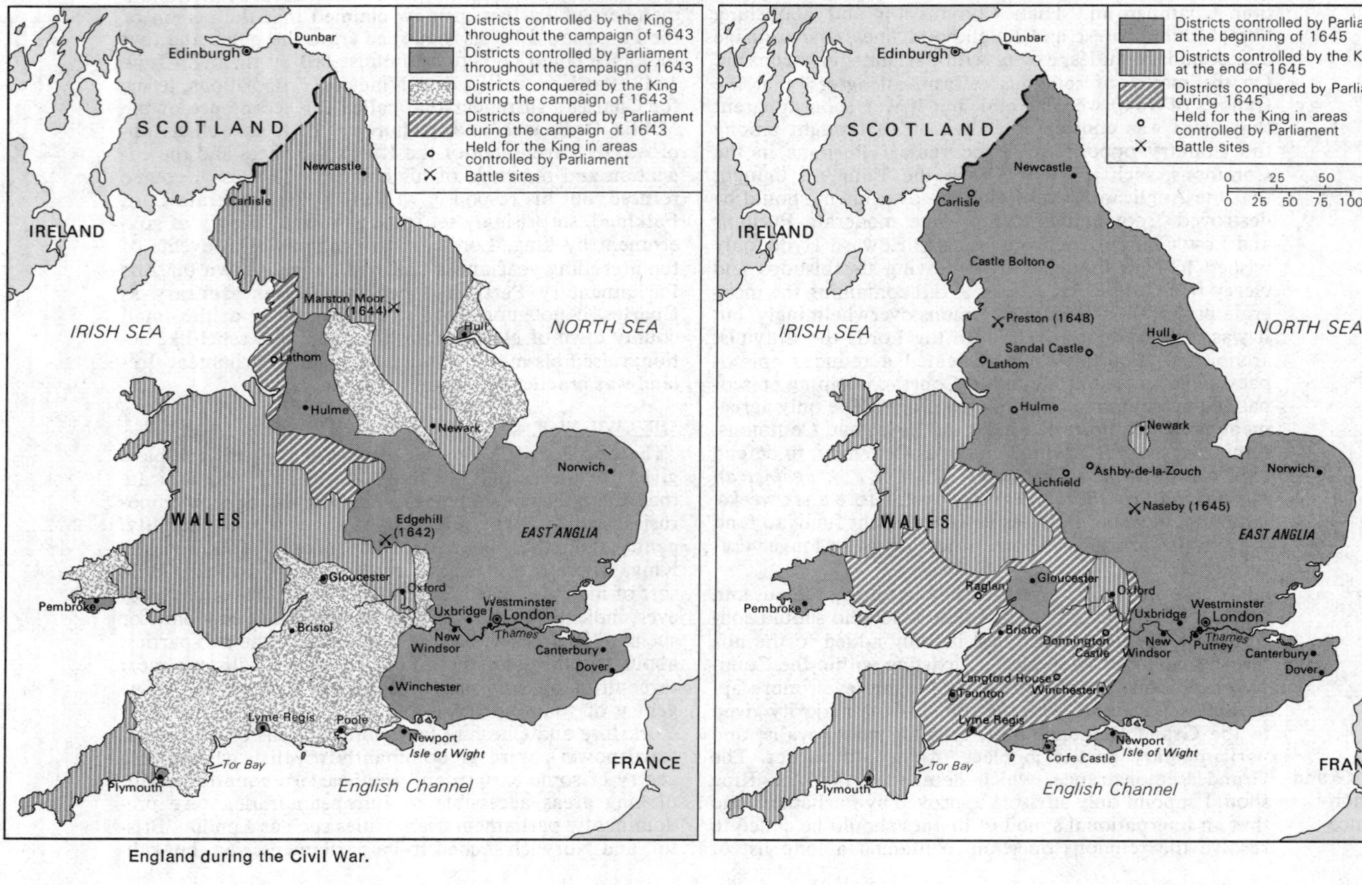

England during the Civil War.

to ally with the Independent Party. The religious Presbyterians in Parliament were successful in replacing the bishops of the Anglican Church with a Presbyterian form of church government, but the Scottish Presbyterians in the assembly called it a "lame Erastian Presbytery" since the Erastians from all parliamentary groups or parties had made sure that Parliament rather than the church would have control over religious affairs. Lieutenant General Cromwell, an Independent in religion and a radical member of the middle group in Parliament, was able, with a corps of Independent chaplains, to establish his religious imprint on the parliamentary forces, which, under the leadership of Sir Thomas Fairfax (later 3rd Baron Fairfax of Cameron), the commander in chief, was remodelled into a well-disciplined fighting unit. The New Model Army—with the motto "If God be for us, who can be against us?"—defeated the King's forces at Naseby (1645). With the King's flight to the Scots in May and the surrender of Oxford to the New Model Army in June 1646, the first phase of the Civil War came to an end.

Naseby

The King, the army, and Parliament. The Scots, Parliament, and the army made successive attempts during the next two years to come to terms with an evasive King determined to play off one suitor against the others. After the failure of negotiations between Charles and the Scots, they turned him over to Parliament. Parliament presented the King with the Newcastle Propositions (very similar to the Uxbridge Propositions), and on May 31 he finally agreed to accept Presbyterianism for a period of three years and to surrender control of the militia to Parliament for ten years. The agreement did not come into effect because the New Model Army seized Charles on June 4. On the following day, disturbed at Parliament's desire to reduce its numbers and send a force to Ireland, the New Model Army issued its Solemn Engagement not to disband until its grievances, including pay in arrears, were redressed. While the quarrel between Parliament and the army progressed, some army officers, especially Cromwell's son-in-law, Commissary General Henry Ireton, made some new proposals to Charles on August 1. The officers' Heads of the Proposals called for a council of state and biennial Parliaments that would control the militia for ten years and a limited toleration as a defense against Presbyterianism. Charles liked the Heads better than the Newcastle Propositions because of the implied admission of episcopacy, but he finally rejected them. Within the New Model Army's rank and file were the Agitators, who drew up an Agreement of the People based upon the views of the Leveller Party leaders: men such as John Lilburne, William Walwyn, and Richard Overton. Lilburne was influenced by the fundamental law of Coke, whereas Walwyn and Overton stemmed from a Christian Humanist tradition. The Agreement set forth ideas that were to be realized in the U.S. Constitution: legislative power as a trusteeship from the people (who are sovereign) and civil and religious rights, based upon natural laws, reserved by the people from the legislature. Although some Levellers, such as Lilburne, wanted to limit voting privileges only to freemen (excluding servants and alms takers), other Levellers, such as Col. Thomas Rainborow, wished to include everyone. For instance, at the army debates over the Agreement at Putney (October 1647), Rainborow said: "The poorest hee that is in England hath a life to live as the greatest hee." To this, Ireton (no Leveller) responded that no one should vote except those with "a permanent fixed interest in the kingdom." However much Puritan Independency may have provided a training ground for Leveller ideas through the election of ministers, the church covenant, and the equality of the saints, the chaplains of the New Model Army preached an Antinomianism (the complete assurance of salvation for God's elect solely through the free gift of the Holy Spirit), which stressed a millennial holy commonwealth ruled over by the lay saints.

The Agreement of the People

While the army was debating the Agreement, Charles fled from its custody to the Isle of Wight, where on December 26 he signed the secret Treaty of Newport with the Scots that was to lead to his undoing. In the treaty the King agreed to eradicate Independency and to establish Presbyterianism for three years, and the Scots agreed to send an army to England to settle a lasting peace should the King, Parliament, and themselves fail to do so. The treaty virtually made a second civil war a certainty. In a huge prayer meeting at New Windsor, Berkshire, the army agreed to bring Charles Stuart, "that man of blood," to account. This took place just before the army defeated the Scots at Preston in mid-August. "Surely," wrote Cromwell, "this is nothing but the hand of God." After Preston the Commons passed the final ordinance establishing the Erastian Presbyterianism. When it appeared that the King and Parliament at long last would sign a peace treaty, Col. Thomas Pride arrested or imprisoned 231 M.P.'s from the Presbyterian Party and the moderate majority of the middle group that previously had been tied to the Independent Party. Pride's Purge left a small Rump Parliament made up of the Independent Party and the radical minority of the middle group, some of whom were religious Presbyterians. The Rump Parliament proceeded to create a wholly unprecedented High Court of Justice to bring Charles to trial for high treason and other crimes. High treason, according to the law, was a crime performed against, not by, the king, but something of a case could be made that Charles had levied war against his subjects. The army, having reached the point where it no longer trusted the King, was determined to show that kings had to be responsible to their subjects. At his trial in late January, Charles refused to recognize the jurisdiction of the court, but he did say, without his usual stammer: "if Power without Law may make Lawes . . . I do not know what subject he is in England, that can be sure of his life or any thing that he calls his own." The King's guilt was a foregone conclusion. On January 30 at Whitehall, Charles Stuart—unlike Edward II, Richard II, and Henry VI, who were deposed before they were killed —was executed as a reigning king. Cromwell attributed the Court's action to "Providence and necessity."

Flight of Charles

Trial of the King

THE COMMONWEALTH (1649–60)

With the abolition of the office of monarchy and the House of Lords in 1649, the Rump proclaimed the "Commonwealth and Free-State," a republican form of government to be directed by the Council of State for the next four years. As Latin secretary for the Council, it was the task of John Milton, the poet, to defend the regicide to the rest of Europe. With Cromwell as commander in chief, the army, after suppressing a Leveller mutiny, weakened the Presbyterian Church settlement by defeating the Scots at Dunbar, East Lothian (1650), and at Worcester (1651). Also, it finally ended the Irish revolt by slaughtering the survivors (including women and children) of the besieged garrisons of Drogheda and Wexford in accordance with contemporary practice. As a result Scotland and England achieved a temporary political union, as James I had wished, and many English landowners acquired property in Ireland, a situation somewhat related to the confiscation and sale of sizable church, crown, and royalist lands in England. The Commonwealth's navy took command of the English Channel in the first of three trade wars fought with the Dutch in the mid-17th century. On matters of religion, the Rump produced no major ecclesiastical changes, but a spate of legislation, including the Blasphemy Act of 1650, dealt with moral and doctrinal laxity, especially in such Puritan sects as the Ranters, Diggers, Muggletonians, and Quakers. The Rump delayed enacting the army's program to abolish tithes, to reform the law, and to hold free elections, so Cromwell entered St. Stephen's Chapel with troops, as Charles I had done, and dissolved the remnant of the Long Parliament (1653). At the advice of Maj. Gen. Thomas Harrison, who was sympathetic to the political millennialism of another Puritan sect known as the Fifth Monarchy Men, Cromwell convoked a small Parliament of 140 Puritan saints chosen by the army with nominations by some Independent churches. The radical millenarians of this Barebones Parliament (named after a member, Praise-God Barbon) abolished the Court of Chancery and planned to abolish ecclesiastical patronage and tithes, so Cromwell, always a conservative in social reform, got the moderate Independents to dissolve the experiment in saintly rule after six months.

The Protectorate. For the next few years the form of government was to be called a Protectorate, as provided by the Instrument of Government (1653), a written constitution (England's first) drawn up by Maj. Gen. John Lambert from Ireton's Heads of Proposals. In addition to making Cromwell the lord protector (an office subsequently to be elective) and commander in chief of the army, the Instrument provided for a council and a single-chamber, triennial Parliament, the redrawn constituencies of which contained a much larger percentage of county seats held by Country gentry. The Instrument designated Christianity as the "public profession" of the nation, but religious toleration was to be extended only to such Puritan groups as the Independents, Presbyterians, Baptists, and some Puritan sectarians (not to Catholics, Anglicans, and licentious people). Cromwell, who allowed the Jews to return to England, was somewhat more tolerant than his two Parliaments, which prosecuted the Socinian (Unitarian) John Biddle for heresy and the Quaker James Nayler for blasphemy. The Protector's preference for Independency was revealed in his personal ordinances to regulate the ministry: a central committee of Triers to admit new ministers and county committees of Ejectors to remove scandalous ministers. Peace with Holland (1654) and a war with Spain (1655), which resulted in the capture of Jamaica, suited the Protector's notion of a Protestant crusade, but he did make an alliance with the France of Cardinal Mazarin. Cromwell also differed with his Parliaments, both of which he purged, over the control and payment of the army, even though taxes, including the excise begun in the 1640s and a new assessment levied directly on property, were higher than they had been under Charles I. In response to a royalist uprising in 1655, the Protector instituted the Rule of the Major Generals, a scheme dividing England into 11 military districts to keep down plots and to enforce the Commonwealth's repressive blue laws. The resentment inspired by the major generals caused Parliament to issue a modified version of the Instrument known as the Humble Petition and Advice (1657). This new constitution would have made Cromwell a king, but, under heavy republican pressure from the army, which he had hoped to reduce in size, he refused the crown while accepting its other provisions providing for the restoration of the "Other House" (*i.e.*, an upper chamber), a hereditary protectorate, and further restrictions on liberty of conscience. On September 3, 1658, Cromwell died, and with him went all hope for a permanent Puritan commonwealth. He had been a brilliant commander of troops, but he had never been able to find a lasting settlement for church and state. "I am as much for government by consent as any man," he once said, "but where will you find that consent?"

The Instrument of Government

The return of the monarchy. The next two years brought about the restoration of the monarchy through a continuation of the steps, in reverse order, by which it had been dismantled. In January 1659 Richard Cromwell, who succeeded his father as lord protector, called his only Parliament, elected by the pre-Instrument constituencies, but in April he dissolved it under pressure from ambitious army officers whose allegiance his inexperience and indecision could not command. Richard resigned as protector, and the army, in need of some legitimate authority, decided to restore the surviving members of the Rump Parliament whom they had expelled in 1653. The Protectorate had come to an end. Despite the appearance of a large number of tracts by Milton, James Harrington, and others in behalf of the "good old cause" of republicanism, an alliance between royalists and Presbyterians was formed. Lambert, acting on behalf of the republicans in the army, dismissed the Rump Parliament in October, but Gen. George Monck, commander of the army in Scotland, decided to intervene. Meanwhile, the Rump, which had been expelled twice, was restored in December for the second time. Lambert's troops were unable to stop Monck's entrance into London in February 1660, whereupon Monck enlarged the Rump Parliament to include all of those surviving members who had been purged by Colonel Pride. This restored Long Parliament, with its Presbyterian party majority, proceeded to implement Presbyterianism and to reaffirm the Treaty of Newport of 1647 as the basis for peace with the crown. After 20 years it finally voted to dissolve itself, as the law prescribed, in favour of a Convention Parliament that called for the return of the Stuarts in the person of Charles II, the son of the executed king. The Convention Parliament accepted without any conditions Charles II's Declaration of Breda (April 4), promising his consent to parliamentary bills relating to land purchases and army arrears in pay, a general pardon to all except those specified by Parliament, and liberty of conscience for all men unless there was a disturbance to the peace of the kingdom. There was something in the declaration for everyone. Because of Richard Cromwell's weakness, because of the differences between the various Parliaments and the army, and because of the divisions within Parliament (at first between republicans and Cromwellians and later between republicans and Presbyterians), Charles II (ruled 1660–85) could safely return to England on May 25, never to embark on his travels again.

The Declaration of Breda

XI. The later Stuarts (1660–1714)

CHARLES II (1660–85)

The Restoration settlement. Charles II quickly addressed himself to the promises in the Declaration of Breda: the crown, the Anglican Church (including bishops in England and Scotland), and some royalist lands in England were restored; a large part of the army was demobilized with full pay in arrears; and only a handful of Independent and sectarian regicides, including Vane and Harrison, were executed. But the liberty of conscience did not come into effect despite the King's efforts. The Sion House Proposals of some leading Presbyterians, including Richard Baxter, for a comprehensive church through Ussher's 1641 plan for a reduced episcopacy were firmly rejected by the 11 surviving Anglican bishops. Charles's Worcester House Declaration, drafted by Edward Hyde (soon to be earl of Clarendon), called for suffragan bishops and Presbyters plus the calling of a national synod on the Anglican prayer book. But these concessions, the most generous ever offered by Anglicans to Puritans, were rejected by the Convention Parliament, some Independent members voting with the majority. The only salve for the Presbyterians was the King's call for a conference to be held at the Savoy (in London) between Presbyterian and Anglican divines, but, before any agreement was reached, the Convention Parliament was superseded by the Cavalier Parliament (1661–79), which was overwhelmingly Anglican. The failure of the Presbyterians at the Savoy Conference was similar to that of their forefathers at Hampton Court.

Religious policies

The Cavalier Parliament set the tone for forthcoming legislation by welcoming the bishops back to the House of Lords with the repeal of the Bishops' Exclusion Act of 1642. This repeal was followed by the passage of the Corporation Act (1661) restricting local political office to Anglicans. Meanwhile, the Convocation of the clergy, after taking over from the Savoy Conference, drafted a new prayer book making slight concessions to the Savoy Presbyterians and to the Laudian Anglicans that became the basis for a new Act of Uniformity (1662). The Caroline Uniformity Act required subscription by the clergy to the new prayer book, the Thirty-nine Articles, the oaths of supremacy and allegiance, and a new oath of nonresistance to the crown. The expulsion of nearly 2,000 ministers (about 20 percent) from their livings meant the end of comprehension, or the policy of including diverse religious groups within the Anglican Church. In the Conventicle Act (1664) the Nonconformists, or Dissenters, as the Puritan community was now called, were prevented, largely out of fear of subversion, from assembling in groups of five or more persons. In the Five Mile Act (1665) they were forbidden from coming within five miles of where they had once preached. The Great Fire of London (1666) destroyed Dissenter meeting houses and Anglican churches, and from the ruins of the city, Inigo Jones developed the Palladian style of church architecture, which ultimately found its way into Christopher Wren's St. Paul's Cathedral.

The foregoing pieces of legislation, inaccurately referred to as the Clarendon Code, had one important consequence: together with the Test Acts of the 1670s, they cut off Dissenters from all avenues of professional advancement—church, politics, education, and the professions—except for business. It may well be that the affinity between Dissent and the business world, so characteristic of the age of the Industrial Revolution, can be explained more by this exclusion than by the Calvinist ethic of Puritan theology. Nor does there seem to have been much affinity between Puritan theology and the "new science," as some historians have claimed, in the founding of the Bacon-inspired Royal Society by Charles II in 1662. Such scientists as William Harvey, Robert Boyle, Isaac Newton, and John Wilkins were latitudinarian in their religious views, tending to gravitate toward the natural theology of the Cambridge Platonists, who reacted strongly against the Puritan doctrines of predestination and election. The policies of the government in economic affairs at the Restoration were an acceleration, rather than a reversal (as in religious affairs) of those underway during the Interregnum. On the question of the king's revenue, for example, Charles agreed to give up purveyance and the feudal dues, abolished during the Interregnum, in exchange for Parliament's retention of the excise started by Pym and continued by Cromwell. A new hearth tax and the traditional tonnage and poundage duties for life did not bring the King up to the proposed annual income of £1,200,000 per year, and he was constantly in debt, as his father had been. Charles II, therefore, was not able to resist Parliament as strongly as he might have wished. In matters of overseas trade, including that with Scotland and Ireland, the government's policy of protectionism was reflected in the Corn Laws, which were to protect producers—instead of consumers, as under earlier acts—through import duties on grain from abroad during bad harvests and by means of bounties on exports to foreign countries during good harvests. Thomas Mun's book *England's Treasure by Forraign Trade* (written earlier but published in 1664), in which he said that the rule is "to sell more to strangers yearly than we consume of theirs in value," reflected the mercantilist idea of the Navigation Acts (1660–63). Patterned after the Cromwellian ordinance of 1651, the Navigation Acts provided for the transportation of all goods to and from the colonies in English or English colonial ships. The exceptions to this principle were (1) certain colonial enumerated commodities that were first to be shipped directly to England and (2) all commodities produced in Europe for the colonies, which were first to be shipped to England, either in ships of England, her colonies, or the originating European country. The Navigation Acts, designed to give the mother country a favourable balance of trade with the colonies, stood for the triumph of the national interest over the special interests of the trading companies. They were also designed to damage the Dutch carrying trade by giving shipping a monopoly, and they contributed heavily to the commercial rivalry, especially in the New Draperies, that was a basic cause of the second Dutch war in 1665. The capture and burning of English naval ships by the Dutch in the Thames in 1667 terminated the war but not before the English capture of New Amsterdam (renamed New York). It also led to the fall of Charles's chief minister, the Earl of Clarendon.

Economic policies

The Cabal. After the fall of Clarendon in 1667, government power passed into the hands of a group of five men, all non-Anglicans, whose initial letters formed the word cabal. Although a Triple Alliance had been signed with Holland and Sweden in 1668, Charles was more interested in a treaty with the France of Louis XIV, whom he admired. Accordingly, the Treaty of Dover was signed in 1670, in which Charles promised to support France in a war with Holland in exchange for a subsidy during the war. But a secret provision, known only to the Cabal's Catholic sympathizers, Thomas Clifford and Lord Arlington, provided for the King, in exchange for another subsidy and troops if necessary, to declare himself a Roman Catholic—a step his brother James, duke of York, had taken the preceding year. A Stop of the Exchequer in 1672, by which the government halted payment to its banker creditors, indicated that the royal treasury was almost bankrupt, so Charles declared war on Holland, gaining the annual subsidy from Louis XIV. Charles did not announce any conversion to Catholicism, but he did resume his attempts at religious toleration with the issuance of a Declaration of Indulgence (1672). As a result the Dissenter John Bunyan was freed from Bedford jail, where he had written most, if not all, of *Pilgrim's Progress* (1678). The Indulgence suspended the penal laws, including the Clarendon Code, in ecclesiastical matters, but it was greeted with reservations by some Dissenters, partly because they questioned this extension of the royal prerogative and partly because they feared that the King's ultimate goal was the advancement of popery. The Cavalier Parliament strongly opposed the Indulgence, largely for the same reasons, so Charles, anxious to get a subsidy from Parliament, cancelled the Indulgence on the advice of a Cabal Dissenter (Lord Ashley, by then earl of Shaftesbury). Not content to stop there, Parliament passed a Test Act (1673) requiring any civil or military officeholder at the national level to take the Anglican holy sacrament and to denounce the Roman Catholic doctrine of transubstantiation. The latter excluded all Catholics, and the former excluded all Dissenters. The King reluctantly signed the bill, and the Duke of York resigned as lord high admiral. The Test Act began the breakup of the Cabal that was completed with the appointment of the Earl of Danby as chief minister (1674).

Treaty of Dover

The Popish Plot. Danby represented a change from the Cabal, for he was pro-Dutch and pro-Anglican in his sympathies. Although he brought the war with Holland to a close and although he was able to arrange the marriage of Mary, the Duke of York's elder Protestant daughter, to William (later King William III of England), the Protestant stadtholder of the United Provinces of the Netherlands, he was obliged to conduct a pro-French foreign policy, including the handling of the French subsidy, in order to remain in office. In the summer of 1678 Titus Oates, a habitual liar, "informed" the Privy Council of an alleged Popish Plot to kill the King and to replace him with his brother, the Duke of York. In September Oates made depositions to this effect before a popular London magistrate, Sir Edmund Godfrey, who in turn revealed them to Edward Coleman, the secretary to the Duchess of York. The arrest of Coleman, who had had a long correspondence of a treasonable nature with the Jesuit confessor to Louis XIV, gave some credence to the plot, but it was raised to near panic proportions with the discovery of Godfrey's body on Primrose Hill in Hampstead. His death still remains a mystery. On the day after Coleman was found guilty of treason (November 28), Oates accused Catherine, Charles's Catholic queen, of treason before the bar of the House of Lords; but Charles, who had sired numerous children by several mistresses throughout his entire marriage, remained cool throughout the whole proceedings and stood loyally behind the Queen. Meanwhile, Parliament passed a second Test Act (1678) requiring all members of either house of Parliament, the Duke of York excepted, to be members of the Anglican Church. In December, Danby was impeached by the House of Commons for arranging a French subsidy for Charles, but the King responded by dissolving the Cavalier Parliament in 1679, 18 years after it had begun.

The Exclusion Controversy. The anti-Catholic atmosphere of the Popish Plot led directly into the Exclusion Controversy. Three short Parliaments during the years 1679–81 were primarily occupied with the efforts of Shaftesbury to exclude the Duke of York from succeeding Charles on the throne. The issue, which caused men to form embryonic political parties, was quite simple: should the future supreme governor of the church and state be a Roman Catholic? The exclusionist supporters

Political parties

of Shaftesbury, who were Dissenter (and frequently Low Anglican) critics of the royal prerogative, were called Whigs. The anti-exclusionist supporters of the Duke of York, who were Anglican, especially High Church (but not Catholic) backers of the royal prerogative, were known as Tories. Even though the situation was by no means as serious as 1641, Charles II, unlike his father when confronted by a Country opposition, made some conciliatory moves: he took Shaftesbury into the government as part of a new Court group, and he offered to place limitations on James. The Whigs, however, would settle only for exclusion in the Parliament of 1679, so the King dissolved it after signing a bill that strengthened procedures in the use of writs of habeas corpus, which safeguarded Englishmen from arbitrary arrest and imprisonment. In the Parliament of 1680, the Whig candidate for the succession was Charles's illegitimate son, the Duke of Monmouth—"that Absalom, ambitious of the Crown" in John Dryden's biblical allegory—but the Whigs failed again with their exclusion bill, mostly because of the opposition in the Lords. The Parliament of 1681 at Oxford, where the King had posted troops, was dissolved within a week, but there was no repetition of the events of January 1642. It was just after the Exclusion Controversy that the philosopher John Locke wrote his book *Two Treatises of Government* (published in 1690), stating that a government could be changed if it no longer represented the interests of the people; Locke's work was later used to justify the overthrow of James II in 1688. For his unflinching support of James and the Catholic succession, Charles was able to obtain another subsidy from Louis XIV, making it unnecessary for him to call any more Parliaments during the remaining four years of his reign, even though this action violated the Triennial Act of 1664, based upon that of 1641. On his deathbed Charles received the last rites of the Catholic Church, at long last fulfilling his promise in the secret Treaty of Dover.

JAMES II (1685–88) AND THE GLORIOUS REVOLUTION

When the Duke of York succeeded his brother Charles as James II (1685–88), he promised both the Privy Council and his only Parliament to preserve the church and state "as it is now by law established," but it was soon apparent that he wanted to re-establish the Catholic religion. An attempt by Monmouth to raise a rebellion in the southwest was crushed a few months later, and Chief Justice George Jeffreys exacted a fearful retribution from Monmouth's Protestant supporters in the "Bloody Assizes." Monmouth himself was put to death. James, determined not to be without Catholic officers in the future, could not get Parliament to repeal the Test Act of 1673. In a court test of the issue in 1686 (*Godden* v. *Hales*), the judges upheld the royal dispensing power for army commissions, clearing the path for James to appoint Catholics elsewhere. Although he did not appoint any Catholics to the episcopal bench, James did create a Commission for Ecclesiastical Causes (somewhat different from the old Court of High Commission), which suspended Bishop Henry Compton, among other clergymen, for disobedience. At the instigation of William Penn, who had introduced religious toleration to the colony of Pennsylvania, James pardoned 1,200 Quakers, and he issued, as Charles II had done, a Declaration of Indulgence (1687). In the preface, James frankly admitted: "We cannot but heartily wish, as it will be easily believed, that all the people of our dominions were members of the Catholic Church." The Earl of Halifax spoke for most Dissenters: "You are therefore to be hugged now, only that you may be squeezed at another time." James's success in appointing Catholics as president and fellows of Magdalen College, Oxford, may have offset any support he may have gained from the Indulgence.

The "Bloody Assizes"

The negative response the King got from county justices of the peace and prominent gentry to questions posed by the lords lieutenant, asking if they would vote to repeal the penal laws and Test Acts if elected to a new Parliament, was the first of several defeats. James issued a second Declaration of Indulgence (April 1688), but this time he required the bishops to have it read in all churches. Seven bishops stated their "averseness" to the Indulgence in a petition to the King because they believed the suspending power was illegal. James brought them to trial for seditious libel. The bishops finally had abandoned nonresistance and passive obedience. During the course of their trial, the Queen gave birth to a male heir, which assured the continuance of a Roman Catholic monarchy. On the same day that the seven bishops were acquitted, seven Whig and Tory peers, including Bishop Compton and Lord Danby, invited William of Orange to assume the throne of England. Some last minute concessions by James came too late. Aided by the so-called Protestant wind, William landed at Torbay (the modern Tor Bay) on November 5, while Louis XIV, hopeful of another long English civil war, sent troops to his eastern border. Unlike the time of Monmouth's invasion, James's army experienced wholesale desertions. Even his old comrade-in-arms, John Churchill (later 1st duke of Marlborough and ancestor of the 20th century's Winston Churchill), deserted his post as lieutenant general of the army for William because, as he put it, "our religion and country were in danger of being destroyed." On December 11 James burned the writs for a new Parliament (already overdue) and fled to France. Although captured, James was allowed to escape, since William had no intention of making James the martyr his father had become. For the second time in 40 years, a king had been toppled from the throne; this time, however, the Church of England had been saved rather than destroyed.

Landing of William and flight of James

WILLIAM III (1689–1702) AND MARY II (1689–94)

The revolutionary settlement. From the various plans put forward for the settlement of the kingdom by Whigs and Tories, the one adopted for political affairs was the moderate Whig plan. The throne was declared vacant because of the King's abdication, and a Convention Parliament offered the throne to William III and Mary II as joint sovereigns subject to certain conditions set forth in a Bill of Rights. A hereditary succession was replaced by a parliamentary succession. With the exception of a few articles guaranteeing individual rights against royal power, the Bill's main provisions were directed toward the king and Parliament. The Bill affirmed free speech, free elections, and frequent meetings of Parliament; it prohibited the levying of taxes or the keeping of a standing army except with the consent of Parliament; and it proscribed ecclesiastical commissions, or courts, and the royal suspending and dispensing power. Subsequent legislation, some of which was sponsored by a new Country Party made up of Old Whigs and New Tories, enlarged upon this essentially conservative settlement by ensuring Parliament's control over the army with a system of courts-martial (1689), regularizing the election of Parliament triennially (1694), permitting a freer press through the lapse of the Licensing Act (1695), providing for the testimony of two witnesses in all treason trials (1696), and creating from the excise tax a fixed Civil List for both the crown's household and administrative expenditures (1698), the latter an enlargement upon the Long Parliament's distinction between the private man and the public office. When the Bill of Rights was enacted into law (1689), Parliament added a provision requiring oaths of fidelity and true allegiance (replacing the old oaths of supremacy and allegiance) to William and Mary, which several bishops (including, ironically, five of the "seditious" seven) refused to take. It also added a provision preventing the sovereign from being a Catholic. Even the new coronation oath required the sovereign to uphold the "protestant reformed religion established by law." A large group of Tory members agreed to support a religious toleration bill when the Whigs agreed to drop a comprehension bill to unite Anglicans and Dissenters in one church. The decline of rigid Calvinism, the weariness with religious strife, and the desire to reward Dissenters for their obedience to the law produced the Toleration Act (1689), which permitted everyone except Catholics, Jews, and Unitarians to worship as he pleased. In 1690 the Scottish Parliament removed the bishops

The Bill of Rights

from the Kirk, ratified the Westminster Confession, and set up the Presbyterian form of church government once again.

The revolutionary settlement brought an end to innovative attempts by Charles II and James II to rule without Parliament and to reintroduce the Catholic religion by religious toleration. In short, it was a vindication of the old Whig policy of exclusion. The Bill of Rights made it obligatory for the king to rule with the assistance of Parliament, and the Toleration Act outlawed Catholicism for all Englishmen. Monumental as the Toleration Act was, it did not repeal the Test and Corporation Acts, which would have allowed Dissenters access to the political and professional life of the nation. The Bill of Rights was neither a forward-looking guarantee of individual rights against the power of a legislative body nor a statement of the natural rights of man, as in the United States and France, respectively, 100 years later. Rather, it had much in common with the medieval charters that set out the rights and privileges of a particular group in society. As Magna Carta had guaranteed the rights of the barons against the crown, so did the Bill of Rights guarantee the rights of the nobility and gentry against the crown. By his interference with voting privileges, army commissions, church benefices, and university fellowships, James II had not only restricted the freedom of the upper orders in English society, but he had also tampered with their freeholds, the privileged social position they regarded as a property right like the ownership of land. Free elections and free speech meant free from influence by the king and the lower orders of society but not free from influence by the nobility or the gentry. Although the revolutionary settlement reasserted that the king was under the law, as Magna Carta had done, by preventing the suspending and dispensing power, it would be a mistake to assume that it effectively transferred sovereign power from the king to Parliament. While it did make Parliament a partner on the important questions of revenue and the army, other aspects of the royal prerogative remained, for the most part, untouched: the waging of war and the making of peace, the conduct of foreign policy, and, above all, the appointment and dismissal of the crown's ministers. The increasing costs of postrevolutionary warfare would increasingly bring even these aspects into the orbit of Parliament's concern.

Effect of the revolutionary settlement on Parliament

William's campaign against France. William's central purpose in assuming the throne of England was to use its men and resources in his life's work of defending Holland against the aggrandizement of France under Louis XIV. As carried out, it meant a sharp reversal in the traditional pro-French and anti-Dutch foreign policy. William's forces, including some 70,000 English troops, lost border fortresses, such as Namur in the Spanish Netherlands, to France during the early years of the War of the League of Augsburg (1689–97), but in Ireland they were successful at the Battle of the Boyne (1690), crushing James II's last hope of regaining his throne. The scale of such operations could not be financed from the tonnage and poundage duties that William's second Parliament (1690–95) had granted for four years. The hearth tax was repealed and replaced by a general land tax, but even that was insufficient. In 1693–94 the Junto group of Court Whigs joined the Cabinet Council (also called the Lords of the Committee when the monarch was absent). The Cabinet Council, or Cabinet, which was smaller than the ungainly Privy Council and designed to handle the daily business of the war, took steps to handle the growing debt—about £14,000,000 from 1688 to 1702. Investors were able to place their money not only with trading companies, which were engaged in war profiteering and speculation, but also with the government. The means to do the latter was the newly chartered Bank of England (1694), a Whig joint-stock company. The Bank raised £1,200,000 in 12 days from the public and loaned it to the government (not the King) at 8 percent interest in exchange for the right to issue bank notes and to discount bills. The loan did not have to be repaid as long as the interest, about £100,000 annually, was raised by import duties. Here was the origin of a funded national debt. The debt precluded future Stops of the Exchequer, as in 1672, and the Bank's loan paid for the recapture of Namur in 1695. The Bank's issuance of notes in excess of deposits, however, led to an inflation that, combined with a depreciated currency through the clipping of silver coins and the need to pay the troops in the Spanish Netherlands, led to a financial crisis in 1696 almost as severe as that of the early 1620s. Some 60 or 70 joint-stock companies, including the Scots' Darién Scheme in Spanish Central America, collapsed. The bank survived through the wealth of its directors; a huge pamphlet debate on monetary policy led to recoinage, rather than devaluation, under the Warden of the Mint, Isaac Newton; the Board of Trade was re-created (1696), after brief starts in 1660 and 1670, to regulate overseas trade; and the war with France was terminated by the Treaty of Rijswijk in 1697. The economy snapped back because it was more diversified and broadly based than in the 1620s, but William was only waiting for the opportunity to form an alliance once more against France.

Establishment of the Bank of England

The last few years of William's life were absorbed with the problem of the succession to the throne of Spain and, to a lesser extent, with the succession to the throne of England. When the new Country Party, together with the Tories, forced out the Whig Junto after the election of 1698, the King's armed forces were drastically reduced; even his Dutch guards were dismissed. William, disgusted with an ungrateful people, threatened to abandon England. His main concern was that the Spanish Netherlands might fall to France upon the death of the childless Spanish king, Charles II the Sufferer. The dying Spanish king's last will provided that his throne and empire should go to Louis's second grandson (Philip V) if the crowns of France and Spain would remain separate. Louis at once accepted the will. In September 1701 the French king's prohibition of imports to France and Spain from England, plus his recognition of the 13-year-old pretender, James III, upon the death of James II, as king of England, swung public opinion behind William's new Grand Alliance against France (1701).

The Spanish succession

The Act of Settlement. Meanwhile, the last surviving child of Princess Anne, the younger daughter of James II, also had died, leaving the English throne—except for Anne—without a successor, since William and Mary had had no children. After the first of two elections in 1701, both won by Tories, including Robert Harley (who had made the passage from Old Whig to New Tory), Parliament passed the Act of Settlement (1701). The act designated the granddaughter of James I, the electress Sophia of Hanover, as Anne's heir and required all future sovereigns to be members of the Anglican Church. Other clauses, which were as much New Tory and Country Party criticism of William as they were to be restrictions upon the Hanoverians, stated that foreign-born kings should not defend their continental possessions without parliamentary consent; that no king should leave the country without parliamentary consent; that all governmental transactions should be handled only in the Privy Council and signed by all who consented (repealed in 1706, thereby continuing the life of the Cabinet); that foreigners could not sit in Parliament and the Privy Council or hold civil or military office; that officeholders could not sit in the Commons (modified in 1706 so that members of the Commons, when appointed to high office, must resign but could be re-elected); that no king could pardon men impeached by the Commons; and that judges held their commissions solely on good behaviour. The last provision gave judges independence from the crown, but it did not give them the right to declare parliamentary legislation unconstitutional. When William died in 1702, the Tory party leaders had assumed the mantle of the Old Whigs as the chief critics of the royal prerogative, whereas the Whig leaders (to a lesser extent with the Junto) had assumed the mantle of the Old Tories as the chief proponents of the royal prerogative.

QUEEN ANNE (1702–14)

The dull, dowdy, and devout princess Anne succeeded William as sovereign, but John Churchill (now earl of

Marlborough), whose witty, beautiful, and free-thinking wife, Sarah, was an intimate friend of the new queen, succeeded William as military commander of the English and Dutch forces in the Grand Alliance. After the parliamentary election of July 1702, Marlborough and Sidney (Lord Godolphin) formed a Tory Cabinet. This election was the third in 20 months and the fifth of nine held between 1695 and 1713. While these frequent and strongly contested elections may have given a certain instability to the English political process, they also provided a healthy polarization of the two parties over issues of the royal prerogative, the war, and the church. As a High Anglican, the Queen supported the efforts of the high Tories, including the Earl of Nottingham and her uncle the Earl of Rochester to pass an Occasional Conformity Bill. Such an act would have prevented Dissenters from qualifying for political office by their occasional attendance at Anglican communion services. Some Latitudinarian bishops regarded occasional conformity as a "healing custom"—a substitute for comprehension, although Daniel Defoe thought it hypocrisy—"playing bopeep with God Almighty." But Anne's support was withdrawn when they tried unsuccessfully to win over moderate Tories to their bill by tacking it on to the land tax measure, Lord Treasurer Godolphin's means to support the European campaigns of Marlborough. The high Tories subsequently were defeated in the election of 1705. Even though the Tories still outnumbered the Whigs by 30 votes in the new Commons, Godolphin wanted the Queen to bring more Whigs into the Cabinet, since they gave stronger support than the Tories to the war, at least in the Spanish Netherlands. The Whigs, together with 100 Queen's Servants—courtiers holding pensions and placemen holding offices—formed the war majority in the Commons. Against the advice of the Tory Harley, who had joined the Cabinet, the Queen reluctantly appointed a few Whigs to her Cabinet because she did not wish to jeopardize the military successes against France.

Marlborough's victories

Gibraltar had been captured in 1704, and Marlborough had won two brilliant victories: at Blenheim in 1704, which saved the Grand Alliance, and at Ramillies in 1706, which removed the French from the Spanish Netherlands. For the first time since the Hundred Years' War, England was a triumphant military power in Europe.

The Act of Union. Godolphin also called on the Whigs to help him carry through Parliament an incorporating union with Scotland that William had recommended on his deathbed. The Scottish Parliament had passed an Act of Security (1703) providing for a Protestant Stuart succession, upon Anne's death, unless the Scottish government was freed from "English or any foreign influence." The English Parliament retaliated with an Aliens Act (1705) prohibiting all Scottish imports to England unless the Scots accepted the Hanoverian succession. In 1706 agreement was reached to an Act of Union passed by both Parliaments the following year. The Scots gained the advantage of free trade within the new British common market of some 7,000,000 people; the English gained increased security, because Scotland could no longer be used by European powers as a base for an attack on England. The Scots were allowed to keep their legal system and the Presbyterian Kirk, but they gave up their Parliament. In return, they received 45 seats in the English House of Commons and could elect 16 lords to the English House of Lords. The Act of Union provided a constitutional means whereby the crown's influence in Parliament could be strengthened through a distribution of patronage to the Scots.

Whigs and Tories. The strong backing of the Whigs for the Act of Union gave them an even stronger claim for additional appointments to the Cabinet.

Whig ascendancy

A kinswoman of Harley (and of the Duchess of Marlborough), Abigail Hill, a lady of the bedchamber for Queen Anne, gave the Tory leader some influence over the Queen, but Harley's attempt in February 1708 to oust Marlborough and Godolphin, who in effect had become Whigs, only resulted in his own resignation from the Cabinet. An invasion scare in March, through Scotland, helped the Whigs in their May election victory even though many people were tiring of the war. In July at Oudenarde, Marlborough defeated a French army, which was saved from annihilation only by darkness, and the navy seized Minorca. The death in October of the prince consort, George of Denmark, opened up additional offices to the Whigs. By the beginning of 1709 the war against France had been won, but the peninsular war against Spain had only endeared Philip V to his subjects. The Whigs entered into peace negotiations with Louis on the slogan "No peace without Spain," but when Louis agreed to all of the Allies' terms except removing Philip V from the throne by force, the English broke off the negotiations. In September Marlborough won the last of his important battles at Malplaquet, but it was with such a heavy loss of life that the French spirit was restored. On November 5 Henry Sacheverell, a High Anglican who had no use for the increasing rationalism in religion, preached an inflammatory sermon against Godolphin, the Whigs, and the settlement of 1689. The Whig leaders of the Commons impeached Sacheverell for high crimes and misdemeanours, but it was a Pyrrhic victory, like Malplaquet, since the Lords convicted him only by 17 votes and gave him a light sentence. With the cry of "Sacheverell and Peace," the Tories won the election of October 1710, but Godolphin had been dismissed from the Cabinet the previous August without any thanks from the Queen, and the Duchess of Marlborough had left the Queen's service in a burst of hysterics the previous April. Only Marlborough, who had been denied his request to be captain general for life, remained at his post.

The efforts of the Tory Cabinet under Harley and Henry St. John were concentrated on a peace settlement. Because the Tories believed, with some truth, that the war's high tax on land was depleting the landed interest, which was predominantly Tory, and that wartime investments were enriching the moneyed interest, which was predominantly Whig, they passed a Parliamentary Property Qualification Act requiring possession of land worth £600 for county members and £300 for borough members. In October, St. John, much to the disgust of George of Hanover (the future George I), negotiated with French diplomats the preliminaries for a separate peace settlement that would leave Philip V on the Spanish throne, give Gibraltar, Minorca, Hudson Bay, Newfoundland, and Nova Scotia to Britain, and provide Britain with certain trading rights with the Spanish colonies in the Americas. While the Whig views on the peace found an outlet in the coffee shops through the journalistic efforts of Joseph Addison (*The Spectator*) and Richard Steele (*The Tatler*), the Tory leaders engaged an Irish Anglican churchman, Jonathan Swift, who defended a "Peace without Spain" in his *Conduct of the Allies* (1711). In the Lords the High Tory, Nottingham, agreed to support an amendment opposing "Peace without Spain" if the Whigs agreed to an Occasional Conformity bill. The Whigs sacrificed the Dissenters in order to overthrow the government, the bill becoming law and the amendment carrying by eight votes. This blow to the Tory government by the Whig lords was overcome by Anne's appointment of 12 Tory peers. The dismissal of Marlborough and the withdrawal of English troops from the field finally brought their Dutch allies to the conference table at Utrecht in 1713. At Utrecht the preliminaries were adopted, plus a line of barrier fortresses for Holland and a guarantee from Louis that the thrones of France and Spain would not be united.

Problem of succession

Although the Tories were able to present a united front to win the election of 1713, on the matter of the succession to the throne there had been growing division, especially between the lord treasurer, Harley (now earl of Oxford) and the secretary of state, St. John (now Viscount Bolingbroke), who became bitter rivals for power in the Tory Party. The serious illness of the Queen in December caused both men to make overtures to the Pretender, the more serious commitment being made by Bolingbroke, but by March it was clear that the Pretender would not give up his Catholicism. In

April suspicious of the policies of their party leaders, a group known as the Hanover, or "Whimsical," Tories, voted with the Whigs against a governmental motion that the Hanoverian succession was not in danger, a sure sign that the Tories were in trouble. With the death of Sophia, her son George became the heir to the throne, and Oxford, now favouring the Hanoverian succession, made a speech in favour of a large reward for the capture of the Pretender. In an effort to embarrass Oxford, who had a Dissenter's background, Bolingbroke brought forward a Schism Bill designed to put an end to all Dissenting academies, the nesting area for future Whigs. The Schism Bill passed the Commons by more than a 100-vote majority, but in the Lords, where Oxford could not bring himself to oppose it, it passed by only five votes. Oxford failed in an attempt to bring corruption charges against Bolingbroke, and on July 27 the Queen dismissed Oxford as lord treasurer, but Bolingbroke did not get the coveted post. When the Queen died on August 1, the bitter struggle for power in the Tory Party was dangerous but far from hopeless.

The achievement of the Stuarts. Queen Anne's death followed by two years that of the Earl of Rochester, whose father, the Earl of Clarendon, had been born six years after James I came to the throne. The two men had witnessed (as had Oliver Cromwell, who was born in 1599, and his son Richard, who died in 1712) the whole succession of Stuart rulers. What were the main outlines of the struggles they had seen? Political and constitutional matters took on a fairly recognizable pattern of development. The struggle for control of the state by the king and Parliament, neither of which had a concern for anything resembling manhood suffrage, was characterized by the increasing claims of both the royal prerogative and parliamentary rights (the latter more than the former) until the 1640s when the office, as well as the holder, of the crown was eliminated and Parliament became the sovereign power in the realm. The reestablishment of the monarchy at the Restoration, foreshadowed in the Cromwellian Protectorate, was not altogether different from what it had been under James I, but the absolutist tendencies of Charles II and particularly James II brought limitations upon the crown through the revolutionary settlement, which laid the basis for the "mixed" government of the 18th century. A somewhat similar pattern can be found in religious matters. The struggle for control of the church by Puritans and Anglicans, both of which had extremists who wanted to put down the royal supremacy, was characterized by Calvinist and Arminian modifications (the former perhaps more than the latter) upon the Elizabethan church settlement until the 1640s, when the Anglican Church was abolished and the Puritans came to power—at first under a state-controlled Presbyterianism and, later, under Cromwell's theocratic establishment. The revival of the Anglican Church at the Restoration, largely along the non-Arminian and Erastian lines of Elizabeth's day, was reinforced by the monopoly of political privileges given only to Anglicans, but the move toward Catholicism under Charles II and James II, together with the enforced separation of the Dissenters from the Anglican Communion, culminated in 1689 in a policy of religious toleration (but not political privileges) for Dissenters that was to remain until the 19th century.

In social and economic matters the pattern is broken. There was no struggle between the various classes in English society at the time of the Civil War; instead, there were divisions to varying degrees within the aristocracy, gentry, and merchants, when it came to choosing sides. Although many aristocrats and some gentry lost political and economic influence during the Interregnum, partly because of the composition of Parliament and the confiscation of lands, after the Restoration they regained their earlier privileged positions. Also, there is some evidence that these social classes were not as strongly represented among the Dissenters as they had been among their Puritan predecessors; conversely, Dissent became more associated with trade and finance. Finally, there is some evidence that the bankers and the merchants after 1689 were to be found more in the Whig Party, which embraced many Dissenters, than in the Tory Party, which embraced the High Anglicans. (L.F.S.)

XII. Great Britain: 1714–1815

THE FIRST HANOVERIANS (1714–60)

When Queen Anne died, George Louis, elector of Hanover, became George I of Great Britain and Ireland under the Act of Settlement. The Revolution of 1688 gave legitimacy to the Hanoverian succession. The Jacobite Party—a few thousand country squires, High Anglicans, and Roman Catholics—were committed to the Stuarts under the doctrine of indefeasible hereditary succession discredited by the Revolution of 1688. Most politicians and place seekers showed acceptance of George I by courting Baron Johann Caspar von Bothmer, the Hanoverian envoy. Immediately upon Anne's death, Caspar revealed to the Privy Council the list of regents; 14 of the 18 were known as Whigs. The liveliest question was not who would oppose the new king but whom he would prefer as his ministers.

The old order crumbled before the King's arrival from Hanover in September. George I had already dismissed the Tory leaders Henry St. John, 1st Viscount Bolingbroke, and James Butler, duke of Ormonde, and had excluded John Churchill, duke of Marlborough, from the regency. Preferring known loyalty, the King sought it among Whigs. Only Charles Howard, 1st earl of Nottingham, and George Talbot, duke of Shrewsbury, represented the ideal of a "mixed ministry" of Whigs and Tories. Charles Viscount Townshend and James Stanhope, 1st Earl Stanhope, secretaries of state, headed the ministry. Passing time and royal decisions virtually eliminated the leaders of the revolutionary generation of both parties.

The changeover went smoothly. The King enjoyed the prerogative right of appointment and dismissal; the only grounds for challenging his appointments were political. The Whigs, led by such men as Charles Spencer, 3rd earl of Sunderland, James Stanhope (after 1717, Earl Stanhope), Lord Townshend, and Robert Walpole, 1st earl of Orford, identified themselves with the security of the Hanoverian succession; and the election of 1715 gave the Whigs a majority of about 150 in the House of Commons. Because Bolingbroke obligingly fled to France, the government did not proceed beyond a resolution of impeachment against former ministeries responsible for the unpopular Treaty of Utrecht ending English participation in the War of the Spanish Succession. Ormonde followed Bolingbroke into exile a few months later; the Earl of Oxford remained in the Tower of London; the Tory minority was leaderless. In France, Bolingbroke became secretary of state to James II's son, James III, the Stuart pretender who was preparing an invasion of Great Britain. The Jacobite Rebellion of 1715–16 (the "Fifteen") and the Whig success in identifying the Tories with it frustrated Tory hopes of recovery. The romantics who surrounded the Pretender in France persuaded him to undertake an invasion that his able half brother Marshal Berwick and Bolingbroke opposed. Stanhope and Townshend were prepared when John Erskine, earl of Mar, led a premature rising in Scotland and an invasion of England. Mar was in retreat even before the Pretender arrived in Scotland in December. A month later they left for France, where the regency encouraged James to go on to Italy. The "Fifteen" was Mar's rebellion, mixed with Scottish politics and religious antipathies, as much as it was a Jacobite rising.

The Whig leaders

The establishment of Whig supremacy. The rising blasted Tory ambitions. The government treated actual rebels with moderation but took political vengeance upon politicians of doubtful loyalty, and, by the spring of 1716, the ministry was purely Whig. Robert Walpole, formerly paymaster of the forces, became first lord of the treasury and chancellor of the exchequer. The Septennial Act of 1716 extended the life of "this present Parliament" four years, postponed the unsettling effects of an early election, and, by providing legal lives of seven years for subsequent Parliaments, gave winners more time to consolidate victories. All politicians would enjoy the benefit of fewer elections and economies in election expenses. The act did not abolish the king's prerogative of dissolution, but it did inaugurate the septennial convention, which during the 18th century was clearly violated only once, in the election of 1784.

Whig factionalism succeeded a long generation of Whig–Tory warfare. After a decade of doubt, scholars again believe that the last two Stuart reigns knew a two-party system based on significant distinctions between the parties. Under the Whig supremacy after 1715, the differences among Whig politicians did not go to the bedrock of English life as had earlier Whig–Tory ones. Between the Townshend–Walpole and Stanhope–Sunderland factions, personal rivalries as well as disagreements over foreign policy created ill feeling, leading to Townshend's demotion and Walpole's resignation in April 1717. In foreign affairs, Stanhope pursued a vigorous continental policy. In 1717 he concluded a Triple Alliance with France and the Dutch that minimized foreign support for the Jacobites and gained for England the valuable diplomatic influence and organization of France in northern Europe. Stanhope's treaty with France was a constant of British policy for 15 years. His forward policy in the Baltic area exposed the controversial question of England's responsibilities toward Hanover, unavoidable in any case. Russia's presence in Europe after its victory over Sweden in the Great Northern War (1700–21) was less threatening to England than to Hanover; England and Russia were able to resolve commercial problems.

Peace with France

During his three years of office, Walpole engaged in factious opposition. In particular, he and Townshend courted the Prince of Wales. During the 18th century, the Hanoverian kings were nearly always at odds with the heir apparent, who constituted a "reversionary interest": unemployed politicians might cluster around the Prince of Wales, especially if the king was old. The game, however, was risky, as the Georges looked suspiciously at the reversionary principle. In 1719 Walpole helped defeat the Peerage Bill, which aimed at restricting the prerogative power to create new peers. The King himself favoured the bill because, if he died, it would prevent his successor from using the prerogative against Stanhope, whom he liked.

By 1720 Stanhope reached the height of his power. He had converted the Elector of Hanover into the king of Great Britain by winning for English ministers that part of the King's confidence formerly given to Hanoverian advisers. The King and the Prince of Wales were reconciled, and Walpole and Townshend accepted Stanhope's foreign policy. By April 1720 an era of good feeling prevailed among Whigs, marked by Walpole's return to the paymastership and Townshend's acceptance of the lord presidency of the council. All of this occurred on the eve of Walpole's accession to leadership. He had political luck as well as ability.

No sooner was Walpole back in office than the government was embroiled in a frenzy of speculation associated with the South Sea Company. Sunderland, first lord of the treasury, sponsored a plan whereby the company took over three-fifths of the national debt in return for trading privileges and a payment to the government of £7,000,000. Anticipations of profits inflated imaginations, and by September 1720 the boom in company shares collapsed. An indignant public opinion and ruined speculators blamed the company and the government. Walpole, however, who had not sponsored the scheme, escaped criticism. In December his plan of salvation, endorsed by the Bank of England and the company, revived public confidence and raised Walpole's prestige. Sunderland and John Aislabie, chancellor of the exchequer, had to resign. Then Stanhope's death in February 1721 vacated the northern secretaryship of the state. The successions were predictable. Walpole, with Townshend, did not acquire full control, however, until Sunderland died a year later and until John, Lord Carteret, the other secretary of state, resigned in 1724 after offending the King's mistress, the Duchess of Kendal. (The office of secretary of state was divided between the northern and southern departments until 1782, when the southern department became the Home Office and the northern department became the Foreign Office.) With Townshend and Thomas Pelham-Holles, 1st duke of Newcastle, as secretaries of state, with disaffected Whigs such as William Pulteney, 1st earl of Bath, and John Carteret (later Earl Granville) powerless, with the Tories in the wilderness, with the ministry united and strong in Parliament and enjoying the King's favour, Walpole by 1725 inaugurated the age of political stability.

The South Sea bubble

Political stability in the 18th century. The English historian J.H. Plumb has defined this stability as "the acceptance by society of its political institutions, and of those classes of men or officials who control them." Three conditions making for stability prevailed by 1725: single-party government; executive control of the legislature; and a sense of identity among those people who possessed social, economic, and political power. The completeness of the Whig monopoly was unprecedented. Besides losing parliamentary seats, Tories suffered purges from local offices and governmental services. Family allegiances became Whig. That politics was a Whig preserve was clear in 1733 when Walpole created a furor of popular protest by his attempt to impose an excise tax on wine and tobacco. But despite the unpopularity of the measure, a Tory government was not a conceivable alternative to Walpole's. At his fall in 1742, the Whigs continued in power; the aristocrats were nearly all Whig, and the hard-core Tories, mainly gentry and squires, numbered only 150 in Parliament. Until the 1780s and the beginning of a new two-party system, the Whigs predominated; ministerial changes were mere Whig reshufflings.

The three conditions of stability

Control of the legislature. Walpole was the first minister to control the legislature with a one-party executive. His steadfast supporters were government officeholders and placeholders whose influence joined with his own, with the King's, and with others', such as the powerful and wealthy Duke of Newcastle, to manage the electoral system. Walpole, Henry Pelham, and Frederick North, Lord North, who had the longest tenures as heads of ministries until the younger William Pitt—21, 11, and 12 years, respectively—had time to perfect this kind of management, which in turn prolonged their tenures of office.

In the 18th century, a ministry needed the king's support. With the exceptions of Charles James Fox and Edmund Burke, who in the political turmoil of 1783–84 were 50 years ahead of their time in asserting the primacy of the House of Commons, politicians accepted the king's prerogative power of appointment and dismissal. Kings, like politicians, distinguished between constitutional and political precepts, conceding the importance of political realities when considering the makeup of ministries. Besides his ultimate powers, the king's patronage power and influence were available to a ministry he favoured. Good relations between ministers and courtiers who could influence the king were also important to ministerial security. George II's queen, Caroline of Ansbach, gave powerful aid, for example, to Walpole. Yet Carteret exaggerated in saying that the crown alone could keep a minister in power. Henry Pelham said more correctly that, in single instances, the king's support could get what a minister wanted; steady control required the support of both king and Parliament.

The king sometimes farmed out his patronage powers to others, such as the Duke of Newcastle, who became known as the "ecclesiastical minister" because of his control over church appointments. Under George II, however, no one mistook the fount of patronage: government, as it had always been, was the king's. The delegation of local administrative work to parish officials and justices of the peace did not lessen the numbers of royal officials. Wars being more costly, more people were needed to collect and manage the growing revenues. Besides money for the debt service (the interest payment on the national debt) and the armed services, Parliament provided the civil list, or the annual payment to the crown, increasing it for George II from £700,000 a year to £800,000. It came in a lump sum, and with it the king paid the costs of the civil side of government, pensions, household support, and the secret service. The political use of the civil list was not so great, however, as gossip had it.

Influence and patronage did not necessarily bribe members of Parliament. Generally, placeholders as well as independent country gentlemen recognized an obligation to support the government in office because it was the king's. In any given House of Commons, two-thirds of the 200 placemen were holdovers free of obligation to the ministry in office. The total consisted of some 40 ministers and administrative officials, 50 court and household officials, 60 officers in the armed service, and the remainder sinecurists and pensioners. The king had 26 ecclesiastical appointments to the House of Lords. Political considerations entered into them, and generally the incumbents supported the government.

The electoral system. Management of the electoral system was the other requisite for control of Parliament. The peers sat in the House of Lords by hereditary right, bishops by virtue of their offices; Scotland was represented in the House of Lords by 16 members elected by their own Scottish peers. The first two Georges used sparingly their prerogative power of creating peers. The House of Lords remained at about 220 members until the 1780s, when George III tried to offset the reduction of his patronage by increasing the appointment to peerages. Some peers were active politicians, and 18th-century cabinets were predominantly aristocratic.

Management of elections

Parliament had taken control of the ancient electoral system in the late 17th century. The politicians preferred to manage the system rather than to tamper with it. The list of borough constituencies and franchise qualifications remained virtually unchanged until the Reform Bill of 1832 (see below). The property-based franchise was fixed by statute in 1430 for the counties and by local custom or charter in the boroughs. The electorate numbered about 400,000 voters distributed unevenly among some 300 constituencies. In only 19 boroughs besides Westminster, London, and Bristol did the electorate exceed 1,000. Yet the management of elections was neither easy nor cheap. Each borough and county had a unique character, history, and personality. Management also meant arrangements for avoiding electoral contests. A general election was a varying number of contests, normally on local issues or personalities, and not a national electorate's judgment on national issues. In the last half of the 18th century, the largest number of contested counties in any election was 11. The absence of contests, as much as electoral victories, attested to good management.

After 1770, radicals increasingly stirred the question of parliamentary reform. They desired a Parliament more representative of the number and distribution of voters, and they hoped to achieve this by more frequent elections, by the redistribution of seats in accord with population, and by adding personal (*i.e.*, not landed) property to the electoral qualifications. The basic complaint was against the preponderance of land in the electoral structure.

Land was only one of the several interests deserving representation. In 1770 Edmund Burke in his *Thoughts on the Causes of the Present Discontents* identified other interests—commercial, official, professional, military, and naval. Actually, close-knit family and political relationships guaranteed representation of the other interests in themselves and through land. The propertyless—the poor, the wage labourers, the people who lacked free agency—were thought to deserve no voice in public affairs. The national consensus on the connection between property and political participation underlay the political stability of the 18th century. In the "balanced" constitution mixing democracy, aristocracy, and monarchy, and resting upon a property base, England enjoyed a closer union of political, constitutional, and social systems than perhaps any other European nation.

The growth of the Cabinet. Stability after 1725, however, was not synonymous with dullness or predictability in politics. The life of every government depended upon good working relations among king, ministers, and Parliament. The appearance of the institution of the Cabinet after the Revolution of 1688 did not solve the problem. Politicians were uncertain of the status or even the name of the executive group that took over the work of the Privy Council, which by 1715 had been reduced to honorary status. A committee of the Privy Council, the Cabinet or Cabinet Council met with the sovereign in its early days. Responsible individually to the king for the business of their offices, ministers only slowly developed a sense of corporate responsibility.

The Cabinet's membership fluctuated and was often too large for effectiveness. It included upward of 20 household and state officers, heads of administrative departments, and prominent persons such as the archbishop of Canterbury. This "nominal" Cabinet lasted into the 1760s. Walpole preferred to work with an inner cabinet made up of the two secretaries of state, the lord chancellor, the lord privy seal, the lord president of the council, and himself as first lord of the treasury and chancellor of the exchequer. But instead of creating the cabinet system, Walpole might have checked its growth had his preference prevailed. His opponents accused him of concentrating authority too narrowly, and later first ministers learned from his experience. After 1762 the "nominal" Cabinet yielded to the "effective" Cabinet, the membership of which, made up out of the Privy Council, for practical and political reasons stabilized at about nine until the 1790s, when it grew to some 12. The composition also became more fixed. By the 1780s the household officers were gone, and the Cabinet consisted of the three great officers of state and heads of administrative departments.

Yet uncertainties remained. The Cabinet had no legal status, but it was politically important and soon became a part of the working constitution. After 1718, George I, who did not speak English, ceased to attend its meetings; the next two kings followed his precedent almost without exception and did not thereby diminish the Cabinet's growing constitutional authority. Historians are cautious against dogmatism on details of Cabinet development and practice, because the sources are sometimes contradictory and seldom full.

The role of the prime minister

The lack of a clearly defined party structure and the uncertain status of the Cabinet left unclear the role of the first, or prime, minister. Politicians said they feared the rise of an all-powerful subject. After the eclipse of the Tories and the prevalence of Whig factionalism, no one person was head of the Whig Party and thus the indubitable first minister. Yet the head of the government was usually identifiable. From Walpole onward he was normally the first lord of the treasury or, if in the House of Commons, chancellor of the exchequer. The term prime minister gradually took hold. The important thing was the substance, not the name, and Walpole provided an example of strong leadership of a relatively well knit government. No 18th-century head of a ministry could be a prime minister in the modern sense, because there was not a disciplined party opposition whose leader was the alternative prime minister. Nevertheless, the difference between Walpole's government after 1724 and its predecessors was striking. The contrast encouraged exaggerations of the maturity of Cabinet, party, and prime ministership and tempted historians in the 19th century to see George III trying to subvert a developed parliamentary government. None could have existed until the 19th century.

Walpole's ministry. *Domestic affairs.* Walpole became first minister after 20 years in Parliament. A proud House of Commons man who mastered its ways, he understood the prejudices and sensitivities of its members. During the first decade of his administration, he concentrated upon domestic matters, leaving foreign affairs to Townshend. Some substance and much political opportunism informed his harassment of Jacobites. Bolingbroke returned from exile in France in 1723 more interested in politics (though excluded from the House of Lords) than in the Pretender. Gathering about him disaffected politicians, notably William Pulteney and the old Tory Sir William Wyndham, and speaking through the newspaper *The Craftsman*, Bolingbroke attacked Walpole. Just as vocal were the "Patriots"—an ironic name given to a group of Whigs whom Walpole had alienated, among them Carteret, Lord Chesterfield (Philip Dormer Stanhope), Lord Cobham (Richard Temple), William Pitt, and Archibald Campbell, 3rd duke of Argyll. Soon after the accession of George II in 1727, the opposition swarmed around Frederick Louis, Prince of Wales, on the reversionary principle. His establishment, Leicester House, was also—in addition to being a centre of political opposition to Walpole—the centre of fashion, and attracted such leading authors as Jonathan Swift, Alexander Pope, John Gay, and Henry Fielding, along with important ladies, including Carteret's mother, Lady Granville.

Opposition to Walpole

The opposition was a varied, interesting group, but Walpole had the votes. The parliamentary elections of 1727 and 1734 were his victories. His parliamentary strength had a core of about 150 men, some of them placeholders, who faithfully attended sessions of Parliament. There were times of stress, like the storm over "Wood's Halfpence" in 1723–25, when an English ironmaster, William Wood, was granted a patent to mint a debased coinage for Ireland. The Irish complained that they had not been consulted and also feared that the new coins would drive out good currency. Swift's "Drapier's Letters" powerfully attacked the deal. Walpole revoked the patent in 1725. The main effect was upon Ireland, where the furor contributed to a political awakening.

The fiasco revealed two of Walpole's weaknessess—stubbornness, as contrasted with persistence, and secretiveness. His conduct over the excise in 1733 also showed these traits. Walpole desired to convert certain customs duties into excises, payable after the sale of goods released from bonded warehouses. Before he revealed his plan, the opposition and *The Craftsman* spread rumours of a general excise the merits of which were not as self-evident as Walpole thought. When he finally introduced a plan for a tobacco excise, the opposition had already misled the public. Though the government retained a majority in the House of Commons, Walpole gave up the scheme in April. "Coerced by clamor and opinion," he retreated, not because he had lost his majority but because he feared he might. But electoral success in 1734 showed that the storm had done no fatal damage.

Walpole's financial achievements

These two episodes are better known than Walpole's solid accomplishments in national finance and commercial policy. Politicians accepted the principles underlying the protectionist commercial system; but Walpole improved its workings. He lowered many import duties, notably on raw materials, in the interest of British manufacturing and exports. Walpole's work on national finances was technical and administrative. He diverted the sinking fund to uses other than debt retirement, thus keeping down taxes. The national debt in 1739, when war began with Spain, was £46,000,000, reflecting a reduction of only £8,000,000 since 1714. But he halved the annual debt service charge by reducing the interest rate. Had he retired the debt, many holders of securities would have been unhappy. Walpole taught England that it could live and prosper with a national debt; he made it a permanent part of the nation's financial structure and of the domestic economy of many private citizens.

Foreign policy. Townshend continued Stanhope's policy of friendship with France against the empire. An alliance in 1725 between Austria and Spain justified distrust of Austria. Fearful for the European balance of power and for British interests in the Mediterranean, Townshend tried unsuccessfully to supplement the old Triple Alliance by new arrangements with Prussia and the northern countries. Walpole's desire for agreement with Austria, however, caused Townshend to resign in 1730 and meant the abandonment of the Stanhope policy. The Treaty of Vienna (1731) was a return to cooperation with the emperor and implied conflict of English–French interests. Commercial, colonial issues between them were growing more tense. The Treaty of Vienna proved immediately useful for Walpole, who found in it an excuse for staying out of the War of the Polish Succession, which erupted in Europe in 1733.

In the 1730s, when England had no staunch continental ally, relations with Spain deteriorated. Both sides complained of violations of trade treaties. English merchants poached upon Spain's protectionist system in the West Indies, and English opinion supported them. In 1739 Capt. Robert Jenkins, who had earlier had his ear cut off by the Spanish coastal patrol, exhibited his severed ear to Parliament. Against his will Walpole had to agree to war against Spain because Parliament, the merchants, and the nation wanted it. The Anglo-Spanish War (the so-called War of Jenkins' Ear) soon blended with the War of the Austrian Succession, a wider European war that broke out after the death of Emperor Charles VI. As a guarantor of the Pragmatic Sanction intended to safeguard the Habsburg patrimony of Charles's daughter Maria Theresa, England granted a subsidy to Austria. Walpole survived the election of 1741 with a reduced majority. He was becoming an anachronism. When he resigned in February 1742, he left the nation in good economic condition, but with military and naval establishments unprepared for war.

The War of Jenkins' Ear

The attacks of the "Patriots" during the preceding decade were against Walpole personally and the concentration of authority in himself, rather than against the ministry. Neither the King nor the opposition expected or desired a clean sweeping. The new ministry was a reshuffling of Whig politicians. The opposition leader, Pulteney, tried to bring the King and Leicester House together and promoted Spencer Compton, earl of Wilmington, for first lordship of the treasury. The King and Newcastle brought in Carteret as secretary of state but kept out Pitt, Chesterfield, and the Grenvilles. "Patriot" stock fell even further when the King and the Prince of Wales made peace. The new government was strong enough to stall attempts to inquire into Walpole's conduct as minister.

The Pelhams. The times at first favoured Carteret. Content to manage foreign affairs, he refused to be angry when, after the death of Wilmington in 1743, the King replaced the latter with Henry Pelham, the brother of Newcastle, instead of Pulteney (now earl of Bath). Carteret, a Europeanist, rejected the Patriots' emphasis upon the colonial–maritime war. His search for a German settlement appeared to the Patriots to be oriented toward Hanover, and Pitt protested vigorously. English aid to Austria helped it regain ascendancy in Italy, which displeased Frederick II of Prussia. His alliance with France shattered Carteret's diplomatic structure. Pelham and Newcastle thought him a political liability. The King's protection was not enough, and Carteret resigned in November 1744.

Pelham tried to make the ministry his own. He brought in some of the Patriots, but the King balked at Pitt, without whom Pelham had trouble controlling Parliament. In February 1746, when the King rejected Pelham's request to appoint Pitt to office, the ministry resigned. It says much for Pelham's success in monopolizing political talent that only Carteret (now Earl of Granville) and Bath were available to the King. When they failed to form a government, Pelham came back on his own terms. In one of his finer moments as king, George II agreed to give his confidence to Pelham and appointed Pitt as paymaster general. For the first time there was a "broad bottomed" Whig ministry, which included all factions.

The ministerial crisis of 1746 occurred against the background of the Jacobite Rebellion of 1745, not because of it. The Young Pretender, Charles Edward, hoped that success in Scotland would bring French reinforcements. The enterprise was hopeless in spite of the Stuart mystique. Charles landed in western Scotland with a few friends and gathered support as he moved eastward. In September 1745 he occupied Edinburgh. He invaded England, reaching Derby unopposed. But his officers, seeing signs of gathering English strength, forced him to

The Jacobite Rebellion

withdraw. The Duke of Cumberland's forces backed Charles into northern Scotland and, on April 16, 1746, destroyed his army at Culloden. Charles then wandered in the Highlands, a refugee, until he left for France in September, committing his cause to romance and dwindling Jacobite sentimentality.

Cumberland and his successor in Scotland, William Keppel, earl of Albemarle, enforced loyalty, or at least submission, to the Hanoverian succession in Scotland. The Lowlands were by now accommodated to the Act of Union of 1707 and the new dynasty. The Highlands had remained apart, dominated by a feudal regime. Clan chieftains enjoyed medieval judicial and military privileges that were frequently in conflict with sterner conceptions of public order. Upheld by acts of Parliament, the government now extended the royal system of shires and judges, as had been done centuries before in Wales. A statute abolished the chieftains' authority to require military service from tenants. Still, the chieftains did not suffer economically; they became landlords over estates formerly held in trust for their clans. The change in the basis of landholding worked a social revolution, to the detriment of the crofters, or tenant farmers. Scottish emigration to the empire increased greatly thereafter. Other statutes required oaths of allegiance from the Episcopalian clergy, forbade the wearing of kilts and tartans, and disarmed the Scots. After the Forty-five Rebellion, Highland Scotland became a part of the United Kingdom and knew peace.

English politics were not peaceful despite the Pelham–Newcastle victory in the 1747 election. Unable to accuse Pelham of acting like Walpole, the opposition instead criticized the excessive influence of the Pelhams and the great Whig families. The opposition took up the idea, advocated by Bolingbroke, of a "patriot king," who would rule above faction and party strife. Never reliable, Pitt courted the Prince of Wales at Leicester House, while Newcastle muttered about Cumberland's influence upon the King. As George II grew older, the reversionary interest became more intriguing. Ironically, however, the Prince of Wales died first, in 1751. Pitt returned to the safety of the ministry in time to support the Regency Act that checked the ascendancy of Cumberland and before Bolingbroke's death completed the discomfiture of Pelham's opponents.

Pelham's last years

Pelham's ministry accomplished a good deal. The Treaty of Aix-la-Chapelle in 1748 ended the war but left colonial issues unsettled. During Pelham's last six years (he died in March 1754), England was officially at peace, and Pelham, an able finance minister, reduced the annual budget from the wartime peak of £10,000,000 to just over £2,500,000. He further reduced the cost of debt service by converting most of the debt to "three per cents." The Gin Act of 1751 took distillers out of retailing. Contemporaries thought the consequent reduction in gin consumption caused a decline of drunkenness, disorder, and crime. Other legislative reforms included the adoption of the Gregorian calendar in 1752 and the Hardwicke Marriage Act of 1753, which checked the racket in secret marriages, whereby younger sons in the aristocracy could inveigle a young heiress into a quick marriage. Against these measures prejudiced and uninformed opinions protested, but never so effectively as in 1753, when, with an election pending (1754), the government repealed its own measure permitting naturalization of Jews.

More than the politicians, George II in his commonsense way had appreciated Pelham's abilities, and he feared political troubles when Pelham died. Newcastle, who overrated his own abilities as much as he underrated his brother's and who confused electioneering with statesmanship, went to the Treasury as head of the ministry. Refusing to pay the price (patronage control) demanded by Henry Fox, 1st Baron Holland, or to meet Pitt's insincere conditions, he entrusted leadership in the House of Commons to two second-rate men, Thomas Robinson, 1st Baron Grantham, and Henry Legge. In 1755, Newcastle brought in Fox as secretary of state, passing over Pitt, whose discomfiture was the greater because he disliked Newcastle's foreign policies. Pitt attacked the Newcastle–Fox combination and was dismissed from his post of paymaster general in 1755.

Pitt and the Seven Years' War. Like the King, Newcastle did not understand the importance of the imperial issue with France, and both were anti-Prussian and pro-Austrian. Anglo-French colonial rivalry came to a head in 1754 over conflicting claims to the Ohio Valley in North America. Already Pitt could point to Gen. Edward Braddock's defeat at Ft. Duquesne in July 1755, by French and Indian forces, as indicative of French strength. Yet Newcastle managed to arrange a system of treaties that was to serve as the base in Europe for Pitt's global strategy. After arranging subsidies for Bavaria, Saxony, and Hesse, Newcastle in September 1755 made a subsidy treaty with Russia. Frederick of Prussia felt the pressure and in January 1756 agreed with England to the Convention of Westminster, providing for mutual territorial guarantees. France completed this "diplomatic revolution" by accepting Austria's overtures. Russia, realizing the incompatibility between England's treaties with Prussia and itself, joined France and Austria. In May 1756, after a French attack on the British in Minorca, Great Britain declared war; within a year all of Europe was plunged into war (see also SEVEN YEARS' WAR).

The "diplomatic revolution"

Pitt saw the potentialities of these treaties more clearly than Newcastle. News of disasters in India, North America, and Minorca added substance to attacks upon the government, which he was freer to make after dismissal from office in November 1755. Fox resigned as secretary of state in October 1756, forcing Newcastle to tell the King that only Pitt could save the government. Pitt, who hated Newcastle, thought he could save England without Newcastle's help. The King yielded in November. The government, nominally headed by William Cavendish, 4th duke of Devonshire, had support in the nation, where Pitt, secretary of state, was popular; but it lacked the King's confidence and the support of the House of Commons. The King dismissed it in April 1757. The weakness of the patchwork ministry that replaced it made possible the obvious solution. Pitt contributed his own popularity and the support of Lord John Stuart Bute and Leicester House. Newcastle offered his patronage support, his personal influence, and his political skill. Fox contributed nothing, but as paymaster he could make a fortune, and the government need not worry about him. Pitt as secretary of state controlled the war effort; Newcastle at the Treasury devoted himself to political management.

When he took over Newcastle's treaty structure, Pitt redirected it from Hanoverian to global ends. Pitt was not unique in his theoretical understanding of the relation between the German war and the imperial conflict with France. But he was foremost in determination and ability to act according to his assessment of priorities. Sea power enabled the British navy to put France upon the defensive throughout the world, preparing the way for the victories that made 1759 the "year of miracles." French naval strength was great enough, however, to threaten invasion of England until the English victory of Quiberon Bay in November 1759. This was two months after the fall of Quebec and one month after the French fleet left India, where the English dominated Bengal and were winning in the Carnatic. These victories followed upon the capture of Guadeloupe and a British surge in the West Indies. English successes continued in 1760. Pitt had united the nation in the greatest war effort in its history. At the close of the war in 1763, Great Britain had become a major world power.

Quiberon Bay victory

George II died on October 25, 1760, in the middle of the war. His last were his best years, in that at crucial moments he subordinated personal preferences to national needs. Whether he chose freely or was a prisoner of the Whig politicians is a much debated question. The accession of his grandson, George III, who at age 22 was far from mature, made everyone ask whether a new king meant new men.

The answer was self-evident because the ministry was a patchwork of factions, and the King's opinions on politics and the war were well-known. Newcastle and his Old Whigs, wearing the Pelham mantle, were the largest active faction, allied with the Court during the late years of George II. Pitt, supported at the moment by his wife's brothers, Richard Grenville-Temple, 1st Earl Temple, and George Grenville, was popular with the Country and in the city of London but lacked parliamentary strength. He had lately neglected Leicester House, where Lord Bute and the Princess Dowager dominated. Under the reversionary principle, both Newcastle and Pitt could expect unfriendly treatment. John Russell, 4th duke of Bedford, headed a growing faction that as a peace party would soon be at odds with Pitt. The hard-working civil servant types by definition were loyal to the King and were ready on the same principle to join with politicians who naturally gravitated toward the King and were known as King's Friends. The Duke of Cumberland, though Fox followed him, was not a factional leader but a political influence in his own right. The politicians feared most Lord Bute's capacity for intrigue and his influence upon the King. Together they represented the old cant of Leicester House, namely, throw the rascals out, eliminate factions, and establish a regime of purity and high-mindedness under a king who was devoted to the public good and an enemy of evil. The program of unemployed politicians was also the substance of the idea of a patriot king, and had Bolingbroke never written the book of that title, George III would have possessed the idea, having been under the moralizing tutelage of Bute.

There were also differences of opinion among the factions over the war. George III desired to end what he called "this bloody and expensive war"; Bute thought England should consolidate its gains before concluding peace; Pitt insisted upon continuing the war vigorously, though he consented to preliminary peace talks with France. Pitt found himself in the minority in favouring immediate war against Spain when its alliance with France became known. Not only the Bedford faction but also Newcastle and Lord George Anson, the talented first lord of the admiralty, opposed him. Pitt resigned. His successor, Lord Bute, as secretary of state with the responsibility for a Cabinet he could not control, had the powerful support of the King and the Princess Dowager. Though England declared war on Spain in January 1762, the government refused to renew the Prussian subsidy treaty and resumed peace talks with France. The Bedford peace party grew in influence as war weariness spread. Newcastle, old and tired, gave way to Bute, who formed a ministry in May 1762. In Paris, Bedford reached agreement on peace terms with France. Pitt opposed these terms violently in the House of Commons in November because he thought they threw away England's war gains. But he had the sense neither of the nation nor of Parliament. The opposition was adrift, and waverers supported the government in the absence of a reversionary interest. The government's victory (319–65) indicated not steady strength but, rather, the absence of a desirable alternative policy. Nonetheless, the nation did not think the less of Pitt for losing on the peace. Contemporaries gave him credit for leading England to heights it had never before attained, and posterity has agreed.

Treaty of Paris

THE REIGN OF GEORGE III TO 1789

Political instability, 1760–70. George III had support from country gentlemen and independent members, from placeholders, from ambitious young men who aspired to political careers and government service, and from factional leaders eager to replace the Old Whigs. Newcastle had no political future, and other Old Whigs such as Devonshire and Hardwicke soon died off. A corps of younger Old Whigs maintained some cohesion and by 1764 looked to the 34-year-old Charles Watson-Wentworth, 2nd marquess of Rockingham, as their leader. Though neither a dynamic personality nor a parliamentary speaker, Rockingham had patience and a character that inspired loyalty.

The national debt and taxes were the most pressing postwar problems. The debt of £114,000,000 continued to increase. The land tax met only one-half of the annual debt service. The government's excise tax on cider was a political blunder and, as a financial expedient, not worth a furor. Pitt and the Old Whigs feared for the liberties of the subject. Though the measure passed easily, Bute quailed. He was too thin-skinned for a front-rank politician. He resigned in April 1763; neither he nor the King saw political danger in a private advisory relationship. The King's alternatives reduced to one—Sir George Grenville, whom he personally disliked. Grenville saw his constitutional duty in serving the King and protecting him from political pressures. Though honest and an able lawyer, Grenville was rigid, dogmatic, and haughty—in short, a poor politician. Grenville's Cabinet, however, was an abler one than Bute's, if for no other reason than that Grenville replaced Bute as first lord of the treasury and the incompetent Sir Francis Dashwood as chancellor of the exchequer.

Miscalculation, bad luck, and his own poor judgment of people doomed Grenville. His measures, such as the Sugar Act of 1764 and the Stamp Act of 1765, to improve the customs service and revenue collections were fiscally sound but as politically explosive as the Proclamation of 1763, a well-intentioned, temporary arrangement for the territories in America newly acquired in the Seven Years' War. The most damaging effects of these measures beset Grenville's successors. Grenville was unlucky enough to be in office when the political agitator John Wilkes, who supported Pitt, burst into prominence. Wilkes, a London demagogue, gave virulent journalistic support to Pitt and the opposition in his newspaper the *North Briton*. Wilkes was given financial assistance by Richard Grenville-Temple, 1st Earl Temple, Grenville's brother, who was, however, hostile to the new ministry. Temple encouraged Wilkes to issue the famous "No. 45" (April 23, 1763) of the *North Briton*, which attacked the King's speech defending the Treaty of Paris. The government reacted by issuing a general warrant under which 48 persons, in addition to Wilkes, were arrested. Sir Charles Pratt, chief justice of common pleas and a friend of Pitt, checkmated the government's assault upon Wilkes by affirming his privilege as a member of Parliament. Later Pratt ruled illegal the "general warrant" under which the government first proceeded against Wilkes. In Parliament the government fared better. The House of Commons voted "No. 45" a seditious libel; the House of Lords declared Wilkes's "Essay on Woman" an obscenity. After Wilkes fled to Paris to escape proceedings under an indictment in the Court of King's Bench, that court outlawed him. The House of Commons expelled Wilkes and overruled Pratt's decision on general warrants. The Rockingham Whigs and Pitt again cried that liberty was in danger and nearly beat the government on the question of general warrants.

Agitation of John Wilkes

Grenville's financial and administrative measures began to take effect by 1765. Wartime finance gave way to peacetime finance. But Grenville embarrassed the King's mother by mishandling the Regency Bill (necessitated by the King's illness). Then Grenville asked the King to keep away from Bute. After dismissing Grenville and failing to enlist Pitt's help, the King had to turn to Rockingham. The Marquess accepted some "king's friends," but his major appointments were from a Rockingham party independent of Pitt's patriots, the Grenvilles, and the Bedford gang. Rockingham appointed Edmund Burke as his secretary, and Burke won election to Parliament in December 1765.

The Rockingham government early met reactions to the Stamp Act. American discontent mingled with English mercantile complaints of declining trade. Though from substantial people, these protests were extramural (*i.e.*, outside Parliament), and they added a new dimension to parliamentary politics. When Parliament assembled in January 1766, Pitt thundered for repeal of the Stamp Act, which he claimed violated the rights of Englishmen by taxing colonials without their consent. Grenville upheld Parliament's right to tax the colonies and demanded enforcement of it. The Rockingham compromise accepted something from each. It repealed the Stamp Act as impolitic and passed the Declaratory Act of 1766 asserting Parliament's right to legislate "in all cases whatsoever." The principle of the Declaratory Act continued to frustrate the empire. Americans, who rejected the principle, eventually ceased to talk about their rights as Englishmen; in 1776 they based their claim to independence upon their rights as men. The British constitution, as most members of Parliament understood it, did not admit autonomy of subordinate assemblies in the empire. The debate on the Stamp Act showed that on questions of constitutional rights, English and American claims were antithetical.

Achievements of Rockingham's ministry

During its short life, the Rockingham ministry accomplished much. It repealed the Cider Act, declared general warrants illegal, and amended the Navigation Acts. Reduction of the levies on West Indian molasses helped the trade and produced a handsome revenue. But the King's open distaste for the ministry encouraged disaffection within it. The nation and some politicians continued to look to Pitt. The King surprised no one when he dismissed the ministry, and the nation learned joyously in midsummer of 1766 that Pitt had consented to save it. At his best, Pitt could not have imposed his reading of the constitution upon Parliament and would have met difficulties in conciliating American opinion. He was at his worst, physically and mentally, after a few months in office. He failed to provide the "patriotic," nonpartisan government the nation expected. Sitting in the House of Lords as the earl of Chatham, Pitt lost touch with the House of Commons. When he was in the country, ill and at times deranged, ministers went their several ways. Prussia and Russia repelled England's advances. Chatham's plan for asserting crown sovereignty over East India Company territories in India became a temporary arrangement whereby the company paid money to the government and continued to expand its responsibilities in India. The Americans found arguments against the quartering of troops in Massachusetts and New York.

The Townshend duties

The chancellor of the exchequer, Charles Townshend, persuaded Parliament in 1767 to levy duties on certain imports into America, which he asserted were palatable as commercial regulations. This casuistry provoked an American challenge to indirect taxation and made tea a symbol of the imperial tyranny.

By autumn 1768, when a pitiful Chatham resigned along with his discouraged secretary of state, the 2nd Earl of Shelburne, the ministry lost whatever Chathamite tinge had lasted beyond Townshend's death and the entry of the Bedfords—except for Augustus, 3rd duke of Grafton, who agreed to carry on the government. John Wilkes continued to embarrass the government. Wilkes had returned from France in March to win election for the county of Middlesex. The Court of King's Bench reversed his outlawry on a technicality, but Wilkes had to spend 22 months in the Tower on other charges. There he lived happily during the storm created by government's efforts to keep him out of the House of Commons. Middlesex re-elected him each time the House of Commons expelled him, until after the fourth election the House of Commons resolved that his opponent, Col. Henry Luttrell, ought to have won and seated him.

The Rockinghams, Grenvilles, and Chathamites supported a petitioning campaign asserting the rights of electors and asking redress of grievances. The King gave them, instead, a new prime minister in January 1770. This was Lord North, a charming man and a skillful parliamentarian but a man who lacked, as Burke said, the "spirit of command that the time required." But in 1770 this deficiency was not yet apparent. North had, at any rate, strong parliamentary support and the King's confidence. Though in time he acquired a following, he never welded into a party the factions that supported him. North did not control the government tightly; each department head had access to the King.

Radical movements and the loss of America. Until the election of 1774, which seated North's government firmly, the ministry survived a sequence of embarrassments. The petitioning movement was followed by a squabble over publication of parliamentary debates. Without conceding the right of publication, the government ceased to prosecute offenders. Wilkes became active in London politics, serving as lord mayor in 1774, the year he won the election to the House of Commons. He contributed to English political history the beginnings of extramural radicalism and the movement for parliamentary reform. When Burke's *Thoughts on the Causes of the Present Discontents* (1770) decried the court's influence over Parliament, it offered as remedy only the Rockingham party as "trustees" for the people. But the radicals, mostly middle class and strongly Protestant Dissenter in tone, preferred parliamentary reform. The Society for the Defence of the Bill of Rights, founded in 1769 to aid Wilkes, was the first in the long history of reform associations. The radicals disagreed on details; most of them connected property with political participation. In 1776 Maj. John Cartwright's pamphlet *Take Your Choice!* demanded universal manhood suffrage. James Burgh's *Political Disquisitions* (1774–75), advocating popular associations for reform, became a source book for radicals.

Agitation outside Parliament

The radicals, rather than the Rockingham Whigs, were the true friends of America in England. Between the Dissenters and the American Puritans was an especially close communion. Richard Price, a Dissenting clergyman, wrote a best selling pamphlet, *Observations on the Nature of Civil Liberty* (1776), linking freedom with autonomy. By that test America was not free. Neither the Rockingham Whigs nor the Chathamites could go so far. The Rockingham party, stuck with the Declaratory Act, hoped that men of goodwill might somehow adjust imperial differences. Burke made it seem that the tax on tea was the problem. Chatham denounced the right to tax but defended the imperial protectionist system. His ideas were out of date by the time the Americans declared their independence.

For the first six years the nation supported the war against America. After France entered the war in 1778 and Spain joined France in 1779, the war took on a new character. The opposition had to support it as a foreign war and could only criticize the government's conduct of it. When North fell in 1782, it was because England had lost the war, not because the country had gotten into it in the first place.

The East India Company

The British Empire in India was another of North's problems. The East India Company exercised sovereign powers in the country. Its financial crises inflamed bitter rivalries within the court of directors and invited parliamentry concern. Between 1770 and 1773 Parliament hardly mentioned American affairs, giving its attention to the Indian question. Two temporary acts passed in 1773. One granted a loan to the company, along with trade concessions that angered American merchants and led to the Boston Tea Party. The Regulating Act altered administrative arrangements in India. The statute's abbiguities, as well as the personalities of the people who directed company affairs in India, produced contentions between the governor general, Warren Hastings, and members of the Bengal council, notably Sir Philip Francis.

By 1780 England's fortunes sank low. High taxes, a mounting debt, talk of financial mismanagement, and the dreary continuation of the war in America worried the country gentlemen whose support North needed. The parliamentary opposition and the radicals outside criticized bitterly. Ireland stirred as the "Volunteers," formed to defend the nation against invasion, changed into a political organization. Concessions to Roman Catholics and to Irish trade in 1778 encouraged demands for more, and in 1779 the government granted them. In April 1780 Henry Grattan in the Irish House of Commons demanded an independent legislature for Ireland. Men saw similarities between America and Ireland. In England the parliamentary reformers revived. In Yorkshire in December 1779, an Anglican clergyman, Christopher Wyvill, led a meeting to endorse a mild parliamentary reform and the idea of corresponding societies to agitate for it nationwide. Edmund Burke announced his plan to reform the king's household and the executive establishment to reduce expenditures and the political influence of the crown. Burke's bill was defeated in March 1780, but on April 6 the House of Commons demanded reduction of the influence of the crown. In the metropolis the Westminster Committee asked for radical parliamentary reform. The Society for Constitutional Information began its effort to educate England to the need for reform to recover "lost rights." In the late spring of 1780, the anti-Catholic feeling mounted. The Protestant Association under Lord George Gordon protested to Parliament against concessions to Catholics. The demonstrations degenerated into mobs, and, during the first two weeks of June, men feared for the very existence of London. Before troops restored order, much property was destroyed.

The Gordon riots

The Gordon riots temporarily discredited extramural associations. Lord North therefore asked for an election. Without much altering the political status quo, it gave North's government a new lease on life.

The country remained troubled. Late in 1781 came news of Cornwallis' surrender at Yorktown. Independent members began to desert North. On March 15, 1782, his majority fell to nine votes, and a few days later he resigned. The angry King accused North of deserting him; in fact, an angry Parliament had overturned a ministry enjoying the King's confidence. Parliament forced upon the King a new ministry under Rockingham and a reform program he did not want. Rockingham held over only one man from North's Cabinet. George III salvaged something by using Shelburne, secretary of state for home and colonial affairs, as royal confidant. Few politicans trusted Shelburne, but Rockingham had to tolerate him because he led the Chathamites who had opposed North. Parliament passed Rockingham's reform program. Burke's economical reform marked an important stage in transferring control of the executive and all but the most intimate parts of the household to parliamentary supervision. Other reform measures disfranchised revenue officers, excluded holders of government contracts from Parliament, and changed the paymaster's office from a private sinecure to a public trust. The grant of legislative independence to Ireland did not terminate England's political control of the Irish administration or oligarchical management of the Irish Parliament.

The Fox–North coalition. Peace negotiations in Paris split the government. Shelburne hoped to hold America within the empire under a revised commercial system. Rockingham's death on July 1 gave George III an opening. Burke and Fox were alone in wanting to fight him for control of appointments to the new ministry. Rather than serve under Shelburne, the King's choice, some Rockingham ministers resigned. The possibility of a drastic change of the constitution disappeared. Shelburne, with his chancellor of the exchequer, the young William Pitt, extended the administrative reforms begun by Rockingham. Shelburne also reached peace terms with France and America, which Parliament rejected as overgenerous in February 1783. The Rockingham Whigs (now headed by William Bentinck, 3rd duke of Portland, and led in the House of Commons by Fox) and Lord North's party, after defeating the treaty, went on to form a government. Again the King had to surrender. The Old Whigs dominated the government headed by Portland, with Fox and North as secretaries of state. Contemporaries established a caricature of an unholy, unnatural coalition, which historians accepted. The coalition had substance. The American Revolution was now history; Fox and North agreed to act independently on parliamentary reform; they agreed on most other current issues; they were personal friends and both hated Shelburne. Among possible combinations, the Fox–North coalition was the most likely.

Reform movement

The coalition survived the embarrassment of passing a peace treaty like the one they had defeated to force Shelburne's resignation. But there was a difference. Shelburne hoped to supplement the treaty with generous trading concessions to the United States. The coalition, like England, revered the protectionist system.

Apart from American affairs, England was looking to the East, where the problem of India was paramount. It had been under study since the acts of 1773. The reports of Burke's Select Committee and the secret committee of Henry Dundas, 1st Viscount Melville, appeared in 1782–83 as mines of information and indictments of company administration. The coalition brought in two bills. The opposition saw the provisions for a board of commissioners, named in the bill and after four years to be appointed by the King, as a coalition effort to monopolize Indian patronage. The bill to tighten English supervision over the administration in India was called unworkable. Fought by the East India interest and the younger Pitt's followers, the bills passed the House of Commons only to meet defeat in the House of Lords on December 17, 1783. Ignoring the coalition's victory in the House of Commons, the King dismissed it and called upon Pitt.

Pitt's ministry. The King's action was irregular and dangerous, but events vindicated him. Pitt hung on throughout the winter as a minority minister, but the minority grew. On March 25, 1784, the King dissolved Parliament in disregard of the septennial convention. Pitt's victory was not that of a homogeneous party but of varied groups and hatred of the coalition. Pitt was not a party leader until 1789, though the Portland Whigs acted steadily in opposition along with a dwindling number of North's men.

Pitt dealt masterfully with accumulated business, aided by able men who had their first chance to lead. Pitt's India Act of 1784 created a Board of Control nominated by the King from among privy councillors. The extent of the board's domination over the company could not be specified, but under Dundas' presidency the board was vigorous. Burke and his opposition friends led the prosecution of Warren Hastings for alleged high crimes and misdemeanours in India. Pitt voted for one crucial charge as a matter for impeachment. Burke won his greatest parliamentary victory when the House of Commons voted for impeachment. In 1788 the trial opened before the House of Lords in Westminster Hall. It went on intermittently until 1795, when the House of Lords acquitted Hastings. If the evidence did not support a conviction, it supported the need for some kind of proceedings to settle doubts.

Pitt's India Act

Pitt pursued administrative and fiscal reform more vigorously than parliamentary reform. He owed an election debt to the parliamentary reformers and brought in a bill in 1785. Not a test of loyalty to him, the bill lost, 248 votes to 174; thereafter Pitt was done with the subject. His commercial reforms went as far as contemporary protectionist sentiment permitted. He carried a commercial treaty with France but failed to win lower duties on American and Irish trade. His customs reforms improved revenue collections and simplified customs administration. Advised by Richard Price, he altered methods of managing the national debt with a new sinking fund. The substantial increase of trade increased the annual revenue by one-half during Pitt's peacetime ministry. Had not war intervened in 1793, his sinking fund could have fulfilled its purpose of orderly debt retirement.

In foreign affairs Pitt raised England from the depths of the early 1780s. In 1788 he engineered a triple alliance with Holland and Prussia against France. Pitt took a strong line in two diplomatic crises. Under threat of war, Spain conceded British fishing and settlement rights on Vancouver Island and thus opened England's future interests in that region. Pitt could not force Russia in 1791 to give up Oczakov on the Black Sea. But this was so far removed that only Turkey was disturbed; in western Europe England's prestige was high. Just before the war of the French Revolution began, Pitt said England was secure and the future looked stable.

By 1789 the political future also appeared secure. The King's illness and mental derangement in the winter of 1788 (according to the latest studies, as the result of porphyria, a hereditary blood disorder) caused a crisis. As regent, the Prince of Wales might use the prerogative powers to replace Pitt with Fox. Pitt hoped by statute to restrict the regent's (not the royal) powers, but the King's recovery halted proceedings on the bill. The bitter partisanship of the debates thoroughly discredited the parliamentary opposition. Pitt emerged a Galahad with a larger and more closely knit majority. The election of 1790 renewed his political strength.

England, celebrating the King's recovery, reacted initially with mixed feelings toward the French Revolution. Enthusiasts, including survivors of the earlier reform movement, welcomed the fall of the Bastille as heralding an era of freedom and brotherhood among men. Speaking to the Revolution Society commemorating the Revolution of 1688, Dr. Price called the French Revolution an example to England and a warning to fulfill the promise of 1688 by reforming Parliament. Few people openly opposed the Revolution. The government, officially neutral, thought France too beset with internal troubles to disturb the peace of Europe. Two months after Pitt recommended a reduction in army appropriations because the future promised peace, France, in April 1792, declared war on Austria, plunging Europe into war.

THE ERA OF THE FRENCH REVOLUTION (1789–1815)

The end of reform. By this time English opinion had become divided. Burke's *Reflections on the Revolution in France* (November 1790) condemned the English reformers and warned of the Revolution's threat to the Christian social order of Europe. Thomas Paine, whose *Rights of Man* (1791) was written in reply to Burke, represented to upholders of the established order the dangers from revived English radicalism and French Jacobinism. Burke and Paine were the extremists in the controversy over the related questions of reform, the Revolution, and war. Pitt and his foreign secretary, William Wyndham Grenville, Baron Grenville, found no English vital interest at stake in the continental war until the winter of 1792–93, when France executed its king, and its Revolutionary armies threatened the independence of the Low Countries and the European balance of power. France spared Pitt a decision by declaring war on England, February 1, 1793.

Fear of Jacobinism

The Revolution and the war strongly affected politics and the movement for parliamentary reform. The old reform societies were middle class and property conscious. The London Corresponding Society, however, founded in 1792 with the shoemaker Thomas Hardy its secretary, brought the lower middle class and the working class into politics. This society, with its affiliates throughout England and Scotland, had organization and a sense of public purpose to distinguish it from mobs of 18th-century England. The Corresponding Societies, unlike the Society for Constitutional Information, asked for universal manhood suffrage. The number of active reformers never numbered more than a few thousand; the established order retained its credit with the nation; it is doubtful that England was on the verge of revolution. But panic spread among some of the governing class and the propertied, encouraged by reformers' indiscretions and excesses of zeal. The Association for the Preservation of Liberty and Property, founded in the winter of 1792–93 in London, had affiliates throughout the country. Authorities broke up reform conventions in Scotland in 1792–93, and the courts sentenced a few of the leaders harshly. English radicals' talk of a convention, for purposes never made quite clear, stimulated the government to act. In May 1794 it seized 12 reform leaders. After the jury acquitted the first three to be tried for high treason, the remaining cases were dropped. Some prosecutions succeeded, but the number before magistrates has never been determined. Parliament enacted some repressive statutes. By 1795 the reform agitation virtually ended, to be revived toward the end of the Napoleonic Wars.

Wartime politics. Like England, the parliamentary opposition divided over reform and war. Fox led the liberal minority—the New Whigs—whom Burke accused of deserting the principles of 1688. The Old Whigs, fearful of splitting the Portland party, only slowly came to accept Burke's views. In 1794 they crossed over. Portland, William Wentworth, 2nd Earl Fitzwilliam, and Burke's disciple William Windham took Cabinet offices. The coalition of 1794 did not essentially change Pitt's policy. Relying on alliances and subsidies, he aimed to preserve the balance of power and England's vital interests rather than overthrow the Revolutionary government. Burke desired a Bourbon restoration in France. The abortive peace negotiations of 1796–97 showed Pitt's willingness to treat with the Revolutionary regime.

The Irish problem flared up in the 1790s. Legislative independence was a mockery when the Lord Lieutenant of Ireland and Pitt's Cabinet leagued with the Irish junto to block reforms, control patronage, and preserve the Protestant ascendancy. Although another extension of civil rights was granted to the Irish in 1793, Catholics were still forbidden to sit in Parliament. Catholic hopes rose late in 1794, when Earl Fitzwilliam became lord lieutenant. His hasty dismissal of junto politicians and his advocacy of Catholic emancipation so alarmed the government that Portland, his superior, recalled him. Ireland drifted toward civil war, as the recently formed Society of United Irishmen took a militant lead. The Rebellion of 1798 was not as dangerous as it was dramatic. French aid supported only a small effort in the northwest of Ireland, while elsewhere English forces quickly suppressed risings. Pitt saw the solution to the Irish problem in a legislative union combined with Catholic emancipation. Cornwallis, the lord lieutenant, agreed. Both parliaments enacted legislative union in 1801, adding 100 Irish seats to the House of Commons and 28 Irish peers and four bishops to the House of Lords at Westminster. The King broadcast his opposition to Catholic emancipation, and Pitt's Cabinet rejected it. For a month in February–March 1801, the King was again deranged. Pitt could not accept responsibility for both the government of the empire and the King's health. He resigned, promising never again to bring up emancipation.

The Irish Rebellion

Besides the Irish business, Pitt resigned because he was weary after 17 strenuous years in office. The contrast between his successes before the war and failures afterward encouraged the judgment that he was only a great peacetime minister. Yet he laid down the lines of war policy that England followed to the end.

Henry Addington (later 1st Viscount Sidmouth) formed a government in March 1801. Country gentlemen in Parliament and a nation anxious for peace supported him. Englishmen persuaded themselves that peace with Napoleon, who had recently come to power, was peace with a stable France. By the Treaty of Amiens (1802), England recognized the republican regime in France and restored all conquests except Trinidad and Ceylon. The election of 1802 registered satisfaction with both the Irish Union and the peace. But relations with France quickly deteriorated. When England declared war in May 1803, men looked to Pitt for leadership. Pitt recommended a nonpartisan ministry. George III detested Fox, but he could accept Grenville, who had deserted Pitt over Catholic emancipation. Pitt reconsidered, dropped Grenville, and formed a conservative government including only ministers personally desirable to the King. The second Pitt ministry, in May 1804, came largely from its immediate predecessor, excluding Addington. The parliamentary opposition was uncomfortably strong just when French invasion threatened and the Third Coalition was forming against Napoleon. When, in August 1805, Austria allied with England and Russia, the danger of invasion had passed, for Admiral Nelson had frustrated Napoleon's plans for controlling the Channel. Nelson's victory at Trafalgar in October 1805 gave England mastery of the seas. Napoleon, however, smashed the Third Coalition after invading Austria.

Battle of Trafalgar

Pitt's death on January 23, 1806, confused English politics. The Cabinet refusing to go on, George III was forced to accept the Fox–Grenville "Ministry of All the Talents," less comprehensive than the name suggests. It was mainly Foxite, if returned Whigs like Fitzwilliam and Windham are so considered, but hardly homogeneous with its inclusion of Addington (Lord Sidmouth) and Thomas Lord Erskine, counsel for the defendants in the treason trials of 1794. Before his death in September 1806, Fox failed to achieve the peace with France that he had always thought men of goodwill could make. Grenville carried on, strengthened by the election of October

1806. With strong radical support, the government abolished the slave trade in March 1807, ending a 20-year campaign that had worn down the opposition. The King, encouraged by Sidmouth, frustrated Grenville's desire to open army careers to Catholics by dismissing the government before Parliament seriously took up the bill. The Duke of Portland was called upon to form a ministry. There was no place in Portland's government for Sidmouth because George Canning would not serve with him. Portland's strong Cabinet included Canning, Spencer Perceval, Lord Hawkesbury (Robert Banks Jenkinson), and Viscount Castlereagh. But personal dislikes and disagreements over the conduct of the war betrayed the ideological harmony. After Canning and Castlereagh resigned, Portland yielded to Perceval in October 1809; the Whigs could only observe. Perceval carried on until an assassin's bullet killed him in May 1812.

Liverpool's ministry

Yet through this period cabinets were remarkably stable. Like Perceval, Lord Liverpool (Hawkesbury) as prime minister continued his predecessor's Cabinet. Canning and Castlereagh were the main problems. With Canning choosing to remain out of office, Castlereagh returned as foreign secretary before Perceval died and continued under Liverpool. Two other men contributed to the stability. The Prince of Wales, regent because of his father's incapacity, wisely gave his confidence to Liverpool. After his powers as regent were made permanent, he broke with his former Whig friends. The choice of Liverpool was a happy one. Considered a man of second-rate abilities in his own time and nearly ever since, Liverpool has recently been recognized for one great talent. He held his government together as a conciliator rather than as a powerful personality. Prime minister until 1827, he molded a party out of the elements that Pitt, Portland, and Perceval had gathered. More than Pitt, Liverpool left a party hehind him, having identified with conservatism the Tory party he inherited.

The conduct of the war. The steady war effort also reveals the continuity of the period of 1807–15. The standoff between French land power and British sea power persuaded Napolean to try economic warfare against England. By his Continental System he aimed to exclude English goods from European markets. England, in turn, blockaded ports its ships could not enter. This warfare hurt England; the trade statistics show that in 1811 England exported to northern European ports goods of only one-sixth the value of exports in 1805. Unemployment grew. The increase in England's Latin American trade only partially made up for the decline in trade with Europe and the United States. The Americans boycotted British goods in retaliation against England's interference with their shipping and neutral rights. The War of 1812 with the United States followed; a central event in American history, the war is only peripherally treated in British history.

The Continental System

Europe also suffered from Napoleon's economic war, and in 1810 he replaced exclusion with high tariffs. His economic policy needed political–military support; Napoleon invaded Russia and the Iberian Peninsula in part to complete his economic system. But England found entry to the Continent in Portugal, where its forces landed in 1808 (see FRENCH REVOLUTIONARY AND NAPOLEONIC WARS). The Peninsular War culminated in Wellington's invasion of France over the Pyrenees in 1813–14. This occurred as the allies penetrated from the east. Never before had Napoleon faced such universal and united opposition. Stressing the need for unity to win victory and a peace settlement imposed by the great powers, Castlereagh avoided piecemeal treaties lacking the force of general agreement. The government and Parliament supported generously the subsidy policy undergirding Castlereagh's diplomacy. The Treaty of Chaumont (March 9, 1814), his great edifice, clarified allied war aims (including the expulsion of Napoleon), tightened allied unity, and promised a general European settlement under supervision of the great powers for 20 years. Napoleon's return from Elba, the Hundred Days ending at Waterloo, and his exile to St. Helena did not interrupt the peacemakers at Vienna or change England's policy.

The end of the wars

The Vienna Congress settlement of 1815 was the concrete manifestation of Castlereagh's definition of British policy: to assure the peaceful conduct of France by not mistreating her, while providing security against her for the Netherlands and northern Italy; to stabilize Germany by strengthening Prussian and Austrian influence in central Europe and the Rhineland; to check the extension of Russian influence westward; and to safeguard England's commercial and colonial interests.

The end of a long generation of war found in office a Tory government proud of England's contribution to war and the peace, secure in its parliamentary strength, but uncertain of its domestic course. A vastly different England than had entered the war in 1793 faced problems only partly to be understood as marking the transition from war to peace. They were also those of the first modern nation to experience the change from rural and agrarian to industrial and urban nationhood.

ECONOMIC, SOCIAL, AND CULTURAL HISTORY (1714–1815)

Population. The dearth of reliable demographic and economic statistics for 18th-century England contrasts with the abundance of contemporary writings on "political arithmetic." A lexicographer in 1710 described its content as the extent and value of land, population, public revenues, commerce, and manufactures, or whatever related to the strength and riches of a nation. Concern with the well-being of the state thus showed a mercantilist bias. The earliest official national census (1801) produced the first dependable population statistics for England, Wales, and Scotland. For the first two the population was 8,893,000 and for Scotland 1,608,000. In 1811 the numbers were 10,164,000 and 1,806,000—a remarkable growth. Just over a century earlier, the statistician Gregory King estimated the population of England and Wales as 5,500,000. Attempts to explain the near doubling of the population during the century produced disputes about numbers and statistical methodology. The population grew slowly, if at all, until the 1740s, rapidly after 1780.

Demographers and economic historians disagree on the reasons for population growth and its effect upon economic growth. The declining death rate, increasing birthrate, improved medical science, and a rise in the standard of living, all offered as explanation, have been challenged. None by itself explains the growth but taken together they mean multiple causation for a complex phenomenon. Statistical evidence is impeachable, contemporary opinions were impressionistic, yet together they suggest a rise in general well-being, whatever the hardships of life.

Equally complex is the relationship between economic and population growth. To say that the latter caused the other oversimplifies and hardly explains increased output per person. Population growth helps account for increased labour supply and consumer demand. Expansion of overseas trade stimulated demand and production. The overall impression is of a growing population and expanding economy buoyed by a confident spirit.

The Industrial Revolution. The word revolution is used to describe economic changes of the past two centuries. Though a few historians place the beginnings in the mid-16th century, most hold that the "takeoff," or the dramatic upturn, of industrial growth began about 1780, with the social impact coming later.

During the 18th century, English society was preindustrial, an agricultural and commercial rural society with one metropolis, London. After 1780 migration to cities increased as manufacturing acquired a factory, power-driven character, especially in the cotton-textile industry. This industry was the bellwether of the Industrial Revolution; by 1815 exports of cotton cloth exceeded woollen by three times. Yet the population, 85 percent in the country or in communities under 5,000 persons during the century, remained officially rural until the census of 1851. In the 18th century the structure of society and distribution of population among classes remained preindustrial. Contrary to older views, the enclosure of common lands to increase efficiency did not depopulate

Urbanization

the countryside. Population growth supplied the surplus from rural areas for the factory system. Migration was toward the towns and industry; in the midlands and north of England, new industry attracted people to once thinly populated areas. Not until the 19th century did the industrial–urban complex exist, emphasizing textiles, iron, and coal. Besides London, the population of which nearly doubled from 1700 to 1801 to a total of 1,000,000 persons, the considerable towns (though none exceeded 80,000) were Liverpool, Birmingham, Sheffield, Norwich, Bristol, and Glasgow. Birmingham doubled between 1770 and 1801.

Much of the rural population engaged in domestic manufactures of textiles or in supplying agricultural, mining, or building needs. Occupational classification was therefore difficult; the census of 1841 was the first to attempt it. Gregory King's groupings were socio-occupational. He thought 70 percent of the population was primarily agricultural, with the family the unit of production. King distinguished between families (511,586) who "increas[ed] to the Wealth of the Kingdom" and the majority (849,000) who decreas[ed] the Wealth of the Kingdom because the cost of living exceeded their incomes. Supplements deriving ultimately from the productive minority made up the difference, for England had an annual economic surplus and more than fed itself.

In King's groupings, the margins of the upper and middle classes and of the lower middle class and the lower class overlapped. Some great traders were wealthier than some peers and most gentlemen. Rich merchants often owned land and almost always aspired to it because land conferred status. Ownership of land was an eligibility requirement for the House of Commons. Below the nobility and gentry, King listed officeholders, merchants, clergy, professional men, freeholders, and farmers. Shopkeepers and artisans occupied the borderland above the lower class. The lower orders—common soldiers and sailors, labourers and servants, cottagers, paupers, and vagrants—constituted the majority who "diminished the wealth of the kingdom." Contemporaries nevertheless considered England a rich nation whose people were better off than any Europeans except the Dutch. Estimates of per capita income—£9 at the beginning of the century, £13 at midcentury, and £22 at the end—suggest a level comparable to that in the wealthier underdeveloped countries in mid-20th century.

Agricultural revolution

By 1815 English agriculture had changed in important ways within a nation becoming an urban and industrial community. Increasing consumer demand stimulated the agricultural revolution and an increasing supply of capital assisted improvement. New techniques of cultivation and of land usage and management as well as new crops not only made land more productive but brought new land into tillage. Between 1700 and 1760, some 300,000 acres were enclosed, and ten times that amount between 1760 and 1800. Under the General Act of 1801, which eliminated the need for private enclosure acts, the transformation to closed fields was nearly complete by 1820. Enclosure facilitated more effective use of arable land and encouraged improvement of breeding by the segregation of livestock. The social effects of enclosure have been debated vigorously and emotionally. Recent studies show that enclosure did not depopulate rural districts. The need for agricultural labour did not decline. The citywide migration was that of the rural surplus. Nor did enclosure eliminate the smallholders. If enclosure costs forced out some, compensation for surrender of ancient common rights often enabled cottagers to acquire small holdings. The post-1815 agricultural depression hurt the smallholders severely. The agricultural revolution, important in itself, sustained and encouraged the Industrial Revolution, providing food for the growing nonagricultural population and supplying some of the capital for industrial expansion.

Commercial revolution

The term commercial revolution usually refers to the two preceding centuries, but important changes occurred in the 18th century. Commerce became securely interlocked with agricultural and industrial expansion. The volume of trade, which increased sevenfold during the century and doubled between 1750 and 1800, also shifted regionally. Domestic exports to Europe declined from 85 to 30 percent of Britain's total, while those to North America increased from 6 to 30 percent and to the West Indies from 5 to 25 percent, all between the opening and the end of the century. Meanwhile imports from Europe declined from 66 to 43 percent of a total of which the West Indies and the East Indies each sent 25 percent. Europe took 85 percent of England's re-exports both at the beginning and the end of the century, but the total was much larger at the end. England was the primary supplier of colonial products to Europe. The monetary gains of the re-export trade were great because British merchants made a profit on the average of about 15 percent on the value of the goods traded. Commerce aided English manufacturing by stimulating domestic and foreign demand, assisting other countries to buy English goods, bringing raw materials to British industry, and contributing to the stock of investment capital.

The Industrial Revolution of the 18th and early 19th centuries was a British phenomenon. Manufacturing increased in Europe but the use of power-driven machinery concentrated in factories was strikingly particular to Britain and especially to the cotton and iron industries. If the history of the cotton industry is not quite the history of the Industrial Revolution from about 1780 to 1840, it is illustrative. The traditional textile industry was woollen; cotton manufacturing became important in the last third of the 18th century. In 1815 England exported £22,000,000 worth of cotton cloth, three times as much as woollen cloth, and over 100 times the value of cotton cloth exports in the early 1760s. This was the result of a sequence of technological innovations in spinning and weaving, beginning in the 1730s. The most sophisticated machine, Edmund Cartwright's power loom (1787), did not come into general use until after 1815. The cotton industry, new and unrestrained by tradition, became the example par excellence of machine work in the factory.

The iron industry was also amenable to technological change. Use of coke for smelting, shown to be practicable by Abraham Darby in 1709, was widespread by midcentury. Henry Cort's puddling process for making bar iron, patented in 1783, increased the supply of wrought iron. James Watt's improvement of the steam engine in 1775 marked the beginning of the machine age. The iron industry was as productive in the reign of Charles I as in 1760. Then came Watt and Cort and the "takeoff." In 1800 England produced 1,000,000 tons of pig iron, of which 60,000 were exported. The export figure alone was twice the total production of 1760. The statistics of coal production, so closely related, are 6,000,000 tons in 1770 and 15,000,000 in 1815.

Growth of transport

Inland transport responded to economic necessity and stimulated industrial growth. The canal age began in 1759, when Francis Egerton, 3rd duke of Bridgwater, linked his Worsley coal mines by canal with Manchester. By the 1820s local capital organized corporately, and ingenious engineers, such as the canal builder James Brindley and the highway builders Thomas Telford and John MacAdam, laced England with canals and improved roads. The history of the Wedgwood potteries, a striking story of entrepreneurial genius, reveals the dependence of manufacturing growth upon safer, cheaper, and faster transportation. New manufacturing techniques increased production, salesmanship and promotion spread the demand for Wedgwood ware, and improved transport brought raw materials to the potteries and carried the ware to consumers. When the age of canal building ended, England had invested £20,000,000 in a system of navigation vital especially to heavy industries but inadequate for the future needs of industry. The railways were to meet the need in the next age.

Effects of industrialization. To the usual list of physical, social, and political causes of the economic revolution should be added a psychological one. England in the 18th and early 19th centuries was as buoyant and confident as Holland in the 17th century or the United

States after the American Civil War. Englishmen responded to challenges, risking loss of capital should an invention prove impracticable, an enterprise be mismanaged, or any number of unforeseen calamities occur. This happened despite the fact that the principle of unlimited liability prevailed, whereby all shareholders were held responsible for any debts incurred by the company. Often the people who suffered worst when a joint-stock enterprise collapsed were small investors, and many were the unhappy partners in failing enterprises. The first 75 years of the Industrial Revolution were years when the spirit of adventure was keen.

The standard of living

The growth of wealth suggests the potential for amelioration of life in this period. Judgments have been influenced by emotional involvement and political opinions. No one denies the existence of poverty and hardship, but some historians stress improvement throughout the period. Economic growth helped the worker directly and made possible greater indirect aid from private and group philanthropy. Parish officials and the magistrates were responsible for enforcement of the Poor Laws, which was spotty in the absence of central supervision; a zealous local official, however, might send the poor to the workhouse, where paupers, sick or well, young or old, were thrown together indiscriminately. The Poor Laws also forbade the destitute to settle outside their own parishes, but these laws were not rigorously enforced, permitting mobility of labour. Economic growth and increased concern for the poor existed together; whether there was merely heightened awareness or an actual increase of poverty, the statistics show a sixfold growth in the amount of poor-rate collections between 1775 and 1825. Part of the increased expenditures went for wage supplements to bring incomes among the poor up to a minimum cost of living. The practice, called the Speenhamland system, spread widely after 1795, when a group of Berkshire magistrates adopted it. To attribute the apparently growing magnitude of the problem of the poor to industrialization and urbanization is to oversimplify the problem and to slight the problem of the poor in preindustrial England. The population trebled between 1700 and 1821, and the urban poor made the problem more visible.

The growth of industry and towns created a serious psychological problem. The pattern of life governed by the seasons, the sun and moon, and the weather gave way to the discipline of the clock and the rhythms of the machines. Neither the laws of nature nor of Parliament, but the laws of the marketplace, determined the times for operating machines. Workers had no preparation for the new industrial discipline. In addition to physical adjustment, they had to make within two generations a radical mental and moral adjustment to a new way of life.

Religion. Religion probably offered less consolation to the labouring poor and the paupers than some might like to think. The churches and organized religion did not deal adequately with problems arising from new urban and industrializing trends. But the churches were not meeting social problems in preindustrial England, and the poor often shirked churchgoing. Statistics are lacking except in scattered localities. Contemporary literature shows the churches as the preserves of the upper and middle classes. Among Protestant Dissenters, the Baptists were thought of as the poorer sort. Quakers, not strictly Dissenters, were in the middle ranks of society, along with Presbyterians, Independents, and Unitarians. The Roman Catholics, a small minority, cut across all ranks of the social structure, as did the Established Church of England.

Methodism

One of the traditional explanations for the rise of Methodism is that it filled a gap in religious life. This was particularly true in Wales, despite the prominence there of Protestant Dissent. Neither Dissent nor the Church of England reached certain areas and groups in England and Wales. Dissent was notoriously intellectual and held "enthusiasm" (which in the 18th century connoted fanaticism) in disfavour as much as did the Established Church. Launched by the brothers Charles and John Wesley and by George Whitefield in 1739, Methodism sought out the neglected and underprivileged. Emotionally and enthusiastically, itinerant preachers offered "the glad tidings of salvation," as John Wesley put it, often in the open air. Edmund Gibson, bishop of London, called Methodists "Rabble." Methodism was not a socially revolutionary force, except by the implication of equality in its teachings about salvation, but it felt the disapproval of the religious establishment. Separation from the Church of England did not come until just after John Wesley's death in 1791, and then on technical grounds. But in spirit and form Methodism was nonconformist long before the separation.

Methodism influenced some earnest Anglicans, the Evangelicals, who deplored the decline of manners in society and the religious lethargy in the Church of England. The Evangelicals promoted social but not political reforms; they worked for the abolition of the slave trade and of slavery; and as social superiors they desired the amelioration of the hard lot of the poor and the oppressed. But Evangelicalism did not try to abolish deference among the lower orders. Sunday schools would teach people to read the Bible and Hannah More's popular tracts that offered patience in this world and the expectation of rewards in Heaven. Literacy was not for absorbing the doctrines of Thomas Paine's *Rights of Man* or his *Age of Reason.*

Dissenters were prominent out of proportion to their numbers in the political-reform movements. The Test and Corporation acts (1673 and 1661) limited the civil rights of non-Anglicans, and Dissenters, often well-educated and prosperous, resented the discrimination. They disliked the preference for land in determining political qualifications, and they abhorred restrictions imposed upon them merely because they were Dissenters. They desired to open careers to men of talent, but they thought especially of opportunities for the middle class. Their campaign for repeal of the Test and Corporation acts lasted a century before it succeeded in the 1820s. It joined that for parliamentary reform to form an important chapter in the history of political and constitutional change in modern England.

The Church of England remained secure in its position of establishment, less torpid than tradition has it, but less vital intellectually than in the 17th century. Its legal position guaranteed involvement of the clergy in politics, if nothing more than in patronage. Deism did not become a strong influence in England, in part because, in its benevolently placid faith in reason, it was not far removed from the Latitudinarianism so prominent in the church.

The Enlightenment. Faith in the power of human reason has been emphasized into a cliché suggesting a monolithic character for 18th-century thought. Recent writings on the Enlightenment qualify this exaggeration. René Descartes, Sir Isaac Newton, and John Locke bequeathed a conception of man's capacity to discover the laws governing the universe and similarly his capacity to understand and apply the laws governing the social order. England enjoyed a reputation, spread by Voltaire and Montesquieu, for having devised a political order that was the envy of Europeans. Englishmen were proud that their "happy constitution" combined freedom with good order, protected property, and responded to the country's needs. It was a unique political system; the great powers of Europe knew only monarchical absolutism even in the later period of Enlightened Despotism.

The Philosophes desired freedom above all, for it was fundamental to human improvement or any concept of perfectibility. They did not seek a particular organization for society, nor were they uniformly optimistic about the powers of human reason to create a perfect social order. English writers, already enjoying freedom, had less at stake than continental Philosophes. England's two most important contributors to the Enlightenment were George Berkeley and the Scot David Hume, whose writings, by demonstrating the limitation of human reason, ironically did much to undermine the Rationalism upon which the Enlightenment was built. There were other anti-Rationalist elements in 18th-century England. The novels of Samuel Richardson contributed to a "cult of sensibility." Edmund Burke wrote on the sublime in an anti-Rationalist approach to aesthetics and art and directly attacked Rationalism in other writings. Burke's emphasis upon history and experience in the development of society, law, and government placed him among the precursors of Romanticism. Jeremy Bentham denied the existence of natural law so prominent in Enlightenment thought and replaced it with utility (the principle of the greatest good for the greatest number) as the guiding principle of the legislator. Thus England contributed to the Enlightenment and exemplified the freedom it desired but at the same time prepared the way for Romanticism and Utilitarianism.

SCOTLAND AND WALES: 1714–1815

The union of England and Scotland in 1707 came exactly a century after Parliament rebuffed James I (James VI) on the issue. The ease with which Scotland accommodated itself to the union contrasts with the difficulties of achieving it. The Jacobite troubles and pro-Stuart feelings lost political force by midcentury. Political realism and economic opportunity attracted Scottish interests to England and the empire. Some facts about Glasgow concentrate the story. A town of 12,000 at the time of union, Glasgow was a commercial centre and becoming an industrial city by 1800, when it reached a population of 70,000 (as large as Liverpool's). Glasgow took eager advantage of opportunities in the imperial commercial system. Old dislikes between Scots and Englishmen lingered, but political and economic self-interest kept them properly subordinated.

History and the Act of Union operated to mesh the political systems in form and function. The Scottish electoral structure resembled England's and also lent itself to management. The office of secretary of state for Scotland was so unnecessary that it was vacant between 1746 and 1885. The best known managers, the 2nd and 3rd dukes of Argyll during the reigns of the first two Georges and Henry Dundas during the first administration of Pitt the Younger, dispensed patronage, influenced elections, and controlled the Scottish votes in Parliament. Normally, the Scottish contingent supported the government.

Areas unaffected by the Act of Union

The union did not dissolve particularities in three important areas—the law, the church, and education. The Scottish legal system was based on Roman law. In substance and form it provided justice admirably under such men as Duncan Forbes of Culloden, lord president of the Court of Session (1737–47). The Presbyterian Church remained the established church, with an influence upon Scottish life much greater than that of the church in England. Though nominally democratic by virtue of the electoral process that brought laymen to its governing bodies, the kirk was authoritarian in its supervision of the morals and the education of the community. About midcentury intolerance lessened, and the outlook of the clergy broadened, but this was a relative matter, subject to important local exceptions when parish clergymen had large moral influence. Yet this could work another way. The revival of patronage in appointment of ministers after 1712—so that some 90 percent of the benefices were filled by appointment by the crown, the nobility, and the gentry—strengthened the influence of patrons' views, generally more enlightened and tolerant than parishioners'. Because, however, congregations retained a formal right to reject nominees, tensions and disputes arose. The secessions of 1740 over personal and doctrinal matters produced four new Presbyterian churches.

The 18th century was a great age in Scottish educational and intellectual history. The church took seriously the duty to provide elementary education, after acquiring it in the time of John Knox. A beneficial result of the Forty-five Rebellion was that the Highlands were opened to the spread of educational facilities, by the church, by supplemental efforts of the Society for Promoting Christian Knowledge, and by some governmental assistance with money from forfeited estates. The English language became the language of instruction in the schools. The Scottish universities won admiring recognition in England, in the colonies, and in Europe. A flourishing intellectual, scientific, and literary life existed in the universities and in Edinburgh. At no time in its history have the names of Scotland's scholars and writers been so prominent in such proportionately large numbers as in the last half of the 18th century and the early 19th century. To name Adam Smith, David Hume, William Robertson, Lord Kames, Francis Hutcheson, and Thomas Reid is to suggest the quality of intellectual leaders of Scotland's golden age. The founding of *The Edinburgh Review* in 1802 by a new generation promised that the intellectual light would continue to glow as the new century opened.

The economic growth of Scotland is directly attributable to the union. Article VI of the Act of Union opened the imperial commercial system to Scots. The progress of Scottish agriculture was less spectacular than the expansion of trade. The most important agricultural development was the growth of livestock and dairy interests, and the benefits came in the next century. Union immediately opened commercial opportunities. The story is properly the history of the merchant class and of energetic individuals. If Glasgow virtually stole the tobacco trade from Bristol and Liverpool, it was the "tobacco lords" who did it. Union offered encouragements for the traditional industries—fishing, linen, and woollens. Later, cotton manufacturing in Scotland shared in the expansion of that new industry in the United Kingdom. An important consequence of the union, and then of the Forty-five Rebellion, was the participation of Scots with great effect in the military–imperial life of the British people. As soldiers, explorers, settlers, and administrators, Scots went with and ahead of the Union Jack. The history of the British Empire after the mid-18th century owes more to Scots than their relative numbers would suggest.

The work of a ruler part Welshman, Henry VIII, accounts for some differences between the histories of Wales and Scotland in the 18th century. Because Henry VIII completed the extension of the English system of law and local government to Wales and enlarged its representation in the House of Commons, there was no later problem of absorbing alien institutions into the English system as in 1707 with Scotland. Wales was a part of the English system when the Reformation occurred, and the religious history of Wales moved along with that of England. Welsh political history in the 18th century was either a part of national history or, as in the English counties, local history. Wales felt the same influences as England in that period, most notably in religion and in economic life. Nonconformity of the Dissenting and then the Methodist variety played a more important part in the intellectual and social life of Wales than of England. In the 19th century it was a strong political influence upon the Liberal and later the Labour parties. Along with England, Wales participated in the agricultural and industrial revolutions. The Welsh terrain and mineral endowments made the raising of livestock, the woollen industries, and later the production of coal and iron of first importance. The history of Wales in the 18th century can be written in the histories of religion and of the economic revolution more meaningfully than as an attempt at separate national political history, so long as proper attention is given to local differences. (C.B.Co.)

XIII. Great Britain: 1815–1914

BRITAIN AFTER THE WARS

The end of the long wars against Napoleon did not usher in a period of peace and contentment. Although both agricultural and industrial production had greatly, if unevenly, increased during the wars, the total national debt had nearly quadrupled since 1793. Of the total annual public revenue after 1815, more than half had to be employed to pay interest on this debt. The abolition of Pitt's income tax in 1816 meant that the debt burden fell on consumers—many of them with low incomes—and on industrialists. The archaic and regressive nature of the national taxation system, associated as it was with a mounting scale of locally levied poor-law rates, provoked widespread anxiety and criticism.

The postwar economy and society. The peace was followed, indeed, by open social conflicts, most of them exacerbated by a postwar slump. As the long-run process of industrialization continued, with a rising population and a cyclical pattern of relative prosperity and depression, many social conflicts centred on questions of what contemporaries called "corn and currency." Others were directly related to the growth of factories and towns and to the parallel development of middle class and working class consciousness.

The agriculturalists, who were predominant in Parliament, attempted to safeguard their wartime economic position by securing, in 1815, a new Corn Law designed to keep up grain prices and rents by taxing imported grain. Their political power enabled them to acquire economic protection. Yet many of them suffered, particularly after 1819, from a serious fall of agricultural prices. Debts contracted during the wars became more onerous as prices fell. There were many complaints of agricultural distress during the early 1820s.

The Corn Law of 1815

Many of the industrialists, an increasingly vociferous group outside Parliament, resented the passing of the Corn Law. Others objected to the return of gold, agreed to by Parliament in 1819 and put into effect in 1821. Whatever their outlook, industrialists were beginning to demand a voice in Parliament. The term middle class began to be used more frequently in social and political debate.

Town and village labourers were also unrepresented in Parliament, and it was they who bore the main brunt of the postwar difficulties. Bad harvests and high food prices left them hungry and discontented, and in the worst years, when bad harvests and industrial unemployment coincided, discontent assumed a political shape. The creation of the sense of a working class followed the emergence of a steam-driven factory system with new rhythms of work and new disciplines of control, a breakdown in traditional family relationships, and the growth of towns with structures of communication quite different from those of villages or preindustrial urban communities. There were radical riots in 1816, 1817, and particularly in 1819, the year of the Peterloo Massacre, when there was a clash in Manchester between workers and troops of the yeomanry, or local citizenry.

Local magistrates, with no adequate police forces at their disposal, were often unsure how to deal either with secret "conspiracy" or with open challenges to authority, while Lord Liverpool's government, with only rudimentary administrative machinery at its disposal, tended to follow a policy of repression. The Six Acts of 1819, associated with Viscount Sidmouth, the home secretary, were designed to reduce disturbances and to check the extension of radical propaganda and organization. They provoked sharp criticism from Whigs as well as from radicals, and they did not dispel the fear and suspicion that were threatening the stability of the whole social order.

There was a revival of confidence after 1821, as economic conditions improved and the government itself embarked on a program of economic reform. Sidmouth retired, to be succeeded by Sir Robert Peel; and Viscount Castlereagh, the foreign secretary, committed suicide. Even the king, George IV (1820–30), who had been drawn into the heart of politics when his discarded queen, Caroline, returned to England in 1820 and for a time became a radical heroine, ceased to be the target for continual radical abuse. Liverpool was a sufficiently able and sensible prime minister to work with new men and to move in new directions. Between 1821 and 1825, duties on raw material imports were reduced and tariff schedules were simplified; and in 1828, one year after Liverpool resigned, the fixed Corn Law of 1815 was replaced with a sliding scale. During this same period, Peel was reforming the law. Even after the collapse of the economic boom of 1824–25, no attempt was made to return to negative policies of repression.

Foreign policy. There was a change of tone if not of principle in foreign policy, as in home affairs, after Castlereagh's suicide. Castlereagh himself, who had represented Britain at the Congress of Vienna in 1815, had refused to follow up the peace settlement he had signed by converting the Quadruple Alliance of the victorious wartime allies into an instrument of police action to suppress liberalism and nationalism anywhere in Europe. His policy was one of nonintervention. His successor at the Foreign Office, George Canning, propounded the British viewpoint in more colourful language and with a strong appeal to British public opinion and emphasized differences between British viewpoints and those of the European great powers as much as their common interests. In 1824 he recognized the independence of Spain's American colonies, declaring in a famous phrase that he was calling "the New World into existence to redress the balance of the Old." In 1826 he used British force to defend constitutional government in Portugal, while, in the tension-ridden area of the eastern Mediterranean, he supported the cause of Greek independence. Although he died in 1827, before the new Greek state came into existence, after having served for a few months as Lord Liverpool's successor as prime minister, his policies and styles were reasserted by Palmerston, who became foreign minister in 1830.

The beginning of political reform. Between the death of Canning and Palmerston's acceptance of office in a government presided over by the aristocratic Whig leader Earl Grey, there had been a major shift in British politics. Canning's weak successor as prime minister, Viscount Goderich, who had been a successful chancellor of the exchequer under Liverpool, was unable to deal adequately with the increasingly complicated tangle of Tory and Whig factions, and he was soon replaced by Wellington, the military hero of the Napoleonic Wars. It was the Wellington ministry that introduced the new Corn Law of 1828 and presented Peel, the Prime Minister's chief henchman, with the renewed opportunity of reforming the law and, in 1829, with the chance of creating a new model police force for London. Yet Wellington, more soldier than politician, had to tackle two very difficult tasks—coping with Irish disorders and holding together in the same government Tories who had supported and opposed Canning.

Irish disorders centred, as they had since 1801, on the issue of Catholic emancipation, a favourite cause of the Whigs, who had been out of power since 1807. During the 18th century, Catholics in England had achieved a large measure of unofficial toleration, but, in Ireland, restrictions against Catholics' holding office were still rigorously enforced. In 1823 Daniel O'Connell, a Dublin Roman-Catholic lawyer, had founded the Catholic Association, the object of which was to give Roman Catholics in Ireland the same political and civil freedoms as Protestants. Employing impressive techniques of organization, he galvanized opinion in Ireland while at the same time mobilizing all his allies in England. In 1828 he won an election in County Clare, Ireland, so convincingly that Wellington, who—like the king—had always opposed Catholic emancipation, came to the conclusion that the government would have to push a measure for emancipation, which Canning had supported, through a Tory-dominated British Parliament. With difficulty he persuaded Peel, who had been tempted to resign, and the king, who had to be bullied, that an emancipation act was necessary and inevitable. Yet 128 "ultra-Tories" voted against the 1829 measure. Tory divisions left an opening for the Whigs, who were themselves divided on tactics if not on objectives. Some of them had joined the Canning ministry, but others had stayed aloof, biding their time. They had considerable support from financial interests and from religious dissenters, whose civil rights were recognized in 1828.

The issue of Catholic emancipation

The death of George IV, in June 1830, speeded up events. After the accession of William IV (1830–37) and an inconclusive general election, Wellington, beset by many enemies, was defeated in November on a relatively unimportant motion on royal expenditure. In a year of renewed economic distress and of revolution in France, when the political reform issue was being raised again at public meetings in different parts of the country, Wellington had not made matters easier for himself by expressing complete confidence in the constitution as it stood. He decided, therefore, to resign, and the king went on to send for Earl Grey, who had been *persona non grata* with George IV, to ask him to form a new ministry. The government Grey assembled was predominantly aristocratic—and it included Canningites as well as Whigs—but the new Prime Minister, like most of his colleagues, was committed to introducing a measure of parliamentary reform. For this reason, 1830 marked a real parting of the ways. At last there was a break in the continuity of regime that led back to Pitt's victory over Fox in the 1780s and that had only temporarily been interrupted in 1806–07. Moreover, the new government, aristocratic or not, was the parent of most of the Whig–Liberal administrations of the next 35 years.

The year 1830 was also one of economic and social grievances, with religion still being thrown into the melee. In many parts of the southern countryside, village labourers, backed, if not instigated, by the popular radical leader William Cobbett, were engaged in acts of violence against landlords and property (the "Captain Swing" disturbances), while in the midland and northern towns and cities, political reform movements were winning the support of the crowds. The Whigs were as afraid of rural riot as the Tories and almost as suspicious of new urban radical leaders in cities like Birmingham. Corn laws, currency laws, poor laws, and game laws were all being attacked, while, in the industrial north, the demand was growing for new laws to protect factory labour. It was in such an atmosphere that the new Whig-led government prepared its promised reform bill.

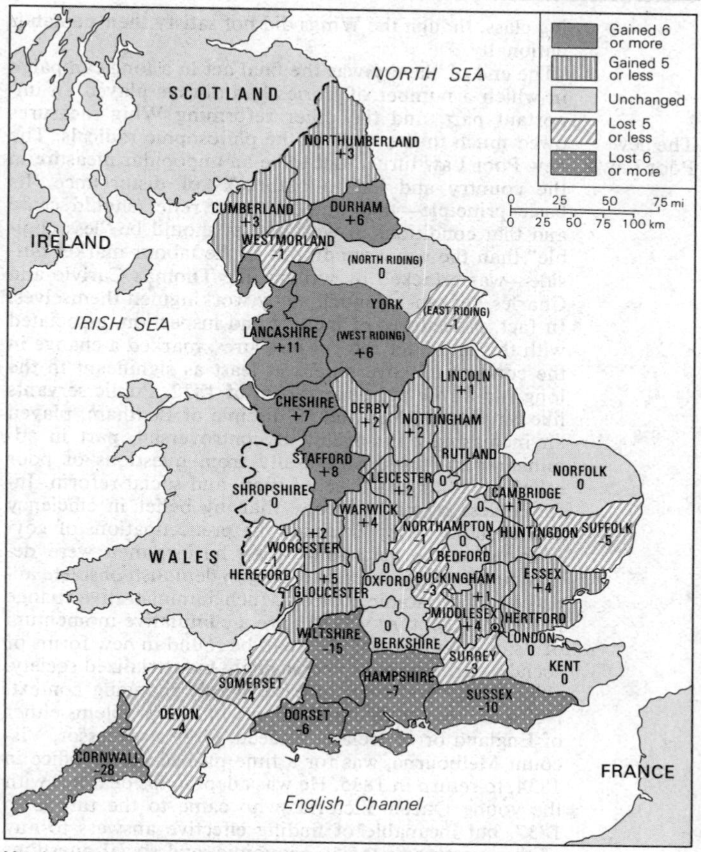

Membership change, by county, in the House of Commons as a result of the Reform Bill of 1832 (England only).

THE POLITICS OF REFORM

Whig interest in parliamentary reform went back to the 18th century, and Grey himself provided a link between two separate periods of public agitation. Yet, in the country as a whole, there were at least three approaches to the reform question. Middle class "reformers" were anxious to secure representation for commercial and industrial interests and for towns and cities, like Birmingham and Manchester, that had no direct voice in Parliament. "Popular radicals," middle class or working class, were concerned with asserting rights as well as with relieving distress. "Philosophic radicals," the followers of the utilitarian philosophy of Jeremy Bentham, were strong ideological protagonists of parliamentary reform but deeply hostile both to the arguments and the tactics of the popular radicals, unless they felt that they were in a position to deploy or control them. It was agitation in the country that kept the reform question on the boil between 1830 and 1832, while Grey, aloof from all forms of agitation, faced unprecedented constitutional difficulties with both the King and Parliament.

Three approaches to reform

The Reform Bill of 1832. A Whig reform bill was introduced in March 1831 and was carried, in its first form in the Commons, by one vote. In mid-April, however, after an opposition amendment had been successfully pressed, Grey induced a reluctant King to dissolve Parliament. At the ensuing general election, the government won a clear majority on the single cry "the bill, the whole bill and nothing but the bill." A second reform bill passed the Commons with no difficulty but was defeated in October in the Lords. Immediately there was a public outcry, with mass meetings of "political unions" and, in some cities, riots. A third bill was then passed by the Commons, only to be thrown out again—on an amendment—in the Lords in May 1832. William refused Grey's request to create a number of new peers who would carry the bill in the Lords, and, in consequence, Grey resigned and Wellington was called in. Such was the public mood, however, that he could not form a ministry, and Grey had to be reappointed, this time with a royal pledge that peers would be created if necessary. The threat was sufficient, and the bill passed, receiving the royal assent on June 7.

The Reform Bill was in no sense a democratic measure. It was concerned with giving the middle classes a stake in responsible government rather than with changing the basis of government. Yet it entailed a substantial redistribution of constituencies and a change in the conditions of the franchise. The total electorate was increased by 217,000, but the artisans, the working classes, and some sections of the lower middle classes still remained outside "the pale of the constitution." No radical demands were met, even if the manner of the passing of the bill had demonstrated the force of organized opinion in the country. Those Tories who had prophesied that it would mean revolution were wrong, since the composition of the new House of Commons differed little from the old. It continued, indeed, for many years to reflect property rather than population, and landed interests remained by far the largest interests represented there. The Tories were nonetheless right in arguing that in the long run there would be a change of system. The Whigs, for their part, were wise in recognizing that if a reform bill were not passed, there might well be real pressure for revolution but unrealistic in arguing that it would satisfy reformers as a final measure.

Achievement of the Reform Bill

Further Whig reforms. In fact, the Whigs, returned with a huge majority at the general election of December 1832, carried out a number of other important reforms. A statute in 1833 ended slavery in the British colonies; in the same year the East India Company lost its monopoly of the China trade and became a purely governing body with no commercial functions. In 1834 a new Poor Law, recommended by a royal commission appointed in 1832, was passed; this law grouped parishes into unions and placed the unions under the control of elected boards of guardians, with a national Poor Law Board in London. In 1835 the Municipal Corporations Act was passed, which swept away old oligarchies in local government. Elected councils were to appoint town clerks and treasurers, and many unincorporated industrial communities were to be granted their first governmental powers. In some towns, religious dissenters became the new governing class, though the Whigs did not satisfy their demands nationally.

The end of slavery was the final act in a long campaign in which a number of Tories had always played an important part, and the other reforming Whig measures owed much to the ideas of the philosophic radicals. The new Poor Law turned out to be an unpopular measure in the country and led to outbreaks of disturbance. Its basic principle—that outdoor poor relief should cease and that conditions in workhouses should be "less eligible" than the worst conditions in the labour market outside—was attacked by writers like Thomas Carlyle and Charles Dickens as much as by workingmen themselves. In fact, procedures of inquiry and inspection, associated with this and later reform measures, marked a change in the conduct of government at least as significant in the long run as the political reform of 1832. Public servants like Sir Edwin Chadwick, a disciple of Bentham, played an increasingly important, if controversial, part in administration, turning naturally from questions of poor relief to public health, education, and social reform. Inspired less by philanthropy than by belief in efficiency and economy, they extended the preoccupations of government at the very time when businessmen were demanding freer trade and seeking to demolish obsolete apparatus of economic control. Much administrative change in the 19th century was to have a cumulative momentum of its own, but its origins are to be found in new forms of social awareness in an increasingly industrialized society.

The new Poor Law

The Whigs were not at ease in this changing context. Nor were they united in dealing with the problems either of England or of Ireland. Indeed, Grey's successor, Viscount Melbourne, was for a time pushed out of office in 1834, to return in 1835. He was adept in his dealings with the young Queen Victoria, who came to the throne in 1837, but incapable of finding effective answers to any of the pressing financial, economic, and social questions of the day. All of these questions multiplied after 1836, when a financial crisis ushered in a period of economic depression accompanied by a series of bad harvests. Social conflicts, never far from the surface, became more open and dramatic. Early Victorian England was turbulent and excited, and if it had not been for Robert Peel, who succeeded Melbourne as prime minister after the general election of 1841 had returned to power the "Conservatives" (as Peel liked to think of his party), there might well have been even greater disorder. The achievements of his Conservative ministry must be considered both within the context of the immediate social and political disturbance and within the perspectives of 19th-century British history as a whole.

SOCIAL CLEAVAGE AND SOCIAL CONTROL IN THE EARLY VICTORIAN YEARS

Chartism and the Anti-Corn Law League. As the economic skies darkened after 1836 and prophets like Carlyle anticipated cataclysmic upheaval, the two most disgruntled groups in society were the industrial workers and their employers. Each group developed new forms of organization and each turned from local to national extraparliamentary action. The two most important organizations were the Chartists and the Anti-Corn Law League. Chartism drew on a multiplicity of working class grievances, extending working class consciousness as it grew; the Anti-Corn Law League, founded as a national organization in Manchester in 1839, was the spearhead of middle class energies, and it enjoyed the advantage not only of lavish funds but also of a single-point program—the repeal of the Corn Laws.

Chartism, which aimed at parliamentary reform, took its name from the People's Charter published in London in May 1838, containing six points, all of them political and all with a radical pedigree—annual parliaments; universal male suffrage; the ballot; no property qualifications for members of Parliament; payment of members; and equal electoral districts. Behind the political demands, however, was a fierce social discontent and a desire to establish working class political power. The new Poor Law of 1834 was a main source of grievance in the provinces; so, too, in Lancashire and Yorkshire, were long working hours in the factories. Earlier localized agitations centring on such grievances were subsumed in Chartism. In addition, the failure to create effective trade unions during the early 1830s directed efforts toward national political action. The Chartists failed to secure any of the six points during the course of their mostly uncoordinated agitation that continued with fluctuating fortunes until the early 1850s. Problems of organization, local differences, disagreements about tactics (including the use of force), arguments about leadership (particularly about the leadership of Feargus O'Connor), and an improvement in economic conditions—first between 1844 and 1846 and then after 1848—dictated the details of the story. One of the few violent incidents was the small "rising" at Newport on the Welsh border in November 1839, like many of the other demonstrations, a demonstration that got out of hand before it failed. In Scotland "moral force" Chartism was particularly strong. In discontented Ireland, which might have provided support for Chartism, it was only after O'Connell's death in 1847 that the Chartists found allies.

Disagreement among Chartists

The middle class Anti-Corn Law League, led by Richard Cobden and John Bright, attempted to secure the repeal of the duties on imported grain, which were believed to raise the price of food for the workingman and benefit only the landowning classes. The League also had its difficulties, particularly at the outset, but it employed every device of propaganda, including the use of new media of communication, such as the penny post, introduced in 1840. The formula of the League was a simple one, designed to secure working class as well as middle class support. Repeal of the Corn Laws, it was argued, would settle the two great issues that faced Britain in the "hungry forties"—securing the prosperity of industry and guaranteeing the livelihood of the poor. The only barrier to salvation was the landlord. Most Chartists were unconvinced by this logic, but, in a landed Parliament, a few Anti-Corn Law Leaguers, led by Richard Cobden, told Peel firmly that he would be "a criminal and a poltroon" if he did not repeal what they regarded as an immoral as well as an economically restrictive piece of legislation.

Peel and the Peelite heritage. Much depended on the nature of Peel's response to the problems of the time. Between 1832 and 1841 he had built up a disciplined party, most members of which accepted 1832 as a *fait accompli.* He himself, though brought up as a Tory, was a child of the Lancashire cotton industry and accepted industrialization as beneficial as well as inevitable. Afraid of violence, he sought, with a strong sense of public duty, to discover practical solutions to the complex issues of an industrializing society. He was the presiding genius of a powerful administration, strictly supervising the business of each separate branch of government, some of which were managed by very able lieutenants. From the start Peel attached top priority to financial reform. Beginning with his budget of 1842, he set about simplifying and reducing tariff restrictions on trade and in the same year he reintroduced income tax. In 1844 his Bank Charter Act laid the foundations of a sound national banking and credit system centred on the Bank of England. Finally, in 1846 he repealed the Corn Laws.

Peel's reforms

In this sequence of changes he alienated many of his followers, and repeal brought all the conflicts within his party to a head. The squirearchy rebelled, roused by the brilliant speeches of an exotic young politician, Benjamin Disraeli, who in his writings had already approached the "condition of England question" in a totally different style from that of Peel. During the crisis, Peel put his sense of duty to his sovereign, to posterity, and to his own conscience first and his obligations to his party second.

The results of repeal were important politically as well as economically. Party boundaries remained blurred until 1859, with the "Peelites" retaining a sense of identity even after Peel's premature death following a riding accident in 1850. Some of them, particularly Gladstone, eventually became leaders of the late-19th-century Liberal Party, which emerged from the midcentury confusion. The protectionists, most of whom abandoned protection after 1852, formed the nucleus (around the Earl of Derby and Disraeli) of the later Conservative Party, but they were unable to secure a majority at any election until 1874. The minority governments they formed in 1852, 1858, and 1866 lacked any secure sense of authority. The Whigs, themselves divided into factions, returned to office in 1847 and held it for most of the midcentury years, but they were often dependent on radical and Irish support. Leadership in these years rested with strong or persuasive personalities, of whom Viscount Palmerston was the most prominent.

There was no time between 1846 and 1866, however, when extraparliamentary agitation assumed the dimensions it had done between 1838 and 1846; and, when revolutions spread throughout Europe in 1848, Britain remained almost immune. Only a fierce outburst of Chartism, this time Chartism with an injection of socialism and of Irish nationalism, disturbed the year. Ireland, positively or negatively, played an important part in the politics of crisis, for it was the failure of the Irish potato crop in 1845–46 and the threat of famine in Ireland that helped sway Peel to repeal the Corn Laws. Unfortunately, disaster was not averted in Ireland itself, and in the course of a few terrible famine years, about 500,000 Irish died and 1,000,000 Irish emigrated. Peel's Whig successor, Lord Russell, had no command over this situation, which challenged all the economic, administrative, and political assumptions of the time.

Irish famine

Social legislation and social control. In Britain, by contrast, steps were taken before and after Peel to assume an increasing measure of social control. The question of public health, raised in the late 18th century and given a high degree of urgency during the 1830s, was the subject of several widely discussed reports before the passing of the first national Public Health Act in 1848. Chadwick was the leading spokesman of "the sanitary idea," which was canvassed vigorously by the novelists Charles Dickens and Charles Kingsley and which was to inspire George Eliot. Industrial questions also figured prominently in the social novels of the 1840s, including those of Disraeli; and statisticians, treated warily by most novelists, provided a different form of ammunition in the social debate. A report on conditions in the mines was followed by legislation, in 1842, forbidding the employment underground of children under ten and of all women. Meanwhile, the reports of factory inspectors, appointed under an act of 1833, were attracting widespread interest; and in 1847, after earlier attempts had proved abortive, a Factory Act was passed, limiting the hours of work of children in textile factories to ten: it was the first of many acts amending abuses and extending the principle of intervention.

Developments in education

In education there were significant new departures, limited in scope by the rivalry between churchmen and dissenters. In 1833 the first government grants had been made to the two main voluntary organizations sponsoring primary education, and in 1839 the first school inspectors had been appointed. J.P. Kay (later Sir James Kay-Shuttleworth), secretary of the Committee of Council on Education, did everything he could to make the most of an admittedly inadequate system of provision, which was extended further with the first grants for teacher training and salaries in 1846. Kay's main object was to encourage the use of education as a means of introducing a measure of order and discipline into the working class population, when older and more traditional methods of wielding authority through subordination had broken down. Yet just as the operation of the deterrent Poor Law directed attention in the long run to the need for more complex welfare policies, so the extension of educational provision, limited and belated though it was, involved the interplay of more varied motives and purposes. That there was no revolution in Britain in 1848, as there was in most countries in Europe, was owing to the character of Britain's social structure. Yet the contemporary prophets of revolution, whether for or against, tended to overlook the effort, local as well as national, to influence conditions of life through conscious policies.

The evolution of such policies was difficult for a number of reasons: first, there were entrenched vested interests, particularly obvious in questions of public health; second, there was a shortage of professional expertise, particularly in engineering and medicine; third, most radicals were highly suspicious of all forms of state intervention, particularly if they involved spending large sums of money or interfering with local freedoms; fourth, the orthodox economic policies of the day stressed the need for private rather than for public initiative. Yet there were aspects of the social structure that encouraged social action. Industrialists were sometimes especially sensitive to the problems of the workers in the countryside, particularly during the heyday of the Anti-Corn Law League, when the Leaguers were attacking "feudalism"; and some landlords, notably the evangelical philanthropist Lord Ashley, were especially sensitive throughout the 1830s and '40s to the problems of town workers. In such circumstances, it was difficult to rest content with things as they were. In the words of one of Disraeli's characters, this was a "high-pressure" age. For the statistician G.R. Porter, whose *Progress of the Nation* (1836–43) went through many editions, all "the elements of improvement" in the country were "working with incessant and increasing energy." He added that in his own lifetime he had seen "the greatest advances in civilisation that can be found recorded in the annals of mankind."

The pace of economic change. Not all of Porter's contemporaries would have agreed about the phrase "the greatest advances in civilisation," for some of them criticized the quality of life in the new society, and others pointed to the social contrasts reflected, for example, in the unequal distribution of incomes. There was a debate between "optimists" and "pessimists," the latter suggesting that the condition of the working classes was actually deteriorating as national wealth increased. Most people were concerned, too, about the rise in population. At the first (defective) census of 1801, the population of England and Wales was around 9,000,000 and that of Scotland around 1,500,000. By 1851 the comparable figures were 18,000,000 and 3,000,000. At its peak between 1811 and 1821, the growth rate for Britain as a whole was 17 percent for the decade. It took time to realize that the fears expressed so eloquently by Malthus that population would outrun subsistence were exaggerated and that, as population grew, national production would grow also.

"Optimists" and "pessimists"

Indeed, national income at constant prices increased nearly threefold between 1801 and 1851, substantially more than the increase in population, and the share of manufacturing, mining, and building in the national accounts of wealth increased sharply, as compared with the share of agriculture. In 1801 agriculture accounted for 34 percent and manufacturing, mining, and building for 28 percent. The comparable figures for 1851 were 21 percent and 40 percent. Cotton textiles remained the dominant new industry, with the cotton factory being thought of by one of its contemporary admirers, Edward Baines, as "the most striking example of the dominion obtained by human science over the powers of nature of which modern times can boast." There were 1,800 cotton factories in 1851. Raw cotton imports had increased unevenly from 101,000,000 pounds in 1815 to 757,000,000 pounds in 1851 and exports of manufactured cotton piece goods from 253,000,000 yards in 1815 to 1,543,000,000 yards in 1851. Similar steam-driven technology accounted for the expansion of the woollen textiles industry over the same period, with Australia, which provided no raw wool for Britain in 1815, providing 30,000,000 pounds in 1851. It was the textiles industry more than any other that illustrated Britain's dependence on international trade, a trade that it commanded not only through the size of the import bill or of manufacturing output but through the strength of its banking and other financial institutions and the extent of its shipping industry. Despite the advance of steam (registered steamship tonnage in 1815, 1,000, and in 1851, 187,000), the tonnage of sailing ships also increased. There was no problem comparable to that of the displaced handloom weavers, the victims of technological progress.

The new technology rested on coal, iron, and steam; it reached its peak in the age of the railway and the steamship. Coal production, about 13,000,000 tons in 1815, increased five times during the next 50 years, and, by 1850, Britain was producing over 2,000,000 tons of pig iron, half the world's output. Both coal and iron exports increased dramatically, with coal exports amounting to 3,300,000 tons in 1851, as against less than 250,000 tons at the end of the French wars. Coal mining was scattered in the coal-producing districts, with few large towns and with miners living a distinctive life with their own patterns of work and leisure. Iron production was associated with larger plants and considerable urbanization. In South Wales, for example, one of the areas of industrial expansion, the Dowlais works were employing 6,000 people and turning out 20,000 tons of pig iron each year during the 1840s. Birmingham, Britain's second largest city, was the centre of a broad range of metallurgical industries, mainly organized in small workshops, very different in character from the huge textile mills of Lancashire and Yorkshire.

Impact of the railroads

Industrialization preceded the coming of the railway, but the railway did much to lower transport costs, to consume raw materials, to stimulate investment through an extended capital market, and to influence the location of industry. The railway age may be said to have begun in 1830, when the line from Liverpool to Manchester was opened, and to have gone through its most hectic phases during the 1840s, when contemporaries talked of a "railway mania." By 1851, 6,800 miles of railway were open, some of them involving engineering feats of great complexity. There was as much argument among contemporaries about the impact of railways as there was about the impact of steam engines in factories, but there was general agreement about the fact that the coming of the railway marked a great divide in British social history. The novelist William Thackeray put it succinctly, when he compared the last years of the stagecoach with the railway age. "Your railroad starts the new era, and we of a certain age belong to the new time and the old one." It was not until the 1870s and '80s that steamships brought this "new time" to its full realization, and by then British engineers and workmen had been responsible for building railways in all parts of the world. By 1890 Britain had more registered shipping tonnage than the rest of the world put together.

The Great Exhibition of 1851. By 1890 it had become apparent that the British industrial revolution, far from being unique, was merely the first in a sequence of industrial revolutions and that Britain's early lead was becoming something of a handicap. In 1851, however, Britain was not only the workshop of the world but the main influence on the industrialization of other nations as well as its own. The Great Exhibition of 1851, in London, symbolized this economic supremacy. The exhibition was housed in a huge glass and iron building called —with a touch of romance—"the Crystal Palace." Here, people from all parts of the world could examine machines of every kind, which Thackeray, once again catching the mood for posterity, described as "England's arms of conquest . . . the trophies of her bloodless war." Part of the success of the exhibition was political as much as economic. Many of the visitors who flocked to London came from European cities that had been racked with revolution only three years before.

Victoria and Albert

The exhibition was a triumph not only for the economy but also for Victoria and her German husband, Albert, whom she had married in 1840. "In England," wrote a continental observer, "loyalty is a passion." Despite outbursts of opposition to Albert, particularly in 1855, the family life of the Victorian court began to be considered increasingly as a model for the whole country. The fact that Albert had appreciated the significance of Peel's achievement and that he put his trust in the advancement of industry and science was as important as the fact that Victoria herself established monarchy on respectable foundations of family life. It was during the 1850s that the word "Victorian" began to be employed to express a new self-consciousness, both in relation to the nation and to the period through which it was passing. The death of Albert in 1861 and the subsequent withdrawal of the Queen from public life led to a decline in the popularity of the court, but in time the Queen's subjects, both at home and overseas, came once again to consider both her developed virtues and her obvious limitations as the very essence of "Victorianism" itself.

MID-VICTORIAN SOCIETY, RELIGION, AND CULTURE

After the excitements of the 1830s and 1840s, mid-Victorian England was relatively quiet, with the family being regarded by most mid-Victorians as the central institution in society. In national social life, a kind of balance was struck between the busy industrial north and midlands and the sleepy countryside described in the novels of Anthony Trollope. A kind of balance was also struck between the traditional ideal of "the gentleman" and the new ideal of the hero of "self-help," with a place being left both for deference and dependence, on the one hand, and for individual advancement and acquisitiveness, on the other. There was far more talk during this period of self-help than there was of class conflict; indeed, the most comfortable social theory of the period rested on the assumption that class dividing lines could and should stay, provided that individuals in each class could move. Social discipline was strong, counting for more, perhaps, than the extension of the local police forces by an act of 1856.

Effects of economic prosperity

Victorian attitudes. All kinds of balance rested, however, on economic as well as on psychological and sociological factors. From the early 1850s to the early 1870s, with occasional years of high unemployment and business failure (bad harvests counted for less as food imports increased), almost all sections of the population seemed to be benefitting from relative prosperity. Profits rose, as did wages and incomes from land. Indeed, those supporters of protection who had argued in the 1840s that free trade would ruin British agriculture were mocked by the mid-Victorian prosperity of agriculture in a golden age of high arable farming. There seemed to be little need in such a society for strong government, and it was only during the Crimean War (1854–56), when even many radicals looked for enemies abroad rather than at home and when the war itself was managed with obvious inefficiency, that either society or government seemed to be under great strain.

It was during these years, when great individual creative power was tapped, that Victorianism, perhaps the only "ism" in history attached to the name of a sovereign, came to represent a cluster of restraining moral attributes —earnestness, respectable comportment and behaviour, "character," "duty," hard work, and thrift. All these were virtues extolled and related to each other in the many books of Samuel Smiles, author of the best seller *Self-Help* (1859). Later in the century, they were to be taken apart and criticized, even lampooned, one by one in the course of a late-Victorian revolt. It is too simple, however, to dismiss them as bourgeois virtues, since many of them were shaped more by religion than by class, and all of them made an appeal, for a time at least, to non-middle-class sections of the population, aristocratic or trade unionist. All of them, moreover, were subjected to contemporary criticism. In the same year as Smiles's *Self-Help*, there appeared John Stuart Mill's essay, *On Liberty*, a powerful attack on conformity and a classic liberal statement of freedom of discussion. Charles Dickens frequently made fun of the Victorian smugness and unwillingness to face unpleasant facts, as represented by Mr. Podsnap in *Our Mutual Friend;* the critics Mathew Arnold and John Ruskin, each arguing from a different point of departure, questioned many of the accepted beliefs and prejudices of the age. Minority communicators in the widely read reviews were often extremely critical, and even Smiles himself, writing for a bigger public, thought that none of the virtues he was extolling came to men naturally nor could any of them

Self-criticism and doubt

be taken for granted in the middle of the 19th century. There was always a Victorian underworld. Belief in the family was accompanied by a high incidence of prostitution, and in every large city there were districts where every Victorian virtue was ignored or flouted. Mill's London was also the London of Henry Mayhew, whose *London Labour and the London Poor* was published in book form in 1862.

Religion. The critical sense of many of the great Victorians—at least as far as opinions were concerned—inevitably involved questions of religion as much as of society or politics, and Victorian doubt was as much an acknowledged theme of the period as Victorian belief. During the year of the Great Exhibition, the poet Tennyson's *In Memoriam* considered the triumphs of 50 years of economic advance against the background of the whole story of man and of the earth. Geology and biology continued to challenge all accepted views of religion handed down from the past. Darwin's *Origin of Species* was another of the great books of the remarkable year 1859. A year later *Essays and Reviews* was published; a lively appraisal of fundamental religious questions by a number of liberal-minded religious thinkers, it provoked the sharpest religious controversy of the century.

Yet, behind such controversies, there were many signs of a confident belief on all sides that inquiry itself, if freely and honestly pursued, would do nothing to dissolve the ideals of conduct that were generally shared. Even those writers who were "agnostic" sought the "religion of humanity" or tried to be good "for good's sake, not God's." There was also a dutiful acceptance of the importance of standards in institutional as well as in private life. These were years when the extension of the civil service involved the development of a remarkable code of institutional morality. Following a report by Sir Charles Trevelyan and Sir Stafford Northcote in 1853–54, a civil service commission was set up. Recruitment and promotion in most parts of the service were to depend on competitive examination. An order-in-council of 1870 made this system mandatory, except for the Foreign Office. The extended civil service that took shape owed little to political patronage and was almost completely free from corruption.

Emphasis on conduct was, of course, related to religion. The English religious spectrum was of many colours. The Church of England was flanked on one side by Rome and on the other by religious dissent. Both were active forces to be reckoned with. The Roman Catholic Church was growing in importance not only in the Irish sections of the industrial cities but also among university students and teachers. Dissent had a grip on the whole culture of large sections of the middle classes, dismissed too abruptly by Arnold as "mutilated and incomplete men." Sometimes the local battle between Church of England and Dissent was bitterly contested, with Nonconformists acting as a militant group, opposing church rates (taxes), challenging closed foundations, and preaching total abstinence and educational reform. A whole network of local voluntary bodies, led either by Anglicans or Dissenters, usually in rivalry, came into existence, a tribute to the energies of the age and to its fear of state intervention.

The Oxford Movement

The Church of England itself was a divided family, with different groups contending for positions of influence. The High Church movement (which emphasized the "Catholic" side of Anglicanism) was given a distinctive character, first by the Oxford Movement, or Tractarianism, which had grown up in the 1830s as a reaction against the new liberal theology, and then by the often provocative and always controversial ritualist agitation of the 1850s and '60s (see ANGLICAN COMMUNION: *19th and 20th centuries*). The fact that prominent members of the Church of England flirted with "Romanism" and even crossed the Rubicon often raised the popular Protestant cry of the "church in danger." Peel's conversion to free trade in 1846 scarcely created any more excitement than John Henry Newman's conversion to Rome the previous year, while, in 1850, Lord John Russell, Peel's successor as prime minister, tried to capitalize politically on violent antipapal feelings stimulated by the Pope's decision to create Roman Catholic dioceses in England.

The Evangelicals, in many ways the most influential as well as the most distinctively English religious group, were suspicious both of ritual and of appeals to any authority other than that of the Bible. Their concern with individual conduct was a force making for social conformity during the middle years of the century rather than for that depth of individual religious experience that the first advocates of "vital religion" had preached in the 18th century. Yet leaders like Ashley were prepared to probe some of the difficult questions of the social order and to stir men's consciences, even if their preoccupation was with saving souls, and their missionary zeal influenced overseas as well as domestic development. There were some members of the church, usually not evangelicals, who urged the cause of what they called "Christian Socialism." Their intellectual leader was the outstanding Anglican theologian Frederick Denison Maurice.

Beyond the influence of both church and chapel there were thousands of people in mid-Victorian England who were ignorant of, or indifferent toward, the message of Christianity, a fact demonstrated by England's one religious census in 1851. Although movements like the Salvation Army, founded by William Booth in 1865, attempted to rally the poor of the great cities, there were many signs of apathy or even hostility. There was also a small but active secularist organization. The great religious controversies of mid-Victorian England were not so much settled as shelved.

The Church of Scotland

In Scotland, where the Church of Scotland had been fashioned by the people against the crown, there was a revival of Presbyterianism in the 1820s and '30s. A complex and protracted controversy, centring on the right of congregations to exclude candidates for the ministry whom they thought unsuitable, ended in schism. In 1843, 474 ministers left the Church of Scotland and established a free church. Within four years they had raised over £1,250,000 and built 654 churches. This was a remarkable effort, even in a great age of church and chapel building. It left Scotland with a religious pattern even more different from that of England and Wales than it had been in 1815. Yet many of the most influential voices in mid-Victorian Britain, including Thomas Carlyle and Samuel Smiles, were Scottish voices, and the conception of the gospel of work, in particular, owed much in content and tone, even if often indirectly, to Scottish Calvinism.

MID-VICTORIAN POLITICS

Religious questions helped divide the limited electorate, with the dissenters encouraging, from their local bases, the development of liberalism, and churchmen often—but by no means universally—supporting the Conservative Party. Party divisions were based on customary allegiance as much as on careful scrutiny of issues, and there was still considerable scope for bribery at election times. The civil service might be pure, but the electors often were not. The Corrupt Practices Act of 1854 provided a more exact definition of bribery than there had been before, but it was not until a further act of 1883 that election expenses were rigorously controlled. During the mid-Victorian years, the way to Parliament often led through the pigsty.

The prestige of the individual member of Parliament was high, and the fragmentation of parties after 1846 allowed him considerable independence. Groups of members supporting particular economic interests, especially the railways, could often determine parliamentary strategies. Contemporaries feared such interests less than they feared what was often called the most dangerous of all interests, executive government. Powerful government and large-scale "organic" reform were considered dangerous, and even those radicals who supported organic reform, like Cobden and Bright, were suspicious of powerful government. For most politicians, politics was identified not with theories or even programs but with pragmatic leadership.

In his interesting analysis of the English constitution (1867), Walter Bagehot considered the cabinet as "a board of control chosen by the legislature, out of persons whom it trusts and knows, to rule the nation." Its primary task was to administer, not to legislate. There was little legislation dealing with public health or trade unions or Irish agrarian problems until the late 1860s, although the Company Act of 1862 consolidated limited liability legislation passed during the 1850s. A judge told a number of men who were convicted of illegal activities during a strike of 1867,

> Everybody knows that the total aggregate happiness of mankind is increased by every man being left to the unbiased, unfettered determination of his own will and judgement as to how he will employ his industry and other means of getting on in the world.

Palmerston. Palmerston, an aristocrat born in 1784, stood out as the dominant political personality in mid-Victorian Britain, precisely because he was opposed to dramatic change and because he knew through long experience how to manoeuvre politics within the half-reformed constitution. In a period when it was difficult to collect parliamentary majorities, he often forced decisions, as at the general election of 1857, on the simple question, "are you for or against me?" He was skillful also in using the growing power of the press in order to reinforce his influence. At a time of party confusion, when the Queen might well have played a key part in politics, Palmerston found the answer to royal opposition in popular prestige, carefully stage-managed. His chief preoccupation was with foreign affairs, and his approach was diametrically opposed to that of the court on several occasions.

There was no contradiction between his views on domestic and foreign policy. He preferred the English system of constitutional government, resting on secure social foundations, to continental absolutism, but, like Canning before him, he was anxious above all else to advance the interests of England as he saw them. The supremacy of British sea power, British economic ascendancy, and political divisions inside each of the main countries of Europe before and after the revolutions of 1848 gave him his opportunity. He liked to appear active. In 1850 he sent a blockading squadron to Greece to enforce payments of debts due to Don Pacifico, a Gibraltar-born British subject, and restated the doctrine of *civis Romanus sum* ("I am a Roman citizen," by which an ancient Roman could proclaim his rights throughout the empire) in a Victorian setting. In 1852, when he helped overturn Russell's shaky government, he had his revenge on Russell, who had dismissed him from his post as foreign secretary in December 1851 for welcoming Napoleon III's coup d'etat in France. In January 1855, after Lord Aberdeen, a Peelite, had shown his incompetence as a war leader during the Crimean War, Palmerston was made prime minister for the first time. His interventions were not confined to Europe. In 1840–41 he forced the China ports open to foreign trade and, by the Treaty of Nanking (1842), acquired Hong Kong for Britain. In 1857 he went to war in China again and, when defeated in Parliament, appealed triumphantly to the country. Although his government was defeated in 1858, he was back again as prime minister, for the last time, a year later.

The Don Pacifico affair

During the remarkable ministry of 1859–65, which included Russell as foreign secretary and the Peelite Gladstone as chancellor of the exchequer, it was impossible for Britain to dominate the international scene as effectively as in previous periods of Palmerstonian power. With efficient military power at his disposal, the Prussian prime minister, Otto von Bismarck, proved more than a match for him. The union of modern Italy, which Palmerston supported; the American Civil War, in which his sympathies were with the South; and the rise of Bismarck's Germany, which he did not understand, were reshaping the world in which he had been able to achieve so much by forceful opportunism. When he died, in October 1865, it was clear that, in foreign relations as well as in home politics, there would have to be what Gladstone described as "a new commencement."

In home politics it had been only the continued influence of Palmerston as prime minister that had delayed overdue reforms. In the large urban constituencies, the demand for a new and active liberalism was gaining ground, and at Westminster itself Gladstone was beginning to identify himself not only with the continued advance of free trade but with the demand for parliamentary reform. In 1864 he forecast new directions in politics when he stated that the burden of proof concerning the case for reform rested not with the reformers but with their opponents. A year later he lost his seat at Oxford University and was returned "unmuzzled" as representative for a populous Lancashire constituency. The death of Palmerston was followed by the reopening of the question of parliamentary reform and by the passing of the Second Reform Bill in 1867.

The Reform Bill of 1867. Yet it was Disraeli and not Gladstone who claimed the credit for the act of 1867. On Palmerston's death, Russell and Gladstone had introduced a modest and colourless bill that was severely mauled both by Conservatives and reform Liberals. The government resigned, and Derby and Disraeli took office. It was difficult to shelve the demand for reform, and the government decided to "dish the Whigs" and "take a leap in the dark." Agitation in the country was more vociferous on the issue than it had been since the days of the Chartists, and organizations, notably the Reform League, were engaged in stirring the public, alongside prominent individuals, notably John Bright. In a Parliament where Disraeli was in a minority, his only chance lay in accepting amendments, however radical, to the bill that he had introduced and in claiming them as his own. All reserves and safeguards were dropped, and, although he lost some of his own supporters, he eventually carried a bill very different from the one he had introduced. It added 938,000 new names to the register, almost a doubling of the electorate, and gave the vote to many workingmen in the towns and cities. The county franchise was not substantially changed, but 45 new seats were created by taking one member from existing borough constituencies with a population of less than 10,000. Disraeli hoped that, in return for passing this measure, urban workingmen would vote for him—he believed rightly that many of them were Conservatives already by instinct and allegiance—but, at the first general election under the new system, it was Gladstone who was returned as prime minister.

The "leap in the dark"

GLADSTONE AND DISRAELI

The choice between Gladstone and Disraeli was the first of many similar choices offered to an extended electorate—the choice between two men who were completely different in temperament and political outlook. Gladstone had made his mark first and lived on far longer (1898) than did his rival (1881). He saw politics in terms of moral principles and, in his ministry of 1868–74, introduced some of the most important Liberal legislation of the 19th century. Disraeli, who combined opportunism and political imagination, carried through an impressive program of social reform and embarked upon an active foreign policy both in Europe and overseas. Yet much of the Liberal legislation was the product of compromise rather than of principle, and much of the significant social legislation of the Conservatives was considered sufficiently politically unimportant by them, at the time, for them to neglect it when they appealed to the electorate in 1880. In both parties, there were new forces stirring at the local level and energetic efforts to organize the electorate and the political parties along new lines. With the development of central party machinery and local organization, the role of the crown was reduced during this period to that of merely ratifying the result of general elections. Although the Queen greatly preferred Disraeli to Gladstone, she could not keep Gladstone out. Her obvious partisanship made some of her acts look unconstitutional, but they would not have been deemed unconstitutional in any previous period of history. The public during this period was more interested in the political leaders than in the Queen, who lived in retirement and was sharply criticized in sections of the press.

Gladstone's first administration. The achievements of Gladstone's first administration were several: the disestablishment and partial disendowment of the Irish Church, accomplished in 1869 in face of the opposition of the House of Lords; the Irish Land Act of 1870, providing some safeguards to Irish tenant farmers; William Edward Forster's Education Act of the same year, the first national act dealing with primary education; the Trade-Union Act of 1871, legalizing unions and giving them the protection of the courts; and the Ballot Act of 1872, introducing secret voting. There were many other important reforms, most of which were designed to broaden the span of individual opportunity or to reform cumbersome administrative machinery. In 1871, for example, the universities of Oxford and Cambridge were opened to Dissenters, while between 1868 and 1873 the cumbrous military machine was renovated by Gladstone's secretary for war, Edward Cardwell. The system of dual responsibility of commander in chief and secretary at war was abolished, and the subordination of the former to the latter was asserted. In 1873 the Judicature Act, amended in 1876, simplified the tangle of legal institutions and procedures.

Administrative reforms

Many of these reforms did not satisfy affected interests. The Irish Church Disestablishment Act failed to placate the Irish and alarmed many English churchmen, while the Education Act was passed only in face of bitter Nonconformist opposition. The Dissenters objected that Forster's system did not break the power of the church over primary education, and, although the act was extended in 1880 when primary education was made compulsory and in 1891 when it became free, there were often noisy struggles between churchmen and Dissenters in the new school boards set up locally under the Forster Act. If the Education Act alienated many Dissenters, the Licensing Bills of 1871 and 1872 alienated their enemies, the brewers. At the general election of 1874, therefore, months after Disraeli had described the Liberal leaders in one of his many memorable phrases as a "range of exhausted volcanoes," the brewers threw all their influence behind the Conservatives. "We have been borne down in a torrent of gin and beer," Gladstone complained.

Disraeli's second administration. Disraeli's ministry embarked upon a sizable program of social legislation. Gladstone, throughout his life, preferred free and cheap government to expensive and socially committed government. He was anxious, indeed, in 1873 to abolish income tax, on which the public finances of the future were to depend. Disraeli had always been interested in "the condition of England question" and, with the assistance of men like Richard Cross, the home secretary, justified at last his reputation as a social reformer. By the Employers and Workmen Act of 1875, "masters" and "men" were put on an equal footing as regards breaches of contract, while by a Trade-Union Act of 1875 that went much further than the Liberal act of 1871, trade unionists were allowed to engage in peaceful picketing and to do whatever would not be criminal if done by an individual. The Public Health Act of 1875, a consolidating piece of legislation, created a public health authority in every area; the Artizans' and Labourers' Dwellings Improvement Act of the same year enabled local authorities to embark upon schemes of slum clearance; a factory act of 1878 fixed a 56-hour week; while further legislation dealt with Friendly Societies (private societies for mutual-health and old-age insurance), the protection of seamen, land improvements carried out by tenants, and the adulteration of food. There was no similar burst of social legislation until after 1906.

Foreign policy. If there were significant, if not fully acknowledged, differences between the records of the two governments on domestic issues, there were open, even strident differences on questions of foreign policy. Gladstone had never been a Palmerstonian. He was always anxious to avoid the resort to force, and he put his trust not in national prejudices but in an enlightened public opinion in Europe as well as England. His object was justice rather than power. In practice, however, he often gave the impression of a man who vacillated and could not act firmly. Disraeli was willing to take risks to enhance British prestige and to seek to profit from, rather than to moralize about, foreign dissensions. His first ventures in "imperialism"—a speech at the Crystal Palace in 1872, the purchase of the Suez Canal shares in 1875, and the proclamation of the Queen as "Empress of India"—showed that he had abandoned the view, popular during the middle years of the century, that colonies were millstones around the mother country's neck. But these moves did not involve him in any European entanglements, nor did the costly if brilliantly led campaigns of Major General Roberts in Afghanistan (1878–80) and the annexation of the Transvaal in South Africa in 1877.

Disraeli's "imperialism"

It was the Near Eastern crisis of 1875–78 that produced the liveliest 19th-century debate on foreign policy issues. In May 1876, Disraeli rejected overtures made by Russia, Austria-Hungary, and Germany to deal jointly with the Turks, who were faced with revolt in Serbia. His pro-Turkish sympathies irritated many Liberals, and, after the Turks had gone on to suppress with great violence a revolt in Bulgaria in 1876, the Liberal conscience was stirred and mass meetings were held in many parts of the country. Gladstone, who had gone into retirement as Liberal leader in 1875, was slower to respond to the issue than many of his followers, but, once roused, he emerged from retirement, wrote an immensely influential pamphlet on the atrocities, and led a public campaign on the platform and in the press. For him the Turks were "inhuman and despotic," and, whatever the national interests involved, Britain, in his view, should do nothing to support them. Disraeli's calculations concerned strategic and imperial necessities rather than ideals of conduct, and his suspicions were justified when the Russians attacked Turkey in April 1877. Opinion swung back to his side, and in 1878 Disraeli sent a British fleet to the Dardanelles. There was a war fever in London—the term jingoism was used to describe it—that was intensified when news reached London that a peace treaty had been signed at San Stefano whereby the Turks accepted maximum Russian demands. Reservists were mobilized in Britain, and Indian troops were sent to the Mediterranean. Disraeli's Foreign Minister, who disapproved of such action, resigned, to be succeeded by Lord Salisbury, who was eventually to serve as prime minister in the last Conservative administrations of the 19th century. The immediate crisis passed, and, at an international conference held in Berlin in June and July 1878, which Disraeli attended, the inroads into Turkish territory were reduced, Russia was kept well away from Constantinople, and Britain acquired Cyprus. Disraeli brought back "peace with honour." But the swings of public opinion continued, and in 1879 Gladstone, starting at Midlothian in Scotland, fought a nationwide political campaign of unprecedented excitement and drama. At the general election of April 1880, the Liberals returned to power triumphantly, with a majority of 137 over the Conservatives. Disraeli, who had moved to the House of Lords in 1876, died in 1881.

LATE VICTORIAN POLITICS

Gladstone and Chamberlain. Yet the second Gladstone administration (1880–85) did not live up to the promise of the election victory. The Cabinet that Gladstone assembled was neither compact nor united. Eight of the members were Whigs, but, of the other three, one—Joseph Chamberlain—was representative of a new and aggressive urban radicalism, less interested in orthodox statements of liberal individualism than in the uncertain aspirations and strivings of the different elements in the mass electorate. Already, as mayor of Birmingham (1873–76), he had embarked upon large-scale schemes of civic improvement, which he did not scruple to call "municipal socialism." At the opposite end of the spectrum, the Whigs were the largest group in the Cabinet, but the smallest in the country. Many of them were already abandoning the Liberal Party; all of them were nervous about the kind of radical program that Chamberlain and the newly founded National Liberal Federation (1877) were advocating and about the kind of caucus-based organization that Chamberlain favoured locally and nationally. In terms of political logic, it seemed likely in 1880 that the Gladstonian Liberal Party would eventually split into Whig and radical components, the latter led by Chamberlain. For the moment, however, Gladstone was the man of the hour, and Chamberlain himself conceded that he was indispensable.

Third Reform Bill

The government carried a number of important reforms culminating in the Third Reform Bill of 1884, which continued the trend toward universal male suffrage by giving the vote to agricultural labourers, thereby tripling the electorate, and the Redistribution Act of 1885, which robbed 79 towns with populations under 15,000 of their separate representation. For the first time, the franchise reforms ignored the claims of the traditional influences of property and wealth and rested firmly on the democratic principle that the vote ought to be given to people as a matter of right and not of expediency.

The most difficult problems continued to arise in relation to foreign affairs and, above all, to Ireland. When, in 1881, the Boers defeated the British at Majuba Hill and Gladstone abandoned the attempt to hold the Transvaal, there was considerable public criticism. And in the same year, when he agreed to the bombardment of Alexandria in a successful effort to break a nationalist revolt in Egypt, he lost the support of the aged radical, Bright. In 1882 Egypt was occupied, thereby adding, against Gladstone's own inclinations, to British imperial commitments. A rebellion in the Sudan, which led to the sending out of British troops in 1883, was the occasion of one of the most terrible tragedies of the decade. Gen. Charles Gordon, who was dispatched to Khartoum, was killed in 1885, two days before the arrival of a mission to relieve him. Large numbers of Englishmen held Gladstone personally responsible, and, in June 1885, he resigned after a defeat on an amendment to the budget.

The Irish Question. The Irish question had loomed ominously as soon as Parliament had assembled in 1880, for there was now an Irish nationalist group of more than 60 members led by Charles Stewart Parnell, most of them committed to Irish Home Rule; in Ireland itself, the Land League, founded in 1879, was struggling to destroy the power of the landlord. Parnell himself embarked on a program of agrarian agitation in 1881, at the same time that his followers at Westminster were engaged in various kinds of parliamentary obstructionism. Gladstone's response was an Irish Land Act, based on guaranteeing "three *fs*"—fair rents, fixity of tenure, and free sale—and a tightening up of the rules of closure in parliamentary debate. The Land Act did not go far enough to satisfy Parnell, who continued to make speeches couched in violent language; a coercion act was passed by Parliament against Irish agitators and Parnell was arrested. He was released, however, in April 1882 after an understanding had been reached that he would abandon the land war and the government would abandon coercion.

The Phoenix Park Murders

Lord Frederick Charles Cavendish, a close friend of Gladstone and brother of the Whig leader, Lord Hartington, was sent to Dublin as chief secretary on a mission of peace, but the whole policy was undermined when Cavendish, along with the permanent undersecretary, was murdered in Phoenix Park, Dublin, within a few hours of landing in Ireland.

Between 1881 and 1885, Gladstone coupled a somewhat stiffer policy in Ireland with minor measures of reform, but in 1885, when the Conservatives returned to power under Salisbury, the Irish question forced itself to the forefront again. Lord Carnarvon, the new lord lieutenant of Ireland, was a convert to Home Rule and followed a more liberal policy than his predecessor. At the general election of November 1885, Parnell secured every Irish seat but one outside Ulster and urged Irish voters in British constituencies—a large group mostly concentrated in a limited number of places like Lancashire and Clydeside in Scotland—to vote Conservative. The result of the election was a Liberal majority of 86 over the Conservatives, almost exactly balanced by the Irish group, who thus controlled the balance of power in Parliament. The Conservatives stayed in office, but when, in December 1885, the newspapers reported a confidential interview with Gladstone's son, in which he had stated (rightly) that his father had been converted to Home Rule, Salisbury made it clear that he himself was not a convert, and Carnarvon resigned. All Conservative contacts with Parnell ceased, and a few weeks later, in January 1886, after the Conservatives had been defeated in Parliament on a radical amendment for agrarian reform, Salisbury resigned, and Gladstone returned to power.

Split of the Liberal Party. Gladstone's conversion had been gradual but profound, and it had more far-reaching political consequences for Britain than for Ireland. It immediately alienated him further from most of the Whigs and from a considerable number of radicals led by Joseph Chamberlain. He had hoped at first that Home Rule would be carried by an agreement between the parties, but Salisbury had no intention of imitating Peel. Gladstone made his intentions clear by appointing John Morley, a Home Rule advocate as Irish secretary, and in April 1886 he introduced a Home Rule bill. The Liberals remained divided, and 93 of them united with the Conservatives to defeat the measure. Gladstone appealed to the country and was decisively beaten at the general election, in which 316 Conservatives were returned to Westminster along with 78 Liberal Unionists, the new name chosen by those Liberals who refused to back Home Rule. The Liberals mustered only 191, and there were 85 Irish nationalists. Whigs and radicals, who had often seemed likely to split Gladstone's 1880 government on left–right lines, were now united against the Gladstonians, and all attempts at Liberal reunion failed.

Chamberlain, the astute radical leader, like many others of his class and generation, ceased to regard social reform as a top priority and worked in harness with Hartington, his Whig counterpart. In 1895 they both joined a Salisbury government. The Liberals were, in effect, pushed into the wilderness, although they held office briefly and unhappily from 1892 to 1895. Gladstone, 82 years old when he formed his last government, actually succeeded in carrying a Home Rule bill in the Commons in 1893, with the help of Irish votes (Parnell's power had been broken as a result of a divorce case in 1890, and he died in 1891), but the bill was thrown out by the Lords. He resigned in 1894, to be succeeded by Lord Rosebery, who further split the party; at the general election of 1895, the Conservatives could claim that they were the genuinely popular party, backed by the urban as well as the rural electorate. Although Salisbury always stressed the defensive aspects of Conservatism, both at home and abroad, Chamberlain and his supporters were able to mobilize considerable working class as well as middle class support for a policy of crusading imperialism.

Rise of the Conservatives

THE EXPANSION OF EMPIRE

The word imperialism was the key word of the 1890s, just as Home Rule had been in the critical decade of the 1880s, and the cause of empire was associated not merely with the economic interests of businessmen, looking for materials and markets, and the enthusiasm of crowds, excited by the adventure of empire, but with the traditional lustre of the crown. Disraeli had emphasized the last of these associations, just as Chamberlain emphasized the first. When Chamberlain deliberately chose to take over the Colonial Office in 1895, he was acknowledging the opportunities, both economic and political, afforded by a vast "undeveloped estate." The same radical energies that he had once devoted to civic improvement were now directed toward imperial problems, with every effort being made at the same time to make the empire meaningful and attractive to children at school and to the newspaper-reading mass electorate.

In fact, however, it was difficult to pull the empire together politically or constitutionally, certainly to move toward federation, since the interests of different parts were already diverging, and in the last resort only British power—above all, sea power—held it together. The processes of imperial expansion were always complex, and there was neither one dominant theory of empire nor one single explanation of why it grew. White colonies, like Canada or New Zealand and the states of Australia, had been given substantial powers of self-government since the Durham Report of 1839 and the Canada Union Act of 1840. Yet India, "the brightest jewel in the British crown," was held not by consent but by conquest. The Indian "mutiny" of 1857 was suppressed, and a year later the East India Company was abolished; thereafter, given the strategic importance of India to the military establishment, attempts were made to justify British rule in terms of benefits of law and order said to accrue to Indians. "The white man's burden," as the poet Rudyard Kipling saw it, was a burden of responsibility.

It was difficult for the British voter to understand or to appreciate this network of motives and interests. Chamberlain himself was always far less interested in India than the white "kith-and-kin dominions" and in the new tropical empire that was greatly extended in area between 1884 and 1896, when 2,500,000 square miles of territory fell under British control. Even he did not fully understand either the rival aspirations of different dominions or relationship between economic development in the "formal" empire and trade and investment in the "informal" empire where the British flag did not fly.

The South African War

Victoria's jubilees in 1887 and 1897 involved both imperial pageantry and imperial conferences, but, between 1896 and 1902, public interest in problems of empire was intensified not so much by pageantry as by crisis. British–Boer relations in South Africa, always tense, were further worsened after the Jameson raid of December 1895, and, in October 1899, war began. The early stages of the struggle were favourable to the Boers, and it was not until spring 1900 that superior British equipment began to count. British troops entered Pretoria in June 1900 and Paul Kruger, the Boer president, fled to Europe, where most governments had given him moral support against the British. Thereafter the Boers followed guerrilla tactics, and the war did not end until May 1902. It was the most expensive of all the 19th-century "little wars," with the British employing 450,000 troops, of whom 22,000 never returned. Just as the Crimean War had focussed attention on "mismanagement," so the South African (Boer) War led to demands not only for greater "efficiency" but for more enlightened social policies in relation to health and education.

While the war lasted, it emphasized the political differences within the Liberal Party and consolidated Conservative–Unionist strength. Rosebery's Liberal imperialism was totally uncongenial to young pro-Boer Liberals like Lloyd George. A middle group of Liberals emerged, but it was not until after 1903 that party rifts were healed. The Unionists won the "khaki election" of 1900 and secured a new lease of power for nearly six years, but their unity also was threatened after the Peace of Vereeniging in May 1902. Salisbury retired in 1902, to be succeeded by his nephew, Arthur Balfour, a brilliant man but a tortuous and insecure politician. There had been an even bigger break in January 1901 when the Queen died, after a brief illness, in her 82nd year. She had ruled for 64 years and her death seemed to mark not so much the end of a reign as the end of an age.

LATE VICTORIAN AND EDWARDIAN BRITAIN

Her successor, Edward VII, 59 years old, had never been on good terms with his mother, whose ways of life were sharply different from his. He, too, gave his name to an age: flamboyant, ostentatious, at times vulgar and strident, with picturesque contrasts of fortune and circumstance. Yet the sharpness of the contrast between "Edwardian" and "late Victorian" should not be exaggerated. The last decade of the 19th century and the first decade of the 20th century had much in common, and there had been bigger breaks in mood and preoccupation between the high-Victorian years and the 1890s.

Darwin's disciple, Thomas Huxley, an influential popularizer of science, had noted during the 1870s that everything was in question—opinions, institutions, and conventions—and the questioning thereafter never stopped. "The disintegration of opinion is so rapid," one writer put it in the 1880s, "that wise men and foolish are equally ignorant where the close of this waning century will find us." The writers of the last decades of the 19th century included iconoclasts like George Bernard Shaw and deviants like Oscar Wilde; for both, as for many others like them, all that was established was now suspect. Some commentators wrote of "a general revolt" against the accepted canons of the midcentury, a revolt influenced by thinkers outside Britain and challenging not only political or social assumptions (for example, about law and will or self-help and respectability) but also 19th-century culture as a whole, the culture of an industrialized society transformed through individual enterprise.

The economy. Changes in economic conditions during the last decades of the century were obviously of crucial importance. Mid-Victorian prosperity had reached its peak in a boom that collapsed in 1873. Thereafter, although national income continued to increase (nearly four times at constant prices between 1851 and 1911), there was a persistent pressure on profit margins, with a price fall that lasted until the mid-1890s. Contemporaries talked misleadingly of a "great depression," but however misleading the phrase was as a description of the movement of economic indexes, the period as a whole was one of doubt and tension. There was anxious concern about both markets and materials, and the fact that there was a retardation in the national rate of growth to below 2 percent per annum was even harder to bear when the growth rates of competitors were rising, sometimes in spectacular fashion.

Slowing of growth rate

The interests of different sections of the community diverged between 1870 and 1900 as they had diverged before the mid-Victorian period of equipoise. In particular, arable and meat-producing farmers felt the full weight of foreign competition in cereals, and many, though not all, industrialists felt the growing pressure of foreign competition both in old and new industries. As a result of improved transport, including storage and refrigeration facilities, and the application of improved agricultural machinery, overseas cereal producers fully penetrated the British market. In 1877 the price of English wheat stood at 56s. 9d. a quarter (1846: 54s. 6d); for the rest of the century it never again came within 10s. of that figure. During the 1890s, therefore, there was a sharp fall of rents, a shift in land ownership, and a challenge to the large estate in the cereal-growing and meat-producing areas of the country. The fact that dairy and fruit farmers flourished did not relieve the pessimism of most spokesmen of the threatened landed interests.

In industry, where there were new forms of power and a trend toward bigger plants and more impersonal organization, there were also moves throughout the period to increase cartels and amalgamations. Britain was never as strong or as innovatory in the age of steel as in the earlier age of iron—by 1896 British steel output was less than that of either the United States or Germany—while the textile industry was declining absolutely. Exports fell between 1880 and 1900 from £105,000,000 to £95,000,000. There were many explanations of what was happening, psychological as well as economic, but none of them was encouraging. Yet the country's economic position would have been completely different, had it not been for Britain's international economic strength as banker and financier. During years of economic challenge at home, capital exports greatly increased, until they reached a figure of almost £200,000,000 per annum before 1914, and investment income poured in to rectify adverse balances on visible trade accounts. During the last 20 years of peace before 1914, when Britain's role as *rentier* was at its height, international prices began to rise again, continuing to rise, with fluctuations, until after the end of World War I.

The rise of labour. Meanwhile, whether prices were falling or rising, labour in Britain was increasingly discontented, more articulate, and more highly organized. Throughout the period, national income per head grew faster than the continuing population growth (which stayed at above 10 percent per decade until 1911, although the birth rate fell sharply after 1900), but neither the growth of income nor the falling level of retail prices until the mid-1890s made for industrial peace. By the end of the century, when pressure on real wages was once again increasing, there were 2,000,000 trade unionists in unskilled unions as well as in skilled unions of the midcentury type, and by 1914 the figure had doubled.

Labour and politics

There were also significant political changes. Some of the new union leaders were confessed socialists, anxious to use political as well as economic power to secure their objectives, and a number of socialist organizations emerged between 1880 and 1900—all conscious, at least intermittently, that, whatever their differences, they were part of a "labour movement." The Social Democratic Federation, influenced by Marxism, was founded in 1884; it was never more than a tiny and increasingly sectarian organization. The Independent Labour Party, founded in Bradford in 1893, had a more general appeal, while the Fabian Society, founded in 1883–84, included intellectuals who were to play a big part in 20th-century labour politics. In February 1900 a labour representation conference was held in London at which trade unionists and socialists agreed to found a committee, with Ramsay MacDonald as first secretary, to promote the return of Labour members to Parliament. This conference marked the beginning of the 20th-century Labour Party, which, with Liberal support, won 29 seats at the general election of 1906. Although until 1914 the party at Westminster for the most part supported the Liberals, in 1909 it secured the allegiance of the "Lib-Lab" miners' members. Financially backed by the trade unions, it was eventually to take the place of the Liberal Party as the second party in the state.

THE RETURN OF THE LIBERALS (1905–14)

The Liberals returned to power in December 1905 after Balfour had resigned. Between the end of the South African War and this date, they had become more united as the Conservatives had disintegrated. In 1903 Chamberlain had taken up the cause of protection, thereby disturbing an already uneasy balance within Balfour's cabinet. He failed to win large-scale middle class or working class support outside Parliament as he had hoped, and the main effect of his propaganda was to draw rival groups of Liberals together to protect free trade. At the general election of 1906 the Liberals won 377 seats, which gave them an enormous majority of 84 over all other parties combined. Their leader was Sir Henry Campbell-Bannerman, a cautious Scot, who had stayed clear of the extreme factions during the South African War. He formed an able cabinet that included radicals and Liberal imperialists, and when he retired in 1908, H.H. Asquith moved from the Home Office to become prime minister.

Social legislation. Social reform had not been the chief cry at the general election, which was fought mainly on the old issues of free trade, temperance reform, and education. In many constituencies there was evidence of Nonconformist grievances against a Balfour education act of 1902 that abolished the school boards, transferred educational responsibilities to the all-purpose local authorities, and laid the foundations of a national system of secondary education. Yet local and national inquiries, official and unofficial, into the incidence of poverty had pointed to the need for public action to relieve distress, and, from the start, the new Liberal government embarked upon a program of social legislation. In 1906 free school meals were made available to poor children; in 1907 a school medical service was founded; in 1908 a Children's Act was passed, along with an Old Age Pensions Act granting pensions under prescribed conditions to people over 70; in 1908 the miners were given a statutory working day of eight hours; and in 1909 trade boards were set up to fix wages in designated industries where there was little or no trade-union strength, and labour exchanges were created to try to reduce unemployment (a subject that was also being investigated locally and nationally) and to increase mobility. The vigour of these reforms owed much to a partnership between Winston Churchill at the Board of Trade and Lloyd George, chancellor of the exchequer.

Lloyd George's budget of 1909 set out deliberately to raise money to "wage implacable warfare against poverty and squalidness." The money was to come in part from supertax on high incomes and from capital gains on land sales. The budget so enraged Conservative opinion, inside and outside Parliament, that the Lords, already hostile to the trend of Liberal legislation, rejected it, thereby turning a political debate into a constitutional one. Passions were as strong as they had been in 1831, yet, at the ensuing general election of January 1910, the Liberal majority was greatly reduced and the balance of power in Parliament was now held by Labour and Irish Nationalist members. The death of Edward in May 1910 and the succession of the politically inexperienced George V added to the confusion, and it proved impossible to reach agreement between the parties on the outlines of a Parliament bill to define or to curb the powers of the House of Lords. After a Liberal Parliament bill had been defeated, a second general election in December 1910 produced similar political results to those earlier in the year, and it was not until August 1911 that the peers eventually passed the Parliament Act by 131 votes to 114. The act provided that money bills could become law without the assent of the Lords and that other bills would also become law if they passed in the Commons and failed in the Lords three times within two years. The act was finally passed only after the Conservative leadership had repudiated the "diehard peers" who refused to be intimidated by a threat to create more peers.

The Parliament Act of 1911

In the course of the struggle over the Parliament bill, strong, even violent, feelings had been roused among lords who had seldom bothered hitherto to attend their house. Their intransigence provided a keynote to four years of equally fierce struggle on many other issues in the country, with different sectional groups turning to noisy direct action. The Liberals remained in power, carrying important new legislation, but they faced so much opposition from extremists, who cared little either about conventional political behaviour or the rule of law, that these years have been called by the American historian, George Dangerfield, "the strange death of Liberal England." The most important legislation was once more associated with Lloyd George—the National Insurance Act of 1911, which provided, on a contributory basis, for limited unemployment and health insurance for large sections of the population.

Liberal difficulties. The National Insurance Act, which Parliament accepted without difficulty, was the subject of much hostile criticism in the press and was bitterly opposed by doctors and duchesses. Nor did it win unanimous support from labour. The parliamentary Labour Party itself mattered less during these years, however, than extraparliamentary trade-union protests, some of them violent in character—"a great upsurge of elemental forces." There was a wave of strikes in 1911 and 1912, some of them tinged with syndicalist ideology, all of them asserting, in difficult economic circumstances for the workingman, claims that had never been made before. Old-fashioned trade unionists were almost as unpopular with the rank and file as capitalists. In June 1914, less than two months before the outbreak of World War I, a "triple alliance" of transport workers, miners, and railwaymen was formed to buttress labour solidarity. In parallel to labour agitation, the suffragettes, fighting for women's rights, resorted to militant tactics that not only embarrassed Asquith's government but tested the whole local and national machinery for maintaining order. The Women's Social and Political Union, founded in 1903, was prepared to encourage illegal acts, including bombing and arson, which led to sharp police retaliation, severe sentences, harsh and controversial treatment in prison, and even martyrdom.

Irish difficulties

The issue that created the greatest difficulties, however, was one of the oldest: Ireland. In April 1912, armed with the new powers of the Parliament Act, Asquith introduced a new Home Rule bill. Conservative opposition to it was reinforced on this occasion by a popular Protestant movement in Ulster; and the new Conservative leader Bonar Law, who had replaced Balfour in 1911, gave his covert support to army mutineers in Ulster. No compromises were acceptable, and the struggle to settle the fate of Ireland was still in full spate when war broke out in August 1914. Most ominously for the Liberals, the Irish Home Rule supporters at Westminster were losing ground in southern Ireland, where in 1913 a militant working class movement entered into close alliance with the nationalist forces of Sinn Féin. Ireland was obviously on the brink of civil war.

The international crisis. The seeds of international war, sown long before 1900, were nourished between the resignation of Salisbury and August 1914. Two intricate systems of agreements and alliances—the Triple Alliance of Germany, Austria-Hungary, and Italy, and the Triple Entente of France, Russia, and Britain—faced each other in 1914. Both were backed by military and naval apparatus (Britain had been building a large fleet, and Richard Haldane had been reforming the army), and both could appeal to half-informed or uninformed public opinion. The result was that a war that was to break the continuities of history started as a popular war cheered by the crowds.

The Liberal government under Asquith faced a number of diplomatic crises from 1908 onward. Throughout a period of recurring tension, its foreign minister, Sir Edward Grey, often making decisions that were not discussed by the Cabinet as a whole, strengthened the understanding with France that had been initiated by his Conservative predecessor in 1903. An alliance had already been signed with Japan in 1902, and in 1907 agreements were reached with Russia. Meanwhile, naval rivalry with Germany familiarized Englishmen with the notion that if war came, it would be with Germany. The 1914 crisis began in the Balkans, an old storm centre, where the heir to the Austro-Hungarian throne was assassinated in June 1914. Soon Austria, backed by Germany, and Russia, supported by France, were arrayed against each other. The British Cabinet was divided, but after the Germans invaded Belgium on August 4, thereby violating a neutrality that Britain was committed by treaty to support, Britain and Germany went to war. Bonar Law pledged full support, as did John Redmond, the Irish leader at Westminster; only a few pacifists, radicals, and socialists stood on one side. Few foresaw a war of attrition or had any intimation of the profound economic, social, and political changes that lay in store. (As.B.)

XIV. Britain since 1914

THE PERIOD OF THE WORLD WARS

World War I. In the political and constitutional areas, the war witnessed many significant modifications in parliamentary and administrative practices required for transforming democratic processes designed for peace into an efficient machine for waging war. Thus, to avoid partisan division on war issues, no elections were held during the war—the general election, provided by law at the latest in 1915, was postponed by parliamentary resolution. There were, nevertheless, shifts in power. The first formal change came in May 1915, when the Liberal government under Asquith, weakened by criticism of the War Office and the munitions shortage and suffering from controversy over strategy between Churchill at the Admiralty and John Fisher, the first sea lord, was reorganized as a "Coalition" government, including Conservatives and one Labourite. But continued discontent in Parliament over the conduct of the war, distrust of Asquith's capacity as a war leader, and the weakening of his control over the Cabinet forced his hand in December 1916, and he was replaced as prime minister by David Lloyd George. Political power became largely concentrated in the War Cabinet of five, with parliamentary support taken for granted. As political processes, these changes were hardly revolutionary—well before 1914, party organization controlling the electorate and tighter discipline within parliamentary parties were elevating the roles of prime minister and Cabinet.

Wartime government

While intervention of the state in economic and social questions had been increasing since the late Victorian era and accelerated after 1906, during 1914–18 governmental controls were greatly expanded in marshalling resources for the war effort. DORA (Defence of the Realm Acts), though usually administered with caution and discretion, authorized regulations "for public safety and defence," control of armament plants, the requisitioning of factories, and the control of production and distribution. But authority was exercised through advisory commissions and was usually limited to establishing priorities. In munitions, coal, and railroads, controls came closest to outright government ownership. Various measures encouraged home food production and regulated prices and wages, but rationing of foodstuffs came only in 1918, and to a limited degree.

The prolongation of the war beyond all initial expectations complicated these problems and added to them. When voluntary enlistment proved insufficient to replace the thinning ranks of the armed forces, after long debate, in May 1916, came military conscription of all males between 18 and 41—the first such in English history. Labour unrest, at a peak at the outbreak of the war and further aroused by fears of the consequences of a war economy, was a constant concern, with serious strikes and stoppages in 1917 and 1918, but government and industry managed to maintain, without compulsion, a fairly satisfactory degree of order. In all ranks of society the tragedy of long casualty lists (of 6,000,000 in uniform from the United Kingdom some 750,000 lost their lives and 1,700,000 others were wounded) made heavy inroads on national morale. With the Lloyd George government a policy of "war to the finish" terminated any prospects for an early end to the war by negotiation, and in some circles, particularly the literary and the intellectual, patriotic support of the war effort turned to one of horror and despair at man's inhumanity to man.

Deterioration of morale

Public morale, however, was periodically fortified by talk of reconstruction, social reform, "a better world." There were indeed winds of change during the war. What peace had not secured for women, the war did: women's suffrage in 1918, and inevitably so because of their role in the war—in the auxiliaries of the armed forces, in the nurses corps, and particularly in industry—in offices, in shops, on the farms, on trams and buses. Because of the heavy reliance on home production of foodstuffs, the status of the farmer and the agricultural labourer attained a respectability unknown for two generations. In general, class lines, so pronounced in Victorian and Edwardian days, were becoming blurred, particularly in matters of dress. Economic inequalities were lessened. There was a sharp decline in servant keeping. A salaried and professional "middle class" grew apace, and the traditional cleavage between landowners and men of commerce disappeared for good. Nonetheless, distinct class lines remained in education, in accent, in class consciousness, and in life style generally.

Lloyd George, always sensitive to public opinion, took the lead in establishing by statute the Ministry of Reconstruction in 1917; investigations of industry, public health, transport, and housing were soon underway. An education act set the school-leaving age at 14, envisioned raising it to 15, and provided for part-time schooling until 16.

The power structure that waged and won the war began as a Liberal government in 1914 and ended as a Coalition dominated by Conservatives, though still under the leadership of a Liberal, Lloyd George. The split in 1916 between those Liberals supporting Asquith and those supporting Lloyd George was widened in May 1918 by Asquith's motion for a committee of inquiry in the Commons to investigate divergent statements of the Prime Minister and the director of military operations in the War Office over the strength of the army. Asquith's motion was defeated, with 100 Liberals voting for his motion and 71 against. But even more important, the composition of the constituencies of the major parties was uncertain, as well as the issues that would divide them after the war.

One matter became increasingly clear. The Labour Party under the leadership of J. Ramsay MacDonald and

Growth of the Labour Party

Arthur Henderson, though still small in numbers in the Commons, was becoming a stronger voice for social democracy. Labour, though somewhat divided by issues of war and peace, managed to maintain its solidarity as a parliamentary party, while moving to the left in social and economic matters. By 1918 Labour had established unity on certain essentials: (1) reorganization of its structure to provide for active membership through individuals, as well as through trade unions and socialist societies; (2) a restatement of purpose in socialist terms—"a new social order based . . . on deliberately planned cooperation in production and distribution for the benefit of all who participate by hand or brain"; (3) a decision to leave the Coalition at the end of the war and contest the next general election as an independent party.

Aftermath of the war (1918–24). World War I ended November 11, 1918. England's mood was one of profound relief and a sense of triumph but also one of optimism for the future. It was perhaps unfortunate that the general election came so promptly (polling day was December 14)—unfortunate in its revival of party bitterness, revelation of personal animosities, and demands for revenge against Germany. But an immediate election was essential; the existing Parliament had been elected in 1910. In the campaign the significant factor was Lloyd George's decision to maintain the Coalition with both Conservative and Liberal support and the arrangement that no Conservative candidate would oppose a Liberal pledged to the Coalition. This divided the Liberal vote, rendering it unlikely that anything approaching proportional representation would result. The main issue was this: should Lloyd George and the Coalition continue? The result was their stunning triumph with some 478 seats out of 707, though the popular vote for their candidates was slightly in excess of their opponents. Asquith Liberals were crushed and Labour emerged, with 59 seats, as the official opposition.

The Coalition continued in power until October 1922. Its tasks and those of the British people were formidable: to negotiate a durable peace mindful of British interests; to restore a peacetime economy favourable to British production and world trade; to absorb the returning armed forces in a changing economy and society; and to solve the problem of Irish national aspirations. These problems were compounded by a conflict of generations (especially between those returning from the trenches and the high seas, and their elders), by an almost irrational desire to forget the war and return to "normalcy," and, thus, by a breakdown of morale.

So it was that the peace treaty negotiated at Versailles was debated in England in a partisan spirit and increased the difficulty of the government in clarifying and achieving policies in the national interest: limited disarmament designed to slow down the arms race; diplomacy by negotiation to relieve international tension; general rehabilitation of Germany. In these years, in spite of some 23 international conferences, questions of disarmament and German reparations seemed without solution.

The postwar economy

As to the economy, no one seemed prepared for the situation that developed. A brief postwar boom rather encouraged the business world in its inclination to return to prewar policies and methods: free trade abroad and laissez-faire at home; restoration of the gold standard, which had been temporarily suspended in 1919; reduction of wages and other costs of production, if necessary to meet foreign competition. But when European markets were opened to the expanding economies of the United States and Asia, Britain suffered a decided decline in production and foreign trade relative to its prewar status. The chief consequence was an alarming rise in unemployment—reaching, in July 1921, 22.4 percent of all insured workers (who comprised nearly the entire work force).

Politics, influenced by uncertainties at home and abroad, tended to become motivated by fear—fear of the other side—and to polarize political groups. A new "Right" sought to erase the old distinction between Liberal and Conservative and to advocate a limited role of the state in society and the economy, to stabilize Europe as a British market, to keep a safe distance from Russia, and to strengthen imperial ties. The "Left," composed of Labour and dissident Liberals, urged nationalization of key industries and government housing, supported collective security and disarmament, encouraged ties with Russia, and was increasingly skeptical about the empire.

Resignation of Lloyd George

The Lloyd George government met the crisis in the coal industry with temporary subsidies, extended unemployment insurance, and established the Irish Free State. But the Coalition steadily weakened; in October 1922 Conservatives voted their independence and Lloyd George resigned. There followed three governments in three years. The first, a Conservative government under Bonar Law, sought to capitalize on the cry for "tranquility"; Law's serious illness soon brought about his replacement (May 1923) not by Lord Curzon, his logical successor, but by Stanley Baldwin, a member of the cabinet only since 1921. He successfully reunited the Conservative Party but failed in his attempt to get party and national support for a protective tariff. As a result of the general election of December 1923, Labour, with 191 seats in the Commons, formed with Liberal support the first Labour government in British history. In its short rule of ten months the only significant change in domestic policy was in legislation establishing new procedures for government housing. MacDonald, foreign minister as well as prime minister, was more active abroad, where he helped set in motion the Dawes Plan for German reparations, which brought evacuation of the Ruhr. Soviet Russia was recognized. But it was its policy toward Russia, including matters of trade, that lost Labour Liberal support; and in the general election of October 1924 Stanley Baldwin and the Conservatives returned to office with 48 percent of the popular poll and 419 seats in the Commons. Labour more than held its own in the popular vote, but the Liberals collapsed, polling but 18 percent of the vote.

Stanley Baldwin as prime minister

Stability and crisis (1924–31). It was perhaps logical that Stanley Baldwin was prime minister, 1924–29. He was fairly typical of Britishers of the 1920s—plain-spoken, rather modest in manner, honest, patient. He did not profess to know all the answers and was committed to no policy. But he did seek stability, tranquility, peace of mind, good will among men; in such an atmosphere, he insisted, problems would find solutions. So it was, to a degree. By mutual consent among parties British armaments were drastically reduced. Austen Chamberlain, foreign secretary, received good marks for his part in deliberations leading to the Pact of Locarno (1925), providing for arbitration of disputes in western Europe. There was little dissent to the creation of the British Broadcasting Corporation as a monopoly in 1926. National health insurance, unemployment insurance—these, in principle, ceased to divide the nation. Under Neville Chamberlain at the Ministry of Health, more social legislation was enacted than by either the Labour government that had preceded or the one that followed. This included implementation of Chamberlain's Housing Act of 1923, with over 400,000 new dwellings, and the Local Government Act of 1929, which abolished the Boards of Guardians.

The General Strike of 1926

In the economy, production went beyond prewar figures and unemployment levelled off at 10 percent. But such favourable signs were illusory; the significant fact was that Britain lagged behind the rest of the industrial world —by 1929 the volume of exports was still below the 1913 figure, and the annual value of exports declined after the return to the gold standard in 1925. That problems of production and of labour were out of control was evident in the General Strike of 1926. This came from the crisis in coal—the largest single industry—where royal commissions produced but temporary measures to deal with rising costs of production. An end to governmental subsidies supplementing wages led to the owners' insistence on wage reductions. Rejection of the new wage scale by the Miners' Federation of Great Britain brought lockout notices, closing down the mines on May 1, 1926. An overwhelming vote of unions affiliated with the national Trades Union Congress (TUC) approved a general strike in support of the miners. In actuality, the General Strike affected about 70 percent of union members and has been aptly described as "a strike under wraps." Most of the strikers had served in the armed forces during the war, and few of them had revolutionary intent. The strike was conducted with little violence and no loss of life. The government's attitude, however, was one of firmness; it declared the strike "unconstitutional" and "illegal" and soon persuaded the general council of the TUC to accept revision of the wage scale after reorganization of the industry. The strike ended May 12, and Baldwin broadcast a message calling for a general reconciliation. It was his greatest hour.

The aftermath of the strike was less successful. The government took no action to bring about reorganization of the coal industry and passed in 1927 a statute that declared sympathetic strikes illegal. Furthermore, the Baldwin government produced no program for dealing with general unemployment and did nothing to revitalize other basic industries such as steel and textiles or to assist agriculture, again in difficulties. Treasury economies stalled advances in secondary education. In foreign policy nothing was done to implement the spirit of Locarno. In imperial affairs, largely due to L.S. Amery at the Colonial Office, policy was more progressive. The Imperial Conference of 1926 adopted Balfour's report calling for abrogation of all British legislative control in the dominions—this became the Statute of Westminster in 1931. In 1927 was created the Simon Commission to review the political situation in India since 1919, when dyarchy had been adopted.

In the general election of May 1929, Labour profited by the inaction of the Baldwin government in many areas and emerged with a plurality in Parliament. The Liberals, now under Lloyd George, who had replaced Asquith as party leader in 1926, made a gigantic effort in support of state action to solve the problems of the economy and finished respectably with 23 percent of the popular vote and 59 seats. Nevertheless, they came in a poor third.

MacDonald's government

MacDonald formed a moderate Labour Cabinet the major accomplishments of which were again in foreign affairs. Philip Snowden, chancellor of the exchequer, helped implement the Young Plan for German payment of reparations; Arthur Henderson, foreign secretary, presided over the commission at The Hague that brought allied evacuation from the Rhineland. Thanks in large part to MacDonald himself, progress was made on naval reduction at the London Naval Conference in 1930. The Round Table Conference was a step toward a federated India. But the record in domestic affairs was found "meagre" by the usually objective British periodical *The Economist.* The Great Depression compounded all of England's problems. Escalating unemployment (23 percent of the insured workers by mid-1931) brought such demands on the Unemployment Insurance Fund that a budgetary and financial crisis threatened the country's international credit. Proposals for drastic cuts in unemployment insurance and other social services divided the Cabinet, and MacDonald resigned in August 1931. Neither Baldwin nor Sir Herbert Samuel (now Liberal leader) were anxious to assume responsibility alone, and MacDonald was persuaded to form a coalition, the so-called National Government (August 24).

The National Government: crisis and recovery (1931–39). The necessary financial credits were secured abroad, and the National Government, formed to deal with an emergency, was overwhelmingly confirmed in office in the general election in October 1931. The Parliamentary Labour Party had, however, repudiated MacDonald and fought the election independently; the result was disastrous—every former cabinet member save one was defeated, and only 52 Labourites were returned. In the election, the National Government made a virtue of the division of opinion in its ranks—voters were merely asked to support "Safety and the Union Jack." Whether diversity of opinion could produce action was soon tested. To meet the problems of finance and trade, the government pushed through a general protective tariff—the Liberal and Labour free traders in the Cabinet were allowed to "differ" both in the debate and in the poll. But the extension of the tariff to imperial preference brought resignation of the free traders.

Continued effects of depression

As to economic matters in general, the Depression continued until 1933 (the drop in production from 1929 to 1932 was 16 percent), with substantial recovery thereafter (by 1937 production was 50 percent above that of 1932). British industry turned to the home market with housing (average annual construction of 270,000 houses) and new industries—automobiles, electrical applicances, industrial chemistry. Recovery, however, was only in relation to the 1920s, for the United Kingdom's share in world trade continued to decline. Unemployment, though reduced, was concentrated in certain areas and trades. The very significant Unemployment Act of 1934 reorganized the system of relief, and for the working classes life was, in general, somewhat better in the 1930s than in the 1920s.

In June 1935 Baldwin replaced MacDonald as prime minister. And a few months later a general election confirmed the National Government, but with considerable gains for Labour. George Lansbury, Labour leader since 1931, but now at odds with his party on foreign policy, resigned; Clement Attlee, who had proved himself as a parliamentarian, became Labour leader. In domestic affairs the most important episode for Baldwin was the abdication crisis. The death of George V in January 1936 led to the succession of Edward VIII. For many months, few outside official circles knew of his friendship with an American-born lady, Mrs. Simpson, already twice married and once divorced. Her second divorce was granted in October. The government, with Labour support, opposed her marriage to the King and held firm against a "King's Party" forming around a strange nucleus including Winston Churchill, Sir Oswald Mosley, and George Bernard Shaw. In a message to Parliament (December 10), Edward VIII abdicated and his brother was proclaimed King George VI. But it soon became clear that the institution of monarchy had not suffered.

Abdication of Edward VIII

After the coronation of George VI in May 1937, Baldwin was replaced as prime minister by Neville Chamberlain, whose administration was largely concerned with meeting the social and economic problems of the late 1930s. The 1930s as a whole were preoccupied with "planning." PEP (Political and Economic Planning) was a nonpartisan agency for research—beginning in 1933 a series of significant reports dealt with iron and steel, cotton, coal, international trade, public health, housing, the press, and other areas of public concern. *Plan or No Plan* (1934), by Barbara Wootton of London University, urged a planned economy. *Reconstruction: A Plan for a National Policy* (1933) and *The Middle Way* (1938), by Harold Macmillan, a Conservative and a future prime minister, urged a minimum wage and partial nationalization of industry. B. Seebohm Rowntree, studying poverty in the city of York, found that 19 percent of the population was existing on a substandard diet. The distribution of national income came in for careful study and led to scholarly studies of unemployment and "the depressed areas." Implementation of some of the ideas did not have to wait. Some 120 railway companies were amalgamated into four systems. The Central Electricity Board purchased current and distributed it through "a grid"—of incalculable importance when war came. With the creation of the Exchange Equalization Fund (1932), the Bank of England was all but nationalized, and the nationalization of coal royalties in 1938 was a long step toward nationalization of that industry. As to steel, a committee from the industry and a committee from the government determined prices and controlled production. Altogether, "nationalization" was well under way before World War II.

Beginning of nationalization

Foreign policy and appeasement (1931–39). In July 1931 each of the party leaders paid pious tribute to the League of Nations, to disarmament, and to the renunciation of war. But statesmanship did not bridge the gap between piety and circumstance. The carefully prepared World Disarmament Conference that convened at Geneva in February 1932 proved a disappointment. Any decisive action to break the deadlock of French and German demands depended on a military commitment that Britain refused to give. On questions of war and peace, the climate of thought in England was negative. A vague pacifism did not consider how peace was to be maintained. Collective security through the League of Nations was generally supported—as long as no obligations were incurred. This seemed to be the purport of the so-called Peace Ballot of 1934, a house-to-house canvass organized by the League of Nations Union, in which 40 percent of those polled favoured disarmament.

In his successful election campaign of 1935, Baldwin advocated collective action by the League in the border dispute between Italy and Abyssinia but added that war was not anticipated. But while government spokesmen were endorsing the League, Sir Samuel Hoare and Pierre Laval, foreign ministers for England and France, were drafting in private the proposal to settle the dispute by handing over half of Abyssinia to Italy. Its disclosure (December 9) brought a flood of protest in the press, the pulpit, and the electorate that forced the government to repudiate the agreement. Hoare resigned, to be succeeded by Anthony Eden. But there was still no will to impose sanctions on Italy, which completed without interference the conquest of Abyssinia.

The Spanish Civil War

The year 1936 was one of crisis. There was the abdication at home, and abroad the unfolding of Nazi policy in Europe and the outbreak of the Spanish Civil War. The usually placid *Annual Register* described British policy as hesitant, indecisive, apologetic, content to drift. The German military occupation of the Rhineland (March 1936) in violation of Versailles was accepted by the British government, with little dissent from Labour, as a *fait accompli;* few favoured sanctions against Germany and many thought Germany was justified. This was the beginning of appeasement.

British policy toward Spain in the civil war between the Loyalists to the Republic and the "nationalist rebels" led by Francisco Franco was hardly more forthright. Britain was the chief sponsor of "nonintervention" by the powers, which was something of a farce since Fascist Italy and Nazi Germany sent military aid to the rebels, and the Soviet Union the same, on smaller scale, to the Republic. In actuality, Britain did take sides—the government sympathized with the rebels, the Labour opposition with the Loyalists. But in public opinion generally, cleavage cut across party lines. In general, the Spanish Civil War marked the end of pacifism as a fashionable attitude.

Neville Chamberlain, as prime minister, dominated foreign policy from May 1937; the subordinate role assigned the Foreign Office contributed to Eden's resignation early in 1938. Policy, determined by Chamberlain and a few advisers, put little faith in collective security and sought direct negotiation with Hitler and Mussolini —compromise and appeasement where necessary—to reduce tensions that might lead to war. In an important interview in November 1937 Lord Halifax told Hitler that Britain would not oppose boundary changes in central Europe if they came by "peaceful evolution." But Chamberlain was not without a strategy of his own: he would settle differences with Mussolini and thus strengthen his hand against Hitler.

But in the event, negotiation tempered by appeasement merely brought a succession of crises. In March 1938 Austria was absorbed into the German *Reich*. In August 1938 the "Runciman mission" failed in its attempt to mediate between Germany and Czechoslovakia over the status of German-speaking Sudetenland, a part of Czechoslovakia. In September, at Munich, Chamberlain, along with the French premier Édouard Daladier, Mussolini, and Hitler, agreed to the cession of the Sudetenland to Germany but accompanied with a guarantee of the integrity of the remainder of Czechoslovakia. When Chamberlain returned to London he proclaimed that the agreement meant "peace for our time." Six months later, however, the Nazis invaded Czechoslovakia and seized control. Now at last Chamberlain denounced Hitler; rearmament was stepped up and policy reversed. Guarantees of support were given to Poland, Romania, and Greece, but Chamberlain's patient efforts to include the Soviet Union in the security system ended abruptly with the signing (August 23) of the German-Soviet Nonaggression Pact. Germany invaded Poland on September 1, and when an ultimatum to Germany calling for a cessation of hostilities went unanswered, Chamberlain broadcast to the nation, Sunday morning, September 3, that Britain was at war.

Munich conference

World War II. World War II was "total war" and, as such, was in many ways a conflict in which the civilian and the man in uniform shared dangers and hardships in common. Air raid warnings began the Battle of London on the first day of the war. Two days before, on September 1, began the evacuation from danger zones, and in three days 1,473,000 persons were relocated. Two million others had already removed themselves privately, some to the country, some to the dominions, others to the United States. Schooling for a time was demoralized, and it is estimated that by the following January 1,000,000 children had not yet been placed in classrooms. Construction began at once on a program of 2,500,000 outdoor household steel shelters designed to protect 10,000,000 persons against air attack. They sold for £5 but were distributed free to low-income families.

Chamberlain broadened his government to include Winston Churchill at his old post in the Admiralty and also Anthony Eden. Hitler's Polish campaign quickly over in September, there followed six months of the "Phony War," with land operations almost at a standstill and national morale in Britain diminished. The British consoled themselves with the conviction that if it were to be an endurance contest control of the seas and blockade of Germany would eventually bring victory. But any complacency was suddenly jolted in April 1940 by the German invasion of Denmark and Norway; the collapse of Norway led to an angry Commons' debate in which some 100 Conservatives refused continued support of Chamberlain, who forthwith resigned (May 10). King George was inclined to Halifax as prime minister, but on Chamberlain's advice he sent for Churchill, who formed a coalition government, with a five-member war cabinet including the Labour leader, Attlee, who became in effect leader of the Commons. Another key appointment was that of Ernest Bevin, a trade union official, as minister of labour and national service.

The wartime government

An inspired Churchill led the country in the "miracle of Dunkirk"; at the end of May, 338,000 Allied troops were evacuated to Britain after the Germans had smashed their way to the French coast. But this episode was soon overshadowed by the Battle of Britain in August and September 1940—the most critical period of the war. Germany threatened invasion, and for that to succeed it must first cripple British defenses—air fields, radar stations, London docks—and attain air supremacy. But the Royal Air Force stood up against all attacks and by September 15 was having the better of it. Some of the most stirring narratives of the war relate the experience of "the Blitz." For a time in the metropolitan area one out of every seven was sleeping in a public shelter—a basement, a railway arch, a "tube" station. From July to December 1940 civilian casualties in air raids numbered 23,000 dead—more than in the armed forces.

The war at home remained grim in the spring of 1941 with aerial attacks on Plymouth (600 killed in five days), in Liverpool (death toll of 1,900 in a week), in London (1,400 deaths in two days and the destruction of the chamber of the Commons), and elsewhere. But 1941 was also the year in which Britain found the answer to the manpower problem in the Registration for Employment Order, which eventually mobilized into the services or into industry 94 percent of all males between the ages of 14 and 64. And in 1941 came "lend-lease" for war supplies from the United States, the Nazi invasion of the Soviet Union, and the Japanese attack on Pearl Harbor. The Grand Alliance was formed, and by the end of 1942—with allied landings in North Africa, the rout of the Germans in Libya, and the counterattack against the Germans in Russia—Churchill could speak of "the end of the beginning."

By 1943 it was clear that the war was bringing change at home. World War II was undoubtedly the most socially levelling experience in modern English history—in the risks of war, in food and shelter, in clothing and amusement, and to a degree in taxation. "Planning," in vogue in the 1930s, now became more systematically applied, for war, of course, but also for peace. Commissions drafted proposals for the use of land in town and country. And the Beveridge Report, December 1942 (Sir William Beveridge was chairman of an interdepartmental committee), outlined a program of social insurance embracing in theory all persons but in application classified according to need, with a "national minimum" of income guaranteed to all. Impressive as it was, the report was merely "welcomed" and not endorsed by the Commons and had to await the end of the war for serious consideration. The most significant piece of legislation not directly associated with the war effort was the Education Act of 1944—for the most part the work of R.A. Butler—which created the Ministry of Education with effective power for developing a national educational policy, raised the school-leaving age (after the war) to 15, and provided for a full range of educational services—primary, secondary, and "further" without fees.

The Beveridge Report

Even as the war was approaching its end, civilians still confronted grave danger. In June 1944, soon after the Allied invasion of Normandy, the first of the "flying bombs"—the V-1s—fell on England; there were nearly 5,500 dead from this weapon by September. And then came the rockets, the V-2s. When the conflict ended September 2, 1945, one day short of six years, civilian casualties numbered about 60,000. Of the armed forces of the United Kingdom, 300,000 lost their lives. And Britain lost one-fourth of its national wealth.

Commonwealth and empire. World War II gave a new direction to Commonwealth affairs. Unlike World War I, the entrance of the dominions in the war in 1939 was their own action; Ireland remained officially neutral. During the course of the war it was clear that equality of status (implicit in the Statute of Westminster of 1931) was being replaced by equality of function. The dominions controlled the employment of their own forces and were usually consulted in matters of strategy. The war strengthened both the bonds of the Commonwealth in a world that seemed destined to be dominated by the United States and the Soviet Union and the conviction of the dominions that as independent nations they were approaching the status of "great powers."

But the growth of this notion of equality within the Commonwealth tended to differentiate more sharply the dominions from India, Burma, and Ceylon, on behalf of which the United Kingdom declared war in 1939. For them the significance of the war lay in its impact upon their future. For India the chief result was internal—the war greatly strengthened Muslim nationalism, which, through the Muslim League lead by Jinnah Mohammad Ali, came into violent conflict with the Indian National Congress led by Jawaharlal Nehru.

BRITAIN SINCE WORLD WAR II

Labour and the welfare state (1945–51). World War II, like World War I, was followed immediately by a general election; and Churchill, like Lloyd George, sought to perpetuate the wartime coalition. But here the parallel ends. In 1945 all parties contested the election independently. During the war, Labour maintained its organization. In 1941 it had issued "Labour in Government: A Record of Social Legislation in War Time," and in 1942, "The Old World and the New Society," a statement of postwar policy. In contrast, the Conservatives had not redefined their policies.

The postwar election

The European war was at an end May 8. Angry with Labour for breaking away from the Coalition, Churchill would not await the end of the Japanese war and resigned May 23. Polling day was set for July 5. The heart of the campaign was a series of evening broadcasts. The British Broadcasting Corporation estimated that on the average 45 percent of the adult population listened, with Churchill's audiences only slightly larger than the others. In his opening broadcast Churchill sought to associate Labour with Socialism and thereby show it to be dangerous. Attlee refused to take this seriously, for Socialism as an ideology was hardly an issue. Nor was the achievement of the war coalition, despite its emphasis by the Conservatives. The important question seemed to be: What of the future? Labour had a comprehensive program; the Conservatives did not. The outcome was a stunning victory for Labour, beyond all prediction, with 393 members of Parliament, a clear majority of 146 over all other parties. Attlee formed a strong cabinet with Bevin at the Foreign Office, Hugh Dalton at the Exchequer, and Herbert Morrison as leader of the Commons.

Labour promptly implemented its program. First came nationalization of the Bank of England, of coal, of electrical power, and of inland transport (railroads, road transport, inland waterways, docks and harbours). Only transport was seriously contested. No private interest was confiscated, and management usually remained in the hands of those who directed the industry when privately owned. As to agriculture, war legislation guaranteeing prices and markets was continued, rendering farming a respected occupation and one that provided a good livelihood. Labour created "the welfare state," or, more accurately, extended in dramatic fashion social services by the state. Legislation provided insurance against unemployment, sickness, industrial injury, old age; supplementary grants were provided for emergencies—pregnancy and maternity care, widowhood, burial. The National Assistance Act provided a weekly benefit for minimum needs. The National Health Service Act (1946)—which did not go into effect until July 1948—provided medical care for all, regardless of ability to pay; as such the act was the outcome of 35 years of piecemeal social legislation. Though all assumed that some kind of national health service was required, the problem was to enact legislation that would satisfy the medical profession without their active participation in its formulation. In the controversy, the medical profession was rent asunder. But by 1950 it was clear that Britain's health service was there to stay—95 percent of the population were enrolled on lists of doctors in the service, who numbered 88 percent of all medical practitioners.

National Health Service

In order to implement the Education Act of 1944, the government by 1951 had trained 35,000 new teachers (one-sixth of those in service), had established 6,300 temporary school rooms and constructed 1,000 new buildings, had extended the school-leaving age to 15 (1947), had expanded part-time technical training schools to nearly 300,000 workers, and had underwritten higher education (73 percent of students in universities were receiving grants-in-aid).

In the economy, Britain's task was clear: to restore and if possible to improve upon its prewar standard of living; to achieve a rate of production that would satisfy consumer demands at home and provide a surplus for export to pay for imported foodstuffs and raw materials; to bolster up sterling. Labour sought to achieve these goals by maintaining controls and powers exercised by the government during the war. While there was full employment, production was unimpressive. And in 1947, partly because the severe winter of 1946–47 interfered with production and transportation, but more especially because of slowdowns in mines and factories from discontented labour, there came a severe economic crisis, British exports falling sharply and the stability of sterling challenged.

But economic policy can hardly be separated from foreign policy, for it became apparent soon after the end of the war that Britain would depend on the United States for economic aid. It was agreed that on the lend-lease war account, Britain incurred no obligation for American aid actually consumed during the war; and, more importantly, outright financial aid through the Marshall Plan began in 1948. But before the end of 1945 it was just as clear that British and Soviet interests in Europe were irreconcilable. From the Baltic to the Adriatic, said Churchill at Fulton, Missouri, March 5, 1946, "an iron curtain has descended across the continent." Eastern European states, including East Germany, became Soviet satellites, and by 1947–48 a state of "cold war" existed between the Soviet Union and the West. In its search for economic recovery and national security, Britain apparently had to choose between Commonwealth ties or European cooperation: it moved cautiously toward Europe. The Dunkirk Treaty of Alliance (1947) allied Britain and France against a possible revival of German militarism; and Belgium, The Netherlands, and Luxembourg joined them in the Brussels Treaty (1948). The most significant event for security in the West was the North Atlantic Treaty Organization (NATO), organized in April 1949, which bound the Brussels signatories with Canada and the United States in a military alliance.

NATO

A veritable revolution began within the Commonwealth. Self-determination had long been pledged to India. Despite tremendous difficulties this was achieved in August 1947, with the creation of India and Pakistan as independent dominions within the Commonwealth. In 1946 Britain terminated its mandate over Transjordan, and in 1948, over Palestine. Rising Egyptian nationalism forced Britain to withdraw its military forces in 1947, except those in the Suez. In 1949 Ireland proclaimed itself a republic and left the Commonwealth.

At the end of 1949, Labour was confronted with a general election. The party's limited success at nationalization and other controls to strengthen the economy and an "austerity" program limiting consumption had somewhat broken Labour's hold on the electorate. Further, there was disaffection in Labour's ranks, particularly against policy at the Foreign Office. The Conservatives had, meanwhile, effectively reorganized. In the February 1950 election Labour's vote was cut sharply by the still active Liberals, and the Labour majority in the Commons was reduced to six. Parliamentary government became a sparring engagement. The steel industry was nationalized, but its methods of operation remained much as before. United Nations support for South Korea brought some rearmament, but this further alienated leftists in the Labour party. Britishers found a brief diversion from their problems in the summer of 1951 in the Festival of Britain on the south bank of the Thames. In the autumn, however, Attlee announced a general election. The Conservatives won a majority of 17, ending the postwar rule of Labour.

The Conservative response to postwar change (1951–64). The Conservative comeback proved genuine, the party winning three elections in succession (1951, 1955, 1959), each with a larger majority. Party leadership changed, first in April 1955 from Churchill to Anthony Eden, and then in January 1957 from Eden to Harold Macmillan. At Buckingham Palace there was also a change—King George VI died in February 1952. Elizabeth II was proclaimed in June 1953 with coronation ceremonies in Westminster Abbey that were televised worldwide.

Coronation of Elizabeth

The Conservatives dominated the 1950s primarily because their domestic program proved more dynamic than that of Labour, which was slow to appreciate the need for new goals and new slogans to replace "full employment," "fair shares," and "nationalization." Furthermore, on foreign policy Labour was seriously divided, with Aneurin Bevan and Harold Wilson leading a strong minority opposed to rearmament.

At first, however, the Churchill government, with its slender control in the Commons, moved slowly, tampering little with Labour legislation, save for denationalizing steel and road transport. R.A. Butler at the Exchequer produced measures designed to reverse the unfavourable balance of international payments—curtailing imports, raising the bank rate for borrowing, and cutting tourist allowances abroad 50 percent. With these measures and favourable conditions abroad, foreign trade by 1953 was on even terms for the first time since the war. The volume of exports steadily increased, and domestic consumption advanced—an increase between 1951 and 1954 of 12 percent, especially noticeable in automobiles and television sets. A matter of great popular interest was the creation in 1955 of the Independent Television Authority, which ended the British Broadcasting Corporation monopoly.

The economy

This record helped the Conservatives increase their majority in the Commons to 58 in 1955.

Although there was talk of affluency, actual growth remained modest. The threat of inflation caused the government to turn again in 1957 to fiscal control—raising the bank rate to 7 percent, increasing sales taxes, reducing food subsidies, and restricting installment buying. The economy accordingly improved; in 1959 industrial production was up 13 percent from 1954, and exports doubled in volume from 1938. By 1960 the rate of growth was about 3 percent annually. The advances in the 1950s came not in the nationalized industries, which under public ownership were only a little more prosperous than under private, but rather in new industries—especially automobiles and aircraft, but also in chemicals, scientific instruments, and electrical equipment. During the decade real wages rose 40 percent, and the average family owned an automobile, a refrigerator, and a television set. In 1959 the Conservatives again scored at the polls, achieving a majority in the Commons of 100.

In the 1950s Britain was faced with foreign policy decisions even more momentous than before. Its greatest task was the liquidation of the empire, which was accomplished peacefully. Most of the newly independent states—including The Sudan, Somalia, the Federation of Malaya (Malaysia), and Malta—chose to remain in the Commonwealth. In Rhodesia (Zimbabwe), however, the movement for independence was marred by intransigence over the status of the vast African majority; and this same issue of white supremacy, along with national consciousness, caused South Africa to proclaim itself a republic and to sever ties with the Commonwealth.

World War II had once more made it clear that Britain was not a part of Europe, but interests of national security persuaded the country to abandon its traditional policy of temporary international agreements for immediate ends and to associate in permanent military union with those who shared its dangers. In Europe, NATO, with the admission of West Germany in 1955, became the Western European Union, and in 1954 Britain, concerned with security in the southwest Pacific, associated itself with SEATO (Southeast Asia Treaty Organization).

Foreign policy in the 1950s

British policy, successful in treaty negotiations, was a failure in Egypt, where Britain was slow in realizing that it did not have sufficient power to implement policy in its own interests. Prime Minister Eden's plan, through a 1954 Anglo-Egyptian treaty, was to create close military cooperation with Egypt by evacuating British troops in stages. In 1956 Britain and the United States hoped that loans for the construction of the Aswān High Dam would counter Communist-bloc influence with the Egyptian leader, Gamal Abdel Nasser, but Nasser's recognition of the People's Republic of China and his encouragement of a Soviet proposal to finance the dam caused the United States and Britain to withdraw their offers. Nasser replied by nationalizing the Suez Canal in July. An Israeli attack across the Egyptian border brought Anglo-French military intervention. Opinion in the United Nations and throughout the world was so generally hostile to the Anglo-French action that they soon halted operations. This abortive intervention made Nasser an Arab hero and cost Britain what remained of Arab confidence. In the next few years it was evident that the Middle East had ceased to be a British "sphere of influence."

In domestic affairs the early 1960s stood in some contrast to the 1950s. The economy, which had been growing, if somewhat unsteadily, came to a standstill. From 1960 to 1962 three chancellors of the exchequer sought to stimulate the economy by old measures (higher bank rates and higher taxes) and new (a "pay pause," *i.e.*, restraints in wages and salaries, and an "incomes policy"). These measures were neither popular nor successful. While British production lagged behind that of other industrial countries, wages and prices rose. For many the future looked brighter when Britain in October 1961 formally applied for membership in the European Economic Community (EEC, or Common Market). There was, to be sure, opposition in Britain, from agricultural interests and from concern over the Commonwealth, as well as from an important section of the Labour Party. But negotiations were actually ended in January 1963, by Gen. Charles de Gaulle, who declared that geography, economy, and trade made it impossible for Britain to join the Common Market.

In 1963 Hugh Gaitskell, the leader of the Labour Party since 1955, died. His successor was Harold Wilson, another academic, around whom leftists in the party had gathered. After failure with the Common Market the Conservative government turned to the National Economic Development Council and to the National Incomes Commission for guidance in a planned economy that would stimulate production and control inflation. Progress in both directions was limited.

The "Profumo Affair"

Macmillan and the Conservatives also suffered in public esteem in the "Profumo Affair," when John Profumo, war secretary, was involved in an unsavory situation. A judicial inquiry found no breach of security but censured the government for failing to make prompt and adequate investigation. Macmillan suffered acute embarrassment in the Commons (June) but made a good comeback in his contributions to the Nuclear Test-Ban Treaty (July). In October, however, after an illness, he resigned. His exit left the Conservatives divided. On his advice Lord Home, foreign secretary, was chosen by the Queen.

The Peerage Act of July 1963 permitted Home to renounce his peerage, and as Sir Alec Douglas-Home he won a vacant seat in Scotland and took his place in the Commons. Of Cabinet rank only since 1957, he soon demonstrated that he was well able to govern. But in 1964 current events were in any case overshadowed by the prospect of a general election called for by law.

Contemporary affairs. The election, long expected, did not come until October; thus there was a long preelection campaign. Douglas-Home's task was to make himself known, while that of Wilson was to overcome complacency within his party, which expected an easy victory. Labour's popularity was waning, but the feeling of "time for a change" prevailed with enough voters to give Labour a majority of four in the Commons. Wilson formed the first Labour Cabinet since 1951.

Despite its slender majority, it started vigorously with an emergency budget but was considerably embarrassed when the foreign-secretary designate, Patrick Gordon Walker, was defeated in a by-election in January 1965. The death of Sir Winston Churchill, aged 90, in January was a solemn moment for Britain and much of the world.

Labour made a determined effort through the National Board for Prices and Incomes to control inflation and in September 1965 unveiled a master plan for attaining a 25 percent increase in production by 1970. With by-elections favourable to Labour, Wilson, in an effort to enlarge his majority, called for a general election in March 1966. Edward Heath, the leader of the Conservatives since July 1965, declared that his party would "lead England into Europe" and through free enterprise would restore the economy. In a low poll, Labour emerged with a solid majority of 97.

Election of 1966

In the years 1966–69 Labour's economic and financial policy was energetic and often bold—with severe budgets, a six-month freeze on wages in 1966 and restraints thereafter, a 14.3 percent devaluation of sterling in November 1967, a firm tone toward labour unions, and proposals for shifting from the principle of universality in welfare to that of selectivity. But it was a policy that achieved little success and that alienated the trade unions and much of Labour's working-class following.

The 1960s proved to be an important decade in education. The school-leaving age was scheduled to rise to 16 in 1970–71, and the "comprehensive school," offering all types of secondary education, was expanding. Goals set by the Robbins Report (1963)—60 universities by 1973–74 as against 32 in 1963, and 390,000 student places in higher education—were pursued. And, prodded by the Franks Report (1966), Oxford and Cambridge, bulwarks of tradition, were undergoing change.

By the end of the decade the Labour government was not winning high marks for its success in dealing with the economy. On the other hand, Heath had hardly made himself credible as a future prime minister. For him a major problem was Enoch Powell, a former Conservative Cabinet member, who thrust the racial issue into politics in 1968 with a demand for a halt to nonwhite immigration from Commonwealth lands.

By 1969 industrial stability seemed threatened by a series of wildcat strikes, democratic processes were being questioned, and student demonstrations illustrated a general social discontent. Wilson's government was forced to abandon two major measures on its agenda: reform of the House of Lords and reform of trade unions. An unforeseen improvement in the nation's foreign trade and modest gains by Labour in by-elections and in public opinion polls led Wilson to call for a general election in June 1970. With only 72 percent of the electorate voting, the lowest since 1945, the result was an unexpected victory for the Conservatives, with a popular swing to its ranks of 4.6 percent and a majority of 30 in the Commons.

(A.F.H./Ed.)

The new Heath government had to deal with the highest unemployment since 1939 and a series of crippling strikes. Meanwhile, unrest continued in Northern Ireland and violence increased (see below *The history of Ireland: Northern Ireland after 1921*). Prime Minister Heath temporarily balanced his difficulties with dramatic success when Britain formally entered the EEC on January 1, 1973, but the debate over this step was by no means over.

Common Market entrance

Economic problems continued—low growth rate, record trade deficits, the oil crisis, demands for higher wages, rising prices—despite strong measures by the Heath (and later the Wilson) government, which included, in 1973, the declaration of a state of emergency, the imposition of a three-day workweek, and an emergency budget. Lack of confidence in the government was reflected by Conservative Party losses in the local elections of that year, and the Prime Minister called for a general election on February 28, 1974. Labour emerged with a slim majority of five seats in Parliament, and Harold Wilson was again asked to form a government. The state of emergency was ended and the five-day workweek resumed. In December the government announced plans to reduce military manpower and bring overseas forces home and also decided to abandon several new civilian programs. Despite these measures the exchange rate for sterling plummeted, inflation reached 25 percent, and industry was in deep recession. The British voted two to one in favour of remaining in the EEC after Wilson had renegotiated more advantageous terms for British membership, and oil began to flow from the North Sea deposits discovered in the 1960s.

In March 1976 Wilson resigned, and he was succeeded in April by the foreign secretary, James Callaghan. Britain's financial woes continued to worsen; the value of sterling dropped below $1.60 in October. In December the International Monetary Fund (IMF) began a rescue operation that sparked a dramatic economic recovery in 1977 and 1978. The increased production of North Sea oil, which by mid-1977 was supplying half of Britain's requirements, was prominent in the recovery. The Labour government, however, had never enjoyed a strong majority in Parliament and was forced to rely on smaller parties, especially the Liberals, to stay in power. Several by-election defeats in 1977, labour unrest in 1978, strikes and layoffs early in 1979, and defeat of the referenda on devolution in Scotland and Wales (see below) led to a no-confidence vote in the House of Commons on March 28, 1979, the first such defeat of a government since 1924. In the general election held May 3 the Conservative Party won a majority, and Margaret Thatcher became Britain's first woman prime minister.

North Sea petroleum

In her first budget Thatcher embarked on a policy of stringent monetarism, characterized by tight control of the money supply; tax cuts, especially to the wealthy; reliance on free-market forces; and heavy cuts in government services, especially housing and education. By the early 1980s Britain was suffering from record interest rates, numerous business foreclosures, and unemployment exceeding 11 percent. A significant political development was the emergence of the Social Democratic Party (SDP) in 1981.

Drawn from Labour Party members and former members of Parliament—including former Labour Cabinet ministers Roy Jenkins, David Owen, and Shirley Williams, who were disgruntled with Labour's shift to the left—the SDP proclaimed a centrist and pro-European policy that the public appeared eager to support. By the end of the year the SDP had 25 members in Parliament, including Williams, its first elected member. In March 1982 Jenkins won a seat in Glasgow, thus officially becoming the SDP leader.

The nonwhite population of 1,000,000 in 1968 had nearly doubled by the end of the 1970s, and racial tensions exploded. Anger was felt most deeply by the West Indians. There were outbreaks of racial violence in London in 1977 and riots in several cities in 1981. During this period, however, Britons twice joined together in unified adulation of the monarchy and unabashed displays of national pride. During the summer of 1977 the entire nation played host to a Silver Jubilee marking the 25th anniversary of Queen Elizabeth II's accession to the throne. The Queen made hundreds of public appearances and also visited several Commonwealth countries. The festivities were repeated in July 1981 when Charles, prince of Wales, married Lady Diana Spencer in an internationally televised ceremony.

(Ed.)

SCOTLAND AND WALES IN THE 20TH CENTURY

Scotland and Wales, though integral parts of the British community, by virtue of their history, language, and local institutions, still preserve something of their individuality. In Scotland national consciousness has tended to be political rather than cultural. The Scots have long had their own national church, and language has almost ceased to be a national symbol. The universities are not zealous for a cultural revival, and the Edinburgh Festival is international.

On the other hand, Scottish legal and school systems and local institutions have survived into the 20th century. To preserve them as such and to seek particular remedies for particular economic problems have inspired in many a revival of nationalism. Around the turn of the century, the idea of "Home Rule All Round" spread from Ireland to Scotland and to Wales, and for a time something like dominion status seemed possible for Scotland. But after World War I this notion was moribund. Scottish demands for a dignified relation with Westminster led to the establishment of a secretary of state for Scotland, with Cabinet status later, based in Edinburgh. But this was insufficient for the nationalists, who, while seldom favouring outright independence, did seek an autonomous Scottish parliament. They formed the Scottish National Party (SNP) in 1934, which achieved considerable success in local elections. In parliamentary politics, where the established parties dominate, the SNP was victorious only in by-elections in 1945 and 1967. But it kept Westminster aware of the Scottish problem. In 1966 a White Paper outlined long-range plans, and in 1968 the government announced a select committee to consider the possibility of a Scottish assembly. Since Aberdeen was one of the major British ports for reception of petroleum from the North Sea fields (see above), Scotland hoped to derive great economic benefit from the exploitation of these fields; this was reflected in a resurgence of the SNP, which in the elections of October 1974 gained 11 seats in Parliament.

Welsh Radicalism

In Wales, Welsh Radicalism—its great objective, that of the disestablishment of the Church of England, having been achieved—virtually came to an end with World War I. Enthusiastic support for one of their own, David Lloyd George, as prime minister, continued after the war. The idea of a Welsh state revived with the formation in 1925 of the Welsh Nationalist Party, later called Plaid Cymru (Party of Wales). By the 1950s it had some 210 local branches, and in 1966 amid much excitement, in a by-election in Carmarthenshire, returned to Parliament the party president, Gwynfor Evans (in October 1974 three Welsh nationalists gained seats). Indeed, in the 1960s issues of devolution and federation were much discussed. In 1968 a poll indicated that 59 percent favoured some kind of Welsh parliament. These developments did not go unnoticed at Westminster—the minister for Welsh affairs, appointed in 1951, became a secretary of state in 1964, and in 1960 a Welsh grand committee was established in the Commons.

The Welsh have been interested in cultural revival, though, with strong differences between the rural north and the industrial south, this concern has not always been unifying. The University of Wales has stimulated Celtic scholarship. Welsh poets use their native tongue. The annual festival, the Eisteddfod, held alternately in North Wales and South, stimulates interest in Welsh poetry and choral singing. But the use of the Welsh language continues to decline—the census of 1971 revealed that only one-fifth of the population could use it.

By 1980, however, the issue of limited home rule (termed "devolution" by Westminster) in Scotland and Wales appeared to be dead. Referenda that would have given each region an elected assembly with limited powers were defeated in March 1979. In addition, only two of the 11 SNP members of Parliament were returned in the May election.

(Ed.)

XV. The history of Ireland

Ireland, lying to the west of Britain, has always been to some extent cut off by it from direct contact with other European countries, especially the area between Sweden and the Rhine. Approach from France, Spain, and Portugal, and even from Norway and Iceland, has been more possible. Internally, the four ecclesiastical provinces into which Ireland was divided in the 12th century realistically denoted the main natural divisions of the country. Of these, the north had in the earliest times been culturally connected with Scotland, the east with Roman Britain and Wales, the south with Wales and France, and the southwest and west with France and Spain. In later times, despite political changes, these associations tended to continue in greater or lesser degree.

The position of Ireland, geographically peripheral to western Europe, became central and thus potentially more important once Europe's horizons expanded, in the 15th and 16th centuries, to include the New World. Paradoxically, however, it was in the earlier period that Ireland won especial fame as a notable and respected centre of Christianity, scholarship, and the arts. After the Middle Ages, subjugation to Britain stultified, or the struggle for freedom absorbed, much of Ireland's native energy. But its influence was always exercised as much through its emigrants as in its achievements as a nation. During the centuries of British occupation the successors of the great missionaries and scholars who, from the 7th to the 9th century, fostered Christianity and learning among the Germanic peoples of the Continent were those who formed a considerable element in the armies and clergy of Roman Catholic countries and had an incalculable influence on the later development of the United States. In British history innumerable great men of Anglo-Irish origin or nurture have, as statesmen or soldiers, played vital parts; the influence of Ireland itself on Britain has been constant and profound.

Ireland's influence

EARLY IRELAND

The human occupation of Ireland did not begin until a late stage in the prehistory of Europe. It has generally been held that the first arrivals were Mesolithic hunter-fisher people, represented largely by flintwork found mainly in ancient beaches in Antrim, Down, Louth, and Dublin. These artifacts have been named Larnian after the type site at Larne, County Antrim; dates from 6000 BC onward have been assigned to them. More recent work, however, casts considerable doubt on the antiquity and affinities of the people who were responsible for the Larnian industry; association with Neolithic remains suggests that they should be considered not as a Mesolithic people but rather as groups contemporary with the Neolithic farmers. The Larnian could then be interpreted as a specialized aspect of contemporary Neolithic culture. Lake and riverside finds, especially those along the River

Medieval Ireland.
From A. Orme, *Ireland*

Bann, show a comparable tradition. A single radioactive carbon date of 5725 ± 110 BC from Toome Bay, north of Lough Neagh, for woodworking and flint has been cited in support of a Mesolithic phase in Ireland, but such a single date cannot be relied on.

The Irish Neolithic. The general pattern of radioactive-carbon determinations suggests that the Neolithic period in Ireland began about 3000 BC. As in Britain, the most widespread evidence of early farming communities is long-barrow burial. The main Irish long-barrow series consists of Megalithic tombs called court tombs because an oval or semicircular open space, or court, inset into the end of the long barrow, precedes the burial chamber. These court tombs number well over 300. They occupy the northern half of Ireland, and the distribution is bounded on the south by the lowlands of the central plain. The development of the design of the tombs and the great densities west of the River Erne indicate a general spread of tomb builders from centres in Sligo and Mayo, across central Ulster, and beyond to western Scotland and the Isle of Man. Timber-built rectangular houses belonging to the court-tomb builders have been discovered at Ballynagilly, County Tyrone, and at Ballyglass, County Mayo.

Megalithic tombs

The court tombs are intimately related to the British long-barrow series of the Severn-Cotswold and chalk regions and probably derive from more or less common prototypes in northwestern France.

In Ireland a second type of Megalithic long barrow—the so-called portal tomb—developed from the court tomb. There are more than 150 examples. They spread across the court tomb area in the northern half of Ireland and extend into Leinster and Waterford and also to west Wales and Cornwall.

A notable feature of the Irish Neolithic is the passage tomb. This Megalithic tomb, unlike the long-barrow types, is set in a round mound, sited usually on hilltops and grouped in cemeteries. The rich grave goods of these tombs include beads, pendants, and bone pins. Many of the stones of the tombs are elaborately decorated with engraved designs. The main axis of the distribution lies along a series of great cemeteries from the River Boyne to Sligo (Boyne and Loughcrew in County Meath, Carrowkeel and Carrowmore in County Sligo). Smaller groups and single tombs occur largely in the northern half of the country and in Leinster—for example, there is a group on the headlands around Fair Head in Antrim and another on the fringe of the Dublin–Wicklow mountains. A specialized group of later, indeed advanced, Bronze Age date, near Tramore, County Waterford, are quite closely akin to a large group on the Scilly Islands and Cornwall. The great Irish passage tombs include some of the most magnificent Megalithic tombs in all Europe—for example, Newgrange and Knowth. While the passage tombs represent the arrival of the Megalithic tradition in its fullest and most sophisticated form, the exact relation between the builders of these tombs and the more or less contemporary long-barrow builders is not clear. The passage tombs suggest rather more clearly integrated communities than do the long barrows.

From the final stages of the Neolithic, single burials are found in Leinster—for example, at Rath, County Wicklow, and Linkardstown, County Carlow. These, while preserving certain of the Neolithic traditions, seem to represent a new influence that presages the Bronze Age single-burial mode. To this final stage of the Neolithic probably belong the rich house sites of both rectangular and circular form at Lough Gur, County Limerick. The pottery shows a strong connection with the tradition of the long barrow (court tomb and portal tomb).

The Irish Bronze Age. Two great incursions establish the early Bronze Age in Ireland. One, represented by approximately 400 Megalithic tombs of the wedge-tomb variety, is associated with beaker pottery. This group is dominant in the western half of the country. Similar tombs also associated with beaker finds are common in Brittany, and the origin of the Irish series is clearly from this region. In Ireland the distribution indicates that these tomb builders sought well-drained grazing land, such as the Burren limestones in Clare, and also copper deposits, such as those on the Cork-Kerry coast and around the Silvermines area of Tipperary.

In contrast, in the eastern half of the country a people in the single-burial tradition dominate. Their burial modes and distinctive pottery, known as food vessels, have strong roots in the beaker tradition that dominates in many areas of western Europe. They may have reached Ireland via Britain from the lowland areas around the Rhine or farther north.

Throughout the early Bronze Age Ireland had a flourishing metal industry, and bronze, copper, and gold objects were exported widely to Britain and the Continent. In the middle Bronze Age (around 1500 BC) new influences brought urn burial into eastern Ireland.

From about 1200 BC elements of a late Bronze Age appear, and by about 800 BC a great late Bronze Age industry was established. A very considerable wealth of bronze and gold is present, an example of which is the great Clare gold hoard. Nordic connections have been noted in much of this metalwork. Unfortunately, as a result of the paucity of habitation and burial sites, many aspects of the culture of these fine metalworkers remain obscure.

The Irish Iron Age. The period of the transition from the Bronze Age to the Iron Age in Ireland is fraught with uncertainties. There is little sign of a continental-like Hallstatt Iron Age in Ireland. La Tène, which may date in Ireland from 300 BC or earlier, is represented in metalwork and some stone sculpture, mainly in the northern half of the country. Connections with northern England are apparent. Hillfort building seems also characteristic of the Iron Age. The problem of identifying archaeological remains with language grouping is notoriously difficult, but it seems on the whole likely that the principal Celtic arrivals occurred during the Iron Age. Irish sagas, which probably reflect the pagan Irish Iron Age, reflect conditions in many respects similar to the descriptions of the ancient classical authors, such as Poseidonius and Julius Caesar.

Early Celtic Ireland. *Political and social organization.* Politically, Ireland was organized into a number of petty kingdoms or *tuatha*, each of which was quite independent under its elected king. Groups of *tuatha* tended to combine, but the king who claimed overlordship in each group had a primacy of honour rather than of jurisdiction. Not until the 10th century AD was there a king of all Ireland (*árd rí Éireann*). A division of the country into five groups of *tuatha*, known as the Five Fifths (Cuíg Cuígí), occurred about the beginning of the Christian era. These were Ulster (Ulaid), Meath (Midhe), Leinster (Laigin), Munster (Muma), and Connaught (Connacht).

The Five Fifths

Surrounding a king was an aristocracy (*airi aicme*, the upper class), whose land and property rights were clearly defined by law and whose main wealth was in cattle. Greater landowners were supported by *céilí*, clients. These and other grades of society, minutely classified and described by legal writers, tilled the soil and tended the cattle. Individual families were the real units of society and exercised collectively powers of ownership over their farms and territory. At law the family (*fine*) did not merely act corporatively but was, by one of the oldest customs, held responsible for the observance of the law by its kindred, serfs, and slaves.

Rural economy and living conditions. There were no urban centres, and the economic basis of society was cattle rearing and agriculture. The principal crops were wheat, barley, oats, flax, and hay. The land was tilled with plows drawn by oxen. Sheep appear to have been bred principally for their wool, and the only animal reared specifically for slaughter was the pig. Fishing, hunting, fowling, and trapping provided further food. Transport of goods by land was by packhorse, for wheeled vehicles appear to have been few. Sea transport was by currach, a wicker-framed boat covered with hides; the normal freshwater craft was the dugout.

The dwellings of the time were built on the post-and-wattle technique, and some, at least, were situated within the protected sites called by archaeologists ring forts. Excavations have shown that some of these may have existed even in the Bronze Age and that they remained a normal place of habitation down to medieval times. Advantage was also taken of the relative security of islands in rivers or lakes as dwelling places; and artificial islands, called crannogs, were also extensively made.

The Irish laws point to a large development of rural industry in the period in which they were first written down, shortly before the Norse invasions beginning at the end of the 8th century. They deal minutely not only with the management of land and animal rearing but with innumerable further details of husbandry, including milling, dyeing, dairying, malting, meat curing, and spinning and weaving. Wool was spun with a wooden spindle weighted with a whorl of bone or stone; and it was woven on a loom. The outer garment worn by both men and women was a large woollen cloak (*brat*), fastened on shoulder or breast with a pin or brooch. The inner garment was a long linen tunic (*léine*), girded at the waist with a belt. Shoes of rawhide or tanned leather were worn, at least by the upper classes and the higher professional ranks. A large amount of metalwork reveals the adaptation by Irish craftsmen of many techniques originating in Britain or on the continent. An instinct for design, added to the skillful use of these techniques, enabled them to produce many superb objects, of which the Tara brooch, dating from about the mid-8th century, is an outstanding example. The chief musical instrument of the period was the harp.

Early political history. The documentary history of Ireland really begins only in the 7th century, which saw the production both in Latin and Irish of sufficiently rich and numerous records of all sorts. For events before that time historians have to rely on literary sources such as the sagas, many of whose characters may represent only poetic imagination and in which the social or political circumstances portrayed reflect the fantasies of their authors rather than historical reality. Nevertheless, the traditions seem to indicate, during the early centuries of the Christian era, a process of political cohesion in Ireland through which the *tuatha* ultimately became grouped into the Five Fifths. Among these, Ulster seems at first to have been dominant; but by the time of Niall of the Nine Hostages (died early 5th century), hegemony had passed to his midland kingdom of Meath, which was then temporarily associated with Connaught. In the 6th century, descendants of Niall, ruling at Tara in northern Leinster, were claiming to be overkings of three provinces, Ulster, Connaught, and Meath. Later, they claimed to be kings of all Ireland, although their power rarely extended over Munster or the greater part of Leinster. Two branches of Niall's descendants, the Cenél nEogain, of the northern Uí Néill, and the Clan Cholmáin, of the southern Uí Néill, alternated as kings of Ireland from 734 to 1002, a fact that suggests a formal arrangement between the two septs. Inevitably, claims to a high kingship came to be contested by the rulers of Munster, who, from their capital at Cashel, had gradually increased their strength, depriving Connaught of the region that later became County Clare. But not until the reign of Brian Boru in the 11th century was Munster sufficiently strong to secure a real high kingship over all Ireland.

The Irish kingship

Irish raids and migrations. From about the middle of the 3rd century Latin writings make frequent reference to raiding expeditions carried out by the Irish, who were now given the new name, Scotti, rather than the older one, Hiberni. Native Irish traditions also suggest that such attacks took place. In the second half of the 4th century, when Roman power in Britain was beginning to crumble seriously, the raids became incessant, and settlements were made along the west coast of Britain and extensively in Wales and Scotland. From the early 5th century the rulers of Dalriada in northern Antrim extended their power over the Irish already settled in Argyll and the neighbouring islands. Ultimately the Scottish kingdom of Dalriada became separated from the Irish; and when, in the 9th century, it overcame the Picts, it gave its name, Scotland, to the whole area.

Early Christianity. *Conversion.* Little is known of the first impact of Christianity upon Ireland. Traditions in the south and southeast refer to early saints who allegedly preceded St. Patrick, and their missions may well have come through trading relations with the Roman Empire. The earliest firm date is AD 431, when St. Germanus, bishop of Auxerre in Gaul, proposed, with the approval of Pope Celestine I, to send a certain Palladius to "the Scots believing in Christ." Subsequent missionary history in Ireland is dominated by the figure of St. Patrick, whose 7th-century biographers, Tirechán and Muirchú, credited him with converting all the Irish to Christianity, and won for him the status of national apostle.

A 9th-century record, the *Book of Armagh*, includes a work by Patrick himself, the *Confessio* ("Confession," a reply to charges made by British ecclesiastics), in which he describes his life at a Roman villa in Britain, his capture by Irish raiders, and his seven years of slavery in Ireland. Recovering his freedom, he was educated and ordained to the priesthood and eventually managed to be sent as a missionary to Ireland. He concentrated on the north and west of the country, achieving remarkable success; he did not himself claim to have converted all Ireland. Confusion exists regarding the chronology of Patrick's life, and it is seriously contended that tradition came to merge the experience of two men, the continental Palladius and the Patrick of the *Confessio*. No sufficient evidence supports the traditional date (AD 432) for the beginning of Patrick's mission, while of the rival dates (AD 461/462 and AD 492/493) given for his death in annals and biographies, the latter is now preferred.

St. Patrick

Irish monasticism. Though monks and monasteries were to be found in Ireland at the time of Patrick, their place was then altogether secondary. But in the course of the 6th and 7th centuries a comprehensive monastic system developed in Ireland, partly through the influence of Celtic monasteries in Britain, such as Candida Casa at

Whithorn in Galloway and Llangarvan in Wales. Early attempts to organize the Irish Church on the usual Roman system—by which each bishop and his clergy exercised exclusive jurisdiction within a diocese—seem to have given way to one in which groups of Christian settlements were loosely linked together, usually under the auspices of some one or other of the great saints. Careful study of the lives of the early saints reveals the manner in which their reputations developed in proportion to the power of the political dynasties that became connected with them.

By the end of the 6th century, enthusiasm for Christianity was leading Irishmen to devote themselves to a most austere existence as monks, as hermits, and as missionaries to pagan tribes of Scotland, in the north of England, and in a great area of west central Europe, particularly between the Rivers Rhine, Loire, and Rhône. St. Columba's foundation (*c.* 563) of the monastery of Iona off the northwest Scottish coast provided the best known base for the Celtic Christianization of Scotland; and its offshoot, Lindisfarne, lying off the coast of the Anglo-Saxon kingdom of Northumbria, was responsible for the conversion of that area. Of the continental missionaries, the best known is St. Columban (died 615), whose monastic foundations at Luxeuil near Annegray in the Vosges and at Bobbio in northern Italy became important centres of learning. Columban, however, by his individualism and austere puritanism, came into conflict not only with the Merovingian rulers of Gaul but also with the local ecclesiastical administration; his limitations exemplify those of the Irish monastic system as a whole and explain why, in the end, it was supplanted by the ordinary administrative system of the Church.

Learning and art. Both at home and abroad the saints were succeeded by scholars, whose work in sacred and classical studies and particularly in elaborating an Irish Christian mythology and literature was to have profound effects upon the Irish language and was to be a major factor in its survival. The Irish monasteries became notable centres of learning; in Ireland itself those of Clonmacnoise (in County Offaly) and Clonard (in County Meath) were among the most famous. Christianity had brought to Ireland the Latin tongue and command of the Latin authors; not only Church Fathers but classical writers were read and studied. Irish scribes produced manuscripts written in the clear hand known as Insular; this usage spread from Ireland to Anglo-Saxon England and to the continental Irish monasteries. Initial letters in the manuscripts were illuminated, usually with very intricate ribbon and zoomorphic designs. The most famous of the Irish manuscripts is the *Book of Kells,* a copy of the Four Gospels dating from about the 8th or 9th century. The earliest surviving illuminated manuscript, the *Book of Durrow*, was probably made about a century earlier.

Illuminated manuscripts

The adoption of Christianity made it necessary to relate the chronology of Irish tradition, history, and genealogies to the events recorded in the Bible. The *Book of Invasions* (*Leabhar Gabhála*), in which Irish history was linked with events in the Old Testament, was a notable example of this process. In this way Latin civilization in Ireland became linked to the Gaelic; and the association became closer under the impact of the Viking wars. Gradually the Latin products of the Christian schools became replaced by Irish works; Latin lives of the saints, for example, are almost always earlier in date than those written in Irish. Recurring bouts of puritanism and reforming movements in the church tended to remove secular literature from monastic control; ultimately, a class of professional families developed, who were its custodians from the 12th to the 17th centuries. The medieval secular writers, employing a degenerate form of Old Irish usually known as Middle Irish, were responsible for a large proportion of Irish literary achievement; their historical works, the annals, and the great genealogies, supplemented by the law collections, have enabled historians to reconstruct early Irish social history.

The Norse invasions and their aftermath. The first appearance of the Norsemen on the Irish coast is recorded in 795. Thereafter the Norsemen made frequent plundering raids, sometimes far inland. They seized and fortified two ports, Annagassan and Dublin, in 838; and the 840s saw a series of large-scale invasions in the north of the country. These invaders were driven out by Aed Finnliath, high king from 862 to 879, but meanwhile the Norse rulers of Dublin were reaching the zenith of their power. They took Waterford in 914 and Limerick in 920. Gradually, without quite abandoning piracy, the Vikings became traders in close association with the Irish and their commercial towns became a new element in the life of the country. The decline of Norse power in the south began when they lost Limerick in 968 and was finally effected when the Scandinavian allies of the king of Dublin were defeated by High King Brian Boru at the Battle of Clontarf in 1014.

Though the Battle of Clontarf removed the prospect of Norse domination, it brought a period of political unsettlement. High kings ruled in Ireland but almost always "with opposition," meaning that they were not acknowledged by a minority of provincial kings. The Viking invasions had, in fact, shown the strength and the weakness of the Irish position. The fact that power had been preserved at a local level in Ireland enabled a maximum of resistance to be made; and although the invaders established maritime strongholds, they never achieved any domination comparable to their control of eastern England or northwest France. After Clontarf they remained largely in control of Ireland's commerce but came increasingly under the influence of neighbouring Irish kings.

In the 11th and 12th centuries the ecclesiastical reform movement of western Europe was extended into Ireland. And as the kings of Munster and Connaught, Leinster and Ulster struggled each to secure the dominant position that had once been held by Brian Boru, they came to realize the value to them of alliance with the forces of church reform. Thus, with the aid of provincial rulers, the reformers were able to set up in Ireland a system of dioceses, whose boundaries were coterminous with those of the chief petty kingdoms. At the head of this hierarchy was established the archbishopric of Armagh, in association with the province of Ulster dominated by the royal family of Uí Néill. But the victory of the reformers was not complete, for the parochial system was not introduced until after the Anglo-Norman Conquest. Moreover, the reformers sought to influence Irish conduct as well as church organization. The enormities of Irish moral behaviour were colourfully described by St. Bernard of Clairvaux in his life of his contemporary St. Malachy, the reforming bishop who introduced the Cistercian monks into Ireland. The reforming popes Adrian IV and Alexander III encouraged Henry II's invasion of Ireland, believing that it would further church reform in that country. In a remarkable account of the conquest, Gerald of Wales provided a lurid description of the archaic Irish civilization that the invaders encountered. The recognition of Henry II as lord of Ireland and the linking of the church to a foreign administration terminated the independence of Gaelic Ireland and reduced the country to a position of subordination for centuries to come.

Church reform

FIRST CENTURIES OF ENGLISH RULE (C. 1166–C. 1600)

The Anglo-Norman invasion. Before the arrival of Henry II in Ireland (October 1171), Anglo-Norman adventurers, including Richard de Clare, earl of Pembroke, subsequently known as "Strongbow," invited by Dermot MacMurrough, a king of Leinster who had been expelled by the high king, Rory O'Connor (Roderic), had conquered a substantial part of eastern Ireland, including the kingdom of Leinster, the towns of Waterford, Wexford, and Dublin, and part of the kingdom of Meath. Partly to avert any chance of Ireland's becoming a rival Norman state, Henry took action to impose his rule there. He granted Leinster to de Clare and Meath to Hugh de Lacy, who had gone to Ireland in the King's army; but he kept the chief towns in his own hands, exacted forms of submission from the Irish kings, and secured from a church synod recognition of his overlordship. During subsequent years the Anglo-Norman sphere in Ireland was extended; and while all the Irish kings, except in the northwest, agreed to recognize his supremacy, Henry was obliged to acquiesce in the establishment of new Norman lordships in Ulster under John de Courci and in Munster under de Cogan, de Braose, and others. By the Treaty of Windsor (1175), O'Connor, the high king, accepted Henry as his overlord and restricted his own style to that of king of Connaught. But he was permitted to exercise some vague authority over the other Irish kings and was charged with collecting from them tribute to be paid to Henry. This arrangement was unsuccessful, for thereafter O'Connor encountered opposition even in his own province, and he was ultimately obliged to abdicate.

King John, who visited Ireland in 1210, established there a civil government independent of the feudal lords, and during the 13th century it became more fully organized. An Irish exchequer had been set up in 1200, and a chancery followed in 1232. The country was divided into counties for administrative purposes, English law was introduced, and serious attempts were made to reduce the feudal liberties of the Anglo-Norman baronage. Parliament started in Ireland, as in England; in 1297 the peers and prelates were joined by representatives of counties, and in 1300 the towns also sent members. But these represented the Anglo-Irish only; the native Irish, to some extent resurgent in Ulster under the O'Neills and O'Donnells, and in southwest Munster under the MacCarthys, were aloof and unrepresented.

The medieval Irish Parliament

The 14th and 15th centuries. A brief threat to English control of Ireland, made by Edward Bruce, brother of King Robert I of Scotland, ended when Bruce was killed in battle at Faughart near Dundalk (1318). English control was reasserted and strengthened by the creation of three new Anglo-Irish earldoms, that of Kildare, given to the head of the Leinster Fitzgeralds; that of Desmond, given to the head of the Munster Fitzgeralds; and that of Ormonde, given to the head of the Butlers, who held lands around Tipperary. But the increased power and lands of the Anglo-Irish brought an inevitable reaction; and the remainder of the 14th century saw a remarkable revival of Irish political power, matched by a flowering of Irish language, law, and civilization. The Gaels recovered large parts of Ulster, the midlands, Connaught, and Leinster, while the Anglo-Irish became increasingly Irish, marrying Irish wives and often adopting Gaelic customs.

The English government, which in any case, because of its aim to curtail feudal privileges, was always to some extent opposed by the Anglo-Norman aristocracy, made an effort to restore control but achieved little more than a definition of the status quo. Edward III's son, Lionel, duke of Clarence, as viceroy from 1361 to 1367, passed in the Irish Parliament the Statutes of Kilkenny (1366), which listed the "obedient" (English-controlled) lands as Louth, Meath, Trim, Dublin, Carlow, Kildare, Kilkenny, Wexford, Waterford, and Tipperary. Intermarriage or alliances with the Irish were forbidden. Although the king's sovereignty over the whole country was not renounced, the independent Irish outside the Pale (the area of English control) were regarded as enemies and were assumed to possess their lands only by usurpation. In practice they were feared, and their attacks were often bought off by almost regular payments. Visits by King Richard II in 1394–95 and 1399 achieved nothing. During the first half of the 15th century Ireland was, in effect, ruled by the three great earls, of Desmond, Ormonde, and Kildare, who combined to dominate the Dublin government. Desmond had sway in Counties Limerick, Cork, Kerry, and Waterford; Ormonde in Tipperary and Kilkenny; and Kildare in Leinster. Although both the Gaels and the Anglo-Irish had supported the Yorkist side in the Wars of the Roses, the Yorkist king Edward IV found them no less easy to subjugate than had his Lancastrian predecessors. Succeeding (1468) in bringing about the attainder and execution for treason of Thomas, earl of Desmond, he was, nevertheless, obliged to yield to aristocratic power in Ireland. The earls of Kildare, who thereafter bore the title of lord deputy (for the English princes who were lords lieutenant), were, in effect, the actual rulers of Ireland until well into the 16th century.

The Kildare ascendancy. The substitution (1485) of Tudor for Yorkist rule in England had no apparent effect in Ireland, where the ascendancy of the Fitzgerald earls of Kildare, established when Thomas, 7th earl, was created lord deputy in 1471, had passed (1477) to his son Garret More (Great Gerald). The fiction of the king's power was preserved by appointing an absentee lieutenant, from whom Kildare held as deputy; in practice, any real power was exercised largely through dynastic alliances with the chief Gaelic and Anglo-Irish lords. Opposition to Kildare was negligible so long as the king was unable to maintain a permanent power to which his opponents might turn; an attempt to displace him was made when Kildare gave support (1487) to Lambert Simnel, a pretender to the English throne. After the advent of a more dangerous pretender, Perkin Warbeck, it was decided (1494) to remove Kildare and rule through an Englishman, Sir Edward Poynings. Poynings subdued Kildare, but he could not reconquer the northern Gaelic Irish. At Drogheda (1494–95) he induced a Parliament to pass an act that came to be known as "Poynings' Law"; it subjected the meetings and legislative drafts of the Irish Parliament to the control of the English king and council. But his administrative expenses were too great, and Henry VII decided in 1496 to restore Kildare.

Sir Edward Poynings

On Kildare's death (1513), the deputyship passed to his son Garret Oge (Young Gerald), 9th earl of Kildare, who continued, though less impressively, to dominate the country. But James, 10th earl of Desmond, intrigued with the emperor Charles V; and Henry VIII became convinced that Kildare had lost the power to keep Ireland neutral. Therefore, when the divorce (1533) of Catherine of Aragon made the danger of imperial intervention particularly acute, the King summoned Kildare to England (1534). There were, thereafter, no Irish-born viceroys for more than a century.

The Reformation period. Rumours that Kildare had been executed precipitated the rebellion of Kildare's son, Lord Thomas Fitzgerald, called Silken Thomas. The rebellion facilitated the transition to the new system. Silken Thomas had opposed Henry VIII's breach with Rome; his execution (1537) caused a revival of the power of the Butlers of Ormonde; Piers Butler, earl of Ossory, helped to secure the enactment of the royal (instead of papal) ecclesiastical supremacy by the Dublin Parliament of 1536–37. As a further step in getting rid of the Pope, in 1541 a complaisant Parliament recognized Henry VIII as king of Ireland (his predecessors had held the title of lord of Ireland). Confiscation of monastic property, as well as the lands of the rebels, met most of the costs of the expanded administration. This loss of land inevitably drove the religious orders and the Anglo-Irish into the arms of the Gaelic Irish, thus weakening the old racial rivalries of medieval Ireland.

Sir Anthony St. Leger, lord deputy in 1540–48 and again in 1550–56, then began a conciliatory policy by which outstanding lords were persuaded, in order to gain new titles and grants of lands, to renounce the Pope and recognize the King's ecclesiastical supremacy. This policy, however, required a steady series of efficient governors and disciplined administrators; in fact, neither in Tudor nor in Stuart times did the English succeed in converting elective chiefs into hereditary nobles holding offices delegated by the crown. Moreover, even those who had recently submitted were often condemned for religious conservatism and deprived of their lands. St. Leger's personal success was all the more remarkable because the first Jesuit mission to Ireland arrived in the north in 1542.

Under Edward VI (1547–53), the Dublin authorities carried out a forward policy in religion as well as in politics, but Protestantism got no support except from English officials. The official restoration of Catholicism under Queen Mary (1553–58) revealed the strength of resentment in Ireland against Protestantism. As in England, the papal jurisdiction was restored, but otherwise the Tudor regulations of authority were observed. The Pope was induced to recognize the conversion of the Tudor Irish lordship into a kingdom. Finally, Mary gave statutory approval for the plantation of Leix, Offaly, and other Irish lordships of the central plain. Her viceroy was Thomas Radcliffe, earl of Sussex, lord deputy (1556–59), who was soon, as lord lieutenant (1559–66) for Elizabeth I, to restore the state's authority over the church.

Ireland under Elizabeth I. The Acts of Supremacy and Uniformity, enforcing the Anglican Church settlement, were passed in Ireland in 1560, but fear of driving the inhabitants of the Pale into alliance with the Gaelic Irish and perhaps with the Spanish made the government lenient in enforcing the terms of the Acts. Political affairs continued to preoccupy the administrators, so that the new Protestant church was unequipped to resist the forces of the Counter-Reformation. This was inevitable in an Ireland only superficially conformed to royal obedience; but the seriousness of the situation was shown by the three great rebellions of the reign, those of Shane O'Neill (1559), of the Fitzgeralds of Desmond (1568–83), and of O'Neill (Tyrone) and O'Donnell (1594–1603).

The rebellion of Shane O'Neill

The first of these rebellions, that of Shane O'Neill, fully exposed the weakness and later the folly of the government. O'Neill's father, Con Bacach (the Lame), who as the "O'Neill" was head of a whole network of clans, had been made earl of Tyrone in 1541, the succession rights of his illegitimate son Feardorchadh (Matthew) being recognized. Shane, younger but the eldest legitimate son, was, nevertheless, elected O'Neill on his father's death (1559), and soon afterward Feardorchadh was killed. O'Neill then took the field against the Dublin government, demanding recognition according to the laws of primogeniture, and he insisted that neither of Feardorchadh's sons, Brian and Hugh, had claims to the earldom. Elizabeth invited O'Neill to London to negotiate, but the opportunity for a statesmanlike settlement was lost. O'Neill was to be "captain of Tyrone" and was encouraged to expel from Antrim the MacDonnell (MacDonald or MacConnell) migrants from Scotland. Returning to Ireland in May 1562, O'Neill routed the MacDonnells as well as the loyal O'Donnells of the northwest, and attempted to secure support from Scotland and France. Eventually the government was saved from a serious situation only through the defeat of O'Neill by the O'Donnells and his murder in 1567 by the MacDonnells.

The lands of the O'Neills and even of loyal Gaelic lords were declared forfeit in 1569, and in a wave of enthusiasm for colonization, various questionable adventurers were permitted to attempt substantial plantations in Munster, Leinster, and Ulster. The folly of this policy was seen when the government, despite its having declared the position of "O'Neill" extinguished, yet allowed the O'Neills to elect Shane's cousin, Turloch Luineach, as their chief. Butlers and Munster Fitzgeralds also combined forcibly to resist the plantations. The only gleam of statesmanship shown in these years by Henry Sidney, lord deputy (1565–71, 1575–78), was that he managed to avoid a major combination against the government's religious policy. The Butlers were induced to submit, the planters were given only limited support, and a head-on collision with Turloch Luineach was averted. When the Ulster plantation plans could not be carried out against Irish resistance, the Queen wisely decided they should be dropped. The pardon of the Butlers pacified Leinster, and although in Munster the earl of Desmond's cousin James Fitzgerald, called "Fitzmaurice," attempted to make the war one of religion, he too was eventually pardoned.

The Desmond wars

Despite his pardon, Fitzmaurice in 1575 fled to the Continent, returning to Ireland in 1579 with papal approval for a Catholic crusade against Queen Elizabeth. Although neither France nor Spain supported it, and Fitzmaurice was surprised and killed in August 1579, the government was extremely apprehensive. Gerald Fitzgerald, 14th earl of Desmond, then assumed direction of the enterprise. As a military commander he was wholly deficient, and his mediocrity may well have kept outstanding figures in the north and west out of the movement. The rebels were defeated, and in November 1580 a force of Italians and Spaniards was massacred at Dún an Óir ("Golden Fort"), Smerwick Harbour, County Kerry.

The end of the Desmond rebellion gave the government the opportunity to confiscate more than 300,000 acres (100,000 hectares) in Munster and initiate more stringent proceedings against Catholics. But the plantation was not a success. A more statesmanlike attitude was displayed in regard to Connaught land titles. When Sir John Perrot was lord deputy (1584–88), a number of agreements were made with individual landowners and chieftains, by which their titles were officially recognized in return for fixed regular payments. This was a step in the process of converting a great part of the country to English tenures. Perrot was less successful in handling the 1585–86 Parliament, in which the government's anti-Catholic program was defeated by the opposition.

The Tyrone war

The origins of the third rebellion, the O'Neill (Tyrone) war, remain in doubt. Both Hugh Roe O'Donnell and Hugh, younger son of Feardorchadh O'Neill, for whom the earldom of Tyrone had been revived in 1585 and who had had himself elected O'Neill on Turloch Luineach's death in 1595, certainly resented the extension of the royal administration, but the religious issue was probably more important. For a generation exiled Catholics had been trained as missionaries in the continental colleges of the Counter-Reformation, and the majority of those who returned to Ireland concluded that Catholicism could only survive there if Elizabeth were defeated. The outbreak of hostilities in Ulster in 1594 was at first confined to the northwest, where O'Donnell and Maguire, lord of Fermanagh, tried to drive out the English troops. The intervention of Hugh O'Neill was expected, if not inevitable. His participation with his brother-in-law O'Donnell proved decisive in the north and west, and the English were defeated both in Ulster and in Connaught. A more intimidating combination thus threatened Dublin than even in Shane O'Neill's time. Even in the Pale, arbitrary exactions and exclusion from offices won Hugh much sympathy, and it was said that he knew of Dublin Castle decisions before they were known in the city. Resentful of O'Neill's alleged ingratitude, Elizabeth became impatient of negotiations with him and finally sent Robert Devereux, earl of Essex, to Ireland (1599) to subdue him. But Essex lost his reputation by his inglorious progress through the country and by the speed with which he returned to England after a private conversation with O'Neill. Before Charles Blount, Lord Mountjoy, arrived (1600) to replace Essex, the Irish leaders had gained the qualified support of Pope Clement VIII and of King Philip III of Spain. But Philip could afford to send only a minimal force to aid the Irish rebels. Its leader Juan del Aguila occupied Kinsale and was besieged (1601) by Mountjoy. O'Neill marched south to relieve Aguila, but a rash attempt to surprise the English lines by night proved disastrous (December 24, 1601); the Irish were defeated and the Spaniards surrounded. O'Neill held out in Ulster for over a year but finally submitted a few days after the Queen's death (March 1603).

Viewed generally, Elizabeth's Irish policy had the distinction of having reduced the country to obedience for the first time since the invasion of Henry II. But the cost was a serious one. The loyalty of the Irish was perennially strained over the religious issue, so that further rebellion was almost inevitable and virtually predictable in 1640 when the English government was embarrassed by the Second Bishops' War with Scotland. Economically, the towns and the countryside were needlessly exploited by the new administrators and planters, while the Queen's expenditure was substantially increased. Commitments in Ireland were at least partly responsible for the poverty of the crown, which was to become a serious factor in precipitating its 17th-century conflict with Parliament.

MODERN IRELAND

The 17th century. *James I (1603–25).* James VI of Scotland, who also became King James I of England and Ireland in 1603, might have pursued an Irish policy more enlightened than that of Elizabeth, who had been committed to war against the papacy and against Spain. He did make peace with Spain, but his policy of guarded religious toleration was nullified by the intransigence of

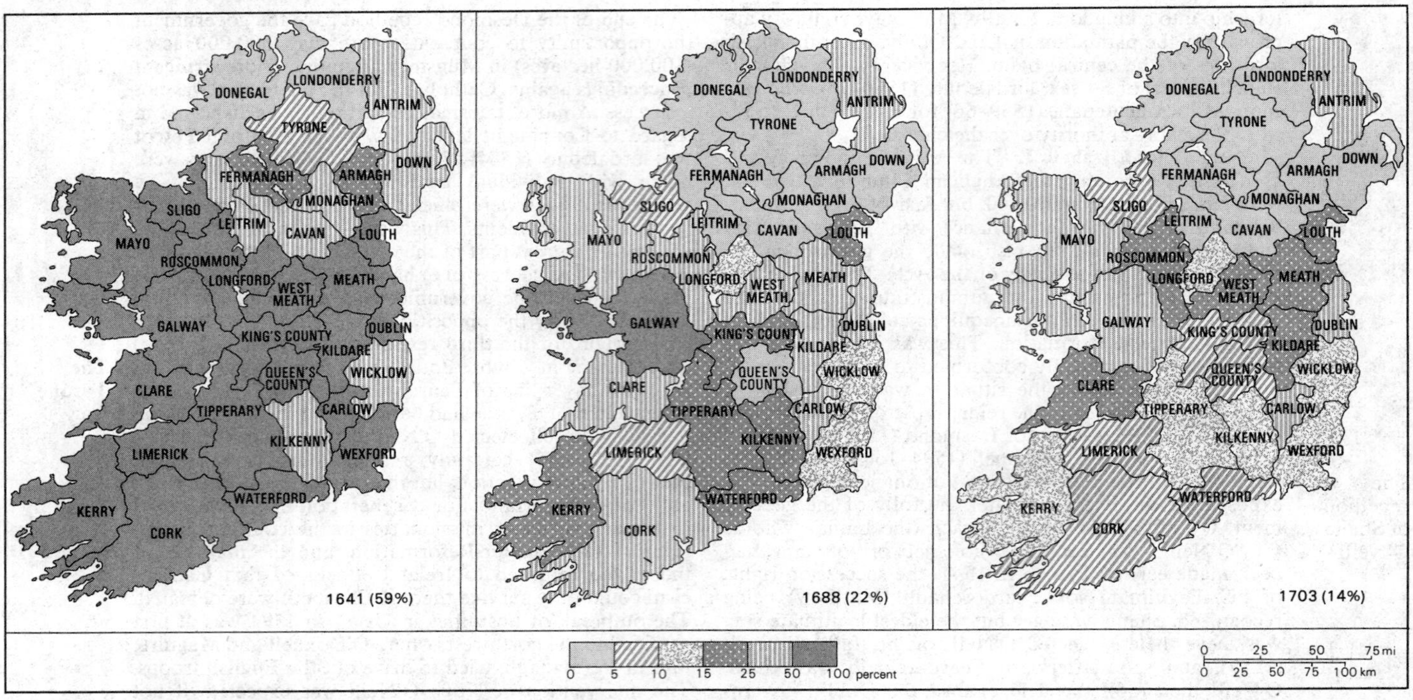

The percentage of land, by county, owned by Roman Catholics in 1641, 1688, and 1703.
The average percentage for all of Ireland is indicated after the year identifying each map.
From A. Orme, *Ireland*

the established Anglican Church and of the papacy. Unfortunately, James allowed Irish policy to be dominated by the interests of the English governing class and also sought to provide in Ireland opportunities for his countrymen. He thereby virtually continued Elizabethan policy, and as a result the steady exodus of Irish soldiers and churchmen to Catholic countries on the continent was unabated. On a short-term basis, their absence contributed to peace; but their influence abroad made the Irish question an international one. In Ireland, the overwhelming majority of the Gaelic Irish and of the old Anglo-Irish remained detached from government in attitude as well as in way of life.

As soon as James's policy became clear, the earls of Tyrone and of Tyrconnel and other Ulster Gaelic lords joined the flight from Ireland. Their departure opened the way for the plantation of Ulster by a new landowning class, which included Scots as well as Englishmen. This proved the most successful British settlement made in Ireland, mainly because British tenantry and labourers were introduced as well as landlords. The newcomers were mainly from the Scottish Lowlands, and at first the English feared them almost more than they feared the Irish. In an attempt to counter their influence, the city of London was involved in the Ulster plantation, its name being combined with that of the historic ecclesiastical settlement of Derry to provide the name of a plantation. The Presbyterianism of the Scottish immigrants was successfully kept at bay until the time of the English Civil War; the Anglican bishoprics in Ireland were well endowed and powerful, and it was not until 1643 that the first presbytery was established in Belfast.

Plantation in Ulster

In the Parliament of 1613–15, summoned to ratify the Ulster plantation, a small Protestant majority was achieved because many new boroughs had been created in the newly planted areas. But government was concerned more with the appearance than the reality of consent, and no Parliament was called again until 1633. In the last years of James's reign, pressure from his Spanish and French allies caused him to concede toleration to the Catholics; and from 1618 a Catholic hierarchy was in residence in Ireland.

Charles I (1625–49) and the Commonwealth (1649–60). Charles I conceived the idea of raising armies and money in Ireland, in return for religious concessions known as "the graces" by which Catholics were allowed to engage in various public activities. But this policy was abandoned by Thomas Wentworth, later earl of Strafford, lord deputy from 1633 to 1640. He set himself to break the power of the great and of trade monopolists, both Irish and English, including the London city companies. He induced the Catholic members of the Irish House of Commons to join in voting large subsidies in the hope of obtaining further concessions but then abolished most of the existing "graces." He thus seriously weakened the loyalty to the crown of the old landowning classes; and later all his enemies in Ireland joined with those in England in bringing about his execution (1641). His Irish Army was disbanded, and control of the Irish government passed to Puritan lords justices.

A general rising of the Irish in Ulster was almost inevitable. It took place in October 1641, and thousands of colonists were murdered or fled. A Catholic confederacy was formed at Kilkenny in 1642, but it did not succeed in welding together the various groups of which it was composed. During the period of the English Civil War there were Irish confederate armies in Ulster and in Leinster; English parlimentary armies operated in the north and south; and Dublin was held by James, duke of Ormonde, commanding an army of Protestant royalists. Negotiations for peace between Ormonde and the confederates were difficult and protracted; and in 1646, when it was clear that Charles I's cause was lost, Ormonde surrendered Dublin to a parliamentary commander. The confederates in isolation could offer little resistance (1649–50) to Oliver Cromwell. By 1652 all Irish resistance was over.

Ireland during the English Civil War and its aftermath

During the Commonwealth and Protectorate, authority in Ireland was exercised by parliamentary commissioners and chief governors. A union of the three kingdoms of England, Scotland, and Ireland, effected in 1653, resulted in Irish representatives attending Parliaments held in London in 1654, 1656, and 1659. By an Act of Settlement, Ireland, regarded as conquered territory, was parcelled out among soldiers and creditors of the Commonwealth, and only those Irish landowners able to prove their constant support of the Parliamentary cause escaped having their estates confiscated. Of these, those who were Catholics were still obliged to exchange land owned to the northeast or south of the River Shannon for land in Connaught. Catholics and Anglicans were forbidden to practice their religion, but the campaign against Irish Cathol-

The English plantation of Ireland in the 16th and 17th centuries.

icism was not successful. After the Restoration (1660) Charles II personally favoured complete religious toleration, but the forces of militant Protestantism sometimes proved too strong for him. The Commonwealth parliamentary union was, after 1660, treated as null and void.

The Restoration period and the Jacobite war. Most significant of the events of the Restoration was the second Act of Settlement (1662), which enabled Protestant loyalists to recover their estates. The Act of Explanation (1665) obliged the Cromwellian settlers to surrender one-third of their grants, providing a reserve of land from which Catholics were partially compensated for losses under the Commonwealth. This satisfied neither group. Catholics were prevented from residing in towns, and local power, in both borough and county, became appropriated to the Protestant interest. But Protestantism itself became permanently split; as in England, the Presbyterians refused to conform to Episcopalian order and practice and, in association with the Presbyterians of Scotland, organized as a separate church.

Under James II, advantage was taken of the King's Catholicism to reverse the tendencies of the preceding reign. After his flight from England to France (1688), James crossed to Ireland, where, in a Parliament, the Acts of Settlement and Explanation were repealed and provision was made for the restoration of expropriated Catholics. When William III landed in Ireland to oppose James, the country divided denominationally, but the real issue was not religion but the land. After his defeat at the Battle of the Boyne (1690) James fled to France, but his Catholic supporters continued in arms until defeated at Aughrim and obliged to surrender (1691) at Limerick. Here, however, they secured either the right to go overseas or, if they accepted William's regime, immunity from discriminatory laws. But civil articles to secure toleration for the Catholics were not ratified, thus enabling later Irish leaders to denounce the "broken treaty" of Limerick. Immediately after Limerick, the Protestant position was secured by acts of the English Parliament declaring illegal the acts of King James's Parliament in Ireland and restricting to Protestants membership of future Irish Parliaments. The sale of the lands forfeited by James and some of his supporters further reduced the Catholic landownership in the country; by 1703 it was less than 10 percent. On this foundation was established the Protestant Ascendancy.

The 18th century. The Protestant Ascendancy was a supremacy of that proportion of the population, about one-tenth, which alone belonged to the established Protestant Episcopalian Church. They celebrated their position as a ruling class by annual recollections of their victories over their hated popish enemies. Not only the Catholic majority but also the Presbyterians and other Nonconformists, whose combined numbers exceeded these of the church establishment, were excluded from full political rights, notably by the Test Act of 1704, which made tenure of office dependent upon willingness to receive communion according to the Protestant Episcopalian (Church of Ireland) rite. Owing to their banishment from public life, the history of the Catholic Irish in the 18th century is concerned almost exclusively with the activities of exiled soldiers and priests, many of whom distinguished themselves in the service of continental monarchs. Details of the lives of the unrecorded Catholic majority in rural Ireland can be glimpsed only from ephemeral literature in English and from the Gaelic poetry of the four provinces.

The Protestant Ascendancy

The Protestant Ascendancy of 18th-century Ireland began in subordination to that of England but ended in asserting its independence. In the 1690s commercial jealousy compelled the Irish Parliament to destroy the Irish woollen export trade, and in 1720 the Declaratory Act affirmed the right of the British Parliament to legislate for Ireland and transferred to the British House of Lords the powers of a supreme court in Irish law cases. By the end of the first quarter of the 18th century, resentment at this subordination had grown sufficiently to enable the celebrated pamphleteer Jonathan Swift to whip up a storm of protest over the affair of "Wood's halfpence." Wood, an English manufacturer, had been authorized to mint coins for Ireland; the outcry against alleged exploitation of the lesser country by arbitrary creation of a monopoly became so violent that it could be terminated only by withdrawing the concession from Wood.

Nevertheless, it was another 30 years before a similar protest was made. In 1751 a group of patriots organized themselves to defeat government resolutions in the Irish Parliament appropriating a financial surplus as the English administrators rather than the Irish legislators saw fit. Although in 1768 the Irish Parliament was made more sensitive to public opinion by provision for fresh elections every eight years instead of merely at the beginning of a new reign, it remained sufficiently controlled by government to pass sympathetic resolutions on the revolt of the American colonies.

The American Revolution greatly influenced Irish politics, not least because it removed government troops from Ireland, and the Protestant Irish volunteer corps, spontaneously formed to defend the country against possible French attack, exercised a coercive influence for reform. A patriotic opposition, led by Henry Flood and Henry Grattan, began an agitation that led in 1782 to the repeal of the Declaratory Act of 1720, and to an amendment of Poynings' Law to give legislative initiative to the Irish Parliament. In this period many of the disabilities suffered by Catholics in Ireland were abolished, and in 1793 the British government, seeking to win Catholic loyalty on the outbreak of war against Revolutionary France, gave them the franchise and admission to most civil offices. The government further attempted to conciliate Catholic opinion in 1795 by founding the seminary of Maynooth to provide education for the Catholic clergy. But the Protestant Ascendancy had become concerned about its position and resisted efforts to make the Irish Parliament more representative. The outbreak of the French Revolution had effected a temporary alliance between an intellectual elite among the Presbyterians and leading middle class Catholics; these, under the inspiration of Theobald Wolfe Tone, founded societies of United Irishmen, a series of radical political clubs. After the outbreak of war, the societies, reinforced by agrarian malcontents, were driven underground. In despair they sought the military support of Revolutionary France, which, between 1796 and 1798, dispatched a series of abortive naval expeditions to Ireland. The United Irishmen were preparing for rebellion; it broke out in May 1798 but was widespread only in Ulster and in Wexford in the south. Although the rebellion was unsuccessful, it brought the Irish question forcibly to the attention of the British Cabinet, and the prime minister William Pitt planned and carried through an amalgamation of the British and Irish Parliaments, merging the kingdoms of Great Britain and Ireland into the United Kingdom. Despite substantial opposition in the Irish Parliament, the measure passed into law, having effect from January 1, 1801. To Grattan and his supporters the Union seemed the end of the Irish nation; the last protest of the United Irishmen was made in Robert Emmet's abortive rebellion of 1803.

The Union with Great Britain

Social, economic, and cultural life in the 17th and 18th centuries. Although the late 16th century saw the destruction of Gaelic civilization in the upper levels of society, it was preserved for more than the next two centuries among the ordinary people of the northwest, west, and southwest, who continued to speak Irish and who maintained a way of life remote from that of the new landlord class.

The 17th-century confiscations made Ireland a land of great estates and, except for Dublin, of small towns decaying under the impact of British restrictions on trade. Except on the Ulster plantations, the tenantry was relatively poor in comparison with that of England and employed inferior agricultural methods. Over large parts of the east and south, tillage farming had given way to pasturage. In the north of Ireland, a somewhat similar tendency, creating a decline in the demand for labour, led in the early 18th century to the migration of substantial numbers of Ulster Scots to North America. In Ulster there gradually emerged a tenantry who compelled their landlords to maintain them in their farms against the claims and bids of Catholic competitors now once again legally entitled to hold land. This purpose immensely strengthened the Orange Order, founded in 1795 in defense of the Protestant Ascendancy. Increasingly it linked the Protestant gentry and farmers, while excluding Catholics from breaking into this privileged ring. Tillage farming was maintained in Ulster more extensively than in the south and west, where there developed on the poorer lands a system of subdivision apparently necessitated by population increase. Little is known of the lives of the ordinary people and even for those of the gentry the evidence, apart from that of estate records, is rarely extensive.

Little need be said of the culture of the Anglo-Irish in the same period, as it followed so closely the traditions of Britain and, very occasionally, those of the rest of Europe. Gradually, during the 18th century, the new landowning class developed some appreciation of the visual arts. But the really original achievement of the period was in literature, particularly in drama, where the rhetorical gifts of the people secured an audience. In this period there was a strong connection between rhetoric and the arts, as between oratory, themes of social decay, and the consoling power of language and form. Such works as Oliver Goldsmith's *Deserted Village* and *Traveller*, Edmund Burke's speeches, and the speeches and plays of Richard Brinsley Sheridan are manifestations of a rhetorical tradition central to Irish feelings.

The 19th and early 20th centuries. By the Act of Union it was provided that Ireland would have in the United Kingdom about one-fifth of the representation of Great Britain, with 100 members in the House of Commons. The union of the churches of England and Ireland as the established denominations of their respective countries was also effected, and the pre-eminent position in Ireland of Protestant Episcopalianism was further secured by the continuation of the British Test Act, which virtually excluded Nonconformists (both Catholic and Protestant) from Parliament and from membership of municipal corporations. Not until 1828–29 did the repeal of the Test Act and the concession of Catholic emancipation provide political equality for most purposes. It was also provided in the Union that there should be free trade between the two countries and that Irish merchandise would be admitted to British colonies on the same terms as British merchandise. But these advantages were not enough to offset the disastrous effect upon Ireland of exposure to the full impact of Britain's industrial revolution. Within half a century agricultural produce dropped in value, estate rentals declined, while the rural population increased substantially. When the potato, the staple food of rural Ireland, rotted in the ground through the onset of blight in the mid-1840s, thousands died of starvation and fever in the Great Famine that ensued, and thousands more fled abroad.

At first, and perhaps for more than one-third of the 19th century, the auguries of success for the Union were favourable. After the defeat of Napoleon at Waterloo (1815), political discontent increased but became concentrated, so far as the Catholics were concerned, on securing their emancipation. Until this was achieved there had not clearly emerged any notable difference in outlook between the Catholics and Presbyterians; but the dramatic manner in which the Catholic Daniel O'Connell was elected for County Clare (1828), subsequently sweeping the emancipation movement into victory, provoked a panic among timid Protestants and led to an alliance between the Presbyterians and their old oppressors, the Protestant Episcopalians. After emancipation, the middle class Catholics and Protestants drifted apart, the latter increasingly clinging to the Union, the former more slowly but at last decisively coming to seek its repeal.

Emergence of Daniel O'Connell

O'Connell's adherence to the cause of repeal did not prevent him from participating actively in British politics. Lord Melbourne, the Whig prime minister, by a bargain known as the Lichfield House Compact (1835), secured O'Connell's support in return for a promise of "justice for Ireland." But meanwhile the Tories, led by Sir Robert Peel, exercised through their control of the House of Lords an effective restriction on promised social and economic reforms for Ireland, and when Peel returned to power in the early 1840s O'Connell, despairing of further concessions, began a massive campaign outside Parliament for repeal of the Union, notably by organizing large popular demonstrations. A climax was reached in October 1843 when troops and artillery were called out to suppress the mass meeting arranged at Clontarf outside Dublin. O'Connell's method of popular agitation within the law proved unavailing, however, and his influence thereafter rapidly declined.

Associated with O'Connell's repeal agitation was the Young Ireland movement, a group connected with a repeal weekly newspaper, *The Nation*, and led by its editor Charles Gavan Duffy, its chief contributor Thomas Osborne Davis, and its special land correspondent John Blake Dillon. But they became increasingly restless at O'Connell's cautious policy after Clontarf and in 1848 became involved in an abortive rising. Its failure, and the deportation or escape from Ireland of most of the Young Ireland leaders, destroyed the repeal movement.

For about 20 years after the Great Famine, political agitation was subdued, while emigration continued to reduce the population every year. The landowners had also suffered severely from inability to collect rents, and there was a wholesale transfer of estates to new owners. Evictions were widespread, and cottages were demolished at once by the landlords to prevent other impoverished tenants from occupying them. The flow of emigrants to the United States was encouraged by invitations from Irishmen already there. And in England, also, the new industrial cities and shipping centres attracted large settlements of hopeless and embittered exiles from Ireland.

Rise of Fenianism. Among the exiles both in the United States and in England, the Fenian movement spread widely. A secret revolutionary society named after the Fianna, the Irish armed force in legendary times, it aimed at securing Ireland's political freedom by exploiting every opportunity to injure English interests.

Imprisonment of Fenian leaders

In Ireland, Fenian ideals were propagated in the newspaper *The Irish People;* and in 1865 four Fenian leaders, Charles Kickham, John O'Leary, Thomas Clarke Luby, and Jeremiah O'Donovan Rossa were sentenced to long-term imprisonment for treasonable writing in it. Gradually, during the next two years plans developed for a projected nationwide rising, financed largely by funds collected in the United States. It took place in March 1867 but was easily crushed and its leaders imprisoned. The prime minister, W.E. Gladstone, at last recognized the necessity for drastic Irish reforms, disestablishing the Protestant Church in Ireland in 1869 and in 1870 introducing the first Irish Land Act, which conceded the principles of secure tenure and compensation for improvements made to property. He may also have been concerned at the cleavage between English and Irish public opinion caused by the execution at Manchester of W.P. Allen, Michael Larkin, and Michael O'Brien for involvement in a Fenian prisoner-rescue operation that resulted in the shooting of a British police sergeant. To most Englishmen the "Manchester murderers" richly deserved their fate; to most Irishmen they were the "Manchester martyrs," celebrated in ballad and legend.

The Home Rule movement and the Land League. Soon afterward, in 1870, a constitutional movement, the Home Government Association (Home Rule League), was founded by Isaac Butt, a prominent Unionist lawyer interested in land reform. In the election of 1874 it returned about 60 members to Parliament. The movement was tolerated rather than encouraged by the various groups of Irish nationalists, and it was not fully supported by the Catholic clergy until the 1880s.

A return of bad harvests in 1879 brought new fears of famine, and Michael Davitt founded the Irish Land League, seeking to achieve for tenants security of tenure, fair rents, and freedom to sell property. A formidable agrarian agitation developed when Davitt was joined by Charles Stewart Parnell, a young landowner and member of Parliament in the Home Rule Party, which soon elected him as its leader in place of Butt. Parnell undertook a tour of North America to raise funds for the Land League; there he was influenced by two Irish Americans, John Devoy, a leading member of Clan na Gael, an effective American Fenian organization, and Pat Ford, whose New York paper *The Irish World* preached militant Socialism and hatred of England. At Westminster Parnell adopted a policy of persistent obstruction, which compelled attention to Irish needs by bringing parliamentary business to a standstill. Gladstone was forced to introduce his Land Act of 1881, conceding fixity of tenure, fair rents, and free sale of the tenant's interest.

Parnell's success was not achieved without serious difficulties, including the ultimate proscription of the Land League by the government and the imprisonment of its leaders. As a result, Parnell used his parliamentary party, then increased to 86, to defeat and thus dismiss from office Gladstone's Liberal government, already unpopular in England as a result of its failure to relieve General Gordon at Khartoum in 1884. For a while Conservatives and Liberals both negotiated with Parnell, but ultimately Gladstone became converted to Home Rule, introducing a bill to bring it into effect after he returned to office in 1886. The bill, however, was defeated by a combination of Conservative Unionists influenced by Irish Orangemen and splinter groups from the Liberal Party. There followed 20 years during which Irish Nationalist ambitions seemed frustrated, partly because Conservative-Unionists were mainly in power and partly because bitter internal rivalries discredited the Irish Nationalist Party after Parnell's involvement (1889) in a divorce suit. Meanwhile, Gladstone's second Home Rule Bill (1893) was rejected in the House of Lords. Only in 1900 was a Parnellite, John Redmond, able to reunite the Nationalists. In the last years of the century, partly in reaction to political frustrations, a cultural nationalist movement developed, led by Douglas Hyde and Eoin MacNeill. Through the Gaelic League much was done to revive interest in the speaking and study of Irish. These cultural movements were reinforced by others, such as that of the Sinn Féin ("Ourselves") movement led by Arthur Griffith, who preached a doctrine of political self-help. It subsequently emerged that a Fenian organization, the Irish Republican Brotherhood, had revived and was secretly recruiting membership through various cultural societies and through the Gaelic Athletic Association, founded to promote specifically Irish sports.

Gladstone's Home Rule bill

Around the close of the century the Conservatives initiated a policy designed to "kill Home Rule by kindness" by introducing constructive reforms in Ireland. Their most important achievement in this field was the Wyndham Land Purchase Act of 1903. This, by providing generous inducements to landlords to sell their estates, effected by government mediation the transfer of land ownership to the occupying tenants.

The 20th-century crisis. After the great Liberal victory of 1906, Redmond decided to force the Liberals to revive Home Rule, and when Lloyd George's radical budget provoked a collision with the House of Lords in 1909, he seized his opportunity. He agreed to support the campaign of the prime minister, H.H. Asquith, against the Lords in return for the promise of a Home Rule bill. The reduction of the power of the Lords by the 1911 Parliament Act seemed to promise success for the third Home Rule bill, introduced in 1912. But in the meantime the Irish Unionists, under their colourful leader Sir Edward Carson, had mounted an effective countermovement, backed by most of the British Unionists. Thousands of Ulstermen signed the Ulster Covenant of resistance to Home Rule (1912), and Carson announced that a provisional government would be formed there. At first planning to reject Home Rule for all Ireland, the Unionists gradually fell back on a demand for Ulster to be excluded from its scope. Redmond's claim that there was "no Ulster question," implying that even among the Ulster members of Parliament there was a majority for Home Rule, hardened the Protestant and Unionist resistance in the areas around Belfast. Down, Antrim, Armagh, and Derry all contained large Unionist majorities; Donegal, Cavan, and Monaghan had strong Home Rule majorities; and Tyrone and Fermanagh had small Home Rule majorities. The Ulster Volunteer Force was organized and boasted of active sympathy among army officers; their boasts became formidable when all the officers in the cavalry brigade at the Curragh suddenly announced (March 1914) that they would resign if ordered to move into Ulster. Meanwhile, to counter the Ulster Volunteers, a nationalist force, the Irish Volunteers, had been launched in Dublin in November 1913. Both forces gathered arms, and Ireland was on the verge of civil war when World War I broke out. Assured of Redmond's support in recruiting for the army, Asquith enacted Home Rule but followed this with a Suspensory Act, delaying implementation until the return of peace.

Meanwhile in Ireland, the revolutionary element gained support from those alienated by Redmond's pro-British attitude. Before the end of 1914 the Irish Republican Brotherhood had made full plans for a revolutionary outbreak. Sir Roger Casement went to Germany to solicit help; but he obtained only obsolete arms and was himself arrested on his return to Ireland on April 21, 1916. When the rising took place three days later, on Easter Monday, only about 2,000 of the small force available were actually engaged. A provisional Republic government was proclaimed. The General Post Office and other parts of Dublin were seized; street fighting continued for about a week

The Easter Rising

until Patrick Pearse and other Republican leaders were forced to surrender. Their subsequent execution aroused Irish public opinion and led to the defeat and virtual extinction of Redmond's constitutional party at Westminster in the general election of December 1918. Their successful opponents, calling themselves Sinn Féin but supporting the Republican program announced in 1916, were led by Eamon De Valera, a surviving leader of the Rising. Again the Republicans set up their provisional government, elected by the Irish members of Parliament at a meeting in Dublin called Dáil Éireann, the "Irish Assembly." This provided a constitutional facade when British government was rapidly breaking down except in the northeastern counties. Simultaneously, the Irish Republican Army (IRA) was organized to resist British Administration and to secure recognition for the Republican government. Its members soon engaged in widespread ambushes and attacks on barracks, while the government retaliated with ruthless reprisals. A large proportion of the Irish police resigned and were replaced by English recruits, known from their temporary uniforms as the Black and Tans.

In this condition of virtual civil war Britain gradually alienated Irish public opinion and was forced, partly under American influence, to pass the Government of Ireland Act (1920). By this measure Ireland was divided into two self-governing areas, Northern Ireland and Southern Ireland. Both were to enjoy, within the United Kingdom, limited powers of self-government. After a general election in Ireland, King George V opened the Parliament of Northern Ireland in Belfast (1921) and in his speech appealed for an end to fratricidal strife. The King's initiative forced the British prime minister Lloyd George to open negotiations with De Valera, but for some time progress proved impossible, because neither side would admit the other's legality. Ultimately, on December 6, 1921 a treaty was signed on behalf of Great Britain by Lloyd George and leading members of his cabinet and on behalf of Ireland by Arthur Griffith, Michael Collins, and other members of the Republican Cabinet.

THE IRISH FREE STATE AND THE REPUBLIC OF IRELAND

Establishment of the Irish Free State. The Anglo-Irish treaty, signed on December 6, 1921, provided that Ireland should in future have the "same constitutional status in the Community of Nations known as the British Empire" as had the dominions of Canada, Australia, New Zealand, and South Africa, "with a Parliament having powers to make laws for the peace, order and good government of Ireland and an Executive responsible to that Parliament." The new dominion was to be known as the Irish Free State. This peace agreement, ratified by the British Parliament, became operative when it had also been passed (January 1922) by a meeting of the Dáil. The new state comprised only 26 of the 32 counties, the northeastern area, known as Northern Ireland, remaining separate.

But the terms of the treaty had been accepted by the Irish signatories only because Lloyd George had threatened war on Ireland if they were rejected. Particularly obnoxious were a prescribed oath of allegiance to the British crown and the provisions allowing Northern Ireland to remain outside the new State. De Valera and the Republicans immediately repudiated the treaty, and after its passage in the Dáil, De Valera resigned the presidency. Michael Collins, chairman of the provisional government set up according to the terms of the treaty, and Arthur Griffith, the new president, desired an immediate general election to obtain a verdict on the treaty; in deteriorating conditions he eventually made with De Valera an agreement known as the Pact (May 20, 1922), in which it was settled that government and Republican candidates would not oppose each other and that De Valera would consider resuming office. But the Pact naturally could not bind other parties, and at the election (June 16) Republicans were ousted in favour of members of a labour party and a farmers' party and by independents, thus reducing the anti-treaty vote to a small minority. Before the Dáil could meet, civil war had broken out between the government and the Republicans, who were allegedly accessories to the assassination (June 22) in London of Field Marshal Sir Henry Wilson soon after his acceptance of the position of military adviser to the government of Northern Ireland. The Republicans in Dublin had occupied the Four Courts (central courts of justice) and eventually, under pressure from Britain, which also provided military equipment, Collins ordered them to retire. Serious fighting ensued for a week, until the Courts were blown up, and Rory O'Connor, the Dublin Republican leader, surrendered. Meanwhile, De Valera, who had escaped to the southwest, was openly supporting the Republicans. Griffith and Collins decided that no further compromise was possible, and military operations were begun. The strain had told so heavily on Griffith that he died suddenly on August 12, while Collins, inspecting the military operations, was killed in an ambush on August 22.

Repudiation of the treaty by the Republicans

The provisional government had thus lost two of its most prominent leaders, and surviving ministers could not appear openly without armed protection. Moreover, there was urgency in that, by the terms of the treaty, the newly elected Dáil was required to frame its constitution before December 6, 1922. It was therefore summoned to meet on September 9, elected as the new president William Thomas Cosgrave, and, in the absence of the Republican deputies, quickly passed the clauses of the constitution defining the relations of the Free State with the British crown and outlining arrangements for imperial defense. Timothy Michael Healy, a veteran follower of Parnell who had later supported Sinn Féin, was then appointed governor general, and Cosgrave became president of the executive council. The new constitution was also ratified at Westminster.

The Cosgrave ministries. Both before and after the ratification of the constitution the government resorted to strong measures to quell disorder and violence. Its decision to execute those found in unauthorized possession of firearms embittered Irish politics for years afterward. Numerous Republican insurgents were also imprisoned, and 77 were executed. Although Republican opposition was at first more bitter than ever, it eventually became less well organized, and by May 1923, on De Valera's recommendation, armed resistance ended.

The fourth Dáil

At the end of August 1923 the fourth Dáil was elected, on a basis of adult suffrage for men and women. De Valera retained his personal following, and his party won 44 seats out of 128. Cosgrave's party won less than half the total number of seats, but as the Republicans refused to sit in the new Dáil, he had a majority among those who did attend. The absence of any effective opposition party greatly strengthened the power of the new government to carry measures quickly, and in the following years it displayed great energy. Despite initial economic difficulties, it pursued an efficient farming policy and carried through important hydroelectric schemes. Government was increasingly centralized, with the elimination of various corrupt borough corporations; Kevin O'Higgins, as minister for justice, carried through many judical reforms, and an efficient civil service was organized, in which competence in the Irish language became an essential qualification for promotion.

The Anglo-Irish Treaty of 1921 had provided that, if Northern Ireland did not enter the Free State, a boundary commission must establish the frontier between the two countries. Two of the six excluded counties, Tyrone and Fermanagh, contained clear, though small, Nationalist majorities, and the southern portions of both Down and Armagh had for years returned Nationalist members. Despite Northern Ireland's reluctance, a commission was established and sat in secret session during 1925. But it only recommended minor changes, which all three governments rejected as less satisfactory than maintaining the status quo.

In the general election of June 1927 Cosgrave's support in the Dáil was further reduced, but he nevertheless formed a new ministry, in which O'Higgins became vice president of the Executive Council. O'Higgins' assassination on July 10 suddenly revived old feuds, and Cosgrave passed a Public Safety Act, declaring all revolutionary societies treasonable. He forced the Republicans to acknowledge allegiance to the crown before being seated in the Dáil, though De Valera decried the oath as an "empty political formula." Shortly thereafter the Republicans, allied with the Labour Party and the National League, almost defeated Cosgrave, who thereupon dissolved the Dáil. In new elections Cosgrave won a slim majority of seats and again formed a ministry. In the depression of the early 1930s, unemployment and general discontent with the government led to its defeat in February 1932. Fianna Fáil won enough seats for De Valera, with support from the Labour Party, to form a new government.

De Valera's governments (1932–48). De Valera entered office with a policy of encouraging industry and improving social services. He abolished the oath of allegiance to the crown and also stopped payment to Britain of interest on the capital advanced under the Land Purchase Acts of the late 19th and early 20th centuries. This refusal led to a tariff war with Britain. The country endorsed his policies in January 1933 by returning him to the Dáil.

De Valera introduced proposals for a new constitution in 1937, taking advantage of British weakness during the crisis over the abdication of Edward VIII. The power of the crown was ended, and the office of governor general was replaced by that of a president elected by national suffrage. The first president was Douglas Hyde, a Celtic scholar who had been associated with the Gaelic revival since 1890. The new constitution did not proclaim an independent republic, but it replaced the title of the Irish Free State with the word Eire (Ireland). The new constitution was ratified by a plebiscite at the 1937 general election (in which De Valera was again victorious) and became operative on December 29, 1937.

Establishment of Eire

An agreement in April 1938 ended British occupation of naval bases at Cork and Berehaven in southwestern Ireland and Lough Swilly in the north, which had been left in British hands by the Anglo-Irish Treaty of 1921. The dispute over the land-purchase annuities was settled, and the economic warfare was abated. In this period government relations with the radical Republicans deteriorated; members of the IRA suspected of complicity in shootings were imprisoned, and some were executed.

At the time of the outbreak of World War II, De Valera renewed his statement, made in 1938, that Ireland would not become a base for attacks on Great Britain. His government, re-elected in 1943 and 1944, remained strictly neutral throughout the war, despite German air raids on Dublin in 1941 and, after the United States entered the war in December 1941, pressure from U.S. president Franklin D. Roosevelt.

Postwar developments. In the general election of 1948 Fianna Fáil won 68 of the 147 seats comprising the Dáil, but De Valera refused to enter a coalition. John A. Costello emerged as the leader of a bloc composed of his own party, Fine Gael, and several smaller groups. Out of office, De Valera toured the world to advocate the unification and independence of Ireland. Fearful of De Valera's prestige, Costello introduced in the Dáil the Republic of Ireland Act, which ended the fiction of Commonwealth membership that had been maintained since 1937. Britain recognized the status of Ireland in 1949 but declared that cession of the six counties could not occur without consent of the Parliament of Northern Ireland. Economic difficulties and a controversy between the ministry and the Catholic hierarchy over the Public Health Act weakened Costello's government, and after the general election of 1951, De Valera again became prime minister. His ministry aroused sufficient discontent for Costello to be returned to power in 1954, but economic troubles enabled Fianna Fáil to win a majority in 1957. The aging De Valera was elected president in 1959 and was succeeded as prime minister by Sean Lemass (1959–66) and Jack Lynch (1966–73). From the mid-1950s until 1962, the government tried to restrain IRA members who were raiding British army posts on the Ulster border; from the late 1960s the worsening situation in Northern Ireland increasingly preoccupied the Irish government. In 1973 a Fine Gael-Labour coalition won control of the Dáil, and Liam Cosgrave (son of William Cosgrave) became prime minister.

The mid-1970s was a period of transition and political instability in Ireland. In 1973 De Valera's last presidential term expired, and his death in August 1975 marked the end of an era. His successor, Erskine Childers, died in 1974; the office passed to Carroll O'Daly, who was forced to resign in October 1976 in a constitutional crisis. He was succeeded by Patrick J. Hillery. The situation in the north continued to trouble Ireland, but economic problems came to dominate and upset the political climate. By 1980 inflation was more than 18 percent, and unemployment was about 9 percent. In 1977 the Fianna Fáil regained the Dáil with a strong majority, and Lynch again became prime minister. He resigned in late 1979 and was succeeded by Charles J. Haughey. In the May 1981 election Haughey was upset by Garrett FitzGerald of Fine Gael. Loss of a budget vote precipitated Haughey's reelection in March 1982.

Ireland, like Britain, suffered setbacks in the 1960s in attempting to join the European Economic Community, but both nations formally entered the EEC on January 1, 1973. Since World War II, the international role played by Ireland has included the contribution of troops for United Nations peace-keeping efforts, notably in the Congo and in Cyprus.

NORTHERN IRELAND AFTER 1921

Under successive prime ministers—Sir James Craig, later Viscount Craigavon (1921–40); John Miller Andrews (1940–43); Sir Basil Brooke, later Viscount Brookeborough (1943–63); Capt. Terence O'Neill, later Lord O'Neill of the Maine (1963–69); Maj. James Chichester-Clark, later Lord Moyola of Castledawson (1969–71); and Brian Faulkner (1971–72)—the Unionist Party ruled the six counties. During that time the two main political factions became identified with the religious affiliations of their adherents. Unionist support had come from two Protestant groups, the Presbyterians (who make up 30 percent of the population) and members of the Church of Ireland (25 percent); opposition had centred in the Roman Catholics (35 percent), most of whom are Irish Nationalists resentful of the partition of Ireland and of their second-class social and economic status.

From the early 1960s more active opposition arose among the younger Catholics, and successive British governments urged Ulster to endorse equality in housing, public employment, and opportunities in general. A militant Protestant group, proclaiming the dangers of popery, secured a strong following among the poorer elements. Upon the launching of a civil-rights campaign in 1968, violence erupted in Belfast and Londonderry. At first, British troops contained the strife, but later they seemed to aggravate it. Bitterness was increased in August 1971 by the internment without trial of several members of the IRA who were suspected of playing leading roles in the uprising. Bombings and shootings increased in frequency for the rest of the year, and in March 1972 the British prime minister, Edward Heath, suspended the constitution and replaced the provincial government by appointing the first of a series of secretaries of state for Northern Ireland.

After elections in June 1973, limited self-government resumed under a moderate Catholic-Unionist coalition. Faulkner became chief of an 11-member executive body. Representatives of Britain, Northern Ireland, and the republic met at Sunningdale, Berkshire, in December 1973, but the Ulster Unionist Council rejected Faulkner's recommendation to endorse the discussions, and he resigned from the party. A general strike by the Unionist workers paralyzed the province in May 1974, the executive body collapsed, and direct British rule was reimposed. In May 1975 a constitutional convention was elected to search for ways to reinstitute home rule. It was heavily dominated by a coalition of Unionist parties who favoured a return to Protestant rule and opposed Catholic participation. Their report, submitted in March 1976, was rejected by the British. Repeated attempts at finding a political solution ended in failure, and direct rule from London continued.

The violence, which had abated somewhat in early 1975, again intensified as the IRA realized the position of the convention. By November 1,000 citizens had died since the resort to violence in 1969. The violence became more directed at the British, and assassinations, including that of Lord Louis Mountbatten in 1979, increased. The IRA also initiated hunger strikes at prisons in an attempt to gain political status and other concessions for IRA prisoners. Although they achieved limited success, the deaths of 10 of the hunger strikers in 1981 greatly increased worldwide awareness of the seriousness of the problems in Northern Ireland.

(R.W.D.E./Ed.)

BIBLIOGRAPHY

General works: The 15 volumes of the *Oxford History of England*, under the editorship of SIR G.N. CLARK (3rd–4th ed., 1934–65), provide a comprehensive survey, with excellent bibliographies. Other multivolume histories include the "Pelican History of England" series, 8 vol., particularly valuable for social history; *The Political History of England*, 12 vol. (1905–10), somewhat antiquated but informative; and CHRISTOPHER BROOKE and D.M. SMITH (eds.), *A History of England*, 8 vol. (1960–). GEORGE MACAULAY TREVELYAN, *History of England*, 2nd ed. (1937; reprinted with minor corrections, 1966), is a beautifully written but highly patriotic survey. A.B. ERICKSON and M.J. HAVRAN, *England: Prehistory to the Present* (1968), is a good one-volume textbook.

The Anglo-Saxon period: (*Sources*): BEDE, *Historia ecclesiastica; Anglo-Saxon Chronicle.* For a translation of and commentary on essential record and narrative material, see DOROTHY WHITELOCK (ed.), *English Historical Documents*, vol. 1 (1955). (*General histories*): F.M. STENTON, *Anglo-Saxon England*, 3rd ed. (1971); P. HUNTER BLAIR, *An Introduction to Anglo-Saxon England*, 2nd ed. (1956); R.H. HODGKIN, *A History of the Anglo-Saxons*, 3rd ed. (1952); H.R. LOYN, *Anglo-Saxon England and the Norman Conquest* (1962); R.I. PAGE, *Life in Anglo-Saxon England* (1970); DOROTHY WHITELOCK, *The Beginnings of English Society*, rev. ed. (1966). (*Works on specific topics*): T.D. KENDRICK, *A History of the Vikings* (1930, reprinted 1968); L.M. LARSON, *Canute the Great* (1912); W.R.W. STEPHENS and W. HUNT (eds.), *A History of the English Church*, vol. 1 (1899); WILHELM LEVISON, *England and the Continent in the Eighth Century* (1946); DAVID KNOWLES, *The Monastic Order in England*, 2nd ed. (1963); J. ARMITAGE ROBINSON, *The Times of Saint Dunstan* (1923); FRANK BARLOW, *The English Church, 1000–1066* (1963); JAMES TAIT, *The Medieval English Borough* (1936, reprinted 1968); R.H.M. DOLLEY (ed.), *Anglo-Saxon Coins* (1961) and *Anglo-Saxon Pennies* (1964); C.S. and C.S. ORWIN, *The Open Fields*, 3rd ed. (1967); C.T. CHEVALLIER and DOROTHY WHITELOCK *et al.*, *The Norman Conquest: Its Setting and Impact* (1966).

England from 1066 to 1485: (*Sources*): CARL STEPHENSON and F.G. MARCHAM (eds.), *Sources of English Constitutional History* (1937), devotes about a third of its coverage to the medieval period. In the new "English Historical Documents Series," see D.C. DOUGLAS and G.W. GREENAWAY (eds.), *English Historical Documents, 1042–1189* (1953); and A.R. MYERS (ed.), *English Historical Documents, 1327–1485* (1969). BERTIE WILKINSON, *The Constitutional History of England, 1216–1399*, 3 vol. (1948–58) and his *Constitutional History of England in the Fifteenth Century, 1399–1485* (1964), are anthologies of documents with extensive commentary by the author. (*General works*): HELEN M. CAM, *England Before Elizabeth*, 2nd rev. ed. (1960); CHRISTOPHER BROOKE, *From Alfred to Henry III, 871–1272* (1961); GEORGE HOLMES, *The Later Middle Ages, 1272–1485* (1962); F.M. STENTON, *English Society in the Early Middle Ages (1066–1307)* (1952), and A.R. MYERS, *England in the Late Middle Ages* (1952), two works that emphasize social history; A.L. POOLE, *From Domesday Book to Magna Carta, 1087–1216*, 2nd ed. (1955); F.M. POWICKE, *The Thirteenth Century, 1216–1307* (1953); MAY MCKISACK, *The Fourteenth Century, 1307–1399* (1959); E.F. JACOB, *The Fifteenth Century, 1399–1485* (1961). (*Special topics*): J.H. CLAPHAM, *A Concise Economic History of Britain, from Earliest Times to 1750* (1949); *The Cambridge Economic History of Europe*, ed. by J.H. CLAPHAM *et al.*, 3 vol. (1941–63; 2nd ed., 1966–); H.C. DARBY (ed.), *An Historical Geography of England Before A.D. 1800* (1936), includes several essays on the medieval period; DAVID KNOWLES, *The Religious Orders in England*, 3 vol. (1948–59), a comprehensive and definitive account; C.H. LAWRENCE (ed.), *The English Church and the Papacy in the Middle Ages* (1965), a volume of essays by specialists; WILLIAM STUBBS, *The Constitutional History of England*, 6th ed. (1897, reprinted 1967), not altogether superseded by modern works such as BRYCE D. LYONS, *A Constitutional and Legal History of Medieval England* (1960). (*1066–1307*): FRANK BARLOW, *The Feudal Kingdom of England, 1042–1216*, 2nd ed. (1961); R. ALLEN BROWN, *The Normans and the Norman Conquest* (1968); C.R. CHENEY, *From Becket to Langton: English Church Government, 1170–1213* (1956); H.W.C. DAVIS, *England Under the Normans and Angevins, 1066–1272* (1905), an old but not completely superseded work; R.H.C. DAVIS, *King Stephen, 1135–1154* (1967), sheds new light on the period of the anarchy; D.C. DOUGLAS, *William the Conqueror* (1964), the best single source on the conquest of England by the Normans; V.H. GALBRAITH, *The Making of Domesday Book* (1961), discusses the Conquest in an analytical statement about the survey of 1086; J.C. HOLT, *Magna Carta* (1965), the latest and most readable scholarly book on the Great Charter; J.E.A. JOLLIFFE, *Angevin Kingship*, 2nd ed. (1963), a challenging thesis that England might have developed into an absolute state in the medieval period if it had not been for the barons who fought John; REGINALD LENNARD, *Rural England, 1086–1135* (1959); H.R. LOYN, *The Norman Conquest* (1965), gives special emphasis to the social and economic impact of the Conquest; F.W. MAITLAND, *Domesday Book and Beyond* (1897), a seminal classic by a great historian; F.M. POWICKE, *King Henry III and the Lord Edward*, 2 vol. (1947); SIR FRANK STENTON, *The First Century of English Feudalism, 1066–1166*, 2nd ed. (1961), not superseded despite a great deal of discussion of the subject in later work; G.O. SAYLES, *The Medieval Foundations of England*, 2nd rev. ed. (1950), an excellent introduction to the history and the primary sources to the time of Edward I. (*The 14th and 15th centuries*): A.R. BRIDBURY, *Economic Growth: England in the Later Middle Ages* (1962); F.R.H. DU BOULAY, *An Age of Ambition* (1970); V.H.H. GREEN, *The Later Plantagenets* (1955), a useful general textbook; P.M. KENDALL, *Richard the Third* (1955) and *Warwick the Kingmaker* (1957); E.F. JACOB, *Henry V and the Invasion of France* (1947), a critical modern treatment; GEORGE MACAULAY TREVELYAN, *England in the Age of Wycliffe*, new ed. (1909), a social and political history of Richard II's reign; R.L. STOREY, *The End of the House of Lancaster* (1966), the best book on the Wars of the Roses.

The 16th century: Standard bibliographies for 16th-century England are CONYERS READ (ed.), *Bibliography of British History: Tudor Period, 1485–1603*, 2nd ed. (1959); and MORTIMER LEVINE's shorter compilation, *Tudor England 1485–1603* (1968). The best political and social surveys are S.T. BINDOFF, *Tudor England* (1950); and G.R. ELTON, *England Under the Tudors* (1955). For the personalities of the sovereigns, see CHRISTOPHER MORRIS, *The Tudors* (1955); and for the European setting, L.B. SMITH, *The Elizabethan World* (1966). Constitutional and institutional development can be studied in CHRISTOPHER MORRIS' short but brilliant *Political Thought in England: Tyndale to Hooker* (1953); JOHN NEALE's classic works on Parliament, *Elizabeth I and Her Parliaments*, 2 vol. (1953–57), and *The Elizabethan House of Commons* (1949); and G.R. ELTON's controversial *The Tudor Revolution in Government* (1953). Social and intellectual change is best sampled in four provocative but important works: W.K. JORDAN, *Philanthropy in England, 1480–1660* (1959); LAWRENCE STONE, *The Crisis of the Aristocracy, 1558–1641* (1965); R.H. TAWNEY, *Religion and the Rise of Capitalism* (1926, reprinted 1962); and E.M.W. TILLYARD, *The Elizabethan World Picture* (1943). The religious crisis of the century is neatly summarized in A.G. DICKENS, *The English Reformation*, rev. ed. (1967); and treated in greater length from a Catholic point of view by PHILIP HUGHES, *The Reformation in England*, rev. 5th ed., 3 vol. (1963). The best works on the Elizabethan period are PATRICK COLLINSON, *The Elizabethan Puritan Movement* (1967); and W.R. TRIMBLE, *The Catholic Laity in Elizabethan England, 1558–1603* (1964), whereas a fine book on religion in pre-Reformation England is HERBERT MAYNARD SMITH, *Pre-Reformation England* (1938). Foreign policy is surveyed by R.B. WERNHAM in *Before the Armada: The Growth of English Foreign Policy, 1458–1588* (1966). Overseas expansion is handled in A.L. ROWSE, *The Expansion of Elizabethan England* (1955).

The 17th century: The starting points for a detailed study of Stuart England from 1603 to 1656 and from 1685 to 1702 are still, for all their Whiggish faults, the respective multivolume studies of two great 19th-century historians, SAMUEL RAWSON GARDINER (continued to 1660 by CHARLES H. FIRTH and GODFREY DAVIES) and T.B. MACAULAY. The best one-volume surveys of the 17th century are GEOFFREY AYLMER, *The Struggle for the Constitution, 1603–1689*, 2nd ed. (1968); CHRISTOPHER HILL, *The Century of Revolution, 1603–1714* (1961); MAURICE ASHLEY, *England in the Seventeenth Century*, 3rd ed. (1961); and JOHN P. KENYON, *The Stuarts* (1958). The best one-volume study of the causes of the English Civil War is PEREZ ZAGORIN, *The Court and the Country* (1969); and of the interregnum, IVAN ROOTS, *The Great Rebellion: 1642–1666* (1966). There are several good three-volume studies: C.V. WEDGWOOD for the reign of Charles I from 1637 to 1649 (1956–66); DAVID OGG for later Stuarts from 1660 to 1702 (1955); and GEORGE

MACAULAY TREVELYAN (1930–34) for the reign of Queen Anne. There are fine biographies: DAVID HARRIS WILLSON, *King James VI and I* (1956); CATHERINE DRINKER BOWEN, *The Lion and the Throne: The Life and Times of Sir Edward Coke* (1957) and *Francis Bacon* (1963); HUGH R. TREVOR-ROPER, *Archbishop Laud, 1573–1645*, 2nd ed. (1962); and C.V. WEDGWOOD, *Strafford, 1593–1641* (1935). There have been several important historiographical controversies on the Stuart period in recent years. The Max Weber thesis on the relationship between Puritanism and economic matters was recast by R.H. TAWNEY in *Religion and the Rise of Capitalism* (1926, reprinted 1962), but it has been challenged in two articles in *Church History* by WINTHROP S. HUDSON (1949) and CHARLES H. GEORGE (1958). For the controversy over the rise of the gentry, see R.H. TAWNEY, *Economic History Review*, 11:1–38 (1941); HUGH R. TREVOR-ROPER, *Economic History Review Supplement* (1953); and JACK H. HEXTER, "Storm over the Gentry," *Encounter*, 10:22–34 (1958); LAWRENCE STONE has analyzed *The Crisis of the Aristocracy, 1588–1641* (1965); and PETER LASLETT has examined the lower orders of society in *The World We Have Lost* (1965). The relationship between Puritanism and democracy has been set forth by WILLIAM HALLER, *The Rise of Puritanism* (1938) and *Liberty and Reformation in the Puritan Revolution* (1955); and A.S.P. WOODHOUSE (ed.), *Puritanism and Liberty*, 2nd ed. (1951), but some of their conclusions have been questioned by MICHAEL WALZER, *The Revolution of the Saints* (1965); and LEO F. SOLT, *Saints in Arms* (1959). The relationship between Puritanism and the New Science was first developed by ROBERT K. MERTON, *Science, Technology and Society in Seventeenth Century England* (1938); and more recently by J.E.C. HILL, *The Intellectual Origins of the English Revolution* (1965), but they have come under attack in articles by HUGH F. KEARNEY and THEODORE K. RABB in *Past and Present* (1964–66) and by the latter in the *Journal of World History*, 7:46–67 (1962). The traditional interpretation of a two-party system in Queen Anne's reign given by WILLIAM T. MORGAN, *English Political Parties and Leaders in the Reign of Queen Anne, 1702–1710* (1920); KEITH FEILING, *A History of the Tory Party, 1640–1714* (1924); and Trevelyan were challenged by the biographical studies of ROBERT WALCOTT, *English Politics in the Early Eighteenth Century* (1956), but the earlier view has been stressed by J.H. PLUMB, *The Growth of Political Stability in England: 1675–1725* (1967); and GEOFFREY S. HOLMES, *British Politics in the Age of Anne* (1967).

1714–1815: T.S. ASHTON, *An Economic History of England: The Eighteenth Century* (1955), a readable introduction for the general reader, and *The Industrial Revolution, 1760–1830* (1948), a classic brief overview; JOHN M. BEATTIE, *The English Court in the Reign of George I* (1967), combines administrative with political history—aids understanding of later Hanoverian reigns; LEWIS B. NAMIER, *The Structure of Politics at the Accession of George III*, 2 vol. (1929; 2nd ed., 1 vol., 1957), an analytical study that destroyed traditional views on 18th-century political history—the starting point for all modern studies of 18th-century politics; JOHN BROOKE, *The Chatham Administration, 1766–1768* (1956), a detailed political history in the Namierite manner; HERBERT BUTTERFIELD, *George III and the Historians*, rev. ed. (1959), historiographical study with extended criticism of Namierite treatment of politics; IAN CHRISTIE, *The End of North's Ministry, 1780–1782* (1958); CARL B. CONE, *Burke and the Nature of Politics*, 2 vol. (1957–64), political biography based on recently available corpus of Burke papers; *The English Jacobins* (1968), narrative account of parliamentary reform before and during the French Revolution; PHYLLIS DEANE, *The First Industrial Revolution* (1965), topically organized work stressing the concept of economic growth; JOHN EHRMAN, *The Younger Pitt* (1969), standard biography; A.S. FOORD, *His Majesty's Opposition, 1714–1830* (1964), on the growth and acceptance of the idea and practice of a formed parliamentary opposition; DEREK JARRETT, *Britain, 1688–1815* (1965), the best short history, mainly political; D.L. KEIR, *The Constitutional History of Modern Britain Since 1485*, 9th ed. (1968), a balanced narrative treatment of this period; W.E.H. LECKY, *A History of England in the Eighteenth Century*, 7 vol. (1899–1901), good on social history but outdated in many respects; DOROTHY MARSHALL, *English People in the Eighteenth Century* (1956), emphasis on social history; RICHARD PARES, *King George III and the Politicians* (1953), a highly regarded analysis that modifies some Namierite interpretations; J.H. PLUMB, *The Growth of Political Stability in England, 1675–1725* (1967), a conceptual study showing how and why stability replaced instability; *Sir Robert Walpole*, 2 vol. (1956–61; vol. 3 in prep.), the definitive biography; NORMAN SYKES, *Church and State in England in the Eighteenth Century* (1934), corrects older views of torpor and inadequacy of the church; J.S. WATSON, *The Reign of George III, 1760–1815* (1960); R.J. WHITE, *The Age of George III* (1968), readable, brief, interpretative, and comprehensive in its coverage; BASIL WILLIAMS, *The Whig Supremacy, 1714–1760*, 2nd ed. (1962); E.N. WILLIAMS (ed.), *The Eighteenth Century Constitution, 1688–1815* (1960), a collection of well-selected documents.

1815–1914: ELIE HALEVY, *Histoire du peuple anglais au XIXe siècle*, 5 vol. (1912–32; Eng. trans., *A History of the English People in the Nineteenth Century*, 2nd ed., 6 vol., 1949–52), is the best general account, although the second half of the century is only partially and sketchily covered. G.M. YOUNG, *Victorian England: Portrait of an Age*, 2nd ed. (1960), is a brilliant essay, as is GEOFFREY BEST, *Mid-Victorian Britain, 1851–1875*, (1971). E.L. WOODWARD, *The Age of Reform, 1815–1870*, 2nd ed. (1962); see also his *Victorian People* (1954) and *Victorian Cities* (1963). R.C.K. ENSOR, *England, 1870–1914* (1936), is a good standard study. ASA BRIGGS, *The Age of Improvement* (1959), is the fullest account of the period from the Industrial Revolution to the Second Reform Bill in all its aspects; and R.K. WEBB, *Modern England: From the 18th Century to the Present* (1969), is the most valuable recent textbook; but also of interest is WALTER HOUGHTON, *The Victorian Frame of Mind, 1830–1870* (1957). There is much that cannot be found elsewhere in *Edwardian England, 1901–1914*, ed. by SIMON H. NOWELL-SMITH (1964). Among a large number of studies of economic history, W.H.B. COURT, *A Concise Economic History of Britain, from 1750 to Recent Times* (1954), provides the most useful introduction, while for Britain's overseas relationships, R.W. SETON-WATSON, *Britain in Europe, 1789–1914* (1937, reprinted 1968); and C.E. CARRINGTON, *The British Overseas*, 2nd ed. (1968), deal with both continental and imperial relationships. On World War I, see ARTHUR MARWICK, *The Deluge* (1965).

Great Britain since 1914: Several works deal in a fairly comprehensive manner with British history since 1914: W.N. MEDLICOTT, *Contemporary England, 1914–1964* (1967); T.O. LLOYD, *Empire to Welfare State: English History 1906–1967* (1970); ALFRED F. HAVIGHURST, *Twentieth-Century Britain*, 2nd ed. (1966). Medlicott emphasizes political and diplomatic history, while the other two are somewhat broader in scope. More detailed is A.J.P. TAYLOR, *English History, 1914–45* (1965), at times extraordinarily perceptive and provocative. The best work on the interwar years is CHARLES LOCH MOWAT, *Britain Between the Wars, 1918–1940* (1955). SIDNEY POLLARD, *The Development of the British Economy, 1914–1967*, 2nd ed. rev. (1969), is reliable; and F.S. NORTHEDGE, *The Troubled Giant: Britain Among the Great Powers, 1916–1939* (1966) and *British Foreign Policy: The Process of Readjustment, 1945–1961* (1962), provide consecutive treatment of diplomatic history. The period may be approached in an interesting manner through diaries and memoirs—*e.g.*, three volumes by HAROLD MACMILLAN: *Winds of Change, 1914–1939* (1966), *The Blast of War 1939–1945* (1968), and *Tides of Fortune, 1945–1955* (1969). Excellent biographies include: HAROLD NICOLSON, *King George the Fifth: His Life and Reign* (1952); ALAN BULLOCK, *The Life and Times of Ernest Bevin*, 2 vol. (1960–67); RANDOLPH CHURCHILL, *Life of Winston S. Churchill*, 2 vol. (1966–67), vol. 3 by MARTIN GILBERT (1971). *The Annual Register of World Events* provides a useful and reliable summary of British and Commonwealth affairs. As a reference book, D.E. BUTLER and JENNIE FREEMAN, *British Political Facts, 1900–1967* (1968), is the best of its kind.

History of Wales: Two standard surveys are DAVID WILLIAMS, *A History of Modern Wales* (1950; reprint, 1965); and WILLIAM REES, *An Historical Atlas of Wales from Early to Modern Times*, new ed. (1959). J.E. LLOYD, *A History of Wales from the Earliest Times to the Edwardian Conquest*, 3rd ed., 2 vol. (1939), remains a valuable survey of the history of Wales to 1282. The results of more recent investigations into the early history of Wales are reflected in I.L. FOSTER and G. DANIEL (eds.), *Prehistoric and Early Wales* (1965); N.K. CHADWICK (ed.), *Studies in Early British History* (1954) and *Studies in the Early British Church* (1958). V.E. NASH-WILLIAMS, *The Roman Frontier in Wales*, rev. ed. by M.G. JARRETT (1969), and *The Early Christian Monuments of Wales* (1950); and E.G. BOWEN, *Saints, Seaways and Settlements in the Celtic Lands* (1969), are major studies. J.G. EDWARDS, "The Normans and the Welsh March," *Proceedings of the British Academy*, 42:155–177 (1956), is of fundamental importance for an understanding of the effect of the Norman invasion. The narrative account of the age of the princes in Lloyd's *History of Wales* has not been superseded; but J.G. EDWARDS, *Littere Wallie* (1940); THOMAS JONES, *Brut y Tywysogyon; or, the Chronicle of the Princes, Peniarth MS. 20 Version* (1955); and H.D. EMANUEL (ed.), *The Latin Texts of the Welsh Laws* (1967), provide key source materials and important critical studies. Chapters relating to Wales are included in F.M. PO-

WICKE, *King Henry III and the Lord Edward*, 2 vol. (1947) and *The Thirteenth Century, 1216–1307* (1953). T. JONES PIERCE, *Medieval Welsh Society: Selected Essays* (1972); or WILLIAM REES, *South Wales and the March, 1284–1415* (1924), are indispensable studies of social and agrarian history. J. CONWAY DAVIES, *Episcopal Acts Relating to Welsh Dioceses*, 2 vol. (1948–53); and GLANMOR WILLIAMS, *The Welsh Church from Conquest to Reformation* (1962), cover ecclesiastical history. J.E. LLOYD, *Owen Glendower* (1931), describes the early-15th-century rebellion; and GLYN ROBERTS, *Aspects of Welsh History* (1969), includes essays dealing with the later Middle Ages. KENNETH O. MORGAN, *Wales in British Politics, 1868–1922*, rev. ed. (1970), treats the principality in its United Kingdom context. *The Dictionary of Welsh Biography down to 1940* (1959) is valuable. *A Bibliography of the History of Wales* (1958; 2nd ed., 1962), with supplements in *The Bulletin of the Board of Celtic Studies*, vol. 20, 22, 23, provides a comprehensive guide to primary and secondary sources, including numerous important essays whose conclusions are not as yet reflected in general works.

History of Scotland: The best general histories are W.C. DICKINSON, *Scotland from the Earliest Times to 1603*, 2nd rev. ed. (1965); and ROSALIND MITCHISON, *A History of Scotland* (1970), which also contain bibliographies. (*Prehistoric and Roman times*): STUART PIGGOTT, *Scotland Before History* (1958), is a good introduction. I.A. RICHMOND (ed.), *Roman and Native in North Britain* (1958), is helpful. (*Dark Age peoples*): ISABEL HENDERSON, *The Picts* (1967), is authoritative. (*Unification and the development of the monarchy*): A.O. ANDERSON, *Early Sources of Scottish History*, 2 vol. (1922), supplies the sources; see also the Scottish chapters in G.W.S. BARROW, *Feudal Britain* (1956). (*The Wars of Independence*): G.W.S. BARROW, *Robert Bruce and the Community of the Realm of Scotland* (1965), is balanced and important. (*The Reformation and the 16th century*): GORDON DONALDSON, *The Scottish Reformation* (1960); and the early chapters of T.C. SMOUT, *A History of the Scottish People, 1560–1830* (1969).

History of Ireland: T.W. MOODY and F.X. MARTIN (eds.), *The Course of Irish history* (1967), a collection of essays by various scholars that provides a good introduction to Irish history, with bibliographies, illustrations, and a useful chronological table; A.J. OTWAY-RUTHVEN, *A History of Medieval Ireland* (1968), essential for the study of medieval Ireland prior to 1496; J.C. BECKETT, *The Making of Modern Ireland, 1603–1923* (1966), a standard textbook for this period, with an excellent critical bibliography, including books on local history; J.F. KENNEY, *Sources for the Early History of Ireland: An Introduction and Guide* (1929 and 1967); R.J. HAYES (ed.), *Manuscript Sources for the History of Irish Civilization*, 11 vol. (1966), an extensive index of manuscript sources on Irish history from the 5th to the 20th century, with a list of microfilms in the National Library of Ireland; SEAN O'RIORDIAN, *Antiquities of the Irish Countryside*, 4th ed. (1964), a good introduction and bibliography; KATHLEEN HUGHES, *The Church in Early Irish Society* (1966), an account of the development of the Irish Church to the 11th century, including bibliography and illustrations; MYLES DILLON (ed.), *Early Irish Society* (1959), an authoritative collection, originally a broadcast discussion; JOHN MACNEILL, *Early Irish Laws and Institutions* (1935) and *Celtic Ireland* (1921); F.X. MARTIN in *Irish Historical Studies* (1948), for a listing of MacNeill's other writings; MAIRE and LIAM DE PAOR, *Early Christian Ireland*, 3rd ed. (1961), a detailed illustrated work; FRANCOIS HENRY, *Irish Art in the Early Christian Period to 800 A.D.*, rev. ed. (1965), a discussion of the art of this period against its historical background, with bibliography and illustrations; LUDWIG BIELER, *Ireland, Harbinger of the Middle Ages* (1963), a study of Irish missions and their influence in Europe; G.H. ORPEN, *Ireland Under the Normans, 1169–1333*, 4 vol. (1911–20, reprinted 1968), remains indispensable for this period; H.G. RICHARDSON and G.O. SAYLES, *The Administration of Ireland, 1172–1377* (1963) and *The Irish Parliament in the Middle Ages* (1952), an important work on the early history of the Irish parliament; RICHARD BAGWELL, *Ireland Under the Tudors*, 3 vol. (1885–90, reprinted 1963), and *Ireland Under the Stuarts and During the Interregnum*, 3 vol. (1909–16, reprinted 1963); and R. DUDLEY EDWARDS, *Church and State in Tudor Ireland* (1935, reprinted 1972), all standard works; L.W. HANSON, *Contemporary Printed Sources for British and Irish Economic History, 1701–1750* (1963), especially valuable because little has been written in this area; K.H. CONNELL, *The Population of Ireland, 1750–1845* (1950), a scholarly account; see also Connell's "Land and Population in Ireland 1780–1845," in D.V. GLASS and D.E.C. EVERSLEY (eds.), *Population in History* (1965); R.B. MCDOWELL, *Public Opinion and Government Policy in Ireland, 1801–46* (1952), a continuation of *Irish Public Opinion, 1750–1800*, with good bibliography; *The Irish Administration, 1801–1914* (1964), a detailed reference work on 19th-century administration; P.S. O'HEGARTY, *A History of Ireland Under the Union, 1801–1922* (1952), an extremely interesting but not wholly objective history of this period; K.B. NOWLAN, *The Politics of Repeal* (1965), an examination of Great Britain–Ireland relations, 1841–50; ANGUS D. MACINTYRE, *The Liberator: Daniel O'Connell and the Irish Party, 1830–1847* (1965), a recent study of O'Connell, with new material added on aspects of Anglo-Irish politics in the 1830s and 1840s; R.D. EDWARDS and T.D. WILLIAMS (eds.), *The Great Famine* (1956), an important compilation by Irish scholars; NICHOLAS MANSERGH, *The Irish Question, 1840–1921* (1965), a revision of *Ireland in the Age of Reform and Revolution* (1940), an interpretation of the effects of various political and social forces on Anglo-Irish relations; J.L. HAMMOND, *Gladstone and the Irish Nation* (1938, reprinted 1964), a standard work on Gladstone's Irish policy, 1869–93; C. CRUISE O'BRIEN (ed.), *The Shaping of Modern Ireland* (1960), a collection of biographical essays on prominent Irish personalities; *Parnell and His Party 1880–90*, rev. ed. (1964), the standard work on Parnell; BASIL CHUBB (ed.), *A Source Book of Irish Government* (1964), a collection of illustrative documents on the nature and background of the Republic of Ireland; T.P. COOGAN, *Ireland Since the Rising* (1966), presents the republican view of Irish history since 1916; F.S.L. LYONS, *Ireland Since the Famine* (1971); and R. DUDLEY EDWARDS, *A New History of Ireland* (1972), two recent interpretative works.

(D.W./M.Has./La.B.S./L.F.S./C.B.Co./As.B./A.F.H./J.B.Sm./J.M.S./R.W.D.E.)

British Columbia

One of the last regions of the North American continent to be explored and settled, British Columbia has become within recent decades one of the major provinces of Canada in population, economic wealth, and overall potentiality. Its 366,255 square miles (948,596 square kilometres) create a diversity of climate and scenery unparalleled in the nation, from the island-studded and fjord-indented coast to the great peaks of the western continental cordilleras with their large interior plateaus. The province is bounded on the west by the Pacific Ocean and the Panhandle of Alaska, on the north by the Yukon and Northwest territories, on the east by Alberta, and on the south by Montana, Idaho, and Washington.

Although the impetus for settlement of the province was the fur trade and the gold that lay in its mountains, British Columbia in the 1970s had a prosperous, modern economy balanced between the forest and mineral wealth of its interior, the hydroelectric production of its rivers, the agriculture of its plateaus and river valleys, the attraction of dramatic and varied scenery for the tourist, and the industry and shipping of its coastal cities. The cities include Vancouver, largest port of Canada and of western North America, and Victoria, the provincial capital, located on the southeastern tip of Vancouver Island. British Columbia, with Alberta and Ontario, was one of Canada's "have" provinces, contributing far more to federal coffers than they received back in grants. The 2,200,000 British Columbians enjoyed a per capita income second only to that of the citizens of Ontario.

Canada's prairie provinces and the Yukon constitute an added factor in British Columbia's prosperity, for they ship a large part of their grain, potash, sulfur, and phosphates from British Columbia's ports. The potential of the Yukon hinterland has been seriously developed only in recent decades. Although British Columbia lies far from the heartland of Canada and is overshadowed in the federal Parliament by the larger representations of Ontario and Quebec, the province has become a major force in the nation's economic, political, and social life. (For information on related topics, see the articles CANADA; CANADA, HISTORY OF; NORTH AMERICA; ROCKY MOUNTAINS; FRASER RIVER; and PACIFIC COAST RANGES.)

THE HISTORY OF BRITISH COLUMBIA

At the time of initial contact with white explorers, Indians in present-day British Columbia numbered about 80,000. The coast was dominated by Coast Salish, Nootkas, Kwakiutls, Bella Coolas, Tsimshians, and Haidas, whose economy was largely based on the products of the sea and on the huge coastal cedars. Expert fishermen, they utilized traps, nets, hooks, spears, and even an ingenious toggling harpoon for hunting down whales. Their clothing was made of skins and cedar bark covered by beautifully patterned blankets woven from the wool of mountain goats. Indian dwellings were large square or rectangular buildings of cedar beams and planks, divided into compartments for families. Houses were located in clusters along beaches suitable for canoe landings and just above the high-water mark. These pre-white Indians were already enterprising traders in copper, blankets, elk hides, furs, shells, candlefish oil, and slaves along the intertribal routes that ran north–south into California and east–west into the interior. They also enjoyed a rich social life in this land of the potlatch. Rival families competed with each other to distribute blankets, food, jewelry, and other favours to guests, often invited from hundreds of miles away, to mark the birth, adolescence, marriage, or death of an important member of the tribe.

Explorations and trading posts. The area that was to become British Columbia first caught the attention of European nations in the late 18th century. Spanish ships visited the coast in 1774, followed by Capt. James Cook, who was searching for the Northwest Passage. The latter's account of the fur wealth of the area stimulated the interest of British and American traders, who soon arrived to trade with the Indians for the highly prized sea otter pelts. The growing interest of Great Britain in the area was indicated by the dispatch of Capt. George Vancouver, who circumnavigated Vancouver Island and charted the mainland's intricate coastline.

Simultaneously, other British fur traders penetrated the region from the east, thereby strengthening Britain's claim to the area. Alexander Mackenzie of the North West Company of Montreal entered the region through its winding waterways; he completed the first overland journey across the entire continent when he arrived at Bella Coola, at the mouth of Dean Channel, in 1793. A fur trade based on fixed posts in the interior followed the establishment, by Simon Fraser in 1805, of the first trading post at McLeod Lake. Three years later he descended the Fraser River to its mouth, the site of present-day Vancouver.

Early dominance of the fur trade

After the southern boundary was fixed at the 49th parallel, Vancouver Island was recognized as solely British territory, following years of near-conflict with the United States. Ft. Victoria became the western headquarters of the Hudson's Bay Company. In 1849 Vancouver Island was made a crown colony by the imperial government, which expected that an orderly settlement in this distant outpost of empire would follow. Settlement, however, ran counter to the best interest of Gov. James Douglas and the fur company, which controlled local policy, and they discouraged it so successfully that in 1855 the total population of European origin in the colony was only 774, most of them involved in the pursuit of the fur trade.

Gold rush and permanent settlements. The gold strike of 1858 and the gold outpourings of the next five years made Ft. Victoria into a city, opened the mainland to settlement, and transformed an unpeopled frontier into a prosperous and dynamic society that was proclaimed the Colony of British Columbia in 1858. Hordes of gold seekers from California, Australia, and other parts of the Pacific community joined with Britishers and Canadians to work the alluvial gold deposits of the Lower Fraser and by 1862 the Cariboo gold country on the Upper Fraser.

By 1865 the gold days were over, and most of the miners had departed with the larger part of nearly $25,000,000 in gold dust. But the palmy days of the rush had attracted an army of ranchers, farmers, hotel operators, storekeepers, and civil servants who, although diminished in numbers, formed a nucleus for an ongoing, settled society. Left behind also was a fairly well-established transportation and communications network. Steamships linked Victoria and points on the Fraser River, and a 400-mile coach road connected Ft. Hope, on the Lower Fraser, with Barkerville, in the Cariboo gold country. The two colonies solved their problem in 1871 by joining Canada as the Province of British Columbia.

Stimulus of the railroads

The arrival of the Canadian Pacific Railway at Port Moody in 1885 opened a new era. Permanent railroad and lumbering settlements sprang up along the railroad route. The extension of the lines into Vancouver in 1886 brought about the incorporation of that city in the same year. The establishment of a steamship line connecting it with the Orient, in 1891, assured its future as a port.

Once the construction of the Panama Canal was assured, British Columbia experienced its first boom since the heady days of the gold rush, a boom based upon the assumption of investors that the province's raw resources would soon be able to compete in the markets of the Atlantic nations. Forest tracts were allotted by the thousands to eager American, British, German, and Canadian investors by a funds-starved provincial government eager to make an impressive fiscal showing and ensure its perpetual re-election. A similar situation prevailed in the mining industry, with the initial prizes going to British investors. Simultaneous with the opening up of these resource industries, the belated but now rapid settlement of the treeless prairies occurred, with its demand for lumber and other supplies best filled from British Columbia. With a revitalized economy the population increased from less than 180,000 to nearly 400,000 between 1901 and 1911, and Vancouver emerged as the leading city, with more than 111,000.

Economic cycles. Postwar dislocation after 1918, a continued shortage of shipping, strikes, and sporadic unemployment fed the flames of anti-Oriental feeling, always strong in Vancouver. Politicians, union leaders, and the *Vancouver Daily World* (now defunct) eagerly laid the blame for lack of prosperity on Oriental workers. Exclusionist legislation was passed by an obliging provincial legislature in 1923 and remained in force until the late 1940s, when Orientals were enfranchised.

But, scarcely recovered from the war years, the province found its newly acquired markets swept away by the economic depression of the 1930s. Recovery was delayed until war once again was declared in 1939. This time, military demands were extensive enough to reach across the continent into the shipbuilding yards, the lumbering communities, and the mines of British Columbia, ensuring the continued prosperity of the province's industry even beyond the war years.

Postwar political consolidation. With postwar economic prosperity came political change. To meet the political threat of the Depression-born Cooperative Commonwealth Federation (CCF), a moderate Socialist party, Conservatives and Liberals combined forces to form a coalition government during the war years. Growing disenchantment with the party in power, however, made inevitable the appearance of a new party as an alternative to the CCF. The Social Credit Party, which won the election of 1952, was formed by dissidents of both old-line parties but chiefly by conservatives, who adopted the name but not the philosophical principles of a highly successful conservative party in power in Alberta. The Social Credit government remained in power until 1972, when it lost the provincial election to the New Democratic Party (reformist successor to the CCF) which increased its standing from 12 to 38 seats in the 55-seat legislature.

THE LANDSCAPE

The natural environment. *Surface features.* The vast territory of British Columbia lies almost entirely within the great mountain system, or cordillera, that stretches along the western edge of the Americas from above the Arctic Circle to Cape Horn, at the southernmost extremity of South America. Its hundreds of rugged, coast-hugging islands—the largest of which are Vancouver Island and the Queen Charlotte Islands—offer a protected waterway along the coastline, which is indented by myriads of narrow fjords that twist inland about the bases of towering mountains. The broad Fraser Delta, behind Vancouver, is the largest of the limited coastal lowlands, while in the interior many of the wide plateaus are cut

The mountains, the sea, and the islands

by deep canyons and entirely surrounded by seemingly endless ranges of mountains.

About 60 percent of the land area is forested, while another one-third consists of barren alpine tundra, snowfields, and glaciers. More than three-quarters of the province is above 3,000 feet in altitude, beyond the limits of agriculture and often useful only for grazing. The Peace River country in the far north, outside the cordillera, contains the only vast areas suitable for large-scale farming, but its high latitudes make the growing season short.

Rivers and lakes. The province contains three main river systems: the Peace in the far north; the Fraser, which drains nearly all of the interior plateau; and the Columbia in the southeastern and south central regions. Lesser rivers, such as the Skeena, Nass, Iskut, and Stikine, drain the northwestern region into the Pacific, while the Laird system drains the northeastern section into the Arctic Ocean.

The Fraser, the only major river that lies entirely within the province, rises in the Rockies near the Yellowhead Pass, flows north along the Rocky Mountain Trench, and then southwestward to Prince George. There it receives the Nechako and turns almost due south for 300 miles, flowing through plateau and mountain valley to Hope, then westward through the lush farmlands of the Lower Fraser to the sea south of Vancouver. The Columbia follows the Rocky Mountain Trench northward, receiving the flow off the Columbia Icefield and the Selkirk glaciers, bends around the northern end of the Selkirk Mountains, and turns south to flow into the Arrow Lakes and then heads southward into Washington and Oregon, where it finds an outlet to the sea.

The Peace also becomes a formidable stream within the Rocky Mountain Trench, but it cuts eastward through the Rockies and into the plains area of Alberta, where it loses itself in the complex Mackenzie River system flowing to the Arctic.

Exploitation of the lakes

Most of the thousands of lakes are small, but they are important for the water they store in an age when hydroelectric power has become a prized resource. The larger lakes are made long and narrow by the north–south mountain ranges that confine them in the deep and narrow valleys in all parts of the province. Atlin and Teslin in the northwest extend into the Yukon. Babine, Stuart, Shuswap, Quesnel, and François, which range from 90 to 200 square miles (230 to 520 square kilometres) in area, are important salmon-spawning lakes. The Arrow Lakes are important storage reservoirs for the Columbia hydroelectric projects downstream while Kootenay Lake fulfills the same function for the generating plants on the Kootenay River.

Climate. Because of the Kuroshio, or Japanese, Current, which warms the coast, and the mountain ranges that make up its topography, British Columbia experiences a widely diverse range of climates. Climatologists claim that, in its temperature, humidity, and variability, the southwestern corner of the province has one of the most favourable climates for man, plants, and animals. There the climate resembles that of European nations in the same latitude, but it is tempered by the warm Kuroshio Current. The prevailing winds from the Pacific, flowing over succeeding mountain ranges, cause a wide variety of precipitation and temperature across the province, but along the coast such variation is negligible. Summers are comfortably cool, while winters are not severe, and 0° F (−18° C) is seldom recorded. In the Okanagan and Cariboo regions to the east, wider ranges are recorded; summers are hot and winters are colder. Still farther east, up against the Rockies, similar temperature ranges prevail but with considerably heavier snowfalls. In the northern interior and Peace River country very cold winters and very hot summers are normal.

British Columbia is well supplied with water, but its distribution is far from ideal. Some coastal towns have average annual rainfalls of 160 inches (4,100 millimetres) or more (perhaps the wettest region on the continent), while Ashcroft and Merritt, only 125 miles from the coast, register only seven and nine inches (180 and 230 millimetres), respectively. Victoria, sheltered by Vancouver Island mountains, receives only 27 inches, but Vancouver, 72 miles across the Strait of Georgia, receives 60 inches, picked up by the winds crossing that body of water.

Human uses of the land. The mountains and waters that surround them have made the British Columbians a race of valley dwellers. Valleys have assumed enormous importance for transportation and communications as well as for settlement, especially in the southern part of the province, where three-quarters of its population lives.

The mountains of Vancouver Island are separated from the Coast Mountains on the mainland by the Strait of Georgia, a saltwater valley along whose rocky slopes, on both sides, are located the province's largest and most important cities: Vancouver, Victoria, New Westminster, Nanaimo, and the pulp and paper centre of Powell River. East of that valley is located the valley and canyon of the Fraser, with such service centres as Hope, Boston Bar, Lytton and Lillooet, while still farther east lie the irrigated fruitlands of the Okanagan Valley and the cities of Salmon Arm, Enderby, Vernon, Kelowna, and Penticton. Beyond and pressing against the Rockies are the parallel mining and lumbering valleys of the West and East Kootenays, with the communities of Rossland, Trail, Nelson, and Fernie.

For the most part, trails, roads, railroads, oil and gas pipelines, and, to a less extent, electric power lines follow the routes of the rivers. Often they lie within yards of each other, so restricted are the narrow passes in much of the province's topography.

THE PEOPLE OF BRITISH COLUMBIA

British Columbia is the most urbanized province of Canada, with more than 80 percent of its citizens living in incorporated municipalities. It is also one of the most racially diverse.

Composition of the populace. The English, Scots, and Northern Irish played the major role in founding the province, and, to this day, they form the controlling elite. Scots dominated the fur-trade settlements before 1858, but, with the arrival of more than 20,000 Americans from California by 1864, the imperial government dispatched large numbers of Northern Irish to serve as the political and administrative arms of the province. With the return of most Americans to California in the mid-1860s, British Columbia became essentially British and remained so until the 1940s, in spite of notable minorities of Chinese, Japanese, Swedes, Norwegians, Italians, and Americans.

The ethnic mix

Since World War II the pattern has been modified somewhat by the arrival of large numbers of Europeans, especially Dutch farmers, attracted to the Fraser Delta lands, Germans, to the cities of the lower mainland, and Italians, to the railroads and construction industry. By the 1970s the people of the province were considerably less than 50 percent British in origin.

The native Indian population of 47,000 has more significant problems than any other minority group. It has been estimated that they numbered about 80,000 in the early 1800s, before tuberculosis, diphtheria, smallpox, and other "white man's diseases" reduced their ranks to 23,600 by 1934. Improved health measures, inaugurated since then, have stemmed their decimation, but they still live in greater poverty and have a much higher mortality rate than the white population. Scores of reservations dot the province's landscape, chiefly in rural areas. The pressure of an increasing population combined with great poverty and a lack of opportunity began driving Indians from reservations into the cities, in which about 30 percent of them lived in the early 1970s. Without education or skills valued by white society, they were relegated, with few exceptions, to permanent unemployment. In 1969 only 34 Indians were enrolled in the province's four universities.

The French-Canadian minority of 80,000 is scattered so thinly throughout the province that only the community of Coquitlam, near Vancouver, has the bilingual school program that prevails throughout much of Canada. Significant numbers of this minority are also found in the forest-industry centres of Terrace, Prince George, Powell River, and Port Alberni. In spite of the pleas of their leaders, French-Canadians in this province most distant from Quebec are singularly unmilitant about the bilingual and bicultural crusade that has so moved French-Canadians in other parts of the nation in recent years.

Although Americans constitute a small minority, they are an influential factor in the industrial life of the province—in manufacturing, mining, ranching, and forestry. During the education boom of the mid-1960s, they became a very important part of the teaching, administration, and research staffs of the universities and colleges.

About 2,500 blacks make up one of the smallest minorities. Most live in the Vancouver area, although a notable pioneer group, originating in a pre-Civil War exodus from the United States, reside in the Gulf Islands near Victoria.

Contemporary migratory patterns. Interprovincial migration, a noteworthy feature of Canadian life, holds particular significance in the rapid growth of British Columbia. During the 1960s it gained about 200,000 inhabitants from elsewhere in the nation, more than twice the number gained by the next-largest magnet, Ontario. Its relative prosperity, high rate of personal income, and mild climate are special enticements for residents of the prairie provinces. The Victoria, Vancouver, and Okanagan areas attract large numbers of older persons, bent on retirement amid a gentler climate and abundant amenities, from the prairies.

Recent influx of people

By contrast, central and northern British Columbia attract a preponderance of young people from the south, as well as from the prairies and eastern Canada. They are able to cope with the rigours of the more severe climate, the lack of good housing, and the absence of many services taken for granted in the south. In return, the north offers them higher wages and the opportunity to establish themselves in a still largely virginal territory, an appealing prospect in a period in which populations increasingly show signs of deserting the crowded and polluted urban centres.

THE PROVINCE'S ECONOMY

Areas of public ownership. The economy of British Columbia is a mixture of public and private enterprise. Two of the three major railroads serving the province are publicly owned. The provincially owned British Columbia Railway (BCR) contributes significantly to the economic viability of the central and northern regions, which are served poorly or not at all by the two national roads. It operates some 1,100 miles of mainline track between North Vancouver and its northern terminal at Fort Nelson; 420 additional miles of track, under construction in the early 1970s, will take it to Dease Lake, about 100 miles from the Yukon border.

The second important public corporation is British Columbia Hydro and Power Authority, which generates, transmits, and distributes electricity in areas containing 90 percent of the province's population and distributes natural gas in the Vancouver and Lower Fraser Valley areas. It also operates transit systems in greater Vancouver and greater Victoria and interurban bus systems between Fraser Valley points and Vancouver and between Vancouver, Victoria, and Nanaimo. On the Peace River the corporation undertook construction of the W.A.C. Bennett Dam, one of the largest in the world, and several others on the Columbia River. By 1973 the Peace River power project, located west of Fort St. John, was to supply 1,800,000 kilowatts of power to Vancouver and southern British Columbia. The Mica, Hugh Keenleyside, and Duncan dams in the Columbia system aided in flood control in the downstream sections of the river in U.S. territory.

The private sector. Of chief interest in the private sphere are forest industries, mining, tourism, shipping, and agriculture. The forests of British Columbia make up more than half of the total Canadian forest resource. The forest industry is dominated by several giant multinational corporations, which usually hold forest-management licenses from the provincial government for sustained-yield forestry, a continuous replanting that is practiced in more than 85 percent of the province's forest area. These companies have integrated the production of timber, lumber, chips, shingles, plywood, and pulp and paper under single corporate organizations for maximum utilization. The chief areas of forest activity are the Georgia Strait area, between Campbell River and Vancouver, where pulp and paper production is particularly important; and the Prince George area, where pine production and pulp and paper predominate. In 1969 the forest industry contributed more than $1,200,000,000 to the province's economy.

Minerals, petroleum, and natural gas worth nearly $520,000,000 were produced in British Columbia in 1971, but the production of petroleum, natural gas, and coal were still in their infancy, with rapid expansion likely in the decade of the 1970s. The most valuable mined products are copper, crude oil, molybdenum, zinc, lead, and natural gas.

The ports of Vancouver, Victoria, Chemainus, Powell River, New Westminster, and Prince Rupert are the chief ones through which the resources of British Columbia and other provinces are exported to the United States, Japan, and other world markets. Most of Vancouver's shipping is carried out from the inner harbour, but Roberts Bank "superport" handles increasingly large shipments of coal and other bulk cargoes, especially for the Japanese market. The National Harbours Board of Canada is responsible for the construction of Roberts Bank, Canada's first superport, located just south of Vancouver at the mouth of the Fraser. Facilities capable of loading thousands of tons an hour have been erected, and berths capable of servicing the world's largest cargo carriers have been set up.

Transportation. Although an elementary system of transportation was established in gold-rush days and most of its routes are still followed, no concerted effort was made to tie the isolated areas of the province together by roads, ferries, and railroads until after World War II. Highways are exceedingly important in a province having the highest number of passenger cars per capita in Canada. This crucial fact was recognized and exploited by the infant Social Credit Party, which adopted an ambitious and controversial program of road building, bridge building, and ferry services as the chief plank of its highly successful political platform. In the 15-year period after 1955, over $1,500,000,000 was spent constructing and repairing over 7,800 miles of highway and building 528 bridges, including such structures as the Alexandra North Arch in the Fraser Canyon, the Port Mann Bridge near New Westminster, the Okanagan Bridge at Kelowna, and the unique four-lane, 2,100-foot Deas Island Tunnel under the Fraser River near Vancouver.

Highway expansion

British Columbia's convoluted landscape makes it a bridge country, with more than 3,000 crossings, and places construction costs of roads in many areas at more than $1,000,000 per mile, apart from the bridges. The Fraser Canyon, north of Hope, includes seven highway tunnels up to 2,000 feet long.

Vancouver Island, with one-sixth of the province's population, represents a special transportation problem. This has been met by the development of one of the world's largest ferry fleets. Most of the ferries connecting Vancouver with Victoria and Nanaimo carry 1,000 passengers and from 140 to 200 cars each.

The province is served by three railroads. The Canadian Pacific Railway (CPR) connects Vancouver with eastern Canada via a mail line through the Crowsnest Pass and maintains a network of branches serving the mining, forest, and agricultural industries throughout southern British Columbia. The Canadian National Railway, like the BCR, is publicly owned. It serves the south and the north with terminals at Vancouver and Prince Rupert. The British Columbia Railway was discussed above.

The vastness of the province combined with difficult terrain and variable weather conditions have offered particular encouragement to the development of air travel. Vancouver International Airport is headquarters for Canadian Pacific Air and Pacific Western Airlines Ltd., Canada's second- and third-largest carriers.

ADMINISTRATION AND SOCIAL CONDITIONS

Structure of government. Parliamentary government in British Columbia dates from the inauguration of the first legislature of the Colony of Vancouver Island, August 12, 1856, but responsible government was not achieved until confederation.

Provincial level. The lieutenant governor, appointed by the government in Ottawa, ostensibly represents the British crown, but in the real sense he represents the federal government. The lieutenant governor calls upon the recognized leader of the majority party in the provincial Legislative Assembly to form a government, with that leader as premier. The premier and his Cabinet, whom he selects from the elected members of the legislature, comprise the Executive Council. The Cabinet is responsible to the Legislative Assembly for the operation of the day-to-day business of the government. The unicameral assembly has 55 members representing 42 electoral districts.

Local government. More than 80 percent of the population resides in municipalities governed by elected mayors and councils. These local governments are the children of the provincial government, which creates them and supervises their activities. Because the senior government has greater access to revenue sources, especially new forms of taxation, funds-starved municipalities are growing more receptive to the requests of the minister of municipal affairs for greater cooperation among them in such areas as education, hospital services, transportation, and even local government. Since the provincial government meets a large part of the municipal budgets outside of the large cities, the minister receives considerable cooperation even in his demands for outright amalgamation of contiguous municipalities.

Justice and law enforcement. The attorney general of the province is responsible for the administration of justice, for the enforcement of the law, and for the administration of the provincial Court of Appeal, Supreme Court, and county courts (except judicial appointment) under terms of the British North America Act. There are two Courts of Appeal registries, in Vancouver and Victoria, and 40 Supreme Court and county registries throughout the province. In addition, at the lower court level, the attorney general controls the appointment of magistrates, family-court judges, coroners, and justices of the peace, all of whose duties are defined by federal and provincial statutes.

By agreement, the Royal Canadian Mounted Police (RCMP) act as the provincial police force under the control of the attorney general. Most cities and district municipalities are responsible for law enforcement within their own boundaries. Most elect to have this function contracted out to the RCMP, but Vancouver, Victoria, and New Westminster maintain independent forces. The RCMP is responsible for all unorganized areas. Legal aid, administered by the British Columbia Law Society on a limited basis to the poor, is paid for chiefly by the attorney general from provincial funds.

Provincial involvement in medical services

The social milieu. *Health and welfare.* The British Columbia Overall Medical Services Plan is available to all residents of the province on a voluntary subscription basis at low, uniform rates. It provides comprehensive medical care coverage, including specified services of physicians, surgeons, certain dental surgeons, the Red Cross, nurses, chiropractors, osteopathic physicians, and others. Hospital care at $1.00 per day is also available under the British Columbia Hospital Insurance Service (BCHIS). Medical care for the aged meets the standards of the Medical Care Act of Canada and receives contributions from the federal government. About 98 percent of the province's population is covered by the plan and by BCHIS. Ninety-four general hospitals operate under BCHIS in addition to eight Red Cross outpost hospitals, five federal hospitals, and 22 special hospitals.

Narcotics addiction is a special medical problem of enormous significance to British Columbia, which has in the past accounted for more than half of Canada's narcotics addicts. Prior to 1908, when narcotics were made illegal, Vancouver legally produced refined opium of high quality. Though supplies now come illegally from Europe rather than China, the problem of addiction has remained serious. The Narcotic Addiction Foundation of British Columbia, located in Vancouver, offers methadone treatment and psychotherapy free of charge, but no unified system of addiction treatment has been established in the province.

Environmental pollution. Environmental health and pollution control are of enormous concern to British Columbians, especially as they affect the Fraser River, the Gulf and Strait of Georgia, and the lakes of the Okanagan and Kootenay regions. Of the 42 communities within the Fraser River watershed, only a handful have adequate waste-disposal units. Consequently, the river is polluted to the point where the important salmon runs are endangered and the usefulness of the river for recreation purposes is being rapidly circumscribed. The only tertiary treatment plant in British Columbia is located in Kelowna, where the plant removes a high percentage of phosphates from sewage effluent dumped into that endangered lake.

The rapid expansion of the raw-resources industries, especially in pulp, paper, and mining since 1960, has produced a problem of mammoth proportions. Each pulp mill releases millions of gallons of toxic effluents into rivers and coastal waters daily and tons of obnoxious air pollutants. Strip-mining of coalfields in the Kootenay Range, to feed the blast furnaces of Japan, are laying waste miles of mountainside, and scores of mines (nine in the Fraser watershed alone) release staggering quantities of toxic substances from mining processes into the tributaries of the Fraser, the Columbia, and other streams.

British Columbia has been slow to enforce pollution control, partly because of the cost and partly out of fear of slowing down investment in the industries responsible for the pollution. Ecologists consider existing control legislation inadequate and government supervision of offending industries lax.

Education. The provincial government spends about 30 percent of its budget on the rapidly expanding education industry of the province. Public school education is free and compulsory to the age of 15. High schools can be found in every part of the province, while two-year junior colleges, operated by local school boards, are located in ten communities. Vocational schools are operated in most districts, and the local school board operates the Vancouver School of Art.

The University of British Columbia, in Vancouver, offers a wide range of advanced studies to upward of 20,000 students. Of special interest are the schools of medicine, forestry, dentistry, oceanography, agriculture, architecture, and Asian studies. A library of nearly 2,000,000 books, manuscripts, and microforms is especially strong in periodical literature, Canadiana, English literature of the 19th and early 20th centuries, and Chinese literature and history. Simon Fraser University, in adjacent Burnaby, has an enrollment of 5,000, as does the University of Victoria. Notre Dame University of Nelson is a small Roman Catholic institution.

CULTURAL LIFE AND INSTITUTIONS

Cultural dominance of the frontier

The majority of cultural activities in British Columbia tend to reflect the pioneer background of the province, the great distances between pockets of population, and the various economic backgrounds of areas still oriented to resource industries and to the outdoors. The Williams Lake Stampede is the great annual event of the white and the Indian populations of the ranching country of the Central Interior. The Kelowna Regatta attracts thousands to that watersports and tourist centre. Even the annual Pacific National Exhibition in Vancouver is largely oriented to the agricultural communities of the Lower Fraser Valley rather than to the urban interest of Vancouver. Other centres hold annual loggers-day festivals, salmon contests, and pioneer events related to outdoor industry and pursuits.

Cultural activities of the larger cities are in a transitional stage, neither frontier nor unabashedly big city. Spectator sports based on monster stadiums and imported professional players made their debut with the building of the Empire Stadium in Vancouver and the establishment of the British Columbia Lions professional football team, later supplemented by the Vancouver Canucks of professional hockey. Vancouver's opera association, both respectable and ambitious, mounts productions featuring artists imported from the world's great opera houses, while its symphony society receives enthusiastic support from a loyal following of citizens. Smaller but important organizations, such as the Vancouver Institute, with its presentation of important speakers of international repute, and the Vancouver History Society, with its growing list of publications on provincial history, are finding increasing support as the city leaves the frontier behind.

Local industrialists have done much to support the recent upsurge in cultural activities through their financial support of such distributing agencies as the Vancouver Foundation and the Koerner Foundation. Private funds are channelled through them into the theatres, orchestras, university libraries, art galleries, and museums, as well as to private artists and scholars.

Cultural activities were given a sharp impetus by the three centennial celebrations of 1958, 1967, and 1971, when millions of dollars were provided by all three levels of government and by foundations and private companies to mark the establishment of the province, the founding of the nation, and the entry of British Columbia into confederation. The centennials fortunately occurred in a period of economic prosperity that found the public and private enterprise in a mood to support the expenditure of large sums on theatres, libraries, museums, planetariums, public squares and fountains, the restoration of historic sites, and similar expressions of unappeased cultural hunger. Among the most noteworthy constructions in Vancouver were the Centennial Museum, Maritime Museum, and H.R. MacMillan Planetarium, the Bloedel Conservatory, the Queen Elizabeth Theatre complex, the Court House square and fountain. In Victoria the McPherson Playhouse–City Hall complex is outstanding, as is the British Columbia Provincial Museum.

In a special place is the continuing restoration of Barkerville, once the thriving centre of the Cariboo gold rush of the 1860s. There the provincial government has rebuilt scores of old buildings to re-create the old gold town as it appeared over a century ago. A noncommercial project, it is probably the most historically faithful restoration of a complete town in the North American West.

The restoration of historic buildings of Victoria is also a notable consequence of a rebirth of interest in the province's cultural heritage. Scores of derelict buildings of historic interest have been restored to their original appearance and rented to merchants. Squares have been opened, and whole streets have been revitalized without recourse to bulldozers or slum clearance. Old buildings have been blended in with new in one of the most expansive and imaginative programs of its kind on the North American continent. Victoria, always a history-conscious city, has demonstrated that the architectural and cultural heritage of the province can be preserved and at the same time be made to serve a day-to-day useful purpose.

PROSPECTS

It is possible to look hopefully at future possibilities for British Columbia because of the ironic juxtaposition within the province of the untamed and the settled, of the promise that lies ahead and the rewards for the past. Urban British Columbia is, in every sense, economically vital and fully a part of western Canada's economy. Close at hand lie frontier and wilderness areas that provide not only spectacular recreational and nonurban-living opportunities but also potentialities for a continued economic development. Environmental damage is perhaps the most serious problem threatening at least a part of the province, unhappily but inevitably the most populated portion. Finally, it remains a question as to how long the province's economy, without pursuing new avenues of innovation, can continue to absorb the influx from other parts of the nation.

BIBLIOGRAPHY. RODERICK HAIG-BROWN, *The Living Land: An Account of the Natural Resources of British Columbia* (1961), a first-rate comprehensive inventory of the natural resources of the province, with a useful outsize map in folder pocket; MARGARET A. ORMSBY, *British Columbia: A History* (1958), a scholarly yet eminently readable account of the historical development of the province, especially rich in the pre–1935 period; REGINALD E. WATTERS (ed.), *British Columbia: A Centennial Anthology* (1958), a literary treatment of the province's many-sided development drawing upon hundreds of diverse sources; *British Columbia Historical Quarterly* (1937–58), a rich source on British Columbia history; *B.C. Studies*, a quarterly periodical presenting scholarly papers about the province's history, geography, archaeology, and economics; HARRY B. HAWTHORNE (ed.), *A Survey of the Contemporary Indians of Canada: Economic, Political, Educational Needs and Policies*, 2 vol. (1966–69), a comprehensive account of one of the most pressing human problems in Canada today; *Canadian Literature*, a scholarly quarterly periodical devoted to the study of Canadian literature (offers excellent coverage of British Columbia's literature); IRENE HOWARD, *Vancouver's Svenskar: A History of the Swedish Community in Vancouver* (1970), a noteworthy first publication of the Vancouver History Society's series on the ethnic groups of British Columbia; E.O.S. SCHOLEFIELD and F.W. HOWAY, *British Columbia from the Earliest Times to the Present*, 4 vol. (1914), full treatment of the province's history up to 1914—dated but valuable (two of four volumes are biographical); GEORGE WOODCOCK and IVAN AVAKUMOVIC, *The Doukhobors* (1968), a scholarly account of an unusual people; *Transactions of the Ninth British Columbia Natural Resources Conference* (1956), the most comprehensive account of the province's resources compiled by government departments.

(J.C.L.)

British Empire and Commonwealth

The development of the British Empire and Commonwealth was long and complicated. Not only did Britain win and lose a number of territories through conquest and cession (*e.g.*, Manila was British from 1762 to 1764; Java, from 1811 to 1816) but the degree of sovereignty Britain possessed over particular territories varied (*e.g.*, there was never any actual sovereignty over Egypt, in spite of British administration for half a century; and in a number of other cases British sovereignty was indirect, being derived from treaties or the proclamation of a protectorate).

The growth of independence by territories of the empire led to a new kind of political organization—the (British) Commonwealth of Nations; and, while later members of this body became independent only after a clear renunciation of sovereignty by Britain, the older members (such as Canada, Australia, and New Zealand) were, between the two World Wars, thought of as still in the British Empire, of which the British Commonwealth of Nations, consisting of self-governing territories, was regarded as part.

THE GROWTH OF THE BRITISH EMPIRE

British voyages of discovery and profit. The beginnings of the British Empire are usually located in the 16th century, when an urge toward overseas trade and settlement developed out of the pioneering voyages of Elizabethan seamen. A succession of voyages followed John Cabot's discovery of Newfoundland in 1497 and the establishment of a flourishing fishing trade there. At first the objects were trade and plunder; settlement had to wait until the beginning of the 17th century, although there were earlier abortive attempts to settle Newfoundland and Virginia. The expansion of Britain's maritime strength, however, paved the way for the establishment of settlements in North America and the West Indies.

Beginnings of the empire

In later centuries, exploration again stimulated imperial expansion, notably through the discoveries of Capt. James Cook in the South Pacific in the latter part of the 18th century and those of David Livingstone, Richard Burton, John Hanning Speke, and other travellers in Africa in the 19th. Apart from these notable cases, however, the 18th- and 19th-century development of the empire was due much more to conquest, international rivalry, and the search for favourable trading opportunities than to direct discovery.

Origins of British expansion. British expansion in the Americas, India, and Africa began in earnest in the 17th century. North America and the Caribbean were the scenes of what is sometimes called "the first British Empire," terminating in the loss of the colonies that became the United States. In nearly all cases, the early settlements arose from the enterprise of particular companies and magnates rather than from any effort on the part of the crown.

In the first half of the 17th century, when Virginia, Maryland, and the colonies of New England were set up, there were also settlements in Nova Scotia, Barbados, the Bermudas, Honduras, Antigua, and certain other West Indian islands. Jamaica was obtained by conquest in 1655. The Hudson's Bay Company established itself in what became northwestern Canada from the 1670s onward. The hold of the crown over these colonies, obtained through the issue of a charter, was slight but greater than that of the British Parliament. As late as 1732, the parliamentary leader Robert Walpole objected to the discussion by Parliament of the charter for Georgia, since it was regarded as part of the royal prerogative.

The crown exercised some rights of appointment and supervision, but the colonies were essentially self-managing, the form of their management depending on the character of those who had established them. No attempt was made to establish a uniform administration, although it was usual for the colonies to have some sort of local legislature and to reproduce the English legal system.

India. In India the beginnings of British influence were similar, though they did not involve settlement. The East India Company, granted its charter in 1600, was content for a long time to establish trading posts without controlling territory. Not until the authority of the Mogul Empire began to disintegrate at the beginning of the 18th century and other European powers, especially France, began actively to look for gains in India did the company set about the series of treaties and conquests that led to the consolidation of the Indian Empire. The Straits Settlements (Penang, Singapore, Malacca, and Labuan) became British through an extension of the East India Company's activities (see INDIAN SUBCONTINENT, HISTORY OF THE: *India and European expansion, c. 1500–1858*).

Africa. The British became involved in Africa later than in the Americas and India, though the first permanent British settlement on the African continent was established on James Island in the Gambia River as early as 1661. Sierra Leone was the scene of Sir John Hawkins' successful slave-trading ventures in 1562, but it did not become a British possession until 1787, after which it was used to resettle slaves from other British colonies. The Gold Coast (later Ghana) was a further example of 17th-century British trading effort, but it did not develop into an administered territory until the 19th century, when Nigeria, by various stages, also became British.

Whereas the main British interest in these western African territories was in trade, in the southern tip of Africa it was in settlement, following the acquisition of the Cape in 1806; the interior was opened up by Boer and British pioneers, ultimately under British control. British administration of what are now Kenya and Uganda, on the eastern coast, did not begin until the 1880s.

Thus the motives that led to British control of great areas far from Britain itself were various. The commercial motive was undoubtedly the strongest at the start, and it remained important; but as time went on, it was augmented by missionary influence and by strategic considerations. It is important to emphasize, however, how unorganized was the extension of the empire. Only rarely was there strong sentiment in Britain in favour of the acquisition of territory as such (the last two decades of the 19th century were one such period). The British tradition was of piecemeal acquisition, each case being treated on its merits, sometimes with the British government being the least willing partner in the enterprise.

Relations between England and the empire

The empire of outposts, to 1763. The sphere in which the crown exercised most control over the colonies in the 17th and 18th centuries was trade and shipping.

Trade in goods. In accordance with the mercantilist philosophy of the time—also adhered to by other European colonial powers—the colonies were regarded as a source of necessary supplies for England and were granted monopolies for their products, such as tobacco and sugar, in the British market. In return, they were expected to conduct all their trade by means of English ships. The Navigation Act of 1651 and further acts after the Restoration provided that no other country could carry goods to or from the colonies, that the main colonial products could be exported only to England, and that only those foreign products that had been brought to England first could be imported into the colonies. This closed economic system caused objections from some of the colonies but guaranteed others that their distinctive products would find a sheltered market in Britain and not be subject to competition from other powers' sugar colonies, especially those of Spain. This arrangement lasted until the combined effects of the Scottish economist Adam Smith's *Wealth of Nations* (1776), the loss of the American colonies, and the growth of a free-trade movement in Britain slowly brought it to an end; but the last Navigation Act was not repealed until 1849.

The slave trade. In the 18th century, most of the colonial economic systems in the Americas rested on the Navigation Acts, on the one hand, and slavery, on the other. The slave trade, begun by Hawkins, had become an economic necessity for the Caribbean colonies and the southern parts of what later became the United States. It was not confined to these British colonies but was common to those of France and Spain, with which the British colonists were in competition. Movements for the ending of the slave trade and of slavery itself had begun in Britain before the loss of the colonies on the eastern American seaboard; they came to fruition in British possessions long before the similar movement in the United States. The trade was abolished in 1807, slavery in 1833. It left behind it, however, many people of African stock who still form the bulk of the populations of the independent states of Jamaica, Trinidad, Barbados, and other Caribbean islands that remain British dependencies.

British sea power. In the 18th century, the Caribbean colonies were important to Britain not only as suppliers of sugar and buyers of slaves but also as strategic possessions in deciding the issue of naval supremacy between Britain, France, and Spain. The admirals George Rodney and Horatio Nelson were as familiar with the waters of the Indies as with those of Europe. Indeed, as hostility continued between Britain and France, colonial possessions became not only bases but also prizes. In the process, Britain gained two of the most important parts of its empire—Canada and India.

British conquests. Fighting between the French and British colonies in North America was endemic in the first half of the 18th century. It was especially fierce during the Seven Years' War (1756–63), which was ended by the Peace of Paris in 1763, whereby British control of Canada became undisputed, with expansion into the west and northwest no longer threatened by a chain of French forts stretching southward from Quebec to Louisiana. Control of a large population of French descent, language, and culture in Quebec was a new experience for Britain, but this did not prevent an eventual consolidation of Canada.

In India, the East India Company was confronted by the French Compagnie des Indes. Under the governor general Joseph-François Dupleix, French influence and conquest flourished while British influence diminished. The balance was redressed in favour of the British by the military genius of Robert Clive and by a change in French policy, which recalled Dupleix. Clive and Eyre Coote went on to further victories against the French and against the rulers of Bengal, thus providing the East India Company with its first massive accession of territory and ensuring that no other European power would challenge British supremacy in India.

Clive's victory at Plassey in India was in 1757; James Wolfe's at Quebec, in 1759. By this time Britain was, of necessity, showing more governmental concern for the colonies. Although the New England colonists in America and the East India Company in India might fight the French on local ground, their doing so was part of the larger struggle between Britain and France and had to be taken into account—sometimes assisted, sometimes muted—by the government in London. For strategic reasons, the government displayed a great interest in acquiring territory at the Treaty of Aix-la-Chapelle in 1748 and the Treaty of Paris in 1763. Yet it could not be said that any great colonial design was manifest in the British demands; the fact that Lord Bute's Cabinet in 1763 discussed whether it would be better to retain the conquered sugar island of Guadeloupe than to keep the French out of Canada indicates the short-term considerations that often governed policy.

Changes in the empire

Losses and gains, 1763–1815. Despite the loss of its colonies in what is now the United States, the empire continued to grow during the late 18th and early 19th centuries.

The loss of the American colonies. Britain lost the 13 colonies in North America because it attempted to interfere in their affairs but lacked the military skill and organization to bring them to heel when they revolted. The war in America dragged on from 1775 until 1783 and was enlarged by the entry of France, Spain, and Holland against Britain. Apart from the loss of the colonies in revolt, some Caribbean islands were lost temporarily to France, and Tobago and Minorca were no longer British after the peace settlement. The blow to British pride was considerable; but the British Empire was soon to show further vitality through the spectacular growth of Upper Canada after the emigration there of loyalists from what had become the United States and through the establishment of new colonies of settlement in the South Pacific.

The first settlements in Australia. In 1770 Capt. James Cook sailed along the previously unknown eastern coast of Australia and around New Zealand, bringing back reports that formed the basis of later settlement. New Zealand did not come under formal British control until 1840; but the settlement of Australia began in New South Wales in 1788, in part due to the loss of the American colonies, which were no longer available as a repository for some of Britain's convicts. Australia's period of transportation lasted only about 60 years, however, and the main mass of the population was derived from free settlement. Tasmania (1803) and Queensland (1824) were convict settlements, and Western Australia, after its inception as a freemen's colony, took convicts for labour from 1849 until 1868; but Victoria (1834) and South Australia (1836) were never convict colonies.

Conquests during the Napoleonic Wars. The Napoleonic Wars (1799–1815) provided further additions of territory to the empire, although only one acquisition—the Cape of Good Hope—became an area of substantial British settlement. By the Treaty of Amiens in 1802 Britain gained Trinidad and Ceylon. By the first Treaty of Paris in 1814 gains included Tobago, Mauritius, St. Lucia, and Malta—each of which had strategic value. At the Cape, however, Britain made its most fateful acquisition. The Dutch had been settling there since 1652, reinforced by French Huguenots. The Boer farmers had developed a distinctive society and an ethos of their own. Britain's interest in retaining the Cape was at first a naval one because of the route to India, but this was soon augmented by the wish to anglicize the Boers through the use of the English language and through added immigration from Britain. Many of the Boers proved recalcitrant.

Certain other additions, made early in the 19th century, were of great future importance. They included Malacca, which came into British hands in 1795, and Singapore—a mudbank with few inhabitants when Sir Thomas Stamford Raffles took it over for the East India Company in 1819, but later a trading port of growing importance. The future shape of Canada was being determined with the settlement of Alberta, Manitoba, and British Columbia. These, like Australia, New Zealand, and the Cape, were fertile and comparatively empty; they were to become areas of substantial British migration. The War of 1812 with the United States provided an impetus to Canadian unity and strengthened Canadian disinclination to become part of the U.S.

In India, the period of the Napoleonic Wars was notable —not for fighting with France but for local wars against French influence and for the acquisition by the East India Company, through conquest and treaty, of the United Provinces of Agra and Oudh and the Central Provinces; East Bengal and Assam were to follow before long.

Further spread of British influence

Expansion in the 19th century. The Crimean War (1854–56) made little or no difference to the British Empire, and Britain had no other wars with European powers between 1815 and 1914. During this long period, British wars were either in India or in the colonial empire—notably in pacification programs in Africa—but also against the Maoris in New Zealand. The most serious conflicts were with the Boers (in 1881 and 1899–1902) and with the Mahdi (*q.v.;* 1884) in the Sudan. For the most part, 19th-century development was a matter of consolidating existing colonies and of extending into new areas, especially in Africa.

Colonial administration and policy. Administration and policy changed during the century from the haphazard arrangements inherited from the 17th and 18th centuries to the relatively sophisticated system characteristic of Joseph Chamberlain's tenure in the Colonial Office (1895–1900). That office, the distinct existence of which can be traced from 1801, was first an appendage of the Home Office and Board of Trade, and then linked with the secretary for war. By the 1850s, it had become a separate department with an increasing staff and something of a continuing policy; it was the means by which discipline and pressure were exerted on the colonial governments (though not upon the East India Company) when such action was considered necessary.

In the main, however, colonial governments were left largely to themselves. In the areas of new settlement in North America, South Africa, and the Pacific, local self-government was soon granted to the settlers. In the Caribbean, however, an opposite movement took place; the powers of most of the long-established legislative bodies were reduced and those of the governors increased so that these became "crown colonies," subject to direct rule. The reason for this was the condition of the islands after the repeal of slavery in 1833. Emancipation, combined with the effects of the withdrawal of the sugar monopoly in Britain after the triumph of Free Trade, made government in the interests of the tiny minority of planters no longer acceptable. When expansion took place in Africa and the Pacific, the crown colony system was again applied.

New Zealand and Oceania. In the Pacific, New Zealand became officially British in 1840, following pressure from the missionaries who were alarmed at the impact on the Christianized Maoris of the small collection of white rogues and vagabonds who had established themselves there. Systematic colonization followed rapidly. Land disputes between the settlers and the Maoris led to the Maori Wars of the 1840s and 1860s; but the eventual settlement satisfied both sides, and British troops were withdrawn. Late in the century British control was extended to other islands in the Pacific—often again because of missionary pressure and sometimes because of international rivalry. Fiji was ceded in 1874. A British High Commission for the Western Pacific Islands was established in 1877. A protectorate was declared over Papua in 1884, following pressure from Queensland, and over Tonga in 1900. Other groups of islands were also taken over. Some of these acquisitions later became the responsibility of Australia and New Zealand.

Asia. The situation in 19th-century India was one of slow but constant extension, first of the East India Company's territory, and then, after the replacement of the company's authority by that of the crown following the Indian Mutiny (1857), of the Indian Empire. The greatest acquisition was that of Burma, completed in 1886; but the conquest of the Punjab (1849) and of British Baluchistan (1854–76) provided substantial territory in the Indian subcontinent itself. The importance of a new route to India, after the opening of the Suez Canal, was signified by the growth of Aden (originally captured by the East India Company in 1839), by a protectorate in Somaliland, and by the extension of British influence among the sheikhdoms of southern Arabia and the Persian Gulf. Cyprus—a link, like Gibraltar and Malta, in the chain of communication with India through the Mediterranean—was occupied by treaty with the Ottoman Empire in 1878.

British influence in the Far East expanded with the development of the Straits Settlements and the federated Malay states. In the 1880s Britain became established in Borneo, with a chartered company at work in British North Borneo and protectorates over Brunei and Sarawak. Hong Kong island became British in 1841, and adjacent territories on the Chinese mainland were acquired in 1860 and 1896. The British also obtained special rights in Shanghai, another great trading port through which Britain's "informal empire" in China operated; this was not a matter of sovereignty, however, and mention of it in the context of the British Empire, while realistic in a sense, is more doubtful in legal terms.

Africa. The greatest development of 19th-century British imperial power took place in Africa. In Egypt, Britain was the acknowledged ruling force from 1882 onward, following a naval bombardment of Alexandria; in The Sudan, formerly a nominal Egyptian province, British control was exercised under the guise of an Anglo-Egyptian joint administration established in 1899. The idea that British power might extend "from the Cape to Cairo" fascinated many people in Britain in the 1880s and '90s—a period of great enthusiasm for the empire, marked by Queen Victoria's two jubilees, by colonial conferences, by the re-establishment of chartered companies to seek out new areas of opportunity, and by mining discoveries and wars in South Africa. On the western coast the Royal Niger Company began the extension of British influence in Nigeria. The Imperial British East Africa Company operated in what are now Kenya and Uganda, and the British South Africa Company in the areas now called Rhodesia, Zambia, and Malawi. Again, missionary influence was strong in the eventual transfer of some of these territories to the crown.

After the South African War (Boer War, 1899–1902), British influence spread northward from the Cape. Natal had become British in 1843. The Orange Free State and the Transvaal swayed back and forth between independence and British suzerainty, but they were annexed after the South African War. Meanwhile, the activities of the British South Africa Company, north of the Transvaal, had ensured a British presence in Southern and Northern Rhodesia. South Africa was the principal source of argument between imperialists and anti-imperialists. To many, British policies there epitomized the misuse of imperial power.

For better or worse, the spread of the British Empire had been so great during the 19th century that it comprised nearly a quarter of the land surface and included more than a quarter of the population of the world. The term empire, however, was obviously used rather for convenience than in any sense equivalent to the older or despotic empires of history. This was due to the high degrees of self-government obtained by the white-dominated colonies.

THE COMMONWEALTH OF NATIONS

Growth of self-government. The beginnings of the self-government movement probably lie with Lord Durham's *Report on the Affairs of British North America* (1839). Following minor rebellions in both Upper Canada (Ontario) and Lower Canada (Quebec), Durham was sent out as governor general to investigate.

Responsible government. Durham's report recommended that responsible government (*i.e.*, the acceptance of the advice of local ministers by governors) be granted to the two Canadas, which should be merged in one. The merger took place immediately, but Durham's advice on responsible government was not accepted until put into effect by his son-in-law Lord Elgin, governor general in 1847. Thereafter, the pattern was applied to other Canadian provinces and to the Australian colonies. The British government's willingness to let the colonies of settlement manage their own affairs was very much in line with its contemporary disavowal of the mercantilist philosophy and with its withdrawal of colonial privileges in the British market.

New South Wales, Tasmania, South Australia, and Victoria had responsible government by the end of 1855, having been invited to draw up their own constitutions by the Australian Colonies Government Act of 1850. Queensland followed in 1859. Western Australia had to wait until 1890. In New Zealand and South Africa, the position of the local colonists was not so strong as in Canada and Australia because in both cases they were still dependent on British troops for protection against natives; moreover, the existence of large native populations in both was an argument used by the Colonial Office (often subject to humanitarian pressure in London) against a too rapid advance toward local autonomy. New Zealand obtained responsible government in all but native matters in 1856; by 1870, when the British troops went home after the Maori Wars, even these reservations had disappeared, and the local settlers were in full charge of the country's affairs. The Cape Colony achieved responsible government in 1872, and Natal in 1893.

Dominion status. Meanwhile, British North America experienced further development in self-government. The union of Upper and Lower Canada developed many stresses by the 1860s. In addition, the maritime colonies were seeking new forms of association with one another and with Upper and Lower Canada. The result, after local conferences, was the British North America Act of 1867, whereby Ontario, Quebec, New Brunswick, and Nova Scotia were brought together in a confederation known as the Dominion of Canada. Manitoba joined in 1870, British Columbia in 1871, and Prince Edward Island in 1873. The continuing development of the prairies brought in Alberta and Saskatchewan in 1905. Of the British North American colonies, this left only Newfoundland outside the confederation—a situation finally adjusted by Newfoundland's entrance in 1949.

The Australian colonies formed a federation in 1901. There was a union of the South African colonies in 1910. In the latter, the defeated Transvaal and Orange Free State were added to the Cape and Natal. By means of these arrangements, each of the three countries (including Canada) obtained a national government that operated in full control of its own affairs, as did that of New Zealand. Britain retained minor powers of veto, which amounted to very little. Its influence lay in its provision of naval defense and its position as a buyer of local products and an investor in local enterprises. In 1907 the countries' special position was recognized by their designation as "dominions," not colonies; by the creation of a special Dominions division in the Colonial Office; and by the regular institution of an Imperial Conference, which they, with Newfoundland, would attend.

Growth of national governments

In World War I, the contribution of the dominions was so substantial that they were given representation in an "imperial cabinet" that, while it did not survive the war, emphasized the degree of autonomy they had attained. At the peace settlement some of the dominions acquired mandatory responsibilities, and all became members of the League of Nations. In the 1920s Canada, South Africa, and the Irish Free State (which had been given the status of a dominion in 1921) applied pressure for a clearer definition of dominion status.

Independence. At the 1926 Imperial Conference this was met by an agreed statement that Great Britain and the dominions were "autonomous communities within the British Empire, equal in status, in no way subordinate one to another in any aspect of their external or domestic affairs, though united by a common allegiance to the Crown and freely associated as members of the British Commonwealth of Nations." Parliament passed the Statute of Westminster in 1931, which embodied this declaration in a self-denying ordinance, whereby legislation concerning the dominions would be enacted only with their consent.

The Commonwealth in operation. The 1926 definition of dominion status, while immediately satisfying to those who had pressed for it, left a number of questions unanswered: Could a dominion secede from the Commonwealth? Did "common allegiance" mean a single crown, or was the crown divisible? Could and should there be more than one foreign policy in the Commonwealth? Could one dominion be at peace while others were at war? These questions were much discussed in the 1930s; they were answered effectively in World War II, when Canada and South Africa made separate, delayed declarations of war, and Ireland remained neutral. As in World War I, there was considerable support for Britain's war effort from the belligerent dominions, though the dispersed nature of the war—especially its Pacific aspect—led to more active diplomacy by some of them. When the war ended, their independence was no longer in question.

Independence for Asian, African, Caribbean, and Oceanic nations

India's independence. At this stage (1945), dominion status still applied only to settler communities. For some time, however, the possibility of India's achieving dominion status had been actively canvassed. India was a special case within the British Empire; by title an empire in its own right, it had a viceroy, a separate secretary of state in London, its own army, and even, to a certain degree, its own foreign policy. Its size alone made it unique—the most notable of Britain's possessions. Since the beginning of the century, however, there had been agitation for greater local autonomy, even though India's communal divisions made this hard for many Englishmen to envisage.

Indian contributions in World War I had led to reforms in 1919, whereby British India was governed under a system called "dyarchy," which gave a good deal of experience to provincial legislatures but stopped far short of self-government. The viceroy still held the keys of power. In the 1920s and '30s, the Indian National Congress, led by Mahatma Gandhi and Jawaharlal Nehru, agitated for independence. The exigencies of World War II led to explicit British promises of dominion status; this entailed splitting the formerly undivided India into two dominions—India and Pakistan—when the move took place in 1947. Ceylon and Burma also obtained their independence at this time, but Burma chose independence outside the Commonwealth.

Changes in Commonwealth relations. The appearance of Asian dominions led to changes of tone and character in the Commonwealth of Nations. No longer was its British quality stressed; even the adjective British was tacitly dropped by British spokesmen when they referred to it. The large-scale Imperial Conferences of the interwar years, intended to display imperial unity, gave way to briefer and more intimate gatherings of prime ministers. The Dominions Office, which had been detached from the Colonial Office in 1925, was amalgamated with the India Office to form a Commonwealth Relations Office with its own secretary of state. The network of diplomatic posts within the Commonwealth grew rapidly, under high commissioners with the status of ambassadors; but the previous assumption of a common foreign policy disappeared. Consultation, not unity, was assumed to be the essence of the Commonwealth tie.

This loosening of the previous connections was taken a stage further in 1949, when India stated its wish to assume the status of a republic but to remain within the Commonwealth. The other members gave approval. The crown thus became an institution applicable to individual Commonwealth countries, which remained realms, but not to the Commonwealth as a whole. Instead, the British monarch, in his or her person, was recognized as "Head of the Commonwealth," a ceremonial position without functions.

The rush toward independence. In the 1950s the remaining British colonies in Africa, Asia, the Caribbean, and the Mediterranean moved at varying speeds toward further self-government. The process was at first hesitant, but it gained speed as international pressure mounted

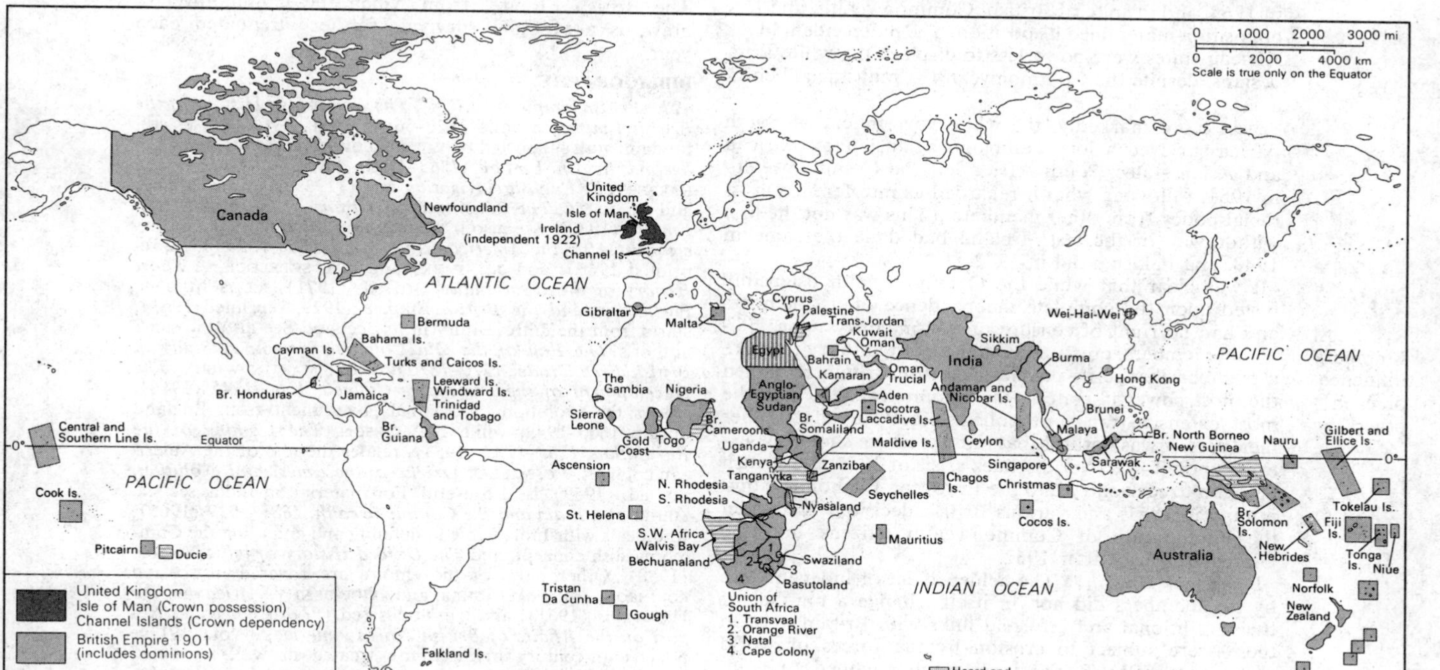

The British Empire, 1901 and 1939.

(notably at the United Nations), as the notion of independence spread in the colonies themselves, and as the British public, no longer actively imperial in its sentiments, accepted the idea of independence as a foregone conclusion. The British political parties no longer argued about whether independence should be granted or not, but about its pace and structure. In some cases—such as Aden, Singapore, Cyprus, and Malta—strategic considerations made independence difficult to contemplate at first; but these concerns were overcome either by special arrangements after independence or by the abandonment of the strategic assumptions that had previously been held. In such other cases as The Gambia and the former High Commission territories of southern Africa (Basutoland, Bechuanaland, and Swaziland), smallness of size and poverty of resources seemed at first to prevent independence; but these considerations, too, were displaced. The experiences of other European colonial powers and the pressure of American opinion also hastened the policy of independence. In nearly all cases, except those in which the complex politics of the Middle East made it impossible (The Sudan, Somaliland, South Arabia, and Palestine), former colonies chose membership in the Commonwealth. Increasingly in the 1960s, they chose also the status of republics, not realms. By the late 1970s the number of Commonwealth members had grown to 36.

Problems within the Commonwealth

The process of colonial independence was not, however, altogether smooth. Kenya, Cyprus, British Guiana, and Malaya experienced violence beforehand. The white settlers of Africa, alarmed not only by the speed of British decolonization but also by the example of the Belgian Congo and French Algeria, saw the Commonwealth increasingly as a means whereby Britain was pushed into granting independence to peoples who were not ready for it, who would misuse it, and who might, through example and subversion, threaten others' privileged position. Such feelings by the settlers of Kenya were successfully overcome. But in Southern Rhodesia they became dominant when the former Federation of Rhodesia and Nyasaland—set up in 1953 and involving, in practice, domination by the Rhodesian settlers—was dissolved in 1963 because of African pressure. The government of Rhodesia made a unilateral declaration of independence in 1965, and in spite of British, Commonwealth, and UN opposition maintained its position. The independent black African states were powerless to displace the white Rhodesians, despite the Commonwealth's "multiracial" character.

Even more markedly, the white government of South Africa survived a long campaign against it by African and Asian states. South Africa left the Commonwealth in 1961, following what it regarded as interference in its racial policy from other members. (This was not the first withdrawal, or the last: Ireland had done the same in 1948, and Pakistan did in 1972.)

Members' influence on each other

It was clear that while the Commonwealth ostensibly rested upon the complete independence of its members and had no right of censure of any majority upon individual members, pressure could be exerted to try to make a member change its policies. Because Britain remained the most powerful state in the Commonwealth, with the most extensive range of policies likely to affect other members, it was natural that most pressure should be exerted upon it—as over the Suez crisis of 1956, the British decision to seek entry into the European Economic Community in 1961, and various British decisions to restrict the immigration of Commonwealth citizens into the United Kingdom after 1962.

Links with Britain. The achievement of independence by the members did not, in itself, change a number of their traditional and informal links with Britain, though these were subject to erosion by the forces of world change generally. British investment remained a significant factor in some members' economies, and British trade did in most (although the widespread but not universal system of preferential trade, set up at a conference in Ottawa in 1932, was greatly eroded by war and postwar changes); the wartime organization of the Sterling Area (countries with most of their exchange reserves in the Bank of England) continued in the 1950s but proved less important in the 1960s and '70s. Migration was considerable from Britain to Australia, New Zealand, and Canada and was matched by a flow into Britain from these countries and from India, Pakistan, and the West Indies in the 1950s and '60s. British educational, sporting, publishing, legal, and professional influence continued to be felt in countries that had been part of the empire.

Commonwealth organization. The formal organization of colonial and Commonwealth affairs changed under the pressure of accelerated independence. The Colonial Office, which had grown in the 1940s and '50s, as the colonies were provided with more elaborate assistance in development and welfare, shrank in the 1960s and was incorporated in the Commonwealth Relations Office (renamed the Commonwealth Office). The Commonwealth Office, in turn, was merged with the Foreign Office, a small section continuing to administer the affairs of the few remaining dependent territories, of which by the 1970s there were none in Africa, only Hong Kong and Brunei in Asia, Gibraltar in the Mediterranean, and certain islands in the Pacific, Indian, and Atlantic oceans, together with some islands in the Caribbean and British Honduras (Belize) in Central America.

Commonwealth Secretariat

Before 1965 there had been no executive for the Commonwealth as such. The British government normally arranged the meetings of Commonwealth prime ministers; otherwise, contacts were at the diplomatic level, with a network of ad hoc bodies in such spheres as scientific and educational cooperation. In 1965 a Commonwealth Secretariat was established in London, with a secretary general and a staff drawn from and supported by the member states. Its duties were the promotion of Commonwealth cooperation and the conduct of Commonwealth meetings, which continued to take place at various levels, from those of prime ministers to those of officials concerned with particular activities such as finance and the promotion of trade and tourism. There was also a certain amount of intra-Commonwealth economic aid, although most aid was bilateral between donors and recipients.

The Commonwealth is now only one of a growing band of international bodies to which its members belong. The British Empire, from which the Commonwealth grew, is a vestigial survival, further attenuated each year.

BIBLIOGRAPHY

The British Empire to 1914: The Cambridge History of the British Empire, 8 vol. (1929–36; 2nd ed., 1963–), is still fundamental, supported by V.T. HARLOW, *The Founding of the Second British Empire, 1763–1793*, 2 vol. (1952–64); L.A. HARPER, *The English Navigation Laws* (1939, reprinted 1964); and A.B. KEITH, *The Constitutional History of the First British Empire* (1930). See also H.T. MANNING, *British Colonial Government After the American Revolution, 1782–1822* (1933, reprinted 1966); and J.H. PARRY and P.M. SHERLOCK, *A Short History of the West Indies*, 3rd ed. (1971). R.L. SCHUYLER, *Parliament and the British Empire* (1929, reprinted 1963), starts from the 16th century in its account. See also the same author's *The Fall of the Old Colonial System: A Study in British Free Trade, 1770–1870* (1945). MARTIN WIGHT, *The Development of the Legislative Council, 1606–1945* (1946), covers the evolution of colonial government from England during 1606–1945, while L.H. GIPSON, *The Coming of the Revolution, 1763–1775* (1954), relates the loss of the American colonies. J.C. MILLER, *Origins of the American Revolution*, rev. ed. (1959), is also useful. For material on India, see S.R. MEHROTRA, *India and the Commonwealth, 1885–1929* (1965), who deals with India's role in defining and enlarging the Commonwealth concept, and *The Oxford History of India*, 3rd ed. (1958). Other parts of the empire are covered in RONALD ROBINSON, JOHN GALLAGHER, and ALICE DENNY, *Africa and the Victorians* (1961); and C.P. LUCAS (ed.), *Lord Durham's Report on the Affairs of British North America*, 3 vol. (1912). Nineteenth-century opinions are treated in W.P. MORRELL, *British Colonial Policy in the Age of Peel and Russell* (1930, reprinted 1966); and C.A. BODELSEN, *Studies in Mid-Victorian Imperialism*, 2nd ed. (1960). See also J.E. TYLER, *The Struggle for Imperial Unity, 1868–1895* (1938).

The Commonwealth after 1914: R.M. DAWSON (ed.), *The Development of Dominion Status 1900–1936* (1937, reprinted

1965); J.A. WILLIAMSON, *A Notebook of Commonwealth History*, 3rd ed. (1967), which deals with the old colonial empire, then the modern empire and the Commonwealth; COLIN CROSS, *The Fall of the British Empire: 1918–1968* (1968), describing the change from empire to commonwealth; J.B. WATSON, *Empire to Commonwealth 1919 to 1970* (1971); A.L. BURT, *The Evolution of the British Empire and Commonwealth, from the American Revolution* (1956); and MAX BELOFF, *Imperial Sunset*, vol. 1, *Britain's Liberal Empire, 1897–1921* (1969), all trace the Commonwealth's emergence. Supplementary works include A.B. KEITH, *Responsible Government in the Dominions*, 2nd ed., 2 vol. (1928), and *The Governments of the British Empire* (1935); and W.K. HANCOCK, *Survey of British Commonwealth Affairs*, 2 vol. (1937–42). ALEXANDER BRADY, *Democracy in the Dominions*, 3rd ed. (1958), examines administration in the dominion countries. H.J. HARVEY, *Consultation and Co-operation in the Commonwealth* (1952), examines the ways Commonwealth countries can communicate and coordinate. Other useful works on the organization's machinery are G.W. KEETON (ed.), *The British Commonwealth: The Development of Its Laws and Constitutions*, 12 vol. (1952–64); P.N.S. MANSERGH, *The Multi-Racial Commonwealth* (1955), and *Survey of British Commonwealth Affairs*, 2 vol. (1952–58); K.C. WHEARE, *The Statute of Westminster and Dominion Status*, 5th ed. (1953), and *The Constitutional Structure of the Commonwealth* (1960); CLIVE PARRY, *Nationality and Citizenship Laws of the Commonwealth and of the Republic of Ireland* (1957); and GEOFFREY MARSHALL, *Parliamentary Sovereignty and the Commonwealth* (1957). Geographical aspects of the Commonwealth are treated in DENNIS AUSTIN, *West Africa and the Commonwealth* (1957); and A.A. MAZRUI, *The Anglo-African Commonwealth* (1967), covering Africa's impact on the Commonwealth's evolution. P.N.S. MANSERGH *et al.*, *Commonwealth Perspectives* (1958); THE ECONOMIST, *Economic Geography of the Commonwealth* (1957); and C.B. HOOVER (ed.), *Economic Systems of the Commonwealth* (1962), deal with the Commonwealth's differing components. The more recent Commonwealth is covered in M.S. RAJAN, *The Post-War Transformation of the Commonwealth* (1963); S.A. DE SMITH, *The New Commonwealth and Its Constitutions* (1964); J.D.B. MILLER, *The Commonwealth in the World*, 3rd ed. (1965), and *Britain and The Old Dominions* (1966); ZELMAN COWEN, *The British Commonwealth of Nations in a Changing World* (1965); and W.B. HAMILTON, KENNETH ROBINSON, and C.D.W. GOODWIN (eds.), *A Decade of the Commonwealth, 1955–1964* (1966). See also H. DUNCAN HALL, *Commonwealth: A History of the British Commonwealth of Nations* (1971), a standard work of the 1920s and 1930s. The CENTRAL OFFICE OF INFORMATION, *The Commonwealth in Brief*, 5th ed. (1970), a short but comprehensive summary; and NICHOLAS MANSERGH, *The Commonwealth Experience* (1968), a critical account of the Commonwealth's development from the mid-19th century to the 1970s. RICHARD BAILEY, *Promoting Commonwealth Development* (1970), suggests the Commonwealth can raise living standards of developing countries; while PAUL STREETEN and HUGH CORBET (eds.), *Commonwealth Policy in a Global Context* (1971), contains collected essays from various sources. See also DEREK INGRAM, *The Commonwealth at Work* (1969). (J.D.B.M.)

British Honduras (Belize)

British Honduras, since 1973 officially named Belize (or Belice to neighbouring Spanish-speaking countries), is a constitutional monarchy on the east coast of Central America. After El Salvador, it is the smallest political unit on the mainland of the Americas. It has an area of 8,867 square miles (22,965 square kilometres) and had an estimated population in 1982 of 150,000. To the north and northwest it is bounded by Mexico, to the south and west by Guatemala, and to the east by the Caribbean Sea, on which it has a 174-mile (280-kilometre) coastline. Belize City was ravaged by a hurricane in 1961, and the capital of the territory was moved in 1970 from there to Belmopan, a new city built about 50 miles southwest. The country gained independence in late 1981 and became a member of the Commonwealth and of the United Nations.

The name "Belize" is traditionally believed to have been derived from the Spanish pronunciation of the last name of Peter Wallace, a Scottish buccaneer who is said to have begun a settlement at the mouth of the Belize River about 1638. It is also possible, however, that the country's name is derived from any of several Mayan words, one of which means "muddy water." (For historical aspects, see CENTRAL AMERICAN STATES, HISTORY OF THE.)

Relief and drainage. Situated at the base of the Yucatán Peninsula, Belize is a land of mountains, swamps, and

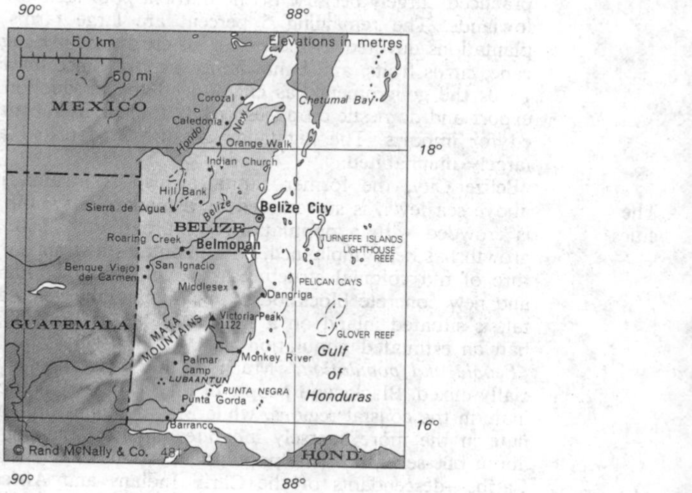

BELIZE

tropical jungle. Southern Belize is dominated by the Maya Mountains, a plateau cut by erosion into hills and valleys that stretch across the frontier from Guatemala in a southwesterly to northeasterly direction. The Cockscomb Mountains, a spur of the Maya range, run toward the sea, culminating in Victoria Peak (3,681 feet [1,122 metres] high), the highest point in Belize. Northern Belize consists of lowlands less than 200 feet above sea level, much of which are swamp. The lowlands are drained by the navigable Belize River (on which stands Belize City), the New River and the Hondo River; the latter forms the northern frontier with Mexico. Both the New and the Hondo rivers drain into Chetumal Bay to the north. South of Belize City the coastal plain skirts the highlands and is crossed by short river valleys. About 15 miles off the coast the second largest barrier reef in the world, underlain by a submarine escarpment, runs parallel to the coast. It is fringed by dozens of small islands, called cays.

The Maya and Cockscomb mountains

Climate. The climate is subtropical, with a well-marked dry season from late February to May and a wet season from June to November that is interrupted from August to September by another dry season. The mean temperature at Belize City is 74° F (23° C) in December and 85° F (29° C) in July. The mean annual rainfall increases from 53 inches (1,350 millimetres) at Corozal on the northern frontier to 180 inches at Barranco on the southern frontier. At Belize City it is 69 inches, but there, as elsewhere, there are considerable yearly variations. Trade winds blow onshore most of the year, but from September to December northerly winds bring cooler, drier air. Hurricanes are an annual threat from July through November.

Temperature and rainfall

Vegetation and animal life. More than two-thirds of Belize consists of forests. There are at least 50 different forest tree species, which include mahogany, Santa Maria (an evergreen tree with shiny leathery leaves and white flowers), cedar, and ironwood. On the limestone soils of the north the forest is deciduous, and sapote (date plum) and mahogany predominate. In the south the forest is taller and is evergreen. Santa Maria, rather than mahogany, flourishes on the plateau, and oak and pine grow on some of the plateau ridges. The rivers are largely bordered by swamp forests. On the southern coastal plain and inland from Belize City, open savanna (grassland) is marked by scattered oaks, pines, and palmetto palms. The coast is fringed with mangrove trees.

The abundant wildlife of Belize includes such animals as deer and the jaguar, puma, tapir, American crocodile, and manatee, as well as many species of turtles, tortoises, birds, reptiles, insects, and fishes.

The land under human settlement. About 15 percent of the land is actively utilized; in the early 1980s agricultural land amounted to about 217,000 acres (88,000 hectares). About 95 percent of the farms are less than 100 acres in area, many of them *milpas* (temporary forest clearings). On most of these farms traditional shifting agriculture is practiced, largely because of the nutrient-poor soils of the lowlands. The remaining 5 percent are large farms or plantations devoted to the raising of crops, mainly sugarcane, citrus fruits, and bananas, for export. Since the late 1970s the government has encouraged the production of export and domestic crops, especially those that substituted for imports. The highlands are mostly forested and largely uninhabited.

The cities

Belize City, the former capital, which is located just above sea level, is surrounded by a mangrove swamp. It is crowded with a population of more than 42,000. Its growth has been unplanned, and it contains a strange mixture of old colonial structures, wooden frame buildings, and new concrete blockhouses. Belmopan, the new capital, is situated inland on a site not liable to flooding; it had an estimated population of 4,500 in 1980.

People and population. Much of the population is racially mixed. Blacks and people of black ancestry predominate in the coastal regions, while Maya Indians predominate in the more sparsely inhabited interior, making up about one-seventh of the population. About 12,000 Black Caribs—descendants of the Carib Indians and Africans exiled from the British West Indian islands in the 18th century—live in settlements on the southern coast. Europeans and Asian Indians, who live in the coastal area, constitute about one-tenth of the total population.

English is the official language, but about three-fourths of the population also speaks Creole. The Indians speak Spanish or one of several Indian languages. Groups of Mennonites, who migrated from northern Mexico in 1958, have established themselves inland on the Belize River at Spanish Lookout and Barton Ramie and at Blue Creek and Shipyard.

Belize, Area and Population

	area		population	
	sq mi	sq km	1970 census	1980 estimate
Districts				
Belize	1,663	4,307	49,000	54,300
Cayo	2,006	5,196	16,000	22,300
Corozal	718	1,860	16,000	18,200
Orange Walk	1,790	4,636	17,000	20,000
Stann Creek	986	2,554	13,000	15,300
Toledo	1,704	4,413	9,000	10,500
Total Belize	8,867	22,965*	120,000	140,600

*Figures do not add to total given because of rounding.
Source: Official government figures.

Forest and agricultural products

The national economy. The export of timber was for years the basis of the Belize economy, but by 1960 the combined value of sugar and citrus exports exceeded that of timber, and since 1965 timber production has steadily declined. Chicle, used in the manufacture of chewing gum, is obtained from the sapodilla tree, and cedar, mahogany, and rosewood have increased in economic importance since the 1970s. Furniture and power and telephone poles are the major products of the forestry industry, which includes about 40 sawmills. Resin, turpentine, and hardwood veneers are also produced.

Sugar is grown in Corozal and Orange Walk districts and is exported to Great Britain, the United States, and Canada. Oranges, grapefruit, and bananas are grown mainly in the Stann Creek and Cayo areas, south of Belize City. In the early 1980s the exportation of sugar and citrus fruits accounted for two-thirds of the total value of exports. Much of the rice is raised on large mechanized farms in the Belize River Valley, while corn (maize), roots and tubers, red kidney beans, and vegetables are raised throughout the country, mostly by small farmers.

The Mennonite community at Spanish Lookout has developed fresh milk and cheese production and has introduced large-scale chicken farming. Beef cattle are raised for the local market and for export to the United States and to other Caribbean nations. Pigs are raised throughout the country for fresh and smoked and cured meat.

Fishing for lobster, shrimp, scale fish, conch, and sea turtles is conducted mainly by six cooperatives, some of which have freezing or canning plants. Much of the fish harvest is exported, more than nine-tenths of the exports going to the United States.

Industrial growth

Manufacturing, accounting for about one-sixth of the national production, is oriented toward both the domestic and export markets. The Belize government has stressed the substitution of imports to promote industrial development. Fertilizer and animal feed plants have been opened, while the numerous sawmills, a wire and nail plant, and a roofing-material plant serve the construction and furniture-manufacturing industries. Footwear, beer, soft drinks, and cigarettes are also produced. Food-processing industries include a sugar refinery at Corozal, citrus-processing plants in the Stann Creek area, beef-packing and rice-processing plants, and fish-freezing and canning factories. Two garment factories utilizing imported fabric produce clothing for the export market.

Transport. Apart from one line used for logging, there are no railroads in the country. Agricultural and forest produce is usually transported by road, although rivers are still used. More than 1,550 mi (2,500 km) of roads constitute a network that extends to all the district capitals, west to the Guatemalan border, and north to the Mexican border. All-weather roads link Belize City and Belmopan with other major population centres in the central and northern areas of Belize and with Punta Gorda on the southern coast.

The ports

Belize City, the main port, has no docks or deepwater quays, and vessels with more than 20 feet (eight metres) draft have had to anchor more than a mile offshore. In 1977, however, construction began on an offshore artificial island, linked to the mainland by a causeway, with docking facilities to accommodate ships of up to 28 feet draft. Another port, at Commerce Bight, handles the citrus exports of the Stann Creek district; smaller ports at Riversdale and Big Creek are used for the export of bananas, and Punta Gorda handles seaborne trade with Guatemala and Honduras.

The Belize International Airport is about 10 miles from Belize City; scheduled flights link it to the United States, Mexico, and Central America, and to the Caribbean through Jamaica. There are scheduled domestic flights to Belmopan, to the district capitals, to Independence (near Big Creek), and to San Pedro on Ambergris Cay.

Administration and social conditions. All of the country's six districts, except Belize, are administered by district commissioners. District town boards have authority over most municipal affairs; in some villages an *alcalde* (headman) is appointed with limited powers. The legal system is based upon the common law of Great Britain.

Under a constitution that came into force on September 21, 1981, Belize achieved independence. The constitution provides for universal suffrage for those over the age of 18, for a bicameral National Assembly composed of an elected House of Representatives and an appointed Senate, and for a Cabinet with the prime minister as chairman. Elections normally take place every five years. The governor general, who represents the British crown, appoints a prime minister and an opposition leader from among members of the House of Representatives.

Education

More than 90 percent of the population over 15 years of age is literate. Primary schooling is compulsory between the ages of six and 14. Most schools are Roman Catholic although some are Methodist or Anglican; the Mennonites operate their own schools by special agreement with the government. All schools are jointly funded by the government and their respective church organizations. There are more than two dozen secondary schools, four vocational secondary schools, four technical colleges, and the Belize Teachers' College. The Belize College of Arts, Science, and Technology was opened in 1980.

The Baron Bliss Institute in Belize City is devoted to the promotion of the arts and drama and houses a museum with a fine collection of Mayan antiquities and a library. The National Library Service operates branch libraries in the district capitals and both local and mobile libraries throughout the country.

The Belize radio broadcasts in Spanish and English. There are two daily newspapers, three weeklies and one Sunday newspaper.

Health and welfare

Medical care is free, and the government operates and staffs hospitals, dental clinics, and child-care facilities in each district, as well as rural health centres and mobile clinics. The government also operates disease control and vaccination projects and dental care programs in the schools. Nurses are trained locally, and in 1975 Belize joined a training program for physicians undertaken by the Caribbean Commonwealth countries. There remains, however, a shortage of doctors and dentists in the rural areas.

A social security program was approved and funded in the late 1970s to replace the program of social assistance formerly available to senior citizens and to extend coverage to sick, disabled, and unemployed workers and to survivors of deceased insured workers. Improvements of the water supply and waste disposal systems were begun during the late 1970s after hurricanes had seriously damaged facilities in the lowlands, leading to an upsurge of gastrointestinal disease, which is a major cause of infant mortality in Belize.

BIBLIOGRAPHY. L. BRADLEY, *Belizean Races and Their Customs,* and *Glimpses of Our Country* (1965), two booklets that provide a good account of contemporary Belize, with a fairly accurate breakdown of the population and the origin of each ethnic strain; J.A. BURDON (ed.), *Archives of British Honduras,* 3 vol. (1931–35), an important collection of official records and local archives from the 17th through the 19th century; O.N. BOLLAND, *The Formation of a Colonial Society* (1977), a thoroughly researched history of Belize from the Mayan period to 1871; D. CARR and J. THORPE, *From the Cam to the Cays: The Story of the Cambridge Expedition to British Honduras 1959–60* (1961), an enjoyable and informative report of the impressions of the members of the expedition; S. COSHINKSY, *Interethnic Relations in Punta Gorda, British Honduras* (1966), a useful study of the Carib race in Toledo district; D.H. ROMNEY (ed.), *Land in British Honduras* (1959), a work that may be used as a starting point for the study of the economy of Belize; A.R. GREGG, *British Honduras* (1968), the first full-length study of political developments in the country during the late 20th century; J. ERIC THOMPSON, *Maya Archaeologist* (1963), a brief account of archaeological work in Belize; D.A.G. WADDELL, *British Honduras: A Historical and Contemporary Survey* (1961), a general work briefly covering all aspects of the subject, with an excellent bibliography; *Caribbean Year Book* (annual); GOVERNMENT OF BELIZE, *Development Plan 1977–1979* (1977); FOREIGN AND COMMONWEALTH OFFICE, *A Yearbook of the Commonwealth* (annual), covering developments in Belize.

(A.E.A./Ed.)

Broadcasting

Broadcasting is the transmission of radio and television programs that are intended for general public reception, as distinguished from private signals that are directed to specific receivers. In its most common form, broadcasting may be described as the systematic dissemination of entertainment, information, educational programming, and other features for simultaneous reception by a scattered audience, individually or in groups, with appropriate receiving apparatus. Broadcasts may be audible only, as in radio, or visual or a combination of both, as in television. Sound broadcasting in this sense may be said to have started about 1920, while television broadcasting began in the 1930s.

The scope of this article is limited to the nontechnical aspects of broadcasting, and the following subjects are covered:

I. History
- Radiobroadcasting
- Television broadcasting

II. Broadcasting systems
- The broadcaster and the government
- The broadcaster and the public

III. Broadcasting operations
- Types of programs and development of studios
- Relations with artists, speakers, authors, and unions
- Internal organization, administration, and policy control
- The state of broadcasting in selected countries

(For a history of the development of radio and a technical description of radio equipment, see RADIO. For similar information about television, see TELEVISION.)

I. History

RADIOBROADCASTING

The United States. The first known radio program in the United States was broadcast by Reginald Aubrey Fessenden from his experimental station at Brant Rock, Massachusetts, on Christmas Eve, 1906. Two musical selections, the reading of a poem, and a short talk apparently constituted the program, which was heard by ship wireless operators within a radius of several hundred miles. Following the relaxation of military restrictions on radio at the conclusion of World War I, many experimental radio stations—often equipped with homemade apparatus—were operated by amateurs. The range of such broadcasts was only a few miles, and the receiving apparatus necessary to hear them was mostly in the hands of other experimenters, who, like the broadcasters, pursued radio as a hobby. Among the leading personalities of this early period was David Sarnoff, later of the Radio Corporation of America and the National Broadcasting Company, who first, in 1916, envisaged the possibility of a radio receiver in every home.

Growth of commercial radio. From this beginning the evolution of broadcasting was rapid; many persons who wanted to hear music from the air soon created a demand for receivers that were suitable for operation by the layman. The increase in the number of listeners in turn justified the establishment of stations especially for the purpose of broadcasting entertainment and information programs. The first commercial radio station was KDKA in Pittsburgh, which went on the air in the evening of November 2, 1920, with a broadcast of the returns of the Harding–Cox presidential election. The success of the KDKA broadcast and of the musical programs that were initiated thereafter motivated others to install similar stations; a total of eight were operating in the United States by the end of 1921.

First commercial radio station

The popularity of these early stations created two possible sources of financial support to offset the operating costs of broadcasting. First, there were possibilities for profit in the manufacture and sale of radio receiving equipment; and, second, the fame attained by the organizations operating the first broadcasting stations called attention to the value of broadcasting as an advertising medium. Advertising eventually became the principal means of support for broadcasting in the United States.

Between 1921 and 1922 the sale of radio receiving sets and of component parts for use in home construction of such sets began a boom that was followed immediately by a large increase in the number of transmitting stations. By November 1, 1922, 564 broadcasting stations had been licensed.

Interconnection of stations. The use of long-distance wire telephone lines in 1922 to connect a radio station in New York City with one in Chicago to broadcast a description of a football game introduced a new idea into radiobroadcasting. In 1926 the National Broadcasting Company purchased WEAF in New York and, using it as the originating station, established a permanent network of radio stations to which it undertook to distribute daily programs. Some of these were sponsored by advertisers and furnished revenue to both the network and its associated stations, while others were supported by the network, with part of the time being set aside for public-service features.

Government regulation. Although the growth of radiobroadcasting in the United States was spectacularly swift, in the early years it also proved to be chaotic, unplanned, and unregulated. Furthermore, business arrangements that were being made between the leading manufacturers of radio equipment and the leading broadcasters seemed to threaten monopoly. Congress responded by passing the Radio Act of 1927, which, although directed primarily against monopoly, also set up the agency that is now called the Federal Communications Commission (FCC) to allocate wavelengths to broadcasters. The government's attack on monopoly resulted eventually in four radio networks—the National Broadcasting Company, Columbia Broadcasting System, Mutual Broadcasting System, and American Broadcasting Company—while the FCC permitted orderly growth and assured the survival of educational radio stations.

The United Kingdom. *Early development.* Radiobroadcasting in Britain eventually developed in quite a different way from that in the United States. The first initiatives after World War I were taken by commercial firms that regarded broadcasting primarily as a means of point-to-point communication. The first successful broadcasting of the human voice, from a transmitter in Ireland across the Atlantic in 1919, led to the erection of a six-kilowatt transmitter at Chelmsford, Essex. From this spot two daily half-hour programs of speech and music, including a well-received broadcast by the opera singer Dame Nellie Melba, were broadcast for about a year between 1919 and 1920. Opposition from the armed services, fear of interference with essential communications, and a desire to avoid the "commercialization" of radio led, however, to a ban on the Chelmsford broadcasts, which the Post Office claimed the right to impose. Experimental broadcasts, the Post Office ruled, had to be individually authorized. Nevertheless, 4,000 receiving-set licenses and 150 amateur transmitting licenses issued by the Post Office by March 1921 were evidence of growing interest. When these amateurs, grouped into 63 societies comprising about 3,000 members, petitioned for regular broadcasts, their request was granted in a very limited form: the Marconi Company was authorized to broadcast about 15 minutes weekly.

First trans-Atlantic broadcast

The first of these authorized broadcasts, from a hut at Writtle, close to Chelmsford, took place on February 14, 1922; the station call signal was 2MT. Shortly thereafter an experimental station was authorized at Marconi House in London, and its first program went on the air May 11, 1922. Other stations were soon to follow.

Formation of the British Broadcasting Company. By this time developments in the United States had demonstrated the commercial possibilities of radio but also suggested a need for greater order and control. The Post Office took the initiative in encouraging cooperation among manufacturers, and on October 18, 1922, the British Broadcasting Company, Ltd., was established as a private corporation. Only bona fide manufacturers were permitted to hold shares, and the directors of the firm, all of whom represented manufacturing interests, met under an independent chairman. The company's revenue came from half of the 10-shilling license fee for receivers and a 10 percent royalty on the sale of receiving sets and equipment. Provincial stations were provided for, and all stations were to broadcast "news, information, concerts, lectures, educational matter, speeches, weather reports, theatrical entertainment. . . ."

Revenue sources of the British Broadcasting Company, Ltd.

Already several precedents had been established that were later followed in many other countries; of these the license revenue was the most important, but the royalty on sets and equipment was also adopted elsewhere, even after its abandonment in Britain. Because the British Broadcasting Company was a monopoly and because British radio as a result developed in a more orderly manner than elsewhere, such problems and issues of broadcasting as control of finance, broadcasting of controversy, relations with government, network organization, and public-service broadcasting became apparent, and solutions were sought in the United Kingdom earlier than elsewhere.

In 1925, upon recommendation of a parliamentary committee, the company was liquidated and replaced by a public corporation, the British Broadcasting Corporation (BBC), answerable ultimately to Parliament but with day-to-day control left to the judgment of the Board of Governors appointed on the basis of their standing and experience and not representing any sectional interests. A key figure, the chief executive of the original company and director general of the corporation, was John Reith (later Lord Reith), whose concept of public-service broadcasting prevailed in Britain and influenced broadcasting in many other countries. The BBC retained its monopoly until the creation of the Independent Television Authority in 1954. Its radio monopoly was finally broken by the government's decision to permit local commercial broadcasts starting in the 1970s.

Radio developments in other countries. Even before the pioneer station in Pittsburgh commenced operations, regular broadcasts began from The Hague, running from November 1919 until 1924. In Canada the first regular broadcasts from Montreal began in 1920, while in Australia a small station in Melbourne opened in 1921, though the official start occurred in Sydney in 1923. In New Zealand several low-powered stations were operating in 1921, though the Radio Broadcasting Company was not founded until 1927. In Denmark experimental amateur stations went on the air in 1921, and the official State Broadcasting System was instituted in 1925. France began regular transmissions from the Eiffel Tower in 1922, and the first Soviet station commenced broadcasts from Moscow in the same year. By the end of 1923 there also were radio stations established in Belgium, Czechoslovakia, Germany, and Spain. The list of countries lengthened rapidly, with Finland and Italy beginning broadcasts in 1924 and Norway, Poland, Mexico, and Japan in 1925. In India organized broadcasting began in 1926; the Indian Broadcasting Company had stations in Bombay and Calcutta in 1927.

In most of these countries, the problem of control arose. In some countries private enterprise was given free rein, subject to licensing by a government department or agency and to agreement upon the wavelengths or frequencies to be used. In others there was closer control (*e.g.*, France) or encouragement to cooperation between potentially conflicting interests (*e.g.*, Germany and Japan). Britain's example was followed in Denmark, Sweden, several Commonwealth countries, and some British colonies. In Canada and France state and private enterprise operated side by side. Private stations were well established in Canada, for example, before the Canadian Broadcasting Commission was formed in 1936.

The problem of control

In France the Administration of Posts and Telegraphs handled early broadcasts; although a state monopoly was declared in 1923 and state broadcasting remained a department of the Administration of Posts and Telegraphs until World War II, some private stations were granted licenses, including Radio Normandy, which broadcast programs and advertising to the United Kingdom. Some of these private commercial stations continued in operation, broadcasting under government control until 1945, when their licenses were withdrawn and radio became a complete state monopoly, independent of the Administration of Posts and Telegraphs but answerable to the government.

In Germany the Ministry of Posts retained control and ownership of all technical equipment, while private companies started programs in various cities. It was not long before the Reich Broadcasting Company acquired controlling interests in these companies; in 1932 all were nationalized.

International conferences. The wavelength problems that created so much confusion in the United States and provided a strong argument for monopoly in Britain arose also internationally, particularly in Europe, where the concentration of heavily populated and advanced sovereign nations compelled international agreement. Telegraphy had led to an early conference in Paris in 1865 that created what became later the International Telecommunications Union. This event was followed by the Berlin conference of 1885 to discuss international telephone communications, two further conferences in Berlin in 1903 and 1906 on radiotelegraph, and still another in London in 1912 to cover the whole field of radio communications. An informal conference of 10 countries held in London in 1925 created the Union Internationale de Radiophonie. The union was based in Geneva, with a BBC representative as president and another as secretary general, and was the first international broadcasting organization. The use of wavelengths, copyright problems, and international program exchanges inevitably were discussed, and a plan was drawn up.

Agreement on wavelength allocation, implemented in November 1926, was based on a formula involving area, population, and the extent of telephone and telegraph traffic. In spite of its dominating position, the BBC, which had been using 20 medium wavelengths, emerged with one long wavelength, 10 medium wavelengths, and five further medium wavelengths shared with others but below the Post Office limit range for broadcasting of between one megahertz and 600 kilohertz (300 and 500 metres). (Long waves range from 30 to 300 kilohertz; medium waves from 300 kilohertz to three megahertz; and shortwaves from three to 30 megahertz.) All of the more advanced of the participating countries (which had risen to 16: Austria, Belgium, Czechoslovakia, Denmark, Finland, France, Germany, Hungary, Ireland, Italy, The Netherlands, Norway, Spain, Sweden, Switzerland, and the United Kingdom) had to make some sacrifices, and some, such as the United Kingdom, had to persuade their post offices to agree to the use of wavelengths outside the broadcasting range; but the principle of international agreement had been established. The Washington Conference of 1927 widened the area of cooperation in respect to radiotelegraph, broadcasting, and the international allocation of wavelengths, or frequencies. It was followed by the Madrid Conference of 1932, which codified the rules and established the official international frequency list. This agreement stabilized the situation until World War II, after which the European scene was substantially changed, and a conference in Copenhagen in 1948 reallocated frequencies in the European Broadcasting Area. The Atlantic City Conference in 1947 had already created the International Frequency Registration Board. A conference in Buenos Aires in 1952 prepared the text of the International Telecommunications Convention. The text was revised at Geneva in 1959, where radio regulations were also revised. Geneva also was the site of the 1963 conference for the allocation of frequency bands for space and Earth–space communications.

International organizations. The International Telecommunications Union, created in 1865, has worldwide membership; within the union are the International Frequency Registration Board, the International Telegraph and Telephone Consultative Committee, and the International Radio Consultative Committee. Apart from the International Telecommunications Union, a number of organizations have been established, primarily on a regional basis, since World War II. When tensions between the East and West made the Union Internationale de Radiophonie almost unworkable, a strong organization, the European Broadcasting Union, was created by the nations of western Europe in 1950, and it has a membership that now includes not only all nations of western Europe but also Cyprus, Greece, Iceland, Israel, Lebanon, Morocco, Tunisia, Turkey, and Yugoslavia; associate members include the United States and most Commonwealth and former French colonial countries, as well as Japan and several Latin-American countries. A parallel organization, also created in 1950, is the International Radio and Television Organization, which serves nearly all Communist countries (excluding Yugoslavia) and allies of the Communist bloc. The European Broadcasting Union is based in Geneva, while the International Radio and Television Organization has its headquarters in Prague.

Asian and African organizations

The Asian Broadcasting Union, which was formally established in 1964 as a union of national broadcasting organizations in Asia and the Pacific, includes Japan, Australia, New Zealand, and the Philippines, as well as Iran, Turkey, Egypt, and most of the non-Communist countries of Asia; its headquarters are in Tokyo. The Union of National Radio and Television Organizations of Africa, which was formed in 1962, includes most former French and British colonies. The union is based in Dakar, Senegal, and has its technical centre at Markala, Mali. The Arab States Broadcasting Union was formed in 1969 as an intergovernmental organization within the framework of the Arab League; the secretariat is in Cairo and the Engineering Center is located in Khartoum, The Sudan. The Asociación Inter-Americana de Radiodifusión covers North, Central, and South America, with a central office in Montevideo. The Commonwealth Broadcasting Association, established in 1945 as a standing association of national public-service broadcasting organizations in the independent countries of the Commonwealth, bases its secretariat in London.

There are other international broadcasting bodies, including the United Nations and the Press and Audio-Visual Information Division of the United Nations Educational, Scientific, and Cultural Organization (UNESCO). The International Broadcast Institute, created in 1968 as a nonprofit-making and nongovernmental association supported by charitable foundations, with headquarters in London, fosters a free flow of communications for informational, cultural, and educational purposes. There are also a substantial number of religious broadcasting bodies, some of regional and some of worldwide proportions; among the most important are the World Association for Christian Communications, set up in 1968 and based in London, and the Association Catholique Internationale pour la Radiodiffusion et la Télévision, based in Brussels. There is also Radio Free Europe, based in Munich, and financed by U.S government funds, which broadcasts pro-Western propaganda to the Communist countries of eastern Europe.

TELEVISION BROADCASTING

Through a series of technical developments in Great Britain, Europe, the Soviet Union, and the United States, television reached a state of technical feasibility by 1931. In that year a research group was established in Britain under Isaac (later Sir Isaac) Shoenberg, an inventor with vast experience in radio transmission in the Soviet Union. He fostered the evolution of a complete and practical television-broadcast system based on a camera tube known as the Emitron and an improved cathode-ray tube for the receiver. Shoenberg saw the need to establish a system that would endure for many years, since any subsequent changes in basic standards could give rise to severe technical and economic problems. He therefore proposed a system that, though ambitious for its day, was fully justified by subsequent events. Shoenberg's electronic scanning proved far superior to the mechanical scanning method that had been developed by the pioneer John Baird. The government authorized the BBC to adopt Shoenberg's standards (405 lines) for the world's first high-definition service, which was launched in London in 1936. So adequate were they that they formed the sole basis of the British service until 1962, when they gradually were superseded by the European continental standard of 625 lines. The first notable outside broadcast by the BBC was the procession of the coronation of King George VI from Hyde Park Corner in November 1937; a portable transmitter mounted on a special vehicle made its first public appearance. Several thousand viewers saw the transmission.

First practical television system

Television developments were slower in the United States. It was not until April 30, 1939, at the opening of the New York World's Fair, that a public demonstration was made by the National Broadcasting Company, which announced in that year that it was ready to begin broadcasting for two hours per week. The Columbia Broadcasting System and the Dumont network began telecasting in 1939 and 1940, respectively. By mid-1940 there were 23 television stations in the United States. World War II, however, brought nearly all activity to an end, as electronics factories were converted to wartime production. The Federal Communications Commission had authorized only limited commercial operation (the first sponsored television broadcasts began in 1941), and gradually stations closed down; only six were left with limited programs to serve the owners of some 10,000 sets. When wartime restrictions governing the manufacture of receivers were removed in 1946, the stage was set in the United States for a rapid growth of the television-broadcasting industry. By 1949 there were 1,000,000 receivers in use; the 10,000,000 mark was passed in 1951 and the 50,000,000 mark eight years later. In England the BBC's television service was resumed in June 1946; by 1949 there were 126,567 television licenses, and by 1950 there were 343,882, equal in proportion to 1,000,000 in the United States.

Other nations did not begin television broadcasting on anything resembling a wide scale until the 1950s. However, by the early 1980s receivers in use throughout the world totalled about 460,000,000; about 169,000,000 were in the United States, 18,000,000 in the United Kingdom, and 11,000,000 in Canada. Japan had about 27,800,000 sets, and the Soviet Union had an estimated 75,000,000 sets.

II. Broadcasting systems

THE BROADCASTER AND THE GOVERNMENT

Most observers recognize that no broadcast organization can be wholly independent of government, for all of them must be licensed in accordance with international agreements. Although broadcasters in democratic countries pride themselves on their freedom in respect to their governments, they are not always free of stockholder or advertiser pressure, nor are producers and editors truly independent if senior executives, under pressure from whatever source, interfere with their editorial functions. Independence, therefore, is a relative term when it is applied to broadcasting.

In a monograph that was written for the European Broadcasting Union, broadcasting systems are classified under four headings: state operated, those that work under the establishment of a public corporation or authority, those whose systems are a partnership blend of public authorities and private interests, and those under private management. A brief summary of these systems provides an indication of the complex variations that have arisen.

State operation. Grouped under this heading are broadcasting systems that are operated by a government department or delegated to an administration, perhaps with a legal personality and even possibly independent in financial and administrative matters, but subject to the government and not essentially autonomous. Under this heading is listed the Soviet Union, where a special committee, set up in 1957, is in charge of Soviet radio and television under the direct authority of the U.S.S.R. Council of Ministers. Similar arrangements prevail in Czechoslovakia and Poland, except that the committees have a legal personality. Romania also delegates broadcasting to a committee attached to the Council of Ministers. All-India Radio is a department of the Ministry of Information and Broadcasting. Similar arrangements prevail in most Communist countries and in most nations that were colonies but have gained their independence since World War II.

Establishment of a public corporation or authority. The BBC has been the prototype of this kind of system. Provided it abides by the charter and terms of the license under which it operates, the BBC has maximum independence as regards the disposal of its funds (although its revenue is subject to governmental decision as to the cost of the license that is required for every television or radio receiver), the production and scheduling of programs, and, above all, editorial control. Certain residual government powers are either hedged around with agreed provisos or never exercised. Its income, save for profits on the sale of programs abroad and the sale of various phonograph records and publications, is exclusively derived from licenses. External broadcasting (*i.e.*, broadcasting to areas outside national boundaries) is separately financed. The chairman and Board of Governors constitute the legal personality of the BBC; they are chosen by the government, not as representatives of sectional interests but on the basis of their experience and standing. Political parties in office have been careful to avoid political prejudice in these appointments.

Canadian Broadcasting Corporation

The Canadian Broadcasting Corporation (CBC)—or Société Radio-Canada—also has substantial independent powers as determined by the Broadcasting Act of 1958, though over the years producers often have been restive due to political pressures, and Canadian broadcasting has been affected by the problems arising from the aspirations of some French-speaking Canadian citizens. The CBC is dependent on an annual parliamentary grant for its finance, supplemented by an income derived from advertising that amounts to nearly a quarter of its annual revenue. Canadian broadcasting as a whole is a mixed system, with private broadcasting companies operating alongside the CBC.

The Japan Broadcasting Corporation, like the BBC, once had a monopoly on broadcasting but has since lost it. By a series of acts in 1950 the Nippon Hōsō Kyōkai (NHK) was charged with the task of conducting "its broadcasting service for the public welfare in such a manner that its broadcasts may be received all over Japan." The NHK Board of Governors is appointed by the prime minister with the consent of both houses of the Diet. The system is financed almost exclusively from the sale of licenses for receiving sets.

Under this heading is also included the Office de Radiodiffusion-Télévision Française (ORTF), although there are substantial differences. The French system has had a monopoly since 1945 but it must contend, in the field of radio, with the so-called *postes périphériques*, which broadcast in French from just outside the French frontiers. The ORTF system is described as a public administration attached directly to the presidency of the council or by delegation of the chief of the government to a minister or secretary of state, normally the minister who is responsible for information. It is, therefore, in its finances and in its editorial policy under closer government control than, for example, its British counterpart. There is an administrative council which is presided over by a president, and the chief executive is the director general. The French system derived its revenue almost exclusively from the sale of receiving-set licenses until 1968, when this source began to be supplemented by advertising.

Though West German broadcasting is properly included in this category, the situation there is substantially different, for the basic radio and television services are not a matter for the Federal government but for the individual states (*Länder*). The nine state broadcasting organizations are also grouped together in a national organization to cooperate in the first television network. In each state, though there are some variations, there is a broadcasting council that is appointed by the legislature or nominated by churches, universities, associations of employers or trade unions, political parties, or the press; an administrative council; and a director general. Their revenue comes from receiving-set licenses and sometimes also from advertising.

Belgian broadcasting

The broadcasting system in Belgium provides an interesting example of a device that has been used successfully for coping with a two-language country. There are three public authorities: one for French broadcasts; a second for Flemish; and a third that owns the property, owns and operates the technical equipment, and is responsible for the symphony orchestra, record library, and central reference library.

Partnership of public authorities and private interests. In many cases this partnership is nominal and historical rather than substantial and actual. The outstanding example is Radiotelevisione Italiana (RAI), originally founded in 1924. In 1927 an agreement was made with the government for a 25-year broadcasting concession. The charter was extended to cover television in 1952, and two years later a government agency acquired control and more than 75 percent of the shares. A board of managers includes 10 members elected by a special parliamentary commission, and the remaining six are chosen by the General Assembly. Inevitably, therefore, RAI is subject to close government surveillance, but an ad hoc committee of 30, appointed from all political parties by the presidents of the two legislative chambers, is responsible for ensuring political independence and objective news reporting. The organization must also prepare an outline of programs on a quarterly basis for approval by the Ministry of Posts and Telecommunications, aided by an advisory committee concerned with cultural, artistic, and educational policies. A separate organization runs the broadcast advertising business, which, together with receiving-set licenses, provides the revenue of RAI. By the early 1980s there were some 500 private television stations operating in Italy alongside the RAI.

Ownership of Swedish radio

In Sweden the broadcasting monopoly is technically a privately owned corporation in which the state has no financial interest, thus emphasizing the independence of Sveriges Radio from the government. The shares of the corporation must be held by the Swedish press (20 percent), large noncommercial national bodies or movements (60 percent), and commerce and industry (20 percent). The board of governors is made up of a chairman and government nominees and an equal number elected by the shareholders; there also are two employee representatives of Sveriges Radio on the board. The government reserves the right to determine the amount of revenue from receiving-set licenses on an annual basis and thus controls both investment and the amount of broadcasting. The government, however, does not control how that revenue is spent. On balance, Sveriges Radio has a substantial measure of freedom.

In Switzerland, too, there are elements of partnership between private interests and public authorities, but the federal constitution, the need to broadcast in three languages, and geographical factors have led to a system by which the Société Suisse de Radiodiffusion et Télévision comprises nine regional societies based in Geneva, Lausanne, Zürich, Bern, Basel, Lugano, Sankt Gallen, Luzern, and Chur.

Private management. Most of the broadcasting organizations under this heading are commercial firms that derive their revenue from advertising, which takes the form of brief announcements scheduled at regular intervals throughout the day. In some cases a program, such as a sports event or concert, may be sponsored by one advertiser or group of advertisers. Methods and degree of government control vary, and no general characteristics may be isolated. Private enterprise radio predominates in the United States and Latin America.

Subject to similar controls in these nations are many nonprofit-making educational stations, financed by universities, private subscriptions, and foundations. There is a public-service network, the Public Broadcasting Service, in the United States.

Other methods of distributing sound and vision programs by wire and cable are not strictly broadcasting. In the main, wire-diffusion enterprises concentrate on giving efficient reception in densely populated areas, large blocks of buildings, and in hotels of programs that are being broadcast. A tall apartment building, for example, may have one television antenna on its roof to which residents may attach their receivers. "Pay TV," the provision of such programs as sports, special events, films, and theatrical performances via direct cable lines to subscribers, has been growing in popularity. Cable television reached some 21,000,000 homes in the United States by the early 1980s and has created two industries in broadcasting: one to hook up homes, the other to supply the programs. Cable television has drawn viewers away from the major commercial television networks, whose share of the prime-time audience has fallen from 93 to 89 percent and was expected to decline further.

THE BROADCASTER AND THE PUBLIC

Nature of the broadcast audience. The psychology and behaviour of a radio or television audience, which is composed principally of individuals in the privacy of their own homes, differs considerably from that of an audience in a theatre or lecture hall. There is none of the crowd atmosphere that prevails in a public assembly, and listeners are only casually aware that they are actually part of a large audience. This engenders a sense of intimacy that causes the listener to feel a close personal association with the speaker or performer. Furthermore, many people will not accept in their own homes many of the candid forms of expression that they readily condone or support on the stage or in literature.

Because it owes its license to operate to the state, if indeed it is not state operated, and because of its intimate relationship to its audience, broadcasting functions in a quasi-public domain, open in all its phases to public scrutiny. It is therefore held to be invested with a moral as well as a legal responsibility to serve the public interest and must remain more sensitive to public sentiment and political opinion than most other forms of public expression.

Audience measurement. For economic reasons, as well as those outlined above, evaluation of audience opinion and response is important to the broadcaster. Audience measurement presents difficult problems, because there is no box office by which to determine the exact number of listeners. Mail received comes principally from those who have the time and inclination to write and cannot be regarded as wholly representative. Audience measurement information may also be obtained by telephone-sampling methods, interviews in the home by market-research organizations, or by special recording devices attached to individual receiving sets. The latter, installed with the owner's consent, record the amount of time the set is used, when it is turned on and off, and the stations tuned in. These devices are expensive, however, and do not necessarily indicate whether someone is actually watching or listening, and they are therefore limited to small samples of the total audience. Whatever the method of rating, commercial broadcasters are quick to alter or discontinue any program that shows lack of audience appeal, and the listeners are thus influential in determining the nature of the programs that are offered to them. In commercial broadcasting sponsored programs also are affected by their apparent success or failure in selling the goods advertised.

Audience-measuring devices

Educational broadcasting. It is difficult to give an account of educational broadcasting in countries where broadcasting is largely or wholly a matter of private management and where the larger and more important stations and networks are private commercial enterprises. Nevertheless, considerable numbers of educational transmissions are made in the United States and Latin America by universities and colleges and sometimes by municipal or state-owned stations. The Public Broadcasting Service in the United States has increased the amount of educational and generally more thought-provoking material available on the air, and in Latin America some countries use broadcasts not only to support the work of teachers in schools but also to combat illiteracy and to impart advice to isolated rural populations in matters of public health, agricultural methods, and other social and practical subjects. The Roman Catholic Church has been in the forefront of the latter activity, operating, for example, the Rede Nacional de Emissôras Católicas in Brazil and the Acción Cultural Popular in Colombia. A similar use of broadcasting is made in most of the tropical nations of Africa and Asia.

Japan's educational broadcasting

Japan's NHK has the most ambitious educational-broadcasting output in the world. Each of its two television and AM radio services is devoted wholly to education, while general television services and FM radio also transmit material of this nature. Japan prepares programs for primary, secondary, and higher education, special offerings for the mentally and physically handicapped, and a wide range of transmissions under the general heading of "social education," which includes foreign languages, vocational and technical instruction, advice on agriculture, forestry, fisheries, and business management, plus special programs for children, adolescents, and women. The educational broadcasts of NHK reach more than 90 percent of Japan's primary and secondary schools.

In Europe the French state broadcasting service devotes more than one-half of its radio output to educational and cultural broadcasts in the arts, letters, and sciences; and on television nearly 14 percent of its first and second networks are devoted to adult education. Primary and secondary instruction is offered, as are refresher courses for teachers and university-level courses.

Although Italian radio devotes less than 1 percent of its output specifically to educational programs for children, nearly 20 percent is given to cultural and allied offerings. Educational television began in Italy in 1958 with courses of a vocational nature, followed by transmissions aimed at secondary schools. In 1966 special programs were initiated for areas where there are no secondary schools. By the early 1980s, 17 percent of Italian television time was devoted to educational and school broadcasts and 4 percent to cultural programs.

Swedish radio offers a comprehensive service of educational and cultural broadcasting, with the output on television higher than that on radio. There is also a substantial output of adult education at the primary, secondary, and university levels, with about 1,400 school broadcasts a year, and Sweden has concentrated on vocational training and refreshment for teachers. German broadcasting, by contrast, has been used much less for formal education. In The Netherlands more than two and a half hours of school and continuing education broadcasting are broadcast weekly on the radio; in addition, nearly eight hours of educational television are transmitted every week.

The BBC pioneered in education; its work, in both radio and television, has steadily expanded. The BBC offers primary and secondary students more than 100 radio series and nearly 40 television series. The BBC also offers biweekly programs especially designed for study in degree courses with the Open University, created and financed by the government, with the broadcast teaching supplemented by publications and correspondence work. By the mid-1970s BBC broadcasts for the Open University averaged 16 hours weekly on radio and more than 18 hours on television. In addition, the Independent Broadcasting Authority in the United Kingdom has required the commercial program companies to contribute educational material both for schools and for adults; by 1970 this amounted to 10 hours weekly during periods totalling 28 weeks of the year.

In Australia there is a small educational output on the commercial stations, both radio and television, but by far the greater part of educational broadcasting is undertaken by the Australian Broadcasting Commission. Educational programming accounts for about 4 percent of radio time and 18 percent of television output, the majority of which is broadcast to schools and kindergartens. The Canadian Broadcasting Corporation is required to provide educational programs in both English and French and does so on its AM and FM radio networks, as well as on television.

Broadcasts for external reception. International broadcasting—the transmission of programs by a country expressly for audiences beyond its own frontiers—dates from the earliest days of broadcasting. The Soviet Union began foreign-language transmissions for propaganda purposes in the 1920s. Fascist Italy and Nazi Germany made such broadcasts at a later date. France, Great Britain, and The Netherlands were next in the field among European countries, though their first use of shortwave broadcasting was aimed at French-, English-, or Dutch-speaking populations overseas. Great Britain began foreign-language broadcasting early in 1938 with a program in Arabic and transmissions in Spanish and Portuguese directed to Latin America. By August 1939 countries broadcasting in foreign languages included Albania, Bulgaria, China, France, Germany, Great Britain, Hungary, Italy, Japan, Romania, the Soviet Union, Spain, the United States, and Vatican City.

Radio propaganda

During World War II foreign-language broadcasting continued; the programs of the BBC in particular, because of their reliability and credibility, had an important effect in maintaining morale among the countries that were under German occupation. The continuance of international tension after World War II led to remarkable growth of foreign-language services. In 1950, for example, although all of the Communist countries of eastern Europe except East Germany had launched external services, these were on a small scale, and even the Soviet Union was transmitting a total of more than 500 hours of broadcasts weekly in all foreign languages. The United Kingdom's output, which had once led the field, had been reduced to slightly more than 600 hours a week and the Voice of America to less than 500 hours per week. By the early 1980s the situation had changed radically. The Soviet Union alone broadcast more than 2,000 hours per week, and the output of all Communist countries of eastern Europe (excluding Yugoslavia) totalled some 1,500 hours. The United Kingdom logged 744 hours in 1981, West Germany 785 hours, and the United States broadcast over the Voice of America, Radio Liberty, and Radio Free Europe 1,925 hours a week. The output of China had risen from 66 hours weekly in 1950 to 1,375 hours by 1981. The increase in Chinese broadcasts reflected in part the rising tension between China and the Soviet Union; significantly, the output of China's ally for much of this period, Albania, rose from 26 to 560 hours weekly during the same period. By the early 1980s Japan was transmitting for 263 hours, while Australia and Canada also sponsored external broadcasts.

Monitoring and transcriptions. A logical development following from external broadcasting is the monitoring of foreign broadcasts and their analysis for intelligence purposes. The BBC in particular has a highly developed monitoring service; this activity often yields quite valuable information. The Central Intelligence Agency of the United States is also active in monitoring and analyzing foreign broadcasts. Transcriptions (recordings) of programs produced in either the domestic or the external services of one country can be acceptable for broadcast in others. Radiobroadcasts of an educational nature can be used in different countries speaking the same language. Although many radio transcriptions are supplied free, in television the situation is different, and there is a substantial trade in television films.

Pirate and offshore stations. In some countries where broadcasting in general or radio alone is a monopoly, radio has had to compete for brief periods with independent commercial stations mounted on ships anchored at sea outside territorial waters. Sweden, Denmark, The Netherlands, and the United Kingdom have been the countries most affected by these stations, which have made use of unauthorized wavelengths, thus endangering other radio communications and operating free of any copyright obligations in respect to any of their broadcast material. Government action gradually has forced closure of such operations: in Sweden a competitive service of popular music proved effective; and in Denmark naval police action (the international legality of which may be questioned), followed by confiscation and heavy penalties, brought an end to the pirate station. The United Kingdom combined legislation penalizing any party who advertised or supplied such ships with the launching by the BBC of Radio 1, substantially a popular music service, to solve the problem. The French have had a particular problem of competition from the so-called *postes périphériques*, which include Europe No. 1 in the Saar and Radio Andorra in the Pyrenees, not to mention the French-language broadcasts of Monaco, Belgium, Luxembourg, and Switzerland. The strongest competition came from Europe No. 1, in which the French government finally purchased a controlling interest.

The problem of *postes périphériques* in France

III. Broadcasting operations

TYPES OF PROGRAMS AND DEVELOPMENT OF STUDIOS

There are a number of distinguishable types of programs that are broadcast, but they often overlap in technique, subject matter, and style. Radio, for example, broadcasts speech and music, but in an endless number of combinations. Television adds the visual element, greatly increasing the number of possible program forms. Most sizable broadcast organizations, however, have several categories for administrative convenience. But the definitions cannot be too precise, and lines of demarcation are necessarily vague.

Entertainment. Entertainment can include comedy, impossible wholly to differentiate from drama; quizzes, not always easily distinguished from relatively serious programs of information and education; popular music, in which the frontier with jazz and serious music is anything but rigid; and variety, or a series of unrelated acts, nearly always linked by a popular presenter or established performer.

From the early days of radio there was a tendency to make use of a variety format, and as this approach represented an extension of old music-hall traditions, success was achieved by many programs in this vein. From the music-hall-variety-type program emerged the "gang show," in which a cast of performers remaining the same from week to week would make use of a series of humorous situations or catchphrases, gradually building up a familiar background against which the incongruities of the script could exploit humour to the full. A further development was the "situation comedy," in which a number of characters, such as the members of a family, remain in the same situation week after week but experience comic adventures. Though these laughter programs lost popularity on radio as television gained popular acceptance, they have become the mainstays of television. A contemporary phenomenon has been the comedy program involving substantial amounts of political and social satire. The situation comedy has also been influenced by this trend.

Situation comedy

The many types of comedy entertainment programs that are produced around the world all have one common characteristic: not only have the performers needed the stimulus of a studio audience, but also the listeners and viewers are stimulated by the laughter and applause of the audience. This has led to some abuses, such as the superimposition of laughter and applause on prerecorded programs, a practice that is frowned upon but still practiced. It has also meant that large studios are required to accommodate not only the performers, frequently including more than one music combination, but also the audience. In television there must be room for settings that have become increasingly ambitious and for dancers and choruses. Broadcasting organizations have generally been able to build studios of appropriate size, though radio-broadcasters in the early days preferred to purchase or rent small theatres.

In their form and structure, children's entertainment shows resemble those for adults. Animated cartoons, however, represent an exception to this rule; the Hungarians, Poles, and French have achieved genuine distinction in this area.

Drama. Radio and television drama is not best produced in a theatre; the nature of the studio is therefore different. Early radio drama was produced in a relatively small studio, often with a single microphone, just as early television plays were produced with a single camera. Radio engineers soon began to employ a control panel with inputs from more than one studio and sound effects ingeniously achieved; their counterparts in television expanded their use of cameras and sets. Mixing in radio from one studio to another and in television from one set to another, plus increasingly sophisticated sound effects and background music, have all become accepted techniques in drama production. Inevitably, television drama has borrowed substantially from the techniques of film production.

Feature films, usually originally made for the cinema, continue to form an accepted and important element in television schedules throughout the world. Both radio and television occasionally broadcast live stage plays from theatres, but there is a general feeling that such offerings do not adequately exploit the advantages of either medium. From the earliest days of radio and television, the studio-produced drama has been an important ingredient in program schedules; in television, as in films, it was not long before shooting on location also became an accepted practice. Offerings have included classical Greek drama, Shakespeare and other Elizabethan dramatists, the Spanish and French theatre, Russian and Scandinavian plays, and modern works.

Serial presentations on television and radio have included adaptations of famous works of literature, such as the novels of Dickens, Balzac, and Tolstoy, the *Forsyte Saga* of John Galsworthy, historical costume dramas based on the lives of such figures as Henry VIII and Elizabeth I of England, and, of course, the romantic melodramas aimed largely at the daytime viewer or listener, known as "soap operas." Radio and television serials of fantasy and adventure are also produced for children.

Three other distinguishable types of drama have achieved almost universal popularity: western adventures; shows involving gangsters, crime, and police; and shows set in hospitals and other medical situations. Violent episodes in some crime and western adventure programs have drawn criticism from those who believe that such violence is harmful to children. In response, many broadcasting organizations have introduced codes of practice to minimize such scenes.

Violence on television

Western adventure programs, largely produced in the United States, have been popular with studios because of their relatively low production costs and ready salability abroad. Dramatic series of this type have been shown all over the world, often with dubbed sound tracks. Although these exported U.S. productions are often much less expensive than home-produced programs, Australia has been able to produce some western-type series, and Canada has exploited its legendary "Mounties." So many U.S. television programs have been exported, however, that broadcasting organizations in some nations, such as Japan and the United Kingdom, have taken steps to assure that home-produced dramas should have priority in terms of percentage of schedule hours and prime time (peak placing).

Spoken word. Spoken-word programs have included entertainment types, such as "This is Your Life" and many of the "talk shows," in which a personality interviewer questions celebrities, sometimes with interludes of music or comedy or with serious discussions, documentaries, or lectures. A fear of controversy, the problem of maintaining an overall impartiality, and sometimes the belief that the mass audience would be alienated by programs demanding a conscious effort and concentration, combined, in the early days of radio, to limit the time given to serious spoken-word programs. It was not long, however, before many broadcasters developed a sense of pride and responsibility in their function and regarded it as their duty to provide information and opinion. In countries where broadcasting achieved a substantial measure of independence, some broadcasters gradually became concerned not only with the exposition of fact and controversy but also with the task of exposing the ills and abuses of their society.

News continues to be the most important element in spoken-word radio. Since it was inescapable that broadcast news would affect the industry, newspaper proprietors in the early days of radio either made efforts to restrict the sources of news and the times at which it could be broadcast or sought themselves to enter the field. In areas where broadcasting was commercialized, the press was further concerned, because radio competed with it for advertising revenues and because radio could almost always get a story to the public before the newspapers could. Nevertheless, there is no evidence that radio news reduced the circulation of newspapers; some have even maintained that radio whetted the appetite of listeners for news and increased newspaper sales. It would seem, however, that television has adversely affected the daily press and, even more so, weekly or monthly magazines. Long before television outstripped radio, broadcasting organizations were employing reporters and special and foreign correspondents and were supplementing the service received from news agencies. Some broadcast reporters became public personalities in their own right.

News broadcasts

Television news presented additional production problems; the announcer at the microphone reading from a script or TelePrompTer was not satisfactory, and it was not long before the greater part of television news was appropriately accompanied by relevant pictures. The need for film shots and the cost and difficulty of obtaining them were, and to some extent remain, serious problems. In spite of substantial expenditure on the supply of such shots, television news is open to the criticism that news values and objectivity are distorted by the availability or nonavailability of pictures.

In general, however, broadcasting organizations have adjusted to the much higher cost of television news. The syndication of film reports, the development of live networks on an international basis, such as Eurovision, and satellite communications have overcome most problems of news reporting on television. On the other hand, it has become apparent that the psychological impact of film

Emotive effect of television news

shots of war and civil disturbance, as of accidents and disasters, is far greater than that of the radio report. Television reports of, for example, the Vietnam War did far more to influence public opinion than radio news bulletins could have done. Radio has the advantage, however, of not requiring the same degree of attention; the trend has been toward frequently repeated short bulletins. In the United States there are radio stations that restrict themselves entirely to news, usually in a continuous magazine format, plus, of course, the advertising spots. The news magazine, or newsreel, in radio was introduced even earlier on BBC. A series of brief reports, interviews, and extracts from speeches, making use of many voices and exploiting the technique of frequent renewal of stimulus, proved to be a successful formula. This technique has spread into news bulletins and is increasingly used in the coverage of current affairs, both in radio and television. In all these programs of news and comment, one of the problems has been that of the anchors, or presenters, and the degree to which they may be given freedom to project their personalities or express their views. In the United States there have been fewer inhibitions in this area than in countries where broadcasting is or has been a monopoly and where the need for and tradition of impartiality have been dominant. In the case of the BBC, newsreaders were long anonymous; but on television the identity of a newsreader, or of the presenter of a magazine of news or comment, cannot be concealed, and these inhibitions have broken down. Nevertheless, in western Europe and Commonwealth countries the impartiality of broadcasting services remains an issue of greater importance than in the United States or Latin America. In Britain, when the Independent Television Authority was created, it was enjoined to see that in the coverage of controversial matters each program should be balanced in itself. The BBC, with greater freedom, makes no effort to ensure balance in any one program, provided that an overall balance in respect of any issue is achieved over a reasonable period of time. In all developed countries elaborate programs are prepared to report the results of elections, though it is in the United States and the United Kingdom that these are most ambitious.

In radio straight talk persists in some countries, though less so than in the heyday of the medium. Nevertheless, some successful lectures at much greater length have been scheduled occasionally on television and in some countries on radio. Straight talk of 10 minutes or more does not lend itself to exciting television production, unless accompanied by filmed illustrations to the point where it all but becomes a documentary.

Another pattern popular in many countries involves a panel of distinguished figures under a chairman, answering questions of a topical nature from members of a studio audience. In some cases a parabolic microphone is employed so that questions may be asked from any part of the studio or hall in which the program is mounted; others may call for written queries in advance so that questioners can be conveniently seated in the first row. Some radio panel programs also solicit queries from members of the listening audience who call them in on the telephone.

The documentary program

Development of the radio documentary stemmed from drama, as writers searched for new material especially appropriate for broadcasting. Not surprisingly, early documentary was in dramatic form, and most of it was based on well-known historical events, of which the programs were in effect dramatic reconstructions. Production of radio documentaries was simplified by the invention of magnetic recording tape that was far easier to edit and use on location than its predecessors, the wax-coated disc and the wire recorder. Ironically, just when these technical advances had made the best form of radio documentary possible, the television documentary on contemporary themes began to supplant its radio counterpart. Documentaries have become more expository of public (current) affairs concerned with international relations, domestic politics, and social problems.

Religion. There have been, in the main, two types of religious program: devotional and information-discussion. The former comprises prayer, religious services, or hymn singing, either mounted in a studio or as outside broadcasts from a church, chapel, or hall. A third type is the dramatization of a religious theme, though the tendency has been to devote a good proportion of religious broadcasting time to documentaries, discussions, and interviews. Some sects have produced broadcasts that combine political and religious material. Missionary bodies, mostly under the control of one of the many international or regional religious broadcasting organizations, either buy time on commercial stations or operate stations in many parts of the world, including Latin America, Africa, and Asia.

Outside broadcasts. Although broadcasts do not constitute a distinct and definable form, they nevertheless have been since the birth of radio the most popular and arresting of all material transmitted on either medium. Sports of every description and ceremonial and political events have exercised an unfailing appeal and, in general, attract the largest audiences. Outside broadcasts have stimulated the imagination and taxed the ingenuity of television-broadcasting engineers to such an extent that they have accustomed the public to feats unimaginable to the pioneers of radio. The improvement of line communications, the development of mobile transmitters, and, above all, the use of satellite communications have given the outside broadcast an elasticity and an almost limitless range, as was strikingly demonstrated by the 1969 telecast of astronauts walking on the Moon.

Music. Radio has had two important effects on the musical life of the world: it has widened the audience for all forms of music and has made easier the development of new forms, such as electronic music. Music remains a staple ingredient of radio in its own right, whereas in television, though there are programs of music as such, it is more often an adjunct to something else, as, for example, dancing, or as a small component of a mixed program. In the field of popular music, radio has immensely aided the rapid changes of fashion, which have coincided with technical advances in the making of records and their popularity and sales. A recognition by record manufacturers of the enormous power of radio in popularizing a song or performer has led to some abuses. In the United States "payola," or bribes, were given to prominent radio personalities by record companies in return for promotion of their songs.

The development of stereophonic sound techniques has revolutionized the record industry and has played an important role on radio, though earliest in the field of serious music. Frequency modulated (FM) radio broadcasts of serious music, and later of other forms of music, have been popular in many areas; some records are broadcast stereophonically but can be received on monophonic radios (see SOUND RECORDING AND REPRODUCING).

Opera, too, has profited from broadcasting, and outside broadcasts from opera houses, as well as studio performances on both radio and television, have done much in European and many other countries to bring this form of music to a large public. Music programs have presented more difficulties than most others in the matter of studios, partly because of the size of studio required for a full symphony orchestra and partly because of the delicate balancing of acoustics for proper reproduction of such performances.

RELATIONS WITH ARTISTS, SPEAKERS, AUTHORS, AND UNIONS

In the early days of radio, problems of fees, royalties, performing rights, copyright, and relations with unions rarely were regarded. Entertainers performed largely for publicity purposes. Only gradually did performers appreciate radio's effect, first, as a threat to their theatre earnings and, second, as a highly lucrative substitute. To try to trace how a modus vivendi was reached in these matters in different countries would present a picture of baffling complexity in the light of the different prevailing laws and different union structures. Generally speaking, copyright issues have revolved around the rights of record manufacturers and fees for composers (see COPYRIGHT LAW). Rates and fees for reproducing recordings often

Copyright fees

have been the subject of disputes with the unions. Radiobroadcasters soon found that purchasing records or making their own recordings from live musical performances meant substantial economies; these, however, came at the expense of the musicians. Consequently, the musicians' unions sometimes attempted to prevent use of phonograph records or recording of live performances. In some countries, such as The Netherlands, the repeat problem has been solved by the performers receiving a fee for each repeat, the fee rising with each successive use of the recording until it ceases to represent an advantage to the broadcaster.

Relations of the broadcasting organizations with their staffs have also been complex. In Canada attempts to exercise a restrictive control have led to revolts and resignations, while in France editors and producers who have been unwilling to conform to government policy have been removed from their jobs, though often under other pretexts. The position of staff is particularly vulnerable in those countries where broadcasting is a state monopoly; an example is Czechoslovakia, where senior broadcasting officials were ousted after the fall in 1968 of Premier Alexander Dubček, who had attempted to liberalize the Communist regime.

INTERNAL ORGANIZATION, ADMINISTRATION, AND POLICY CONTROL

The organization and administration of broadcasting bodies can, in the case of a small independent station, be relatively simple, and the policies can be implemented with ease. Sizable organizations, however, have a complex problem because it is not possible to determine success or failure purely on the basis of financial returns. Monopoly organizations, though in theory their sole purpose is public service, in practice often must take into account the views of the government. In the case of nonprofit–public-service operations dependent upon license fees for revenue but with commercial competition, ratings cannot be completely ignored, and these organizations must compete for mass audiences to some extent in order to justify their existence at the expense of the listening and viewing public.

Functions of the broadcast administration

The broadcasting administration has two essential functions: first, programming—*i.e.*, allocation of funds and setting of schedules—and, second, production, the preparation of programs. The former is in effect a branch of direction, and those in charge of planning program schedules and allocating funds have a power that if not checked can be absolute. On the other hand, these planners are dependent on the goodwill of the production and supply departments.

A main problem arises in the treatment of controversial subjects in the field of current affairs. Where broadcasters are under no obligation to be impartial, as in The Netherlands, or where, as in totalitarian countries, only one point of view may be aired, the problem does not arise. In democratic countries, however, where the broadcaster has independence and where there is a need to achieve an overall impartiality, the problem is very serious. Even though decisions may be reached by discussion and a consensus of opinion, the responsibility usually has to be carried by one person. No broadcasting organization has been able to find a complete solution to the problem that does not involve rigid control and intrusion on the independence of the editorial and production staff.

Administration must also deal with routine matters, such as staff pay and conditions of service, recruitment, finance, accounting, negotiations with unions, procurement of equipment, and provision of office and studio space. In general, it has been found best to subordinate such routine management operations to the needs of those directly concerned with the principal function of broadcasting. Much the same may be said of engineering and technical staff, though their research work and technical advances influence the decisions of direction and development of broadcasting.

THE STATE OF BROADCASTING IN SELECTED COUNTRIES

Argentina. Broadcasting in Argentina is wholly controlled by the government but only partly operated by government agencies. Partly for historical reasons, the method of control is not clear-cut: all broadcasting is subject to the approval of the Consejo Federal de Radio y Televisión (Federal Radio and Television Council), a body working under the State Secretary of Communications, though the Secretary of Information can and does intervene on behalf of the president of the republic. All political activities were suppressed between 1966 and 1971, and, even after the government of Alejandro Agustín Lanusse lifted the ban, the restored freedom was not reflected in broadcasting. Of the approximately 150 radio stations in the country, nearly half are grouped into two large networks: an official cultural noncommercial network with 29 stations, some strategically placed in relation to broadcasts from other countries; and a government-controlled commercial network. There are more than 50 private commercial stations; some are small and low-powered. All television, though commercial, is administered by the state. LS82 Canal 7 in Buenos Aires is state owned; the other three stations in that city have separately owned provincial affiliates. Argentina has more than 30 television stations.

Sources of Argentine programs

Early television in Argentina depended on U.S.-produced telefilms dubbed into Spanish, and, although U.S.-dubbed feature films are still used, Argentine-produced programs dominate the market. Some material comes from Spain, Italy, and the United Kingdom. Argentine-produced programs can rarely be exported, because the Argentine accent in Spanish, particularly that of Buenos Aires, is not acceptable elsewhere in Latin America. There are more than 10,000,000 radio sets and 4,500,000 television receivers.

Australia. Australian broadcasting is under the supervision of the Australian Broadcasting Control Board. The principal organization is the Australian Broadcasting Commission, which is financed by parliamentary appropriations, revenue from the sale of publications, profits from public concerts, and subsidies for symphony orchestras. The government derives considerable income from the sale of receiving-set licenses, of which there are nearly 3,000,000 for radio and television combined. The Australian Broadcasting Commission, as well as the commercial stations, has a fair measure of freedom, though consultation with government and officials occurs frequently. The commission operates about 90 radio stations; two in each state capital are "metropolitan," five serve Papua New Guinea, 11 are shortwave stations broadcasting to inland Australia, and the rest are "regional" stations in the states, including Tasmania and Northern Territory, except for the 14 transmitters for the external services (Radio Australia). The domestic stations are grouped into three networks. The Australian Broadcasting Commission is required by law to broadcast all sessions of the Federal Parliament, which it does on its First network of seven stations. There are, in addition, 125 commercial radio stations, of which 25 are in state capitals. These are associated in the Federation of Australian Commercial Broadcasters, and many are grouped in various networks. The Australian Broadcasting Commission has more than 50 television stations, six in state capitals. Nearly half their output is imported, and of the total almost 25 percent is drama, 19 percent news and "public interest" programs, nearly 13 percent sports, and about 7 percent cultural, excluding education. There are 43 members of the Federation of Australian Commercial Television Stations, 15 in state capitals. Imported programs account for much of the commercial output, and of the total 45 percent is drama; 9 percent news, information, and current affairs; and 26 percent light entertainment. There are an estimated 7,250,000 radio sets and more than 5,500,000 television receivers in Australia.

Brazil. There are some 1,500 radio and more than 100 television stations in Brazil; the majority are commercial. In general they are under the authority of the Ministry of Communications. All broadcasting is subject to censorship, and any station that runs counter to the government's wishes can be closed. There are radio stations of the Ministry of Education in Rio de Janeiro and Brasília; some of the states have official radio outlets, and a few have television installations. There are also some university radio stations and a few television stations, apart from the Roman Catholic educational radio network (see above *Educational broadcasting*). The remaining stations are private commercial enterprises, operating independently or linked to one of the networks, of which the best known are associated with large newspaper concerns, such as Diarios Associados or O Globo. The larger radio networks use shortwave broadcasting, which permits simultaneous transmissions on medium-wave provincial stations. Provincial television stations prepare their newscasts, often in cooperation with a local newspaper and radio station. The others employ film, telefilm, and videotape to supplement local production. All radio stations must devote one hour each day to "The Voice of Brazil," a government news program supplied by the official Agencia Nacional; radio stations must also broadcast at least five hours a week of educational programs. Television stations may be called upon to broadcast programs produced by the Agencia Nacional, consisting mainly of government statements and ministerial and presidential speeches. In 1975 the government created Radiobras, the Brazilian Broadcasting Company, which broadcasts to the remote regions of the Amazon Basin, bringing those regions into closer contact with the political and cultural mainstream of Brazil. Television entertainment consists substantially of Brazilian-produced serials, supplemented by U.S.-produced and dubbed films and telecine programs. The number of radio sets in Brazil is about 39,000,000, and the total number of television receivers is estimated at more than 12,000,000.

Official news on Brazilian stations

Canada. The principal broadcasting organization is the Canadian Broadcasting Corporation (CBC), which has one main television network in French and another in English and one main AM radio network in each language. In addition, there are small FM networks and some shortwave transmission. There are several regional networks, including two for French television, five for English television, two for French radio, and eight for English radio. The CBC has 38 principal radio stations and 324 low-power relay transmitters; in addition, 52 privately owned stations are affiliated with it and are paid for transmitting its output. For the French television service there are 10 stations and some 172 privately owned affiliates. The English television service has 17 principal stations and 539 privately owned affiliates. Public and private broadcasting in Canada, apart from educational broadcasts, consists of information, including news, public affairs, and religion (25 percent on radio and 34 percent on television); light entertainment, including light music and drama (65 percent on radio and 47 percent on television); cultural programs, including serious music and drama (4 percent on radio and 2 to 3 percent on television); and sports and various ethnic programs accounting for the remainder. There are some 11,000,000 television receivers in the country.

Two-language broadcasting in Canada

External services are smaller than in most comparable countries; there are broadcasts on shortwave to the Canadian armed forces overseas and an international service in English, French, German, Spanish, Portuguese, Czech, Slovak, Hungarian, Polish, Ukrainian, and Russian for listeners in Europe and Latin America. Apart from the CBC, there are more than 400 radio and nearly 100 television stations, privately owned and commercial.

France. The broadcasting system in France has been outlined above. The Office de Radiodiffusion Télévision Française (ORTF) broadcasts on three national radio networks: (1) France-Inter, a 24-hour service of entertainment and news, integrated with Inter-Variétés on regional transmitters carrying programs produced by regional stations and France-Inter Paris, a morning program of popular music and news flashes for Paris and the surrounding area; (2) France-Culture, with information and public affairs along with cultural programs; and (3) France-Musique, a network of musical programming. Regular television service began in 1938, was interrupted by World War II, and recommenced in 1945. Colour television was inaugurated in 1967.

Regional broadcasting is organized in 11 regions; these control 30 program production centres and 23 news offices. The purpose of the regional structure in France is to communicate the news and artistic and cultural developments in each region to its residents, as well as to integrate a reflection of the region in the national networks. Regional coordination and liaison are the responsibility of a special group working directly under the national office, which is also responsible for broadcasting in the overseas departments and territories of France.

French regional broadcasts

Although the largest contribution to the revenue of ORTF continues to be the proceeds of receiving-set licenses, it is active in promoting commercial activities, including the sale of publications, records, and films, and is authorized to derive revenue from advertising on a limited scale both on television networks and on the France-Inter radio network. The ORTF distinguishes between *publicité de marques* (advertising of named products) and *publicité collective* (advertising of types of products on behalf of manufacturers' associations or state monopolies); France-Inter may carry only the latter. Two committees, appointed for radio and television, advise the central administrative body on programs, schedules, and the balance between the different categories of output and may be called upon to comment on future projects and make proposals. Approximate percentages of the total radio output devoted to the main program categories, excluding the educational, are as follows: news, information, and sports, 14 percent; light entertainment, 33 percent; arts, letters, and science, 38 percent; drama and literary programs, 8 percent. There is only a small radio sports output, but the use of radio for traffic control on a national scale (Radio-guidage) is particularly effective during the late summer, when children travel home from school vacations. Television output in France is more difficult to classify, but about 42 percent is devoted to news, information, and sports; 9 percent to documentaries; 10 percent to light entertainment; 5 percent to drama and theatre; and 5 percent to youth programs, excluding school broadcasts. Practically all homes have radios, and there are about 15,000,000 television receivers.

France's external services have a weekly output of roughly 100 hours, of which half is in French. Radio-France internationale regularly broadcasts to North and Central America, Germany, and Africa.

Italy. The origin and development of Radiotelevision Italiana (RAI) is covered above. Regular television broadcasts began in January 1954. RAI has three radio services on national networks on AM and FM: a First, or National, Program offering a balanced output; a Second Program essentially of entertainment; and a Third Program. In addition, there is a substantial regional output. There are two television services: the first, on VHF (very high frequency), broadcasting 63 hours weekly, is the National Program; the Second Program also transmits 63 hours weekly on UHF (ultrahigh frequency). The RAI provides limited regional television on special occasions only, except for a daily one and one-half hours in German for the German-speaking minority of the Trentino-Alto Adige region. RAI has 18 production centres and 21 regional offices. The Trieste and Bolzano offices are responsible, respectively, for radio output weekly in Slovene for the Friuli-Venezia Giulia region and, apart from the German television output, for broadcasts in German and in Ladin (Romansh) for the Trentino-Alto Adige region. RAI's revenue comes from a proportion, determined by the government, of the proceeds of the sale of radio- and television-receiving licenses and from advertising. Advertising is closely regulated and may not "prejudice the good quality of programs"; it is guided by a code, and the percentage of time given to it is limited. RAI devotes 70 percent of its radio output to light entertainment, 16 percent to news and information, 4 percent to cultural programs, and 1 percent to youth and educational programs. On television 36 percent is news and information, 19 percent is entertainment, 4 percent is cultural, and 17 percent is programs for schools and education. There are about 12,600,000 television receivers in Italy.

Italy's external services use medium wave for broadcasting to the Mediterranean basin in Arabic, English, and

German and shortwave for services to Africa, the Americas, Australasia, Europe, and the Middle East in Italian and nearly 30 other languages; the total output, including external broadcasts in Italian, amounts to some 218 hours weekly.

Japan. The basic structure of Nippon Hōsō Kyōkai (NHK) is covered above. NHK has two television and three radio networks (two AM and one FM), of which one television and one AM network are almost entirely devoted to education. The General Television program gives a balanced service, as does the First (AM) Radio service, while the FM (VHF) service is concerned mainly with cultural and local music programs. There is relatively little political broadcasting in Japan, and the first occasion on which candidates for election to the Japanese Diet were able to present their political views on television was in December 1969. NHK output in program categories is summarized in the Table.

NHK Program Categories—Percentages of Total Output (1979)

	general television (GTV)	educational television (ETV)	First Radio	Second Radio	FM radio
Education	16.3	78.6	2.9	76.3	7.6
Reports	37.5	2.0	42.1	11.6	14.4
Culture	23.3	19.4	28.5	12.1	42.6
Entertainment	22.9	—	26.5	—	35.4
Total hours of daily output	18	18	19	18.5	18

Japanese program scheduling

NHK has installed a system of computerized automation for its scheduling, resource allocation, and transmitting operations, probably the most advanced in the world, with a view to giving its production staff a maximum freedom for creative work. In 1978 the organization installed the 12,000,000,000-hertz (2.5-centimetre) wave for metropolitan area broadcasting and broadcasting two television sound outputs simultaneously so that a single television image can be received with sound in either of two languages. NHK has 173 medium-wave transmitters for the First Radio network, 141 for the Second, and 474 for the VHF-FM network. General and educational television use about 2,800 transmitters each, most of which are rebroadcasting or relay stations. The so-called regional broadcasting is not so much regional as local and concerned mainly with news and practical information. Local television output averages one and a half hours and local radio averages more than three and a half hours daily. In addition to NHK there are 85 broadcasting organizations that are members of the National Association of Commercial Broadcasters in Japan. They offer 489 VHF-TV stations 4,115 UHF-TV stations, 45 AM radio stations, and four FM stations. There are about 27,800,000 television receivers in Japan.

NHK is responsible also for Japan's external services, which are divided into a general service—*i.e.*, a worldwide service in English and Japanese that broadcasts a total of seven hours daily—and a regional service for the Americas, Europe, Asia, Africa, and Australasia, in some two dozen languages.

Mexico. There are some 380 radio stations in Mexico, of which about 50 are FM stations. Most are commercial, and about 130 are grouped into two nationwide networks. There is a smaller number of television stations, constantly growing, many of which are grouped into networks of varying size, of which the largest and only nationwide network is Televisa, which combined the former Telesistema Mexicano and Televisión Independiente de Mexico. Television, too, is nearly all commercial, though there are some university stations, of which the best known is Radio Universidad, run by the Universidad Nacional Autónoma de México in Mexico City; in addition, the Instituto Politécnico Nacional operates a cultural station in the capital. In theory there is no government control over broadcasting, but in practice there is no political broadcasting critical of the government or of the leading political party. Most stations carry the Hora Nacional, an hour-long officially produced program, every Sunday morning. The government has the right to use 12.5 percent of the total transmitting time of all radio and television stations. This right so far has not been fully exercised, though the announced intention is that the Comisión de Radiodifusión should acquire the resources to make full use of the time. Except for the few noncommercial stations, the majority of radio stations do little more than broadcast recorded popular music, news, and spot advertisements.

Television, with few exceptions, is substantially devoted to entertainment; a good proportion of material originates in the United States, though the government has banned some of the more violent shows, and some comes from the United Kingdom. Production of programs for other Spanish-speaking countries is on the increase, with programs made for Puerto Rico, the Dominican Republic, Central American countries, Venezuela, Peru, Colombia, Ecuador, Argentina, Chile, and the Hispanic community in the United States. The government has proposed a network of officially operated small stations to provide cultural and educational programs. There are estimated to be about 14,000,500 radio and 6,000,000 television receiving sets in the country.

The Netherlands. In all democratic countries governments have found it difficult to reflect minority views in broadcasting. The Netherlands has made perhaps the most determined attempt to deal with this problem. The Dutch system basically consists of one national organization, the Nederlandse Omroep Stichting (The Netherlands Broadcasting Corporation), which is responsible for the transmission of all programs, and a number of broadcasting societies (or organizations) that, through the size of their membership, have earned the right to produce a proportion of the foundation's output. The Netherlands Broadcasting Corporation also has responsibility for the production of the so-called joint programs, which account for 25 percent of the radio and 40 percent of the television transmissions. The Broadcasting Act of 1966 called upon the responsible minister to allocate time on the air, in both radio and television, to bodies that fulfill certain conditions, in particular a sufficient membership, and that, by October 1971, included: broadcasting societies or organizations, groups aspiring to recognition as broadcasting societies, the churches, associations of a nature comparable to churches, political parties, other reputable associations of approved purpose, an advertising foundation, and educational bodies. As far as the full-fledged societies are concerned, the amount of time they have on the air is determined by their category, in turn dependent upon the number of subscribers, whose subscriptions pay for a weekly program bulletin. Some of the other bodies with time on the air may prepare their own programs or have them produced by groups with more experience. Organizations with at least 60,000 members may petition to broadcast from one hour per week to four hours. The government, however, has moved to restrict access to broadcasting, with legislation requiring aspirant broadcasting groups to offer innovative proposals to the existing range of programs in order to qualify. The financing of broadcasting, when production time is allocated among so many, presents a complex problem of accountancy. The revenue comes from the sale of receiving-set licenses and from advertising profits.

Dutch broadcasting societies

The Netherlands has six radio services, in addition to the Nederlandse Omroep Stichting, and three independent television services. There is no regional television, but there are several regional radio organizations. The main categories of overall radio output are 25 percent news, public affairs, and information; 22 percent classical music; 14 percent light music; and 28 percent entertainment and other light programs. Television output is more diversified, with 32.3 percent entertainment (of which more than half is of foreign origin); 2.9 percent Dutch-produced drama; 5 percent films, mostly foreign; and 31.2 percent news, public affairs, and information. There are about 5,100,000 television receivers.

The Dutch external services broadcast some 45 daily hours of shortwave transmissions to most areas of the world in Dutch and seven other languages (Portuguese, Spanish, Papiamento, Arabic, English, French, and Indonesian).

New Zealand. In New Zealand the relatively small population (fewer than 3,200,000) means that broadcasting personnel are closely in touch with their audience, whose demand for a high-standard broadcasting service presents financial problems. The National Broadcasting Service, a government department set up in 1936, was faced by the competition of the National Commercial Broadcasting Service a year later. The two were amalgamated and reorganized as a government department, the New Zealand Broadcasting Service, in 1946. The service had some degree of independence from the start, and the inauguration of a television service in June 1960 provided the opportunity for the Broadcasting Act of 1961, by which was created the New Zealand Broadcasting Corporation, with a far greater constitutional autonomy. It is financed by license fees and advertising revenue. In 1979 the Broadcasting Corporation of New Zealand was created, incorporating two previously independent networks. Radio New Zealand has one radio medium-wave network and two television networks with a mixed output, mainly in English, while radio includes some broadcasts in Maori, Samoan, Tongan, Nivean, and Tokelauan. The corporation has more than 50 radio stations in 32 cities and towns and some 15 television stations with more than 30 relay stations, mainly low-powered. The corporation is also responsible for the Foreign Service (Radio New Zealand), which broadcasts to Australia, the Pacific Islands, and the Ross Dependency in the Antarctic in English, twice a week to Samoa in Samoan, and once a fortnight to the Cook Islands, in Rarotongan, and to Niue, in Niuean. There are nine private radio stations.

New Zealand's external services

Soviet Union. The State Committee for Television and Radio Broadcasting operates a substantial undertaking under the Soviet Union's Council of Ministers. The chairman of the committee has four deputies, one each for television, external services, domestic radio, and for administration and finance, and there is an editorial board of 13 members. The committee controls output and is responsible for the equipment of television centres and for all personnel, but all lines, radio stations, and studios are under the control of the Ministry of Communications. Under the committee, domestic radio is run by seven Chief Editorial boards: program planning and presentation; propaganda; information (news); children; youth; literature and drama; and music, comedy, and satire. There is a joint radio and television department for sports. No program may go on the air without the approval of the editor in chief (or his deputy) of the appropriate editorial board. Though regional stations have a measure of autonomy, the committee controls the work of the regional committees handling radio in the various republics, regions, and districts. Radio in the Soviet Union requires between 300 and 400 transmitters for its networks and regional broadcasts. To achieve maximum coverage, it makes use of long waves, medium waves, and shortwaves, as well as FM. Moscow is responsible for five outputs as follows:

Program I is a mixed program covering the entire union; Program II is a 24-hour service with news and commentaries every half-hour, also covering the entire population; Program III is primarily for the European regions of the Soviet Union and reaches more remote regions by shortwaves and FM. There is also a local output of some three half-hours a day for the Moscow area on some of the channels used for Program III. Program IV is on FM and offers classical music nine hours a day. Program V is directed toward Soviets abroad. The regional effort is impressive, with broadcasts in almost 70 languages in use within the territory of the Soviet Union. There are 23 principal regional stations. With so diverse an output there is no means of making a meaningful percentage breakdown of program categories, but Soviet radio on the whole devotes more time to information, educational, and cultural programs and less to entertainment than other countries.

The Moscow television station began broadcasting in 1939 and claims to have been the first European television station to renew operation after the World War II interruption. Colour was introduced in 1967. About four-fifths of the population are within reach of a television signal, for which there are 280 main and about 2,000 relay transmitters. In most of the principal cities there are at least two outputs to choose from. The satellites Molniya I and Ekran, combined with 82 Orbita ground and relay stations, has greatly increased the size of the potential audience. At the Moscow television centre, Ostankino, there is a 1,739-foot (530-metre) tower used for television and other communications. The services broadcast cannot be easily analyzed, and it is claimed that from Moscow six can be broadcast simultaneously. Of the four main channels, one is for the Moscow area only, a second is sent to most of the other republics of the union, and a third is educational at primary, secondary, and university levels. The fourth channel features social and political issues, the arts, and sports. There is also a substantial output originated in the regional centres. There were estimated to be, by 1980, some 75,000,000 television receivers in the Soviet Union.

The external services described above are probably the largest of any country. The output can be divided into six types: (1) for foreign countries from Moscow; (2) for foreign countries from regional stations; (3) relays of domestic services for listeners abroad; (4) broadcasts for Soviets abroad, under the aegis of the Committee for Cultural Relations; (5) a service for the Merchant Marine and for fishermen; and (6) the "Peace and Progress" station. It is the Moscow output, supplemented by the foreign services from the regional stations, that has the widest coverage and makes use of nearly 70 languages, including more for Africa and Asia than any other country and including even, for example, Quechua (for Peru). The "Peace and Progress" output is in German for Europe; in various Chinese languages, Mongolian, and English for Asia; in Yiddish, Arabic, and Hebrew for the Near East; and in Spanish, Portuguese, Creole (for Haiti), and Guaraní (for Paraguay) for Latin America. In 1978 Soviet broadcasting initiated its "World Service in English."

Soviet foreign-language transmissions

Sweden. The historical background of Sveriges Radio, the Swedish broadcasting monopoly, is described above. Two important developments occurred in 1967, embodied in the Broadcasting Law, effective from July 1 of that year. Public authorities and agencies were specifically forbidden to examine programs in advance or to attempt to prevent them from being broadcast; this meant that the government had not even the power of veto. The legal responsibility for any program rests not on the organization, its board of directors, or even the director general but on the program supervisor, and no program may be broadcast against his will. Program content is ultimately controlled by the Radio Council, which supervises both radio and television. The Radio Council may only rule on shows that have already been aired, thus avoiding a role of censorship. The financing is entirely from licenses for receiving sets, but the proceeds are allocated by Parliament to Sveriges Radio, which produces most of the programs; the Swedish Telecommunications Administration, which transmits them; and the Swedish General Services Administration, which is responsible for the construction of broadcasting facilities.

Sweden has three radio and two television networks. A substantial number of stations and transmitters on long waves, medium waves, and shortwaves ensures national coverage of the three radio services, as well as allowing for regional broadcasting. Twenty-four regional stations have a substantial autonomy and their own budgets, but they must negotiate with the heads of the national networks to opt out, with their own regional programs, for up to a total of 25 percent of the network programming. In radio one network broadcasts spoken-word programs almost exclusively with some serious music during the day; the second consists of education and light as well as serious music in the evening, and the third, a 24-hour operation, features popular music, news, light entertainment, and regional broadcasts. The two television net-

Sweden's television networks

works offer a wide variety of features, which include information (17.9 percent), drama and film (13.6 percent), entertainment (13.1 percent), programs for children (10.8 percent), news (9.6 percent), sports (9.5 percent), and education (8.9 percent). Colour television was inaugurated in April 1970. There are estimated to be some 3,100,000 television receivers.

Sveriges Radio is also responsible for Sweden's external services, the cost of which (as with the cost of educational broadcasts) is separately budgeted and paid for from government funds. The broadcasts are in Swedish and six foreign languages: English, French, German, Spanish, Portuguese, and Russian. They are beamed as appropriate to all parts of the world.

United Kingdom. *British Broadcasting Corporation.* A monopoly until 1954, the BBC has four radio networks: Radio 1, broadcasting mostly popular music, mainly during the day; Radio 2, primarily transmitting light music and entertainment; Radio 3, broadcasting mainly serious music during the day, educational programs in the early evening, and cultural programs in the late evening; and Radio 4, scheduling spoken word primarily, school programs in the midmorning and early afternoon, and a mixed program in the evenings. The main ingredients of overall output are: 42.9 percent entertainment and music; 21.2 percent serious music; 9.1 percent news and outside broadcasts; 4.8 percent drama; 3.6 percent education; and 2.2 percent features. Some 20 local radio stations have been added to the BBC since 1967. The BBC has two television services, the first of which transmits 82 hours a week and the second 42; both have mixed programs that are coordinated to avoid conflicts. The main ingredients are news, documentaries, and information (31 percent); British and foreign films and series (15.5 percent); outside broadcasts, substantially sports, and sports news (14 percent); drama (8 percent); "family" programs and light entertainment (13.5 percent); education (11.1 percent); and religion (2.2 percent).

There is substantial regional activity in both media. Of the six regions in the kingdom that formerly operated with a fair degree of autonomy, only the "national" regions remain for Scotland, Wales, and Northern Ireland. In place of the other three regions, North, Midland, and West and South, there are 20 production centres for both radio and television. Regions broadcast their own programs by opting out of Radio 4 or BBC 1 and using their own section of the corresponding network. There are special broadcasts in the Welsh language for Wales. There are about 50 local FM (VHF) stations as authorized by the government: these are mostly placed to cover the larger city areas. Twenty-five competitive commercial local stations have been set up under the supervision of the Independent Broadcasting Authority.

The BBC is also responsible for the United Kingdom's external services, which are paid for by annual grants-in-aid from the treasury. Though no longer among the leaders in quantity of output, it remains among them in terms of penetration. Seventy transmitters, of which 26 are overseas relay stations, provide a shortwave worldwide service and a medium-wave service in many areas, including Europe (from Berlin and Munich), western Asia, and the eastern Mediterranean. Of the weekly output of about 740 hours, roughly one-third in the World Service is in English, and the remainder is in nearly 40 foreign languages, of which the main ones are Arabic (119 hours), French for Europe and Africa (more than 45), Russian and German (55 and 30), Spanish for Spanish-speaking America (28), Polish and Czech (24 and 15), Hungarian (16), and Portuguese for Brazil and Portugal (23).

Independent Broadcasting Authority. The Independent Broadcasting Authority (originally called Independent Television Authority) was established by act of Parliament in 1954; broadcasting began under its control a year later. Although the authority has substantial independence, it does not produce any programs or advertising; these tasks are performed by commercial program companies. These latter, organized on a regional basis, supply all the material broadcast except for news, for which a separate group, Independent Television News, was created, jointly owned and financed by the program companies.

Control of the British program companies

The program companies are under a substantial measure of control from the Independent Broadcasting Authority, which is responsible for the appointment of program companies, control of program and advertising output, and its transmission. The authority enforces codes with respect to advertising and violence on the screen. The 15 television companies broadcast throughout the week within their respective areas, except for two that share the London area. The program companies are entirely financed by spot advertising (sponsored programs are forbidden by law) in "natural breaks" in and between programs; they pay a rental to the authority to cover the latter's transmitting and administrative costs and a fiscal levy to the exchequer. The program companies cooperate in a network committee, and a substantial number of the principal programs are broadcast by all companies. The contribution to the network made by each company varies in accordance with its size and resources. The revenue of each company is substantially dependent upon the number of homes with television receivers able to receive the Independent Broadcasting Authority signal in the area it covers, which varies from 32,000 in the Channel Islands to 2,630,000 in the Midlands and 4,300,000 in the London area. So diversified an output makes valueless any percentage analysis of program categories; but the principal types of output, in order of size, are as follows: drama, including telefilm series; news, news magazines, features, and documentaries; sports; entertainment; feature films (British and foreign); education; children's programs; and religion. The Television Act of 1964 established the present authority situation for 12 years, and its license has since been extended. The authority has also been given the task of supervising local commercial radio (hence its change of name).

United States. So great is the broadcasting operation in the United States, so many are the stations, both radio and television, and so extensive the ramifications and links with other industries, that it is not possible to produce a summary on the lines of those for countries where broadcasting has been more tightly organized. Some idea of the magnitude of the broadcasting scene is provided by the number of broadcasting stations in operation in June 1981, as authorized by the Federal Communications Commission: radio AM, 4,619; radio FM, 3,324; educational radio FM, 1,106; commercial television UHF, 242; commercial television VHF, 522; educational television UHF, 162; educational television VHF, 107; television relay stations UHF, 1,681; television relay stations VHF, 2,616—a total of some 14,000 stations. In most categories more stations have been authorized than are operating. The largest proportional increase has been in educational radio FM. Commercial broadcasting on television, as on radio in the past, is dominated by the three great national networks: the American Broadcasting Company, Columbia Broadcasting System, and the National Broadcasting Company. In radio, where the networks are no longer dominant, there is also the Mutual Broadcasting System; the majority of radio stations are as independent of the large networks as of the government, and many of the commercial stations specialize in a single type of output, which may be one or other of various kinds of popular music, classical music, news, or even traffic information. A few are owned by or affiliated with the national networks or with smaller local networks; some even are small local stations offering a basic fare of neighbourhood gossip interspersed with recorded music and spot advertising. After a slump following the major onset of television, radio, even network radio, has again become profitable. In television the three major networks own and operate their own stations in some of the larger cities and substantially control a majority of affiliates.

Noncommercial broadcasting has risen in the United States. The National Association of Educational Broadcasters serves educational stations with transcriptions produced by its members and by other domestic as well as foreign broadcasters. The National Public Radio is also largely educational, supported by donations from foundations and other sources. There are radio stations supported by donations and subscriptions from listeners, in particular the Pacifica group. The Public Broadcasting Service has a loose organization. Its production facilities are not jointly organized, and it makes use of noncommercial stations for its network. Its revenue is uncertain; it received $137,000,000 in 1982 from a congressional appropriation, which must be renewed annually, and the rest from foundations, public contributions, and individual stations.

Another system is community antenna television (CATV), increasingly known as cablevision, or cable TV, originally set up in areas of poor reception or where the choice of receivable television services was poor and cablevision could offer additional choices from elsewhere. By 1964, 1,000 such systems were in operation. At the time, no one thought of "cablecasting"—*i.e.*, that the cablevision companies should originate their own programs—but in many areas cablecasting has proved a success. Even a relatively small enterprise such as the Twin County Trans Video, of Allentown, Pennsylvania, for example, more than doubled its subscribers in little more than a year after it began originating its own local program. Cablevision, transmitted via direct cables connected to each television set, offers viewers a large choice of programs, as well as excellent reception. There are estimated to be some 169,000,000 television receivers in the United States.

Official external services are operated by the Board for International Broadcasting, known as the Voice of America. They are broadcast to all parts of the world and have a number of relay stations overseas. Apart from English, 29 languages are used. There are also two foreign-based organizations, Radio Free Europe and Radio Liberty. In addition there is the International Broadcast Station, KGES, offering a shortwave service to Latin America in English, Spanish, and German and in Russian to Asia; Radio New York World Wide, with a commercial service to Europe and Africa in English and to the Caribbean in English and Spanish; and World International Broadcasters, whose shortwave commercial service with a religious background is broadcast in English to Europe, the Near East, and North Africa. The American Forces Radio and Television Service has a network of shortwave stations broadcasting a worldwide service; stations are located in Alaska, Canada, Europe, North Africa, Ethiopia, the Caribbean, the Far and Near East, Antarctica, the North Atlantic, and the Pacific.

West Germany. Though Germany was one of the first countries to begin radio transmissions (October 1923), the state organization owes nothing to earlier development. It was the occupying powers at the end of World War II that established the present system based on nine state (*Länder*) organizations. All state organizations have a First Radio service on medium wave, supported by FM. All have a Second and Third Radio service on FM, and the Cologne group has a Fourth. Berlin has an AM channel, as well as FM for each of its three radio services. In many cases, two or more *Länder* organizations cooperate and broadcast simultaneously a single output on one of their FM services. The latter in most cases is broadcast for only three to four hours daily and is substantially, sometimes entirely, devoted to foreign languages for foreign workers in West Germany. The output of the First and Second Radio services is to some extent mixed, but there is a tendency for the more serious output, especially good music, to be found on the Second rather than the First. The Saar's First service, for example, is entirely popular light music and hourly news bulletins, and the Second is cultural.

Germany's provincial organizations

The First German Television service is nationally coordinated with contributions from each *Land* organization. Each organization broadcasts a substantial amount of regional material for its own audience. The Second Television service is centrally planned and produced, with headquarters in Mainz; schedules are coordinated to give the viewer a maximum choice. Each organization has also a Third Television service for only a few hours a day, often of an educational nature; this service, like the radio Third service, is sometimes produced and simultaneously broadcast by groups of two or three *Länder* organizations. The Federal government has no authority for the control of broadcasting within the West German territory, and legislative and administrative competence for broadcasting rests with the *Länder*. But even the *Land* governments and parliaments are legally barred from intervening beyond a statutory supervision and may not interfere with the basic independence of the broadcasting organizations. There are estimated to be some 20,300,000 radio receivers and about 20,500,000 television receivers in West Germany.

There are two external service organizations. Deutschlandfunk has a First Program in German on medium wave and long wave and a Second on medium wave only, broadcasting for France, the United Kingdom, The Netherlands, and northern and eastern Europe. Deutschlandfunk also broadcasts in Dutch, English, French, Italian, Romanian, Serbo-Croatian, Hungarian, Czech, Slovak, Polish, Norwegian, Swedish, and Danish. Deutsche Welle broadcasts in 30 foreign languages to most areas of the world for a total of nearly 800 hours weekly.

BIBLIOGRAPHY. ERIK BARNOUW, *A History of Broadcasting in the United States*, 3 vol. (1966–70), a lively journalistic and revealing account of the development of broadcasting in the United States, and *Tube of Plenty: The Evolution of American Television* (1975), a condensation and update of his three-volume work; WILLIAM A. BELSON, *The Impact of Television: Methods and Findings in Program Research* (1967); HANS BRACK, *Organisation und wirtschaftliche Grundlagen des Hörfunks und des Fernsehens in Deutschland* (1968; Eng. trans., *German Radio and Television: Organization and Economic Basis*, 1968); ASA BRIGGS, *The History of Broadcasting in the United Kingdom*, 4 vol. (1961–79), a solid and detailed history of broadcasting in the United Kingdom; BRITISH BROADCASTING CORPORATION, *BBC Audience Research in the United Kingdom* (1961), and *Violence on Television: Programme Content and Viewer Perception* (1972); LES BROWN, *Televi$ion: The Business Behind the Box* (1971), a critical look at network policies in programming; JEAN CAZENEUVE, *Sociologie de la radio-télévision*, 2nd ed. (1965); GEORGE COMSTOCK *et al.*, *Television and Human Behavior* (1978), a summary of research findings; LIDIA DE RITA, *I contadini e la televisione* (1964), on the impact of television on an agricultural community; J.D. HALLORAN, *Problems of Television Research* (1966), a progress report of the Television Research Committee; W.V. HANEY, *Communication: Patterns and Incidents*, rev. ed. (1967), a study concentrating on misunderstandings; SYDNEY W. HEAD (ed.), *Broadcasting in Africa* (1974), a comprehensive survey, including a bibliography; HILDE T. HIMMELWEIT, A.N. OPPENHEIM, and PAMELA VINCE, *Television and the Child* (1958), an authoritative study of the impact of television on children; ELIHU KATZ *et al.*, *Broadcasting in the Third World: Promise and Performance* (1977), an analysis of broadcasting in developing countries; WILLIAM E. MCCAVITT (ed.), *Broadcasting around the World* (1981), generally useful, though the chapter on the Soviet Union should be read with caution; GERHARD MALETZKE, *Psychologie der massen Kommunikation* (1963), a psychological study of the relationship between communicator and recipient; ALBERT NAMUROIS, *Problems of Structure and Organization of Broadcasting in the Framework of Radiocommunications* (1964); BURTON PAULU, *British Broadcasting: Radio and Television in the United Kingdom* (1956), and *Radio and Television Broadcasting on the European Continent* (1967); EUGÈNE PONS, *General Considerations on License Fees for Radio and Television Sets* (1964); *A Public Trust: The Report of the Carnegie Commission on the Future of Public Broadcasting* (1979); HARRY J. SKORNIA, *Television and Society* (1965), a critical view of broadcasting in the United States; ANTHONY SMITH (ed.), *Television and Political Life* (1979), a collection of essays describing patterns of control over television broadcasting in six European countries; R.J. THOMSON, *Television Crime-Drama* (1959), a study of the impact of violence on children and adolescents; U.S. SURGEON GENERAL'S SCIENTIFIC ADVISORY COMMITTEE ON TELEVISION AND SOCIAL BEHAVIOR, *Television and Growing Up: The Impact of Televised Violence* (1972); BRUNO VASARI, *Financial Aspects of Broadcasting* (1965); E.G. WEDELL, *Broadcasting and Public Policy* (1968), a critical view of broadcasting in the United Kingdom; RAYMOND WILLIAMS, *Britain in the Sixties: Communications* (1962), on the role of mass media in dissolving class structure.

The handbooks, yearbooks, annual reports, and occasional monographs of broadcasting organizations, supervisory bodies, and international organizations (particularly, the European Broadcasting Union in Geneva) are invaluable sources of basic and statistical information.

(J.A.Ca.)

Broglie, Louis-Victor, duc de

A French theoretical physicist, Louis de Broglie was responsible for the then far-reaching idea that the electron and other material constitutents of the atom possess wavelike properties. In 1923, when Broglie put forward this idea, there was no experimental evidence whatsoever that the electron, the corpuscular properties of which were well established by experiment, might under some conditions behave as if it were radiant energy. Broglie's suggestion, his one major contribution to physics, thus constituted a triumph of intuition.

Wide World Photos

Broglie, 1958.

Early life

Born in Dieppe, France, on August 15, 1892, Broglie was the second son of a member of the French nobility. From the Broglie family, whose name is taken from a small town in Normandy, have come high-ranking soldiers, politicians, and diplomats since the 17th century. In choosing science as a profession, Louis de Broglie broke with family tradition, as had his brother Maurice (from whom, after his death, Louis inherited the title of duc). Maurice, who was also a physicist and made notable contributions to the experimental study of the atomic nucleus, kept a well-equipped laboratory in the family mansion in Paris. Louis occasionally joined his brother in his work, but it was the purely conceptual side of physics that attracted him. He described himself as "having much more the state of mind of a pure theoretician than that of an experimenter or engineer, loving especially the general and philosophical view. . . ." He was brought into one of his few contacts with the technical aspects of physics during World War I, when he saw army service in a radio station in the Eiffel Tower.

Broglie's interest in what he called the "mysteries" of atomic physics—namely, unsolved conceptual problems of the science—was aroused when he learned from his brother about the work of the German physicists Max Planck and Albert Einstein, but the decision to take up the profession of physicist was long in coming. He began at 18 to study theoretical physics at the Sorbonne, but he was also earning his degree in history (1909), thus moving along the family path toward a career in the diplomatic service. After a period of severe conflict, he declined the research project in French history that he had been assigned and chose for his doctoral thesis a subject in physics.

Theory of electron waves

In this thesis (1924) Broglie developed his revolutionary theory of electron waves, which he had published earlier in scientific journals. The notion that matter on the atomic scale might have the properties of a wave was rooted in a proposal Albert Einstein had made 20 years before. Einstein had suggested that light of short wavelengths might under some conditions be observed to behave as if it were composed of particles, an idea that was confirmed in 1923. The dual nature of light, however, was just beginning to gain scientific acceptance when Broglie extended the idea of such a duality to matter.

Broglie's proposal answered a question that had been raised by calculations of the motion of electrons within the atom. Experiments had indicated that the electron must move around a nucleus and that, for reasons then obscure, there are restrictions on its motion. Broglie's idea of an electron with the properties of a wave offered an explanation of the restricted motion. A wave confined within boundaries imposed by the nuclear charge would be restricted in shape and, thus, in motion, for any wave shape that did not fit within the atomic boundaries would interfere with itself and be cancelled out.

The first publications of Broglie's idea of "matter waves" had drawn little attention from other physicists, but a copy of his doctoral thesis chanced to reach Albert Einstein, whose response was enthusiastic. Einstein stressed the importance of Broglie's work both explicitly and by building further on it. In this way the Austrian physicist Erwin Schrödinger learned of the hypothetical waves, and on the basis of the idea, he constructed a mathematical system, wave mechanics, that has become an essential tool of physics. Not until 1927, however, did Clinton Davisson and Lester Germer in the United States and George Thomson in Scotland find the first experimental evidence of the electron's wave nature.

Later career and writings

After receiving his doctorate, Broglie remained at the Sorbonne, becoming in 1928 professor of theoretical physics at the newly founded Henri Poincaré Institute, where he taught until his retirement in 1962. He also acted, after 1945, as an adviser to the French Atomic Energy Commissariat.

For his discovery of the wave nature of the electron, Broglie was awarded the 1929 Nobel Prize for Physics. He also received, in 1952, the Kalinga Prize, awarded by the United Nations Economic and Social Council, in recognition of his writings on science for the general public. He was a foreign member of the British Royal Society, a member of the French Academy of Sciences, and, like several of his forebears, of the Académie Française.

Broglie's keen interest in the philosophical implications of modern physics found expression in addresses, articles, and books. The central question for him was whether the statistical considerations that are fundamental to atomic physics reflect an ignorance of underlying causes or whether they express all that there is to be known; the latter would be the case if, as some believe, the act of measuring affects, and is inseparable from, what is measured. For about three decades after his work of 1923, Broglie held the view that underlying causes could not be delineated in a final sense, but, with the passing of time, he returned to his earlier belief that the statistical theories hide "a completely determined and ascertainable reality behind variables which elude our experimental techniques."

BIBLIOGRAPHY. Some of the popular writings of Broglie have been translated into English: *Matter and Light: The New Physics* (1939); *The Revolution in Physics* (1953); *Physics and Microphysics* (1960); and *New Perspectives in Physics* (1962). An account of his work may be found in BARBARA LOVETT CLINE, *The Questioners: Physicists and the Quantum Theory* (1965).

(B.L.C.)

Bromeliales

The characters that separate the order Bromeliales, with its single family (Bromeliaceae), from other orders of monocotyledons (one of the two large classes of flowering plants) are the regular three-parted flowers of its members and the mealy endosperm (starchy nutrient tissue) of their seeds. The presence of water-absorbing scales on their leaves is an even more distinctive character and the one most generally used for quick identification of the group.

Within the above limits, the family (and therefore the order, since there is only the one family) has tremendous variation, as is shown by the contrast of its two best known members, the pineapple (*Ananas comosus*) and the Spanish moss (*Tillandsia usneoides*). The great majority of species are like those popular in cultivation, with a rosette of leaves that usually holds water and an inflorescence (flower cluster) that owes its colour and beauty more to its bracts (usually leaflike appendages associated with flowers) than to its flowers.

There are well over 2,000 known species in the family Bromeliaceae, and all but one are confined to the New World. Their habitat ranges from the wettest of rain forests to the driest of deserts and from just above tidemark to treeless mountain tops.

GENERAL FEATURES

Size range and diversity of structure. In size, bromeliads (*i.e.*, members of the family Bromeliaceae) range from the 30-foot (9-metre) *Puya raimondii* to the one-to two-inch high *Tillandsia bryoides* that is found roosting on it. The great majority of species, however, have flowering shoots between one and five feet high.

Although most bromeliads are "stemless" rosette plants, a good number have stems much longer than their leaves, and these stems vary from the massive pillars of *Puya raimondii* to the fine hanging threads of Spanish moss.

Most bromeliad leaves are spiny throughout or completely unarmed. The unarmed leaves are generally of two types, narrowly triangular with a dense coat of gray scales or strap-shaped with inconspicuous scales. The first type stores water in its tissues and is adapted to arid conditions. The leaves of the second form a watertight tank and adapt the plants bearing them to life in the rain forest.

Drawing by M. Moran based on A. Engle and K. Prantl, *Die naturlichen Pflanzenfamilien*

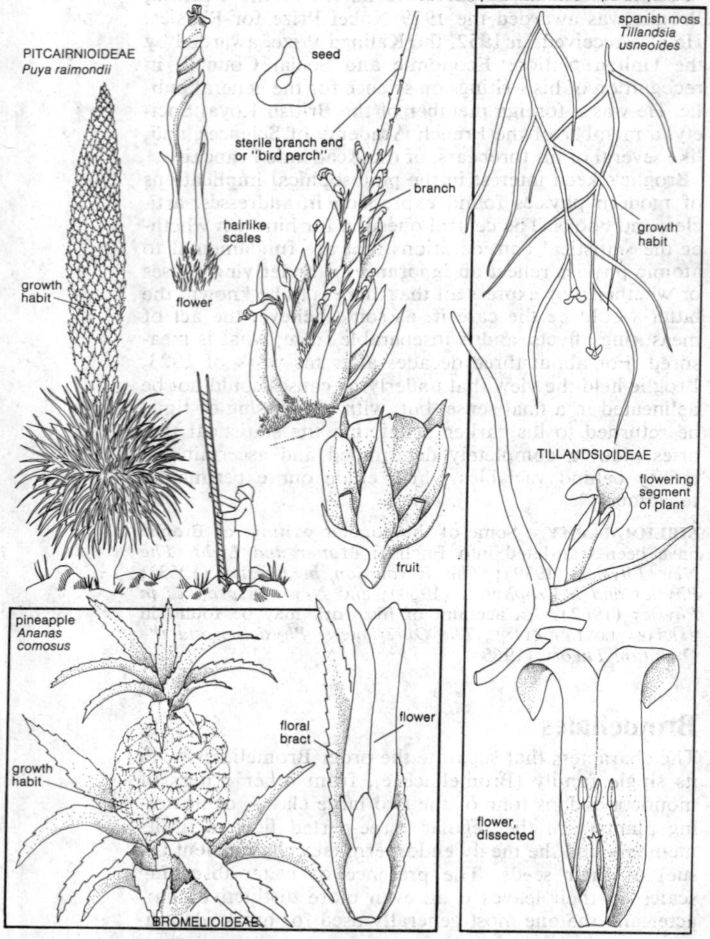

Plants and plant parts showing characteristics of the three subfamilies in the order Bromeliales.

Distribution and abundance. The range of the whole family very nearly coincides with that of Spanish moss, extending from coastal Virginia through southeastern United States, Mexico, and the West Indies to central Argentina and Chile. Spanish moss is a prominent part of the vegetation in the southeastern United States. Species of *Tillandsia* form great masses in the coastal desert of Peru, and *Deuterocohnia* covers large areas of the arid Andes of northwestern Argentina. Elsewhere, bromeliads tend to be relatively inconspicuous to a man on foot, though the story is much different when the rain forest is viewed from a helicopter or becomes dwarfed. In the rain forest, bromeliads present the greatest bulk of epiphytic vegetation, although orchids are much richer in number of species. (Epiphytes are plants that grow upon tree branches or on other aerial supports; they are not rooted in soil.)

Economic, medical, and other importance. The pineapple is by far the most important crop plant in the family Bromeliaceae and the only one that is regularly cultivated. As in the case of most other crop plants, the pineapple has thrived best far from its home, probably because it has escaped its natural enemies in this way. As far as can be determined, it evolved in the interior of South America but is best cultivated in Hawaii. At the time Columbus landed, the pineapple had already been spread by the Indians, but for use as a fibre, not as a fruit. In arid northeastern Brazil, the caroa (*Neoglaziovia*) is cropped regularly from wild growth and used as fibre in coarse bagging. Pineapple cultivation

Spanish moss has a small but constant cropping for use as cushion filling, and the Indians have used species of *Bromelia* and *Aechmea* for fibre and the leaf-spines of *Puya* for fish hooks.

Medicinally, the bromeliads have some slight drug values, but they also harbour malaria carriers in their water-tight rosettes.

NATURAL HISTORY

Life cycle. Nearly all types of pollen dispersal are represented in the family Bromeliaceae. The majority of species are insect pollinated, but there is a large amount of pollination by hummingbirds, particularly of the red-flowered species. Probably unique are the sterile branch-ends of the *Puya raimondii* group that enable pollination by perching birds. As might be suspected, some bad-smelling night-blooming species prove to be bat-pollinated. Finally, *Fosterella* is thought to be wind-pollinated, judging by the yellow cloud of pollen the flowers emit when jarred.

There are no elaborate mechanisms effecting cross-pollination, such as are found in the orchids, but there is self-sterility, differential maturity of stamens and pistil (male and female reproductive structures), and the isolation of the sexes of functionally unisexual flowers on separate plants, as in *Hechtia*. On the other hand, the flowers of some species of *Guzmania* do not open and are doubtless cleistogamous (*i.e.*, they are self-fertile and set seed without the necessity of opening to permit cross-fertilization).

Seed dispersal is by wind in the case of species with winged or plumose seeds, although some of the river-bank and deep rain forest species are thought to be waterborne. *Navia*, with no seed appendages and an unappetizing dry capsular fruit, is also thought to depend on water. Its highly localized species would indicate that its means of dispersal is extremely poor. Species with unappendaged seeds but edible baccate (berry-like, pulpy throughout) fruits depend chiefly on birds for distribution, but some dispersal by bats is also indicated. Seed dispersal

Vegetative reproduction is tremendously important in bromeliads, many species increasing mostly by this method and many more making a balanced combination of vegetative and sexual means. The rosette-forming species send out basal offsets, often in regular patterns, such as those that zig-zag up tree trunks with a rosette at every angle. The long-stemmed species elongate, branch, and break apart, with the air-borne Spanish moss the extreme example. There are a number of species, including *Tillandsia latifolia* of the Peruvian coastal desert, that are viviparous, producing small plants in place of flowers.

Establishment usually is most critical in the early seedling stage. Once past this, the chances of survival are better, although growth may be very slow. Viviparous plants bypass this stage, but thereby miss the benefits of cross-pollination.

Ecology. Bromeliads have an external ecology like all other plants, but, in addition, the tank-forming species have an almost unique internal ecology as well. In their external relation to the environment, they show a greater range of adaptation than most flowering plants. Even the most primitive genera show a great range of adaptation. *Fosterella* is a forest type with small requirements of light, but large requirements of water and temperature. *Puya*, growing on bare Andean mountain summits, receives a maximum of light, but endures a summer-to-winter extreme in temperature cycle every twenty-four hours. Many species of *Puya* have adapted by covering their flowers with large bracts and a dense mat of wool formed by finely divided scales. *Encholirium* and *Dyckia* in Brazil and *Deuterocohnia* and *Abromeitiella* in Argentina usually grow on bare rock in the full sun. They have adapted by developing thick tough leaves with well-protected stomata (microscopic openings in leaf surfaces) that ensure a minimum moisture loss. In its different species, the genus *Pitcairnia* runs the full range of habitats from rain forest to extreme aridity, which latter environment has given rise, in a number of cases, to species with deciduous leaves. *Pitcairnia* and *Brocchinia* show the beginnings of adaptation to epiphytism. It is only a slight beginning, however, because, in their very wet rain forest, there is not such a great difference between living conditions on the ground and in the crotch of a tree trunk.

Adaptations to the environment

The subfamily Tillandsioideae shows the greatest diversity of all in adaptation to different environments. A large part of the genus *Tillandsia* has adapted to extreme aridity by the development of highly efficient leaf scales that absorb water and transmit it to the interior of the leaf blade. This characteristic is usually correlated with a long stem, as in Spanish moss. The remainder of the genus *Tillandsia* and practically all species of the other genera of Tillandsioideae have adapted in the opposite direction, with the development of tank rosettes and scales that are concentrated more on the leaf sheaths. A few species of *Tillandsia* have combined the arid type of leaf scale with a bulbous rosette.

The subfamily Bromelioideae has also adapted in both directions, but not so extremely toward aridity. There, as in the genus *Bromelia*, the development has been to a heavy thickened leaf like that of the primitive members of the subfamily Pitcairnioideae. The majority of genera have adapted to humidity by producing a tank that varies from a broad basin to a narrow tube.

With the development of the tank rosette, bromeliads have attained a second ecological relationship practically unknown in other plants. As epiphytes, they supplement their scanty food supply from the excreta and remains of a host of small plants and animals, many of which live or breed only in bromeliad tanks. Thus, they have coevolved with their aquatic guests to a very close ecological relationship.

The plant colonies in bromeliad tanks range all the way from unicellular algae to the insectivorous bladderworts (*Utricularia*), which are among the most highly developed of flowering plants. With the exception of certain mosses, no plant species are known to be limited to the tank habitat.

The species of animals in bromeliad tanks are much more numerous than those of plants and form a much more important relationship with the bromeliads. These animals range from unicellular protozoa to vertebrates, and their relationship goes from complete life history to breeding to occasional seeking of shelter. The spread of totally tank-adapted species from one bromeliad to another is not always easy to explain. Protozoa are easily spread by wind and rain, especially in the encysted state, but the dispersal of the ostracod crustacean, *Elpidium*, is more difficult to account for. This tiny animal, which measures about a tenth of an inch long and looks like a shrimp enclosed in a clam shell, has no means of locomotion out of water, yet manages to inhabit the great majority of tanks in southern Brazil. Crabs, such as *Sesarma miersii*, which are found in salt to brackish water from the West Indies to Uruguay, not unsurprisingly, turn up in bromeliads growing a few feet above high tide mark. *Metopaulias depressus*, a crab species of Jamaica, however, is found in bromeliads above the 2,500-foot (800-metre) elevation.

As elsewhere, insects outnumber all other classes of animals in the tanks in number of species and individuals. Best represented is the order Diptera (flies), especially mosquitoes, but a good number of other insect orders are commonly found. Several species of Odonata (dragonflies and damselflies) breed there, with their larvae preying on the mosquito larvae. All the strictly aquatic larvae are adapted to living in water that is more than half mud, but the mosquito larvae of bromeliads, unlike their terrestrial relatives, do not have to surface for air. They simply pick up oxygen given off by the leaf sheaths. The order Hymenoptera (bees, wasps, and ants) is represented chiefly by ants, but only after the tank, or at least its outer leaves, is drained. Whether the ants contribute to the bromeliad's growth is being investigated, but it does not appear to be as advantageous to the plant as the presence of aquatic species. The ants also appear to prevent occupation of the rosettes by mosquitoes.

Frogs and salamanders are the only vertebrates using the tank itself, although snakes are sometimes found sheltering in the rosettes. The amphibians not only breed there, but the mostly nocturnal adults shelter there during the daylight hours. Probably the greatest adaptation is reached by a frog in semi-arid northeastern Brazil that inhabits the long tubes of certain species of *Billbergia*. It not only holes up there during the day but very effectively plugs the hole with its hard-topped head, thereby keeping the tube more humid, to its own advantage and to that of the plant.

Snakes in rosettes

FORM AND FUNCTION

Vegetative characteristics. Roots are normal in form and function in the primitive subfamily Pitcairnioideae; that is, they absorb food and moisture through the root hairs and pass it up through the larger roots to the rest of the plant. In the species that grow on rock, however, the larger roots take on the function of adhesion. The roots are basal in most Pitcairnioideae, but in species of *Puya* with prostrate stems they may sprout anywhere, each piercing several leaf sheaths before reaching the ground. In several species of *Navia*, the roots emerge all along the erect stem, but turn down and stay within the cortex (outer plant sheath) until reaching the ground.

In the subfamilies Tillandsioideae and Bromelioideae, the roots have lost most of their absorptive function and become mere holdfasts, the leaves taking over as absorbing organs. Finally, in several species of *Tillandsia*, such as the Spanish moss, the roots have lost even the function of adhesion and have disappeared. In some species of *Bromelia*, the roots have no contact with the ground, but end in the leaf-axils (upper angles between leaf and stem), where a mat of coarse scales gives them considerable moisture.

Stems of bromeliads are solid and have scattered vascular bundles as in a corn stalk. In long-stem types as diverse as the pineapple and the Spanish moss, the stem can be fragmented, each part capable of living and forming a new plant. The "stemless," or rosette, types have a very short, broadly conical stem that usually gives rise to offshoots ranging from short ascending shoots to long, slender, and scaly rhizomes (horizontal, creeping stems, rootlike in appearance).

Leaf arrangement and structure

Leaves of bromeliads are spirally arranged and usually occur in many ranks, but in a number of tillandsias (genus *Tillandsia*) and a few species of the subfamily Bromelioideae they are two-ranked. Nearly always the sheath and leaf blade are distinct. In the primitive subfamily Pitcairnioideae and in the long-stemmed species of *Tillandsia* the sheaths are tightly overlapping and lack scales on the covered parts. The tank types have sheaths that make watertight contact along their edges, but they have considerable open space elsewhere, and they have a greater concentration of scales than do the blades. The leaf blades also vary in shape and function. The greatest variation in form occurs in the genus *Pitcairnia*, with every gradation from the broad petiolate (stalked) blades of species in the deep jungle to the grasslike deciduous ones on sun-drenched rocks. Their function, however, is relatively simple, the position and number of stomata being adjusted to the best use of sunlight and moisture. In the genus *Tillandsia* there is much less variation in form, but more in function, through the development of scales that imbibe salts as well as water, and thus take over the functions of roots.

Flower and fruit characteristics. The scape, or stalk, of the inflorescence is usually well-developed and is located at the terminal end of the stem. Functionally, it is a specialized stem that feeds the inflorescence. Like the stem, it contains no living cells at maturity except in the genus *Deuterocohnia*. In that group, just below the cortex, there is a sheath of live tissue, like the cambium (a zone of cell division contributing to growth in stem thickness) of dicotyledons, but which has no ability to form rings of wood and bark. Instead, it keeps the axis of the inflorescence active and enables it to put forth new branches year after year as old ones wither and fall. In most cases the scape is covered with brightly coloured bracts that quickly distinguish it from the stem, and, in many species of the subfamily Bromelioideae, these provide the most beautiful part of the plant.

The inflorescence varies in form from a much branched cluster to a single flower. Nearly always the bracts are more showy than the flowers. The flowers consist of three sepals, three petals, six stamens in two series, and a pistil of three carpels (segments of the female reproductive unit). The ovary runs all the way from wholly superior (*i.e.*, the sepals, petals, and stamens attach at the base of the ovary) to wholly inferior (*i.e.*, the other flower parts appear to attach at the upper end of the ovary their fused basal parts enclosing it) in the genus *Pitcairnia* alone, but its position usually is significant in determining the limits of the genera. The ovules are appendaged in most cases, but in all members of the subfamily Bromelioideae the appendage is lost in the mature seed, and in the subfamily Pitcairnioideae it develops into a wing or tail, and in the subfamily Tillandsioideae into a plume. The fruit can be a regularly opening capsule or a berry, or have an intermediate form that is dry like a capsule and has winged seeds but only ruptures irregularly with age.

EVOLUTION

Fossil record. Six species of fossil plants have been ascribed to the family Bromeliaceae. The only one from the New World is almost certainly a cycad. The remaining five are all European and thus are not very likely to be bromeliads, as judged on a geographical basis, and they show no really distinctive bromeliad character in any case. Thus fossil evidence is no help in determining the evolution of the group.

Phylogeny. Without the support of any good fossil evidence, the phylogeny (evolutionary history) of the family Bromeliaceae must be inferred from morphology (form and structure) with some help from geographical distribution. It is generally agreed that primitive flowers have numerous simple free parts spirally arranged and that evolution has taken place by the reduction, specialization, and merging of these parts and their change to a whorled or opposite position of like parts. On such a basis, bromeliads, with whorled reduced flower parts, are not primitive, but neither are they very far advanced. Whether their farinose (mealy) endosperm places them above or below the family Liliaceae is purely speculation, but the separation must have been far back in the evolution of the monocotyledons.

Criteria used to determine evolutionary status in flowers

Geographical evidence is confusing when applied to the evolution of the whole family, but is clearer when correlated with its internal development. If the Bromeliaceae family is as primitive as its floral morphology would indicate, why has it not spread further in the Old World, like some of its more specialized associates, such as the families Xyridaceae (order Commelinales), Eriocaulaceae (Eriocaulales), and Commelinaceae (Commelinales)? Like the families Rapateaceae and Mayacaceae (both in the order Commelinales), it has a single species native to Africa. This spanning of the South Atlantic may be viewed as fortification of the hypothesis of continental drift, but it is doubtful if the families are old enough to have been present when the continents were supposedly joined.

It is generally agreed that within the family Bromeliaceae, evolution has developed three well-marked subfamilies, with the Pitcairnioideae the most primitive, and the Tillandsioideae and Bromelioideae derived separately from their ancestral stock, which is thought to have been not greatly different from the living genera *Fosterella*, *Puya*, and *Pitcairnia*. In *Brocchinia paniculata* the solid seed wing of the Pitcairnioideae shows a tendency to split, like the plumose seed of the Tillandsioideae; but the advanced characteristics of *Brocchinia* indicate that this must be a case of parallel evolution and not of direct descent.

Pitcairnia shows a development in the direction of the Bromelioideae, with some Amazonian species having nearly or quite inferior ovaries. They retain their appendage, however, when the ovule matures into a seed.

Arguments as to which of the two advanced subfamilies is closest to the Pitcairnioideae depend upon which characteristics are emphasized. Primitive species of *Tillandsia* have superior ovaries, appendaged seeds, and dehiscent (splitting open along definite lines) fruits, like primitive species of Pitcairnioideae. On the other hand, the subfamily Bromelioideae has spiny leaves and the same type of epidermal (surface) scales as the subfamily Pitcairnioideae.

Centres of distribution

Geographic evidence shows a centring of the primitive genera of the Pitcairnioideae and Tillandsioideae subfamilies in the northern Andes. It is almost impossible to say just which genera of the Bromelioideae are primitive, but the subfamily as a whole centres on eastern Brazil. Within genera, expansion patterns are so clear that evolution must have been very recent or is still rapidly continuing, as in *Dyckia*, in which species are very fluid and difficult to define.

CLASSIFICATION

Distinguishing taxonomic features. In the order of their importance, the distinguishing characteristics of the family Bromeliaceae are the definite number of flower parts, the form of the flower parts, the farinose character of the endosperm, and the highly evolved epidermal scales. The exact number of flower parts distinguishes them from the primitive monocotyledons. The uniformity of these parts and their lack of specialization separate them from both the higher monocots such as the orchids and from most of their immediate relatives as well. Their farinose endosperm separates them from the family Liliaceae (lilies) and related families, and finally their absorptive leaf scales are practically unique.

Annotated classification. The Bromeliaceae were very early recognized as a distinct family, and recent studies have only led to their further isolation, going from the order Farinosae in earlier classification systems to an order of their own in modern arrangements. The division into three subfamilies has been almost unanimously accepted since its first appearance in a monograph in 1896. In 1929 one authority proposed *Navia* as a fourth and most primitive group because of its lack of a seed appendage, but later studies have shown that the seed appendage is actually present in early stages and is later lost; thus, the genus is now considered to be advanced rather than primitive.

ORDER BROMELIALES

Largely herbaceous perennials, rarely shrubby, the more advanced floral types largely epiphytic. Roots usually present, but their absorptive function often taken over by the leaves. Leaves spirally arranged, usually rosulate, and with distinct sheaths and blades, bearing peltate (shieldlike) scales that serve to absorb and transmit moisture. Inflorescence simple or compound, usually bearing brightly coloured conspicuous bracts. Flowers perfect (both sexes present) or sometimes functionally unisexual and dimorphic (male and female flowers exhibit different forms), radially symmetric or nearly so. Perianth (sepals and petals) of 2 unlike series, the sepals and petals free or connate (fused). Stamens 6 in 2 series; filaments free or variously joined. Ovary superior to inferior, 3-celled; placentae axile (ovule attachment to a central stalk in ovary). Fruit capsular or baccate. Seeds winged, plumose, or naked. Embryo small, located at the base of the copious, mealy endosperm. About 2,000 species, all but 1 confined to the New World.

Family Bromeliaceae

The only family in the order, it has the characters of the order.

Subfamily Pitcairnioideae (including Navioideae)

Usually terrestrial, herbaceous or shrubby. Leaves mostly spinose-serrate (*i.e.,* the serrations or marginal teeth end in spines). Ovary superior to (rarely) inferior. Fruit usually capsular. Seeds with entire appendages (lost in *Navia*).

Subfamily Tillandsioideae

Usually epiphytic, herbaceous. Leaves always unarmed; cells of the leaf scales symmetrical, arranged in groups of 4. Ovary usually superior. Fruit capsular. Seeds with plumose appendages.

Subfamily Bromelioideae

Largely epiphytic herbs. Leaves usually spinose-serrate. Ovary inferior. Fruit baccate. Seeds unappendaged.

Critical appraisal. It is doubtful if further research will do more than solidify subfamily lines, but there are large opportunities to clarify generic and subgeneric relationships. Studies of pollen in the subfamily Bromelioideae, for example, although necessarily limited to broad sampling, have already disclosed both correlations and contradictions. Complete studies of the substomal openings (the tissue structure in the region of the stomata, tiny openings in the leaves) in certain genera show uniformity in some and variation along species limits in others.

BIBLIOGRAPHY. For articles emphasizing the horticultural aspects of bromeliads, see *The Bromeliad Society Bulletin*, vol. 1–20 (1951–70), continued as *Journal of the Bromeliad Society*, vol. 21– (1971–); J.L. COLLINS, *The Pineapple* (1960), a complete detailed account; C. MEZ, "Bromeliaceae," in A. ENGLER and K. PRANTL (eds.), *Das Pflanzenreich IV*, 32: 1–667 (1934–35), in Latin, the latest complete taxonomic monograph; L.B. SMITH, "Bromeliad Malaria," *Smithsonian Report for 1952*, pp. 385–398 (1953), a brief report with essential bibliography.

(L.B.Sm.)

Brontë Family

The Brontë sisters survive as living figures in the popular imagination because their lonely and tragic lives were imbued with the same emotional intensity as the heroes and heroines of their novels. Charlotte Brontë, whose *Jane Eyre* and other novels achieved the most immediate influence, presented with frankness and ardour women in conflict with their natural desires and their social condition. Emily Brontë, the best poet of the three, wrote the fierce and tragic *Wuthering Heights*, eventually acclaimed both as the first social revolutionary novel and the predecessor of the novel of flux and sensation. And Anne Brontë, with none of her sisters' fire, has found champions to defend the quiet strength and the integrity and realism of *Agnes Grey*.

LIVES

Their father was Patrick Brontë, an Irishman from County Down, who was able to attend Cambridge despite his humble birth through his own savings and help of the Wesleyan Methodists. Allusions to Methodism are infrequent but significant in the sisters' writings, and their passion has been interpreted as a Methodist passion transferred to secular objects. Patrick Brontë took his degree in 1806. While a curate at Hartshead, Yorkshire, he met and married Maria Branwell in 1812, and there his elder daughters Maria (1813–25) and Elizabeth (1814–25) were born. He then served at Thornton, Yorkshire, where Charlotte was born on April 21, 1816; Patrick Branwell on June 26, 1817; Emily Jane on July 30, 1818; and Anne on January 17, 1820. Three months after

The Brontë sisters (left to right) Anne, Emily, and Charlotte, oil painting by P.B. Brontë (their brother) *c.* 1835. In the National Portrait Gallery, London.
By courtesy of the National Portrait Gallery, London

Anne's birth, the father became rector of Haworth, near Bradford, Yorkshire, where he remained for the rest of his life. There Mrs. Brontë died of cancer on September 15, 1821.

Early childhoods

After Mrs. Brontë's death, her sister Elizabeth Branwell joined the household at Haworth. Branwell was her favourite, but she instructed the girls, especially in needlework, and did her duty by them. She never became close to them, however, and her austere Methodism oppressed them, especially Anne. Branwell was educated by his father, a man of marked intelligence (he published some books of poetry and miscellaneous prose and stimulated his children's intellectual interests), fond of his family but eccentric and unsocial in his habits, though a conscientious parson. Thus the children were left very much to themselves. They read whatever they could lay their hands on, including newspapers, and rambled on the moors. They were happy and very precocious, but this sequestered upbringing left the girls with a crippling shyness and deprived Branwell of the companionship of his peers, which might have proved steadying.

In 1824 the father sent Maria and Elizabeth to school at Wakefield but soon transferred them to the recently opened Clergy Daughters' School at Cowan Bridge, near Kirkby Lonsdale, Lancashire, where Charlotte and then Emily joined them. The fees were low, the food unattractive, and the discipline harsh. When Charlotte recorded her memories of this school in the Lowood of *Jane Eyre*, she was unaware of exaggerating. Her description was challenged, however, and the subject has been much debated. It is agreed that, during the months the Brontë sisters were there, the school was badly run and the girls sickly. What exaggeration existed was derived from the keen sensibilities of a highly intelligent and passionate child, who had seen her two elder sisters sicken and taken home to die, an experience that left deep traces on both Charlotte and Branwell.

Creation of fantasies

Charlotte and Emily returned home in June 1825, and for over five years the children learned and played there. There they began those sustained imaginative games that led to an enormous output of midget books written in minute script, which have attracted much attention. The four children created the imaginary Kingdom of Angria and jointly elaborated its wars, its politics, and its aristocracy and their feuds and loves. At some time, probably in 1831 when Charlotte was sent to Miss Wooler's school at Roe Head, near Huddersfield, Emily and Anne seceded and founded their own Kingdom of Gondal, leaving Charlotte and Branwell to conduct the affairs of Angria. These complex romantic sagas were kept going by the sisters well into their 20s. Negligible as literature, they were the training ground of the Brontë genius. Themes and situations in their published works were first adumbrated there and worked on at all stages from adolescence to maturity. Many Angrian chronicles are extant, but all the Gondal prose has been destroyed. It is plain, however, from the manuscripts that many of Emily's poems are dramatic utterances of Gondal characters, and from them it has proved possible to draw a dubious outline of the lost corpus. The Angrian and Gondal daydreams have a deep psychological interest. Charlotte early recognized the compensatory nature of her dream and was troubled by guilt at the discrepancy between it and the sober, restricted life before her. There is no sign that Emily felt this division. She filled Gondal with the growing weight of her own thoughts and emotions until the fantastic husk fell off and Gondal was revealed as Yorkshire. Anne wrote Gondal verse and prose, but her novels are strictly and responsibly realistic, bearing no trace of the dream, which may have become, for her, chiefly a medium of communication with Emily. Branwell's tragedy seems to have been that he ceased to be able to distinguish between obsessive daydream and reality.

At Roe Head, where she stayed a year, Charlotte made some lasting friendships; her correspondence with one of her friends, Ellen Nussey, which continued till her death, has provided much of our knowledge of her. In 1832 she came home to teach her sisters, and for three years they lived, studied, and wrote together at Haworth. The whole family delighted in drawing, and all except Charlotte were musical. The moors, with their changes of weather and season, were their exhilarating playground. In all their books the Brontës show themselves to be country women. In 1835 Charlotte returned to Roe Head as a teacher. She wished to improve her family's position, and this was the only outlet that was offered to her unsatisfied energies. Branwell, moreover, was to start on his career as an artist, and it became necessary to supplement the family resources. Emily accompanied Charlotte as a pupil but was too homesick to remain, and her place was taken by Anne. The work, with its inevitable restrictions, was uncongenial to Charlotte. She fell into ill health and melancholia and took fright at the state of health of the always delicate Anne, who left at the end of 1837. In the summer of 1838 Charlotte terminated her engagement. Emily, who had spent six exhausting months as teacher in Miss Patchett's school at Law Hill near Halifax, had also resigned her post, and the sisters were at home again.

In 1839 Charlotte declined a proposal from the Rev. Henry Nussey, her friend's brother, and some months later one from another young clergyman. She and Anne also made brief and unsuccessful experiments as governesses in 1839. The hardships and anomalies of the position are reflected in their novels and impressed public opinion, but it is doubtful if Charlotte, touchy and inhibited by her duties from imaginative creation, could ever have been contented in such a post. Anne endured better and presently established herself with the Robinsons at Thorpe Green, near Boroughbridge, Yorkshire, where she stayed for four years (1841–45). At the same time Charlotte's ambition to make the practical best of her talents and the need to pay Branwell's debts urged her to spend some months as governess with the Whites at Upperwood House, Rawdon. Branwell's talents for writing and painting, his good classical scholarship, and his social charm had engendered high hopes for him. He had sent specimens of his writing to Wordsworth but had received no encouragement; Charlotte, at about the same time (January 1837), had had a similar experience with Robert Southey. At the end of 1837 Branwell had set up as a portrait painter in Bradford and had worked steadily for a year; but he was fundamentally unstable, weak willed, and intemperate, and the venture collapsed. After six months as a tutor in Broughton-in-Furness, he was working as clerk in charge at Sowerby Bridge on the Leeds and Manchester Railway (September 1840) and from there was transferred to Luddenden Foot but was dismissed in January 1842 for culpable negligence.

Meanwhile his sisters had planned to open a school together, which their aunt had agreed to finance, and in February 1842 Charlotte and Emily went to Brussels as pupils to improve their qualifications in French and acquire some German. Emily also studied and later taught the piano. The talent displayed by both brought them to the notice of Constantin Héger, a fine teacher and a man of unusual perception. Charlotte was on the whole happy, though as a staunch Protestant she despised her Catholic surroundings. Emily, while working with stubborn resolution, pined for the liberty of home. The death of Miss Branwell in October summoned them to Haworth. She had bequeathed each of her nieces a sum that may have amounted to £300 (specification is lacking), but they put their money aside for a greater need. Emily remained at Haworth to keep house while Branwell joined Anne as tutor at Thorpe Green and Charlotte returned to Brussels as pupil-teacher. She stayed there during 1843 but was lonely and depressed. Her friends had left Brussels, and Madame Héger appears to have become jealous of her. The nature of Charlotte's attachment to Héger and the degree to which she understood herself have been much discussed. His was the most interesting mind she had yet met, and he had perceived and evoked her latent talents. His strong and eccentric personality appealed both to her sense of humour and to her affections. She offered him an innocent but ardent devotion, but he tried to repress her emotions. The letters she wrote to him after her return may well be called love letters. When, however, he suggested that they were open to misapprehension, she stopped writing and applied herself, in silence, to disciplining her feelings. Shirley's indignation at Moore's assumption that she loves him (in Charlotte's novel *Shirley*) may well reflect part of the author's reaction. However they are interpreted, her experiences at Brussels were crucial for her development. She received a strict literary training, became aware of the resources of her own nature, and gathered material that served her, in various shapes, for all her novels.

Education in Brussels

In 1844 Charlotte attempted to start a school she had long envisaged in the parsonage itself, as her father's failing sight precluded his being left alone. Prospectuses were issued, but no pupils were attracted to distant Haworth. In 1845 Anne left the Robinsons, and soon afterward Branwell was dismissed, charged with making love to his employer's wife. The sisters believed the fault lay with Mrs. Robinson. Charlotte transmitted this view to Elizabeth Gaskell, the novelist, who embodied it in the first edition of her *Life of Charlotte Brontë* (1857) but was forced by Mrs. Robinson's representatives to withdraw and apologize for the passages in question. Whatever happened, it finished Branwell. He spent the last three years of his life at Haworth, incurring debts, drinking, taking opium, alternately blaspheming and repenting until he died of his excesses—a profound grief to his father and sisters, an obstacle to his sisters' hopes, and a great and tragic stimulus to their genius.

First publications

In the autumn of 1845 Charlotte came across some poems by Emily, and this led to the publication in 1846 of a joint volume of *Poems by Currer, Ellis and Acton Bell;* the pseudonyms were assumed to preserve secrecy and avoid the special treatment they believed reviewers accorded to women. The book was issued at their own expense. It received few reviews and only two copies were sold. Nevertheless, a way had opened to them, and they were already trying to place the three novels they had written. By midsummer of 1847 Emily's *Wuthering Heights* and Anne's *Agnes Grey* had been accepted for publication by T.C. Newby, but Charlotte had failed to place *The Professor*. She had, however, nearly finished *Jane Eyre,* begun in August 1846 in Manchester where she was staying with her father, who had gone there for an eye operation. When Smith, Elder and Company, declining *The Professor*, declared themselves willing to consider a three-volume novel with more action and excitement in it, she completed and submitted it at once. It was accepted, published less than eight weeks later (on Oct. 16, 1847), and had an immediate success. In December Newby brought out *Wuthering Heights* and *Agnes Grey,* and in June 1848 Anne's *Tenant of Wildfell Hall*, which sold well. Reviewers had already suggested that *Wuthering Heights* was an earlier work by Currer Bell, Charlotte's pseudonym. Now Newby offered the American rights of *The Tenant* as by the author of the successful *Jane Eyre*, and in July Charlotte and Anne were forced to go to London to acknowledge their identities to their publisher.

The year that followed was a tragic one. On September 24 Branwell died. Emily caught cold at his funeral, came down with acute tuberculosis, refused all medical help, and died on December 19. Immediately afterward Anne, Emily's closest friend, sickened of the same disease; Charlotte put aside *Shirley*, on which she was working, to nurse her. Anne submitted dutifully to treatment but died on May 28, 1849, at Scarborough. Charlotte completed *Shirley* in the empty parsonage, and it appeared in October. In 1850 Smith, Elder and Company republished *Wuthering Heights* and *Agnes Grey* with Charlotte's "Biographical Notice" of her sisters. In the following years Charlotte went three times to London as the guest of her publisher, George Smith, and his mother, met Thackeray and other literary men and women, and sat for her portrait by George Richmond. She went twice to the Lake Country, where she stayed in 1851 with Harriet Martineau, the writer, went to Scotland, and visited Mrs. Gaskell in Manchester and entertained her at Haworth. *Villette* came out in January 1853. Meanwhile, in 1851, she had declined a third offer of marriage, this time from James Taylor, a member of Smith, Elder and Company. Her father's curate, Arthur Bell Nicholls (1817–1906), an Irishman, was her fourth suitor. It took some months to win her father's consent, but they were married on June 29, 1854, in Haworth church. They spent their honeymoon in Ireland and then returned to Haworth, where her husband had pledged himself to continue as curate to her father. He did not share his wife's intellectual life, but she was happy to be loved for herself and to take up her duties as his wife. She began another book, *Emma*, of which some pages remain. Her pregnancy, however, was accompanied by exhausting sickness, and she died on March 31, 1855. Nicholls stayed in Haworth until Patrick Brontë's death in 1861, when he went back to Ireland.

ASSESSMENT

The absorbing personal history of the Brontë family has stimulated many writers. Haworth is a place of pilgrimage and Haworth parsonage a Brontë museum. Plays and novels have been written about them. Each of the family has had partisans and, in the attempt to define their distinct natures, the close bonds of temperament, conviction, imagination, and pooled experience have sometimes been undervalued. Emily, the least known and praised in her lifetime, has proved the most interesting for modern biographers and critics. There has been a corresponding tendency to withhold justice from Charlotte as a writer and a woman. Yet without Charlotte's ambition we should not have had Emily's writings. Her editing of them, now under censure, was aimed at removing obstacles between the contemporary reading public and work that she deeply admired. In what she wrote of her sisters, she had it in mind to defend their "dear names" against the charges of coarseness and brutality that had been launched at their novels.

Emily's poems, often unfinished and very unequal, show the influence of Scott and the Border ballads but at their rare best transmit the flavour of a unique and powerful personality. She had a strong lyrical note, a beautifully spontaneous and flexible metre, and, at her best, a powerful and precise—though limited—diction. Her work on *Wuthering Heights* cannot be dated, and she may well have spent a long time on this intense, solidly imagined novel. It is distinguished from other novels of the period by its dramatic and poetic presentation, its abstention from all comment by the author, and its unusual structure. It recounts in the retrospective narrative of an onlooker, which in turn includes shorter narratives, the impact of the waif Heathcliff on the two families of Earnshaw and Linton in a remote Yorkshire district at the end of the 18th century. Embittered by abuse and by the marriage of Cathy Earnshaw—who shares his stormy nature and whom he loves—to the gentle and prosperous Edgar Linton, Heathcliff plans a revenge on both families, extending into the second generation. Cathy's death in childbirth fails to set him free from his love–hate relationship with her, and the obsessive haunting persists until his death; the marriage of the surviving heirs of Earnshaw and Linton restores peace.

Wuthering Heights

The way the tale begins at the 11th hour may derive from French classical tragedies that Emily read in Brussels. The method of direct narrative, heard in oral storytellers, is used with deliberate effect to recount an action that culminates through two generations, for which the model may have been Shakespeare's later romantic plays. There is no confusion, though some awkwardness. Everything is thoroughly worked out. Sharing her sisters' dry humour and Charlotte's violent imagination, she diverges from them in making no use of the events of her own life and showing no preoccupation with a spinster's state or a governess's position. Working, like them, within a confined scene and with a small group of characters, she constructs an action, based on profound and primitive energies of love and hate, which proceeds logically and economically, making no use of such coincidences as Charlotte relies on, requiring no rich romantic similes or rhetorical patterns, and confining the superb dialogue to what is immediately relevant to the subject. The sombre power of the book and the elements of brutality in the characters affronted some 19th-century opinion. Its supposed masculine quality was adduced to support the claim, based on the memories of Branwell's friends long after his death, that he was author or part author of it. While it is not possible to clear up all the minor puzzles, neither the external nor the internal evidence offered is substantial enough to weigh against Charlotte's plain statement that Emily was the author or a reference to Branwell's extant writings. Modern interest in myth and symbol has stimulated fresh approaches. Lord David Cecil (*Early Victorian Novelists*, chapter 5, 1934) regards Emily's characters as types of the cosmic forces of storm and calm, which replace the principles of good and evil; both are good in their proper relations, but tragedy results from their mismating. A widely different approach has been made by David Wilson ("Emily Brontë: First of the Moderns," *Modern Quarterly Miscellany*, number 1, 1947), who interprets the story of Heathcliff and Catherine Earnshaw as a metaphor of the social struggle going on in the turbulent Pennine district under Emily's eyes—a struggle in which she saw evil and degradation on both sides. This illuminating suggestion has been carried further by other writers who insist on Emily's conscious social passion. These studies give a new dimension to the book but should not obscure the depth of her imaginative response to the wild and remote nor the fact that what matters most to her is the freedom and energy, in love and hate, of the individual human spirit. *Wuthering Heights* masters the reader by its passion and fullness of meaning; its rapid, concrete presentation; its resonant, concise dialogue; and the courage, unparalleled in the contemporary novel, with which it accepts the tragic logic of its assumptions. It is not a flawless masterpiece, but it is unexhausted.

Critical interpretations

Anne is commonly described as gentle and pious. In chaste and shapely verse she examines her thoughts and feelings in the light of moral and religious truth. Her novel *Agnes Grey*, probably begun at Thorpe Green, records with limpidity and some humour the life of a governess. George Moore called it "simple and beautiful as a muslin dress." *The Tenant of Wildfell Hall* presents an unsoftened picture of a young man's debauchery and degradation and sets against it her Arminian belief, opposed to Calvinist predestination, that no soul shall be ultimately lost. Her outspokenness raised some scandal, and Charlotte deplored the subject as morbid and out of keeping with her sister's nature, but the vigorous writing indicates that Anne found in it not only a moral obligation but also an opportunity of artistic development.

Charlotte's first novel, *The Professor* (published posthumously, 1857), shows her extreme reaction from the Angrian indulgences of her girlhood. Sober in colouring and discreet in action, it is nevertheless satirically lively and, like all her fiction, prickles with personality. Told in the first person by an English tutor in Brussels, it is based on Charlotte's experiences there, with a reversal of sexes and roles. The necessity of her genius, reinforced by reading her sister's *Wuthering Heights*, modified this restrictive self-discipline; and, though there is plenty of satire and dry, direct phrasing in *Jane Eyre*, what carried it to success was the fiery conviction with which it presented a thinking, feeling woman, craving for love but able to renounce it at the call of impassioned self-respect and moral conviction. Jane Eyre, an orphan and governess to the ward of Mr. Rochester, falls in love with her Byronic and enigmatic employer. Her love is reciprocated, but on the wedding morning it comes out that Rochester is a married man and keeps a mad and depraved wife in the attics of his mansion. Jane leaves him, suffers hardship, and finds work as a village schoolmistress. When Jane learns, however, that Rochester has been maimed and blinded, trying vainly to rescue his wife from the burning house she set afire, Jane seeks him out and marries him. There are melodramatic naïvetés in the story, and Charlotte's elevated rhetorical passages—though genuine and powerful in their kind—do not much appeal to modern taste, but she maintains her hold on the reader. The novel is subtitled *An Autobiography*, and Charlotte follows Anne in putting her tale in the mouth of a governess, but, except in Jane's impressions of Lowood, the autobiography is not Charlotte's. Personal experience is fused with suggestions from widely different sources and the Cinderella theme may well come from Samuel Richardson's *Pamela*. The action is carefully motivated, and apparently episodic sections, like the return to Gateshead Hall, are seen to be necessary to the full expression of Jane's character and the working out of the threefold moral theme of love, independence, and forgiveness. The landscape background, geared closely to the phases of the action, carries into the novel a lyricism only partially anticipated by Ann Radcliffe and Sir Walter Scott.

Jane Eyre

Charlotte intended *Shirley* to be "real, cool and solid," avoided melodrama and coincidences, and widened her scope. Setting aside Maria Edgworth and Scott as national novelists, *Shirley* is the first regional novel in English, full of shrewdly depicted local material—Yorkshire characters, church and chapel, the cloth workers and machine breakers of her father's early manhood, and a sturdy but rather embittered feminism. It is not, however, easy to elicit a dominant theme. Of her two heroines, Shirley, on Mrs. Gaskell's authority, was a "representation" of Emily in ampler circumstances, and Caroline, at least in some parts, approximates Anne. While Charlotte was writing, both sisters died, and it is arguable that the course of the novel was diverted. Caroline, who in the earlier chapters seems marked for the spinsterhood that was so much in Charlotte's and Anne's minds, is dismissed to married happiness, while Louis Moore, abruptly introduced in the last third of the book, carries out with Shirley the master–pupil love relationship that occurs in all Charlotte's novels.

Villette

In *Villette* she recurs to the Brussels setting and the first-person narrative, disused in *Shirley;* the characters and incidents are largely variants of the people and life at the Pension Héger. Against this background she sets the ardent heart, deprived of its object, contrasted with the woman happily fulfilled in love. The action is seen through the personality of the sober-seeming governess Lucy Snowe, whose struggle for detachment stimulates the reader to attain it. Charlotte said her heroine was morbid and unamiable and refused to divert tragedy from her but allowed her to achieve a useful and honourable independence.

The influence of Charlotte's novels was much more immediate than that of *Wuthering Heights*, which was described for many years as without posterity. Charlotte's combination of romance and satiric realism had been the mode of nearly all the women novelists for a century. Her fruitful innovations were the presentation of a tale through the sensibility of a child or young woman—in which Dickens followed her; her lyricism—in which the genius of romantic poetry entered the novel; and the picture of love from a woman's standpoint—with which she unwittingly startled a section of Victorian opinion. The two sides of her nature were never fully harmonized and this results in what Virginia Woolf called the "jerking of the planes." Her special mastery lies in her intense participation in her story and its transmission to readers.

MAJOR WORKS

POETRY: *Poems by Currer, Ellis and Acton Bell* (1846). Separate editions of the *Complete Poems* of Charlotte and Anne Brontë were published in 1923 and of Emily Brontë in 1924.

NOVELS: CHARLOTTE BRONTE (pseudonym Currer Bell): *Jane Eyre: An Autobiography*, ed. by Currer Bell, 3 vol. (1847); *Shirley: A Tale*, 3 vol. (1849); *Villette*, 3 vol. (1853); *The Professor: A Tale* (1857); *Emma* (1860), a fragment, published in *The Cornhill Magazine*.

EMILY BRONTE (pseudonym Ellis Bell): *Wuthering Heights*, 2 vol. (1847).

ANNE BRONTE (pseudonym Acton Bell): *Agnes Grey* (1847); *The Tenant of Wildfell Hall*, 3 vol. (1848).

BIBLIOGRAPHY. LIONEL STEVENSON, "The Brontës," in the *New Cambridge Bibliography of English Literature*, vol. 3, pp. 864–873 (1969), lists bibliographies, collections and composite works, editions, and critical and biographical books and articles from 1846 to 1966.

Manuscripts: Letters and literary manuscripts of the Brontës are preserved in the following centres in England: Brontë Parsonage Museum, Haworth; British Museum; the libraries of Manchester and Leeds universities; Fitzwilliam Museum Library, Cambridge; and in the United States: the Berg Collection, New York Public Library; Harry Elkins Widener Memorial Library, Harvard University; Wren Library, Texas University; Henry F. Huntingdon Library and Art Gallery, San Marino, California; J. Pierpont Morgan Library, New York City; and the Bonnell Collection, Philadelphia.

Editions: The best working edition is *The Shakespeare Head Brontë*, 19 vol. (1932–38).

Biography and criticism: E.C. GASKELL, *The Life of Charlotte Brontë*, 2 vol. (1857, many later editions), raised controversy and was modified in the third edition. It is indispensable. See MARGARET LANE, *The Brontë Story: A Reconsideration of Mrs. Gaskell's Life of Charlotte Brontë* (1953, reprinted 1971). The Haworth edition, *The Life and Works of Charlotte Brontë and Her Sisters*, 7 vol. (1899–1900), was edited by C.K. SHORTER and H. WARD, who had access to material in the hands of Mr. Nicholls and published all of Charlotte's available letters in C.K. SHORTER, *The Brontës: Life and Letters*, 2 vol. (1908). The first supplement, however, was provided by T. WEMYSS REID in *Charlotte Brontë: A Monograph* (1877). During the 20th century a formidable body of biographical and critical investigation and assessment appeared. The publication *in extenso* of the early writings began with *Legends of Angria*, ed. by FANNIE E. RATCHFORD and W. CLYDE DE VANE (1933), and Miss Ratchford has studied them in *The Brontës' Web of Childhood* (1941) and *Gondal's Queen* (1955). The Brontë manuscripts have yielded fresh verse by Emily and Anne, and their complete poems have been published. The first biography of Emily by A.M.F. ROBINSON, *Emily Brontë* (1883), to which Ellen Nussey contributed information but did not approve the conclusions, was followed by ROMER WILSON, *All Alone: The Life and Private History of Emily Jane Brontë* (1928); MURIEL SPARK and DEREK STANFORD, *Emily Brontë: Her Life and Work* (1953); JACQUES BLONDEL, *Emily Brontë* (1955); and JOHN HEWISH, *Emily Brontë* (1969). Other studies include: ADA HARRISON and DEREK STANFORD, *Anne Brontë: Her Life and Work* (1959); and WINIFRED GERIN, *Anne Brontë* (1959), *Branwell Brontë* (1961), *Charlotte Brontë* (1967), and *Emily Brontë* (1971). *The Clue to the Brontës* by G. ELIZABETH HARRISON (1948), follows up the Brontës' Methodist connections. The Brontë Society publications (1895–) include biographical, topographical, and critical contributions. The following studies are important: MAY SINCLAIR, *The Three Brontës* (1912); E. DIMNET, *Les Soeurs Brontë* (1910; Eng. trans., *The Brontë Sisters*, 1927); IRENE COOPER WILLIS, *The Authorship of Wuthering Heights* (1936); LAURA L. HINKLEY,

The Brontës, Charlotte and Emily (1945); PHYLLIS E. BENTLEY, *The Brontës* (1947) and *The Brontë Sisters* (1950); LAURENCE and E.M. HANSON, *The Four Brontës* (1949); INGA STINA EWBANK, *Their Proper Sphere: A Study of the Brontë Sisters As Early-Victorian Female Novelists* (1966); and W.A. CRAIK, *The Brontë Novels* (1968).

(J.M.S.T.)

Brown, Robert

Robert Brown is best known for establishing the concept of the continuous motion of minute particles suspended in a fluid, the Brownian movement, as a property of both organic and inorganic matter. In addition, he recognized the fundamental distinction between the conifers and their allies (gymnosperms) and the flowering plants (angiosperms), recognized and named the nucleus as a constant constituent of living cells in most plants, and improved the natural classification of plants by establishing and defining new families and genera. He contributed substantially to knowledge of plant morphology, embryology, and geography, in particular by his original work on the flora of Australia.

By courtesy of the National Portrait Gallery, London

Brown, drawing by W. Brockedon, 1849. In the National Portrait Gallery, London.

Brown was born on December 21, 1773, at Montrose, Scotland, the son of a Scottish Episcopalian clergyman. He studied medicine at the universities of Aberdeen and Edinburgh and, at the age of 21, joined the British Army as an ensign and assistant surgeon. During the five years his regiment spent in Ireland, he divided his time between his official medical duties and self-education.

A visit to London in 1798 brought Brown to the notice of Sir Joseph Banks, president of the Royal Society, whose herbarium at Soho Square contained many Australian plants that, together with his rich botanical library, were readily accessible to visiting scientists. Banks had travelled with Capt. James Cook on the 1768–71 voyage of the "Endeavour" and had thereby acquired a lasting interest in New Holland, as Australia was then called. By December 1800, the Admiralty had prepared plans for a surveying voyage along the northern and southern coasts of Australia under the command of Matthew Flinders. Impressed by Brown's enthusiasm and abilities, Banks recommended him for the post of naturalist aboard Flinders' ship, "Investigator."

Expedition to Australia

Brown promptly accepted and sailed with the expedition on July 18, 1801. A duplicate set of herbarium specimens of Australian plants given him by Banks enabled him to obtain an intimate knowledge of many plants of Australia before his arrival there. The "Investigator" reached King George's Sound, Western Australia, an area of great floristic diversity, on December 8, 1801. Until June 8, 1803, and while the ship circumnavigated Australia, Brown made extensive plant collections, which were portrayed by the great botanical artist Ferdinand Bauer.

Returning to England on October 13, 1805, Brown devoted his time to classifying the approximately 3,900 species he had gathered. The results of his Australian trip were partially published in 1810 as his *Prodromus Florae Novae Hollandiae* . . ., a classic of systematic botany and his major work, which contains much information relevant to plant taxonomy as a whole. Disappointed by its small sale, however, he published only one volume. Brown's close observation of minute but significant details was also shown in his publication on *Proteaceae*, in which he demonstrated how pollen-grain characters could assist the definition of genera. In 1810 Banks appointed Brown as his librarian and in 1820 bequeathed him a life interest in his collections. Brown transferred them to the British Museum in 1827, when he became keeper of its newly formed botanical department.

In 1828 he published a pamphlet, *A Brief Account of Microscopical Observations* . . ., in which he recorded that, after having noticed moving particles within living pollen grains of *Clarkia pulchella*, he examined both living and dead pollen grains of many other plants and found similar particles. Experiments with organic and inorganic substances, reduced to powder and suspended in water, then revealed such motion to be a general property of matter in that state. This phenomenon has long been known as Brownian movement (*q.v.*). In 1831, while dealing with the fertilization of *Orchidaceae* and *Asclepiadaceae*, he noted the existence of a structure within cells that he termed the nucleus of the cell. These observations testify to the range and depth of his pioneering microscopical work and his ability to draw far-reaching conclusions from isolated data or selected structures.

Brownian movement and the cell nucleus

Brown died in London on June 10, 1858.

BIBLIOGRAPHY. There is no definitive biography but J.B. FARMER, "Robert Brown, 1773–1858," in F.W. OLIVER (ed.), *Makers of British Botany*, pp. 108–125 (1912); and W.T. STEARN, "Brown, Robert," in the *Dictionary of Scientific Biography*, vol. 2, pp. 516–522 (1970), provide concise outlines of his career and major scientific achievements.

(W.T.S.)

Brownian Movement

Brownian movement is a term used to describe many physical phenomena in which some quantity is constantly undergoing small, random fluctuations. The oldest example, described by the discoverer, Scottish botanist Robert Brown, in 1827, is the motion of microscopic particles suspended in a liquid or gas. In 1900 L. Bachelier published his "Théorie de la Speculation," in which the variation of prices on the Paris Bourse was analyzed in terms of random fluctuations. Bachelier's work anticipated many results obtained decades later by physicists and mathematicians.

Examples of Brownian movement. A homely example of Brownian movement is the relative position of one individual within a stream of pedestrians moving along a sidewalk. His position will undergo random fluctuations; over a period of time, he may gradually drift toward the front or the back or the centre of the stream. In biology the size of a large population of any living organism undergoes constant fluctuations as individuals are born and die, and, therefore, a gradual increase or decrease may be studied as an example of Brownian motion. Any electrical instrument is subject to random fluctuations in input, for example, because of unpredictable variations in the electrical current. These variations can result in an oscillation or Brownian motion of the output, or dial reading, of the instrument, so that the theory of Brownian motion is not only important in electrical engineering but also imposes limitations on the attainable accuracy of scientific measurements.

Basic process

If a number of particles subject to Brownian movements are present in a medium and there is no preferred direction for the random oscillations, then over a period of time the particles will tend to be spread evenly throughout the medium. Thus, if A and B are two adjacent regions and, at time t, A contains twice as many particles as B, at that instant the probability of a particle leaving A to enter B is twice as great as the probability that a particle will leave B to enter A. A physical process in which a substance tends to spread steadily from regions of high concentration to regions of lower concentration is called diffusion. Thus, diffusion is a macroscopic manifestation of Brownian motion on the microscopic level. As a consequence, it is possible to study diffusion by simulating the motion of a Brownian particle and computing its average behaviour; this example illustrates the Monte Carlo method that has been made possible by high-speed computing machines. A few examples of the countless diffusion processes that are studied in terms of Brownian motion include the diffusion of pollutants through the atmosphere, the diffusion of "holes" (minute regions in which the electrical charge potential is positive) through a semiconductor, and the diffusion of calcium through bone tissue in living organisms.

History of explanations. By "classical Brownian motion" is meant the random movement of microscopic particles suspended in a liquid or gas. Brown was investigating the fertilization process in *Clarkia pulchella*, a newly discovered species of flower, when he noticed a "rapid oscillatory motion" of the pollen grains suspended in water under the microscope. Others had noticed this phenomenon (Georges de Buffon [1707–88] and Lazzaro Spallanzani [1729–99] appear to have been aware of it), but Brown was the first to study it. Initially, he believed that such activity was peculiar to the male sexual cells of plants, but then he was startled to observe that pollen of plants dead for over a century showed the same movement, and he called this a "very unexpected fact of seeming vitality being retained by these 'molecules' so long after the death of the plant." Further study revealed that the same motion could be observed not only with particles of other organic substances but even with chips of glass or granite or particles of smoke.

Early explanations attributed the motion to thermal convection currents in the fluid. When observation showed that nearby particles exhibited totally uncorrelated activity, however, this simple explanation was abandoned. By the 1860s theoretical physicists had become interested in Brownian movement and were searching for a consistent explanation of its various characteristics: a given particle appeared equally likely to move in any direction, further motion seemed totally unrelated to past motion, and the motion never stopped. An experiment (1865) in which a suspension was sealed in glass for a year, showed that the Brownian motion remained unchanged. More systematic investigation in 1889 determined that small particle size and low viscosity of the surrounding fluid resulted in faster motion.

Since higher temperature (Figure 1) also led to more rapid Brownian motion, in 1877 it was suggested that its cause lay in the "thermal molecular motion in the liquid environment." The idea that molecules of a liquid or gas are constantly in motion, colliding with each other and bouncing back and forth, is a prominent part of the kinetic theory of matter developed in the third quarter of the 19th century by the physicists J.C. Maxwell, L. Boltzmann, and R.J.E. Clausius in explanation of heat phenomena.

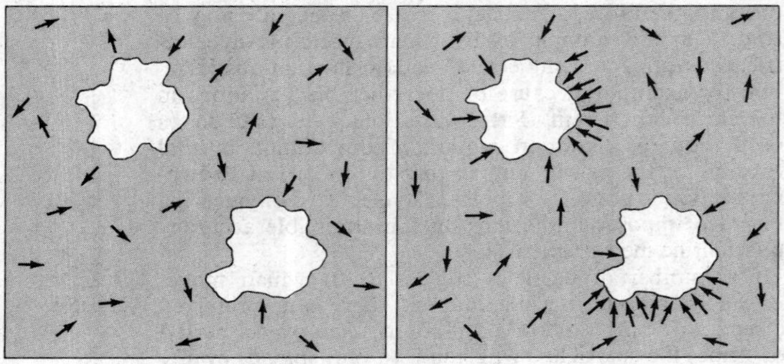

Figure 1: (Left) Random motion of a Brownian particle. (Right) Random discrepancy between the molecular pressures on different surfaces of the particle that cause motion.

According to the theory, the temperature of a substance is proportional to the average kinetic energy with which the molecules of the substance are moving or vibrating (any body in motion has kinetic energy). It was natural to guess that somehow this motion might be imparted to larger particles that could be observed under the microscope; if true, this would be the first directly observable effect that would corroborate the kinetic theory. This line of reasoning led Albert Einstein in 1905 to produce his quantitative theory of Brownian motion. Similar studies were carried out on Brownian movement, independently and almost at the same time, by M. Smoluchowski, who used methods somewhat different from Einstein's, and the contributions of both have been fundamentally important in subsequent developments.

Einstein's calculations

Calculations. Einstein wrote later that his major aim was to find facts that would guarantee as much as possible the existence of atoms of definite finite size. In the midst of this work, he discovered that, according to atomistic theory, there would have to be an observable movement of suspended microscopic particles. Einstein did not realize that observations concerning the Brownian motion were already long familiar.

Reasoning on the basis of statistical mechanics, Einstein showed that for such a microscopic particle the random difference between the pressure of molecular bombardment on two opposite sides would cause it constantly to wobble back and forth. A smaller particle, a less viscous fluid, and a higher temperature each would increase the amount of motion one could expect to observe. Over a period of time, the particle would tend to drift from its starting point, and on the basis of kinetic theory it is possible to compute the probability (P) of a particle moving a certain distance (x) in any given direction (the total distance it moves will be greater than x) during a certain time interval (t) in a medium whose coefficient of diffusion (D) is known, D being equal to one-half the average of the square of the displacement in the x-direction. This formula for probability "density" allows P to be plotted against x. The graph is the familiar bell-shaped Gaussian "normal" curve (Figure 2), which typically arises when

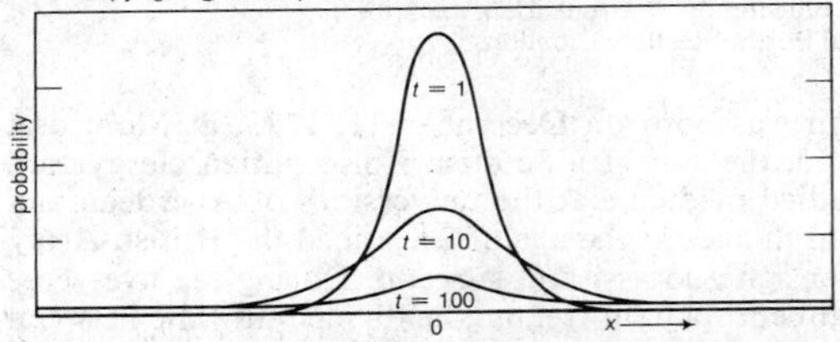

Figure 2: Bell-shaped curves showing probable position of a Brownian particle. The horizontal axis of the graph denotes the distance travelled in a given direction, assuming that at a time $t = 0$ the particle is at point $x = 0$. The vertical axis measures the probability that the particle will be at any given point (x) at time $t = 1$, 10, and 100 seconds, respectively, for the three curves.

the random variable is the sum of many independent, statistically identical random variables, in this case, the many little pushes that add up to the total motion. The equation for this relationship is

$$P = \frac{e^{-x^2/4Dt}}{2\sqrt{\pi Dt}}.$$

Each value of t gives us a different graph for P and x. For increasing values of t, the graphs become flatter and more spread out because the longer the elapsed time the greater the likelihood that the particle will travel far from its starting point. On the other hand, for any t, the point $x = 0$ always has the greatest probability density, since the particle is likelier to be near its starting point than near any other particular point. One formula obtained by Einstein shows that the diffusion of a particle is speeded by a rise in temperature and by a reduction in the size of the particle and in the viscosity of the liquid. The complete equation for the coefficient of diffusion, D, is

$$D = \frac{RT}{6\pi N_A \eta r},$$

in which R is the universal gas constant, T is absolute temperature, η is the viscosity of the liquid, r is the radius of the particle (assumed to be a sphere), and N_A is Avogadro's number (the number of molecules in a gram-molecular weight of gas). Einstein invited the experimentalists to subject his calculations to the test.

Perrin's experiments

The introduction of the ultramicroscope in 1903 aided quantitative studies by making visible small colloidal particles whose greater activity could be measured more easily. R. Zsigmondy (1905) and T. Svedberg (1911) made important measurements of this kind. J. Perrin was successful in verifying Einstein's analysis, and for this work he was awarded the Nobel Prize for Physics in 1926. Perrin's most famous accomplishment was the application of Einstein's formula to compute Avogadro's number, N_A. In order to do this, it was necessary to know D and r as accurately as possible; the other quantities in the formula are easily measurable or are well-known universal constants. To determine D, Perrin used an automatic camera to record the positions of a particle at 30-second intervals. Squaring the successive displacements along each axis, averaging, and dividing by two, one obtains an experimental value for D. To control r, he used a technique of fractional centrifuging to obtain highly uniform particles. Their size could be determined by coagulating them into chains whose length could be accurately measured and whose links could be counted. A second determination of Avogadro's constant was made by studying rotational Brownian movement—that is, the random change in spatial orientation, that is, rotation, of a particle because of molecular bombardment. Einstein derived a formula that determines the average of the square of the rotation per unit time ($RT/4\pi N_A \eta r^3$). To check this formula, it was necessary to use particles so large that they could be observed under an ordinary microscope, for the ultramicroscope shows each suspended particle only as a speck of light, not as a solid object. Perrin used particles of mastic, a natural gum, about $\frac{1}{2,000}$ inch in diameter, with occlusions of foreign matter below their surfaces as index marks. Thus he was able to observe the rotational motion of the particles, finding an average rotation of 14.5° per minute, as compared with a theoretical value of 14°. Perrin obtained no less than four independent measurements of Avogadro's number. His work established the physical theory of Brownian motion and ended the skepticism about the existence of atoms and molecules as actual physical entities.

Wiener's theory

Although Perrin's experiments confirmed the physical theory of Brownian motion, from a mathematical viewpoint there were still grave difficulties to be faced. While the expected displacement of a Brownian particle could be explained by the Einstein–Smoluchowski theory, this was far from true with respect to the random motion of an individual particle. Such a motion was in some sense chosen at random from a certain set of possible motions. To explain precisely what was meant by choosing at random from the uncountably infinite set of possible motions was a mathematical challenge of major proportions. The U.S. mathematician Norbert Wiener in 1918 and following years gave the first rigorous meaning to the notion of a random motion or a random curve. An idea of what is involved can be obtained by supposing that only finitely many speeds are permitted, and changes in speed are permitted only at multiples of a fixed time interval. Then only finitely many polygonal paths would be possible, and evidently one could in some appropriate way assign a probability to each path, with a total probability of one. If a small enough time interval is chosen and a large enough collection of possible speeds, then any continuous motion can be approximated by one of the finitely many polygonal motions. But to use this idea to assign probabilities to the set of all continuous paths is far from easy. Wiener set up a mathematical model satisfying the following laws:

(1) For each time t greater than 0, there is given a random variable $X(t)$, which is "normally distributed" (*i.e.*, the probability that $X(t)$ is between any two numbers a and b equals the area bounded by a bell-shaped curve, the lines $x = a$, $x = b$, and the X-axis).

(2) At time $t = 0$ the value of X is 0.

(3) At all future times t, the expected (mean) value of the random variable X is 0.

(4) If (t_1,t_2) and (t_3,t_4) are any two nonoverlapping time intervals, then the increment $x(t_2) - x(t_1)$ is independent of the increment $x(t_4) - x(t_3)$.

It should be clear that such a stochastic (random) process is a mathematical idealization of physical Brownian motion. The first and greatest difficulty that had to be overcome in Wiener's theory was to establish that such a family $x(t)$ actually exists—that is, to establish that the assumptions (1) to (4) are not contradictory. Wiener's original proof has subsequently been simplified and modernized by several authors. From assumptions (1) to (4) it can be shown that a single parameter, σ^2, suffices to determine completely the properties of a Wiener process. In the interpretation of the Wiener process as physical Brownian motion, σ^2 is the mean square displacement of the particle per unit time and equals twice the diffusivity of the medium. For some applications the assumption (3) has to be modified. If, for example, it be supposed that a Brownian particle, in addition to its random oscillation, undergoes a steady drift due to some constant force such as gravity, then, if the X-axis is vertical, the expected position at time t will be μt, where the constant μ is the distance the particle is pulled in unit time by the force field.

One of Wiener's most striking results was his theorem that the random path $X(t)$ is almost certain to be continuous but nowhere smooth. That is, its graph has a sharp corner at every time t. This mathematical result had been foreshadowed by Perrin's comment that the erratic paths of the particles he watched reminded him of the weird, continuous, but nowhere differentiable curves of the pure mathematicians.

Other properties of the paths in Wiener's process are less appealing to the intuition. It turns out that, with probability one, the particle traverses an infinite distance in every finite time interval, however short. This is nothing more than an inevitable consequence of the hypothesis; the trouble is that, on a very small time scale, the hypothesis of independent increments is physically unrealistic. (The next push occurs before viscosity has quite had time to damp out the last push.) The physicists L. Ornstein and G. Uhlenbeck in 1930 developed a more refined model for Brownian motion, in which velocities remain finite, although accelerations are still infinite.

The mathematics of Brownian motion has had a great influence in quantum mechanics. The path integral method of R. Feynman uses a formalism closely analogous to the computation of the probability of sets of continuous curves in Wiener's theory.

In pure mathematics the study of stochastic processes is now a major subject. The Wiener process continues to occupy a central role in this study, and mathematicians have contributed to the subject, which has established profound connections between probability, differential equations, and functional analysis.

BIBLIOGRAPHY. J.B. PERRIN, *Les Atomes* (1913; Eng. trans., 2nd ed., 1923); ALBERT EINSTEIN, *Investigations on the Theory of the Brownian Movement*, ed. by R. FURTH (1956); N. WAX (ed.), *Selected Papers on Noise and Stochastic Processes* (1954), a collection of famous articles by Chandrasekhar, Ornstein, Uhlenbeck, Wang, Rice, and Kac; E. NELSON, *Dynamical Theories of Brownian Motion* (1967), an up-to-date mathematical treatment; R. HERSH and R.J. GRIEGO, "Brownian Motion and Potential Theory," *Scient. Am.*, 220:66–74 (1969), a popular mathematical account.

(R.H.)

Browning, Robert

Although his popularity has fluctuated, Robert Browning remains one of the great poets of the Victorian Age. His poetic genius is most evident in his mastery of the dramatic monologue as a technique for powerful poetic narrative and rich psychological portraiture.

By courtesy of the Gernsheim Collection, the University of Texas at Austin

Robert Browning, photograph by Julia Margaret Cameron.

Life. Browning was born on May 7, 1812, at Camberwell in southeast London. His father, a clerk in the Bank of England, could afford to indulge his artistic and literary tastes and had a large and varied collection of books, which he encouraged his son to explore. Thus, in his youth Browning's reading was unsystematic but exceptionally wide, especially in the drama and in works of history and scholarship. It was in his father's library that he acquired the extraordinary range of interests that was to distinguish his writing; an even more powerful immediate effect was exerted by a volume of Shelley's lyrics that he read in 1826. Following Shelley's example Browning temporarily declared himself a vegetarian and an atheist, but the book had a more profound literary influence, for it introduced Browning to Keats and the other Romantic poets and thus determined the course of his life. Browning recognized that poetry was his profession. It was his fortune that he was able to devote his life to his chosen career without depending for his livelihood on the money he made by writing.

Browning's formal education was slight, although his father gave him a grounding in Greek and Latin. His mother, Sarah Anna Wiedemann, who was born in Scotland of German parentage, was an earnest Congregationalist and ensured that her son's religious education was not neglected, but his nonconformity barred him from the older English universities. In 1828 he attended classes at the University of London but left after half a session. Apart from a journey to St. Petersburg in 1834 with George de Benkhausen, the Russian consul general, and two short visits to Italy in 1838 and 1844, he lived with his parents in London until 1846, first at Camberwell and after 1840 at Hatcham. During this period (1832–46) he wrote his early long poems and most of his plays.

Browning's first published work, *Pauline: A Fragment of a Confession* (1833, anonymous), although formally a dramatic monologue, embodied many of his own adolescent passions and anxieties. A well-known Radical editor, W.J. Fox, who had already seen an earlier volume of Browning's work *Incondita* (1824, privately circulated), reviewed *Pauline* enthusiastically. Browning, however, was far more deeply affected by the unpublished criticisms of John Stuart Mill, who condemned the poet's exposure and exploitation of his own emotions and his "intense and morbid self-consciousness." It was perhaps Mill's critique that determined Browning never to confess his own emotions again in his poetry but to write objectively. Certainly in his later work he used the impersonality afforded by the dramatic form to safeguard himself against any revelation of his intimate affairs. Similarly, he objected to attempts to treat his poetry as autobiography, insisting that his poems though often lyric in expression were always "dramatic in principle, and so many utterances of so many imaginary persons, not mine."

Paracelsus, Sordello, and the plays

In 1835 he published *Paracelsus* and in 1840 *Sordello,* both poems dealing with men of great ability striving to reconcile the demands of their own personalities with those of the world. *Paracelsus* was well received, but *Sordello,* which made exacting demands on its reader's knowledge, was almost universally declared incomprehensible. Nevertheless, Browning's powers were recognized by several of the leading poets of the day, and he moved on friendly and equal terms among many young writers and artists.

Encouraged by the actor Charles Macready, Browning devoted his main energies for some years to verse drama, a form that he had already adopted for *Strafford* (1837). Between 1841 and 1846, in a series of pamphlets under the general title of *Bells and Pomegranates,* he published seven more plays in verse, including *Pippa Passes* (1841), *A Blot in the 'Scutcheon* (produced in 1843), and *Luria* (1846). These, and all his earlier works except *Strafford,* were printed at his family's expense. Although Browning enjoyed writing for the stage because of its objectivity and the close contact with his audience, he was not successful in the theatre, since his strength lay in depicting, as he had himself observed of *Strafford,* "Action in Character, rather than Character in Action." The third and seventh pamphlets in the series (1842 and 1845) were devoted to short poems, including "My Last Duchess," "Waring," "The Pied Piper of Hamelin," "Home Thoughts, from Abroad," and many others that prefigure the work of his maturity.

Elizabeth Barrett

By 1845 the first phase of Browning's life was near its end. In that year he met Elizabeth Barrett. In her *Poems* (1844) Miss Barrett had included lines praising Browning, who wrote to thank her (January 1845). In May they met and soon discovered their love for each other. Miss Barrett had, however, been for many years an invalid, confined to her room and thought incurable. Her father, moreover, was a dominant and selfish man, jealously fond of his daughter, who in turn had come to depend on his love. When her doctors ordered her to Italy for her health and her father refused to allow her to go, the lovers, who had been corresponding and meeting regularly, were forced to act. They were married secretly in September 1846; a week later they left for Pisa.

Throughout their married life, although they spent holidays in France and England, their home was in Italy, mainly at Florence, where they had a flat in Casa Guidi. Their income was small, although after the birth of their son, Robert, in 1849 Mrs. Browning's cousin John Kenyon made them an allowance of £100 a year, and on his death in 1856 he left them £11,000. Thereafter they were never harassed by lack of money, and their life was full but tranquil. Browning was not as passionately devoted as his wife to the cause of a united Italy, but he loved his adopted country and wrote many of his finest poems on Italian subjects.

On the whole, however, Browning produced comparatively little poetry during his married life. Apart from a collected edition in 1849 he published only *Christmas-Eve and Easter-Day* (1850), an examination of different attitudes toward Christianity, perhaps having its immediate origin in the death of his mother in 1849; an introductory essay (1852) to some spurious letters of Shelley, Browning's only considerable work in prose and his only piece of critical writing; and *Men and Women* (1855). This was a collection of 51 poems—dramatic lyrics such as "Memorabilia," "Love Among the Ruins," and "A Toccata of Galuppi's"; the great monologues such as "Fra Lippo Lippi," "How It Strikes a Contemporary," and "Bishop Blougram's Apology"; and a very few poems in which implicitly ("By the Fireside") or explicitly ("One Word More") he breaks his rule and speaks of himself and of his love for his wife. Before the book appeared he wrote, "I am writing—a first step towards popularity for me—lyrics with more music and painting than before, so as to get people to hear and see." *Men and Women*, however, had no great sale, and many of the reviews were unfavourable and unhelpful. Disappointed for the first time by the reception of his work, Browning wrote to Ruskin, "A poet's affair is with God, to whom he is accountable, and of whom is his reward." In the following years he wrote little, sketching and modelling in clay by day and enjoying the society of his friends at night. At last Mrs. Browning's health, which had been remarkably restored by her life in Italy, began to fail. On June 29, 1861, she died in her husband's arms. He at once decided to "go away, break up everything, go to England, and live and work and write." In the autumn he returned slowly to London with his young son.

His first task on his return was to prepare his wife's *Last Poems* for the press. At first he avoided company, but gradually he accepted invitations more freely and began to move in society. Another collected edition of his poems was called for in 1863, but *Pauline* was not included. When his next book of poems, *Dramatis Personae* (1864)—including "Abt Vogler," "Rabbi Ben Ezra," "Caliban Upon Setebos," and "Mr. Sludge, 'The Medium' "—reached two editions, it was clear that Browning had at last won a measure of popular recognition. After the death in 1866 of his father, who had lived in Paris since 1852, the poet shared his house in Warwick Crescent with his sister Sarianna.

The Ring and the Book and later poems

In 1868–69 he published his greatest work, *The Ring and the Book*, based on the proceedings in a trial for murder in Rome in 1698. Grand alike in plan and execution, it was at once received with enthusiasm, and Browning was established as one of the most important literary figures of the day. For the rest of his life he was much in demand in society, dining out so frequently that many observers remarked on the difficulty of reconciling his intensely imaginative poetic life with his life as a high-spirited man of the London world, who appeared to have no serious occupation except planning his son's education and later advancing him in his career as an artist. He spent his summers with friends in France, Scotland, or Switzerland or, after 1878, in Italy. While he was in Scotland in 1869 he stayed with the rich and attractive Lady Ashburton and proposed to her, explaining candidly that their marriage would be of advantage to his son. When Lady Ashburton refused him Browning was distressed less by his rejection than by the subsequent gossip and recriminations.

The most important works of his last years, when he wrote with great fluency, were the long narrative or dramatic poems, often dealing with contemporary themes, such as *Prince Hohenstiel-Schwangau* (1871), *Fifine at the Fair* (1872), *Red Cotton Night-Cap Country* (1873), *The Inn Album* (1875), and the two series of *Dramatic Idyls* (1879 and 1880). He wrote a number of poems on classical subjects, including *Balaustion's Adventure* (1871) and *Aristophanes' Apology* (1875), and made a translation of the *Agamemnon* of Aeschylus (1877), which, it was said, could be understood quite easily with the help of the Greek. In addition to many collections of shorter poems—*Pacchiarotto and How He Worked in Distemper* (1876), *Jocoseria* (1883), *Ferishtah's Fancies* (1884), and *Asolando: Fancies and Facts* (1889)—Browning published toward the end of his life two books of unusually personal origin—*La Saisiaz* (1878), at once an elegy for his friend Anne Egerton-Smith and a meditation on mortality, and *Parleyings with Certain People of Importance in Their Day* (1887), in which he discussed books and ideas that had influenced him since his youth.

While staying in Venice in 1889, Browning caught cold and became seriously ill; he had time to learn of the favourable reception of *Asolando* before he died on December 12. Public recognition of his eminence, which had been successively shown by honorary degrees from the University of Oxford, an honorary fellowship of Balliol College, and presentation to the Queen, was fittingly completed by his burial in Westminster Abbey.

Characteristics of Browning's poetry. Few poets have suffered more than Browning from hostile incomprehension or misplaced admiration, both arising very often from a failure to recognize the predominantly dramatic nature of his work. The bulk of his writing before 1846 was for the theatre; thereafter his major poems showed his increasing mastery of the dramatic monologue. This consists essentially of a narrative spoken by a single character and amplified by his comments on his story and the circumstances in which he is speaking. From his own knowledge of the events described (as in "An Epistle of Karshish" and "Cleon") or by inference from the poem itself (as in "Andrea del Sarto"), the reader provides a quasi-dramatic context for the poem and is eventually enabled to assess the intelligence and honesty of the narrator and the value of the views he expresses. Thus the dramatic monologue, since it depends on the unconscious provision by the speaker of the evidence by which the reader is to judge him, is eminently suitable for the ironist. Equally, it offered the technical impersonality of the dramatist to a poet who, like Browning, distrusted the romantic exploitation of the writer's own personality. Browning's fondness for the form has, however, encouraged the two most common misconceptions of the nature of his poetry—that it is deliberately obscure and that its basic "message" is a facile optimism. Neither of these criticisms is groundless; both are incomplete.

Use of the dramatic monologue

Browning is not always difficult. In many poems, especially short lyrics, he achieves effects of obvious felicity, while even in his thorniest poems there are many passages that give an immediate poetic pleasure and many in which the force of his imagination is perfectly conveyed by the rough vigour of his language. Nevertheless, his superficial difficulties, which prevent an easy understanding of the sense of a passage, are evident enough: his attempts to convey the broken and irregular rhythms of speech, running the sense on from line to line, yet often stressing an unusual or arresting rhyme, so that it is almost impossible to read the verse quickly; his elliptical syntax, which disconcerts and sometimes confuses the reader but which can be mastered with little effort; the demands he makes on his readers' knowledge, as in *Sordello* or "Old Pictures in Florence," poems that require for full appreciation a considerable acquaintance with their subjects; and his fondness for putting his monologues into the mouths of charlatans and sophists, such as Mr. Sludge or Napoleon III, thus obliging the reader to follow a chain of subtle or paradoxical arguments—all these stand in the way of easy reading. Further, Browning frequently indulges his taste for the grotesque and yields to the temptation to display his prodigality of technical invention. Yet while there is admittedly much hasty and slipshod writing, much overcleverness, and much distortion of language into conformity with an arbitrary rhyme scheme, the surface difficulties of Browning are no greater than those of most of his successors.

But even when individual problems of style and technique have been resolved, the poem's interest is seldom exhausted. First, Browning often chooses an unexpected point of view, especially in his monologues, thus forcing the reader to accept an unfamiliar perspective. Secondly, he is capable of startling changes of focus within a poem. For example, he chooses subjects in themselves insignificant, as in "Fra Lippo Lippi" and "Master Hugues of Saxe-Gotha," and treats through them the eternal themes of poetry. This transition from particular observation to transcendental truth presents much the same challenge to the reader as do the metaphysical poets of the 17th century and much the same excitement. Thirdly, as Browning seldom presents a speaker without irony, there is a constant demand on the reader to appreciate exactly the direction of satiric force in the poem. Even in a melodious poem such as "A Toccata of Galuppi's," the valid position must be distinguished from the false at every turn of the argument, while in the major casuistic monologues, such as "Bishop Blougram's Apology," the shifts of sympathy are subtler still.

Browning's poetry, then, is seldom simple, but its complexity is a legitimate source of poetic pleasure since it springs not from a desire to mystify and impress but from the seriousness of Browning's attitude toward his art. He wrote in 1868, "I can have little doubt that my writing has been, in the main, too hard for many I should have been pleased to communicate with; but . . . I never pretended to offer such literature as should be a substitute for a cigar, or a game at dominoes, to an idle man."

It has also been objected that Browning uses his poetry as a vehicle for his philosophy, which is not of itself profound or interesting, being limited to an easy optimism. Against this it may be argued, in the first place, that since Browning seeks to win imaginative rather than speculative conviction it is inadmissible to judge his poetry simply as versified metaphysics. Secondly, Browning's dramatic monologues must, as he himself insisted, be recognized as the utterances of fictitious persons drawing their strength from their appropriateness in characterizing the speaker, and not as expressions of Browning's own sentiments. Thus his great gallery of imagined characters is to be regarded as an exhaustive catalog of human motives, not as a series of self-portraits. Nevertheless, certain fundamental assumptions are made so regularly that they may be taken to represent Browning's personal beliefs.

Religious values

Browning normally considers the existence of a God and of a life after death as certain beyond the need of proof and often, especially in his early years, accepts the central beliefs of the Christian faith. Readers who cannot follow him in this complain that this leads him to view the human situation with an equanimity not far removed from complacency. Yet in many poems he allows his speakers to debate at length the problem of reconciling the unhappiness of mankind with the providence of a benevolent God. The solutions that he accepts in "Abt Vogler" or "Rabbi Ben Ezra," for example, may often seem too easy, but it is significant that he at least starts from a recognition that misery and evil are at large in the world; in his best work, notably *The Ring and the Book* and *La Saisiaz*, he makes such answers as a poet may to the manifold perplexities that beset men of faith.

In matters of human conduct his sympathies are with those who show loving hearts, honest natures, and warmth of feeling; certainly these qualities are never satirized. He is in general on the side of those who commit themselves wholeheartedly to an ideal, even if they fail. By itself this might suggest rather a naïve system of values, yet he also, sometimes even in the same poem, shows his understanding of those who have been forced to lower their standards and accept a compromise. Thus, although Browning is far from taking a cynical or pessimistic view of man's nature or destiny, his hopes for the world are not simple and unreasoning but qualified and considered.

Browning did not share the prevailing Romantic interest in nature, declaring that men and women interested him far more. Consequently the diversity and external picturesqueness of the settings of his poems are unimportant compared with his abiding interest in the springs of human conduct. Thus he was able to find subjects fit for poetry in the life of his own times as well as in the events of the past. In the long poems of his prime, from 1855 to 1880, he demonstrated that sustained narrative in verse was still possible in an age that furnished the poet with none of the materials of the conventional heroic poem. In these works he wrote, as none of the other great poets of the 19th century chose to write, about contemporary life, and, as nearly as he could, he used the language of his time. If this makes his poetry unmistakably Victorian, its Victorianism is its strength rather than its weakness. Even *The Ring and the Book* was felt by its first readers to be a modern poem, since it recognized that to urban readers in industrial civilizations the truly heroic action was not that which showed most strength and courage but that which showed the greatest moral resolution and intellectual power. In this poem Browning displays all his distinctive qualities. He allows a dramatic monologue to each character he portrays—to the man on trial for murder, to his young wife, whom he has mortally wounded, to her protector, to various Roman citizens, to the opposing lawyers, and to the pope, who ultimately decides the accused's fate. Each deals with substantially the same occurrences, but each, of course, describes and interprets them differently. By permitting the true facts to emerge gradually by inference from these conflicting accounts, Browning reveals with increasing subtlety the true natures of his characters. As each great monologue illuminates the moral being of the speaker, the meanness and triviality of the subject are seen to be irrelevant, for it becomes clear that nothing less than the whole ethical basis of human actions is in question. For over 20,000 lines Browning explores his theme, employing an unfaltering blank verse, rising often to passages of moving poetry, realizing in extraordinary detail the life of 17th-century Rome, and creating a series of characters as diverse and fully realized as those in any novel. Indeed, Browning's achievement in this and in his other long poems, which show his genius to the full, is most fittingly compared with that of the great 19th-century novelists, particularly Balzac.

Reputation and influence

During his lifetime his reputation was slow to recover from the general rejection of *Sordello;* even his plays were financially unsuccessful. After 1864 critical recognition came rapidly; and, while his books never sold as well as his wife's or Tennyson's, he had a considerable and enthusiastic public for the rest of his life and, what he valued more, a large circle of friends and distinguished admirers, including Carlyle, Rossetti, Benjamin Jowett, and a French critic, Joseph Milsand. In the 20th century, his reputation, along with those of the other great Victorians, has declined and his work has not enjoyed a wide reading public, perhaps in part because of increasing skepticism of the values implied in his poetry. He has, however, influenced many modern poets, such as Robert Frost and Ezra Pound, partly through his development of the dramatic monologue, with its emphasis on the psychology of the individual and his stream of consciousness, but even more through his success in writing about the variety of modern life in language that owed nothing to convention.

Critical assessments of Browning have varied widely, but as long as technical accomplishment, richness of texture, sustained imaginative power, and a warm interest in humanity are counted virtues, he will be numbered among the great English poets.

MAJOR WORKS

POETRY AND VERSE DRAMA: *Pauline: A Fragment of a Confession* (1833); *Paracelsus* (1835); *Strafford* (1837), historical tragedy; *Sordello* (1840); *Bells and Pomegranates* (eight numbers): no. 1, *Pippa Passes* (1841), a drama; no. 2, *King Victor and King Charles* (1842), a tragedy; no. 3, *Dramatic Lyrics* (1842), including "Waring," "My Last Duchess," and "The Pied Piper of Hamelin"; no. 4, *The Return of the Druses* (1843), a tragedy; no. 5, *A Blot in the 'Scutcheon* (1843), a tragedy; no. 6, *Colombe's Birthday* (1844), a play; no. 7, *Dramatic Romances and Lyrics* (1845), including "Home Thoughts, from Abroad"; and no. 8, *Luria* and *A Soul's Tragedy* (1846); *Christmas-Eve and Easter-Day* (1850); *Men and Women*, 2 vol. (1855), including "Two in the Campagna," "Bishop Blougram's Apology," "Fra Lippo Lippi," and "Love Among the Ruins"; *Dramatis Personae* (1864), including "Abt Vogler," "Rabbi Ben Ezra," "Caliban upon Setebos," and "Mr. Sludge, 'The Medium' "; *The Ring and the Book*, 4 vol. (1868–69); *Balaustion's Adventure* (1871); *Prince Hohenstiel-Schwangau, Saviour of Society* (1871); *Fifine at the Fair* (1872); *Red Cotton Night-Cap Country; or Turf and Towers* (1873); *Aristophanes' Apology* (1875), including a *Transcript from Euripides: Being the Last Adventure of Balaustion; The Inn Album* (1875); *Pacchiarotto and How He Worked in Distemper* (1876), with other poems; *The Agamemnon of Aeschylus* (1877), a translation; *La Saisiaz: The Two Poets of Croisic*, 1 vol. (1878); *Dramatic Idyls* (1879, first series; 1880, second series); *Jocoseria* (1883); *Ferishtah's Fancies* (1884); *Parleyings with Certain People of Importance in Their Day* (1887); *Asolando: Fancies and Facts* (1889).

BIBLIOGRAPHY. L.N. BROUGHTON, C.S. NORTHUP, and R. PEARSALL (comps.), *Robert Browning: A Bibliography, 1830–1950* (1953) is the standard work. PARK HONAN gives a full descriptive account of Browning studies up to 1966 in chapter 3 of F.E. FAVERTY (ed.), *The Victorian Poets: A Guide to Research*, 2nd ed. (1968). The manuscripts of *Paracelsus* and *Christmas-Eve and Easter-Day* are in the Victoria and Albert Museum; that of *The Ring and the Book* in the British Museum; and that of *Dramatis Personae* in the Pierpont Morgan Library, New York, which also holds the manuscript of *Asolando*. With this exception the manuscripts of all Browning's works published after 1870 are held by Balliol College, Oxford. The Armstrong Browning Library, Baylor University, Waco, Texas, has important Browning collections and publishes *The Browning Newsletter*.

Editions: Of the many editions of Browning's works, the most complete is that of AUGUSTINE BIRRELL (1915). A variorum edition edited by R.A. KING *et al.* is in progress.

Letters: T.L. HOOD (ed.), *Letters of Robert Browning* (1933); R. CURLE (ed.), *Robert Browning and Julia Wedgwood* (1937); W.C. DEVANE and K.L. KNICKERBOCKER (eds.), *New Letters of Robert Browning* (1950); E.C. MCALEER (ed.), *Dearest Isa: Robert Browning's Letters to Isabella Blagden* (1951); *Learned Lady: Letters from Robert Browning to Mrs. Thomas FitzGerald, 1876–1889* (1966); P. LANDIS and R.E. FREEMAN (eds.), *Letters of the Brownings to George Barrett* (1958); G.R. HUDSON (ed.), *Browning to His American Friends* (1965); E. KINTNER (ed.), *The Letters of Robert Browning and Elizabeth Barrett Browning, 1845–1846*, 2 vol. (1969).

Biography: W.H. GRIFFIN (completed by H.C. MINCHIN), *The Life of Robert Browning*, 3rd ed. rev. (1938, reprinted 1966), is the standard biography, now rather dated. M. WARD, *Robert Browning and His World*, 2 vol. (1967–69), is the best modern life. Two lively accounts of Browning that make no attempt at impartiality are G.K. CHESTERTON's sympathetic *Robert Browning* (1903) and B. MILLER's hostile *Robert Browning: A Portrait* (1952). HENRY JAMES, *William Wetmore Story and His Friends*, 2 vol. (1903), gives the most vivid picture of Browning as he appeared to those who knew him.

Criticism: W.C. DEVANE, *A Browning Handbook*, 2nd ed. (1955), is an indispensable commentary on every aspect of the poems. R.W. LANGBAUM, *The Poetry of Experience* (1957), relates Browning's handling of the dramatic monologue to modern literary ideas. R.D. ALTICK and J.F. LOUCKS, *Browning's Roman Murder Story* (1968), is a detailed study of *The Ring and the Book*. More general accounts of Browning's poetry may be found in R.A. KING, *The Focusing Artifice* (1969); W.D. SHAW, *The Dialectical Temper* (1968); and P. DREW, *The Poetry of Browning: A Critical Introduction* (1970). B. LITZINGER and D. SMALLEY (eds.), *Robert Browning: The Critical Heritage* (1970), presents in chronological order the most important reviews and studies of Browning by his contemporaries. A selection of more recent critical work may be found in B. LITZINGER and K.L. KNICKERBOCKER (eds.), *The Browning Critics* (1965); and P. DREW (ed.), *Robert Browning: A Collection of Critical Essays* (1966).

(Ph.D.)

Bruckner, Anton

A composer of strikingly original symphonic works, Anton Bruckner is less well known for his sacred music, in which the great tradition of Austrian church music, in the view of many music historians, reached its final and most perfect consummation. To Bruckner, composition had the significance of a liturgical art, and he brought to it the same zeal that a God-fearing priest might bring to the enactment of the sacred rites. It is precisely this spiritual content that has caused his music to remain a closed book to many people, even when the passage of time has swept away many of the misconceptions about the composer. Bruckner's intense devoutness was an essential component of his personality, for he appears to have felt most acutely that he was an instrument of God. A measure of his greatness lies in the purely altruistic nature of his life and work, undefiled by materialistic values.

Creative influences. (Josef) Anton Bruckner was born in Ansfelden, a small village near Linz in Upper Austria, on September 4, 1824. His musical talent was soon recognized, and in the spring of 1835 he was sent to Hörsching to learn the organ from his godfather. His father's illness brought this interlude to a sudden end, and Bruckner returned to Ansfelden to assist his father in his duties as

Bruckner, portrait by Ferry Bératon, 1889. In the Österreichische Nationalbibliothek, Vienna.
By courtesy of the Osterreichische Nationalbibliothek, Vienna

village schoolmaster and organist. After his father's death in June 1837, Bruckner was accepted as a choirboy by the prior of Sankt Florian Abbey near Linz. Here he spent the next three years, receiving a broad general education, with particular emphasis on musical instruction. Following in his father's footsteps, he undertook a teachers' training course in 1840–41, after which he received appointments as an assistant teacher in Windhaag, 1841–43, Kronstorf, 1843–45, and, finally, once again at Sankt Florian.

Bruckner's second stay at Sankt Florian, from 1845 to 1855, was a critical period in his artistic life. The turning point in the gradual transition from the life of a teacher to that of a musician and composer was probably his appointment—provisionally in 1848, officially in 1851—as organist of Sankt Florian Abbey. Nevertheless, during the early 1850s, Bruckner attended a teachers' training course at Linz and went a stage further in 1855 by successfully completing the necessary examination for a high school teacher's certificate. The advice and encouragement of several people, however, convinced Bruckner that his future lay in music. Finally, in 1856, he secured the position of cathedral organist in Linz.

A few months earlier, Bruckner had been accepted as a pupil by Simon Sechter, a musician known for his contrapuntal works, and with him, between 1855 and 1861, he pursued an intensive course of counterpoint, undertaken partly by correspondence and partly during his visits to Vienna during holidays. The course culminated in a final examination, the main part of which was a practical examination. An initially skeptical panel of judges, consisting of some of Vienna's most prominent musicians, was left with no doubts of Bruckner's capabilities as both a performer and an improviser.

Bruckner's 12 years in Linz were years of both happiness and disappointment. His happiness lay in his numerous friendships and in his association with the Frohsinn choir, which he conducted in 1860–61 and 1868. He was aware also of an increasing facility in composition, particularly after 1861, when as part of a course in musical form and orchestration he undertook a thorough study of Richard Wagner's opera *Tannhäuser*. This was Bruckner's first acquaintance with the music of the composer before whom in later years he would stand in awe. The Wagnerian example provided a perfect foil to Sechter's contrapuntal training and led to the composition of his first major works—the three great masses, the *Overture in G Minor*, *Symphony No. 0 in D Minor*, and *Symphony No. 1 in C Minor*. Bruckner's disappointments in the Linz years stemmed largely from his failure to find a

Influence of Wagner

suitable marriage partner. His many proposals of marriage were rejected without exception, and his strong religious convictions made it impossible for him to enter into any physical relation outside of marriage.

Opposition and final recognition. In 1867 Sechter died and Bruckner, having recovered from a nervous breakdown, applied for the vacant position of organist at the *Hofkapelle* in Vienna. His application was rejected, but he was offered a professorship of harmony and counterpoint at the Vienna Conservatory and an unpaid provisional appointment as court organist. Ten more years were to elapse before Bruckner was made a full member of the *Hofkapelle*, and his attempts to secure a lectureship at the University of Vienna were to be unsuccessful until 1875. The latter delay was caused largely by the hostility of the powerful Viennese critic and dean of the University's music faculty, Eduard Hanslick, who was a champion of the German composer Johannes Brahms and antipathetic toward Wagner. For years, Bruckner was quite erroneously branded as a disciple of the latter.

The last 28 years of Bruckner's life were spent in Vienna, devoted to the composition of symphonies 2 to 9, the last of which remained unfinished, the *String Quintet in F Major*, the *Te Deum*, *Psalm CL*, *Helgoland*, and several smaller sacred and secular choral works. He rarely moved far from the capital, except for visits to France in 1869 and to England in 1871 to represent Austria as an organ virtuoso. In the 1880s and early 1890s he travelled to various German towns to hear performances of his symphonies and major sacred works. During these years he had to battle against the apathy of the public and the hostility of many critics besides Hanslick. His pupils and others sympathetic to his cause stood by him, however, and he gradually gained recognition. In 1891 the University of Vienna put the official seal on this recognition by conferring on him the honorary degree of doctor of philosophy. He died in Vienna on October 11, 1896.

MAJOR WORKS

Orchestral works

SYMPHONIES: *No. 0 in D Minor* (1864, rev. 1869); *No. 1 in C Minor* (first or "Linz" version, 1865–66; second or "Vienna" version, 1890–91); *No. 2 in C Minor* (1871–72, rev. 1875–76, and later); *No. 3 in D Minor* (*Wagner Symphony*), five versions (1873–90); *No. 4 in E flat Major* (*Romantic*), four versions (1874, 1877–78, 1878–80, 1887–88); *No. 5 in B flat Major* (1875–76, rev. 1876–78, and later); *No. 6 in A Major* (1879–81); *No. 7 in E Major* (1881–83, rev. 1885); *No. 8 in C Minor*, three versions (1884–85, 1886–87, 1888–90); *No. 9 in D Minor* (finale in sketch only; first three movements, 1887–94; finale 1894–96).

Chamber music

String Quintet in F Major (1878–79), rev. 1883–84, and later.

Vocal music

LARGE-SCALE SACRED WORKS: *Short Chorale Mass in C Major*, for contralto, two horns, and organ (*c.* 1842); *Chorale Mass in F Major*, for Maundy Thursday, for unaccompanied four-part chorus (1844); *Requiem in D Minor*, for chorus, orchestra, and organ (1848–49, rev. 1894); *Psalm CXIV*, for five-part chorus and three trombones (1852); *Missa Solemnis in B flat Minor*, for solo voices, chorus, and orchestra (1854); *Mass No. 1 in D Minor*, for soprano, chorus, and orchestra (1864, rev. 1876 and later); *Mass No. 2 in E Minor*, for eight-part chorus and wind instruments (1866, rev. 1876 and later); *Mass No. 3 in F Minor* (*Grosse Messe*), for solo voices, chorus, orchestra, and organ (1867–68, rev. 1876–90); *Te Deum*, for soprano solo, chorus, orchestra and organ (1881, rev. 1883–84); *Psalm CL*, for soprano solo, chorus, orchestra, and organ (1892).

SMALLER SACRED WORKS: *Pange Lingua in C Major*, for four-part chorus (1835, rev. 1891); *Ave Maria*, for four-part chorus and organ (1856); offertory, *Afferentur*, for four-part chorus and trombones (1861); *Pange Lingua*, for chorus in the Phrygian mode (1868); antiphon, *Tota pulchra es*, for tenor, chorus, and organ (1878); *Ecce Sacerdos*, for chorus, three trombones, and organ (1885).

CANTATAS: Festive cantata, *Preiset den Herrn*, for solo voices, male chorus, brass and woodwind instruments, and timpani (1862); *Germanenzug* (1863), *Das deutsche Lied* (1892), and *Helgoland* (1893), all three for male-voice choir, with brass instruments.

BIBLIOGRAPHY. The main repository of Bruckner's autograph scores, personal papers, and memorabilia is the Music Section of the Austrian National Library in Vienna. Bruckner's letters have been published in two collections, *Gesammelte Briefe*, ed. by M. AUER and ed. by F. GRAFLINGER (both works 1924). The standard biography is A. GOLLERICH and M. AUER, *Anton Bruckner: Ein Lebens-und Schaffensbild*, 4 vol. (1922–37). Other important biographies include those by M. AUER, 6th ed. (1966); F. BLUME in *Die Musik in Geschichte und Gegenwart*, vol. 2 (1952); R. HAAS (1934); E. KURTH, 2 vol. (1925); L. NOWAK (1947, 1964); A. OREL (1925); H.F. REDLICH, 2nd ed. (1963); and H.H. SCHONZELER (1970). Critical evaluations of Bruckner's symphonies have been made by W. ABENDROTH, *Die Symphonien Anton Bruckners* (1940); A. HALM (1914); and R.W.L. SIMPSON, *The Essence of Bruckner* (1967); of his sacred works by M. AUER (1927); further critical studies may be found in *Bruckner-Studien*, ed. by FRANZ GRASBERGER (1964).

(A.C.H.)

Bruegel, Pieter, the Elder

Generally accepted as having been the greatest Flemish painter of the 16th century, Pieter Bruegel has, from his own day to the present, been one of the most popular painters of any period or country. With a seemingly inexhaustible power of narrative inventiveness, his canvases wittily expose human shortcomings and folly, often in bold images of peasant life. Bruegel often, but not exclusively, depicted erring mankind under the images of peasants, which not only earned him the nickname "Peasant Bruegel" but also led to the belief that he was a peasant himself. The discovery of his close personal association with such leading humanists of his time as the Antwerp geographer Abraham Ortelius has put an end to this legend and focussed attention on aspects of his work that reveal him as a man well-versed in the humanities. Recent studies of the religious and philosophical implications of his imagery have aligned him in spirit to the Dutch humanist–writer Desiderius Erasmus, to the great French writer François Rabelais, and to such Dutch religious reformers as the philosopher, politician, and engraver Dirck Coornhert (1522–90). In addition, Bruegel has come now to be seen not as the last of the Flemish primitive painters but as the greatest artist of northern Europe within a wider so-called Mannerist tendency that dominated much of the art of the later 16th century throughout most of Europe. If occasionally he used the fantastic subject matter, the demons and the monsters, and even the manner of depiction, of a Dutch painter of allegory, Hieronymus Bosch, it is now clear that this was simply a matter of his own deliberate choice. Deliberate, too, was the apparently primitive form of his human figures, reductions to basic, cubic shapes more characteristic of 20th-century art, and certainly very different from those of his Flemish contemporaries.

Relation to the humanistic tradition

By courtesy of the Kunsthistorisches Museum, Vienna

"Hunters in the Snow," oil on panel by Pieter Bruegel, the Elder, 1565. In the Kunsthistorisches Museum, Vienna.

Studies of nature in the Impressionistic painting of the late 19th century have led to a renewed appreciation of the freshness and beauty of Bruegel's landscape paintings. Despite his own pessimistic view of mankind, he saw nature as a great positive and eternal force untouched in its purity by the doings of man. Throughout his life, landscape played a large part in his work; and in all the history of landscape painting, he is counted among the great creators of new types. He was not content merely to continue the Flemish tradition of the vast panoramic view, though his keen observation endowed it with greater credibility and reality of detail. He discovered and portrayed in his paintings and drawings a great variety of landscape forms, from magnificent alpine scenery to the lowlands and the stormy seas on which, to a considerable extent, Dutch landscape art of the 17th century was based. The Flemish painter Peter Paul Rubens, who owned 12 paintings by Bruegel, also came under his spell both in landscape and in some figural compositions. It is a measure of Bruegel's historical importance that he exerted a strong influence on the painting of the Low Countries for a long time and that his landscapes and other works of varied subject matter were endlessly imitated.

Early influences. Though there is sufficient evidence for the high esteem Bruegel enjoyed among his contemporaries and in the following generation, there is but little information about his life. Only the main outlines can be drawn, from a few surviving documents and the biography contained in Karel van Mander's *Het Schilderboeck* (*Book of Painters*) published in Amsterdam in 1604, 35 years after Bruegel's death. Neither the place nor the date of Bruegel's birth has been established with certainty. Rather than trusting van Mander's somewhat confused reference to a village called Breughel, of which there are several in the Low Countries, many scholars are now inclined to accept the city of Breda, now in The Netherlands, as his birthplace. A contemporary and, on the whole, well-informed source, Lodovico Guicciardini's *Descrittione di tutti i Paesi Bassi* (1567; "Description of All the Low Countries"), refers to the artist as Pietro Brueghel di Breda. Bruegel was received as a master into the Antwerp painters' guild in 1551. Assuming that he had undergone the usual period of apprenticeship of the time, he was probably born around 1525, possibly as late as 1530.

According to van Mander, Bruegel was apprenticed to Pieter Coecke van Aelst, a leading Antwerp artist who had located in Brussels a few years before his death in December 1550. The head of a large workshop, Coecke was a sculptor, architect, and designer of tapestry and stained glass. He had travelled in Italy and in Turkey and was a person with wide, mainly humanistic, interests. By translating and publishing architectural books of the contemporary Italian architect Sebastiano Serlio and of the ancient Roman Vitruvius, he contributed greatly to the spread of the ideas of the Italian Renaissance in the Low Countries. Although Bruegel's earliest surviving works show no stylistic dependence on Coecke's Italianate art, connections with Coecke's compositions can be detected in later years, particularly after 1563, when Bruegel married Coecke's daughter Mayken. In any case, the apprenticeship with Coecke represented an early contact with a humanistic milieu. Through Coecke Bruegel became linked indirectly to another tradition as well. Coecke's wife, Maria Verhulst Bessemers, was a painter known for her work in watercolour or tempera, a suspension of pigments in egg yolk or a glutinous substance, on linen. The technique was widely practiced in her hometown of Mechelen (Malines) and was later employed by Bruegel. It is also in the works of Mechelen's artists that allegorical and peasant thematic material first appear. These subjects, unusual in Antwerp, were later treated by Bruegel. His work in 1551 on the wings of an altarpiece (now lost) for the chapel of the glovemaker's guild in the Church of St. Rombaut at Mechelen undoubtedly gave him the opportunity to enhance his knowledge of the art of this city. At this time Bruegel was an assistant to the Antwerp master Pieter Baltens, who, though an older artist, later came himself under the influence of Bruegel.

The influence of the artistic traditions of Mechelen

Italian pilgrimage. In 1551 or 1552, Bruegel set off on the customary northern artist's journey to Italy, probably by way of France. From several extant paintings, drawings, and etchings, it can be deduced that he travelled beyond Naples to Sicily, possibly as far as Palermo, and that in 1553 he lived in Rome for some time where he worked with a celebrated miniaturist, Giulio Clovio, an artist greatly influenced by Michelangelo and later a patron of the young El Greco. The inventory of Clovio's estate shows that he owned a number of paintings and drawings by Bruegel as well as a miniature done by the two artists in collaboration. A seascape with many ships and a burning town, inserted in the decorative framework of a major miniature by Clovio (Towneley Lectionary, New York Public Library), has recently been attributed to Bruegel. It was also in Rome, in 1553, that Bruegel produced his earliest signed and dated painting, a "Landscape with Christ and the Apostles at the Sea of Tiberias." The holy figures in this painting were probably done by Maarten de Vos, a painter from Antwerp then working in Italy.

Thus the earliest surviving works, including two drawings with Italian scenery that were sketched on the southward journey and dated 1552, are landscapes. A number of drawings of Alpine regions, produced between 1553 and 1556, indicate the great impact of the mountain experience on this man from the Low Countries. With the possible exception of a drawing of a mountain valley by Leonardo da Vinci (Royal Library, Windsor Castle, England), the landscapes produced as a result of this journey are almost without parallel in European art for their rendering of the overpowering grandeur of the high mountains. Very few of the drawings were done on the spot, and several were done after Bruegel's return, at an unknown date, to Antwerp. The vast majority are free compositions, combinations of motifs sketched on the journey through the Alps. Some were intended as designs for engravings commissioned by Hieronymus Cock, an engraver who was Antwerp's foremost publisher of prints.

Impact of the mountains on his work

From imitation to independence. Bruegel was to work for Cock until his last years, but, from 1556 on, he concentrated, surprisingly enough, on satirical, didactic, and moralizing subjects, often in the fantastic or grotesque manner of Bosch, imitations of whose works were very popular at the time. Other artists were content with a more or less close imitation of Bosch, but Bruegel's inventiveness lifted his designs above mere imitation and he soon found ways to express his ideas in a much different manner. His early fame rested on prints published by Cock after such designs. But the new subject matter and the interest in the human figure did not lead to the abandonment of landscape. Bruegel, in fact, extended his explorations in this field. Side by side with his mountain compositions, he began to draw the woods of the countryside, turned then to Flemish villages, and, in 1562, to townscapes with the towers and gates of Amsterdam (drawings in Musée des Beaux-Arts, Besançon and Museum of Fine Arts, Boston).

The double interest in landscape and in subjects requiring the representation of human figures also informed, often jointly, the paintings Bruegel produced in increasing number after his return from Italy. All of his paintings, even those in which the landscape appears as the dominant feature, have some narrative content. Conversely, in those that are primarily narrative, the landscape setting often carries part of the meaning. Dated paintings have survived from each year of the period except for 1558 and 1561. Within this decade falls Bruegel's marriage to Mayken Coecke in the Church of Notre-Dame de la Chapelle in Brussels in 1563 and his move to that city in which Mayken and her mother were living. His residence recently was restored and turned into a Bruegel museum. There is, however, some doubt as to the correctness of the identification.

In Brussels, Bruegel produced his greatest paintings, but only few designs for engravings, for the connection with Hieronymus Cock may have become less close after Bruegel left Antwerp. Another reason for the concentration on painting may have been his growing success in this field. Among his patrons was Cardinal Antione Perrenot de Granvelle, president of the council of state in the Netherlands, in whose palace in Brussels the sculptor Jacques Jonghelinck had a studio. He and Bruegel had travelled in Italy at the same time, and his brother, a rich Antwerp collector, Niclaes, was Bruegel's greatest patron, having by 1566 acquired 16 of his paintings. Another patron was Abraham Ortelius, who in a memorable obituary called Bruegel the most perfect artist of the century. Most of his paintings were done for collectors, and although these included works of a religious character, no commissions for churches are known after the Mechelen altarpiece. Bruegel received what would have been his most honourable commission and an act of public recognition from the Brussels city council, a series of works commemorating the digging of the Brussels–Antwerp Canal. According to van Mander, death interfered with the project. No painting forming part of the series is known, nor is there information on whether he completed any part of the commission.

Bruegel died on September 5/9, 1569, and was buried in Notre-Dame de la Chapelle in Brussels. He was survived by his wife and two sons, Pieter (1564–1638) and Jan (1568–1625). Both of them became painters, Pieter known as "Hell Brueghel," Jan, as "Velvet Brueghel." Through them their father, known to history as Pieter Bruegel the Elder, became the ancestor of a dynasty of painters that survived into the 18th century. Jan honoured his parents' memory by erecting over their tomb an epitaph, which he had adorned by Rubens with a painting of "Christ Giving the Keys to St. Peter."

The dynasty of Bruegels

Artistic evolution and affinities. In addition to a great many drawings and engravings by Bruegel, 45 authenticated paintings from a much larger output now lost have been preserved. Of this number, about a third is concentrated in the Vienna Kunsthistorisches Museum, reflecting the keen interest of the Habsburg princes in the 16th and 17th centuries in Bruegel's art. Since Bruegel signed and dated many of his works, it is not difficult to trace his artistic evolution. In his earliest surviving works he appears as essentially a landscape artist, indebted to, but transcending, the Flemish 16th-century landscape tradition as well as to Titian and to other Venetian landscape painters. After his return from Italy, he turned to multifigure compositions, representations of crowds of people loosely disposed throughout the picture and usually seen from above. Here, too, antecedents can be found in the art of Hieronymus Bosch and of other painters closer in time to Bruegel.

By courtesy of the Detroit Institute of Arts

"The Wedding Dance in the Open Air," oil on panel by Pieter Bruegel, the Elder, 1566. In the Detroit Institute of Arts.

In 1564 and 1565, under the spell of Italian art and especially of Raphael, he reduced the number of figures drastically, the few being larger and placed closely together in a very narrow space. In 1565, however, he turned again to landscape with the celebrated series known as "Labours of the Months." In the five of these that have survived, he subordinated the figures to the great lines of the landscape. Later on crowds appear again, disposed in densely concentrated groups.

Bruegel's last works often show a striking affinity with Italian art. The diagonal spatial arrangement of the figures in "Peasant Wedding" recalls Venetian compositions. Though transformed into peasants, the figures in such works as "Peasant and Bird Nester" (1568; Kuntshistorisches Museum, Vienna) have something of the grandeur of Michelangelo. In the very last works, two trends appear; on the one hand, a combined monumentalization and extreme simplification of figures and, on the other hand, an exploration of the expressive quality of the various moods conveyed by landscape. The former trend is evident in his "Hunters in the Snow" (1565; Kunthistorisches Museum, Vienna), one of his winter paintings. The latter is seen in the radiant, sunny atmosphere of "The Magpie on the Gallows" and in the threatening and sombre character of "The Storm at Sea," an unfinished work, probably Bruegel's last painting.

The influence of other artists on Bruegel's work, rather than detracting from its greatness, showed his wide familiarity with contemporary art and his ability to adapt it for his own purposes. In fact, his work reflects his constant observation, exploration, and experimentation. He studied the changes in nature's moods brought about by the seasons in the series of "The Months," his feeling for nature transforming and enlivening a traditional subject. Particularly attracted by winter, he captured its various aspects in at least four paintings besides the famous "Hunters in the Snow" in the series "The Months."

Works of nature and of man

Range of vision and interest. He was no less interested in observing the works of man. Noting every detail with almost scientific exactness, he rendered ships with great accuracy in several paintings and in a series of engravings. A most faithful picture of contemporary building operations is shown in the two paintings of "The Tower of Babel" (one, 1563, Kunsthistorisches Museum, Vienna; the other, not dated, Museum Boymans-van Beuningen, Rotterdam). The Rotterdam "Tower of Babel" illustrates yet another characteristic of Bruegel's art, an obsessive interest in rendering movement. It was a problem with which he constantly experimented. In the Rotterdam painting, movement is imparted to an inanimate object, the tower seeming to be shown in rotation. Even more strikingly, in "The Magpie on the Gallows," the gallows apparently take part in the peasants' dance shown next to them. The several paintings of peasant dances are obvious examples, and others, less obvious, are the processional representations in "The Way to Calvary" and in "The Conversion of St. Paul." The latter work also conveys the sensation of the movement of figures through the constantly changing terrain of mountainous regions. This sensation had appeared first in the early mountain drawings and, later, in different form, in "The Flight into Egypt" (1563; Count Seilern Collection, London). Toward the end of his life, Bruegel seems to have become fascinated by the problem of the falling figure. His studies reached their apogee in a rendering of successive stages of falling in "The Parable of the Blind." The perfect unity of form, content, and expression marks this painting as a high point in European art.

The subject matter of Bruegel's compositions covers an impressively wide range. In addition to the landscapes, his repertoire consists of conventional biblical scenes and parables of Christ, mythological subjects as in "Landscape with the Fall of Icarus" (two versions, Musées Royaux des Beaux-Arts and D.M. van Buuren Collection, Brussels), the illustrations of proverbial sayings in "The Netherlandish Proverbs" and several other paintings. His allegorical compositions are often of a religious character, as the two engraved series of "The Vices" (1556–57) and "The Virtues" (1559–60), but they included profane social satires as well. The scenes from peasant life are well known, but a number of subjects that are not easy to classify include "The Fight between Carnival and

Lent" and "Children's Games" (1559 and 1560, both Kunsthistorisches Museum, Vienna) and "Dulle Griet" also known as "Mad Meg" (1562; Musée Mayer van den Bergh, Antwerp).

Although the surface meaning of Bruegel's works generally is obvious, modern research has called attention to some deeper significance that is not always easily elucidated. There seems to be much justification in the words in Ortelius's obituary of Bruegel, "In all his works more is implied than is depicted." Moreover, van Mander speaks of drawings that Bruegel asked that his wife burn when he was on his deathbed, either from remorse or for fear that she might get into trouble. These destroyed drawings might have been political, directed against the Spanish oppression of the Low Countries, or religious, against the Roman Catholic Church. Considering the biographer's remarks in the light of the extant works and their general character, there seems to be no possibility for believing these works to have contained political implications. The one painting that has been assumed to refer to the Spanish Duke of Alba's reign of terror, "The Massacre of the Innocents" (two versions, Hampton Court, England, and Kunsthistorisches Museum, Vienna) was probably painted shortly before Alba's arrival in the Low Countries in 1567.

Religious views

As for religious unorthodoxy, which Bruegel expressed in a veiled way, it has been suggested that the painter may have been associated with the "Familia Caritatis" or "Family of Love," a contemporary heretical movement indulging in mysticism. If Bruegel's religious convictions were in fact unorthodox, it is more likely that he shared the views of Dirck Coornhert, a friend of Ortelius and one of the engravers working for Cock. It has recently been shown how closely many of Bruegel's works mirror the moral and religious ideas of Coornhert, whose writings on ethics show a rationalistic, commonsense approach. He advocated a Christianity free from the outward ceremonies of the various denominations, Roman Catholic, Calvinist, and Lutheran, which he rejected as irrelevant. In an age of bitter conflicts arising out of religious intolerance, Coornhert pleaded for toleration. Bruegel, of course, castigated human weakness in a more general way, with avarice and greed as the main targets of his criticism that was ingeniously expressed in the engraving "The Battle Between the Money Bags and Strong Boxes." This would have been in keeping with Coornhert's views as well, which permitted taking part outwardly in the old forms of worship and accepting the patronage of Cardinal Granvelle.

MAJOR WORKS

"The Adoration of the Kings" (*c.* 1556; Musées Royaux des Beaux-Arts, Brussels); "The Fight Between Carnival and Lent" (1559; Kunsthistorisches Museum, Vienna); "The Netherlandish Proverbs" (1559; Staatliche Museen Preussischer Kulturbesitz, Berlin); "The Triumph of Death" (*c.* 1562; Prado, Madrid); "The Suicide of Saul" (1562; Kunsthistorisches Museum, Vienna); "View of Naples" (*c.* 1562–63; Galleria Doria-Pamphili, Rome); "The Tower of Babel" (1563; Kunsthistorisches Museum, Vienna); "The Way to Calvary" (1564; Kunsthistorisches Museum, Vienna); "The Adoration of the Kings" (1564; National Gallery, London); "Labours of the Months" (1565; three in Vienna, one in Prague, and one in New York); "The Massacre of the Innocents (*c.* 1565–67; Hampton Court, Middlesex, England); "The Wedding Dance" (1566; Detroit Institute of Arts); "The Sermon of St. John the Baptist" (1566; Budapest Museum of Fine Arts); "The Conversion of St. Paul" (1567; Kunsthistorisches Museum, Vienna); "The Cripples" (1568; Louvre, Paris); "Peasant Wedding" (*c.* 1567; Kunsthistorisches Museum, Vienna); "The Parable of the Blind" (1568; Museo e Gallerie Nazionali di Capodimonte, Naples); "The Magpie on the Gallows" (1568; Hessiches Landesmuseum, Darmstadt); "The Storm at Sea" (Kunsthistorisches Museum, Vienna).

BIBLIOGRAPHY

Bibliographies: E. MICHEL, *Bruegel* (1931); *Musée National du Louvre: Catalogue raisonné des peintures . . . flamandes du XVᵉ et du XVIᵉ siècle* (1953); F. GROSSMANN, "Pieter Bruegel, the Elder," *Encyclopedia of World Art*, vol. 2, col. 632–651 (1960); R.H. MARIJNISSEN, *Bruegel le vieux* (1969; Eng. trans., *Bruegel the Elder*, 1969).

Biographical and critical studies: G. GLUCK, *Das grosse Bruegel-Werk* (1951; Eng. trans., *The Large Bruegel Book*, 1953), contains the most complete catalog of Bruegel's paintings; F. GROSSMANN, *Bruegel: The Paintings*, 2nd ed. rev. (1966), a detailed biography including a review of contemporary and later opinions and new interpretations; C.G. STRIDBECK, *Bruegelstudien* (1956), an iconographic study concentrating on an examination of Coornhert's philosophy and its relevance for Bruegel; C. DE TOLNAY, *Pierre Bruegel l'Ancien* (1935), the first biography in which Bruegel's humanistic connections are discussed in detail; *Die Zeichnungen Pieter Bruegels*, 2nd ed. (1952; Eng. trans., *The Drawings of Pieter Bruegel the Elder*, 1952), a fundamental, critical study of the drawings, with catalog; L. MUNZ, *Pieter Bruegel: The Drawings* (1961), a new assessment of Bruegel's drawing technique, catalog differing partly from Tolnay's; H.A. KLEIN (ed.), *Graphic Worlds of Peter Bruegel the Elder* (1963), the only survey in English of the engravings after Bruegel, useful though not based on original research; J. GRAULS, *Volkstaal en volksleven in het werk van Pieter Bruegel* (1957), a detailed study of Netherlandish folklore illustrated by Bruegel; L. LEBEER, *Catalogue raisonné des estampes de Bruegel l'Ancien* (1969), the latest scholarly catalog of the engravings after Bruegel.

(F.G.)

Brunei

Brunei is a small, British-protected Islāmic sultanate situated on the north coast of Borneo. It has an area of only 2,226 square miles (5,765 square kilometres) and a population of about 136,000. It is bounded to the north by the South China Sea and on all other sides by the Malaysian state of Sarawak, which also divides the state into two separate and unequal enclaves; the western enclave is the larger. The capital is Bandar Seri Begawan (formerly the city of Brunei).

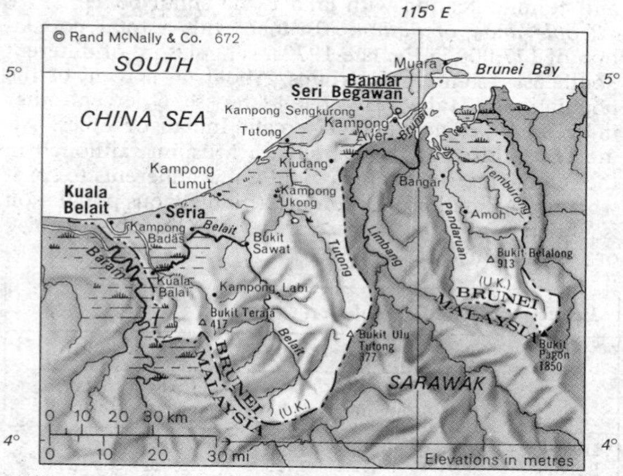

BRUNEI

Brunei is one of the largest oil producers in the British Commonwealth and enjoys one of the highest standards of living in Southeast Asia. It is one of the few remaining countries in the world without personal income tax.

Relief, drainage, and soils. Except for the narrow coastal plain, the country is rugged and hilly, with maximum altitudes of a little more than 3,000 feet in the southeast. The country is drained by the Belait, Tutong, Brunei, and Temburong rivers, all of which flow generally northward to the sea. The Belait is the largest river in the country. In the hilly region soils are mainly infertile laterites (red soils with a high content of iron oxides and aluminum hydroxide), but a narrow coastal stretch has alluvial and peat soils deposited by the rivers.

The rivers

Climate. The climate is governed by the equatorial monsoons (rain-bearing winds). The average range of temperatures is between 76° and 86° F (24° and 30° C). The annual rainfall varies from 100 inches in the coastal areas to more than 200 inches in parts of the interior. Most of the rainfall is brought by the northeast monsoon in November and March. From June to August the southwest monsoon season is relatively dry.

Vegetation and animal life. About 75% of the country is covered with tropical rain forest, characterized by a large variety of hardwood species; large stretches of forest are inaccessible. Along the coast, hardwood casuarinas (often planted as shade trees) grow in the sandy soils, while peat and mangrove swamps occur along the poorly drained upper Belait and Tutong rivers and around Muara, a town in the extreme northeast portion of western Brunei. In 20 percent of the area, primary forest has been cleared for temporary cultivation, after which a secondary forest growth has occurred. The forests are inhabited by lions, tigers, and monkeys as well as by a variety of birds, insects, lizards, and snakes.

The landscape under human settlement. The interior is sparsely populated by indigenous peoples who clear areas of the forest for temporary cultivation. Permanent settlers and cultivators—Malays, Ibans, Kadazans (or Dusuns), and a few Chinese—occupy the river valleys and coastal areas. They live in thatched-roofed wooden or bamboo houses raised on stilts and cultivate rice, pepper, or sago on small farms. Coconut palms and a few fruit trees are planted around their houses, and, occasionally, rubber is grown on small holdings. In coastal areas fishing supplements agriculture. Farmers are poor, for agricultural productivity is low.

Urban settlement

Most of the population lives near the oil fields at Seria and Kuala Belait. The largest concentration of urban population is at Bandar Seri Begawan, the capital, which is situated nine miles up the Brunei River. Whereas wooden houses are found in the rural areas, the city has apartment buildings, hotels, a shopping centre, a commercial centre, and port facilities. Alongside the modern section of the city is the older section known as Kampong Ayer, where 10,000 Brunei Malays live in small houses on stilts along the inlets of a broad, winding river. These houses are interconnected by footbridges, and communication with land is via small boats.

People and population. Brunei, with a total population of 177,000 in the late 1970s, is a mixture of different Southeast Asian ethnic groups. About 66 percent of the population is Malay, 23 percent Chinese, 6 percent other indigenous peoples, and 5 percent Indian or other. Almost two-thirds of the people are Muslims, although in the remote interior there are still a few adherents to spirit worship. A small proportion of the indigenous population is Christian, and the Chinese are usually Buddhist, Taoist, or Confucianist.

Brunei, Area and Population

	area		population	
	sq mi	sq km	1971 census	1975 estimate
Districts				
Belait	1,052	2,725	42,400	51,300
Brunei and Muara	220	570	72,800	87,200
Temburong	450	1,166	5,200	6,100
Tutong	503	1,303	15,900	17,700
Total Brunei	2,226*	5,765*	136,300	162,400*

*Details do not add to total given because of rounding.
Source: Official government figures.

During the 1960–71 intercensal period, the annual rate of population increase was 4.5 percent; more than a quarter of the total increase (52,000 persons), however, was attributable to immigration. The natural growth of the population was thus estimated to be a rather high 3.3 percent per annum. The high rates of natural increase and immigration continued into the late 1970s but were easily outpaced by the increase in oil revenues, allowing the standard of living to rise rapidly.

The national economy. Petroleum, discovered in 1929, now forms the backbone of Brunei's economy, accounting for 99 percent or more of its export earnings and giving its inhabitants the highest per capita income in East Asia, exceeding even that of the Japanese. Brunei draws crude oil from the original onshore well at Seria and from offshore wells that stretch for 700 miles between Bandar Seri Begawan and Seria and ships it by pipeline to the Lutong refinery in Sarawak. Production is increasing, and total reserves are estimated at 1,900,000,000 barrels.

Oil production

New fields continue to be found offshore, and prospecting continues on land. The main sources of revenue are taxes on and royalties from oil and investments abroad.

Agricultural and forestry products—rubber, pepper, wood, and cork—account for less than 1 percent of the export earnings. Rubber is mainly a smallholder crop, and only small amounts are produced on estates; productivity is generally low. Pepper is cultivated at Labi in Belait district. Other agricultural crops—rice, sago, and local fruits—are grown on a small scale. Production does not meet local demand; hardly more than a quarter of the rice requirement is produced locally. Sago—grown in the remote areas for food, sago flour, and thatching materials—is cultivated in peaty swamps and takes from eight to 10 years to mature.

Accessible forest regions supply an expanding timber industry, which exports sawn timber.

Transport. Road transport is poorly developed. A main trunk road links the capital to the oil towns of Seria and Kuala Belait, while another road links the coast to the pepper-growing district at Labi. Elsewhere in the interior, rivers are the main means of communication.

Brunei is served by two river ports—at Bandar Seri Begawan and at Kuala Belait—and both have wharves. A deepwater port at Muara was completed in 1973. Passenger ferry services are in operation between Bandar Seri Begawan and Labuan, in Malaysia, and between Bandar Seri Begawan and Bangar. At Bandar Seri Begawan there are an airport and several landing strips for helicopters. Royal Brunei Airlines and other airlines operate passenger service to and from Brunei, and domestic services are provided by the defense forces.

Administration and social conditions. In accordance with Brunei's first written constitution (1959), as amended in 1965, there are a Privy Council (which advises the sultan), a Council of Ministers, and an elected Legislative Council of 20 members and a speaker appointed by the sultan. Executive authority belongs to the *mentri besar* (chief minister), who is an ex-officio member of the Legislative Council and the Council of Ministers. The sultan presides over the Council of Ministers, on which also sits the high commissioner, representing the United Kingdom. Elections are officially held every five years, but the last were held in 1965 and further elections were postponed indefinitely.

Internal security is maintained by the Royal Brunei Malay Regiment, equipped with armoured vehicles, helicopters, air-cushion vehicles, and coastal and riverine patrol boats. The 6th Gurkha Battalion is stationed there.

Social welfare

Brunei is a welfare state, and social facilities are well developed. Medical services for rural areas include a "flying doctor" service to the villages, outdoor clinics, and travelling dispensaries. Education at the primary and secondary levels is available in English, Malay, and Chinese. Primary education is universal, and tuition is free. Free hostel accommodation and free transport are provided for pupils in remote areas. There is a pension scheme for the aged, disabled, and sick.

Future prospects. Brunei is making rapid progress with the aid of its income from petroleum. Lack of trained labour, however, constitutes a drawback.

BIBLIOGRAPHY. The Economist Intelligence Unit's *Quarterly Economic Review, Malaysia, Singapore, and Brunei* (no. 33), quarterly with an annual suppl., is a source of information on Brunei's economy, including data on its sources of revenue, trading partners, and petroleum industry. The first biennial *Brunei Statistical Yearbook,* published by the STATE SECRETARIAT, ECONOMIC PLANNING UNIT, STATISTICS DIVISION, covered the period 1973/74–1974/75 and provided official data on all aspects of the country's economic and social life. STATE SECRETARY, *State of Brunei Annual Report* (1946–), offers a basis for evaluating the success of the development plan (although published several years after the title year recorded in it); it also gives a concise account of social, economic, political, and cultural aspects of Brunei's national life. For financial analysis, STATE SECRETARY, *Estimates of Revenue and Expenditure* (annual, 1955–), provides insight into domestic and international factors that influence Brunei's economy.

(Ha.Se./Ed.)

Brunelleschi, Filippo

Although the renown of the architect Filippo Brunelleschi springs from his achievement in constructing the celebrated dome of Florence Cathedral (Duomo) and from his designs for the other buildings that were the prelude to Renaissance architecture in Italy, he began his career as a goldsmith and sculptor, went on to invent ingenious machines and mechanical devices, and founded the systematic application of the rules of scientific perspective. Brunelleschi also concerned himself with problems of time and motion (he reportedly made clocks), statics, hydraulics, and mathematics. Although some documents relating to Brunelleschi's professional activities have survived from the 15th century, they provide little information of a personal nature about the man who is regarded as one of the pioneers of Italian Renaissance art. Most of what is known about Brunelleschi's life and career is based on a biography written in the 1480s by an admiring younger contemporary identified as Antonio di Tuccio Manetti. Despite its inaccuracies and the fact that it was written four decades after Brunelleschi's death in 1446, Manetti's *Vita di Filippo Brunelleschi* remains the richest source of information about the great Renaissance master.

Alinari

Interior of S. Spirito, Florence, designed by Filippo Brunelleschi, begun 1436.

Early years. Filippo Brunelleschi was born in 1377 in Florence, the second of three sons of Ser Brunellesco di Lippo Lapi, a notary of some distinction, and Giuliana Spini. After training as a goldsmith and sculptor, he applied for registration in the Arte della Seta and in 1401 was designated a master. Although no documented works remain from Brunelleschi's earliest creative period, some of the small figures representing prophets and Church Fathers that adorn a silver alter in the Cathedral of Pistoia have convincingly been attributed to the young artist and dated *c.* 1399. Brunelleschi competed with Lorenzo Ghiberti and five other sculptors in 1401 to obtain the commission to make the bronze reliefs for the door of the Baptistery of Florence. Brunelleschi's trial panel depicting "The Sacrifice of Isaac" (Bargello, Florence) is the high point of his career as a sculptor. His ability to arrest narrative action at the moment of its greatest dramatic impact and the vigorous gestures and animated expressions of the figures account for the merit of his panel. It was Ghiberti, however, who was declared the winner, although the facts surrounding the jury's decision cannot be interpreted clearly. Brunelleschi's extreme disappointment at losing the commission probably accounted for his decision to concentrate his talents on architecture instead of sculpture. It also resulted in a lifelong hostility toward Ghiberti, although this resentment did not prevent them from collaborating on other projects when it was expedient. Brunelleschi did not, however, abandon his skill as a sculptor. No documented works after the competition panel remain, but the following are attributed to him: from the period 1410–15 a wood crucifix (Gondi Chapel, Sta. Maria Novella, Florence), a polychrome wood statue of Mary Magdalene (lost in a fire in 1471), and a small gilded metal figure produced jointly with Donatello in 1415 (lost); from the 1440s are the polychrome terra-cotta reliefs of the four Evangelists (beneath the dome of the Pazzi Chapel, Sta. Croce, Florence). The style of Brunelleschi's sculpture in the four decades between the Pistoia altar figures and the reliefs of the Pazzi Chapel underwent little change. He expressed himself primarily in the style of late Gothic art, creating attenuated figures wrapped in liquid draperies and placed in shallow layers of space. His most direct models have been traced to the late medieval workshops of French 14th-century goldsmiths.

Competition with Ghiberti

While still in the early phase of his architectural career (probably *c.* 1410–15) Brunelleschi rediscovered the principles of linear perspective construction known to the Greeks and Romans but buried along with many other aspects of ancient civilization during the Middle Ages. Brunelleschi demonstrated his findings with two painted panels, now lost, depicting Florentine streets and buildings. From Manetti's descriptions it is clear that Brunelleschi had understood the concept of a single vanishing point, toward which all parallel lines drawn on the same plane appear to converge, and the principle of the relationship between distance and the diminution of objects as they appear to recede in space. By using the optical and geometric principles upon which Brunelleschi's perspective devices were based, the artists of his generation were able to produce works of astonishing realism. On two-dimensional surfaces they were able to create extraordinary illusions of three-dimensional space and tangible objects, so that the work of art appeared to be either an extension of the real world or a mirror of nature. Although the laws governing perspective construction were brought to light by Brunelleschi, they were codified for the first time by the Humanist architect Leon Battista Alberti. In 1435 Alberti set them down in *Della pittura*, his famous treatise on painting, which included a warm dedication to Brunelleschi—undoubtedly an expression of Alberti's debt to his friend's revolutionary discovery.

Rediscovery of linear perspective

Solving complex problems of engineering and statics was another facet of Brunelleschi's wide-ranging abilities. His renowned mechanical inventions were immortalized in the Latin epitaph inscribed on his tomb in Florence Cathedral:

> How valiant Filippo the Architect was in the Daedalian art both the wonderful vault of this celebrated temple and the many machines invented by his divine genius document.

While most of his technical inventions related to the construction of the dome of Florence Cathedral, some of them reached as far afield as theatre production. One of Brunelleschi's most famous machines, probably invented around 1435–40, provided the setting for a liturgical drama celebrating the mystery of the Annunciation in the church of S. Felice in Florence. Suspended from the rafters of the church, the apparatus represented the dome of heaven. It contained complex movable sections and was operated by a hidden windlass.

Architectural career. The machines that Brunelleschi invented for the construction of the soaring dome of the Florence Cathedral and its lantern (a structure set on top of the dome to help illuminate the interior) and his scheme for the construction itself, represent his greatest feats of technological ingenuity. The cathedral was begun in 1296; during the 14th century the nave was completed and work commenced on the complex octagon of the east end. By 1418 construction reached the stage at which the technical problems of constructing a vault above the enormous dimensions of the octagon had to be solved. These problems had involved previous generations of cathedral architects in bitter disputes. It was Brunelleschi who worked out a successful method to vault the dome, invented the machinery necessary to carry it out, and designed the structure's crowning lantern and its lateral tribunes (semicircular structures). He was named chief architect (*capomaestro*) of the dome project in 1420 and remained in that office until his death in 1446.

Florence Cathedral commission

In 1418 the cathedral officials announced a prize for models presenting technical devices for the construction of the dome, designed in the late Gothic period as an eight-sided vault of pointed curvature without exterior buttresses (structures built for additional support). Brunelleschi, along with many others (including his arch rival Ghiberti) submitted a model. In 1420 a decision was reached in favour of Brunelleschi's model, which demonstrated that the dome could be constructed without the traditional armature, or skeletal framework, by placing the brickwork in herringbone patterns between a framework of stone beams. This construction technique had been evolved by the ancient Romans and had possibly been first observed by Brunelleschi on his supposed trip to Rome (*c.* 1401) with his friend the sculptor Donatello, when both of these giants of early-Renaissance art are believed to have studied classical sculpture and architure. In 1420 Brunelleschi's dome was begun; in 1436 the completed structure was consecrated, and in the same year his design for its lantern was approved. (The lantern, however, was not completed until after his death.) The imagination and the engineering calculations that led to the successful erection of the dome established Brunelleschi's fame.

Mid-20th-century criticism has modified the earlier approach to Brunelleschi's buildings as the foundations of Renaissance architecture. They are now understood in the context of two worlds—that of the waning Gothic period and also of the incipient Renaissance. Brunelleschi, therefore, is seen as an artist still profoundly dependent on Gothic forms of architecture and construction but with a vision of art and science that was based on the Humanistic concept of the ideal. This is borne out by his first major architectural commission, the Ospedale degli Innocenti (Hospital of the Innocents, or Foundling Hospital), where it is not clear whether his contribution was restricted to the arcaded portico that forms the building's facade or extended to the design of the rear portions of the building. Although Brunelleschi's name first appears in the hospital's construction records in 1421, he was probably at work on the building as early as 1419–20. His last documented association with the project was in 1426. After he left the project it was completed with deviations from his original plan, but his portico was generally regarded as the first example of the Renaissance style in architecture. This judgment must now be qualified to accommodate changing perspectives of the Renaissance. Although the portico is composed of many novel features, morphologically it still is related to traditions of Italian Romanesque and late Gothic architecture. The truly revolutionary aspects of the building emanated from Brunelleschi's intuitive sense of the formal principles of the classical art of antiquity. The Innocenti facade offered a new look in Florentine architecture and a marked contrast to the medieval buildings that preceded it. Its lingering late-medieval echoes were subordinated to the new style that provided the facade with its antique air: a wall delicately articulated with classical detail (such as Corinthian capitals, pilasters, tondi, and friezes), modular construction, geometrical proportions, and symmetrical planning.

Association with the Medici

By the early 1420s Brunelleschi was the most prominent architect in Florence. At this time the powerful and influential Medici family commissioned him to design the sacristy of S. Lorenzo (known as the Old Sacristy to distinguish it from Michelangelo's "new" 16th-century sacristy in the same church) and the basilica of S. Lorenzo itself. Work was begun in 1421. The sacristy was completed (without its decoration) by 1428. Construction on the basilica was halted at that time but began again in 1441 and lasted into the 1460s.

The S. Lorenzo structures are considered keystones of the early Renaissance architectural style. In form the church did not depart from the traditional basilican church with nave (central aisle), side aisles, and apse (a semicircular projection at the end of the nave). What Brunelleschi added to the conventional format was a new vocabulary using his own interpretation of antique designs for the capitals, friezes, pilasters (rectangular columns set into the wall), and columns. Further, his design of the church as a whole was one of unusual regularity, where the separate parts of the church rationally corresponded to each other and created a profound visual and intellectual harmony.

Brunelleschi designed the Old Sacristy (originally intended as a Medici family mausoleum) as a cube vaulted with a hemispherical dome. The structural and decorative units that delineate the architectural surface of the walls of the Old Sacristy and of the basilica proper are of particular elegance and restraint characteristic of Brunelleschi's work at this time.

Work for the Pazzi family

Around 1429 another wealthy and influential Florentine family, the Pazzi, commissioned Brunelleschi to design a chapel adjacent to the monastic church of Sta. Croce that was intended to be a chapter house (a place of assembly for monks to conduct business). Work probably did not begin before 1442; the building still was not complete in 1457. Modern archaeological investigation has revealed that the porch, famous for the beauty of its design and the elegance of its elaborate ornamentation, is not part of Brunelleschi's original project and that he intended to leave visible the outer curve of the barrel-vaulted sections of the roof, now covered by masonry. Brunelleschi used mathematical modules and geometric formulas for the plan and elevation of the Pazzi Chapel, as he had in S. Lorenzo, but he arranged the space in a more complex and sophisticated manner in the later building. A hemispherical dome covers a central square, which is extended on either side so that the square forms the centre of a rectangle. The minor spatial compartment, opening off a third side of the main square, is a corresponding square apse covered by a dome and containing the altar. The creamy wall surface of the Pazzi Chapel is marked off in geometric patterns by dark gray stone. The clarity, coolness, and elegance for which Brunelleschi's architecture is noted are seen in this small, harmoniously proportioned chapel.

Another example of Brunelleschi's experiments with central planning is one of his most enigmatic buildings, Sta. Maria degli Angeli, built for the Camaldolese monastery in Florence. It was begun in 1434 but left incomplete in 1437 (remaining in an unfinished state until the 1930s, when it was completed in a controversial manner). The building was planned as a central octagon with a 16-sided exterior. A chapel opened on each of the eight sides of the interior octagon, terminating in a deeply recessed apse at the end. Eight niches were cut into alternate facets of the exterior walls. Sta. Maria degli Angeli was Brunelleschi's most revolutionary design. It represented a perfectly centralized structure, more formally consistent than the Old Sacristy. Brunelleschi's model for this building has not been agreed upon by the critics, who have variously suggested monumental vaulted remains of ancient Roman architecture, such as the Temple of Minerva Medica in Rome or the late-medieval chapel-ringed octagon of Florence Cathedral. Instead of emphasizing the two-dimensional quality of his earlier works, Brunelleschi asserted the malleable nature of the wall mass and the plasticity of the structural and decorative architectural units. Many scholars therefore regard Sta. Maria degli Angeli as the beginning of a mature phase of Brunelleschi's architectural career, a phase dominated by solid rather than plane geometry and by sculptural space-molding elements. The late date, however, of the flat Pazzi Chapel, and the simultaneous construction of many of Brunelleschi's projects, tend to invalidate sharp distinctions between early and late styles in his career.

Brunelleschi's church of S. Spirito in Florence was designed either in 1428 or 1434, depending on the interpretation of the documents. The architect devised several unusual features for this building; one of the most interesting was a facade oriented to provide the building with a large entrance square overlooking the Arno River (this early example of Renaissance urban planning was never realized). Work on the church was begun in 1436 and proceeded through the 1480s. In 1486 the present facade with three portals was agreed upon in place of Brunelleschi's original scheme for a four-portal facade.

A basilican church with a centrally planned eastern end, S. Spirito is ringed by semicircular chapels opening off the dome-vaulted side aisles, the transept, and the apse. These chapels accounted for a unique aspect of the design, for the exterior walls of the church were meant to conform to the shape of the chapels in a sequential series of curves. After Brunelleschi died, however, the protruding round chapels were walled over with the flat conventional exterior now visible. Rather than creating its walls as flat surfaces onto which are pressed thin rectilinear members (pilasters), a style perfected in S. Lorenzo and the Pazzi Chapel, Brunelleschi designed S. Spirito with a feeling for its weight, gravity, and plasticity. The building, therefore, can be associated stylistically with Sta. Maria degli Angeli, and also with the four semicircular tribunes above the sacristies of Florence Cathedral. Brunelleschi's model for these tribunes was approved in 1439; the first one was completed in 1445, and the remaining three were finished in the 1460s. They are composed of deeply concave semicircular niches crowned with a shell device and separated by thick walls to which have been applied Corinthian half columns with projecting entablatures. In form and in mood, the tribunes were closer to monumental antique architecture than anything constructed in Florence up to that time, and they foreshadowed the strong profiles and massive grandeur of the buildings of Leon Battista Alberti and Donato Bramante (1444–1514).

Role as a residential and military architect

Brunelleschi's role as architect of residential buildings is difficult to assess, although Manetti relates that he was summoned from far and wide to design palaces. No documentary evidence exists for the houses and palaces with which biographers and scholars have credited him, the most significant of which (all in Florence) are the Pitti Palace, a rejected plan for the Palazzo Medici–Riccardi, and the Palazzo Bardi–Busini. Each of these palaces contains novel features that are tempting to attribute to Brunelleschi's inventiveness, but definitive proof of his influence or authorship has not been offered.

The manifold architectural abilities of Brunelleschi also are attested to by his military architecture, some of which is partially extant. He is associated with the building and rebuilding of fortifications in Pisa, Rencine, Vicopisano, Staggia, Castellina, Rimini, and Pesaro. In 1430 he was involved in a plan to convert the city of Lucca into an island by building a dam and deflecting the Arno River.

Brunelleschi was active through the early 1440s, and probably continued to be until shortly before his death. He died in Florence on April 15, 1446, and he is buried in Florence Cathedral. His burial place is marked by a wall monument composed of a marble half-length figure in relief, an idealized portrait of the architect carved by his adopted son, Andrea di Lazzaro Cavalcanti, and by the epitaph composed by the Florentine Humanist Carlo Aretino (Carlo Marsuppini).

Private life and assessment. An image of the personality of Brunelleschi can be pieced together from fragments contained in surviving source materials and documents. Although he never married, he was devoted to his adopted son and heir, Andrea di Lazzaro Cavalcanti (known as Il Buggiano), a sculptor, whose career he promoted. Many pieces of church furniture (pulpits, tabernacles, altar tables, lavabos, etc.) attributed to Brunelleschi were in fact designed by Brunelleschi but executed by Il Buggiano. Brunelleschi was an irascible and argumentative man, and he was secretive, believing it imprudent to share his inventions and ideas. These characteristics were consistent with the highly competitive atmosphere of early-15th-century Florence. He not only sustained his bitter rivalry with Ghiberti throughout his lifetime but he also had acrimonious arguments with many other artists, including his friend Donatello. Brunelleschi also wrote sonnets, which seem to have been largely inspired by anger; for his known sonnets were created as public invectives against his enemies.

Above all, Brunelleschi was a practical man. Not inclined to theorizing or codifying, he changed the course of architecture through persistent attention to problems of structure and space. Although he was respected and admired by the greatest Humanists of his generation, his approach to antiquity was not academic or doctrinaire. Using the classicizing elements of Tuscan medieval architecture as the medium through which he approached the venerated classical world, he imparted to his buildings a unique elegance and grace that were uncharacteristic of ancient Roman architecture. Convincing prototypes for his buildings can be discovered in the Byzantine-influenced structures of northeastern Italy, in Tuscan Romanesque and Italian late Gothic architecture, as well as in the ruins of ancient Rome. The most impressive symbol of the synthesis of Brunelleschi's two worlds is the harmonious juxtaposition of the "Gothic" dome of Florence Cathedral and its Renaissance tribunes, these structures being brilliantly unified by the ingenuity of "the valiant Filippo."

MAJOR WORKS

Spedale degli Innocenti (Foundling Hospital), Florence (1419–26); Barbadori Chapel, Sta. Felicita, Florence (*c.* 1420); Palazzo di Parte Guelfa, Florence (facade and grand salon, *c.* 1420); dome of Florence Cathedral (1420–36); Old Sacristy, S. Lorenzo, Florence (1421–28); basilica of S. Lorenzo, Florence (1421–29, 1441–60s); Sta. Maria degli Angeli, Florence (1434–37, unfinished); lantern of Florence Cathedral (1435 ff.); S. Spirito, Florence (1436–80s); tribunes of Florence Cathedral (1439 ff.); Pazzi Chapel, Sta. Croce, Florence (?1442–60s).

BIBLIOGRAPHY. The most important biography of Brunelleschi, informatively annotated, is ANTONIO MANETTI, *Vita di Filippo di Ser Brunellesco* (1812 and later editions; Eng. trans., *The Life of Brunelleschi*, ed. by H. SAALMAN, trans. by C. ENGGASS, 1970). Fundamental studies of Brunelleschi and his work, not translated, are CORNELIUS VON FABRICZY, *Filippo Brunelleschi: Sein Leben und seine Werke* (1892); L.H. HEYDENREICH, "Spatwerke Brunelleschis," *Jahrbuch der Preussischen Kunstsammlungen*, 52:1–28 (1931); P. SANPAOLESI, *Brunelleschi* (1962); and E. LUPORINI, *Brunelleschi, Forma e Ragione* (1964); in English are F.D. PRAGER and G. SCAGLIA, *Brunelleschi: Studies of His Technology and Inventions* (1970); C. ARGAN, "The Architecture of Brunelleschi and the Origins of Perspective Theory," *Journal of the Warburg and Courtauld Institute*, 9:96–121 (1946); P. SANPAOLESI, biography of Brunelleschi in the *Encyclopedia of World Art*, vol. 2 (1960), with bibliography; and P.J. MURRAY, *Architecture of the Italian Renaissance* (1963).

(I.Hy.)

Bruno, Giordano

Giordano Bruno, a 16th-century philosopher, astronomer, and mathematician, is significant for his theories of the infinite universe and the multiplicity of worlds, in which he rejected the traditional geocentric (or Earth-centred) astronomy and intuitively went beyond the Copernican heliocentric (Sun-centred) theory, which still maintained a finite universe with a sphere of fixed stars. Bruno is, perhaps, chiefly remembered for the tragic death he suffered at the stake because of the tenacity with which he maintained his unorthodox ideas at a time when both the Roman Catholic and the Reformed churches were reaffirming rigid Aristotelian and Scholastic principles in their struggle for the evangelization of Europe.

Unorthodox ideas

Early career in Italy and Geneva. Bruno was born in 1548 at Nola, Italy, near Naples, the son of a professional soldier. He was named Filippo at his baptism and was later called "il Nolano," after the place of his birth. In 1562 Bruno went to Naples to study the humanities, logic, and dialectics (argumentation). He was impressed by the lectures of G.V. de Colle, who was known for his tendencies toward Averroism—*i.e.*, the thought of a number of Western Christian philosophers who drew their inspiration from the interpretation of Aristotle put forward by the Muslim philosopher Averroës—and by his own reading of works on memory devices and the arts of memory (mnemotechnical works). In 1565 he entered the Dominican convent of San Domenico Maggiore in Naples and assumed the name Giordano. Because of his unorthodox attitudes, he was soon suspected of heresy. Nevertheless, in 1572 he was ordained as a priest. During the same year he was sent back to the Neapolitan convent to continue his study of theology. In July 1575 Bruno completed the prescribed course, which generated in him an annoyance at theological subtleties. He had read two forbidden commentaries by Erasmus and freely discussed the Arian heresy, which denied the divinity of Christ; as a result, a trial for heresy was prepared against him by the provincial father of the Order, and he fled to Rome in February 1576. There he found himself unjustly accused of a murder. A second excommunication process was started, and in April 1576 he fled again. He abandoned the Dominican Order, and, after wandering in northern Italy, he went in 1578 to Geneva, where he earned his living by proofreading. Bruno formally embraced Calvinism; after publishing a broadsheet against a Calvinist professor, however, he discovered that the Reformed Church was no less intolerant than the Catholic. He was arrested, excommunicated, rehabilitated after retraction, and finally allowed to leave the city. He moved to France, first to Toulouse—where he unsuccessfully sought to be absolved by the Catholic Church, but was nevertheless appointed to a lectureship in philosophy—and then in 1581 to Paris.

Career in France, England, and Germany. In Paris Bruno at last found a congenial place to work and teach. Despite the strife between the Catholics and the Huguenots (French Protestants), the court of Henry III was then dominated by the tolerant faction of the Politiques (moderate Catholics, sympathizers of the Protestant king of Navarre, Henry of Bourbon, who became the heir apparent to the throne of France in 1584). Bruno's religious attitude was compatible with this group, and he received the protection of the French king, who appointed him one of his temporary *lecteurs royaux*. In 1582 Bruno published three mnemotechnical works, in which he explored new means to attain an intimate knowledge of reality. He also published a vernacular comedy, *Il Candelaio* (1582; "The Candlemaker"), which, through a vivid representation of contemporary Neapolitan society, constituted a protest against the moral and social corruption of the time.

In the spring of 1583 Bruno moved to London with an introductory letter from Henry III for his ambassador Michel de Castelnau. He was soon attracted to Oxford, where, during the summer, he started a series of lectures in which he expounded the Copernican theory maintaining the reality of the movement of the Earth. Because of the hostile reception of the Oxonians, however, he went back to London as the guest of the French ambassador. He frequented the court of Elizabeth I and became associated with such influential figures as Sir Philip Sidney and Robert Dudley, the earl of Leicester.

In February 1584 he was invited by Fulke Greville, a member of Sidney's circle, to discuss his theory of the movement of the Earth with some Oxonian doctors; but the discussion degenerated into a quarrel. A few days later he started writing his Italian dialogues, which constitute the first systematic exposition of his philosophy. There are six dialogues, three cosmological—on the theory of the universe—and three moral. In the *Cena de le Ceneri* (1584; "The Ash Wednesday Supper"), he not only reaffirmed the reality of the heliocentric theory but also suggested that the universe is infinite, constituted of innumerable worlds substantially similar to those of the solar system. In the same dialogue he anticipated his fellow Italian astronomer Galileo Galilei by maintaining that the Bible should be followed for its moral teaching but not for its astronomical implications. He also strongly criticized the manners of English society and the pedantry of the Oxonian doctors. In the *De la causa, principio e uno* (1584; Eng. trans., *Concerning the Cause, Principle, and One*, 1950) he elaborated the physical theory on which his conception of the universe was based: "form" and "matter" are intimately united and constitute the "one." Thus, the traditional dualism of the Aristotelian physics was reduced by him to a monistic conception of the world, implying the basic unity of all substances and the coincidence of opposites in the infinite unity of Being. In the *De l'infinito universo e mondi* (1584; Eng. trans. *On the Infinite Universe and Worlds*, 1950), he developed his cosmological theory by systematically criticizing Aristotelian physics; he also formulated his Averroistic view of the relation between philosophy and religion, according to which religion is considered as a means to instruct and govern ignorant people, philosophy as the discipline of the elect who are able to behave themselves and govern others. The *Spaccio de la bestia trionfante* (1584; Eng. trans., *The Expulsion of the Triumphant Beast*, 1964), the first dialogue of his moral trilogy, is a satire on contemporary superstitions and vices, embodying a strong criticism of Christian ethics—particularly the Calvinistic principle of salvation by faith alone, to which Bruno opposes an exalted view of the dignity of all human activities. The *Cabala del cavallo Pegaseo* (1585; "Cabal of the Horse Pegasus"), similar to but more pessimistic than the previous work, includes a discussion of the relationship between the human soul and the universal soul, concluding with the negation of the absolute individuality of the former. In the *De gli eroici furori* (1585; Eng. trans., *The Heroic Frenzies*, 1964), Bruno, making use of Neoplatonic imagery, treats the attainment of union with the infinite One by the human soul and exhorts man to the conquest of virtue and truth.

The Italian dialogues

Polemics against mathematicians and philosophers

In October 1585 Bruno returned to Paris, where he found a changed political atmosphere. Henry III had abrogated the edict of pacification with the Protestants, and the King of Navarre had been excommunicated. Far from adopting a cautious line of behaviour, however, Bruno entered into a polemic with a protégé of the Catholic party, the mathematician Fabrizio Mordente, whom he ridiculed in four *Dialogi*, and in May 1586 he dared to attack Aristotle publicly in his *Centum et viginti articuli de natura et mundo adversus Peripateticos* ("120 Articles on Nature and the World against the Peripatetics"). The Politiques thereupon disavowed him, and Bruno left Paris.

He went to Germany, where he wandered from one university city to another, lecturing and publishing a variety of minor works, including the *Articuli centum et sexaginta* (1588; "160 Articles") against contemporary mathematicians and philosophers, in which he expounded his conception of religion—a theory of the peaceful coexistence of all religions based upon mutual understanding and the freedom of reciprocal discussion. At Helmstedt, however, in January 1589 he was excommunicated by the local Lutheran Church. He remained in Helmstedt until the spring, completing works on natural and mathematical magic (posthumously published) and working on three Latin poems—*De minimo*, *De monade*, and *De innumerabilibus sive de immenso*—which re-elaborate the theories expounded in the Italian dialogues and develop Bruno's concept of an atomic basis of matter and being. To publish these, he went in 1590 to Frankfurt am Main, where the senate rejected his application to stay. Nevertheless, he took up residence in the Carmelite convent, lecturing to Protestant doctors and acquiring a reputation of being a "universal man" who, the Prior thought, "did not possess a trace of religion" and who "was chiefly occupied in writing and in the vain and chimerical imagining of novelties."

Final years in Venice and Rome. In August 1591, at the invitation of the Venetian patrician Giovanni Mocenigo, Bruno made the fatal move of returning to Italy. At the time such a move did not seem to be too much of a risk: Venice was by far the most liberal of the Italian states; the European tension had been temporarily eased after the death of the intransigent pope Sixtus V in 1590; the Protestant Henry of Bourbon was now on the throne of France, and a religious pacification seemed to be imminent. Furthermore, Bruno was still looking for an academic platform from which to expound his theories, and he must have known that the chair of mathematics at the University of Padua was then vacant. Indeed, he went almost immediately to Padua and, during the late summer of 1591, started a private course of lectures for German students and composed the *Praelectiones geometricae* and *Ars deformationum*. At the beginning of the winter, when it appeared that he was not going to receive the chair (it was offered to Galileo in 1592), he returned to Venice, as the guest of Mocenigo, and took part in the discussions of progressive Venetian aristocrats who, like Bruno, favoured philosophical investigation irrespective of its theological implications. Bruno's liberty came to an end when Mocenigo—disappointed by his private lessons from Bruno on the art of memory, and resentful of Bruno's intention to go back to Frankfurt to have a new work published—denounced him to the Venetian Inquisition in May 1592 for his heretical theories. Bruno was arrested and tried. He defended himself by admitting minor theological errors, emphasizing, however, the philosophical rather than the theological character of his basic tenets. The Venetian stage of the trial seemed to be proceeding in a way that was favourable to Bruno; then, however, the Roman Inquisition demanded his extradition, and on January 27, 1593, Bruno entered the jail of the Roman palace of the Sant'Uffizio (Holy Office). During the seven-year Roman period of the trial, Bruno at first developed his previous defensive line, disclaiming any particular interest in theological matters and reaffirming the philosophical character of his speculation. This distinction did not satisfy the inquisitors, who demanded an unconditional retraction of his theories. Bruno then made a desperate attempt to demonstrate that his views were not incompatible with the Christian conception of God and creation. The inquisitors rejected his arguments and pressed him for a formal retraction. Bruno finally declared that he had nothing to retract and that he did not even know what he was expected to retract. At that point, Pope Clement VIII ordered that he should be sentenced as an impenitent and pertinacious heretic. On February 8, 1600, when the death sentence was formally read to him, he addressed his judges, saying: "Perhaps your fear in passing judgment on me is greater than mine in receiving it." On February 17 he was brought to the Campo di Fiori, his tongue in a gag, and burned alive.

Denounced to the Inquisition

Influence. Bruno's theories influenced 17th-century scientific and philosophical thought, and since the 18th century, have been absorbed by many modern philosophers. As a symbol of the freedom of thought, Bruno inspired the European liberal movements of the 19th century, particularly the Italian Risorgimento (the movement for national political unity). Because of the variety of his interests, modern scholars are divided as to the chief significance of his work. Bruno's cosmological vision certainly anticipates some fundamental aspects of the modern conception of the universe; his ethical ideas, in contrast with religious ascetical ethics, appeal to modern humanistic activism; and his ideal of religious and philosophical tolerance has influenced liberal thinkers. On the other hand, his emphasis on the magical and the occult has been the source of criticism as has his impetuous personality. Bruno stands, however, as one of the important figures in the history of Western thought, a precursor of modern civilization.

BIBLIOGRAPHY

Editions: Modern editions of Bruno's works are (*Latin*): *Opera latine conscripta*, ed. by FRANCESCO FIORENTINO *et al.*, 3 vol. in 8 parts (1879–91, reprinted 1962), supplemented by *Due dialoghi sconosciuti e due dialoghi noti* (1957) and "*Praelectiones geometricae*" e "*Ars deformationum*" by GIOVANNI AQUILECCHIA (1964), which were unknown to the previous editors. (*Italian*): *Dialoghi Italiani*, by GIOVANNI GENTILE, 3rd ed. by GIOVANNI AQUILECCHIA (1958), is the standard edition of the six dialogues. "Concerning the Cause, Principle and One," in SIDNEY GREENBERG, *The Infinite in Giordano Bruno* (1950); *Cause, Principle and Unity*, by JACK LINDSAY (1962); "On the Infinite Universe and Worlds," in DOROTHEA WALEY SINGER, *Giordano Bruno: His Life and Thought* (1950); *The Expulsion of the Triumphant Beast*, anon. (1713) and by A.D. IMERTI (1964); *The Heroic Frenzies*, by P.E. MEMMO, JR. (1964).

Biography: VINCENZO SPAMPANATO, *Vita di Giordano Bruno* (1921), with an appendix of documents reprinted with new documents in *Documenti della vita di Giordano Bruno*, ed. by VINCENZO SPAMPANATO and GIOVANNI GENTILE (1933); *Il sommario del processo di Giordano Bruno*, ed. by ANGELO MERCATI (1942), a summary and partial transcription of the minutes of the trial; GIOVANNI AQUILECCHIA, *Giordano Bruno* (1971), a synthetic but exhaustive biography, with a bibliographical appendix that substantially brings up to date that contained in VIRGILIO SALVESTRINI, *Bibliografia de Giordano Bruno, 1582–1950*, 2nd posthumous ed. by LUIGI FIRPO (1958).

Critical studies: GIOVANNI GENTILE, *Il pensiero italiano del Rinascimento*, 4th ed. (1968), which considers Bruno as a precursor of the 19th- and 20th-century philosophical Idealism; P.H. MICHEL, *La Cosmologie de Giordano Bruno* (1962), which reacts to the metaphysical interpretation of Bruno's system; PAUL O. KRISTELLER, *Eight Philosophers of the Italian Renaissance* (1964); FRANCES A. YATES, *Giordano Bruno and the Hermetic Tradition* (1964), which reacts to the progressive interpretation of Bruno's thought by considering it as belonging to the occult tradition based on the texts of the pseudo-Hermes Trimegistus; and *The Art of Memory* (1966), which includes a study of Bruno's mnemotechnic works considered against their historical and philosophical background; and FULVIO PAPI, *Antropologia e civiltà nel pensiero di Giordano Bruno* (1968), which includes an original discussion of Bruno's views on human attitudes and civilization.

(G.A.)

Brussels

Brussels in the early 1970s consisted of an agglomeration of more than 1,000,000 inhabitants, divided into 19 administratively autonomous communes centring on Inner Brussels, the capital of the Kingdom of Belgium. Though the average visitor might remain unaware of this dispersal of local government powers, it implies many disadvantages for the inhabitants and holds the key to an understanding of much of the condition of life in the contemporary city. It has impeded the harmonious development of the spreading built-up areas that reflect the continued population influx which has occurred since 1830, and a rational solution to the traffic problem—a crucial difficulty for more than half a century—has been rendered practically impossible.

The importance of local government powers

A further major problem arises from the geographic location of the city, which places it in the Flemish linguistic zone, only a few miles north of the invisible "frontier" separating the Flemish community and the French-speaking community, which between them constitute the Belgian nation. The majority of residents in the Brussels agglomeration, however, speak French, and the area has been the principal venue for often-disruptive clashes between Flemings and Walloons, which have served as a real threat to national unity.

In spite of these difficulties, the historic city, in addition to acting as a major European tourist and cultural attraction, functions simultaneously as regional metropolis, national capital, and international centre. The last-named role has flourished since the city became host to the European communities (made up of the European Economic Community, or European Common Market; the European Coal and Steel Community; and the European Atomic Energy Community) as well as to the North Atlantic Treaty Organization (NATO) headquarters. Over 80 ambassadors are now accredited to the king of the Belgians, to the European Common Market, or to NATO.

HISTORY

Brussels owes its origin to the establishment, in the 6th century, of a fortified castle on a little island in the River Senne (Flemish Zenne), a tributary of the Schelde (French Escaut) flowing from south to north, and to an east–west economic route linking the Rhenish towns with those in the county of Flanders.

A market and bartering place developed under the protection of the dukes of Brabant, at the point where road and river crossed. Craftsmen and merchants settled in

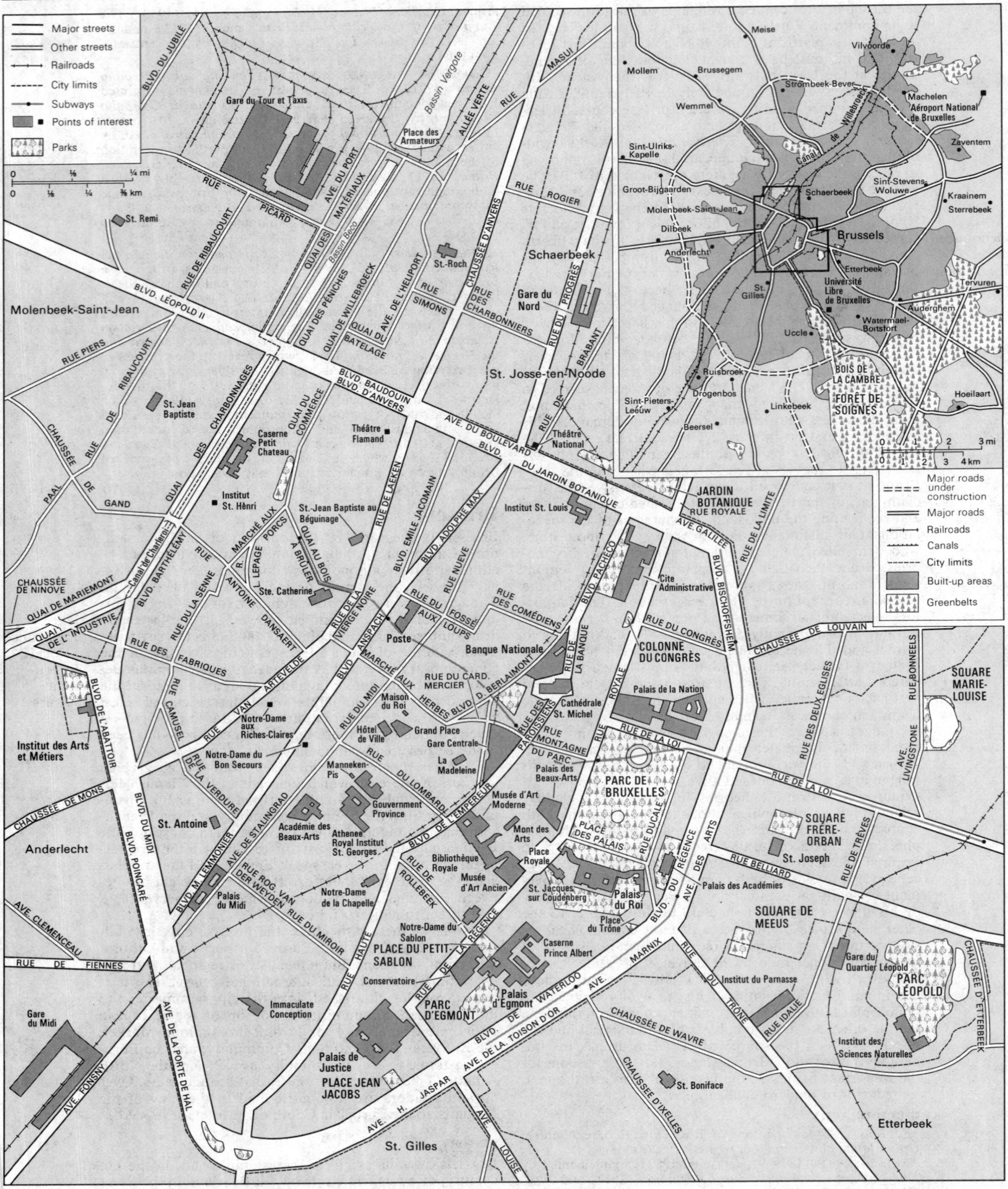

Central Brussels and (inset) its metropolitan area. For most places, French names have been used; Flemish equivalents have equal official standing.

increasing numbers in the locality, which they called Bruoc-sella (the Settlement in the Marshes). By the 11th century the little community was protected by encircling ramparts with towers and seven fortified gateways.

During the 12th, 13th, and 14th centuries the manufacture of luxury fabrics, exported to fairs in the Champagne region of France, Paris, Venice, and elsewhere, occupied thousands of workers. It also made fortunes for a few enterprising merchant families, who developed into seven dynasties that, with the help of the duke of Brabant, acquired a position of complete political mastery. In control of business and municipal affairs, they also exercised power as magistrates, giving rulings on disputes and conflicts arising among the inhabitants; the prevailing regime was, in fact, strongly plutocratic in nature.

Abuse of such powers provoked violent popular uprisings, in 1280, in 1303, in 1421. This last upheaval led to a more democratic system, with local powers divided between the patrician families, on the one hand, and the emergent guilds of craftsmen and other workers, on the other.

Events of particular significance in the 14th century were the invasion of the duchy of Brabant by the Count of Flanders' troops, their occupation of Brussels, the town's liberation, and the construction immediately afterward (1357) of huge surrounding fortified walls, which survived until 1830.

Burgundian era

In 1430 the duchy was merged in the possessions of the duke of Burgundy. The Burgundian period, which lasted until 1477, was one of political and artistic prestige. Brussels became the seat of the central administrative bodies for the ducal possessions in the Low Countries, which constituted a rich centre of art and culture. Pictures by Rogier van der Weyden, the officially appointed town painter, sculptures in wood, large tapestries with historic motifs, plate, jewelry, and other products by Brussels craftsmen came to be exported in all directions.

Brussels began to beautify itself: by the marketplace, the Hôtel de Ville (Town Hall) (1402–54) rose proudly, with its tall perforated steeple surmounted by a statue of the archangel Michael, the city's patron saint. Various Gothic churches and cathedrals—the Cathedral of St. Michel and Ste. Gudule, Notre-Dame du Sablon, Notre-Dame de la Chapelle—and the ducal Coudenberg Palace, with its extensive park, added to the architectural splendour.

Brussels retained its position as a capital during the reign of Charles V (1515–55), Holy Roman Emperor. The three government councils (the Council of State, the Privy Council, and the Finance Council) were established there permanently. The population reached nearly 50,000. In the later part of the 16th century the Canal de Willebroeck (Kanaal van Willebroek) was dug to provide a direct link with the Rupel and the Schelde rivers; in other words, with the port of Antwerp. Replacing the sandy little river, this channel was to play an important commercial role.

The reign of Archduke Albert and Isabella (1598–1633) left its mark on the urban surroundings with the construction of a series of fine churches in the Italo-Flemish Baroque style: St. Jean Baptiste au Béguinage, Notre-Dame aux Riches-Claires, Notre-Dame du Bon Secours, and others, nearly all of which are still in existence. The second half of the 17th century witnessed repeated invasions by the armies of Louis XIV of France. During a bombardment by his troops in 1695, hundreds of buildings were destroyed by fire, including the various craft headquarters. Out of this catastrophe there arose the new guild houses, constituting the architectural marvels now surrounding Grand Place, the heart of the Old Town.

Baroque churches

Three-quarters of a century later, the upper part of the town was the scene of urban planning on a large scale, which resulted in the Place Royale (Royal Square) and a park on the French model, perfectly symmetrical, surrounded by Neoclassic buildings lining rue Royale, rue Ducale, rue de la Loi, and the Place des Palais. The former Court Chapel was replaced by the church of St. Jacques sur Coudenberg. The largest building in the rue de la Loi has served as national Parliament since 1830; it houses the Chamber of Representatives and Senate.

The Hôtel de Ville (Town Hall) in the Grand Place, Brussels, built 1402–54.
By courtesy of Sabena Belgian World Airlines

Following the Brabant revolt against the government of Emperor Joseph II of Austria, the French republican armies made their appearance, and the Belgian principalities were annexed to France. Under the Napoleonic empire, Brussels was reduced to the rank of chief town of the French *département* of the Dyle, losing into the bargain all authority over its satellite villages.

One of the consequences of Napoleon's defeat at Waterloo was the creation of the Kingdom of The Netherlands, which lasted 15 years (1815–30). During this period Brussels shared the status of capital with The Hague. Its appearance changed appreciably, above all because of the demolition of the city walls and their replacement by treelined boulevards, as well as the digging of the Canal de Charleroi, which from 1832 onward made waterborne transport possible from as far as the province of Hainaut to the port of Antwerp via the capital.

Independence of Belgium

In 1830 came revolution; Belgium won its independence, and, in the constitution adopted by the National Congress, Brussels, which had played a major role in the fighting, was named the capital of Belgium and the seat of government.

MODERN BRUSSELS

Topography. Since Belgium became an independent kingdom in 1830, Brussels has been transformed, in the Old Town as well as in the surrounding communes. The determining factor in this metamorphosis has been incessant population pressure, which caused a building boom and the development of an ever-widening network of streets, avenues, and roads crisscrossing the countryside, urbanizing the neighbouring villages.

At first the urban tentacles only pushed forward along the seven or eight routes radiating from the city's toll gates, but subsequently they also spread out along many new roads after the toll system was abolished, in 1860.

The suburbs expanded rapidly beyond the town gates, so that by the end of the 19th century the territory of several of the first ring communes was completely or almost completely covered by residential building. The expansion, moreover, continued vigorously in the following century, in spite of enemy occupation during World Wars I and II. All four points of the compass were involved: north and south along the valley of the Senne, east and west on the undulating plateaus separated by the tributaries of the Senne (Maalbeek, Woluwe, and others).

As a result, the landscape was entirely changed. With rare exceptions, the ponds and pools of earlier days were filled in, most of the hollows were banked up, the clear streams covered over and converted into sewers, the small woods cut down, fields, pastures, and orchards parcelled out for development, and footpaths eliminated. The River Senne became a main sewer running under the wide, straight boulevards of Inner Brussels, linking the North (1841) and the South (1869) railway stations.

Greater Brussels is not entirely built over, mainly because, with the increasingly common use of rapid means of transport, urban development has been by means of leapfrogging to satellite communities rather than by continuous, uninterrupted expansion. If the Middle Ages had endowed Inner Brussels with a geometric pentagonal configuration, modern times gave the sprawling metropolis the appearance of an amoeba. Its boundaries are continually changing, though legislation in the latter third of the 20th century on the linguistic problem may cause the outlines to be fixed rigidly (the laws being popularly known as the *carcan*, or "straitjacket").

Inner Brussels is divided between the commercial quarter and the upper town, where the principal governmental buildings are situated. The commercial quarter extends from the western outer boulevards to a little east of the central boulevards and includes the Grand Place. This square is occupied on its south side by the town hall and on its north by the ornate Maison du Roi (almost entirely rebuilt during 1873–95), which contains the historical museum. One of the curiosities of this quarter is the Manneken-Pis Fountain (1619), noted for a bronze statue of a boy urinating and known to the people of Brussels as their oldest "citizen."

The upper town is the remaining eastern area of the city proper. It is crossed from southwest to northeast by a thoroughfare formed by the rue de la Régence, which, at the Place Royale, becomes the rue Royale. On this street are the Palais du Roi and the Palais de la Nation. The latter was erected (1779–83) by the Austrian governors and after independence became the home of the Senate and the Chamber of Representatives. It stands at the intersection of the rue Royale and the rue de la Loi, an area that has become a symbol for the national government. Between the Palais de la Nation and the Palais du Roi is a large public park, extending along the rue Royale, and nearby are the Bibliothèque Royale (Royal Library), the Musée d'Art Moderne (Museum of Modern Art), and the Musée d'Art Ancien (Museum of Ancient Art).

The people. In the Old Town (the Pentagon), population continued to grow until 1890, reaching 159,374 from 99,552 inhabitants in 1831. The numbers then decreased successively from 141,558 in 1900 to 104,718 in 1930, 66,570 in 1961, and 60,000 in 1966.

A period of expanding population was thus followed by a very marked decline in density. Inner Brussels was partially emptied of inhabitants. By annexing some adjacent areas (in 1853, 1864, and again in 1921), the losses were nevertheless counterbalanced, and the total reached 200,433 in 1930. A decline set in thereafter, and in 1970 the figure had gone down to just over 160,000.

The same phenomenon of rising density followed by a fall occurred in the inner ring of abutting communes, the turning point occurring in 1910. These seven communes, which among them had only 21,338 inhabitants in 1831, contained a population of more than 500,000 in 1961. In the second ring of communes, during the period 1831 to 1961 the population rose from 16,283 to 350,309.

20th-century immigration

The immigrants came from all over: at first from the villages of Brabant, then from farther afield—whether from the Walloon provinces or the Flemish provinces—and from beyond the national frontiers, from European countries and overseas. In 1961 the number of inhabitants of foreign nationality amounted to 31,000 (French, Italian, Dutch, German, British, Spanish, American).

The influx of foreigners has proceeded apace since then. It has been calculated that between 1962 and 1966, for example, the number of people arriving from abroad to settle in one of the 19 communes of Brussels just exceeded 100,000. In this four-year period the largest contingents of newcomers originated from Spain, North Africa (Algerians, Moroccans, Tunisians), France, and Italy. In some of the decaying areas of Brussels a solid group of foreigners replaced the original residents. In the St. Gilles area, for example, the proportion of foreigners, mainly Spanish, reached one-third by the 1970s, and some primary schools had more foreign children than Belgian children. The former city-centre inhabitants moved outward toward more open areas on the outskirts. It is here that the well-to-do families, the officials of the European institutions, and the representatives of Brussels subsidiaries of important foreign firms establish themselves: the detached single-family house and the luxury villa, with its green lawns, flower beds, and trees, are multiplying, contrasting with the burgeoning inner-city skyscrapers.

The economy. In the early days of national independence, in the 1830s, food markets in the Old Town were supplied by the neighbouring villages. These have since been urbanized, and there are hardly any peasants left. Industrial, commercial, and service activities have been substituted for rural work.

On Greater Brussels' south–north axis, along the valley of the Senne, where canals and docks servicing the port of Brussels have been developed and where the railway lines run, an exclusively industrial zone has sprung up, which is being extended year by year both northward and southward. A maritime station and huge warehouses have been erected near the docks. At the same time, domestic and foreign banking institutions and insurance companies have appeared in the commercial centre in increasing numbers.

Economic and financial importance of the city

Most of the big Belgian industrial and commercial concerns have their registered offices in Brussels, so it constitutes the decision-making centre for economic and financial affairs. All the more so since, with the establishment of the European Common Market, many multinational corporations have set up their regional coordinating offices there.

United States companies with offices in Brussels numbered well over 400 by the early 1970s, and nearly a fifth of them functioned as European headquarters. An indication of Brussels' economic importance can be derived from the fact that there were well over 25,000 employers in the metropolis and nearly 500,000 manual workers, clerks, and shop assistants. There are also many independent craftsmen working in the flourishing luxury trades.

In sum, Brussels has developed into an international economic centre, with an important stock exchange and annual commercial fair.

Political and governmental institutions. A de facto capital since the 15th century, Brussels became the de jure capital of the Kingdom of Belgium in 1830. The king has his palace there, facing the Palais de la Nation, which houses the Chamber of Representatives and the Senate. For a long time the various ministries were close by, but several have migrated to the Résidence Palace and to an enormous functional administrative block.

The Belgian constitution stipulates that matters concerning individual communes only are to be settled by the local council, according to principles laid down in the constitution. In 1836 Parliament passed the "organic" communal law, which provided for the autonomy of each commune. This explains why Greater Brussels for long was governed by 19 separate authorities and not by one single authority.

Constitutional change of 1970

In December 1970 Parliament drastically amended the constitution to provide for the recognition of five large urban agglomerations (Brussels, Antwerp, Ghent, Liège, and Charleroi), as well as federations of communes. This paved the way for the administration of Greater Brussels by an "Agglomeration Council" empowered to deal with a series of technical problems involving the 19 communes as a whole. Five of the new federations of communes surround Greater Brussels. Each of the 19 communes of Brussels continued, however, to have its own council, municipal establishments, burgomaster, and alderman.

The council is a deliberative assembly whose members are elected by universal suffrage; the aldermen are chosen by the councillors from among themselves; the burgomaster is appointed by the king, being usually selected from among the councillors. Representing the head of state in the commune, it is his duty to see that general and provincial laws and regulations are carried out. He acts as local chief of police, and in emergencies he can take whatever steps are necessary to maintain or restore public order. The burgomaster of Brussels is a political figure of importance.

Local government employees in the communes are under the control of either the council and college or the registrar or the burgomaster. The most important official is the communal secretary, serving the council, the aldermen, and the burgomaster and coordinating the work of the various administrative departments.

Public services. Brussels' communal services have proliferated since 1830 under the impact of increased population and the demands of modern technological civilization. The effect of larger scale and faster speed has inevitably meant staff inflation in existing administrative departments as well as the creation of many new ones, such as the water, gas, and electricity administrations and the departments for youth and sports, for the aged, for burial services, and for education and the fine arts. Inner Brussels has played an exemplary role in setting up scholastic institutions, most notably its generous contributions to the foundation in 1834 of the Université Libre de Bruxelles (Free University of Brussels) and to its development.

Several of the communal industrial administrations have been replaced by intercommunal corporations (water, gas, electricity). The public transport services (trams and buses) have been entrusted to a corporation of this kind. The construction and maintenance of motorways, however, is the responsibility of the Belgian state; that is to say, the Ministries of Public Works and of Communications, which has developed a "semimetro" network (electric train routes running half underground) designed to cover Greater Brussels.

Responsibility for the Belgian railway system, of which Brussels is the focal point, is entirely in the hands of a national company. The electrified lines to neighbouring countries all pass through Brussels stations. A special line links the Gare Centrale (Central Station) and the Aéroport National de Bruxelles (Brussels National Airport) in less than 20 minutes.

Recreation and cultural life. Brussels is an artistic and tourist centre, with a wide variety of cultural activities. In addition to the Free University—divided into a French-speaking university and a Flemish-speaking university—the Institut Saint Louis faculties (Catholic), the royal academies of science, medicine, French language and literature, and Flemish language and literature, and various other institutes of higher learning are based there, as are the Military College, the Albert I Library, and many communal and national museums.

Educational institutions

The Palais des Beaux-Arts provides a cultural centre for those interested in painting, sculpture, films, music, literature, and the theatre. It is the headquarters of the Philharmonic Society and the National Federation of Youth and Music. The Queen Elizabeth International Music Competition attracts connoisseurs every year. Midday poetry readings and midday concerts are held weekly. Most of the communes in the agglomération have, on the model of the Palais des Beaux-Arts, established cultural centres that organize exhibitions, various stage shows, and concerts.

Foremost among some 30 theatres is the Théâtre National (National Theatre). Théâtre Royal de la Monnaie, with a long-standing reputation, has been rejuvenated by a dynamic management. Cinemas are still plentiful, in spite of television competition.

Many secular and religious monuments of architectural interest embellish the Old Town and some of the suburbs. And not far from the urban centre are scenic walks in the magnificent beech groves of the Forêt de Soignes and its offshoot, the Bois de la Cambre.

BIBLIOGRAPHY. The standard books are: A. HENNE and A. WAUTERS, *Histoire de la ville de Bruxelles*, 3 vol. (1845, reprinted 1970), with detailed coverage of monuments; A. WAUTERS, *Histoire des environs de Bruxelles . . .* , 3 vol. (1851–57); and G. DES MAREZ, *Guide illustré de Bruxelles, monuments civils et religieux*, 4th ed. brought up to date and supplemented by A. ROUSSEAU (1958), an excellent handbook. For further reading: P. GOUROU, *L'Agglomération bruxelloise, eléments de géographie urbaine* (1958), a study by a leading French urban geographer; L. VERNIERS, *Bruxelles et son agglomération de 1830 à nos jours* (1958) and *Un Millénaire d'historie de Bruxelles, depuis les origines jusq'en 1830* (1965), a general view of urban evolution; R. MOLS, *Bruxelles et les Bruxellois* (1961); G. JACQUEMYNS, *Histoire contemporaine du Grand-Bruxelles* (1936).

(L.Ve.)

Bryopsida

The mosses are comparatively small green plants, most of which are comfortably visible to the unaided eye but much better seen with a hand lens. They constitute the class Bryopsida of the division Bryophyta. Commonest in moist, shady locations, mosses are perhaps best known for those species that carpet woodland and forest floors. Mosses, which number about 600 genera and 15,000 species, have trailing or erect stemlike structures called caulids and leaflike appendages called phyllids, organs that differ in many respects from the stems and leaves of higher plants.

The name moss often has been misapplied to other plants, among them Spanish moss (a flowering plant), club mosses (fern relatives), sea mosses (marine algae or seaweeds), and reindeer moss and beard moss (lichens). A phylum of marine invertebrates consists of creatures so mosslike in appearance that they are called Bryozoa, meaning "moss-animal."

In spite of little direct economic importance, with the exception of peat mosses (*Sphagnum*) discussed later, mosses are of interest scientifically because they exhibit a conspicuous alternation of generations, provide clues to past floras, and are valuable plants for studies in plant physiology. They also play a role in the natural biotic community and even an esthetic one for man.

GENERAL FEATURES

Mosses range in size from the microscopic terrestrial forms (*Ephemerum, Nanomitrium*), difficult to see without a hand lens, to the robust, erect moss *Dawsonia* of Australia and neighbouring areas, which may be over two feet tall, with "leaves" an inch long.

Common names are infrequent for the mosses, but some kinds are named for their interesting form (Figure 1): tree moss (*Climacium*); wind-blown moss (*Dicranum*); feather moss (*Ptilium*); extinguisher moss (*Encalypta*); turkish-slipper moss (*Diphyscium*); rose moss (*Rhodobryum roseum*); bug-on-a-stick (*Buxbaumia*), which lacks an easily visible leafy stem; and elfin-gold (*Schistostega*), a stage of which contains lens-shaped cells that can reflect available light from the crevices of caves or cellars.

Geographic distribution

Mosses are found almost everywhere except in marine water or salt waters. They occur from the Antarctic to the Arctic; in the latter they are an important part of the tundra vegetation. They also are abundant in tropical and temperate rain forests, where they may hang in festoons from the trees and form deep cushions on soil, logs, and boulders. They are scarce but not absent in

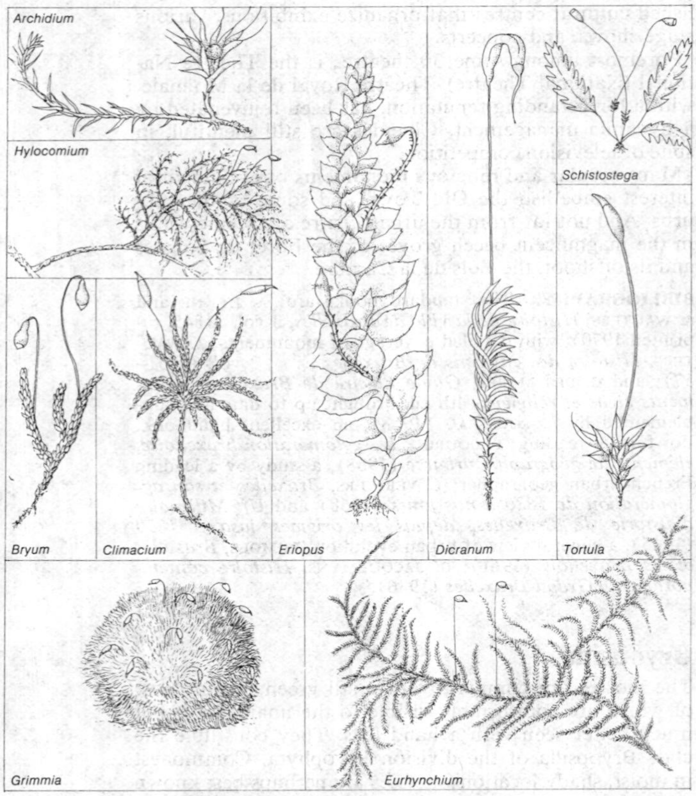

Figure 1: Diversity among bryid mosses.
Drawing by M. Pahl based on *An Evolutionary Survey of the Plant Kingdom* by R.F. Scagel, G.E. Rouse, J.R. Stein, R.J. Bandoni, W.B. Schofield, T.M.C. Taylor. © 1965 by Wadsworth Publishing Company, Belmont, California. Reprinted by permission of the publisher.

deserts, and aquatic forms are frequent in seeps, springs, brooks, and on the margins of freshwater bodies. A very few (*e.g., Grimmia maritima*) are found on rocks along the seashore, above the tideline.

Although much of the literature implies that mosses are widely dispersed over the world, most of them have distribution patterns that more or less match those of seed plants. Some, such as *Gollania turgens,* have peculiar ranges not easily explained on a basis of presently known facts; such species may be useful in testing the validity of long-range dispersal, persistence in microenvironments when other larger plants have been eliminated, and other theories in plant geography.

Useful mosses

Only the bog or peat mosses in the genus *Sphagnum* have significant direct economic value. They are the chief components of peat bogs, often covering acres and filling lakes and kettle holes left by glacial activity. Through slow decomposition these mosses change into peat as the older growth is pushed under water by new growth at the top. Under compression in nature, peat can be changed into lignite, which is used as fuel in peaty areas. Some *Sphagnum* species absorb and retain 35 times their dry weight of water and synthesize sphagnol, chemically akin to phenol and somewhat effective as an antiseptic.

Bog water used to be carried on long sea voyages because it only very slowly became stagnant. *Sphagnum* moss is still used locally by primitive people for diapers and menstrual pads and as recently as World War I was a component of many surgical dressings. Peat is useful in conditioning soils, for packing nursery stock and cut flowers, and as litter in animal quarters, where it absorbs odour as well as moisture.

Other mosses were used rather extensively in the past. Pigeon wheat, or hair-cap moss (*Polytrichum*), and carpet moss (*Hypnum*) have been used as filler in bedding. Pigeon wheat, often over a foot high, has been used in making brooms and dusters, and the stems stripped of their leaves and outer layers were plaited into baskets and other articles. Mosses have been used as ornaments, especially on women's hats, and for Christmas decorations in Latin America, where bales of mosses are gathered and shipped from the mountains each December. Some mosses retard erosion; species of *Pogonatum* forming extensive feltlike mats are particularly effective in stabilizing exposed slopes.

Some mosses are used in landscaping, especially in the moss gardens of Japan, notably in Kyōto. While most mosses are very sensitive to pollution, one species, *Tortula pagorum*, seems to do better in a polluted atmosphere than in clean air. Mosses have been used as indicators of forest conditions; their abundance may reveal unpolluted fog zones and layers of humid air.

NATURAL HISTORY

Life cycle. The mosses, like the liverworts, exhibit a well-defined alternation of generations between a gametophyte phase, whose cells contain a single set of chromosomes (n), and a sporophyte phase, whose cells contain a double set of chromosomes (2n). It is convenient to begin discussion of the moss life cycle with the spore (Figure 2). When a spore (n) alights in a favourable spot, it germinates into an inconspicuous threadlike network called a protonema, a juvenile gametophyte. In time, the protonemata produce buds that give rise to adult gametophytes (n).

The adult gametophyte is the conspicuous leafy green, photosynthetic plant popularly called moss. It contains, at maturity, two kinds of sex organs: the archegonia, or female organs, each of which can produce a single, large egg (n); and the antheridia, or male organs, each of which produce numerous small motile sperm (n). The zygote, or fertilized egg (2n), formed in the basal portion of the archegonium by the union of an egg and a sperm, begins the sporophyte phase.

The young sporophyte (2n), embedded in the nutritive tissue of the enlarged archeogonium (now called the calyptra), grows very rapidly. Eventually its needlelike seta ruptures the top part of the calyptra and carries it aloft like a hood, beneath which the spore capsule (sporangium) develops. At maturity, sporocytes, or spore

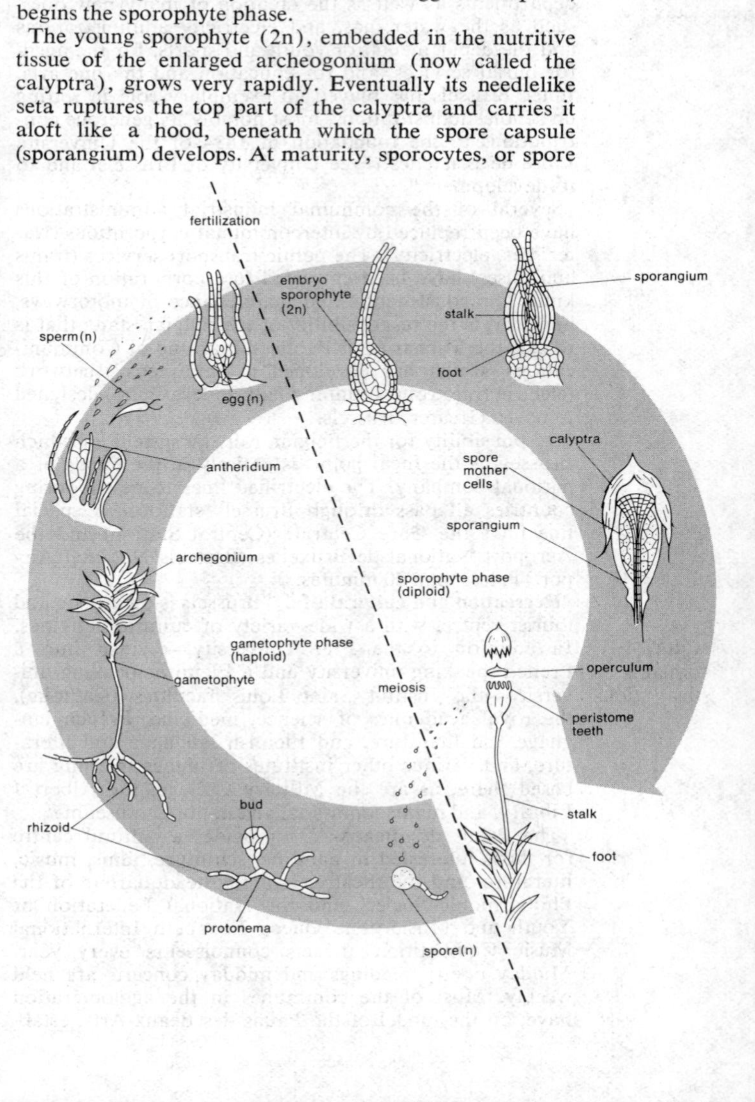

mother cells (2n) in the sporangium, undergo reduction division (meiosis) and produce spores (n). The spores are then shed, and the cycle repeats.

Habitat range. Mosses restricted to a particular type of rock or to the bark of a specific kind of tree cannot, of course, extend beyond the range of these substrates. Mosses such as the silvery bryum (*Bryum argenteum*), the cord moss (*Funaria hygrometrica*), and the horn-tooth moss (*Ceratodon purpureus*) are common and almost cosmopolitan in distribution. Some species, however, are characteristic of vegetation types; *Anomodon rugelii* seems restricted to the eastern deciduous forest of North America, and the stair-step moss (*Hylocomium splendens*) is seldom found outside the northern coniferous forest and the tundra.

Special habitat restrictions

There are many curious restrictions to habitats among the mosses. Members of the family Splachnaceae, which require much nitrogen, are usually found on dung, badly decayed carcasses, and owl pellets; the most extensive growth known occurs on the soil at Point Barrow, Alaska, where whales were once butchered by the Eskimos. Another group, of which *Merceya* is an example, is called the "copper mosses"; they are usually found on or near copper-containing soil, but it is not clear whether copper or sulfur, or a combination of the two, is a prerequisite for their growth. *Didymodon tophaceus, Fissidens grandifrons, Eucladium verticillatum,* and additional moss species seem to grow best on limestone rocks in waters heavily charged with calcium salts. In the Americas, *Pleurochaete squarrosa* is characteristic of limestone in *Juniperus* barrens.

In some forests, tree seeds seem to germinate better in a moss carpet. Mosses, along with liverworts, lichens, and often algae, are usually the first plants to colonize new or recently exposed substrates. In new mineral soils, such as volcanic sand, they build up organic material. On logs they delay water loss, facilitating the growth of decay organisms. Rocks are more rapidly fragmented by the freezing of water retained by mosses and by the actions of chemicals secreted by these plants. Mosses serve as habitats for mites, tardigrades, and insects and are used as materials for some bird nests. Mice and lemmings harvest the spore capsules of the larger mosses for food.

FORM AND FUNCTION

The gametophyte. *The protonemal phase.* Almost as remarkable as the contrast between the gametophyte and the sporophyte phase is the difference between the juvenile gametophyte, or protonema, and the adult gametophyte. The almost microscopic protonemata may be thalloid (irregularly leaflike or ribbonlike) or threadlike; they often resemble richly branching algal webs, especially in the order of Bryales. After a period of growth and the attainment of a certain size and maturity, a protonema produces buds that will develop into adult gametophytes.

The adult gametophyte. The individual moss plant that one usually observes is the green plant with narrow leaflike phyllids arranged spirally along a stemlike caulid. The gametophytes of some mosses resemble tiny trees with clusters of branches on the tip of the main shoot; others are unbranched and erect or branched at the base of the caulid, with parallel shoots; still others recline along the ground and branch irregularly. The phyllids are usually of simple outline and often resemble true leaves; they are usually one cell thick.

At certain times of the year, sex organs develop among the phyllids at the lip of a caulid: the flask-shaped female archegonium and the elongated male antheridium. In some species, called homothallic, both kinds of sex organ occur on the same individual gametophyte; other species are heterothallic, the archegonia occurring on one individual and the antheridia on another.

In the acrocarpous mosses, archegonia are borne terminally on the main stem; in the pleurocarpous forms they occur on very short lateral branches. The former are more often erect plants, the latter, prostrate.

Use of the phyllids in identification

In identifying mosses by use of the gametophyte, the phyllids are more useful than the caulids. Variations occur in the shape of the phyllids, the nature of their margins, and the presence or absence of a midrib (costa). Also of interest is the apex of the phyllid: it may be rounded, acute, or extremely slender, sometimes ending in a hair. The bases sometimes may form short wings down the caulid and at times have areas of specialized alar cells in the angles. Phyllids of *Aloina* have short, upright filaments on top, and those of the Polytrichaceae have ribbonlike plates (lamellae) of green cells longitudinally attached by one edge to the upper surface. The size and shape of cells in the phyllid, and the thickness of the cell walls, are useful characters, as is the nature of the external surface of the phyllid, which may be smooth or covered with minute or larger "pimples" (papillae). In a few species (*Thelia*) the papillae are unusually large, and with fantastic shapes.

The sporophyte. The moss sporophyte, in contrast to that of the liverwort, usually elongates gradually throughout its development. The mature sporophyte is embedded in the basal portion of the archegonium by a "foot," through which nutrients may diffuse from the gametophyte. The sporange is usually elevated on a stemlike seta (absent in a few species), which sometimes has a differentiated central strand that may serve as a conductive tissue (water, however, seems to diffuse into the plants through most surfaces).

The sporangium is often cylindrical (sometimes curved) but in some species is spherical or ovoid. Usually under the calyptra is a differentiated lid (operculum), which falls off at maturity. The operculum may be a short cone or, at the other extreme, a very slender, beaked "dunce cap." When it falls, the opening left sometimes is naked but more often is surrounded by one or two rings (peristomes) of slender, triangular teeth; the absence or presence of peristomes and, if present, whether they are composed of one or two rows of teeth are highly significant in identifying mosses. These teeth flare outward when dry, apparently enhancing wind dissemination of the spores. The shape of the peristome teeth and their markings (whether smooth, punctate, or striated) are useful, as is the presence or absence of stomates with guard cells in the basal half of the sporange.

The spore-bearing tissue is in the shape of a hollow cylinder surrounding a central column (columella) of sterile cells. The spores are unicellular and small, usually much less than 1/10 millimetre in diameter. Some germinate within the sporange and give the appearance of being multicellular. Nearly all spores have chloroplasts, which increase in number as the protonema develops. In most mosses the spores appear uniform; but in at least one species of *Macromitrium* there are two size types, which may reflect an incipient heterospory characteristic of the higher plants, the larger spore apparently giving rise to female gametophytes and the smaller to male gametophytes.

Asexual reproduction

Perhaps the most frequent type of reproduction in the mosses (and in some the only method known) is asexual. Each cell of the gametophyte and most cells of the sporophyte seem capable of developing into a new gametophyte if provided with a suitable environment. Often specialized cells or groups of cells (gemmae, propagula, or brood bodies) grow from the caulids or phyllids and when broken loose may grow into new plants. Most amazing is the growth under certain conditions of a sporophyte from some vegetative portion of the gametophyte—for instance, from the tip of a phyllid. Segments of developing sporophytes can give rise to new protonemata, which form gametophytes with twice the usual number of chromosomes per nucleus.

The chromosomes of mosses are small, and the number per nucleus is relatively low. The basic number ranges between 6 and 13 (with the exception of *Sphagnum*, which has 21) with the commonest probably being 11. One of the curiosities of mosses is the occurrence of tiny "m" chromosomes, of unknown significance.

The mosses have proved to be valuable cytological and

genetic material because it is relatively easy to double the number of chromosomes per nucleus by using segments of a young sporophyte in culture as the source of new protonemata.

Some mosses exhibit sex chromosomes, which often control size as well as sex of gametophytes. In one species of *Homaliadelphus* the male gametophytes are small enough that they can grow as epiphytes upon the phyllids of the female.

Physiological responses. Mosses respond physiologically in much the same manner as higher plants. Both gametophytes and sporophytes are provided with chloroplasts, which photosynthesize to produce carbohydrates and starch grains. Food also may be stored in spores and gemmae in the form of oil droplets.

The requirements of mosses for various minerals are not essentially different from those of vascular plants. Mosses can grow, however, in dilute cultures or even in distilled water for some time. Most of them respond to changes in light quality, intensity, and periodicity. Two of the most easily observed responses are the formation of buds on the protonema and the growth of these buds into leafy gametophytes, which are influenced by the factors mentioned above and also by growth promoting and regulating substances and other chemicals. *Funaria hygrometrica, Physcomitrium turbinatum,* and related species are mosses most commonly grown in culture.

Terrestrial gametophytes grown at low light intensities or high humidities or both become spindly and yellow, with elongated caulids and reduced phyllids, much as do the stems and leaves of seed plants under such conditions. This response may help explain why it is frequently difficult to identify the various forms of a single species developed in different habitats.

Resistance to fungi and insects

Mosses seem to resist infestations by most fungi and are not usually seriously damaged by insects. They do possess an antibiotic material not yet fully identified and exploited, which may account for their antifungal properties. Some fungi (*Pleurotus* and *Pestalozzia* species), however, do parasitize mosses, and others can intermingle with protonema to form lichen-like associations.

Mosses can withstand extremes of temperature and of desiccation. They have the remarkable ability to remain dormant under very warm environments or dry environments or both and quickly revive and grow again under suitable conditions. This is true in the case of the remarkable black species of *Grimmia* and other genera that grow on hot, dry, exposed rocks.

EVOLUTION AND CLASSIFICATION

Fossil distribution. Not many mosses are known from the geological record. Fossils from Permian rocks in the U.S.S.R. resemble the modern genera *Mnium, Bryum,* and *Sphagnum*, but no reproductive structures have been found. *Sphagnum* has been reported also from Jurassic and Cretaceous beds. The largest number of fossil mosses, and the best preserved, are found in the peats of the Pliocene and Pleistocene beds, many of which can be related to modern genera and some to species still living today.

Distinguishing taxonomic features. The characters that separate the class Bryopsida (mosses) from the rest of the Bryophyta and that distinguish the subclasses, primarily, are those found in the sporophyte, particularly the sporange. They include the presence or absence of a slowly elongating seta, or pseudopodium (a false seta formed as a specialized branch of the gametophyte), the degree of specialization in the exterior of the sporange, the amount of its internal differentiation, and the nature of the opening through which the spores are dispersed. The nature of the protonema, the first structure formed following spore germination, is also significant.

Annotated classification. The following classification is modified from a classical taxonomic scheme.

CLASS BRYOPSIDA

Protonema usually filamentous; seta or pseudopodium gradually elongating; the sporange with a tough epidermis, opening by a deciduous operculum or by 4 slits down the side (rarely without either), and with a sterile columella in the centre. Mature gametophyte never thalloid. About 600 genera and 15,000 species.

Order Sphagnales (peat or bog mosses)

Protonema thalloid, at maturity usually erect and much branched with many phyllids, very absorbent by reason of many large, empty cells with pores in the walls. Seta lacking, but sporophyte borne on a pseudopodium. Sporange spherical with operculum, but no peristome. Spore-bearing tissue thimble-shaped over a domelike columella. Usually found in bogs or on wet acid substrates. A single genus, *Sphagnum.*

Order Andreaeales (granite mosses)

Protonema thalloid; at maturity usually erect, small, dark, with many compactly arranged phyllids. Seta lacking, but sporophyte borne on a short pseudopodium. Capsule cylindrical without operculum, opening by 4 equidistant, longitudinal slits. Spore-bearing tissue shaped like an elongated thimble over a finger-shaped columella. Usually found on exposed, noncalcareous rock; occasionally on sand in bed of intermittent streams at high latitudes. Represented by the genus *Andreaea,* with about 100 species, and a problematical species or two.

Order Bryales (true mosses)

Protonema filamentous; at maturity, erect, ascending or prostrate, usually with many phyllids, variously coloured. Seta present in most species (pseudopodia always absent). Sporange cylindrical to spherical usually with a deciduous operculum beneath which is the peristome (occasionally lacking). Spore-bearing tissue shaped like a hollow cylinder around a sterile, central columella. Stomata frequently present in the basal half of the capsule. Found on various substrata in many environments. The bulk of the genera (500) and species of mosses; including *Bryum, Mnium, Eriopus, Hylocomium,* and *Funaria.*

Critical appraisal. An earlier, time-honoured classification still enjoying currency places the mosses in the class Musci of the division Bryophyta. Some systems have restricted the division Bryophyta to include only the mosses (the liverworts then becoming the Hepatophyta). The mosses have enough characters in common with the liverworts to indicate that they are rather closely related, however, and should be placed together in the division Bryophyta. The classification used in this article is one of several that may find wider acceptance as more information accumulates.

The order Bryales, in contrast to the other two orders, is much more variable in all respects and may be subdivided into families in several ways. It has been suggested that some families (*e.g.,* Polytrichaceae) be given the rank of an order. When the great diversity within the Bryales is considered, it seems more manageable to retain these divergent forms within this order. Some botanists would raise the orders Sphagnales, Andreaeales, and Bryales to subclass or class rank. Until more is known about their origin and more data is available about extant species, no taxonomic arrangement can be made with security; perhaps it may never be done.

BIBLIOGRAPHY. Works concerned with the botanical details of mosses include: W.T. DOYLE, *The Biology of Higher Cryptograms* (1970); N.S. PARIHAR, *An Introduction to Embryophyta,* 5th ed., vol. 1, *Bryophyta* (1965); W.C. STEERE, "Evolution and Speciation in Mosses," *Am. Nat.,* 92:5–20 (1958); and E.V. WATSON, *The Structure and Life of Bryophytes* (1964). References helpful in the identification of mosses include: H.S. CONARD, *How to Know the Mosses and Liverworts* (1956), a good manual for American mosses; A.J. GROUT, *Mosses with a Hand-Lens,* 4th ed. (1947), a field guide to American mosses, *Moss Flora of North America, North of Mexico,* 3 vol. (1928–40), a more complete account, with bibliography; and P.W. RICHARDS, *A Book of Mosses* (1950), a small popular book on selected British and European mosses, with delightful watercolour plates.

(A.J.Sh.)

Bryozoa

The bryozoans, also called polyzoans or ectoprocts, comprise the phylum Bryozoa of which there are about 4,000 extant species. The bryozoans are a widely distributed, aquatic, invertebrate group, members of which form colonies composed of numerous units called zooids. Until the mid-18th century, bryozoans, like corals, were regarded as plants; hence their name, which means "moss animals." Seventy-five years later, the bryozoans (then called Polyzoa) were distinguished from the coelenterates, and the characteristic structure of the zooid was first described.

Bryozoans may be separated into three classes: Phylactolaemata (freshwater dwelling); Stenolaemata (marine); and Gymnolaemata (mostly marine). The order Cheilostomata (class Gymnolaemata), containing 600 genera, is the most successful bryozoan group.

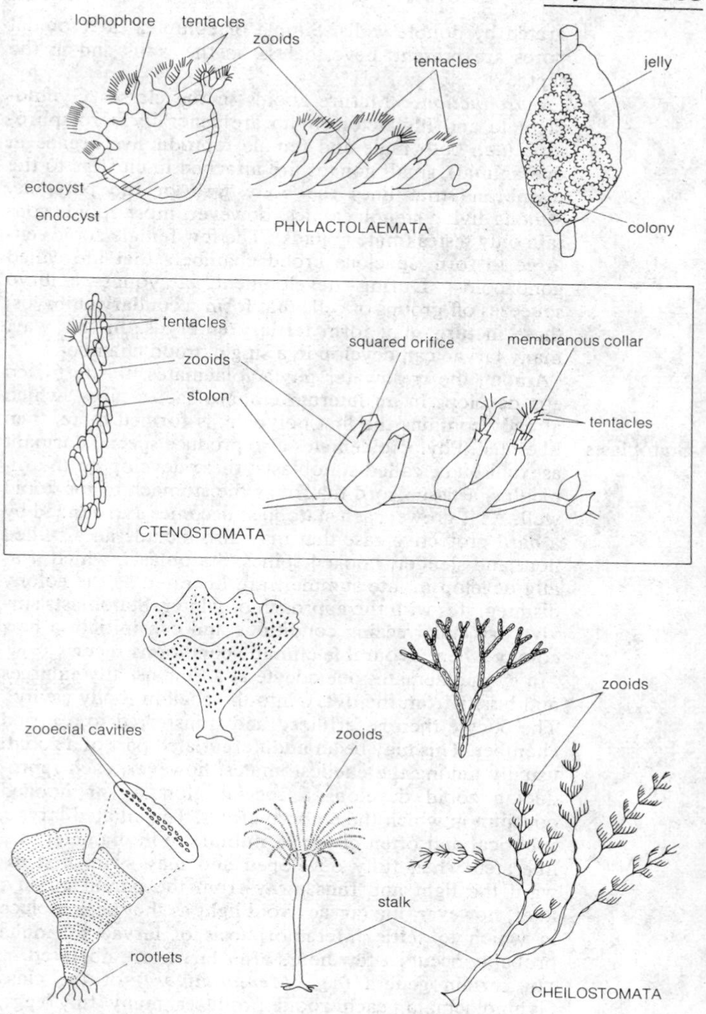

Figure 1: Growth forms of bryozoan colonies.

GENERAL FEATURES

Bryozoan colonies are found in both fresh and salt waters, almost invariably as growths or crusts on other objects. Freshwater bryozoans, which are frequently inconspicuous, are found among vegetation in clear, quiet, or slowly flowing water. Marine species range from the shore down to the ocean depths but are most plentiful in the shallow waters of the continental shelf. They cover seaweeds, form crusts on stones and shells, hang from boulders, or rise from the seabed. Bryozoans readily colonize submerged surfaces, including ship hulls and the insides of water pipes.

The zooid walls, which constitute the matrix (or substance in which living cells are embedded) of the colony, generally are calcareous (*i.e.*, impregnated with calcium carbonate) and bryozoans, therefore, have left a fossil record. The phylum has a long geological history, and many earth strata, from the Ordovician onward (*i.e.*, from about 500,000,000 years ago), are characterized by bryozoan fossils.

Size range. Bryozoan colonies vary in size. The very small genus *Monobryozoon*, which lives between marine sand particles, consists of little more than a single zooid less than one millimetre in height. The coralline genus of European seas *Pentapora*, however, is found in clumps that occasionally are one metre or more in circumference; and a warm-water genus, *Zoobotryon*, hangs from harbour pilings in chains or clumps that may be one half metre in length. Colonies that form crusts generally cover only a few square centimetres; erect colonies may rise only two to five centimetres.

Appearance. The texture of the colonies is variable. Some colonies, especially those in fresh water and on sea shores, are gelatinous or membranous; others are tufted, with flat fronds (leaflike structures) or whorls of slender branches, whose horny texture results from light deposits of lime in zooid walls. Still other colonies are hard and have calcified skeletons. Such colonies may form rough-surfaced, reddish patches or may rise in slender branching twigs (such as those that form a network in the beautiful lace corals *Retepora* or *Sertella*).

Colonies

The colonies, diverse and complex in structure, are composed of individual zooids or compartments; and each zooid is a complete and well-organized animal. A bryozoan colony usually has many zooids, which may be of one type or of types that differ both functionally and structurally. Neighbouring zooids are united and may communicate by tiny pores present in the zooids' walls. Many zooids have slender tentacles at one end on which are found cilia (hairlike projections) that propel tiny particles of food toward the zooid mouth. The mouth opens into a digestive tract that is divided into several regions and terminates at an anus, which is outside (but near) the tentacles. If zooids are disturbed, they withdraw their tentacles inside the body cavity. Only if the zooids have transparent walls, such as in the *Bowerbankia* and the *Membranipora*, is the digestive tract visible. The tentacles and digestive tract together are called the polypide of the zooid.

NATURAL HISTORY

Primary zooid

Life cycle. *Budding.* A colony is formed by asexual budding, from initially either a primary zooid (or ancestrula) or a resting bud. The ancestrula originates from a sexually produced larva. New zooids then are budded to produce colonies of definite shape and growth habit. In the freshwater class Phylactolaemata, the primitive zooids are cylindrical in form, and the budding pattern results in a branched colony. In more highly evolved phylactolaemates, colonies are compact, and discrete zooids can be recognized only with difficulty. New polypides (*i.e.*, tentacles plus digestive tract), which originate by ingrowth of a cell layer called the epithelium, remain suspended within a common colonial coelom, or body cavity.

Among living members of the primitive (and mainly fossil) marine class Stenolaemata, the long and slender zooids have calcified tubular skeletons. A larva metamorphoses into a hemispherical primary disk (or proancestrula). A cylindrical extension grows from the proancestrula, and the matrix of the colony then is built up by repeated divisions of the zooidal walls. Internal walls of the colony are termed septa. The growth and budding zones of the colony are found at its outer edges. Cells from the surface epithelium push inward to produce the polypide, and the septa create a chamber around the polypide. The walled portion of a zooid is termed the cystid.

In the class Gymnolaemata, in which the zooids frequently are flattened, budding occurs as transverse septa form and cut off parts of the primary zooid (or other parent zooid); each part is called a daughter cystid. As each cystid enlarges to become a zooid, a polypide forms inside. In the important order Cheilostomata, budding usually produces rows of identical zooids that radiate from the primary zooid and adhere to each other. Although the rows divide periodically to keep pace with the increasing circumference of the colony, they maintain their adherence to each other. Successive zooids in a row are separated by transverse septa, but adjoining rows are separated by double walls. Simple or complex interzooidal pores are present, nevertheless, in the walls and in the septa.

Reproduction. Mature zooids in the classes Gymnolaemata and Phylactolaemata are generally hermaphroditic (*i.e.*, both male and female reproductive organs in one animal); small gonads are attached in clusters to the membrane that lines the body wall or the polypide. Among living stenolaemates, however, most zooids contain only testes (male gonads). The few female zooids enlarge to form spacious brood chambers that are called gonozooids. During development, a young embryo squeezes off groups of cells that form secondary embryos; these in turn may form tertiary embryos. In this way, many larvae can develop in a single brood chamber.

Among the freshwater phylactolaemates, the fertilized egg develops in an internal embryo sac; a larva, which already contains the first polypide, is formed there, then liberated. Phylactolaemates also produce special dormant asexual buds, called statoblasts; these develop on the funiculus, a tissue cord that links the stomach to the zooid wall. As it grows, each statoblast becomes surrounded by a hard protective case that may also include an air-filled float and slender, hooked spines. Statoblasts, which usually develop in late summer, are liberated as the colony disintegrates with the approach of winter. Statoblasts survive dry and freezing conditions and can initiate a new colony when favourable climatic conditions recur.

Statoblasts

In gymnolaemates one oocyte at a time usually enlarges and bursts from the ovary into the coelom (body cavity). The oocyte then is fertilized and transferred to a brood chamber. This may be an undifferentiated part of a zooid; usually among the cheilostomates, however, each reproducing zooid develops a special globular or hooded ooecium in which the embryo grows. The ciliated larvae, spherical and often about ¼ millimetre in diameter, are liberated when fully developed and may swim first toward the light and thus away from the parent colony; later, however, the larvae avoid light as they seek a place in which to settle. Metamorphosis of larvae to adults probably occurs a few hours after larvae are liberated.

In certain genera (*e.g.*, *Membranipora*) of the class Gymnolaemata, each zooid produces many tiny eggs, which are fertilized by sperm from another zooid as they are shed directly into the sea. The fertilized eggs develop into triangular, bivalved larvae, known as cyphonautes, which for several weeks live among, and feed on, plankton. Larvae from brood chambers and cyphonautes settle in a similar way; *i.e.*, both locate a suitable surface and explore it with sensory cilia. Attachment is achieved by flattening a sticky holdfast, which pulls the larva down on top of it. As metamorphosis proceeds, larval organization degenerates, and the first polypide develops inside a primary zooid.

Ecology. *Freshwater bryozoans.* Freshwater bryozoans live mainly on leaves, stems, and exposed tree roots in shallow water; before drinking water was filtered, however, freshwater bryozoans regularly polluted water supply pipes. Though not uncommon, freshwater bryozoans are inconspicuous in pools, lakes, or gently flowing rivers, especially in slightly alkaline water. The few species of the freshwater class Phylactolaemata tend to be widely distributed, presumably as a result of the ease with which statoblasts can be scattered.

Bryozoans along shores

Marine bryozoans. The most familiar marine bryozoans are those that inhabit shores, though they occur in greater numbers below tidemarks. Dredge hauls of stones and shells yield colonies in abundance. Colonies also occur on the ocean bed, even at great depths, but the frequently muddy bottom of the oceanic abyss is an unfavourable habitat. A few species tolerate hypersaline or brackish waters; on the other hand, the predominantly marine Gymnolaemata have a freshwater representative, *Paludicella.*

Shallow, sheltered channels that have currents but are protected from severe waves are typical bryozoan habitats. Open coastlines support fewer species, but noncalcareous species occur abundantly on intertidal algae in temperate waters. A familiar genus is the lacy *Membranipora* (class Gymnolaemata), found throughout the world and well adapted to living on kelp weeds at, and just below, the low-water mark. Although the zooid walls of *Membranipora* colonies are calcified, they contain flexible joints, which allow the colony to bend as the alga sways in the waves. *Membranipora,* which may cover large areas with a million or more zooids, always grows predominantly toward the youngest part of an algal frond. Overhangs, which form when soft rock erodes along a shoreline, and the shaded pilings of jetties and piers are other favoured bryozoan habitats. Since they do not require light and can grow in dark places, bryozoans can avoid competition from algae that could smother them. Sea slugs and sea spiders appear to be the principal predators of bryozoans.

FORM AND FUNCTION

Zooids. The details of zooid structure vary from class to class. Among the zooids of the freshwater class Phylactolaemata, the lophophore (*i.e.*, the ridge from which the tentacles originate) is generally horseshoe shaped, and the tentacles are more numerous than are those in the gymnolaemates (*e.g.*, *Bowerbankia*). The body wall is muscular, and there are no transverse parietal muscles. In zooids of the class Stenolaemata, the walls form a slender calcareous tube, which cannot be pulled inward to turn the tentacles outward; instead, body fluid is forced from one part of the zooid to another by internal muscles.

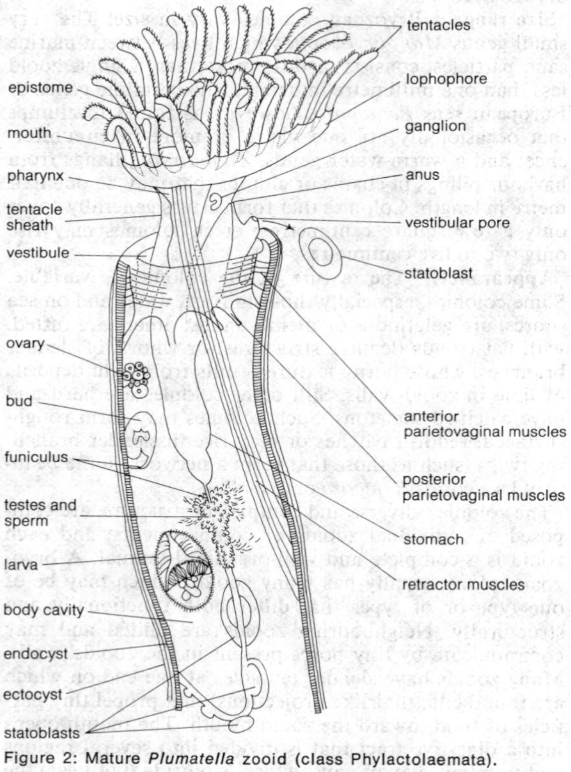

Figure 2: Mature *Plumatella* zooid (class Phylactolaemata).

Zooids rarely are longer than one millimetre. Since the most primitive type is cylindrical, the bryozoan ancestor probably was wormlike. Tentacles, spread to form a funnel at the free end of the zooid; arise from the lophophore, which surrounds the mouth. In *Bowerbankia* (class Gymnolaemata), the digestive canal forms a deep loop; the pharynx descends to the gizzard and stomach, and the rectum rises to an anus, which lies just outside the lophophore. Although the walls of the zooid are covered by a cuticle and are protective in function, they lead to the lophophore by means of a structure called a tentacle sheath (or introvert). When feeding zooids are disturbed, powerful retractor muscles withdraw the tentacles, by pulling them down inside the introvert. The inrolled end of the zooid then terminates in an opening called an orifice. The tentacles leave the sheath by an indirect mechanism. Contraction of muscles called the transverse parietal muscles pulls the zooid wall inward and compresses the internal fluid, the resulting increase in pressure pushing the tentacles out again as the retractor muscle relaxes.

In shape, *Bowerbankia* is not typical of the class Gymnolaemata. During gymnolaemate evolution, a transition from tall cylindrical zooids to short flattened zooids probably occurred. During the evolution of zooids typical of certain genera of the order Ctenostomata to the rigid zooids typical of the order Cheilostomata, for example, a critical development may have been calcification of lateral walls. Primitive cheilostomes (*e.g.*, *Membranipora*) have box-shaped zooids with rigid side walls but a flexible membranous front. The mechanism for turning the tentacles outward is dependent upon this membrane. Transverse parietal muscles span the coelom from the side walls to the frontal membrane; their contraction pulls the membrane inward and creates the pressure increase necessary to push out the tentacles.

Although the anascan suborder represented by *Membranipora* is an abundant and successful group, these animals are only a starting point in the cheilostome trend toward stronger and better protected zooids. In the diversified and even more successful ascophoran suborder represented by *Schizoporella*, for example, the frontal membrane, which appears to be absent, actually has been converted into, or perhaps replaced by, a delicate membranous sac (called an ascus) that fulfills the same function; *i.e.*, it communicates with the exterior through a small opening at the orifice. The transverse parietal muscles are inserted on the ascus, and their contraction dilates it. Water from outside flows into the ascus as it expands, while the coelomic fluid is simultaneously compressed. The ascophoran frontal wall has both cellular and cuticular covering layers and is penetrated by tissue-filled structures called pseudopores. Further calcification can take place outside that already present, so that the wall grows thicker with time without affecting the inner volume of the zooid.

Zooid polymorphism in cheilostomes

Zooid polymorphism exists among the colonies of the Cheilostomata, and the operculum, a flap that functions as a pivotal lid at the orifice of most cheilostomes, seems to have been of particular significance in the evolution of the specialized zooids of this order. The avicularium type of zooid has a small body and a rudimentary polypide; the operculum, however, is proportionally larger, has strong adductor (closing) muscles and has become, in fact, a jaw. Avicularia are found among normal zooids but usually are smaller and attached to normal zooids, as in *Schizoporella*. In *Bugula* the avicularia are moveable on short stalks, and closely resemble miniature birds' heads; hence the name avicularium. Another specialized form of zooid is the vibraculum, in which the operculum has become a whiplike seta (*i.e.*, hairlike projection). The functions of avicularia and vibracula are not yet known with certainty, but both types of zooids may help to keep the colony free from particles and epizoites (*i.e.*, organisms that attach to the surface of the colony but do not parasitize it).

Physiology. Respiratory, circulatory, and excretory systems are absent in bryozoans. The capture of plankton is the major role of tentacles, which spread in a manner similar to that of a funnel, with the mouth at the vertex. Long lateral cilia (*i.e.*, hairlike projections) create a water current that flows into the top of the funnel and out between the tentacles. Shorter frontal cilia direct food particles toward the mouth; from there they are sucked into the gut by the pharynx. Diatom shells, if ingested, are pulverized in the gizzard of those species that have one; digestion and absorption occur in the stomach. Although digested products must be transmitted from one zooid to another, the mechanism by which this process occurs is not yet known with certainty.

The polypide degenerates periodically during the lifetime of a zooid, and a compact mass, called a brown body, frequently remains in its place. A new polypide soon differentiates from living cells of the cystid.

The small nervous system of bryozoans is associated largely with the tentacles. It is not yet known if any interzooidal nervous coordination occurs. There are no special sense organs.

EVOLUTION AND PALEONTOLOGY

The Bryozoa have a long history. From the Lower Ordovician (430,000,000 to 500,000,000 years ago) onward, a majority of limestone formations, especially those with shale alternations, are rich in bryozoan fossils. The skeletons of calcified bryozoans are easily preserved. Stenolaemates are found abundantly as fossils; after their appearance in the Lower Cretaceous (110,000,000 years ago), cheilostome fossils also are abundant. The soft-bodied phylactolaemates, on the other hand, have left no fossil record, and fossilized ctenostomes are rarely found.

Oldest bryozoan fossil

The most ancient stenolaemate or bryozoan of any kind is the genus *Archaeotrypa*, believed to be a ceramoporoid bryozoan from the Upper Cambrian (about 500,000,000 years ago). The ceramoporoids, a group belonging to the order Cystoporata, flourished during the Ordovician and were certainly the earliest established bryozoan group to leave a fossil record. Although they declined during the Silurian (395,000,000 to 430,000,000 years ago), the ceramoporoids evidently were the progenitors of a more advanced group, the fistuliporoids, which were successful until the end of the Permian (225,000,000 to 280,000,000 years ago).

Dominant among the early Paleozoic (225,000,000 to 570,000,000 years ago) stenolaemates, however, was the order Trepostomata, which evolved rapidly during the Ordovician and attained its peak of evolutionary development during the upper part of the same period. The long, slender zooids of trepostomes grew together to form large, solid colonies. As a zooid grew longer and longer, diaphragms (or transverse partitions) were deposited. The trepostomes declined in importance after the Ordovician, perhaps as a result of competition from the cryptostomes, and were extinct by the close of the Permian (225,000,000 years ago).

The geological history of the order Cryptostomata contrasts markedly with that of the Trepostomata. Cryptostomes evolved rapidly during the Ordovician, without matching the early success of the trepostomes; thereafter, however, the cryptostomes flourished for millions of years and were the dominant bryozoans during the Devonian (345,000,000 to 395,000,000 years ago), the Carboniferous (280,000,000 to 345,000,000 years ago), and Permian periods. Then suddenly (in geological terms), and for reasons not yet explained, the cryptostomes dwindled, and the order became extinct soon after the end of the Paleozoic Era (225,000,000 years ago).

Primitive cryptostomes were similar to the trepostomes but evolved a freely erect, more delicate kind of colony that was flat and leaflike in one group, the ptilodictyoids, with two zooid layers placed back to back; in another group, the rhabdomesoids, colonies were a branching arrangement of slender stems, in which the zooids were disposed around a central axis. Fronds formed a lacy network in a third group called the fenestelloids, originating either as a fan or funnel, in *Fenestella*, or as a spiral, in *Archimedes*.

The Cyclostomata were unimportant during the Paleozoic, although living tubuliporoid genera like *Berenicea* and *Stomatopora* first appeared during the Ordovician. Alone among the Stenolaemata, however, the cyclostomes survived into the Mesozoic Era (225,000,000 to 65,000,000 years ago), diversified, and flourished during the Jurassic (136,000,000 to 190,000,000 years ago) and Lower Cretaceous. Several new groups evolved and still survive.

Although the ctenostomes (class Gymnolaemata) have never been very numerous, they apparently gave rise (during the Early Cretaceous) to the cheilostomes, thus far the most successful group of bryozoans to have evolved. The more primitive anascan type, with calcified side walls but a frontal membrane, was successful. An early offshoot, in which the membrane is covered by a shield of modified spines, was abundant but then declined. An ascophoran type also evolved from the anascans early in cheilostome history.

CLASSIFICATION

Distinguishing taxonomic features. Both colony type and zooid morphology are used to classify bryozoans. Zooidal characters, however, are more reliable. The cylindrical zooids are of rather uniform appearance throughout the Stenolaemata, and classification, therefore, is difficult. Wall structure and the morphology of the embryo chambers are important taxonomic characters. In cheilostomes the skeletal features of the zooids, particularly the presence, extent, and structure of the frontal wall—together with shape of the orifice, type of ooecia, and zooid polymorphism—provide the most important distinguishing taxonomic criteria. Among ctenostomes and phylactolaemates, whose zooids lack skeletal features, colony form is more important. Statoblasts are of taxonomic value. Internal characters have been used less, but the presence or absence of a gizzard, number of tentacles, and colour of developing embryos are considered to be of taxonomic significance.

Annotated classification.

PHYLUM BRYOZOA

Sedentary, aquatic invertebrates; form colonies of zooids by budding; each zooid with circular or crescentic lophophore surrounding a mouth from which slender, ciliated tentacles arise; anterior part of body forms an introvert within which the lophophore can be withdrawn; alimentary canal deeply looped; anus opens near mouth but outside lophophore; excretory organs and a blood vascular system absent; each zooid secretes a rigid or gelatinous wall to support colony; about 4,000 extant species.

Class Phylactolaemata

Zooids basically cylindrical, with a crescentic lophophore and an epistome (hollow flap overhanging mouth); body wall non-calcareous, muscular, used for everting the lophophore; coelom continuous between zooids; new zooids arise by replication of polypides; special dormant buds (statoblasts) are produced; zooids monomorphic; exclusively freshwater; cosmopolitan; apparently primitive, but with no certain fossil record; about 12 genera.

Class Stenolaemata

Fossil except for some Cyclostomata; zooids cylindrical; body wall calcified, without muscle fibres; not used for everting the lophophore; zooids separated by septa; new zooids produced by division of septa; limited polymorphism; marine; Ordovician to present; about 550 genera.

Order Cyclostomata

Orifice of zooid circular; lophophore circular; no epistome; zooids interconnected by open pores; sexual reproduction involves polyembryony, usually in special reproductive zooids; Ordovician to present; all seas; about 250 genera.

Order Cystoporata

Zooid skeletons long and tubular, interconnected by pores and containing diaphragms (transverse partitions); cystopores (not pores but supporting structures between the zooid skeletons) present; Ordovician (?Cambrian) to Permian; about 50 genera.

Order Trepostomata

Colonies generally massive, composed of long tubular zooid skeletons with lamellate calcification; without interzooidal pores; orifices polygonal; sometimes with numerous diaphragms, zooid walls thin proximally, thicker distally; Ordovician to Permian; about 100 genera.

Order Cryptostomata

Colonies mostly with foliaceous or reticulate fronds or with branching stems; zooid skeletons tubular, shorter than in trepostomes; without pores; with diaphragms; proximal portions thin walled, distal portions funnel-like and separated by extensive calcification; Ordovician to Triassic; about 130 genera.

Class Gymnolaemata

Zooids cylindrical or squat, with a circular lophophore; no epistome; body wall sometimes calcified; nonmuscular; eversion of lophophore dependent on deformation of body wall by extrinsic muscles; zooids separated by septa or duplex walls; pores in walls plugged with tissue; new zooids produced behind growing points by formation of transverse septa; zooids polymorphic; mainly marine; all seas; Ordovician to present; about 650 genera.

Order Ctenostomata

Zooids cylindrical to flat; walls not calcified; orifice terminal or nearly so, often closed by a pleated collar; no ooecia or avicularia; Ordovician to present; about 40 genera.

Order Cheilostomata

Zooids generally shaped like a flat box, walls calcified; orifice frontal, closed by a hinged operculum; specialized zooids, such as avicularia, commonly present; embryos often developing in ooecia (brood chambers). Cretaceous to present; about 600 genera.

Critical appraisal. Classification of bryozoans began in 1837 when the freshwater and marine Bryozoa were separated as Lophopoda and Stelmatopoda, respectively. These names were replaced by Phylactolaemata and Gymnolaemata in 1856. Although division into two classes became generally accepted and is retained by some zoologists, studies on cyclostomes led to the naming of the third class, the Stenolaemata, formerly part of the Gymnolaemata. The cyclostomes and the fossil trepostomes were placed in the new class, which was acceptable to many paleontologists. In recent years, the work of geologists has settled the position of the cryptostomes (in the Stenolaemata). The most satisfactory system, therefore, separates the bryozoans into three classes, distinct since the beginning of the fossil record.

Most of the bryozoan orders were named many years ago: Cheilostomata, Ctenostomata, and Cyclostomata in 1852; Trepostomata in 1882; and Cryptostomata in 1883. In 1964, a Russian bryozoologist introduced a new order, Cystoporata, to include the Paleozoic ceramoporoids and fistuliporoids. The limits of the Cystoporata have not yet been satisfactorily defined. One modification may occur in the future; that is the segregation of the fenestelloid and non-fenestelloid cryptostomes into separate orders.

BIBLIOGRAPHY. E. ANNOSCIA, *Briozoi* (1968), an introduction to the study of Bryozoa (in Italian), but including an extensive and valuable glossary of special terms with their equivalents in English, French, German, Russian, and Spanish; R.S. BASSLER, "Bryozoa," in R.C. MOORE (ed.), *Treatise on Invertebrate Paleontology*, pt. G (1953), a useful book with definitions of all known bryozoan genera, although in need of revision; P. BRIEN, "Bryozoaires," in P.P. GRASSÉ (ed.), *Traité de zoologie*, 5:1054–1335 (1960), an advanced zoological treatise in French, with an especially good account of the Phylactolaemata; L.H. HYMAN, *The Invertebrates*, vol. 5, *Smaller Coelomate Groups*, pp. 275–515 (1959), an advanced zoological treatise; J.S. RYLAND, *Bryozoans* (1970), a general survey of the phylum for the nonspecialist, including both fossil and living bryozoans, and *Phylum Bryozoa* in T.J. PARKER and W.A. HASWELL, *Text-Book of Zoology*, 7th ed., vol. 1 (1971), an up-to-date textbook.

There is no comprehensive account of the geological history and stratigraphic distribution of Bryozoa, although there are some fine monographs on the bryozoan fauna of particular formations. These can be traced from the bibliographies of the works listed here, or from sect. 8 of the *Zoological Record*, published annually.

(J.S.R.)

Buber, Martin

Martin Buber, the German-Jewish and Israeli religious philosopher, biblical translator and interpreter, and master of German prose style, was one of the most influential figures in 20th-century spiritual and intellectual life. As one of the last great figures of German Jewry, he is comparable with the first one, the 18th-century philosopher Moses Mendelssohn. Each of them not only benefitted from German culture but also enriched it by his lifeworks, including a translation of the Hebrew Bible into German. But whereas Mendelssohn's translation of the Pentateuch (the first five books of the Bible) was partly intended to teach Jewish youth pure German, Buber's translation of the whole Bible (begun in collaboration with Franz Rosenzweig) preserved a Hebrew flavour to lead the reader to the original word and to the life and spirit that it expressed.

Buber.
By courtesy of Israel Information Services

From Vienna to Jerusalem. Buber was born February 8, 1878, in Vienna, Austria, to Carl Buber, an agronomist, and his wife—both assimilated Jews. When Martin was three his mother left his father, and the boy was brought up by his grandparents in Lemberg (now Lvov, Ukrainian S.S.R.). The search after the lost mother became a strong motive for his dialogical thinking—his I–Thou philosophy (see below).

Galician boyhood and university days

Solomon Buber (1827–1906), the Lemberg grandfather, a wealthy philanthropist, dedicated his life to the critical edition of Midrashim, a part of the nonlegal rabbinic lore. His works show him as a Hebrew gentleman-scholar who was also interested in Greek linguistic parallels. His wife, Adele, was even more a product of the 19th-century Enlightenment movement among east European Jewry that sought to modernize Jewish culture. Though influenced by both, and taught Hebrew by Solomon, young Martin was drawn more to Schiller's poems than to the Talmud. His inclination toward general culture was strengthened by his grammar school education, which provided him with an excellent grounding in the classics. During his adolescence his active participation in Jewish religious observances ceased altogether.

In his university days—he attended the universities of Vienna, Berlin, Leipzig, and Zürich—Buber studied philosophy and art. His doctoral dissertation (Vienna, 1904) dealt with the theories of individuation in the thought of two great mystics, Nicholas of Cusa and Jakob Böhme, but it was Friedrich Nietzsche's proclamation of heroic nihilism and his criticism of modern culture that exerted the greatest influence on Buber at that time. The Nietzschean influence was reflected in Buber's turn to Zionism and its call for a return to roots and a more wholesome culture. On the invitation of the Zionist leader Theodor Herzl, in 1901 he became editor of the Zionist weekly *Die Welt* ("The World"). But soon a significant difference of opinion developed between the two men. Buber favoured an overall spiritual renewal and, at its core, immediate agricultural settlements in Palestine, as against Herzl's emphasis on diplomacy to bring about the establishment of a Jewish homeland secured by public law.

Consequently, Buber resigned his post the same year he assumed it; he remained a Zionist but generally stood in opposition to official party policies and later to official state policies of Israel. He was among the early protagonists of a Hebrew university in Jerusalem.

In 1916 Buber founded the influential monthly *Der Jude* ("The Jew"), which he edited until 1924 and which became the central forum for practically all German-reading Jewish intellectuals. In its pages he advocated the unpopular cause of Jewish-Arab cooperation toward a binational state in Palestine.

After his marriage (1901) to a non-Jewish, pro-Zionist author, Paula Winckler, who converted to Judaism, Buber took up the study of Ḥasidism. His *Chassidischen Bücher* (1927) made the legacy of this popular 18th-century east European Jewish pietistic movement a part of Western literature. In Ḥasidism Buber saw a healing power for the malaise of Judaism and mankind in an age of alienation that has shaken three vital human relationships: those between man and God, man and man, and man and nature. They can be restored, he asserted, only by man's again meeting the other person or being who stands over against him, on all three levels—the divine, human, and natural. Buber maintained that early Ḥasidism accomplished this encounter and that Zionism should follow its example.

Study of Ḥasidism

In *Paths in Utopia* (English translation of the original Hebrew; 1949) he referred to the Israeli kibbutz—a cooperative agricultural community the members of which work in a natural environment and live together in a voluntary communion—as a "bold Jewish undertaking" that proved to be "an exemplary non-failure," one example of a "utopian" socialism that works. Yet he did not ascribe ultimate success to it. His reservation stemmed from the fact that, generally, members of the kibbutz disregarded the relation between man and God, denying or doubting the existence or presence of a divine counterpart. In the interpersonal area they fulfilled God's commandment to build a just community while yet denying the divine origin of the implicit imperative. Buber as an educator tried to refute these ideological "prejudices of youth," who, he asserted, rightly criticize outworn images of God but wrongly identify them with the imageless living God himself.

Buber's pedagogical work reached a climax under the new conditions created by the Nazi assumption of power. In November 1933 he became head of the newly reopened Freies Jüdisches Lehrhaus for Jewish adult education in Frankfurt am Main. In 1934 he became director of the whole organization of Jewish adult education and retraining of Jewish teachers in Nazi Germany, where Jewish teachers and students were being progressively excluded from the educational system. He was a courageous spokesman of spiritual resistance. As against the Nazi nationalism of "blood and soil," he stressed that, while the Jew must maintain his authentic Jewish existence, the educational aim could not be racist (*Völkisch*). His old slogan "to be human in a Jewish way" was now completed by the demand to be Jewish in a humane way.

After the Nazi secret police forbade his public lectures and then all of his teaching activities, he immigrated as a man of 60 to Palestine. He activated his Hebrew and soon took part in the social and intellectual life of the Palestinian Jewish community. He was appointed to a professorship in social philosophy at Hebrew University in Jerusalem, a post he held until 1951. He was the first president of the Israeli Academy of Sciences and Arts. After the establishment of the State of Israel and with the beginning of mass immigration from the Islāmic countries, Buber initiated the founding of the Teachers Training College for Adult Education in Jerusalem and became its head (1949). This college trained what were probably the best educators for the immigrants from the Middle East and North Africa, many of them having been chosen from among the immigrants.

Years in the Holy Land

As a teacher of adults, Buber enjoyed the cooperation of his political adversaries and sometimes also of his religious adversaries. Though he denied the obligatory character of Jewish religious Law and emphasized a nonlegalistic prophetic type of religion, some of the Orthodox also worked with him. Buber's endeavours in adult education were based on his insight that adults again become educable when crisis threatens their spurious security.

From mysticism to dialogue. Buber's manifold activities were inspired by his philosophy of encounter—of man's meeting with other beings. An early mystical period culminated in *Daniel* (1913), five dialogues on "orientation" and "realization," man's two basic stances toward the world. Orientation takes the world as a static state of affairs governed by comprehensible laws. It is a receptive, analytical, or systematizing attitude. Realization, on the other hand, is a creative, participative attitude that realizes the possibilities in things, experiencing through one's own full reality the full reality of the world. It operates within an open horizon of possibilities.

The *Reden über das Judentum* (1923; "Talks on Judaism") mark another step in his development. The early "Talks" were delivered in 1909–11 before large Zionist student audiences in Prague; each of the speeches tries to answer its opening question: "Jews, why do we call ourselves Jews?" To half-assimilated Zionists in search of a rationale for their Jewish existence, Buber offered his theories regarding the essence of Judaism, basing his quest for it on his listeners' assumed identity as "Jews." In some of the "Talks," as well as in *Daniel,* the mystic element still prevails, but Buber later abandoned the notion of a mystical union between man and God and embraced instead the notion of their encounter, which presupposes and preserves their separate existence.

This basic view underlies Buber's mature thinking; it was expressed with great philosophic and poetic power in his famous work *Ich und Du* (1923; *I and Thou*). According to this view, God, the great Thou, enables human I–Thou relations between man and other beings.

Ich und Du

Their measure of mutuality is related to the levels of being: it is almost nil on the inorganic and botanic levels, rare on the animal level, but always possible and sometimes actual between human beings. A true relationship with God, as experienced from the human side, must be an I–Thou relationship, in which God is truly met and addressed, not merely thought of and expressed.

Between man and man, the I–Thou relationship into which both parties enter in the fullness of their being—as in a great love at its highest moment or in an ideal friendship—is an exception. Generally, we enter into relationships not with the fullness of our being but only with some fraction of it. This is the I–It relationship, as in scholarly pursuits in which other beings are reduced to mere objects of thought or in social relations (*e.g.,* boss and worker) wherein persons are treated largely as tools or conveniences. This form of relationship enables the creation of pure and applied science as well as the manipulation of man by man. Buber's ethical concept of the "demarcation line"—to be drawn anew every day between the maximum of good that can be done in a concrete situation and the minimum of evil that must be done in it—calls for an I–Thou relation whenever possible and settles for an I–It relation whenever necessary —*e.g.,* for the purpose of human survival and security.

Toward God, any type of I–It relationship should be avoided, be it theoretical by making him an object of dogmas, juridical by turning him into a legislator of fixed rules or prayers, or organizational by confining him to churches, mosques, or synagogues. Buber's so-called religious anarchism—his rejection of any fixed rules of behaviour in the relation between man and God—

Buber's "religious anarchism"

opened to him new insights in his works on the Bible but also served as a block to an objective evaluation of biblical, let alone Talmudic, Law. He saw the Bible as originating in the ever-renewed encounter between God and his people, followed by a tradition that authentically reflected this experience and another that distorted it to serve later ideological aims. He ascribed most of the legal prescriptions of the Talmud to the "spurious" tradition removed from the Thou relation with God. This interpretation has been criticized as one-sided and subjective; Buber mitigated it somewhat in his later years.

After the religious philosopher Franz Rosenzweig, Buber's friend and fellow translator of the Bible, read *Ich und Du,* he remarked: "Buber gives more recognition to the 'Thou' than anybody before him, but he wrongs the 'It'." To this Buber replied, many years later, that had he lived in a time when the Thou was flowering, he would have "sounded the praises of the It," but that in his time, when the Thou was withering, he had to do the reverse. This argument between Buber and his closest and greatest friend indicates his attitude toward normative Judaism. While Rosenzweig tried to live it as much as possible and became more and more a practicing Jew, Buber stood his ground as one who embodied his Judaism in no prescribed, special manner. This, in addition to his political views (*i.e.,* his opposition to Zionist policy toward the Arabs), set him apart from his own people. It made him, however, their main spokesman in the Jewish–Christian dialogue. In his *Zwei Glaubensweisen* (1950) he construed two religious types according to their approach to God: one called by the Hebrew term for trust, *emuna,* spelling mutual confidence between

Dialogue with Christians

God and man (I and Thou), and the other called by the Greek term for faith, *pistis,* spelling the belief in the factuality of crucial events in salvation history—*e.g.,* Paul's statements about Jesus' life, death, and Resurrection. Judaism for Buber was the classical example of *emuna* and Christianity of *pistis,* although there was a good deal of *pistis* in historical Judaism and a good deal of *emuna* in historical Christianity. His Christian opponents on this and other matters still found a common ground with Buber, because he agreed to a dialogically open, if not dogmatically defined, universe of discourse in which they could talk fruitfully with one another.

The final years. In his last years a group of kibbutz members turned to him with their personal and communal problems. *Siḥot loḥamin* (1967; Eng. trans., *The Seventh Day,* 1970), published by them shortly after the Six-Day War, testifies to Buber's living spirit by its self-searching attitude on ethical questions of war and peace and on Arab–Jewish relations.

Buber died June 13, 1965. An unprecedented event occurred at his funeral in Jerusalem, a high state function: a delegation of the Arab Students' Organization placed a wreath on the grave of one who strove mightily for peace between Israel's and Palestine's two peoples.

MAJOR WORKS

Some of Buber's works were written in Hebrew and later translated into German or English or both. Other works, particularly collections of essays, were published originally in German and later translated into English. Those of his writings that appeared only in Hebrew are not listed here.

PHILOSOPHICAL WORKS: *Ich und Du* (1923; *I and Thou,* 1937 and 1970); *Rede über das Erzieherische* (1926); *Bildung und Weltanschauung* (1935); *Die Frage an den Einzelnen* (1936); *Netivot be-uṭopya* (1947; *Paths in Utopia,* 1949; *Pfade in Utopia,* 1950); *Das Problem des Menschen* (1948; published in *Dialogisches Leben,* 1947; "What Is Man?" in *Between Man and Man,* 1947); *Zwei Glaubensweisen* (1950; *Two Types of Faith,* 1951); *Zwischen Gesellschaft und Staat* (1952); *Bilder von Gut und Böse* (1952; *Images of Good and Evil,* 1952; *Good and Evil, Two Interpretations,* 1953); *Eclipse of God* (1952; *Gottesfinsternis,* 1953).

BIBLICAL AND RELIGIOUS WORKS: *Daniel: Gespräche von der Verwirklichung* (1913; rev. ed. 1919); *Die Schrift,* 15 vol. (1926?–?37; rev. ed., 1954–62), a translation of the Hebrew Bible into German; *Königtum Gottes,* vol. 1 of *Das Kommende* (1932; Eng. trans. from the 3rd German ed. of 1956, *Kingship of God,* 1966); *Gog u-megog* (1941; *For the Sake of Heaven,* 1945; *Gog und Magog,* 1957); *Torat ha-nevi'im* (1942; *The Prophetic Faith,* 1949; *Der Glaube der Propheten,* 1950); *Moshe* (1945; *Moses,* 1946 and 1952); *Ha-tzedeq we-ha'awon* (1950; *Right and Wrong,* 1952); *Elija: ein Mysterienspiel* (1963).

HASIDISM: *Die Geschichten des Rabbi Nachman* (1906, rev. ed. 1955; *The Tales of Rabbi Nachman,* 1956); *Die Legende des Baalschem* (1908; *The Legend of the Baal-Shem,* 1955); *Die chassidischen Bücher* (1927; Eng. trans. in 2 vol., *Tales of the Hasidim,* 1947–48; later German ed. *Die Erzählungen der Chassidim,* 1949); *Der Weg des Menschen nach der Chassidischen Lehre* (1948; *The Way of Man, According to the Teachings of Hasidism,* 1950; 2 vol., *Hasidism and the Way of Man,* 1958, 1960).

OTHER WORKS: *Ben 'am le-'artzo* (1945; *Israel und Palästina,* 1950; Eng. trans. from the German, *Israel and Palestine,* 1952); *Bücher und Menschen* (1952); *An der Wende* (1952; *At the Turning,* 1952); *Der Mensch und sein Gebild* (1955).

BIBLIOGRAPHY. MOSHE CATTANE (comp.), *A Bibliography of Martin Buber's Works (1897–1957)* (1958).

Biographies: HANS KOHN, *Martin Buber: Sein Werk und seine Zeit* (1930; new ed. with a postscript by ROBERT WELTSCH, 1963), the authoritative biography; "My Way to

Hasidism" in *Hasidism and Modern Man* (1958); "Autobiographical Fragments: Martin Buber," in SCHILPP and FRIEDMAN, ch. 1 (cited below); AUBREY HODES, *Martin Buber: An Intimate Portrait* (1971), worthwhile reading, though not fully reliable in all factual details.

Writings on Buber: PAUL ARTHUR SCHILPP and MAURICE FRIEDMAN (eds.), *The Philosophy of Martin Buber* (1967), 30 critical essays by different authors on Buber's impact on such fields as theology, philosophy, Zionism, Ḥasidism, and education; SIDNEY and BEATRICE ROME (eds.), "Interrogation of Martin Buber," in *Philosophical Interrogations*, new ed. (1970), queries by various thinkers and scholars with answers by Buber; HANS URS VON BALTHASAR, *Einsame Zwiesprache: Martin Buber und das Christentum* (1958; Eng. trans., *Martin Buber and Christianity: A Dialogue Between Israel and the Church*, 1961), a Roman Catholic scholar's friendly but critical answer to *Two Types of Faith;* ARTHUR A. COHEN, *Martin Buber* (1957), a critical appreciation from a more traditional Jewish standpoint; MALCOLM L. DIAMOND, *Martin Buber: Jewish Existentialist* (1968), an empathetic analysis of one central aspect of Buber's thought; MAURICE FRIEDMAN, *Martin Buber: The Life of Dialogue* (1960), the pioneer work on Buber in English; WILL HERBERG, *The Writing of Martin Buber* (1956), an excellent introduction and a good selection of quotations from Buber's work; ROY OLIVER, *The Wanderer and the Way: The Hebrew Tradition in the Writings of Martin Buber* (1968), a personal testimony of a former follower and student of Gandhi for whom Buber's biblical work became a turning point; GRETE SCHAEDER, *Martin Buber: Hebräischer Humanismus* (1966), a standard work, partly done under Buber's personal supervision; AKIBA ERNST SIMON, "Jewish Adult Education in Nazi Germany As Spiritual Resistance," in *Yearbook I* of the Leo Baeck Institute, pp. 68–104 (1956), deals largely with Buber's initiative, educational philosophy, and practical leadership; "Martin Buber and German Jewry," in *Yearbook* III, pp. 3–39 (1958), deals *inter alia* with Buber's relation to Herzl, H. Cohen, and F. Rosenzweig.

(A.E.Si)

Bucer, Martin

Martin Bucer, an important Protestant Reformer of the 16th century, who is best known by scholars for his ceaseless attempts to make peace between conflicting reform groups, influenced not only the development of Calvinism (one of the three classical Reformation groups—the other two being Lutheranism and Anglicanism) but also the liturgical development of the Anglican Communion.

Bucer, medal by Friedrich Hagenauer, 1543. In the Archives et Bibliothèque de la Ville de Strasbourg.
By courtesy of the Archives et Bibliotheque de la Ville de Strasbourg

Born at Schlettstadt, Alsace, France, on November 11, 1491, Bucer entered the Dominican monastic order in 1506. He was sent to study at the University of Heidelberg, Germany, where he became acquainted with the works of the great Humanist scholar Erasmus and Martin Luther, the founder of the Protestant Reformation. In 1521 Bucer withdrew from the Dominicans and entered the service of the count palatine of the Rhine, one of the seven electors of the Holy Roman emperor. The following year he became pastor of Landstuhl, where he married a former nun. Excommunicated by the church in 1523, he made his way to Strassburg, where his parents' citizenship assured him of protection. His personal charm, intellectual abilities, and zeal eventually gained him a position of leadership in Strassburg and southern Germany.

Early career as a Protestant Reformer

Under the influence of Erasmus, he had accepted the ideals of Christian Humanism and the Renaissance, which called for a rebirth of what the Humanists believed was the true good, the original rightness, in man and society.

When caught up in the enthusiasm of the Reformation that was rapidly spreading in northern Europe, Bucer became a Protestant Reformer. He envisioned a renewal of man and society that was based on his earlier Humanist views, and he believed that such a renewal would result from the preaching of the true gospel and from faithful adherence to the divinely given pattern of living found in the Bible. This reform through conversion, piety, and discipline found its fullest expression in the massive program for the reformation of England that he presented to King Edward VI of England in 1551.

Bucer's adopted city, Strassburg, lay between the area influenced by the most important Swiss Reformer, Huldrych Zwingli—south Germany and Switzerland—and the area influenced by Luther—north Germany. After 1524 Luther and Zwingli clashed over the meaning of the words, "This is my body," a central phrase in the liturgy of the Lord's Supper. Summoned to Marburg by the landgrave, Philip of Hesse, in 1529, the two leading Reformers and other Reformers engaged in a colloquy to settle the dispute. Luther held to the traditional view that Christ was "really present" in the bread and wine of the sacrament of the Lord's Supper; Zwingli espoused a "spiritual" interpretation that was common among the Humanists; Bucer believed that the two opposing views could be reconciled. But when, at the end of the colloquy, Zwingli and Bucer proffered their hands in fellowship to Luther, he refused.

Bucer as mediator

Believing that the rift between the two reform movements could be bridged, Bucer participated in nearly every conference on religious questions held in Germany and Switzerland between 1524 and 1548. In the various colloquies between Protestants and Catholics or between German Lutheran and Swiss Reform churchmen, Bucer often advocated the use of obscure language and ambiguous formulas when explicit agreement between the opposing parties was impossible to attain. His justification for the use of ambiguity was that he believed that the essential goal was the reform of the people and the doctrinal issues could be worked out later. At Basel, in 1536, Bucer participated in the writing of the First Helvetic Confession, a document that was considered by many Reformed theologians to veer too much toward Luther's views, especially regarding the Lord's Supper. At Wittenberg, Germany, in the same year, Bucer took part in a conference between Lutheran and Reformed theologians, including the Lutheran Philipp Melanchthon, a Humanist theologian with whom he has often been compared. It appeared for a time as though Bucer and Melanchthon were about to achieve their goal of ending the dispute over the Lord's Supper, a dispute that had split the Reformation on the Continent into two major groups. Luther, in satisfaction over the apparent agreement that Bucer and Melanchthon had helped to bring about, declared, "We are one, and we acknowledge and receive you as our dear brethren in the Lord." Bucer is reported to have shed tears at Luther's words. Melanchthon subsequently drew up the Wittenberg Concord incorporating the agreement, but, to Bucer's and Melanchthon's disappointment, it failed to effect a lasting union. The Swiss were unhappy that Bucer had made concessions that leaned toward the doctrine of the real presence, and some thought that he should formally recant his statements as they were incorporated in the Wittenberg Concord.

Even though Bucer was criticized for his evasive approach and concealment of the issues in the controversies between the adherents of Zwingli and Luther, the civil authorities in many south German areas sought his advice and guidance in arranging compromises based on edicts by local authorities. Since Bucer regarded these compromises as tailored to local circumstances, he soon was charged by all parties as having no conviction except that the end justifies the means. In his defense he claimed that each of these compromises was only a temporary measure, that he hoped that further changes gradually would be made. Bucer's policy of agreement by compromise was seen in a better light when it was applied to the problem of religious toleration. Under Bucer's policies there was less persecution of Anabaptists—the left wing of the early Reformers who espoused revolutionary concepts in political and social organization—and other minority groups in Strassburg than in most of Europe.

Bucer's policy of pragmatic solutions of problems proved to be especially difficult in the case of the bigamy of Philip, landgrave of Hesse. Philip, who had given much support to Luther, Bucer, and other Reformers, had serious marital problems but thought it inadvisable to divorce his wife. Bucer helped him to persuade Luther, Melanchthon, and others to sanction a second wife, on the basis of Old Testament plural marriages. In an effort to keep the scandal of Philip's bigamy secret, falsehoods were told, and the matter caused much damage to the Reformers' reputations.

Apart from promoting intra-Protestant union, Bucer had long dreamed of healing the Protestant–Catholic rift, and in this effort he engaged in secret negotiations with certain liberal, reform-minded Catholics. The emperor Charles V, for political reasons, was pursuing similar aims. Fearing a Turkish invasion of central Europe, he wanted, at almost any price, to restore unity between the princes of Germany. He accordingly called for the Colloquy of Regensburg, between Catholics and Protestants, in 1541. Charles selected three Catholic and three Protestant theologians (including Bucer) to discuss the anonymous Regensburg Book, which proposed steps toward Catholic–Protestant union. When Charles used Bucer's rather far-reaching concessions in his secret negotiations with the liberal Catholics as the basis for an official solution of the controversy over the Reformation, Bucer, taken by surprise, denied any participation in a scheme for union. Both Catholics and Protestants rejected the Regensburg Book. Charles settled the matter for a time by subduing the Protestant powers, which would not accept any religious compromise by military force, and by enforcing his own compromise scheme, the Augsburg Interim of 1548.

Although the Augsburg Interim did not concede much more to Catholicism than some of his own earlier compromise solutions had, Bucer vigorously opposed its acceptance by Strassburg. His view was that even a poor compromise was justified if it made some progress toward reform but that if Strassburg accepted the Augsburg Interim it would be a step backward. The armies of Charles, however, prevailed, and Strassburg discharged Bucer and several other Protestant ministers, all of whom were invited to England by the Archbishop of Canterbury, Thomas Cranmer. There Bucer supported the official, cautious reform program of Cranmer and Nicholas Ridley against the more radical reform of the English Church urged by the Zwinglian John Hooper and the Scottish Reformer John Knox. *The First Prayer Book of Edward VI* (1549), the liturgical book of the newly reformed English Church that contained evidence of Lutheran influence, was submitted for formal criticism to Bucer, who could not speak English. His assessment, the *Censura,* delivered to the Bishop of Ely a month before Bucer died, pointed out the vague Lutheranisms of the prayer book. *The Second Prayer Book of Edward VI* (1552), utilizing Bucer's criticism, offended the conservatives in the English Church and did not satisfy the more radical Reformers; it remained in force for about eight months. Bucer's influence as a mediator, however, continued to have its effect in subsequent attempts at compromise in the English Church in the 16th century. He died in England on February 28, 1551.

BIBLIOGRAPHY. The standard biography in English is HASTINGS EELLS, *Martin Bucer* (1931). MIRIAM U. CHRISMAN, *Strasbourg and the Reform* (1967), provides a good history of the city in Bucer's time. FRANCOIS WENDEL, *Calvin: Sources et évolution de sa pensée religieuse* (1950; Eng. trans., *Calvin: The Origins and Development of His Religious Thought,* 1963), discusses Bucer's influence upon Calvin. WILHELM PAUCK (ed.), *Melanchthon and Bucer,* pp. 155–394 (1969), gives an English translation, with an excellent introduction and commentary, of Bucer's *On the Kingdom of Christ,* presented to King Edward VI for the reform of the whole of English society. CONSTANTIN HOPF, *Martin Bucer and the English Reformation* (1946), is a scholarly study of Bucer's role in England and is supplemented on liturgical matters by G.J. VAN DE POLL, *Martin Bucer's Liturgical Ideas* (1944). Among the few monographs in English on Bucer's theology is W. PETER STEPHENS, *The Holy Spirit in the Theology of Martin Bucer* (1970). Each of the above works contains an extensive bibliography. The definitive edition of the collected works of Bucer is now in progress, the Latin works edited by FRANCOIS WENDEL *et al.* (1955–), and the German works edited by ROBERT STUPPERICH *et al.* (1960–).

(L.J.T.)

Bucharest

Bucharest (Romanian Bucureşti), capital of Romania and the most easterly of European capitals except Moscow, stands in the Romanian Plain on the Dîmboviţa River, a tributary of the Argeş (itself a tributary of the Danube), 25 miles (40 kilometres) from the southern frontier of the country. Its physical development reflects the long and eventful history of the region, which has archaeological remains dating from the earliest periods of European prehistory and architectural survivals that serve as a reminder of the long period of Ottoman domination. Following Romanian independence (1878), the city underwent an extensive, planned transformation as the political, economic, administrative, and cultural centre of Romania. With its suburban communes, the city now covers an area of 234 square miles (605 square kilometres). In 1977 its population was 1,934,025, or 9 percent of the total population of the whole country, compared with 340,000 in 1912. (For information on related topics, see BALKANS, HISTORY OF THE; OTTOMAN EMPIRE AND TURKEY, HISTORY OF THE; ROMANIA.)

The site. The winding course of the Dîmboviţa was straightened and diked in 1882 to open the way for urban development along the once marshy floodplain, lying only some 175 to 260 feet (53 to 82 metres) above sea level. The river actually runs for 15 miles (24 kilometres) through the city, dividing it into almost equal halves.

The climate is moderately continental, temperatures averaging 73° F (23° C) in summer and 27° F (−3° C) in winter. Occasionally there are particularly hot summers, usually followed by exceedingly cold winters. The well-watered nature of the region, together with favourable climate and soil conditions, has created a flourishing growth of vegetation. Bucharest is renowned for the number and extent of its green areas, and it is fringed by attractive natural landscapes with meadows and oak groves. A chain of nine landscaped lakes lying to the north, along the Colentina Valley, further enhances the area. All of these beauty spots are much used for rest and recreation.

Historical development. The physical growth of Bucharest took place in several stages, each reflecting historical conditions, in particular the long (15th to 19th century) period of direct and indirect Turkish and Greek domination.

The earliest period. Apart from fortified monasteries and churches on small "islands" in the floodplain, the first recorded urban development took place on the terraces marking the northern slopes of the Dîmboviţa Valley. But the first settlement is much older than the Middle Ages. According to one tradition, the town was founded by a shepherd named Bucur; according to another, the founder was a fisherman. Recent archaeological excavations, revealing remains of the Paleolithic, Bronze, and Iron ages as well as Roman and early medieval relics, have demonstrated that the area now covered by the city has experienced a very long period of almost continuous occupation. Continuity of settlement

The medieval period and its legacy. The first written appearance of the name Bucureşti dates from September

20, 1459, when it was recorded in a document of Vlad Ţepeş (Vlad IV the Impaler), whose rule (1456 to 1462, and again in 1476–77) of Walachia offered the area a brief respite from the ever-present Turkish threat. The Prince appreciated the strategic situation of the ancient settlement, located as it was on a trade route between Braşov (a town to the north that commanded the far side of the Predeal Pass) and the Danube River. He built the fortress of Bucharest—the first of many fortifications—with the aim of holding back the Turks who were threatening the existence of the Walachian state and particularly its then capital, Tîrgovişte, 43 miles away to the northwest, on the exposed southern flank of the Carpathians. Further fortifications were erected during the mid-16th-century reign of Mircea Ciobanul (Mircea the Shepherd), who built what became known later as the Curtea Veche (Old Court), part of which survives as the city's oldest building. This structure was sited in the vicinity of the present-day Piaţa de Flori (Flower Square).

Under the Ottoman suzerainty that was eventually established, Bucharest developed rapidly as the main economic centre of Walachia, becoming the capital in 1659. This growth was accompanied by changes in the physical appearance of the town and also in its social structure. The town spilled over its early limits, spreading across to the right, or southern, bank of the river, although growth in this zone of low hills, rising to just over 300 feet (90 metres), was very modest until the 19th century. Within the old core, the population continued to grow, with tradesmen and craftsmen—and their new, taller buildings—becoming more and more numerous. The names of some streets—Uliţa Blănarilor (Furriers' Lane), Uliţa Şelarilor (Saddlemakers' Lane), Uliţa Şepcarilor (Capmakers' Lane)—testify to the emergence of guild organizations. Uliţa Lipscanilor was named after the annual fair held in the German city of Leipzig, where many Bucharest merchants traded their goods. As early as the reign (1688–1714) of Prince Constantin Brâncoveanu (Brîncoveanu), large, broad thoroughfares were built. These were known as *poduri* ("bridges"—*i.e.,* streets paved with logs), and they were of significance in forming the present street patterns of the city.

Development of guilds

The census of 1798 recorded that the town had more than 6,000 houses and about 50,000 inhabitants. Strong class distinctions were reflected in the living conditions. At this time government was no longer in the hands of native princes but was controlled instead by Phanariotes (*i.e.,* Greeks originating in the Phanar district of Constantinople) appointed by the authorities of the Sublime Porte.

The 19th and 20th centuries. In 1821 a popular uprising, led by the great Walachian national hero Tudor Vladimirescu, ended Phanariote rule. Bucharest, like many European cities, entered a period of effervescence; the people of Bucharest, for example, played an important role in the revolutions that shook the continent of Europe in 1848. Again, in 1859, civic unrest played a part in forcing the union of Walachia and Moldavia, followed in 1862 by the proclamation of Bucharest as the capital of the Romanian state. These events, coupled with a land reform in 1864 and the final achievement of national independence in the war of 1877–78, gave a strong impetus to the economic development of both the nation and its capital city.

Popular unrest

The increasing number of financial transactions focussed on the city resulted in the establishment of the National Bank (1880) and other banking institutions. In the last 15 years of the 19th century, important public edifices were built, many of them along the main thoroughfare known as Calea Victoriei (Victory Avenue), the name celebrating the newly won independence. The new structures included the Romanian Athenaeum (1888), the Post Office (1900), and the Savings Bank. Nearby are the National Bank and the Palace of Justice (1895; in French neo-Renaissance style). Further progress was signified by the introduction of the first electric tramway, operated along the new thoroughfare called Obor-Cotroceni.

After World War I, Bucharest strengthened its position as the most important economic, political, and cultural centre of a greatly enlarged country. The architectural legacy is very clear, with some modern villas and public buildings incorporating traditional elements as a reaction to the more anonymous "international" styles used for many of the apartment buildings.

Further growth took place after World War II, and since the nationalization of land in 1948 this has been characterized by large-scale projects and a marked architectural uniformity.

World War II and after

On the evening of March 4, 1977, Bucharest was shaken by a severe earthquake (7.2 on the modified Richter scale), which killed some 1,400 people and injured 7,600. The central part of the city was hardest hit, many apartment buildings, hospitals, and cultural institutions being destroyed or seriously damaged.

The economy. Modern industries were introduced in the late 19th century to supplement the workshops of the artisans. During the 1920s and '30s industrialization continued, largely on the basis of private enterprise. Following the nationalization of industry in 1948, many of the old enterprises were amalgamated and re-equipped. In addition, many new factories have been built. By the 1970s, the reordered urban economy concentrated on the production of engineering products, notably machine tools and agricultural machinery, as well as electrical and automotive equipment, buses, trolleybuses, and a wide variety of other goods, including consumer goods. Some 18 percent of the entire industrial production of Romania stems from Bucharest, which is also the largest commercial centre of the country, with about 5,900 state and cooperative trading units.

Educational and cultural life. By the later 1970s Bucharest had 50 faculties of higher education, serving about 71,000 students, compared with 13 faculties and 18,000 students in 1940. There were 13 specialized institutions of higher education, with curricula ranging from agronomy to fine arts. The most important centres for higher education were the "Gh. Gheorghiu-Dej" Polytechnic Institute (founded 1819) and the University of Bucharest (founded 1864). In addition, there were several important academies in both arts and sciences, as well as numerous research institutes conducting scientific work. Bucharest has three central libraries (the Library of the Academy of the Socialist Republic of Romania and the Central State Library, both with many valuable manuscripts, and a central university library) and many public library units.

There are 19 theatres, some of which—for example, the National Theatre "I.L. Caragiale" and the Theatre of Opera and Ballet of the Socialist Republic of Romania—have long traditions. Bucharest is also the seat of the state philharmonic orchestra and many other professional and amateur musical groups, many of them with a strong folk interest. Every third year, the Georges Enesco International Festival (for violin, piano, and vocal music) takes place in the city. Among the many museums are the Museum of the History of the City of Bucharest and the Art Museum of the Socialist Republic of Romania, the latter being the largest of its kind in the country, maintaining large collections of national, European, and Oriental art. Among other notable museums is a highly original ethnographic collection, the Village Museum (founded 1936), made up of peasant houses brought from various parts of the country, complete with outbuildings, furniture, and the household objects appropriate to each region.

The city has a great number of churches, usually small, in Byzantine style. Apart from the Curtea Veche (Old Court) Church, the Antim Monastery (1715) and the churches of SS. Stavropoleos (1724) and Spiridon (1747) are of considerable architectural interest. There are also a Roman Catholic cathedral, several Protestant churches, and a number of synagogues.

The city is a medical centre, providing a variety of medical services, generally free of charge. For recreational purposes, there are also numerous sports grounds, covered gymnasiums, and stadiums, the largest (the "23

August") having nearly 100,000 seats. The large expanse of parkland on the northern edge of the city, surrounding the lakes of the Colentina Valley, is also an important recreational asset.

Town planning and the contemporary topography. Major works in town planning were carried out in the late 19th century, and since the 1930s development has been coordinated by an urban plan, periodically updated. The present plan envisages a maximum urban area of some 38,400 acres (15,500 hectares), to contain the population of 2,300,000 expected by the year 2000. The main trend in recent years has been the construction of new residential districts in outlying areas, each with a planned modern aspect including a variety of services. New avenues have been opened, other streets have been rebuilt, and important new buildings have appeared on the major city thoroughfares.

Republic Square—with the new palace hall, seating 3,000 people, and other new buildings as well as the historic Creţulescu Church (1722)—has become one of the most beautiful squares of the town. It is harmoniously linked to Palace Square, which is surrounded by an imposing group of administrative, political, and cultural buildings including the headquarters of the Communist Party of Romania, the Art Museum (housed in the former Royal Palace), and the massive round building of the Romanian Athenaeum, notable for its columned facade. Nearby, in the heart of Bucharest, lies the junction of the almost straight thoroughfares that traverse the city from north to south (Nicolae Bălcescu Boulevard and 1848 Boulevard) and from east to west (Republicii Boulevard and Gh. Gheorghiu-Dej Boulevard). Here, near the university, rise the National Theatre "I.L. Caragiale" and the 25-story Intercontinental Hotel.

Large areas of old housing in the inner city, however, await redevelopment, and this must be given high priority in the immediate future, to prevent a further outward expansion of the built-up area.

Municipal services

Bucharest was among the first cities in the world to be lighted by kerosine (1856) and gas (1871), and this lighting system was maintained, in part, until after World War II. After 1950 electric lighting was extended over the whole urban area, and the number of paved streets was greatly enlarged and the water and sewerage systems were expanded.

Bucharest has become a modern city, whose complexity can be illustrated by taking the route into the city from the international airport at Otopeni. After 10 miles, the road enters the city on the main north–south thoroughfare, passing the smaller Băneasa Airport. After crossing a bridge over Lake Herăstrău, in the vicinity of the Museum of Folk Art "Dr. N. Minovici" (1905), the large Scînteia Square is reached. In the background, on the right, stands Scînteia House, with the largest printing enterprise in the country, a monument to Soviet influence by virtue of its architecture and the circumstances of its construction. Ahead lies the hall housing the national economy exhibition, and on the left is the Park of Culture and Rest, at 470 acres the largest park in the city, encompassing the Village Museum, an open-air theatre (seating 2,800 people), and a number of other facilities including a flower exhibition. From Scînteia Square the main thoroughfare passes by a triumphal arch (built in the 1930s to commemorate the achievement of Greater Romania after World War I), crosses a public garden (the Kisselef Park, modelled on the Parisian Champs-Élysées), and enters Victory Square. This square is dominated by the modern building of the Council of Ministers, near which rises a natural history museum. From Victory Square, streets lead in several directions. To the left, passing by the Dinamo Sports Park, Ilie Pintilie Boulevard leads to the Ştefan cel Mare Highway, which goes to the old Obor Market, now the site of a large market hall, and, farther, to the modern Titan district. To the right, an older avenue leads to Griviţa Road and the North Railway Station. Ahead appears, on the one hand, a series of modern boulevards: Ana Ipătescu, General Magheru, Nicolae Bălcescu, and 1848, the latter leading to Union Square, dominated by the hill on which the Palace of the Grand National Assembly stands, with Liberty Park beyond. On the other hand, by contrast, lies Victory Avenue, one of the oldest thoroughfares, originally dating from 1702.

The heart of the city

These old and new streets are crossed in the heart of the city by other avenues forming the east–west axis. To the west of the university—near which are the Museum of the History of the City of Bucharest and the oldest hospital of the town, the Coltea, founded in 1704, a visitor crosses Victory Road and reaches the attractive Cişmigiu Lake and Garden, which have dominated the city centre for more than a century. In the western part of the Gh. Gheorghiu-Dej Boulevard (formerly Vest–Est Boulevard), not far from the Romanian opera building and the building of the Faculty of Medicine (1903), rises the Pioneers' Palace, headquarters of the Communist organization for children. The same quarter—Cotroceni—is dominated by the building of the Military Academy, and behind it extends Drumul Taberei, a modern residential quarter. Farther west, the route passes the botanical garden (1884) and the largest clothing factory in the country, and then, surrounded by factories and apartment buildings, merges with the highway leading northwest to the city of Piteşti.

Eastfoto

Palace Square near the heart of Bucharest, Romania. The former Royal Palace (foreground) now houses the Art Museum of the Socialist Republic of Romania.

A further issue in planning concerns the wider city region. This includes the suburban communes, which together account for 130,000 people (compared with 1,930,000 for the whole municipality of Bucharest); much of the increase in population anticipated by 1990 may be accommodated in these peripheral districts. An important question is the extent to which agricultural land should be preserved, a consideration that is especially important on the western side of the city, where favourable conditions of soil, topography, groundwater, and microclimate are reflected in extensive irrigation works and hothouses. Planners are discussing, on the one hand, the merits of a deeper suburban belt all around the city against, on the other, the attractions of expanding the city along certain axes enjoying road and rail communications. Bucharest has enormous physical capacity for expansion, and, although the high cost of dispersal is likely to result in continued high-density development, there are many possibilities to consider in deciding the future urban form.

BIBLIOGRAPHY

ION SADOVEANU, *Bucharest* (1964), a prose tribute to the city accompanies photographic views of contemporary Bucharest; C.C. GIURESCU, *Istoria Bucureştilor* (1966), and N. IORGA, *A History of Roumania* (1925), deal with historical aspects; WALTER STARKIE, *Raggle-Taggle: Adventures with a Fiddle in Hungary and Roumania* (1933, reprinted 1964), provides a picture of Bucharest in the 1930s; GEORGE OPRESCU, *Oriental Art in Rumania* (1963), 140 reproductions of objects from the Art Museum of the Socialist Republic of Romania, Bucharest, and other collections, with an introduction by the author.

(V.Mi./D.T.)

Budapest

Regarded as one of the most beautiful international cities of the modern period, Budapest, the capital of Hungary, has a unique reputation and character. Strategically located on the Danube River, commanding the approaches to the Great Hungarian Plain (the Great Alföld), it dominates most aspects of Hungarian national life and, with a resident population exceeding 2,000,000 in 1976, is the third largest city in the Soviet bloc, after Moscow and Leningrad. In addition to its economic importance, the contemporary status of Budapest is enhanced by a magnificent natural setting, offering fine panoramas across the city; by its historic relics, museums, and noted thermal baths; by a unique and friendly atmosphere; and by an international accessibility.

As the political, administrative, industrial, and commercial centre of the Hungarian People's Republic, Budapest has close ties with the rest of the country. These links are facilitated by its position at the focal point of the Hungarian road and rail systems. That it is the seat of the Hungarian government and Parliament reflects its national political and administrative role, while its local functions are mirrored in its being the administrative centre of Pest County (*megye*) and Buda rural district (*járás*). Budapest also acts as the host to a number of international bodies: the Danube Commission has its headquarters in the city as do the World Federation of Democratic Youth and several permanent committees of the Council for Mutual Economic Assistance (Comecon), the east European economic and trade organization. The European significance of Budapest is reflected in its international transport links; it lies on a waterway connecting eight countries, and transcontinental highways and railways converge upon it. Budapest is also the centre of an industrial agglomeration of 44 smaller settlements that are linked to the city for planning purposes.

International bodies in the city

The capital acquired the name Budapest in 1873 when the communities of Pest (on the left bank of the Danube), Buda (on the right bank), and Óbuda (Old Buda) to the north were amalgamated. During the subsequent hundred years, the functions of the former royal boroughs were integrated and most of the neighbouring settlements were also included within the city boundary. The city has, in fact, fulfilled an administrative role almost without interruption since Buda emerged as the royal residence in the aftermath of the Mongol invasion of 1241.

Six road bridges, including the Széchenyi Chain Bridge (Széchenyi Lánchíd, built by the Scottish engineer Adam Clark), two railway bridges, and a tunnel carrying the east–west underground railway link Buda with Pest. All the bridges were demolished by the retreating German forces at the end of World War II but have since been rebuilt. Elizabeth Bridge (Erzsébet-híd), reconstructed as a suspension bridge, crosses the Danube in one span.

One-fifth of the population of Hungary resides in the capital, and a further 200,000 to 300,000 commute to work in the city each day. In the mid-1970s about 512,000 were employed in the industries of the city, an 18 percent reduction from 1968, after the decentralization of plants to provincial centres began to reduce this number.

Historical development. From early times the significance of the site of Budapest has been appreciated, combining as it does a defensive with a communications function; the river was always fordable at this point. Archaeological evidence shows that the site has been continuously settled since at least the 3rd millennium BC, and Copper, Bronze, and Iron Age man lived there. The Eravisci tribes, of Celtic origin, lived at the foot of Gellért Hill, 771 feet (235 metres) above sea level, and also farther north in what was to become Óbuda. This settlement was called Ak-Ink, meaning "ample water," from which was derived Aquincum, the name given to the civilian town and military camp established by the Romans at the end of the 1st century AD. By the time the Magyar tribes entered the Pannonian Basin in the 9th century, Aquincum, over which had flowed the great Eurasian migrations that followed the fall of the Roman Empire, had ceased to exist. Although there is evidence that some of the Roman buildings were used as shelter, the focus of settlement moved south.

The Roman settlement

This shift was consolidated by the construction of a stone fortress on a rocky spur overlooking the west bank of the Danube by King Béla IV, in the years following the Mongol invasion of 1241. The fortress became known as Buda Castle and the spur as Castle Hill (Várhegy). Soon a settlement sprang up at its base and another on the riverbank opposite, which were to grow respectively into the towns of Buda and Pest. In the 15th century Buda emerged as the most important handicraft and trading centre of the country, and during the reign (1458–90) of Matthias I Corvinus it also became a seat of learning. Buda and Pest were occupied by the Turks in 1541, and during the ensuing period of Turkish domination (to 1686) both towns declined.

During the more stable years of the early 18th century, the two towns again prospered, and by the 1790s Buda had become the seat of national government. Buda, Pest, and a re-emergent Óbuda now began to follow separate paths of economic specialization. Buda and Óbuda were characterized mainly by handicrafts and agriculture; Pest, which was increasingly identified with industry and commerce, rapidly outstripped its neighbours in significance. Throughout the centuries, Buda and Pest had suffered considerably from winter and spring flooding. As a result of the great disaster of 1838, when both towns were devastated, it was decided to regulate the Danube by constructing an extensive series of embankments; these did much to mold subsequent urban layout. The introduction of steamship navigation on the Danube in 1830 and the beginnings of railway construction (the first railway line, from Pest to Vác, was opened in 1846) further assisted the industrial development of Pest. In addition to the industrial and trading companies, numerous cultural institutions also emerged during this period, including the Hungarian National Museum (Magyar Nemzeti Múzeum) and the Hungarian Academy of Sciences (Magyar Tudományos Akadémia), paving the way for the declaration of Pest as the official capital of Hungary in 1848.

Two events occurring within five years of each other provided the institutional framework for urban expansion in the second half of the 19th century. The first was the Compromise (Ausgleich) of 1867 with Austria, which formally recognized Hungarian independence within the political framework of the Dual Monarchy, Austria–Hungary; this agreement was instrumental in increasing

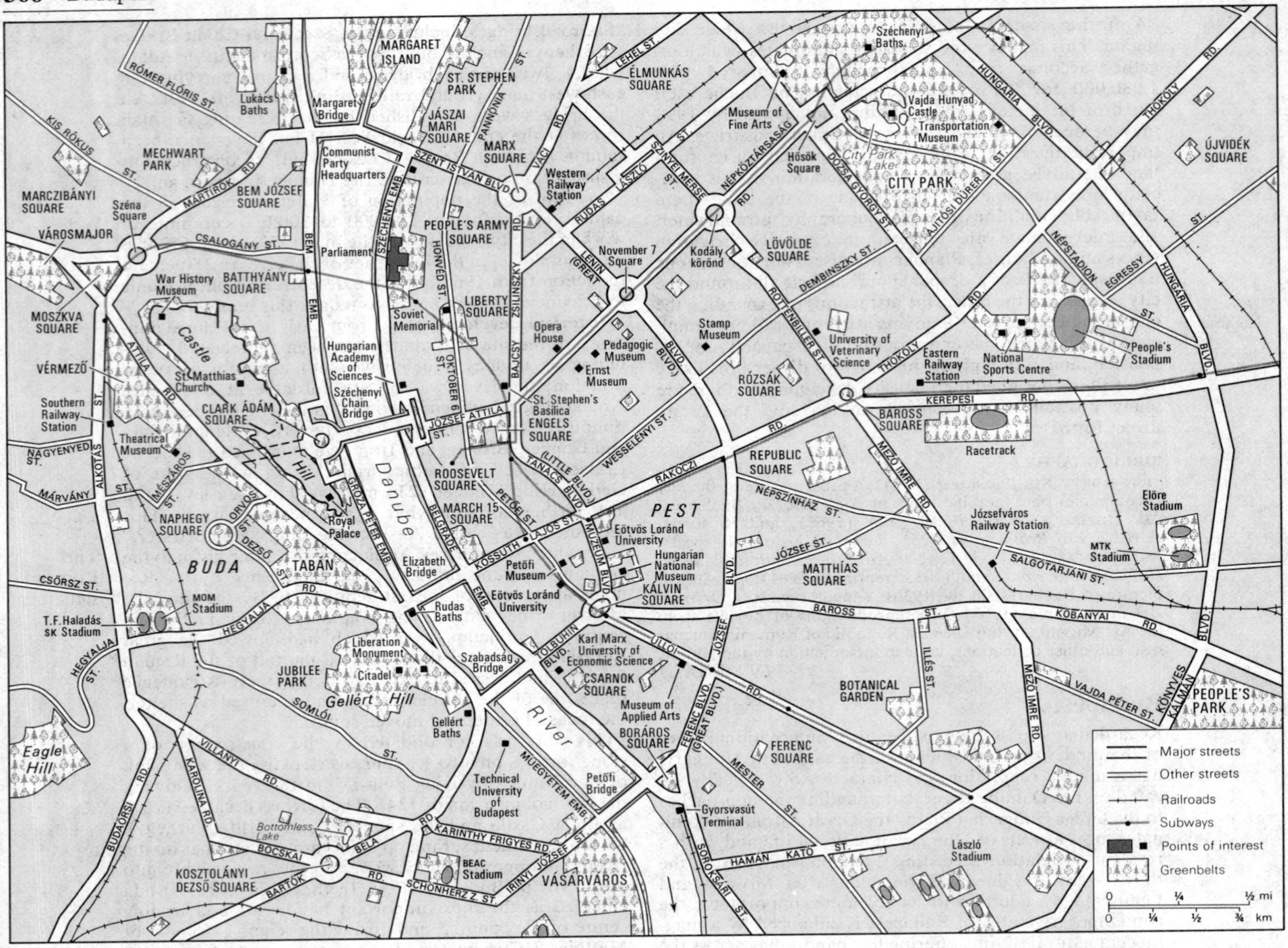

Central Budapest.

both the administrative and financial roles of the city. The second was the formal recognition of the strong mutual ties between Buda, Pest, and Óbuda with their amalgamation into one administrative unit in 1873, since when Budapest has developed as an organic whole. Concurrently, mechanization was providing the stimulus for further industrialization. Budapest was evolving into one of the most important centres for the production of agricultural machinery in Europe, and as a consequence engineering had become a dominant component in the urban economy by the end of the 19th century. Industrial zones emerged on the northern, eastern, and southern outskirts of the city, turning the former settlements of these areas into industrial suburbs.

Amalgamation

From a relatively small town of 54,000 in 1800, the population of Budapest expanded to 302,000 by the time of the first census in 1869, and thereafter rose at a rate of almost 4 percent per year to total 1,110,000 by 1910. It was during this phase of explosive growth that present Budapest took shape. The last four decades of the century saw the construction of the Great Boulevard (Nagykörút), the Little Boulevard (Kiskörút), and important radial arteries such as the present People's Republic (Népköztársaság) Road. The restored Royal Palace, the new Parliament building (1904), together with the Danube bridges succeeded in blending the architectural heritage of the past with the needs of an expanding modern city.

At the outbreak of World War I, Budapest fulfilled well the role of capital of a country of more than 18,000,000 people. This situation was radically changed in 1920 when, as a result of the Treaty of Trianon, which created new nation-states from the former territories of Austria–Hungary, Budapest found itself the overly large capital of a country with a population of less than 8,000,000. No other town was sufficiently large to counterbalance the magnetic pull of Budapest in all aspects of Hungarian life, a state of affairs that exists to this day. As a consequence, even though grave economic problems confronted the country during the interwar years—partly because of loss of territory and the need to adjust the economy accordingly, and later as a result of the world depression —Budapest still managed to grow in terms of population, industry, and built-up area. Four more city districts were added to the 10 that were formed at the time of the union of Buda, Pest, and Óbuda, and by 1941 the population had grown to 1,713,000.

World War II

The city suffered severe damage during World War II. Nine in 10 of the factories were partly or totally destroyed, and 85 percent of all dwellings were demolished or seriously damaged. Practically all forms of transport were destroyed, and by the end of the siege in 1945 the population had fallen by between a quarter and a third.

The first phase of the postwar era was thus one of reconstruction. In 1950 the area of the city was extended to include the outer industrial suburbs and was divided into the 22 districts that still provide the framework for local government. Services were gradually extended to the outer suburbs, which are linked to the central area by a rapid and cheap public transport system. Nevertheless there are still many peripheral parts of the city, both on the Buda side and in Pest, that lack paved streets and public utilities such as sewerage and piped water. Morphologically these areas are of rural rather than urban aspect. The industrialization of the city continued during the 1950s and early '60s; thereafter attempts were made to decentralize industry to provincial towns, although many enterprises have expressed opposition to this policy. The pattern of industrial development is, however, changing, moving away from labour-intensive heavy industry to more modern sectors that are capital-intensive.

Urban structure plan

Since 1971 the development of the city has been guided by the principles embodied in a revised urban structure plan. The structure plan does not contain detailed planning objectives but rather defines the general zoning of land use within the city. According to its conception, new high-density residential areas will dominate the northern sector of the city, residential neighbourhoods will be separated from industrial districts, office employment will be removed from the central city to the suburbs, and industry will be distributed more evenly throughout the urban area to reduce pollution.

The setting. Budapest lies across the Danube at the centre of the Carpathian Basin on the ancient route linking the Great Hungarian Plain with northern Transdanubia. The city contains marked topographic contrasts. Pest is situated on a flat and featureless plain, the Pest Plain, on the left, or eastern, bank of the river; Buda, by contrast, is located on the higher river terraces and slopes of the Buda Hills where they sweep down to the western bank of the Danube. The summit of Gellért Hill in Buda is surmounted by the Liberation Monument and the former citadel, which now houses a tourist hotel, a restaurant, and a museum. The Castle Hill district, 554 feet (169 metres) above sea level, provides the setting for the restored Royal Palace, which is now a combined museum, library, and picture gallery. John's Hill (János hegy), 1,736 feet (529 metres) above sea level, is the highest point in the Buda Hills. Easily reached by chair lift, the lookout tower at the summit provides a panoramic view of the whole city. The Danube, in addition to its transport function, supplies some of the most appreciated recreational settings for the population. The more prosperous citizen can build his second home along the Danube Bend, some 22 miles (35 kilometres) upstream. Trade-union organizations have workers' rest homes along the Roman Shore, on the northern outskirts of the city, while Margaret (Margit) Island is a favourite place for walking and sports.

A fault running under the Danube is the source of numerous thermal springs, the waters of which range in temperature from 63° to 165° F (17° to 74° C) and contain radium. Medicinal baths—among them the Gellért, Rudas, Lukács, and Széchenyi baths—have been built where the waters (which were known and used as long ago as Roman times) reach the surface.

The climate of Budapest is transitional between the more extreme continental conditions of the Great Hungarian Plain and the climate of Transdanubia, which is more temperate and western European, with abundant precipitation. Mean annual temperature is 52° F (11° C), ranging from a July average of 72° F (22° C) to 30° F (−1° C) in January. Mean annual precipitation is 24 inches (600 millimetres).

Open lands

Budapest covers a total of 203 square miles (525 square kilometres), of which only 45 percent is the built-up area of the city; the remainder comprises agricultural land and open country, largely wooded. The network of roads and streets is 2,274 miles (3,660 kilometres) in length, and parks, of which the most important are Margaret Island, City Park (Városliget), and People's Park (Népliget), cover more than 3,000 acres (1,230 hectares).

The people. Average residential density in the city is approximately 10,100 persons per square mile (3,915 per square kilometre), ranging from 70,000 per square mile in the inner-city districts of tall apartment buildings (districts I, V, VI, VII, and VIII) to 3,500 per square mile in the outer areas (districts XVI, XVII and XXII). Although the explosive phase of population increase ended in 1910, the rate of growth remained relatively high during the interwar period and subsequently to the mid-1960s. Throughout that period the migration to the city of people from rural areas and other towns was the primary component of growth. After 1964 the influx of migrants declined significantly, a product of the combined effects of an acute housing shortage and deliberate policy; as deaths also exceeded births in a number of years, the rate of population growth slowed down markedly.

Within the city important shifts of population have been taking place as a result of inner-city redevelopment and the construction of new residential areas in the outer suburbs. The redevelopment of Óbuda as a residential quar-

Bernard P. Wolff—Photo Researchers

Parliament Building and the town of Pest on the eastern bank of the Danube, seen from the castle of Buda.

ter of uniform multistory apartment buildings, housing many thousands of families, was virtually complete by 1976, and major slum clearance had begun in Józsefváros. The focus of new construction moved south to Pesterzsébet and Kelenföld and north to Újpalota, Káposztásmegyer, and Békásmegyer. Despite the large investment in these projects and the use of modern prefabricated techniques of construction, however, the housing shortage remains severe, and there is evidence of considerable overcrowding in the city. The net effect of these changes is a steady shift of people from the inner city, where some districts are declining in population, to the suburban periphery.

Employment

The economy. Wage earners comprise two-thirds of the population of the capital, and two-fifths of them are employed in industry. The tertiary sector, however, is undergoing the most dynamic development and by the mid-1970s employed a quarter of all workers. The growing administrative role of Budapest has also meant a commensurate rise in the number and proportion of civil servants, who by that time represented more than 11 percent of total wage earners. Industrial development has been an important stimulus to the growth of Budapest. Initially food processing, primarily milling, was predominant. By the first decade of the 20th century, heavy industry had outstripped other forms of production, and the engineering factories, which still play an important role in the city's economy, date from this time. Light industry, particularly textiles, telecommunications, and instrument manufacture, became significant branches during the interwar years, and after World War II many of the new technologically based industries, such as electronics and vacuum engineering, took their place in the expanding urban economy.

The decentralization of industry after the mid-1960s meant a steady reduction in the proportion of the nation's industrial workers employed in Budapest, from more than 50 percent of the national total in 1938 to 28 percent in 1975. Many of the capital's large plants participated in this process by setting up new branches in the provinces instead of expanding in Budapest. Although the number of industrial jobs in the capital is actually contracting, selective expansion of those sectors that cannot function efficiently elsewhere—especially the technologically advanced, the exporting, and the urban supply industries—will continue. The overall result should be a significant extension of industrial land use to enable existing industry to spread itself as new processes and improved factory amenities are introduced, to facilitate the removal of plant from the city centre, to make provision for new space-extensive processes such as the manufacture of prefabricated housing units, and to allow a reduction in the average length of journeys between residence and factory.

Concentration in the central business district

Budapest is a monocentric city in which commerce is overwhelmingly located in and around the central business district. In consequence, the suburbs generally possess a lower level of facilities per capita than many rural areas do. Another consequence is that the central business district is finding it increasingly difficult to function efficiently; competition for existing space is intense, and traffic congestion is severe. The resolution of these problems lies in the creation of a network of suburban service centres, and major centres, each serving 150,000 to 300,000 inhabitants, are planned for Óbuda, Moszkva Square, Lágymányos, Újpest, Zugló, and Kispest.

As in other metropolitan areas, agriculture is a low-grade activity in the immediate environs of Budapest, although market gardening and the cultivation of flowers and peach orchards on the southern slopes of the Buda Hills meet some of the city's requirements.

Transportation. Budapest plays a vital role in the transport and communications services of Hungary. The main highways and railways radiate from the city, and traffic on the Danube also stresses its centrality. The largest railway stations and busiest freight yards are found there, and long-distance buses provide regular services to most of the towns and cities of Hungary. Csepel Free Port handles international freight traffic on the Danube, and there vessels of the member countries of the Danube Commission can dock, negotiate cargoes, and take on supplies. All the Danubian countries maintain shipping agencies in Budapest, whose authority covers the free port. In addition to the conventional facilities of modern freight yards, cold storage, and warehouses, the free port is equipped to handle container traffic.

The Csepel Free Port

The urban transport system consists of a network of bus, tram, and trolley-bus routes, while suburban railways connect outlying districts with the city centre. Although car ownership is rising rapidly, city policy is to improve public transport still further and thus prevent the deterioration seen in so many Western cities. At the core of this policy is the construction of a rapid-transit rail system, mostly underground, and its integration with existing modes of transport. The first link was completed in 1973 when the east–west Metro from the Southern Railway Station to the Fehér Road interchange in south Zugló was opened. In the same year the Millennium Underground, completed in 1896, was extended. The second phase of the program is a north–south artery from Újpest to Kispest, expected to be finished in 1985. A south Buda section to Kelenföld and Budafok was planned to follow.

International commerce is also important. Budapest has gained a reputation for its international fairs and industrial and agricultural exhibitions. The city is also the centre of most foreign trade companies and embassies.

Cultural life, administration, and services. Budapest is a cultural, scientific, and artistic centre. Almost all the activities of the Hungarian Academy of Sciences are conducted there, and about 50,000 students, including 1,000 from abroad, study at the city's universities and colleges. The 20 theatres and three concert halls confirm a lively interest in the arts, and the museums and art galleries contain valuable and extensive collections. The city is also the centre of Hungarian sports life, and many world competitions have been held in People's Stadium (Népstadion) and at other nearby grounds and halls.

Tourism

Tourists contribute a sizable income to the city. Their needs for accommodation are catered to by 31 hotels, including the Duna Intercontinental and the Budapest, whose construction was partly financed by Western capital, by two camping sites, and by rooms in private dwellings let through the state travel agency (IBUSZ). A Hilton Hotel in the Castle District was also partly financed by Western interests.

Overall control of local government is exercised by Budapest Metropolitan Council; executive decisions affecting the whole city and the maintenance of essential services (upkeep of roads, etc.) are its responsibility. Routine administration, however, is the task of the 22 directly elected metropolitan district councils (for instance, the collection of property taxes and planning permission for new private residential development). Members of the Budapest Metropolitan Council are elected by the Metropolitan district councillors. Public utilities are generally up to European standards. Health centres, dispensaries, and hospitals, operating under the national health scheme, provide for public health.

Following the postwar reconstruction of the city and the continuing struggle to cope with the 19th-century legacy of slums and backward outer districts, the Budapest of the late 1970s has taken on a more modern appearance. Extensive housing developments have gone a long way to improve the living conditions of the city's population, although the fulfillment of the aim that every family should have its own dwelling is still some distance away. Significant improvements, mapped out in long-term city plans, will continue to be made in the decades ahead.

(Z.A./P.A.C.)

BIBLIOGRAPHY

General: MARTON PECSI and BELI SARFALVI, *The Geography of Hungary* (1964), includes useful statistical data on Budapest; ZOLTAN HALASZ (ed.), *Hungary*, 2nd rev. ed. (1963), contains a geographical summary of Budapest; IVAN BOLDIZSAR (ed.), *Hungary: A Comprehensive Guidebook for Visitors and Armchair Travellers*, 6th ed. (1969), provides tourist information on Budapest, with several illustrations and maps; THOMAS SCHREIBER, *Hongrie* (1957; Eng. trans., 2nd ed., 1964), has information on Budapest and environs, including a folding map of the city.

The past: EMERIC TRENCSENYI (comp.), *British Travellers in Old Budapest* (1937), descriptions of Budapest by five British travellers beginning with Edward Brown in the 17th century; GRACE HUMPHREY, *Come with Me Through Budapest* (1933), gives a picture of Budapest as it was before World War II; ALEXANDRA ORME, *By the Waters of the Danube* (Eng. trans. 1951), a highly personal account of life in Budapest in 1945.

Art: KLARA GARAS, *Masterpieces from Budapest* (1961) and *Selected Paintings from the Old Picture Gallery, Budapest Museum of Fine Arts* (1967), two selections of reproductions in colour from the notable paintings at the Budapest Museum of Fine Arts; DENES PATAKY, *Master Drawings from the Collection of the Budapest Museum of Fine Arts, 19th and 20th Centuries* (Eng. trans. 1959), excellent reproductions in a well-produced book.

Chiefly photographic: MIKLOS REV, *Budapest: The Life of a City in Snapshots* (1960), shows the principal buildings of the city and the people in their daily life; JANOS REISMANN (ed.), *Budapest: The Hungarian Capital in Pictures* (1956), panoramas and closer views of the city and surrounding countryside.

Buddha

The Buddha, Siddhārtha Gautama, was the founder of Buddhism, one of the great world religions and philosophical systems that, in turn, produced a great culture with its own peculiar art, architecture, sculpture, and enormous literature in Pāli, Sanskrit, Chinese, Tibetan, and many other languages.

The term buddha, literally meaning "awakened one" or "enlightened one," is not a proper name but rather a title, such as messiah (the christ). Thus, the term should be accompanied by an article, such as "the Buddha" or "a buddha" (because of a belief that there will be innumerable buddhas in the future as there have been in the past). The personal name of the Buddha known to the history of this present world is Gautama (in Sanskrit), or Gotama (in Pāli). Therefore, in using the term the Buddha, it is generally assumed that it refers to Gautama the Buddha.

The story of the Buddha's life, as recorded here, is based on the Pāli texts of the *Tipiṭaka* (the "Triple Canon," or the "Three Baskets"), which is recognized by scholars as the earliest extant record of the Buddha's discourses, and their Pāli commentaries. Thus, in this article the Pāli as well as the Sanskrit spellings will be used for most names and terms. In the ancient Pāli texts the Buddha is designated Gotama. The style and technique of these ancient texts, followed in this biography, provide a record—sometimes symbolical, sometimes legendary, and always graphic—of the life of the revered Teacher. Just as there has been a vigorous search for the "historical Jesus" by Christian and other Western-oriented scholars, so also among some Western Orientalists there has been a scholarly search for the "historical Buddha," the history of whom the Buddhists themselves never questioned and which had never interested them or posed a problem of importance for them. This article will concentrate on Gautama the Enlightened One as depicted in the Buddhist scriptures and legends that developed about the man, his teachings, and his activities.

THE BIRTH AND EARLY LIFE OF THE BUDDHA

The Buddha was born about the year 563 BC in the kingdom of the Sakyas (on the borders of present-day Nepal and India). As the son of Śuddhodana, the king, and Mahāmāyā, the queen, the Buddha thus came from a Kṣatriya family (*i.e.*, the warrior caste or ruling class).

Mother's dream of the birth of the Buddha

The story of the Buddha's life, however, begins with an account of a dream that his mother Mahāmāyā had one night before he was born: a beautiful elephant, white as silver, entered her womb through her side. Brahmins (Hindu priests) were asked to interpret the dream, and they foretold the birth of a son who would become either a universal monarch or a buddha. Ten lunar months after the conception, the Queen and her retinue left Kapilavastu, the capital of the Sakya kingdom, on a visit to her parents in Devadaha. She passed through Lumbinī, a park that was owned jointly by the people of both cities. There, she gave birth to the Buddha in a curtained enclosure in the park on the full-moon day of the month of Vesākha (May). The site of his birth, now called Rummindei, lies within the territory of Nepal. A pillar placed there in commemoration of the event by Aśoka, a 3rd-century-BC Buddhist emperor of India, still stands.

Immediately upon hearing of the birth of the Buddha, the sage Asita (also called Kāḷa Devala), who was King Śuddhodana's teacher and religious adviser, went to see the child. From the auspicious signs on the child's body, Asita recognized that this child would one day become a buddha, and he was overjoyed and smiled. Because he was very old, however, he grew sad and wept, knowing that he would not remain alive to see the child's subsequent enlightenment. Śuddhodana, because of this strange display of alternate emotions, was concerned about possible dangers to the child, but Asita explained why he had first smiled and then wept and reassured the King about the child's future. Both the sage and the King then worshipped the child.

On the fifth day after birth, for the name-giving ceremony, 108 Brahmins were invited, among whom eight were specialists in interpreting bodily marks. Of these eight specialists, seven predicted two possibilities: if the child remained at home, he would become a universal monarch; if he left home, he would become a buddha. But Koṇḍañña, the youngest of the eight, predicted that he would definitely become a buddha. Later, this same Koṇḍañña became one of the Buddha's companions and was one of his first five disciples. The child was given the name Siddhārtha (in Sanskrit), or Siddhattha (in Pāli), which means One Whose Aim Is Accomplished.

On the seventh day after his birth, his mother died, and the child was brought up by her sister Mahāprajāpatī Gautamī, Śuddhodana's second consort.

Signs of the Buddha's eventual career

A significant incident in the Buddha's boyhood is recorded in ancient Pāli commentaries. One day, the little Siddhārtha was taken to the state plowing festival, in which the King, with his ministers and the ordinary farmers, took part, according to the traditional custom of the Sakyas. The boy was left with his nurses in a tent under a *jambu* tree. The nurses, attracted by the festivities, left the Prince alone in the tent and went out to enjoy themselves. When they returned, they found the boy seated cross-legged, absorbed in a trance (Sanskrit *dhyāna;* Pāli *jhāna*). The king was immediately informed and saw his little son in the posture of a *yogin* (a practitioner of psychological, physiological meditation techniques). Upon seeing his son sitting in this fashion, he worshipped the child a second time. Many years later, the Buddha himself, in one of his discourses (the *Mahā-Saccaka-sutta*, "The Great Discourse to Saccaka," of the *Majjhima Nikāya*, or the "Collection of the Middle Length Sayings of the Buddha"), briefly mentions his attaining to the first *dhyāna* under the *jambu* tree.

The young prince was brought up in great luxury, but his father, always worried that his son might leave home to become a homeless ascetic as the Brahmins had predicted, took every care to influence him in favour of a worldly life. According to the *Aṅguttara Nikāya* ("Collection of the Gradual Sayings of the Buddha"), a canonical text, the Buddha himself is reported to have said later about his upbringing:

"*Bhikkhu*s [monks], I was delicately nurtured, exceedingly delicately nurtured, delicately nurtured beyond measure. In my father's residence lotus-ponds were made: one of blue lotuses, one of red and another of white lotuses, just for my sake. . . . Of Kāsi cloth was my turban made; of Kāsi my jacket, my tunic, and my cloak . . . I had three palaces: one for winter, one for summer and one for the rainy season. *Bhikkhu*s, in the rainy season palace, during the four months of the rains, entertained only by female musicians, I did not come down from the palace."

At the age of 16, Siddhārtha married his cousin, a princess named Yasodharā, also 16 years old. Although Śuddhodana tried his utmost to make Siddhārtha content by providing him with luxury and comfort, the young prince's thoughts were generally elsewhere, occupied with other concerns.

THE FOUR SIGNS OF THE GREAT RENUNCIATION

The effect of suffering on the young Siddhārtha

The Four Signs. The turning point in Gautama's life came when he was 29 years old. One day, while out driving with his charioteer, the prince Siddhārtha saw "an aged man as bent as a roof gable, decrepit, leaning on a staff, tottering as he walked, afflicted and long past his prime." The charioteer, questioned by the Prince as to what had happened to the man, explained that he was old and that all men were subject to old age if they lived long enough. The Prince, greatly perturbed by this sight, went back to the palace and became absorbed in thought. Another day, again driving with his charioteer, he saw "a sick man, suffering and very ill, fallen and weltering in his own excreta, being lifted up by some . . . ." Because Siddhārtha was perturbed, the charioteer explained, as before, that this was a sick man and that all men are subject to sickness. On a third occasion the Prince saw a dead body and again the charioteer provided the explanation. Finally, Siddhārtha saw "a shaven-headed man, a wanderer who has gone forth, wearing the yellow robe." Impressed with the man's peaceful and serene demeanour, the Prince decided to leave home and go out into the world to discover the reason for such a display of serenity in the midst of misery.

This account should probably not be taken literally. It is difficult to believe that by the age of 29 Siddhārtha had not seen an old man or a sick man, even if the sight of a corpse is excluded. A psychological factor, however, should be taken into consideration: a common phenomenon may one day, unexpectedly, produce in a man a psychological crisis because of various combining circumstances. Old age, sickness, and death, in this account, symbolically represent human suffering in general. Siddhārtha, touched by the suffering of humanity and out of compassion for the world, decided to leave home and go in search for a solution to the problem of suffering.

On his way back to the palace after seeing the yellow-robed ascetic, Siddhārtha received the news of the birth of his son, whom he named Rāhula.

The great renunciation. Upon receiving this news, the Prince decided to make what is known as the great renunciation: giving up the princely life to become a wandering ascetic. Waking up in the middle of the night, he ordered Channa, his charioteer and companion, to saddle his favourite horse, Kanthaka, and went to the bedchamber to have a last look at his sleeping wife and their son. He did not enter the chamber for fear of awakening his wife, which would be a sure obstacle to his plan. He thought he would one day come to see them again.

Beginning of the quest for the truth

That night Siddhārtha left the city of Kapilavastu, accompanied by his companion Channa. By dawn he had crossed the Anomā River. He then gave all his ornaments to Channa, assumed the guise of an ascetic, and sent Channa and Kanthaka back to his father.

As an ascetic, Gautama (henceforth, he will be called Gautama) went south, where centres of learning and spiritual discipline flourished, and arrived at Rājagaha (modern Rājgīr), the capital of the Magadha kingdom. Bimbisāra, the king of Magadha, was impressed by the handsome appearance and the serene personality of this strange ascetic and visited him when he was seated at the foot of a hill. The King, after he discovered that the ascetic was a former prince, offered him every comfort and suggested that he should stay with him to share his kingdom. Gautama, however, rejected the King's offer, saying that he had no need again of those things that he had renounced and that he was in search of truth. Bimbisāra then requested that, when Gautama obtained the Enlightenment, he return to visit Rājagaha again, to which Gautama agreed.

THE SEARCH FOR THE TRUTH AND THE GREAT ENLIGHTENMENT

The search for the truth. Leaving Rājagaha, Gautama went in search of teachers to instruct him in the way of truth. Two of them the Buddha himself mentioned by name in several discourses. He first went to Āḷāra Kālāma, a renowned sage, and expressed his wish to follow Āḷāra's system; Āḷāra gladly accepted Gautama as his pupil. Gautama studied and rapidly mastered Āḷāra's whole system and then asked his teacher how far the master himself had realized that teaching. Āḷāra told him that he had attained the "sphere of no-thing" (*ākiñcaññāyatana*). Gautama soon attained the same mystical state himself. Āḷāra admitted that that state was the highest he could teach and declared that Gautama and himself were now equals in every respect—in knowledge, practice, and attainment—and invited the Sakyan ascetic to guide, along with him, the community of his disciples. The Buddha spoke of this occasion in the *sūtra* (or *sutta*, "discourse"): "In this way, *bhikkhus*, did Aḷāra Kālāma, my teacher, set me, his pupil, on the same level as himself and honoured me with the highest honour." Gautama, however, was not satisfied with attaining the "sphere of no-thing," though it was a very high mystical state. He was in quest of absolute truth, Nirvāṇa, and thus he left Āḷāra Kālāma.

He then went to Uddaka Rāmaputta, another great teacher, who taught him to attain the "sphere of neither-perception-nor-nonperception" (*nevasaññā-nāsaññāyatana*), a higher mystical state than the former. Gautama, however, was not satisfied with this either and searched further for the truth.

Travelling through the Magadha country, Gautama arrived at a village, called Senānigama, near Uruvelā, and, according to his own words, found "a beautiful stretch of land, a lovely woodland grove, and a clear flowing river with a pleasant ford, and a village for support close by." He was joined there by a group of five ascetics, among whom was Koṇḍañña, the Brahmin who had predicted at the name-giving ceremony that the child Siddhārtha would definitely become a buddha one day.

The Buddha's practice of asceticism

Gautama's real struggle in his search for the truth began at Uruvelā. Here, for nearly six years, he practiced various forms of severe austerities and extreme self-mortifications. These austerities were vividly described in detail by the Buddha himself in several discourses (*e.g.*, in the *Majjhima Nikāya*). What he looked like and what happened to him as a result of these austerities is depicted in the following words from the ancient text:

> Because of so little nourishment, all my limbs became like some withered creepers with knotted joints; my buttocks like a buffalo's hoof; my back-bone protruding like a string of balls; my ribs like rafters of a dilapidated shed; the pupils of my eyes appeared sunk deep in their sockets as water appears shining at the bottom of a deep well; my scalp became shrivelled and shrunk as a bitter gourd cut unripe becomes shrivelled and shrunk by sun and wind; . . . the skin of my belly came to be cleaving to my back-bone; when I wanted to obey the calls of nature, I fell down on my face then and there; when I stroked my limbs with my hand, hairs rotted at the roots fell away from my body . . . .

A Gandhāra (Greco-Buddhist) statue (of between the 2nd and 4th centuries AD) depicts the Buddha in this emaciated state.

As a consequence of all these severe bodily austerities, Gautama became so weak that he once fainted and fell down and was believed by some to be dead. By these experiences, he realized that such mortifications could not lead him to what he sought; he thus changed his way of life and again began to eat proper amounts of food.

His five companions, who had much faith and confidence in him, were disappointed at his rejection of extreme asceticism and left him in disgust. Gautama thus remained alone in Uruvelā, regained his health and strength, and then followed his own path to enlightenment.

The great Enlightenment. One morning, seated under a banyan tree, Gautama accepted an offering of a bowl of milk rice from Sujātā, the daughter of the landowner of the village Senānigama. This was his last meal before his Enlightenment. He spent the day in a grove of sal trees and in the evening went to the base of an *assattha* tree, now known as *bodhi* tree (*Ficus religiosa*), and sat cross-legged, determined not to rise without attaining enlightenment.

At that point, the greatest of Gautama's struggles began: Māra, the evil one, the tempter who is the lord of the world of passion, determined to defeat him and prevent him from attaining enlightenment; he approached Gautama with his hideous, demonic hordes. Gautama, however, sat unmoved in meditation, supported only by the ten *pāramitā*s ("great virtues") that he had perfected during innumerable past lives as a *bodhisattva* ("buddha-to-be") in order to attain enlightenment. (In order to attain buddhahood, all *bodhisattva*s ["buddhas-to-be"—*i.e.*, those who aspire to become buddhas] have to perfect, during innumerable lives, these ten *pāramitā*s: charity, morality, renunciation, wisdom, effort, patience, truth, determination, universal love, and equanimity.) Māra was thus vanquished and fled headlong with his armies of evil spirits.

The struggle with Māra, the tempter

The battle with Māra is graphically and vividly described in the old commentaries and depicted in painting on the walls of Buddhist temples. In the *Padhānasutta* ("Discourse on the Exertion") of the *Suttanipāta*, one of the earliest canonical texts, the Buddha states that, when he was practicing austerities by the River Nerañjarā in Uruvelā, Māra approached him, speaking such words as: "You are emaciated, pale, you are near death. Live, Sir, life is better. Do meritorious deeds. What is the use of striving?" After some preliminary words, Gautama replied to Māra:

"Lust is your first army; the second is dislike for higher life; the third is hunger and thirst; the fourth is craving; the fifth is torpor and sloth; the sixth is fear (cowardice); the seventh is doubt; the eighth is hypocrisy and obduracy; the ninth is gains, praise, honour, false glory; the tenth is exalting self and despising others. Māra, these are your armies. No feeble man can conquer them, yet only by conquering them one wins bliss. I challenge you! Shame on my life if defeated! Better for me to die in battle than to live defeated . . . ." Māra, dejected and overcome with grief, then disappeared. The fight with Māra was a mythologized struggle between good and evil, an inner struggle.

Having defeated Māra, Gautama spent the rest of the night in deep meditation under the tree. In the first watch of the night (6 PM to 10 PM), he gained the knowledge of his former existences (*pubbenivāsānussati-ñāṇa*). In the middle watch (10 PM to 2 AM), he attained the "superhuman divine eye" (*dibba-cakkhu*), the power to see the passing away and rebirth of beings. In the last watch (2 AM to 6 AM), he directed his mind to the knowledge of the destruction of all cankers and defilements and realized the Four Noble Truths. In the Buddha's own recorded words: "My mind was emancipated, . . . Ignorance was dispelled, science (knowledge) arose; darkness was dispelled, light arose."

The realization of the Four Noble Truths

Thus, Gautama, at the age of 35, attained the Enlightenment, or Awakening, and became a supreme buddha during the night of the full-moon day of the month of Vesākha (May), about the year 528 BC, at a place now called Buddha Gayā, or Bodh Gayā.

Contemplation on the truth. After his Enlightenment the Buddha spent several weeks (five or seven weeks according to different accounts) in Uruvelā, meditating on the various aspects of the *dhamma* ("truth") that he had realized, particularly on the most important and difficult doctrine of causal relations, known as the dependent origination or the conditioned genesis (*paṭiccasamuppāda*). This doctrine views everything as relative and interdependent and teaches that there is no eternal, everlasting, unchanging, permanent, or absolute substance, such as the soul, the self, or the ego, within or without man.

Four weeks after his Enlightenment, again seated under a banyan tree, the Buddha is reported to have thought to himself: "I have realized this Truth which is deep, difficult to see, difficult to understand . . . comprehensible by the wise. Men who are overpowered by passion and surrounded by a mass of darkness cannot see this Truth which is against the current (*paṭisotagāmin*), which is lofty, deep, subtle and hard to comprehend."

With these thoughts in mind, the Buddha hesitated trying to explain to the world the truth that he had just realized. He then compared the world to a lotus pond: In a lotus pond there are some lotuses still under water; there are others that have risen only up to the water level; and there are still others that stand above water and are untouched by it. In a similar way, in this world there are men of different levels of development. Some of them would understand the truth; the Buddha thus decided to teach what he had comprehended in the great Enlightenment.

Decision to teach the truth

His problem, however, was concerned with whom he should first teach this *dhamma*, this truth. He first thought of his two former teachers, Āḷāra Kālāma and Uddaka Rāmaputta; but they had already died by this time. He then thought of the five companions who had left him and were now staying in Isipatana near Bārāṇasī (now Vārānasi) and decided to go there.

On meeting the five ascetics, the Buddha told them that now he was a "perfected one" (*arahant*), a "fully awakened one" (*sammāsambuddha*), that he had realized the "immortal" (*amata*), and that he wished to instruct and teach them the *dhamma*. They replied to him:

> But, Reverend Gautama, even by all that conduct, that practice, that austerity, you did not realize this supreme knowledge, this supreme state. So how can you now realize it when you live in abundance, when you have given up striving and have reverted to a life of abundance?

The Buddha denied to them that he had given up striving and that he had reverted to a life of abundance. He requested again that they listen to him. Again, however, they replied in a similar manner. A third time the Buddha repeated what he said before and asked them to listen to him, and they repeated their remark.

The Buddha then asked them a very personal question: "Do you admit, monks, that I have never spoken anything like this before?" They were struck by such straightforwardness and knew how sincere and earnest he was. Convinced that he had attained what he claimed to have attained, they no longer addressed the Buddha as "Reverend Gautama," but changed their attitude toward him and answered him: "Lord, you have not." The Buddha then delivered to them his first sermon, known as the "Dhammacakkappavattana-sutta" ("Setting in Motion the Wheel of Truth"), at Isipatana, now called Sārnāth (near Vārānasi, [Benares]), where an ancient *stūpa* (building containing a religious relic) marks the spot.

The substance of this *sūtra* is as follows: a man who has left home and gone forth (*pabbajita*) should not follow two extremes, namely self-indulgence and self-mortification. Avoiding these two extremes, the Tathāgata (He Who Has Discovered the Truth—*i.e.*, the Buddha) has discovered the "middle path" (*majjhimā paṭipadā*) leading to vision, to knowledge, to calmness, to awakening, to Nirvāṇa. This middle path is known as the Noble Eightfold Path consisting of right view, right thought, right speech, right action, right mode of living, right endeavour, right mindfulness, and right concentration. The first noble truth is that man's existence is *dukkha*, full of conflict, dissatisfaction, sorrow, and suffering. The second noble truth is that all this is caused by man's selfish desire; *i.e.*, craving or *taṇhā*, "thirst." The third noble truth is that there is emancipation, liberation, and freedom for man from all this, which is Nirvāṇa (Pāli Nibbāna). The fourth noble truth, the Noble Eightfold Path, is the way to this liberation.

The teaching of moderation and the Eightfold Path

THE FOUNDING OF THE SANGHA

At the end of the sermon, these five monks, the Buddha's first disciples, were admitted by him as *bhikkhu*s and became the first members of the *sangha* ("order"). A few days later, this sermon was followed by the *Anattalakkhaṇa-sutta*, dealing with the doctrine of no-self, at the conclusion of which all five *bhikkhu*s became *arahant*s ("perfected ones").

The Buddha spent about three months in Vārānasi. During this period an important and influential wealthy young man named Yasa became his disciple and entered the order. His father and mother, along with his former wife, also were converted. They were the first lay disciples to take refuge in the "Triple Jewel": the Buddha, the *dhamma* (truth), and the *sangha* (the order). Later, four of Yasa's close friends followed his example and entered the order. Enthusiasm for this new movement became so impelling that 50 of their friends also joined them in the *sangha*. All these became *arahants* in due course, and the Buddha soon had 60 disciples who were perfected ones.

Conversions to the Buddha's teachings

The Buddha addressed this group in the following words and sent them out into the world to spread his message of peace, compassion, and wisdom:

> Bhikkhus, I am freed from all fetters, both divine and human. You, too, are freed from all fetters, both divine and human. Wander forth, bhikkhus, for the good of the many, for the happiness of the many, out of compassion for the world. . . . Let not two of you go by one road [*i.e.*, go in different directions]. Teach the *Dhamma* which is good at the beginning, good in the middle, and good at the end. . . . There are people who will understand the *Dhamma*. I, too, bhikkus, will go to Uruvelā to teach the *Dhamma*.

The 60 disciples went in various directions to spread the teaching of the Buddha. The Buddha himself set out for Uruvelā. On the way he converted 30 young men, who then entered the order. In the region of Uruvelā he also converted three leading ascetics along with a large number of their disciples. To these ascetics, formerly known as "matted hair" (*jaṭilas*), the Buddha delivered the famous "Fire Sermon" (the "Ādittapariyāya-sutta"), which states that all man's existence is burning with the fire of lust, the fire of hate, and the fire of delusion. This *sūtra* ("discourse") is perhaps better known to the Western world as the source of Section III of the poem *The Waste Land* by the U.S.-born English poet T.S. Eliot.

From Uruvelā the Buddha went on to Rājagaha, the capital of Magadha, fulfilling his promise to visit King Bimbisāra after his Enlightenment. Large numbers of people, including the King, became his lay disciples. The King offered his park, Veḷuvana, as a monastery site to the Buddha and his order. During this visit a very important event that had far-reaching effects took place: Sāriputta and Moggallāna, two Brahminic ascetics who later became the Buddha's two chief disciples, joined the order. Sāriputta had first heard of the Buddha and his new teaching from Assaji, one of the original 60 disciples. At the express request of his father, the Buddha visited Kapilavastu with a large number of his disciples. In that city, where as prince he had once lived in great splendour and luxury, he went about begging for his food from house to house. His father, King Suddhodana, was grieved and upset by this, but, upon learning that this was the custom of all buddhas, he conducted the Blessed One and his disciples to eat a meal at the palace.

Conversion of members of the Buddha's family

All the ladies of the court went to him to offer reverence, except his former wife Yasodharā. She refused, saying that the Blessed One himself would come to her if he thought that she had any virtue in her and that she would then worship him. The Buddha, with his two chief disciples and the King, went to see her in her apartment. She fell at his feet, clasped his ankles with her hands, and put her head on his feet.

The Buddha's father, his aunt Mahāpajāpatī, Yasodharā, and large numbers of Sakyans (members of the Buddha's clan) became his followers. On the following day he ordained his half-brother Nanda and a few days later his son, Rāhula. All this troubled the old King so much that he personally requested the Buddha to lay down a rule that no son should be ordained without the consent of his parents. Accordingly, the rule was formulated, and it continues to be followed up to the present by the *sangha*.

Anāthapiṇḍika, a banker of Sāvatthi, the capital of Kosala kingdom, had met the Buddha at Rājagaha and had become deeply devoted to him. He invited the Blessed One to his city, where he built for him the famous monastery at Jetavana. This monastery in Sāvatthi virtually became the headquarters of the Buddha's activities. Here, he spent most of his time and delivered most of his sermons. The Buddha and his new teaching became so popular that monasteries were built for him and his *sangha* in almost all the important cities in the valley of the Ganges, and the number of his followers among all classes of people increased rapidly.

The order of nuns, *bhikkhunī-sangha*, was instituted, after some hesitation. Ānanda, the Buddha's cousin and later his chief attendant and constant companion, pleaded with the Master on behalf of women. The Buddha's own aunt Mahāpajāpatī Gautamī and her friends were the first women to enter the order.

Members of some hostile sects, who became jealous of the Buddha's success and popularity, made several attempts to vilify him.

Attacks against the Buddha's authority

Devadatta, one of the Buddha's cousins, an ambitious man of ability and guile, was his rival from early days. He too joined the order but was never sincerely devoted to the Master. He became popular and influential with some people, however, and, about eight years before the Buddha's death, Devadatta conceived the idea of becoming the Buddha's successor and suggested to him that the leadership of the *sangha* should be handed over to him in view of the Master's approaching old age. The suggestion, however, was rejected. The Buddha stated that he would not pass on the leadership of the order to anyone, not even to Sāriputta or Moggallāna. Thus, no one was named as the future leader of the *sangha*, which was established on democratic principles, and everything was (and is) decided by majority vote. Its constitution was (and is) the *vinaya* (the "discipline," consisting of rules to guide the material and spiritual and the individual and communal life of the members of the order), which was laid down by the Master.

After this rebuttal Devadatta vowed vengeance. He made three cleverly designed attempts on the life of the Buddha, all of which failed. Devadatta next tried to bring about a schism in the *sangha*, taking with him a group of newly ordained monks to establish a separate community. All those who were misled by Devadatta, however, were later persuaded to go back to the Master by Sāriputta and Moggallāna. After this event Devadatta became very seriously ill and died after about nine months of illness.

THE DEATH OF THE BUDDHA

After the Buddha had trained learned, well-disciplined followers and his mission was fulfilled, at the age of 80, with a group of *bhikkhus*, he set out on his last journey, from Rājagaha toward the north. As usual, he passed in leisurely fashion through cities, towns, and villages, teaching the people on his way and stopping wherever he wished.

The Buddha's attempt to recover his health

In due course he arrived at Vesālī, the capital city of the Licchavi. The Buddha spent that rainy season not in the park in Vesālī, which had just been donated to him by Ambapālī, the celebrated courtesan of that city, but in an adjoining village called Beluvagāma. There the Buddha became seriously ill, almost dying (*māraṇantika*). He thought, however, that it was not right for him to die without preparing his disciples who were near and dear to him. Thus, with courage, determination, and will, he bore all his pains, got the better of his illness, and recovered; but his health was still poor.

After the Buddha's recovery, Ānanda, his most devoted attendant, went to his beloved Master and said:

> Lord, I have looked after the health of the Blessed One. I have looked after him in his illness. But at the sight of his illness, the horizon became dim to me, and my faculties were no longer clear. Yet there was one little consolation: I thought the Blessed One would not pass away until he had left instructions concerning the Order of the Sangha.

The Buddha, full of compassion and feeling, replied:

> Ānanda, what does the Order of the Sangha expect from me? I have taught the *dhamma* without making any distinction as to exoteric and esoteric. With regard to the Truth, the Tathāgata has nothing like the 'closed fist of a teacher' (*ācariya-muṭṭhi*), who keeps something back. Surely, Ānanda, if there is anyone who thinks that he will lead the *sangha* and that the *sangha* should depend on him, let him set down his instructions. But the Tathāgata has no such idea. Why should he then leave instructions concerning the *sangha?* I am old now, Ānanda . . . eighty years old. As a worn-out cart has to be kept going by repairs, so, it seems to me, the body of the Tathāgata can only be kept going by repairs. . . . Therefore, Ānanda, dwell by making yourselves your island, making yourselves, not anyone else, your refuge; making the *dhamma* your island, the *dhamma* your refuge, nothing else your refuge.

The Buddha's decision to die

Later on, the Buddha told Ānanda that he had decided to die after three months and asked him to assemble in the hall at Mahāvana all the *bhikkhu*s who were at that time residing in the neighbourhood of Vesālī. At this meeting, the Buddha first advised the monks to follow what he had taught them and to spread it abroad for the good of the many, out of compassion for the world, and then announced that he had decided to die after three months.

Leaving Vesālī, the Buddha gazed at the city in which he had stayed on many occasions and said: "This will be the last time, Ānanda, that the Tathāgata will behold Vesālī. Come, Ānanda, let us proceed. . . ."

Stopping at several villages and townships, the Buddha eventually arrived at Pāvā and stayed in the park of Cunda the goldsmith, who was already one of his devoted followers. At his invitation the Buddha and the *bhikkhu*s went to his house for a meal. Cunda had prepared, besides various delicacies, a dish called *sūkara-maddava.* This is interpreted in the ancient Pāli commentaries in several ways: (1) as pork (this is generally accepted), (2) as bamboo sprouts trodden by pigs, (3) as a kind of mushroom growing in a spot trodden by pigs, (4) as a rice pudding rich with the essence of milk, or (5) as a special preparation (an elixir?) intended by Cunda to prolong the Buddha's life. Whatever it might have been, the Buddha asked Cunda to serve him with *sūkara-maddava* and to serve the *bhikkhu*s with other dishes. At the end of the meal, the Buddha requested Cunda to bury in a hole whatever was left of the *sūkara-maddava*, saying that no one would be able to assimilate it except a Tathāgata. This was the Buddha's last meal.

After it the Buddha became sick and suffered violent pains but bore them without complaint. He set out for Kusinārā, accompanied by Ānanda and other *bhikkhu*s. Explaining that he was tired, he stopped and rested in two places. On the way, the Buddha said to Ānanda:

> Now it may happen, Ānanda, that someone should stir up remorse in Cunda by saying that the Tathāgata died after eating his meal. Any such remorse in Cunda should be dispelled. Tell him, Ānanda, that you heard directly from my mouth that there are two offerings of food which are of equal fruit, of equal profit: the offering of food before the Enlightenment and the offering of food before the *Parinibbāna* (the passing away) of a Tathāgata. Tell him that he has done a good deed. In this way Ānanda, you should dispel any possible remorse in Cunda.

The Buddha arrived at Kusinārā (the modern Kasia, also called Kuśinagara) toward evening, and, on a couch between two sal trees in the park Upavattana of the Mallas, he "laid himself down on his right side, with one leg resting on the other, mindful and self-possessed." This was the full-moon day of the month of Vesākha (May).

Final conversations with Ānanda and other monks

Ānanda inquired of the Buddha how and what they should do with his remains. He told Ānanda they should not occupy themselves with honouring the remains of the Tathāgata but rather to be zealous in their own spiritual development. The lay devotees, he said, would busy themselves with that task.

Ānanda, in remorse, left the immediate area and cried out: "My Master is about to pass away from me—he who is so kind to me." The Buddha inquired where Ānanda was and, on being told that he was weeping, called to him and said: "No, Ānanda, don't weep. Haven't I already told you that separation is inevitable from all near and dear to us? Whatever is born, produced, conditioned, contains within itself the nature of its own dissolution. It cannot be otherwise." Then, the Master spoke to the *bhikkhu*s in praise of Ānanda's wonderful qualities and abilities. The Mallas, clansmen, of Kusinārā came with their families to pay homage to the Blessed One. A wandering ascetic named Subhadda asked for permission to see the Buddha, but Ānanda refused, saying that the Blessed One was tired and that he should not be troubled. The Buddha, overhearing the conversation, called Ānanda and asked him to allow Subhadda to see him. After an interview with the Buddha, Subhadda joined the order the same night, thus becoming his last direct disciple.

The Buddha then addressed Ānanda:

> It may be, Ānanda, that to some of you the thought may come: 'Here we have the Word of the Master who is gone; our Master we have with us no more.' But, Ānanda, it should not be considered in this light. What I have taught and laid down, Ānanda, as *Dhamma* (Truth, Doctrine) and as *Vinaya* (Discipline), this will be your Master when I am gone. . . . If the Sangha (Order) wish it, Ānanda, let them, when I am gone, abolish lesser and minor precepts (rules).

The Buddha next addressed the *bhikkhu*s and requested them three times to ask him if they had any doubt or question that they wished clarified, but they all remained silent. The Buddha then addressed the *bhikkhu*s: "Then, *bhikkhu*s, I address you now: transient are all conditioned things. Try to accomplish your aim with diligence." These were the last words of the Tathāgata. A week later, his body was cremated by the Mallas in Kusinārā.

A dispute over the relics of the Buddha between the Mallas and the delegates of rulers of several kingdoms, such as Magadha, Vesālī, and Kapilavastu, was settled by a venerable old Brahmin named Doṇa on the basis that they should not quarrel over the relics of one who preached peace. With common consent, the relics were then divided into eight portions to the satisfaction of all. *Stūpa*s were built over these relics, and feasts were held commemorating the Buddha.

ASSESSMENT OF THE PERSONALITY AND CHARACTER OF THE BUDDHA

Not much information is available about the physical appearance of the Buddha. Caṅkī, a highly respected Brahmin leader, is reported to have said that "the recluse Gotama is lovely, good to look upon, charming, possessed of the greatest beauty of complexion, of a sublime colour, a perfect stature, noble of presence."

The reputation of the Buddha in his own time

He had a unique reputation as a great teacher and a trainer of men. His conversion and taming of Aṅgulimāla, a murderer and bandit who was a terror even to the King of Kosala, is an example of his great powers and abilities. People who went to see and hear him were fascinated and so quickly converted to his new teaching that his opponents described him as having some "enticing trick" (*āvaṭṭanī-māyā*). The King of Kosala said that those who went with the idea of confounding the Buddha in debate became his disciples at the end. Full of compassion (*karuṇā*) and wisdom (*paññā*), he is recognized as knowing how and what to teach each individual for his own benefit according to the level of his capabilities. He is known to have walked long distances to help one single person.

The Buddha, affectionate and devoted to his disciples, was always inquiring after their well-being and progress. When he was staying in a monastery, he paid daily visits to the sick ward. Once, he himself attended a sick monk neglected by others and on that occasion said: "He who attends on the sick attends on me."

The Buddha as a social reformer

As a social reformer, the Buddha condemned the caste system that was a long-established and respected institution in India and recognized the equality of man. He also perceived the connection between economic welfare and moral development. Trying to suppress crime through punishment, he said, was futile. Poverty (*dāḷiddiya*), according to the Buddha, was a cause of immorality and crimes; therefore, the economic condition of people should be improved.

He appreciated both natural and physical beauty. On several occasions he was moved aesthetically, as he told Ānanda how delightful certain places were to him. At Vesālī he told the *bhikkhu*s that, if they had not seen the *deva*s (gods) of Tāvatiṃsa (Heaven), they should look at the handsome Licchavis, beautifully and elegantly dressed in different colours.

The Buddha was a strict "disciplinarian." King Pasenadi could not understand how the Buddha maintained such order and discipline in the community of *bhikkhu*s, when he, a king, with the power to inflict punishment, could not maintain it as well in his court. The Buddha, however, kept order and discipline on the basis of a mutual love, affection, and respect that exists between teacher and pupil.

Many miraculous powers were attributed to the Buddha, but he did not consider these of any importance. Once, when one of his disciples performed a miracle in public, the Buddha reproached him and laid down a rule that his disciples should not perform miracles before the laity. In his view, the greatest miracle was to explain the truth and to make a man realize it.

Behind his philosophy and strict ethics, the Buddha had a quiet sense of humour. A conceited Brahmin, who was in the habit of discrediting others, questioned him as to the qualities of a true Brahmin. In a list of such high qualities as freedom from evil, purity of heart, the Buddha gently included "not discrediting."

The portrait of the Buddha, as can be inferred from the lines of the ancient texts, is thus one of a man of both great wisdom (*mahāpaññā*) and great compassion (*mahākaruṇā*) moved by the spectacle of human suffering and determined to free men from its fetters by a rational system of thought and a way of life.

BIBLIOGRAPHY

Canonical sources: The Collection of the Middle Length Sayings (*Majjhima-nikāya*), vol. 1, trans. by I.B. HORNER, "Pali Text Society Translation Series No. 29 (1954): "Discourse on the Ariyan Quest" (*Ariyapariyesana-sutta*, No. 26); and the "Greater Discourse to Saccaka" (*Mahāsaccaka-sutta*, No. 36), contain the story of the Buddha from the great renunciation up to the first sermon, including some aspects of the Buddha's private life; in the same volume, the "Great Discourse on the Lion's Roar" (*Mahāsīhanāda-sutta*, No. 12), contains a vivid description of the Buddha's severe austerities before the Enlightenment. *The Book of the Discipline*, vol. 4 (*Mahāvagga*), pp. 1–28, trans. by I.B. HORNER, ("Sacred Books of the Buddhists Series," vol. 14, 1962), includes an account from the Enlightenment up to the time of sending out the first 60 disciples as missionaries. "The Book of the Great Decease" (*Mahāparinibbāna-sutta*, No. 16) in the *Dialogues of the Buddha* (*Dīgha-nikāya*), vol. 2, trans. by T.W. and C.A.F. RHYS DAVIDS (1910; 3rd ed. reprinted 1966, "Sacred Books of the Buddhists Series," vol. 3), contains a fairly detailed narration of the final stage of the Buddha's life and his last journey.

Commentaries and later works: The *Buddhist Birth Stories* (*Jātaka* commentary), trans. by T.W. RHYS DAVIDS (1880; new ed. by MRS. RHYS DAVIDS, 1925), in the introductory section relates the Buddha's life with accompanying legends and miracles up to the time of his acceptance of the Jetavana monastery in Sāvatthi. See also HENRY CLARKE WARREN, *Buddhism in Translations* (1896, reprinted 1963).

Modern works: Information according to Tibetan sources may be found in W.W. ROCKHILL, *The Life of the Buddha* (1884). Information from some Sanskrit and Chinese sources is available in SAMUEL BEAL, *The Romantic Legend of Sâkya Buddha* (1875). EDWIN ARNOLD, *The Light of Asia* (1961), is a popular retelling in poetic form of the life and teaching of the Buddha. ALFRED FOUCHER, *La Vie du Bouddha d'après les textes et les monuments de l'Inde* (1949; abridged Eng. trans., *The Life of Buddha*, 1963), is a study according to both ancient texts and monuments of India. HERMANN OLDENBERG, *Buddha: His Life, His Doctrine, His Order* (1882), is a standard work, although some of its opinions and ideas expressed are now outdated. E.J. THOMAS, *The Life of Buddha As Legend and History* (1927; 3rd ed. rev., 1949, reprinted 1969), critically examines the original sources, sometimes advancing unnecessary speculations and theories, probably because of a lack of contact with the living traditions and their interpretations, and contains a useful bibliography. A modern Hindu philosopher's estimation may be found in SARVEPALLI RADHAKRISHNAN, *Gautama the Buddha,* (1945, reprinted in his translation of the *Dhammapada*, 1950).

(Wa.R.)

Buddhism

Buddhism is a pan-Asian religion and philosophy that has played a central role in the spiritual, cultural, and social life of the Eastern world. This article surveys Buddhism as a whole, in its various aspects, schools, and areas. (For a specific discussion of the philosophical aspect, see also BUDDHIST PHILOSOPHY.)

The article is divided into the following sections:

I. General observations

Buddhism originated in India in the 5th century BC in an area that extended roughly from Vārānasi to Gayā, Rājagṛha, Pāṭaliputra, Vaiśālī, Kuśinagara, and Pāvā (*i.e.*, in the regions of Magadha, the Malla, the Kāśī, and the Vṛjji) and in a period of great fervour in speculative, mystical, and religious life. There was an ongoing codification of sacrificial ritual (Brāhmaṇa), not without philosophical insights; a deepening of the theory of *karman* (deeds and their results in future existences); and a formulation of the initial insights of the *Upaniṣads* (ancient Hindu treatises), which declared the only reality to be an inner entity, *ātman*, which is either unique or the reflex in an individual of a single principle (*brahman*), outside of which all is only temporal—fleeting, changing, unreal. Ascetic branches were perfecting theories and practices of great antiquity (which came together in Yoga), not only native to India but analogous to certain magical and psychotherapeutic traditions throughout most of Asia—from India to China. Other schools held that any effort intended to modify life's destiny was in vain and that all ends with death. The Jaina school, having a tradition perhaps more ancient than Buddhism's classified the number and correlations of the various *karman.*

Buddhism developed in two directions. One, usually called Theravāda by its present-day adherents, remained relatively faithful to what it considered to be the true tradition of the Buddha's teachings. The other is called Mahāyāna, "the means of salvation adapted to a larger number of people," by its followers, who call the first Hīnayāna, "the means of salvation restricted to a smaller number of people" (or simply the greater and lesser vehicles). Both paths lead to Nirvāṇa (salvation); what matters is to be inside Buddhist doctrine, not outside it.

In its spread, Buddhism influenced the currents of thought and religion in other countries. Following the diverse religious aspirations and the passage of time, the iron law of *karman* was replaced by more yielding principles or devotional ecstasies. Finally there developed in India a movement called Tantra, the aim of which was to obtain liberation more speedily and which was influenced by gnostic and magical currents pervasive at that time.

For all the discussion on the two paths of salvation—the gradual and the instant—and the various ways of interpreting the key Mahāyāna concepts of the "void" and the mind-element, the ethics remain fundamentally the same. The monastic organizations suffered the influence of diverse historical situations, yet their structure remains the same. The Buddha, the original teacher, is always the revealer of the esoteric doctrine. In the later doctrines, his preaching is not just that given to his first disciples: he multiplies himself in numberless epiphanies—all manifestations of a single immutable reality—and he emphasizes the certainty of the void and the relativity of all appearances. He reinforces the belief in the presence of the Buddha within men.

In spite of all these vicissitudes, Buddhism did not negate its basic principles. Instead they were reinterpreted, rethought, and reformulated, bringing to life an immense literature that has always been regarded by followers of the Mahāyāna and Tantra as *Buddhavacana,* the word of the Buddha. Consequently, from the first sermon of the Buddha at Sārnāth to the last recent derivations, there is an indisputable continuity—a development or metamorphosis around a central nucleus—by virtue of which Buddhism is not confused with other religions. Thus, in spite of its diffusion, the discussion of Buddhism should proceed not by countries but by branches—branches of a single trunk, as is done in the presentation below.

II. The foundations of Buddhism

THE LIFE AND TEACHINGS OF THE BUDDHA

Life of the Buddha. Little is known of the life of Gotama (Gautama) Siddhattha (Siddhārtha), the founder of Buddhism. The term Śākyamuni, by which he is often called, designates a sage of the Śākyas, a warrior clan of the southern borderland of Nepal. Born about 563 BC, Gautama soon became aware of the futility of social life and was convinced that excessive philosophical discourse keeps men from the most important thing—right living. He saw that the shadow of death rests on all living creatures and that nothing is eternal. Legend attributes his final decisive renunciation to encounters with a sick man, an old man, a dead man, and, finally, a serene mendicant ascetic. It also tells of the repeated attempts by his father to turn him from his purpose. At last, he abandoned his home, wife, and son and associated with the most famous spiritual masters of his time. He learned Yoga, a meditative discipline, which he practiced in the extreme until he realized that to be effective meditation requires a healthy body. Thus he discovered the path that leads to the correct knowledge of the nature of persons and things and of their appearance and disappearance.

Gautama's path to Enlightenment

Under the pipal tree in Gayā (subsequently called Bodh Gayā) in about 525 BC, he achieved Enlightenment (*bodhi*), and thus became a (or the) Buddha (Enlightened One). The question then arose: should he keep for himself the truth he had discovered or should he preach it to others? The Hindu gods Indra and Brahmā, according to legend, descended from their heavens and begged him to reveal his liberating doctrine to all. This he did, preaching without rest until his death in about 480 BC at Kuśinagara.

Teachings of the Buddha. The teaching attributed to the Buddha was transmitted orally by his disciples prefaced by the phrase, *evaṃ mayā śrutam* ("Thus have I heard"); therefore, it is difficult to say whether his discourses were related as they were spoken. They usually allude, however, to the place, time, and community where he preached; and there is concordance between various versions. An attempt was made by Buddhist councils in the first centuries after the Buddha's death to establish his true and original teachings (see BUDDHISM HISTORY OF, *Early Buddhist Councils*).

The basic Buddhist terms below are given in both Pāli and Sanskrit at their first appearance where they differ (*e.g., anicca, anitya*) and thereafter in Sanskrit, which is more familiar in Western literature.

Impermanence, no-self, and misery. According to the Buddha, all is impermanent (*anicca, anitya*), a flowing reality, whether of external things or the psychophysical totality of human individuals; thus a succession and concatenation of microseconds called *dhamma, dharma* (hereafter, *dharmas*; not to be confused with *dharma,* meaning "law" or "teaching"). The Buddha departed from the main lines of traditional Indian thought in not asserting an essential or ultimate reality in things. Moreover, contrary to the theories of the *Upaniṣads* (Hindu sacred treatises), Gautama maintained that an *ātman* ("self" or "soul") does not exist: there is nothing within us that is metaphysically real. Thus, along with impermanence, he affirms the theory of *anattā, anātman,* or *nairātmya,* the nonexistence of an eternal "I," or *ātman.* Yet human beings are caught in the cycle of births and deaths (*saṃsāra*) because the extinction of life—if the effect of a completed deed (*karman*) has not been stopped—does not mean the end of existence but a projection toward a new existence. He also perceived and taught that existence is subject to misery connected with the unpleasant, especially sickness and death, and separated from the pleasant.

The Four Noble Truths. Awareness of these fundamental realities led the Buddha to formulate the Four Noble Truths: the truth of misery (*dukkha, duḥkha*); the truth that misery originates within us from the craving for pleasure and for being or nonbeing; the truth that this craving can be eliminated; and the truth that this elimination is the result of a methodical way or path that must be followed. Thus, there must be an understanding of the mechanism by which man's psychophysical being evolves; otherwise men would remain indefinitely in *saṃsāra,* in the continual flow of transitory existence.

Misery and its cure

The law of dependent origination. Hence the Buddha formulated the law of dependent origination (*paṭiccasamuppāda, pratītya-samutpāda*), whereby one condition arises out of another, which in turn arises out of prior conditions. Every mode of being presupposes another immediately preceding mode from which the subsequent mode derives, in a chain or series of causes. The original condition is ignorance (*avijjā, avidyā*); then come the cooperating karmic agents (*sankhāra, saṃskāra,* literally "aggregates" or "compounds"; mental qualities, dispositions, and habits); then consciousness (*viññāna, vijñāna*); and then "name and form" (*nāma-rūpa*), the naming and materiality of things. The five sense organs and the mind (*satāyatana, ṣaḍāyatana*), thereupon condition contact (*phassa, sparśa*). Contact in turn causes the psychic, mental, or emotional response to sense objects (*vedanā*). This is the antecedent of the ensuing craving evoked by the objects (*taṇhā, tṛṣṇā*). From this comes the grasping for, or attachment to, those same objects (*upādāna*), an essential condition because it determines *bhava,* coming into existence, and, hence, *jāti*, "birth," with its consequent *jarā-maraṇa*, "old age" and death, and, so, misery. Thus, the misery that is bound up with all sensate existence is accounted for by a methodical chain of causation.

The *pratītya-samutpāda* is the law of interdependence or reciprocal conditioning of phenomena within the totality of physical, psychic, and psychosomatic existence. It is the subject of solitary meditation by the Buddhist aspirant. It is initiated by one's own ignorance, together with the cooperating karmic agents representing the inheritance from the past. Present life is the effect constituted by consciousness and its derivatives, the mental faculties and corporeity (*nāma* and *rūpa*), the six sensory "bases," contact or impression, and the psychic or mental response. In the present state, man accumulates a karmic charge projected into the future. This is caused by craving for enjoyment, grasping for sensuous impressions, the notion of "I" and "mine," and attachment to false theories; thus, the law of dependent origination takes men again into space and time (*bhava*), with consequential birth and death (their future). Consciousness, therefore, is the ripening (*vipāka*) of the past life. It has five different ways of apprehending: with the eye, ear, nose, tongue, and body; thus, it bears the responsibility for a new rebirth (*patisandhi-viññāna*). It also conditions *nāma-rūpa*, name and form; "name," because this presupposes an awareness of the things named (*i.e.*, mental faculties, or mind), and "form" because without bodily or material form sensate beings would not exist. Corporeity is reduced to the physical elements that exist both in external things and in the body: earth, water, fire, air, and the forces that join them—solidity, fluidity, heat, and motion—to which correspond the five sense organs and the five sense fields.

Consciousness and its consequences

The law of dependent origination of the successive states of life and understanding remains invariable and fundamental in all schools of Buddhism, although there are diverse interpretations of it.

The Eightfold Path. Given the awareness of this law, the question arises as to how one may escape the continually renewed cycle. Here ethical conduct enters in. It is not enough to know that misery pervades all existence and the way in which life evolves; there must also be a purification that leads to the overcoming of this process. Such a liberating purification is effected by following, with a sincerity reinforced by continual meditation, the noble Eightfold Path: the right mode of seeing things, right thinking, right speech, right action, right mode of living, right effort in every mode of being, right mindfulness, right meditation. The term right (true or correct) is used to distinguish sharply between the precepts of the Buddha and other teachings.

Nirvāṇa. The ultimate goal to be achieved through following the Eightfold Path is Nibbāna, Nirvāṇa; but the Buddha does not explain what it is or what it is not because it cannot be expressed in general terms and escapes all definitions. Nirvāṇa is a condition that is realized when *karman* and the consequential succession of lives and births (*saṃsāra*) have been definitely overcome. Expositions of the subtleties of the doctrine of Nirvāṇa largely deal with this process.

Saṅgha (community). The disciples gathered around the Buddha made up the *saṅgha* (community). They could possess nothing and lived on alms. The Buddha was the "Teacher" (*sattha, śāstṛ*), or, borrowing a word from the world of merchants, among whom Buddhism fared especially well, the "head caravaneer," the guide along the route that leads to salvation. The *saṅgha* was the group of properly ordained disciples. Its members comprised neophytes (*sāmaṇera, śrāmaṇera*) and fully ordained monks (*bhikkhu, bhikṣu*). The most excellent member was the *arahant, arhat* ("saint," or worthy one") who had achieved the complete detachment that leads to Nirvāṇa. The Buddha provided the example that the others could follow. The power of his attraction was in his being an Enlightened One who kindled faith (*saddhā, śraddhā*) in others.

The "Three Jewels" and the Threefold Refuge. The force of his conviction and example exalted the disciples; consequently, the three factors of adherence to the Teacher were: faith in the Buddha, in the law or doctrine taught by him (*dhamma, dharma*), and in the community (*saṅgha*), the repository of his teaching. These are the Three Jewels in which a devout layman (*upāsaka* if male, *upāsikā* if female) takes refuge (*sarana, śaraṇa*). "I take refuge in the Buddha, I take refuge in the law, I take refuge in the community," is the traditional Buddhist affirmation.

The traditional Buddhist affirmation

The appeal of the Buddhist teaching. According to the Buddha's teaching, the universal aim is salvation, the attainment of Nirvāṇa; this, however, requires a great span of time (the *Jātaka* stories, which tell about the previous lives of the Buddha, demonstrate this); but the important thing is that the way has been found, that "one has set out on the path." Several features favoured the rapid success of the Buddha and of his doctrine. Buddhism was open to all, regardless of caste (an important factor in Indian society), because the Buddha did not recognize any essential difference among men; the difference among them, in his view, derived solely from their diverse moral and karmic maturity.

THE ANCIENT SCHOOLS

Buddhism may be divided into three main branches: (a) the ancient schools (currently represented by Theravāda), (b) Mahāyāna, and (c) Tantrism, the esoteric branch, which, though distinctive, is inseparable from Mahāyāna. Each branch has several subgroups. According to the ancient chronicles, the Buddhist community had broken up into a number of schools, the so-called 18 schools (although there were more than 18) during its first three centuries.

The development of the most important schools of Buddhism is summarized in the chart.

The various schools or branches were not limited to a particular region. Mahāyāna and Tantrism flourished side by side with Theravāda for many centuries in Ceylon (now Sri Lanka) and Southeast Asia. In the 7th century, various sects coexisted in Central Asia, India (often in the same area), and Southeast Asia.

Theravāda (Sthaviravāda). The Theravāda (Sanskrit, Sthaviravāda) school is regarded as the transmitter of ancient Buddhism. Hence it is of fundamental importance to consider its main doctrines and practices.

Cosmology. In the Theravāda view there is a plurality of universes surrounded by water and mountain chains. Every universe has three planes: (a) the "sphere of desire" (*kāmadhātu*); (b) the sphere of material form (*rūpadhātu*) but removed from sensuous desire; and (c) the sphere of immateriality or the formless (*arūpadhātu*). On the plane of desire, creatures and their mode of being are divided into five or six species: demons; *preta*, a species of wandering, famished ghosts; animals; men; gods; and a sixth group not universally acknowledged, the *asura* (demigods). The matter of the world is made up of four elements: earth, water, fire, and air, held together in various combinations.

Plurality of universes, planes, and cycles

Time moves in cycles (*kalpa*s), involving a period of involution (destruction by fire, water, air), of stability, of renewal, and of duration, at the end of which the cycle moves again into a period of destruction and repetition of the subsequent periods. The *kalpa*s are made up of four ages (*yuga*s)—Kṛta, Tretā, Dvāpara, and Kali—of progressively decreasing happiness and life-span.

Human existence is a privileged state because the Buddha is born only among men. Moreover, man has the capability of choosing that which can lead him to do good works (which will result in a good birth) or bad works (and thus a bad birth); and, above all, he has the possibility of becoming a Buddha. All of these capacities and activities are reduced to a series of *dharma*s, instant points in continual motion or changing states, subject to appearing, aging, and disappearing.

Classification of dharmas. *Dharma*s are divided and subdivided into many groups. The essential ones that concern man's psychophysical person are the five components (*khandha, skandha*), the 12 bases (*āyatana*), and the 18 sensory elements (*dhātu*). The five components, or

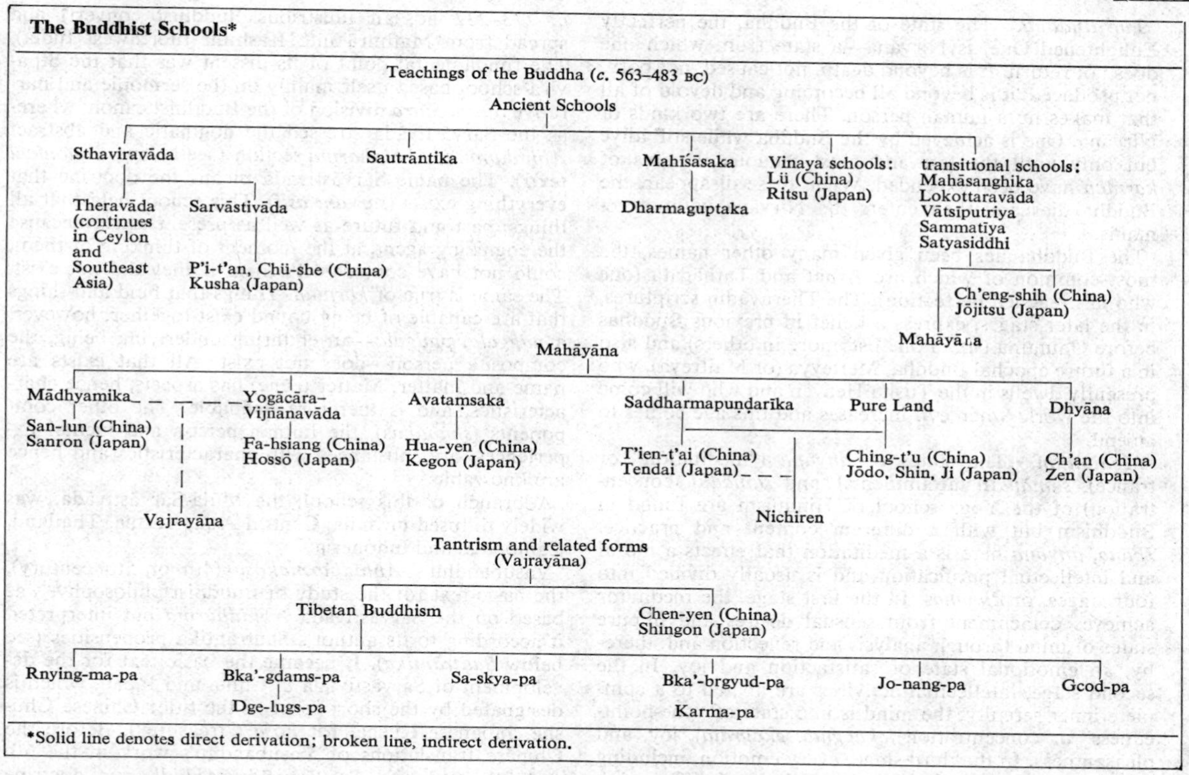

skandhas, are: a) *rūpa*, materiality, or form; b) *vedanā*, feelings of pleasure or pain or the absence of either one; c) *saṃjñā*, cognitive perception; d) *saṃskāra*, the forces that cooperate to condition the psychic activity of an individual, from tactile sensations to emotions, memory, the disposition for concentration (*samādhi*), and the reasoning faculty (*pañña, prajñā*)—*i.e.*, all of the impulses and conscious factors that determine the psychic inclination and volitional tendency of thought; and e) *vijñāna*, the six modes of apprehension related to the five senses, in addition to the general mind organ (*manas*), and consciousness as such.

The 12 bases, or *āyatanas*, include the five sense organs, such as the eye; the five related sense fields, such as the visible world; and *manas*, the general mind organ, or instrument of thought, and that toward which it is turned—*i.e.*, not things as such but things as they are reflected in mental perception.

The 18 elements, or *dhātus*, comprise the five sense organs and the *mano-dhātu* (mind element), their six correlated objects, and the six consciousnesses (*vijñāna*) of the eye, ear, nose, tongue, body, and *manas*.

Thus the classification of *dharmas* is an increasing elaboration of the psychophysical components of the human person and their corresponding objects. These lists may converge, but repetitions are derived from different codifications of the original teaching. For example, also listed are the faculties (*indriyas*) through which one comes to components of major importance: the five sense organs and the mind mentioned above; vitality; the experience of passion, pain, joy, sadness, or indifference; masculine and feminine potentialities; and faith (*śraddhā*), energy, mindfulness, concentration (*samādhi*), and wisdom—the five moral or spiritual faculties. The last three are of particular importance to the Buddhist.

Clearly in this ancient (Theravāda) version, Buddhism is not concerned with metaphysical problems but with man in his psychosomatic components, because only through his awareness of their interrelation, combination, and operation, and of the way to cultivate some and to suppress others can he arrive at the state of an *arhat* ("worthy one"). Its aim is not to promulgate a metaphysics but to liberate man by employing his psychic mechanism in a way to stop his *karman*.

Through the classification of *dharmas* a person comes to be seen as an aggregate of many elements working together, ruled in his becoming by the law of *karman*, whether good or bad, and thus destined to suffer good or bad consequences. All of this rests on the presupposition that there is no metaphysical entity such as an "I" or *ātman* outside of time, but that there is a psychosomatic aggregate situated in time, the freedom of choice of which allows it to perform this or that act, which can be with or without overflows and thus capable or not capable of consequences.

Knowledge of *dharmas* a step toward liberation from rebirth

Such classifications do not have a doctrinal goal; rather, they are preparatory distinctions that guide whoever accepts the teaching of the Buddha in passing from the temporal to the atemporal plane and overcoming the cycle of rebirths. Here enter the seven factors of Enlightenment: clear memory, the exact investigation of the nature of things, energy and sympathy, tranquillity, impartiality, and a disposition for concentration. These are assisted by subsidiaries, such as love for all living creatures, compassion, delight in that which is good or well done, and, again, impartiality. The last four are known as the "incommensurables," the necessary preconditions for liberation from *karman* and *saṃsāra*.

The stages leading to arhatship. The way that leads the disciple to the stages of *arhat*ship traverses an immense number of lives, during which the aspirant gains true insight into the nature of things.

One who believes in the teachings of the Buddha and practices them passes through four stages. (1) He who has entered into the stream; *i.e.*, begun the process leading to release from rebirth, can take two paths: that of devotion and that of intellectual discipline. His chances of rebirth are reduced greatly. (2) After that comes the stage of one who returns only once. (3) The third stage is that of one who does not return again, for he has freed himself from the lower bonds (belief in a permanent self, doubt, belief in mere morality or rites, sensual passion, and malice). He can obtain liberation in the time that runs from death until rebirth in a paradise, or even while in this existence. (4) The *arhat* gains freedom from death because he has accomplished all that he proposed and had to do in order to achieve his condition. He is free from all bonds, even desire for existence in the formed or formless worlds, excitability, ambition, and ignorance.

Nirvāṇa

The Buddha. The state of the Buddha, the perfectly Enlightened One, is Nirvāṇa—a state from which one does not return. It is beyond death, not caused, not born, not produced; it is beyond all becoming and devoid of all that makes up a human person. There are two kinds of Nirvāṇa. One is achieved by the Buddha while still alive but only until the last and most tenuous remains of *karman* have been expended. When these disappear, the Buddha dies and then enters the Nirvāṇa without remains.

The Buddha has been given many other names, the most common of which are Arhat and Tathāgata (one who has reached perfection). The Theravādin scriptures, in the later stages, express a belief in previous Buddhas before Gautama (six in one list, more in others) and also in a future epochal Buddha, Metteyya (or Maitreya), who presently dwells in the Tuṣita Heaven and who will come into the world when evil increases and this age comes to an end.

Meditation. The states of *dhyāna* ("meditation" or trance), *samāpatti* (attainments), and *samādhi* (concentration) of the Yoga school of Hinduism are found in Buddhism but with a different content and practice. *Jhāna, dhyāna* here is a meditation that effects a moral and intellectual purification and is usually divided into four stages, or *dhyāna*s. In the first stage, the meditator achieves detachment from sensual desires and impure states of mind through analysis and reflection and, thereby, an emotional state of satisfaction and joy. In the second stage, intellectual activities are abated to a complete inner serenity; the mind is in a state of "one-pointedness" or concentration (*ekaggatā, ekāgratā*), joy, and pleasantness. In the third stage, every emotion, including joy, has disappeared, leaving the meditator indifferent to everything while remaining completely conscious; he is in a state of well-being. The fourth stage is the abandoning of any sense of satisfaction, pain, or serenity because any inclination to a good or bad state of mind has disappeared. The meditator thus enters a state of supreme purity, indifference to everything, and pure consciousness.

At this point the meditator begins the *samāpatti*s (or further *dhyāna*s). Beyond all perception of form, withdrawn from the influence of perception, immune to the perception of plurality, concentrating on infinite space, he reposes in the condition of spacial infinity. Going beyond this stage and concentrating on the limitlessness of consciousness, he remains in that state. Proceeding further and concentrating on the nonexistence of everything whatsoever, he remains in a state in which there is absolutely nothing. Even further on, he remains in a state in which there is neither perception nor nonperception.

Psychic emptying out and nullification

This kind of meditation is somewhat different from the mystical contemplation of other Indian schools. It comprises the quiescence of all psychic activities and the transcending of contemplation itself. A progressive nullifying of every psychic activity and emotional or mental faculty, with the attainment of each successive stage of *dhyāna* or *samāpatti*, this form of meditation does not aim at finding or realizing a presence already contained within us but at the cessation of the more subtle aspects of consciousness. Thus it is an empty solitude that gradually liberates until it equals the immovable, uncreated, and infinite vastness of space, wherein the very factors that led one there dissolve because their function has been exhausted. The goal of the states of concentration is to attain supernatural consciousness and, finally, that mental jump into what is called Nirvāṇa.

Also to be noted in this connection is the notion of the unconditioned (*asamkhata, asaṃskṛta*), a *dharma* that is produced without depending on any cause; *i.e.*, something that is not born, does not last, does not change, and does not cease to be. In Theravāda, Nirvāṇa is regarded as an *asaṃskṛta*; other schools include space (*ākāśa*), *tathatā*, the "suchness of things," and *dharmatā*, the "being of things" among *asaṃskṛta*s.

Sarvāstivāda (P'i-t'an, Chü-she/Kusha). This group detached itself from the Sthavira school, the precursor of Theravāda, around the time of Aśoka (emperor of India c. 273–232 BC, an illustrious Buddhist convert) and spread from Mathurā into Kashmir (northwest India). The fundamental point of its dissent was that the Sthavira school based itself mainly on the sermonic and narrative *Sutta, Sūtra* division of the Buddhist canon, whereas the Sarvāstivāda stressed the dogmatic and abstract *Abhidamma, Abhidharma* section (see below, *Canonical texts*). The name Sarvāstivāda means the doctrine that everything exists (*sarvam asti*). This school held that all things, past and future as well as present, exist, because the cognizing agent, at the moment of thinking of them, could not have contact with them if they did not exist. The same is true of *karman*. Things that bind and things that are capable of being bound exist together; however, a *puggala, pudgala*—an enduring underlying being, the composite person—does not exist. All that exists are name and matter. Matter (*rūpa*) has aspects, hence characteristics, and is therefore definable. The other components (*skandha*s), the human person and mental experiences, are substances with characteristics and hence are knowable.

A branch of this school, the Mūla-Sarvāstivāda, was widely diffused in India, Central Asia, Burma, Thailand, Cambodia, and Indonesia.

Vasubandhu's *Abhidharmakośa* (4th or 5th century), the basic text for the study of Buddhist philosophy, was based on the Sarvāstivāda *Abhidharma* but interpreted it according to its author's Sautrāntika propensities (see below *Sautrāntika*). It became the basic text for the development of Sarvāstivāda in China and Japan, which is designated by the short form of the title: Chinese Chü-she, Japanese Kusha, for *kośa* ("treasure"). Before the Chinese translations of Vasubandhu's work in the 6th and 7th centuries, Sarvāstivāda *Abhidharma* doctrine was represented in China by the P'i-t'an school, based on texts of the Gandhāra and Kashmir branch of Sarvāstivāda (P'i-t'an is the Chinese abbreviation for *Abhidharma*). Summarizing, interpreting, and confuting the theories of various masters in regard to external and psychosomatic *dharma*s, time, and categories, the *Abhidharmakośa* has always been regarded as the basis of Buddhist dogma in China, as also in Tibet.

Sautrāntika. This school is so named (*sūtra* plus *anta*, "end") because it gave pre-eminence to the *sūtra* portion of the canon. Its followers trace their school back to Ānanda, a close disciple of the Buddha. For them, the karmic factors (*saṃskāra*) are insubstantial and momentary, disappearing as soon as they have been manifested only to reappear again to give rise to a new aggregate. There is continual motion by virtue of which a person passes from one condition to another. Thus there exists not only a continuum of psychic states but also the modification of them, since each series arises at each instant distinct from any other but corresponding to the initial force of the impulse. Again, however, the individual being (*pudgala*) does not exist in an absolute sense. Nor does the past or future exist in a direct sense. Between one state and another there exists the same connection that there is between a seed and the fruit, which is manifested by means of the tree. Every thought or act is pervaded by a sort of very subtle impregnation that in turn is capable of impregnating the subconscious so as to generate new correlated psychic situations. The school is of great importance because its tenets were precursors of the Vijñānavāda (see below *Yogācāra/Vijñānavāda*).

Mahīśāsaka. The Mahīśāsaka (Pāli Mahiṃsāsaka) apparently took its name from its founder (but according to others, from the name of a place). Its origins go back to a disagreement concerning disciplinary rules that occurred at the first Council of Rājagṛha (483 BC); however, some of their theses seem to have developed later than the Sarvāstivāda. The Mahīśāsakas felt that the state of an *arhat* is irreversible, and they did not accept the existence of a transmigrating being. They were especially numerous in southern India.

Dharmaguptaka. This branch separated from the Mahīśāsaka school toward the end of the 2nd or the beginning of the 1st century BC. It recognized as its original master Maudgalyāyana, one of the first disciples of the Buddha, although its actual founder may have been Dharmagupta (3rd century BC?). It was still to be found in scattered places in the 7th century. The Dharmaguptakas added two new "baskets," or collections (*piṭaka*), a *Bodhisattvapiṭaka* and *Dhāraṇīpiṭaka*, to the regular *Tripiṭaka* of the Buddhist canon (see below *Canonical texts*). They held that the Buddha was not part of the *saṅgha*—consequently, a gift given to him is infinitely superior to one given the *saṅgha*—and that the body of an *arhat* has no karmic outflows. They emphasized the merit that derives from the cult of the *stūpa*—a mound, often containing relics—which is a centre of devotion in lay Buddhism. The individual person (*pudgala*) is purely nominal because a person is nothing but his psychophysical components. States of contemplation and meditation of the past and future are without objects. The path of the Buddha and the *bodhisattva* is distinct from that of the *śrāvaka* (disciple). Perhaps due to its connection with the Mahāsāṅghika school (see below), its tenets contain foreshadowings of the Mahāyāna version of Buddhism.

Sammatīya. This branch, a derivation of the Vātsīputrīya school founded in the 3rd century BC, had a wide diffusion. According to the reports of Chinese Buddhist pilgrims in the 7th century, its followers were numerous along the Ganges Valley; and the school flourished in Gujarāt and in eastern India, as well as in Campā (or Champa, later Indochina); a 16th-century Tibetan account states that it still flourished during the Pāla dynasty that ruled Bengal up to the end of the 11th century. The Sammatīyas maintained that the rejection of moral infections is gradual and that there is a complete awareness. An act vanishes but it leaves a thrusting, a commitment to fructify, to have consequences. A person (*pudgala*) is an essence not wholly identical with his components. The knowable is at the same time both describable and indescribable. An *arhat* can fall from his state. The Sammatīyas have tendencies toward an ontological concept of the *pudgala*—that it is real though undefinable. They insist on the merit that stems from generosity; *i.e.*, gifts of food or things useful to everyone (for example, a hospital or a well). They posit an intermediate existence between death and rebirth.

Sammatīya doctrines

Canonical texts. The above schools possessed a canon of which only the Theravāda version is entirely extant in the original. Of the versions of other schools, such as the Mūla-Sarvāstivāda, parts of the Vinaya section and fragments of other works in Sanskrit or local dialects exist.

The canon consists of three *piṭaka*s ("baskets," or collections) hence called *Tripiṭaka* (Pāli *Tipiṭaka*): (1) *Vinaya*, a collection of disciplinary rules not always stated directly but often introduced through a story referring to the earlier lives of the Buddha to show the results of a good or bad act. (2) *Sūtra*, sermons and dicta attributed to the Buddha. (3) *Abhidharma*, the dogmatic section, abstract and impersonal in form and content.

In China the Buddhist scriptures were also collected in a *Tripiṭaka* (Chinese *Ta-ts'ang Ching*, "Great Storehouse Scripture," or *San-ts'ang*, "Three Collections"), accepted also in Korea and Japan but divided into different and more numerous sections. Because of the prevalence in it of Mahāyāna works, the Chinese *San-ts'ang* has little in common with the Pāli *Tripiṭaka* of the Theravāda. It was composed of works (many now lost) that came from India, Central Asia, or Tibet and were translated into Chinese with commentaries and critical treatises by Chinese and Korean authors.

The Tibetan canon

The Tibetan canon consists not of three but of two collections, the *Bka'-'gyur*, or *Kanjur* ("Translation of the Buddha-word") and the *Bstan-'gyur*, or *Tanjur* ("Translation of Teachings"). The *Bka'-'gyur* [pronounced Kanjur] contains all that has been attributed to the revelation of the Buddha, consisting predominantly of Mahāyāna and Tantric works. The *Bstan-'gyur* [pronounced Tenjur] includes works by interpreters and commentators, with Indian treatises on non-Buddhist subjects, such as poetry, grammar, astrology, and medicine.

The first texts of Theravāda Buddhism were introduced in Ceylon by Mahinda, Aśoka's son, and they were written in Pāli. Pāli is considered to be a form of Māgadhī, the language of the Magadha region, spoken by the Buddha himself but modified by the time of Aśoka. In any case, it was adopted as the canonical language by the Buddhists of Ceylon, Burma, Thailand, Cambodia, and Laos. The oral tradition was written down at the order of the Ceylonese king Vaṭṭagāmani in the 1st century BC and revised by Buddhaghosa, an Indian monk-scholar of the 4th–5th century AD who was the author of the *Visuddhi-magga*, ("Way to Purity"), a systematic work on the whole *Tripiṭaka*, regarded as orthodox Theravāda teaching.

Vinaya schools: Lü/Ritsu. The development of schools based on an emphasis on the *Abhidharma* and *Sūtra* "baskets" has been indicated above in the presentation of Sarvāstivāda and Sautrāntika. As for the Vinaya, however, although it constituted an integral part of the *Tripiṭaka* and regulated and consecrated the norms of monastic life, it gave rise to a school of its own only in China and Japan, apparently without any Indian precedent. The Lü-tsung (Vinaya school) originated in China in the 7th century during a period of highly intellectualist Buddhism and stressed observance of the ethical precepts and disciplinary rules. In the following century it was introduced into Japan by the famous Chinese priest Chien-chen (Japanese Ganjin) at the invitation of the Japanese emperor and was known as Risshū or Ritsu (Japanese for Vinaya). The emphasis of Vinaya in Japan was on the correctness and validity of ordination (initiation) into the *saṅgha*, especially for monks and nuns; and controversy ensued between those who stressed the formal, external aspect and those who stressed the spiritual, internal aspect of vows and discipline. A reformed Ritsu school was established in the 13th century, based on a "self-vow discipline," marking a return to the validity of spontaneous vows, beyond any formalism, in accordance with Mahāyāna teachings. The Vinaya Lü-tsung, with its ethical, disciplinary emphasis, so congenial to the Chinese mind, continued to play a vital part in Chinese Buddhism down to modern times; Ritsu, whose teachings were in principle accepted by most Japanese Buddhists, still had its temples and following at mid-20th century.

THE TRANSITIONAL SCHOOLS

Mahāsaṅghika. According to traditional accounts, the Mahāsaṅghikas (Adherents of the Great Order, or Assembly) split off from other Buddhists in the 3rd century BC, in what may here been the original schism. Their emphasis was on a more open community, a less strict version of the discipline, and a metaphysical view of the Buddha, all of which were later developed by Mahāyāna (see below). They focussed not on the historical Buddha and his teachings but on the transcendent Buddha. In their view, the Buddha is *lokottara* ("transcending the world"), indestructible, completely devoid of all worldly impurities, with stainless *karman*. Pronouncing a single word the Buddha can be heard by all creatures, whose understanding of his words, however, depends on their karmic purity. His body is perfect, for the body through which he reveals himself is not his true body; it is instead an apparitional body (*nirmāṇakāya*). Being above the world, he has boundless power and life; he neither sleeps nor dreams. Even in the state of a *bodhisattva*, prior to his final birth, the Buddha entered the maternal womb completely pure. All *bodhisattva*s can remain as long as they will among the inferior creatures (beasts, demons, etc.) for the purpose of leading creatures to salvation. The knowledge of things occurs in a single instant: all is void (*śūnya*) and without self; the ultimate end of the way of seeing is an instantaneous recognition that reveals the singular and proper character of all things.

The *lokottara* ("transcendent") Buddha

The Ekavyāvahārika, a branch of Mahāsaṅghika, asserts that everything is a representation, that *saṃsāra*, Nirvāṇa, and the *dharma*s of the world in which we exist (*laukika*), as well as those that transcend the world, are nothing but mere designations.

Lokottaravāda. The only surviving part of the Mahāsaṅghika canon, the *Mahāvastu*, is derived from Lokottaravādins, who stem from the Mahāsaṅghikas. They assert that things of this world do not possess any reality at all; on the contrary, they exist as atemporal *dharmas* beyond this world. Two principles are absolutely real, the two kinds of void (*śūnyatā*): of persons and of things. The way that leads to the overcoming of a given stage is real and its result also because it provides us with the knowledge of those two kinds of "voidness." The (or a) Buddha is completely supramundane (*lokottara*, hence the name Lokottaravāda) and his historical life and actions are mere appearance, convention, mental image. This is the docetic view of the Buddha.

Vātsīputrīya. The Vātsīputrīyas (or Pudgalavādins) split off in the first half of the 3rd century BC. They affirmed the existence of an enduring person (*pudgala*) distinct from both the conditioned (*saṃskṛta*) and the unconditioned (*asaṃskṛta*); the sole *asaṃskṛta* for them is Nirvāṇa. The *pudgala* really exists and can transmigrate from life to life, unlike all other things, none of which possess this property. The Vātsīputrīyas refer to a text in which the Buddha speaks of a "bundle," (*i.e.*, the components of a human being, the *skandhas*) and of one "who carries the bundle." If consciousness exists, there must be a subject of consciousness, the *pudgala;* it is this alone that transmigrates. The Vātsīputrīyas recognized an intermediate life between death and rebirth, and they did not exclude the possibility that a *bodhisattva* can become a Buddha in this existence.

The Sammatīya school, which also propounded these doctrines. is regarded variously as an offshoot of the Vātsīputrīya, the origin of the latter, or synonymous with them. It is sometimes regarded as one of the four main ancient schools, under which all the rest may be grouped.

Satyasiddhi. The Satyasiddhi school, probably derived from the earlier Sautrāntika school, is based on the *Satyasiddhi-śāstra*, a book attributed to Harivarman, a 3rd–4th century Indian writer, and known only in its Chinese version (4th–5th century). It gave birth to a school in China (Ch'eng-shih) and Japan (Jōjitsu) that maintained all things are merely designations devoid of reality. Men are enveloped in the illusion that either the ego (*pudgala*) or the world (*dharmas*) is real, whereas neither is. The past does not exist, the future has not yet come to be; and the present, as soon as it comes into being, disappears. Hence, the sense of continuity is illusory.

Harivarman, like the Lokottaravādins, postulates a void, both of the *dharmas* and of the ego: no *dharmas* of any sort exist, though from the point of view of relative truth *dharmas* may appear to exist. In China this doctrine was sharply attacked as destructive nihilism by the San-lun school (see below *San-lun*). It is perhaps improper to speak of Satyasiddhi as a school; it refers rather to certain centres that attached particular importance to the *Satyasiddhi-śāstra* without ignoring the rest of the Buddhist teachings. (In Japan, Jōjitsu is considered part of the Sanron school.)

III. Mahāyāna

Arising in India, the Mahāyāna version of Buddhism spread to Central Asia, China, Japan, Java, Sumatra, and even Ceylon (Abhayagiri monastery). It became the pan-Asiatic form of Buddhism and involved basic shifts in doctrine and approach for which, however, there were precedents in earlier schools. It taught that neither the self nor the *dharmas* exist. Moreover, for the elite *arahant* ideal it substituted the *bodhisattva*; *i.e.*, he who possesses the innate tendency to attain Enlightenment (*bodhi*), to become a Buddha—a disposition inherent in all men. In Mahāyāna, love for creatures is exalted to the highest; a *bodhisattva* can offer the merit he derives from good deeds for the good of others, not being concerned only with his own salvation. The mystic tension that agitated India also entered the Mahāyāna.

NATURE AND CHARACTERISTICS

Mahāyāna is not merely a metaphysics, dealing with the basic structure and principles of reality. It is rather a theoretical propaedeutic to the achievement of a desired state or condition that entered into the yogic-magical Indian tradition; hence, the coexistence of theoretical investigation and supreme experience: the former, the premise; the latter, the consequence. The convergence of meditative exercises leads to an emptying of thought to reach a point in which one proceeds from voidness to voidness and finally to the ultimate where even the most attenuated thought vanishes. Rational activity is exercised until it becomes quiescent: *prajñā* itself, the supreme wisdom, by successive emptying becomes nullified, and only in doing so does it identify with the unutterable ultimate reality; thus a state is acquired that is the summit of the meditative quest that empties itself more and more of all content, the achievement of an irreversible transcendence of the mind. It is a continuation of the rarefaction of thought that, expanding in emptiness, is nullified by an action because an "other" has entered in its place. According to the various schools, Nirvāṇa, the state of the Buddha, is also called the *dharma-kāya*, Buddhahood, the *tathatā*, the essence of the Buddha, and the absolute. It comprises an omniscience that is not knowledge in the ordinary sense but clear consciousness in which, as in a mirror, is reflected the play of appearances that do not exist. Such a state is the voidness that in Tantrism the meditator finds in his heart and, through a meditative process, brings from it the divine worlds, the infinite Buddhas, and the divinities—because that voidness is the mother of the "non-self," of what appears and what is not.

Mahāyāna as a theoretical propaedeutic to a desired state

BASIC TEACHINGS

The Buddha: divinization and multiplicity. The Buddha is viewed not merely as a human master and model, as was the historical Buddha but as a transcendent being. He multiplies himself and is reflected in a pentad of Buddhas: Vairocana, Akṣobhya, Ratnasambhava, Amitābha, Amoghasiddhi; some of these, taking the place of Śākyamuni, are revealers of doctrines and elaborate, complicated liturgies; Amitābha (or Amitāyus) is probably a fusion of ancient Indian ideas and Iranian conceptions. Dīpaṅkara, the first of the 24 Buddhas traditionally held to have preceded Gautama, is depicted with a flame rising from his shoulders, as in the religious and iconographic traditions of kingship of Iran and Central Asia. As Mahāyāna developed, a great deal of literature called *Buddhavacana* (Revelation of the Buddha)was circulated, but it had nothing to do with the ancient canons; on the contrary, it was proposed as the highest revelation, superseding prior texts. In this literature the teaching is viewed not as merely of one kind but as on various levels, each adapted to the intellectual capacity and karmic propensities of those who hear it. The Buddha is no longer the historical sage of the Śākyas but is now supramundane (*lokottara*). Even the *saṅgha* is of two types: that of this world and that beyond it.

The bodhisattva ideal. The essential premise of the *bodhisattva* ideal is to generate in one's own self the thought of Enlightenment and to fulfill the vow to become a Buddha, foregoing entrance into Nirvāṇa in order to remain in the world as long as there are creatures to be saved from suffering. With that vow the aspirant begins the career of a *bodhisattva*, which traverses 10 stages or spiritual levels (*bhūmi*) and purifies him through the practice of the 10 perfections (*pāramitā*). These levels, which become progressively higher and higher, elevate the *bodhisattva* to the condition of a Buddha. The first six levels are preliminary, representing the true practice of the six perfections (generosity, morality, patience, vigour, concentration, and wisdom), an indispensable condition because the *bodhisattva* should have complete mastery over ecstasies and the various modes of concentration through constant exercise, so that those sublimations become his own manner of being. Irreversibility occurs as soon as he reaches the 7th stage. From that moment the *bodhisattva* assumes the true Buddha nature, even though his nature is to be further purified and fortified in the stages that follow; this is the moment when, having performed his duty, he engages in activity aimed at completely fulfilling the obligations of a *bodhisattva.* The difference between this and the preceding six

The ten spiritual stages (*bhūmi*) and the ten perfections (*pāramitā*)

stages is that now his activity is explained as an innate and spontaneous impulse manifested unconstrainedly and therefore not subjected to doubts; this can happen because his behaving in such a manner is by now of his very nature. Everything for him is now uncreated, ungenerated; his body becomes identified more and more completely with the essential body (*dharma*), Buddhahood, omniscience.

The three Buddha bodies. The three bodies (*tri-kāya; i.e.*, modes of being) of the Buddha, which became a subject of major discussion in the Mahāyāna, are rooted in the Theravāda teachings: the physical body consisting of four elements, the mental body, and the body of the law. It is with the Mahāyāna, however, that the theory of the three bodies enters into the salvation process and assumes central significance in the doctrine. The phenomenal body (*nirmāṇakāya*) is a manifestation of the Buddha among creatures to teach them the path to liberation, even though for some schools it is nothing but an illusory appearance of eternal reality. The enjoyment (or bliss) body (*sambhogakāya*) is the body to which contemplation can ascend, in particular supramundane contemplative stages where that body manifests to the *bodhisattva* its splendor and reveals doctrines unintelligible to unenlightened men. The unmanifested body of the law (*dharmakāya*) already appears in the *Saddharmapuṇḍarīka*, or *Lotus Sūtra*, a transitional text that became central in many Mahāyāna devotional schools (see below *Saddharmapuṇḍarīka* and *Nichiren*); in many Mahāyāna texts Buddhas are infinite, but all partake of an identical nature—the *dharmakāya*. As anticipated in ancient schools, the Buddha is the law (*dharma*). "He who sees the law sees me; he who sees me sees the law." There is identification of the Buddha with an eternal *dharma*, with Enlightenment (*bodhi*), and hence with Nirvāṇa; later, real existence will be opposed to the mere appearance of existence, and voidness, the "thingness of things," an undefinable condition, present and immutable within the Buddhas, will be stressed. All is in the *dharmakāya;* nothing is outside of it, just as nothing is outside of space; transcendence and immanence come together. Other schools posit a presence innate within men even if it is not perceived, like a gem hidden in dross, which shines in its purity as soon as the veil of ignorance is removed: but it is differentiated into five Buddhas who constitute the elements (*skandhas*) of the person; it then is the "diamond body" since the beginning, but also the supreme beatitude that is expressed in the symbol of the union of the god and his consort. It is omnipresent. Above the multiplicity of all the Buddhas exists the Ādi-Buddha, the primeval Buddha. Various "families" of divinities are derived from the Buddhas, an expansion of the One into a multiplicity; so that, through meditation, man can reverse the way and go from multiplicity back to the One. Besides these three bodies, there is another one, the body in itself (*svābhāvikakāya*), because in the Buddhas is inherent the very nature of Buddha-being.

Buddha as *dharma*

New revelations. New revelations are made not only to men on earth but also in the heavenly paradises by Śākyamuni and other Buddhas. The teaching evolves uninterruptedly in the universe because worlds and paradises are infinite and all Buddhas are consubstantiated with the essential body. The assemblies to which they speak consist not only of *śrāvakas* (disciples) but also of *bodhisattvas*, gods, and demons. The authors of the new doctrines were captivated by exaltations that often make their discourses logically implausible: phantasmagoria of celestial choruses, fabulous visions in which shine flashes of new speculations, and trains of thought under the influence, more or less conscious, of speculative and mystical Indian traditions. The texts, from which new trends spring, overflow with repetitions and modulate the same arguments with variations in reading; but they are considered as teachings to be propagated when the time is ripe.

The task of Mahāyāna thinkers was very difficult because it was not easy to produce a completely logical arrangement from this prolix literature. The appearance of some of these books is surrounded with legend. The *Prajñāpāramitā* and the *Avataṃsaka-sūtras*, for instance, are said to have been concealed by the *nāgas*, demigods living at the bottom of lakes and rivers, in miraculous palaces. There are various *Prajñāpāramitā* ("Perfection of Wisdom") texts, from those having 100,000 verses to those having a single verse. The *Prajñāpāramitā-sūtras* announce that the world as it appears to us does not exist; reality is the indefinable "thingness of things" (*tathatā, dharmaṇām dharmatā*), voidness (*śūnyatā*) is "the absolute," "that without signs or characteristics" (*animitta*). The fundamental assumption of the *Prajñāpāramitā* is expounded in a famous verse (*Vajracchedikā*): "like light, a mirage, a lamp, an illusion, a drop of water, a dream, a lightning flash; thus must all compounded things be considered." Not only is there no "self," but all things lack a real nature (*svabhāva*) of their own. There are two truths: relative truth, which "applies to things as they appear," and absolute truth, the intuition of voidness (it can be of 10, 14, 18, or 20 kinds).

The "Perfection of Wisdom" (*Prajñāpāramitā*) *sūtras*

THE MAHAYANA SCHOOLS

Mahāyāna comprises the following main schools: the Mādhyamika, the Yogācāra or Vijñānavāda (Vijñaptamātratā), the Avataṃsaka, the school of the identity of the paths to salvation (*ekāyana*) represented by the *Saddharmapuṇḍarīka* (Lotus of the True Law), the various devotional (Pure Land) schools, and the Dhyāna school (Ch'an in China, Zen in Japan).

Mādhyamika (San-lun/Sanron). Mādhyamika or Madhyamaka (Doctrine of the Middle View) also known as Śūnyavāda (Theory of Negativity or Relativity) is an important philosophical school of Buddhism founded by the great Indian logician Nāgārjuna probably in the 2nd or 3rd century AD. His teachings and those of his close disciple Āryadeva attempt to assume a middle position between the extremes of existence and nonexistence or affirmation and negation, by revealing the contradictory nature of various philosophies and yet not assuming a dogmatic stance themselves. In the 5th century two rival Mādhyamika groups debated Nāgārjuna's intentions. One group, led by Bhāvaviveka, believed that Mādhyamika should assume a philosophical position of its own against other systems of thought. The second group, headed by Buddhapālita, preached the reduction of philosophical arguments, including one's own, to absurdity, in the hope that this process would lead to an intuitive realization of a reality beyond all ordinary and relative cognition. This latter branch of Mādhyamika was supported by the 7th-century commentator, Candrakīrti, whose works reinforced the belief that this doctrine of *reductio ad absurdum* was originally taught by Nāgārjuna.

The Mādhyamika school of thought was spread to China from India by the missionary translator of Indian-Kuchan parentage Kumārajīva, in the 5th century. Among the many texts that he translated from Sanskrit into Chinese were *Mahāprajñāpāramitā-śāstra* ("Great Perfection of Wisdom Treatise") attributed to Nāgārjuna, and his *Mādhyamika Kārikā* ("Treatise of the Middle Way"), and *Dvādaśamukha-* or *Dvādaśa-dvāra-śāstra* ("The Twelve Topics or Gates Treatise"), and also Āryadeva's *Śata-śāstra* ("One Hundred Verses Treatise"). The latter three works became the basic texts of the Chinese San-lun (Japanese Sanron) or Three Treatise school of Mādhyamika. For a brief period of time this school was challenged by a more positivistic form of Mādhyamika called the Ssu-lun or "Four Treatise" school, which also accepted the *Mahāprajñāpāramitā-śāstra* as a basic text. This school, however, was soon overwhelmed by San-lun as taught by Kumārajīva's disciple, Seng-chao, and later by Chi-tsang. Both of these Chinese Mādhyamika masters restated Nāgārjuna's thesis in numerous influential commentaries. A Korean disciple of Chi-tsang named Ekwan (Hui-kuan) then spread San-lun (Korean Samnŏn) to Japan in 625, thus completing the rapid spread of Mādhyamika thought from India to China and to Japan. This school, however, never gained popularity among the masses; it remained rather the basis for logical and philosophical thought among the learned few, rarely forming a separate or independent sect. As a basic philosophical thesis of Buddhism, Mādhyamika is still intensely studied by Japanese monks.

The middle way

Nāgārjuna and his followers attempted to arrive at a middle position, devoid of name and character and beyond all thought and words, by first employing a rigorous logic to demonstrate the absurdity of various philosophical positions, including Brahmanic (early Hindu), Hīnayāna, and Mahāyāna thought. On the assumption that any contradiction is proof of error, Nāgārjuna took any point of view that would reveal the error of his opponents. Yet, he did not therefore accept the opposing point of view but only used it as a means to show the relativity of the system he was attacking. He was just as willing to refute his first position. In this way he claimed adherence to no doctrine.

With this method of reduction to absurdity or contradiction, Nāgārjuna attempted to prove that all worldly thought is empty (*śūnya*) or relative and to point to his belief that the true path is that of the middle, between, or more correctly, above extremes. This has been called the doctrine of emptiness of all things; but, as has been pointed out, this too is relative and should be seen only as a means of argumentation, later to be transcended.

Nāgārjuna revealed this middle path most clearly in his paraphrase of the Eightfold Truth of Buddhism. He stated:

> Nothing comes into being, nor does anything disappear. Nothing is eternal, nor has anything an end. Nothing is identical, nor is anything differentiated. Nothing moves here, nor does anything move there.

In presenting these pairs of opposites, Nāgārjuna taught that anything that can be conceptualized or put into words is relative. This led to the Mādhyamika identification of Nirvāṇa and *saṃsāra*. Both are empty concepts with the truth lying somewhere beyond.

After the emptiness or relativity of the world has been proved, the question arises how man is to go beyond this position. Nāgārjuna answered that men are not irreconcilably caught in this world, for this world can be used as a ladder leading to the absolute—beyond all duality. The transition that can be effected from this world to salvation has been called Nāgārjuna's doctrine of two truths. The relative truth is of this existence. By the logical method all propositions can be destroyed. This leads to the realization that all is emptiness and from this to the intuition of an absolute truth beyond all conceptions. The link between these two truths—the relative and the absolute—is the Buddha. He experienced the absolute truth, which is *niṣprapañca*—*i.e.*, inexplicable in speech and unrealizable in ordinary thought; and yet he returned to point to this truth in the phenomenal world. By following this path, man can be saved.

Nāgārjuna's doctrine of two truths

Thus, Nāgārjuna taught that through the middle path of Mādhyamika, which is identified as the Buddha's true teachings, man is guided to an experience beyond affirmation and negation, being and nonbeing. Mādhyamika is a philosophy that can rightly be called a doctrine of salvation, for it claims to present man with a system that leads to rescue from his situation.

Yogācāra/Vijñānavāda (Fa-hsiang/Hossō). The Yogācāra (or Vijñānavāda) school is traditionally ascribed to the brothers Asaṅga and Vasubandhu (5th century AD), to which may be added Sthiramati (6th century). These writers were systematizers of doctrines already being taught and contained in such literature as the *Laṅkāvatāra-sūtra* and the *Mahāyāna-śraddhotpada-śāstra* (attributed to Aśvaghoṣa, but probably an apocryphal book written in Central Asia or in China). Yogācāra explored and propounded basic doctrines that were to be fundamental in the future development of Mahāyāna and that influenced the rise of Tantrism (see below).

Its central doctrine is that only consciousness (*vijñāna-mātra;* hence the name Vijñānavāda) is real; that thought or mind is the ultimate reality. External things do not exist; nothing exists outside the mind. The common view that external things exist is due to an error or misconception that is removable through a meditative process that brings a complete withdrawal or "revulsion" from these fictitious externals and an inner concentration and tranquillity; that is, through the practice of Yoga (hence, the alternative name Yogācāra, or Yoga practice).

A store consciousness (*ālaya-vijñāna*) is postulated as the receptacle, or storehouse, of the imprint of thoughts and deeds, the *vāsanā* (literally, "perfuming") of various karmic seeds (*bījas*). The "seeds" develop into touch, mental activity, feeling, perception, and will, corresponding to the five *skandhas*. Then ideation (*manas*) develops, which sets off a self or mind against an outer world. Finally comes the awareness of the objects of thought via sense perceptions and ideas. The store consciousness must be purified of its subject-object duality and notions of false existence and restored to its pure state, equivalent to the absolute, "suchness," Buddhahood, the undifferentiated.

Store consciousness (*ālaya-vijñāna*)

Corresponding to this process of false imagination (*vikalpa*), right knowledge, and suchness are the three modes in which things are, the *svabhāvas*: (1) the mere fictions of false imagination (*parikalpita-svabhāva*); (2) the relative existence of things, under certain conditions or aspects (*paratantra-svabhāva*); and (3) the perfect mode of being corresponding to right knowledge (*pariniṣpanna-svabhāva*). The latter state of consciousness and being is that ultimately attained by the *bodhisattva* in Buddhahood. Corresponding to this threefold version of the modes of being and awareness is the *tri-kāya* doctrine of the Buddha noted above (the apparitional, enjoyment, and *dharma* bodies), a doctrine that was put into its systematic, developed form by Yogācāra thinkers.

The special characteristics of Yogācāra are its emphasis on meditation and a broadly psychological analysis, in contrast with the other great Mahāyāna system, Mādhyamika, where the emphasis is on logical analysis and dialectic.

The ideation (or consciousness) school of thought, called Yogācāra (or Vijñānavāda) in India, was represented in China primarily by the Fa-hsiang (or Dharmalakṣaṇa) school, called Hossō in Japan. The basic teachings of Yogācāra became known in China primarily through the work of Paramārtha, a 6th-century Indian missionary-translator (he also made known the teachings of the opposite Abhidharma or Kusha realist school). His translation of the *Mahāyāna-saṃparigraha-śāstra* provided the foundation for the She-lun school, which preceded the Fa-hsiang school as the vehicle of Yogācāra thought in China. Fa-hsiang was founded by Hsüang-tsang, a 7th-century Chinese pilgrim-translator, and his main disciple, K'uei-chi. Hsüang-tsang went to India and studied the doctrines derived from Dharmapāla (died 507) and taught at the Vijñānavāda centre at Valabhī. When he returned to China he translated Dharmapāla's *Vijñapti-mātratā-siddhi* and many other works. His teachings mainly followed the line of Dharmapāla but also included the ideas of other Indian teachers (Dignāga, Sthiramati, etc.); they were expressed systematically in his works *Fa-yuan-i-lin-chang* and *Wei-shih-shu-chi*, the basic texts of the Fa-hsiang school.

Fa-hsiang is the Chinese translation of the Sanskrit *dharmalakṣaṇa* (characteristic of *dharma*), referring to the school's basic doctrine of the peculiar characteristics (*lakṣaṇa*) of the *dharmas* that make up the world that appears in human ideation, rather than to their essential nature (*svabhāva*). The connection of this so-called idealist school with the "realist" Abhidharma-Kusha school (see above *Sarvāstivāda*) is evident, though many new elements are introduced. There are five categories of *dharmas*: (1) eight mental *dharmas* (*cittadharma*), comprising the five sense consciousnesses, cognition, the cognitive faculty, and the store consciousness; (2) 51 mental functions or capacities, dispositions, and activities (*caitaśikadharma*); (3) 11 elements concerned with material forms or appearances (*rūpa-dharma*); (4) 24 things, situations, and processes not associated with the mind—*e.g.*, time, becoming (*citta-viprayuktasaṃskāra*); and (5) six noncreated or nonconditioned elements (*asaṃskṛta-dharma*)—*e.g.*, space or "suchness" (*tathatā*).

Characteristic of *dharmas* (*dharma-lakṣaṇa*)

Hsüang-tsang's work *Ch'eng wei-shih lun* explained how there can be a common empirical world for individuals who construct or ideate particular objects and who possess distinct bodies and sensory systems: the universal "seeds" in the store consciousness account for the common appearance of things and particular "seeds" for the differences.

Fa-hsiang was brought to Japan on various occasions, according to the traditional accounts: first by Dōshō, a Japanese priest who visited China, studied under Hsüang-tsang, and established the teaching (now called Hossō) at Gangō-ji monastery, and then by other priests, Japanese and Korean, who studied in China under Hsüang-tsang, K'uei-chi, or their disciples. Thus, the Japanese claim to have received the Hossō teaching in a direct line from its originators, and it continues to have a living and significant role in Japanese Buddhism.

Identity of proximate and ultimate

Avataṃsaka (Hua-yen/Kegon). In contrast with the Fa-hsiang (Hossō) concentration on the specific characteristics, the differentiations of things, and its separation of facts and ultimate principles, the Avataṃsaka school (called Hua-yen in China, Kegon in Japan) stressed the sameness of things, the presence of absolute reality in them, and the identity of facts and ultimate principles. It took its name from the *Avataṃsaka-sūtra* ("Wreath *sūtra*" or "Garland *sūtra*"), which, according to traditional legend, was first preached by the Buddha Vairocana expressing the perfect truth revealed in his Enlightenment but then kept secret when it proved incomprehensible to his hearers, being replaced with easier doctrines. The *sūtra* tells of the pilgrimage of a young man in a quest to realize *dharma-dhātu* ("totality" or "universal principle"). Extant are three Chinese versions and one Sanskrit original (the *Gaṇḍavyūha*) of the last section only. There is no trace of an Indian sectarian development and the school is known only in its Chinese and Japanese forms.

The school was preceded in China by the Ti-lun school, based on a translation (early 6th century) of Vasubandhu's *Daśabhūmika-sūtra*, concerning the 10 stages of a *bodhisattva* on the way to Buddhahood; since this work was related to the *Avanaṃsaka-sūtra*, the Ti-lun adherents readily joined the Hua-yen school established in the late 6th century (?) by Tu-shun (Fa-shun), the first patriarch (died 640). Fa-tsang (or Hsien-shou), the third patriarch (died 712), is considered the real founder because he systematized the teachings; hence, it is also called the Hsien-shou school. His student, Ch'eng-kuan (of Ch'ing-liang monastery; died *c.* 820 or *c.* 838), wrote famous commentaries on the *Avataṃsaka-sūtra* and defended the purity of the faith against heresy. After the death of the fifth patriarch, Tsung-mi, in 841, Hua-yen declined, during the general suppression of Buddhism that ensued in China. But it greatly influenced the development of Neo-Confucianism (a significant movement in Chinese thought beginning in the 11th century) and is regarded as the most highly developed form of Chinese Buddhist thought. It was brought into Japan by pupils of Fa-tsang and an Avataṃsaka missionary from Central India during the period *c.* 725–740, and began a vital and important development there that has continued down to the present day.

Causation by "totality" (*dharma-dhātu*)

The main doctrine of this school is the theory of causation by *dharma-dhātu; i.e.*, that all of the elements arise simultaneously, that the whole of things creates itself, further, that ultimate principles and concrete manifestations are interfused, and that the manifestations are mutually identical. Thus, in Fa-tsang's example of the golden lion in the Imperial palace, gold is the essential nature or principle (*li*) and lion is the particular manifestation or form (*shih*); moreover, as gold, each part or particle expresses the whole lion and is identical with every other part or particle. Applied to the universe, this model means that all phenomena are the expressions of absolute reality, the ultimate suchness or voidness, while still retaining their phenomenal character; each is both "all" and "one." All the constituents of the world (the *dharmas*) are interdependent, cannot exist independently; and each possesses a sixfold nature: universality, speciality, similarity, diversity, integration, differentiation.

The ideal is a harmonious totality of things encountered in the perfectly enlightened Buddha. The Buddha-nature is present potentially in all things. There are an infinite number of Buddhas and Buddha realms. There are myriads of Buddhas in every grain of sand and a Buddha realm at the tip of a hair.

The Japanese priest Myōe (1173–1232), venerated as the restorer of the Kegon sect, depicted at his daily meditation while seated in a tree near his monastery. Detail of a hanging scroll, light ink and colour on paper, 13th century. In the Kōzan-ji, Kyōto, Japan.
From Dietrich Seckel, *The Art of Buddhism* (1964); reproduced by permission of Holle Verlag

The universe is fourfold: a world of factual, practical reality; a world of principle or theory; a world of principle and facts harmonized; and a world of factual realities interwoven and mutually identified. The latter is the harmonious whole taught by Hua-yen/Kegon, while the first three are the peculiar emphasis of other schools. Hua-yen/Kegon classifies various grades or aspects of Buddhist teachings, ranging from the most elementary to the most complete—the doctrine taught by Hua-yen/Kegon and expressing the perfect knowledge attained by the Buddha Vairocana and communicated in the *Avataṃsaka-sūtra*.

Saddharmapuṇḍarīka (T'ien-t'ai/Tendai). The T'ien-t'ai/Tendai school is one of the most important developments in Chinese and Japanese Buddhism; it is significant not only for its doctrines, which in many respects are similar to Hua-yen/Kegon, but also for its practical devotional influence. Its doctrines and practices are focussed on the Indian *Saddharmapuṇḍarīka-sūtra* ("Lotus of the True Law *sūtra*") or *Lotus Sūtra*, also central in the Nichiren school (see below), and recited in Zen temples; the *sūtra* is one of the best known and most popular of Mahāyāna Buddhist texts. (The *Mahāparinirvāṇa* and *Mahāprajñāpāramitā-sūtra*s were also important in the development of T'ien-t'ai/Tendai.) The school, which apparently had no separate development as such in India, is sometimes also called Lotus (Fa-hua in Chinese; Hokke in Japanese) but is usually known as T'ien-tai in China and Tendai in Japan, after the mountain in southeast China where the basic interpretation of the *Lotus Sūtra* was first propounded in the 6th century. Prior to this, the original Sanskrit text was studied extensively in China; it was translated into Chinese early in the 5th century by Kumārajīva, and it was taught in North

China by the monks and first patriarchs, Hui-wen and Hui-ssū. The latter's student, Chih-i, who settled on Mt. T'ien-t'ai and established a famous monastery there, is regarded as the true founder of the school because he propounded the systematic and definitive interpretation of Lotus doctrines. These later became known in Japan, where Saichō (later Dengyō Daishi), a Buddhist priest who studied them first in Japan and then on Mt. T'ien-t'ai, founded a new Tendai Lotus Sect (early 9th century) and a monastery on Mt. Hiei that was to become a great centre of Buddhist learning. With Shingon (see below), with which it was closely connected, it became perhaps the most important religious and philosophical influence on the Japanese spirit. Tendai has been markedly syncretistic, striving to include various Buddhist tendencies, from Vinaya to Shingon and Zen, and also Shintō, the Japanese national cult.

The one way that includes all ways

The *Lotus Sūtra*'s main purpose is to establish the one way (or "vehicle" or "career") for attaining salvation (Buddhahood). It claims to be the definitive and complete teaching of the Buddha, here presented as a transcendent eternal being, surrounded by myriad *arhat*s, gods, *bodhisattva*s, and other figures; one who propounds the true doctrines through sermons, lectures, imaginative parables, and miracles. Religious merit is attributed to preaching, reciting, and hearing the *sūtra*, which is not merely a statement of the nature of things but a central object of devotion. The three ways of salvation preached by the Buddha are adjusted to the level and situation of the hearers and all are expressions of the one way: *śrāvakayāna*, the way of the disciples (*śrāvaka*s), aimed at being *arhat*s; *pratyekabuddhāyana*, the way of those who aim at salvation for themselves alone; and *bodhisattvayāna*, the way of those (the *bodhisattva*s) who on the point of attaining salvation give it up to work for the salvation of all other beings. All are forms of the one way, the *buddhāyana*. Being a Buddha is the one aim for all.

As systematized in the T'ien-t'ai/Tendai version of the *Lotus Sūtra*, the Buddha's teachings are divided into five periods and eight doctrines. The periods are: (1) The Avataṃsaka, or Hua-yen/Kegon, propounded vainly immediately after the Buddha's Enlightenment; (2) the *Āgama*s (scriptures), or Deer Park period, preachings to reach those of ordinary human capacities; (3) the *Vaipulya*, or Fang-teng, broad and equal, or development period, Mahāyānistic teachings intended for all men; (4) Mahāprajñāpāramitā, or Ta-pan-jo-po-lo-mi-to, preaching absolute voidness and the falsity of all distinctions; and (5) the *Saddharmapuṇḍarīka* and the *Mahāparinirvāṇa-sūtra*, or Wisdom period, teaching the identity of contrasts, unity of three "vehicles," and supreme character of the *Lotus Sūtra*. The classification of doctrines is: abrupt, gradual, secret or mystic, indeterminate, Piṭaka or Hīnayāna, common, special, and round or perfect. These characterizations of doctrines are applied to the five periods to classify more precisely the vast materials of Buddhist teaching.

The threefold truth

Central to T'ien-t'ai/Tendai doctrine is the threefold truth principle (following Nāgārjuna's [?] commentary on the *Mahāprajñāpāramitā*): (1) that all things are void, without substantial reality, (2) that all things have temporary existence, and (3) that all things are in the mean or middle state, synthesizing voidness and temporary existence, being both at once. The three truths are a harmonious unity, mutually including one another, and the mean or middle truth is equivalent to the absolute thusness. The world of temporary appearances is thus the same as absolute reality.

T'ien-t'ai/Tendai propounds an elaborate cosmology of 3,000 realms. First are the 10 basic realms, respectively, of Buddhas, *bodhisattva*s, *pratyeka-buddha*s, *śrāvaka*s, heavenly beings, fighting spirits (*asura*), men, hungry spirits or ghosts (*preta*), beasts, and depraved hellish beings. Since each includes the other nine and their characteristics, the 10 are squared to 100 realms. Each of these in turn is characterized by the 10 features of thusness manifested through phenomena: form, nature, substance, power, action, cause, condition, effect, compensation, and ultimacy; so the 100 realms are re-multiplied to 1,000. Furthermore, each of the 1,000 realms comprises three divisions; living beings, space, and the aggregates (*skandha*s); hence, the whole of things consists of 3,000 realms.

These 3,000 realms interpenetrate one another, are mutually immanent, and are immanent in one moment of thought; "one thought is the three thousand worlds." The universe is not produced by thought or consciousness but is manifest in it, and thereby also the absolute Thusness: hence, the central importance on concentration (*chih*) and insight (*kuan*) in T'ien-t'ai, to realize the unity of things and their manifestation of the ultimate.

Pure Land (Sukhāvatī/Ching-t'u/Jōdo, Shin, and Ji). The main text of the Pure Land schools is the *Sukhāvatīvyūha* (*Pure Land Sūtra*) written in northern India probably before the beginning of the 2nd century AD. (There are two original versions of the *Sukhāvatīvyūha*. The longer one includes an emphasis on good works; the shorter version emphasizes faith and devotion alone.) This *sūtra* tells of a monk, Dharmākara, who heard the preaching of Lokeśvararāja Buddha many aeons ago and asked to become a Buddha. After millions of years of study, Dharmākara promised to fulfill a number of vows if he finally attained Buddhahood. He vowed to establish a Pure or Happy Land (Sanskrit Sukhāvāti; Chinese Ching-t'u; Japanese Jōdo), also known as the Western Paradise, where no evil would exist, the people would be long-lived, and would receive whatever they desired, and from where they might attain Nirvāṇa. Dharmākara then revealed in a number of vows the means by which this Pure Land can be reached. Several of these vows emphasize meditation and good works on earth as a prerequisite, but the 18th one (a famous vow in the later development of the Pure Land school) states that one may merely call the name of the Buddha at death to be reborn in the Pure Land. Many years after these vows, Dharmākara attained Buddahood and now sits in his Pure Land fulfilling his promises of helping men achieve salvation. Here he is known as the Buddha of Unlimited Light (Sanskrit Amitābha; Chinese O-mi-t'o-fo; Japanese Amida) or the Buddha of Unlimited Lifespan (Amitāyus). He is flanked by Avalokiteśvara (Chinese Kuan-yin; Japanese Kannon) on his left and Mahāsthāmaprāpta on his right, who assist Amitābha in bringing the faithful to his Pure Land.

The Buddha of Unlimited Light

The Amitābhist doctrine spread from India to China by the 3rd century AD, where, through the work of five patriarchs, a sect based on it gradually became the most popular form of Buddhism. The sect was then transferred to Japan by the followers of the Tendai school, who attempted to weld the many sects of Buddhism into one system. By the 13th century AD, the Pure Land sect had separated from the Tendai school and spread among the common people of Japan through the work of two outstanding figures, Hōnen and Shinran.

The basic doctrines of the Pure Land sect differ widely from the doctrines of the early Buddhists. The Pure Land's leaders have generally taught that a man reaches salvation from this Earth not by individual effort or the accumulation of merits but through faith in the grace of the Buddha Amitābha. The main practice of those who follow the Pure Land teachings is not the learning of the texts, nor meditation on the Buddha but rather the constant invocation of the name Amitābha. This practice, based on the 18th vow of Amitābha, is called *nien-fo* in Chinese and *nembutsu* in Japanese (see also below *Nichiren*). Furthermore, in Pure Land Buddhism, the attainment of Nirvāṇa is not the goal; it is rather to become reborn in the Pure Land of Amitābha.

Invocation of the name (*nembutsu*)

These doctrines and the practice of invoking the name Amitābha gained great popularity in China and Japan, where it was believed that the world had reached a degenerate period, in which the Buddhist doctrines were no longer clear and men no longer possessed the purity of heart or determination to attain salvation by self-endeavour. Therefore, all men of every section of society could only hope to be saved by the grace of Amitābha. As the Pure Land sect spread from India to China and then to Japan, this doctrine of grace became more and more radical until individual actions were said to play no part in the attainment of salvation.

There is little available data on the practices of the Amitābhist believers in India, but scholars hold that while *nembutsu* was used, the main emphasis was upon meditation and worship of the Buddha. In China this stress on meditation and rites weakened, as indicated in the teachings of the three most important Pure Land patriarchs, T'an-luan, Tao-ch'o, and Shan-tao, during the 6th–7th centuries. T'an-luan was originally a follower of Taoism, who, while searching for the elixir of immortality, was converted to the Pure Land doctrine by an Indian monk. Dedicating his life to the spread of this doctrine, T'an-luan preached the invocation of the name Amitābha and declared that even evil men were eligible for the Pure Land if they sincerely uttered the *nembutsu*. He warned, however, that the lowest hell awaited those who reviled the Buddhist *dharma*.

T'an-luan was followed by Tao-ch'o, who argued that in this degenerate age men must take the "easy path" to salvation of complete trust in Amitābha, for men no longer possessed the capacity to follow the more difficult path of the saints. His disciple, Shan-tao, believed by the Japanese Pure Land sect to be the incarnation of Amitābha, was primarily responsible for shaping the doctrines of Pure Land Buddhism. This evangelist distributed many copies of the *Pure Land Sūtra* and wrote a famous commentary in which he taught that rebirth in the Western Paradise is effected primarily by *nembutsu*. This must be supplemented, however, by the chanting of *sūtra*s, meditation on the Buddha, worshipping of Buddha images, and singing his praises.

Salvation by Amitābha's grace: Hōnen and Shinran

The work of Shan-tao inspired Hōnen, the founder of the Pure Land sect (Jōdo-shū) in Japan, to declare that in this evil period man must put complete faith in the saving grace of Amitābha Buddha and constantly invoke his name. Hōnen, who was a very learned scholar and well-versed in Buddhist knowledge, wrote a treatise (*Senchaku hongan nembutsu-shū*) expressing his beliefs. While this treatise proved popular among the common people, as were his teachings generally, it was burned by the monks of Mt. Hiei and his teachings were vigorously opposed by the established Buddhist priesthood. One of his disciples, Shinran, who was exiled at the same time, was the founder of a more radical sect named the True Pure Land sect (Jōdo Shinshū, or Shin). Shinran married, with Hōnen's consent, proving that one need not be a monk to attain the Pure Land; and he popularized his doctrines by preaching in Japanese villages. In his teachings he rejected all *sūtra*s except the *Pure Land Sūtra* and rejected the vows of Amitābha in this *sūtra*, that stress individual merit. Basing his doctrines on the 18th vow, Shinran discouraged any attempt to accumulate merits, for he felt that this stood in the way of absolute faith and dependence on Amitābha. Furthermore, he rejected Hōnen's practice of continual invocation of Amitābha, believing that the faithful need only say the *nembutsu* once in order to attain salvation. Any repetition after this *nembutsu* must be seen as praise of Amitābha and not as bringing merit or affecting one's salvation. Thus it can be seen that with Shinran the doctrine of grace, which had little meaning in early Indian Buddhism, gained total ascendancy. A third Pure Land sect grew up around the itinerant teacher, Ippen. He travelled throughout Japan, advocating the chanting of Amida's name at set intervals throughout the day, hence his school was called the Ji ("Times") sect, or Ji-shū.

Music, dance, drama (Nō plays), and the tea ceremony have been important forms of expression of Shin. Since the late 19th century it has engaged in extensive educational and social welfare programs and played a significant role in Japanese life. It is the largest single Buddhist sect in Japan.

Nichiren. The indigenous Japanese Nichiren school is related both to the *Lotus Sūtra* and Pure Land schools, for it, too, is centred on the "Lotus of the True Law" and also emphasizes fervent faith and the repetition of a key phrase. Hence it has been aptly called "Lotus-pietism" by a famous scholar in Japanese Buddhism. Its distinctiveness is rooted in the extraordinary personality and character of its founder; significantly, it is named after a man, a historical person, not after a book or a doctrine. Nichiren (1222–82), the son of a poor fisherman, became a monk at an early age and studied at Mt. Hiei, the centre of the Tendai school. Nichiren was frustrated, however, by the many paths of Buddhism promising salvation and left Mt. Hiei for 10 years to search for the true path. When he emerged from his independent studies he taught that the *Lotus Sūtra* (*Saddharmapuṇḍarīka-sūtra*) contains the final and supreme teaching of the Buddha Śākyamuni (Gautama) and offers the only true way to salvation. According to Nichiren's interpretation of this *sūtra*, the three forms of the Buddha—the universal or law body (*dharmakāya*), the enjoyment body (*sambhoga-kāya*), and the phenomenal body (*nirmāṇakāya*)—should be granted equal respect, as they are important aspects of the Buddha Śākyamuni. Also, following the teachings of Chih'i, the Chinese founder of T'ien-t'ai/Tendai, that the *Lotus Sūtra* is the essence of Buddhism, Nichiren held that this same Buddha-nature was possessed by all men and could be realized only by proper worship of the *Lotus Sūtra*. Furthermore, Nichiren felt that his time, which was marked by political upheaval and unrest, was the period of degeneration known in the *Lotus Sūtra* as the time of the latter-day *dharma* (*Mappō*). During this time the purity of the Buddhist doctrines could be kept only by the *bodhisattva*s. Nichiren identified himself as an incarnation of several of these *bodhisattva*s, especially the *bodhisattva* of supreme conduct (Viśiṣṭacāritra; Japanese Jōgyōbosatsu) and believed that his mission was to propagate the true teachings of the *Lotus Sūtra* in Japan, which he felt would become the new repository of the Buddhist *dharma*.

Nichiren's life and teachings

In attempting to guide Japan to the Buddhist *dharma* as he interpreted it, Nichiren drew great criticism for his strong-willed and uncompromising attitude. In one treatise Nichiren wrote that the unrest in Japan was caused by the chaotic state of religious beliefs, a condition that could be corrected only by adopting the teachings of the *Lotus Sūtra*. He taught that if men turned to this *sūtra*, they would realize their true Buddha-nature, perceive that suffering is illusion, and see that this world is a paradise. If men—*i.e.*, the Japanese—did not follow the teachings of the *Lotus Sūtra*, however, natural disasters and invasions would result. With firm confidence in the righteousness of his cause, Nichiren attacked the Shingon and Amida sects of Buddhism for neglecting the true Buddha of the *Lotus Sūtra*, Śākyamuni, and attacked Zen for placing stress only upon Śākyamuni's historical form. These sharp criticisms led Nichiren to be exiled twice and almost brought his execution, from which he was saved in a miraculous fashion, according to his account and the belief of his adherents.

The two main religious practices advocated by Nichiren

Nichiren advocated two main religious practices based on his interpretation of the *Lotus Sūtra*. The first is the worship of the *honzon* (or *gohonzon*), a *maṇḍala* (symbolic diagram) designed by Nichiren, representing the Buddha-nature that is in all men as well as the three forms of the Buddha Śākyamuni. The second is the repetition of the phrase *namu Myōhōrenge-kyō* (salutation to the *Lotus Sūtra*), a practice called *daimoku* ("title"), as the affirmation of the devotee's belief in the teaching and efficacy of the *Lotus Sūtra*. This repetition was not only to be done orally but in every action of the true believer. Nichiren also taught that there should be a sacred place of ordination (*kaidan*) where the believer could receive training in the doctrines of the *Lotus Sūtra* in order that he might keep the true spirit of this document. This sacred place might be seen as wherever the believer in the *Lotus Sūtra* lives, for there is the Buddhist truth. The *honzon*, *daimoku*, and *kaidan* comprise "the three great secret laws" (or "mysteries") that are regarded as the essential teaching of Nichiren—the *sandai-hihō*.

Nichiren's fervent faith brought him wide fame and many devotees, and at his death he chose six disciples to continue his work. This sect was simply known as Nichiren-shū (Sect of Nichiren). It still controls the main temple founded by Nichiren at Mt. Minobu. One of his disciples, Nikkō, however, soon began another sect known as the Nichiren-shō-shū (True Sect of Nichiren), which taught that Nichiren, not Śākyamuni, was the saviour and that the *maṇḍala* painted by Nichiren was alone efficacious in saving mankind. In the 20th century these sects have gained many devotees. Within the Nichiren-shū the Reiyū-kai (Association of the Friend of the Spirit) arose in 1925. This sect, which preaches a combination of ancestor cult and the doctrines of Nichiren, places faith not in the Buddha or *bodhisattva*s but in the *maṇḍala*, in which all saving power is concentrated. The Risshō-Kosei-Kai (Society for Establishing Righteousness and Friendly Relations) split from Reiyū-kai in 1938. This sect teaches the recitation of the *daimoku* as an affirmation of faith in the teaching of the *Lotus Sūtra*, and the worship of the Buddha Śākyamuni. Like Reiyū-kai, it also allows the veneration of ancestral spirits. Risshō-Kosei-Kai gained many converts after World War II, but its success was soon eclipsed by Sōka-gakkai, the lay movement of Nichiren-shō-shū. Sōka-gakkai (Value Creation Society) was founded by Makiguchi Tsunesaburo in 1930, dedicated to educational research and the extension of Nichiren-shō-shū. Its founder insisted on the practical values of worldly gain and satisfaction as well as the attainment of goodness and beauty and taught that Nichiren was to be worshipped as the True Buddha predicted in the *Lotus Sūtra*. The members also fervently practice *daimoku* and worship the *honzon* as the repository of magical power. After World War II, Sōka-gakkai, under the leadership of Toda Jōsei, grew rapidly through a technique of evangelism called *shakubuku* ("break and subdue") in which the resistance of the other person is destroyed by forceful argument. A zealous missionary movement, it has spread to many foreign countries, including the United States. Thus, Nichiren's teaching and personality are still strong influences today.

Sōka-gakkai

Dhyāna (Ch'an/Zen). The Dhyāna (Chinese, Ch'an; Japanese, Zen) school of Buddhism emphasizes meditation as the way to immediate awareness of ultimate reality, an important practice of Buddhism from its origin in India, and derives its name from the Sanskrit term for meditation, *dhyāna*. The meditative emphasis in other schools of Indian origin, such as Yogācāra, has been noted above. Ch'an, with its special training techniques and doctrines and its Taoist influence, however, is generally considered a specifically Chinese product.

While scholars point out that 4th–5th-century Chinese Buddhist monks, such as Hui-yüan and Seng-chao, were teaching doctrines and practices similar to those of the Ch'an school before the traditional date of its arrival in China, standard Chinese texts name a South Indian monk, Bodhidharma, who came to China about AD 520, as its founder. Bodhidharma is held by Ch'an devotees to be the 28th patriarch of the Indian meditational school, which began with the monk Kāśyapa, to whom the Buddha Śākyamuni revealed his supreme teaching. This teaching is found in the *Laṅkāvatāra-sūtra*, an important text for the early Ch'an school, which relates that all beings possess a Buddha-nature, often equated with *śūnya* (the void) in Ch'an, and that realization of this fact is Enlightenment (Chinese Wu; Japanese Satori). The truly enlightened one cannot explain this ultimate truth or reality, for it is beyond the ordinary duality of subject and object. Books, words, concepts, and teachers cannot convey it. It must be realized in direct personal experience.

The Enlightenment experience: Satori

Bodhidharma, who came to be known as the first patriarch of Ch'an in China, passed his mantle to Hui-k'o; and this line of transmission continued to the fifth patriarch, Heng-jen. After his death a schism occurred between the adherents of the Northern school founded by Shen-hsui, which held that Enlightenment must be attained gradually, and the Southern school of Hui-neng, which taught that true wisdom, as undifferentiated, must be attained suddenly and spontaneously. Furthermore, the Southern school tended to neglect rituals and literature and rely on teaching passed from master to pupil, adopting as well an iconoclastic attitude toward the Buddha. It was reasoned that if all things contain the Buddha-nature, then the Buddha could rightfully be equated with a dung heap. The two schools had fundamentally differing views of the Buddha-mind or Buddha-nature. Eventually the Southern school won out, and its victory is attested in the standard Chinese Ch'an texts, which name Hui-neng as the true and only sixth patriarch, as opposed to the counterclaim of Shen-hsui and the Northern school. Hui-neng's *Platform Scripture* (Chinese: *T'an Ching*) became a key text of the Ch'an school.

Two branches of Ch'an Buddhism developed from the Southern school in the 9th century: Lin-chi (Japanese Rinzai) and Ts'ao-t'ung (Japanese Sōtō). The former relied heavily on the *kung-an* (Japanese *koan*), a paradoxical question or answer that aimed at inducing the student to realize that all conceptualization is wrong and led him suddenly beyond this to Enlightenment. The *kung-an* were often accompanied by shouts and slaps from the master to provoke anxiety and, from this, an instant realization of the truth. This consisted of sitting in meditation under the direction of a master and allowing the mind to be free of all notions. Both schools followed the doctrine of Hua-hai, who taught that a monk who did not work would not eat. This practice not only made the Ch'an schools self-sufficient, helping to save them from the purge of parasitic Buddhist monks by the government in 845, it expressed the Ch'an stress on acting naturally and spontaneously in whatever task one is performing. This emphasis on spontaneity and naturalness greatly influenced Chinese painters and writers, who devoted long hours to the practice of technique so that they might act spontaneously when an inspiration arose.

The *kung-an* or *koan*

Most scholars believe that Ch'an Buddhism was influenced by Taoism. Like the Buddha-nature, the Tao (Way) was thought by the Taoists to reside in all beings. Moreover, its realization could not be taught, as it was above all duality and conceptualization. This doctrine, like that of the Ch'an school, led the Taoists to the use of paradoxes in an endeavour to point to the truth. Furthermore, the Taoists' emphasis on the natural life might have influenced the Ch'an practices. But Ch'an, independently of Taoist influence, developed many ideas already present in Indian Buddhism, such as meditation and the Buddha-nature, to fit the Chinese mentality.

Ch'an (Zen) Buddhism was introduced into Japan as early as the 7th century, but it did not flower until the 12th century, in the work of two monks, Eisai and Dōgen. Eisai, founder of the Rinzai school in the 12th century, was a Tendai monk who wished to restore pure Buddhism to Japan and with that aim visited China. When he returned, he taught a strict meditational system based on the use of the *koan* phrases; however, this was taught as only one element in the Tendai system. Unlike the Ch'an schools, Eisai also taught that Zen should defend the state and could observe ceremonial rules and offer prayers and incantations. These teachings influenced the warrior class and led to a Zen influence over the martial arts of archery and swordsmanship. Zen influence can also be seen in the Nō play, in poetry, flower arrangement, and the tea ceremony, all of which stress grace and spontaneity.

Dōgen, who established the Sōtō school in Japan in the 13th century, joined the Tendai monastery of Mt. Hiei at an early age, after the death of his mother and father had dramatically taught him the transitoriness of life. Searching for the true path of Buddhism, he, like Eisai, journeyed to China, where he fell under the influence of a Chinese Ch'an master. Upon his return to Japan he taught a discipline of "sitting straight" (*zazen*) without any effort being directed toward achieving of Enlightenment. Unlike his Chinese counterparts, however, Dōgen studied scriptures and criticized those who did not. These Zen sects still exist in Japan and deeply influence its culture. By mid-20th century Zen had become perhaps the best known of the Buddhist schools in the Western world.

Zazen

IV. Tantrism and related forms

TANTRISM (VAJRAYANA, MANTRAYANA)

Tantrism, also known as Vajrayāna (the Diamond Vehicle) or Mantrayāna (the Path of the Sacred Formulas), is a school of Buddhism that gained prominence in various parts of India and Ceylon. Scholars infer that, because of the esoteric nature of Tantric practice and doctrine, this school might have been developing quietly from the 2nd or 4th centuries AD, when Buddhist tradition associates Nāgārjuna or Asaṅga with its origins. Although a modified version of Tantrism, apparently without sexoyogic practices, spread to China and then to Japan where it became known as Shingon (see below *Shingon*), most scholars associate the Tantric tradition with Tibet (see below *Tibetan Buddhism*).

Identity and unity of opposites

Although Tantrism is essentially nonspeculative, describing numerous yogic or contemplative stages that an aspirant must experience before achieving Enlightenment, rather than elaborating doctrines, it holds the Mahāyāna identification of Nirvāṇa and *saṃsāra* as a basic truth. Tantrism carries this identification of the world of misery and the state of Enlightenment further by teaching that Nirvāṇa as *śūnyatā* (voidness) is one side of a polarity that must be resolved with *karuṇā* (compassion of the *bodhisattva*). *Karuṇā* is the means (*upāya*) or dynamic aspect of this world, whereas *śūnyatā* is seen as passive wisdom (*prajñā*) that possesses an absolutely indestructible or diamond-like (*vajra*) nature beyond all duality. Enlightenment arises when these seeming opposites are realized to be in truth one. This realization, which is known experientially and not through a purely cognitive process, is portrayed in Tantric imagery and practice as the union (*maithuna*) of the passive female deity (*yum*), which signifies wisdom or voidness, with the dynamic male (*yab*), signifying compassion without attachment. Such a union, called *yab-yum* (father-mother) in Tibetan, is not a satisfaction of physical impulses but a symbol of the unity of opposites that brings eternal bliss (*mahāsukha*) or Enlightenment.

Tantrists believe that as all things are in truth of one nature—the void—the physical-mental processes can be used as a vehicle for Enlightenment. In the *Kālacakra Tantra* it is written that the Buddha taught that in this age of degeneration (*Kali yuga*) one must achieve Enlightenment through one's own body, which contains the whole cosmos. This doctrine is taught in all the Tantras. Tantric specialists warn, however, that in order to use correctly the body's processes to achieve an identification of the void with compassion, the aspirant must follow absolutely the instructions of a master or teacher who has been initiated into the mysteries of Tantrism. Such a master alone can direct the pupil's every step so that he learns to control his mental and physical processes instead of being dominated by them. Therefore, the first step toward Enlightenment in Tantric practice is the undergoing of initiation (*abhiṣekha*) by an initiated master.

The path to initiation

The master first endeavours to direct the student to compassion through meditation on the transitoriness of life, the relation of cause and effect of one's actions, and the general suffering of mankind. After this sympathy for the suffering of mankind is aroused, the master guides his pupil in yogic, or contemplative, exercises that help to produce inner experiences that correspond to the various stages of spiritual growth. This process of advancement toward Enlightenment involves the identification of the initiate with gods or goddesses that represent various cosmic forces. These gods are first visualized with the help of *mudrās* (meditative gestures and postures), *mantras* (sacred syllables and phrases), and icons, all of which are believed to possess the essence of the divinities to be invoked. The icons are portrayed in a *maṇḍala*, a sacred design that represents the universe as an aid to meditation. After this visualization, the initiate identifies with the divinities and finds that each in turn is *śūnyatā*, or voidness.

The culmination of this process, called *vajrasattva yoga*, gives the initiate a diamond-like body beyond all duality. Four stages in the process are described in four different groups of *tantras*, the *Kriyātantra*, *Caryātantra*, *Yogatantra*, and *Anuttarayogatantra*. These four stages are likened to the fourfold phases of courtship: the exchange of glances, a pleasing or encouraging smile, the holding of hands, and consummation in the sexual act. The first stage involves external ritual acts, whereas the second combines these outward acts with contemplation. The third stage involves only contemplation and the fourth is the unification of all dualities in the sexual act. This last stage, however, is divided into two phases. The first involves the use by the initiate of his controlled imagination, which allows him to experience the union on an ideational level. The second phase is the *maithuna*, or sexual coupling. This act, however, cannot be construed as an ordinary physical mating, because the initiate has already realized the voidness of all things, allowing him to act with perfect control over his emotions and without attachment. Whereas the ordinary sexual act gives rise to only momentary pleasure, this *maithuna* is the symbol for the attainment of Enlightenment and eternal bliss.

Tantric Buddhist priest performing a ritual, holding a hand-drum and a bell.
William MacQuitty, London

These Tantric practices have been unjustly condemned as a degeneration of Buddhism by those who do not look beyond the surface to the depth of Tantric doctrines. It is quite easy to misinterpret the *Guhyasamāja Tantra* when it states that adultery and eating of human flesh are actions of the *bodhisattva* (*bodhisattvacaryā*) if one does not realize that this imagery points to the belief that voidness alone exists, beyond good or evil, or that the initiate must act only with compassion for the benefit of the salvation of the world. Once the true depths of Tantric doctrines and practices are perceived, this school can be designated as a development of Buddhist thought that emphasizes the attainment of Enlightenment through a graduated process of meditation under the direction of an initiated teacher.

TIBETAN BUDDHISM

The distinctive form of Buddhism that developed in Tibet is a synthesis of Mahāyāna and Vajrayāna thought, both of which were current in north India during the main period of transmission to Tibet (7th to 11th century). The two traditions complemented and interacted with one another, the first stressing the gradual understanding of an established body of doctrine and the other the use of mystical means to achieve a more sudden transformation. Tibetan Buddhism has adopted also in modified form many practices from the pre-existing Bon cult, such as oracular priests, some local divinities, and a notion of divine kingship (see also below *Buddhism and other Asian religions: Buddhism and Tibetan religion*).

History. Buddhism, according to the Tibetan tradition, was first given recognition in Tibet during the reign (620?–649) of Srong-brtsan-sgam-po, two of whose wives were early patrons of the religion and later regarded in popular tradition as incarnations of the Buddhist saviouress, Tārā. The religion received active encouragement from Khri-srong-lde-btsan during whose reign (775–797) the first monastery was built at Samye, the first seven monks were ordained, and the celebrated Tantric master Padmasambhava was invited from India. A great deal of legend surrounds Padmasambhava, who was a *mahāsiddha* ("master of miraculous powers"); he is credited with subduing the Bon spirits and demons and subjugating them to the service of Buddhism. Contemporaneous with Padmasambhava was another Indian monk, Śāntirakṣita, whose disciple, Kamalaśīla, represented the Indian point of view in the debate at the Council of Samye (792–94) as to whether the Indian or Chinese (Ch'an) forms of Buddhism should be followed in Tibet; the Indian side (according to the orthodox view) was proclaimed the winner. Buddhism also received encouragement from Ral-pa-can (reigned 815–838), the third of the "religious" (*i.e.*, Buddhist) kings; but after his assassination in 838 it suffered a period of suppression.

The 10th to 11th century revival in Tibet

Buddhism was again revived in the 10th to the 11th century by the ruling noblemen in western Tibet, who encouraged the travel by Tibetans to India in quest of books and masters and the translation of sacred texts. Foremost among the great translators was Rin-chen bzang-po. With the arrival in 1042 of the renowned Indian master Atīśa, Buddhism became firmly established as the dominant religion of Tibet. Atīśa, like other Mahāyāna masters, emphasized the importance of monastic discipline and direct transmission of doctrine from master to disciple.

By the 14th century the Tibetans had translated all of the Buddhist literature they could obtain and had produced their own canon, the *Bka'-'gyur* (*Kanjur* or *Kagyur;* "Translation of the Buddha-word") and the *Bstan-'gyur* (*Tenjur* or *Tangyur;* "Translation of Teachings"). Separate orders of monks began to develop around particular masters and, as the growing monastic establishments acquired temporal power, intense rivalries arose. In the struggles—more often motivated by a contest for political power than by religious differences—rival monasteries allied themselves with one or another powerful clan. In the 17th century the head of the Dge-lugs-pa order—who belonged to the series of those believed to be reincarnated abbots, known by the honorific title of Dalai Lama—appealed to the Mongol chieftain Güühri Khan for help in the struggle against the rival Karma-pa sect, whose patrons were the rulers of Gtsang. After Güühri Khan's defeat of the Gtsang forces, he awarded the country of Tibet to the Dalai Lama as a religious gift. From 1642 until Chinese Communist occupation of the country in the 1950s, the Dge-lugs-pa has been the dominant sect in Tibet and the Dalai Lama the effective ruler.

Sects. *Bka'-gdams-pa.* The Bka'-gdams-pa (Kadampa, Those Bound By Precept) was a sect based on the teachings of Atīśa and founded by his chief disciple, 'Brom-ston, who emphasized austere discipline. The central practice of the sect was the purification of the mind, which required the elimination of intellectual and moral blemishes in order for a clear vision of the "emptiness" (*śūnyatā*) to be obtained. The sect relied on the *Prajñāpāramitā* and related texts and also made use of *mantras*. The Bka'-gdams-pa order was absorbed in the 15th century by the Dge-lugs-pa sect, described below.

Sa-skya-pa. The Sa-skya-pa order derives its name from the Sa-skya monastery founded in 1073 by 'Khon Dkon-mchog rgyal-po. The first five Sa-skya-pa masters promoted a great translating activity from Sanskrit and prepared the ground for Bu-ston, a 13th- to 14th-century scholar who revised the translated texts in order to ascertain their authenticity and to eliminate the dubious versions. Under the abbot 'Phags-pa, in the 13th century, the Sa-skya-pa enjoyed considerable political power. 'Phags-pa conferred initiation according to the *Hevajra Tantra* on Kublai Khan (founder of the Mongol dynasty in China) and in turn was appointed *ti-shih* (Chinese: Imperial preceptor) and invested with the authority to govern Tibet, though under the control of the Mongol court.

The Sa-skya-pa system

The Sa-skya-pa system is also called the "path and its fruit" (*lam-'bras*). The Buddhist path as presented here evolves in three stages: (1) the actual moment, the particular existence in which the seeker finds himself; (2) the road to be followed, during which he learns what is to be accepted or rejected and the mystical experiences that are realizable with the help of various forms of meditation and Yoga; and (3) the result, the attainment of Buddhahood. This experience can be attained through meditation while travelling on the path or during the intermediate stage between death and a new life.

In Tibetan Buddhism, everything is centred on the *sems* (Sanskrit *citta*), the mind element, which is exalted in a "body of sublime knowledge" and thus, through successive moments, can be transformed into the diamond body; *i.e.*, Buddhahood. This *sems* is not only a mind element; it is also light, and it is precisely on the question of the relationship between the two—the mind element and the light—that notable differences between the various Tibetan schools become apparent. Whereas the Sa-skya-pa consider light as a specific characteristic of the mind element, the Dge-lugs-pa, for example, assert that light is its very nature.

There was no aspect of Buddhist thought with which the Sa-skya-pa did not occupy themselves. They attempted a classification of the Tantras (the Tantric scriptures) even before that made by Mkhas-grub-rje in the 14th and 15th centuries. The Sa-skya-pa established branches in many parts of Tibet and gave rise to a subsect, the Ngor-pa, founded by Kun-dga' bzang-po in 1429.

Bka'-brgyud-pa. The Bka'-brgyud-pa (Transmitted Command) stresses the direct transmission of esoteric teaching from master to pupil, without which the teaching would be lost. The order traces its spiritual lineage from the Indian master Tilopa, who transmitted the teachings to the Indian yogi Nāropa, who in turn was the master of Mar-pa, the 11th-century householder-teacher who in turn was the master of Mi-la ras-pa, the most renowned poet of Tibet and a great ascetic. The latter's songs are the profound expression of his inner spiritual experiences and are often difficult to understand. Mi-la ras-pa's follower, Sgam-po-pa, had several disciples who established separate subschools based on his teaching, one of which was the influential Karma-pa.

The Bka'-brgyud-pa stressed, among other techniques, the exercises of Haṭha Yoga (a Yoga emphasizing breathing and special postures) and posited as the supreme goal the *mahāmudrā* (the "Great Seal") or the overcoming of dichotomous thought in the very being of Buddhahood.

Nāropa's "Six Teachings"

Frequent reference is made by the Bka'-brgyud-pa to the "Six Teachings of Nāropa." These techniques for attaining Enlightenment, either in this life or at the moment of death, deal with (1) self-produced heat; (2) the illusory body; (3) dreams; (4) the experience of the light—*i.e.*, the mind; (5) the state of existence intermediate between death and rebirth (Bardo); and (6) the passing over from one existence into another.

Rnying-ma-pa. The Rnying-ma-pa (Nyingmapa; the Old Order) claim to most purely preserve the spirit of the teachings of the 8th-century miracle worker Padmasambhava. It makes fuller use than the other schools of a group of "rediscovered" texts said to have been hidden since the period of Buddhist persecution following the assassination of Ral-pa-can, the third religious king, in the 9th century; the texts began to reappear in the 14th century.

The school divides revelation into nine progressively superior groups and also subdivides the Tantras in a somewhat different manner from the traditional classification. Six groups are enumerated: (1) *kriyā*, or ritual; (2) *upayoga*, convergence of the two truths and meditation on the pentad of Buddhas; (3) *yoga*, the evocation of the god and identification of the self with the god; meditation on the *maṇḍala* (ritual drawing); (4) *mahāyoga*, meditation on the factors of human consciousness (*skandhas*) as divine forms; (5) *anuyoga*, secret initiation into the presence of the god and his consort; meditation on the "voidness" in order to destroy the illusoriness of things; (6) *atiyoga*, meditation on the union of the god and his consort, leading to the experience of bliss. Those initiated into the *kriyātantra* can attain Buddhahood after seven lives; the *upayoga*, five lives; the *yoga*, three lives; the *mahāyoga* in the next existence; the *anuyoga* at death; and the *atiyoga* in the present existence.

Jo-nang-pa. The Jo-nang-pa takes its name from the Jo-nang monastery founded by Shes-rab rgyal-mtshan (1292–1361), whose master had been a disciple of Candranātha, a Kashmiri. The school reflects the direction taken by Indian Buddhism during its last centuries; and in the formulation of its doctrine of emptiness suggests possible parallels, however indirect, with the Hindu schools of Śaivism and Vedāntic philosophy. As a consequence, it was considered heterodox by the other schools, and its monasteries were forced to close. The Jo-nang-pa assert that the only reality is the *tathāgata-garbha* (the Matrix of the Buddhas) present in each person. Things are empty: he who meditates and that on which he meditates are but the luminous mind element, essentiality itself. To talk of the fruit of meditation is only a way of speaking, for the effect is already inherent in the cause. Blemishes are illusory appearances. Liberation is not a new situation but rather the liberation of essentiality from such blemishes. The *tathāgata-garbha* is emptiness itself; in other words, it is devoid of all that is other than itself. In fact, if the blemishes were inherent in the mind element, they could not be cancelled, for the mind element would disappear with the cancellation of the blemishes.

The *tathāgata-garbha*

Gcod-pa. The Gcod ("cut off") rite and school developed out of Zhi-byed-pa, brought to Tibet from India in the 11th century by Pha-dam-pa Sangs-rgyas. It assumes that the dichotomous process by which thoughts flow keeps man away from awareness of "voidness." All opposites, good and evil, life and death, must therefore be cancelled through the symbolic sacrifice of the body. This is accomplished by meditations performed at night in cemeteries or in places where corpses are exposed. The practitioners of Gcod conjure up imagined demons until they are able to bring before themselves the terrible-appearing forms of Tibetan iconography. Then the practitioners eliminate the demons by reabsorbing them in the heart, thus demonstrating their nonexistence.

Dge-lugs-pa. The Dge-lugs-pa (Gelugpa, the Virtuous) constitute the reformed sect in Tibet; its members are commonly known as Yellow Hats from the colour of their head cover. Their founder, Tsong-kha-pa, attended the most important schools in 14th-century Tibet, the Sa-skya-pa, Bka'-brgyud-pa, and Bka'-gdams-pa. His own school is considered the continuation of the Bka'-gdams-pa. Tsong-kha-pa was prompted to initiate the reform of monastic discipline by what he considered to be a general laxity of morals, an increasingly less rigorous observance of monastic rules, and the prevalence of deviations in the interpretation of the Tantras. He imposed respect for the traditional rules of the Vinaya and placed renewed emphasis on dogmatics and on logic as aids to salvation. His treatise, the *Lam-rim chen-mo* ("The Great Gradual Path"), is based on the *Bodhipathapradīpa* by Atīśa. In it Tsong-kha-pa presents the process of mental purification leading to victory, ascending through the 10 spiritual levels (*bhūmi*) to Buddhahood. The essential points of such a process are the state of quiescence and the state of enhanced vision. Tsong-kha-pa attributed great importance to the study of logic and instituted the regular holdings of debates at monasteries. Competing monks sought to reach, by means of formal logic and in the presence of an abbot of great learning, an unassailable conclusion on a chosen topic. Various ranks of monks were established on the basis of examinations, the highest being that of *dge-bshes* (the philosophers).

Tsong-kha-pa's account of the stages of the path

This insistence on doctrinal and logical problems did not exclude interest in the Tantras, and Tsong-kha-pa's *Sngags-rim chen-mo* ("The Great Gradual Tantric Path") deals with Tantric ritual. The Tantric schools, however, were open only to those students who had previously mastered theoretical learning. The literature of the Dge-lugs-pa is enormous, including also the gigantic collections of the Dalai and Panchen Lamas, both of whom are members of this school.

The Dge-lugs-pa assert that the nature of the mind element (*sems*) is light, which constitutes the cognitive capacity. The continuum of each person, therefore, is a thinking and luminous energy, which is in either a coarse or subtle state, the latter state achieved only after purification through meditation and contemplation.

SHINGON

Shingon (Chinese Chen-yen) or True Word Buddhism is an esoteric Sino-Japanese school that derives its name from the Japanese term for *mantra* (Sanskrit; a mystical doctrine or formula; hence, Mantrayāna). This school, which flourished most prominently in Japan from the 9th century, when it was introduced by the monk Kūkai, appears to be closely associated with the late (Tantric) form of Mahāyāna Buddhism called Mantrayāna that was transported from India to China in the 7th and 8th centuries notably by three Buddhist monks: Śubhakarasiṃha, Vajrabodhi, and Amoghavajra. Śubhakarasiṃha brought Mantrayāna to China from the famous Indian centre of Buddhist learning at Nālandā and was instrumental in translating into Chinese the *Mahāvairocana-sūtra* the most important text of Shingon Buddhism. Soon after Śubhakarasiṃha, a second monk, Vajrabodhi, arrived from Nālandā and translated another important Shingon text, the *Vajraśekhara-sūtra* ("Diamond Peak *sūtra*"). His pupil, Amoghavajra, taught the Chinese monk Hui-kuo, who in turn passed his learning on to Kūkai, the founder of Shingon in Japan.

Kūkai, better known by his posthumous name Kōbō Daishi (Great Master Who Propagated the *Dharma*), was an exceptional scholar, poet, painter, and calligrapher who early in life wrote a treatise comparing Confucian, Taoist, and Buddhist thought, naming the latter as superior. Although he had trained for government service, he experienced a change of heart and became a Buddhist monk. In pursuit of the pure Buddhist doctrine, he, like many great monks of his time, journeyed to China, where he met the Chen-yen master Hui-kuo, who recognized Kūkai's potentiality and bestowed upon him the esoteric teachings of his school. After the death of Hui-kuo, Kūkai returned to Japan to receive many governmental honours and to establish a monastery on Mt. Kōya as the centre of Shingon Buddhism.

In propagating the teachings of his sect, Kūkai wrote many important texts, including the *Jūjū shinron* ("The Ten Stages of Consciousness") and the *Sokushin-jōbutsugi* ("The Doctrine of Becoming a Buddha with One's Body During One's Earthly Existence"). In the first of these documents, Kūkai presented a theory of the development of the spiritual life of human beings by placing the teachings of Buddhist schools and several other religions into a hierarchical system. Kūkai taught that the first stage of human spiritual development was one in which man is completely controlled by his instincts. In the second stage, which Kūkai identifies with Confucian teachings, man attempts to live a proper moral existence. The third stage is that of Brahmanism and Taoism, where the individual strives for supernatural powers and heavenly rewards. The fourth and fifth stages of spiritual development are taught by the Hīnayāna schools and are characterized by man's striving for self-enlightenment. The next stages, from six to nine, are Mahāyānist paths identified with the teachings of Hossō, Sanron, Tendai, and Kegon, which lead the individual to compassion for others. The zenith of spiritual development is identified by Kūkai with the esoteric teachings of Shingon.

The hierarchy of religions

The Shingon school preached that it possessed the highest and purest doctrine, for its beliefs were not based on the teachings of the historical Buddha Śākyamuni, who expounded the doctrine with limitations of his audience in mind, but on the timeless and immutable teachings of the Buddha in his *dharmakāya*, or cosmic body. This

Buddha, named Mahā-Vairocana, was felt to be beyond all earthly dualism and impurity but at the same instant to be within all things as their Buddha-nature.

In Shingon the realization that one's own Buddha-nature is identical with Mahā-Vairocana is Enlightenment. This Enlightenment, as depicted in the title of Kūkai's treatise mentioned above, can be achieved in this world while possessing a human body. In order to achieve this enlightened state, however, one must be given the secret doctrine of Shingon. The gift of this doctrine is handed down to the aspirant only orally by the Shingon master. The truth that the master reveals is founded on the three ritual mysteries of the body, speech, and mind. These mysteries invoke the cosmic forces embodied in the form of Buddhas and *bodhisattva*s with which the aspirant identifies until he can become one with Mahā-Vairocana. The mystery of the body involves *mudrā*s: various devotional gestures of the hands and fingers in accordance with the Buddha to be invoked, postures of meditation, and the handling of such sacred instruments as the *vajra* (diamond) and the lotus. The mystery of speech involves the recitation of *dhāraṇi*s or *mantra*s, which are mystical verses and sounds believed to be the essence of the cosmic forces with which one wishes to commune. The mystery of the mind involves yogic contemplation of and absorption in the Buddha Mahā-Vairocana and his attendants.

The three ritual mysteries of Shingon

The aspirant was further helped in his quest to identify his Buddha-nature with the cosmic Buddha by means of two sacred drawings, or *maṇḍala*s, often placed on the Shingon altar. These *maṇḍala*s, believed to contain all the power of the cosmos, were drawn in accordance with the teaching of Hui-kuo that the doctrines of the Buddha Mahā-Vairocana were so deep and abstruse that their meanings could be conveyed only in art. One *maṇḍala*, known as the *vajra-dhātu* (Japanese *kongō-kai*), portrayed the Buddha Mahā-Vairocana sitting upon a white lotus in deep contemplation, surrounded by the Buddhas of the four regions. This symbolized Mahā-Vairocana's indestructible, immutable, or potential aspect. The second *maṇḍala*, the *garbha-dhātu* (Japanese *taizō-kai*) or womb-world, revealed Mahā-Vairocana sitting on a red lotus surrounded by innumerable Buddhas, *bodhisattva*s, and Hindu gods, with consorts. This represents the cosmic Buddha's dynamic manifestation in which he is immanent in everything. Through the correct meditation on these two *maṇḍala*s it was believed that the aspirant would realize the unity beyond the diversity of the world.

The emphasis of Shingon upon ritual, symbolism, and iconography, coupled with the government's praise of Kūkai and the bestowal upon him of the shrine for the protection of the country, led to a great popularity of Shingon among the Japanese. Many people came to use Shingon rites, believed to control the forces of the cosmos, to ward off evil and bring supernatural help in everyday life. The popularity of Shingon was one of the causes for the growth of Ryōbu Shintō (Two Aspects Shintō), which identified Shintō gods with *bodhisattvas*. While this combination of more this-worldly concerns with esoteric Buddhism led to some schisms in Shingon, it has continued in the 20th century as one of Japan's strongest Buddhist sects.

V. Practices and institutions

ETHICS

Buddhist ethics from the beginning have been committed to the middle way between asceticism and hedonism that was announced in the noble Eightfold Path. In affirming the Threefold Refuge in the Buddha, *dharma*, and *saṅgha*, the Buddhist adherent commits himself to achieving a certain way of life, to which the Buddha pointed the way.

Although Buddhism on the whole eschews mandatory dogmas and specific injunctions to which the adherent must conform, there are traditional precepts that list the obligations or moralities (*śīla*s) to be observed. The five precepts (*pañca-śīla*) for the layman prohibit killing, stealing, engaging in sexual misconduct, lying, and drinking intoxicating liquor. There are five additional precepts for monastic novices and laity committed to this stricter regime: not to eat during prohibited hours; not to take part in festivals and amusements; not to use garlands, perfumes, or ointments; not to use a bed (or chair) that is too large or luxurious; not to accept money (for oneself). Taken together, these comprise the ten precepts (*dasa-śīla*). In many, but not all, traditions, the injunction against sexual misconduct has been interpreted as enjoining celibacy for monks and nuns. Although Buddhism distinguishes between non-Buddhists, members of the *saṅgha*, and lay devotees, there is no distinction of caste, social class, or ethnic origin.

The ten precepts

By emphasizing the obligatory nature of charity, hospitality, and love for every living being, Buddhism revalues ethics as the foundation of society. The *Dhammapada*, a popular ethical text, states, "Abstention from sin, doing good works, and purifying one's mind, this is the teaching of Buddhism," and, furthermore: "One does not repay evil with evil, but one repays evil with good." The fact that no distinction is made among men except on spiritual grounds and that, among the essential virtues, one finds love, compassion, joy, and equanimity for all that which is good—all this makes for deep human warmth. Buddhism is characterized by an acute psychological sense, which acknowledges that men are not all capable of understanding the law in the same manner, hence the necessity for the masters or the preachers (*dharma-bhāṇaka*) to adapt themselves to the moral and intellectual preparation or capacity of the person to whom they are speaking. Education cannot be a single and generic teaching but rather a gradual, individual process. Perfection is attained not through an instant flash but through continuous exercise and example; hence the necessity for spending time with helpful persons who can cooperate toward the aspirant's internal purification. Obstinate attachment to a single point of view, whether good or bad, is to be avoided. Conformism of any kind is an obstacle to serenity of spirit.

India has often been suffocated by the metaphysics that sees everything as illusion; for in illusion one runs the risk of no longer caring either for good or for evil. Some might say that this danger also threatened Mahāyāna when it asserted that everything is "voidness," that there is neither good nor bad. Mahāyāna, however, even in its metaphysical flights, did not fall short of the ethical values of ancient Buddhism. On the contrary, it enlarged the horizons of Buddhism by stressing the importance of the *bodhisattva* state as the ultimate ideal for men in this life, foregoing Buddhahood for the time being. This implied the renunciation of extinction in the Nirvāṇa in order to stay in life for the purpose of serving as an example to others, to spread the word of the Buddha, to sacrifice oneself for the triumph of the law, that is, for the happiness of everyone. Thus, there is emphasis on the value of sympathy (*maitrī*), of compassion (*karūṇa*), and of joyful participation (*muditā*) in the good performed by others, an ideal of love and fellowship toward every living being, to which the past lives of the Buddha (as told in the *Jātaka* tales) serve as an incentive. Admittedly, the exaltation of the acts of heroism and charity of the *bodhisattva*s ran the risk of provoking a momentary ardour without its thereby being translated into continuous everyday practice. Nevertheless, the ideal capacity of transferring the merit of one's own actions for the benefit of others is a brake to egoism, especially self-serving spiritual egoism, and stimulates fellow feeling.

Triumph of the ethical over the metaphysical emphasis

The gift and the sacrifice remain always at the top of the ten "perfections." A gift does not only mean charity; it is primarily the gift of the law, that is, the teaching of the law for everyone's benefit. From the time of Aśoka, Buddhists have been promoters of works destined to the common good: construction of wells, irrigation projects, bridges, hospitals, shelters for both men and animals. In fact, Buddhism extends its solidarity also to wild animals, since they also participate in the nature of the Buddha. This was not a new principle in India, where the injunction against harming any form of life (*ahiṃsā*) is an ancient norm; but Buddhism conferred upon it a greater extension. Also pre-eminent is another "perfection," the moral energy (*vīrya*), the unshakable tenacity, the active

Social ethics and good works

responsibility, the courage of one's own ideas, and the perseverance to struggle for the common good.

All of this tends to develop in the faithful a spirit of social cooperation and active participation in society, fostered by the *saṅgha*, which radiates upon all people the benefit of its prayers. The monasteries traditionally have been centres of education and medical service for laymen. The teaching inculcates the fear of the consequences of sin and stimulates the imitation of ideals of humaneness or of compassion. The Buddhist is required to be always alert and aware of what he does, thinks, and says because sin is threefold: physical, mental, and verbal. Although he is solicitous of his own salvation, he cannot isolate himself from the infinite crowd of converts and those who can be converted. Thus, the sense of human solidarity is strengthened. Both men and women participate in the Buddhist society.

A certain laxity did not fail to manifest itself when the certainty of the maturation of *karman* became weak in people's minds. Among the devotional and Tantric schools the confidence that with prayers, hymns, and liturgies man could purify himself from the evil he committed stifled the old moral rigour. The devotee dreamed of redemptions instead of the strict and implacable law of *karman* and was also able to abdicate the responsibilities with which it had been invested by the Buddha.

Relaxations of the "moralities"

In this new dispensation, the use of meat and alcoholic beverages (in former times strictly forbidden) was tolerated. It was normal for some Tantric monks to cohabitate with women who were not their wives, but this can not be considered a relaxation of moral standards; the Tantric adept was no longer bound by common morality, and in any case the sexual act was undergone as a ritual act with symbolic meaning, not for the pleasures of the senses. According to the new rules one might even kill when it became necessary, not for personal advantage, but to prevent a sinner from committing other crimes and thus render his own *karman* heavier. This authorized Buddhists to resort to weapons when the community was threatened. The monasteries themselves became great economic and political powers and waged war against one another (in Tibet and Japan). The assertion of one's own individuality inspires the anticonformism of Ch'an (Zen), which is supreme freedom. Without the authority of a god to command man to be good, and without even the future lure of reward after death (the *bodhisattva* renounces immediate participation in Nirvāṇa in order to bring salvation to others), Buddhism places an autonomous value on one's actions. The good is good for its own sake. Above all, the ever-present thought of death, the certainty of the common misery, and the awareness that everything will unfailingly pass away have induced in the hearts of Buddhists a serenity of spirit (see also BUDDHIST PHILOSOPHY: *Buddhist Ethics*).

MONASTIC INSTITUTIONS

Traditionally, Buddhists have expressed their faith by taking refuge in the Buddha, in his teachings (*dharma*), and in the *saṅgha*. The *saṅgha* is the assembly of Buddhist monks that has, from the origins of Buddhism, authoritatively studied, taught, and preserved the teachings of the Buddha. In their communities monks have served the laity through example and, as directed by the Buddha, through the teachings of morality (*śīla*). In exchange for their service the monks have received support from the laity, who thereby earn merit. Besides serving as the centre of Buddhist propaganda and learning, the monastery offers the monk an opportunity to live apart from worldly concerns, a situation that has usually been believed necessary or at least advisable in order to follow strictly the path of the Buddha to release.

The origin and development of the saṅgha. According to scholars of early Buddhism, at the time of the Buddha in northeastern India there existed numerous religous mendicants or almsmen who wandered and begged individually or in groups. These men had forsaken the life of a houseowner and the attachment with worldly affairs that this involves in order to seek a doctrine that would meaningfully explain life and offer salvation. When such a seeker met someone who seemed to offer such a salvatory message, he would accept him as a teacher (guru) and wander with him. The situation of these mendicants is summed up in the greeting with which they met other religious wanderers. This greeting asked, "Under whose guidance have you accepted religious mendicancy? Who is your master (*sattha*)? Whose *dharma* is agreeable to you?"

The yearly rain retreat

These groups of mendicants that formed around one teacher broke their wanderings during the rainy season (*vassa*) from July through August. At this time they gathered at various rain retreats (*vassavāsa*), usually situated near villages. Here they would beg daily for their few needs and continue their spiritual quest. The Buddha and his followers appear to have been one of the many groups that founded such a yearly rain retreat. After the Buddha's death, however, his followers did not separate but continued to wander and enjoy the rain retreat together. In their retreats the followers of the Buddha's doctrines probably built their own huts and lived separately, but their sense of community with other Buddhists led them to gather fortnightly at the time of the full and new moons to recite the *Pātimokkha* or assertion of their faith in the Buddha's *dharma*. This ceremony, in which the laity also participated, was called the *uposatha*.

Within the first several centuries of the Buddha's death, the rain retreats were forsaken for permanent monastic settlements (*vihāra*s). There appear to be two major reasons for this change in the mode of living. First, the followers of the Buddha were able, through their confession of a common faith, to build up a certain coherent organization. Secondly, the laity gave meritorious gifts of land and raised buildings in which the followers of the Buddha might live permanently, assured of a supply of the staples of life and also fulfilling the Buddha's directive to minister to the laity. In this manner small *vihāra*s were raised in northeastern India, where Buddhism remained a rather parochial sect of monks and laymen until the rise of the Mauryan empire and the reign of King Aśoka around 250 BC. This king, who controlled or was honoured in much of India, was a follower of the Buddha's doctrine, and Aśoka's active help and prestige gave Buddhism a more universal perspective.

From the practice of a few monks living together, sometimes in hillside caves, there developed in about the 5th century AD *mahāvihāra*s, or great monasteries, serving as universities, such as Nālandā. These universities served as centres of Buddhist learning and propaganda, drawing monks from China and Tibet and sending forth missionaries to these lands. These institutions were open to the outside influence of a resurgent Hinduism, however, which is one of the factors that weakened Buddhism and led to its disappearance from India in the 13th century.

The monks that such *mahāvihāra*s attracted and sent out spread Buddhist monasticism to Southeast Asia, Tibet, China, and Japan. While the new environments led to architectural changes, including such minor ones as the introduction of new guardian deities derived from the indigenous folklore, and major changes such as the meditational hall or the hall for the recitation of the name of Amida serving Ch'an (Zen) and Pure Land monks, respectively, the monasteries continued to serve as (1) centres of missions and learning and (2) as retreats. These are the two important functions of monasteries throughout the Buddhist world. It should be noted, however, that in China there are two distinct types of monasteries: the large public monasteries and the small hereditary institutions. The former, populated by only 5 percent of the monks in China, are orthodox institutions following rules that are essentially the same as Buddhist monasteries in other lands. The hereditary monasteries serve the rural area and on the average are manned by only five monks. They are hereditary institutions in the sense that the abbot of the small monastery adopts a monk who inherits the endowment and responsibilities of the monastery.

Continuing functions of the monasteries

Internal organization of the saṅgha. The development of the *saṅgha* from a group of wandering mendicants loosely bound together by their faith in the Buddha and his teachings, to monks living closely together in a permanent monastery necessitated the development of rules and a degree of hierarchical organization. It appears that the earliest organization within Indian monasteries was democratic in nature. This democratic nature arose from two important historical factors. First, the Buddha did not, as was the custom among the teachers of his time, designate a human successor. Instead, the Buddha taught that each monk should strive to follow the path that he had preached. This decision of the Buddha placed every monk on the same footing. There could be no absolute authority vested in one person, for the authority was the *dharma* of the Buddha. Secondly, the region in which Buddhism arose was noted for a system of tribal democracy, or republicanism. When a serious question demanded attention in the region, the male inhabitants would meet to decide upon a course of action, often electing a temporary ruler. This republican tradition, which supported the anti-authoritarian nature of the Buddha's teaching, was adopted by the early *saṅgha.*

Democracy and hierarchy in the *saṅgha*

When an issue arose, all the monks of the monastery assembled. The issue was put before the body of monks and discussed. If any solution was forthcoming, it had to be read three times, with silence signifying acceptance. If there was debate, a vote might be taken or the issue referred to committee or the arbitration of the elders of a neighboring monastery. As the *saṅgha* developed, a certain division of labour and hierarchical administration was adopted. The abbot became the head of this administrative hierarchy and was vested with almost unlimited powers over monastic affairs. The anti-authoritarian character of Buddhism, however, continued to assert itself. In China, for instance, the abbot continued to refer all important questions to the assembled monks, who have elected him as their leader. Similarly, in Southeast Asian countries Buddhism shows a great dislike for hierarchy, making rules difficult to enforce in the numerous almost independent monastic units.

As the Buddhist *saṅgha* developed, specific rules and rites were enacted that differ very little in all Buddhist monasteries even today. The rules by which the monks are judged and the punishments that should be assessed are found in the Vinaya texts (Vinaya literally means "That Which Leads"). The *Vinaya Piṭaka* of the Theravāda canon, which is the most complete of the various Buddhist schools, contains precepts that were supposedly given by the Buddha as he judged a particular situation. While in the majority of cases the Buddha's authorship can be doubted, the attempt is made to refer all authority to the Buddha and not to one of his disciples. The heart of the Vinaya texts is the *Pātimokkha*, originally a statement of faith, which, in the course of the *saṅgha*'s development, became a list of monastic rules. The rules are recited by the assembled monks every fortnight, with a pause after each one, so that any monk who has transgressed this rule may confess and receive his punishment. While the number of rules in the *Pātimokkha* differs in the various schools, with 227, 250, and 253, respectively in the Pāli, Chinese, and Tibetan canons, the rules are essentially the same. The first part of the *Pātimokkha* deals with the four gravest sins, which necessarily lead to expulsion from the monastery. They are sexual intercourse, theft, murder, and exaggeration of one's miraculous powers. The other rules, in seven sections, deal with transgressions of a lesser nature, such as drinking or lying.

The novice's way

In the Theravāda countries—Ceylon (modern Sri Lanka), Burma, Thailand, and Cambodia—the Buddhist community is composed of monks (*bhikṣus*) and nuns (*bhikṣuṇīs*), male and female novices (*śrāmaṇeras* and *śrāmaṇerīs*), and laymen and laywomen (for ceremonies of initiation or ordination, see below *Ceremonies and festivals*). In some Theravādin countries, notably Burma and Thailand, almost every layman must join the monastery for a period of instruction and meditation. Thus, all men in these countries can to a certain extent be considered monks. This increases lay participation in monastic affairs. In the Mahāyānist countries of Tibet and China there is a stage of one year before the aspirant can become a novice. This is a year of probation when the aspirant does not receive tonsure and remains subject to governmental taxation and service, while receiving instructions and performing menial tasks within the monastery. At the end of this one-year probationary period, the aspirant must pass a test, including the recitation of part of a well-known *sūtra*—the length depending upon whether the applicant is male or female—and a discussion on various doctrinal questions. In China, one usually does not progress beyond the novice stage unless he or she is of exceptional character or is affiliated with the government.

According to Vinaya rules, entry into the *saṅgha* is an individual affair, dependent upon the wishes of the individual or his family. In China, however, ordination has often been under the control of the state. During some dynasties, the state conducted the examinations held to determine entry or advancement in the *saṅgha.* Ordination could be obtained not only through such examinations but also by the favour of the emperor or through the purchase of an ordination certificate from the government. This selling of ordination certificates was at times abused by the government in order to fill its treasury.

The life of a Buddhist monk was originally one of wandering, poverty, begging, and strict sexual abstinence. The monks were supposed to live only on alms, to wear clothes made from cloth taken from rubbish heaps, and to possess only three robes, one girdle, an alms bowl, a razor, a needle, and a water strainer used to filter insects from the drinking water (so as not to kill or imbibe them). Most Buddhist schools still stress celibacy, although the Shin sect of Japan has encouraged abolition of the monastic discipline and some Tantric schools have allowed sexual intercourse as symbolic of the attainment of release. Begging, however, has tended in all schools to become merely a symbolic gesture used to teach humility or compassion or to raise funds for special purposes. Also, the growth of large monasteries has often led to compromises on the rule of poverty. While

Relaxation of poverty rule

Fujihira—Monkmeyer

Burmese Buddhist monks receiving rice from a laywoman, while making their daily rounds of alms.

the monk might technically give up his property before entering the monastery—although even this rule is sometimes relaxed—the community of monks might inherit wealth and receive lavish gifts of land. This acquisition of wealth has led at times not only to a certain neglect of the Buddhist monastic ideal but to the attainment of temporal power. This factor, added to the self-governing nature of Buddhist monasteries and the early Buddhist connection with Indian kingship, has encouraged the interaction of the *saṅgha* and the state.

The saṅgha and the state. The early Buddhist *saṅgha* in India appears to have been treated by Indian rulers as a self-governing unit not subject to their power unless it proved subversive or was threatened by internal or external disruption. Aśoka, the Buddhist king whose personal faith and prestige helped Buddhism grow from a regional to a universal religion, appears to have been applying this policy of protection from disruption when he intervened in Buddhist monastic affairs to expel schismatics. He came to be remembered, however, as the Dharmarāja, the great king who protected and propagated the teachings of the Buddha. His was looked upon as a golden age, and in Theravāda countries Aśoka's image as a supporter and sponsor of the faith is used to judge political authority. In general, Buddhism in Theravāda countries is either heavily favoured or officially recognized by the government, so that the golden age of interaction of the government and monks can be viewed as an obtainable goal. The *saṅgha*'s role in this interaction is to preserve the *dharma* and to act as the spiritual guide and model, revealing to the secular power the need for furthering the welfare of the people. While the *saṅgha* and the government appear as two separate structures, there is some intertwining, for monks (often of royal heritage) act as temporal advisers; and the king, as all laymen—at least in Thailand—spends some time in the monastery. It should also be pointed out that Buddhist monastic institutions serve as a link between the rural peoples and the urban elites, helping to unify the various Theravāda countries.

In China, the relationship between the *saṅgha* and the state has fluctuated. At times Buddhism has been seen as a foreign religion, a state within a state or a drain on national resources of men and wealth. This attitude has led to sharp purges of Buddhism and to rules to curb its influence. Some of the rules attempted to limit the number of monks and to guarantee governmental influence in ordination through state examinations and the granting of ordination certificates. Buddhism, however, especially that of the Ch'an school, which taught that a monk must work daily or not eat, survived these rules and purges. At other times, such as during the T'ang dynasty (7th to 10th century AD), Buddhism was considered almost the state religion. The government created a commissioner of religion to earn merits for the state by erecting temples, monasteries, and images in honour of the Buddha.

In Japan from the 10th to the 13th century, monasteries gained great landed wealth and temporal power. They formed large armies of mercenaries and monks that took part in wars with rival religious groups as well as in temporal struggles. In Japan such monastic power waned in the 14th century; but in Tibet, the Dge-lugs-pa order was able to gain such power—mainly through negotiating with the invading Mongols—that its leader, known as the Dalai Lama, became the centre for both religious and secular power. This power lasted from the 17th century until the flight of the Dalai Lama from the Chinese occupation forces in 1959.

CEREMONIES AND FESTIVALS

The religious year. *Uposatha.* The four monthly holy days of ancient Buddhism continue to be observed in the Theravāda countries of Southeast Asia. The *uposatha* days—the new moon and full moon days of each lunar month and the eighth day following the new and full moons—have their origin, according to some scholars, in the fast days that preceded the Vedic-*soma* sacrifices. Laymen and monk alike pay strict attention to the observance of religious laws during the *uposatha* days. Laymen may choose to visit a monastery and to give alms to the monks. The *uposatha* service typically includes the repetition of the precepts, offering of flowers to the Buddha image, the recitation of Pāli *sutta*s, and a sermon by one of the monks for the benefit of the visitors. The more pious laymen may vow to observe the eight precepts for the duration of the *uposatha*. These are the five precepts normally observed by all Buddhists—not to kill, steal, lie, take intoxicants, or commit sexual offenses—upgraded to include complete sexual continence, plus injunctions against eating food after noon, attending entertainments or wearing bodily adornments, and sleeping on a luxurious bed. The monks observe the *uposatha* days by assembling in pairs for mutual confession of sins and by listening to the recitation by one of their members of the *Pātimokkha*, or rules of conduct, contained in the *Vinaya Piṭaka*.

Anniversaries. The three major events of the Buddha's life—his birth, Enlightenment, and entrance into final Nirvāṇa (*i.e.*, death)—are invariably commemorated in all Buddhist countries but not everywhere on the same day. In the Theravāda countries the three events are all observed together on Vesak, the full moon day of the sixth lunar month (Vaiśākha), which usually occurs in April. (The Māgha Pūjā takes place three months earlier—on the full moon of February—and celebrates the Buddha's first exposition of the *Pātimokkha*.)

Commemorations of Buddha's birth, Enlightenment, and final Nirvāṇa

In Japan and other Mahāyāna countries, the three anniversaries of the Buddha are observed on separate days (the birth April 8, the Enlightenment December 8, and the death February 15). Festival days honouring other Buddhas and *bodhisattvas* of the Mahāyāna tradition are also observed, and considerable emphasis is placed on anniversaries connected with the patriarchs of each sect. Padmasambhava's anniversary, for example, is especially observed by the Rnying-ma-pa sect in Tibet; and the birthday of Nichiren is celebrated by his followers in Japan.

Vassa. The beginning of *vassa*, the three-month, rainy-season retreat from July to October, and its conclusion are two of the major festivals of the year among Theravāda Buddhists, particularly in Burma, Cambodia, Thailand, and Laos. The retreat has largely been given up by Mahāyāna Buddhists. It is an accepted practice in countries such as Thailand for a layman to take monastic vows for the *vassa* period and then to return to his lay life. Commonly, the number of years a monk has spent in monastic life is expressed by counting up the number of *vassa*s he has observed.

The end of *vassa* is marked by joyous celebration. The month following is a major occasion for presenting gifts to monks and acquiring the consequent merit. The *kaṭhina*, or robe-offering ceremony, is a public event during this period and usually involves a collective effort by a village or group of villages to bestow gifts on an entire monastery. A public feast and display of the robes and other presents on a "wishing-tree" are the usual components of the ceremony. The *kaṭhina* season is climaxed by the making and presentation of the *mahākaṭhina* ("great robe"), a particularly meritorious gift that requires the cooperation of a number of people, for the entire operation of producing the robe—from symbolically spinning the thread to stitching the cloth—is supposed to be completed in a single day and night. The robe commemorates the act of the Buddha's mother, who on hearing that he was about to renounce worldly life, wove his first mendicant robes in one night.

All Souls festival. The importance of the virtues of filial piety and the reverence of ancestors in China and Japan has established Ullambana, or All Souls Day, as one of the major Buddhist festivals in those countries. In China, worshippers in Buddhist temples make "boats of the law" (*fa-ch'uan*) out of paper, some very large, which are then burned in the evening. The purpose of the celebration is twofold: to remember the dead and to free and let ascend to heaven the *preta*. The *preta* are the spirits of those who died as a result of an accident or a drowning and as a consequence were never buried; their presence among men is thought to be dangerous. Under the guidance of Buddhist temples, societies (*hui*, *Yu-lan-hui*) are formed to carry out ceremonies for the *preta*—lanterns are lit, monks are invited to recite sacred verses, and offerings of fruit are presented. An 8th-century Indian monk, Amoghavajra, is said to have introduced the ceremony into China, from where it was transmitted to Japan. During the Japanese festival of Bon, two altars are constructed, one to make offerings to the spirits of dead ancestors and the other to the souls of those dead who have no peace. Invocations to Amida and Odori-nembutsu (the chanting of invocations accompanied by dancing and singing) are features of the Bon celebrations.

Remembrance of the dead and liberation of the unquiet spirits

Popular traditions. *New Year's and harvest festivals.* The New Year's festival—like the harvest festival, funeral rites, and exorcistic ceremonies—is an example of Buddhism's involvement in pre-existing local traditions. On the occasion of the New Year, images of the Buddha are in some countries taken in procession through the streets. Worshippers visit Buddhist sanctuaries and circumambulate the *stūpa*, or sacred image, and monks are fed and presented gifts. One of the most remarkable examples of the absorption of local custom was the Smonlam festival in Tibet, celebrated on a large scale in Lhasa until the beginning of Chinese Communist rule in the 1950s. The festival was instituted in 1408 by Tsong-kha-pa, the founder of the predominant Dge-lugs-pa sect, who transformed an old custom into a Buddhist festivity. Smonlam took place at the beginning of the winter thaw, when caravans began to set out once again and the hunting season was resumed. The observances included exorcistic ceremonies, performed privately within each family to remove evil forces lying in wait for individuals as well as for the community as a whole, and propitiatory rites, performed to ward off evil such as droughts, epidemics, or hail, during the coming year. During the more public propitiatory rites, the *saṅgha* cooperated with the laity by invoking the merciful forces that watch over good order; and processions, fireworks, and various amusements created an atmosphere of hopefulness. Through the collaboration of the monastic community and the laymen, a general reserve of good *karman* was accumulated to see everyone through the dangerous moment of passage from the old year to the new.

The harvest festival celebrated in the Tibetan villages during the eighth lunar month was quite different in nature from the New Year ceremonies. Most commonly, offerings of thanks were made to local deities in rites that were only externally Buddhist. The same interplay between Buddhism and folk tradition is observable elsewhere. In Sri Lanka at harvest time, for example, there is a "first fruits" ceremony that entails offering the Buddha a large bowl of milk and rice.

An integral part of the harvest celebrations in many Buddhist countries is the sacred performance of an episode in the life of a Buddha or a *bodhisattva*. In Tibet, troupes of actors specialize in performances of Buddhist legends. In Thailand, the recitation of the story of Phra Wes (Sanskrit Viśvāntara) constitutes one of the most important festival events of the agricultural calendar.

Pilgrimages. Many local temples have their own festivals, associated with a relic enshrined there or an event in the life of a sacred figure. Some of these, such as the display of the tooth relic at Kandy, Sri Lanka, are occasions for great celebrations, attracting many pilgrims. Other favourite pilgrimage sites are the Buddha's birthplace at Lumbinī in Nepal; the spot where he achieved Enlightenment, at Bodh Gayā, Bihār state; where he preached his first sermon "setting in motion the wheels of the law" at Sārnāth, near Vārānasi; and the site of his death, at Kuśinagara, near Gorakhpur, Uttar Pradesh. In China, each of the four sacred mountains—O-mei, Wu-t'ai, P'u-t'o, and Chiu-hua—is dedicated to a different *bodhisattva*, whose temples and monasteries are located on the mountainside. Pilgrimages to distant shrines are often undertaken in fulfillment of a vow, as for example after recovery from an illness.

Passage rites. *Ordination.* Admission to the *saṅgha* involves two distinct acts, *pabbajjā, pravrajyā*, which consists of renunciation of secular life and acceptance of monasticism as a novice (*sāmaṇera, śrāmaṇera*) and *upasaṃpadā*, the official consecration as a monk (*bhikkhu, bhikṣu*). The evolution of the procedure is not entirely clear; in early times, the two acts probably occurred at the same time. Subsequently, the Vinaya established that *upasaṃpadā*, or full acceptance into the monastic community, should not occur before the age of 20, which, if the *pravrajyā*, ceremony took place as early as the age of 8, would mean after 12 years of training. Ordination could not occur without the permission of the aspirant's parents. The initial Pāli formula was *ehi bhikkhu*, "Come, O monk!"

The rite established in ancient Buddhism remains essentially the same in the Theravāda tradition. To be accepted, the postulant shaves his hair and beard and dons the yellow robes of the monk, leaving his right shoulder uncovered. He bows to the abbot or senior monk, to whom he makes his petition for admittance, and then seats himself with legs crossed and hands folded, pronouncing three times the formula of the Triple Refuge ("I take refuge in the Buddha, I take refuge in the *dharma*, I take refuge in the *saṅgha*.") He repeats after the officiating monk the Ten Precepts, and vows to observe them. Thereafter, in the presence of at least 10 monks (fewer in some cases) the postulant is questioned in detail by the abbot—as to the name of the master under whom he studied, whether he is free of faults and defects that would prevent his admission, has committed any infamous sins, is diseased, mutilated, or in debt. The abbot, when satisfied, thrice proposes acceptance of the petition; the chapter's silence signifies consent. The ceremony is basically the same for ordination as a nun.

The *Upasaṃpadā* rite

Bodhisattva vows. In Mahāyāna Buddhism, new rituals were added onto the ceremony of ordination prescribed by the Pāli Vinaya. The declaration of the Triple Refuge is as central an assertion as ever, but special emphasis is placed on the candidate's intention to achieve Enlightenment and his undertaking of the vow (*praṇidhāna*) to become a *bodhisattva*. Five monks are required for the ordination: the head monk, one who guards the ceremony (*karmācārya*), a master of secrets (the esoteric teachings, such as *mantras*), and two assisting officiants.

Abhiṣeka. The esoteric content of Vajrayāna tradition requires a more complex ceremony of consecration. In addition to the other ordination rites, preparatory study, and training in Yoga, the Tantric neophyte receive *abhiṣeka* (literally, "sprinkling," of water). This initiation takes several forms, each of which has its own corresponding "wisdom" (*vidyā*), rituals, esoteric formulas, and one of the five Buddhas of the supreme pentad. The initiate meditates on the *vajra* ("thunderbolt") as a symbol of Vajrasattva Buddha (the Admantine Being), on the bell as a symbol of the void, and on the *mudrā* (ritual gesture) as "seal." The intent of the initiation ceremony is to produce an experience that anticipates the moment of death. The candidate emerges reborn as a new being, a state marked by his receipt of a new name.

Tonsure ceremony. In some Theravāda countries, such as Burma and Thailand, the first part of the ordination into the monastic community, the *pabbajjā*, is an experience normally undergone by every male child and constitutes, in effect, the principal rite of passage into adulthood. The ceremony generally takes place at puberty, from about the age of eight onward. In commemoration of Sākyamuni's renunciation of his princely heritage, the child is first dressed in rich garments. Then, after a ritual bath, he puts on monastic garb and his head is shaved. After the ceremony he spends some time in a monastery receiving religious instruction and leading the life of a novice; then he returns to his parents' home and his regular education.

Funeral rites. The origin of the Buddhist funeral observances can be traced back to Indian customs. The cremation of the body of the Buddha and the subsequent distribution of his ashes are told in the *Mahāparinibbāna Sutta* ("Sūtra on the Great Final Deliverance"). The early Chinese travellers, such as Fa-hsien, described cremations of venerable monks. After cremation, the ashes and bones of the monk were collected and a *stūpa* built over them. That this custom was widely observed is evident from the large number of *stūpa*s found near monasteries.

With less pomp, cremation is also used for ordinary monks and laymen, though not universally. In Sri Lanka, for example, burial is the more usual method. In Tibet also, because of the scarcity of wood, cremation is rare. The bodies of great lamas, such as the Dalai and Panchen Lamas, are placed in rich *stūpa*s in attitudes of meditation, while lay corpses are exposed in remote places to be devoured by vultures and wild animals.

Buddhists generally agree that the thoughts held by a person at the moment of death are of essential significance. For this reason, sacred texts are read to the dying man to prepare his mind for the moment of death or to the newly dead, since the conscious principle is thought to remain in the body for about three days following death. In Tibetan, Mongolian, and Chinese lamaseries, a lama recites the famous *Bardo Thödrol* (commonly referred to in English as *The Tibetan Book of the Dead*).

Beliefs about the state and journey of the dead

The dead are believed to experience the supreme void as pure, colourless light. If the dead cannot retain that realization and thus secure release from rebirth, the second most desirable state is rebirth in the paradise of Amitābha. Accordingly, officiating monks invoke the mercy of Amitābha Buddha and of his assistant, the compassionate *bodhisattva*, Avalokiteśvara. Another book frequently read during funeral ceremonies is the *Bhaiṣajya-guru-vaiḍūrya-prabhāsa*, which expounds the 12 vows made by the Buddha in his previous lives to come to the aid of suffering creatures. Those who honour the vows for a year and three months and follow the precepts of the book are thought to be reborn in the paradise of Amitābha. At the moment of death eight *bodhisattvas* will come to show the dead the way, or Amitābha himself may descend from his Pure Land and come to meet the dead who have invoked him sincerely. The event is frequently depicted in Chinese, Japanese, and Tibetan iconography.

Protective rites. Buddhism does not exclude, even in the Theravāda, exorcistic and magical rites. In South Asian countries, notably Sri Lanka, a monk is frequently called in during crises such as a serious illness or death to recite the *Parittas*. These consist of various verses, any one of which is considered to be efficacious in providing protection against a variety of dangers, by instilling in the minds of the listeners a suitably calm state. At least one of the spells is alleged to have been given by the Buddha himself—the *Khanda Paritta*, providing protection against snakebite.

SYMBOLISM AND ICONOGRAPHY

The Buddha image. *Aniconic symbols.* In early Buddhist art (prior to the 1st century AD), the Buddha was never represented in human form. On the relief sculptures decorating *stūpa* railings and gateways at Bhārhut and Sāñchī (2nd–1st century BC) his presence was indicated by aniconic (imageless) symbols such as footprints, a throne, the Bo tree under which he achieved Enlightenment, and the *stūpa*, which symbolized his final deliverance, or death. Some symbols, first used to represent the Buddha in a particular event, later continued to symbolize an aspect of his doctrine, *e.g.*, the *dharma-cakra* ("wheel of law"), used to indicate the Buddha's presence in early reliefs depicting his first sermon at Sārnāth (Uttar Pradesh; near Vārānasi), is also used to symbolize his law. Numerous literary references and representations in art attest to the worship of these symbols: the *stūpa-pūjā* was essentially worship (*pūjā*) of the Buddha, inasmuch as the *stūpa* represented the Buddha.

Origin of the human image. The growing popular expressions of devotionalism, encouraged by the *bhakti* (devotional) movements current within Hinduism in the centuries immediately preceding the beginning of the Christian Era, presumably led to a demand for more approachable representations of the Buddha. The earliest images of the Buddha in human form date from the 1st century AD and come from the Gandhāra region (broadly speaking, northwest Pakistan and eastern Afghanistan) and Mathurā (in present-day Uttar Pradesh, India), both areas then under the rule of the Kuṣāṇas, an Indo-Scythian dynasty. Though the question of the origin of the Buddha image has aroused considerable controversy in the past, the evidence now available suggests independent development in the two regions. The Gandhāran sculptors drew upon Greco-Roman models and portrayed the Buddha with a youthful Apollo-like face, sometimes dressed in robes similar to the Roman toga, whereas the Mathurā images were based on prototypes of Indian *yakṣa* (nature deity) images and exhibited a similar sense of inner power, with wide shoulders and legs firmly planted.

The Gandhāra (Greco-Roman) and Mathurā (Indian *yakṣa*) components

The first artists were guided also by the Indian conception of the *mahāpuruṣa*, or "great soul" (one destined to become either a universal teacher or—as in the case of the Buddha—a spiritual teacher). The *lakṣaṇas*, or "signs" that a *mahāpuruṣa* bore on his body, were enumerated in Indian texts and included features that were adapted by the developing Buddhist iconography. Among these, the *uṣṇīṣa* (protuberance on the top of the cranium), the *ūrṇā* (mole in the middle of the forehead), and symbolic signs on the hands and the feet are the most distinctive.

The Buddha images that came into being at Gandhāra and Mathurā influenced each other, and there gradually developed in the Gupta period (4th–7th century AD) workshop of Mathurā and Sārnāth the classic representation of the Buddha that was to spread throughout the Buddhist world. This shows the Buddha with a serene, inward-looking expression, slightly smiling lips, hair arranged in a series of spiral curls, dressed in a monastic robe most often covering both shoulders, backed by a nimbus and, if seated, generally in a cross-legged posture and on a lotus throne.

Standard forms. The Buddha is depicted standing, sitting, or, less commonly, stretched out on his right side in the position of *parinirvāṇa* (final deliverance; *i.e.*, death). His distinctive hand positions (*mudrās*) serve to call to mind particular episodes in the life of the Buddha or attitudes expressed by him, the most popular being the preaching of the law (*dharmacakra-mudrā*), the calling of the Earth to witness (*bhūmisparśa-mudrā*), reassurance (*abhaya-mudrā*), meditating (*dhyāna-mudrā*), and gift bestowing (*varada-mudrā*).

In addition to this stylized iconographic image, the Buddha is also represented in narrative scenes. Of these, the events associated with his conception and birth, his Enlightenment, his preaching, and his death are particularly popular. The reliefs of the Gandhāra school drew in great detail upon the Buddha life and legend, as did the reliefs of Amarāvati in southeast India.

Mahāyāna and Vajrayāna elaboration. The various Buddhas of the past were represented in early Indian art by means of their aniconic symbols, particularly the trees associated with each of them. When the figural representation of Śākyamuni Buddha came into being, these other Buddhas also began to be represented. At first there was little to distinguish the image of one Buddha from that of another, but in the course of time each came to be known by specific sets of gestures and symbols. Very similar was the development of the various *bodhisattva* images. The compassionate Avalokiteśvara and the *bodhisattva* of wisdom, Mañjuśrī, were particularly popular; and to them were added a whole pantheon, each distinguished by his own specific attributes, just as Mañjuśrī, who in one of his forms is provided with a book, a sword, and a lion mount.

Bodhisattva images

The movement toward a progressively complex and conventional iconography culminated in medieval Indian art and in the arts of Tibet and Nepal. A fivefold ordering of celestial, or self-born, Buddhas was established and linked to other sets of five. When each of the celestial Buddhas is associated with two *bodhisattvas*, a triad is formed (*e.g.*, the Buddha Amitābha, often shown in the company of the *bodhisattvas* Avalokiteśvara and Mahāsthāmaprāpta). Vajrayāna Buddhism further elaborated upon the idea of associated "families" of Buddhas by including a feminine consort and a pacific and horrific aspect of the various Buddhist divinities.

What appears at first glance to be the product of a feverish and bizarre imagination may be understood rather as symbolic representation of doctrine. An image such as the fierce Vajrabhairava, the terrifying aspect of the *bodhisattva* Mañjuśrī—nine-headed, heavily armed, locked in sexual embrace with his consort while trampling on various creatures underfoot—was not generally intended for the view of the uninitiated. Written commentaries relate its nine faces to nine parts of the scripture, its 34 arms to multiple facets of Enlightenment, its sexual embrace to the union of *upāya* (means), symbolized as male, with *prajñā* (wisdom), symbolized as female. It is an esoteric vocabulary given visual expression.

Architectural forms. Buddhism has three main types of architectural buildings and monuments: the *stūpa*, basically a commemorative relic mound; the *caitya*, a temple enshrining a *stūpa* or an image of the Buddha; and the *vihāra*, or monastery, a residence for monks and, strictly speaking, a secular building. Often, however, *stūpa*s or images are incorporated in the monastery or the monastery complex, thus giving it a sacred character. In Buddhism, large monastic establishments have developed that possess *stūpa*s, *caitya*s, a number of monastic residences, and a variety of other buildings to cater to the needs of a particular monastic community. Sometimes, as at Nālandā (near modern Patna, Bihār state, India), they became great centres of learning.

The stūpa. The *stūpa* is the single most important monument in Buddhism, built to house relics of the Buddha or of his disciples, or to commemorate an event or place in Buddhist legend or history. Sometimes, as at Gilgit (in Jammu) and in Tibet, texts were enshrined in *stūpa*s, so that two "bodies" come together: the *stūpa* as the symbol of the spiritual body of the Buddha and the books as his verbal body.

Structure of the *stūpa*

The *stūpa* consists of a hemispheric cupola resting on a base, encircled by a balustrade that may be intersected by four gateways (*toraṇa*s). On the cupola rests a square railing or boxlike structure (*harmikā*) from which rises a shaft of metal or wood, supporting umbrellas. It may be seen in its most characteristic form at Sānchī, Madhya Pradesh, India (1st century BC–3rd century AD); and with variations is found throughout the Buddhist world.

In Sri Lanka, where it is referred to as *dāgaba* (heart of *garbha* [womb]), the form closely follows the early Indian model. In Burma, the cupola, usually gilded, rests on a steep, high base mounted by stairs. In Thailand, the cupola is often bell-shaped. In Tibet, an important type is the *stūpa* of "many doors" (*sgo-mang*), so called because it has many chapels with frescoes depicting the deities of the various Tantric cycles. The pagodas of China and Japan—derived in part from the storied watch tower and polygonal buildings already known in China and also possibly inspired by Kaniṣka's tall *stūpa* at Peshāwar, with its wooden scaffolding—are essentially turreted *stūpa*s.

The most magnificent example of a later *stūpa* is the monument (*c.* 800 AD) at Borobuḍur, in central Java; the walls of the galleries built for circumambulation are covered with stately bas-reliefs illustrating events from Buddhist scriptures. The structure is a monumental *stūpa* and a huge architectural *maṇḍala* (ritual diagram), containing meditating images of the five celestial Buddhas.

The caitya. A *caitya* originally meant "that worth being looked at"; *i.e.*, "worshipful," and referred to sacred objects such as the Bo tree as well as to *stūpa*s. In time the word came to be applied to sacred buildings or temples generally consisting of a hall containing a sacred object to be worshipped, such as a small *stūpa* or a Buddha image. Sometimes the *caitya* was carved into a cave, as at Ajantā in western India, which has ensured its preservation and has provided a clear idea of the ancient forms.

The vihāra. A monastery (*vihāra, ārāma*) was at first characteristically rectangular or square in plan, with the cells arranged around a large central courtyard. Chapels for images were also provided, and a *stūpa* sometimes placed in the centre of the court, which also served as a place for instruction. In some cases, special units called *dhamma-maṇḍapa* or *dhamma-sālā* ("*dharma*-porch") were built for assemblies prescribed by the disciplinary rules. The basic scheme, which is described in Pāli sources and confirmed by archaeological and documentary findings, was increasingly elaborated and underwent considerable variation in accordance with special needs such as climate or local architectural tradition. Some monasteries were excavated in rock, as at Ajantā and at Tun-huang, in northwestern China. In Tibet, the earliest religious buildings consisted of a rectangular hall, with the statue of the divinity placed at one end on a high pedestal and a *pradakṣiṇā* (circumambulatory) path around it.

As the communities grew to as many as 6,000–7,000 monks, veritable monastic cities developed, with assembly halls, offices for monastery functionaries, and temples, each with its own "secret" chapel for its fierce tutelary deities (*mgon khang*). In China, the monastic compound was walled and oriented to the south, with a great gateway covered by one or more roofs. This gave access to a courtyard in which stood a pagoda (comparable in function to the Indian *stūpa*) with several roofs, tapering to a pinnacle at the top. Beyond was the hall for worship and, further on, outside the "sacred area," the refectory and dormitory. This same architectural style was introduced to Korea and to Japan; the 7th-century Hōryū-ji near Nara in Japan gives a clear idea not only of the Japanese style but also of Chinese architectural models no longer standing.

The Chinese monastic compound

Ritual use of images and other supports of worship. *Image worship.* The Theravāda Pāli canon enjoins three objects of reverence for the Buddhist: relics of the Buddha's person, generally enshrined in the *stūpa;* relics of belongings, such as his alms bowl; and images of his likeness. Worship (*pūjā*) consists of presenting offerings of flowers, incense and light, of bowing down, and (in the case of *stūpa*s) of circumambulation. Worship does not necessarily imply deification of the Buddha but reverence for his teachings and for his example.

In Mahāyāna and Vajrayāna Buddhism, images, enshrined in household altars as well as in temples and monasteries, increased in importance. In the meditational schools concentration on an image of a Buddha or of a *bodhisattva* became a way of realizing spiritual truths, practiced in combination with other meditational supports, such as the *dhāraṇī, mantra, mudrā, sādhana, dhyāna*, and *maṇḍala*.

Dhāraṇī and mantra. A *dhāraṇī* is a short statement of a doctrine that sums up the essential significance of the longer text and serves as an aid to its retention. By means of a *dhāraṇī* an adept symbolically evokes the truth of a revealed text without reciting the whole of it. Though the *dhāraṇī* is, for those capable of spiritual disciplines, primarily an aid to meditation, the *dhāraṇī* serves the common man much as a magical formula, to be worn in a locket as a talisman or inserted in a sacred image to "confer life on it" (in the ceremony of consecration known as *prāṇapratiṣṭhā*). The *dhāraṇī* may sound to the uninitiated like a series of largely unintelligible words—its esoteric meaning is often transmitted directly by a teacher to his pupil.

Aids to meditation and magical formulas or sounds

The *mantra* is an even further reduction of the *dhāraṇī*, sometimes to a single syllable, the *bīja-* ("seed-") *mantra*, which is the representation in sound, just as the image is the visual representation, of the deity invoked. For example, the whole of the *Prajñāpāramitā* literature is ultimately concentrated in the *bīja-mantra* consisting of one syllable, *pram*. Repetition of this syllable, when uttered with the right insight, ritual, and concentration, is considered equivalent to recitation of an entire 8,000-stanza text.

The recitation of *mantra*s plays an important part in the devotional worship of the Pure Land and Nichiren Buddhist sects. In esoteric Buddhism (Tantra and related forms) the *mantra* also implies belief in the mystical efficacy of sound. If pronounced incorrectly or inattentively, the divinity may not be invoked, may not appear before the worshipper, or may even do him harm.

Mudrā. In Vajrayāna Buddhism, the liturgical act, to be efficacious, must include the *mantra*, properly intoned according to the respiratory methods of Yoga, accompanied by the proper symbolic ritual gesture, or *mudrā*. The various meanings of the word *mudrā* include the sense of a "sign" or "seal." The principal *mudrā*s are related to the gestures and attitudes expressed by the Buddhas in the iconographic tradition but have multiplied along with the growth of the Mahāyāna pantheon. Each divinity is invoked by a particular *mudrā* associated with that divinity.

Sādhana. A *sādhana* is a spiritual exercise, a means of attaining an inner mystical state by first evoking a divinity, then realizing an identity with the divinity, thus experiencing the meditator's own divine nature. The *sādhana* texts give specific instructions on how to visualize a particular divinity, such as its colour, pose, ornaments, attributes, and attendants and thus also serve as manuals on iconography for the makers of images. The meditator, after undergoing preparatory rites of purification, commences concentrating until he has an inner vision of the divinity invoked, either in his own heart (the "heart" is a synonym of the void) or appearing before him, according to the specific technique employed. The *sādhanas* are methods of self-suggestion by means of which the meditator—corresponding to the void—emanates from himself the divinities and then reabsorbs them, thus achieving the awareness that all is void. The *sādhanas* differ from the *dhyānas* of meditation, which require the progressive discontinuance of thought and emotion.

Realization of divinity

Maṇḍala. A *maṇḍala* is a psychocosmogram in which the essence of a Tantric text is represented by syllables or visual symbols. Understanding of a *maṇḍala* requires both initiation and long periods of contemplation, but the spiritually adept gain from the diagram the same significance as from the sacred text. The various types of *maṇḍalas* are all basically ways of representing the projection of the one into the many (the *garbhadhātu*, or "womb-world" *maṇḍala*) or conversely, the many into the one (the *vajradhātu*, or "diamond-world" *maṇḍala*), the two characteristic forms of *maṇḍalas* used in the Shingon sect of Japan. In Tibetan initiation ceremonies *maṇḍalas* are drawn on the floor of the consecration hall with the aid of cords that have been dipped in coloured powders. *Maṇḍalas* are also painted on cloth in Nepal, Tibet, and in Japan as aids of contemplation. In certain instances the body itself may be conceived as a *maṇḍala*, with the heart as its centre, man (the microcosm) thus symbolically identified with the universe (the macrocosm).

Regional variations. As Buddhism spread—in the south by sea to Sri Lanka, Indonesia, and Indochina and in the north by the various land trade routes to Central Asia, Tibet, China, Korea, and Japan—the image of the Buddha and the iconography of other sacred figures remained substantially the same, though the artistic traditions of each country and age produced some modifications, as did the growth of new cults.

Tibet. Many specifically Tibetan aspects of Buddhist symbolism have already been noted. Also of interest is the manner in which local gods and goddesses have been assimilated to Buddhism, for nowhere is this more apparent than in Tibet. There deities of pre-Buddhist (Bon) and of Indian origin were "conquered" by Buddhist priests and pressed into service as "guardians of the doctrine" (*dharmapāla*). They are represented in art as ferocious in appearance, brandishing weapons in multiple hands and dressed in ornaments of skulls and bones taken from vanquished enemies, in keeping with their role as protectors of the faith.

Assimilation of non-Buddhist images

Central Asia. Through Central Asia passed the great caravan routes connecting India with China and western Asia, frequented by merchants and by Buddhist pilgrims, particularly in the period 400 to 700 AD. During the early centuries of the Christian Era, Central Asia was a meeting ground of many diverse religious movements, including Manichaeism and Nestorian Christianity with its Iranian substratum. The Tantric forms of Buddhism never took hold there as they did in Nepal and Tibet, and Central Asian art is generally more serene than the art of those two regions. Along the trade route into China many impressive Buddhist monuments were built, as for example at Bāmiyān (near modern Kābul), where in the 4th–5th century colossal statues of the Buddha were carved out of the rocky cliff. Khotan (a stronghold of Mahāyāna Buddhism) on the southern route, Kucha (the main centre of Hīnayāna) and Turfan on the northern, and Tunhuang, in northwest China at the eastern terminus of both routes, are sites of important monasteries, containing rock-cut sanctuaries embellished with wall painting and sculpture.

East Asia. In China, popular devotion to the Buddha Amitābha (Chinese O-mi-t'o; Japanese Amida) and the hope of rebirth after death in his Sukhāvatī (the Happy Land) gave occasion to many representations of the Buddha and of his Pure Land. The depictions of Amitābha's Pure Land, in wall paintings and in scrolls, are based on passages in the *Sukhāvatīvyūha-sūtra* and *Amitāyurdhyāna-sūtra* that describe the Buddha in the midst of celestial splendour, sitting on a lotus throne, flanked by the *bodhisattvas* who assist him, and surrounded by images of other Buddhas and *bodhisattvas*, palaces, lotus ponds, jewelled trees, and flowers. The Chinese representations of Sukhāvatī exhibit a typically Chinese sense of hierarchy and ordered arrangement. The Tun-huang caves are rich in paintings on this theme, which was popular in Japan also, a notable example being the frescoes in the Hōryū-ji near Nara (unfortunately destroyed by fire in 1949). In Japan, the vision of Amitābha descending from his paradise accompanied by his *bodhisattvas* Avalokiteśvara and Mahāsthāmaprāpta to welcome the newly dead to Sukhāvatī is expressed in a type of painting known as Amida *raigō* ("Amida coming to welcome").

Amitābha's companion, the *bodhisattva* Avalokiteśvara, became immensely popular in China and Japan as an independent saviour figure. In a process that is not clearly understood by scholars, Kuan-yin, as the *bodhisattva* is known in China (Kannon in Japan), apparently merged with local myths of goddesses and, in the popular mind at least, from about the 11th or 12th century was increasingly conceived as a female figure. A certain ambiguity regarding the sexual representation of the *bodhisattva* is in keeping with the view that a *bodhisattva* has reached a state of perfection that has transcended sexual differentiation, along with all other oppositions of the phenomenal world. Another explanation given in Buddhist scriptures is that the *bodhisattva* has the power to assume whatever identity—male, female or animal—is necessary to relieve suffering.

The figure of Kuan-yin in Sino-Japanese art

The Ch'an (Japanese Zen) sect, with its emphasis on direct, intuitive experience, brought a radically different approach to the representation of the Buddha and other sacred figures. A favourite theme was that of Śākyamuni returning from solitude after having given up the ascetic life as a means of achieving Enlightenment. Śākyamuni is shown in a realistic pose far removed from the immobile, inward-looking, meditating icons. In China in the mid-Sung period, Ch'an art developed into the "untrammeled" school of painting, the final result being a free, spontaneous style with which Ch'an found much affinity. The emphasis in Ch'an Buddhism on the direct transmission from master to pupil led to a demand for realistic portraits of the teachers, which were presented to the pupils at the end of their instruction. Such paintings were carried back from China by Japanese monks; and the style was continued in Japan, with the paintings of the patriarchs honoured in the Zen monasteries. This interest in the expression of inner spirituality through an individualized human person is magnificently realized in the carved portrait of Asaṅga (Japanese Mujaku) by the sculptor Unkei in Kōfuku-ji, in Nara.

VI. Buddhism and other Asian religions

BUDDHISM, HINDUISM, AND JAINISM

Buddhism is one branch of the multitudinous variety of Indian religion and speculation. It began in the spiritual excitement (at the time of the Buddha) in a region agitated with religious and speculative ardour and ended by dissolving into Hinduism. The growth of Buddhism was pervaded by a social and human sensibility less developed in other Indian religious and philosophical systems. Its missionary tendencies and direct communication with the people broke the bonds of Brahmanic orthodoxy. It did not sanction caste privileges or social monopolies, and it passed beyond the borders of India. Just as it accepted with unusual tolerance the religious, cultural, and magical traditions of many countries as it spread, it was unable to avoid compromise in India with local cults or to remain apart from the evolution of Indian speculation. There were exchanges of thought between Buddhist and Hindu schools. The Mādhyamika and Yogācāra schools had a significant influence on Hindu thought. Little by little, however, Buddhism succumbed because it ended up saying the same things as Śivaism and Vedānta, albeit in different terms. It was difficult for many to see how the void was anything but a somewhat different version of the *Paramaśiva*, an undefinable reality that transcended all in its absolute indescribable essence.

The Hinduization of Buddhism

Buddha, from a human teacher, became a supramundane being and multiplied himself in infinite refractions, bringing a symbiosis in both inconographic representation and in the details of symbolism between Śiva and Avalokiteśvara. Tantrism, in both its Hindu and Buddhist forms, shelters the most primitive and ancient gods of Indian religious experience. Mystical experiences, meditational procedures, a common heritage of chants, Yoga (which in the course of time assumed the complex forms of Haṭha Yoga)—these are the basics of various methods of mental purification and exaltation that arouse the secret possibilities latent within. They transmute the indissoluble unity of the psychophysical complex into a new mode of being, so that the body, once considered by mystics of the Hīnayāna and Mahāyāna schools in their meditation on a cadaver to be an impure thing or a burden and obstacle, became in Śaivist and Buddhist schools the means of salvation.

Many of the 84 *siddha*s, "those who have reached what they desired, those who have become perfect," in Tibetan lists also appear in Hindu lists among the greatest masters of esoterism. Like the branches of the Bo tree (*aśvattha*), Buddhism returned to its roots. The masses sought an easier, quicker way to salvation, less speculative and more devotional or magical. Instead of solitary men like the *arahant* or the *bodhisattva*, who required incalculable stretches of time to reach Nirvāṇa, they preferred the immediate, solacing presence of a being, adored and invoked, who would lighten the heavy burden of *karman*—Amitābha, Lokanātha, Avalokiteśvara, Tārā. Man no longer relied on his own powers; there were gods who, if propitiated, would save him.

Mahāyāna separated into a cold dialectic or into devotional or esoteric schools that expressed the same aspirations as those of Hinduism. It took refuge in Nepal and Indonesia and mingled with Tantric cults in which *Śakti* had a notable part, as in the Sahajiyā or among the followers of *Dharma-maṅgal* in Bengal, still found today. When Islām conquered India, Buddhism withdrew into itself and became even more influenced by the current speculative, magical, and Tantric aspirations. Since the liberation of the India-Pakistan subcontinent, many "untouchables" have renounced the old religion that excluded them from civil society and have favoured Theravāda Buddhism because it emphasizes the ethical values that have overcome obsolete cults in post-Gandhian India.

Jainism kept a greater distance from Buddhism, despite its very ancient speculative heritage and common "heretical" past. More archaic, it lacked the mystical anxiety of Mahāyāna Buddhism. According to the Jainas *karman* is a ponderable and measurable element. There is for them no distinction between voluntary and involuntary sin, and above all they believe in the presence in matter of a soul (*jīva*).

BUDDHISM AND ISLAM

Islām pushed aside both Hinduism and Buddhism because they lacked a revealed book. While resisting in Zābulistān the first Arab conquest of Afghanistan, in one of the later Tantras, the *Kālacakra* (Wheel of Time), Buddhism advanced, as an attempt at monotheism, the doctrine of Ādi-Buddha, the Buddha who is above all else. The *Kālacakra* speaks of Mecca and introduces Islāmic formulas into *mantras*. After India was conquered by the Muslims, who extended themselves as far as Bengal, one of the oldest Bengali books, the *Gorakhavijaya*, which deals with the intricacies of Yoga and narrates the life of a celebrated *siddha*, Gorakṣa, was written by 'Abd-ul-Karīm, a Muslim. Muslims were the authors of many *padyāvalī*s, poems singing the love of Kṛṣṇa and Rādhā. Through the villages there circulated anonymous and apocryphal Tantras, some even attributed to Nāgārjuna, and among the *mantra*s and incantations are found Islāmic formulas. Thus for a long time the two religions coexisted in some parts of India. All the same, Buddhism suffered destructions caused by Islām, which knew only the Mahāyāna school with its manifold gods and complicated rituals—things all remote from the Islāmic concept of God. Yet there are instances of encounters between Buddhist soteriology and Islām; *e.g.*, in certain Ismāʿīlī texts such as the *Umm al-kitāb*. In Sri Lanka, Theravāda Buddhism, Islām, Hinduism, and Christianity coexist. This is due in part to the innate tolerance of a Buddhism that sees Buddha, Allah, and Jesus as different manifestations of the same entity.

BUDDHISM AND CHINESE RELIGION

Obstructions to the spread of Buddhism in China

Buddhist proselytism in China was not easy. It met with a millenary culture, a tradition of rationalism, as in Confucianism, a solid social structure, the cult of the family and, at the summit, the authority of the state. And there was Taoism, in its literary and speculative form reserved for the few and in its magical form for the many. Thus, the introduction of Buddhism came about slowly. It was often obstructed by a distinctly different mode of posing thought and expression. At first there were ambiguities and misunderstandings. Taoist and Confucian words were used that had nothing to do with the Buddhist concepts they were to express. Moreover, monastic organization represented a dangerous innovation that withdrew men from the service of the state and had a negative effect on the national wealth. Hesitancy was also caused by the fact that the new religion was foreign, the religion of "barbarians," even though in some circles Lao-tzu and the Buddha were considered identical. The doctrine of *karman* was not comprehensible because the Chinese maintained that after a certain time the soul died. On the other hand, the aspiration toward serenity and peace and the rejection of violence were easily understood by the Taoist masters. The populace, moreover, gave in to the attraction of a gospel that opened new hopes to all in the *bodhisattva* ideal and a way to an easy salvation, as promulgated by the devotional schools. Buddhism gained strength during the 2nd century AD crisis in Confucianism. Buddhism at first remained on the outside, isolated in small communities; but by the 4th century it had brought about a new ferment of ideas in China.

Interplay between Buddhism and Taoism

Translations of Mahāyāna works in the 2nd century had used Taoist expressions for key Buddhist terms, and certain Buddhist schools were formed whose discussions must be understood on the basis of the Taoist lexicon, which carried into the Buddhist camp the problem of the relation between "being" (*yu*) and "nonbeing" (*wu*). Seng-chao (AD 384–414) wrote the *Book of Chao*, an attempt to conciliate between Buddhism and Neo-Taoism. Until the T'ang dynasty, with its greatest flowering of Buddhism in China, Neo-Taoism had remained the basis of speculation; and many masters who converted to Buddhism did not forget the teachings of the Taoist sage Chuang-tzu.

Lu Ch'eng (AD 425–494) showed clearly the fundamental difference between the Indian mentality, inclined toward gradual Enlightenment, and the Chinese disposition to know the truth by intuition, without the meditation of a progressive psychic catharsis. This explains why certain texts celebrated in India and Tibet, such as those on logic, had little diffusion in China. Peculiar Indian philosophic trends were elaborated in China by Paramārtha and of Hsüang-tsang, mainly concerning the *Vijñapti-mātratā-siddhi* of Vasubandhu, which Hsüang-tsang had translated and glossed. During the period in which Buddhism was flourishing, before the great setback of the persecution of 845, there was a fruitful dialogue between Buddhist and traditional Chinese thought, as evident in the Neo-Confucianism of Chu Hsi (1130–1200). At the same time, there were original Chinese contributions to Buddhism, as, for example, in the schools of Ch'an and Hua-yen.

During the Yüan dynasty, 'Phags-pa, the lama of the Sa-skya monastery, introduced the Tibetan form of Buddhism; but seeing that Tantric literature (*i.e.*, the *Hevaj-*

ra) was unsuited to Chinese propensities, he limited himself to sending the Mongol princes short epistles, succinct summaries of the essential Buddhist dogmas.

BUDDHISM AND TIBETAN RELIGION

Things were quite different in Tibet. When Buddhism arrived, it did not find a culture deserving of that name. Tibet's conquest of Central Asia and its contact with India, China, and Nepal, however, plus the influx of Buddhist missionaries, created an intellectual fervour that sprouted out of a cultural vacuum. Bon, the native religion of Tibet, was largely magical, a defense against invisible powers present everywhere and harmful if not placated. Every place, every mountain pass was presided over by a spirit: the *klu*, whose abode was water and springs; the *sa-bdag*, ("soil masters"), who abide in the ground; the *btsan*, without fixed abode; or the *lha*, which was usually a sacred mountain from which the ancestral god of the family that dominated the territory had descended to earth or fallen from heaven.

The native Tibetan religion: Bon

The innate tendency toward magic, of which Bon was the oldest expression; rites that did not exclude the sacrifice of animals and even humans in ancient times; black magic to cause hail to fall on an enemy's field or bring about his death; and the rites of redemption from demonic forces—all these favoured the spread of Tantric texts, especially those in which magic predominated. And yet, the Tibetans, without a cultural heritage, slaves of century-old superstition, suddenly awoke and also translated, comprehended, and explicated the most difficult works of Mahāyāna speculation, carrying on the tradition of the most famous monasteries of India. Tibet represents a genuine case of cultural transplantation that presupposes an uncommon gift for dialectic and speculation, yet the Tibetans added nothing to what they were taught. They were interpreters, explainers, and lucid commentators; but except for the monks, who wrote enormous works, the masses, protected by the sacredness of the *saṅgha*, still lived under the fruitful shadow of local deities that must be propitiated and of evil forces waiting always and everywhere in ambush. Thus converged abstract speculation, formal logic, abstruse dogmatics, magic, and the ineradicable remains of an ancient religion varying from place to place, though always with strong similarities.

BUDDHISM AND JAPANESE RELIGION

Japan also did not have any genuine speculation when Buddhism arrived. Shintō was dominant, with its complicated cosmology and theogony, in which the god Izanagi and the goddess Izanami were paramount. They created the island in the ocean, descended to it, married, and produced Amaterasu-Ō-mikami, the great goddess of the radiant sky and the sun. Each thing or being invested with some sacredness was called a *kami*, descending in a scale from Amaterasu to a stone or a worm. The *kami* were generally not represented by icons, only casually by symbols. Instead of a priestly class there were guilds of the "pure" that maintained contact with sacred objects. Others could communicate with the gods and would deliver their oracles to the chieftains.

The indigenous Japanese religion: Shintō

When Buddhism entered Japan it had to define its relationship to the indigenous religion. The common feature was the magical character that Buddhism attributed to its rites and the reading of sacred texts. Buddhism arrived sporadically in the 4th century through Korean refugees and craftsmen. When the ruler of the Korean kingdom of Paekche sent an image of the Buddha and Buddhist books and monks, along with Confucian texts, in the 6th century, this aroused the opposition of certain powerful families. One ancient family (Soga), however, favoured the new religion.

Its entry became definite in the conversion of Prince Shōtoku Taishi (573–621), who became its chief spokesman and propagator. Three different elements met: the native religion of Shintō, Confucianism, and a Buddhism at first just vaguely comprehended. In the beginning Buddhism was expounded to protect the state and the emperor against calamities and diseases. In the course of time funeral customs changed, the law of *karman* and the possibility of rebirth came to be accepted, the philosophical schools were introduced, and so Buddhism gradually became the principle component of Japanese thought, inspiring art and shaping the spirit, as in Tibet.

Very technical schools such as the Hossō and the Sanron trained the Japanese mind in the subtleties of Mahāyāna literature. At the same time, Shintō found analogues with its magical use of the reading of sacred texts. The aim of protecting persons and things tended to be the same, and thus compromises came about that led to a symbiosis between Shintō and Buddhism.

To encourage its own acceptance, Buddhism accepted local divinities and made them objects of worship as incarnations of the Buddha or of *bodhisattva*s, Shintō chapels were often found in Buddhist temples; and many *kami* were adopted as protectors of the law. The emperor Shōmu (reigned 724–748) dreamed that the goddess Amaterasu appeared to him and declared that Japan was the land of the gods and all should be venerated, since their nature was the same as Vairocana Buddha's. The *kami* were nothing but the temporal manifestations of the Buddha and the *bodhisattva*s. In 767 an imperial decree proclaimed that the *kami* were guarding the Law of the Buddha, and Buddhist monks were authorized to officiate in Shintō temples along with Shintō priests. This was the beginning of Ryōbu Shintō ("Two Aspects Shintō"). All this led to a closer tie between the state and the various Buddhist sects, which later was broken because of the great power acquired by the monasteries.

The *kami* as protectors of the law and manifestations of Buddhas and *bodhisattvas*

The work of assimilation was advanced by Dengyō Daishi, founder of Japanese Tendai, and Kōbō Daishi, the Shingon founder. Before Dengyō founded the Tendai monastery on Mt. Hiei he recognized the Shintō gods as protectors of the temple. Kōbō Daishi strengthened the alliance of the two religions through the esoteric aspect of his school. Basing itself on the twofold division of being and appearance, Shingon advanced a classification of things in two groups, finally arriving at the identification of Amaterasu with Mahā-Vairocana, the cosmic Buddha, which was accepted among the adherents of Shintō.

Along with Confucianism, which was diffused more widely in later periods, Buddhism is obviously one of the leading elements of Japanese thought, so much so that Japan may consider it as its spiritual patrimony.

VII. Buddhism in contemporary Asia

BUDDHISM AND NATIONALIST MOVEMENTS

Buddhism as a political force. Buddhism assumed a significant role in the movements to establish or reassert national independence in modern Asia. In these movements, Buddhism represented the basis of the national culture, notwithstanding the coexistence of certain minority sects, In Burma, where the king had been the protector of the Buddhist *saṅgha*, Buddhism took an active political role in forging the new nationalism, justifying its presence by the claim that it was the custodian of the spiritual and cultural values of the people. For decades it had proclaimed itself as being egalitarian and democratic. In 1913 Anāgārika Dharmapāla, a Buddhist leader from Ceylon (now Sri Lanka), declared that the teaching of the Buddha is primarily social and liberates man from materialistic instincts. Laksmi Narasu, an Indian Buddhist leader, maintained that the Buddha was anti-capitalist. U Nu, an eminent Burmese Buddhist statesman, said that Socialism is a corollary of the social and ethical principles of the Buddha and approved the law nationalizing landholdings. While others were of the opinion that Karl Marx had been influenced by the Buddha, U Ba Swe, another Burmese Buddhist leader, held that Marxism was the relative truth and Buddhism the absolute truth. If capitalism exists it is because man has forgotten the teachings of the Buddha.

Buddhism viewed as an egalitarian, democratic, and Socialist force

Similarly, in Ceylon, the Mahāsaṅghasabhā movement, aiming at a united front of orthodox Buddhists, was a reaction to Western interests and the ruling class, for the most part Catholics or Protestants. Buddhism underwent Socialist and also Marxist influences, and it was even said that Marxism is a page extracted from the book of Buddhism but misinterpreted.

In such (largely Theravāda) places it is argued that Buddhism is a practice and an ethical philosophy more than a religion because it does not worship a god. Śākyamuni is a teacher, even if the masses lacking comprehension honour him as a god. Buddhism regards all men as equal because they are all subject to the same destiny of misery. It seeks to explain what causes misery and the means of liberation from it. In placing among the "Perfections" gifts, charity, and compassion, to be understood as active abnegation and a sense of sympathy for creatures, the Buddha promoted a solidarity that renders one happy by the happiness of others. Thus he had anticipated the modern methods of assistance, aid, and the elimination of social and economic inequalities in a world based on economic relations. Buddhism is not, therefore, a religion derived from a feudal culture (as some Chinese Communist writers have asserted on certain occasions) but stems from the people and works for the people. Arguments such as these, put forth most often in Burma and Ceylon, led Buddhist statesmen such as U Nu and S.W.R.D. Bandaranaike (see below *Ceylon*) to seek accords between Buddhism and Marxism, proclaiming Buddhism as the inalienable spiritual heritage of the country.

Burma. The great diffusion of Theravāda in Burma began at the time of Anawrahta (reigned 1044–1077); it enjoyed the protection of successive kings and its fortunes increased when Burma obtained its independence in 1948. Under Prime Minister U Nu the *saṅgha* was extremely powerful and Buddhism became the state religion (1961). In the following year, when General Ne Win took over the supreme control of the state, Buddhism lost much of its political influence. Ne Win followed a program of moderate socialism aimed at modernizing the country as much as possible. The Buddhists have adapted themselves to the new situation and proclaim the necessity of acting and working for social welfare, not merely in a Burmese or Buddhist society, but for mankind as a whole.

Ceylon. In Ceylon (after 1972, Sri Lanka) the People's United Front, which was supported by those who had received European educations or were non-Buddhists for the most part, was accused of not having taken proper account of Buddhism, a historical reality. When Bandaranaike became prime minister, he included the extreme left party of Gunawardena in the government. He proclaimed Buddhism to be the religion of Ceylon, set up universities on European models, established a ministry for cultural affairs, and proposed the nationalization of schools, hoping to harmonize the needs of modern and traditional instruction. Yet the *saṅgha* perceived in these measures a menace to its power; and groups linked both to financial and monastic interests formed a conspiracy that entrusted a monk with the job of assassinating Bandaranaike, who earlier had actually been considered a *bodhisattva*. He was succeeded by his widow, Sirimavo Bandaranaike, the nationalization of schools was accomplished, and a law was proposed whereby monasteries would not be exempt from taxation, while monks were advised not to participate in political life. Mme Bandaranaike's government fell; but after an interregnum of the United National Party, she was re-elected with a leftist program in 1970. A commission was set up to draft a new constitution and proclaim Ceylon an independent republic; and relations were established with China, North Vietnam, and North Korea.

Conflict between state and *saṅgha* in Ceylon

Thailand. Theravāda Buddhism is the state religion of Thailand. Since the reign of King Chulalongkorn (1873–1910) it has been considered a peaceful means for bringing unity to the country, though in the north tribal groups (Karen, Meo, Lua, Yao, and others) have remained faithful to their ancestral beliefs. The centralized church directs and coordinates the activity of missionaries whose task is to travel about during the dry season, not only to preach the law but also to cooperate in the development of the country and to teach in village schools. The work of the Thammacarik, or Dhammacarika ("pilgrims of the *dhamma*"), is to spread Buddhism among the tribal groups; but they seem to have had little success because of the independent spirit of those tribes.

Interior of the Temple of the Dawn, Thon Buri, Thailand, during Wesak, the festival commemorating the birth, enlightenment, and death of the Buddha.
Ewing Galloway

Presently two sects are found in Thailand: Mahānikāya ("the larger sect") and Dhammayuttika-Nikāya ("sect of the followers of the *dhamma*"). A patriarch is selected by the heads of the two sects; but he is officially named by the king, on the advice of the minister for religious affairs. He is assisted by a cabinet of 10 persons responsible for four bureaus, for the administration of religious property, education, propaganda, and public works, respectively. Thus, the *saṅgha* is state-directed and carries out a social function.

Vietnam, Cambodia, and Laos. Both Mahāyāna and Theravāda are to be found in Vietnam; Mahāyāna is represented by the Thien (Chinese Ch'an) and by the Tin-do sects (followers of Amitābha). While the division between the two sects was formerly strict, in recent years the two have tended to converge under the impact of lay movements that have promoted a kind of Buddhist modernism. This movement started with the Association for the Study of Buddhism founded in 1932 in Saigon and in 1934 in Hue and Hanoi. The new generation was encouraged to take up social work and ultimately to intervene in politics, under the inspiration of the General Buddhist Association for Vietnam, which was established to unite all the various Buddhist associations of Vietnam. After the political division of the country in 1954 there was a split in the Association also; the General Association of Buddhists of Vietnam remained in Saigon while the United Association of Buddhists became its counterpart in Hanoi. These associations also were joined after the death of Ngo Dinh Diem (1963), by the Theravādins (most numerous among the Khmer population). This was the beginning of the United Buddhist Congregation of Vietnam, which had above it a High Spiritual Institute of Vietnam (Vien Tang Thong) that was responsible for the behaviour of the monks and an Institute for the Expansion of Buddhism (Vien Hao Dao). All of these groups were linked with provincial or local organizations; the two highest monks were alternatively a Mahāyānist and a Theravādin, but this situation came to an end in 1966. Meanwhile, the younger generation, both laymen and monks, had become increasingly involved in politics; they had tried to enlarge the mutual understanding among the sects and to involve Buddhists in social welfare activities. It was at this time, inspired by a Chinese tradition (chiefly connected with the *Saddharmapuṇḍarīka*), that monks began to commit suicide by burning themselves to death. As regards the situation of Buddhism in Hanoi, there is little certain information.

Monastic compounds in Cambodia

In Cambodia, where Theravāda was introduced in ancient times, and which maintained frequent contacts with Ceylon, there are Theravāda centres with monasteries in which Pāli is taught. There are common hermitages for men and women who live in separate cells for periods of variable length, but residence is obligatorily in the rainy season. It is not necessary for all the inhabitants of the monastic compounds to be monks or nuns; many of them are lay persons and practice meditation in a rather elementary way. In 1955 Prince Norodom Sihanouk established the Sang Kum Restr Niyum (or Sangkum; People's Socialist Community), which aimed to restore in a new form the ancient Trinity of nation, religion, and king. The Sangkum considered Buddhism to be a Socialist religion, an unremitting struggle against evil, and hence an essential element in the formation of a Socialist party. In both Cambodia and Laos, Buddhism and, therefore, the monks have played a significant role, with a tendency toward the left politically. The destructive conflict in Vietnam and adjacent areas in the 1960s and 1970s has made monastic life difficult. Buddhists, whether clerics or laity, were obliged to participate actively in national affairs, involving themselves in the various political currents, with a tendency toward pacifistic and pro-Communist alignments. The frequent suicides by immolation in South Vietnam were a protest against the war by monks dedicated to the Buddha's ideal of peace; they sacrificed themselves thus to exemplify and stimulate a stronger resistance against the war.

Tibet. Kuomintang China, under Chiang Kai-shek, which had never renounced its sovereignty over Tibet, even though Tibet had declared its independence in 1913 under the 13th Dalai Lama, sought to maintain good relations with it. The Nationalists had a permanent mission (not an embassy) at Lhasa, the Tibetan capital. On the occasions of annual festivals, they would distribute considerable sums of money to the most important monasteries.

Relations between Communist China and Tibetan Buddhism

As for the People's Republic of China, its constitution assured its citizens of freedom of religion. It was announced that the functions of the Dalai Lama would continue in Tibet, and the customs of the peoples and the temples would be respected. China could not forget that a great part of Asia was Buddhist and that any anti-Buddhist measures would create an unfavourable impression. In 1952 some Buddhists were invited to take part in a Peace Conference of the Asian Peoples, and in 1953 a Buddhist association was set up under the presidency of Shes-rab rgya-mtsho [pronounced Sherapgyatso], who affirmed that Buddhism was a doctrine of revolutionary character and hence not opposed to the new democracy. Thus monks were directed to participate in reforms, combat reactionaries and imperialists, and to adapt their religion to the new social situation.

Buddhist monks were permitted to receive a delegation from Laos in 1956; some temples were restored and a Buddhist academy was founded. But in 1959 the Chinese authorities proclaimed that the religion had to be gradually weakened and ultimately suppressed. In that year the Dalai Lama fled Tibet. During the disorders caused by that event, many temples were destroyed.

Chinese policy toward Tibet changed from one of toleration to one of re-education. Monks were forced to teach and to work side by side with secular persons. The new social and economic structure, the required attendance at Chinese schools, and the presence in Tibet of many Chinese (not just military) are intended to modify, if not eliminate, a tradition of centuries. In China itself, many monasteries have been closed or adapted for other uses, whereas those of historical and artistic interest have been restored at state expense as national monuments.

Before the Cultural Revolution that began in 1966, work was begun on an inventory of Chinese objects of artistic value conserved in the monasteries; excavations were begun and two archaeological journals of considerable interest were published. Large volumes were also dedicated to Tun-huang and its caves. These activities were suspended during the Cultural Revolution, but have since been resumed.

Sōka-gakkai

Japan. In Japan, new schools with political tendencies have grown out of the better known ones. Such is the Sōka-gakkai, the lay association of the Nichiren-shō-shū sect, which has its principal centre at Taiseki-ji on the lower slope of Mt. Fuji. The Sōka-gakkai was founded by Makiguchi Tsunesaburō in 1930, and through the efforts of Toda Jōsei and Daisaku Ikoda it has won over 10,000,000 adherents and has representatives in the Diet. Its three principal elements of worship are: (1) the *gohonzon*, a *maṇḍala* before which one recites; (2) the *daimoku*, or salutation to the *Lotus Sūtra*; and (3) the *kaidan*, or platform, from which one receives the teaching during assemblies at Taiseki-ji for recitation of the *daimoku* and some chapters of the Hokke-kyō (*Lotus Sūtra*).

This is the religious basis of the political activity that began in a victorious confrontation with the mine owners of Hokkaido, where the Sōka-gakkai movement had infiltrated among the workers. Its political ideas are those of Nichiren: harmony between religion and the interests of national life, with a militant, well-organized type of nationalism and a vigorous conversion technique (*shakubuku*, "break and subdue"). Its political arm is the Kōmeitō (Clean Government Party), which has adopted the principle of *Buppō minshū-shugi* (Buddhist Democracy) and opposed rearmament in defense of the "peace constitution."

THE PROSPECTS FOR THE FUTURE

Buddhism in Asia finds itself in a state of contentious contradiction, except in Burma. In countries in which it is the traditional religion it supports nationalist movements and opposes colonialism in all its forms, past and present. Though retaining tolerance, it is inclined to a certain distrust of other religions, especially of Christianity, which it sees as a rival, a reaction to the historical effects of its alliance with colonialism. Nevertheless, Buddhism is imitating Christianity's methods; *e.g.*, by organizing its own missionaries in Ceylon and Thailand. Since the last decades of the 19th century it has modified its structures to encourage associations under various titles, both local and international in scope, with the aim of disseminating the teachings of the Teacher throughout the world. Many Buddhists and sympathizers with Buddhism in the West have encouraged and spurred on the messianic spirit that gives this movement life. Opposed to this activist position is a conservative attitude that seems to arise from the *saṅgha*'s fear that Buddhism will lose its prestige. Caught between the old and the new, Buddhism finds itself in an ambiguous situation. In Ceylon there was opposition to nationalization of the schools and establishment of a university on the European model, open to both monks and laymen. The dispute was resolved by the establishment of the University of Anuradhapura solely for monks. Although the liberal wing maintains that there is nothing in Buddhism that is contrary to science, when a renowned archaeologist of Ceylon, S. Paranavitana, declared that the traditional account of the Buddha's visit there was pure legend, the monks were scandalized. In countries such as Laos and Cambodia the custom continued of regarding the king as chief patron of the law and the *saṅgha* (comparable to the *Dharmarāja* in India and the *cos-rgyal* in Tibet). In

The *saṅgha*'s opposition to modernity

Vietnam, the conflict there has been a great blow to Buddhism. The choice is inevitable: whether to be for or against the reforms required by the new social order, even at the risk of harm to Buddhism itself.

The hesitancy of the *saṅgha* and its division into contending groups have made the younger generations skeptical, doubtful, or fanatical. Buddhism anticipated certain modern ideas: the negation of God and the soul is a basic concept in the Theravāda school. Buddhism has always lived under the protective shadow of the state; or it has been sufficiently powerful to govern on its own, as in Tibet. When protection was lacking during changes of dynasties, the *saṅgha* withdrew into itself, attempting, if the new conditions permitted, to live off its own properties or charity in exchange for spiritual protection, prayers, exorcisms, and education provided by temple schools. After the persecution of 845 in China, Buddhism recovered; but it never again achieved the splendour it had in Wei and T'ang times (6th–10th centuries). It survived and there were still important thinkers and very notable mystics, but on the whole the *saṅgha* declined.

In various ways the same thing was happening in the 1970s to both Mahāyāna and Theravāda. The Mahāyāna offered less possibility of resistance because of its apparent polytheism (few understand the symbolic meaning of the images found in the temples). In Japan its prospects were better. There is a multiplicity of sects there, many of which are identified with national aspirations or have even sparked them, and the devotional schools inspire faith and comfort; Zen and the followers of Nichiren encourage self-control and freedom of action. The chances of a resurgence of Theravāda in the contemporary world are better, however, because of its innate rationalism, its ethical foundations, and its lack of myths and symbols. Yet the *saṅgha* in Theravāda countries also is being abandoned or is losing its power of attraction. If it is not able to compete with the state in education, in social service, and in genuine contributions to the economic improvement of the masses, the number of monks will continue to decline.

University students, caught up in the agony of Southeast Asia, are looking for more rewarding occupations and are not attracted by the monastic life. Yet it should not be said that Buddhism is destined to lose ground. As a mode of spiritual behaviour it still has great vitality outside the *saṅgha* itself. This can increase if Buddhism returns to its origins, to the original teaching of the Buddha, freed of the monastic structure and of the dogmatic and theological complexities that have encrusted it in the course of time. One cannot even exclude the possibility that it may carry its basic ethical message to a West uncertain and full of doubt in the face of the collapse of seemingly irrefutable values. This would seem to be indicated by the constantly increasing interest aroused by Buddhism in the West, not simply as an object of scholarly research but as the inspiration for an acceptance, not bound by worn-out or moribund traditions, of the teaching contained in the word of the Teacher—capable of renewed spiritual energy—like a sermon the Buddha continually repeats for anyone who understands it and applies it to life.

BIBLIOGRAPHY. The bibliography on Buddhism is vast; see the *Bibliographie Bouddhique* (annual since 1928). Encyclopaedias on this subject are primarily in Japanese: *Bukkyô Dai-jiten*, ed. by TOKUNO ODA (1917); *Bukkyô Dai-jiten* 5 vol., (1932–36), well indexed; and *Mikkyō Dai-jiten* (1931–33; French trans., *Hôbôgirin: Dictionnaire encyclopédique du Bouddhisme . . .*, 4 vol. to date, 1937–67). The government of Ceylon (now Sri Lanka) has undertaken the *Encyclopaedia of Buddhism*, ed. by GEORGE P. MALALASEKERA, 3 vol. to date (1961–). Since Buddhism has been diffused over a large part of Asia, scholarly works on it are generally limited to an individual country or to the areas in which the authors are specialized. A good book for the nonspecialist is CHARLES ELIOT, *Hinduism and Buddhism: An Historical Sketch*, 3 vol. (1921, reprinted 1962). The best summary of Indian Buddhism is ETIENNE LAMOTTE, *Histoire du bouddhisme indien, des origines à l'ère Śaka* (1958); see also EDWARD J. THOMAS, *The History of Buddhist Thought*, 2nd ed. (1951); and on the sects, ANDRE BAREAU, *Les Sectes bouddhiques du petit véhicule* (1955), and *La Vie et l'organisation des communautés bouddhiques modernes de Ceylon* (1957).

For an understanding of Indian Buddhism, the following accounts of the Chinese pilgrims should be consulted: HERBERT A. GILES, *The Travels of Fa-hsien* (1886, reprinted 1923); THOMAS WATTERS, *On Yuan Chwang's Travels in India, 629–645 A.D.*, 2 vol. (1904–05, reprinted 1971); and I TSING, *A Record of the Buddhist Religion As Practised in India and the Malay Archipelago (A.D. 671–695)*, trans. by JUNJIRO TAKAKUSU (1896).

A good book on the life of the Buddha is HERMANN OLDENBERG, *Buddha: His Life, His Doctrine, His Order* (1882); also EDWARD J. THOMAS, *The Life of Buddha As Legend and History*, 3rd ed. rev. (1949, reprinted 1969). An easy-to-read survey of Buddhist thought is HELMUTH VON GLASENAPP, *Der Buddhismus: Eine atheistische Religion* (1966; Eng. trans., *Buddhism: A Non-Theistic Religion*, 1970); ANDRE BAREAU, *Recherches sur la biographie du Buddha dans les Sūtrapitaka et les Vinayapiṭaka anciens* (1963), is a more technical study. For the oldest and most strictly dogmatic form of Buddhism, see NYANTILOKA MAHATHERA, *Guide Through the Abhidamma-Pitaka, Being a Synopsis of the Philosophical Collection Belonging to the Buddhist Pali Canon, Followed by an Essay on the Paticca-Samppāda*, 2nd ed. rev. by NYANAPONIKA THERA (1957); and for the history and the ritual, WALPOLA RAHULA, *History of Buddhism in Ceylon* (1956).

For Buddhism with respect to China, the work of FUNG YU-LAN, *A History of Chinese Philosophy*, 2nd ed. 2 vol. (Eng. trans. 1952–53), is valuable although only some aspects of Chinese Buddhism are considered. For the encounter between Taoist and Buddhist thought, see WALTER LIEBENTHAL, *The Book of Chao: A Translation from the Original Chinese, with Introduction, Notes and Appendices* (1948); ERIK ZURCHER, *The Buddhist Conquest of China*, 2 vol. (1959); and ARTHUR F. WRIGHT, *Buddhism in Chinese History* (1959); for a general survey, KENNETH K.S. CH'EN, *Buddhism in China* (1964). The recent history of Buddhism in China is discussed by WING-TSIT CHAN in *Religious Trends in Modern China* (1953).

For Korea and Japan, in addition to the book by Eliot that has already been cited, see his *Japanese Buddhism* (1935, reprinted 1959); AUGUST K. REISCHAUER, *Studies in Japanese Buddhism* (1917, reprinted 1970); GEORGE B. SANSOM, *Japan: A Short Cultural History*, rev. ed. (1946); EDWIN O. REISCHAUER, *Ennin's Travels in T'ang China* (1955), and (trans.), *Ennin's Diary: The Record of a Pilgrimage to China in Search of the Law* (1955); and JUNJIRO TAKAKUSU, *The Essentials of Buddhist Philosophy*, 3rd ed. (1956). On Zen the following studies are recommended: D.T. SUZUKI, *Essays in Zen Buddhism*, new ed., 3 series (1927–61); *The Training of the Zen Buddhist Monk* (1934); and the studies by HEINRICH DUMOULIN: *Zen: Geschichte und Gestalt* (1959; Eng. trans., *A History of Zen Buddhism*, 1963); *Wu mên-kuan: Der Pass ohne Tor* (1953); *Die Entwicklung des chinesischen Ch'an nach Huinêng in Lichte des Wu-mên-Kuan* (1953; Eng. trans., *The Development of Chinese Zen After the Sixth Patriarch in the Light of Mumonkan*, 1953); and *The Sutra of Wei Lang or Hui Nêng*, new ed. (1947).

For the influence of Buddhism on the economic life of China, see JACQUES GERNET, *Les Aspects économiques du Bouddhisme dans la société chinoise du Ve au Xe siècle* (1956).

A study relevant to Tibet and Mongolia that demonstrates the synthesis of Tibetan culture and its religious tradition is ROLF A. STEIN, *La Civilisation tibétaine* (1962; Eng. trans., *Tibetan Civilization*, 1972); on the schools of religion, see HELMUT HOFFMANN, *Die Religionen Tibets* (1956; Eng. trans., *The Religions of Tibet*, 1961); GIUSEPPE TUCCI and WALTHER HEISSIG, *Die Religionen Tibets und der Mongolei* (1970); and ROBERT J. MILLER, *Monasteries and Culture Change in Inner Mongolia* (1959); on the Tibetan tradition, HERBERT V. GUENTHER, *Tibetan Buddhism Without Mystification* (1966); and A. BHARATI, *The Tantric Tradition* (1965).

Works on Buddhist iconography include B.T. BHATTACHARYYA, *The Indian Buddhist Iconography*, 2nd ed. (1958); A.K. COOMARASWAMY, *Elements of Buddhist Iconography* (1935); GIUSEPPE TUCCI, *Tibetan Painted Scrolls*, 3 vol. (1949) and *Teoria e pratica del mandala* (1949; Eng. trans., *The Theory and Practice of the Maṇḍala*, 2nd ed., 1969); and FERDINAND LESSING, *Yung-Ho-Kung: An Iconography of the Lamaist Cathedral in Peking* (1942). On Buddhism and art, see ALFRED C. FOUCHER, *La Vie du Bouddha d'après les textes et les monuments de l'Inde* (1949; abridged Eng. trans., *The Life of Buddha*, 1963); HAROLD INGHOLT and ISLAY LYONS, *Gandhāran Art in Pakistan* (1957); JOHN M. ROSENFIELD, *The Dynastic Arts of the Kushans* (1967); J. LEROY DAVIDSON, *The Lotus Sūtra in Chinese Art* (1955); ALEXANDER SOPER and LAURENCE SICKMAN, *The Art and Architecture of China* (1956); and TOSHIO NAGAHIRO, *Yün-kang, the Buddhist Cave-Temples of the Fifth Century in North China* (1951–56).

For Southeast Asia, GEORGE COEDES, *Les États hindouisés d'Indochine et Indonésie*, rev. ed. (1964; Eng. trans., *The Indianized States of Southeast Asia*, 1968); S.J. TAMBIAH, *Buddhism and the Spirit Cults in North-East Thailand* (1970); and KENNETH W. MORGAN (ed.), *The Path of the Buddha* (1956).

The relationship between western thought and Buddhism and the actual position of Buddhism in East Asia is discussed in HENRI DE LUBAC, *La Rencontre du Bouddhisme et de l'Occident* (1952); GEORG SIEGMUND, *Buddhismus und Christentum* (1968); KOSHO YAMAMOTO, *Buddhism in Europe* (1967); GUY R. WELBON, *The Buddhist Nirvāna and Its Western Interpreters* (1968); HARRY THOMSEN, *The New Religions of Japan* (1963); DONALD E. SMITH (ed.), *South Asian Politics and Religion* (1969); CLARK B. OFFNER and HENRY VAN STRAELEN, *Modern Japanese Religions* (1963); and RICHARD LOWENTHAL (ed.), *Issues in the Future of Asia* (1969).

(Gi.T.)

Buddhism, History of

Originating in northern India in the 6th century BC under the leadership of Siddhārtha Gautama, the Buddha, Buddhism arose as a reaction to certain aspects of Hinduism. Spreading over much of India, and then suffering there a decline, Buddhism expanded over much of Central and Southeast Asia, China, Korea, and Japan, influencing the social, cultural, economic, and political life of the lands in which it gained prominence.

This article is divided into the following sections:

Basic characteristics and problems in the study of the history of Buddhism
Origins and early developments
  The cultural context
  The founding of Buddhism
  Early developments of Buddhism in India
Buddhism in India
  Early Buddhist councils
  Early sectarian schisms
  Expansion of Buddhism
  The decline of Buddhism in India
Buddhism in Central Asia and China
  Developments in Central Asian kingdoms
  Developments in China
Buddhism in Korea and Japan
  Developments in Korea
  Developments in Japan
Buddhism in Tibet and the Himalayan kingdoms
  Developments in Tibet
  Developments in the Himalayan kingdoms
Buddhism in Ceylon and Southeast Asia
  Developments in Ceylon
  Developments in Southeast Asia
Buddhism in the late 19th and 20th centuries

BASIC CHARACTERISTICS AND PROBLEMS IN THE STUDY OF THE HISTORY OF BUDDHISM

After centuries of fanciful speculation, European scholars in the 19th century began to display a disciplined curiosity about the history of the Buddhist religion. As a result of this disciplined approach, rather than mere whimsical theorizing, the foundations for the modern scientific study of Buddhism were laid. Throughout the 19th century there was a great variety of opinion regarding the nature of Buddhism and the original message of its founder, Siddhārtha Gautama, the Buddha. The analysis of even so fundamental a Buddhist concept as Nirvāṇa (annihilation, bliss, rectitude, or the release from individuality) deeply divided scholarly opinion and significantly influenced the subsequent reconstruction of Buddhist thought and piety. Some scholars, such as Jules Barthélemy-Saint-Hilaire, a French philosopher and statesman, and F. Max Müller, an Anglo-German comparative philologist, were puzzled by a religion that seemed to be both nihilistic and atheistic. Others, such as Albrecht Weber, a German Orientalist, proclaimed its founder to be a simple moralist and social reformer. The quest for the historical Buddha—in method and intent similar to the quest for the historical Jesus in Christianity—played a crucial role in all Buddhological studies because of the tendency among scholars to judge the later developments in Buddhism in terms of its "earliest gospel." (Unfortunately, many scholars have tended to identify what they regarded as the earliest scriptural traditions with the actual words of the Buddha.)

Western schools of interpretation

Modern studies of Buddhism in the West, according to Edward Conze, a German-British Buddhologist, can be divided into three schools of interpretation: the Anglo-German school; the Leningrad school; and the Franco-Belgian school. The Anglo-German school, headed by T.W. Rhys Davids, an eminent English Buddhologist, and Hermann Oldenberg, a German scholar, concentrated on the Pāli canon, the Buddhist scriptures written in an ancient Indian language, of Theravāda (Way of the Elders) Buddhism and emphasized the moral, less mystical, and practical aspects of the religion and its founder. The Leningrad school, led by Fyodor Shcherbatskoy, a Russian scholar, took its clue from Bu-ston, a historian of Tibetan Buddhism, and divided the history of Buddhism into three consecutive periods: pluralism, monism, and idealism. Relying upon the later commentatorial literature, especially the *Abhidharmakośa* ("Treasury of Higher Law") written in the 4th century AD by Vasubandhu, a founder of the Yogācāra (Idealist) school of Mahāyāna (Greater Vehicle) Buddhism, Shcherbatskoy concentrated on how the concepts of *dharma* (norm, law) and the *dharma*-elements unfolded in Buddhist thought. The result was a brilliant overemphasis on the metaphysical aspects of Buddhism. The Franco-Belgian school, to which are associated many scholars in the 20th century, was initiated by such scholars as Louis de la Vallée-Poussin, a French Buddhologist who regarded Buddhism not as a system of ideas based on the *Upaniṣads*, Hindu philosophical books (often pre-Buddhist), but as an ascetic, religious, and Indian institution based on *yoga*, a physical–psychological meditation discipline. Aware that Theravāda Buddhism was only one of about 18 early Buddhist sects, each having its own scriptural traditions, Franco-Belgian Buddhologists like Jean Przyluski, Sylvain Lévi, Paul Demiéville, and Étienne Lamotte no longer rely solely on the Pāli scriptures of the Theravādins for their reconstruction of early Buddhism. Though it may be impossible to discover the actual words of the Buddha, these scholars believe the earliest traditions of the Buddhist community can be uncovered by a careful comparative study of the existing literature of all the known early sects. When accounts in the Pāli canon and the extant Sanskrit accounts of the Sarvāstivādins (members of a sect who believe everything is real) agree, for example, a conclusion may be reached that these accounts contain a tradition antedating the split within the orthodox monastic order, the Sthāviras (from Sanskrit: the "elders"), into the Theravādins (Pāli *thera*, "elders") and Sarvāstivādins (*c.* 250 BC). Likewise, when these accounts agree with those recorded in the literature of the more liberal Mahāsaṅghikas (members of the Great Saṅgha, or Community), the conclusion may be made that scholars now have a record of what was generally accepted by nearly all early Buddhists about 140 years after the Buddha's death when the schism between the Mahāsaṅghikas and the Sthāviras took place (*c.* 340 BC).

Non-textual sources

In addition to this variety of textual resources, Buddhologists (in the latter part of the 20th century) rely more heavily upon archaeological, iconographic, and sociological fieldwork than previously was the case. This plurality of approaches, introduced by the Franco-Belgian Buddhologists, has had a constructive effect on all aspects of Buddhist studies. The scriptural tradition is now recognized as only one aspect of a much larger religiocultural complex. No longer can the doctrines and values of a monastic elite, who produced the scriptures, be equated with Buddhism per se. Nor is it any longer possible to regard the several historical forms of Buddhism that emerged across Asia, from India to Japan, as "deviations" from some pristine form of the faith. Everywhere, Buddhism has grown into symbiotic relationships with the religion of the folk (*e.g.*, apotropaic magic; and rituals of fertility, family, and healing) and the nation (*e.g.*, sacred kingship). The fact is that scholars simply do not know whether Buddhism was originally a popular cult or the spiritual philosophy of a religious virtuoso that only later became the religion of the common man.

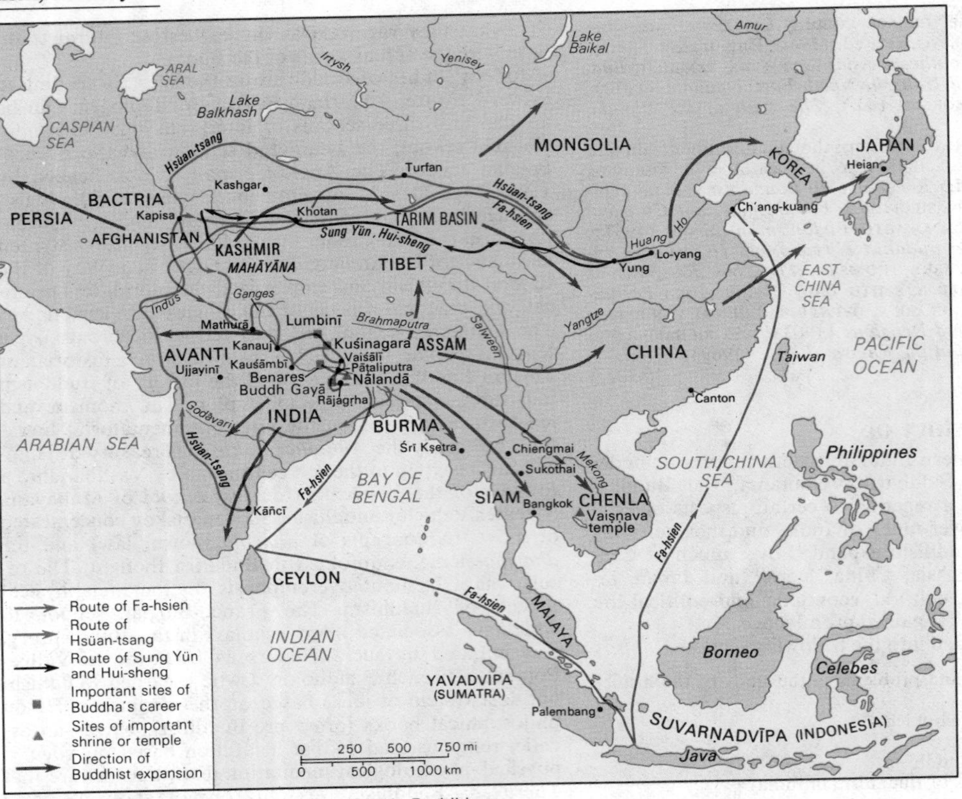

Important sites and routes of expansion of early Buddhism.

ORIGINS AND EARLY DEVELOPMENTS

The cultural context. During the period of the Buddha (*c.* 560–*c.* 480 BC), the northeastern region of India was virtually alive with small religious movements composed of charismatic yogic leaders who influenced people by the force of their spiritual qualities, of a community rule, or laws, and of members of the community; *i.e.*, followers of a particular teacher and his rule. This pattern later was taken over by the Buddhists as the *tri-ratna* ("three jewels"): (1) the Buddha, (2) the *dharma* ("rule"), and (3) the *saṅgha* ("community"). At this time in India, many were no longer content with the external formalities of Brahmanic (Hindu high caste) sacrifice and ritual. Giving up their place in society, their sacred threads (*upavīta*), and the sacred tuft of hair (*śikhā*), many of the discontented adopted the life of wandering almsmen. In northwestern India such itinerant ascetics tried to go beyond the Vedas (Hindu sacred scriptures). In the literature that grew out of this movement, the *Upaniṣads*, a new emphasis on renunciation and transcendental knowledge can be found. But northeastern India, which was little influenced by the Aryans who had developed the main tenets and practices of the Hindu faith, became the breeding ground of most heterodox sects. Society in this area was troubled by the breakdown of tribal unity and the expansion of several petty kingdoms. Religiously, this was a time of doubt, turmoil, and experimentation. New sects abounded, including various kinds of skeptics (*e.g.*, Sañjaya Belaṭṭhiputta), atomists (*e.g.*, Pakudha Kātyāyana), materialists (*e.g.*, Ajita Keśakambalin), and antinomians; *i.e.*, those against rules or laws (*e.g.*, Pūraṇa Kāśapa). Among the most important sects to arise at the time of the Buddha were the Ājīvikas, who emphasized the rule of fate (*niyati*), and the Jainas, an ascetic movement stressing the need to free the soul from matter. Though the Jainas, like the Buddhists, have often been regarded as atheists, their beliefs are actually more complicated. Unlike early Buddhists, both the Ājīvikas and Jainas believed in the permanence of the elements that constitute the universe, as well as the existence of the soul.

Religious movements flourishing in the 6th century BC

A proto-Sāṃkhya sect (a Hindu school of thought founded by Kapila) teaching the dualism of spirit (*puruṣa*) and matter (*prakrti*) was dominant where Buddhism later arose and probably had some impact on early Buddhist thought. Despite the bewildering variety of religious communities, many shared the same vocabulary—Nirvāṇa, *yoga*, *karma* (causality), *tathāgata* ("thus-gone," or "he who has thus attained"), *buddha* (enlightened), *saṃsāra* (eternal recurrence, becoming), and *dharma*—and most were based on the practice of *yoga*.

The founding of Buddhism. According to tradition, the Buddha himself was a *yogin; i.e.*, a miracle-working ascetic. After leaving his home in Kapilavastu in northern India (present Nepal), the young Siddhārtha went to Rājagṛha, the capital of Magadha (an ancient kingdom in northeastern India), and studied under two *yogins*, Ālāra Kālāma and Uddaka Rāmaputta. Because he found that their teaching did not satisfy his spiritual needs, he moved to a grove near Uruvelā, not far from Buddh Gayā. There Siddhārtha spent nearly seven years practicing yogic austerities. Finally realizing that he had been overemphasizing these practices, he adopted a milder course, called the Middle Way, or Path (Mādhyamika). One night, he entered into a yogic trance, during which he first recollected his own previous existences. During the second watch of the night, he entered into a second trance, in which he acquired the "divine eye," enabling him to envisage the death and rebirth of all creatures. During the third watch he entered an even higher state of trance, during which the "outflows" of his life—his ignorance and desires—were finally quelled. He then grasped what were called the Four Noble Truths and the principle of dependent origination. The crux of Siddhārtha's discovery was that suffering and death can be overcome only when ignorance and craving have been put aside. After his Enlightenment the Buddha (Enlightened One) could have remained a "silent one" in a permanent state of bliss. Instead, he chose to return and work for the salvation of others. During the remaining years of his life, he devoted himself to establishing a community that would be based on selfless, compassionate "right action." After spending approximately 43 years in preaching, begging, and labouring within this community, the Buddha became ill with dysentery and passed into a final state of Nirvāṇa near Kuśinagara (in northeast India).

The Enlightenment of Siddhārtha Gautama, the Buddha

From this sketch of the Buddha's life, it is apparent that

Pilgrims praying at the site of the Buddha's Enlightenment at Buddh Gayā in India, a place of pilgrimage for Buddhists of all sects. The Bo tree at left is believed to be a descendant of the one under which the Buddha sat during the night before his Enlightenment.
Foto Features

Buddhist Enlightenment is deeply rooted in the practice of *yoga*. *Yoga*, a complex of ecstatic spiritual techniques going back to the earliest period of Indian civilization, was preserved in India's hinterlands, such as the Nepalese–Indian frontier where the Buddha was born. Together with other indigenous elements in the country's religious history (*e.g.*, *pūjā*, offerings to gods, and *bhakti*, or devotionalism), *yoga* was a concrete and experimental form of religious experience. Many shamanistic elements (*i.e.*, healing practices and psychic transformations) seem to be reflected in its practice, as well as in the myths and legends that grew up around the person of the *yogin*. Among these are initiatory ordeals, celestial flights, descent into the underworld, and other magicoreligious feats. In the Buddha's legendary biography are found numerous yogic–shamanistic elements. According to some stories, he was able to fly through the air. He also is reported to have dismembered his body, letting his limbs fall to the ground and then magically reassembling them. In a previous life, he is said to have given his body to feed starving animals and demons. Texts describe him as "burning," a term reflecting the heat-fire symbolism common to both the Vedic and yogic–shamanistic traditions. Early Buddhist thought likewise exhibits aspects of the pre-Aryan inheritance; for example, the five classes of "superknowledge" (*abhijñā*) that included: (1) miraculous or magical powers, (2) the "divine eye," (3) "divine hearing," (4) knowledge of another's thoughts, and (5) recollection of one's previous existences. As noted above, the Buddha himself, on the night of his Enlightenment, was able to recollect all of his previous existences, and later in the night he acquired the "divine eye" enabling him to see the death and rebirth of all creatures.

Early developments of Buddhism in India. Perhaps as a response to the crisis in the traditional ethos of Indian culture in northeastern India, Buddhism creatively revalorized tribal and folk traditions. In the *Mahāparinibbāna Sutta* (a Buddhist text in sermonic or dialogue form), the Vajjian tribal confederacy is made the model for the Buddhist community. The practical aspects of the new Buddhist *dharma* were soon appropriated by the emerging trading class, largely of the Vaiśya (Hindu merchant) caste. The layman was an integral part of the early Buddhist community, not only because he supported the monastics but also because he himself could become a "streamwinner" destined only for happy rebirths in heaven (*sagga*) and, finally, Enlightenment. The early Buddhist community (*saṅgha*) included monks, nuns, laymen, and laywomen alike. The layman's ethic, though not identical with that of the monks, was nevertheless "Buddhist." Even the scriptures gave him practical advice, such as how to avoid clever people who want only to deceive and cheat him. Greediness was believed to stem from laziness, and not from ambition. The ideal of the Buddhist merchant was, therefore, not simply to avoid the wasting of money but also to make it. Still, the layman was not as concerned about Nirvāṇa as he was about winning a better rebirth. For him, the Buddha as saviour and lord (Bhagavat) was more important than the *dharma*. From the piety of these lay Buddhists arose such well-established Buddhist practices as *Buddha-pūjā* (worship), the veneration of relics, and the building of *stūpa*s (reliquaries).

Influence of the *bhakti* movement

A crucial influence on early Buddhism was the *bhakti* movement, a pietistical development in Indian religious life going back to the time of Śākyamuni (Sage of the Śākyas, Gautama Buddha). *Bhakti* stressed the need for faith in and devotion to a saviour-deity, who, in turn, provided the faithful with the means of salvation. This was a radically different outlook from that of the Buddha, who insisted that, after his decease, his disciples should follow only the *dharma*. *Bhakti*'s emphasis on faith is seen even in the "Three Refuges" common to all branches of Buddhism; *i.e.*, the vow to take refuge in Buddha, *dharma*, and *saṅgha*. The Buddha became the Lord (Bhagavat) who actively sets about saving the faithful. This led to the actual worship of the Buddha (*Buddha-pūjā*). In this worship the *stūpa* became of prime importance. Pilgrims, coming from great distances, circumambulated the *stūpa* (originally, a reliquary mound), bearing flowers and incense to be offered as gifts to the Lord.

BUDDHISM IN INDIA

From the beginning, there was a close relationship between monks and laymen. The early Buddhist monastic community was not regarded as something set apart from the world but, rather, as the means for promoting the "welfare and happiness of the many." Originally, the wandering ascetics moved about constantly, settling down only during the monsoon season. Only in the Buddhist community did it become the rule (probably by the 4th century BC) to live together during the three months of inclement weather. From this experience was born the ritual affirmation of the community rule (Pātimokkha). Gradually, these rain retreats (*vassāvāsa*s) gave way to permanent monastic settlements. Only when the differences between monk and layman were later emphasized did there arise the notion of an exchange of layman's support for monk's merit. By the time of the Muslim invasion of India (10th century AD), laymen had little interest in the restoration of Buddhism. Jainism, on the other hand, continued to maintain close relations between monk and layman and perpetuated its traditional discipline even among the uncloistered. This was one reason why Jainism survived the Muslim invasions of India, and Buddhism did not.

Early Buddhist councils. The early Buddhist councils (*saṅgīti*s, or "recitals") were largely concerned with the purity of the faith and practice of the monastic community. Unfortunately, the councils pose an enormous problem to the historian because each major sect has its own account and opinion of them. Legend and even myth have so coloured these accounts that scholars cannot be sure when and where they took place or even who may have taken part in them. Though many scholars deny its very existence, all Buddhist traditions maintain that a council was called at Rājagṛha immediately after the death of the Buddha. According to the legend, this council (comprising 500 *arhat*s, or monks) was responsible for the composition of the *vinaya* (monastic discipline), under the monk

Upāli, and the *dhamma* (*i.e.*, the *sūtra*s), under the monk Ānanda, even though the latter was supposedly brought to trial at the same council. Though there were memorizers of *sūtra*s (*sūtra-dhara*) and the *vinaya* (*vinaya-dhara*), as well as authorized commentators (*mātṛkā-dhara*) at work in the community during the period of the first three Buddhist councils, the scriptures as such existed only in an inchoate oral (yet normative) form. More scholars are prone to accept the historicity of the second council that was held at Vaiśālī when a controversy broke out between a certain Yasa and the monks of Vajji. The ten points of discipline observed by the Vajjian monks, and opposed by Yasa, permitted storing salt in a horn, eating in the afternoon, and drinking buttermilk after meals. These and other lax rules were condemned by the council. According to tradition, a third council was called by King Aśoka at Pāṭaliputra (Patna) about 250 BC. According to some accounts, the *Tripiṭaka* (Buddhist canon) was completed by this council and missionaries were sent out to various countries. Moggaliputta Tissa, president of the council, supposedly completed his *Abhidhamma* (Higher Dharma) treatise, the *Kathāvatthu* ("Points of Controversy"), during this council. More significant was the controversy that arose between the Sarvāstivādins and the Vibhajyavādins (usually identified with the early Theravādins) over the reality of past and future states of consciousness (*citta*s). After the Sarvāstivādin view that such states actually exist was condemned, the sect withdrew from the lower Ganges Valley to Madhurā in the northwest. There it appears to have continued to develop as a transitional school between the older, more conservative schools and the nascent Mahāyāna (Greater Vehicle) movement. A fourth council was believed to have been held under King Kaniṣka, probably in the 1st century AD, at Jalandhar or in Kashmir. This council seems to have been limited to the composition of commentaries. Because there is no evidence of Mahāyāna at this council, and because only Sarvāstivādin and Sthaviravādin viewpoints seem to have been represented, scholars generally conclude that this was actually a sectarian synod rather than an actual ecumenical Buddhist council. At any rate, the fourth council, whose work was recorded in Sanskrit, has never been recognized by southern Buddhists.

The work of the third council

Early sectarian schisms. About 140 years after the Buddha's death, the Buddhist community, which had long been divided into many informal factions, became openly divided between two sects, the Mahāsaṅghika (Great Council) and the Sthāviras (those who stood for the tradition of the elders at the council of Pāṭaliputra). These were the forerunners of the great split of Buddhism into Mahāyāna (Greater Vehicle) and Theravāda, or Hīnayāna (Lesser Vehicle), respectively—southern Buddhists prefer Theravāda, rather than the designation Hīnayāna, which, they believe carries with it a negative connotation. The Sthāviras, in turn, later gave rise to the Sarvāstivādins (those who teach that "everything" exists; *i.e.*, space, past, present, future, and Nirvāṇa) and the Sautrāntikas (who rejected the *Abhidharma* in favour of the *sūtra*s). Another line of descent led from the Sthāviras to the Theravādins of Ceylon and Southeast Asia.

Origins of Mahāyāna and Hīnayāna (Theravāda) Buddhism

Theravādins. The Theravādins (Way of Elders) maintained that the ideal Buddhist is the *arhat*, the accomplished ascetic who wins Nirvāṇa through his own efforts. Actually, he is a monk within the monastic *saṅgha.* Though the Theravādin *arhat* naturally "took refuge in the Buddha," his emphasis was not on the grace of the Saviour, but on his *dharma.* In its "theology," Theravāda tended to make distinctions. It insisted that Nirvāṇa was beyond the realm of empirical reality and that the Buddha (Gautama or Śākyamuni Buddha, who attained final Nirvāṇa in the 5th century BC) was separable from the *dharma* that he taught. It maintained that the *arhat* and layman have different roles to play both in society and in religion.

Mahāyānists. These distinctions were broken down by Mahāyāna. Arising in areas where Buddhists no longer could control the state, Mahāyānists focussed their attention on celestial Buddhas, Buddhafields, and *bodhisattvas* (Buddhas-to-be). In fact, the *bodhisattva* now became the ideal Buddhist. He was a man—monk or layman—who postponed his own enjoyment of Nirvāṇa in order to win salvation for all sentient creatures. To this end, he took vows in the presence of a Buddha that, having crossed the stream of suffering, he would ferry others across. His aim is not merely to attain the "wisdom" of the Theravādin *arhat* but rather to practice compassion and selflessness. He was said to fulfil six perfections: charity, morality, forbearance, striving, meditation, and wisdom. Though the *bodhisattva* ideal was not new with Mahāyāna, it did receive a new emphasis and a new ontological (theory of Being) foundation in this school. The compassion of the *bodhisattva* breaks down the distinctions that Theravāda insists upon. Finding the elitist split between *arhat* and layman intolerable, Mahāyānists teach that, as long as the "accomplished one" is distinguished from others, he is still susceptible to the pride that breeds illusion and suffering. Mahāyāna finds the solution to this problem in the identity of the phenomenal world (*saṃsāra*) and Nirvāṇa, both growing out of the Void (*śūnyatā*). In the Void all discriminations, all theories, all contradictory projects, and ideas have their ground. All dualisms are abolished. Subject does not differ from object, yes from no, saint from sinner. Thus, the *bodhisattva*, in his compassion, breaks down all distinctions and pride, dissolving them in emptiness.

One extremely complicated school of Mahāyāna Buddhism was known as Yogācāra (*yoga* practice) or Vijñānavāda (consciousnessism, or mind-only). According to the teachings of this school, subjects and objects do not exist. Only mind exists. The regularity of sense impressions men have of the world is because of a perceptual "storehouse" (*ālaya-vijñāna*) that has been inherited from all previous impressions. Salvation consists in reducing this "storehouse" to absolute reality, or suchness. Two brothers, Asaṅga and Vasubandhu, who lived in the 4th century AD, were the founders of Vijñānavāda. The younger, Vasubandhu, wrote the well-known Hīnayāna work, the *Abhidharmakośa* ("Treasury of the Higher Law"), before being converted to the mind-only position by his brother.

Another school of great historical importance was the Mādhyamika, or school of the Middle Path or Way, founded by Nāgārjuna in the 2nd century AD. By using very subtle, if not devious, logic, Nāgārjuna sought to reduce all other doctrines and theories to self-contradictions. At the same time, he refused to offer alternatives to the positions taken up by opponents. His aim was, by confounding all doctrines, to point to the essential emptiness (*śūnyatā*) of all things. Stated negatively, his position was that nothing comes into being, nor does anything disappear. Nothing is infinite or finite. Nothing is identical or different; nothing moves hither, nothing moves thither. By means of such negative feats of logic, Nāgārjuna tried to free men from all contradictory entanglements. Salvation, not a more refined philosophy, was his ultimate goal.

Expansion of Buddhism. *Buddhism under the Mauryan dynasty.* To the rulers of the kingdoms and republics arising in northeast India, the patronage of heteroprax (differing practices) sects was one way of avoiding the meddling of Brahmins (high-caste Hindus) in the affairs of state. The first Mauryan emperor, Candragupta (*c.* 321–*c.* 297 BC), patronized Jainism and finally became a Jain monk. His grandson, Aśoka, who ruled over the greater part of the subcontinent from 269–238 BC, became the archetypal Buddhist king. Aśoka attempted to establish a "true *dharma*" in his realm based on the virtues of self-control, impartiality, cheerfulness, truthfulness, and goodness. Though he did not found a state church, he did attempt to make for the state a church that would include Hindu, Jaina, Ājīvika, and Buddhist alike. His aim was to create a religious and social milieu that would enable all "children of the King" to live happily and attain heaven in the next life. Thus, he created a "welfare state" by setting up medical assistance for men

The goals of Aśoka

and beasts, maintaining reservoirs and canals, and promoting trade. A system of *dharma* officers (*dhamma-mahāmattas*) was set up to provide for the empire magistrates, district attorneys, preachers, bureaucrats, social workers, and spies. The lay ethic preached by the King of the *dharma* (*dhamma-rāja*) and his officers was focussed on the layman's obligations in this world. Though Aśoka created a new ideal of kingship that would have powerful repercussions in Ceylon and Southeast Asia, the various problems posed by a state of such vast dimensions in India proved greater than could be solved by even such an inspired ideology. Soon after Aśoka's death, the Mauryan Empire began to crumble.

Developments under the Gupta dynasty. Though Buddhism was spreading through Central Asia, Ceylon, and China, in India there was a concurrent revival of Brahmanism and a steady growth of *bhakti*. Gradually, Buddhism absorbed various elements from these Indian traditions so that, by the time of the Gupta period (*c.* AD 300–*c.* 600), some Hindus were practicing *Buddha-pūjā*, regarding the Buddha as an *avatar* (incarnation) of the important Hindu deity Viṣṇu (Vishnu). Under the Guptas, some monasteries lost the spirit of the cloister and merged with other like-minded centres to form monastic clusters (*mahāvihāras*), functioning as liberal-arts institutions. The most famous of these was built at Nālandā, where the curriculum went far beyond canonical Buddhism. Nālandā soon became the leading centre for the study of Mahāyāna, which was fast becoming the dominant sect in India.

Visits of Chinese pilgrims. Though Buddhist institutions seemed to be faring well under the Guptas, various Chinese pilgrims, visiting India between AD 400 and 700, could discern an internal decline in the Buddhist community and the beginning of the reabsorption of Indian Buddhism by Hinduism. Among these pilgrims were Fa-hsien, Sung Yün, Hui-sheng, Hsüan-tsang, and I-ching.

The travelogues of these Chinese travellers provide the historian with invaluable information about Asian cultures from the Sāsānian (Persian) Empire in the west to Sumatra and Java in the east, and from Turfan in Central Asia to Kāñcī in the south of India. In 399 Fa-hsien left China, crossed the Gobi Desert, and visited various holy places in India. He then returned to China via Ceylon and Java, taking with him numerous Buddhist scriptures and statues. The most famous of the T'ang (a Chinese dynasty that ruled from AD 618–907) travellers was the monk Hsüan-tsang, who left China in 628 without imperial permission. Like Fa-hsien, he found both Hīnayānists and Mahāyānists in Central Asia. In 630 he attended an assembly of various Buddhist sects at Kapisa. When he arrived in northwest India, he found "millions of monasteries" reduced to ruins by the Huns, a Central Asian nomadic people who had even reached the gates of Rome in the 5th century. Many of the remaining Buddhists were turning to Tantrism, an esoteric psychic–physical system of belief and practice. In the northeast, he visited various holy places and studied Yogācāra, a Mahāyāna system, and Indian philosophy at Nālandā. After visiting Assam and southern India—intending to study Hīnayāna in Ceylon but being prevented from doing so by civil wars in that country—he returned to China with about 600 *sūtras*. After being received by the Chinese emperor T'ai-tsung in 645, he spent the rest of his life translating and studying the scriptures he had brought back. Another Chinese traveller, I-ching, went to Sumatra, Śrivijaya, and Malaya. In India, he visited Bodh Gayā and other Buddhist sites and, like Hsüan-tsang, studied at Nālandā. In 695, after an absence of 24 years, he returned to China.

The journeys of Hsüan-tsang

The decline of Buddhism in India. After the destruction of numerous Buddhist monasteries in the 6th century AD by the Hūṇa (Hun) king Mihirakula, Buddhism revived but moved east, where it flourished for a time under the Buddhist Pāla kings (8th–12th centuries AD). These kings continued to protect the monastic centres (*mahāvihāras*), building such new centres as Odantapurī, near Nālandā, and establishing a system of supervision for all such institutions. Under the Pālas, Tantrism (*i.e.*, Vajrayāna) became the dominant sect. Adepts of this sect, called *siddhas*, identified Nirvāṇa with the passions, maintaining that one could "touch the deathless element with his body." Though some of its practices seemed excessive, scholars of this school sought to revalorize some of the most archaic elements in Indian religion, by means of the techniques of Yogācāra and the philosophy of the Mādhyamika school. During this period, the university of Nālandā became a centre for the study of Tantra and the practice of Tantric magic and rituals. Under the Pāla kings, contacts with China decreased as Indians began to turn their attention to Tibet and Southeast Asia.

Causes for the decline

Scholars do not know all of the factors that contributed to the disappearance of Buddhism from India. Some have maintained that Buddhism was so tolerant of other faiths that it was simply reabsorbed by the dominant Hindu tradition. This did occur, although Indian Mahāyānists occasionally displayed a hostile attitude toward *bhakti* and Hinduism in general. Buddhism in India, having become mainly a monastic movement, probably paid little heed to the laity. Some monasteries became wealthy enough to have slaves and hired labourers to care for the monks and tend the lands they owned. Thus, after the Muslim invaders sacked the Indian monasteries in the 12th century AD, Buddhism became a minority in India. After the destruction of the monasteries, the Buddhist laity showed little interest in restoring the "Way."

In India, Buddhism began to spread under the Maurya dynasty from its place of origin in Magadha and Kośala. The next major Buddhist centres to arise were probably Mathurā and Ujjayinī to the west. About 100 years after the demise of the Buddha, invitations were supposedly sent out for the Council at Vaiśālī to such far-off places as Patheya, Avanti, Kauśāmbī, Kanauj, and Sankasya. Buddhism lost its royal patronage with the rise of the Śuṅgas, but by this time the religion had won a popular footing, as is witnessed by the Kārlī caves and the Sāñchī and Bharhūt *stūpas*, all built during the Śuṅga-Kāṇva period (185–28 BC). It was also at this time that King Menander and many Yavanas (Greeks) living in northwest India are said to have been converted. By the 1st century AD, Buddhism flourished under King Kaniṣka in Afghanistan, Bactria, Kashgar, Yarkand, Khotan, and Kashmir. At this time, the religion was spreading throughout Central Asia. During the first Christian centuries the Chinese became acquainted with the "Way" of the Buddha.

Missionaries had been sent out under King Aśoka in the 3rd century BC to Ceylon and Southeast Asia. In the latter area, the Mon peoples were among the first to adopt Buddhism, later transmitting the faith to their conquerors, the Burmese, Khmer, and Thai. Buddhism probably passed from India to Southeast Asia both by land, through Assam, and by sea. Another line of penetration, more difficult to reconstruct, ran from Central Asia through southern China down into Southeast Asia. Such peoples as the Thai were already familiar with Buddhism by the time they arrived in the peninsula in the 9th century AD. Mahāyāna was introduced in the southern part of the peninsula, in the kingdom of Funan in the 5th century AD, and passed to the Khmer by the 6th century. Before the 5th century, Buddhism had penetrated as far as Java and Sumatra.

In the north, Mahāyāna spread from China to Korea by the 4th century AD. From Korea it was introduced in Japan by the 6th century AD, and, by the 7th century, it had been introduced in Tibet.

BUDDHISM IN CENTRAL ASIA AND CHINA

Developments in Central Asian kingdoms. The spread of Buddhism from India to China through Central Asia is still not completely understood by historians. In the Tarim Basin in Central Asia, there was a confusing welter of languages, religions, and cultures, and, as the new religion passed through this area, it took on a new look. Some Mahāyānist *sūtras* were probably written or edited here. Shamanism, Zoroastrianism (an Iranian religion founded by Zoroaster, a *c.*-7th–6th-century-BC prophet), Nestorian Christianity (an Eastern heretical church that

Syncretistic developments

did not accept the orthodox decrees of the Council of Chalcedon, 451), and, later, Islām all penetrated these lands. There is evidence of some degree of syncretism between Buddhism and Manichaeism, an Iranian dualistic religion that was founded in the 3rd century AD. Some of the Mahāyāna *bodhisattvas*, such as Amitābha, Avalokiteśvara, Mañjuśrī, and Kṣitigarbha, may have been inspired, in part, by Zoroastrian influence. The missionary expansion of northern Indian schools into Central Asia was greatly aided by the support given by the Indo-Scythian King Kaniṣka (?78–103 AD) of the Kuṣāṇa (Kushan) dynasty. In addition to purportedly calling together a Buddhist council, he also patronized the art of Gandhāra, an Indian kingdom now in Pakistan, which had introduced Persian and Greek elements into Buddhist iconography. By the 1st century BC, Buddhism had probably been introduced in Eastern Turkistan, where there were numerous Indian colonies. According to tradition, a son of Aśoka founded the kingdom of Khotan around 240 BC. The grandson of this king supposedly introduced Buddhism in Khotan, where it became the state religion. In the northern part of Chinese Turkistan, Buddhism spread from Kucha to the kingdoms of Agnideśa (Karashahr), Kao-ch'ang (Turfan), and Bharuka (Aksu). Even after the decline of these states, Buddhism continued to flourish under the patronage of the Uighur Turks until the 11th century. Chinese travellers noted that Hīnayānists were strongest in Turfan, Shanshan, Kashgar, and Kucha, and Mahāyāna was found in Yarkand and Khotan. In some places both were to be found. After the rise of Islām (7th century AD) and the decline of the T'ang dynasty (618–907) in China, Central Asia ceased to be the important crossroads of Indian and Chinese culture it once had been.

Developments in China. Though there are reports of Buddhists in China as early as the 3rd century BC, Buddhism was not actively propagated in that country until the early centuries of the Christian Era. Tradition has it that Buddhism was introduced after the Han emperor Ming (AD 58–76) had a dream of a flying golden deity that was interpreted as a vision of the Buddha. Accordingly, the Emperor dispatched emissaries to India who subsequently returned to China with the *Sūtra in Forty-two Sections*, which was deposited in a temple outside the capital of Lo-yang. In actuality, Buddhism entered China gradually, first through Central Asia and, later, by way of the Malay Archipelago (around the 6th–7th centuries AD).

Buddhism during the Han dynasty (206 BC–AD 220). The Buddhism that first became popular in China during the Han dynasty was deeply coloured with magical practices, making it congruent with popular Chinese Taoism (a combination of folk beliefs and practices and philosophy). Instead of the doctrine of no-soul, early Chinese Buddhists taught the indestructability of the soul. Nirvāṇa became a kind of immortality. They also taught the theory of *karma*, the values of charity and compassion, and the need to suppress the passions. Until the end of the Han dynasty, there was a virtual symbiosis between Taoism and Buddhism and a common propagation of the means for attaining immortality through various ascetic practices. It was widely believed that Lao-tzu, the founder of Taoism, had been reborn in India as the Buddha. Many Chinese emperors worshipped both Lao-tzu and the Buddha on the same altar. The Buddhist *sūtras* that were translated first into Chinese—namely those dealing with such topics as breath control and mystical concentration—utilized a Taoist vocabulary to make the Buddhist faith intelligible to the Chinese. After the Han period, in the north of China, Buddhist monks were often used by non-Chinese emperors for their political–military counsel as well as for their skill in magic. At the same time, in the south, Buddhism began to penetrate the philosophical and literary circles of the gentry. One of the most important contributions to the growth of Buddhism in China during this period was the work of translation. The most important of the early translators was the learned monk Kumārajīva, who, before he was brought from Tibet in AD 401, had studied the Hindu Vedas, the occult sciences, and astronomy, not to mention both the Hīnayāna and Mahāyāna *sūtras*. His translations paved the way for the rise of the Chinese school of Mādhyamika (San-lun, or the Three Treatises, school).

Developments during the 6th century. In the 6th century, an important school arose in China that sought to integrate the various schools and *sūtras* of Buddhism. The T'ien-t'ai sect (a rationalist school of thought), under the leadership of Chih-i, sought to arrange the bewildering plethora of *sūtras* according to "five periods and eight teachings" of the Buddha. The effect of this was to demonstrate that these teachings had evolved from the "simple" truths of Hīnayāna to the more "advanced" insights of Mahāyāna. The highest wisdom was the recognition that in every particle of dust, in every moment of thought, the whole universe is contained.

Origins of T'ien-t'ai and Pure Land Buddhism

At about the same time, the school of Amitābha pietism, known as Pure Land Buddhism, was also making progress in China. In India, believers in the devotional cult that emphasized the worship of Amitābha (Chinese O-mi-t'o) Buddha taught that one can win rebirth in the Pure, or Happy, Land after death by various methods, such as (1) hearing the name of Amitābha, (2) by arousing the thought of Enlightenment and meditating as few as ten times on Amitābha, or (3) by showing a simple desire to be born in the Western Paradise (Sukhāvatī, or "Happy Land"). Thus, one had to cooperate with the "other-power" of Amitābha—it was not simply a matter of "salvation by faith alone." In China, the Pure Land school emphasized what it called the "easy path," one that was appropriate for what it regarded as the "latter days" of the *dharma*, which, it was widely believed, began around AD 550. Coming after the age of the "True Dharma" and that of the "Counterfeit Dharma," this final age was regarded as a period of decadence during which the earlier "path of the saints" had become too difficult for men to follow. According to one of the leaders of the Pure Land school, Shan-tao (7th century), the "primary act" that would lead to rebirth in the western paradise was the recitation of the name of O-mi-t'o. Nevertheless, "secondary acts," such as meditation, *sūtra* chanting, and singing, should also be practiced. Primitive Buddhism had generally emphasized "self-power," as can be seen in such important sayings of the Buddha as, "Be ye lamps *unto yourselves*, be ye a refuge *unto yourselves*." The "other-power" of O-mi-t'o taught by Pure Land Buddhism was based on the doctrine of *pariṇāmanā*, or the transfer of merits from a Buddha or *bodhisattva* to a sentient being. This kind of "pietism" was deeply influenced by the folk tradition. Under the influence of Tantra, Pure Land's principal *bodhisattva*, Avalokiteśvara, was transformed into a feminine deity and was homologized with the Tibetan mother-goddess, White Tara. This *bodhisattva* was known as Kuan-yin in China and as Kannon in Japan.

Developments during the T'ang dynasty (618–907). The golden age of Buddhism in China occurred during the T'ang dynasty. Though the T'ang emperors were usually Taoists themselves, they tended to favour Buddhism, which had become extremely popular. Under the T'ang, the government extended its control over the monasteries and the ordination and legal status of monks. From this time forward, the Chinese monk styled himself simply *ch'en*, or "a subject." This new age saw the rise of several new Buddhist schools in China—San-lun (Three Treatises school), Fa-hsiang (Dharma-characteristic), Hua-yen (Flowery Splendour), and Pure Land under Shan-tao. There was a great expansion in the number of Buddhist monasteries and temple lands. This was also the age of many pilgrimages to India, heroic journeys that greatly enriched Buddhism in China both by the *sūtras* and the spiritual and intellectual inspiration brought back from "the Country of the Elephant."

The Ch'an sect—better known in the West by its Japanese name, Zen—traces its history back to Bodhidharma, who came from India to Canton in 470 and then went to North China in 520. It is said that he was able to meditate so deeply that once, while facing a wall in meditation for nine years, his legs fell off, and that he once cut off his eyelids to prevent them from disturbing his meditation. Ch'an, or Zen, combines the metaphysics of Śūnyavāda and Vajrayāna (especially their emphasis on the Void and the identity of *saṃsāra* and Nirvāṇa) with the doctrine of sudden Enlightenment taught by the Chinese monk Tao-sheng in the 5th century. Ch'an was violently antitraditional, insisting that awakening (*wu;* Japanese *satori*) had nothing to do with reciting scriptures. The Ch'an master I hsüan told his disciples,

Origins and teachings of Ch'an, or Zen, Buddhism

> kill everything that stands in your way. If you should meet the Buddha, kill the Buddha. If you should meet the Patriarchs [of Ch'an], kill the Patriarchs. If you should meet the *arhats* on your way, kill them too.

In the Lin-chi branch of Ch'an, the disciple was subjected to beatings and verbal paradoxes called *kung-an* (*kōan* in Japanese). The Ts'ao-tung branch, however, emphasized "sitting in meditation." Though early Ch'an seems to have admitted there could be stages of Enlightenment, the school gradually began to emphasize a sudden awakening. In contrast to other Buddhist monks, Ch'an monks engaged in physical labour. They had the rule: "one day no work, one day no food." This had the fortunate result of making them less dependent on the rulers and laity of China and may be the reason why they were the only sect to survive the persecution of Buddhism in 845 in fairly good stead, when 4,600 Buddhist temples, 40,000 shrines, and 260,500 monks and nuns succumbed to a governmental proscription.

Developments during the Sung dynasty (960–1279). During the Sung dynasty, Ch'an had a decisive impact on landscape painting. Artists used flowers, rivers, and trees, executed with sudden deft strokes, as symbols of the flux and emptiness at the bottom of all things. The bamboo was a typical symbol of this sort, its straight, hard wood representing rectitude, its hollow centre, the Void.

As Buddhism spread through China, it naturally absorbed the spirit of the people. Its genius, compared with that of Indian Buddhism, was pragmatic and this-worldly. Monasteries operated oil presses and general stores, maintained roads, planted trees, and indulged in commerce and moneylending. In the face of the opposition it met from the Chinese family system, Buddhists could spread the ideal of celibacy only by emphasizing the merit that a monk brought to his whole family. In China, the comparatively democratic, or anarchic, Indian *saṅgha* was gradually transformed into a monastic system rigidly controlled by the state. Monks were granted their ordination certificates in government offices staffed by Confucian bureaucrats. More important, however, were the changes made in the basic symbols and ideas of the religion: the affirmation of the soul, belief in countless Buddha-worlds and Buddhas, the harmonization of the various sects (in T'ien-t'ai), and the emphasis on an easy or sudden Enlightenment (Pure Land and Ch'an). These tendencies seem to reflect the general tendency of the Chinese to concretize the abstract and harmonize the contradictory.

BUDDHISM IN KOREA AND JAPAN

Developments in Korea. Buddhism was first introduced into Korea when that peninsula was still divided into the three kingdoms of Paekche, Koguryŏ, and Silla. After Buddhism was brought to the northern kingdom of Koguryŏ from China in the 4th century, it gradually spread throughout the other Korean kingdoms. As often happened, the new faith was first accepted by the court and then extended to the people. After the unification of the country by the kingdom of Silla in the 660s, Buddhism began to flourish throughout Korea. The monk Wonhyo (flourished 7th century) was one of the most impressive scholars and reformers of his day. He was married and taught a kind of "ecumenical" version of Buddhism that included all branches and sects. He tried to use music, literature, and dance to express the meaning of Buddhism. Another scholar of the Silla era was Uisang, who went to China and returned to spread the Hwaom sect in Korea. The Chinese Ch'an sect (Zen) was introduced in the 8th century and, by absorbing the Korean versions of Huayen, T'ien-t'ai, and Pure Land, gradually became the dominant school of Buddhism in Korea, as it did in Vietnam.

Early Korean Buddhism was characterized by a this-worldly attitude. It emphasized the pragmatic, nationalistic, and aristocratic aspects of the faith. Still, an indigenous tradition of shamanism influenced the development of popular Buddhism throughout the centuries. Buddhist monks danced, sang, and performed the rituals of shamans. During the Koryŏ (Koryŭ) period that followed (935–1392), Korean Buddhism reached its zenith, but then began to decline. During the first part of this period, the Korean Buddhist community was active in the publication of the famous *Tripitaka Koreana*, one of the most inclusive editions of the Buddhist *sūtras* up to that time. After 25 years in research, a monk by the name of Uich'on published an outstanding three-volume bibliography of Buddhist literature. Uich'on also sponsored the growth of the T'ien-t'ai sect in Korea. He emphasized the need for cooperation between Ch'an and the other "Teaching" schools of Korean Buddhism. Toward the end of this period, Buddhism began to suffer from internal corruption and external persecution, especially that promoted by the Neo-Confucianists. The government now began to put limits on the privileges of the monks, and Confucianism replaced Buddhism as the religion of the state. Though the Yi dynasty (1392–1910) continued these restrictions, Buddhist monks and laymen fought bravely against the invasion of the Japanese armies under Toyotomi Hideyoshi (1537–98) in 1592 and 1596. In the decade before the annexation of Korea by Japan (1910), some effort was made to unify Korean Buddhism. These efforts, as well as the subsequent efforts of Buddhist "missionaries" from Japan, were largely in vain.

Characteristics of early Korean Buddhism

Developments in Japan. *Introduction of Buddhism to Japan.* Though Buddhism in China sent its roots down into the subsoil of the family system, in Japan it found anchorage in the nation itself. The Buddhism that was initially introduced into Japan in the 6th century from Korea was regarded as a talisman (charm) for the protection of the country. The new religion was accepted by the powerful Soga clan but was rejected by others, thus causing controversies that resembled the divisions caused by the introduction of Buddhism in Tibet. In both countries, some believed that the introduction of Buddhist statues had been an insult to the native deities, resulting in plagues and natural disasters. Only gradually were such feelings overcome. Though the Buddhism of the Soga clan was largely magical, under the influence of Prince Shōtoku, who became regent of the nation in 593, Buddhism recovered part of the religious depths that it had lost in its initial transmission to Japan. Shōtoku lectured on various scriptures that emphasized the ideals of the layman and monarch, and he composed a "Seventeen Article Constitution" in which Buddhism was adroitly mixed with Confucianism as the spiritual foundation of the state. In later times, he was widely regarded as the incarnation of the *bodhisattva* Avalokiteśvara.

Early sectarian developments. During the Nara period (710–784), Buddhism actually became the religion of the state. Emperor Shōmu actively propagated the faith, making Nara—with its "Great Buddha" statue (Daibutsu)—the national cult centre. Provincial temples (*kokubunji*) made the system effective at the local level. The Kegon sect (the Japanese version of the Chinese Hua-yen)—a sect that emphasized the doctrine of the interpenetration of all things—provided the ideology for the new Buddhist state. During the Nara period there were six different sects that were active. Two of these schools were of Hīnayāna extraction: Kusha, a Sarvāstivādin sect based on Vasubandhu's *Abhidharmakośa* ("Treasury of Higher Law"), and Jōjitsu, a Sautrāntika school, which made use of Harivarman's *Satyasiddhi* ("Completion of Truth"). Sanron was the Japanese version of the Chinese Three Treatises school (San-lun) that was based, as the name implies, on three fundamental texts: the *Mādhyamika-śāstra* ("Treatise on the Middle Way"), the *Śata-śāstra* ("One-hundred Verses Treatise"), and the *Dvādaśa-dvāra*

Sects active during the Nara period

("Twelve Gates"). The numerous texts of the Hossō sect were summarized in the *Vijñaptimātratāsiddhi* ("Completion of Mere Ideation") by Dharmapala. Kegon (similar to the Hwaom sect in Korea) was a cosmotheistic sect, emphasizing that every existence in the universe can commune with the cosmic soul embodied in the Buddha's person, which concentrated on the *Avataṃsakasūtra* ("Wreath Scripture"). The Ritsu school was mostly concerned with maintaining the *vinaya* discipline. Except for Kegon and Hossō, these schools were merely academic alternatives. At this time, the ideal of universal salvation, taught by the *Lotus Sūtra*, and emphasis on the role of the layman, as taught in the *Vimalakīrti-sūtra*, were officially propagated. It soon became obvious to the throne that ecclesiastics were becoming too active in politics. During the reign of Shōmu's daughter, the monk Dōkyō, who was acting as her regent (or "king of the *dharma*"), tried to become emperor. Only the resistance of the aristocracy saved Japan from becoming a Buddhist theocracy on the order of Tibet. Partly because of this pressure from the monastic community, the court decided to move to Heian-kyō (Kyōto) in 794.

In 804 the monk Saichō was sent to China and returned to Japan later to preach the doctrines of T'ien-t'ai (Japanese Tendai). Though the Hossō sect had taught that there were some who could not be saved, Tendai stressed a gospel of universal salvation. The nationalistic overtones of Japanese Buddhism continued to be heard in the new schools of the Heian period. Tendai's monastic complex on Mt. Hiei was known as the "Chief Seat of the Buddhist Religion for Ensuring the Security of the Country." Shingon Buddhism was a form of Tantrism that was introduced into Japan by the monk Kūkai in the early 9th century. Shingon (True Word) Buddhism emphasizes the unity of the believer with the Buddha as he performs various esoteric rites. The two *maṇḍalas* (picture-charts, or cosmoplans) called the "thunder-bolt-element-circle" and the "womb-element-circle" are of primary importance in Shingon Buddhism. With Tendai and Shingon, Dual Shintō, the joint worship of the Shintō gods (*kami*) and Buddhist deities and Buddhas, began.

Shingon Buddhism

Development of Japanese Pure Land sects. Though Japanese Amida (Sanskrit Amitābha) pietism can be traced back to Hui-yüan (333–416) in China, it was Ennin (794–864) who first brought the practice of *nembutsu* (recitation of Amida's name) to Japan. The Tendai sect nourished the new piety and the Tendai monk Kūya (903–972) taught a communal recitation of Amida's name. His movement was later restored by another shamanistic Amidist, Ippen (1239–89). This resulted in the formation of the Ji (Times) sect, so called because it stressed the recitation of the hymn of Shan-tao six times every day. Another Amidist leader was Ryōnin (1072–1132), who founded the Yūzū Nembutsu (All-Permeating Amida Buddha) sect, in which the teachings of the *Lotus Sūtra* were blended with Amida piety. The popular Shugen-dō (mountain religion) became deeply impregnated with the practice of *nembutsu*, which was regarded as a prophylactic against evil spirits (*goryō*). Thus, long before the Kamakura period (1192–1333), when it became truly popular, the cult of Amida had taken root in the religious subsoil of Japanese folk piety. The Pure Land school (Jōdo-shū) was systematized in Japan by Hōnen (1133–1212), and his follower, Shinran (1173–1262), gave a new and radical emphasis to the teachings of the sect. Shinran, who married and lived "neither as a monk nor layman," began a movement that has been compared to the Lutheran Reformation in Christianity. Rejecting the entire merit-*karma* way of thinking, Shinran taught that men could be saved even by a single invocation of Amida. But even then, he maintained, it was Amida who inspired the invocation. This marked what could be called the high point of *tariki* (salvation by faith in other powers) in the history of Buddhism. In the 15th century. Rennyo shaped Shinran's teachings and followers into a sect that came to be called True Pure Land (Jōdo-Shinshū). This sect had its own armies and extensive temple lands. In the 20th century the Pure Land sects have more adherents than any other Buddhist group in Japan.

Development of Nichiren and Zen Buddhism. In the 13th century, Japanese Buddhism produced its one "prophet," the monk Nichiren (1222–82). This charismatic and abrasive leader taught that salvation could be won by reciting the words *namu Myōhōrengekyō* ("salutation to the *Lotus Sūtra*") and did not hesitate to attack other, contradictory doctrines. the fulfillment of his prediction of the Mongol attacks on Japan brought him fame throughout the country. Much of his nationalistic spirit lives on today in the followers of Sōka-gakkai (Value Creation Society).

During the Kamakura period Zen (Chinese Ch'an) began to be popular in Japan. The Lin-chi (Japanese Rinzai) school was introduced by the monk Eisai (1141–1215), who also wrote a tract called "Propagate Zen, Protect the Country." In the 13th century, Dōgen (1200–53) introduced the Ts'ao-tung school of Zen (Sōtō, in Japanese) with its emphasis on "sitting in meditation" (za-zen). The Fuke sect, a community of wandering monks, was founded by Kakushin in 1255. Zen soon became associated with the most important facets of medieval Japanese art and culture, infusing them with its own unique spirit. Because it taught its followers a direct and unhesitating style of life, Zen became popular with Japan's military class. Later, in 1654, the Ōbaku school of Zen was established by the Chinese priest Yin-yüan Lung-ch'i (Japanese Ingen Ryūki). This school showed similarities to Rinzai, but also made use of Amidist practices.

During the chaos of the Ashikaga period (1338–1573), many Buddhist monasteries took up arms to protect themselves and to extend their holdings. An exception to this was the Zen sects that were active even during this period, developing and refining Japanese culture and aesthetics and introducing Neo-Confucianism to Japan—a doctrine that would later turn upon Buddhist patrons with a vengeance. Christianity, another rival of Japanese Buddhism, was introduced in 1549 by Francis Xavier.

Developments during the Tokugawa period (1603–1867). Under the Tokugawa shogunate (a feudal system), Buddhism became an arm of the government. Temples were used for registering the populace—one way of preventing the spread of Christianity that the feudal government regarded as a political menace. This association with the Tokugawa regime made Buddhism quite unpopular at the beginning of the Meiji period (1868–1912), at least among the elite. At that time, in order to set up Shintō as the new state religion, it was necessary for Japan's new ruling oligarchy to separate Shintō from Buddhism. This led to the confiscation of temple lands and the unfrocking of many Buddhist priests. During the period of ultranationalism (*c.* 1930–45), Buddhist thinkers called for uniting the East in one great "Buddhaland" under the tutelage of Japan. After the war, however, Buddhist groups, new and old alike, began to emphasize Buddhism as a religion of peace and brotherhood. During the postwar period, the greatest visible activity among Buddhists has been among the "New Religions" such as Sōka-gakkai and Risshō-Kōsei-kai (Society for Establishing Righteousness and Friendly Relations). During this period, Sōka-gakkai entered politics with the same vigour it had traditionally shown in the conversion of individuals. Because of its highly ambiguous but conservative ideology, the Sōka-gakkai-based political party (the Kōmei-tō) is regarded with both suspicion and fear by many Japanese. In spite of a certain measure of ecumenical cooperation between some of the "New Religions," Japan today abounds with a plurality of Buddhist sects as does no other Buddhist country in the world.

Buddhism as a state religion

BUDDHISM IN TIBET AND THE HIMALAYAN KINGDOMS

Developments in Tibet. Tantra was not very important in China or Japan, though it did exist in these countries. In Tibet, however, it played a more important role. Buddhism was introduced in Tibet by the 7th century, but, only by the middle of the following century, with the arrival of Padmasambhava, a Tantric master from India, did the religion begin to dominate the indigenous shamanistic practices called Bon. It was at this time that the Tibetans decided to follow Indian rather than Chi-

Grand finale to a Sōka-gakkai gathering in Tokyo, 1967. Great numbers of followers make formations on the field, while others in the stands hold placards spelling out "world peace."

By courtesy of Soka Gakkai, Tokyo

nese Buddhism. A curious mixture of shamanism, Tantrism, and Indian Mādhyamika gradually became the core of what came to be known erroneously as Lamaism, the religion of the "superior ones." A persecution of Buddhism under King Glang-dar-ma in the 9th century was a great setback for Tibetan Buddhism, and it was not until the 11th century, with the arrival of the Indian monk Atīśa, that the religion began to prosper once again. During the 11th century the famous Sa-skya monastery of the "Yellow Hats" sect rose to prominence.

The role of the Lamas

Under the Mongols, the abbots of this monastery became the theocratic rulers of Tibet. Known as Dalai Lamas (Great Ocean Lamas), these rulers were regarded as incarnations of Avalokiteśvara. The head of the Tashilhunpo monastery, west of Lhasa, was known as the Paṇchen Lama (Wise and Great Lama) and was thought to be the incarnation of Amitābha. Unlike the Dalai Lama, the Paṇchen Lama was thought to be merely a spiritual ruler. Tibetan monasteries were controlled by aristocratic abbots who were free to marry and pass along their monastic possessions to their sons. Monks often played the role of warriors and the monasteries themselves became armed fortresses. The history of Tibetan Buddhism is filled with intrigue and the lust for power. The Manchus in the 18th century and, after them, the Nationalist Chinese, the Chinese Communists, and the British have all tried to exploit the division of power between the Paṇchen and Dalai Lamas for their own ends. In 1959, after the Dalai Lama fled to India, the Chinese Communists took over his temporal powers.

Developments in the Himalayan kingdoms. *Nepal.* Buddhism in Nepal has been influenced both by India and Tibet. Though the Buddha was born in the southern part of the country at Lumbinī, about 15 miles (24 kilometres) from Kapilavastu, the Buddhist religion seems to have been actively propagated only later, probably under Aśoka. By the 8th century AD, Nepal had fallen into the cultural orbit of Tibet. A few centuries later, as a result of the Muslim invasions of India, both Hindus (such as the Brahmanic Gurkha aristocracy) and Buddhists took refuge in the country. In modern times, Buddhist prayer wheels and flags are reminders of the direct influence of Tibetan Buddhism. The Indian heritage is especially evident in the caste system that embraces Buddhists and non-Buddhists alike The Siva *liṅga* (phallic symbol), so popular in Nepalese Hinduism, is regarded by Buddhists as the lotus in which Ādi-Buddha was revealed to Mañjuśrī and the early Buddhas.

Bhutan. In Bhutan, a Tibetan Lama introduced Buddhism and a Tibetan style of hierarchical theocracy in the 17th century AD. The Duk-pa ('Brug-pa) sect of Buddhism that arose in Bhutan was a kind of "unreformed" Lamaism. The Tibetan Bka'-brgyud-pa sect, which stressed the magical benefits of living in caves, had a direct influence on Bhutanese Buddhists. Few monks in this country are celibate.

Sikkim. In Sikkim, most of the population originally came from Nepal and preserved their ancient Nepalese castes (or tribal identity). Tibetan and Bhutanese tribes are also present, having brought with them their native religious traditions. In the 17th century AD, Tibetans usurped the government, with the result that even the aboriginal Lepchās were influenced by Tibetan Buddhism.

BUDDHISM IN CEYLON AND SOUTHEAST ASIA

Developments in Ceylon. In Ceylon, Theravāda Buddhism took shape as a complete religiosocial system, and from Ceylon, beginning in the 11th century, a reformed Theravāda Buddhism spread to Southeast Asia. In spite of its reputation for staunch orthodoxy, the history of Theravāda in Ceylon was one of constant struggle against Hinduism, Tantrism, and various types of Mahāyāna. Though the Mahāyānist influence was strongest in the 4th century, by the 8th century esoteric Buddhism had become powerful enough on the island to have some impact on the development of Mantrayāna in both India and China. Under Tamil kings from South India, Sinhalese Buddhism was threatened with reabsorption by both Hinduism and Mantrayāna from the 9th through the 11th centuries. Three times in the history of the island the valid Theravāda ordination lineage had to be renewed by foreign ecclesiastics (in the 11th and 15th centuries, when monks were brought to Ceylon from Burma, and again in the 18th century, when Thai monks from Ayutthaya restored the succession).

Transmission of Buddhism by Mauryan missionaries

Buddhism took root in Ceylon with the arrival of Aśoka's son Mahinda and his six companions. Sent as missionaries by the Mauryan emperor, these travellers converted King Devānampiya Tissa and many of the nobility. Under King Tissa, the Mahāvihāra monastery was built, an institution that was to become the centre of Sinhalese orthodoxy. After Tissa's death (*c.* 207 BC) Ceylon fell into the hands of the Tamils until the time of Duṭṭhagāmaṇī (101–77 BC), a descendant of Tissa, who overthrew the Tamil king Eḷāra. During this time, as a reaction to the threat posed by the Tamils, Buddhism and Sinhalese nationalism became closely intertwined. Again, it was probably because of this danger that the Pāli canon was first written down under King Vaṭṭagāmaṇī Abhaya in the 1st century BC. This king also built the Abhayagiri monastery, the main centre of the various Mahāyāna movements in Ceylon. These heterodox tendencies, which provoked a popular rebellion, were openly supported by King Mahāsena (AD 276–303). Under Mahāsena's son, Śrī Meghavarṇa, the "Tooth of the Buddha" was brought to Abhayagiri and made the national palladium. Next to the Pāli canon itself, the Theravāda faith was probably most clearly spelled out by the scholar Buddhaghosa in the 5th century AD. Studying a Mahāvihāra, Buddhaghosa translated Sinhalese works into Pāli and wrote exegetical works of his own. In the 11th century, King Vijayabāhu sought to reform the *saṅgha* by appointing a *saṅgharāja* (ruler of the order) to rule over all monastics on the island and by re-establishing the valid line of ordination.

In modern times, Ceylon fell prey to the Western colonial powers (to the Portuguese in 1505–1658, the Dutch in 1602–1796, and finally the British in 1796–1947). Under King Kittisiri Rājasiha (1747–81) the ordination lineage was once again renewed by monks dispatched from Thailand. The monastic community in Ceylon (now Sri Lanka) is divided into three major bodies: (1) the Siam Nikaya, founded in the 18th century, a conservative and wealthy sect that admits only members of the Goyigama, the highest Sinhalese caste; (2) the Amarapura sect, founded in the 19th century, which has opened its ranks to members of lower castes; and (3) the reformed splinter group from the Siam Nikaya called the Ramanya sect. Only the Amarapura and Ramanya sects have been active in politics, the Siam sect becoming involved only when its own interests have been threatened.

Characteristics of Ceylonese Buddhism

As conservative as it may be, the Theravāda tradition of Ceylon cannot be regarded as "pure" Buddhism. It includes the worship of Hindu gods as well as local spirits. The main-line tradition that emerged on the island was characterized by an emphasis on the historical person of the founder (and not on his transcendent or cosmological nature). As for religious practice, the *bodhisattva* ideal never seemed to detract from the emphasis laid upon being a disciple (*śrāvaka*) of the Buddha. By regarding them as a means of recalling the life of the founder, images and relics were made "theologically" acceptable. The *dharma* became equated with the new Pāli canon. Because of the *dharma*-power they contained, the scriptures were often chanted as spells to ward off evil. One of the most outstanding features of Sinhalese Buddhism has been its nationalistic spirit. The Sinhalese Buddhist kings perpetuated the ideals of Aśokan kingship. They also enlarged this ideology by promoting the popular homologization of the figure of the Buddhist king with the Buddha and *bodhisattva*. In particular, it was Maitreya (the only *bodhisattva* generally recognized by Theravādins) who was most frequently associated with the king.

Developments in Southeast Asia. The peoples of Southeast Asia have not been mere satellites of the more powerful Indian and Chinese civilizations. On the contrary, the cultures that arose in these three vast areas might better be thought of as developments within a greater Austroasiatic civilization, sometimes referred to as "Asia of the monsoons." For this reason, the transmission of Buddhism and Hinduism to Southeast Asia can be regarded as the spread of the religious symbols of the more "advanced" elements within this Austroasiatic cluster to peoples sharing some of the basic religious presuppositions and traditions.

Chinese influence in the area was more or less limited to what is now North Vietnam (ancient Annam). In contrast to the Chinese penetration of the area, the Indian influence was spread peacefully, by merchants and missionaries. In the 2nd century BC India's trade routes in Central Asia had been cut off by the Romans, who, at the same time, showed an interest in purchasing spices, gold, and fine wood from Indian merchants. These merchants turned to Southeast Asia for these products. From that time until the beginning of the 14th century, there were close relations between India, Ceylon, and the Indianized states of Southeast Asia in both trade and culture.

Conversion of Burmese and Khmer peoples to Theravāda

Burma. In the region that is now central Thailand and southern Burma, the Mons were among the first to be influenced by Indian culture and Buddhism. They subsequently played an important role in the conversion of the Burmese and Khmer peoples to Theravāda. By the 3rd century AD, the Pyu, a Tibeto-Burmese tribe, had established themselves in Lower Burma and had made their capital, Śrī Kṣetra, a centre of Theravāda learning. In spite of inroads made by Mūla (fundamental)-Sarvāstivādin and Mahāyāna ideas, the Pyu kingdom remained a stronghold of Theravāda until its fall in the 9th century. In Upper Burma at this time, the Aris, a Tantric sect, flourished. The Mahāyāna *bodhisattva*s Avalokiteśvara, Maitreya, and Mañjuśrī were also known in this area. Under King Anawrahta (1044–77) Upper and Lower Burma were united in a new Theravāda state. Burmese Buddhism was soon troubled by a controversy over ordination that lasted for 300 years. One school held that its ordination pedigree, going back to missionaries sent out by Aśoka, was valid. Another insisted that only ordinations in the line of succession established by the Sinhalese monastery of Mahāvihāra should be recognized. King Dhammazedi (reigned 1472–92) settled the controversy in favour of the Sinhalese faction. This crucial decision contributed to the development of the conservative orthodoxy of Burmese Buddhism.

Thailand. The Thai, who had begun to move into Southeast Asia by the 9th century AD, originated in China, where they came into contact with Mahāyāna Buddhism. By the 12th and 13th centuries, they had come under the spell of the reformed Sinhalese form of Theravāda that was then sweeping through Southeast Asia. In the 13th century, Thai kingdoms were set up at Sukothai and Chiengmai, the capital of the Lan Na Thai kingdom. By the 14th century the Pāli tradition had been taken over from Sukothai, and, by the 16th century, Chiengmai had become a leading centre of the Theravāda. Under King Tiloka (reigned 1442–87), the "Emerald Buddha" was adopted as the national palladium (*cf.* the "Tooth of the Buddha" in Ceylon). In 1350 a powerful Thai kingdom arose at Ayutthaya. This kingdom conquered Angkor, the Khmer capital, in 1431, and from the conquered Khmer people the Thais of Ayutthaya absorbed elements from the Brahmanic tradition that continued to be an asset to Thai statecraft even in the kingdom of Bangkok established by King Rama I (reigned 1782–1809). The kingdom of Bangkok became the dominant Thai state after the fall of Ayutthaya to the Burmese in 1769.

Indochina. In Laos, Buddhist statues of Mahāyāna inspiration have been discovered dating from the 11th and 12th centuries AD. Initially, Laotian Buddhism came under the influence of the Khmers, and both Mahāyāna and Theravāda traditions were recognized. Later, in the 14th century, Theravāda became the dominant faith. In 1356, King Fa Ngum, at the prompting of his wife, invited a Theravāda mission from Cambodia to visit Laos.

At the southern extremity of the Indochinese Peninsula, one of the earliest known states was Funan. A Sanskrit variety of Hīnayāna was first introduced here. Later, under King Kaundinya Jayavarman in the 5th century, Hinduism and Mahāyāna were introduced. The Khmer kingdoms at Chenla (6th century) and at Angkor (9th century) inherited many items from the culture of Funan. At these two capitals Śaivism (worship of the Hindu god Śiva) was the basis of the state cult, though Vaiṣṇavism (worship of the Hindu god Viṣṇu) and Mahāyāna Buddhism were also to be found. In the 11th and 12th centuries Śaivism declined, and Vaiṣṇavism and Mahāyāna seemed to increase in strength (witness the Vaiṣṇava temple at Angkor Wat in Cambodia). Under Jayavarman VII (reign dates 1181–*c.* 1215, possibly as late as 1219) the power of the Khmer Empire reached its apex. A Brahmanic–Mahāyāna Buddhism became the foundation of the state. A radical change soon took place when the conquered Mons began to spread Theravāda (*c.* 1200–1350) among the Khmers. By the time of the capture of Angkor in 1431, the conversion of the Khmers to Theravāda seems to have been complete.

Vietnamese Buddhism

Vietnam is the only country in Southeast Asia where both Theravāda and Mahāyāna continue to exist side by side. Theravāda seems to have been introduced by the Khmer minority in the country and is still found mainly on the Cambodian border. The Mahāyāna sects were limited, for the most part, to varieties of Zen and Pure Land. The first *dhyāna*, or "meditation," school was introduced by Vinitaruci, an Indian monk who had come to Vietnam from China in the 6th century. In the 9th century a school of "wall meditation" was introduced by the Chinese monk Vo Ngon Thong. A third major Zen school was established in the 11th century by the Chinese monk Thao Durong. From 1414 to 1428, Buddhism in Vietnam was persecuted by the Chinese, who had again conquered the country. Tantrism, Taoism, and Confucianism were also filtering into Vietnam at this time. Even after the Chinese had been driven back, a Chinese-like bureaucracy closely supervised the Vietnamese monasteries. The clergy was divided between the highborn and Sinicized (Chinese-influenced), on the one hand, and those in the lower ranks who often were active in peasant uprisings.

Indonesia. With the help of Indian missionaries, such as the monk Guṇavarman, Buddhism had gained a foothold on Java well before the 5th century AD. The religion was also introduced at about this time in Sumatra, and, by the 7th century, the King of Śrīvijaya on the island was a Buddhist. When the Chinese traveller I-ching visited this kingdom in the 7th century, he noted that Hīnayāna was dominant in the area but that there were also a few Mahāyānists. It was also in the 7th century that the great scholar Dharmapala of Nālandā university visited Indonesia, or Suvarṇadvīpa as it was called. The Śailendra dynasty, which ruled over the Malay Peninsula and a large section of Indonesia from the 7th to the 9th century, promoted Mahāyāna and erected Buddhist monuments at Mendut, Kalasan, and Borobuḍur in Java. From the 7th century onward, Tantrism spread throughout Java and Sumatra, coming originally from Bengal. King Kertanagara of Java (reigned 1254–92) was especially devoted to Tantrism. Buddhism was also introduced in Bali and Borneo, but local variations of Hinduism ultimately dominated the religious life of these islands.

BUDDHISM IN THE LATE 19TH AND 20TH CENTURIES

Both the character of the various national and religious traditions and the kind of encounter experienced with Western colonial powers conditioned the response of Buddhism to the challenges of the modern age. The adequacy of this response and the strength of Buddhism in the various Asian cultures are difficult to measure, because the vitality of a religion cannot be measured in terms of its institutions alone and also because no accurate index of secularization is available. In some areas, such as in China, the historian is hindered by a simple lack of information, but he does know, however, that the Buddhist community suffered considerable damage during the rampages of the Red Guard (1966–69) especially in Tibet.

Of the Buddhist nations, only Thailand and Japan escaped colonization by Western powers. Thus, Buddhism could not help becoming involved in the struggle against colonialism and the creation of new polities all over Asia. In Ceylon there were only five ordained monks left after the expulsion of the Portuguese. Under the less fanatical Dutch and British, the Sinhalese began to convert to Christianity, often for pragmatic reasons. In the second half of the 19th century, Buddhism produced a counteroffensive movement led by Mohottivatte Gunananda, who studied the Christian Scriptures and the Western critics of Christianity and then challenged the Christian missionaries to debates. The Buddhist Theosophical Society, founded by Col. Henry S. Olcott, an American, in 1880, and the Maha Bodhi Society, founded in 1891 by the monk Dharmapala (David Hewavitarane), made significant contributions to the revival of Buddhism in Ceylon. Once again the Buddhist nationalism of the medieval kings became the inspiration of Sinhalese politics. After the British withdrawal from the island (1947), S.W.R.D. Bandaranaike, leader of the Sri Lanka Freedom Party, became prime minister in 1956 with the help of Buddhist nationalists. Unable to control the excessive demands of extremists, violence erupted between Buddhists and the Tamil minority (1958–59). Though monks campaigned for him during this election, disenchanted monks were also responsible for his assassination in 1959. He was succeeded by his wife, during whose regime (1960–65 and 1970–) Ceylon moved far to the left politically.

Influence of Western colonialism

Cambodia's prince Norodom Sihanouk and Burma's former prime minister U Nu have also been outstanding, if ultimately unsuccessful, Buddhist nationalists. In Ceylon and Southeast Asia, Buddhist politicians have leaned toward neutralism and have professed a religious commitment to peaceful coexistence. The Aśokan welfare state has been the model for Buddhist Socialism. In Japan, however, the Kōmei-tō, the political wing of Sōka-gakkai, has made accommodations with capitalism and an extreme form of nationalism.

In India, Buddhist politics is virtually synonymous with the name Bhimrao Ramji Ambedkar, leader of the untouchable, or scheduled, caste of Mahārāshtra. As early as 1935, Ambedkar had decided that he could never find justice for his people within Hinduism. Still, it was only in 1956, two months before his death, that Ambedkar, together with as many as 600,000 followers, converted to Buddhism at a mass conversion ceremony held at Nagpur. Since 1930, Ambedkar had regarded Gandhi as an enemy of the scheduled caste (Gandhi believed that India could not survive without a reformed "four caste" system, minus untouchables). Today, Ambedkar's Buddhism is often regarded as the external religious rhetorical form of his Republican Party.

Buddhists often have been forced into the political arena. In Vietnam, the Buddhist community was not politically activated until it was mistreated by the excessively partisan Roman Catholic and anti-Buddhist Ngo Dinh family. In 1963, the government forbade the flying of the Buddhist flag during the May 8 celebration of Buddha's birthday, though Roman Catholics were allowed to fly their flag. The riot that erupted because of this order was put down by well-armed government troops. Understandably, the coup against the Diem regime on November 1, 1963, was actively supported by militant Buddhists. Buddhists in this country have been divided between a moderate group led by Thich Tam Chau and a more militant wing led by Thich Tri Quang. Usually claiming to be politically neutral, the Buddhist call for peace has often been treated by the Saigon government as weakness in the face of Communism. Since 1963 there have been over 30 self-immolations of monks in South Vietnam protesting the ruin of their country.

In spite of its alleged otherworldliness, Buddhism, under certain circumstances, has contributed to the modernization of Asian cultures. In Thailand, Buddhist kings of the Chakri dynasty, together with a reform movement within the monastic community (the Thammayutika Nikaya), contributed strongly to the modernization of the country. Members of the Thammayutika sect have been able to control half of the key positions in the *saṅgha,* though they make up less than 5 percent of the total membership. In Ceylon and Southeast Asia, great efforts have been made to improve the content and relevance of monastic education.

Though poorly educated monks have lost respect among the Western-educated Buddhist elite, new movements have arisen that give the layman a greater religious role. Laymen's meditation groups have been formed, and in Japan powerful new sects, such as Sōka-gakkai and Risshō-Kōsei-kai, have developed as lay movements. The religious education of the layman has lately received more attention, as in the founding of the Buddhist Sunday School Movement in Thailand in 1958. The traditional virtues of the layman, such as compassion (*karuṇā*) and love (*mettā*), have been deemed to be more relevant in the modern world than virtues practiced in the cloister. Above all, the *bodhisattva* ideal has played a dominant role in Buddhist social thought.

Role of the laity in modern Buddhism

One of the great benefits of the World Fellowship of Buddhists, founded in 1950 by G.P. Malalasekera, has been the role it opened up to laymen. Under the auspices of this ecumenical movement, layman and monk, Mahāyānist and Theravādin, have enjoyed an unprecedented encounter. Parallel to the Buddhist ecumenical movement has been the consolidation of national Buddhist communities. Several Buddhist nations, especially Ceylon, Thailand, and Japan, have shown a new interest in Buddhist missions abroad. Probably the most ambitious undertaking of contemporary Buddhism was the sixth great Buddhist Council held in Rangoon, Burma, 1954–56, which, among other accomplishments, re-edited the sacred scriptures of Buddhism.

Some Buddhist writers have gone to great lengths to promote Buddhism as a rational, scientific alternative to the antinomies exposed in Western thought by the battles between Christian dogma and science. They have been quick to point out the Buddha's "empirical" attitudes, the Buddhist concepts of cause and effect, and the flux of elements in Buddhist metaphysics as anticipations of modern scientific views. Still, it cannot be said that Buddhism has generally come to grips with the intellectual problems posed by modern philosophy and science. There are exceptions to this, of course, such as the Zen philosophies of the late Nishida Kitarō (1870–1945) and Nishitani Keiji.

BIBLIOGRAPHY

Buddhism in general: Comparatively recent, concise but scholarly, are the following treatments of Buddhism in general: E. CONZE, *Buddhism: Its Essence and Development* (1951 and 1959); R.H. ROBINSON, *The Buddhist Religion: A Historical Introduction* (1970); and KENNETH K.S. CH'EN, *Buddhism: The Light of Asia* (1968). A helpful aid is E.

ZURCHER, *Buddhism: Its Origin and Spread in Words, Maps and Pictures* (1962). Older studies are H. OLDENBERG, *Buddha: Sein Leben, sein Lehre, sein Gemeinde* (1890; Eng. trans., *Buddha: His Life, His Doctrine, His Order*, 1882); and C.A.F. RHYS DAVIDS, *Buddhism: A Study of the Buddhist Norm* (1912). CHARLES ELIOT, *Hinduism and Buddhism: An Historical Sketch*, 3 vol. (1921, reprinted 1962), especially when considered together with his *Japanese Buddhism* (1935, reprinted 1959), comprises a major historical account of the whole of Buddhism in English. An important and scholarly study of the earlier development of doctrine is E.J. THOMAS, *The History of Buddhist Thought*, 2nd ed. (1951). GUY WELBON, *The Buddhist Nirvāna and Its Western Interpreters* (1968), traces and interprets the history of the West's attention to and study of Buddhism.

Buddhism in India: Among the various works on the life of the Buddha are E.J. THOMAS, *The Life of the Buddha in Legend and History*, 3rd rev. ed. (1949, reprinted 1969); and ALFRED FOUCHER, *La Vie de Bouddha*, (1949; abridged Eng. trans., *The Life of Buddha*, 1963). A.K. COOMARASWAMY wrote of this and other topics in Buddhism from a Hindu perspective in *Buddha and the Gospel of Buddhism* (1916, reprinted 1964). For a very good study of Buddha's life and the subsequent history, see SUKUMAR DUTT, *The Buddha and Five After-Centuries* (1957). Dutt's *Buddhist Monks and Monasteries of India* (1962), traces the early history of the *sangha*, especially on the basis of archaeological remains in India. For a study of yoga techniques in Buddhism, see the chapter by that title in MIRCEA ELIADE, *Le Yoga: immortalité et liberté* (1954; Eng. trans., *Yoga: Immortality and Freedom*, 1958). For materials and discussion of the early Buddhist councils and their effect upon the development of the various Buddhist schools, see ANDRE BAREAU, *Les Premiers conciles bouddhiques* (1955); E.J. THOMAS, *The History of Buddhist Thought* (1933); and LOUIS DE LA VALLEE POUSSIN, "Councils (Buddhist)," in vol. 4 of the *Encyclopaedia of Religion and Ethics*, ed. by JAMES HASTINGS. Indispensible for the development of doctrine is E. CONZE, *Buddhist Thought in India* (1962).

Theravāda Buddhism: For Buddhism in Ceylon, see WALPOLA RAHULA, *History of Buddhism in Ceylon: The Anuradhapura Period, 3rd century B.C.–10th Century A.C.* (1956). An important recent study of religion and society in Ceylon is H. BECHERT, *Buddhismus, Staat und Gesellschaft in den Ländern des Theravāda Buddhismus*, vol. 1, *Gerundlagen, Ceylon* (1966). For recent developments in Ceylon, see "Religious Revival and Cultural Nationalism," in W.H. WRIGGINS, *Ceylon: Dilemmas of a New Nation* (1960). For Southeast Asia, see GEORGE COEDES, *Les États hindouisés d'Indochine et d'Indonésie*, 3rd ed. (1964; Eng. trans., *The Indianized States of Southeast Asia*, 1968), and *Les Peuples de la Peninsule Indochinoise* (1966; Eng. trans., *The Making of Southeast Asia*, 1967), which discuss the impact both of Indian civilization and of Buddhism on this area of Asia. Many important studies of the relationship between Buddhism and society in particular Southeast Asian nations have recently appeared. For Burma, see especially E. SARKISYANZ, *Buddhist Backgrounds of the Burmese Revolution* (1965); DONALD E. SMITH, *Religion and Politics in Burma* (1965); and MELFORD E. SPIRO, *Buddhism and Society: A Great Tradition and Its Burmese Vicissitudes* (1970). Other valuable studies of Burmese Buddhism are NIHAR RAJAN-RAY, *An Introduction to the Study of Theravāda Buddhism in Burma* (1946); and KENNETH E. WELLS, *Thai Buddhism: Its Rites and Activities*, rev. ed. (1960). The best studies of Buddhism in Vietnam are in French; see especially essays by DURAND and MAI-THO-TRUYEN in *Présence du Bouddhisme*, ed. by R. DE BERVAL (1959). For a discussion of some contemporary problems of Asian Buddhism in general and Theravāda in particular, see ERNST BENZ, *Buddhas Wiederkehr und zie Zukunft Asiens* (1963; Eng. trans., *Buddhism or Communism: Which Holds the Future of Asia?*, 1965).

Mahāyāna Buddhism: For Mahāyāna Buddhism in China and its development from its earliest days to modern times, see KENNETH K.S. CH'EN, *Buddhism in China: A Historical Survey* (1964), which includes an extensive bibliography. For a thorough presentation of doctrinal development, see E. ZURCHER, *The Buddhist Conquest of China*, 2 vol. (1959), a superb study of the history of Chinese Buddhism until 400 AD. See also ARTHUR F. WRIGHT, *Buddhism in Chinese History* (1959), a lucidly written scholarly account. The philosophical ideas of Mahāyāna as these developed in the various sects of China and Japan are presented in JUNJIRO TAKAKUSU, *The Essentials of Buddhist Philosophy*, 3rd ed. (1956). For a presentation of a Japanese monk's acute observations of Buddhism in China in the 9th century, see E.O. REISCHAUER, *Ennin's Travels in T'ang China* (1955). HOLMES WELCH, *The Practice of Chinese Buddhism, 1900–1950* (1967), is an important study of contemporary Buddhist monasticism in China. ALICE GETTY's illustrated *The Gods of Northern Buddhism*, 2nd ed. (1928, reprinted 1962), is one of the best presentations of the history of the Buddhist icon in China, Tibet, Korea, and Japan. HEINRICH DUMOULIN, *Zen: Geschichte und Gestalt* (1959; Eng. trans., *A History of Zen Buddhism*, 1963), is an account of the history of the Zen school in both China and Japan. Of the many writings on Zen by D.T. SUZUKI, see especially his *Essays in Zen Buddhism*, 3 series (1927–61), and his *Zen and Japanese Culture* (1959). Two standard works include Buddhism in the course of a presentation of the range of religious history in Japan; they are M. ANESAKI, *History of Japanese Religion* (1930, reprinted 1963); and the more recent *Religion in Japanese History* by J.M. KITAGAWA (1966), which includes a bibliography of works in Japanese and Western languages.

Tibetan Buddhism: HELMUT HOFFMANN, *Die Religionen Tibets* (1956; Eng. trans., *The Religions of Tibet*, 1961), a scholarly and standard work, also treats the relationship between Buddhism and the older Bon religion of Tibet. W.Y. EVANS-WENTZ, a theosophist who lived and studied for years in Tibet, introduced some important and interesting Tibetan works to the West; see his *Tibetan Book of the Great Liberation* (1954) and *Tibetan Book of the Dead*, 3rd ed. (1960). See also DAVID L. SNELLGROVE, *Buddhist Himalaya: Travels and Studies in Quest of the Origins and Nature of Tibetan Religion* (1957) and *Himalayan Pilgrimage: A Study of Tibetan Religion by a Traveller Through Western Nepal* (1961); and GIUSEPPE TUCCI, *Tibetan Painted Scrolls*, 3 vol. (1949).

Translated sources: A translation from the Pāli texts is HENRY CLARKE WARREN, *Buddhism in Translations* (1896, reprinted 1963), old but still very useful. Another good source is *Buddhist Texts Through the Ages*, ed. by E. CONZE (1954). The *Edicts of Asoka*, have been translated by N.A. NIKAM and RICHARD MCKEON (1958). Many important Buddhist texts may be found in translation in the "Sacred Books of the East." In this series the *Sutta Nipata* is in vol. 10; the *Vinaya Texts* in vol. 13, 17, and 20; the *Saddharma Pundarika* or *The Lotus of the True Law* in vol. 21; and *Mahāyāna Texts* in vol. 49. An important Ch'an (Zen) text of China is *The Platform Sutra of the Sixth Patriarch*, newly translated with a valuable introduction by PHILIP B. YAMPOLSKY (1967). An important Japanese Zen text is one by DOGEN, recently translated and made available as *A Primer of Sōtō Zen* by R. MASUNAGA (1971). GARMA C.C. CHANG's translation, *The Hundred Thousand Songs of Milarepa* (abridged edition 1962), is a lucid representation of the poetry and prose of a classic of Tibetan Buddhism.

(J.M.K.)

Buddhist Mysticism

Mysticism in Buddhism is a definite, recognizable form of experience and type of awareness that may be approached and interpreted in various ways. Mysticism is found in all forms of Buddhism—in Theravāda ("Way of the Elders," also known as Hīnayāna, or "Lesser Vehicle"), the predominant form in present-day Southeast Asia and Ceylon; in Mahāyāna (or "Greater Vehicle"), the predominant form in east Asia; and in Tantric (magical) and Tibetan Buddhism, prevailing at present in the Himalayan regions. In the course of history the mystical element in Buddhist thought became ever more clearly emphasized. The climax was reached when, about the 1st century AD, the transition from early Buddhism into Mahāyāna had been effected. Early Buddhism was codified selectively in the Theravāda canon and remained static; the latter proliferated into distinct lines of thought. Buddhist mysticism will be dealt with here in terms of its distinctive nature, its regional interpretations, and its techniques of realization.

NATURE AND GOALS

Ineffability and timelessness

Universal mystical aspects. Buddhist mysticism, like other forms of mysticism, insists on the ineffability of the mystical experience, because it defies expression in terms that are intelligible to anyone who has not had analogous experience. The knowledge involved is never merely intellectual but is a kind of felt knowledge in which things are seen in a different perspective and take on a new significance. Related to its ineffability is the timeless quality of this experience, which means that the mystic seems to be outside of time and space, oblivious to his surroundings and the passage of time.

The earliest Buddhist mysticism was concerned with the

emptying of subjective Being, considered to be the greatest obstacle to the individual's spiritual growth. This passing into a new dimension of Being was described in terms of a flame going out: it was merely extinguished; it could not be said that it had gone somewhere. In this emptying process the limits that constitute the individual's being, as defined by an analysis of both physical and mental components, were transcended, although all these components were said to be retained. The experience of this new dimension of being was a vision in marked contrast to normal perception—"beyond the reach of mere logic."

The timelessness of the mystical experience underlines the verifiable fact that those experiences that are felt to be most profound and significant cannot be adequately described in terms of past, present, and future or of "earlier than" and "later than." All that the texts say is that there exists a sense of something "unborn, not become, not made, uncompounded" and that the feeling of being born and transitory serves to re-emphasize the timeless and ineffable reality.

Most characteristic, even of the earliest form of Buddhism as codified in the Tipiṭaka, the Theravāda canon, is the emphasis on the path that man must traverse in order to attain his goal. The path is not so much an inert link between two points, such as *saṃsāra* (the bondage to the circumstances of existence) and Nirvāṇa (enlightenment or escape from *saṃsāra*), as the individual's effort to free his being from alien constraints and to break through into a new and more rewarding dimension of Being. This effort presupposes the ability to use and even to know the different modes of Being. Knowledge of Being, not absorption of the self into divine or cosmic Being, is therefore the keynote of Buddhist mysticism. In order to know who the mystic is, one must know what he represents; in order to know what he represents, one must know what it means for man to be; and in order to know what it means for man to be, one must know the difference modes of Being, since they are all that there is or can be. This noetic or cognitive quality of the mystic experience in Buddhism, referred to by the term "eye of knowledge" (*jñānacakṣur*), contains within it moments or facets of appreciation and evaluation. In this immediate apprehension of Being there is no sense of union with the divine, conceived in terms of personality or superpersonality (as in the Hindu *Ātman-Brahman* concept, which posits the identity of the self and the cosmos).

While early Buddhism was analytical in its attempt to free Being from the imposition of subjectivity, Mahāyāna continued the analytical process by extending it to objective Being. In its rejection of subjectivism and objectivism, it emphasized the nature of Being-as-such, which was experienced in enlightenment (*bodhi*). While the various philosophical trends associated with the emergence and development of Mahāyāna dealt with the intellectual problem of being, shorn of all its positive and negative qualifications, the *Tantras* (forming the literature of Mantrayāna—"vehicle of magical spells"—or Vajrayāna—"vehicle of the thunderbolt of awareness"—commonly referred to as Tantric Buddhism) dealt with the existential problem of how it is or feels to be. The Mahāyāna may be said to look at Being, Tantric Buddhism to act through Being.

Peculiarly Buddhist character. Inasmuch as Buddhist mysticism is a mysticism concerned with the analysis of existence, the effort to free Being from alien constraints centres on the separating of some portions of existence and then placing them in relevant relation to one another inside Being. This is done, for example, by contemplative concentration (*dhyāna*) on a particular item (a coloured patch, for example), which then is seen as a unique instance. Such concentration is closely related to aesthetic or intrinsic perception. In contemplative concentration, the practitioner does not see something different, but he sees differently the same thing that others see. This implies the ability to perceive the ineffable, that which cannot be put into words. Trying to force it into words changes it and makes it something other than it is, something that may be like it yet is different from it. The critique of the earlier forms of comtemplative concentration by the later Buddhists, particularly by those belonging to Japanese Zen or the schools close to Zen, with their emphasis on enlightenment (Satori) itself, merely reaffirms the ineffability of the mystic experience. While the earlier forms of Buddhism fixed their gaze on particular phenomena, the later ones took the whole of the psychic energy or mind as the meditative object. Concentration—that is, becoming grounded in the real and not running after the ephemeral—is itself asceticism in the original meaning of practice, not in the subsidiary meaning of mortification of the flesh. As a rule, the Buddhists rejected mortification, although such instances also occurred and may have been due to imitation of essentially non-Buddhist practices.

Contemplative concentration

Goals of Buddhist mysticism and meditation. All meditational techniques aim at enabling the practitioner to come closer to his being, which, in its fulfillment, is felt as an enrichment of the personality with corresponding loss of fear (*abhaya*, "fearlessness") and anxiety, generally referred to as "liberation" (*mokṣa*, *vimokṣa*, *mukti*). It is a kind of self-actualization in the sense that the practitioner becomes more integrated and less split, more independent of his lower needs, less ego centred as a thing of the world. The self-actualization culminates in "integration" (*samādhi*), which does not imply a molding or shaping according to some preconceived postulates. In order to actualize his own potentialities, the practitioner has to traverse the path discriminately. What the final actualization is said to be depends on the particular goal that a man sets himself. Here the different attitudes of earlier and later Buddhism are of decisive importance. The former is self-contained, the latter all-encompassing in orientation.

Means of achieving the goals. The most common means is referred to by the Indian term *yoga* (physical and mental discipline), which in Buddhist mysticism has the specific connotation of harnessing all that is in man to a certain goal and never implies a union with a postulated absolute. Breathing techniques (*prāṇāyāma*) and recitations of *mantras* (magical spells) form an important part, inasmuch as they help to "protect mind from going astray into its own fictions." Similarly, evocative formulas (*dhāraṇī*) are used in the empathetic visualization (*sādhanā*) of the psychic powers appearing in the polarities of male and female. Inasmuch as the aspirant tries to pattern his life after the envisaged content of enlightenment, he adopts certain postures (*mudrās*) that outwardly seem to be gestures and attitudes but, seen from within, are said to be the "imprints" of Being on the aspirant's individual being.

REGIONAL HISTORY

In India and Southeast Asia. The growth of Buddhist mysticism in India coincides with the development of the various Buddhist philosophical schools, particularly with the Yogācāra—which held that only consciousness itself is real—and Mādhyamika—which held both subject and object to be unreal and whose central doctrine is *śūnyatā* ("emptiness")—systems and their interactions (see also BUDDHIST PHILOSOPHY). These disciplines formed the intellectual framework of Tantric Buddhism, the climax of Buddhist mysticism, which spread from Kashmir and Bengal throughout Asia. Applied mysticism, as distinguished from philosophical mysticism, is represented by the "great accomplished ones" (*mahāsiddas*) in India. Tradition counts 84 *mahāsiddhas*. Very little is known about their lives and times, except that they ranged over the whole period of Mahāyāna in India and that they came from different walks of life. Among the *mahāsiddhas* notable for the spread of mysticism are the Brahmin Saraha; the hunter Śabarī; the prince Nāropa and his teacher, the oil-maker Tilopa; and King Indrabhūti and his sister Princess Lakṣmīṃkarā. All of them expressed their experiences in songs, many of them recorded in the Indian vernacular languages. Only fragments have been preserved in the original; for the rest the Tibetan translations are invaluable. It is evident that such songs, or lyric poems—vague in doctrinal content but rich in suggestive imagery—can be used by any group for its spe-

Mahāsiddhas

cific exegesis. In this way Buddhist mysticism exerted a lasting influence on Hinduism and in India was finally absorbed by it. Thus Matsyendranātha, the semimythical founder of the Nātha Yogis—a group of wandering Hindu ascetics still found in present-day India—is claimed by both Buddhists and Hindus as their follower.

While in India the mystic element remained linked to the renunciative trend (even though its symbol language had erotic overtones, which by analogy pointed to the ecstatic feeling tone of the mystical experience), in Southeast Asia Buddhist mysticism blended with political ideas. Hīnayāna Buddhism had come to Southeast Asia in the 4th century, and by the 7th century, Sumatra was an important Buddhist centre. In 717 Vajrabodhi introduced Tantric forms of worship. The mystic genius of the Śailendra period (*c.* 752–832) in Java found its expression in the famous Borobuḍur monument depicting simultaneously the cosmos and the personality. Southeast Asian mysticism is furthermore marked historically by the syncretism of Hinduism—as embodied in both Vaiṣṇavism (worship of the Hindu god Viṣṇu [Vishnu]) and Śaivism (worship of the Hindu god Śiva [Shiva])—and Tantric Buddhism.

In Cambodia, the syncretism of Vaiṣṇavism and Śaivism under Suryavarman II (1113–50) was further advanced by a blending with Mahāyāna Buddhism, which ultimately gave rise to a mystical cult of Śiva-Buddha. Today, however, Theravāda Buddhism dominates Southeast Asia.

In Central Asia and Tibet. It is now a well-established fact that Buddhism had reached Central Asia by the 2nd century AD, but a clear picture of its tenets in the Central Asian oasis states is provided only by sources dating from the 4th century. One of the most important centres was Kucha (China), where Hīnayāna and Mahāyāna existed side by side, with each trend alternately dominating the scene between the 4th and 7th centuries. Afterward it remained predominantly committed to Hīnayāna Buddhism. The existence of mystical Buddhism by the 4th century is well attested. The monk Fo T'u-ch'eng, reaching northern China in 310, was famous for his magic formulas. Between 402 and 412 Kumārajīva translated *dhāraṇī* texts (evocative formulas), and the Indian monk Dharmakṣema is said to have taught sexual practices, which are believed by certain people to constitute or lead to mystical experiences, among the northern Liang. In view of the fact that Kumārajīva translated Hīnayāna, Mahāyāna, *dhāraṇi*, and *dhyāna* (meditation) texts, great tolerance seems to have prevailed, and the mystically minded person could choose any suitable formulation for expressing his experience.

Buddhism was present in Tibet during the reign of Srong-brtsan-sgam-po (died 650), whose Chinese and Nepalese wives were devout Buddhists. At first Buddhism was restricted to the court, and the priests were Indian and Chinese. In the 8th century the two trends of Buddhism—the one conventionally academic and monastic, represented by Śāntirakṣita and Kamalaśīla, two Indian scholars active in Tibet; the other unconventional, mystical, and ritualistic, initiated by the Indian missionary Padmasambhava—were well established. The 11th and 12th centuries were singularly important for the development of mysticism. Foremost is the Bka'-brgyud-pa school, spiritual head of which was Mar-pa (1012–96), disciple of the Indian Nāropa. He was succeeded by Mila Ras-pa, a strict ascetic whose teaching was transmitted by Sgam-po-pa (1079–1153). The latter's disciples subsequently established no less than six famous schools. During the second half of the 11th century, Dam-pa Sangs-rgyas, a Brahmin from South India, visited Tibet; but, although he wrote nothing, he bestowed Tantric initiations upon suitable persons. One of his followers was Lab-kyi sgron-ma, who lived sometimes as a nun and sometimes as a married woman. Her teaching, the *gcod-yul*, is still practiced today. This teaching aims at curbing the emotions by practicing compassion and cultivating discrimination between the real and the illusory. While there are no essential differences in doctrine between the various orders, the techniques of realization and the attachment to particular tutelary deities are the distinguishing features.

Tibetan Bka'-brgyud-pa school

In China, Japan, and Korea. Buddhist mysticism was brought to China by monks from Central Asia as early as the 3rd century, when Chu Lü-yen translated some *dhāraṇīs* (AD 260). Mysticism spread during the 4th and 5th centuries, when Fo T'u-ch'eng and Dharmarakṣa translated many Indian texts. It flourished during the T'ang period (618–907) and disappeared with the general decline of Buddhism due to its persecution in 845.

Philosophical mysticism was represented by the Ch'an meditative school (Japanese Zen), whose origin is mythical. Other schools in which the mystical element is very strong are the T'ien-t'ai (Japanese Tendai), founded by Hui-wen (550–577), and the Hua-yen (Japanese Kegon, Sanskrit Avatamsaka), initiated by Tu-shun (also known as Fa-shun; 557–640), systematized by Fa-tsang (640–712), and restored to its original purity by Ch'eng-kuan (*c.* 760–820/838). Although deriving their impetus from Indian sources, all these schools are purely Chinese developments. Applied mysticism, the "True Word" (Chinese Chen-yen, Japanese Shingon) school, also known as "Secret Doctrine," though of importance in Japan, was never a school in itself in China. Its origin goes back to the monk Śrīmitra (between 335 and 342), who translated into Chinese several texts containing *dhāraṇīs*.

Indian mystics in China

The real mystical movement began with three able Indian teachers: Śubhakarasiṃha (637–735); Vajrabodhi (633–733), and his disciple Amoghavajra (705–774), who became the instructor of three successive Chinese emperors.

I-hsiang (625–702) from Silla, a state of Korea, founded the first Hua-yen school in Korea, where Buddhism had already arrived in 372. The totalistic principle by which the emperor Shōmu (reigned 724–748) intended to govern Japan was that of this school, which had been brought to Japan in 730 by Fa-tsang's disciple Tao-hsüan. This principle implies that in the same way as the various Buddhas are representations and manifestations of the Buddha Mahāvairocana, so the government organization is the representation of the Emperor. Today the Tōdai-ji temple at Nara, still the largest wooden structure in the world, is the only prominent monastery belonging to this school. The Tendai (Chinese, T'ien-t'ai) school in Japan was founded by Dengyō Daishi, disciple of the school's sixth patriarch, Chan-jan (712–782). At present there are three branches, Sammon, Jimon, and Shinsei. The founder of the "True Word" school in Japan was Kōbō Daishi (Kūkai; 774–835). His is the mystical doctrine called Tōmitsu, as distinguished from Taimitsu, handed down by Jikaku Daishi (784–864) of the Tendai school. Both schools are alike in emphasizing the possibility of becoming a Buddha in this life, in considering the phenomenal world as the self-representation of the absolute, and in upholding the idea that the absolute, its manifest as well as its functional aspects are mutually interpenetrating, but they differ in their teaching of these tenets. The Tōmitsu makes use of two *maṇḍalas* (ritual meditation diagrams), the *vajradhatu-maṇḍala* and the *mahākaruṇagarbha-maṇḍala*, while the Taimitsu recognizes a third, the *susiddhi-maṇḍala* which in the Tōmitsu forms part of the *Mahākaruṇagarbha-maṇḍala*. Or, the Taimitsu may employ the *mahākaruṇagarbha-maṇḍala* and the *susiddhi-maṇḍala* at the exclusion of the *vajradhātu-maṇḍala*. Zen was introduced to Japan several times. While all these schools are still flourishing in Japan, in Korea, Zen achieved the dominant role. The Hua-yen school also flourished for some time in the Korean kingdom of Silla, but the Tantric form does not seem to have been widespread.

TECHNIQUES OF REALIZATION

The relationship between man and reality. Since throughout its history Buddhism in its mystical aspect represents an existence-mysticism with a strong poetic quality, the problem of what man is going to be has loomed large and has been the guiding principle of the Buddhist path. Early Buddhism conceived of its goal in terms of the *arhat*—"he who has overcome the enemy."

the enemy being the triad of passion, hatred, and ignorance and the fetters that they have created in man. In his approach to this goal the aspirant frees himself successively from ten fetters. He does so by pursuing four stages and enjoying the fruition of each. By "entering the stream" (that will carry the aspirant to his goal) and then having become a "person in the stream," he rids himself of three fetters, namely, the view that his physical existence is the whole truth, skepticism or doubting, and the belief that rites and observances have any effect. In becoming a "once-returner," he rids himself of two other fetters, sensuality and the desire for sensuous and sensual relations, which tie him down to this world, and ill will, which grudges others what they have. As a "non-returner" he frees himself from any attachment to the world of sensuous forms and also from the desire for formlessness. An *arhat* becomes free from conceit, self-righteousness, and ignorance (the inability to understand reality, not the failure to know something). According to the intensity of this experience, nine varieties of mystic accomplishment are distinguished, while from the noetic point of view six types are recognized. The first five are prompted by faith rather than by intellectual acumen and therefore are unable to maintain this experience; hence the aspirant lapses from his exalted state. Only those who, by their superior intellectual acumen, are able to continue in this mystical state are never relapsing and "unperturbable" (*akopya*).

Concepts of Buddhahood

With the emergence of the Mahāyāna school the interiorization of the problem of what man is going to be resulted in the ideal of Buddhahood. For Mahāyāna the central question was what was the experience that has made the historical Buddha worthy of the name "The Enlightened One"? It was this Buddhahood experience that he wanted his disciples to gain for themselves through his teaching and that by implication was attainable by everyone. The term buddha, a participle of the Sanskrit verbal root *budh*, "to awake," has been interpreted in different ways, most commonly as "awareness" and "awakening" (*bodhi*), the characteristics of an "Enlightened One (Buddha). The awareness is all-encompassing, while the awakening comprises self-awakening, as from deep sleep; the rousing of others from the sleep of ignorance; and the unity of the awakening process with ultimate reality or Being-as-such. In this sense, the attainment of Buddhahood is a self-validating moment that carries its own intrinsic value. Negatively, it is an escape from the fog caused by conflicting emotions and primitive beliefs about reality; positively, it is an awareness that sees reality as it becomes manifest in a system of concepts or words or relations without getting lost in it. There are thus two kinds of awareness: one seeing reality in its intrinsic uniqueness, the other remaining aware of the danger of losing the possibility of seeing reality with complete freshness when—as happens ordinarily—things are seen by classifying, comparing, evaluating, and using them.

This existential experience is known on the basis of the above two approaches as *vimuktikāya* (existence in freedom) and *dharmakāya* (existence in infinite richness). The doctrine of the Buddha's *kāya*s (literally "bodies"), realms or forms of existence, which range in number from three to ten, is one of the most complicated problems of Buddhist studies and is still largely unsolved. The triad (*tri-kāya*) of *dharmakāya* ("existence body"), *sambhogakāya* ("enjoyment body"), and *nirmāṇakāya* ("transformation body") figures most commonly in the description of Buddhahood as an existential experience. The *dharmakāya* is an end experience, while the other two *kāya*s are means-experiences. The *dharmakāya*, referring to the mystic experience of wholeness, is a name for an absolute value-fact. In its realization, reality is felt to be absolutely positive, good, and valuable, and this value-sense communicates itself through the means-experiences of *sambhogakāya* and *nirmāṇakāya*. The *sambhogakāya* is twofold: referential (*parasambhogakāya*) and nonreferential (*svasambhogakāya*). In its latter aspect, it is self-sufficient and not in need of anything, a continuous delight as may be felt in the perception of an aesthetic object; in the former, this delight communicates with other experiences. *Nirmāṇakāya* is a term for genuine existence that itself becomes a stimulus for others to find their own true being. It therefore may manifest itself in any guise. All three *kāya*s (none of which is literally a "body" in any real sense of the word) represent existential patterns or functions. They are not separate entities but fuse with each other and form a unity that in philosophical terms is called *svābhāvikakāya* (the state of Being itself). Even here the experience of absoluteness has been instrumental in coining this term, as it indicates the autonomy, self-sufficiency, and self-containedness of the experience of Being. Ultimately, therefore, the *kāya*s are facets of Being rather than parts of it.

Tri-kāya

The mystic experience not only makes perception richer and permits the person to see all the intrinsic qualities of the object simultaneously and to see also that they are necessary to each other, but the experience also is emotionally more satisfying, because it has gone beyond any ordinary needs and drives. This aspect was termed *mahāsukhakāya* ("existence in absolute bliss") and was developed within Tantric Buddhism. It is not an innovation or additional form of existence. Already in the Pāli canon, *Nirvāṇa* had been described as bliss, quite distinct from any other ordinary feeling of happiness.

Special characteristics of Tantric mysticism

Peculiar to Tantric Buddhism is the idea that Buddhahood can be realized during a person's lifetime by various practices and that Buddhahood is not merely the realization of a wider vision but also a physical phenomenon; body and mind, in Tantric Buddhism, are abstractions from a uniquely vivid reality, not different and differently evaluated entities. This idea constitutes an unconditional acceptance of Being. Each individual represents and constitutes reality. Consequently, what in other Buddhist disciplines were considered as obstacles and had to be suppressed are here utilized for the realization of Buddhahood.

An important concept used in Tantric and non-Tantric contexts is *mahāmudrā* (the "Great Seal"). It is the leitmotiv of the Tibetan Bka'-brgyud-pa school, which was organized by sGam-po-pa, the famous disciple of Mi-la Ras-pa, disciple of Mar-pa who studied under the Indian Nāropa, and has theoretical and practical content. Theoretically, as the "Great Seal," it is a term for the absolute unity of reality, for "seal" denotes a pattern that serves as an integrating focus for a wide range of specific activities; and it also indicates that there is no going beyond reality. Practically, it teaches the way to secure an inner immunity that cannot be assailed by hopes and fears. In the process of "sealing" reality the experiential character is evident. Reality, which comprises man and the world not as correspondences but as a unity, is "bliss" (*sukha*) and also an "utter openness" (*śūnya*). In this unity Buddhist mysticism combines its philosophical conclusion that there can be no ontology (theory about the nature of being), in the traditional Western way, with its experiential quality of absolute positiveness.

Means and modes of the relationship. *Concepts of action.* The means of attaining the goal have been laid down in the various canonical texts, the large *Mahāyāna-sūtra*s (texts), and, above all, in the literature of the *Tantras* (the texts of Tantric Buddhism), which uses a highly technical and symbolic language that has remained a stumbling block to understanding for noninitiates. Inasmuch as the mystic sees the world in a different light and therefore also draws different conclusions in the sphere of conduct, his actions in the world will necessarily be influenced accordingly and will constitute a way of life not always sanctioned by society. The mystic's conduct (*caryā*) involves both intelligence (*prajñā*) and a moral framework (*upāya*). Intelligence is a discriminative and appreciative function of the mind, which sees men and things as transitory and hence unsuited to serve as a reliable basis for an adequate way of life and which pays attention to the open dimension (*śūnyatā*) out of which the transitory things emerge and in which they participate. The moral framework is the application to goal achievement of this insight. In order to be able to perceive and attend to the open dimension, it is necessary that the noetic function is itself as nothing or utterly open (*śūnya*); and since in the mystic experience at its peak the only possible emotions are kindliness (*maitrī*) and compassion (*karuṇā*), the mystic's reaction to the world is compassion in an absolute sense (*mahākaruṇā*). Foreshadowed in early Buddhist literature, this idea was elaborated in Mahāyāna and Tantric texts: "Enlightenment is the indivisibility of (cognitive) openness and (active) compassion."

Multiple approaches. The classification of the essentially mystical works, the *Tantras*, is mainly based on the different approaches to goal realization, which is nothing less than Buddhahood. Traditionally four kinds of *Tantras* have been distinguished: *Kriyātantra*, *Caryātantra*, *Yogatantra*, and *Anuttarayogatantra*. *Kriyātantra* is basically ritualistic and devotional in character and is counted the lowest because of the emphasis Buddhist mysticism places on the intellectual acumen (*prajñā*) of the aspirant; in this case, faith (*śraddhā*) predominates over intelligence, and the relation of the aspirant toward the powers that motivate him and appear to him in the guise of gods and goddesses is that of servant to master. In the second kind of *Tantra*—*Caryātantra*—faith and intelligence are evenly distributed. Intelligence as the discriminative function moves to its apex in the last two kinds of *Tantras*. In the *Caryātantra*, the dependence relation of master and servant has given way to a feeling of friendship in which each partner is equally respected. In the *Yogatantra*, the contemplative and discriminative processes are even more developed, and this produces a greater intimacy between friends, approximating to a feeling of identity.

The four kinds of *Tantras*

The *Anuttarayogatantra* is divided into the so-called *Father Tantra*, *Mother Tantra*, and *Nondual Tantra*. In all of them the symbolic approach to the realization of the goal is the outstanding characteristic. The *Father Tantra* emphasizes the developing stage (*utpannakrama*), which is a vision of the world and those that live in it in a transfigured way. The so-called physical world is said to be a heavenly mansion, and those that live in it are gods and goddesses. The technique of producing the developing stage corresponds to the active part (*upāya*) of the imaginative process. In the *Mother Tantra* the fulfillment stage (*sampannakrama*) is the main topic. It is the appreciation of the vision in all its beauty and splendour, and this corresponds to the appreciative part (*prajñā*) of the same imaginative process that operates in the developing stage. In the *Nondual Tantra* both stages are experienced as a unity. Here the mystic experience culminates in a feeling of absolute identity. Paradoxically, the highest attainment of identity or selfhood is simultaneously a transcending of itself, a going beyond selfhood.

The symbolic approach to Buddhahood, which characterizes Buddhist mysticism, is described in a code language that can be interpreted by the aspirant either literally or metaphorically, according to his own intellectual level of understanding. It is important to know that this code language—precisely because it is a code language—does not refer to any objective existence of what is pointed to. The physical and symbolical codes belong to two different logical levels. This applies in particular to the various *yoga* techniques, where the *yogic* body is conceived of as a structural pyramid or cone in which the central part of an imaginary chart consists of focal points of experience (*cakra*), innervated by the awakening of sensations moving along certain bodily channels (*nāḍi*, *lalanā*, *rasanā*, and *avadhūti*).

An important role is played by the *maṇḍala* ("circle"), which is a blueprint of orientation in the development of the mystical vision. On the one hand, it is a projection of the mystic's vision of his universe in terms of a divine mansion and its gods and goddesses; on the other, it is an evocative means to assist in the creation of the vision. According to the Hua-yen school and the Tantric forms of Buddhist mysticism, a *maṇḍala* is an ornament of the Buddha-mind.

There are many different approaches, depending on the aspirant's temperament and abilities, and much misunderstanding has been due to the interpretation of the code language in a one-sided manner. This happened in the case of the use of *mudrās* (gestures and positions). Apart from gestures, this term can also be interpreted both as "woman" and "imprint." Failing to realize the ambiguous character of the code language, Easterners and Westerners alike have interpreted the code terms of Buddhist mysticism in a literal sense and have created the idea of an "eroticized" Buddhism that actually existed only in their own minds. Even the male–female icons (*yab-yum*) of Tibet and Nepal do not evoke erotic feelings in practitioners of Buddhist mysticism but are always understood as polarity symbols, illustrating the intimate relationship between appreciation (*prajñā*) and action (*upāya*).

The states of achievement. Although the ultimate achievement was Buddhahood, throughout its development, Buddhist mysticism recognized various states. Such were, in the early phase, the *arhat* and the Pratyeka-buddha—a person who had realized Buddhahood but did not communicate his realization to others. When the ideal shifted from self-centredness to altruistic participation, the *bodhisattva* (Buddha-to-be) concept was elaborated and ten stages were codified. The first stage of joyfulness initiates the path of seeing, on which the nonontological character of self and nonself is realized, is related to liberality (*dāna*), and thereby opens the way to further progress. The subsequent stages are related to the other perfections (*pāramitā*) such as discipline (*śīla*), patience with and acceptance of things as they are (*kṣānti*), endeavour and perseverance (*vīrya*), concentration (*dhyāna*), and insight (*prajñā*). These are followed by the higher stages of morally significant action (*upāya*), of commitment to gain enlightenment (*praṇidhāna*) by not being taken in by conventional characteristics, of the ten powers of Buddhahood (*bala*), and of being able to communicate the highest realization to all the world equally (*jñāna*).

The ten stages of Buddhahood

The last stage is, for all practical purposes, already the attainment of Buddhahood. Since Buddhist mysticism eschewed a static conception of its goal, additional stages were named. This was essentially a device to prevent the aspirant from becoming complacent, and it also presented a vast picture of the world in which everyone could feel at home. Ultimately, the various stages and the achievements of each of them indicate the manner in which reality manifests itself in and before the human mind, just as the moon takes various shapes in the waves of the ocean.

BIBLIOGRAPHY. S. SPENCER, *Mysticism in World Religion* (1963); and F.C. HAPPOLD, *Mysticism* (1964), contain valuable samplings of Buddhist mysticism in relation to other forms of mysticism. A. BHARATI, *The Tantric Tradition* (1965), deals with Hindu and Buddhist mysticism with a valuable bibliography. Historical rather than doctrinal works include: K.K.S. CH'EN, *Buddhism in China* (1964); D.L. SNELLGROVE and H.E. RICHARDSON, *A Cultural History of Tibet* (1968); and CHARLES ELIOT, *Japanese Buddhism* (1935, reprinted 1959). Though obsolete, this work is not yet superseded. D.T. SUZUKI, *Essays in Zen Buddhism*, 3 series (1927–61), is devoted exclusively to Zen. H.V. GUENTHER, *The Life and Teaching of Nāropa* (1963), *Tibetan Buddhism without Mystification* (1966), and *The Royal Song of Saraha* (1969), include standard translations with important analyses of mystical techniques. J. TAKAKUSU, *The Essentials of Buddhist Philosophy*, 3rd ed. (1956), emphasizes the philosophical aspects.

(H.G.)

Buddhist Mythology

Buddhist mythology consists of the numerous legends, myths, and tales of Buddhism throughout Asia. The mythology may be divided into two basic types: (1) myths concerning the historical Buddha, Gautama (late 6th–early 5th century BC) called here by his clan name Śākyamuni ("Sage of the Śākya dynasty") and (2) myths concerning celestial Buddhas and *bodhisattvas* ("Buddhas to be"). Fundamental to Buddhist mythology is the simple story of Śākyamuni's attainment of enlightenment or Nirvāṇa—the release or escape from the endless cycle of rebirths inherent in ordinary human destiny—despite a variety of temptations brought forth by an evil tempter named Māra. All of the major sectarian forms of Buddhism, such as Theravāda ("Way of the Elders," also called Hīnayāna, or "Lesser Vehicle," the predominant school in Southeast Asia), Mahāyāna ("Greater Vehicle," the predominant school in East Asia), Tantric (magical), and Tibetan Buddhism, have such mythological dimensions. Sources for mythology are found in literature, in art, and in archaeology.

ROLES AND FUNCTIONS OF MYTH

Myth has played an essential and all-pervading role in the history of Buddhism. Its analysis was already a delicate task in the early historical period (*c.* 500–100 BC). Myth became far more complex in the classical Mahāyāna period (*c.* 100 BC–AD 800) and evaded altogether precise presentation, as Buddhism, already a complex cultural growth, coalesced in its varying stages of development with local indigenous beliefs throughout the whole of Asia (*c.* AD 100 onward). Since the 19th century it has begun to coalesce with Western rationalizing and liberal thought, resulting in a new demythologized version of the historical Buddha Śākyamuni's teachings.

Myths in Buddhism

In Buddhism three different kinds of myth are found: (1) fundamental cosmological myth—*e.g.*, the "dogma" of continual rebirth together with the whole imagined structure of phenomenal existence (see *Cosmological myths* below); (2) fundamental religious myth, or myth employed as symbolic expression of a radical religious insight—*e.g.*, the myth of the Buddha, the perfected or "divinized" man, or again of Māra, the devil, who represents the force of spiritual evil; and lastly (3) myth as a deliberate fabrication from legends and fragmentary myths, put together in order to justify or to explain certain traditionally accepted beliefs, an example of this being the early traditional account of the first Buddhist council at Rājagṛha, which was invented very early in order to prove that the sacred scriptures in the forms that the different sects preserved them were actually the recited word of Śākyamuni himself. Except for the third kind, myth is not fictitious and may often be true in its intended symbolic sense. Thus by treating Buddhism as a mythology, one detracts in no way from its positive value as one of the great religions of the world.

TYPES AND SOURCES OF MYTH

Śākyamuni Buddha in traditional literary accounts. The traditional biographies of Śākyamuni, in whatever language they are written, all derive ultimately from early Indian extracanonical rearrangements of the still earlier, scattered canonical accounts of his great acts, which were supposedly recited at Rājagṛha together with the rest of the canon within a year of his decease. The best known of the Indian "biographies" are the Sanskrit works, the *Mahāvastu* and the *Lalitavistara;* the Chinese *Abhiniṣkramaṇa-sūtra*, translated from an Indian original; and the Pāli *Nidānakathā*, as well as the commentary on the *Buddhavaṃsa*. These early works themselves are the result of a continual traditional growth, and to ascertain the dates of their final versions helps in no way to estimate the actual age or reliability of much of the material they contain. All that can be said is that this material agrees substantially with the earliest known fragmentary canonical accounts on the one hand, while on the other, once presented in coherent biographical form, it shows little or no change in the later "national" versions of the story. The later Singhalese, Thai, Burmese, and Cambodian stories are all firmly based on the earlier Pāli versions. The Koreans and Japanese have derived their accounts direct from the Chinese, which in turn are derived, via Central Asia, from Indian sources. The Tibetans, who represent the extreme limits of Indian Buddhist developments, draw their versions from the same earlier Indian versions. The biography of Śākyamuni included by the Tibetan historian Bu-ston (1290–1364) in his *History of Buddhism* differs from other traditional accounts only by its listing of the later Mahāyāna doctrines as part of Śākyamuni's teaching program on earth. All in all, the unity of the mythological and quasi-historical interpretations of the life and death of the "historical" Buddha, in whatever Buddhist country they have been retold, remains very impressive.

Myths and biographies of the Buddha

The claim of the Theravādin Buddhists of Ceylon, Burma, and Thailand to represent unadulterated "original Buddhism" is really based not on their possession of early traditions lost to the Mahāyāna countries but rather on their having remained faithful to the early enthusiastic acclamation of Śākyamuni as the one and only Buddha of the present world age. It certainly cannot be based on the often wrongly supposed, greater historical plausibility of their canonical literature, as preserved in Pāli since the 1st century BC. The only other early canonical literature surviving in an Indian language in any great substance is the *Vinaya* (the rules of monks) of a northwest Indian sect, the Mūla-Sarvāstivādins; and internal textual evidence suggests that in some places this has priority over the Pāli version. The comparative lateness of the appearance of such texts as these does not mean that they do not contain some of the very earliest traditional material.

All of the early canonical accounts agree in describing Śākyamuni's experience of enlightenment as a definitive victory over Māra, the Evil One, and as resulting in a threefold knowledge, that of his own previous births, that of the births and deaths of all other sentient beings, combined with the saving knowledge of his final release from the whole unhappy process. However symbolically one may treat the descriptions of the various possible spheres of rebirth among gods, men, animals, ghosts (*preta*), and the denizens of hell, belief in the cosmological myth of continual rebirth is fundamental to Buddhism. Śākyamuni was acclaimed "Great Sage" (Mahāmuni) and Lord (Bhagavat) not because he achieved a state of spiritual equilibrium in the present life but because he attained the supramundane state of Nirvāṇa. There are no textual indications that he was ever regarded by his followers as a kind of Socratic sage but rather as a typical perfected *yogin* (ascetic with magical powers) of his day, possessed as was then expected of miraculous powers and divine insight, combined with an altogether extraordinary concern for the spiritual advancement of others. Thus from the first his state of enlightenment or Buddhahood was recognized as "transcendent" (*lokottara*), and as the living transient embodiment of such supramundane knowledge. Śākyamuni was identified with the pre-Buddhist Indian myth of the "Great Man" (*mahāpuruṣa*), now conceived of as the predestined religious genius who appears on earth whenever the circumstances are ripe. He was thus accepted as the seventh in an imagined series of previous Buddhas. Why the seventh is not known, unless the number was derived from astronomical association, and the question may be pointless from the mythical viewpoint. His contemporary, Mahāvīra, leader of the Jains, was linked to a similar series of 24. The essential mythical idea consists not in the numbers but in the notion of predestination and fulfillment. The title Tathāgata, meaning probably "the one who has reached such (perfection)," is regularly used by Śākyamuni of himself, and it would seem likely (whatever 19th-century demythologizing scholars might say to the contrary) that he did indeed use this title. Apart from such utter confidence in his achievement, his religious movement would doubtless have died with him.

The appearances of Buddhas

Not only do Buddhas appear at predestined times but the final appearance of any Buddha is the culmination of a whole series of previous lives, during which he gradually advances towards enlightenment. Such a belief accords with the whole world view in which Buddhism had its origin, and it may be supposed fairly that Śākyamuni believed this of himself. In any case the earliest known Buddhist tradition most certainly presented him as so believing, and it is scarcely disputable that Śākyamuni inspired the belief. The essential Buddha myth thus belongs to the very origins of the religion, and the cult of the living master is logically followed by the cult of the deceased master who has passed into the transcendent state of Buddhahood. Popular mythology soon set to work to give some tangible substance to the fundamental myth, and no scholar would doubt that the stories of

Śākyamuni's previous lives (*Jātaka*), included in such profusion in the early canonical texts, are later accretions, culled haphazardly from Indian folk literature in order to fill the gaps in general knowledge concerning "dogma" that was fundamental to faith in the Buddha.

Another example of fundamental myth that is subsequently decked out in the trappings of popular mythology is Māra, the Evil One, who represented the force of spiritual evil that Śākyamuni was conscious of having confronted and overcome. Māra is explicitly identified as Concupiscence and as Death, the twin foes of all those who strive toward the tranquil and immortal state of Nirvāṇa. At the same time he is identified popularly with all of the demons and evil spirits of popular belief, and the texts usually describe him in these terms. The close relationship of fundamental myth as based on a radical religious insight and of popular mythological expression has been well illustrated by the eminent British student of Buddhism, Trevor O. Ling (see *Bibliography*). One notes that the definitive victory over Māra, on whatever spiritual or popular level this may be understood, remains an inalienable element of the myth and is just as important as the belief, universally attested in the earliest traditions of all Buddhists, in the omniscience and the miraculous powers of Śākyamuni.

Since Śākyamuni's followers were interested in him as a marvellous being and a transcendent Buddha, such historical reminiscences as may have been preserved in the story are incidental to the recounting of such things as the great acts of his previous lives, his miraculous birth in his last life, the drama of his final enlightenment while sitting under the pipal (Bo) tree, his stupendous decision to convert and save others (as symbolized by his first sermon in the Deer Park near Banaras), and his final decease at Kuśinagara. The historical sites of these four main events appear to have been clearly remembered. Śākyamuni may well have been born of noble (Kṣatriya) lineage, but the whole story of Śākyamuni's early life is a concoction of legends. The 45 years that he seems to have spent as head of his religious order can be reconstructed only in the most general terms, lacking all chronology. The description of his last journey and death appears to have a recognizable historical basis. Whether the human figure of a gentle religious sage created by means of careful, rational selection from all of the available material has any historical value at all is, however, seriously open to doubt (see also BUDDHA).

Śākyamuni Buddha in Asian art and archaeology. The primary Buddhist monument, both in time and in Buddhist usage to this day, is the *stūpa*, originally a reliquary mound or tumulus. The cult of the *stūpa* may be attested archaeologically from the 3rd century BC onward, but the canonical literary tradition of all Buddhist lands links this all-important cult to the great events associated with Śākyamuni's decease. Mythologically it becomes the supreme symbol of the Buddha in his transcendent state of immortality. Carved stonework preserved from the 2nd century BC onward, especially from the ancient *stūpas* of Sāñchī and Bhārhut in India, reveal the total identity of the great Buddha myth, as revealed in the texts and the monuments. The scenes portrayed are those not only of the great events of Śākyamuni's last life but also the great events of his previous births (*Jātaka*). It is noteworthy that in the earliest period (viz., the centuries BC) the transcendent lord is represented by symbols, a tree indicating his enlightenment, a wheel his first preaching, and a miniature *stūpa* his final Nirvāṇa. Such was felt to be the sanctity of his being, that even as *bodhisattva* of the *Jātaka* stories and of the last life up to the great enlightenment, he was at first not physically portrayed. The tree cult was itself an ancient pre-Buddhist mythology which coalesced with the act of the enlightenment as performed beneath the Bo tree (pipal or *ficus religiosa*). The wheel was both the symbol of the universal monarch (*cakravartin*) and of the Buddha as universal guide and teacher. The *stūpa* cult, with its extraordinary preoccupation with human relics, may have been a special Buddhist development, related to the clearly expressed faith in Nirvāṇa as a transcendent immortal state. It is in

Depiction of the Buddha through symbols

Devotees worshipping at a *stūpa*, the monument that symbolizes the Buddha's *parinirvāṇa*, or final transcendence. Detail of a Bhārhut *stūpa* railing, mid-2nd century BC. In the Indian Museum, Calcutta.
Pramod Chandra

marked contrast with the usual Hindu (Brahmanic) horror of mortal remains as unclean. Śākyamuni began to be figured in sculpture in northwest India from about the 1st century BC onward, and stereotyped presentations of him soon became the model for future use throughout Asia. Common types of Buddha image are that of his calling the earth to witness against Māra by touching it with the finger tips of the right hand, the meditating Buddha protected by a cobra's hood, or Buddha lying on his right side as he enters final Nirvāṇa. The Buddha protected by a cobra's hood represents a coalescing of the Buddha myth with the pre-Buddhist cult of snakes as protecting divinities (the *nāga* cult), but it was justified canonically by a special early legend. This particular image and the "earth witness" one have been very popular in Southeast Asian lands. Iconographically, the Buddha image was adapted to all of the main scenes of Śākyamuni's life, and while the later *stūpas* in India and Southeast Asia achieve ever greater artistic splendour, they remain fundamentally the symbols of Śākyamuni's transcendence, and they continue to be decorated by scenes from his previous lives as well as from his last life. Famous examples are Amarāvatī in South India, *c.* 3rd century AD (some of its stone carvings are preserved in the British Museum), and Borobuḍur in Java, 9th century AD. Borobuḍur is "Mahayānist" in that it is also the symbol of the Five Celestial Buddhas (of which more below), but it reveals the close association between later developments and the great Buddha myth of Śākyamuni.

Temples and indeed whole monasteries hewn out of the rock were used by Buddhists at least from the 2nd century BC until the 8th century AD and probably later. Early ones, famous for their temples with internal *stūpas* set in a kind of sanctuary, are Bhājā, Bhedsa, and Kārlī, all within reach of Bombay; others famous for the development of the iconography of the Buddha figure are Kanheri (near Bombay), Nāsik, Ellora, and, especially, Ajantā. At Ajantā are also preserved fine murals dating from the 1st century BC to the 9th century AD. These mainly represent Śākyamuni in his last and in his previous lives as a compassionate *bodhisattva*.

The traditions of imagery relating to Śākyamuni thrive to this day chiefly in Ceylon and the other Buddhist lands of Southeast Asia where Theravādin Buddhism prevails, but even in the Mahāyāna countries of Nepal, Tibet, China, Japan, Mongolia, and Korea the same iconographic traditions are preserved whenever an image or painting of Śākyamuni is required. Nowhere, thus, are they really lost so long as Buddhism remains.

Celestial Buddhas and bodhisattvas in literary sources. The starting point of all of the later developed Buddhology was the great Buddha myth under one aspect or another. The early idea of a series of Buddhas in time, first seven and later 24, allowed very soon for the idea of a future Buddha, the *bodhisattva* Maitreya. Next was mooted the possibility of other Buddhas in other Buddha lands elsewhere through endless space. Vague popular knowledge in northwest India of the great Iranian divinity Ahura Mazdā seems to have led to the general belief in a Great Buddha of the West, known as "Boundless Light" (Amitābha) or "Boundless Life" (Amitāyus). From its beginnings in northwest India this particular cult spread across Central Asia to China, Korea, and Japan, where it has had an enormous influence to this day. In Indian beliefs this Western Buddha was balanced with the Buddha of the East, the "Imperturbable" (Akṣobhya), who iconographically is identical with Śākyamuni in the "earth-witness" posture. The cult of the "Imperturbable" Buddha probably derives from the actual Buddha cult at Bodh Gayā, the historical place of enlightenment. In addition to Amitābha of the West and Akṣobhya of the East, there are three others—Vairocana, Ratnasambhava, and Amoghasiddhi—that comprise the Five Celestial Buddhas (for the centre of the universe and the four compass points). Vairocana, the "Resplendent" (centre), is the universal sage or *cakravartin* Buddha, indicated by his gesture of preaching and by the symbol of the wheel. Ratnasambhava, the "Jewel Born" (South), represents the Buddha's selfless giving and is indicated by the gesture of giving gifts—right hand open, pointing outward and downward. Amoghasiddhi, "Infallible Success" (North), represents his miraculous power to save and is indicated by the hand gesture of giving protection—right hand raised, palm outward and pointing upward. The Five Celestial Buddhas, also sometimes called Dhyāni Buddhas, seem to be hypostases (concrete manifestations) of Śākyamuni.

Five Celestial Buddhas

From Ryujun Tajima, "Les Deux Grands Mandalas et la Doctrine de l'Esoterisme Shingon," *Bulletin de la Maison Franco-japonaise* (Nouvelle serie, VI); published by Presses Universitaires de France, Paris, 1959

The five celestial Buddhas, shown in the centre and at the four points of the compass, with *bodhisattvas* (Buddhas-to-be) seated on the petals in between. Central section of a *garbha-dhātu maṇḍala* (Japanese *taizō-kai*), a ritual drawing used in worship of the Japanese Shingon sect.

The cult of Śākyamuni in his previous lives as future Buddha (*bodhisattva*) likewise develops manifold forms. Maitreya, the Buddha yet to come, is already known in the earlier period, but from the 1st century onward there is a great cult of celestial *bodhisattva*s, who respond to the same human needs of Buddhists as do the great gods of the developing Hindu pantheon for other Indian devotees. Especially popular are Mañjughoṣa ("Gentle Voice") or Mañjuśrī ("Glorious Gentle One"), the representative of divine wisdom; Avalokiteśvara, the "Lord of Compassion"; and Vajrapāṇi, "the one who wields the ritual thunderbolt (*vajra*)" and as lord of *yakṣas*, a class of local Indian divinities, enters the pantheon as a great protector. In accord with later developments, these three *bodhisattvas* are associated with the three primary Buddhas, Śākyamuni Vairocana, Amitābha, and Akṣobhya. With the development of the set of Five Buddhas, attendent *bodhisattva*s are allocated symmetrically to each. Such a balanced systematization was, however, a gradual process and can be traced in the main Mahāyāna *sūtra*s (texts).

"The Lotus of the Good Law" (*Saddharmapuṇḍarīka*), a text existing before the 2nd century AD, reveals a great theophany (divine manifestation) of Śākyamuni as glorified lord of the universe. The text of the *Sukhāvatī-vyūha* recounts the wonders of Amitābha's Western "Land of Bliss" (Sukhāvatī). The *Karunāpuṇḍarīka* ("The White Lotus of Compassion") is a text concerned with a Buddha Padmottara of the southeast direction but treats also of other Buddhas, especially Amitābha and Śākyamuni, as well as of their previous manifestations as *bodhisattvas*. An important distinction is made between Pure Buddha Lands, like that of Amitābha, and Impure Buddha Lands, such as the present world in which Śākyamuni appeared. Śākyamuni is praised as the more noble because out of his great compassion he chose an Impure Land. A whole new mythology, of great importance in Far Eastern Buddhism, developed in association with the Pure Buddha Lands. In popular aspiration these replaced for Buddhists the paradises of the ordinary Indian gods, which already formed part of the fivefold or sixfold "wheel of life"—a metaphor for and diagrammatic schematization of the cycle of rebirths. But in the case of the Pure Buddha Lands there was the great added advantage of never falling back into unhappy states of existence. Faith alone suffices to ensure one's rebirth in Amitābha's Western paradise. This particular Buddhist devotion may have begun in northwest India whence it certainly reached China via Central Asia. It had some following in India and Nepal, whence it passed to Tibet, but Amitābha usually remains in later Indian tradition as merely one important member of the Five Buddha group. The "Five Buddha" complex finds its primary expression in a text known as the "Symposium of Truth of All the Buddhas" (*Sarvātathāgatattvasaṃgraha*), in which Śākyamuni, as Vairocana, appears as the central Buddha. Another related text is the *Mahāvairocana-sūtra*, important for Japanese Tantric Buddhism (Shingon). The set of Five Buddhas represents the limits of Mahāyāna Buddhological developments, preparing the way for the psychophysical theories of the *Tantra*s. The set of five was correlated not only with the centre and four compass points, viz, the macrocosm, conceived as a unity of the Five Great Elements but also with the microcosm of the human personality with the Five Components (*skandhas*)—*rūpa* (material qualities) *vedanā* (feeling or sensation), *saṃjñā* (perception), *saṃskāra* (components of consciousness), and *vijñāna* (consciousness)—and with the Five Great Evils (Ignorance, Wrath, Desire, Malignity, and Envy), typifying normal phenomenal existence. At this stage mythology is developed as a psychological symbolism. These developments had a great vogue in India from the 8th century onward, thus overlapping with Mahāyāna proper. They spread to Southeast Asia, especially Java and Sumatra, to Nepal, and to Tibet. Tantric Buddhism reached China also in the 8th century, and, before dying out, it passed on to Japan, where as Shingon it still exists. Ceylon, Burma, Siam, and Cambodia were less affected, even by the Mahāyāna forms, because of the extraordinary combative strength of Theravādin Buddhism.

With the *Tantra*s, Buddhist mythology begins at last to part company with the original Buddha myth and clearly links up with the Hindu mythology in a scarcely disguised form. Akṣobhya, thus, has as his fierce Tantric form what is in effect the fierce form of the Hindu god Śiva (Shiva), given, however, his fierce names special to Buddhist Tantric tradition. Known as Heruka, Hevajra, or Saṃvara, he is all one and the same. He is known in Japan in this fierce form as Fudō ("Imperturbable"). The Indian god Bhairava, a fierce bull-headed divinity, adopted by Tantric Buddhists as Vajrabhairava, also known as Yamāntaka "Slayer of Death," and identified as the fierce form of the gentle Mañjuśrī, was accorded quasi-Buddha rank.

Objects of special devotion

Some *bodhisattvas* have become the object of very special devotion. Chief of these is Avalokiteśvara, the Lord of Compassion, who as patron saint of Tibet is believed to reincarnate in the Dalai Lamas. As Kuan-yin in China, Kwannon in Japan, and Kwandyeieum in Korea, this *bodhisattva* is confused with his feminine counterpart Tārā (of whom more below) and becomes a kindly madonna. The *bodhisattva* Kṣitigarbha ("womb of the earth"), who was of no great significance in India and hence of none in Nepal and Tibet, seems to have attracted a cult of himself as lord of the underworld in Central Asia, whence it spread to China and the Far East generally. Known as Ti-ts'ang in Chinese and Jizō in Japanese, he is Lord of hell and so the centre of afterdeath liturgies. Popular cross identifications occur everywhere in Buddhism in the case of minor divinities but seldom with those of quasi-Buddha rank.

Celestial Buddhas and bodhisattvas in art and archaeology. It is mainly from archaeological and artistic remains that scholars are able to trace the remarkable spread of Mahāyāna Buddhist mythology throughout the whole of Asia from the 1st century AD onward. The main points of departure were northwest India for Central Asia and the Far East, and the Bay of Bengal, especially the port of Tāmraliptī. Early Mahāyāna developments also affected South India, and thence Ceylon, Burma, and Siam, and rediscovered images of Avalokiteśvara indicate the earlier popularity of this *bodhisattva* in what are now Theravādin lands. But Bihar and Bengal remained Buddhist, largely late Mahāyāna and Tantric until the 13th century, and there is ample evidence in Java and Sumatra from iconographic remains of the popularity of the Buddhas, *bodhisattvas*, and fierce quasi-Buddha figures mentioned above. There are even traces at Pagan (Burma) in the form of images and paintings of late Mahāyāna and Tantric divinities. Alone in Southeast Asia, the island of Bali still retains a living but mixed Hindu–Tantric Buddhist culture.

Paintings and figures unearthed during the 20th century in Central Asia (Chinese Turkistan) have revealed the manner in which Buddhist architecture, iconography, and painting passed from northwest India to China and the Far East. Especially important are the paintings of Buddhas and *bodhisattvas* in the caves of Tun-huang (4th to 10th century AD). Especially popular in China, and hence in Japan and Korea, are Amitābha–Amitāyus, Vairocana, Maitreya, Mañjuśrī, Kṣitigarbha, and Avalokiteśvara (as the goddess Kuan-yin). Most of these figures were also frequently portrayed in both painting and sculpture in western Tibet, especially during the 10th to 12th centuries AD, and were made known only in the 1930s as a result of the expeditions of the eminent Italian scholar Giuseppi Tucci. In all of these cases the source of the tradition was northwest India.

The main repository of Mahāyāna and Tantric iconographic traditions is Tibet, where Buddhism travelled direct from India, mainly via Nepal, from the 8th to the 13th centuries. Until the Communist take-over of 1959 the Tibetans preserved Indian (Pala) styles of iconography, ancient techniques and styles of Indian Buddhist painting, modified and enriched in some schools by very much later Chinese influence, and the vast range of the late Mahāyāna and Tantric pantheon of deities.

RECURRENT MYTHIC THEMES

Cosmological myths. Śākyamuni is represented according to early tradition as denying all importance to the enquiry whether the universe is infinite or not, eternal or not. It was enough to realize that normal existence consisted of a wretched process of continual death and rebirth, from which, by following his teachings, one might procure one's release. Such an ordinance did not prevent his followers from accepting the general cosmological beliefs of their time, modified by conclusions drawn from his specific moral and religious teachings.

It was thus believed that the present world system, like all others throughout space, goes through the inevitable process of creation, duration, and destruction. Thus nothing of the "realm of desire" (*kāmadhātu*), in which the gods, humans, and lower creatures live, has any permanence, not even the "creator god" Brahmā, who is merely the first being to appear and the last to disappear with every recurrent cycle. Brahmā's life, of course, covers a vast period of time by human reckoning. The present world system consists of various stages, becoming, as one descends, more impure and more unhappy. First come six graded heavens, occupied by corresponding orders of gods. Next comes the world of human beings. This consists of four "continents" (*dvīpa*) that surround the central mountain (Meru), on which the gods dwell. The southern "continent," named Jambudvīpa, vaguely represents India and surrounding lands. The other living creatures, such as animals, birds, fishes, and insects, which share the world of men, are thought of as leading even more miserable lives than men do. Still more unhappy are the tormented spirits (*preta*) who help to make life still more troublesome for mankind. Below the world of men are the terrible hells in which the most excruciating torments await evildoers.

Five conditions of rebirth

Depending upon their actions men are reborn in any of these five conditions: as gods, men, animals, tormented spirits, or in the hells. Later, a sixth condition, that of Titans, was added. These five or six states represent the ever-revolving wheel of life. When the world system comes to an end, the combined potency of previous actions (*karman*) restarts the whole process, just as present individual actions (which become *karman* in the future) result in a continuous series (*santāna*) of apparently personal existences. Thus, for practical purposes, the process of existence appears as infinite, and only the practice of Buddhist teachings can bring it to an absolute end, which is the deathless state of enlightenment.

It must be stressed that Buddhists are never agnostic in any Western sense. They are justified in believing in gods, troublesome spirits, and the hells, at least to the extent that they believe in the everyday life of the ordinary world. Ultimately everything is impermanent, but at least the gods have a much longer spell of life than men do and so need to be taken into account, as do troublesome spirits, in everyday affairs. Only the contemplative sage can afford to regard them as unreal, just as he regards the world of men as a mere empty flux. Thus the pursuit of the myth of the origin and destruction of the cosmos, of the time process (*saṃsāra*), and of release from it (Nirvāṇa) is a privilege of a special elite; and Buddhist layfolk and indeed the majority of ordinary monks usually have been content to accept on faith the various findings of their philosophers, realizing meanwhile that they have to come to terms first of all with the transient phenomenal world, with its gods and its spirits, and with the prospect, not of final release but of a new life in what may be worse circumstances than the present.

With the change in philosophy from the phenomenalism of the early schools to the monistic idealism of the Mahāyāna, the process of origin and destruction was diagnosed by the elite as an illusive mental construct deriving from the apparent operation of *karman*. Thus in theory the whole time process (*saṃsāra*) is pure imagination in essence, although as a means toward release one may have to act as though taking it seriously. So long as one is still on the path toward enlightenment the perception of the higher knowledge of an absolute kind has to be tempered by actions, words, and thoughts, relative to the empirical needs of oneself and of others.

Myths of Buddhas and bodhisattvas. The Buddhas, celestial *bodhisattvas*, and the fierce quasi-Buddha manifestations recognized by the followers of the *Tantras* all transcend phenomenal existence in their absolute state while readily involving themselves in it for the sake of suffering living creatures. Although this idea was only fully developed by the Mahāyāna, it has already been noted that the same fundamental conception of a Buddha as transcendent in essence, but at the same time operative as world saviour in an imminent sense, belongs to the great Buddha myth constructed around Śākyamuni by the first Buddhist believers. Thus, while a small contemplative elite may always regard any Buddha as the impersonal symbol of the ineffable state of enlightenment, most of the faithful have been equally justified in approaching him as a divine saviour. Buddhism has always been a religion of faith, whether of faith in the realizability of final enlightenment or of faith in the Buddhas and *bodhisattvas* as helpers along the way. The Mahāyāna and certainly the Tantric schools vastly increased the available means of progress to suit all local tastes and propensities, but the fundamental psychology of an accepted dual approach remains scarcely changed. The mystical-philosophic approach aims at comparatively rapid results and risks wholesale denials, both bodily and mental. The slow approach, through devotion to Buddhas and *bodhisattvas* as divine beings and through the practice of morality in the everyday world, posits religious realities that the spiritual elite in theory deny but in practice readily accept, for they know their very denial is as relative to the desired end as the actual acceptance (see also *Celestial Buddhas and bodhisattvas in literary sources* above).

Local gods and demons. While the contemplative elite may deny the real existence of gods and demons together with all the rest of phenomenal existence, the majority of Buddhists from the earliest times in India, and in whatever country north to south where Buddhism has spread, have never neglected indigenous religious beliefs. It has already been noted how Māra, the manifestation of spiritual evil, is presented in the earliest literature in the terms of local demonological beliefs. It is also to be noted that the early *stūpas* and entrances to cave temples were decorated with local male and female divinities (usually referred to as *yakṣa* and *yakṣinī*) who were presumably already conceived as converted defenders of the new faith. This proved the easier way of justifying the continuance of the cult of local divinities, and it has been employed in varying degrees in every Buddhist land.

Buddhism as a religion of faith

There thus began to develop a pantheon of minor divinities, which from a common original stock has continued to take in new members wherever Buddhism has become an established religion. The Mahāyāna has given them a more ready official welcome, even admitting their cult as a subsidiary part of liturgies in honour of Buddhas and *bodhisattvas*. Such favoured ones are Mahākāla, the great black divinity; the mother goddess Hārītī; Kuvera, the god of wealth; and especially Hayagrīva, a fierce horse-faced god, who, now converted to the Buddhist doctrine, is very powerful in driving off unconverted demonic forces. A favourite myth, originating probably in northwest India or even in Central Asia and well established in Tibet and Mongolia, China, Korea and, Japan, was that of the Great Kings (Sanskrit: *mahārāja;* Tibetan: *rgyal-chen*) of the four quarters, who defend the frontiers of Buddhist religion. They are regularly depicted on the walls of the entrance halls of temples. Their Sanskrit names are Kuvera (north), Dhṛtaraṣṭra (east), Virūḍhaka (south), and Virūpākṣa (west).

It is commonly believed by Tibetans related in their history books that Buddhism began to become established in their land in the 8th century only as a result of a wholesale subjugation of opposing local divinities. Some have continued to be hostile throughout the centuries and must be placated by offerings or quelled by suitable fierce rites. The indigenous priests, known as *bon*, increasingly replaced by Buddhist Tantric sorcerers, are thought to have the best control over these troublesome intruders. The same situation has existed in China, where a vast variety of local divinities has been kept in check, where possible, by Taoist priests, assisted sometimes by Buddhists, and likewise in Japan, where the local Shintō gods have never lost their power.

Quite as much in Theravādin as in Mahāyāna countries, Buddhism has everywhere had to come to terms with local beliefs, and in their everyday lives Buddhists have continued to be more preoccupied with placating local divinities or avoiding their ill effects than with worshipping the Buddha in his temple. After all, the Buddha is known to be benign. Much has been written of the power of the *nat* in Burma, the *phi* of Siam, and the various local spirits of Cambodia and Laos. Nor is Buddhism any more pure in this respect in Ceylon, where small shrines of converted Hindu and local Ceylonese divinities may be placed in the vicinity of a Buddhist temple. In all of the lands within easy reach of India—namely Ceylon, Burma, Siam to the south, and Nepal to the north—Indian (Hindu) divinities have been accepted without any sense of contradiction on the part of those who call themselves Buddhists.

Local spirits in Buddhist countries

Feminine divinities. The presence of minor feminine divinities of the kind described above, allowed to exist as "protectors" on the fringe of the religion, presents no special problem. But the elevation of feminine figures to Buddha rank requires special comment. The appearance of a universal mother goddess in Indian Buddhism is not surprising and was easily rendered "theologically" acceptable. She appears in Mahāyāna Buddhism under two aspects, as the personification of Supreme Wisdom and as the Mother of all Buddhas, as manifest especially in Mahāmāyā, the virgin mother of Śākyamuni. As universal mother, she is known as Tārā the Saviouress, may be identified with Supreme Wisdom (*Prajñāpāramitā*), and thus far is pure and chaste. In all this there is nothing that contravenes the notions of celibacy, which have in fact remained typical of Buddhist monasticism everywhere, despite occasional aberrations. The majority of Mahāyānists have never gone beyond this point, and the devotion to Kuan-yin in China, Japan, and Korea as a great mother goddess belongs to the generally acceptable Indian Mahāyāna tradition.

From the 7th century, however, a whole riot of feminine divinities began to find their way into certain circles of Buddhist *yogins*, where they were actually represented by women partners in a special kind of sexual *yoga* (physical and mental discipline). The whole process, both the actual rites as well as the actual feminine divinities, was gradually interpreted as an internal form of celibate *yoga*, for in accordance with Mahāyāna theory, enlightenment was achieved by the union of Wisdom and Method, now conceived of symbolically as female and male. Thus it became possible to present supreme Buddhahood, as represented pre-eminently by the Five Supreme Buddhas, as a union of pairs. So it came about that every celestial Buddha or quasi-Buddha might be represented as a male and female pair (Tibetan *yab-yum*). The actual sexual ritual was certainly performed at one time in India and Nepal, seemingly to a very limited extent in Tibet, and perhaps not at all in China and Japan, although the symbolism became known there and the Japanese Shingon sect has adopted it. This whole Tantric iconography very soon came to represent an esoteric and often quite grotesque symbolism, which Mahāyāna Buddhists have simply taken for granted as part of their received tradition. This particular "myth" has achieved its fullest iconographic and artistic expression in Tibet, where it has been left to Westerners and more recently to Communist Chinese to marvel at so extraordinary a development.

Kings and yogins. The great Buddha myth is a combination of the ideals of universal kingship and universal religious pre-eminence. This is clearly expressed in the myth of the prophetic utterance of future greatness by the sage Asita—an astrologer who examined auspicious signs on the infant Śākyamuni—over the child *bodhisattva*. Also in his previous life as Viśvantara, Śākyamuni had already realized the perfection of the extraordinary combination of kingship and all-abandoning asceticism. As crown prince, Viśvantara is famed for his vast generosity, and, becoming the despair of his more practical-minded father, he accepts banishment to the forest, where he attains the ultimate of self-abnegation in giving away his children and his wife and in some accounts even his own eyes. These and all else are restored to him miraculously, and responding to the demands of his countrymen he returns home to become the best of kings. Similarly, the last life of Śākyamuni, up to the time of his great renunciation, is told entirely as a royal story.

Although the practice of Buddhist religion strictly required withdrawal from the world, or at least renunciation of its pleasures, Buddhist monks were, understandably enough, anxious to win royal support. They always needed benefactors, and what better benefactor than a king. Any suggestion of royal benefaction thus resulted in the revival of the "myth" of the vastly generous monarch. Whenever Mahāyāna tendencies were at work, also in the notion of his sanctity, he represented, in one important aspect, that of generous giving, the ideal of the *bodhisattva*. The most famous example is the Indian emperor Aśoka (3rd century BC), who certainly facilitated the spread of Buddhism and concerning whom vast legends have grown up. Among other things he is credited with having built 84,000 *stūpa*s. Surrounding countries all claim to have received Buddhism through his mediacy. On a smaller scale legends embellish the life of King Tissa of Ceylon (same period), who presided over the arrival of Buddhism. In the same context one may mention Prince Shōtoku Taishi of Japan (died AD 621) and Srong-brtsan-sgam-po of Tibet (died AD 650), noting, however, that the enthusiasm of the first for Buddhism is genuinely historical. This is also true of Tibet's two other great "kings of religion." Khrisong Detsan (second half of 8th century) and Ral-pa-chem, assassinated by enemies of the faith in AD 836.

The role of emperor Aśoka

The great *stūpa* of Borobuḍur, already mentioned, deliberately represents the self-identification of the ruling monarch of Java with the aspiration toward Buddhahood. The king presents himself as the *bodhisattva* par excellence. At the other side of the Buddhist world, the Tibetans developed the same idea when they identified their reincarnating Dalai Lama as a manifestation of their patron "saint," the *bodhisattva* Avalokiteśvara. Seen in its total Buddhist context, this idea is not as strange as Europeans appear to find it. Also by polite mythical fiction the Manchu emperors of China were regarded as manifestations of the *bodhisattva* Mañjuśrī; so too (with far more justice) was the great Tibetan religious reformer Tsong-kha-pa (1357–1419). As a result of the more limited nature of their doctrines, Theravādin countries lag far behind in these interesting developments. There such kings as Dammazed of Pegu (died 1491) or Mindon of Burma (died 1878), and even great religious ascetics, remain transient mortal beings of flesh and blood.

Under the aspect of the pre-Buddhist Indian myth of the ideal perfected *yogin*, possessed of miraculous powers, however, the greatness of the Buddhist ascetic is a theme well suited to Buddhism everywhere. The early disciples of Śākyamuni, known as *arhat*s when they achieved perfection, were conceived of as miracle-working *yogin*s, and the early canonical literature presents them in this way. This same ideal was acknowledged in Theravādin Ceylon, and the Ceylonese claim their share of *arhats*. But it is in Tibet, which drew on the more developed Indian myth of the "great yogin" (*mahāsiddha*) of the Tantric period (8th to 12th centuries AD) that this theme shows its most luxurious development. Especially famous are Padmasambhava (also called Guru Rimpoche), an 8th-century Indian *yogin* credited with having quelled the evil spirits of Tibet, and again the strange figure of Dam-pa Sangs-rygas, a Brahmin of South India who became a Buddhist and visited Tibet and possibly China in the 11th century. Doubtless historical, Dam-pa Sangs-rygas passes right out of history into myth with his fantastic powers and equally fantastic longevity. Better known in Europe is the story of the Tibetan *yogin* Mi-la Ras-pa also 11th century. During its earlier period in China, Buddhism was more of a gentlemanly cultural pursuit than an enthusiastic religious movement, but the same mythical tendencies were soon at work. Bodhidharma (6th century), founder of Ch'an (Zen) Buddhism, is also an Indian *yogin*, appearing in quasi-historical, quasi-mythical guise. Subsequently the ideal of the Buddhist sage, as typified by the *arhat*s, is confused in Chinese thought with the Taoist immortals; and here, as in so much else, Far Eastern Buddhism developed new forms of the religion as it coalesced increasingly with the great non-Buddhist mythologies of China and Japan.

*Arhat*s and *mahāsiddha*s

SIGNIFICANCE

Myth in Buddhism is used at various intellectual levels in order to give symbolic and sometimes quasi-historical expression to apprehended or presumed religious truths. Accepted on its own terms, Buddhism is a supernatural religion in the sense that without a Buddha to reveal them, the truths remain unknown. Only after a man has received the Buddha revelation can he proceed apparently by his own efforts. This teaching was explicit in the early schools, in which the revelation was still thought of as historically related to Śākyamuni's mission in the world. Gradually the idea formed in some schools of the Buddha's continuous revelation and gracious assistance, deriving from his glorified state of time-transcending enlightenment. Thus the comparatively simple mythology of the great Buddha myth developed into the far more elaborate mythology of the Mahāyāna. The acceptance of the mythology, whether early or fully developed, depends upon faith. Without faith the whole religion crumbles to nothing, and nothing is left but a demythologized supposedly historical figure who has no special revelation to give. He becomes a wandering ascetic of 6th–5th century India BC, like the many others known to scholars, and his religion has no explanation. One must, thus, emphasize that it was the extraordinary combination of the historical Śākyamuni and the relevant myth that he was seen to fulfill that set the whole great religious tradition known as Buddhism on its varied historical course. It has been observed also how myth is continually used at second or even third remove to bolster the primary myth and to give it a more convincing expression, at least for those who do not have the means of checking the validity of the traditional materials employed. This subsidiary form of myth—*e.g.*, the stories about the recitation of the Buddhist canon soon after Śākyamuni's decease, the details of his previous lives, the stereotyped descriptions of the six spheres of rebirth—can be shown up as an artificial, imagined construction. Mahāyāna Buddhist philosophy performed precisely this task, although with arguments very different from those of modern scholarship. Yet knowledge of the relative and artificial nature of this subsidiary mythology does not necessarily destroy the fundamental myth, which is the story of salvation achieved by means that rest on premises that are always provisional but, insofar as they serve the gaining of the chief objective, never really false. Thus the state of the intelligent Buddhist believer must always be ambivalent.

BIBLIOGRAPHY. Two major general works are *Mythologie asiatique illustrée*, introduced by P.L. COUCHOUD (1928), covering the whole subject except for Ceylon and the Theravādin countries of Southeast Asia, with good illustrations; and *New Larousse Encyclopaedia of Mythology*, introduced by ROBERT GRAVES (1959), containing relevant articles on Indian, Chinese, and Japanese mythology.

Other important works include: BU-STON, *History of Buddhism*, trans. by E.E. OBERMILLER, 2 vol. (1931–32), an important short history of Indian Buddhism as seen from the traditional Mahāyāna viewpoint; PERCY BROWN, *Indian Architecture*, vol. 1, *Buddhist and Hindu Periods*, 3rd rev. ed. (1965), a standard work for tracing the development of Buddhist mythology in art and architecture; R.S. COPLESTON, *Buddhism: Primitive and Present in Magadha and Ceylon* (1908), a readable, informative account quoting traditional Buddhist sources, still very useful; CHARLES ELIOT, *Japanese Buddhism* (1935, reprinted 1959), a classical work and a useful survey; ALFRED FOUCHER, *La vie du Bouddha d'après les textes et les monuments de l'Inde* (1949; abridged Eng. trans., *The Life of Buddha*, 1963), a unique study of the legends surrounding Śākyamuni, *Les vies antérieures du Bouddha* (1955), a readable survey of Buddha's previous lives; ALICE GETTY, *The Gods of Northern Buddhism*, 2nd rev. ed. (1928), a useful description of Buddhism's chief divinities; H. KERN, *The Lotus of the True Law* (Eng. trans. 1963), a discussion of the type of Mahāyāna *sūtra* which expressed the developing Buddhological myth; ETIENNE LAMOTTE, "La Légende du Bouddha," in *Revue de l'histoire des religions*, 134:37–71 (1947–48), an important article, arguing the futility of trying to discover an historical figure acceptable to modern expectations; T.O. LING, *Buddhism and the Mythology of Evil: A Study of Theravada Buddhism* (1962), a short and brilliant study of one particular aspect of Buddhist mythology; PAUL MUS, *Borobudur* (1935), a lengthy detailed work, covering the whole complex mythology of later Buddhism; WALPOLA RAHULA, *History of Buddhism in Ceylon* (1956), a useful survey of the period 3rd century BC to 10th AD; K.J. SAUNDERS, *Buddhism and Buddhists in Southern Asia* (1923), a brief readable account of the more external features of Buddhism in Ceylon, Burma, and Siam; D.L. SNELLGROVE, *Buddhist Himalaya* (1957), a survey of Buddhism as a living mythology as it passed from India via Nepal to Tibet, and (ed. and trans.), *Four Lamas of Dolpo* (1967), a study of the daily lives of four Tibetan lamas; F. STARR, *Korean Buddhism* (1918), three essays on the history of Buddhism in Korea, its actual condition, and on Buddhist art (a slight work, but useful where so little information is available); E.J. THOMAS, *The Life of Buddha as Legend and History*, 3rd ed. rev. (1949, reprinted 1969), an important standard work; GIUSEPPE TUCCI, *Indo-Tibetica*, 4 vol. (1932–41), an essential, well-illustrated work for any serious student of late Indian Mahāyāna and Tantric art, *Tibetan Painted Scrolls*, 2 vol. (Eng. trans. 1949), an essential work, including much historical material; L. DE LA VALLEE POUSSIN, *Le dogme et la philosophie du Bouddhisme* (1930), a very important short work, drawing the necessary distinction between Buddhist philosophy, and mythology as expressed in dogma, and showing how in practice one does not contradict the other; and ISSHI YAMADA, *Karunāpundarīka*, 2 vol. (1968), an important discussion of the development of Mahāyāna beliefs concerning celestial Buddhas and their paradises.

(D.L.S.)

Buddhist Philosophy

Buddhist philosophy is both a system of thought and a set of ethical norms offering practical guidance in everyday social affairs. This article deals with the Buddhist views regarding metaphysics and epistemology, the problems of human existence, eschatology and soteriology, ethics, psychology, and logic.

Buddhist metaphysics and epistemology. *The fundamental attitude.* Buddhism sought reform by rejecting the authority of established religions and teaching an independent ethical morality.

Buddhists are enjoined to follow the path prescribed by the Buddha. Faith is indispensable, but it is only a preliminary requirement for practicing the way. Faith, for the Buddhist, should not be in contradiction to reason. Faith unexamined by reason becomes superstition. Buddhists have accepted two standards for the truth (veracity) of a statement: it must be in accordance with the Buddhist canonical scriptures, and it must be proved true by reasoning. No Buddhist is expected to believe anything that does not meet these two tests.

The *dharmas*

Buddhism presupposes universal laws called *dharmas*, which govern human existence and may be known by reason. Personal relations should be brought into harmony with the universal norms, which apply to all existence, regardless of time and space. Metaphysical speculation concerning problems not related to human activities and the attainment of Enlightenment, such as whether the world is infinite or finite and whether the soul and the body are identical or different from each other, is discouraged.

Throughout the Buddhist world, the community has never been organized around a central authority that could decree doctrines or practices that must be observed by all followers. Buddhists of all types have been comparatively individualistic and unwilling to submit to a rigid outer authority. Agreement as to the doctrines to be held and the practices to be followed has been reached by discussion within the community, guided by the scriptures accepted as a basis for their faith. Only in Japan are there marked sectarian differences, but the authorities of the extant sects are not coercive.

All metaphysical views are only partial apprehensions of the whole truth, which lies beyond rational analysis. Only a buddha can apprehend the whole truth. Rational analysis is useful in making clear the limitations of rationality, but it is by detaching oneself from philosophical oppositions that one is able to grasp the truth. Thus, the doctrine of the Buddha is not a system of philosophy in the Western sense but is rather a path. A buddha is simply one who has walked this path and can report to others on what he has found.

The Buddha's doctrine is called a vehicle in the sense that it is like a ferryboat. One enters the Buddhist vehicle to cross the river of life from the shore of worldly experience, spiritual ignorance, desire, and suffering to the other shore of transcendental wisdom, which is liberation from bondage and suffering. If a man builds a raft and by this means succeeds in attaining the other shore, then he should abandon the raft. In the same way the vehicle of the doctrine is to be cast away and forsaken, once the other shore of Enlightenment has been attained. Just as the difference in shape, weight, and material among rafts does not matter, difference in teachings does not matter. This point of view is set forth both in Theravāda and in Mahāyāna, the major divisions of Buddhism, the former being the earlier form, prevalent in South Asia, and the latter the more liberal, prevalent in China and Japan.

The ways of faith and insight

Faith is an introductory means to the attainment of truth, not an acceptance of definite dogmas. When one takes refuge in the Three Jewels (Buddha, the teaching, and the order), it is a partial turning away from the visible to the invisible. Faith does not necessarily mean the realization of truth itself; it is important only insofar as it opens the door of the ideal state. Throughout Buddhist history there have been two currents, the devotional approach and the approach through inner knowledge, insight. The approach through the inner vision has always been regarded as the truer one, while the devotional approach has been more or less regarded as a means for the common people. The only outstanding exceptions to this have been Pure Land Buddhism (a Chinese and Japanese sect stressing worship of Amitābha Buddha—the Buddha of infinite life and splendour) and the Nichiren sect (followers of the 13th-century nationalist saint Nichiren). For them, faith is made supreme and is essential to deliverance.

The universe. Buddhism declares that everything has been brought about by causes, that there is no permanent substratum of existence. There is general agreement that the only true method of explaining any existing thing is to trace one cause back to the next, without the desire or need to explain the ultimate cause of all things. For Buddhism there is no divine creator. It asserts that the universe is uncreated, without beginning or end, and that origination, duration, destruction, and annihilation succeed one another in recurrent cyclic change.

According to Buddhist dogmatics there are three spheres, or planes, where living beings stay: (1) the immaterial plane (sphere) of existence (*arūpadhātu*), where pure spirits without material body live; (2) the material plane of existence (*rūpadhātu*), where ethereal living beings live; (3) the plane of desire (*kāmadhātu*), where living beings of gross material live and which, roughly speaking, corresponds to the natural world. The world in which human beings live, the plane of desire, is made up of four elements: earth, water, heat, and wind (later theories add space and intelligence).

Buddhist beliefs concerning the nature of the universe were shaped by belief in *karman* and rebirth. In accordance with the admittance of the doctrines of transmigration and *karman*, the Buddhists had to assume good and bad places—heavens and hells—in which people could be born according to their deeds. The Buddha did not deny the existence of divine beings and their realm. Common people preferred to look for a better world beyond, which ritualism would ensure to them. Though the traditional Buddhist cosmology is held only nominally by present-day Buddhists who have training in modern sciences, the underlying premise remains the same. The structure of the natural world is not essential in Buddhism: the Buddha's essential concern was human conduct.

The categories of living beings

Living beings. Living beings in the plane of desire are divided into five categories, two good and three bad, called "kinds of existence" (*gati*). They are (1) heavenly beings (gods), (2) men, (3) departed spirits (*preta*), (4) animals (beasts), and (5) the hellish creatures (depraved men) who live in numerous hells. Sometimes another category of existence, that of the *asura* (a demon, warlike, fighting spirit), also is predicated between gods and men. These beings, including the gods, belong to the sphere of transmigration. One result of this theory of the world has been that the Buddhist attitude toward animals has been one of kindness to fellow beings. In some countries, people visiting temples make a practice of releasing birds or fish that have been captured. There have always been many Buddhists who were vegetarians.

Birth as a human being is essential for the appreciation of the *dharma* for Enlightenment. Gods are too happy to feel a dislike for conditioned things and live too long to have any appreciation for the doctrine of impermanence. Animals, departed spirits, demons, and the damned lack sufficient clarity of mind to enable them to overcome their ignorance; therefore, the human state is in general more favourable than any other for the attainment of Enlightenment. Man is distinguished from other beings by his aptitude for goodness, a love for the *dharma*, and, consequently, by love or compassion (*mettā*) for other beings.

Problems of human existence. Always and everywhere through its long history, Buddhism has stressed the fact of human suffering. Existence is painful. The conditions that make an individual are precisely those that also give rise to suffering. Individuality involves limitation; limitation ends in suffering.

Existence as suffering

Desire causes suffering, since what is desired is transitory, changing, and perishing. It is the impermanence of the object of our craving that causes disappointment and sorrow. These desires are caused by ignorance, from which men can be freed by following the "path" taught by the Buddha. The Buddha's doctrine was not one of despair. Living amid the impermanence of everything and being himself impermanent, man searches for the way of deliverance, for that which shines beyond the transitoriness of human existence—in short, for Enlightenment. The only significant variation from the teaching that man must work out his own salvation has been the dependence of the Pure Land sect of China and Japan upon the help of the external power.

The theory of nonself. The teaching of *anātman* (Pāli *anatta*, "nonego" or "nonself") has been regarded as characteristic of Buddhist thought. The Sanskrit *ātman* is translated as "ego" or "soul," though its more literal meaning is "self," for even in early Buddhism a distinction was frequently made between the ego and the true self. The Buddha did not want to assume that there is any metaphysical substance. Life is a stream of becoming, a series of manifestations and extinctions. The concept of the individual ego is a popular delusion; the objects with which man identifies himself—fortune, social position, family, body, and even mind—are not his true self. There is nothing permanent, and, if only the permanent deserved to be called the self, or *ātman*, then nothing on Earth is self. There can be no individuality without a putting together of components. This is becoming different, and there can be no way of becoming different without a dissolution, a passing away.

The constituents of human existence

To make clear the teaching of nonego, Buddhists set forth the theory of the five aggregates or constituents (*skandha*s) of human existence: (1) corporeality or physical forms (*rūpa*), (2) feelings or sensations (*vendanā*), (3) ideations (Sanskrit *saṃjñā;* Pāli *saññā*), (4) mental formations or dispositions (Sanskrit *saṃskāra;* Pāli *sankhara*), (5) consciousness (Sanskrit *vijñāna;* Pāli *viññāna*). Human existence is only a composite of the five aggregates (*skandha*s), none of which is the self or soul. A person is in a process of continuous change, with no fixed underlying entity. In this way Buddhism swept away the traditional conception of a substance called soul, or ego, which had theretofore dominated the minds of the superstitious and the intellectuals alike.

In daily life the assumption is made that something is "mine," that "I" am something, or that something is "myself." According to Buddhism, this is erroneous. Properly applied, the method of reflection on the *skandha*s has a tremendous power to disintegrate unwholesome experience and can contribute much to a person's mental development by helping him set up the habit of viewing all things impersonally.

Denial of the ego

In early Buddhism those who got rid of the notion of ego were highly praised. Such a denial, however, does not connote nihilism or materialism. The Buddha clearly expressed what the self is not, but he did not give any clear account of what it is. The Buddha did not want to assume the existence of souls as metaphysical substances, but he admitted the existence of the self as the subject of action in a practical and moral sense. The Buddha neither affirms nor denies the existence of *ātman*. As "body" (corporeality) is a name for a system of some functions, even so "soul" is a name for the sum of the states that constitute a person's mental existence. Without functions there can be admitted no soul.

The true self. In early Buddhism "one who knows the self" was highly esteemed. The virtue of relying upon oneself also was highly stressed. The Buddha taught his disciples, "Be a refuge to yourself." On another occasion he asked a group of young men who were searching for a missing woman: "Which is better, for you to go seeking the woman, or to go seeking the Self?" It is to be noted that he did not say "your selves"; he did not think that each individual had its own self as an entity. There are two selves: the empirical self in daily life that is to be subdued and the religious self. The realization of Nirvāṇa can be explained as taking refuge in one's own true self. On this point the Buddha's assertion suggests a comparison with Hindu Vedānta philosophy. But the self (*ātman*) of the Vedāntists was rather metaphysical, while the Buddha's self was genuinely practical.

Mahāyāna Buddhism developed the idea of a "Buddha-nature" latent in everyone's existence. This concept of the Great Self was especially emphasized in the Mahāyāna text, the *Mahāparinirvāṇa-sūtra* (an account of the Buddha's last days, of which only the Chinese versions are extant), and was generally admitted in Vajrayāna (*i.e.*, Tantric Buddhist) texts. The idea is commonly held by Chinese, Korean, and Japanese Buddhists but not by Theravāda Buddhists, who criticize the concept for its similarity to Vedāntic philosophy.

Inquiry into the cause of suffering. The Buddha inquired into the cause of worldly suffering on the practical, psychological level and found out that the real cause of human suffering is ignorant craving (*tṛṣṇā*). Just as a physician must study a disease in order to determine a cure, so also the Buddha studied the range of suffering, its origin, its cessation, and the way that leads to its cessation.

The Four Noble Truths

His conclusions were expressed in the doctrine of the Four Noble Truths: (1) the noble truth of suffering: birth, decay, disease, death, union with the unpleasant, separation from the pleasant, and not obtaining what one wishes—all are suffering; in brief, the five aggregates that spring from clinging (that is, the conditions of individuality) are suffering. (2) The noble truth of the origin of suffering: it is the craving thirst that causes rebirth, accompanied by sensual delights; this thirst seeks satisfaction (now here, now there) as a craving for lust, for existence, or for nonexistence. (3) The noble truth of the cessation of suffering: suffering ceases with the complete cessation of that craving—the giving up, the getting rid of, the release from, and the detachment from this craving thirst. (4) The noble truth of the way that leads to the cessation of suffering: the noble Eightfold Path consists of right views, right intention, right speech, right conduct, right livelihood, right effort, right mindfulness, and right concentration. The path pointed out by Gautama is called the noble Eightfold Path; the truths enumerated are called the Four Noble Truths. All the items of the Four Noble Truths were commented upon in full detail by later dogmaticians.

The sufferings and afflictions of man originate spontaneously from the impetus of his innermost condition of nonknowing. The distress of craving is based upon this nonknowing or fallacious understanding, on thinking that there is something real in satisfying these desires in the mundane world. It is this mistake about the true essence of reality that is the cause of all the sufferings that affect man's life. Ignorance and false desires are the theoretical and the practical sides of one fact; in actual life the two are one. When ultimate Enlightenment dispels ignorance, the successive constituents of the individual cease to operate, and suffering as well as transmigration ends.

The formula of "dependent origination"

It was by the attainment of this supreme Enlightenment, or wisdom, that Gautama became a buddha. In its simplest form it can be expressed thus: because of ignorance (lack of knowledge), man suffers. Because of knowledge (*i.e.*, disappearance of ignorance), man does not suffer. Between the two extremes of ignorance and suffering, Buddhist thinkers have found and formulated several intermediate conditions, expressed finally in the following formula: (1) the condition of ignorance leads to (2) will-to-action (*saṃskāra*), which in turn leads to (3) consciousness, which leads to (4) psycho-physical existence, which leads to (5) the six organs of sense (eye, ear, nose, tongue, body or sense of touch, and mind), which leads to (6) contact, which leads to (7) sensation (or feeling), which leads to (8) craving, which leads to (9) attachment (or grasping), which leads to (10) becoming (or worldly existence), which leads to (11) birth, which leads to (12) decay, death, grief, lamentation, physical suffering, dejection, and despair.

This formula, called origination through dependence or "dependent origination" (Sanskrit *pratītyasamutpāda;* Pāli *paṭiccasamuppāda*), is repeated in many scriptural passages, together with elaborate explanations of each.

It is noteworthy that the law of dependent origination was taught without regard to the authority of buddhas. As expressing a universal truth, it was considered as valid externally and from eternity, independently of the advent of buddhas or action by a deity.

The term dependent origination became very popular in later Buddhism. All schools of Buddhism accepted the importance of the chain of causation, but not all interpreted dependent origination in the same way. One definition of the term widely accepted in the ancient schools, especially in the Sarvāstivāda (All Exists school), is the interconnection according to causal laws of all the elements cooperating in the formation of life through continuing cycles of progress from birth to death and from death to rebirth in successive lives. In Mahāyāna, especially in the Mādhyamika (Middle View) school, dependent origination meant the interrelational existence of all things or the relationality of things and ideas. The Vijñānavāda (Consciousness Only) school occasionally took it to mean the process of manifestation of all phenomena out of the fundamental consciousness (*ālaya-vijñāna*). The Hua-yen (Kegon) school in China and Japan interpreted the term as the interpenetration of all things in the universe throughout the past, the present, and the future, asserting that nothing can exist separately from other things and that all things are interrelated.

Voidness (*śūnyatā*). The concept of voidness (*śūnyatā*) appeared already in the ancient schools of Buddhism, but it was not elaborately theorized. Mahāyāna Buddhism found in dependent origination the basis for voidness. There is no real existence; all things are but appearances and are in truth empty. Voidness or emptiness is neither nothingness nor annihilation but is that which stands right in the middle between affirmation and negation, existence and nonexistence, eternity and annihilation. The void is all-inclusive; having no opposite, there is nothing that it excludes or opposes. It is living void because all forms come out of it, and whoever realizes the void is filled with life and power and the Bodhisattva's compassion of all beings. Voidness, which is nothing but ultimate reality, is called by other terms, such as suchness (*tathatā*) or the basis of reality (*bhūtakoṭi*).

The belief in rebirth

Karman (*freedom and determination*). The belief in rebirth—of an endless series of worldly existences repeated by every being—was in pre-Buddhist India already associated with the doctrine of *karman* and was generally accepted by both the Theravāda and the Mahāyāna traditions. According to the doctrine of *karman* (literally meaning "act" or "deed"), good conduct brings a pleasant and happy result and creates a tendency toward similar good acts, while bad conduct brings an evil result and creates a tendency toward repeated evil actions. This furnishes the basic condition for moral improvement of the individual.

Some *karman*s bear fruit in the same life in which they are committed, others in the immediately succeeding one, and others in future lives more remote. The individual is the result of a multitude of causes carried over from his past existence and intimately related to all other causes in the world. The interconnection between one individual and the whole universe is stressed in the Buddhist doctrine of *karman*.

Most Buddhists have attached much importance to the way of dying, in the belief that the nature of the rebirth corresponds to the nature of a person's thoughts in the moments preceding death. The Shin sect of Japan differs from this general view by asserting that the destiny of each person after death is fixed by his faith during his lifetime.

The acceptance by Buddhists of the belief in *karman* and rebirth while holding to the doctrine of nonself gave rise to a difficult problem: how can rebirth take place without a permanent subject to be reborn? Indian non-Buddhist philosophers attacked this vulnerable point in Buddhist thought, and many modern scholars have also considered it to be an insoluble question. The relation between existences in rebirth has been explained by the analogy of fire, which maintains itself unchanged in appearance and yet is different in every moment—what may be called the continuity of an ever changing identity. In order to meet this vulnerable point, some Buddhists later assumed a sort of soul, though calling it by different names. This assumption finally gave rise to the conception of the fundamental consciousness (*ālaya-vijñāna*) of the Yogācāra (Practice of Yoga, also called Vijñānavāda, or Doctrine of Consciousness Only) school in Mahāyāna.

Buddhist eschatology and soteriology. *The ideal state* (*Nirvāṇa*). The aim of religious practice is to be rid of the delusion of ego, thus freeing oneself from the fetters of this mundane world. He who is successful in doing so is said to have overcome the round of rebirths and to have achieved Enlightenment. This is the final goal—not a paradise or a heavenly world.

Extinction of illusion

The living process is likened to a fire burning. Its remedy is the extinction of the fire of illusion, passions, and cravings. The buddha, the enlightened one, is one who is no longer kindled or enflamed. Many poetic terms are used to describe the state of the enlightened man—the harbour of refuge, the cool cave, the place of bliss, the further shore. The term that has become famous in the West is Nirvāṇa, translated as Dying Out; that is, the dying out in the heart of the fierce fire of the three cardinal sins—sensuality, ill will, and infatuation. But Nirvāṇa is not extinction, and indeed the craving for annihilation or nonexistence (*vibhave-taṇhā*) was expressly repudiated by the Buddha. Buddhists search not for mere cessation but for the eternal, the immortal. Though Nirvāṇa is often presented negatively as "release from suffering," it is to be considered in a more positive fashion: as an ideal state, as happiness, as bliss.

The Buddha left indeterminate questions regarding the destiny of the man who has attained this ideal state or the existence of the purified saint after death, for such judgments are inapplicable to this present existence.

Though it is true that the Buddha avoided discussion of the ultimate reality that lay beyond the categories of the phenomenal world, he did not seem to have had any doubts about the absolute. He said, "There is an unborn, an unoriginated, an unmade, an uncompounded; were there not, there would be no escape from the world of the born, the originated, the made and the compounded." The Buddha believed in something that endures beneath the shifting appearances of the visible world. The positive character of Nirvāṇa is inexpressible in any terms of finite experience of human beings, for its reality transcends the realm of birth and death.

In deliverance there is no discrimination. The Buddha declared: "Just as the great ocean has one taste only, the taste of salt, just so have this doctrine and discipline but one flavour only, the flavour of emancipation." Those monks who exert themselves in the religion can be saved; they will never be reborn into suffering. But the attainment of the ideal state should be realized not only after death but also now, in this life—the "Nirvāṇa here and now."

The goal of the Buddhist

The Mahāyānistic, especially Zen, understanding of the ideal state is not as something concrete, or seizable, but as the proceeding onward toward an always elevated goal. The man who has attained deliverance should continue his actions in this world, working for the welfare of others.

In Theravāda Buddhism the goal of a monk is to attain the *arahant* state (roughly, "sainthood"); he cannot hope to become a buddha. Laymen are not expected to attain that state but may be reborn in one of the heavens. Mahāyāna Buddhism, on the other hand, professes that anyone is entitled to become a buddha, although he might have to pass through many births. According to the Pure Land school, even a layman can become a buddha by virtue of the grace of Amitābha Buddha. There is no concept of the eternally damned; both Theravādins and Mahāyānists believe that even a most vicious person can ultimately attain Enlightenment.

The buddha. The person who has attained wisdom or who has realized the universal norm (the *Dharma*, not to be confused with *dharmas*) is called the enlightened one or the awakened one (buddha). At the beginning of Buddhism, the Buddha was merely a man and nothing more, but with the lapse of time he came to be extolled more and more highly. Many miraculous powers, such as supernatural memory and levitation, were ascribed to the Buddha. From the point of view of doctrine, the magical powers were of no great importance, but they played an important role with the common people. Even the relics of the Buddha came to be esteemed for their magical potency.

Buddhism admits the existence not only of one Lord Buddha but also of other buddhas. References are made in the Pāli scriptures to seven or to 24 buddhas, though the most popular is Śākyamuni (Gautama), the founder of Buddhism. In Theravāda Buddhism devotion is paid almost exclusively to Gautama Buddha. Mahāyānists, although they remember the historic Gautama Buddha also, regard him as one of many buddhas—all of whom are manifestations of one eternal and primordial Buddha—who teach variously according to the needs of living beings in their different realms. Maitreya Buddha, the buddha of the future, was highly revered in the past throughout all the Buddhist world, though not so much in modern times. Pure Land Buddhism prefers Amitābha Buddha to Śākyamuni, though it pays homage to the latter, while Vairocana Buddha, the primordial Buddha, has been the object of much devotion in esoteric Buddhism.

Mahāyāna substitutes the eternal Buddha for the historical Buddha. According to Mahāyāna doctrine, his existence in the earthly form is not his true and proper mode of being; his historical existence seems to be quite temporary.

Threefold body of the Buddha

Mahāyāna Buddhism developed the idea of the threefold body (*tri-kāya*) of the Buddha: (1) the body of the law (*dharma kāya*)—voidness, the formless reality beyond words and thoughts, the cosmic body; (2) the body of enjoyment (*sambhogakāya*)—the void, absolute reality, enjoyed as a result of merits earned by working for the salvation of others, the perfected body; (3) the body of transformations (*nirmāṇakāya*)—the corporeal, preaching buddha, such as Śākyamuni, revealed in the empirical world, the saviour body.

Mahāyāna admits the existence of innumerable buddhas engaged in the work of saving as many suffering creatures as they can. While the concept of a saviour is not allowed in Theravāda Buddhism, it is accepted in Mahāyāna. The saviour does not bring beings directly to Nirvāṇa but makes the path easier and brings the disciple to a heaven where he may hear the preaching of the doctrine that leads the way to Enlightenment. The only exception to this concept in Mahāyāna is Pure Land Buddhism in China and Japan, which says that to be born into the Pure Land is the same as attaining Nirvāṇa.

The arhat. In Theravāda, *arhats* (Pāli *arhants*)—monks who have attained Nirvāṇa—have always been highly revered, and the *arhat* state is regarded as the ultimate goal of the monk. The *arhat* seeks to show that it is humanly possible to reach Nirvāṇa by his own personal efforts and to encourage others to tread the path. On the other hand, Mahāyāna Buddhists have often charged that it is selfish to seek the state of *arhat*, to seek Enlightenment for oneself rather than to work for the salvation of others.

The bodhisattva. A *bodhisattva* is a "being destined for Enlightenment," often translated "buddha-to-be." A *bodhisattva* was originally in ancient Buddhism one who was on the way to the attainment of perfect knowledge, a candidate for Enlightenment. This concept of a *bodhisattva* has been retained in Theravāda Buddhism. In Mahāyāna the altruistic inclinations and activities of the *bodhisattva* have been emphasized. The *bodhisattva* is one who has taken a vow to delay his own buddhahood in order to work for the good of others. From the outset, he identifies his ego absolutely and entirely with that of his neighbours. A *bodhisattva* renders help to others through perfecting himself in the six virtues (*pāramitās*) of generosity, morality, patience, vigour, concentration (in meditation), and wisdom.

The concept of the *bodhisattva* affected the doctrine of *karman*. Whereas some ancient schools (the Theravāda and its offshoots) held that the state of a *bodhisattva* is a result of the merits accumulated in his past lives, the Mahāsaṅghika (Great Assembly) school and the Mahāyāna schools held that a *bodhisattva* is born in this life freely and by his own intention—out of compassion for living beings, not as a result of past *karmans*.

Stages of the path. Several stages on the path to Enlightenment have generally been recognized. Theravāda Buddhism has clearly defined the four stages of spiritual attainment that must be passed through before a man can become an *arhat*: (1) entering into the stream of sanctification; (2) not being reborn on Earth (the realm of desires) more than once; (3) not returning to Earth; and (4) being in the state of *arhat*.

Mahāyāna Buddhism also assumed the existence of many steps for getting to buddhahood, the number of stages varying with different *sūtras* and sects. Some Mahāyānists, however, asserted that the intermediate steps could be skipped and man could attain to buddhahood directly. Zen, for instance, teaches that Enlightenment comes about by means of the direct intuition of one's own nature. Japanese Tendai and Shingon sects expressed similar ideas, while Pure Land Buddhists profess that it comes by means of the grace of Amitābha Buddha.

Buddhist ethics. *The middle path.* The ethics of Buddhism have stressed the universal norms that are constant, apply to everyone, and do not conflict with human nature. The way of Gautama Buddha is called the middle path because it avoids both the extremes of the outright pursuit of worldly desires and the practice of severe disciplines of self-mortification followed by ascetics. The universal norms of human life are constant, although in each case they must be adjusted to the infinitely varying circumstances of actual life. Otherwise, there would be a danger that detailed and petty regulations might encroach unduly on the moral autonomy of the individual. This same fundamental approach to ethical problems has been preserved up to modern times throughout the Buddhist world, although its application has differed in various historical periods and areas.

Norms of human conduct

Evil actions are to be avoided by following the middle path, or the right way of ethical practice. Only Pure Land Buddhism, with its belief that all living beings are sinful and are saved by the compassionate grace of Amitābha Buddha, departs from this view.

Compassion. The fundamental principle of Buddhist ethics is that all men should develop an attitude of compassion—a very highly esteemed virtue in Buddhism. True wisdom consists not in metaphysical sophistication but in practical knowledge expressed in compassion as the fundamental principle in social life. Compassion or love in Sanskrit is *maitrī* (Pāli *mettā*), derived from *mitra* ("friend"). Thus, the term embodies the meaning "true friendliness." If one allows the virtue of compassion or love to grow in him, it will not occur to him to harm anyone else any more than he would willingly harm himself. By widening the boundaries of what one regards as his own, he breaks down the barriers that separate him from others.

This altruistic attitude is attained by meditation on one's *dharma*s (the elements that constitute one's self). Such meditation dissolves the existence of one's self into a conglomeration of impersonal and instantaneous elements. By dissolving human existence into component parts, one is rid of the notion of self and, through that meditation, led to a limitless expansion of the self in a practical sense, because one identifies oneself with more and more living beings. The whole world and all individuals are intimately and indissolubly linked.

The practice of compassion

Love is accompanied by other mental attitudes, often described as the sublime conditions (*brahma-vihāra*). The four are love, sorrow at the sorrows of others, joy in the joys of others, and equanimity as regards one's own joys and sorrows. Each of these feelings should be deliberately practiced, beginning with a single object and gradually increasing until the whole world is suffused with such kinds of feeling.

The problem of evil. Men are always afflicted by their own evils. The most dangerous obstacles to the good life have customarily been listed in Theravāda Buddhism as the 10 bonds: (1) delusions about the existence of the ego, (2) doubt, (3) reliance upon works (ascetic discipline), (4) sensuality, (5) ill will, (6) desire for rebirth on Earth, (7) desire for rebirth in heaven, (8) pride, (9) self-righteousness, and (10) ignorance.

These evil dispositions should be conquered. The overcoming of ignorance, the last of the bonds and the fundamental principle motivating man's mundane existence, finally leads to release. The disciples of the Buddha, both clergy and laity, must gradually rid themselves of these evils through their own efforts. Having attained the final "assurance," there can then be no permanent relapse; the view of Theravāda Buddhists is that sooner or later, in this or another birth, final salvation is assured.

The five most heinous crimes are: (1) matricide, (2) patricide, (3) the murder of an *arhat*, (4) the wounding of a buddha, and (5) the creation of a schism in the order (*saṅgha*). The 10 immoral actions are: (1) killing, (2) stealing, (3) unchastity, (4) lying, (5) slandering, (6) harsh language, (7) frivolous talk, (8) covetousness, (9) ill will, and (10) false views. This definition of the moral problem has been generally accepted throughout all Buddhism.

These evil actions are to be avoided by following the right path. To the Buddha, evil is something to be conquered; inhibition should be observed assiduously. Viewed from the religious standpoint, good action as such is never a means to the final end. Yet devout Buddhists practice good actions spontaneously, without considering the results of actions concerned. In the Buddhist faith there is no conception of original sin. Eternal damnation is inconceivable for the Buddhists; even such hideous crimes as patricide are forgiven by deep repentance. The path of religion leads through morality, but, when one approaches the goal, one enters into an entirely different realm; the saint who has attained the calm of Nirvāṇa is said to be "beyond good and evil." What is called good in daily life is very often defiled with worldly desire. The ideal situation should be perfectly pure, so it is said to transcend secular good and evil (this idea was especially emphasized in Mahāyāna).

Ethical disciplines. The disciplines that create a spirit of compassion have always been stressed in Buddhism. The evil passions must be calmed, the senses must be restrained, and constant awareness of one's feelings and desires must be developed. Meditation, which is the discipline for the path to Enlightenment, was also adopted as a discipline for the ethical life, as the means for developing the awareness that checks attachment to the senses.

Secular versus monastic life

Early Buddhism stressed the necessity for monastic life to enable one to follow the disciplines necessary for attainment of the ethical ideal and for attaining Enlightenment. The rules for the layman were far less stringent than for the monk; withdrawal from the life of the householder was considered a necessity if one wished to devote himself to following the path. If the monasteries' monks would devote all their time to meditation and study, attachment to food and clothes could be curbed, sexual attachments could be eliminated, and all actions could be guarded. This otherworldly ideal has been preserved in Theravāda Buddhism to this day in the Saṅgha (the monastic order), which is still central in Buddhist life. In Tibet, too, the monastery remained the most important aspect of Buddhist community life and the centre for Buddhist disciplines—at least until Chinese rule.

On the other hand, some Mahāyāna scholars have argued that the moral disciplines could be followed and that the absolute could be comprehended in secular life. It was this type of Buddhism that was selected by the Japanese and the Nepalese and, to a large extent, by the Chinese. Even when other doctrines were accepted, the Japanese managed to impress upon them the stamp of this-worldliness. Although resignation and nonattachment may have characterized Buddhist life in Asia in general, they were often specifically repudiated by the Japanese not only in modern times but also in the remote past.

The Japanese have put heavy emphasis upon activity in human relationships. This attitude accounts for the absence of the all-inclusive monastic order in Japan, the disapproval of begging as a discipline, marriage of the priests, and similar practices that distinguish some of the features of Japanese and Nepalese Buddhism from those of the Theravāda countries.

Service. Another distinction between the ethical practices of Buddhism in the southern countries and in the northern Mahāyāna countries lies in the field of service. The this-worldly character of Japanese and Nepalese Buddhism brought the priests into close contact with the common people and their needs. In South Asian countries, where climate, rainfall, and natural fertility combine to bring harvests without great human labour, the ethics of distribution rather than of production have been emphasized. That is why, for example, almsgiving was considered so important in southern Buddhism. But in countries such as Japan, where production is of vital importance, stress has been placed on the ethics of hard work to produce the necessary food. Even monks and priests have engaged in productive labour as an expression of their Buddhist ethical principles.

One result of this attitude has been that the responsibility for service in Theravāda Buddhism has been placed largely on the individual monk as a personal matter, with comparatively less of the emphasis on social institutions that has been characteristic of Mahāyāna Buddhism. Individual householders feel free to come to the monastery for help in time of need in Theravāda countries, and many acts of mercy are performed by the monks. But in China and Japan there have been many institutions such as hospitals, orphanages, and schools that have been motivated by the Buddhist spirit.

The five precepts and virtues

Ethics for laymen. In both Theravāda and Mahāyāna countries the monks and priests are responsible for the spiritual guidance of the laymen, and the laymen are responsible for the support of the religious institutions. The basic ethics taught to laymen are the same in all Buddhist countries. The laymen should obey the five precepts that admonish him (1) not to kill, (2) not to take what is not given, (3) to refrain from unlawful sexual intercourse, (4) not to tell lies, and (5) not to drink intoxicating liquors. (In Tibet, Nepal, and Japan the fifth precept is often minimized.) The duties that are stressed are those between parents and children, pupils and teachers, husband and wife, friend and friend, master and servants, and laymen and monks.

The virtues stressed are (1) generosity, (2) benevolence, (3) cooperation, and (4) service; these four are regarded as the fundamental ones for social life. Courtesy, sympathy, honesty, and other virtues are also encouraged.

Economic ethics. At the council of Vaiśālī, held about 100 years after the death of the Buddha, one of the issues was whether monks could accept money as a gift by laymen. The Sthaviravāda, or Theravāda (school of the Elders; precursors of the modern Buddhism of South Asia), did not permit such gifts, but monks of the Mahāsaṅghika (Great Assembly) and, later, of the Mahāyānas did.

Theravāda Buddhist monks were not permitted to engage in economic activities, to cultivate land, or to be involved in making profit. They lived only on alms. This attitude has been preserved in most Asian countries with the exception of China and Japan. In China Ch'an (known in Japan as Zen) monks began to engage in manual labour. As early as the 8th century AD, they began to cultivate fields attached to their own temples in order to secure foods. "If one did not work on a day, one should not eat on that day" became one of their favorite mottos. In China some monks engaged in philanthropic activities; they formed groups of Buddhists to lend money to people in need. The spirit of labour and service was encouraged.

This way of life was introduced into Japan. In Japan monks of many sects engaged even in such kinds of philanthropic activity as constructing roads, resthouses, hospitals, ponds, and harbours. In Japan today, priests are not prohibited from engaging in economic activities.

Meditation. In order to acquire the calmness of mind necessary for travelling the path to Enlightenment, Buddhism has always recommended meditative practices derived from ancient *yoga*, stripped of its ascetic character. Meditation practices that were originally influenced by Indian *yoga* have been followed in Theravāda Buddhism by laymen as well as by monks in Tibet, China, and Japan —nowadays chiefly through the influence of Zen.

Equality of men. From the time of the Buddha, Buddhism has stressed the equality of man. Buddhism removed all restrictions of caste and placed upon all members the same requirements. There was no discrimination among the monks in the early Buddhist order. This sense of equality has been theoretically preserved throughout most Buddhist orders, although it has often been impaired because of political reasons.

Removal of caste barriers

Tolerance. Tolerance has been an outstanding characteristic of Buddhism from earliest times. Buddhism has attempted to arrive at the truth not by excluding its opposites as falsehood but by including them as another form of the same truth. Although Buddhism was predominant in many Asian countries, there is no record of any persecution by Buddhists of the followers of any other faith. They waged no religious war. It is very difficult to have a firm conviction and at the same time to be tolerant, but the Buddha himself and many of his followers have achieved such tolerance.

Buddhists are generally noted for their liberal attitude toward other religions, whether polytheistic, monotheistic, or non-theistic. This feature is found in all Buddhist countries. Buddhists admit the truth of any moral and philosophical system, whether primitive or developed, provided only that it is capable of leading men at least part way toward their final goal.

Buddhist psychology. The psychological analysis of one's own existence was not yet systematized in early scriptures. It was due to the efforts by Abhidharma (scholastic) teachers that various aspects of human existence were elaborately analyzed and schematized.

In the Sarvāstivāda school, especially, a complex system of psychology was developed, according to which all constituent elements of human existence were classified as 75 in number. These 75 were divided into two major groups: (1) cooperating, impermanent elements (*saṃskṛta*) and (2) non-cooperating, immutable elements (*asaṃskṛta*). The former is divided into four major groups: (1) matter, (2) mind, or pure consciousness without content, (3) the 46 mental elements or faculties intimately connected with the element of consciousness, and (4) the forces that can be included neither among material nor among spiritual elements. Matter is further subdivided into the organs of sight, sound, smell, taste and touch and their sense data, and the unmanifested matter that is the vehicle of moral qualities. The 46 mental elements are divided into six groups: (1) 10 general mental faculties present in every moment of consciousness, namely, feeling (pleasant, unpleasant, and indifferent), conceptualization, will or conscious effort, sensation (caused by "contact" between object, sense organ, and consciousness), desire, intelligence, memory, attention, ascertainment, and concentration; (2) 10 universally "good" moral forces present in every favourable moment of consciousness, namely, the faculties of belief, courage in good actions, equanimity or indifference, modesty (being ashamed with reference to oneself), feeling disgust with reference to other peoples' objectionable actions, absence of greed, absence of hatred, causing no injury, mental dexterity, and endeavouring to acquire good qualities; (3) six universally "obscured" elements present in every unfavourable moment of consciousness (these are not always absolutely bad; they sometimes may be indifferent for the spiritual progress, but they are nevertheless always "obscured" in a selfish tendency), namely, the faculties of infatuation or ignorance, laziness, mental heaviness, non-believing, sloth or indolent or inactive temperament, and being addicted to pleasure; (4) two universally "bad" elements present in every unfavourable moment of consciousness, namely, the faculties of irreverance or want of humility and of not feeling indignant at offenses done by others; (5) 10 vicious elements of limited occurrence, namely, the faculties of anger, hypocrisy, envy, jealousy, approving objectionable things, causing harm, breaking friendly feeling, deceit, trickery, and complacency; and (6) eight elements not having any definite place in the above system but capable of entering into various combinations, namely, the faculties of repenting, absentmindedness, a searching state of mind, an ascertaining state of mind, attachment by mind, hatred, pride, and doubting.

The fourth group of impermanent elements, those that are neither material nor spiritual, are further subdivided into forces that effect the acquisition of the elements in an individual existence, occasionally keep some elements in abeyance in an individual existence, produce generality or homogeneity of existences, transfer an individual into the realms of conscious trance, and stop consciousness, producing either an unconscious trance or the highest trance; in addition, there are the forces of life duration, origination, subsistence, decay, and extinction, as well as the forces imparting significance to words, to sentences, and to articulate sounds. The immutable elements consist of (1) space for all *dharma*s, (2) the suppression of the manifestations of elements through the action of intelligence, and (3) the same cessation produced not through the action of intelligence. This scheme of 75 elements was developed and enlarged to that of 100 elements by the Yogācāra idealists.

The scheme of elements

One item that is noteworthy from the psychological viewpoint is that the Yogācāra advocated the theory of the eightfold consciousness: the visual consciousness, auditory consciousness, odour consciousness, taste consciousness, touch consciousness, the conscious mind, the subconscious mind (the substrate of self-consciousness), and the "store-consciousness," which is the fundamental consciousness.

According to the orthodox thought of the 6th-century Indian monk Dharmapāla, conveyed by the 7th-century Chinese pilgrim Hsüan-tsang to China and Japan, where it became known as the Fa-hsiang (Japanese Hossō) school, these are separate consciousnesses, existing as different entities, and the first seven of these consciousnesses are collectively termed the transformed consciousnesses. The She-lun school of China (now merged with Fa-hsiang) regarded the store-consciousness that has become pure and taintless as thusness (*tathatā*) and gave it a special name, "taintless consciousness," designated as the ninth consciousness. Generally speaking, Buddhist psychology is highly tinged with ethical and soteriological evaluations.

Buddhist logic. Buddhist logic in its incipient stage can be noticed in 4th-century texts such as Maitreya's *Yogācārabhūmi-śāstra* ("The Science of the Stages of Yoga Practice") and Asaṅga's *Abhidharma-samuccaya* (a summary of *abhidharma,* or scholastic, doctrine), Vasubandhu's *Vādavidhi* ("Method of Dispute"), and *Vādavidhāna* ("Rule of Dispute").

The founder of the Buddhist new logic, as against the old logic set forth in the Nyāya school, was Dignāga (*c.* 400–485). He established the three-proposition syllogism, replacing the five-proposition syllogism prevalent before his time. The older, five-proposition formula consists of: (1) proposition (*pratijñā*)—*e.g.,* sound is impermanent; (2) reason (*hetu*)—because it is produced by causes; (3) example (*dṛṣṭānta*)—it is like pots; (4) application (*upanaya*)—pots are produced by causes and are impermanent in the same way as sound is also; and (5) conclusion (*nigamana*)—therefore, sound is impermanent.

In the threefold formula by Dignāga, propositions (4) and (5) are omitted. The whole scheme of syllogism is deductive, but in (3) the inductive method also is implied. The theory of the nine reasons or types of argument was also set forth by Dignāga. *Nyāyapraveśa,* by the South Indian Śaṅkarasvāmin, is a brief introduction to Dignāga's logic. In China and Japan this work was regarded as almost the only authority and was studied in great detail by traditional scholars of Buddhist logic.

The logic of Dignāga and Dharmakīrti

The logic and epistemology (really fused together) of Dignāga was elaborated upon in the 7th century by the Indian Buddhist logician Dharmakīrti. Among Indian and Tibetan thinkers he was regarded as the representative Buddhist philosopher. He admitted only two kinds of valid knowledge; *i.e.,* direct perception and inference. He asserted that in the function of mind, cognition and the cognized belong to different moments.

Dharmakīrti denied the authority of scriptures but in another way admitted Buddha as the source of all knowledge. According to him, every being is transitory, and each person assumes the continuous existence of an individual, who is nothing but a continuation of moments and who is constructed by imaginative and discriminative thinking. Objects of inference are universals, whereas objects of perception are particulars, which are nothing but moments. He distinguished between analytic inference and synthetic inference. Nonperception was limited to purely epistemological significance; relation between subject and object in cognition was a secondary one.

In Japan the traditional scholarship of Buddhist logic as conveyed by the Buddhist pilgrim Hsüan-tsang to China in the 7th century has been preserved, especially in the old capital of Nara. Zen took exactly the opposite standpoint to the formal logic of Buddhist logicians. In the Rinzai school of Zen, meditation on paradoxes (*koan*) is used to awaken intuitive insight into what transcends logical distinctions. In popular Japanese speech, Zen dialogue, or *mondo,* is equivalent to what is not understandable or what is illogical.

BIBLIOGRAPHY

On Buddhism in general: P.V. BAPAT (ed.), *2500 Years of Buddhism* (1956), a collaboration by different scholars sponsored by the government of India; EDWARD CONZE, *Buddhism: Its Essence and Development* (1951 and 1959), a good introduction for beginners; CHARLES ELIOT, *Hinduism and Buddhism: An Historical Sketch,* 3 vol. (1921, reprinted 1962), a very detailed and sound survey; JUNJIRO TAKAKUSU, *The Essentials of Buddhist Philosophy,* 3rd ed. (1956), rather technical but very valuable as a reference work; HAJIME NAKAMURA, *Ways of Thinking of Eastern Peoples,* rev. and ed. by PHILIP P. WIENER (1964), a discussion of adaptation in various Asian countries; ALICIA MATSUNAGA, *The Buddhist Philosophy of Assimilation* (1969), on the theory of Honji-suijaku.

On Indian Buddhism: EDWARD J. THOMAS, *The History of Buddhist Thought,* 2nd ed. (1951), a standard work; EDWARD CONZE, *Buddhist Thought in India* (1962), a good survey; A.B. KEITH, *Buddhist Philosophy in India and Ceylon* (1923), a brief introduction.

On early Buddhist philosophy: GOVIND CHANDRA PANDE, *Studies in the Origins of Buddhism* (1957), the most advanced study on this subject; K.N. JAYATILLEKE, *Early Buddhist Theory of Knowledge* (1963), a very detailed study on Buddhist epistemology, highly welcomed by Western readers; G.P. MALALASEKERA, *Dictionary of Pali Proper Names,* rev. ed., 2 vol. (1960); KOGEN MIZUNO, *Primitive Buddhism* (Eng. trans. 1969), written by the greatest authority on early Buddhism in Japan.

Later Buddhist philosophy: THEODOR STCHERBATSKY, *The Central Conception of Buddhism and the Meaning of the Word "Dharma"* (1923, reprinted 1956), a pioneering work on the philosophy of the Sarvāstivādins; *The Conception of Buddhist Nirvāna* (1927, reprinted 1965), the standard work on the philosophy of Nāgārjuna and the Mādhyamika school; *Buddhist Logic,* 2 vol. (1932, many reprints), the standard work on Buddhist logic; T.R.V. MURTI, *The Central Philosophy of Buddhism* (1955), a remarkable contribution on Nāgārjuna's philosophy; W.M. MACGOVERN, *A Manual of Buddhist Philosophy* (1923); S.B. DASGUPTA, *An Introduction to Tāntric Buddhism,* 2nd ed. (1958), a unique contribution.

On Buddhism in South Asia: R.H.L. SLATER, *Paradox and Nirvana* (1950), an authoritative discussion of some essential points of Buddhist philosophy; W.L. KING, *A Thousand Lives Away: Buddhism in Contemporary Burma* (1964).

On Tibetan Buddhism: W.Y. EVANS-WENTZ (ed.), *The Tibetan Book of the Dead,* 3rd ed. (1960); D.L. SNELLGROVE, *Buddhist Himalaya* (1957), especially valuable with regard to esoteric Buddhism; HELMUT HOFFMANN, *Die Religionen Tibets* (1956; Eng. trans., *The Religions of Tibet,* 1961), based upon his textual studies; F.D. LESSING and ALEX WAYMAN, *Mkhas grub rje's Fundamentals of the Buddhist Tantras* (1968).

On Chinese Buddhism: ARTHUR F. WRIGHT, *Buddhism in Chinese History* (1959), a brief but illuminating discussion in consideration of the social background; KENNETH K.S. CH'EN, *Buddhism in China* (1964), a reliable and authoritative historical survey; FUNG YU-LAN, *A History of Chinese Philosophy,* 2nd ed., 2 vol. (Eng. trans. 1952–53), Buddhist philosophy is discussed partly.

On Japanese Buddhism: MASAHARU ANESAKI, *History of Japanese Religion* (1930, reprinted 1963), the standard work; CHARLES ELIOT, *Japanese Buddhism* (1935, reprinted 1959); HONPA HONGWANJI MISSION OF HAWAII, *The Shinshu Seiten: The Holy Scripture of Shinshu,* 2nd ed. (1961); SHINSHO HANAYAMA, *A History of Japanese Buddhism* (1960), an authoritative work; SHOKO WATANABE, *Japanese Buddhism: A Critical Appraisal* (1964), severely critical of Japanese Buddhism; SHOJUN BANDO *et al.* (eds.), *A Bibliography on Japanese Buddhism* (1958); R.H. COATES and R. ISHIZUKA, *Hōnen: The Buddhist Saint* (1925), based upon the authorized biography of Hōnen; HEINRICH DUMOULIN, *Die Entwicklung des chinesischen Ch'an nach Huinêng in Lichte des Wu-mên-Kuan* (1953; Eng. trans., *The Development of Chinese Zen After the Sixth Patriarch in the Light of Mumonkan,* 1953); *Zen: Geschichte und Gestalt* (1959; Eng. trans., *A History of Zen Buddhism,* 1963), the most objective description; D.T. SUZUKI, *Essays in Zen Buddhism,* 3 series (1927–61), essays by a well-known master.

Bibliography: Bibliographie Bouddhique (annual since 1928); SHINSHO HANAYAMA, *Bibliography of Buddhism* (1961).

Dictionary: DAITO SHUPPANSHA, *Japanese-English Buddhist Dictionary* (1965).

(H.Na.)

Buddhist Sacred Literature

Buddhist sacred literature is the name given to a vast number of works ranging from what are supposed to have been the original discourses of the Buddha—a prince who gained enlightenment in the 6th century BC—to the exegetical works that were inspired by the Buddha's teachings and to the religious and philosophic thought that, in turn, contributed to the growth of a variety of philosophical and religious works. Buddhist sacred literature consists of the religious texts of all major forms of Buddhism, including Theravāda (Way of the Elders, also known as Hīnayāna, or "Lesser Vehicle"), the predominant form in present-day Southeast Asia and Ceylon; Mahāyāna (Greater Vehicle), the predominant form in East Asia; and Tantric (magical) and Tibetan Buddhism, prevailing at present in the Himalayan regions. Included in this literature are works dealing with the regulations for the monastic life and manuals about the techniques of meditation. The following sur-

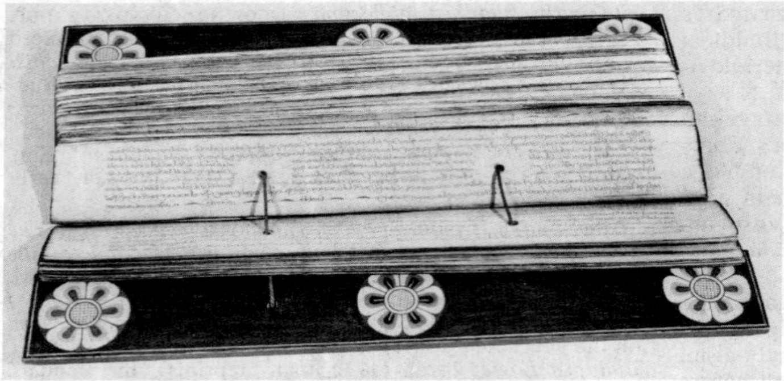

Buddhist Pāli manuscript from Kandy, Sri Lanka (former Ceylon), about 45 centimetres (18 inches) long. The palm-leaf pages are threaded with twine, and the covers are wood with painted decoration. In the Newberry Library, Chicago.
By courtesy of the Newberry Library, Chicago

vey will describe the beginnings and the development of this literature in India as well as its diffusion through the rest of Asia by means of translations into the major Asian languages. In addition, it will touch upon the indigenous contributions of the Tibetans, Chinese, Mongolians, and Japanese. Since Buddhist literature not only significantly molded the ways of thinking and the life of the peoples of Asia but also influenced the fine arts, which, in turn, gave new impetus to thought, this interrelationship between literature and the fine arts is also examined briefly. Obviously only works that had an enduring influence can be mentioned. This article will deal with the general aspects of Buddhist sacred literature, its major texts, its significance in the life of the peoples of Asia, and its relation to the fine arts. The article is divided into the following sections:

I. Types and forms of texts
II. Major Buddhist texts
- The Pāli canon and its Asian translations: *Tipiṭaka* (*Tripiṭaka*)
  - *Vinaya Piṭaka*
  - *Sutta Piṭaka*
  - *Abhidhamma Piṭaka*
- Important noncanonical texts in Pāli
  - *Milinda-pañha*
  - Writings of Buddhaghosa
  - Writings of Buddhadatta
  - Writings of Dhammapāla
  - Ceylonese chronicles
- Mahāyāna texts
  - *Prajñāpāramitā* literature
  - Mādhyamika texts
  - *Avataṃsaka-sūtra*
  - *Saddharmapuṇḍarīka-sūtra*
  - *Sukhāvati-vyūha-sūtra*
  - Other Mahāyāna texts
- Tantric and Tibetan texts
  - *Tantras*
  - Tibetan literature
  - Mongolian texts
- Chinese and Japanese texts
- Other important texts

III. Ritual use and influence of Buddhist texts

I. Types and forms of texts

Buddhist literature originated within the community of monks and served its members as an aid to a goal realization. By striving for a goal the character of which changed in the course of time—the early ideal of becoming an *arhat* (saint) changing to that of realizing Buddhahood (the state of enlightenment as a Buddha)—the aspirant was setting an example that could be emulated, first by other monks (and nuns), and then also by the laity. This striving found its expression in what was to become the acknowledged sacred literature of the Buddhists, which, therefore, comprises both Hīnayāna and Mahāyāna works, the former concerned with the ideal of sainthood, the latter with Buddhahood through the intermediate stage of *bodhisattva*hood (the state of being a Buddha-to-be). Although it is customary to refer to Buddhist sacred literature either by the term Pāli canon or *Tripiṭaka* (Pāli *Tipiṭaka*, Chinese *san-ts'ang*, "The Three Collections"), these terms can strictly be applied only to works representing the texts that have been recognized by the *thera* ("elders") or Vibhajyavādins (Theravādins) of Ceylon. The Mahāyānists do not repudiate the *Tripiṭaka*, but for them it is but the revered foundation on which they built. The Mahāyāna works attempt to elucidate the meaning of the early texts and this elucidation has two aspects, the one theoretical and doctrinal (*i.e.*, how do human beings perceive and what is meant by this or that term) and the other reflected in the *Tantra*s (see below). When emphasis is laid on what is supposed to have been said and done by the Buddha, as is the practice of the Theravādins, a text is a "canon" or part of a set of sacred scriptures; but when emphasis is laid on interpretation and meaning, it is a religious and philosophical text, but not a canon.

Although tradition claims that a fivefold division into *nikāya*s ("collections") was worked out with the assistance of Ānanda, cousin and favourite disciple of the Buddha, at the first council (said to have been held in 483 BC), this account, apart from its legendary character, is contradicted by the opening words "Thus I have heard," which indicate that there was a long oral tradition before the discourses were put down in writing. Since, moreover, everyone was allowed to study the Buddha-word in his own dialect, there is no one version but a continuous replacement of one vernacular version by other local ones, and intermediate ones of a mixture of vernaculars and Sanskrit that finally replaced every kind of vernacular writing. It is impossible to say exactly when the oral tradition was written down.

Classification of Buddhist texts

A major problem that faced the collectors of the Buddhist texts was the classification of this extremely diverse material. The most obvious solution was the classification into "The Three Collections," reflecting the general nature of the contents. Another division into nine *aṅgā*s ("parts") is related to the literary form and specific contents. It is found in both Pāli and early Sanskrit works, although differences are noticeable. The Pāli denominations of these *aṅgā*s (with their Sanskrit equivalents in parenthesis, where applicable) are (1) *sutta* (*sūtra*), a connected narrative or collection of verses on one subject; (2) *geyya* (*geya*), a composition of mixed prose and verse; (3) *veyyākaraṇa* (*vyākaraṇa*), an "exposition" containing the whole *Abhidharma* (scholasticism or "higher subtleties of the religion"), the *sūtra*s that have no verse, and the words of the Buddha not included in the other eight *aṅgā*s; (4) *gāthā*, unmixed verses; (5) *udāna*, ecstatic utterances; (6) *itivuttaka* (*ityukta*, wrongly *itivṛttaka*), a collection of *sūtra*s beginning with the words "Thus the Buddha spoke"; (7) *Jātaka*, stories of the Buddha's previous births; (8) *abbhutadhamma* (*adbhutadharma*), discourses relating wonderful (*adbhuta*) conditions and events such as accompanying the birth of a Buddha; and (9) *vedalla* (*vaipulya*), questions posed after feeling a pleasant emotion. In Sanskrit texts, three more varieties are added: *nidāna*, a group of works that were written in response to a request or a certain event; *avadāna*, stories; and *upadeśa*, instruction. The former two are well represented in the Pāli canon but not counted as separate *aṅgās*; the *upadeśas* deal with esoteric doctrines and the instruction of promising disciples and indicate that esotericism was present in Buddhism at a very early stage. As to the *vaipulya*, these works have nothing but the name in common with the Pāli *vedalla*. Dealing with the acquisition of goods in this world (*artha*) and of the world to come (*dharma*), the *Vaipulya-sūtras* are distinguished from the older *sūtras* by a different approach and by the change of idiom. They comprise a prose version, followed by one in verse, the latter being more or less a repetition of the former or the source of the prose narrative. The Tibetans classified the whole material into "Translation of the Buddha Word" and "Translation of Treatises" and in this great division were free to arrange the material according to content.

From the 2nd century AD onward, Mahāyāna authors wrote "treatises" (*śāstras*) in their own names. They quoted the *sūtras* in support of their interpretations of Buddhist ideas and in so doing stimulated the composition of new *sūtras*. Another form presented the didactic material in "memorial verses" (*kārikās*) that sometimes had an explanation (*vrtti*) by the author himself, on which others wrote commentaries and subcommentaries (*vyākhyā, bhāṣya*) or word by word explanations (*ṭīkā*). Mahāyāna authors excelled in devotional and edifying literature in both prose and verse form. The poetical compositions in praise of the Buddha or the ideas of Buddhism are known as *stotra* (hymns).

II. Major Buddhist texts

THE PALI CANON AND ITS ASIAN TRANSLATIONS: TIPITAKA (TRIPITAKA)

The earliest systematic and most complete collection of early Buddhist sacred literature is the Pāli *Tipiṭaka* ("The Three Collections"). Its arrangement reflects the importance that the early followers attached to the regulations of the monastic life (*Vinaya*), to the discourses of the Buddha (*Sutta*), and subsequently to the interest in scholasticism (*Abhidhamma*).

There is no complete canon of Buddhist books preserved in Sanskrit. It seems that the Sarvāstivāda school —an early sect that believed not only present mental elements or states of mind to be real but also past and future ones as well—did have the *āgamas* corresponding to the Pāli *nikāyas* and also a set of *Abhidharma* (Sanskrit form of *Abhidhamma*) texts, corresponding only in number to the Pāli set. The Mūla-Sarvāstivādins—who upheld the doctrine that "all exists really" whether transitorily or eternally, and who were closely related to the Sarvāstivādins, sharing the same ideas—possessed a *Vinaya Piṭaka* ("Basket of Discipline"), large sections of which are preserved in manuscripts found in Gilgit (Pakistani-occupied Jammu and Kashmir). Different schools of Buddhism esteemed different texts. Thus the noncanonical *Mahāvastu* ("Great Subjects") is claimed to be a book on *Vinaya* belonging to the Lokottaravādins (who held that the Buddhas are "exalted above the world" and only seem to participate in this world), but its subject matter is extremely varied and in it are found *sūtras* corresponding to those in other kinds of texts. These divergences in tradition show that over the centuries Buddhism lost its early sectarian character and became an all-embracing spiritual movement.

The three "baskets" into which the 32 texts of the Pāli canon are divided are *Vinaya Piṭaka* ("Basket of Discipline"), *Sutta Piṭaka* ("Basket of Discourse"), and *Abhidhamma Piṭaka* ("Basket of Scholasticism").

Vinaya Piṭaka. The Pāli *Vinaya Piṭaka*, which is still in theory the rule in Theravāda monasteries, although large sections have fallen into disuse, is divided into five major parts grouped into three divisions—*Sutta-vibhaṅga* ("Division of Rules"), *Khandhakas* ("Sections"), and *Parivāra* ("Accessory").

Sutta-vibhaṅga. *Sutta-vibhaṅga* is a commentary on the *Pātimokkha-sutta* ("Obligatory Rules"), which forms the nucleus of the *Vinaya Piṭaka*. It is the oldest part of the Pāli canon in an archaic language. It consists of two parts, the *Bhikkhu-pātimokkha* ("Rules for Monks") and the *Bhikkhunī-pātimokkha* ("Rules for Nuns"). The offenses a monk or nun is likely to commit are listed according to their gravity, as, for instance, those warranting permanent expulsion from the order (*pārājika*), those entailing temporary suspension, and those (*pācittiya*) of which a guilty person can be absolved by a formal confession before the monastic order. The commentary on the *Pātimokkha* is divided into the *Mahā-vibhaṅga* ("Great Division"; 227 rules for monks) and *Bhikkhunī-vibhaṅga* ("Division Concerning Nuns"). The latter lists additional specific rules and regulations.

Rules for monks and nuns

Khandhaka. *Khandhaka* consists of two parts, the *Mahāvagga* ("Great Grouping") and the *Cullavagga* ("Small Grouping"). The topics dealt with in these two sections have not always been clearly distinguished and also lack logical sequence. They contain rules for ordination; "observance" days, when all monks resident within the district were required to assemble for recitation of the *Pātimokkha*; descriptions of rainy-season retreats, clothing, food, and medicines; judicial rules; miscellaneous rules; instruction of nuns; and so forth. While the *Mahāvagga* can be regarded as the history of the developing Buddhist community, the *Cullavagga* supplements the details of the former to make an authoritative compilation of the Buddha's sayings, compiled in order to suppress a relaxation of disciplinary rules. This, however, led to a schism, the majority rejecting the suppressive rulings.

Parivāra. *Parivāra* contains summaries and classifications of the disciplinary rules. It is a later supplement intended not only to help monks or nuns to remember the rules but also to make them aware of the circumstances that would bring them within the orbit of these rules.

Sutta Piṭaka. By far the largest "basket" is the *Sutta Piṭaka* ("Basket of Discourse"), which consists of five collections (*nikāyas*) containing the discourses of the Buddha. Although, from a literary viewpoint, many of the discourses seem to be drawn out and repetitive, they nevertheless make rewarding reading because of the sublimity of thought and the richness and beauty of the illustrative similes that they contain. The discourses, reported by the Buddha's disciples, begin with the affirmative statement "Thus I have heard" and then relate the place and occasion of the discourse. At the end, the listener acknowledges the validity of the Buddha's exposition and asks to be counted henceforth among his followers. It is obvious that these discourses do not represent the exact words of the Buddha, although some phrases may have been his words. Still, they reveal the personality, the didactic technique, and the spirit of Buddhism. The discourses are chiefly in prose, except for stanzas illustrating or summing up a particular point. The grouping of the discourses into *nikāyas* ("collections") does not rest on a rational basis. Apparently there existed two groups of teachers (*bhāṇakas*), who memorized certain *sūtras* and handed them down to their disciples orally. Reciters of lengthy verses were called Dīghabhāṇakas, and reciters of medium length verses, Majjhimabhāṇakas. The other two *nikāyas* (*Saṃyutta* and *Aṅguttara*) seem to reflect a later development, their aim being to rearrange the topics dealt with in the *Dīgha* and *Majjhima Nikāyas*.

Discourses of the Buddha

Dīgha Nikāya. The *Dīgha Nikāya* ("Collection of Long Discourses") contains 34 *suttas*, some of considerable length, presenting a vivid picture of the different aspects of life and thought at the Buddha's time. Divided into three books, it contrasts superstitious beliefs, various doctrinal and philosophical speculations, and ascetic practices with Buddhist ethical ideas, which are elucidated with the help of similes and examples taken from the everyday life of the people. By far the best *suttanta* ("discourse") is the *Mahāparinibbāna Sutta*, which gives an account of the last days of the Buddha and stresses the importance of striving for emancipation.

Majjhima Nikāya. *Majjhima Nikāya* ("Collection of Medium-Length Discourses") contains 152 *suttas* in its present version, while the Chinese one, preserving the lost Sarvāstivāda collection, has 222, some of which are also found in other *nikāyas* of the Pāli canon, and some of which cannot be traced. On the whole, there is not much difference in content between the two versions. Like the *Dīgha*, the *suttas* in the *Majjhima* present Buddhist ideas and ideals, illustrating them by similes of great literary beauty.

Saṃyutta Nikāya. *Saṃyutta Nikāya* ("Collection of Kindred Discourses") has altogether 2,941 *suttas*, classed in 59 divisions (called *saṃyutta*) grouped in five parts (*vagga*). The first *vagga* has *suttas* that contain stanzas. The *suttas* begin with a description of the particular occasion when the stanzas were spoken; the stanzas themselves represent a kind of questioning and answering. The second *vagga* deals with the important principle of dependent origination—the chain of cause and effect affecting all things. The third *vagga* presents the *anātman* (no-self) doctrine, which is the rejection of an abiding principle that could be termed a self or a pure ego. The fourth *vagga* is very similar to the previous one, but here it is not the philosophical principle underlying the analysis that is stressed but the transitoriness of the elements constituting reality. The fifth *vagga* is devoted to a discussion of the basic principles of Buddhist philosophy, religion, and culture.

Aṅguttara Nikāya. *Aṅguttara Nikāya* ("Collection of Item-More Discourses") contains as many as 2,308 small *suttas* arranged according to the number of topics discussed, ranging from one to eleven. One *sutta* relates that loving kindness practiced for a fraction of a second only will yield great merit. Other *suttas* state that there are three areas in which training is needed—in conduct, concentration, and insight—and that there are eight worldly concerns—gain, loss, fame, blame, rebuke, praise, pleasure, and pain. Here, too, similes enliven an otherwise dry presentation.

The 15 "small texts"

Khuddaka Nikāya. *Khuddaka Nikāya* ("Collection of Small Texts") comprises 15 separate titles:

1. *Khuddaka-pāṭha* ("Small Reading"), the smallest book in the entire *Tipiṭaka*. Compiled for use by primary trainees, its contents are used on various occasions. Two *suttas* have been borrowed from the *Suttanipāta* (see below), and their recitation is regarded as very auspicious.

2. *Dhammapada* ("Verses on the *Dharma*"—the law). This work contains 423 verses in 26 chapters. Presenting the maxims of Buddhist ethics, it not only occupies an eminent place in the religious life of the peoples in Buddhist countries but is also of universal appeal, as it recommends a life of peace and nonviolence and declares that enmity can never be overcome by enmity, only by kindness.

3. *Udāna* ("Utterances"). This contains 80 utterances attributed to the Buddha or his chief disciples, when they had achieved the bliss of their emancipation or spoke in appreciation of a sublime state.

4. *Itivuttaka* ("Thus Said"). This contains 112 short pieces dealing with ethical principles, such as generosity, good and evil, greed, passion, and malice, that are considered to be the actual words of the Buddha.

5. *Suttanipāta* ("Collection of *Suttas*"). This is one of the most important books in the *Khuddaka Nikāya*. It is partly in verses, partly in a mixed style of prose and verses. The verse part is of high poetic quality.

6. *Vimānavatthu* ("Tales of Heavenly Mansions"). This book describes the different abodes of deities, male and female, who are born in the heavens as a result of their former meritorious deeds.

7. *Petavatthu* ("Tales of Ghosts"). This work gives an account of the various purgatories and the woes of the beings reborn there as a result of their wicked deeds.

8. *Theragāthā* ("Hymns of the Elders"). This collection contains songs attributed to 264 personal disciples of the Buddha. The songs are said to have been composed when their authors experienced the bliss of emancipation. The verses stress the abstract teachings of Buddhism.

9. *Therīgāthā* ("Hymns of the Senior Nuns"). These are the songs attributed to about 100 female disciples of the Buddha. They provide rich material for the study of the position of women at the time of the Buddha. Their merit consists in their revealing the deep impression the Buddha's teaching made upon their life. A personal tone is unmistakable.

10. *Jātaka* ("Lives [of the Buddha]"). Only the verses are considered to be canonical, while the 547 tales of the Buddha's previous lives are considered a later addition. The prose stories contain legends, fables, humorous anecdotes, and short sayings, as well as lengthy romances.

11. *Niddesa* ("Exposition"). This work, consisting of two parts, *Mahāniddesa* and *Cullaniddesa*, actually belongs to the group of commentaries. The last two chapters comment on the *Suttanipāta*.

12. *Paṭisambhidā-magga* ("The Way of Analysis"). This is a kind of encyclopaedia of the philosophical ideas in the *Sutta Piṭaka*. It is primarily meant for reference and intensive study.

13. *Apadāna* ("Stories"). This is a collection of stories of the previous lives of the Buddha, the Pratyeka-buddhas (who attain enlightenment by themselves and are unconcerned about the enlightenment of others), the chief disciples, and other important figures. The concluding sentence of the collection is intended to show that even the smallest meritorious act has the potentiality of giving vast positive results even after a long time. All the stories are in verses put into the mouths of saints (both male and female).

14. *Buddhavaṃsa* ("Lineage of the Buddha"). This work relates the lives of 24 previous Buddhas, of Śākyamuni (the historical Buddha), and of Maitreya (the future Buddha), presented as being told by the Buddha himself.

15. *Cariyā Piṭaka* ("Basket of Conduct"). This collection retells several *Jātakas* (stories of Buddha's previous lives) in verse form, illustrating the *bodhisattva*'s (Buddha-to-be's) practice of the ten perfections (*pāramitās*) necessary for the attainment of Buddhahood.

Abhidhamma Piṭaka. The *Abhidhamma Piṭaka* ("Basket of Scholasticism") comprises seven works that, although based on the contents of the Buddha's discourses, deal with selected and specific topics that form the basis for the later philosophical interpretations.

The Pāli Abhidhamma Piṭaka. The Pāli version is a strictly Theravāda collection and has little in common with the *Abhidharma* works recognized by other schools of Buddhism. Since the Theravādins were concerned with preserving what they believed to have been the Buddha's words and not with developing Buddhist ideas, the Pāli *Abhidhamma* has had little influence outside the Theravāda tradition. It consists of seven works: (1) *Dhammasaṅgaṇi* ("Summary of *Dharma*"), an enumeration of the entities constituting reality; (2) *Vibhaṅga* ("Division"), a definition of these entities from various points of view; (3) *Dhātukathā* ("Discussion of Elements"), a classification of the elements of reality according to various levels of organization; (4) *Puggalapaññatti* ("Designation of Person"), an interesting psychological typology in which people are classified according to their intellectual acumen and spiritual attainments; (5) *Kathāvatthu* ("Points of Controversy"), a later work discussing the controversial doctrinal points among the various Hīnayāna schools, mentioning the general doctrines of the Mahāsaṅghikas—"those belonging to the great order of monks"—an early Buddhist sect from which Mahāyāna Buddhism later developed; (6) *Yamaka* ("Pairs"), dealing with basic sets of categories arranged in pairs of questions; and (7) *Paṭṭhāna* ("Activations"), a voluminous work discussing 24 kinds of causal relations.

The Sanskrit texts. While the Pāli *Abhidhamma* is significant only for the Theravādins, the Sanskrit *Abhidharma*, considered to be canonical by the Sarvāstivādins, is of much greater importance for the development of Buddhist philosophy. The Sanskrit *Abhidharma* also has seven works that are attributed to distinct authors, some of them living several centuries after the Buddha. This authorship, however, is not uniform in the Tibetan and Chinese traditions. The seven works recognized are (1) *Jñāna-prasthāna* ("Method of Knowledge"), by Kātyāyanīputra, not well organized, but interesting for the history of ideas. (2) *Prakaraṇa* ("Treatise"), by Vasumitra, an important work that is often quoted in the *Abhidharmakośa* ("Treasure of the *Abhidharma*"), by Vasubandhu, a monumental work on Buddhist philosophy or metaphysics. (3) *Vijñāna-kāya* ("Synopsis of Consciousness"), by Devaśarman, dealing with the controversial topic of the idea of an individual (*pudgala*). (4) *Dharma-skandha* ("Collection on the law"), by Buddha's disciple Śāriputra (by Maudgalyāyana—another of Buddha's disciples—according to the Chinese tradition), a collection of *sūtras* the Buddha delivered in the Jetavana, a park in Sāvatthi (Śrāvasti). (5) *Prajñapti-śāstra* ("Treatise on Communication"), by Maudgalyāyana, in three parts, dealing with cosmology and causality. (6) *Dhātu-kāya* ("Synopsis of Elements"), by Pūrṇa (by Vasumitra, according to the Chinese tradition), listing the *dharmas* (mental elements) of the Sarvāstivādins; the classification was accepted by all other schools, although they differed in their interpretations of the logical status of these *dharmas*. (7) *Saṅgītiparyāya* ("Discourse and Rehearsal of Sacred Tenets"), by Mahākauṣṭhila (by Śāriputra, according to the Chinese tradition), a version of the *Saṅgīti Suttanta* in the *Dīgha Nikāya*.

IMPORTANT NONCANONICAL TEXTS IN PALI

The noncanonical literature of Hīnayāna Buddhism consists, to a large extent, of commentaries on the *Tripiṭaka* texts but also includes independent works that are invaluable for the understanding of ancient Indian history and thought. Among the Pāli writers and exponents of Hīnayāna Buddhism who attempted to harmonize the apparently conflicting teachings and to grasp the inner meaning of the doctrine, four names stand out—Nāgasena, Buddhadatta, Buddhaghosa, and Dhammapāla. Nothing is known of Nāgasena except that he was the learned debater with the Greco-Bactrian ruler Menander related in the famous literary work *Milinda-pañha*. Buddhadatta and Buddhaghosa were 5th-century contemporaries, deeply versed in the Pāli tradition, while Dhammapāla was slightly later but followed the same tradition.

Milinda-pañha. Nāgasena is supposed to have compiled the *Milinda-pañha* ("Questions of King Menander"). It is generally assumed that this work was written either at the time of Menander (150 BC) or shortly afterward but certainly before the time of Buddhaghosa (AD 400), who very often quotes this work as an authority. As the work stands today, it contains seven chapters. Of these the first is largely personal and historical, the others doctrinal. Since its different chapters are written in more than one style, it seems probable that some are later additions. The Chinese translation, made between AD 317 and 420 and known as the *Nāgasena-sūtra*, contains only the first three chapters of the Pāli version. Furthermore, at the end of the third chapter it is stated that the questions of King Menander have come to an end. It is, of course, likely that different versions of the text were available and that a later redactor welded them together into a single work.

Writings of Nāgasena

The *Milinda-pañha* is undoubtedly a great literary achievement in the field of Indian prose writing. The author begins his work with an account of the past lives of himself and King Menander, which is the reason that the two are to meet again in this life. Menander, a well-informed scholar and keen debater, was disheartened when he could find no one to solve his metaphysical problems. But one day he saw Nāgasena going on his begging round. The monk's serenity made a deep impression on the King, and the latter visited him in his monastery. They had a conversation that was later resumed at the palace and which forms the subject matter of the *Milinda-pañha*. The *Milinda-pañha* presents a profound and comprehensive exposition of Buddhist metaphysics, ethics, and psychology. It is in this work that is found the famous statement that just as the parts of a chariot put together in a specific way constitute the chariot, and that there is no chariot as such over and above its parts, similarly the different components of an individual make up the individual and there is no other additional entity to hold the components together.

Writings of Buddhaghosa. Buddhaghosa is undoubtedly the most prolific and important writer in the Pāli language. There are different views about his birthplace. Certainly, he stayed at Buddh Gaya, in eastern India, for a long time, and this brought him into contact with the Ceylonese monks, because the *vihāra* (monastery) there had been built with the permission of Emperor Samudra Gupta (*c.* AD 330–380) for Ceylonese pilgrims. These monks retained Pāli as their sacred language, while India had already switched over to Sanskrit, with the Theravāda doctrine and the Pāli language dwindling into insignificance. Buddhaghosa started for Ceylon and stayed at the Mahāvihāra ("great monastery"), with its rich commentary literature, probably in Old Sinhalese. The first work he wrote was his famous *Visuddhi-magga* ("Way to Purity"), a compendium of the whole of the *Tripiṭaka*. No chronological order can be established for his other works. Using the *Mahā-aṭṭakathā* ("Great Commentary"), he wrote commentaries on the *Vinaya*, the four principal *nikāyas*, and on the seven books of the *Abhidhamma Piṭaka*. He is also credited with having written commentaries on the *Dhammapada*, *Khuddaka-pāṭha*, *Suttanipāta*, and *Jātaka*. It is now generally assumed, however, that the commentaries on the *Suttanipāta* and *Khuddaka-pāṭha* are not his work. There are also doubts—on stylistic grounds—concerning his authorship of the commentary on the *Dhammapada*. The *Jātakaṭṭhakathā* ("Commentary on the *Jātaka*") is an extensive work. The introduction to the work, the *Nidānakathā* ("Narrative of the Beginnings"), is the only biography of the Buddha in Pāli. It states that the period of the *bodhisattva*'s existence from the time of the mythical Buddha Dīpaṅkara up to his birth as a Tuṣita (a class of celestial beings) god is the "distant epoch," his descent from the Tuṣita Heaven to his enlightenment is the "intermediate epoch," and the early teaching career up to his meeting with his patrons Anāthapiṇḍika and Viśākhā is the "proximate epoch." The reference to Viśākhā's former existence sets the scene for the 547 *Jātaka* tales, which are a mine of information about the cultural life at the time of the author. The pattern of these stories is quite stereotyped. For example, an incident during the Buddha's life is explained by an episode in one of his previous lives. In all cases the *bodhisattva* (Buddha-to-be) has the leading role. The stories range from short narratives to full-fledged romances. Their themes have exerted a tremendous influence on the fine arts and subsequent narrative literature. In a large number of these stories, the *bodhisattva* is an animal caring for his fellow animals. The general tone is one of charity and self-sacrifice, which finds its climax in the *Vessantara-jātaka* ("Birth as Vessantara"), where the *bodhisattva* parts not only with his material possessions but also with his wife and children, with whom he is, of course, reunited in reward for his self-denial.

Stories of the Buddha's previous lives

Writings of Buddhadatta. Buddhadatta, a contemporary of Buddhagosa, was a native of Uragapura, the present Uraipur, South India. He had gone to Ceylon to study at the Mahāvihāra (great monastery) in Anuradhapura. On his return he wrote his works in a monastery on the banks of the Kaveri River. His *Abhidhammāvatāra* ("The Coming of the *Abhidhamma*"), although a summary of Buddhaghosa's commentaries on the *Abhidhamma Piṭaka*, stands supreme. In no way did he follow Buddhaghosa blindly. He reduced Buddhaghosa's five metaphysical ultimates—*i.e.*, form, feeling, sensations, motivations, and perception—to four, namely, mind, mental events, forms, and Nirvāṇa (enlightenment or emancipation). This creative classification, similar to that of the Sarvāstivādins, makes him a philosopher in his own right rather than a commentator who merely restates things in new terms.

Writings of Dhammapāla. Dhammapāla, probably a South Indian, is credited with having written commentaries on all the works left untreated by Buddhaghosa, whom he mentions in his work, the *Paramattha dīpanī*

("Elucidation of the True Meaning"). In the *Paramattha Mañjūsā* ("Jewel Box of the True Meaning"), his commentary on Buddhaghosa's *Visuddhi-magga* ("Way to Purity"), he quotes a verse from the Hindu scripture *Bhagavadgītā* and frequently mentions the views of other schools and teachers. This work provides valuable information about intellectual activity in Hīnayāna circles.

Ceylonese chronicles. At the close of the 4th century AD there existed in Ceylon an older work, a kind of chronicle, of the history of the island from its legendary beginning onward. It probably formed part of the *Mahā-aṭṭhakathā*, the commentary literature of the canonical writings that formed the basis of the works by Buddhaghosa and others. The historical information therein is reflected in the *Dīpavaṃsa* ("History of the Island"), which appears to be a poor redaction in Pāli of an older Old Sinhalese version. The *Mahāvaṃsa* ("Great Chronicle") by Mahānāma, continued in the *Cūlavaṃsa* ("Little Chronicle"), shows much greater skill in the use of the Pāli language and makes liberal use of other material. It is an artistic composition containing rich historical material.

MAHAYANA TEXTS

Only a small part of the vast Mahāyāna literature in Sanskrit has been preserved in its original version; for the most part translations into various Central Asian languages as well as into Chinese and Tibetan are the only sources. This literature can be divided into a philosophical one, stimulating the development of different schools of thought, and an edificatory literature that greatly appealed to the masses.

Prajñāpāramitā literature. The *Prajñāpāramitā* ("Perfection of Wisdom") literature is not an innovation but an exposition of the profounder meaning of the Buddha's teachings. There is evidence to suggest that the *Aṣṭasāhasrikā* ("In 8,000 *Śloka*s," *śloka*s in the context of a prose work meaning a unit of 32 syllables) is the oldest and most basic text, from which there have been such expansions as the *Śatasāhasrikā* ("In 100,000 *Ślokas*") and the *Pañcaviṃśatisāhasrikā* ("In 25,000 *Śloka*s") and abridgements, the *Saptaśatikā* ("In 700 *Ślokas*"), *Adhyardhaśataka* ("In 150 *Ślokas*"), *Vajracchedika* ("Diamond Cutter"), and even the *Prajñapāramitāhṛdayasūtra* ("The Essence of the Perfection of Wisdom"), which consists of only a few lines. In this literature a philosophical absolutism expressed through the dialectics of negation (*śūnyatā*) of all empirical notions and speculations is established. While in earlier Buddhism it was shown that the notion of a self was untenable, here the same critique is applied to those elements of reality other than the self. The origin of this literature falls into the period of the 1st century BC, if not earlier; by the second century AD it was sufficiently famous to be translated, the earliest translation into Chinese of the *Aṣṭasāhasrikā* having been made by the Yüeh-chih (Indo-Scythian) Lokarakṣa in AD 172.

Mādhyamika texts. The Mādhyamika ("middle way") system—which held both subject and object to be unreal—is the systematized form of the doctrine of *śūnyatā* (cosmic emptiness) contained in the *Prajñāpāramitā* literature. The most famous exponent of this system was the Indian philosopher Nāgārjuna, author of the voluminous *Mahā-prajñāpāramitā-śāstrā* ("The Great Treatise on the Perfection of Wisdom"), preserved in its Chinese translation (402-05) by Kumārajīva; of the *Mūlamadhyamakakārikā* ("The Basic Memorial Verses of the Middle Doctrine"), which is the Mādhyamika work par excellence; of the *Śūnyatā-saptati*, expounding the unreality of all elements of reality; of the *Vigrahavyāvartanī*, a refutation of possible objections to the doctrine of *śūnyatā*; of the *Vyavahārasiddhi*, teaching that absoluteness and relativity can coexist in practice; and of the *Yukti-ṣaṣṭika*, dealing with relativity. It is likely that Nāgārjuna is also the author of the *Ratnāvalī*, of the *Pratītyasamutpādahṛdaya*, and of the *Sūtrasamuccaya*, besides many other works attributed to him. Nāgārjuna's chief pupil was Āryadeva. His main work, the *Catuḥśataka*, not only criticizes the early form of Buddhism but also the classical Sanskrit philosophical systems. Together with his teacher Nāgārjuna, Āryadeva is the real founder of the Mādhyamika system.

Works of Nāgārjuna and Āryadeva

A new phase in this system was initiated during the 5th–6th century by Buddhapālita and Bhāvaviveka, the founder of a subschool that sought to prove the correctness of Mādhyamika doctrines by means of independent arguments. The former, commenting on the *Mādhyamika-śāstra*, developed the method of reducing to absurdity the arguments of an opponent on principles acceptable to him; the latter, author of the philosophical work *Tarkajvālā* ("Firebrand of Logical Investigation"), the *Mādhyamikārthasamgraha* ("Summary of the Mādhyamika Doctrine"), and the *Mādhyamikāvatārapradīpa* ("Lamp of the Mādhyamika Descent"), as well as the *Karatalaratna* ("Jewel in the Hand"), was a more liberal philosopher, and his works, now lost in the original, have been extremely influential. The Buddhist logician Candrakīrti (6th- or 7th-century-AD), author of the *Prasannapadā* ("The Clear-Worded"), a commentary on the *Mādhyamika Kārika*, and of the *Mādhyamikāvatāra* ("Descent of the Mādhyamika Teaching"), and Śāntideva, author of the *Śikṣā-samuccaya* ("Summary of Training") and the *Bodhicaryāvatāra* ("The Coming of the *Bodhisattva* Way of Life"), two of the most popular works in the whole Mahāyāna literature, continued the orthodox line of the Mādhyamika system; while Śāntirakṣita, a celebrated Indian teacher, who visited Tibet (8th century AD), author of the *Tattvasaṃgraha* ("Summary of the Essentials"), and the *Mādhyamikālaṅkāra Kārikā* ("Verses on the Ornament of the Mādhyamika Teaching"), on which his disciple Kamalaśīla wrote a commentary, represents the liberal line, which had great impact on Tibetan Buddhism.

The strict orthodox line is continued in such *sūtra*s as the *Samādhiraja-sūtra*, in which *śūnyatā* is explained in *samatā* (self-sameness), and the *Suvarṇabhāsottama-sūtra*, of which various versions existed and which introduced significant ideas concerning the *Buddhakāya*s—the various "bodies" of the Buddha.

The Mādhyamika system must be viewed in relation to the mentalistic philosophy of the Yogācāras, who held that only consciousness itself is real and who, too, accepted the *śūnyatā* of the *Prajñāpāramitā*s but interpreted it experientially rather than primarily metaphysically. Their leading exponent is Maitreyanātha (270–350), represented by his illustrious disciple Asaṅga (*c.* 350), author of the *Mahāyāna-sūtrālaṅkāra, the Dharmadharmatā-vibhaṅga*, and the *Madhyānta-vibhāga.* Important for the development of Japanese Zen Buddhism—a meditative school that emphasizes sudden enlightenment—was the *Laṅkāvatāra-sūtra* ("The Buddha's Descent on Ceylon *Sūtra*"), which combines both the absolutism of the Mādhyamikas and the mentalism of the Yogācāras (see also BUDDHIST PHILOSOPHY; NAGARJUNA).

Avataṃsaka-sūtra. There exists a vast collection of Buddhist scriptures known as the *Mahāvaipulya-Buddhāvataṃsaka-sūtra* ("The Great and Vast Buddha Garland *Sūtra*"), or, briefly, as the *Avataṃsaka-sūtra.* The only part that has been studied in detail is the *Daśabhūmika-sūtra* ("The *Sūtra* on the Ten Spiritual Levels"), dealing with the ten stages of a *bodhisattva;* another part is the *Gaṇḍavyūha-sūtra* ("The Compact Display *Sūtra*"). The latter dates back to the 1st century AD, and the text is probably of South Indian origin. The important centre of *Avataṃsaka* Buddhism, where the process of accretion and combination of various texts took place, was, however, in Central Asia, particularly Khotan. The *Avataṃsaka-sūtra* already existed in parts in China before the first complete translation was finished (AD 418–420). Among the early translations, a work called *Tou-sha-ching* ("Tuṣita [Heaven] *Sūtra*"), a somewhat shorter version of the *Ju-lai ming hao p'in* ("Section on the Tathāgata's [Buddha's] Names") of the later *Avataṃsaka* translation, has been attributed to Lokakṣema (AD 168–188). A fragmentary translation of the *Gaṇḍavyūha*, attributed to the monk Sheng-chien, belongs to the period of the reign of the emperor Hsiao-wu (AD 373–385) of the Eastern Chin dynasty. Between 418 and 421 the North Indian

Central Asian translations

monk Buddhabhadra made the first translation of the entire text, which had been imported from Khotan in 60 volumes (*chüan*). In AD 680 the monk Divākara retranslated a small part of the *Gaṇḍavyūha* in order to fill a gap in Buddhabhadra's work. In 699 a second translation was completed under the direction of the Khotanese monk Śīkṣānanda. This new translation in 80 *chüan* was also made from a text imported from Khotan. In AD 796–798 the monk Prajña translated a *Gaṇḍavyūha* manuscript in 40 *chüan*. The central theme of the *Avataṃsaka-sūtra* is the meaning of true enlightenment. Since the *Gaṇḍavyūha*, which relates the travels of the youth Sudhana in search of enlightenment (assisted by numerous spiritual friends, all of whom belong to different walks of life), is an integral part of the *Avataṃsaka-sūtra*, the elucidation of the complicated system of different stages of spiritual attainment is the secondary theme. The end of the *Gaṇḍavyūha* is formed by the *Samantabhadracarī-praṇidhāna-gāthā*, or, briefly, *Bhadracaryā*. In 62 verses the devotee makes a pious vow to follow the exemplary conduct of the *bodhisattva* Samantabhadra. From the available evidence of different translations, the incorporation of the *Bhadracaryā* into the *Gaṇḍavyūha* came at a later date. The *Avataṃsaka-sūtra* is the basic work of the Hua-yen (Japanese Kegon) school, with its theory of universal causation and its belief that there is a universal, immutable mind that is the basis of all phenomena.

Saddharmapuṇḍarīka-sūtra. One of the most popular early texts of the Mahāyānists is the *Saddharmapuṇḍarīka-sūtra* ("The Lotus of the Good Law")—popularly known as the *Lotus Sūtra*—which is the basic text of the Tendai (Chinese T'ien-t'ai) sect—which emphasized the possibility of universal salvation and the Buddha-nature that is inherent in all beings—and the Nichiren sect (founded by the 13th-century prophetic reformer Nichiren) in Japan. The *Lotus Sūtra* is also recited in the temples of the Zen sect of Japan. Manuscripts have been found in Nepal, Central Asia, and Gilgit (Kashmir). The earliest Chinese translation (AD 286) is by Dharmarakṣa (a Yüeh-chih), born in Kansu but educated farther west. The text was next translated by Kumārajīva, a Buddhist missionary from Kucha (an oasis on the northern trade route through Central Asia) to China, in AD 406. A third translation (AD 601) by Jñānagupta and Dharmagupta follows the Nepalese version. In the 4th century AD a commentary in four volumes had already been completed by Chu Fa-ch'ung, a learned Chinese monk. Kumārajīva's translation had 27 chapters (as has the extant Sanskrit version), but the Chinese Buddhist monk and traveller Fa-hsien (flourished AD 399–414) found in Khotan another chapter, which he had translated by Fa-i, an Indian. This chapter deals with Devadatta, Buddha's cousin and enemy, and was added to the 27-chapter version in the Chinese rendering.

Purpose of the work

The aim and object of the work is to establish the "one spiritual pursuit" (*ekāyāna*). There are three successive stages, or "vehicles," in the attainment of *ekāyāna:* (1) the Śrāvakayāna, the vehicle for disciples (*Śrāvaka*s) who become saints through hearing the teachings of the Buddha and are unconcerned with the salvation or enlightenment of others; (2) *Pratyekabuddhayāna*, the vehicle for those who attain salvation or enlightenment by themselves and are unconcerned with the salvation of others; (3) *Bodhisattvayāna*, the vehicle for those who are ready to become enlightened but postpone their enlightenment in order to save all other beings first. The work also contains the Buddha's plans for imparting training to those having different mental capacities and inclinations due to their past deeds. Another point is the emphasis on the immense merit a person derives from reading, copying, or propagating this *sūtra*. Being mainly devotional, this text avoids the philosophical aspects of Buddhism; but when they are touched upon, they are the same as those expounded in the other Mahāyāna *sūtra*s that deal with *śūnyatā*. The ultimate aim is Buddhahood, and for its attainment the practice of the six *pāramitā*s, or perfections (liberality, morality, patience, energy, concentration, and wisdom), is recommended; the sixth, the *Prajñāpāramitā* (perfection of wisdom), is identical with omniscience. Along with the practice of the *pāramitā*s the *bodhisattva* must lead a well-controlled life, showing kindness and compassion. This practice is not restricted to monks and nuns but can be performed equally well by householders. It is in this work that are found the famous parables of the burning house (from which the father lured his children by promising them toys and different carriages, but when they came out they saw there was only one carriage), the rich man's son (who, having returned home destitute, does not recognize his father, but whose inheritance is revealed at the end of his father's life), and the wise caravan leader (who lets his travellers rest before leading them on to the final destination).

Sukhāvatī-vyūha-sūtra. Of purely devotional character is the *Sukhāvatī-vyūha-sūtra* ("Pure Land *Sūtra*"), which exists in two versions, a larger and a smaller one. It was translated into Chinese by Lokarakṣa (a Yüeh-chih) in the latter half of the 2nd century, by Chih-ch'ien (also a Yüeh-chih) in the second half of the 3rd century, by Saṅghavarman (from Sogdiana, in Central Asia, shortly after 250), and by Kumārajīva around 400. The first three translations closely resemble each other and the larger *Sukhāvatīvyūha*, while Kumārajīva's version corresponds to the smaller *Sukhāvatīvyūha*. Apart from these important works, a number of other translations are still extant. In these texts the Buddha reigning over the Western Paradise is called Amitābha ("of measureless light") to denote his character of infinite light and Amitāyus ("of measureless life") to indicate his infinite life. His paradise, Sukhāvatī ("Pure Land"), is the most beautiful one. Those who have lived in purity or have called on his name he will welcome to his paradise at the moment of their death. This work is basic to the most widespread form of Buddhism, the Pure Land school (Ch'ing t'u) in China—characterized by the belief that salvation consisted in attaining the Pure Land or Western Paradise of the Buddha Amitābha and is attainable through faith in Amitābha—and the Jōdo schools (Amidism) in Japan (Japanese Pure Land schools).

Other Mahāyāna texts. As early as the 1st century AD, the *Lalitavistara* ("The Detailed Narration of the Sport [Play] of the Buddha"), in mixed Sanskrit and Sanskritized vernacular, telling the life story of the Buddha up to his first discourse, was translated into Chinese and followed by other translations. The *Kāśyapa-Parivarta-sūtra* ("Kāśyapa's Discourse *Sūtra*"), existing before AD 200, contributed much to the development of the Mādhyamika system; while the *Śrīmālādevī-siṃhanāda-sūtra* ("*Sūtra* of Srīmālādevī Whose Discourse is Like the Roaring of a Lion") emphasizes the "one spiritual pursuit" and the *bodhisattva* ideal, thus being close to the *Saddharmapuṇḍarīka-sūtra*. The *Daśabhūmika-sūtra*, in particular, deals with the stages of development of the *bodhisattva* ideal. The *Amitāyurdhyāna-sūtra* ("*Sūtra* on the Meditation on Amitāyus") has been influential for meditation on the celestial Buddha Amitābha-Amitāyus. The *Vimalakīrtinirdeśa-sūtra*, explaining Ultimate Enlightenment by a householder and containing a subtle satire on those who avoided involvement in daily life, has been popular even in Zen circles. Lastly, the 2nd-century Buddhist saint and scholar Aśvaghoṣa's *Buddhacarita* ("The Life of the Buddha"), the life story of the Buddha, and his *Saundarānanda-kāvya* ("The Poetic Narration of Sundarī and Nanda"), having the Buddha's disciple Nanda's infatuation with women's beauty as its theme—both in highly poetic style—must be mentioned. The *Divyāvadāna* ("Heavenly Heroic Deeds") is a collection of narratives extolling the Buddhist virtues of sacrifice and kindness, the *Avadāna-śataka* ("A Hundred Stories of Heroic Deeds") is a collection of edifying tales, and Āryaśūra's *Jātakamālā* ("Garland of *Jātaka*s [Birth Stories]") is a poetic treatment of some of the stories of the Buddha's previous lives.

Works of Aśvaghoṣa

TANTRIC AND TIBETAN TEXTS

While the *sūtra*s cannot be underestimated in the development of Buddhist thought and of the various philosophical systems, there exists another kind of literature that is concerned with the inner experience of the Buddhist ideas and ideals. The *sūtras*, therefore, can be said to represent the theoretical and speculative aspect of Buddhism; while the *Tantras* ("Treatises"), written in a highly figurative language, express Buddhism as individually lived. The *Tantras* are essentially individual works that apply to larger groups of persons because of the similarity of the experiences described in them. The individual spiritual development occurs through symbols that must not be reduced to signs; a symbol always points beyond itself. Because of this symbolic character, the *Tantras* have usually been kept secret, and a literalist interpretation of such texts has usually failed to make any sense out of them.

Tantras. The *Guhyasamāja-tantra* ("Treatise on the Sum Total of Mysteries"), also known as the *Tathāgataguhyaka* ("The Mystery of Tathāgatahood [Buddhahood]"), is the earliest known written *Tantra*. It is by tradition ascribed to the renowned Indian scholar Asaṅga (*c.* 4th century AD), the propounder of the Yogācāra philosophy. Usually the *Tantras* do not give an explanation of the technical or symbolic terms, as this explanation is left to the teacher, but the *Guhyasamāja-tantra* devotes a very long chapter to the elucidation of these terms. An important feature of all *Tantras* is a polarity symbolism, which on the physical level appears as the union of male and female, on the ethical level appears as beneficial activity and insight into and appreciation of what there is as it is, and on the philosophical level appears as the dynamic aspect of enlightenment as absolute Being and absolute compassion. It is to be noted that in Buddhist *Tantras* the female component in the nature of reality is an appreciative awareness (*prajñā*), an inspiration, not a power (*śakti*) through which a male superbeing attempts to dominate, as in Hinduism. Another feature is the idea of the *maṇḍala* (ritual drawing), which is both a projection of an ordering and a visual aid to the psychological orientation process, which is a kind of seeing the world and oneself in transfiguration. While the *sūtras* often create the impression of a negative approach to life, the *Tantras* insist on the absolute value of what there is. In order to realize this value, a strict discipline is demanded. The rich symbolism of the *Tantras* is already indicated in the opening of the *Guhyasamāja*, when the absolute in its polarity symbolism manifests itself in various *maṇḍalas*, each related to one of the celestial, meditational Buddhas—Akṣobhya, Vairocana, Ratnasambhava, Amitābha, and Amoghasiddhi—each of whom again represents a polarity, portrayed in iconographic works as being in union with their female consorts (see BUDDHIST MYTHOLOGY). The symbolism involved is further elaborated by the development of the idea that spirituality is existentiality and vice versa and that spirituality and existentiality are also communication.

Tantric symbolism

The ideas presented in the *Guhyasamāja-tantra* became in the course of time more and more clearly elaborated. Because the *Tantras* reflect an individual process of growth, the centre toward which this process gravitates and from which it is also fed appears in various symbols given various designations. Thus, there is the *Hevajra-tantra*, in which the sustaining life force is called *Hevajra*, and the *Mahā-Vairocana-tantra*, in which it is Mahā-Vairocana ("The Great Resplendent One"; in Japan, identified with the Sun) as distinguished from Vairocana belonging to a lower level.

In view of the fact that the *Tantras* may emphasize either "beneficial activity" or "appreciative awareness" or their "unity," the Tantric literature has been divided into the so-called *Father Tantra* (emphasizing activity), the *Mother Tantra* (emphasizing appreciation), and the *Nondual Tantra* (dealing with both aspects unitively). Almost all these works have been lost in their original Sanskrit versions, but their influence is noticeable in such works as the great Tantric teacher Indrabhūti's (*c.* 687–717) *Jñānasiddhi* ("Attainment of Knowledge"), the 8th-century Indian writer Anaṅgavajra's *Prajñopāyaviniścayasiddhi* ("The Realization of the Certitude of Appreciative Awareness, and Ethical Action"), and the songs of the 84 *mahāsiddhas* ("great accomplished ones," who were spiritual adepts). One of the last Sanskrit works to have been written in Central Asia is the *Kālacakra-tantra*. Its penetration into India may be dated AD 966. The central theme is the Ādi-Buddha—primeval Buddhahood—manifesting itself as a continuum of time (*kāla*) and space (*cakra*).

Tibetan literature. The vast mass of Buddhist literature, mostly lost in India, has been preserved in its Tibetan and Chinese translations, from which many translations into other Asian languages have been made. The translation techniques varied; first the attempt was made to render the spirit of the texts rather than their exact words. This technique was employed by the Chinese under the influence of Kumārajīva. The Tibetans, too, first rendered the spirit of the texts, but these early translations are not found in the standard collection, which utilized only those translations of texts that had been made under the influence of the translator Rin-chen bzang-po (11th century). This later translation technique was more concerned with the exact words of the original. The earlier version, still very little known, is of much greater importance for the study of the history of the development of Buddhist thought, while the later translation reflects the final stage of Buddhism. It is important to remember that there are more texts than the number contained in the Tibetan collections, known as the *Bka'-'gyur* ("Translation of the Buddha-Word") and *Bstan-'gyur* ("Translation of Teachings"). There are different editions, mostly differing in the arrangement of the texts; the oldest edition is the so-called Cone edition, which was the prototype for the Derge edition, on which, in turn, the Peking edition of 1411 is based. These are very good editions. The Narthang edition (printed by Tibetan monks in the 18th century) was made in a hurry and is full of mistakes. The following analysis follows the arrangement of the Peking edition.

Classification of Tibetan texts

Bka'-'gyur ("Translation of the Buddha-Word"). This collection, containing the works that are supposed to represent the Buddha's words, is divided into six sections, containing 1,055 titles in 92 volumes. The arrangement is (1) *Tantra;* (2) *Prajñāpāramitā;* (3) *Ratnakūṭa*, a collection of 49 small Mahāyāna texts; (4) *Avataṃsaka;* (5) *Sūtra*, mostly Mahāyāna *sūtras* but also a number of Hīnayāna ones; and (6) *Vinaya*.

Bstan-'gyur ("Translation of Teachings"). This collection of 224 volumes with 3,626 texts is divided into three major groups: (1) *Stotras* (hymns of praise) in one volume, including 64 texts; (2) commentaries on *Tantras* in 86 volumes, including 3,055 texts; and (3) commentaries on *sūtras* in 137 volumes, including 567 texts.

Commentaries on the *sūtras* include *Prajñāpāramitā* commentaries (16 volumes), Mādhyamika treatises (17 volumes), Yogācāra treatises (29 volumes), *Abhidharma* (eight volumes), miscellaneous (four volumes), *Vinaya* commentaries (16 volumes), narrative literature and drama (four volumes), and technical works—logic (21 volumes), grammar (one volume), lexicography and poetics (one volume), medicine (five volumes), chemistry and sundry other "sciences" (one volume), and a supplement (old and recent translations, indices, 14 volumes).

Other Tibetan texts. Tibetan Buddhist literature developed in intimate relationship with the translation work that brought new ideas and interpretations to a people who were singularly gifted at assimilating and developing. By the time that the Indian texts became widely available, Buddhism in India was on the wane, but it found new life with the Tibetans, who disseminated Buddhist ideas into Mongolia, which, in turn, contributed to the flowering of Buddhist thought. Perhaps the greatest stimulus to this development was the arrival of the great Indian teacher Atīśa in Gu-ge, an ancient kingdom in western Tibet, in AD 1042. Although his favourite disciple, 'Brom-ston (1008–64), avoided publicity of all kinds, even refraining from giving instruction, the strictness of his conduct and his earnest attention to the Buddhist axioms of transitoriness, frustration (resulting from believing that something would last forever when it may break at any moment), and the ethical obligations that derive from seeing the world in its true light left an indelible impression on his followers, who became known as the Bka'-gdams-pa, "those bound by command." The *Bka'-gdams gces-bsdus* ("Collection of the Sayings of the Bka'-gdams-pa Saints") has preserved their utterances, which often are of high poetic quality. In this religiously saturated climate, the first school, or order, to be established was the Sa-skya-pa, named after the monastery of Sa-skya, which had been founded in AD 1073 by Dkon-mchog rgyal-po, a disciple of 'Brog-mi, an eccentric mystic. It was Dkon-mchog rgyal-po's son and successor, the great Sa-skya-pa Kun-dga' snying-po (1092–1158), who formulated the teachings received. His *Legs-bshad* ("A Treasury of Aphoristic Jewels"), a collection of maxims, is one of the most famous works, also highly appreciated by other Tibetan schools. The indigenous contributions to Buddhist thought were contained in the *gsung-'bum* (collected works) of the great lamas. They are of prime importance for evaluating the Tibetan and Mongolian achievement in every field of knowledge. It is not possible, however, to deal with these works exhaustively because no systematic survey has been made as yet. The topics that are dealt with in these collected works range from explanations of the *Prajñāpāramitā*, *Mādhyamika*, *Vinaya*, and *Abhidharma* to contributions to epistemology, *Tantra*, ritual, and philosophical surveys. The latter present the whole of Buddhism as a gradation and are known under the name *Lam-rim* ("Stages on the Path"). One of the earliest works of this kind is Sgam-po-pa's (1079–1153) *Thar-rgyan* ("Jewel Ornament of Liberation"), in which he embodied teachings of religious practices of his master Mi-la ras-pa (Milarepa). It has become the manual of the Bka'-brgyud-pa ("those who transmit the Buddha-Word") order. Mi-la ras-pa (1040–1123) himself is known from his beautiful songs expounding his religious experiences.

Writings of Tsong-kha-pa

Widely known for his learning was Tsong-kha-pa (1357–1419), founder of the Dge-lugs-pa order—the dominant order of Tibetan Buddhists, who wear yellow hats. His religious views seem to have taken their final form when at the age of 40 he joined the great Bka'-gdams-pa monastery of Ra-sgreng. There he wrote his voluminous *Lam-rim chen-mo* ("The Great Account of the Stages on the Path"), which he later supplemented by the *Sngags-rim chen-mo* ("The Great Account of the Stages on the Tantric Path"), a highly technical work of ritual and mystical practices. His *Lam-rim chen-mo* became the pattern after which subsequent lamas molded their accounts of the Buddhist Path, such as the *Myur-lam* ("Quick Path") by the third Dalai Lama (1543–88)—Dalai Lamas were spiritual and temporal rulers of Tibet before 1959—on which countless commentaries were written.

A famous writer and historian was Tāranātha (born AD 1575). He belonged to the Jo-nang-pa school, a sect whose monasteries were eventually destroyed and whose books were burned by the Dge-lugs-pas. Tāranātha's writings are still extant, however, and his *Rgya-gar chos-'byung* ("History of Buddhism in India") has been highly appreciated even by modern scholars.

Padma dkar-po is the main representative of the 'Brug-pa suborder of the Bka'-brgyud-pa. His systematic approach to all aspects of Buddhism makes him one of the greatest scholars.

Outstanding among the rNying-ma-pa ("The Old Order")—followers of the earliest Tibetan Buddhist traditions—are Klong-chen rab-'byams-pa (1308–63), whose *Klong-chen-mdzod-bdun* ("Seven Treasures of Klong-chen") reflects the profoundest thought of Tibet, and Mi-'pham of Khams (1846–1914), who wrote elaborate commentaries on the canonical texts.

Thu-kwan Blo-bzang chos-kyi nyi-ma (1737–1802) is the author of a history of the doctrines of the various Buddhist and other heterodox schools in India, Tibet, China, and Mongolia.

A very erudite work is the *Grub-mtha'shel-gyi me-long* ("History of the rNying-ma-pa") by Dudjom Tulku Rimpoche (1964).

Mongolian texts. In Mongolia there have been three propagations of Buddhism, the earliest through Li-yul (Khotan, Sogdiana, or the Tocharian kingdom), the middle and later ones through Tibet. The contribution of the Mongols to Buddhism has been enormous, both as regards the *Lam-rim* literature and the *Tantras*. Lcang-skya qutuγtu Ngag-dbang blo-bzang chos-ldan (1642–1714) and Lcang-skya qutuγtu Rol-pa'i rdo-rje (1717–86) were both prodigious scholars, the latter making a fundamental contribution toward the creation of a classical Mongolian language into which to translate Buddhist texts.

The masterly manuals by 'Jam-dbyangs-bzhad-pa I, Ngag-dbang-brtson-'grus (1648–1721), are highly esteemed by the Dge-lugs-pa and studied in Tibet and Inner and Outer Mongolia by the Buryats and Kalmuks. 'Jam-dbyangs-bzhad-pa II, Dkon-mchog-'jigs-med dbang-po (1728–81), is noted for his concise exposition of philosophical systems. The many works in the Tibetan language composed by the Mongols have been acclaimed even in Tibet and are testimony to the rich literary activity inspired by Buddhism.

CHINESE AND JAPANESE TEXTS

By the end of the T'ang dynasty (618–907), the composition of the Chinese *Tripiṭaka* (*Ta-ts'ang Ching*, "Great Scripture Store") was practically completed. Sporadic translations were still made during the Sung period (960–1279), but they did not add anything new. The standard modern edition, *Taishō Shinshū Daizōkyō*, contains 2,184 texts arranged in 24 sections as follows: (1) *Āgama* section, containing the Long, Medium, Kindred, and Item-More (*i.e.*, numerically graded) *Āgamas*, as well as some individual texts corresponding to sections of the Pāli *Khuddaka Nikāya;* (2) story section—*Jātakas*, lives of various Buddhas, fables, and parables; (3) *Prajñāpāramitā* section; (4) *Saddharmapuṇḍarīka* section, three complete versions of this famous *sūtra* together with some doctrinally related *sūtras*; (5) *Avataṃsaka* section; (6) *Ratnakūṭa* section, 49 Mahāyāna *sūtras*, some in more than one translation; (7) *Mahāparinirvāṇa* section, the Mahāyāna version of the Buddha's last days; (8) Great Assembly section, containing texts similar to the *Ratnakūṭa* section but more varied in content; (9) *sūtra*-collection section, a miscellany of *sūtras*, mostly Mahāyāna; (10) *Tantra* section; (11) *Vinaya* section, the disciplinary codes of various early Buddhist groups (some texts deal with the *bodhisattva* discipline); (12) commentaries on *sūtras* by Indian authors; (13) *Abhidharma* section, scholastic works of various early Buddhist groups; (14) Mādhyamika section; (15) Yogācāra section; (16) collection of *śāstras*; (17) commentaries on *sūtras* by Chinese authors; (18) commentaries on the *Vinaya* by Chinese authors; (19) commentaries on *śāstras* by Chinese authors; (20) Chinese sectarian writings; (21) history and biography; (22) encyclopaedias and dictionaries; (23) non-Buddhist doctrines, including non-Buddhist philosophies of India and Manichaean and Nestorian Christian writings; and (24) catalogs of earlier compilations.

As Buddhism permeated the way of thinking of the peoples of the Far East, the tendency to concentrate on the study of one particular scripture or group of scriptures led to significant contributions by the most brilliant minds of China, Japan, and Korea. Apart from such early scholars as Seng-chao (AD 384–414), Tao-sheng (5th century AD), and Tao-an (AD 312–385), Chi-tsang (549–623), who had a Parthian father and a Chinese mother, greatly elaborated and systematized the Mahāyāna teachings. His influence extended to the 8th century, after which his school rapidly declined. Of more lasting fame was the Chinese development of the Indian Yogācāra school by Hsüan-tsang (596–664), who, in his *Ch'eng wei-shih lun* ("Dissertation on Consciousness-Only"), selected, summarized, and systematized the ideas of ten great philosophers of India. Although this school also declined after the 9th century, it is on these ideas that such modern philosophers as Hsiung Shih-li (1885–1968) and T'ang Chün-i (1907–   ) base their own philosophies. Chih-k'ai (or Chih-i, 538–597), a southerner with a distinctly intellectual background, under the influence of his teacher the monk Hui-ssu (*c.* 514–577), gave both a con-

Early Chinese writers

templative and an intellectual interpretation of the *Saddharmapuṇḍarīka-sūtra*. *Ta-ch'eng chih-kuan fa-men* ("The Method of Concentration and Insight in the Mahāyāna"), by Hui-ssu, and *Fa-hua Hsuan-i* ("The Profound Meaning of the *Saddharmapuṇḍarīka*"), by Chih-k'ai, are important works for the T'ien-t'ai school, characterized by the belief that all men can become the Buddha, since all men possess the Buddha nature. Significant contributions to the development of the Hua-yen (Japanese Kegon; Sanskrit Avataṃsaka) school—which stresses the doctrine that all things in the universe are representations of the same supreme mind—were made by Tu-shun (557–640), the nominal founder, and Fa-tsang (643–712), who is considered to be the real founder and whose treatise *Chin shih-tzu chang* ("The Golden Lion") is one of the most lucid expositions of the Hua-yen philosophy. Tsung-mi (780–841), revered as the fifth and last patriarch of both the Hua-yen school and the Ho-tse branch of the Southern school of Ch'an (Zen) Buddhism (see below), was the author of the *Yüan jen lun* ("Treatise on the Original Nature of Man"). In this work his own spiritual development—early training in classical Chinese studies, conversion to Ch'an Buddhism in his early twenties, and introduction in his early 30s to Hua-yen philosophy by Ch'eng-kuan, the fourth patriarch of the school—as well as his critical evaluation of the principal schools of thought of his time is clearly reflected. The Pure Land Buddhism found able interpreters in T'an-luan (476–542), commenting on the *Sukhāvatīvyūha;* in Tao-ch'o (died AD 645), a T'ien-t'ai monk, in his *Ching t'u lun* ("Compendium on the Happy Land"); and in Shan-tao (613–681), who is known for his pietism and the influence he exerted on the Pure Land schools in Japan.

Works of Ch'an school

Among the works of the Ch'an school, which began with the study of the *Laṅkāvatāra-sūtra* but gradually split into a Northern school stressing gradual enlightenment and Southern school advocating sudden enlightenment, *T'an Ching* ("The Platform Scripture") of the sixth patriarch, Hui-neng (died AD 713), is a highly esteemed work said to represent a collection of sermons and the autobiography of Hui-neng as transmitted by his disciple Fa-hai. It is the only Chinese noncanonical work called a *sūtra* (*ching*). The original version, found at Tun-huang in northwest Kansu, is rather primitive, while the current one has been greatly extended and revised. The stories of the Ch'an masters, recording their sayings and short paradoxical stories about them, which are said to indicate the depth of their understanding, are collected in the *Ching-te ch'uan-teng lü* ("Records of the Transmission of the Lamp"), AD 1004.

Writings of Saichō and Kūkai

In Japan, Saichō (or Dengyō Daishi, 767–822), of Chinese descent, based his teaching on the *Lotus Sūtra,* which he had studied in China; and the Tendai sect, founded by him, upheld the "one spiritual pursuit" idea as the real meaning of Mahāyāna Buddhism. His writings, undistinguished in style, reveal his earnestness and sincerity. At first he was on friendly terms with Kūkai (Kōbō-daishi, 774–835), but a rift occurred when the latter asked Saichō to become his regular disciple, if he wanted to study the esoteric form of Buddhism. Kūkai's first major work was *Sangō-shiiki* ("The Indications to the Three Teachings"), in which he treats Confucianism, Taoism, and Buddhism in a somewhat superficial way. In AD 804 Kūkai sailed for China, where he met the great master Hui-kuo (746–805), who took him as his chosen disciple. His greatest contribution is the systematization of esoteric "True Word" (Shingon) Buddhism—which considered the cosmic Buddha Mahā-Vairocana to be the source of the whole universe. His *Jūju shinron* ("The Ten Stages of Consciousness") was written entirely in Chinese in an ornate poetical style.

The sudden collapse of the Kyōto court in the 12th century coincided with a crisis in the religious life of the Japanese, which found its expression in the growth and spread of Pure Land Buddhism. Forerunners of this movement had been Kūya (903–972), the "saint of the streets"; Ryōnin (1072–1132), who promulgated the *nembutsu*—the constant repetition of Amida Buddha's [illegible] (1239–89) who believed that the grace of Amida was found everywhere. The popularization of this faith owes much to Genshin (942–1017) through his famous work *Ōjō-yōshū* ("Essentials of Salvation"), in which he describes the torments of hell and the bliss of the Pure Land of Amida Buddha. The Pure Land Buddhism as a separate school owes its existence to Hōnen (1133–1212) through his epoch-making *Senchaku-shū* ("Original Vow of Amida") and to Shinran (1173–1262), who later claimed to be Hōnen's true disciple. The writings of the prophetic reformer Nichiren (1222–82) introduce a rather militant tone. The writings of Dōgen (1200–53) are important for the Sōtō school of Zen, as are the writings of Hakuin (1685–1768) for the modern Rinzai school of Zen.

OTHER IMPORTANT TEXTS

A unique work that has often been quoted and that played an important role in the formulation of Hua-yen thought is the *Mahāyāna-Śraddhotpāda* ("The Awakening of Faith in Mahāyāna"). Its one-time attribution to the famous Indian poet and dramatist Aśvaghoṣa is certainly wrong. Since the philosophical ideas so clearly presented in it are rather an amalgamation of Buddhist and Taoist ideas, a Central Asian or Chinese origin is more likely. The *Sādhanamālā* ("Garland of Successful Visualizations") contains more than 300 visualizations —prescriptions for both mental images and actual temple images—of Buddhist deities and is invaluable for the study of Buddhist iconography. A favourite of Zen scholars has been the *Pi-yen lu* (Japanese *Hekigan-roku,* "Blue Cliff Records"), a collection of one hundred short stories of Zen teachers who had lived and taught in various parts of China for over 400 years.

III. Ritual use and influence of Buddhist texts

Because the practice of Buddhism has demanded detachment from the turmoil of daily life and has insisted on disciplined study, any use of the Buddhist texts for non-study purposes is purely incidental and a concession to popular demand. The Buddhist monks officiate at funerals, perform ceremonies in the monastery temples, and instruct the young. Each ceremony, whether in Hīnayāna or Mahāyāna countries, begins with the invocation of the Three Jewels (the Buddha, the *dharma*—the law—and the *saṅgha*—the monastic order or community) and what follows varies with the wealth and the piety of the person asking for a recitation of the sacred texts or arranging a specific ceremony. In Tantric ceremonies the choice of texts that are recited depends not only on the occasion and the nature of the ceremony but also on the tradition a particular monastery follows.

Buddhist sacred literature has had a lasting influence on the fine arts, which, in the case of painting, were applied to illustrate the manuscripts. The overwhelming majority of works of Buddhist art are cult images, representing sacred figures either individually or in groups. It is the nature of the cult image that it signifies the absolute as revealed to the observer; at the same time it is at the service of Buddhahood, goodness, and salvation. The simplest form of the cult image is the Buddha either in his shape as the Enlightened One or as the *bodhisattva.* When the psychological process of enlightenment became the focus of attention, since everyone is capable in principle of attaining Buddhahood, it was only natural that this process, manifesting itself in symbolic forms, was made visible in the many Tantric deities who are but formulated psychic energies, incorporated in the texts dealing with them as visual aids. As cult images there must also be counted the many representations of the Pure Land of Amitābha, whose description is found in the *Sukhāvatīvyūha*. In contrast to the cult images, the narrative image depicts the ordinary world in such a way that the beholder is reminded of the fact that the world can be overcome. The most frequent themes in telling a tale are taken from the *Jātaka*s, as can be seen in the illustrative paintings in the Ajantā caves of India. A specifically favoured theme in China and Japan was the *bodhisattva*'s self-sacrifice to save a starving tigress and her cubs. This scene is found in the cave temples of

Mai chi shan and on the Tamamushi Shrine in the Hōryūji. From among the *sūtra*s it was the *Vimalakīrtinirdeśa-sūtra* that stimulated the artists to paint the domestic scene in which the rich householder Vimalakīrti discourses with the *bodhisattva* Mañjuśrī on the central subject of the Mādhyamika system.

Illustration of texts

Just as the sacred Buddhist texts inspired artists to paint and carve cult images and narrative images, the texts themselves are also illustrated. The most famous texts to be illustrated were the *Saddharmapuṇḍarīka-sūtra* and the *Avataṃsaka-sūtra*, the last part of which, the *Gaṇḍavyūha*, inspired the Borobuḍur temple complex in Java. Other famous *sūtra*s that were illustrated were the *Sanzen Butsu-myō-kyō* ("*Sūtra* of the Three Thousand Names of the Buddha"), the *Prajñāpāramitā-sūtra*, and, in Japan, the *Yakushi hongan-kyō* ("The *Sūtra* of the Original Vow of Bhaiṣajyaguru [Buddha of Healing]"). A special illustrative method, which was also applied to secular subjects, is the Japanese hand scroll, *emaki* or *emakimono*. Here the pictorial part is not merely a short illustration interspersed in the texts but is itself a narrative. Portraits of priests frequently were used to illustrate the texts they wrote or to whose development they contributed.

BIBLIOGRAPHY. MORIZ WINTERNITZ, *Geschichte der indischen Litteratur*, vol. 2 (1913; Eng. trans., *A History of Indian Literature*, vol. 2, 1933), still the only general survey of Buddhist sacred literature in Sanskrit and Pāli; LOKESH CHANDRA (ed.), *Materials for a History of Tibetan Literature*, 3 vol. (1963), a valuable beginning for assessing the voluminous Tibetan literature; and LOKESH CHANDRA, *Eminent Tibetan Polymaths of Mongolia* (1961).

(H.G.)

Budgets, Governmental

A governmental budget is the forecast by a government of its expenditures and revenues for a specific period of time. In national finance, the period covered by a budget is usually a year, known as a financial or fiscal year, which may or may not correspond with the calendar year. The word budget is derived from the Old French *bougette* ("little bag"). When the British chancellor of the exchequer makes his annual financial statement, he is said to "open" his budget or receptacle of documents and accounts.

Budgeting and control

Government budgetary institutions in the West grew up largely as a result of the struggle for power between the legislative and executive branches of government. With the decline of the feudal system, it became necessary for kings and princes to obtain resources for their ventures from taxation rather than dues. The disappearance of the old feudal bonds meant that taxpayers demanded to be consulted before they paid. In England this was written into Magna Carta (1216), which stated:

> No scutage or aid shall be imposed in the Kingdom unless by the common council of the realm, except for the purpose of ransoming the King's person, making his first-born son a knight, and marrying his eldest daughter once, and the aids for this purpose shall be reasonable in amount.

This related to taxes; the control of expenditures came much later. For centuries, Parliament seemed content to restrict the amounts that the sovereign levied while letting him spend the money as he pleases. Only after the controversies of the 17th century culminated in the Revolution of 1688 and the Bill of Rights did Parliament extend its concern to the question of expenditure control. The tradition grew up that expenditures must flow from appropriations, and appropriations were to be made for specific purposes.

In France, the struggle between the monarchy and the nobility over control of tax revenues was one of the causes of the Revolution of 1789 that led to the overthrow of both the monarchy and the nobility. Financial crises have been turning points in the history of many other countries.

The United States budget system also evolved out of controversy. In the early days of the republic there was a famous dispute between Alexander Hamilton and Thomas Jefferson as to the amount of discretion that the executive branch should exercise in the spending of public funds. Jefferson's victory enabled Congress to assert its authority by making appropriations so highly specific as to hinder efficient executive action. Had Hamilton won, the treasury would have attained extraordinary power in relation both to Congress and to the president. As it was, Congress assumed authority with respect to both expenditures and revenue.

A budget in the 20th century, however, is not simply a matter of raising money to pay for government expenditures. In many countries budget policy has become an important part of general economic policy. With the great increase in government expenditures, raising and spending money have come to have a significant impact on the functioning of the national economy. A deficit or a surplus in the government budget may have inflationary or deflationary consequences; it may even mean the difference between prosperity and recession (see FISCAL AND MONETARY POLICY).

BUDGETS AND THE REDISTRIBUTION OF INCOME

Impact of budgets on different groups

Government budgets almost inevitably affect the distribution of income—that is, the purchasing power of different sections of the population. The very act of transferring resources from the private sector to the public sector has a different impact on some groups than on others. In many cases the redistribution of income is one of the goals of public policy. For example, payments to the poor, the sick, or the aged are generally financed through taxes that bear more heavily on those with higher incomes. But the budget may redistribute income indirectly through taxes and subsidies that bear differentially on different sectors of the economy. A protective tariff redistributes income in favour of protected industries at the expense of those that remain exposed to the competition of the world market. Subsidies to miners or farmers redistribute income in their favour. Such measures may bear little relation to personal need, and in many cases they result in greater personal inequality.

A third type of redistribution is regional. Most governments are exposed to strong pressures to give economic support to poorer regions of the country through grants-in-aid, government contracts, or public works. Regions like the South of the United States or the Northeast of Brazil thus receive very favourable treatment in their national budgets, though income disparities may remain wide.

PROGRAM BUDGETING

Budgeting and the allocation of resources

A relatively new development in budgeting is the attempt to use the budgetary process as a method of achieving an allocation of national resources that is efficient in the economic sense. This has come along with the great expansion in the economic role of most governments since World War II, and the enormous increase in the size of government budgets relative to the national product. As budgets rose, so did political and economic expectations. Governments were faced with multiple demands upon their resources, ranging from social welfare to foreign aid, and from the building of schools to vast military expenditures. No budget can please everyone. Good budgeting, it may be said, should result not in general contentment but in equally distributed discontent among rival groups. The more efficiently resources can be allocated among competing uses, the more nearly everyone can be satisfied. The need for economizing in this sense gave rise to the program budgeting movement, which originated in the United States in the area of military planning.

Program budgeting (or so-called systems analysis) is an attempt to apply the economics of choice to public decision making. Its basic assumption is that explicit choice among alternative courses of action leads to better results than do other methods of decision making. At the highest governmental levels difficult choices must be made that involve the use of a portion of the nation's resources. But the same principles apply to decision making at lower levels. The problem of allocating resources within a specific field, such as health or education, are conceptually similar to those faced in drawing up the national budget.

Program budgeting also takes account of the time dimension in many government programs. New undertakings often take time to come into operation. A typical new program may have to pass through a research and development phase and an investment or construction phase before it reaches the operating phase. Alternative programs may differ considerably in this respect. The process of choosing among alternatives frequently involves trading the present against the future. One alternative may require ten years before it yields results; another may yield smaller results but more quickly. The kinds of choices made in government often involve alternatives that cannot be measured in terms of market value. For this reason governmental decisions involve much more uncertainty than do most business decisions.

A governmental program must therefore be frequently revised in the light of unfolding circumstances. Indeed, every year should be thought of as the first year of a new program. Pervasive uncertainty also requires a high degree of flexibility and a capacity for program revision. A number of options should be held open, particularly in the development phase. Even though this may appear costly, it is less costly than commitment to a design that proves to be inappropriate because of circumstances that could not be foreseen in the early stages.

Program budgeting should be thought of not as a method of reaching definitive conclusions but rather as a method of organizing discussion and marshalling evidence. The situation is analogous to that of a legal trial, in which, if the rules of evidence are followed and both sides are well represented, the decision is more likely to be good than bad.

This is admittedly imprecise. Various efforts have been made to provide more specific criteria for choosing among programs. One of the best known approaches is that of cost-benefit analysis.

Criteria for choosing among programs

Cost-benefit analysis. This attempts to do for government programs what the forces of the marketplace do for business programs: to measure, and compare in terms of money, the discounted streams of future benefits and future costs associated with a proposed project. If the ratio of benefits to costs is considered satisfactory, the project should be undertaken. "Satisfactory" means, among other things, that the project is superior to any available public or private alternative. Or, if funds are limited, public investment projects may be assigned priorities according to their cost-benefit ratios.

One difficulty with cost-benefit analysis is that every government agency has an incentive to estimate favourable ratios for its own projects. It must, after all, compete with other agencies for funds. No one can be certain as to the returns to be expected from an irrigation canal or a highway. Private investors have also been known to exaggerate their claims in appealing to stockholders, but they are generally subject to market sanctions that encourage them to err on the side of caution. It is only human for estimators to be optimistic—however professionally competent they are.

The most important difficulty, however, is that in public undertakings some of the expected benefits are likely not to be measurable in money. Water projects, for example, are designed to produce a variety of benefits ranging from electric power and irrigation to employment and recreation. The cost of training a high school dropout is not to be measured only against the income he will earn but also against the social benefits of making him a productive member of society. In other areas, such as defense and conservation, economic standards are applicable either not at all or only to a small extent.

The theory of public goods. Economists have sought to provide objective criteria for public expenditures through the so-called theory of public goods. It is generally recognized that some goods needed by the public cannot be provided through the private market (lighthouses are a classic example). While everyone wants such goods, everyone has an incentive to let someone else pay for them. Consequently, government action is required. Economists have tried to devise voting procedures that would guide the public authorities in providing these goods in the desired quantities.

The difficulty with this approach is that it rests on the assumption of fixed consumers' tastes and holds that the function of government is to give effect to those fixed tastes. But the private economy is actively engaged in changing individual tastes; and the government is similarly engaged, whether or not it ought to be. It would be absurd to say that the consumer has a taste for national defense and that it is the job of the government to satisfy it. The task of national leaders is to evolve a defense policy and persuade the public to accept it. Similarly, conservationists must attempt to awaken the public to the importance of parks and wildlife. In the context of public policy, the efficient allocation of resources consists not merely of distributing funds in the pursuit of given objectives but involves determining the objectives themselves. For this reason budgeting has become an essential component of the decision-making process.

ALTERNATIVE APPROACHES TO THE BUDGET

The various forms a budget may take

In order to deal with the problems discussed above, most countries have experimented with various kinds of budgets for different purposes. In the current American terminology these are: the administrative budget, the cash budget, the capital budget, the national income accounts budget, the unified budget, the full-employment budget, and the program budget.

Administrative budget. The administrative budget is the traditional one. It contains the executive's recommendations concerning the raising of what the Magna Carta referred to as "scutage or aid," and the disposal of it for purposes of government. This kind of budget is designed to control expenditure; accordingly, it emphasizes the salaries and tasks of civil servants rather than the results that they are supposed to achieve.

The objective of control naturally gives rise to the doctrine that the administrative budget should be balanced. Deficits imply irresponsibility. Surpluses imply the imposition of unwarranted tax burdens on the public.

The limitations of the administrative budget are that some important items receive less than adequate attention or are excluded from it entirely. Military procurement is one example. Neither budget offices nor appropriations committees are well equipped to scrutinize the actual procurement of ships or aircraft. Consequently, in most countries large expenditures on military items are often treated perfunctorily while the activities of civil servants receive an inordinate amount of attention.

The administrative budget generally does not include all governmental receipts and expenditures. Those of trust funds are often excluded. Trust funds are used to finance contributory old age and unemployment insurance; taxes are paid directly into the funds and disbursements made out of them. The theory is that the government acts as trustee for the public and that the public is protected by having its social security taxes put in a separate fund. (The same idea has been used to ensure that gasoline and highway taxes are used for highway construction.)

Other items may be included in the budget on a net rather than a gross basis. For instance, the total receipts and expenditures of the post office usually do not appear, only the postal deficit or surplus. The theory justifying this treatment is, first, that business management is not well performed by legislative committees and, second, that so long as a business undertaking pays its way, its conduct is not a matter of public concern.

Capital budget. In many countries, some items are regarded as inappropriate for the administrative budget and are included "below the line." The rule of budget balance is not applied to them; instead, it is permissible to finance them by borrowing.

In the United Kingdom, all government loans to other public bodies and to nationalized industries are included below the line on the ground that since the loans are repayable they need not be covered by current taxation. The government's own borrowing can be repaid out of the loan repayments it receives.

By similar reasoning, direct public works are regarded by most countries as suitable for loan financing on the ground that they are productive assets that will yield a revenue sufficient to cover their cost. They may do so either directly, as in the case of a toll highway, or indirectly by increasing the general economic welfare, as in the case of a free highway. In many cases, however, governments succumb to the temptation of including in their capital budgets items such as free playgrounds, which, however socially desirable, are not productive in the economic sense.

Another reason for loan financing is that some expenditures are so "lumpy" that it is neither feasible nor equitable to saddle the contemporary taxpayer with the full costs of the undertaking. This applies particularly to war expenditures, but the same is true of the construction of schools and hospitals by local governments.

The federal government of the United States has resisted the idea of a capital budget, even though there was strong pressure for one in the 1930s when economists and politicians wanted to legitimize the government deficit. Among U.S. state and municipal governments, however, loan financing of public works is the regular practice, for two reasons. First, those bodies are usually unable to finance their projects by current taxation; second, they do not want to because the projects are generally of a long-term nature.

Most national governments have now become accustomed to thinking in terms of national economic policies in which the amount of borrowing to be undertaken depends on current requirements for stability and growth. This makes capital budgeting less attractive, particularly if the government wishes to use the budget to supplement the national flow of savings. The more need there is to increase saving the smaller should be the amount of government borrowing. On the other hand, government borrowing is justified when private savings tend to exceed private capital requirements.

Cash budget. The consolidated cash budget has the merits of simplicity and comprehensiveness. As used in the United States, it presents total payments by the federal government to and from the public (including other levels of government). It is thus similar to the cash flow account of a modern business. Trust fund expenditures and receipts are included, as well as cash payments and receipts involved in loan transactions. Government business undertakings such as the post office, however, are still included on a net basis.

The cash budget suffers from the defect that it is not directly tied to government decision making. Liabilities incurred do not synchronize completely with payments. This is because government expenditures result from appropriations and other forms of commitments; cash expenditures may follow appropriations and other commitments of money only after a considerable lag, notably in the case of construction and procurement. Appropriations relate to actions in the future. Expenditures result from past decisions. Both kinds of information are needed for a complete appraisal.

National accounts budget. It is useful to have a budget that is constructed in terms of the national income accounts. From the point of view of aggregate economic analysis, the accounts of the public sector should mesh with those of the private sector. The "national accounts budget" differs from the cash budget principally by excluding loans made by the government and also repayments to the government. While this is justified by the need for consistency with the national income accounts, which do not consider lending as an expenditure or a receipt, the total exclusion of government loans does not make much sense from the point of view of analyzing government operations. In terms of its effects on the economy, an excess of loans over repayments in a government lending agency cannot readily be distinguished from an excess of expenditures over receipts of other types of government business organization.

Unified budget. The United States government, in an effort to reduce public confusion over the foregoing array of concepts, has adopted a so-called unified budget concept that is more logical than the cash budget but differs from it only in some details that do not materially affect the budget aggregates.

Full-employment budget. A concept that is gradually seeping into budget discussions is that of the receipts and expenditures that would prevail under conditions of full employment. This approach views the actual expenditures and receipts for the coming year as of secondary importance; it assigns primary importance to the influence of the budget on the national economy. In time of recession a budget deficit may thus be presented as a necessary step toward achieving a balanced budget at full employment. Ideally, the budget should include estimates of expenditures and revenues at full employment, and also estimates of the same items at the anticipated level of employment. These ideas have been extensively used in the United States by the Council of Economic Advisers.

An analogous procedure could be used with respect to inflation. Expenditures and receipts would then be estimated on the assumption of little or no inflation, and supplementary estimates would show the effects on the budget of the amount of inflation actually expected. This idea is still far from acceptance, since governments are no less reluctant to anticipate inflation than they are to budget for unemployment.

Program budget. Traditionally, government expenditures have been considered as inputs rather than outputs. This is because, in the classical 19th-century conception, the well-run government does not produce a marketable output. The program budget is a new departure; it attempts to classify expenditures in terms of the outputs to which they are devoted. For example, a traditional school budget would categorize expenditures in terms of teachers, books, and buildings, and what came out of the process would be left to the reader's intuition or experience. The program budget, in contrast, attempts to assign expenditures to specific outputs, categorizing them according to numbers of children completing various programs.

In government, budgets have traditionally been constructed according to departments and agencies of government. This may be justified on historical or administrative grounds, but it does not necessarily correspond to the structure of activity. Every country organizes the civilian and military components of its foreign policy in separate departments—but this is frequently a serious obstacle to effective policy making. Again, the requirements of good administration suggest that there should be a single department of agriculture. But that department's activities impinge on those of others, both in domestic and foreign policy. A budget constructed according to actual programs would cut across departmental boundaries.

Difficulties in defining output, and the obvious conflicts with organizational structure, suggest that program budgets of governmental scope will never fully replace the traditional administrative approach.

THE BUDGETARY PROCESS

The United States. Since 1921 the budget of the United States has been the responsibility of the president. It is prepared under his direct authority by the Office of Management and Budget (OMB). The process begins when the various departments and agencies prepare their appropriation requests, based on expenditures required under existing law and those estimated under new legislation to be proposed by the president. These requests are carefully scrutinized by the OMB. In case of disagreement, cabinet officers negotiate directly with the president, who is ultimately responsible.

Unlike the budgets of many countries, that of the U.S. deals mainly with expenditures. Revenue is covered in much less detail. Great significance is ascribed to the size of the expected deficit or surplus, even though there is no legal requirement that the budget be in balance.

The budget is submitted in January and normally applies to appropriations for the fiscal year beginning July 1. These must normally be spent in the following two years. For some items, such as construction or procurement of military hardware, appropriations are made to cover expenditures for the whole construction period.

The Appropriations Committees of Congress

When the budget reaches the House of Representatives, it is distributed among the subcommittees of the Appropriations Committee. Each subcommittee is concerned with a particular organizational unit. There is virtually no consideration of the budget as a whole by the committee as a whole. Revenues fall under the jurisdiction of the Ways and Means Committee of the House and are considered separately and possibly even at a different time from appropriations. The upper house of Congress, the Senate, plays a secondary role with respect to the budget. Its Appropriations Committee acts as a kind of court of appeal from the House Appropriations Committee. These procedures allow more coordination than appearance would suggest. The committee chairmen are among the most influential members of Congress, and the committee staffs are very experienced and skillful.

Economic impact of the budget. The president sends three documents to Congress in January: the State of the Union Message, the Budget, and the Economic Report. The first is addressed to broad national policy, whereas the Economic Report is concerned with economic policy alone. In particular, it seeks to assess the economic impact of the budget and its effect on employment and prices. The Economic Report was instituted by the Employment Act of 1946, which requires the president to report to Congress on the state of the economy and to recommend policies to promote "maximum employment, production and purchasing power."

The record in this respect is a mixed one. The most serious problems stem from inflation, which in turn is the result of governmental budget deficits incurred during periods when the economy is at a high level of activity. Once inflation is allowed to get under way, attempts to correct it seem to result in high levels of unemployment.

Budget makers in the U.S. must also consider the international balance of payments. This is a relatively new problem for the United States, which historically enjoyed a balance-of-payments surplus until the 1960s. A declining trade balance, coupled with heavy military commitments abroad, now requires that budgetary and other economic measures be designed with international as well as national economic balance in mind.

Effect of the budget on resource allocation. There is no formal machinery for ensuring that the budget strikes a satisfactory balance among the different programs contained in it. But the alternatives receive a good deal of scrutiny. Cabinet officers have their clienteles in the public and in Congress and through them can bring political power to bear in the competition for funds. Similarly, the congressional committees are able to exert some influence on the budget during its preparation. The president for his part is not passive; he has a political position of his own that permits him to assert his conception of the national interest. Other pressures come from the taxpayers, who are able to express their stand on expenditures both to Congress and to the president.

A satisfactory outcome for the allocative process depends on the evenness with which these competing forces are balanced. Opinions will differ. It can be said that the process of decision making is at least an open one, even though vested interests have entrenched themselves in particular areas.

Even though amendments to the budget are usually minor, the influence of Congress is not negligible. The prospect of facing Congress is a sobering one to the officers of government. And departmental budget recommendations are often strongly influenced by the views of congressional committees. The secretary of agriculture, for example, often has a relationship with the Agricultural Committees of Congress that is friendlier and more intimate than his relationship with the president.

The United Kingdom. The British budget is submitted to Parliament by the chancellor of the exchequer, who is responsible for its preparation. The emphasis of the chancellor's budget speech is on taxation and the state of the economy, rather than on the detail of expenditures; public discussion likewise is devoted mainly to the chancellor's tax proposals. The estimates of expenditures are sent to Parliament with less fanfare, where they are reviewed by the select committee on estimates of the House of Commons. The review of the committee hardly touches matters of policy. While the committee does not amend the budget, it is influential through its criticism and advice.

Britain: the power of the treasury

In the preparation of the budget, the treasury appears to have virtually complete authority over the government departments on matters of detail. Major issues are settled in Cabinet discussions, the records of which are not available. The British system thus vests extensive controls in the treasury bureaucracy.

A major part of the budget speech by the chancellor of the exchequer is addressed to forecasts of employment, prices, and the balance of payments, together with a discussion of fiscal and monetary policies. Economic analysis is a continuing preoccupation of the Treasury. Forecasts are prepared three times a year; a budget committee composed of important financial and economic officials meets continously to discuss policy matters. Their attention, however, is focused on tax, borrowing, and monetary policies rather than on the details of government spending.

In the 1960s the attempt was made to plan government expenditures on a long-term basis. Emphasis was placed on the predetermination of expenditures, over a five-year period, in accordance with the expected (or desired) rate of growth of the economy. Planned expenditures are broken down by major functional categories such as defense, education, health and welfare, housing, and so forth, which are to serve as guides in the preparation of annual budgets. The functional breakdown is also intended to assist legislative discussion.

Japan. Under Japan's 1947 constitution the Cabinet has the responsibility of preparing the national budget, which must then be submitted to the lower house of the Diet. Taxes can be imposed or modified only as prescribed by laws enacted by the Diet.

The budget is prepared on a fiscal-year basis by the budget division of the Ministry of Finance. The centre of the budget system is the general account, which theoretically includes all revenue and expenditure directly applicable to the overall fiscal operation of the government. There is also a system of special accounts for the operation of government enterprises and other special aspects of government finance. Theoretically, each special account is self-balancing. In actual practice, however, there have at times been substantial deficits in the special accounts that have had to be covered by direct government appropriations, borrowings, and transfers of funds from one account to another.

Under the Public Finance Law of 1947, the general account of the national budget must be either balanced or in surplus. The government cannot increase its net long-term debt without special legislation, and then the increase must be tied to some specific investment use.

The budget under central planning

Soviet budgeting practices. In the Soviet Union and some other countries having Communist governments, economic activity is either carried on by state enterprises or is subject to central control. The national budgets therefore have a much broader scope than in countries where most economic activity is in the private sphere. In the Soviet Union well over 90 percent of capital investment is financed by the government; in the United States the corresponding figure is less than 25 percent, and in Great Britain it is less than 50 percent. There are two main sources of revenue: the profits of state-owned enterprises and the turnover tax on the sales of enterprises. The relative proportions of the funds drawn from enterprises under these two headings vary; there has been a long-term tendency for the share of the turnover tax to decline and for profit transfers to increase.

The budget is essentially a part of the national economic plan. It is drawn up by the Ministry of Finance and presented to the Supreme Soviet for consideration and approval every calendar year. Revenues and expenditures are usually in close balance. The budget is implemented by the Ministry of Finance, which scrutinizes the operations of the state enterprises in accordance with the economic plan.

BIBLIOGRAPHY

General works: HERBERT BRITTAIN, *The British Budgetary System* (1959); JESSE BURKHEAD, *Government Budgeting* (1956); R.W. DAVIES, *The Development of the Soviet Budgetary System* (1958); C.J. HITCH and R.N. MCKEAN, *The Economics of Defense in the Nuclear Age* (1960, reprinted 1965); R.N. MCKEAN, *Efficiency in Government Through Systems Analysis, with Emphasis on Water Resources Development* (1958); R.A. MUSGRAVE, *Fiscal Systems* (1969), *The Theory of Public Finance* (1959); ARTHUR SMITHIES, *The Budgetary Process in the United States* (1955); A.B. WILDAVSKY, *The Politics of the Budgetary Process* (1964).

Program budgeting: H.H. HINRICHS and G.M. TAYLOR (comps.), *Program Budgeting and Benefit-Cost Analysis: Cases, Text, and Readings* (1969); DAVID NOVICK (ed.), *Program Budgeting* (1965); E.S. QUADE and W.I. BOUCHER (eds.), *Systems Analysis and Policy Planning* (1968); U.S. CONGRESS, *Planning, Programming, Budgeting*, Inquiry of the Subcommittee on National Security and International Operations, Senator Henry M. Jackson, Chairman, Committee on Government Operations, 90th and 91st Congress, 1st sess. (1970), a compilation of hearings, reports, and committee prints.

Buenos Aires

Buenos Aires, the capital of Argentina, is the largest city in the Southern Hemisphere and the sixth-largest in the world. Located on the western shore of the Río de la Plata, the city proper, which is also the federal district, covers an area of 77 square miles (200 square kilometres) and has a population of about 3,000,000. The total metropolitan area, however, extends over 1,500 square miles and has about 8,400,000 inhabitants. According to tradition, 16th-century Spanish sailors named the port for their patron saint, St. María del Buen Aire (St. Mary of Good Air). Today, the citizens of Buenos Aires call themselves *porteños* ("people of the port").

The city is the national centre of commerce, industry, politics, and culture. Its wealth and influence overshadow the life of the rest of the nation and confront Argentina with its greatest economic and social problems. Since its nomination as the head city of the Río de la Plata government (a dependent of the viceroyalty of Peru) in the 18th century, Buenos Aires has been the region's administrative and financial capital; in addition, because of its location, it has also often been a focus for political and social unrest outside of its borders. The Argentine poet and philosopher Martínez Estrada has called the city "The Head of Goliath," a metaphor that illustrates its imbalance in relation to the rest of the country, much like a large-headed giant with a feeble body.

Buenos Aires is beset with the same problems encountered by other large cities. Increased industry is causing increased pollution; limited land area in the city proper has led to the construction of high-rise buildings with resultant congestion; rapid expansion is hampered by inadequate public services; increased migration from the countryside is creating a growing urban population composed of the poor and unskilled. There is at the same time, however, a feeling of progress and burgeoning strength. (For an associated physical feature, see PLATA, RIO DE LA.)

HISTORY

Foundation of the city

Pedro de Mendoza—the first Spanish governor general of the Río de la Plata region—established a *real*, or provisionary settlement, at the mouth of the Riachuelo River in 1536. The poorly fortified settlement was soon besieged by the surrounding Indian population, and the settlers were forced to flee northward up the Río de la Plata to Asunción. From there, Juan de Garay led an expedition back to the original site and founded the Ciudad de la Trinidad (Trinity City) and the Puerto de Santa María de Buen Aire in 1580. Streets and city blocks were laid out on a rectilinear plan, urban and rural lands were granted to the expedition's members, and the conquered Indians were divided as slaves among the larger landholders.

For two centuries Buenos Aires was a poor city in the extreme south of the opulent viceroyalty of Peru. Since Spanish policy decreed that all trade be carried out through the Pacific Ocean port of Lima, Buenos Aires was not able to engage in direct commerce with Europe or North America. There was, however, an active trade in all manner of contraband. In 1776 the viceroyalty of the Río de la Plata was created, with its seat in Buenos Aires, after which the city began to grow.

After fighting off several attacks by pirates in the 18th century, the city's population defended itself against British attacks in 1806 and 1807 without any help from the Spanish government. In 1810, when Napoleon invaded Spain and placed his brother, Joseph Bonaparte, on the Spanish throne, the city felt little allegiance toward the new government. It therefore deposed the viceroy and established its own government in the name of the deposed Spanish king. A constitutional congress subsequently met in San Miguel de Tucumán and, in 1816, declared independence from Spain. A Directory, or provisional government, was created, and Buenos Aires was named the capital of the United Provinces of the Río de la Plata. Ten years later, the presidential republic was formed, and the capital district of Buenos Aires came into existence. After much political wrangling, interspersed with threats of secession, the state was reconstituted in 1860 and consolidated in 1880 as the Argentine Republic with Buenos Aires as its capital. The towns of San José de Flores and Belgrano were added to the federal district in 1887, bringing it to its present size.

The city's development

In the mid-1800s Buenos Aires was more an overgrown village than a city. Houses were low built and widely spaced, and public utilities were at a minimum. The population was almost totally Spanish. Between 1860 and the outbreak of World War I, however, the city received a continuous influx of European immigrants, largely from Italy and Spain. During that period the population grew by about 500 percent. Because land was inexpensive and readily available in all directions except the east, the newcomers spread out in barrios, or self-contained neighbourhoods, that were usually identified with a particular ethnic group. Some barrios were located outside the federal district and formed part of what later became Gran (Greater) Buenos Aires. The original site became dotted with collective houses known as *conventillos*, where the poor lived under slum conditions in tiny rooms connected by long open corridors.

The expansion of the city was accompanied by a program of beautification and improvement without a proper city plan. Trees were planted in the squares, streets were paved and lighted, and old buildings were replaced with new until little remained of the original city. Buenos Aires also developed as the political, cultural, and economic centre of the country, completely overshadowing other Argentine cities. Rapid industrialization after World War II increased the city's attraction for immigrants from abroad, as well as for migrants from within the country. Buenos Aires is now a cosmopolitan, sprawling megalopolis, faced with a problem of economic and social imbalance.

THE CITY SITE

Location and natural environment. The federal district is located mostly on the southeastern corner of the plain that stretches between the Río Reconquista to the west and the Riachuelo (Matanza) River to the southeast; it is bordered by the Río de la Plata to the east, the Riachuelo River to the southeast, and the Province of Buenos Aires to the west and north. The city slopes eastward from its centre at Villa Ortúzar, which is 82 feet above sea level, to the *barrancas*, or ravines, which rise to 15 feet above sea level. Between the ravines and the Río de la Plata are two large coastal zones in the flat Matanza River Valley and the estuary margin. The areas are flooded during abnormally high tides; they have been partially reclaimed with landfill and developed as residential and recreational areas. Gran Buenos Aires is composed of the federal district and 22 adjacent municipalities in the Province of Buenos Aires.

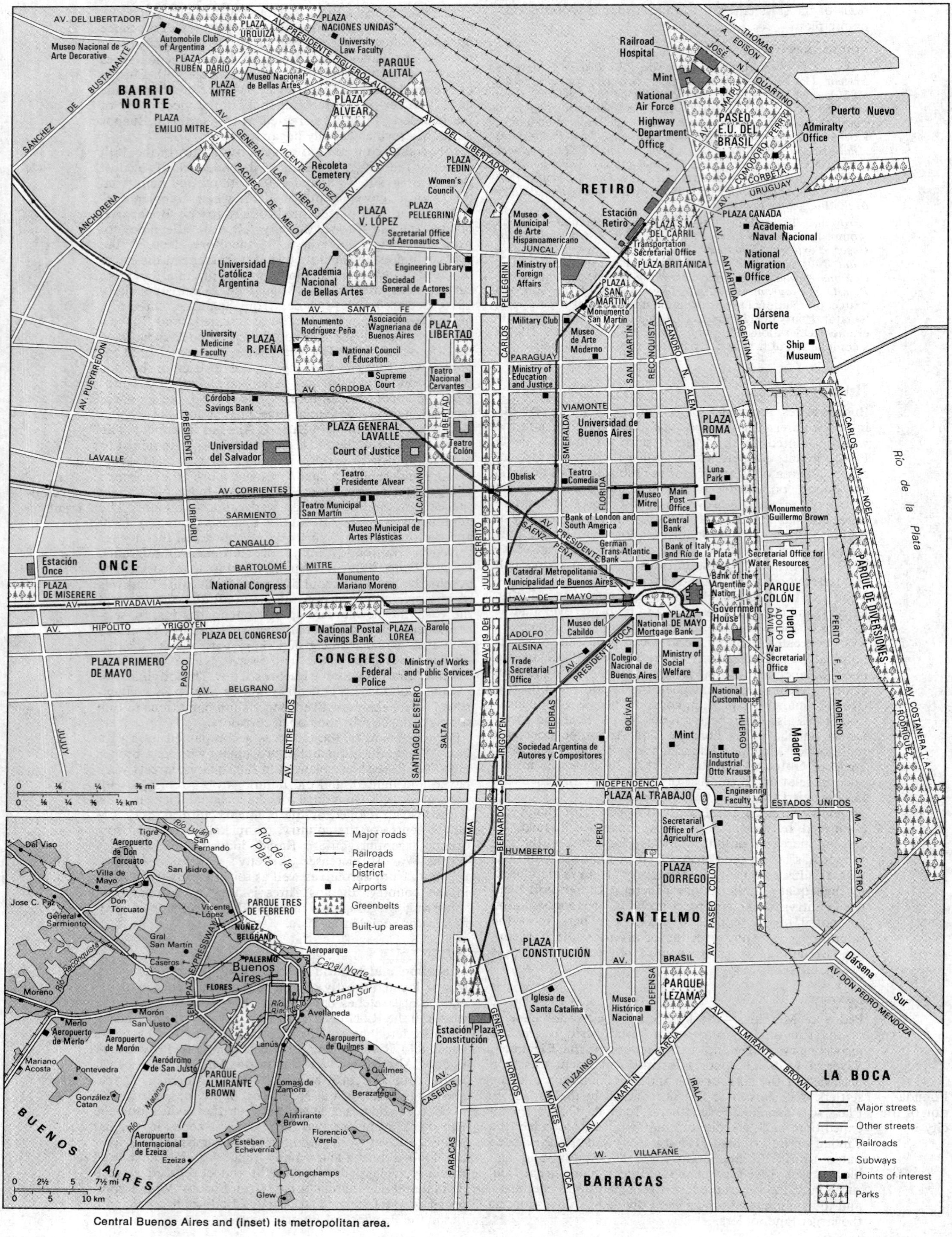

AV. DEL LIBERTADOR
Museo Nacional de Arte Decorative
Automobile Club of Argentina
PLAZA URQUIZA
PLAZA NACIONES UNIDAS
University Law Faculty
AV. PRESIDENTE FIGUEROA ALCORTA
PLAZA RUBÉN DARÍO
Museo Nacional de Bellas Artes
PLAZA MITRE
PARQUE ALITAL
BARRIO NORTE
PLAZA EMILIO MITRE
PLAZA ALVEAR
AV. BUSTAMANTE
SÁNCHEZ DE
AV. GENERAL LAS HERAS
VICENTE LÓPEZ
A. PACHECO DE MELO
Recoleta Cemetery
CALLAO
AV. DEL LIBERTADOR
PLAZA TEDIN
Women's Council
PLAZA PELLEGRINI
PLAZA V. LÓPEZ
Secretarial Office of Aeronautics
ANCHORENA
RETIRO
Railroad Hospital
Mint
National Air Force
Highway Department Office
AV. THOMAS A. EDISON
JOSÉ N. QUARTINO
MAIPÚ
PASEO E.U. DEL BRASIL
COMODORO PERRY
CORBETA
URUGUAY
Puerto Nuevo
Admiralty Office
PLAZA CANADA
Academia Naval Nacional
Estación Retiro
PLAZA S.M. DEL CARRIL
Transportation Secretarial Office
PLAZA BRITÁNICA
National Migration Office
Museo Municipal de Arte Hispanoamericano
JUNCAL
Ministry of Foreign Affairs
Universidad Católica Argentina
Academia Nacional de Bellas Artes
Engineering Library
Sociedad General de Actores
AV. SANTA FE
PELLEGRINI
PLAZA SAN MARTÍN
Monumento San Martín
Dársena Norte
AV. ANTÁRTIDA ARGENTINA
AV. LEANDRO N. ALEM
Monumento Rodríguez Peña
Asociación Wagneriana de Buenos Aires
PLAZA LIBERTAD
Military Club
Museo de Arte Moderno
University Medicine Faculty
PLAZA R. PEÑA
National Council of Education
CARLOS
PARAGUAY
Ship Museum
AV. PUEYRREDÓN
Supreme Court
Teatro Nacional Cervantes
Ministry of Education and Justice
SAN MARTÍN
RECONQUISTA
AV. CÓRDOBA
Córdoba Savings Bank
VIAMONTE
PRESIDENTE
LIBERTAD
PLAZA GENERAL LAVALLE
Universidad de Buenos Aires
PLAZA ROMA
AV. CARLOS M. NOEL
Río de la Plata
Universidad del Salvador
Court of Justice
Teatro Colón
ESMERALDA
LAVALLE
Teatro Presidente Alvear
Obelisk
Teatro Comedia
Luna Park
AV. CORRIENTES
FLORIDA
Museo Mitre
Main Post Office
Teatro Municipal San Martín
URIBURU
SARMIENTO
TALCAHUANO
Museo Municipal de Artes Plásticas
Bank of London and South America
Central Bank
Monumento Guillermo Brown
AV. PRESIDENTE SÁENZ PEÑA
CANGALLO
CERRITO
German Trans-Atlantic Bank
Bank of Italy and Río de la Plata
Secretarial Office for Water Resources
Estación Once
ONCE
BARTOLOMÉ MITRE
JULIO
Catedral Metropolitana
Municipalidad de Buenos Aires
Bank of the Argentine Nation
PARQUE COLÓN
PARQUE DE DIVERSIONES
PLAZA DE MISERERE
National Congress
Monumento Mariano Moreno
AV. DE MAYO
AV. RIVADAVIA
Government House
Puerto
ADOLFO DÁVILA
PERITO F. P. MORENO
AV. HIPÓLITO YRIGOYEN
PLAZA DEL CONGRESO
National Postal Savings Bank
PLAZA LOREA
Barolo
ADOLFO
Museo del Cabildo
PLAZA DE MAYO
National Mortgage Bank
ALSINA
AV. PRESIDENTE ROCA
Trade Secretarial Office
Colegio Nacional de Buenos Aires
Ministry of Social Welfare
War Secretarial Office
PLAZA PRIMERO DE MAYO
CONGRESO
Ministry of Works and Public Services
AV. 9 DE JULIO
Federal Police
PASCO
AV. BELGRANO
National Customhouse
AV. ENTRE RÍOS
SANTIAGO DEL ESTERO
SALTA
IRIGOYEN
PIEDRAS
BOLÍVAR
Mint
HUERGO
Madero
AV. COSTANERA T. A. RODRÍGUEZ
JUJUY
Sociedad Argentina de Autores y Compositores
Instituto Industrial Otto Krause
AV. INDEPENDENCIA
PLAZA AL TRABAJO
Engineering Faculty
ESTADOS UNIDOS
0 1/8 1/4 3/8 mi
0 1/8 1/4 3/8 1/2 km
LIMA
BERNARDO DE
PERÚ
Secretarial Office of Agriculture
M. A. CASTRO
HUMBERTO I
PLAZA DORREGO
AV. PASEO COLÓN
SAN TELMO
PLAZA CONSTITUCIÓN
AV. BRASIL
DEFENSA
PARQUE LEZAMA
Dársena Sur
AV. DON PEDRO MENDOZA
Iglesia de Santa Catalina
Museo Histórico Nacional
Estación Plaza Constitución
GENERAL HORNOS
AV. ALMIRANTE BROWN
AV. MARTÍN GARCÍA
ITUZAINGÓ
IRALA
LA BOCA
AV. CASEROS
AV. MONTES DE OCA
W. VILLAFAÑE
PARACAS
BARRACAS
Major streets
Other streets
Railroads
Subways
Points of interest
Parks
Río Luján
Tigre
San Fernando
Río de la Plata
Del Viso
Aeropuerto de Don Torcuato
San Isidro
Villa de Mayo
Don Torcuato
Jose C. Paz
General Sarmiento
Vicente López
PARQUE TRES DE FEBRERO
NÚÑEZ
BELGRANO
Gral San Martín
GEN. PAZ EXPRESSWAY
Aeroparque
Caseros
PALERMO
Buenos Aires
Canal Norte
Río Reconquista
FLORES
Canal Sur
Moreno
Río Riachuelo
Merlo
Morón
San Justo
Avellaneda
Aeropuerto de Merlo
Aeropuerto de Morón
Aeropuerto de Quilmes
Lanús
Aeródromo de San Justo
Mariano Acosta
Pontevedra
Quilmes
PARQUE ALMIRANTE BROWN
Lomas de Zamora
González Catan
Berazategui
Río Matanza
Almirante Brown
BUENOS AIRES
Florencio Varela
Aeropuerto Internacional de Ezeiza
Esteban Echeverría
Ezeiza
Longchamps
Glew
0 2½ 5 7½ mi
0 5 10 km
Major roads
Railroads
Federal District
Airports
Greenbelts
Built-up areas

Central Buenos Aires and (inset) its metropolitan area.

Soil and water. The soils of the urban region are composed of loess (a brownish mixture of clay, silt, and sand deposited by the wind) in the plains area and marine sands in the river valleys. The granite base is covered by compacted layers of clay to a depth of 1,000 feet. Subterranean water is found at various depths; most of it is potable and is used in industry. Numerous streams flow beneath the city; some of the plazas and public gardens were once lagoons or water-filled depressions.

Underground water

Climate. The temperate climate of the Pampas (the vast Argentinian plain) that is characteristic of the Río de la Plata's coastal area is marked by a long summer (December–March) and abrupt temperature changes in autumn (March–June) and spring (September–December). Temperature differences within a 24-hour period can be as great as 22° F (12° C). The average annual temperature is slightly higher than 60° F (16° C); frosts occur from May to September. June and July are the coldest months, with mean temperatures of 52° F (11° C), and January the warmest, with a mean temperature of 75° F (24° C). Winds are generally of low velocity and are more frequent during the electrical storm season between September and March. Humid southeastern ocean winds bring the rains, accompanied by occasional windstorms, that result in a prodigious rise in the Río de la Plata, and northeastern winds bring warm air from Brazil. The northern winds are suffocatingly hot; those from the east are relatively fresh. The rare southwestern winds, or *pamperos*, may occur at any time of the year and usually follow winds from the north. They cool the air and clear it of humidity. Rainfall is greatest during March; the average annual rainfall is about 37 inches. The relative humidity is high throughout the year and averages 76 percent.

Vegetation and animal life. The original vegetation of the coastal forests has been practically eliminated and replaced by foreign and domestic exotic plants. The city is dotted with trees, including the jacaranda, the large-coned araucaria, the caranday palm, and the foreign eucalyptus. Various species of birds live in the city parks and along the coast. The coastal waters abound in edible fish such as the pejerrey, or silversides, which is related to the gray mullet.

Pollution. Air and water pollution have not yet reached serious proportions, but the tributaries of the Río de la Plata contain increasing amounts of urban and industrial waste. The air is also affected by automobile exhaust and domestic and industrial smoke.

The plan of the city. Buenos Aires has expanded without the benefit of urban planning, and its growth patterns have been determined largely by real-estate values. Zoning laws have been subject to constant modification. There is progressive congestion in the centre of the city, as well as in those areas reached by railroad, bus, or subway. Older *barrios jardines* ("garden neighbourhoods") are being replaced by high-rise apartment buildings.

The overall layout of the city corresponds to the quadrangular pattern decreed by the laws of the Indies—a body of legislation codified in 1680 for all the Spanish colonies. The streets run at right angles to one another and enclose city blocks that are, on the average, 330 feet square.

The centro. The *centro*, or the city centre, coincides with the original settlement. The streets are narrow, running from north to south and from east to west. Beginning in 1826, every fourth street was widened to form larger quadrangles of avenues enclosing groups of 16 city blocks. The widest avenue in Buenos Aires, the Nueve de Julio (9th of July), runs from north to south and helps to alleviate traffic congestion.

The capital zone

Part of the *centro* is known as the capital zone, because it contains the Government House (Casa de Gobierno), the National Congress (Congreso Nacional), the Palace of Justice, and other government buildings, as well as the official banks, the city cathedral, the Museo del Cabildo, and the larger newspapers and commercial concerns. This area developed along the Avenida de Mayo from east to west and along the Paseo Colón and Leandro N. Alem from north to south. These streets and the diagonal ones nearby converge on a wide, green space composed of the Plaza de Mayo and the Parque Colón, which comprise the urban core.

The barrios. There are more than 50 distinguishable barrios in the city, most of which were founded in the 19th century. The two oldest—the cathedral barrio and San Telmo, in the *centro*—coincide with Juan de Garay's original city. La Boca, on the waterfront, is largely an Italian community; Flores was originally a country village founded in 1804. Other barrios of importance include Barracas, Concepción, Montserrat, Balvanera, and Retiro, all of which surround the *centro* and originally formed the outskirts, or *orillas*, of the viceregal city. Their inhabitants were called *orilleros* to distinguish them from the original port settlers, the *porteños.* Belgrano (originally La Calera), Once, Almagro, Caballito, Floresta, Liniers, Colegiales, Ortúzar, Coghlan, Núñez, Saavedra, Urquiza, and Villa del Parque grew up in the last half of the 19th century around rail and tram lines. La Recoleta, or Barrio Norte, became a focus for the upper-income group, as it moved out of the *centro;* since the 1960s, however, the wealthier families have left the city proper to settle farther north along the Río de la Plata in provincial municipalities.

Gran Buenos Aires. There are numerous towns within the greater metropolitan area. Those with more than 100,000 inhabitants include Matanza (San Justo) and Morón to the west; Lanús, Lomas de Zamora, and Almirante Brown to the south; Avellaneda and Quilmes to the east; Vicente Lopez, San Isidro, and San Fernando to the north; and San Martín and General Sarmiento to the northwest. There are also six smaller towns within the area.

THE PEOPLE

Population growth

Demography. The dominant feature of the city's development has been its rapid population growth since the end of the 19th century. In 1855 there were 100,000 inhabitants, and by 1862 the population doubled to 200,000. By 1905 the city had outgrown its boundaries, and 15 percent of its 1,000,000 citizens lived in adjacent communities. By 1927 the metropolitan area included 2,000,000 people, and by 1947 it had grown to about 4,700,000, of whom less than 3,000,000 lived within the federal district. By 1960 the city proper housed nearly 3,000,000 people, about two-thirds of whom were native-born. By 1970, 5,400,000 people lived in the suburbs, while the population of the city itself remained constant, bringing the total metropolitan population to 8,400,000.

Between 1860 and 1900, this prodigious growth was due to a large European migration. The city's position as the national political, commercial, and industrial centre attracted migrants from other parts of Argentina, which resulted in further expansion. New arrivals moved into existing population centres and also settled on small rural subdivisions known as *loteos*, as well as on public and private lands, thereby creating *villas miserías* (slum districts).

The demographic composition of the city is similar to that of other large cities. There are more women than men and more adults than children. The average family is small; almost half the population is employed.

Ethnic composition. The population is almost entirely European. Spanish and Italians predominate, but there are also sizable English, French, and German communities. There are smaller groups of Poles, Russians, Portuguese, Syrians, and Turks; and the Negro and mulatto population is negligible in size. Although some ethnic groups tend to congregate in particular areas of the city, strictly defined or officially sanctioned ghettos do not exist. The Argentine identity tends to override specific cultural loyalties but is flexible enough to allow ethnocentric mutual-aid societies and social clubs to emerge. Even the dominant Spanish language has been affected by the acceptance of other European cultures and has undergone pronunciation and grammatical changes; in the slums and waterfront districts an italianized dialect has emerged. Italian cuisine is popular in the city, and pasta dishes appear on almost all restaurant menus.

Cultural and linguistic influences

Buenos Aires, with the Congreso Nacional building and the Plaza de Mayo in the foreground.
Carl Frank

Perhaps the most important social difference is that between the *porteños* and the *orilleros*. Since the city's inception, the established families of the original town site have retained political and social power; they are still identified with the federal-district area, even though some are now moving to northern residential suburbs. The *porteño* identification has also been expanded to include all those born in the city, as opposed to immigrants or visitors. The *orilleros*, now suburbanites, often belong to the lower income groups living in the industrialized communities that surround the city.

Housing. *Building types.* The one-family home of one or two stories, with an interior patio and a garden, predominates. In the *centro* and in the centres of the barrios, apartment buildings ranging from five to 20 stories are common and result in congestion and insufficient services. Large, one-family dwellings or apartments, built according to official plans, are found throughout the city and contrast with the congested buildings around them. In old Flores, the municipal government is developing a large area where homes in the form of large flats are interspersed with public parks. In areas not developed under municipal guidance, the construction code permits the building of compact apartment buildings on small lots of land. Skyscrapers are permitted on slightly larger lots, thus improving hygienic conditions, although at the cost of an extremely high population density. Older barrios—such as Belgrano, Palermo, and Núñez—are conglomerations of multistoried buildings, many of which are of excellent architectural quality; they are raised above the ground and have ample gardens at street level.

Rents have been fixed by law since 1943. This has resulted in a large quantity of low-rent apartments being made available but has also bankrupted some building owners and discouraged building improvement. Many streets appear to be run-down even though they are not old. Since 1948, however, the Horizontal Property Law has stimulated the renovation of entire urban areas with thousands of new apartment flats financed by private banks.

Architecture. In the coastal barrios of Barracas and La Boca, the one- and two-story buildings are made of wood and corrugated-metal roofing and are almost all over 100 years old. They are painted in various primary colours and are graced with flower-laden patios. Caminito Street, in La Boca, is maintained by the municipal government as an example of late-19th- and early-20th-century prefabricated architecture. By contrast, the Barrio Norte contains luxurious palaces from the same era, many of which have been converted into embassies, museums, elegant clubs, and public institutions. Among these are the Chancellory (formerly Anchorena Palace), the Military Club (formerly Paz Palace), and the Museo Nacional de Arte Decorativo (National Museum of Decorative Arts, formerly Errazuriz Palace).

Buildings of the Spanish period

Almost all of the few remaining relics of the Spanish viceregal period are churches, convents, and religious schools found in the *centro* and its surrounding barrios. The best architectural examples from this period are the Cabildo, or Town Hall, and the Metropolitan Cathedral. In San Telmo and Centro Sur barrios are old tiled homes, one of which served as the residence of viceroy Santiago Liniers and is now a national historic monument.

Buildings of the 20th century are interspersed with those from earlier years. New buildings are usually eclectic in design, are sometimes capricious in conception, and can be of debatable functional or aesthetic value. Within the banking zone of the *centro*, Neoclassical bank buildings are crowded together with the Bank of London and South America, a structure of painted, reinforced concrete with vast windows and exposed gas and water pipes built in 1969. There are many notable examples of functional, high-quality architecture in the city, including the numerous office and apartment "towers" built during the 1960s and large housing units called monoblocks, scattered about the *centro* area.

THE ECONOMY

Industrial and commercial trends

Industry. Gran Buenos Aires represents about 80 percent of Argentina's investment in industry, labour, and business. Industrial establishments are usually large factories with modern equipment, although smaller units do exist. During the 1950s, there was great emphasis on the production of consumer goods, and the city now meets its own needs. Main industries include food processing (meat, fish, grain), metalworks, automobile assembly, and oil refining, as well as printing, and the manufacture of textiles, beverages, paper, paint, and chemicals. Service industries are important, especially in the suburban areas, and the metropolitan area consumes more than half of all the electric and natural gas energy produced in the country. Inside the city proper are many larger industrial and manufacturing establishments, mostly in the barrio of Barracas.

Commerce. The national banking system is controlled by the Banco Central de la República Argentina (Central Bank of the Argentine Republic). Five government banks represent the official banking board, to which all private banks are responsible. Many of the private banks are associated with foreign banks or are subsidiaries of provincial banks. Numerous credit corporations provide funds for small businesses, while larger credit organizations are concerned with national and international enterprises. Federally controlled savings and loan associations finance home building.

Financial quotations are available from the stock exchange and the stock market. There are also specialized markets for meat, cattle, fruit, and grain. Insurance companies are backed by the Instituto Nacional de Reaseguros (National Re-insurance Institute).

More than 40 percent of all imports and 30 percent of all exports in Argentina pass through the port of Buenos Aires. Large warehouses and *barracas* ("huts") store the goods and act as national distributing houses. The administrative centres of the country's large agricultural, industrial, and mining enterprises are located in the city.

Transportation. *Roads.* The highway system is composed of five expressways that radiate out from the *centro* to connect it with the General Paz Expressway, which circles most of the city, thus forming a pattern resembling the sticks of a fan. Since 1886, the Riachuelo River and Avenida General Paz have defined the city's inland limits. Other main avenues penetrate to the Plaza de Mayo, in the heart of the city.

Railways and subways. The city is the terminus of every major railway in the country. There are four main railway stations within the urban area—Constitución, Once, Federico Lacroze, and Retiro. There are also two electric lines connecting the city with the towns of Tigre and Moreno. The city's five subway lines are interconnected and also connect the railway stations. They run for a total distance of 22 miles through tunnels decorated with murals made of multicoloured tiles.

Air services. The two international airports of Ezeiza and Don Torcuato, as well as the military airport, are respectively located outside the city limits in the municipalities of Matanza, Tigre, and Morón. They are connected to the city by expressways. The Buenos Aires City Airport lies within the federal district and services all the domestic airlines, as well as those that operate to and from Chile, Uruguay, and Paraguay.

The port of Buenos Aires

Port facilities. Buenos Aires is one of the world's largest ports, and its harbour is entirely man-made. Ships reach the port facilities through a twisting channel in the Río de la Plata, which must be continuously dredged because of shifting sand. The port stretches for five miles along the city's waterfront in a series of five interlocking basins and docks, which are connected to the main channel by smaller branch channels with a maximum depth of 30 feet. Puerto Nuevo (New Port) contains six open docks. It is the main passenger port and an important freight centre because of its large grain elevators and its proximity to the railway yards of Retiro. Located between Puerto Nuevo and Puerto Madero, the other major port facility, is Dársena Norte (North Dock), the naval operations base. Southward along the waterfront are Puerto Madero, which accommodates the river trade; Dársena Sur (South Dock), which handles all combustible materials; and two miles of wharves at the mouth of the Riachuelo, the original anchorage site for sail ships, called "la Boca."

Traffic. Though most city traffic is regulated by automatic traffic lights, the city's residents are notorious for ignoring them. Since the early 20th century, two major streets have been closed to motorized traffic during part of the day to allow for a free flow of pedestrians. More than 400,000 automobiles are registered in the city, and thousands of other vehicles enter and leave the city daily. Since trams were eliminated in the 1950s, *colectivos* (microbuses) and taxis have added to the steady flow of traffic.

ADMINISTRATIVE AND SOCIAL CONDITIONS

Political and governmental institutions. Buenos Aires, as mentioned, is the national capital, and the city proper is the federal district. The seven main national parties maintain their headquarters in the city. The president of the republic controls the municipality, and the National Congress is responsible for all legislation pertaining to it. The president appoints the mayor, who is his official representative. Over the years an elected city council has functioned only intermittently.

The administrative districts

The city territory is divided into 46 administrative districts, which coincide approximately with the traditional barrios. Each district has a neighbourhood junta, or council, composed of representatives from institutions such as the Lions and Rotary clubs, trade and industry groups, and workers' syndicates, who deal with various problems of public concern.

Many of the provincial governments maintain provincial houses in the city, which act as information and promotion centres; most of these are also concerned with relations between province and capital.

Public utilities. *Organization of services.* Almost all public-service facilities are in the hands of nonmunicipal organizations, functioning independently of the city administration. The municipal government is in charge only of the construction and maintenance of pavements and sidewalks, and parks. Because of population growth and uncontrolled building, the public services are severely overtaxed. There is also a lack of cooperation among individual public services, although the municipality indirectly exercises a coordinating role.

Types of services. Sanitary facilities—water supply, drainage, sewers—are the responsibility of the General Administration of Sanitary Works of the Nation (OSN), which services the greater part of Gran Buenos Aires. The large water-purification plant in Palermo Park treats water from the Río de la Plata and sends it underground through tunnels to four reservoirs in different parts of the city. This water is used for drinking, bathing, laundry, irrigation, fire fighting, public fountains, and industry. Electricity is provided by the Stock Company of Electrical Services of Gran Buenos Aires (SEGBA) and the Italian–Argentine Electrical Company (CIAE). Four main thermal centres are located in the port area with other stations in the urban area. These are fuelled by nationally produced oil, coal, and natural gas. All are interconnected with the thermic centre of San Nicolás and the nuclear centre of Atucha, both on the Paraná River coast. The National Tele-Communications Enterprise (ENTEL) operates about 70 centres and provides telephone service for the capital and its surrounding areas. International service is operated via satellite and national intercommunication by microwave. Natural gas is provided for all of Gran Buenos Aires by the State Gas Corporation from oil fields to the north, south, and west of Argentina through gas ducts and pipelines.

Health and security. *Public health.* The city has almost 600 municipal and private hospitals, as well as numerous dispensaries, pharmacies, and social hygiene centres in the various barrios. A relatively high number of hospital beds are maintained in order to accommodate the many patients from other parts of Argentina who travel to Buenos Aires for specialized treatment.

The waste-disposal system includes garbage-burning centres, but most wastes are used to fill lowlands along the Río de la Plata. The reclaimed areas are converted into parks, sports areas, and construction sites.

Safety. The federal police are responsible for maintaining public order and ensuring personal safety; the force is administered by the National Ministry of Internal Affairs. The police control traffic and regulate parking; traffic infractions are referred to the municipal tribunal. There are 50 district police stations in the capital's barrios, the central office is in the *centro*, and the mounted police headquarters is in Barrio Norte.

The fire department is under the jurisdiction of the federal police. There are several volunteer-firemen groups in the different barrios.

The military

The headquarters of the National Military Defense system is in Buenos Aires, as are the main offices of the Defense Ministry's navy, army, and airforce secretariats. The chiefs of staff of the coast guard and the frontier (national) guard are also located in the city, as are the barracks of the *patricios* and *granaderos*. The *granaderos*, a regiment created in 1812 by General San Martín, constitute the President's guard and cavalry. The *patricios*, created in 1810 by General Cornelio Saavedra, is the first army national corps.

Education. *Administration*. Educational institutions at all levels—nursery, primary, secondary, and university—are under the jurisdiction of the National Council of Education. The municipal government is in charge of a few nursery schools and some trade schools. Public schools are administered by the National Council of Education; and private schools are under the jurisdiction of an inspection department of the Secretariat of Culture and Education.

The school system. Primary education is obligatory and uniform for children in both public and private schools; it lasts for seven years. There are over 1,000 primary schools, with an attendance of about 290,000 students, as well as almost 600 nursery schools.

Secondary education is mandatory for three out of a possible five years. More than 450 secondary schools either prepare future teachers or serve as college-preparatory schools. The public schools are not usually coeducational, although most private schools are. The boys' schools are called *colegios nacionales* and the girls', *liceos*. Several secondary schools specialize in such subjects as fine arts, languages, or technical training. The University of Buenos Aires (Universidad de Buenos Aires) runs two preparatory schools—the Carlos Pellegrini Commercial School (Escuela Superior de Comercio "Carlos Pellegrini"), which is affiliated with the Faculty of Economics, and the Colegio Nacional de Buenos Aires (National College), both coeducational since 1965.

The universities

There are more than 40 universities in the city. The University of Buenos Aires, the principal university in the country, was founded in 1821. The Universidad Tecnológica Nacional (National Technological University) was founded in 1959 and offers courses in construction, engineering, and metallurgy. Important private universities include the Universidad Católica Argentina (Catholic University of Argentina), the Universidad del Salvador (University of Salvador), the Universidad de Belgrano, and the Universidad del Museo Social Argentino. Several faculties of the National University have been moved to an area on the Río de la Plata in an attempt to create a university campus. The Universidad Católica Argentina is located on the Riachuelo River at the opposite end of Buenos Aires, in Almirante Brown Park. The armed forces operate several technical schools and institutes, such as the Military Geographical Institute, which specializes in cartography.

CULTURAL LIFE

Buenos Aires has an active cultural life. The major newspapers and magazines publish cultural supplements, and numerous institutes, sports clubs, and labour unions offer cultural and recreational programs.

The arts. *Music and literature*. Varied activities include performances given by the Wagnerian Association and the Argentine Mozart Society, as well as literary presentations by the Writer's House and the Theatre House. Performances of folk songs and dances, known as *peñas*, are extremely popular. The tango originated in the city's ancient barrios "orilleros."

Entertainment. The most important of the city's 40 theatres is the Teatro Colón opera house, which attracts famous artists during its June to August season. It is also the headquarters of the national ballet and the national symphony. The Teatro San Martín houses three simultaneously available stages as well as an art gallery; the Teatro Alvear offers performances almost daily. Another theatre of note is the Teatro Nacional Cervantes. Amateur theatre groups present their works in rooms donated by businesses or labour organizations, and there is an open-air stage in the Boca barrio.

The city offers numerous tea rooms and cabarets. Along one of the streets in La Boca, dozens of Italian cantinas specialize in pasta and fish dishes and offer music and singing in which the clients merrily participate. Most of the modern nightclubs are located along the roads leading into the city. There are also more than 100 commercial movie houses.

Museums. The city's 16 museums—six of which are run by the municipal government—house varied collections. The Argentine Museum of Natural Sciences possesses an exceptionally rich fossil collection and runs a scientific institute. The National Museum of Fine Arts contains collections of world masters and of Argentine painters and sculptors, while the National Museum of Decorative Arts houses tapestries and antiques. The Museum of Spanish-American Art contains antique silver objects in a replica of a colonial home. Other art collections include Spanish, Italian, and modern works, and there are several historical museums and documentary centres. Museums of lesser importance are annexed to various public and private institutes, and there are 11 national academies of arts and sciences.

Libraries. The public municipal libraries, distributed throughout the city, are complemented by larger scholastic and institutionally sponsored libraries. The largest is the National Library, and others of importance include those of the Mitre Museum, the National College, the National Congress, the Women's Council, the National Council of Education, the Central Bank, and the Argentine Centre of Engineering. All of the universities maintain libraries, and numerous private foundations present public scientific and cultural programs.

The media. *The press*. The press includes hundreds of daily newspapers edited in Buenos Aires. Morning papers of long standing and of national importance are *La Prensa*, *La Nación*, and the country's oldest English-language paper, *The Standard*. The *Clarín* is also an important morning paper, and *La Razón* and *La Crónica* are published in the evening. Numerous others are published by professional groups, unions, and associations.

Television. All television stations are commercial. There are four local television stations, and the city also receives broadcasts from La Plata.

Radio. There are 13 local radio stations, two of which belong to the government. The most important commercial stations are Radio El Mundo, Radio Argentina, Radio Belgrano, Radio Splendid, Radio Excelsior, and Radio Mitre. Programs from Uruguayan stations are also received.

Recreation. *Parks*. The city is ringed with *espacios verdes* ("green areas"), which include plazas, parks, and tree-lined boulevards. Two extensive parks that were built on reclaimed floodlands are the Almirante Brown Park in the Riachuelo Valley, and the Parque Tres de Febrero, on the Río de la Plata. Palermo, the oldest park, has an area of 1,500 acres and contains Bosque de Palermo, or Palermo Forest.

Nueve de Julio Avenue, which is about 460 feet wide and has a strip of grass and trees down its centre, forms, in effect, a mile-long park running through the city centre. In general, however, available public recreational space has been reduced by the use of a large portion of the marginal parks for sports installations and other municipal development.

Sports facilities. The Club River Plate has built a gigantic stadium in Parque Tres de Febrero, where the Riding School of the Argentine Equestrian Club is also located. Other facilities include the National Race Track, the zoological and botanical gardens, the National University campus, the public baths, various nautical and sports clubs, the planetarium, the Lago Theatre, the Rose Walk of Palermo, and the northern coastal highway, which is lined with small restaurants, or *carritos*, specializing in steaks.

In Almirante Brown Park is the Autodromo Municipal—the city automobile race track—as well as a vast reservoir, used for boating, and a public recreation area.

In Costanera Park, near the port, reclaimed land is used for a football stadium, for exhibitions, and for a public park. Other sports clubs have their headquarters and stadiums in the urban area proper.

Gardens. Buenos Aires is one of the most tree-filled cities in the world, and the fondness of the population for flowers and plants is evident from the aspect of patios, balconies, and flower-covered terraces.

BIBLIOGRAPHY. DIRECCION NACIONAL DE ESTADISTICA Y CENSO, various statistical publications with census figures from 1869, 1895, 1914, 1947, and 1960; also provisional census figures from 1970 dealing with population, housing, and education; the Municipality of Buenos Aires City, various publications on historic and present development; IPRU (Institute of Regional and Urban Planning of Buenos Aires), various publications dealing with urban development and land use, particularly for the years 1950 to 1965; JUAN AGUSTIN GARCIA, *La ciudad indiana*, 2nd ed. (1909), a description of 19th-century Buenos Aires; BERNARDO CANAL FEIJOO, *Teoría de la ciudad argentina* (1951), a penetrating discussion of the role of Greater Buenos Aires within the country's structure; EZEQUIEL MARTINEZ ESTRADA, *La cabeza de Goliath* (1940, various editions), an explanation of the difference between Buenos Aires and other Argentinian cities.

(J.M.F.P./Jo.B.)

Buffon, Georges-Louis Leclerc, Comte de

Buffon was a French naturalist famous for his comprehensive work on natural history. He is also remembered for his celebrated *Discours sur le style* (1753), in which he said, "Le style c'est l'homme même" ("The style is the man himself").

Buffon, engraving by C. Baron, 1761, after a painting.
By courtesy of the Hunt Botanical Library, Carnegie-Mellon University, Pittsburgh, Pennsylvania

Early years

He was born Georges-Louis Leclerc on September 7, 1707, at Montbard in Burgundy. The name Buffon came from an estate that he inherited from his mother at about the age of 25. His father, Benjamin Leclerc, was a state official in Burgundy; his mother was a woman of spirit and learning, and he was fond of saying that he got his intelligence from her.

Beginning his studies at the College of Godrans in Dijon, which was run by the Jesuits, he seems now to have been only an average student but with a marked taste for mathematics. His father wanted him to have a legal career, and in 1723 he began the study of law. In 1728, however, he went to Angers, where he seems to have studied medicine and botany as well as mathematics.

He was forced to leave Angers after a duel and took refuge at Nantes, where he lived with a young Englishman, the Duke of Kingston. In his correspondence he gives an impression of the town, where "one lives very well and drinks excellent wine." The two young men travelled to Italy, arriving in Rome at the beginning of 1732. They also visited England, and while there Buffon was elected a member of the Royal Society.

The death of his mother called him back to France. He settled down on the family estate at Montbard, where he undertook his first research in the calculus of probability and in the physical sciences. Buffon at that time was particularly interested in questions of plant physiology. In 1735 he published a translation of Stephen Hales's *Vegetable Staticks*, in the preface of which he developed his conception of scientific method. Maintaining an interest in mathematics, in 1740 he published a translation of Sir Isaac Newton's *Fluxions*. In his preface to this work he discussed the history of the differences between Newton and Leibniz over the discovery of the infinitesimal calculus. He also made researches on the properties of timbers and their improvement in his forests in Burgundy.

In 1739, at the age of 32, he was appointed keeper of the Jardin du Roi and of the museum that formed part of it through the patronage of the minister of marine, J.-F.-P. de Maurepas, who realized the importance of science and was anxious to use Buffon's knowledge of timber for the shipbuilding projects of the French government. Maurepas also charged Buffon to undertake a catalog of the king's museum, which Buffon's ambition transformed into an undertaking to produce an account of the whole of nature. This became his great work, *Histoire naturelle, générale et particulière*.

The *Histoire naturelle*

Though he laboured arduously on it—he spent eight months of the year on his estate at Montbard, working up to 12 hours a day—he was able to publish only 36 of the proposed 50 volumes before his death. He had several collaborators. In the preparation of the first 15 volumes, which appeared in the years 1749–67, he was assisted by several associates. The next seven volumes formed a supplement to the preceding and appeared in 1774–89, the most famous section, *Époques de la nature* (1778), being contained in the fifth of them. They were succeeded by nine volumes on birds (1770–83), and these again by five volumes on minerals (1783–88). The remaining eight volumes, which complete the first edition, appeared after Buffon's death; they covered reptiles, fishes, and cetaceans. To keep the descriptions of the animals from becoming monotonous, Buffon interspersed them with philosophic discussions on nature, the degeneration of animals, the nature of birds, and so forth.

He was elected to the Académie Française, where he delivered his *Discours sur le style* on August 25, 1753. He was also treasurer to the Académie des Sciences. During the brief trips he made each year to Paris, he frequented the literary and philosophical salons. Though he was a friend of Diderot and d'Alembert, he did not collaborate on their *Encyclopédie*. He enjoyed his life at Montbard, living in contact with nature and the peasants and managing his properties himself. He built a menagerie and a large aviary there. He also transformed one of his outbuildings into a laboratory, with a furnace large enough to conduct experiments on the nature of fire.

Buffon's wife died in 1769, leaving him with a five-year-old son. The boy showed signs of brilliance; and when he was 17 Buffon asked the naturalist J.-B. Lamarck to take him along on his botanical travels across Europe. But the younger Buffon was not interested in study. He developed into a spendthrift, and his imprudences were to lead him to the guillotine during the Revolution (1794).

In 1785 Buffon's health began to decline. To his physical disabilities were added family cares, particularly the public liaison between his son's wife and the Duc d'Orléans. At the beginning of 1788, feeling his end near, he returned to Paris. Unable to leave his room, he was visited each day by his "sublime friend" Mme Necker, the wife of the finance minister Jacques Necker. He died on April 16. Mme Necker, who was with him to the very end, is said to have understood him to murmur, "I declare that I die in the religion in which I was born. . . . I declare publicly that I believe in it."

Buffon's position and influence

Buffon's position among his contemporaries was by no means assured. Though the public was nearly unanimous in its admiration of him, he met with numerous detractors among the learned. The theologians were aroused by his conceptions of geological history; others criticized his views on classification; the philosopher Étienne de Condillac disputed his views on the faculties of animals; and many took from his work only some general philosophical ideas about nature that were not faithful to what he had written. Voltaire did not appreciate his style, and d'Alembert called him "the great phrasemonger." According to the writer J.-F. Marmontel, Buffon had to put up with snubs from the mathematicians, chemists, and astronomers, while the naturalists themselves gave him little support and some even reproached him for writing ostentatiously in a subject that required a simple and natural style. He was even accused of plagiarism but made no reply to his detractors, writing to a friend that "I shall keep absolute silence . . . and let their attacks fall upon themselves."

In some areas of natural science Buffon had a lasting influence. He was the first to reconstruct geological history in a series of stages, in *Époques de la nature* (1778). With his notion of lost species he opened the way to the development of paleontology. He was the first to propose the theory that the planets had been created in a collision between the Sun and a comet. While his great project opened up vast areas of knowledge that were beyond his powers to encompass, his *Histoire naturelle* was the first work to present the previously isolated and apparently disconnected facts of natural history in a generally intelligible form.

BIBLIOGRAPHY. Buffon's collected writings are in *Oeuvres complètes de Buffon*, 12 vol. (1853–55), rev. and annotated by PIERRE FLOURENS; *Oeuvres philosophiques de Buffon*, ed. by JEAN PIVETEAU (1954), including a detailed bibliography; and *Histoire naturelle, générale et particulière*, 44 vol. (1749–1804; Eng. trans., *Natural History, General and Particular*, 20 vol., 1781–1812).

Evaluations of his work are in E. GEOFFROY SAINT-HILAIRE, *Fragments biographiques, précédés d'études sur la vie, les ouvrages, et les doctrines de Buffon* (1838, Pillot edition); PIERRE FLOURENS, *Buffon: histoire de ses travaux et de ses idées* (1844); F. GOHIN (ed.), *Buffon: discours et vues générales* (1905); D. MORNET, *Les Sciences de la nature en France au XVIIIe siècle* (1911), essential to the study of Buffon, particularly the bibliography and the chapter on the controversial Buffon; L. ROULE, *Buffon et la description de la nature* (1924), emphasizes the scientific value of his work and the introduction of the idea of time into the study of nature; and EMILE GUYENOT, *Les Sciences de la vie aux XVIIe et XVIIIe siècles: l'idée d'évolution* (1941), which contains lengthy passages on Buffon, notably on the origin of the idea of evolution, the idea of transformism in Buffon, and Buffon as the precursor of Lamarck. For an analysis of the contribution of Buffon's thought to the doctrine of evolution, see A.O. LOVEJOY, "Buffon and the Problem of Species," *Pop. Sci. Mon.* 79:464–473, 554–567 (1911); and J.S. WILKIE, "Buffon, Lamarck and Darwin: The Originality of Darwin's Theory of Evolution," in P.R. BELL (ed.), *Darwin's Biological Work* (1964).

(J.Piv.)

Building Construction

Protection from inclement weather, human enemies, and animals has always been one of man's basic needs. His first attempts to provide such shelter were crude, involving such primitive constructions as screens and windbreaks made of interwoven branches, reeds, and animal skins. Man seems always to have understood the elementary principles of building and to have been blessed with a sense of structure; with similar raw materials—mud, stone, and timber—widely scattered groups often built the same type of structure. As time passed, man refined his knowledge through practical experience; advances in structural techniques roughly paralleled those in industrialization and mathematics.

This article is divided into the following sections:

I. History of construction

ANCIENT CONSTRUCTION MATERIALS AND METHODS

Reed and straw construction. Before the ancient Egyptians began to quarry stone, little material was available for building other than the reeds, rushes, and mud of the Nile Valley. In a few cases, date-palm stems were used. In building reed houses (Figure 1), the reeds, which grew

From Norman Davey, *A History of Building Materials* (1961); reproduced by permission of Phoenix House, London

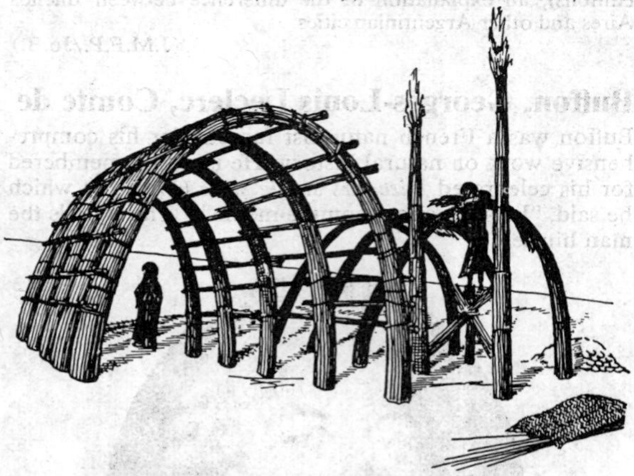

Figure 1: Reed dwellings under construction.

up to 20 feet (six metres) in height, were cut and tightly bound into bundles to form long tapering pillars that were set vertically in two parallel rows of holes about two and a half feet (75 centimetres) deep. Next, a tripod five to six feet (150 to 180 centimetres) high was made from cut and bound reed bundles. Standing on this rigid structure, a man would reach up, bring the tops of two parallel reed columns together and bind the ends securely with the twisted edges of a sedge leaf. The tripod was then moved to the next pair of columns, and the process was repeated until a series of high parabolic arches had been made. When the arches were complete, slender bundles of reeds were tied horizontally to them, and the entire structure was covered with reed matting. Finally, other tapered pillars were set up at the ends of the structure to support an end wall of alternating matting and trelliswork. This construction principle has survived for 6,000 years and can be seen in the modern reed dwellings in the Mesopotamian marshes of southern Iraq.

Use of reed ceilings

Reeds have also been used for reinforcing and constructing roofs, floors, and ceilings. A flat ceiling in a house at Eutresis in ancient Greece was made by placing a layer of clay reinforced with reeds upon closely spaced timbers spanning the main beams. Matting was then laid over the secondary beams, followed by a layer of reed, a second layer of matting, and a mixture of mud and chopped straw. These materials were made watertight by applying bitumen. According to Vitruvius, the Roman architect and engineer, the Romans used reeds in constructing curved ceilings. Parallel laths of cypress wood were placed not more than two feet (60 centimetres) apart and bent to the shape of an arch. Reeds were then bound to the ribs with cords of Spanish broom. After completion of the arches and their interweaving with reeds, the undersurface was finished with mortar (made with sand and hair) or marble.

Reeds were used in England until about 1850 in plaster

floor construction (Figure 2). A layer of reeds or straw was placed across floor joists, secured with batten strips (light strips of wood), and covered with about three

From N. Davey, *A History of Building Materials*, Drake Publishers

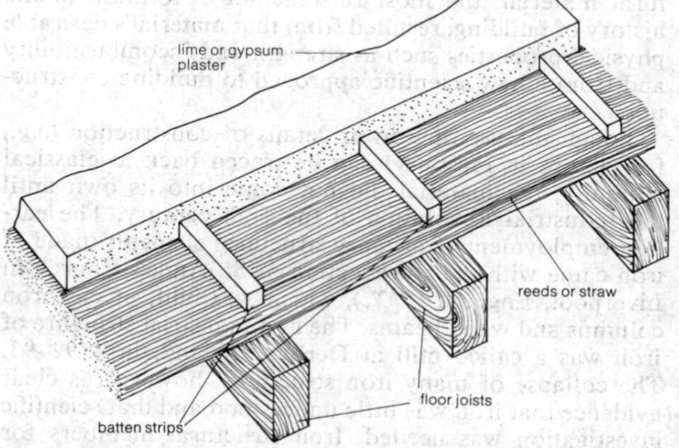

Figure 2: Lime or gypsum over reed or straw floor construction in England about 1850 (see text).

inches (75 millimetres) of lime or gypsum plaster. In some cases, ashes, sand, or crushed brick were included in the mix. Reeds and straw have also been employed in wall construction; the reeds were placed vertically, staggered, and tied to horizontal ribs about two inches (five centimetres) in diameter. A mixture of clay and chopped straw was then pressed into the voids and the wall surface finished with a clay coating.

Thatching. Thatching involves covering the rafters or beams of flat roofs with some vegetable material held in place by various methods. Depending upon locality, brushwood, grass, broom, bracken, or heather may serve as thatch; it may be sewn direct to the battens, nailed to the rafters, held down with rods secured by ropes stretched over the surface with ends tied and weighted, held by ropes fixed by pegs; or held by knotting the ends of the sheaves or bundles and thrusting them into or between turves (bundles of turf). Layers of mud or a straw-mud mixture may be used to fill any voids.

Where turves were used, as in Ireland, they were cut in long strips, sometimes 20 feet (six metres) or more in length and up to two feet (60 centimetres) in width, and about two to three inches (50–75 millimetres) thick. They were sewn with grass upward onto the battens and purlins (horizontal timbers supporting the rafters) of the roof structure. Where there were no battens or purlins, a layer of straw, woven to form a mat, was used, and the sheaves or bundles of thatch were attached.

Rope thatching methods

Rope thatching is still done in Scotland and Ireland. The straw, which in these countries may be heather, flax, or rye straw, is placed in layers on a sloped roof and held down by ropes. The ropes are sometimes tied to stones projecting from the wall at the eave, or they may be weighted by stones. In the Soviet Union, particularly in the Ukraine, the roof is covered with small bound sheaves or bundles of straw placed with the ears downward, except at the eaves, where the sheaves are placed with the ears upward. The sheaves are then tied to the battens with twisted straw.

Wood construction. *Trunks and staves.* During the period of reed and straw construction (about 5500–2500 BC), men in warmer climates where timber was plentiful (Britain, for example), began to construct rectangular dwellings with single or multiple rows of posts to support the roof. Interiors were often subdivided by partitions into compartments or rooms, whereas the floors were often covered with roughhewn timber planking, and occasionally with birch bark. From about 2500 to 1500 BC, walls in Europe were built of split trunks or planks. A variation of this type of construction, which included upright planks or staves embedded in a wall trench, was later found in Danish fortresses and churches such as the 11th-century AD St. Maria Minor at Stavkyrkaus. In this structure timbers were grooved along their sides, and tongues of wood were let in. One of the few remaining stave churches (built about AD 1013) stands near Ongar, Essex, in England.

Logs. Where straight-trunked trees, such as pine, fir, and beech, were available, as in Scandinavia, the French and Swiss Alps, northern Italy, Czechoslovakia, the Soviet Union, and the Himalayas, log-cabin-type construction began to appear. Gaps between the timbers were filled with wood chips and mud. In a dwelling of this type near Stockholm, the roof at the eave has a special board that projects above the roof line to retain the heavy snow and thus to provide additional insulation in the winter. Log cabins in the Ukraine consisted of roughly squared full logs coated with clay both on the interior and exterior. In another Russian method, the underside of the log was hollowed over its entire length so that it rested on the log beneath. Moss was then stuffed into the joists.

Wood frames. Since log cabins used large amounts of timber, a wood frame or structure with a wattle and clay daub in-fill was more economical in areas where timber was scarce. Chopped straw or grass was often added to the clay daub to act as a binder and lessen the effects of shrinkage cracking. By the 16th century this had evolved into half-timber construction, in which the timber was vertical, closely spaced, and mortised into horizontal wall plates and sills. Uprights were grooved from top to bottom; split oak lath was wedged into these grooves. In other cases, square-panelled construction was preferred. The uprights were more widely spaced and horizontal timbers were introduced. Since durability was a problem with wattle and clay daub, a good roof overhang was required; in the case of a two-story dwelling, the second-floor beams and walls overhung the wall of the first story. For a complete description of wood frame construction, including the various joints used, see CARPENTRY. Wooden bridges and their construction are described in BRIDGES, CONSTRUCTION AND HISTORY OF.

Roofs. During the late 17th century, four major types of roofs—the gable, gambrel, hipped, and rainbow—were in use. The gable roof, which was the simplest, consisted of two planes sloped on each side of a ridge, usually but not always centred on the short dimension of the dwelling. The gambrel was a gable roof in which one plane broke about half-way down from the ridge to slope at a steeper pitch. The hipped roof sloped to all four sides of the dwelling; and in the rainbow roof, the side planes normally bowed out in a convex curve. Another rather common type of roof, found in the New England region of America, was the single-pitch or lean-to, typically used to cover an extension to the house.

Masonry construction. *Egypt.* Though brick and stone, or masonry, construction can be traced as far back as the 3rd millennium BC, it did not achieve real development until the Middle Ages. The earliest stone buildings—palaces, temples, tombs, and monuments—are recorded in Egypt during the 4th millennium BC. Cut slabs of limestones were used for lining and roofing of small chambers. Probably the earliest complete stone building that can be dated accurately is the pit chamber of the tomb of King Khasekhemui of the 2nd dynasty (*c.* 2890–*c.* 2686 BC). Sandstone was also used in ancient Egypt but in no great quantity until the 18th dynasty (1567–1320 BC); granite, alabaster, basalt, and quartzite were reserved mainly for monumental and decorative purposes. The most remarkable of Egyptian masonry constructions were the pyramids, made mostly of rough-dressed limestone cased with fine white limestone.

Greece. The ancient Greeks demonstrated considerable versatility in masonry construction, fitting blocks together with remarkable precision and artistry. Early types of stone walling used by the Greeks were built with very large and heavy pieces, irregular in shape, roughly trimmed, piled skillfully, and wedged together by filling the interstices with smaller pieces of stone, sometimes bedded in clay. With the development of mortar that attained considerable strength on hardening, it became possible to construct walls with a concrete core capable of taking most of the load and to face them with stones

Development of mortar

smaller than those used previously. This was done mainly for appearance and convenience. Later, the Greeks constructed concrete walls by placing stones in layers inside formwork, pouring mortar over each layer, and inserting string courses (narrow layers of stone or tile at the same height in a wall) every three or four feet (90 to 120 centimetres) to improve stability. By the 2nd century BC, concrete was being produced by incorporating stone in a mortar mix.

Brick. Bricks came into use because of their strength and durability, ease of production from readily obtainable clays, and lower cost in comparison to stone. In some areas, builders were compelled to use small units of material such as bricks because the local geology did not supply stone in blocks sufficiently large. The Chaldeans, for example, developed brick arches for the openings in their buildings, whereas the Greeks and Egyptians were able to find large blocks of stone to span wide openings. Modern brick construction had its most rapid development in the American colony of Virginia in the 17th century. The most skilled brick masons in the colony were the Dutch, who became the first to use and build with glazed brick and tile. Their work is exemplified by Bacon's Castle, a monumental house built about 1655 in Surry County, Virginia.

Arch, vault, and dome. The arch is primarily used for spanning intervals of space in one major vertical plane by means of inclined or curved masonry, as opposed to horizontal beams. When masonry forms based on the arch are used to cover extended spatial compartments, the result is a vault. Within the limits of masonry construction, arches have two advantages over horizontal beams: they can span much greater distances and they can carry much greater loads. In all likelihood, the arch was conceived by accident when a lack of large stones compelled builders to use bricks and other small units of material. The true or radiating arch, in which each voussoir (wedge-shaped piece) is stepped upward and outward (corbelled) away from its support, dates from the period of Etruscan architecture, about 750 BC. It was in Roman Italy during the late republican period that the arch was first exploited on a grand scale both as a structural device (in aqueducts) and as a symbolic form (in triumphal arches).

The arch in Gothic buildings

During the four and a half centuries from 1100 to 1550 arches were most widely used in European architecture, especially in churches and monastic buildings whose ribbed vaults and flying buttresses reveal the arch as the first principle of Gothic structural engineering. Churches of that period became veritable systems of arches in which walls, windows, and roofs served only as screens against the weather. Though the arch was undoubtedly used during this period for its structural advantages, its symbolic value in making churches splendid structures was important as well.

A dome is an ovoidal or hemispherical vault, or a vault of polygonal plan that resembles the round dome in shape. Masonry dome construction was important during Roman times; the Pantheon, built under Hadrian between AD 120 and 124, with a diameter of about 125 feet (38 metres), displayed a masterful command of large-scale domical construction in brick, with an intricate system of built-in relieving arches. The construction was heavy, the only opening being a great "eye" at the top. A great advance in domical construction was made by Byzantine architects when they developed the pendentive (a triangular segment of a spherical surface filling in the upper corners of a room in order to form, at the top, a circular support for a dome), enabling them to dome over a plan of any shape. The greatest Byzantine dome was that over the basilica-plan church of Hagia Sophia at Constantinople (originally built 532–537). So skillfully and subtly was the weight of this 100-foot-wide, 180-foot-high (30 by 55 metres) dome transferred through pendentives to side walls and buttresses, that on the interior it gave what a contemporary described as the effect of being "suspended on a golden cord from heaven." Muslim builders, under Byzantine influence, used the dome in a lavish form but on a small scale in Spain and North Africa, and they developed it along Byzantine lines in Egypt, Persia, India, and Turkey.

THE DEVELOPMENT OF MODERN MATERIALS AND METHODS

Metal construction. The adoption of iron as a structural material, the most far-reaching revolution in the history of building, resulted from that material's desirable physical properties such as strength and incombustibility and from a new scientific approach to building construction.

Though the use of iron in details of construction (*e.g.*, for clamps in masonry) can be traced back to classical antiquity, the material did not come into its own until the Industrial Revolution of the 18th century. The earliest employment of primary structural elements made of iron came with the construction of St. Anne's Church in Liverpool, England (1772), which was built of cast-iron columns and wood beams. The first industrial structure of iron was a calico mill at Derby, England, in 1792–93. The collapse of many iron structures, however, is clear evidence that iron was little understood and that scientific investigation was needed. Iron structural members for buildings were introduced in the United States in Philadelphia and New York. Though iron-fronted and iron-framed buildings continued to be erected through the 19th century, their number dwindled after the American Civil War.

Growth of the railroads created a demand for fire-resistant bridges capable of spanning relatively large distances and carrying substantial loads; iron met these requirements. The iron arch was created, followed by the iron truss, which first appeared in a railroad bridge built in Manayunk, Pennsylvania, in 1845. A truss is an assemblage of members such as beams in triangular combinations to form a rigid framework; adoption of the iron truss in railroad bridges spurred experimentation with this new device, leading to several different designs and the use of the truss in iron-framed buildings.

First use of iron truss

The forms and techniques of the new large-scale urban building were largely developed in Chicago, where the Auditorium Building of 1889 employed elliptical trusses with a maximum span of 117 feet (36 metres) to carry its ceiling and flat trusses to support the roof over the theatre, the ceilings of the main dining room and banquet hall of the former hotel (now a university building), and the ceiling of the rehearsal hall above the theatre. The remainder of the hotel and office areas were framed in iron within the granite and limestone piers of the exterior walls. The final step in the creation of the framing that made the modern skyscraper possible came with the Home Insurance Company Building (1885) erected in Chicago, in which an internal skeleton and curtain wall were used for the first time in a rigorously functional high office building. The most advanced features of the framing system in this building were the method of supporting each bay of the wall on a shelf angle and the introduction of steel into the building frame. Four years after the Home Insurance Company Building was complete, the steel-framed skyscraper had totally evolved in Chicago. The final step in the creation of the modern skyscraper came with the construction of the second Rand McNally Building in 1890. The frame of this high office building was wholly freed from its masonry parts and built entirely of steel.

By 1894, the problem of foundations had been solved with the placing of concrete caissons extending to bedrock. The structural culmination was reached with the Reliance Building (1895), erected in Chicago, which was braced by 24-inch- (60-centimetre-) deep girders, supporting exterior panels (spandrels), to provide portal bracing, and two-story columns erected with staggered joints to increase the rigidity of the vertical members.

A rigid frame is one that has triangularly arranged members and moment-resisting joints; *i.e.*, they resist tendencies to produce motion. Such a frame can be designed so that under a vertical load the tensile and compressive stresses arising from the deflection of a beam are distributed equally among three members rather than concentrated in the horizontal member. Though originally used in bridges, the rigid frame was adopted for buildings in the early 1930s. A three-dimensional arrangement of trusses is known as a space frame; an early structure with such a frame, designed for maximum rigidity and minimum weight, was the George Washington Bridge (1927–31) in New York City. Another important innovation in steel construction was welding, used to its greatest potential in the Inland Steel Building (1955–57) of Chicago, in which all the floors and roof loads are carried by 58-foot (18-metre) transverse girders to seven pairs of columns outside the wall planes of the long elevations.

Although the dome had disappeared for the most part as an element in building construction, it reappeared in the 20th century in a number of functional designs to shelter the maximum area at the least cost. The idea of metal shells and stretched membrane, or stressed skin, found its way into specialized construction; this technique combined curtain wall and roof in a single continuous enclosure by stretching a thin aluminum skin over a framework of ribs.

Invention of the geodesic dome

Perhaps the most heralded structural invention of the 20th century is the geodesic dome, patented by R. Buckminster Fuller in 1947. Fuller's primary intention was to substitute a great number of light, mass-produced, hand-assembled elements for the heavy ribs and purlins of the conventional steel-framed dome. The dome is a thin cover of aluminum or plastic pinned to a framework of steel or aluminum tubing arranged in a pattern of triangles or hexagons. By the nature of triangles and hexagons, the structure is a rigid framework theoretically limited to compressive stresses. In 1958, an immense geodesic dome was designed to house the car-repair facilities of the Union Tank Car Company at Baton Rouge, Louisiana. The first use of a plastic skin was at a botanical conservatory built in St. Louis between 1961 and 1962.

Concrete construction. Though concrete is the oldest synthetic material used in building construction, there was a period of about 13 centuries when knowledge of it was wholly lost in Europe. The Romans were known to have employed concrete made from pozzolana, a clean, sandy earth, to construct domes, vaults, and walls; these were faced with brick, stone, alabaster, porphyry, and other marbles. In conjunction with brick and stone casing, concrete gave uniformity of style to Roman architecture. Concrete was used by Mayan builders as early as the 11th century, but this work had no influence on later building in the New World.

Not until the late 16th century was concrete rediscovered as a result of systematic investigations carried on by the English civil engineer John Smeaton preceding the reconstruction of the Eddystone Lighthouse off the Plymouth coast. Though concrete was used in construction from that time, the modern scientific age of concrete did not begin until 1871, when the American David O. Saylor patented an equivalent of Portland cement, built a production centre, and studied its physical properties and structural behaviour in a systematic manner. By 1880, concrete, either poured in place or cast as blocks, had come to be used for a wide variety of simple structural elements such as piers, walls, and footings. The pioneer concrete multistory building was the Ponce de Leon Hotel (1886–88), in St. Augustine, Florida. The footings, foundations, main exterior walls, and some interior walls were monolithic concrete with a shell aggregate. Concrete was also applied successfully to bridges and dams.

Unlike iron construction, the technology of reinforced concrete developed rather rapidly. Reinforced masonry had spread from France to England and the United States in the early half of the 19th century. Not until 1854 did the idea arise of strengthening concrete in a similar manner; in 1867, concrete was first reinforced with iron bars. The first building constructed of reinforced concrete was a residence in Port Chester, New York, erected between 1871 and 1876. With such progress in reinforced concrete construction, engineers, especially in France and Germany, began adapting the new techniques to arch bridges. A more efficient design was now possible because the reinforcing metal could do the work formerly done by large volumes of concrete.

The first skyscraper of reinforced concrete was the 16-story Ingalls Building in Cincinnati, Ohio, erected between 1902 and 1903. The main tendency in American concrete construction was to meet larger loads simply by increasing the size of structural members. Employing reinforced concrete made it possible to eliminate long beams and trusses, an important advantage in warehouses and freight-handling facilities where overhead space is quite valuable. Known as flat-slab construction, this technique eventually reached the point of maximum simplicity, marked by slabs of uniform depth and columns of uniform section, that freed the vertical space entirely of beams, capitals, and other structural details.

Building systems. Though the construction industry constantly innovates, changes tend to be incremental and evolutionary rather than revolutionary. Perhaps the greatest change in recent years has been the emergence of building systems (mass production of prefabricated buildings) immediately following the end of World War II in Europe. Among the most important contributing causes to the replacement of traditional hand methods by industrialized building systems were the shortage of manpower, especially skilled craftsmen; the extensive demand for housing units due to bombing destruction; the need to reduce costs while erecting buildings rapidly; and the participation of national governments in public housing programs. Generally speaking, industrialized building systems have made their swiftest progress in countries such as France and the United Kingdom, where a large percentage of the total construction program is financed by the national government; slower progress has been made in such nations as Germany and Italy, where the private sector is stronger. About 25 percent of new construction in western Europe employs building systems, whereas for eastern Europe, approximately 60 percent is estimated.

Currently, hundreds of specific systems are available for use throughout Europe, differing in details such as materials used, dimensions of panels, and intended end use (*e.g.*, single story, multi-story; residential, school). Development of a building system is commonly initiated by contractors, engineers, clients, or manufacturers. To date, contractors and engineering organizations dominate the field.

Open and closed systems

A system may be either open or closed. In an open system, the components are interchangeable with those of other systems with which they are dimensionally coordinated. Conversely, a closed system is one in which the components are designed and coordinated only for that system. The trend today is toward open systems, which offer the architect greater flexibility.

Though building systems are widely used in the United States, they are usually not so identified. All home manufacturers, metal-building producers, mobile-home manufacturers, and some industrial firms, for example, have their own building systems encompassing design, manufacture, transportation of components, erection, and finishing. Generally speaking, United States systems employ lighter building materials than their European counterparts and emphasize single-family dwelling units and other low-rise structures rather than medium and high-rise structures.

Box systems. Basically a modular volumetric unit composed of some combination of walls, roof, and/or floor, the box system is usually prefabricated in a plant; its degree of factory finish and the extent of mechanical services included varies considerably among manufacturers. The box can be transported to a site and stacked, hung, inserted, or grouped according to project requirements. The system is relatively new; considerable interest was stirred by the Canadian government's Habitat, a box system displayed at Montreal in 1967.

Panel systems. The panel system utilizes either load-bearing exterior walls, load-bearing cross-wall construction, or a combination of exterior and interior load-bearing panels. Basic sizes of these panels vary considerably from small sections to room size. The lower cost, cross-wall type of construction is currently quite popular; its major advantage is that since the interior walls, floors, and roofs resist both vertical and lateral loads, a non-load-bearing facade panel can be used that permits exterior design flexibility.

Frame systems. Almost any curtain-wall building can be classified as a frame-system building; this system is used more than any other. Pre-engineered frame-system buildings can be used for dormitories, apartments, and industrial or commercial structures.

II. Modern building construction

PRECONSTRUCTION PLANNING

Before any building project can be undertaken, numerous decisions must be made. The design program must be resolved. The site must be chosen and economic feasibility determined. Finally, a completed design for the building must be made. Each of these elements is important; none can be considered in isolation of the others.

Design programming. Frequently a decision is made to construct a building before much has been determined about its function. In the case of a residence, little information is needed to make the decision to build. In the case of other buildings, such as offices or retail stores, questions of actual need may arise, and a market analysis (see below) may be performed. Once need has been determined, it is necessary to develop guidelines for designing and building the structure. The first step in this process is to determine how the building is to be used—its overall function and the purposes various spaces within it must serve. In a residence, for example, the potential occupant must determine his needs: living, sleeping, food preparation, dining, bathroom, storage areas, and special design features, such as a fireplace, wood panelling, and air conditioning. Typically, a residence does not require very comprehensive programming or study. The potential owner or occupant may do nothing more than describe his desires to an architect or builder, who then translates them into design sketches.

Larger buildings, such as offices, schools, and industrial buildings, require more comprehensive programming. School planners, for example, may attempt to project future student population in order to determine the size of the building. Present and future curricula may be analyzed before a specific design program, including classrooms, gymnasium, library, etc., is drawn up.

Determination of future needs

In most countries, if a project under development is to be sold or leased, the ability of the owner to market the project at a reasonable return will be critical in determining the project's feasibility. Marketing analysis is undertaken for projects such as multifamily housing, office, commercial, and selected industrial buildings, and even new towns. The method used can be either simple or comprehensive and complex. The approach will vary with the type of construction. In determining the market for a housing project, for example, analysts may examine the supply of housing in the area, projected population and employment, and the levels of income expected by future residents. In this way both the extent and market value of housing demand can be estimated. The extent of market competition is usually also analyzed.

Site selection and land acquisition. Before the market analysis can be completed, there must be a decision on the approximate geographic location of the project. To make this decision, specific information is needed on such points as land value; tax rates; availability of utilities; drainage; relationship to the transportation network; zoning, if any; and number of workers in the immediate area of the site. This kind of information is typically obtained and organized in map form. Another important map tool is a diagram showing areas of accessibility to home, to work, or to a shopping centre. In considering a shopping centre, for example, the distance of the site from potential shoppers is of major importance. In a project such as a general office building, the distance of the site from major transportation lines is usually a consideration.

Maps used in planning

As the market analysis progresses, various site advantages and disadvantages can be considered. Finally, one site is given priority over others under consideration. Final site selection is generally delayed until the financial feasibility study is well underway.

Architectural design, specifications, and bidding. *Schematic design.* During financial-feasibility analysis, and before any construction-cost analysis is made, simple schematic design sketches are prepared to illustrate the design-program requirements. Generally, these sketches as well as the more detailed design, construction drawings, and specifications are prepared by an architect.

The purpose of schematic design sketches is to assist the client in his understanding of the design program, to illustrate possible solutions within the shortest possible time and at a minimum expense, and to assist the client in determining the feasibility of the project. A series of sketches, sometimes a long series, is made in the process of studying the possibilities of the problem and in attempting to find an acceptable solution within the imposed financial limits. Schematic sketches include building plans, elevations, perspectives, and site utilization. Three-dimensional models can facilitate the study of mass, proportion, scale, and the relation of parts. When the project is a part of a larger development, such as a master plan of a downtown area or a university, the relationship should be indicated and explained.

Besides the sketches, other information is developed by the architect, such as the ratio of the gross floor area to the area to be used for the purpose of the building. For some types of building, calculations of floor area per occupant or per unit of production are useful. In addition, a preliminary cost estimate is prepared by taking data available from recent similar projects and applying unit costs (*e.g.*, per square foot or metre, per cubic foot or metre, per bed, per student) to the proposed project to determine the estimated cost. If there is a variance in number of stories, type of construction or finish, mechanical equipment, labour or material costs, the unit cost is modified.

At the time the schematics are being developed, the architect considers applicable zoning restrictions. In most countries, zoning controls are regulatory tools used by local governments to guide land-use development. Typically, a zoning ordinance prescribes how each parcel of land in a community may be used and covers land use, population density, and building bulk. Many zoning regulations divide uses into three categories: residential, commercial, and industrial. Population density is also controlled by setting a minimum required size for each lot. In other cases, the number of families per acre or hectare may be limited. Building bulk is limited by limiting building height, the proportion of lot area that may be covered by buildings, and open spaces along lot boundaries. The architect is expected to take these and other requirements into consideration during the design stages.

National or local building codes are also important at this stage of planning. A building code is a series of standards and specifications designed to establish minimum safeguards in the erection and construction of buildings, to protect against fire and other hazards, and to establish regulations to further protect the health and safety of the public.

Building codes

Detailed design development. Once the schematic design has been approved by the client, detailed design development goes forward, comprising drawings of plans, elevations, building cross sections, perspectives, and in some cases three-dimensional models. This stage includes illustration and description of the site development, materials, structural system, mechanical equipment, and even interior furnishings. In studying and developing the design for these components, it is necessary to have at least tentative data concerning the location, kind, and size of structural members (*e.g.*, wood, steel, or concrete); location and size of heating and air-conditioning components; elevators and moving stairways; plumbing; illumination; acoustical system (*e.g.*, acoustical ceiling and materials in theatres); and general colour scheme.

During the design-development stage, the architect typically collaborates with other consultants, such as a landscape architect, structural engineers, mechanical engineers, and cost consultants. Also during this stage, outline specifications are prepared. Thus, a more definite basis is provided for a more detailed cost estimate, which should also be prepared. The method used for preparing this cost estimate is similar to that employed in preparing the cost estimate during the schematic-design stage. It is based upon unit cost per square foot or metre, unit cost per cubic foot or metre, or cost per occupancy unit.

Working drawings and specifications. Once the detailed design has been approved by the client, the architect may move into the development of working drawings and specifications. These are essentially the contract documents, upon which depend exactness in construction-cost estimating and the effectiveness of the contractor to determine the current market price by competitive bidding. A good set of working drawings is clear and simple, arranged in an orderly and readable manner on the sheet, and accurately drawn, so that scaled measurements agree with the illustrations. In general, the working drawings include the design, location, and dimensions of the elements of the building.

The plans and elevations prepared during the design development can be used for the working drawings if they are at the same scale. As the working drawings develop, details of parts of the building are made at large scale (in some cases full scale) to indicate how the various materials and parts fit together. Dimensions are established as soon as possible, so that those working on other phases of the project can use them.

In addition, schedules included on the working drawings present information on room finishes, wall finishes, floor finishes, hardware, opening lintels and arches, columns and footings, doors and frames, lighting fixtures, kitchen equipment, and laboratory equipment.

During the development of the working drawings, a detailed set of specifications is prepared. Specifications, the written description of the work to be done, form part of the contract and describe the quality of materials, workmanship, and the scope of the work to be performed in constructing the building. Typically, the sections are arranged in the order in which the respective building trades normally begin their work. Specifications also facilitate the assignment of the work to subcontractors and separate contractors; for example, for special equipment to be installed in a hospital or laboratory. Each section includes a description of the scope of the work and a description of the various categories of material and labour.

Arrangement of specifications

After the award of the contract, the construction phase begins, and a list of subcontractors and a cost breakdown are furnished by the successful contractor. At this point the contractor becomes a part of the team with the owner and the architect; one of the first tasks during the construction phase is the preparation of the necessary formal agreements among the different parties and supplying of bonds to guarantee performance of work.

ELEMENTS OF BUILDING CONSTRUCTION

Surveying procedures. The first step in beginning any actual building at the site is either a land survey or laying out the building foundation on the site. If a large parcel of land is involved in a proposed development and it is necessary to establish new boundaries or if it is necessary to establish subboundaries inside the land acquired for the project, a land survey is undertaken. Laying out the building on the site is done by marking each corner of the proposed building and running string lines from corner to corner.

In laying out a building foundation, the first step is to locate one corner of the building. This first corner can be located by measuring a specified distance from a curb or other given point, depending upon the site layout in the architectural drawings. At this point a stake can be driven. A transit or level can then be set up over the first stake and the building lines set. Once the lines are set, wood batter boards (two horizontal boards nailed to stakes approximately 4 to 10 feet [one to three metres] outside the corners of the building) may be erected. The actual excavation line may then be laid out using string with the ends tied to the batter boards. At this point the site is ready for excavation.

Foundations and footings. Those portions of a building resting upon the earth or rock are known as the foundations or footings. The foundation is closely dependent upon the design and weight of the building and on the conditions and behaviour of the subsoils involved. As a result, detailed study must be given to calculating the size of the foundation and its strength as well as determining the characteristics and resistance of the earth or bed upon which they rest. Thus, the two sets of forces—those applied by the structure itself and those applied by the subsoil beneath the structure—must balance with each other. If the subsoil is unable to develop the needed forces of resistance to the forces of the building, functional failure will occur in the form of excessive or unequal settlement.

Three methods are employed to achieve the proper size of foundation for supporting a building. In the first, foundations may be spread to distribute the load over the earth or bed so that the safe bearing capacity of the bed per square foot is not exceeded. Alternatively, excavations can be made through unstable materials until a stratum of soil or bed of rock is reached, the bearing power of which is sufficient to carry the loads. The foundations as a whole or the footings under individual walls and columns are then built upon this base. These footings may also be spread to distribute the load. In the third method, long shafts of wood or concrete known as piles are driven into the ground until they are sufficiently embedded to carry the loads without further sinkage or until their lower ends rest upon rock. The footings and column bases are then built upon the tops of these piles.

Testing the earth under a structure

The first element of foundation construction is to test the strength of the material upon which the proposed foundation is to sit. Several methods of testing in common use involve determining not only the nature of the materials that might be encountered but also what underlies them and at what depths water or rock might be encountered. The four typical methods of testing are test pits, auger borings, wash borings, and core borings. Test pits may be dug in the ground to explore the actual conditions. Auger borings are made with an ordinary two-inch or 2½-inch auger fastened to a pipe or rod. The auger may be removed after a few turns, exposing samples of the strata. A wash boring may be used when the material is too compact for good results with an auger. The equipment for a wash boring consists of a pipe, two to four inches (five to ten centimetres) in diameter, driven into the soil and containing a smaller jet pipe through which water is forced. The flow of the water washes the material at the bottom up to the surface, where it is collected and examined. Core borings, however, are probably the most dependable. These can penetrate to great depths, through all materials, including rock, and bring up complete cores of the material they pass through.

Footings and foundations for light buildings. Probably the simplest and most common foundation is the masonry-wall foundation, used under light wood-frame construction in such buildings as residences and apartment houses. The foundation can be rather shallow, extending only to below the frost line, or quite deep, acting as the basement wall. It must be of sufficient thickness to carry the imposed loads of the structure above and must also resist the lateral forces of the earth that push on the outside face. The footing for such a wall foundation is usually plain concrete when the loads are small or reinforced concrete when the loads become heavier. Often a rectangular section having a depth of twice the projection from the face of the wall is adequate. Concrete masonry units of eight or 12 inches (20 or 30 centimetres) in thickness are then laid on top of the footing. Often the concrete masonry is reinforced with metal bars spaced 12 feet (3.7 metres) on centres and running from the footing to the top of the foundation wall.

When girders or roof trusses are supported on a wall, it is often necessary to thicken the wall, the foundation wall, and the footing to provide sufficient strength to carry the concentrated loads. In other cases a wide footing may be required to distribute the load from a wall so that the bearing capacity of the soil per square foot or metre is not exceeded. To save concrete and reinforcement the footing may be stepped from the width of the wall to the width required for the footing.

Footings for heavy buildings. Whenever a building—through its walls, piers, or columns—transmits such loads to the foundations that it is not economical or practical to use plain concrete footings, these may be combined or counterbalanced, and steel beams or reinforced concrete must be used. Although walls may at times be so loaded as to require reinforcement in the wall footings, heavy buildings are generally constructed so that they transmit their loads to the foundations through columns. These columns may be supported by a slab footing, a spread footing, a mat, or raft, foundation, or a pier. The slab footing and the spread footing are similar to that described above for light buildings. Of mat, or raft, foundation, there are two types—the beam-and-slab type and the flat-slab type. The beam-and-slab type is composed of beams running from column to column in both directions and slabs spanning from beam to beam; it is similar to a beam-and-slab floor construction except that the forces are inverted. The slabs lie on the underside of the beams and may be calculated as flanges of inverted T beams. An additional slab is constructed over the beams to provide a basement floor. The flat slab is similar to an inverted flat-slab floor construction except that a drop or slab thickening is placed under the slab at the column. The advantage of such a foundation is that the building will settle more uniformly. If the columns rested upon independent footings, some of which sank farther than others, severe cracking might occur throughout the structure.

Where piles are used, timber, precast or prestressed reinforced-concrete, or steel bearing piles are driven into the ground by a single-acting hammer or a drop hammer. The pile is driven down to a depth at which the soil resistance is adequate to resist the forces of the structure. The individual piles are designed to have the capability of transferring the load down to the point of sufficient soil resistance. Cast-in-place pier systems are excavated by the use of a mechanical auger in which concrete is placed. The Fondedile pile (Figure 3) is very much the same in principle. Here, a cutting ring is attached to a length of casing. The casing is then fed down to cut through the soil. Unlike ordinary cast-in-place piling, the Fondedile pile can reach to great depths by simply adding length of casing. The necessary reinforcing is then lowered into place and grout (waterproof cement) is forced to the bottom of the casing by pressure. As the grout rises, the drilling water also rises until it is expelled when the grout reaches the surface. The casings are then withdrawn one by one.

From R. Hammond, *Modern Foundation Methods;* Applied Science Publisher

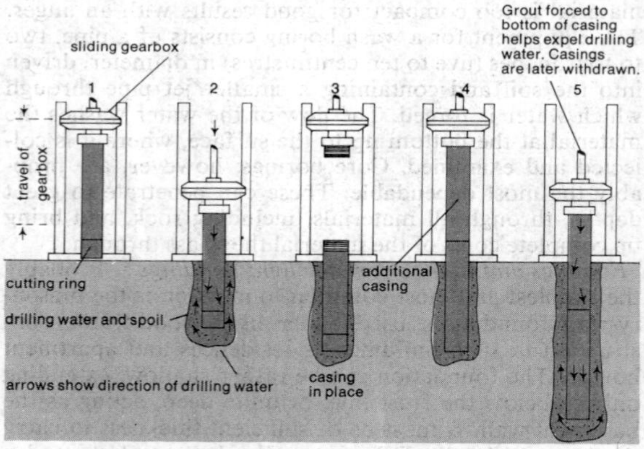

Figure 3: Sequence of operations for boring Fondedile pile in planting building foundations (see text).

Floating or caisson foundation

In areas where the soil condition is poor, a floating foundation or caisson foundation is used. There large areas are excavated in relatively deep positions. The floating foundation, or caisson, can be sufficiently rigid to resist all moments (tendencies toward movement) applied by the distribution of concentrated loads over its surface. Its function is to reduce the overall loading at any given point by relieving the weight of soil originally lying above such point and then replacing the soil by a structure of approximately the same weight or slightly more. The result is that the soil is in the same condition as before excavation began and settlement is greatly diminished.

The structural frame. The selection of one particular structural frame system over another is determined by consideration of the many elements that prevail in the basic design of any building. Understanding the primary uses of the structure will obviously determine the required clear distances between supporting walls or columns and the necessary live and dead loads that are imparted.

For small structures, such as residences, a 12- to 20-foot (3.7- to 6-metre) clear span may be common. In a two- or three-story office building, spans may commonly approach 25 feet (eight metres). Because these types of structures carry a relatively light load, the design may call for a wall-bearing (weight-carrying) structure, either masonry or wood, with the interior bearing on light steel columns or masonry walls. If the structure is to be a warehouse or one where machinery is housed, it may be necessary to design a reinforced concrete or steel frame, even if there are only two or three stories, because of the large concentration of load. In one-story structures in which the structural frame is not required to carry a heavy load, long-span light steel or laminated-wood roof supports bearing on masonry walls or steel columns may be used. In certain instances, fireproofing and soundproofing of the structural frame may be needed, in which case a light steel frame may not be adequate.

Though building codes often restrict the designer to a limited number of structural approaches, many systems are available; one must be selected that will most closely fit requirements of strength, economy, and quality of design. The availability and cost of materials and labour, and the efficiency of the frame in regard to the architectural concept are other important considerations that must be made in selecting the structural frame.

Wood frame. The wood frame, being light and simple, is most common in residences, apartments, and other small structures. The first step in wood-frame construction is a solid concrete or masonry foundation. On top of the foundation wall or basement wall rests a wood member called the sill, usually a nominal two inches (five centimetres) thick and having approximately the same width as the supporting foundation wall. It is bolted into the wall at equal intervals to prevent it and the members it supports from pulling away.

Balloon and platform frames

There are two common methods of constructing the exterior walls of a wood-frame building: the balloon frame and the platform frame. The essential characteristics of the balloon frame—a less rigid system than the platform but one that saves in labour and materials—are the studs (vertical framing members) that rest on the sill and extend in one piece from it to the top plate, regardless of whether it is one story or two. Studs are usually two inches thick by four inches wide (five by ten centimetres) spaced at intervals of 12, 16, or 24 inches (30, 40, or 60 centimetres). At the upper ends of the studs is the horizontal plate, which supports the ends of the roof rafters. The first-floor joists rest on the sill, and the upper floor joists rest on one- by six-inch (25- by 150-millimetre) ribbon boards that are placed, horizontally, between the inner faces of the studs and the corner posts. The top plate is a four- by four-inch (ten- by ten-centimetre) member and carries the roof rafters. The exterior wall is usually covered with some type of sheathing material such as insulation board or plywood, which is, in turn, covered with a finished surface such as wood siding, stucco, or brick veneer. The interior surface is usually covered with plaster or wood panelling. The roof rafters are covered with a roof decking, consisting of a plywood sheathing, and a finished material such as asphalt or wood shingles, tile, or metal. The floor joists are covered first by a subflooring material such as plywood or particle board and then by a finished flooring. The primary advantage of the balloon frame is its relatively smaller vertical shrinkage.

The main feature of the platform frame is that the entire first-floor construction can be completed before work is started on the framing for the first-story exterior walls and the interior partitions. This condition is achieved by first placing the floor joists on the sill and covering them with a sheathing material such as wood or plywood. The first-floor wall studs are then placed, including a top and bottom two- by four-inch plate. The second-floor platform can then be constructed before the second-story studs and roof rafters are raised. The primary advantage of the platform frame over the balloon frame is that it provides a work platform. Both the balloon frame and the platform frame can be modified to meet special conditions.

For more elaborate residences and small office buildings, a light steel frame or a structural masonry exterior wall is often used. These support open-web steel joists on which the roof or floor rests.

Steel frame. For many years, building codes limited tall structures over a certain height to steel frames. Although there have been many advances in concrete design and changes in codes allowing the use of the concrete frame for tall structures, there are still many advantages to steel construction. First, steel is easily and quickly assembled. Second, steel is physically less bulky than concrete. Third, steel is lighter in weight than concrete, an advantage in areas of poor soil bearing conditions.

The I beam

The most common structural-steel shapes used in building construction are wide flange beams, I beams, channels, T beams, angles, and plates. Of these, the I-shaped form is the most popular. It is economical for its weight because a large proportion of the steel is concentrated in the top and bottom flanges at which points the greatest stresses occur and can be resisted. Steel channels are convenient in certain locations in which design considerations are limited to size or in which overall strength can be reduced. Steel angles—which may be used as beams for short spans and light loads and especially as lintels over openings supporting brick, concrete block, or stone masonry—are also important as members of built-up sections such as columns, trusses, and girders and as connection members. Steel T sections are often used as top and bottom chords of welded steel trusses and as framing members for roof systems. Steel plates are used for webs of built-up girders and columns and as flange and web reinforcement. There are two general forms of wide-flange shapes. The narrow and deep forms are more suitable for beams and girders, and the nearly square forms for column sections. These various shapes are fabricated in the shop by rivetting and welding when a desired built-up section is needed. Each member is cut to the proper dimension and shape and fastened together to form a complete member.

A structural-steel building frame consists of a series of columns, girders, and beams. The column is a vertical support while the girders and beams are horizontal members. Thus, the column supports the weight transferred to it from the girders and any other materials attached directly to it such as masonry, precast concrete, or metal panels. The girders in turn support the beams that carry the floor loads, including interior partitions, ceiling systems, and mechanical systems, the interior live load including the building occupants and furnishings, and such added loads as wind or snow. The sizes and spacing of these members are dependent upon engineering calculations that take all of the load factors into consideration. In order to minimize total cost and to have an efficient floor plan, the size and spacing of these members are maximized in terms of the building's function and cost.

In wall-bearing construction, the exterior and interior walls serve as the end support for the steel beams that carry the weight of the subfloors, finish floors, interior partitions, ceiling systems, mechanical systems, building occupants, and interior furnishings, as well as the roof deck and finish roofing membrane. In such cases, the bearing walls eliminate the necessity for columns and girders.

Field erection of these steel members is accomplished by raising them into position by a crane and temporarily bolting them. Once these members are finally positioned, final rivetting, bolting, or welding can take place. As the framing progresses upward, other required secondary steel framing members are attached, such as the subfloor, exterior wall system, roof system, ceiling system, finish floor, and interior partitions.

Lift-slab system

Probably one of the most unique forms of steel-frame construction is the lift-slab system, a combination of steel frame and concrete flooring. The steel columns are first erected, and the floor slabs are cast on the ground, one on top of the other, separated by a membrane of melted paraffin. At each column location, a steel collar is integrally cast with the slab as a means of securing the floor slab to the column when it has been lifted to its permanent position. When the floor slabs have been cured (set) sufficiently, usually 10 to 14 days, they are individually lifted into position by means of a hydraulic jack placed on top of each column. The last slab cast is the first to be raised, and when it reaches its proper height, the steel collar in the slab is welded to the column. The remaining slabs are then raised and secured in the same manner. Column spacing of 20 to 24 feet (six to seven metres) is the most economical and should not exceed 12 columns for any one lift.

Concrete frame. For a long time the design of concrete structures imitated the typical steel design of column, girder, and beam. With technological advances in structural concrete, however, its own form began to evolve. Concrete has the advantages of lower cost than steel, of not requiring fireproofing, and of its plasticity, a quality that lends itself to free flowing or boldly massive architectural concepts. On the other hand, structural concrete, though quite capable of carrying almost any compressive (vertical) load, is extremely weak in carrying significant tensile loads. It becomes necessary, therefore, to add steel bars, called reinforcement, to concrete, thus allowing the concrete to carry the compressive forces and the steel to carry the tensile (horizontal) forces.

Reinforced-concrete framing

Structures of reinforced concrete may be constructed with load-bearing walls, but this method does not use the full potentialities of the concrete. The skeleton frame, in which the floors and roofs rest directly on exterior and interior reinforced-concrete columns, has proven to be most economical and popular. Reinforced-concrete framing is seemingly a quite simple form of construction. First, wood or steel forms are constructed in the sizes, positions, and shapes called for by engineering and design requirements. The steel reinforcing is then placed and held in position by wires at its intersections. Devices known as chairs and spacers are used to keep the reinforcing bars apart and raised off the formwork. The size and number of the steel bars depends completely on the imposed loads and the need to transfer these loads evenly throughout the building and down to the foundation. After the reinforcing is set in place, the concrete, a mixture of water, cement, sand, and stone or aggregate of proportions calculated to produce the required strength, is placed, care being taken to prevent voids or honeycombs.

Building codes require that test samples of the concrete that is used in every placement be made so that the actual strength of the concrete is determined and compared to the required strength needed to carry the imposed loads. After the concrete has set and cured for a specified period of time, the forms may be removed and moved to a new location for the next placement. As the finished frame moves upward, the exterior walls on the lower floors may be erected. These walls may be placed between or over the face of the exterior columns and are non-load-bearing. They are often concrete or masonry panels or even glass and metal curtain-wall systems. The interior partitions, also non-load-bearing, can then be erected. The floor and roof are integral parts of the building frame and need only to receive the finish materials.

One of the simplest designs in concrete frame is the beam and slab. This system follows ordinary steel design but uses concrete beams that are cast integrally with the floor slabs. The beam-and-slab system is often used in apartment buildings and other structures where the beams are not visually objectionable and can be hidden. The reinforcement is simple, and the forms for casting can be utilized over and over for the same shape. The system, therefore, produces an economically viable structure.

With the development of flat-slab construction, exposed beams can be eliminated. In this system reinforcing bars are projected at right angles and in two directions from every column supporting flat slabs spanning 12 or 15 feet (four or five metres) in both directions.

Prestressing and posttensioning

Reinforced concrete reaches its highest potentialities when it is used in prestressed or posttensioned members. Spans as great as 100 feet (30 metres) can be attained in members as deep as three feet (90 centimetres) for roof loads. The basic principle is simple. In prestressing, reinforcing rods or high tensile strength wires are stretched to a certain determined limit and then high-strength concrete is placed around them. When the concrete has set, it holds the steel in a tight grip, preventing slippage or sagging. Posttensioning follows the same principle but the reinforcing is held loosely in place while the concrete is placed around it. The reinforcing is then stretched by hydraulic jacks and securely anchored into place. Prestressing is done on individual members in the shop and posttensioning as part of the structure on the site.

In some instances in which long clear spans must be met, heavy wood construction offers advantages. A heavy post-and-beam frame may hold up two- or three-ply laminated-wood floors. Another important use of wood is in the laminated-wood arch or truss. The arch is made up of several thicknesses of wood glued together and shaped into the required form. All shapes and sizes are possible and spans of 120 feet (40 metres) can be achieved. One of the greatest advantages of the heavy wood arch is its resistance to heat as compared to that of steel. In extreme heat, steel loses its strength quickly, and the possibility of its collapse increases. Wood, however, chars slowly and therefore loses its strength slowly.

Other frame systems. There are also other structural frame systems, which, although they differ in appearance from the wood, steel, or concrete frames, use many of the same principles. Framing methods such as the dome, the arch, and the vault are most common. Domes are frequently used as roofs for structures requiring large circular floor areas. They are constructed of self-supporting reinforced-concrete shells or may be made of various types of wood, steel, and aluminum sections arranged in a great variety of patterns. A dome exerts a force outward around its entire perimeter. These forces are resisted by what is known as a tension ring. The dome and tension ring are usually supported on columns spaced around the perimeter and braced to add lateral stability.

The arch is a common system used to span openings in walls or areas in square or rectilinear buildings. The concept of the arch is to transfer overhead loads down on either side of the opening or clear area. Masonry components of brick or stone are used to span door or window openings; and wood, steel, or reinforced concrete are used to span large clear areas. Arches may be formed in many shapes (Figure 4) and hinged in many ways to carry the imposed loads. A vault, an arch that runs continuously from one end of the roofed area to the other, is usually constructed of reinforced concrete, solid-arch ribs, or trussed-arch ribs of steel or wood.

From W.C. Huntington, *Building Construction: Materials and Types of Construction*, 3rd ed., Copyright 1929, 1941 by Whitney C. Huntington, Copyright © 1963 by John Wiley & Sons, Inc.; reprinted by permission

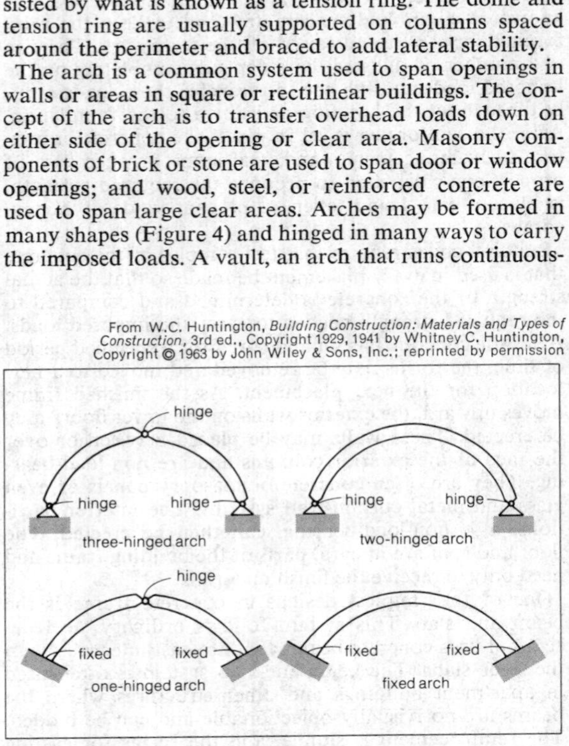

Figure 4: Selected types of arches.

Floor systems. The primary purpose of the floor system in any building is to support the weight of the functions and activities to be carried out there. Thus, the floor system must be capable of supporting the occupants; the interior furnishings and equipment; and the weight of the materials in the floor system itself and of other interior partitions. In addition to this function a floor system must work together with the structural frame to stiffen the structure and to help the frame resist the loads placed upon it. Before the design of a floor system can be finally determined, several factors must be considered.

Requirements for a good floor system

Besides being able to support the imposed loads and providing stiffness to the structural frame, a floor system must be capable of transmitting its load to the structural frame; must meet the code requirements concerning fire resistance and strength; must lend itself to the placing of any auxiliary systems such as elevators, stairs, or electrical and plumbing systems; and must meet certain cost limitations imposed by the building budget.

Wood floor systems. For light frame construction such as residences or apartments, the most common floor system consists of wood or steel joists supporting both subflooring and finish flooring. The joists are usually nominal two-inch- (five-centimetre-) thick wood members, the depth depending on their span, but spaced 12, 16, or 24 inches (30, 40, or 60 centimetres) apart. In heavy wood construction, joists may be three or four inches (75 or 100 millimetres) in thickness. In other cases open-web steel joists may be used. Their actual dimensions may vary from the wood joist dimensions but the spacing may be similar.

The subflooring first provides a working surface during construction and later provides support for the finish floor, which is typically thinner and considerably more expensive than the subfloor. The subfloor may also be more fire-resistant and provide additional soundproofing. It may be ordinary wood sheathing in nominal one-inch- (25-millimetre-) thick boards or plywood panels in four- by eight-foot (1.2- by 2.4-metre) sheets.

Just as the floor system provides lateral stiffness to the frame, cross bridging (*i.e.*, nailing small diagonal crosspieces between joists) provides stiffness to the floor joists. Cross bridging also helps in distributing loads over the entire floor.

Steel or composite floor systems. In steel-framed buildings the floor system is typically supported by open-web steel bar joists or steel beams. The spacing of these members is dependent upon the same factors described above for steel frames. A variety of floor decks may be placed over the bar joists or beams. This deck is typically ribbed or cellular and varies in depth from 1½ to 7½ inches (40 to 190 millimetres). In the erection process it follows the placement of the bar joists or steel beams with the advantage that it can be used as a working platform during construction and can serve as the formwork for the finish concrete. It is also capable of carrying electrical wiring and can act as an air duct if its rib is deep enough. The most common metal deck is the cellular floor section. It is typically 1½ or three inches (40 or 75 millimetres) in depth and may be covered on the bottom by sheet metal. As a result, an open channel is formed inside the panel. Although the deck comes in various lengths, it is most economical in relation to span and thickness at about ten feet (three metres) in length. Once the deck is in place and all work in relation to it is completed, the deck is covered with concrete.

Use of precast concrete slabs

Besides the steel deck, a precast concrete slab or precast hollow-core concrete slab may be used. The precast concrete slab may be relatively small in dimension (two-foot [60-centimetre] widths) and supported by the steel joists or beams at the ends. The longitudinal joists between the slabs are usually filled with a high-strength grout. As a result, the concrete panels accept a superimposed load more uniformly.

Similar to the concrete panel is the precast hollow-core concrete slab, six or eight inches (15 or 20 centimetres) in depth and 16 or 24 inches in width. The length varies according to the span. Hollow cores that run the length of the panel tend to lighten the dead load and also provide a conduit for electrical wiring or heat. Similar to their precast-concrete counterpart, these panels are supported by the steel beams, and, because of a metal plate cast into the ends of the panels, they can be tack welded to the steel beams to prevent shifting during construction.

Reinforced-concrete floor systems. The floor system in a reinforced structure is commonly constructed in a monolithic manner with the framing system. In buildings with heavy floor loads, a system known as flat-slab construction is common, in which a concrete slab is reinforced in two directions and supported only by the structural columns. It becomes practical in systems in which the floor panels, as defined by the location of the columns, are approximately square. The tops of the columns may be built up with a capital and a drop panel that help transfer the floor loads down the column (Figure 5).

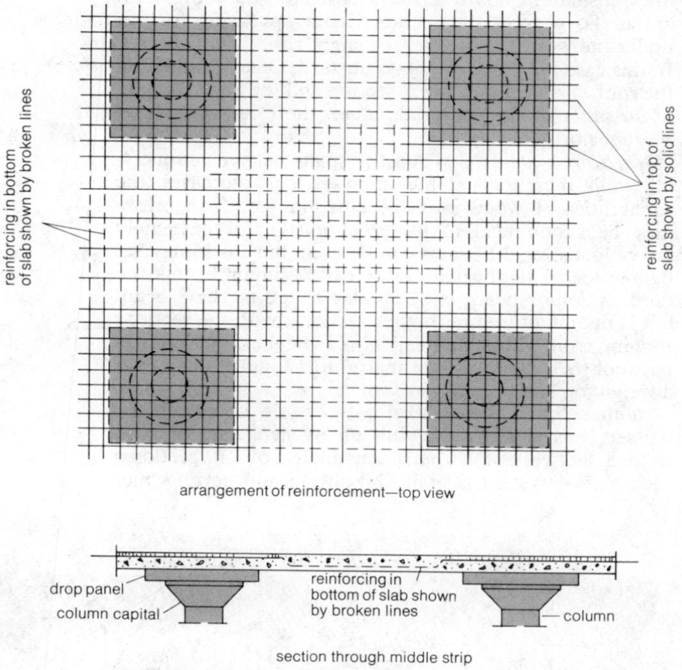

Figure 5: Two-way flat-slab construction with capital and drop panel (see text).

In structures with lighter loads, a flat-plate floor system is often used, similar to the flat-slab system except that the capital and drop panel are removed and the underside of the floor slab is uninterrupted. Its advantage is that for the same ceiling height in any other system, flat-plate construction results in a much lower story height. Another type of floor system is the slab band, which employs the wide and shallow beam that runs continuously over each row of columns. It is placed in a monolithic manner with the slabs that span between.

In the flat-slab, flat-plate, and slab-band systems, a large part of the concrete on the lower side is unnecessary; to save on concrete and reinforcing steel and in effect reduce the weight of the slab, ribbed-slab systems have been developed that remove this material. These ribs are made wide enough to resist the shearing stresses and to carry the necessary tensile steel. If it becomes necessary to support the slab on all four sides, ribs are placed in two directions. The ribbed-slab system is appropriate for spans of ten to 35 feet (three to 11 metres) but can be used for longer spans. As with the steel-deck system, these ribbed slabs can help carry wiring and air-conditioning and heating ducts.

Floor finishes. A variety of materials are available for the floor finish or wearing surface. This surface is applied over the wood or concrete subfloor. The most popular materials for light frame construction are wood, tile, terrazzo, and resilient tile or sheet. Typical materials for commercial and industrial building construction are resilient tile or sheet, concrete, terrazzo, and tile.

Flooring materials

Oak, yellow pine, and maple are the woods most generally used, for they have the highest resistance to wear in comparison to other woods. Matched flooring, plank-finished flooring, parquet flooring, and wood-block flooring are the most common shapes and finishes of wood flooring used. The most common resilient floorings are asphalt tile, linoleum, and vinyl or rubber tile or sheet. Asphalt tile is made from asphalt or resinous binders, asbestos fibre, mineral pigments, and inert fillers by combining them under heat and pressure. The sheets are then cut into tiles that are resilient, nonabsorbent, reasonably stain proof and acid proof, moisture proof, and relatively inexpensive. Linoleum is composed of oxidized linseed oil, ground cork, wood flour, and a colouring material pressed to a burlap back at great pressure. Linoleum may be plain or solid in colour or may be stamped or printed with a pattern on the surface. It is sanitary, easily cleaned, resilient, and inexpensive. Rubber tile is made of synthetic rubber combined with fillers such as cotton fibre, various minerals, and colour pigments at high temperatures. Rubber tile is attractive, elastic, noiseless, durable, easily cleaned, but more expensive than asphalt tile or linoleum. Vinyl asbestos tile has asbestos fibres added to the combination of materials. Vinyl sheet is composed of thermoplastic binders, plasticizers, and granular mineral fillers and pigments in the required proportions to give the desired properties and colours. Vinyl tile is wear resistant, impervious, resilient, easily maintained, and attractive. The method of securing all these materials is by cementing directly to the wood or concrete floor.

Where moisture and dirt collection is a problem, finish floor materials such as terrazzo and glazed or unglazed ceramic tile may be used. Terrazzo consists of a mixture of cement, sand, and marble chips applied in a two-inch (five-centimetre) thickness over a concrete slab. To minimize possible cracking over a large area, small metal divider strips are inserted in the terrazzo finish every 24 to 30 inches (60 to 75 centimetres). Both glazed and unglazed tile, also frequently used, are made in many different colours and are quite wear resistant. Common styles of floor tile are semivitreous quarry tile, ceramic mosaic tile, and glazed tile. If these materials are applied on the floor, adhesive may be used. A thin set method consists of applying an adhesive to the concrete or wood, placing the tile, and filling the joints between the tile with a mortar. Another technique consists of applying a cement mortar bed over the concrete, placing the tile, and filling the joints between the tiles with a grout. Wall application of these tiles is similar.

Roof systems. Roof systems have the same type of structural support as floor systems: wood, steel, concrete. In addition, roof systems may be classified by their pitched or flat slope. Typical roof types are flat with wood rafters, flat with steel framing, flat with concrete framing, pitched with wood rafters, and pitched with steel framing. Flat roofs are used extensively on nonresidential buildings; these are sloped only slightly to insure drainage. Pitched roofs are used more frequently on residences and apartments. Common pitched roofs—such as shed, lean-to, gable, hip, gambrel, mansard, and deck—are illustrated in Figure 6. In selecting a particular roof system, the primary considerations are the materials used as the structural framing; the character and amount of the loads; the span; the degree of fire resistance; and the general character employed to meet economically the requirements of the entire building.

Wood roof systems. Many of the small structures being built today, such as houses and apartments, have wood framing. Loads are light; the frame is composed of many light members spaced close together, each carrying a relatively small load. The roof framing is supported on members (rafters) two inches (five centimetres) thick

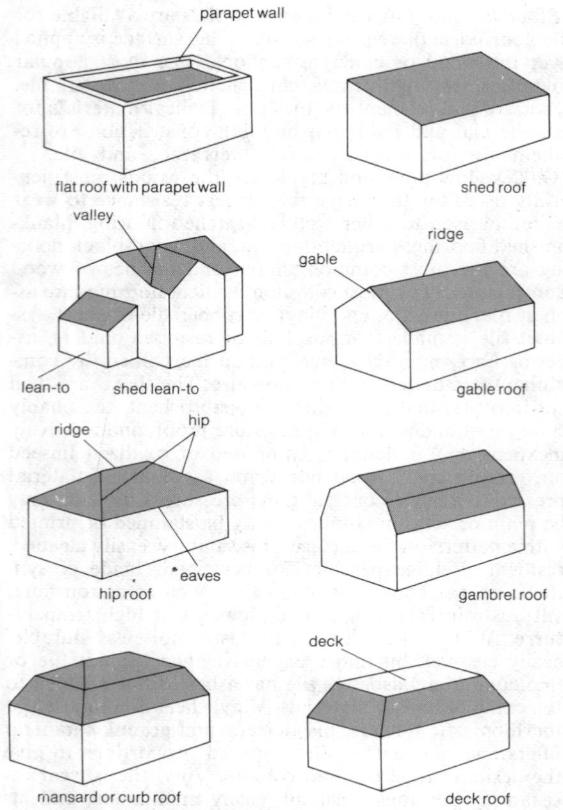

Figure 6: Common roof types.
From W.C. Huntington, *Building Construction: Materials and Types of Construction*, 3rd ed., Copyright 1929, 1941 by Whitney C. Huntington, Copyright © 1963 by John Wiley & Sons, Inc.; reprinted by permission

by four to 14 inches (ten to 35 centimetres) deep, usually spaced 12 to 24 inches (30 to 60 centimetres) apart, depending upon the imposed load. The rafters rest on the top wall plate and meet opposing rafters at the ridge (centre line of a house) or valley rafter. The outward thrust imposed on the rafters by the loads that each carries is counteracted by the ceiling joists that act as ties or collar beams. For great spans, it may be necessary to support the rafters to help carry the added loads. In many cases attic partitions or posts may be adequate for support. More frequently, trusses are used.

Wooden trusses

Trusses are composed of a number of triangles framed together. A triangle cannot change its shape without a change in the length of one of its sides. Therefore, in the truss composed of many triangles, every member is pulling or pushing against another—*i.e.*, is in tension or compression. In analyzing the loads imposed on a given truss, these individual members can be sized accordingly and be so made to keep the truss from failing or collapsing. There are many types of trusses; the proper one is determined by the length of span, the material of which it is constructed, and the manner of loading (Figure 7). Another important point about truss construction is that the truss is always designed so that the end reactions are vertical upon the supporting members. Horizontal movement may take place by sliding or rolling on the bearing plate. If the truss is designed so that the loads are transmitted in the direction of the slope of the truss, horizontal movement is restricted and causes the bearing structures to lean in an outward direction and the truss to act in the same manner as an arch. These considerations are common for both wood and steel trusses.

The usual method of constructing roofs with trusses is to space the trusses at regular intervals and to accommodate the loading and the particular size of the roofing material. Support between trusses is accomplished by purlins (horizontal members) that run from truss to truss.

A new development in spanning clear areas is the trussed rafter. Here, a truss of light material, usually wood two inches thick by four inches wide or two inches thick by six inches wide, is placed two feet apart and the roofing material is nailed directly to it. These trusses can be fabricated on the ground, in a shop, or on the site and then erected as a whole. They eliminate the need for interior bearing walls, thus considerably reducing labour and material costs. Trussed rafters have become ideal for spans of 20 to 40 feet.

Reinforced-concrete roof systems. A reinforced-concrete roof system is similar to the reinforced-concrete floor system, as described above. Typically, a reinforced-concrete roof system is a basic part of a total concrete structural frame. The roof system consists of a roof slab that is either flat or with ribs or joists underneath. A one- or 1½-inch- (25- or 40-millimetre-) thick insulation board, together with a built-up roof, is laid over the roof slab.

As well as a poured-in-place concrete roof system, a series of precast prestressed concrete T sections may be used, particularly for a one- or two-story building. These units may be single T or double T cross sections capable of spanning sizable distances. The sections provide a flat roof surface capable of carrying one- to 1½-inch-thick insulation board as well as a built-up roof membrane. To prevent the sections from appearing to give under the weight, a camber, or slight rise, is built into it. In this case the T section bows upward. Once installed on the roof, the weight of the T section and the added weight of the other roofing materials causes the T section to level out but not sag.

Steel roof systems. When the spans between supporting walls increase and the imposed load increases, the capabilities of wood joists become limited. It therefore may be economical to use steel joists. For extremely heavy loads, steel I beams can be used, but for somewhat lighter loads, lightweight joists called junior beams are used. A junior beam is of similar shape to the I beam but is manufactured in thinner sections, with the sections ranging from six inches deep with a weight of 4.4 pounds per foot (6.5 kilograms per metre) to 12 inches deep with a weight of 11.8 pounds per foot.

Another form of the steel joist is the open-web, or trussed, joist (Figure 8), built up of steel bars or rods welded between flat bars, channels, or T sections; such a roof system is light and strong and permits me-

From W.C. Huntington, *Building Construction: Materials and Types of Construction*, 3rd ed., Copyright 1929, 1941 by Whitney C. Huntington, Copyright © 1963 by John Wiley & Sons, Inc.; reprinted by permission

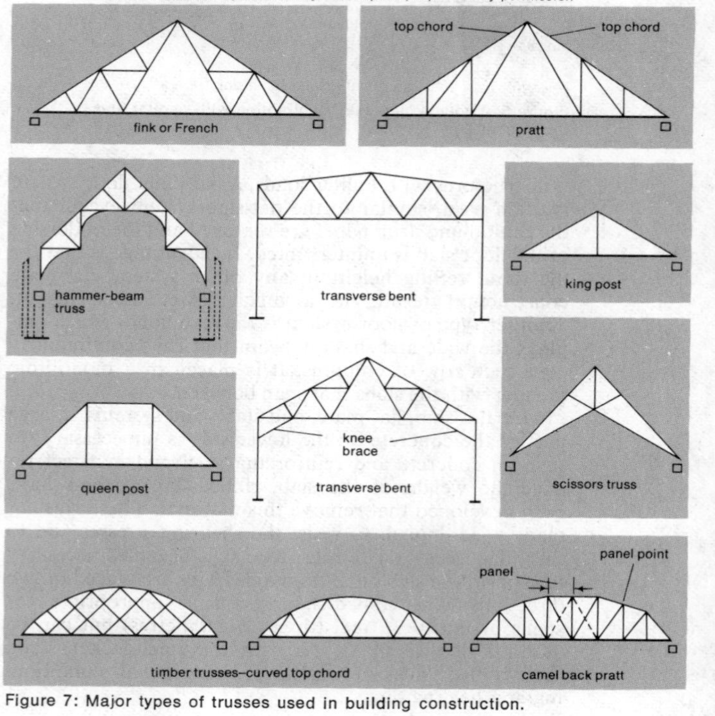

Figure 7: Major types of trusses used in building construction.

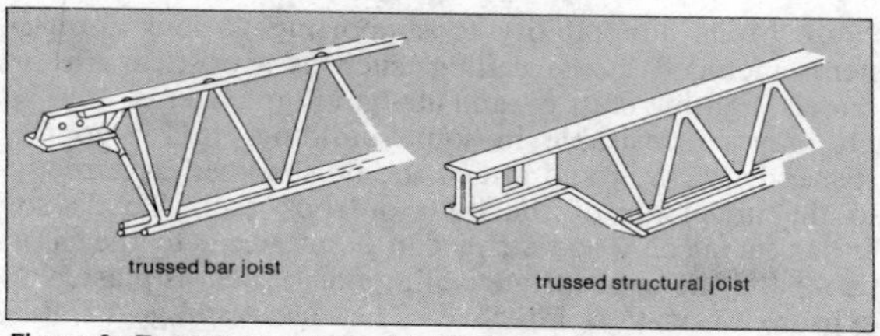

Figure 8: Two types of trussed joists for roof and floor supports.
From H.E. Parker *et al.*, *Materials and Methods of Architectural Construction* (1958); John Wiley & Sons, Inc.

chanical systems to occupy its open spaces. These are commonly called bar joists. Bar joists placed 12 to 30 inches (30 to 75 centimetres) apart are braced laterally to prevent them from twisting and often support a thin concrete slab reinforced in both directions. Wood nailing strips running perpendicular to the joists can be fastened on to permit laying of the finish roofing material.

Finish roof materials. A roof is covered with a finished material to provide protection from the elements. Many materials have proved to be satisfactory. The most generally approved types of materials are shingles of wood, asphalt, or asbestos; slate; tile; glass and sheet metal including tin, copper, lead, zinc, aluminum, steel, Monel metal, stainless steel; and built-up roofing (see below).

Wood shingles, used primarily in residential construction, vary in lengths and have random widths. They are laid horizontally, each row overlapping the preceding row and nailed to wood slats four or five inches apart.

Asbestos shingles

Asphalt shingles (made of asphalt-impregnated felt covered with crushed slate of various colours) are commonly used in residential construction because they frequently cost less and are more fire-resistant. Because the butt ends are relatively thin, a roof covered with this material gives a flat appearance.

Asbestos shingles, also used primarily in residential construction, are made to imitate wood shingles in shape and size and, to a slight degree, in appearance. Very durable and very fire-resistant because they are formed under great pressure and composed of about 15 percent asbestos fibre and 85 percent cement, these are nailed to plywood sheathing covered with felt or waterproof paper.

Slate, because of its very marked layers, is easily split into thin sheets. The slate sheets are drilled so that they may be nailed to felt covered sheathing. Slate is fire-resistant and durable but very heavy, so that the roof rafters or trusses must be designed to carry the additional load.

Clay roofing tile is made of wet clay pressed in molds and fired in kilns. It is fastened with copper nails to the roof surface, which is covered with an asphalt felt. Quarry tile, a large, red, unglazed rectangular or square tile, is laid in a bed of cement mortar spread over the top layer of built-up roofing.

Tin, copper, zinc, and lead have been used as roofing materials for many years. They are especially useful on flat roofs with too little slope for conventional shingles and on curved roofs. Tin roofing is made by coating sheets of iron or steel with tin, the sheets being laid over felt covered sheathing and the joints, either flat or standing seams, soldered tight. If tin roofing is kept well painted, it can successfully resist corrosion for as long as 50 years.

Probably the most popular of the metal roofing materials is copper. Although initially more expensive than tin, it requires no maintenance after installation because when it oxidizes it thus provides a protective coating for itself. Laid much as tin roofing, its seams are not soldered because the copper expands and contracts.

Lead roofing, long an accepted roofing material, is quite pliable and can be stretched to meet any surface requirements without being cut or soldered. Its weight and tendency to creep have long been disadvantages, but in the 1960s hard lead was developed with more tenacity and less expansion, reviving interest in lead roofing. Lead is also laid in much the same manner as tin and copper.

Flat glass is used for roofing greenhouses, and ribbed or prism glass may be inserted in domes or on the roofs of public buildings. Corrugated glass is often adapted to industrial buildings. When strength is required, wire glass is employed. High strength polyester plastic sheets have been developed for roofing: flat or corrugated; transparent, translucent, or opaque; in a wide variety of colours; and readily formed into many shapes.

Other roofing materials

Built-up roofing, which has been proved best adapted to flat roofs having great open areas, adjusts well to expansion and contraction, is considerably less expensive than sheet-metal roofing, and when properly laid may last for many years. It is composed of three to five layers of felt saturated with coal-tar pitch or with asphalt, each layer set in tar or asphalt. The top layer is finished with a covering of crushed slag or clean gravel or with a layer of flat quarry tile. It may be laid on wood-plank roof, concrete slabs, or cinder-concrete roof fill.

Space-enclosure systems. Space-enclosure systems are the exterior or interior walls or panels used in a structure to delineate the interior space; they may be classified as load-bearing or non-load-bearing. Load-bearing walls are capable of carrying structural loads imposed by the floor or roof, while non-load-bearing walls do not carry any additional load imposed by the structure. As a result, load-bearing walls can be used on the exterior to support the ends of the floor or roof joists or on the interior, if it is more economical than having the floor or roof joists span the entire width of the building. Non-load-bearing walls may also be used interchangeably. When non-load-bearing walls are used on the exterior, however, they either cover the face of the structural frame and are supported by the structural frame or they are in-fill panels that bear on the floor.

Load bearing and non-load bearing walls

Wood. Wood wall systems can be either load-bearing or non-load bearing and, thus, can be used either on the exterior or interior. They typically consist of two- by four-inch (five- by ten-centimetre) studs, 16 inches (40 centimetres) on centre, which bear on a sill and are capped by a wood top plate. In the case of exterior walls, an insulation bat or blanket is used to fill a portion of the void between the studs to provide adequate insulation, particularly in northern climates. The exterior finish consists of one or more materials such as insulation board, wood or plywood siding, cement plaster or stucco, aluminum siding, brick, stone, or plastic siding or paneling. The interior finish of the exterior wall typically consists of gypsum drywall, plywood, or plaster. These same finishes are also usually applied to the interior walls (Figure 9A). If it is necessary to minimize the amount of floor area consumed by interior partitions, the wood stud may be turned so that its narrower dimension is used for the wall thickness. To cover any construction joints which typically occur at the floor, at doors, and at windows, wood trim is most often used. At the floor, however, a rubber or vinyl base approximately four inches high may be employed, particularly in kitchens and bathrooms, in which water and moisture might be splashed against the base.

From W.C. Huntington, *Building Construction: Materials and Types of Construction*, 3rd ed, Copyright 1929, 1941 by Whitney C. Huntington, Copyright © 1963 by John Wiley & Sons, Inc.; reprinted by permission

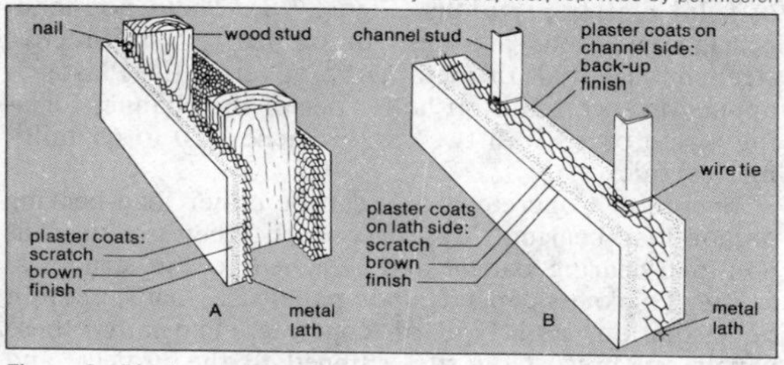

Figure 9: *Plaster construction.*
(A) Metal lath and plaster on wood studs; (B) metal lath and plaster solid partitions (see text).

Masonry. Masonry walls may be either load-bearing or non-load-bearing. If the walls are load-bearing, they should be thick enough to support loads without exceeding the compressive strength of the masonry units. If the wall is non-load-bearing, the thickness should be related to the unsupported height of the wall. In either case, there should be sufficient lateral support and, if necessary, wire-mesh reinforcing added to maintain wall integrity and strength. The masonry units most often used, individually or in combination, are brick, concrete block, structural clay tile, glazed tile, gypsum block, and stone, including granite and marble. If these materials are used in combination in the same wall, it is necessary to connect them, often by interlocking one material, such as brick, with a back-up material, such as concrete block or structural clay tile, a system that bonds the materials together. Sometimes a mechanical bond such as a wire or thin piece of metal is employed. If wood panelling, gypsum drywall, or plaster is applied over the masonry, a thin wood strip is attached to the masonry and the wood panelling or gypsum drywall is fastened to the strip. Plaster may be applied to a gypsum lath board in the same manner or directly to the masonry.

Use of mullions

Metal. In modern architectural design, the desire for large glass areas in the exterior wall has stimulated the use of prefabricated panels in curtain walls that are simply building skins with no load-bearing characteristics. Extruded aluminum or steel sections (called mullions) similar to I beams are placed over the frame. Between these mullions, windows and spandrel panels of aluminum, structural glass, marble, or precast concrete are attached. The spandrel panel is located between the head of one window and the sill of the window above. Great care must be taken by the contractor to make this system airtight and watertight.

The three basic types of curtain-wall systems are custom walls, commercial walls, and industrial walls. Custom walls are designed specifically for one building. Commercial walls are made up of members standardized by a manufacturer and assembled in stock patterns. In industrial walls, preformed sheets in stock sizes are used for the major surfaces along with standard metal windows.

For interior wall use, steel studs have become popular. These bear on galvanized runners at both the floor and ceiling and are spaced at 16-inch (40-centimetre) intervals. Four- by eight-foot (1.2- by 2.4-metre) sheets of gypsum drywall are fastened to the metal studs by concealed clips. Just as in the wood stud partition, the gypsum drywall is taped and covered with a joint compound or covered with decorative battens. In some cases, particularly in office buildings, metal panels are applied over the steel studs. These panels are typically designed so that they can be dismounted, moved, and reassembled in a new location. The concept is to provide a flexible interior and a low-cost wall system.

Another means of saving floor area is through the use of solid plaster partitions (Figure 9B). These non-load-bearing partitions are built of ¾-inch (19-millimetre) steel channel studs or metal lath, set vertically. Plaster is applied to metal lath on both sides of the channel forming a reinforced wall two to 2½ inches (50 to 65 millimetres) thick.

Concrete. Concrete panels can be either load-bearing or non-load-bearing. Most frequently, they are used as non-load-bearing panels and attached to the structural frame. Thickness depends upon panel size, loads, amount of insulation, and type of concrete. Typically, these panels are precast off site, shipped to the project, and raised in place by a crane. In relatively small structures, these precast concrete panels can be tilted into position—a method known as tilt-up construction. The panels in many cases are cast on site.

Surface treatment may consist of various forms of texturing or, in some cases, application of an aggregate to provide an even coarser texture. Where insulation is included in the precast concrete panel, the insulation material may be a polystyrene or polyurethane foam or cellular glass.

Ceiling systems. A finished ceiling is often hung at some distance below the underside of the floor system. In accomplishing this, a 1½-inch (40-millimetre) metal channel, called the runner channel, is hung from the floor system by rods, bars, or wires. This system has become quite popular, particularly in commercial buildings, because of its adaptability to supporting various components included in the ceiling, such as acoustical tile or panels, lighting fixtures, and air-handling systems.

It may be desirable in some buildings to forego the suspended ceiling and attach the finished ceiling directly to the underside of the floor or roof deck. To do so, either metal or wood strips can be attached to the floor deck, and the appropriate ceiling finish such as plaster or gypsum drywall is attached. The disadvantage of this method is that any deep girders or beams will project below the ceiling line and lighting fixtures must be suspended from the ceiling. Most designers prefer to conceal structural members, lighting fixtures, and mechanical equipment by suspending the ceiling or finishing around them.

Finish hardware. Hardware, an important aspect of the finish of any building, includes door knobs, locks, hinges, door closers and stops, push bars and plates, kick plates, thresholds, and door openers. Because these materials are in constant use and contact by the occupants, the designer chooses the hardware that will reflect and conform to the overall design of the structure. Hardware is made of materials that withstand a great deal of abuse and wear—such as stainless steel, chrome plating, aluminum, and bronze. Usually door knobs, lock face plates, strike plates, and cylinder faces are of noncorrosive metal. Hinges on the interior of the building are usually cold-rolled wrought steel, while on the exterior they are a noncorrosive metal with nonremovable pins. Automatic door-opening devices may be operated electrically, pneumatically, or hydraulically. An actuating mechanism starts a hydraulic or air pump or an electric motor that opens the door. The same type of device or a spring may shut the door.

Auxiliary systems. Another important element in building design and construction is the mechanical, or auxiliary, system—plumbing; heating, ventilating, and air conditioning; electrical wiring; vertical transportation; and chimneys and flues.

Plumbing systems. The purpose of the plumbing system in any building, whether residential, commercial, or industrial, is to provide clean water for drinking, cleaning, washing, and sanitary facilities and to remove and dispose of wastes. Governments long ago recognized the importance of plumbing and have taken steps to insure proper facilities through building codes. As a result, the codes are very specific as to the design and installation of the system. Pipe sizes, materials, connections, number of fixtures for both sexes, sewer lines, septic tanks, and drain or leaching fields are covered in great detail for all buildings and their type of occupancy.

In structures such as auditoriums, theatres, plants, and office buildings, sanitary facilities are based on the number of occupants expected to use the building in relation to the total usable floor area. In multifamily dwellings, facilities are determined by the number of families housed and the amenities demanded. In addition to providing water supply and liquid waste disposal for the occupants, it is also important to provide for cleaning facilities for both interior and exterior areas, air-conditioning equipment and heating systems, and for fire fighting.

Plumbing system planning

In designing plumbing facilities for any one building, the designer, besides considering the convenience of the occupants and the codes, must always keep the flexibility of the system in mind. Allowances must often be made for expansion to meet the requirements of an increasing need and use. These allowances are usually made by oversizing the initial equipment. Such advanced planning is valuable when expansion of the building is made or if the type of occupancy changes. These considerations can add to the resale or leasing value of the building.

In a sanitary waste system, it has been good practice to use extra heavy cast-iron soil pipe above and below the ground inside the building and to a point approximately five feet (1.5 metres) outside the building. From that point extra strength vitrified clay pipe may be used outside the building. Galvanized-iron, copper, or plastic pipe is typically used inside the building. Plastic pipe has become popular, however, because of its lower cost, limited maintenance, and resistance to corrosion. Horizontal sanitary pipes are laid at a slope, usually ⅛ inch per foot (about one centimetre per metre), to insure proper drainage and to prevent backup. Sanitary lines or drain lines have traps incorporated in the line to prevent the backup of unwanted gases into the building. These gases are vented through pipes that run vertically through the building and discharge through the roof to the outside. Vent pipe is usually galvanized iron, copper, or plastic. Codes are very specific about vents and vent sizes and how they are to be connected to various fixtures to help prevent gas and sewerage backup in the main sewerage lines.

Although storm water is also a form of waste, storm water and sanitary drains are kept separate. If the two are connected, the line may become overloaded during a heavy rainstorm thus overflowing, and bringing both storm water and sewage back into the building. Consideration is also being given to the size of the storm drain required in the particular geographic area in which the building is located. If the area is one of heavy rainfall, the lines are sized accordingly. Storm drains are usually galvanized or cast iron.

In buildings that have drains below the city's sanitary and storm sewer lines, sewage ejectors and sump pumps are employed. These are actuated by float valves that activate the motor when the collection of water and sewage has reached a certain level. The pumps, with waterproof motors, are capable of disposing all the waste and storm water into the city's lines. These pumps are usually made of special iron or bronze, ideal materials for such equipment in heavy use areas.

Cold-water supply systems usually use bituminous-coated cast-iron piping for the service between the street mains and the building. Inside the building, the distribution piping is usually galvanized iron, copper piping or tubing, or 85 percent red brass.

The hot-water system parallels the cold-water system except that a heat exchanger or a hot-water tank is used to warm the water. In some cases the system may be designed in a loop and a circulating pump used. Such a system returns the water to the generator to be reheated to provide hot water at the outlets. The hot-water tank is usually steel lined with a noncorroding coating. It contains controls that regulate the flow of the heating medium that in turn heats the surrounding water. The hot-water distribution piping is galvanized iron, copper, or red brass.

Though galvanized piping has been extensively employed in hot- and cold-water supply systems, the corrosive action of hard water on it has led to a preference for copper pipe or to treatment (softening) facilities or to both. Hard water contains a great quantity of dissolved minerals that deposit and collect on the walls of iron or steel pipe, as well as carbon dioxide that combines with water to form carbonic acid, the cause of most corrosion in iron or steel piping. Water can be softened at a centralized water-treatment plant or at the individual building with special equipment.

Necessity of system testing

In all the systems mentioned above, tests must be conducted before the system is closed in or covered over during construction. Water supply lines, for example, may be placed under abnormally high pressure to test strength and tightness. Waste and vent lines are filled with water or a pungent odor; lowering of the water level or the detection of the strong odor will indicate a leak. All water supply systems are tested to determine the actual flow rate as compared to the required flow rate.

Codes also require the installation of water systems for fire-fighting purposes in buildings having a high concentration of occupants or valuable contents. These systems are completely independent from the regular plumbing system. A common fire-fighting installation is the standpipe that consists of a vertical riser of black iron pipe, the size of which is determined by code according to the height of the building. The standpipe is connected to a permanent source of water and has an outlet at every floor. The number of standpipes, also set by code, is determined by the total floor area and building dimensions. The sources of permanent water are rooftop tanks or pumps connected to an outside main or other source.

For positive fire protection in high-risk areas, sprinkler systems are designed so that they may discharge water in spray form directly into the fire from outlets located in the ceiling. The spray outlets are opened when a small metal plug that holds the outlet closed is melted away by the heat. These plugs melt at temperatures from 135° to 165° F (57° to 74° C) and are often connected to an alarm system so that when the outlet is opened it will actuate a fire alarm (see also FIRE PREVENTION AND CONTROL).

Heating, ventilation, and air conditioning. Almost every modern building receives some form of heating, ventilation, and air conditioning, depending on the climate, the size of the building, and the availability and comparative cost of various fuels. To determine the proper system, the designer considers several factors. Of primary importance is the use of the building and the location and climate of the site. Based upon these factors the designer determines the desired inside temperature and the maximum variations in outside temperatures. Through the use of established equations and tabular data, the designer can determine the amount of heating or cooling needed to sustain such an inside temperature. Of course, consideration is given to the materials used and the quality and quantity of insulating material.

Central heating systems

In northern climates a central heating plant is generally used. In residences, apartment buildings, or small commercial buildings, the heating plant can be either a hot-water or steam boiler, or a forced-warm-air plant. In a hot-water system, hot water is circulated through either wall or baseboard convectors. These units are designed to transmit heat by moving air over and through their warm surfaces and are thermostatically controlled, and, as a result, the entire heating system can be adapted to zone heating, in which different areas can receive different amounts of heat.

In radiant heating, hot water is circulated in pipe coils placed in a concrete floor slab or in the ceiling. This system involves a danger of pipe leakage, however, and the difficulty and expense of repair.

In steam heating, steam is generated in a centrally placed boiler and transported through pipes to various locations in the building. Heat transfer then takes place in a manner similar to the hot-water system. As the heat is withdrawn from the steam, the steam condenses to water and flows back to the boiler.

A forced-air heating unit heats the surrounding air. The air is forced by a fan through ducts to the individual rooms. Cooled air is then returned to the plant through cold-air return ducts for reheating, thus keeping the air circulating. Fresh air is added directly from the outside or by air that infiltrates around windows and doors. Warm air from a forced-air system can be humidified by passing it through water. Furthermore, the system can be readily adapted to receive air conditioning. If the required heating load is low, floor furnaces, which are self-contained heating units installed under the floors, can be used.

For the small multiple-dwelling or business buildings, the calculation of heat load is the same in principle as that for a residence. The choice of the heating unit is, to some extent, dependent on whether or not the building is air conditioned. In general, an oil- or gas-fired hot-water or low-pressure steam boiler is used. Large areas are often heated by unit heaters in which air is blown by fans through coils which carry the hot water or steam.

In large office buildings, design of the heating unit is tied in with the ventilating and cooling systems. The basic calculations for heat loads are the same, but consideration is also given to prevailing winds and sun. Because the heating is closely associated with the ventilating and cooling systems, the heat is always transmitted by means of air that is warmed by passing over warm surfaces and blown into the desired spaces. The air is then recirculated and fresh air added mechanically. The heating plant can be a low-pressure hot-water or steam boiler, a heat exchanger, or a high-pressure steam plant that supplies steam for turbine-driven compressors for air conditioning and uses the "left over" low-pressure steam for heating. If electrical energy is economical, a low-pressure boiler is most practical. These systems are usually prefabricated units that are ready to install. If electrical energy is not economical and other fuels are, a high-pressure steam plant may be used that runs the air-conditioning compressors and heats the building. The distribution of the heat depends on the total design of the air-conditioning systems. In some instances the hot water or steam is sent to a series of window units around the perimeter of the building. These units then force air over the warmed surfaces. In other instances, the hot water or steam is supplied to coils located at central fan systems that blow air over the coils and then force the warm air through ducts to the desired areas.

Air-conditioning factors

Air-conditioning plants vary in size and capacity but all work on the same principle (for a detailed description of various systems, see HEATING, VENTILATING, AND AIR CONDITIONING).

In large buildings, certain areas may require heat while others require cooling. To supply each properly, the designer divides the building into zones and provides individual heating and cooling units for each zone. The number of zones required is determined by the climate, the orientation of the building, and the amount of wind.

Air conditioning also raises the problem of location of the plant in the building. It may conveniently be sited on the basement level or on the roof. If it is placed in the basement the structural frame does not need to be strengthened to carry the additional load, and installation and service are easier. The boiler stack and condenser lines, however, must carry to the roof, thus eliminating valuable space, and there may be basement waterproofing problems. Among the advantages of roof placement are the fact that the condenser water and the chilled water lines are at a minimum because the cooling tower and the fan units are close by and that centralized maintenance and controls are facilitated. Utility lines must be extended to the roof, however, and the structural frame and floors must be completed before installation. An increasing number of new high-rise buildings are placing their air-conditioning plants on the roof.

Air-distribution methods

There are four methods of distributing air that are generally used. The first is the high- and low-pressure system. Here, small diameter air ducts are run up the perimeter of the building along the exterior columns. The ducts carry warm or cool air at a fairly high velocity. The air is carried to induction perimeter units that further heat or cool the air and then release it into the space. For interior conditions, large ducts carry air at low velocity to ceiling louvres or diffusers. A single-duct system is often used in small buildings. The air is distributed to the floors by means of two vertical ducts, sent through a tempering coil, and distributed into every space by ceiling diffusers. A third system is the double-duct, a complex of main vertical and branch horizontal ducts that carry high-pressure warm air and a parallel series carrying high-pressure cool air. The horizontal ducts end in mixing boxes located in the ceilings in every area that is controlled by a thermostat. Fourth, is the perimeter window unit. These units consist of a series of coils that carry either hot or cold water. Thin metal fins are bonded to these coils so that the maximum metal surface is presented to the air that flows over them. The air that comes from the vertical high-pressure riser ducts enters a large chamber under the coils where its pressure is reduced. As the fresh warm or cool air blows over the coils, its velocity induces room air to enter the chamber and mix with it.

The entrance of fresh air is provided by a ceiling plenum reinforced by exhaust ducts running in the hung ceiling space. A ceiling plenum is the space between the underside of the floor and the top of the hung ceiling. The exhaust air moves into this space through ceiling exhaust louvres. It is pushed in by the incoming conditioned air and is circulated by fans to vertical risers that empty into the outside air.

Other important factors supplemental to the total design of the heating and cooling systems are sound abatement, water treatment, and the control system. The control systems are the most important, because they must be able to maintain predetermined temperatures and humidities during all seasons and for every work activity. The system performs this task by first measuring the changes in temperature and humidity in the various areas or zones. It then must convert the observed changes into energy impulses, either pneumatic or electrical, and, finally, correct the system by means of the controlling devices.

Electrical systems. An electric current in buildings typically is carried by a wire of copper, aluminum, or other metal, but liquid or gas may also conduct electricity. To provide for interchangeability of electrical appliances and devices and for low cost, voltage ratings have been standardized, though the standards vary in the United States, western Europe, and elsewhere. Higher voltages are required for air-conditioning systems, pumps, fans, and elevators than for lighting.

Electrical services may be as simple as those installed in a single-family residence or as complicated as those that are installed in hospitals or nuclear power plants. Whatever the installation, the designer should always make provisions for expansion of the system. Even in the single-family residence, with its increasing number of electrical appliances, it is difficult for a designer to predict the extent of any future expansion.

Electrical service is delivered to a building by dropping service wires to a meter, usually outside the building. Wiring fed through the wall to the panel box is distributed to the various circuits through circuit breakers or fuses, the function of which is to prevent overload. In office buildings the designer must consider the many machines that will be used in great quantities, such as typewriters and calculators, or devices that draw an extremely large load, such as computers. In manufacturing plants such equipment demands heavy electrical loads. By determining a total electrical load for the building, the designer can make the necessary provisions for installing transformers of the proper size. These transformers will carry the total load and reduce it to the required service load needed. The basic theory behind the reduction in current by the transformer is that the higher the voltage coming into the transformer the more efficient the transmission of electricity to the various outlets. From the transformer the electrical service is brought to panel boxes similar to those used in residential construction but providing many more circuits. The circuits are fused and distributed to the area where the service is needed.

Circuit wiring

Circuit wiring can be brought to the area between the suspended ceiling and the structural floor or it can even be brought through the floor itself if it is composed of a steel deck or concrete components with sufficient cell space. Wiring can also be brought through the interior partitions if there is a hollow base suitable for distributing the wire. Where a heavy use of electrical current is needed, provisions may be made for under-floor raceways that may be tapped at desired locations. The raceway can be incorporated in the floor system, or it can be a separate duct laid over the structural floor. Bus ducts are sometimes used that contain four copper or aluminum bus bars—rectangular, round or tubular—used as conductors for very high currents. The bus ducts are prefabricated and can be bolted together to form any length.

Interior illumination of a building is often the most important consideration in designing the electrical service. An office or industrial building requires nonglare, evenly distributed lighting. Lighting level requirements vary for many reasons, but a level of 65 to 85 footcandles of illumination is usually adequate for office buildings. Drafting or design work areas require higher levels. Illumination levels must be analyzed for every situation and designed to fit the need. Important considerations are: the type of work performed, ceiling height, spacing of fixtures, the quality of light, and the size of the fixture. Other considerations such as the design of the fixture and the lens and its maintenance factor are also important. Well-proven formulas and tabulated data have been prepared to help the designer study these factors and make a decision that will be advantageous to the owner and those who live or work in the building (see also LIGHTING AND LIGHTING DEVICES).

Vertical transportation systems. The two most common types of vertical public transportation are the passenger elevator and the escalator. The freight elevator and the dumbwaiter are the primary types used for materials handling. The need for elevators became evident when high-rise buildings began; advances in elevator design have enhanced the flexibility of multistory buildings.

The essential characteristics of an ideal vertical transportation system are prompt availability of cars at any level and in either direction; minimum delay in starting; rapid and comfortable acceleration; constant high speed after acceleration; rapid and comfortable deceleration; quick levelling at the landing; and rapid opening of the doors. All this should be achieved with smoothness, quietness, and complete safety to passengers.

Elevator handling capacity

An initial consideration in the design stage is the handling capacity per elevator. The elevators must be capable of transporting a certain percentage of the total occupancy of a building at peak travelling times within a certain time span. The designer must also determine the number of passengers the elevators are likely to carry and the round trip time of the elevators. It has been determined that the number of passengers per trip never normally exceeds 80 percent of the carrying capacity of the elevator, because many passengers alight at intermediate floors. Given the rate of speed of the needed elevator, the designer can calculate that 80 percent of the capacity of that elevator will be carried in the time it takes for a total round trip, or x amount of people in the assumed time span. If a certain percentage of the total occupancy is to be transported in this assumed time span, he can, therefore, determine the number of elevators required. By dividing the round trip time of the elevator by the number of elevators, the designer can determine the waiting interval between elevators. A specification for a 20- to 30-story high-rise building may call for: as many as six cars with 3,500-pound (1,600-kilogram) capacity travelling at 1,000 feet (300 metres) per minute. Such a specification provides much flexibility for shifting floor occupancies.

The requirements for a freight elevator differ. Freight elevators are used primarily for transporting office supplies, janitorial equipment and personnel, and heavy or bulky loads. A single freight elevator, consisting of a 4,000-pound (1,800-kilogram) car travelling at 500 feet (150 metres) per minute, is generally adequate for a multistory office building of about 600,000 square feet. A freight elevator must be much larger in physical dimensions and total carrying capacity, however, than the passenger elevator.

The mechanical equipment used for elevators in high-rise buildings are the geared traction machine or the gearless traction machine. The geared traction machine consists of a high-speed electric motor that drives a hoisting sheave by means of a worm-and-gear reduction unit. It is run on alternating current (ac) which comes directly from the power lines. Alternating current, though economical, causes a jerky ride, and levelling the car is difficult, creating a hazard to the occupants. A direct current (dc) motor provides flexibility in speeds and a smooth ride. The gearless traction machine consists of an ac–dc motor generator that drives the dc hoisting motor. The hoisting motor is directly connected to a sheave over which hoisting cables travel to raise and lower the car and counterweight. Such machines can easily handle elevators of 10,000-pound (5,000-kilogram) capacity and 1,800-feet- (550-metre-) per-minute travelling speed. The gearless traction machine gives a great flexibility in speed and smooth operation. It is advantageous in handling large numbers of passengers in a short period of time. Freight elevators are always operated by geared traction because of their heavy use.

Elevators are always equipped with safety devices that are positive and "failsafe." No car can start unless the outer and inner doors are closed, thereby closing the operating circuit. If a person or object is in the door opening, an electric eye or a pressure-activated door edge reverses the motion of the door and causes it to open again. This device provides added safety for the individual passenger. The cables are of special steel designed to take continual bending and stretching. They are wrapped around both a primary and secondary sheave to prevent slippage. The counterweight is usually equal to the weight of the car plus 40 percent of the car capacity. It helps in relieving the motor of the full load, and if the motor does fail with a less than 40 percent load, it carries the car to its uppermost point. Limit switches, governor cables, and brakes control the speed of the car if it starts to travel faster than its present speed. An additional safety measure is hydraulic or heavy spring bumpers placed in the elevator pit that can absorb much of the force of a falling car.

The overall speed of the elevator service depends in great part on the operation of the door mechanisms. Door speeds of seven seconds for opening and closing time are usually accepted for a good operating system. A dc motor drives both doors through a gear reduction unit that enables the doors to open or close smoothly and completely. The doors are supported by rigid door hangers and move on sheave wheels; as they close, a projecting vane on the inner doors disengages, actuating the interlock mechanism which closes the electrical circuit and permits the car to proceed.

In modern elevators the pushbutton calling devices indicate the floor called until it has been reached and the direction in which the car is moving. Audible signalling devices are also sometimes used to indicate that the car is stopping.

The escalator

The escalator has become an increasingly valuable means of vertical circulation. It involves no waiting time, and a great number of people can be continually moved. A 48-inch- (1.2-metre-) wide escalator moving at 120 feet (40 metres) per minute can move between 6,700 and 10,700 people per hour. Escalators can be placed in a variety of patterns, depending on available space, the desired direction of circulation, and economics.

The mechanism is composed of a running gear or moving steps that carry the passengers. On either side is a fixed balustrade with a handrail on top that moves at the same speed as the steps. The equipment is supported on a track and a steel truss. Movement is supplied by a dc motor that provides a smooth and even ride. Since the escalator is continually moving, the electrical consumption is much lower than that of the elevator. There are basically two types of escalators, the flat-step and the cleat-step type. Both operate in the same manner, but the difference is in the method of entering and leaving. The flat step consists of a number of steps which are held flat forming a moving platform. The passenger enters on the platform and gradually the steps are formed as the escalator moves upward. At the top, this pattern is reversed. This type requires added floor area at the top and bottom. The cleat step has longitudinal cleats, and by a combing action, they appear and disappear without the use of a platform. This enables the passenger to step directly on and off the escalator with greater ease and safety and eliminates the need for additional floor area.

Chimney and flues. To produce a given amount of heat in a building, fuel must be burned at a given rate. To do this a definite weight of air must be supplied for combustion. In this process air must flow through the fuel bed. The force causing the air flow in a natural draft plant is the chimney. It is capable of producing a draft that is caused by the difference between the atmospheric pressure and the pressure existing at any point in the furnace or in the flue. The intensity of draft that a chimney is capable of producing at the base is a function of its height, temperature of the flue gas, and the outside air temperature.

In designing a chimney several factors are considered—grate surface area, size of breeching (smoke pipe), and the rate of combustion. By using selected formulas, the flue area can be calculated. Height of the flue should be sufficient to prevent any downdrafts through the flue caused by adjacent roofs at the same height.

Chimneys may be constructed from concrete, masonry, or steel. Masonry chimneys, particularly for smaller buildings, such as residences, should be lined with a terra-cotta flue liner to prevent combustion fumes from penetrating the building through cracks in the mortar. The chimney for a high-rise building is a special case. Available formulas or manufacturers' recommendations, especially in the case of prefabricated chimneys, should be used to design them.

BIBLIOGRAPHY. The early history of building materials and building techniques is best covered by NORMAN DAVEY, *A History of Building Materials* (1961); and RENE ALLEAU, *Histoire des grandes constructions* (1966; Eng. trans., *History of the Great Building Constructions*, 1967). BANISTER FLETCHER, *A History of Architecture (on the Comparative Method)*, 18th ed. (1975), characterizes the many architectural styles through time and describes many of their influential factors; while SIGFRIED GIEDION, *Space, Time, and Architecture*, 5th ed., rev. and enlarged (1967), contrasts architectural styles and building techniques with an incisive analysis. CARL CONDIT, *American Building* (1968), narrates the history of building materials and techniques in the United States from the beginning of the Colonies. ROLLAND B. GUY *et al.*, *The State of the Art of Prefabrication in the Construction Industry* (1968), describes the trends toward prefabrication and the potential for building systems in the United States. Other references describing the history of construction are HENRY COWAN, *An Historical Outline of Architectural Science* (1966); GAVIN MAXWELL, *A Reed Shaken by the Wind* (1957); A.W. LAWRENCE, *Greek Architecture*, rev. ed. (1975); VITRUVIUS, *Ten Books on Architecture* (Eng. trans. 1914); JOHN H. BATEMAN, *Materials of Construction* (1950); and DON A. HALPERIN, *Building with Steel*, 2nd ed. (1966). LAURENCE E. REINER, *Methods and Materials of Construction* (1970); HARRY PARKER, CHARLES M. GAY, and JOHN W. MACGUIRE, *Materials and Methods of Architectural Construction*, 3rd ed. (1958); and JOHN L. SCHMIDT, WALTER H. LEWIS, and HAROLD B. OLIN, *Construction: Principles, Materials and Methods* (1970), present a description of materials and techniques currently used in the various functional areas (*e.g.*, foundations, structural frames, roofs, floors, space enclosure, and finishes) in residential and nonresidential construction. WILLIAM J. MCGUINESS *et al.*, *Mechanical and Electrical Equipment for Buildings*, 5th ed. (1975), provides the same type of detailed analysis relative to auxiliary systems, such as plumbing, electrical heating, ventilating, and air conditioning, as well as vertical transportation. PHILIP KISSAM, *Surveying*, 2nd ed. (1956); LOUIS C. RIPA, *Surveying Manual* (1964); W. FISHER CASSIE, *Fundamental Foundations* (1968); W.H. ELGAR, *Foundations for Houses and Other Small Structures* (1951); ROLT HAMMOND, *Modern Foundation Methods* (1967); LEONARD MICHAELS, *Contemporary Structure in Architecture* (1950); WHITNEY C. HUNTINGTON, *Building Construction*, 4th ed. (1975); THEODORE CRANE, *Architectural Construction*, 2nd ed. (1956); and T. BAUMEISTER and LIONEL MARKS, *Standard Handbook for Mechanical Engineers*, 8th ed. (1977), treat individual elements of construction (*e.g.*, surveying, foundations, and structural frame) in considerable detail. Structures with special construction problems are discussed in PETER BLAKE, "Cape Kennedy," *Architectural Forum*, 126:58–59 (1967); HARRY A. KULJIAN, *Nuclear Power Plant Design* (1968); and J.F. MUNCE, *The Architect in the Nuclear Age* (1964). The role of the architect and the design professions is well described in the AMERICAN INSTITUTE OF ARCHITECTS, *Handbook of Architectural Practice*, latest ed.; and *Comprehensive Architectural Services: General Principles and Practice* (1965). The role of the contractor and subcontractor, as well as the bidding process, is described in RICHARD H. CLOUGH, *Construction Contracting*, 3rd ed. (1975).

(J.R.Ha./D.C.Hu.)

Bulgaria

A Communist country of southeastern Europe, the People's Republic of Bulgaria occupies the eastern portion of the Balkan Peninsula, crossed by historically important routes from northern and eastern Europe to the Mediterranean Basin and from western and central Europe to the Middle East. The home of some 8,730,000 people at the time of the census of 1975, Bulgaria is remarkable for its variety of scenery, its rugged mountains and modern Black Sea resorts alike attracting an increasing flow of tourists from other countries. Historical, cultural, and political ties connect the republic with the Soviet Union, and long-term alliances also bind Bulgaria to other Soviet-bloc countries that are members of Comecon, the east European mutual economic development program, and the Warsaw Treaty Organization.

A nation of some 43,000 square miles (111,000 square kilometres), Bulgaria is bounded by Romania on the north, the border being marked by the Lower Danube River. The Black Sea lies to the east, Turkey and Greece to the south, and Yugoslavia to the west. The capital, Sofia, lies in a mountainous basin in the west, commanding important trans-European routes and near the geographical centre of the whole Balkan region.

This article is concerned with the contemporary country Bulgaria. For historical aspects, see BALKANS, HISTORY OF THE; see also DANUBE RIVER and SOFIA.

THE LAND

Topography. Within a relatively small compass, the Bulgarian landscape exhibits striking topographic variety. Open expanses of lowland alternate with broken mountain country, cut by deep river gorges and harbouring, often unexpectedly, such upland basins as that in which Sofia lies. The bewildering detail tends to conceal a series of crescent-shaped basic structural and physiographic divisions that run east–west.

Topographic variety

The Danubian Plain. All but a small section of the northern frontier of Bulgaria is marked by the Lower Danube, the abrupt and often steep Bulgarian bank contrasting with the swamps and lagoons of the Romanian side. A fertile, hilly plain, with rivers flowing northward from the Balkan Mountains to join the Danube, borders the river. The average altitude of the region is 584 feet (178 metres), and it covers 12,171 square miles (31,523 square kilometres).

The Balkan Mountains. The Balkan Mountains border the Danubian Plain on the south, their rounded summits having an average height of 2,368 feet and rising to 7,795 feet (2,376 metres) in Botev, the highest peak. Parallel to this main chain (its Bulgarian name, Stara planina, means Old Mountains, "old" signifying its greater extent compared to the adjacent ranges) lies a transitional region of very complex relief. Block faulting—the raising or lowering of great structural segments along regular lines of crustal weakness—has produced here the Sredna gora (*gora* means "hill" and *planina* means "mountain," or "mountain range"), Vitosha Mountains, Lisa planina, a number of sheltered structural basins, and the Upper Thracian and Tundzha lowlands.

The Rila–Rhodope massif. Another mountain mass covers southern Bulgaria. This includes the alpine Rhodope (Rodopi in Bulgarian, Rodhópis in Greek) Mountains, which rise to 7,188 feet (2,191 metres) in Golyam Perelik Peak; the Rila Mountains, rising to Musala Peak, at 9,596 feet (2,925 metres) the highest in the country and indeed in the whole Balkan Peninsula; the Pirin Mountains, with Vikhren Peak reaching 9,560 feet (2,914 metres); and a frontier mountain range known as the Belasitsa.

These majestic ranges discharge meltwater from montane glaciers throughout the summer, and their sharp outlines, pine-clad slopes, and, in the Rila and Pirin ranges, several hundred glacial lakes combine to form some of the most beautiful of Bulgarian landscapes.

The Black Sea coast. Trending north–south at the eastern fringe of the other regions, the narrow Black Sea coastal region has few bays (exceptions being the fine harbours of Varna and Burgas) but does have extensive stretches of sandy beach that have led to the growth of a number of picturesque seaside resorts.

Drainage. Bulgaria has a complex drainage pattern characterized, with the notable exception of the Danube, by relatively short rivers. The major rivers are the Maritsa (Marica), draining the lowlands to the north of the Rila–Rhodope massif before turning away southward at the Greek–Bulgarian–Turkish frontier; the Iskŭr (Iskâr), draining the Sofia Basin before turning northward toward the Danube in a deep gorge through the Balkan Mountains; the Struma, running southward toward the Aegean through a valley paralleling Bulgaria's western frontier; the Arda, of the central Rhodope; the Tundzha, running

Rivers

east along the southern flank of the Balkan Mountains; and the Yantra, flowing north to the Danube.

Overall, 57 percent of the runoff drains to the Black Sea and 43 percent to the Aegean. Northern areas subject to continental influences have a spring runoff maximum, while transitional Mediterranean influences give a winter runoff maximum farther south. Bulgaria's numerous lakes may be coastal (as the large lakes around Varna and Burgas), glacial (as in the southern mountains), structural, or karst in origin. A distinctive feature is the 500 or so mineral springs, half of which are warm or hot (reaching 215° F [101° C] at Sapareva Banya), which are used for bathing or drinking or both, the waters being considered healthful. Many dams have been constructed in the mountains.

Soils. The varied Bulgarian natural environment has produced about 20 soil types and subtypes, which may be grouped into three main regions. Northern Bulgaria is characterized by the fertile black-earth soils known as chernozems and also by gray soils of forest origin. Southern Bulgaria has forest soils with acidic (cinnamonic) traces—by far the most extensive single category—as well as the modified chernozems known as chernozem-smolnitzas (a dark-coloured zonal soil with a deep and rich humus horizon). Finally, the rugged high mountain regions have brown forest, dark mountain forest, and mountain meadow soils.

Climate. The greater part of Bulgaria has a moderate continental climate, which is tempered by Mediterranean influences in the south. The average annual temperature is 51° F (10.5° C), but this conceals a wide variation; temperatures as low as —37° F (—38° C) and as high as 113° F (45° C) have been recorded. Mean annual precipitation ranges from about 18 inches (450 millimetres) in the northeast to more than 47 inches (1,200 millimetres) in the highest mountains. This abundant rainfall is brought by thunderstorms in the spring and summer, and damaging hailstorms are also common.

Precipitation

Five climatic regions may be broadly distinguished. The north and northwest have a moderately continental climate, with cold winter winds from the European interior and the northeast sweeping over the Danubian Plain. A transitional version of this climate, with continental extremes moderated somewhat, affects the west, southwest, and central regions.

A 25-mile-wide belt on the Black Sea coast has a warmer winter but a cooler summer. The Mesta and Struma river valleys and the southeast have a transitionally Mediterranean climate, often with summer drought. Finally, regions above about 3,000 feet have a severer mountain climate.

Vegetation and animal life. The relatively large number of Bulgarian plant and animal species reflects the country's border situation adjoining several of the great Eurasian biogeographical zones. During the Ice Age, life in the region was not destroyed by advancing glaciers as occurred in much of Europe; it was actually enriched by the immigration of species from the north, some of which still survive. Influences from the steppes of western Asia also penetrated the region at that time. Nonetheless, the greater part of the plant and animal life is central European, mixed with a type that blends Arctic and alpine characteristics in the high mountains. Steppe species are most characteristic of the northeast and southeast, while the south is rich in sub-Mediterranean and Mediterranean species. To the east, the organisms of the Black Sea coastal fringe are of the steppe type along with some thermophilic, or heat-loving, species, while the Black Sea waters contain chiefly Mediterranean elements combined with some from the Caspian Sea.

In keeping with an awakening worldwide interest in the natural environment, the Bulgarian government has introduced a number of conservation measures, including steps to protect soil, water, and air from pollution and to establish protected areas of outstanding interest to naturalists. A council for the protection of the natural environment was set up in 1971, and 81 recreational areas, seven national parks, and 39 places of special interest were designated for protection in 1973.

Conservation

The human imprint. The natural environment of Bulgaria falls into three basic regions: North Bulgaria, including the Danubian Plain and the Balkan Mountains; South Bulgaria, including the Rila–Rhodope massif; and a transitional area between them. Each of these traditional regions over the centuries has been subjected to the actions of man, whether in the remoter mountains, where national culture was cherished and the seeds of nationalism were sown during the long Ottoman domination; or in the Danubian Plain, where agriculture has been practiced from ancient times. By the mid-1970s, Bulgarian settlements had been officially classified into 214 urban areas and some 5,441 villages, the latter including more than 500 small hamlets, about 350 clusters of farmsteads, and, deep in the mountains, a handful of historic monasteries.

Urban settlement patterns. Bulgarian towns have roots in the Middle Ages and in remotest antiquity, although new, modern settlements are being created each year; the urban population overtook the rural for the first time in 1969. Contemporary towns can best be classified according to their economic functions; thus, Sofia, Dimitrovgrad, and Pernik have a preponderance of industry, while other towns specialize in transportation or services.

The rapid urbanization now transforming much of the Bulgarian landscape is planned, each new or modernized town having its own development plan. The neighbourhood unit is a characteristic feature of this process. The rapid increase in the population of the capital and the largest towns has created a severe housing shortage, which the government did not seriously attack till 1970. The average size of a town increased from just over 16,000 people in 1946 to more than 26,000 by the early 1970s, when there were 14 towns with populations of more than 50,000, including seven major cities with more than 100,000 inhabitants. In spite of this transformation, many Bulgarian towns preserve their ancient charm and are rich in cultural monuments; in the remoter areas, they offer a slower pace of life than can be found in the cities.

Sofia, the capital, is the largest city; with almost 1,000,000 people in its built-up area, it dominates the national economic and cultural life. Plovdiv, with more than 300,000 inhabitants, enjoys a scenic location on the Maritsa River and is another major industrial and cultural centre, where an international trade fair is held annually. Varna (ancient Odessus), with 252,000 inhabitants, is a resort on the shores of the Black Sea. The newer seaside resort of Zlatni Pyassŭtsi (Golden Sands), nearby, is attracting an increasing international tourist trade. On the Danube, Ruse, with more than 150,000 inhabitants, is the largest Bulgarian river port; there the Friendship Bridge leads to the Romanian city of Giurgiu. Burgas, with a population of well over 130,000, is Bulgaria's largest Black Sea port and a major industrial (petrochemicals), cultural, and resort centre. Stara Zagora, the Roman Augusta Trajana, lies on the southern flanks of the central Sredna gora, is the home of more than 110,000 persons, and is famous for its archaeological and architectural remains.

Major cities

Rural settlement patterns. The numerous contemporary Bulgarian villages are either compactly clustered or relatively scattered. Since World War II, they have undergone a radical transformation from the sleepy, backward, and poverty-stricken settlements that typified much of the region for centuries. By the early 1970s, 90 percent of the rural population was living in villages with a water supply, and electricity was available to virtually all communities; from 70 to 75 percent of the houses were recent constructions, replacing the older lath and plaster structures. Most of the villages have paved and asphalted streets and new community centres. Industrial plants have been set up in the larger villages, and the agro-industrial economic complexes and detailed regional planning that is a part of government policy helps relate these developments to the needs of specific areas. Smaller villages (fewer than 500 inhabitants) nevertheless form nearly half of the total, although less than 7 percent of the rural population is found there. Administratively, the villages have undergone extensive amalgamation.

THE PEOPLE

Ethnic, religious, and linguistic background. Ethnically, the population is fairly homogeneous, Bulgarians making up more than 88 percent of the total.

The origins of the Bulgarians

The Slav tribes that settled in the eastern part of the Balkan Peninsula in the 6th and 7th centuries AD, thereby assimilating the local Thracian tribes, formed a basic ethnic group. The group known as the proto-Bulgarians, who, together with the Slavs, formed the Slav-Bulgarian state in 681, formed another component. With the gradual obliteration of fragmented Slav tribes and also of the ethnic differences in the territory of the first Bulgarian state (covering Moesia, Thrace, and Macedonia) in the 9th and 10th centuries, proto-Bulgarians and Slavs consolidated into a unified Slav people who thence retained the name of Bulgarians. This national unity, present in embryonic form during the long Ottoman domination, flowered in the independence struggles of the 19th century, and the Bulgarians today share a unity unassailed by either ethnographic or linguistic differences.

The majority of religious Bulgarians (the church is separate from the state) are Eastern Orthodox, with small numbers of Catholics, Protestants, and Muslims, the latter including those Muslim Bulgarians who were forced to adopt Islām in the 16th and 17th centuries but who have nevertheless retained Bulgarian language and customs. The Turks, Bulgaria's largest minority, live in some regions of the northeast and in the eastern Rhodope. Gypsies and Macedonians are two other sizable minorities (though the government does not consider Macedonians as such, regarding them as ethnically Bulgarian), and there are a few thousand Russians, Armenians, and Greeks (mostly in the towns) and Romanians and Tatars (mostly in the villages).

Minorities

The Bulgarian language belongs to the South Slavic group, along with Serbo-Croatian, Slovene, and Macedonian (the last, however, considered to be a dialect of Bulgarian by the Bulgarian government). A number of dialects remain in the common speech.

Contemporary demography. *Birth and death rates.* As a result of social and economic changes after World War II, notably the introduction of free medical care and the improvement of working conditions, Bulgaria's mortality rate dropped from 13.4 per 1,000 in 1939 to 10.3 in 1975, with infant mortality dropping from 139 to 23.1 per 1,000 over the same period. The birth rate dropped from 21.4 per 1,000 in 1939 to 16 in 1970, rising to 16.6 in 1975, and was about the same in town and country. Nat-

MAP INDEX

Political subdivisions

Blagoevgrad.....42·01n 23·06e
Burgas..........42·30n 27·28e
Gabrovo.........42·52n 25·19e
Khaskovo........41·56n 25·33e
Kŭrdzhali.......41·39n 25·22e
Kyustendil......42·17n 22·41e
Lovech..........43·08n 24·43e
Mikhaylovgrad...43·25n 23·13e
Pazardzhik......42·12n 24·20e
Pernik..........42·36n 23·02e
Pleven..........43·25n 24·37e
Plovdiv.........42·09n 24·45e
Razgrad.........43·32n 26·31e
Ruse............43·50n 25·57e
Shumen..........43·16n 26·55e
Silistra........44·07n 27·16e
Sliven..........42·40n 26·19e
Smolyan.........41·35n 24·41e
Sofia (Grad)....42·41n 23·19e
Sofiya..........42·41n 23·50e
Stara Zagora....42·25n 25·38e
Tolbukhin.......43·34n 27·50e
Tŭrgovishte.....43·15n 26·34e
Varna...........43·13n 27·55e
Veliko Tŭrnovo..43·04n 25·39e
Vidin...........43·59n 22·52e
Vratsa..........43·12n 23·33e
Yambol..........42·29n 26·30e

The names of the political subdivisions do not appear on the map because they are the same as the names of their capital cities.

Cities and towns

Akhtopol........42·06n 27·57e
Alfatar.........43·57n 27·17e
Ardino..........41·35n 25·08e
Asenovgrad......42·01n 24·52e
Aytos...........42·42n 27·15e
Balchik.........43·25n 28·10e
Bansko..........41·50n 23·29e
Batak...........41·57n 24·13e
Belene..........43·39n 25·07e
Belogradchik....43·38n 22·41e
Berkovitsa......43·14n 23·07e
Blagoevgrad.....42·01n 23·06e
Bobovdol........42·22n 23·00e
Borovan.........43·26n 23·45e
Botevgrad.......42·54n 23·47e
Bratsigovo......42·01n 24·22e
Bregovo.........44·09n 22·39e
Brest...........43·38n 24·35e
Breznik.........42·44n 22·54e
Brezovo.........42·21n 25·05e
Burgas..........42·30n 27·28e
Butan...........43·39n 23·45e
Byala...........42·53n 27·54e
Byala...........43·27n 25·44e
Byala Slatina...43·28n 23·56e
Chepelare.......41·44n 24·41e
Cherven Bryag...43·16n 24·06e
Chirpan.........42·12n 25·20e
Devin...........41·45n 24·24e
Devnya..........43·13n 27·33e
Dimitrovgrad....42·03n 25·36e
Dolni Dŭbnik....43·24n 24·26e
Dolni Lom.......43·31n 22·47e
Drenovets.......43·42n 22·59e
Dryanovo........42·58n 25·27e
Dulovo..........43·49n 27·09e
Durankulak......43·42n 28·31e
Dve Mogili......43·36n 25·52e
Elena...........42·56n 25·53e
Elin Pelin......42·40n 23·36e
Elkhovo.........42·10n 26·34e
Etropole........42·50n 24·00e
Gabrovo.........42·52n 25·19e
General Toshevo.43·42n 28·02e
Gigen...........43·42n 24·29e
Gorna
Oryakhovitsa....43·07n 25·41e
Gotse Delchev...41·34n 23·44e
Gramada.........43·50n 22·39e
Grudovo.........42·21n 27·10e
Gulyantsi.......43·38n 24·42e
Gyueshevo.......42·14n 22·28e
Ikhtiman........42·26n 23·49e
Isperikh........43·43n 26·50e
Ivaylovgrad.....41·32n 26·08e
Kalofer.........42·37n 24·59e
Karlovo.........42·38n 24·48e
Karnobat........42·39n 26·59e
Kavarna.........43·25n 28·20e
Kazanlŭk........42·38n 25·21e
Kharmanli.......41·56n 25·54e
Khaskovo........41·56n 25·33e
Klisura.........42·42n 24·27e
Knezha..........43·10n 24·05e
Kostenets.......42·16n 23·49e
Kotel...........42·53n 26·27e
Kozloduy........43·47n 23·44e
Krichim.........42·03n 24·28e
Krivodol........43·23n 23·29e
Krumovgrad......41·28n 25·39e
Kubrat..........43·48n 26·30e
Kula............43·53n 22·31e
Kŭrdzhali.......41·39n 25·22e
Kyustendil......42·17n 22·41e
Lekhchevo.......43·32n 23·32e
Levski..........43·22n 25·08e
Lom.............43·49n 23·14e
Lovech..........43·08n 24·43e
Lukovit.........43·12n 24·10e
Lyubimets.......41·50n 26·05e
Madan...........41·30n 24·57e
Malko Tŭrnovo...41·59n 27·32e
Maritsa.........42·02n 25·50e
Medkovets.......43·37n 23·10e
Mezdra..........43·09n 23·42e
Michurin........42·10n 27·51e
Mikhaylovgrad...43·25n 23·13e
Mikre...........43·02n 24·31e
Momchilgrad.....41·32n 25·25e
Nesebŭr.........42·39n 27·44e
Nikopol.........43·42n 24·54e
Nova Zagora.....42·29n 26·01e
Novi Pazar......43·21n 27·12e
Obnova..........43·26n 24·59e
Omurtag.........43·06n 26·25e
Opaka...........43·27n 26·10e
Orekhovo........43·45n 23·57e
Panagyurishte...42·30n 24·11e
Pavlikeni.......43·14n 25·18e
Pazardzhik......42·12n 24·20e
Pernik..........42·36n 23·02e
Peshtera........42·02n 24·18e
Petrich.........41·24n 23·13e
Pirdop..........42·42n 24·11e
Pleven..........43·25n 24·37e
Plovdiv.........42·09n 24·45e
Polski Trŭmbesh.43·22n 25·38e
Pomorie.........42·33n 27·39e
Popintsi........42·25n 24·17e
Popovo..........43·21n 26·13e
Pordim..........43·23n 24.51e
Preslav.........43·10n 26·49e
Provadiya.......43·11n 27·26e
Pŭrvomay........42·06n 25·13e
Radnevo.........42·18n 25·56e
Radomir.........42·33n 22·58e
Razgrad.........43·32n 26·31e
Razlog..........41·53n 23·28e
Rudozem.........41·29n 24·51e
Ruse............43·50n 25·57e
Samokov.........42·20n 23·33e
Sandanski.......41·34n 23·17e
Sapareva Banya..42·17n 23·16e
Septemvri.......42·13n 24·06e
Sevlievo........43·01n 25·06e
Shabla..........43·32n 28·32e
Shumen..........43·16n 26·55e
Silistra........44·07n 27·16e
Simitli.........41·53n 23·06e
Sliven..........42·40n 26·19e
Slivnitsa.......42·51n 23·02e
Smolyan.........41·35n 24·41e
Sofia...........42·41n 23·19e
Sozopol.........42·25n 27·42e
Stanke Dimitrov..42·16n 23·07e
Stara Zagora....42·25n 25·38e
Svilengrad......41·46n 26·12e
Svishtov........43·37n 25·20e
Svoge...........42·58n 23·21e
Telerig.........43·51n 27·40e
Tervel..........43·45n 27·24e
Teteven.........42·55n 24·16e
Tolbukhin.......43·34n 27·50e
Topolovgrad.....42·05n 26·20e
Troyan..........42·51n 24·43e
Trŭn............42·50n 22·39e
Trŭstenik.......43·31n 24·28e
Tryavna.........42·52n 25·30e
Tsenovo.........43·32n 25·39e
Tŭrgovishte.....43·15n 26·34e
Tutrakan........44·03n 26·37e
Tvŭrditsa.......43·42n 25·52e
Ugŭrchin........43·06n 24·25e
Varna...........43·13n 27·55e
Veliko Tŭrnovo...43·04n 25·39e
Velingrad.......42·04n 24·00e
Vetovo..........43·42n 26·16e
Vetren..........42·16n 24·03e
Vidin...........43·59n 22·52e
Vratsa..........43·12n 23·33e
Vŭlchedrŭm......43·42n 23·27e
Vŭrshets........43·12n 23·17e
Yakoruda........42·02n 23·40e
Yambol..........42·29n 26·30e
Zafirovo........44·00n 26·50e
Zavet...........43·46n 26·40e
Zlatitsa........42·43n 24·08e
Zlatni Pyassŭtsi..43·17n 28·02e
Zlatograd.......41·23n 25·06e
Zornitsa........42·23n 26·56e

Physical features and points of interest

Aladzha,
Manastir,
monastery......43·17n 28·01e
Arda, *river*.......41·35n 26·08e
Balkan
Mountains......43·15n 25·00e
Batak, yazovir,
reservoir........41·59n 24·11e
Belasitsa,
mountains......41·21n 22·50e
Black Sea.......42·40n 29.00e
Botev, *mountain*..42·43n 24·55e
Burgaski zaliv,
bay.............42·30n 27·33e
Cherni vrŭkh,
mountain.......42·34n 23·17e
Danube, *river*....44·14n 27·15e
Dobrudzhansko
plato, *plateau*...43·32n 27·50e
Dobruja,
historic region...43·50n 28·00e
Emine, nos, *cape*.42·42n 27·51e
Golyama
kamchiya, *river*. 43·03n 27·29e
Golyam Perelik,
mountain.......41·36n 24·34e
Iskŭr, *river*.......43·44n 24·27e
Iskŭr, yazovir,
reservoir........42·30n 23·30e
Kaliakra, nos,
cape............43·21n 28·27e
Kamchiya, *river*..43·02n 27·53e
Kom, *mountain*..43·10n 23·03e
Kotlenski
prokhod, *pass*...42·53n 26·27e
Lisa planina,
mountains......43·02n 26·20e
Luda kamchiya,
river............43·03n 27·29e
Marica, see
Maritsa
Maritsa, *river*....41·43n 26·19e
Mesta, *river*......41·28n 24·02e
Midzhur,
mountain.......43·23n 22·42e
Mochuritsa, *river*.42·31n 26·32e
Musala,
mountain.......42·11n 23·34e
Osŭm, *river*......43·42n 24·51e
Petrokhanski
prokhod, *pass*...43·08n 23·08e
Pirin, *mountains*..41·40n 23·30e
Rhodope
Mountains......41·30n 24·30e
Rila, *mountains*..42·08n 23·33e
Ruen, *mountain*..42·10n 22·31e
Shipchenski
prokhod, *pass*...42·46n 25·19e
Sredna gora,
mountains......42·30n 25·00e
Stara planina,
mountains......43·15n 25·00e
Struma, *river*....41·21n 23·17e
Sŭrnena gora,
mountains......42·32n 25·48e
Troyanski
prokhod, *pass*...42·47n 24·37e
Tundzha, *river*...41·52n 26·32e
Varnenski zaliv,
bay.............43·11n 27·56e
Veleka, *river*.....42·04n 27·58e
Vikhren,
mountain.......41·46n 23·24e
Vitosha,
mountains......42·33n 23·15e
Yantra, *river*.....43·38n 25·34e

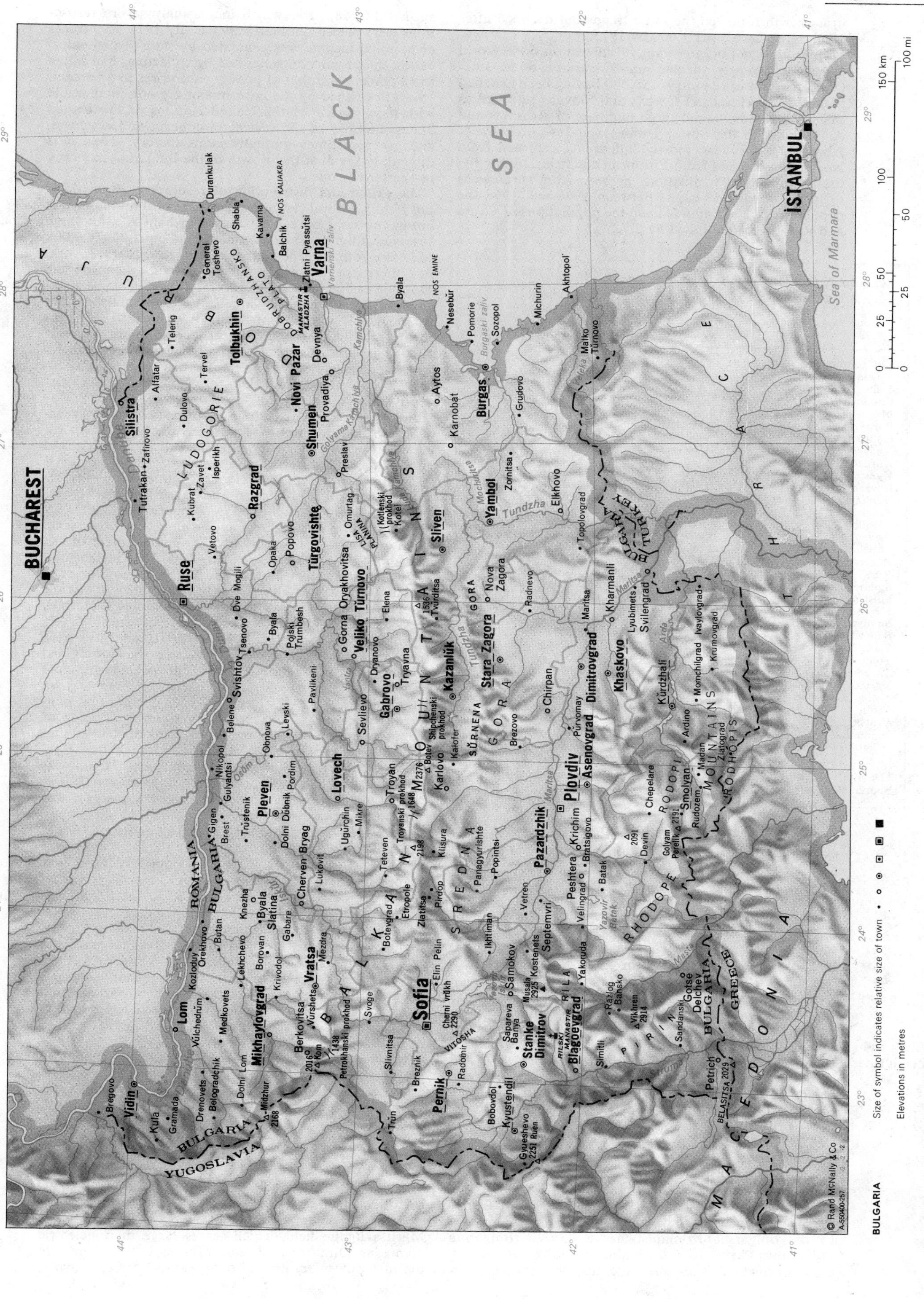
BLACK SEA
BUCHAREST
ROMANIA
BULGARIA
YUGOSLAVIA
GREECE
TURKEY
İSTANBUL
Sea of Marmara
Danube
Sofia
Plovdiv
Varna
Burgas
Ruse
Stara Zagora
Pleven
Tolbukhin
Sliven
Shumen
Pernik
Khaskovo
Yambol
Pazardzhik
Blagoevgrad
Veliko Türnovo
Vratsa
Gabrovo
Vidin
Kazanlŭk
Kyustendil
Mikhaylovgrad
Lom
Silistra
Razgrad
Türgovishte
Lovech
Dimitrovgrad
Asenovgrad
Kŭrdzhali
Smolyan
Stanke Dimitrov
Novi Pazar
Karlovo
Svishtov
Nikopol
Tutrakan
Balchik
Kavarna
Shabla
Durankulak
Nesebŭr
Pomorie
Sozopol
Michurin
Akhtopol
Malko Türnovo
Aytos
Karnobat
Provadiya
Devnya
Preslav
Samokov
Petrich
Sandanski
Gotse Delchev
Bansko
Razlog
Peshtera
Velingrad
Batak
Ardino
Madan
Svilengrad
Kharmanli
Topolovgrad
Elkhovo
Nova Zagora
Chirpan
Sevlievo
Troyan
Botevgrad
Ikhtiman
Svoge
Breznik
Trŭn
Slivnitsa
Dupnitsa
DOBRUDZHANSKO PLATO
LUDOGORIE
DOBRUDZHA
BALKAN MOUNTAINS
STARA PLANINA
SREDNA GORA
SŬRNENA GORA
RILA
PIRIN
RHODOPE MOUNTAINS
RODOPI
VITOSHA
MACEDONIA
THRACE
NOS KALIAKRA
NOS EMINE
Burgaski zaliv
Varnenski zaliv
Maritsa
Iskŭr
Tundzha
Struma
Mesta
Arda
Yantra
Osŭm
Kamchiya
Musala 2925
Vikhren 2914
Botev 2376
Cherni vrŭkh 2290
Midzhur 2168
Belasitsa 2029
Shipchenski prokhod
Petrokhanski prokhod
Troyanski prokhod
Kotlenski prokhod
Rilski Manastir
Manastir Aladzha
Yazovir Batak
0 25 50 100 150 km
0 25 50 100 mi
Size of symbol indicates relative size of town
Elevations in metres
© Rand McNally & Co
A-550400-257
BULGARIA

ural growth followed the same trends but declined after 1968, reaching 6.3 per 1,000 by 1975.

Emigration and immigration. Emigration since World War II has mostly affected non-Bulgarians. Some 190,000 Turks left the country, 155,000 having been expelled in 1949–51. Almost all Czechs and Slovaks returned to their homelands, as did large numbers of Russians and Armenians (to the Soviet Union) and Jews (to Israel). About 35,000 others, mostly Bulgarians, returned from North America and from European countries. Internally, the movement of population has been from rural areas to larger towns and cities. Between 1946 and 1968 the population of Sofia doubled and the populations of Varna and Ruse were multiplied by 2.7.

Bulgaria, Area and Population

	area		population	
	sq mi	sq km	1965 census*	1975 estimate
City commune (*gradska obshtina*)				
Sofia	401	1,038	895,000	1,066,000
Provinces (*okrŭzi*)				
Blagoevgrad	2,496	6,464	303,000	324,000
Burgas	2,936	7,605	381,000	421,000
Gabrovo	798	2,068	169,000	176,000
Khaskovo	1,556	4,029	290,000	293,000
Kŭrdzhali	1,552	4,020	284,000	288,000
Kyustendil	1,159	3,002	197,000	199,000
Lovech	1,594	4,129	217,000	217,000
Mikhaylovgrad	1,384	3,585	241,000	236,000
Pazardzhik	1,691	4,379	297,000	314,000
Pernik	909	2,355	181,000	175,000
Pleven	1,615	4,184	352,000	359,000
Plovdiv	2,159	5,591	645,000	721,000
Razgrad	1,022	2,646	198,000	204,000
Ruse	1,013	2,624	273,000	294,000
Shumen	1,303	3,374	243,000	254,000
Silistra	1,111	2,876	171,000	177,000
Sliven	1,440	3,729	227,000	238,000
Smolyan	1,358	3,518	160,000	163,000
Sofiya	2,851	7,385	318,000	322,000
Stara Zagora	1,893	4,902	352,000	390,000
Tolbukhin	1,810	4,689	236,000	250,000
Tŭrgovishte	1,063	2,754	178,000	179,000
Varna	1,475	3,820	367,000	430,000
Veliko Tŭrnovo	1,811	4,690	339,000	350,000
Vidin	1,201	3,110	181,000	179,000
Vratsa	1,616	4,186	309,000	312,000
Yambol	1,607	4,162	223,000	207,000
Total Bulgaria	42,823†	110,912†	8,228,000†	8,734,000†

*De jure. †Figures do not add to total given because of rounding.
Source: Official government figures.

Population distribution. Bulgaria's geographical variety is reflected in the distribution of its population. The most densely populated areas are the Danubian Plain, the Upper Thracian Basin, the Burgas plain, and the intermontane basins of southwestern Bulgaria. Areas of lowest density are the east and southeast of the country, the Strandzha and Dobruja regions, and the higher mountain areas. Of a total population of more than 8,700,000 in 1975, just over half lived in cities, as compared to a quarter in 1946 (see above *The human imprint: Urban settlement patterns*).

Birth and death rates

Demographic trends. Urbanization continues to have an effect on the demographic structure; a large segment of the urban population is of a young working age, and this has an effect on the rising birth rates of the 1970s and the natural growth of the towns. Because relatively more older adults remain in the villages, the birth rate there continues to be lower and the mortality rate higher.

THE NATIONAL ECONOMY

The Bulgarian economy is based on the premise that all means of production should be owned by the state. Economic activities are centrally planned and supervised by the Council of Ministers—assisted by several ministries for specific aspects of the economy—along lines indicated by the Bŭlgarska Komunisticheska Partiya (Bulgarian Communist Party). Industry is almost wholly state owned, though private artisans were tolerated, and even encouraged, till 1968, after which increasingly severe restrictions were placed on their activities. By 1975, 83 percent of national income was generated by state-owned enterprises; the proportion generated by collectives had fallen to 12 percent and that of private enterprises to 5 percent.

Statistics issued by the government are not comparable with those issued by the United Nations or the United States, because of differences in concept and coverage, and are sometimes mutually contradictory. Thus it is difficult to speak of the growth of the Bulgarian economy in Western terms.

Coals

The extent and distribution of resources. Bulgaria is not rich in natural resources. Deposits of bituminous and anthracite coal have been almost exhausted, but large reserves of lignite (said to amount to about 3,000,000,000 tons) are found in the Maritsa Basin near Stara Zagora, and there are promising deposits of coking coal in the Dobruja region. Oil and gas are produced in small quantities in the Danubian Plain. Iron comes mainly from Kremikovtsi, northeast of Sofia. Government reports indicate mining of the important steel-alloying minerals (manganese, chromium, and molybdenum), but imports of these are also reported. Nonferrous metals—particularly copper, lead, and zinc—are apparently more extensive than ferrous.

Biological resources include the forests, meadow vegetation, edible mushrooms and the fruits of other plants, plant products used in the pharmaceutical industry, and fish, game, and mussels and oysters.

Lignite provides the basic local source for power requirements and feeds most of the power stations. Hydroelectric resources are limited in comparison.

Sources of national income. *Mining and quarrying.* Coal output—mostly lignite, with a large content of ash and moisture—was around 34,097,000 tons in the mid-1970s, more than meeting Bulgaria's own requirements. About 20 quarrying enterprises provide chiefly materials for production of cement and other building materials; there are also eight marble and granite quarries.

Manufacturing. Before World War II, industries were of minor importance in Bulgaria. Under the Communist system, industrialization became one of the principal aims of economic policy, with particular emphasis on basic industries such as electric power, ferrous and nonferrous metallurgy, and chemicals. Central planning of management, production, and investment channelled into industry a steadily increasing part of the national resources, and by 1975 industrial output was 55 times as great as before World War II and accounted for 66 percent of the national income. Industrial expansion was slowing, however.

Postwar industrialization

Before the war, shipbuilding at Varna and foundries at Sofia, Plovdiv, Ruse, and Pernik were the most important metallurgical industries. Those developed after the war include iron and steel works at Pernik, based upon local brown coal and iron ore from the Sofia district; a large steel project at Kremikovtsi; a lead and zinc works at Kŭrdzhali; and a copper and sulfuric acid plant at Pirdop. A chemical industry has developed at Dimitrovgrad, and chemical plants were also built at Stara Zagora, Vratsa, Devnya, and Vidin, and a petrochemical plant at Burgas. Machine building is a priority branch of the national economy. Its relative share of industrial production jumped from 2.4 percent in 1939 to 17.8 in 1966 and to 25 in 1975.

Textile industries before World War II were mainly to be found in the central part of the country—*e.g.*, Gabrovo, Sliven, Kazanlŭk, Khaskovo—together with Sofia, Varna, and Ruse. These used locally produced wool, cotton, or silk. Under the five-year plans, large new mills were built at Sofia, Sliven, and Plovdiv, and the total output of textile fabrics by 1966 rose to 16 times what it was in 1939. Other industries that have increased since World War II are food processing and consumer goods industries such as footwear, pottery, and furniture.

Energy. The major source of energy in Bulgaria is the Maritsa lignite field, which serves large thermoelectric plants at Dimitrovgrad and Maritsa-Iztok; there are thermal power stations also at Pernik, Sofia, Plovdiv, and Burgas. About 90 hydroelectric stations generate about 9 percent of the total electricity output, but planners are giving considerable emphasis to developing the quite substantial potential power in the country's rivers, particularly in the Rhodope Mountains. Nuclear energy is provided from a station at Kozloduy (constructed with Soviet aid), which began operation in 1974 and has a capacity of 1,760,000 kilowatts. Transmission lines serve most parts of the country.

Agriculture, forestry, and fishing. A cooperative movement developed in Bulgaria before World War II, and after the war it spread further, until probably more than 80 percent of the arable land was in cooperative farms. In 1957 there were 3,202 cooperative and state farms, which by 1970 had been merged into about 1,000 large state and collective units. Agriculture had grown unevenly, however, and in that year these were consolidated into 170 large agro-industrial complexes (later consolidated still further) to take better advantage of mechanization, including automation, supply, etc. Agriculture accounts for about 18 percent of the national income.

Crops

Cereal crops are grown on almost three-fifths of the sown land. Wheat is by far the most important (32 percent of sown land), followed by corn (maize) with nearly 15 percent and barley with 11 percent; rye, oats, and rice are also grown. Other food crops are varied, as farmers produce most of their own vegetables and fruits.

Industrial crops are important, especially tobacco, a good-quality Oriental type grown mainly in the south. Sunflower seed is the chief (about 90 percent) oil-seed crop; after extraction of the oil, the pulp is made into cattle feed. Sunflowers, like sugar beets, grow mainly in the north and were introduced after 1918. Bulgaria has become a leading exporter of grapes and tomatoes. Animal husbandry accounts for about 43 percent of the agricultural output.

Financial services. About half of the national expenditure goes toward financing the economy and about a quarter for education, science, culture, and social services. Around three-quarters of the budget is financed from the profits of the state-owned economy. The Bulgarian National Bank (Bŭlgarska Narodna Banka) is the principal banking institution, although a Bulgarian Foreign Trade Bank (Bŭlgarskata Vŭnshnotrgovska Banka) was set up in 1964, and the State Saving Bank (Dŭrzhavna spestovna kasa) and the State Insurance Institute (Dŭrzhaven zastrakhovatelen institut) are also incorporated into the financial and credit system.

Imports and exports

Foreign trade is a state monopoly. Capital goods make up some 47 percent and consumer goods (a large proportion of agricultural origin) 53 percent of the export total, while for imports the corresponding figures are 87.5 and 12.5 percent. The export of machinery and equipment is rising and accounts for more than a quarter of the value of all exports. About 70 percent of foreign trade is with Comecon member countries (half of the total foreign trade being with the Soviet Union) and 17 percent with the developed capitalist countries.

Management of the economy. *The state role.* The national economy is managed by the state, as noted above. The drafts of the five-year plans and of the budgets (including the budgets for local governments) are worked out by the Council of Ministers (the government) and approved by the National Assembly. The Council of Ministers organizes, directs, and controls the implementation of plan and budget, with the National Assembly regularly receiving progress reports on the work done.

Taxation. The main sources of revenue are the turnover tax and deductions made from the profits produced by public enterprises. The turnover tax is based on a fixed rate and goes immediately into the budget after the sale of products by state enterprises. In this way the state budget is ensured a regular and uniform source of revenue to finance the undertakings called for in the economic plan. The turnover tax is dependent on the size, variety, and sale of manufactured products; ultimately it is passed on to the consumer. The profit deduction tax from state enterprises, unlike the turnover tax, is not at a fixed rate. It comes from each enterprise's net income after deduction of the turnover tax. The profit shown by an enterprise is the difference between income and maintenance expenses. In the mid-1970s, 42 percent of an enterprise's profit was left for its own disposal after subtracting the two taxes.

Budget. The size of the state budget increased nearly eightfold between 1949 and 1969. Some of this was accounted for by loans from the Soviet Union, but the size of these loans is not generally known; they must be large enough to suggest that the deferred repayment for Bulgaria's industrialization policy will be the responsibility of several generations of Bulgarians in the future. The national budget finances most capital investments, enterprises under direct central management, and a number of social and cultural needs (*e.g.*, higher educational institutions, research institutes, etc.). It also covers defense and the central government departments. People's council budgets—those of the district, municipality, and village people's councils—maintain a variety of educational, health, and cultural institutions, urban development and planning, and various other services. The state social insurance budget covers expenditure for employees' pensions, temporary incapacity to work, maternity leave, maintenance of rest homes, family allowances, etc.

State loans

The national budget allots around 50 percent of its revenues to developing the national economy, a large portion of this going to development of heavy industry. It also provides funds for capital investment in industrial enterprises and provides them with turnover funds. Large credits are allocated to agricultural development and the supply of farm equipment. Budgetary credits are also used to finance long-term investment projects (*e.g.*, power generation, forestry, ferrous metallurgy, and land improvement and water conservation projects). About a third of all investment comes from state budgetary credits, and two-thirds is covered by local enterprises' funds and bank credits. About 30 percent of the budgetary expenditure goes to social services and about 2 percent to administration.

The role of trade unions. The Dimitrov Constitution of 1947 proclaimed the trade unions to be "mass, nonparty public organizations of the workers and employees." In fact, however, the trade unions all belong to one organization, the Central Council of Trade Unions (Tsentralen sŭvet na profesionalnite sŭyuzi), founded in 1944 with 264,000 members; by the mid-1970s, it had some 3,324,000. The whole of Bulgaria's labour force is under state control and theoretically not allowed to strike or to disobey the government. Evidence suggests that theory and practice sometimes differ; worker discontent and strikes occurring during early 1971 were followed by a broad purge of the top leadership of the Central Council of Trade Unions. Such administrative response to workers' discontent may not be effective in the long term; the workers' dislike for totally dependent bureaucratic organizations that in their view have done little to protect their interests tends to refute the official line that "the trade union is the chief organizer of the working people in the struggle for fulfilling the economic plan [and it is its duty to] see to labour safety and do its best to improve and meet the working people's social and communal needs, defending and representing their interests in the conclusion of labour contracts."

Transportation. The development of the Bulgarian economy has required the expansion of the transportation system. The relationship among the various components of the system is changing rapidly; by the mid-1970s, road transport accounted for 88 percent of all the freight carried (on a tonnage basis) and for about five-sixths of all passenger traffic.

Roads and railways. Roads and railways together account for all but a small fraction of both freight and passengers carried. Road mileage by the 1970s was more than double that before World War II. An expressway ring linking Sofia–Plovdiv–Burgas–Varna and Sofia–Pleven–Varna was under construction, and the E-5 European International Highway, crossing the country toward Istanbul, had been thoroughly reconstructed in the Kalotina–Kapitan Andreevo section.

By the mid-1970s, railway track mileage was only a fifth that of roads, though half as much again as the pre-World War II total. The main lines connect Sofia with the Black Sea coast, and electrification is underway.

Water and air transport. The Danube is used for both internal and international traffic, Ruse and Lom being the main river ports. The chief seaports are Varna and Burgas, and there is a regular international merchant service on the Black Sea. Bulgaria has international airports at Sofia, Varna, and Burgas, and internal air services are growing; scheduled international service showed a considerable increase during the 1960s and '70s.

Airports

ADMINISTRATION AND SOCIAL CONDITIONS

The constitutional framework. The People's Republic of Bulgaria is one of the states of the Communist bloc of eastern Europe. Power in this people's democracy, according to the constitution of May 18, 1971 (which replaced the so-called Dimitrov Constitution of 1947), resides in "the working people in town and countryside," and the Bulgarian Communist Party is "the leading force in society and in the state" ("leading" is permissible, since one other party is tolerated). The nominal supreme organ of power is the one-chamber National Assembly (Narodno Sŭbranie), which consists of 400 representatives elected for five-year terms from constituencies with equal numbers of inhabitants and which meets for very short sessions three times a year. The highest constantly functioning organ of state power is the State Council (Ministerski Sŭvet), theoretically responsible to the National Assembly, which has both legislative and executive functions. The Council of Ministers is the official executive and administrative organ.

The country is divided into 28 districts (*okrŭzi*, singular *okrŭg*), which are subdivided into municipalities (further divided, if large, into urban constituencies, or *rayoni*) and villages (grouped together to form rural constituencies, or *obshtini*). Organs of government paralleling those at the national level exist at the local levels.

In practice, the Bulgarian Communist Party exercises legislative and executive control at all levels of government.

The political process. Elections to the various representative bodies are open to all citizens who have attained the age of 18, and representatives are theoretically accountable to the electorate. There are two political parties. The ruling party is the Bulgarian Communist Party (Bŭlgarska Komunisticheska Partiya, or BKP), founded in 1891 as the Bulgarian Social Democratic Party, with about 790,000 members by 1976. The other party that is permitted to function is the Bulgarian Agrarian Union (Bŭlgarski Zemedelski Sŭyuz, or BZS), founded as a peasant organization in 1899, with some 120,000 members in the mid-1970s. The Fatherland Front (Otechestvenofront), founded in 1942 by several political parties and some independents, was transformed in 1948 into the largest mass organization, with some 3,770,000 members in the mid-1970s. The Dimitrov Young Communist League has a membership of about 1,300,000.

Bulgarian Communist Party

Justice and the armed forces. The judiciary is part of the government structure, ranking below the executive and legislative branches. The system of court organization distinguishes between general (district) courts, special courts (for the armed forces and transport facilities), and a Supreme Court. Supreme Court judges are elected by the National Assembly for terms of five years, judges of district courts for three years; judges of people's courts, on the lowest level, are elected by the general electorate for the same three–year period. All judges are subject to removal by the agency that elected them.

Individual court decisions (apart from those of the Supreme Court) are not a source of law and are binding only in the case for which they are rendered. Even judicial practice does not constitute a source of law. Decisions are important only for the elucidation of the contents of law and its application. A decision of the Supreme Court, however, taken at its civil, criminal, or military division, is considered binding upon the lower courts and a source of Bulgarian law.

According to a ruling of 1953, "the courts correctly understand and carry out the policy of the Bulgarian Communist Party and people's democratic power [*i.e.*, government] for a merciless struggle against the crimes as defined in the Criminal Code."

Bulgarian military forces are made up of the Bulgarian People's Army and the troops of the Ministry of the Interior, both under the State Council; the Bulgarian People's Army is under the immediate command of the Ministry of National Defense, most of whose members are military officers. The term of obligatory national service is two years, except in the naval forces, in which it is three. The army is well equipped with modern weapons and integrated with the forces of other Warsaw Treaty Organization member countries.

Military forces

Also under the Ministry of National Defense are the Border Troops, responsible for the integrity of the frontiers. The Construction Troops, which provide labour under military discipline and organization, are directly under the Council of Ministers. The Ministry of Internal Affairs supervises the activities of the People's Militia, who act as local police, and the state security police, who deal with crimes against national security or those presenting a threat to society.

Services. *Education.* Education is the responsibility of a government ministry and of the educational councils of local people's councils, while higher education is supervised by a special state committee. Education is free for all types and levels (for financing, see above *The economy: Management of the economy: Taxation*) and is obligatory for children from seven to 16 years of age. Since 1959, general education includes polytechnical subjects and vocational training. There are 21 semi-higher institutions and more than 30 higher institutions. The Sofiiski Universitet "Kliment Ohridski" (founded in 1888 as the Sofia Higher Institute) is the oldest body of higher learning and was the only university till 1971, when two teacher-training institutes in Plovdiv and Veliko Tŭrnovo were elevated to university status. There is a ratio of 1,800 students to 10,000 inhabitants, and the educational system compares well with other countries of Europe.

Health and welfare services. The health service, directed by a health ministry, provides free medical assistance of all types. By the mid-1970s there were more than 180 hospitals, with one bed per 130 inhabitants. In addition, a number of specialized establishments took care of tuberculosis patients and children. Medical social services are supported by an insurance plan that consists of a consolidated fund of contributions from state and cooperative enterprises and institutions and similar bodies. It is directed by the Central Council of Trade Unions and covers practically all of the working population.

Housing. Some 15 percent of the total capital investment in Bulgaria in the mid-1970s was going into housing, reflecting a program adopted in 1970 to try to alleviate the severe housing shortage caused by rapid urbanization. An amount equal to about 10 percent of the capital investment program is spent on individual housing construction, with the state granting to individuals loans that can be repaid over periods of up to 25 years.

Urban housing shortage

Social conditions. Since both wages and retail prices are controlled by the government, they are kept relatively stable in relation to one another. The highest annual wages are those in the building trades, lowest in agriculture. Monthly children's allowances, pensions, and sick pay in some cases add considerably to the income from wages alone.

Industrialization is having its effect on the socio-economic categories of the population: some 33.5 percent were engaged in industry in 1975, compared with 21.9 percent in 1960 (and 7.8 percent in 1934), while the share of agriculture declined from 54.7 to 27.6 percent over the same period. There has also been a rise in the numbers employed in education, culture, and art (from 3.4 percent in 1960 to 6.1 percent in 1975) and in the health services (1.6 percent to 3.6 percent). The percentage of women workers continues to rise, having reached 47.4 percent overall by 1975 and as high as 73.2 percent in finance, banking, and insurance.

CULTURAL LIFE AND INSTITUTIONS

Contemporary Bulgarian culture is a lively blend of the millennium-old folk traditions of the region; a more formal culture, which played a vital role in the emergence of national consciousness and the development of a modern state; and, since World War II, the development of a strong Communist element.

Socialist Realism

The fine and decorative arts and architecture. Socialist Realism now dominates Bulgarian painting, with its theme of building Communism. There is, nevertheless, much variety in individual forms and styles, ranging from satirical drawings and cartoons to portrait painting, genre pictures, and woodcuts. In applied arts—wood carving, ceramics, textiles, wrought iron, and embroidery—a number of artists are striving to blend contemporary artistic requirements with the old national traditions.

A new content has imbued architecture as a result of housing and public building programs and the development of professional and experienced architects. Many communities are changing their appearance, with well-planned housing developments replacing the often dilapidated older structures. The Black Sea coast has seen some of the more spectacular vacation and health resort developments, notably those of Zlatni Pyassŭtsi (Golden Sands) and Slunchev Bryag (Sunny Beach). Modern industrial architecture has also made headway, succeeding a rigid, monumental style imposed in the 1940s and '50s. The new industrial towns of Dimitrovgrad, Madan, and Rudozem are cited as examples of all-round planning.

Folklore and literature. Bulgaria is a country of rich, orally disseminated folklore; contemporary folklore, while preserving its old forms, is being enriched with a new content reflecting both the guerrilla movement of World War II and ensuing programs of reconstruction. There is a noticeable coming together of folklore and the general body of literature: folklore authors master the techniques and forms of personal poetry, while the contemporary writer is enriched by the poetic folklore heritage. Folklore is widely disseminated by books, radio, television, folk song and dance ensembles, and amateur folklore groups.

Bulgarian written literature dates from the 9th century AD, when SS. Cyril and Methodius created alphabets for Old Bulgarian (or Old Church Slavonic) and translated the Bible into that language. Their disciples created a literature that influenced the writers of Serbia, Russia, and Romania. From the 15th to the 18th century, Bulgarian literature suffered under Ottoman oppression. The literature of the ensuing Bulgarian revival was characterized by a democratic and realistic spirit and served the cause of national awakening and general cultural advance. It reached its climax in the poetry of Khristo Botev. After the liberation from the Turks in 1878 came the period of Critical Realism, of which Elin Pelin was probably the best example. The novels and poems of Ivan Vazov spanned the period before and after liberation, and the poetry of Pencho Slaveykov and Peyo Yavorov is also regarded as being of very high standard. The 1930s and '40s saw a number of anti-Fascist and antimilitarist works joining a growing undercurrent of working class and Marxist literature and criticism. Socialist Realism dominated the scene after World War II, and historical themes, as well as the anti-Fascist struggle, were accorded much attention by writers and critics. Among the writers should be mentioned the poets Elisaveta Bagryana and Valery Petrov and the prose writers Dimitr Talev, Dimitr Dimov, Emilian Stanev, and Nikolay Khaytov, as well as the humorist Yordan Radichkov and Blaga Dimitrova, author of both poetry and prose.

Bulgarian revival

Music and the theatre. By 1975 there were seven state opera houses, a number of orchestras, an operetta theatre, and state choreographic schools. Choir singing, instrumental music, and amateur activities are particularly developed, with such groups as the S. Obretenov Choir, the State Folk and Dance Ensemble, and the Bodra Smyana pioneer children's choir achieving international reputations. The two basses Boris Khristov and Nikolay Ghiaurov are probably the singers best known in the West.

The theatre has always had a strong tradition of Realism, and its principles were consolidated by N.O. Massalitinov, who studied at the Moscow Art Theatre and exerted a powerful influence as head of the Ivan Vazov National Theatre from 1925 to 1944. The "Krastju Sarafov" Higher Institute of Dramatic Art was set up in Sofia in 1948, and there are some three dozen state drama theatres, a dozen or so puppet theatres, and three Turkish variety theatres active in the country.

The cinema and the mass media. Prior to 1944, motion-picture production was limited, but during the ensuing decade a number of films were produced by a highly talented group. Major productions ranged from *Alert* (1951), concerning the problem of an individual person's neutrality in World War II, to *Farewell Friends* (1970), which was about the education of young people in a Communist society. The popularity of film going is reflected in high attendance rates.

By the mid-1970s some 498 newspapers, 830 periodicals, and 3,700 book titles were coming out regularly each year, and circulation figures reflected the high readership interest. Most of the newspapers are issued rather infrequently, however; only 13, for example, are dailies, all of them published in Sofia and all reflecting official views in their treatment of the news. Radio and television broadcasting—all operated by the state—by the mid-1970s reached, respectively, 262 and 168 persons per 1,000 population.

Institutions. There are some 10,500 libraries, with a total holding of about 59,460,000 volumes, and more than 180 museums. There are an additional 4,270 *chitalishchas,* which resemble reading rooms, found in even the smallest villages, that are a special Bulgarian form of cultural and educational activity. It first emerged in 1856 in Svishtov during Turkish bondage and has a very fine record in broadening the consciousness of a wide cross section of the community.

THE OUTLOOK

Techno-cratic manage-ment

By the early 1970s, the question of improving the technical and organizational standards of production, labour, and management was being raised with the greatest urgency. In this connection, automated managerial systems began to appear as early as 1968, and within a few years a number of electronic computer centres were under construction. One of Bulgaria's basic problems has been the lack of raw materials, and efforts have been directed toward increasing local supplies, which accounted for only half the total by the 1970s. An extended long-term forecast for power generation and an improvement of the national fuel and energy balance envisages heavy dependence on nuclear power plants (about a quarter of total electricity production by 1980).

Underproduction by workers, a consequence of lack of incentive, is considered by Western observers to be a serious problem. Continued urbanization will have marked effects on the demography of the country and the provision of social services. Overall coordination of all aspects of economic and social life will continue to be controlled by the state planning apparatus. It is hoped that the process will take into account the need for safeguarding the national heritage of a rich and distinctive culture.

BIBLIOGRAPHY. General works include SPASS ROUSSINOV, *Bulgaria: Land, Economy, Culture* (Eng. trans. 1965) and *A Race Against Time* (Eng. trans. 1962), on economic policy (both published in Sofia), and *Economic Development of Bulgaria after the Second World War* (1969); BULGARIAN NATIONAL COMMITTEE, *Bulgaria* (1964). Statistical data may be found in the *Statistical Yearbook of the People's Republic of Bulgaria*; and additional sources of information in MARIN V. PUNDEFF, *Bulgaria: A Bibliographic Guide* (1969). Also useful are EUGENE K. KEEFE *et al., Area Handbook for Bulgaria* (1974); BERNARD NEWMAN, *Bulgarian Background* (1961), the author's extensive travels in Bulgaria reflected in a comprehensive and balanced picture; BOGOSLAV DOBRIN, *Bulgarian Economic Development Since World War II* (1973); GURSHARAN SINGH, *Co-operative Farming in Bulgaria* (1959); NISSAN OREN, *Revolution Administered: Agrarianism and Communism in Bulgaria* (1973). (F.W.C./Ed.)

Bullfighting

Bullfighting is the Spanish national spectacle. It developed in Spain, the country that still is the hub of *la fiesta brava*, but there is also keen interest in it in Mexico, Peru, Colombia, and Venezuela. The Spanish name is *corrida de toros*, from the Latin *currere*, "to run," and *taurus*, "bull." Bulls used in *corridas de toros* are not the commonly known variety of meat or milk cattle, which are basically domesticated, but a distinctly savage breed.

Combats and spectacles with bulls were common in ancient Crete, Thessaly, and imperial Rome but depended on the inherent trait of domesticated cattle to flee their attackers; the distinguishing trait of savage Iberian stock is its spirited and continuous attack without the slightest provocation.

Iberia's savage horned beasts

History. Even before the Punic Wars the Celtiberian people knew the peculiarities of the savage cattle that inhabited their forests, having developed their hunt into a game and also having used them as an auxiliary in war. Thus, when in 228 BC the Carthaginian Hamilcar Barca marched on Ilici and blockaded the city, the defenders gathered a great herd of the beasts, attached wagons loaded with resinous wood to them, which they lighted with torches, and drove them at the enemy. In the ensuing battle Hamilcar was killed and his army annihilated. Carthaginians and Romans, disputing the known world between them, were astounded by accounts of Barca's annihilation. They were equally amazed at subsequent tales of games held in Baetica (the Spanish province of Andalusia) in which men exhibited dexterity and valour before dealing the death blow with ax or lance to a savage horned beast. The Iberians were reported to use skins or cloaks to avoid the repeated attacks of their savage bulls before killing them.

Conquest of the Iberian Peninsula by Vandals, Swabians (Sueves or Suebi), and Visigoths modified the customs of the people. Three centuries of Visigoth rule (AD 415–711) evolved a spectacle featuring brute strength of men over bulls (*forcados* or *pegadores*), later adopted by the Lusitanos (Portuguese) and still retained as one of their specialties. The Muslims from Africa who overran Andalusia in AD 711 gradually modified the existing games. As the Muslims were great horsemen, their dignity demanded that they take the lance from their vassals, relegating the peons to the inferior position of simply manoeuvring the animals on foot so that their mounted masters might perform to better advantage. The crumbling Roman amphitheatres of Seville, Cordova, Toledo, Tarragona, Mérida, and Cádiz were rebuilt and embellished. Tournaments developed as a result of the rivalry between Moorish chieftains and Christian Iberian knights, and, except in large cities that boasted amphitheatres, most festive occasions were held in the city square or plaza, from which all bullrings derive their names, or in the open fields outside the town.

The first Castilian to lance a bull from horseback is thought to have been Rodrigo Díaz de Vivar, "El Cid Campeador" (1043–99). After the Muslims were driven from Spain in the 15th century, bull-lancing tournaments continued to be the favourite sport of the aristocracy. By the time of the Austrian accession it had become an indispensable accessory of every court function, and Charles V endeared himself to his subjects by lancing a bull on the birthday of his son Philip II. During the reign of Philip IV the lance was discarded in favour of the *rejoncillo* (short spear) and the leg armour (still worn by the picadors) was introduced. As knowledge of the nobles' prowess spread, they were invited to competitive jousts in provincial tournaments. The nobles' unfamiliarity with the spirit of bulls other than their own caused the vassals to gain greater experience and fame than their masters. By 1700 they were performing on foot and had relegated their peons to a subordinate role on horseback (picador). By the early 1700s bull breeding had become financially profitable, and herds were bred for specific characteristics. The royal houses of Spain, France, Portugal, Italy, and even the Roman Catholic Church in Spain competed to present the best specimens in the ring.

First professional bullfighters: introduction of the sword

Papal threats of excommunication gradually wrought a radical transformation in the character of the *lidia* (bull joust), forcing the nobles to relinquish their role to professional subordinates who, because of class consciousness, discarded the lance in favour of the sword. One of the first great professional *espadas*—*i.e.*, the man who actually kills the bull—was Francisco Romero of Ronda in Andalusia (about 1700), who introduced the *estoque* (the sword still used to kill the bull) and the muleta (small, heart-shaped red worsted serge-type cloth cape folded lengthwise over a 56-cm staff), used in conjunction with the *estoque*. At the height of his fame, the artist Francisco José de Goya y Lucientes (1746–1828) designed a distinctive professional uniform (worn only on commemorative gala occasions in Goya-style *corridas* or *corridas goyescas*). Performers began using a net to hold back their shoulder-length hair, later tying it in a knot at the base of the skull for protection in falls when tossed by the bull, just as, before the innovation of the helmet, football players used their hair to protect the head. This hair style later developed into the *moña y coleta*, the satin-covered semispherical cork headpiece and short queue that became the distinguishing mark of the profession. Expense and lack of native spirited stock prevented bullfighting from taking root in France proper (though *corridas* are held in southern France) and Italy. Portugal retained the *rejoneadores* or *cabaleiros en praça* (lancers mounted on highly trained horses) who, with the *forcados* or *pegadores* and *salteadores* (men who pole-vault over a charging bull), comprise what is known as Portugal's *corridas* in which the bull's horns are padded or brass-ball tipped; thus the horses and bulls are rarely killed. After the introduction of railways, the *plazas de toros* in Spain, Portugal, and Latin America (where the conquistadors introduced *corridas* in the early 1500s) greatly multiplied. Spain in the second half of the 20th century had about 400 *plazas de toros* of all sizes, from those of Madrid and Barcelona, seating about 20,000 spectators each, to those of the small towns accommodating 1,500. The arena floor never varies more than several metres, those at higher altitudes being smaller than those at sea level to help compensate for altitude fatigue. The *plaza de toros* in Mexico City, inaugurated during the 1945–46 season, seats approximately 50,000.

Bull breeding. The bulls used in *corridas* are invariably of pedigreed lineage reared on special ranches (*ganaderías*), the most celebrated being those of Miura, from Seville, which have killed more famous matadors, including the great Manolete, than any others. Shortly after weaning, vaccinating, and branding, the yearling males are tested in the open fields (*tienta de acoso y derribo*, hazing and tumbling), and only those displaying the proper spirit are retained for future *corridas*. Some yearlings of remarkable pedigree, true coloration, and fine physical construction are separated and when three years old are put through a series of tests (*tentadero de sementales*, stud tests) designed to prove the animal's spirit beyond a doubt. If acceptable, such bulls are then used exclusively at stud, usually 15 years; if not, they are sent to the slaughterhouse. At two to three years the heifers are tested in a small ring at the ranch (*tentadero de vaquillas*, test of heifers to be used for breeding) through all the phases of the *corrida* and only those acceptable are used; the rejects or culls go to the slaughterhouse. Royalty attended these tests, which became fortnightly social events at which famous matadors practiced new manoeuvres.

Bulls are never used a second time in the *corrida*. First, their memory is remarkable and former experience would not permit the type of performance expected; and second, to be acceptable for a *corrida*, they must be physically virgin as well as virgin of contact with any phase of the *corrida*. All cattle are colour blind. The colour red has been adopted for the work cape and muleta since it minimizes the sight of blood and other

(Left) Manolete (Manuel Rodríguez) executes a natural, a close *pase* with the muleta in the left hand. (Right) Matador Carlos Arruza places *banderillas* from horseback.

(Left) Barnaby Conrad, (right) C. Don Mengason

stains and produces a more colourful spectacle; the inside of the cape is yellow and the bulls charge just as readily at it as they do the red.

Performers. *Toreros* or professional bull men consist of matadors; *banderilleros*, assistants on foot who work with the cape and also place *banderillas*; and picadors, mounted assistants with pike poles, or lances. Six bulls usually are killed during one *corrida*, the matadors, whose *cuadrillas* or troupes consist of two or three *banderilleros* and two or three picadors to each, alternating in the performance according to seniority in the profession. Matadors must pass through a trying novitiate as *novilleros* (professional novices) before receiving the *alternativa*, the ritualistic ceremony in which the senior matador confers on the novice professional status and acceptance as a professional equal, capable of dispatching any bull properly.

The ceremony. The *corrida* begins with the grand entry procession of the *cuadrillas* led by one or two mounted *alguaciles* (bailiffs in 16th-century costume). The matadors wear short jackets, waistcoats, and knee-length, skintight trousers of silk and satin, richly embroidered in gold, silver, and silk; dress capes of satin, heavily embroidered in gold, silver, and silk, or combinations of them, worn only during the entry procession; handdrawn linen lace shirtwaists: coral-pink heavy silk stockings; flat, heelless black slippers; and *monteras* or hats made of tiny black silk chenille balls hand sewn in special designs on heavy buckram. *Banderilleros* wear similar garments, lacking only the gold embroidery, which is reserved exclusively for the matadors. Picadors wear broad-brimmed, low-crowned, heavy, beige-coloured hats called *castoreños*, jackets and waistcoats similar to those of the matadors but not as ornate, hip-to-ankle armour of steel one-eighth inch thick on the right leg, and knee-length left-leg armour covered by tightly fitting trousers of heavy cream-coloured chamois and heavily protected chamois ankle boots.

Opening ceremonies

After the opening procession has crossed the arena, the *presidente municipal* (the mayor or his legal representative) throws down to one of the *alguaciles* the key to the *toriles* or bull pens. When the *cuadrillas* not performing with this bull have left the arena and the others have taken their respective positions, the *toril* door is opened. As the bull passes through the *toril* door, an attendant perched above attaches a silken rosette made of the ranch colours into the shoulder muscles of the bull. A *banderillero* capes the bull with one hand only, so that the matador may judge whether the bull shows marked preference in the use of either horn or attacks equally from both sides. Then the matador goes into the arena and performs the initial passes, usually the basic *verónica*, working as gracefully and as close to the horns as possible. During the cape work, a bugle signals the entrance of the picadors, the beginning of the first of the three main divisions or acts (*tercios*) that constitute the fight—the *pic*-ing, the planting of the *banderillas*, and the kill. The picadors move into position, and when the bull charges the horse it is the picador's duty to fend off the attack by the use of his pike pole, planting the point in the bull at the junction of the neck and shoulder blades. Because of shocking and unnecessary disembowelment of the horses, complete protective armour made of three-inch thick compressed cotton encased in leather and canvas, encouraged by Sidney Franklin, the first U.S.-born professional matador, was officially adopted in March 1930, thus virtually eliminating harm to the horses.

The three matadors vie in series of passes (*quites*) as gracefully as possible, taking turns in order of seniority (the matador performing with this bull coming first, the others following in turn). This is done a minimum of two times and a maximum of four, stamina and spirit of the bull dictating the number. A bugle call announces the *tercio de banderillas*, and the picadors retire from the arena. *Banderilleros* alternate in planting two to four pairs of *banderillas* (72-centimetre staves decorated with coloured paper and with a 3-centimetre barb at one end) in the bull's shoulders at the junction with the neck. This is done by attracting the bull's attention with violent gestures and shouts from a distance of 20 to 30 yards. As the bull charges, the *banderillero* runs forward and slightly to one side, and as both come together, the *banderillas* are deftly planted, the man spins away to safety, and the bull's momentum takes it out of goring range. The basic object of both the *banderillas* and the picador's use of the pike pole is to weaken the great neck muscle of the bull so that his head will be low enough at the end of the fight for the matador to kill him with the sword. Some matadors, especially the Mexicans, are highly skilled with the *banderillas* and plant their own.

The Hour of Truth

Another trumpet call signals the third and final *tercio*, the killing, known as the Hour of Truth. This is done by the matador alone, his *banderilleros* being present only in case of emergency or should he request their assistance. The matador takes a position below the *presidente's* box and with *montera* held aloft in his right hand, muleta and *estoque* in his left, he formally requests permission to *brindar* (dedicate) the bull to some personage or friend to whom he tosses his *montera*. After the matador has performed many dangerous and graceful passes with the bull to prove complete mastery (using only the muleta, which may be spread wider with the *estoque*), he prepares for the kill. This is done *al volapié*, or "fleet-foot," in which man and bull attack each other from a standstill position; or *recibiendo*, in which the man stands still and receives the bull. The latter is rarely done because of the great precision and courage required for its successful completion. At no time is the matador permitted to touch the bull with the *estoque* except for the kill. Improper ethics on the part of any *torero* during a *corrida* may result in heavy fines or jail sentences, or both.

The kill

The kill is executed by the matador thrusting forward the muleta with his left hand, causing the bull to lower his head in quest of his adversary, while with his right hand the matador sinks the *estoque* between the bull's shoulder blades at the junction with the neck. The blade should penetrate diagonally, severing the aorta, or great artery; the thrust, if well executed, causes almost instant death.

After the kill the matador, if acclaimed, circles the arena with his *banderilleros* to the applause of the spectators. Then he returns to the person honoured by his *brindis* to retrieve his *montera*, which invariably is returned with money or a gift. If the performance has been excellent the matador receives, as a token of popular esteem, one ear of the bull. If it has been exceptional he receives two ears. If his success should be extravagant, he receives both ears and the tail. While the matador is being acclaimed, a *puntillero* (an attendant armed with a short blade) severs the bull's spinal cord at the base of the skull, and the carcass is dragged from the arena, quartered, and dressed. Sometimes the bull's meat is given to the poor, but usually it is sold right at the *plaza de toros*. The ring is raked over, the next bull is introduced, and the spectacle begins anew.

A specific and colourful vocabulary has evolved to describe each of the actions and manoeuvres of the participants, the performance of the bull, and other aspects of the spectacle. Many of the terms, which are Spanish, derive from slang used by Gypsies (*caló*). Glossaries of bullfighting terms may be found in the references cited in the bibliography, below.

Great matadors. The star performer of this spectacle, the matador, can be and often is a wealthy man. When Manolete was killed at the age of 30 in 1947, he had made the equivalent of $4,000,000 U.S. Many *toreros* (never "toreadors," a word popularized by the French composer Georges Bizet in his opera *Carmen*) risk their lives for 10 years or so, amass a fortune, and then retire to a large ranch where they raise bulls for younger men to fight, as Juan Belmonte did.

Juan Belmonte

It was Belmonte who truly revolutionized the ancient spectacle about 1914. Formerly, the main object of the fight had been only to prepare the bull for the sword thrust; Belmonte, a small, frail Andalusian, emphasized the danger to the man by close and graceful capework, and the kill became secondary. He worked closer to the horns than people had ever believed possible and became an overnight sensation. The crowd does not actually wish to see a man killed, but the possibility of death and the man's disdain of it and his skillful avoidance of injury thrills a crowd.

The audience is not interested in simply seeing a man go into an arena, kill an animal in the safest manner, and emerge unscathed; they want to see skill, grace, and daring. Therefore a *corrida* is not really a struggle between a man and a bull but rather the struggle of a man with himself: how close will he dare to let the horns come, how far will he go to please the crowd?

Joselito (José Gómez), Belmonte's great friend and rival, considered the greatest bullfighter of all time, gave his life for the crowds in 1920, as have many men. Virtually every matador is gored at least once a season in varying degrees of severity. Belmonte was gored more than 50 times. Of the approximately 125 major matadors (since 1700), more than 40 have been killed in the ring; this figure does not include beginning matadors, *banderilleros*, and picadors who have been killed.

The greatest matadors of the 20th century have been the Mexicans Rodolfo Gaona, Armillita Chico (Fermín Espinosa), and Carlos Arruza; and the Spaniards Belmonte, Joselito, Domingo Ortega, and Manolete (Manuel Rodríguez). Perhaps the man who made the largest sum of money was El Cordobés (Manuel Benítez), who dominated bullfighting from 1963 until his retirement.

C. Don Mengason

Matador Jaime Bolaños faces the bull for the kill.

Women bullfighters

There have been several women bullfighters but no great ones. The first mention of a *torera* occurred in 1654. Later, one of Goya's etchings depicted "the manly courage of La Pajuelera" as she performed in the arena at Zaragoza. Even a nun, Doña María de Gaucín, supposedly left a convent in an unknown year to become a *torera*. Around the turn of the 20th century, "La Reverte" became famous as a *señorita matadora*, but in 1908 the government of Spain declared it illegal for women to perform in bullrings, so that "La Reverte" was forced to doff his wig and reveal himself as a man. In modern times two young American women, Bette Ford and Patricia McCormick, attracted publicity by fighting as *novilleras* with a modicum of success. The finest female bullfighter, however, is generally agreed to have been Conchita Cintrón, who achieved great success in Peru, Mexico, and Spain in the late 1930s and early '40s, fighting both on horseback in the Portuguese style and on foot. She was the only woman of any nationality to be taken seriously by both spectators and fellow bullfighters. While women are allowed to fight bulls on foot in Latin America, such practice is prohibited on the Iberian Peninsula, where, however, they may still perform on horseback.

BIBLIOGRAPHY. ERNEST HEMINGWAY, *Death in the Afternoon* (1932); REX SMITH, *Biography of the Bulls: An Anthology of Spanish Bullfighting* (1957); BARNABY CONRAD, *La Fiesta Brava: The Art of the Bull Ring* (1953), *Gates of Fear* (1957), *The Death of Manolete* (1958), and (ed.), *Encyclopedia of Bullfighting* (1961); CARLOS ARRUZA, *My Life as a Matador* (1956); JUAN BELMONTE, *Juan Belmonte, Killer of Bulls* (1937); ANGUS MACNAB, *The Bulls of Iberia: An Account of the Bullfight* (1957); KENNETH TYNAN, *Bull Fever*, 2nd rev. ed. (1966).

(B.C.)

Bultmann, Rudolf

Perhaps the leading New Testament scholar of the 20th century and certainly the one who occasioned the most controversy, Rudolf Bultmann was best known for his program to "demythologize" the New Testament. He held that its essential message was expressed in mythical terms derived from the mythological context of its time and place, and he proposed to interpret these "myths" (*e.g.*, virgin birth, incarnation, Resurrection) in terms of the categories of 20th-century Existentialist philosophy in order to give meaning to the message for modern man. Both his view of the New Testament texts as essentially mythical rather than historical and his explicit use of

Existentialist philosophy to interpret them aroused intense discussion. Bultmann was also a major figure in the general theological field, one of the giants of the period between the two World Wars. His theological position also aroused controversy, because he claimed, following his interpretation of Paul the Apostle and John the Evangelist, that Christian faith is, and should be, comparatively uninterested in the historical Jesus and centred instead on the transcendent Christ. Christian faith, he asserted, is faith in the *kērygma* ("proclamation") of the church, into which Jesus may be said to be risen (Bultmann's understanding of the Resurrection), and not faith in the historical Jesus.

Rudolf Karl Bultmann was born on August 20, 1884, at Wiefelstede, Germany, the son of a Lutheran pastor and the grandson of a missionary. He always intended to

By courtesy of James M. Robinson

Rudolf Bultmann.

follow an academic theological career, and at 19 he began his theological studies at the University of Tübingen. By 1912 he had completed his qualifying studies and was appointed a lecturer at the University of Marburg. There followed appointments at Breslau (1916) and Giessen (1920). In 1921 he was appointed professor of New Testament at Marburg, where he remained until his retirement in 1951. He continued his residence in Marburg after his retirement.

Early works

In 1921 Bultmann published his *Geschichte der synoptischen Tradition* (*History of the Synoptic Tradition*), an analysis of the traditional material used by the Evangelists Matthew, Mark, and Luke and an attempt to trace its history in the tradition of the church prior to their use of it. This proved to be a seminal work, and it established Bultmann's reputation as a scholar. He followed it with a book on Jesus (*Jesus*, 1926; English translation, *Jesus and the Word*, 1934), in which the beginning of his own theological position can be traced. Between 1922 and 1928 he had as a colleague at Marburg the German Existentialist philosopher Martin Heidegger, whose *Sein und Zeit* (*Being and Time*) was published in 1927. Heidegger was enormously influential upon Bultmann, in part because Bultmann felt that he was developing, in philosophical terms, an analysis of human existence that was strikingly parallel to the understanding of human existence implied by the theologies of Paul and John, as Bultmann interpreted them. It was during these years of discussion with Heidegger that Bultmann developed his own theological position, which found its earliest expression in two essays, "Der Begriff der Offenbarung im Neuen Testament" ("The Concept of Revelation in the New Testament"), written in 1929, and "Die Geschichtlichkeit des Daseins und der Glaube" ("The Historicity of Man and Faith"), written in 1930. His position was to remain constant thereafter, and all his subsequent work, including his demythologizing proposal made in 1941, developed consistently out of it.

During the Hitler years in Germany, Bultmann refused to modify his teaching in any way to suit Nazi ideology, and he supported the Confessing Church, the German Protestant movement organized to resist Nazi church policy. But, in his own words, he "never directly and actively participated in political affairs"; *i.e.*, he did not directly oppose the Nazi regime. With the resumption of contacts between the German universities and the rest of the world after World War II, Bultmann became a major international academic figure. His pupils came to occupy leading positions in German universities, and his views were the subject of discussion around the world. All New Testament scholars found themselves in dialogue with him, and among theologians his position became the point of departure for major developments in both Germany and the United States. He himself gave an extremely influential series of lectures in Britain in 1955 (*History and Eschatology: The Presence of Eternity*) and in the United States in 1958 (*Jesus Christ and Mythology*), and his demythologizing program became the subject of a multivolume series with the title *Kerygma und Mythos* (*Kerygma and Myth*).

Assessment

Bultmann was an outstanding teacher, and he encouraged independence of mind among his students. The result was two major developments within the "Bultmann school." In 1954 Ernst Käsemann raised "the question of the historical Jesus" (*i.e.*, the question of the significance of knowledge of the historical Jesus for Christian faith), and a number of Bultmann's pupils developed a position independent of their teacher's on the matter. Then Ernst Fuchs and Gerhard Ebeling, building on Bultmann's Existentialist analysis, developed a method of interpreting the New Testament that emphasized the linguistic mode of human existence. This is the so-called new hermeneutic.

Bultmann himself took part in these discussions among his pupils for as long as his health permitted, later living quietly in Marburg, where he died on July 30, 1976.

BIBLIOGRAPHY. There is no formal biography of Bultmann, although some discussions of his theology include a biographical sketch and there is "Autobiographical Reflections" in C.W. KEGLEY (ed.), *The Theology of Rudolf Bultmann* (1966), in itself a series of dialogues between Bultmann and other scholars. Collections of essays by and about Bultmann include H.W. BARTSCH (ed.), *Kerygma und Mythos*, 4th rev. ed. (1960; Eng. trans., *Kerygma and Myth I*, 1961, and . . . *II*, 1962); C.E. BRAATEN and R.A. HARRISVILLE (eds.), *Kerygma and History* (1962), and *The Historical Jesus and the Kerygmatic Christ* (1964), and SCHUBERT M. OGDEN (ed.), *Existence and Faith* (1973), a collection of Bultmann's shorter writings. Important discussions of his theology are found in SCHUBERT M. OGDEN, *Christ Without Myth* (1961); R. MARLE, *Bultmann et l'interprétation du Nouveau Testament* (1956); W. SCHMITHALS, *Die Theologie Rudolf Bultmanns: Eine Einführung* (1967; Eng. trans., *An Introduction to the Theology of Rudolf Bultmann*, 1968); and G. HASENHUTTL, *Der Glaubenvollzug* (1963). Popularly written are N. PERRIN, *The Promise of Bultmann* (1969), J.M. ROBINSON, *A New Quest of the Historical Jesus* (1959; there are important changes in the German versions *Kerygma und historischer Jesus*, 1960; rev. ed., 1967); and J.M. ROBINSON and J.B. COBB (eds.), *The New Hermeneutic* (1964), details the developments within the "Bultmann school."

(N.P.)

Buñuel, Luis

Probably the most controversial of film makers, Luis Buñuel owes his fame to his absolute sincerity. Ignoring fashions and conventions, he has pursued his career in his native Spain, in France, in the United States, and in Mexico for a half century, mostly working within the limitations of the film industry. Yet, no other film maker has been more personal, more frank in expressing his continuing obsessions with social injustice, religious excess, gratuitous cruelty, and eroticism—themes as evident in his first film, the avant-garde Surrealist classic *Un Chien andalou* (1928; *An Andalusian Dog*), as in his greatest international success, *Tristana* (1970).

Buñuel.
Camera Press—Publix

The eldest of seven children, Buñuel was born on February 22, 1900, at Calanda, in northeastern Spain. From his father, Leonardo Buñuel, a businessman, who had left home at the age of 14 to join the army and fight in Cuba in the Spanish-American War (1898), Luis inherited an adventurous spirit. He excelled at school, in Saragossa, spending only his holidays in Calanda. He was also good at sports, such as boxing, and in playing the violin. He attended a Jesuit college in Saragossa, until at 17 he entered the University of Madrid, where he became a friend of the painter Salvador Dalí and the poet Federico García Lorca. In 1920 Buñuel founded the first Spanish movie club and wrote critiques of the films shown there.

Early interest in film

Having discovered Freudian psychoanalysis and having broken away from religion, he went to Paris in 1925 and entered film-producing circles, feeling that films would become his true medium of expression.

In 1926 he became an assistant director, and in 1928 he directed his first picture, *Un Chien andalou*, in collaboration with Dalí. It created a sensation: at a time when movies tended to be dominated by the natural and the literal, Buñuel discovered the cinema of instinct, which issued through him from the Surrealist movement. Spain always remained the background of his films, the moral and poetical content of which was expressed in terms of Surrealism.

His next two films—*L'Age d'or* (1930; *The Golden Age*), a radically anticlerical and antibourgeois film made in France, and *Las Hurdes* (1932; English title, *Land Without Bread*), a documentary about a particularly wretched region of Spain—asserted his concern with the freedom to dream and to imagine, his revolutionary attitude toward social problems, his aggressive sense of humour, and his contempt for traditional logic.

In Spain, Buñuel acted as producer of a number of commercial films in an attempt to build a native industry. When the Spanish Civil War began in 1936, he volunteered to the republican government in Paris, and in 1938, he acted as a technical adviser for two Hollywood films about the Spanish Republic. In the United States he experienced his greatest difficulties. He did some film editing and worked briefly for the Museum of Modern Art, in New York City, until it became known that he had directed the atheistic *L'Age d'or*, and he was allegedly forced to resign. In 1947 he settled in Mexico with his wife and two sons.

Exile from Spain

There he began a new career, directing pictures designed to have box-office appeal, into which he introduced one or two freely creative sequences. The success of one of these, *El gran calavera* (1949; *The Great Madcap*), allowed him to make a personal film, *Los olvidados* (1950; *The Young and the Damned*), a fascinating argument in favour of juvenile offenders.

Buñuel exercised more and more freedom in allowing the "free" sequences to invade otherwise conventional films, and his own blasphemous but tender world reappeared more often. Soon all his films, even those imposed upon him by producers, such as *Robinson Crusoe* (1952), rendered the Buñuelian universe—a dreamland in which strange and unwonted happenings occur. The most sincere poetry is combined with an aggressiveness, born of tenderness, in his work. His great films from this Mexican period include *Ensayo de un crimen* (1955; *The Criminal Life of Archibald de la Cruz*) and *Nazarin* (1958), about an unworldly priest.

In 1960 Buñuel was allowed to return to Spain to make *Viridiana;* the Spanish authorities, however, found the completed film to be anticlerical and tried to suppress it. Nonetheless, it was smuggled out to be shown at the Cannes Festival, where it was awarded the top prize. In 1962, in Mexico, he made another major work, *El ángel exterminador* (*The Exterminating Angel*), about a formal dinner party from which the guests find themselves powerless to depart; it too was interpreted as having powerful anticlerical connotations.

Now acclaimed throughout the world, Buñuel was again free to make films as he chose, as he had not been since his first period in France. Critics everywhere declared him to be among the authentic creative geniuses in film, one of the few capable of achieving popular as well as critical success.

Implications of Buñuel's success

Buñuel's late films offer a remarkable diversity of themes: *Le Journal d'une femme de chambre* (1964; *The Diary of a Chambermaid*) deals with problems of social status; the 42-minute *Simón del desierto* (1965; *Simon of the Desert*) and *La Voie lactée* (1969; *The Milky Way*) contain humorous reflections on religion; and *Belle de jour* (1966) and *Tristana* show the destruction of dream and reality, the confusion of true and false, of the rational and the imaginary. Buñuel's late works are increasingly calm and serene, avoiding all spectacular technical effects in favour of clear and simple expression that is still surprising and complex in its inner meaning.

MAJOR WORKS

Un Chien andalou (1928; *An Andalusian Dog*); *L'Age d'or* (1930; *The Age of Gold*); *Las Hurdes* (1932; *Land Without Bread*); *Los olvidados* (1950; *The Young and the Damned*); *Robinson Crusoe* (1952); *El* (1952); *Ensayo de un crimen* (1955; *The Criminal Life of Archibaldo de La Cruz*); *Nazarin* (1958); *Viridiana* (1961); *El ángel exterminador* (1962; *The Exterminating Angel*); *Le Journal d'une femme de chambre* (1964; *The Dairy of a Chambermaid*); *Simon del desierto* (1965; *Simon of the Desert*); *Belle de jour* (1966); *Tristana* (1970).

BIBLIOGRAPHY. The most complete monographs are ADONIS KYROU, *Luis Buñuel*, 4th French ed. (1970; Eng. trans., 1963); FRANCISCO ARANDA, *Luis Buñuel* (1969), in Spanish; RAYMOND DURGNAT, *Buñuel* (1967); and FREDDY BUACHE, *Luis Buñuel* (1970), in French. Buñuel's works have amply been studied in general publications dealing with different aspects of the cinema. His Surrealist character is analyzed by J.B. BRUNIUS, Buñuel's assistant in the production of *The Age of Gold*, in *En Marge du cinéma français* (1954). ADONIS KYROU, *Le Surréalisme au cinéma* (1963), places Buñuel's works in the Surrealist context of the 1920s and 1930s. Buñuel wrote fascinating film reviews in the periodical *Cahiers d'Art* in 1927, and poetical texts by him appeared in Surrealist magazines of that time: "Une Girafe," a poem in prose, in *Le Surréalisme au Service de la Révolution* (May 15, 1933), and "Réponse à un questionnaire sur l'amour," in *La Révolution Surréaliste* (December 15, 1929).

(A.Ky.)

Bunyan, John

John Bunyan, English Puritan minister and preacher, was the author of *The Pilgrim's Progress*, a work of universal appeal and the most characteristic expression of the Puritan religious outlook. Born in November 1628, at Elstow near Bedford, in the heart of the agricultural midlands, he declared that he had been brought up "among a multitude of poor plowmen's children"; his father Thomas Bunyan was a brazier, or travelling tinker. He learned to read and write at a local grammar school, but he probably left school early to learn the family trade.

Early life. Bunyan's mind and imagination were formed in these early days by influences other than those of formal education. He absorbed with delight the popular tales of adventure that appeared in chapbooks and were sold at fairs like the great one held at Stourbridge near Cambridge (it provided the inspiration for Vanity Fair in *The Pilgrim's Progress*). In these works, such as *Bevis of Hampton* and *The Seven Champions of Christendom*, the heroes of medieval romance entered the lives

Influences on Bunyan

of the common people. He also became acquainted with the varied popular literature of the English Puritans: plain-speaking sermons, homely moral dialogues, books of melodramatic judgments and acts of divine guidance, and Foxe's *Book of Martyrs* with the fearsome woodcuts of the Elizabethan edition. Above all he steeped himself in the English Bible; the Authorized Version was but 30 years old when he was a boy of 12. As a child whose parents were "of the national church," he was not cut off by a narrow piety but brought up on the general store of

By courtesy of the trustees of the British Museum

Bunyan, pencil drawing on vellum by Robert White (1645–1704). In the British Museum.

country lore and tradition. He had seen the shot bird tumble headlong from the tree; his mind was stocked with proverbs: both visual experience and popular saying were to go into his later works.

Bunyan speaks in his autobiography of being troubled by terrifying dreams. It may be that there was a pathological side to the nervous intensity of these fears; in the religious crisis of his early manhood his sense of guilt took the form of delusions. But it seems to have been abnormal sensitiveness combined with the tendency to exaggeration that caused him to look back on himself in youth as "the very ringleader of all . . . that kept me company into all manner of vice and ungodliness."

In 1644 a series of misfortunes separated the country boy from his family and drove him into the world. His mother died in June, his younger sister Margaret in July; in August his father married a third wife. The Civil War had broken out, and in November he was mustered in a parliamentary levy and sent to reinforce the garrison at Newport Pagnell. The governor was Sir Samuel Luke, immortalized as the Presbyterian knight of the title in Samuel Butler's *Hudibras.* In Newport Bunyan remained till July 1647; it is likely that he saw little fighting, though once when he was "drawn out to go to such a place to besiege it" (probably Leicester), a comrade took his place and was shot, so that later he felt he had been preserved by divine providence.

His military service, even if uneventful, brought him in touch with the seething religious life of the left-wing sects within Cromwell's army, the preaching captains, and those Quakers, Seekers, and Ranters who were beginning to question all authority except that of the individual conscience. Luke had trouble with many such religious agitators passing through his garrison; in this atmosphere Bunyan became acquainted with the leading ideas of the Puritan sectaries, shared alike by Cromwell and his meanest trooper. They believed that the striving for religious truth meant an obstinate search, often from sect to sect, relying on free grace revealed to the individual, and condemning all forms of public organization as "legal and dark." The devotion of the New Model Army both in prayer and action left an indelible impression on him; it is recalled in *The Holy War* in the preaching, drilling captains of Emanuel's army, Credence and Boanerges.

Some time after his discharge from the Army (in July 1647) and before 1649, Bunyan married. He says in his autobiography *Grace Abounding* that he and his first wife "came together as poor as poor might be, not having so much household-stuff as a dish or spoon betwixt us both." His wife came from a godly family and she brought to him as her dowry two evangelical books, Arthur Dent's *The Plain Man's Path-way to Heaven* and Lewis Bayly's *The Practice of Piety;* the former taught him that even a religious tract could employ racy colloquialisms and salt its precepts with homely proverbs. Their first child, a blind daughter Mary, was baptized in July 1650. Three more children, Elizabeth, John, and Thomas, were born to Bunyan's first wife before her death in 1658. The record of Elizabeth's birth in the transcript register of Elstow shows that she, too, was baptized in the parish church there in 1654, though by that time her father had been baptized by immersion as a member of the Bedford separatist church.

Bunyan's family

Conversion and ministry. Bunyan's conversion was a gradual process in the years following his marriage (1650–55); it is dramatically described in his autobiography. After an initial period of legal conformity in which he went regularly to church and looked with awe at the "priest" and his "vestments" (probably at this period a plain Geneva gown), he gave up, slowly and grudgingly, his favourite recreations of dancing and bell ringing and sports on the village green, and began to concentrate solely on his inner life. Then came agonizing temptations to spiritual despair lasting for several years. The "storms" of temptation, as he calls them, buffeted him with almost physical violence; voices urged him to blaspheme; the texts of scriptures, which seemed to him to threaten damnation, took on personal shape and "did" pinch him very sore." Finally one morning he believed that he had surrendered to these voices of Satan and had betrayed Christ: "Down I fell as a bird that is shot from the tree." In his psychopathic isolation and despair he presents all the features of the divided mind of the maladjusted as they have been analyzed in the 20th century; Bunyan, however, had a contemporary psychological instrument for the diagnosis of his condition, the pastoral theology of 17th-century Calvinism, which interpreted the grim doctrine of election and predestination in terms of the real needs of souls, the evidence of spiritual progress in them, and the covenant of God's grace. Both techniques, that of the modern analyst and that of the Puritan preacher, have in common the aim of recovering the integrity of the self; and this was what Bunyan achieved as he emerged, slowly and painfully, from his period of spiritual darkness, gradually beginning to feel that his sin was "not unto death" and that there were texts to comfort as well as to terrify. He was aided in his recovery by association with the Bedford separatist church and its dynamic leader John Gifford. He entered into full communion with this church about 1655.

The Bedford community practiced adult baptism by immersion but unlike the strict Baptists it did not insist on this as a condition of church membership; its position was closer to that of modern Congregationalists: it was an open-communion church, admitting all who professed "faith in Christ and holiness of life."

Bunyan as preacher

Bunyan soon proved his talents as a rousing lay preacher. Fresh from his own spiritual troubles, he was fitted to warn and console others: "I went myself in Chains to preach to them in Chains, and carried that Fire in my own Conscience that I persuaded them to beware of." He was also active in visiting and exhorting church members, but his main activity in 1655–60 was in controversy with the early Quakers, both in public debate up and down the market towns of Bedfordshire and in his first printed works, *Some Gospel Truths Opened* (1656) and *A Vindication of Some Gospel Truths Opened* (1657). The Quakers and the open-communion Baptists were rivals for the religious allegiance of the "mechanics" or small tradesmen and artificers in town and country; much alike in class attitude, stress on salvation by free grace, and separation from the world, they were divided, apart from the strains of evangelical competition, by the Friends' doctrine of the inner light. Bunyan's passionate conviction was always expressed in an orthodox, objective theology with a clear frontier drawn between the realms of God and man. This explains the violence of his protest against what seemed to him the dangerously blurred and self-centred mysticism of the Quaker preacher Edward Burrough. He soon became recognized as a leader among the sectaries. Already in 1659 a letter to George Fox speaks of "Bunyan and his people."

The Restoration of Charles II brought to an end the 20 years in which the separated churches had enjoyed freedom of worship and exercised some influence on government policy. On Nov. 12, 1660, at Lower Samsell in South Bedfordshire, Bunyan was brought before a local magistrate and, under an old Elizabethan act, charged with holding a service not in conformity with those of the Church of England. He refused to give an assurance that he would not repeat the offense, was condemned at the assizes in January 1661, and imprisoned in the county jail in Bedford. In spite of the courageous efforts of his second wife (he had married again in 1659) to have his case brought up at the assizes, he remained in prison for 12 years. A late-17th-century biography, added to the early editions of *Grace Abounding*, reveals that he relieved his family by making and selling "many hundred gross of long Tagg'd laces"; prison conditions were lenient enough for him to be let out at times to visit friends and family and even to address meetings.

Bunyan's imprisonment

Literary activity. During this imprisonment Bunyan wrote and published his spiritual autobiography (*Grace Abounding*, 1666). In the effort to recall the state of his soul with complete accuracy and absolute honesty he achieved a remarkable prose instrument for subjective analysis. He describes his inner life in a style rich in powerful physical imagery; the text that seemed to spell out his damnation "stood like a mill-post at my back." The imaginative vitality of his subsequent work, *The Pilgrim's Progress*, springs from a blending of the musical flow of this dreamlike, introspective style with the popular sermon style of the "mechanic preacher," which draws on the common life and culture of the countryside; his comparisons always appeal to common experience, as witness the rustic reality of his portraits of hypocrites:

> His house is as empty of Religion as the white of an egg is of savour . . . a saint abroad and a devil at home.

Bunyan's release from prison came in March 1672 under Charles II's Declaration of Indulgence to the Nonconformists. The Bedford community had already chosen him as their pastor in January, "after much seeking God by prayer" (Bedford Church Book) and a new meeting-house was obtained. In May he received a license to preach together with 25 other Nonconformist ministers in Bedfordshire and the surrounding counties. His nickname "Bishop Bunyan" suggests that he became the organizing genius in the area. When persecution was renewed he was again imprisoned for illegal preaching; the circumstances of this imprisonment have remained more obscure than those of the first, though it does not appear to have lasted longer than six months. A bond of surety for his release, dated June 1677, has survived, so it is likely that this second detention was in the first half of that year. Since *The Pilgrim's Progress* was published soon after this, in February 1678, it is probable that he had begun to write it not in the second imprisonment but in the first, soon after the composition of *Grace Abounding*, and when the examination of his inner life contained in that book was still strong upon him.

The Pilgrim's Progress

The Pilgrim's Progress was published by Nathaniel Ponder in 1678. There is an intense life-or-death quality about the story of Christian's pilgrimage through danger and distraction to the Celestial City in this first part of the allegory. Personal experience has been translated into solid characters and presences, the pompous snob Worldly Wiseman, Apollyon the demon, Vanity Fair, the Valley of the Shadow of Death, the smug young man Ignorance, the Delectable Mountains where the pilgrims rest before the final crossing of the River of death—all these creations have entered fully into the mainstream of the English imagination because they are observed from life with a sharp objective eye, as well as having been germinated in the depths of personal spiritual growth. The book was instantly popular with all classes, though it was perhaps the last great expression of the folk tradition of the common people before the divisive effects of modern enlightened education began to be felt. It may in the present age seem a paradox that Bunyan wrote simply as a physician of souls and yet created a work of art, but this is a measure of his wholeness as a human being.

Bunyan continued to tend the needs of the Bedford church and the widening group of East Anglian churches associated with it. As his fame as a preacher increased with his literary reputation, he also preached in Congregational churches in London. In 1672–73 he entered into controversy with William Kiffin and other London Baptists for his open-communion principles. *The Life and Death of Mr. Badman* (1680) is more like a realistic novel than an allegory, giving an insight into the problems of money and marriage when the Puritans were settling down after the age of persecution and beginning to find their social role as an urban middle class. Some of the strongest writing in the book is found in the short anecdotes related by Wiseman, the narrator, to illustrate particular vices.

Later writings

The Holy War (1682), Bunyan's second allegory, has a carefully wrought epic structure and is correspondingly lacking in the spontaneous inward note of *The Pilgrim's Progress*. The town of Mansoul is besieged by the hosts of the devil, relieved by the army of Emanuel, and later undermined by further diabolic attacks and plots against his rule. The metaphor works on several levels; it represents the conversion and backslidings of the individual soul, as well as the story of mankind from the Fall through to the Redemption and the Last Judgment; there is even a more precise historical level of allegory relating to the persecution of Nonconformists under Charles II.

The Pilgrim's Progress, Second Part (1684), tells the story of the pilgrimage of Christian's wife, Christiana, accompanied by her children. It gives on the whole a more social and humorous picture of the Christian life than the First Part, but the great concluding passage on the summoning of the pilgrims to cross the River of death is perhaps the finest single thing in Bunyan.

In spite of his ministerial responsibilities Bunyan found time to publish a large number of doctrinal and controversial works in the last ten years of his life. He also composed rough but workmanlike verse of religious exhortation; one of his most interesting later volumes is the children's book *A Book for Boys and Girls* (1686), vigorous poems serving as comments on emblematic pictures.

Under James II, when there was a renewal of the persecution of dissenters, Bunyan protected his family by a deed of gift transferring all his property to "my well-beloved wife, Elizabeth Bunyan" (December 1685). When the Protestant dissenters were being wooed in order that James might obtain toleration for Roman Catholics, Bunyan shrewdly resisted the blandishments of the royal agent Lord Aylesbury, who offered him an official position; at the same time he secured seats for members of his church on the reorganized corporation of Bedford. He died on Aug. 31, 1688, in London, after one of his preaching visits; he had ridden out of his way through heavy rain to Reading to settle a quarrel between father and son and contracted a fever (probably pneumonia). He was buried in Bunhill Fields, the Nonconformists' traditional burying ground.

Reputation. Until the decline of religious faith and the great increase in books of popular instruction in the 19th century, Bunyan, like the Bible, was to be found in every English home and was known to every ordinary reader. In literary estimation, however, he remained beyond the pale of polite literature during the 18th century, though his greatness was acknowledged by Swift and Johnson. After the Romantic movement he was recognized as a type of the natural genius and placed alongside Homer and Robert Burns. Twentieth-century scholarship has made it possible to see how much he owed to the tradition of homiletic prose and to Puritan literary genres already developed when he began to write. But the sublime tinker remains sublime, if less isolated from his fellows than was formerly thought; the genius of *The Pilgrim's Progress* remains valid. Nothing illustrates better the profound symbolic truth of this noted work than its continuing ability, even in translation, to evoke responses in readers belonging to widely separated cultural traditions.

MAJOR WORKS

RELIGIOUS ALLEGORIES: *The Pilgrim's Progress*, 1678, and *The Pilgrim's Progress, . . . The Second Part*, 1684 (published together in modern editions); *The Life and Death of Mr. Badman*, 1680; *The Holy War . . . for . . . Mansoul*, 1682.

AUTOBIOGRAPHY: *Grace Abounding to the Chief of Sinners*, 1666; *A Relation of the Imprisonment of Mr. John Bunyan* (included in later editions of *Grace Abounding*), 1765.

THEOLOGICAL PAMPHLETS AND DEVOTIONAL WORKS: *Some Gospel-truths Opened*, 1656; *Profitable Meditations*, 1661?; *The Barren Fig-tree*, 1673?; *Instruction for the Ignorant*, 1675; *Come and Welcome, to Jesus Christ*, 1678; *Solomon's Temple Spiritualiz'd*, 1688; *Mr. John Bunyan's Last Sermon* (included in later editions of *The Holy War*), 1689; *An Exposition of the First Ten Chapters of Genesis*, 1692.

VERSE: *A Book for Boys and Girls* (retitled *Divine Emblems, or, Temporal Things Spiritualized*, 1724 onward), 1686.

BIBLIOGRAPHY

Editions: The first collected edition of his works was *The Works of that Eminent Servant of Christ, Mr. John Bunyan*, ed. by C. DOE (1692). Because of copyright difficulties, only vol. 1 of what was to have been a complete edition appeared; 2nd ed., 2 vol. (1736). The standard complete edition is still that by G. OFFOR, *The Works of John Bunyan*, 3 vol. (1853, 1862). Editions of single works include: *The Pilgrim's Progress*, ed. by J.B. WHAREY, rev. by R. SHARROCK (1960, rev. ed. 1968); *Grace Abounding*, ed. by R. SHARROCK (1962); *The Life and Death of Mr. Badman*, ed. by G.B. HARRISON (1928); *The Holy War*, ed. by J.F. FORREST (1967).

Bibliography: F.M. HARRISON, *A Bibliography of the Works of John Bunyan*, suppl. to the *Transactions of the Bibliographical Society*, no. 6 (1932).

Biography and Criticism: LORD MACAULAY in *Critical and Historical Essays*, vol. 1 (1843), a general and biographical essay; J. BROWN, *John Bunyan, His Life, Times and Work* (1885; rev. by F.M. HARRISON, 1928), a heavily documented life; W.Y. TINDALL, *John Bunyan, Mechanick Preacher* (1934), on the background of the sects; H.A. TALON, *John Bunyan (1628–1688) l'homme et l'oeuvre* (1948; Eng. trans., 1951), a French critic's view; R. GREAVES, *John Bunyan* (1969), on Bunyan's theology; R. SHARROCK, *John Bunyan*, rev. ed. (1968), a concise critical account; R.M. FRYE, *God, Man and Satan* (1960), theological comparison of Milton and Bunyan. O.E. WINSLOW, *John Bunyan* (1961), a straightforward and readable biography; R. SHARROCK, *John Bunyan: "The Pilgrim's Progress"* (1966), a critical study.

(R.S.)

Burckhardt, Jacob

One of the first great historians of art and culture, Jacob Burckhardt was an outstanding representative of historical scholarship in the classical period of that discipline, around the middle of the 19th century. After much controversy, his general concept of an original European culture in the age of the Renaissance and much of his philosophy about the course of world history have been absorbed into the basic outlook of the present generation of historians. In the German originals the literary style of his works remains masterly and inimitable.

Education

Jacob Christopher Burckhardt was born in Basel, Switzerland, on May 25, 1818, the son of a Protestant clergyman. The thriving Burckhardt family was among the most respected in town. For three centuries some of its members had earned wealth in international trade and the manufacture of silk and with their wealth had gained political power, while others had served the community as professors and pastors. Basel's excellent grammar school provided Burckhardt with a humanistic education. His first studies at the local university, supplemented by a stay in Neuchâtel, were dominated by a devotion to Greek. But, before the philological and increasingly historical orientation of his interests could fully assert itself, Burckhardt spent three years in the study of formal theology. Although he never regretted this concession to the professional traditions of his father and grandfather, Burckhardt took up divinity without a calling and after a prolonged crisis abandoned it, together with the explicit profession of Christian faith. Henceforth, he was always to avoid clarification of his religious position, which may be described as a kind of pantheism. Markedly romantic at first, in later years Burckhardt's religious ideas revealed their classical inspiration and, evincing a profound respect for human destiny, came to underlie his concept of history.

Burckhardt, 1892.
By courtesy of the Universitats-Bibliothek Basel

From 1839 to 1843 Burckhardt studied at the University of Berlin, where his talents were acknowledged by two eminent teachers of ancient history, August Boeckh and Johann Gustav Droysen. But it was under the influence of two other professors—Franz Kugler and Leopold von Ranke—that his appreciation of ancient and modern history came into balance in his efforts to comprehend the past as a whole. Art and architecture had fascinated Burckhardt from childhood. Now Franz Kugler provided a formal introduction to the fledging discipline of art history, which profoundly appealed to the German Romantics. The achievements of painters and architects not only directed Burckhardt's attention toward Italy and the Renaissance; they also helped to reduce law, politics, and diplomacy to a somewhat inferior status in his concept of the past. At Berlin, Burckhardt's developing priorities accounted for an ambiguous relationship with the most famous among all his teachers, Leopold von Ranke. Ranke, the master of diplomatic history, assigned an autonomous and exalted function to statehood and nationhood and consequently cast his lot with Prussian and German nationalism, forces that Burckhardt would later denounce with growing violence. Since Ranke and Burckhardt are often used to illustrate diametrically different approaches to historiography, it is important to note that Burckhardt respected the scholarly achievements of his great teacher, and Ranke recognized and commended the ability of his student. Burckhardt was later offered a chair at Berlin, but he declined it.

After the chill of two Berlin winters, Burckhardt permitted himself a summer term at the young and modest University of Bonn, where he passed many of his most romantic and imaginative hours among the circle that met in the home of Gottfried Kinkel, a fellow art historian who had in the past, like Burckhardt, given up theology but would, unlike his Swiss friend, become a leader in the unsuccessful liberal revolution that erupted in Germany in 1848–49, by which time their friendship had cooled completely. Burckhardt's political creed is as hard to define as his religious one. The spirit of his hometown and upbringing was democratic, although tempered with patrician arrogance. His love of freedom was supreme, but he soon came to despise the aspirations of political liberalism in Switzerland and Germany. For

Burckhardt 1848–49 was a turning point. Romantic indulgence and political hopes were now dead; his German friends were almost forgotten. With complete concentration he turned to his studies and his teaching. He was a conservative by now, but his conservatism was cultural rather than political. His own time was, he thought, hopelessly superficial. He felt increasingly out of touch with it and concentrated all his energies on reclaiming a past that seemed incomparably deeper and richer. Also in 1849, Margarethe Stehlin, the only woman for whom he ever seems to have had any deep affection, married a Basel banker. He suppressed his feelings without too much difficulty and never again considered marriage, stating that he had no wish to beget children "who would be tutored by a proletarian."

The University of Basel awarded Burckhardt the degree of Ph.D. *in absentia*, and after his return from Berlin in 1843 he was quickly authorized to give private lectures. Lecture he did, but for two years he had to earn his living as the editor of the *Basler Zeitung*, a conservative daily. In 1846–47 he returned to Berlin to prepare, in conjunction with his friend and teacher Kugler, substantially enlarged new editions of Kugler's two textbooks of art history. The winter of 1847–48 was spent in Rome.

University career

Thereafter he resumed his teaching at Basel. The university was small and, on the whole, undistinguished. Burckhardt's lectures, by far the largest component of his life's work and also the most accomplished, were normally delivered before a mere handful of students. Never did his academic audience reach 50; only when he addressed the Basel public at large, as he often did with series of evening lectures, was the attendance more substantial. In 1855 Burckhardt left Basel to teach art history at the newly founded Federal Institute of Technology in Zürich, but in 1858 he returned to his home university and henceforward occupied Basel's only chair of history. For another 20 years, however, he also had to teach in his former grammar school. Only from 1874 could he divide his time evenly between his university lectures in history and art history. From 1886 until his retirement in 1893 he taught art history exclusively. In his courses he covered the entire range of European civilization from ancient Greece to the French Revolution.

Burckhardt, who had learned Italian, in 1837 first crossed the southern frontier of his country, hiking all the way from Basel and back. In the following summer he returned for a month-long tour of northern and central Italy. Thereafter and until 1883, travel in Italy and elsewhere was a regular feature of Burckhardt's bachelor life.

Burckhardt's most successful books are unthinkable without his familiarity with the historical sites and art treasures of Europe. His first important work, however, like the last, attested to his deep interest in ancient civilization. In *Die Zeit Konstantins des Grossen* (1853; Eng. trans., *The Age of Constantine the Great*, 1949) Burckhardt presented a picture of a transitional age, unhealthy and immoral but teeming with religious and cultural activity. While he recognized that the rise of Christianity was inevitable and that it was necessary for the development of an original culture during the Middle Ages, his sympathies lay clearly with the waning forces of the ancient world. *Der Cicerone* (1855; Eng. trans. 1873) is a comprehensive study of Italian art, geographically arranged in the form of a travel guide. It went through many editions, but Burckhardt reacted to the popularity of his work with growing aloofness.

Burckhardt's concept of the Renaissance

Burckhardt's next book, *Die Kultur der Renaissance in Italien* (1860; Eng. trans., *The Civilization of the Renaissance in Italy*, 1878), is the major source of his fame. Using programmatic subheadings (the discovery of world and man; the development of individuality; the state as a work of art; the modern sense of humour), Burckhardt deftly analyzed the daily life of Renaissance Italy, its political climate, and the thought of its outstanding minds. His sources—often contemporary chronicles and tales—were in print and readily available yet frequently ignored by historians. He approached them with newly conceived questions in mind. Although Burckhardt emphasized many contrasts between the Middle Ages and the Renaissance, he did not underrate medieval achievements. His concept of history left no room for the idea that the Renaissance or any other period was characterized by general progress over the preceding epoch. If Raphael's art presented the Renaissance at its best, the ingenious and ruthless mechanism of Renaissance politics reminded Burckhardt of "the works of a clock." Here he perceived the beginnings of the modern state, a precision instrument of mass control, without consideration for the creative freedom of individuals and minorities.

Art was to Burckhardt the saving grace of the Renaissance, but in his *Die Kultur* this vital subject was not treated. Burckhardt hoped to cover it in a separate monograph, but that hope found only partial fulfillment in *Die Geschichte der Renaissance in Italien* (1867), which deals with architecture only. If eventually Burckhardt's study of the Renaissance provided a basic model for the treatment of cultural history in general, the implications for art history were best realized by his pupil and successor Heinrich Wölfflin. Styles of art followed one another as did historical periods. They were determined by common features derived from the general character of a period and in turn helped to define the period's culture. Among Burckhardt's minor publications, a small but precious collection of poetry in the Alemannic dialect may be noted: *E Hämpfeli Lieder* (1853).

Burckhardt died at Basel on August 8, 1897. Friends edited his last great work, four volumes of an uncompleted survey of Greek civilization—*Griechische Kulturgeschichte* (1898–1902; abridgment in Eng. trans., *History of Greek Culture,* 1963)—and some essays in art history: *Erinnerungen aus Rubens* (1898), *Beiträge zur Kunstgeschichte von Italien* (1898). Of particular significance are two later posthumous publications. *Weltgeschichtliche Betrachtungen* (1905; Eng. trans., *Force and Freedom: Reflections on History*, 1943) epitomizes his philosophy of history. *Historische Fragmente* (1929 in *Gesamtausgabe*; Eng. trans., *Judgments on History and Historians,* 1958) selects highlights from his lecture manuscripts and demonstrates impressively Burckhardt's gift for visualizing history as a whole. Both books contain passages that can be interpreted as prophetic visions of the violent totalitarian states of the 20th century; but more important than Burckhardt's prophecies of the future is his vision of the past, which offers, he said, "experience to make us, not shrewder (for the next time), but wiser (for ever)."

BIBLIOGRAPHY. A critical edition of Burckhardt's collected works, *Gesamtausgabe*, 14 vol., ed. by E. DURR *et al.* (1929–34), is now being followed by a critical edition of his letters, *Briefe*, ed. by MAX BURCKHARDT, 7 vol. (1949–). See also WERNER KAEGI, *Jacob Burckhardt, eine Biographie*, 4 vol. (1947–67); WALLACE K. FERGUSON, *The Renaissance in Historical Thought* (1948); and *Jacob Burckhardt and the Renaissance, 100 Years After* (1960), papers read at a meeting of the Central Renaissance Conference.

(P.G.B.)

Bureaucracy

In everyday usage the term bureaucracy connotes the "red tape" and inefficiency that one often experiences in dealings with large-scale organizations, especially with a state administration. As a sociological concept, the term has a less pejorative, a more "neutral" meaning. It simply refers to a type of formal organization. By formal organization is meant a social unit that is established in a more or less deliberate manner for the attainment of a specific goal (in contrast to such social units as a friendship group or a neighbourhood that seem to emerge in a spontaneous, unplanned manner). Thus *purposive design* and *goal specificity* seem to be the two crucial criteria differentiating formal organizations from other types of social groupings. A business firm, a modern political party, and a trade union, for instance, are typical examples of formal organizations, and all such organizations coordinate their activities and other resources in a highly deliberate manner in order to achieve a number of specific goals.

This article is divided into the following sections:

I. The character of bureaucracy and bureaucratization

THE CLASSICAL OR "IDEAL" CONCEPTION OF BUREAUCRACY

Not all formal organizations are bureaucratic. Bureaucracy refers to a special type of formal organization whose structure has a number of specific characteristics. These characteristics were first formulated in a systematic manner by the German sociologist Max Weber (1864–1920), whose definition and theories on bureaucracy have set the foundations for all subsequent work on the subject. They refer to (1) the division of labour in the organization, (2) its authority structure, (3) the position and role of the individual member, and (4) the type of rules that regulate the relations between organizational members.

Division of labour

A highly developed division of labour and specialization of tasks is one of the most fundamental features of bureaucracy. This is achieved by a precise and detailed definition of the duties and responsibilities of each position or office. The allocation of a limited number of tasks to each office operates according to the principle of fixed jurisdictional areas that are determined by administrative regulations.

The bureaucratic organization is characterized by a "rational" and impersonal regulation of inferior-superior relationships. In traditional types of administration (feudal, patrimonial), the inferior-superior relationship is personal, and the legitimation of authority is based on a belief in the sacredness of tradition. In a bureaucracy, on the other hand, authority is legitimized by a belief in the correctness of the process by which administrative rules were enacted; and the loyalty of the bureaucrat is oriented to an impersonal order, to a superior position, not to the specific person who holds it.

When one shifts the focus of attention from the organization as a whole to the role and status of the individual member, the following features characterize the bureaucrat's position. Starting with the mode of recruitment, the bureaucrat is not selected on the basis of such particularistic considerations as family position or political loyalties. His recruitment is based on formal qualifications (diplomas, university degrees) that testify that the applicant has the necessary knowledge to accomplish effectively his specialized duties. Once a candidate enters the bureaucratic organization, his office is his sole—or at least his primary—occupation. It constitutes a *career*. That is to say, it is not accepted on an honorary or short-term basis; it implies stability and continuity, a "life's work." Moreover, there is usually an elaborate system of promotion based on the principles of both seniority and achievement.

Insofar as the mode of remuneration is concerned, the bureaucrat usually receives a salary based not so much on his productivity performance as on the status of his position. Contrary to some forms of traditional administration, in the bureaucratic case the civil servant cannot sell his position or pass it on to his sons. There is a clear-cut separation between the *private* and the *public* sphere of the bureaucrat's life. His private property is sharply distinguished from the "means of administration" that do not belong to him.

Rational rules

The most important and pervasive characteristic of bureaucracy (one that to some extent explains all the others) is the existence of a system of control based on rational rules—that is, rules meant to design and regulate the whole organization on the basis of technical knowledge and with the aim of achieving maximum efficiency. According to Max Weber, "Bureaucratic administration means fundamentally the exercise of control on the basis of knowledge. This is the feature of it which makes it specifically rational" (*The Theory of Social and Economic Organization*, 1947, p. 339).

These are briefly the major features of Weber's ideal type of bureaucracy. The type is "ideal" in the sense that the characteristics included in it are not to be found, in their extreme form, in all concrete bureaucracies. Real organizations can be more or less bureaucratic according to their degree of proximity to their ideal formulation.

THE BUREAUCRATIZATION OF THE STATE IN WESTERN EUROPE

Although the ideal type refers to all types of formal organizations (religious, political, economic), Weber formulated this concept having in mind mainly the administrative apparatus of the modern state. Being primarily concerned with explaining the unique features of Western civilization, he wanted to examine the processes that made the state apparatus of western European societies approach so closely his ideal type of bureaucracy. For Weber thought that although bureaucratic administrative systems existed in many state societies of the past, only in western Europe did the bureaucratization of the state apparatus reach its fullest form. For this reason, the concept of bureaucracy can perhaps be best understood if seen comparatively and within a context of long-term historical developments. Such a historical examination can be important not only for a better comprehension of the notion of bureaucracy itself but also for an understanding that the bureaucratization of the state set the initial and fundamental framework for further bureaucratization in all other institutional areas. Although such bureaucratic organizations as the Roman Catholic Church and the political organization of medieval cities did exist in Europe before the emergence of the modern state, it was only after a strong bureaucratic state had established a unified and centralized political community over an extended territory that bureaucracy, as a form of organization, could spread and prevail in all spheres of social life.

Political origins of bureaucracy

Differentiation between state and royal household administration. The origin of the main administrative departments in western European countries is to be found in the royal household. Initially there was no differentiation between state activities and the administration of the king's court. Royal income and expenses, for instance, were hardly distinguished from state finances, and all public officials were household dependents directly supported from the king's stores. In a typically nonbureaucratic manner, the administration of the realm was discharged by the same people who were in charge of the main functions of the household.

The gradual ascendancy of the crown and the ensuing increasing volume and complexity of administrative tasks initiated a process of differentiation between household and state administration. To take England as an example, the first major department to be separated from the royal court was the treasury in the 12th century. Because at that time the royal household still had an itinerant character, it was becoming increasingly difficult—even from a purely physical point of view—for the moving court to carry the treasury with it. Thus its headquarters were fixed at Westminster, and clergymen, leading a communal life under the leadership of the Exchequer, were its first officials.

The chancery, originally in charge of the king's correspondence, was the second important department that "went out of court." This development, which started under Henry III (reigned 1216–72), was completed only with the administrative reforms of Edward II (reigned 1307–27), when the accounts of the chancery were finally separated from the king's accounts.

A similar process of differentiation took place in continental countries. With the extension of royal authority, administrative tasks became more numerous and complex and royal officials increased in number; hence it became more and more difficult for the royal household to provide for the needs of such a large population of officials; officials had gradually to establish their own households.

The expansion of the state administration. If the emergence of the state administration out of the royal household constitutes the first big step toward bureaucratization, the subsequent spectacular expansion of the state administration, and its continuous acquisition of new functions by its encroachment on local self-government, contributed greatly to further bureaucratization in the administrative field.

In England this process was very slow, especially after the failure of the Tudor and Stuart dynasties to establish an absolutist system of rule in the 16th and 17th centuries. The powerful nobility managed through Parliament to check effectively the state administration's expansive tendencies. Thus English local government remained for a long time in the hands of nonprofessional noblemen, the justices of the peace. It was on the Continent that administrative expansion reached impressive dimensions quite early. This expansion was linked with the rise of royal absolutism and the gradual curbing of the political autonomy of the nobility and of the towns. The French monarchy and its administration, as it was finally shaped under Louis XIV (reigned 1643–1715), has been the prototype of European absolutist rule, a model imitated all over Europe. Until the 17th century the French nobility managed to maintain some political functions by exercising constitutional opposition to the crown through the States General and the local *parlements*. But the Bourbons, unlike the English kings of the time, managed gradually to reduce the nobles' power. The provincial governing positions ceased to be the hereditary fiefs of the nobility, and by the Edict of 1641 the autonomy of the local *parlements* was destroyed, their powers being relegated to the Royal Council. The famous *intendants*, the crown representatives to the provinces, first appeared in the 16th century. After their powers were extended by cardinal de Richelieu in the 1620s and '30s, they gradually managed to weaken self-government until they became the effective masters of all local affairs. Town autonomy disappeared in a similar fashion under Louis XIV.

Influence of absolutism on bureaucratization

The continual expansion of the French state apparatus was temporarily checked toward the end of the 18th century with the weakening of royal power. During the so-called feudal reaction after the death of Louis XIV, an attempt was made to revive the local *parlements*. But the revival was both partial and short-lived. The French Revolution and later Napoleonic rule (1789–1815), with its hostility to all "intermediate powers," promoted and consolidated a political system in which the central state apparatus was all dominant—all local self-governing bodies being considered an interference to the direct relationship that the state should have with its citizens.

In Prussia the process of bureaucratic expansion followed essentially similar lines. The ruling Great Elector —or king, as he was later titled—managed to build up a strong state administration by curbing the power of the nobility and their representative bodies. The *Regierungen*, the equivalent of the French *parlements*, were reduced to insignificance as most of their functions were gradually absorbed by the central administration. This process was momentarily arrested by Frederick the Great (reigned 1740–86), who, in his attempt to reinvigorate the Prussian nobility and to fight the increasing dominance of the state bureaucracy, tried to revive the local *Regierungen*. But the attempt, as in France, was short-lived and basically unsuccessful.

The aristocratization and commercialization of office. In many ways administrative expansion meant bureaucratization: the increasing complexity and volume of administrative tasks made a minimum of rationalization imperative. Spheres of competence had to be more rigorously defined; specialization within and between departments was becoming more necessary; and at least a partial opening of posts to professionally trained people had to be effected. But if the process of administrative growth was fairly continuous, the process of bureaucratization, at least in terms of some Weberian characteristics of bureaucracy, was less so. In fact, following Weber, it is more precise to say that the public administrations of the *ancien régime* were "patrimonial" bureaucracies because they were characterized by a peculiar mixture of patrimonial and bureaucratic elements. Of course, in the long term, the patrimonial elements were declining in importance and bureaucratic ones were becoming more dominant. But this process of bureaucratization was never a unilinear, direct movement. Drawbacks and temporary processes of debureaucratization were both numerous and persistent.

The entry of aristocrats into bureaucratic government

In order to understand such processes, one must examine the relationship of the public administration both to the upper classes and to its royal head. If the nobility failed in resisting the growth of the central authority and administration, it was much more successful, once this growth was consolidated, in advancing its own interests within the new bureaucratic framework of the central state. The destruction of the aristocratic self-governing bodies by no means implied the destruction of the nobility as a class. Despite the loss of their political autonomy, European aristocracies proved flexible and remarkably resilient. For a very long time they managed to maintain their economic advantages and even to exercise effective political power—not anymore by opposing the state administration but by occupying the top positions within it.

This partial aristocratization of the state administration, though a common feature of all *ancien régime* European societies, is nowhere more clearly seen than in the administrative development of Prussia. During the initial stage of administrative expansion, the Great Elector, facing serious aristocratic opposition to centralizing policies, had to open the gates of the growing administration to commoners, especially to those having a legal training. Talented officials of common origin could reach top administrative positions and exercise great influence in the formation of policy. Of course noblemen who were prepared to change camps and to join forces with the king also were welcomed. Thus a delicate balance between aristocrats and commoners, between a nonbureaucratic inheritance system and a bureaucratic merit system of recruitment, was achieved.

The three forces of king, aristocracy, bureaucracy

At a later stage of development, however, when the state administration had been well established and the aristocratic opposition had started to wane, the administration rather than the aristocracy started to create problems for the king: the entrenched bureaucrats became as difficult to control as the previously recalcitrant aristocracy. Thus Frederick the Great, in his frantic attempts to exercise effective control over the state bureaucracy, resorted to the aristocracy. He made it a policy to reserve all the key administrative positions for noblemen. This policy was never completely realized, because certain positions required trained skills not always easy to find among those of noble birth. Moreover, restrictions were watered down by the process of ennoblement: successful officials of common origin aspired to and often achieved aristocratic status. Nevertheless, despite these reservations, the process of debureaucratization temporarily succeeded and was even reinforced after Frederick's death, as the sponsors of the Prussian Legal Code of 1794 tried to "improve" the merit system of recruitment by setting aside all important state positions for the aristocracy. These legal restrictions were abolished during the great administrative reforms at the beginning of the 19th century. Ultimately, the highest ranking Prussian bureaucrats, whether of noble or common origin, developed into a self-conscious, self-recruiting status group striving to promote its own interests and achieving considerable autonomy vis-à-vis both the various social strata (including the "nonbureaucratic" aristocracy) and their royal master. In the long drawn-out triangular contest between the aristocracy, the king, and the bureaucracy, the bureaucrats were the ultimate victors. Although some of these developments were indeed peculiar to Prussia, the mixture of the ascriptive and merit system of recruitment was a common feature of all European bureaucracies up to the 18th and even into the 19th century.

Apart from aristocratization, the commercialization of offices was another "nonbureaucratic" feature that persisted for a long time in the public administrations of western Europe. Although in England the practice lasted longer, it was in France that the system of buying and selling of public offices reached extraordinary dimensions and with quite disastrous consequences. Francis I systematized the sale of offices by establishing in 1522 the Bureau des Parties Casuelles, which was literally an "office-selling" bureau. At the beginning, attempts were made to limit the sales to financial posts only. Gradually, however, judicial as well as most other offices of the royal administration could be bought. Such offices could become hereditary through payment of an annual fee. Moreover, at times of financial crisis, offices were created en masse for the sole purpose of raising additional funds. Office selling became at certain periods the main source of state revenues. Thus between 1620 and 1632, for instance, one third of the French state's income came from office transactions.

Looking at the aristocratization and commercialization of the public office in power terms, one can say that both phenomena enhance the autonomy of the officials vis-à-vis their royal master (although this type of autonomy, based on status and money, is quite different from the "contractual" autonomy that the modern bureaucrat enjoys vis-à-vis his superiors). Consequently they impose a certain rigidity on the administrative structure because the ruler cannot rely on the continuous cooperation and obedience of his officials in the policies that he wants to pursue. Of course, this situation varied according to the relative power of the king. In England, where the crown was never as powerful as in some continental countries, the autonomy of a sinecure owner was considerable. In France, before the weakening of royal authority in the 18th century, the situation was quite different. Proprietorship rights were no full guarantee against royal arbitrariness. At times of grave financial crisis, the crown often arbitrarily abolished sinecure rights or refused to pay the holders of sinecures; often the latter were forced to provide loans to the government or to pay for their office a second and third time.

Despite these variations in the power relationships between officials and their rulers, one could risk the generalization that *ancien régime* European administrations enjoyed a relatively high degree of autonomy vis-à-vis their rulers. This becomes obvious if one compares them with certain cases of oriental rule (as among the Ottomans or Mongols), in which officials were subjugated to a despotic ruler. On the other hand, this administrative autonomy in Europe did not reach the point of jeopardizing the whole political framework of society. In that sense European administrations never went through the "feudalization" processes that typically occur during the decline of highly centralized empires—that is, such processes as the total paralysis of the ruler's power and the usurpation of the means of administration by various local officials who become totally autonomous.

Further bureaucratization. The sales of offices and the various other types of ascriptive recruitment started to decline at the end of the 18th century. As a result of revolution (as in France) or of various reform movements initiated by officials striving for more autonomy and self-regulation and by extrabureaucratic groups fighting against the privileged access to public office, public administration in western Europe gradually took a more rational-bureaucratic character. The purchase of sinecures was abolished; examinations as well as the systematic requirement of formal qualifications for office became the standard mode of selection; and departmental divisions were established on a more rational basis.

Formalizing the selection and tenure of bureaucrats

Moreover, as the nation-state developed further and as *subjects* became *citizens* and as more and more people were actively drawn into the political process, public administration ceased to be an instrument at the personal service of a king or a privileged group. It became, at least in the minds of the people, a service rendering "neutral" organization at the service of all citizens. As such, it had to be protected and "insulated" from all pressures that might attempt to divert the bureaucrat from the professional and disinterested performance of his task. As a matter of fact, the gradual establishment of various legal guarantees (such as tenure for life under "civil service" rules) has succeeded in protecting the bureaucrat against his master's arbitrariness and against powerful external groups, which, in their efforts to promote their narrow interests, might put pressure on the public official to abandon his "neutral" position.

Thus public officials, as a group, managed to achieve a relatively high degree of autonomy and self-regulation, though this autonomy, in contrast to the *ancien régime* patrimonial bureaucracies, is based neither on aristocratic status nor on the strong economic position of the bureaucrat. It is mainly based on the general developments mentioned above and on the fact that the bureaucrat's expertise and administrative experience place him in a position of strength vis-à-vis his master, who has increasingly become simply a high-level decision maker in administrative matters.

For some theorists of bureaucracy this autonomy and "insulation" of modern bureaucracy has gone too far—in the sense that the public bureaucracy, instead of being a neutral tool at the service of the people and its legitimate leaders, has become itself the real master. The problem of the position of the state administrative apparatus in the power structure of modern society requires an examination of the classical theories of bureaucracy that placed this problem at the centre of their preoccupations.

II. Theories of bureaucracy

CLASSICAL THEORIES OF BUREAUCRACY

Despite the variety of sources from which the classical writings in bureaucracy have sprung, it is possible to identify in all of them a recurrent theme: the impact of large-scale organizations on the power structure of society. In what way does "big" government or "big" business influence the political institutions of modern industrial societies? Or, on the level of the individual, in what ways do such developments affect man's chances for a free and meaningful existence? In other terms the problem is to find out whether bureaucracy, despite its dimensions, is still an administrative apparatus for the implementation of socially useful goals or whether it has lost its neutral and instrumental character; whether from a tool in the hands of the legitimate policy-making body it has become itself the master dictating policies of narrow self-interest.

In a way, most students of modern society deal directly or indirectly with such problems. Among the various writings, it is possible to identify three major perspectives, three outstanding contributions, that constitute the key elements in the development of the classical literature of bureaucracy: the Marxist, the Weberian, and what may be called the oligarchic theories.

The Marxist theories. Although the concept of class rather than the concept of bureaucracy is at the centre of Karl Marx's work, his theory of the state bureaucracy is a crucial starting point for understanding future debates on the problem of bureaucratization in modern society. Marx studied bureaucracy in the context of the capitalist state and its administrative apparatus. His main thesis about the nature and development of modern bureaucracy derives from his general theory on the dynamics and future of the class struggle in capitalist society.

The withering away of bureaucracy under communism

For Marx, the state, with its bureaucratic administration, is a mere instrument in the hands of the dominant social class. It is the division of society into classes that explains the existence and growth of the state apparatus. More specifically, the bureaucracy of the state is one of the main means by which the exploiting class manages to consolidate and perpetuate its domination over the masses. The greater the divisions and the interclass struggles in society, the more oppressive the state apparatus becomes. In fact, according to Marx, the increasing bureaucratization of the state in capitalist societies is a reflection of increasing tension in the sphere of production, of the mounting intensity of the class struggle.

It follows, according to Marxists, that with the advent of socialism and the gradual abolition of class divisions, a process of debureaucratization will gradually take place. The state and its oppressive apparatus will ultimately wither away in the communist classless society of the future. For in such a society, since there will be no oppressors and no oppressed, the state apparatus will become superfluous.

The Weberian theories. For Max Weber bureaucracy rather than class becomes the key concept of modern society. Weber elaborated his concept of bureaucracy within the context of his political sociology—in discussing ideal types of domination. According to him, a system of domination is mainly characterized by (1) a number of beliefs that legitimize the exercise of power and (2) an administrative apparatus that operates as a bridge between the ruler and the ruled. Weber distinguishes three types of domination: the charismatic, the traditional, and the legal.

Charismatic domination

Types of domination. Charisma, from the Greek, means literally "gift of grace." A leader with charisma is someone who has, or is believed to have, extraordinary personal qualities that become the basis of his domination. Thus beliefs in the extraordinary capacities of the ruler legitimize power in the charismatic type of domination. The administrative apparatus, whenever it exists, consists simply of the leader's immediate disciples.

Belief in the sacredness of tradition, respect for the old and established ways of doing things, is the basis of legitimation in the traditional type of domination. The traditional ruler commands by virtue of his inherited status. His orders are personal and arbitrary but within limits fixed by custom. His subjects obey out of personal loyalty to him or out of respect for his traditional status. When this type of domination, typical in the patriarchal household, is extended over many people and a wide territory, the ensuing administrative apparatus ideally can take the *patrimonial* or the *feudal* form. In the patrimonial administration the officials are personal retainers (servants, relatives, favourites), usually dependent on their master for remuneration. On the other hand, the feudal apparatus has a greater degree of autonomy for the officials in relation to the master. The feudal officials are not personal dependents but allies giving an oath of fealty to their lord. By virtue of this type of contract they exercise independent jurisdiction, they usually own their administrative domain, and they are not dependent on their superior for remuneration and subsistence.

Finally, belief in the rightness of law constitutes the basis for legitimation in the legal type of domination. Here the ruled obey the ruler not because he possesses exceptional qualities or hereditary status but because he came to occupy his position by following certain properly enacted rules to which both the ruler and the ruled adhere. Bureaucracy is the typical administrative apparatus in the legal type of domination.

Weber's "ideal" bureaucrat

The power position of the bureaucrat. In a typically bureaucratic administration a ruler's arbitrariness is seriously curtailed by the existence of legal norms that regulate in great detail the relations between him and the bureaucratic officials. Thus for instance, with the acquisition of tenure it is very difficult, if not impossible, to dismiss a recalcitrant bureaucrat. Dismissal is only possible in exceptional circumstances, and such circumstances are stipulated by impersonal regulations, not by any superior official. The bureaucrat, moreover, can refuse to obey orders that go against some generally accepted rules or professional standards of job performance. He can equally refuse commands that directly impinge on his private sphere of existence, for a superior's authority is to be strictly limited to the office situation.

If, however, the bureaucrat is enjoying a high degree of autonomy vis-à-vis his superior in terms of job security and the application of professional standards, in all other respects he is supposed to follow faithfully orders coming from above, even if such orders go against his personal opinions and beliefs. In other terms, insofar as general policy making is concerned, the bureaucrat should be a mere tool; he should put aside his own preferences and execute in a highly "neutral" manner his master's will.

This delicate balance between professional autonomy and political neutrality is, of course, an ideal formulation; it refers to things as they ought to be, not to things as they actually are. Weber saw clearly that such a balance could easily be shattered in actual situations. As a matter of fact, in the legal type of domination there is a built-in tension between the bureaucrat and his legitimate ruler: as the complexity of administrative problems increases and as their solution requires more expert knowledge, it becomes increasingly difficult for the ruler, usually a nonexpert in administrative matters, to exercise effective control. The expert bureaucrat can easily boycott the ruler's policies by withholding information or by judging any undesirable policy as technically unfeasible.

On the other hand, in this struggle between the ruler and his administrative apparatus, the ruler is not always at the complete mercy of his "servants." His position is strengthened by the internal struggles between bureaucrats. Their intensive competition for promotion often enables the ruler to control an obstructive bureaucrat with the help of his antagonistic colleagues. Thus, although not an expert, the ruler can use the rivalries between experts in order to check the concealment or distortion of facts. In many cases such collegiate bodies as state councils or ministerial cabinets can be used as a forum in which rival experts express their opinions, thus enabling the ruler to get a more balanced view on a problem.

In conclusion, according to Weber, inherent in the legal type of domination are tendencies that could destroy the ideal balance of professional autonomy and political neutrality between bureaucracy and its master. This balance can be shattered either by way of a total subjugation of the bureaucracy to its master or by way of its total dominance. Whether the balance shall be maintained or not and whether it will tip on the side of the master or of the bureaucrat depends on the specific configuration of forces surrounding the bureaucracy in each actual situation.

The bureaucratization of all spheres of life

The future of bureaucracy. Although the power position of bureaucracy can vary from case to case, according to Weber, its permanence and technical indispensability in modern society is beyond doubt. Revolutions in modern times can change radically the power position of various groups, including the bureaucracy, but they can never abolish it. Whatever the political regime and whatever the sociopolitical changes in modern society, bureaucracy is here to stay. Thus Weber did not agree with Marx's prediction of the eventual disappearance of bureaucracy. According to Weber, not only will the state bureaucracy not wither away but the bureaucratic form of organization will spread and become dominant in all spheres of life. Whether in the religious, educational, or economic domain, Weber predicted the proliferation of large-scale organizations, the concentration of the means of administration at the top of the hierarchy, and generally the adoption of the bureaucratic type of organization. The modern army, the church, the university, and other institutions are gradually losing their traditional aspects. They are increasingly administered by impersonal and rational rules aiming at maximum efficiency.

But if Weber did not share Marx's optimism, neither did he share the pessimism of subsequent writers (see below) who have predicted the inevitability of the bureaucrat's political dominance as a result of the spreading and technical indispensability of bureaucracy in modern society. For Weber bureaucratic indispensability does not automatically imply political dominance. The slaves also were technically indispensable in some ancient societies, but they had no political power whatsoever. Bureaucracy's impersonality makes it a tool that can serve many masters.

Oligarchic theories of bureaucracy. If for Marx bureaucracy was an oppressive tool in the hands of the dominant class and for Weber an efficient one in the hands of whoever knows how to control it, subsequent writers, impressed by the increasing bureaucratization of modern society and by the rise of totalitarian regimes in East and West, have seen bureaucracy as an oligarchic system of political domination: bureaucracy ceases to be a tool; it becomes the master, the politically dominant group in a new type of society that is neither capitalist nor socialist. If for Weber the political domination of bureaucracy was problematic, for the German sociologist Robert Michels (1876–1936) and other writers having a similar orientation it became an inevitable outcome, inherent in the internal dynamics of bureaucracy.

Michels' "iron law of oligarchy." Michels was one of the first theorists who tried systematically to link increasing bureaucratization with the oligarchic tendencies in modern society. He focussed his attention primarily on the internal political structure of large-scale organizations. His main thesis, the famous "iron law of oligarchy," postulates that with the increasing complexity and bureaucratization of modern organizations all power is concentrated at the top, in the hands of an organizational elite that rules in a dictatorial manner. This is so even if oligarchy, as in the German Socialist party, which he extensively studied, runs against the ideals and intentions of both rulers and ruled.

In fact, the increasing size of modern organizations and the increasing complexity of the problems with which they have to deal makes technically impossible the participation of the rank and file in the taking of decisions. Moreover, given the ensuing apathy of the members and the increasing concentration of the means of communication at the top, the power position of the leader becomes impregnable. Not only can the leader manipulate information and use the communication network against any potential rival but also, by the exercise of his functions, he acquires specialized knowledge and political skills that make him almost irreplaceable to the organization. In this way both the structural position of the rulers and the ruled lead to a political system that perpetuates the leadership of the person in power and alienates the rank and file from the political process.

Once in control, according to Michels, the organizational oligarchy always has as its primary aim the consolidation of its own power position. Whenever this aim clashes with the more general aims of the rank and file, the elite will sacrifice the latter rather than jeopardize its own privileges. It is in this way that Michels explains the decline in radicalism of the established Socialist parties whose bureaucratic conservatism serves more the interests of the leaders and less the masses whose interests they are supposed to represent.

Finally, for Michels, organizational oligarchy brings societal oligarchy. If the political systems of such voluntary organizations as trade unions and political parties cannot work democratically, then the democratic institutions of the whole society are undermined at their very roots. Indeed, a society dominated by large-scale oligarchic organizations eventually develops an oligarchic political regime. Organizational elites, together with other social elites, having a common interest in the maintenance of the status quo, form a strong power group determined to oppose any demand for change coming from the masses.

Other oligarchic theories. Michels' theory focusses mainly on the bureaucratization of "voluntary" organizations, such as political parties. Other theorists, sharing his pessimism about the future of democracy, point more to the increasing size and bureaucratization of the state administration or of the capitalist enterprise as the main threats to the parliamentary institutions of Western societies.

On the one hand, such liberal German economists as Ludwig von Mises and Friedrich von Hayek are alarmed at the proportions of the state bureaucracy and its increasing intervention in the economic sphere. For them, it is the government's "levelling" tendencies, its insatiable appetite for expansion that gradually destroys free enterprise and undermines democratic institutions.

Alleged effects of expanding government

On the other hand, there are those who attribute increasing bureaucratization and the decline of democracy not to the state's interference but to the internal dynamics of the capitalist economic system. According to this view, the technological changes under a capitalist system necessitate the formation of huge corporations that dominate the market and destroy any kind of competition. Under such circumstances, economic power is concentrated in the hands of a few monopolists who become a "state within a state." Thus, there is an opinion, for instance, that extreme monopolization of the German economy was responsible for bringing the Nazis to power (Franz Neumann, *Behemoth*, 1942). A similar opinion holds that business concentration favours totalitarianism and that, because economic concentration is as strong in some democratic states (Great Britain, United States) as it has been in totalitarian ones (prewar Japan, Germany, Italy), democracy is endangered in the Anglo-Saxon countries (Robert A. Brady, *Business as a System of Power*, 1943).

The other centre of similar debates has been among Marxists trying to understand the nature of the increasingly bureaucratized Soviet society and its deviance, not from democratic but from Marxist principles. What all Marxists now accept is that instead of the withering away of the bureaucratic state predicted by Marx, in the newly founded socialist order one witnesses the exact opposite: the state and its apparatus have expanded in an unprecedented manner.

Theories on the nature of Soviet bureaucratization

For Lenin the increasing bureaucratization of the Soviet state was seen as a sign of the "immaturity of socialism." The civil war and the ensuing chaotic state of the economy, the persistence of internal and external foes of the regime, were used to explain to a great extent the increasing bureaucratization of the state. But such a trend, in Lenin's view, was bound to be a transient phenomenon. As soon as industrialization had transformed the infrastructure and consolidated the regime, debureaucratization would set in and Marx's prediction would come true. Leon Trotsky, who wrote later, at a time when bureaucratization had reached its peak under the dictatorship of Joseph Stalin, explained bureaucratization by the fact that the Soviet economy, being predominantly agricultural, was totally inimical to a socialist regime. This did not mean that the Russian revolution was premature. It simply meant that it had to be expanded in other more industrialized countries through permanent, worldwide revolution. Stalin's policy to build socialism in one country only and his attempt to impose a socialist superstructure on a non-industrial society explained both the expansion and the increasing oppression of the party and the state bureaucracy.

For Trotsky, as for Lenin, bureaucratization had a transient character. The bureaucrats did not constitute a new social class, since they did not directly own the means of production. Their position in the productive process was not "organic" and permanent as was that of a "real" class. If they regulated the production and distribution of goods, it was by *delegation*, not by direct ownership. Therefore, Trotsky believed, as had Lenin, in their eventual decline and loss of power. For Lenin this could come about through intensive industrialization; for Trotsky a new proletarian revolution was needed for the overthrow of the bureaucrats.

Whereas Lenin and Trotsky could not admit that bureaucracy had a permanent and "organic" position in the Soviet system, other Marxists have thought that it was at its centre and that it defined more than anything else the very nature of the regime. Thus if the former tried to accommodate Soviet reality to Marx's specific predictions about the withering away of the state, the latter dismissed such predictions and tried to analyze the Soviet reality by using a fundamentally Marxist conceptual framework. From their point of view, bureaucracy is not only a privileged oppressive group but a new exploiting class, a class characterized by a new type of oligarchic regime that is neither socialist nor capitalist and that is rapidly spreading both in the East and in the West.

The first systematic elaboration of this position was attempted by the Italian Marxist Bruno Rizzi in *The Bureaucratisation of the World* (1939). For Rizzi the Soviet bureaucracy constituted a new ruling class that exploited the proletariat as much as the capitalists had in the past. It differed from capitalism only in that the new type of domination was based not on individual but on group ownership of the means of production. In fact, in the Soviet system the means of production represent not "socialism" but "stateism." They do not belong to the whole collectivity but to the state and to the bureaucrats who control it. In the last analysis, it is these bureaucrats —the technicians, directors, and specialists holding key positions in the party and state administration—who exploit the proletarians and steal the surplus value of work. According to Rizzi this new type of regime, which he called bureaucratic collectivism, was not limited to the Soviet Union. Similar tendencies could be discerned in fascist countries and even in the "welfare state" type of capitalist democracies. The Yugoslav Communist Milovan Djilas in *The New Class* (1957), a later criticism of the Yugoslav Socialist regime, used arguments similar to Rizzi's.

The managerial revolution

The American philosopher and critic James Burnham proposed a theory of the "managerial revolution" that was more or less an elaboration of Rizzi's ideas. According to his theory, technological progress and the growth of large-scale economic as well as political bureaucracies deprived the old capitalist class of the control of the means of production. The effective control of the economy and of political power had passed to the managers —that is, to the production executives and to the administrators of the state bureaucracy. He predicted that at a later stage of development, private ownership would be abolished and the bureaucrats would appropriate collectively, through the state, the means of production. Thus, according to Burnham, both in the East and the West the managers would impose a new type of oligarchic order.

The classical theories in review. The classical writings on bureaucracy constitute a coherent body of thought with a well-defined pattern of development—a pattern that reflects the changing character of the problems posed by the increasing spread of large-scale organizations in modern society. Indeed, the Marxist, Weberian, and oligarchic theories of bureaucracy could be placed along an optimism-pessimism continuum.

For Marx, bureaucratization was a transient phenomenon, to disappear with the advent of socialism-communism. Marx's optimism and his faith in a classless society prevented him from identifying organizational problems that are common in all advanced industrial societies, whether capitalist or not. In this sense the subsequent analysis of Weber is complementary to the Marxist critique of the strictly capitalist aspects of modern society that come to the fore. Weber saw clearly the permanence and indispensability of the state bureaucracy in modern society without, however, deducing from this indispensability its ultimate political dominance.

Finally, such writers as Michels, Rizzi, and Burnham saw bureaucracy as a system of political domination arising from a shift of power from the legitimate sources of authority to those officeholders (whether in the big corporation or in the government) who achieve de facto dominance because of their strategic position and their acquisition of specialized knowledge.

Merits and defects of the classical theories of bureaucracy

If one tries to identify common elements among the classical theories of bureaucracy, the most basic one is the broad scope attempted by all of them. Their analysis of bureaucracy was not placed, as in many modern studies, in a political and social vacuum. It was systematically linked with the social structure as a whole. Moreover, most of the classical writers had a broad historical perspective. In dealing with the problems of bureaucracy and bureaucratization, they were fully aware that such problems can be understood only when the societies within which they arise are studied dynamically in their long-term historical development and change.

Of course, the broadness of scope or the all-inclusiveness of the classical approach has its shortcomings. By attempting to embrace all the aspects of the problem, the classical theorists offered analyses that often lacked the rigour and precision that can be achieved by a more limited, less ambitious approach. Thus, sometimes they formulated sweeping generalizations that clearly are half-truths or that are valid only under certain conditions that remain unspecified by classical theory. From this point of view, more recent writers, preoccupied with the same problems, try to refine these generalizations by examining in a more limited and empirical manner the specific conditions under which classical statements hold true.

Such a re-examination has, on the whole, dispelled some of the "gloom" characterizing the oligarchic theories of bureaucracy. Michels' law of oligarchy, for instance, was empirically re-examined by a group of American sociologists (Seymour M. Lipset, Martin A. Trow, and James S. Coleman, *Union Democracy*, 1956). In an intensive study of the International Typographical Union, a voluntary organization effectively run in a democratic manner, they tried to identify the conditions accounting for the initiation and maintenance of the union's two-party political system. Among other factors, they found that the relatively high autonomy of the local branches of the union was one of the most relevant conditions. As a matter of fact, a decentralized system of authority increased the power of the locals and thus constituted the basis of a pluralistic system of power. Another important factor was the degree of participation and interest of the rank and file in union affairs. Such an interest was enhanced in the union by the existence of a strong occupational "community" that provided members with many occasions for meeting and discussing union problems.

Such a study challenges effectively the overly deterministic character of Michels' theory. It shows clearly that under certain conditions increasing bureaucratization does not inevitably lead to organizational oligarchy. In defense of Michels, however, it must be mentioned that most empirical studies do support his theory. Thus not only most trade unions and political parties but even such voluntary organizations as cooperatives, professional associations, and churches are oligarchically run.

Nevertheless, in spite of the undeniable fact that large-scale organizations do have an oligarchic political system, many modern writers refuse, simply because of this fact, to accept Michels' pessimistic conclusions as to the meagre chances of democratic institutions in modern society. They argue that such oligarchic large-scale organizations as unions and even political parties can very well constitute autonomous and antagonistic centres of power. Such forces, in the pursuit of their particular interests, sustain the pluralistic system of democratic regimes.

It is because of this pluralistic system of power, indeed, that the structural differentiation (accentuated by the growth of large bureaucracies) between masses and elites does not necessarily lead to the unlimited manipulation of the former by the latter. The so-called elitist theory of democracy maintains that even though the masses do not actively participate in the political process, competing elites do need electoral support and are forced to take into consideration interests other than their own.

The debate does not end here. "Democratic pluralism" is attacked by those who think that a multiplicity of centres of power is an insufficient condition for democracy. As one critic put it, "It is one of the political myths of our age that democracy is protected and sustained principally or solely by the competition between elites, which balance and limit each other's power." (From T.B. Bottomore, *Elites and Society*, 1964.) Democracy, according to such an argument, is meaningful only if decisions are *not* taken at the top by a unified or a pluralistic establishment and only if an environment is created in which the people can effectively participate in all decisions concerning their daily life.

MANAGERIAL THEORIES OF ORGANIZATION

"Taylorism," or scientific management

The second major tradition of organization writings starts with the American engineer Frederic W. Taylor (1856–1915) and the movement of "scientific management." Here the problem of productivity rather than the problem of power is the dominant preoccupation. If the classical theorists were worried about the impact of large-scale organizations on the power structure of society, writers in the managerial tradition are much more concerned with finding out ways of running such organizations in the most efficient manner. What is problematic here is not the chances of freedom in an increasingly bureaucratized environment but whether the environment can be made even more rational and bureaucratic in the interests of increased productivity. As the problems change so does the basic conceptual framework underlying such theories: Taylor's main unit of analysis is not society as a whole but the individual at the workplace. In fact, Taylor is concerned with the individual more as an isolated unit than as an organizational member. A brief examination of his theories and their organizational implications, however, is necessary for understanding subsequent theoretical developments that try to support or refute Taylorism.

The scientific management movement. The basic aim of Taylorism is the more rational utilization of human and material resources at the workplace. In order to realize this goal, Taylor advocated the empirical and experimental approach to the problems of workshop management. He believed that for every process, every task in industry, there is one best way of doing it. In order to discover this unique way, one has to study work in a "scientific" way: one has to examine in a highly detailed and objective manner the actual ways in which workers were working. On the basis of such an examination, a more rational method of doing the job can be found. In this way, Taylor thought that scientific knowledge could replace intuition and the rule-of-thumb method in organizations.

Time-and-motion studies

It is this basic drive of rationalization that underlies such well-known techniques of scientific management as the time-and-motion study. Very briefly, such a technique consists in the following processes. By the detailed analysis and registration of a worker's movements, the whole working process is broken down to simple operations, all operations being timed. Then, by a systematic analysis of the data thus obtained, the unnecessary movements are corrected and the whole work process is reconstructed in a more simplified and rational manner. Finally, the standard time of the new way of doing the job is calculated by adding up the time units of each operation and the "idle" times (rest and other unavoidable delays). Once the "best way" of doing the job is discovered, the next step is to teach the new work method to the workers. For Taylor, this can easily be achieved by an incentive system that rewards the fast and pliant workers and penalizes the slow or recalcitrant ones.

Taylor and most of his followers, being engineers, approached the organization mechanistically. In analyzing the organization member at work and in building up standard procedures, they concentrated on the instrumental aspects of human behaviour. Indeed, the organization member was conceived as an instrument of production to be handled as easily as any other tool (provided that one knows the laws of scientific management). In such a conception there is no consideration of the feelings, attitudes, and private goals of the individual; neither is there any realization that the worker is a social being influenced by his colleagues and by the social structure and culture of the groups within which he finds himself. Briefly, Taylorism neglected the psychological and sociological variables of organizational action.

Formal theories of administration. Despite Taylor's concern with spreading the methods of scientific management throughout the whole organization, the workshop remained his chief field of investigation. Formal theories of administration are in many ways complementary to Taylorism. They shift the concern for rationalization and efficiency from the shop floor to the administrative problems of management. The aim of such theories is the discovery of principles enabling the manager to build up and administer an organization in the most efficient manner.

The design of organizational networks

Formal theories of administration conceive the structure of the organization in terms of the rights and responsibilities attached to each position and in terms of the prescribed ways by which various positions are linked with one another. On the basis of such a conception of structure, the problem is (given the goals of the organization) to find the best way of designing the organizational blueprint, and principles are sought that can help the manager in this task. The principle of a "flat" hierarchy, for instance, suggests that levels of authority should be kept at a minimum so that communications are facilitated. Another well-known principle suggests that the number of people under the control of a superior should be quite small for the supervision to be effective. Similar principles are formulated insofar as the general process of management is concerned. Their aim is to help the manager at his everyday work by rationalizing such managerial activities as coordination, planning, control, and so forth.

Administrative theories of this type concentrate on the formal aspects of the organization. The emphasis is not on actual relations between groups or individuals but on prescribed relations. It is not on actual behaviour and motivation but on design and rules to be recorded in an organizational chart or manual. One is not concerned with how actual managers are acting and trying to solve problems but with the "best" ways of acting, which are exclusively related to the formal goals and functions of the organization. This highly formalistic perspective explains to a great extent why such theories of administration have failed in their major endeavour of formulating universally valid principles of management. The principles, and more generally the whole literature of this school, do not give the impression of a growing body of knowledge; they give more the image of a mosaic of definitions and redefinitions and of common-sense formulations of rules that make little significant contribution to knowledge of how real organizations function.

The human relations school. The "human relations school," by introducing the social sciences in the study of the workplace, can be seen as a reaction both to Taylor's mechanistic approach and to the sterile formalism of those who tried to discover universal principles of management.

Informal organization

The comprehensive approach. The school has its starting point in studies undertaken in 1927 at the Hawthorne Western Electric plant in Cicero, Illinois. The chief objective of this research was the examination of work conditions and their relevance to workers' performance on the job. At the beginning the approach was not very different from Taylor's. The investigators tried to relate the workers' performance to such variables as illumination, ventilation, fatigue, and so forth. Because the results were inconclusive and confusing, the Hawthorne researchers started gradually to realize that such variables as illumination or humidity cannot be treated separately from the meaning that individuals assign to them or from their attitudes and preoccupations about them. This insight made the investigators turn their attention to the psychological and finally to the sociological determinants of the work situation. Indeed, at the last stage of their long research, they realized that they must look for the explanation of workers' behaviour in the social organization of the plant. Thus, they started examining, by direct observation and through interviews, a group of operators at work. They soon found out that workers' activities were not regulated by formal managerial policies and directives but by a system of informal norms that were in direct opposition to management's rules and objectives. There were rules, for instance, regulating the pace of work with informal sanctions against any worker producing above a stipulated maximum.

Such rules and patterns of behaviour, emerging spontaneously through the daily interaction of people working together, constitute the informal organization of a plant. This new concept has far-reaching implications for the study of organizations. The worker is no longer perceived as an isolated unit of production but as a social being, as a group member whose actions are very much influenced by the social organization of the workplace. According to the Hawthorne students, this new perspective also has important implications for the practical theory of management. Usually management operates on the basis of assumptions not far removed from those of Taylor and the formalists. The informal organization is ignored, and workers are seen as isolated production units, solely motivated by economic rewards. Management's logic of economic rationality, because it does not take into consideration the psychological and sociological dimensions of the situation, clashes with the workers' "logic of sentiments." As a result, communications break down and industrial conflict becomes inevitable. The remedy for such a situation should be a radical reorientation of managerial conceptions and attitudes toward the workers. Once managers cease to see the worker as a *Homo oeconomicus* and once they turn their attention to the informal organization of work groups, they will be more capable of bringing the informal aims of workers and the formal goals of the firm closer together.

The approach adopted at the final stage of the Hawthorne investigations has been followed by many subsequent studies that attempt to account, in the most detailed and comprehensive way, for the patterns of relations and norms that emerge spontaneously in the work situation. Because such informal patterns are not immediately visible to an outsider, their study necessitates an intimate and long-term acquaintance with the persons and events involved. For this reason, researchers usually limit themselves to the study of a restricted area within an organization (such as a work group). Within this limited context, the informal organization is studied as a social system, as a whole of interdependent parts that emerges within the formal framework of the larger organization.

The "abstractive" phase. The exhaustive study of a single work group, even though it gives insights into the unobtrusive workings of an organization, nevertheless has serious limitations, too—the most important being that the findings in one such case cannot be generalized. One cannot be sure about their applicability and relevance in other cases. For such reasons, human relations students at a later stage abandoned the comprehensive one-case approach and attempted, by abstracting a few variables from the group situation, to examine the relations of these variables in many organizational settings. They hoped that the loss in comprehensiveness could be compensated by findings that would be more valid.

Styles of bureaucratic leadership

Thus an attempt was made to establish correlations between productivity and such variables as characteristics of the worker (*e.g.*, age, sex, social background) or characteristics of the work group (cohesion, type of supervision). The most representative writings of this type were concerned with the relation between the supervisor's style of leadership and group productivity. Their conclusions were that a "democratic," nonauthoritarian style of supervision was positively correlated with high productivity and morale. Strict "punishment-oriented" supervision was conducive to poor work performance. On the basis of such findings human relations students started advocating the training of supervisors in social skills as a solution to the problems and conflicts arising at work.

Such optimism was short-lived. Not only did training schemes for foremen not have the anticipated results, but also correlations between styles of supervision and productivity were put in doubt by subsequent studies that found no consistent relations between them. It was shown, for example, that technology may influence the type of leadership style that will be more effective. When the technological setting involves repetitive and routine tasks, strict rather than permissive supervision seems to be more conducive to high productivity. It was also realized that in order to understand the relation between style of leadership and productivity, one should focus not only on the work group; wider organizational factors also must be taken into account. It was found, for instance, that the supervisor's position within the managerial hierarchy is very important in understanding his effectiveness as a leader. Only the supervisor having a certain influence with his superiors can effectively adopt a permissive style of leadership; without such influence, permissive leadership fails.

As a result of such developments, it was gradually realized that it was not possible to establish valid generalizations by abstracting a few variables and studying their relations in a number of organizations—ignoring, thus, the organizational and group context in which such variables are embedded.

Return to a more comprehensive approach. Thus at a third stage of the development of the human relations school, there was a return to the more inclusive approach of the Hawthorne studies. Moreover, with the new emphasis on technology and with the gradual shifting of attention to organizational variables, human relations writings started to lose their distinctive character. They gradually became indistinguishable from post-Weberian bureaucracy studies (see below *Converging trends*) or from other writings in industrial sociology that are not in the human relations tradition.

Criticism of the human relations approach

The fundamental weakness of the human relations approach is its narrow focus. Human relations students, wishing to avoid the vagueness and imprecision of broader theories, concentrated their attention on the individual and the small group. Such an emphasis on the individual and the group, however, prevented them from taking into consideration certain crucial aspects of industrial organizations that can be clearly seen only if one shifts the focus to the organization as a whole and to the wider societal context in which organizations are embedded. This is apparent if one examines the way in which human relations students have studied organizational conflict. By studying it on the individual and group level, they have stressed mainly its psychological dimensions. They have viewed it as bad interpersonal relations or as misunderstandings arising out of bad leadership. In this way conflict became a technical problem that allegedly could be solved by human relations training in social skills. Social conflict—the conflict of different interests arising out of the structure of work organizations and the wider society—was ignored.

Not surprisingly, therefore, the various remedies that the human relations people proposed have not always been effective. Neither better knowledge of the informal organization nor more skillful supervision can alter the fundamental fact that workers and managers in advanced industrial societies have conflicting interests arising ultimately from the general distribution of power in such societies. If this fundamental proposition is accepted, it becomes clear that methods of conflict resolution, which might be partially effective on the individual and group level, cannot work on the organizational and societal level. A permanent resolution of conflict on those higher levels, if at all possible, would certainly require a radical redistribution of power in modern societies. Of course such ideas are completely alien to human relations writers who accept the status quo.

The criticism above does not invalidate all human relations research. Although human relations students have not given definite answers to the problems they posed, they have introduced the social and psychological sciences to the study of work organizations and have thus broken through the mechanistic and formalistic approach of previous theories.

The decision-making approach. Decision-making theory, as applied to the study of bureaucracies or formal organizations, constitutes a distinct development and must be seen as a reaction to the shortcomings and opposing perspectives of the human relations school, the formal administration theories, and some economic theories of the firm. Its leading exponent is the American social scientist Herbert Simon.

According to this approach, human relations students, by emphasizing the importance of the informal organization, have neglected what is most distinctive about formal organizations—their "formalness," the fact that they are set up in a highly purposive manner for the attainment of specified objectives. By their emphasis on "sentiments," human relations students have completely underrated the fact that people in organizations, whatever their feelings, must solve problems and make rational decisions in their day-to-day work. On the other hand, those disciplines that focus strongly on the rational aspects of action, usually go to the other extreme. They build up ideal models of a perfectly rational man with unlimited capacities for computation and prediction. Thus, for example, in economic theory, economic man, when faced with a problem, is supposed (1) to know in an omniscient way all the alternative courses of action, (2) to predict all ensuing consequences, and (3) to rank automatically all consequences from the least to the most desired according to a system of preferences. In this way economic man always makes optimal choices. This model, of course, does not tell us anything about how real people make decisions. It tells us only how people should decide if they were perfectly rational and omniscient beings. As for the formal theories of administration, they have a similar bias. In trying to formulate principles of good management, they are more concerned with how managers ought to decide and less with how managers actually decide and solve problems.

Decision-making theory represents an attempt to bridge the gap between the extreme positions by formulating a framework of organizational action that can effectively integrate all previous approaches to the study of organizations.

The social psychology of organizational decision making. The decision maker's environment can be seen as a set of premises upon which his decision can be based. There are *factual* premises, subject to empirical testing for their vadility, and *value* premises, which (because they do not refer to what *is* but what *ought* to be) are not subject to such tests. From this point of view, a rational decision can be seen as the right conclusion reached from these two kinds of premises.

The search for solutions in decision making

In economic theory, the decision maker is supposed to have all factual premises (complete knowledge of alternatives and consequences) and value premises (preference ordering) that are relevant to his problem. In real situations these premises are not given. He has to search for them. In the search process, there are all sorts of limitations reducing both the quantity and the quality of such premises. Thus the habits, skills, and reflexes of the decision maker, his feelings and value orientations, as well as his basic knowledge and available information, will limit seriously the "rationality" of his decisions. In fact, because of such limitations, he will not achieve or seek an optimal but a satisfactory solution. He is not the *maximizing* man of economics but the *satisfying* man; that is to say, as soon as he finds a satisfactory solution, he will stop the search for alternatives.

As soon as the organizational decision maker joins the organization, his decisional autonomy is reduced. The organization shapes and limits his decision-making environment in a way that both simplifies problem solving and ensures the general coordination of all decision making activities. Thus the division of labour, by assigning to each member a limited area of responsibility, limits the problems for which he must make a decision. The organizational hierarchy is another crucial factor in structuring the decision maker's environment. The broad and crucial policy decisions are taken at the top. They are subsequently transmitted to the lower echelons and become the value premises that the subordinate will use in making decisions of a more detailed and procedural character.

Thus the division of labour, the authority structure, and other organizational features shape the decisional environment of the individual. They do not necessarily deprive him of all initiative, rather they determine some of the value and factual premises of his environment.

Decision making and organizational structure. When decision-making theorists shift the focus of analysis from the individual problem solver to the organization as a whole, they usually conceptualize it in two ways.

In the first way, attention is paid to the relation of the organization to its external environment. The total organization is seen as a decision maker that tries to give "satisfactory" solutions to organizational problems. As in economics, an attempt is made to build up models of how economic organizations behave in different market situations. But in contrast to the ideal models of economics, decision making theorists attempt to build "realistic" models of how organizations, given the limitations imposed by their own structure and environment, actually take major decisions about such matters as prices and output.

In the second way of conceptualizing the whole organization, the focus shifts more to internal structure. The organization is seen not as a decision-making *unit* but as a decision-making *system*—as a network of decision centres linked together through communications channels. Here cybernetic concepts are used. The organization is seen as a self-controlled communication system with feedback mechanisms. These ensure that whenever a deviation occurs (that is, whenever decisions taken by individuals are not promoting organization goals), information is fed back to the centres and corrective decisions are taken and then implemented.

Criticism of decision-making theory

Decision-making theory, by re-emphasizing formal structure and the rational problem-solving aspects of organizations, has definitely made a significant contribution. It was a healthy reaction against all those psychologically oriented students who were considering the formal structure as something unreal or irrelevant in contrast to the "real" feelings and relations arising spontaneously at work. Moreover, being highly empirical, it has shown the sterility and formalism of those management theories that try to elaborate principles of formal structure without any previous research on how formal organizations are actually structured.

When decision-making theorists claim that they have a conceptual framework within which all previous approaches to the study of organizations can be accommodated, however, their claims are not well founded. It is true that it is somewhat possible to fit all sorts of variables into their decision-making framework when a single individual is making decisions. On the level of the individual, informal values, technology, elements of the formal structure, interest groups, and even societal institutions can be accounted for as premises limiting or expanding the decisional environment of the organizational member. But when the focus becomes broader and shifts from the individual to the organization as a whole, the conceptual framework loses its "integrative" capacity. In fact, when the organization is seen as a system of decision centres and when a vocabulary borrowed from cybernetics is used to account for processes common to all kinds of self-regulated systems (machines, biological organisms, etc.), then the specifically sociological dimensions of organizations are lost.

This does not mean that, on the organizational level, the approach is useless. It can be fruitful insofar as one does not accept in an uncritical manner analogies between self-controlled machines, organisms, and organizations and insofar as one does not forget its partiality and limitations. Otherwise it might lead to gross misrepresentations. There is a tendency among "communication" theorists (especially in industrial contexts), for instance, to reduce all difficulties and troubles in an organization to communication problems, which could supposedly be solved by improving communication channels, correcting "feedback" procedures, and so forth. Although such techniques may be successful in some cases, they are not effective whenever the real trouble lies not in bad communication engineering but elsewhere—for instance, in the rivalry of different departments or bureaus. In such a case, the eventual breakdown in communications is a result, not the cause of the trouble. Under such circumstances, the solution of the conflict (if a solution is possible) is not technical, as would be a problem in communication engineering, but is primarily political, and the political solution will improve communications, rather than the other way round. Consequently, if one wants to discover the organizational conditions under which communication engineering is effective and those under which it is irrelevant, one certainly needs an organizational model that is more inclusive than the "cybernetic" one.

Problems in communication theory

CONVERGING TRENDS

Classical and managerial theories compared

The two lines of organizational writings so far examined have diametrically opposed starting points. Classical theories of bureaucracy, by focussing on the whole social structure, are meant to reveal the impact of increasing bureaucratization on the power structure of modern societies. Managerial theories have relegated the problems of power and social conflict to the background and have tended to look at the industrial organization as a basically harmonious unit whose efficiency one should improve.

As already suggested, however, certain developments on both sides have narrowed the gap between the two different lines of thought. As more and more social scientists become interested in organizational problems, and as they freely choose their conceptual tools from a variety of sources, boundaries between schools become increasingly uncertain; an interchange of ideas and methods constitutes a distinctive feature of recent organization theory. Thus, for instance, post-Weberian theories of bureaucracy use extensively informal organization concepts (a distinctive contribution of the human relations school) in order to challenge Weber's assumption about the rationality of bureaucratic organizations. Moreover, most writings seem to avoid both the short-sighted focus of the social-psychological studies and the all-inclusive society-wide framework of classical theories. Increasingly, the main focus of analysis becomes the organization itself, as a whole.

The problem then is how one sees this whole. Some writers, putting more emphasis on the systemic and integrative aspects of the organization, see it as a system having to fulfill certain functions or needs in order to survive; they examine organizational parts and try to see to what extent various processes inhibit or promote the fulfillment of organizational goals. Other writers, emphasizing organizational conflict, are interested not so much in how an organization solves its systemic problems but, rather, in the configuration of groups within an organization and in the strategies by which they try to promote their usually conflicting interests.

Functionalist theories. Weber's ideal type of bureaucracy has been the starting point of many modern functionalist theories of bureaucracy. Weber argued that the bureaucratic type of organization is technically the most efficient mode of administration. Indeed, the closer that an organization can approach the ideal characteristics of bureaucracy (impersonality, concentration of the means of administration at the top, etc.), the more efficient it will become. In a way, a large part of the post-Weberian literature on bureaucracy tries to show that this hypothesis does not always hold—that very often an accentuation of bureaucratic elements makes an organization not more but less efficient.

(In fairness to Weber, it must be pointed out that many of these criticisms may be misplaced. Weber used a very broad historical perspective and tried to contrast bureaucracy with other types of state administrations. On such a level of analysis, bureaucracy is probably the most rational and efficient organizational instrument ever invented by man. And such a position does not deny that in viewing single bureaucratic organizations one can find and acknowledge bureaucratic inefficiencies.)

The "red tape" image of bureaucracy

Dysfunctional aspects of bureaucracy. The American Robert K. Merton was among the first sociologists to emphasize systematically the other side of the bureaucratic picture—its red tape and inefficiency. According to Merton, if, as Weber thought, the predominance of rational rules and their close control of all actions favours the reliability and predictability of the bureaucrat's behaviour, it also accounts for his lack of flexibility and his tendency to turn means into ends. Indeed, the emphasis on conformity and strict observance of the rules induces the individual to internalize them. Instead of simply means, procedural rules become ends in themselves. Thus a kind of "goal displacement" occurs. The instrumental and formalistic aspect of the bureaucratic role becomes more important than the substantive one, the achievement of the main organizational goals. According to Merton, when one leaves the sphere of the ideal and studies a real organization, one can see that a certain bureaucratic characteristic (such as strict control by rules) can both promote and hinder organizational efficiency; it can have both functional effects (predictability, precision) and dysfunctional effects (rigidity).

Many writers after Merton have tried to study these inefficient, "nonrational" aspects not portrayed in the ideal type of organization. This emphasis on dysfunctions is strongly linked with the key concepts elaborated by the human relations school—that of the formal and the informal organization. Within a formal framework, informal arrangements among workers can go against the fulfillment of organizational goals and, from that point of view, are dysfunctional. Or at least they are dysfunctional from the point of view of management; from the point of view of the workers the informal organization can be functional, since it increases their degree of autonomy and self-regulation. Thus what is functional for one group can be dysfunctional for another group, in the same way that policies promoting one type of goal can hinder the fulfillment of other organizational goals.

The unanticipated consequences of formal controls. Another concept central to functionalist theories of bureaucracy and linked with the formal-informal, functional-dysfunctional concepts is that of the unintended consequences of purposive action. People consciously coordinate their activities in order to achieve specific goals, and the existence of a formal structure clearly reflects purposiveness. But purposive action can have unpredicted consequences. Although formal rules are designed to control everyone's activities in the interest of organizational productivity, they apply not to inert materials or tools but to human beings and thus can never succeed in controlling a situation completely. Contrary to the hopes of Taylorism, human beings can never be turned into perfect machines. They have goals of their own that do not always coincide with the formally prescribed organizational objectives.

The humanness of human beings

The recalcitrance of human beings reluctant to accept full bureaucratic control generates unanticipated "informal" consequences, which in their turn bring forth a renewed attempt to control the situation by additional formal rules. Thus, in a schematic way, the following dialectic pattern seems to be present in many bureaucratic situations: formal control by bureaucratic rules leads to unanticipated consequences of action that in turn lead to renewed formal control.

In one study of a U.S. employment agency, for instance

(reported in Peter Blau, *The Dynamics of Bureaucracy*, 1955), there was an example of an attempt to increase organizational productivity by introducing statistical records of the daily quantity of work of each employee. This formal attempt to control work behaviour had unanticipated consequences. Although productivity was increased, the quality of the work performance deteriorated. Employees were so keen on showing a good record of performance, dealing with as many cases as possible every day, that they ceased giving adequate attention to the case of each particular client. This unanticipated event created the need for a further elaboration of formal controls to change the quality of services. New rules modified the statistical records to take into consideration the nonquantitative aspects of an employee's performance.

The imposition of rules has another dysfunctional aspect: as A. Gouldner has pointed out in his *Patterns of Industrial Bureaucracy*, the detailed definition of unacceptable behaviour in lists of rules increases the employee's knowledge about what behaviour of his is minimally acceptable. This may tend to incite the bureaucrat to accomplish the minimum work required. Such an attitude of course is detrimental to the productivity of the organization. One consequence may be that supervisors will increase their activities and controls and thus increase interpersonal conflict and tension.

Some sociologists believe that the central dilemma in bureaucracy arises out of the need to delegate power to organizational subsystems. The increasing complexity of organizational tasks makes decentralization and the delegation of responsibility to intermediaries inevitable. But such a measure can bring forth a divergence of interests between the central system and its decentralized subunits. There is a tendency for the subunits to neglect the overall organizational goals in favour of their limited subgoals. In this way subgoals become ends in themselves rather than simply means. This situation makes the need for centralized control stronger, and the circle may start all over again. (This circular pattern of rationalization in bureaucracy may be merely a tendency that can be more or less checked by countervailing forces.)

The Parsonian theory of organizations. The formal-informal dialectic outlined above helps the student to study the organization dynamically, as a "going concern," as a system of tensions that produce short-term change. As a conceptual framework, however, it is too simplistic. It cannot in itself account in a thorough and systematic manner for all the complex aspects of an organization. Within the context of functionalist theories, the American sociologist Talcott Parsons has attempted to provide a more comprehensive framework. In applying his general sociological theories to the field of formal organizations, he has attempted to account systematically for the various organizational processes and for the ways in which such processes are linked with one another and with the larger society.

Parsons has seen the organization as a system made up of various subsystems (groups, departments) and embedded in larger systems (community, society). The point of departure and the main emphasis in his theory of organizations is on values. Primarily, organizational values legitimize the major goals of the organization. At a lower level of generality, these values are differentiated and institutionalized in the form of more detailed norms that regulate the various organizational activities. More precisely, these norms regulate the processes that carry out the functions of the organization. According to Parsons, as in every other social system, an organization has four functional requirements or problems that it has to cope with if it wants to survive. These are the problems of adaptation, goal achievement, integration, and latency.

Adaptation, goal achievement, integration, and latency

The adaptation problem points to every organization's need to acquire all the material and human resources necessary for its proper functioning. The institutionalized norms and processes designed to cope with this problem constitute the adaptation sector of the organization. Thus, for instance, norms regulating personnel recruitment will be placed within the adaptation sector.

The goal-achievement sector refers to all norms that contribute to the mobilization of resources to achieve organizational goals. This is basically the problem of fitting means (resources provided by the adaptation sector) to ends. It is in this sector that Parsons places the major power aspects of the organization; in this sector are found the norms regulating the crucial decision-making processes that set the major goals and policies for the organization.

Integration, the third functional problem, refers to the need of every organization to coordinate and keep together its various subsystems (groups, departments). The latency problem, finally, is basically one of "socialization." The latency sector contains all the processes designed to ensure that individual members have adequate training and a motivational commitment for the performance of organizational tasks.

All organizations have the same four functional problems, according to Parsons. What differentiates one from another is that, depending on their goals, they solve these problems in different ways, and the systematic study of such different institutionalized solutions should be one of the major aims of organization theory.

In another context Parsons has been less concerned with functional problems and has paid more attention to the hierarchical structure of an organization. In this respect he distinguishes three subsystems: the technical, the managerial, and the institutional. The technical is concerned with all those activities that contribute directly to the achievement of the organization's goal—such as the processing of raw material in a factory or the actual teaching in a school. The managerial system administers the internal affairs of the organization and mediates between the technical subsystem and outsiders by procuring the necessary resources and by finding "customers" for the disposal of organizational products. The institutional subsystem operates as a link between the technical-managerial subsystem and the larger society. Thus, for instance, in a business bureaucracy the plant would correspond to the technical subsystem, the office or administration to the managerial, and the board of directors to the institutional.

Criticisms of the Parsonian approach

Although Parsons' conceptual framework helps one to understand the system of norms that maintain an organization as a functioning whole, it does not help one to understand how these norms came about nor how they can change. It says little about the concrete actors, collective or individual, who actually create and transform such norms. In fact, in talking continuously about values and norms as regulating processes and solving problems, Parsons gives the impression that such values exist in a social vacuum. His approach, for instance, does not acknowledge that norms regulating the remuneration of personnel are often a reflection of the power position of various groups within an organization. As the power of such groups changes, so do the remuneration norms. To speak of norms without reference to the distribution of power and other scarce resources among organizational groups not only gives a partial view of an organization but also makes impossible the study of organizational change.

Conflict theories. A group of theorists has rejected the functional approach and contended that organizations must be seen as configurations of antagonistic groups that aim, through various strategies, to promote their conflicting interests. Although these theorists do view the organization "as a whole," they see that the parts of the whole are not institutional norms but instead are groups that, according to their power position, can influence policies. Obviously such an approach can deal more easily with social conflict and change than the previous one, which emphasizes integration or equilibrium.

This emphasis on organizational conflict, being a relatively recent development, is far from having a conceptual framework that can be compared with the Parsonian one in thoroughness and sophistication. Nevertheless, some of the recent work on the problems of power and conflict provides useful insights that may constitute a basis for the elaboration of a more general theory. Thus the American sociologist Melville Dalton, in a book based on his long experience as a participant and observer in six business firms (*Men Who Manage*, 1959), offered a revealing picture of organizational structure in terms of conflicting cliques and their interminable struggles for gaining more power and ensuring a greater share of organizational rewards. Even if sometimes exaggerated, this analysis showed in a striking way to what extent organizational members and groups can be primarily interested in the pursuit of their narrow interests and the consolidation and improvement of their own power position, even at the expense of wider organizational interests. Moreover, it showed the pervasiveness of the ensuing struggles and their impact on every aspect of organizational life. It showed, too, how this intense political activity can be scrupulously and skillfully camouflaged so that the resulting policies appear to be in harmony with the official ideology.

Organizations as networks of cliques and power-seeking groups

This emphasis on the "dirty linen" aspect of the organization, its incessant intricacies and petty struggles, caused Dalton to assign less importance to such larger antagonisms as "staff versus line" or "management versus workers." According to Dalton, although such broad divisions can be identified in the organizational structure, neat lines of demarcation are blurred because numerous cliques within and across the major blocks emerge and fight each other—without regard to abstract ideologies overall. Thus the organizational image that finally emerges from such an analysis is a bewildering kaleidoscope of swiftly changing and conflicting cliques, which cut across departmental and other traditional loyalties and which ultimately account for organizational order or disorder.

The French sociologist Michel Crozier's study of two French government agencies (*The Bureaucratic Phenomenon*, 1963; Eng. trans. 1964) was another important step in the analysis of organizational power and conflict. In Crozier's analysis, the social structure consists of highly cohesive occupational groups, each presenting a unified and rather hostile front toward the others. (Contrary to Dalton, Crozier ignores the existence of cliques within and across these occupational groupings.) Each group's strategy consists in manipulating the rules in order to enhance its own prerogatives and secure its independence from every direct and arbitrary interference by those higher up. Because rules obviously can never cover everything, "areas of uncertainty" always emerge that constitute the focal points around which collective conflicts become acute and instances of direct dominance and subordination develop. The group that, by its position in the occupational structure, can control the "unregulated" area, has a great strategic advantage that it naturally uses in order to improve its power position and to ensure a greater share of organizational rewards.

Conflict studies, as illustrated by the work of Dalton and Crozier, point to the central importance of an organization's political structure and thus open a new perspective in the analysis of bureaucracy. To the image of the organization man as a person of sentiments seeking friendship and emotional security and to the image of the problem solver and decision maker is added the new image of a "political man" primarily interested in the collective and individual pursuit of power for the promotion of his own interests. So long as it is not followed single-mindedly, this new dimension should contribute to a more inclusive and realistic approach to the study of organizations.

Finally, insofar as conflict theories emphasize concrete *actors* and their strategies rather than *systems* and their impersonal functioning, they come close to such new trends in sociological theory as phenomenology and symbolic interactionism. These trends have already had a limited impact on organization theory. Symbolic interactionists reject the functionalist approach which views organizational processes and activities in terms of system needs. For them to speak of system or organizational needs, as distinct from the needs of concrete social actors, is to postulate a mystical social entity over and above the existence of organizational members. Thus, for instance, the English sociologist David Silverman in his book *The Theory of Organisations* (1970) placed social actors rather than system parts as the centre of organizational analysis. According to him, organizational order as well as disorder can only be understood if one refers to the meaningful activities of concrete individuals and groups interacting with each other. In fact, social actors, in attaching meanings to their own actions and to the actions of others and in pursuing various strategies for the achievement of their goals, create, sustain, and change social reality. The action frame of reference has been implicit, at least partly, in many organization writings; but its clear theoretical formulation is a useful, although somewhat exaggerated, reaction against those system theorists who tend to dissociate the study of social reality from the human beings who are involved.

Symbolic interaction

General conclusion. On the level of a general theory of organizations, what is needed most at the present time is a synthesis of the integration-functionalist and the conflict-action frames of reference—a conceptual framework that would help the student to study as *inseparably interrelated phenomena* both normative integration and the conflict of interests, both system requirements and actors' orientations. It has become clear in general sociological theory that one cannot deal adequately with social conflict without considering normative arrangements that limit and regulate it. Inversely, one cannot understand system formation and change without reference to group strategies and conflicts, to the contests of power that determine to a great extent the concrete ways in which norms are institutionalized and de-institutionalized.

BIBLIOGRAPHY. For general reviews of the literature on bureaucracy and formal organizations, see P. BLAU and W.R. SCOTT, *Formal Organizations: A Comparative Approach* (1962); J. MARCH and H.A. SIMON, *Organizations* (1958); N.P. MOUZELIS, *Organisation and Bureaucracy: An Analysis of Modern Theories* (1967); and S.N. EISENSTADT, "Bureaucracy and Bureaucratization: A Trend Report and Bibliography," *Current Sociology*, 7:99–164 (1958).

For historical works on state bureaucracies, *cf.* H. ROSENBERG, *Bureaucracy, Aristocracy, and Autocracy: The Prussian Experience 1660–1815* (1958); S.N. EISENSTADT, *The Political Systems of Empire: The Rise and Fall of the Historical Bureaucratic Societies* (1963); and OTTO HINTZE, *Staaf und Verfassung*, 2nd ed. (1962).

For an extensive exposition of Marx's views on bureaucracy and the state, see P. NAVILLE, *Le Nouveau Leviathan*, pp. 70–127 (1957). For attempts to confront Marx's prediction of the withering away of the state bureaucracy with Soviet reality, see VLADIMIR I. LENIN, *The State and Revolution* (1964; orig. pub. in Russian, 1917); and LEON TROTSKY, *The Permanent Revolution* (1965; orig. pub. in Russian, 1930), *The Revolution Betrayed* (1937). The writings of MAX WEBER on bureaucracy include his *Theory of Social and Economic Organization* (1957; orig. pub. in German, 1922), and *From Max Weber: Essays in Sociology*, trans. and ed. by H.H. GERTH and C.W. MILLS (1946), a critical analysis of his ideal type; various other definitions of bureaucracy may be found in M. ALBROW, *Bureaucracy* (1970).

The classical work on the oligarchic tendencies of modern bureaucratic organizations is R. MICHELS, *Political Parties* (1949; orig. pub. in German, 1925). A more recent and popular work along similar lines is J. BURNHAM, *The Managerial Revolution* (1960). The major themes of the scientific management movement may be found in F. TAYLOR, *The Principles of Scientific Management* (1964). The Hawthorne experiments, which are considered the starting point of the human relations school, are extensively reported in F.J. ROETHLISBERGER and W.J. DICKSON, *Management and the Worker: Technical vs. Social Organization in an Industrial Plant* (1934); some of the broader philosophical and sociological assumptions of the human relations tradition may be found in ELTON MAYO, *The Social Problems of an Industrial Civilisation* (1945); for a reappraisal of the Hawthorne experiments and of the more recent human relations literature, see H. LANDSBERGER, *Hawthorne Revisited: Management and the Worker* (1958). A representative work of the decision-making approach is H.A. SIMON, *Administrative Behavior*, 2nd ed. (1957). For theories with a marked functionalist orientation, see R.K. MERTON, "Bureaucratic Structure and Personality," in *Reader in Bureaucracy*, pp. 261–372 (1952); A. GOULDNER, *Wildcat Strike* (1954); P. BLAU, *The Dynamics of Bureauc-*

racy: A Study of Interpersonal Relations in Two Government Agencies (1955); and TALCOTT PARSONS, "Suggestions for a Sociological Approach to the Theory of Organizations," *Administrative Science Quarterly*, 1:63–85, 227–239 (1956). Other significant works are P. SELZNICK, *TVA and the Grass Roots: A Study in the Sociology of Formal Organization* (1949); and A. ETZIONI, *A Comparative Analysis of Complex Organisations* (1961).

(N.P.M.)

Burgundy, History of

The name of Burgundy (French Bourgogne) has designated several political formations that have at various times occupied the region of the Rhône and Saône rivers in eastern France. In modern times the name has been limited to the region lying between the Saône, the Loire, and the upper Seine—that is, to the former duchy of Burgundy (see below)—but in the Middle Ages the name was applied to a Burgundian kingdom later called the kingdom of Arles, and to the countship of Burgundy, later known as the Franche-Comté.

Early kingdoms. The Burgundians were a Scandinavian people whose original homeland lay on the southern shores of the Baltic, where the island of Bornholm (Burgundarholm, in the Middle Ages) still bears their name. About the 1st century AD they moved into the lower valley of the Vistula, but, unable to defend themselves there against the Gepidae, they migrated westward to the borders of the Roman Empire. There, serving as *foederati*, or auxiliaries, in the Roman army, they established a powerful kingdom, which by the early 5th century extended to the west bank of the Rhine. Their king Gundahar (Gundicar or Gunther), who seems to have had his capital at Worms, became involved in hostilities with the Romans about 435. The Roman general Aetius, using the Huns as allies, nearly annihilated the Burgundians the following year. The massacre of the royal family by the Huns is recounted in the great medieval German epic, the *Nibelungenlied*. In 443 Aetius transferred the surviving Burgundians to Sapaudia (Savoy) in the vicinity of Lake Geneva.

As Rome's hold over its Western Empire declined in the second half of the 5th century, the Burgundians gradually spread their control over areas to the north and west of Savoy, and then throughout the Rhône and Saône valleys. This second Burgundian kingdom reached its zenith under the lawgiver and king Gundobad (474–516), who promulgated a written code of laws, the Lex Gundobada, for the Burgundians and a separate code, the Lex Romana Burgundionum, for his Gallo-Roman subjects. Although Gundobad was a Christian of the heretical Arian sect, he and his people lived on good terms with the Gallo-Roman bishops. Gundobad's son Sigismund, who was later canonized, converted to Catholicism and founded the monastery of Saint-Maurice d'Agaune. Under Sigismund the Burgundians were attacked by the powerful Frankish kingdom founded by Clovis to the north and east of Burgundy. Sigismund was killed by Chlodomer, son of Clovis, in 524, but Burgundy remained independent under his brother Gundomar until 534, when the Franks occupied the kingdom, extinguishing the royal dynasty.

Conquest by the Franks

With the death of Clotaire I in 561, however, the Frankish kingdom was partitioned among members of the Merovingian dynasty, and one of Clotaire's sons, Guntram, secured the *regnum Burgundiae*, or kingdom of Burgundy. This *regnum* eventually included not only all the former Burgundian lands but also the diocese of Arles in Provence, the Val d'Aosta east of the Alps, and even extensive territory in north central France. It remained a separate Merovingian kingdom until Charles Martel, the grandfather of Charlemagne, subjugated it to Frankish Austrasia early in the 8th century.

The Carolingians made several partitions of Burgundy before Boso, ruler of the Viennois, had himself proclaimed king of all Burgundy from Autun to the Mediterranean in 879. The French Carolingians later recovered the country west of the Saône and north of Lyons from him, and the German Carolingians recovered Jurane, or Upper, Burgundy (*i.e.*, Transjurane Burgundy, or the country between the Jura and the Alps, together with Cisjurane Burgundy, or the Franche-Comté). Boso and his successors, however, were able to maintain themselves in the kingdom of Provence, or Lower Burgundy—sometimes also, rather misleadingly, called Cisjurane Burgundy—until about 933.

Creation of the last Burgundian kingdom

In 888 Rudolf I (died 912) of the German Welf family was recognized as king of Jurane (Upper) Burgundy, including much territory in what is now Switzerland. His son and successor Rudolf II was able in *c.* 931 to conclude a treaty with Hugh of Provence, the successor of Boso's son Louis the Blind, whereby he extended his rule over the entire *regnum Burgundiae* except the areas to the west of the Saône. This union of Upper and Lower Burgundy was bequeathed in 1032 to the German king and emperor Conrad II and became known from the 13th century as the kingdom of Arles (the name Burgundy being increasingly reserved for the county and for the duchy of Burgundy).

Adapted from R. Treharne and H. Fullard, (eds.), *Muir's Historical Atlas: Ancient, Medieval and Modern*, 9th ed. (1964); George Philip & Son, Ltd., London

Burgundy in the 11th century.

The county of Burgundy to 1335. The rulers of the kingdom of Burgundy had little control over the local counts in Cisjurane Burgundy, where effective authority passed more and more into the hands of the counts of Mâcon. In 1127 the new count Raynald III refused to do homage to the German king Lothair III. Lothair then tried to set up Conrad of Zähringen in Raynald's place, but after ten years of conflict Raynald was victorious. Thereafter he was the *franc-comte* ("free count"), and his territory known as the Franche-Comté.

The emperor Frederick I (Barbarossa) married Raynald's heiress, Béatrix, in 1146, hoping that the possession of the countship would strengthen his influence in Germany. The countship, however, passed on Béatrix's death to her third son, Otto I (died 1200), then to his daughter Béatrix and her husband Otto II (died 1234) of the house of Meran. Their son Otto III was succeeded in 1248 by his sister Alix, whose husband, Hugh, of the house of Chalôn, was descended from a brother of Raynald III. Their son, Otto IV, heavily in debt after a long conflict with the Emperor, agreed in two treaties (1291 and 1295) with the French king Philip IV to surrender the county to the French crown. Otto's daughter married the future Philip V of France, and their daughter's marriage to the Burgundian duke Eudes IV in 1335 temporarily succeeded in reuniting the duchy and the county of Burgundy.

The duchy of Burgundy to 1335. The duchy of Burgundy was that part of the *regnum Burgundiae* west of the Saône that was recovered from Boso by the French Carolingians and remained a part of the kingdom of France. Boso's brother Richard, called the Justiciar, count of Autun, was invested with a command against the Norman invaders who devastated the duchy in 888–889. Richard expelled them and then organized the greater part of the territory under his own authority. His son Rudolph (Raoul), who succeeded him in 921, was elected king of France in 923. On Rudolph's death in 936 the Carolingian king Louis IV and Hugh the Great, duke of the Franks, detached Sens, Troyes, and Langres from Burgundy, and Hugh secured the succession to the duchy for his two sons. The younger of these, Henry I (Eudes-Henry), who died without issue in 1002, had adopted his stepson Otto William, but the king of France, the Capetian Robert II, who was Henry's nephew, refused to acknowledge Otto William as heir to Burgundy and conquered the duchy (1003–06). Robert made his son Henry duke of Burgundy, to which Dijon (separated from the duchy with Langres) was restored in 1016, though the countships of Nevers and Auxerre were detached from it. In 1032, after Henry's accession to the French crown, his brother became duke as Robert I (died 1075).

The duchy under the Capetians

The duchy formed in 1016, though smaller than its 10th-century predecessor, was stronger and remained in the Capetian family until 1361. In their foreign policy the Capetian dukes adhered loyally to their cousins the kings of France and in internal affairs enlarged their domain and enforced obedience from their vassals. Burgundy came to be recognized as the premier peerage of the French kingdom. Hugh III (died 1192) commanded the French forces in the Holy Land in the Third Crusade after King Philip II Augustus returned home. His successor, Eudes III (duke 1192–1218), fought against the Albigensian heretics and supported Philip Augustus against John of England. Hugh IV was prominent in the reign of St. Louis. Robert II (duke 1272–1306) and Eudes IV (duke 1315–49) were the most powerful French barons of their time, being allied by marriage to the royal house and often directing royal policy.

The development of feudal institutions within the two Burgundies proceeded at an unequal pace. Central authority over the vassals was much stronger in the duchy than in the county, which had been plagued by dynastic rivalry, and judicial institutions such as the *grand jours* (ducal assizes) and courts of appeal were organized sooner and more thoroughly within the duchy. The towns prospered: Dijon became an important market town; a fair was held at Chalon-sur-Saône, where merchants from the south of France met northern traders; and Italian merchants came to Burgundy to buy its wool, which rivalled that of England. Pilgrims flocked to Vézelay and Autun, where in 1146 a magnificent church was built around the tomb of St. Lazare. Burgundian monasteries were famous: Cluny (founded 910) became the centre of an order of monks extending from England to Spain; and in 1098 the monastery of Cîteaux was founded and with it a new religious order, the Cistercian.

Growth of towns

Unification under the Valois dukes. The reunification of the two Burgundies effected in 1335 was ended in 1361 with the death of Eudes IV's grandson Philip of Rouvre. The king of France, John II the Good, reunited the duchy to the domain of the crown, while Franche-Comté went to the Count of Flanders. A new period of Burgundian history opened under King John, who in 1363 granted the duchy to his son Philip the Bold; then in 1369 Philip married the heiress of the county, Margaret of Flanders. In 1384, when his father-in-law died, Philip inherited Nevers, Rethel, Artois, and Flanders, as well as the Franche-Comté. The two Burgundies formed the southern part of a state, the northern possessions of which extended over the Netherlands, the valley of the Meuse, and the Ardennes. In the north expansion was to continue (Hainaut, 1428: Brabant, 1430; Luxembourg, 1443), but the south, from which Nevers was again detached in 1404, became less and less important. Philip the Bold, however, who lived in Burgundy, built the monastery Chartreuse de Champmol at Dijon. He also purchased the southern territory of Charolais in 1390.

John the Fearless succeeded Philip in 1404 and devoted most of his energies to the struggle with his rival Louis, duc d'Orleans, and with Louis' supporters under the Count of Armagnac, who devastated the southern borders of Burgundy between 1412 and 1435. John was assassinated in 1419, and his son Philip the Good continued the struggle against the Armagnacs and threw his support to the English during the Hundred Years' War. The Treaty of Arras (1435), which established peace between Burgundy and Charles VII, added greatly to the Burgundian domain. Even so, mercenary bands continued their depredations in Burgundy until 1445, after which the duchy enjoyed peace until Philip's death in 1467.

The next duke, Charles the Bold, was constantly in conflict with the French king Louis XI. Charles's aim was to unite the northern and southern sections of the kingdom by annexing Lorraine, and he demanded from the Emperor the title of king of Burgundy. Charles was thwarted in these efforts by the persistent efforts of Louis XI, who conducted several campaigns against him and subjected Burgundy to an economic blockade.

Economic decline

The two Burgundies suffered from the ravages of the Black Death in 1348 and from the mercenaries' bands of the Hundred Years' War. The population declined perceptibly and put a heavy strain on production in the 15th century. The lucrative trade in grain, wines, and finished wool was threatened, and the market-fairs lost some of their importance. But on the whole the two Burgundies seem to have enjoyed more security than much of Europe during the 14th and 15th centuries. The Valois dukes (1363–1477) introduced new institutions into the Burgundies: in the duchy the Chambre des Comptes ("chamber

Adapted from R. Treharne and H. Fullard, *Muir's Historical Atlas: Ancient, Medieval and Modern* (1964); George Philip & Son, Ltd., London

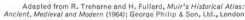

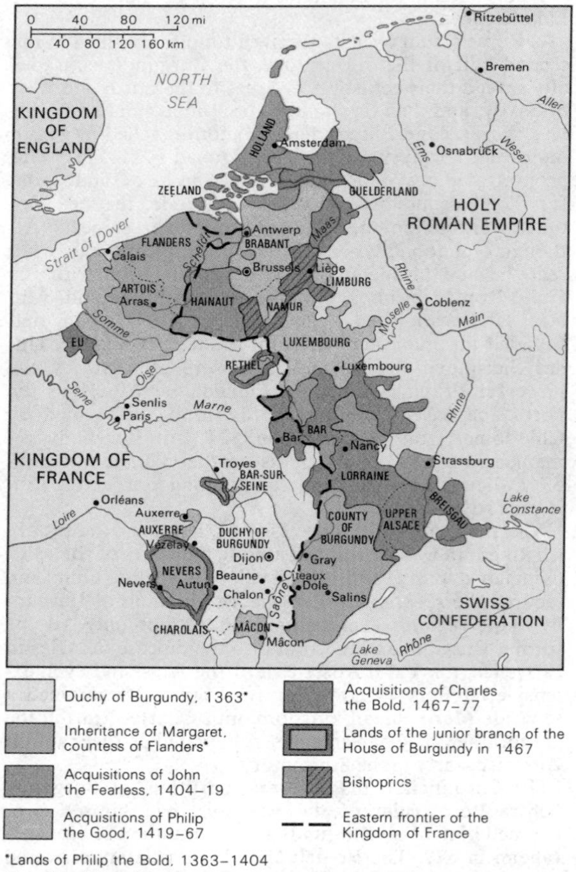

Growth of the domain of the House of Burgundy in the 14th and 15th centuries.

of accounts") was organized in Dijon in 1386, and the *grand jours* were transformed by Charles the Bold as a *parlement*, or permanent court, which met alternately at Beaune and at Dôle (which also became the meeting place for the estates of the Franche-Comté). The "lands of Burgundy" were administered by a single governor but remained separate in fiscal matters. The Burgundian nobility profited from the rule of the Valois dukes as state servants.

Later history. After the death of Charles the Bold in 1477, his heiress married the Austrian archduke Maximilian of Habsburg (later Holy Roman emperor), thus disappointing French hopes that she would marry Louis XI's son Charles, the future Charles VIII of France. The Treaty of Arras (1482), however, ceded the Franche-Comté to Charles on his betrothal to Mary's daughter Margaret of Austria. When he broke this engagement, he had to cede the Franche-Comté to Austria by the Treaty of Senlis in 1493.

The Franche-Comté. For the next 185 years the Franche-Comté was a possession of the Habsburgs. By the Treaty of St. Jean-de-Losne (1522) with France, the neutrality of the county was ensured during the wars between the Habsburgs and the last French kings of the Valois line. Its ensuing prosperity, enhanced by industrial development, can be judged by the splendid Renaissance architecture of its towns. Civil disturbances, however, came with the Reformation, when bands of Protestants entered the predominantly Catholic county from Germany and Switzerland. The Franche-Comté passed to the Spanish Habsburgs through the emperor Charles V's partition of his dominions in 1556. Under Philip II of Spain a forceful repression of Protestants took place, and Henry IV of France, in his war with Philip, violated the Franche-Comté's neutrality. From 1598 to 1635 peace was maintained, but French fear of Habsburg encirclement led Louis XIII to attempt to annex the county. He invaded and ravaged the area annually from 1636 to 1639, but the Peace of Westphalia (1648) confirmed Habsburg control.

Annexation by the French

Conquered in 1668 by the prince de Condé during the War of Devolution but returned to Spain by the Peace of Aix-la-Chapelle (Aachen; May 2, 1668), the Franche-Comté was finally conquered for France by Condé in the last of the so-called Dutch Wars, the French annexation being recognized by the Peace of Nijmegen in 1678. Louis XIV transferred the capital of the new province to the former imperial city of Besançon. In 1790, along with the rest of France, the Franche-Comté was divided into three separate *départements* of Jura, Doubs, and Haute-Saône.

The province of Burgundy. After the death of Charles the Bold (1477), the duchy was annexed by the French crown. During the 16th century it was devastated by the Wars of Religion. The towns had to be fortified, and mercenaries roamed the country. As Catholic supporters of the Holy League during the wars, the towns did not recognize the former Protestant Henry IV as king until 1595. The duchy was again ravaged in the Thirty Years' War, and also during the aristocratic revolt known as the Fronde (1648–53) led by the great Condé. Not until the French annexation of the Franche-Comté in 1678 were peace and security restored. From 1631 to 1789 the duchy was governed by the princes de Condé. After the French Revolution the province of Burgundy disappeared, divided into the *départements* of Côte-d'Or, Saône-et-Loire, and Yonne.

BIBLIOGRAPHY. Although the history of the Burgundian lands has been the subject of several general works, including A. KLEINCLAUSZ, *Histoire de Bourgogne*, 2nd rev. ed. (1924); J. RICHARD, *Histoire de la Bourgogne* (1957); and E. PRECLIN, *Histoire de la Franche-Comté* (1947), none of these works satisfies the demands of present research. Major works have been devoted to different periods of Burgundian history. M. CHAUME, *Les origines du duché de Bourgogne*, 4 vol. (1925–37), covers the Roman period to the end of the 11th century. This may be supplemented by R. GUICHARD, *Essai sur l'histoire du peuple burgonde* (1965); R. POUPARDIN, *Le royaume de Bourgogne* (1907); and on ducal Burgundy, J. RICHARD, *Les ducs de Bourgogne et la formation du duché du XIe au XIVe siècle* (1954). The Valois dukes and the formation of their state is the subject of R. VAUGHAN, *Philip the Bold: The Formation of the Burgundian State* (1962), *John the Fearless: The Growth of Burgundian Power* (1966), *Philip the Good: The Apogee of Burgundy* (1970); and J. BARTIER, *Charles le Téméraire* (1970), all of which give references to additional studies. The history of Burgundy and Franche-Comté in the 16th century has been studied by L. FEBVRE, *Philippe II et la Franche-Comté* (1911); and H. DROUOT, *Mayenne et la Ligue en la Bourgogne*, 2 vol. (1937). For a discussion of the crisis of the 17th century, see G. ROUPNEL, *La Ville et la campagne au XVIIe siècle* (1922), a study of the ascendancy of Dijon over the surrounding countryside. A good city history is C. FOHLEN (ed.), *Histoire de Besançon*, 2 vol. (1964–65). Essential material is furnished by numerous critical articles and reviews, recorded in the *Bibliographie bourguignonne* (annual); and in C. FOHLEN (ed.), *Bibliographie franc-comtoise, 1940–1960* (1961).

(J.B.R.)

Burke, Edmund

British statesman, parliamentary orator, and political thinker, Edmund Burke played a prominent part in all major political issues from 1765 to his death in 1797 and remains an important figure in the history of political theory.

By courtesy of the National Portrait Gallery, London

Burke, oil painting from the studio of Sir Joshua Reynolds, 1771. In the National Portrait Gallery, London.

Early life and career. Burke was Irish, born in Dublin probably on January 12 (January 1, old style), 1729. His father, a solicitor, was Protestant, his mother Roman Catholic. He encountered a third religious tradition at his boarding school, run by a Yorkshire Quaker. He entered Trinity College, Dublin, in 1744 and moved to London in 1750 to begin his studies at the Middle Temple. There follows an obscure period in which Burke lost interest in his legal studies, was estranged from his father, and spent some time wandering about England and France. In 1756, he published anonymously and in the style of the statesman and man of letters Viscount Bolingbroke *A Vindication of Natural Society in a Letter to Lord . . ., by a Late Noble Writer*, a satire aimed at both the destructive criticism of revealed religion and the contemporary vogue of "return to Nature." A contribution to new trends in aesthetic theory, *A Philosophical Enquiry into the Origin of Our Ideas of the Sublime and Beautiful*, which appeared in 1757, gave him some reputation in England and was noticed abroad, among others by Denis Diderot, Immanuel Kant, and G.E. Lessing, the German dramatist and man of letters. In agreement with the publisher Robert Dodsley, Burke initiated *The Annual Register* as a yearly survey of world affairs; the first volume appeared in 1758 under his (unacknowledged) editorship, and he retained his connection with it for about 30 years.

In 1757 Burke married Jane Nugent, the daughter of an Irish Catholic doctor. From this period also date his numerous literary and artistic friendships, including those with Dr. Samuel Johnson, Oliver Goldsmith, Sir Joshua Reynolds, and David Garrick.

Secretary to Marquess of Rockingham

After a first unsuccessful venture into politics, Burke was appointed secretary, in 1765, to the Marquess of Rockingham, leader of one of the Whig groups, the largely liberal faction in Parliament, and entered the House of Commons. Burke remained Rockingham's secretary until the latter's death in 1782, exercising great influence on his upright and disinterested, if not very forceful, patron. He worked with some success to inspire with a sense of unity and common principle the group that formed round Rockingham. Mostly in opposition, this group was to be the vehicle of Burke's parliamentary career.

Political life. Burke soon took an active part in the domestic constitutional controversy of George III's reign. The revolution settlement after the accession of William and Mary to the throne in 1689 had enlarged the role of Parliament, but while placing specific limitations on the royal prerogative it had left many aspects of constitutional practice undefined. The main problem during the 18th century was whether king or Parliament controlled the executive. George III was seeking to reassert a more active role for the crown, which had lost some influence in the reigns of the first two Georges, without infringing the revolution settlement. Burke's chief comment on this issue is his pamphlet "Thoughts on the Cause of the Present Discontents" (1770). He argued that George's actions were against not the letter but the spirit of the constitution. Choice of ministers purely on personal grounds was favouritism; public approbation by the people through Parliament should determine their selection. The community and its accredited representatives must be presumed capable of rational choice, provided that the independence of the House of Commons was maintained. But changed circumstances of government meant that a restoration of the past, such as a return to triennial Parliaments, was no remedy; what was needed was a more active intervention of the electorate in defense of its powers. The pamphlet includes Burke's famous, and new, justification of party, defined as a body of men united on public principle, which could act as a constitutional link between king and Parliament, providing consistency and strength in administration, or principled criticism in opposition.

Member of Parliament

In 1774 Burke was elected a member of Parliament for Bristol, then the second city of the kingdom and an open constituency requiring a genuine election contest. He held this seat for six years but failed to retain the confidence of his constituents. For the rest of his parliamentary career he was member for Malton, a pocket borough of Lord Rockingham's. It was at Bristol that he made the well-known statement on the role of the member of Parliament. The elected member should be representative, not delegate. The electors are capable of judging his integrity, and he should attend to their interest; but, more importantly, he must address himself to the general good of the whole community, acting according to his own judgment and conscience, unfettered by mandates or prior instructions from those he represents.

Burke gave only qualified support to the parliamentary reform movements, his main concern being curtailment of the crown's powers. However, he accepted the possibility of widening political participation, provided that there was evidence of rationality, restraint of aggressive partiality, and dedication to the common good; he rejected any doctrine of mere rule of numbers. Apart from holding general principles on this subject, Burke made a practical attempt to reduce the influence of the crown as one of the leaders of the movement for economical reform, which pressed for parliamentary control of royal patronage and expenditure. When the Rockingham Whigs took office in 1782, bills were passed reducing pensions and emoluments of offices, including Burke's own. Burke was specifically connected with an act regulating the civil list, the amount voted by Parliament for the personal and household expenses of the sovereign.

Colonial policies. A second great issue that confronted Burke in 1765 was the quarrel with the American colonies. Their prodigious development in the 18th century had produced strains in the system of imperial political and economic regulation that came to a head after the Seven Years' War. The imposition of a stamp duty by George Grenville in 1765, along with other measures, provoked unrest and opposition, which soon swelled into disobedience, conflict, and secession. English policy was vacillating; determination to maintain imperial control ended in coercion, repression, and unsuccessful war. The Rockingham group opposed coercion, basing their American policy on their actions in their short administration of 1765–66 when they repealed the Stamp Act, while asserting the imperial right to impose taxation by the Declaratory Act.

Views on American policy

Burke's best known statements on this issue are two parliamentary speeches, "On American Taxation" (1774) and "On Moving His Resolutions for Conciliation with the Colonies" (1775), and "A Letter to . . . the Sheriffs of Bristol, on the Affairs of America" (1777). British policy, he argued, had been both imprudent and inconsistent, but above all legalistic and intransigent, in the assertion of imperial rights. Authority must be exercised with respect for the temper of those subject to it, if there was not to be collision of power and opinion. This truth was being ignored in the imperial quarrel; it was absurd to treat universal disobedience as criminal: the revolt of a whole people argued serious misgovernment. Burke made a wide historical survey of the growth of the Colonies, the special traditions and circumstances that had formed their character, the revolutionary changes in the recent past, and their economic problems. In the place of narrow legalism he called for "legislative reason," an imaginative reinterpretation of the values enshrined in the imperial relation in the light of these new factors. The claims of circumstance, utility, and moral principle should be considered, as well as precedent. And as a prerequisite of reconciliation, a conciliatory temper must be shown by the imperial Parliament with readiness to meet American complaints and measures to restore colonial confidence. His proposal was an extension of the forms of the British constitution to the imperial relation, so far as circumstances allowed it.

In view of the magnitude of the problem, the adequacy of Burke's specific remedies is questionable, but the principles on which he was basing his argument were the same as those underlying his "Present Discontents": government should ideally be a cooperative, mutually restraining relation of rulers and subjects; there must be attachment to tradition and the ways of the past, wherever possible, but equally, recognition of the fact of change and the need for a comprehensive and discriminating response to it, reaffirming the values embodied in tradition in new circumstances.

Ireland was a special problem in imperial regulation. It was in strict political dependency on England and internally subject to the ascendancy of an Anglo-Irish Protestant minority, owning the bulk of the land. Roman Catholics were excluded by a penal code from political participation and public office. To these oppressions were added widespread rural poverty and a backward economic life aggravated by commercial restrictions resulting from English commercial jealousy. Burke was always concerned to ease the burdens of his native country. He consistently advocated relaxation of the economic and penal regulations, and steps toward legislative independence, at the cost of alienating his Bristol constituents and of incurring suspicions of Catholicism and charges of partiality.

The remaining imperial issue, to which he devoted many years, and which he ranked as the most worthy of his labours, was that of India. The commercial activities of a chartered trading concern, the British East India Company, had created an extensive empire. Burke in the 1760s and 1770s opposed interference by the English government in the company's affairs as a violation of chartered rights. However, he learned a great deal about the state of the company's government as the most active member of a select committee that was appointed in 1781 to investigate the administration of justice in India but which soon widened its field to that of a general inquiry. Burke concluded that the corrupt state of Indian government could be remedied only if the vast patronage it was bound to dispose of was in the hands neither of a company nor of the crown. He drafted the East India Bill of 1783 (of which the Whig statesman Charles James Fox was the nominal author), which proposed that India should be governed by a board of independent commissioners in London. Two of Burke's best known speeches were on Indian affairs, "On Mr. Fox's East India Bill" (1783) and "On a Motion Made for the Papers Relative to the Nabob of Arcot's Debts" (1785). After the defeat of the bill, Burke's indignation came to centre on Warren Hastings, governor general of Bengal from 1772 to 1785. It was at Burke's instigation that Hastings was impeached in 1787 and he challenged Hastings' claim that it was impossible to apply Western standards of authority and legality to government in the East. He appealed to the concept of the Law of Nature, the moral principles rooted in the universal order of things, to which all conditions and races of men were subject. The impeachment dragged on for eight years and ended with Hastings' acquittal on all charges. The proceedings resulted in an authoritative statement of the principle of responsible rule in imperial affairs; but it is generally regarded as an act of injustice to Hastings, who had been, despite questionable methods, a disinterested servant of the company and the British name in India.

Hastings impeached

Burke's political judgment. The impeachment is the most conspicuous illustration of the failings to which Burke was liable throughout his public life, including his brief periods in office as paymaster general of the forces in 1782 and 1783. His political positions were sometimes marred by gross distortions and errors of judgment. His Indian speeches fall at times into a violence of emotion and abuse, lacking restraint and proportion. His reliance on the opinions of Sir Philip Francis, one of Hastings' most pertinacious enemies, illustrates his inability to accurately judge personality. His parliamentary activities were at times irresponsible or factious. Nor did he escape the charge, in Indian affairs, of personal interest. Throughout his career he was associated financially and politically with his brother Richard and a putative kinsman William Burke, both doubtful characters known to be unsuccessfully speculating in East India stock. The Burkes' joint finances were indeed always in a precarious state, and as Edmund was ever eager to forward his kinsmen's political fortunes it is understandable that he appeared in some hostile eyes as hardly more than one of a clan of Irish adventurers.

It can plausibly be argued that these failings were defects of Burke's virtues rather than an impurity in those virtues themselves. It has not been shown that he himself was a speculator in company stock; it seems rather that he was rendered blind or oblivious to the nature of his relatives' proceedings by family partiality. Nor do his political lapses, even at their worst, appear to spring from self-interest or unworthy motives but from his failure to control and balance his unusually sensitive and powerful emotional nature. Burke's weaknesses therefore lie close to what is best in his character and career: the capacity to illuminate practical politics by general principles in a synthesis at once intellectual and emotive, the intensity of his dedication and industry in public affairs, the constancy of his humanitarian struggle against injustice and suffering, the readiness and generosity of his help in need (of which the poet George Crabbe and painter James Barry are the best known recipients), the distinction of his numerous literary and political friendships, and the happiness of his family life and kinship ties.

Writings on French Revolution. The outbreak of the French Revolution in 1789 was initially greeted in England with much enthusiasm. Burke, after a brief suspension of judgment, was both hostile to it and alarmed by this favourable English reaction. He was provoked into writing his *Reflections on the Revolution in France* (1790) by a sermon of the Protestant dissenter Richard Price welcoming the Revolution. Burke's deeply felt antagonism to the new movement propelled him to the plane of general political thought; it provoked a host of English replies, of which the best known is Thomas Paine's *The Rights of Man* (1791–92).

Reflections on the Revolution in France

In the first instance Burke discussed the actual course of the Revolution, examining the personalities, motives, and policies of its leaders. More profoundly, he attempted to analyze the fundamental ideas animating the movement and, fastening on the Revolutionary concepts of "the rights of man" and popular sovereignty, emphasized the dangers of democracy in the abstract and the mere rule of numbers when unrestrained and unguided by the responsible leadership of a hereditary aristocracy. Further, he challenged the whole rationalist and idealist temper of the movement. It was not merely that the old social order was being pulled down. He argued, further, that the moral fervour of the Revolution, and its vast speculative schemes of political reconstruction, were causing a devaluation of tradition and inherited values and a thoughtless destruction of the painfully acquired material and spiritual resources of society. Against all this, he appealed to the example and the virtues of the English constitution: its concern for continuity and unorganized growth, its respect for traditional wisdom and usage rather than speculative innovation, for prescriptive, rather than abstract, rights, its acceptance of a hierarchy of rank and property, its religious consecration of secular authority and recognition of the radical imperfection of all human contrivances.

As an analysis and prediction of the course of the movement, Burke's French writings, though frequently intemperate and uncontrolled, were in some ways strikingly acute; but his lack of sympathy with its positive ideals concealed from him its more fruitful and permanent potentialities. It is for the criticism and affirmation of fundamental political attitudes that the *Reflections* and *An Appeal from the New to the Old Whigs* (1791) retain their freshness, relevance, and force.

Appeal from the New to the Old Whigs

Burke opposed the French Revolution to the end of his life, demanding war against the new state, and gaining a European reputation and influence. But his hostility to the Revolution went beyond that of most of his party and in particular was challenged by Fox. Burke's long friendship with Fox came to a dramatic end in a parliamentary debate (May 1791). Ultimately the majority of the party passed with Burke into support of William Pitt's government. In 1794, at the conclusion of Hastings' impeachment, Burke retired from Parliament. His last years were clouded by the death of his only son, on whom his political ambitions had come to centre. He continued to write, defending himself from his critics, deploring the condition of Ireland, and opposing any recognition of the French government (notably in "Three Letters Addressed to a Member of the Present Parliament on the Proposals for Peace, with the Regicide Directory of France" (1796–97). Burke died at Beaconsfield, Buckinghamshire, on July 9, 1797.

Burke's political thought. Burke's writings on France, though the most profound of his works, cannot be read as a complete statement of his views on politics. Burke, in fact, never gave a systematic exposition of his fundamental beliefs but appealed to them always in relation to specific issues. His consistency during his political career has therefore been debated. He himself repudiated the charge of inconsistency, and it is possible to regard his writings as an integrated whole in terms of constant principles underlying his practical positions.

Those principles are, in essence, an exploration of the concept of "Nature." Burke conceives the life of feeling and the spiritual life of man as a harmony within the larger order of the universe. Natural impulse, that is, contains within itself self-restraint and self-criticism; the moral and spiritual life is continuous with it, generated from it and essentially sympathetic to it. It follows that society and state make possible the full realization of human potentiality, embody a common good, and represent a tacit or explicit agreement on norms and ends. The political community acts ideally as a unity. Political participation will naturally differ from one part of society to another, and from period to period, but it should always exclude aggressive self-interest and allow expression of rational self-interest compatible with the good of the whole. Burke therefore does not reject the concept of natural right, but he does not give it any simple or direct political implication.

This interpretation of nature and the natural order implies deep respect for the historical process and the usages and social achievements built up in time. Therefore, social change is not merely possible but inevitable and desirable. But the scope and the role of thought operating as a reforming instrument on society as a whole is limited. It should act under the promptings of specific tensions or specific possibilities, in close union with the detailed process of change, rather than in large speculative schemes involving extensive interference with the stable, habitual life of society. Also, it ought not to place excessive emphasis on some ends at the expense of others; in particular, it should not give rein to a moral idealism that sets itself in radical opposition to the existing order. Such attempts cut across the natural processes of social development, initiating uncontrollable forces or provoking a dialectical reaction of excluded factors. Burke's hope, in effect, is not a realization of particular ends, such as the "liberty" and "equality" of the French Revolution, but an intensification and reconciliation of the multifarious elements of the good life that community exists to forward.

Assessment and influence. Burke's system is in essence a defense of God's goodness and omnipotence in the face of the existence of evil. Burke is not a Christian political thinker in the sense that the tenets of Christian faith, or unity of Christian worship, are integral elements in his political thought, as is the case with Richard Hooker. But of all earlier English political thinkers, his closest affiliations, in historical situation, in tone, and in many details of thought, are with Hooker; and both belong to the tradition of political thought whose greatest figures are St. Thomas Aquinas and Aristotle.

In his own day, Burke's writings on France were an important inspiration to German and French counterrevolutionary thought. His influence in England has been more diffuse, more balanced, and more durable. He stands as the original exponent of long-lived constitutional conventions, the idea of party, and the role of the member of Parliament as free representative, not delegate. More generally, his remains the most persuasive statement of certain inarticulate political and social principles long and widely held in England: the validity of status and hierarchy and the limited role of politics in the life of society. As for the contemporary relevance and ultimate validity of his thought, this hinges on the question as to how far his particular conception of "nature" can still be found consonant with subsequent social experience and speculation.

BIBLIOGRAPHY. There are 19th-century editions of Burke's *Works* but no modern edition. The most recent edition of *Reflections* is that of C.C. O'BRIEN (1969), using the critical edition of W.B. TODD (1959). The most detailed up-to-date biography is C.B. CONE, *Burke and the Nature of Politics*, 2 vol. (1957–64). Discussions of Burke's thought, or phases of it, in relation to the political issues of his career are J. MORLEY, *Edmund Burke: A Historical Study* (1867); G.W. CHAPMAN, *Edmund Burke: The Practical Imagination* (1967); H.C. MANSFIELD, JR., *Statesmanship and Party Government: A Study of Burke and Bolingbroke* (1965); and R.R. FENNESSY, *Burke, Paine, and the Rights of Man* (1963). Attempts to restate Burke's ideas as a systematic political philosophy in the tradition of Natural Law are: C.W. PARKIN, *The Moral Basis of Burke's Political Thought* (1956); P.J. STANLIS, *Edmund Burke and the Natural Law* (1958); and F.P. CANAVAN, *The Political Reason of Edmund Burke* (1960). A. COBBAN, *Edmund Burke and the Revolt Against the Eighteenth Century*, 2nd ed. (1960), is an interpretation of Burke's place in intellectual history. J.T. BOULTON, *The Language of Politics in the Age of Wilkes and Burke* (1963), is a special study analyzing the relation of style and content in the political writings of Burke and his contemporaries.

(C.W.Pa.)

Burma

Burma is an independent republic in Southeast Asia, with an area of 261,789 square miles (678,034 square kilometres) and, early in the 1970s, a population of some 27,000,000. It is bordered by Thailand and Laos on the east, by China (the autonomous region of Tibet and the province of Yunnan) on the north and northeast, by India on the northwest, on the west by Bangladesh and the Bay of Bengal, and on the southwest and south by the Gulf of Martaban and the Andaman Sea.

Burma stretches from latitude 10° N to about 28° 30′ N; almost half the country is, therefore, situated outside the tropics, but, because of its configuration, it is generally considered to be a primarily tropical country. The country is in the shape of a diamond, with a long tail—running south along the Malay Peninsula—attached to it. Its total length from north to south is 1,300 miles; its width, at the widest part, is 575 miles from east to west.

Burma's historic tradition

In ancient and medieval times, Burma was regarded as a gateway to the Indochinese Peninsula, as well as to China; it was known as the Golden Land, because of its abundant natural resources and the wealth that its control of trade routes generated. In the 11th century it became the homeland of Theravāda Buddhism (one of the two great schools of Buddhism, the other being Mahāyāna) at a time when that faith was being suppressed in other countries. After being annexed by the British in 1886, it fell under Japanese rule for a period during World War II; British rule ended in 1948, when Burma regained its sovereign independence.

Burma is individualistic in its social structure and nationalistic in its outlook. As one of the original nonaligned countries—maintaining independence from both Eastern and Western power blocs—Burma achieved some international importance in the first decade after its independence; in the early 1970s, however, it had for some years tended to remain aloof and isolated from the international community. The land and air battles that were waged throughout the country during World War II destroyed many towns and villages and dislocated the economy. In the early 1970s Burma still exported rice but was no longer, as it once was, the foremost rice-exporting country in the world. The wounds of war had not completely healed, partly because of lack of capital and partly because of insurgency and political unrest. Since independence, some modest industrialization programs have been embarked upon, but the country remains primarily agricultural. (See the city article RANGOON; for associated physical features, see ANDAMAN SEA; BENGAL, BAY OF; IRRAWADDY RIVER; MEKONG RIVER; and YANGTZE RIVER; for historical aspects, see BURMA, HISTORY OF.)

THE LANDSCAPE

The natural environment. *Relief.* The country slopes from north to south, from an elevation of 19,578 feet (5,967 metres) at Hkakabo Razi peak in the extreme north to sea level at the Irrawaddy and Sittang deltas. The mountain ranges are longitudinal, running from north to south. The country as a whole can be divided into five landscape regions—the northern mountains, the western mountains, the eastern plateau, the central basin, and the coastal strips.

The five landscape regions

The northern mountains consist of a series of ranges forming a complex knot, with peaks of nearly 20,000 feet. It is in this region that the sources of such great rivers as the Irrawaddy, Salween, Mekong, and Yangtze arise in swirling torrents. They flow through deep gorges within a few miles of each other, separated by peaks rising sheer into the sky. It was across this wild and forbidding region that the ancestors of the present-day Burmese travelled from their original homeland in Tibet.

The western ranges, which originate in the northern mountain knot, continue southward as far as Cape Negrais, the southern tip of the Arakan Peninsula, where they run under the sea, reappearing as the Andaman

Islands. Their average height is about 6,000 feet, although some peaks rise to 10,000 feet and more. They are folded mid-Tertiary ranges (formed about 20,000,000 to 40,000,000 years ago), with a core of old crystalline rocks surrounded by hard, tightly folded sedimentary rocks on either side. Forming the border between India and Burma, they are given different names according to locality—being known successively as the Patkoi, Lushai, Naga, Manipur, and Chin hills. The southern portion of these mountains lies entirely within Burma, forming the Arakan Yoma (*yoma* in Burmese means "main bone"). They separate the Arakan coastal strip from the central plain.

The Shan Plateau in the east rises abruptly from the central basin, often in a single step of 2,000 feet. Occupying the whole of the east of the country, it is deeply dissected, with an average height of 3,000 feet. The plateau was formed during the Mesozoic Era (65,000,000–225,000,000 years ago) and thus is much older than the western mountains. But the plateau also shows intensive folding, with north–south longitudinal ranges with heights of 6,000 to 8,600 feet, rising abruptly from the plateau surface. Northward, the plateau merges into the northern ranges, and southward it continues into the Tenasserim Yoma, a series of parallel ranges with narrow valleys. The central basin, lying between the Arakan Yoma and the Shan Plateau, is structurally connected with the folding of the western mountains. The basin was deeply excavated by the predecessors of the Irrawaddy, Chindwin, and Sittang rivers; the ancient valleys are now occupied by these rivers, which cover the ancient soft sandstones, shales, and clays with their new alluvial deposits. In the deltaic regions formed by the Irrawaddy and Sittang (total area 12,000 square miles), the landscape is absolutely flat, and the monotony is relieved only by a few blocks of erosion-resistant rocks, never more than 60 feet high. The basin is cut into two unequal halves, the larger Irrawaddy Valley and the smaller Sittang Valley, by the complex folded range of Pegu Yoma.

In the centre of the basin and structurally connected with the Pegu Yoma and its northern extension is a line of extinct volcanoes with small crater lakes and eroded cones, the most impressive being Popa Hill, 4,984 feet (1,519 metres).

The coastal strips consist of the narrow Arakan and Tenasserim coastal plains, which are backed by the high ranges of the Arakan Yoma and Tenasserim Yoma and are fringed with numerous islands of varying sizes.

Drainage and soil. Like the mountains, the rivers run from north to south. About two-thirds of Burma's surface is drained by the Irrawaddy (*q.v.*) and its tributaries.

The rivers

Flowing through the entire length of Burma, it is 1,300 miles long and is navigable for 872 miles. At the apex of its delta, it breaks up into a network of streams and empties into the Andaman Sea through nine mouths. Its great tributary, the Chindwin, drains the western region. The Bassein River drains the southern Arakan Yoma, and the Rangoon River drains the Pegu Yoma, both entering the Irrawaddy at the delta. The Sittang flows into the Gulf of Martaban of the Andaman Sea and, in spite of its comparative shortness, has a large valley and a huge delta. The Shan Plateau is drained by the Salween, which enters Burma from Yunnan in China and empties into the Gulf of Martaban south of the Sittang. It is deeply entrenched and crosses the plateau in a series of deep gorges. Many of its tributaries are more than 300 miles long and enter the Salween in cascades. The Arakan coastal plains are drained by short, rapid streams, which, after forming broad deltas, flow into the Bay of Bengal. The Tenasserim plains are drained also by short and rapid rivers, which make right-angled turns to enter the Gulf of Martaban.

The highland regions of Burma are covered with laterite (red soil, leached of silica and containing iron oxides and hydroxide of aluminum). Protected by the forest cover, it absorbs heavy rain, but, once the forest is cleared, it erodes quickly. The lowland regions are covered with alluvial soil—mainly silt and clay. Low in potash, lime, and organic matter, it is improved by fertilizers. In the central-region dry belt, the alluvial soil develops into a black soil rich in calcium and magnesium. In the same region, however, when the soil has a low clay content, it becomes saline under high evaporation and is recognizable by its yellow or brown colour.

Climate. Burma belongs to the monsoon (rain-bearing wind) region of Asia, but its climate is greatly modified by its geographical position and its relief. Although the cold-air masses of Central Asia bring snow to the northern tip for two months of the year, the mountain wall prevents them from moving farther south, so that Burma lies primarily under the influence of the monsoon winds. The north and south alignment of ranges and valleys forces the northeast monsoon to blow from the north. When the southwest monsoon winds blow from the Indian Ocean, this alignment of ranges and valleys creates alternate zones of heavy and scanty rainfall.

Elevation and distance from the sea affect both the temperature and the rainfall; although a tropical country, temperatures are not high. Daily range of temperature is negligible everywhere, and no locality in Burma has a continental type of climate. Even at Mandalay, in the centre of the dry belt, the annual range is only 22° F (12° C) compared with 11° F (6° C) at Rangoon and 7° F (about 4° C) at Moulmein; the average temperature is 82° F (28° C) compared to 81° F (27° C) at Rangoon, 79° F (26° C) at Sittwe (Akyab) in Arakan, and 71° F (22° C) at Lashio on the Shan Plateau.

There are three seasons: the cool dry season, from October to February; the hot dry season, from March to the middle of May; and the rainy season, from May to October. The coastal regions and the mountains receive annually 200 inches of rain, while the delta regions receive nearly 100. The central region is not only away from the sea but also in the rain shadow of the Arakan Yoma. Rainfall gradually decreases northward until in the dry zone it is only between 20 and 40 inches. The Shan Plateau, because of its elevation, receives about 65 inches.

Vegetation and animal life. Even after centuries of rice cultivation involving clearing of forest, 67 percent of Burma is covered with forests of various types, depending on elevation and the amount of rainfall. Above the frost line at 3,000 feet, evergreen forests of oak and pine are to be found. In the northern mountains at heights above 6,000 feet are forests of rhododendrons. In regions with more than 80 inches of rainfall, there occur evergreen tropical forests. The trees are of hardwood but of little commercial value. In regions where the rainfall is between 40 and 80 inches, there appear monsoon forests, the trees of which shed their leaves in the hot season. They produce valuable cabinet wood, including teak. Where rainfall is less than 40 inches, the forests gradually merge into scrubland. There are no real grasslands, but, when a patch of forest has been cleared, bamboo, bracken, and coarse grass grow. In the Irrawaddy and Sittang deltas are tidal forests of mangrove trees, growing as high as 100 feet and supplying firewood and charcoal, as well as bark for tanning.

The forests

In the jungles of Burma are the homes of pheasants, parrots, peacocks, wild fowl, and grouse. The Asiatic two-horned rhinoceros, wild buffalo, bison, and various kinds of deer were once plentiful but are now reduced in numbers and protected. Elephants are numerous, a number of them being caught annually to be trained to work. Tigers, leopards, and wild cats are still common. Bears are found in hilly regions, and gibbons and monkeys of various kinds inhabit the thicker parts of the forests. Snakes include pythons, cobras, and vipers, and crocodiles are found in the deltas. Turtles live in coastal regions, and edible fishes abound in every stream.

The landscape under human settlement. *Traditional regions.* The Burmese live in the plains and the tribal peoples in the hills. In the plains, the division between Upper and Lower Burma dates from early history, not only because of differences in the geography but also because the Mons, now a small minority, lived in Lower Burma. The division became more marked during the period from 1852 to 1885, when Lower Burma became British Burma. The Arakan and Tenasserim coastal plains are traditional regions; the people there speak Burmese in a dialect retaining archaic features.

The villages

Urban and rural settlement. Burma is a land of villages. Except for Rangoon (*q.v.*), which has 2,449,000 people, Mandalay, which has 473,000, and Moulmein, 295,000, there are few large cities, and the towns are merely overgrown villages. The hill peoples, although practicing a shifting agriculture, have settled in villages perched near the tops of mountains and at some distance from the fields. On the Shan Plateau and the plains, the fields adjoin the villages. Older villages are circular in shape, but along the banks of the delta streams and along the railway line the villages are rectangular. Burmese houses are built of timber and bamboo, the roofs thatched or tiled. Typical Burmese houses were built on piles, the original purpose being protection from wild animals or floods. The style persists in many villages, especially those on the hills, and farm animals are kept under the houses at night. In small towns the piles have given way to a supporting brick structure with cement flooring, the upper story still being made of timber. Houses entirely of brick were few in number before 1942, but many have since sprung up in Rangoon, Mandalay, and larger towns on the rubble of buildings destroyed during World War II. Life in villages and towns is still communal because of tribal custom, the influence of Buddhism, and the "classless" nature of Burmese society. Even once-cosmopolitan Rangoon regained its Burmese atmosphere after independence.

PEOPLE AND POPULATION

Language groups

Linguistic and other groups. More than 100 indigenous languages—as distinct from mere dialects—are spoken in Burma, most of them by the hill peoples. The common language is Burmese, spoken by both the people of the plains and the hill peoples. All of these languages belong to only three groups. The Burmese language itself, and most of the other languages, belong to the Tibeto-Burman subfamily of the Sino-Tibetan family. The Shan language belongs to the Tai family. Languages spoken by the Mons of Lower Burma and by the Was and Palaungs of the Shan Plateau are members of the Mon-Khmer subfamily of the Austro-Asiatic family.

Until colonial times, only the Burmese, Mons, and Shans had written languages, and, even today, writing systems for Karen, Kachin, and Chin are still being developed. The archaic Burmese spoken in Arakan and Tenasserim, when written down, shows no difference from the Burmese spoken in the plains. To the majority of the hill peoples, Burmese is the second mother tongue.

During the colonial period, English became the official language, but Burmese survived as the second official language. Both English and Burmese were made compulsory subjects in schools and colleges, and although a knowledge of English became an asset, and many learned to speak it, no English-speaking elite emerged. Burmese remained the language of commerce, and Burmese literature also survived. After independence, English ceased to be the official language and lost its importance in

MAP INDEX

Political Subdivisions

Arakan	19·00n	94·15e
Chin	22·00n	93·30e
Irrawaddy	17·00n	95·00e
Kachin	26·00n	97·30e
Kawthule	17·30n	97·45e
Kayah	19·15n	97·30e
Magwe	23·00n	95·00e
Mandalay	22·00n	96·00e
Mon	16·30n	97·35e
Pegu	18·00n	96·30e
Rangoon	16·50n	96·10e
Sagaing	24·00n	95·00e
Shan	22·00n	98·00e
Tenasserim	13·00n	99·00e

Cities and towns

Allanmyo	19·22n	95·13e
Amarapura	21·54n	96·03e
An	19·47n	94·02e
Anin	15·40n	97·46e
Athok	17·12n	95·05e
Bassein	16·47n	94·44e
Baw	23·19n	95·50e
Bawlake	19·11n	97·21e
Bawmi	17·19n	94·35e
Bhamo	24·16n	97·14e
Bilin	17·14n	97·15e
Bogale	16·17n	95·24e
Chauk	20·54n	94·50e
Chi-Kyaw	20·17n	93·54e
Falam	22·55n	93·40e
Gangaw	22·11n	94·07e
Gwa	17·36n	94·35e
Haka	22·46n	93·51e
Heho	20·43n	96·49e
Henzada	17·38n	95·28e
Homalin	24·52n	94·55e
Hsipaw	22·37n	97·18e
Hsuphang	20·18n	98·42e
Insein	16·53n	96·07e
Inywa	23·56n	96·17e
Kalagwe	22·31n	96·31e
Kalaw	20·38n	96·34e
Kaletwa	21·45n	92·48e
Kalewa	23·12n	94·17e
Kanbalu	23·12n	95·31e
Kanbe	16·42n	96·01e
Kani	22·26n	94·50e
Kansau	23·50n	93·35e
Katha	24·11n	96·21e
Kayan	16·54n	96·34e
Ke-hsi Mansam	21·56n	97·50e
Keng Hkam	21·01n	98·29e
Keng Hkam	21·27n	97·03e
Keng Tung	21·17n	99·36e
Konglu	27·16n	97·56e
Kontha	19·30n	96·03e
Kunhing	21·18n	98·26e
Kutkai	23·27n	97·56e
Kyaikto	17·18n	97·01e
Kyaukme	22·32n	97·02e
Kyaukpadaung	20·50n	95·08e
Kyaukpyu	19·05n	93·52e
Kyaukse	21·33n	96·06e
Kyauktaw	20·51n	92·59e
Kyindwe	20·58n	93·51e
Kyondo	16·35n	98·03e
Kyunhla	23·21n	95·18e
Kywebwe	18·42n	96·25e
Labutta	16·09n	94·46e
Lahe	26·20n	95·26e
Lashio	22·56n	97·45e
Lenya	11·28n	99·00e
Loi-kaw	19·41n	97·13e
Lonton	25·06n	96·17e
Magwe	20·09n	94·55e
Makaw	26·27n	96·42e
Malan	25·37n	96·21e
Male	23·02n	95·58e
Maliwun	10·14n	98·37e
Mandalay	22·00n	96·05e
Man Hpang	22·41n	98·36e
Man Na	23·27n	97·14e
Martaban	16·32n	97·37e
Ma-Ubin	16·44n	95·39e
Maungdaw	20·50n	92·21e
Mawlaik	23·38n	94·24e
Maymyo	22·02n	96·28e
Meiktila	20·52n	95·52e
Mergui	12·26n	98·36e
Minbu	20·11n	94·52e
Mogaung	25·18n	96·56e
Mogok	22·55n	96·30e
Mong Hai	20·46n	99·49e
Mong Hawm	23·51n	98·20e
Mong Hsat	20·32n	99·15e
Mong Ma	21·37n	99·54e
Mong Mit	23·07n	96·41e
Mong Nai	20·31n	97·52e
Mong Nawng	21·39n	98·08e
Monywa	22·05n	95·08e
Moulmein	16·30n	97·38e
Moulmeingyun	16·23n	95·16e
Myaing	21·37n	94·51e
Myanaung	18·17n	95·19e
Myaungmya	16·36n	94·56e
Myebon	20·03n	93·22e
Myingyan	21·28n	95·23e
Myitkyina	25·23n	97·24e
Naba	24·15n	96·11e
Nai Ga	27·48n	97·30e
Namhkam	23·50n	97·41e
Namlan	22·15n	97·24e
Namtu	23·05n	97·24e
Nankye	14·20n	98·11e
Nathkaw	26·53n	96·13e
Natkyizin	14·55n	97·57e
Nyaunglebin	17·57n	96·44e
O-mu	22·58n	99·18e
Pa-an	16·53n	97·38e
Pakokku	21·20n	95·05e
Palauk	13·16n	98·38e
Paleik	21·49n	96·03e
Paletwa	21·18n	92·51e
Panghkam	23·53n	97·37e
Pantha	23·49n	94·33e
Papun	18·04n	97·27e
Pauk	21·27n	94·27e
Paungde	18·29n	95·30e
Pawota	17·46n	97·17e
Pegu	17·20n	96·29e
Pinlaung	20·08n	96·47e
Putao	27·21n	97·24e
Pyapon	16·17n	95·41e
Pye (Prome)	18·49n	95·13e
Pyinmana	19·44n	96·13e
Pyu	18·29n	96·26e
Rangoon	16·47n	96·10e
Sagaing	21·52n	95·59e
Samka	20·09n	96·57e
Sandoway	18·28n	94·22e
Shwebo	22·34n	95·42e
Sinbaungwe	19·43n	95·10e
Singkaling Hkamti	26·00n	95·42e
Sittwe (Akyab)	20·09n	92·54e
Syriam	16·46n	96·15e
Taikkyi	17·19n	95·58e
Tamu	24·13n	94·18e
Tangyan	22·29n	98·24e
Taungdwingyi	20·01n	95·33e
Taunggon	23·38n	96·32e
Taunggyi	20·47n	97·02e
Taungup	18·51n	94·14e
Tavoy	14·05n	98·12e
Tazungdam	28·02n	97·35e
Tenasserim	12·05n	99·01e
Thagyettaw	13·45n	98·09e
Tharrawaddy	17·39n	95·48e
Thaton	16·55n	97·22e
Thaungdut	24·26n	94·42e
Thayetmyo	19·19n	95·11e
Thazi	20·51n	96·05e
Thongwa	16·46n	96·32e
Thonze	17·38n	95·47e
Tilin	21·42n	94·04e
Tingkawk Sakan	26·04n	96·44e
Tongta	21·20n	99·16e
Toungoo	18·56n	96·26e
Wadat Ga	26·00n	97·00e
Wakema	16·36n	95·11e
Wan Namton	22·03n	99·33e
Yamethin	20·26n	96·09e
Yandoon	17·02n	95·39e
Ye	15·15n	97·51e
Yebyu	14·15n	98·12e
Yenangyaung	20·28n	94·52e
Ye-ngan	21·09n	96·27e
Ye-u	22·46n	95·26e
Yinmabin	22·05n	94·54e
Ywamun	20·31n	95·25e

Physical features and points of interest

Andaman Sea	12·00n	95·00e
Arakan Yoma, *mountains*	19·00n	94·40e
Bassein, *river*	15·56n	94·18e
Bengal, Bay of	18·00n	93·00e
Bilauktaung Range	13·00n	99·00e
Bluff Cape	18·00n	94·26e
Cheduba Island	18·48n	93·38e
Chindwin, *river*	21·26n	95·15e
Chin Hills	22·30n	93·30e
Coco Channel	13·45n	93·00e
Coco Islands	14·05n	93·18e
Combermere Bay	19·37n	93·34e
Dawna Range	16·50n	98·15e
Gangew Taungdan, *mountains*	24·55n	96·35e
Great Tenasserim, *river*	12·24n	98·37e
Hkakabo Razi, *mountain*	28·20n	97·32e
Irrawaddy, *river*	15·50n	95·06e
Kaladan, *river*	20·09n	92·57e
Kennedy Peak	23·19n	93·45e
Kumon Range	26·30n	97·15e
Lemro, *river*	20·25n	93·20e
Mali Hka, *river*	25·43n	97·29e
Mangin Range	24·20n	95·42e
Martaban, Gulf of	16·30n	97·00e
Maw Taung, *mountain*	11·39n	99·35e
Mekong, *river*	20·28n	100·10e
Mergui Archipelago, *islands*	12·00n	98·00e
Mon, *river*	20·20n	94·54e
Moscos Islands	14·00n	97·45e
Mu, *river*	21·56n	95·38e
Myittha, *river*	23·12n	94·17e
Namnoi, Khao, *mountain*	10·36n	98·38e
Negrais, Cape	16·02n	94·12e
Nmai Hka, *river*	25·42n	97·30e
Pegu Yoma, *mountains*	19·00n	95·50e
Pezawa Taung, *mountain*	19·33n	94·31e
Popa Hill	20·55n	95·15e
Preparis Island	14·52n	93·41e
Preparis North Channel	15·27n	94·05e
Preparis South Channel	14·40n	94·00e
Purian Point	15·50n	94·24e
Ramree Island	19·06n	93·48e
Rangoon, *river*	16·29n	96·21e
Salween, *river*	16·31n	97·37e
Shan Plateau	22·00n	98·00e
Sittang, *river*	17·10n	96·58e
Taungnyo Range	15·38n	97·56e
Taungup Pass	18·40n	94·45e
Tavoy Point	13·32n	98·10e
Tenasserim Yoma, *mountains*	13·00n	98·45e
Thaungyin, *river*	17·50n	97·42e
Victoria, Mount, *mountain*	21·14n	93·55e
Zami, *river*	16·09n	97·58e

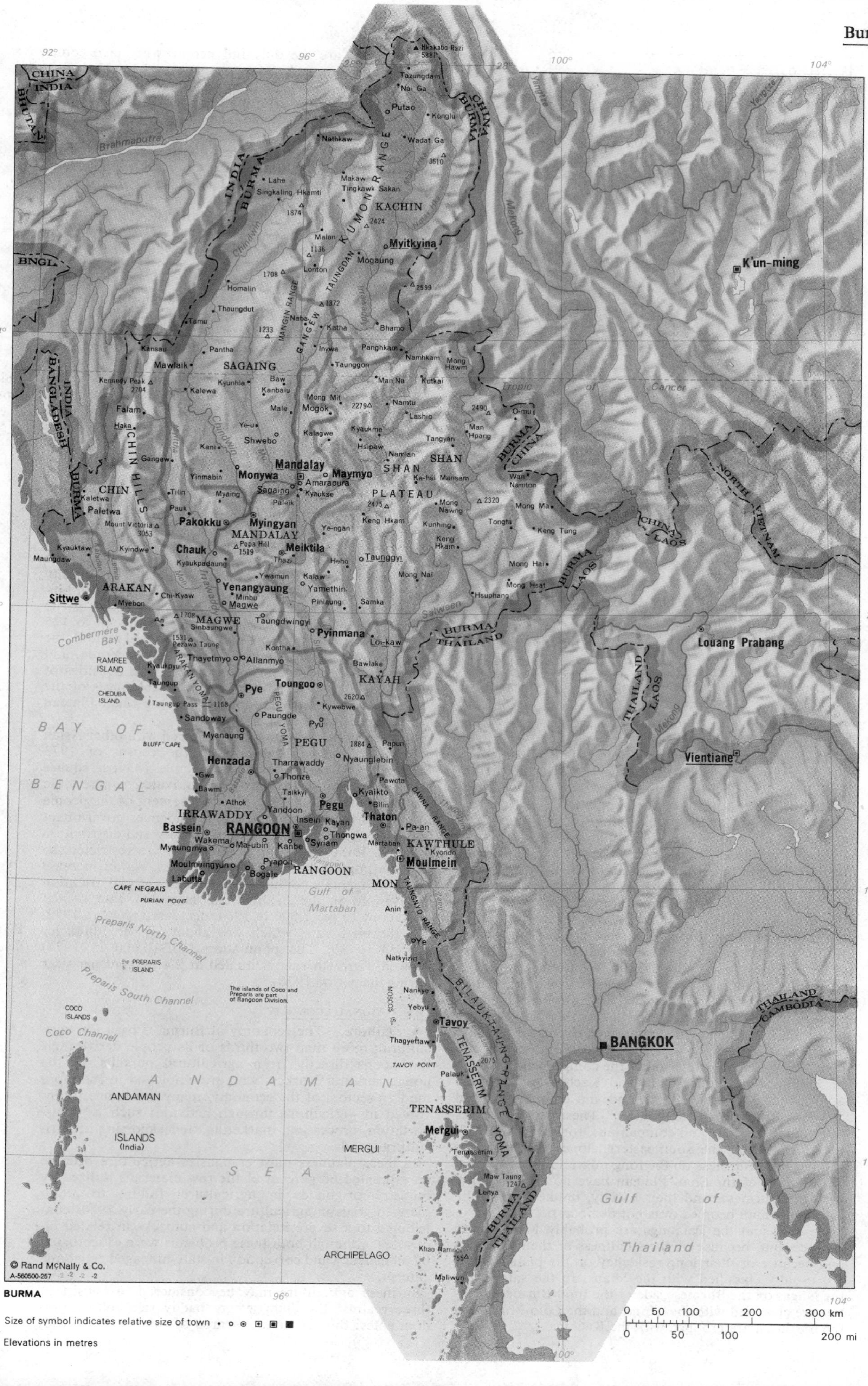

BURMA

Size of symbol indicates relative size of town • ○ ⊙ ⊡ ▣ ■

Elevations in metres

© Rand McNally & Co.
A-560500-257

| 0 | 50 | 100 | 200 | 300 km |
| 0 | 50 | 100 | 200 mi |

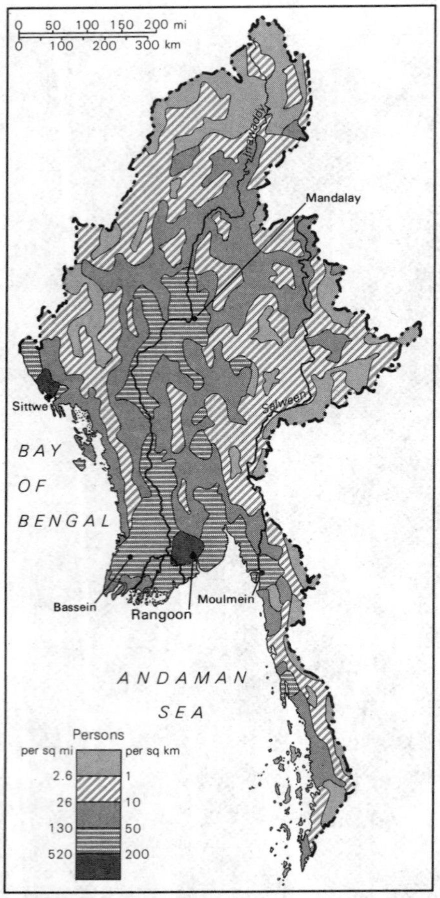

Population density of Burma.

schools and colleges, although an elementary knowledge of English is still required.

Ethnic groups. The original home of the Burmese in the dry zone established the ethnic character of the entire Irrawaddy Valley and the coastal strips. These areas hold three-fourths of the population.

The Irrawaddy and Sittang deltas were once peopled by the Mons, who entered the country from their kingdoms in the Chao Phraya River Valley in Thailand. They were conquered in the 11th century by the Burmese, a less cultured race at the time. The Mons attempted from time to time to throw off the Burmese yoke, but by the end of the 18th century they had been largely absorbed by the Burmese, mainly through intermarriage but partly through suppression. A few hundred thousand still remain in the Sittang Valley and in Tenasserim; although they still call themselves Mon, many of them have Burmese blood and no longer speak their original language.

The tribal peoples

In the western hills and the valley of the Chindwin are various tribes called by the comprehensive name of Chin. The Upper Irrawaddy Valley and the northern hills are occupied by tribal groups under the comprehensive name of Kachin. The names Chin and Kachin are Burmese and indicate, respectively, "friend and companion" and "dancing friend and companion." These tribal peoples were indeed friends and companions, for they lived with the Burmese on the southeastern slopes of Tibet and followed the Burmese on the long migration into Burma.

The Shans of the Shan Plateau have no racial affinity with the Burmese, and their society, unlike that of the Tibeto-Burman peoples, was not democratic.

The Was and the Palaungs are probably Mon-Khmer by race, but, because of the smallness of their numbers and because of their long residency on the plateau, they are usually classified with the Shans. In the same way, the Nāgas on the Burmese side of the Indo-Burmese frontier are classified with the Chins, and the Lolo-Muhsos in the northeast are grouped with the Kachins.

The Karens are the only hill people who have come down to the plains. Although racially and linguistically they are Tibeto-Burman, they were closely associated with the Mons. They are found in the deltas among the Burmese, on the Pegu Yoma, and along both sides of the lower Salween River.

The Kayahs, who live on the southern edge of the Shan Plateau, were known as Red Karens, or Karenni, from their red robes. Although racially and linguistically Karens, they tend to have their own identity.

In the mid-1970s there were estimated to be about 3,000,000 Karens, some 1,500,000 Shans, about 1,000,000 Chins and Kachins, and 100,000 Kayahs. These were unofficial estimates, made in the absence of any published official figures. The number of Indians and Chinese decreased as a result of an exodus at the outbreak of World War II and of a second exodus in 1963, when commerce and industry were nationalized. There are now about 120,000 Indians, Pakistanis, and Bengalis and some 400,000 Chinese.

Buddhist population

Religious groups. About 85 percent of the population is Buddhist. The Burmese are Buddhists except for minimal numbers of Christians and Muslims; the Shans are also Buddhists. Among the Karens, there are twice as many Buddhists as Christians, and the remainder are animists. All of the other hill peoples are animists except a few Kayah Buddhists and Kachin and Chin Christians.

Demography. The density of population in each region depends upon its suitability for agriculture. The most thickly populated regions are therefore the Irrawaddy Delta and the dry zone, which have 126 to 200 persons per square mile (49 to 77 per square kilometre); in the upper delta, between Rangoon and Henzada, the density reaches 250 (97). The Sittang Delta, the sedimented hinterland of Akyab, and the regions of both sides of the lower Chindwin have densities ranging from 76 to 125 (29 to 48). Arakan (except the Sittwe [Akyab] region), the west bank of the Irrawaddy behind Arakan Yoma, and Tenasserim are all sparsely populated, with densities of 26 to 75 (10 to 29). The more inaccessible parts of the western and northern mountains and the Shan Plateau have a density of less than 25 (10).

Burma is underpopulated as compared with other Asian countries. Its overall density at the census of 1973 was only 110 persons per square mile (43 per square kilometre), and its density per cultivated square mile was only about 500 (190). Only 16 percent of the people lived in urban areas. Since independence, government policy has been to preserve these density and distribution patterns. Immigration and emigration are restricted, so that the population remains indigenous. As an increase in the indigenous population is desired, special attention is given to public health. The mortality rate, which was about 19 per 1,000 in 1964, decreased to 12 in 1972, and the birth rate, which was about 37 per 1,000, increased to 39. The population (30,310,000 in 1974) showed a growth rate estimated at 2.4 percent per year during the period 1970–75.

Birth and death rates

THE NATIONAL ECONOMY

Agriculture. The economy of Burma is basically agricultural; more than two-thirds of its people derive their livelihoods directly from agricultural pursuits; of the nonagricultural workers who are employed in the more modern sectors of the economy, many are indirectly involved in agriculture through activities such as transportation, processing, marketing, and exporting of agricultural goods.

Burmese planners must emphasize agriculture because an estimated 60 percent of the raw materials utilized by industry originates in agriculture; failure to attain planned goals in agriculture during the early 1970s contributed to a severe inflation and cutbacks in related industries, although both these problems were exacerbated by inefficiency and corruption in state-managed economic enterprises.

Burmese agriculture may be considered to consist of three realms: the delta, where paddy rice culture predominates; the dry zone, an area of mixed agriculture;

and the hill country, where forestry and shifting agriculture have been the rule.

Although the agriculture of the dry zone has been most typically Burmese in the past, it is the rice culture of the delta that now provides from 40 to 50 percent of the country's export earnings and the staple diet of the country's people and on which the short- and long-term health of the economy depends. About 60 percent of the land in agricultural use is devoted to rice culture, and despite a climate that would permit much more extensive double cropping, only about 10 percent of the land is actually so managed. The delta's traditional agriculture consisted primarily of rice in normal years, with the substitution of millet in drier years when there was insufficient moisture for rice; both grains yielded good returns on the alluvial soils of the delta. After Burma was officially annexed to British India in 1886, colonial policy called for a more commercially oriented and extensive cultivation of rice; since the indigenous Burmese labour force was insufficient to support this new economy, officially encouraged immigration of Indian and Chinese labourers and their families took place during the early decades of the 20th century. By 1942, first-generation immigrants composed about 13 percent of the total population. Despite relatively low growth in rice production since World War II, it still remains both the basic food and the basic export of Burma.

Agriculture in the dry zone is much more diversified than that of the delta. Its major products include, in addition to rice, other grains (wheat, millet, and corn, or maize), peanuts (groundnuts), sesame, legumes, tea, and rubber. However, to cultivate much of this land successfully, irrigation is required. The construction of the earliest known Burmese irrigation works, in Kyaukse and Minbu districts, can be dated from the 11th century, and although their maintenance has not been a continuing concern of governments throughout Burmese history, many are still in active service. As in the delta, the arrival of the British led to increased commercial and public works activities; British authorities renewed and extended many of these ancient systems and, in addition, built new ones during the early years of the 20th century, including the Mandalay (1903), Shwebo (1906–12), Mon (1912), and Salin (1926). About five-sixths of Burma's irrigated land is in the dry zone, and even here about 90 percent is cultivated in rice. The portions of the dry zone that are not irrigated are utilized for the production of crops that are less sensitive to the seasonality or irregularity of rainfall than rice. In addition to the crops mentioned above, cotton and sugarcane are cultivated in this zone, although neither is of considerable significance. Cattle are also raised in the dry zone.

Irrigation

The third zone of agriculture, the hill country, occupies perhaps two-thirds of the area of Burma, and, although it is of much less economic significance than the other two, it is the home of many of the non-Burmese peoples of the country. Their agriculture has been, and to a considerable extent still is, a type of slash-and-burn agriculture called *taungya*, although more sedentary traditional modes also exist and others are imposed with the advance of agricultural technology and central planning. Outside the forest areas of these highlands, the principal foods raised are rice, yams, millet, with swine and poultry ubiquitous. Possibilities, largely unrealized, exist for commercial agriculture in the more fertile river and lake basins.

Bullocks and buffalo are used as beasts of burden, and goats, pigs, and poultry are raised for food in all parts of the country.

Fisheries. The second most important element in the Burmese diet after rice is fish—fresh, preserved, or prepared as *ngapi*, a sort of paste that is eaten with rice. Marine fisheries are not well developed, although the reported commercial catch of 320,000 metric tons is more than twice as great as the reported catch from inland waters. The latter, however, provide much private, noncommercial fishing in virtually every type of permanent, seasonal, or artificial body of water of any size. Two nonindigenous fish, the European carp and the tilapia of Thailand, have been imported and breed very well in impounded waters.

Forestry. Forestry is particularly important to economic planners, since exports of teak yield more than a quarter of all export earnings. Burma has been estimated to contain up to three-quarters of the world's exploitable teak supplies. The trees are found in the mixed deciduous forests of the hills and commonly comprise about 12 percent of forests of which they are a part. The forests are state-owned, and the responsibility for their management and exploitation belongs to the State Timber Board.

Minerals. Burma's rich mineral deposits are not fully exploited. Deposits of silver, lead, and zinc are located in the northern Shan Plateau; tin and tungsten are found in Tenasserim. Ruby mines in the northern Shan Plateau were worked to exhaustion during colonial times. Jade is found in the northern mountains, but for some years the output has been negligible. There are petroleum fields in the dry zone; installations and several surveys for offshore oil deposits have been undertaken. Coal of an inferior quality is found in the upper Chindwin Valley.

Manufacturing and power. There was little industrialization until after independence, when a limited program began. Rangoon, Myingyan (in the dry zone), and Arakan division (now state) were selected to become the new industrial centres. There are textile factories at Rangoon and Myingyan and one near Paleik in the central region. Rangoon also has steel-processing and pharmaceutical plants, and there is a paper mill in Arakan. Existing food-processing plants (mainly rice mills) and lumber mills have been improved and expanded. Cottage industries are encouraged by subsidies.

After independence the government built a large thermal power plant in Rangoon and undertook the development of hydroelectric power plants on the Balu Chaung, a tributary of the Salween; at Taikkyi near Pegu; and in northern Arakan. The Balu Chaung plant serves Rangoon and many surrounding villages.

Trade. In the first few years of independence, trade, which had been totally abandoned during the Japanese occupation, showed definite signs of revival; after 1963, however, a steady decline occurred, partly because of inexperience after nationalization but mainly because of the virtual collapse of the international rice market. In 1974 the chief items of export by value were rice (41 percent), teak (26 percent), and oil cake (5 percent). The exports have been fairly evenly distributed among India, Sri Lanka, the People's Republic of China, Japan, Indonesia, West Germany, Singapore, the United Kingdom, Hong Kong, and Malaysia. Imports were mainly machines and spare parts, defense stores, industrial raw materials, and consumer goods from the United States, Japan, the United Kingdom, the People's Republic of China, India, France, West Germany, the Soviet Union, and Australia. Because of the shortage of foreign exchange, imports were balanced against exports.

Trading partners

Management of the economy. All large industrial enterprises, the banking system, insurance, foreign trade, domestic wholesale trade, and 90 percent of the retail trade were nationalized in 1962 and 1963. Small-scale industry (consisting mainly of food and beverage processing, miscellaneous manufacturing, and cottage industries), agriculture, and fishing were left in the private sector. Further nationalization, however, took place in medium-sized industries in the late 1960s and early '70s.

Enterprises remaining in the private sector after nationalization account for only about 10 percent of the nation's tax income. The balance is collected from the public sector. The principal sources of revenue are income, customs, and commercial taxes. There is also a land tax, applicable to the private sector only, and, applicable to both, excise, forest, mineral, fishery, and miscellaneous taxes.

There are no trade unions or employer associations. Strikes are not permitted; labour disputes are submitted to local conciliation committees consisting of labour officers and selected workers. A network of workers' councils has been formed to complement the conciliation committees in the implementation of general government policy toward workers that includes a wage policy.

The overall economic objective is the establishment of a fully socialized state. Policy measures include the diversification of agricultural production to promote exports; the substitution, wherever feasible, of essential commodities for imports; the utilization of existing industrial plants to full capacity by providing spare parts and adequate raw materials; and the assignment of priority to mining and petroleum exploration both on land and offshore. The pace of development is based on the availability of foreign exchange.

The problems of the economy, which are both structural and serious, arise from lack of experience. Inefficiency in the nationalized sectors is apparent in both production and distribution; allocation is often inequitable, and pricing policies are sometimes artificial. There are deficits in the balance of payments and a sharp decline in foreign reserves, and the international rice market has deteriorated.

TRANSPORTATION

River transport. The Irrawaddy River is the backbone of the transport system. Trade in rice, which is still the basis of the country's economy despite the decline in exports, is dependent on water transport. There has never been any need for grain elevators, as small country boats can reach any rice field that has surplus rice to sell.

Navigable streams

The Irrawaddy is navigable up to Bhamo, a distance of some 900 miles (1,450 kilometres) from the sea; the next stretch of another 90 miles to Myitkyina is navigable only during the dry season when there are no rapids. The Chindwin is navigable for 380 miles (610 kilometres) from its confluence with the Irrawaddy below Mandalay. The many streams of the Irrawaddy Delta, with a total length of 2,000 miles (3,200 kilometres), are navigable, and there is a system of connecting canals with a total length of 60 miles (97 kilometres). The Sittang, in spite of its silt, is usable by country boats; the Salween, in spite of its rapids, is navigable up to 74 miles (119 kilometres) from the sea. Small steamers and country boats also serve the coasts of Arakan and Tenasserim.

Railways. The first railway line, running from Rangoon to Pye (Prome) and built in 1877, followed the Irrawaddy Valley. At that time Upper Burma was still a kingdom, and Pye was just a few miles from the frontier between British Burma and the Kingdom of Burma. The line was not extended to Mandalay; instead, after 1886 a new railway from Rangoon up the Sittang Valley was constructed, meeting the Irrawaddy at Mandalay. From Mandalay it crosses the river and, avoiding the Irrawaddy Valley, goes up the Mu Valley to connect with the Irrawaddy again at Myitkyina. A short branch line connects Naba to Katha on the Irrawaddy below Bhamo.

The Rangoon–Mandalay–Myitkyina railway is the main artery, and from it there are branch lines connecting the northern and central Shan Plateau with the Irrawaddy. Other branches run from Pyinmana across the Pegu Yoma to Kyaukpadaung, which in the early 1970s was being extended to the oil fields on the Irrawaddy River, and from Pegu to Moulmein to Ye. The Pye–Rangoon railway has a branch line crossing the apex of the delta to Henzada and Bassein. There are no railways in Arakan and Tenasserim. The entire railway system had 2,400 miles (3,860 kilometres) of narrow-gauge track in the mid-1970s.

Roads. The road system was built without plan or policy, and, until independence, it was confined to the Irrawaddy and Sittang valleys, duplicating the railway route. A road goes from Pye along the Irrawaddy to the oil fields. Government policy is to improve and extend existing highways and to construct new ones connecting Burma proper with its six sister states.

There were originally three international roads in use during World War II—the road from Lashio to K'unming in China, the road between Myitkyina and Assam in India, and the road between Kentung in the southern Shan Plateau and northern Thailand. The road between Assam and Myitkyina has now disappeared, and the other two roads have been neglected and are only in partial use.

Airways and ports. The Union of Burma Airways runs frequent domestic flights from Rangoon to some 50 towns and regular flights to Hong Kong, Bangkok, Dacca, Calcutta, and Kāthmāndu. Rangoon and Mandalay have international airports. Rangoon, as the terminus of road, rail, and river transport systems, is an international port with up-to-date equipment and facilities. Bassein, Moulmein, and Sittwe are also international ports.

ADMINISTRATION AND SOCIAL CONDITIONS

Constitution of 1974. A new constitution was approved by a referendum in December 1973 and came into force on January 4, 1974, the 26th anniversary of Burmese independence. The country also assumed a new official name, the Socialist Republic of the Union of Burma. General elections were held in January and February, and a new government was established on March 2, 1974, the 12th anniversary of the coup that had established a military government.

The new constitution provides for seven states (Arakan, Chin, Kachin, Kawthule, Kayah, Mon, and Shan) and seven divisions of Burma proper (Irrawaddy, Magwe, Mandalay, Pegu, Rangoon, Sagaing, and Tenasserim), with "local autonomy under central leadership." The supreme power is the Pyithu Hlutdaw, which exercises legislative, executive, and judicial authority. The adoption of the name Hlutdaw (or Hluttaw; literally "place of release") is significant. Under the Burmese kings the Hlutdaw was a supreme council discharging legislative, executive, and judicial functions, but as the historical Hlutdaw was a royal institution the new designation is Pyithu ("People's") Hlutdaw. Thus, Pyithu Hlutdaw is the People's Council at the national level as distinct from the People's Council at the division or state, township, and ward or village levels. Elections to the Hlutdaw and to the local council are held simultaneously, members being elected for four-year terms.

Pyithu Hlutdaw

Central government structure. The organs of the 450-member Pyithu Hlutdaw are the Council of State, the Council of Ministers, the Council of People's Justices, the Council of People's Attorneys, and the Council of People's Inspectors. The Council of State consists of an elected representative from each state and division, an equal number elected by the Pyithu Hlutdaw as a whole, and the prime minister as an ex-officio member. The Council of State elects its own chairman, who is ex-officio president of the republic, and its own secretary. The president, Ne Win, and the secretary, Gen. San Yu, are also, respectively, the chairman and the secretary general of the Burma Socialist Programme Party. The Council of State appoints senior civil servants and deputy ministers and submits lists of names for election by the Hlutdaw of the prime minister, his Cabinet, and the councils of justices, attorneys, and inspectors. The number of ministers can fluctuate, but the three councils have five members each. The Council of People's Justices is the equivalent of a supreme court in a parliamentary democracy; the Council of People's Attorneys is comparable to an attorney general (but members do not need legal qualifications or experience) and the Council of People's Inspectors to an auditor general.

Local government structure. The local People's Council follows the pattern of the Hlutdaw; every council has an Executive Committee and a Judicial Committee. All but the village or ward councils also have a Committee of Inspectors. The Committee of Judges, not necessarily composed of lawyers, sits as the local court, exercising criminal and civil jurisdiction.

Civil service and political parties. There is a civil service, and military officers are drafted into it. All political parties are illegal except the official party, the Burma Socialist Programme Party. Membership is by election after preliminary service as a "friend of the party" and then as an "auxiliary." It was at first restricted to cadres, but the party held its first national assembly in 1971, when its membership was widened so that it be-

One-party system

came a national party. Civil servants and members of the armed forces, as well as workers and peasants, are members, and senior military officials and civil servants are included in the party's hierarchy.

Armed forces. The Burmese fighting forces consist of a trained and well-equipped army, a small navy, and a small air force. The Defense Service Academy is located at Maymyo. The police force, although armed and equipped and often used as a branch of the army in emergencies, remains essentially civilian in character and regional in organization; it deals with the day-to-day maintenance of law and order.

Public welfare. In social welfare measures, the government has given special attention to workers and peasants and to the hill peoples. The National Housing Board was retained after the coup in 1962, and, in spite of a shortage of imported building materials, the housing problem is not acute. A high mortality rate, especially among infants, has been lowered substantially, and every village has a health unit and access to a hospital.

Education. The literacy rate has always been at a high level and continues to improve. Education is free in the primary schools, and in secondary schools and universities fees are nominal. The number of children attending school doubled between 1960 and 1970, and the number of students attending universities and institutions of equivalent status tripled in the same period. The University of Rangoon and its branch at Mandalay were separated in 1958 into autonomous units now known as the Rangoon Arts and Science University and the Mandalay Arts and Science University. Various institutes and colleges teach medicine, technology, agriculture, economics, etc.

Burmese folk culture

Cultural life and institutions. Burmese culture is essentially a folk culture. Buddhism, which originated in a rural setting such as that of Burma, has pervaded Burmese life since the 11th century and has blended harmoniously with folk culture. The emphasis given by Buddhism to equality among all men and women and to the liberty and dignity of the individual fits in with Tibeto-Burman social tradition. The Feast of Merit in Chin animism, for example, has the same folk background as that of a Buddhist Burmese alms-giving ceremony; the dancing, singing, music, and general gaiety of a Kachin sacrificial celebration are reflected in the Burmese ceremony initiating a boy as a novice in the Buddhist order of monks; and the animals, monsters, trees, flowers, and abstract designs carved on the central post of a Kachin men's club are similar to those carved on the doors of the palace of the kings. Some observers maintain that Burmese culture is animistic; others, that it is Buddhist; but all agree that it is Burmese.

Ewing Galloway

Burmese dancers performing in traditional costume.

Burmese drama in 1886 appeared to be dying with the passing of the old kingdom. As it was essentially a folk drama, however, it survived and with the regaining of independence gathered new strength.

Wood-carving, lacquerwork, goldwork, and silverwork, the sculpture of Buddhist images and mythological figures, and temple architecture also survived under colonial rule; there has been a revival of these indigenous art traditions under the patronage of the Ministry of Culture. The arts of bronze casting among the Burmese and of making bronze drums among the Karens, however, both disappeared. The Burmese puppet show also declined, although occasionally there are attempts to revive it. The cinema is the one Western art form that has been accepted in the cultural life of the Burmese people.

Literature

Burmese literature remained alive throughout the colonial period, and, both in verse and in prose, native traditions continue to prevail. A later development is biography, which has become more popular than fiction. The Burma Translation Society, which is sponsored by the government, annually awards substantial cash prizes for the best translation, the best novel, and the best biography. There are state schools of Burmese dance, music, and drama, as well as state schools of fine arts, at Rangoon and Mandalay. The National Museum is at Rangoon, and there are regional museums at Mandalay and at the state level. (See also SOUTHEAST ASIAN PEOPLES, ARTS OF.)

There were 12 Burmese-language and two English-language newspapers at the time of the coup in 1962. Only one Burmese newspaper remains in private hands, the others having been nationalized. The government has its own official newspaper, *The Working People's Daily*. Broadcasting is under the control of the government information department. (M.H.Au./Ed.)

PROSPECTS FOR THE FUTURE

Burma has been passing through a period of political change and economic recession. Faced with internal problems, the country remains aloof from the rest of the world. The international community was at first intrigued by this tendency but then lost interest. An English newspaper report summed up the situation by suggesting that, if Burma could do without the world, then the world could very well do without Burma. Its three complex and interrelated problems are insurgency, the economy, and resultant social ills. The various insurgencies, Communist and ethnic, which led in 1962 to the Socialist revolution of military officers, were made worse by the Communist victories in Indochina in 1975. The second and central problem was the economy. Where growth occurred after 1962 it was slight and usually swallowed up by population growth. To obtain improvement in this area, Burma must initiate more effective central planning; end dependence of the export market on a very few commodities and the isolationism that prevents foreign assistance; and combat unemployment and inflation. The concomitant social ills include labour unrest, poor public health, and a black market, smuggling, and hoarding.

Some concessions by the government to increased private participation in the economy, especially in the important transportation sector, indicated a willingness in the government to consider alternatives to doctrinaire socialism in the resolution of the country's predicament.

Despite the strains, however, the country looks to a new generation, which has gained fresh experience in technology and management, to build a new economy. At the same time Burmese society seeks to preserve the old values of individual liberty and social justice within a tribal framework. (Ed.)

BIBLIOGRAPHY. E.H.G. DOBBY, *Southeast Asia*, 10th ed. (1967), gives a general description of Burma as a part of Southeast Asia and also contains a special section on the country itself, with detailed maps. O.H.K. SPATE, *Burma Setting* (1943), gives a brief but detailed introduction to the physical and social geography of Burma and some details of the economic geography of Burma up to the outbreak of World War II. H.L. CHHIBBER, *Physiography of Burma* (1933) and *Geology of Burma* (1934), are standard works on the Burmese landscape. R. KAULBACK, *Salween* (1939); and L.D. STAMP, "Irrawaddy River," *Geogrl. J.*, 95:329–356 (1940), describe the drainage system of Burma. J.R. ANDRUS, *Burmese Economic Life* (1948); and J.S. FURNIVALL, *Political Economy of Burma*, 2nd rev. ed. (1938), describe the economy during the colonial period. FRANK N. TRAGER, *Burma: From Kingdom to Republic* (1966), contains an account of the economy before and after independence, up to the years of extensive nationalization in 1962–63. MAUNG HTIN AUNG, *A History of Burma* (1967), gives the historic background and contains accounts of Burmese society and culture.

(M.H.Au./Ed.)

Burma, History of

Burma lies on the western edge of the peninsula of Indochina and forms part of the region of Southeast Asia. In prehistoric times it was traversed, both along its coasts and down its river valleys, by band after band of migrating peoples on their way farther eastward and southward. During the first ten centuries of the Christian Era the overland trade route between China and India passed through Burma's borders, and merchant ships from India, Ceylon, and even farther west converged on its ports, which were also the termini of the portage routes across the narrow isthmus from what is now the Gulf of Thailand. Thus, Burma was the gateway of Southeast Asia.

The Indian merchants brought with them not only precious cargoes but also great cultural gifts in the form of religious, political, and legal ideas; and within a few decades Indian cultural traditions had remolded native society, native thought, and native arts and crafts. Although the new cultural treasures passed through to Southeast Asia, Burma never allowed its own native culture to be overwhelmed.

Surrounded on three sides by mountain walls and on the fourth by the sea, Burma has always been insular; and as a consequence, Burmese culture, in spite of the many Indian influences and in spite of its close affinity with the cultures of the other countries of Southeast Asia, has remained distinct and separate. For example, it rejected the Hindu Indian theory of a divine king and insisted that men and women are born free and equal.

The first area in Southeast Asia to receive Buddhism, because of its proximity to India, Burma became the centre of Theravāda Buddhism almost overnight in the 11th century, when the faith was being assailed not only in India and Southeast Asia but in the whole of Asia itself. The Buddhist doctrine of the equality of all men and women was superimposed with grace and harmony on the native tradition of social equality.

The unique nature of Burmese society and culture was noticed at the time of the British conquest (late 19th century) even by humble privates, whose conception of Burma as a "cleaner, greener land" was embodied by the British author Rudyard Kipling in "Mandalay." The historian G.E. Harvey wrote in *British Rule in Burma* that "there is, in Burmese life, not only a beauty that delights the eye but also a dignity which makes one proud of the human race."

BURMA UNTIL THE ADVENT OF BRITISH RULE (TO 1885)

The origins of civilization in Burma. The Irrawaddy River, flowing southward through the entire length of Burma, divides the country in two and its valley forms the central plain. The first human settlements in Burma appeared some 5,000 years ago in the middle portion of the Irrawaddy Valley. The stone and fossilized-wood tools used by those Paleolithic and Proto-Neolithic people have their own distinguishing features, and anthropologists have given their culture its own name—Anyathian (Burmese *anya*, "Upper Burma"). A discovery in 1969 by the Department of Archeology of the Burmese government of some cave paintings and stone tools in the eastern part of Burma's Shan State shows that that area, too, had Paleolithic and Proto-Neolithic settlements. Crude shards and ringstones found at the site appear to have been attached to stonecutting tools, to make them more suitable for digging; and woodcutting tools were probably used in clearing patches of the forest for cultivation, which would indicate that the shift to agriculture had already begun.

The first human settlements in Burma

The Anyathian people probably migrated down the Irrawaddy River, and the Shan cave people down the Salween. Thus, even during the stone ages, the general pattern of human migration and settlement for both Burma and the rest of mainland Southeast Asia had been fixed—tribal groups coming from the north over the mountains and then down the great rivers: the earlier or stronger groups settling in the valley to learn the art of wet-rice cultivation and the later or weaker groups being pushed into the mountainous parts to learn only the method of "slash and burn" rice growing. In those early times the Irrawaddy had not yet formed its great delta; and at its huge mouth and along the coast, the country was stormy, wild, and desolate.

The Stone Age Anyathians stayed far from the sea. The earliest arrivals on Burma's coast were Negritos, a fact remembered in Burmese folktales, which tell of dark-skinned, short-statured, fuzzy-haired, and human-flesh-eating ogres who dwelled at the mouths of great rivers and on islands in the sea; a Buddhist legend describes how monk-missionaries sent from India saved the people of Thaton from ogres who lived on nearby islands and raided the city in quest of human flesh. As to the Anyathians, even folk memory no longer knows them, and it cannot be said whether they died out or merged with the later arrivals in the Irrawaddy Valley. (For a discussion of associated physical features, see IRRAWADDY RIVER.)

The Mons of Lower Burma. The first people in Burma to leave definite traces of their settlement were the Mons. Speaking an Austro-Asiatic language, they were close cousins of the Khmers, with whom they originally came down the Mekong River. Later the Khmers followed the river southeastward to what is now Cambodia, and the Mons veered southwestward toward the source of the Me Nam River (Mae Nam Chao Phraya) and went down its valley. By at least the 3rd century BC the Mons not only occupied the entire Me Nam Valley but had also spread to the Sittang Valley, doubtless through the gaps in the eastern mountain wall of Burma. Their port capital was Thaton, not far from the isthmian portage routes; and through this window to the sea they saw India, in its full glory, united and peaceful under the emperor Aśoka and a flourishing centre of Theravāda Buddhism.

Origin of the Mons

Introduction of Indian culture. Aśoka sent a mission of Buddhist monks to Suvarnabhūmi, "the Golden Land"; although a few scholars still remain unconvinced, it seems definite that the Golden Land was the three Mon regions of Upper Me Nam, Lower Me Nam, and the Sittang Valley. The ancient monastic settlement of Kelasa, situated a few miles from Thaton and claimed by Burmese and Mon chronicles to have been founded by Aśoka's missionaries, was mentioned in early Ceylonese records as being represented at a great religious ceremony held in Ceylon in the 2nd century BC.

With the expansion of Indian commerce in Southeast Asia in the 1st century AD, Thaton's prosperity and importance increased. The expansion was sudden and revolutionary but peaceful, and the Indian merchants and seamen came to Thaton as friends rather than as conquistadores or colonists. Their numbers were never great, and their settlements were only temporary. Until the 8th century, when there was a scramble for the new lands of the Irrawaddy Delta, no conflicts developed between the Indians and the Mons. As a result, the Indians' cultural gifts were found acceptable.

Blending of Indian and native cultures. The Mons saw to it that their native culture was not abandoned or displaced, and they worked for a harmonious blending of the old and new cultures. They brought many of their native animistic beliefs into the fold of Theravāda Buddhism. They enhanced the power and prestige of their king by adopting the Hindu ritual of coronation. They developed a new art of sculpture by blending the native tradition of wood carving with the Greco-Indian conventions of making images of the Buddha. They built *stūpas* on the Indian model and then developed new forms of temple architecture by a mixture of native and Indian traditions.

Mon culture

Within a few decades the Mons became the most advanced people in Southeast Asia, and they assumed the role of teachers to their neighbours, spreading Theravāda Buddhism and their new culture over the entire region. Their cousins, the Khmers, were the first to benefit, followed by the Burmese. Even in the 13th century, when their glory had passed and they were a conquered people in the Me Nam Valley, the Mons freely shared their cultural heritage with the new arrivals, the Tais.

The Tibeto-Burmese invasions. About the time the Mons were reaching the Me Nam Valley, some Tibeto-Burmese tribes were leaving their homeland on the southeastern slopes of the Tibetan Plateau. They had reached quite a high level of culture, but their way of life and their social values of individual equality were being threatened by the rival kingdoms of Tibet and China. Preferring physical hardship to political bondage, they started a long trek across the northern mountains of Burma; they entered the Upper Irrawaddy Valley, perhaps by the time of the Buddha (*c.* 500 BC). By Aśoka's time their spearhead, the Pyus and allied tribes, had founded their city-kingdoms, perhaps at Tagaung and certainly at Halingyi. They gradually moved southward, leaving along the way settlements that later became city-kingdoms. They stopped for a while at Taungdwingyi, and some tribes crossed the river and the mountains to Arakan. They finally reached the vicinity of modern Prome, only a few miles from what was then the apex of the Irrawaddy's mouth. At about the time of Christ, they founded the city of Śrī Kṣetra near modern Prome.

The Pyu state of Upper Burma. For long there had been a trade route between China and India that passed through northern Burma and then across the Chindwin Valley. The Pyus had gained full control of this route and had even provided an alternative routing—down the Irrawaddy to Śrī Kṣetra and then by sea to India and also to the portage routes and the islands. Because the Pyus were in control of the whole Irrawaddy Valley, Roman embassies to China in AD 97 and 121 chose the overland route through Burma for their journey.

Doubtless in the beginning the Pyus learned much from the Mons, but later they came into direct contact with Indian culture. They were so prosperous and powerful that they became the overlords of the Mon kingdom of Thaton and the portage routes. Chinese historical records noted that the Pyus claimed sovereignty over 18 kingdoms, many of them to the south of Burma.

Pyu life

The same Chinese records emphasized the humane nature of Pyu government and the elegance and grace of Pyu life. Fetters, chains, and prisons were unknown, and punishment of criminals was a few strokes with the whip. Gaily dressed in blue, the men wore gold ornaments on their hats and the women wore jewels in their hair. The Pyus lived in houses built of timber and roofed with tiles of lead and tin; they used golden knives and utensils and were surrounded by art objects of gold, green glass, jade, and crystal. The walls, the palace, and the monasteries were of glazed brick. Amid this luxury, the Pyus were devout Theravāda Buddhists. Their architects evolved the vaulted temple, which later found its golden age at Pagan. Their sons and daughters were disciplined and educated in monasteries or convents as novices.

Despite their power over the neighbouring regions and the elegance of their life, the Pyus remained a loosely knit medley of tribes. Retaining their old tribal values, the Pyus remained more democratic than the Mons, who possessed the institution of a hereditary chieftain (later king) and a hereditary nobility; but as a consequence, the Pyus were less united and disciplined. There were conflicts between Pyu tribal groups, resulting in changes of dynasties at Śrī Kṣetra.

The huge delta became silted up, and the Pyu city swiftly became inaccessible from the sea. The Mons—politically organized as the confederacy of Ramanna and embracing the three kingdoms of Thaton, Dvaravati, and Haripunjaya—asserted their claim to the newly emerged island of Pegu, in the mouth of the Irrawaddy, by attacking both the Pyus and the Indian merchant ships in the vicinity. In the 6th century a tribal war forced the Pyus and their loyal allies to abandon Śrī Kṣetra. There was a fresh merger of tribes, and in the process the Burmese, a people subject to the Pyus, became prominent for the first time.

Advent of the Pagan Burmese. The Pyus and their allies moved to Upper Burma, where they set up a new capital. The Burmese, still loyal, established a small settlement of their own. Early in the 9th century the Tai-Shans from their kingdom of Nanchao in South China mounted a series of raids on the cities of Indochina and even besieged Hanoi. The Mon and Khmer cities held firm, but the Pyu capital fell. The leadership of the Tibeto-Burmese tribes passed to the Burmese, and in 849 they founded their own city of Pagan and built a wall around it.

The founding of the city of Pagan

The Pagan kingdom (849–1287). By that time the Mons had become supreme in Lower Burma. They had occupied the whole of the Irrawaddy Delta, building the port of Bassein in the west and founding the city of Pegu in the centre. They could have stepped into the vacuum caused by the destruction of the Pyu kingdom, but they were not politically ambitious and perhaps did not relish going up the river into arid country.

Subjugation of Upper and Lower Burma. The Mons' reluctance allowed the infant Burmese kingdom to survive and grow. The Burmese had learned much from the Pyus, but they were cut off from the fountain of Buddhist culture, now transferred to Ceylon. Theravāda Buddhism had disappeared from India, and in its place were Mahāyāna Buddhism, its offshoot Tantrism, and a resurgent and aggressive Hinduism. The Burmese still controlled the overland route; along it from China and Nanchao came Mahāyāna Buddhism, and from Bengal came Tantrism. There was also a return to native animistic beliefs.

In 1044 Anawrahta came to the throne at Pagan, and his accession coincided with the seemingly final defeat of Theravāda Buddhism in Southeast Asia; the islands and the Khmers went over completely to Hinduism, and the Theravāda Mons were pressured by their neighbours into accepting certain Hindu beliefs. An orthodox monk, Shin Arahan, fled in protest to Pagan, where he was able to convert the young king to the Theravāda faith. The people also accepted it because there was still a vague remembrance that the Pyus had been Theravādins and because the faith's emphasis on the equality and dignity of the individual fitted their society and their prevailing mood. Anawrahta, declaring himself the champion of Theravāda Buddhism, challenged and subdued the Mahāyānist kingdom of Nanchao, annexed the animistic Shan Plateau, and conquered the Theravāda Mons. He united the whole of Burma into a single kingdom and founded the first Burmese empire. His work was continued by his great commander Kyanzittha, who was elected king; and the latter was followed by another great ruler, his grandson (Anawrahta's great-grandson), Alaungsithu.

The first Burmese empire

Anawrahta's subjugation of the Shans checked the flood of Tai-speaking mercenaries and migrants into Southeast Asia, and the strength of his kingdom brought peace to the region, now divided into two great empires, Khmer and Burmese. Anawrahta's dynasty of kings lasted until the 13th century. By that time, their great temples had been built and their message of Theravāda Buddhism had been carried not only to the Shans but also to the Khmers.

Destruction by the Mongols. A malaise seemed to have set in by the middle of the 13th century. Then came a demand for submission and tribute by the Mongol Kublai Khan. The proud Burmese refused and made a valiant effort to stem the tide of invasion that followed; but it was unavailing, and Pagan fell to the Mongol armies in 1287.

Cultural changes in the Pagan period. Pagan was a fabulous kingdom even to its contemporaries, and Marco Polo was impressed by its splendour. Its many temples and monasteries testified to the prosperity of its people and the richness of its culture. The conquest of Thaton was the foundation of both its economy and its culture. All the ports of the country were in Burmese hands, and Pagan's temples were built by free artisans, who were paid their wages not only in money but also in kind and whose clothing, shelter, health, comfort, and safety were the responsibility of their employers (as evidenced by contemporary inscriptions, giving the monetary details connected with the construction and endowment of a temple).

Mon craftsmen, artisans, artists, architects, goldsmiths, and wood carvers—captured at Thaton—were taken to Pagan to teach their skills and arts to the Burmese, whose artistic traditions, inherited from the Pyus, had been lying dormant. The Burmese learned quickly and soon were able to stand shoulder to shoulder with Mon and Indian craftsmen. Mon monks and scholars taught the Burmese the Pāli language and the Buddhist scriptures; and the Burmese soon became scholars themselves, making Pagan the centre of Theravāda learning. Some of their religious commentaries came to be accepted as part of the Pāli canon by all Theravādins. The women of Pagan took part in all these activities, their freedom and equality doubly guaranteed by tribal usage and by Buddhist doctrine.

Devout and orthodox, the people of Pagan made Buddhism their way of life but retained those animistic beliefs that were found compatible with Buddhism. They set a pattern of religion, government, and society that later generations of Burmese followed almost without change. Temple frescoes show the Pagan people to have been simply dressed. Their utensils and implements were not of gold, and so their life was not so elegant as that of the Pyus (see also PAGAN).

Burma c. 1300–c. 1750. During the reigns of the last kings of Pagan, many Shans entered royal service as mercenaries. After the fall of Pagan these Burmanized Tai-speaking soldiers of fortune drove out the Mongols; but instead of restoring the fallen dynasty, they founded small kingdoms for themselves. Before invading Burma, Kublai Khan had conquered Nanchao and turned it into the Chinese province of Yunnan; when his armies had withdrawn, he encouraged the Shans to leave their old homeland and attack the Burmese and the Khmers. The consequence was the rise of a number of Tai-speaking kingdoms in the Me Nam Valley and the restoration of the kingdom of Pegu by the Mons of Lower Burma. In 1368 Upper Burma was unified under one kingdom, that of Ava, whose kings were half-Burmese and half-Shan and who proudly regarded themselves as Anawrahta's successors. They encouraged scholarship and learning, making their period a great age of Burmese literature. They wasted their resources, however, by waging a long war against the Mons.

The Shans of the Me Nam Valley fought both Pegu and Ava. In the meantime the small settlement of Burmese refugees at Toungoo, on the Pegu-Ava frontier, sought survival by playing Mon against Shan. The Shan refugees from Nanchao who were waiting in the north of Burma for an opportunity to win back their old kingdom decided to conquer Ava instead. They had not been won over to Buddhism; and in 1540 there was a massacre of monks, resulting in an exodus of Burmese to Toungoo. In the meantime the Mons at Pegu were achieving another golden age under wise rulers. Under Dhammazedi, Pegu became the centre of Theravādin scholarship and it also entered into close commercial relationship with Malacca, on the Malay Peninsula, an Islāmic kingdom before 1511 and a Portuguese possession thereafter. In 1531 Tabinshwehti became king of Toungoo, and within a few years he conquered Upper Burma from the Shans and Lower Burma from the Mons. Transferring his capital to Pegu, he made a great attempt to unite Burmese, Mon, and Shan into a single nation. He died in 1551 and was succeeded by his brother-in-law Bayinnaung. The Shans in the Me Nam Valley had consolidated their power under the kingdom of Ayutthaya (Siam), and they cast their eye on the Shan Plateau and Mon Lower Burma. Bayinnaung marched on to Ayutthaya and conquered the entire Me Nam Valley, thus founding the second Burmese empire. He used Portuguese mercenaries and Portuguese cannon, but he was determined to keep the Portuguese out of mainland Southeast Asia.

The second Burmese empire

Bayinnaung was a very able king, but after his death the empire broke up. Manipur (which had been subjugated in 1560) declared itself a free kingdom. Then the Mons revolted, the Siamese not only regained their independence but also ravaged Lower Burma, and the Portuguese founded a kingdom at Syriam. Bayinnaung's grandson, Anaukpetlun, in 1605 overcame all three and restored the Burmese kingdom, including Lower Burma. The Burmese, tired of war and international commerce, shifted their capital back to Ava. There were no more Mon rebellions and the kingdom remained at peace. Eventually, the kings became weak and power passed to the ministers.

The fall of the Ming dynasty in China (mid-17th century) resulted in occupation of Burmese territory by the armies of the fallen emperor and also by the pursuing armies of the new emperor. The raja of Manipur sent his raiders into Burma for loot. The Mons rose in rebellion, encouraged by the French in India. Assailed from all sides, Ava fell to the Mons in 1752; and the whole of Burma passed under Mon rule.

The Alaungpaya dynasty. It was soon proved, however, that only the Burmese king and his ministers had been defeated and not the people; before the year had ended a popular leader, Alaungpaya, drove the Mons out of Upper Burma and regained the Shan States. By 1758 he had regained Manipur and defeated the Mons and their French garrisons. The Siamese became alarmed and attempted to rouse the Shan chiefs to rebel. Alaungpaya retook Tenasserim, the site of the old portage kingdoms, and invaded Siam. Although his invasion failed and he himself died during the retreat in 1760, the Burmese now felt that, unless Siam were conquered, their kingdom would be insecure. The defeats suffered in 1752 had embittered them, and they decided to pursue a policy of aggrandizement and repression. Alaungpaya's son and successor, Hsinbyushin, sent his armies into Siam in 1766; they captured Ayutthaya in 1767. China, alarmed over the growing power of the Burmese, unsuccessfully invaded Burma four times during the period 1766–69.

The Burmese then reconquered Arakan (on the northwest coast of Burma) and occupied Assam, thus coming face to face with the British power in India. The result was the First Anglo-Burmese War (1824–26), in which Siam fought on the British side. The Burmese eventually had to sue for peace and lost Assam, Manipur, Arakan, and Tenasserim. (For a further discussion on British India, see also ASSAM.)

The Anglo-Burmese wars

The Second Anglo-Burmese War (1852) was provoked by the British, who wanted to close the gap in their coastline stretching from Calcutta to Singapore; it left the Burmese kingdom high and dry in Upper Burma. As the British became more and more interested in trade with China through its back door, they waited for a suitable pretext and in 1885 declared war on the Burmese for the third time. To meet international criticism of their action, the British gave the excuses that the last independent Burmese king, Thibaw (ruled 1878–85), was a tyrant and that he was intriguing to give France greater influence over the country. Neither of these charges seems to have had much foundation.

The administration of traditional Burma. In the government of old Burma the king was the chief executive and the final court of appeal, but there were checks on his power. He could not make laws, only edicts that would lapse with his death. Custom was the only recognized source of law, and even the king could be sued for civil wrongs. In addition, following the old tribal requirement that each chieftain was to be elected by the council of elders, the king had to be elected by the previous king's council of ministers. With the advent of strong kings, generally the election was merely a formality; but in times of crisis there were real elections.

The king was also the patron of Buddhism and was expected to act as a humane ruler. Buddhist monks were not organized into a church, but there was a primate who, although appointed by the king, often proved to be his sternest critic. Although monks were outside the sphere of politics, they had the right to give sanctuary in that they could ask for the life of a condemned criminal. In practice this right was exercised only when there was some miscarriage of justice. Because monasteries also served as schools for all children, the monks were the teachers of the people and molded public opinion regarding the king's justice.

As a corollary to the centuries-old Burmese insistence that all men and women were born free and equal, there were no hereditary nobles. The king's officials were appointed, at least in theory, on their character and talent alone; and their appointments lapsed with the king's death.

The centre of government

The High Court of Justice was the centre of government. It had three wings—the treasury, the executive, and the judiciary. The judicial wing was the final court of appeal; in theory and often in practice the king presided over its deliberations. All proclamations and appointments that were made by the king became valid only when orders giving effect to them were issued by the executive wing.

Every province had a governor, to whom were delegated certain powers by the High Court of Justice; but there was always a right of appeal against all his decisions to the High Court. Local government was in the hands of "group-village headmen." Villages were grouped together according to their size and geography. Each village in a group was under an elected elder, and these elders together elected the headman, who was then given his appointment by the king. The institution of headman was almost hereditary: because of the need for continuity and experience, the elders usually gave preference to the son, brother, daughter, or even the widow of the former headman. The headman, like a governor, had the right of immediate audience with the king.

THE EMERGENCE OF MODERN BURMA (SINCE 1885)

The Third Anglo-Burmese War lasted but a week; the Burmese never expected that hostilities would break out, and, realizing the hopelessness of the situation because of the disparity in arms, they offered no resistance. They also believed that the British aim was merely to replace King Thibaw with a Burmese prince who had been sheltered and groomed in India for the throne; and this belief seemed to be confirmed when the British commander called upon the High Court of Justice to continue to function. The British finally decided, however, not only to annex the whole kingdom but also to make it a province of India (effective January 1, 1886).

Burmese anti-Indian feelings

This was a bitter blow to Burmese pride. The Burmese had always been prejudiced against the Indians, calling them *kala* ("caste people"). In addition, they remembered that in Burma's three wars with the British, Indian troops had fought for their British masters. It was true that, after the war of 1824, Arakan and Tenasserim had been placed under British commissioners responsible to the British government of India and that, after the province of Pegu had been annexed in 1852, the whole territory of British Burma had been placed under a chief commissioner also responsible to the government of India. But these were temporary and makeshift arrangements, to be reconsidered in the light of experience. Burma seemed too big a territory to be attached to India, and moreover the Burmese were different from the Indians in race, language, society, way of life, attitude, and temperament. The Buddhist culture the Burmese had received from India had been modified and transformed so that it had become Burmese-Buddhist culture, while in India, Buddhism had been suppressed and discarded many centuries

British territorial acquisitions in Burma.
Adapted from F. Trager, *Burma, From Kingdom to Republic* (1966); Praeger Publishers, Inc.

before. Even little Ceylon, despite its cultural, racial, and linguistic ties with India, was never made an Indian province.

The effects of colonialism. The Burmese refused to accept the British victory as final, and they resorted to guerrilla warfare against the British army of occupation. There were spontaneous uprisings all over the country, led by former officers of the disbanded royal army, former officials (including village headmen), and princes of the blood. They considered themselves soldiers still fighting the Third Anglo-Burmese War; but to the British the war had ended with the annexation of the kingdom and the fighters were rebels and bandits. For the next four years, although no martial law was proclaimed, the British military officers acted as both judge and jury in dealing with captured guerrillas. Villagers who aided the rebels were also sternly punished. There were mass executions and even cases of wholly massacred villages.

British attempts to end the rebellion

As the guerrillas fought on, the British tried to force the people into submission. Villages were burned; families who had supplied villages with their headmen were uprooted from their homes and sent away to Lower Burma; and strangers were appointed as headmen for the new villages the British had set up. The guerrillas resorted to cruel and desperate measures against the new village officials. Finally, the might of the British army prevailed, and by 1890—with thousands of guerrillas killed or executed—the struggle was over.

Although the British were successors to the Burmese kings, they did not wish to favour any one religion over another, and they were reluctant to patronize Burmese Buddhism. Queen Victoria, as empress, had proclaimed strict British neutrality in religious affairs of the Indian peoples; but the position in India was different: it was the home of two rival religions, Hinduism and Islām. The patronage of Burmese Buddhism did not mean financial support, of which Burmese Buddhist monks were in no need (they could own no property, and such simple needs as robes, food, books, and medicine were met by donations from the public). Patronage involved authority; and although the king had been required to kneel before even a freshly ordained monk visiting him, it had been the king's right to appoint the primate, who exercised supervision and discipline among the ranks of the clergy all over the kingdom. The king had also had the right to attach two royal officials to the primate—the commissioner of ecclesiastical lands and the ecclesiastical censor. The duty of the commissioner had been to see that ecclesiastical lands were exempted from payment of taxes; but at the same time, he had seen to it that bogus and illegal endowments did not escape taxation. The duty of the censor had been to maintain a register of monks, which had given the king an indirect control over the clergy. The power of disrobing a wayward monk had lain only with the primate, but the same result could have been achieved by the censor scratching the monk's name from the register. This arrangement was designed to prevent unworthy persons from taking advantage of the people's respect and devotion for the clergy.

The British refusal of a plea by the clergy and the elders to continue this arrangement resulted in the appearance of pseudo-monks, who lowered the prestige of the Buddhist clergy and contributed to the failure of an attempt by Sir Arthur Phayre (chief commissioner of Lower Burma, 1862–67) to build a modern educational system using the monastic schools as its foundation. Phayre's successors recommended the foundation of government schools, but only a few were actually established. The government of India preferred to encourage foreign Christian missions to found schools by offering them "grants-in-aid."

Education under the British

Many mission schools were founded to which parents were forced to send their children because there were no alternatives. Because the teachers were missionaries, the lessons they gave were marked by repeated criticism of Buddhism and its culture. In the government schools the first teachers, British and Indian, were mere civil servants, unable and unwilling to continue the older traditions of education.

The British impact on the Burmese economy proved disastrous. This was not so much due to the usual economic exploitation of a country by a foreign ruler (the British were milder in this respect than were other colonial powers) as it was to the British policy of laissez-faire and to Burma's being made an Indian province. The British dream of a golden road to China through Burma could not be realized, but the opening of the Suez Canal in 1869 was equally golden, for it increased international demand for Burma's rice, which had never before been an important item of export. This development came in the wake of a change in Burma from a barter economy to a money economy. The Burmese peasant was both psychologically unprepared for and inexperienced in the use of cash; and under Burmese law, capital accumulations were almost impossible because the Burmese possessed no right of disposing property by will, so that a family estate had to be divided after the death of the parents among all sons and daughters.

The Irrawaddy Delta was swiftly cleared of its mangrove forests to become covered with rice fields. Even in 1857 the price of rice increased 25 percent; by 1890 the 1857 price had more than doubled and it continued to increase until the Depression in 1930. Tempted by the prevailing rice prices, the Burmese flocked to the delta; but in order to prepare the land for cultivation they had to borrow capital from Indian moneylenders from Madras at an interest rate of some 120 percent. The British banks would not grant loans on mortgage of rice land, and the British government had no policy for establishing land-mortgage banks or for making agricultural loans. Prevailing prices were high in the international market, but the local price was kept down by a handful of British firms that controlled wholesale trade and by Indian and Chinese merchants who controlled retail trade. Although the Burmese economy developed rapidly from 1890 to 1900, the Burmese people did not benefit from it. A railway had been built through the entire valley of the Irrawaddy, and hundreds of steamboats plied the entire length of the river; but the railway and the boats belonged to British companies. Roads had been built by the government, but they were meant for the swift transport of troops during frequent rebellions. A British company worked the ruby mines until they became exhausted. The extraction of oil and timber was monopolized by two British firms. The balance of trade was always in favour of Burma; but this was only on paper because there was no control or even record of foreign exchange remittances to their home countries by the British and Indian troops; the British, Indian, and Chinese merchants; the British and Indian civil servants; and the Indian labourers who came in thousands without any restrictions because they were merely travelling from one part of the Indian empire to another. With land values and rice prices soaring, the Indian moneylenders foreclosed mortgages at the earliest opportunity. The dispossessed farmers could not find employment even on their lost lands because, with a higher standard of living, they could not compete with Indian labourers. Burmese villagers, unemployed and lost in a disintegrating society, took to petty theft and robbery and soon acquired the reputation of being lazy and undisciplined.

The emergence of nationalism. Those Burmese who attended the new schools managed to gain admission to the clerical grades of government service, but even in those lower grades there was competition from Indians. Because science courses were not available, the professions of engineering and medicine were closed to the Burmese. Those who advanced to the government liberal arts college at Rangoon entered the middle grades of the civil service; a few went on to London to study law. When these young barristers returned to Burma they were looked upon as their new leaders by the people. Their sojourn in the liberal atmosphere of London had convinced these new leaders that some measure of political independence could be regained by negotiation. They first gave their attention to the national religion, culture, and education; in 1906 they founded the Young Men's Buddhist Association (YMBA) and established a number of schools supported by private donations and government grants-in-aid (the movement was not antigovernment). That same year the British, attempting to pacify the Indian National Congress, introduced some constitutional reforms in India. Only a few inferior changes were made in the Burmese constitution, but these confirmed the young leaders' faith in British liberalism. In 1920, however, when it was found that Burma would be excluded from new reforms introduced in India, the barristers led the people in a nationwide protest, which involved a boycott of British goods. In 1886, to humiliate the Burmese, the British had made Burma a part of India; they now found they could not exclude Burma from sharing benefits granted to India.

The new Burmese leaders

The following December, Rangoon College was raised to the status of a full university; but because its control was vested in a body of British professors and government nominees, its students went on strike. Younger schoolboys and schoolgirls followed suit. The strikers camped in the courtyards of monasteries, reviving memories of days when education was the concern of the monks. The general public and the Buddhist clergy gave full support to the strike. The University Act was amended, and the strike was settled; but many strikers refused to go back to mission and government schools. The YMBA schools, now calling themselves "National" schools, opened their doors to the strikers.

Constitutional reforms were finally granted in 1923; but the delay had split the leaders, some of whom, like the masses, were beginning to doubt whether political freedom could be attained by peaceful protest. In the University of Rangoon itself, students began to resent their

Thakin movement

British professors. A radical student group began protests, which came to be known as the Thakin movement (a term of derision, from *thakin*, "master," by which Burmese were required to address the British).

(M.H.Au.)

In 1931 Burmese peasants, under their leader Saya San, rose in rebellion. Armed only with swords and sticks, they resisted British and Indian troops for two years. The young Thakins won the trust of the villagers and emerged as leaders in place of the liberals. In 1936 university students again went on strike, and two of their leaders, U Nu and Aung San, joined the Thakin movement, adding strength to it. In 1937 the British government separated Burma from India, but the masses interpreted this as proof that the British planned to exclude Burma from the next phase of Indian reform.

When World War II broke out in Europe in 1939, the Burmese sympathized with Britain, but they wanted to bargain with the government before giving their support. A warrant was issued for the arrest of Aung San, but he escaped to China, where he attempted to contact radical groups for support. Japanese assistance was offered instead; he returned to Burma in secret, recruited 29 young men, and took them to Japan, where the "Thirty Comrades" received military training. The Japanese promised independence for Burma; hence, when Japanese troops reached Bangkok, Aung San announced the formation of the Burma Independence Army. Independence was not declared, however, and Aung San and his army began to conspire against Japan. When the Japanese administration learned of the plot, they disbanded the Independence Army and formed a smaller Burma Defense Army, with Aung San still as commander.

Ba Maw, the first prime minister under the 1937 constitution and later the leader of the opposition, was appointed head of state, with a Cabinet including Gen. Aung San and U Nu. In 1943, when the tide of battle started to turn against the Japanese, they declared Burma a fully sovereign state. But the Burmese government was still a mere facade, with the Japanese army ruling. Aung San contacted Lord Mountbatten, the Allied commander in Southeast Asia, offering cooperation, and in March 1945, on receiving Mountbatten's "go ahead," Aung San and his army joined the British side.

The AFPFL

After the liberation of Rangoon, Aung San and the Thakins formed a coalition of all parties under the name Anti-Fascist People's Freedom League (AFPFL). At this critical moment the British military administration showed their old prejudices. But Lord Mountbatten hastily sent a major general, Sir Hubert Rance, to head the administration; and Rance, with a conciliatory attitude, regained for the British the trust of Aung San and the general public. When the war ended, the military administration was withdrawn, and Rance was replaced by the former civilian governor, who formed a Cabinet consisting of older and more conservative politicians. The new administration arrested Aung San on a criminal charge. Surprised and angered, the Burmese people prepared for rebellion; but the British government in London wisely replaced the governor with Rance, now retired from the army. Rance formed a new Cabinet, including Aung San, and discussions for a peaceful transfer of power began. These were concluded in London in January 1947, when the British agreed to Burma's independence and its leaving the Commonwealth of Nations.

The Communist and conservative wings of the AFPFL were dissatisfied with the agreement. The Communists broke away and went underground, and the conservatives went into opposition. In July Aung San and most members of his Cabinet were assassinated by gunmen sent by U Saw, a former prime minister and now a conservative. Rance asked U Nu to form a new Cabinet. On January 4, 1948, Burma became the Union of Burma, a sovereign independent republic.

Burmese independence

The national period. With its economy shattered and its towns and villages destroyed during the war, independent Burma needed some years of peace; a foreign policy of neutrality was decided upon, but because of internal strife no peace resulted. The Communists were the first insurgents, followed by Aung San's veterans, and then the Karens, the only ethnic minority on the plains; but the other minorities—Chins, Kachins, and Shans—who had been ruled separately by the British but who had enthusiastically joined the union, stood firm.

A division of Chinese Nationalist troops occupied parts of the Shan Plateau after China had fallen to the Communists in 1949; and because of the United States' general support for Nationalist China, Burma stopped accepting American aid and became prejudiced against all foreign aid. At the UN, Burma endeavoured to show impartiality. It was one of the first countries to recognize Israel and also the People's Republic of China.

In 1958 Burma was well on the road to internal peace and economic recovery when the ruling AFPFL was divided by personal quarrels between U Nu and his closest associates. Amid rumours of a military takeover, U Nu invited the army chief of staff, Gen. Ne Win—who had been a Thakin, one of the Thirty Comrades, and Aung San's second in command—to take the premiership. Ne Win prepared the country for general elections, which took place in February 1960. The opponents were the two sections of the AFPFL, and U Nu was returned to office with an absolute majority. His followers now quarrelled among themselves, however.

Socialist takeover. In March 1962 Gen. Ne Win led a coup d'etat and arrested U Nu, the chief justice, and Cabinet ministers. Suspending the constitution, he ruled the country with a revolutionary council made up of senior military officers. His stated purpose was to make Burma a socialist state. Land had been nationalized in U Nu's administration, and now all commerce and industry were nationalized as well; the economy did not improve, however. A one-party (Burma Socialist Programme Party) system was established, and measures were introduced to decentralize the administration. In April 1972 Gen. Ne Win and other members of the revolutionary council retired from the army.

New constitution

U Ne Win promised a new constitution, and in September 1971 representatives of the party's central committee, of the country's various ethnic groups, and of other interest groups were appointed to draft a document. Committee members toured extensively, inviting criticism and suggestions. A referendum to ratify the new constitution was held in December 1973, with more than 90 percent of nearly 15,000,000 eligible voters signifying approval. Elections to the Pyithu Hlutdaw (People's Council)—the supreme legislative, executive, and judicial authority—and to local People's Councils were held early in 1974; the new government was established on March 2 with U Ne Win as president of the Socialist Republic of the Union of Burma.

Despite the new political organization, Burma's economy continued to stagnate in the late 1970s. Student and worker unrest erupted periodically, and Communist and ethnic insurgency continued in the eastern part of the country.

(Ed.)

BIBLIOGRAPHY. U AUNG THAW, "Neolithic Culture of Padhalin Caves," *Journal of Burma Research Society*, vol. 52 (1969), contains a good account of the Stone Age in Burma. See also the articles by G.H. LUCE on the Pyus, Mons, and Early Burmese, *ibid.*, vol. 27 (1932), vol. 34 (1950), and vol. 43 (1959); to be read with MAUNG HTIN AUNG, *Burmese History Before 1287: A Defence of the Chronicles* (1970). A.P. PHAYRE, *A History of Burma* (1883, reissued 1969); and G.E. HARVEY, *A History of Burma* (1925, reissued 1969), are standard works for the pre-British period (*i.e.*, to 1824). G.E. HARVEY, *British Rule in Burma, 1824–1942* (1946; reprinted 1974), attempts to justify British rule. DOROTHY WOODMAN, *The Making of Burma* (1962); MAUNG MAUNG, *Burma in the Family of Nations*, 2nd ed. rev. (1957); and MAUNG HTIN AUNG, *The Stricken Peacock: Anglo-Burmese Relations, 1752–1948* (1965), deal with the history of Anglo-Burmese relations. H. TINKER, *The Union of Burma*, 4th ed. (1967); and FRANK N. TRAGER, *Burma: From Kingdom to Republic* (1966), give the history for the post-independence (1948) period. The only book dealing comprehensively with Burmese history is MAUNG HTIN AUNG, *A History of Burma* (1967). D.G.E. HALL, *A History of Southeast Asia*, 3rd ed. (1968), contains chapters on Burmese history that give the British view.

(M.H.Au.)

Burns, Robert

Robert Burns is the poet of the realized moment of experience, of human feelings purged of all the accretions and falsifications of idealization and generalization. The greatest Scottish poet after the Middles Ages, he is his country's national poet, celebrated annually with rites associated with no other man of letters anywhere.

Burns, oil painting by Alexander Nasmyth (1758–1840). In the National Portrait Gallery, London.
By courtesy of the National Portrait Gallery, London

LIFE

Burns was born at Alloway, Ayrshire, on Jan. 25, 1759. His father had come to Ayrshire from Kincardineshire in an endeavour to improve his fortunes, but though he worked immensely hard first on the farm of Mount Oliphant, which he leased in 1766, and then on that of Lochlea, which he took in 1777, ill luck dogged him, and he died in 1784, worn out and bankrupt. It was watching his father being thus beaten down that helped to make Robert both a rebel against the social order of his day and a bitter satirist of all forms of religious and political thought that condoned or perpetuated inhumanity. He received some formal schooling from a teacher as well as sporadically from other sources; he acquired a superficial reading knowledge of French and a bare smattering of Latin, and he read most of the important 18th-century English writers as well as Shakespeare, Milton, and Dryden. His knowledge of Scottish literature was confined in his childhood to orally transmitted folk songs and folk tales together with a modernization of the late 15th-century poem "Wallace," a work that "poured a Scottish prejudice in my veins, which will boil along there till the flood-gates of life shut in eternal rest." Burns also studied biblical history, world geography, and English grammar; and he learned some physics, astronomy, and botany from such books as William Derham's *Physico-Theology* and *Astro-Theology* and John Ray's *The Wisdom of God Manifested in the Works of the Creation*, which presented scientific facts as arguments for the existence of God as a benevolent designer. Burns's religion throughout his adult life seem to have been a humanitarian deism.

Proud, restless, and full of a nameless ambition, the young Robert Burns did his share of hard work on the family farm. After his father's death he was head of the household and tenant of the farm of Mossgiel to which the family moved. But he had already started writing poetry, in which the tone of Scottish folk song and that of 18th-century sentimental and meditative poetry were strangely mingled. Early in 1783 he began to keep a commonplace book in which he entered his first poem (a song, written for a specific folk tune) in April, preceded by the comment: "There is certainly some connection between Love and Music and Poetry . . . I never had the least thought or inclination of turning Poet till I once got heartily in Love, and then Rhyme and Song were, in a manner, a spontaneous language of my heart." The poem is an unpretentious, lilting piece written in an English tipped with Scots, but it becomes pure neoclassic English in the final stanza. Shortly afterward he entered in the commonplace book sentimental, melodramatic, or melancholy pieces whose thought reflected the family misfortunes of the time and whose vocabulary and manner derived from minor 18th-century English poets. He was cultivating, in a heavily self-conscious way, a gloomy sensibility. But suddenly we come across a lively, swinging piece deriving from the Scottish folk tradition rather than from contemporary English sentimentalists: "My father was a farmer upon the Carrick border O." This was entered in the commonplace book in 1784, with an apologetic note that it was "miserably deficient in Versification." Meanwhile, his father's death freed him to seek male and female companionship where he would. He took sides against the dominant extreme Calvinist wing of the church in Ayrshire and championed a local gentleman, Gavin Hamilton, who had got into trouble with the Kirk Session for sabbath breaking. He had an affair with a servant girl at the farm, Elizabeth Paton, who in 1785 bore his first illegitimate child, and on the child's birth he welcomed it with a lively poem. This poem was written in a stanza that had had a long history in Scottish poetry and had been used by Allan Ramsay and Robert Fergusson. Even more purely in the Scottish literary tradition is "The Death and Dying Words of Poor Mailie," entered in the commonplace book in June 1785; this is a "mock testament" put into the mouth of a dying sheep, done with shrewd, ironical humour and considerable technical adroitness. Burns by now had available to him not only the Scottish folk tradition but also at least some of the traditions of Scottish "art" poetry, both as they came to him through Fergusson and as he found them for himself in 18th-century collections of older Scottish poetry.

First poetry

Burns developed rapidly throughout 1784 and 1785 as an "occasional" poet who more and more turned to verse to express his emotions of love, friendship, or amusement or his ironical contemplation of the social scene. But these were not spontaneous effusions by an almost-illiterate peasant. Burns was a conscious craftsman; his entries in the commonplace book reveal that from the beginning he was interested in the technical problems of versification. If he never learned to distinguish emotional control from emotional self-indulgence in 18th-century English poetry, he did learn to appreciate economy, cogency, and variety in the work of Pope and others, and, most important of all, he learned from older Scots literature to handle Scottish literary forms and stanza patterns, particularly in descriptive and satirical verse, with assurance and cunning. From the oral folk tradition he learned a great deal about song rhythms and the fitting of words to music; and out of his own Ayrshire speech, his knowledge of older Scots, and his reading in standard English, he fashioned a flexible Scots–English idiom which, though hardly a literary language in the sense that Robert Henryson's or William Dunbar's language was in 15th- and 16th-century Scottish verse, proved to be an effective medium for a poetry that was distinctly Scottish without being antiquarian.

Though he wrote poetry for his own amusement and that of his friends, Burns remained restless and dissatisfied. He won the reputation of being a dangerous rebel against orthodox religion, and when in 1786 he fell in love with Jean Armour, her father refused to allow her to marry Burns even though a child was on the way and under Scots law mutual consent followed by consummation constituted a legal marriage. Jean was persuaded by her father to go back on her promise; Robert, hurt and enraged, took up with another girl, Mary Campbell, who died soon after; on September 3 Jean bore him twins out of wedlock. Meanwhile, the farm was not prospering, and Burns, harassed by insoluble emotional and economic problems, thought of emigrating to Jamaica. But he first wanted to show his country what he could do. In the midst of his troubles with the Armours (Armour threatened to sue him to provide for the upkeep of Jean's as yet unborn child) he went ahead with his plans for publishing a volume of his poems at the nearby town of Kilmarnock. It was entitled *Poems, Chiefly in the Scottish Dialect,* and appeared on July 31, 1786. Its success was immediate and overwhelming. Simple country folk and sophisticated Edinburgh critics alike hailed it, and the upshot was that Burns set out for Edinburgh on Nov. 27, 1786, to be lionized, patronized, and showered with well-meant but dangerous advice.

The Kilmarnock poems

The Kilmarnock volume was a remarkable mixture. It included a handful of first-rate Scots poems: "The Twa Dogs," "Scotch Drink," "The Holy Fair," "An Address to the Deil," "The Death and Dying Words of Poor Mailie," "To a Mouse," "To a Louse," and some others, including a number of verse letters addressed to various friends. There were also a few Scots poems in which he was unable to sustain his inspiration or that are spoiled by a confused purpose. In addition, there were six gloomy and histrionic poems in English, four songs, of which only one, "It Was Upon a Lammas Night," showed promise of his future greatness as a song writer, and, what to contemporary reviewers seemed the stars of the volume, "The Cotter's Saturday Night" and "To a Mountain Daisy."

Burns selected his Kilmarnock poems with care: he was anxious to impress a genteel Edinburgh audience. In his preface he played up to contemporary sentimental views about the natural man and the noble peasant, exaggerated his lack of education, pretended to a lack of natural resources (which was ridiculous in the light of the careful craftsmanship that his poetry displays), and in general acted a part. The trouble is that he was only half acting. He was uncertain enough about the genteel tradition to accept much of it at its face value, and though, to his ultimate glory, he kept returning to what his own instincts told him was the true path for him to follow, far too many of his poems are marred by a naïve and sentimental moralizing. "The Cotter's Saturday Night," which has stanzas of quiet beauty and impressive craftsmanship, also contains passages of intolerable histrionics and others where sharply etched realism and grandiose theatrical generalizations stand oddly side by side: Burns was not certain whether he was projecting a picture of Scottish peasant life from the inside or showing off the Scottish peasant for the edification of connoisseurs of sentimental beauties in Edinburgh.

Edinburgh unsettled Burns, and after a number of amorous and other adventures there, and several trips to other parts of Scotland, he settled in the summer of 1788 at a farm in Ellisland, Dumfriesshire, leased to him by an admirer who was nevertheless a shrewd landlord. At Edinburgh, too, he arranged for a new and enlarged edition (1787) of his poems, but little of significance was added to the Kilmarnock selection. Substantially, it was by the Kilmarnock poems that Burns was known in his lifetime. He found farming at Ellisland difficult, though he was helped by Jean Armour, with whom he had been reconciled and whom he finally married in 1788, to the annoyance of Mrs. Agnes Maclehose (the "Clarinda" of the poems), an Edinburgh woman, separated from her husband. Burns had been carrying on a violent flirtation with her, which produced some indifferent lyrics and, at the final parting, one great song, "Ae Fond Kiss."

Marriage

In Edinburgh Burns had met James Johnson, a keen collector of Scottish songs who was bringing out a series of volumes of songs with the music, and enlisted Burns's help in finding, editing, improving, and rewriting items. Burns was enthusiastic and soon became virtual editor of Johnson's *Scots Musical Museum.* Later, he became involved with a similar project for George Thomson, but Thomson was a more consciously genteel person than Johnson, and Burns had to fight with him to prevent him from "refining" words and music and so ruining their character. The six volumes of Johnson's *Scots Musical Museum* (1787–1803) and the eight parts of Thomson's *Select Collection of Original Scotish Airs for the Voice* (1793–1818) contain the bulk of Burns's songs. Burns spent the latter part of his life in assiduously collecting and writing songs to provide words for traditional Scottish airs and to keep Johnson and Thomson going. He regarded his work as service to Scotland and quixotically refused payment. The only poem he wrote after his Edinburgh visit that showed a hitherto unsuspected side of his poetic genius was *Tam o'Shanter,* a spirited, narrative poem in brilliantly handled eight-syllable couplets based on a folk legend associated with Alloway Kirk.

Meanwhile, Burns corresponded with and visited on terms of equality a great variety of literary and other people who were considerably "above" him socially. He was an admirable letter writer and a brilliant talker, and he could hold his own in any company. At the same time, he was still a struggling tenant farmer, and the attempt to keep himself going in two different social and intellectual capacities was wearing him down. After trying for a long time, he finally obtained a post in the excise service in 1789 and moved to Dumfries in 1791, where he lived until his death on July 21, 1796, caused by rheumatic heart disease contracted in his youth as a result of too much physical exertion on an inadequate diet. (The myth that Burns died of drink has long since been exploded.) His life at Dumfries was active. He wrote numerous "occasional" poems on contemporary political and other events and did an immense amount of work for the two song collections, in addition to carrying out his duties as exciseman. The outbreak of the French Revolution excited him, and some indiscreet outbursts nearly lost him his job at a time when the excesses of the French revolutionaries had provoked the fiercest political reaction in Scotland. But his reputation as a good exciseman and a politic but humiliating recantation saved him. It was his attitude to the French Revolution, too, that estranged him from Mrs. Dunlop, an elderly female admirer who was genuinely fond of Burns and had been a real friend to him.

ASSESSMENT

Burns was a man of great intellectual energy and force of character who, in a class-ridden society, never found an environment in which he could fully exercise his personality. After his death the lively literary lady Maria Riddell wrote a character sketch of him in the *Dumfries Journal* in which she said that his powers of conversation, his impromtu wit, his ability to grasp new ideas, his intolerance of stupidity and arrogance, his capacity for devastating ironic comment were in her opinion even more impressive than his poetry. But it was not only the class structure of his society, which led to his being alternately patronized and sentimentalized over, that constricted him. The fact is that Scottish culture in his day could provide no intellectual background that might replace the Calvinism that Burns rejected. The Edinburgh literati of Burns's day were second raters. But the problem was more than one of personalities. The only substitute for the rejected Calvinism seemed to be a sentimental deism, a facile belief in the good heart as all, and this was not a creed rich or complex enough to nourish great poetry. That Burns in spite of this produced so much fine poetry shows the strength of his unique and remarkable genius, and that he has become the Scottish national poet is a tribute to his hold on the popular imagination.

Burns perhaps exhibited his greatest poetic powers in his satires. There is also a remarkable craftsmanship in his verse letters, which display a most adroit counterpointing of the colloquial and the formal. But it is by his songs that Burns is best known, and it is his songs that have carried his reputation round the world. Burns is without doubt the greatest song writer Britain has produced. He found Scottish song in a confused and fragmentary state. Scottish airs had been popular since the latter part of the 17th century, and many collections of Scottish songs and song tunes appeared both in Edinburgh and London in the 18th century. But the great majority of older songs survived only in fragments.

Songs

Burns's aim was to recover as many airs and sets of words as he could, and where the existing words were fragmentary, impossibly coarse, or equally impossibly genteel, to re-create the song in the true spirit of the folk tradition. It was a staggering program, nothing less than the single-handed re-creation of the whole body of Scottish folk song. Further, Burns undertook to provide words to tunes that now existed only as dance tunes. He was anxious that all Scotland should be represented, and in his journeys scrupulously collected such songs and fragments as he could find to rework them into complete songs. His journeys can be traced in the provenance of the songs: a fisherman's song from Fife, an old Aberdeen folksong, a song about an alehouse keeper by the Moray Firth and innumerable love songs connected with particular hills, valleys, streams, and woods in various Scottish counties. If Burns had not been uncannily in tune with the folk spirit in Scottish song, he would be execrated today for having spoiled the original fragments by artificial improvements. But in fact he did not spoil them; he saved them from total corruption and disappearance and gave them new life and meaning and popularity.

Burns wrote all his songs to known tunes, sometimes writing several sets of words to the same air in an endeavor to find the most apt poem for a given melody. Many songs which, it is clear from a variety of evidence, must have been substantially written by Burns he never claimed as his. He never claimed "Auld Lang Syne," for example, which he described simply as an old fragment he had discovered, but the song we have is almost certainly his, though the chorus and probably the first stanza are old. (Burns wrote it for a simple and moving old air that is *not* the tune to which it is now sung, as Thomson set it to another tune.) The full extent of Burns's work on Scottish song will probably never be known.

It is positively miraculous that Burns was able to enter into the spirit of older folk song and re-create, out of an old chorus, such songs as "I'm O'er Young to Marry Yet," "Green Grow the Rashes, O," and a host of others. It is this uncanny ability to speak with the great anonymous voice of the Scottish people that explains the special feeling that Burns arouses, feelings that manifest themselves in the "Burns cult." But his songs are not all in a simple folk idiom, though most of them have that air of simplicity (whatever the subtleties below the surface) so necessary to a sung poem. There is the symbolic colour and imagery of "Open the Door to Me Oh" that so impressed William Butler Yeats:

The wan moon sets behind the white wave,
And time is setting with me, Oh!

A wonderful mixture of tenderness and swagger appears in "A Red, Red Rose," Burns's rewriting of an old fragment. In the controlled historical melancholy of the Jacobite songs Burns gives this romantic lost cause a new meaning in terms of human emotion:

Now a' is done that men can do,
And a' is done in vain:
My Love and Native Land fareweel,
For I maun cross the main, my dear,
For I maun cross the main.

In contrast there is a brilliant counterpointing of folk feeling and high ceremony, of simple emotion and pageantry, in the poem beginning "Go fetch to me a pint o' wine," where the whole atmosphere of medieval romance and ballad is concentrated in two stanzas. There is the magical tenderness of "O Lay Thy Loof in Mine Lass" though there the tune is particularly important. There is the lilting love song he composed to one of his wife's favourite airs, "The Posie":

O luv will venture in where it daur na weel be seen,
O luve will venture in where wisdom ance has been; . . .

There is that sprightly piece of ironic self-compliment, "There Was a Lad Was Born in Kyle." There is the moving benedictory cadence, so perfectly wrought together with the music, in "Ca' the Yowes to the Knowes":

Ghaist nor bogle shalt thou fear;
Thou'rt to Love and Heaven sae dear,
Nocht of Ill may come thee near,
My bonnie Dearie.

and the protective gentleness of "Oh, Wert Thou in the Cauld Blast," written as he lay dying for Jessie Lewars who helped nurse him, to her favourite air, "Lennox Love to Blantyre." Here the dying man reversed the actual roles of himself and the girl and wrote as the protecting male. (All excerpts from James Kinsley, *The Poems and Songs of Robert Burns;* Claredon Press, Oxford, 1968).

Lyrical diversity

Love songs, work songs, drinking songs—Burns achieved brilliant success in all three varieties. He is one of the few love poets who relates sex to paternity and maternity, who links the sexual ecstasy with the prospect of children, who never isolates sexual passion into a Platonic ideal removed from given human relationships but keeps it always grounded in the known facts of experience. And he could sing the songs of either sex. Where else in English—or Scottish—literature can be found the happy audacity of the song beginning "O Wha my babie-clouts will buy," the song he put into the mouth of Jean Armour when she was about to bear his child, which expresses both the female joy in sexual surrender and the female joy in maternity? Burns does not idealize lust, but he localizes and even domesticates it, something much more difficult to do. His bawdiest songs, derived from Scottish folk material, had to wait until 1965 before they were published for the general public in *The Merry Muses of Caledonia.* (A semiprivate edition had appeared six years earlier.) He is not a "romantic" poet. He never waxes enthusiastic over the mountains or the sea (he never mentions the former and very rarely the latter), but he sees the landscape of the countryside as a context within which the rhythms of human emotions and the farmer's year act themselves out.

MAJOR WORKS

Burns's first collection of *Poems, Chiefly in the Scottish Dialect* (July 1786; "the Kilmarnock edition"), contains 44 of Burns's best-known poems. The Edinburgh edition of April 1787 adds 22 poems, including "Address to the Unco Guid, or the Rigidly Righteous," "The Brigs of Ayr," and "Tam o' Shanter." The last edition to be supervised by Burns, 2 vol. (February 1793), adds another 19. James Johnson's collection, *The Scots Musical Museum*, 6 vol. (1787–1803), includes some 200 songs and fragments, with some airs, written, revised, or collected by Burns. More than 70 songs are included in George Thomson's *A Select Collection of Original Scotish Airs for the Voice*, 8 pt. (1793–1818).

BIBLIOGRAPHY. J.W. EGERER, *A Bibliography of Robert Burns* (1964), is the most complete listing of all the appearances of Burn's poetical and prose works between 1786 and 1802 and of all "formal" editions (including translations) up to the date of publication.

Editions: Many of Burns's poems and songs remained unpublished or uncollected in his lifetime; a full and definitive text of all those both acknowledged by him as his and now thought to be his may be found only in JAMES KINSLEY (ed.), *The Poems and Songs of Robert Burns*, 3 vol. (1968), containing full critical apparatus and commentary. A one-volume abridged edition without the apparatus and commentary appeared in 1969. Some famous earlier editions that include valuable biographical commentary are: J. CURRIE, *The Works of Robert Burns, with an Account of His Life and a Criticism on His Writings*, 4 vol. (1800); R. CHAMBERS (ed.), *The Life and Works of Robert Burns*, 4 vol. (1856–57), a work of massive scholarship, and its revision by W. WALLACE (the famous "Chambers-Wallace" edition, 1896), both of which are classics; and the centenary edition, W.E. HENLEY AND T.F. HENDERSON (eds.), *The Poetry of Robert Burns*, 4 vol. (1896–97), including valuable notes. The standard edition of Burns's letters is J. DE L. FERGUSON (ed.), *The Letters of Robert Burns*, 2 vol. (1931): Ferguson also has a useful one-volume *Selected Letters* (1953).

Biography and criticism: J.G. LOCKHART, *The Life of Robert Burns* (1828), was long a popular classic but contains some inaccuracies, The standard modern biography is F.B. SNYDER, *The Life of Robert Burns* (1932); although R.T. FITZHUGH, *Robert Burns: The Man and the Poet* (1970), adds some factual details and is very full. J. DE L. FERGUSON, *Pride and Passion: Robert Burns, 1759–1796* (1939), is an admirable portrait of Burns the man. D. DAICHES, *Robert Burns*, rev. ed. (1966), gives a full account of both the man and the poetry, while the same author's *Robert Burns and His World* (1971), sets the man and his work clearly in the context of his time and place. T. CRAWFORD, *Burns: A Study of the Poems and Songs* (1960), is a critical and scholarly study for the student.

(D.Da.)

Burns

Burns are a major and unique problem in the field of injury and surgery. In the majority of other injuries or forms of surgery, a person usually remains in a precarious balance between life and death for only a few days and then either recuperates or succumbs. After one has experienced deep or extensive burns, his life remains in jeopardy for weeks; and he must receive intelligent and unremitting care if he is to survive.

The problems encountered in the treatment of burns were so great and so unfathomable that until recently only a few doctors would devote the time required to caring for burn patients. Probably in no other field of medicine has so little progress been made and treatment been so mismanaged. Only after World War II have there been significant advances in the theory and practice of burn trauma management.

Early treatments of burns

Since ancient times, burns have been mishandled. Emollient preparations with bizarre ingredients were placed on the burn wound as a standard form of treatment. Purgation and bleeding were popular treatments throughout the Middle Ages. Until recently the best form of treatment prescribed consisted of washing the burn wound with soap and water, leaving it exposed to the air, and giving the patient salt water to drink.

In 1607, Fabricius Hildanus recognized three degrees of burns. In 1750 David Cleghorn recognized that purgation was harmful to the patient. By 1905, some physicians were cognizant of the fluid and salt losses sustained by the burn patient. In some medical circles, intravenous salt solutions were prescribed. More appreciation of the enormous quantities of water, salt, and protein losses was shown by Frank Pell Underhill in 1930, by Oliver Cope and F.D. Moore in 1947, and by E.T. Evans in 1952. Although it had been performed earlier, skin grafting came upon a firm basis through the work of Jacques Louis Reverdin in 1869; Karl Thiersch in 1874; and Blair, Brown, and Davis in 1939.

Local treatments of all types have been tried through the centuries. No local treatment that was not actually harmful was used, however, until Alexander Burns Wallace, Truman Graves Blocker, and Edwin J. Pulaski popularized the exposure method of burn treatment in the late 1940s. This method had previously been described but had been discarded in favour of methods such as treatment with tannic acid, gentian violet, and concentrated silver nitrate.

The Brooke Army Surgical Research Group in San Antonio, Texas, emphasized in 1953 that septicemia was a major cause of death in burns. Probably the most important recent advance in the treatment of burns has been the local application of bacteriostatic agents. The Brooke Army Group also popularized homografting (grafts taken from another person) and heterografting (grafts taken from animals) as a means of temporary physiologic coverage of the burn wound. The patient with a deep burn must eventually be covered with his own skin, however, as skin from other people or animals is rejected, just as other transplants tend to be rejected, except among identical twins.

CLASSIFICATION OF BURNS

Depth. In the past, the depth of a burn has usually been classified as being one of three degrees: first, second, or third degree. The first-degree burn is a redness of the skin such as is seen in sunburn; the second-degree burn is a partial-thickness burn with blister formation such as is seen in hot-water burns; the third-degree burn is a full-thickness burn such as is seen in clothing burns (Figure 1).

Classification of burns by degree

The first and third classifications have remained essentially accepted but, in recent years, many different depths have been observed within the second-degree burn classification—the partial-thickness burns. E.R. Crews subdivides the second-degree classification into "superficial second-degree burns" and "deep second-degree burns." In part, this differentiation in classification within the second-degree burn category arose from the observation that spontaneous healing or epithelization occurs in some burned areas that, upon initial examination, appear to be full-thickness burns.

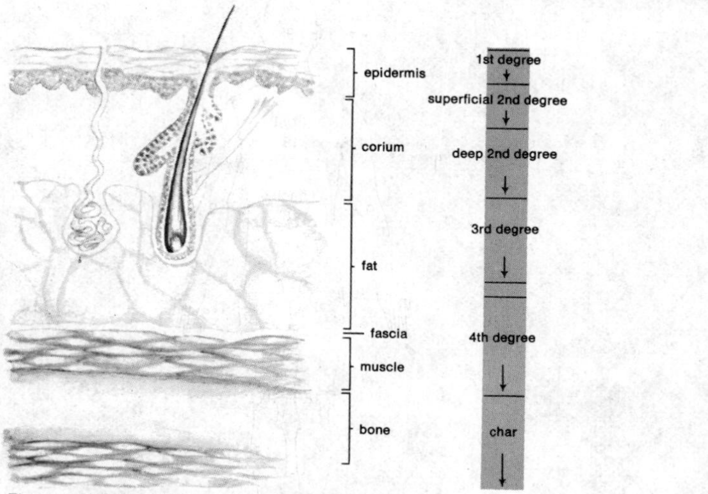

Figure 1: Depth of burn as classified by degree.
By courtesy of E.R. Crews, *A Practical Manual for the Treatment of Burns*, 1st ed. (1964); Charles C. Thomas

With newer drugs and improved methods in the use of bacteriostatic local agents (agents that suppress bacterial growth in the wound), the bacterial flora has been reduced to such an extent that there is little interference with spontaneous healing. Even though some of the deeper second-degree burns do not epithelize within the usual time (40 days), the grafting area is reduced and the graft takes are better, with a more satisfactory end result. In the past, partial-thickness burns were converted to full-thickness burns because of infection. Third-degree burns, or full-thickness burns, result in coagulation necrosis (death) of all layers of the skin. Deeper burns that involve fat, muscle, and bones may be classified as fourth-degree burns.

Without infection, superficial second-degree burns will heal in approximately two weeks. Deeper second-degree burns are not usually healed within three weeks; but within 21 to 30 days the crust is separated and one may observe deep layers of skin (corium) with a pigskin appearance, in contrast to raw or granulation tissue that is observed at this time in third-degree or full-thickness burns.

Area and relationship to survival. The area of the burn, the depth of the burn, and the age of the patient generally determine the survival of the burned patient. Except in the aged, the physician may expect survival with a much more extensive second-degree burn than in a full-thickness burn. Patients with second-degree burns over 70 percent of the body commonly survive. Patients with third-degree burns of this magnitude usually succumb; only rarely does a patient with a 50 percent or greater third-degree burn survive.

There are generally two methods of measuring the extent of the burn. Figure 2 illustrates the "Rule of Nines." With this method the physician can make an immediate gross estimate of the percentage of the body surface that is burned. Figure 3, the Lund and Browder method, illustrates a way of determining the exact percentage of the burn with greater precision. The latter method is more accurate in infants and children, since the proportional area of the head becomes less while the proportional area of the thighs and legs becomes greater with increasing age. A deep burn of 15 to 30 percent in the elderly patient will frequently be fatal because of the long periods of relative immobility, the lowered resistance among the elderly, and the more frequent complications.

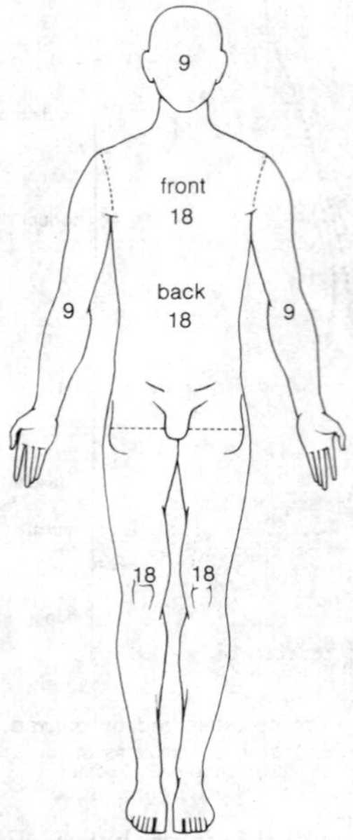

Figure 2: Estimation of percentage burn, rule of nines method.

Courtesy of E.R. Crews, *A Practical Manual for the Treatment of Burns* (1967); Charles C. Thomas

To some extent, though not as much as in the past, the area of the body whereon a patient is burned determines somewhat his chances of survival and freedom from infection. Burns of the upper thighs, buttocks, perineum, and back more commonly become infected than other areas of the body. Circumferential burns are more prone to infection, and thus the incidence of morbidity and mortality is higher.

Occasionally burns deeper than a full thickness of the skin are incurred, as when a person or a part of his body is entrapped in a flame and not immediately extricated. Electrical burns are usually deep burns. These deep burns frequently go into the subcutaneous tissue and, at times, beyond and into the muscle, fascia, and bone. Such burns are of the fourth degree, also called black (because of the typical colour of the burn), or char, burns. Fourth-degree burns are of grave prognosis, particularly if they involve more than a small portion of the body. In these deep burns toxic materials may be released into the bloodstream. If the char burn involves only a small part of the body, it should be excised down to healthy tissue. If an extremity is involved, amputation may be indicated.

Respiratory burns are rare; when they do occur, they, too, are of grave prognosis. Smoke inhalation burns are more common. These burns occur in enclosed places from which a person cannot free himself within a few minutes. Carbon particles are inhaled into the tracheobronchial tree and cause much irritation of the tracheobronchial mucosa. There is a high instance of pneumonic complications in this type of burn. When smoke inhalation occurs with an extensive burn, it worsens the chances of survival.

PATHOLOGIC CHANGES AND PHYSIOLOGIC RESPONSES

The pathologic effects resulting from a burn are due mainly to the intensity and the duration of the heat. For example, if an area burned by boiling water is exposed to the air, the heat (100° C) is quickly dissipated, with a resultant superficial second-degree burn. Gasoline explosions, while of high heat intensity, are momentary and usually result in superficial burns. Hot cereal, hot tar, or prolonged immersion in hot water will inflict a deeper burn. Flaming clothes (fire burn) are of high-intensity heat, and clothing takes a relatively long time to burn completely. Such burns are usually full-thickness or deep second-degree burns. Other less common causes of burns include chemicals, chiefly strong acids and alkalies; X-radiation; and ultraviolet light. Internal burns are occasionally seen, such as the burning of the esophagus from swallowing lye.

Fluid losses in second-degree burns

Superficial second-degree burns. When the physician first observes superficial second-degree burns, often 30 minutes or more after burning, there is already blister formation with surrounding areas of redness. Some of the blisters are likely to have been ruptured. This is commonly called a "weeping burn," since fluid continues to weep from the surface for 24 to 36 hours. If a thick gauze dressing is applied, the dressing will usually become wet throughout within eight hours. In this type of burn, there is usually destruction of the epidermis. Contrary to popular belief, the visible fluid losses constitute only a small fraction of the total amount of fluid that is functionally lost; greater fluid losses occur deep in the wound. Underneath the wound surface, there is vasodilatation, loss of capillary integrity, with capillary permeability into the tissue spaces. This causes a leakage of fluid into the area immediately beneath the burned skin.

The fluid is mainly a salt solution, the composition of which approximates that of blood plasma. There is also some leakage of plasma, mainly of the albumin fraction; but this is of no great consequence in superficial burns. Thrombosis of small vessels in and around the wound is of little consequence in this type of burn. Fluid losses in the burn wound cease within 36 to 48 hours, and after 48 hours the fluid is slowly reabsorbed. Within approximately one week, the vascular continuity is restored. It takes approximately two weeks for this type of burn to heal if it does not become infected. The fluid and salt loss from the vascular system is considerable. This loss varies according to the percentage of the body surface area affected.

Courtesy of E.R. Crews, *A Practical Manual for the Treatment of Burns* (1967); Charles C. Thomas

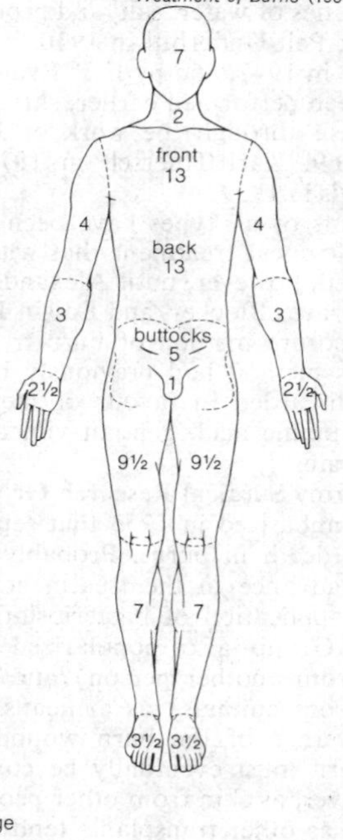

areas variable with age

	birth	1 year	5 years	10 years	15 years	adult
head	19	17	13	11	9	7
both thighs	11	13	16	17	18	19
both legs	10	10	11	12	13	14

areas not variable with age

neck	2	genitalia	1	both forearms	6
anterior trunk	13	both buttocks	5	both hands	5
posterior trunk	13	both upper arms	8	both feet	7

Figure 3: Estimation of percentage burn, Lund and Browder method (see text).

Deep burns. All burns deeper than a superficial second-degree burn will be described herein as deep burns. This includes deep second-, third-, and fourth-degree burns. The pathologic physiology of these burns will be described as a unit, since the fluid losses are similar, although the destruction and stages of repair are different.

In these deep burns, there is an immediate coagulation necrosis of the skin. There is very little weeping from the surface. Immediately under the skin, in the subcutaneous tissue, there is a loss of integrity of the capillaries, the venules, and arterioles, with vascular occlusion and thrombosis. There is agglutination of red cells within all the surrounding small vessels. The deeper the burn, the more pronounced and widespread the thrombosis. As a result, there is generalized sludging of blood within the blood vessels in and around the area of the burn, causing decreased blood flow with hypoxia to the area of the burn. In deep burns, the nerve endings are destroyed, and there is little or no pain in the region of the burn.

The resultant injury causes a leakage of salt-rich and plasma-like fluid into the burn beneath the burn surface. This loss is uncontrollable, rapid, and persistent. Until it is reabsorbed by the body, this fluid remains stagnant; and there is almost no circulation underneath the burn wound surface. The body's immediate reaction is comparable to that seen with acute hemorrhage; there is rapid pulse, generalized vasoconstriction, and thirst; but there is not much immediate loss of red blood cells.

Loss of salts, proteins and plasma

The predominant losses in this injury are salt, water, and plasma proteins. The composition of the electrolyte loss approximates that of blood plasma. The plasma loss is mainly of the albumin fraction, since this molecule is smaller than that of the globulin. This loss approximates three grams per litre in the extravasated fluid. The body reacts by withdrawing salt water from the unburned interstitial tissue spaces until adequate intravenous fluid treatment has been given. The kidney stops functioning almost completely immediately after an extensive burn.

With these previously mentioned electrolyte and plasma protein losses, there is an increase in blood viscosity accompanied by a high hematocrit, or ratio of volume of packed cells to volume of whole blood. There is generalized impairment of blood flow throughout the body with a resultant generalized low oxygen level, dehydration, hyponatremia (low serum sodium), and metabolic acidosis. As a result, there is increased heart rate, vasoconstriction, decreased cardiac output, decreased venous return, and decreased pulse pressure and blood pressure. Because of increased peripheral resistance, increased blood viscosity, and hemoconcentration, there is a decreased effective blood volume.

Systemic reactions to deep burns

Within about an hour, in a large burn, if fluid replacement has not been adequately instituted, these losses begin to impair important organ functions. Signs of shock become manifest: there is paleness, coolness, restlessness, thirst, rapid pulse with evidence of impaired circulation, and a drop in blood pressure. If treatment is not begun early, or if it is given in inadequate measure, protective stress hormones are evoked in increasing quantities. These hormones, while protective during the immediate shock period, may cause an adverse effect once adequate treatment has been begun.

Fluid losses are greatest within the first few hours after burning. Thereafter, the losses are less rapid but continue and are persistent for 36 to 48 hours. These losses cease when the tissue pressure rises and equals that of capillary hydrostatic pressure and the capillary endothelium returns to normal beneath the damaged area. The degree of homeostatic pathologic change that occurs is determined by the time elapsing after the burn until intravenous fluid treatment is instituted and by the adequacy of the fluid treatment given. If treatment is adequate, with rapid replacement of a balanced salt solution, there is minimal alteration of physiologic responses, although some pathological body changes are inevitable—continued high hematocrit, high urinary specific gravity, rapid heart rate, and decreased cardiac output—with present methods of treatment.

If treatment is inadequate, there will be continued withdrawal of salt solutions from the unburned extravascular and extracellular spaces to replace the unremitting losses into the sequestered burn wound. There will be continued inadequate renal blood flow, with low urinary output and protracted inadequate circulation throughout the body. The longer this impaired circulation persists, the more damage to important organ functions will be incurred. This detriment may be reflected later in the course of the burn treatment.

After about the 48th hour, there is a sealing of the capillaries, and reabsorption of the extravasated fluid begins, chiefly by the way of the lymphatics. This reabsorption of fluids is slow and, in uncomplicated cases, takes approximately three to four days. The reabsorption of fluids is delayed if there is infection, and infection spreads rapidly with impaired circulation in the burn wound.

Clinically, one may observe the maximum accumulation of fluid in the tissues at the end of 24 hours after the occurrence of the burn. This may be most evident when a patient has been burned on the head and face. At this time, the head and face resemble a basketball, with the eyes completely closed. After reabsorption of fluid occurs, the contours of the burned surface become relatively normal.

In deep burns, the loss of integrity of the skin causes marked increase in water vaporization from the burn surface. This vaporization causes heat loss, and these processes continue until the integrity of the skin is regained either by re-epithelization or by skin grafting.

From the onset in a large burn, there is marked catabolism, or breakdown, with a negative nitrogen balance that continues until the patient has received a skin graft or until epithelization occurs. There are many obvious explanations for this, including caloric loss from evaporization, hypermetabolic stress due to adrenocortical hyperfunction, and the obvious need for reparative processes. Infection also increases catabolism.

There is a loss of potassium from both the burned tissues and hemolysis (or destruction) of erythrocytes. This results in early transient hyperkalemia (high blood potassium), which is usually of no clinical significance. After about the fourth day after the burn, there may be potassium depletion that requires replacement.

In a deep second-degree burn, a "crust" is formed out of the dried secretions from the burn wound. The dead skin in a third-degree burn is called an eschar. The crust or the eschar starts separating from the wound edges in about 14 days, and there is a continued slow separation thereafter between this dead tissue and the underlying healthy tissue. The separation may become complete in 21 to 40 days. Even after removal of the crust or eschar, there usually will remain numerous strands of dead tissue that must be removed before grafting. When removal of the crust is complete in a deep second-degree burn, the tissue has a pigskin appearance and numerous areas of deep skin follicles are evident. This tissue may epithelize if the burn is superficial, but if it is deep it will usually not heal without the aid of grafting. In full-thickness burns, when the removal of the eschar is complete, raw or granulation tissue is evident.

If there is infection in a deep second-degree burn, the septic growth may destroy the deeper skin (corium) and convert the injury to a full-thickness burn. If there is infection in a third-degree burn, it may invade deeper tissues and cause systemic infection or septicemia. Skin grafts usually are not successful on an infected wound.

Complications: liver, heart, lung, and gastrointestinal damage

As mentioned above the most obvious sign of enormous fluid losses in large burns is an almost complete renal shutdown. This is a reflection not only of the losses into the burn wound but also of the massive withdrawal of salt-containing fluid from the unburned tissue spaces throughout the body with resultant extreme dehydration. If fluid replacement is not prompt and adequate, the patient may succumb from the ensuing shock. Renal failure is a direct result of inadequate or late fluid replacement.

Liver damage, heart damage, and lung and brain damage are the result of prolonged impaired circulation acidosis, and lack of oxygenation to the cells of these organs. Low levels of serum proteins always result from a large burn even though plasma has been used in the fluid treatment of the burn. This results in a low osmotic pressure in the vascular system. In the early stages of such a burn, treatment of shock with intravenous electrolytes is of primary importance. When sufficiently large amounts of electrolytes have been given intravenously to restore circulation and to produce adequate urinary output, and this urinary output is maintained, the physician may presume that he has mastered the shock phase of the treatment of the burn patient.

Gastrointestinal complications are common in large burns. Patients often suffer paralytic ileus (nonmechanical bowel obstruction) for several days following an extensive burn. The larger the burn, the more prolonged will be the ileus. Patients usually will not tolerate any liquids by mouth for one or two days after an extensive burn. They ordinarily will not tolerate any type of high-calorie diet for at least a week after their burn. Stomach swelling is a complication sometimes seen in burns. Patients with extensive burns have poor appetites, and it is extremely difficult to keep them in good nutrition; forced tube feeding may be required.

Not infrequently, patients with extensive burns develop ulcerations of the upper gastrointestinal tract called "Curling's ulcers." Such ulcers are most commonly seen in the stomach and duodenum, and frequently result in massive hemorrhage; they also may perforate into the abdominal cavity. Antacids and anticholinergic drugs have not been found to be of significant benefit. Gastrectomies often are necessary to control massive hemorrhage. These ulcerations usually manifest themselves during the first week but may occur later. The incidence of these ulcers in large burns, observed by a surgical research unit over a period of 13 years, was 13 percent. This complication carries a very high rate of mortality. It is E.R. Crew's opinion that these ulcers are of stress origin and are the result of late or inadequate fluid treatment during the shock phase.

Patients with large burns have a high metabolic rate and remain in negative nitrogen balance until their burn wounds are covered with a graft or epithelize. Avitaminosis is common, and these patients must receive large doses of vitamins, particularly B-complex and C.

Because the physician must give intravenous fluids over a prolonged period, thrombophlebitis—inflamation of the vein with formation of an obstructing blood clot—is common. This condition is usually chemical in nature; if there is also infection, the vein should be excised. Pulmonary emboli may occur but are rare.

In the infant, special care must be given to the administration of fluids as there is danger of overload or underload. Infants and children are also difficult feeding problems.

The aged suffer a high mortality and morbidity rate even with less extensive burns. Older people have low cardiopulmonary reserve and can be easily overloaded with fluids. Aging affects all the organs of the body; there is lowered resistance to infection. Old people do not tolerate remaining in one position over a prolonged period. They are difficult feeding problems and frequently become disoriented.

Complications: respiratory injury, infection

Respiratory burns are extremely serious. They are usually associated with large body burns. The inhaled heat does not commonly cause a burn below the vocal cords but will cause internal thermal injury of the mouth, posterior pharynx, and upper larynx. The ensuing edema usually necessitates tracheostomy. Smoke inhalation commonly is seen when a patient is trapped in an enclosed burning building. The carbon particles that are deposited throughout the tracheobronchial tree cause severe irritation to the tracheobronchial mucosa and predispose to pneumonic complications. Pneumonia, as a cause of death in burns, seems to be increasing even when there is no respiratory tract damage from the burn.

Burn-wound sepsis and septicemia are, at present, the most common cause of death in large burns. Sepsis during the first week after the burn is most commonly caused by *Staphylococcus aureus*. Later, after the second week, the most common causative organism of burn wound sepsis and septicemia is *Pseudomonas aeruginosa*. Other organisms commonly causing infection in burns are *Streptococcus, Proteus vulgaris, Aerobacter aerogenes,* and *Escherichia coli*. Viral and fungus septicemias are rare complications.

There are two major difficulties in treating deep infections in burns: first, the early recognition of an infective process and the determination of the causative organism in order to select the proper antibiotic; and, second, the prompt administration of the selected antibiotic. Thus, early burn symptoms such as disorientation, anorexia, gastric distention, and fever are indications for the administration of antibiotics that are effective against *Staphylococcus aureus*. Later deep infections, usually caused by *Pseudomonas,* are frequently manifested by purulent exudate, a discoloured and unhealthy appearance of the burn wound, redness surrounding the burn wound, and general deterioration of the patient's condition. The patient's temperature may be elevated or subnormal. Unfortunately, these later invaders of the burn wound, particularly *Pseudomonas,* are not particularly susceptible to any of the antibiotics now available. For this reason, it should be emphasized that intensive prophylactic local care of the burn wound is of prime importance in order to suppress the growth of these organisms before they become uncontrollable.

There are particular complications that occur when specific areas are burned. The ears are frequently burned when the head is burned. The skin over the ears is thin and chondritis is a common complication. Chondritis usually causes the loss of the structure of the ear, namely, the cartilage. Burns of the eyelids are not uncommon and, if deep, cause ectropion, which prevents the eyelids from closing. This necessitates suturing the lid margins together and early grafting of the eyelids.

In deep circumferential burns of an extremity, there is often a tourniquet-like effect that causes loss of circulation to the hands and feet. In these circumstances, incision through the eschar (escharotomy), particularly over the joints, is necessary to release this constricting effect and allow free blood flow to the distal part.

Cystitis may be a side effect because prolonged catheterization is necessary. At times, bladder stones are formed.

Deep burns often involve structures deeper than the skin, such as bones and joints. They occur with prolonged exposure to fire and also are seen in electrical burns. They are extremely difficult to treat and usually cause marked loss of function of the part. They are prone to infection and should have early excision for purposes of drainage. Repeated debridements are usually necessary.

Burns of the hands are common and are crippling if not treated correctly. The skin of the back of the hands and fingers is thin; if the tendons and joints are to be salvaged, intensive physical therapy and early grafting are necessary. Frequently hand burns are associated with extensive body burns, and it is often difficult to give adequate treatment simultaneously to the hands and to the body as a whole.

Contractures are a common complication of burns and usually occur over joints. The contractures are not as severe or disabling if grafting is done early. When contractures are severe or disabling, plastic surgery may be necessary later.

TREATMENT

Specialized treatment facilities. The care of burns requires dedication from doctors, nurses, and attending personnel. Burned patients are among the most difficult nursing problems in the field of medicine. Large burns require constant attention. During the shock phase, hourly recordings of intake and output of fluids are necessary, with a need for frequent adjustment of intravenous fluids. Cleanliness, isolation technique, nutrition, dressing changes, and the like are daily necessities throughout the course of burn treatment. To treat a hospitalized burn adequately, special treatment facilities should be available and should include doctors and nurses with knowledge of burn care. Since burn patients require isolation and special attention, they should be kept in the same area of the hospital where nurses are trained in burn care.

Burn treatment centres; emergency measures

Several large burn disasters in recent years have indicated the necessity for burn treatment centres. Truman Graves Blocker, in Galveston, and the Brooke Army Group, in San Antonio, Texas, established the world's first well-known burn unit in the late 1940s. More recently, numerous burn units have been established. The Shriners have built, and support, three centres in the United States for the treatment of burned children. In Europe, burn centres or services exist in Rome; Birmingham, England; Edinburgh; and Prague.

Types of treatment. The depth of the burn is due in part to the duration of the heat; hence the burned area is cooled immediately to stop this process. If the burn is small, application of ice cubes is most beneficial. If the burn is large, the patient may be put in a shower or covered with towels soaked in ice water. No ointment or preparation of any type should be applied to the burn wound. The physician will have to clean the burn wound as part of the treatment, and it is much easier and less painful if the wound has not been covered by any preparation. If the clothes are in flames, a blanket may be wrapped around the body to extinguish the flames. The cooling procedures mentioned above are then followed.

After shock therapy (intravenous fluids) has been started, the burn wound and the body in general are thoroughly cleansed with a warm detergent solution and the dead tissue is debrided. This procedure is performed with the patient under intravenous narcotic analgesia. The patient is not given a general anesthetic.

In superficial burns of less than 15 percent of the body surface, except in infants and the aged, intravenous fluids are not necessary. The patient may drink a soda-salt solution for replacement.

In larger burns, intravenous replacement with a salt solution is a necessity. There is some disagreement among groups regarding the composition of the electrolytes that should be given and whether plasma expanders (dextran) should be used. The majority of authorities favour electrolytes that approximate the concentrations seen in blood plasma, namely, lactated Ringer's solution, since this is the composition of the loss in the burn wound. The rate of administration of intravenous fluids and the quantity given vary with the extent of the burn and the size or weight of the individual patient.

Many formulas have been devised for the rate and quantity of fluids that should be given during the first and second days after the burn, but none apply exactly to a particular patient. These formulas are useful only as a rough guide. Generally, the intravenous fluids are infused rapidly the first few hours; and when the urinary output approaches normal (50 cc per hour for an adult and 25 cc per hour for a child), the rate of administration of fluids is decreased. The kidney or the urinary output remains the most reliable indicator of adequate hydration.

Intravenous fluid regimens

In large burns, the rate of administration of fluids the first hour or two may approximate one or two litres per hour. Thereafter, when urinary output approaches normal or becomes excessive, the intravenous intake is sharply curtailed.

Many centres continue to use an intravenous fluid regimen consisting entirely of lactated Ringer's solution. Others simultaneously administer plasma after the first few hours of electrolyte administration. Some centres use dextran for this purpose, though more than two litres of this solution may cause a tendency to bleed.

In the aged or the infirm, central venous catheters are inserted into the superior vena cava to measure pressures in order to insure that overloads of fluid are not administered. Fluids in the amount of 10 to 20 percent of the patient's body weight may be necessary in the first two days of treatment of patients with extensive burns.

Generally, no more electrolytes or plasma are given after 48 hours. Intravenous fluids in the form of five percent glucose in water are continued after this time, and the patient is allowed oral fluids as desired. Intravenous fluids are continued until the patient can drink an adequate amount of water. Food is given as desired.

During the reabsorption phase, large amounts of urine that contain concentrated electrolytes are excreted. No attempts are made to force the patient to eat during the first week after a large burn, as a paralytic ileus continues during this time. Frequent feedings are encouraged when the patient is able to tolerate them.

"Closed" treatment and "exposure"

Accepted methods of treatment of "superficial second-degree burns" are either the closed treatment or the exposure treatment. The initial treatment consists of thorough cleansing of the burn wound with a warm detergent solution, copious irrigation, and debridement of the dead or blistered skin. This is usually done with intravenous narcotic analgesia. All of the blistered skin is removed and the burn and surrounding skin are thoroughly cleansed. If the burn patient is to be admitted to the hospital, the burn wound is exposed to the air. The wound and the surrounding skin are cleansed daily with a detergent solution. The dried secretions form a crust that falls away in about two weeks. If the patient is to be treated as an outpatient, the closed treatment is preferable. This consists of a water-soluble ointment dressing covered with a bulky gauze dressing and bandages securely applied. Most of these burns heal without incident in 14 days. Occasionally, such a burn will become infected; the patient will then require hospitalization for treatment of the infection.

Early forms of treatment

Before 1965, the most popular treatments for "deep burns" were the closed treatment and the exposure treatment. The closed treatment had many deficiencies. The physician was unable to sterilize the burn wound no matter how long he washed or whatever the agent used. The bacteria in the sweat glands and hair follicles could not be reached. The warm, moist environment on the burn surface in an enclosed dressing was an ideal situation for bacterial growth, and deep burns almost invariably became infected when the closed treatment was used. With the exposure type of treatment, better results were obtained, as in full-thickness burns there was a dry, hard eschar and in deep second-degree burns a dry, hard crust was formed. The dryness of the exposed wound inhibited bacterial growth. There were deficiencies in this type of treatment also; namely, when the patient was forced to lie on his burn (a circumferential burn) the warmth and moisture promoted bacterial proliferation. Furthermore, the dried eschar or crust did not promote epithelization in the deep second-degree burns. If there was any infection present in deep second-degree burns, they were readily converted into full-thickness burns.

In deep burns, before 1965, grafting was usually delayed until all the eschar and all the necrotic tissue was removed. This delay could last 25 to 40 days, and during this time many distressing complications could occur. Part of the wound would be debrided and the granulations exposed to infection, and part would still be covered with an eschar. Grafts would not take on the granulations at this time unless exposed to the air. When the surgeon finally completed his debridement in large burns, he would find that there was not enough donor skin on the patient's body to cover the exposed raw area. He would then graft whatever he could cover and would, of necessity, await re-epithelization from the donor areas (21 days), in order to reharvest additional grafts. If the original grafts took well, there was a chance of recovery. If they did not take, there was disaster. Meanwhile, during this interval of awaiting regrafting, the exposed granulation would become less receptive to grafting, and the patient's general condition would deteriorate. Homografts were used to solve some of these problems of coverage of the raw tissue. These grafts also had disadvantages as, if these homografts took as grafts, they would begin to be rejected by the body after the 15th day. One could not then graft these areas for an additional month.

The surgeon did not usually attempt to debride these large burn eschars surgically as there was always infection underneath, and surgery would predispose to a breakdown of the body defenses and open avenues to invasive infection that would usually cause septicemia and death of the patient.

Newer treatments

In 1965 two new forms of local treatment for burns evolved. One of these, was the use of silver nitrate wet soaks to cover the burn wound. The originator observed that concentrated silver nitrate, while it would kill bacteria, would also destroy live tissue. He recommended a dilute silver nitrate solution (0.5 percent), as this would inhibit bacterial growth and would not destroy living tissue. This treatment was to be given immediately after wound cleansing and debridement. The patient's burn wounds were completely wrapped in thick gauze bandages, and this gauze was kept saturated with the silver nitrate solution at all times. The treatment retarded bacterial growth and allowed epithelization in deep second-degree burns. The bacteriostatic effect was only on the surface of the burn wound and did not penetrate.

The second new treatment advocated was by the research group at Brooke Army Hospital. This treatment was with mafenide (Sulfamylon) in a water-soluble ointment applied to the burn wound with the gloved hand. The ointment was spread twice daily over the burn wound in a thin layer. The excess and dried ointment was removed once or twice daily in a Hubbard tank, an agitated bath that has been developed for this purpose. This treatment caused a marked diminution in bacterial growth on the burn wound and, particularly, it inhibited growth of *Pseudomonas.* The sulfa would penetrate the burn wound eschar or crust and be an effective bacteriostatic agent in the subcutaneous tissue. The surgeon could place grafts on granulation tissue alongside the eschar and the grafts would take.

A third form of treatment is credited to the Brooke Army Group. This is known as temporary homografting. As mentioned above, homografting (skin grafts taken from another person) had been used for a number of years, but it had disadvantages. The Brooke Army Group observed that if homografts were placed on the granulating tissue and were removed within four to five days, the grafts would not take and they could be reapplied in a similar manner indefinitely, being removed each time after four or five days. This procedure offered an excellent physiological coverage and eliminated the water vaporization and caloric loss and also eliminated bacterial growth from the wound.

The above forms of treatment were notable advances. Each has saved many lives that otherwise would have been lost. As with other forms of treatment, however, each of these forms has its imperfections, and there are elements of danger if the treatment is not used by experts familiar with the possible side effects.

Silver nitrate withdraws sodium, chloride, potassium, and calcium from the burn wound in direct proportion to the extent of the burn. These elements must be replaced daily, either orally or parenterally. The dressings must be constantly wet to avoid cauterization of newly formed epithelium. Silver nitrate stains everything it touches. This type of treatment is time-consuming and requires attentive nursing care.

Mafenide is absorbed and blocks carbonic anhydrase in the kidney, causing acidosis. The respiratory rate is increased during treatment. Pneumonia is not uncommon and, if it occurs, the treatment must be stopped or delayed. Mafenide also retards epithelization to some extent.

Temporary homografts are ideal if the physician or burn team can procure them or has the time to collect them. These homografts are usually taken from the body of a person recently deceased. Permission to do so must be secured, and the homografts must be taken in the operating room under sterile conditions. Acquiring these grafts takes considerable time and effort. If the grafts are used as "temporary homografts," large quantities of the grafts must be used and this requires many donors.

Only one institution, the Brooke Army Hospital, is geared to taking these grafts in quantities necessary for the treatment of many burns in this fashion, although other institutions are employing temporary homografts to a lesser extent.

Freeze-dried skin also is useful as a physiologic dressing or coverage, but its use is restricted because of limited facilities. Heterografts (skin grafts taken from animals) also have been used as temporary coverage.

Other types of local treatment are being developed to combat local infection; namely, other types of local bacteriostatic ointments such as gentamicin and silver sulfadiazine.

To expand donor skin coverage, grafts may be "meshed." Small slits are cut in the skin graft by a machine and, when expanded, form a type of lace network increasing the coverage two to three times the width of the graft.

Although antibiotics play an important role in the treatment of burns, antibiotics are rather ineffective once burn wound sepsis or septicemia has developed, particularly if *Pseudomonas* is the causative organism.

Nutrition and nursing care

Burned patients require a high intake of vitamins. Adults require supplemental B-complex and C vitamins. Infants and children require additional A and D vitamins.

Patients with large burns cannot be force-fed during the first week. The larger the burn, the more prolonged will be the paralytic ileus that accompanies all large burns. Hourly liquid feedings in small amounts are given after the second day.

After a week, or sooner if the burn is less extensive, the patient is placed on a high-calorie diet with frequent feedings. These patients must be kept well nourished if they are to survive. They generally stay in a negative nitrogen balance and continue to lose weight until they receive grafts.

These patients have little appetite and must be encouraged to eat more than they really desire. Numerous high-protein feedings have been devised in the past years, but all have been failures. They are unpalatable; and if given in large quantities or by tube feeding, they cause vomiting and diarrhea. Whole food has been found to be the feeding of choice. Even in infants, the choice of feedings, either orally or by tube, is strained baby food mixed with small quantities of milk. For adequate nutrition, nurses, aides, and even the family play an important role. Extensive burns usually involve the upper extremities, and the patients have no use of their hands and must be fed. Frequently, it may require an hour to get an adequate meal into a patient. Also, the patient may have particular likes and dislikes for certain foods. These food preferences must be catered to.

A patient with a large burn becomes extremely dependent upon those who care for him. He requires close nursing attention throughout the day and night. He is in constant discomfort. Tranquillizers are of benefit to lessen the discomfort.

After grafting, if the grafts take well, there is a dramatic psychological change in the behaviour of the patient. Whereas he has been querulous and dissatisfied, he now becomes smiling and good-natured and has an excessive appetite. In spite of cosmetic and functional deformities that may exist, he remains optimistic and is glad to be alive.

The surgical treatment employed in burns consists mainly of debridement, grafting, and plastic repairs after healing.

Skin grafts taken for burn coverage are split-thickness grafts taken between 0.008 and 0.012 inch in thickness. These usually are taken with an electric or air-driven dermatome. The donor areas commonly are covered with one layer of bandage gauze and exposed to the air. The recipient area is covered with the graft. This may be placed on the granulating surface of the wound with or without suturing. The grafted area either may be enclosed in a dressing or left exposed. There are many different techniques and dressing complexes used in grafting, but once the graft has been put in place, no slippage must occur. Mesh-grafting and homografting have been previously discussed.

PROGNOSIS

Factors that affect prognosis

The prognosis in burn patients depends upon many factors: the extent of the burn, the depth of the burn, the age of the patient, the hospital facilities for the care of burns, and the knowledge and attention of the physicians and nurses who care for these patients. Expert care of burns decreases scarring, contractures, cosmetic deformities, hospitalization time, and morbidity and mortality.

In general, the aged succumb to a lesser burn than do young or middle-aged patients. Infants have a higher mortality rate than children or adults. The adequacy of early treatment of the shock phase alters the prognosis greatly. The health of the individual at the time of the burn varies the prognosis. Cardiovascular, renal, or liver dysfunction increases the mortality rate.

It has been established that at present the principal cause of death in large burns is infection. Hundreds of methods have been tried over the past years to combat or control infection, but it was not until 1965 that appreciable progress was made in this direction. Mafenide, silver nitrate dressings, gentamicin ointment, silver sulfadiazine ointment, and other bacteriostatic agents have shown promise in reducing infection in burn patients. Homografting and heterografting also are useful in combatting infection and are helpful as temporary coverage for the burn wound.

The prognosis with a deep burn covering 50 percent of the body surface is good in centres equipped to treat burns. The prognosis also is good for a superficial burn covering 70 to 80 percent of the body surface.

Formerly, when a person with what appeared to be a full-thickness burn that was caused by fire was admitted to a hospital, the burn actually became a full-thickness injury eventually; and the only epithelization that occurred came from the edges of the burn wound. At present with local infection controlled by bacteriostatic agents, many of these apparently deep burns turn out to be deep second-degree injuries that in many instances will epithelize and thus will not require grafting. Hospitalization time is now shortened, deformities decreased, and the results are much improved in the treatment of burns.

In spite of all the advances that have been made in the treatment of burn patients, large burns are still a catastrophe. Such burns average the most prolonged hospital time of any injury, and the cost of treating a burn is the greatest of any type of trauma or surgical event.

The yearly meetings of the American Burn Association, formed in 1967, attract personnel who are interested in burn care. This has added greatly to the dissemination of knowledge and has stimulated much research. The International Burn Society was established in 1965; this society meets every four years to disseminate current knowledge of burn therapy world wide.

It is now possible to save many more persons with extensive burns than in previous years; and as proficiency in saving patients with large burns grows, it becomes certain that most of the patients with smaller burns can be salvaged. Unfortunately, the more sophisticated regimens of burn treatment cannot be employed in many parts of the world. The local preparations mentioned as bacteriostatic agents are expensive and cannot be afforded in many countries even if these agents are available.

BIBLIOGRAPHY. C.P. ARTZ and J.A. MONCRIEF, *The Treatment of Burns* (1969), a thorough and comprehensive text on the problems, pathology, treatment, and complications of burns, including research performed at Brooke Army Hospital; W.P. COCKSHOTT, "The History of the Treatment of Burns," *Surg., Gynec., Obstet.*, 102:116–124 (Jan. 1956), the most comprehensive article available on the history of burns prior to 1956; E.R. CREWS, *A Practical Manual for the Treatment of Burns*, 2nd ed. (1967), a useful guide on methods of treatment of burns for nurses, residents, and doctors; includes a thorough discussion of exposure treatment, for use in situations where only limited facilities are available; I. FELLER, *International Bibliography on Burns* (1969), a comprehensive list of articles on burns and related subjects that have been written since 1950; L. GOLDMAN and R.E. GARDNER (eds.), *Burns: A Symposium* (1965), contains present-day knowledge on the problems and treatment of burns; C.A. MOYER, L. BRENTANO, and W.W. MAFANO, "Treatment of Large Burns with 0.5 Percent Silver Nitrate Solution," *Arch. Surg.* 90:812 (1965), a detailed and informative article by the originator of the treatment of large burns with dilute silver nitrate solution; S.E. ORDER and J.A. MONCRIEF, *The Burn Wound* (1965), an illustrated and graphic description of the pathology of the burn wound with emphasis on burn wound infection with *Pseudomonas aeruginosa*.

(E.R.C.)

Bursa

Synovial and other bursas

A bursa is any small pouch or sac within the body. The bursas have been classified as adventitious, subcutaneous, and synovial. Adventitious, or accidental, bursas arise in soft tissues as a result of repeated subjections to unusual shearing stresses, particularly over bony prominences. Subcutaneous bursas ordinarily are ill-defined clefts at the junction of subcutaneous tissue and deep fasciae (sheets of fibrous tissue); these bursas acquire a distinct wall only when they become abnormal, and they are classified as adventitious by some authorities. Synovial bursas are thin-walled sacs that are interposed between tissues such as tendons, muscles, and bones, and are lined with synovial membrane, so called because it exudes synovia, a lubricating fluid. This article is concerned chiefly with the synovial bursas.

The precise number of bursas in man is not known. Some estimates are as high as 300; *Nomina Anatomica* lists 52. In Alexander Monro's classic treatise (1799), 156 are listed as recognizable with the naked eye, but this figure is probably excessive because it includes what later came to be distinguished as tendon sheaths, which differ from bursas only in that they envelop tendons. Most bursas are located near the large joints of the arms and legs. Three are present at the larynx.

Bursitis. The term "bursitis" comprehends all types of inflammation of the bursas. Bursas sometimes are involved along with the joints and tendon sheaths in rheumatoid arthritis and gout. Infectious agents introduced by penetrating wounds or borne by the bloodstream also may result in bursitis, but this is unusual. Tuberculous lesions restricted to bursas are rare occurrences and represent instances of infections borne by the bloodstream; more often the bursas are affected because they are next to centres of tuberculous infection in adjacent bones. The prepatellar bursa, located on the lower part of the kneecap, is especially subject to involvement in brucellosis (undulant fever). Although earlier medical literature described inflammation of the synovial membrane and bursitis as manifestations of early acquired syphilis, this view is not accepted today.

Causes of bursitis

The cause of most cases of bursitis appears to be one or another local mechanical irritation. Often the injury is of occupational origin and accordingly has been known for centuries as weaver's bottom (ischiogluteal bursitis); nun's or housemaid's knee (prepatellar bursitis); and soldier's heel (Achilles bursitis). A little less than 60% of cases occur in the shoulder region, a little over 20% at the knee, a little over 15% near the hip, and 5% elsewhere. The inflammatory reaction is not a distinctly particularized one and may or may not include deposition of calcium salts. The borderline between bursitis and other painful rheumatic conditions of the soft tissues is indistinct in many instances.

The commonest form of bursitis affects the subdeltoid bursa, which lies above the shoulder joint. Bursitis in this circumstance is not the primary abnormality, but results from degeneration and calcification of the adjacent rotator tendon. Direct injury is not usually the cause of calcium deposits and inflammation in the tendon; indeed, heavy labourers are less frequently affected than persons engaged in less strenuous occupations. The possibility that there is a constitutional predisposition to this type of degeneration has been considered, but little is known about such a cause. The bursa proper is affected only when debris from the tendon extends into it, this intrusion being the principal cause of an acutely painful shoulder. The condition occurs most often in middle age and is infrequent among young children. Women are twice as likely to have the condition as men. The onset may be sudden and unprovoked. Pain and tenderness are great and there is difficulty in raising the arm. The calcium deposits can be seen in X-ray films of the shoulder. No single method of dealing with the disorder in all affected persons is known, and response varies widely among individuals. Resting the arm and use of analgesics tend to lessen the discomfort, corticosteroids may reduce inflammation, and carefully graduated exercises may be used to lessen the possibility of lasting stiffness of the shoulder. Many months may pass before complete recovery is attained. Chronic inflammation of the bursa at the side of the hip joint—trochanteric bursitis—has a similar course.

The more clearly traumatic forms of bursitis are exemplified by "beat knee," a bursitis that develops below the kneecap of miners who must kneel over long periods to work the narrow coal seams of England. Bloody fluid distends the bursa and, unless removed early, may cause the walls of the bursa to become thickened permanently. Treatment, which involves protection from further irritation to the extent that this is possible, is otherwise similar to that for subdeltoid bursitis. A fair proportion of these lesions become infected as a consequence of injury to the overlying skin.

A bunion is an adventitious bursa that develops on the inner side of the base of the great toe in association with hallux valgus (deviation of the first toe so that it lies on top of or below the other toes). Wearing narrow, pointed shoes is a major contributory factor. Mild cases are relieved by use of proper shoes and care of the feet, but surgery may be necessary for correction of severe deformities.

Diseases of the bursa also occur in domestic animals. Capped elbow and capped hock are examples of chronic bursitis in horses, resulting from lying on hard floors, kicks, and similar injuries.

Tumours. Malignant synovial tumours typically arise from tissues about the joints proper rather than within them. The tissues around the joints must include bursas as well as the capsule and tendon sheaths, but synovial tumours confined to a bursa have not been recognized. A benign, tumourlike condition of synovial tissue, called pigmented villonodular synovitis, has occasionally been reported in bursas. So, too, has synovial chondromatosis, a rare disorder in which cartilaginous nodules proliferate in the lining of the sac.

BIBLIOGRAPHY. E.G. BYWATERS, "The Bursae of the Body," *Ann. Rheum. Dis.*, 24:215–218 (May 1965), a brief evaluation of contemporary knowledge of bursae in historical perspective of Monro's treatise; J.L. HOLLANDER (ed.), *Arthritis and Allied Conditions* (1966), an authoritative textbook of rheumatology that includes several chapters dealing with bursitis.

(L.S.)

Burton, Sir Richard

One of the greatest British scholar-explorers of the 19th century, Sir Richard Burton, in a world in which there seemed to be little left to be discovered, sought out its few remaining mysteries. He was the first European to explore the forbidden Muslim city of Harer in Somaliland, he penetrated the secret cities of Mecca and Medina, and he discovered Lake Tanganyika. He was also a soldier, poet, botanist, geologist, and a leading ethnologist, linguist, and translator. Late in life his passion became the study and translation of the erotica and folk literature of the East, and today he is best known for his work in this field for which his Victorian contemporaries condemned him and for his still unexcelled translation of the *Arabian Nights*.

Early life and career. Born in Torquay, Devonshire, March 19, 1821, the son of Lieutenant Colonel Joseph Netterville Burton and Martha Baker, Burton was of mixed English, Irish, and possibly French ancestry. His father, retiring early from an unsuccessful army career,

Burton, oil painting by Lord Leighton, 1876. In the National Portrait Gallery, London.

By courtesy of the National Portrait Gallery, London

chose to raise his two sons and daughter in France and Italy, where young Richard developed his astonishing talent for languages to such an extent that before matriculating at Trinity College, Oxford, in 1840, he had become fluent in French, Italian, and the Béarnais and Neapolitan dialects, as well as in Greek and Latin. But his continental upbringing left him ambivalent about his national identity. He called himself "a waif, a stray . . . a blaze of light, without a focus," and complained that "England is the only country where I never feel at home."

Offices in India

Expelled from Oxford in 1842 because of a minor breach of discipline, he went to India as subaltern officer in the 18th Regiment of Bombay Native Infantry during England's war with the Sind (now a province of West Pakistan). He mastered Arabic and Hindi and during his eight-year stay became proficient also in Marathi, Sindhi, Punjabi, Telugu, Pashto, and Miltani. Eventually in his travels over the world he learned 25 languages, with dialects that brought the number to 40.

As a favoured intelligence officer of Sir Charles James Napier, commander of the English forces in the Sind, Captain Burton went in disguise as a Muslim merchant in the bazaars, bringing back detailed reports. Napier in 1845 asked him to investigate the homosexual brothels in Karāchi; his explicit study resulted in their destruction; it also resulted, after Napier's departure, in the destruction of Burton's promising career, when the report was forwarded to Bombay by an unfriendly officer who hoped to see Burton dismissed in disgrace. Though the effort failed, Burton realized his reputation was irreparably clouded and returned, ill and disconsolate, to England.

From his 29th to his 32nd year he lived with his mother and sister in Boulogne, France, where he wrote four books on India, including *Sindh, and the Races That Inhabit the Valley of the Indus* (1851), a brilliant ethnological study, published before the new science of ethnology had a proper tradition against which its merits could be evaluated. Meanwhile he perfected his long-cherished plans for going to Mecca.

Exploration in Arabia. Disguising himself as a Pathan, an Afghanistan Muslim, in 1853 he went to Cairo, Suez, and Medina, then travelled the bandit-ridden route to the sacred city of Mecca, where at great risk he measured and sketched the mosque and holy Muslim shrine, the Ka'bah. Though not the first non-Muslim to penetrate and describe the "mother of cities," Burton was the most sophisticated and the most accurate. His *Pilgrimage to El-Medinah and Mecca* (1855–56) was not only a great adventure narrative but also a classic commentary on Muslim life and manners, especially on the annual pilgrimage. Instead of returning to London to enjoy his sudden fame, however, he organized a new expedition in 1854 to the equally forbidden East African city of Harer and became the first European to enter this Muslim citadel without being executed. He described his adventures in *First Footsteps in East Africa* (1856).

By this time Burton had become fascinated by the idea of discovering the source of the White Nile and planned an expedition with three officers of the British East India Company, including John Hanning Speke in 1855, intending to push across Somaliland. Natives attacked the party near Berbera, however, killing one member of the party and seriously wounding Speke. Burton himself had a javelin hurled through his jaw and was forced to return to England. After recovery, in July 1855, he went to the Crimea to volunteer in the war against Russia. At the Dardanelles he helped train Turkish irregulars but saw no action at the front.

The Crimean War over, he turned again to the Nile search, leading an expedition inland from Zanzibar with John Speke in 1857–58. They suffered almost every kind of hardship Africa could inflict. When they finally arrived on the shores of Lake Tanganyika, Burton was so ill from malaria he could not walk, and Speke was virtually blind. Ailing, and disappointed by native information that the Rusizi River to the north poured into rather than out of the lake, Burton wished to return and prepare a new expedition. Speke, however, who had recovered more quickly, pushed on alone to the northeast and discovered Lake Victoria, which he was convinced was the true Nile source. Burton's unwillingness to accept this theory without further exploration led to quarrels with Speke and their eventual estrangement.

Discovery of Lake Tanganyika

Speke was the first to return to London, where he was lionized and given funds to return to Africa. Burton, largely ignored and denied financing for a new exploration of his own, felt betrayed. His *Lake Regions of Central Africa* (1860) attacked Speke's claims and exacerbated their by now public feud.

In 1860 Burton went off unexpectedly to the United States, where he travelled by stagecoach to the Mormon capital, Salt Lake City. The resulting volume, *City of the Saints* (1861), showed that he could write with sophistication about the nature of the Mormon Church, compose a vivid portrait of its leader, Brigham Young, and also be dispassionate about the Mormon practice of polygamy, which was then outraging most Americans. Shortly after his return from the United States, in January 1861, he and Isabel Arundell, the daughter of an aristocratic family, whom he had been courting since 1856, were married secretly.

Foreign office. Burton now entered the British Foreign Office as consul in Fernando Po, a Spanish island off the coast of West Africa. During his three years there, he made many short trips of exploration into West Africa, gathering enough material to fill five books. His explicit descriptions of tribal rituals concerning birth, marriage, and death, as well as fetishism, ritual murder, cannibalism, and bizarre sexual practices, though admired by modern anthropologists, won him no favour with the Foreign Office, which considered him eccentric if not dangerous.

Returning to London on leave, September 1864, Burton was invited to debate with Speke before the British Association for the Advancement of Science. Speke, who with the British soldier and explorer James Augustus Grant had made a memorable journey from Zanzibar to Lake Victoria and then down the whole length of the Nile, was expected to defend his conviction that Lake Victoria was the true Nile source. After the preliminary session on September 15, Speke went hunting, dying mysteriously as a result of a shotgun wound in his chest. The coroner's jury ruled the death an accident, but Burton believed it to be a suicide. He wrote in anguish to a friend, "The charitable say that he shot himself, the uncharitable say that I shot him."

Burton spent the next four years as consul in Santos, Brazil, where he wrote a book on the highlands of Brazil (1869) and translated *Vikram and the Vampire, or Tales of Hindu Devilry* (1870). He also began translating the works of the romantic Portuguese poet-explorer Luís de Camões, with whom he felt a deep sense of kinship. Yet his work did not help him to overcome his increasing aversion for Brazil. He took to drink, and finally he sent his devoted wife to London to obtain a better post for him. She succeeded in persuading the Foreign Secretary to appoint Burton consul in Damascus.

Back in the Near East, which he loved, Burton for a time was highly successful as a diplomat; but Muslim intrigue, complicated by the proselytizing indiscretions of his devoutly Catholic wife, resulted in his humiliating dismissal in August 1871. The details of this traumatic failure were recorded by Isabel Burton in her lively, defensive *Inner Life of Syria* (1875).

Dismissal from Damascus

Trieste. In 1872 Burton reluctantly accepted the consulate at Trieste, and although he considered it an ignominious exile, he eventually came to cherish it as his home. There he stayed until his death, publishing an astonishing variety of books. He wrote a book on Iceland, one on Etruscan Bologna, reflecting his passion for archaeology, a nostalgic volume on the Sind, two books on the gold mines of the Midian, and one on the African Gold Coast (now Ghana), none of which matched the great narratives of his earlier adventures. His *Book of the Sword* (1884), a dazzling piece of historical erudition, brought him no more financial success than any of the others. In 1880 he published his best original poetry, *The Kasidah*, written under a pseudonym and patterned after the *Rubáiyát of Omar Khayyám*.

In Trieste, Burton emerged as a translator of extraordinary virtuosity. He translated and annotated six volumes of Camões, a volume of Neopolitan Italian tales by Giambattista Basile, *Il Pentamerone*, and Latin poems by Catullus. What excited him most, however, was the erotica of the East. Taking it upon himself to introduce to the West the sexual wisdom of the ancient Eastern manuals on the art of love, he risked prosecution and imprisonment to translate and print secretly the *Kama Sutra of Vatsyayana* (1883), *Ananga Ranga* (1885), and *The Perfumed Garden of the Cheikh Nefzaoui* (1886). He also published openly, but privately, an unexpurgated sixteen-volume edition of the *Arabian Nights* (1885–1888), the translation of which was so exceptional for its fidelity, masculine vigour, and literary skill that it has frightened away all competitors. Moreover, he larded these volumes with ethnological footnotes and daring essays on pornography, homosexuality, and the sexual education of women. He railed against the "immodest modesty," the cant, and hypocrisy of his era, displaying psychological insights that anticipated both Havelock Ellis and Sigmund Freud. His *Nights* were praised by some for their robustness and honesty but attacked by others as "garbage of the brothels," "an appalling collection of degrading customs and statistics of vice."

Burton as translator

In February 1886 Burton won belated recognition for his services to the crown when Queen Victoria made him Knight Commander of St. Michael and St. George. He died of a heart attack in Trieste on Oct. 20, 1890. His wife, fearful lest her husband be thought vicious because he collected data on what Victorian England called vice, at once burned the projected new edition of *The Perfumed Garden* he had been annotating. She then wrote a biography of Burton in which she tried to fashion this Rabelaisian scholar-adventurer into a good Catholic, a faithful husband, and a refined and modest man. Afterward she burned almost all of his 40-year collection of diaries and journals. The loss to history and anthropology was monumental; the loss to Burton's biographers, irreparable.

BIBLIOGRAPHY. Burton wrote 43 volumes on his explorations and travels and over 100 articles, as well as almost 30 volumes of translations. These are meticulously listed in NORMAN PENZER, *Annotated Bibliography of Sir Richard Francis Burton* (1923, reprinted 1970). Some of the manuscript material that escaped Lady Burton's burning is now housed in the Royal Anthropological Institute of Great Britain and Ireland, London, which also has Burton's private library. ISABEL BURTON, *The Life of Captain Sir Richard F. Burton*, 2 vol. (1893), though highly romanticized, remains the best single source book. THOMAS WRIGHT, *The Life of Sir Richard Burton*, 2 vol. (1906, reprinted 1968), is largely hostile; that by Burton's niece GEORGIANA STISTED, *The True Life of Capt. Sir Richard F. Burton* (1896), is a panegyric, with the hostility reserved for Burton's wife. For short but vivid and perceptive portraits, see FRANK HARRIS, *Contemporary Portraits* (1920) and *My Life and Loves* (1963); and an excellent account by ALAN MOOREHEAD, *The White Nile* (1960). Biographies by FAIRFAX DOWNEY, *Burton, Arabian Nights Adventurer* (1931); HUGH J. SCHONFIELD, *Richard Burton, Explorer* (1936); and SETON DEARDEN, *Burton of Arabia* (1937), are superficial; BYRON FARWELL, *Burton* (1963), is not. FAWN M. BRODIE, *The Devil Drives: A Life of Sir Richard Burton* (1967), is thoroughly documented and defines the psychological complexities of Burton's personality.

(F.M.B.)

Burundi

Burundi is a landlocked republic in eastern Africa south of the Equator; it has an area of 10,759 square miles (27,865 square kilometres) and a population of more than 3,500,000. Together with its neighbour Rwanda (*q.v.*), it is the most densely populated state in Africa, with more than 350 people to the square mile (135 per square kilometre). To the north it is bounded by Rwanda, to the east and south by Tanzania, to the southwest by Lake Tanganyika, and to the west by Zaire. The most southerly source of the Nile is considered to be the Kagera River, and the ultimate headstream of the Kagera, the Kigira-Mukasenyi, is located within the borders of Burundi. The capital is Bujumbura (population 110,000). Before independence in 1962, Burundi, called Urundi, was part of the United Nations Trust Territory of Ruanda–Urundi under Belgian administration.

For coverage of associated physical features, see EAST AFRICAN LAKES; EAST AFRICAN MOUNTAINS; and NILE RIVER; for coverage of historical aspects, see EAST AFRICA, HISTORY OF.

Burundi is a mountainous country, lying across the dividing crest of the Nile and Congo watersheds; most of

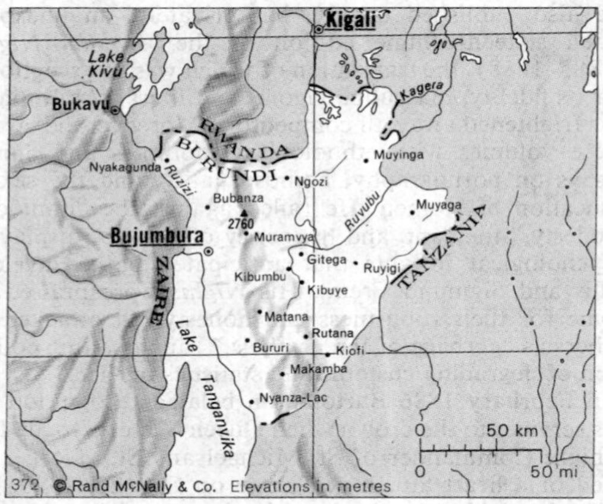

BURUNDI

the country lies at an altitude of more than 5,000 feet (1,500 metres) above sea level. The people live primarily by subsistence agriculture; coffee is grown for export. Industry is little developed. Among the countries that help Burundi, Belgium provides the most important aid.

Historical note

Burundi as a political entity is about 400 years old; it came into existence when the tall, cattle-owning Tutsi (Batutsi), a Nilotic people from the north, established their rule over the original Hutu (Bahutu) population and a small number of Twa (Batwa) Pygmy inhabitants. Once dominated by its more powerful Tutsi-ruled sister state of Rwanda to the north, Burundi was administratively separated from it when a German colonial occupation was proclaimed in 1897. During World War I the country was occupied, in 1916, by Belgian forces from the Congo; after the war the League of Nations mandate for the two kingdoms was given to Belgium, which administered them jointly with the Congo. After World War II the two kingdoms were given the status of a United Nations trust territory. Bujumbura (then Usumbura) was the capital.

On July 1, 1962, the two territories became independent separately. Unlike Rwanda, where the *mwami* (king) was deposed before independence, a Tutsi *mwami* continued to rule in Burundi until 1966, when the country became a republic.

While more intermarriage has occurred between the Tutsi (less than one-fifth of the population) and the Hutu (more than four-fifths) in Burundi than it has in Rwanda, tension between the two groups has nevertheless led to repeated political upheavals.

Relief and drainage. Burundi mostly consists of a high plateau of ancient Precambrian rock standing on the eastern side of the East African Rift System that runs from north to south throughout eastern Africa. The Ruzizi River to the west and Lake Tanganyika to the southwest lie in the trough of the rift valley. From the lake the land rises steeply to the Congo–Nile divide, which reaches altitudes of about 8,500 feet. To the east of the divide, plateau surfaces slope gently toward the east and southeast at altitudes of between 5,000 and 6,500 feet (1,500–2,000 metres). The valley of the Ruvubu River, which flows to the northeast, cuts into the plateau. The Kigira-Mukasenyi is a tributary of the Ruvubu, one of the headstreams of the Kagera River, which forms part of the Rwanda–Burundi frontier. To the north, along the frontier with Rwanda, there are a few valleys occupied by shallow lakes.

The Congo–Nile divide

Climate, vegetation, and animal life. The climate is tropical, although moderated by altitude. The annual rainfall averages more than 55 inches (1,400 millimetres) in the highest parts of the country and less than 40 inches (1,000 millimetres) in the southwest, on the shores of Lake Tanganyika. The dry season lasts from May to August, and sometimes to September, although some rain occurs in August. Irregular rainfall sometimes adversely affects the crops and has caused famines. The average temperature on the plateau is about 70° F (21° C), with a maximum temperature of 91° F (33° C) and a minimum of 43° F (6° C) below 6,500 feet.

The mountain slopes, which are wetter and cooler than the rest of the country, are forested. On the plateau, wooded savanna is found at higher altitudes, giving way to more open savanna on the lower slopes. The animal life is varied and includes elephant, lion, leopard, hippopotamus, crocodile, buffalo, warthog, baboon, and antelope.

The landscape under human settlement. On the plateau, dwellings are dispersed, each house being surrounded by a plantation of banana trees, the fruit of which is used for brewing. There are virtually no villages. Of the total land area of the country, about 40 percent is under cultivation and another 26 percent is fallow; about 25 percent is used for pasture; the remainder is either forest or wasteland.

Bujumbura, the capital, is a port city standing at the northern end of Lake Tanganyika and is renowned for the scenic beauty of its setting. Belgians and Greeks are prominent in the commerce of its central business district; the Asian district is near the port, as is also the industrial sector. Numerous suburbs make up an unbroken sequence of African dwellings.

People and population. The population is primarily composed of three ethnic groups—the Hutu, the Tutsi, and the Twa. There is considerable intermarriage between the Hutu and Tutsi, whose social systems are not dissimilar. The Hutu, who constitute 85 percent of the population, are a Bantu people who, it is believed, originally came from the Chad–Niger area and appear to have entered central and eastern Africa in about the 2nd century AD. They are primarily agriculturists. The Tutsi, who originally came from the Nile Valley, or perhaps Ethiopia, and are related to the Galla peoples of eastern Africa, entered Burundi between the 15th and the 18th century. Averaging about five feet nine inches in height, they are cattle raisers; their cattle have characteristically lyre-shaped horns. The Twa are Pygmies; they were the first inhabitants of the country and are thought to have

Ethnic groups

entered it from the Congo. They were once forest dwellers and today are hunters and potters.

Three further minority groups are also to be found in the country. These are Europeans, who are mostly businessmen, missionaries, or technical assistance personnel; Africans from other countries, among whom refugees from Rwanda and Zaire are the most numerous; and Asians, who constitute the smallest minority of all and are engaged in commerce.

Kirundi and French are the official languages of Burundi, but Swahili is also spoken, and English is taught in some schools. Kirundi is spoken not only in Burundi but also in Rwanda and in other neighbouring countries. It has been estimated that, apart from 7,000,000 people who speak it in Burundi and Rwanda, it is also spoken by about 2,000,000 Tanzanians and about 1,000,000 people in the Bukavu area of Zaire, as well as by a smaller group in southern Uganda.

The principal forms of religion are the traditional religion, which is based on the veneration of ancestors, and Christianity, primarily Roman Catholicism. Christianity, to which the majority of the population adheres, is slowly displacing the traditional religion.

The rate of population growth is rapid, with a rate of increase of about 2 percent a year. Out of the total population of about 3,544,000, it is estimated that almost half are under the age of 15.

Burundi, Area and Population

	area		population	
	sq mi	sq km	1965 census	1970 estimate
Provinces				
Bubanza	...	...	395,500	437,000
Bujumbura	...	...	96,700	107,000
Bururi	...	...	384,800	425,000
Gitega	...	...	534,800	590,000
Muramvya	...	...	351,100	388,000
Muyinga	...	...	470,700	520,000
Ngozi	...	...	662,800	732,000
Ruyigi	...	...	313,600	346,000
Total Burundi	10,759	27,865	3,210,000	3,544,000*

*Figures do not add to total given because of rounding.
Source: Official government figures.

Agriculture

The national economy. The economy is primarily agricultural. The main cash crops are arabica coffee, most of which is sold to the United States and which accounts for more than 80 percent of the value of exports, and cotton, which represents another 8 percent. In order to diversify the economy, the European Development Fund is financing the establishment of tea plantations. Subsistence crops include millet, maize, beans, yams, potatoes, manioc, and other crops, as well as such tropical fruits as bananas, mangoes, papayas, and oranges. Cattle raising is regarded as particularly important since ownership of cattle has a social as well as an economic significance, and cattle are also used as security for contracts. Apart from cattle, sheep, goats, pigs, and poultry also are raised. Fish are caught in Lakes Tanganyika, Cohoba, and Rweru. Fishing usually takes place at night, except when there is a full moon, and traditional methods are employed; some commercial fishing, using modern techniques, also has been begun. Mining and manufacturing represent only a small sector of the economy. A small amount of bastnaesite (a weakly radioactive mineral), cassiterite (tin ore), and gold is worked, and manufacturing industries include brewing, soapmaking, and cotton milling. There is also a construction industry. Governmental revenue is raised principally from taxes and customs duties; Belgian aid is also significant. Additional aid for development has been received from the United States, West Germany, and United Nations agencies.

Transport. A network of roads and dirt tracks covers the country; there are no railroads. There is a good road from Bujumbura to Bukavu in the Congo, and other principal routes lead from Bujumbura to Gitega (formerly Kitega, once the seat of the *mwami* and for a brief period after independence, the capital) and to Kigali in Rwanda. An international airport is located at Bujumbura, connected by regular flights to East African, Congolese, and European airports. There are four small airports for local flights situated at Nyanza-Lac, Kiofi, Gitega, and Nyakagunda. Steamers on Lake Tanganyika sail regularly between Bujumbura and the ports of Kalemi (Albertville) in Zaire, and Kigoma in Tanzania.

Administration and social conditions. There are eight provinces, each administered by a governor appointed by the administration. Each province is divided into two or three districts (arrondissements), each of which is administered by a commissioner. Each district is divided into communes, to each of which an administrator is appointed. There are 18 districts and 78 communes. Since the proclamation of the republic in November 1966, Col. Michel Micombero has been president of the government. He is assisted by the General Assembly of the party. The sole political party is the Parti de l'Unité et du Progrès National du Burundi (Uprona).

There are local tribunals of customary law. Other courts, including courts of first instance and appeal, operate under codified law.

In the late 1960s there were about 183,000 pupils in primary schools, about 4,000 in secondary schools, and 4,200 in vocational schools. There is one university, the Université Officielle de Bujumbura. Both Catholic and Protestant missions conduct literacy courses for adults.

The country has about one doctor for every 58,000 people. Malaria is endemic, although its incidence has been reduced. Sleeping sickness does not occur on the plateau, but pulmonary diseases, particularly tuberculosis, are quite widespread. In the public health sector there is one main hospital and eight more hospitals or medical centres; there are also eight private hospitals, and more than 80 medical dispensaries.

Cultural life. National culture is traditional rather than written. It is composed in part of a considerable body of oral literature consisting of stories, legends, and fables, as well as poetry and songs. Music is played on various instruments, such as the harp (*inanga*), the *dingidi* (a single-stringed fiddle) and the *ikimbe* (a linguaphone). Burundi folk dancing is internationally famous. Newspapers in Bujumbura include a daily, and the national radio station, which broadcasts in Kirundi, French, and Swahili, is located there.

Prospects for the future. While economic development is progressing, its rapid growth is precluded by Burundi's landlocked situation: Dar es-Salaam in Tanzania, the nearest ocean port, is 710 miles away from Bujumbura. An increase in exports would lessen the country's dependence upon Belgian aid; it is hoped that the newly introduced tea plantations, which are being subsidized by the European Development Fund of the European Economic Community (EEC), as well as by the International Monetary Fund, may eventually earn as much export revenue for Burundi as is now obtained from coffee. Meanwhile, the rapid and continuing rate of population growth poses a further challenge to development planners. The strategic situation of Bujumbura, the capital, at the head of Lake Tanganyika guarantees it increasingly regional as well as national importance.

BIBLIOGRAPHY. A.C. VEATCH, *The Evolution of the Congo Basin* (1935); W. ROBYNS, "La Flore et la végétation du Congo Belge," *Revue Quest. Scient.*, 97–98:261–299 (1930); J. MAES and O. BOONE, *Les Peuplades du Congo Belge* (1935); P. GOUROU, *La Densité de la population au Ruanda-Urundi* (1953); H.M. STANLEY, *The Congo and the Founding of Its Free State*, 2 vol. (1885); "Décolonisation et indépendance du Rwanda et du Burundi," in *Chronique de politique étrangère*, vol. 16 (1963), a governmental report including texts of constitutions; A.L. LATHAM-KOENIG, "Ruanda-Urundi on the Threshold of Independence," *World Today*, 18:288–295 (1962); UNITED NATIONS VISITING MISSION TO EAST AFRICA, *Report on Ruanda-Urundi 1948–1960*, 5 vol. (1949–60).

(P.-C.N.)

Business Associations, Law of

Business associations, from a legal viewpoint, are undertakings with more than one member, at least when they are formed, having assets distinct from the private assets of the members and a formal system of management, which may or may not include members of the association. The first feature, initial plurality of membership, distinguishes the business association from the business owned by one man; the latter does not need to be regulated internally by law because the single owner can do as he pleases with its assets; since he is personally liable for debts and obligations incurred in connection with the business, no special rules are needed to protect its creditors beyond the ordinary provisions of bankruptcy law. The second feature, the possession of distinct assets (or a distinct patrimony, as European lawyers would say), is essential for two purposes: to delimit the assets to which creditors of the association can resort to satisfy their claims (though in the case of some associations, such as the partnership, they can also compel the members to make good any deficiency), and to make clear what assets the managers of the association may use to carry on business for the members' benefit. The assets of an association are contributed directly or indirectly by its members: directly if a member transfers a business or property or investments of his own to the association in return for a share in its capital, and indirectly if a member pays the amount of his share of capital in cash and the association then uses his contribution and like contributions in cash made by other members to purchase a business, property, or investments. The third essential feature, a system of management, varies greatly. In a simple form of business association the members who provide the assets are entitled to participate in the management, and each member has an equal voice in management decisions unless otherwise agreed. In the more complex form of association, such as the company or corporation of the Anglo-Saxon countries, members have no immediate right to participate in the management of the association's affairs, though they are able to appoint and dismiss the managers, known in this case as directors, presidents, or administrators, and their consent is required for major changes in the company's structure or activities, such as reorganizations of its capital and mergers with other associations. Because the role of a member of a company or corporation is basically passive, he is known as a shareholder or stockholder, the emphasis being placed on his investment function. The managers of a business association, however, do not in law comprise all the persons who exercise discretion or make decisions. Even the senior executives of big corporations or companies are often merely employees, and like manual or clerical workers their legal relationship with the corporation is of no significance in considering the law governing the corporation. Whether an executive is a director, president, or administrator, and so an element in the company or corporation's legal structure, depends on purely formal considerations; if he is named as such in the document constituting the corporation, or if he is subsequently appointed or elected to hold such an office, it is irrelevant that his actual functions in running the corporation's business and the power or influence he wields are great or small. Nevertheless, for certain purposes, such as liability for defrauding creditors in English law and liability for deficiencies of assets in bankruptcy in French law, people who act like directors and participate in the management of the company's affairs are treated as such although they have not been formally appointed.

Essential features of business associations

FORMS OF BUSINESS ASSOCIATION

Partnerships. The most important forms of business association, because the most numerous, are the partnership and the company or corporation. The distinguishing features of the partnership are the personal and unrestricted liability of each partner for the debts and obligations of the firm (whether he assented to them being incurred or not) and the right of each partner to participate in the management of the firm and to act as an agent of it in entering into legal transactions on its behalf. The civil law systems of the European countries have additionally always permitted a modified form of partnership, the limited partnership (*société en commandite, Kommanditgesellschaft, società in accomandita*) in which one or more of the partners are liable for the firm's debts only to the extent of the capital they contribute or agree to contribute, but such limited partners are prohibited from taking part in the management of the firm, and if they do, they become personally liable without limit for the debts of the firm, together with the general partners. Anglo-Saxon common law refused to recognize the limited partnership, and in the United States at the beginning of the 19th century only Louisiana, which was governed by French civil law, permitted such partnerships. During the 19th century, however, most of the states enacted legislation allowing limited partnerships to be formed, and in 1907 Great Britain adopted the limited partnership by statute, but it has not been much used there in practice. Another distinction between kinds of partnership made by the civil law system, which has no equivalent in Anglo-Saxon countries, is between civil and commercial partnerships. This distinction depends on whether the purposes for which the partnership is formed fall within the list of commercial activities in the country's commercial code or not. These codes always make manufacturing, dealing in, and transporting goods commercial activities, while professional and agricultural activities are always noncommercial. Consequently, a partnership of lawyers, doctors, or farmers is a civil partnership, governed exclusively by the civil code of the country concerned and untouched by its commercial code. No such distinction is made in the Anglo-Saxon countries, where professional and business partnerships are subject to the same rules as trading partnerships, with the one difference that only partners in a trading partnership have implied power to borrow on the firm's behalf.

Companies or corporations. The company or corporation, unlike the partnership, is formed not simply by an agreement entered into between its first members; it must also be registered at a public office or court designated by law, or otherwise obtain official acknowledgment of its existence. Under English and American law the company or corporation is incorporated by filing the company's constitution (memorandum and articles of association, articles or certificate of incorporation) signed by its first members at the Companies Registry in London or, in the U.S., at the office of the state secretary of state or corporation commissioner. In France, Germany, and Italy and the other countries subject to a civil law system, a notarized copy of the constitution is filed at the local commercial tribunal, and proof is tendered that the first members of the company have subscribed the whole or a prescribed fraction of the company's capital, and that assets transferred to the company in return for an allotment of its shares have been officially valued and found to be worth at least the amount of capital allotted for them. English and American law, together with the laws of the Netherlands and the Scandinavian countries, provide only one category of business company or corporation (in the Netherlands the *naamloze vennootschap*, in Sweden the *aktiebolag*), although all these systems of law make distinctions for tax purposes between private, or close, companies or corporations on the one hand and public companies or corporations on the other. English law also distinguishes between private and public companies for some purposes of company law; for example, a private company cannot have more than 50 members and cannot advertise subscriptions for its shares. Under the other civil law systems, however, a fundamental distinction is drawn between the public company (*société anonyme; Aktiengesellschaft; società per azioni*) and the private company (*société à responsabilité limitée, Gesellschaft mit beschränkter Haftung* [*G.m.b.H.*], *società a responsabilità limitata*), and in Germany the two kinds of company are governed by different enactments, as they were in France until 1966. Functionally, however, public and private companies are the same in all countries. Private companies are formed when there is no need to appeal to the public to subscribe for the company's shares or to lend money to it, and often they are little more than incorporated partnerships whose directors hold all or most of the company's shares. Public companies are formed—or more usually created by the conversion of private companies into public ones—when the necessary capital cannot be supplied by the directors or their associates and it is necessary to raise funds from the public by publishing a prospectus and, in Great Britain and the British Commonwealth countries, obtaining a stock exchange listing for the shares or other securities offered. In a typical public company the directors hold only a small fraction of its shares, often less than 1 percent; and in Great Britain and the United States, at least, it is not uncommon for up to one-half of the funds raised by the company to be represented not by shares in the company but by loan securities such as debentures or bonds.

In Anglo-Saxon countries, public and private companies account for most of the business associations formed, and partnerships are now entered into only for professional activities. In European countries, the partnership in both its forms is still widely used for carrying on commercial undertakings, and in Germany a popular form of association combines both the partnership and the company. This is the *G.m.b.H. & Co.*, which is a limited partnership whose general partner (nominally liable without limit for the partnership's debts) is a private company and whose limited partners are the same persons as the shareholders of the company. The limited partners enjoy the benefit of limited liability for the partnership's debts, and by ensuring that most of the partnership's profits are paid to them as limited partners and not to them as shareholders in the private company, they largely avoid the incidence of corporation tax.

Other forms. Besides the partnership and the company or corporation there are a number of other forms of business association, of which some are developments or adaptations of the partnership or company, some are based on contract between the members or on a trust created for their benefit, and others are purely statutory creations. The first of these classes includes the cooperative society; the building society or home loan association and its German equivalent, the *Bausparkasse;* the trustee savings bank or people's or cooperative bank; the friendly society or mutual insurance association; and the American mutual fund investment company. The essential features of these associations are that they provide for the small or medium investor; and although they originated as contractual associations, they are now governed in most countries by special legislation and not by the law applicable to companies or corporations. The second class comprises the English unit trust and the European *fonds d'investissements* or *Investmentfonds*, which fulfill the same functions as the American mutual funds; the Massachusetts business trust (now little used, but providing a means of limiting the liability of participants in a business activity like the limited partnership); the foundation (*fondation, Stiftung*), a European organization with no equivalent in Anglo-Saxon countries, which has social or charitable objects and often carries on a business whose profits are devoted to those objects; and, finally, the cartel or trade association, which regulates the business activities of its individual members and is itself extensively regulated by antitrust and antimonopoly legislation. The third class of associations, those wholly created by statute, comprise corporations formed to carry on nationalized business undertakings (such as the Bank of England and the German Federal Railways) or to coexist with other businesses in the same field (such as the Italian Istituto per la Ricostruzione Industriale) or to fulfill a particular governmental function (such as the Atomic Energy Commission and the Tennessee Valley Authority). Such statutory associations usually have no share capital, though they do raise loans from the public. They are regarded in European law as being the creatures of public law, like departments and agencies of the government. In recent years, however, a hybrid between the state corporation and the privately owned corporation or company has appeared in the form of the mixed company or corporation (*société mixte*). In this kind of organization part of the association's share capital is held by the state or a state agency and part by private persons, this situation often resulting from a partial acquisition of the association's shares by the state. In only France and Italy are there special rules governing such associations; in Great Britain and Germany they are subject to the ordinary rules of company law.

HISTORY OF COMPANY LAW

From partnership to limited liability

Space precludes more than an outline of the history of the law governing business associations. Although a primitive form of partnership, the *societas*, existed under Roman law, it was not until the Middle Ages that the germ of the modern partnership and company appeared in Italy and France and spread by imitation to England and the countries of northern Europe. By the 16th century, the law relating to general and limited partnerships had been extensively developed in the Mediterranean countries and in some places codified, but the selective adoption of parts of this law by the courts in England and the complete exclusion of the limited partnership left the Anglo-Saxon common law in this field largely inarticulate. In the 16th and 17th centuries, overseas trading by the newly emerged nation-states was conducted mostly by privileged companies of merchants chartered by the monarch or the state, such as the English and Dutch East India companies and the French Mississippi Company, and in the 17th century the practice of incorporating companies by charter was extended to domestic undertakings which could afford to pay for the privilege. Merchants and lawyers, however, soon learned how to adapt the partnership so as to gain most of the benefits of incorporation by charter, and by the end of the 17th century unincorporated companies with transferable shares and elected boards of directors, which in law were merely large partnerships, became common. In France such companies were tolerated and partly regulated by the *Ordonnance de Commerce* of 1673, but in England they were legally suppressed by the Bubble Act of 1720, a measure enacted to stop the orgy of speculation in the shares of chartered and unincorporated companies.

The nineteenth century. Until the Bubble Act was repealed in 1825, no real development took place in English company law, though unincorporated companies had been extensively formed throughout the 18th century, and in the 1820s the shares of over a hundred of them were dealt in by stockbrokers who were members of the London Stock Exchange. In France, on the other hand, the law governing all forms of commercial companies and partnerships had been codified in the Commercial Code of 1807, and although it was not possible to form a public company or *société anonyme* without the authorization of the state until 1863, the French supreme court held in 1832 that a *société en commandite*, formed simply by an agreement registered in the local commercial court, could have freely transferable shares like the *société anonyme*. This heralded the *société en commandite par actions*, the prototype of the limited liability company in Europe. Meanwhile, New York State had enacted legislation in 1811 that permitted manufacturing companies to be incorporated and to obtain the benefit of limited liability merely by filing with the secretary of state a certificate setting out the essential features of the company's constitution. During the 19th century, all the states of the U.S. enacted similar legislation extending to all kinds of companies, but, because the corporation laws of the different states were enacted at different times and independently of each other, there was great diversity between them. In Great Britain, the incorporation of companies by mere registration at a public office was not authorized by legislation until 1844, and until 1855 members of such registered companies were liable personally for the company's debts like partners, the privilege of limited liability only being obtainable by special act of Parliament. In 1855 this privilege was made available to all registered companies, and in 1856 and 1862 there were enacted the major Companies Acts on which modern British company law is based. France enacted its major companies legislation in 1867, in many respects following the English pattern, though retaining distinctive features from the Commercial Code of 1807. Prussia adopted legislation based on the French Commercial Code in 1843, but it was not until 1870 that Germany permitted limited liability companies with transferable shares to be formed merely by registration. In one respect Germany took the lead, however, for it was the first country to establish the private company (*G.m.b.H.*) as a distinct category. This was done in 1892; Great Britain followed suit in 1907, but France not until 1925.

The twentieth century. The 20th century has been a period of continuous reform and modification of company law in all industrial countries. In the United States, some measure of correspondence between the legislation of the different states has been achieved, and in California an attempt has been made to codify corporation law. Despite the publication of a Uniform Business Corporation Act in 1928 and the American Bar Association's Model Business Corporation Act in 1946, however, there is still much diversity between the corporation laws of the different states, and the only area where complete uniformity prevails is in federal legislation governing the public issue of corporations' shares and bonds, the operation of the securities markets, the organization and conduct of mutual fund companies, and the terms of issue of corporation bonds and the protection of bondholders.

MANAGEMENT AND CONTROL

The structure of management

The simplest form of management is the partnership. In the Anglo-Saxon and the European civil law countries every partner is entitled to take part in the management of the firm's business, unless he is a limited partner; however, a partnership agreement may provide that an ordinary partner shall not participate in management, in which case he is a dormant partner but is still personally liable for the debts and obligations incurred by the other managing partners.

Corporations. The management structure of companies or corporations is more complex. The simplest is that envisaged by English, Belgian, Italian, and Scandinavian law, by which the shareholders of the company periodically elect a board of directors who collectively manage the company's affairs and reach decisions by a majority vote but also have the right to delegate any of their powers, or even the whole management of the company's business, to one or more of their number. Under this regime it is common for a managing director (*directeur général; direttore generale*) to be appointed, often with one or more assistant managing directors, and for the board of directors to authorize them to enter into all transactions needed for carrying on the company's business, subject only to the general supervision of the board and to its approval of particularly important measures, such as issuing shares or bonds or borrowing. The American system of management is a development of this basic pattern. By the laws of most of the states it is obligatory for the board of directors elected periodically by the shareholders to appoint certain executive officers, such as the president, vice president, treasurer, and secretary. The two latter have no management powers and fulfill the administrative functions that in an English company are the concern of its secretary; but the president, and in his absence the vice president, have by law or by delegation from the board of directors the same full powers of day-to-day management as are exercised in practice by an English managing director.

Public companies. The most complex management structures are those provided for public companies under German and French law. The management of private companies under these systems is confided to one or more managers (*gérants, Geschäftsführer*) who have the same powers as managing directors. In the case of public companies, however, German law imposes a two-tier structure, the lower tier consisting of a supervisory committee (*Aufsichtsrat*) whose members are elected periodically by the shareholders and the employees of the company in the proportion of two-thirds shareholder representatives and one-third employee representatives (except in the case of mining and steel companies where shareholders and employees are equally represented), and the upper tier consisting of a management board (*Vorstand*) comprising one or more persons appointed by the supervisory committee, but not from their own number. The affairs of the company are managed by the management board, subject to the supervision of the supervisory committee, to which it must report periodically and which can at any time require information or explanations. The supervisory committee is forbidden to undertake the management of the company itself, but the company's constitution may require its approval for particular transactions, such as borrowing or the establishment of branches overseas, and by law it is the supervisory committee that fixes the remuneration of the managers and has power to dismiss them. The French management structure for public companies offers two alternatives. Unless the company's constitution otherwise provides, the shareholders periodically elect a board of directors (*conseil d'administration*), which "is vested with the widest powers to act on behalf of the company," but which is also required to elect a president from its members who "undertakes on his own responsibility the general management of the company," so that in fact the board of directors' functions are reduced to supervising him. The similarity to the German pattern is obvious, and recent French legislation carries this further by openly permitting public companies to establish a supervisory committee (*conseil de surveillance*) and a management board (*directoire*) like the German equivalents as an alternative to the board of directors-president structure. In recent years Dutch and Italian public companies have tended to follow the German pattern of management, although it is not expressly sanctioned by the law of those countries. The Dutch *commissarissen* and the Italian *sindaci*, appointed by the shareholders, with legal functions not dissimilar from those of the auditors of companies in the Anglo-Saxon countries in the days before professional accountants took over audit work, have, probably because of the spread of professional auditing, taken over the task of supervising the directors and reporting on the wisdom and efficiency of their management to the shareholders.

The making of transactions

Contractual authority. A person who enters into a transaction with a partnership or company is less concerned with the structure of its management than with ensuring that the representatives of the firm he negotiates with have authority to bind it legally. In the case of a partnership, the Anglo-Saxon and civil law systems agree that the firm is bound if the representative is a partner (other than a limited one) and the transaction is relevant to the kind of business the firm carries on. The fact that the other partners repudiate the transaction or were not consulted beforehand, or that the partnership agreement restricts the authority of the partner who negotiates the transaction, does not prevent the transaction from binding the firm, though in the latter event in Anglo-Saxon law the other party to the transaction must have been ignorant of the restriction. The law is not so simple in the case of transactions negotiated by directors of companies, although in respect of transactions entered into on behalf of private companies the directors or managers individually have the same power to bind the company under French, German, and Belgian law as partners have to bind their firm. In the case of other companies, the powers of directors are, with some exceptions, limited first by the rule that the transaction in question should be relevant to the kind of business the company is authorized to carry on by its constitution, and secondly by the rule that the transaction must be authorized by the board of directors collectively. The first rule has been carried to extremes by Anglo-Saxon common law, which in effect obliges the person dealing with the company to inspect the company's constitution and to ensure at his peril that the transaction is authorized by it, though in some states of the U.S. legislation has made even unauthorized transactions valid if the person dealing with the company is unaware that they are beyond the company's powers, and in all the states the transaction is binding if one of the parties has fulfilled his obligations under it. European civil law has always adopted a more generous attitude. By French law the transaction is valid if "within the limits of the objects of the company," which is interpreted as meaning if it is appropriate to carrying on the kind of business mentioned in the company's constitution. By German law the transaction is binding in all cases, even if totally unconnected with the company's business, unless the person dealing with the company conspired with its representative to defraud it. The second rule, requiring the collective approval of the board of directors for a transaction to bind a company, obviously does not apply to transactions entered into by the company's managing director or president or by an individual director to whom the board has delegated its authority, nor does it apply to transactions entered into by the president or management board of a French or German public company. But any other director has no more power than a shareholder to negotiate a transaction individually on behalf of his company, and in this respect his position is far weaker than that of a partner. The two rules here considered illustrate the difficulty experienced by the courts of different countries in trying to reconcile the conflicting claims of the shareholders—that their company's assets should only be used to satisfy obligations properly incurred on its behalf in conformity with its constitution— and of the outsider who deals in good faith with one or more directors or managers. On the whole, the law of the Anglo-Saxon countries has favoured the shareholders' claim, while civil law has favoured the outsider's.

Powers and duties

Directors. Company legislation in all countries imposes specific duties on directors, such as the duty to call a general meeting of shareholders once a year and on other occasions when demanded by a certain fraction of the shareholders. It also imposes certain prohibitions on directors, such as the absolute prohibition on borrowing from the company imposed by English and French law and the law of many states of the U.S. But over and above these specific provisions, every system of law also imposes on partners and directors general fiduciary duties to exercise their powers in the interests of the partnership or company and not for their private gain, and to avoid situations where their private interests conflict with those of their firm. American law has gone farthest in enlarging these almost ethical obligations. Like some other systems of law, it has made directors return unreasonably large remuneration and account for profits made out of business opportunities that they have diverted from the company to themselves. Also it has gone farther than many other systems by making directors compensate the company for any loss it has sustained from their competing with it or taking interests in competing firms, and by rendering them accountable to the company for personal gains made out of such activities and out of carrying on business activities in fields related to the company's into which the company may wish to expand in the future. English law does not go this far. Although it makes directors accountable for personal gains from use of the company's property, including trade secrets, knowledge of its customers and "know-how" generally, there is nothing to prevent a director from competing with the company unless he has contracted not to do so or has agreed to devote all his time to managing the company. European law has dealt with the question of competition by directors in express legislative provisions. German law prohibits members of the management board of a public company from carrying on any other business alone or in partnership, and from engaging in transactions in the company's business field, unless the supervisory committee consents; and Italian law prohibits all directors from competing with their company unless the shareholders resolve that they may. French law achieves the same result indirectly by forbidding any person from being president or a member of the management board of more than two public companies, or a member of the board of directors or supervisory committee of more than eight. In addition to his fiduciary duties, a director is, under all systems of law, subject to a duty to act carefully in managing his company's affairs, and he is liable to compensate it for all loss sustained as a result of his carelessness. Some legal systems have sought to establish the standard of care required by legislation. Under German law, the members of the management board and the supervisory committee of a public company must "exercise the care of a competent and conscientious business manager," and by Italian law all directors must exhibit "the diligence of a salaried agent." English law has not defined directors' duties of care in this way, and the courts have long held that they are not required to bring more skill to the performance of their functions than they in fact possess, nor to exercise more care than a reasonable man could be expected to do in handling his own affairs. In particular, under English law, directors are not obliged to supervise their fellow directors or to take any action against them unless they have cause to suspect their honesty. American common law is more exacting than this; it requires directors to show the same standard of care as is expected of the ordinary prudent director or businessman, and in some states their duty has been codified by legislation in similar terms.

The rights of ownership

Shareholders. The beneficiaries of sound management are the shareholders, and by the same token the shareholders are the primary sufferers if a company's affairs are mismanaged or badly managed. For this reason all systems of law make directors answerable to the shareholders to a greater or lesser degree. The first means of making this responsibility meaningful is the requirement imposed by the laws of all countries that a general meeting of shareholders be held annually, before which the directors must lay the company's audited annual accounts (balance sheet and profit and loss account, and sometimes group accounts if the company has subsidiaries) and a report by the directors on the company's activities during its last financial year and on its present position. Since directors are elected or re-elected by shareholders at these annual general meetings, the shareholders can express their disapproval of the directors' management of the company's affairs by electing a new board, or if only a fraction of the directors retire each year, by not re-electing those of them who present themselves for re-election. Where the company has a two-tier management structure, as have French and German public companies and American and English companies whose presidents or managing directors are appointed by the board of directors and not by the shareholders, a change in the composition of the board or supervisory committee does not result immediately in a change in the president, managing director, or management board, but since most systems of law permit the removal of the latter for any reason (though subject to the payment of damages if there is no good cause for the removal, or if it amounts to a breach of contract), the new board or supervisory committee may quickly effect a change in the management body. The statutory power of removal extends under all systems of law to the board of directors or supervisory committee as well, and can be exercised by the shareholders at extraordinary general meetings held at any time, so that to this extent the directors' answerability to the shareholders is continuous and not merely periodic. It is rare for most of the shareholders of big companies to attend annual or extraordinary general meetings personally; instead they avail themselves of the right given by all systems of law to appoint proxies to attend and vote on their behalf. The directors and opposing groups of shareholders who seek to displace them assiduously solicit proxy appointment from uncommitted shareholders by sending them circulars setting out their respective cases well in advance of the general meeting in question, and English and German law and the federal law of the United States confer limited rights on individual shareholders or minority groups of shareholders to have their solicitation material circulated by the company itself. The outcome of a contest for control of the board of directors in such cases is usually known shortly before the general meeting is held when the time for notifying proxy appointments expires; the outcome is determined by the number of proxies each side has been able to obtain, and the meeting is then purely a formality. In Anglo-Saxon countries it is uncommon for shareholders to give proxies for more than one general meeting at a time unless they are members of an opposition group that acts collectively by forming a voting pool, but in Europe it is not uncommon for shareholders to authorize the banks with which they deposit their shares to exercise the voting rights attached to them for an indefinite period. To discourage this, the German law governing public companies provides that such an authority expires after 18 months, though it may be renewed by the shareholder, and the depositary bank must seek the instructions of the shareholder as to how it is to vote on each occasion a general meeting is held, and it may vote as it thinks fit only if he gives no instructions.

Shareholders' suits. The second way shareholders may call directors to account is by suing them for damages or other appropriate remedies. Under the law of the Anglo-Saxon countries, directors' duties are owed to the company, not to the shareholders individually, and so proceedings can be brought only if a general meeting of shareholders so resolves, or if the case is one where the law exceptionally permits one or more shareholders to sue on behalf of all of them to enforce the company's claim. In English law such representative actions can be brought only if the directors have infringed the fundamental provisions of the company's constitution, or if they control a majority of votes that can be cast at a general meeting and have been guilty of fraud or breach of fiduciary duty. American law is more liberal in allowing representative actions (known as derivative suits because the claim that is being enforced is derived from the company). Generally a shareholder may bring such an action if he has requested the directors and a meeting of shareholders to sue in the company's name and they have refused, and the only limitations imposed are that the shareholder must not be motivated by bad faith and the matter must not be the exercise of a reasonable business discretion by the directors. Under European law, legislation gives shareholders who hold a certain fraction of a public company's shares, usually one-tenth, the right to sue to enforce any claim of the company against its directors, and in France, Belgium, and Italy (but not in Germany) they may also sue individually to recover compensation for the fall in the value of their shares caused by mismanagement. Although English common law gives only very restricted rights to individual shareholders to remedy wrongs done to their company, legislation does permit them to petition the court for any appropriate form of relief if the persons who control the company (whether directors or not) have treated them oppressively over a period of time, and the court can, among other things, order the purchase of the petitioners' shares at a fair value by the persons in control, or the sale of the latter's shares so as to break up their control. American common law now recognizes that persons in control of a company do owe a fiduciary duty to minority shareholders and so are liable to compensate them if they sell their controlling shareholding to persons whom they know are likely to loot or mismanage the company, but there are as yet no legislative provisions in any of the states, or in any European country either, that go as far as the English provision for judicial relief against oppression.

SHARES AND OTHER SECURITIES

How company shares differ from those in a partnership

Under all systems of law a partner may assign his share or interest in a partnership to anyone he wishes unless the partnership agreement forbids this, but the assignment does not make the assignee a partner unless all of the other partners agree. If they do not, the assignee is merely entitled to receive the financial benefits attached to the share or interest without being able to take part in the management of the firm, but neither is he personally liable for the debts of the firm.

The shares of a company are quite different. In the first place, they are freely transferable unless the company's constitution imposes restrictions on their transfer, or, in French and Belgian law, unless the company is a private one, in which case transfers require the consent of the holders of three-quarters of the company's issued shares. The constitution of an English private company must always restrict the transfer of its shares for the company to qualify as private. The restriction is usually that the directors may refuse to register a transfer for any of several reasons, or that the other shareholders shall have the right to buy the shares at a fair price when the holder of them wishes to sell. In American law similar restrictions may be imposed, but unreasonable restrictions are disallowed by the courts. According to French and German law, the transfer of shares in public companies may be restricted only by being made subject to the consent of the board of directors or of the management board, but under French law if the directors do not find an alternative purchaser at a fair price within three months their consent is considered as given.

Limited liability. In the second place, shares in a company do not expose the original holder or a person to whom they have been transferred to unlimited liability in the way a partner (other than a limited one) is liable for the debts of his firm. Under all systems of law, except those of Belgium and some of the states of the U.S., all shares must have a nominal value expressed in money terms, such as $10, £1, DM. 50 or Fr. 100, the latter two being the minimum permissible under German and French law. Although a company may issue shares for a subscription price greater than this nominal value, the excess being known as a share premium, it generally cannot issue them for less than that nominal value, and any part of the nominal value and the share premium that has not so far been paid is the measure of the shareholder's maximum liability to contribute if the company becomes insolvent. If shares are issued without a nominal value (no par value shares), the subscription price is fixed by the directors and is the measure of the shareholder's maximum liability to contribute. Usually the subscription price of shares is paid to the company fairly soon after they are issued; the period for payment of all the installments is rarely more than a year in Anglo-Saxon countries, and it is not uncommon for the whole subscription price to be payable when the shares are issued. The actual subscription price is influenced by general market factors, by the company's profit record and prospects, and by the market value of the company's existing shares. Although directors have a duty to obtain the best subscription price possible, they can offer new shares to existing shareholders at favourable prices, and those shareholders can benefit either by subscribing for the new shares or by selling their subscription rights to other persons. Under European legislation directors are bound to offer new shares to existing shareholders in the first place unless they resolve to forgo their pre-emptive rights. In most states of the U.S. (but not in Great Britain) such pre-emptive rights are implied if the new shares belong to the same class as existing shares, but the rights may be negated by the company's constitution.

The third difference between shares in companies and interests in partnerships is that a partner is automatically entitled to his share of profits of the firm as soon as they are ascertained, but a shareholder is only entitled to a dividend out of the company's profits when it has been declared. Under English law, dividends are declared at annual general meetings of shareholders, though the company's constitution usually provides that the shareholders cannot declare higher dividends than the directors recommend. Under American law dividends are usually declared by the directors, and if shareholders consider, in view of the company's profits, that too small a dividend has been paid, they may apply to the court to direct payment of a reasonable dividend. German law similarly protects shareholders of public companies against niggardly dividends by giving the annual general meeting power to dispose as it wishes of at least half the profit shown by the company's annual accounts before making transfers to reserve, and with the same object Swedish law empowers the holders of 10 percent of a company's shares to require at least one-fifth of its accumulated profits and reserves to be distributed as a dividend, provided that the total distribution will not exceed one half of the profits of its last financial year.

Classes of shares. Companies may issue shares of different classes, the commonest classes being ordinary and preference, or in American terminology, common and preferred shares. The latter are entitled by the terms on which they are issued to payment of a dividend of a fixed amount (usually expressed as a percentage of their nominal value) out of the profits of the company before any dividend is paid to the ordinary shareholders. If the shares are cumulative preference shares, any unpaid part of a year's dividend is carried forward and added to the next year's dividend, and so on repeatedly if necessary until the arrears of preference dividend are paid off. The accumulation of arrears of preference dividend naturally depreciates the value of the ordinary shares, whose holders cannot be paid a dividend until the arrears of preference dividend have been paid. Consequently, it has been common in the United States (but not in Great Britain) for companies to issue noncumulative preference shares, giving their holders the right to a fixed preferential dividend each year if the company's profits are sufficient to pay it, but limiting the dividend to the amount of the profits of the year if they are insufficient to pay the preference dividend in full. Preference shares are not common in Europe, but under German and Italian law they have the distinction of being the only kind of shares that can be issued without voting rights in general meetings, all other shares carrying voting rights proportionate to their nominal value by law.

Bonds and debentures. In addition to shares, which constitute its capital, a company may issue debentures or bonds to raise loans, and since by their terms such loans are often repayable only 15 or 20 years after they are raised, the debentures or bonds of a company are referred to as its loan capital. Debentures or bonds may be issued to a few persons, but public companies often issue them to the investing public at large, and the problem then arises of providing for the representation of the bondholders by one or two persons who may enforce their rights on their behalf and may agree to, or call meetings of bondholders to consent to, modifications of any security given for the bonds. In Anglo-Saxon countries this is done by appointing a trustee for the bondholders or debenture holders and by vesting in it any security for the bonds, such as a mortgage of the company's land or, under British practice, a general charge on all the company's assets. In European countries, the bondholders by law have to be represented by an agent who is under a duty to protect the bondholders' interests and has the power to call meetings of bondholders so that they may consent to certain limited modifications of the company's obligations. The duties of trustees for bondholders or debenture holders have not been codified by statute in the United States or Great Britain, but in the United States they are now extensively governed by federal legislation. Because of the worldwide rise in commercial interest rates in recent years, American, British, and European companies have increasingly issued convertible bonds and debentures carrying a lower rate of interest than ordinary debentures but entitling the holder to convert them into ordinary shares of the company (expected to rise in value) at a specified rate of exchange on specified future dates or during a specified future period. The conversion rights, not yet protected by legislation in the United States and Great Britain, were by French and German law to ensure that they were not diluted by further issues of the company's shares or by it taking action adverse to the bondholders' interests.

CURRENT AND FUTURE PROBLEMS

Mergers. Of the many current and likely future developments in the laws of the industrialized countries, mergers, and employee participation call for particular mention, as also does the tendency of the company laws of the western European countries toward uniformity in all respects.

The most dramatic development in the field of business associations in recent years has been the wave of mergers of small and large companies with other concerns that have made "take-over" or "tender" bids. Until recently, the laws of few countries regulated such bids; probably the earliest was legislation in Great Britain in 1928 that enabled a bidding company, which had acquired 90 percent or more of the shares bid for, to acquire the outstanding shares at the bid price even against the wishes of their holders. The regulation of take-over bids is still more extensive in Great Britain than in any other country, and the law is supplemented by the rules of the stock exchanges (which are adhered to since bidding companies do not wish to lose the listing or quotation of their shares) and by the Code on Take Overs and Mergers (which is a set of rules for the fair conduct of take-over operations and the fair treatment of investors in the bidding company and the company that is bid for, conformity with these rules being ensured by the action of the banks and underwriters who participate). The law does little beyond requiring the bidding company to give full information about recent dealing prices in its shares and the shares bid for in the circular containing its offer to buy those shares or exchange them for shares newly issued by itself, and also to disclose in that circular any special arrangements it has with the directors of the company bid for in respect of their retirement or the acquisition of their shares. The detailed rules of the game are contained in the Code, which requires the bid to be notified to the board of the company bid for before it is published and to be kept secret until it is sent out simultaneously to all the shareholders concerned; forbids both companies and their associates from engaging in dealings in the shares of either company, which may create a false market; permits the bidding company to buy shares of the other company on the market outside the bid, but only on paying shareholders who accept the bid the average price paid for its market purchases if that is higher than the bid price; forbids a bidding company from declaring its bid unconditional and binding unless it has received so many acceptances that it holds more than half the votes that can be cast at a general meeting of the company bid for; enables an accepting shareholder to retract his acceptance if the bid is not declared unconditional within three weeks after it is made; requires the bidding company to allow a further period for late acceptances after the bid is declared unconditional; and finally, requires all shareholders to whom the bid is addressed to be treated with absolute equality, and in particular, if a bid for less than all the shares of a class is made and acceptances exceed the number of shares bid for, that the acceptances shall be scaled down proportionately. The Code probably sets the pattern of future legislation on this subject. As yet United States federal law has only required the filing and circulation of certain information in connection with tender bids and has not regulated the conduct of bids in detail, although the general provisions of federal law directed against fraud and fraudulent manipulations of security prices apply to the conduct of such bids as they do to other transactions in securities. European law has made no provision in respect of tender bids, beyond that in the German legislation enabling a public company that has acquired 95 percent of the shares of another company to acquire the remainder. Nevertheless, the Paris Stock Exchange and the Belgian Banking Commission do in fact exercise some control over tender bids.

"Take-over" and "tender" bids

Participation and profit sharing. The second topic that is likely to be of increasing significance in the future is participation by employees in the direction of the companies for whom they work. English and American law have so far only dealt with this matter by permitting companies to establish share subscription schemes under which employees may acquire shares in their employing company at favourable prices, and share bonus schemes by which a fraction of the company's profits are set aside annually and used to acquire shares in the company for the benefit of employees by subscription or by purchase in the market. Although such schemes may involve a company financing the acquisition of shares in itself, they are recognized as lawful by legislation in Great Britain and several of the states of the U.S. But schemes of this kind are optional, and their outcome is simply that the number of shareholders of the company is increased; shares held by employees carry no special rights, and in any case they are either issued without votes in general meetings or carry only a small fraction of the votes that may be cast. European law has led the way toward a more positive position. As already stated, one-third (or in the mining and steel industries, one-half) of the members of the supervisory committee of German public companies are elected by its employees from a list of candidates nominated by the works council (*Betreibsrat*), an obligatory elected body of employees, which, among other things, manages employees' pension funds and has to be consulted on management measures affecting employees. The provisions relating to works councils and the election by employees of representatives to the supervisory committee also apply to private companies employing more than 500 persons, and their management structure consequently is the same as that of public companies. French law is weaker than German in providing for direct employee participation in management. It, too, provides for elected works councils (*comités d'entreprise*) where a business employs 50 or more persons, but employees are represented on the board of directors only if the company is a public one, and even then only by two nonvoting representatives appointed by the works council. On the other hand, French law is more advanced in entitling the employees of a company to share in its profits by making it compulsory for companies to establish share bonus schemes under which shares are periodically allotted to employees and paid for out of the company's profits. These shares carry the full rights of ordinary shares, but are nontransferable for five years after they are issued.

Uniform legislation in Europe. Another matter of current and future importance is the tendency in recent years for the companies legislation of the western European countries to become more homogeneous, largely as a result of the setting up of the European Economic Community (EEC). Most countries and states of the U.S. have long permitted companies formed in other countries or states to carry on business in their own territory, usually subject to filing particulars of the foreign company's constitution and periodic reports on its activities. But the law of the foreign country or state where the company was incorporated or where it has its central management still governs it, and inevitably there will be conflicts with the host country's laws and gaps in the application of the host country's own companies legislation to its foreign company. Moreover, it is usually impossible for companies formed in different countries to merge under the laws governing any of them, and the nearest practicable approach to a merger is the formation of parallel companies in each of the countries concerned and the distribution of their shares to the original shareholders of the merged businesses. Such difficulties would be overcome if a uniform companies law were enacted by each country or state, but this has proved impossible to achieve in the United States, though recently accomplished by the six states of Australia. Progress toward uniformity in western Europe is likely to be slow and will more likely come from the conscious adoption of the best provisions of other countries' legislation by the respective national legislatures than by the imposition of a uniform law by the authorities of the EEC. Draft legislation for the creation of companies of European type (*societas europea*) is under consideration by the EEC member states at the present time, and if adopted it will provide facilities for the formation of companies that will be subject to uniform rules and wll have uniform powers throughout the EEC.

BIBLIOGRAPHY

English law: L.C.B. GOWER, *The Principles of Modern Company Law* (1970); and R.R. PENNINGTON, *Company Law*, 2nd ed. (1967), are textbooks written primarily for students but may also be used by practitioners. They are, nevertheless, suitable for the reader who has some basic knowledge of business associations. R.R. PENNINGTON, *The Investor and the Law* (1968), is primarily a comparative study of the laws of the U.S. and the western European countries on investment law, with consideration given to questions relevant to business associations. M.A. WEINBERG, *Take-Overs and Amalgamations*, 2nd ed. (1967), is a practitioners' textbook on English Law. Two works intended for the general reader are A. RUBNER, *The Ensnared Shareholder* (1965); and G. GOYDER, *The Responsible Company* (1961).

American law: *Ballantine on Corporations*, rev. ed. (1946); G.D. HORNSTEIN, *Corporation Law and Practice* (1959); and *Lattin on Corporations*, 3rd ed. (1959), are standard student textbooks. The last two works contain more detail and are more up-to-date. E.R. ARANOW and H.A. EINHORN, *Proxy Contests for Corporate Control*, 2nd ed. (1968), is a detailed practitioner's book that the experienced reader will find interesting. A.A. BERLE and G.C. MEANS, *The Modern Corporation and Private Property*, rev. ed. (1968), is written on a more elementary level.

Other countries: W.G. FRIEDMANN and R.C. PUGH (eds.), *Legal Aspects of Foreign Investment* (1959); R.R. PENNINGTON, *Companies in the Common Market* (1970); and E.M. CHURCH, *Business Associations under French Law* (1960), are suitable works for the reader who has no knowledge of the company law of overseas countries. G. RIPERT and R. ROBLOT (eds.), *Traité Elémentaire de Droit Commercial*, 6th ed., vol. 1 (1968); A. HUECK, *Gesellschaftsrecht*, 13th ed. (1965); and A. GRAZIANI, *Diritto delle società*, 5th ed. (1963), are standard students' textbooks on French, German, and Italian company law. They presuppose a knowledge of basic European law.

(R.R.P.)

Business Cycles

Business cycles are best defined as fluctuations in the general level of economic activity, or more specifically, in the levels of employment, production, and prices. The Figure shows fluctuations in wholesale prices in four Western industrialized countries over the period from 1790 to 1940. Though some regularities in price movements are apparent, it is possible to ask whether the movements are regular enough to be called cycles.

The word cycle derives from the Greek word for circle. An object moving around a circle returns to its starting point; a wave motion, with upward and downward curves, may also be considered a cycle. The various movements characteristic of economic activity are not always as regular as waves, and for this reason some prefer to call them fluctuations.

The varieties of cycles

There are many types of economic fluctuations. Because of the complexity of economic phenomena, it may be that there are as many types of fluctuations or cycles as there are economic variables. There are daily cycles in commuter traffic or the consumption of electricity, to cite only two examples. Almost every aspect of economic life displays seasonal variations: sales of coal or ice, deposits in savings banks, monetary circulation, agricultural production, purchases of clothing, travel, and so on. As one lengthens the span of observation, one finds new kinds of fluctuations such as the hog cycle and the wheat cycle, the inventory cycle, and the construction cycle. Finally, there are movements of general economic activity that extend over periods of years.

THE STATISTICAL STUDY OF CYCLES

Early observations. Modern economic history has recorded a number of periods of difficult times, often called depressions, during which the business economy was marked by sudden stock market declines, commercial bankruptcies, bank failures, and mounting unemployment. Such crises were once looked upon as pathological incidents or catastrophes in economic life, rather than as a normal part of it. The notion of a "cycle" implies a different view.

Juglar's eight-year cycle. The first authority to explore economic cycles as periodically recurring phenomena

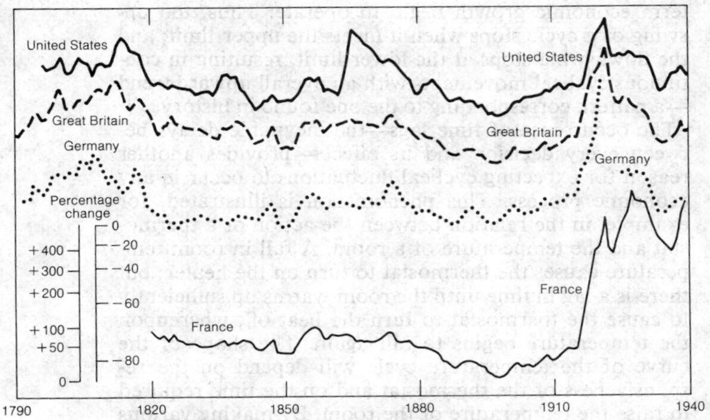

Wholesale price indexes for United States, Great Britain, Germany, and France, 1790–1940.
Reprinted from A. Burns and W. Mitchell, *Measuring Business Cycles;* by permission of National Bureau of Economic Research

was probably a French physician, Clément Juglar, in 1860. Other writers who developed Juglar's approach suggested that the cycles recur every nine or ten years, and distinguished three phases, or periods, of a typical cycle: prosperity, crisis, and liquidation. Subsequent analysis has tended to designate 1825, 1836, 1847, 1857, 1866, 1873, 1882, 1890, 1900, 1907, 1913, 1920, and 1929 as initial years of crisis. If that is correct, then the average interval between them was eight years, rather than nine or ten as suggested by Juglar. In the years since 1929, the regularity of business fluctuations has been somewhat offset by government anticyclical policies.

The wealth of data

The so-called Juglar cycle has often been regarded as the true, or major, economic cycle, but several smaller cycles have also been distinguished. Close study of the interval between the peaks of the Juglar cycle suggests that partial setbacks occur during the expansion, or upswing, and that there are partial recoveries during the contraction, or downswing. These smaller cycles generally coincide with changes in business inventories, lasting an average of 40 months. Other small cycles result from changes in the demand for and supply of particular agricultural products such as hogs (three to four years), cotton (two years), and beef (five years in the Netherlands). Hide and leather production fluctuates in an 18-month cycle.

Kondratieff's waves. Longer cycles have also been studied. The construction industry has been found to have cycles of 17 to 18 years in the United States, and of 20 to 22 years in England. Finally, there are the long waves, or so-called Kondratieff cycles, named for a Russian economist, Nikolai D. Kondratieff, who showed that in the major Western countries during the 150 years from 1790 to 1940 it was possible to distinguish three periods of slow expansions and contractions of economic activity averaging 50 years in length:

1. 1792–1850	Expansion: 1792–1815	23 years
	Contraction: 1815–50	35 years
2. 1850–96	Expansion: 1850–73	23 years
	Contraction: 1873–96	23 years
3. 1896–1940	Expansion: 1896–1920	24 years
	Contraction: 1920–40	20 years

Only these three Kondratieff waves have been observed.

Some students of business cycles have analyzed them by statistical methods, in the hope of finding regularities that are not immediately apparent. One speculative theory has held that the larger cycles were built up from smaller ones. Thus, two seasonal cycles would produce a two-year cycle, two of which would produce a four-year cycle; two four-year cycles would become an eight-year, or Juglar, cycle, and so on. The hypothesis is not widely accepted.

Depressions and upswings. Cycles of varying lengths are closely bound up with economic growth. In 19th-century Germany, for example, upswings in total economic activity were associated with the growth of the railroad, metallurgy, textile, and building industries. Periodic crises brought slowdowns in growth. The crisis of 1873 led to a wave of financial and industrial bankruptcies; recovery started in 1877, when iron production ceased to fall, and by 1880 a new upswing was underway. The recession of 1882 was less severe than the previous one, but a slump that began in 1890 led to a serious depression, with complaints of overproduction.

Cycles in history

The year 1890 was also one of financial crisis in England and the United States. The British banking house of Baring Brothers failed, partly because of a revolution in Argentina. English pig-iron production fell from 8,300,000 tons in 1889 to 6,700,000 in 1892, and unemployment increased. That depression might have been less severe but for the international financial crisis, especially intense in the United States, where, in 1893, a stock market panic led to widespread bank failures.

The recession of 1900 was followed by an unusually vigorous upsurge in almost all of the Western economies. U.S. pig-iron production increased by more than 150 percent during the expansion, which lasted until 1907; building permits more than doubled; and freight traffic rose by more than 50 percent. Prices rose more and more rapidly as the U.S. economy approached full employment.

Deviations from cycle patterns. Cycles are compounded of many elements. Historical fluctuations in economic activity cannot be explained entirely in terms of combinations of cycles and subcycles; there is always some factor left over, some element that does not fit the pattern of other fluctuations. It is possible, for example, to analyze a particular fluctuation into three principal components: a long component or trend; a very short, seasonal component; and an intermediate component, or Juglar cycle. But these components cannot be found exactly recombined in another fluctuation because of a residual element in the original fluctuation that does not have a cyclical form. If the residual is small, it might be attributed to errors of calculation or of measurement. Or, the residual might be regarded as the result of such accidental events as epidemics, floods, earthquakes, riots, strikes, revolutions, or wars, which obviously cannot be fitted into a recurring pattern. On a more sophisticated statistical level, it can be treated as "random movement." If the random element is always present, it becomes an essential element of the analysis to be dealt with in terms of probability.

A more rigorous analysis has to go even further. One difficulty in separating out the components of economic movements is that the components are not perfectly independent of each other. The determination of a long component or trend assumes that the Juglar component is already known. In the same way, determining the Juglar component requires isolating it from the long-term component. Probably only the seasonal component can be isolated independently of the others, and that because it is immediately related to such noneconomic factors as climate or custom. To avoid such difficulties, researchers have tried looking for "hidden periodicities," using a mathematical technique known as harmonic analysis, or Fourier series. Two alternative methods are open to them: they may assume a certain periodicity and try to fit the statistical data to the resulting equation; or they may ask mathematicians to supply all of the possible periodicities contained in the data and then determine which are the most probable.

Problems of analyzing cycles

For practical purposes, it would be useful to know the typical shape of a cycle and how to recognize its peak and trough. A great amount of work has been done in what may be called the morphology of cycles. In the United States, Arthur F. Burns and Wesley C. Mitchell have based such studies on the assumption that at any specific time there are as many cycles as there are forms of economic activity or variables to be studied and have tried to measure these in relation to a "reference cycle," which they artificially constructed as a standard of comparison. The object in such studies was to describe the shape of each specific cycle; to analyze its phases; to measure its duration and velocity; and to measure the amplitude or size of the cycle.

In studying various cycles, it has been possible to construct "lead and lag indicators"—that is, statistical series with cyclical turning points consistently leading or lagging behind the turns in general business activity. Researchers using these methods have identified a number of series, each of which reaches its turning point from two to ten months before the turns in general business activity; and another group of series, which has followed the turns in business by two to seven months. Examples of leading series include published data for new business orders, residential building contracts, the stock market index, business failures, and the length of the average workweek. These and other leading indicators are widely used in economic forecasting.

THE DYNAMIC ANALYSIS OF CYCLES

Factors that may engender fluctuations

A satisfactory explanation of cycles must isolate the forces and relationships that tend to produce these recurrent movements. There have been many theories of the business cycle. An understanding of them requires analysis of some of the factors that can cause cyclical movements.

The multiplier and the accelerator. One such factor is the relationship between investment and consumption. Any new expenditure—*e.g.*, on building a road or a factory—generates several times as much income as the expenditure itself. This is so because those who are paid to build the road or factory will spend more of what they receive; their expenditures will thus become income for others, who will in their turn spend most of what they receive. Every new act of investment will, thus, have a stimulating effect on aggregate income. This relationship is known as the *investment multiplier*. Of itself, it cannot produce cyclical movements in the economy; it merely provides a positive impulse in an upward direction.

To the relationship between investment and consumption must be added that between consumer demand and investment. An increase in demand for refrigerators, for example, will eventually require increased investment in the facilities for producing them. This relationship is known as the *accelerator;* and it implies that an increase in national income will stimulate investment. As with the multiplier, it cannot of itself explain cyclical movements; it merely accounts for a fundamental instability.

It can be shown, however, that the multiplier and accelerator in combination may produce very strong cyclical movements. Thus, when an increase in investment occurs, it raises income by some larger amount, depending on the value of the multiplier. That increase in income may in turn induce a further increase in investment. The new investment will stimulate a further multiplier process, producing additional income and investment. In theory, the interaction might continue until a point is reached at which such resources as labour and capital are being fully utilized. At that point—with no increase in employment and, therefore, no rise in consumer demand—the operation of the accelerator would cease. That halt in demand, plus the lack of new capital, would cause new investment to decline and workers to be laid off. The process thus would go into reverse. The fluctuations in national income could take various forms, depending on the characteristics of the economy and the way in which the population allocated its income between consumption and savings. Such spending habits, of course, affect both the levels of consumer demand and capital investment. This theoretical analysis does not explain actual economic fluctuations; it is merely an aid to understanding them.

Other dynamic factors. The analysis can be made more realistic by taking into account three other factors. First, since the theoretical, wide-swinging cycles engendered by the interaction of the multiplier and the accelerator are observed to occur only within narrow limits, one may assume that although the economy has an inherent tendency to swing very widely there are limits beyond which it cannot go. The upper limit to the swings would be the point at which full employment or full capacity is reached; the lower limit is more difficult to define, but it would be established when the forces that make for long-term economic growth begin to operate. Thus, the upswing of a cycle stops when it meets the upper limit; and the downswing stops at the lower limit, resulting in continuous cyclical movements with an overall upward trend—a pattern corresponding to the one found in history.

Upper and lower limits to swings

The occurrence of time lags—the inevitable delays between every decision and its effects—provides another reason for expecting cyclical fluctuations to occur in any economic process. This phenomenon is illustrated, for example, in the relation between the action of a thermostat and the temperature of a room. A fall in room temperature causes the thermostat to turn on the heater; but there is a lag in time until the room warms up sufficiently to cause the thermostat to turn the heat off, whereupon the temperature begins to fall again. The shape of the curve of the temperature cycle will depend on the responsiveness of the thermostat and on the time required to raise the temperature of the room. By making various adjustments, it is possible to minimize the cycle, but it can never be eliminated entirely. In economic life, there are many such time lags: between the decision to invest and the completion of the project; between the farmer's decision to raise hogs and the arrival of pork chops at the store; between prices at the time of a decision and prices at the time the action is completed.

Random shocks, or what economists call exogenous factors, constitute the third type of phenomena affecting business cycles. These are such external disturbances to the system as weather changes, unexpected discoveries, political changes, wars, and so on. It is possible for such external impulses to cause cyclical motions within the system, in much the same way that striking a rocking horse with a stick will cause the horse to rock back and forth. The length of the cycle will be determined by the internal relationships of the system, but its intensity is governed by the external impulse.

THEORIES OF THE BUSINESS CYCLE

The analytic concepts above may be found in most of the realistic attempts to explain economic fluctuations. Theories of the business cycle, or, more properly, of economic fluctuations, may be classified in two groups: those that ascribe cyclical movements to external forces (exogenous factors); and those that attribute the fluctuations to internal forces (endogenous factors).

Exogenous theories. *Agricultural.* Perhaps the oldest theories of the business cycle are those that link their cause to fluctuations of the harvest. Since crops depend upon soil, climate, and other natural factors that in turn may be affected by biological or meteorological cycles, such cycles will transmit their effects through the harvests to the rest of the economy. The 19th-century English economist William Stanley Jevons thought he had found the key to such a process in the behaviour of sunspots, which seemed to display a ten-year cycle. His naive explanation could not long withstand critical examination. It had a certain interest, however, in suggesting a causal factor that was completely detached from the economic system and one that could not be influenced by it in turn.

Psychological. A number of writers have explored mass psychology and its consequences for economic behaviour. Individuals are strongly influenced by the beliefs of the group or groups to which they belong. There are times when the general mood is optimistic, and others when it is pessimistic. An English economist, Arthur C. Pigou, in his *Industrial Fluctuations* (1927), put forward a theory of "noncompensated errors." He pointed out that if individuals behave in a completely autonomous way their errors in expectations will tend to offset each other. But if they imitate each other, their errors will accumulate until they acquire a global magnitude that may have powerful economic effects. This follow-the-crowd tendency obviously operates as a factor in the ups and downs of the stock exchanges, financial booms and crashes, and the behaviour of investors. One can say, however, that the psychological factor is not enough to explain economic fluctuations; moods of optimism and pessimism must themselves rest upon economic factors.

Effects of wars and taxes

Political. Some observers have maintained that economic fluctuations result from political events. It is obvious that such events as the Napoleonic Wars, World Wars I and II, and even the Korean War of 1950–53 have had strong economic consequences. Even the imposition of a tax or an import restriction may have some dynamic effect upon the economy. The question is whether such political factors are capable of producing cyclical movements.

Technological. Ever since the Industrial Revolution at the end of the 18th century, technical innovations have followed each other without end but not without pause. There have been periods of innovation and quieter periods in which the innovations were being absorbed. The world has passed through the era of steam, the era of petroleum, and the era of electricity and has entered the era of atomic energy. It is possible that if a rhythm could be found in these waves of change, the same rhythm might be responsible for corresponding movements in the economy. But it is equally possible that the technical innovations themselves have been dictated by the prior needs of the economy.

Demographic. Even population has been postulated as a cause of economic fluctuations. There are, undeniably, cyclical movements of population; it is possible to find fluctuations in the rates of marriage, birth, mortality, and migration; but the extent to which such fluctuations may have been caused by economic conditions is not clear.

Endogenous theories. *Monetary.* Some writers have ascribed economic fluctuations to the existence of money. Changes in the money supply do not always conform to underlying economic changes, and it is not difficult to see how this lack of coordination could produce disturbances in the economic system. Thus, an increase in the total quantity of money, if it is not matched by an increase in economic activity, will tend to produce higher prices; the higher prices in turn may stimulate an investment boom, and so on.

The banking system, with its ability to expand the supply of credit in a time of boom and to contract the supply of credit in time of recession, may in this way amplify small economic fluctuations into major cycles of prosperity and depression. Some theorists have emphasized the influence of the rate of interest: if the rate fixed by the banking system does not correspond to the "natural" rate dictated by the requirements of the economy, the disparity may of itself induce an expansion or contraction in economic activity.

Underconsumption. In a progressive economy, production tends to expand more rapidly than consumption. The disparity results from the unequal distribution of income; the rich do not consume all their income, while the poor do not have sufficient income to meet their consumption needs. This imbalance between output and sales has led to theories that the business cycle is caused by overproduction or underconsumption. But the basic, underlying cause is society's inadequate provision for an even flow of savings out of the excess of what is produced over what is consumed. In other words, saving is out of step with the requirements of the economy; it is improperly distributed over time.

Imbalance between output and sales

Investment. The fact that changes in the supply of savings, or loanable funds, are not closely coordinated with changes in the rest of the economy lies at the heart of the numerous theories that link investment imbalance to the business cycle. Savings accumulate when there is no immediate outlet for them in the form of new investment opportunities. When times become more favourable, these savings are invested in new industrial projects, and a wave of investment occurs that sweeps the rest of the economy along with it. It is in this context that the tools of analysis—the accelerator and the multiplier—find their application: the new investment creates new income, which in turn acts as a further stimulus to investment. An early observer of this phenomenon, a Russian economist, Mikhayl Tugan-Baranovsky, in 1894 published a study of industrial crises in England in which he maintained that the cycle of investment continues until all the capital funds have been used up. Bank credit expands as the cycle progresses. Disproportions then begin to develop among the various branches of production as well as between production in general and consumption. These imbalances lead to a new period of stagnation and depression.

CYCLES AND PUBLIC POLICY

Controlling and damping the business cycle

The study of business fluctuations leads naturally to the question of what government and society can do to offset, or control them. Any action must begin with prediction. The problem of predicting business fluctuations is that they are not cycles in the sense that they display a regular and recurring pattern. The past serves as no sure guide to the future.

Forecasting. Much study has gone into the development of techniques for forecasting economic events—both for a whole national economy and for individual industries (see ECONOMIC FORECASTING). The best known approach involves finding statistical series that are leaders in an upturn or downturn; *i.e.*, the leading indicators such as stock prices or residential building contracts mentioned earlier. But these are easier to recognize in hindsight than at the time of occurrence because the behaviour of economic statistics is not always consistent—leading series do not always lead. Furthermore, it is not always easy to tell whether a downturn in a particular series is really a downturn or simply a minor irregularity in a continuing upward movement.

Another approach to the understanding and control of the cycle is through rather elaborate econometric models employing many simultaneous equations that describe the relationships of statistical series to one another over time. With modern computers, the necessary calculations can be made very quickly, and, to the extent that the equations themselves are an accurate representation of the economy and of the way its human components behave, the forecasts will be accurate (see ECONOMETRICS).

Regulation of the cycle. The econometric approach has been useful as an instrument of policy making. A Dutch economist, Jan Tinbergen, has distinguished three types of economic variables: those that cannot be influenced directly by government action; those that may be regarded as the targets of government action or policy (such as employment and national income); and those upon which a government can exert a direct influence (wage rates, government expenditures, tax rates, profit margins, and so forth). The aim of policy is to minimize cyclical fluctuations, not in the hope of making them disappear but in the belief that it is possible to avoid the extremes of inflation and depression.

There are various ways of doing this. Monetary policies seek to increase or decrease the money supply to counter the contracting or expanding phases, respectively, of a cycle; this is accomplished through the operation of the central banking system. The government can also influence the economy fiscally by raising or lowering taxes and expenditures, thereby stimulating business activity or damping it down; it can lower tax rates and spend more freely in times of recession and raise taxes and reduce its spending in times of inflation (see FISCAL AND MONETARY POLICY). The government may also intervene more directly in the economy by attempting to control wages, prices, and profits, or by stimulating or discouraging investment.

Postwar era of mild recessions

Since World War II, cycles have flattened out; the recessions have been mild; and the upswings have not proceeded to the extremes of former times. Over the years 1949–70, the Western industrial countries and Japan experienced a remarkable period of economic growth that showed no sign of abating. That record seemed to be attributable in part to countercyclical policies the governments had pursued. The increased proportion of governmental revenue expenditure in most national economies also tended to level the peaks and valleys of the cycle. Much of this fiscal weight acts countercyclically, automatically offsetting cyclical changes in income and expenditure. During a recession, income tax receipts fall off, while government expenditures on unemployment compensation and relief rise. Conversely, during an upswing, government income tax revenues rise faster than the level of economic activity and, as a damper on private spending, they thus help to restrain the upward movement of the economy.

Cycles under a planned economy. It has often been suggested that cycles and fluctuations might be eliminated altogether by thoroughgoing economic planning. In this view, the business cycle is a disease of the market economy; in a planned economy, there would be no market and hence no possibility of a cycle. The planning authority would map out the growth of the economy in advance for five or seven years, and it would control the execution of the plan so that there would be no serious disparity between expectations and results. It is not likely that any plan will ever be fulfilled exactly; in the history of planned economies, there are always discrepancies between what was originally planned and what was finally attained. These have to be corrected through new plans.

A particularly severe fluctuation occurred in the planned economy of Czechoslovakia in 1963. Difficulties became apparent in 1961, when planned production targets for basic industries were not met. Shortages in basic industries were communicated to other industries dependent on them. When the difficulties increased in 1962, the government decided to abandon the five-year plan (then half way through its second year) and replace it with a one-year plan to allow for reorganization; a seven-year plan, beginning in 1964, followed. Investments for the interim year of 1963 were slashed, and only a 1-percent increase in production was planned. But economic difficulties grew, made worse by a transportation crisis. To these troubles were added an unusually harsh winter and a drought-ridden summer, with the consequence that industrial output in 1963 fell below the level of 1962. In subsequent years, the economy swung upward again.

Fluctuations and cycles may be inherent in modern economies, whatever the nature of the controls imposed by society. It is possible that an economy in which there were no cycles would be incapable of growth.

BIBLIOGRAPHY. Good introductions to the study of business cycles include: A.H. HANSEN, *Business Cycles and National Income*, enl. ed. (1964); R.A. GORDON, *Business Fluctuations*, 2nd ed. (1961); R.C.O. MATTHEWS, *The Business Cycle* (1962); E. LUNDBERG (ed.), *The Business Cycle in the Post-War World* (1955); and H. GUITTON, *Fluctuations et croissance économiques*, 3rd ed. (1969). Famous surveys of business cycle theories are J.A. SCHUMPETER, *Business Cycles: A Theoretical, Historical, and Statistical Analysis of the Capitalist Process*, 2 vol. (1939; abridged ed., 1964); and G. HABERLER, *Prosperity and Depression*, 5th ed. (1964); J. TINBERGEN, *Statistical Testing of Business Cycle Theories*, 2 vol. (1939, reprinted 1968), attempts to verify the theories surveyed in Haberler's work by econometric analysis. The nontheoretical approach to business cycle research is set forth in A.F. BURNS and W.C. MITCHELL, *Measuring Business Cycles* (1946); further developed in G.H. MOORE (ed.), *Business Cycle Indicators* (1961). Important articles are collected in the AMERICAN ECONOMIC ASSOCIATION, *Readings in Business Cycle Theory* (1944), and *Readings in Business Cycles* (1965).

(H.Gu.)

Butler, Samuel

The certainties of the Victorian Age met their match in Samuel Butler, the English novelist, essayist, and critic, whose *Erewhon* ("nowhere" rearranged) foreshadowed the collapse of the illusion of eternal progress as later exemplified in the satiric utopias of Aldous Huxley's *Brave New World* (1932) and George Orwell's *Nineteen Eighty-four* (1949), while his *Way of All Flesh* helped turn the tide against excessive parental dominance and religious rigidity.

The son of the Rev. Thomas Butler and grandson of Samuel Butler, headmaster of Shrewsbury School and later bishop of Lichfield, Butler was born at Langar Rectory, Nottinghamshire, on Dec. 4, 1835. After six years at Shrewsbury he went to St. John's College, Cambridge, and graduated in 1858. His father wished him to be a clergyman, and young Butler actually went as far as to do a little "slumming" in a London parish by way of preparation for holy orders. But the whole current of his

Butler, oil painting by Charles Gogin, 1896. In the National Portrait Gallery, London.

By courtesy of the National Portrait Gallery, London

highly independent and heretical nature was carrying him away from everything his father stood for: home, church, and Christianity itself—or what Christianity had appeared to mean at Langar Rectory. Butler returned to Cambridge and continued his musical studies and drawing, but after an unpleasant altercation with his father he left Cambridge, the church, and home and emigrated to New Zealand, where (with funds advanced by his father) he set up a sheep run in the Canterbury settlement.

Reaction to Darwin

When Darwin's *Origin of Species* (1859) came into his hands soon after his arrival in New Zealand, it took him by storm; he became "one of Mr. Darwin's many enthusiastic admirers," and a year or two later he told a friend that he had renounced Christianity altogether. Yet, as it proved, Christianity had by no means finished with him. For the next 25 years it was upon religion and evolution that Butler's attention was mainly fixed. At first he welcomed Darwinism because it enabled him to do without God (or rather, without his father's God). Later, having found a God of his own, he rejected Darwinism itself because it left God out. Thus, he antagonized both the church and the orthodox Darwinians and spent his life as a lonely outsider, or as Butler called himself after the biblical outcast, "an Ishmael." To the New Zealand *Press* he contributed several articles on Darwinian topics, of which two—"Darwin Among the Machines" (1863) and "Lucubratio Ebria" (1865)—were later worked up in *Erewhon*. Both show him already grappling with the central problem of his later thought: the relationship between mechanism and life. In "Darwin Among the Machines" he tries out the consequences of regarding machines as living organisms competing with man in the struggle for existence and so likely to win that they must at once be destroyed. In the "Lucubratio" he takes the opposite view that machines are extracorporeal limbs and that the more of these a man can tack on to himself the more highly evolved an organism he will be.

Return to England

Having doubled his capital in New Zealand, Butler returned to England (1864) and took the apartment in Clifford's Inn, London, which was to be his home for the rest of his life. In 1865 his *Evidence for the Resurrection of Jesus Christ . . . Critically Examined* appeared anonymously. For a few years he studied painting at Heatherley's art school and tried to convince himself that this was his vocation. Until 1876 he exhibited occasionally at the Royal Academy. One of his oil paintings, "Mr. Heatherley's Holiday" (1874), is in the Tate Gallery, London, and his "Family Prayers," in which the ethos of Langar Rectory is satirically conveyed, is at St. John's College, Cambridge. Later he tried his hand at musical composition, publishing *Gavottes, Minuets, Fugues and Other Short Pieces for the Piano* (1885), and *Narcissus*, a comic cantata in the style of Handel—whom he rated high above all other composers—in 1888; *Ulysses: An*

Oratorio appeared in 1904. It was typical of Butler to use his native gifts and mother wit in such exploits, and even in literature, his rightful territory, much of his work is that of the shrewd amateur who sets out alone to sling pebbles, small but lethal, at various Goliaths of the establishment. "I have never," he once said, "written on any subject unless I believed that the authorities on it were hopelessly wrong"; hence his assault on the citadels of orthodox Darwinism and orthodox Christianity; hence, later, his attempt to prove that the *Odyssey* was written in Sicily by a woman (*The Authoress of the Odyssey*, 1897); and hence his new interpretation of Shakespeare's sonnets (*Shakespeare's Sonnets Reconsidered, and in Part Rearranged*, 1899).

Erewhon

Erewhon (1872) made whatever reputation as a writer Butler enjoyed in his lifetime; it was the only one of his many books on which he made any profit worth mentioning, and he only made £69 3*s.* 10*d.* on that. Yet it was received by many as the best thing of its kind since *Gulliver's Travels*—that is to say, as a satire on contemporary life and thought conveyed by the time-honoured convention of travel in an imaginary country. The opening chapters, based upon Butler's recollections of the upper Rangitoto Mountains in New Zealand, are in an excellent narrative style; and a description of the hollow statues at the top of the pass, vibrating in the wind with unearthly chords, makes a highly effective transition to the strange land beyond. The landscape and people of Erewhon are idealized from northern Italy; its institutions are partly utopian and partly satiric inversions of our own world. Butler's two main themes, religion and evolution, appear respectively in "The Musical Banks" (churches) and in chapters called "Some Erewhonian Trials" and "The Book of the Machines." The Erewhonians have long ago abolished machines as dangerous competitors in the struggle for existence, and by punishing disease as a crime they have produced a race of great physical beauty and strength.

The Fair Haven (1873) is an ironical defense of Christianity, which under the guise of orthodox zeal undermines its miraculous foundations. Butler was dogged all through life by the sense of having been bamboozled by those who should have been his betters; he had been taken in by his parents and their religion; he was taken in again by friends, who returned neither the money nor the friendship they accepted from Butler for years; life itself, and the world, sometimes seemed to him a hollow sham. Was Darwin himself, his saviour from the world of Langar Rectory, now to prove a fraud as well? This was the suspicion that dawned upon him while writing *Life and Habit* (1878) and envenomed the series of evolutionary books that followed: *Evolution, Old and New* (1879), *Unconscious Memory* (1880), and *Luck or Cunning* (1887). Darwin had not really explained evolution at all, Butler reasoned, because he had not accounted for the variations on which natural selection worked. Where Darwin saw only chance, Butler saw the effort on the part of creatures to respond to felt needs. He conceived creatures as acquiring necessary habits (and organs to perform them) and transmitting these to their offspring as unconscious memories. He thus restored teleology to a world from which purpose had been excluded by Darwin, but instead of attributing the purpose to God he placed it within the creatures themselves as the life force.

The Way of All Flesh

Many regard *The Way of All Flesh*, published in 1903, the year after Butler's death, as his masterpiece. It certainly contains much of the quintessence of Butlerism (though the *Note-Books* are necessary to supplement it). This largely autobiographical novel tells, with ruthless wit, realism, and lack of sentiment, the story of Butler's escape from the suffocating moral atmosphere of his home circle. In it, the character Ernest Pontifex stands for Butler's early self and Overton for his mature self; Theobald and Christina are his parents; Towneley and Alethea represent "nice" people who "love God" in Butler's special sense of having "good health, good looks, good sense, experience, and a fair balance of cash in hand." The book was influential at the beginning of the anti-Victorian reaction, and Butler was saluted by G.B. Shaw as "the greatest English writer of the latter half of the nineteenth century." He died in London on June 18, 1902.

MAJOR WORKS

TOPOGRAPHICAL: *A First Year in Canterbury Settlement*, 1863 (ed. by R.A. Streatfield, with other early essays, 1914); *Alps and Sanctuaries of Piedmont and the Canton Ticino*, 1882; *Ex Voto: An Account of the Sacro Monte or New Jerusalem at Varallo-Sesia*, 1888.

SATIRICAL AND THEOLOGICAL: *The Evidence for the Resurrection of Jesus Christ, as Given by the Four Evangelists, Critically Examined*, 1865 (anon.); *Erewhon; or, Over the Range*, 1872 (anon.); *The Fair Haven*, 1873; *Erewhon Revisited*, 1901; *God the Known and God the Unknown*, 1909.

SCIENTIFIC: *Life and Habit: An Essay After a Completer View of Evolution*, 1878; *Evolution, Old and New*, 1879; *Unconscious Memory*, 1880; *Luck or Cunning as the Main Means of Organic Modification?*, 1887.

NOVEL: *The Way of All Flesh*, 1903.

MISCELLANEOUS: *A Lecture on the Humour of Homer*, 1892; *The Life and Letters of Dr. Samuel Butler*, 2 vol., 1896; *The Authoress of the Odyssey*, 1897; *The Iliad of Homer, Rendered into English Prose*, 1898; *Shakespeare's Sonnets Reconsidered, and in Part Rearranged*, 1899; *The Odyssey, Rendered into English Prose*, 1900; *Essays on Life, Art and Science*, 1904; *The Note-Books of Samuel Butler* (ed. H. Festing Jones), 1912.

MUSICAL COMPOSITIONS: *Gavotte, Minuets, Fugues and Other Short Pieces for the Piano*, 1885 (in collaboration with H. Festing Jones); *Narcissus*, 1888 (a comic cantata in the style of Handel); *Ulysses: An Oratorio*, 1904.

BIBLIOGRAPHY. The standard biography is H. FESTING JONES, *Samuel Butler, Author of Erewhon (1835–1902): A Memoir*, 2 vol. (1919). Studies on different aspects of Butler as man and writer include: M.R. GARNETT, *Samuel Butler and His Family Relations* (1926); C.G. STILLMAN, *Samuel Butler: A Mid-Victorian Modern* (1932); MALCOLM MUGGERIDGE, *The Earnest Atheist: A Study of Samuel Butler* (1936); P.N. FURBANK, *Samuel Butler, 1835–1902* (1948); PHILIP HENDERSON, *Samuel Butler: The Incarnate Bachelor* (1953); BASIL WILLEY, *Darwin and Butler: Two Versions of Evolution* (1960); U.C. KNOEPFLMACHER in *Religious Humanism and the Victorian Novel*, ch. 7–8 (1965); also essays in J.B. YEATS, *Essays, Irish and American* (1918); H. KINGSMILL, *After Puritanism, 1850–1900* (1929); DESMOND MACCARTHY, *Collected Essays II* (1932). There is a bibliography of Butler's works and of books about him (up to 1919) in vol. 1 of Jones's *Memoir* (cited above). See also A.J. HOPPE, *A Bibliography of the Writings of Samuel Butler (Author of "Erewhon") and of Writings About Him* (1925, reprinted 1967); and S.B. HARKNESS, *The Career of Samuel Butler, 1835–1902: A Bibliography* (1955).

(B.W.)

Byrd, Richard E.

Rear Admiral Richard E. Byrd of the United States Navy, a 20th-century pioneer aviator and polar explorer, first won fame by his long-distance flights in the Arctic and over the Atlantic and is best known for his well-organized expeditions to the Antarctic, where he conducted scientific explorations, survived a winter alone near the South Pole, and, from his base, named Little America, on the edge of the Ross Sea, Antarctica, flew over and named hitherto undiscovered tracts of territory. The knowledge and experience he gained was of substantial benefit to subsequent expeditions to the south polar regions.

Byrd was born at Winchester, Virginia, on October 25, 1888. After attending Shenandoah Military Academy, the University of Virginia, and the U.S. Naval Academy, he learned flying at the U.S. Naval Air Station, Pensacola, Florida, and served in the navy with distinction until the end of World War I. After the war he turned his attention to developing navigational aids for aircraft; he developed plans for the first NC flying boat transatlantic flights, but he was deprived of a place in the principal aircraft. He also assisted with dirigibles built for transatlantic crossings. His polar career began in 1924 when he had command of a small naval aviation detachment with Comdr. D.B. MacMillan's Arctic expedition to western Greenland, based at Etah.

The experience of flying over sea ice and glaciers in

Byrd, 1925.
By courtesy of the National Geographic Society, © 1925 National Geographic Society

west Greenland had fired Byrd with the ambition to fly over the North Pole. He claimed this accomplishment on May 9, 1926, while acting as navigator, with a compatriot, Floyd Bennett, as pilot. According to his records, the return journey from King's Bay, Spitsbergen, took 15½ hours, with no mishaps beyond an oil leak from the starboard engine of his Fokker tri-motor airplane. For this feat he was awarded the U.S. Congressional Medal of Honor. (In the early 1970s, however, grave doubts were cast upon these records and, indeed, upon Byrd's claim to have reached the pole at all.) He later aided the U.S. aviator Charles A. Lindbergh with navigational training and the use of the specially extended runway for Lindbergh's transatlantic solo flight in May 1927.

Byrd next decided to make an attempt to fly the Atlantic from west to east; and in June 1927, with three companions, he made the flight in 42 hours, crash-landing in bad weather at Ver-sur-Mer on the coast of Brittany, France. For this successful flight he was made a Commandant of the French Legion of Honour; he and his crew also received the Medal for Valor from the Mayor of New York City.

In 1928 he announced his decision to explore the unknown regions of the Antarctic from the air. With large financial backing from such wealthy Americans as Edsel Ford and John D. Rockefeller, Jr., his fame was such that he could inspire the American public to contribute liberally to the estimated cost of the venture, which was about $400,000.

At Little America

His expedition, the largest and best equipped that ever had set out for the Antarctic, sailed south in October 1928. A substantial and well-supplied base, called Little America, was located on the face of the Ross Ice Shelf, a wide plain of shelf ice fronting the Ross Sea near an indentation in the ice cliff named the Bay of Whales. Flights were made from this base over the Antarctic continent. A range of high mountains, named the Rockefeller Mountains, was discovered; and a large tract of hitherto unknown territory beyond them was named Marie Byrd Land, after Byrd's wife. The following spring—*i.e.*, in November 1929, according to the Antarctic season—Byrd, as navigator, with three companions, flew from Little America to the South Pole and back in 19 hours with no mishap, except that a few of their provisions had to be thrown overboard in order to lighten the plane.

In 1933 a second Byrd expedition visited Little America with the aim of mapping and claiming land around the pole; he extended the exploration of Marie Byrd Land and continued his scientific observations. During the winter of 1934 (from March to August), Byrd spent five months alone in a hut at a weather station named Bolling Advance Base, buried beneath the Barrier face 123 miles (196 kilometres) south of Little America, enduring temperatures between −58° and −76° F (−50° and −60° C) and sometimes much lower. He was finally rescued in a desperately sick condition, suffering from frostbite and carbon-monoxide poisoning. This was perhaps his most controversial exploit.

Byrd led three subsequent expeditions while serving as director of U.S. government expeditions. For brief periods on each trip he continued personally to take an active part in exploration. At the request of Pres. Franklin D. Roosevelt he took command of the U.S. Antarctic service, which was terminated after its first year because of the approach of World War II. Bases were located at Little America and Stonington Island, Antarctic Peninsula. Byrd's discovery of Thurston Island greatly decreased the length of unexplored coast of the continent.

During World War II Byrd served on the staff of the chief of naval operations and, among other duties, evaluated Pacific islands as operational sites. His talent for organization and administration and his influence and skill in public relations led him to serve in many important governmental, patriotic, and humanitarian capacities.

After World War II Byrd was in charge of a program known as Operation High Jump, which claimed to have discovered and mapped 537,000 square miles (1,390,000 square kilometres) of Antarctic territory. Byrd flew into Little America from the deck of the aircraft carrier "Philippine Sea" north of the icepack, about 700 miles from the camp. He made a second flight over the South Pole and took part in several other flights. In 1955 Byrd was made officer in charge of the United States Antarctic programs, the senior authority for government Antarctic matters. He accompanied naval Operation Deep Freeze aboard the icebreaker "Glacier" and took his last exploratory flight over the heartland of Antarctica and once again over the South Pole on January 8, 1956.

Byrd's achievement

Byrd's major achievement was to apply the airplane, radio, and other modern technical resources to polar exploration. He did not agree with the Norwegian explorer Roald Amundsen (1872–1928) that the airplane one day would supplant exploration by the traditional means of using sledges and dogs. Rather, he believed that modern techniques of exploration should supplement the traditional methods that would always have the advantage of guaranteeing greater certainty and accuracy. All of his expeditions, therefore, carried dog teams, sledges, and personnel to handle them—a combination that was to prove efficient and to achieve results of great scientific value.

It is in his book *Alone*, which describes his experiences at Bolling Advance Base, that the character of the man can be glimpsed rather than in the more official account, *Little America*. The picture that emerges is that of a simple, homely man, devoted to his family and always full of consideration for others. There is no doubt that men trusted him and followed him, that his ability inspired confidence. He was officially cited 20 times for bravery or conspicuous conduct.

Byrd was also competent in public relations. Indeed, perhaps inevitably, his expeditions were surrounded by a glare of publicity that aroused criticism, particularly by commentators abroad. Press accounts of a "million dollar expedition" conveyed an impression of unlimited funds and profligate expenditure. But the impression was not true. Byrd was as pressed for money as any other polar explorer, and he had to rely largely on the public to provide the funds. Hence the tumult and the shouting. The U.S. public saw in him the virtues they most admired and placed their trust in him. Although Byrd himself knew the value of publicity, he always kept in mind his goal of professional achievement. When he died in Boston on March 11, 1957, he was an international hero. He was buried in Arlington National Cemetery, Virginia, with full military honours.

BIBLIOGRAPHY. RICHARD E. BYRD, *Little America* (1930), is an account of his aerial exploration in the Antarctic and his flight to the South Pole; *Skyward* (1928) is the official report of his 1928 to 1930 expedition to the Antarctic, and his report of the flight to the North Pole and flight across the Atlantic; *Alone* (1938) describes his experiences at Bolling Advance Base. Works about Byrd include: CHARLES J.V. MURPHY, *Struggle: The Life and Exploits of Commander Richard E. Byrd* (1928), a biography; F. GREEN, *Dick Byrd, Air Explorer* (1928); and RICHARD MONTAGUE, *Oceans, Poles and Airmen* (1971), disputing Byrd's claim that he flew to the North Pole.

(F.D.O.)

Byrd, William

The greatest English composer of the age of Shakespeare, William Byrd excelled in music that was religious in character and possessed a power and originality transcending the purely liturgical. Of his origins and early life virtually nothing is known; he was born in 1543, possibly in Lincolnshire. He was a pupil and protégé of the organist and composer Thomas Tallis. Byrd's first authenticated appointment was as organist at Lincoln Cathedral (February 27, 1563). In 1572 he moved to London to take up his post as a gentleman of the Chapel Royal, where he shared the duties of organist with Tallis.

Early life

William Byrd, engraving by Nicola Francesco Haym, after a portrait by Gerard van der Gucht.

By courtesy of the trustees of the British Museum; photograph, J.R. Freeman & Co. Ltd.

The close personal and professional relationship between the two men had important musical consequences. In 1575 Elizabeth I granted them a joint monopoly for the importing, printing, publishing, and sale of music, and the printing of music paper. The first work under their imprint appeared in that year—a collection of *Cantiones Sacrae* dedicated to the Queen; of the 34 motets, Tallis contributed 16 and Byrd 18.

In 1577 Byrd moved to Harlington, Middlesex, where he and his family lived for the next 15 years. As a devout and lifelong Catholic he probably preferred the greater privacy of living outside London. Yet in spite of his close social contact with many other Catholics, some of whom were certainly implicated in treasonable activities, his own loyalty to the government was never questioned.

In 1585 Tallis died, and in the following year Byrd's wife, Julian. These sad events may have prompted him to set his musical house in order, for in the next three years he published four collections of his own music: *Psalms, Sonets, & songs of sadnes & pietie* (1588), *Songs of sundrie natures* (1589), and two further books of *Cantiones Sacrae* (1589 and 1591). The two secular volumes were dedicated, respectively, to Sir Christopher Hatton, the lord chancellor, and to Lord Hunsdon, the lord chamberlain and first cousin to the Queen. Both volumes of motets were dedicated to prominent Catholics: the Earl of Worcester, a great friend and patron of Byrd's, whose loyalty to the crown was unimpeachable, and Lord Lumley. Also in 1591 a manuscript volume of Byrd's keyboard music was prepared for "my Ladye Nevell" (probably Rachel, wife of Sir Edward Nevill), while many more keyboard pieces found their way into the volume known as the *Fitzwilliam Virginal Book*, copied by another well-known Catholic, Francis Tregian, during his imprisonment in the Fleet.

First collections of works

In 1592 or 1593 Byrd moved with his family to Stondon Massey, Essex, where he lived for the rest of his life. At the accession of James I the Catholics' prospects temporarily brightened, and this probably prompted Byrd's next three publications. In his collection of three masses and two books of *Gradualia* (1605, 1607), he attempted to provide single-handed a basic liturgical repertory, comprising music for the ordinary (*i.e.*, the unvarying parts of the mass) and for the proper (*i.e.*, the parts of the mass that vary according to the day or the feast) of all main feasts. It is significant that the dedicatees of both books of *Gradualia* were prominent Catholics ennobled within the first years of James's reign: the Earl of Northampton and Lord Petre of Writtle, another close friend of Byrd's. One further publication came from Byrd, the *Psalmes, Songs and Sonnets* of 1611, containing English sacred and secular music. He died on July 4, 1623.

Byrd's musical stature can hardly be overrated. He wrote extensively for every medium then available except, it seems, the lute. His virginal and organ music brought the English keyboard style to new heights and pointed the way to the achievements of other English composers, such as John Bull, Giles Farnaby, Orlando Gibbons, and Thomas Tomkins. In music for viol consort he also played an extremely important role, pioneering the development of the freely composed fantasia, which was to become the most important form of Jacobean and later composers. Although he admired Italian madrigals and as a publisher helped introduce them to England, Byrd's own secular vocal music is distinctly conservative; much of it is conceived for the old-fashioned medium of solo voice accompanied by viol consort, later abandoned by the English madrigalists, with Thomas Morley (Byrd's pupil) at their head. Byrd sometimes added texts to the polyphonic accompaniments of these songs, in effect making them madrigals.

Achievement and significance

Byrd's religious beliefs did not prevent him from composing a great deal of church music to English words, most of which has survived only in manuscript. Although this is of generally high quality it cannot be denied that Byrd maintained his highest consistent level in his Latin sacred music. Of this, the 1589 and 1591 sets of *Cantiones Sacrae* (mostly designed for the private edification of the Catholic circles Byrd moved in and therefore unrestricted by liturgical considerations) have an intensity unrivalled in England and a breadth of scale unknown on the Continent. Although the *Gradualia* are necessarily more concise and superficially more similar to the work of Giovanni da Palestrina and Tomás Luis de Victoria, with which Byrd was well acquainted, closer examination reveals their real individuality as well as an astonishingly consistent level of inspiration.

MAJOR WORKS

Roman Catholic church music

MASSES: Masses for three, four, and five voices.

MOTETS: Motets for from three to nine voices in *Cantiones Sacrae*, 1575; *Cantiones Sacrae*, books 1 and 2, 1589 and 1591; *Gradualia*, two books, 1605 and 1607.

Anglican church music

ANTHEMS: More than 20 motets, for from three to six voices, and for solo voice and viols, most in *Songs of sundrie natures*, 1589; and in the collection *Teares or Lamentations of a Sorrowful Soul* of Sir William Leighton, 1614.

PSALMS: About 20 in *Psalmes, Sonets, & songs of sadnes & pietie*, 1588; and *Songs of sundrie natures*, 1589.

MISCELLANEOUS: Litany for four voices; two complete services; two magnificats and a Nunc Dimittis; prayers and responses.

Songs and madrigals

MADRIGALS: About 50 madrigals in *Psalmes, Sonets, & songs of sadnes & pietie*, 1588; *Songs of sundrie natures*, 1589; *Musica Transalpina*, 1588; and *The first sett of Italian Madrigalls*, 1590.

SONGS: Songs for voices and viols in *Songs of sundrie natures*, 1589; and in *Psalmes, Songs, & sonnets of sadnes & pietie*, 1611; over 30 for voices and instruments in manuscript; about 40 rounds and canons.

Instrumental music

VIOLS: Fantasias in three to six parts; In nomines; pavans and galliards.

KEYBOARD: About 140 pieces for keyboard in *Parthenia*, manuscript collection written *c.* 1611; *My Ladye Nevells Booke*, manuscript collection written in 1591; *The Fitzwilliam Virginal Book*, manuscript collection written in *c.* 1612–19; and in *Will Forster's Book*, manuscript collection written in 1624.

BIBLIOGRAPHY. *The Collected Vocal Works of William Byrd*, 2 vol., ed. by E.H. FELLOWES (1937–50); and a more scholarly edition of the sacred works in vol. 2, 7, and 9 of *Tudor Church Music* (1921–28). See also E.H. FELLOWES, *William Byrd*, 2nd ed. (1948).

(J.J.No.)

Byron, Lord

The English poet and satirist Lord Byron was a colourful figure whose poetry and personality captured the imagination of Europe; his name became a symbol for the deepest romantic melancholy on the one hand and for the aspirations of political liberalism on the other. Renowned as the "gloomy egoist" of his autobiographical poem *Childe Harold's Pilgrimage* during most of the 19th century, he is now more generally esteemed for the satiric realism of his *Don Juan* and the facetious wit of his letters.

By courtesy of the National Portrait Gallery, London

Byron, portrait by Richard Westall, 1813. In the National Portrait Gallery, London.

Early life. The poet's grandfather, second son of the fourth Lord Byron, was an admiral in the British navy, and his father was the handsome and profligate Capt. John Byron, who first seduced and later married the Marchioness of Carmarthen. On the death of his first wife (who bore him a daughter Augusta), the Captain married Catherine Gordon of Gight, an only child of a proud Scottish family that traced its ancestry to James I of Scotland. Mrs. Byron, after following her husband to Paris while he squandered most of her fortune, returned to England, where her son was born with a clubfoot on January 22, 1788, in London. She took her child, George Gordon, to Aberdeen, where they lived in lodgings on a meagre income. Her husband died in France in 1791. The boy, who early developed an extreme sensitivity to his lameness, attended the Aberdeen grammar school. His nurse, May Gray, helped to awaken precocious passions in him when he was only nine. This experience and a quite different one—his idealized love for his distant cousin Mary Duff at about the same period and a similar feeling for his cousin Margaret Parker—shaped his parallel and paradoxical attitudes toward women through the rest of his life.

In 1798, at the age of ten, George Gordon inherited the title and estates of his great-uncle, the "wicked" Lord Byron. His mother proudly took him to England. The boy fell in love with the ghostly halls and spacious grounds of Newstead Abbey, which had been presented to the Byrons by Henry VIII, and he and his mother lived in its ruins for a while. He was privately tutored in Nottingham, and his clubfoot was doctored by a quack named Lavender. John Hanson, Mrs. Byron's attorney, rescued him from the pernicious influence of May Gray, the tortures of Lavender, and the uneven temper of his mother. He took him to London, where a reputable doctor prescribed a brace and later a special boot, and in the autumn of 1799 Hanson sent him to a school at Dulwich.

Education

In 1801 Byron went to Harrow, one of England's most prestigious schools. His first years were marked by battles with the boys and quarrels with the masters, but later his friendships with younger boys fostered a romantic attachment to the school. It is possible that these friendships gave the first impetus to his sexual ambivalence, which became more pronounced at Cambridge and in Greece. The Rev. Joseph Drury, the headmaster, won his confidence and encouraged his participation in the "Speech Day" recitations that stimulated his early ambition to become a parliamentary orator. He spent the summer of 1803 with his mother at Southwell, near Nottingham, but he soon escaped to Newstead and stayed with his tenant, Lord Grey, while he courted his distant cousin, Mary Chaworth, at nearby Annesley Hall. This first adolescent love kept him from returning to Harrow in the autumn, and when Mary, already engaged, grew tired of "that lame boy," he indulged his grief by writing melancholy poetry; and she became the symbol of idealized and unattainable love.

Byron took "super-excellent" rooms at Trinity College, Cambridge, in 1805 and piled up debts at a rate that alarmed his mother. But after indulging in the conventional vices of the undergraduates, which did not much engross him, he spent his time with a few favourites and with a devoted chorister, John Edleston, for whom he developed "a violent, though *pure*, love and passion." After the first term, Byron indulged in dissipations in London that put him further into debt. He returned in the summer of 1806 to Southwell where he gathered his early poems in a volume privately printed in November with the title *Fugitive Pieces*. The following June his first published poems, *Hours of Idleness*, appeared. When he returned to Trinity for the autumn term, he formed a close friendship with John Cam Hobhouse, who stirred his interest in liberal Whiggism. At the beginning of 1808, he entered into "an abyss of sensuality" in London that threatened to undermine his health as well as his finances. A sarcastic critique of his *Hours of Idleness* that appeared in *The Edinburgh Review* caused Byron to revise a satire he had begun (modelled on the *Dunciad* of Alexander Pope) and to add some lines on Francis Jeffrey, the *Review*'s editor, whom Byron erroneously assumed to have been the reviewer. In the autumn he regained possession of Newstead from his tenant, furnished some of the empty halls, and entertained his friends there. On reaching his majority in January 1809, he took his seat in the House of Lords, published his satire anonymously as *English Bards and Scotch Reviewers*, and then embarked with his friend Hobhouse on a grand tour.

Travel abroad. They sailed on July 2, 1809, on the Lisbon packet, crossed Spain to Seville and Cádiz, and proceeded by Gibraltar to Malta. There Byron fell in love briefly with a married woman and almost fought a duel on her account. Byron and Hobhouse next landed at Préveza in western Greece and made an inland voyage to Janina (Ioánnina) and later to Tepelene in Albania to visit the cruel but mild-mannered despot Ali Pasha. On their return Byron began at Janina an autobiographical poem, *Childe Harold*, which he continued during the journey to Athens where they arrived on Christmas day. They lodged with a widow, whose daughter, Theresa Macri, Byron celebrated as "The Maid of Athens." In

Visit to Greece

March 1810 he sailed with Hobhouse for Constantinople by way of Smyrna, and, while becalmed at the mouth of the Hellespont, Byron visited the site of Troy and swam the channel from Sestos to Abydos in imitation of Leander. After two months in Constantinople, Byron returned to Athens, and Hobhouse went back to England. Byron's sojourn in Greece made a lasting impression on his mind and character. The "clime of the East," the freedom and open frankness in contrast to the English reserve and hypocrisy, had entered his blood, broadened his views of men and manners, and contributed to his lifelong nostalgia for that "land of the Sun." After visiting Veli Pasha, ruler of the Peloponnesus, at Tripolitza (Trípolis), he took lodgings in a Capuchin monastery in Athens. He bathed in the sea, made a journey to Soúnion—which inspired his "Isles of Greece"—and delighted in the sunshine and the moral tolerance of the people.

Return to England. Byron arrived in London on July 14, 1811, and his mother died on August 1 before he could reach her at Newstead. He was further shocked to learn that John Edleston, the beloved choirboy, had died in his absence. During the autumn, he met the poets Thomas Moore and Samuel Rogers, who introduced him to Holland House, the great literary and political centre. On February 27, 1812, he made his first speech in the House of Lords on the frame-breaking bill, going beyond even the radical Whigs in his humanitarian plea for the Nottingham weavers. At the beginning of March, *Childe Harold's Pilgrimage* was published by John Murray and took the town by storm. Besides furnishing a poetic travelogue of picturesque lands, it gave vent to the moods of melancholy and disillusionment of the post-Revolutionary and Napoleonic eras. And the poem voiced with a frankness unprecedented in the literature of the time the disparity between the romantic ideal and the world of reality. Byron was lionized in Whig society. The handsome poet with the clubfoot, curly auburn hair, pale face, and pouting lips, who had bared his soul in the melancholy verses of *Childe Harold*, was swept into a liaison with the passionate and eccentric Lady Caroline Lamb, daughter-in-law of Lord and Lady Melbourne. Although her open defiance of conventions shocked him and he was ultimately repelled by her reckless indiscretions, the scandal of an elopement was barely prevented by Hobhouse. Byron took consolation in the "autumnal charms" of Lady Oxford, who encouraged his political radicalism.

Publication of *Childe Harold's Pilgrimage*

During the summer of 1813, Byron apparently entered into intimate relations with his half sister Augusta Leigh. His confidante, Lady Melbourne, encouraged his flirtation with Lady Frances Webster as a diversion from this dangerous liaison. The agitations of these two love affairs and the sense of mingled guilt and exultation they aroused in his mind are reflected in the Oriental tales he wrote during the year, *The Giaour* and *The Bride of Abydos.* Despite his admiration for the objectivity and verbal skill of Pope's balanced satire, Byron indulged in the romantic concept of poetry as "the lava of the imagination whose eruption prevents an earthquake." He "spared" Lady Frances while their relations remained still platonic, but it was not so easy to break with Augusta. The affair went on through the winter and summer of 1814, while his emotions found vent in the gloomy and remorseful Oriental tales, *The Corsair* (which sold 10,000 copies on the day of publication) and *Lara*.

Marriage

Seeking escape in marriage, in September he proposed to and was accepted by Lady Melbourne's niece, Anne Isabella (Annabella) Milbanke, only child of Sir Ralph and Lady Judith (*née* Noel) Milbanke. She had met Byron at Melbourne House in 1812 and had intrigued him by her innocence and her serious conversation. He had proposed to her through Lady Melbourne when he was trying to extricate himself from the affair with Caroline Lamb. She refused but later renewed the correspondence that led to the second proposal. The marriage took place on January 2, 1815. After a honeymoon "not all sunshine," the Byrons, in March, settled in a large house at 13 Piccadilly Terrace, London. Delays in negotiations to sell Newstead left them financially embarrassed and before long bailiffs were in the house. Byron escaped to the house of John Murray, his publisher, where he met Walter Scott, and to the Theatre Royal in Drury Lane, where he had become one of the subcommittee of management. Augusta had come for a visit to Piccadilly Terrace, and Byron, exasperated by debts, irritated by Annabella's humourless sensitivity, and liberated by drink, talked wildly and hinted at past sins.

Lady Byron gave birth to a daughter, Augusta Ada, on December 10, and on January 15 she left with the child for a visit to her parents. Two weeks later Byron received word from her father that she would not return to him. The reasons for her decision were never given and rumours began to fly, most of them centring on Byron's relations with Augusta Leigh. When the rumours grew, Byron signed the legal separation papers, parted fondly from Augusta, and went abroad, never returning to England.

Exile abroad. After visiting the battlefield of Waterloo, which inspired some stanzas of a new canto of *Childe Harold*, he followed the Rhine into Switzerland. At the Villa Diodati, near Geneva, he was on friendly terms with Shelley and his entourage, which included William Godwin's daughter Mary, who was Shelley's wife, and Godwin's stepdaughter by a second marriage, Claire Clairmont, who had insinuated herself into a liaison with Byron before he left England. A boat trip to the head of the lake with Shelley gave Byron material for his "Prisoner of Chillon," and he completed the third canto of *Childe Harold* at Diodati (published November 18, 1816). The French writer Madame de Staël, whom he visited at Coppet, tried to effect a reconciliation between him and his wife but was rebuffed by Lady Byron. At the end of the summer the Shelley party left for England, Claire carrying Byron's illegitimate daughter (born January 12, 1817, and named Allegra by Byron). A tour of the Bernese Oberland with Hobhouse provided the scenery for *Manfred* (published June 16, 1817), a Faustian poetic drama that reflected Byron's brooding sense of guilt and remorse and the wider frustrations of the romantic spirit doomed by the reflection that man is "half dust, half deity, alike unfit to sink or soar."

Friendship with Shelley

On October 5 Byron and Hobhouse left Diodati for Italy. After a stop in Milan, they arrived in Venice on November 10. Byron was not disappointed in the seagirt city, which had always been, he wrote, "(next to the East) the greenest island of my imagination." He took lodgings in the house of a draper with whose dark-eyed wife, Marianna Segati, he proceeded to fall in love. He studied Armenian at the monastery of S. Lazzaro and occasionally attended the literary and artistic gatherings of the Countess Albrizzi, "the de Staël of Venice." In May he joined Hobhouse in Rome and rode over the ruins, gathering impressions that he recorded in a fourth canto of *Childe Harold* (published April 28, 1818). At a summer villa at La Mira on the Brenta River, he also wrote *Beppo*, a rollicking satire on Italian manners. There he met Margarita Cogni, wife of a baker, who followed him to Venice and eventually replaced Marianna Segati in his affections. When he leased the Palazzo Mocenigo on the Grand Canal in May 1818, she became his housekeeper. His descriptions of the vagaries of this "gentle tigress" are among the most entertaining passages in his letters from Italy. During the summer he completed the first canto of *Don Juan* (cantos I and II published July 15, 1819), a picaresque verse satire in the manner of *Beppo*, with more pointed references to his own experiences. In *Don Juan* he freed himself from the excessive melancholy of *Childe Harold* and the mannered style that accompanied those romantic moods and revealed other sides of his character and personality—his satiric wit, and his unique view of the comic rather than the tragic discrepancy between reality and appearance, desire and fulfillment. Claire had sent his illegitimate daughter Allegra for him to raise and was continually annoying him with admonitions. The sale of Newstead Abbey in the autumn of 1818 for £94,500 finally cleared most of his debts, which had risen to £34,000, and left him with

First work on *Don Juan*

an income of £3,300. And since he had come abroad, his yearly earnings from writing had averaged more than £2,000.

Shelley and other visitors, in 1818, had found Byron grown fat, with hair long and turning gray, looking older than his years, and sunk in sexual promiscuity. A chance meeting with the Countess Teresa Guiccioli in April 1819 changed the course of his life. In a few days he fell completely in love with Teresa, who was only 19 and married to a wealthy and eccentric man nearly three times her age. Byron followed her to Ravenna, and, later in the summer, she accompanied him back to Venice and stayed at his villa at La Mira until her husband called for her. In October Byron presented Thomas Moore, who came for a visit, with the manuscript of his memoirs, which Moore sold to Murray for 2,000 guineas but which was burned at the insistence of Hobhouse and Murray after Byron's death. Byron returned to Ravenna in January 1820, as Teresa's accepted *cavalier servente* (gentleman-in-waiting). He won the friendship of her father and brother, the Counts Ruggero and Pietro Gamba, who initiated him into the secret revolutionary society of the Carbonari. In Ravenna he was brought into closer touch with the life of the Italian people than he had ever been in Venice. He gave arms to the Carbonari and alms to the poor. It was one of the happiest and most productive periods of his life. He wrote there *The Prophecy of Dante;* cantos III, IV, and V of *Don Juan;* the poetic dramas *Marino Faliero*, *Sardanapalus*, *The Two Foscari*, and *Cain* (all published in 1821); and his satire on the poet Robert Southey, *The Vision of Judgment*. When Teresa's father and brother were exiled for their part in an abortive uprising and she, now separated from her husband, was forced to follow them, Byron reluctantly removed to Pisa where Shelley had rented the Casa Lanfranchi on the Arno River for him. He arrived on November 1, 1821, having left his daughter Allegra in a convent near Ravenna where, despite the protests of Claire, he had sent her to be educated.

Byron paid daily visits to Teresa, whose father and brother had found temporary asylum in Pisa. Suspected and watched by government spies as a dangerous revolutionary, he made no friends among the natives. The death of his mother-in-law in January 1822 gave him an additional income of £3,000. By the terms of the will, he henceforth took the name of Noel Byron. The comfortable routine into which he had settled was broken in March by an unfortunate affray ending with the stabbing of a dragoon by one of Byron's servants. Close upon this came word of the death of Allegra in the convent on April 20. Shelley had rented a house on the Bay of Lerici, and Byron leased a villa near Leghorn for the summer, taking Teresa and the Gambas with him.

Work with Shelley and Hunt on *The Liberal*

There the poet and essayist Leigh Hunt found him on July 1, when he arrived from England to join with Shelley and Byron in the editing of a new periodical. Shelley came from Lerici to help install Hunt and his family in the lower floor of Byron's house in Florence. At the same time, the Gambas were expelled from Tuscany, and Byron returned with Teresa to Pisa. The drowning of Shelley on July 8 left Hunt entirely dependent on Byron, who had already "loaned" him £250 for his passage and furnished an apartment for him and his family. Byron found Hunt an agreeable companion, but their relations were somewhat strained by Mrs. Hunt's moral condescension and by the depredations of her six uninhibited children. Byron contributed his *Vision of Judgment* to the first number of the new periodical, *The Liberal*, which was published in London by Hunt's brother John (October 15, 1822). At the end of September he moved his entire household to a suburb of Genoa, where the Gambas had found asylum and had taken a large house for him. Mary Shelley had leased another house nearby for herself and the Hunts.

Byron's interest in the periodical had waned, but he continued to support Hunt and to give manuscripts to *The Liberal*. After a quarrel with his publisher, John Murray, Byron gave all his later work, including cantos VI to XVI of *Don Juan*, *The Age of Bronze*, and *The Island*, to John Hunt. Restive in the domesticity of his life with Teresa Guiccioli and longing for the opportunity for some noble action that would vindicate and redeem him in the eyes of his countrymen, Byron seized eagerly the offer from the London Greek Committee, which came in April 1823, to act as its agent in aiding the Greeks in their war for independence from the Turks. He prepared to take supplies and money to the scene of the struggle. In the meantime, the arrival in Genoa of the Countess of Blessington and her party turned his thoughts nostalgically to England. His last weeks in Italy were made hectic by quarrels with Leigh Hunt and Mary Shelley and by the emotional strain of the final parting from Teresa.

Role in war for Greek independence

On July 16, Byron left Genoa on a chartered ship, the "Hercules," accompanied by the adventurer Edward Trelawny and the young count Pietro Gamba, Teresa's brother. They arrived at the Ionian island of Cephalonia on August 2, and Byron settled in the village of Metaxáta to await developments. After a trip to Ithaca, he tried to promote the floating in London of a loan for the Greeks. He was avidly wooed by the Greek factions, all eager for his cash and influence. Finally, he sent £4,000 of his own money to prepare the Greek fleet for sea service and then sailed for Missolonghi (Mesolóngian) on December 29 to join Prince Aléxandros Mavrokordátos, leader of the forces in western Greece.

With tremendous energy he entered into the plans to attack the Turkish-held fortress of Lepanto. He employed a fire master to prepare artillery and took under his own command and pay the Suliote soldiers, reputedly the bravest of the Greeks. In addition he made efforts to unite eastern and western Greece by effecting a reconciliation of the factions. But a serious illness on February 15, 1824, followed by the usual remedy of bleeding, weakened him at the same time that an insurrection of the Suliotes opened his eyes to their cupidity. Though his enthusiasm for the Greek cause was undiminished, he had thenceforth a more realistic view of the obstacles and was often depressed. He was also suffering from the emotional strain of an unequal friendship with Loukas Chalandritsanos, a Greek boy, whom he had brought as a page from Cephalonia and to whom he addressed his last agonized poems, including his lines on completing his 36th year. He still fixed his hopes on the Greek loan and the uniting of the dissident parties. He was planning to attend a conference with Odysseus and other leaders at Salona when, drenched by a sudden downpour during his daily ride, he contracted a fever, which was aggravated by the bleeding insisted on by the doctors. After a painful and pathetic illness of ten days, he died on April 19, 1824. Deeply mourned throughout the land, he became a symbol of disinterested patriotism and a Greek national hero. His body was brought back to England and, refused burial in Westminster Abbey, was placed in the vault of his ancestors in Hucknall Torkard Church near Newstead. Ironically, 145 years after his death, in 1969, a memorial to Byron was finally placed on the floor of the Abbey.

MAJOR WORKS

Hours of Idleness: A Series of Poems, Original and Translated (1807); *English Bards and Scotch Reviewers: A Satire* (1809); *Childe Harold's Pilgrimage: A Romaunt*, cantos i and ii (1812); canto iii (1816); canto iv (1818); *The Giaour: A Fragment of a Turkish Tale* (1813); *The Bride of Abydos: A Turkish Tale* (1813); *The Corsair: A Tale* (1814); *Lara: A Tale*, with *Jacqueline: A Tale*, by Samuel Rogers (1814); *The Siege of Corinth: A Poem*, pub. with *Parisina: A Poem* (1816); *Poems* (1816); *The Prisoner of Chillon, and Other Poems* (1816); *The Lament of Tasso* (1817); *Manfred: A Dramatic Poem* (1817); *Beppo: A Venetian Story* (1818); *Mazeppa: A Poem* (1819); *Don Juan*, cantos i and ii (1819); cantos iii–v (1821); cantos vi–viii, cantos ix–xi, and cantos xii–xiv (all 1823); cantos xv–xvi (1824); *Marino Faliero: Doge of Venice*, pub. with *The Prophecy of Dante: A Poem* (1821); *Sardanapalus: A Tragedy; The Two Foscari: A Tragedy; Cain: A Mystery* (1821); *The Vision of Judgment*, first pub. in *The Liberal* (1822).

BIBLIOGRAPHY. The fullest bibliography of first editions is T.J. WISE, *A Bibliography of the Writings in Verse and Prose of . . . Byron . . .*, 2 vol. (1932–33, reprinted 1963);

for first, later, and foreign editions see that by E.H. COLERIDGE in vol. 7 of his edition of the poetry (cited below). For Byroniana, see SAMUEL C. CHEW, *Byron in England* (1924); and E.J. LOVELL, "Byron," in FRANK JORDAN (ed.), *The English Romantic Poets: A Review of Research and Criticism* (1971).

Editions: The standard edition of the works remains *Letters and Journals*, ed. by R.E. PROTHERO, 6 vol. (1898–1901); *Poetry*, ed. by E.H. COLERIDGE (1898–1904). The best 1-volume edition is *The Complete Poetical Works . . .*, ed. by PAUL ELMER MORE (1905). Other accessible editions include: *Poems*, ed. by G. POCOCK, Everyman's Library, rev. ed., 3 vol. (1948); *Selections . . .*, ed. by PETER QUENNELL, the Nonesuch edition (1949); *The Selected Poetry . . .*, ed. by L.A. MARCHAND, Modern Library edition (1951; rev. ed., 1967); *Selected Poetry and Letters*, ed. by E. BOSTETTER (1951). For *Don Juan*, the fullest critical edition is *Byron's Don Juan: A Variorum Edition*, by T.G. STEFFAN and W.W. PRATT, 4 vol. (1957); the best 1-volume edition is *Don Juan*, ed. by L.A. MARCHAND (1958). Additional letters are in *Lord Byron's Correspondence . . .*, ed. by JOHN MURRAY, 2 vol. (1922); and *Byron: A Self-Portrait . . .*, ed. by PETER QUENNELL, 2 vol. (1950).

Biographical works: The definitive modern biography is L.A. MARCHAND, *Byron: A Biography*, 3 vol. (1957); supplemented and updated in *Byron: A Portrait* (1970). Memoirs by contemporaries include: R.C. DALLAS, *Recollections of the Life of . . . Byron (1808–1814)* (1824); T. MEDWIN, *Journal of the Conversations of . . . Byron . . . at Pisa* (1824; ed. by E.J. LOVELL, 1966); P. GAMBA, *A Narrative of . . . Byron's Last Journey to Greece* (1825); W. PARRY, *The Last Days of . . . Byron* (1825); J.H. LEIGH HUNT, *Lord Byron and Some of His Contemporaries*, 2nd ed. (1828); T. MOORE, *Letters and Journals of . . . Byron: With Notices of His Life*, 2 vol. (1830), the first "official" biography; COUNTESS OF BLESSINGTON, *Conversations of Lord Byron* (1834; ed. by E.J. LOVELL, 1969); E.J. TRELAWNY, *Recollections of the Last Days of Shelley and Byron* (1858); E.J. LOVELL, JR. (ed.), *His Very Self and Voice: Collected Conversations of . . . Byron* (1954). Among later biographies and biographical studies should be noted: J. CORDY JEAFFRESON, *The Real Lord Byron*, 2 vol. (1883); E. MAYNE, *Byron* (1924), and *The Life and Letters of . . . Lady Noel Byron* (1929); HAROLD NICOLSON, *Byron: The Last Journey* (1924; rev. ed., 1940); ANDRE MAUROIS, *Don Juan; ou, la vie de Byron* (1930; Eng. trans., *Byron*, 1930); P. QUENNELL, *Byron: The Years of Fame* (1935; new ed., 1967) and *Byron in Italy* (1941); W.A. BORST, *Lord Byron's First Pilgrimage* (1948); IRIS ORIGO, *The Last Attachment* (1949), the story of Byron and the Countess Guiccioli; C.L. CLINE, *Byron, Shelley and Their Pisan Circle* (1952); G. WILSON KNIGHT, *Lord Byron: Christian Virtues* (1952) and *Lord Byron's Marriage* (1957). See also DORIS L. MOORE, *The Late Lord Byron* (1961), on the posthumous reputation of Byron; and MALCOLM ELWIN, *Lord Byron's Wife* (1962), based on the Lovelace Papers (Lady Byron's papers).

Criticism: E.J. LOVELL, *Byron: The Record of a Quest* (1949); A. RUTHERFORD, *Byron: A Critical Study* (1961), and (comp.), *Byron: The Critical Heritage* (1970), a collection of 19th-century critiques; P. WEST (ed.), *Byron: A Collection of Critical Essays* (1963), 20th-century views; L.A. MARCHAND, *Byron's Poetry: A Critical Introduction* (1965); JEROME J. MCGANN, *Fiery Dust: Byron's Poetic Development* (1968); M.K. JOSEPH, *Byron, the Poet* (1964); on *Don Juan*, E.F. BOYD, *Don Juan: A Critical Study* (1945); G.M. RIDENOUR, *The Style of Don Juan* (1960).

(L.A.M.)

Byzantine Empire

The very name Byzantine illustrates the misconceptions to which the empire's history has often been subject, for its inhabitants would hardly have considered the term appropriate to themselves or to their state. Theirs was, in their view, none other than the Roman Empire, founded shortly before the beginning of the Christian Era by God's grace to unify his people in preparation for the coming of his Son. Proud of that Christian and Roman heritage, convinced that their earthly empire so nearly resembled the heavenly pattern that it could never change, they called themselves Romaioi, or Romans. Modern historians agree with them only in part. The term East Rome accurately described the political unit embracing the Eastern provinces of the old Roman Empire until 476, while there were yet two emperors. The same term may even be used until the last half of the 6th century, as long as men continued to act and think according to patterns not unlike those prevailing in an earlier Roman Empire. These same centuries nonetheless witnessed changes so profound in their cumulative effect that after the 7th century state and society in the East differed markedly from their earlier forms. In an effort to recognize that distinction, historians traditionally have described the medieval empire as "Byzantine."

Origin of the designation "Byzantine"

The latter term is derived from the name Byzantium, borne by a colony of ancient Greek foundation on the European side of the Bosporus, midway between the Mediterranean and the Black Sea: the city was, by virtue of its location, a natural transit point between Europe and Asia Minor (Anatolia). Refounded as the "new Rome" by the emperor Constantine in 330, it was endowed by him with the name Constantinople, the city of Constantine. The derivation from Byzantium is suggestive in that it emphasizes a central aspect of Byzantine civilization: the degree to which the empire's administrative and intellectual life found a focus at Constantinople from 330 to 1453, the year of the city's last and unsuccessful defense under the 12th Constantine. The circumstances of the last defense are suggestive, too, for in 1453 the ancient, medieval, and modern worlds seemed briefly to meet. The last Constantine fell in defense of the new Rome built by the first Constantine. Walls that had held firm in the early Middle Ages against German, Hun, Avar, Slav, and Arab were breached finally by modern artillery, in the mysteries of which European technicians had instructed the most successful of the Central Asian invaders: the Ottoman Turks. In short, the Byzantine Empire, by virtue of its geographical position and its long continuity, unites a number of worlds: geographically, that of Asia and that of Europe; chronologically, that of classical antiquity and that of the Renaissance.

The fortunes of the empire thus were intimately entwined with those of peoples whose achievements and failures constitute the medieval history of both Europe and Asia. Nor did hostility always characterize the relations between Byzantines and those whom they considered "barbarian." Even though the Byzantine intellectual firmly believed that civilization ended with the boundaries of his world, he opened it to the barbarian, provided that the latter (with his kin) would accept Baptism and render loyalty to the emperor. Thanks to the settlements that resulted from such policies, many a name seemingly Greek disguises another of different origin: Slavic, perhaps, or Turkish. Barbarian illiteracy, in consequence, obscures the early generations of more than one family destined to rise to prominence in the empire's military or civil service. Byzantium was a melting-pot society, characterized during its earlier centuries by a degree of social mobility that belies the stereotype, often applied to it, of an immobile, caste-ridden society.

A source of strength in the early Middle Ages, Byzantium's central geographical position served it ill after the 10th century. The conquests of that age presented new problems of organization and assimilation; and these the emperors had to confront at precisely the time when older questions of economic and social policy pressed for answers in a new and acute form. Satisfactory solutions were never found. Bitter ethnic and religious hostility marked the history of the empire's later centuries, weakening it in the face of new enemies descending upon it from east and west. The empire finally collapsed when its administrative structures could no longer support the burden of leadership thrust upon it by military conquests it had won in the European and Asian worlds.

Sources of Byzantine history. Research in Byzantine history can be as frustrating as it is fascinating, thanks to certain unique characteristics of the sources. First of all, linguistic problems are monumental. Since the historical experience of almost all medieval peoples impinged upon that of Byzantium, the historian may have to consult materials written in a bewildering array of languages. Even Byzantine Greek itself is a double language: the "pure" language of the intellectual class, rooted in the Greek of ancient Athens and the New Testament, and the demotic, or popular living tongue, spoken in city and

Problems of Byzantine historiography

village. Second, the historical record is far from satisfactory for all places and all periods. As a result of the high degree of centralization in Constantinople, most materials (whether literary, legal, or economic) are concerned with the affairs of that city and not of the provinces. Nor are all periods equally well represented. From the end of the 6th century to the second half of the 8th century, the record must be pieced together from an extremely small number of chronicles, legal codes, ecclesiastical documents, and saints' lives. After about 800, the sources become increasingly abundant, permitting the historian to investigate a much wider range of problems, including even the economic and social conditions of specific villages. Third, the sources frequently display no sense of historical development or even any high degree of historical consciousness. The Byzantine intellectual often described his own world in terms of the past, borrowing whole passages from earlier authors to delineate contemporary practice. The modern historian, in consequence, may be misled in one of two ways: either he may read long-vanished patterns into a later era, or, more insidiously, he may assume that nothing Byzantine ever changed, forgetting that, if the Byzantine people were overly conscious of the past and of an almost burdensome cultural heritage, the struggle for survival had made pragmatists of them. They had learned to observe clearly the world of the outsider as well as their own, however little they liked or respected the stranger outside their gates.

This article contains the following sections:

I. The empire to 867

THE ROMAN AND CHRISTIAN BACKGROUND

Unity and diversity in the late Roman Empire. The Roman Empire, the ancestor of the Byzantine, remarkably blended unity and diversity, the former being by far the better known since its constituents are the predominant features of Roman civilization. The common Latin language, the coinage, the "international" army of the Roman legions, the urban network, the law, and the Greco-Roman heritage of civic culture loomed largest among those bonds that Augustus and his successors hoped would bring unity and peace to a Mediterranean world exhausted by centuries of civil war. To strengthen these sinews of imperial civilization, the emperors hoped that a lively and spontaneous trade might develop among the several provinces. At the pinnacle of this world stood the emperor himself, the man of wisdom who would shelter the state from whatever mishaps fortune had darkly hidden. The emperor alone could provide this protection since, as the embodiment of all the virtues, he possessed in perfection those qualities displayed only imperfectly by his individual subjects.

The Roman formula of combatting fortune by reason and therewith assuring unity throughout the Mediterranean world worked surprisingly well in view of the pressures for disunity that time was to multiply. Conquest had brought regions of diverse background under Roman rule. The Eastern provinces were ancient and populous centres of that urban life that for millennia had defined the character of Mediterranean civilization. The Western provinces had only lately entered upon their own course of urban development under the not always tender ministrations of their Roman masters.

Each of the aspects of unity enumerated above had its other side. Not everyone understood or spoke Latin. Paralleling and sometimes influencing Roman law were local customs and practices, understandably tenacious by reason of their antiquity. Pagan temples, Jewish synagogues, Christian baptisteries attest to the range of organized religions with which the official forms of the Roman state, including those of emperor worship, could not always peacefully coexist. And far from unifying the Roman world, economic growth often created self-sufficient units in the several regions, provinces, or great estates.

Given the obstacles against which the masters of the Roman state struggled, it is altogether remarkable that Roman patriotism was ever more than an empty formula, that cultivated gentlemen from the Pillars of Hercules to the Black Sea were aware that they had "something" in common. This "something" might be defined as the Greco-Roman civic tradition in the widest sense of its institutional, intellectual, and emotional implications. Grateful for the conditions of peace that fostered it, men of wealth and culture dedicated their time and resources to glorifying that tradition through adornment of the cities that exemplified it and through education of the young who they hoped might perpetuate it.

Greco-Roman civic tradition

Upon this world the barbarians descended after about AD 150. To protect the frontier against them, warrior emperors devoted whatever energies they could spare from the constant struggle to reassert control over provinces where local regimes emerged. In view of the ensuing warfare, the widespread incidence of disease, and the rapid turnover among the occupants of the imperial throne, it would be easy to assume that little was left of either the traditional fabric of Greco-Roman society or the bureaucratic structure designed to support it.

Neither assumption is accurate. Devastation was haphazard, and some regions suffered while others did not. In fact, the economy and society of the empire as a whole during that period was more diverse than it had ever been. Impelled by necessity or lured by profit, men moved from province to province. Social disorder opened avenues to eminence and wealth that the more stable order of an earlier age had closed to the talented and the ambitious. For personal and dynastic reasons, emperors favoured certain towns and provinces at the expense of others, and the erratic course of succession to the throne, coupled with a resulting constant change among the top administrative officials, largely deprived economic and social policies of recognizable consistency.

The reforms of Diocletian and Constantine. The definition of consistent policy in imperial affairs was the achievement of two great soldier-emperors, Diocletian (ruled 284–305) and Constantine (324–337), who together ended a century of anarchy and refounded the Roman state. There are many similarities between them, not the least being the range of problems to which they addressed themselves: both had learned from the 3rd-century anarchy that one man alone and unaided could not hope to control the multiform Roman world and protect its frontiers; as soldiers, both considered reform of the army of prime necessity in an age that demanded the utmost mobility in striking power; both found the old Rome and Italy an unsatisfactory military base for the bulk of the imperial forces. Deeply influenced by the soldier's penchant for hierarchy, system, and order, a taste that they shared with many of their contemporaries as well as the emperors who preceded them, they were appalled by the lack of system and the disorder characteristic of the economy and the society in which they lived. Both, in consequence, were eager to refine and regularize certain desperate expedients that had been adopted by their rough military predecessors to conduct the affairs of the Roman state. Whatever their personal religious convictions, both, finally, believed that imperial affairs would not prosper unless the emperor's subjects worshipped the right gods in the right way.

Rule of succession

The means they adopted to achieve these ends differ so profoundly that the one, Diocletian, looks to the past and ends the history of Rome; the other, Constantine, looks to the future and founds the history of Byzantium. Thus, in the matter of succession to the imperial office, Diocletian adopted precedents he could have found in the practices of the 2nd century AD. He associated with himself a co-emperor, or Augustus. Each Augustus then adopted a young colleague, or Caesar, to share in the rule and eventually to succeed the senior partner. This rule of four, or tetrarchy, failed of its purpose, and Constantine replaced it with the dynastic principle of hereditary succession, a procedure generally followed in subsequent centuries. To divide administrative responsibilities, Constantine replaced the single praetorian prefect, who had traditionally exercised both military and civil functions in close proximity to the emperor, with regional prefects established in the provinces and enjoying civil authority alone. In the course of the 4th century, four great "regional prefectures" emerged from these Constantinian beginnings, and the practice of separating civil from military authority persisted until the 7th century.

Contrasts in other areas of imperial policy are equally striking. Diocletian persecuted Christians and sought to revive the ancestral religion. Constantine, a convert to the new faith, raised it to the status of a "permitted religion." Diocletian established his headquarters at Nicomedia, a city that never rose above the status of a provincial centre during the Middle Ages, while Constantinople, the city of Constantine's foundation, flourished mightily. Diocletian sought to bring order into the economy by controlling wages and prices and by initiating a currency reform based upon a new gold piece, the aureus, struck at the rate of 60 to the pound of gold. The controls failed and the aureus vanished, to be succeeded by Constantine's gold solidus. The latter piece, struck at the lighter weight of 72 to the gold pound, remained the standard for centuries. For whatever reason, in summary, Constantine's policies proved extraordinarily fruitful. Some of them—notably hereditary succession, the recognition of Christianity, the currency reform, and the foundation of the capital—determined in a lasting way the several aspects of Byzantine civilization with which they are associated.

Yet it would be a mistake to consider Constantine a revolutionary or to overlook those areas in which, rather than innovating, he followed precedent. Earlier emperors had sought to constrain groups of men to perform certain tasks that were deemed vital to the survival of the state but that proved unremunerative or repellent to those forced to assume the burden. Such tasks included the tillage of the soil, which was the work of the peasant, or *colonus;* the transport of cheap bulky goods to the metropolitan centres of Rome or Constantinople, which was the work of the shipmaster, or *navicularius;* and services rendered by the *curiales,* members of the municipal senate charged with the assessment and collection of local taxes. Constantine's laws in many instances extended or even rendered hereditary these enforced responsibilities, thus laying the foundations for the system of *collegia,* or hereditary state guilds, that was to be so noteworthy a feature of late-Roman social life. Of particular importance, he required the *colonus* (peasant) to remain in the locality to which the tax lists ascribed him.

THE 5TH CENTURY: PERSISTENCE OF GRECO-ROMAN CIVILIZATION IN THE EAST

Whether innovative or traditional, Constantine's measures determined the thrust and direction of imperial policy throughout the 4th century and into the 5th. The state of the empire in 395 may, in fact, be described in terms of the outcome of Constantine's work. The dynastic principle was established so firmly that the emperor who died in that year, Theodosius I, could bequeath the imperial office jointly to his sons, both of whom were young and incompetent: Arcadius in the East and Honorius in the West. Never again would one man rule over the full extent of the empire in both its halves. Constantinople had probably grown to a population of between 200,000 and 500,000; in the 5th century the emperors sought to restrain rather than promote its growth. After 391 Christianity was far more than one among many religions: from that year onward, imperial decree prohibited all forms of pagan cult, and the temples were closed. Imperial pressure was often manifest at the church councils of the 4th century, with the emperor assuming a role he was destined to fill again during the 5th century in defining and suppressing heresy.

Economic prosperity

Economic and social policies. The empire's economy had prospered in a spotty fashion. Certain provinces, or parts of provinces such as northern Italy, flourished commercially as well as agriculturally. Constantinople, in particular, influenced urban growth and the exploitation of agricultural frontiers. Balkan towns along the roads leading to the great city prospered, while others not so favoured languished and even disappeared. Untilled land in the hilly regions of northern Syria fell under the plow to supply foodstuffs for the masses of Constantinople. As the 4th century progressed, not only did Constantine's solidus remain indeed solid gold, but evidence drawn from a wide range of sources suggests that gold in any form was far more abundant than it had been for at least two centuries. It may be that new sources of supply for the precious metal had been discovered; perhaps in spoils plundered from pagan temples, perhaps from mines newly exploited in western Africa and newly available to the lands of the empire, thanks to the appearance of camel-driving nomads who transported the gold across the Sahara to the Mediterranean coastline of North Africa.

The extreme social mobility noted in the late 3rd and early 4th centuries seems less characteristic of the second half of the latter century. Certainly the emperors continued their efforts to bind men collectively to their socially necessary tasks, but the repetition of laws tying the *colonus* to his estate, the *navicularius* to his ship, and the *curialis* to his municipal senate suggests that these edicts had little effect. Indeed, it would be a mistake to conclude from such legislation that Roman society was universally and uniformly organized in castes determined in response to imperial orders. There was always a distinction between what an emperor wanted and what he could obtain, and, as the foregoing survey has suggested, there were distinctions among the provinces as well.

Even before the end of the first quarter of the 5th century, these provincial differences were visible; and, in no small degree, they help to explain the survival of imperial government and Greco-Roman civilization in the East while both eventually perished in the West. Throughout the Eastern provinces, population levels seem to have remained higher, and the emperors in Constantinople never had to search (at least until the 6th century) for men to fill the ranks of their armies. As might be expected in those eastern lands in which urban civilization was several centuries old, cities persisted and, with them, a merchant class and a monetary economy. Eastern merchants, known in the sources as Syrians, assumed the carrying trade between East and West, often establishing colonies in the beleaguered cities of the latter region.

Most important, the emperor in the East never lost access to, or control over, his sources of manpower and money. An older and probably more wealthy senatorial class, or aristocracy, in the West consolidated its great estates and assumed a form of protection or patronage over the labouring rural classes, depriving the state of desperately needed military and financial services. The senatorial class in the East seems to have been of more recent origin, its beginnings to be found among those favourites or parvenus who had followed Constantine to his new capital. By the early 5th century, their wealth seems to have been, individually, much less than the resources at the disposal of their Western counterparts; their estates were far more scattered, their rural dependents less numerous. They were thus less able to challenge the imperial will and less able to interpose themselves between the state, on the one hand, and its potential soldiers or taxpayers, on the other.

Relations with the barbarians. These differences between Eastern and Western social structures, together with certain geographical features, account for the different reception found by the Germanic invaders of the 4th and 5th centuries in East and West. Although the Germanic people had eddied about the Danube and Rhine frontiers of the empire since the 2nd century, their major inroads were made only in the latter half of the 4th century, when the ferocious Huns drove the Ostrogoths and Visigoths to seek refuge within the Danubian frontier of the empire. The initial interaction between Roman and barbarian was far from amicable; the Romans seemed to have exploited their unwelcome guests, and the Goths rose in anger, defeating an East Roman army at Adrianople in 378 and killing the Eastern emperor in command. Emperor Theodosius (ruled 384–395) adopted a different policy, granting the Goths lands and according them the legal status of allies, or *foederati*, who fought within the ranks of the Roman armies as autonomous units under their own leaders.

Battle of Adrianople

Neither in West nor East did Theodosius' policy of accommodation and alliance prove popular. The Goths, like most Germanic peoples with the exception of the Franks and the Lombards, had been converted to Arian Christianity, which the Catholic, or Orthodox, Romans considered a dangerous heresy. The warlike ways of the Germans found little favour with a senatorial aristocracy essentially pacifist in its outlook, and the early 5th century is marked in both halves of the empire by reactions against Germanic leaders in high office. At Constantinople in 400, for example, the citizens rose against the senior officer of the imperial guard (*magister militum*), Gainas, slaughtering him together with his Gothic followers. Although this particular revolt was, in many respects, less productive of immediate results than similar episodes in the West, and the Germanic leaders later reappeared in roles of command throughout the East, the latter acted thenceforth as individuals without the support of those nearly autonomous groups of soldiers that western barbarian commanders continued to enjoy.

Furthermore, the East made good use of its resources in gold, in native manpower, and in diplomacy, while quickly learning how best to play off one enemy against another. In the reign of Theodosius II (408–450), the Huns under their chieftain Attila received subsidies of gold that both kept them in a state of uneasy peace with the Eastern Empire and may have proved profitable to those merchants of Constantinople who traded with the barbarians. When Marcian (ruled 450–457) refused to continue the subsidies, Attila was diverted from revenge by the prospect of conquests in the West. He never returned to challenge the Eastern Empire, and, with his death in 453, his Hunnic empire fell apart. Both Marcian and his successor, Leo I (ruled 457–474), had ruled under the tutelage of the Alan, Aspar, until Leo resolved to challenge Aspar's pre-eminence and the influence of the Goths elsewhere in the empire by favouring the warlike Isaurians and their chieftain, Tarasicodissa, whom he married to the imperial princess, Ariadne. The Isaurian followers of Tarasicodissa, who was to survive a stormy reign as the Emperor Zeno (474–491), were rough mountain folk from southern Anatolia and culturally probably even more barbarous than the Goths or the other Germans. Yet, in that they were the subjects of the Roman emperor in the East, they were undoubtedly Romans and proved an effective instrument to counter the Gothic challenge at Constantinople. In the prefecture of Illyricum, Zeno ended the menace of Theodoric the Amal by persuading him (488) to venture with his Ostrogoths into Italy. The latter province lay in the hands of the German chieftain Odoacer, who in 476 had deposed Romulus Augustus, the last Roman emperor in the West. Thus, by suggesting that Theodoric conquer Italy as his Ostrogothic kingdom, Zeno maintained at least a nominal supremacy in that western land while ridding the Eastern Empire of an unruly subordinate.

Dissolution of the Western Empire

With Zeno's death and the accession of the Roman civil servant Anastasius I (ruled 491–518), Isaurian occupation of the imperial office ended, but it was not until 498 that the forces of the new emperor effectively took the measure of Isaurian resistance. After the victory of that year, the loyal subject of the Eastern Roman emperor could breathe easily: Isaurians had been used to beat Germans, but the wild mountain folk had, in their turn, failed to take permanent possession of the imperial office. Imperial authority had maintained its integrity in the East while the Western Empire had dissolved into a number of successor states: the Angles and Saxons had invaded Britain as early as 410; the Visigoths possessed portions of Spain since 417, and the Vandals entered Africa in 428; the Franks, under Clovis, had begun their conquest of central and southern Gaul in 481; Theodoric was destined to rule in Italy until 526.

Religious controversy. If ethnic hostility within the empire was less a menace around the year 500 than it had often been in the past, dissensions stemming from religious controversy seriously threatened imperial unity, and the political history of the next century cannot be understood without some examination of the so-called Monophysite heresy. The latter was the second great heresy in the Eastern Empire, the first having been the dispute occasioned by the teachings of the Alexandrian presbyter Arius, who, in an effort to maintain the uniqueness and majesty of God the Father, had taught that he alone had existed from eternity, while God the Son had been created in time. Thanks in part to imperial support, the Arian heresy had persisted throughout the 4th century and was definitively condemned only in 381 with promulgation of the doctrine that Father and Son were of one substance and thus coexistent.

The Monophysite heresy

If the Fathers of the 4th century quarrelled over the relations between God the Father and God the Son, those of the 5th century faced the problem of defining the relationship of the two natures—the human and the divine—within God the Son, Christ Jesus. The theologians of Alexandria generally held that the divine and human natures were united indistinguishably, whereas those of Antioch taught that two natures coexisted separately in Christ, the latter being "the chosen vessel of the Godhead . . . the man born of Mary." In the course of the 5th century, these two contrasting theological positions became the subject of a struggle for supremacy among the rival sees of Constantinople, Alexandria, and Rome. Nestorius, patriarch of Constantinople in 428, adopted the Antiochene formula, which, in his hands, came to stress the human nature of Christ to the neglect of the divine. His opponents (first the Alexandrian patriarch, Cyril, and later Cyril's followers, Dioscourus and Eutyches) in reaction emphasized the single divine nature of Christ, the result of the Incarnation. Their belief in Monophysitism, or the one nature of Christ as God the Son, became extraordinarily popular throughout the provinces of Egypt and Syria. Rome, in the person of Pope Leo I, declared in contrast for Dyophysitism, a creed teaching that two natures, perfect and perfectly distinct, existed in the single person of Christ. At the Council of Chalcedon (451), the latter view triumphed thanks to the support of Constantinople, which changed its position and condemned both Nestorianism, or the emphasis on the human nature of Christ, and Monophysitism, or the belief in the single divine nature.

More important for the purposes of military and political history than the theological details of the conflict was the impact Monophysitism produced on the several regions of the Mediterranean world. Partly because it provided a formula to express resistance to Constantinople's imperial rule, Monophysitism persisted in Egypt and Syria. Until these two provinces were lost to Islām in the 7th century, each Eastern emperor had somehow to cope with their separatist tendencies as expressed in the heresy. He had either to take arms against Monophysitism and attempt to extirpate it by force, to formulate a creed that would somehow blend it with Dyophysitism, or frankly to adopt the heresy as his own belief. None of these three alternatives proved successful, and religious hostility was not the least of the disaffections that led Egypt and Syria to yield, rather readily, to the Arab conqueror. If ever the East Roman emperor was to reassert his authority in the West, he necessarily had to discover a formula that would satisfy Western orthodoxy while not alienating Eastern Monophysitism.

The empire at the end of the 5th century. In the reign of Anastasius I (491–518), all these tendencies of the 5th century found their focus: the sense of *Romanitas*, which demanded a Roman rather than an Isaurian or a German emperor, the conflict between orthodoxy and Monophysitism, and the persisting economic prosperity of the Eastern Roman Empire. Acclaimed and elected as the Roman and orthodox emperor who would end both the hated hegemony of the Isaurians and the detested activity of the Monophysite heretics, Anastasius succeeded in the first of these objectives while failing in the second. While he defeated the Isaurians and transported many of them from their Anatolian homeland into Thrace, he gradually came to support the Monophysite heresy despite the professions of orthodoxy he had made upon the occasion of his coronation. If his policies won him followers in Egypt and Syria, they alienated his orthodox subjects and led, finally, to constant unrest and civil war.

Anastasius I

Anastasius' economic policies were far more successful; if they did not provide the basis for the noteworthy achievements of the 6th century in military affairs and the gentler arts of civilization, they at least explain why the Eastern Empire prospered in those respects during the period in question. An inflation of the copper currency, prevailing since the age of Constantine, finally ended with welcome results for those members of the lower classes who conducted their operations in the base metal. Responsibility for the collection of municipal taxes was taken from the members of the local senate and assigned to agents of the praetorian prefect. Trade and industry were probably stimulated by the termination of the *chrysargyron*, a tax in gold paid by the urban classes. If, by way of compensating for the resulting loss to the state, the rural classes had then to pay the land tax in money rather than kind, the mere fact that gold could be presumed to be available in the countryside is a striking index of rural prosperity. In the East, the economic resurgence of the 4th century had persisted, and it is not surprising that Anastasius enriched the treasury to the extent of 320,000 pounds of gold during the course of his reign.

With such financial resources at their disposal, the Emperor's successors could reasonably hope to reassert Roman authority among the western Germanic successor states, provided they could accomplish two objectives: first, they must heal the religious discord among their subjects; second, they must protect the eastern frontier against the threat of Sāsānian Persia. Since the 6th century was, in fact, to witness concurrent warfare on both fronts, some knowledge of the age-old rivalry between Rome and Persia is essential to an understanding of the problems confronted by the greatest among Anastasius' successors, Justinian I (ruled 527–565), as he undertook the conquest of the West.

In 224 the ancient Persian Empire had passed into the hands of a new dynasty, the Sāsānians, whose regime brought new life to the enfeebled state. Having assured firm control over the vast lands already subject to them, the Sāsānians took up anew the old struggle with Rome for northern Mesopotamia and its fortress cities of Edessa and Nisibis, lying between the Tigris and the Euphrates. In the course of the 4th century, new sources of hostility emerged as East Rome became a Christian empire. Partly by reaction, Sāsānian Persia strengthened the ecclesiastical organization that served its Zoroastrian religion; intolerance and persecution became the order of the day within Persia, and strife between the empires assumed something of the character of religious warfare. Hostilities were exacerbated when Armenia, lying to the north between the two realms, converted to Christianity and thus seemed to menace the religious integrity of Persia. If small-scale warfare during the 4th and 5th centuries rarely erupted into major expeditions, the threat to Rome nonetheless remained constant, demanding vigilance and the construction of satisfactory fortifications. By 518, the balance might be said to have tipped in the favour of Persia as it won away the cities of Theodosiopolis, Amida, and Nisibis.

The rise of Sāsānian Persia

THE 6TH CENTURY: FROM EAST ROME TO BYZANTIUM

The 6th century opens, in effect, with the death of Anastasius and the accession of the Balkan soldier who replaced him, Justin I (ruled 518–527). During most of Justin's reign, actual power lay in the hands of his nephew and successor, Justinian I (527–565). The following account of these more than 40 years of Justinian's effective rule is based upon the works of Justinian's contemporary, the historian Procopius. The latter wrote a laudatory account of the Emperor's military achievements in his *History of the Wars* and coupled it in his *Secret History* with a venomous threefold attack upon the Emperor's personal life, the character of the empress Theodora, and the conduct of the empire's internal administration. Justinian's reign may be divided into three periods: (1) an initial age of conquest and cultural achievement extending until the decade of the 540s; (2) ten years of crisis and near disaster during the 540s; and (3) the last decade of the reign, in which mood, temper, and social realities more nearly resembled those to be found under Justinian's successors than those prevailing throughout the first years of his own reign. After 550, it is possible to begin to speak of a medieval Byzantine, rather than an ancient East Roman, empire. Of the four traumas that eventually transformed the one into the other—namely, pestilence, warfare, social upheaval, and the Arab Muslim assault of the 630s—the first two were features of Justinian's reign, and these the following account will emphasize.

The accession of Justinian I

The years of achievement to 540. Justinian is but one example of the civilizing magic that Constantinople often worked upon the heirs of those who ventured within its walls. Justin, the uncle, was a rude and illiterate soldier; Justinian, the nephew, was a cultivated gentleman, adept at theology, a mighty builder of churches, and a sponsor of the codification of Roman law. All these accomplishments are, in the deepest sense of the word, civilian, and it is easy to forget that Justinian's empire was almost constantly at war during his reign. The history of East Rome during that period illustrates, in classical fashion, how the impact of war can transform ideas and institutions alike.

The reign opened with external warfare and internal strife. From Lazica to the Arabian Desert, the Persian frontier blazed into action in a series of campaigns in which many of the generals later destined for fame in the West first demonstrated their capacities. The strength of the East Roman armies is revealed in the fact that, while containing Persian might, Justinian could nonetheless dispatch troops to attack the Huns in the Crimea and to maintain the Danubian frontier against a host of enemies. In 532 he abandoned military operations for diplomacy, negotiating, at the cost of considerable tribute, an "Endless Peace" with the Persian king, Khosrow, which freed the Roman's hands for operations in another quarter of the globe. Thus Justinian attained the first of the objectives needed for reconquest in the West: peace in the East.

Even before his accession, Justinian had aided in the attainment of the second. Shortly after his proclamation as emperor, Justin had summoned a council of bishops at Constantinople. The council reversed the policies of Anastasius, accepted the orthodox formula of Chalcedon, and called for negotiations with the pope. Justinian had personally participated in the ensuing discussions, which restored communion between Rome and all the Eastern churches save Egypt. No longer could a barbarian king hope to maintain the loyalties of his Catholic subjects by persuading them that a Monophysite emperor ruled in the East.

The Nika Revolt

In the same year of 532, Justinian survived a revolt in Constantinople, stemming from the Nika (*i.e.*, "conquer") riots, which initially threatened his life no less than his throne but, in the event, only strengthened his position. To understand the course of events, it is essential to remember that Constantinople, like other great East Roman cities, had often to depend upon its urban militia, or demes, to defend its walls. Coinciding with divisions within the demes were factions organized to support rival charioteers competing in the horse races: the Blues and the Greens. In addition to their sporting and military functions, the Blues and the Greens also played a political role during the emperor's appearance at the horse races in the Hippodrome. In a rhythmical chant, they would present popular grievances, thereby serving as the only effective channel of protest whereby popular discontent could reach the emperor's ordinarily inaccessible ear. The Blues tended to draw their leadership from the landholding senatorial aristocracy, a class usually orthodox in its sympathies; the Greens, in contrast, found their leaders among men whose wealth was based upon trade and industry and whose theological sympathies lay with the Monophysites. Given these social and religious differences, accentuated by residence in different quarters of Constantinople, it is not surprising that Blues and Greens were often at each other's throats.

The Nika riot of 532 was one of the rare occasions when the two factions united in opposition to the imperial government. Angered at the severity with which the urban prefect had suppressed a riot, Blues and Greens first freed their leaders from prison and then insisted that Justinian dismiss from office two of his most unpopular officials: John of Cappadocia and Tribonian. Even though the Emperor yielded to their demands, the crowd was not appeased, converted its riot into a revolt, and proclaimed a nephew of Anastasius as emperor. Justinian was saved only because the empress, Theodora, refused to yield. Justinian's able general, Belisarius, sequestered the rebels in the Hippodrome and slaughtered them to the number of 30,000. The leaders were executed, and their estates passed, at least temporarily, into the Emperor's hands.

After 532 Justinian ruled more firmly than ever before. With the subsequent proclamation of the "Endless Peace," he could hope to use his earlier won reputation as a champion of Chalcedonian orthodoxy and appeal to those Western Romans who preferred the rule of a Catholic Roman emperor to that of an Arian German kinglet. In these early years of the 530s, Justinian could indeed pose as the pattern of a Roman and Christian emperor. Latin was his language, and his knowledge of Roman history and antiquities was profound.

Promulgation of legal code

In 529 his officials had completed a major collection of the laws and decrees of the emperors promulgated since the reign of Hadrian. Known as the Code of Justinian and partly founded upon the 5th-century Code of Theodosius, this collection of imperial edicts pales before the Digest completed under Tribonian's direction in 533. In the latter work, order and system was found in (or forced upon) the contradictory rulings of the great Roman jurists; to facilitate instruction in the schools of law, a textbook, the Institutes, was designed to accompany the Digest. Meanwhile, architects and builders worked apace to complete the new Church of the Holy Wisdom, Hagia Sophia, designed to replace an older church destroyed in the course of the Nika riots. In five years they had constructed the edifice, and it stands today as one of the major monuments of architectural history.

In 533 the moment had clearly come to reassert Christian Roman authority in the West, and Vandal North Africa seemed the most promising theatre of operations. Although a major expedition mounted under Leo I had failed to win back the province, political conditions in the Vandal monarchy had lately altered to the Eastern emperor's favour. When King Hilderich was deposed and replaced, Justinian could rightfully protest this action taken against a monarch who had ceased persecution of North African Catholics and had allied himself with Constantinople. The Eastern merchants favoured military action in the West, but Justinian's generals were reluctant; possibly for that reason, only a small force was dispatched in tentative fashion under Belisarius. Success came with surprising ease after two engagements, and in 534 Justinian could set about organizing this new addition to the provinces of the Roman Empire.

These were, in fact, years of major provincial reorganization, and not in North Africa alone. A series of edicts dated in 535 and 536, clearly conceived as part of a master plan by the prefect, John of Cappadocia, altered administrative, judicial, and military structures in Thrace and Asia Minor. In general, John sought to provide a simplified and economical administrative structure in which overlapping jurisdictions were abolished, civil and military functions were sometimes combined in violation of Constantinian principles, and a reduced number of officials were provided with greater salaries to secure better personnel and to end the lure of bribery.

In the prefaces to his edicts, Justinian boasted of his reconstituted authority in North Africa, hinted at greater conquests to come, and—in return for the benefits his decrees were to provide—urged his subjects to pay their taxes promptly so that there might be "one harmony between ruler and ruled." Quite clearly the Emperor was organizing the state for the most strenuous military effort, and, later (possibly in 539), reforms were extended to Egypt, whence the export of grain was absolutely essential for the support of expeditionary armies and Constantinople.

Campaigns in Italy

Developments during 534 and 535 in Ostrogothic Italy made it the most likely victim after the fall of Vandal North Africa. When Theodoric died in 526, he was succeeded by a minor grandson for whom Theodoric's daughter, Amalasuntha, acted as regent. Upon the boy's death, Amalasuntha attempted to seize power in her own right and contrived at the assassination of three of her chief enemies. Her diplomatic relations with the Eastern emperor had always been marked by cordiality and even dependency; thus, when Amalasuntha, in turn, met her death in a blood feud mounted by the slain men's families, Justinian seized the opportunity to protest the murder.

In 535, as in 533, a small, tentative expedition sent to the west—in this instance, to Sicily—met with easy success. At first the Goths negotiated; then they stiffened their resistance, deposed their king, Theodahad, in favour of a stronger man, Witigis, and attempted to block Belisarius' armies as they entered the Italian peninsula. Here the progress of East Roman arms proved slower, and victory did not come until 540 when Belisarius captured Ravenna, the last major stronghold in the north, and—with it—King Witigis, a number of Gothic nobles, and the royal treasure.

All were dispatched to Constantinople, where Justinian was presumably thankful for the termination of hostilities in the West. Throughout the 530s, Justinian's generals almost constantly had to fight to preserve imperial authority in the new province of North Africa and in the Balkans as well. In 539 a Gothic embassy reached Persia, and the information it provided caused the king, Khosrow, to grow restive under the constraints of the "Endless Peace." During the next year (the same year [540] that a Bulgar force raided Macedonia and reached the long walls of Constantinople), Khosrow's armies reached even

Antioch in the pursuit of booty and blackmail. They returned unhurt, and 541 witnessed the Persian capture of a fortress in Lazica. In Italy, meanwhile, the Goths chose a new king, Totila, under whose able leadership the military situation in that land was soon to be transformed.

The crisis of midcentury. At last the menace of simultaneous war on two fronts threatened Justinian's plans. During the 550s, his armies were to prove equal to the challenge, but a major disaster prevented them from so doing between 541 and about 548. The disaster was the bubonic plague of 541–543, the first of those shocks, or traumas, mentioned earlier, that would eventually transform East Rome into the medieval Byzantine Empire. The plague was first noted in Egypt, and from there it passed through Syria and Asia Minor to Constantinople. By 543 it had reached Italy and Africa, and it may also have attacked the Persian armies on campaign in that year. In East Asia, the disease has persisted into the 20th century, providing medical science with an opportunity to view its causes and course. Transmitted by fleas to men from infected rodents, the plague attacks the glands and early manifests itself by swellings (buboes) in armpit and groin, whence the name bubonic. To judge from Procopius' description of its symptoms at Constantinople in 542, the disease then appeared in its more virulent pneumonic form, wherein the bacilli settle in the lungs of the victims. The appearance of the pneumonic form was particularly ominous: the latter may be transmitted directly from man to man, spreading the infection all the more readily and producing exceptionally high mortality rates. Comparative studies, based upon statistics derived from incidence of the same disease in late-medieval Europe, suggest that between one-third and one-half the population of Constantinople may well have died, while the lesser cities of the empire and the countryside by no means remained immune.

Outbreak of bubonic plague

The short-term impact of the plague may be seen in several forms of human activity during the 540s. Justinian's legislation of those years is understandably preoccupied with wills and intestate succession. Labour was scarce, and workers demanded wages so high that Justinian sought to control them by edict, as the monarchs of France and England were to do during the plague of the 14th century. In military affairs, above all, the record of those years is one of defeat, stagnation, and missed opportunities. Rather than effective Roman opposition, it was Khosrow's own weariness of an unprofitable war that led him to sign a treaty of peace in 545, accepting tribute from Justinian and preserving Persian conquests in Lazica. Huns, Sclaveni, Antae, and Bulgars ravaged Thrace and Illyricum, meeting only slight opposition from Roman armies. In Africa, a garrison diminished by plague nervously faced the threat of Moorish invasion. In Italy, Totila took the offensive, capturing southern Italy and Naples and even (546) forcing his way into Rome despite Belisarius' efforts to relieve the siege. Desperately, Justinian's great general called for reinforcements from the east; if ever they came, they were slow in arriving and proved numerically less than adequate to the task confronting them.

The last years of Justinian I. After about 548, Roman fortunes improved, and, by the mid-550s, Justinian had won victories in most theatres of operation, with the notable and ominous exception of the Balkans. A tour of the frontiers might begin with the east. In 551 the fortress of Petra was recovered from the Persians, but fighting continued in Lazica until a 50 years' peace, signed in 561, defined relations between the two great empires. On balance, the advantage lay with Justinian. Although the latter agreed to continue payment of tribute in the amount of 30,000 solidi a year, Khosrow, in return, abandoned his claims to Lazica and undertook not to persecute his Christian subjects. The treaty also regulated trade between Rome and Persia, since rivalry between the two great powers had always had its economic aspects, focussed primarily upon the silk trade. Raw silk reached Constantinople through Persian intermediaries, either by a land route leading from China through Persia or by the agency of Persian merchants in the Indian Ocean. The need to break this Persian monopoly had led Justinian to search for new routes and new peoples to serve as intermediaries: in the south, the Ethiopian merchants of the kingdom of Aksum; in the north, the peoples around the Crimea and in the Caucasian kingdom of Lazica, as well as the Turks of the steppes beyond the Black Sea. Other valuable commodities were exchanged in the Black Sea region, including textiles, jewelry, and wine from East Rome for the furs, leather, and slaves offered by the barbarians; yet, silk remained the commodity of prime interest. It was fortunate, then, that before 561 East Roman agents had smuggled silkworms from China into Constantinople, establishing a silk industry that would liberate the empire from dependence on Persia and become one of medieval Byzantium's most important economic operations.

The silk trade

In the West, Justinian's successes were even more spectacular. By 550 the Moorish threat had ended in North Africa. In 552 the armies of Justinian had intervened in a quarrel among the Visigothic rulers of Spain, and the East Roman troops overstayed the invitation extended them, seizing the opportunity to occupy on a more permanent basis certain towns in the southeastern corner of the Iberian Peninsula. Most important of all, Italy was recovered. Early in the 550s, Justinian assembled a vast army composed not only of Romans but also of barbarians, including Lombards, Heruli, and Gepids, as well as Persian deserters. Command of this host eventually was given to an unlikely but, as events were to prove, able commander: the eunuch and chamberlain Narses. In two decisive battles (Busta Gallorum and Mons Lactarius), the East Roman general defeated first Totila and then his successor, Teias. The Goths agreed to leave Italy. Despite the continued resistance of certain Gothic garrisons, coupled with the intervention of Franks and Alamanni, after 554 the land was essentially a province of the East Roman Empire.

In view of the wide mixture of peoples that descended upon it, the Balkans present a far more complex situation, and the Romans used a wider variety of tactics to contain the barbarians. After the Kutrigur Bulgar attack of 540, Justinian worked to extend a system of fortifications that ran in three zones through the Balkans and as far south as the Pass of Thermopylae. Fortresses, strongholds, and watchtowers were not, however, enough. The Slavs plundered Thrace in 545 and returned in 548 to menace Dyrrhachium; in 550 the Sclaveni, a Slavic people, reached a point about 40 miles (60 kilometres) from Constantinople. The major invasion came in 559, when the Kutrigur Bulgars, accompanied by Sclaveni, crossed the Danube and divided their force into three columns. One reached Thermopylae; a second, the Gallipoli Peninsula near Constantinople; and the third, the suburbs of Constantinople itself, which the aged Belisarius had to defend with an unlikely force of civilians, demesmen, and a few veterans. Worried by Roman naval action on the Danube, which seemed to menace the escape route home, the Kutrigurs returned north and found themselves under attack from the Utigurs, a people whose support Justinian's agents had earlier connived at and won by suitable bribes. The two peoples weakened each other in warfare, of which the episode of 559 was not the first instance, and this was precisely the result at which Byzantine diplomacy was aimed.

Balkan affairs

As long as the financial resources remained adequate, diplomacy proved the most satisfactory weapon in an age when military manpower was a scarce and precious commodity. Justinian's subordinates were to perfect it in their relationships with Balkan and south Russian peoples. For, if the Central Asian lands constituted a great reservoir of people, whence a new menace constantly emerged, the very proliferation of enemies meant that one might be used against another through skillful combination of bribery, treaty, and perfidy. East Roman relations in the late 6th century with the Avars, a Mongol people seeking refuge from the Turks, provide an excellent example of this "defensive imperialism." The Avar ambassadors reached Constantinople in 557, and, if they did not receive the lands they demanded, they were loaded with precious gifts and allied by treaty with the empire. The Avars moved westward from south Russia, subjugating Utigurs, Kutrigurs, and Slavic peoples to the profit of the empire; at the end of Justinian's reign, they stood on the Danube. They were a nomadic people hungry for lands and additional subsidies and by no means unskilled themselves in a perfidious diplomacy that would help them pursue their objectives.

Impact of the bubonic plague

No summary of the quiet, but ominous, last years of Justinian's reign would be complete without some notice of the continuing attacks of bubonic plague and the impact they were to continue to produce until the 8th century. As have other societies subjected to devastation from warfare or disease, East Roman society might have compensated for its losses of the 540s had the survivors married early and produced more children in the succeeding generations. Two developments prevented recovery. Monasticism, with its demands for celibacy, grew apace in the 6th century, and the plague returned sporadically to attack those infants who might have replaced fallen members of the older generations.

The resulting shortage of manpower affected several aspects of a state and society that perceptibly were losing their Roman character and assuming their Byzantine. The construction of new churches, so noteworthy a feature of the earlier years, ceased as men did little more than rebuild or add to existing structures. An increasing need for taxes, together with a decreasing number of taxpayers, evoked stringent laws forcing members of a village tax group to assume collective responsibility for vacant or unproductive lands. This, contemporary sources avow, was a burden difficult to assume, in view of the shortage of agricultural workers after the plague. Finally, the armies that won the victories described above in east and west were largely victorious only because Justinian manned them as never before with barbarians: Goths, Armenians, Heruli, Gepids, Saracens, and Persians—to name only the most prominent. It was far from easy to maintain discipline among so motley an army; yet, once the unruly barbarian accepted the quieter life of the garrison soldier, he tended to lose his fighting capacity and prove, once the test came, of little value against the still warlike barbarian facing him beyond the frontier. The army, in short, was a creation of war and kept its quality only by participating in battlefield action, but further expansive warfare could hardly be undertaken by a society chronically short of men and money.

In summary, the East Roman (or better, the Byzantine) state of the late 6th century seemed to confront many of the same threats that had destroyed the Western Empire in the 5th century. Barbarians pressed upon it from beyond the Balkan frontier, and peoples of barbarian origin manned the armies defending it. Wealth accumulated during the 5th century had been expended; and, to satisfy the basic economic and military needs of state and society, there were too few native Romans. If the Byzantine Empire avoided the fate of West Rome, it did so only because it was to combine valour and good luck with certain advantages of institutions, emotions, and attitudes that the older empire had failed to enjoy. One advantage already described, diplomatic skill, blends institutional and attitudinal change, for diplomacy would never have succeeded had not the Byzantine statesmen been far more curious and knowing than Justinian's 5th-century predecessor about the habits, customs, and movements of the barbarian peoples. The Byzantine's attitude had changed in yet another way. He was willing to accept the barbarian within his society provided that the latter, in his turn, accept orthodox Christianity and the emperor's authority. Christianity was often, to be sure, a veneer that cracked in moments of crisis, permitting a very old paganism to emerge, while loyalty to the emperor could be forsworn and often was. Despite these shortcomings, the Christian faith and the ecclesiastical institutions defined in the 6th century proved better instruments by far to unite men and stimulate their morale than the pagan literary culture of the Greco-Roman world.

Christian culture of the Byzantine Empire. Justinian's legislation dealt with almost every aspect of the Christian life: entrance into it by conversion and Baptism; administration of the sacraments that marked its several stages; proper conduct of the laity to avoid the wrath God would surely visit upon a sinful people; finally, the standards to be followed by those who lived the particularly holy life of the secular or monastic clergy. Pagans were ordered to attend church and accept Baptism, while a purge thinned their ranks in Constantinople and masses of them were converted by missionaries in Asia Minor. Only the orthodox wife might enjoy the privileges of her dowry; Jews and Samaritans were denied, in addition to other

Byzantine morality

From *Grosser Historischer Weltatlas*, vol. 1, *Vorgeschichte und Altertum* (1972); Bayerischer Schulbuch-Verlag, Munich

The Byzantine Empire at the death of Justinian in AD 565.

civil disabilities, the privilege of testamentary inheritance unless they converted. A woman who worked as an actress might better serve God were she to forswear any oath she had taken, even though before God, to remain in that immoral profession. Blasphemy and sacrilege were forbidden, lest famine, earthquake, and pestilence punish the Christian society. Surely God would take vengeance upon Constantinople, as he had upon Sodom and Gomorrah, should the homosexual persist in his "unnatural" ways.

Justinian regulated the size of churches and monasteries, forbade them to profit from the sale of property, and complained of those priests and bishops who were unlearned in the forms of the liturgy. His efforts to improve the quality of the secular clergy, or those who conducted the affairs of the church in the world, were most opportune. The best possible men were needed, for, in most East Roman cities during the 6th century, imperial and civic officials gradually resigned many of their functions to the bishop, or patriarch. The latter collected taxes, dispensed justice, provided charity, organized commerce, negotiated with barbarians, and even mustered the soldiers. By the early 7th century, the typical Byzantine city, viewed from without, actually or potentially resembled a fortress; viewed from within, it was essentially a religious community under ecclesiastical leadership. Nor did Justinian neglect the monastic clergy, or those who had removed themselves from the world. Drawing upon the regulations to be found in the writings of the 4th-century Church Father St. Basil of Caesarea, as well as the acts of 4th- and 5th-century church councils, he ordered the cenobitic (or collective) form of monastic life in a fashion so minute that later codes, including the rule of St. Theodore the Studite in the 9th century, only develop the Justinianic foundation.

Probably the least successful of Justinian's ecclesiastical policies were those adopted in an attempt to reconcile Monophysites and orthodox Chalcedonians. After the success of negotiations that had done so much to conciliate the West during the reign of Justin I, Justinian attempted to win over the moderate Monophysites, separating them from the extremists. Of the complicated series of events that ensued, only the results need be noted. In developing a creed acceptable to the moderate Monophysites of the East, Justinian alienated the Chalcedonians of the West and thus sacrificed his earlier gains in that quarter. The extreme Monophysites refused to yield. Reacting against Justinian's persecutions, they strengthened their own ecclesiastical organization, with the result that many of the fortress cities noted above, especially those of Egypt and Syria, owed allegiance to Monophysite ecclesiastical leadership. To his successors, then, Justinian bequeathed the same religious problem he had inherited from Anastasius.

If, in contrast, his regulation of the Christian life proved successful, it was largely because his subjects themselves were ready to accept it. Traditional Greco-Roman culture was, to be sure, surprisingly tenacious and even productive during the 6th century and was always to remain the treasured possession of an intellectual elite in Byzantium; but the same century witnessed the growth of a Christian culture to rival it. Magnificent hymns written by St. Romanos Melodos mark the striking development of the liturgy during Justinian's reign, a development that was not without its social implications. Whereas traditional pagan culture was literary and its pursuit or enjoyment thereby limited to the leisured and wealthy, the Christian liturgical celebration and its musical component were available to all, regardless of place or position. Biography, too, became both markedly Christian and markedly popular. Throughout the countryside and the city, holy men appeared in legend or in fact, exorcising demons, healing the sick, feeding the hungry, and warding off the invader. Following the pattern used in the 4th century by Athanasius to write the life of St. Anthony, hagiographers recorded the deeds of these extraordinary men, creating in the saint's life a form of literature that began to flower in the 6th and 7th centuries.

The rise of popular Christian culture

The vitality and pervasiveness of popular Christian culture manifested themselves most strongly in the veneration increasingly accorded the icon, an abstract and simplified image of Christ, the Virgin, or the saints. Notable for the timeless quality that its setting suggested and for the power expressed in the eyes of its subject, the icon seemingly violated the Second Commandment's explicit injunction against the veneration of any religious images. Since many in the early centuries of the church so believed, and in the 8th century the image breakers, or iconoclasts, were to adopt similar views, hostility toward images was nearly as tenacious an aspect of Christianity as it had been of Judaism before it.

The contrasting view—a willingness to accept images as a normal feature of Christian practice—would not have prevailed had it not satisfied certain powerful needs as Christianity spread among Gentiles long accustomed to representations of the divinity and among Hellenized Jews who had themselves earlier broken with the Mosaic commandment. The convert all the more readily accepted use of the image if he had brought into his Christianity, as many did, a heritage of Neoplatonism. The latter school taught that, through contemplation of that which could be seen (*i.e.*, the image of Christ), the mind might rise to contemplation of that which could not be seen (*i.e.*, the essence of Christ). From a belief that the seen suggests the unseen, it is but a short step to a belief that the seen contains the unseen and that the image deserves veneration because divine power somehow resides in it.

Men of the 4th century were encouraged to take such a step, influenced as they were by the analogous veneration that the Romans had long accorded the image of the emperor. Although the first Christians rejected this practice of their pagan contemporaries and refused to adore the image of a pagan emperor, their successors of the 4th century were less hesitant to render such honour to the images of the Christian emperors following Constantine. Since the emperor was God's vicegerent on Earth and his empire reflected the heavenly realm, the Christian must venerate, to an equal or greater degree, Christ and His saints. Thus the Second Commandment finally lost much of its force. Icons appeared in both private and public use during the last half of the 6th century: as a channel of divinity for the individual and as a talisman to guarantee success in battle. During the dark years following the end of Justinian I's reign, no other element of popular Christian belief better stimulated that high morale without which the Byzantine Empire would not have survived.

The successors of Justinian: 565–610. Until Heraclius arrived to save the empire in 610, inconsistency and contradiction marked the policies adopted by the emperors, a reflection of their inability to solve the problems Justinian had bequeathed his successors. Justin II (565–578) haughtily refused to continue the payment of tribute to Avar or Persian, thereby preserving the resources of the treasury, which he further increased by levying new taxes. Praiseworthy as his refusal to submit to blackmail may seem, Justin's intransigence only increased the menace to the empire. His successor, Tiberius (578–582), removed the taxes and, choosing between his enemies, awarded subsidies to the Avars while taking military action against the Persians. Although Tiberius' general, Maurice, led an effective campaign on the eastern frontier, subsidies failed to restrain the Avars. They captured the Balkan fortress of Sirmium in 582, while the Slavs began inroads across the Danube that would take them, within 50 years, into Macedonia, Thrace, and Greece.

Justin II

The accession of Maurice in 582 inaugurated a reign of 20 years marked by success against Persia, a reorganization of Byzantine government in the west, and the practice of economies during his Balkan campaigns that, however unavoidable, would destroy him in 602. Byzantine efforts against Sāsānian Persia were rewarded in 591 by a fortunate accident. The lawful claimant to the Persian throne, Khosrow II, appealed to Maurice for aid against the rebels who had challenged his succession. In gratitude for this support, Khosrow abandoned the frontier cities and the claims to Armenia, the two major sources of contention between Byzantium and Persia. The terms of the treaty gave Byzantium access, in Armenia, to a land rich in the soldiers it desperately needed and, equally important, an opportunity to concentrate on other frontiers where the situation had worsened.

The exarchate of Carthage and Ravenna

Confronted by a Visigothic resurgence in Spain and by the results of a Lombard invasion of Italy (568), which was steadily confining Byzantine power to Ravenna, Venice, and Calabria-Sicily in the south, Maurice developed a form of military government throughout the relatively secure province of North Africa and in whatever regions were left in Italy. He abandoned the old principle of separating civil from military powers, placing both in the hands of the generals, or exarchs, located, respectively, at Carthage and Ravenna. Their provinces, or exarchates, were subdivided into duchies composed of garrison centres that were manned not by professional soldiers but by conscript local landholders. The exarchate system of military government seems to have worked well: North Africa was generally quiet despite Moorish threats; and in 597 the ailing Maurice had intended to install his second son as emperor throughout those western possessions in which he had clearly not lost interest.

But the major thrust of his efforts during the last years of his reign was to be found in the Balkans, where, by dint of constant campaigning, his armies had forced the Avars back across the Danube by 602. In the course of these military operations, Maurice made two mistakes: the first weakened him; the second destroyed him together with his dynasty. Rather than constantly accompanying his armies in the field, as his 7th- and 8th-century successors were to do, Maurice remained for the most part in Constantinople, losing an opportunity to engage the personal loyalty of his troops. He could not count on their obedience when he issued unwelcome commands from afar that decreased their pay in 588, ordered them to accept uniforms and weapons in kind rather than in cash equivalents, and, in 602, required the soldiers to establish winter quarters in enemy lands across the Danube, lest their requirements prove too great a strain on the agricultural and financial resources of the empire's provinces south of the river. Exasperated by this last demand, the soldiers rose in revolt, put a junior officer named Phocas at their head, and marched on Constantinople. Blues and Greens united against Maurice, and the aged emperor watched as his five sons were slaughtered before he himself met a barbarous death.

The ensuing reign of Phocas (602–610) may be described as a disaster. Khosrow seized the opportunity offered him by the murder of his benefactor, Maurice, to initiate a war of revenge that led Persian armies into the Anatolian heartland. Subsidies again failed to restrain the barbarians north of the Danube; after 602 the frontier crumbled, not to be restored save at the cost of centuries of warfare. Lacking a legitimate title, holding his crown only by right of conquest, Phocas found himself confronted by constant revolt and rebellion. To contemporaries, the coincidence of pestilence, endemic warfare, and social upheaval seemed to herald the coming of the Antichrist, the resurrection of the dead, and the end of the world.

But it was a human saviour who appeared, albeit under divine auspices. Heraclius, son of the Exarch of Africa, set sail from the western extremes of the empire, placing his fleet under the protection of an icon of the Virgin against Phocas, stigmatized in the sources as the "corrupter of virgins." In the course of his voyage along the northern shores of the Mediterranean, Heraclius added to his forces and arrived at Constantinople in 610 to be hailed as a saviour. With the warm support of the Green faction, he quickly bested his enemy, decapitating Phocas and, with him, those the latter had advanced to high civil and military office. There were, in consequence, few experienced counsellors to aid Heraclius, for, among the men of prominence under Phocas—and earlier under Maurice—few survived to greet the new emperor.

THE 7TH CENTURY: THE HERACLIANS AND THE CHALLENGE OF ISLAM

Heraclius and the origin of the themes. The most threatening problem Heraclius faced was the external menace of the Avars and the Persians, and neither people abated its pressure during the first years of the new reign. The Avars almost captured the Emperor in 617 during a conference outside the long walls protecting the capital. The Persians penetrated Asia Minor and then turned to the south, capturing Jerusalem and Alexandria (in Egypt). The great days of the Persian Achaemenid Empire seemed to have come again, and there was little in the recent history of the Byzantine emperors that would encourage Heraclius to place much faith in the future. He clearly could not hope to survive unless he kept under arms the troops he had brought with him; yet, the fate of Maurice demonstrated that this would be no easy task, given the empire's lack of financial and agricultural resources.

Three sources of Heraclius' strength

Three sources of strength enabled Heraclius to turn defeat into victory. The first was the pattern of military government as he and the nucleus of his army would have known it in the exarchates of North Africa or Ravenna. As it had been in the West, so it now was in the East. Civil problems were inseparable from the military: Heraclius could not hope to dispense justice, collect taxes, protect the church, and assure the future to his dynasty unless military power reinforced his orders. A system of military government, the exarchate, had accomplished these objectives so well in the West that, in a moment of despair, Heraclius sought to return to the land of his origins. In all likelihood, he applied similar principles of military rule to his possessions throughout Asia Minor, granting his generals (*stratēgoi*) both civil and military authority over those lands that they occupied with their "themes," as the army groups, or corps, were called in the first years of the 7th century.

Secondly, during the social upheaval of the past decade, the imperial treasury had doubtless seized the estates of prominent individuals who had been executed either during Phocas' reign of terror or after the latter's death. In consequence, though the treasury lacked money, it nonetheless possessed land in abundance, and Heraclius could easily have supported with grants of land those cavalry soldiers whose expenses in horses and armament he could not hope to meet with cash. If this hypothesis is correct, then, even before 622, themes, or army groups—including the guards (Opsikioi), the Armenians (Armeniakoi), and the Easterners (Anatolikoi)—were given lands and settled throughout Asia Minor in so permanent a fashion that, before the century was out, the lands occupied by these themes were identified by the names of those who occupied them. The Opsikioi were to be found in the Opsikion theme, the Armeniakoi in the Armeniakon, and the Anatolikoi in the Anatolikon. The term theme ceased thereafter to identify an army group and described instead the medieval Byzantine unit of local administration, the theme under the authority of the themal commander, the general (*stratēgos*).

When Heraclius "went out into the lands of the themes" in 622, thereby undertaking a struggle of seven years' duration against the Persians, he utilized the third of his sources of strength: the religious. The warfare that ensued was nothing less than a holy war: it was partly financed by the treasure placed by the church at the disposal of the state; the Emperor's soldiers called upon God to aid them as they charged into battle; and they took comfort in the miraculous image of Christ that preceded them in their line of march. A brief summary of the campaign unfortunately gives no idea of the difficulties Heraclius encountered as he liberated Asia Minor (622), fought in Armenia with allies found among the Christian Caucasian peoples, the Lazi, the Abasgi, and the Iberians (624), and struggled in far-distant Lazica while Constantinople withstood a combined siege of Avars and Persians (626). An alliance with the Khazars, a Turkic people from north of the Caucasus, proved of material assistance in those years and of lasting import in Byzantine diplomacy.

Defeat of the Persians

Heraclius finally destroyed the main Persian host at Nineveh in 627 and, after occupying Dastagird in 628, savoured the full flavour of triumph when his enemy, Khosrow, was deposed and murdered. The Byzantine emperor might well have believed that, if the earlier success of the Persians signalized the resurrection of the Achaemenid Empire, his own successes had realized the dreams of Caesar, Augustus, and Trajan.

Yet this was a war fought by medieval Byzantium and not by ancient Rome. Its spirit was manifest in 630, when Heraclius triumphantly restored the True Cross to Jerusalem, whence the Persians had stolen it, and—even more—when Constantinople resisted the Avar–Persian assault of 626. During the attack, the patriarch Sergius maintained the morale of the valiant garrison by proceeding about the walls, bearing the image of Christ to ward off fire, and by painting upon the gates of the western walls images of the Virgin and child to ward off attacks launched by the Avars—the "breed of darkness." The Avars withdrew when Byzantine ships defeated the canoes manned by Slavs, upon whom the nomad Avars depended for their naval strength. The latter never recovered from their defeat. As their empire crumbled, new peoples from the Black Sea to the Balkans emerged to seize power: the Bulgars of Kuvrat, the Slavs under Samo, and the Serbs and Croats whom Heraclius permitted to settle in the northwest Balkans once they had accepted Christianity.

As for the Byzantine defenders of Constantinople, they celebrated their victory by singing Romanos' great Akithistos hymn, with choir and crowd alternating in the chant of the "Alleluia." The hymn, still sung in a Lenten service, commemorates those days when Constantinople survived as a fortress under ecclesiastical leadership, its defenders protected by the icons and united by their liturgy. This they sang in Greek, as befitted a people whose culture was now Greek and no longer Latin.

The successors of Heraclius: Islām and the Bulgars. In the same year that Heraclius went out into the themes, Muḥammad made his withdrawal (*hijrah*) from Mecca to Medina, where he established the *ummah*, or Muslim community. Upon the Prophet's death in 632, the caliphs, or successors, channelled the energies of the Arab Bedouin by launching them upon a purposive and organized plan of conquest. The results were spectacular: a Byzantine army was defeated at the Battle of the Yarmūk River (636), thereby opening Palestine and Syria to Arab Muslim control. Alexandria capitulated in 642, removing forever the province of Egypt from Byzantine authority. The Arabs had, meanwhile, advanced into Mesopotamia, capturing the royal city of Ctesiphon and, eventually, defeating an army under command of the Persian king himself. So ended the long history of Persia under Achaemenids, Parthians, and Sāsānians; further conquests were shortly to initiate that region's Islāmic phase (see further IRAN, HISTORY OF; CALIPHATE, EMPIRE OF THE).

The rise of Islām

At least three aspects of the contemporary situation of Byzantium and Persia account for the phenomenal ease with which the Arabs overcame their enemies: first, both empires, exhausted by wars, had demobilized before 632; second, both had ceased to support those client states on the frontiers of the Arabian Peninsula that had restrained the Bedouin of the desert for a century past; third, and particularly in reference to Byzantium, religious controversy had weakened the loyalties that Syrians and Egyptians rendered to Constantinople. Heraclius had sought in 638 to placate Monophysite sentiment in these two provinces by promulgating the doctrine of Monothelitism, holding that Christ, although of two natures, had but one will. Neither in the East nor in the West did this compromise prove successful. The victorious Muslims granted religious freedom to the Christian community in Alexandria, for example, and the Alexandrians quickly recalled their exiled Monophysite patriarch to rule over them, subject only to the ultimate political authority of the conquerors. In such a fashion the city persisted as a religious community under an Arab Muslim domination more welcome and more tolerant than that of Byzantium.

The aging Heraclius was unequal to the task of containing this new menace, and it was left to his successors—Constantine III (ruled 641), Constans II (641–668), Constantine IV (668–685), and Justinian II (685–695, 705–711)—to do so. This bare list of emperors obscures the family conflicts that often imperilled the succession, but gradually the principle was established that, even if brothers ruled as co-emperors, the senior's authority would prevail. Although strife between Blues and Greens persisted throughout the century, internal revolt failed to imperil the dynasty until the reign of Justinian II. The latter was deposed and mutilated in 695. With the aid of the Bulgars, he returned in 705 to reassume rule and wreak a vengeance so terrible that his second deposition, and death, in 711 is surprising only in its delay of six years. From 711 until 717 the fortunes of the empire foundered; in that year, Leo, *stratēgos* of the Anatolikon theme, arrived as a second Heraclius to found a dynasty that would rescue the empire from its new enemies, the Arab Muslims and the Bulgars.

Three features distinguish the military history of the years 641–717: first, an increasing use of sea power on the part of the Arabs; second, a renewed threat in the Balkans occasioned by the appearance of the Onogur Huns, known in contemporary sources as the Bulgars; third, a persisting interest among the emperors in their western possessions, despite the gradual attrition of Byzantine authority in the exarchates of Carthage and Ravenna. Thanks to the control that the Arabs gradually asserted over the sea routes to Constantinople, they climaxed their earlier assaults on Armenia and Asia Minor with a four years' siege of the great city itself (674–678). Defeated in this last attempt by the use of Greek fire, an inflammable liquid of uncertain composition, the Arabs signed a 30 years' truce, according to which they agreed to pay tribute in money, men, and horses. Lured by the unsettled conditions following upon Justinian's second deposition, they renewed their assaults by land and sea, and the year 717 found the Arabs again besieging Constantinople.

The Bulgar menace

On the Balkan frontier, meanwhile, the Bulgars assumed the role abdicated by the Avars after 626. A pagan people whom the Khazars had forced toward the Danube Delta in the latter part of the 7th century, they eluded Constantine IV's attempts to defeat them in 681. By virtue of a treaty signed in that year, as well as others dating from 705 and 716, the Bulgars were recognized as an independent kingdom, occupying (to the humiliation of Byzantium) lands south of the Danube down into the Thracian plain. While the Bulgars had thus deprived the empire of control in the north and central Balkans, the Byzantines could take comfort in the expeditions of 658 and 688 launched by Constans and Justinian II into Macedonia and in the formation of the themes of Thrace (687) and Hellas (695), evidence that Byzantine authority was beginning to prevail along the peninsular coastline and in certain parts of Greece where Slavs had penetrated.

In the West, the situation was less reassuring. Monothelitism had evoked a hostile reception among the churches of North Africa and Italy, and the resulting disaffection had encouraged the exarchs of both Carthage (646) and Ravenna (652) to revolt. By the end of the century, Africa had been largely lost to Muslim conquerors who would, in 711, seize the last outpost at Septem. For the moment, at least, Sicily and the scattered Italian possessions remained secure. Constans, in fact, undertook operations against the Lombards, and he apparently intended to move his capital to Sicily, before his assassination ended the career of the last Eastern emperor to venture into the West. In summary: Leo in 717 ruled over an empire humiliated by the presence of pagan barbarians upon Balkan soil rightfully considered "Roman," threatened by an attack upon its Anatolian heartland and its capital, and reduced, finally, in the West to Sicily and the remnants of the Ravenna exarchate.

Economics and institutions

However dismal the military record, institutional and economic developments had permitted the empire to survive and were to provide foundations for greater success in the centuries to come. The themal system had taken root and, with it, probably the institution of soldiers' properties. Military service was a hereditary occupation: the eldest son assumed the burden of service, supported primarily by revenues from other members of the family who worked the land in the villages. This last was a task easier to accomplish at the end of the 7th century thanks to the colonies of Slavs and other peoples brought into the empire and settled in the rural areas by Heraclius, Constantine IV, and Justinian II. In the 8th and 9th centuries, other emperors, including Leo III, Constantine V, and Nicephorus I, were to continue the practice, thus ending the population decline that had long eroded the ranks of Byzantine society. There are unmistakable signs of agricultural expansion even before 800; and, at about that time, urban life, which had never vanished in Asia Minor, began to flourish and expand in the Balkans. To judge from the evidence of the Farmer's Law, dated in the 7th century, the technological base of Byzantine society was more advanced than that of contemporary western Europe: iron tools could be found in the villages; water mills dotted the landscape; and field-sown beans provided a diet rich in protein. None of these advances was to characterize western European agriculture until the 10th century. Byzantine agriculture enjoyed the further advantage of a highly developed tradition of careful farming that persisted even in the darkest days, enabling the peasant to make the most of the soil upon which he worked. The invasions had even provided a form of stimulus to development: having lost first its Egyptian granary and, later, its North African and Sicilian resources, the empire had to live essentially, although not totally, from whatever it could produce in the lands remaining to it. The invasions had also, in all probability, broken up many a large estate, and the small peasant holding seems to have been the "normal" form of rural organization in this period. Although collective village organization persisted in the form of the rural commune and, with it, certain collective agricultural practices, the state seems to have made little or no attempt to bind the peasant to the soil upon which the tax registers had inscribed him. While Byzantium remained a slave-owning society, the *colonus* of the later Roman Empire had vanished, and a greater degree of freedom and mobility characterized agricultural relationships during the 7th and 8th centuries.

So it was, too, in trade and commerce. After the loss of Egypt and North Africa, the grain fleets manned by hereditary shipmasters disappeared; in their place there emerged the independent merchant, of sufficient importance to call forth a code of customary law, the Rhodian Sea Law, to regulate his practices. Military and religious hostilities failed to check him as he traded with the Bulgars in Thrace and, through Cyprus, with the Arabs. Despite constant warfare, this was, in short, a healthier society than the late Roman, and its chances of survival were further increased when the sixth general council (681) condemned Monotheletism and anathematized its adherents. With Egypt and Syria under Muslim rule, it was no longer necessary to placate Eastern Monophysitism, and it seemed that doctrinal discord would no longer separate Constantinople from the West. Events were to prove otherwise.

THE AGE OF ICONOCLASM: 717–867

For more than a century after the accession of Leo III (717–741), a persisting theme in Byzantine history may be found in the attempts made by the emperors, often with wide popular support, to eliminate a practice that had earlier played a major part in creating the morale essential to survival: namely, the veneration of icons.

The veneration of icons

The latter sentiment had grown in intensity during the 7th century: the council in Trullo of 691–692 had decreed that Christ should be represented in human form rather than, symbolically, as the lamb. The reigning emperor, Justinian II, had taken the unprecedented step of placing the image of Christ on his coinage while proclaiming himself the "slave of God." Evidence of a reaction against such iconophile (or image venerating) doctrines and practices may be found early in the 8th century, but full-fledged Iconoclasm (or destruction of the images) emerged as an imperial policy only when Leo III issued his decrees of 730. Under his son, Constantine V (ruled 741–775), the iconoclastic movement intensified, taking the form of violent persecution of the monastic clergy, the foremost defenders of the iconophile position. The Council of Nicaea in 787 restored iconophile doctrine at the instigation of the empress Irene, but military reversals led Leo V to resurrect in 815 the iconoclastic policies associated with Constantine V, one of Byzantium's most successful generals. Not until 843 were the icons definitively restored to their places of worship and icon veneration solemnly proclaimed as orthodox belief. Even this brief summary suggests that the Emperor's fortunes on the battlefield were of no small moment in determining his attitude toward the icons, those channels whence superhuman power descended to man. An account of the age of Iconoclasm opens appropriately, then, with its military history.

The reigns of Leo III (the Isaurian) and Constantine V. Almost immediately upon Leo's accession, the empire's fortunes improved markedly. With the aid of the Bulgars, he turned back the Muslim assault in 718 and, in the intervals of warfare during the next 20 years, addressed himself to the task of reorganizing and consolidating the themes in Asia Minor. Thanks to the assistance of the traditional allies, the Khazars, Leo's reign concluded with a major victory, won again at the expense of the Arabs, at Acroinon (740). His successor, Constantine, had first to fight his way to the throne, suppressing a revolt of the Opsikion and Armeniakon themes launched by his brother-in-law Artavasdos. During the next few years, internal disorder in the Muslim world played into Constantine's hands as the ʿAbbāsid house fought to seize the caliphate from the Umayyads. With his enemy thus weakened, Constantine won noteworthy victories in northern Syria, transferring the prisoners he had there captured to Thrace in preparation for the wars against the Bulgars that were to occupy him from 756 to 775. In no fewer than nine campaigns, he undermined Bulgar strength so thoroughly that the northern enemy seemed permanently weakened, if not crushed. Even the venom used by the iconophile chroniclers of Constantine's reign cannot disguise the enormous popularity his victories won him.

In later centuries, the folk of Constantinople would stand by his tomb, seeking his aid against whatever enemy imperilled the city's defenses.

Constantine's weak successors. His successors all but let slip the gains won by the great iconoclast. Constantine's son Leo IV died prematurely in 780, leaving to succeed him his ten-year-old son, Constantine VI, under the regency of the empress Irene. Not much can be said for Constantine, and Irene's policies as regent and (after the deposition and blinding of her son at her orders) as sole ruler from 797 to 802 were all but disasterous. Her iconophile policies alienated many among the themal troops, who were still loyal to the memory of the great warrior emperor, Constantine V. In an effort to maintain her popularity among the monkish defenders of the icons and with the population of Constantinople, she rebated taxes to which these groups were subject, as well as reducing the customs duties levied outside the port of Constantinople, at Abydos and Hieros. The consequent loss to the treasury weighed all the more severely since victories won by the Arabs in Asia Minor (781) and by the Bulgars (792) led both peoples to demand and receive tribute as the price of peace. A revolt of the higher palace officials led to Irene's deposition in 802, and the so-called Isaurian dynasty of Leo III ended with her death, in exile, on the isle of Lesbos.

The empress Irene

In the face of the Bulgar menace, none of the following three emperors succeeded in founding a dynasty. Nicephorus I (ruled 802–811), the able finance minister who succeeded Irene, reimposed the taxes that the Empress had remitted and instituted other reforms that provide some insight into the financial administration of the empire during the early 9th century. In the tradition of Constantine V, Nicephorus strengthened the fortifications of Thrace by settling, in that theme, colonists from Asia Minor.

Taking arms himself, he led his troops against the new and vigorous Bulgar khan, Krum, only to meet defeat and death at the latter's hands. His successor, Michael I

Rangabe (811–813), fared little better; internal dissensions broke up his army as it faced Krum near Adrianople, and the resulting defeat cost Michael his throne. In only one respect does he occupy an important place in the annals of the Byzantine Empire. The first emperor to bear a family name, Michael's use of the patronymic, Rangabe, bears witness to the emergence of the great families whose accumulation of landed properties would soon threaten the integrity of those smallholders upon whom the empire depended for its taxes and its military service. The name in question seems a Hellenized form of a Slav original (*rokavu*), and, if so, Michael's ethnic origin and that of his successor, Leo the Armenian (ruled 813–820), provide evidence enough of the degree to which Byzantium in the 9th century had become not only a melting-pot society but, further, a society in which even the highest office lay open to the man with the wits and stamina to seize it. Leo fell victim to assassination, but before his death events beyond his control had improved the empire's situation. Krum died suddenly in 814 as he was preparing an attack upon Constantinople, and his son, Omortag, arranged a peace with the Byzantine Empire in order to protect the western frontiers of his Bulgar empire against the pressures exerted by Frankish expansion under Charlemagne and his successors. Since the death of the caliph, Hārūn ar-Rashīd, had resulted in civil war in the Muslim world, hostilities from that quarter ceased. Leo used the breathing space to reconstruct those Thracian cities that the Bulgars had earlier destroyed. His work indicates the degree of gradual Byzantine penetration into the coastal fringes of the Balkan Peninsula, as does the number of themes organized in that same region during the early 9th century: those of Macedonia, Thessalonica, Dyrrhachium, Dalmatia, and the Strymon.

Michael II and Thomas the Slav

The new emperor, Michael II, the Amorian, was indeed able to establish a dynasty, his son Theophilus (829–842) and his grandson Michael III (842–867) each occupying the throne in turn, but none would have forecast so happy a future during Michael II's first years. One Thomas the Slav, Michael's former comrade in arms, gave himself out to be the unfortunate Constantine VI and secured his coronation at the hands of the Patriarch of Antioch, with the willing permission of the Muslim caliph under whose jurisdiction Antioch lay. Thomas thereupon marched upon Constantinople at the head of a motley force of Caucasian peoples whose sole bonds were to be found in their devotion to iconophile doctrine and their hatred of Michael's Iconoclasm. Assisted by Omortag and relying upon the defenses of Constantinople, Michael defeated his enemy, but the episode suggests the tensions beneath the surface of Byzantine society: the social malaise, the ethnic hostility, and the persisting discord created by iconoclasm. All these may explain the weakness displayed throughout Theophilus' reign, when a Muslim army defeated the Emperor himself (838) as a prelude to the capture of the fortress of Amorium in Asia Minor. It may also explain the concurrent decline of Byzantine strength in the Mediterranean, manifest in the capture of Crete by the Arabs (826) and in the initiation of attacks upon Sicily that finally secured the island for the world of Islām. Iconoclasm certainly played its part in the further alienation of East from West, and a closer examination of its doctrines will suggest why this may have been.

The Iconoclastic Controversy. Iconoclasts and iconophiles (or iconodules) agreed on one fundamental point: a Christian people could not prosper unless it assumed the right attitude toward the holy images, or icons. They disagreed, of course, on what that attitude should be. Each could discover supporting arguments in the writings of the early church, and it is essential to remember that the debate over images is as old as Christian art. The fundamentals of Iconoclasm were by no means an 8th-century discovery. The ablest defender of the iconophile position was, however, the 8th-century theologian St. John of Damascus. Drawing upon Neoplatonic doctrine, John suggested that the image was but a symbol; the creation of the icon was justified since, by virtue of the Incarnation, God had himself become man.

The iconoclasts responded by pointing to the express wording of the Second Commandment. The condemnation therein contained of idolatry seems to have weighed heavily with Leo III, who may have been influenced by Islām, a religion that strictly prohibited the use of religious images. The latter point is debatable, as is the contention that Iconoclasm was particularly an expression of religious sentiment to be found in the eastern themes of the empire. There is little doubt, however, that Monophysitism influenced the ideas of Constantine V and, through him, the course of debate during the last half of the 8th century. In the eyes of the Monophysite, who believed in the single, indistinguishable, divine nature of Christ, the iconophile was guilty of sacrilege. Either he was a Nestorian, reducing the divine nature to human terms in the image, or he was a Chalcedonian Dyophysite, radically distinguishing that which man could not distinguish. Still another consideration favouring iconoclasm may be found in the intimate connection of iconoclastic doctrine with the emperor's conception of his role as God's vicegerent on Earth. During the late 6th and 7th centuries, iconophile emperors had viewed themselves in a "pietistic" fashion, emphasizing their devotion and subservience to God. Constantine V, on the other hand, pridefully replaced the icons with imperial portraits and with representations of his own victories. Viewed in this light, Iconoclasm signalled a rebirth of imperial confidence; and, so deservedly great was Constantine's reputation, so dismal the accomplishments of his successors, that a Leo V, for one, could easily believe that God favoured the iconoclastic battalions.

Under Constantine V, the struggle against the icons became a struggle against their chief defenders, the monastic community. The immediate destruction wrought by Constantine and his zealous subordinates is, however, of less moment than the lasting effect of the persecution on the orthodox clergy. Briefly put, the church became an institution rent by factions, wherein popular discontent found a means of expression to replace the Blues and the Greens, whose significance steadily waned during the 8th century. Intransigent iconophiles looked for their leaders among the monks of the monastery of Stoudion, and they found one in the person of the monastery's abbot, St. Theodore the Studite (759–826). In the patriarch Ignatius (847–858; 867–877) they discovered a spokesman after their own hearts: one drawn from the monastic ranks and contemptuous of all the allurements that the world of secular learning seemed to offer. More significant than the men to be found on the other extreme, iconoclast patriarchs including Anastasius and John Grammaticus, were the representatives of the moderate party: the patriarchs Tarasius, Nicephorus, Methodius, and Photius. Although iconophile in sympathy, the latter group enjoyed little rapport with the monastic zealots. Unlike the average monk, they were often educated laymen, trained in the imperial service and ready to compromise with imperial authority.

Byzantine relations with Catholic Europe

Not only was Iconoclasm a major episode in the history of the Byzantine, or Orthodox, Church, it also permanently affected relations between the empire and Catholic Europe. The Lombard advance, it may be remembered, had restricted Byzantine authority in Italy to the Exarchate of Ravenna, and to that quarter the popes of the 7th century, themselves ordinarily of Greek or Syrian origin, turned for protection against the common enemy. During the 8th century, two issues alienated Rome from Constantinople: Iconoclasm and quarrels stemming from the question of who should enjoy ecclesiastical jurisdiction over Illyricum and over Calabria in south Italy. Pope Gregory II refused to accept the iconoclastic doctrines of Leo III; and his successor, Gregory III, had openly to condemn them at a council. Once Ravenna fell to the Lombards, and the exarchate ceased to exist in 751, the Pope had to seek a new protector. This he found in the person of the Frankish leader Pepin III, who sought some form of sanction to legitimize his seizure of the crown from the feeble hands of the last representative of the Merovingian dynasty. Thus Pope Stephen anointed Pepin as king of the Franks in 754, and the latter entered Italy to take arms against the Lombard king. Even the restoration of icon veneration in 787 failed to bridge the differences between orthodox Byzantium and Catholic Europe, for the advisers of Pepin's son and successor, Charlemagne, condemned the iconophile position as heartily as an earlier generation had rejected the iconoclast decrees of Leo III. Nor could the men of Charlemagne's time admit that a woman—the empress Irene—might properly assume the dignity of emperor of the Romans. For all these reasons, Charlemagne, king of the Franks and Lombards by right of conquest, assented to his coronation as emperor of the Romans on Christmas Day, 800, by Pope Leo III. No longer a barbarian king, Charlemagne became, by virtue of the symbolism of the age, a new Constantine. This the Byzantine chancery could not accept, for, if there were one God, one faith, and one truth, then there could be but one empire and one emperor; surely that emperor ruled in Constantinople, not in Charlemagne's Aachen. Subsequent disputes between Rome and Constantinople seemed often to centre upon matters of ecclesiastical discipline; underlying these differences were two more powerful considerations, neither of which could be ignored. According to theory there could be but one empire; clearly, there were two. And between Rome and Constantinople there stood two groups of peoples open to conversion: the Slavs of central Europe and the Bulgars in the Balkans. From which of the two jurisdictions would these people accept their Christian discipline? To which, in consequence, would they owe their spiritual allegiance?

The reign of Michael III

The reign of Michael III draws together these and other threads from the past. Veneration of the icons was definitely rehabilitated in 843, in so diplomatic a fashion that the restoration, in itself, produced no new rifts although old factionalisms persisted with the appointment of a monk, Ignatius, as patriarch. The latter's intransigent zealotry found little favour with Caesar Bardas, Michael's uncle, who had seized power from the Empress Regent in 856. Two years later, Ignatius was deposed and replaced by a moderate: the scholar and layman Photius. No single person better exemplifies the new age, nor, indeed, did any other play a larger part in the cultural rebirth and missionary activity among the Slavs, Bulgars, and Russians that marks the middle of the 9th century. The same aggressive and enterprising spirit is manifest in the military successes won on the Asia Minor frontier, culminating in Petronas' victory at Poson (863) over the Muslim emir of Melitene.

In Sicily, and throughout the Mediterranean, Byzantine arms were less successful, but, thanks to Photius' diplomatic skill, the see of Constantinople maintained its position against Rome during the so-called Photian Schism. When Pope Nicholas I challenged Photius' elevation to the patriarchate, deploring as uncanonical the six days' speed with which he had been advanced through the successive ranks of the hierarchy, the Byzantine patriarch refused to bow. He skillfully persuaded Nicholas' delegates to a council, summoned at Constantinople to investigate the matter, that he was the lawful patriarch despite the persisting claims of the rival Ignatian faction. Nicholas, alleging that his men had been bribed, excommunicated Photius; a council at Constantinople responded (867) by excommunicating Nicholas in turn. The immediate issues between the two sees were matters of ecclesiastical supremacy, the liturgy, and clerical discipline; behind these sources of division lay the question, mentioned above, of jurisdiction over the converts in Bulgaria. And behind that question may be found centuries of growing separation between the minds and institutions of the eastern and the western Mediterranean worlds, symbolized in the roles assumed by two among the major protagonists in the Photian Schism. It was the supreme spiritual authority, the pope, who hurled anathemas from the west, but it was God's vicegerent on Earth, the emperor Michael III, who presided at the council of 867.

Michael did not long survive this moment of triumph. In that very year, he was murdered by his favourite, Basil, who, on his bloody path to the throne, had earlier disposed of Caesar Bardas. As had Heraclius and Leo III before him, Basil came to found a dynasty, in this instance the Macedonian house. Unlike his predecessors, he came not as a saviour but as a peasant adventurer, to seize an already sound empire whose next centuries were to be its greatest. (J.L.Te.)

II. From 867 to the Ottoman conquest

THE MACEDONIAN ERA: 867–1025

Under the Macedonians, at least until the death of Basil II in 1025, the empire enjoyed a golden age. Its armies regained the initiative against the Arabs in the East, and its missionaries evangelized the Slavs, extending Byzantine influence in Russia and the Balkans. And, despite the rough military character of many of the emperors, there was a renaissance in Byzantine letters and important developments in law and administration. At the same time there were signs of decay: resources were squandered at an alarming rate; there was growing estrangement from the West; and a social revolution in Anatolia was to undermine the economic and military strength of the empire.

Founding of the dynasty

The empire was in theory an elective monarchy with no law of succession. But the desire to found and perpetuate a dynasty was strong, and it was often encouraged by popular sentiment. This was especially true in relation to the Macedonian dynasty, the founder of which Basil I, murdered his way to the throne in 867. Probably of Armenian descent, though they had settled in Macedonia, Basil's family was far from distinguished and can hardly have expected to produce a line of emperors that lasted through six generations and 189 years. But, having acquired the imperial crown, Basil tried to make sure that his family would not lose it and nominated three of his sons as co-emperors. Though he was his least favourite, through the scholarly Leo VI, who succeeded him in 886, the succession was at least secure. Even the three soldier-emperors who usurped the throne during the Macedonian era were conscious, in varying degrees, that they were protecting the rights of a legitimate heir during a minority: Romanus I Lecapenus for Constantine VII, the son of Leo VI; and Nicephorus Phocas and John Tzimisces for Basil II, the grandson of Constantine VII.

The Macedonian Emperors, 867–1025

name	reign dates
Basil I	867–886
Leo VI	886–912
Constantine VII	913–959
Romanus I*	919–944
Romanus II	959–963
Nicephorus II	963–969
John I	969–976
Basil II	976–1025

*Ruled in Constantine's name.

Military revival. A reassertion of Byzantine military and naval power in the East began with victories over the Arabs by Michael III's general Petronas in 856. From 863 the initiative lay with the Byzantines. The struggle with the Arabs, which had long been a struggle for survival, became a mounting offensive that reached its brilliant climax in the 10th century. By 867 a well-defined boundary existed between the Byzantine Empire and the territory of the ʿAbbāsid caliphate. Its weakest point was in the Taurus Mountains above Syria and Antioch. Basil I (reigned 867–886) directed his operations against this point, recovered Cyprus for a while, and campaigned against the Paulicians, a heretical Christian sect whose anti-imperial propaganda was effective in Anatolia. But the conflict with Islām was one that concerned the whole empire, in the West as well as in the East, by sea as well as by land. In 902 the Arabs completed the conquest of Sicily, but they were kept out of the Byzantine province of South Italy, for whose defense Basil I had even made some effort to cooperate with the Western emperor Louis II. The worst damage, however, was done by Arab pirates who had taken over the island of Crete. In 904 they plundered Thessalonica, carrying off quantities of loot and prisoners. Leo VI sent a naval expedition to Crete in 911, but the Muslims drove it off and humiliated the Byzantine navy off Chios in 912.

Success of Eastern offensive

On the eastern frontier, the Byzantine offensive was sustained with great success during the reign of Romanus I Lecapenus by an Armenian general John Curcuas (Gurgen), who captured Melitene (934) and then Edessa (943), advancing across the Euphrates into the caliph's territory. It was Curcuas who paved the way for the campaigns of the two soldier-emperors of the next generation. In 961 Nicephorus Phocas, then domestic (commander) of the armies in the West, reconquered Crete and destroyed the Arab fleet that had terrorized the Aegean for 150 years; he thereby restored Byzantine naval supremacy in the eastern Mediterranean. In 962 his strategy achieved unexpected triumphs all along the eastern frontier and culminated in the capture of Aleppo in Syria. When he was proclaimed emperor in March 963 Nicephorus appointed another Armenian general, John Tzimisces, as domestic of the East, though he retained personal command of operations against the Arabs. By 965 he had driven them out of Cyprus and was poised for the reconquest of Syria. The revived morale and confidence of Byzantium in the East showed itself in the crusading zeal of Nicephorus Phocas and John Tzimisces for the reconquest of Syria and the Holy Land. The ground lost to Islām in the 7th century was thus fast being regained; and although Jerusalem was never reached, the important Christian city of Antioch, seat of one of the patriarchs, was recaptured in 969. These victories were achieved largely by the new cavalry force built up by Nicephorus Phocas. In the areas recovered from the Arabs, land was distributed in military holdings with the interests of the cavalry in mind. But the victories were achieved at the expense of the western provinces, and an attempt to recover Sicily ended in failure in 965.

The campaigns of John Tzimisces, who usurped the throne in 969, were directed against the Emir of Mosul on the Tigris and against the new Fāṭimid Caliph of Egypt, who had designs on Syria. By 975 almost all of Syria and Palestine, from Caesarea to Antioch, as well as a large part of Mesopotamia far to the east of the Euphrates, was in Byzantine control. The way seemed open for Tzimisces to advance to the ʿAbbāsid capital of Baghdad on the one hand and to Jerusalem and Egypt on the other. But he died in 976 and his successor, Basil II, the legitimate heir of the Macedonian house, concentrated most of his resources on overcoming the Bulgars in Europe, though he did not abandon the idea of further reconquest in the East. The Kingdom of Georgia (Iberia) was incorporated in the empire by treaty. Part of Armenia was annexed, with the rest of it to pass to Byzantium on the death of its king. Basil II personally led two punitive expeditions against the Fāṭimids in Syria, but otherwise his eastern policy was to hold and to consolidate what had already been gained. The gains can be measured by the number of new themes (provinces) created by the early 11th century in the area between Vaspurakan in the Caucasus and Antioch in Syria. The annexation of Armenia, the homeland of many of the great Byzantine emperors and soldiers, helped to solidify the eastern wall of the Byzantine Empire for nearly a century.

Relations with the Slavs and Bulgars. Although imperial territory in the East could be reclaimed only by military conquest, in the Balkans and in Greece the work of reclamation could be assisted by the diplomatic weapon of evangelization. The Slavs and the Bulgars could be brought within the Byzantine orbit by conversion to Christianity.

Conversion of the Slavs

The conversion of the Slavs was instigated by the Patriarch Photius and carried out by the monks Cyril and Methodius from Thessalonica. Their invention of the Slavonic alphabet (Cyrillic and Glagolitic) made possible the translation of the Bible and the Greek liturgy, and brought literacy as well as the Christian faith to the Slavic peoples. The work began in the Slavic Kingdom of Moravia and spread to Serbia and Bulgaria. Latin missionaries resented what they considered to be Byzantine interference among the northern Slavs, and there were repeated clashes of interest that further damaged relations between the sees of Rome and Constantinople. The conversion of the Bulgars became a competition between the two churches and was ably exploited by the Bulgar king Boris until, in 870, he opted for Orthodox Christianity on condition of having an archbishop of his own.

Bulgarian wars. The trade with Constantinople that followed the missionaries whetted the appetites of the Slavs and Bulgars for a larger share in the material wealth of Byzantium. Symeon of Bulgaria, who succeeded his father Boris in 893 and who had been educated at Constantinople, proved to be an even more dangerous enemy than the Arabs. His efforts to become emperor dominated Byzantine history for some 15 years. In 913 he brought his army to the walls of Constantinople, demanding the imperial title. The patriarch, Nicholas Mysticus, appeased Symeon for a time, but it was Romanus Lecapenus who, by patience and diplomacy, undermined the power of the Bulgars and thwarted Symeon's ambitions. Symeon died in 927, and his son Peter came to terms with Byzantium and married a granddaughter of Romanus.

Relations with Russia. The Russians lay far outside the Roman jurisdiction. Their warships, sailing down the Dnepr from Kiev to the Black Sea, first attacked Constantinople in 860. They were beaten off, and almost at once Byzantine missionaries were sent into Russia. The Russians had been granted trading rights in Constantinople in 911. But in 941 and 944, led by Prince Igor, they returned to the attack. Both assaults were repelled and Romanus I set about breaking down the hostility and isolationism of the Russians by diplomatic and commercial contacts. In 957 Igor's widow Olga was baptized and paid a state visit to Constantinople during the reign of Constantine VII; her influence enabled Byzantine missionaries to work with greater security in Russia, thus spreading Christianity and Byzantine culture. Olga's son Svyatoslav was pleased to serve the empire as an ally against the Bulgars in 968–969, though his ambition to occupy Bulgaria led to war with Byzantium in which he was defeated and killed. In 971 John Tzimisces accomplished the double feat of humiliating the Russians and reducing Bulgaria to the status of a client kingdom. Byzantine influence over Russia reached its climax when Vladimir of Kiev, who had helped Basil II to gain his throne, received as his reward the hand of the Emperor's sister in marriage and was baptized in 989. The mass conversion of the Russian people followed, with the establishment of an official Russian Church subordinate to the patriarch of Constantinople.

Bulgar revolt. The Bulgars, however, were not content to be vassals of Byzantium and rebelled under Samuel, youngest of the four sons of a provincial governor in Macedonia. Samuel made his capital at Ochrida and created a Bulgarian empire stretching from the Adriatic to the Black Sea and even, for a while, into Greece, though Thessalonica remained Byzantine.

Bulgars crushed by Basil II

The final settlement of the Bulgar problem was worked out by Basil II in a ruthless and methodical military campaign lasting for some 20 years, until, by 1018, the last resistance was crushed. Samuel's dominions became an integral part of the Byzantine Empire and were divided into three new themes. At the same time the Slav principalities of Serbia (Rascia and Dioclea) and Croatia became vassal states of Byzantium, and the Adriatic port of Dyrrhachium came under Byzantine control. Not since the days of Justinian had the empire covered so much European territory. But the annexation of Bulgaria meant that the Danube was now the only line of defense against the more northerly tribes, such as the Pechenegs, Cumans, and Magyars.

Estrangement from the West. The extension of Byzantine interests to the Adriatic, furthermore, had raised again the question of Byzantine claims to South Italy and, indeed, to the whole western part of the old Roman Empire. The physical separation of that empire into East and West had been emphasized by the settlement of the

Slavs in the Balkan Peninsula and in Greece, and since the 7th century the two worlds had developed in their different ways. Their differences had been manifested in ecclesiastical conflicts, such as the Photian Schism. The conversion of the Slavs had produced bitterness between the agents of the rival jurisdictions. But the re-establishment of Byzantine authority in Greece and eastern Europe, added to the gains against the Muslim powers in Asia, reinforced the Byzantine belief in the universality of the empire, to which Italy and the West must surely be reunited in time. Until that time came, the fiction was maintained that the rulers of western Europe, like those of the Slavs, held their authority by virtue of their special relationship with the one true emperor in Constantinople.

It was sometimes suggested that a marriage alliance might bring together the Eastern and Western parts of the empire and so provide for a united defense against the common enemy in Sicily—the Arabs. In 944 Romanus II, son of Constantine VII, married a daughter of Hugh of Provence, the Carolingian claimant to Italy. Constantine VII also kept up diplomatic contact with Otto I, the Saxon king of Germany. But the case was dramatically altered when Otto was crowned emperor of the Romans in 962, for this was a direct affront to the unique position of the Byzantine emperor. Otto tried, and failed, to establish his claim, either by force in the Byzantine province in Italy or by negotiation in Constantinople. His ambassador Liudprand of Cremona wrote an account of his mission to Nicephorus Phocas in 968 and of the Emperor's scornful rejection of a proposed marriage between Otto's son and a Byzantine princess. The incident vividly demonstrates the superior attitude of the Byzantines toward the West in the 10th century. John Tzimisces relented to the extent of arranging for one of his own relatives to marry Otto II in 972, though the arrangement implied no recognition of a Western claim to the empire. Basil II agreed that Otto III also should marry a Byzantine princess. But this union was never achieved; and subsequently Basil reorganized the administration of Byzantine Italy and was preparing another campaign against the Arabs in Sicily at the time of his death in 1025. The myth of the universal Roman Empire died hard.

Holy Roman Empire founded in the West

Culture and administration. The Iconoclastic Controversy had aggravated the estrangement of the Byzantine Church and Empire from the West. But it helped to define the tenets of Orthodoxy; and it had an effect on the character of Byzantine society for the future. On the one hand, the church acquired a new unity and vitality: its missionaries spread the Orthodox faith in new quarters of the world, its monasteries proliferated, and its spiritual tradition was carried forward by the sermons and writings of the Patriarch Photius in the 9th century and of Symeon the New Theologian in the 10th and 11th centuries. On the other hand, the empire became more aware of its Greco-Roman heritage. Interest in classical Greek scholarship revived following the re-organization of the University of Constantinople under Michael III. The revival was fostered and patronized particularly by the scholar-emperor Constantine VII Porphyrogenitus, who saw to the compilation of three great works on the administration, the court ceremonies, and the provinces of his empire. He also commissioned a history of the age to which he contributed a biography of his grandfather Basil I. The age produced little original research, but lexicons (such as the 10th-century *Suda*), anthologies, encyclopaedias, and commentaries (such as the *Lexicon* and *Bibliotheca* of Photius) were produced in great number. The soldier-emperors of the 10th century were less interested in intellectual pursuits, but scholarship received a new impetus in the 11th century with Michael Psellus.

The founder of the dynasty, Basil I, and his son Leo VI, made plain their intention to inaugurate a new era by a restatement of the imperial law. Basil hoped to make a complete revision of the legal code, but only a preliminary textbook (*Procheiron*) with an introduction (*Epanagoge*) appeared during his reign. Leo VI, however, accomplished the work with the publication of the 60 books of the *Basilica*, which Hellenized the legal code of Justinian and made it more intelligible and accessible to lawyers. Additions and corrections to meet the needs of the time were incorporated in Leo's 113 *Novels*, which represent the last substantial reform of the civil law in Byzantium. Enshrined in this legislation was the principle of the absolute autocracy of the emperor as being himself the law. The Senate, the last vestige of Roman republican institutions, was abolished. Only in the matter of the spiritual welfare of his subjects did the emperor recognize any limits to his authority. The ideal relationship of a dyarchy between emperor and patriarch, the body and the soul of the empire, was written into the *Epanagoge* of Basil I, in a section probably composed by Photius.

Growth of bureaucracy

The administration in this period was ever more closely centralized in Constantinople, with an increasingly complex and numerous bureaucracy of officials who received their appointments and their salaries from the emperor. The emperor also controlled the elaborate machinery of the foreign and diplomatic service. Some of his civil servants, however, were powerful enough to play the part of kingmakers, notably Basil, the chamberlain who engineered the ascent to the throne of Nicephorus Phocas and John Tzimisces. Order and the regulation of trade, commerce, and industry in the capital were in the hands of the Prefect of the City, whose functions are outlined in the 9th-century *Book of the Eparch*. He was responsible for organizing and controlling the guilds or colleges of craftsmen and retailers, whose legal rights and duties to the state were strictly circumscribed and supervised. The provinces in Europe and Asia were administered according to their territorial division into themes, which, by the 10th century, numbered over 30. The themes, though subdivided and reduced in size, retained their military character. Their governors, or *stratēgoi*, combined military and civil authority and were directly answerable to the emperor, who appointed them. The army and the navy were, for the most part, recruited from the ranks of soldier-farmers who held hereditary grants of land within the territory of each theme. The border districts were protected by contingents of frontier troops, led by their own officers or lords of the marches. Their exploits and adventures were romanticized in the 10th-century folk-epic of *Digenis Akritas*. But warfare was studied and perfected as a science, and it was the subject of treatises such as the *Tactica* of Leo VI, derived from the *Strategicon* of the emperor Maurice.

Social and economic change. The wars of reconquest on the eastern frontier in this period and the general military orientation of imperial policy brought to the fore a new class of aristocracy, whose wealth and power was based on land ownership and who held most of the higher military posts. Trade and industry in the cities were so rigidly controlled by the government that almost the only profitable form of investment for private enterprise was the acquisition of landed property. The military aristocracy, therefore, took to buying up the farms of free peasants and soldiers and reducing their owners to varying forms of dependence. As the empire grew stronger, the rich became richer. Given the system of agriculture prevailing in Anatolia and the Balkans, every failure of crops, every famine, drought, or plague produced a quota of destitute peasant-soldiers willing to turn themselves and their land over to the protection of a prosperous and ambitious landlord. The first emperor to see the danger in this development was Romanus I Lecapenus, who, in 922 and 934, passed laws to defend the small landowners against the acquisitive instincts of the "powerful"; for he realized that the economic as well as the military strength of the empire depended on the maintenance within the theme system of the institution of free, yet tax-paying, soldier-farmers and peasants in village communities. (Only freemen owed military service.)

Growth of land-holding aristocracy

Successive emperors after Romanus I enforced and extended his agrarian legislation. But the cost of the campaigns of reconquest from the Arabs had to be met by higher taxation, which drove many of the poorer peasants to sell their lands and to seek security as tenant-farmers. Nicephorus Phocas, who belonged to one of the aristocratic landowning families of Anatolia, was naturally reluctant to act against members of his own class, though he adhered to the principle that the rights of the poor should be safeguarded. His laws about land tenure were particularly directed towards the creation of a more mobile force of heavy-armed cavalry recruited from those who could afford the equipment, which inevitably brought changes in the social structure of the peasant militia. On the other hand, Nicephorus took a firm line to prevent the accumulation of further land by the church, and he forbade any addition to the number of monasteries, whose estates, already extensive, were unproductive to the economy.

The last emperor to attempt to deal with the problem of land ownership seriously was Basil II, whose rise to the throne had involved the empire in a bitter and costly war against the aristocratic Sclerus and Phocas families. In 996 Basil promulgated comprehensive punitive legislation against the landed families, ordering the restitution of land acquired from the peasantry since 922 and requiring proof of title to other land going back in some cases as far as 1,000 years. Further, the system of collective responsibility for the payment of outstanding taxes known as the *allelengyon* now devolved not on the rest of the village community but on the nearest large landowner, whether lay or ecclesiastical. Basil's conquest of Bulgaria somewhat altered the social and economic pattern of the empire, for new themes were created there in which there was no long tradition of a landed aristocracy as in Anatolia. After his death in 1025 the powerful hit back, and the government in Constantinople was no longer able to check the absorption of small freeholders by the great landowners and the consequent feudalization of the empire.

This process was particularly disastrous for the military establishment. The success and prestige of the Byzantine Empire in the Macedonian era to a large extent depended on the unrivalled efficiency of its army in Anatolia. A professional force, yet mainly native to the soil and so directly concerned with the defense of that soil, it had no equal in the Western or the Arab world at the time. And yet it was in this institution that the seeds of decay and disintegration took root; for most of the army's commanders were drawn from the great landowners of Anatolia, who had acquired their riches and their status by undermining the social and economic structure on which its recruitment depended. Basil II had restrained them with such an iron hand that a reaction was inevitable after his death. Indeed, it is doubtful if Byzantine society could have tolerated another Basil II, for all his triumphs. Soured by long years of civil war at the start of his reign, ascetic and uncultured by nature, Basil embodied the least attractive features of Byzantine autocracy. Some have called him the greatest of all the emperors. But the virtue of philanthropy, which the Byzantines prized and commended in their rulers, was not a part of his greatness; and the qualities that lent refinement to the Byzantine character, among them a love of learning and the arts, were not fostered during his reign. Yet, while Basil was busily earning his title of Bulgaroctonus (Bulgar Slayer), St. Symeon the New Theologian was exploring the love of God for man in some of the most poetic homilies in all mystical literature.

BYZANTINE DECLINE AND SUBJECTION TO WESTERN INFLUENCES: 1025–1260

Basil II never married. But after his death his relatives remained in possession of the throne until 1056, less because of their efficiency than because of a general feeling among the Byzantine people that the prosperity of the empire was connected with the continuity of the Macedonian dynasty. When Basil's brother Constantine VIII died in 1028, the line was continued in his two daughters, Zoe and Theodora. Zoe was married three times: to Romanus III Argyrus (ruled 1028–34), to Michael IV (1034–41), and to Constantine IX Monomachus (1042–55), who outlived her. When Constantine IX died in 1055, Zoe's sister Theodora reigned alone as empress until her death a year later.

The later Macedonians

The great emperors of the golden age, not all of them members of the Macedonian family, molded the history of that age. The successors of Basil II were rather the creatures of circumstances in that they did not make and seldom molded. In the 56 years from 1025 to 1081, there were 13 emperors. An attempt made by Constantine X Ducas to found a new dynasty was disastrously unsuccessful. Not until the rise of Alexius I Comnenus to power, in 1081, was stability restored by an ensured succession in the Comnenus family, which ruled for more than 100 years (1081–1185).

11th-century weakness. The state of the Byzantine Empire in the 11th century may be compared to that of the Roman Empire in the 3rd century, when, after a long period of secure prosperity, new pressures from beyond the frontiers aggravated the tensions that were latent in society. The brief reigns of Basil II's heirs reflected, and were often the product of, a division in the ruling class, a conflict between the military aristocracy of the provinces and the civilian aristocracy, or bureaucracy, of Constantinople. Each faction put up rival emperors. The sophisticated urban aristocracy generally favoured rulers who would reverse the militaristic trend of the empire, and

The Byzantine Empire in 1025.

who would expand the civil service and supply them and their families with lucrative offices and decorative titles. The military families, whose wealth lay not in the capital but in the provinces, and who had been penalized by Basil II's legislation, favoured emperors who were soldiers and not civil servants. In this they were more realistic, for in the latter part of the 11th century it became ever clearer that the empire's military strength was no longer sufficient to hold back its enemies. The landowners in the provinces appreciated the dangers more readily than the government in Constantinople, and they made those dangers an excuse to enlarge their estates in defiance of all the laws passed in the 10th century. The theme system in Anatolia, which had been the basis of the empire's defensive and offensive power, was rapidly breaking down at the very moment when its new enemies were gathering their strength.

On the other hand, the urban aristocracy of Constantinople, reacting against the brutalization of war, strove to make the city a centre of culture and sophistication. The university was endowed with a new charter by Constantine IX in 1045, partly to ensure a steady flow of educated civil servants for the bureaucracy. The law school was revived under the jurist John Xiphilinus; the school of philosophy was chaired by Michael Psellus, whose researches into every field of knowledge earned him a reputation for omniscience and a great following of brilliant pupils. Psellus—courtier, statesman, philosopher, and historian—is in himself an advertisement for the liveliness of Byzantine society in the 11th century. What he and others like him failed to take into account was that their empire was more and more expending the resources and living on the reputation built up by the Macedonian emperors.

Arrival of new enemies. The new enemies that emerged in the 11th century, unlike the Arabs or the Bulgars, had no cause to respect that reputation. They appeared almost simultaneously on the northern, the eastern, and the western frontiers. It was nothing new for the Byzantines to have to fight on two fronts at once. But the task required a soldier on the throne. The Pechenegs, a Turkic tribe, had long been known as the northern neighbours of the Bulgars. Constantine VII had thought them to be valuable allies against the Bulgars, Magyars, and Russians. But after the conquest of Bulgaria, the Pechenegs began to raid across the Danube into what was now Byzantine territory. Constantine IX allowed them to settle south of the river, where their numbers and their ambitions increased. By the mid-11th century they were a constant menace to the peace in Thrace and Macedonia, and they encouraged the spirit of revolt among the Bogomil heretics in Bulgaria. It was left to Alexius I to avert a crisis by defeating the Pechenegs in battle in 1091.

Seljuq Turks in the East

The new arrivals on the eastern frontier were the Seljuq Turks, whose conquests were to change the whole shape of the Muslim and Byzantine worlds. In 1055, having conquered Persia, they entered Baghdad, and their prince assumed the title of sultan and protector of the ʿAbbāsid caliphate. Before long they asserted their authority to the borders of Fāṭimid Egypt and Byzantine Anatolia. They made their first explorations across the Byzantine frontier into Armenia in 1065 and, in 1067, as far west as Caesarea in central Anatolia. The raiders were inspired by the Muslim idea of holy war, and there was at first nothing systematic about their invasion. They found it surprisingly easy, however, to plunder the countryside and isolate the cities, owing to the long neglect of the eastern frontier defenses by the emperors in Constantinople. The emergency lent weight to the military aristocracy in Anatolia who, in 1068, finally secured the election of one of their own number, Romanus IV Diogenes, as emperor. Romanus assembled an army to deal with what he saw as a large-scale military operation. It was a sign of the times that it was mainly composed of foreign mercenaries. In August 1071 it was defeated at Manzikert, near Lake Van in Armenia. Romanus was taken prisoner by the Seljuq sultan, Alp Arslan. He was allowed to buy his freedom after signing a treaty, but the opposition in Constantinople refused to have him back as emperor and installed their own candidate, Michael VII. Romanus was treacherously blinded. The Seljuqs were thus justified in continuing their raids and were even encouraged to do so. Michael VII invited Alp Arslan to help him against his rivals, Nicephorus Bryennius and Nicephorus Botaneiates, each of whom proclaimed himself emperor at Adrianople in 1077 and at Nicaea in 1078. In the four years of ensuing civil war there were no troops to defend the eastern frontier. By 1081 the Turks had reached Nicaea. The heart of the empire's military and economic strength, which the Arabs had never mastered, was now under Turkish rule.

Battle of Manzikert

The new enemies in the West were the Normans, who began their conquest of South Italy early in the 11th century. Basil II's project of recovering Sicily from the Arabs had been almost realized in 1042 by the one great general of the post-Macedonian era, George Maniaces, who was recalled by Constantine IX and killed as a pretender to the throne. The Normans thereafter made steady progress in Italy. Led by Robert Guiscard, they carried all before them; in April 1071, Bari, the last remaining Byzantine stronghold, fell after a three-year siege. Byzantine rule in Italy and the hope of a reconquest of Sicily were at an end.

The disasters at Manzikert and at Bari, at opposite extremes of the empire, in the same year 1071, graphically illustrate the decline of Byzantine power. The final loss of Italy seemed to underline the fact of the permanent division between the Greek East and the Latin West, which was now not only geographical and political but also increasingly cultural and ecclesiastical. In 1054 a state of schism had been declared between the churches of Rome and Constantinople. The political context of the event was the Norman invasion of Italy, which at the time was a matter of as much concern to the papacy as it was to Byzantium. But the event itself, the excommunication of the patriarch Michael Cerularius by Cardinal Humbert in Constantinople, symbolized an irreconcilable difference in ideology. The reform movement in the Roman Church had emphasized an ideal of the universal role of the papacy that was wholly incompatible with Byzantine tradition. Both sides also deliberately aggravated their differences by reviving all the disputed points of theology and ritual that had become battle cries during the Photian Schism in the 9th century. The schism of 1054 passed unnoticed by contemporary Byzantine historians; its significance as a turning point in East–West relations was fully realized only later.

Schism between churches

Alexius I and the First Crusade. But even the events of 1071 had not made the decline of Byzantium irretrievable. The shrinking of its boundaries reduced the empire from its status as a dominating world power to that of a small Greek state fighting for survival. That survival now depended on the new political, commercial, and ecclesiastical forces in the West, for it could no longer draw on its former military and economic resources in Anatolia. The civil aristocracy of Constantinople yielded with a bad grace. After four years of civil war, the military lords triumphed with the accession of Alexius I Comnenus, the greatest soldier and statesman to hold the throne since Basil II. The history of his reign was written in elegant Greek by his daughter Anna Comnena; and, as she remarks, it began with an empire beset by enemies on all sides. The Normans captured Dyrrhachium in 1081 and planned to advance overland to Thessalonica. Alexius called on the Venetians to help him, but Robert Guiscard's death in 1085 temporarily eased the Norman problem. The following year the Seljuq sultan died, and the sultanate was split by internal rivalries. Fortune thus played into Alexius's hands by ridding him of two of his besetting enemies. By his own efforts, however, he defeated the Pechenegs in 1091.

The Venetians had been pleased to help drive the Normans out of the Adriatic Sea but demanded a heavy price. In 1082 Alexius granted them trading privileges in Constantinople and elsewhere on terms calculated to outbid Byzantine merchants. This charter was the cornerstone of the commercial empire of Venice in the eastern Mediterranean. But it fed the flames of Byzantine resentment against the Latins; and it provoked the rich, who might have been encouraged to invest their capital in shipbuilding and trade, to rely on the more familiar security of landed property.

The terms that Alexius made with his enemies in the first ten years of his reign were not meant to be permanent. He fully expected to win back Anatolia from the Seljuqs; his plans, however, were not given time to mature, for matters were precipitated by the arrival in the East of the first Crusaders from western Europe (1096). Alexius had undoubtedly solicited the help of mercenary troops from the West but not for the liberation of the Holy Land from the infidel. The urgent need was the protection of Constantinople and the recovery of Anatolia. The Byzantines were more realistic about their Muslim neighbours than the distant popes and princes of the West. Jerusalem had finally been taken by the Seljuqs in 1077, but the most immediate threat to Byzantium came from the Pechenegs and the Normans. Alexius was tactful in his dealings with the pope and ready to discuss the differences between the churches. But neither party foresaw the consequences of Pope Urban II's appeal in 1095 for recruits to fight a Holy War.

Involvement in the First Crusade

The response in western Europe was overwhelming. The motives of those who took the cross as crusaders ranged from religious enthusiasm to a mere spirit of adventure or a hope of gain; and it was no comfort to Alexius to learn that four of the eight leaders of the First Crusade were Normans, among them Bohomund, the son of Robert Guiscard. Since the crusade had to pass through Constantinople, however, the emperor had some control over it. He required its leaders to swear to restore to the empire any towns or territories they might conquer from the Turks on their way to the Holy Land. In return, he gave them guides and a military escort. Still, the cost was enormous, for the crusaders had to be supplied with food or live off the land as they went.

Nicaea fell to them in 1097 and was duly handed over to the emperor in accord with the agreement. In 1098 they reached, and captured, Antioch. Here the trouble started. Bohomund refused to turn over the city and instead set up his own principality of Antioch. His example was imitated in the establishment of the Latin Kingdom of Jerusalem, which fell to the crusaders in 1099, and of the counties of Edessa and Tripoli. The crusaders settled down to colonize and defend the coast of Palestine and Syria and to quarrel among themselves. While they did so, Alexius was able to establish a new and more secure boundary between Byzantium and Islām through the middle of Anatolia. Full advantage was taken of the prevailing rivalry between the Seljuq sultans at Konya and the Dānishmends emirs at Melitene; and a limit was set to the westward expansion of the Turks.

The First Crusade thus brought some benefits to Byzantium. But nothing could reconcile the emperor to Bohomund of Antioch. In 1107 Bohomund, who had returned to the West, mounted a new invasion of the empire from Italy. Alexius was ready for him and defeated him at Dyrrhachium in 1108. Byzantine prestige was higher than it had been for many years, but the empire could barely afford to sustain the part of a great power. Alexius reconstituted the army and re-created the fleet, but only by means of stabilizing the gold coinage at one-third of its original value and by imposing a number of supplementary taxes. It became normal practice for taxes to be farmed out, which meant that the collectors recouped their outlay on their own terms. People in the provinces had the added burden of providing materials and labour for defense, communications, and provisions for the army, which now included very large numbers of foreigners. The supply of native soldiers had virtually ceased with the disappearance or absorption of their military holdings. But Alexius promoted an alternative source of native manpower by extending the system of granting estates in *pronoia* (by favour of the emperor), and tying the grant to the military obligation. The recipient of a *pronoia* was entitled to all the revenues of his estate and to the taxes payable by his tenants (*paroikoi*), on condition of equipping himself as a mounted cavalryman with a varying number of troops. He was in absolute possession of his property until it reverted to the crown upon his death. Similarly, Alexius tried to promote more profitable development of the estates of the church by granting them to the management of laymen as *charisticia* or benefices. As an expedient, the *pronoia* system had obvious advantages both for the state and for the military aristocracy who were its main beneficiaries. But in the long term it inevitably hastened the fragmentation of the empire among the landed families and the breakdown of centralized government that the 10th-century emperors had laboured to avert.

The *pronoia* system

Later Comneni. The domestic and foreign policies of Alexius I were continued by his son John II (reigned 1118–43) and his grandson Manuel I Comnenus (reigned 1143–80). The 12th century saw a growing involvement of the Western powers in the affairs of the East, as well as an increasingly complex political situation in Europe. In Asia, too, matters were complicated by the continuing conflict between the Seljuqs and the Dānishmends (a rival Turkish dynasty) by the emergence of the kingdom of Lesser Armenia in Cilicia, and by the activities of the crusader states. Foreign relations and skillful diplomacy became of paramount importance for the Byzantines. John II tried and failed to break what was fast becoming the Venetian monopoly of Byzantine trade, and he sought to come to terms with the new kingdom of Hungary, to whose ruler he was related by marriage. Alexius I had seen the importance of Hungary, lying between the Western and Byzantine empires, a neighbour of the Venetians and the Serbs. More ominous still was the establishment of the Norman Kingdom of the Two Sicilies under Roger II in 1130. But John II astutely allied himself with the Western emperor against it.

Manuel I realized even more clearly that Byzantium could not presume to ignore or offend the new powers in the West, and he went out of his way to understand and to appease them. Certain aspects of the Western way of life appealed to Manuel. His first and second wives were both Westerners, and Latins were welcomed at his court and even granted estates and official appointments. This policy was distasteful to most of his subjects; and it was unfortunate for his intentions that the Second Crusade occurred early in his reign (1147), for it aggravated the bitterness between Greeks and Latins and brought Byzantium deeper than ever into the tangled politics of western Europe. Its leaders were Louis VII of France and the emperor Conrad III, and its failure was blamed on Byzantine treachery. The French king discussed with Roger of Sicily the prospect of attacking Constantinople; and in 1147 Roger invaded Greece. But Manuel retained the personal friendship and the alliance of Conrad III against the Normans and even planned a joint Byzantine-German campaign against them in Italy.

Appeasement of the West

No such cooperation was possible with Conrad's successor, Frederick I Barbarossa, after 1152. To Frederick, the alliance between the Holy Roman Empire and what he called "the kingdom of the Greeks" was not one between equals. Manuel launched a vain invasion of the Norman kingdom on his own account in 1154; but it was too late for a revival of Byzantine imperialism in the West. It was hard for the Byzantines to accept the fact that their empire might soon become simply one among a number of Christian principalities.

In the Balkans and in the Latin East Manuel was more successful. His armies won back much of the northwest Balkans and almost conquered Hungary, reducing it to a client kingdom of Byzantium. The Serbs, too, under their leader Stephen Nemanja, were kept under control, while Manuel's dramatic recovery of Antioch in 1159 caused the crusaders to treat the Emperor with a new respect. But in Anatolia he overreached himself. To forestall the formation of a single Turkish sultanate, Manuel invaded the Seljuq territory of Rūm in 1176. His army was surrounded and annihilated at Myriocephalon. The battle marked the end of the Byzantine counteroffensive against the Turks begun by Alexius I. Its outcome delighted the Western emperor, Frederick Barbarossa, who had supported the Seljuq sultan of Rūm against Manuel and who now openly threatened to take over the Byzantine Empire by force.

Manuel's personal relationships with the crusaders and with other Westerners remained cordial to the end. But his policies had antagonized the Holy Roman Empire, the papacy, the Normans, and, not least, the Venetians. His effort to revive Byzantine prestige in Italy and the Balkans, and his treaties with Genoa (1169) and Pisa (1170), roused the suspicions of Venice; and in 1171, following an anti-Latin demonstration in Constantinople, all Venetians in the empire were arrested and their property was confiscated. The Venetians did not forget this episode. They, too, began to think in terms of putting Constantinople under Western control as the only means of securing their interest in Byzantine trade.

Manuel's policies antagonized many of his own people as well. His favouritism to the Latins was unpopular, as was his lavish granting of estates in *pronoia.* A reaction set in shortly after his death in 1180, originated by his cousin Andronicus Comnenus, who ascended to the throne after another anti-Latin riot in Constantinople. Andronicus murdered Manuel's widow and son Alexius II. He posed as the champion of Byzantine patriotism and of the oppressed peasantry. But to enforce his reforms he behaved like a tyrant. By undermining the power of the aristocracy he weakened the empire's defenses and undid much of Manuel's work. The King of Hungary broke his treaty; Stephen Nemanja of Serbia declared his independence from Byzantium and founded a new Serbian kingdom. Within the empire, too, disintegration proceeded. In 1185 Isaac Comnenus, governor of Cyprus, set himself up as independent ruler of the island. In the same year the Normans again invaded Greece and captured Thessalonica. The news prompted a counter-revolution in Constantinople and Andronicus was murdered.

He was the last of the Comnenian family to wear the crown. His successor Isaac II Angelus was brought to power by the aristocracy. His reign, and, still more, that of his brother Alexius III, saw the collapse of what remained of the centralized machinery of Byzantine government and defense. Isaac tried at least to keep his foreign enemies in check. The Normans were driven out of Greece in 1185. But in 1186 the Bulgars began a rebellion that was to lead to the formation of the Second Bulgarian Empire. Matters were not made easier by the arrival of the Third Crusade, provoked by the loss of Jerusalem to the Muslim leader Saladin in 1187. One of its leaders was Frederick Barbarossa, whose avowed intention was to conquer Constantinople. He died on his way to Syria. But Richard I the Lion-Heart of England appropriated Cyprus from Isaac Comnenus, and the island never again reverted to Byzantine rule.

The Fourth Crusade and the establishment of the Latin Empire. In 1195 Isaac II was deposed and blinded by his brother Alexius III. The Westerners, who had again blamed the failure of their crusade on the Byzantines, saw ways of exploiting the situation. The emperor Henry VI had united the Norman kingdom of Sicily with the Holy Roman Empire. He inherited the ambitions of both to master Constantinople, and his brother, Philip of Swabia, was married to a daughter of the dethroned Isaac II. Alexius bought off the danger by paying tribute to Henry. But Henry died in 1197. The idea had now gained ground in the West that the conquest of Constantinople would solve a number of problems and would be of benefit not only to trade but also to the future of the crusade and the church. In 1198 Innocent III was elected pope. The new rulers of Hungary, Serbia, and Bulgaria all turned to him for the recognition of the sovereignty that Byzantium would not give them.

Conquest and colonization by the West

It was under Innocent's inspiration that the Fourth Crusade was launched, and it was by the diversion of that crusade from its purpose and objective that the conquest and colonization of the Byzantine Empire by the West was realized. A multiplicity of causes and coincidences led up to the event; but the ambition of Venice, which supplied the ships, must rank high among them. A plausible excuse was offered by the cause of restoring Isaac II, whose son Alexius IV had escaped to the West to seek help, and who made lavish promises of reward to his benefactors. But when, in 1203, the crusaders drove Alexius III out of Constantinople, Isaac II and his son proved incapable either of fulfilling the promises or of stifling the anti-Latin prejudice of their people, who proclaimed an emperor of their own in the person of Alexius V. The Venetians and crusaders therefore felt justified in taking their own reward by conquering and dividing Constantinople and the Byzantine provinces among themselves. The city fell to them in April 1204. They worked off their resentment against the inhabitants in an unparalleled orgy of looting and destruction, which did irreparable damage to the city and immeasurable harm to East–West understanding.

The Venetians, led by their doge, Enrico Dandolo, gained most from the enterprise by appropriating the principal harbours and islands on the trade routes. The crusaders set about the conquest of the European and Asiatic provinces. The first Latin emperor, Baldwin I, was the suzerain of the feudal principalities that they established in Thrace, Thessalonica, Athens, and the Morea (Peloponnese). He soon came into conflict with the ruler of Bulgaria. Still more serious was the opposition offered by the three provincial centres of Byzantine resistance. At Trebizond (Trabzon) on the Black Sea, two brothers of the Comnenian family laid claim to the imperial title. In Epirus in northwestern Greece Michael Angelus Ducas, a relative of Alexius III, made his capital at Arta and harrassed the crusader states in Thessaly. The third centre of resistance was based on the city of Nicaea in Anatolia, where Theodore I Lascaris, another relative of Alexius III, was crowned as emperor by a patriarch of his own making in 1208. Of the three, Nicaea lay nearest to Constantinople, between the Latin empire and the Seljuq sultanate of Rūm; and its emperors proved worthy of the Byzantine traditions of fighting on two fronts at once and of skillful diplomacy. Theodore Lascaris and his son-in-law John III Vatatzes built up at Nicaea a microcosm of the Byzantine Empire and church in exile. The Latins were thus never able to gain a permanent foothold in Anatolia; and even in Europe their position was constantly threatened by the Byzantine rulers of northern Greece, though in the centre and south of the country their conquests were more lasting.

The most successful of the Latin emperors was Baldwin's brother, Henry of Flanders, after whose death in 1216 the Latin empire lost the initiative and the recovery of Constantinople became a foreseeable goal for the Byzantines in exile. The Latin regime was prolonged less by its own vitality than by the inability of the successor states of Epirus and Nicaea to cooperate. In 1224 Theodore Ducas of Epirus, who had extended his territories across the north of Greece and far into Bulgaria, wrested Thessalonica from the Latins and was crowned emperor there in defiance of the Emperor in Nicaea. In 1230, however, he was defeated in battle against the Bulgars before reaching Constantinople; and his defeat gave John Vatatzes the chance to extend his own empire into Europe, to ally with the Bulgars, and so to encircle Constantinople. Theodore's successor was made to renounce his imperial title, and Thessalonica surrendered to the empire of Nicaea in 1246. The Mongol invasion of Anatolia, which had meanwhile thrown the East into confusion, was of great benefit to Nicaea, for it weakened the Seljuq sultanate and isolated the rival empire of Trebizond.

John Vatatzes might well have crowned his achievements by taking Constantinople had he not died in 1254. When his son Theodore II Lascaris (1254–58) died in 1258, leaving an infant son, John IV, the regency and then the throne in Nicaea were taken over by Michael VIII Palaeologus (reigned 1259–82). Michael came of one of the aristocratic families of Nicaea whom Theodore II had mistrusted. But it was he who carried the work of the Lascarid emperors to its logical conclusion. The Byzantine state in Epirus had revived under Michael II Ducas, who set his sights on Thessalonica. Despite several efforts to reach a diplomatic settlement, the issue between the rival contenders had finally to be resolved in

The accession of Michael Palaeologus

battle at Pelagonia in Macedonia in 1259. Michael II was supported by William of Villehardouin, the French prince of the Morea, and by Manfred, the Hohenstaufen king of Sicily. The victory went to the army of Nicaea. Two years later a general of that army entered Constantinople. The last of the Latin emperors, Baldwin II, fled to Italy; and the Venetians were dispossessed of their lucrative commercial centre. In August 1261 Michael VIII was crowned as emperor in Constantinople; the boy heir to the throne of Nicaea, John IV Lascaris, was blinded and imprisoned. In this way, the dynasty of Palaeologus, the last to reign in Constantinople, was inaugurated.

THE EMPIRE UNDER THE PALAEOLOGI: 1261–1453

The empire in exile at Nicaea had become a manageable and almost self-sufficient unit, with a thriving economy based on agriculture and, latterly, on trade with the Seljuqs. It had no navy but the land frontiers in Anatolia, policed by well-paid troops, were stronger than they had been since the 12th century. By stretching the frontiers into Europe the empire had not dissipated its strength; for the possession of Thessalonica balanced that of Nicaea. When the seat of government was moved from Nicaea to Constantinople, that balance was upset, the economy was re-oriented, and the defense system in Anatolia began to break down. Constantinople was still the New Jerusalem for the Byzantines. To leave it in foreign hands was unthinkable. But after the dismemberment of the empire by the Fourth Crusade, the city was no longer the focal point of an integrated structure. It was more like an immense city-state in the midst of a number of more or less independent provinces. Much of Greece and the islands remained in French or Italian hands. The Byzantine rulers of Epirus and Thessaly, like the emperors in Trebizond, refused to recognize Michael VIII as emperor. His treatment of the Lascarid heir of Nicaea, for which the patriarch Arsenius excommunicated him, appalled many of his own subjects and provoked what was known as the Arsenite schism in the Byzantine Church. Many in Anatolia, loyal to the memory of the Lascarid emperors who had enriched and protected them, condemned Michael VIII as a usurper.

Michael VIII. The new dynasty was thus founded in an atmosphere of dissension. But its founder was determined that it should succeed. He took measures for the rehabilitation, repopulation, and defense of Constantinople. He stimulated a revival of trade by granting privileges to Italian merchants. The Genoese, who had agreed to lend him ships for the recovery of the city from their Venetian rivals, were especially favoured; and soon they had built their own commercial colony at Galata opposite Constantinople, and cornered most of what had long been a Venetian monopoly. Inevitably, this led to a conflict between Genoa and Venice, of which the Byzantines were the main victims. Some territory was taken back from the Latins, notably in the Morea and the Greek islands. But little was added to the imperial revenue; and Michael VIII's campaigns there and against Epirus and Thessaly ate up the resources that had been accumulated by the emperors at Nicaea.

Threat of reconquest by the West

The dominating influence on Byzantine policy for most of Michael's reign was the threat of reconquest by the Western powers. Charles of Anjou, the brother of the French king Louis IX, displaced Manfred of Sicily and inherited his title in 1266, organizing a coalition of all parties interested in re-establishing the Latin empire and posing as the pope's champion to lead a crusade against the schismatic Greeks. Michael VIII countered this threat by offering to submit the Church of Constantinople to the see of Rome, thereby inviting the pope's protection and removing the only moral pretext for a repetition of the Fourth Crusade. The offer to reunite the churches had been made as a diplomatic ploy to previous popes by previous emperors, but never in such compelling circumstances. Pope Gregory X accepted it at its face value; and at the second Council of Lyons in 1274 a Byzantine delegation professed obedience to the Holy See in the name of their emperor. Michael's policy, sincere or not, was violently opposed by most of his people; and he had to persecute and imprison large numbers of them in order to persuade the papacy that the union of the churches was being implemented. Later popes were not convinced by the pretense. In 1281 Charles of Anjou invaded the empire. His army was beaten back in Albania, but he at once prepared a new invasion by sea, supported by Venice, Serbia, Bulgaria, and the separatist rulers of northern Greece. His plans, however, were wrecked in 1282 by a rebellion in Sicily known as the Sicilian Ves-

From W. Shepherd, *Historical Atlas;* Barnes & Noble Books, New York

The remnants of the Byzantine Empire in 1265.

pers and by the intervention of Peter III of Aragon, which the Byzantines encouraged. Michael VIII died at the end of the same year. He had saved his empire from its most persistent enemy, but he died condemned by his church and people as a heretic and a traitor.

Whatever sins he may have committed in the eyes of the Orthodox Church, it is true that Michael VIII, by concentrating on the danger from the West, neglected, if he did not betray, the eastern provinces where he had come to power. Frontier defense troops in Anatolia were withdrawn to Europe or neglected, and bands of Turkish raiders, driven westward by the upheaval of the Mongol invasion, began to penetrate into Byzantine territory. Like the Seljuqs in the 11th century, the new arrivals found little organized opposition. Some of the local Byzantines even collaborated with them out of their own antipathy to the emperor in Constantinople. By about 1280 the Turks were plundering the fertile valleys of western Anatolia, cutting communications between the Greek cities; and their emirs were beginning to carve out small principalities. Michael VIII's network of diplomacy covered the Mongols of Iran and of the Golden Horde in Russia, as well as the Mamlūks of Egypt. But diplomacy was ineffective against Muslim *ghāzīs* (warriors inspired by the ideal of holy war); by the time the threat from Italy was removed in 1282, it was almost too late to save Byzantine Anatolia, even by military measures.

Neglect of Eastern defenses

Nor was it possible to raise armies to fight in Europe and Asia simultaneously. The native recruitment fostered by the Comnenian emperors had fallen off since 1261. Estates held in *pronoia* had now become hereditary possessions of their landlords, who ignored or were relieved of the obligation to render military service to the government. The knights of the Fourth Crusade had found many familiar elements of feudalism in the social structure of the Byzantine provinces. By the end of the 13th century the development had gone much further. The officers of the Byzantine army were still mostly drawn from the native aristocracy. But the troops were hired, and the cost of maintaining a large army in Europe, added to the lavish subsidies that Michael VIII paid to his friends and allies, crippled the economy.

Andronicus II. Michael's son Andronicus II (reigned 1282–1328) unwisely attempted to economize by cutting down the size of the army and disbanding the navy. Unemployed Byzantine sailors sold their services to the new Turkish emirs, who were already raiding the Aegean islands. The Genoese became the suppliers and defenders of Constantinople by sea, which excited the jealousy of the Venetians to the pitch of war and led to the first of a series of naval battles off Constantinople in 1296. In reaction against his father's policy, Andronicus II pursued a line of almost total isolation from the papacy and the West. The union of Lyons was solemnly repudiated and Orthodoxy restored, to the deep satisfaction of most Byzantines. But there were still divisive conflicts in society. The Arsenite schism in the church was not healed until 1310; the rulers of Epirus and Thessaly remained defiant and kept contact with the successors of Charles of Anjou in Italy; and the people of Anatolia aired their grievances in rebellion. As the Turks encroached on their land, refugees in growing numbers fled to the coast or to Constantinople, bringing new problems for the government. In 1302 a band of Turkish warriors defeated the Byzantine army near Nicomedia in northwestern Anatolia. Its leader, Osman I, was the founder of the Osmanlı or Ottoman people, who were soon to overrun the Byzantine Empire in Europe. His activities were so far on a smaller scale than those of some of the other Turkish emirs. But Nicomedia was dangerously near to Constantinople.

Appearance of Ottoman Turks

In 1303 Andronicus hired a professional army of mercenaries, the Catalan Company, who had been fighting in Sicily. The Catalans made one successful counterattack against the Turks in Anatolia. But they were unruly and unpopular; and when their leader was murdered they turned against their employers. For some years they used the Gallipoli Peninsula as a base from which to ravage Thrace, inviting thousands of Turks to come over and help them. The Catalans finally moved west; in 1311 they conquered Athens from the French and established the Catalan Duchy of Athens and Thebes. The Turks whom they left behind were not ejected from Gallipoli until 1312. The cost of hiring the Catalans, and then of repairing the damage that they had done, had to be met by desperate measures. The face value of the Byzantine gold coin or *hyperpyron* was lowered when its gold content was reduced to a mere 50 percent; and the people had to bear still greater burdens of taxation—some extracted from the landlords of Macedonia and northern Thrace, some payable in kind by farmers. Inflation and rising prices led to near famine in Constantinople, the population of which was swollen by vast numbers of refugees. Unscrupulous merchants made great black-market profits.

Cultural revival. Materially, the empire seemed almost beyond hope of recovery in the early 14th century, but spiritually and culturally it showed a remarkable vitality. The church, no longer troubled over the question of union with Rome, grew in prestige and authority. The patriarchs of Constantinople commanded the respect of all the Orthodox Churches, even beyond the imperial boundaries; and Andronicus II, himself a pious theologian, yielded to the patriarch the ancient right of imperial jurisdiction over the monastic settlement on Mt. Athos, which prospered at a time when other centres of Byzantine monasticism were being occupied by the Turks. There was a new flowering of the Byzantine mystical tradition in a movement known as Hesychasm, whose chief spokesman was Gregory Palamas, a monk from Athos. The theology of the Hesychasts was thought to be heterodox by some theologians; and a controversy arose in the second quarter of the 14th century that had political undertones and was as disruptive to the church and state as the Iconoclastic dispute had been in an earlier age. It was not resolved until 1351.

Mysticism and scholarship

The revival of mystical speculation and the monastic life may have been in part a reaction against the contemporary revival of secular literature and learning. Scholarship of all kinds was patronized by Andronicus II, whose court was likened to the Lyceum of antiquity. As in the 11th century, interest was mainly centred on a rediscovery of ancient Greek learning. The scholar Maximus Planudes compiled a famous anthology and translated a number of Latin works into Greek, though knowledge of Latin was rare and most of the Byzantine scholars prided themselves on having in their Hellenic heritage an exclusive possession that set them apart from the Latins. A notable exception was Demetrius Cydones who, like Michael Psellus, managed affairs of state for a number of emperors for close to 50 years. Cydones translated the works of Thomas Aquinas into Greek; he was the forerunner of a minority of Byzantine intellectuals who joined the Roman Church and looked to the West to save their empire from ruin. More typical of his class was Theodore Metochites, the Grand Logothete or chancellor of Andronicus II, whose encyclopaedic learning rivalled that of Psellus. His pupil Nicephorus Gregoras, in addition to his researches in philosophy, theology, mathematics, and astronomy, wrote a history of his age. The tradition of Byzantine historiography, maintained by George Acropolites, the historian of the Empire of Nicaea, was continued in the 14th century by George Pachymeres, by Gregoras, and finally by the Emperor John VI Cantacuzenus, who wrote his memoirs after his abdication in 1354.

Andronicus III and John Cantacuzenus. The histories they wrote tell more of politics and personalities than of the underlying social and economic tensions in their society that were to find expression in a series of civil wars. Trouble broke out in 1320 when Andronicus II, purely for family reasons, disinherited his grandson Andronicus III. The cause of the young emperor was taken up by his friends and there was periodic warfare from 1321 to 1328, when the older Andronicus had to yield the throne. It was in some ways a victory for the younger generation of the aristocracy, of whom the leading light was John Cantacuzenus. It was he who guided the empire's policies during the reign of Andronicus III (1328–41). They were men of greater drive and determination, but the years of fighting had made recovery still more difficult and given new chances to their enemies. In 1329 they fought and lost a battle at Pelekanon (near Nicomedia) against Osman's son, Orchan, whose Turkish warriors went on to capture Nicaea in 1331 and Nicomedia in 1337. Northwestern Anatolia, once the heart of the empire, was now lost. There seemed no alternative but to accept the fact and to come to terms with the Ottomans and the other Turkish emirs. By so doing, Andronicus III and Cantacuzenus were able to call on the services of almost limitless numbers of Turkish soldiers to fight for them against their other enemies: the Italians in the Aegean islands, and the Serbs and the Bulgars in Macedonia and Thrace.

The power of Serbia, which Andronicus II had managed to control by diplomatic means, grew alarmingly after the accession of Stefan Dušan to the Serbian throne in 1331. Dušan exploited to the full the numerous embarrassments of the Byzantines and in 1346 announced his ambitions by having himself crowned as emperor of the Serbs and Greeks. The greatest practical achievement of Andronicus III was the restoration to Byzantine rule of the long separated provinces of Epirus and Thessaly. But only a few years later, in 1348, the whole of northern Greece was swallowed up in the Serbian Empire of Stefan Dušan.

Outbreak of civil war

When Andronicus III died in 1341, civil war broke out for a second time. The contestants on that occasion were John Cantacuzenus, who had expected to act as regent for the boy-heir John V, and his political rivals led by his former partisan Alexius Apocaucus, the patriarch John Calecas, and the empress-mother Anne of Savoy, who held power in Constantinople. Cantacuzenus, befriended and then rejected by Dušan of Serbia, was crowned as the Emperor John VI in Thrace in 1346; and, with the help of Turkish troops, he fought his way to victory in the following year. Like Romanus Lecapenus, he protested that he was no more than the protector of the legitimate heir to the throne, John V Palaeologus. His brief reign, from 1347 to 1354, might have turned the tide of Byzantine misfortunes had not the second civil war provoked unprecedented social and political consequences. In the cities of Thrace and Macedonia the people vented their dissatisfaction with the ruling aristocracy by revolution. It was directed mainly against Cantacuzenus and the class that he represented. The movement was most memorable and lasting in Thessalonica, where a faction known as the Zealots seized power in a coup d'etat and governed the city as an almost independent commune until 1350.

The second civil war was consequently even more destructive of property and ruinous to the economy than the first. At the same time, in 1347, the Black Death decimated the population of Constantinople and other parts of the empire. John VI Cantacuzenus, nevertheless, did what he could to restore the economy and stability of the empire. To coordinate the scattered fragments of its territory he assigned them as appanages to individual members of the imperial family. His son Manuel took over the province of the Morea in 1349 with the rank of despot and governed it with growing success until his death in 1380. His eldest son, Matthew, was given a principality in Thrace; while the junior emperor John V, who had married a daughter of Cantacuzenus, ruled in Thessalonica after 1351. This somewhat feudal system of imperial government was to be continued by the successors of John VI, sometimes making for stability but more often for rivalry between the various princes or Despots.

Cantacuzenus also tried but failed to weaken the economic stranglehold of the Genoese by rebuilding a Byzantine war fleet and merchant navy. The effort involved him in warfare, first on his own and then as an unwilling partner of the Venetians against the Genoese, from which Byzantium emerged as the loser. The revenue of the Genoese colony at Galata, derived from custom dues, was now far greater than that of Constantinople. The empire's poverty was reflected in dilapidated buildings and falling standards of luxury. The crown jewels had been pawned to Venice during the civil war, and the Byzantine gold coin, hopelessly devalued, had given place in international trade to the Venetian ducat. More and more, Byzantium was at the mercy of its foreign competitors and enemies, who promoted and exploited the political and family rivalries among the ruling class. John Cantacuzenus was never popular as an emperor, and feeling against him came to a head when some of his Ottoman mercenaries took the occasion of the destruction of Gallipoli by earthquake to occupy and fortify the city in March 1354. It

The Byzantine Empire in 1355.

was their first permanent establishment in Europe, at the key point of the crossing from Asia. In November of the same year John V Palaeologus, encouraged by the anti-Cantacuzenist Party, forced his way into Constantinople. In December Cantacuzenus abdicated and became a monk. Though his son Matthew, who had by then been crowned as co-emperor, fought on for a few years, the dynasty of Cantacuzenus was not perpetuated.

Turkish occupation of Gallipoli

Turkish expansion. John Cantacuzenus's relationship with the Turks had been based on personal friendship with their leaders, among them Orchan, to whom he gave his daughter in marriage. But once the Turks had set up a base on European soil and had seen the possibilities of further conquest, such relationships were no longer practicable. Stefan Dušan, who very nearly realized his ambition to found a new Serbo-Byzantine empire, was the only man who might have prevented the subsequent rapid expansion of the Turks into the Balkans, but he died in 1355 and his empire split up. The new emperor, John V, hoped that the Western world would sense the danger and in 1355 he addressed an appeal for help to the Pope. The popes were concerned for the fate of the Christian East but guarded in their offers to Constantinople so long as the Byzantine Church remained in schism from Rome. In 1366 John V visited Hungary to beg for help, but in vain. In the same year his cousin Amadeo, count of Savoy, brought a small force to Constantinople and recaptured Gallipoli from the Turks, who had by then advanced far into Thrace. Amadeo persuaded the emperor to go to Rome and make his personal submission to the Holy See in 1369. On his way home, John was detained at Venice as an insolvent debtor; and, during his absence, the Turks scored their first victory over the successors of Stefan Dušan on the Marica River near Adrianople in 1371. The whole of Macedonia was now open to them. The remaining Serbian princes and the ruler of Bulgaria became their vassals; and in 1373 the Emperor was forced to do the same.

Byzantium was now a vassal state of the Turks, pledged to pay tribute and to provide military assistance to the Ottoman sultan. The possession of Constantinople thereafter was disputed by the Emperor's sons and grandsons in a series of revolutions, which were encouraged and sometimes instigated by the Turks, the Genoese, or the Venetians. John V's son Andronicus IV, aided by the Genoese and the sultan Murad I, mastered the city for three years (1376–79). He rewarded the Turks by giving back Gallipoli to them, and Murad made his first European capital at Adrianople. The Venetians helped John V to regain his throne in 1379, and the empire was once again divided into appanages under his sons. Only his second son, Manuel, showed any independence of action. For nearly five years, from 1382 to 1387, Manuel reigned as emperor at Thessalonica and laboured to make it a rallying point for resistance against the encroaching Turks. But the city fell to Murad's army in April 1387. When the Turks then drove deeper into Macedonia, the Serbs again organized a counteroffensive, but were overwhelmed at Kossovo in 1389.

Manuel II and respite from the Turks. The loss of Thessalonica and the Battle of Kossovo sealed Constantinople off by land. The new sultan Bayezid I (1389–1402) intended to make it his capital; when Manuel II came to that throne at his father's death in 1391, the Sultan warned him that he was emperor only inside the city walls. The Turks already controlled the rest of Byzantine Europe, except for the south of Greece.

In 1393 Bayezid completed his conquest of Bulgaria, and soon afterward he laid siege to Constantinople. The blockade was to last for many years, though the city could resist so long as its walls remained intact. Manuel II, like his father, pinned his hopes of rescue on the West. A great crusade against the Turks was organized by the King of Hungary; but it was defeated at Nicopolis on the Danube in 1396. In 1399 the French marshal, Boucicaut, who had been at Nicopolis and had returned to the relief of Constantinople with a small army, persuaded Manuel to travel to western Europe to put the Byzantine case in person. From the end of 1399 to June 1403 the Emperor visited in Italy, France, and England, leaving his nephew John VII in charge of Constantinople. Manuel's journey did something to stimulate Western interest in Greek learning. His friend and ambassador in the West, Manuel Chrysoloras, a pupil of Demetrius Cydones, was appointed to teach Greek at Florence. The Pope instituted a defense fund for Constantinople, even though Manuel did not offer to submit the Byzantine Church to Rome as an incentive. Interest and sympathy were forthcoming, but little in the way of practical help. During Manuel's absence, however, the Ottomans were defeated at Ankara by the Mongol leader Timur (Tamerlane) in July 1402. Bayezid was captured and his empire in Asia was shattered. His four sons contended with each other to secure possession of the European provinces, which had been little affected by the Mongol invasion, and to reunite the Ottoman dominions. In these wholly unexpected circumstances the Byzantines found themselves the favoured allies first of one Turkish contender, then of another. The blockade of Constantinople was lifted. Thessalonica—with Mt. Athos and other places—was restored to Byzantine rule; and the payment of tribute to the sultan was annulled. In 1413 Mehmed I, helped and promoted by the emperor Manuel, triumphed over his rivals and became sultan of the reintegrated Ottoman Empire.

Appeals of Manuel II in western Europe

During his reign, from 1413 to 1421, the Byzantines enjoyed their last respite. Manuel II, aware that it could not last, made the most of it by strengthening the defenses and administration of the fragments of his empire. The most flourishing province in the last years was the Despotate of the Morea. Its prosperity had been built up first by the sons of John Cantacuzenus (who died there in 1383), and then by the son and grandson of John V—Theodore I and Theodore II Palaeologus. Its capital city of Mistra became a haven for Byzantine scholars and artists and a centre of the last revival of Byzantine culture, packed with churches, monasteries, and palaces. Among its scholars was George Gemistus Plethon, a platonist who dreamed of a rebirth of Hellenism on Hellenic soil.

Final Turkish assault. When Murad II became sultan, in 1421, the days of Constantinople and of Hellenism were numbered. In 1422 Murad revoked all the privileges accorded to the Byzantines by his father and laid siege to Constantinople. His armies invaded Greece and blockaded Thessalonica. The city was then a possession of Manuel II's son Andronicus, who in 1423 handed it over to the Venetians. For seven years Thessalonica was a Venetian colony, until, in March 1430, the Sultan assaulted and captured it. Meanwhile, Manuel II had died in 1425, leaving his son John VIII as emperor. John, who had already travelled to Venice and Hungary in search of help, was prepared to reopen negotiations for the union of the churches as a means of stirring the conscience of Western Christendom. His father had been skeptical about the benefits of such a policy, knowing that it would antagonize most of his own people and arouse the suspicion of the Turks. The proposal was made, however, at the Council of Florence in 1439, attended by the emperor John VIII, his patriarch, and many Orthodox bishops and dignitaries. After protracted and difficult discussions, they agreed to submit to the authority of Rome. The union of Florence was badly received by the citizens of Constantinople and by most of the Orthodox world. But it had its notable adherents, such as the bishops Bessarion of Nicaea and Isidore of Kiev, both of whom retired to Italy as cardinals of the Roman Church. Bessarion's learning and library helped to encourage further Western interest in Greek scholarship. The union of Florence also helped to stimulate a crusade against the Turks. Once again it was led by the king of Hungary, Vladislaw III of Poland, supported by George Branković of Serbia and by János Hunyadi of Transylvania. But there were disagreements among its leaders, and the Christian army was annihilated at Varna in 1444.

Fall of Thessalonica

The Byzantine collapse and the Ottoman triumph followed swiftly thereafter. In 1448 Constantine XI, the last emperor, left Mistra for Constantinople when his brother

John VIII died without issue. His two other brothers, Thomas and Demetrius, continued to govern the Morea, the last surviving Byzantine province. In 1449 the new sultan, Mehmed II, began to prepare for the final assault on Constantinople. No further substantial help came from the West, and the formal celebration of the union of the Churches in Hagia Sophia in 1452 was greeted with a storm of protest. Even in their extremity, the Byzantines would not buy their freedom at the expense of their Orthodox faith. They found the prospect of being ruled by the Turks less odious than that of being indebted to the Latins. When the crisis came, however, the Venetians in Constantinople, and a Genoese contingent commanded by Giovanni Giustiniani, wholeheartedly cooperated in the defense of the city, though the Genoese at Galata declared their neutrality. Mehmed II laid siege to the walls in April 1453. His ships were obstructed by a chain that the Byzantines had thrown across the mouth of the Golden Horn. The ships were therefore dragged overland to the harbour from the seaward side, bypassing the defenses. The Sultan's heavy artillery continually bombarded the land walls until, on May 29, some of his soldiers forced their way in. Giustiniani was mortally wounded. The emperor Constantine was last seen fighting on foot at one of the gates.

The Sultan allowed his victorious troops three days and nights of plunder before he took possession of his new capital. The Ottoman Empire had now superseded the Byzantine Empire; and some Greeks, like the contemporary historian Critobulus of Imbros, recognized the logic of the change by bestowing on the Sultan all the attributes of the emperor. The material structure of the empire, which had for long been crumbling, was now under the management of the sultan-basileus. But the Orthodox faith was less susceptible to change. The Sultan acknowledged the fact that the church had proved to be the most enduring element in the Byzantine world; and he gave the Patriarch of Constantinople an unprecedented measure of temporal authority by making him answerable for all Christians living under Ottoman rule.

The last pockets of resistance were eliminated soon after 1453. Athens fell to the Turks in 1456; and in 1460 the two Despots of the Morea surrendered. Thomas fled to Italy, Demetrius to the Sultan's court. In 1461 Trebizond, capital of the last Greek empire, which had maintained its precarious independence by paying court to Turks and Mongols alike, finally succumbed; and the transformation of the Byzantine world into the Ottoman world was at last complete. (D.M.N.)

BIBLIOGRAPHY. The following surveys and analyses provide brief introductions to Byzantine history and civilization: N.H. BAYNES and H. ST. L.B. MOSS (eds.), *Byzantium: An Introduction to East Roman Civilization* (1948); J.M. HUSSEY, *The Byzantine World*, 3rd rev. ed. (1967); R.J.H. JENKINS, *Byzantium and Byzantinism* (1963); and P.D. WHITTING, *Byzantium: An Introduction* (1971). Brief general characterizations of various aspects of Byzantine civilization may be found in the collected essays of two masters of Byzantine studies: N.H. BAYNES, *Byzantine Studies and Other Essays* (1955); and FRANZ DOLGER, *Byzanz und die europäische Staatenwelt* (1953) and *Paraspora* (1961). Deeper study of Byzantine history should begin with GEORGE OSTROGORSKY, *Geschichte des byzantinischen Staates* (1965; Eng. trans., *History of the Byzantine State*, 2nd ed., 1968); and may continue with *The Cambridge Medieval History*, vol. 4, pt. 1–2, *The Byzantine Empire*, 2nd ed. (1966–67), a collective survey of uneven quality that suffers from its adoption of the year 717 as a starting point for Byzantine history. Geographical relationships are discussed in ALFRED PHILIPPSON, *Das byzantinische Reich als geographische Erscheinung* (1938); and its church and theology in H.G. BECK, *Kirche und theologische Literatur im byzantinischen Reich* (1959). By far the most profound and extensive work in Byzantine studies before World War I had been completed in imperial Russia, A.A. VASILIEV, *History of the Byzantine Empire, 324–1453*, 2nd ed. rev. (1952, reprinted 1964; orig. pub. in Russian, 1917), provides a thorough bibliography; M.V. LEVCHENKO, *Byzance des origines à 1453* (1949; orig. pub. in Russian, 1940), illustrates the Marxist approach in the Soviet Union, where, since World War II, Byzantine history has undergone a renaissance. Current work is published in a number of periodicals of international character: *Byzantinische Zeitschrift* (Munich); *Byzantion* (Brussels); *Byzantinoslavica* (Prague); *Dumbarton Oaks Papers* (Washington, D.C.); *Travaux et Mémoires* (Paris); *Vizantiiskii Vremennik* (Moscow and Leningrad).

The Roman and Christian background: The first two chapters, by Moss and Matthews, in *The Cambridge Medieval History*, vol. 4, will introduce the reader to the problems discussed in this section. Further reading might include the brief and extremely provocative sketch by PETER BROWN, *The World of Late Antiquity* (1971), excellent for cultural history; and at the other extreme of length, A.H.M. JONES, *The Later Roman Empire, 284–602: A Social, Economic, and Administrative Survey*, 2 vol. (1964), which will probably remain one of the monuments of 20th-century scholarship on the period.

The 5th and 6th centuries: Two older works provide a more extensive coverage than that found in Jones's *Later Roman Empire:* J.B. BURY, *History of the Later Roman Empire from the Death of Theodosius I. to the Death of Justinian (A.D. 395 to A.D. 565)*, 2nd ed., 2 vol. (1923, reprinted 1958); and ERNST STEIN, *Histoire du Bas-Empire*, 2 vol. (1949–59). The 1960s and early 1970s saw the publication of a number of new works on Justinian of varying merit: BERTHOLD RUBIN, *Das Zeitalter Justinians*, vol. 1 (1960); J.W. BARKER, *Justinian and the Later Roman Empire* (1966); ROBERT BROWNING, *Justinian and Theodora* (1971); and THOMAS FITZGERALD, *Justinian the Great: Roman Emperor of the East* (1970). The conclusions presented herein are justified in detail in JOHN L. TEALL, "The Barbarians in Justinian's Armies," *Speculum*, 40:294–322 (1965). Since the end of the century was first studied in a sophisticated fashion by ERNST STEIN, *Studien zur Geschichte des byzantinischen Reiches* (1919), it has received less attention than it should.

The 7th century and the Heraclian reforms: A general overview of the age and its problems will be found in *Dumbarton Oaks Papers*, vol. 13 (1959), a collection of papers, including important studies by Ostrogorsky on the significance of the Slavic invasions and on the cities, by Charanis on ethnic mixture, and by Lopez on trade. R.J.H. JENKINS, *Byzantium: The Imperial Centuries, A.D. 610–1071* (1966), provides a survey of this and the following three centuries that, though founded on sound scholarship, reads like a novel. For a contrasting opinion on the foundation of the themes, see PAUL LEMERLE, "Esquisse pour une histoire agraire de Byzance," *Revue historique*, 219:32–74, 254–284 and 220:43–94 (1958), an important survey of agrarian institutions from the 4th to the 11th century. A detailed defense of the position taken above, with references to other studies, will be found in JOHN L. TEALL, "The Byzantine Agricultural Tradition," *Dumbarton Oaks Papers*, 25:33–59 (1971), which also deals with agricultural technology and problems of land settlement. Byzantium's position in eastern Europe is presented in masterly fashion by DIMITRI OBOLENSKY, "The Empire and Its Northern Neighbors," *The Cambridge Medieval History*, vol. 4, and in the same author's *Byzantine Commonwealth* (1971). A convenient history of Iconoclasm is E.J. MARTIN, *A History of the Iconoclastic Controversy* (1930).

The 9th century: The standard survey remains J.B. BURY, *A History of the Eastern Roman Empire . . ., A.D. 802–867* (1912, reprinted 1965); but to FRANCIS DVORNIK must be given much of the credit for the subsequent revision of views on the period, particularly on the significance of the reign of Michael III. A number of Dvornik's important works have recently been reprinted with new introductions: *Les Légendes de Constantin et de méthode vues de Byzance*, 2nd ed. (1969); *Les Slaves, Byzance et Rome au IXème siècle* (1926, reprinted 1970); and *The Photian Schism* (1948, reprinted 1970); see also his *Byzantine Missions Among the Slavs* (1970). The work of another distinguished revisionist is summarized in, but not well represented by, the chapter he prepared for *The Cambridge Medieval History*, vol. 4: HENRI GREGOIRE, "The Amorians and Macedonians, 842–1025." Arab-Byzantine warfare is narrated in A.A. VASILIEV, *Byzance et les Arabes*, vol. 1, *La Dynastie d'Amorium, 820–867* (1935).

The Macedonian dynasty (867–1025): J.B. BURY, *The Imperial Administrative System in the Ninth Century* (1911, reprinted 1958); FRANCIS DVORNIK, *The Photian Schism* (1948, reprinted 1970); J.M. HUSSEY, *Church and Learning in the Byzantine Empire, 867–1185* (1937, reprinted 1963); R.J.H. JENKINS, *Byzantium: The Imperial Centuries, A.D. 610–1071* (1966); STEVEN RUNCIMAN, *A History of the First Bulgarian Empire* (1930), *The Eastern Schism* (1955), and *The Emperor Romanus Lecapenus and His Reign* (1929, reprinted 1963); GUSTAVE SCHLUMBERGER, *L'Epopée byzantine à la fin du Xᵉ siècle*, 3 vol. (1896–1905); A.A.VASILIEV, *Byzance et les Arabes*, vol. 2, pt. 1–2 (1950–68); ALBERT VOGT, *Basile Iᵉʳ, Empereur de Byzance (867–886) et la civilisation byzantine à la fin du IXᵉ siècle* (1908).

Byzantine decline and subjection to Western influence (1025–1260): C.M. BRAND, *Byzantium Confronts the West, 1180–*

1204 (1968); FERDINAND CHALANDON, *Les Comnènes*, vol 1, *Essai sur le règne d'Alexis Ier Comnène, 1081–1118* and vol. 2, *Jean II Comnène, 1118–1143, et Manuel I Comnène, 1143–1180* (1900–13); ALICE GARDNER, *The Lascarids of Nicaea* (1912); R.J.H. JENKINS, *The Byzantine Empire on the Eve of the Crusades* (1953); OKTAWIESZ JUREWICZ, *Andronikos I. Komnenos* (1962; Eng. trans., 1970); D.M. NICOL, *The Despotate of Epiros* (1957); GEORGE OSTROGORSKY, *Pour l'histoire de la féodalité byzantine* (1954), and "Agrarian Conditions in the Byzantine Empire in the Middle Ages," in *The Cambridge Economic History of Europe*, 2nd ed., vol. 1, ch. 5 (1966); D.I. POLEMIS, *The Doukai: A Contribution to Byzantine Prosopography* (1968); STEVEN RUNCIMAN, *A History of the Crusades*, 3 vol. (1951–54, reprinted 1962–66); K.M. SETTON (ed.), *A History of the Crusades:* vol. 1, *The First Hundred Years*, ed. by M.W. BALDWIN; vol. 2, *The Later Crusades, 1189–1311*, ed. by R.L. WOLFF and H.W. HAZARD (1955, 1962).

The empire under the Palaeologi (1261–1453): FRANZ BABINGER, *Mehmed der Eroberer und seine Zeit* (1953; French trans., 1963); J.W. BARKER, *Manuel II Palaeologus (1391–1425): A Study in Late Byzantine Statesmanship* (1969); U.V. BOSCH, *Kaiser Andronikos III. Palaiologos* (1965); D.J. GEANAKOPLOS, *Emperor Michael Palaeologus and the West, 1258–1282* (1959); H.A. GIBBONS, *The Foundation of the Ottoman Empire* (1916, reprinted 1968); JOSEPH GILL, *The Council of Florence* (1959); OSKAR HALECKI, *Un Empereur de Byzance à Rome* (1930); JEAN LONGNON, *L'Empire latin de Constantinople et la principauté de Morée* (1949); WILLIAM MILLER, *The Latins in the Levant: A History of Frankish Greece, 1204–1566* (1908), and *Trebizond, the Last Greek Empire* (1926); D.M. NICOL, *The Byzantine Family of Kantakouzenos (Cantacuzenus) ca. 1100–1460* (1968) and *The Last Centuries of Byzantium 1261–1453* (1972); A.T. PAPADOPOULOS, *Versuch einer Genealogie der Palaiologen, 1259–1453* (1938); L.P. RAYBAUD, *Le Gouvernement et l'administration centrale de l'empire byzantin sous les premiers Paléologues (1258–1354)* (1968); STEVEN RUNCIMAN, *The Sicilian Vespers* (1958), *The Fall of Constantinople, 1453* (1965), *The Great Church in Captivity* (1968), and *The Last Byzantine Renaissance* (1970); K.M. SETTON, "The Byzantine Background to the Italian Renaissance," *Proceedings of the American Philosophical Society*, 100:1–76 (1956); ORESTE TAFRALI, *Thessalonique au quatorzième siècle* (1913); GUNTER WEISS, *Joannes Kantakuzenos, Aristokrat, Staatsmann, Kaiser und Mönch* (1969); ERNST WERNER, *Die Geburt einer Grossmacht—die Osmanen, 1300–1481* (1966); PAUL WITTEK, *The Rise of the Ottoman Empire* (1938, reprinted 1965); D.A. ZAKUTHENOS, *Le Despotat grec de Morée*, 2 vol. (1932–53), and *Crise monétaire et crise économique à Byzance du XIIIe au XVe siècle* (1948).

(D.M.N./J.L.Te.)

Cabral, Pedro Álvares

Though other Europeans had preceded him to that part of the world, Pedro Álvares Cabral is generally credited with discovering Brazil, in 1500. Cabral, who lived from 1467 or 1468 to 1520, was one of the foremost of the Portuguese navigators who brought fame to their homeland during the Age of Discovery.

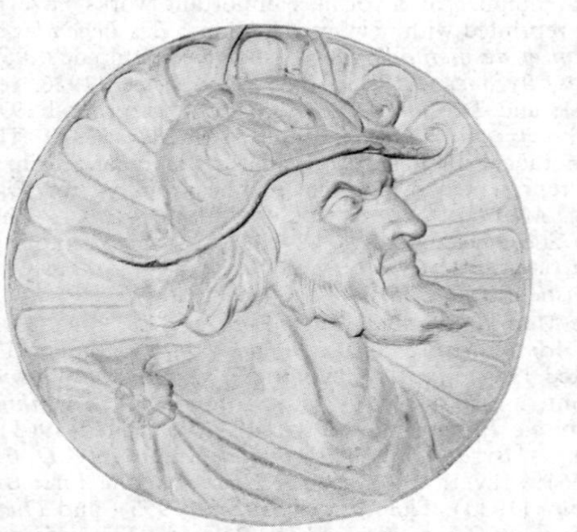

Cabral, medallion by an unknown artist, 16th century. From the Mosterio dos Jerónimos, Portugal.
By courtesy of the Secretaria de Estado da Informacao Cultura Popular e Turismo, Lisbon

Born in Belmonte, Portugal, the son of Fernão Cabral, a nobleman, and of Isabel de Gouveia, he was heir to a long tradition of service to the throne. He himself enjoyed the esteem of King Manuel I of Portugal, from whom he received various privileges in 1497; these included a personal allowance, the title of counsellor to his highness, and the habit of the military Order of Christ. Three years later the King entrusted him with the command of the second major expedition to India, expressing "the great confidence we have in Pedralvares de Gouveia, nobleman of our household." Cabral was named admiral in supreme command of 13 ships, which set out from Lisbon on March 9, 1500. He was to follow the route taken earlier by Vasco da Gama, to strengthen commercial ties, and to further the conquest his predecessor had begun.

The expedition to India

In accordance with da Gama's instructions, based on his experiences during the first voyage, Cabral was to sail southwest so as to bypass the becalmed waters of the Gulf of Guinea. This course, which later became known as the "circle around Brazil," had the added advantage of providing the Portuguese with opportunity to reconnoitre along the coast of the lands to the west, which they had previously sighted and which belonged to them in accordance with the Treaty of Tordesillas (1494).

Sailing westward under favourable conditions, on April 22, Cabral discovered the land he named Island of the True Cross. Later renamed Holy Cross by King Manuel, the country ultimately took its modern name, Brazil, from a kind of wood it produces, *pau-brasil*, which is used in dye processing.

Discovery of Brazil

Cabral is reported to have made a special effort to treat the natives kindly, receiving them on board his caravel. Nonetheless, he took formal possession of the country and dispatched one of his ships to Portugal to inform the King. Henceforth, maps of the region showed Portugal as ruler of a great expanse of land with vaguely defined boundaries that came to serve as a point of call on the long voyage from Europe to the Cape of Good Hope and the Indian Ocean.

After a stay of only ten days in Brazil, Cabral sailed for India, in a voyage that was plagued by a series of misfortunes. On May 29, while the fleet was rounding the Cape of Good Hope, four ships were lost with all hands aboard; Bartolomeu Dias, the Portuguese who had discovered the cape in 1488, was one of those who perished in this disaster. The remaining ships cast anchor on September 13, 1500, at Calicut, India, where the *zamorin* (Muslim ruler) welcomed Cabral and allowed him to establish a fortified trading post. Disputes with Muslim traders soon arose, however, and on December 17 a large Muslim force attacked the trading post. Most of the Portuguese defenders were killed before reinforcements could arrive from the Portuguese fleet lying at anchor in the harbour.

Cabral retaliated by bombarding the city, and then by capturing ten Muslim vessels and executing their crews. He then sailed for the Indian port of Cochin, farther south, where he was affably received and permitted to trade for precious spices, with which he loaded his six remaining ships. Cabral also made port at Carangolos and Cananor on the same coast, completed his cargo, and on January 16, 1501, began the return voyage to Portugal. On his way, however, two ships foundered, and it was with only four vessels that Cabral finally reached the mouth of the Tagus River in Portugal on June 23, 1501.

King Manuel was pleased at the outcome of the undertaking, in spite of the misfortunes that had beset it; he is said to have at first favoured making Cabral head of a new and more powerful expedition, but in the end it was Vasco da Gama and not Cabral who was appointed to that command. Accounts differ as to the reason for the King's change of heart. One chronicler attributes it to disagreement over division of authority within the new fleet; another offers the explanation that da Gama opposed the appointment of Cabral on the grounds that da Gama himself already held the title admiral of all the fleets that might leave Portugal for India and that the disasters of Cabral's expedition should disqualify him for the new mission.

Rivalry with Vasco da Gama

Whatever the true explanation, the discoverer of Brazil

held no further position of authority at the Portuguese court. He retired to his estate in the Beira Baixa province of Portugal and spent his remaining years there. He died in 1520 in Santarém, Portugal, where his tomb was identified in 1848 by the Brazilian historian Francisco Adolfo Varnhagen.

In 1968, the year that marked the fifth centenary of the birth of Cabral, Brazil and Portugal honoured the memory of the "admiral of the fleet" in joint festivities. Both Rio de Janeiro and Lisbon have erected monuments in his honour.

BIBLIOGRAPHY. PEDRO CALMON, *História do Brasil*, 7 vol. (1959); WILLIAM BROOKS GREENLEE (ed. and trans.), *The Voyage of Pedro Alvares Cabral to Brazil and India from Contemporary Documents and Narratives*, works issued by the Hakluyt Society, 2nd series, no. 81 (1938); D. ANTONIO PEREIRA, *Pedralvares* (1968); JOSE CARLOS AMADO, *Pedro Alvares Cabral* (1968).

(P.Ca.)

Cactales

The cacti are curious, often spiny, fleshy-stemmed plants constituting the family Cactaceae, order Cactales, characteristic of and well adapted to dry regions. Although the cacti are native to the Americas—with one possible exception (see below)—they are cultivated widely throughout the world for their bizarre forms and often striking blossoms. Cacti are easily grown from cuttings or from seeds; they are adapted to warm, arid indoor conditions and require little care once established.

General features. *Importance.* Cacti are economic plants in Mexico, parts of Central and South America, and the Caribbean region. Various species are cultivated for food, including vast complexes of prickly pears, especially of *Opuntia ficus-indica*, and torch cacti (*Cereus*). Drinks prepared from some cactus fruits have been a popular native medicine for fevers. In Mexico, leaves of chollas, resembling string beans, are eaten. In Latin America, species of *Opuntia*, *Cereus*, and other genera are planted around houses, often forming an impenetrable barrier. Barrel cacti (*Echinocactus* and *Ferocactus*) are a source of water in emergencies.

Cacti are cultivated chiefly for their ornamental features and general hardiness. They can be grafted easily, and many rare species are propagated by grafting upon more vigorous stocks. Many small cacti are suitable for home cultivation. Without water, most cacti persist but do not grow. Some species, however, do require periodic drought. Many species grow well in warm weather in full sun, provided there is adequate soil moisture, but others require some shade.

Appearance. Most cacti are composed of stems and have no leaves. The leaves, when present, are usually greatly reduced; they may occur only temporarily at the growing end of the plant. Only in the genera *Pereskia* and *Pereskiopsis*, restricted to the tropics, do the leaves fit the popular conception of leaves.

Size range

Cacti vary greatly in size and general appearance, from button-like peyote (*Lophophora*) and low clumps of prickly pear (*Opuntia*) to upright columns of barrel cacti (*Ferocactus* and *Echinocactus*) and the imposing saguaro (*Cereus giganteus* or *Carnegiea gigantea*) trees. Some of the climbing tropical species—such as those of the leaf cactus (*Epiphyllum*) and some species of *Rhipsalis*—have thin, flattened stems. Regardless of its shape, degree of elongation, or branching, the cactus stem is succulent (having fleshy, moisture-conserving tissue) and greatly enlarged as storage tissue. The appearance of the plant varies also according to whether the stem surface is smooth or ornamented with protruding tubercles, ridges, or grooves.

Distribution. The Cactaceae are native through most of the length of North and South America, from British Columbia and Alberta southward. The northernmost limit is along the Peace River in Canada; the southernmost limit extends far into Chile and Argentina. The only representatives of the family possibly native to the Old World are members of the genus *Rhipsalis*, occurring in East Africa, Madagascar, and Ceylon. Whether these plants are native or were introduced in these tropical areas is a matter of disagreement, as is the possibility of dispersal of this highly specialized group from the Western Hemisphere to the Eastern Hemisphere.

Various species of *Opuntia* and some other genera have been introduced into the Mediterranean region, and some have grown wild there since shortly after the discovery of America. Species of *Opuntia* are widely naturalized in India, the Malayan region, Hawaii, and Australia. In Australia and eastern Cape Province in South Africa, they have become pests difficult to eradicate.

Natural history. *Life cycle.* The characteristic feature of cactus seedlings is the pair of large seed leaves (cotyledons), which tend to be succulent, sometimes markedly so. From seed some species reach the flowering stage in two or three years, and both flowers and fruits may be developed even on stems that still retain juvenile characters. (This curious feature led to the naming of many supposed species on the basis of plants that seemed to be mature because of reproduction but that did not have the expected type of spines.)

Usually within a few years the succulent stem assumes the characteristic form and appendages for the species. In the prickly pears, in which the adult stem is composed of flattened joints arranged end to end, the portion developed in the first year of growth is cylinder-like for several months, the upper portion gradually becoming flattened, and the joints developed later being flat.

Most cacti reach a considerable relative size within five or ten years, but some grow much slower. Information concerning the age of older plants usually is lacking because the woody parts are very thin; counting of growth rings requires sectioning and careful study with a compound microscope. The saguaro, or giant cactus, is estimated to attain ages in the hundreds of years.

Pollination is mostly by insects or birds, though sometimes by other animals such as bats. Because there is no precise mechanism governing the pathway of pollinators, the process of pollination tends to be haphazard, at least in most of the larger flowers of the open as opposed to the tubular types. Most flowers open in the daytime and are visited by day-flying insects or birds, but many, and especially such species as the saguaro and the various species of *Cereus*, open at night. As with other night-pollinated plants the night blooming cacti tend to be white flowered.

Ecology. Cacti are admirably adapted to dry environmental conditions through such features as the thick water-retaining stem, extensive root system, and lack of leaves.

Adaptations to arid conditions

The stems of prickly pears concentrate water over the flat surfaces of the joints that either drips or streams from the curved lower margins, thereby increasing the amount of water in the soil just under the plant. Some species of cacti have spines that point downward; water collected on the spines, even from light mists, is directed in droplets to the ground. The saguaro's downward-pointed spines during its earlier years of growth collect water and repel rodents that might eat the succulent stems to secure water. In older saguaros the stem above about the four- or five-foot level produces another not downward-directed type of spine. For plants growing near the lower edge of a rock or a crack between rocks, the amount of water available from a relatively light rain may be greatly increased, as it would for a plant living under the edge of a roof.

The root systems of cacti are shallow and widespreading. They remain receptive to moisture through many months of dry weather and immediately soak up even the scantiest rainfall. Substances from the roots of some desert plants, and perhaps some of the cacti, prevent the invasion of any other plants nearby, thus increasing the chance of continued survival for established plants. The absence of leaves reduces the ratio of plant surface to internal plant volume, as does the thickening of the stems, thus aiding water retention.

Within their natural range, cacti occur in a wide variety of soil types. Frequently, a species is restricted to a particular type of rock formation, such as limestone or igne-

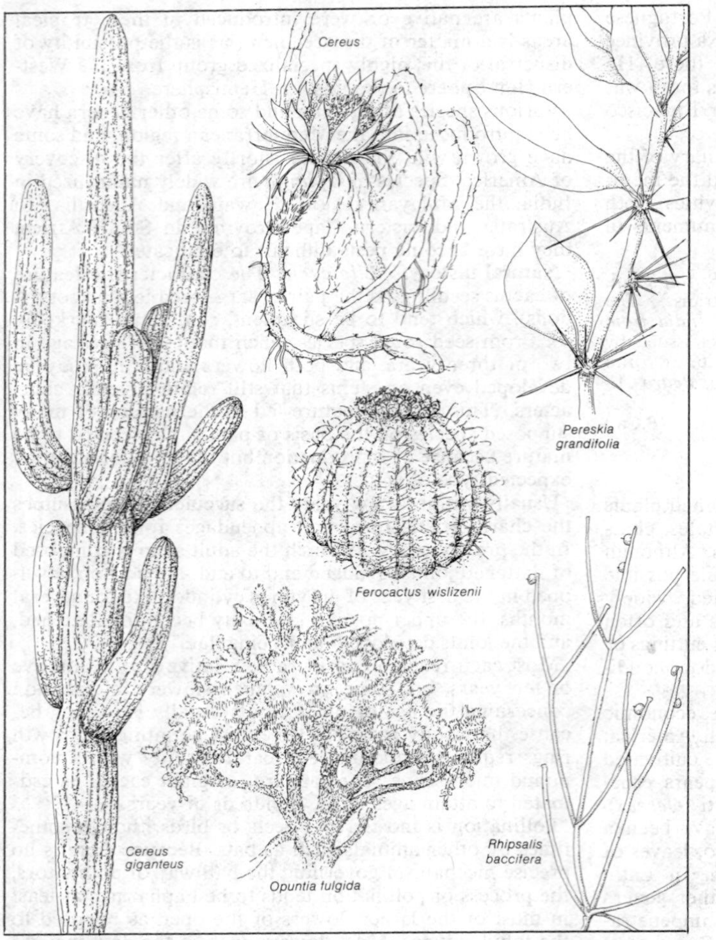

Representative cacti.
Drawing by M. Pahl

ous rock. A few species are confined to localized rock outcroppings, a limitation particularly striking in the genus *Pediocactus*, in which eight of its 11 species are found on special rock ledges on the Colorado Plateau or on gypsum-rich soil.

Some species are associated with tropical rain forests, as in the Everglades in Florida, where species of *Opuntia* and *Cereus* occur at points at which the water table may be only a few inches below the surface. Most species are sensitive to cold, but many grow in regions with cold winters, as in the United States on the Great Plains and in the Great Basin and the Rocky Mountains.

Form and function. *Vegetative characteristics.* Many other plants, succulent and essentially leafless, are often confused with cacti. A large group of spurges (*Euphorbia* species) occurring in Africa includes many plants with long cylindroid stems similar in appearance to cacti. These plants, common in cultivation, are distinguished readily by their milky juice, a feature rare in cacti and supposedly absent in cacti with elongated stems. Yuccas and the century plants (*Agave* species) often are confused with cacti, but they are distinguished readily by succulence of the leaves rather than the stems.

Distinctive structure

Cacti can be distinguished from all other succulent plants by the presence of spines in areoles, special clearly defined areas, each developed from a lateral bud of the stem. Areoles are universal in the cactus family (at least in the juvenile phase) and have so far not been found in any other plant family. Almost all species of cactus have tufts of stiff sharp spines. In some species the mature plant may not have spines, but it does have areoles, which are filled with hair or sharp, barbed structures called glochids. The more obvious characters of the cactus family, in combination with areoles, are reduction or lack of leaves, unusual floral formation, and distinctive fruit and seed.

The leaves, if discernible, are reduced in size (except in *Pereskia*, as indicated above). In *Opuntia* they appear only on young joints of the stem and fall off after a month or more of growth. They are relatively small and succulent and range from conical to elongated and cylindroid. In most genera the leaves are not visible to the unaided eye but are represented by a hump of tissue just below a spine-bearing areole.

Reproductive characteristics. Frequently the flowers are large, attractive, and white or brightly coloured. All the genera have a floral tube that invests the ovary, and, except in *Pereskia*, adheres to its surface. The portion of the tube covering the ovary usually develops small, inconspicuous scales, which increase gradually in size upward on the free portion of the floral tube above the ovary. They grade into sepaloid flower parts and, farther up, into petaloid parts. There are many conspicuous stamens (pollen-bearing organs) and three to 20 or more stigmas (parts that receive pollen) arising from a single style. In some groups, especially *Opuntia*, there is only a short floral tube above the ovary, but in others, as with some species of *Cereus*, the tube may be very long. The fusion of the floral tube with the surface of the ovary occurs in all species of cacti except *Pereskia* and in many other flowering plants. A flower which has this feature is described as epigynous, and its ovary is said to be inferior.

The ovary and the investing floral tube may develop into a fleshy and often edible fruit. It is one-chambered, and the numerous ovules borne on the walls give rise to numerous seeds. The ovules usually are campylotropous; that is, curved between the hilum (point of attachment to the stalk) and the opening through which the pollen tube enters (micropyle).

The flowers usually are associated with a spine-bearing areole, but in *Mammillaria* (fishhook cacti) they may be produced in a special areole between the elongated tubercles of the stem surface or they may be in this position but have no visible connection with an areole. The flowers develop either inside the spine-bearing part of the areole or in an area either merging with it or remote from it and connected by an isthmus.

Evolution and relationships. Because of the lack of fossils, the evolutionary course of the cacti is difficult to trace. One *Opuntia*-like fossil has been uncovered, but evidence suggests that it may not represent a cactus at all. Primitive living cacti may suggest lineage. The greatest number of primitive features is preserved in *Pereskia.* The flowers of some species are perigynous (floral tube surrounds the ovary) instead of epigynous; the stems are only moderately succulent; the leaves, though succulent, are similar to those of many other plants. The wood and reproductive parts reveal other primitive features. Of particular significance is the similarity of the carpels of *Pereskia pititache* to those of the primitive tropical woody plants of the buttercup order of other taxonomic systems (Ranales). The carpels are unsealed, which may indicate origin of the cacti from a very primitive stock and an early separation in evolutionary development from the Ranales or from developmental lines ancestral to the Ranales and to related groups. One of these lines of development may have branched off long ago to the ancestors of the order Caryophyllales, as indicated by the features held in common between that order and the cacti.

Origin of cacti

The numerous differences between these two groups indicates that they separated as far back as the Late Mesozoic Era (about 130,000,000 years ago).

Classification. *Distinguishing taxonomic features.* The features used in separating cacti from other succulents are listed above (see *Form and function*). The family Cactaceae apparently is not closely related to any other plant family.

Annotated classification. The Cactaceae are considered by some authorities as the sole family of the order Cactales, as in this article. Certain plant taxonomists, however, group the Cactaceae with the families of the pink order (Caryophyllales). The proper disposition of the family, therefore, has not been clearly determined; unless future research reveals otherwise, it seems appropriate to consider it as constituting a distinct order.

ORDER CACTALES

Coextensive with the family Cactaceae.

Family Cactaceae

Stems succulent, ranging from minute to as much as 50 feet long and up to 2½ feet in diameter, smooth or covered with ribs and tubercles (knobby projections). Leaves usually absent in adult plants; when present, they are large, flat, and persistent (*Pereskia* and *Pereskiopsis*) or conical to cylindroidal and short-lived. Areoles are present in the leaf axils or their structural equivalents and are arranged spirally on the surface of a smooth stem or on the apices of the tubercles, when present, and bear spines (spines rarely absent on the adult stem but present in juvenile stages). Flowers and fruits develop within or associated with a spine-bearing areole. The flower, except in some species of *Pereskia*, is epigynous, but of different origin than the epigyny of other flowering plants; the floral tube is developed from the receptacle, usually bears scale leaves and areoles; the superior floral tube or cup (the part above and free from the ovary) sometimes tubular; scale leaves of the floral tube show a gradation into the sepaloid outer perianth parts and these grade into the petaloid inner perianth parts. Stamens are numerous, spirally arranged. Carpels (structures constituting the innermost whorl of the flower), from 3 to 20, are arranged in a circle; one style; stigmas as many as the carpels; the ovary at maturity with one chamber; numerous ovules and seeds; ovules usually campylotropous (curving between the hilum and the micropyle) or sometimes amphitropous or orthotropous. Fruit variable; seeds of various colours (usually brown, black, reddish, gray, or white) and shapes. From 800 to 1,500 valid species. Distributional centres—Mexico and the South American deserts. The better known genera include *Melocactus* (melon-thistle, or Turk's-cap, cactus), *Ferocactus* and *Echinocactus* (barrel cacti), *Echinocereus* (hedgehog cactus), *Cereus* (torch cactus), *Mammillaria* and *Coryphantha* (fishhook, or pincushion, cacti), *Epiphyllum* (leaf cactus), *Opuntia* (prickly pears and chollas), and *Pereskia.*

Critical appraisal. The cacti stand alone, not being related closely to any other group of flowering plants. They do share some features in common with the orders Ranales, Myrtales, Rosales, and others, but the relationship to any of them is not close.

Similarities to other plant groups

The order Cactales, consisting of the single family Cactaceae, has been included recently by several authorities in the Caryophyllales. This proposed alliance first arose from the obvious succulence of the Cactaceae and a subfamily of the family Aizoaceae. These families are similar to the cacti in features of the pollen grains, in the development of the embryo sac (megagametophyte), and in the campylotropus ovules with the food in reserve in the perisperm. In the cacti, however, the ovules may be in a variety of positions other than the campylotropous condition. Betacyanin pigments occur in the Caryophyllales as well as in the Cactaceae, indicating a link between the groups; they have been assumed to occur in no other groups of plants.

The Aizoaceae, despite similarities, lack a number of the characteristic features of the cacti. Leaves of the Aizoaceae usually are opposite; those of the Cactaceae are alternate. The leaves are conspicuously succulent, while in cacti the stems are succulent. The Aizoaceae do not have spines in areoles, as do cacti. The flowers are superficially similar, but in the Aizoaceae there are no leaves on the floral cup (tube) and leaves do not grade into sepaloid and petaloid parts. In the Aizoaceae the fruit has partitions at maturity, unlike the cacti. There is more than one style instead of the single style in the Cactaceae.

Similarities of the cacti and other groups, accompanied by numerous differences, indicate the derivation of these groups from a common ancestry. The major taxa and even the species of living flowering plants were mostly derived from ancestors that were wholly or partly displaced and that usually have become extinct, leaving no recognizable remains behind.

BIBLIOGRAPHY. For a conservative treatment of the genera, see F. VAUPEL, *Cactaceae* in A. ENGLER and K. PRANTL, *Die natürlichen Pflanzenfamilien*, 2nd ed., vol. 21, pp. 594–651 (1925); for a more radical but general consideration of the entire family, see N.L. BRITTON and J.N. ROSE, *The Cactaceae*, 4 vol. (1919–23; 1937; reprinted in 2 vol., 1963); a supplement to Britton and Rose's work, W.T. MARSHALL and T.M. BOCK, *Cactaceae* (1941); FRANZ BUXBAUM, *Morphology of Cacti*, 3 vol. (1950–55); and VERA HIGGINS, *The Study of Cacti*, 2nd ed. (1946); for a discussion of species native in the United States, see LYMAN BENSON, *The Cacti of Arizona*, 3rd ed. (1969); *The Native Cacti of California* (1969); and "Cactaceae," in C.L. LUNDELL, *Flora of Texas*, vol. 2 (1969).

The following works are of value for horticultural aspects: CURT BACKEBERG, *Die Cactaceae*, 6 vol. (1958–62), with good photographs of many species; J. BORG, *Cacti*, 4th ed. (1970); W. HAAGE, *Das praktische Kakteenbuch in Farben* (1961; rev. Eng. trans., *Cacti and Succulents: A Practical Handbook* 1963).

(L.Be.)

Caesar, Julius

A Roman general, dictator, and statesman, Caesar changed the course of the history of the Greco-Roman world decisively and irreversibly. The Greco-Roman society has been extinct for so long that most of the names of its great men mean little to the average, educated modern man. But Caesar's name, like Alexander's, is still on people's lips throughout the Christian and Islāmic worlds. Even people who know nothing of Caesar as a historic personality are familiar with his family name as a title signifying a ruler who is in some sense uniquely supreme or paramount—the meaning of *Kaiser* in German, *tsar* in the Slavonic languages, and *qayṣar* in the languages of the Islāmic world.

Caesar's gens (clan) name, Julius (Iulius), is also familiar in the Christian world; for in Caesar's lifetime the Roman month Quintilis, in which he was born, was renamed "July" in his honour. This name has survived Caesar's assassination and the fall of the Roman Empire. So has Caesar's reform of the calendar. The old Roman calendar was inaccurate and manipulated for political purposes. Caesar's calendar, the Julian calendar, is still partially in force in the Eastern Orthodox Christian countries; and the Gregorian calendar, now in use in the West, is the Julian, slightly corrected by Pope Gregory XIII.

FAMILY BACKGROUND AND EARLY CAREER

Caesar's gens, the Julii, were patricians; *i.e.*, members of Rome's original aristocracy, which had coalesced in the 4th century BC with a number of leading plebeian (commoner) families to form the nobility that had been the governing class in Rome since then. By Caesar's time, the number of surviving patrician gentes was small; and in the gens Julia the Caesares seem to have been the only surviving family. Though some of the most powerful noble families were patrician, patrician blood was no longer a political advantage; it was actually a handicap, since a patrician was debarred from holding the paraconstitutional but powerful office of tribune of the plebs. The Julii Caesares traced their lineage back to the goddess Venus, but the family was not snobbish or conservative-minded. It was also not rich or influential or even distinguished.

Alinari

Caesar, marble bust. In the Capitoline Museum, Rome.

A Roman noble won distinction for himself and his family by securing election to a series of public offices, which culminated in the consulship, with the censorship possibly to follow. This was a difficult task for even the ablest and most gifted noble unless he was backed by substantial family wealth and influence. Rome's victory over Carthage in the Second Punic War (218–201 BC) had made Rome the paramount power in the Mediterranean basin; an influential Roman noble family's clients (that is, protégés who, in return, gave their patrons their political support) might include kings and even whole nations, besides numerous private individuals. The requirements and the costs of a Roman political career in Caesar's day were high, and the competition was severe; but the potential profits were of enormous magnitude. One of the perquisites of the praetorship and the consulship was the government of a province, which gave ample opportunities for plunder. The whole Mediterranean world was, in fact, at the mercy of the Roman nobility and of a new class of Roman businessmen, the equities ("knights"), which had grown rich on military contracts and on tax farming.

Military manpower was supplied by the Roman peasantry. This class had been partly dispossessed by an economic revolution following on the devastation caused by the Second Punic War. The Roman governing class had consequently come to be hated and discredited at home and abroad. From 133 onward there had been a series of alternate revolutionary and counter-revolutionary paroxysms. It was evident that the present misgovernment of the Roman state and the Greco-Roman world by the Roman nobility could not continue indefinitely and it was fairly clear that the most probable alternative was some form of military dictatorship backed by dispossessed Italian peasants who had turned to long-term military service.

The traditional competition among members of the Roman nobility for office and the spoils of office was thus threatening to turn into a desperate race for seizing autocratic power. The Julii Caesares did not seem to be in the running. It was true that Sextus Caesar, who was perhaps the dictator's uncle, had been one of the consuls for 91; and Lucius Caesar, one of the consuls for 90, was a distant cousin, whose son and namesake was consul for 64. In 90, Rome's Italian allies had seceded from Rome because of the Roman government's obstinate refusal to grant them Roman citizenship, and, as consul, Lucius Caesar had introduced emergency legislation for granting citizenship to the citizens of all Italian ally states that had not taken up arms or that had returned to their allegiance. The Julii Caesares

Whoever had been consul in this critical year would have had to initiate such legislation, whatever his personal political predilections. There is evidence, however, that the Julii Caesares, though patricians, had already committed themselves to the antinobility party. An aunt of the future dictator had married Gaius Marius, a self-made man (*novus homo*) who had forced his way up to the summit by his military ability and had made the momentous innovation of recruiting his armies from the dispossessed peasants.

The date of Caesar the dictator's birth has long been disputed. The day was July 12 or 13; the traditional (and perhaps most probable) year is 100; but if this date is correct, Caesar must have held each of his offices two years in advance of the legal minimum age. His father, Gaius Caesar, died when Caesar was but 16; his mother, Aurelia, was a notable woman, and it seems certain that he owed much to her.

In spite of the inadequacy of his resources, Caesar seems to have chosen a political career as a matter of course. From the beginning, he probably privately aimed at winning office, not just for the sake of the honours but in order to achieve the power to put the misgoverned Roman state and Greco-Roman world into better order in accordance with ideas of his own. It is improbable that Caesar deliberately sought monarchical power until after he had crossed the Rubicon in 49, though sufficient power to impose his will, as he was determined to do, proved to mean monarchical power.

In 84 Caesar committed himself publicly to the radical side by marrying Cornelia, a daughter of Lucius Cornelius Cinna, a noble who was Marius' associate in revolution. In 83 Lucius Cornelius Sulla returned to Italy from the East and led the successful counter-revolution of 83–82; Sulla then ordered Caesar to divorce Cornelia. Caesar refused and came close to losing not only his property (such as it was) but his life as well. He found it advisable to remove himself from Italy and to do military service, first in the province of Asia and then in Cilicia. Sulla

In 78, after Sulla's death, he returned to Rome and started on his political career in the conventional way, by acting as a prosecuting advocate—of course, in his case, against prominent Sullan counter-revolutionaries. His first target, Gnaeus Cornelius Dolabella, was defended by Quintus Hortensius, the leading advocate of the day, and was acquitted by the extortion-court jury, composed exclusively of senators.

Caesar then went to Rhodes to study oratory under a famous professor, Molon. En route he was captured by pirates (one of the symptoms of the anarchy into which the Roman nobility had allowed the Mediterranean world to fall). Caesar raised his ransom, raised a naval force, captured his captors, and had them crucified—all this as a private individual holding no public office. In 74, when Mithridates VI Eupator, king of Pontus, renewed war on the Romans, Caesar raised a private army to combat him.

In his absence from Rome, Caesar was made a member of the politico-ecclesiastical college of pontifices; and on his return he gained one of the elective military tribuneships. Caesar now worked to undo the Sullan constitution in cooperation with Pompey (Gnaeus Pompeius), who had started his career as a lieutenant of Sulla but had changed sides since Sulla's death. In 69 or 68 Caesar was elected quaestor (the first rung on the Roman political ladder). In the same year his wife, Cornelia, and his aunt Julia, Marius' widow, died; in public funeral orations in their honour, Caesar found opportunities for praising Cinna and Marius. Caesar afterward married Pompeia, a distant relative of Pompey. Caesar served his quaestorship in the province of Farther Spain (modern Andalusia and Portugal).

Caesar as political figure

Caesar was elected one of the curule aediles for 65, and he celebrated his tenure of this office by unusually lavish expenditure with borrowed money. He was elected pontifex maximus in 63 by a political dodge. By now he had become a controversial political figure. After the suppression of Catiline's conspiracy in 63, Caesar, as well as the millionaire Marcus Licinius Crassus, was accused of complicity. It seems unlikely that either of them had committed himself to Catiline; but Caesar proposed in the Senate a more merciful alternative to the death penalty, which the consul Cicero was asking for the arrested conspirators. In the uproar in the Senate, Caesar's motion was defeated.

Caesar was elected a praetor for 62. Toward the end of the year of his praetorship, a scandal was caused by Publius Clodius in Caesar's house at the celebration there of the rites, for women only, of Bona Dea (a Roman deity of fruitfulness, both in the Earth and in women). Caesar consequently divorced Pompeia. He obtained the governorship of Farther Spain for 61–60. His creditors did not let him leave Rome until Crassus had gone bail for a quarter of his debts; but a military expedition beyond the northwest frontier of his province enabled Caesar to win loot for himself as well as for his soldiers, with a balance left over for the treasury. This partial financial recovery enabled him, after his return to Rome in 60, to stand for the consulship for 59.

The first triumvirate and the conquest of Gaul. The value of the consulship lay in the lucrative provincial governorship to which it would normally lead. On the eve of the consular elections for 59, the Senate sought to allot to the two future consuls for 59, as their proconsular provinces, the unprofitable supervision of forests and cattle trails in Italy. The Senate also secured by massive bribery the election of an anti-Caesarean, Marcus Calpurnius Bibulus. But they failed to prevent Caesar's election as the other consul.

Caesar now succeeded in organizing an irresistible coalition of political bosses. Pompey had carried out his mission to put the East in order with notable success, but after his return to Italy and his disbandment of his army in 62, the Senate had thwarted him—particularly by preventing him from securing land allotments for his veterans. Caesar, who had assiduously cultivated Pompey's friendship, now entered into a secret pact with him. Caesar's master stroke was to persuade Crassus to join the partnership, the so-called first triumvirate. Crassus—like Pompey, a former lieutenant of Sulla—had been one of the most active of Pompey's obstructors so far. Only Caesar, on good terms with both, was in a position to reconcile them. Early in 59, Pompey sealed his alliance with Caesar by marrying Caesar's only child, Julia. Caesar married Calpurnia, daughter of Lucius Piso, who became consul in 58.

As consul, Caesar introduced a bill for the allotment of Roman public lands in Italy, on which the first charge was to be a provision for Pompey's soldiers. The bill was vetoed by three tribunes of the plebs, and Caesar's colleague Bibulus announced his intention of preventing the transaction of public business by watching the skies for portents whenever the public assembly was convened. Caesar then cowed the opposition by employing some of Pompey's veterans to make a riot, and the distribution was carried out. Pompey's settlement of the East was ratified *en bloc* by an act negotiated by an agent of Caesar, the tribune of the plebs Publius Vatinius. Caesar himself initiated a noncontroversial and much-needed act for punishing misconduct by governors of provinces.

Another act negotiated by Vatinius gave Caesar Cisalpine Gaul (between the Alps, the Apennines, and the Adriatic) and Illyricum. His tenure was to last until Feb. 28, 54. When the governor-designate of Transalpine Gaul suddenly died, this province, also, was assigned to Caesar at Pompey's instance. Cisalpine Gaul gave Caesar a military recruiting ground; Transalpine Gaul gave him a springboard for conquests beyond Rome's northwest frontier.

Caesar's Roman strategy

Between 58 and 50, Caesar conquered the rest of Gaul up to the left bank of the Rhine and subjugated it so effectively that it remained passive under Roman rule throughout the Roman civil wars between 49 and 31. This achievement was all the more amazing, considering that the Romans did not possess any great superiority in military equipment over the north European barbarians. Indeed, the Gallic cavalry was probably superior to the Roman, horseman for horseman. Rome's military superiority lay in strategy, tactics, discipline, and military engineering. In Gaul, Rome also had the advantage of being able to deal separately with dozens of relatively small, independent states. Caesar conquered these piecemeal, and the concerted attempt made by a number of them in 52 to shake off the Roman yoke came too late.

Great though this achievement was, its relative importance in Caesar's career and in Roman history has been overestimated in Western tradition (as have his brief raids on Britain). In Caesar's mind his conquest of Gaul was probably carried out only a means to his ultimate end. He was acquiring the military manpower, the plunder, and the prestige that he needed to secure a free hand for the prosecution of the task of reorganizing the Roman state and the rest of the Greco-Roman world. This final achievement of Caesar's looms much larger than his conquest of Gaul, when it is viewed in the wider setting of world history and not just in the narrower setting of the Greco-Roman civilization's present daughter civilization in the West.

In 58 Rome's northwestern frontier, established in 125, ran from the Alps down the left bank of the upper Rhône River to the Pyrenees, skirting the southeastern foot of the Cévennes and including the upper basin of the Garonne River without reaching the Gallic shore of the Atlantic. In 58 Caesar intervened beyond this line, first to drive back the Helvetii, who had been migrating westward from their home in what is now central Switzerland. He then crushed Ariovistus, a German soldier of fortune from beyond the Rhine. In 57 Caesar subdued the distant and warlike Belgic group of Gallic peoples in the north, while his lieutenant Publius Licinius Crassus subdued what are now the regions of Normandy and Brittany.

In 56 the Veneti, in what is now southern Brittany, started a revolt in the northwest that was supported by the still unconquered Morini on the Gallic coast of the Straits of Dover and the Menapii along the south bank of the lower Rhine. Caesar reconquered the Veneti with some difficulty and treated them barbarously. He could not finish off the conquest of the Morini and Menapii before the end of the campaigning season of 56; and in the winter of 56–55 the Menapii were temporarily expelled from their home by two immigrant German peoples, the Usipetes and Tencteri. These peoples were exterminated by Caesar in 55. In the same year he bridged the Rhine just below Koblenz to raid Germany on the other side of the river, and then crossed the Channel to raid Britain. In 54 he raided Britain again and subdued a serious revolt in northeastern Gaul. In 53 he subdued further revolts in Gaul and bridged the Rhine again for a second raid.

Vercingetorix

The crisis of Caesar's Gallic war came in 52. The peoples of central Gaul found a national leader in the Arvernian Vercingetorix. They planned to cut off the

Roman forces from Caesar, who had been wintering on the other side of the Alps. They even attempted to invade the western end of the old Roman province of Gallia Transalpina. Vercingetorix wanted to avoid pitched battles and sieges and to defeat the Romans by cutting off their supplies—partly by cavalry operations and partly by "scorched earth"—but he could not persuade his countrymen to adopt this painful policy wholeheartedly.

The Bituriges insisted on standing siege in their town Avaricum (Bourges), and Vercingetorix was unable to save it from being taken by storm within one month. Caesar then besieged Vercingetorix in Gergovia near modern Clermont-Ferrand. A Roman attempt to storm Gergovia was repulsed and resulted in heavy Roman losses—the first outright defeat that Caesar had suffered in Gaul. Caesar then defeated an attack on the Roman army on the march and was thus able to besiege Vercingetorix in Alesia, to the northwest of Dijon. Alesia, like Gergovia, was a position of great natural strength, and a large Gallic army came to relieve it; but this army was repulsed and dispersed by Caesar, and Vercingetorix then capitulated.

During the winter of 52–51 and the campaigning season of 51, Caesar crushed a number of sporadic further revolts. The most determined of these rebels were the Bellovaci, between the rivers Seine and Somme, around Beauvais. Another rebel force stood siege in the south in the natural fortress of Uxellodunum (perhaps the Puy d'Issolu on the Dordogne) until its water supply gave out. Caesar had the survivors' hands cut off. He spent the year 50 in organizing the newly conquered territory. After that, he was ready to settle his accounts with his opponents at home.

Antecedents and outcome of the civil war of 49–45. During his conquest of Gaul, Caesar had been equally busy in preserving and improving his position at home. He used part of his growing wealth from Gallic loot to hire political agents in Rome.

Dissolution of the triumvirate

Meanwhile the cohesion of the triumvirate had been placed under strain. Pompey had soon become restive toward his alarmingly successful ally Caesar, as had Crassus toward his old enemy Pompey. The alliance was patched up in April 56 at a conference at Luca (Lucca), just inside Caesar's province of Cisalpine Gaul. It was arranged that Pompey and Crassus were to be the consuls for 55 and were to get laws promulgated prolonging Caesar's provincial commands for another five years and giving Crassus a five-year term in Syria and Pompey a five-year term in Spain. These laws were duly passed. Crassus was then eliminated by an annihilating defeat at the Parthians' hands in 53. The marriage link between Pompey and Caesar had been broken by Julia's death in 54. After this, Pompey irresolutely veered further and further away from Caesar, until, when the breach finally came, Pompey found himself committed to the nobility's side, though he and the nobility never trusted each other.

The issue was whether there should or should not be an interval between the date at which Caesar was to resign his provincial governorships and, therewith, the command over his armies and the date at which he would enter his proposed second consulship. If there were to be an interval, Caesar would be a private person during that time, vulnerable to attack by his enemies; if prosecuted and convicted, he would be ruined politically and might possibly lose his life. Caesar had to make sure that, until his entry on his second consulship, he should continue to hold at least one province with the military force to guarantee his security.

This issue had already been the object of a series of political manoeuvres and countermanoeuvres at Rome. The dates on which the issue turned are all in doubt. As had been agreed at Luca in 56, Caesar's commands had been prolonged for five years, apparently until Feb. 28, 49, but this is not certain. In 52, a year in which Pompey was elected sole consul and given a five-year provincial command in Spain, Caesar was allowed by a law sponsored by all ten tribunes to stand for the consulship *in absentia*. If he were to stand in 49 for the consulship for 48, he would be out of office, and therefore in danger, during the last ten months of 49. As a safeguard for Caesar against this, there seems to have been an understanding—possibly a private one at Luca in 56 between him and Pompey—that the question of a successor to Caesar in his commands should not be raised in the Senate before March 1, 50. This manoeuvre would have ensured that Caesar would retain his commands until the end of 49. However, the question of replacing Caesar was actually raised in the Senate a number of times from 51 onward; each time Caesar had the dangerous proposals vetoed by tribunes of the plebs who were his agents—particularly Gaius Scribonius Curio in 50 and Mark Antony in 49.

The issue was brought to a head by one of the consuls for 50, Gaius Claudius Marcellus. He obtained resolutions from the Senate that Caesar should lay down his command (presumably at its terminal date) but that Pompey should not lay down his command simultaneously. Curio then obtained on Dec. 1, 50, a resolution (by 370 votes to 22) that both men should lay down their commands simultaneously. Next day Marcellus (without authorization from the Senate) offered the command over all troops in Italy to Pompey, together with the power to raise more; and Pompey accepted. On Jan. 1, 49, the Senate received from Caesar a proposal that he and Pompey should lay down their commands simultaneously. Caesar's message was peremptory, and the Senate resolved that Caesar should be treated as a public enemy if he did not lay down his command "by a date to be fixed."

Caesar crosses the Rubicon

On Jan. 10–11, 49, Caesar led his troops across the little river Rubicon, the boundary between his province of Cisalpine Gaul and Italy proper. He thus committed the first act of war. This was not, however, the heart of the matter. The actual question of substance was whether the misgovernment of the Greco-Roman world by the Roman nobility should be allowed to continue or whether it should be replaced by an autocratic regime. Either alternative would result in a disastrous civil war. The subsequent partial recuperation of the Greco-Roman world under the principate suggests, however, that Caesarism was the lesser evil.

The civil war was a tragedy, for war was not wanted either by Caesar or by Pompey or even by a considerable part of the nobility, while the bulk of the Roman citizen body ardently hoped for the preservation of peace. By this time, however, the three parties that counted politically were all entrapped. Caesar's success in building up his political power had made the champions of the old regime so implacably hostile to him that he was now faced with a choice between putting himself at his enemies' mercy or seizing the monopoly of power at which he was accused of aiming. He found that he could not extricate himself from this dilemma by reducing his demands, as he eventually did, to the absolute minimum required for his security. As for Pompey, his growing jealousy of Caesar had led him so far toward the nobility that he could not come to terms with Caesar again without loss of face.

The first bout of the civil war moved swiftly. In 49 Caesar drove his opponents out of Italy to the eastern side of the Straits of Otranto. He then crushed Pompey's army in Spain. Toward the end of 49, he followed Pompey across the Adriatic and retrieved a reverse at Dyrrachium by winning a decisive victory at Pharsalus on Aug. 9, 48. Caesar pursued Pompey from Thessaly to Egypt, where he was murdered by an officer of King Ptolemy. Caesar wintered in Alexandria, fighting with the populace and dallying with Queen Cleopatra. In 47 he fought a brief local war in northeastern Anatolia with Pharnaces, king of the Cimmerian Bosporus, who was trying to regain his father Mithradates' kingdom of Pontus. Caesar's famous words, *Veni, vidi, vici* ("I came, I saw, I conquered"), are his own account of this campaign.

Caesar then returned to Rome, but a few months later,

now with the title of dictator, he left for Africa, where his opponents had rallied. In 46 he crushed their army at Thapsus and returned to Rome, only to leave in November for Farther Spain to deal with a fresh outbreak of resistance, which he crushed on March 17, 45, at Munda. He then returned to Rome to start putting the Greco-Roman world in order. He had less than a year's grace for this huge task of reconstruction before his assassination in the Senate House at Rome on March 15, 44 (the Ides of March).

Caesar's death

Caesar's death was partly due to his clemency and impatience, which, in combination, were dangerous for his personal security. Caesar had not hesitated to commit atrocities against "barbarians" when it had suited him, but he was almost consistently magnanimous in his treatment of his defeated Roman opponents. Thus clemency was probably not just a matter of policy. Caesar's earliest experience in his political career had been Sulla's implacable persecution of his defeated domestic opponents. Caesar amnestied his opponents wholesale and gave a number of them responsible positions in his new regime. Gaius Cassius Longinus, who was the moving spirit in the plot to murder him, and Marcus Junius Brutus, the symbolic embodiment of Roman republicanism, were both former enemies. *Et tu, Brute* ("You too, Brutus") was Caesar's expression of his particular anguish at being stabbed by a man whom he had forgiven, trusted, and loved.

There were, however, also a number of ex-Caesareans among the 60 conspirators. They had been goaded into this volte-face by the increasingly monarchical trend of Caesar's regime and, perhaps at least as much, by the aristocratic disdain that inhibited Caesar from taking any trouble to sugar the bitter pill. Some stood to lose, rather than to gain, personally by the removal of the autocrat who had made their political fortunes. But even if they were acting on principle, they were blind to the truth that the reign of the Roman nobility was broken beyond recall and that even Caesar might not have been able to overthrow the *ancien régime* if its destruction had not been long overdue. They also failed to recognize that by making Caesar a martyr they were creating his posthumous political fortune.

If Caesar had not been murdered in 44, he might have lived on for 15 or 20 years. His physical constitution was unusually tough, though in his last years he had several epileptic seizures. What would he have done with this time? The answer can only be guessed from what he did do in the few months available. He found time in the year 46 to reform the Roman calendar. In 45 he enacted a law laying down a standard pattern for the constitutions of the *municipia*, which were by this time the units of local self-government in most of the territory inhabited by Roman citizens. In 59 Caesar had already resurrected the city of Capua, which the republican Roman regime more than 150 years earlier had deprived of its juridical corporate personality; he now resurrected the other two great cities, Carthage and Corinth, that his predecessors had destroyed. This was only a part of what he did to resettle his discharged soldiers and the urban proletariat of Rome. He was also generous in granting Roman citizenship to aliens. (He had given it to all of Cisalpine Gaul, north of the Po, in 49.) He increased the size of the Senate and made its personnel more representative of the whole Roman citizenry.

At his death, Caesar was on the point of starting out on a new military campaign to avenge and retrieve Crassus' disastrous defeat in 53 by the Parthians. Would Caesar have succeeded in recapturing for the Greco-Roman world the extinct Seleucid monarchy's lost dominions east of the Euphrates, particularly Babylonia? The fate of Crassus' army had shown that the terrain in northern Mesopotamia favoured Parthian cavalry against Roman infantry. Would Caesar's military genius have outweighed this handicap? And would Rome's hitherto inexhaustible reservoir of military manpower have sufficed for this additional call upon it? Only guesses are possible, for Caesar's assassination condemned the Romans to another 13 years of civil war, and Rome would never again possess sufficient manpower to conquer and hold Babylonia.

PERSONALITY AND REPUTATION

Caesar was not and is not lovable. His generosity to defeated opponents, magnanimous though it was, did not win their affection. He won his soldiers' devotion by the victories that his intellectual ability, applied to warfare, brought them. Yet, though not lovable, Caesar was and is attractive, indeed fascinating. His political achievement required ability, in effect amounting to genius, in several different fields, including administration and generalship besides the minor arts of wire pulling and propaganda.

In all these, Caesar was a supreme virtuoso. But if he had not also been something more than this he would not have been the supremely great man that he undoubtedly was.

Caesar was great beyond—and even in conflict with—the requirements of his political ambition. He showed a human spiritual greatness in his generosity to defeated opponents, which was partly responsible for his assassination. (The merciless Sulla abdicated and died in his bed.)

Speeches and writings

Another field in which Caesar's genius went far beyond the requirements of his political ambition was his writings. Of these, his speeches, letters, and pamphlets are lost. Only his accounts (both incomplete and supplemented by other hands) of the Gallic War and the civil war survive. Caesar ranked as a masterly public speaker in an age in which he was in competition first with Hortensius and then with Cicero.

All Caesar's speeches and writings, lost and extant, apparently served political purposes. He turned his funeral orations for his wife and for his aunt to account, for political propaganda. His accounts of his wars are subtly contrived to make the unsuspecting reader see Caesar's acts in the light that Caesar chooses. The accounts are written in the form of terse, dry, factual reports that look impersonal and objective, yet every recorded fact has been carefully selected and presented. As for the lost *Anticato*, a reply to Cicero's eulogy of Caesar's dead opponent Marcus Porcius Cato, it is a testimony to Caesar's political insight that he made the time to write it, in spite of the overwhelming military, administrative, and legislative demands on him. He realized that Cato, in giving his life for his cause (46), had made himself posthumously into a much more potent political force than he had ever been in his lifetime. Caesar was right, from his point of view, to try to put salt on Cato's tail. He did not succeed, however. For the next 150 years, Cato the martyr continued to be a nuisance, sometimes a menace, to Caesar's successors.

The mark of Caesar's genius in his writings is that though they were written for propaganda they are nevertheless of outstanding literary merit. A reader who has seen through their prosaic purpose can ignore it and appreciate them as splendid works of art.

Caesar's most amazing characteristic is his energy, intellectual and physical. He prepared his seven books on the Gallic War for publication in 51 when he still had serious revolts in Gaul on his hands, and he wrote his books on the civil war and his *Anticato* in the hectic years between 49 and 44. His physical energy was of the same order. For instance, in the winter of 57–56 he found time to visit his third province, Illyria, as well as Cisalpine Gaul; and in the interval between his campaigns of 55 and 54 he transacted public business in Cisalpine Gaul and went to Illyria to settle accounts with the Pirustae, a turbulent tribe in what is now Albania. In 49 he marched, within a single campaigning season, from the Rubicon to Brundisium and from Brundisium to Spain. At Alexandria, probably aged 53, he saved himself from sudden death by his prowess as a swimmer.

Caesar's physical vitality perhaps partly accounts for his sexual incontinence. His sexual escapades were out of the ordinary, even by contemporary Greek and Roman standards. It was rumoured that during his first visit to the East he had had homosexual relations with King Nicomedes of Bithynia. The rumour is credible, though not proved, and was repeated throughout Caesar's life. There is no doubt of Caesar's heterosexual affairs, many of them with married women. Probably Caesar looked upon these as trivial recreations. Yet he involved himself at least twice in escapades that might have wrecked his career. If he did in fact have an affair with Pompey's wife, Mucia, he was risking his entente with Pompey. A more notorious, though not quite so hazardous, affair was his liaison with Cleopatra. By dallying with her at Alexandria he risked the loss of what he had just won at Pharsalus. By allowing her to visit him in Rome in 46 he flouted public feeling and added to the list of tactless acts that, cumulatively, goaded old comrades and amnestied enemies into assassinating him.

Caesar's achievement

This cool-headed man of genius with an erratic vein of sexual exuberance undoubtedly changed the course of history at the western end of the Old World. By liquidating the scandalous and bankrupt rule of the Roman nobility, he gave the Roman state—and with it the Greco-Roman civilization—a reprieve that lasted for more than 600 years in the East and for more than 400 years in the relatively backward West. Caesar substituted for the Roman oligarchy an autocracy that could never afterward be abolished. If he had not done this when he did, Rome and the Greco-Roman world might have succumbed, before the beginning of the Christian era, to barbarian invaders in the West and to the Parthian Empire in the East. The prolongation of the life of the Greco-Roman civilization had important historical effects. Under the Roman Empire the Near East was impregnated with Hellenism for six or seven more centuries. But for this the Hellenic element might not have been present in sufficient strength to make its decisive impact on Christianity and Islām. Gaul, too, would have sunk deeper into barbarism when the Franks overran it, if it had not been associated with the civilized Mediterranean world for more than 500 years as a result of Caesar's conquest.

Caesar's political achievement was limited. Its effects were confined to the western end of the Old World and were comparatively short-lived by Chinese or ancient Egyptian standards. The Chinese state founded by Shih Huang Ti in the 3rd century BC still stands, and its future may be still greater than its past. Yet, even if Caesar were to prove to have been of lesser stature than this Chinese colossus, he would still remain a giant by comparison with the common run of human beings (see also ROME, ANCIENT).

MAJOR WORKS

Military Commentaries: in seven books, *Commentarii de bello Gallico,* covering the years 58–52 BC, written in 52–51 BC (*The Gallic War,* 1917); in three books, *Commentarii de bello civili,* covering the year 49–48 BC, written probably in 45 BC (*The Civil Wars,* 1914; *Caesar's War Commentaries,* 1953).

De bello Alexandrino (*The Alexandrian War,* 1955); *De bello Africo* (*The African War,* 1955); and *De bello Hispaniensi* (*The Spanish War,* 1955), though ascribed by the manuscripts of Caesar, are generally regarded as of uncertain authorship. Caesar's speeches, letters, and pamphlets are all lost.

A translation of Caesar's works is available in the Loeb series (1914–55), and in the Penguin Classics series (1951 and 1967).

BIBLIOGRAPHY

Ancient works: CAESAR, *De bello Gallico,* books i–vii (Book viii, covering events of 51 BC, was written after Caesar's death by AULUS HIRTIUS), ed. by T. RICE HOLMES (1914); *De bello civili,* books i–iii. The *Bellum Alexandrinium* (the wars of 47 BC), ed. by F. KRANER *et al.,* 12th ed. (1959), *De bello Africo,* and *De bello Hispaniensi* are all anonymous but contemporary with Caesar and included with his works; CICERO, various letters and speeches (see CICERO, MARCUS TULLIUS: *Bibliography*); SALLUST, *Epistulae ad Caesarem* (the authenticity of these two memoranda addresses to Caesar has, however, been questioned); APPIAN, *Civil Wars,* book ii; CASSIUS DIO, books xxxvii–xliv; PLUTARCH, *Lives of Caesar, Pompey, and Crassus;* SUETONIUS, *Divus Julius;* VELLEIUS PATERCULUS, ii, 41–56.

Modern works: THEODOR MOMMSEN, *Römische Geschichte,* 3 vol. (1854–56; Eng. trans., *The History of Rome,* vol. 4–5, rev. ed., 1895); G. FERRERO, *Grandezza e decadenza di Roma,* 5 vol. (1902–07; Eng. trans., *The Greatness and Decline of Rome,* vol. 1–2, 1907–09); T.R.E. HOLMES, *Caesar's Conquest of Gaul,* 2nd ed. (1911), and *Ancient Britain and the Invasions of Julius Caesar,* esp. ch. 6–8, 2nd ed. (1936); E. MEYER, *Caesars Monarchie und das Principat des Pompejus,* 3rd ed. (1922); M. CARY *et al.,* in *Cambridge Ancient History,* vol. 9, ch. 11–13 and 15–18 (1932); J. CARCOPINO, *Histoire romaine,* vol. 2, *César,* 2nd ed. (1940); R. SYME, *The Roman Revolution* (1939); L.R. TAYLOR, *Party Politics in the Age of Caesar* (1949); M. GELZER, *Caesar: Der Politiker und Staatsmann,* 6th ed. (1960; Eng. trans., *Caesar: Politician and Statesman,* 1968); and A.H. MCDONALD, *Republican Rome* (1966).

(A.J.T.)

Cairo

Cairo (al-Qāhirah, meaning Victorious), capital of Egypt, with more than 5,000,000 people and a metropolitan population of more than 8,000,000 in the early 1980s, is Africa's largest city. This ancient metropolis (more than 1,000 years on the same site with the same name) stands on the banks of the Nile, primarily on the eastern shore, some 500 miles (800 kilometres) downstream from the Aswān High Dam, and just before the lower Nile separates into the Rosetta and Damietta branches.

The environment

Cairo is a place of vivid contrasts. Along the well-irrigated shoreline, lush tropical vegetation, tall palms, flowering flame trees, and white skyscrapers are profiled against a cloudless sky; the older inland quarters to the east, beneath the foothills of the Arabian Desert and the rocky promontories of the Muqaṭṭam Hills and the Red Mountain (al-Jabal al-Aḥmar, with its petrified forest), are brown- and ochre-coloured. The typical desert climate contrasts daytime dry heat (summer highs, 90°–110° F [32°–43° C]) with cool summer nights (65°–75° F [18°–24° C]) freshened by Nile breezes. During the brief winter, days are warmed by the strong Tropic of Cancer sun, but nights are quite cool and often damp. A healthful climate has long made Cairo a renowned winter resort.

The city juxtaposes ancient and new, East and West. The Great Pyramids near Memphis stand at the southwestern edge of the metropolis, and an obelisk in the northeast marks the site of Heliopolis (where Plato once studied); among modern landmarks are the elegant Sheraton and Meridien hotels overlooking the Nile. Between these extremes are other architectural monuments dating from Roman, Arab, and Turkish times. In addition to department stores, cinemas, hotels, and town houses, Cairo contains a large functioning bazaar and an extensive medieval city liberally endowed with more than 400 registered historic monuments (mosques, mausoleums, crenelated walls, and massive gateways) dating from AD 130 to the early 19th century—the largest number in any African or Middle Eastern city.

Inhabitants are equally diverse. Africans, Turks, and Arabs have long mingled at this geographic crossroad. Unsophisticated peasants from the rural hinterland pass bankers, lawyers, and turbanned shaykhs. Some workers run steel mills and textile factories, while others hand hammer and inlay delicate metal trays in tiny workshops. A small proportion of women still wrap themselves in black, but fashionable pantsuits are as common. The crowded streets form a common meeting ground for all these various elements.

HISTORY

Although ruined Memphis, 14 miles south of Cairo, was a metropolis 5,000 years ago, and about 2,000 years ago the Romans occupied a town on the site of Cairo called Babylon (now the Miṣr al-Qadīmah quarter), the seed from which contemporary Cairo sprang was the town of al-Fusṭāṭ, founded in AD 641 by ʿAmr ibn al-ʿĀṣ, commander of the Arabs who brought Islām to Egypt. Successor dynasties added royal suburbs (al-ʿAskar, founded in 750 by the Umayyads; al-Qaṭāʾiʿ, founded in 870 by Aḥmad ibn Ṭūlūn) to the increasingly prosperous commercial and industrial port city of al-Fusṭāṭ. Little remains of these early developments in the southern part of the city, except the tower of Trajan (AD 130), the mosques of ʿAmr ibn al-ʿĀṣ (641) and Aḥmad ibn Ṭūlūn (878), and the partially excavated mounds covering the site of al-Fusṭāṭ.

The Mosque of as-Sulṭān Ḥasan, built c. 1361, with modern Cairo in the background.
Annan Photo Features

In 969 adherents of a dissident Islāmic sect, the Fāṭimids, invaded Egypt from what is now Tunisia. The conquering general, Jawhar, established a new rectangular walled city northeast of existing settlements. Initially named al-Manṣūrīyah, the city was rechristened al-Qāhirah in 973–974 when the Fāṭimid caliph al-Muʿizz arrived to make it the capital of a dynasty that lasted for 200 years. Al-Qāhirah and al-Fusṭāṭ coexisted until 1168, when unfortified al-Fusṭāṭ was set on fire to protect Cairo from the crusaders. The crusaders were driven off by a Sunnī (orthodox Islāmic) army from Syria, after which the victorious commander, Saladin, founded the Ayyūbid dynasty, which controlled a vast empire from Cairo.

The Mamlūk era

Even though al-Fusṭāṭ was partially rebuilt, Cairo was transformed from a royal enclave into an imperial city. Saladin further extended the 11th-century walls built by a high official called Badr al-Jamālī (the northern and southern walls and three main gates, Bāb al-Futuḥ, Bāb an-Naṣr, and Bāb Zuwaylah, are still extant) and constructed a citadel on the Muqaṭṭam spur (now dominated by the Muḥammad ʿAlī Mosque). After 1260, when Baybars I became the first Mamlūk sultan of undisputed legitimacy, Cairo served as the capital of the Mamlūk empire, which governed Egypt and the Fertile Crescent until 1516.

Medieval Cairo reached its apogee during the Mamlūk era. By about 1340, almost 500,000 people lived in an area five times greater than the original Fāṭimid walled city, and Cairo had become the greatest city of Africa, Europe, and Asia Minor. Its al-Azhar University was the principal seat of Islāmic learning. The city was a key link in the profitable East–West spice trade and the recipient of tribute from a wealthy empire. Most of Cairo's greatest architectural masterpieces were built during this epoch.

Decline set in thereafter—sporadically at first, and then precipitously. The population was decimated by plagues, including the Black Death in 1348. Timur Lenk (Tamerlane) ravaged the eastern frontier in about 1400. The spice trade monopoly was broken by Vasco da Gama's voyage to India (1498). Finally, political autonomy was lost to the conquering Turks, who, after 1517, reduced Cairo to a provincial capital. In 1798, when Napoleon's campaigns brought him to Cairo, less than 300,000 people were living in the city and its two port suburbs, Miṣr al-Qadīmah and Būlāq. The Turks returned after Napoleon's defeat in 1801. In 1805 Muḥammad ʿAli, commander of an Albanian contingent, was appointed pasha, thus founding the dynasty that ruled Egypt until his great-great-grandson, Farouk I, abdicated in 1952.

Modern urban growth began in the 1830s, but only during Ismāʿīl's reign (1863–79) was the city fundamentally transformed. Eager to westernize Cairo and influenced by Baron Haussmann's renovation of Paris, Ismāʿīl ordered the construction of a European-style city to the west of the medieval core. French city-planning methods dominated the design of the districts of Azbakīyah (with its new park), ʿAbdīn, and Ismāʿīlīyah—all now central zones of contemporary Cairo. By the end of the century these districts were well developed, but with the rise of British hegemony from 1882 onward, they became transformed into a colonial enclave. Following the overthrow of the monarchy in 1952, however, the number and power of foreign residents declined.

During the 20th century Cairo grew spectacularly in both population and area. Transport improvements fostered the growth of suburban Heliopolis and al-Maʿādī; flood control permitted riverfront development; bridges encouraged settlement of islands (Rawḍah and az-Zamālik) and of the western bank. By mid-century the city was growing northward into the fertile Delta, a trend further encouraged by industrialization. The most dramatic postrevolution addition to Cairo is Naṣr City, a planned community reclaimed from the desert near Heliopolis, which has the capacity to house some 500,000 residents.

THE CONTEMPORARY CITY

Cairo is fan-shaped, narrowest in the south, where the river valley is wedged between desert escarpments, and widest in the north, where the valley blends into the Delta. Expansion into the desert is blocked by terrain and by the expense of irrigation. Over the centuries the city grew toward the river, on the newly flood-free land left by a receding river channel, chiefly on the east bank. Recently, however, in response to heightened demand, the city has been elongated to the north and south and has developed an expanding annex on the western shore.

The governorate (*muḥāfaẓah*) of Cairo is one of 25 major districts into which Egypt is administratively divided. The boundaries of the governorate do not encompass the entire urbanized area of the metropolis and include some agricultural zones. Ḥulwān, an industrial satellite in the extreme south, is included, but the industrial satellites in the far north (such as Shubrā al-Khaymah) and the developed western bank are excluded. At least 300,000,000 people live in the urbanized area outside the governorate boundaries.

The organization of the metropolitan complex is under-

Sectors of the city

standable only in the context of the city's history. The three oldest areas constitute an interior slum virtually surrounding the westernized core. The largest of these is the Fāṭimid city with its pre-19th-century extensions (al-Jamālīyah, ad-Darb al-Aḥmar, Bāb ash-Shaʿriyah, eastern as-Saiyīdah Zīnab, northern al-Khalīfah). In this densely settled zone containing the oldest buildings are most of Cairo's historic monuments, from the Mosque of Baybars I at the northern edge to Saladin's Citadel in the south. Among the major bazaars near al-Azhar Mosque in the central walled city are the Khān al-Khalīlī (1390) and the markets for gold articles, copper ware, textiles, rugs, amber, spices, and leather goods. Two major thoroughfares run north–south: Muʿizz li-Dīn Allāh, which bisects the old city and contains the major mosques and markets; and Khalīj Street (now Port Said), which runs along the bed of an ancient canal that once marked the western border of Fāṭimid Cairo. Only two streets connect the old city with the modern central business district: Mūskī Street (built in the 19th century) and al-Azhar Street (1931). A final diagonal, Qalʿah Street, formerly Boulevard Muḥammad ʿAlī, built in 1874, links the central business district with the Citadel. Most other streets are narrow and twisting and they often dead-end. Motor vehicles are confined to major thoroughfares.

The other two old quarters are Būlāq and Miṣr al-Qadīmah (al-Fusṭāṭ), formerly port suburbs of Cairo. Būlāq, an island until 1340 and the main port by 1560, became an industrial quarter in the early 19th century. It contains small workshops, the National Press, textile factories, and trade schools. A poor population, including many village migrants, is housed there at extremely high densities (about 171,000 persons per square mile [66,000 per square kilometre]). The mosques of Abū al-ʿAlā' and Sinān Pasha are among the few historic buildings remaining. Miṣr al-Qadīmah is an even poorer quarter, although only a small section is ancient. The walled compound of Babylon, with its semi-submerged Roman bastion, its Coptic churches and museum, and its ancient synagogue and houses, is virtually intact, as is the reconstructed ʿAmr Mosque nearby. The area is inhabited by extremely poor town dwellers, by potters whose simple kilns overlook ruined al-Fusṭāṭ, and by farmers who till the rich soil between Cairo and Ḥulwān. Only suburban al-Maʿādī, built by the British, interposes a contemporary note.

In sharp contrast is the modern downtown area of Cairo (Azbakīyah) and the elegant associated commercial-residential sections of Ismāʿīlīyah, Qaṣr an-Nīl, and Garden City, which stretch between the old city and the Nile and spread onto the island of az-Zamālik just offshore. Particularly along the river, near the Qaṣr an-Nīl bridge (still flanked by statues of lions placed there in Ismāʿīl Pasha's time) is situated the district that constitutes the "showcase" of Cairo. The major thoroughfare is al-Kūrnīsh (the Corniche), a highway paralleling the river, built since the overthrow of the monarchy. From north to south are aligned the imposing Television Building, the Arab League Headquarters, the Baladīyah (Municipality) Buildings, the Nile Hilton Hotel (with the Egyptian Museum of Antiquities behind it), and the Shepheard's hotel. Also in the vicinity are the intricately curved streets of Garden City, lined with tall apartment houses. Az-Zamālik, opposite al-Kūrnīsh, is the site of hotels, the Cairo Tower, fairgrounds, gardens, a racetrack, and sporting and officers' clubs, as well as elegant housing.

Between the imposing Nile front and the ancient inland quarters is a transitional zone (al-Mūskī, Bāb al-Lūq, eastern ʿAbdīn, an-Naṣrīyah, al-Ḥilmīyah) of lower middle-class status. Chiefly developed in the 19th century, it contains the National Library, the Museum of Islāmic Art, and the Qasr al-Gumhūriah (Presidential Palace) and archives.

"The City of the Dead"

Along the eastern edge of the metropolis are extensive cemeteries—a zone known as "the City of the Dead," which has no counterpart outside Egypt. In a vast, dusty, ochre-coloured zone unserviced by municipal utilities are found exquisite shrine-mosques and mausoleums of early religious leaders (such as that of Imām ash-Shāfiʿī, an al-Fusṭāṭ resident and founder of Egypt's major legal tradition) and of Mamlūk sultans (among the most beautiful are the memorials of Qā'it Bāy, Barqūq, and Qalā'ūn). More modest and recent structures are also found there. Particularly since the population increase that occurred during World War II, housing and shops have been added to the City of the Dead. About 250,000 Cairenes live there, for the most part without government sanction.

The northern and western peripheries have grown dramatically in the past several decades, and most of Cairo's population lives in these newer quarters. On the west bank, and on the island of Rūḍah, land has been converted from agricultural to urban use. In these areas are located developed residential quarters (ad-Duqqī and al-Jīzah, or Giza), the Zoological and Botanical Gardens, the Agricultural Museum, and the campus of the University of Cairo. Large-scale housing projects built there include the Workers' City in Imbābah, as well as Madīnāt al-Muhandisīn (Engineers' City), and Madīnat al-Awqāf (Waqf City). Expansion has also taken place to the north. Beginning about 1905 but expanding substantially in the 1920s, the northern quarters of Rawḍ al-Faraj, Shubrā, Sharabīyah, al-Qubbah, al-ʿAbbāsīyah, al-Maṭarīyah, az-Zaytūn, and Miṣr al-Jadīdah (Heliopolis) gained population. By 1927 they contained some 300,000 of Cairo's 1,000,000 residents. Since that time urban developments have increasingly encroached on agricultural land and have been extended into the desert periphery by elaborate irrigation schemes. Heliopolis, first conceived in 1905, and Naṣr City, a new town begun in 1958, are examples of this. By the late 1970s the northern quarters contained more than 2,000,000 people. Income levels of the inhabitants of Rawḍ al-Faraj along the Nile are at a lower level than of those living in az-Zaytūn; income levels rise still further in Shubrā and are highest in Heliopolis. A rural population still inhabits the northern fringe.

Architectural styles. Building styles in Cairo are related to the historic period during which each quarter developed. In the oldest sections, two- to four-story structures prevail, most built of fired brick covered with plaster and sometimes shored with half-timbering. Wood, being rare, is used frugally. Some of the oldest homes have windows covered with delicately turned wooden lattices (*mashrabīyah*) and massive wooden doors decorated with inlay, brass, or iron nailheads, indicating past elegance. The traditional dwellings (of which only a few remain intact) open onto fountained courtyards and have separate quarters for men and women; the traditional workshops and warehouse inns (of which more have survived) have galleries overlooking the interior court.

European architectural influences

Parts of Cairo built in the 19th century reveal exaggerated European influences—highly ornate stone exteriors, cupolas, and Romanesque doorways. While this ungainly style, darkened with time, predominates in the transitional zone, perhaps the most outlandish examples are the later Palace of Sakākīnī (northeast of Baybars I Mosque) and the Hindu Versailles of Baron Empain, founder of Heliopolis.

In the more modern Western quarters, built at the turn of the century, the architectural style is Parisian; most of the moderately tall buildings are of stone or poured concrete. Closer to the Nile and on the islands, a contemporary Mediterranean style predominates. Tall reinforced concrete and glass structures with balconies are decorated with tile. In these less derivative forms, Egyptian architectural genius, so noticeable in the clean, almost stark lines of the ancient temples, seems to be reemerging.

The monuments of the eastern cemeteries are Mamlūk in design, each topped by a plain or fluted dome; the lesser tombs are simpler rectangles. Houses there and in the rural fringe areas are habitually of mud or of crudely fired brick, resembling village housing in the hinterland.

In the newest quarters on the west and north the more elegant districts have both handsome elevator apartments and one- or two-story "villas," with high walls enclosing colourful gardens. Lower middle and working-class housing consists exclusively of concrete multiflat structures, gray or yellow-beige in colour, often with shops occupying the ground floor. The poorest zones contain three- to five-story walk-ups, often of crudely fired redbrick.

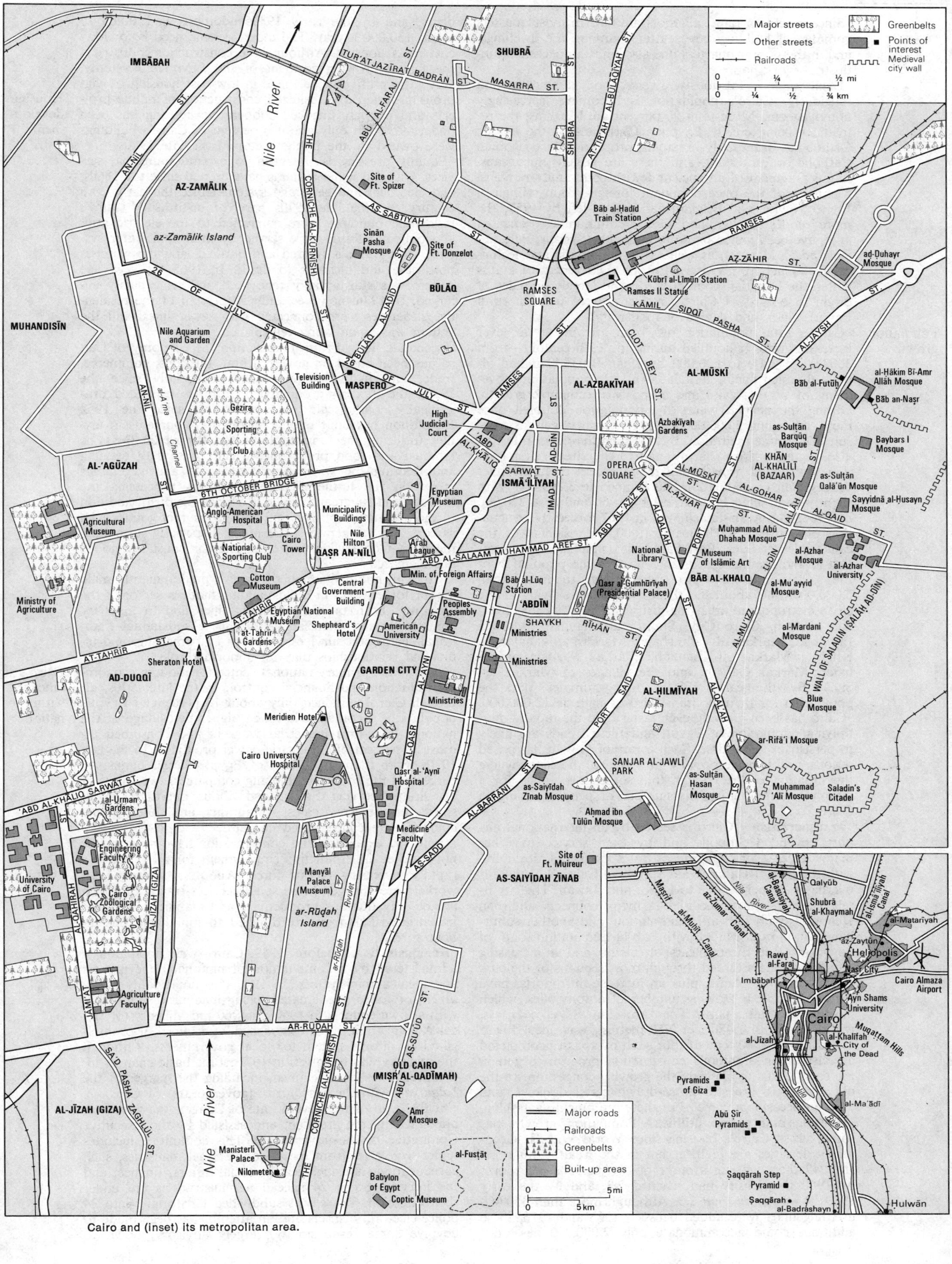
Major streets
Other streets
Railroads
Greenbelts
Points of interest
Medieval city wall
0 ¼ ½ mi
0 ¼ ½ ¾ km
IMBĀBAH
SHUBRĀ
TUR'AT JAZĪRAT BADRĀN ST.
MASARRA ST.
AL-BULĀQIYAH ST.
AT-TIR'AH
SHUBRA ST.
Nile River
AN-NĪL ST.
ABŪ AL-FARAJ ST.
THE CORNICHE (AL-KURNĪSH) ST.
AZ-ZAMĀLIK
az-Zamālik Island
Site of Ft. Spizer
AS-SABTIYAH ST.
Sinān Pasha Mosque
Site of Ft. Donzelot
BŪLĀQ AL-JADĪD ST.
BŪLĀQ
Bāb al-Ḥadīd Train Station
RAMSES ST.
RAMSES SQUARE
Kūbrī al-Limūn Station
Ramses II Statue
AZ-ZĀHIR ST.
ad-Duhayr Mosque
KĀMIL ṢIDQĪ PASHA ST.
AL-JAYSH ST.
CLOT BEY ST.
26 OF JULY ST.
MUHANDISĪN
Nile Aquarium and Garden
Television Building
MASPERO
AL-AZBAKĪYAH
AL-MŪSKĪ
al-Ḥākim Bī-Amr Allāh Mosque
Bāb al-Futūḥ
Bāb an-Naṣr
AN-NĪL
al-A'ma Channel
Gezira Sporting Club
High Judicial Court
'ABD AL-KHĀLIQ SARWAT
AD-DĪN
Azbakīyah Gardens
as-Sulṭān Barqūq Mosque
Baybars I Mosque
AL-'AGŪZAH
6TH OCTOBER BRIDGE
ISMĀ'ĪLIYAH
'IMĀD
OPERA SQUARE
KHĀN AL-KHALĪLĪ (BAZAAR)
as-Sulṭān Qalā'ūn Mosque
Sayyidnā al-Ḥusayn Mosque
AL-MŪSKĪ ST.
AL-GOHAR ST.
AL-QAID ST.
AL-AZHAR ST.
Egyptian Museum
Anglo-American Hospital
Agricultural Museum
Municipality Buildings
Cairo Tower
Nile Hilton
Arab League
QAṢR AN-NĪL
National Sporting Club
ABD AL-SALAAM MUHAMMAD AREF ST.
'ABD AL-'AZĪZ ST.
AL-QAL'AH
PORT SAID
Muḥammad Abū Dhahab Mosque
National Library
Museum of Islāmic Art
al-Azhar Mosque
al-Azhar University
Ministry of Agriculture
Cotton Museum
Min. of Foreign Affairs
Central Government Building
Bāb al-Lūq Station
Qaṣr al-Gumhūrīyah (Presidential Palace)
BĀB AL-KHALQ
al-Mu'ayyid Mosque
AT-TAHRĪR ST.
Egyptian National Museum
at-Tahrir Gardens
Shepheard's Hotel
American University
Peoples Assembly
'ABDĪN
SHAYKH RĪḤĀN ST.
Ministries
al-Mardani Mosque
WALL OF SALADIN (ṢALĀḤ AD-DĪN)
Sheraton Hotel
AD-DUQQĪ
GARDEN CITY
AL-HILMĪYAH
AL-MU'IZZ
Blue Mosque
Meridien Hotel
Cairo University Hospital
Qaṣr al-'Aynī Hospital
AL-'AYNĪ
AL-QAṢR
ar-Rifā'ī Mosque
SANJAR AL-JAWLĪ PARK
as-Saiyidah Zīnab Mosque
as-Sulṭān Ḥasan Mosque
Muhammad 'Alī Mosque
Saladin's Citadel
'ABD AL-KHĀLIQ SARWAT ST.
al-Urman Gardens
Aḥmad ibn Ṭūlūn Mosque
AL-BARRĀNĪ ST.
Medicine Faculty
Engineering Faculty
University of Cairo
Cairo Zoological Gardens
AL-QAHIRAH
AL-JĪZAH (GIZA)
Manyāl Palace (Museum)
ar-Rūḍah Island
ar-Rūḍah Rivulet
AS-SADD
Site of Ft. Muireur
AS-SAIYIDAH ZĪNAB
Agriculture Faculty
JĀMI'AT
AR-RŪḌAH ST.
ABŪ AS-SU'ŪD ST.
OLD CAIRO (MIṢR AL-QADĪMAH)
SA'D PASHA ZAGHLŪL ST.
AL-JĪZAH (GIZA)
'Amr Mosque
Manisterli Palace
Nilometer
al-Fusṭāṭ
Babylon of Egypt
Coptic Museum
Major roads
Railroads
Greenbelts
Built-up areas
0 5mi
0 5km
Qalyūb
al-Basusiyah Canal
Masrif
az-Zumar Canal
al-Muḥīṭ Canal
Shubrā al-Khaymah
al-Ismā'īliyah Canal
al-Maṭarīyah
az-Zaytūn
Heliopolis
Rawḍ al-Faraj
Imbābah
Naṣr City
Cairo Almaza Airport
'Ayn Shams University
Cairo
al-Jīzah
al-Khalīfah
City of the Dead
Muqaṭṭam Hills
Pyramids of Giza
Abū Ṣīr Pyramids
al-Ma'ādī
Ṣaqqārah Step Pyramid
Ṣaqqārah
al-Badrashayn
Ḥulwān

Cairo and (inset) its metropolitan area.

Since it seldom rains, all roofs are flat. In most quarters commercial buildings are scattered among the dwellings, and in the poorer quarters one also finds an occasional industrial workshop.

Demography. Previously diverse, both ethnically and religiously, Cairo's population is becoming increasingly homogeneous. More than 90 percent are Muslims, the remainder being chiefly Egyptian Christians of the Coptic Orthodox faith. Only a small proportion are Roman Catholic or Protestant, and these are largely Europeans. A tiny fragment of an ancient Jewish community remains. Members of the once dominant foreign groups (English, French, Swiss, and Belgian) had mostly left by 1957; the more modest Italian and Greek communities remained and have been joined by Arab nationals (Syrians, Palestinians, and Sudanese), as well as by diplomatic and technical personnel from eastern Europe. Differences of status within the Egyptian population depend largely on place of origin (one-third of Cairo's residents were born in rural Egypt), class, and degree of modernity.

Population growth

Cairo's total population has been growing at an ever increasing rate. It doubled during the 19th century—from 300,000 in 1800 to 600,000 by 1900. By 1930 it had almost doubled again, stimulated by the population movements of World War I and by postwar economic growth. During the next 20 years the population doubled once more, exceeding 2,000,000 by 1947, again largely as a result of wartime migration. By this time the death rate had also begun to drop sharply, and to the stream of migration was added growth due to an excess of births over deaths. Cairo's population had climbed to 3,353,000 (with slightly contracted boundaries) by 1960 and to 4,220,000 by 1966. The Arab–Israeli War in 1967 forced the evacuation of between 500,000 and 1,000,000 residents of the canal cities of Suez, Port Said, and Ismailia. Most resettled in and around Cairo, and by 1976 the population of the governorate of Cairo had grown to more than 5,000,000, and about 8,000,000 people were living in the city's metropolitan area (the districts Jīzah City and Markaz al-Jīzah, Cairo City, Shubrā al-Khaymah, Markaz Imbābah, Markaz al-Badrashayn, Markaz al-Kanater al-Khairia, Markaz al-Khānkah, Markaz Shebein al-Kanater, Markaz Qalyūb, and the villages of Markaz aṣ-Ṣaff). By the early 1980s some estimates put the population for metropolitan Cairo as high as 12,000,000.

Cairo has been growing even faster than the rapidly multiplying population of Egypt, and these trends are likely to persist for some time. Such a rate of growth has posed serious problems, especially in terms of housing, where the situation is dire enough that some have called for a permit system limiting the number of people settling in Cairo.

Transportation. Cairo is served by an international airport beyond Heliopolis and by train service to other major cities. Air-conditioned trains connect Alexandria with the Bāb al-Ḥadīd Train Station in Cairo, and there is overnight sleeper service to Luxor and Aswān. The city itself has mass-transit facilities. A metro connects suburban Heliopolis with Bāb al-Ḥadīd station, and another suburban train links al-Maʿādī with Bāb al-Lūq station south of downtown. Electric tramcars, streetcars, and an increasing number of buses thread through most sections of the city. Local assembly plants, plus an increase in imports, have made available a growing number of automobiles, which has led to traffic jams. The ʿAmr ibn al-ʿAs overpass, with a length of 1,480 feet (450 metres), was opened near Old Cairo in 1980, one of four such overpasses completed as part of an ambitious construction program begun in the early 1970s to alleviate the growing congestion. In the old city there are still horse-drawn carts, donkeys, and even an occasional camel, but these are quickly vanishing.

Housing and public utilities. Population growth has sorely taxed Cairo's housing since World War II. Occupancy densities are high, except in the wealthy quarters. In 1947 there was an average of two persons per room; by 1960 the density had reached 2.3, and by the early 1980s it was more than 2.5. Although more than 350,000 dwelling units were added between 1966 and 1976, these additions could accommodate only 2,000,000 new residents, and by the early 1980s additions had fallen to about 130,000 a year. The most pressing need is for low-cost mass housing. Although the construction industry is the fastest growing segment of the Egyptian economy, very little profit can be made in low-cost housing. A vigorous program of subsidized construction of public projects and publicly financed cooperative housing has been undertaken, but only about 6 percent of Cairo's buildings were owned by the public sector in the late 1970s.

Housing development

Equally pressing is the need to expand municipal services. Gas and water systems have existed since the 1860s, and electrical and sewerage systems since the early 20th century. By the late 1970s barely four-fifths of Cairo's residential buildings were connected to the electric grid, and only two-thirds were served by municipal water systems. Nile water is filtered and purified, and tap water is both safe and pleasant to drink. In 1965 the sewerage system was substantially renovated and its capacity enlarged. In 1976, however, only 58 percent of the residential structures were connected with sewer lines, and the system was again being refurbished.

Economic life. From its inception the economy of Cairo has been based on governmental functions, commerce, trade, and industrial production. Especially since the 1920s, the modern productive sector has expanded dramatically. Large-scale industrialization since the 1952 Revolution has built upon previous developments in textiles (utilizing the long-staple cotton for which Egypt is famous) and food processing, which consists of canning and freezing the wide variety of fruits and vegetables grown in the fertile Delta, as well as processing the tobacco and sugarcane grown in Upper Egypt. In addition to the production of iron and steel, consumer goods, such as cars and refrigerators, are made. Especially since 1956 the output of a wide variety of smaller consumer goods has increased.

Although about one-half of Cairo's predominantly male labour force works in the expanding modern sector of the economy, both on the assembly lines and in auxiliary commercial and financial institutions, a substantial traditional sector still survives, in which craftsmanship and individual relationships play an important role.

Cairo's significance within the nation

Cairo is the primary national centre for modern economic production and financial control. In the late 1970s, although Cairo contained only about 13 percent of Egypt's population, it contained a much higher percentage of the nation's large-firm industrial workers and consumed almost 35 percent of all electric power produced. In the late 1970s more than 80 percent of Egypt's larger banks, 46 percent of the country's shipping companies, two-thirds of all airlines serving Egypt, and about one-third of all sports, amusements, cafés, restaurants, and hotels in the country were concentrated in Cairo.

Industrial expansion and concentration have nevertheless not resulted in productive employment for all of Cairo's rapidly increasing labour force. About one-third of all workers are engaged in personal services, many of which are of only dubious productivity and viability. Five-year industrialization plans are directed to mobilizing this labour force.

Administration. Before 1949 Cairo was anomalously administered by a combination of national policymakers and local administrators. In 1949 the municipality (*baladīyah*) of Cairo was created, being inaugurated, together with a town council, in 1950. In 1960 the Ministry for Local Administration was established, after which it promulgated a uniform system for local governments. Although the ministry was dissolved in 1971, some basic changes introduced have been retained, including the merger of the *baladīyah* with the *muḥāfaẓah* (governorate) of Cairo.

At the head of the governorate of Cairo is the governor, appointed by the president and assisted by the Executive Committee of the governorate. This committee includes under-secretaries from the major national ministries, such as education, housing, health, social affairs, finance, and the interior. Some 24 special administrations are under their direction. The city is subdivided territorially into 24 police-electoral districts and an attempt has been made to devolve some responsibility, largely advisory, down to these sub-areas. The Municipal Council (Majlis Muḥāfaẓah al-Qāhirah), consisting of both elected representatives and members ex-officio, was dissolved in 1971 and replaced by the Peoples Assembly (al-Majlis al-Shaʿabī), in which only elected representatives can vote. Fiscal powers, however, still reside primarily with the ministries of the central government. The development of a metropolitan government coordinating those portions of the urbanized area that fall within the governorates of Giza and Qalyubiyah remains an unfinished but needed task.

Health, security, and education. The number of health and medical facilities concentrated in Cairo contrasts with those available elsewhere in the country. There are about a dozen government general hospitals, including the enormous general hospitals of Qaṣr al-ʿAynī and Dimardāsh and the mental hospital at ʿAbbāssīyah. The city is also served by numerous smaller private hospitals (such as Dār al-Shifā', the Italian Hospital, and the Anglo-American hospital). In the early 1970s there were more than 100 family-care societies. There are some 100 maternity and child-welfare clinics, and the 65 social units that operate in Cairo have taken on additional functions as birth-control centres. Special clinics and public hospitals are devoted to prevalent eye diseases (chiefly trachoma).

Cairo has a relatively low crime rate, and a similarly low number of persons are incarcerated in Cairo's prisons. Fire rates are also low, possibly due to the absence of wood-frame construction and the low utilization of electrical appliances. A large municipal police force, mostly for traffic, and a relatively small fire protection department suffice for the city's needs.

Primary education is compulsory, and the illiteracy rate has dropped dramatically. By the late 1970s only one-third of the population 10 years of age or older was illiterate. In the early 1970s Cairo had almost 120 nursery schools. In addition to primary and secondary schools, educational facilities include technical institutes, pre-university superior schools, and foreign schools. The total number of students enrolled in primary schools in 1972 was about 500,000. Since then, both the number of schools and, even more, the number of pupils has risen markedly.

Higher education

Cairo is also the centre of higher education in the country and attracts students not only from Egypt but also from other Arab countries. The various faculties of the University of Cairo produce the country's largest number of college graduates and specialized professionals (doctors, lawyers, engineers). In the academic year 1980–81, almost 91,000 students were enrolled on its campuses. The second largest institution was ʿAin Shams, with an enrollment of more than 86,000. Al-Azhar University previously specialized in religious subjects and language and literature, but it expanded in 1961 to include teaching in the sciences on its new supplementary campus in Naṣr City. It is the nation's third most important university, with more than 43,000 students in 1980–81. The considerably smaller privately run American University in Cairo offers instruction in English in various arts and sciences.

Cultural life, mass media, and recreation. Cairo is the cultural capital of the Middle East as well as the region's chief mass-media centre. For many centuries the region's major religious and cultural institutions have been concentrated there. During the 19th century European cultural institutions, such as theatre and opera, were added. The Baroque Opera House (destroyed by fire in 1971), where music by Egyptian composers was sometimes heard, was home to the Cairo Symphony Orchestra and host to guest ballet and opera companies, including the indigenous Reḍā Folklore Ballet Troop.

Egypt has long been famous for its musical and dramatic talent. Particularly in recent years there has been a renaissance of the legitimate Arabic theatre. Virtually all Arabic films (except some from Beirut) are produced by Cairo's five major companies or by smaller and shorter lived Cairene companies. The leading cinema stars, as well as the most popular musical entertainers of the Arab world (such as ʿAbd al-Wahhāb, Yūsef Wahbī, and Taḥīya Kariukā), make Cairo their headquarters. Egyptian radio, especially the influential "Voice of the Arabs" program, is beamed throughout North Africa, into the Fertile Crescent, and south into Africa.

Cairo, with its computerized printers and data systems, is the publishing centre of the Middle East, and the city's press exercises a wide influence in the Arabic-speaking countries. Cairo's daily newspapers—the semi-official organ *al-Ahrām*, *al-Jumhūrīyah*, and *al-Akhbār*—circulate abroad as well as throughout Egypt, as do such weeklies as the politically oriented *Rose al-Yūsuf*. Most books in circulation in the Middle East are printed by one of the five largest publishing houses in Cairo. Since 1959 Cairo has had television; three channels, two government-owned and a privately owned channel, were transmitting a combined 20 hours daily in the early 1980s.

Cairo is rich in museums, such as the Egyptian (National) Museum on Maydān Taḥrīr, which displays the treasures of Tutankhamen; the Coptic Museum in Miṣr al-Qadīmah, specializing in pre-Islāmic icons, textiles, and stones; the Museum of Islāmic Art in Bāb al-Khalq, with Mamlūk Qur'āns and objects of wood, brass, inlay, and glass; the War (Citadel) Museum; and the Turkish-style Manyal Palace Museum (on ar-Rūḍah). The mosques of Cairo offer as rich a store as any museum.

The Cairo Zoological Gardens in al-Jīzah contain extensive collections of rare tropical animals in a garden setting. Popular public haunts include al-Kūrnīsh, Azbakīyah, and the Botanical Gardens. Entertainment facilities available include sailboat trips up the Nile, as well as innumerable Nile-front cafés, restaurant boats, and nightclubs. In addition to the older sporting facilities on az-Zamālik (racetracks, swimming clubs, gardens), there is a racetrack at Heliopolis. Naṣr City has playing fields as well as the Cairo Stadium.

BIBLIOGRAPHY. JANET ABU-LUGHOD, *Cairo: 1001 Years of the City Victorious* (1971), a scholarly historical and sociological study; JAMES ALDRIDGE, *Cairo* (1969), general and anecdotal; MARCEL CLERGET, *Le Caire: étude de géographie urbaine et d'histoire économique*, 2 vol. (1934), a scholarly work on the city from its origins to 1927; DEBORAH COWLEY and ALEYA SEROUR, *Cairo: A Practical Guide*, 3rd ed. rev. and updated by SHANTHA ARULANANTHAN and JEAN O'HANLON (1981), an interesting and concise compilation of information on many aspects of life in Cairo; STANLEY LANEPOOLE, *The Story of Cairo* (1902), heavily architectural; DESMOND STEWART, *Cairo: 5500 Years* (1968), a beautifully written, brief history with contemporary vignettes; CAIRO MINISTRY OF CULTURE, *Cairo: Life Story of 1000 Years, 969–1969* (1969), mostly illustrations.

(J.L.A.-L.)

Calcium Products and Production

A metallic element, calcium was so named by the English chemist Sir Humphry Davy because of its occurrence in chalk. Though it does not occur in the free state, its compounds are widely distributed. It is the fifth most abundant element in the Earth's crust, constituting 3.63 percent of the igneous rocks and 3.22 percent of the entire crust of the Earth. It is found in gypsum and related minerals.

Natural occurrence of calcium

Forms of calcium occur as fluorite and (with calcium phosphate) as apatite. Many minerals, notably feldspars and zeolites, contain calcium silicates. Asbestos is composed of calcium magnesium silicate. Calcium phosphate is the principal inorganic constituent of bones; it also occurs as the mineral phosphorite. Calcium carbonate (calcite) occurs in limestone, chalk, marble, dolomite, eggshells, pearls, coral, stalactites, stalagmites, and the shells of many marine creatures.

Production. In 1808 Davy showed that lime is a compound of oxygen and a metal, which he named calcium. While calcium was formerly produced by electrolysis of anhydrous calcium chloride, practically all commercial production now is by the reduction of lime by aluminum in heated retorts under low pressures. Calcium distills out of the reaction mass and is collected in a cool section of the retort or in a condenser. Calcium metal is costly and production is small.

Uses. Calcium is used in making alloys of aluminum, copper, lead, magnesium, and other base metals. It is an important deoxidizer for chromium–nickel, chromium–nickel–iron, and related resistance high-temperature alloys and for nickel, steel, and tin bronzes. It is an evacuating agent (getter) to remove residual gases in the production of high-vacuum products such as electron tubes. It has been employed as a reducing agent in the preparation of chromium, thorium, uranium, zirconium, and other metals from their oxides; as a dehydrating agent for organic liquids; a desulfurizer for petroleum fractions; and a decomposing agent for thiophenes and mercaptans. As calcium–lead, it is employed on telephone cables and in storage batteries.

Calcium is necessary in the human diet and a deficiency of it leads to diseases of the body resulting from the lack of material for bone formation.

Compounds. Calcium carbonate (calcite, $CaCO_3$) occurs in all limestones, other minerals, and in some naturally hard waters. Precipitated chalk is calcium carbonate prepared by mixing solutions of calcium chloride and a soluble carbonate. Tooth powders, white polishes, and cements are made with calcium carbonate.

Lime, calx, or quicklime is calcium oxide (CaO), a strongly caustic ingredient used for making mortars and plasters. Calcium hydroxide [$Ca(OH)_2$], slaked lime, is important in the production of mortars, plasters, and cements. In these materials, which set as they dry, the hydroxide combines with carbon dioxide in the air to form calcium carbonate. Lime has many uses in industry as a cheap alkali and in agriculture as an agent for removing excess soil acidity.

Calcium peroxide (CaO_2) is obtained by the addition of hydrogen peroxide to limewater; the resulting calcium hydrate ($CaO_2 \cdot 8H_2O$) loses water on being heated to 130° C and forms the peroxide—a pale, buff-coloured powder sometimes used for bleaching and antiseptic purposes.

Calcium phosphide (Ca_3P_2), a dangerous fire hazard, is obtained by passing phosphorus vapour over strongly heated lime. It is used in marine signal lights because it decomposes on contact with water to produce spontaneously inflammable hydrogen phosphide.

Calcium phosphate

Calcium phosphate [$Ca_3(PO_4)_2$] is the principal inorganic constituent of bones and of bone ash; it occurs as phosphorite [$Ca_3(PO_4)_2$] in Florida, Tennessee, parts of the western United States, and northern Africa. The acid salt [$CaH_4(PO_4)_2$] is obtained by evaporating a solution of the normal salt in hydrochloric or nitric acid; it is very soluble and, with calcium sulfate, is a superphosphate plant food, produced by treating mineral phosphates with sulfuric acid. In medicine calcium phosphate is used as a source of phosphorus. It is used as a polishing powder in dentifrices. Calcium phosphate is used in manufacturing milk glass, porcelains, pottery, and enamelling. It is a mineral supplement in animal feeds.

Calcium sulfate ($CaSO_4$) occurs in nature as gypsum, alabaster, anhydrite, satin spar, selenite, and terra alba. In water it is one of the salts causing permanent hardness; *i.e.*, hardness not removed by boiling. Calcium sulfate, a white polishing powder, is used to make plaster of Paris, which is a semihydrate ($CaSO_4 \cdot \frac{1}{2}H_2O$), and cements, particularly Keene's cement. It is a white pigment in paints. In paper manufacturing it is used as filler, size, and glaze.

Calcium sulfide (CaS), erroneously called sulfurated lime, is produced by heating the sulfate with charcoal or by heating lime in a current of hydrogen sulfide. Calcium sulfide has been used medically to treat acne and boils. It is a depilatory in leather manufacturing. Luminous calcium sulfide, called Canton's phosphorus, used in luminous paints and varnish, is made by igniting a mixture of calcium carbonate and sulfur with tiny amounts of bismuth or manganese salts.

Calcium chloride

Calcium chloride ($CaCl_2$), water soluble and moisture absorbing (deliquescent), occurs in many natural waters and is a by-product of several industrial processes. The crystals may contain two, four, or six molecules of water for each gram molecular weight of the salt. The hexahydrate and dihydrate are used for antifreeze and refrigerating solutions and for laying dust on roads. The anhydrous chloride, obtained by heating the crystals above 200° C in a current of hydrogen chloride, is used as a drying agent. Bleaching powder is usually a mixture of the basic chloride [$CaCl_2 \cdot Ca(OH)_2(H_2O)$] and the basic hypochlorite [$Ca(OCl)_2 \cdot 2Ca(OH)_2$]. It is made by exposing thin layers of slaked lime to chlorine at 30° to 40° C.

Calcium fluoride (CaF_2) occurs as the mineral fluorite and can be prepared as a white precipitate by mixing solutions of calcium chloride and sodium fluoride. It is used to increase the fluidity of the waste products (slag) in ferrous metallurgy. Single pure crystals are made for use in spectroscopy.

Calcium hydride (CaH_2), sometimes called hydrolith, is obtained by heating the metal in a current of hydrogen. This compound is easily transported and on treatment with water yields hydrogen. It is used as a portable source of hydrogen. Calcium hydride is used to reduce rare metals from their oxides and as a drying agent.

Calcium silicide, calcium boride, and calcium carbide are used in metallurgical work as gas-removing agents, as reducing agents, and as sources of calcium for alloys. Often, however, in (highly specialized) alloy work, examples of which are the nickel–chromium and nickel–chromium–iron materials for high-temperature service, these compounds may introduce undesirable materials from which the metallic calcium is free.

Alloys. Calcium–silicon, made in the electric furnace from lime, silica, and carbon, is a deoxidizer and degasifier for iron, steel, and high-tensile-strength cast irons. It is added either to the furnace in the final stages of processing or at the time of casting. Both calcium and silicon are active deoxidizers and their reaction products are a slag with a low melting point, giving a clean steel ingot with improved fluidity and freedom from holes (blowholes) caused by captured gases.

Calcium–manganese–silicon, also made in the electric furnace, similar to calcium–silicon but with manganese ore as an addition, is sometimes preferred to calcium–silicon for the additional effect of the manganese.

BIBLIOGRAPHY. C.L. MANTELL, "The Alkaline Earth Metals: Calcium, Barium and Strontium," in C.A. HAMPEL (ed.), *Rare Metals Handbook*, 2nd ed. (1961), describes recent technological processes involving calcium, barium, and strontium; C.L. MANTELL, *Industrial Electrochemistry*, 3rd ed. (1950), includes operating details for calcium products processes; W.A. HAMMOND, "Calcium Compounds," *Kirk-Othmer Encyclopedia of Chemical Technology*, 2nd rev. ed., vol. 4, pp. 1–27 (1964), is a general technical approach.

(C.L.M.)

Calcutta

Calcutta, the capital of West Bengal, is India's largest city and one of its major ports. It is located on the east bank of the River Hooghly, an arm of the Ganges River, about 80 miles (128 kilometres) upstream from the head of the Bay of Bengal; here the port city developed as a point of transshipment from water to land and from river to sea. A city of commerce and manufacture, it is the dominant urban centre of eastern India. It has a population estimated to be about 3,100,000.

Origin of the name

The city's name is an anglicized version of Kalikātā. According to some, Kalikātā is derived from the Bengali word Kālīkshetra (field of the goddess Kālī); others hold that the name is derived from the Sanskirt word *kola* ("hog"), because there were many hogs near the settlement and a hog market nearby. Still another version is that Calcutta derived its name from a village industry in which *kali* (slaked lime) was prepared from *kātā* (burnt shells). For an associated physical feature, see GANGES RIVER.

HISTORY

While the village of Calcutta was recorded as existing in 1596, its history as a British settlement dates from the establishment of a trading post there by Job Charnock, an agent of the English East India Company, in 1690. Charnock had previously had disputes with officials of the Mughal Empire at the river port of Hooghly and had been obliged to leave, after which he attempted unsuccessfully to establish himself at other places down the river. When the Mughal officials, not wishing to lose what they had gained from the English company's commerce, permitted Charnock to return once more, he chose Calcutta as the seat of his operations. The site was apparently carefully selected, being protected by the Hooghly River on the west and by salt lakes three miles to the east. Rival Dutch and French settlements were higher up the river on the west bank, so that access from the sea was not threatened, as it was at the port of Hooghly. The river at this point was also wide and deep; the only disadvantage was that the marshes to the east made the spot unhealthy. Moreover, before the coming of the English, three local villages—Sutanati, Kalikātā, and Govindpore, which were later to become parts of Calcutta—had been chosen as places to settle by Indian merchants who had migrated from the silted-up port of Satgaon, farther upstream. The presence of these merchants may have been to some extent responsible for Charnock's choice of the site.

Ft. William

By 1696, when a rebellion broke out in the nearby district of Burdwān, the Mughal provincial administration had become friendly to the straggling settlement. The servants of the company, who asked for permission to fortify their trading post, or factory, were given permission in general terms to defend themselves. The rebels were easily crushed by the Mughal government, but the settlers' defensive structure of brick and mud remained and, in 1700, came to be known as Ft. William. In 1698 the English obtained letters patent that granted them the privilege of purchasing the zamindari right (the right of revenue collection; in effect, the ownership) of the three villages.

The grant of trade rights. In 1717 the Mughal emperor granted the East India Company freedom of trade in return for a yearly payment of 3,000 rupees; this arrangement gave a great impetus to the growth of Calcutta. A large number of Indian merchants flocked to the city. The servants of the company, under the company's flag, carried on a duty-free private trade. When the Marāthās from the southwest began incursions against the Mughals in the western districts of Bengal in 1742, the English obtained permission from the Nawab (ruler) of Bengal to dig an entrenchment to form a moat on the land side. This came to be known as the Maratha Ditch. Although it was not completed to the southern end of the settlement, it marked the city's boundary on the landward side.

In 1756 the Nawab's successor, Sirāj-ud-Dawla, captured the fort and sacked the town. Calcutta was recaptured in 1757 by Robert Clive, one of the founders of British power in India, and by the British admiral Charles Watson. The Nawab was defeated shortly afterward at Plassey, after which British rule in Bengal was assured. Govindpore was cleared of its tiger jungle, and the new Ft. William was built on its present site, overlooking the Hooghly at Calcutta, where it became the symbol of British military ascendancy.

The capital of British India. Calcutta did not become the capital of British India until 1772, when the first governor general, Warren Hastings, transferred all important offices to the city from Murshidābād, the provincial Mughal capital. In 1773 Bombay and Madras became subordinate to the government at Ft. William. A supreme court administering English law began to exercise original jurisdiction over the city as far as the Maratha Ditch (now Circular Road, both Upper and Lower).

In 1706 the population of Calcutta was about 10,000 to 12,000. By 1752 it had increased to about 118,000 and by 1822 to 300,000. The White (British) Town was built on ground that had been raised and drained. There were so many palaces in the British sector of the city that it was named the "city of palaces." Outside the British town were built the mansions of the newly rich, as well as clusters of huts. The names of different quarters of the city—such as Kumartuli (the potters' district) and Sankaripara (the conch-shell workers' district)—still indicate the various occupational castes of the people who became residents of the growing metropolis. Two cities—one British, one Indian—came to coexist in Calcutta.

Calcutta at this time was described as a pestilential town. There were few good roads. In 1817 a Lottery Committee was constituted to finance public improvement by means of lotteries, and between 1817 and 1836 it took some effective measures to improve conditions. Some wide paved roads—Cornwallis Street, College Street, Wellington Street, Wellesley Street, and Wood Street—were constructed, as also were several squares, including Cornwallis Square, College Square, and Wellesley Square.

Development of the port

From trade to empire. By successive stages, as British power extended over the subcontinent, the whole of northern India became a hinterland for the port of Calcutta. There was a seemingly limitless market for the manufacturers of England, and Calcutta was the port of entry. The abolition of inland customs duties in 1835 created an open market. The construction of railways further quickened the tempo of business life. British merchants in Calcutta specialized in the jute, coal, iron, and plantation industries. British banking and insurance also flourished. The Indian sector of Calcutta also became a busy hub of commerce and was thronged with merchants from all parts of India and many other parts of Asia. As the administrative headquarters of British India, Calcutta also became the intellectual centre of the subcontinent.

20th-century problems. The 20th century marked the beginning of Calcutta's woes. Lord Curzon partitioned Bengal in 1905, making Dacca the capital of eastern Bengal and Assam. Insistent agitation led to the annulment of this partition, but in 1912 the capital of British India was removed from Calcutta to Delhi, where the government could enjoy relative calm. Last came the blow of the second partition of Bengal in 1947.

As the century progressed and Calcutta's population grew larger, social problems also became more insistent, as did demands for home rule for India. Communal riots occurred in 1926, and, when Gandhi called for noncompliance with unjust laws, serious riots occurred in 1930. In World War II, Japanese air raids upon the Calcutta docks caused heavy loss of life. The most serious riots of all took place in 1946, when the partition of British India became imminent, and tensions between Muslims and Hindus reached their height. In 1947 the partition of Bengal between India and Pakistan constituted a serious setback for Calcutta, which became the capital of West Bengal only, losing the trade of a part of its former hinterland. At the same time, millions of refugees from East Pakistan flocked to Calcutta, aggravating social problems and increasing overcrowding, which had already assumed serious proportions.

THE CONTEMPORARY CITY

The setting. The city site, as already mentioned, appears to have been originally selected partly because of its easily defensible position and partly because of its favourable trading location. The low, swampy, hot, and humid riverbank otherwise has little to recommend it. Its maximum elevation is 30 feet above sea level. Eastward from the river the land slopes away to marshes and swamplands. Similar topography on the west bank of the river has confined the metropolitan area to a strip three to five miles wide on either bank of the river. Reclamation of lowland is now in progress; the success of the Salt Lake Reclamation Project on the northeastern fringe of the city has demonstrated that the limits of land use and occupation can be expanded.

Size and suburbs

The city proper has an area of about 40 square miles (about 100 square kilometres), but the metropolitan area as a whole consists of about 500 square miles (about 1,300 square kilometres), consisting of 3 corporations, 1 cantonment, 26 municipalities, and 44 municipal urban areas located on both banks of the Hooghly. The principal suburbs of Calcutta are Howrah (on the west bank), Baranagar to the north, South Dum Dum to the northeast, the South Suburban Area (Behāla) to the south, and Garden Reach in the southwest. The whole area forms a single metropolis held together by close economic ties.

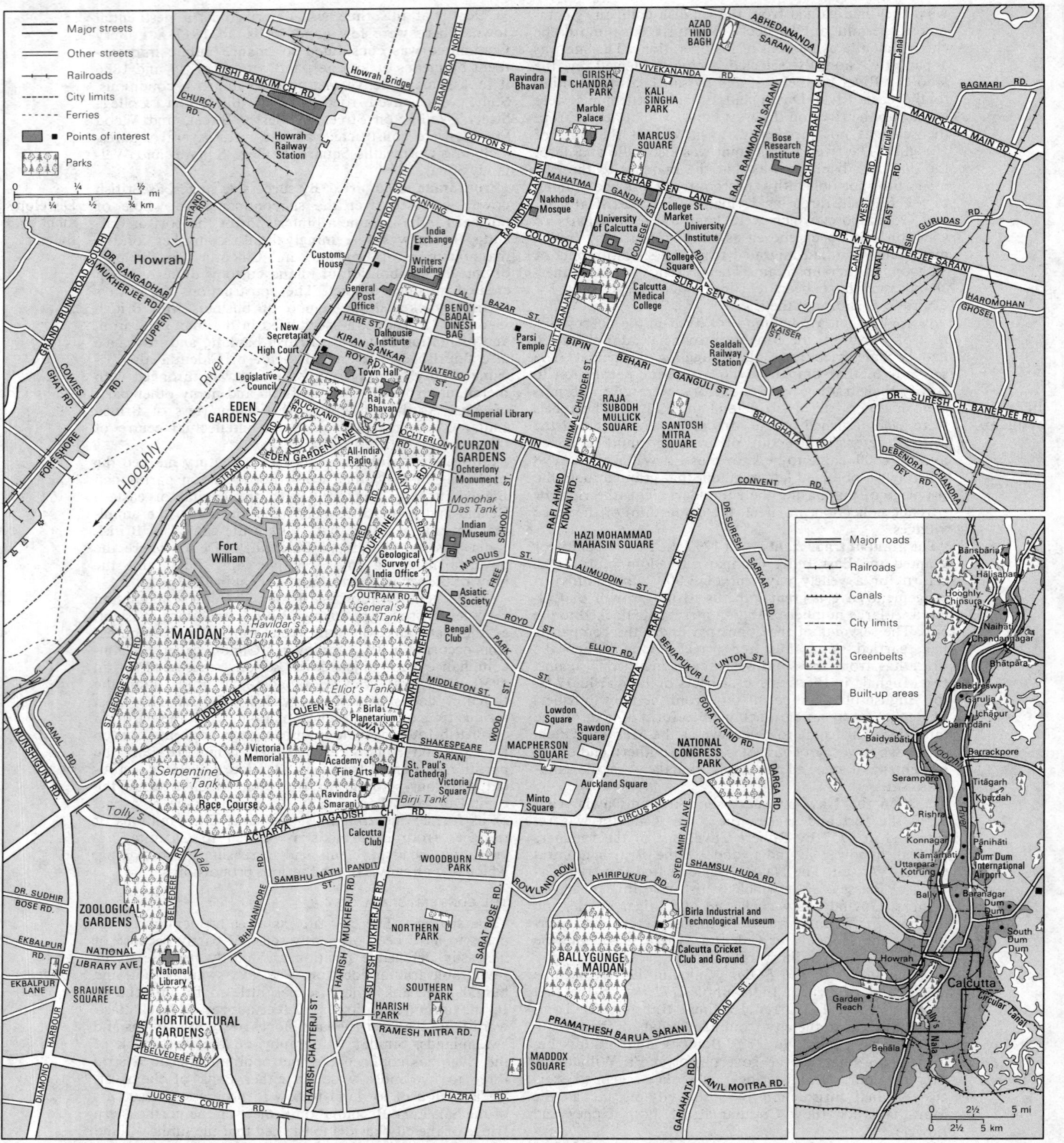

Central Calcutta and (inset) its metropolitan area.

Climate. Calcutta has a subtropical climate with a seasonal regime of monsoons (rain-bearing winds). The maximum temperature reaches about 108° F (42° C) and the minimum temperature about 44° F (7° C). The average annual rainfall is 64 inches. About 80 percent of this falls from June to September, the period of the monsoon. These months are very humid and sometimes sultry. During October and November the rainfall dwindles. The winter months, from about the end of November to the end of February, are pleasant and rainless; fogs and mists occasionally reduce visibility in the early-morning hours at this season, as also do thick blankets of smog in the evenings. The atmospheric pollution has increased by from 50 to 100 percent since 1951. Thermal-generating stations, which burn coal, are a primary cause of this pollution, but monsoon winds act as cleansing agents by bringing in fresh air masses and also hastening the removal of water pollution.

The city plan, streets, and land use. Calcutta, with the exception of certain areas where Europeans formerly lived, has grown haphazardly, and until recently systematic planning was unknown. This haphazard development is most noticeable in the fringe areas around the central core formed by the city of Calcutta and the suburb of Howrah. It has encouraged the development of a pattern of daily commuting that has overburdened Calcutta's roads, utilities, and other municipal facilities.

The street plan

Local streets are narrow. Motorized transport is a recent development. There is only one expressway—the Calcutta to Dum Dum highway. In 1967 there were about 116 miles of main roads in Calcutta and Howrah and about 185 miles in the rest of the metropolitan district. These main roads form a grid pattern in central Calcutta, but elsewhere road planning has a haphazard character. Part of the reason for this has been the difficulty of providing enough river crossings; for the same reason, most streets and highways have a north to south orientation. Nullahs (watercourses) and canals that require bridging have also been important factors in influencing the road pattern.

Transportation. *Urban transport.* While the city, with its immediate suburbs, has a total of about 500 miles of surfaced roads, their poor condition poses an acute problem. The mass-transportation system, which is entirely on the surface until completion of the Dum Dum–Tollyganj subway (see below), depends on trams and buses. In Calcutta and Howrah there are 26 tram routes, consisting of about 40 miles of double-track tramways. Trams are under government management. Buses are run by the state government and by private companies. The public-transport system generally has about 1,100 buses and 450 trams in service; they carry about 1,000,000,000 passengers a year.

Construction began in 1973 on India's first subway system, a 10.3-mile (16.5-kilometre) north–south line between Dum Dum and Tollyganj that was to be completed in about six years and that would serve 1,390,000 persons daily in its first year of operation.

The connection between Calcutta and its hinterland to the west depends upon two bridges over the Hooghly—the Howrah Bridge and, farther north, the Bally Bridge. Construction of a third bridge is planned. The Howrah Bridge, Calcutta's main link with the hinterland, carries eight lanes of vehicular traffic, has two tramway tracks in the centre, and is one of the most heavily used bridges in the world.

Intercity transport. The Grand Trunk Road (National Highway No. 2) is one of the oldest road routes in India. It runs for about 1,000 miles, from Calcutta to Kashmir, and is the main route connecting the port with northern India. Other national highways connect Calcutta with the west coast of India, the northern part of West Bengal, and the frontier with Bangladesh.

Two railway stations—Howrah on the west bank and Sealdah on the east—serve the railway networks running north and south as well as those running east and west. More than 250,000 suburban passengers arrive and depart daily from these two stations.

Calcutta's major air terminal, at Dum Dum, serves about 120 international and domestic flights each day. (For the role of sea transport, see below *Economic life*.)

Demography. According to the 1971 census the population of the city of Calcutta was 3,150,000, although the population of the entire metropolitan area is over 7,000,000. The transient population, of which a considerable proportion is commuters, numbers about 1,000,000. The total population of the city during daylight hours may therefore be estimated at about 4,000,000. At the time of the 1971 census, Hindus numbered 2,620,000, Muslims 450,000, and Christians 40,000, with Sikhs, Jains, Buddhists, and others accounting for the rest. The Bengali-speaking population represented (in 1961) 66 percent of the whole, Hindi-speaking 20 percent, Urdu-speaking 9 percent, Oriya 2 percent, and others 3 percent. Calcutta is not only an Indian city: it is also cosmopolitan. Apart from Indians, other groups present include Bengalis, British, Nepalis, Chinese, Americans, Australians, Burmese, Armenians, Africans, Portuguese, Irish, Dutch, French, Italians, Danes, Israelis, and Iranians.

The density of population is about 78,000 per square mile—about 160 persons per developed acre and 300 persons per residential acre. But averages are misleading. In a district known as Ward No. 72, for example, density is 127 persons per residential acre, while in some of the wards (districts) in north Calcutta the density is above 1,000 per acre. In 20 wards of north Calcutta, density was 590 persons per acre in 1961. There are few multistoried buildings in this area. People live mostly in single-, double-, or three-storied buildings. Overcrowding has reached virtually intolerable proportions.

A socio-economic survey of the city of Calcutta made during the decade of the 1950s drew attention to certain demographic features in the city. There was a large number of migrants, who fell into one of two categories. Ordinary migrants were those who came from other states of India in search of employment—mostly from Bihār, Orissa, and eastern Uttar Pradesh. They were male and married but led a single life in Calcutta. Most of them were unskilled manual workers, but some were skilled labourers or traders. Deprived of family life, though married, they lent an element of instability to the city's life. This also explained the excessive predominance of males—1,900,000, as compared with 1,200,000 females, at the time of the 1971 census. The second category of migrants included refugees from East Pakistan (Bangladesh); in 1967 these numbered about 400,000 in Calcutta and its immediate neighbourhood.

The housing shortage

Housing. The city is faced with an immense housing shortage. In 1973 it was estimated that there were at least 200,000 pavement dwellers in the city. Of 366,000 persons living in institutional shelters in the Calcutta metropolitan district, probably more than two-thirds live in the city itself. There are more than 600,000 housing units in the city, about three-quarters used for dwelling purposes only. The average number of persons per household is almost five, and the average number of persons per room is about three. Most of the units are very small.

There are 3,000 bustees, or slums, housing 189,000 families. A bustee is officially defined as "a collection of huts standing on a plot of land of at least one-sixth of an acre." There also are bustees built on less than one-sixth of an acre. The majority of huts are unventilated single-story rooms, often dilapidated. They have few sanitary facilities, and there is very little open space. The government is sponsoring a bustee-improvement program.

Architectural features. In contemporary Calcutta the skyline is broken in some areas by skyscrapers and tall multi-story blocks. The cityscape is changing very rapidly. Chowringhee area in central Calcutta, once a row of palatial houses, has been given up to offices, hotels, and shops. In north and central Calcutta, buildings are still mainly two or three stories high. In south and south central Calcutta, multi-storied apartment buildings prevail.

In 1875 there were 21 Christian churches and chapels listed in Calcutta; today some of them are in ruins. Calcutta is full of temples, both large and small; most of them are shrines attached to houses, which explains the absence of monumental temples to the Hindu deities.

Western architectural influences

Western influence is dominant in Calcutta's old architectural monuments. Government House (now Raj Bhavan) is an imitation of Kedleston Hall in Derbyshire; the High Court resembles the Cloth Hall at Ypres, Belg.; the Town Hall is in Grecian style with Doric-Hellenic portico; St. Paul's Cathedral is of Indo-Gothic-style architecture; the Writers' Building is of Gothic-style architecture with statuary on top; the Indian Museum is in Italian style; and the General Post Office, with its majestic dome, has Corinthian columns. The beautiful column of the Ochterlony Monument is 165 feet high—its base is Egyptian, its column Syrian, and its cupola in the Turkish style. The Victoria Memorial represents an attempt to combine classical Western influence with Mughal architecture; the Nakhoda Mosque is modelled on Akbar's Tomb at Sikandra; the Birla Planetarium is based on the Buddhist stupa (monument) at Sāñchī.

The West Bengal Legislative Council is a dignified building in the modern architectural style. The Ramakrishna Mission Institute of Culture, the most important example of post-independence construction, represents an attempt to interpret the cultural heritage of India.

Economic life. Calcutta is eastern India's financial headquarters, as well as a great commercial entrepôt, and the centre of an industrial urban district. Its port provides an outlet for the products of the tea gardens of Assam and Meghalaya and West Bengal's jute industry. Although Calcutta's economy is inseparably connected with the Calcutta conurbation and with the hinterland as a whole, few industries, except for jute, are linked directly to the port.

The port of Calcutta. In normal years the Calcutta port handles—in terms of value—25 percent of India's import cargoes and 40 percent of its export cargoes. Some decline in traffic occurred in the late 1960s, partly because of problems encountered in dredging silt from the river and partly because of labour problems. Calcutta imports better quality steel and iron and exports crude steel and pig iron. Other commodities imported include salt, petroleum, asphalt, bitumen, cement, fertilizers, machinery, and railway materials. Among commodities exported are coal, ores, gunnies (jute sacking), tea, sugar, bones and bone meal, scrap iron, and other cargo. Import of food grains, formerly the largest single import in terms of total tonnage, was expected to end in 1972. Transport, storage, wholesaling, and retailing requirements for all these exports and imports are concentrated in Calcutta. The Calcutta port accounts for the bulk of India's foreign exchange.

Imports and exports

Banking and commerce. Of the foreign banks in India, almost one-third are in Calcutta. They account for somewhat more than 33 percent of all deposits in foreign banks in India and almost the same percentage of all advances. The Calcutta stock exchange plays an important part in the organized financial market of the country.

In addition, the controlling agency for coal mines is in Calcutta. Jute mills and large-scale engineering industries are also controlled from the city. The Bengal Chamber of Commerce and Industry, the Bengal National Chamber of Commerce and Industry, and the Indian Chamber of Commerce are based in Calcutta. The products of Calcutta's hinterland include coal, iron, manganese, mica, petroleum, tea, and jute. Calcutta is the eastern region's shipping centre; it is also a major centre for printing, publishing, and newspaper circulation, as well as for recreation and entertainment.

Manufactured products

Industry. Calcutta is the world's largest processor of jute; the city also manufactures, processes, and distributes such consumer goods as rice products, wheat, flour products, sweetmeats, dairy products, edible oils, tobacco, betel nuts, nonalcoholic drinks, toilet and textile products, hosiery goods, bedding materials, and footwear. Its factories also produce tires, tubes, transport vehicles, electric motors, electroplated wares, type foundries, dyes, varnishes, chemicals, plywood, tea chests, soap, ink, pencils, iron and steel goods, paper, and textiles.

Overall economy. That the city's economy is primarily mercantile is reflected in the fact that almost 40 percent of all workers are employed in the distributive trades. There are, however, 40,000 workers on the payrolls of the port authorities alone. Other important occupational classifications include public service in different government departments, the armed forces, the police, the banks, and the Life Insurance Corporation of India. Private services include the stock exchange, medical and educational services, legal services, accountancy and credit firms, chambers of commerce, various public utility services, such as the municipal corporation, electricity and gas companies, tramways, bus service, and construction works. The number of persons with unearned incomes has diminished with the abolition in 1954 of the zamindars (revenue-collection) system. The problem of unemployment in Calcutta is, to a considerable extent, educated unemployment—that is, unemployment among people educated for clerical and other white-collar jobs.

Administration and social services. *Governmental institutions.* As Calcutta is the capital of West Bengal, the governor resides in the city in the historic Raj Bhavan. The state Legislative Assembly is located in the city, as is also the Secretariat, known as Writers' Building, housing the state ministries in charge of different departments. The Calcutta High Court, exercising original jurisdiction over the city and appellate jurisdiction over West Bengal, is also located there. A number of government of India institutions, including the National Library, the Indian Museum, the Geological Survey of India, and the Indian Meteorological Department, are also in the city.

Municipal government is carried on by the Municipal Corporation of Calcutta, which is composed of 100 members representing the 100 wards into which the city is divided and who are elected on the basis of adult franchise. The members annually elect a mayor, a deputy mayor, and a number of committees to conduct the activities of the corporation. A commissioner, the executive head of the corporation, is responsible to its elected membership.

Other important governmental institutions are the Calcutta Improvement Trust, the Calcutta Metropolitan Planning Organization, the Calcutta Metropolitan Water and Sanitation Authority, and the Calcutta Metropolitan District Authority, which has executive functions.

Public utilities. A daily total of 116,000,000 gallons of filtered water is supplied from the main waterworks located 22 miles from the city, as well as from 175 major wells and some smaller wells. It has been estimated, however, that the total supply of filtered water required to meet the city's needs is 240,000,000 gallons per day. High salinity of the water supply in the dry months results from the use of the Hooghly River. The construction of Farakka Barrage on the Ganges, 240 miles upriver from Calcutta, due for completion in 1973, will ensure a saline-free water supply for the city. About 80,000,000 gallons of unfiltered water per day are supplied for watering the city streets and for use by the fire brigade, but many bustee residents use this water for their daily needs. This circumstance was largely responsible for the former prevalence of cholera during the summer months; chlorination of unfiltered water and cholera inoculation have now brought this disease under control. The total elimination of the unfiltered water supply has been recommended.

Water supplies

Municipal Calcutta has more than 400 miles of sewers and less than 400 miles of surface drains, about 44 percent of the total area of the city still remaining unsupplied with sewers. Accumulation of silt has narrowed many sewer channels. The system of removing garbage and of garbage dumping is unsatisfactory and needs improvement. Unsanitary methods of human-waste disposal persist in the unsewered part of the city.

Although Calcutta is supplied with electricity by the Calcutta Electric Supply Corporation, West Bengal State Electricity Board, Durgapur Power Station, Bandel Thermal Power Station, and Damodar Valley Corporation Grid, there is still a gap between generating capacity and potential demand.

Health and safety. Malaria has been eradicated from the city, and death from enteric fever has been brought under control. Death rates from cholera, smallpox, influenza, and tuberculosis have declined. There are 36 hospitals, apart from private clinics, as well as free dispensaries run by the Municipal Corporation of Calcutta and charitable trusts. There are four medical colleges. The city has about 7,000 registered medical practitioners, both men and women, practicing modern medicine, almost 800 practicing traditional Hindu medicine, and 600 practitioners of homeopathic medicine. The number of doctors per 1,000 people is greater in Calcutta than in most parts of the country, but the city is also a medical centre for the northeast region of India, and the hospitals are always overcrowded. For those who can afford them, there are also many nursing homes.

Medical facilities

Administration of the Calcutta police force is vested in the city's commissioner of police, as is direction of the suburban police force. The city is divided into four police divisions. The fire brigade, with a fleet of vehicles and well-trained personnel, has its headquarters in central Calcutta.

Jawaharlal Nehru (formerly Chowringhee) Road, a main street in Calcutta overlooking the Maidan, the city's largest park.
J. Allan Cash

Public safety had become a serious problem in the 1970s, when there was an alarming increase in crimes and murders as a result of interparty clashes. The city's police force was considerably strengthened in consequence.

Education. Almost 70 percent of the primary education age group (six to ten years) attend primary schools; of these, one-third attend free primary schools run by the municipal corporation. The rest attend recognized schools that are under private management. About 60 percent of boys and 40 percent of girls from the ages of 11 to 14 receive secondary education; about 30 percent of boys and 20 percent of girls in the age group 14 to 16 receive education in recognized schools, both governmental and private. All recognized schools, in both the secondary and higher-secondary categories, are supervised by the Board of Secondary Education.

The universities

The three universities are the University of Calcutta, Jadavpur University, and Rabindra Bharati University. The University of Calcutta has 50 colleges in the city, as well as many outside. It has faculties of agriculture, arts (humanities), commerce, dental science, education, engineering, fine arts and music, home science, journalism, law, library science, technology, social welfare, business management, and veterinary science. Besides these colleges, university colleges of arts (humanities), science, and medicine specialize in postgraduate teaching and research. Jadavpur University has three faculties—arts (humanities), science, and engineering. Rabindra Bharati University specializes in humanities and the fine arts (dance, drama, and music). The colleges are all overcrowded.

Research institutions include the Indian Statistical Institute, the Indian Association for the Cultivation of Science, the Bose Research Institute (natural science), and the All-India Institute of Hygiene and Public Health.

Cultural life. Calcutta is the most important cultural centre of India. Besides the three universities, the Asiatic Society of Bengal, the Bangiya Sahitya Parishad, the Ramakrishna Mission Institute of Culture, the Academy of Fine Arts, the Birla Academy of Art and Culture, the Maha Bodhi Society, the Iran Society, and the Calcutta Historical Society are among the organizations that contribute to the cultural life of the city. All branches of the arts are pursued, and crafts play an important role. Cinematic films are produced in the city's film studios.

Rabindranath Tagore in 1937 inaugurated the first All-Bengal Music Conference in Calcutta, and a number of music conferences are held every year. The Society of Working Artists, the Society of Progressive Artists, the Society of Oriental Art, the Painters' Front, and other bodies present annual shows.

Theatre and films

There is no permanent English-language theatre in Calcutta, but English plays are staged by amateur dramatic clubs, and there are six theatres that regularly stage Bengali dramas. There are almost 80 cinemas. English, Bengali, Hindi, and Urdu films are regularly shown.

The Indian Museum on Jawaharlal Nehru Road (formerly Chowringhee Road) is the oldest in India. The archaeology and numismatic sections contain the most valuable collections. The exhibits at Victoria Memorial Hall trace Britain's relations with India. The Asutosh Museum of Indian Art in the University of Calcutta has exhibits of the folk art of Bengal among its collections.

Valuable library collections are to be found in the Asiatic Society, Bangiya Sahitya Parishad, and the University of Calcutta; special mention should be made of the National Library, which is the largest in India, with holdings of 10,000,000 books and 2,000 original manuscripts.

Press, radio, and television. Three English-language daily newspapers and six Bengali-language dailies are published in Calcutta and have large circulations throughout eastern India. Hindi daily newspapers number five and Urdu dailies four; there is also a Punjabi-language daily. Bengali-language periodicals are more numerous than ever before. There are some English-language weeklies and monthly magazines. Akashbani Bhavan, the All-India Radio station, is located in the city, and the establishment of a television station is planned.

Recreation. There are 170 parks, squares, and open spaces maintained by the Corporation of Calcutta. There is, however, very little open space in the overcrowded parts of the city. The Maidan (1,283 acres) is the most famous open space; the major soccer, cricket, and hockey fields are located there. Adjacent to the Maidan is one of the oldest cricket fields in the world, in the Eden Gardens. There are two racecourses and two golf courses within the city. Rowing at the Lake Club and at the Bengal Rowing Club is popular. The Zoological Gardens are spread over an area of 45 acres. The Indian Botanical Gardens, on the western bank of the river, cover an area of about 270 acres and have a river frontage of almost 6,000 feet. Their famed herbarium contains about 40,000 species of plants.

BIBLIOGRAPHY. Early historical works include: W.K. FIRMINGER, *Historical Introduction to the Bengal Portion of the Fifth Report* (1917); J. LONG, *Selection from Unpublished Records of Government for the Years 1748 to 1767 Inclusive, Relating Mainly to the Social Condition of Bengal*, vol. 1 (1869); A.K. ROY, *Calcutta Town and Suburbs* (1902); and C.R. WILSON, *Early Annals of the English in Bengal*, 3 vol. (1896–1917). The BENGAL CHAMBER OF COMMERCE, *West Bengal: An Analytical Study* (1971), describes the city's present crisis. See also the CALCUTTA CORPORATION, *Handbook 1969–70*, on municipal government, health, and mortality; reports of the CALCUTTA METROPOLITAN PLANNING ORGANISATION on housing, public utilities, traffic, and transport; N.R. KAR, "Calcutta Conurbation," in R.L. SINGH (ed.), *India Regional Studies* (1968), for geographical data; MITRA ASOK, *Calcutta: India's City* (1963); *Census of India, 1951*, vol. 6, pt. 3, *Calcutta City* (1954); B. RAY, *Census of India 1961, West Bengal Census Handbook*, vol. 2 (1966); N. MUKHERJEE, *The Port of Calcutta: A Short History* (1968), for export and import figures; S.N. SEN, *The City of Calcutta: A Socio-Economic Survey, 1954–55 to 1957–58* (1960), for economic life, occupational structure, and other findings; N.K. SINHA, *Economic History of Bengal*, 3 vol. (1961–70); and P. SINHA, "The City as a Physical Entity," *Bengal Past and Present*, 89:264–276 (1970).

(N.K.S.)

Calder, Alexander

Alexander Calder, known throughout the world as the artist who made sculpture move, was one of the few artists in history who could lay claim to the creation of a new art form. This form, the mobile, greatly extended the limits and possibilities of the art of sculpture. Although isolated experiments in the introduction of motion into sculpture had preceded his work, Calder was the first to realize the full implications of the element of motion and explored these implications in hundreds of variations.

Alexander Calder was born on July 22, 1898, in Lawnton, Pennsylvania, now a part of the city of Philadelphia. He was the son and grandson of sculptors, and his mother was an accomplished painter; he grew up in the atmosphere of American academic art of the early 20th century. Despite this environment, he seems to have had little inclination to become an artist himself. Aside from an unusual amount of travelling and moving around, necessitated in part by his father's health, Calder's youth and interests were typical of middle-class American boys growing up in the early years of the century. His reminiscences of his early activities—which are remarkable for their completeness—have to do largely with family affairs, sports, and relations with his classmates. Perhaps the only indication of his subsequent career lay in his facility for making things and his enjoyment of gadgets.

Early interests

After study at the Stevens Institute of Technology in Hoboken, New Jersey, he graduated in 1919 with a degree in mechanical engineering. For a time he travelled widely and held various engineering jobs. In 1922 he took drawing lessons at a night school in New York and in 1923 entered the Art Students League, where he was influenced by painters of the New York scene, the so-called Ashcan School, of which the painters John Sloan and George Luks were among the leaders. At this point, his aspirations, like those of many American artists of the time, did not extend much beyond securing a well-paying job in illustration or commercial art. In 1924 he began doing illustrations for the *National Police Gazette*, for which he covered prize fights and the circus.

© Karsh—Rapho Guillumette

Calder, photograph by Yousuf Karsh, 1966

After several other routine commercial illustrating jobs, Calder decided in 1926 to go to Paris, the world centre for modern art. In Paris, while working on sculpture, he began, for his own amusement, to make toylike animals of wood and wire. Out of these he developed a miniature circus (Whitney Museum of American Art, New York City), performances of which were attended by many of the leading artists and literary figures in Paris. The little circus figures, as well as his interest in continuous line drawings, led Calder to the creation of wire sculptures, such as the figure of a woman seven feet high entitled "Spring" and "Romulus and Remus," a group that included a she-wolf 11 feet long.

Creation of wire sculpture

Among the artists he met in Paris through his circus exhibitions, perhaps the most crucial for his subsequent career was the Spanish Surrealist painter Joan Miró. Although Surrealism was reaching its first major peak in the late 1920s, Calder does not seem to have been conscious of the movement; in fact throughout his career he isolated himself from the "art world." With Miró, however, he established an immediate rapport, and a lasting friendship was formed.

In 1930 Calder met the Dutch painter Piet Mondrian and visited his studio, an event that made him suddenly aware of the modern movement in painting and that influenced his work in the direction of the abstract. In the winter of 1931–32 he began to make motor-driven sculptures, consisting of various geometrical shapes. The name mobile was given to them by Marcel Duchamp. Aesthetically, movement, because of the changing relationships between the various elements, gave the sculpture a continually changing composition. The following year, when Calder exhibited similar works that did not move, Jean Arp described them as stabiles, a term that Calder continued to use. Beginning in 1932 most of his mobiles were given their movement by air currents.

In 1931, while fashioning a wedding ring for his marriage, Calder formed an interest in making jewelry. Also in 1931 he produced illustrations for an edition of the *Fables of Aesop*. Illustrations for a number of other books followed in the 1940s.

During the 1930s Calder further developed the concept of the mobile. The first major manifestation of his work was at the Paris World's Fair of 1937, where he created his so-called mercury fountain for the Spanish pavilion. In this sculpture, movement was introduced by a stream of mercury striking a plate that was attached to a swivelling rod. From this point, Calder's reputation expanded continually through annual exhibitions in Europe and America, climaxed by a showing at the Museum of Modern Art in New York City in 1943.

First major mobiles

Although Calder's early mobiles and stabiles were on a relatively small scale, he increasingly moved toward monumentality in his later works. One very large stabile organization was an acoustical ceiling, which he designed in 1952 for the auditorium of the Universidad Central de Venezuela in Caracas. In 1961 an exhibition on motion in art, which originated at the Stedelijk Museum in Amsterdam, emphasized the work of Calder and his followers. During the 1960s his accomplishments were recognized through major exhibitions in Kassel, West Germany; at the Solomon R. Guggenheim Museum, New York City; and at the Musée d'Art Moderne de la Ville de Paris.

In 1931, Calder was married to Louisa Cushing James, and after their marriage the Calders travelled continually, not only between France and the United States but to South America and Asia. In 1955 and 1956 they visited India, where Calder created 11 mobiles.

In the 1970s Calder's studio was at Saché, near Tours. There he designed his major stabiles and experimented with free-form drawings and paintings. His normal method with large-scale works was to create a small model, the enlargement of which he supervised at a foundry in Tours. Although Calder lived most of the time in France, he maintained a home in Roxbury, Connecticut, where his house and his studio were filled with mobiles and stabiles. He died of a heart attack in New York City on November 11, 1976.

MAJOR WORKS

"Josephine Baker" (1926; private collection); "Romulus and Remus" (1928; Solomon R. Guggenheim Museum, New York); "Helen Wills" (1928; collection of the artist); "The Horse" (1928; Museum of Modern Art, New York); "Spring" (*c.* 1929; Solomon R. Guggenheim Museum, New York); "Portrait of Shepard Vogelgesang" (1930; Shepard Vogelgesang Collection, New York); "Kiki's Nose" (1931; private collection, Paris); "Dancing Torpedo Shape" (1932; Berkshire Museum, Pittsfield, Massachusetts); "Calderberry Bush" (1932; private collection, New York); "White Frame" (1934; collection of the artist); "A Universe" (1934; Museum of Modern Art, New York); "The Circle" (1934; Agnes Rindge Claflin Collection, Poughkeepsie, New York); "Steel Fish" (1934; Virginia Museum of Fine Arts, Richmond, Virginia); "Hanging Mobile" (1936; Meric Callery Collection, New York); "Dancers and Sphere" (1936; collection of the artist); "Whale" (1937; Museum of Modern Art, New York); "Tight Rope" (1937; collection of the artist); "Lobster Trap and Fish Tail" (1939; Museum of Modern Art, New York); "Spherical Triangle" (1939; collection of the artist); "Thirteen Spines" (1940; collection of the artist); "Black Beast" (1940; collection of the artist); "Hour Glass" (1941; Catherine White Collection, New York); "Cockatoo" (1941; C. Earle Miller Collection, Downingtown, Pennsylvania); "Red Petals" (1942; The Arts Club of Chicago); "Little Tree" (1942; Edgar Kaufmann, Jr., Collection, New York); "Horizontal Spines" (1942; Addison Gallery of American Art, Phillips Academy, Andover, Massachusetts); "Constellation with Red Object" (1943; Museum of Modern Art, New York); "The Water Lily" (1945; Pauling Donnelly Collection, Chicago); "Bayonets Menacing a Flower" (1945; Washington University Gallery of Art, St. Louis, Missouri); "Red and White on Post" (1948; collection of the artist); "Jacaranda" (1949; Wallace K. Harrison Collection, New York); "Blériot" (1949; Ida Chagall Collection, Paris); "El Corcovado" (1951; José Luis Sert Collection, Lattingtown, Long Island, New York); "Universe" (1974; Sears Tower, Chicago).

BIBLIOGRAPHY. ALEXANDER CALDER, *An Autobiography with Pictures* (1966), dictated by Calder to his son-in-law Jean Davidson, is perhaps the best picture of the artist as an individual. It suggests his personality and includes most of the details concerning his life and career. H.H. ARNASON, *Calder* (1966), is a critical biography with photographs by PEDRO E. GUERRERO that traces the development of Calder as an artist; H.H. ARNASON and UGO MULAS, *Calder* (1971), is a photographic document with anthology, comments, and quotations from Calder and many friends who knew him throughout his career. This work and the preceding one contain bibliographies by and about the artist. JAMES J. SWEENEY, *Alexander Calder* (1951), an exhibition catalog of the Museum of Modern Art, New York, is the first major study of Calder with the most complete bibliography to 1951.

(H.H.A.)

Calderón de la Barca, Pedro

The dramatist and poet Pedro Calderón de la Barca, who was to succeed Lope de Vega as the greatest Spanish dramatist of his age, was born at Madrid on Jan. 17, 1600. His father, a fairly well-to-do government official who died in 1615, was a man of harsh and dictatorial temper. Strained family relations apparently had a profound effect on the youthful Calderón, for several of his plays show a preoccupation with the psychological and moral effects of unnatural family life, presenting anarchical behaviour directly traced to the abuse of paternal authority.

Career. Destined for the church, Calderón matriculated at the University of Alcalá in 1614 but transferred a year later to Salamanca, where he continued his studies in arts, law, and probably theology until 1619 or 1620. Abandoning an ecclesiastical career, he entered the service of the constable of Castile and in 1623 began to write plays for the court, rapidly becoming the leading member of the small group of dramatic poets whom Philip IV gathered around him. In 1636 the King made him a Knight of the Military Order of St. James. Calderón's popularity was not confined to the court, for these early plays were also acclaimed in the public theatres, and on the death of Lope de Vega (1635) Calderón became the master of the Spanish stage. On the outbreak of the Catalan rebellion he enlisted in 1640 in a cavalry company of knights of the military orders and served with distinction until 1642, when he was invalided out of the army. In 1645 he entered the service of the Duke of Alba, probably as secretary. A few years later an illegitimate son was born to him; nothing is known about the mother, and the idea that sorrow at her death led him to return to his first vocation, the priesthood, is pure surmise. He was ordained in 1651 and announced that he would write no more for the stage. This intention he kept as regards the public theatres, but at the King's command he continued to write regularly for the court theatre. He also wrote each year the two Corpus Christi plays for Madrid (see below *Religious plays*). Appointed a prebendary of Toledo cathedral, he took up residence in 1653. The fine meditative religious poem *Psalle et sile* ("Sing Psalms and Keep Silent") is of this period. Receiving permission to hold his prebend without residence, he returned to Madrid in 1657 and was appointed honorary chaplain to the king in 1663. He died in Madrid on May 25, 1681.

Ordination

Aesthetic milieu and achievement. The court patronage that Calderón enjoyed constitutes the most important single influence in the development of his art.

The court drama grew out of the popular drama, and at first there was no distinction in themes and style between the two. The construction, however, of a special theatre in the new palace, the Buen Retiro, completed in 1633, made possible spectacular productions beyond the resources of the public stage. The court plays became a distinctive Baroque genre, combining drama with dancing, music, and the visual arts and departing from contemporary life into the world of classical mythology and ancient history. Thus Calderón, as court dramatist, became associated with the rise of opera in Spain. In 1648 he wrote *El jardín de Falerina* ("The Garden of Falerina"), the first of his zarzuelas, plays in two acts with alternating spoken and sung dialogue. In 1660 he wrote his first opera, the one-act *La púrpura de la rosa* ("The Purple of the Rose"), with all of the dialogue set to music. This was followed by *Celos aun del aire matan* (1660; "Jealousy Even of the Air Can Kill"), an opera in three acts with music by Juan Hidalgo. As in the Italian tradition, the music was subordinate to the poetry, and all of Calderón's musical plays are poetic dramas in their own right.

Calderón's drama must be placed within the context of the court theatre, with its conscious development of an unrealistic and stylized art form. For two centuries after his death his pre-eminence remained unchallenged, but the realistic canons of criticism that came to the fore toward the end of the 19th century produced a reaction in favour of the more "lifelike" drama of Lope de Vega. Calderón appeared mannered and conventional: the structure of his plots artificially contrived, his characters stiff and unconvincing, his verse often affected and rhetorical. Although he used technical devices and stylistic mannerisms that by constant repetition became conventional, Calderón remained sufficiently detached to make his characters, on occasion, poke fun at his own conventions. This detachment indicates a conception of art as a formal medium that employs its artistic devices so as to compress and abstract the externals of human life the better to express its essentials.

Dramaturgy and craftsmanship

In this direction Calderón developed the dramatic form and conventions established by Lope de Vega, based on primacy of action over characterization, with unity in the theme rather than in the plot. He created a tightly knit structure of his own, while leaving intact the formal framework of Lope's drama. From the start he manifested his technical skill by utilizing the characters and incidents of his plots in the development of a dominant idea. As his art matured his plots became more complex and the action more constricted and compact. The creation of complex dramatic patterns in which the artistic effect arises from perception of the totality of the design through the inseparability of the parts is Calderón's greatest achievement as a craftsman. *The Painter of His Own Dishonor* (*c.* 1645) and *La cisma de Ingalaterra* (*c.* 1627; "The Schism of England") are masterly examples of this technique, in which poetic imagery, characters, and action are subtly interconnected by dominant symbols that elucidate the significance of the theme. Although rhetorical devices typical of the Spanish Baroque style remained a feature of his diction, his verse developed away from excessive ornamentation toward a taut style compressed and controlled by a penetrating mind.

Secular plays. The difficulties that Calderón's art presents to the modern reader have tended to obscure the originality of his themes. Accepting the conventions of the comedy of intrigue, a favourite form on the Spanish stage, he used them for a fundamentally serious purpose: *The Phantom Lady* (1629) is a neat and lively example. In *Casa con dos puertas, mala es de guardar* (1629; "A House with Two Doors Is Difficult to Guard") the intrigues of secret courtship and the disguises that it necessitates are so presented that the traditional seclusion of women on which these intrigues are based is shown to create social disorder by breeding enmity and endangering love and friendship. *No siempre lo peor es cierto* (*c.* 1640; "The Worst Is Not Always True") and *No hay cosa como callar* (1639; "Silence Is Golden") mark the peak of this development: although the conventions of comedy remain, the overtones are tragic. Both plays also implicitly criticize the accepted code of honour. Calderón's rejection of the rigid assumptions of the code of honour is evident also in his tragedies. In the famous *The Mayor of Zalamea* (*c.* 1640), the secrecy and the vengeance demanded by the code are rejected. This play also presents a powerful contrast between the aristocracy and the people: the degeneration of the aristocratic ideal is exposed, wealth is associated with manual labour, and honour is shown to be the consequence and prerogative of moral integrity regardless of class. Yet Calderón's humanity has been questioned in connection with *The Surgeon of His Honour* (1635). The critics who allege that he approves of the murder of an innocent wife because honour demands it overlook the fact that the horror one feels at this deed is precisely what he intended.

Calderón's tragic view of life is, however, wider than his preoccupation with the social code of honour. A keynote is his deep-seated realization that a man can be responsible through his own wrongdoing for the wrongdoing of another. This realization probably derives from Calderón's own family experience. In *Devotion to the Cross* (*c.* 1625) and *Three Judgments at a Blow* (*c.* 1637) the heart of the tragedy lies in the fact that the greatest sinner is also the most sinned against—in that others, before he was born, had begun to dig his grave. *The Painter of His Own Dishonor* (*c.* 1645) is built on a similar plot.

Contrasts of human values in secular plays

The human predicament, as seen by Calderón, lies in the fact that while each man is separated from all other men, his fate is ineluctably intertwined with theirs. He is caught in circumstances that are the collective responsibility of all, yet, being the prisoner of his own limited vision, he cannot perceive the consequences of these circumstances. Connected with this is another keynote of Calderón's drama, that of "confusion," the difficulty of seeing clearly and choosing correctly from among the maze of possibilities that life offers. In *Life Is a Dream* (1635) the material and social advantages that life can bestow are shown to be dreamlike and transient.

The fully developed court plays are best represented by *La hija del aire* (1653; "The Daughter of the Air"). This play in two parts dramatizes the legend of Semiramis (the warrior queen of Babylon whose greed for political power led her to conceal and impersonate her son on his accession). It is often considered Calderón's masterpiece. Highly stylized, it conveys a strong impression of violence. It presents, with considerable complexity, the contrast between passion and reason. Passion, in its self-seeking, in its grasping for power and devouring of everything in the urge to domination, breeds disorder and leads to destruction; reason, in its sacrificing of self-interest to justice and loyalty, produces order. This basic contrast underlies the themes of Calderón's last period, its various aspects being expanded in a number of interesting variations, many directly concerned with the positive values of civilization. Though none has the intensity of *La hija del aire,* most exemplify a thoughtful, dignified, and restrained art. Mythological themes predominate, with a more or less allegorical treatment, as in *Eco y Narciso* (1661; "Echo and Narcissus"), *La estatua de Prometeo* (1669; "The Statue of Prometheus"), and *Fieras afemina amor* (1669; "Wild Beasts Are Tamed by Love").

Religious plays. Calderón's vision of the human world in his secular plays is one of confusion and discord arising out of the inevitable clash of values in the natural order—honour in conflict with love, ambition with loyalty, peace with justice, and so on. The values underlying his thought in these plays are based on natural reason: prudence and social cooperation through unselfishness, trust, and love. His religious plays round off his view of life by confronting natural values with supernatural ones. The most characteristic of these religious plays, following the tradition established outside Spain by the Jesuit drama, are based on stories of conversion and martyrdom, usually of the saints of the early church. One of the most beautiful is *The Constant Prince* (1629), which dramatizes the martyrdom of Prince Ferdinand of Portugal. *The Wonder-Working Magician* (1637) is a more complex religious play; *The Two Lovers of Heaven* (date unknown); and *El Joséf de las mujeres* (*c.* 1640; "The Joseph of Womankind") are the most subtle and difficult. The basic human experience upon which Calderón relies for rational support of religious faith is decay and death and the consequent incapacity of the world to fulfill its promise of happiness. This promise is centred in such natural values as beauty, love, wealth, and power that, although true values if pursued with prudence, cannot satisfy the mind's aspiration for truth or the heart's longing for happiness. Only the apprehension of an "infinite Good" can assuage the restlessness of men.

This religious philosophy is given its most moving expression, in terms of Christian dogma, in the *autos sacramentales.* Seventy-six of these allegorical plays, written for open-air performance on the Feast of Corpus Christi, are extant. In them Calderón brought the tradition of the medieval morality play to a high degree of artistic perfection. The range of his scriptural, patristic, and scholastic learning, together with the assurance of his structural technique and poetic diction, enable him to endow the abstract concepts of dogmatic and moral theology with convincing dramatic life. At their weakest the *autos* tend to depend for their effect upon the ingenuity of their allegories, but at their best they are imbued with profound moral and spiritual insight, and with a poetic feeling varying from tenderness to forcefulness. *Belshazzar's Feast* (*c.* 1630) and *The Great Theatre of the World* (*c.* 1635) are fine examples of the early style; the greater complexity of his middle period is represented by *No hay más fortuna que Dios* (*c.* 1652; "There Is No Fortune but God") and *Lo que va del hombre a Dios* (1652–57; "The Gulf Between Man and God"). But his highest achievement in this type of drama is to be found among those *autos* of his old age that dramatize the dogmas of the Fall and the redemption, notably *La Viña del Señor* (1674; "The Lord's Vineyard"), *La nave del mercader* (1674; "The Merchant's Ship"), *El nuevo hospicio de pobres* (1675; "The New Hospital for the Poor"), *El día mayor de los días* (1678; "The Greatest Day of Days"), and *El pastor fido* (1678; "The Faithful Shepherd"). Here is found Calderón's most moving expression of his compassionate understanding of human waywardness.

Religious allegorical plays

To have found a dramatic form that conveys the doctrines of the Christian faith gives Calderón a special place in literature. But his greatness is not confined to this; the depth and consistency of his thought, his supremely intelligent craftsmanship and artistic integrity, his psychological insight, and the rationality and humanity of his moral standards make him one of the major figures of world drama.

MAJOR WORKS

COMEDIAS: Of Calderón's more than 100 *comedias* the following are some of the best known. *La devoción de la cruz* (*c.* 1625; *Devotion to the Cross* in *Four Plays*, trans. by E. Honig, 1961); *La cisma de Ingalaterra* (*c.* 1627); *El purgatorio de San Patricio* (*c.* 1628; *The Purgatory of St. Patrick* in *Calderón's Dramas*, trans. by D.F. MacCarthy, 1873); *El príncipe constante* (1629; *The Constant Prince* in *Six Plays*, trans. by D.F. MacCarthy, rev. by H.W. Wells, 1960); *Casa con dos puertas, mala es de guardar* (1629); *La dama duende* (1629; *The Phantom Lady* in *Four Plays*); *De una causa dos efectos* (*c.* 1631–32); *La banda y la flor* (1632); *Amar después de la muerte* (1633; *Love After Death*, trans. by Roy Campbell, 1960); *La vida es sueño* (1635; *Life Is a Dream*, trans. by Roy Campbell, 1959); *A secreto agravio, secreta venganza* (1635; *Secret Vengeance for Secret Insult* in *Four Plays*); *El médico de su honra* (1635; *The Surgeon of His Honour*, trans. by Roy Campbell, 1960); *Las tres justicias en una* (*c.* 1637; *Three Judgments at a Blow* in *Eight Dramas of Calderón*, trans. by E.E. Fitzgerald, 1906); *El mágico prodigioso* (1637; *The Wonder-Working Magician* in *Six Plays*); *La niña de Gómez Arias* (*c.* 1638); *No hay cosa como callar* (1639); *El alcalde de Zalamea* (*c.* 1640; *The Mayor of Zalamea*, trans. by W.E. Colford, 1958); *El Joséf de las mujeres* (*c.* 1640); *No siempre lo peor es cierto* (*c.* 1640); *El pintor de su deshonra* (*c.* 1645; *The Painter of His Own Dishonor* in *Eight Dramas of Calderón*); *El jardín de Falerina* (1648), the first of Calderón's zarzuelas, plays in two acts with alternating spoken and sung dialogue; *La hija del aire*, 2 pt. (1653); *La púrpura de la rosa* (1660), one-act opera; *Celos, aun del aire matan* (1660), three-act opera with music by Juan Hidalgo, some of which has not come to light; *Eco y Narciso* (1661); *Fieras afemina amor* (1669); *La estatua de Prometeo* (1669). For other English translations, see those by D.F. MacCarthy (ten plays and *autos*, 1853–73), rev. by H.W. Wells (1960); and *Eight Dramas of Calderón*, which is freely translated by E.E. Fitzgerald (1906).

AUTOS SACRAMENTALES: Seventy-six of these allegorical plays, written for open-air performance on the Feast of Corpus Christi, are extant. The following are some of the best known: *La cena de Baltasar* (*c.* 1630; *Belshazzar's Feast* in *Six Plays*); *El gran teatro del mundo* (*c.* 1635; *The Great Theatre of the World*, trans. by R.C. Trench, 1856); *No hay más fortuna que Dios* (*c.* 1652); *Lo que va del hombre a Dios* (1652–57); *La viña del Señor* (1674); *La nave del mercader* (1674); *El nuevo hospicio de pobres* (1675); *El pastor fido* (1678); *El día mayor de los días* (1678).

BIBLIOGRAPHY. *Biblioteca de autores españoles*, vol. 7, 9, 12, 14 (1944–45); *Obras completas*, new ed., vol. 1, *Dramas*, vol. 2, *Comedias*, both ed. by A. VALBUENA BRIONES; and vol. 3, *Autos sacramentales*, ed. by A. VALBUENA PRAT (1960–67). These editions are not critical or scholarly. Annotated editions, of varying quality, are the 5 vol. (1951–56) of *Selected Comedias and Autos* in the *Clásicos Castellanos*, and 3 vol. of *Tragedies*, ed. by F. RUIZ RAMON (1967–69). Scholarly texts are to be found only among editions of individual plays, for which see *Calderón de la Barca Studies, 1951–69*, ed. by J.H. PARKER and A.M. FOX, pp. 25–59 (1971).

The only attempt at a full biography is E. COTARELO Y MORI, *Ensayo sobre la vida y obras de D. Pedro Calderón de la Barca* (1924). The best general studies are: of the *Autos*, A.A. PARKER, *The Allegorical Drama of Calderón* (1943, reprinted 1968), and E. FRUTOS, *La filosofía de Calderón en sus Autos Sacramentales* (1952); of the *Comedias*, A.E. SLOMAN, *The Dramatic Craftsmanship of Calderón* (1958), and *Critical Essays on the Theatre of Calderón*, ed. by B.W. WARDROPPER (1965).

Calderón's art and thought are being re-assessed in studies still confined to journals. A critical guide to these is (for 1940–58) in the article by H. FLASCHE in *Deutsche Vierteljahrsschrift für Literaturwissenschaft und Geistesgeschichte*, vol. 32, pp. 613–643 (1958); and (for 1951–69) in *Calderón de la Barca Studies*. The University of Hamburg publishes, under the direction of H. FLASCHE, as a subsection of its *Hamburger Romanistische Studien*, a series of studies, including critical editions of *autos*, under the title of *Calderoniana;* 6 vol. have so far (1971) appeared. The existence of an Anglo-American school of criticism has been affirmed and its principles discussed by R.D.F. PRING-MILL in *Litterae Hispanae et Lusitanae*, ed. by H. FLASCHE (1968).

(A.A.P.)

Calendar

A calendar is a means of grouping days in ways convenient for regulating civil life and religious observances and for historical and scientific purposes. The word is derived from the Latin *calendarium*, meaning interest register, or account book, itself a derivation from *calendae* (or *kalendae*), the first day of the Roman month, the day on which future market days, feasts, and other occasions were proclaimed.

The development of a calendar is vital for the study of chronology, since this is concerned with reckoning time by regular divisions, or periods, and using these to date events. It is essential, too, for any civilization that needs to measure periods for agricultural, business, domestic, or other reasons. The first practical calendar to evolve from these requirements was the Egyptian, and it was this that the Romans developed into the Julian calendar that served western Europe for more than 1,500 years. The Gregorian calendar was a further improvement and is now almost universally adopted because it satisfactorily draws into one system the dating of religious festivals based on the phases of the Moon and seasonal activities determined by the movement of the Sun. Such a calendar system is complex, since the periods of the Moon's phases and the Sun's motion are incompatible; but by adopting regular cycles of days and comparatively simple rules for their application, the calendar provides a year with an error of less than half a minute.

This article is divided into the following sections:

I. Early calendar systems
  Standard units and cycles
  Time determination by stars, sun, and moon
  Complex cycles
  The early Roman calendar
  The Jewish calendar
  The Muslim calendar
II. The western calendar and calendar reforms
  The Julian calendar
  The Gregorian calendar
  Calendar reform since the mid-18th century
III. Ancient Middle Eastern calendar systems
  Lunisolar calendars in antiquity
  Ancient Greek calendars in relation to the Middle East
  The Egyptian calendar
IV. The Far East
  The Hindu calendar
  The Chinese calendar
V. Calendar systems of the Americas
  The Maya calendar system
  The Mexican (Aztec) calendar
  Peru: The Inca calendar
  North American Indian time counts

I. Early calendar systems

STANDARD UNITS AND CYCLES

The basic unit of computation in a calendar is the day, and although days are now measured from midnight to midnight, this has not always been so. Astronomers, for instance, from about the 2nd century AD until 1925 counted days from noon to noon. In earlier civilizations and among primitive peoples, where there was less communication between different settlements or groups, different methods of reckoning the day presented no difficulties. Most primitive tribes used a dawn-to-dawn reckoning, calling a succession of days so many dawns, or suns; and this system was continued by the Babylonians and Greeks, who counted a day from sunrise to sunrise. In Egypt, a midnight-to-midnight reckoning was adopted; the Jews and, later, the Italians counted from sunset to sunset. The Teutons counted nights, and from them the grouping of 14 days called a fortnight is derived.

Divisions of the day

There was also great variety in the ways in which the day was subdivided. The Sumerians, for example, divided it into six watches, three during daylight and three during the night; the Jews adopted a similar method. The length of the watches was not constant but varied with the season, the day watches being the longer in summer and the night watches in the winter. Such seasonal variations in divisions of the day became customary in antiquity since they corresponded to the length of the Sun's time above the horizon, at maximum in summer and minimum in winter. Only with the advent of mechanical clocks in western Europe at the end of the 13th century did seasonal (unequal) hours become inconvenient.

Most early Western civilizations used 24 seasonal hours

in the day—12 hours of daylight and 12 of darkness. This was the practice of the Greeks, the Egyptians, and the Romans, and of Western Christendom so far as civil reckoning was concerned. The church adopted its own canonical hours for reckoning daily worship: there were seven of these—matins, prime, terce, sext, none, vespers, and compline—but in secular affairs the system of 24 hours held sway. This number, 2 × 12, or 24, was derived from the Sumerian sexagesimal method of reckoning, based on gradations of 60 (5 × 12 = 60) rather than on multiples of 10, even though the 24-hour-day itself was an Egyptian invention. The Babylonians—the successors of the Sumerians—used a 12-hour division of the day, and their hours were double hours, with only 12 to cover both day and night. They were among the few to have hours of the same length throughout the year because the Babylonians believed the Sun and Moon to travel through the same number of divisions in the sky during each day and night period.

Origins of the week

Once the day is divided into parts, the next task is to gather numbers of days into groups. Among primitive peoples, it was common to count moons (months) rather than days, but later a shorter period than the month was thought more convenient, and an interval between market days was adopted. It varied widely. In West Africa some tribes used a four-day interval; in central Asia five days was customary; the Assyrians adopted six days and the Egyptians, ten days, whereas the Babylonians attached particular significance to the days of the lunation that were multiples of seven. In ancient Rome there was a *nundinae*, or nine-day, period between weekly markets, although because of the Roman method of inclusive numeration a *nundinae* contained what would now be called eight days.

The seven-day week may owe its origin partly to the four (approximately) seven-day phases of the Moon and partly to the Babylonian belief in hebdomadism—the sacredness of the number seven—which itself was probably related to the seven planets. Moreover, by the 1st century BC the Jewish seven-day week seems to have become adopted throughout the Roman world, and this exerted its due influence on Christendom. The origin of the names of the days of the week appears to be astrological and to have been derived from the Latin or Scandinavian god whose hour started the day.

Table 1: Weekday Names

planets	Latin name	French name	Saxon usage	English name
Sun	Dies Solis	Dimanche	Sun's Day	Sunday
Moon	Dies Lunae	Lundi	Moon's Day	Monday
Mars	Dies Martis	Mardi	Tiw's Day	Tuesday
Mercury	Dies Mercurii	Mercredi	Woden's Day	Wednesday
Jupiter	Dies Jovis	Jeudi	Thor's Day	Thursday
Venus	Dies Veneris	Vendredi	Frigg's Day	Friday
Saturn	Dies Saturni	Samedi	Saterne's Day	Saturday

The month is based on the lunation, that period in which the Moon completes a cycle of its phases. Lasting approximately 29½ days, it is easy to recognize and short enough for the days to be counted without using large numbers. In addition, it is very close to the menstrual period of women and also to the duration of cyclic behaviour in some marine creatures. Thus, the month possessed great significance and was often the governing period for religious observances, of which the dating of Easter is a notable example. All early calendars were, essentially, collections of months, the Babylonians using 29- and 30-day periods alternately, the Egyptians fixing the duration of all months at 30 days, with the Greeks copying them, and the Romans in the Julian calendar having a rather more complex system using one 28-day period with the others of either 30 or 31 days.

The seasons

The month is not suitable for determining the seasons, for these are a solar, not a lunar, phenomenon. Seasons vary in different parts of the world—in tropical countries there are just the rainy and dry periods, but elsewhere there are successions of wider changes. In Egypt, the annual flooding of the Nile was followed by seeding and then harvest, and three seasons were recognized; but in Greece and other more northern countries there was a succession of four seasons of slightly different lengths. However many there seemed to be, it was everywhere recognized that seasons were related to the Sun and that they could be determined from solar observations. These might consist of noting the varying length of the midday shadow cast by a stick thrust vertically into the ground or follow the far more sophisticated procedure of deducing the Sun's position against the background of the stars. In either case the result was a year of 365 days, a period incompatible with the 29½-day lunation. To find some simple relationship between the two was the problem that faced all calendar makers from Babylonian times onward.

TIME DETERMINATION BY STARS, SUN, AND MOON

Celestial bodies provide the basic standards for determining the periods of a calendar. Their movement as they rise and set is now known to be a reflection of the Earth's rotation, which, although not precisely uniform, can conveniently be averaged out to provide a suitable calendar day. The day can be measured either by the stars or by the Sun. If the stars are used, then the interval is called the sidereal day and is defined by the period between two passages of a star (more precisely of the vernal equinox, a reference point on the celestial sphere) across the meridian: it is 23 hours, 56 minutes, 4.10 seconds of mean solar time (see below). The interval between two passages of the Sun across the meridian is a solar day. In practice, since the rate of the Sun's motion varies with the seasons, use is made of a fictitious Sun that always moves across the sky at an even rate. This period of constant length, far more convenient for civil purposes, is the mean solar day, which has a duration in sidereal time of 24 hours, 3 minutes, 56.55 seconds. It is longer than the sidereal day because the motion of the Earth in its orbit during the period between two transits of the Sun means that the Earth must complete more than a whole revolution to bring the Sun back to the meridian. The mean solar day is the period used in calendar computation.

Measurement of the day, the month, and the year

The month is determined by the Moon's passage around the Earth, and, as in the case of the day, there are several ways in which it can be defined. In essence, these are of two kinds: first, the period taken by the Moon to complete an orbit of the Earth and, second, the time taken by the Moon to complete a cycle of phases. For astronomically primitive societies, orbital measures were too sophisticated, and the month was determined by noting the interval between the appearance of one thin crescent Moon and the next—in other words, from one new Moon to another. But however the phases are defined, the interval is now known to be 29.53059 days. Known as the synodic month, it is longer than the orbital month, just as the solar day is longer than the sidereal, and for a similar reason. It grew to be the basis of the calendar month.

The year is the period taken by the Earth to complete an orbit around the Sun and, again, there are a number of ways in which this can be measured. But for calculating a calendar that is to remain in step with the seasons, it is most convenient to use the tropical year, since this refers directly to the Sun's apparent annual motion north and south; it is defined as the interval between successive passages of the Sun through the vernal equinox (*i.e.*, when it crosses the celestial equator late in March) and amounts to 365.242199 mean solar days.

The tropical year and the synodic month are incommensurable, 12 synodic months amounting to 354.36706 days, almost 11 days shorter than the tropical year. Moreover, neither is composed of a complete number of days, so that to compile any calendar that keeps in step with the Moon's phases or with the seasons it is necessary to insert days at appropriate intervals; such additions are known as intercalations.

In primitive lunar calendars, intercalation was often achieved by taking alternately months of 29 and 30 days. When, in order to keep dates in step with the seasons, a solar calendar was adopted, some greater difference between the months and the Moon's phases was bound to occur. And the solar calendar presented an even more fundamental problem—that of finding the precise length of the tropical year. Observations of cyclic changes in plant or animal life were far too inaccurate, and astronomical observations became necessary. Since the stars are not visible when the Sun is in the sky, some indirect way had to be found to determine its precise location among them. In tropical and subtropical countries it was possible to use the method of heliacal risings. Here the first task was to determine the constellations around the whole sky through which the Sun appears to move in the course of a year. Then, by observing the stars rising in the east just after sunset it was possible to know which were precisely opposite in the sky, where the Sun lay at that time. Such heliacal risings could, therefore, be used to determine the seasons and the tropical year. In temperate countries, the angle at which stars rise up from the horizon is not steep enough for this method to be adopted, so that there wood or stone structures were built to mark out points along the horizon to allow analogous observations to be made.

Locating the Sun among the stars

Stonehenge

The most famous of these is Stonehenge in Wiltshire, England, where the original structure appears to have been built about 2000 BC and additions made at intervals several centuries later. It is composed of a series of holes, stones, and archways arranged mostly in circles, the outermost ring of holes having 56 marked positions, the inner ones 30 and 29, respectively. In addition, there is a large stone—the heel stone—set to the northeast, as well as some smaller stone markers. Observations were made by lining up holes or stones with the heel stone or one of the other markers and watching for the appearance of the Sun or Moon against that point on the horizon that lay in the same straight line. The extreme north and south positions on the horizon of the Sun—the summer and winter solstices—were particularly noted, while the inner circles, with their 29 and 30 marked positions, allowed "hollow" and "full" (29- or 30-day) lunar months to be counted off. To obtain other astronomical information, such as the advent of eclipses, observations were made from various different positions, especially those on the outer circle of stones. More than 600 contemporaneous structures of an analogous but simpler kind have been discovered in Britain and Brittany. It appears, then, that astronomical observation for calendrical purposes was a widespread practice in some temperate countries three to four millennia ago.

Today a solar calendar is kept in step with the seasons by a fixed rule of intercalation. But although the Egyptians, who used the heliacal rising of Sirius to determine the annual inundation of the Nile, knew that the tropical year was about 365.25 days in length, they still used a 365-day year without intercalation. This meant that the calendar date of Sirius' rising became increasingly out of step with the original dates as the years progressed. In consequence, while the agricultural seasons were regulated by the heliacal rising of Sirius, the civil calendar ran its own separate course. It was not until well into Roman times that an intercalary day once every four years was instituted to retain coincidence. Without such a rule, the agricultural calendar had to be determined solely by astronomical observation.

COMPLEX CYCLES

Although the incommensurability of months and years and the fact that neither occupied a whole number of days was recognized quite early in all the great civilizations, it was also appreciated that the difference between calendar dates and the celestial phenomena due to occur on them would first grow and then diminish and that a time would come when they were once more in coincidence. The succession of differences and coincidences would be cyclic, recurring time and again as the years passed. An early recognition of this was the Egyptian Sothic cycle. The 365-day year used in the Egyptian calendar was in error with respect to the heliacal risings of the star Sirius (Sothis) by one quarter of a day per tropical year. This amounted to one day every four tropical years, or one whole Egyptian calendar year every 1,460 tropical years (4 × 365), which was equivalent to 1,461 Egyptian calendar years. After this period the heliacal rising and setting of Sothis would again coincide with the calendar dates (see below, *The Egyptian calendar*).

The main use of cycles was to try to find some commensurable basis for lunar and solar calendars, and the most famous of all the early attempts was that usually attributed to Cleostratus of Tenedos (*c.* 500 BC) and Eudoxus of Cnidus (390–*c.*340 BC), often known as the *octaëteris*. Modern scholarship shows Cleostratus to be a somewhat shadowy figure, and it has also become clear that a cycle of this kind was adopted in Babylon between 529 and 504 BC. Whatever its exact origins, the cycle covered eight years, as its name implies; and since in the 6th century BC the year was accepted to be 365 days in length, the *octaëteris* amounted to 8 × 365, or 2,920 days. This was very close to the total of 99 lunations (99 × 29.5 = 2,920.5 days), so this cycle gave a worthwhile link between lunar and solar calendars. When, in the 4th century BC, the accepted length of the year became 365.25 days, the total number of solar calendar days involved became 2,922, and it was then realized that the *octaëteris* was not so satisfactory a cycle as supposed, since the 29.5-day lunation period was still used.

The *octaëteris*

The saros

Another early and important cycle was the saros, essentially an eclipse cycle. There has been some confusion over its precise nature because the name is derived from the Babylonian word *shār* or *shāru*, which could mean either "universe" or the number 3,600 (*i.e.*, 60 × 60). In the latter sense it was used by Berosus (*c.* 290 BC) and a few later authors to refer to a period of 3,600 years. Its first astronomical use appears in an anonymous encyclopaedia called the *Suda Lexicon* (*Suidas Lexicon*), of about 1000 AD. There it was said to be a measure of 222 months used by the Chaldeans, and, although this cannot be quite correct, it is certainly clear that by the 4th century BC the Babylonians did know something of an 18-year or 216-month (18 × 12) cycle of eclipses. What is now known as the saros and appears as such in astronomical textbooks (still usually credited to the Babylonians) is a period of 18 years 11⅓ days (or with one day more or less, depending on how many leap years are involved), after which a series of eclipses is repeated (see ECLIPSE, OCCULTATION, AND TRANSIT).

In Central America an independent system of cycles was established (see below *Calendar systems of the Americas*).

The Metonic cycle

The most significant of all the early attempts to provide some commensurability between a religious lunar calendar and the tropical year was the Metonic cycle. This was first devised about 430 BC by the astronomer Meton of Athens. Meton worked with another Athenian astronomer, Euctemon, and made a series of observations of the solstices, when the Sun's noonday shadow cast by a vertical pillar, or gnomon, reaches its annual maximum or minimum, to determine the length for the tropical year. Taking a synodic month to be 29.5 days, they then computed the difference between 12 of these lunations and their tropical year, which amounted to 11 days. It could therefore be removed by intercalating a month of 33 days every third year. But months were measured in whole days, and Meton and Euctemon wanted a long-term rule that would be as accurate as they could make it, so they settled on a 19-year cycle. This cycle consisted of 12 years of 12 lunar months each and seven years each of 13 lunar months, a total of 235 lunar months. If this total of 235 lunations is taken to contain 110 hollow months of 29 days and 125 full months of 30 days, the total comes to (110 × 29) + (125 × 30), or 6,940 days. The difference between this lunar calendar and a solar calendar of 365 days amounted to only five days in 19 years and, in addition, gave an average length for the tropical year of 365.25 days, a much-improved value that was, however, allowed to make no difference to daily reckoning in the civil calendar. But the greatest advantage of this cycle was that it laid down a lunar calendar that possessed a definite rule for inserting intercalary months and kept in step with a cycle of the tropical years. It also gave a more accurate average value for the tropical year and was so successful that it formed the basis of the calendar adopted in the Seleucid Empire (Mesopotamia) and was used in the Jewish calendar and the calendar of the Christian Church; it also influenced Indian astronomical teaching.

The Metonic cycle was improved by both Callippus and Hipparchus. Callippus of Cyzicus (*c.* 370–300 BC) was perhaps the foremost astronomer of his day. He formed what has been called the Callippic period, essentially a cycle of four Metonic periods. It was more accurate than the original Metonic cycle and made use of the fact that 365.25 days is a more precise value for the tropical year than 365 days. The Callippic period consisted of 4 × 235, or 940 lunar months, but its distribution of hollow and full months was different from Meton's. Instead of having totals of 440 hollow and 500 full months, Callippus adopted 441 hollow and 499 full, thus reducing the length of four Metonic cycles by one day. The total days involved therefore became (441 × 29) + (499 × 30), or 27,759, and 27,759 ÷ (19 × 4) gives 365.25 days exactly. Thus the Callippic cycle fitted 940 lunar months precisely to 76 tropical years of 365.25 days.

Precession of the equinoxes

Hipparchus, who flourished in Rhodes about 150 BC and was probably the greatest observational astronomer of antiquity, discovered from his own observations and those of others made over the previous 150 years that the equinoxes, where the ecliptic (the Sun's apparent path) crosses the celestial equator (the celestial equivalent of the terrestrial Equator), were not fixed in space but moved slowly in a westerly direction. The movement is small, amounting to no more than 2° in 150 years, and it is known now as the precession of the equinoxes. Calendrically, it was an important discovery because the tropical year is measured with reference to the equinoxes, and precession reduced the value accepted by Callippus. Hipparchus calculated the tropical year to have a length of 365.242 days, which was very close to the present 365.242199 days; he also computed the precise length of a lunation, using a "great year" of four Callippic cycles. He arrived at the value of 29.53058 days for a lunation, which, again, is comparable with the present-day figure, 29.53059 days.

The calendar dating of historical events, and the determination of how many days have elapsed since some astronomical or other occurrence are difficult for a number of reasons. Leap years have to be inserted, but not always regularly, months have changed their lengths and new ones have been added from time to time, years have commenced on varying dates and their lengths have been computed in various ways. Since historical dating must take all these factors into account, it occurred to the 16th-century French classicist and literary scholar Joseph Justus Scaliger (1540–1609) that a consecutive numbering system could be of inestimable help. This he thought should be arranged as a cyclic period of great length and he worked out the system that is known as the Julian period, in honour of his father Julius Caesar Scaliger (1484–1558). He published his proposals in Paris in 1583 under the title *De Emendatione Temporum*.

The Julian period is a cycle of 7,980 years. It is based on the Metonic Cycle of 19 years, a "solar cycle" of 28 years, and the Indiction cycle of 15 years. The so-called solar cycle was a period after which the days of the seven-day week repeated on the same dates. Since one year contains 52 weeks of seven days, plus one day, the days of the week would repeat every seven years were no leap year to intervene. A Julian calendar (see below) leap year cycle is four years, therefore the days of the week repeat on the same dates every 4 × 7 = 28 years.

Cycle of Indiction

The cycle of the Indiction was a fiscal, not an astronomical, period. It first appears in tax receipts for Egypt in AD 303, and probably took its origin in a periodic 15-year taxation census that followed Diocletian's reconquest of Egypt in AD 297. By multiplying the Metonic, solar, and Indiction cycles together, Scaliger obtained his cycle of 7,980 years (19 × 28 × 15 = 7,980), a period of sufficient length to cover most previous and future historical dates required at any one time.

Scaliger, tracing each of the three cycles back in time, found that all coincided in the year 4713 BC, on the Julian calendar reckoning. On the information available to him, he believed this to be a date considerably before any historical events. He therefore set the beginning of the first Julian period at Jan. 1, 4713 BC. The years of the Julian period are not now used, but the day number is still used in astronomy and in preparing calendar tables, for it is the only record where days are free from combination into weeks and months.

Non-astronomical cycles

A number of non-astronomical natural signs have also been used in determining the seasons. In the Mediterranean area, such indications change rapidly, and Hesiod (*c.* 800 BC) mentions a wide variety: the cry of migrating cranes, which indicated a time for plowing and sowing; the time when snails climb up plants, after which digging in vineyards should cease; and so on. An unwitting approximation to the tropical year may also be obtained by intercalation, using a simple lunar calendar and observations of animal behaviour. Such an unusual situation has grown up among the Yami fishermen of Botel-Tobago Island, near Taiwan. They use a calendar based on phases of the Moon, and some time about March (the precise date depends on the degree of error of their lunar calendar compared with the tropical year) they go out in boats with lighted flares. If flying fish appear, the fishing season is allowed to commence, but if the lunar calendar is too far out of step with the seasons, the flying fish will not rise. Fishing is then postponed for another lunation, which they insert in the lunar calendar, thus having a year of 13 instead of the usual 12 lunations.

THE EARLY ROMAN CALENDAR

This originated as a local calendar in the city of Rome, supposedly drawn up by Romulus some seven or eight centuries BC. The year began in March and consisted of ten months, six of 30 days and four of 31 days, making a total of 304 days: it ended in December, to be followed by what seems to have been an uncounted winter gap. Numa Pompilius, traditionally the second king of Rome (715?–673? BC), is supposed to have added two extra months, January and February, to fill the gap and to have increased the total number of days by 50, making 354. To obtain sufficient days for his new months, he is then said to have deducted one day from the 30-day months, thus having 56 days to divide between January and February. But since the Romans had, or had developed, a superstitious dread of even numbers, January was given an extra day; February was still left with an even number of days, but as that month was given over to the infernal gods, this was considered appropriate. The system allowed the year of 12 months to have 355 days, an uneven number.

The so-called Roman Republican calendar was supposedly introduced by the Etruscan Tarquinius Priscius (616–579 BC), traditionally the fifth king of Rome. He wanted the year to begin in January since it contained the festival of the god of gates (later the god of all beginnings), but expulsion of the Etruscan dynasty in 510 BC led to this particular reform being dropped. The Roman Republican calendar still contained only 355 days, with February having 28 days; March, May, Quintilis (July), and October 31 days each; January, April, June, Sextilis (August), September, November, and December 29 days. It was basically a lunar calendar and short by 10¼ days of a 365¼-day tropical year, so in order to prevent it from becoming too far out of step with the seasons, an intercalary month, Intercalans, or Mercedonius (from *merces* meaning wages, since workmen were paid at this time of year), was inserted between February 23 and 24. It consisted of 27 or 28 days and was added once every two years; and in historical times at least, the remaining five days of February were omitted. The intercalation was therefore equivalent to an additional 22 or 23 days, so that in a four-year period the total days in the calendar amounted to (4 × 355) + 22 + 23, or 1,465: this gave an average of 366.25 days per year.

Intercalation was the duty of the Pontifices, a board that assisted the chief magistrate in his sacrificial functions. The reasons for their decisions were kept secret, but because of some negligence and a measure of ignorance and corruption, the intercalations were irregular, and seasonal chaos resulted. In spite of this and the fact that it was over a day too long compared with the tropical year, much of the modified Roman Republican calendar was carried over into the Gregorian calendar now in general use. (C.A.R.)

THE JEWISH CALENDAR

The structure of the calendar. The Jewish calendar in use today is lunisolar, the years being solar and the months lunar, but it also allows for a week of seven days. Because the year exceeds 12 lunar months by about 11 days, a 13th month of 30 days is intercalated in the third, sixth, eighth, 11th, 14th, 17th, and 19th years of a 19-year cycle. Arrangements akin to this procedure are well attested in ancient Babylon (see below *Sumero-Babylonian Calendars*). Among the Jews, however, a regular sequence of intercalation in fixed intervals is stated in the sources to have been introduced as late as the 4th century of the Christian Era and dates from the period of Exile. For practical purposes—*e.g.*, for reckoning the commencement of sabbaths—the day begins at sunset; but the calendar day of 24 hours always begins at 6 PM. The hour is divided into 1,080 parts (*ḥalaqim;* this division is originally Babylonian), each part (*ḥeleq*) equalling 3⅓ seconds. The *ḥeleq* is further divided into 76 *regaʿim*.

"Full" and "defective" months

The synodic month is the average interval between two mean conjunctions of the Sun and Moon, when these bodies are as near as possible in the sky, which is reckoned at 29 days 12 hours 44 minutes 3⅓ seconds; a conjunction is called a *molad*. This is also a Babylonian value. In the calendar month, however, only complete days are reckoned, the "full" month containing 30 days and the "defective" month 29 days. The months Nisan, Sivan (Siwan), Av, Tishri, Shevaṭ, and, in a leap year, First Adar are always full; Iyyar, Tammuz, Elul, Ṭevet, and Adar (known as Second Adar, or Adar Sheni, in a leap year) are always defective, while Ḥeshvan (Ḥeshwan) and Kislev (Kislew) vary. The calendar, thus, is schematic and independent of the true New Moon. The number of days in a year varies. The number of days in a synodic month multiplied by 12 in a common year and by 13 in a leap year would yield fractional figures. Hence, again reckoning complete days only, the common year has 353, 354, or 355 days and the leap year 383, 384, or 385 days. A year in which both Ḥeshvan and Kislev are full, called complete (*shelema*), has 355 or (if a leap year) 385 days; a normal (*sedura*) year, in which Ḥeshvan is defective and Kislev full, has 354 or 384 days; while a defective (*ḥasera*) year, in which both these months are defective, has 353 or 383 days. The character of a year (*qeviʿa*, literally "fixing") is described by three Hebrew letters, the first and third giving, respectively, the days of the weeks on which the New Year occurs and Passover begins, while the second is the initial of the Hebrew word for defective, normal, or complete. There are 14 types of *qeviʿot*, seven in common and seven in leap years. The New Year begins on Tishri 1, which may be the day of the *molad* of Tishri but is often delayed by one or two days for various reasons. Thus, in order to prevent the Day of Atonement (Tishri 10) from falling on a Friday or a Sunday and the seventh day of Tabernacles (Tishri 21) from falling on a Saturday, the new year must avoid commencing on Sundays, Wednesdays, or Fridays. Again, if the *molad* of Tishri occurs at noon or later, the new year is delayed by one or, if this would cause it to fall as above, two days. These delays (*deḥiyyot*) necessitate, by reason of the above-mentioned limits on the number of days in the year, two other delays.

The seasons in the Jewish calendar

The mean beginning of the four seasons is called *tequfa* (literally "orbit," or "course"); the *tequfa* of Nisan denotes the mean Sun at the vernal equinox, that of Tammuz the mean Sun at the summer solstice, that of Tishri the mean Sun at the autumn equinox, and that of Ṭevet the mean Sun at the winter solstice. As 52 weeks are the equivalent to 364 days, and the length of the solar year is nearly 365¼ days, the *tequfot* move forward in the week by about 1¼ days each year. Accordingly, reckoning the length of the year at the approximate value of 365¼ days, they are held to revert after 28 years ($28 \times 1\frac{1}{4} = 35$ days) to the same hour on the same day of the week (Tuesday, 6 PM) as at the beginning. This cycle is called the great, or solar, cycle (*maḥzor gadol or ḥamma*). The present Jewish calendar is mainly based on the more accurate value 365 days, five hours, 55 minutes, $25\frac{25}{57}$ seconds—in excess of the true tropical year by about 6 minutes, 40 seconds. Thus, it is advanced by one day in about 228 years with regard to the equinox.

To a far greater extent than the solar cycle of 28 years, the Jewish calendar employs, as mentioned above, a small, or lunar, cycle (*maḥzor qaṭan*) of 19 years, adjusting the lunar months to the solar years by intercalations. Passover, on Nisan 15, is not to begin before the spring *tequfa*, and so the intercalary month is added after Adar. The *maḥzor qaṭan* is akin to the Metonic cycle, a 19-year cycle proposed by the Athenian astronomer Meton in about 432 BC in which seven months were intercalated, and is based on the nearly correct notion that 235 lunar months are equal to 19 solar years. As, however, 19 "years" of 12 lunar months contain only 228 lunar months, seven intercalations are needed at the intervals set forth above in a 19-year cycle to bring it up to the required 235 months.

The Jewish Era in use today is that dated from the supposed year of the Creation (designated *anno mundi* or AM) with its epoch, or beginning, in 3761 BC. The Jewish year 5735 AM, the 16th in the 302nd lunar cycle and the 23rd in the 205th solar cycle, is a regular year of 12 months, or 354 days. The *qeviʿa* is, using the three respective letters of the Hebrew alphabet as two numerals and an initial in the manner indicated in the second paragraph above, GKH, which indicates that Rosh Hashana (New Year) begins on the third (G = 3) and Passover on the fifth (H = 5) day of the week and that the year is regular (K = *ke-sidra*); *i.e.*, Ḥeshvan is defective—29 days, and Kislev full—30 days. This Jewish year (1974–75 of the Christian Era) begins September 17, 1974, and ends September 5, 1975. Neglecting the thousands, current Jewish years AM are converted into years of the current Christian Era by adding 239 or 240—239 from the Jewish New Year (about September) to December 31 and 240 from January 1 to the eve of the Jewish New Year. The adjustment differs slightly for the conversion of dates of now-antiquated versions of the Jewish Era of the Creation and the Christian Era, or both. Tables for the exact conversion of such dates are available.

Months and important days. The months of the Jewish year and the notable days are as follows:

Tishri: 1–2, Rosh Hashana (New Year); 3, Fast of Gedaliah; 10, Yom Kippur (Day of Atonement); 15–21, Sukkot (Tabernacles); 22, Shemini Atzeret (Eighth Day of Solemn Assembly); 23, Simḥat Torah (Rejoicing of the Law).
Ḥeshvan.
Kislev: 25, Ḥanukka (Festival of Lights) begins.
Tevet: 2 or 3, Ḥanukka ends; 10, Fast.
Shevaṭ: 15, New Year for Trees (Mishna).
Adar: 13, Fast of Esther; 14–15, Purim (Lots).
Second Adar (Adar Sheni) or ve-Adar (intercalated month); Adar holidays fall in ve-Adar during leap years.
Nisan: 15–22, Pesaḥ (Passover).
Iyyar: 5, Israel Independence Day.
Sivan: 6–7, Shavuot (Feast of Weeks [Pentecost]).
Tammuz: 17, Fast (Mishna).
Av: 9, Fast (Mishna).
Elul. (E.J.Wi.)

The calendar in Jewish history. For the months of the Jewish year and the notable days of the Jewish calendar see JEWISH RELIGIOUS YEAR. Present knowledge of the pre-exilic Jewish calendar is both limited and uncertain. The Bible refers to calendar matters only incidentally, and the dating of components of Mosaic Law remains doubtful. The earliest datable source for the Hebrew calendar is the Gezer Calendar, written probably in the age of Solomon, in the late 10th century BC. The inscription indicates the length of main agricultural tasks within the cycle of 12 lunations. The calendar term here is yereaḥ, which in Hebrew denotes both "moon" and "month." The second Hebrew term for month, *ḥodesh*, properly means the "newness" of the lunar crescent. Thus, the Hebrew months were lunar. They are not named in pre-exilic sources except in the biblical report of the building of Solomon's Temple in I Kings, where the names of three months, two of them also attested in the Phoenician calendar, are given; the months are usually numbered rather than named. The "beginning of the months" was the month of the Passover. In some passages, the Passover month is that of *ḥodesh ha-aviv*, the lunation that coincides with the barley being in the ear. Thus, the Hebrew calendar is tied in with the course of the Sun, that determines ripening of the grain. It is not known how the lunar year of 354 days was adjusted to the Sun year of 365 days. The Bible never mentions intercalation. The year *shana*, properly "change" (of seasons), was the agricultural and, thus, liturgical year. There is no reference to the New Year's day in the Bible.

After the conquest of Jerusalem (587 BC), the Babylonians introduced their cyclic calendar (see below *Sumero-Babylonian calendars*) and the reckoning of their regnal years from Nisanu 1, about the spring equinox. The Jews now had a finite calendar year with a New Year's day, and they adopted the Babylonian month names, which they continue to use. From 587 BC until AD 70, the Jewish civil year was Babylonian, except for the period of Alexander the Great and the Ptolemies (332–200 BC), when the Macedonian calendar (see below *Ancient Greek calendars in relation to the Middle East: Earliest sources*) was used. The situation after the destruction of the Temple in Jerusalem in AD 70 remains unclear. It is not known whether the Romans introduced their Julian calendar or the calendar that the Jews of Palestine used after AD 70 for their business transactions. There is no calendar reference in the New Testament; the contemporary Aramaic documents from Judaea are rare and prove only that the Jews dated events according to the years of the Roman emperors. The abundant data in the Talmudic sources concern only the religious calendar.

Use of the New Moon

In the latter, the commencement of the month was determined by the observation of the crescent New Moon, and the date of the Passover was tied in with the ripening of barley. The actual witnessing of the New Moon and observing of the stand of crops in Judaea were required for the functioning of the religious calendar (see below *Muslim calendar*). The Jews of the Diaspora, who generally used the civil calendar of their respective countries, were informed by messengers from Palestine about the coming festivals. This practice is already attested for 143 BC. After the destruction of the Temple in AD 70, rabbinic leaders took over from the priests the fixing of the religious calendar. Visual observation of the New Moon was supplemented and toward AD 200, in fact, supplanted by secret astronomical calculation. But the Diaspora, or Dispersion, was often reluctant to wait for the arbitrary decision of the calendar makers in the Holy Land. Thus, in Syrian Antioch in AD 328–342, the Passover was always celebrated in (Julian) March, the month of the spring equinox, without regard to the Palestinian rules and rulings. To preserve the unity of Israel, the patriarch Hillel II, in 358/359, published the "secret" of calendar making, which essentially consisted of the use of the Babylonian 19-year cycle with some modifications required by the Jewish ritual.

The application of these principles occasioned controversies as late as the 10th century AD. In the 8th century, the Karaites, following Muslim practice, returned to the actual observation of the crescent New Moon and of the stand of barley in Judaea. But some centuries later they also had to use a precalculated calendar. The Samaritans, likewise, used a computed calendar.

Because of the importance of the sabbath as a time divider, the seven-day week served as a time unit in Jewish worship and life. As long as the length of a year and of every month remained unpredictable, it was convenient to count weeks. The origin of the biblical septenary, or seven-day, week remains unknown; its days were counted from Sunday on. A visionary, probably writing in the Persian or early Hellenistic age under the name of the prediluvian Enoch, suggested the religious calendar of 364 days, or 52 weeks, based on the week, in which all festivals always fall on the same weekday. His idea was later taken up by the Dead Sea Scrolls people. (E.J.Bi.)

THE MUSLIM CALENDAR

The Muslim Era is computed from the starting point of the year of the emigration (Hegira); that is, from the year in which Muḥammad, the prophet of Islām, migrated from Mecca to Medina, 622 AD. The second caliph, ʿUmar I, who reigned 634–644, set the first day of the month Muḥarram as the beginning of the year (see table of months and days); that is, July 16, 622, which had already been fixed by the Qur'an as the first day of the year.

Table 2: Muslim Months and Days

	days		days
Muḥarram	30	Rajab	30
Ṣafar	29	Sha ʿbān	29
Rabīʿ I	30	Ramaḍān	30
Rabīʿ II	29	Shawwāl	29
Jumādā I	30	Dhū al-Qa ʿdah	30
Jumādā II	29	Dhū al-Ḥijjah	29

The years of the Muslim calendar are lunar and always consist of 12 lunar months alternately 30 and 29 days long, beginning with the approximate New Moon. The year has 354 days, but the last month (Dhū al-Ḥijjah) sometimes has an intercalated day, bringing it up to 30 days and making a total of 355 days for that year. The months do not keep to the same seasons in relation to the Sun, because there are no intercalations of months. The months regress through all the seasons every 32½ years.

The names of the months and the number of days in each are given in the accompanying Table.

Ramaḍān

Ramaḍān, the ninth month, is observed throughout the Muslim world as a month of fasting. According to the Qur'an, Muslims must see the New Moon with the naked eye before they can begin their fast. The practice has arisen that two witnesses should testify to this before a *qāḍī* (judge), who, if satisfied, communicates the news to the *muftī* (the interpreter of Muslim law), who orders the beginning of the fast. It has become usual for Middle Eastern Arab countries to accept, with reservations, the verdict of Cairo. Should the New Moon prove to be invisible, then the month Shaʿbān, immediately preceding Ramaḍān, will be reckoned as 30 days in length, and the fast will begin on the day following the last day of this month. The end of the fast follows the same procedure.

The era of the Hegira is the official era in Saudi Arabia, Yemen, and the principalities of the Persian Gulf. Egypt, Syria, Jordan, and Morocco use both the Muslim and the Christian eras. In all Muslim countries, people use the Muslim Era in private, even though the Christian Era may be in official use.

Some Muslim countries have made a compromise on this matter. Turkey, as early as 1088 AH (AD 1677), took over the solar (Julian) year with its month names but kept the Muslim Era. March 1 was taken as the beginning of the year (commonly called *marti year*, after the Turkish word *mart*, for March). Late in the 19th century, the Gregorian calendar was adopted. In the 20th century, Pres. Mustafa Kemal Atatürk ordered a complete change to the Christian Era. Iran, under Reza Shah Pahlavi (reigned 1925–41), also adopted the solar year but with Persian names for the months and keeping the Muslim Era. March 21 is the beginning of the Iranian year. Thus, the Iranian year 1349 began on March 21, 1970. This era is still in use officially. (N.A.Z.)

II. The western calendar and calendar reforms

The calendar now in general worldwide use had its origin in the desire for a solar calendar that kept in step with the seasons and possessed fixed rules of intercalation. Because it developed in Western Christendom, it had also to provide a method for dating movable religious feasts, the timing of which had been based on a lunar reckoning. To reconcile the lunar and solar schemes, features of the Roman Republican calendar and the Egyptian calendar were combined.

The Roman Republican calendar was basically a lunar reckoning and became increasingly out of phase with the seasons as time passed. By about 50 BC the vernal equinox that should have fallen late in March fell on the Ides of May, some eight weeks later, and it was plain that this error would continue to increase. Moreover, the behaviour of the Pontifices made it necessary to seek a fixed rule of intercalation in order to put an end to arbitrariness in inserting months.

In addition to the problem of intercalation, it was clear that the average Roman Republican year of 366.25 days would always show a continually increasing disparity with the seasons, amounting to one month every 30 years, or three months a century. But the great difficulty facing any reformer was that there seemed to be no way of effecting a change that would still allow the months to remain in step with the phases of the Moon and the year with the seasons. It was necessary to make a fundamental break with traditional reckoning to devise an efficient seasonal calendar.

THE JULIAN CALENDAR

In the mid-1st century BC Julius Caesar invited Sosigenes, an Alexandrian astronomer, to advise him about the reform of the calendar, and Sosigenes decided that the only practical step was to abandon the lunar calendar altogether. Months must be arranged on a seasonal basis, and a tropical (solar) year used, as in the Egyptian calendar, but with its length taken as 365¼ days, a value more accurate than the Egyptians' 365.

To remove the immense discrepancy between calendar date and equinox, it was decided that the year known in modern times as 46 BC should have two intercalations. The first was the customary intercalation of the Roman Republican calendar due that year, the insertion of 23 days following February 23. The second intercalation, to bring the calendar in step with the equinoxes, was achieved by inserting two additional months between the end of November and the beginning of December. This insertion amounted to an addition of 67 days, making a total intercalation for the year of 90 days, and causing the beginning of March, 45 BC in the Roman Republican calendar, to fall on what is still called January 1 of the Julian calendar.

Previous errors having been corrected, the next step was to prevent their recurrence. Here Sosigenes' suggestion about a tropical year was adopted and any pretence to a lunar calendar rejected. The figure of 365.25 days was accepted for the tropical year, and to achieve this by a simple civil reckoning, Caesar directed that a calendar year of 365 days be adopted and that an extra day be intercalated between February 23 and 24 every fourth year. Since February ordinarily had 28 days, February 23 was the sixth day before the Kalendae, or beginning of March, and known as the *sexto-kalendae;* the intercalary day, when it appeared, came the day after, and was therefore called the *bis-sexto-kalendae*. This practice led to the term bissextile being used to refer to such a leap year.

Leap year

The name leap year is a later connotation, probably derived from the Old Norse *hlaupa* ("to leap") and used because, in a bissextile year, any fixed festival after February leaps forward, falling on the next weekday but one to that on which it fell the previous year, not on the next weekday as it would do in an ordinary year.

In Caesar's edict, the intercalary day was known as a *punctum temporis* (point of time), and anyone born that day had subsequent birthdays on February 23 (the day before); but lawyers then and in medieval times raised a number of arguments about its precise interpretation. Also, the Pontifices misinterpreted the edict and inserted the intercalation too frequently. The error arose because of the Roman practice of inclusive numbering, so that an intercalation once every fourth year meant to them intercalating every three years, because a bissextile year was counted as the first year of the next four year period. This error continued undetected for 36 years, during which period 12 days instead of nine were added. The emperor Augustus made a correction by omitting intercalary days between 8 BC and AD 4. In consequence it was not until 48 years after 45 BC that the Julian calendar came into proper operation, a fact that is important in chronology but is often forgotten.

Months of the Julian calendar

It seems that the months of the Julian calendar were taken over from the Roman Republican calendar but were slightly modified to give a more even pattern of numbering. The Republican calendar months of March, May, and Quintilis (July), which had each possessed 31 days, were retained unaltered. Although there is doubt about the details, changes seem probably to have occurred as follows. Except for October, all the months that had previously had only 29 days had either one or two days added. January, September, and November received two days, bringing their totals to 31, while April, June, Sextilis (August), and December received one day each, bringing their totals to 30. October was reduced by one day to a total of 30 days, and February increased to 29 days, or 30 in a bissextile year. With the exception of February, the scheme resulted in months having 30 or 31 days alternately throughout the year. And in order to help farmers, Caesar issued an almanac showing on which dates of his new calendar various seasonal astronomical phenomena would occur.

These arrangements for the months can only have remained in force for a short time, because in 8 BC changes were made by Augustus. In 44 BC, the second year of the Julian calendar, the Senate had decided to alter the name of the month Quintilis to Julius (July), in honour of Julius Caesar, and in 8 BC Augustus prevailed upon them to change the name of Sextilis to Augustus (August), in his honour. Perhaps because Augustus felt that his month must have at least as many days as Julius Caesar's, February was reduced to 28 days and August increased to 31. But because this made three 31 day months (July, August, and September) appear in succession, Augustus is supposed to have reduced September to 30 days, added a day to October to make it 31 days, reduced November by one day to 30 days, and increased December from 30 to 31 days, giving the months the lengths they have today.

Divisions of the month

The Julian calendar retained the Roman Republican calendar method of numbering the days of the month. Compared with the present system, the Roman numbering seems to run backward, for the first day of the month was known as the Kalendae, but subsequent days were not enumerated as so many after the Kalendae but as so many before the following Nonae ("nones"), the day called nonae being the ninth day before the Ides (from *iduare*, meaning "to divide"), which occurred in the middle of the month and were supposed to coincide with the full moon. Days after the Nonae and before the Ides were numbered as so many before the Ides, and those after the Ides as so many before the Kalendae of the next month.

There were no weeks in the original Julian calendar, but days were designated either *dies fasti* or *dies nefasti*, the former being business days and days on which the courts were open: this had been the practice in the Roman Republican calendar. Julius Caesar designated his additional days all as *dies fasti,* and they were added at the end of the month so that there was no interference with the dates traditionally fixed for *dies comitiales* (days when public assemblies might be convened) and *dies festi* and *dies feriae* (religious festivals and holy days). Originally, then, the Julian calendar had a permanent set of dates for administrative matters. The official introduction of the seven-day week by the Emperor Constantine I in the 4th century AD disrupted this arrangement.

It appears, from the date of insertion of the intercalary month in the Roman Republican calendar and the habit of designating years by the names of the consuls, that the calendar year had originally commenced in March, which was the date when the new consul took office. In 222 BC the date of assuming duties was fixed as March

15, but in 153 BC it was transferred to the Kalendae of January, and there it remained. January therefore became the first month of the year, and in the western region of the Roman Empire, this practice was carried over into the Julian calendar. In the eastern provinces, however, years were often reckoned from the accession of the reigning emperor, the second beginning on the first new year's day after the accession; and the date on which this occurred varied from one province to another.

Fixing of January as the first month

THE GREGORIAN CALENDAR

The Julian calendar year of 365.25 days was too long, since the correct value for the tropical year is 365.242199 days. This error of 11 minutes 14 seconds per year amounted to almost one and a half days in two centuries, and seven days in 1,000 years. Once again the calendar became increasingly out of phase with the seasons. From time to time, the problem was placed before church councils, but no action was taken because the astronomers who were consulted doubted whether enough precise information was available for a really accurate value of the tropical year to be obtained. By 1545, however, the vernal equinox, which was used in determining Easter, had moved ten days from its proper date; and in December, when the Council of Trent met for the first of its sessions, it authorized Pope Paul III to take action to correct the error. Correction required a solution, however, that neither Paul III nor his successors were able to obtain in satisfactory form until nearly 1572, the year of election of Pope Gregory XIII. Gregory found various proposals awaiting him and agreed to issue a bull that the Jesuit astronomer Christopher Clavius (1537–1612) began to draw up, using suggestions made by the astronomer and physician Luigi Lilio (also known as Aloysius Lilius; died 1576).

The papal bull appeared in February 1582. First, in order to bring the vernal equinox back to March 21, the day following the Feast of St. Francis (that is, October 5) was to become October 15, thus omitting ten days. Second, to bring the year closer to the true tropical year, a value of 365.2422 days was accepted. This value differed by 0.0078 days per year from the Julian calendar reckoning, amounting to 0.78 days per century, or 3.12 days every 400 years. It was therefore promulgated that three out of every four centennial years should be common years, that is, not leap years; and this practice led to the rule that no centennial years should be leap years unless exactly divisible by 400. Thus, 1700, 1800 and 1900 were not leap years, as they would have been in the Julian calendar, but the year 2000 will be. The bull also laid down rules for calculating the date of Easter.

The date of Easter; epacts. Easter was the most important feast of the Christian Church, and its place in the calendar determined the position of the rest of the Church's movable feasts. Because its timing depended on both the Moon's phases and the vernal equinox, ecclesiastical authorities had to seek some way of reconciling lunar and solar calendars. Some simple form of computation, usable by non-astronomers in remote places, was desirable. There was no easy or obvious solution, and to make things more difficult there was no unanimous agreement on the way in which Easter should be calculated, even on a lunar calendar.

Easter, being the festival of the Resurrection, had to depend on the dating of the Crucifixion, which occurred three days earlier and just before the Jewish Passover. The Passover was celebrated on the 14th day of Nisan, the first month in the Jewish religious year—that is, the lunar month the 14th day of which falls on or next after the vernal equinox. The Christian churches in the eastern Mediterranean area celebrated Easter on the 14th of Nisan on whatever day of the week it might fall, but the rest of Christendom adopted a more elaborate reckoning to ensure that it was celebrated on a Sunday in the Passover week.

Dependence on the Passover

To determine precisely how the Resurrection and Easter Day should be dated, reference was made to the Gospels; but even as early as the 2nd century AD, difficulties had arisen since the synoptic Gospels (Matthew, Mark, and Luke) appeared to give a different date from the Gospel According to John for the Crucifixion. This difference led to controversy that was later exacerbated by another difficulty caused by the Jewish reckoning of a day from sunset to sunset. The question arose of how the evening of the 14th day should be calculated, and some—the quintadecimans—claimed that it meant one particular evening, but others—the quartadecimans—claimed that it meant the evening before, since sunset heralded a new day. Both sides had their protagonists, the Eastern churches supporting the quartadecimans, the Western churches the quintadecimans. The question was finally decided at the Council of Nicaea, in 325, in favour of the quintadecimans, and the Western church agreed. The Eastern churches decided to retain the quartadeciman position, and the church in England, which had few links with the European churches at this time, retained the quartadeciman position until Roman missionaries arrived in the 6th century, when a change was made. The dating of Easter in the Gregorian calendar was based on the decision of the Council of Nicaea, which decreed that Easter should be celebrated on the Sunday immediately following the Full Moon that fell on or after the vernal equinox, which they took as March 21. The Council also ordered that if this Sunday either coincided with the Jewish Passover or with the Easter Day of the quartadecimans, the festival should be held seven days later.

With these provisions in mind, the problem could be broken down into two parts: first, devising a simple but effective way of calculating the days of the week for any date in the year and, second, determining the date of the Full Moons in any year. The first part was solved by the use of a letter code derived from a similar Roman system adopted for determining market days. For ecclesiastical use, the code gave what was known as the Sunday, or dominical, letter.

Dominical letters

The seven letters A through G are each assigned to a day, consecutively from January 1 so that January 1 appears as A, January 2 as B, to January 7 which appears as G, the cycle then continuing with January 8 as A, January 9 as B, and so on. Then in any year the first Sunday is bound to be assigned to one of the letters A–G in the first cycle, and all Sundays in the year possess that dominical letter. For example, if the first Sunday falls on January 3, C will be the dominical letter for the whole year. No dominical letter is placed against the intercalary day, February 29, but since it is still counted as a weekday and given a name, the series of letters moves back one day every leap year after intercalation. Thus, a leap year beginning with the dominical letter C will change to a year with the dominical letter D on March 1; and in lists of dominical letters, all leap years are given a double letter notation, in the example just quoted, CD. It is not difficult to see what dominical letter or letters apply to any particular year, and it is also a comparatively simple matter to draw up a table of dominical letters for use in determining Easter Sunday. The possible dates on which Easter Sunday can fall are written down—they run from March 22 through April 25—and against them the dominical letters for a cycle of seven years. Once the dominical letter for a year is known, the possible Sundays for celebrating Easter can be read directly from the table. This system does not, of course, completely determine Easter; to do so, additional information is required.

This must provide dates for Full Moons throughout the year, and for this a lunar cycle like the Metonic cycle was originally used. Tables were prepared, again using the range of dates on which Easter Sunday could appear, and against each date a number from 1 through to 19 was placed. This number indicated which of the 19 years of the lunar cycle would give a Full Moon on that day. From medieval times these were known as golden numbers, possibly from a name used by the Greeks for the numbers on the Metonic cycle or because gold is the colour used for them in manuscript calendars.

Golden numbers

The system of golden numbers was introduced in 530, but they were arranged as they should have been if adopted at the Council of Nicaea two centuries earlier; and the cycle was taken to begin in a year when the New

Moon fell on January 1. Working backward, this date was found to have occurred in the year preceding AD 1, and therefore the golden number for any year is found by dividing the year by 19, then adding one to the remainder. If the result is zero, the golden number for the year is 19.

To compute the date of Easter, the medieval chronologer computed the golden number for the year and then consulted his table to see by which date this number lay. Having found this date, that of the first Full Moon after March 20, he consulted his table of dominical letters and saw the next date against which the dominical letter for that year appeared; this was the Sunday to be designated Easter. The method, modified for dropping centennial leap years as practiced in the Gregorian calendar, is still given in the English prayer book, although it was officially discarded when the Gregorian calendar was introduced.

The system of golden numbers was eventually rejected because the astronomical Full Moon could differ by as much as two days from the date they indicated. It was Lilius (see above *The Gregorian calendar*) who had proposed a more accurate system based on one that had already been in use unofficially while the Julian calendar was still in force. Called the epact—the word is derived from the Greek *epagein*, meaning "to intercalate"—this was again a system of numbers concerned with the Moon's phases, but now indicating the age of the Moon on the first day of the year, and from which the age of the Moon on any day of the year may be found, at least approximately, by counting, using alternately months of 29 and 30 days.

The epact as previously used was not, however, completely accurate because, like the golden number, it had been based on the Metonic cycle. This cycle occupied a period of 6,939.75 days, whereas it should have lasted for 6,939.9 days; and although the difference is small, it does amount to one day in a little over 307 years, so that after this period, New Moons occur one day earlier than indicated. When the Gregorian calendar was adopted, this difference was taken into account. It was assumed, for convenience, that the error of one day could be said to occur once every 312½ years, so that an eight-day error appeared once every 2,500 years. A one-day change on certain centennial years was then instituted by making the computed age of the Moon one day later seven times, at 300-year intervals, and an eighth time after a subsequent 400 years. This operation was known as the lunar correction, but it was not the only correction required; there was another.

Lunar and solar corrections

Because the Gregorian calendar used a more accurate value for the tropical year than the Julian calendar and achieved this by omitting most centennial leap years, Clavius (see above *The Gregorian calendar*) decided that when the cycle of epacts reached an ordinary centennial year, the number of the epact should be reduced by one; this reduction became known as the solar correction.

One advantage of the epact number was that it showed the age of the Moon on January 1 and so permitted a simple calculation of the dates of New Moon and Full Moon for the ensuing year. Another was that it lent itself to the construction of cycles of 30 epact numbers, each diminishing by one from the previous cycle, so that when it became necessary at certain centennial years to shift from one cycle to another, there would still be a cycle ready that retained a correct relationship between dates and New Moons.

For determining Easter, a table was prepared of the golden numbers, 1 through 19, and below them the cycles of epacts for about 7,000 years; after this time, all the epact cycles are repeated. A second table was then drawn up, giving the dates of Easter Full Moons for different epact numbers. Once the epact for the year was known, the date of the Easter Full Moon could be immediately obtained, while consultation of a table of dominical letters showed which was the next Sunday. Thus, the Gregorian system of epacts, while more accurate than the old golden numbers, still forced the chronologer to consult complex astronomical tables.

Adoption in various countries. The derivation of the term style for a type of calendar seems to have originated some time soon after the 6th century as a result of developments in calendar computation in the previous 200 years. In AD 463, Victorius (or Victorinus) of Aquitaine, who had been appointed by Pope Hilarius to undertake calendar revision, devised the Great Paschal (*i.e.*, Passover) period, sometimes later referred to as the Victorian Period. It was a combination of the solar cycle of 28 years and the Metonic 19-year cycle, bringing the Full Moon back to the same day of the month, and amounted to 28 × 19, or 532 years. In the 6th century, this period was used by Dionysius Exiguus (Denis the Little) in computing the date of Easter, because it gave the day of the week for any day in any year, and so it also became known as the Dionysian period. Dionysius took the year now called AD 532 as the first year of a new Great Paschal period and the year now designated 1 BC as the beginning of the previous cycle. In the 6th century it was the general belief that this was the year of Christ's birth, and because of this Dionysius introduced the concept of numbering years consecutively through the Christian era. The method was adopted by some scholars but seems only to have become widely used after its popularization by the Venerable Bede of Jarrow (?673–735), whose reputation for scholarship was very high in Western Christendom in the 8th century. This system of BC/AD numbering threw into relief the different practices, or styles, of reckoning the beginning of the year then in use. When the Gregorian calendar firmly established January 1 as the beginning of its year, it was widely referred to as the New Style calendar, with the Julian the Old Style calendar. In Britain, under the Julian calendar, the year had first begun on December 25 and then, from the 14th century onward, on March 25.

The Great Paschal period

Because of the division of the Eastern and Western Christian churches and of Protestants and Roman Catholics, the obvious advantages of the Gregorian calendar were not accepted everywhere, and in some places adoption was extremely slow. In France, Italy, Luxembourg, Portugal, and Spain, the New Style calendar was adopted in 1582, and by most of the German Roman Catholic states as well as by Belgium and part of the Netherlands by 1584. Switzerland's change was gradual, beginning in 1583 and being completed only in 1812. Hungary adopted the New Style in 1587, and then there was a pause of more than a century before the first Protestant countries moved over from the Old Style calendar. In 1699–1700, Denmark and the Dutch and German Protestant states embraced the New Style, although the Germans declined to adopt the rules laid down for determining Easter, preferring to rely on astronomical tables and specifying the use of the *Tabulae Rudolphinae* (*Rudolphine Tables*), based on the 16th-century observations of Tycho Brahe. They acceded to the Gregorian calendar rules for Easter only in 1776. Britain adopted the New Style in 1752 and Sweden in 1753, although, because the Swedes had in 1740 followed the German Protestants in using their astronomical methods for determining Easter, they declined to adopt the Gregorian calendar rules until 1844. Japan adopted the New Style in 1873; Egypt in 1875; and between 1912 and 1917 it was accepted by Albania, Bulgaria, China, Estonia, Latvia, Lithuania, Romania, Turkey, and Yugoslavia. Soviet Russia adopted the New Style in 1918; Greece in 1923.

Adoption of the New Style by Protestant countries

In Britain and the British dominions, the change was made when the difference between the New and Old Style calendars amounted to 11 days, by naming the day after September 2, 1752, as September 14, 1752; but there was much public misunderstanding, and in Britain rioters demanded "give us back our 11 days," even though legislation authorizing the change had been framed to avoid injustice and financial hardship. Alaska retained the Old Style calendar until 1867, when it was transferred from Russia to the United States.

CALENDAR REFORM SINCE THE MID-18TH CENTURY

The French Republican calendar. In late-18th-century France, with the approach of the French Revolution, demands began to be made for a radical change in the civil calendar that would divorce it completely from any ecclesiastical connections. The first attacks on the Gregorian calendar and proposals for reform came in 1785 and 1788, the changes being primarily designed to divest the calendar of all its Christian associations. After the storming of the Bastille in July 1789, demands became more vociferous, and a new calendar, to start from "the first year of liberty," was widely spoken about. In 1793 the National Convention appointed Charles-Gilbert Romme, president of the committee of public instruction, to take charge of the reform. Technical matters were entrusted to the mathematicians Joseph-Louis Lagrange and Gaspard Monge and the renaming of the months to the Paris deputy to the convention, Fabre d'Eglantine. The results of their deliberations were submitted to the convention in September of the same year and were immediately accepted, it being promulgated that the new calendar should become law on October 5.

The French Republican calendar, as it came to be known, was taken to have begun on September 22, 1792, the day of the proclamation of the Republic and, in that year, the date also of the autumnal equinox. All future years were to begin on the same date. The total number of days in the year was 365, the same as in the Julian and Gregorian calendars, and this was divided into 12 months of 30 days each, the remaining five days being devoted to festivals and vacations. These were to fall between September 17 and 22 and were specified, in order, to be festivals of virtue, genius, labour, opinion, and rewards. In a leap year an extra festival was to be added—the festival of the Revolution. Leap years were retained at the same frequency as in the Gregorian calendar, but it was enacted that the first leap year should be year 3, not year 4 as it would have been if the Gregorian calendar had been followed precisely in this respect. Each four-year period was to be known as a *Franciade*.

Weeks and *décades*

The seven-day week was abandoned, and each 30-day month was divided into three periods of ten days called *décades*, the last day of a *décade* being a rest day. It was also agreed that each day should be divided into decimal parts, but this was not popular in practice and was allowed to fall into disuse.

The months themselves were renamed so that all previous associations should be lost, and Fabre d'Eglantine chose descriptive names as follows (the descriptive nature and Gregorian calendar dates for 1793–95 are given in parentheses): Vendémiaire ("vintage," September 22 to October 21), Brumaire ("mist," October 22 to November 20), Frimaire ("frost," November 21 to December 20), Nivôse ("snow," December 21 to January 19), Pluviôse ("rain," January 20 to February 18), Ventôse ("wind," February 19 to March 20), Germinal ("seedtime," March 21 to April 19), Floréal ("blossom," April 20 to May 19), Prairial ("meadow," May 20 to June 18), Messidor ("harvest," June 19 to July 18), Thermidor ("heat," July 19 to August 17), and Fructidor ("fruits," August 18 to September 16).

The French Republican calendar was short-lived, for while it was satisfactory enough internally, it clearly made for difficulties in communication abroad because its months continually changed their relationship to dates in the Gregorian calendar. In September 1805, under the Napoleonic regime, the calendar was virtually abandoned, and on January 1, 1806, it was replaced by the Gregorian calendar. The lack of success of the French Republican calendar has no doubt decided other regimes against adopting any similar system, for when Soviet Russia undertook its calendar reform in February 1918, it merely moved from the Julian calendar to the Gregorian, with a loss of 13 days, so that February 1 became February 13. In 1929, a Revolutionary calendar was proposed for the U.S.S.R., but never put into use.

Modern schemes for reform. The current calendar is not without defects, and reforms are still being proposed. Astronomically, it really calls for no improvement, but the seven-day week and the different lengths of months are unsatisfactory to some. Clearly, if the calendar could have all festivals and all rest days fixed on the same dates every year, as in the original Julian calendar, this arrangement would be more convenient, and two general schemes have been put forward—the International Fixed Calendar and the World Calendar.

The International Fixed Calendar is essentially a perpetual Gregorian calendar, in which the year is divided into 13 months, each of 28 days, with an additional day at the end. Present month names are retained, but a new month named Sol is intercalated between June and July. The additional day follows December 28 and bears no designation of month date or weekday name, while the same would be true of the day intercalated in a leap year after June 28. In this calendar, every month begins on a Sunday and ends on a Saturday.

It is claimed that the International Fixed Calendar does not conveniently divide into quarters for business reckoning; and the World Calendar is designed to remedy this deficiency, being divided into four quarters of 91 days each, with an additional day at the end of the year. In each quarter, the first month is of 31 days and the second and third of 30 days each. The extra day comes after December 30 and bears no month or weekday designation, nor does the intercalated leap year day which follows June 30. In this calendar January 1, April 1, July 1, and October 1 are all Sundays. Critics point out that each month extends over part of five weeks, and each month within a given quarter begins on a different day. Nevertheless, both these proposed reforms seem to be improvements over the present system that contains so many variables. (C.A.R.)

III. Ancient Middle Eastern calendar systems

LUNISOLAR CALENDARS IN ANTIQUITY

The lunisolar calendar, in which months are lunar but years are solar—that is, are brought into line with the course of the Sun—was used in the early civilizations of the whole Middle East, except Egypt, and in Greece. The formula was probably invented in Mesopotamia in the 3rd millennium BC. Study of cuneiform tablets found in this region facilitates tracing the development of time reckoning back to the 27th century BC, near the invention of writing. The evidence shows that the calendar is a contrivance for dividing the flow of time into units that suit man's current needs. Though calendar makers put to use time signs offered by nature, say the Moon phases, they rearranged reality to make it fit man's constructions.

Sumero-Babylonian calendars. In Mesopotamia the natural year (that is, the Sun year) was divided into two seasons, the "summer," which included the barley harvest in the second half of May or in the beginning of June, and the "winter," which roughly corresponded to today's fall–winter. Three seasons (Assyria) and four seasons (Anatolia) were counted in northerly countries, but in Mesopotamia the bipartition of the year seemed natural. As late as *c.* 1800 BC, the prognoses for the welfare of the city of Mari, on the middle Euphrates, were taken for six months.

The months began at the first visibility of the New Moon. In the 8th century BC, court astronomers still reported to the Assyrian kings the observation of the New Moon. The names of the months differed from city to city, and within the same Sumerian city a month could have several names: derived from festivals, from tasks (*e.g.*, sheepshearing) usually performed in the given month, and so on, according to the needs of the respective group or office. On the other hand, as early as the 27th century BC, the Sumerians had used artificial time units in referring to the tenure of some high official—*e.g.*, on N-day of the turn of office of PN, governor. The Sumerian administration also needed a time unit comprising the whole vegetation cycle; for example, from the delivery of new barley and the settling of pertinent accounts to the next crop. This financial year began about two months after barley cutting. For other purposes, a year began before or with the harvest. This fluctuating and discontinuous year was not precise enough for the meticulous accounting of Sumerian scribes, who by 2400 BC already used the schematic year of $30 \times 12 = 360$ days.

The royal year

At about the same time, the idea of a royal year took precise shape, beginning probably at the time of barley harvest, when the king celebrated the new (agricultural) year by offering first fruits to gods in expectation of their blessings for the year. When, in the course of this year, some royal exploit (conquest, temple building, and so on) demonstrated that the fates had been fixed favourably by the celestial powers, the year was named accordingly; for example, as the year in which "the temple of Ningirsu was built." Until the naming, a year was described as that "following the year named (after such and such event)." The use of the date formulas was supplanted in Babylonia by the counting of regnal years in the 17th century BC. But, up to the end of their state (612 BC), the Assyrians kept the naming of years after the official called the eponym (known as *limmu*), because the lot by which he was annually chosen was inscribed with a blessing: "May (god Ashur) prosper the crops of Assyria in the year of *limmu* PN."

The use of lunar reckoning began to prevail in the 21st century BC. The lunar year probably owed its success to economic progress. A barley loan could be measured out to the lender at the next year's threshing floor. The wider use of silver as the standard of value demanded more flexible payment terms. A man hiring a servant in the lunar month of Kislimu for a year knew that the engagement would end at the return of the same month, without counting days or periods of office between two dates. At the city of Mari in about 1800 BC, the allocations were already reckoned on the basis of 29- and 30-day lunar months. In the 18th century BC, the Babylonian Empire standardized the year by adopting the calendar of the Sumerian sacred city of Nippur. The power and the cultural prestige of Babylon assured the success of the lunar year, which began on Nisanu 1, in the spring. When, in the 17th century BC, the dating by regnal years became usual, the period between the accession day and the next Nisanu 1 was described as "the beginning of the kingship of PN," and the regnal years were counted from this Nisanu 1.

It was necessary for the lunar year of about 354 days to be brought into line with the solar year of approximately 365 days, which determines the growth of vegetation. This was accomplished by the use of an intercalated month. Thus, in the 21st century BC, a special name for the intercalated month *iti dirig* appears in the sources. The intercalation was operated haphazardly, according to real or imagined needs, and each Sumerian city inserted months at will; *e.g.*, 11 months in 18 years or two months in the same year. Later, the empires centralized the intercalation, and as late as 541 BC it was proclaimed by royal fiat. Improvements in astronomical knowledge eventually made possible the regularization of the calendar by the insertion of extra months; and, under the Persian kings (*c.* 380 BC), Babylonian calendar calculators succeeded in computing an almost perfect equivalence in a lunisolar cycle of 19 years and 235 months with intercalations in the years 3, 6, 8, 11, 14, 17, and 19 of the cycle. The new year's day (Nisanu 1) now oscillated around the spring equinox within the period of 27 days. (The corresponding figure for the present Easter cycle is 35 days.)

Babylonian months

The Babylonian month names were Nisanu, Ayaru, Simanu, Du'uzu, Abu, Ululu, Tashritu, Arakhsamna, Kislimu, Tebetu, Shabatu, Adaru. The month Adaru II was intercalated six times within the 19-year cycle but never in the year that was 17th of the cycle, when Ululu II was inserted. Thus, the Babylonian calendar until the end preserved a vestige of the original bipartition of the natural year into two seasons, just as the Babylonian months to the end remained truly lunar and began when the New Moon was first visible in the evening. The day began at sunset. The night and the daylight period were each divided into three watches and 12 hours. Sundials and water clocks served to count hours.

The influence of the Babylonian calendar was seen in many continued customs and usages of its neighbour and vassal states long after the Babylonian Empire had been succeeded by others. In particular, the Jewish calendar in use at relatively late dates employed similar systems of intercalation of months, month names, and other details (see above *The Jewish calendar*). The Jewish adoption of Babylonian calendar customs dates from the period of Exile (586–516 BC).

Other calendars used in the ancient Near East. *The Assyrians and the Hittites.* Of the calendars of other peoples of the ancient Near East, very little is known. Thus, though the names of all or of some months are known, their order is not. The months were probably everywhere lunar, but evidence for intercalation is often lacking; for instance, in Assyria. For accounting, the Assyrians also used a kind of week, of five days, as it seems, identified by the name of an eponymous official. Thus, a loan could be made and interest calculated for a number of weeks in advance and independently of the vagaries of the civil year. In the city of Ashur, the years bore the name of a yearly official *limmu.* As late as about 1070 BC, his installation date was not fixed in the calendar. From about 1100 BC, however, Babylonian month names began to supplant Assyrian names, and, when Assyria became a world power, it used the Babylonian lunisolar calendar.

The calendar of the Hittite Empire is known even less well. As in Babylonia, the first Hittite month was that of first fruits, and, on its beginning, the gods determined the fates.

Iran. At about the time of the conquest of Babylonia in 538 BC, Persian kings made the Babylonian cyclic calendar standard throughout the Persian Empire, from the Indus to the Nile. Aramaic documents from Persian Egypt, for instance, bear Babylonian dates besides the Egyptian. Similarly, the royal years were reckoned in Babylonian style, from Nisanu 1. It is probable, however, that at the court itself the counting of regnal years began with the accession day. The Seleucids and, afterward, the Parthian rulers of Iran maintained the Babylonian calendar. The fiscal administration in northern Iran, from the 1st century BC, at least, used Zoroastrian month and day names in documents in Pahlavi (the Iranian language of Sāsānian Persia). The origin and history of the Zoroastrian calendar year of 12 months of 30 days, plus five days (that is, 365 days), remain unknown. It became official under the Sāsānian dynasty, from about AD 226 until the Arab conquest in 621. The Arabs introduced the Muslim lunar year, but the Persians continued to use the Sāsānian solar year, which in 1079 was made equal to the Julian year by the introduction of the leap year.

The Zoroastrian calendar

ANCIENT GREEK CALENDARS IN RELATION TO THE MIDDLE EAST

Earliest sources. The earliest sources (clay tablets of the 13th century BC, the writings of Homer and Hesiod) imply the use of lunar months; Hesiod also uses reckoning determined by the observation of constellations and star groups; *e.g.*, the harvest coincides with the visible rising of the star group known as the Pleiades before dawn. This simultaneous use of civil and natural calendars is characteristic of Greek time reckoning. In the classical age and later, the months, named after festivals of the city, began in principle with the New Moon. The lunar year of 12 months and about 354 days was to be matched with the solar year by inserting an extra month every other year. The Macedonians used this system as late as the 3rd century BC, although 25 lunar months amount to about 737 days, while two solar years count about 730 days. In fact, as the evidence from the second half of the 5th century BC shows, at this early time the calendar was already no longer tied in with the phases of the Moon. The cities, rather, intercalated months and added or omitted days at will to adjust the calendar to the course of the Sun and stars and also for the sake of convenience, as, for instance, to postpone or advance a festival without changing its traditional calendar date. The calendric New Moon could disagree by many days with the true New Moon, and in the 2nd century BC Athenian documents listed side by side both the calendar date and that according to the Moon. Thus, the lunar months that were in principle parallel might diverge widely in different cities. Astronomers such as Meton, who in 432 BC calculated a 19-year lunisolar cycle, were not heeded by the politicians, who clung to their calendar-making power.

Civil and natural years compared

The year. The civil year (*etos*) was similarly dissociated from the natural year (*eniautos*). It was the tenure term of an official or priest, roughly corresponding to the lunar year, or to six months; it gave his name to his time period. In Athens, for instance, the year began on Hekatombaion 1, roughly midsummer, when the new archon entered his office, and the year was designated by his name; *e.g.*, "when Callimedes was archon"—that is, 360–359 BC. There was no new year's festival.

As the archon's year was of indefinite and unpredictable length, the Athenian administration for accounting, for the dates of popular assemblies, etc., used turns of office of the sections (prytanies) of the Council (Boule), which each had fixed length within the year. The common citizen used, along with the civil months, the seasonal time reckoning based on the direct observation of the Moon's phases and on the appearance and setting of fixed stars. A device (called a *parapēgma*) with movable pegs indicated the approximate correspondence between, for example, the rising of the star Arcturus and the civil date.

After Alexander's conquest of the Persian Empire, the Macedonian calendar (see above *Earliest sources*) came to be widely used by the Greeks in the East, though in Egypt it was supplanted by the Egyptian year at the end of the 3rd century BC. The Seleucids, from the beginning, adapted the Macedonian year to the Babylonian 19-year cycle (see above *Sumero-Babylonian calendars*). Yet, Greek cities clung to their arbitrary system of time reckoning even after the introduction of the Julian calendar throughout the Roman Empire. As late as *c.* AD 200, they used the antiquated *octaëteris; i.e.*, the intercalation of three months in eight years, to keep the calendar roughly in step with the solar year.

Months, days, seasons. The Athenian months were called Hekatombaion (in midsummer), Metageitnion, Boedromion, Pyanepsion, Maimakterion, Poseideion, Gamelion, Anthesterion, Elaphebolion, Mounychion, Thargelion, and Skirophorion. The position of the intercalary month varied. Each month, in principle, consisted of 30 days, but in roughly six months the next to last day, the 29th, was omitted. The days were numbered within each of the three decades of the month. Thus, for example, Hekatombaion 16th was called "6th after the 10th of Hekatombaion." The Macedonian months were Dios (in fall), Apellaios, Audynaios, Peritios, Dystros, Xanthikos, Artemisios, Daisios, Panemos, Loos, Gorpiaios, and Hyperberetaios. In the Seleucid calendar, Dios was identified with the Babylonian Tashritu, Apellaios with Arakhsamna, and so on.

On the Babylonian pattern, the daylight time and the night were divided into four "watches" and 12 hours each. Thus, the length of an hour oscillated between approximately 45 and 75 present-day minutes, according to the season. Water clocks, gnomons, and, after *c.* 300 BC, sundials roughly indicated time. The season division was originally bipartite as in Babylonia—summer and winter—but four seasons were already attested by about 650 BC. (E.J.Bi.)

THE EGYPTIAN CALENDAR

The ancient Egyptians originally employed a calendar based upon the Moon, and, like many peoples throughout the world, they regulated their lunar calendar by means of a star. For them the year was governed by the star Sirius (Egyptian, Sothis, *Spdt*) and corresponded closely to the true solar year, being 12 minutes shorter. Certain difficulties, however, are inherent in any lunar calendar because the Moon's motion around the Earth in terms of days is not an equal divisor of the 365¼-day solar year. To solve this problem the Egyptians invented a schematized civil year of 365 days divided into three seasons, each of which consisted of four months of 30 days each. To complete the year, five intercalary days were added at its end, so that the 12 months were equal to 360 days plus five extra days. This civil calendar was derived from the lunar calendar (using months) and the agricultural, or Nile, fluctuations (using seasons); it was, however, no longer directly connected to either and thus was not controlled by them. The civil calendar served government and administration, while the lunar calendar continued to regulate religious affairs and everyday life.

The civil year

In time, the discrepancy between the civil calendar and the older lunar structure became obvious. Because the lunar calendar was controlled by the rising of Sirius, its months would correspond to the same season each year, while the civil calendar would move through the seasons because the civil year was about one-fourth day shorter than the solar year. Hence, every four years it would fall behind the solar year by one day, and after 1,460 years it would again agree with the lunisolar calendar. Such a period of time is called a Sothic cycle.

The Sothic cycle

Because of the discrepancy between these two calendars, the Egyptians established a second lunar calendar based upon the civil year and not, as the older one had been, upon the sighting of Sirius. It was schematic and artificial, and its purpose was to determine religious celebrations and duties. In order to keep it in general agreement with the civil year, a month was intercalated every time the first day of the lunar year came before the first day of the civil year; later, a 25-year cycle of intercalation was introduced. The original lunar calendar, however, was not abandoned but was retained primarily for agriculture because of its agreement with the seasons. Thus, the ancient Egyptians operated with three calendars, each for a different purpose.

The only unit of time that was larger than a year was the reign of a king. The usual custom of dating by reign was: "year 1, 2, 3 . . ., etc., of King So-and-So," and with each new king the counting reverted back to year One. King lists recorded consecutive rulers and the total years of their respective reigns.

The civil year (*rnpt*) was divided into three seasons, commonly translated: Inundation, when the Nile overflowed the agricultural land; Going Forth, the time of planting when the Nile returned to its bed; and Deficiency, the time of low water and harvest.

The months (*3bdw*) of the civil calendar were numbered according to their respective seasons and were not listed by any particular name—*e.g.*, third month of Inundation—but for religious purposes the months had names. How early these names were employed in the later lunar calendar is obscure.

Designation of days

The days (*hrw*) in the civil calendar were also indicated by number and listed according to their respective months. Thus a full civil date would be: "Regnal year 1, fourth month of Inundation, day 5, under the majesty of King So-and-So." In the lunar calendar, however, each day had a specific name and from some of these names it can be seen that the four quarters or chief phases of the Moon were recognized, although the Egyptians did not use these quarters to divide the month into smaller segments, such as weeks. Unlike most people who used a lunar calendar, the Egyptians began their day with sunrise instead of sunset because they began their month, and consequently their day, by the disappearance of the old Moon just before dawn. Others calculated their month by the first sighting of a new moon or new crescent after sunset and thus began their day in the evening.

The hours (*wnwt*) of the day were divided into two parts, 12 hours of daylight and 12 hours of darkness. An hour was not 1/24 of the entire day, but was 1/12 of the actual time between sunrise and sunset or 1/12 of the time between sunset and sunrise. Because of the variation in the amount of daylight and darkness between summer and winter, the length of the Egyptian hour changed accordingly. Both water clocks and sundials were constructed with notations to indicate the hours for the different months and seasons of the year. The standard hour of constant length was never employed in ancient Egypt. (J.D.Sc.)

IV. The Far East

THE HINDU CALENDAR

While the Republic of India has adopted the Gregorian calendar for its secular life, its Hindu religious life continues to be governed by the traditional Hindu calendar.

This calendar, based primarily on the lunar revolutions, is adapted to solar reckoning.

Early history. The oldest system, in many respects the basis of the classical one, is known from texts of about 1000 BC. It divides an approximate solar year of 360 days into 12 lunar months of 27 (according to the early Vedic text Taittirīya Saṃhitā 4.4.10.1-3) or 28 (according to the Atharvaveda, the fourth of the Vedas, 19.7.1.) days. The resulting discrepancy was resolved by the intercalation of a leap month every 60 months. Time was reckoned by the position marked off in constellations on the ecliptic in which the Moon rises daily in the course of one lunation (the period from New Moon to New Moon) and the Sun rises monthly in the course of one year. These constellations (*nakṣatra*) each measure an arc of 13°20′ of the ecliptic circle. The positions of the Moon were directly observable, and those of the Sun inferred from the Moon's position at Full Moon, when the Sun is in opposition to the Moon. The position of the Sun at midnight was calculated from the *nakṣatra* that culminated on the meridian at that time, the Sun then being in opposition to that *nakṣatra*. The year was divided into three thirds of four months, each of which would be introduced by a special religious rite, the *cāturmāsya* (four-month rite). Each of these periods was further divided into two parts (seasons or *ṛtu*): spring, (*vasanta*) from mid-March until mid-May; summer (*grīṣma*), from mid-May until mid-July; the rains (*varṣa*), from mid-July until mid-September; autumn (*śarad*), from mid-September until mid-November; winter (*hemanta*), from mid-November until mid-January; and the dews (*śiśira*), from mid-January until mid-March. The spring months in early times were Madhu and Mādhava, the summer months Śukra and Śuci, the rainy months Nabhas and Nabhasya, the autumn months Īṣa and Ūrja, the winter months Sahas and Sahasya, and the dewy months Tapas and Tapasya. The month, counted from Full Moon to Full Moon, was divided into two halves (*pakṣa* "wing") of waning (*kṛṣṇa*) and waxing (*śukla*) Moon, and a special ritual (*darśapūrṇamāsa*, "new and full moon rites") was prescribed on the days of New Moon (*amāvasya*) and Full Moon (*pūrṇimās*). The month had theoretically 30 days (*tithi;* see below), and the day (*divasa*) 30 hours (*muhūrta*).

The *naksatra*

This picture is essentially confirmed by the first treatise on time reckoning, the *Jyotiṣa-vedāṅga* ("Vedic auxiliary [text] concerning the luminaries") of about 100 BC, which adds a larger unit of five years (*yuga*) to the divisions. A further old distinction is that of two year moieties, the *uttarāyaṇa* ("northern course"), when the Sun rises every morning farther north, and the *dakṣiṇāyana* ("southern course"), when it rises progressively farther south.

The classical calendar. In its classic form (*Sūrya-siddhānta*, 4th century AD) the calendar continues from the one above with some refinements. With the influence of Hellenism, Greek and Mesopotamian astronomy and astrology were introduced. Though astronomy and time reckoning previously were dictated by the requirements of rituals, the time of which had to be fixed correctly, and not for purposes of divination, the new astrology came into vogue for casting horoscopes and making predictions. Zodiacal time measurement was now used side by side with the older *nakṣatra* one. The *nakṣatra* section of the ecliptic (13°20′) was divided into four parts of 3°20′ each; thus, two full *nakṣatra*s and a quarter of one make up one zodiac period, or sign (30°). The year began with the entry of the Sun (*saṃkrānti*) in the sign of Aries. The names of the signs (*rāśi*) were taken over and mostly translated into Sanskrit: *meṣa* ("ram," Aries), *vṛṣabha* ("bull," Taurus), *mithuna* ("pair," Gemini), *karkaṭa* ("crab," Cancer), *siṃha* ("lion," Leo), *kanyā* ("maiden," Virgo), *tulā* ("scale," Libra), *vṛścika* ("scorpion," Scorpius), *dhanus* ("bow," Sagittarius), *makara* ("crocodile," Capricornus), *kumbha* ("water jar," Aquarius), *mīna* ("fish," Pisces).

The precession of the vernal equinox from the Sun's entry into Aries to some point in Pisces, with similar consequences for the summer solstice, autumnal equinox, and winter solstice, has led to two different methods of calculating the *saṃkrānti* (entry) of the Sun into a sign: the precession (*ayana*) is not accounted for in the *nirayana* system (without *ayana*), which thus dates the actual *saṃkrānti* correctly but identifies it wrongly with the equinox or solstice, and the *sāyana* system (with *ayana*), which thus dates the equinox and solstice correctly but identifies it wrongly with the *saṃkrānti*.

While the solar system has extreme importance for astrology, which, it is claimed, governs a person's life as an individual or part of a social system, the sacred time continues to be reckoned by the lunar *nakṣatra* system. The lunar day (*tithi*), a thirtieth part of the lunar month, remains the basic unit. Thus, as the lunar month is only about 29½ solar days, the *tithi* does not coincide with the natural day (*ahorātra*). The convention is that that *tithi* is in force for the natural day that happened to occur at the dawn of that day. Therefore, a *tithi* beginning after dawn one day and expiring before dawn the next day is eliminated, not being counted in that month, and there is a break in the day sequence.

The names of the *nakṣatra*s, to which correspond the *tithi*s in the monthly lunar cycle and segments of months in the annual solar cycle, are derived from the constellations on the horizon at that time and have remained the same. The names of the months have changed: Caitra (March-April), Vaiśākha (April-May), Jyaiṣtha (May-June), Āṣāḍha (June-July), Śrāvaṇa (July-August), Bhādrapada (August-September), Āśvina (September-October), Kārttika (October-November), Mārgaśīrṣa (November-December), Pauṣa (December-January), Māgha (January-February), and Phālguna (February-March).

Month names

In this calendar the date of an event takes the following form: month, fortnight (either waning or waxing Moon), name (usually the number) of the *tithi* in that fortnight, and the year of that era which the writer follows. Identification, particularly of the *tithi*, is often quite complicated, since it requires knowledge of the time of sunrise on that day and which thirtieth of the lunar month was in force then.

Eventually, India also adopted the seven-day week (*saptāha*) from the West and named the days after the corresponding planets: Sunday after the Sun, *ravivāra*; Monday after the Moon, *somavāra*; Tuesday after Mars, *maṅgalavāra*; Wednesday after Mercury, *budhavāra*; Thursday after Jupiter, *bṛhaspativāra*; Friday after Venus, *śukravāra*; and Saturday after Saturn, *śanivāra*.

A further refinement of the calendar was the introduction into dating of the place of the year according to its place in the revolution of the planet Jupiter, called *bṛhaspati* in Sanskrit. Jupiter has a sidereal period (with respect to the "fixed" stars) of 11 years, 314 days, and 839 minutes, which brings it in nearly 12 years back into its conjunction with the stars from which it began its orbit. Its synodic period brings it into conjunction with the Sun every 398 days and 88 minutes, a little more than a year. Thus, Jupiter in a period of almost 12 years passes about the same series of *nakṣatra*s that the Sun passes in one year and, in a year, about the same *nakṣatra*s as the Sun in a month. A year then can be dated as the month of a 12-year cycle of Jupiter, and the date is given as, for example, grand month of Caitra. This is extended to a unit of five cycles, or the 60-year cycle of Jupiter (*bṛhaspaticakra*), and a "century" of 60 years is formed. This system is known from the 6th century AD onward.

At the other end of the scale, more precision is brought to the day. Every *tithi* is divided into two halves, called *karaṇas*. The natural day is divided into units ranging from a *vipala* (0.4 seconds) to a *ghaṭikā* (24 minutes) and an "hour" (*muhūrta*) of 48 minutes; the full natural day has 30 such hours. The day starts at dawn; the first six *ghaṭikās* are early morning, the second set of six midmorning, the third midday, the fourth afternoon, the fifth evening. Night lasts through three units (*yāma*) of time: six *ghaṭikās* after sundown, or early night; two of midnight, four of dawn.

All Hindu festivals and almost all Indian festivals are dated according to the above calendar.

The sacred calendar. There are a few secular state holidays (*e.g.*, Independence Day) and some solar holidays, such as the entry of the Sun into the sign of Aries (*meṣa-saṃkrānti*), marking the beginning of the new astrological year, which in 1958–59 fell on January 14; the Sun's entry into the sign of Capricornus (*makara-saṃkrānti*), which marks the winter solstice but has coalesced with a hoary harvest festival, which in southern India is very widely celebrated as the Poṅgal festival; and the *mahāviṣuva* day, which is New Year's Eve. But all other important festivals are based on the lunar calendar. As a result of the high specialization of deities and events celebrated in different regions, there are hundreds of such festivals, most of which are observed in smaller areas, though some have India-wide followings. A highly selective list of the major ones, national and regional, follows.

The Gregorian dates given are, except as noted, those valid for 1958–59.

Rāmanavamī ("ninth of Rāma"), on Caitra Ś. (= *śukla*, "waxing fortnight") 9 (in the Gregorian calendar of 1957–58, April 8), celebrates Rāma's restoration to the throne of Ayodhyā.

Rathayātrā ("pilgrimage of the chariot"), Āṣāḍha Ś. 2, June 29, is the famous Juggernaut (Jagannātha) festival of the temple complex at Puri, Orissa.

Janmāṣṭamī ("eighth day of the birth"), Śrāvaṇa K. (= *kṛṣṇa*, "waning fortnight") 8, August 19, is the birthday of the god Kṛṣṇa.

Gaṇeśacaturthī ("fourth of Gaṇeśa"), Bhādrapada Ś. 4, August 28, is observed in honour of the elephant-headed god Gaṇeśa, a particular favourite of Mahārāshtra.

Durgā-pūjā ("homage to Durgā"), Āśvina Ś. 7–10, September 30–October 3, is special to Bengal, in honour of the destructive and creative goddess Durgā.

Daśahrā ("ten days"), or Dussera, Āśvina 7–10, September 30–October 3, is parallel to Durgā-pūjā, celebrating Rāma's victory over Rāvaṇa, and traditionally the beginning of the warring season.

Lakṣmīpūjā ("homage to Lakṣmī"), Āśvina Ś. 15, October 8; is the date on which commercial books are closed, new annual records begun, and business paraphernalia honoured; for Lakṣmī is the goddess of good fortune.

Dīpāvalī, Dīwālī ("strings of lights"), Āśvina K. 14 and Kārttika Ś. 1, October 21–22, is the festival of lights, when light is carried from the waning to the waxing fortnight and presents are exchanged.

Mahā-śivarātri ("night of great Śiva"), Māgha K. 14, February 16, is when the dangerous but, if placated, benevolent god Śiva is honoured on the blackest night of the month.

Dolāyātrā ("swing festival"), Phālguna S. 15, March 5, is the scene of the famous hook-swinging rites of Orissa.

Holī (name of a demoness), Phālguna S. 15, March 26–27, is a fertility and role-changing festival, scene of great fun-poking at superiors.

Gurū Nānak Jayantī, Kārttika S. 15, November 26, is the birthday of Nānak, the founder of the sect of Sikhism.

The eras. Not before the first century BC is there any evidence that the years of events were recorded in well-defined eras, whether by cycles, as the Olympic Games in Greece and the tenures of consuls in Rome, or the Roman year dating from the foundation of the city. Perhaps under outside influence, eras were begun but were without universal appeal, and few have remained influential. Among those are (1) the Vikrama era, begun 58 BC; (2) the Śaka era, begun 78 AD (these two are the most commonly used); (3) the Gupta era begun 320 AD; (4) the Harṣa era, begun 606 AD. All these were dated from some significant historical event. Of more mythological interest is the Kali era (Kali being the latest and most decadent period in the system of the four *Yugas*), which is supposed to have started at the dawn of February 18, 3102 BC. (J.A.B.v.B.)

THE CHINESE CALENDAR

Evidences from the Shang oracle bone inscriptions show that at least by the 14th century BC the Shang Chinese had established the solar year at 365¼ days and lunation (the time between New Moons) at 29½ days. In the calendar that the Shang people used, the seasons of the year and the phases of the Moon were all supposedly accounted for. One of the two methods that they used to make this calendar was to add an extra month of 29 or 30 days, which they termed the 13th month, to the end of a regular 12-month year. Evidence also suggests that the Chinese developed the Metonic cycle (see above *Early calendar systems: Complex cycles*), *i.e.*, 19 years with a total of 235 months, about a century ahead of Meton's first calculation (no later than the early spring and autumn period, 722–481 BC). During this cycle of 19 years there were seven intercalations of months. The other method, which was abandoned soon after the Shang people started to adopt it, was to insert an extra month between any two months of a regular year. Possibly, a lack of astronomical and arithmetical knowledge allowed them to do this.

By the 3rd century BC, the first method of intercalation was gradually falling into disfavour, while the establishment of the meteorological cycle, the *erh-shih-ssu chieh-ch'i*, during this period officially revised the second method. This meteorological cycle contained 24 points each beginning one of the periods named consecutively the Spring Begins, the Rain Water, the Excited Insects, the Vernal Equinox, the Clear and Bright, the Grain Rains, the Summer Begins, the Grain Fills, the Grain in Ear, the Summer Solstice, the Slight Heat, the Great Heat, the Autumn Begins, the Limit of Heat, the White Dew, the Autumn Equinox, the Cold Dew, the Hoar Frost Descends, the Winter Begins, the Little Snow, the Heavy Snow, the Winter Solstice, the Little Cold, and the Severe Cold. The establishment of this cycle required a fair amount of astronomical understanding of the Earth as a celestial body, and without elaborate equipment it is impossible to collect the necessary information. Modern scholars acknowledge the superiority of pre-Sung Chinese astronomy (at least until about the 13th century AD) over that of other, contemporary nations, yet in its earliest stage the only tool used was an upright pillar with which the sky was measured.

Names of the points

The 24 points within the meteorological cycle coincide with points 15° apart on the ecliptic (the plane of the Earth's yearly journey around the Sun or, if it is thought that the Sun turns around the Earth, the apparent journey of the Sun against the stars). It takes about 15.2 days for the Sun to travel from one of these points to another (because the ecliptic is a complete circle of 360°), and the sun needs 365¼ days to finish its journey in this cycle. Supposedly, each of the 12 months of the year contains two points, but, because a lunar month has only 29½ days and the two points share about 30.4 days, there is always the chance that a lunar month will fail to contain both points, though the distance between any two given points is only 15°. If such an occasion occurs, the intercalation of an extra month takes place. For instance, one may find a year with two "Julys" or with two "Augusts" in the Chinese calendar. In fact, the exact length of the month in the Chinese calendar is either 30 days or 29 days—a phenomenon which reflects its lunar origin. Also, the meteorological cycle means essentially a solar year. The Chinese thus consider their calendar as *yin-yang li*, or a "lunar–solar calendar."

The *yin-yang li*

Although the *yin-yang li* has been continuously employed by the Chinese, foreign calendars were introduced to the Chinese, the Hindu calendar, for instance, during the T'ang dynasty (618–907), and were once used concurrently with the native calendar. This situation also held true for the Muslim calendar, which was introduced during the Yüan dynasty (1279–1368). The Gregorian calendar was taken to China by Jesuit missionaries in 1582, the very year that it was first used by Europeans. Not until 1912, after the general public adopted the Gregorian calendar, did the *yin-yang li* lose its primary importance.

One of the most distinguished characteristics of the Chinese calendar is its time-honoured day-count system. By combining the ten celestial stems, *kan*, and the 12 terrestrial branches, *chih*, into 60 units, the Shang Chinese counted the days with *kan–chih* combinations cyclically. For more than 3,000 years, no one has ever tried to discard the *kan–chih* day-count system. Out of this method there developed the idea of *hsün*, ten days, which some scholars would render into English as "week." The *kan–chih* combinations probably were adopted for year count by Han emperors during the 2nd century AD.

The *yin-yang li* may have been preceded by a pure lunar calendar because there is one occurrence of the "14th month" and one occurrence of the "15th month" in the Shang oracle bone inscriptions. Unless there was a drastic change in the computation, it is quite inconceivable that an extra 90 days should have been added to a regular year. Julius Caesar had made 45 BC into a year of 445 days for the sake of the adoption of the Julian calendar in the next year. Presumably, the Shang king could have done the same for similar reasons. From the above discussion on the intercalation of months, it is clear that within the *yin-yang li* the details of the lunar calendar are more important than those of the solar calendar. In a solar calendar the 24 meteorological points would recur on the same days every year. Moreover, if a solar calendar were adopted first, then the problem of intercalation would be more related to the intercalation of days rather than intercalation of months.

Many traditional Chinese scholars tried to synchronize the discrepancy between the lunation and the solar year. Some even developed their own ways of computation embodying accounts of eclipses and of other astronomical phenomena. These writings constitute the bulk of the traditional almanacs. In the estimation of modern scholars, there were at least 102 kinds of almanacs known, some used regularly. The validity or the popularity of each of these almanacs depends heavily on the author's proficiency in handling planetary cycles. In the past these authors competed with one another for the position of calendar master in the Imperial court, even though mistakes in their almanacs could bring them punishment, including death. (Ch.L.)

V. Calendar systems of the Americas

THE MAYA CALENDAR SYSTEM

The basic structure of the Maya calendar is common to all calendars of Meso-America (*i.e.*, the civilized part of ancient Middle America). It consists of a ritual cycle of 260 named days and a year of 365 days. These cycles, running concurrently, form a longer cycle of 18,980 days, or 52 years of 365 days, called a "Calendar Round," at the end of which a designated day recurs in the same position in the year.

The "Calendar Round"

The native Maya name for the 260-day cycle is unknown. Some authorities call it the *tzolkin* (Count of Days); others refer to it as the Divinatory Calendar, the Ritual Calendar, or simply the day cycle. It is formed by the combination of numerals 1 through 13, meshing day by day with an ordered series of 20 names (see figure). The names of the days differ in the languages of Meso-america, but there is enough correspondence of meaning to permit the correlation of the known series, and there is reason to think that all day cycles were synchronous. The days were believed to have a fateful character, and the Tzolkin was used principally in divination. Certain passages in the *Dresden Codex*, one of the three Maya manuscripts that survived the conquest, show various Tzolkins divided into four parts of 65 days each, or into five parts of 52 days. The parts are in turn subdivided into a series of irregular intervals, and each interval is accompanied by a group of hieroglyphs and by an illustration, usually depicting a deity performing some simple act. The hieroglyphs apparently give a prognostication, but just how the Maya determined the omens is not known.

The 365-day year was divided into 18 named months of 20 days each, with an additional five days of evil omen, named Vazeh. In late times, the Maya named the years after their first days. Since both the year and the number (20) of names of days are divisible by five, only four names combined with 13 numbers could begin the year. These were called Year Bearers and were assigned in order to the four quarters of the world with their four as-

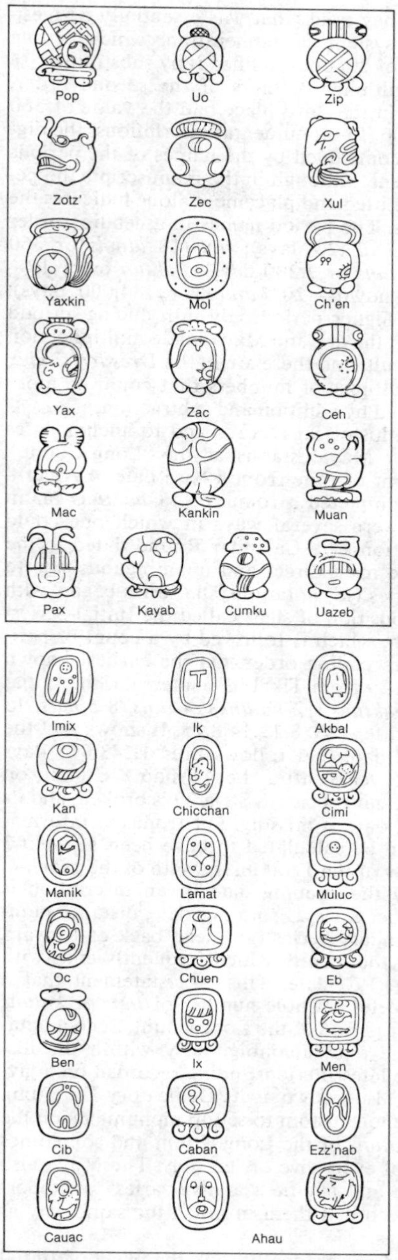

The Maya calendar.
(Top) Month signs. (Bottom) Day-signs.
By courtesy of the trustees of the British Museum

sociated colours. Unlike day cycles, years were not synchronous in all regions. They began at different times and in different seasons, and even among Maya-speaking peoples there was imperfect concordance of the months. Some differences may be due to postconquest attempts to keep the native year in step with the Christian calendar; others no doubt have an earlier origin.

The manner of recording historical dates is peculiar to the ancient Maya calendar. The Maya did not use the names of years for this purpose. To identify a date of the Calendar Round, they designated the day by its numeral and name, and added the name of the current month, indicating the number of its days that had elapsed by prefixing one of the numerals from 0 through 19. A date written in this way will occur once in every Calendar Round, at intervals of 52 years.

This was not good enough to link events over longer periods of time. Maya interest in history, genealogy, and astrology required accurate records of events far in the past. To connect dates to one another, the Maya expressed distances between them by a count of days and their multiples. They used what was essentially a vigesimal place-value system of numeration, which is one based on a count of 20, but modified it by substituting 18 for 20 as the multiplier of units of the second order, so that each unit in the third place had the value of 360 days instead of 400. In monumental inscriptions, the digits are usually accompanied by the names of the periods their units represent, although in the manuscripts the period names are omitted and placement alone indicates the value of the units. The period names in ascending order are: *kin* (day); *uinal* (20 days); *tun* (18 *uinals* or 360 days); *katun* (20 *tuns* or 7,200 days); *baktun* or cycle—native name unknown—(20 *katuns* or 144,000 days); and so on up to higher periods. By introducing an odd multiplier to form the *tun*, the Maya made multiplication and division difficult, and there are in the *Dresden Codex* long tables of multiples of numbers that could be more simply manipulated by addition and subtraction.

Period names

To correlate all historical records and to anchor dates firmly in time, the Maya established the "Long Count," a continuous count of time from a base date, 4 Ahau 8 Cumku, which completed a round of 13 *baktuns* far in the past. There were several ways in which one could indicate the position of a Calendar Round dated in the Long Count. The most direct and unambiguous was to use an Initial-Series (IS) notation. The series begins with an outsized composition of signs called the Initial-Series-introducing glyph, which is followed by a count of periods written in descending order. On the earliest known monument, Stela 29 from Tikal in Guatemala, the Initial Series reads: 8 *baktuns*, 12 *katuns*, 14 *tuns*, 8 *uinals*, 15 *kins*, which is written: IS. 8.12.14.8.15. It shows that the Calendar Round date that follows falls 1,243,615 days (just under 3,405 years) after the 4 Ahau 8 Cumku on which the Long Count is based. Stela 29 is broken, and its Calendar Round date is missing, but from the information above, it can be calculated to have been 13 Men 3 Zip (the 195th day of the Tzolkin, the 44th of the year).

Normally, only the opening date of an inscription is written as an Initial Series. From this date, distance numbers, called Secondary Series (SS), lead back or forward to other dates in the record, which frequently ends with a Period-Ending (PE) date. This is a statement that a given date completes a whole number of *tuns* or *katuns* in the next higher period of the Long Count. Such a notation identifies the date unambiguously within the historic period. The latest Period Ending recorded on a given monument is also known as its Dedicatory Date (DD), for it was a common custom to set up monuments on the completion of *katuns* of the Long Count and sometimes also at the end of every five or ten *tuns*. The Maya also celebrated *katun* and five-*tun* "anniversaries" of important dates and recorded them in much the same way as the period endings.

Period-Ending dates gradually took the place of Initial Series, and, in northern Yucatán, where Mayan sites of the latest period are located, a new method of notation dispensed with distance numbers altogether by noting after a Calendar Round date the number of the current *tun* in a Long Count *katun* named by its last day. Long Count *katuns* end with the name Ahau (Lord), combined with one of 13 numerals; and their names form a Katun Round of 13 *katuns*. This round is portrayed in Spanish colonial manuscripts as a ring of faces depicting the Lords. There are also recorded prophesies for *tuns* and *katuns*, which make many allusions to history, for the Maya seem to have conceived time, and even history itself, as a series of cyclical, recurring events.

The discontinuance of Initial-Series notations some centuries before the conquest of Mexico by Spain makes all attempted correlations of the Maya count with the Christian calendar somewhat uncertain, for such correlations are all based on the assumption that the Katun Round of early colonial times was continuous with the ancient Long Count. The correlation most in favour now equates the 4 Ahau 8 Cumku that begins the Maya count with the Julian day 584,283 (see above *Complex cycles*). According to this correlation, the *katun* 13 Ahau that is said to have ended shortly before the foundation of Mérida, Yucatán, ended on November 14, 1539, by the Gregorian calendar, and it was the Long Count *katun* 11.16.0.0.0. 13 Ahau 8 Xul. Some tests of archaeological material by the radiocarbon method corroborate this correlation; but results are not sufficiently uniform to resolve all doubts, and some archaeologists would prefer to place the foundation of Mérida in the neighbourhood of 12.9.0.0.0. in the Maya count. Correlations based on astronomical data so far have been in conflict with historical evidence, and none has gained a significant degree of acceptance.

The basic elements of the Maya calendar have little to do with astronomy. A lunar count was, however, included in a Supplementary Series appended to Initial-Series dates. The series is composed of hieroglyphs labelled Glyphs *G*, *F*, *E* or *D*, *C*, *B*, and *A*, and a varying number of others. Glyph *G* changes its form daily, making a round of nine days, possibly corresponding to the nine gods of the night hours or Mexican Lords of the Night. Glyph *F* is closely associated with Glyph *G* and does not vary. Glyphs *E* and *D* have numerical coefficients that give the age of the current Moon within an error of two or three days; Glyph *C* places it in a lunar half year; and Glyph *A* shows whether it is made up of 29 or 30 days. The meaning of Glyph *B* is unknown. There are discrepancies in the lunar records from different sites, but during a period of about 80 years, called the Period of Uniformity, a standard system of grouping six alternating 29- and 30-day moons was used everywhere.

Lunar correlations

Occasionally included with the Supplementary Series is a date marking the conclusion of an 819-day cycle shortly before the date of Initial Series. The number of days in this cycle is obtained by multiplying together 13, 9, and 7, all very significant numbers in Maya mythology.

It has been suggested that certain other dates, called determinants, indicate with a remarkable degree of accuracy how far the 365-day year had diverged from the solar year since the beginning of the Long Count, but this hypothesis is questioned by some scholars. The identification of certain architectural assemblages as observatories of solstices and equinoxes is equally difficult to substantiate. So far, it has not been demonstrated how the Maya reckoned the seasons of their agricultural cycle or whether they observed the tropical or the sidereal year.

In colonial times, the star group known as the Pleiades was used to mark divisions of the night, and the constellation Gemini was also observed. A computation table in the *Dresden Codex* records intervals of possible eclipses of the Sun and Moon. Another correlates five revolutions of the planet Venus around the Sun with eight 365-day years and projects the count for 104 years, when it returns to the beginning Tzolkin date. Three sets of month positions associated with the cycle suggest its periodic correction. Other computations have not been adequately explained, among them some very long numbers that transcend the Long Count. Such numbers appear also on monuments and indicate a grandiose conception of the complexity and the almost infinite extent of time.

THE MEXICAN (AZTEC) CALENDAR

The calendar of the Aztec was derived from earlier calendars in the Valley of Mexico and was basically similar to that of the Maya. The ritual day cycle was called Tonalpohualli and was formed, as was the Maya Tzolkin, by the concurrence of a cycle of numerals 1 through 13 with a cycle of 20 day names, many of them similar to the day names of the Maya. The Tonalpohualli could be divided into four or five equal parts, each of four assigned to a world quarter and a colour and including the centre of the world if the parts were five. To the Aztec, the 13-day period defined by the day numerals was of prime importance, and each of 20 such periods was under the patronage of a specific deity. A similar list of 20 deities was associated with individual day names, and, in addition, there was a list of 13 deities designated as Lords of the Day, each accompanied by a flying creature, and a list of nine deities known as Lords of the Night. The lists of deities vary somewhat in different sources. They were probably used to determine the fate of the days by the Tonalpouhque, who were priests trained in calendrical divination. These priests were consulted as to lucky days whenever an important enterprise was undertaken or when a child was born. Children were often named after the day of their birth; and tribal gods, who were legendary heroes of the past, also bore calendar names.

The Aztec and Maya systems compared

The Aztec year of 365 days was also similar to the year of the Maya, though probably not synchronous with it. It had 18 named months of 20 days each and an additional five days, called *nemontemi*, which were considered to be very unlucky. Though some colonial historians mention the use of intercalary days, in Aztec annals there is no indication of a correction in the length of the year. The years were named after days that fall at intervals of 365 days, and most scholars believe that these days held a fixed position in the year, though there appears to be some disagreement as to whether this position was the first day, the last day of the first month, or the last day of the last month, as was suggested by a distinguished Mexican scholar. Since 20 and 365 are both divisible by five, only four day names—Acatl (Reed), Tecpatl (Flint), Calli (House), and Tochtli (Rabbit)—figure in the names of the 52 years that form a cycle with the Tonalpohualli. The cycle begins with a year 2 Reed and ends with a year 1 Rabbit, which was regarded as a dangerous year of bad omen. At the end of such a cycle, all household utensils and idols were discarded and replaced by new ones, temples were renovated, and human sacrifice was offered to the Sun at midnight on a mountain top as people awaited a new dawn.

The year served to fix the time of festivals, which took place at the end of each month. The new year was celebrated by the making of a new fire, and a more elaborate ceremony was held every four years, when the cycle had run through the four day names. Every eight years was celebrated the coincidence of the year with the 584-day period of the planet Venus, and two 52-year cycles formed "One Old Age," when the day cycle, the year, and the period of Venus all came together. All these periods were noted also by the Maya.

Where the Aztec differed most significantly from the Maya was in their more primitive number system and in their less precise way of recording dates. Normally, they noted only the day on which an event occurred and the name of the current year. This is ambiguous, since the same day, as designated in the way mentioned above, can occur twice in a year. Moreover, years of the same name recur at 52-year intervals, and Spanish colonial annals often disagree as to the length of time between two events. Other discrepancies in the records are only partially explained by the fact that different towns started their year with different months. The most widely accepted correlation of the calendar of Tenochtitlán with the Christian Julian calendar is based on the entrance of Cortés into that city on November 8, 1519, and on the surrender of Cuauhtémoc on August 13, 1521. According to this correlation, the first date was a day 8 Wind, the ninth day of the month Quecholli, in a year 1 Reed, the 13th year of a cycle.

The Mexicans, as all other Meso-Americans, believed in the periodic destruction and re-creation of the world. The famous "Calendar Stone" in the Museo Nacional de Antropología (National Museum of Anthropology) in Mexico depicts in its central panel the date 4 Ollin (movement), on which they anticipated that their current world would be destroyed by earthquake, and within it the dates of previous holocausts: 4 Tiger, 4 Wind, 4 Rain, and 4 Water.

PERU: THE INCA CALENDAR

So little is known about the calendar used by the Inca that one can hardly make a statement about it for which a contrary opinion cannot be found. Some workers in the field even assert that there was no formal calendar but only a simple count of lunations. Since there was no written language used by the Inca, it is impossible to check contradictory statements made by early colonial chroniclers. It is widely believed that the quipus of the Inca contain calendrical notations, but no satisfactory demonstration of this is possible.

Most historians agree that the Inca had a calendar based on the observation of both the Sun and the Moon, but it is not clear how the lunar count was related to the year. Names of 12 lunar months are recorded, as well as their association with festivities of the agricultural cycle; but there is no suggestion of the use of a numerical system for counting time, although a quinary decimal system, with names of numbers at least up to 10,000, was used for other purposes. The organization of work on the basis of a week of nine days suggests the further possibility of a count by triads that could result in a formal month of 30 days.

A count of this sort was described by Alexander von Humboldt (see below *Bibliography*) for a Chibcha tribe living in the mountainous region of Colombia. The description is based on an earlier manuscript by a village priest, and one authority has dismissed it as "wholly imaginary," but this is not necessarily the case. The smallest unit of this calendar was a numerical count of three days, which, interacting with a similar count of ten days, formed a standard 30-day "month." Every third year was made up of 13 moons, the others having 12. This formed a cycle of 37 moons, and 20 of these cycles made up a period of 60 years, which was subdivided into four parts and could be multiplied by 100. A period of 20 months is also mentioned. Although the account of the Chibcha system cannot be accepted at face value, if there is any truth in it at all it is suggestive of devices that may have been used also by the Inca.

Attempts to identify calendrical matter in the archaeological remains of the central highlands have not been successful, although at one time the Gateway of the Sun at Tiahuanaco and the Echenique Plaque were much discussed in this regard. Assertions by early historians that the Inca observed solstices and equinoxes are somewhat suspect, too, as is also, particularly, the mention by one investigator of a vertical shadow pole set in a circular space presumably to measure the passage of the seasons by the lengths of the shadow. It is generally conceded, however, that planting seasons were fixed by the observation of the Sun against rows of small square masonry towers built on the skyline to the east and west of Cuzco, in Peru.

In one account, it is said that the Inca Viracocha established a year of 12 months, each beginning with the New Moon, and that his successor, Pachacuti, finding confusion in regard to the year, built the sun towers in order to keep a check on the calendar. Since Pachacuti reigned less than a century before the conquest, it may be that the contradictions and the meagreness of information on the Inca calendar are due to the fact that the system was still in the process of being revised when the Spaniards first arrived.

NORTH AMERICAN INDIAN TIME COUNTS

No North American tribe had a true calendar—a single integrated system of denoting days and longer periods of time. Usually, intervals of time were counted independently of one another. The day was a basic unit recognized by all tribes, but there is no record of aboriginal names for days. A common device for keeping track of days was a bundle of sticks of known number, from which one was extracted for every day that passed, until the bundle was exhausted. Longer periods of time were usually counted by moons, which began with the New Moon, or conjunction of the Sun and Moon. Years were divided into four seasons, occasionally five, and when counted were usually designated by one of the seasons; *e.g.*, an Indian might say that a certain event had happened ten winters ago. Among sedentary agricultural tribes, the cycle of the seasons was of great ritual importance, but the time of the beginning of the year varied. Some observed it about the time of the vernal equinox, others in the fall. The Hopi tribe of northern Arizona held a new-fire ceremony in November. The Creek ceremony, known as the "Busk," was held late in July or in August, but it is said that each town set its own date for the celebration.

As years were determined by seasons and not by a fixed number of days, the correlation of moons and years was also approximate and not a function of a daily count. Most tribes reckoned 12 moons to a year. Some northern tribes, notably those of New England, and the Cree tribes, counted 13. The Indians of the northwest coast divided their years into two parts, counting six moons to each part, and the Kiowa split one of their 12 moons between two unequal seasons, beginning their year with a Full Moon.

The naming of moons

The naming of moons is perhaps the first step in transforming them into months. The Zuni Indians of New Mexico named the first six moons of the year, referring to the remainder by colour designations associated with the four cardinal (horizontal) directions, and the zenith and the nadir. Only a few Indian tribes attempted a more precise correlation of moons and years. The Creeks are said to have added a moon between each pair of years, and the Haida from time to time inserted a "between moon" in the division of their year into two parts. It is said that an unspecified tribe of the Sioux or the Chippewa made a practice of adding a "lost moon" when 30 moons had waned.

A tally of years following an important event was sometimes kept on a notched stick. The best known record commemorates the spectacular meteoric shower (the Leonids, see METEOR) of 1833. Some northern tribes recorded series of events by pictographs, and one such record, said to have been originally painted on a buffalo robe, and known as the "Lone-dog Winter Count," covers a period of 71 years beginning with 1800.

Early explorers had little opportunity to learn about the calendrical devices of the Indians, which were probably held sacred and secret. Contact with white people and their Christian calendar doubtless altered many aboriginal practices. Thus, present knowledge of the systems used in the past may not reflect their true complexity. (T.P.)

BIBLIOGRAPHY. Little material on the calendar is available in English. The main detailed and readable book on both the development of the calendar and its calculation and possible reform is ALEXANDER PHILIPS, *The Calendar: Its History, Structure and Improvement* (1921), which does not, however, contain some of the more recent results of investigations into Babylonian, Roman, and earlier calendar methods. A shorter and more up-to-date reference is the section on the calendar in the *Explanatory Supplement to the Astronomical Ephemeris and the American Ephemeris and Nautical Almanac* (HMSO, 1961). A standard text by F.K. Ginzel, *Handbuch der mathematischen und technischen Chronologie das Zeitrechnungswesen der Völker*, 3 vol. (1906–14), is even older than Philips' book and the same criticism applies.

Sumero-Babylonian: A comprehensive and up-to-date study of Sumerian and Babylonian calendars is lacking. See references to special studies in E.J. BICKERMAN, *Chronology of the Ancient World* (1968). On astronomy and calendar, see OTTO NEUGEBAUER, *The Exact Sciences in Antiquity*, 2nd ed. (1957); and his chapter on "Ancient Mathematics and Astronomy," in the *History of Technology*, ed. by CHARLES SINGER *et al.*, vol. 1 (1954). On the later Babylonian calendar cycle, see RICHARD A. PARKER and WALDO H. DUBBERSTEIN, *Babylonian Chronology 626 B.C.–A.D. 75* (1956). Current bibliography is published in the quarterly review *Orientalia.*

Neighbours of Babylonia: (*Assyria*): HILDEGARD LEWY, *The Cambridge Ancient History*, 3rd ed., vol. 1, pt. 2, ch. 25 (1971), learned and whimsical; and on the "week," see also *The Assyrian Dictionary*, vol. 5 (1956). (*Hittites*): ALBRECHT GOETZE, *Kleinasien* (1933, reprinted 1957). (*Ugarit*): CYRUS H. GORDON, *Ugaritic Textbook* (1965). (*Phoenicians*): JOHN B. PECKHAM, *The Development of the Late Phoenician Scripts* (1968). (*Mari*): *Archives royales de Mari XII*, vol. 2 (1964). (*Iran*): E.J. BICKERMAN in *The Cambridge History of Iran*, vol. 3.

Jewish: The oldest systematic and complete book on the present fixed Jewish calendar is the work of ABRAHAM BAR HIYYA (born *c.* 1065), known as Savasorda of Barcelona, that bears the title *Sefer ha-ʿIbbur*, ed. by HERSCHELL FILIPOWSKI (1851). A précis of this is contained in a section (ch. 6–10) in book 3, treatise 8—"Sanctification of the New Moon"—in *The Code of Moses Maimonides* (1135–1204); English by SOLOMON GANDZ in the "Yale Judaica Series" (YJS), vol. 11 (1956), with notes by the translator, and "Astronomical Commentary" by OTTO NEUGEBAUER; rev. and suppl. in the relevant parts of "Addenda and Corrigenda" by ERNEST WIESENBERG, in YJS, vol. 14 (1961). Additional details of the Jewish calendar of both the rabbinic and sectarian varieties have been outlined by JACOB LICHT and E.J. WIESENBERG in *Encyclopaedia Judaica*, vol. 5, pp. 43–53 (1971).

Early Egyptian: NEUGEBAUER (*op. cit.*) is easy to understand; see also his *Commentary on the Astronomical Treatise* (1969), which is well done and recent; and "The Origin of the Egyptian Calendar," *J. Near Eastern Stud.*, 1:396–403 (1942), important for its discussion of the origin of the older lunar calendar. OTTO NEUGEBAUER and RICHARD A. PARKER (eds. and trans.), *Egyptian Astronomical Texts*, 3 vol. (1960–69), is detailed, but does have some good general discussions. RICHARD A. PARKER, *The Calendars of Ancient Egypt* (1950), is the best on the subject—all older material is out of date; his "Lunar Dates of Thutmose III and Ramesses II," *J. Near Eastern Stud.*, 16:39–43 (1957), is important for later lunar dates. H.E. WINLOCK, "The Origin of the Ancient Egyptian Calendar," *Proc. Am. Phil. Soc.*, 83:447–64 (1940), is also an important discussion.

Early Greek: For the *octaëteris*, D.R. DICKS, "Solstices, Equinoxes, and the Presocratics," *J. Hellenic Stud.*, 86:26–40 (1966), is the best recent discussion of the subject; see also his *Early Greek Astronomy to Aristotle* (1970). STERLING DOW and ROBERT F. HEALEY, *A Sacred Calendar of Eleusis* (1965), is good for another calendar besides that of Athens. BENJAMIN D. MERITT, *The Athenian Year* (1961), contains the latest reconstruction of the Athenian civil years. For a discussion of water clocks, see OTTO NEUGEBAUER and H.B. VAN HOESEN, *Greek Horoscopes* (1959). WILLIAM K. PRITCHETT, *Ancient Athenian Calendars on Stone* (1963), is good for the Athenian calendar. See also his "Gaming Tables and I.G., I², 324," *Hesperia*, 34:131–147 (1965); and, with OTTO NEUGEBAUER, *The Calendars of Athens* (1947), still the most important on the subject, with only minor changes—one should use with it BICKERMAN (*op. cit.*); and ALAN E. SAMUEL, *Greek and Roman Chronology* (1972).

India: The most complete account of the lunar-solar calendar of India may be found in "Indian Calendar," ch. 5 of the *Calendar Reform Committee Report* of the Government of India (1955). A good summary of the materials was published by JEAN FILLIOZAT in "Notions de chronologie," an appendix of the encyclopaedic work on Indian history and culture, *L'Inde classique* by LOUIS RENOU and JEAN FILLIOZAT, vol. 2 (1953).

Chinese: CH'EN CHIH-WU, *Yin li yang li yin-yang li* (1957); CHU WEN-HSIN, *Li fa t'ung chih* (1945); the definitive history of science in China, JOSEPH NEEDHAM and WANG LING, *Science and Civilisation in China*, vol. 3 (1959); T'UNG TSO-PIN, *Yin li pu* (1945).

Pre-Columbian: The following are useful and authoritative references for the Maya calendar: SYLVANUS G. MORLEY, *An Introduction to the Study of the Maya Hieroglyphs* (1915); the most complete and authoritative account is J. ERIC S. THOMPSON, *Maya Hieroglyphic Writing: An Introduction*, 2nd ed. (1960). For the Mexican calendar: ALFONSO CASO, "El Calendario Mexicano," *Memorias de la Academia Mexicana de la Historia*, vol. 17, no. 1 (1958); and *Thirteen Masterpieces of Mexican Archaeology* (1938). For the Inca calendar: ALEXANDER VON HUMBOLDT, *Vues des cordillères, et monuments des peuples indigènes de l'Amérique*, 2 vol. (1816); A.L. KROEBER, "The Chibcha," in *The Handbook of South American Indians*, ed. by JULIAN H. STEWARD, vol. 2 (1946); and JOHN HOWLAND ROWE, "Inca Culture at the Time of the Spanish Conquest. Astronomy and the Calendar," *ibid.*

For North American Indian chronologies, see the chapter by CYRUS THOMAS, "Calendar," in *The Handbook of American Indians North of Mexico*, ed. by FREDERICK W. HODGE, vol. 1 (1907).

(C.A.R./J.D.Sc./E.J.Bi./E.J.Wi./N.A.Z./J.A.B.v.B./Ch.L./T.P.)

Calhoun, John C.

John Caldwell Calhoun, United States congressman, secretary of war, vice president, senator, secretary of state, and perennial seeker after the presidency, served in public life constantly from the time he was elected to Congress in 1811 as a war hawk from South Carolina until his death in 1850. He has become the symbol of the Old South, of whose undoing, many have thought, he was the chief agent. Certainly the Civil War was too vast an event for the main responsibility to be placed upon any one man, but it may well be argued that Calhoun contributed as much to its coming as did William Lloyd Garrison, the Abolitionist, and Abraham Lincoln.

Calhoun, daguerreotype by Mathew Brady, *c.* 1849.
By courtesy of the Library of Congress, Washington, D.C.

The man himself is an enigma. A staunch nationalist during the first half of his public life, one who told Alexander Hamilton's son in 1823 that his father's attempt to develop a strong federal government "as developed by the measures of Washington's administration is the only true policy for this country," Calhoun became in the latter part of his career an unwavering champion of states' rights as laid down in the Constitution. Yet he said shortly before his death, "If I am judged by my acts, I trust I shall be found as firm a friend of the Union as any man in it. . . . If I shall have any place in the memory of posterity it will be in consequence of my deep attachment to it."

Early years

Calhoun was born on March 18, 1782, in Abbeville district, South Carolina, into a well-to-do Scots–Irish pioneer family that had recently migrated from Pennsylvania to the Carolina Piedmont. Two years after enrolling in a local academy at age 18, he entered the junior class at Yale, where he graduated with distinction. After spending a year at a law school at Litchfield, Connecticut, and further study in the office of a prominent Federalist in Charleston, he was admitted to the bar but abandoned its practice after his marriage in 1811 to his cousin, Floride Bonneau Calhoun, an heiress whose modest fortune enabled him to become a planter-statesman. An ardent Jeffersonian Republican who called for war with Britain as early as 1807, he was elected to the state legislature in 1808 and in 1811 to the national House of Representatives. There he functioned as one of Speaker Henry Clay's main lieutenants, and, in his capacity as chairman of the foreign relations committee, he introduced the declaration of war against Britain in June 1812. His service as majority floor leader during the hostilities led a colleague to call him the "young Hercules who carried the war on his shoulders."

Political career. In the postwar session he was chairman of the committees that introduced the bills for the second Bank of the United States, a permanent road system, and a standing army and modern navy; he also vigorously supported the protective tariff of 1816. Thus, during this period, Calhoun was the intellectual father of American nationalism. In 1817 President Monroe appointed Calhoun secretary of war, and his distinguished performance in that post, as well as his previous legislative prominence, led his friend John Quincy Adams, then secretary of state, to declare that his Carolina colleague "is above all sectional and factious prejudices more than any other statesman of this Union with whom I have ever acted."

Calhoun had won rapid recognition by his parliamentary skill as one of the ranking leaders of the Republican Party; yet his eagerness for personal advancement, his glib exuberance in debate, and his egotism aroused an undercurrent of distrust. Former secretary of the treasury Albert Gallatin, commenting on Calhoun's nomination for president in 1821 by a rump group of northern congressmen, called him "a smart fellow, one of the first among second-rate men, but of lax political principles and a disordinate ambition not over-delicate in the means of satisfying itself."

To a degree not exceeded by that of any of his contemporaries, Calhoun was consumed by a burning passion to achieve the presidency. He vigorously sought the office three times, and, each time he thought he had a chance. During each attempt to attain the office, an anonymous eulogistic biography appeared in print. These were largely autobiographies, written in the third person, the last of them published in 1843.

Champion of states' rights. In the 1830s Calhoun became as extreme in his devotion to strict construction of the Constitution as he had earlier been in his support of nationalism. In the summer of 1831 he openly avowed his belief in nullification, a position which he had three years earlier anonymously advanced in the *South Carolina Exposition and Protest.* Each state was sovereign, Calhoun contended, and the Constitution was a compact among the sovereign states. Therefore, any one state (not the Supreme Court) could declare an act of Congress unconstitutional. The proponents of the nullified measure, according to the theory, would then have to get an amendment to the Constitution—which requires a two-thirds vote of each house of Congress and ratification by three-fourths of the states—confirming the power of Congress to take such action.

Although the tariff was the specific issue in the nullification crisis of 1832–33, what Calhoun was actually fighting for was protection of the South's "peculiar institution," Negro slavery, which someday might be abolished by a northern majority in Congress, perhaps with financial compensation to the owners, as the British Parliament decreed in 1833. The tariff, Calhoun put forth in one of his public letters, is "of vastly inferior importance to the great question to which it has given rise . . . the right of a state to interpose, in the last resort, in order to arrest an unconstitutional act of the General Government."

To Calhoun's chagrin, a majority of the Southern states formally and vehemently rejected his abstruse doctrine of nullification. Even Jefferson Davis, who believed in the right of a state to secede from the Union, denied the right of a state to nullify a Congressional act. And the octogenarian former president James Madison, whose Virginia Resolution of 1798 Calhoun used as his authority, publicly refuted him.

A genius unto himself, Calhoun lacked the capacity for close friendship and eventually drove most of his associates into active enmity, not least among them Pres. Andrew Jackson. His banishment by Jackson was, however, mainly a matter of bad luck. No one did more to make Jackson president than Calhoun, and his prospects in 1828 were most promising. "I was a candidate for re-election (as vice president) on a ticket with General Jackson himself," he wrote later, "with a certain prospect of the triumphant success of the ticket, and a fair prospect of the highest office to which an American citizen can aspire." But through his wife, Calhoun became involved in a boycott by the wives of the Cabinet members of the wife of the Secretary of War, and in the end Jackson fired his whole Cabinet and broke with the Vice President. Late in 1832 Calhoun resigned his post, was elected to the Senate, and vainly debated Daniel Webster in defense of his cherished doctrine of nullification. The last 20 years of his life he spent in the Senate working to unite the South against the radical Abolitionist attack on slavery. His efforts were in vain, however. His exuberant defense of slavery as a "positive good" aroused a strong

Quarrel with President Jackson

anti-Southern feeling in the free states, and at the same time he never did unify the South.

Assessment. After his death, in Washington, D.C., on March 31, 1850, his protégé, James H. Hammond, said that

> pre-eminent as he was intellectually above all the men of this age as I believe, he was so wanting in judgment in the managing of men, was so unyielding and unpersuasive, that he never could consolidate sufficient power to accomplish anything great, of himself and [in] due season . . . and the jealousy of him—his towering genius and uncompromising temper, has had much effect in preventing the South from uniting to resist [evil].

Calhoun as political theorist

Calhoun's two books on government, published posthumously, and his many cogent speeches in Congress have gained for him a reputation as one of the nation's foremost original political theorists. He preceded Karl Marx in advancing the economic interpretation of history, but most of his basic ideas, particularly that of nullification, he acquired outright from James Madison, who was 30 years his senior. Calhoun is remembered as the defender of minorities, but he had no use for any minority—certainly not labourers or Abolitionists—except the Southern minority. His solution for the problem of the preservation of the Union was to give the South everything that it demanded. He was truly devoted both to the Union and to the South, and, fortunately, he died before he had choose between them. But with rare insight, in 1850 he told a friend that the Union was doomed to dissolution: "I fix its probable occurrence within twelve years or three Presidential terms."

In his thinking, Calhoun worked the problem back as if from the answer at the end of a mathematics primer. With his objective in mind he chose a seemingly innocuous premise and then proceeded with hard logic to the desired conclusion. The historian William P. Trent said in the 1890s that he "started with the conclusion he wanted and reasoned back to the premises. . . . Calhoun led thought rather than men, and lacking imagination, he led thought badly."

Calhoun's life was a tragedy in both the Greek and the Shakespearean sense. The gods thirsted after him, but he helped them along. Almost his last words were "The South! The poor South!" The poet Walt Whitman heard a Union soldier say shortly after Appomattox that the true monuments to Calhoun were the wasted farms and the gaunt chimneys that were scattered throughout the Confederacy.

BIBLIOGRAPHY

Writings: Works, ed. by RICHARD K. CRALLE, 6 vol. (1854–57); *Papers of John C. Calhoun,* ed. by W. EDWIN HEMPHILL, 3 vol. (1959–67); *Annual Report of the American Historical Association for the Year 1899,* vol. 2 (1900), contains his correspondence.

Biographies: CHARLES M. WILTSE, *John C. Calhoun,* 3 vol. (1944–51), with an excessive pro-Calhoun bias; MARGARET L. COIT, *John C. Calhoun: American Portrait* (1950), also laudatory; GERALD M. CAPERS, *John C. Calhoun, Opportunist: A Reappraisal* (1960), brief and critical; RICHARD N. CURRENT, *John C. Calhoun* (1963), emphasis on the significance of Calhoun's thought for the present. See also RICHARD HOFSTADTER, "Calhoun: The Marx of the Master Class," in *The American Political Tradition and the Men Who Made It,* ch. 4 (1948), an incisive essay; and "From Calhoun to the Dixiecrats," *Social Research,* 16:135–150 (1949).

(G.M.C.)

California

During the 1960s immigration to California was so great that it was described as giving a westward tilt to the United States. California surpassed New York as the most populous state in the nation, and its personal income is one of the highest in the world. The fluid nature of its social, economic, and political life, so much affected by the influx of people from other states, gives California the aura of a laboratory for testing new modes of living.

The more than 23,600,000 Californians recorded by the census of 1980 make up the most urban population in the nation, centred mainly along the coast, with more than a third of it in the Los Angeles and San Francisco metropolitan areas. As in most of the nation's larger states, the capital, Sacramento, is not a major population or economic centre.

California has an area of 158,693 square miles (411,013 square kilometres), exceeded only by Alaska and Texas. The state is bounded on the north by Oregon, on the east by Nevada and Arizona, on the south by the Mexican state of Baja ("lower") California, and on the west by the Pacific Ocean.

The state's physical contrasts

Since its admission to the Union in 1850 as the 31st state, California has been recognized as a land of stunning physical contrasts: from the rainy northern coast to the parched Colorado Desert of the south. The Sierra Nevada exceeds the Rocky Mountains in height. Within 85 miles (137 kilometres) of each other lie Mt. Whitney and Death Valley, respectively 14,494 and 282 feet (4,418 and 86 metres) above and below sea level, the highest and lowest points in the 48 coterminous states. Despite its urbanization, California is also the principal agricultural state of the nation, though only about 15 percent of its area is urban or cultivated. Almost half of its land is federally owned, with national parks and monuments in every part of the state devoted to irreplaceable forest, desert, mountain, and other natural resources. (For related information see UNITED STATES OF AMERICA; UNITED STATES, HISTORY OF THE; PACIFIC COAST RANGES; SIERRA NEVADA RANGE; DEATH VALLEY; SAN FRANCISCO; and LOS ANGELES.)

THE HISTORY OF CALIFORNIA

Exploration. Modern California derives from the discovery of gold at Sutter's Mill in 1848, just nine days before Mexico signed the Treaty of Guadalupe Hidalgo, ceding to the United States a vast area of the Southwest that included all of present-day California. The region had received little attention from Europeans for more than three centuries after its first sighting in 1542 by the Spanish navigator Juan Rodríguez Cabrillo. The merchant Sebastián Vizcaíno sailed the southern California coast in 1602, naming San Diego, Santa Catalina Island, Santa Barbara, and Monterey Bay. Despite these early explorations, California was left to its Indian population—estimated at 130,000 when Spanish explorers reached California in 1542.

Establishment of the Spanish missions

Settlement. Pressure for settlement came from missionaries anxious to convert the Indians and from the intrusion of Russian and British traders, primarily in search of sea-otter pelts. In 1769 the Spanish viceroy dispatched land and sea expeditions from Baja California, and the Franciscan friar Junípero Serra established the first mission at San Diego. Gaspar de Portolá set up a military outpost in 1770 at Monterey. Colonization began after 1773 with the opening of an overland supply route across the southwestern deserts.

The 21 missions established by Serra and his successors were the strongest factors in developing California. While attempting to Christianize the Indians, the padres taught them farming and crafts. With the labour of the Indians, the padres irrigated vast ranches and traded hides, tallow, wine, brandy, olive oil, grain, and leatherwork for the manufactured goods brought by Yankee trading vessels around Cape Horn.

U.S. colonization and acquisition. Secularization of the missions was sought by Spanish–Mexican settlers known as Californios when Mexico became independent of Spain in 1821. Between 1833 and 1840 the mission ranches were parcelled out to political favourites by the Mexican government. The padres withdrew, and the Indians, decimated by European diseases and driven off the mission lands, were cruelly exploited and diminished. In 1841 the first wagon train of settlers left Missouri for California. The colony grew slowly, but in 1846 the Northwest became a part of the United States, and settlers at Sonoma proclaimed an independent California republic. In May the United States declared war on Mexico, and in July the U.S. flag was raised at Monterey. Only minor skirmishes occurred before the Californios surrendered to troops under John C. Frémont near Los Angeles in January 1847. Within a year the form of the present-day United States was nearly cast.

The Gold Rush. Early in 1848 James Wilson Marshall, a carpenter from New Jersey, picked up nuggets of gold from the American River at the site of a sawmill he was building near Coloma. By August the hillsides above the river were strewn with the tents and wood huts of the first 4,000 miners. From the East, prospectors sailed around Cape Horn or risked disease in hiking across the Isthmus of Panama. The hardiest took the 2,000-mile overland route, where cholera proved a greater killer than Indians. About 40,000 came to San Francisco by sea in 1849. Some 6,000 wagons, carrying about 40,000 more, moved west that year over the California Trail. Few of the prospectors struck it rich. The work was hard, prices were high, and living conditions were primitive. The wiser emigrants became farmers and storekeepers.

Gold hastened statehood in 1850, and though the Gold Rush peaked in 1852, the momentum of settlement did not subside. Nearly $2,000,000,000 in gold was taken from the earth before mining became almost totally dormant, yet in 1979 alone the income from California's agriculture was triple that of all the gold ever mined there.

Growth as a state. As gold had buoyed statehood, so statehood buoyed immigration. Cheap land and the hope of a fresh start lured soldiers west after the U.S. Civil War. Service on the first transcontinental railroad began in 1869. The tide of immigration first moved toward southern California around 1900, spurred by citrus, oil, and some wariness of San Francisco after the earthquake and fire of 1906. Land booms came and went. Agriculture in inland valleys and industry in the cities boomed. During World War II aircraft plants and shipyards expanded, and in the 1950s research and educational facilities burgeoned as the movement of people to the West Coast came to include an unusual share of scientists and academicians. The state has nearly doubled in population every 20 years since 1860. San Francisco remains the financial and corporate centre, while the southern one-third of the state exceeds the rest in population.

Early 20th-century immigration

THE NATURAL LANDSCAPE

California offers startling contrasts of landscape and examples of physical diversity. Summer temperatures in its low-lying southern desert compare with the highest of Africa's Sahara, and winter temperatures atop the Sierra Nevada are Arctic. Rainfall ranges from extremes of 174 inches (4,420 millimetres) in the northwest to traces in the southeastern desert, but moderate temperatures and rainfall prevail along the coast. The average annual temperature is about 65° F (18° C) in Los Angeles and 57° F (14° C) in San Francisco. Annual precipitation averages about 14 inches in Los Angeles and 21 inches in San Francisco.

The moderate climate has been a major factor in the concentration of settlement along the coast, where cool ocean breezes hold off heat, and temperatures seldom exceed 90° F (32° C) or drop to freezing. Low humidity usually prevails. Climate changes rapidly with the altitude extremes of California, and the coastal cities are only hours away from mountain skiing or desert sports.

Coast ranges. The long coastline is mountainous, most dramatically in the Santa Lucia Range south of San Francisco, where the homes of Big Sur perch on cliffs 800 feet above the sea. Hills of lesser height flank entrances to the coast's three major natural harbours, at San Diego, San Francisco, and Eureka. Coastal mountains, made up of many indistinct chains, are from 20 to 40 miles in width and from 2,000 to 8,000 feet in height.

The mountains of California

Sierra Nevada. The eastern portions of the state, particularly in the south and extreme northeast, are occupied by sparsely settled desert, high in the north and low and increasingly hot in the south. The majestic Sierra Nevada rises to the west of this desert, extending for 430 miles. The eastern escarpment is sheer, dropping 10,000 feet within 10 miles near Owens Lake. On the west the range slopes to the Central Valley, comprising the San Joaquin and Sacramento valleys, in gradually declining foothills. From the wall that rises near volcanic Lassen Peak in the north, the Sierra Nevada extends south for 430 miles to the fringes of Los Angeles. It is 50 to 80 miles in width and 27,000 square miles in area. Aside from Mt. Whitney, 10 other peaks exceed 14,000 feet in altitude. East–west passes are few and high, some at more than 9,000 feet.

The largest lake of the Sierra Nevada and one of the loveliest in the United States is Lake Tahoe, astride the California–Nevada border at 6,229 feet. A mountain-ringed Alpine lake almost 200 square miles in area, it ranks 11th in the world in average depth: the 1,200-foot line runs near shore, and the maximum depth exceeds 1,600 feet. Elsewhere in the Sierra lie hundreds of smaller lakes, some above the timberline in regions of tumbled granite and smooth-walled canyons. There are three national parks in these highlands: Kings Canyon, Sequoia, and Yosemite—the latter rising from the purplish foothills of the Mother Lode gold country through ice-carved valleys of the Merced and Tuolumne rivers, with their waterfalls and granite domes.

Central Valley. In a north–south arc through the centre of California, the Central Valley runs for 450 miles, forming a deep trough between the Coast Ranges to its west and the Sierra Nevada to its east. The valley constitutes the state's agricultural heartland. Its single opening is the delta through which the Sacramento and San Joaquin rivers drain into San Francisco Bay. The valley is sealed off at the northeast by the Cascade Range and at the northwest by the Klamath Mountains. This far north the terrain is rugged and sparsely populated, heavily timbered and wet on its coastal side and drier and barren in the higher northeast. In the south the Central Valley is closed off by the transverse ranges, notably the Tehachapi Mountains, which are regarded as a dividing wall between southern and central California.

Coastal settlement and forests. Southern California's dense settlement lies along a coastal plateau and in valleys ranging from 40 to 60 miles inland. North of the Tehachapis, where the Coast Ranges move closer to the shore, population becomes sparser along the coast. The populous coastal area around San Francisco Bay gives way to the less developed northern coast, where lumbering and fishing villages lie beside creeks and rivers flowing from the Coast Ranges. This is the area of coastal redwood forests and Redwood National Park. These trees, among the tallest in the world, may reach 300 feet in height, 15 to 35 feet in diameter, and 4,000 years in age. Before European settlement the redwoods covered an estimated 1,500,000 acres (607,000 hectares) of California. Most redwood forests have been cut, but 109,000 acres of redwoods are protected in state and national parks.

The redwood forests

Deserts. Temperature contrasts in the deserts are great. The Colorado Desert of southeastern California has summer temperatures of up to 130° F (54° C), almost the highest temperatures recorded on Earth, with annual rainfall averaging 3 to 4 inches. More than 4,000 square miles of this desert lie below sea level. The 300-square-mile inland Salton Sea, below sea level, was created in 1905–07 when the Colorado River broke out of its channels. Northward, in the higher Mojave Desert, temperatures are somewhat less oppressive. Still relatively untouched by development, this area of more than 25,000 square miles reaches from the Tehachapi and Sierra Nevada to the Colorado River. It has some mining, several military reservations, and aviation test facilities. Farther north, the eastern desert lies from 2,000 to 7,400 feet above sea level, with temperatures ranging from 75° F (24° C) to −25° F (−32° C). It remains sparsely populated.

Water resources. Water is chronically scarce in southern California and the desert regions, but excesses of rain and snowmelt cause winter flooding along the rivers of the northern coast. More than 70 inches of rain falls at Crescent City, near the Oregon border, about 370 miles north of San Francisco; and the village of Honeydew, in the redwoods of Humboldt County, has received as much as 174 inches in a year. Southern California, in contrast, has 60 percent of the state's population and about 2 percent of its water, with an average annual rainfall of 15 inches, entirely in the winter months. Complex systems of dams and aqueducts move water from north to south, but not without citizen protests. The Colorado River Aqueduct moves water from the river, at the Arizona border, across the southern California desert and mountains to serve 119 communities. The California State Water Project, launched in 1960, is the largest water-transfer system ever undertaken. It is designed to deliver an additional 3,338,800,000 gallons (12,638,000,000 litres) daily from the Feather River to communities as far south as the Mexican border.

Long-distance transportation of water

THE PEOPLE OF CALIFORNIA

Spanish and Indian heritages. The Indians and the Spanish settlers of the 18th and 19th centuries are of only vestigial importance in contemporary California. Spanish influence is evident in architecture and place-names. The many Californians with Spanish surnames reflect largely the 20th-century immigration from Mexico—to escape that nation's revolution (1910–17) or to find agricultural jobs. Indians are increasing in number. Of the Indian population in 1980—slightly more than 201,000—some 12,500 lived on 78 reservations totalling more than 450,000 acres.

The historical mix. The first settlers from the California Trail were mostly Midwestern farmers of Anglo-Saxon descent. With the Gold Rush a more cosmopolitan mix appeared. Ships sailed into San Francisco from the Atlantic Seaboard, Europe, and the Orient. In 1850 more than half of the Californians were in their 20s, typically male and single. Only a few hundred Chinese lived in the state in 1850, but two years later one resident out of 10 was Chinese; most performed menial labour. Irish labourers came with the railroad-construction boom during the 1860s. The Irish, French, and Italians tended to settle in San Francisco. As Los Angeles began to grow at the end of the 19th century, it lured Mexicans, Russians, and Japanese, but primarily an additional influx of Anglo-Saxons from the Midwest.

Racial discrimination. Discrimination grew strong, especially against Orientals. An alien land law intended to discourage ownership of land by Orientals was not ruled unconstitutional until 1952. At one time the testimony of Chinese in courts was declared void. Separate schools for Orientals were authorized by law until 1936, and not until 1943 was the Chinese Exclusion Act repealed by Congress. As discrimination against the Chinese flared, Japanese were encouraged to immigrate, and in 1900 alone more than 12,000 entered California. Prospering as farmers, they came to control more than 10 percent of the farmland by 1920, while comprising only 2 percent of the population. Los Angeles became the centre of the nation's Japanese community, while San Francisco's Chinatown became the nation's largest Chinese settlement.

Discrimination against the Japanese smoldered until World War II, when about 93,000 Japanese-Americans lived in the state. Some 60 percent were American-born citizens known as Nisei; most of the others were Issei, older adults who had immigrated before Congress halted their influx in 1924. Never eligible for naturalization, the Issei were classed as enemy aliens. During 1942 almost all of California's Japanese-Americans, both Nisei and Issei, were moved from their farms and homes to isolated inland camps and held under guard until 1945. At the end of the war they found their property sold for taxes or storage fees and their enclaves overrun. After years of litigation about 26,000 claimants were reimbursed for their losses at about one-third of the claimed valuation. About 85 percent of the Japanese-Americans had been farmers, but with their land gone they became gardeners or went into businesses and professions.

The third generation of Japanese-Americans, the Sansei, plays a prominent role in southern California. The Japanese-American community of Los Angeles is estimated to be in excess of 150,000. More than a third of the 806,000 Chinese in the country live in California, predominantly in San Francisco. With a stream of refugees from Hong Kong and Taiwan, the population of San Francisco's Chinatown rose between 1950 and 1970 from about 25,000 to more than 70,000.

Blacks and Mexicans. Few blacks settled in California until World War II, but between 1940 and 1980 the black population of San Francisco rose from about 5,000 to about 86,000, and in Los Angeles from 64,000 to more than 900,000, more than 12 percent of the population. California has had among the largest gains of any state in black population, with those leaving the Southern states attracted to such cities as Los Angeles and Oakland despite unemployment rates there exceeding 30 percent.

More than half the nation's Mexican-Americans, or Chicanos, live in California. Chicano communities in the 1970s experienced increasingly frequent confrontations with police and other officials, especially in Los Angeles, in protests against discrimination and unemployment. None reached the proportion, however, of the black riots that levelled much of Los Angeles' Watts area in 1965.

Religion. Both traditional churchgoing and an interest in flamboyant mystical or evangelical sects declined steadily in California in the years following World War II. In 1971 about one-third of Californians listed church affiliations, a proportion far below the national average. Judaism is strongest in the Fairfax and Beverly Hills areas of the Los Angeles Basin, Roman Catholicism in San Francisco, and fundamentalist Protestant sects in those parts of southern California inhabited by migrants from the South and Southwest. Many of the conventional faiths in California resort to unconventional techniques, advertising worship services in newspapers, offering free bus service, and employing public relations counsellors.

Los Angeles is notorious for its exotic cults. Aimee Semple McPherson, whose Angelus Temple boasted 35,000 members, is the best remembered of such evangelists; she died in 1944 after an overdose of sedatives. Faith healers still are popular. Scientology, calling itself "the common people's science of life betterment," thrived in southern California under the leadership of a former film writer, L. Ron Hubbard. Zen Buddhism enjoyed popularity in San Francisco during the 1950s, with English-born Alan Watts serving as its Occidental interpreter to a following that included the "Beat Generation" of that era, forerunner of the hippies.

Demography. Native-born Americans remained the dominant factor in California's growth phenomenon in the mid-20th century. Many workers who flooded the defense industries during World War II remained as residents, along with hundreds of thousands who first visited the state as servicemen. Los Angeles grew from 1,500,000 to almost 3,000,000 between 1940 and 1980. About three-fifths of the population is concentrated south of the Tehachapi Mountains in about one-fourth of the state's area, with the greatest concentration in the small coastal area.

Present-day migratory patterns

By 1970, however, net immigration was showing annual declines. This trend was accompanied by a decline in the birth rate equal to the national average, and the state's growth began to level off. Later migration took place from the crowded cities of California to rural areas and cities of the Rocky Mountain states. Demographers predict continued population increases for California, which is likely to maintain its rank as the nation's most populous state, but these predictions have been scaled down from earlier years.

THE STATE'S ECONOMY

In economic terms California is more aptly compared with nations than with states. In 1980 its personal income exceeded $259,551,000,000, a total surpassed only by that of the United States as a whole and of a few other industrialized nations. In the recession of 1969–71, with rising unemployment in the aerospace and film industries, the California economy was bulwarked by diversification. Federal spending has been high throughout California's history, but it has undergone a transition from that of colonization-type funds to the present expenditures that involve both the state's natural resources and its wealth of human resources.

Economic overview

Since the Gold Rush, Californians have shown ingenious mastery of the state's resources, and their innovative society has created its own economic momentum. Industry has triumphed over remoteness; lacking iron and coal deposits, it has developed light industry. Financiers have been imaginative in seeking and employing capital, and many of the nation's largest banks and corporations are

California-based, the latter principally involved in aerospace, electronics, computers, and oil and gas. California supplanted New York in 1965 as the leading state in the export of manufactured goods. The state is dominant in aerospace, agriculture, wine making, and the film and television industries. Despite soaring taxes, the California climate and its social freedoms continue to attract high-income immigration and technologically oriented industry.

Agriculture. The foundation of California wealth lies in agriculture. Its fields and orchards yield more than 200 agricultural products of astonishing diversity from more than 7,800,000 acres of irrigated farmland. In 1979 cattle ranked first in value, followed by milk and cream, cotton, and grapes. California produces about one-third of the nation's canned and frozen vegetables and fruits. The state is first in production of tomatoes, sugar beets, and strawberries. In 1978 annual cash farm receipts were $10,500,000,000. About half of this output comes from the Central Valley, which is irrigated through a labyrinth of dams, canals, and power and pumping plants.

The state's agricultural supremacy dates from 1947, when its farm output first exceeded that of any other state. Due to the growing season of nine to 10 months, Fresno, Imperial, Kern, and Tulare counties rank among the top five counties in the nation in value of farm produce. Most farms are huge, and more than two-thirds of farm income is earned by less than 15 percent of the farms. Many large landholdings have derived from federal land grants to railroads, notably the Southern Pacific, which in 1919 was the state's largest landowner. Such farms have tended to become agricultural assembly lines with absentee owners, high mechanization and productivity, and persistent labour strife. Most farms specialize in one or two crops: almonds grow north of Sacramento; cotton and forage crops, figs, and grapes near Fresno; and in the wet delta, asparagus, tomatoes, rice, safflower, and sugar beets. Such specialization has been enhanced by agricultural research at the University of California at Davis; this institution also counsels the California wine industry in its production of 80 percent of the wine consumed in the United States. The citrus industry, almost destroyed in the 1940s by a virus, ranks second to that of Florida in production of oranges.

Farming as big business

Premium wine grapes grow in the picturesque Napa and Sonoma valleys north of San Francisco and in adjacent areas. The Imperial Valley in the Colorado Desert in the extreme south, though smaller in area than the Central Valley, has about 500,000 irrigated areas of farmland. Other major farming areas include the Coachella Valley near Palm Springs, where dates and grapefruit grow, and the Salinas Valley and Monterey Bay region.

The farm-labour pool is made up of low-income labourers, including the many migrants and Mexican nationals crossing the border in harvest seasons. Long abused, migrant labourers organized in the late 1960s under the leadership of César Chavez and began lengthy strikes that drew nationwide support in the form of consumer boycotts. In the 1970s, however, Chavez' United Farm Workers lost much of its membership to the Teamster Union.

Mineral resources. Petroleum production grew rapidly after 1895, with oil strikes in the Los Angeles–Long Beach area. California led all states in petroleum production from 1900 to 1936 and ranked third in 1978. Although in 1968 production reached an all-time daily high of more than 1,000,000 barrels, reserves were being depleted at a rapid rate, and fuel and natural gas were being imported. Petroleum continued, however, to exceed the total of all other minerals in value of production. Gold mining is now insignificant. Other production includes natural gas, cement, sand and gravel, borate, soda, and salt.

Fisheries and forestry. California ranked third among states in 1979 in the value of commercial fish products. Largely ocean fish, the yield included albacore and bluefin tuna, mackerel, sole, squid, sardine, and salmon. Forest industries employ nearly 70,000 workers. Ownership of commercial forest land is almost equally divided between public agencies and private interests, with a total of almost 17,000,000 acres in use.

Industry, tourism, and the military. The aircraft plants and shipyards were supplemented after World War II by branch plants of many Eastern and Midwestern industries. Federal research-and-development funds allocated to California organizations also contributed to the dynamic postwar economy. Despite mercurial rises and declines responding to the shifting population, construction became a major industry. In 1980 about $25,000,000,000 was spent by almost 40,000,000 travellers and tourists.

All federal military services have major facilities in California, significantly affecting both the social and economic life of the state. San Diego, Long Beach, and San Francisco have home-port naval bases. Recruit training is the major role of naval and marine corps bases in San Diego, and infantry training takes place at Fort Ord near Monterey. Camp Pendleton, a marine base, encompasses the last large undeveloped area along the southern California coast. Air force activity centres around the Vandenberg base on the central coast and six other air commands, including the remote and esoteric test facilities on the Mojave Desert.

Transportation. Transportation, primarily by automobile and airplane, is in part both the cause and the product of the restless mobility of Californians, who move their residences more often than the average American and travel considerably more both for business and pleasure. California has the greatest concentration of motor vehicles on Earth and the most extensive system of multilane divided freeways. By 1979 there were more than 15,500,000 registered motor vehicles and almost 180,000 miles of roads. Compact San Francisco has about 7,000 cars per square mile. The BART (Bay Area Rapid Transit) system, completed in the early 1970s, provides ample transportation for residents in the Bay area.

The freeway system is so extensive that one can drive on arterials from San Diego almost 500 miles northward through Los Angeles and the Central Valley without encountering any traffic signals or stop signs. Freeway construction has continued despite growing public opposition based on ugliness, pollution, and usurpation of private and community property rights. The rise of the freeway system after World War II coincided in Los Angeles with the demise of a 1,200-mile interurban rail system that had once been the longest such system in the nation. The lack of a conventional urban core in Los Angeles, along with low population densities, dims the prospects for any rapid-transit system.

The freeway system

Transport of goods in California is predominantly by trucks, and agricultural and trucking lobbies have joined those of the automobile clubs, freeway builders, and the oil industry to perpetuate freeway development. The intricate canals and waterways of the Sacramento River Delta carry some waterborne freight traffic, and there is some coastal freight traffic.

Air commuting has increased phenomenally. The air corridor connecting San Francisco, Los Angeles, and San Diego has a greater volume than that linking Washington, D.C., New York City, and Boston. Air-traffic congestion has grown critical, but not yet so dire as that of the ground traffic around airports.

ADMINISTRATION AND SOCIAL CONDITIONS

Structure of government. California is governed under a constitution framed in 1878–79, its detail reflecting the disillusionment of the period with rampant graft. Before a series of deletions began in 1966, it had grown longer than any governmental constitution except those of Louisiana and India. Reform has often been undertaken in California through constitutional amendment. Those instituted by Gov. Hiram Johnson in 1911 included provisions for voter initiative of and referendum on legislation, recall of elected officials, the direct primary, women's suffrage, and a unique system that allowed candidates to run in primaries of opposing political parties. Since 1962 constitutional revision may be made by voters without calling a convention. In 1966 voters approved a great number of additional amendments.

State executive officers are elected for four-year terms, with members of more than 50 boards and commissions being appointed by the governor. The legislature comprises the Senate, with 40 members, and the General Assembly, with 80 members. Reapportionment in the mid-1960s gave legislative dominance to populous southern California at the expense of rural areas.

The judicial system has five levels, including the seven-member Supreme Court, district courts of appeal, and superior, municipal, and justice courts. Superior courts are the major trial courts, whereas the more numerous municipal districts hear lesser matters.

Local government is conducted through almost 4,000 agencies, including 58 counties and more than 360 incorporated cities, a lower number than in other populous states. Under the constitution counties and cities may establish charters or accept general-law provisions and statutory laws. Cities operate under variations of mayor–council–manager control. Los Angeles and San Francisco operate under mayor–council, while San Diego and San Jose employ city managers, who assume a large share of administrative duty.

Politics. Volunteer party organizations often have usurped roles ordinarily fulfilled by the Democratic and Republican party structure. The parties are forbidden to endorse any candidate prior to the primary, but unofficial organizations do so and are often better funded and organized than the party structure. To overcome this party ineffectiveness, candidates turn to professional campaign managers to enhance their public images.

Amorphousness of state politics

Attempts at machine politics have proven ineffectual because of voter mobility, lack of party entrenchment, and the prime role of civil service in bestowing jobs. The vastness of the state and the political cleavages between the liberal north and the conservative south make it difficult for one party to sweep statewide offices, even with majority registration. Before abolition of cross-filing in 1959, candidates of one party sometimes avoided facing general elections by sweeping the primary elections of both parties. Traditional party alignments seem less significant to many Californians, and crossovers are common despite heavy Democratic pluralities in registration.

Finances. In 1978 voters approved Proposition 13, which mandated a 57 percent reduction in property taxes. Property taxes continue to provide the chief source of local revenue, however. Rising income, sales, and gasoline taxes support state expenditures dominated by highway building, education, and welfare costs. The California budget for 1978 was estimated at nearly $25,000,000,000.

Education. California is oriented toward tax-supported public education. The two-year junior or community college was introduced in California in 1907, and by 1979 there were about 100 such colleges with more than 250,000 full-time students. Nineteen four-year state colleges, with 307,000 students, and the nine-campus University of California system, with more than 130,000 students, completed the public higher-education structure, with a state budget of nearly $3,000,000,000 by the late 1970s. The University Extension system claims 200,000 enrollments in more than 9,000 courses at more than 300 locations throughout the state. Less than 10 percent of California schoolchildren and a slightly higher percentage of college-age students attend private schools.

Higher education

A landmark in California higher education was achieved in 1960 with a master plan that attempted to avoid overlapping roles in the complex system of public colleges and universities. In general the top one-third of high school graduates is eligible to enroll at one of the 14 university campuses, which retain supervision over doctoral degrees. Four-year state colleges also draw from among the top one-third of high school graduates. High school graduates from the lower two-thirds of their classes attend two-year colleges and often are able to transfer at the end of that period to one of the four-year campuses.

During a period of rapid expansion in the 1960s, University of California campuses were developed at Irvine, Santa Cruz, and San Diego, augmenting older campuses at Berkeley, Los Angeles, Davis, Riverside, Santa Barbara, and San Francisco. The campuses at Santa Cruz and San Diego were established on variations of the Oxford University system of numerous small independent colleges sharing limited central facilities or services. By 1972 budget restrictions had severely hampered the scheduled development of new colleges within these two campuses, and student enrollment had fallen below projections; consequently, the addition of new colleges dropped behind schedule. Among new colleges opened was a third college at San Diego that emphasized minorities studies and had large black and Chicano enrollments. The college immediately became embroiled in community and academic controversy, with critics challenging its somewhat lower scholastic standards of admission. Other campuses at all levels were increasing minorities studies, usually within existing frameworks.

The original campus at Berkeley was founded in 1868 and has remained one of the most prestigious academic communities in the nation. This campus was the scene of militant demonstrations beginning in 1964 with the Free Speech Movement, which led in 1967 to dismissal by university regents of Clark Kerr, the respected university president who had been the major architect of the master plan of 1960 and of the new campuses.

By 1980 the university system had 16 Nobel Prize laureates on its faculties. It encompasses three nuclear laboratories, more than 100 research libraries, and about 100,000 employees. It was involved in overseas projects in more than 50 nations, and it offered some 1,000 courses.

Health and welfare. By 1978 almost 2,800,000 Californians—about 12 percent of the population—were receiving Medi-Cal (health) benefits. In 1979, with about 10 percent of the U.S. population, California had 13 percent of the nation's recipients of aid to families with dependent children and about 8 percent of the nation's food stamp recipients.

California long has been considered a liberal state in the extent of its health and welfare statutes. Its mental health programs have been expanded. State funds are dispersed through four major systems: aid to families with dependent children, aid to the totally disabled, aid to the blind, and old-age security. The rapidly increasing cost of these programs between 1960 and 1979 made continuation of California's traditionally generous posture a matter of fierce political debate. As governor, Ronald Reagan proposed welfare reforms, and some curtailment of benefits was legislated. Poverty, however, especially among Mexican-Americans and blacks—many of them immigrants to California—continued as a blemish on the general economic prosperity, and funding of these programs continued to mount. In 1978 state contributions to public welfare in California totalled more than $6,200,000,000.

In Watts, a district of south Los Angeles where the nation's first modern socially directed violence took place in 1965, poverty worsened between 1960 and 1965 at a time when family incomes in southern California rose 10 percent. In predominantly black Watts, about one-half of the families received less than poverty-level income in 1965. Unemployment remained high in Watts, and a majority of its residents received public assistance. There were similar pockets of poverty in all other major California cities. In East Los Angeles, Mexican-Americans made up about 90 percent of the population in 1970; unemployment decreased in subsequent years, but living conditions for a large proportion of the population are considered marginal.

Innovation distinguishes the structure of California's health and welfare programs. The number of mentally ill in state hospitals declined sharply from 1965 to 1977, partly through the introduction of psychotropic drugs and the availability of federal funds for nursing home care, but also through a marked expansion of state-funded mental health programs at the community level. In 1968 the legislature established a county-operated community mental health service in each county with populations exceeding 100,000. In 1969 a landmark act allowed the involuntary treatment of chronic alcoholics and those who are gravely disabled or dangerous to themselves or others.

In the beleaguered Medi-Cal program of medical aid, computer systems were established in 1973, enabling rapid processing of claims. Uniform identification cards were issued in 1971 to control services and validate claims.

These and other procedures were an attempt to eliminate abuse and delay that had nearly caused the program to founder.

CULTURAL LIFE AND INSTITUTIONS

It is too soon to speak of any cultural tradition rooted in California. As a state it has harboured—and given birth to—a notable procession of creative people in all the arts, yet much of their work cannot be associated with the region.

California's culture has not yet taken form. It is marked by widespread public involvement with the arts and enthusiasm for cultural trappings as symbols of achievement, often in the form of lavish expenditures to erect galleries, museums, and concert halls. There is an antipathy toward traditional culture among some segments of the population.

Literature. Early writers associated with California came from outside the state: Bret Harte, born in New York; Mark Twain, in Missouri; Joaquin Miller, in Indiana; and Ambrose Bierce, in Ohio. But the San Francisco of the Gold Rush days provided an eager audience for their writing, as it did for theatre and music. There followed a line of writers who came as close to establishing a regional tradition as have artists in any medium. Jack London, chronicler of men amidst frontier violence, was born in San Francisco. Frank Norris and Upton Sinclair, who opposed the social ills of their times in a foreshadowing of the later work of John Steinbeck and, to a lesser degree, of William Saroyan, were California-born but left the state in the 1940s. The naturalist John Muir, the progenitor of a school of environmental writers that became prominent in the 1960s and 1970s, extolled the state's natural wonders. Robinson Jeffers, who lived in California from 1914 until his death in 1962, was the state's most renowned poet. An influx of literary figures as screenwriters into Hollywood in the 1930s and 1940s established little in the way of regional cultural tradition, and the California milieu became instead a favourite target of satire in such novels as Nathanael West's *The Day of the Locust* and Evelyn Waugh's *The Loved One*, and in works by F. Scott Fitzgerald, Budd Schulberg, Raymond Chandler, and Ross Macdonald.

Visual and performing arts. San Francisco has produced such painters as David Park, Elmer Bischoff, and Richard Diebenkorn. Los Angeles seems more successful as a marketplace for art, with a thriving colony of galleries along La Cienega Boulevard comparable to Manhattan's Madison Avenue. The numerous wealthy art collectors in southern California are prominent in funding the Los Angeles County Museum of Art, which opened in 1965 and had more than twice as many visitors in its first year as the Louvre in Paris during that same period. The Music Center of Los Angeles County is a concert and theatre complex that was constructed during the 1960s by private contributions.

The California Arts Commission was given the task in 1963 of establishing "the paramount position of this state in the nation and in the world as a cultural center." Its contribution was hobbled by a low budget, however, and it has been limited largely to inventorying the arts in California and to providng token sponsorships. Tax-supported state institutions, most prominently the University of California and its extension program, are active in presenting dance recitals, plays and films, concerts, and lectures. The Theater Group of the University of California at Los Angeles is one of the most innovative in the nation. Experimental theatre in San Francisco has bloomed from time to time, especially with the Actor's Workshop between 1952 and 1965, after which the company moved to New York City. An often distinguished mixture of light and avant-garde theatre is offered throughout the year at several theatres, including the community-sponsored Old Globe Theater in San Diego. Amateur theatrical groups are everywhere, as are community orchestras, chamber-music societies, and weekend artists. Carmel, Big Sur, and Sausalito have harboured communities of workers in diverse arts. The symphony orchestras of San Francisco and Los Angeles have achieved international recognition, as has the San Francisco Opera Company. San Diego supports a fine symphony orchestra, opera, and ballet company through voluntary donations to a combined-arts council.

Mass media. Hollywood still is responsible for the bulk of the national movie and television output, and as such it remains an international symbol of glamour. An increasing number of national magazines and periodicals emanate from editorial offices that are located in California. Metropolitan California newspapers have decreased in number, but their total circulation has grown, led by the *Los Angeles Times*, with the largest number of readers in the state.

PROSPECTS

Some patterns of California development once seemed innovative—ranging from those of campus revolt to branch banking and the professional management of political campaigns, from youth cultism to the ranch-style house and the submergence of the two-party political system. Since so many Californians have come from other states, presumably in search of new lifestyles, the appearance of such patterns has led to the popular image of California as a state where acute observers may apprise future directions of life in the United States. Valid or not, that image has placed California affairs under scrutiny both in the popular media and scholarly research.

In the 1970s, however, the Californian's tolerance for innovation and social experiment was viewed by some as an invitation to the destruction of its institutions. Welfare abuses and campus militancy became rallying points of conservatives who deplored the permissiveness of California society. Political alliances seemed to be in flux, with spokesmen for emerging minorities seeking common ground with environmentalists. Critical state budgetary problems threatened advances in education and social improvement. So strong had sentiment become against continued rapid growth that even selective taxes aimed at new immigrants were proposed in 1971. It appeared that the period of boosterism in California had finally come to an end.

BIBLIOGRAPHY. For general points of view on California, see NEIL MORGAN, *The California Syndrome* (1969), and *The Pacific States*, rev. ed. (1970). Older but invaluable are CAREY MCWILLIAMS, *Southern California: An Island on the Land* (1946, reissued 1973), and *California: The Great Exception* (1949, reprinted 1976).

Early California histories by H.H. BANCROFT and T. HITTELL are excellent. Bancroft's voluminous works include: *History of California, 1542–1890*, 7 vol. (1884–90); *California Pastoral, 1769–1848* (1888); *California Inter Pocula, 1848–56* (1888); and *Popular Tribunals*, 2 vol. (1887). Hittell's is *History of California*, 4 vol. (1885–97). Other California histories include: J.W. CAUGHEY, *California: A Remarkable State's History*, 3rd ed. (1970); WALTON BEAN, *California: An Interpretive History*, 2nd ed. (1973); ANDREW F. ROLLE, *California: A History*, 3rd ed. (1978); and ROBERT GLASS CLELAND, *From Wilderness to Empire: A History of California*, ed. by GLENN S. DUMKE (1959). An outstanding regional overview is EARL POMEROY, *The Pacific Slope* (1965).

Of detailed value but variable accuracy is the FEDERAL WRITERS' PROJECT, *California: A Guide to the Golden State*, rev. ed. (1939, reprinted 1974). More accurate guidebooks are *Northern California*, 3rd ed. (1970), and *Southern California*, 3rd ed. (1970), published by SUNSET BOOKS; and ANDREW HEPBURN, *Complete Guide to Northern California*, and *Complete Guide to Southern California* (both 1962).

For geography and landscape, see DAVID W. LANTIS, RODNEY STEINER, and ARTHUR E. KARINEN, *California: Land of Contrast* 3rd ed. (1977). Among JOHN MUIR's many important works on California is *The Mountains of California* (1898, reprinted 1975). MICHAEL W. DONLEY *et al.*, *Atlas of California* (1979), provides a wealth of geographic, demographic, and economic data; WILLIAM L. KAHRL, *The California Water Atlas* (1979), is a comprehensive account of the state's extensive water resources. Among the best books on San Francisco's earthquake is WILLIAM BRONSON, *The Earth Shook, The Sky Burned* (1959). FRANCIS P. FARQUHAR combines history and geography in *History of the Sierra Nevada* (1965). A photographic study of Yosemite is ANSEL ADAMS, *Yosemite and the Range of Light* (1979).

A still-outstanding work on immigration to California is MARY R. COOLIDGE, *Chinese Immigration* (1909, reprinted

1969). The problems of the Japanese in California are addressed in ROGER DANIELS, *The Politics of Prejudice: The Anti-Japanese Movement in California and the Struggle for Japanese Exclusion*, 2nd ed. (1977). Important works are BERNARD DEVOTO, *The Course of Empire* (1952), *Across the Wide Missouri* (1947), and *The Year of Decision: 1846* (1942). A large bibliography of Gold Rush history may be found in JOHN WALTON CAUGHEY, *Gold Is the Cornerstone* (1948, reissued under the title *The California Gold Rush*, 1975). A notable primary source is *The Gold Mines of California:* Two Guidebooks (1849, reprinted 1974). A good guidebook is *Gold Rush Country* (1967).

The Watts riots of 1965 are analyzed in *The Los Angeles Riots: A Socio-Psychological Study*, ed. by NATHAN COHEN (1970).

An early economic history of California is that by ROBERT G. CLELAND and OSGOOD HARDY, *March of Industry* (1929). Economic affairs are discussed in NEIL MORGAN, *Westward Tilt* (1963). For railroad history, see OSCAR LEWIS, *The Big Four* (1938, reprinted 1981); on labour, see IRA B. CROSS, *A History of the Labor Movement in California* (1935, reprinted 1974).

An excellent book about California politics is GLADWIN HILL, *Dancing Bear: An Inside Look at California Politics* (1968). An overview of California politics is found in GEORGE E. MOWRY, *The California Progressives 1900–1920* (1951); and FRANK H. JONAS, *Western Politics* (1961). A fine novel of California politics is EUGENE BURDICK, *The Ninth Wave* (1956). (N.Mo.)

Californian Indians

Native peoples found in California were only generally circumscribed by the present state boundaries. Some of the peoples within these boundaries were culturally intimate with other areas neighbouring California. The Colorado River groups, such as the Mohave and Yuma, shared traditions with both the Southwest (Arizona and New Mexico) and southern California, whereas the peoples of the Sierra Nevada, such as the Washo, shared traditions with the Great Basin peoples. In northern California were found native traditions of the Northwest Coast (see SOUTHWEST AMERICAN INDIANS; NORTH AMERICAN GREAT BASIN INDIANS; and NORTHWEST COAST INDIANS). The remaining native groups occupied the greater part of California and represented indigenous cultural developments.

A conservative estimate of the pre-Spanish population of California is 275,000, making it one of the most populous culture areas of native North America. Various ecological features—seacoasts, tidelands, rivers and lakes, valleys, deserts, and foothills—and various historical traditions contributed to a great cultural diversity. Thus there existed a seemingly endless variety of local environmental niches, each contributing advantages and disadvantages to human adaptation.

The peoples of California were politically stable, sedentary, and conservative and less in conflict with one another than was usually the case in other areas of North America; and neighbouring groups often developed elaborate systems of economic exchange of goods and services. The Californian Indians reached peaks of cultural attainment rarely seen among peoples depending almost wholly for subsistence on hunting, fishing, and the gathering of wild plant foods.

TRADITIONAL CULTURE PATTERNS

Local and territorial organization. California was occupied by a large number of cultural groups that have been described as ethnic nationalities—that is, groups of people sharing common linguistic, social, and cultural traditions and recognizing themselves as part of a single culture distinct from that of other groups. Except for the Colorado River peoples (Mohave and Yuma) and perhaps some Chumash groups, these ethnic nationalities had no centralized governmental structures; instead, each group comprised independent territorial and political units that may be termed tribelets, tightly organized polities that were smaller than the average groupings in most other parts of North America. Populations in these tribelets

"Tribelet" organization

From H. Driver *et al.*, *Indiana University Publications in Anthropology and Linguistics* (1953)

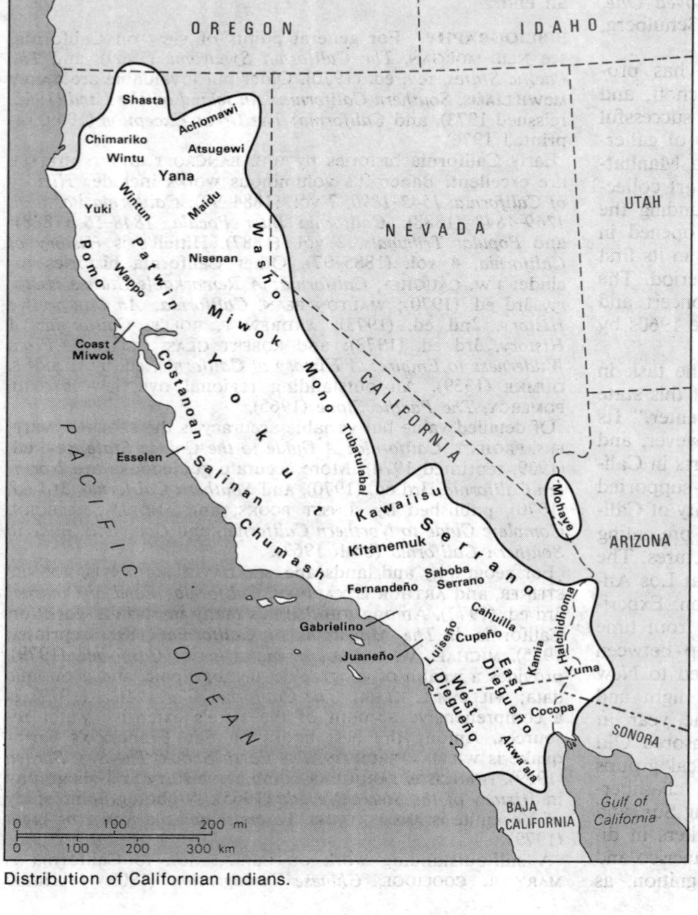

Distribution of Californian Indians.

ranged from a hundred to a few thousand people, depending on the richness of locally available resources; tribelet territories ranged in size from about 50 to 1,000 square miles (150 to 3,000 square kilometres).

Within each tribelet there might be only one principal village in which all the people lived and from which some of them ranged for short periods of time to collect food, hunt, or visit other tribelets for ritual or economic purposes. In some tribelets there was a principal village surrounded by settlements of people who came to the principal village for ritual, social, economic, and political occasions. In other tribelets there were two or more villages, each having various satellite settlements and one serving as a "capital" or central village. Here a principal chief would usually reside, and major rituals and political and economic affairs would be held.

Community organization of tribelet villages was varied, but basic patterns are discernible. Among the Miwok and the peoples south of them, village ownership was usually based on clan arrangements, whereas in northern California land ownership was based more on territorial principles than on kinship ties. Bilateral or nonlineal descent organization usually occurred where village land ownership was not clan based, as in the case of the southeastern desert-dwelling peoples, although exceptions to this occurred in the far northern part of the state.

Kinship and status patterns. Marriage was almost always a matter arranged by the families because it created long-range economic and social bonds between families. Generally the families exchanged goods at the time of the marriage, the bulk of goods coming from the husband's family. In most cases the wife resided with the husband's family and was taught the ways of the husband's group by the mother-in-law. Levirate (widow marriage to the brother of the deceased) and sororate (widower marriage to the sister of the deceased) were widely observed, maintaining relationships between already connected families and stabilizing child-care conditions. Men could often have more than one wife; this was particularly true of chiefs and shamans (medicine men) because heavy social responsibilities were required of their offices and because political ties between groups could thereby be established.

The aged served as the teachers and advisers. Young adults were active in subsistence, and the elders prepared the children for adulthood. The aged made most of the decisions concerning legal disputes and economic crises.

Role of the chief

The role of chief was generally an inherited position providing political stability to the group (though in northern California no formal chief appears to have existed). Women in some groups, such as the Pomo, were chosen as chiefs or "little chiefs." The chief was an economic administrator whose instructions to his people ranged from very general admonitions to very specific directions for particular tasks, such as indicating where food was available and how many people it would require to collect it. He redistributed the economic resources of his community and, through donations from members of the village, maintained resources from which emergency needs of individuals could be met. He was the major decision maker and the final authority in most villages, but he had the aid of a council consisting of such persons as heads of extended families, ritualists, assistant chiefs, and shamans. In some areas the chief functioned as a priest, maintaining the ceremonial house and ritual artifacts.

The chief was generally a conspicuously different person, wealthier, more elaborately dressed, and frequently displaying the symbols of his office. He was treated with great respect. Chiefs' families, in fact, formed a superstratum of the community elites, especially in areas in which lineage development was present.

Shamans and ritualists

Shamans served not only as healers and diviners but also as psychiatrists, artists, and poets. They defined and described the world of the sacred and regulated the fortune of souls before and after death, thereby serving as mediators between the profane and sacred worlds. Most tribelets in California had one or more shamans, usually men. Shamans were active in political life, working with other leaders and placing their powers at the disposal of the community.

Alongside chiefs and shamans in native California there were ritualists—dancers, singers, fire tenders—who were carefully trained in their crafts, and they functioned intimately within the political, economic, and religious spheres of their communities. They were men or women who acquired considerable respect and often wealth because of their skills and placement in the social structure. In effect, they were members of the power elite. When performing, ritualists were usually costumed in headdresses, dance skirts, wands, jewelry, and other items.

Socialization and education. Formal learning was a continuous process in native California life. Older persons instructed children through elaborate tales containing lessons concerning behaviour and values. Constant supervision—provided by adults, older siblings, or other relatives—instructed and reminded the child about how things should be done.

Rites of passage

The dramatic time of the educational process occurred during rites of passage, when individuals were graduating into new status positions. The girls' puberty ceremony, for example, generally consisted of a time of isolation because the girl was considered very dangerous when she began to menstruate. During this time, which varied from several days to several weeks, an older woman would care for the girl and instruct her in her role as an adult. Ceremonies for boys' initiation were less common and, when carried out, were usually less formal, involving instruction in the manly things to do and prediction of the boys' future religious, economic, or political careers.

Sometimes education was quite institutionalized. Young Chumash men, for instance, purchased positions from guildlike associations of specialists in order to receive apprenticeship as professional artisans of some kind, while young Pomo men were charged a fee to be trained as apprentices by recognized professional craftsmen.

Leaders and specialists continued their training on a less formal level throughout their lifetimes. A man destined to become chief received his learning from others (such as ritualists and shamans) and continued to receive such instruction even after assumption of office.

Economic systems. *Settlement patterns.* In most of California the villages were occupied the year round, with small groups moving out only for short periods of time to hunt or collect food. In areas poor in economic resources, people moved more frequently, only temporarily gathering together in large groups for such activities as antelope drives and piñon-nut harvests. Riverine and coastal peoples as a rule enjoyed more stable settlements than those living in the desert and foothills.

Housing

House types varied throughout California from permanent, carefully constructed houses occupied for a lifetime or more to the most temporary type of structure, such as a brush shelter, as dictated by circumstances. Types of houses ranged from wood-framed (northern California), earth-covered (various areas), semi-subterranean (Sacramento area), and brush (desert areas) to thatched palm (southern California). Communal and ceremonial houses were found throughout the region and were often large enough to hold several hundred people for rituals or festivals. Domestic houses ranged in size from five or six feet (almost two metres) in diameter to apartment-style houses in which several families lived together in adjoining units. Another common type of housing consisted of the sweathouses, earth-covered permanent structures that were used by most Californians (the Colorado River groups and the northern Paiute, on the margins of California, were exceptions); sweating was usually a daily activity for men.

Patterns of production and technology. Food production in native California centred on hunting, fishing, and collecting wild plant foods. Men usually hunted and fished while women collected plant foods and small game. Hunting and fishing equipment such as bows and arrows, throwing sticks, fishing gear, snares, and traps were made by men; women manufactured clothing, nets, baskets, pots, and other cooking utensils. Older people commonly made the productive equipment, whereas younger adults performed the harder labours of production using the implements.

For coastal Californians, shellfish, deep-sea fish, surf fish, acorns, and game were the main subsistence staples; peoples in the riverine and lake areas relied on fish, acorns, tule, game, and waterfowl. Native groups of the foothills, valleys, and plains depended on acorns, tule, game, and fish; and those living in the desert regions sought piñon nuts, mesquite, and game (especially antelope and rabbit) and practiced some marginal agriculture.

Special technologies

There were also various special technological devices. The Chumash of southern coastal California made large seagoing plank canoes, which allowed them to hunt large sea mammals. Peoples living on the bays and lakes used tule balsas or rafts, while riverine groups had flat-bottom dugouts (canoes made by hollowing out large logs). Techniques of food preservation included drying, hermetic sealing, and leaching of some foods high in acid content. Milling and grinding equipment was common.

Property and exchange systems. Concepts of property tended to vary in degree rather than kind throughout California. Everywhere, property was owned by individuals, family groups, lineages, communities, or larger political groups such as clans. In general, socially defined groups (such as clans and villages) owned the land and protected it against infringement from other groups. Individuals, lineages, or extended families usually owned exclusive rights only to certain food-collecting, fishing, and hunting areas. Such resources as obsidian mines or areas where medicinal plants grew might be owned by either groups or individuals. Individual articles could be acquired by manufacture, inheritance, purchase, or gift.

Goods and foodstuffs were distributed through two main institutions—reciprocal exchange between kin and "trade fairs," often ritualized. Both operated similarly in that they served as a redistribution and banking system for spoilable foodstuffs; a group with a surplus of foods, that is, would bring it to another group and exchange it for goods (such as shells), which could be used in the future to acquire foodstuffs in return.

There were professional traders in most California groups who travelled long distances among many ethnic nationalities. Goods from as far away as Arizona and New Mexico were exchanged by coastal peoples. Generally, shells from the coastal areas were valued and exchanged for products of the inland areas, such as obsidian or food. Medicines, manufactured goods such as baskets, and other objects were also commonly exchanged in these systems.

Religion. Throughout native California religious institutions were intensely and intimately associated with all other institutions—political, economic, social, and legal. In all the groups there were shamans, religious leaders who served as intermediaries between the supernatural world and the world of man. Priests and other ritualists were common in many groups.

Kuksu and Toloache religions

Two religious systems—the Kuksu and the Toloache—were associated with social organizations into which initiates were formally indoctrinated. In the Kuksu religion common to northern California (as among the Pomo, Yuki, Maidu, Wintun), members "impersonated" spiritual beings and engaged in very distinctive, colourful, and dramatic rituals with special paraphernalia, costumes, and equipment, usually in large public communal houses. Within the Toloache religion of southern California (as among the Luiseño and Diegueño), initiates performed while drinking a hallucinogenic decoction made of Datura meteloides, which put them in a trance and allegedly provided them with supernatural knowledge about their future life and role as members of the sacred societies. In both religions special instruction was a significant factor in the recruitment of members into the ritual society. Members exercised considerable economic, political, and social influence.

Religions on the Colorado River differed slightly because they were not concerned with developing formal organizations and recruitment procedures. Individuals received religious information through dreams; and members recited long narrative texts, explaining the creation of the world, the travel of culture heroes, and the adventures of historic figures.

In the northwest there was another informally structured religious system. It was associated with rituals concerned with world renewal (as in the white-deerskin dance), in which privately owned myths were recited. One communal need served by these ceremonies was that of restructuring relationships in societies lacking the rigid social ordering found in many other native California groups. The display of costumes and valuable possessions (such as white deerskins or delicately chipped obsidian blades) reaffirmed social ranking, and the success of the ritual reaffirmed the orderly relationship of man to the supernatural.

Use of magic

The use of supernatural power to control events or transform reality was basic to every California group. Generally, magic was used in attempts to control the weather, increase the harvest of crops, and foretell the future. Magic was deemed not only the cause of sickness and death but also the principal means of curing many diseases. Sometimes magic was considered as an agent to protect oneself, to punish wrongdoers, or to satisfy personal ends.

Arts and crafts. Oral literature was the art form for which native California was most renowned—especially esoteric and elaborate creation tales and epic poems. There were also songs with accompanying narratives, tales of victory, recollections of recent events or daily activities, and airs of love. Songs were usually short but could, in narrative form, last for days. Singing was accompanied by the sounds of rattles, whistles, or drums.

Visual art forms ranged from decoration on items of daily use (such as baskets and tools) to elaborate rock paintings and rock engravings. California natives are generally most remembered for their exquisite basketwork, though pottery in the eastern desert was shaped and decorated handsomely. Costuming, particularly in relation to the Kuksu religion, involved the creation of elaborate headdresses, skirts, feathered costumes, and so on, which were often symbolic of supernatural beings. Body painting was also popular.

Incising or pecking designs into rock was practiced in various parts of the area, and rock paintings were widespread. They were associated probably with individual and group rituals and hunting and gathering activities on the one hand and served as simple trail markers or indicators of food or water on the other.

EVOLUTION OF CULTURES TODAY

Depressed economic conditions in many areas

Today native Californians are rural peoples residing mainly on reservations or rancherias. There is, however, a long-established pattern of individuals moving to urban areas to find work when necessary but considering their reservation or rancheria as "home," as a place where they will be welcomed upon return. In this manner many native Californians may live away from their lands for the better part of a lifetime and yet come back at last to a way of life compatible with their cultural ideals and involving their family and friends. Many individuals come and go sporadically, depending upon economic conditions; some live only seasonally on the reservations. Native Californians move from depressed areas to towns, villages, and cities, however, not only to find employment but also to arrange for schooling for their children and to find the amenities of life that are often totally lacking in the more remote Indian lands.

As industries have moved into some rural areas, the nearby reservations have become more attractive; people can now often find regular work at home the year round. In many areas, the permanent populations of reservations are expanding, particularly with more young people with children. In other more remote rural areas, the economic situation remains bleak, and few people are able to subsist on the lands that once maintained their parents and grandparents. The main problem seems to be the dwindling water supply. Whereas 75 years ago rural natives could maintain a living by farming, stock raising, hunting, and gathering, today the giant urban areas have siphoned off much of the water, leaving many mountain valleys dry and unsuitable for agriculture. Several legal suits to stop this are now in the California courts.

According to California state-government sources, there are approximately 80 Indian settlements defined as either reservations or rancherias, each with a population varying from a few people to several hundred. Within each there may be tribal lands, which belong in common to all of the members; allotted lands, which are owned by individuals or collections of individuals through inheritance; and assigned lands, which are owned by the reservation as a group but assigned to the specified use of certain individuals.

Since the United States government withdrew most federal responsibility for native Californians in 1955, reservations have become relatively autonomous. Each reservation or rancheria has an elected body of officials, known variously as a business committee or tribal council, which acts as a liaison between the people and such outside interests as the U.S. Bureau of Indian Affairs, business corporations desiring the purchase or lease of reservation lands, public utilities concerned with seeking rights-of-way across lands, and individuals having some form of business with the group. The council acts with the advice and consent of the people in dispersing tribally owned assets such as the lands or funds, and it also acts as the receiving agent for grants from various economic-development or relief organizations of the government. It is often involved in litigation with the government or other agencies concerning tribal grievances, and today it almost invariably participates directly in planning economic and social development programs for the future protection of the group's assets.

Generally speaking, native Californians have adopted much of the ways of the European world. In clothing, housing, transportation, education, and often religion, they are not significantly distinguishable from other people residing in California. In more subtle ways, however, native culture, attitudes, ritual, and psychology are still viable throughout the state from north to south. Wherever there are native populations, one finds ceremonial houses, ritual, and the continued use and manufacture of ritual materials, as well as occasional use of native foods. Many arts and crafts, especially basket weaving, have been maintained. The Indian languages, though spoken less and less as first languages, are being maintained and revived for cultural and nostalgic reasons. On some reservations there are cultural centres and museums helping to preserve the culture and languages, and on other reservations and in some local school districts classes in native languages and culture are being offered to both children and adults. Various organizations of native Californians, such as the American Indian Historical Society and the California Indian Education Association, are aggressively examining, criticizing, and providing new teaching materials for schoolteachers who deal with native Californians in the classrooms.

Attempts to preserve the cultural heritages

On the other hand, few if any traces of traditional cultures remain in some areas of California today. These areas generally coincide with what are today the major population centres of California, from San Francisco and Oakland south to San Diego. A new form of native American cultural development is under way, however, as Indians from all over the United States, not only from rural California but also from reservations in the central great plains of the United States and the Southwest, gravitate to these major urban areas, bringing with them diverse tribal and cultural backgrounds that add up to a new measure of cultural diversity in urban life. Many of these people came in large numbers during World War II, often to work in defense industries, while others came in large numbers after the war as part of the aggressive planning and development of the Bureau of Indian Affairs in the 1950s. These moves led to serious problems among some of the relocatees because Bureau of Indian Affairs coordination was ineptly carried out, with the result that many native American groups have had to develop their own self-help organizations to care for their people in the cities. A pattern of replicating the institutions of the cultural groups they came from is apparent throughout the state. Dance groups as well as educational and political groups have developed generally along lines of cultural similarity. There are, for example, Navajo clubs, Hopi clubs, and so on.

BIBLIOGRAPHY. A.L. KROEBER, *Handbook of the Indians of California*, 2nd ed. (1953); ROBERT F. HEIZER and M.A. WHIPPLE (eds.), *California Indians: A Source Book*, 2nd ed. (1971); and EDWARD S. CURTIS, *The North American Indian*, vol. 15–16 (1907, reprinted 1970), provide the most general summaries of native California cultures, although each source is not wholly representative of the latest thoughts. More recent accounts appear in various publications of the University of California, such as *Anthropological Records, University of California Publications in American Archaeology and Ethnology*, and the *Reports of the University of California Archaeological Research Facility*. Many new interpretations of native California cultures are also contained in the *Annual Reports of the Archaeological Survey of the University of California at Los Angeles*. Several books of interest containing new theoretical views or data, which are more representative of current scholarly views, are RAYMOND C. WHITE, *Luiseño Social Organization* (1963); LOWELL JOHN BEAN, *Mukat's People* (1972); JACK D. FORBES, *Native Americans of California and Nevada* (1968); and ROBERT F. HEIZER and ALAN ALMQUIST, *The Other Californians* (1971). Books recently prepared for the non-specialist, which are very readable, are THEODORA KROEBER, *Ishi i tuå världar* (1963; Eng. trans., *Ishi in Two Worlds*, 1964); and ROBERT F. HEIZER and THEODORA KROEBER, *Almost Ancestors* (1968). B.W. and E.G. AGINSKY, *Deep Valley* (1967), provides a readable fictional account of the Pomo Indians.

(Lo.J.B.)

Caliphate, Empire of the

The Empire of the Caliphate, or Caliphal Empire, was a state comprising the entire Islāmic community and the lands under Muslim domination in the centuries following the death of the Prophet Muḥammad (AD 632). In the name of Allah and Islām, Arab armies extended the theocracy founded by Muḥammad and his successors, the caliphs, beyond its original home in western Arabia until, by the early 8th century, it included most of Southwest Asia, North Africa, and Spain. The impetus of expansion enabled the Patriarchal and Umayyad caliphs (632–750) to maintain the unity of the empire. Once the state reached its territorial limits under the ʿAbbāsid dynasty (750–1258), however, the inadequacies of the central government and the cultural tensions between Arabs and non-Arabs became evident. A slow process of disintegration set in as rival caliphates and local dynasties sprang up in various parts of the Islāmic world. By the early 10th century the ʿAbbāsids no longer had any real political power, though most Muslims continued to regard them as religious leaders until the extinction of their line. Later, the ideal of a politically united Islām remained strong, but was never again achieved.

The article contains the following sections:

I. The rise of the Arab empire, 622–750

THE CONSOLIDATION OF ISLAM AND ARAB EXPANSION

The foundation of the Muslim community (622–632). The political and moral climate of Arabia at the time of Muḥammad's mission was propitious for the rise of a firm, nationalistically Arab faith (see ARABIA, HISTORY OF). The civilization of the Himyarites in South Arabia was in full decay, and outside powers (*e.g.*, Ethiopia and Persia) were contending for control there. The region to the north of Arabia had been for several centuries a battleground between Persia on the one side and Rome and its successor Byzantium on the other. Shortly before Muḥammad died, in 632, the Byzantines, by a great military effort, secured the upper hand, but both these world empires were now exhausted and could no longer ward off the nomads of the Arabian Peninsula, who for centuries had been pressing on the fringes of the Fertile Crescent but who were now fired by the dynamic religion of Islām. Within the peninsula, ancient paganism was moribund, mourned by few but leaving a certain spiritual void. The ethos of the old Bedouin society of Arabia was based on a nexus of kin obligations, but the growth of city life in the western region of the peninsula (the Hejaz), with an incipient commercial economy in Mecca flourishing on the Yemen–Syria caravan trade, may have created some tensions in society, for the resolution of which the traditional ways offered no guidance. All in all, conditions favoured the appearance of a new religious system; and the catalyst for this was to be a religious figure of genius, the Prophet Muḥammad.

Arabia before Islām

Muḥammad began the public proclamation of his belief that God had chosen him to be a prophet and "warner" to his fellow Meccans in 613 or shortly thereafter. But, though there was some response to his preaching from members in the second rank of Meccan society, there were few converts from the leading clans, such as ʿAbd Shams (or Banū Umayyah). This was to have important consequences after Muḥammad's death, when that clan achieved supreme political power in Islām, forming the dynasty of Umayyad caliphs (see below *The Umayyad Caliphate, 661–750*); the Umayyads were never able to shake off the stigma of having been late and lukewarm converts to Islām. When Muḥammad began to attack the pagan gods of Quraysh, the tribe inhabiting Mecca, the Qurayshite chiefs became openly hostile to Muḥammad and his followers.

In September 622 Muḥammad and some 70 of his supporters slipped away from Mecca to the agricultural centre of Yathrib, or Medina, 200 miles (300 kilometres) to the north. This event is known among Muslims as the *hijrah*, or "migration," and the Muslims taking part in it are called *muhājirūn*, or "emigrants"; under the second caliph, ʿUmar I, the beginning of the Arab year in which the *hijrah* took place (*i.e.*, July 15 or 16, 622, in the Julian calendar) was adopted as the beginning of the Muslim era. Muḥammad had prepared the way by meetings with the representatives of the Medinans. It may be that the Medinans, through contact with their local Jewish community, were familiar with the idea of an inspired, messianic leader, but it is more likely that they hoped that Muḥammad, because of the superior wisdom that went with prophetal status, would act as an impartial arbiter in the internecine feuds rife within Medina; moreover, Muḥammad had connections with Medina through his mother.

The *hijrah*

The exact definition of Muḥammad's status in Medina soon became important, for there was some conservative opposition there to him, political rather than religious in inspiration. He was certainly not an unchallenged ruler in Medina but only an invitee, with no authority over the internal affairs of the Medinan clans. There has been preserved in early Islāmic sources a document commonly referred to as the "Constitution of Medina." In its present form it is patently a compilation, but it is undoubtedly based on two agreements made between the Prophet and the Medinans soon after the *hijrah*. This "constitution" is mainly political. It establishes the *muhājirūn* as a tribal group at the side of the eight clans of the Medinans (henceforth often called the *anṣār*, or "Helpers"), but all nine tribes are described as forming an *ummah* or community of Muslims; thus, the term seems to have a religious and theocratic connotation also. The Jews of Medina are described as a separate, protected group. Muḥammad is simply the head of one of the component groups of the Muslim *ummah*, with no coercive powers outside that group; but there is the religiopolitical provision that disputes are to be referred "to God and to Muḥammad." The implication here is that guidance will come either from a Qur'ānic revelation (*i.e.*, from the Qur'ān, or sacred writing) or from Muḥammad's own special wisdom and insight. Though restricted in its scope at the time, this provision was to have great consequences later: by the later Medinan period, Muḥammad was to demand obedience not only to God but also to himself as God's Prophet, a demand buttressed by his added prestige as a successful war leader and skillful negotiator with outlying Bedouin tribes.

As Muḥammad's position grew stronger in Medina, he was able to deal with internal opposition there and elevate his position beyond that of a first among equals. Muḥammad had expected that the Medinan Jews would recognize him as the prophet promised in their own scriptures, but, when the Jews failed to respond, he became openly hostile to them. Certain originally Jewish features in early Islāmic practice were abandoned, and, in the years after 624, the three main Jewish tribes in Medina either were expelled and much of their property confiscated or, in the case of the third tribe, their males slaughtered and the women and children enslaved. The conservative opposition in Medina, the so-called Hypocrites, had been allies of the Jews, and its prestige now suffered a decisive blow.

Muḥammad was accordingly free to deal with external opposition, particularly the pagan Meccans. The *muhājirūn* in Medina contrived to live by plundering Meccan caravans travelling between the Hejaz and Syria. The Meccans retaliated by organizing coalitions of Bedouins against Medina in 625 and 627. These attacks failed, and, with the damage being done to their commercial interests, the more farsighted of the Meccan leaders began to think about coming to terms with the Prophet. Muḥammad had no desire utterly to humiliate the Meccans, for he wished to make the Meccan shrine of the Kaʿbah the centre of his faith, the restored pure religion of Abraham. When at the opening of 630 he led an army against Mecca, opposition to him was negligible, and the Meccan chief Abū Sufyān, head of the clan of Umayyah, speedily made peace.

Absorption of Mecca

The last years of Muḥammad's life were devoted to consolidating the nascent Muslim community in the Hejaz and then to extending his personal links with tribes in the more distant parts of Arabia. These were the years in which the Islāmic cult was systematized, and institutions such as the poor tax, fasting, the veiling of women, and the performance of the pilgrimage to Mecca were given the sanction of Qur'ānic revelation. Thus, the Muslim community acquired a certain ideological infrastructure, the basic features of which were to endure under the caliphate, when the faith and law of Islām became vastly more complex. The conquest of Mecca gave Muḥammad an access of prestige. Delegations of tribesmen began to make their way to Medina, where they received Islām and recognized the dual obligation of obedience to God and his Prophet. From being a mere city-state in Medina, the Muslim community became what has been called a supertribe, a confederation of Arab tribes cemented together by adherence to the Islāmic faith rather than by the old basis of blood kinship.

A noteworthy feature of these last years of Muḥammad is the organization of raids and reconnaissances to the northern frontiers of Arabia, especially against the territories of the Byzantines and their Arab allies. The doctrine that Muḥammad had brought the pure, uncorrupted version of God's scripture meant that his revelation was potentially valid for all mankind and not a narrow, nationalistically Arab one. Hence arises the obligation of *jihād*, or holy war, against idolaters and polytheists, un-

Beginning of external expansion

til they are either exterminated or submit to Islām; and this impulse, compounded of religious enthusiasm and a love of plunder, became the driving force behind the expansion of the Arabs outside their peninsula and the formation of the empire of the caliphate. Herein lay Muḥammad's genius: he strove for internal peace within Arabia and unified the Arabs under the banner of their own religion and their own sacred book; at the same time, he provided an outlet for the energies thus aroused with a policy of external expansion.

The four "Patriarchal Caliphs," 632–661. *Abū Bakr, 632–634.* Muḥammad's death at Medina in 632 caused considerable dismay and confusion. A successor as military and political head of the community was urgently required, but there could be no question of a second religious leader like Muḥammad, for Muḥammad had been the Seal of the Prophets, the culmination of the line. The *muhājirūn* leaders hurriedly imposed Abū Bakr, an early Muslim and the Prophet's father-in-law, as head of the whole Muslim community, thus forestalling the *anṣār*, or Medinans, from choosing a separate head of their own and thereby splitting the community of the faithful. The fact that Abū Bakr, the first caliph (632–634), was from the Prophet's tribe of Quraysh established a precedent in the eyes of future generations, excepting the adherents of certain minority sects, that the head of the community had to be from Quraysh. The caliphate remained in the hands of persons of Qurayshite descent down to 1517, and descent from Muḥammad's clan of Hāshim was the basis of a claim to the caliphate put forward by the Hāshimite *amīrs* of Mecca in 1924 after the abolition of the Ottoman caliphate in Turkey. The actual title caliph (*khalīfah*) came from Qur'ānic usage, and Abū Bakr used the title *khalīfat Rasūl Allāh* ("successor of the Messenger of God"). The second caliph, ʿUmar, first styled himself "successor of the successor of the Messenger of God," but the clumsiness of this title led to adoption of the simple title of caliph, or successor. ʿUmar further styled himself *amīr al-muʾminīn*, "commander of the faithful" (or, possibly, "counsellor of the faithful"). The preservation of the caliphate within Quraysh during this period and subsequently reflected customary Arab practice, in which leadership of a tribe remained within the leading family; that is, the family possessing the requisite leadership qualities. But within that family any senior, capable male member might be chosen. Abū Bakr's nomination also preserved to some extent the idea of election by the whole community, in that the leaders of the Muslim community could claim to be acting on behalf of the masses. Later, some show of election and acclamation by the great men and religious scholars was usually sought at the succession of a new caliph; in this way, a certain sop to democracy could be offered.

Abū Bakr and his three successors are called by the Muslims the *rāshidūn*, literally "rightly guided" or "orthodox" caliphs, but a better term is that of patriarchal caliphs. Later generations of Muslims looked back on them and the first generation of Muslims, the Prophet's Companions, as the founding fathers of the community and regarded their age as a golden one in which a pristine Islām flourished, undefiled by later corruptions and luxury; modern reform movements in Islām have often tried nostalgically to go back to this period of "classical" Islām.

Abū Bakr's prime tasks were to uphold the religious heritage of the Prophet and to maintain the political hegemony of the capital, Medina. At this time, the supporters of Muḥammad may be divided into three groups: a devoted nucleus of Muslim enthusiasts, without whose support Muḥammad could not have persevered in the face of so much indifference and opposition; a larger group, composed of those who were religiously lukewarm but who had joined the Muslim *ummah* because of the advantages that it offered; and the Bedouins, who were only nominally Muslim but who were attracted to the war leader Muḥammad by the prospects of plunder outside Arabia. When Muḥammad died, this latter group saw little reason to keep up an allegiance that had been purely personal. Hence follows the period of the *riddah*, or "apostasy" (though this term, with its theological overtones, is unsuitable for a movement that was mainly one of political renunciation), in which the outlying parts of Arabia refused taxes to Medina. In the east and south, local prophets did arise; apparently, there was a feeling that Islām could be countered only by another faith. But the only serious contenders here were the followers of the veiled prophet of Yemen, al-Aswad (the Black One), and, above all, Musaylimah in the Yamāmah region of eastern Arabia, who seems to have had a genuine religious mission contemporaneous with Muḥammad's in western Arabia. Musaylimah, however, was killed at the Battle of ʿAqrabāʾ or the Yamāmah in 633. Abū Bakr sent out commanders to suppress the *riddah* outbreaks; the tribes of western Arabia were less actively hostile to Medina and generally remained faithful, if without much enthusiasm, to the Muslim connection. The result of the successful campaigns of Abū Bakr's generals against the rebels was that, for the first time, Islām became a military and political force throughout Arabia. Abū Bakr died in 634 and on his deathbed nominated as his successor ʿUmar, another Qurayshite and father-in-law of the Prophet.

The period of the *Riddah*

ʿUmar I, 634–644. The caliph ʿUmar I (634–644) was the great consolidator of the Islāmic empire as it expanded during his reign. Far from being the pious conservative of Muslim tradition, ʿUmar I was a bold innovator in the fields of administration and military organization; he was a puritanical, iron ruler who tried to prevent the Muslim community, now being presented with riches beyond its wildest dreams, from being too embroiled in materialism. During ʿUmar's caliphate, the momentum of conquest outside Arabia increased severalfold. As soon as the *riddah* outbreaks had been quelled, the Arab generals and the tribesmen under their command directed their attention to the settled lands to the north. Thus, the chief of the tribe of Bakr, al-Muthannā ibn Ḥārithah, and the Qurayshite aristocrat Khālid ibn al-Walīd, later known as "the Sword of God," operated in the northeast against Iraq. In 633, Ḥīrah, the capital of the old Lakhmid Arab dynasty, former allies of the Persians, was attacked. Iraq, or Mesopotamia, was at this time part of the Persian Empire, and the Sāsānid dynasty actually had its capital at Ctesiphon, near the site of the later Baghdad; but the population of Iraq was ethnically Semitic (rather than Persian), Syriac speaking, and largely Christian. There was certainly no cordial attachment to the Sāsānids, and, after the decisive battle of al-Qādisīyah, in 636 or 637, all Iraq fell to the Arabs. Subsequently, control of Iraq was ensured by the foundation of military centres at Kūfah and Basra; these served as concentration points for Bedouins from Arabia, and from these were organized expeditions into Armenia, the Caucasus, and Persia proper. The Iranian plateaus and mountains, topographically broken and climatically harsh, were unfavourable terrain for the Arab cavalrymen, and the Persians, proud possessors of an ancient imperial heritage, resisted strongly. Gradually, however, the last Sāsānid emperor Yazdegerd III was driven back, until he was finally killed at Merv, in Khorāsān, in 651; his son Fīrūz fled to China but was never able to organize a successful revanche. The Persian state religion of Zoroastrianism was deprived of support from the secular arm, and, through the Persian land-owning class of *dehqāns*, the Islāmization of Persia began.

Conquest of Iraq and Persia

The overrunning of Jordan, Palestine, and Syria took place at the same time as that of Iraq, under commanders such as the Qurayshite ʿAmr ibn al-ʿĀṣ and Khālid, now transferred by Abū Bakr from Iraq. The enemy in these places was Byzantium, recently triumphant over the Persians but exhausted and overstretched in resources. The Muslims defeated Theodorus, the brother of the Byzantine emperor Heraclius, at Ajnādayn, in Palestine, but were temporarily halted by the siege of Damascus. The city, however, fell to Khālid in 635, and, after a final unsuccessful effort in 636 by Heraclius at the Battle of the Yarmūk, a tributary of the Jordan, all Syria and Palestine lay open to the Muslims. They spread northward to Antioch and into al-Jāzirah, the steppeland of what is

Conquest of Syria–Palestine

now northeastern Syria and northern Iraq, but the natural barrier of the Taurus Mountains prevented further advance into Anatolia, and the frontier there with the Greeks remained stable for more than two centuries. As in Iraq, the Arabs were operating in an ethnically Semitic region into whose fringes Arab settlers had long been infiltrating. The Arabs were undoubtedly helped in Syria and Palestine by indigenous opposition to the Greek ruling class of officials and clergy and to the attempts of the Greek Church to impose their orthodoxy on the Christian churches of the East. The Samaritans in Palestine are reported to have made themselves so useful to the Arabs that they gained in return certain tax exemptions.

The way into Egypt was now open, and ʿAmr marched into the land, defeating a Byzantine army at Heliopolis in 640. The Arabs took advantage of the confused internal state of the country, for the Byzantines had been trying to force a formula of theological reconciliation on the unwilling Coptic Church. ʿAmr negotiated with Cyrus, patriarch of Alexandria, for peace. Alexandria fell in 642 and again, after a Byzantine reoccupation, in 645. Soon after the first fall of Alexandria, ʿAmr made his capital in Egypt at the new army camp of Fusṭāṭ, the later Old Cairo. As elsewhere, the Muslims benefitted from local hostility to Hellenism and an outside imperial power, and they were wise enough to leave local administration and tax collecting in native hands. Possession of Egypt gave the Muslims access to a rich supply of grain, and, to facilitate the export of grain to Arabia, ʿAmr had the pharaonic canal between the Nile and Suez cleaned out and brought into use again. The Muslims also gained the dockyards of Alexandria and soon became a naval power in the eastern Mediterranean, harassing the Byzantine coasts and islands there. From the Nile Delta, Muslim columns moved along the Libyan coast and overran Barqah (modern Cyrenaica). In 647 they defeated an army under the Byzantine governor, or exilarch, Gregory at Subayṭilah (Sbeitla), in Tunisia, but internal divisions within the caliphate necessitated a withdrawal, and the real conquest of North Africa belongs to the succeeding Umayyad period.

ʿUthmān, 644–656. ʿUmar was assassinated by a Persian slave in 644 and was succeeded by ʿUthmān ibn ʿAffān, an early Muslim from the Umayyad clan and a son-in-law of the Prophet; he was actually chosen by the *shūrā*, a committee of six appointed by the dying ʿUmar. ʿUthmān incurred much obloquy from the pietists in Medina, from the non-Umayyad aristocracy of Quraysh, and from the Bedouin tribesmen of the army. This unpopularity resulted from defects in the state and society that were none of ʿUthmān's creation but that were rather the outcome of policies initiated by his predecessor; hence, much of the opposition to ʿUthmān was opposition to ʿUmar's system, now given a religious colouring.

Internal dissension

The rate of external conquest was beginning to slow, although, to occupy the tribesmen and keep up the inflow of plunder, ʿUthmān organized fresh expeditions into North Africa, Armenia, and Persia. Much of the fighting was now in difficult regions in the Caucasus and in the mountain fringes of eastern Persia and Afghanistan, where plunder came in only slowly and where troops were separated for long periods from their families in Iraq. One of ʿUmar's most brilliant innovations had been the institution of the *dīwān*, or pensions list. Since fixed plunder from the conquered lands, such as landed property, could not easily be divided among the Arab warriors, the state left the original owners and cultivators in possession in return for a rent or property tax. Out of this, the state paid fixed pensions to the free Arab warriors registered on the *dīwān*, these pensions being hereditary. But by ʿUthmān's time the soldiers realized that the state was paying back to them only a part of the moneys collected and keeping back the rest, and this became a source of resentment. There was also jealousy of the wealth and ostentation displayed by certain of the Quraysh aristocracy who had done well out of the wars by exploiting opportunities for trading and slave dealing in the conquered lands. There was also opposition to ʿUthmān's appointment of relatives to high offices such as provincial governorships. Ostensibly religious grievances included those over ʿUthmān's collection of the Qurʾān and production of an authoritative text (see below), but these were really a cloak for political opposition.

Egypt and Iraq were the main centres of discontent, and in 656 Egyptian troops entered Medina, besieged the Caliph in his house, and then murdered him as he was reading the Qurʾān. This tragedy had momentous consequences. For the first time, Muslims had laid hands on the head of their own community and had disregarded the Qurʾānic injunction not to shed believers' blood. ʿUthmān's murder originated an age of *fitnah*, or civil strife; hence, he is termed in Arabic sources "the opened door" (*i.e.*, to civil violence).

ʿAlī, 656–661. Already at Muḥammad's death, his cousin ʿAlī ibn Abī Ṭālib had hoped to secure the caliphate for himself, as a member of the Prophet's clan of Hāshim and husband of his daughter Fāṭimah. These hopes were disappointed, and, during the subsequent three caliphates, ʿAlī played no significant part in public life. During the killing of ʿUthmān he remained passive and was then hailed as caliph (656–661). His supporters were the notables and pietistic elements of Medina, plus the Iraqi tribesmen, who hoped to make ʿAlī their creature; ʿAlī did in fact move his capital to al-Kūfah, and the caliphate never returned to Arabia. But conservative elements of Quraysh, who feared an upsurge of tribal anarchy in the caliphate, rose against ʿAlī at the so-called Battle of the Camel near Basra (656); but the ringleaders were killed and the Prophet's widow ʿĀʾishah exiled to Medina.

Yet the cry of vengeance for ʿUthmān proved disastrous for ʿAlī, who was, with justice, accused of implicit agreement to the assassination. The avenger proved to be another member of the Umayyad family, Muʿāwiyah, son of Abū Sufyān, who for some 20 years had served as an energetic and successful governor of Syria; he accordingly represented the interests of Syria against ʿAlī and Iraq. Muʿāwiyah refused homage to ʿAlī, and the forces of the two sides clashed at Ṣiffīn, on the upper Euphrates, in 657. The confrontation was drawn out and indecisive, but Muʿāwiyah's supporter ʿAmr ibn al-ʿĀṣ managed to secure arbitration over the question of who had the superior right to the caliphate. This in itself was a blow to ʿAlī's prestige, for he was the incumbent caliph, whereas Muʿāwiyah had nothing to lose. Indeed, a section of ʿAlī's more intransigent supporters withdrew from his army and formed the violently hostile group of the Khārijites, or Seceders. These Khārijites later evolved into a radical, egalitarian sect that denied the intrinsic right of Quraysh to the caliphate and insisted that piety, not birth, was the sole qualification of leadership of the Muslim world. Militarily, they came to be a thorn in the flesh of the Umayyads and early ʿAbbāsids in Iraq and Persia for almost two centuries. A Khārijite sympathizer assassinated ʿAlī himself in 661. Before this, ʿAlī's prestige had dwindled, his sphere of authority confined mainly to Arabia and Iraq, while Muʿāwiyah consolidated his position in Syria and Egypt, backed by a disciplined military force tested in warfare with Byzantium. ʿAlī's lightweight son al-Ḥasan was raised to the caliphate in Iraq on his father's death—the first appearance in the caliphate of the principle of hereditary succession—but was quickly bought out by Muʿāwiyah, who thus in 661 became generally recognized as caliph, the first of the Umayyad line.

The Khārijites

THE UMAYYAD CALIPHATE, 661–750

The consolidation of the caliphate, 661–684. *Muʿāwiyah I, 661–680.* Muʿāwiyah and his two successors form the Sufyānid line of Umayyads. The rule of the Umayyads cemented the grip of the Qurayshite aristocracy on the caliphate. Indeed, the Umayyads' rivals, such as the partisans of ʿAlī's family and the Zubayrids, were equally from this social group, as was the succeeding dynasty of the ʿAbbāsids. During the period of the Patriarchal Caliphs, succession had been by nomination or election, accompanied, however, by dissent and, latterly, by violence. The Umayyads held the caliphate for 90 years, with the succession only occasionally passing from father to eldest son; often it passed to brothers or to cousins of collateral lines. Nevertheless, a greater continuity in policy was now achieved, and under the Umayyads the Arab empire reached almost to its farthest extent, so that by the early 8th century Arab warriors stood on the Atlantic shores in Morocco and Portugal and the Indus banks in Sind.

The deep impression Muʿāwiyah made on contemporaries is shown by the prominent part he plays in Arabic lore and literature. A skillful organizer of warfare against the Byzantines, he was also a consummate statesman, famed for his shrewdness and his *ḥilm*—a compound of firmness, magnanimity, and conciliatoriness. After persuading al-Ḥasan to abdicate, he arranged to secure Iraq and despatched his general ʿAmr ibn al-ʿĀṣ to govern Egypt again; hence, 661 is celebrated as the "year of reunion," when a measure of peace and unity was restored to the empire. Syria and its capital, Damascus, became the centre of Umayyad power until almost the end of the dynasty. There the caliphs could command the loyalty of Syrian tribesmen long familiar with settled life in the region. In Syria, too, relations with the *dhimmī*s, or "protected peoples" (*i.e.*, Christians and Jews), were more relaxed than in other parts of the caliphate. The family of Muʿāwiyah's wife Maysūn was Christian, as was his favourite court poet, al-Akhṭal. Iraq, on the other hand, was deeply divided confessionally, ethnically, and politically, while, within Arabia, Mecca and Medina no longer commanded the wealth and manpower to aspire to a political role comparable with that of the lands farther north.

Restoration of Muslim unity

The westward orientation of the caliphate enabled the war with Byzantium to be prosecuted with fresh vigour, the conquest of Constantinople being the perpetual goal. There was raiding in the Taurus region, where a string of frontier fortresses was established between Tarsus and Malatya; naval operations were pursued in the Mediterranean and Aegean, and as early as 665, while Muʿāwiyah was still governor of Syria, a Muslim fleet had won the "Battle of the Masts" off the Lycian coast. In 669 Constantinople itself was besieged by Muʿāwiyah's son Yazīd, the future caliph, and further attacks were made during the protracted war of 674–680, when Constantinople is said to have been saved by the use of Greek fire, or naphthalene, hurled at the Arabs. Rhodes and Crete were temporarily occupied (672, 674); the Arabs had already carried off the famous Colossus of Rhodes and sold its bronze as scrap.

Internally, Muʿāwiyah faced the task of securing peace in the east; *i.e.*, Iraq and its administrative dependency of Persia. Here he showed his skill in choosing capable subordinates and delegating his authority to them. He appointed al-Mughīrah ibn Shuʿbah as governor of turbulent al-Kūfah, and it was the latter who in 662 reconciled to Muʿāwiyah the capable Ziyād ibn Abīhi (literally, "son of his father"; *i.e.*, bastard), formerly one of ʿAlī's partisans. Ziyād had a certain claim on the Umayyads in that Abū Sufyān was his reputed father. Muʿāwiyah came to value his talents so highly that in 665 he publicly adopted Ziyād as his half brother. Ziyād now became governor of Basra and, on al-Mughīrah's death, of al-Kūfah also, becoming the dominant figure in the eastern caliphate. He governed with exemplary firmness, suppressing sedition in Iraq and reorganizing the financial system among the tribesmen there, until his death in 673. In particular, he harried the Khārijites and kept careful watch over the partisans of ʿAlī, who were especially strong in al-Kūfah. Noteworthy is the fact that al-Mughīrah and Ziyād, and slightly later, al-Ḥajjāj were from the town of aṭ-Ṭāʾif near Mecca; the Thaqīf, or people of aṭ-Ṭāʾif, had an urban tradition and could produce administrators of this calibre. The *anṣār*, with their Medinan peasant background, generally fade as a distinctive group from public life after ʿAlī's caliphate, largely merging with the "pious opposition" inimical to the Umayyads and all their works.

Muʿāwiyah recognized that, besides threats from the tribesmen and schismatics of the east, there was a threat to his dynasty from the ambitious and disappointed non-Umayyad aristocracy. He therefore endeavoured to safeguard the transition of power after his death by nominating Yazīd as heir apparent. About 676 he solicited provincial centres for their agreement, though it required some effort by his governor in the Hejaz, Marwān ibn al-Ḥakam, to secure assent in Mecca and Medina. The precedent was thus established by which a caliph named his successor, whether a son or brother or other kinsman, during his own lifetime, securing an oath of allegiance to him. The practice certainly minimized the risk of succession strife, but it ran counter to the old democratic instincts of the Arab tribesmen and smacked of Byzantine and Persian autocracy. Hence, the Umayyads' enemies held it against them; pietist circles and later historians (most of these last with a pro-ʿAbbāsid or pro-ʿAlid bias) stigmatize the Umayyads as *malik*s, or "kings," not true caliphs, and their rule as *mulk*, "temporal kingship," and not a *khilāfah nabawīyah* ("caliphate in succession to the Prophet").

Safeguarding the succession

Yazīd I, 680–683. When Muʿāwiyah died, at an advanced age, his son succeeded as Yazīd I (680–683). The expected storm was not long in breaking out, with opposition coming from the Khārijites, the ʿAlids, and the Qurayshite aristocracy in Medina. All these had ostensibly religious grievances, aimed at the restoration of a true *khilāfah* in accordance with the Qurʾān and the Prophet's *sunnah*, or "example"; but they all also expressed a hatred of strong, centralized government, a desire for provincial autonomy, and a dislike of the privileged position of Syria. ʿAlī's son al-Ḥasan had retired to a life of luxury, and it was probably from his excesses that he eventually died. Headship of the legitimate progeny of ʿAlī now devolved on al-Ḥasan's brother al-Ḥusayn. The latter refused to acknowledge Yazīd as caliph and was persuaded to rebel against him by emissaries from the anti-Umayyad stronghold of al-Kūfah; Ziyād's son ʿUbayd Allāh, governor of Basra, easily suppressed the outbreak, and al-Ḥusayn was killed as the rebel he undoubtedly was at the Battle of Karbalāʾ, in central Iraq (680). The symbolic importance of this event was later to prove out of all proportion to its significance at the time. Al-Ḥusayn was considered a martyr, and, under this emotional stimulus, political support for the claims of the ʿAlid family to the caliphate began to take on a more definitely religious flavour. Thus, it came to be held that ʿAlī had been the only possible successor to Muḥammad, for the Prophet had specifically designated ʿAlī as his spiritual as well as his temporal heir. According to this view, the first three Patriarchal Caliphs had actually been usurpers. Furthermore, the divine light dwelling in ʿAlī was transmissible to his descendants; hence, they alone were the true *imām*s ("exemplars," "religious leaders") as well as the true caliphs, or temporal leaders. In this way there evolved the Shīʿah, or Party, of ʿAlī, who set this authoritarian theory of government, the guidance of an infallible *imām*, against the majority, Sunnite theory that the caliphate was a temporal benefit and convenience for the Muslims and that the consensus of the Muslim community was the ultimate authority in religious disputes unresolvable by resort to the Qurʾān or *sunnah*. Though the ʿAlids were frequently to rise in revolt against the Umayyads and early ʿAbbāsids, the Shīʿites did not achieve widespread political power until the decline of the caliphate in the 10th century.

The Shīʿah minority

Another strand of opposition to Yazīd was that eventually led by the Qurayshite ʿAbd Allāh ibn az-Zubayr, son of one of the leaders against ʿAlī at the Battle of the Camel. Stories were circulated in the Hejaz of Yazīd's dissolute life, his love of hunting and wine, of music and poetry—all of these anathema to the pious. Mecca and Medina rose and expelled the Umayyad representatives. A Syrian army marched southward, defeated the Medinans outside their city at the Battle of the al-Ḥarrah, and plundered Medina; it then marched on Mecca and besieged it, destroying the shrine of the Kaʿbah (683). But the news arrived of Yazīd's death in Syria, and, since it was uncertain who would succeed him, the army lifted the siege. The Syrian general al-Ḥuṣayn ibn Numayr, indeed, offered to recognize Ibn az-Zubayr as caliph if he would go to Syria and establish his authority there; but the latter was uncertain of his reception and preferred a safer if more circumscribed power in Arabia. Hence, Ibn az-Zubayr remained as an anticaliph in Arabia, with his authority recognized not only in Arabia but also in Egypt, Iraq, and the east and even in parts of Syria. The Umayyads did not dislodge him for nine years.

Muʿāwiyah II, 683–684. Back in Syria, Yazīd's eldest son, the youthful Muʿāwiyah II, succeeded briefly as caliph (683–684) but died within a few months; as one chronicler says, "none of his deeds merit record." Yazīd's reputation was inevitably blackened by later authors, for he had not only slain ʿAlī's son, al-Ḥusayn, but also had attacked the sacred cities of the Hejaz; hence the epithet frequently given to him, "the accursed." In reality, Yazīd seems to have had a good share of his father's famed quality of *ḥilm.* He had distinguished himself against the Byzantines, and but for his premature death the ensuing crisis of 684 would have been avoided.

The zenith of Umayyad power, 684–715. *The advent of the Marwānids.* The year 684 was one of deep crisis. The childless Muʿāwiyah II had refused to name an heir. He had a brother, but the army leaders in Syria preferred a stronger and more experienced leader, if necessary outside the direct line of Abū Sufyān. Some Syrians favoured Ibn az-Zubayr, but the choice finally fell on Marwān ibn al-Ḥakam, of a collateral branch of the Umayyads, formerly secretary and adviser to ʿUthmān. Under the Marwānids, ʿUthmānid sentiment seems to have been deliberately cultivated to the detriment of the Sufyānids' memory, though the attachment of the Syrian populace to the Sufyānids was enduring; in early ʿAbbāsid days, when Syria had lost its position of primacy in the empire, many Syrians looked for the appearance of a Sufyānid political messiah.

The short reign of the aged Marwān (684–685) was filled with violence. Much of Muʿāwiyah's diplomatic skill had gone into stilling tribal rivalries in Syria and al-Jazīrah. The older established Arab immigrants, mainly of the Kalb group and accounted South Arabian in genealogy, had different interests and attitudes from the North Arabs of the Qays group, more recently arrived from Arabia and controlling al-Jazīrah; these last, in turn, feared that the Umayyads would allow further emigration into the lands that they considered their own special ones. As Qurayshites, the Umayyads themselves were technically North Arabs, but Muʿāwiyah had largely depended on the Kalbites who settled in southern Syria and Palmyra; through his wife Maysūn he had become allied with the influential family of Ibn Baḥdal, so that the Baḥdalites were reckoned as the supporters *par excellence* of the Umayyads. The end of the Sufyānids saw now a recrudescence of tribal warfare, the bane of the ancient Arabs before the unifying bond of Islām and the distraction of external expansion had come along.

The position of Marwān and his supporters was perilous, for the leader of the Qaysites in Syria, aḍ-Ḍaḥḥāk ibn Qays, finally threw in his lot with Ibn az-Zubayr, and was crushed by Marwān only after a fierce battle at Marj Rāhiṭ, near Damascus (684). After this, all Syria and Egypt returned to Umayyad allegiance, and Marwān was firmly established there. Yet the tribal divisions engendered at this time continued later to erupt sporadically into violence all over the empire, from Spain to Khorāsān; and the watchwords of Qays and Yemen have been used by factions in such parts of the Arab world as Syria, Palestine, and Arabia almost to modern times.

ʿAbd al-Malik, 685–705. Marwān died shortly afterward, and the caliphate passed to his son ʿAbd al-Malik (685–705), thus cementing the succession in the Marwānid line. Four of ʿAbd al-Malik's sons eventually became caliph, so that he became known as Abū al-Mulūk, Father of Kings. His 20-year reign was comparable to that of Muʿāwiyah in importance and splendour, once the multiplicity of rebels in various parts of the empire had been mastered; and in this work of pacification and unification the role of the Caliph's right-hand man, al-Ḥajjāj ibn Yūsuf, was decisive. For several years, Ibn az-Zubayr's brother Muṣʿab nominally controlled Iraq on behalf of the anticaliph, but from 684 to 687 Iraqi politics were dominated by an adventurer from aṭ-Ṭāʾif, al-Mukhtār ibn Abū ʿUbayd, who had begun his career as a Shīʿite, attempting to secure support for al-Ḥusayn's son ʿAlī and then for ʿAlī's son by a slave wife, Muḥammad ibn al-Ḥanafīyah, and had then for a time been a supporter of Ibn az-Zubayr. In 685 al-Mukhtār took advantage of simmering discontent in al-Kūfah to raise the standard of revolt. He appealed primarily to pro-Shīʿite sentiments among the Arab tribesmen, to messianic hopes circulating in Iraq at the time, and, to a lesser extent, to the social grievances of the clients, or *mawālī*, non-Arab converts who had become affiliated with Arab tribes but who were nevertheless regarded with contempt by the genuine Arabs. Not until 687 did Muṣʿab manage to kill al-Mukhtār.

Al-Mukhtār's revolt

ʿAbd al-Malik himself could not move against his opponents—the rival caliph Ibn az-Zubayr and various Khārijite movements in Iraq and al-Jazīrah—until he had secured his rear by making peace with the Byzantines, agreeing to pay a tribute of 1,000 dinars a week. In 691 he invaded Iraq, and his forces defeated and killed Muṣʿab at the Battle of Dayr al-Jāthalīq (Monastery of the Catholicos). Ibn az-Zubayr's power was now on the wane. He had remained supinely in the Hejaz, devoting his energies to the rebuilding and enlarging of the Kaʿbah and its enclosure. In 692 al-Ḥajjāj appeared at Mecca with an army, and after a siege of several months, in which the Kaʿbah was again bombarded with catapults, the city was stormed and Ibn az-Zubayr killed. Because of the ending of the rival caliphate, the year 692 is famed as a second "year of reunion."

Al-Ḥajjāj campaigned in other parts of Arabia against Khārijite rebels until in 694 he arrived in al-Kūfah and took over the governorship of Iraq, which he proceeded to rule with a firm hand, suppressing a revolt of the Zanj, or black agricultural slaves, in Lower Iraq. He sent his general al-Muhallab ibn Abī Ṣufrah into Persia to combat the extremist Khārijites of the Azraqite sect; he also was confronted with the serious rebellion of the "Peacock Army." This last was really a revolt of the old Arab tribal aristocracy under the leadership of Ibn al-Ashʿath of the noble tribe of Kindah, but it expressed many of the grievances of the Iraqi tribesmen against the Umayyads and their privileged Syrian troops, for the Peacock Army (so called because of the splendour of its original array) had been sent to restore the Arab position in the remote region of southeastern Afghanistan, where the Arab advance had been halted by the resistance of a powerful local ruler, the Zunbīl (Rutbīl). Rejecting al-Ḥajjāj's attempts to station them there permanently, the troops rebelled and marched back to Iraq until they were crushed in 701 and Ibn al-Ashʿath later himself killed. Seeing that both Basra and al-Kūfah had supported the insurgents and regarding the Iraqis as chronically rebellious, al-Ḥajjāj in 702 founded a new fortified camp, Wāsiṭ, midway between the two earlier camps, and garrisoned it with Syrian troops. Thereafter, he kept Iraq substantially quiet until the end of his governorship and death, in 714. Al-Ḥajjāj's draconian measures against rebellion and schism should not obscure the vigorous positive measures that he took for the restoration of agriculture and irrigation in Iraq and his enlightened patronage of poets and scholars, aspects of his policy insufficiently stressed by later, anti-Umayyad historians.

The "Peacock Army"

ʿAbd al-Malik's power was thus firmly grounded, and he devoted the latter part of his reign to a renewal of the war with Byzantium and to matters of administrative and financial reorganization, all aimed at increasing the Arabization and centralization of the empire and at ensuring within it the dominance of the Arabs. Syria flourished under his rule, and in 691 he erected the magnificent Dome of the Rock in Jerusalem, the third holiest city of Islām, being generally accepted as the goal of the Prophet's "night journey," or miraculous ascent to heaven; some sources state that the caliph hoped to divert pilgrims to Jerusalem because Ibn az-Zubayr barred the way to the Hejaz, but this seems improbable. In his youth in Medina, ʿAbd al-Malik had been famed for his piety, and this interest in religious and cultural affairs was not abandoned when he became caliph.

Al-Walīd, 705–715. ʿAbd al-Malik's eldest son, al-Walīd, succeeded him as caliph (705–715). ʿAbd al-Malik had in fact planned to exclude from the succession his brother ʿAbd al-ʿAzīz, whom Marwān had designated as next in line, but ʿAbd al-ʿAzīz died before ʿAbd al-Malik himself did. Al-Walīd had the advantage of a full treasury left by his father, and the prosperity of the empire was further assured by a great rise in the inflow of plunder and revenue from the new conquests, which outbalanced the decline in revenue from the older conquered lands, such as Iraq. Internally, the empire enjoyed peace. Al-Ḥajjāj continued to secure order in the east, and al-Walīd recovered some popularity for his house by appointing his cousin, the pious and pacific ʿUmar ibn ʿAbd al-ʿAzīz (the future caliph), as governor of the Hejaz (705–712). The holy cities there were beautified with new buildings, and the pilgrimage routes across Arabia were policed and supplied with wells and rest houses. In Damascus, al-Walīd indulged his love of building by erecting the splendid Umayyad Mosque (on the site of the former Christian Cathedral of St. John), which must have been at that time the supreme wonder of the Islāmic world.

But it is the fresh surge in the movement of external conquest, beginning in ʿAbd al-Malik's reign with the restoration of internal peace and reaching its climax under al-Walīd, that especially marks these years.

Conquest of North Africa

The raids along the coast of North Africa into what came to be called by the Arabs the Maghrib (Western Land) were renewed only when Muʿāwiyah had restored peace after the civil wars. The dominating figure in this adventure was the Qurayshite warrior ʿUqbah ibn Nāfiʿ, who later became a semilegendary figure and was almost regarded as the patron saint of Islām in the Maghrib. In 670 or perhaps a few years previously, he penetrated into Ifrīqīyah (present Tunisia) and founded the military settlement of al-Qayrawān (Kairouan), which became the bastion of Muslim arms in the west. The Byzantines were still in the coastal towns, while the indigenous Berber tribes of the interior resisted fiercely; in 683 their leader Kusaylah defeated and killed ʿUqbah near Biskra, and the Arabs were hurled out of Ifrīqīyah. It was not until ʿAbd al-Malik's caliphate that they were able to return, and, with the help of a Muslim fleet, Ḥassān ibn Nuʿmān captured Carthage from the Byzantines in 698 and overcame the Berbers' resistance under their woman leader Kāhinah ("Soothsayer," "Priestess"). In the following year, Mūsā ibn Nuṣayr extended Muslim power as far as Tangier, and the Maghrib was now administratively separated from Egypt and made a separate province directly dependent on Damascus. The Islāmization of the indigenous Berbers, attracted by the superior Arabic culture, now proceeded apace.

Muslim Spain

It was Mūsā who in 711 allowed his freedman Ṭāriq ibn Ziyād to raid across the Strait of Gibraltar into Spain. The Muslims took advantage of a local revolt against the Visigothic king Roderick, and within three years the Visigothic state collapsed. The Muslims overran the peninsula as far as Galicia and the Cantabrian Mountains (modern Cordillera Cantábrica), whither the Visigothic remnant retreated, forming a defensive redoubt that over the following centuries was to be the launching pad for the Christian reconquest of Spain from the Moors (see SPAIN, HISTORY OF). Berber settlers temporarily colonized Galicia, and the Muslims crossed the Pyrenees and occupied the region of Narbonne, in southern France. Raiding parties penetrated into Aquitaine, attracted by the rich abbeys and monasteries of France, but an expedition directed at the shrine of St. Martin at Tours was halted near Poitiers in 732 by the Carolingian Charles Martel, and the Muslims made no further serious attempts to occupy territory beyond the Pyrenees. In any case, it is dubious whether any permanent annexations in France were contemplated; even the conquest of Spain itself seems to have been unplanned, though it was helped by the fact that climatically and topographically the Iberian Peninsula is an extension of North Africa. The utter collapse of the Visigothic ruling class was probably facilitated by the passivity of the Hispano-Roman populace in the face of the Arabs, while the much-persecuted Jewish minority may have welcomed the invaders. Yet unlike North Africa, where Christianity eventually disappeared totally, and unlike Egypt, Syria, and Iraq, where it was reduced to a minority faith, many of the Christians of the Iberian Peninsula held fast to their Latin cultural heritage and Christian religion, forming the so-called Mozarab community; perhaps a half or two-thirds of the former Hispano-Roman population refused to succumb to the blandishments of Islām and its civilization.

In the east the impelling urge for plunder and, above all, for slaves led the Arabs across the Caucasus and beyond the Iranian plateau. Control of the Caucasus region was disputed with the Khazars, a powerful Turkish people who occupied the South Russian and Ciscaucasian steppes and who raided into Georgia and Armenia during the caliphates of Yazīd I and ʿAbd al-Malik. At this period all the Arabs could do was to hold on to their footholds in Armenia. On the far eastern fringes of the Arab empire, however, the frontier was more open and the opportunities for potential expansion greater, although the Arabs faced tenacious opponents there also, including the Hephtalites, or White Huns, in Afghanistan, the West Turkish Khans of Central Asia, and, beyond them, the might of the T'ang emperors of China, who claimed a vague suzerainty over Central Asia and the Iranian frontier lands.

Central Asian campaigns

Soon after the collapse of the Sāsānid monarchy during ʿUthmān's caliphate, Arab troops raided across the Oxus into Transoxania (modern Uzbek S.S.R.), attracted by the agricultural and commercial richness of such centres as Bukhara and Samarkand. Yet for many decades to come these were only summer raids, after which the Arabs returned to their camps at Merv and elsewhere in Khorāsān. In the earliest period there seems to have been no intention to colonize Khorāsān itself with Arab settlers, for the tribesmen disliked long periods of service away from their families in Iraq, and discontent over these absences contributed, as noted above, to the rising of Ibn al-Ashʿath and the Peacock Army of Seistan (Sīstān). It was Muʿāwiyah's governor in the east, Ziyād, who first began the planting of Arab families in Khorāsān on a large scale (671). The governorship of Khorāsān also included that of Seistan, but the Arabs were unable to push farther because of the resistance of the local Hephtalite ruler of Zābulistān (the region of modern Qandahār and Ghaznī). More successful was an expedition from Shīrāz in Persia through the barren region of Makrān (*i.e.*, southern Baluchistan) into Sind by al-Ḥajjāj's son-in-law Muḥammad ibn al-Qāsim, who in 711 captured the port of Daybul at the mouth of the Indus. Within two years he had advanced up the Indus valley to Multān and laid the foundations of an Arab colonization of the province of Sind, which for three centuries remained the Muslim foothold in the Indian subcontinent.

Progress in Central Asia was slow, for the local Iranian and Turkish rulers there were redoubtable foes. The conquests there are especially associated with Qutaybah ibn Muslim, an appointee of al-Ḥajjāj and governor of the east (704–715). Tukharistan, or Bactria, in northern Afghanistan, submitted, Samarkand and Bukhara were occupied, the ancient kingdom of Khwārezm on the lower Oxus was reduced to obedience, and an advance was made through Farghāna (modern Fergana) to the borders of what later became Chinese Turkistan. Yet in these regions the Islāmic faith made only slow progress in the face of indigenous religions such as Buddhism, Zoroastrianism, and Christianity. Transoxania was very remote from Syria and communication lines inordinately long. Above all, progress was hampered by the internal divisions of the Arabs in Khorāsān, for the tribal enmities of Syria and Iraq had been imported to the east. It was not at all surprising that, just before his death in

720, the caliph ʿUmar II ordered a general withdrawal of the Arabs from Transoxania.

The later Umayyads, 715–750. *Sulaymān, 715–717.* Al-Walīd was followed by his brother Sulaymān (715–717). Some sources stress his gluttony and lasciviousness. Others, however, praise him for his reversal of the stern policies of al-Ḥajjāj (who had died just before al-Walīd himself): he released political prisoners, recalled troops from distant garrisons, and, above all, appointed his cousin ʿUmar ibn ʿAbd al-ʿAzīz as his successor. Certainly, Sulaymān instituted a general change of governors, a move aimed at ending the general domination of North Arabs or Qaysites in high office (al-Ḥajjāj's own tribe of Thaqīf was accounted North Arab). Qutaybah, governor of the east, foresaw that al-Walīd's demise would mean a change of direction in the state and tried unsuccessfully to raise a rebellion (715). Muḥammad ibn al-Qāsim was recalled from Sind and executed. Iraq and then Khorāsān were given to Yazīd ibn al-Muhallab of the Yemenite tribe of Azd. It is possible that the shadowy but influential figure of Rajāʾ ibn Ḥaywah was behind Sulaymān's "new order," as he undoubtedly was behind that of ʿUmar II. Rajāʾ had been active under ʿAbd al-Malik as head of the chancery, and he may have had a direct hand in ʿUmar's financial reforms (see below *ʿUmar II, 717–720*). The outstanding military event of Sulaymān's reign was the great effort made against Constantinople, the culmination of early Islāmic attacks on the second Rome. For a whole year (716–717) an enormous army and fleet under the Umayyad prince Maslamah ibn ʿAbd al-Malik (who would certainly have made an outstanding caliph had his mother not been a slave, which had the effect at this time of excluding him from the succession) invested the city. The Byzantine emperor Leo III the Isaurian, however, vigorously defended it. Sulaymān died, and ʿUmar called off the siege. Not until 1453 did the Muslims return to the attack, this time with lasting success, under the Ottoman sultan Mehmed I the Conqueror.

The role of Rajāʾ ibn Ḥaywah

ʿUmar II, 717–720. Against the wishes of his family, Sulaymān designated ʿUmar ibn ʿAbd al-ʿAzīz as the next caliph (717–720). Possibly Sulaymān realized that the empire was heading for an economic and social crisis that could be averted only by a decisive change of leadership and attitudes. ʿUmar II's caliphate became famed as an interval of pious and ascetic rule amid the general frivolity and godlessness of the Umayyads. The Hungarian Orientalist Ignác Goldziher called him "the Hezekiah of the Umayyads," and, in the exhumation and burning of the Umayyads' corpses by the vengeful ʿAbbāsids, ʿUmar's corpse escaped. In fact, ʿUmar was a realist and also a true Umayyad who wished to preserve his family's rule and the domination of the Arabs by making timely concessions and adjustments. Influenced by his Medinan upbringing and the general deepening of religious feeling in the caliphate, he saw the urgent need for a politico-religious reform that would reverse his predecessors' policy of putting state interests first; that would reconcile the claims of piety with political realities; and that would divert the rising tide of grievances against the state by removing the disabilities and complaints of a large element of the empire's population, the converts.

The problem of converts

In order to comprehend ʿUmar's policy, it is necessary to go back several decades. In the first days of the Patriarchal Caliphs, the terms Muslim and Arab had been almost coterminous. The state did not go out of its way to encourage conversions, despite the universality of Muḥammad's message, and the comparatively small number of converts were absorbed into the Muslim *ummah* and admitted to some of the Arabs' financial privileges. But, once the advantages of membership of the *ummah* became apparent, the trickle of conversions swelled to a torrent. Peasants fled from the countryside, where they had been bound to the soil in a serflike condition (the change of masters after the coming of Islām often making little difference there), to the anonymity of the towns and garrisons, contributing to the socially turbulent populations of the latter. It was a major source of chagrin to the converts, or *mawālī* ("clients"), that, though they had adopted a faith in which all men were supposed to be equal through piety, they were regarded by the Arabs with contempt, discriminated against socially, and, above all, still held liable for such burdens as the poll tax, or *jizyah*, supposedly due from non-Muslims only. In defense of the attitude of the state, one must note that the volume of conversions and the loss of taxes badly affected a province such as Iraq; the revenue of Iraq declined sharply toward the end of the 7th century, and this was only partly counterbalanced by the inflow of plunder from the new conquests. The state therefore continued, as far as it could, to exact the poll tax from converted non-Arabs, but it could do little to prevent the exodus from the countryside to the towns, where taxes could be less easily collected.

Hence ʿUmar's dilemma: how to balance the claims of religion and justice with state policy. He tried first of all to still faction and schism by continuing Sulaymān's policy of reducing the ascendancy of one particular party in the state and by refusing to take sides. He tried to conciliate the Shīʿah by ending the public cursing of ʿAlī from the pulpits. Most important, however, was his financial policy, known from a fiscal proclamation circulated to his governors. In this he asserts, among other things, that the prime duty of the state is to extend the faith—"God sent Muḥammad to preach the faith, not to act as a tax-collector." Also, he asserts the obligatory nature of the poor tax, or *zakāt;* the state's duty to put its statutory fifth of all captured plunder for the benefit of the Muslim community; the prohibition of land liable to land tax being diverted into private, tax-exempt land grants for the Muslims; and the right of peasants to migrate to the towns and not be sent back, though they were still to be liable to the *jizyah* on their land. The absence of a categorical provision against exacting the poll tax from converts is probably explicable by the multiplicity of financial practices and systems prevailing in the empire: no general principle could be enunciated. The basic principle, however, was reasserted that converts were liable only to the taxes leviable on Muslims in like occupations, and ʿUmar's encouragement of converts to migrate to the towns, where they could be free of the *jizyah* when it was part of the global land tax, did remove a fertile source of grievance from al-Ḥajjāj's time.

Yazīd II, 720–724. With the end of ʿUmar's short reign, the caliphate returned to the sons of ʿAbd al-Malik in the person of Yazīd II (720–724), famed as a lover of the arts and music. The reforms of ʿUmar were quietly dropped. There was now a return to the policies associated with al-Ḥajjāj and the Qaysite ascendancy, for Yazīd was related by marriage to al-Ḥajjāj's family. One aspect of this was the overthrow of Yazīd ibn al-Muhallab and Yemenite power in the east. Yazīd rose in rebellion at the beginning of the new reign but was defeated and killed by the caliph's half brother Maslamah, and the power of his tribe, the Azd, was severely curtailed in Khorāsān.

Hishām, 724–743. On Yazīd II's death—allegedly of grief at the death of his favourite slave girl—Hishām succeeded smoothly, the fourth son of ʿAbd al-Malik to achieve the caliphate (724–743). Hishām's 20-year reign was comparable in prosperity to those of his father and of Muʿāwiyah. Yet the position of the Umayyad caliphate and the Arab ascendancy was now perceptibly altered. Over the preceding decades the Arab empire had expanded enormously and had virtually reached its limits; the basic difficulty now was to transform this dynamism into a stable, permanent regime; that is, to provide what had hitherto been an essentially military organization with the administrative institutions of a settled state. In order to achieve this, the Umayyad caliphs, from Muʿāwiyah onward, had developed the power of the state, their own personal rule, against centrifugal tribalism and the ambitions of rival Arab families such as the Zubayrids. ʿUmar II had tried to reverse the process of secularization and modify that of centralization but had failed.

Hishām, accordingly, had to follow the traditional Umayyad pattern of rule but at the same time endeavour to make it more palatable, especially as the bases of Umayyad power were narrowing, and Hishām could only depend militarily on the numerically limited Syrian army and the new professional troops being organized by his cousin Marwān ibn Muḥammad, the future caliph Marwān II.

Hishām was clearly aware of all these trends and of the dangers to the Arab ascendancy. Personally frugal, hardworking, and devoted to the orderly conduct of affairs, Hishām kept a balance between Qaysites and Yemenites in the allocation of offices and favours. He is said to have been interested in introducing Sāsānid Persian administrative techniques into his government, though this could hardly endear him to the religious classes. In fact, Hishām was strongly orthodox in religion; he enjoyed the company of the *ʿulamāʾ*, or religious scholars, and it was during his reign that the state intervened directly in religious affairs and the first executions for heresy took place. It seems probable that he followed ʿUmar II's example of reorganizing the fiscal system in response to the grievances of the *mawālī*, though few details are known.

Internal quiet under Hishām

Internally, the empire enjoyed much peace under Hishām. For the greater part of his reign Iraq was ruled by Khālid al-Qasrī, a governor of the calibre of Ziyād and al-Ḥajjāj; it was only in 738 that Qaysite intrigues brought about his downfall and eventual death. Under Khālid, security in Iraq was re-established, and many valuable irrigation and land reclamation projects were carried out. The Khārijites were put down, and a rising of the ʿAlid Zayd ibn ʿAlī at al-Kūfah was later suppressed (740). In the east it was realized that the process whereby the Arab troops in Khorāsān were becoming assimilated to the Persians around them could not be halted. Hishām's policy was to disperse these Arab settlers in various parts of the province and to reinforce them by fresh, unassimilated tribesmen from Iraq plus a Syrian force. Even so, in 734 discontented Arab tribesmen rebelled in Gūzgān in northern Afghanistan under al-Ḥārith ibn Surayj, who held out on these eastern fringes for over ten years with help from the Khan of the Türgesh, or western Turks. The prime task of Hishām's governors in the east was, indeed, to maintain and consolidate the conquests of Qutaybah in the face of strong counterattacks by the Turks from beyond the Jaxartes in the years up to 737.

There was similar pressure from the Turkish Khazars in the Caucasus region, where Maslamah and Marwān ibn Muḥammad campaigned vigorously. The Khazars invaded Armenia and Azerbaijan in 730, reaching al-Jazīrah, before Maslamah hurled them back and himself raided as far as the Khazar capital on the lower Volga or possibly to the lower Don. The Arabs left garrisons at strategic points such as Derbend on the western Caspian shore; but, although agreements for peace and the payment of tribute were frequently made with the local Caucasian rulers, no enduring political control was possible.

In the Muslim west, it soon became difficult to exert control from Damascus. Arab financial exploitation and arrogance sparked off a Berber revolt all over the west (740–742). In the Maghrib, the Arabs were reduced to control of the area round al-Qayrawān. The driving force behind this revolt was anti-Umayyad egalitarianism, which the sources equate with Khārijism. Whatever its connection with the Khārijism of the east, this feeling became a strong current in Berber North Africa down to the 10th century and has left traces today in the shape of the Ibāḍite Khārijite communities of southern Algeria, Jarbah, and Tripolitania. Muslim Spain, or al-Andalus, was in these years ruled by a succession of Arab governors. In 741 a fresh wave of Syrian troops arrived to suppress Berber unrest, and it was the presence of large numbers of Umayyad clients that in 756 enabled the fugitive Umayyad prince ʿAbd ar-Raḥmān I, grandson of Hishām, to achieve power in Spain and set up a revived Umayyad kingdom in rivalry to the ʿAbbāsids.

Disintegration of the Umayyad Caliphate

The last Umayyads. After the passing of Hishām's strong hand, the Umayyad Caliphate began to show signs of disintegration. In the years 743 and 744 there were three ephemeral caliphs. The principle of the caliph being of pure, free Arab stock was breached by the accession in 744 of Yazīd III, a son of al-Walīd I by a Persian slave mother. The financial crisis apparently deepened at this time. On accession, Yazīd III promised to reduce government expenditure; not to spend money on palaces and irrigation works; not to divert funds from the provinces, where they were to be spent on local defense and development; and not to drive the non-Muslims to desperation by overharsh taxation. Such a program, if put into execution, might have stayed the tide of discontent, but Yazīd died after a six-month reign, amid such chaos and civil strife as would have "turned a baby's hair white," as one chronicler puts it.

The last Umayyad caliph, Marwān II (744–750), a grandson of Marwān I, was a resolute commander, nicknamed "the Wild Ass" from that animal's proverbial hardiness, but he faced appalling difficulties. The mainstay of his power was that of the Qaysites of al-Jazīrah, and it was to Ḥarrān in that region that Marwān transferred his capital and administration, the better to watch the storm centre of Iraq. At this time the Khārijites controlled much of Iraq, while in Arabia the Khārijite leader Abū Hamza at one point occupied Medina. Khorāsān had since 739 been governed by the capable Naṣr ibn Sayyār, who restored Arab authority in Transoxania. Yet the internecine tribal feuds of the Arabs continued in Khorāsān, and, because of the region's remoteness from Syria, Naṣr had difficulties in getting reinforcements sent out. When Abū Muslim's revolution started in Merv, Naṣr addressed a last despairing appeal to Marwān (747), but the Caliph was at that point involved with a rising in Syria itself.

The ʿAbbāsid revolt. The movement that toppled the Umayyads was that of the ʿAbbāsid *daʿwah*, or underground propaganda campaign. Al-ʿAbbās had been the Prophet's uncle, but the family had played no significant role in politics during the earlier Umayyad period. From *c.* 718 onward, however, the ʿAbbāsids, from their centre at Ḥumaymah, in southern Jordan, organized a network of secret agents in al-Kūfah and thence in the Merv oasis of Khorāsān, which, unlike Iraq, was remote from Umayyad surveillance. It seems that the ʿAbbāsid head, Muḥammad ibn ʿAlī, secured the transfer to his line of the claim to the imamate of one of the various ʿAlid groups active in Iraq, that of Muḥammad ibn al-Ḥanafīyah and his son Abū Hāshim, and with this took over an extremist sectarian group, the Hāshimiyah (*i.e.*, partisans of Abū Hāshim). The whole movement was working for the overthrow of the Umayyads and the establishment of a caliph-*imām* who was unspecified but who would obviously be from the Hāshimite clan, comprising descendants of both al-ʿAbbās and ʿAlī.

During Hishām's caliphate, his governors successfully repressed overt activity by ʿAbbāsid agents, but propaganda intensified after 743, with the Umayyads' enforced neglect of Khorāsānian affairs, under the direction of two political organizers of genius—Abū Salamah of al-Kūfah and the Persian Abū Muslim al-Khorāsānī. Abū Muslim arrived at Merv in 746 and skillfully took advantage of the factions of the Arabs. Abū Muslim himself represented the extremist wing of the Hāshimīyah, and he appealed to messianic hopes current among both the Shīʿites and the Persian *mawālī*, resentful of Arab social dominance, hopes symbolized perhaps by the adoption of black flags as the emblems of revolution. Nevertheless, it seems that his main support came originally from assimilated Arab settlers in the Merv oasis who had lost many of the financial privileges of the Arab warriors and had come under the control of the Persian landowning class, the *dehqāns*; traditions of Persian support for the movement appear only later. The moderate Shīʿite groups had erupted in Iraq in 744 under the ʿAlid ʿAbd Allāh ibn Muʿāwiyah, but, when this claimant fled to Khorāsān, Abū Muslim had him executed and thus eliminated a possible rival.

In 747 came open revolt. Merv fell, and ʿAbbāsid forces drove Naṣr ibn Sayyār into western Persia, where he died. In 749 ʿAbbāsid troops entered al-Kūfah, where Abū Salamah became provisional head of the political movement. Abū Salamah invited various members of the house of ʿAlī to become commander of the faithful (*i.e.*, caliph) with secular authority only, but this limitation of power was unacceptable to them, for they wanted the imamate, religious primacy, as well as the caliphate. Hence, in a *fait accompli*, the agents in al-Kūfah of the Khorāsānian wing of the revolution under Abū Muslim proclaimed the ʿAbbāsid Abū al-ʿAbbās as-Saffāḥ as caliph (749). Thus it was the ʿAbbāsid family and not the ʿAlids who gained the fruits of revolution. The latter realized that they had been cheated, and the familiar pattern of ʿAlid risings resumed under the early ʿAbbāsids. Marwān II's forces rallied in al-Jazīrah but were defeated at the Battle of the Great Zāb near Mosul in 750. Marwān himself fled to Egypt, where he was killed, and the majority of the Umayyad family were massacred in Syria by the ʿAbbāsids.

Open revolt by the ʿAbbāsids

Thus ended the Umayyads and the purely Arab ascendency in the empire. Except for their later years, the Umayyads had not lacked capable and far-sighted rulers. Yet the evolution of the Islāmic community, with the growth of the religious institution and the yearning for a return to the virtues of primitive Islām, real or imaginary, and the demands of the growing numbers of non-Arab converts for an equal share in power and status, had worked against them. It was the achievement of the ʿAbbāsids to gather up diverse strands of discontent, and the resulting momentum of opposition overwhelmed the Umayyads.

GOVERNMENT AND SOCIETY, 632–750

Administration of the Arab lands. The Arabs in the conquered lands formed a military aristocracy, a thinly spread minority over the subject population. Accordingly, there could be no question of their taking over direct administration of the territories, except that Qurayshites and other Arabs with a comparatively sophisticated urban background filled provincial governorships, with ultimate responsibility for the collection of taxes. Day-to-day administration remained in the hands of the existing officials—Greek, Coptic, Persian, and Nabataean—so that the economic prosperity of the conquered lands was substantially preserved. In the decades after 632, the bellicosity of the Bedouins, to whom the concept of settled government and, above all, the payment of taxes were anathema and who would have turned the rich lands of the Fertile Crescent into pasture for their herds if left unchecked, was diverted against the unbelievers in the "land of war." The Qurʾān laid down that Muḥammad (hence, after his death, the state) was entitled to one-fifth of all captured booty; this provision was in fact merely the modified continuation of pre-Islāmic practice. The state utilized its fifth to fill the public treasury and to finance the increasingly complex work of administration; it also took over the old Byzantine and Sāsānid state domains and those lands vacated by the flight of their owners. The Arab warriors' share was physically divided out, for example, in the case of movables and captives (the *ghanīmah*), but this was clearly not feasible in the case of landed property. The state therefore drew the rents from this property (the *fay*ʾ), compensating the warriors by a system of pensions listed in a register, or *dīwān*, beginning with the Prophet's widows and family, the earliest Muslims, and so on down to the ordinary warriors (see above). The *dīwān* was ʿUmar's invention, and he further showed his administrative wisdom by appointing, in certain provinces, governors with experience of civil affairs instead of pure soldiers. He also founded the two great garrison cities of Iraq, Basra and al-Kūfah, into which Bedouins poured from the desert and were then diverted to the northern and eastern fronts. Within the Arab warrior class, the tribe remained the basic organization now and throughout the Umayyad period, with the tribal chiefs leading their contingents into battle.

ʿUmar's achievements

The system was nationalistically Arab and, in effect, one of military exploitation. This did not necessarily mean that the non-Arabs were worse off than under their old masters; indeed, ʿUmar's interposition of the state between the masses and the Arab warriors over the *fay*ʾ probably protected them to some extent. Nor did the state encourage wholesale conversions to Islām. The only way for non-Muslims to secure admittance to the Muslim *ummah* was by conversion and enrollment as clients (*mawālī;* singular, *mawlā*) of Arab tribes, a lowly status. This process presented few problems in the early years, when clients might find a place on the *dīwān*, or pensions list. But in the Umayyad period the rate of conversions accelerated, while the state's revenue from taxes on the non-Muslims decreased.

Treatment of non-Muslim peoples

The point here was that Islāmic law, based here on the Qurʾān, allowed the "people of the Book" (*i.e.*, those possessing written scriptures, essentially comprising the Jews and Christians, though peoples such as the Zoroastrians and Hindus later claimed this status) to retain their faith and accept a subordinate role in society provided that they paid the *jizyah*, or poll tax, supposedly in lieu of the military service to which all free Arabs were liable. When these "protected peoples," or *dhimmīs*, became Muslim, they naturally expected to become free of the poll tax and to be liable only for the property tax, or *kharāj* (the technical terminology of these taxes is actually vague and shifting in this early period), that Muslims paid on lands acquired by them. The Umayyad caliphs had to resist this process, at its most acute in Iraq, al-Jazīrah, and Egypt. A further aspect was that peasants abandoned their lands, where they had often been liable for corvées, or forced labour, for the shelter of the towns, leaving the remaining, reduced rural population to find the same global amount of tax. The governor of Iraq and Persia, al-Ḥajjāj (see above), therefore adopted a policy of sending back runaways to their villages. There was a counterfeeling among religious circles that conversion to Islām ought not to be discouraged, but it was only ʿUmar II, imbued with a sense of both his governmental and religious responsibilities, who tried to resolve the dilemma by his fiscal reforms. Nevertheless, although he reversed the policy of compulsory resettlement of runaways for a time, the old policies were revived by his successor, and there was still no clear ruling that conversion to Islām meant exemption from the *jizyah*. The grievances of the converts therefore continued to contribute to anti-Umayyad feeling, especially as many converts and their descendants were becoming as learned in the faith as the original Arabs and were entering the ranks of the influential religious scholars and canon lawyers. A typical figure here is Ḥasan al-Baṣrī (died 728), of Persian *mawlā* stock, famed for his sermons and moralistic sayings.

The Umayyad caliphs at first ruled like desert tribal chiefs, *sayyids*. Muʿāwiyah allowed free access to himself for the weak and oppressed and acted as a conciliator and arbiter of disputes; indeed, he owed his position to his role of avenger of ʿUthmān in accordance with pre-Islāmic obligations of blood revenge. But the ruler was bound to have new responsibilities as caliph and commander of the faithful. The trend gradually began whereby the caliph withdrew himself from unfettered public access, protected by his chamberlain. Court ceremonial developed, though to nothing like the degree it was to attain under the ʿAbbāsids, who were to become despots enthroned far above the masses. On the other hand, the office of vizier, the caliph's chief executive minister, did not develop until ʿAbbāsid times. The complexity of government required to control the far-flung empire, to finance external war, and to curb internal sectarian or factional violence, all compelled the Umayyads into centralizing policies that exalted the position of their own family, the only reliable force in the state for continuity and stability. Both ʿAbd al-Malik and Hishām showed an interest in Persian administrative procedures, and the caliphate of the latter, in particular, saw a trend toward Persianizing ways that anticipated the Orientalization of the empire under the ʿAbbāsids. Muʿāwiyah is credited

Growth of responsibilities of the caliph

with the establishment of a chancery for correspondence, the "department of the seal," and ʿAbd al-Malik with that of a government postal and intelligence service, the *barīd*, clearly a development from a similar Byzantine and Persian institution. The need for stability after the first civil war (656–661) explains the Sufyānids' care to regulate the succession. As one historian says, "fearing to leave the community of Muḥammad like sheep without a shepherd," Muʿāwiyah vested the succession in his son Yazīd (see above). Thereafter, one finds the Umayyads vacillating between the principles of the seniorate, succession among the capable elder members of the family, and straight father–son succession, the latter becoming more normal under the ʿAbbāsids.

All these tendencies contributed to the accusation that the Umayyads were mere kings, *malik*s, and not true caliphs; but in reality the Umayyads were by no means unaffected by the general penetration of society by the Islāmic religious ethos. They considered their rule as God-given, and they presided at the Friday mosque worship and delivered the sermon there. ʿUmar II's famed piety was not an isolated phenomenon, for both he and ʿAbd al-Malik consulted Ḥasan al-Baṣrī for spiritual advice. Hishām gave the education of his son to the traditionist az-Zuhrī. Hishām himself inclined to the determinist current of thought in Islām and executed a member of the opposing sect of Qadarites, the partisans of free will.

The two processes of Islāmization and Arabization continued throughout the Umayyad period, the latter more slowly than the former. Conversions to Islām grew once the social and financial advantages of this became apparent. But many peoples retained their ancestral faith. The Christians, Jews, and Zoroastrians were necessary to the caliphs as officials, tax collectors, physicians, and technicians. Zoroastrians persisted in the more mountainous and remote parts of Persia, such as Fars, Azerbaijan, and the Caspian region. The Copts in Egypt and especially the Hispano-Romans in Spain were tenacious of their faith. In these areas, as well as in Syria and Palestine, the Muslims in this period undoubtedly remained a minority. Since Syria was the seat of the Umayyads' power, the caliphs were conciliatory toward the large Christian population there. ʿUthmān's wife Nāʾilah had been a Christian, as was Muʿāwiyah's wife Maysūn, mother of Yazīd I. Under Muʿāwiyah the Damascus Melkite Christian family of Sarjūn (Sergius) filled some of the highest financial offices in the land; one of this family, St. John of Damascus (died 748), was originally a financial official and, in his unregenerate days, a drinking companion of Yazīd I. Certain Arab tribes in Syria and al-Jazīrah, such as the Banū Taghlib, had become Christian in pre-Islāmic times, and some retained their faith until early ʿAbbāsid times, even producing martyrs from among their number. Iraq, in particular, was a melting pot of races and faiths, with relics of ancient beliefs such as Gnosticism and Manichaeism surviving among the generally Christian and Muslim population; it is not surprising that it was so turbulent a region in the early centuries of Islām.

Arabization was slower, though ʿUmar I had shown the way by his expulsion to Iraq of the Christians of Najrān in Yemen, in defiance of the agreement they had made with the Prophet. Toward the end of the 7th century a tendency toward Arabization in the administration is visible, connected with ʿAbd al-Malik's renewed warfare with the Byzantines. The story of the Arabization of the coinage is traditionally linked with a series of Byzantine and Muslim threats and counterthreats over the official headings guaranteeing the authenticity of papyrus exported from Egypt to Byzantium, which had Christian inscriptions, and over the coinage, which the Arabs had in the past continued to mint on the pattern of the Greek gold solidus. Around 697–699 a change was made to the so-called Reform coinage, which still followed Byzantine gold and Sāsānid silver patterns but with the divine name and Qurʾānic inscriptions on it (in fact, Muʿāwiyah seems to have made an abortive attempt to introduce such a coinage nearly 40 years before). ʿAbd al-Malik also changed the language of the government offices and registers from Greek and Persian to Arabic, though the Coptic, Greek, and Persian officials remained unchanged; these adopted Arabic and came to excel the Arabs themselves in knowledge of the language and its literature.

Social classes

The main elements of social classes in Umayyad times have already been delineated: the rentier class of Arab warriors; the converts, increasingly clamorous for a greater say in affairs; and the numerically still important body of *dhimmīs*, or "people of the Book," useful to the Arabs as a reservoir of taxable wealth and as a professional class. In the 8th century the Bedouins were no longer the backbone of the Umayyads' troops, for there was a trend toward professionalism there, supplementing the caliphs' Syrian troops. This process is especially associated with Marwān ibn Muḥammad, the future caliph, during Hishām's reign, and it is said that he introduced the battle tactic of compact bodies of troops instead of the old unbroken line. It is difficult to discern as yet a clearly defined urban bourgeoisie and merchant class, but the bases for this class, prosperous and influential in ʿAbbāsid society, must have been laid. Many of the early conquerors benefited from the opportunities for slave dealing, and the demand for domestic slaves continued to be brisk throughout the empire. But it is also probable that external trade with East Africa, India, and the Far East was already providing a livelihood for the merchants of places such as Basra and its port, Ubulla, for very mixed populations, including colonies of Indians and Malays, were to be found at the head of the Persian Gulf by early ʿAbbāsid times.

Cultural life under the Umayyads. One aspect of the Arabization of the empire was the spread of the Arabic language, though this made only slow progress in the first century or so of Islām. Adoption of Arabic was easiest in regions such as Syria, Palestine, and Iraq, where the indigenous populations spoke Syriac, a Semitic language akin to Arabic. Coptic in Egypt was more resistant and Spanish in al-Andalus even more so. In North Africa, Berber was a nonliterary language; hence, the Berbers quickly adopted Arabic as the language of culture and religion, while retaining Berber as a spoken tongue. Pahlavi, or Middle Persian, went underground, as it were, during this period, as a language of culture, only reappearing two or three centuries later in its New Persian form. In all parts of the empire, Arabic acquired an unassailable prestige as the language of the victors and of the Qurʾān, even where local populations retained their vernaculars, and Arabic culture often became as attractive to non-Muslims as to Muslims. The bursting forth of the Arabs from their peninsula and their mingling with non-Arabic speakers started immediately the transition from the earliest, classical stage of Arabic, that of the desert, to a somewhat simpler, more flexible, spoken version of the tongue, which probably served as a lingua franca in the socially and ethnically mixed garrison cities (the beginnings of that stage of the language known as Middle Arabic). Nevertheless, the classical tongue, in all its richness of vocabulary and expression, remained for centuries the normal vehicle of literary expression, buttressed by the fact that God's own word, the Qurʾān, had been revealed in it.

Spread of Arabic

The period of the initial conquests, that of the Patriarchal Caliphs, was unfavourable to artistic and cultural expression of any kind; the overpowering example of the Qurʾān seems to have inhibited literary production, but, above all, Arab energies were being expended on carving out an empire, though it is strange that no epic emerged on this eminently suitable subject. The culture of the pre-Islāmic Arabs had been pre-eminently a literary one (as might be expected from a largely nomadic race, for whom cultivation of the visual and plastic arts was difficult), centred on their fluent and expressive poetry, of which a fair amount has come down to the present via later generations of Muslim scholars. Under the Umayyads, literature retained this primacy, above all, poetry, although prose tales of the tribal battles of the old Arabs and scraps of Hellenistic and Persian romances from the common Near Eastern heritage also circulated. The civil wars of 656 onward and the growth of sectarian religious strife and political faction, all contributed to the rebirth of poetry, which became the favoured mode of expression for these divergent views. The Khārijites were famed for their poets and orators, such as ʿImrān ibn Ḥiṭṭān (died 703); some poets had Shīʿite sympathies, such as Kuthayyir (died *c.* 723) and al-Kumayt (died after 743) and were moved to eloquence by the martyrdoms and tribulations of the ʿAlids. Political motivation is equally apparent in the work of the three greatest poets of the Umayyad period: al-Akhṭal (died toward 710), Jarīr (died *c.* 729), and al-Farazdaq (died *c.* 728 or 730). These poets were active at the courts of the caliphs and their governors and served as mouthpieces and defenders of the regime. Al-Akhṭal was a Christian and a strenuous defender of the policies of Muʿāwiyah, Yazīd, and ʿAbd al-Malik; because al-Akhṭal's faith put him outside the sectarian conflicts of the Muslim community, Yazīd could, for instance, use him to satirize the *anṣār* of Medina. Jarīr and al-Farazdaq were enemies, though both from the same tribe, and their satires against each other provide brilliant examples of this genre. Indeed, the ethos of these poets was still basically that of the *jāhilīyah*, or pre-Islāmic, period, only partly tinged with Islāmic influences in that they emphasized in their poems praising the Umayyad caliphs the religious nature of their rule as successors to the Prophet.

Rebirth of poetry

Arabia itself became a backwater during the Umayyad period, and Bedouin poets lament the desertedness of once-populous encampments, now that the most vital elements had migrated northward. But the former capital, Medina, in spite of its subordinate political importance, became, on the one hand, a centre for luxury and dissolute living and, on the other, the headquarters of the pietistic party and especially of the scholars of law and tradition (Ḥadīth). It was in Medina that a new school of romantic love poetry, revolving round ʿUmar ibn Abī Rabīʿah (died 712 or 721), arose, and Medina and Damascus were the homes of singing and dancing, where slave girls were trained in these accomplishments. The encouragement of the caliphs was as notable here as in regard to poetry. Yazīd I and al-Walīd II were good poets, and most of the caliphs had their courts thronged with singers and musicians as well as poets, for singers, too, could have a propagandist role, spreading verses and messages favourable to the Umayyad cause.

Islāmic religion was little formalized and institutionalized in the Umayyad period, this being a process that came to fruition in the succeeding ʿAbbāsid period. Under the Umayyads did occur, however, the development of sectarianism, the legacy of the first civil wars, as has been shown above in the delineation of political events. During this period of personal uncertainty and separation from the tribal past, the Shīʿites came to look for an inspired charismatic leader from the house of ʿAlī. The Khārijites, however, saw salvation only within the holy community of Khārijite believers and cut themselves off, physically and intellectually, from the main body of Muslims; they evolved into a politically radical, socially egalitarian sect, emphasizing the brotherhood of all Khārijite faithful, whether from the noblest Arab tribe or a Negro slave. Between these extremes, the mainstream community of orthodox, or Sunnite, Islām contained within itself currents of opinion rather than distinct sects—such informal groups as the Qadarites, or partisans of free will, and the Murjiʾites, those who postponed judgment on the status in the next life of those guilty of great sins.

Rise of sectarianism

A body of Qurʾān readers, the *qurrāʾ*, arose soon after Muḥammad's death to spread knowledge of the sacred book. There was therefore an acute need for a definitive text of the Qurʾān. This was produced between 650 and 656 for the caliph ʿUthmān by a group of experts under Zayd ibn Thābit and variant texts that had circulated in the provinces were destroyed. There now began the intensive study and interpretation of the Qurʾān text, including such questions as the investigation of the occasion for specific revelations, once the generation of the Prophet's Companions, with their firsthand memories, had died out. The science of Ḥadīth, the collection of traditions from the Prophet and early Muslims, on which much of Islāmic law came to be based, was still in its formative stage, but to the Umayyad period belong such important collectors of traditions as ʿUrwah ibn az-Zubayr (died 712 or 717) and az-Zuhrī (died *c.* 741). Nevertheless, Islāmic religion as an institution and as the motivating force behind individual lives of piety did begin slowly to permeate society, despite the strength of pre-Islāmic attitudes; hence, the change to the ostentatious religiosity of the ʿAbbāsids was by no means as abrupt as some of the later historians indicated.

The establishment of the Arabs in the conquered lands made them heirs of the settled civilizations of the Fertile Crescent and Persia. They now had an opportunity to cultivate the arts of peace and enjoy the comforts of sedentary life. At first, everything was strange, and the historians tell amusing stories of the Bedouins' behaviour when first they entered the Persian capital of Ctesiphon in 637; they mistook camphor for salt, thought that the familiar silver was more precious than the unfamiliar gold, and cut up among themselves a jewel-encrusted carpet. After a generation or so, however, such aspects of settled life as permanent settlements and residences appear. The first buildings of the Arabs in Iraq and Egypt were quite primitive, utilizing only such materials as palm trunks and sun-dried brick; it was Ziyād who first built mosques in Basra (665) and al-Kūfah (670) worthy of the name, probably with the help of Persian craftsmen. Conditions, however, were more advantageous in Syria and Jordan, where there remained fine buildings from the Hellenistic and Roman periods and where there was an abundance of building stone. It is not, therefore, surprising that the oldest surviving monument of Islāmic architecture is ʿAbd al-Malik's Dome of the Rock in Jerusalem (completed in 691); this was followed in al-Walīd I's reign by the Umayyad Mosque of Damascus, on a site that had gone through the successive stages of accommodating a pagan temple, a Christian church, and then a church and mosque side by side.

Architecture

The Umayyad caliphs were, indeed, enthusiastic builders and developers of large estates in the Syro-Jordanian region. The remains of their fortified palaces and settlements are dotted all over there, some in fertile, naturally well-watered districts (*e.g.*, Khirbat al-Mafjar, near Jericho; Khirbat al-Minyah, near Tiberias in Palestine; and ʿAnjar, in the Biqāʿ Valley, between the Lebanon and Anti-Lebanon mountains) but the majority on the desert fringes, where complex irrigation systems were necessary (*e.g.*, the two Qaṣr al-Ḥayrs, in south central Syria; Mshattā and Qaṣr ʿAmrah, in Transjordan). Nevertheless, this last group did not comprise exclusively desert hunting palaces, as was once believed, though some of them had extensive enclosures for game (*ḥayr*s); for one thing, they were not in the deep desert and, for another, they clearly formed the centre of rich agricultural estates, producing such things as olives and vines, and with a continuity of occupation and agricultural exploitation from Roman and Greek times. Indeed, the Umayyads were probably continuing some of the traditions of the pre-Islāmic Arab kings of Ghassān in this same area. Many of these palaces can be associated fairly certainly with specific caliphs, such as al-Walīd I with Minyah and al-Walīd II with Qaṣr aṭ-Ṭūbah in eastern Transjordan and the unfinished Mshattā. Above all, Hishām was a great builder, preferring to live outside Damascus, where plague was endemic. Associated with him are al-Mafjar and the two Qaṣr al-Ḥayrs; the eastern one of these last is probably to be identified with Hishām's capital of Ruṣāfah. The massive, fortified architectural style of these buildings is impressive, and the decorations are often splendid, if not quite comparable to the unique glass mosaics of the Umayyad Mosque. Mafjar includes a remarkable floor mosaic, while the bath at Qaṣr ʿAmrah is outstanding for its mural paintings, depicting hunting scenes, the signs of the zodiac, and, above all, the figures of the enemies of Islām, including the Byzantine and Persian emperors, the Negus of Abyssinia, and the Visigothic king Roderick—a striking demonstration of the fact that in earliest Islām there was no religious bar to representing the human form, as arose later. Yet, despite the Umayyads' special attachment to Syria, the provinces of Egypt, the Hejaz, al-Jazīrah, and Iraq were by no means neglected by their governors. The efforts to improve irrigation and agriculture by governors such as Ziyād and al-Ḥajjāj have been noted, and Maslamah ibn ʿAbd al-Malik and Hishām undertook extensive works in al-Jazīrah, adjacent to Hishām's own palace of Ruṣāfah, and in Iraq.

II. The ʿAbbāsid Empire

THE ʿABBASID CALIPHATE 750–945

The establishment of the new dynasty, 750–786. The movement in the eastern provinces of the caliphate that swept the ʿAbbāsids to power is often characterized as a revolution, more exactly in the Arabic terminology of the time, "a turn of fortune, a change in the ruling authority." It is indeed true that after 750 there is discernible a new climate of thought and opinion in the Islāmic empire. The Umayyads had in many ways continued the patriarchal traditions of the "orthodox," or "rightly-guided," caliphs who had immediately succeeded the Prophet; their outlook had remained that of Arab tribal leaders presiding over an Arab military aristocracy geared to the financial and social exploitation of the empire's subject populations. Geographically, the Umayyad caliphate had been oriented toward the Mediterranean, with Byzantium as its supreme enemy. The ʿAbbāsids moved the capital of the empire from Syria to Iraq, because their victory had been essentially that of the Arab tribesmen settled in the east and of the non-Arab clients (*mawālī*), Nabataean and Persian, in Iraq and Persia. Their empire was in some ways a reconstitution of the pre-Islāmic Persian empires that had united the plains of Iraq with the plateaus and mountains of Iran, so that one recent authority has called the Umayyad caliphate "neo-Byzantine" and the ʿAbbāsid one "neo-Sāsānid." The political and military power of the old Arab ruling class was now inevitably reduced; from the caliphate of al-Muʿtaṣim, the old feudal forces of Arab cavalrymen were no longer kept up but replaced by slave troops and mercenaries, prominent among whom were the Turks. The Arabs, however, retained their unassailable social and cultural prestige as the people who had given birth to the Prophet and as speakers of the language in which the Qurʾān, God's own word, had been revealed to men.

ʿAbbāsid shift to the east

There was a further difference in the general ethos of the caliphate and the caliphs' life style after 750. Their actual behaviour did not differ all that much. Yet they and their propagandists adroitly projected a new and changed image of the Commanders of the Faithful as being not only caliphs, secular heads of the Muslim community, but also *imāms*, religiously buttressed figures who were responsible for guiding aright their subjects and ensuring their souls' salvation. The old idea of the Muslim community electing the caliphs still had some validity in men's minds, but in practice the ʿAbbāsids derived their authority from their self-perpetuating momentum and from the concept of responsibility for power to God alone, since Islāmic law was never able to define, much less enforce, explicit limits to the caliph's power.

Religious aura of the caliphs

To bolster the idea that they were the shadows of God on earth, the power of the ʿAbbāsids was given a religious aura. The caliphs frequented the company of the scholars, or *ʿulamāʾ*, and the men of religion and were deferential to them. Even so, these religious leaders rarely had the moral prestige, let alone the practical power, to oppose the caliphs, and on the rare occasions when they did, the caliphs could usually quietly ignore them. One manifestation of the ʿAbbāsids' new religiosity was the innovation of throne names expressing reliance on God or the assurance of his support, such as al-Manṣūr, al-Muntaṣir ("He who is made victorious by God"), al-Mutawakkil ("He who depends on God"), and al-Mustaʿīn ("He who seeks help from God"). This role of the ʿAbbāsids as theocratic rulers seems today a somewhat hypocritical pose. Undoubtedly, there was some disillusionment among people at the time, who grumbled that the "justice" of the ʿAbbāsids was worse than the "tyranny" of the Umayyads; but one should not imagine that contemporaries as a whole saw here elements of conscious dissimulation. Official publicists and scholars dependent on the regime proclaimed in the early ʿAbbāsid period that a new era of justice and piety had dawned, and this undoubtedly secured general assent. The way of life and the social customs of the ʿAbbāsid court reflected the increased influence of the easterners, Persian and Iraqi soldiers and officials. There was, moreover, a hierarchy of courtiers and ministers, with an elaborate ceremonial, and with the caliph screened from the gaze of the vulgar and only approachable in audience through his chamberlain. The caliph's favour or disapproval could make or break a man instantly; hence there was a gradual evolution of the caliph into something resembling the capricious oriental despot familiar from the pages of *The Arabian Nights*.

As-Saffāḥ, 749–754. When Abū al-ʿAbbās as-Saffāḥ ("the lavisher"; whether of largesse or of blood is uncertain) was hailed as caliph in Kūfah at the end of 749, he owed his throne to a political conspiracy and a military rising that had embraced many diverse expectations and hopes, but that had been made in the deliberately vague name of "one who shall be chosen from the House of the Prophet." These different elements of support nevertheless agreed generally upon a belief in the claims of Muḥammad's cousin and son-in-law ʿAlī and his offspring to the temporal caliphate and the imamate, or spiritual direction of the community. The supporters of the ʿAbbāsid revolution, however, had included both an extremist wing that attached itself to the ʿAbbāsid family, as being the ultimate spiritual heirs of one of ʿAlī's children by a slave wife, and also a more moderate wing that expected that the legitimate and direct descendants of ʿAlī would now assume the caliphal office. These last were the nucleus of the so-called Shīʿah, or "party" of ʿAlī. The skillful manoeuvres of the ʿAbbāsids and their partisans now meant that the expectations of these adherents of the claims of ʿAlī's direct progeny were bitterly dashed. The caliphate fell to the ʿAbbāsids, relatives of the Prophet through their ancestor al-ʿAbbās, Muḥammad's uncle, hence more distantly connected than the ʿAlids proper. The mood of frustration and anger engendered among the numerous ʿAlids and their followers was to persist for centuries to come; it was to cause periodic ʿAlid risings and martyrdoms of ʿAlid claimants. More important in the long run was that it brought about the crystallization of vague, emotional feelings for the ʿAlids into a distinct sect, the Shīʿah, with its own separate theology and body of law and hostile to the orthodox majority of Sunnīs (adherents of the *sunnah*, or example of the Prophet). The existence of these irreconciliable elements was to be a source of political and religious weakness in the ʿAbbāsid caliphate. Various caliphs were to abandon persecution for attempts at reconciliation or at least an understanding with the Shīʿah, but this deep-rooted division within the community of Islām has lasted down to modern times.

The ʿAlids

As-Saffāḥ speedily removed various of the men who had aided his rise to power but who might now come forward as rivals for power or focuses for discontent; thus in 750 his vizier (*wazīr*, "helper") Abū Salamah was murdered. Meanwhile, the surviving members of the Umayyad family were mercilessly hunted down and exterminated and the graves of almost all their past caliphs desecrated. Only one Umayyad of consequence escaped, Hishām's grandson ʿAbd ar-Raḥmān. He made his way through North Africa to Spain, where he was hailed as *amīr* by the Arab troops. He thereby became the first ruler of an Umayyad line in Spain, which was to rival the ʿAbbāsids in splendour and which was to endure till 1031.

Al-Manṣūr, 754–775. As-Saffāḥ's brother and successor, al-Manṣūr, had to consolidate the shaky authority of the new dynasty, for too many of the former participants in the ʿAbbāsid revolution had by now become alienated from the ʿAbbāsids. Thus the Persian Abū Muslim, the leader to victory in Khorāsān and a political organizer of genius, was killed by him in 755. ʿAlid revolts in Arabia and Iraq began almost immediately, and extremist Shīʿites and former partisans of Abū Muslim, now inspired by messianic beliefs in his return from the dead, caused further trouble. Security considerations must have influenced al-Manṣūr in his decision to move from the region of turbulent Kūfah to a new capital on the west bank of the Tigris at the ancient settlement of Baghdad, which lay in a fertile and relatively healthy part of central Iraq and which was a centre for communications with both Syria and Persia. By 763 the caliph was able to take up residence in the "City of Peace," more specifically in the "Round City," a circular, walled, and fortified compound comprising a palace, a mosque, residences, barracks, and markets. This garrison compound was soon outgrown; flourishing commercial quarters grew up outside its walls, the right bank was settled, and a bridge of boats linked the two halves of the new capital of the Islāmic world. Until the rise of Cairo under the rival Fāṭimid caliphs of Egypt and Syria (969–1171), Baghdad retained a commercial, social, and cultural primacy among the cities of Islām.

Movement of the capital to Baghdad

Thanks to al-Manṣūr's policies, the stability and continuance of the ʿAbbāsid caliphate were assured. Within his own lifetime he had settled the succession on his son, the future caliph al-Mahdī, ensuring that the caliphate remained within the ʿAbbāsid family. There was never, however, any formal enunciation of the principle of primogeniture. Any suitable male adult member of the family might be designated as heir; hence, as had been the case among the later Umayyads, struggles for the succession within the ʿAbbāsid house were on occasion to lead to civil war and strife. Al-Manṣūr acquired a reputation for meanness, with the nickname of Father of Farthings, but the result of this carefulness was that he had a treasury of several million dinars to leave to his successor.

Al-Mahdī, 775–785. Al-Mahdī attempted a rapprochement with the moderate Shīʿah, but his attempts to win acceptance for the idea that the ʿAbbāsids' ancestor al-ʿAbbās had been specifically designated by Muḥammad as leader of the Muslim community after his death not surprisingly failed. Shīʿite unrest continued, and a rising in Transoxania (Central Asia) and eastern Persia under al-Muqannaʿ ("the Veiled One") combined extremist Shīʿite messianic ideas with older Iranian currents of thought and social protest at the domination of the Arab and Persian landowning class. After the brief reign of al-Mahdī's son al-Hādī (785–786), there succeeded to the caliphate another son, Hārūn, called ar-Rashīd ("the Rightly-Guided one").

The Shīʿite revolt

The ʿAbbāsids at their zenith, 786–861. *Hārūn, 786–809.* Hārūn's reign has gained a somewhat spurious glamour as the one in which the apogee of caliphal splendour and might was reached. In fact, the empire was racked by unrest and revolt in many regions, notably in Syria, where loyalty to the Umayyads' memory was still strong; in Egypt, where harsh financial measures led to periodic rebellions of the indigenous Christians, or Copts; in the Persian province of Daylam, to the south of the Caspian Sea, where ʿAlid claimants had taken refuge; and in eastern Persia, the provinces of Khorāsān and Seistan, where a radical, egalitarian Muslim sect, the Khārijites, took advantage of local grievances against caliphal tax collectors and mounted a revolt that lasted for over two decades. The remote North African province of Ifrīqīyah (modern Tunisia) was in 800 given to Ibrāhīm I ibn al-Aghlab to govern in return for annual tribute. Ibrāhīm subsequently obtained the right to nominate his son as governor after himself and in this fashion set up an autonomous line that endured for over a century (800–909). A precedent was thereby established for the falling away from caliphal allegiance of peripheral provinces, a process that began in earnest toward the end of the 9th century (the Muslim far west, which later became Morocco, had already become fully independent under a descendant of ʿAlī, who had escaped the various massacres of ʿAlids and had in 789 formed the Idrīsid principality, based on Fez). Where Hārūn did distinguish himself personally was in *jihād* (holy war) against Byzantium, leadership in *jihād* being considered in orthodox eyes as one of the key duties of the caliph. Hārūn clearly took this responsibility seriously; in his youth he had already led an expedition that had penetrated through Anatolia and reached the shores of the Bosporus (781–782). It was also in Hārūn's reign that certain obscure diplomatic exchanges took place between the caliph and the Frankish emperor Charlemagne, the latter apparently aiming at securing some privileges for the Latin clergy in Jerusalem; these events are documented, however, exclusively from the Christian side.

Closely associated with the early ʿAbbāsid caliphs were the fortunes of the Barmakid, or Barmecide, family of secretaries and ministers, a family of eastern Iranian Buddhist origin who had come to the fore in the times of as-Saffāḥ and al-Manṣūr and who typified the "new men" raised to high official positions by the ʿAbbāsids. Distrusting the old Arab aristocracy and the ambitious members of their own family, the caliphs preferred to bring up their servants from obscurity, some of these officials becoming officially designated as vizier or chief executive minister. The dominance of this secretarial class, largely Persian in origin and imbued with Persian conceptions of kingship and official procedure, contributed markedly to the orientalization of the caliphate, even though the Barmakids themselves fell from power in 803, when Hārūn decided to assert his personal authority. One aspect of the continued vitality of non-Islāmic beliefs in Iraq and the east is the prevalence among certain circles at this time of dualist beliefs, survivals of Manichaeism, and of messianic expectations combined with advanced social ideas, continuing the doctrines of the pre-Islāmic Persian heresiarch Mazdak; inquisitory tribunals had to be set up in Iraq to ferret out these dissidents, the *zindīqs*.

The Barmakid family

In two measures promulgated in 802, the so-called Meccan documents, Hārūn made arrangements for the future of the empire. Briefly, his son by a noble Arab wife of ʿAbbāsid lineage, the later caliph al-Amīn, was to have the caliphate and the western lands; while another son by a Persian slave mother, the later caliph al-Maʾmūn, was to govern the eastern half of the empire under his brother's general overlordship and be next in line for the succession. Hārūn died in 809, but his carefully laid plans soon went awry. Al-Amīn, although clearly the less capable of the two, determined to assert his direct authority over his half-brother and further decided to vest the succession in his own son and thus exclude al-Maʾmūn. Civil war resulted; Baghdad underwent a fearful siege by al-Maʾmūn's Persian army (812–813), and al-Amīn was deposed and murdered, so that al-Maʾmūn became caliph of a united empire.

Civil war over succession

Al-Maʾmūn, 813–833. If any caliphate deserves to rank as the golden age of Arab civilization, it is that of al-Maʾmūn. Personally brave, he led further expeditions against the Byzantines and coped with rebellions in Egypt, Syria, Armenia, and Khorāsān. Al-Maʾmūn's triumph over al-Amīn has often been viewed as a victory of the Iranian east against the Arab interests represented by the deposed caliph, and this is in large measure true; al-Maʾmūn brought with him Persian troops and ministers, and the Persianizing tendencies in administrative practice discernible in previous reigns were now intensified. Al-Maʾmūn also had a questing intellect; he took an interest in disputations between the adherents of various faiths; he built observatories and encouraged the study of astronomy and geometry; and he founded a "House of Wisdom" (Bayt al-Ḥikmah) in Baghdad devoted to the translation of scientific and philosophical works from the original Greek.

The Caliph seems further to have had in mind a great design, the vision of a united Islām, with the deep rift between the Sunnīs and the Shīʿah healed; in this way, the political unity of the caliphate would be assured and internal peace and prosperity favoured. His sympathies with the Muʿtazilite group of theologians, who were concerned with the defense of Islām by rational arguments against heresy and infidelity (see below), also led to an irenical approach to the Shīʿah, who shared certain attitudes with the Muʿtazilah. The middle portion of al-Maʾmūn's reign is accordingly marked by the adoption in

Attempts at religious unity

817 of the Shīʿite 8th *imām*, ʿAlī ar-Riḍā, as his heir. In the event, the *imām* himself died shortly afterwards, and the episode does not necessarily mean that the caliph planned permanently to divert the succession to the ʿAlids; he may have intended to enlarge the field of capable candidates, ʿAbbāsid and ʿAlid alike, who might then succeed according to personal merit. Attempts like this to win over the Shīʿah were to be followed by other caliphs of the 9th century (notably, al-Muntaṣir and al-Muʿtadid), but the breach between the two wings of Islāmic belief was unbridgeably wide. A predictable result of al-Maʾmūn's policies of favouring the Muʿtazilah and Shīʿah was a sharp reaction among the orthodox Sunnī *ʿulamāʾ* and lawyers, led by Aḥmad ibn Ḥanbal, founder of one of the more conservative law schools of Sunnī Islām (see below). He and others stood firm against the inquisitorial methods of the tribunal set up by al-Maʾmūn to compel agreement to certain theological ideas of the Muʿtazilah, even though these methods were continued with increased vigour under al-Maʾmūn's two successors.

Al-Muʿtaṣim, 833–842. The caliphate of another son of Hārūn ar-Rashīd, al-Muʿtaṣim, was notable for a renewal of the war with the Byzantines, culminating in a famous victory at Amorium (Ammūrīyah; 838), the last serious campaign into Anatolia undertaken by the Arabs; over the next two centuries, it was the Byzantines who were generally to assume the offensive. A 20-year-old rebellion by the heretic Bābak was also crushed in Armenia and Azerbaijan. But the significance of al-Muʿtaṣim's reign lies more in the general military and political trends of the time. The ʿAbbāsids still gloried in their Arab descent, but the percentage of Arab blood in their veins was by now decreasing rapidly. After Hārūn's time, the caliphs ceased to contract formal marriages with free wives, and all the caliphs from al-Maʾmūn onward were born of non-Arab slave mothers—Persian, Turkish, Armenian, Greek, etc. The caliphs soon became physically as well as intellectually removed from the masses of their Arab subjects in Iraq. Already in al-Maʾmūn's caliphate, the Khorāsānian troops were being supplemented by Turkish slave soldiers from Central Asia. Al-Muʿtaṣim turned this unsystematic practice into deliberate policy, purchasing large numbers of Turks, and even Berbers and Slavs, for his palace guard. The violence and unpopularity of these troops in Baghdad made the caliph determine in 836 to move to a new capital at Sāmarrāʾ, 60 miles north of Baghdad. He and subsequent caliphs laid out over several miles of the east bank of the Tigris a vast complex of palaces, barracks, and other buildings. Though only occupied for some 60 years, the ruins of these buildings remain impressive, attesting to advanced ideas of city planning, bold architectural techniques, and a high level of material culture and comfort.

Decline of Arab heritage in the caliphate

Al-Wāthiq, 842–847, and al-Mutawakkil, 847–861. The policies of al-Muʿtaṣim were continued by his son al-Wāthiq, and in particular the *miḥnah*, or tribunal for enforcing Muʿtazilite doctrines, was continued in full vigour. But there was a decisive change of attitude under the energetic al-Mutawakkil. He determined to take full personal charge of affairs, ruling for some time without a vizier, and endeavoured to reduce the influence in the state of the Turkish praetorian guards and the officials who were unscrupulously manipulating them. This entailed a conscious return to pro-Arab, orthodox Sunnī policies. The pro-Muʿtazilite measures of his predecessors were permanently reversed, as were the attempts at conciliating the Shīʿah. The orthodox *ʿulamāʾ* came to the fore, and discriminatory laws against the "People of the Book," primarily Jews and Christians, were revived, including the requirement of distinctive dress. The standard ʿAbbāsid execration of the defeated Umayyads was relaxed, and in 858 al-Mutawakkil temporarily moved his court to the old Umayyad capital of Damascus. But a conspiracy to murder him, successfully hatched by his son al-Muntaṣir, the next caliph, and the Turkish guards, removed these last hopes of reviving the caliphate and of turning its orientation back toward the Arab lands rather than toward the Persian ones.

Sunnī revival

Increasing difficulties and decline, 861–945. A period of anarchy followed al-Mutawakkil's death, with the Turkish generals making and unmaking caliphs, so that four of them, al-Muntaṣir, al-Mustaʿīn, al-Muʿtazz and al-Muhtadī, succeeded in rapid succession (861–870). Civil strife grew in Iraq, including a second siege of Baghdad by rivals for power. This paralysis and lack of continuity at the centre inevitably tempted governors and military leaders in the provinces to rule without reference to the caliphs. From 869 onward, southern Iraq was racked by a great rebellion of Negro agricultural slaves, the Zanj, who, under a leader claiming ʿAlid descent, held ʿAbbāsid armies at bay for some 14 years, seriously disrupting agriculture and commerce in lower Iraq and in the adjacent regions of Khuzistan, in southwestern Persia, and of eastern Arabia. Not long after the suppression in 883 of the Zanj revolt, much of the Syrian Desert and Arabian Peninsula fell under the control of the bitterly anti-ʿAbbāsid Qarmaṭians, a body of radical, egalitarian sectaries connected with the extremist Shīʿah; by 930

The Zanj slave revolt

From S. Ronart and N. Ronart, *The Concise Encyclopedia of Arabic Civilization*, vol. 1

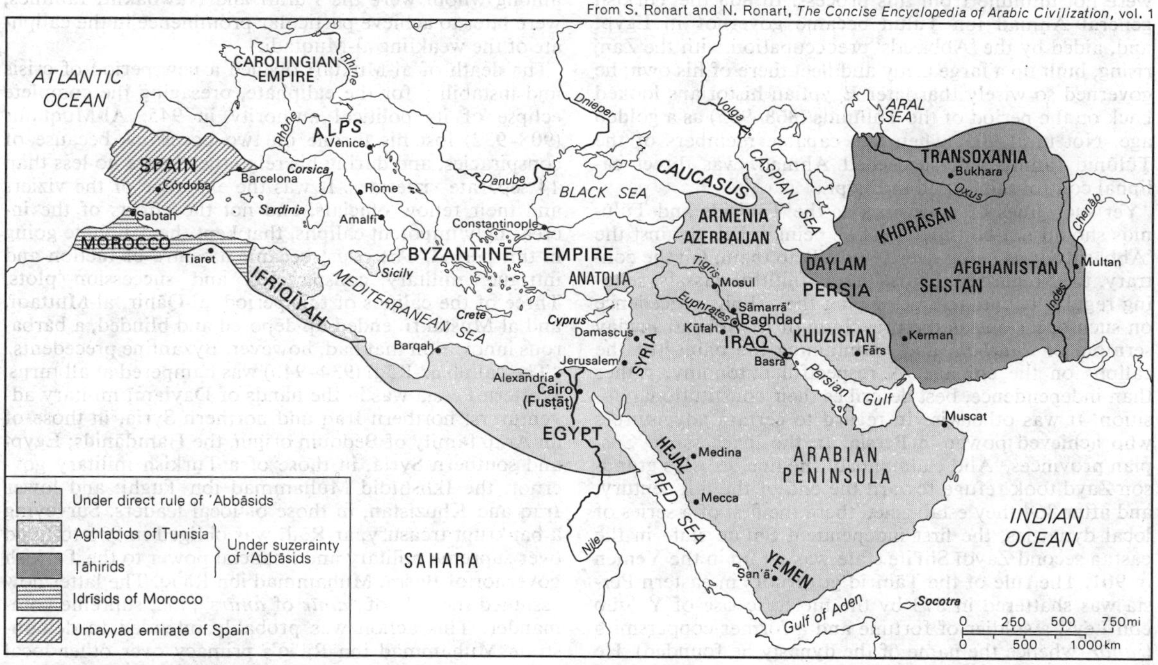

The ʿAbbāsid caliphate in the 9th century.

these Qarmaṭians were bold enough to raid the holy city of Mecca itself and carry off the Black Stone from the Kaʿbah.

Growth of provincial autonomy. The assumption of autonomous powers, if not full independence, by provincial governors was a growing trend of the later 9th century. The problem of holding together such disparate and scattered regions as those making up the Islāmic empire had long been a problem for the strongest monarchs. Control had usually been maintained through the awe and terror inspired by the caliphs themselves and the retributive power of the armies at their command, and through a communications network organized by local intelligence officers (the *barīd* system). As the century progressed, the coercive ability of the caliphs decreased, although they still retained their religious and moral aura as heads of the community of the faithful.

Arabized governors in Persia

In the eastern parts of Persia, a line of Arabized Persian governors, the Ṭāhirids, succeeded each other hereditarily (821–873), while other members of the family held important military and administrative posts in Iraq until the 10th century. In the remote province of Transoxania, the land beyond the Oxus (modern Soviet Central Asia), a local Iranian family, the Sāmānids, governed first as subordinates of the Ṭāhirids, but after 875 and the end of Ṭāhirid rule in Persia, they became directly responsible for Transoxania to the Baghdad caliphs; in the 10th century, they built up a prosperous and powerful amirate, in practice independent, in Transoxania and Khorāsān. Similarly, in Azerbaijan and Armenia, a short line of Arabized Persian governors, the Sājids, exercised power (879–930) in a region that had a long history of heretical and sectarian outbreaks and that presented special problems through the independent aspirations of the local Armenian princes.

A similar process is discernible in the Muslim west. It has been noted that an Umayyad survivor had assumed power in Muslim Spain as far back as 756. The amirate grew in strength under capable rulers until, in the 10th century, the *amīr* ʿAbd ar-Raḥmān III (912–961) actually declared himself caliph in rivalry to the enfeebled representative of the ʿAbbāsids in Baghdad. North Africa was hardly less remote from Iraq than Spain, and local dynasties such as the Idrīsids, Rustamids, and Aghlabids controlled it until the early 10th century and the rise of the Fāṭimids (see below); it was the Aghlabids who in 827 began the conquest of Sicily, turning it into a Muslim province for over two centuries. The lands immediately to the west of Iraq—*i.e.*, Syria, Palestine, and Egypt—were not immune from this process. In 868 the Turkish general Aḥmad ibn Ṭūlūn became governor in Egypt and, aided by the ʿAbbāsids' preoccupation with the Zanj rising, built up a large army and fleet there of his own; he governed so wisely that later Egyptian historians looked back on the period of the Ṭūlūnids (868–905) as a golden age. Not until 905, when less capable members of the Ṭūlūnid family had succeeded Aḥmad, was direct caliphal control reimposed in Egypt.

Yet such lines of governors as the Ṭāhirids and Ṭūlūnids should not be thought of as being rebels against the ʿAbbāsids or as being overtly hostile to them. On the contrary, they regarded themselves as faithful vassals, sending regular tribute to Iraq, giving the caliphs precedence on such occasions as the preaching of the formal Friday sermon, or *khuṭbah*, and maintaining the names of the caliphs on the coinage. A respectful autonomy, rather than independence, best describes their constitutional position. It was otherwise in regard to certain adventurers who achieved power in Persia. In the inaccessible Caspian provinces, ʿAlid claimants of the line of ʿAlī's grandson Zayd took refuge toward the end of the 8th century, and after 864 they established there the first of a series of local dynasties, the first independent Shīʿite state in the east; a second Zaydī Shīʿite state was set up in the Yemen in 901. The rule of the Ṭāhirid governors in eastern Persia was shattered in 873 by the meteoric rise of Yaʿqūb

Rise of the Ṣaffārids

ebn Leyṡ, a soldier of fortune and a former coppersmith (*ṣaffār*, whence the name of the dynasty he founded). He and his brother ʿAmr assembled a vast, if transient, military empire in southern and eastern Persia and in what is now Afghanistan, based on their native province of Seistan. The plebeian Ṣaffārids hated the aristocratic ʿAbbāsids and did not disguise their contempt for them. Yaʿqūb planned to march on Baghdad, and in 876 his army came within 50 miles of this goal before being defeated. The Ṣaffārids were only reduced to the role of purely local princes in Seistan by the efforts of the pro-ʿAbbāsid Sāmānids of Transoxania (910).

The Baghdad caliphs, 861–945. The ʿAbbāsid caliphate in Baghdad survived the decade of chaos after al-Mutawakkil's death, but with impaired prestige and seriously diminished resources. The falling away of outlying provinces decreased the inflow of revenue from them, and the upkeep of a sumptuous court and a large but undisciplined army were drains on what money could be collected. During the nominal caliphate of al-Muʿtamid (870–892), effective power was exercised by his much more capable brother al-Muwaffaq (died 891), who mastered the Zanj rebels by 883 and repulsed the Ṣaffārids from Iraq, although he had to leave Aḥmad ibn Ṭūlūn in control of Egypt. Al-Muwaffaq's son al-Muʿtaḍid (892–902) and grandson al-Muktafī (902–908) were the last ʿAbbāsid caliphs to wield real power until the caliphal revival of the later 11th and 12th centuries. One Muslim author calls al-Muʿtaḍid "the closing point of the dynasty," and the reigns of both these capable caliphs were regrettably brief. Al-Muʿtaḍid aimed at securing internal peace through a program of religious conciliation, and he also had to stave off attacks from the Byzantines, now ruled by the vigorous dynasty of Macedonian emperors (867–1057); al-Muktafī in 905 regained control of Egypt.

The twelfth and last "open" *imām* (*i.e.*, successor to ʿAlī) of the Shīʿites disappeared in mysterious circumstances in al-Muʿtamid's time. Certain strands of the extremist Shīʿah now began to adopt conspiratorial and revolutionary methods that made them greatly feared and were a further menace to the stability of the caliphate and to the fabric of Sunnī orthodoxy. Among these groups were the Qarmaṭians of Syria and Arabia, already mentioned, and the Fāṭimids in North Africa, who claimed descent from ʿAlī and his wife Fāṭimah and who drew support from the "Sevener," or Ismāʿīlī, Shīʿah group, the partisans of the seventh *imām*, Ismāʿīl. Within the very caliphate itself, certain Shīʿite elements were at work, for in an effort to restore financial and administrative stability, al-Muʿtaḍid had recruited a group of Shīʿite secretaries and treasury officials; this group, notable among whom were the Furātī and Nawbakhtī families, were later to achieve particular prominence in the caliphate of the weakling al-Muqtadir.

Shīʿah terrorism

The death of al-Muktafī opened a new period of crisis and instability for the caliphate, presaging the complete eclipse of its political authority in 945. Al-Muqtadir (908–932) lost his throne on two occasions because of conspiracies, and during his reign there were no less than 14 separate vizierates. It was the expertise of the viziers and their fellow officials, and not the efforts of the increasingly impotent caliphs, that kept the caliphate going in this period. The court became a centre of faction and intrigue, military conspiracies, and succession plots. Three of the caliphs of this period, al-Qāhir, al-Muttaqī, and al-Mustakfī, ended up deposed and blinded, a barbarous innovation that had, however, Byzantine precedents.

The caliph ar-Rāḍī (934–940) was hampered at all turns. Western Persia was in the hands of Daylamī military adventurers; northern Iraq and northern Syria, in those of an Arab family of Bedouin origin, the Ḥamdānids; Egypt and southern Syria, in those of a Turkish military governor, the Ikhshīdid Muḥammad ibn Tughj; and lower Iraq and Khuzistan, in those of local leaders. Surveying a bankrupt treasury, ar-Rāḍī was obliged in 936 to hand over supreme military and financial power to the Turkish governor of Basra, Muḥammad ibn Rāʾiq. The latter now assumed the title of "*amīr* of *amīrs*"; *i.e.*, supreme commander. This action was probably intended to demonstrate Muḥammad ibn Rāʾiq's primacy over other local military leaders, but at the same time it symbolized the

The "*amīr* of *amīrs*"

existence of a dual system, with the *amīr* exercising political and military power and leaving to the caliph only his moral authority as spiritual head of Sunnī Islām. A few years later, the Daylamī Aḥmad ebn Būyeh (Buwayh), later to receive the honorific title of Muʿizz ad-Dawlah from the caliph, entered Baghdad and himself assumed Muḥammad ibn Rāʾiq's old title of "*amīr* of *amīrs*" (945). Thus, effective control in the capital and in Iraq passed to a non-Arab, Shīʿite potentate, and for over a century the ʿAbbāsids were little more than puppets.

THE ECLIPSE OF THE ʿABBASIDS AND THE GROWTH OF PROVINCIAL DYNASTIES, 945–1258

The Būyids. The family of Muʿizz ad-Dawlah, that of the Būyids, or Buwayhids, was comprised of soldiers of fortune from the backward region of Daylam in northwestern Persia who took advantage of the disorders in the caliphate to set up a loose confederation of three amirates in southern and western Persia and Iraq. Their rise to power is only one aspect of a wider phenomenon in the eastern Islāmic world at this time, the appearance on the stage of Middle Eastern history of hitherto submerged Iranian peoples, notably the Daylamīs and the Kurds. Hence the period 900–1050 has been termed by the noted historian of Persia, Vladimir Minorsky, "the Daylamī interlude," a period in which Persia threw off rule by Arab or Arabized governors and was actually ruled by native Iranians, until the general triumph of Turkish generals and soldiers in the central and eastern lands of the caliphate again placed Persia under outside domination.

The "Daylamī interlude"

The installation of the Būyids in Baghdad in 945 presented the ʿAbbāsids with a potentially grave threat to their continued existence. The Būyids were rough tribesmen, not long converted to Islām and likely to be contemptuous of Arabic culture and the position of the ʿAbbāsids as heirs to much of this culture. Moreover, they had come to adopt the Shīʿite form of Islām, thanks to the earlier efforts of ʿAlid missionaries in the Caspian provinces. It was not improbable, therefore, that the Būyids might fulfill the dreams of generations of martyred ʿAlids and sweep away the ʿAbbāsid oppressors, regarded by convinced Shīʿites as usurpers of the rightful throne of the Shīʿite *imāms*. In fact, the Būyids were political realists. The Shīʿah were certainly favoured, and this is the period in which their distinctive theology and law, previously somewhat vague and unsystematic, began to take formal shape. But the Būyids made no move to abolish the ʿAbbāsid caliphate, for the latter, now deprived of independent political power and control over revenue, existed only as pensioners of the Būyids. Deposition of the ʿAbbāsids would have provoked a violent Sunnī reaction, and the Shīʿah, in any case, were a small minority compared with the Sunnīs.

Nor did ideological considerations affect the Būyids' external policy. Their main enemies in the west were both Shīʿite powers, the Ḥamdānids of Mosul and the Fāṭimids of Egypt and Syria—the latter, it is true, of the extremist Ismāʿīlī persuasion, whereas the Būyids adhered to the moderate Twelver variety of Shīʿism. Culturally, the attractions of Arabic civilization proved irresistible to the Būyids, and in their time Arabic literature and culture reached new heights; thus the great *amīr* ʿAḍud ad-Dawlah was the patron of al-Mutanabbī, commonly considered by the Arabs as their greatest poet. Hence the ʿAbbāsids continued to live modestly in Baghdad on the revenues that the Būyids allowed them and on the proceeds from the granting of honours and titles. They still retained their moral and spiritual prestige as heads of Sunnī Islām, and in this regard the Būyids had to tread circumspectly. One of the original triumvirate of the Būyid brothers, Rukn ad-Dawlah (ruler of the northern Persian amirate of Jibāl, 947–977), had employed on his coins the ancient Iranian title *shāhanshāh* ("emperor of emperors"), which to orthodox Muslim ears sounded blasphemous, as applicable to God alone. When the Būyid *amīr* of Iraq Jalāl ad-Dawlah (1025–44) wanted the title *shāhanshāh* to be included among all his other ones read out publicly by the official preachers in Baghdad, the populace was outraged at this presumption in the very capital of Islām. It was the caliph al-Qāʾim who quieted uneasy consciences over the title's legitimacy, thereby implicitly upholding the principle that it was the caliph who had the sole right to grant to secular rulers their titles and honours. Also, the Būyids used the prestige of the caliphate and the orthodox Sunnī *ʿulamāʾ* in their rivalry with the Fāṭimids, encouraging denunciations of the Fāṭimids' claim to genuine ʿAlid descent.

The Būyids reached their peak under ʿAḍud ad-Dawlah (949–983), who toward the end of his reign united under his sole rule all the Būyid lands in Persia and Iraq, conquering Kerman and even Oman in eastern Arabia, and pursuing an aggressive policy against the Ḥamdānids and the Daylamī Ziyārids of Ṭabaristān in the Caspian region. After his death there was much strife within the family, and the unitary rule hard won by ʿAḍud ad-Dawlah was lost, with separate Būyid lines emerging in Fārs and Khuzistan; in Kerman; in Jibāl, or northwestern Persia; and in Iraq. In the time of ʿAḍud ad-Dawlah, the ʿAbbāsids had been necessarily quiescent, and one of them, the caliph al-Ṭāʾiʿ (974–991), was deposed by ʿAḍud ad-Dawlah's son Bahāʾ ad-Dawlah (989–1012). But subsequent caliphs held office for unprecedentedly long periods, notably al-Qādir (991–1031) and al-Qāʾim (1031–75), indicative of the later Būyid relaxation of control over the ʿAbbāsids; Muslim historians praise these two caliphs both for their piety and for their gradual reassertion of the prerogatives of office.

Zenith of Būyid strength

The Sāmānids. Meanwhile, the northeastern fringes of the Islāmic world were ruled until 999 by the Sāmānid *amīrs*, faithful Sunnīs who were deferential to the ʿAbbāsids. Their provinces of Khorāsān and Transoxania enjoyed a remarkable material prosperity, and their court of Bukhara was a centre for Arabic scholarship and for the renascent New Persian language and literature alike. Much of this prosperity derived from the Sāmānids' control of the trade in Turkish slaves from the Central Asian steppes. Turks were highly prized for their fighting qualities and their hardiness, and by the 10th century it had become accepted dogma over much of the Islāmic world, outside of the extreme west, that mercenary troops and slave guards were more reliable supports for a ruler than feudal levies or tribal forces. With the aid of loyal troops, a ruler could place himself high above his subjects, centralize his power, and rule despotically. Turkish commanders and governors thereby acquired positions of high influence within the state, and these positions left them well placed for seizing full executive power. This largely explains how from the 11th century much of the Islāmic world was transformed by the installation of Turkish potentates and a Turkish military ruling class.

Use of Turkish troops

The founder of the powerful Ghaznavid empire, which dominated the eastern fringes of the Islāmic world in the first half of the 11th century, arose from the Turkish slave guard of the Sāmānids. The slave's son, the famous Sultan Maḥmūd of Ghazna (998–1030), assembled the most powerful military empire known in the East since the palmiest days of the Arab caliphate, with territories extending from northern Persia and Central Asia to the Ganges basin in India; one of Maḥmūd's great claims to fame as a Muslim hero was his role as "hammer" of the infidel Hindus. Almost all the Turkish dynasties that arose in the Islāmic world were strongly Sunnī; hence the Ghaznavids were hostile to a Shīʿite power like the Būyids on grounds both of political rivalry and religion. The sultans often spoke of mounting a great crusade in the west that would liberate the ʿAbbāsids from the tutelage of the Iraq Būyids and then go on to attack the Fāṭimids of Syria and Egypt; and Maḥmūd did succeed in overthrowing (1029) the Būyid amirate of Jibāl. The Ghaznavids assiduously cultivated links with the caliphs, sending rich presents from the Indian plunder and persecuting Muslim heretics, receiving in exchange the legitimation of their power as heirs of the Sāmānids and grandiloquent titles emphasising their support for and dependence on the ʿAbbāsids. In this way, the caliphal fiction that all secular rulers in the provinces derived their authority from an act of delegation by the caliph was preserved.

The rise of the Ghaznavid empire

Sunnī dynasties like the Ghaznavids, and shortly after them, the Seljuqs, maintained this deference to the caliphs as the ultimate legitimizers of temporal authority, even though the Seljuqs were to follow Būyid precedent in trying to exclude the ʿAbbāsids from exercising practical power. And, as noted earlier, the moderate Shīʿite Būyids found it expedient to leave the ʿAbbāsids as the focus of orthodox moral and spiritual aspirations rather than risk difficulties that would certainly have arisen had the caliphate been abolished or transferred to the ʿAlids.

The Fāṭimids. There arose in the 10th century, however, an impressive power in the west that not only opposed the ʿAbbāsids politically but also denied the religious and moral validity of their claim to the caliphate. It is uncertain whether the Fāṭimids really were of ʿAlid descent, connected in some still-unelucidated way with the seventh *imām*, Ismāʿīl; their Sunnī opponents generally denied the claim. At the beginning of the 10th century, Ismāʿīlī Shīʿite agents were spreading their propaganda in North Africa. With the support of Berber troops, the Fāṭimids speedily overthrew such local dynasties as the Aghlabids and Rustamids and reduced the Idrīsids to vassal status. A great new capital was built in 920 at al-Mahdīyah in Ifrīqīyah, and this was later to be the base for the Fāṭimids' eastward drive against Egypt. The Fāṭimids styled themselves caliphs of the true line of ʿAlī and openly stigmatized the ʿAbbāsids as usurpers who must be extirpated. They thus marked themselves off decisively from other dynasties that had acquired independence in practice but that continued to acknowledge the nominal suzerainty of the ʿAbbāsids.

Assumption of the title of caliph by the Fāṭimids

In fact, the Fāṭimids were not the only ones in the Muslim west to assume the title of caliph at this time. The Spanish Umayyad ʿAbd ar-Raḥmān III adopted the designations of caliph and Commander of the Faithful in 928, partly as a counterblast to Fāṭimid pretensions, partly to show that the Spanish Umayyads were now strong enough to take up once more the caliphal dignity that had anciently belonged to their house. Soon after this, even the petty Midrārid ruler of Sijilmāssah, on the Saharan fringes of Morocco, styled himself caliph. The extreme Muslim west was so remote from Iraq that not even the fiction, let alone the reality, of a united caliphate could be maintained; later Muslim political theorists were compelled reluctantly to admit that there might be more than one caliph of the Faithful, provided that they were widely separated geographically.

The family of the Ikhshīdid Muḥammad ibn Ṭughj had continued to govern Egypt as vassals of the ʿAbbāsids, latterly under the skillful regency of the black eunuch Kāfūr, until in 969 they were swept away by the Fāṭimid invasion of Egypt. The Fāṭimid caliph al-Muʿizz was proclaimed there, and a new capital, that of New Cairo, was begun. It has already been noted that the Fāṭimids were more than unruly governors with independent aspirations. They were heads of a great religious movement, that of extremist Shīʿite Ismāʿīlism, whose agents were active in widely scattered regions of the Islāmic world and which was dedicated to the subversion of the ʿAbbāsid caliphate and its replacement by an Ismāʿīlī one. For over a century, the Fāṭimid caliphs pursued this aim vigorously, by secret propaganda and by force of arms. The organization of their army followed prevalent trends in that its personnel were multinational, with mercenaries and slave guards from several races. Palestine and southern Syria were occupied and the Syrian territories of the Ḥamdānids then taken over, so that the Fāṭimid frontier reached the southern boundary of the Byzantine Empire. Attempts were made to extend Fāṭimid rule into Iraq, and in 1059 a rebellious Turkish general for a while proclaimed the Fāṭimid caliph al-Mustanṣir (1036–94) in Baghdad itself. Ismāʿīlī missionaries worked in, among other places, Syria and Persia, where, toward the end of the 11th century, several inaccessible strongholds were seized and held against the ruling powers there. It was these Ismāʿīlīs who became known to the Frankish crusaders as the Assassins, or "hashish eaters," and who, by their policy of political assassination, spread a terror disproportionately greater than their actual numbers.

The Assassins

The Fāṭimid caliphate flourished culturally and economically, and the caliphs' commercial policy aimed at diverting the Indian and Far Eastern maritime trade from the Persian Gulf and Iraq to South Arabia and the Red Sea route. The splendour of the Fāṭimid court in Cairo far overshadowed that of the poverty-stricken ʿAbbāsids in Baghdad, and Cairo assumed the position of cultural leadership in the Arab world that it still holds today. But the Fāṭimids could not escape the path of decline already trodden by their ʿAbbāsid rivals. Ambitious generals rebelled; there were succession disputes; the Ismāʿīlī movement lost impetus and was rent by various schisms (the Druze sect of southern Syria grew out of the extravagant policies of the caliph al-Ḥākim, 996–1021); and the Fāṭimids' eastern flank was potentially jeopardized after 1099 by the injection of a new element, that of the crusaders. It did not prove difficult in 1171 for the Kurdish general Saladin to end the now feeble Fāṭimid caliphate. Sunnī orthodoxy was restored in Egypt; it returned to the spiritual overlordship of the ʿAbbāsids, and the traces of Fāṭimid rule there were speedily obliterated.

The Seljuq Turks. In 1055, the ʿAbbāsids were released from the tutelage of the Būyids by the Seljuq Turks, whose nomadic bands had been raiding for several years through Persia into Anatolia (where they eventually overlaid Byzantine rule) and into Iraq. The Seljuqs were enthusiastic Sunnīs and at an early point in their career had styled themselves by the stereotyped formula of Clients of the Commander of the Faithful. Orthodox opinion, to some extent, favoured them in their struggle with the Būyids, and eventually their leader, Toghrïl Beg, entered Baghdad and had his title of sultan (*i.e.*, "temporal ruler," a title already well-known in the eastern Islāmic world) confirmed by the caliph al-Qāʾim. Very soon al-Qāʾim married a Seljuq princess, although he held out as long as possible against the idea of the barbarian Toghrïl marrying one of his own daughters. The enfeeblement of the last Būyids had already allowed the caliph tentatively to reassert his authority. For long, the Būyids' close control had deprived the caliphs of the necessity for viziers. In 1045, al-Qāʾim felt strong enough to appoint a vizier who was strongly Sunnī and anti-Būyid, Ibn al-Muslimah. The spread of the Seljuqs over the greater part of the Middle East finally crystallized the new division of power in the central Islāmic lands, a division that had already taken shape in the Būyid period, between the caliph-*imām*s as spiritual heads and the Seljuq sultans as temporal rulers; this duality ultimately had to be recognized in Islāmic constitutional theory. Even so, the ʿAbbāsids were by no means freed from all outside constraint. The Seljuqs controlled much of the caliphal income, and it was through financial pressure that Toghrïl was finally able to compel al-Qāʾim to grant his daughter's hand.

Division between spiritual and temporal rule

The great Seljuq Empire reached its zenith under Malik-Shāh (1072–92) and his famous vizier Niẓām al-Mulk. The latter played a leading role in furthering the general revival of Sunnī orthodoxy in the Islāmic world, a revival favoured by the triumph of the Seljuqs and the decline of the Fāṭimids after 1094. The education and training of a specifically orthodox class of scholars and officials was promoted by the spread of *madrasah*s, or colleges, in conscious rivalry to the Shīʿite centres of learning founded by the Fāṭimids for training Ismāʿīlī missionaries. Despite this broadly Sunnī policy of the Seljuqs, specific contacts between the sultans and caliphs were by no means always harmonious. The ʿAbbāsids and their viziers were beginning to chafe at restrictions that they had previously endured in enforced silence. Malik-Shāh married the caliph al-Muqtadī's daughter in 1087, but relations so deteriorated that, just before his death, Malik-Shāh was contemplating making Baghdad his own winter capital and expelling the ʿAbbāsids from it.

The last ʿAbbāsids. After Malik-Shāh's death, the unity of the great Seljuq sultanate began to crack, and the last century of its life was marked by frequent succession disputes and the rivalries of ambitious Turkish generals. The real power of the ʿAbbāsids now increased proportionately to the weakening of the Seljuqs. They had the services of several capable viziers, such as Ibn Hubayrah, vizier for 16 unbroken years to al-Muqtafī (1136–60) and al-Mustanjid (1160–70). Ibn Hubayrah also threw his weight behind the revived influence within Baghdad of the strictly orthodox Ḥanbalī law school, whose resurgence parallels that of the caliphate itself. The energetic al-Muqtafī built up a professional army of his own and fortified Baghdad, so that he was able to extend his political influence over central and southern Iraq to a degree unknown since the early 10th century; and he intervened on various occasions in the internal quarrels of the Seljuq family as legitimizer of one or another claimant's power.

The caliph an-Nāṣir (1180–1225) became a central figure in the diplomacy and politics of his age. The ʿAbbāsids had paid little attention to events in Syria and the Levant coastlands, where the crusaders had been entrenched since the opening of the 12th century, beyond giving moral encouragement to Muslim princes fighting there; outside of the eastern Mediterranean itself, the crusaders had attracted little interest in the Islāmic world at large. An-Nāṣir's main preoccupation was with the east, where an aggressive Turkish dynasty from Central Asia, that of the Khwārezm-Shāhs, was moving through Persia and threatening Iraq; at one point, the Khwārezm-Shāh Moḥammad seems to have toyed with the idea of putting an ʿAlid on the caliphal throne. The danger was such that the appearance of Genghis Khan's Mongols in Central Asia in 1217 was not unwelcome news to the caliph, relieved that Khwārezmian pressure in the west would now be relaxed; certain later Muslim historians allege that he deliberately incited the Mongols against the Shāh. An-Nāṣir sought to buttress his personal authority by becoming patron of the *futūwah*, or chivalric orders of Islām, using these organizations as a basis for bringing both Sunnī and moderate Shīʿite princes together in an informal union under his own leadership; in this regard, a striking success of his was the return to the orthodox fold in 1211–12 of the Ismāʿīlī Grand Master of the Assassins of Alamūt in northern Persia.

Mongol invasion

An-Nāsir weathered the storm of the first wave of Mongol invasions, but the last ʿAbbāsid of Baghdad, al-Mustaʿṣim (1242–58), was less fortunate. He was unable to ward off, by diplomacy or any other means, the second wave of Mongol onslaughts under Hülegü Khan, and in 1258 the Mongols sacked Baghdad and murdered the Caliph, thus extinguishing the ʿAbbāsid line there. A few years later, the Mamlūk Turkish sultan in Egypt invited a scion of the ʿAbbāsid family to establish himself in Cairo as spiritual head of Islām, but members of this new line of Cairo ʿAbbāsids were puppets and complete nonentities, and the dynasty was ended for all time when the Ottomans invaded Egypt in 1517. The Ottomans eventually styled themselves caliphs as well as sultans, but there is no truth in the story that became current in the 19th century that the last ʿAbbāsid had formally transferred his office to Sultan Selim in 1517.

ECONOMIC AND SOCIAL LIFE UNDER THE ʿABBASIDS

The medieval Islāmic world had an almost closed economy, producing for itself all the essentials for nourishment and comfort of life, with the exception of certain luxury articles imported from outside, such as slaves from Central Asia, Europe, and black Africa; furs from Siberia; and some spices and other tropical products from farther east. The strength of the Islāmic economy is attested by the vigour of city life, with large concentrations of people in Cairo, Baghdad, and Damascus and a network of smaller urban centres, and by the flourishing agricultural lands of the Fertile Crescent, the Nile Valley, Syria, and Mesopotamia, together with the oases of North Africa, Persia, and Central Asia. Only this richness, in the face of frequent natural disasters, such as floods and earthquakes, and in the face of such human interference as the tramplings of armies and the excessive mulcting of people for taxes, explains the resilience and continuity in Islāmic life. It also provides a key to the paradox that, in the ʿAbbāsid Caliphate, economic and cultural progress were not necessarily correlated with political expansion or integration of the state. It was the 10th century, the age of caliphal decline and disintegration, that was characterized by the Swiss orientalist Adam Mez as that which witnessed the social and cultural "renaissance of Islām." In this period, provincial centres for cultural activity and economic production came to replace the more centralized pattern of early ʿAbbāsid times, but without any overall deterioration in the quality of life and the level of achievement.

10th-century "renaissance"

The economy. It was not that this economic florescence of the caliphate was based on the exploitation of slave labour. With the advent of the ʿAbbāsids, the great conquests slowed down and finally ceased. Since Muslims could not in theory be enslaved, slaves had to be imported from outside the Islāmic world and, consequently, commanded high prices. Moreover, their main use was as domestic slaves and, from the 9th century onward, as elite troops. The only place where large-scale agricultural slavery was known was in lower Iraq, where Negro slaves were employed to remove the topsoil and desalinate and denitrify the earth. This region was the epicentre of the Zanj revolt of 869–883 (see above). Yet this was not a rebellion against the institution of slavery as such; the Zanj themselves had their own slaves, as had the egalitarian Qarmaṭians of eastern Arabia.

Among the regions of the caliphate, the fertile and densely populated Nile Valley and the Euphrates–Tigris basin stand out as the most intensely cultivated ones. Egypt had the advantages of reliable harvests from the Nile floods, a centralized bureaucratic tradition to direct agricultural operations, and excellent river and sea transport. Hence, the Egyptian farmers (*fellahin*) produced the sinews of war for dynasties such as the Ṭūlūnids and Fāṭimids, together with a normal surplus for export. But it was the richness of Mesopotamia, what was known as the Sawād, or "black region" (of dark-coloured vegetation, contrasted with the dazzling whiteness of the desert), that for long gave the caliphate such a firm financial base and supplied the populous capital, Baghdad, with its produce. Here, as everywhere in the Islāmic world, the availability of water was the key to life, and a highly complex system of irrigation canals and hydraulic machinery underlay the prosperity of the Sawād. "Bringing land to life" by irrigating and populating it was a traditional duty of caliphs and governors. Unfortunately, from the 10th century onward, the Fertile Crescent suffered from the incursions of nomads (Bedouins and, later, Turkmen) who cared nothing for agriculture or irrigation systems; and the political decline of the caliphate, with a drying up of its financial resources, must have adversely affected agriculture in Iraq. But it was probably long-term economic and cultural change in the Levant that accounted for the reversion to desert, during the early ʿAbbāsid period, of certain formerly flourishing oases in the Syrian and Iraq deserts (settlements whose surviving buildings were for long erroneously believed to be "hunting palaces" of the caliphs).

The wealth of Mesopotamia

The products of Islāmic agriculture were as diverse as the topographical and climatic divisions of the Islāmic world. On the whole, the staples of Muslim diet were bread made from wheat or barley and milk, rather than the rice eaten by peoples further east, and cereals were grown in such regions as the plains of North Africa, Egypt, Syria, and northern Iraq. Rice, however, could be grown in damp and low-lying places, such as the Jordan Valley, lower Iraq, and the Caspian coastlands. Lower Iraq and eastern Arabia were also noted for their dates, of which hundreds of varieties were enumerated, and Syria for its olives and its fruits. Sugarcane had been introduced to the Persian Gulf region from India; Khuzistan, the Jordan Valley, and the Syrian littoral were the main centres where this highly prized plant was grown (it was, of course, to be passed on to Europe at the time of the Crusades). A wide range of vegetables and fruit was grown almost everywhere. Fish was less a staple of life than a delicacy, but the coasts of Arabia and the great rivers did provide fish extensively, although no curing and preserving industry on the northern European scale arose. The existence of easy communications by land and, especially, by sea and river and the needs of urban centres of consumption favoured trade in products that were especially desirable and not immediately perishable. In al-Wāthiq's caliphate, melons were exported from Khwārezm (Khwārazm) in Central Asia all the way to Baghdad in leaden containers packed with snow. Coveted varieties of dates were exported from the Persian Gulf coastlands to more temperate parts of the Middle East, where dates would not grow, while North African dates were sent across the Sahara to pay for slaves and gold from the Niger basin.

The industrial raw materials of the Islāmic world, such as metals, minerals, timber, and building stone, were distributed unevenly and were to be found mainly in the mountainous fringes. As in ancient times, the lack of iron and shortage of timber for fuel and building continued to be the two great bottlenecks hampering technological advance, but the converse of this was the stimulation of internal trade in these commodities. The metal-rich Iranian and Armenian highlands and the Atlas Mountain region of North Africa provided valuable metals, such as silver and mercury, as well as iron and copper; but it was still worthwhile in 964 for the metal-hungry Qarmaṭians of Arabia to carry back with them iron from ar-Raqqah on the upper Euphrates, including the town gates and the shopkeepers' weights.

The availability through trade of these raw materials and the fact that cotton, flax, wool, and silk were produced in abundance in several parts of the Islāmic world favoured small-scale industrial production in the towns and villages, above all of textiles, cloth, and carpets. Almost every town of note had its own specialty here, as the English names of certain types of cloth bear witness; *e.g.*, damask from Damascus, muslin from Mosul, dimity conceivably from Damietta, in northern Egypt. The manufacturer or artisan was often a petty trader also, the markets being centres for both production and retailing. Manufacturing was thus essentially small-scale. The state intervened to organize large-scale production only in cases such as that of the *ṭirāz*, gold-embroidered cloth for ceremonial and official usage. Groups of merchants trading on a larger scale, with ample capital resources, did, however, exist from middle ʿAbbāsid times onward, when the high level of consumption and luxury could support long-distance trading operations. Islām had begun in the mercantile centre of Mecca, and the merchant was an honoured figure in Islāmic society. In addition to extensive internal caravan traffic converging on cities like Baghdad, there were routes into the little-known pagan lands of Siberia, northern India, and sub-Saharan Africa. The volume of Islāmic coins of the 9th and 10th centuries, amounting to hundreds of thousands, found in Russia, the Baltic regions, and even Iceland testifies to the existence of steady trade connections between the northern fringes of the Islāmic world and inner Eurasia and eastern Europe; here, the most prized products were furs, hides, honey, wax, and, above all, slaves.

Absence of large-scale production

If available, sea transport was in many ways less hazardous than land travel, where brigandage, tolls, and other vexations were frequent. The products of the Far East were tapped by Arab and Persian sailors in the earliest Islāmic period, for in the 8th century there was a flourishing Muslim colony in Canton, although, thereafter, Malaysia tended to be the limit of Muslim navigation. But the products of China continued to arrive; much Chinese porcelain of the T'ang dynasty (618–907) has been found in the ruins of Sāmarrāʾ, which was occupied for only five or six decades in the 9th century. Commerce in the Mediterranean came to be shared with the Christians, especially the traders of Venice and Amalfi. The Cairo Geniza records, those of one of the local Jewish communities, covering essentially the Fāṭimid period and just beyond, show much of the trade between Egypt and Tunisia in the hands of Jewish merchants. As well as being entrepreneurs, Jews were at this time acting as something like central bankers to certain Islāmic rulers. In the financial crisis of the ʿAbbāsids in the early 10th century, the caliph's ministers had recourse to Iraqi Jewish financiers; and the Fāṭimid caliphate owed some of its financial stability to the availability of capital and skilled financial advice from Jewish and Christian sources.

ʿAbbāsid society. Social life and organization under the caliphate was in one respect controlled by the state but in others remarkably uncircumscribed. The state or ruling institution was the chief corporate body in Islāmic society; there was no formally constituted church, as in medieval Europe, and the existence of lesser corporate bodies within the state was discouraged. Hence, in the economic field, although practitioners of a particular skill or craft might have their own quarter or market and a loose association for common interests, they had—at least in the first four or five centuries of Islām—no corporative organization comparable to the European trade guilds, with their initiation ceremonies and hierarchies of membership. On the wider plane, this meant that the Islāmic cities, despite a populousness and richness far exceeding that of Dark Age European towns, never evolved corporate identities of their own. Accordingly, there is nothing in the history of the caliphate corresponding to the evolution of the Italian trading republics or the Flemish communes; the state could brook no rivals.

On the other hand, the ordinary Muslim was left very much to himself, provided that he paid the requisite taxes and avoided heretical or seditious activities; the caliph or provincial ruler might be a despot, but his regime was not totalitarian. The non-Muslim communities, Jews, Christians, and Zoroastrians, normally subsisted in peace, provided that they made themselves as unobtrusive as possible and obeyed the official heads of their communities, who were normally confirmed in office by the Muslim ruler. Furthermore, despite the disapproval of pious Muslims, Christians and Jews continued to fill high financial and secretarial offices in the bureaucracy of the ʿAbbāsids and of such dynasties as the Fāṭimids, because of their expertise and probity.

Treatment of non-Muslims

The Bedouins of the Arabian, Syrian, and North African deserts performed certain functions for society, such as escorting caravans and supplying the products of their pastoral way of life, but they were rightly regarded by the sedentaries as predatory nuisances, outside the mainstream of Islāmic civilization and life. After the Arab conquests, the most active elements among the Arabs migrated to the garrison cities of the occupied territories, and the Arabian peninsula became a backwater. Now, with the general conversion of the indigenous peoples in the conquered lands, a population evolved in the ʿAbbāsid period that was culturally and religiously homogeneous, if not ethnically so. It was in the social field that Arabic racial superiority lasted longest, as shown by the *shuʿūbīyah* movement among the non-Arabs (see below).

Islāmic civilization came to be based essentially on the towns, which flourished, as has been noted, during the ʿAbbāsid period; indeed, it came to be tacitly assumed that the good Muslim life could be properly lived only in a town. The villager lived in a very closed world, at little above subsistence level and hence at the mercy of many natural catastrophes. Rural prosperity depended on a strong government for maintaining irrigation and other essential services, for suppressing banditry, and for protecting the peasantry from exploitation by local landlords. The decay of ʿAbbāsid power in the 10th century had a deleterious effect on the agriculture of Iraq. The financial straits of the caliphs and of their successors the Būyids and Seljuqs compelled them to pay their servants in grants of land (*iqṭāʿ*s), so that the central government lost its rights of supervision over the land, and the grantee was left free to exploit his estates to the hilt. The town dwellers were somewhat more secure; hence, urban populations were always being swollen by runaway peasants. In the towns there resided the ruling class of soldiers and officials and the religious classes of *ʿulamāʾ* and lawyers. Below these were the merchants and then the artisans and proletariat, a socially unstable group that, in many Islāmic towns, was likely to erupt periodically under the banners of social or religious faction: the frequent riots

Primacy of urban life

of Sunnīs and Shīʿites in Baghdad are a typical instance of this. Islāmic society was, thus, a rich mosaic of ethnic and social groupings whose positions in life and whose characteristic skills were often handed down hereditarily. All this tended to perpetuate the status quo and to freeze existing patterns of behaviour. Yet in some ways there was less class consciousness and more social mobility than in feudal Europe. A slave guard in a ruler's service might enjoy a high rank in society, independent of his technically servile status. In any case, Muslims were always very conscious of the transience of worldly things: the vizier or even caliph of today might be a pauper tomorrow, while the humble coppersmith might rise to become head of a great military empire, as happened with Yaʿqūb ebn Leys̄ in Seistan (see above).

CULTURAL LIFE UNDER THE ʿABBASIDS

It was under the ʿAbbāsids that Islāmic civilization achieved its full flowering. The Umayyad period had been one of external conquest and of internal sectarian and tribal strife; while the religious institution was beginning to take shape, and the first steps in the systematization of the Sharīʿah, the body of Islāmic theological doctrines and legal practices, were made during that time, it was only under the ʿAbbāsids that these processes came to maturity. After 750 there was, broadly speaking, external peace, and, though sectarian violence continued to erupt in various parts of the caliphate, a general consensus of thought and belief emerged among Muslims, at least among those of the Sunnī majority. The racial arrogance of the Arabs was now less of an obstacle to the assimilation of non-Arab ideas and practices, for the victory of the ʿAbbāsids had ended the Arabs' monopoly of political and military power, if not of social privilege. The characteristic ʿAbbāsid culture was to be an amalgam of Arab, Persian, and Greek elements. On the material plane, the economic buoyancy of the caliphate produced a leisured class of courtiers and urban bourgeoisie who could patronize and enjoy literature and music. The political decay of the later 9th century and after did not affect adversely this cultural florescence. The republic of science and letters was unhindered by political boundaries and probably benefitted from the existence of a welter of rival courts. It is in this period that are found two familiar figures, the sectarian missionary, or propagandist, and the wandering scholar obeying the Prophet's injunction, "Seek knowledge, even as far as China."

Religion. In Umayyad times, there had been signs of increasing religiosity among the caliphs and of a growing influence of the religious classes; the first executions for heresy took place in the early 8th century. Under the ʿAbbāsids, the religious institution became an influential body, comprising theologians, canon lawyers, and traditionists (*i.e.*, those concerned with the handing down and evaluation of the traditions or sayings of the Prophet and the early Muslims), although it never became strong enough to challenge the caliphs for secular power, as did the papacy in medieval Europe in regard to the emperors; respect for the vicegerents of the Prophet and the fear of anarchy were always uppermost. The founders of the four great rites of Islāmic law, which survive today, all flourished in the later 8th and 9th centuries; namely, Abū Ḥanīfah (died 767), founder of the Ḥanafī rite; Mālik ibn Anas (died 795), founder of the Mālikī rite; Muḥammad ash-Shāfiʿī (died 820), founder of the Shāfiʿī rite; and Aḥmad ibn Ḥanbal (died 855), founder of the Ḥanbalī rite. Generally speaking, the Mālikī and Ḥanbalī rites represented a more conservative interpretation of the bases of Islāmic law, the Qur'ān and the *sunnah*, or example of the Prophet; but the differences among the rites were at the outset geographical rather than ideological. Thus, the Mālikī rite represented the custom of Medina and the rugged simplicity of life in the Arabian peninsula; the Ḥanafī rite represented the more flexible practice of Iraq, where society and institutions were more complex and of greater antiquity than those of the Hejaz. In any case, there was no unified, agreed system of basic legal principles; the different rites evolved piecemeal according to the needs of the time and place.

The four great rites of Islāmic law

Islāmic religion in the earliest period was more a body of rituals and practices than one of set beliefs and creeds. But questions of faith had already evoked discussion and dissension in the Umayyad period, as seen in the birth of such sectarian movements as Khārijism. By the end of the 9th century, the Khārijites had ceased to be a vital force, but the Shīʿite schism was more lasting and shows how persistent has been the interweaving in Islām of religion with political and social questions. The split with the Sunnī majority revolved round the question of the caliph-*imām*, with the Shīʿah representing the authoritarian view. For them, the imamate was a necessity for the community, not a matter of convenience, and the imamate resided in the pure and immaculate descendants of ʿAlī, who had been designated by Muḥammad himself. It may be that the emotions engendered around the person of ʿAlī and his martyred progeny provided an element of faith for some Muslims lacking in the rather matter-of-fact Sunnī form of Islām. The revolts of the ʿAlids and their persecution by the ʿAbbāsids have been noted above; but it is worth mentioning that the moderate Shīʿites often managed to live at peace with the orthodox majority and that many of the Shīʿite *imāms* themselves, down to the disappearance of the 12th one, lived respected and unmolested lives. It was the extremists, like the Ismāʿīlīs (from whom sprang the later Assassins) and the Qarmaṭians, who abandoned the apolitical stance of the *imāms* in favour of direct political action, who inevitably brought down upon themselves the full wrath of the Sunnī state. The mainstream of moderate Shīʿism also produced such a commanding figure as the Aristotelian and Neoplatonist philosopher-theologian al-Fārābī (died 950), called "the second teacher" (Aristotle being the first), who ended his days among the Shīʿite Ḥamdānids of Aleppo in northern Syria.

Growth of theology

With the consolidation and elaboration of the Sunnī, the majority form of Islām, this last now acquired a formidable body of theological doctrine. The challenge of other faiths, such as Christianity, had some part in this process, but most significant was the influence of Greek philosophy and logical methods, leading to the enunciation of a systematic Islāmic theology (*kalām*). These stimuli are all seen at work in the theological movement of the Muʿtazilah, which arose in Basra and flourished in early and middle ʿAbbāsid times, although its attitudes remained influential for several centuries afterward. The Muʿtazilah originally may have had some affiliations with the ʿAbbāsid revolution. They soon showed themselves zealous in defense of the faith against outside religions, such as Christianity and Manichaean Dualism, and, in constructing this defense, they defined Islāmic dogmas in Greek theological terms. Politically, they seemed to have aimed at organizing moderate support for the ʿAbbāsid caliphate by broadening its bases of support and compromising on certain details; hence, they favoured an accommodation with the Shīʿah. The caliphs of the period from al-Ma'mūn to al-Wāthiq (813–847) were all enthusiastic patrons of the Muʿtazilah, and they endeavoured to make Muʿtazilite views generally accepted. This provoked a reaction of the orthodox, disturbed by the introduction of Hellenistic methods into sacred theology, and this reaction was symbolized by Aḥmad ibn Ḥanbal's stand in defense of the orthodox doctrine of the uncreated Qur'ān. Al-Mutawakkil restored the primacy of orthodoxy, and the Muʿtazilah henceforth played no significant role in practical affairs.

The orthodox reaction showed the strength of traditional Islām among the masses in Baghdad and other cities. Ḥanbalism was not mere obscurantism: it simply refused to admit the validity of rational arguments in matters of faith, views so dogmatically asserted by the Muʿtazilah. Other groups in orthodox Islām, such as the Ḥanafīs, were also anti-Muʿtazilite, and the 9th and early 10th centuries saw the composition of several Ḥanafī creeds. The noted theologian as-Ashʿarī (died 935/936) adhered to Ḥanbalism, combatted the arguments of the Muʿtazilah, and was, above all, concerned to uphold the sovereignty of God, but he did admit the use, with due care, of rational methods; his great service, it has been said, was to utilize the basic elements of Greek thought without compromising the central dogmas of Sunnī Islām. The outstanding figure in medieval Islāmic thought—according to some judges, the greatest Muslim after Muḥammad—was al-Ghazālī (died 1111), who lived at a time when the ʿAbbāsid caliphate was beginning to throw off Seljuq control and who was, above all, concerned to show that the ecstasies of the Ṣūfī mystics (whose movement was to evolve into definite orders in the course of the 12th century) could be harmonized with faithful observance of the external practices of the Sharīʿah. Finally, the raising of the study of the traditions of the Prophet and early Muslims (the *ḥadīth*s) to the level of a science should be noted as an important aspect of the consolidation of orthodoxy in the middle ʿAbbāsid period. Such figures as al-Bukhārī (died 870) and Muslim (died 875) used critical methods to sift the vast corpus of traditions that had accumulated since early times and to eliminate the patently spurious.

Greek and Iranian influences. The branches of knowledge mentioned above made up some of the native "Arab sciences"; paralleling their development was the growth of *adab* literature and what were termed the "foreign sciences," in effect, the Greco-Persian elements in Islāmic culture. The ʿAbbāsids' dependence on Persian soldiers and on a class of Persian officials and secretaries (the *kuttāb*) led to the adoption of many Persian administrative practices and literary modes into Islām. A pioneer figure in this movement was the Persian Ibn Muqaffaʿ (died *c.* 756), who produced his *Kalīlah wa-Dimnah* from a Middle Persian text going back to the Indian *Panchatantra* collection of animal fables and who also made an Arabic version of the Persian royal chronicle, the *Book of Kings*. Gradually there grew up a body of polite learning, called *adab*, cultivated by persianizing officials and the leisured classes, and this speedily became recognized as a necessary part of a polished education. Virtually nothing was alien to *adab;* the writings of the polygraph al-Jāḥiẓ of Basra (died 869) show him to have been interested in almost every aspect of life, from psychology and anthropology to politics and natural history. It was the Persians who were in the forefront of the Shuʿūbīyah, the "movement of the nations," in the 9th century, in protest against the cultural and social pretensions of the Arabs, especially now that their political and military dominance was a thing of the past. This battle of the books was certainly not, on the Shuʿūbī side, anti-Islāmic. But the Persian and Greek Shuʿūbīs did quote the glories of their past civilizations, compared with the miserable desert origins of the Arabs, and thus, from a claim to equality with the Arabs, they soon passed to a claim of superiority. The defenders of the Arabs stemmed in considerable measure from the scholars of Arabic grammar and lexicography, with their great schools of Basra, Kūfah, and Baghdad, for the Arabic language was regarded as the foundation stone of Arab ideals. Yet surprisingly enough, some of the staunchest defenders of the Arab cause were themselves descendants of Persian clients, or *mawālī*, among them the writer Ibn Qutaybah (died 889). The echoes of the Shuʿūbīyah controversy lingered on long after this; in the later 11th century, a Spanish Muslim Shuʿūbī, Ibn Garcia, wrote against Arab pretensions.

Arab-Persian debate

The Greek heritage showed itself primarily in the fields of philosophy and science and was introduced to the Islāmic world through the activities of schools of translators in Syria, Iraq, and Alexandria, many of whom were Christian; indeed, many Greek texts came into Arabic thirdhand via Syriac. Alone among the infidel countries, Byzantium was profoundly respected by the Muslims as the inheritor of ancient Greek civilization. But it was Greek philosophy, science, and mathematics, and not imaginative literature and history, that interested the Arabs; in these latter fields, Persian influence remained paramount. The translation movement received an impetus from the caliph al-Maʾmūn when he founded his "House of Wisdom," undoubtedly in imitation of the old medical academy of Gondēshapūr (Jundīshāpūr) in Khuzistan. Notable among Nestorian Christian translators was Ḥunayn ibn Isḥāq al-ʿIbādī (died 873), at one time the private physician to al-Mutawakkil and reputedly the translator of the medical works of Galen, Dioscorides, and Hippocrates, as well as of several works of Aristotle and of the Old Testament. The pagan community of Ḥarrān in northern Syria carried on the traditions of Greek astronomy and mathematics, and Thābit ibn Qurrah (died 901) and his family provided, among much else, translations of Archimedes and Apollonius of Perga. Eventually, a considerable body of Aristotle's works, including, however, many apocryphal ones, was available to the Muslims, and Aristotle became a dominant influence in Islāmic philosophy. This was to prove of incalculable significance in the 12th and 13th centuries, when knowledge of Aristotle and other Greek authors was to be passed to medieval Europe through Arabic intermediacy.

Translations of Greek texts

On the basis of translations such as these, Muslim scholars worked on the harmonization of Greek philosophy with Islāmic ideas and began to make their own original contributions to knowledge, above all in the fields of astronomy, mathematics, alchemy, and medicine. Al-Maʾmūn, again, was interested in problems of astronomy and mensuration, and, from a base on the plains of northern Syria, his scholars achieved a surprisingly accurate figure for the circumference of the earth. Al-Kindī of Baghdad (died *c.* 870) won for himself the title "philosopher of the Arabs," and it was he who began the assimilation of Aristotelian and Neoplatonist philosophical ideas, but he was equally brilliant as an astronomer and theoretician of music. This tradition of the scientific polymath was continued by such figures as ar-Rāzī, or Rhazes (died in the 920s or 930s), outstanding as a medical clinician, whose medical encyclopaedia, the *Kitāb al-ḥāwī*, was translated into Latin in the 13th century; and Ibn Sīnā, or Avicenna (died 1037), who produced two great encyclopaedias, one on science and philosophy, the *Kitāb al-shifāʾ* ("Book of Healing"), with a basically Neoplatonist standpoint, and his *Qānūn fī al-ṭibb* (*Canon of Medicine*), the standard medical textbook in later medieval Europe. The views of men like Avicenna easily made them suspected of heresy or even infidelity by the pious; and the only attempt to make an encyclopedic survey of all branches of knowledge was undertaken in the collection of epistles by an Ismāʿīlī group in 10th-century Basra, the Brethren of Purity.

Interaction of Greek and Islāmic thought

Arab literature. The ʿAbbāsid period is generally considered to be the golden age of Arabic literature. By 750, the desert ideals that had inspired the work of the pre-Islāmic and Umayyad poets were becoming anachronistic; the audience for literature was now largely one of city dwellers, who lived far from the harshnesses of desert life and did not particularly want to be reminded of the early Arab past. Only for antiquarian-minded grammarians and lexicographers did poetry cast in the ancient mold still have attraction. A "new wave" in poetry is clearly discernible in the late 8th and 9th centuries. The penetration of Islāmic religious ideals is apparent in the religiously inspired verse of Abū al-ʿAtāhiya (died 825 or 826). The libertine Abū Nuwās, drinking companion of Hārūn ar-Rashīd, developed the earlier erotic poetry that had sprung up in the pleasure haunts of Medina and the Hejaz into a more refined but equally lascivious verse, much of it being homosexual in tone. Abū Tammām (died 845 or 846), compiler of, among other things, a famous anthology of Arabic verse, the *Ḥamāsa*, consciously proclaimed his poetic superiority to the ancients, as did Ibn ar-Rūmī (died 896) shortly afterward.

In the following century appeared al-Mutanabbī, perhaps the greatest of all Arab poets, whose panache, lauding of the heroic virtues and sententiousness alike, have commended him to all succeeding generations of Arabs. Poets such as these could not have flourished without the patronage and favour of contemporary rulers and governors, yet their verse had an appeal beyond that of this limited class of great men and officials and of the scholars; the verses of al-Mutanabbī, for example, spread, within his own lifetime, through popular acclaim to all

The work of the poet al-Mutanabbī

corners of the Islāmic world, and many of their phrases quickly became proverbial.

With the stimulus of the ideal of the *adīb*, the man with an all-round education, Arabic prose takes shape during the ʿAbbāsid period, beginning with the translations and epistles of Ibn al-Muqaffaʿ but best exemplified in the many-sided work of al-Jāḥiẓ, with his acute observation of the quirks of human nature. The danger of the *adab* style lay in its being pushed too far into preciousness and artificiality. Signs of this trend are observable in the spread of rhymed prose instead of the straightforward, almost conversational style of a writer like al-Jāḥiẓ; and, toward the end of the 10th century, there appeared the highly artificial and stylized dramatic sketch, the *maqāmah*, popularized by Badīʿ az-Zamān al-Hamadhānī (died 1008) and perfected by al-Ḥarīrī (died 1122).

Literature, rather than painting and sculpture, has always been the typical expression of the Arab creative spirit. It was not that Islām absolutely forbade representation of living forms, as is clearly demonstrated by some of the murals in the Umayyad hunting palaces and the ʿAbbāsid palaces at Sāmarrāʾ and by the representations of rulers on coins and medals; it was only later that a hostility to figural art developed, especially in the Arab parts of Islām. The desire to give concrete expression to the creative impulse expressed itself rather in such forms as ceramics and metalwork; in calligraphy as a work of art, not merely as a writing technique; and, of course, in architecture, where abstract decorative motifs in stucco, glass mosaic, etc., were widely used in mosques, madrasas, and palaces. In ʿAbbāsid architecture—as seen in a typical selection from its surviving monuments, such as the Sāmarrāʾ ruins (9th century), the mosque of Aḥmad ibn Ṭūlūn in Cairo (late 9th century), and the recently reconstructed Mustanṣirīyah *madrasah* in Baghdad (early 13th century)—there was a basic functional severity much more emphatic than in contemporary Byzantine architecture or that of medieval Europe a little later, yet a severity at the same time relieved by this tasteful decoration. The eastward orientation of the ʿAbbāsid caliphate after 750 had its echoes in architecture also, in that indigenous traditions of Iraqi and Sāsānid Persian architecture came to the fore; but there was an artistic regression in the use of building materials, as compared with the solid-stone Syrian Umayyad structures: ʿAbbāsid buildings of a site such as Sāmarrāʾ were run up hastily from fired and even from stucco-covered, sun-dried brick.

BIBLIOGRAPHY. PHILIP K. HITTI, *History of the Arabs, from the Earliest Times to the Present*, 8th ed. (1963), a detailed, standard work, good for the basic facts and for cultural, artistic, and scientific topics; BERNARD LEWIS, *The Arabs in History*, 4th ed. (1966), brief but full of insight and penetrating interpretations; JOHN J. SAUNDERS, *A History of Medieval Islam* (1965), sets out, in a very readable fashion, the results of recent researches; G.E. VON GRUNEBAUM, *Der Islam in seiner klassischen Epoche, 622–1258* (1963; Eng. trans., *Classical Islam: A History, 600–1258*, 1970), a stimulating interpretation of Islām as a civilization, with special emphasis on the basic cultural and intellectual themes; D. and J. SOURDEL, *La Civilisation de l'Islam classique* (1968), an outstanding synthesis of the latest information, including sections on political history, intellectual life, and economic and social history, this last section being especially valuable in the absence of any other adequate single work on the topic—also includes 224 excellently-reproduced plates and a descriptive bibliography; P.M. HOLT, A.K.S. LAMBTON, and BERNARD LEWIS (eds.), *The Cambridge History of Islam*, vol. 1, *The Central Islamic Lands*, vol. 2, *The Further Islamic Lands: Islamic Society and Civilization* (1971), a massive, detailed treatment of the whole of Islāmic history—parts 1 (on the history of the caliphate) and 8 (on culture) are relevant; CLIFFORD E. BOSWORTH, *The Islamic Dynasties: A Chronological and Genealogical Handbook* (1967), a reference guide to Islāmic dynasties, with tables of rulers and their dates, together with a brief history of each treated; REUBEN LEVY, *The Social Structure of Islam* (1957), good for social life, political administration, and military organization; CARLETON S. COON, *Caravan: The Story of the Middle East*, rev. ed. (1958), an anthropologist's treatment of the basic themes of Middle Eastern life that contains material relevant to social and economic conditions under the caliphate; THOMAS W. ARNOLD, *The Caliphate* (1924), describes the evolution and history of the institution; M.A. SHABAN, *Islamic History A.D. 600–750 (A.H. 132): A New Interpretation* (1971), a recent book that deals specifically with the Umayyad period, based on a re-reading and re-examination of the original sources; J. OBERMANN, "Early Islam," in R.C. DENTAN (ed.), *The Idea of History in the Ancient Near East* (1955), emphasizes the continuity of Arab life in the Umayyad period with the tribal past and examines the birth of historical writing among the Muslims; C.H. BECKER, "The Expansion of the Saracens," in *The Cambridge Mediaeval History*, vol. 2 (1913), a lucid and informative account of the Arab conquests, carrying the story down to the campaigns against Sicily and Italy in the 10th and 11th centuries; ADAM MEZ, *Die Renaissance des Islams* (1922; Eng. trans., *The Renaissance of Islam*, 1937), a classic on the cultural and social life of the caliphate in the 10th century, abounds in curious and recondite items of information from the Muslim sources; W. MONTGOMERY WATT, *A History of Islamic Spain* (1965), a general account of the eight centuries of independent Arab rule in Spain—contains several good plates of Spanish Islāmic art and architecture; R.A. NICHOLSON, *A Literary History of the Arabs*, 2nd ed. (1930, reprinted 1962), weaves the development of Arabic literature into the political events affecting it; W. MONTGOMERY WATT, *Islamic Philosophy and Theology* (1962) and *Islamic Political Thought* (1968); and N.J. COULSON, *A History of Islamic Law* (1964), three concise guides to these subjects; HENRY G. FARMER, *A History of Arabian Music to the XIIIth Century* (1929, reprinted 1967), technical information on music, and also much on the role of music and dancing in social life under the caliphs; D. TALBOT RICE, *Islamic Art* (1965), a general treatment of the subject, well illustrated; K.A.C. CRESWELL, *A Short Account of Early Muslim Architecture* (1958), deals with Umayyad and with ʿAbbāsid architecture.

(C.E.B.)

Calligraphy

Calligraphy is writing as an art. The term derives from the Greek words for "good" or "beautiful" and for "writing" or "drawing" and refers to what writing masters called the art of fair writing. It implies a sure knowledge of the correct forms of letters—*i.e.*, the conventional signs by which language can be communicated—and the skill to inscribe them with such ordering of the various parts and harmony of proportions that the cultivated, knowing eye will recognize the composition as a work of art. In East Asia, calligraphy by long and exacting tradition is considered a major art, equal to painting. In Western culture the simpler Greek and Latin-derived alphabets and the spread of literacy tend to make handwriting theoretically "everybody's art," though in a few instances, especially since the Renaissance, it either has aspired to or attained the status of calligraphy. For the study of ancient Greek and Latin handwriting as a discipline of historical research, see PALEOGRAPHY. (Ra.N.)

This article is divided into the following sections:

I. European handwriting and calligraphy
  Greek handwriting
  Latin handwriting
II. Aramaic, Hebrew, and Arabic handwriting and calligraphy
  Early Semitic and Hebrew writing
  Spread of Aramaic to the Near East and Asia
III. East Asian handwriting and calligraphy
  Chinese calligraphy
  Korean calligraphy
  Japanese calligraphy

I. European handwriting and calligraphy

GREEK HANDWRITING

Origins to the 8th century AD. The oldest Greek writing, syllabic signs scratched with a stylus on sun-dried clay, is that of the Linear B tablets found in Knossos, Pylos, and Mycenae (1400–1200 BC). Alphabetic writing, in use before the end of the 8th century BC, is first found in a scratched inscription on a jug awarded as a prize in Athens. The consensus is that the Homeric poems were written down not later than this time; certainly from the time of the first known lyric poet of ancient Greece, Archilochus (7th century BC), individuals committed their works to writing. But the vehicles of literary writing have perished. Scratchings on pottery or metal and then texts deliberately cut in

Papyrus from Dervéni, Macedonia, 4th century BC (Archaeological Museum, Thessaloníki, Greece).
By courtesy of the Thessaloniki Museum, Greece

bronze or marble or painted on vases are, until *c.* 350 BC, the only immediate evidence for the way the Greeks wrote, and their study is normally treated as the province of epigraphy. A find in 1962 at Dervéni, in Macedonia, of a carbonized roll of papyrus (Archaeological Museum, Thessaloníki, Greece) offers the oldest and only example of Greek handwriting preserved in the Greek peninsula (end of the 4th century BC). From then until the 4th century AD, there are countless texts, especially on papyrus. Found in Egypt, and, with a few exceptions, written there, these texts have given a firm foundation for knowledge. From outside Egypt there is a Greek library buried in Herculaneum, AD 79; and papyri and parchments from Owrāmān, Kurdistan, 1st century BC; from Doura-Europus on the Euphrates, 3rd century BC to 3rd century AD; from Nessana, 6th century AD; and from the Dead Sea area (Qumrān, 1st centuries BC and AD; Murabbaʿat and ʿEn Gedi, 2nd century AD). A number of original vellum manuscripts have survived from the 4th century AD onward, preserved in libraries such as the monastery of St. Catherine at Mt. Sinai. These materials of diverse origin suggest that the forms and shape of Greek handwriting were remarkably constant throughout the Greek world, wherever writing was practiced and whatever the material used; within this consistent framework it is occasionally possible to distinguish local variations (as between the contract hands of 1st-century-AD Doura and of Egypt).

Oldest Greek hand-writing

Writing materials

The principal vehicles for writing were wax tablets incised with a stylus or a prepared surface of skin, such as leather and vellum, or of papyrus written on with a pen. Other surfaces—*e.g.*, broken pieces of pottery, lead, wood, and even cloth—were also used. To some extent the forms of letters were affected by the resistance of the material to the writing instrument. It is likely that the use as a pen of a hard reed, split at the tip and cut into a nib (which must be constantly sharpened), is an invention of the Greeks. Egyptian scribes used a soft reed, with which ink was brushed on.

Until about AD 300, ink was normally made of a carbon such as lampblack, mixed with gum and water, which even today retains its black lustre. After that time, because of the increasing popularity of vellum, iron inks (*e.g.*, of oak galls), better suited to vellum, tended to replace carbon. The iron inks have faded with age and often have eaten by chemical action into the vellum. Erasures could be made on wax with the blunt end of the stylus, on papyrus by wiping with a sponge; but, on vellum written in iron ink, erasures could be made only by rubbing with pumice or scraping with a knife. Texts from which a previous writing was deliberately erased to provide writing material are termed palimpsests.

Papyrus was normally sold in rolls (*volumina*) made up of 20 or 50 glued sheets: the horizontal fibres of the papyrus are placed on the inside of the roll, on which side (the recto) each gummed sheet overlaps the next when the roll is held horizontally. Leather, similarly, was for long made into rolls (the Dead Sea Scrolls). Shortly after the beginning of the Christian Era, the custom began of folding a single sheet (or several superposed sheets, a quarternion or quire) down the middle and stitching the quires into a binding case to give a book of modern form (codex, originally a set of wax tablets coupled with a thong). Tradition associated this invention with Pergamum.

Development of the book

The decisive impetus to the use of this form came from the early Christians, who deliberately chose the commercial vellum notebook (*membranae*) in which to circulate the Christian Gospels in preference to the traditional Jewish roll. Almost without exception the earliest texts of the New Testament are in codex form, even though written on papyrus, which is less able than vellum to bear repeated bending. In the 2nd century AD pagan works of literature also appeared in this format, which gained ground in the 3rd century, often in small or utility sizes. By the 4th century it became the predominant form, and codices with handsome margins, of dazzling white vellum, and of sufficient size to contain the whole Bible (*e.g.*, the Codex Sinaiticus) were being produced.

By courtesy of the trustees of the British Museum

Codex Sinaiticus (British Museum, London; Add. MS. 43725, fol. 260).

Book hands

The fundamental distinction in types of handwriting is that between book hands and documentary hands. The former, used especially for the copying of literature, aimed at clarity, regularity, and impersonality and often made an effect of beauty by their deliberate stylization. Usually they were the work of professionals, who may have multiplied copies to dictation, though ancient evidence on this subject is unreliable, and the evidence of scribal errors is equivocal (since the ancients invariably read out loud, a scribe copying by eye in solitude is likely to have pronounced the words of his exemplar). Outstanding calligraphy is not common among papyrus finds, perhaps because they are mainly provincial work. But the British Museum Bacchylides or the Bodleian

By courtesy of the curators of the Bodleian Library, Oxford

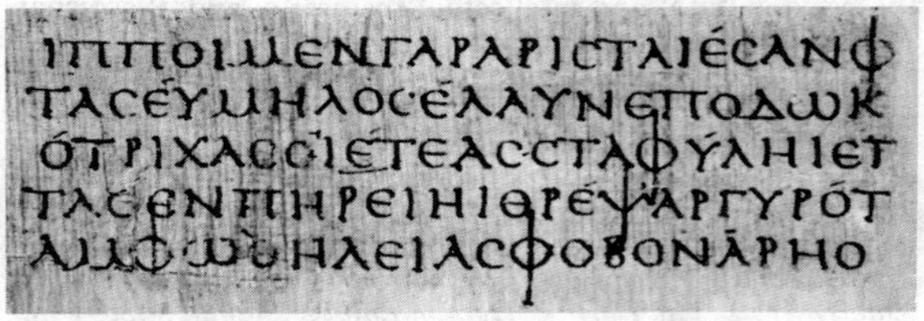

Greek book hand. Bodleian Library Homer, passage from the *Iliad*, copied in the 2nd century AD (Bodleian Library, Oxford; MS. Gr. class A.1 (P)).

Library Homer can stand comparison with any later vellum manuscript from outside Egypt. Book texts are written in separately made capitals (often called uncials, but in Greek paleography, except for the time-hallowed class of biblical uncials, the term is better avoided) in columns of writing, with ample spaces between columns and good margins at head and foot. Punctuation (usually by high dot) is minimal or completely absent; accents are inserted only in difficult poetic texts or as practice by

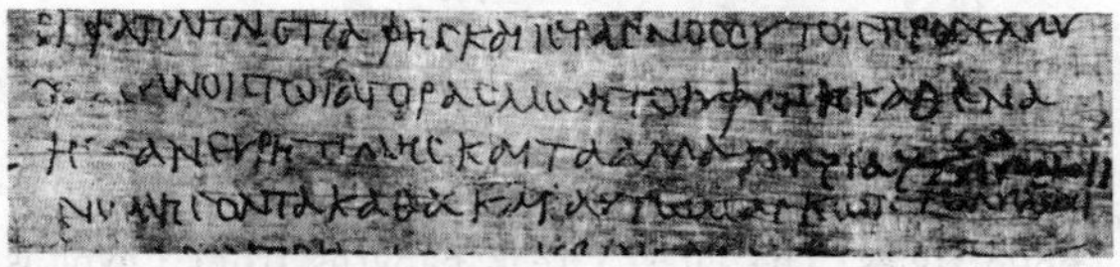

Greek documentary hand. An authorization for the sale of slaves, late 1st century AD (British Museum, London; P. Oxy. 94).

By courtesy of the trustees of the British Museum

schoolboys; and letters are not grouped into separate words.

Documentary hands

Documentary hands show a considerable range: stylized official "chancery" hands; the workaday writing of government clerks or of the street scribes who drew up wills or wrote letters to order; the idiosyncratic or nearly illiterate writing of private individuals. The scribe's aim was to write quickly, lifting his pen very little and consequently often combining several letters in a continuous stroke (a ligature); from the running action of the pen, this writing is often termed cursive. He also made frequent use of abbreviations. When the scribe was skillful in reconciling clarity and speed, such writing may have much character, even beauty; but it often degenerates into a formless, sometimes indecipherable, scrawl.

Both types of hands, in spite of the different styles they assume at different periods, show remarkable uniformity and continuity in the shapes of letters. Behind both lies an unvarying basic alphabetic form taught in the schools. The more skillful a book-hand scribe was, the harder it is to date his work. Documents in the ancient world carried a precise date; books never did. To assign dates to the latter, the paleographer takes account of their content, the archaeological context of their discovery, and technical points of book construction (*e.g.*, quires, rulings) or modes of abbreviation. But he finds of great service: (1) a stylistic comparison with those dated documentary hands that show resemblances to book hands; and (2) those cases where a roll was reused —*i.e.*, has a literary text on its recto and a dated document on its verso (in which case there is a *terminus ante quem* for the literary text, often estimated at 50 years before the date of the verso) or has a dated document on the recto and a book hand on the verso (which gives a *terminus post quem* for the literary text, not more than 25 years after the document). The number of illustrated manuscripts of this period is small; their quality is varied; and there is no agreement between specialists about the sources from which illustrations were taken.

Any historical sketch is bound to be a simplification. At certain epochs several different styles of handwriting existed simultaneously, so that there is no straight line of development. Moreover, owing to the arbitrariness of finds, generalizations are based mainly on provincial work; and, even in that, examples of book hand belonging to the 2nd century BC and the 5th century AD are still relatively rare.

Ptolemaic period. In the roll from Dervéni, Macedonia, dated on archaeological grounds to the 4th century BC, lines and letters are well spaced, and the letters carefully made in an epigraphic, or inscription, style, especially the square Ε, four-barred Σ, and arched Ω; the whole layout gives the effect of an inscription. In the Timotheus roll in Berlin (dated 350–330 BC on archaeological grounds) or in the curse of Artemisia in Vienna (4th century BC), the writing is cruder, and ω is in transition to the form that is afterward the invariable written form. Similar features can be seen in the earliest precisely dated document, a marriage contract of 311 BC. It has indeed been argued that a documentary hand of cursive type had not yet been developed and that it was a creation of the Alexandrian library. Plato, however (*Laws* 810), speaks of Athenian writing whose aim was speed; and later on, when a cursive hand had certainly been developed, documentary scribes often chose to use separate capitals.

Characteristic of its period is the contrast of size between long letters (*e.g.*,) and narrow letters (or , , or). And characteristic forms are to be seen in the letters (with its long crossbar, often with initial stroke); (upsilon) with long shallow bowl; or in three or four strokes; in three strokes; (alpha) raised off the line and its last vertical not finished; small round (with internal dot or tiny stroke); and broad epigraphic and . These same features, written with more regularity, appear in the contemporary book hand of a fragment of a Thucydides manuscript (Staats- und Universitätsbibliothek, Hamburg). In documentary cursive hands of this

By courtesy of Staats- und Universitatsbibliothek, Hamburg

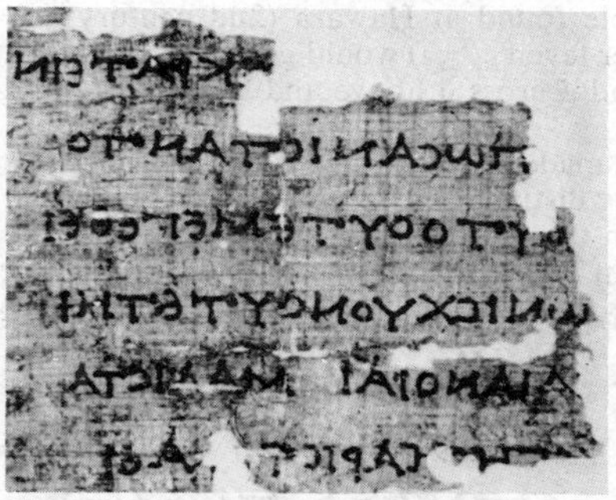

Thucydides manuscript, 3rd century BC (Staats- und Universitätsbibliothek, Hamburg; P. Hamburg 163).

period, letters seem to hang from an upper line: (alpha) often turns into a mere wedge, and (nu) lifts its second vertical above the line. In the 2nd century BC the contrast between long letters and narrow letters disappears, the writing grows rounder, and letters are often linked by ligatures at the top of their last vertical (*e.g.*,). In a loan contract of 99 BC (The John Rylands University Library of Manchester), in which capitals and cursive are mixed, this irregular

By courtesy of The John Rylands University Library of Manchester

Legal text of a loan contract, 99 BC (The John Rylands University Library of Manchester; Rylands Greek Pap. 586).

roundness is clearly seen. Note the ε with detached crossbar and the exaggerated serifs ( ) which have been elevated by some paleographers into a criterion of a special style, though in fact they are always apt to occur.

Roman period. Half a century or so passes after 30 BC before a definitely Roman manner is established. In documentary hands the tendency to roundness continues. Documentary cursive may be influenced in various ways (*e.g.*, by Latin forms such as those of *e* and *d*, or by the exaggeration of verticals practiced by chancery scribes), may lean over in either direction, or may be reduced to tiny proportions. In the 2nd century the cursive hand tends to be round and sprawling, in the 3rd century

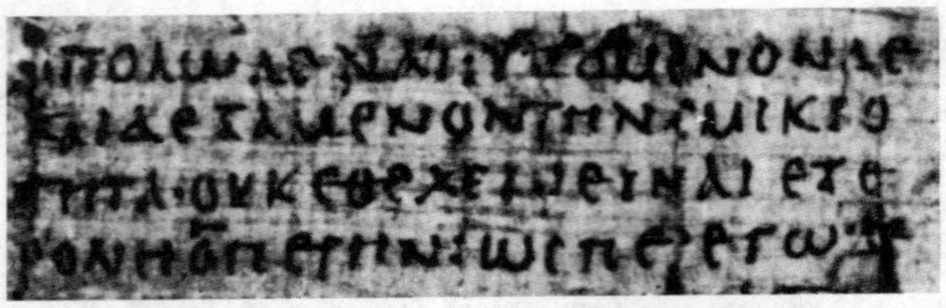

Phaedo, by Plato, copied in AD 100 (Egypt Exploration Society, London; P. Oxy. 1809).

By courtesy of the Egypt Exploration Society, London

to become more angular, and in the 4th century to become characterless and to combine letters into ligatures that distort the forms of the letters concerned. The book hand of a manuscript of Plato's *Phaedo* (*c.* AD 100; Egypt Exploration Society, London) shares its informality but regularizes the letter forms. Written on a larger scale and with more formality, this round hand can be very beautiful. In an example found at Hawara (2nd century AD), almost every letter (even ρ, τ, ι) would go into an identical square; only ϕ and ψ cross it above and below, μ, ω, and π horizontally.

If this writing is made to lean to the right, and to revive the 3rd-century-BC distinction between narrow and broad letters, it takes on the aspect of the "severe" style of the Bacchylides roll in the British Museum (2nd century AD).

By courtesy of the trustees of the British Museum

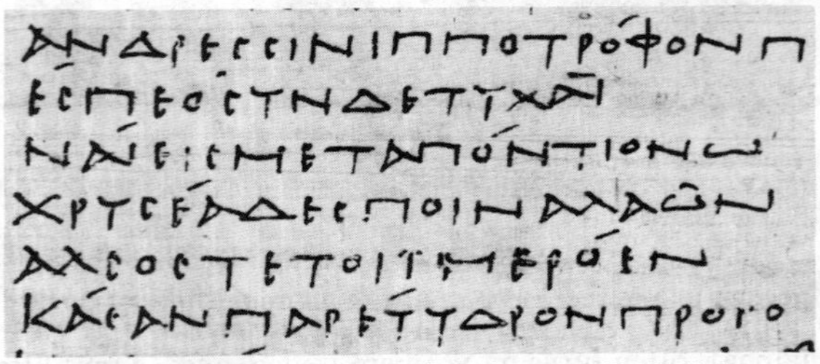

The "severe" style. Bacchylides roll, 2nd century AD (British Museum, London; P. 733).

Biblical uncial

If, however, the scribe makes his verticals or obliques thicker and his horizontals thinner, the hand is called biblical uncial, so named because this type is used in the three great early vellum codices of the Bible: Codex Vaticanus and Codex Sinaiticus of the 4th century and Codex Alexandrinus of the 5th century. It is now certain that this style goes back to the 2nd century AD. In the Dioscorides herbal in Vienna, written in AD 512, the writing is rigid and lumbering; the thick strokes are overdone; and blobs of ink terminate the horizontals of, for example, δ, ϵ, σ, τ. Such heavy decoration is also a feature of the Coptic style, of which there are examples as early as the 2nd century AD. This hand may be thought of as constituting a special case of biblical uncial.

Byzantine period. For the paleographer the significant division is not the founding of Constantinople in 330 but the 5th century, from which a few firmly dated texts survive. At its close a large-sized, exuberant, and florid cursive is found fully established for documents; in the 7th and 8th centuries, it slopes to the right, becomes congested, and adopts some forms of letters that anticipate the minuscule hand (*e.g.*, the π and λ in an 8th-century list of names preserved in the Aberdeen University Library). No new book hand was invented. A favourite informal type of the 6th century is shown in an acrostic poem by Dioscorus of Aphrodito, in the British Museum; it bears a clear relationship to the Menander *Dyskolos* hand, which was probably written in the later 3rd century AD. Similar pairs could be found to illustrate the continuity in transformation of the biblical uncial and Coptic styles. The latest Greek papyrus from Egypt is not later than the 8th century. There is a considerable lapse of time before the history of Greek writing resumes at Byzantium. (E.G.T.)

By courtesy of Osterreichische Nationalbibliothek, Vienna

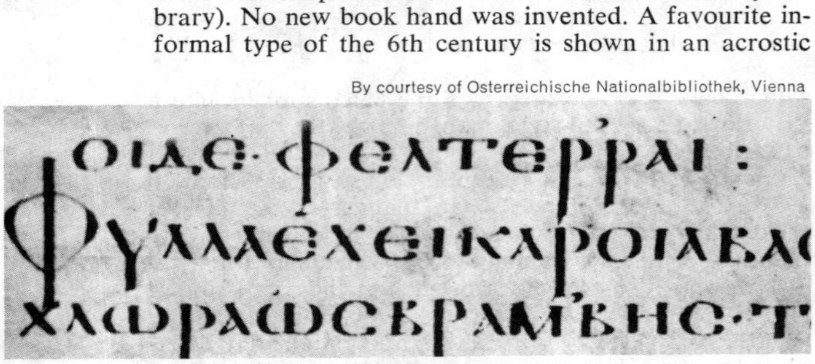

Biblical uncial. Dioscorides herbal, AD 512 (Österreichische Nationalbibliothek, Vienna; Med. Gr. 1).

By courtesy of the Aberdeen University Library, Scotland

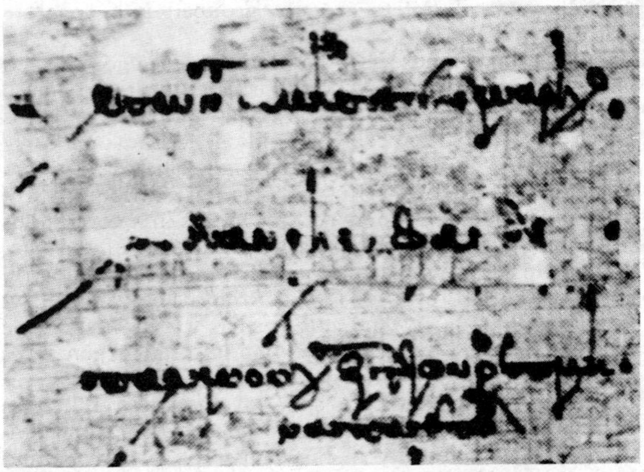

Byzantine documentary hand that is a precursor of minuscule. List of names, 8th century AD (Aberdeen University Library, Scotland; P. 72a).

8th to 16th centuries AD. To judge when and where a Greek manuscript was written is as difficult in this as in the earlier period, but for different reasons. The material for study is admittedly more extensive; manuscripts produced in the Middle Ages and Renaissance have been preserved in very large numbers (more than 50,000 whole volumes survive, of which probably 4,000 or 5,000 are explicitly dated); and they include work from most parts of the Byzantine Empire as well as from Italy. The difficulty of the paleographer lies in the essential homogeneity of the material, which is largely the result of the conditions in which the manuscripts were produced.

The fully developed Byzantine Empire of the 8th to the mid-15th centuries was extraordinarily uniform in its culture. Its contraction in space after the Arab conquests of the 7th century, which cut off the more distant and ethnically differentiated provinces of Syria, Palestine, and Egypt, made it a relatively compact geographical entity. The continuity and comparative stability of a single empire not divided into distinct national states such as evolved in the West resulted in a strength and unity of tradition of which the Byzantines were always conscious and that shows in their habits of writing no less than in their literature and art. Distinct local styles and sharp breaks in ways of writing in different periods cannot, therefore, be looked for; characteristics that may be spe-

By courtesy of the trustees of the British Museum

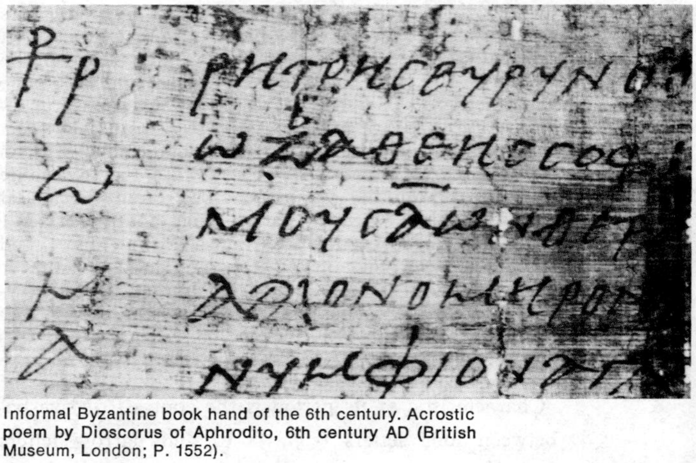

Informal Byzantine book hand of the 6th century. Acrostic poem by Dioscorus of Aphrodito, 6th century AD (British Museum, London; P. 1552).

cially typical of one period come in gradually and disappear equally slowly. A more potent factor than date or place in producing divergencies in the style of writing is the purpose for which a manuscript was designed and what type of scribe wrote it.

Late uncial, 9th to 12th centuries. There is a gap in the evidence covering the 7th and 8th centuries, because of the Arab conquest of Egypt, the perpetual wars on all fronts in the 7th century, and the iconoclastic struggle among Eastern Christians during the 8th and early 9th centuries, so that no literary texts (and very few others) have survived that can actually be dated to this period.

During this time the evolution of writing in capitals (not very aptly named uncial) probably continued toward a greater formality and artificiality. But this natural tendency was hastened by the introduction and spread of minuscule as the normal way of writing, after which the purpose of uncial changed completely. From an everyday hand in which all books were naturally written, it became a ceremonial hand used only for special copies and therefore grew increasingly stylized and artificial. In the 9th century a still elegant style was used for both patristic and classical works in splendid volumes destined for the imperial library or for presentation copies, such as the copy of Gregory of Nazianzus (Bibliothèque Nationale, Paris) made for the emperor Basil I between 879 and 883. By the 11th and 12th centuries, capitals were used only for liturgical books, mainly lectionaries, which had to be read in dimly lit churches; but the increasing tortuousness of the style must in the end have reduced its usefulness, and, by about 1200, uncial was dead.

Change of purpose of uncial

By courtesy of the Bibliotheque Nationale, Paris

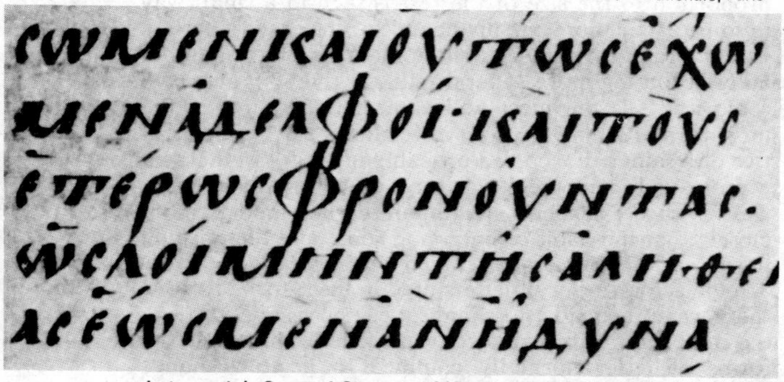

Late uncial. Copy of Gregory of Nazianzus, AD 879–883 (Bibliothèque Nationale, Paris; Grec. 510, fol. 61v).

Earliest minuscule, 8th to 10th centuries. By far the most important development that took place during the 7th–8th-century gap was the introduction of minuscule. There is no incontrovertible evidence of how this came about, or where. What scraps of evidence there are (a few documents from the gap, a few sentences in lives of the abbots of Stoudion of that time, and the first dated manuscript written in true minuscule) point to its development from a certain type of documentary hand used in the 8th century and to the likelihood that the monastery of the Stoudion in Constantinople had a leading part in its early development. Though its origins are obscure, the reasons that led to its introduction and rapid spread are obvious: poverty induced by wars and persecutions coincided with a shortage of papyrus after the Arab conquest of Egypt in the middle of the 7th century to induce a search for a more economical use of the relatively expensive vellum; the polemics of the iconoclastic controversy demanded a speedy, informal style of writing; and, finally, when peace was restored in the middle of the 9th century, the revival of learning, with the reorganization of the university, brought the need for multiplying plain workmanlike texts for scholarly purposes.

Reasons for the rapid spread of minuscule

The earliest dated example of true minuscule (and it is probably one of the oldest extant examples altogether) is a copy of the Gospels written in 835 (Leningrad Library), probably in the monastery of the Stoudion. Here are found all the characteristics of the earliest minuscule, which is called pure minuscule because there is as yet no admixture of uncial forms, except occasionally at line

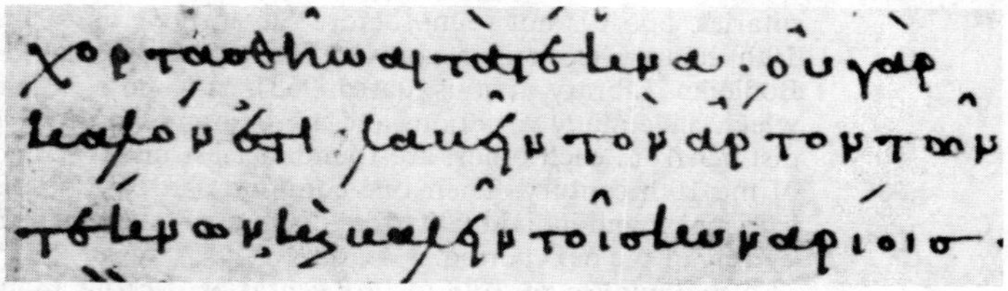

Earliest dated true minuscule. Copy of the Gospels supposedly done at the monastery of Stoudion, AD 835 (Leningrad, Bibl. Publ. 219, fol. 124).

ends. The letters are even and of a uniform size; letters are joined or not joined to each other according to strict rules, sometimes by ligatures in which part of each letter is merged in the other, but not to the extent of distorting the shape of either letter. There is no division between words, for the divisions are only those that arise from the rules for joining or otherwise of individual letters, and at this stage any letter that can be joined to the next one nearly always is joined to it. Breathings are square, either ⊢ ⊣ or ∟ ⌋, and accents are small and neat; abbreviations are very few, usually confined to the established contractions for *nomina sacra* (the names and descriptions of the Trinity and certain derivatives), omitted ν at line ends, a few of the conventional signs for omitted case endings, and S sometimes for $\kappa\alpha\grave{\iota}$. The writing either stands on the ruled lines or is merely guided by them.

Absolutely pure minuscule did not last long. Gradually, uncial forms of those letters that had specifically minuscule forms began to be used alongside the minuscule forms: λ was the first to appear, followed by ξ and then κ, all by the end of the 9th century. Then from about 900 onward, γ, ζ, ν, π, and σ were used regularly, while α, δ, ε, and η were used sometimes. Not before about 950 were β, μ, υ, ψ, and ω used, and still comparatively rarely. But by the end of the 10th century, the interchangeability of all uncial and minuscule forms was complete, though all the alternative forms are not necessarily found in any one manuscript. Perhaps the earliest dated manuscript with any uncial form in it is of 892/893 (Sinai, St. Catherine, MS. 375 + Leningrad, Bibl. Publ. MS. 343, Chrysostom), but pure minuscule continued to be used, in probably the majority of manuscripts, up to 900, and thereafter mainly in provincial manuscripts until the last dated example in 969 (Meteora, Metamorph. MS. 565, John Climacus). Besides the intrusion of uncial letters, some other characteristics of the earliest minuscule were modified during the 10th century. Rounded breathings, ‟, are first found in manuscripts of the last half of the century, interspersed with square ones. From about 925 the practice of making the writing hang from the ruled lines began to prevail. Although in most manuscripts abbreviations were confined to a few forms used at line ends only, a few copies dated in the last part of the century used nearly all the conventional signs.

First changes in minuscule

In spite of these developments—the gradual disappearance of pure minuscule and the other changes that accompanied it—the same general styles of writing persisted until about the end of the 10th century. Broadly considered, three styles can be distinguished. There is a rather primitive-looking, angular, cramped style that may perhaps be associated with the Stoudion monastery, in which a certain number of mainly patristic texts were written *c.* 880–*c.* 980 (*e.g.*, Paris, Bibliothèque Nationale, MS. grec 1470, a menologion of 890). Secondly, there is a plain, neat, workmanlike style (seen in a commentary on Gregory of Nazianzus copied in 986 that is preserved in the Bibliothèque Nationale at Paris), which continued in use at least until the end of the 10th century. In it were written several of the important classical manuscripts that are now the oldest texts of some ancient Greek authors (*e.g.*, Aeschylus, Sophocles, Aristophanes) but are unfortunately not explicitly dated. Thirdly, a consciously elegant, even mannered, style was used in books made for the imperial library or for wealthy dignitaries, but it is not found before the early years of the 10th century (seen in a copy of Basil on Isaiah in the Bodleian Library that is dated 953). All these styles, which have many variations and are by no means always distinct from each other, are found at least until the end of the 10th century. Their one common characteristic is a crispness and individuality that distinguishes them from writing of the next period.

Formal minuscule, 10th to 14th centuries. From about the middle of the 10th century, a smoother, almost mechanical appearance can be noticed in an increasing number of manuscripts; the hands seem more stereotyped, less individual. They are not immediately distinguishable from the plainer styles of the earlier part of the century, and their evolution during the next four centuries was very gradual. A few distinct types can be singled out from time to time. A bold, round, heavy liturgical style, fully established in the 11th century, was one of the most enduring types (*e.g.*, London, British Museum Add. MS. 19,352, a psalter of 1066); it became more and more stereotyped and mechanical until, in the 15th century, a branch of it was transplanted to Italy.

By courtesy of (top, centre) the Bibliotheque Nationale, Paris, (bottom) the curators of the Bodleian Library, Oxford

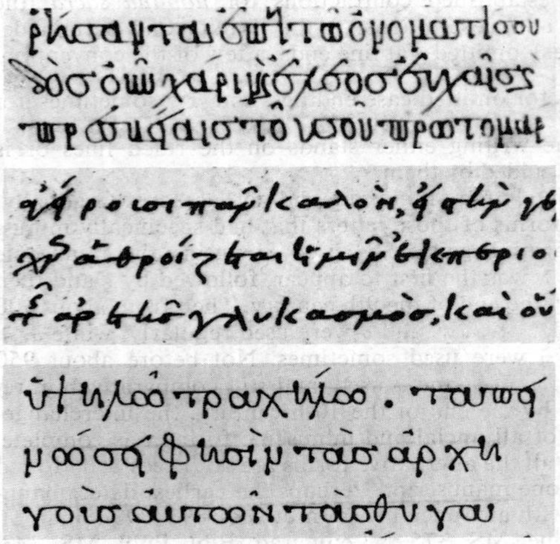

9th–10th century Greek hands.
(Top) Stoudion minuscule, AD 890 (Bibliothèque Nationale, Paris; MS. grec. 1470, fol. 168). (Centre) Commentary on Gregory of Nazianzus, AD 986 (Bibliothèque Nationale, Paris; MS. suppl. grec. 469 a, fol. 7). (Bottom) Commentary on Isaiah by Basil, AD 953 (Bodleian Library, Oxford; MS. Auct. E.2.12, fol. 80).

The style most widely used for biblical and patristic texts from the end of the 10th century, probably mainly in monastic houses in Constantinople, was one with plain, neat, rounded letters; this style became known as *Perlschrift* from its likeness to small, round beads strung together. A very plain, businesslike, rather staccato style was used in manuscripts with musical notation, most commonly in the 12th and 13th centuries (*e.g.*, Leningrad, Bibl. Publ. MS. 789, a sticherarion of 1106).

Manuscripts written outside Constantinople are recognizable, if at all, usually by a rougher, provincial appearance. Only two styles can be assigned to a specific provincial centre. One, a small unpretentious hand used by St. Nilus, the founder of many monasteries in south Italy at the end of the 9th century, was used for a time by others in that part of the world (*e.g.*, a copy of the works of Dorotheus made by Nilus in 965). Later, in the heyday of the reorganized Greek monasteries there in the 12th century, another elegant, rather mannered style, which almost certainly had its origin in Constantinople, is nevertheless often found in manuscripts known to have been written in south Italy and Sicily (*e.g.*, Paris, Bibliothèque Nationale MS. grec 83; Gospels copied in Sicily in 1167).

These particular styles, however, are not really as typical of the period as the less distinctive plain hands in which the majority of the manuscripts are written, at least in the 11th and 12th centuries (*e.g.*, a collection of canon law copied in 1042 in the Bodleian Library).

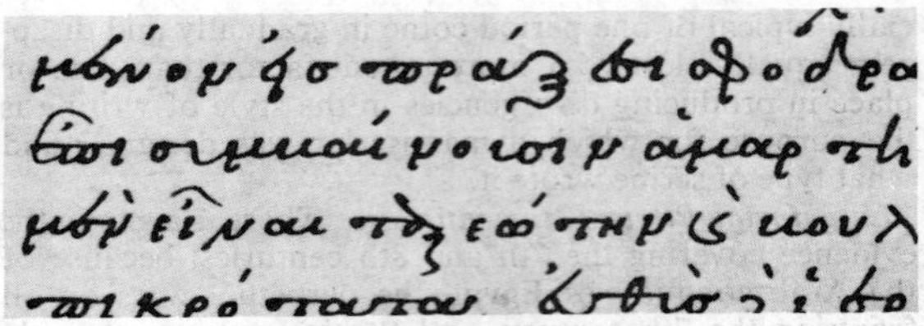

11th and 12th century plain hand. Collection of canon law, 1042 (Bodleian Library, Oxford; MS. Barocci 196, fol. 253).
By courtesy of the Bodleian Library, Oxford

Changes dating from the 11th century

The comparatively uniform type of writing of which all these were minor variations was remarkably enduring and widely dispersed, but, from the 11th century onward, certain changes may be observed that help to date manuscripts written in all types of formal minuscule. One change in its general appearance may be noticed as the 12th century advances: an increasing lightness of touch and a lessening of the closely knit, rather thick appearance that is characteristic of the 11th century. But the most noticeable change in this period is the breakdown in the evenness and regularity of the writing, which is partly attributable to the influence of documentary and the later personal hands. It is not, however, entirely so attributable, for a tendency to enlarge some letters out of proportion to the size of the rest is seen in a small way in some of the more personal hands of the earliest period. But it is rare in formally written manuscripts, only gradually becoming more general until, in the 12th and 13th centuries, it is the most noticeable feature of even the most formal hands (*e.g.*, a synaxarion, or a short narrative of a saint's life, copied probably in 1329). In the 14th century and later, there was a return to less flamboyant ways with the tendency to imitate earlier models more closely, but the habit of enlarging some and diminishing the size of other letters never died out.

In the actual forms of letters used in these formal styles, there was practically no change; very occasionally, from the end of the 10th century onward, one of the "modern" forms of letter normally confined to personal hands found its way into a formal manuscript. Much the same is true of ligatures. The tendency from the 11th century onward is to use ligatures and to join letters less automatically than in earlier times. The permissive rules and most of the forms remain unchanged, for, already in the 10th century, most of the distorting forms (notably those in which the *ε* is represented only by a C-shaped stroke; e.g., 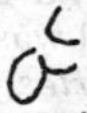 for *σε*) were well established, and in formal manuscripts these, with the earlier forms, continued in use until they were illogically taken over by the first printers of Greek. Time did, however, gradually increase the tendency to join letters by insetting them in or superimposing them upon each other. Abbreviations were even more conservatively used, only the oldest conventional forms being admitted, and often only a very few and those only at line ends.

The rule that the writing should hang from the ruled lines, already applied in most manuscripts by the mid-10th century, became invariable by the middle of the 11th. Square breathings (used indiscriminately among the round ones) were gradually eliminated, though they did not completely disappear from formal manuscripts until the middle of the 12th century. The practice of joining accents with breathings and also with the letters to which they belonged spread from personal hands to formal writing in the 13th century, but it was far more often avoided altogether.

Apart from the actual writing, one development is common to all manuscripts written in this period: the use of paper instead of vellum, which occurred first perhaps in the late 11th century and was common by the 13th century whenever economy was a major consideration.

These are the main criteria by which a formally written manuscript can be assigned to an earlier or a later part of this period. But the problem of distinguishing different styles and their dates, and their places of origin, remains most difficult for these Greek manuscripts.

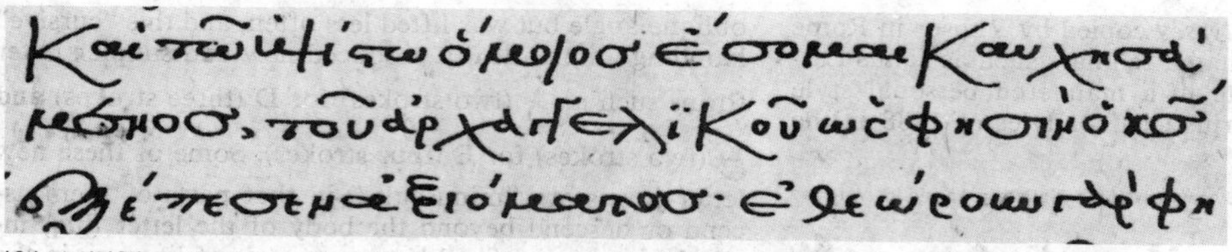

12th and 13th century formal hand. A synaxarion, probably AD 1329 (Bodleian Library, Oxford; MS. Auct. E.5.10, fol. 73v).
By courtesy of the Bodleian Library, Oxford

Personal hands, 12th to 14th centuries. From the beginning of minuscule, there were obviously educated individuals who occasionally copied texts for their own use in a formal hand that nevertheless had a distinctive personal flavour; indeed, professional scribes occasionally used a less formal style than usual. Several dated examples of this type of hand survive from the 10th, 11th, and early 12th centuries, but they are rarities. Toward the end of the 12th century, however, the prosperity and comparative stability of the Comnenan age (named from the dynasty of Byzantine emperors bearing the name Comnenus), with its brilliant literary and artistic achievements, gave way to increasing internal chaos and the hostile encirclement of Byzantium that was a prelude to the Fourth Crusade and the sack of Constantinople by the Western powers in 1204. Scholars perhaps already felt the pinch of poverty, which naturally grew greater during the exile of the Byzantium court (1204–61) and culminated in the economic crises of the 14th century.

Copying by scholars

Certainly, a change in writing habits began slowly to take place. Instead of commissioning professional scribes to copy manuscripts, some scholars began to make copies for themselves, and, in place of the smooth, mechanical styles of the professionals, they used the sort of writing that they presumably already used for personal notes. This was an adaptation (for greater clarity) of the type of writing that had been standardized in official documents from the beginning of the Byzantine period. Its chief characteristic was the greatly exaggerated size of certain letters or parts of letters, particularly letters with rounded bows such as *β*, *ε*, *ζ*, *θ*, *κ*, *ξ*, *ο*, *υ*, *φ*, and *ω*, and the excessive size of these letters is made to look even more unbalanced by some exceptionally small forms of, for example, *η*, *ι*, *ν*, or *ρ*. This essentially unbalanced, "wild" look was transplanted to literary manuscripts written by scholars for their own use.

Along with this exaggerated contrast in size between letters, they took from the documentary hands several new forms of letters that had gradually evolved from the originally common forms of both hands. In the 12th century the new scholarly hands began to use 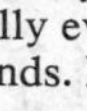 with separate small bows; , with a broken back; 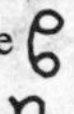, which had lost its high first stroke; and 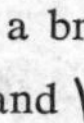, which had dropped its first long downstroke; and, by the end of the 13th century, 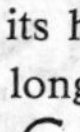, with a short embryonic tail. The old forms of ligature were kept basically the same but, in some cases, were reduced to a barely recognizable minimum (*e.g.*, 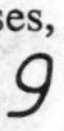 or  for *ει*) and, in others, distorted by the general flourishing tendency of the script (*e.g.*, 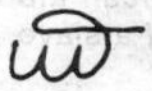 for *επ*). Abbreviations were naturally used with great frequency in all positions; the ancient conventional signs for suppressed syllables, which had acquired rounded and more flourished shapes, were used alongside a certain amount of "arbitrary" abbreviation in which a large part of a word was omitted and replaced simply by a general sign that some abbreviation had taken place.

Use of abbreviations

Accents and breathings joined with each other, with letters, and with abbreviation marks are found earlier and more frequently in scholarly than in formal manuscripts. The only exception to the rule of round breathings in this type of manuscript is in cases of deliberate archaism such as practiced by Demetrius Triclinius (died *c.* 1340).

One of the earliest datable examples of these scholarly productions is the copy of his commentary on the *Odyssey* (Biblioteca Nazionale Marciana, Venice) written *c.* 1150–70 by Eustathius, the scholar-archbishop of Thessalonica. In the 13th century, the exaggeration of specially round features reached its height (*e.g.*, in a copy of Euthymius Zigabenus on the Psalms, of 1279 [Bodleian Library, Oxford; MS. Roe 7]), while, in the 14th century, the tendency, as in the formal styles of writing, was toward less ebullience and exaggeration, and the writing of scholars such as Triclinius is compact and sober (*e.g.*, his copy of Aphthonius and other grammatical works, of 1308). For these hands the problem is not to discover centres of writing or styles for different uses but to identify the hands of individual scholars.

By courtesy of the Biblioteca Nazionale Marciana, Venice

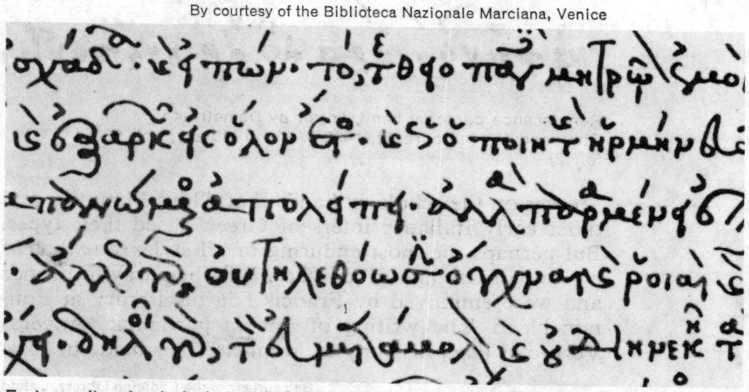

Early medieval scholarly hand. Commentary on the *Odyssey*, written by Eustathius *c.* 1150–70 (Biblioteca Nazionale Marciana, Venice; MS. Marc. Gr. Z. 460 [coll. 330], fol. 79).

By courtesy of New College, Oxford

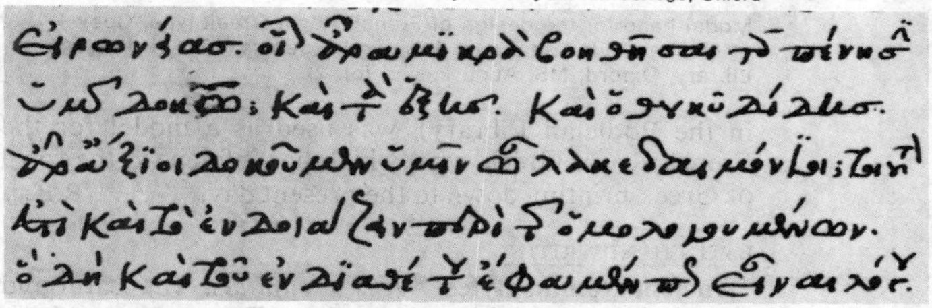

Late medieval scholarly hand. Grammatical works copied by Triclinius, AD 1308 (New College, Oxford; MS. 258, fol. 205).

The Italian Renaissance. By the end of the 14th century, Italian scholars were learning Greek, and they were bringing back Greek manuscripts from Constantinople. At this time Greek scholars had also begun to teach in Italy. The Greek that the earliest Italians learned to write was a clear, simple style taught originally by Manuel Chrysoloras (died 1415). But, although they copied a number of manuscripts for themselves in this hand, the style had no influence beyond their small circle. Before long, Greek scribes began to go to Italy, and both scholars and scribes arrived in increasing numbers as the Turks pressed in round the Byzantine capital until it finally fell in 1453. They brought with them, naturally, the two styles of writing that had persisted throughout the history of the empire. On the one hand, professional scribes such as Joannes Rhosus (died *c.* 1500), the majority of them from Crete, copied an astonishing number of manuscripts in the formal, now glib and stereotyped "liturgical" style of writing (*e.g.*, London, British Mu-

Copies in "liturgical" style

seum Harl. 5658, an *Odyssey* copied by Rhosus in Rome in 1479). On the other hand, scholars such as Janus Lascaris continued to write in a mannered personal style (*e.g.*, a letter of Demetrius Chalcondyles of 1488 in the Vatican Library).

By courtesy of the Biblioteca Apostolica Vaticana

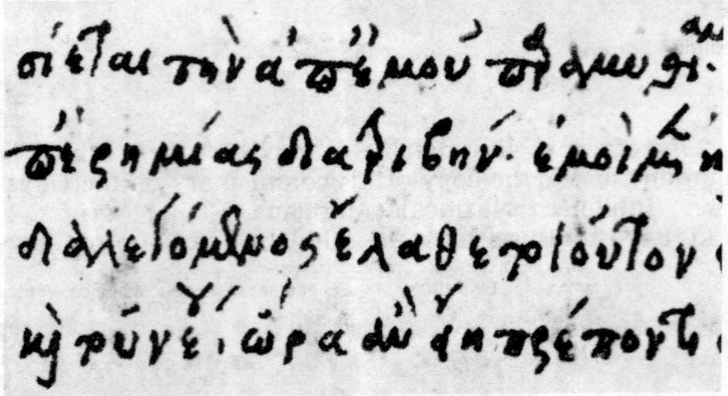

Renaissance personal hand. Letter by Demetrius Chalcondyles (autograph), 1488 (Vatican Library; Lat. 5641, fol. 2).

It was on the scholarly hands that Aldus Manutius and other early Italian printers of Greek based their types. But perhaps the most enduring of all styles was that of a group of Cretan scribes who made their way to France and were employed by Francis I in his library at Fontainebleau. The writing of one in particular, Angelus Vergecius (*e.g.*, his copy of Manuel Philes made in 1564

By courtesy of the Bodleian Library, Oxford

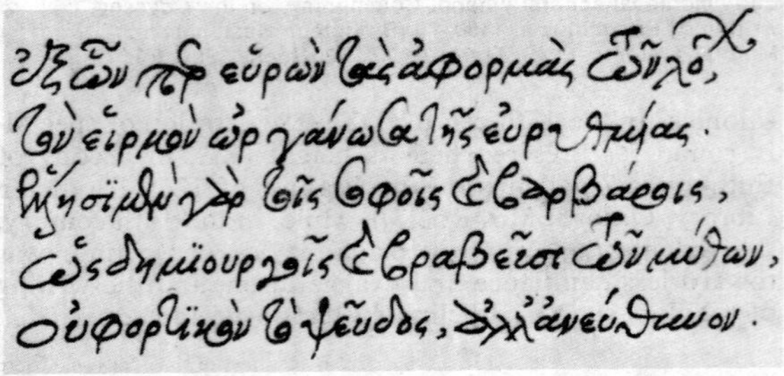

Model hand for the design of French Royal Greek type. Copy of Manuel Philes, made by Angelus Vergecius, 1564 (Bodleian Library, Oxford; MS. Auct. F.4.15, fol. 2).

in the Bodleian Library), was used as a model for the French Royal Greek type, which has influenced the form of Greek printing down to the present day. (R.Ba.)

LATIN HANDWRITING

Ancient Roman styles. *Rustic capitals.* The Latin and vernacular handwriting of western Europe descends in an unbroken line to the present day from the point at which it is first observed, in the 1st century AD. The script used throughout the Roman Empire at that time for books and occasionally for formal documents is known as rustic capitals. The pen was cut with a broad end and held so that its thickest strokes fell at an oblique angle to the line of writing, and it was lifted several times in the formation of a single letter. The rustic capital alphabet is "majuscule," in that all the letters are contained between a single pair of horizontal lines. The use of this elaborate script, whose letter forms were the natural outcome of using a broad pen held obliquely, was extended to certain sorts of inscription on stone and other materials, and it is called rustic only by comparison with the magnificent square capitals characteristic of Roman imperial inscriptions, whose forms were governed by the use of the chisel. Square capitals were seldom used in manuscripts except for titles. Rustic capitals continued in use for literary manuscripts until the 6th century, especially for texts of Virgil, but thereafter they appear only in titles, down to the 12th century.

Roman book hand

Cursive capitals. The business hand of the 1st century, used for correspondence and for most documents, private and official alike, is known as cursive capitals. Here the pen, cut to a sharp point, was held at the same oblique angle but was lifted less often, and this "cursive" handling automatically produced new and simpler letter forms such as d (two strokes) for D (three strokes) and e (two strokes) for E (four strokes). Some of these new letter forms are "minuscule," in that parts of them ascend or descend beyond the body of the letter (h,q) instead of being confined between a pair of lines, as in the majuscule rustic capitals (H,Q).

Roman business hand

From the 2nd to the early 4th century, parchment was replacing papyrus as the standard writing material for books, and the codex was replacing the roll as their standard form. The evidence that survives from this period, during which biblical and other Christian literature was beginning to be copied extensively, is fragmentary, and its interpretation is still controversial. The main line of development, however, is clear enough. The elaborate letter forms of rustic capitals, with their numerous pen lifts, began to be abandoned, and experiments were made with new book hands in which the simplified letter forms of cursive capitals were written with a broad pen, sometimes held obliquely in the traditional way and sometimes held "straight," so that its thickest strokes fell at right angles to the line of writing. It was probably the use of a straight pen that produced, for example, the conversion of cursive capital d (axis oblique) into the fully minuscule d (axis vertical).

Uncials, half uncials, and cursive minuscule. At the end of this period of transition, in the 4th and 5th centuries, when the evidence becomes more abundant, two new book hands and a new business hand are found in use. The older of the book hands, called uncials (the name dates only from the 18th century), was originally written with a slightly oblique pen; but, from the 6th century onward, a straight pen was used, and the hand began to look rounder and more contrived. Although it incorporates several of the cursive letter forms (d, e, h) of cursive capitals and has two forms peculiar to itself (a, m), it also preserves certain forms, such as B, N, R, S, which differ only a little from the forms of rustic capitals; and all three kinds of letters are treated as majuscules, being confined as far as possible between one pair of lines.

By courtesy of (top) the Biblioteca Apostolica Vaticana (bottom) the trustees of the British Museum

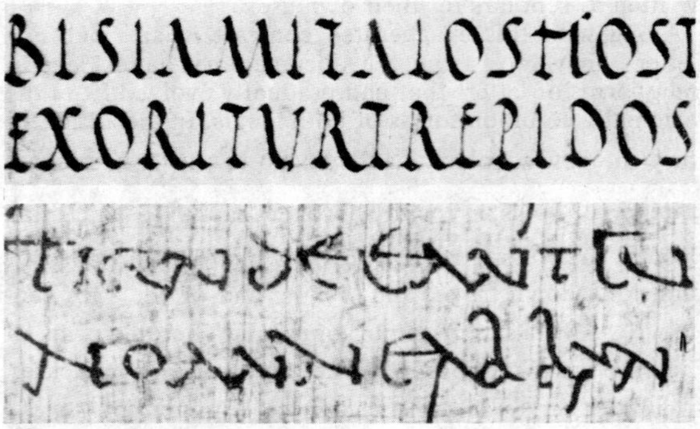

Early Roman capitals.
(Top) Rustic capitals. Codex Palatinus, Virgil, 4th–5th century AD (Vatican Library; Pal. Lat. 1631). (Bottom) Cursive capitals. Sale of a slave, AD 166 (British Museum, London; Pap. CCXXIX).

From the 4th to the early 7th century, most Christian books—biblical, patristic, and liturgical—were written in the uncial script, and even for pagan literature it almost entirely superseded rustic capitals. It survived the collapse of the Roman book trade. And, after the 6th century, when the production of all books, pagan as well as Christian, was taken over by the church—notably by the monasteries, such as the Vivarium founded in southern Italy by Cassiodorus, a scholar whose aim was to perpetuate Roman culture, and the houses that observed the Rule of St. Benedict—uncial script survived in many centres, especially for biblical and liturgical texts, down to the 9th century. Thereafter, like rustic capitals, uncials

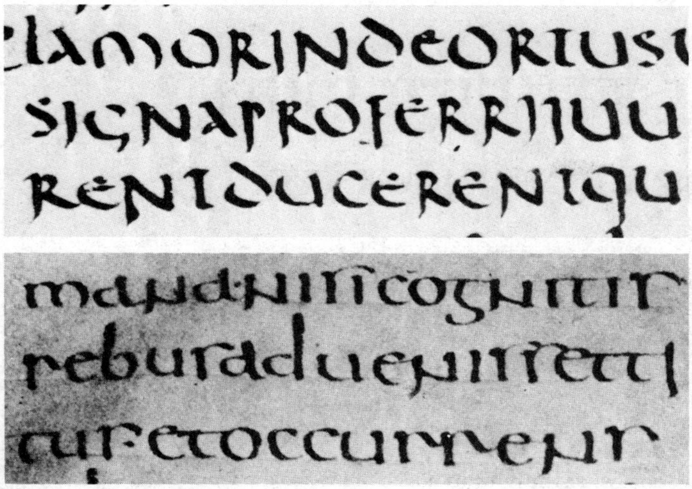

4th–5th century Roman book hands.
(Top) Uncials. Livy, 5th century AD (Bibliothèque Nationale, Paris; Lat. 5730). (Bottom) Half uncials. *De bello Judaico*, Hegesippus, 5th–6th century AD (Biblioteca Ambrosiana, Milan; C.105 inf.).
By courtesy of (top) the Bibliotheque Nationale, Paris, (bottom) the Biblioteca Ambrosiana, Milan

were used only for titles, and they, too, disappeared in the 12th century.

The younger of the two new book hands is called half uncial. This script was less popular than uncials and never broke their monopoly of biblical and liturgical texts, although like them it was still being written in the 8th century and even, as a display script for certain purposes, in the 9th. The artificial name half uncial tells nothing about the origin or nature of the script. It differs from early uncials in being written with a perfectly straight pen. One letter (N) remains more or less unchanged from the capital form, but the rest of the alphabet is cursive in origin. The letter forms that differ most from uncials are *a, b, d, g, m, r, s;* and the alphabet as a whole is frankly minuscule, since no attempt is made to confine it between a single pair of lines.

Cursive minuscule as a business hand

The new business hand of the 4th century and after is known as cursive minuscule. Like cursive capitals it was written with a pointed pen, but the pen was held more or less straight. It, too, is a frankly minuscule alphabet and uses basically the same letter forms as half uncials, although the frequency in cursive minuscule of ligatures between letters tends to conceal the fundamental likeness between the two hands.

By courtesy of the Bibliotheque Nationale, Paris

Cursive minuscule. Avitus of Vienne, 6th century AD (Bibliothèque Nationale, Paris; Lat. 8913 and 8914).

The letter forms that distinguish cursive minuscule and half uncials from rustic and cursive capitals and from uncials were evolved during the obscure period between the 1st and 4th centuries. The question of whether these forms were evolved in the sphere of the book hands or of the business hands is still undecided, but, whatever their origin, their importance for the subsequent history of European handwriting is paramount. They provided the material on which the Caroline (Carolingian) minuscule, first developed in the late 8th century, was based; and that script dominated Europe, in spite of severe modifications, until the end of the Middle Ages. Only in one other period were new letter forms evolved, between the 13th and the 15th centuries, in the group of scripts known as Gothic cursives; and the influence of these late innovations was ultimately cancelled out, thanks to the revival of Caroline minuscule in a pure form by the Italian Humanists at the beginning of the 15th century.

(T.J.Br.)

The Anglo-Celtic, or Insular, and other "national" styles (5th to 13th centuries). From the 5th century the relaxation of imperial Roman authority brought on a reassertion and growth of native cultures—that is, wherever the people were not wholly occupied in a savage struggle against barbarians for mere existence. The most isolated places such as the province of Britain responded strongly to this opportunity and at the same time were able to conserve important elements of the Roman civilization. With Ireland, which was never under occupation by the legions, it offered during Europe's darkest age comparative peace and shelter for the development of the richest and most original of book styles.

Anglo-Celtic monastic centres of manuscript copying and illumination

The Insular manuscripts were produced at monasteries that were often on a barren rock in the sea or at an equally inaccessible site. According to tradition, the earliest centre of Christian learning in Ireland was established by the Romano-British apostle St. Patrick (flourished 5th century AD). A great successor, St. Columba, or Columcille (*c.* 521–597), whom legend credits with divine scribal powers, founded monastic houses at Derry and Durrow and then journeyed to the Inner Hebrides to found one on the lonely island of Iona in 563. St. Columban, another Irish missionary, in much the same period was founding monasteries on the Continent: *c.* 590 in Gaul (modern France) the Burgundian centre Luxeuil, from which Corbie in Picardy was organized, and St. Gall in Switzerland and Bobbio in Italy about the years 612 to 614. From Iona a daughter house was founded in 635 on St. Cuthbert's holy isle of Lindisfarne just off the Northumbrian coast of England. To the south the Northumbrian monk, later abbot and saint, Benedict Biscop (*c.* 628–690) established the twin monasteries of St. Peter at Wearmouth in 674 and St. Paul at Jarrow in 682. He endowed them with splendid collections of books and pictures gathered during repeated visits to Rome, so that, in the late 7th and early 8th centuries, they comprised the most flourishing centre of Christian scholarship in western Europe and the meeting place of Hiberno-British and continental influences.

For the fine books made in the Anglo-Celtic centres, the majuscular script called Insular half uncial was deemed suitable rather than the pointed, more cursive Irish minuscule used for documents and vernacular texts. There is a high degree of conformity, attesting to their stylistic maturity, among such manuscripts as the Book of Kells (Trinity College, Dublin) and the Lindisfarne Gospels (British Museum, London) individual as they are in detail and ornament. After all, there is room for infinite variation where, in one-quarter of a square inch, 158 interlacements have been traced unerringly—by angels, it is said. The Book of Kells, Codex Cenannensis to paleographers, was probably produced at Iona around 800. It has 339 leaves, 13 by ten inches (33 by 25 centimetres) of noble script in single column, jet black on well-made parchment, through which runs the most spirited and colourful of ornamentation, ranging from the red-dotted outlining of letters, which is as much a feature of the style as the wedge-topped ascenders, to the wildly extravagant full-page initials at the opening of Gospels. The other masterpiece of Anglo-Celtic calligraphy and illumination, the Codex Lindisfarnensis, was written in honour of St. Cuthbert shortly after his death in 687. It displays the same lively inventiveness, the love of fantastic animal and bird forms (zoomorphs), intricate interlacing, and even, rhythmic script, set off by generous margins.

The earliest of all extant manuscripts of the Insular style is the *Cathach* ("Battler") of St. Columba (Royal

Insular Half Uncial. The Book of Kells, *c.* AD 800. In the collection of Trinity College, Dublin.
By courtesy of The Board of Trinity College, Dublin

Irish Academy, Dublin), who, according to legend, wrote it himself and, in the judgment of scholars, may actually have done so. Housed in its *cumhdach* (a sort of ark), it was carried into battle to ensure victory.

Besides the proud witness of such books as these to the Anglo-Celtic contribution, there were also the productions of continental centres influenced by St. Columban and his disciples, as well as books mainly in the Roman tradition but carrying the unmistakable sign of Insular influence. For instance, there are three that scholars believe were written in the 7th century at Bobbio, in the monastery of St. Columban. They are Codex Usserianus Primus, now a treasure of Trinity College, Dublin, and two manuscripts preserved in the Biblioteca Ambrosiana, Milan, known as Codex Ambrosianus C.26 sup. and Codex Ambrosianus D.23 sup. There is another, Codex Amiatinus (Biblioteca Medicea-Laurenziana, Florence), of 1,030 leaves measuring 20 by 13½ inches (51 by 34 centimetres), made in Northumbria in the 8th century. It is continental Roman in style with no concession to the Insular habit of ornamentation. This is understandable, for it was designed for presentation to the pope.

Though the Insular minuscule was ready to hand, the majuscular half uncial as the senior script was always given the place of honour and the preference for the fine Latin books of the Anglo-Celtic monasteries. Nevertheless, by the 8th century the minuscule was developing into a disciplined book hand, as seen in the copy of Bede's *Historia Ecclesiastica* (*c.* 731; Cambridge University Li-

By courtesy of the trustees of the British Museum

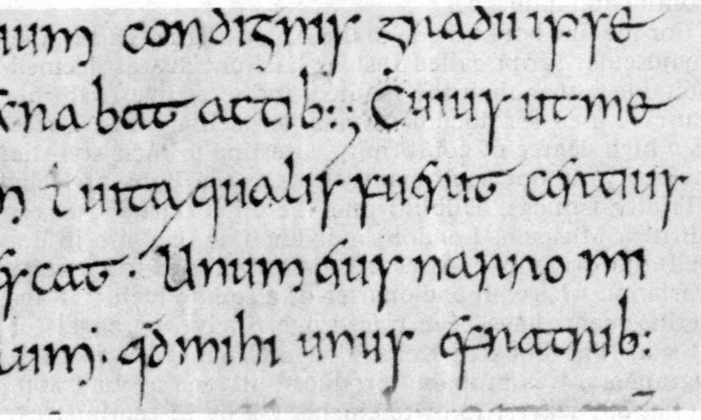

Insular minuscule. *Historia Ecclesiastica*, by Bede, 8th century AD (British Museum, London; Cotton Tiberius C.11).

brary). The spiky, ligatured, compactly written style migrated early to the Continent and, by the beginning of the 8th century, was at home in the Anglo-Saxon foundation of Echternach, in Luxembourg. Fulda and Würzburg, in Germany, were other important centres abroad of Insular culture and book production in this style.

Merovingian and Visigothic scripts

The Merovingian, in France, and the Visigothic, in Spain, are two more varieties of minuscular script that grew out of Latin cursive after the withdrawal of the Roman authority. In the Luxeuil monastery, in Burgundy, the minuscule attained in the 7th century the characteristics of a fine book hand, but for only a short period, when the reforms under Charlemagne took effect. In the Iberian Peninsula, the Visigothic style was in use from at least the 8th to the 12th century. It has the verticality of emphasis that is common to the other hands out of the same cursive background, when deliberately written, with weighted ascenders carefully topped by flat serifs.

The South Italian script of the style called Beneventan, nurtured in the motherhouse of the Benedictine Order at

By courtesy of the trustees of the British Museum

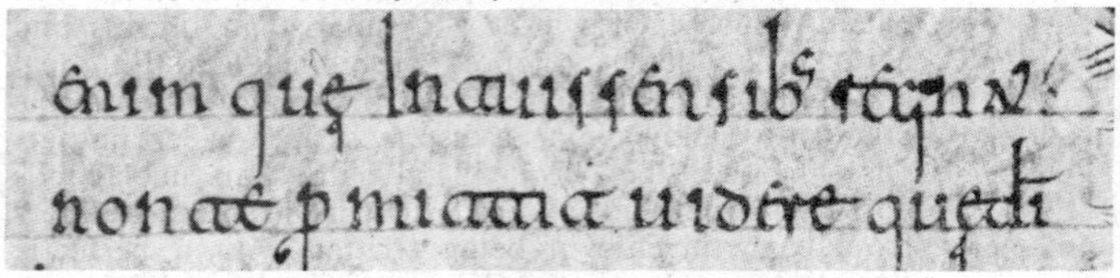

Visigothic minuscule. "Passionale," AD 919 (British Museum, London; Add. 25,600).

Monte Cassino, was the "national" hand that rose to the status of calligraphy and held its position well into the 13th century, an active literary life of more than 500 years. It has a peculiar jerky rhythm and retains individual cursive forms, which, together with the abundance of abbreviations and ligatures, make reading difficult.

Carolingian reforms in the scriptorium (8th and 9th centuries). The literary reforms carried on in the latter part of the 8th century and early 9th century by order of the Holy Roman emperor Charlemagne set the highest of standards for the making of books throughout his Western Empire. The extensive educational program, looking forward to new authorized versions of the Vulgate, the missal, and other liturgical works, he placed in charge of the learned English cleric Alcuin of York. The Emperor persuaded Alcuin to leave his position at the head of the cathedral school of York and the excellent library he had gathered there, first to become master of the palace school at Aachen, then at Tours as abbot of St. Martin's to conduct the literary activities centred at the well-established scriptorium (writing room) there.

Contributions of Alcuin

Before taking up the abbacy in 796, Alcuin was responsible for, or at least inspirer of, the most precious of Carolingian codices, the so-called Golden Gospels. These were a series of illuminated masterpieces mainly written in gold and often on purple-stained vellum. The most famous is the Godescalc Evangeliarium (Bibliothèque Nationale, Paris), written before 783 for Charlemagne, the body of the text in uncials and the dedication in Carolingian minuscule. The most luxurious is the Saint-Médard Gospel Book (Bibliothèque Nationale, Paris), written entirely in gold uncials and illuminated with full miniatures, initials, etc. in gold and silver on purple ground.

Alcuin carried forward the work of the St. Martin scriptorium in the spirit of a true classical renascence. Each variety of traditional letter form was studied with a view to finding its norm by careful comparison with

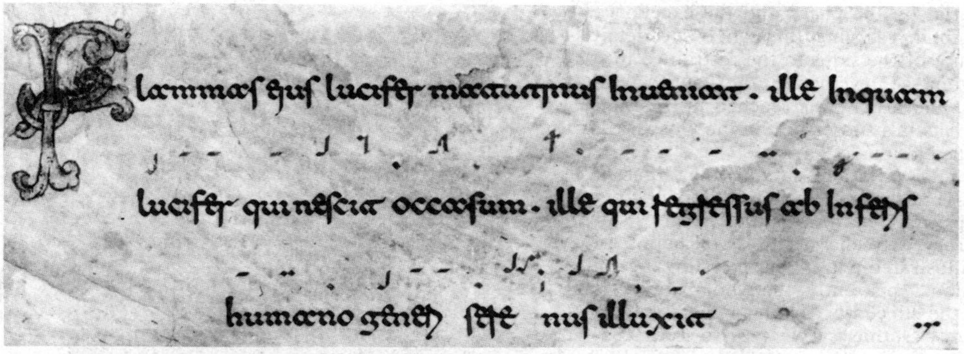

Beneventan script. Exultet Roll from Monte Cassino, Italy, late 11th or early 12th century AD (British Museum, London; MS. 30377).
By courtesy of the trustees of the British Museum

archetypes in ancient monuments and books. Thus, the square capitals, at the top of the hierarchy of scripts, were modelled on Augustan inscriptions. For rustic capitals (*capitales rusticae*), the reformers adopted the style of those used for the text of such fine old codices as the Virgil fragment now in the Vatican. The roman uncial was restored to its simple dignity, as in well-made books of the 6th century, and the minor, or half, uncial was likewise restored to the plain elegance of that earlier period, after the degeneracy of the 7th century.

The model for the most valuable and characteristic of all the Alcuinian contributions, the Carolingian minuscule, has never been precisely determined. It may well have been a local variety of cursive or, more probably, a mixture of half uncial and cursive, in which Alcuin discerned the possibilities of his clear, round, flexible but disciplined script, comfortable to both scribe and reader. For, as regularized at the scriptorium of St. Martin, the minuscule was written with the shaft of the pen pointing somewhat to the right instead of straight back over the shoulder; though the letters were formed deliberately, even and round, stroke by stroke the same way every time by rule, the writing brought relative ease for the hand and eye. With the years some cursive features became more prominent—*e.g.*, a tendency nearly to join certain letters and an occasional hint of "italic" in the slightly sloping, even, well-spaced lines. The incipits (the opening words of the text) were celebrated by means of display letters and a decorative initial that might come from any one of a number of sources, including Insular, Byzantine, and Merovingian scripts. Otherwise, the classic calm was maintained, supported by the superb ar-

Carolingian minuscule

By courtesy of the Bibliotheque Nationale, Paris

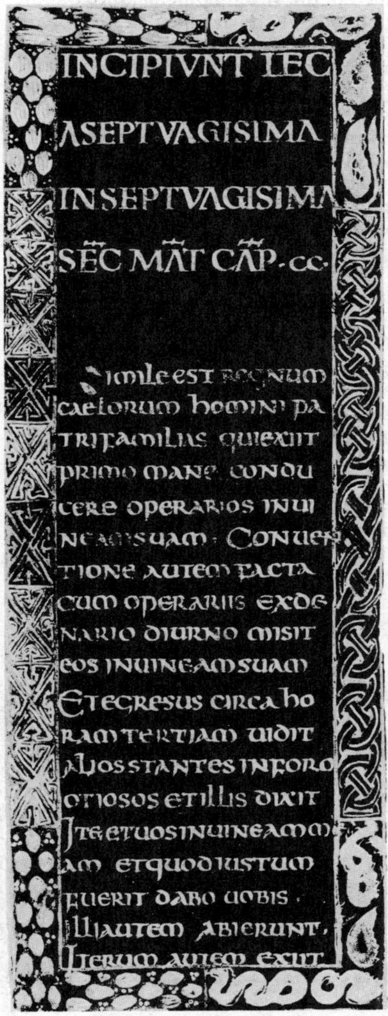

Uncial script. Godescalc Evangeliarium, before AD 783 (Bibliothèque Nationale, Paris; Evangéliaire de Charlemagne, fol. 23).

By courtesy of the Bibliotheque Nationale, Paris

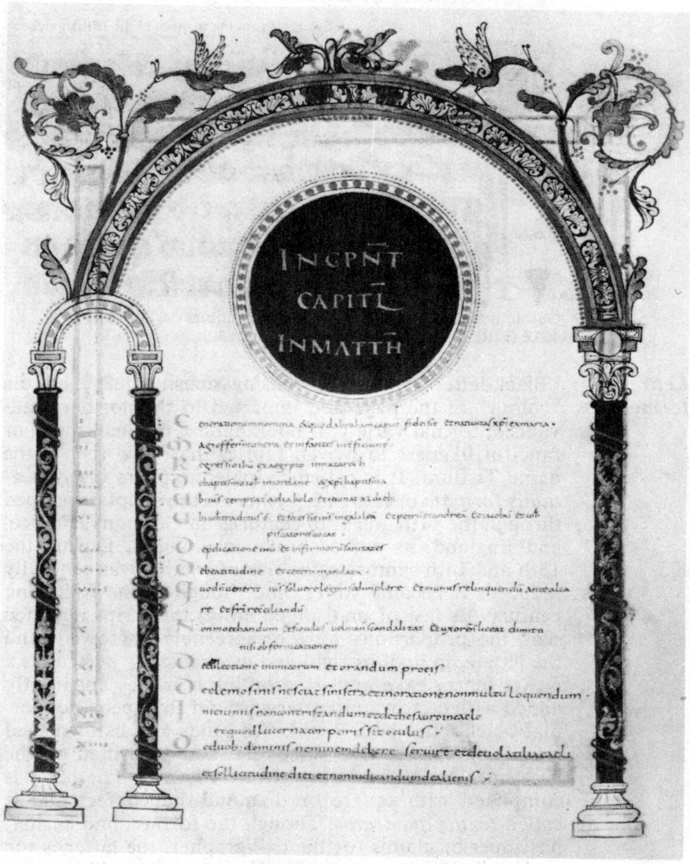

Gospels of Lothair, *c.* AD 850 (Bibliothèque Nationale, Paris; MS. Lat. 266, fol. 19).

rangement of material on the pages and the excellence of the craftsmanship in carrying through every detail from the manufacture of the skins to the restrained illumination. The crowning achievement of the Tours school of scholars, scribes, and artists was reached in the mid-9th century, under Alcuin's successors, in the Gospels of Lothair (Bibliothèque Nationale, Paris).

There are observable variations among the different Carolingian schools, but these are generally in small details. The most surprising departure is the Utrecht Psalter (University Library, Utrecht), written at Rheims, in rustic capitals and illustrated with fluent pen drawings in the Hellenistic fashion. Apparently, the whole work was devotedly copied in the 9th century from an old model.

The black-letter, or "Gothic," style (9th to 15th centuries). Carolingian minuscule remained the unrivalled book hand of western Europe through the 9th century, or nearly so. Then a trend away from the official imperial standards set in. It can be observed progressing in the manuscripts written at St. Gall, in Switzerland, near the end of the 9th century and during the 10th. There is a tendency toward lateral compression of the letters. This begins as the natural result of an easier motion of the pen held in a slanting position—*i.e.*, with the shaft out to the side rather than pointing back over the right shoulder. At such an angle of holding the pen, a nib cut straight across does not deliver body strokes of full thickness to the letters. But the scribes learned to adjust this matter by cutting the pen's writing edge obliquely so that it would be parallel to the top of the page anyway; even though the shaft was held in the slanting position, the nib so cut would yield a perpendicular stroke of maximum width. They were led on by the attractive novelty of bolder and bolder contrasts that eventually were to appear to the eyes of the Italian Humanists in the Renaissance so brutal as to deserve the bad name of Gothic. Nevertheless, the more condensed, compact writing allowed significant economies in the amount of time taken in writing the books and the quantity of materials used and, therefore, in the cost of finished manuscripts.

By courtesy of the trustees of the British Museum

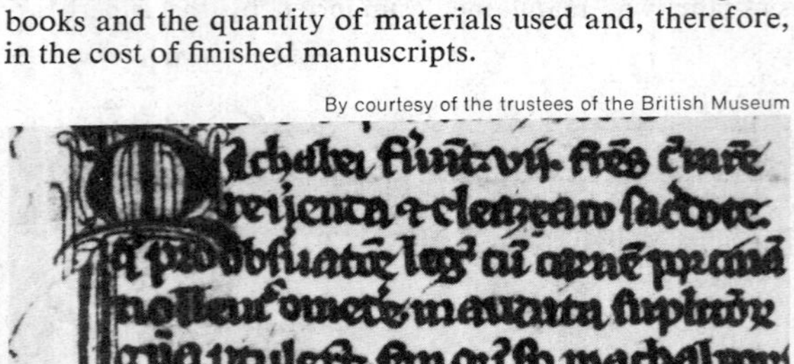

Gothic book hand. *Legenda aurea* by Jacobus de Voragine, 1312 (British Museum, London; Add. 11,882).

Lettre de forme

Black-letter style of increasing density deepened the "colour" of the page and imparted to the northern, advanced, formal variety of book hand a matted aspect, or fanciful likeness to woven fabric, that gave rise to the name Textura. It is called by paleographers *littera textualis formata* or *lettre de forme*. As the script developed through the 11th and 12th centuries in Germany, France, and England, its curves broke into angles. During the 13th and 14th centuries, the size of writing was generally reduced. It became stiffer, and though in the following century (its last of undisputed sway) the script regained size, the proportions were disagreeably narrowed, and the letters, in lines as rigid and mechanically perfect as a picket fence, have angles sprouting hairlines apparently added with a crow quill afterward. Of this species of formal black-letter book hand, two kinds are distinguished by paleographers. One stands flat and unseriffed on the base line and is known as *textus prescissus*. The other is completed with square or diamond-shaped feet and is called *textus quadratus*. Though the former, and earlier, has superior claims for the calligrapher, the latter is the variety that was carried into printing types and hence into much wider use.

Textus prescissus by Brother Tickhill. "Beatus" page from the Tickhill Psalter, *c.* 1310. In the collection of the New York Public Library.

By courtesy of the New York Public Library, the Spencer Collection, Astor, Lenox and Tilden Foundations

In Italy the writing during the same period took on weight, but the curves of comparable book script never became angles. The senior script there was the Rotunda, heavy but not pointed. The form persisted for liturgical work both as writing and printing type until late in the Renaissance.

Lettre bâtarde

The north and the south had, of course, their other kinds of writing for court and business or personal uses. A cursive hand that literally flourished in France, Flanders, and England rose to favour in the 15th century as a vernacular book script. This *littera bastarda*, or *lettre bâtarde* as it is termed in the vexed nomenclature of paleography, for all its high style as attained in fashionable books, was close kin to the epistolary "running secretary" commonly written by northern Europeans and early American settlers until it grudgingly yielded in the 17th century to italic script.

The scripts of Humanism (14th to 16th centuries). Under the inspiration of the 14th-century Italian poet Petrarch, who started the collecting of ancient manuscripts, coins, medals, and other "antiques," the essentially literary movement called Humanism engaged a group of scholars at Florence in the latter part of the 14th century and opening decades of the 15th. Their growing enthusiasm for antiquity led them on an ever-widening search for Latin books and ancient monuments, in order that they might restore the lost heritage of Rome. Classical authors written in the clear Carolingian minuscule with display lines in lapidary style (*i.e.*, in the style of ancient inscriptions cut on stone) appealed to them as though straight from the time of Cicero instead of from the 10th to 12th centuries. Reverently, Coluccio Salutati, the late-14th-century chancellor of Florence who followed Petrarch as leader of the movement, and his fellow Humanists imitated the old script, which they spoke of as the *lettera antica* to distinguish it from the ordinary *moderna* that belonged to the black-letter style.

Lettera antica and *moderna*

By courtesy of the Pierpont Morgan Library, New York

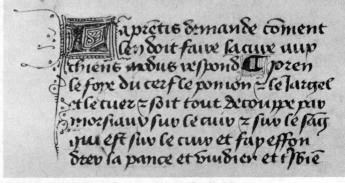

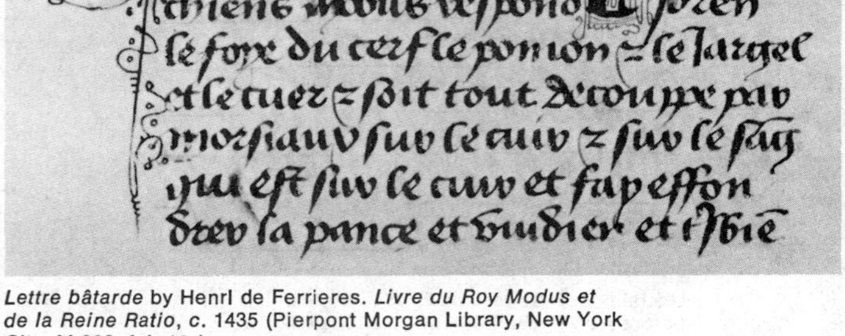

Lettre bâtarde by Henrl de Ferrieres. *Livre du Roy Modus et de la Reine Ratio*, *c.* 1435 (Pierpont Morgan Library, New York City, M.820, fol. 16v).

Two protégés of Salutati are credited with developing, on the basis of these studies and experiments among old manuscripts, the two fundamental scripts of Humanism. Poggio, at the very beginning of the 15th century, produced the round, formal writing that, after further polishing by a generation of scribes, served the new art of printing as prototype of "roman" fonts. He promptly followed up this achievement by introducing into his manuscripts the square capital letters as used on ancient monuments. Later in the century, the rage for epigraphic inscriptions brought such enthusiasts as Cyriacus of Ancona, Felice Feliciano of Verona, and his fellow townsman Giovanni Giocondo into the field and, from Padua, Giovanni Marcanova, Bartolomeo Sanvito, and Andrea Mantegna. They compiled the fruit of their researches in great *sillogi*, or anthologies, which, among other uses, served calligraphers with precious authoritative patterns for letter forms, ornament, and the correct spacing and placing of all display elements in their books. Feliciano, a calligrapher fond of ornament and fertile in invention, about 1460 demonstrated for the first time how to construct the monumental roman capitals according to geometrical rules.

By courtesy of (top) the Biblioteca Medicea Laurenziana, Florence, (bottom) the Biblioteca Nazionale, Florence

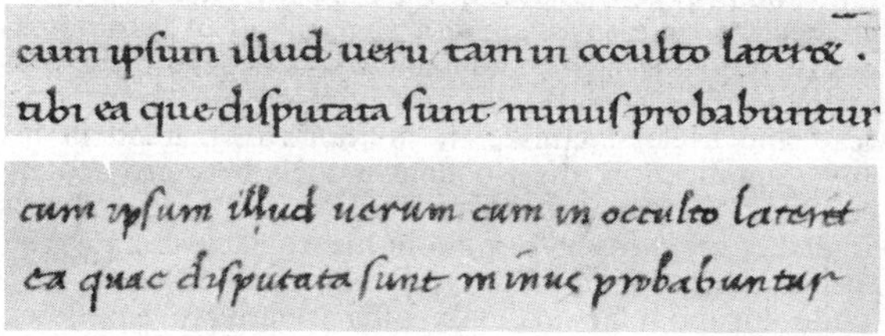

Humanistic scripts.
(Top) *De oratore*, by Cicero, calligraphy by Poggio, *c.* 1425 Laurentian Library Florence; Ms. Laur, Plut. 50.31. C. 166).
(Bottom) *Cicero*, calligraphy by Niccolò Niccoli, *c.* 1423 (Biblioteca Nazionale Centrale, Florence; Soppr., 1.1.14).

The second style of Humanistic script appears earliest in the writings of Poggio's friend Niccolò Niccoli, who was also an accomplished scribe. His slightly inclined cursive, written with a fairly narrow rounded nib at a good rate of speed, was to be to the printers' "italic" what the Poggian hand became to their "roman." Niccoli's innovation employed movements and rhythms close to those of the ordinary black-letter cursive familiar in everyday affairs. Indeed the script contains a sprinkling of current black-letter mannerisms and lends itself similarly to the joining or tying together of letters. The special character of this *antica corsiva* results from the narrowing of the bodies of letters due to the rapid up and down movement of the pen, facilitated by its being held with the shaft pointing at an angle away from the shoulder instead of straight back, producing this ╳, not ┼. As in italic fonts to this day, the form of *a* is distinctive; and *f*, *g*, *k*, and *ſ* (long *s*) are all more or less reminiscent of black-letter current habits. For his headings Niccoli preferred roman capitals "italicized" by a slight inclination to the right.

Antica corsiva

Both scripts were at once taken up and spread by other able scribes working at Florence in the first half of the 15th century, of whom the work of Giovanni Aretino, Giacomo Curlo, and Antonio di Mario, among others, is well recognized.

Poggio himself in 1403 had promptly carried his new script to Rome, where he later became papal secretary. Both scripts were devoted exclusively to the service of Latin literature, but there was a difference. Poggio used his hand as a calligrapher, while Niccoli used his as a copyist. The manuscripts of the former are set forth on fine parchment with meticulous care to formal details, such as even lines at the right-hand margin, and with handsome embellishment. Those of the latter are on paper, compactly and rapidly written, with attention to legibility and textual accuracy above all. There is an interesting parallel in the printed books of the following century. Ambitious Renaissance folios are set in fine roman types, while the well-edited but cheap little student books are just as naturally set in italic.

Influence of printing

Typographic printing displaced the copyists. At the same time it gave impetus and new significance to the work of calligraphers. They accepted the challenge of mechanized writing and for a while responded by turning out the finest of Humanistic masterpieces. In the late 15th and early 16th centuries, the Paduan Sanvito and Pierantonio Sallando of Mantua, for instance, not only wrote the round Humanistic script in a fashion worthy of the richest miniatures and illumination, but they also honoured the slender proportioned "italic" script by promoting it to a place in some of their most proud and precious manuscripts.

Sanvito's folio and octavo classics in the Humanistic cursive are also celebrated for vellum pages stained purple, yellow, green, or salmon pink and for lines of inscriptional capitals alternating gold, blue, lake, purple, violet, and green. The *antica corsiva* perfected by 15th-century papal scriptors for rapidly inditing briefs issued by the chancery also won its way as the chosen medium of polite correspondence. Thus, in the 16th century, the versatile *lettera da brevi*, or *cancellaresca* (chancery cursive), lively yet disciplined, responsive to wide variety in cut of nib and speed of movement, attainable by the novice and gratifying to the adept either as book or epistolary hand, became a vehicle of the new learning throughout Christendom.

Cancelleresca, or chancery cursive

As written by the early-16th-century calligrapher and printer Lodovico degli Arrighi of Vicenza, the *cancelleresca* can range from eye-arresting contrasts of almost

By permission of the controller of H.M. Stationery Office, Crown copyright reserved

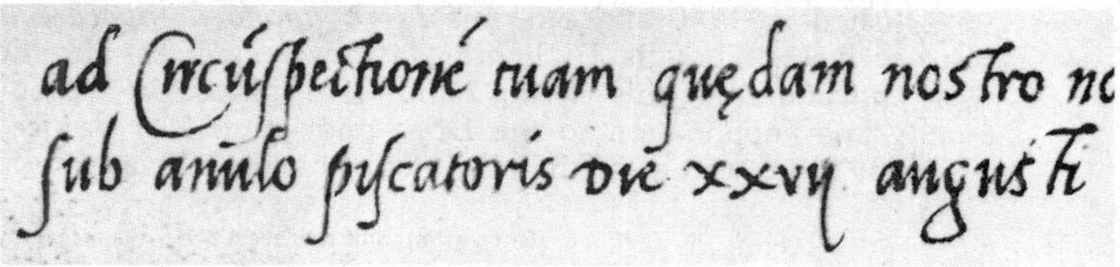

Littera cancellaresca. Brief of Pope Leo X, ascribed to Lodovico degli Arrighi, 1519 (Public Record Office, London; S.P. 1/19).

Gothic thick and thin strokes to a delicate, supple monotone tracery. The ascending letters, instead of terminating in serifs as with Sanvito or Sallando, now wave plumelike to the right, and the descenders are tending to balance them with a swing to the left. In 1522 Arrighi published at Rome his modest though revolutionary work *operina da imparare di scrivere littera cancellaresca.* This, the earliest of printed writing manuals, or copybooks, held out to the public clear, simple directions with woodcut examples and invited everyone to learn in a few days how to write this fashionable hand for themselves. In effect, it announced the end of the era of the scriptorium and the beginning of the era of the writing master. Dependence upon attracting pupils and gaining a reputation with the public was thereafter reflected in the tendency to exploit novel or flashy scripts and extravagant ornament.

Writing manuals and copybooks (16th to 18th centuries). The Arrighi *Operina's* devotion to the chancery cursive is matched in single-mindedness only by Gerardus Mercator's *Literarum Latinarum* (1540). Arrighi's second publication, *Il modo de temperare le penne* (1523), is a more normal performance for the calligrapher, notary, printer, and erstwhile scriptor of apostolic briefs in the role of writing master. Here the scripts described are as follows: *littera a merchanti*, cursive black-letter mercantile hand; *littera per notari*, small cursive semi-black-letter style, slightly inclined; *littera da bolle*, large carefully formed black-letter cursive; *littera da brevi*, chancery cursive; roman capitals, large Humanistic round hand; round black-letter interlaced initials; ribbon initials; large inscriptional roman capitals; large decorated formal Gothic minuscule; large round outline Gothic; *littera formata*, black-letter in two sizes. The specimens are completed with another page of smaller interlaced Gothic initials and two pages of type speci-

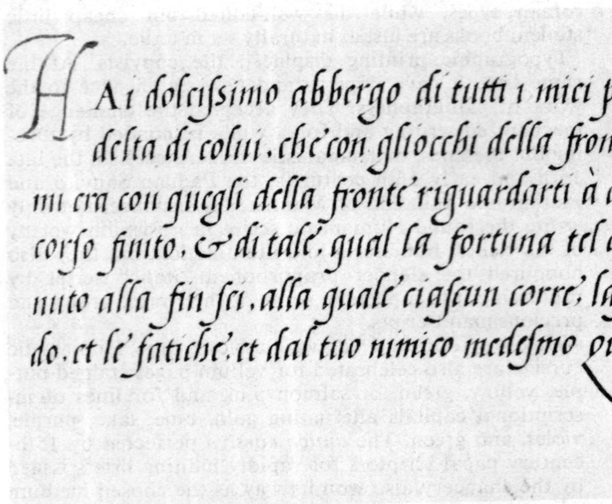
HAi dolcissimo abbergo di tutti i miei piaceri, maladetta sia la cru
delta di colui, che con gliocchi della fronte hor miti fa uedere; assai
mi era con quegli della fronte riguardarti à ciascuna hora. tu hai el tuo
corso finito, & di tale, qual la fortuna tel concedette ti se spacciato, ue
nuto alla fin sei, alla quale ciascun corre; lasciate hai le miserie del mó
do. et le fatiche, et dal tuo nimico medesmo quella sepultura hai. &

Cancellaresca formata by Giovanni Battista Palatino. Manuscript specimen book, *c.* 1550 (Bodleian Library, Oxford; MS. Canon. Ital. 196, fol. 44r).
By courtesy of the Bodleian Library, Oxford

mens, including the cramped italic as seen in books produced by the Aldine Press in Venice and the free calligraphic style first shown here. This book redresses the balance in favour of the popular scripts.

Arrighi's elder contemporary and possible mentor, Giovanni Antonio Tagliente, writing master to the Venetian chancery, published his *Presente libro* in 1524, two years after the *Operina;* and Giovanni Battista Palatino published in 1540 at Rome his *Libro nuovo d'imparare a scrivere.* Though Tagliente was master of an elegant *cancellaresca*—his "living hand" is displayed in a holograph supplication to the Doge and council of Venice, 1491—as well as of the black-letter hands, he was out of date and prey to the vices of the old professional; *e.g.,* his chancery specimens include a page of script leaning excessively to the right, and facing it is a page of similar script leaning away to the left, almost equally hard to read and useless. Unlike the author's own hand in his 1491 supplication, the woodcut models here are acutely pointed. Palatino at the same time exhibits a rigid, sharp-angled *cancellaresca formata* in his excellent manuscript specimen (Bodleian Library, Canon. Ital. 196 fol. 44r), while his popular manuals offer relatively easygoing models for learners. In particular, the Palatino *cancellaresca romana* is a normal even-toned script, modest as to bulbed ascenders (*testegiatta*) and angle of inclination, displaying in its forms hospitality for *bastarda* variations (*i.e.,* Gothicizing *g, h, k, r*). The fact that Palatino's *Libro nuovo,* besides being the most complete, was the most widely disseminated of mid-16th-century books on writing, bespeaks certain latitudinarian qualities along with marvellous virtuosity. The summit of absurdity in 16th-century writing manuals was reserved for Ferdinando Ruano, a Spanish scribe working in the Vatican Library, whose *Sette alphabeti* (1553) demonstrated by means of diagrams how to construct the chancery letters geometrically.

By courtesy of the trustees of the British Museum

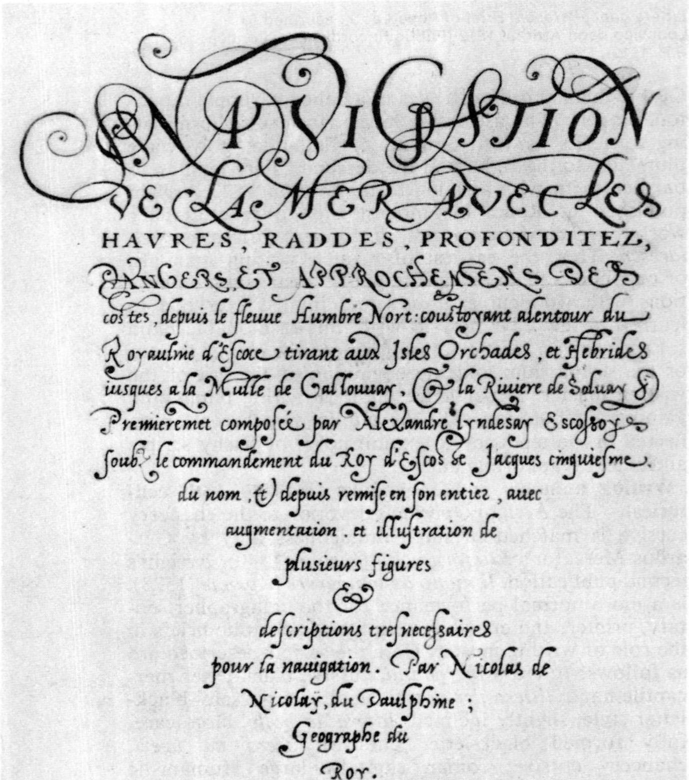
NAVIGATION
DE LA MER AVEC LES
HAVRES, RADDES, PROFONDITEZ,
DANGERS, ET APPROCHEMENS DES
costes, depuis le fleuue Humbre Nort: coustoyant alentour du
Royaulme d'Escoce tirant aux Isles Orchades, et Hebrides
iusques a la Mulle de Gallouuay, & la Riuiere de Soluay
Premieremet composée par Alexandre Lyndesay Escossoys
soub. le commandement du Roy d'Escos Ie Jacques cinquiesme
du nom, & depuis remise en son entier, auec
augmentation. et illustration de
plusieurs figures
&
descriptions tresnecessaires
pour la nauigation. Par Nicolas de
Nicolay, du Daulphine;
Geographe du
Roy.

Chancery cursive attributed to Pierre Hamon. *Navigation,* title page from the Harleyian manuscript, *c.* 1560 (British Museum, London; MS. 3996, fol. 1).

Spread of chancery cursive

The propagation of the chancery cursive abroad was furthered by native manuals too. The Latin letters called italics were introduced into Germany by Casper Neff's *Thesaurium artis scriptoriae* (1549); into Spain by a disciple of Palatino, Juan de Yciar, in his *Recopilacion subtilissima* (1548); into France by Pierre Hamon's *Alphabet de l'invention des lettres en diverses escritures* (1561); and into England by means of *A Booke Containing Divers Sortes of Hands* (1570) by Jean de Beauchesne and John Baildon. This last was a translation of the French senior author's *Thrésor d'escripture,* believed to have been published at Lyons 20 years earlier; since no copy has been found, first place goes by default to the Hamon book.

The pure Italian chancery hand was the favourite of court circles and Humanist scholars through the second half of the 16th century. In England Roger Ascham, mid-16th-century schoolmaster to kings and queens, wrote and taught an exemplary *cancellaresca,* as did the late-16th-century Cambridge don Bartholomew Doding-

By courtesy of the trustees of the British Museum

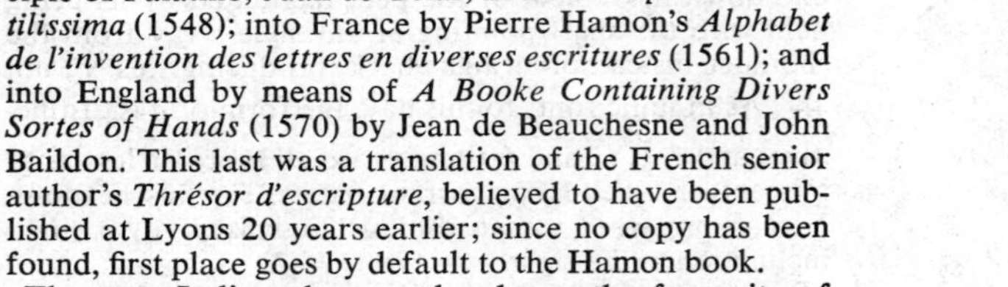
And I pray god, my habilitie may
my purpose is earnestlie bent to mynde

Running secretary hand. Letter by Roger Ascham, 1552 (British Museum, London; Landsdowne 3).

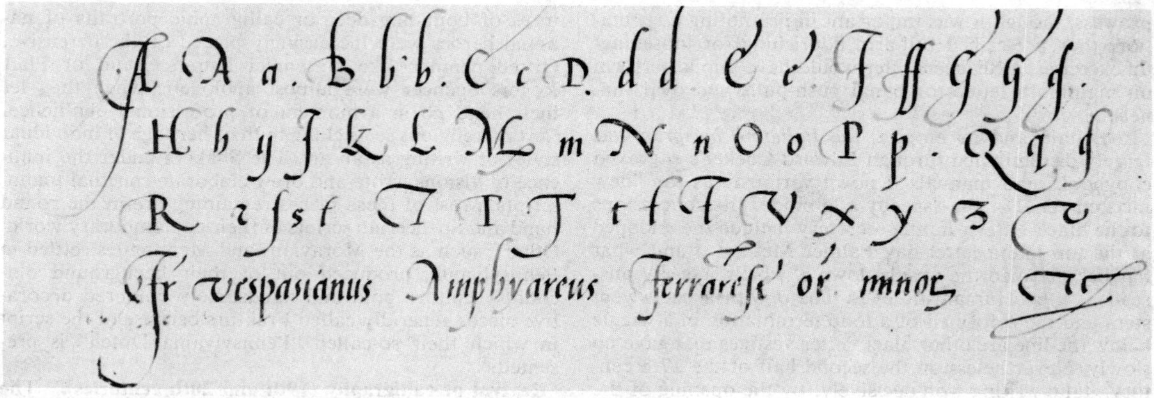

Bastarda script. Writing manual by Vespasiano Amphiareo (Albertacci), *c.* 1548. In the Harvard College Library, Cambridge, Massachusetts.
By permission of the Harvard College Library, Cambridge, Massachusetts, Department of Printing and Graphic Arts

ton. These and other educated Europeans generally wrote the black-letter "running secretary," too, the script of Shakespeare, who gave voice to no more than a sturdy nationalism when he poked fun at the newfangled "sweet Roman hand." For their part, the writing masters, in striving to reach an ever larger public, increasingly emphasized the compromise script intended to bring learners already indoctrinated in the common Gothic cursive to command more readily the fashionable italic style. The *Opera nella quale si insegna a scrivere*, of Vespasiano Amphiareo (Albertacci), had already offered at Venice in 1554 models that combined the overdisciplined strokes of Palatino with elements of black-letter mercantile hands (*e.g.*, loops and running ligatures); to this hybrid *cancellaresca* that he claimed as his own invention, Amphiareo gave the accurate name of *bastarda*. Then Gianfrancesco Cresci of Milan, a Vatican scriptor, published his *Essemplare* (1560), to herald the oncoming Baroque and to reject vehemently the works and ways of Palatino and all his academic sort. He replaced their most stylish broad, chisel-bevelled nib and meticulous building up of disjoined strokes with a narrow, rounded-off pen flexible enough to respond to pressure and fluent in dashing off his much-inclined italic *bastarda* topped off dramatically with bulbous *testegiatta*. It is not too much to say that Cresci's script, with the handsome set of swash capitals (to borrow the typographic term for these free-swinging forms), not only established a revolutionary front for 17th-century calligraphy but also contained the germs of 18th-century "copperplate" and even Spencerian scripts. Cresci, by the way, was the first in Italy to take advantage of the sleek allurements of copperplate engraving, though Giuliantonio Hercolani's *Lo Scrittor Utile* (1574; plates engraved in 1571) was a close rival.

Importance of Cresci

By courtesy of the Biblioteca Apostolica Vaticana

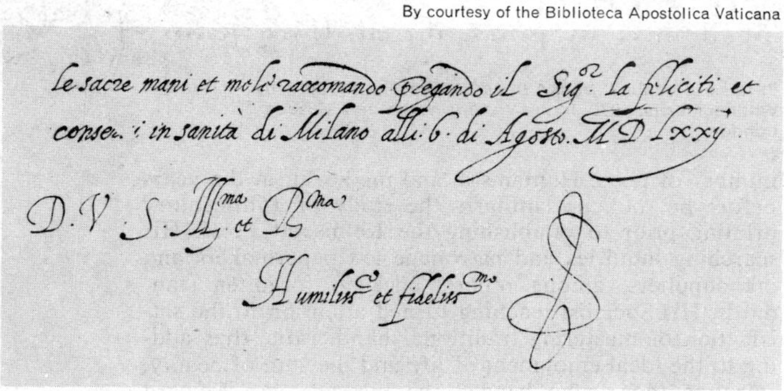

Italic *bastarda*. Letter by Gianfrancesco Cresci, 1572 (Vatican Library; Lat. 6185, fol. 135 R).

The principal French hands of the period were the national black-letter cursive called *lettre françois* or *financière*, used in ordinary affairs, and the aristocratic *italienne bastarde*. In the Low Countries, examples of excellence are provided by Clement Perret in his *Exercitatio alphabetica* (1569), and by Jan van de Velde in his work *Spieghel der Schriftkonste* (1605), the fame of which was carried down through generations of English penmen.

It was the period of elaborate and bold "striking" of decorative figures and fanciful shapes by "command of hand." The writing masters did not regard such ornamental work as mere vain show or necessary proof of

By courtesy of the Columbia University Libraries, New York

Spieghel der Schriftkonste, calligraphy by Jan van de Velde, 1605. In the Columbia University Libraries, New York.

prowess, though it was important in promoting a reputation; they prescribed full-arm flourishing for loosening-up exercises, as teachers later would have pupils perform on mammoth letters or banal push-pulls and oval tunnels.

In Britain and its empire, the *italienne bastarde* was largely disseminated through Edward Cocker's engraved copybooks and manuals. Known variously as the "new mixt current" or the "speedy à la mode," its concessions to the black-letter running secretary include the *e* looped at the top like a latter-day Palmer Method *o* and what has been termed the upside-down *r*, which is easily misread as *u* by Humanistic eyes. The *d* with a backswept stem and the *h* formed of a loop terminating in a wiggle below the line are other black-letter vestiges that gave up slowly. Nevertheless, in the second half of the 17th century, italic writing won decisively. By the opening of the 18th century, a chastened, businesslike version was developed in London by John Ayres and his younger contemporary writing masters eager to serve commercial demands. The small, narrow variety of Italian-French script was relegated to ladies' use as something suited to frail capacities, while the robust strain was considered fit to dominate an epoch of trade supremacy. The former came to be known as the Italian hand simply, while the latter took charge of affairs throughout the world as English round hand or "copperplate."

By courtesy of Dover Publications, Inc.

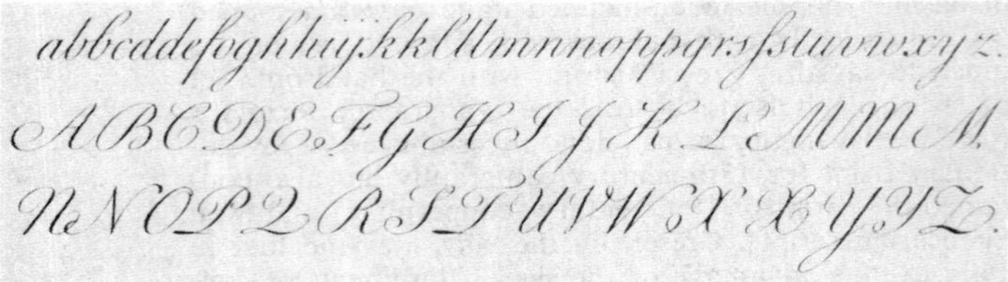

Copperplate, or English round hand. From *The Universal Penman*, Philip Hofer (ed.), engraved by George Bickham, 1743. Facsimile edition, Dover Publications, Inc., 1941.

Penmanship in colonial America

Though the transition from black-letter had been even more accelerated in the American colonies, Boston in New England was one of the last bastions of calligraphy in the trend toward countinghouse and commercial-college penmanship. The traditional foundations were laid solidly by the 18th-century writing master Abiah Holbrook, who raised a group of young Bostonian proficients at the South Writing School and left a fine manuscript, *The Writing Master's Amusement* (1767), in personal testimony.

By permission of the Harvard College Library, Cambridge, Massachusetts, Department of Printing and Graphic Arts

The Writing Master's Amusement, by Abiah Holbrook, 1767. In the Harvard College Library, Cambridge, Massachusetts.

As the 19th century advanced, the competition constantly mounted among systematists emphasizing the plain, practical business hand and decrying the "ornamental branches." Those who loved to flourish quill pictures of bounding deer or calligraphic portraits of national heroes were increasingly placed on the defensive. Gifted penmen like Nathaniel Duren Gould or Platt Rogers Spencer were almost apologetic when they let their hand go in a moment of professional ebullience. Certain religious sects clung to their heritage of individual styles of writing as an art. The Shakers under the influence of visions wrote and drew elaborate spiritual manuscripts. Most of these pieces remaining are in the round hand and Spencerian scripts of their contemporary world. Others, such as the Moravians and Mennonites settled in Pennsylvania, produced out of their background old-country culture bold and handsomely coloured decorative pieces generally called Frakturs because of the script in which their so-called "Pennsylvania Dutch" is presented.

Revival of calligraphy (19th and 20th centuries). The revival of calligraphy at the end of the 19th century was part of an artistic revolt against the mechanization of life. A nostalgic sense of the social losses resulting from industrialization was expressed in social-reformist and arts and crafts movements. About 1870 the English writer and artist William Morris had begun to concentrate attention on the ancient practice of scribes and to study with pen on parchment the means of achieving similar results. In this fashion he wrote out and illuminated a

By courtesy of the Victoria and Albert Museum, London

"Praise of Venus," from *A Book of Verse*, calligraphy by William Morris, 1870. In the Victoria and Albert Museum, London.

number of texts, Humanistic and medieval, in the years before he took up similarly the study of 15th-century printing prior to establishing the Kelmscott Press. His searching inquiries and patronage led papermakers and ink suppliers, among others, back to forgotten standards. His Socialist teaching turned attention to the satisfaction of mastering traditional handicrafts, thus adding to the ideal enjoyment of life and the sum of beauty.

Influence of Edward Johnston

Among those who heeded the message was Edward Johnston. He abandoned studies for an intended medical career for those of a scribe. On the basis of the Morris investigations and guided particularly by Sydney Cockerell, Morris' secretary, he rediscovered how to cut and

By courtesy of the Newberry Library, Chicago, the Wing Collection

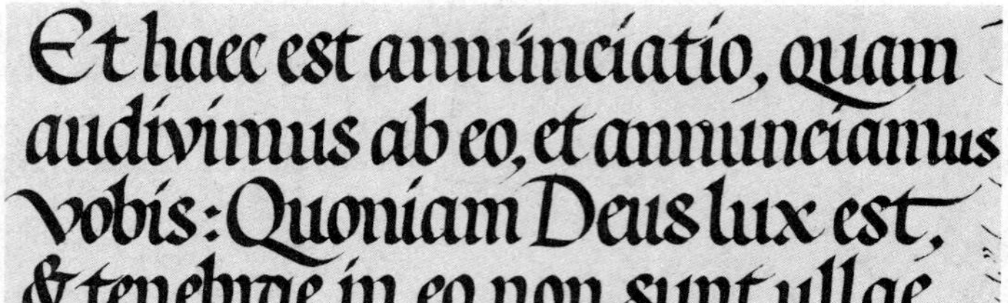

Manuscript copy sheet by Edward Johnston, 1918. In the Newberry Library, Chicago.

sharpen reeds and quills, how to hold the chisel-nibbed pen so as to produce the kinds of writing that had become familiar in his study of old manuscripts, and every detail of how to make manuscripts. In 1899 he began teaching in London, first at the Central School of Arts and Crafts and, two years later, at the Royal College of Art. His early pupils soon became esteemed designers of lettering and influential calligraphers—*e.g.*, Anna Simons, Eric Gill, Noel Rooke, Graily Hewitt, and Percy

Smith. In 1906 he published the basic manual *Writing and Illuminating, and Lettering*, 500 pages profusely illustrated with his own and Rooke's drawings and with reproductions from historic manuscripts. It contains, among other things, a chapter by Gill on cutting inscriptions in stone and material on gilding by the specialist Hewitt. In 1910 the book was published in Germany, where it supported the work independently begun by Rudolf von Larisch in Vienna and carried on by Rudolf Koch and Anna Simons. Under the Nazi regime, the Gothic exponents enjoyed a resurgence, but, after the war, such skilled young German calligraphers as Hermann Zapf led the way back to roman and italic script styles. Jan Tschichold's work has been influential in the appreciation of classical letters for present-day uses.

Art schools everywhere gradually followed the Royal College of Art in offering courses in lettering and writing; these, along with sound forms, instilled a sense of responsibility to a rich heritage. Type design passed from the control of engineers into the hands of artists and calligraphical scholars, such as Stanley Morison, Jan van Krimpen, Akke Kumlien, Bruce Rogers, Frederic W. Goudy, Victor Hammer, Berthold Wolpe, and Warren Chappell. The "freezing" of fine alphabets as font material stabilizes them and multiplies their influence. The effects were not limited to the printed or manuscript page or to book covers and jackets; all kinds of private and public markers and memorials, addresses, diplomas, and even the politicians' ubiquitous testimonial "scrolls" were touched by reform or at least by some consciousness of shortcoming. The stylish lapidary capitals, italics, and sloped letters engraved on boxwood by Reynolds Stone for printing or cut on tablets of wood or stone by John Howard Benson, Will Carter, or David Kindersley are at once distinctively contemporary and lambent with tradition.

Revival of calligraphy in the United States

Though the United States was a decade behind Britain in organizing an arts and crafts movement, four years before the Johnston Bible a Boston architect, Frank Chouteau Brown, brought out a surprisingly sophisticated book, *Letters and Lettering: A Treatise with 200 Examples* (1902). He praised Morris' initiative but wished for more classical balance; he pointed to the neglect of italics and gave them generous space, including specimens from the Lucas 1577 *Arte de escrivir*, "letra del Grifo," *bastarda*, and others. In 1905 *The Parable of the Prodigal Son*, fashioned like a Humanistic manuscript by William Addison Dwiggins and printed from photoengraved plates, was offered for sale. Dwiggins, as illustration for a talk on early writing books, copied a page out of the 1542 Tagliente he had picked up in Europe and passed out prints of it at the December 29, 1913, meeting of the Society of Printers—thereby leading the revival of *cancellaresca*. Other graphic artists concerned in the movement included Thomas Maitland Cleland and Rudolph Ruzicka.

Edward Johnston's pupils, and their pupils, organized in 1921 the Society of Scribes and Illuminators, "zealously directed toward the production of books and documents" by hand and the advancement of the crafts of member scribes, gilders, and illuminators. The program of this professional group based in London is conducted by means of lectures, publications, and exhibitions. In the 1930s exhibits travelled to five American centres, as well as to Paris and Copenhagen. Members representing the several crafts have collaborated in the making of the rolls of honour for the Royal Air Force and United States Air Force, at St. Clement Danes Church, London. The society has served as a model for similar activities abroad, notably the organization in The Netherlands under the leadership of Jan van Krimpen. In 1952 the British society, with Alfred Fairbank as president, recognized the rising popular interest in italic handwriting by instituting the Society for Italic Handwriting, which soon attracted a large international membership of teachers and amateurs.

In the United States individual enthusiasts and informal groups fostered calligraphy outside the art schools. Ernst F. Detterer in Chicago, who had lessons from Johnston in 1913, headed such a group at the Newberry Library for many years and, when he died in 1947, was succeeded by James Hayes. In Portland, Oregon, the instruction and copybooks of Lloyd J. Reynolds, a professor of art in Reed College, had significant influence. For decades Paul Standard in New York practiced and preached *cancellaresca corsiva* and saw the italic reform gain.

20th-century writing manuals and copybooks

Since Johnston a series of manuals and copybooks centring attention on handwriting improvement have proceeded from the espousal of the rather heavy Humanistic hand he admired to an italic that at least implies more speed. Stanley Morison presciently picked out a model for his own hand from Johnston's *Writing and Illuminating, and Lettering* as early as 1913, and a scholar of calligraphy, James Wardrop, called that manuscript "the fons et origo" of his paleographical studies; it is, as Johnston says, a semiformal 16th-century Italian cursive, skillful but a bit colourless to the eye. The fullest and most practical work on the italic is by Alfred John Fairbank, *A Handwriting Manual* (1932). The author places before his book as frontispiece a page of the *bastarda* of Lucas, *Arte de escrivir*, 1577. J.H. Benson's work *The First Writing Book* (1955) consists of the text and examples of the Arrighi *Operina* translated and admirably written out by the editor and furnished with practical clarifications and notes for the learner. Since Johnston calligraphical research and publishing activities have also produced a handsome and scholarly shelfful of books on related forms, most notably the Renaissance capitals.

(Ra.N.)

II. Aramaic, Hebrew, and Arabic handwriting and calligraphy

EARLY SEMITIC AND HEBREW WRITING

During the 2nd millennium BC, various Semitic peoples at the eastern end of the Mediterranean were experimenting with alphabetic writing. Between 1500 and 1000 BC, alphabetic signs found in scattered sites showed a correspondence of form and provided material for sound translations. Bodies of writing from this period are fragmented: a few signs scratched on sherds or cut in stone. Few of these are celebrated in terms of aesthetic value.

One interesting set of Semitic inscriptions was discovered in 1905 at an ancient mining site on the Sinai Peninsula. A sphinx from that discovery yields the taw, nun, taw, or t, n, t, meaning "gift." It is evident that the nun, or n, sign is a rendering of a serpent. Most of the early Semitic alphabetic signs were similarly derived from word signs of more ancient vintage. Early Semitic inscription letters are somewhat stiff in visual quality.

The several Semitic peoples in the Near East area spoke languages that were closely related, and this enabled them to use the same set of alphabetic signs. After some experimentation the alphabet was reduced to 22 signs for consonants. There were no vowel signs. The tribes of Canaan (Hebrews, Phoenicians, and Aramaeans) were important in the development of alphabetic writing, and all seemed to be employing the alphabet by 1000 BC.

Phoenician contributions

The Phoenicians, living along a 20-mile (30-kilometre) strip on the Mediterranean, made the great sea their second home, giving the alphabet to Greeks in the mutual trading area and leaving inscriptions in many sites. One of the finest Phoenician inscriptions exists on a bronze

By courtesy of the Cliche Musees Nationaux, Paris

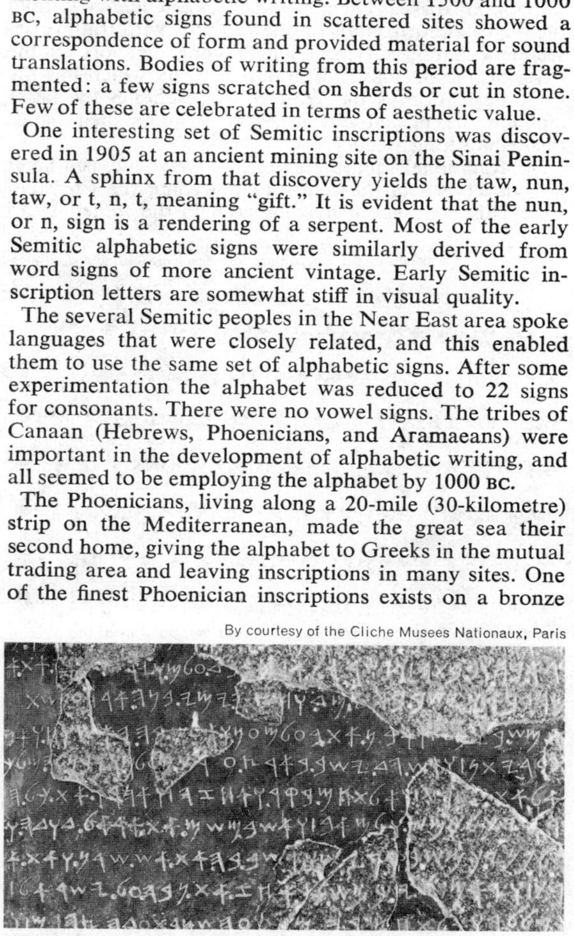

The Moabite Stone, *c.* 850 BC (Louvre, Paris; AO 5066).

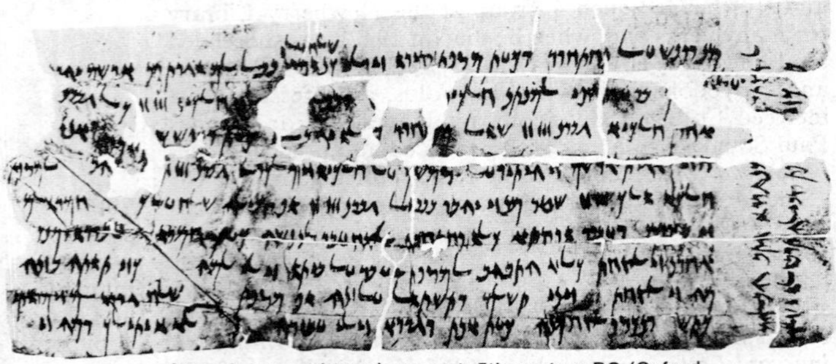

Aramaic pen-written document, 5th century BC (Oxford, Bodleian Library; MS. Pell. Aram. XIV).
By courtesy of the Bodleian Library, Oxford

cup from Cyprus called the Baal of Lebanon (Louvre, Paris) dating from *c.* 800 BC. The so-called Moabite Stone (Louvre, Paris), *c.* 850 BC, has an inscription that is also a famous example of early Semitic writing.

Old Hebrew existed in inscription form in the early centuries of the 1st millennium BC. The pen-written forms of the Old Hebrew alphabet are best preserved in the 13th century AD documents of the Samaritan sects.

The period of exile suffered by the Israelites (586–538 BC) dealt a heavy blow to the Hebrew language, since, after their return from exile, Aramaic was the dominant language of the area, and Hebrew existed as a second and scholarly language. Aramaic pen-written documents begin to appear in the 5th century BC and are vigorous interpretations of inscription letters. As may be observed in the Aramaic document (MS. Pell. Aram. XIV) in the Bodleian Library at Oxford, the penman has cut the pen wide at the tip to produce a pronounced thick and thin structure to the line of letters. The penman's hand was rotated counterclockwise more than 45 degrees relative to vertical, so that vertical strokes were thinner than the horizontal strokes. Then, too, there is a tendency to hold these strong horizontals on the top line, with trailing descenders finding a typical length, long or short on the basis of ancient habits. The *lamed* form, which has the same derivation as the Western L, resembles the latter and can be picked out in early Aramaic pen hands through its long ascender.

Merubbaʿ script

The traditional square Hebrew, or *merubbaʿ*, pen hand was developed in the centuries preceding the Christian Era. This early script may be seen in the famed Dead

By courtesy of the Shrine of the Book, The Samuel and Jeane H. Gottesman Centre for Biblical Manuscripts, The Israel Museum, Jerusalem

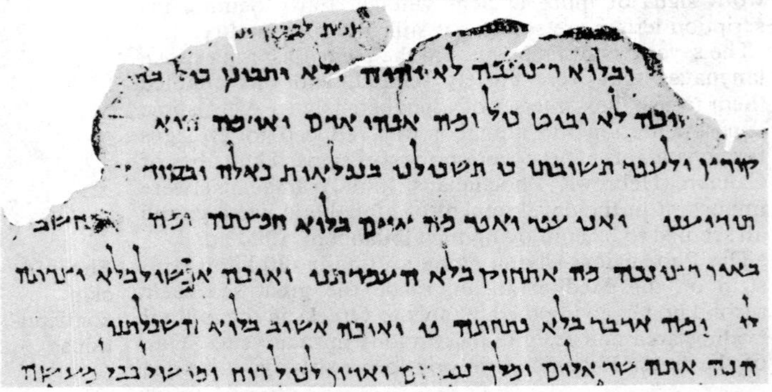

Merubbaʿ pen hand. The *Thanksgiving Psalms*, portion of the Dead Sea Scrolls, *c.* 1st century AD (the Shrine of the Book, Jerusalem; vol. 10).

Sea Scrolls discovered in 1947. These scrolls are associated with a group of dissident Jews who founded a religious commune on the northwestern shore of the Dead Sea about 180 BC. The commune had an extensive library. Pens were the instruments of writing, and, as in earlier Aramaic documents, leather provided the surface. Again the *lamed* form is visually prominent.

There are no Hebrew manuscripts from the first half millennium of the Christian Era. Most of the development in the square Hebrew script occurred between AD 1000 and 1500. The earliest script to emerge from the Dead Sea writing was the Early Sefardic (Spharadic), with examples dating between AD 600 and 1200. The Classic Sefardic hand appears between the years AD 1100 and 1600. The Ashkenazic style of Hebrew writing exhibits French and German Gothic overtones of the so-called black-letter styles (see above) developed to write western European languages in the late Middle Ages. German black-letter with its double-stroked heads and feet was difficult for the scribe. Hebrew scripts from this period exhibit some of the same complicated pen stroking and change of pen slant within individual characters. Some of the decorative qualities of medieval French writing are seen embodied in this Hebrew script.

The Sefardic and Ashkenazic styles

It is generally recognized that Hebrew typefaces have in large measure been imitations of various hand scripts and are more slavish in this imitation than those occurring in other language cultures. One of the finest of the

By courtesy of the Biblioteca Apostolica Vaticana

Medieval Hebrew scripts.
(Left) Sefardic script, before AD 1331; in the Vatican Library (7. Vat. heb. 12. Hagiographa). (Right) Ashkenazic script, AD 1295; in the Vatican Library (6. Urbinas heb. 1. Biblia).

early Hebrew types is credited to the Frenchman Guillaume Le Bé, the excellent 16th-century punch cutter.

SPREAD OF ARAMAIC TO THE NEAR EAST AND ASIA

Aramaic was the mother of many languages in the Near East and Asia. Generally, the Canaanite-Phoenician influence went west from Palestine, while Aramaic became an international language spreading east, south, and north from the eastern end of the Mediterranean Sea. Never sponsored by great political power, the Aramaic script and language succeeded through inherent efficiency and because the Aramaeans were vigorous traders and extensive travellers in the millennium preceding the birth of Christ.

Syriac. One of the important languages to derive from Aramaic was Syriac. It was spoken over large areas to the north and east of Palestine, but the literature emerged from a strong national church of Syria centred in the city of Edessa. The development of Syriac scripts occurred from the 4th to the 7th century AD, and its most important script is called Estrangela.

By courtesy of the trustees of the British Museum

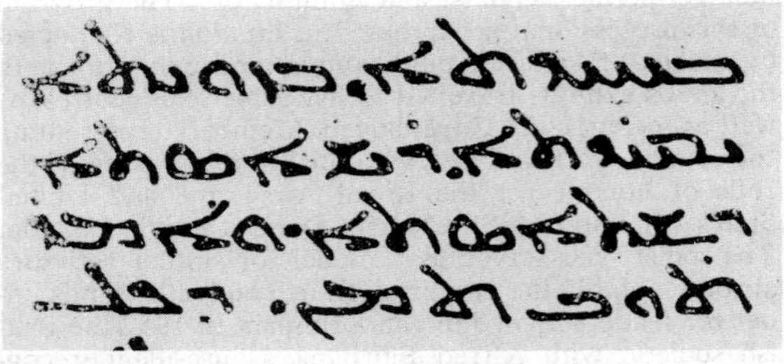

Estrangela script, *c.* AD 474 (British Museum, London; Add. 17,182, Aphraatis demonstrationes Edessa exar.).

Eastern Christendom was riddled with sects and heretical movements. After 431 the Syriac language and script split into eastern and western branches. The western branch was called Serta and developed into two varieties, Jacobite and Melkite. Vigorous in pen graphics, Serta

Serta and Nestorian writing

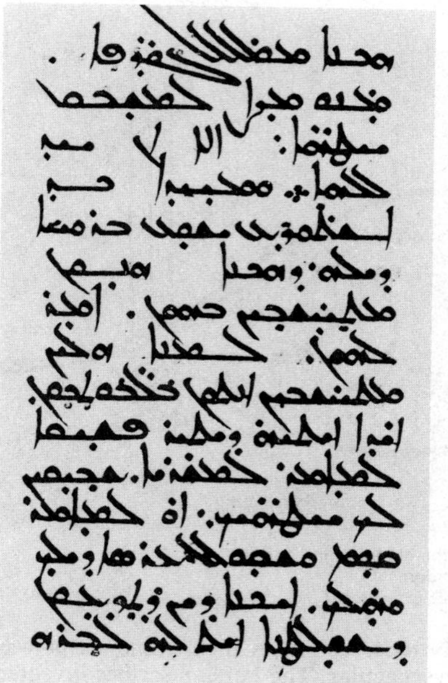

Jacobite script, AD 1481 (Vatican Library; 30.b Vat. syr. 18).
By courtesy of the Biblioteca Apostolica Vaticana

writing shows that, unlike the early Aramaic and Hebrew scripts, characters are fastened to a bottom horizontal. Modern typefaces used to print Syriac, which has survived as a language, have the same characteristic. Eastern Syriac script was called Nestorian after Nestorius, who led a secession movement from the Orthodox Church of Byzantium. The Nestorian church flourished in Persia and spread along trade routes deep into Asia, a fact observed by Marco Polo. (D.An.)

Arabic calligraphy. In the 7th and 8th centuries AD, the Arab armies conquered for Islām territories stretching from the shores of the Atlantic to Sind (Now in Pakistan). Besides a religion, they brought to the conquered peoples a language both written and spoken. The Arabic language was a principal factor in uniting peoples who differed widely in race, language, and culture. In the early centures of Islām, Arabic was not only the official language of administration, but also was and has remained the language of religion and learning. The Arabic alphabet has been adopted by the Islāmic peoples' vernaculars just as the Latin alphabet by the Christian West.

The Muslim believes that God (Allāh) revealed the Qur'ān to the prophet Muḥammad through the Archangel Gabriel as intermediary. For him, not only the sense but also the very words of the sacred text are inspired; and that is why in the Islāmic world the Qur'ān is recited not in the vernacular but in the original Arabic. The apparent great respect for the written word of God clearly explains the reason why calligraphy was accorded a high rank among the arts and why copying the Qur'ān was esteemed a most meritorious act. The names recorded of those who excelled in the art of writing far outnumber those of architects, painters, and craftsmen.

The Arabic script was evolved probably during the 6th century AD from Nabataean, a dialect of Aramaic current in northern Arabia. The earliest surviving examples of Arabic before Islām are inscriptions on stone.

Arabic is written from right to left and consists of 17 characters, or outlines, certain of which by the addition of dots placed above or below the character provide the 28 letters of the Arabic alphabet. Short vowels are not included in the alphabet, being indicated by signs placed above or below the consonant or long vowel that they follow. Certain characters may be joined to their neighbours, others to the preceding one only, and others to the succeeding one only. When coupled to another, the form of the character undergoes certain changes.

These features, as well as the fact that there are no capital forms of letters, give the Arabic script its particular character. A line of Arabic suggests an urgent progress of the characters from right to left. The nice balance between the vertical shafts above and the open curves below the middle register induces a sense of harmony. The peculiarity that certain letters cannot be joined to their neighbours provides articulation. For writing, the Islāmic calligrapher uses a reed pen (*qalam*) with the working point cut on an angle. This produces a thick downstroke and a thin upstroke with an infinity of gradation in between. The line traced by a skilled calligrapher is a marvel of fluidity and sensitive inflection, communicating the very action of the master's hand. Even in monumental inscriptions, whether on stone or some other intractable material, the craftsman still tries to retain this sense of the guiding hand by graduating the thickness of his line.

Kūfic script

Broadly speaking, there are two distinct scripts in the early centuries of Islām: cursive script and Kūfic script. For everyday purposes a cursive script was employed: typical examples are to be seen in the Arabic papyri from Egypt. Rapidly executed, the script does not appear to have been subject to formal and rigorous rules; and not all the surviving examples are the work of professional scribes. Kūfic script, however, seems to have been developed for religious and official purposes. The term Kūfic means the script of Kūfah, an Islāmic city founded in Mesopotamia in AD 638; but the actual connection between the city and the script is not clear. Kūfic is a more or less square and angular script. In monumental and funerary inscriptions in stone, the angular forms may be partly dictated by the material. Professional copyists employed a particular form for reproducing the earliest copies of the Qur'ān that have survived. These are written on parchment and date from the 8th to the 10th century. They are mostly of an oblong as opposed to codex format. The writing is often large, especially in the early examples, so that there may be as few as three lines to a single page. The script can hardly be described as stiff and angular; rather, the pace is majestic and mea-

By courtesy of R. Pinder-Wilson

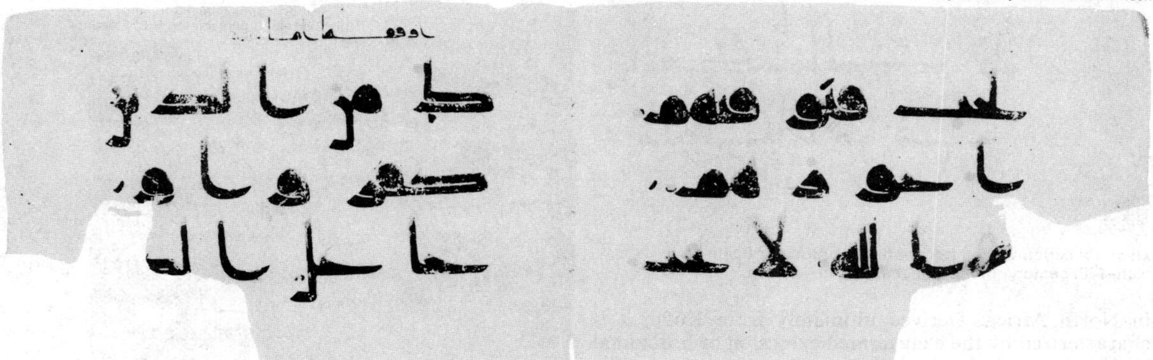

Kūfic script. Double page opening of a Qur'ān from Syria, 9th century AD. In the collection of R. Pinder-Wilson.

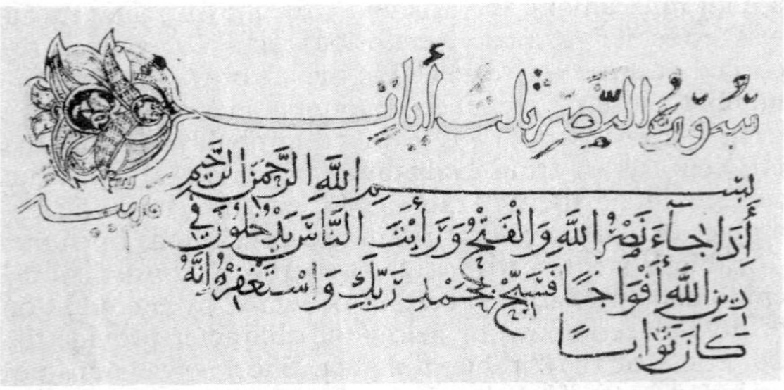

Naskhī script. Baghdad Qur'ān copied by Ibn al-Bawwāb *c.* 1000 (Chester Beatty Library, Dublin; MS. 1431, fol. 283).
By courtesy of the Chester Beatty Library, Dublin

sured. Arab scholars writing in this early period record numerous scripts. Unfortunately, their descriptions do not allow us to determine the precise nature of these.

Kūfic went out of general use about the 11th century, although it continued to be used as a decorative element contrasting with those scripts that superseded it. About AD 1000 a new script was established and came to be used for copying the Qur'ān. This is the so-called *naskhī* script, which has remained perhaps the most popular script in the Arab world. It is a cursive script based on certain laws governing the proportions between the letters. The two names associated with its development are Ibn Muqlah and Ibn al-Bawwāb, both of whom lived and worked in Mesopotamia. Of the latter's work a single authentic example survives, a manuscript of the Qur'ān in the Chester Beatty Library, Dublin. *Naskhī* was used for copying the Qur'ān from the 11th century onward.

Establishment of *naskhī* script

The conception of proportional relationships between the letters gave rise to other scripts, more or less variants on *naskhī;* these include the large and majestic *thuluth* script, which came to be adopted for many of the large copies of the Qur'ān produced from the 13th century. In Mamlūk Egypt of the 14th and 15th centuries, the *ṭūmār* script was also used for large Qur'āns.

Distinctive scripts were developed in particular regions. In Spain, the *maghribī* ("western") script was evolved and became the standard script for Qur'āns

By courtesy of the trustees of the British Museum

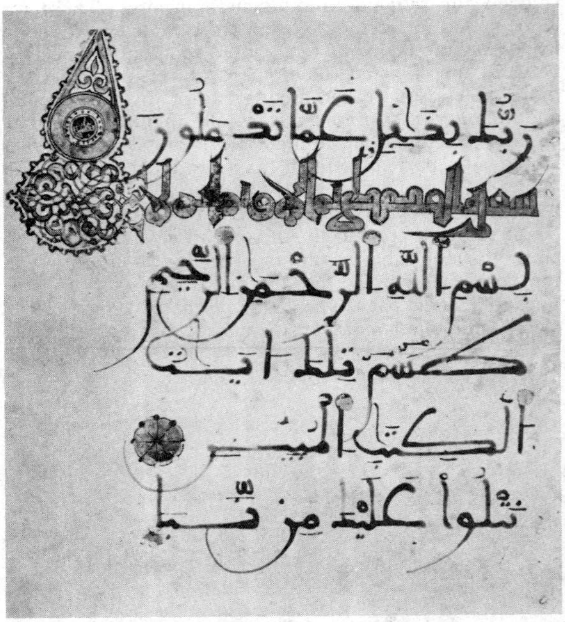

Maghribī script. Qur'ān from northwest Africa or Spain, 13th–14th century. In the British Museum, London.

in North Africa. Derived ultimately from Kūfic, it is characterized by the exaggerated extension of horizontal elements and of the final open curves below the middle register, as well as by certain orthographic peculiarities.

Both Persia and Turkey made important contributions

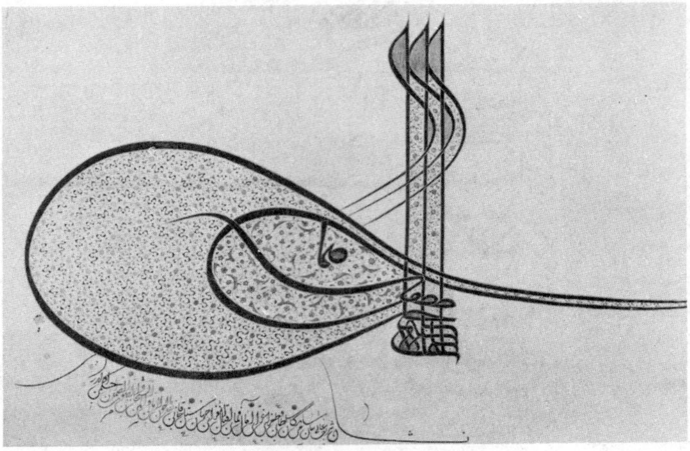

Tuğra of Süleyman the Magnificent, 16th century. In the British Museum, London.
By courtesy of the trustees of the British Museum

to calligraphy. In these countries the Arabic script was adopted for the vernacular. The Persian scribes invented the *taʿlīq* script in the 13th century. The term *taʿlīq* means "suspension" and aptly describes the tendency of each word to drop down from its preceding one. At the close of the same century, a famous calligrapher, Mīr ʿAlī of Tabriz, evolved *nastaʿlīq*, which, according to its name, is a combination of *naskhī* and *taʿlīq.* Like *taʿlīq* this is a fluid and elegant script, and both were popularly used for copying Persian literary works.

Development of *taʿlīq* and *nastaʿlīq* in Persia

A characteristic script developed in Ottoman Turkey was that used in the chancellery and known as *divani.* It is highly mannered and difficult to read. Peculiar to Turkish calligraphy is the *tuğra* (*tughrā*), a kind of royal cipher based on the names and titles of the reigning sultan and worked into an intricate and beautiful design. A distinctive *tuğra* was created for each sultan and affixed to imperial decrees by a skilled calligrapher, the *neshanı.*

There has always existed in the Islāmic world a keen appreciation of fine handwriting, and, from the 16th century, it became a practice to assemble in albums specimens of penmanship. Many of these assembled in Turkey, Persia, and India are preserved in museums and libraries. Calligraphy, too, has given rise to quite a considerable literature such as manuals for professional scribes employed in chancelleries.

In its broadest sense, calligraphy also includes the Arabic scripts employed in materials other than parchment, papyrus, and paper. In religious buildings, verses from the Qur'ān were inscribed on the walls for the edification of the faithful, whether carved in stone or stucco or executed in faience tiles. Religious invocations, dedications, and benedictory phrases were also introduced into the decoration of portable objects. Generally speaking, there is a close relationship between these and the scripts properly used on the conventional writing

By courtesy of the trustees of the British Museum; photograph, R.B. Fleming

Kharoṣṭī inscription on leather, 3rd century AD (British Museum, London; Find Spot n. N.XV. 350).

materials. It was often the practice for a skilled penman to design monumental inscriptions. (R.H.P.-W.)

Indic calligraphy. The most important examples of calligraphy to develop from Aramaic writing in its dissemination through southern and Central Asia were the scripts of India, especially of Sanskrit, the ancient Indo-European language of the subcontinent. Indic writing first appeared in the 3rd century BC during the reign of Aśoka (*c.* 273–232 BC). Leader of a great empire, Aśoka turned from military success to embrace the arts and religion. Aśoka's edicts were committed to stone. These inscriptions are stiff and angular in form. Following the Aśoka style of Indic writing, two new calligraphic types appear: Kharoṣṭī and Brāhmī. Kharoṣṭī was used in the northwestern regions of India from the 3rd century BC to the 4th century of the Christian Era, and it was used in Central Asia until the 8th century. It is characterized by a vigorous pen letter, reflecting the influence of Near East calligraphy.

Kharoṣṭī and Brāhmī scripts

Copper was a favoured material for Indic inscriptions. In the north of India, birch bark was used as a writing surface as early as the 2nd century AD. Many Indic manuscripts are written on palm leaves, even after the Indian languages were put on paper in the 13th century. Both sides of the leaves were used for writing. Long rectangular strips were gathered on top of one another, holes were drilled through all the leaves, and the book was held together by string. Books of this manufacture were common to Southeast Asia. The palm leaf was an excellent surface for penwriting, making possible the delicate lettering used in many of the scripts of southern Asia.

Visually, Sanskrit is associated most closely with the alphabetic form named Devanāgarī. In a 15th-century pen-written manuscript in the Freer Gallery at Washington, D.C., it can be observed that the pen's nib is cut wide, giving a considerable difference in thick and thin

Devanāgarī script

By courtesy of the Smithsonian Institution, Washington, D.C., Freer Gallery of Art

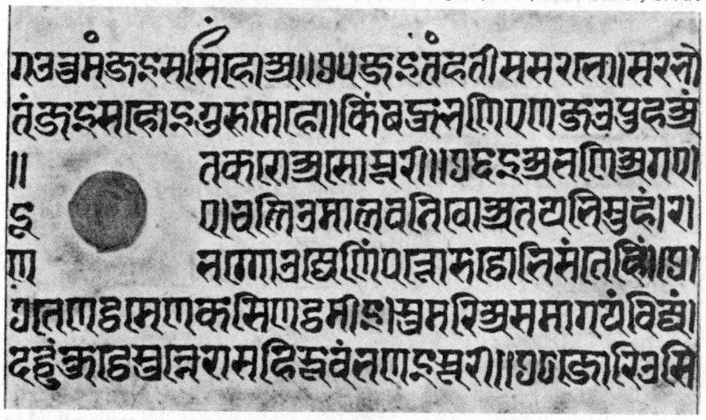

Sanskrit pen-written document, 15th century AD (Freer Gallery, Washington, D.C.; MS. 23.3).

strokes. The alphabetic signs hang down from a strong horizontal top line that may become connected. Through the years the strong horizontal and vertical emphasis of inscription writing has been preserved in the Devanāgarī script, and modern typefaces and teaching manuals stress this stiffness of execution. In informal documents this historical script can have more warmth and grace. (D.An.)

III. East Asian handwriting and calligraphy

In China, Korea, and Japan, calligraphy is a form of pure art. Chinese, Korean, and Japanese calligraphy derive from the written form of the Chinese language. Chinese is not an alphabetical language; each character is composed of a number of differently shaped lines within an imaginary square. The early Chinese written words, like the Egyptian hieroglyphs, were pictorial images, though not so close to the objects they represented as in the ancient Egyptian writing. Rather, they were simplified images, indicating meaning through suggestion or imagination. These simple images were flexible in composition, capable of developing with changing conditions by means of slight variations.

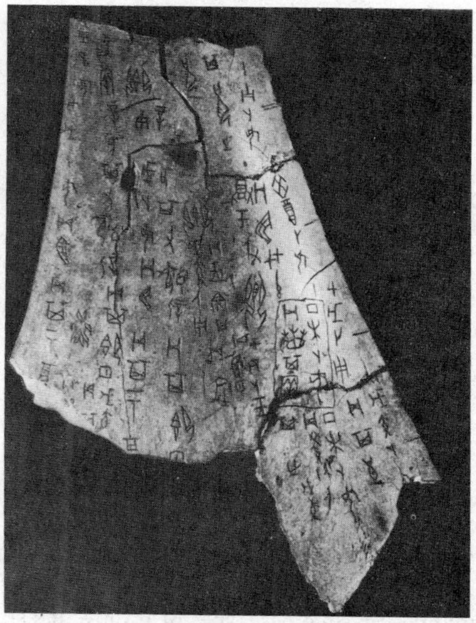

Chinese bone script, Shang dynasty (*c.* 1766–*c.* 1122 BC). In the East Asian Library, Columbia University, New York.

By courtesy of the East Asian Library, Columbia University, New York

CHINESE CALLIGRAPHY

The earliest known Chinese ideographs are engraved on the shoulder bones of large animals and on tortoise shells. The piece illustrated contains a number of the early ideographs; each seems to have been carefully composed before being engraved on the bones or shells. Although they are not entirely uniform in size, the variations are not great. The figures must have evolved from rough and careless scratches in the still more distant past. This *chia-ku-wen*, or bone-and-shell script (dated *c.* 1766–*c.* 1123 BC), is the earliest stage of development in Chinese calligraphy.

Bone-and-shell script

It was said that Ts'ang Chieh, the legendary inventor of Chinese writing, got his ideas from observing animals' footprints and birds' claw marks on the sand as well as other natural phenomena. He then started to work out simple images from what he conceived as repsenting different objects such as those that are given below:

Surely, the first images the inventor drew of these few objects could not have been quite so stylized but must have undergone some modifications to reach the above stage. Each image is composed of a minimum number of lines and yet is easily recognizable. Nouns no doubt came first. Later, new ideographs had to be invented to record actions, feelings, and differences in size, colour, taste, etc. Something was added to the already existing ideograph to give a new meaning. The ideograph for deer, for instance, is 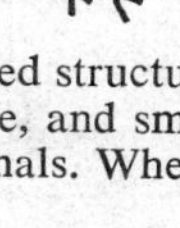, not a realistic image but a very much simplified structure of lines suggesting a deer by its horns, big eye, and small body, which distinguish it from other animals. When two such simple images 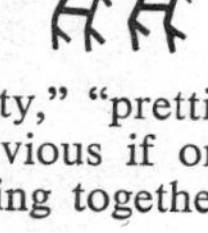 are put side by side, the meaning is "pretty," "prettiness," "beautiful," "beauty," etc., which is obvious if one has seen two such elegant creatures walking together. But, if a third image is added above the other two, as , it means "rough," "coarse," and even "haughty." This interesting point is the change in meaning through the arrangement of the images. If the three stags were not standing in an orderly manner, they could become rough and aggressive to anyone approaching them. From the aesthetic point of view, three such images could not be arranged side by side within an imaginary square without cramping one another, and in the end none would look like a deer at all.

Bronze script

After the bone-and-shell script came writing on bronze vessels, known as bronze script. In the early days of divination, when the kings of the Shang dynasty (*c.* 1766–*c.* 1122 BC) tried to solve their problems by consulting their ancestors and deities, the latter's answers were engraved on bones and on tortoise shells for perpetual preservation. Later, bronze was used to make cooking utensils and wine vessels for the special ceremonies of ancestral worship, raw or cooked food being offered up in them. So sacred were these ancestor-worshipping ceremonies that the best types of bronze utensil were specially designed and cast for such purposes, and, in addition, inscriptions, from a few words up to several hundred, were incised inside the bronzes. The words of the engravings could not be roughly formed or even just simple images; they had to be well worked out to go with the decorative ornaments outside the bronzes, and in some instances they almost became the chief decorative design in themselves. Though they preserved the general structure of the bone-and-shell script, they were considerably elaborated and beautified. Each bronze or set of them may bear a different type of inscription, not only in the wording but also in the manner of writing. Hundreds of them were created by different artists. The bronze script represents another stage of development in Chinese calligraphy, known as *chin-wen* or *ta chuan*, or the big-seal style.

Before long a unification of all types of the bronze script was enforced when China was united for the first time in the 3rd century BC. The first emperor of Ch'in, Ch'in Shih Huang Ti, could be regarded as one of the most terrible dictators in the history of mankind, for he burned Confucian books, buried Confucian scholars alive, and sacrificed thousands and thousands of lives to build the Great Wall to protect himself and his empire; but he did one great thing for the Chinese in unifying their writing, and by this they have been bound together ever since. The First Emperor's prime minister, Li Ssu, was given the task of working out the new script, and no other type was allowed to be used. Here are some common words that can be compared with similar words in bone-and-shell script mentioned above:

This was the third step forward in the development of Chinese calligraphy, known as *hsiao chuan*, or the small-seal style.

The *hsiao chuan*, or small-seal style

In the small-seal style of writing, all lines are drawn of even thickness, and more curves and circles are employed. Each word tends to fill up an imaginary square, and a passage written in small-seal style has the appearance of a series of equal squares neatly arranged in columns and rows, each of them balanced and well-spaced. The Chinese practice the small-seal style when aiming at future attainments in calligraphy. They use only the tip of a long-haired brush, which is almost suspended in the air; no light pencil sketches can be drawn first. It is a hard task and good training.

The uniformity of writing in China was established chiefly for the purpose of meeting the growing demands for documented records. Unfortunately, the small-seal style could not be written speedily and was therefore not entirely suitable. Another stage of development was needed—the fourth stage, which is called *li shu*, or official style. The Chinese word *li* here means "a petty official" or "a clerk"; *li shu* means a style specially devised for the use of clerks. If examined carefully, *li shu* is found to contain no circles and very few curved lines. In other words, all the circles became squares, and the curved parts of the lines became angular. Short straight lines, vertical and horizontal, are chiefly used. Because of the speed needed for writing, the brush in the hand tends to move up and down, and an even thickness of line cannot be enforced. As the thickness varied, artist-writers could concentrate more on the artistic shaping of the lines. Thus, a door opened for developments in Chinese calligraphy.

The *li shu*, or official style

Li shu is thought to have been invented by Ch'eng Miao (240–207 BC), who had offended the First Emperor of Ch'in and was serving a ten-year sentence in prison. He spent his time in prison working out this new development, which not only facilitated speed in writing but opened up seemingly endless possibilities for later calligraphers. According to their own artistic insight, they evolved new variations in the shape of lines and also in construction. The words in *li shu* style tend to be square or slightly rectangular horizontally. Though the even thickness of lines is relaxed, the rigidity in the shaping of them is still there; for instance, the vertical lines had to be shorter, and the horizontal ones longer. As this curtailed the freedom of hand for individual artistic taste, another stage of development came into being—the fifth stage, which is called *chen shu* (*k'ai shu*), or regular style. There is no record of who invented this style, but it must have been in evolution for a long time, at least since the 1st century AD if not earlier. The Chinese still use this regular style of writing today; in fact, what is known as modern Chinese writing is almost 2,000 years old, and the written words of China have not changed since the first century of the Christian Era.

Development of the *chen shu*, or regular style

Since about 1950, it has been claimed that the formation of the Chinese written language has changed. This is a serious misunderstanding; the only change is that a certain number of words can now be written and printed with a simplified construction. Most of those simplifica-

By courtesy of Chiang Yee

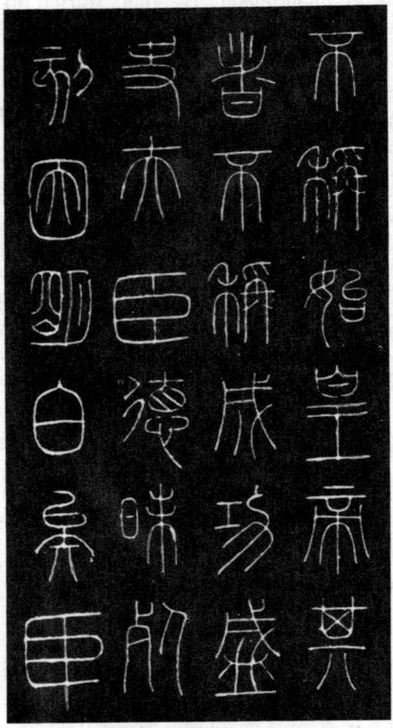

Hsiao chuan ("small seal style"). Rubbing of a copy of Li Ssu's writing engraved on a stone epitaph, Ch'in dynasty (221–206 BC).

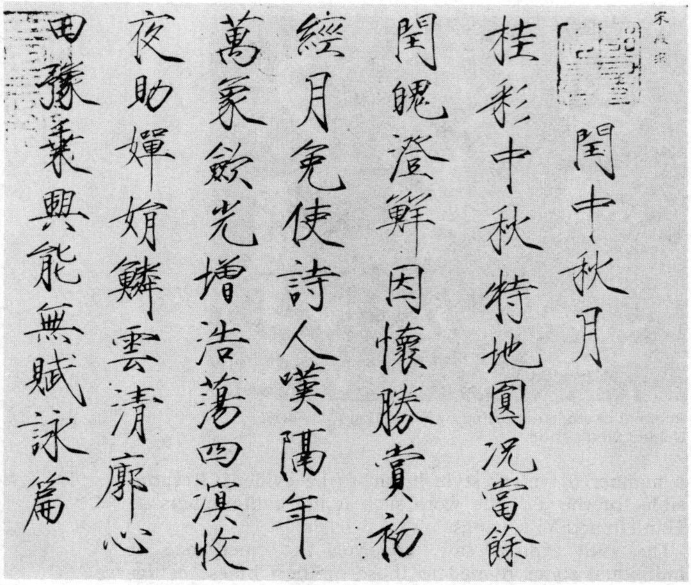

Chen shu ("regular style") written by Emperor Hui Tsung (1082–1135), Sung dynasty. In the National Palace Museum, Taipei.
By courtesy of the National Palace Museum, Taipei

tions had long been in use in the grass style of writing dating back as far as the regular style, but they were not permitted in documents and records, in books, and in making type for printing. Only those who had never been familiar with the grass style of writing mistook them for newly invented forms.

Before coming to the grass style, the regular style, or *chen shu*, must be explained. "Regular" here means "proper"—"the proper style of Chinese writing" used by all Chinese for government documents, printed books, public and private dealings in important matters ever since its establishment. Since the regulations for the civil-service examination enforced in the T'ang period (AD 618–907), each candidate had to be able to write a good hand in regular style. This Imperial decree deeply influenced all Chinese who wanted to become scholars and enter the civil service. This examination was abolished in 1905, but most Chinese still try to acquire a hand in regular style even to the present day.

In *chen shu* each line, each square or angle, and even each dot can be shaped according to the will and taste of the calligrapher. Indeed, a Chinese word in regular style presents an almost infinite variety of problems of structure and composition, and, when executed, it presents to the onlooker a design whose abstract beauty can draw the mind away from the literal meaning of the word itself.

The greatest exponents of Chinese calligraphy were Wang Hsi-chih (died 379) and his son Wang Hsien-chih in the 4th century. Few of their original works have survived, but a good number of their writings were engraved on stone tablets, and rubbings were made from them. Many great calligraphers imitated their styles, but none ever surpassed them. Since the 7th century there have been many master calligraphers such as Ou-yang Hsün (557–641), Sun Kuo-t'ing (died 688), Ch'u Sui-liang (596–658), Yen Chen-ch'ing (709–785), Liu Kung-ch'üan (778–865), Su Tung-p'o (1036–1101), Huang T'ing-chien (1045–1105), Mi Fei (1051–1107), the Sung emperor Hui Tsung (1082–1135), and Chao Meng-fu (1254–1322). A noted modern calligrapher was Yü Yu-jen (1878–1964).

Wang Hsi-chih not only provided the greatest example in the regular style of writing but also relaxed the tension somewhat in the arrangement of the strokes in the regular style by giving easy movement to the brush to trail from one word to another. This is called *hsing shu*, or running style, as if the hand were walking fast while writing. This, in turn, led to the creation of *ts'ao shu*, or grass style, which takes its name from its appearance—as if the wind had blown over the grass in a manner disorderly yet orderly. The English term cursive writing cannot describe the Chinese grass style, for even a cursive hand can be deciphered without very much difficulty.

The *hsing shu*, or running style, and the *ts'ao shu*, or grass style

But Chinese words in grass style are greatly simplified forms of the regular style and can be deciphered only by those who have practiced calligraphy for years. It is not a style for general use but for the calligrapher who wishes to produce a work of abstract art.

Technically speaking, there is no mystery in Chinese calligraphy. It depends on the skill and imagination of the writer to give interesting shapes to his strokes and to compose beautiful structures from them without any retouching or shading and, most important of all, with well-balanced spaces between the strokes. This balance needs years of practice and training.

The tools for Chinese calligraphy are very few—good ink, ink stone, a good brush, and good paper (some prefer silk). Even a child can fill up a squarish space with lines—straight or curved or circular—but to fill it so as to liberate the visual beauty of the linear shapes and composition depends on artistic insight and the training of a master.

By courtesy of the National Palace Museum, Taipei

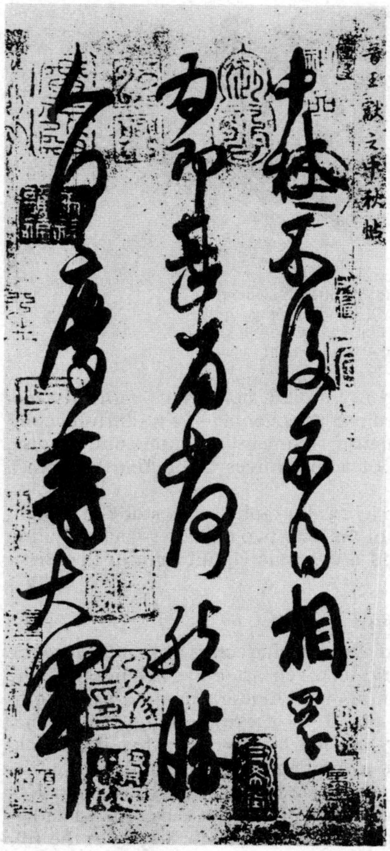

Hsing shu ("running style") and *ts'ao shu* ("grass style") by Wang Hsien-chih (AD 344–388), Six Dynasties period. In the National Palace Museum, Taipei.

The fundamental inspiration of Chinese calligraphy, as of all arts in China, is nature. In *chen shu*, or regular style, each stroke, even each dot, suggests the form of a natural object. As every twig of a living tree is alive, so every tiny stroke of a piece of fine calligraphy has the energy of a living thing. This is very different from the strokes in a printed word. Printing does not admit the slightest variation in the shapes and structures, but strict regularity is not tolerated by Chinese calligraphers, especially those who are masters of the *ts'ao shu*. A finished piece of fine calligraphy is not a symmetrical

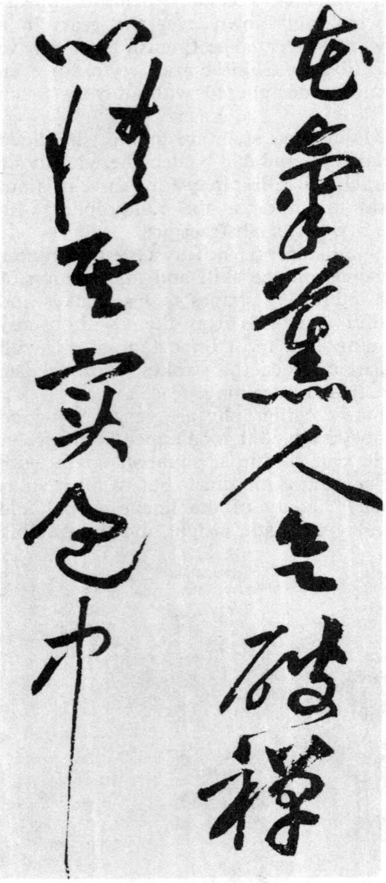

Ts'ao shu ("grass style") written by Huang T'ing-chien (1045–1105), Sung dynasty. In the National Palace Museum, Taipei.
By courtesy of the National Palace Museum, Taipei

arrangement of conventional shape but, rather, something like the coordinated movements of a skillfully composed dance—impulse, momentum, momentary poise, and the interplay of active forces combining to form a balanced whole.

The study of Chinese calligraphy is the study of a highly advanced form of art with two keynotes—a simulation in every stroke and a dynamic equilibrium in the structure. (C.Y.)

KOREAN CALLIGRAPHY

Koreans have used Chinese characters probably since the 2nd or 3rd century AD. Even after the invention of the Korean alphabet in 1447, Chinese was used as the official script until the 19th century. Thus, traditional Korean calligraphy was in Chinese rather than in Korean.

A few inscribed stone monuments remain from the Three Kingdoms period (*c.* 57 BC–AD 668). Ancient Koreans, eager to adopt Chinese culture, developed a calligraphy reflecting contemporary Chinese styles. In the following Unified Silla dynasty (668–935), a devotion and adherence to the T'ang culture of China gave birth to such great masters of calligraphy in Korea as Kim Saing and Choi Ch'i-wŏn, whose styles of writing basically followed those of the Chinese calligraphers Ou-yang Hsün and Yü Shih-nan.

The *chao* style

The angular, squarish style of Ou-yang Hsün, Shih-nan, and Yen Chen-ching, inherited from the Silla dynasty, continued in the Koryŏ period (918–1392) until around 1350, when the rounded, fluent style of the Chinese calligrapher Ch'ao Meng-fu, of the Yüan dynasty, was introduced and became the vogue. Since that time the *chao* style has remained the basic undercurrent in Korean calligraphy.

At first the calligraphy of the Yi dynasty (1392–1910) followed the *chao* style, but, early in the 16th century,

Rubbing of stone engraving by Kim Saing (711–791), Unified Silla period.

a mannered, vulgar style began to be evident. Responsible for the Yi style were such noted calligraphers as Han Ho and Yi Kwangsa.

The 19th century saw, however, the emergence of individual styles related to those of the Chinese calligraphers Su Shih and Mi Fei of the 11th century, Wen Cheng-ming of the 16th century, and Tung Ch'i-ch'ang of the late 16th and early 17th century. The new trend was due to Korea's close cultural contacts with Ch'ing China.

The greatest master of the Yi period was Kim Chŏng hi, who established the so-called *ch'usa* style. His calligraphy is derived from the *li shu* script of China, but his sense of pictorial composition, harmony within asymmetry, and animation by unmatched, forceful strokes gave him a style completely his own.

By courtesy of the National Palace Museum, Taipei

Chao style. *Hs'ing-tsu* written by Chao Meng-fu (1254–1322). In the National Palace Museum, Taipei.

A few calligraphers survived from the Yi dynasty into the early decades of the present century. One distraction was the influence of Japanese calligraphy, which began to be felt about 1920.

Since World War II, traditional calligraphy has survived only as a minor art. A new trend since the 1960s is an effort to exploit calligraphy in the Korean alphabet, a result of the government policy of eliminating Chinese characters from the Korean language. (W.-Y.K.)

JAPANESE CALLIGRAPHY

The art of calligraphy has long been highly esteemed in Japan as in China. There is no definite record of when the Japanese began to use Chinese words—called *kanji* in Japanese. It is known that a Korean scribe named Wani brought some Chinese books of Confucian classics, such as the *Analects*, *Great Learning*, and *Book of Mencius*, to Japan near the end of the 4th century AD.

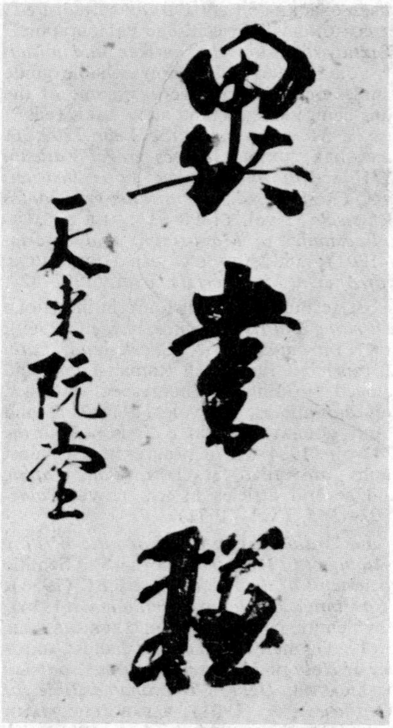

Ch'usa style written by Kim Chong hi (1786–1856), Yi period.

Modern calligraphy by Hisamatsu Shinichi. In the collection of Masao Abe, Kyōto.
By courtesy of Masao Abe, Kyoto

Kanji script

From the 7th century onward, many Japanese scholars, particularly Buddhist monks, went to China, and some Chinese came to Japan. As Indian Buddhism reached Japan via Korea and China and took root there, the use of *kanji* in Japan gradually grew. Eventually, *kanji* became the official system of writing in Japan, because it was the instrument for the transmission of Chinese Buddhism.

Most of the Chinese Buddhist monks who went to live in Japan were scholars and good calligraphers; their writings on the Buddhist scriptures and other subjects were highly admired and esteemed not only for their aesthetic value as calligraphy but also because they were the work of devout personalities and induced a sense of religious awe in the onlookers.

Many of the early Japanese emperors were ardent Buddhists and also acquired a masterly hand in *kanji* writings. So did many Japanese Zen priests, whose calligraphy tended to exercise a religious effect upon the Japanese mind. Theirs became a special type of calligraphy in Japan, namely, Japanese Zen calligraphy, or *bokuseki*.

Naturally, it was unsuitable for Japan to adopt an entire foreign language like Chinese, and Japanese thinkers began to devise a new, native script known as *hira-gana*, which was often referred to as "women's hand," or *onna-e* in Japanese. It was used particularly in the writing of Japanese poetry and had an elegant and graceful appearance. Thus, in Japanese calligraphy there are two different and distinctive types of writing, one in *kanji* and the other in *hira-gana*. Among the best known Japanese calligraphers are Kūkai (Kōbō Daishi), Emperor Saga, Michikaze, Fujiwara Yukinari, the Zen priest Daitō, and Ryōkan. The modern living Zen authority Hisamatsu Shinichi has been the unique calligrapher of the present age in Japan.

Hira-gana calligraphy

There are many outstanding pieces of Japanese calligraphy in *kanji*, but they are not distinctive when compared with their Chinese counterparts. Japanese *hira-gana* calligraphy, however, stands out prominently and proudly, especially in the style of *remmen-tai*, in which the *hira-gana* are written continuously and connected together without break, and in *chōwa-tai*, in which some *kanji* words join hands with the *hira-gana*. Japanese calligraphy in *remmen-tai* or in *chōwa-tai* has some resemblance to the Chinese grass style, but the two are easily distinguishable. In Chinese grass style, although the words are greatly simplified and several words can be joined together with trailing strokes, each separate word normally still retains its regular spacing within an imaginary square, big or small. But Japanese *hira-gana* cannot be spaced so separately and evenly. Therefore, a whole piece of *remmen-tai* calligraphy looks like a big bundle of beautiful silk strings hanging down confusedly yet artistically, as if the calligrapher had arranged them quite unconsciously. They were arranged consciously of course, but the calligrapher seems to have let his hand move swiftly of its own accord. The separate strokes

Types of Japanese Zen Calligraphy

kanji	*hira-gana*	transliteration	description
印可狀	いんかじよう	*inkajō*	document of permit approval
字號	じごう	*jigō*	name or title given a monk by his master
法語	ほうご	*hōgo*	words of the law or words of admonition
偈頌	げじゆ	*geju*	gatha or hymn or short moral poem
遺偈	ゆいげ	*yuige*	a will in the form of a gatha or hymn
進道語	しんどうご	*shindōgo*	instruction or words leading disciples to practice the dharma or law
詩	し	*shi*	poetry
額字	がくじ	*gakuji*	tablet with a few words inscribed horizontally
書簡	しよかん	*shokan*	letter or written communication

and dots have no distinctive shape but join other strokes and dots in the following *hira-gana*. The strokes or lines in *hira-gana* are not shaped like living things, nor are they of even thickness; but there must be good spacing between the strokes or lines and between one *hira-gana* and another, so that there is no confusion or blur in the completed piece. This is a highly demanding art, and the whole piece has to be executed with speed and without hesitation. *Hira-gana* requires solid training and artistic insight.

To complete the whole piece with its strokes or lines not too varied in shape yet not too even in thickness needs a special training; to keep the tip of the brush at an even distance from the paper, the writer must cultivate a steady hand. It is said that some Japanese calligraphers trained themselves by supporting the arm with a cord hanging from the ceiling, so that the hand would remain at a fixed distance from the paper. (C.Y.)

BIBLIOGRAPHY

Calligraphy in the West: DOROTHY MINER *et al., 2,000 Years of Calligraphy* (1965), a comprehensive and well-illustrated catalog of the ambitious three-part exhibition in Baltimore devoted to regions using the Latin alphabet, with especially valuable notes and references from the 1st century down to the 19th; EDWARD JOHNSTON, *Writing and Illuminating, and Lettering*, 14th ed. (1925, continuously reprinted), the gospel of the modern revival by its chief apostle; his *Formal Penmanship, and Other Papers*, ed. by HEATHER CHILD from the master's earlier searching for form (1971); DAVID DIRINGER, *The Hand-Produced Book* (1953), an untidy storehouse of information gathered from acute, far-ranging investigations sketchily indexed; JAN TSCHICHOLD, *Geschichte der Schrift in Bildern* (Eng. trans., *An Illustrated History of Writing and Lettering*, 1946), the brief, perceptive, and personal account by an eminent designer; HERMANN DEGERING (ed.), *Die Schrift* (1929; Eng. trans., *Lettering: A Series of 240 Plates Illustrating Modes of Writing in Western Europe from Antiquity to the End of the 18th Century*, 1929, reprinted 1965), a standard survey of scripts; BERTHOLD L. ULLMAN, *The Origin and Development of Humanistic Script* (1960), the result of reading thousands of documents in the Vatican by a veteran teacher and scholar; JAMES WARDROP, *The Script of Humanism* (1963), by the author of the first-rate studies of papal scriptors in *Signature:* no. 12 (1939, Arrighi); new series, no. 2 (1946, P. Sallando and G. Pagliarlo); no. 5 (1948, Ruano and Cresci); no. 8 (1949, Tagliente); no. 14 (1952, Palatino); JOHN HOWARD BENSON, *The First Writing Book: An English Translation and Facsimile Text of Arrighi's Operina* (1954), all written out in the translator's exemplary italic hand and with his introduction and valuable practical notes; ALFRED FAIRBANK, *A Handwriting Manual*, 3rd ed. rev. (1961), by a British leader of the italic reform movement; ALFRED FAIRBANK and BERTHOLD WOLPE, *Renaissance Handwriting: An Anthology of Italic Scripts* (1960); ALFRED FORBES JOHNSON "A Catalogue of Italian Writing-Books of the Sixteenth Century," in *Signature*, New Series, no. 10 (1950), and reprinted in part by OSCAR OGG (ed.) in *Three Classics of Italian Calligraphy* (1953); SIR AMBROSE HEAL, *The English Writing-Masters and Their Copy-Books, 1570–1800* (1931), the fundamental biographical and bibliographical work, well illustrated and with an important essay by STANLEY MORISON; RAY NASH, *American Writing Masters and Copybooks* (1959), history and bibliography through the colonial period, with 36 plates; and *American Penmanship, 1800–1850* (1969), a historical essay and bibliography of works with miniature reproductions of title pages.

Greek: E.G. TURNER, *Greek Manuscripts* of the *Ancient World* (1971), the best general work on the subject (well-illustrated); FRANCHI DE CAVALIERI and JOHANNES LIETZMANN, *Specimina Codicum Graecorum Vaticanorum* (1910), 50 Greek manuscript specimens in the Vatican Library; *Codex Alexandrinus*, 5 vol. (British Museum, 1909–57), a facsimile in reduced size; *The Codex Sinaiticus and the Codex Alexandrinus*, notes by H.J.M. MILNE and T.C. SKEAT (1963), on the origins of the two great Greek unical Bibles in the British Museum; *Facsimile of the Washington Manuscript of Deuteronomy and Joshua in the Freer Collection* (1910); *Ilias Ambrosiana* (1953), beautiful facsimile of the Homeric codex in the Biblioteca Ambrosiana, Milan (elegant uncial writing).

Greek palaeography—8th to 16th centuries: The standard works on Greek palaeography are of little practical use. The development of different styles and characteristics of writing is more precisely mapped in short surveys; *e.g.*, PAUL MAAS, "Griechische Paläographie," in *Einleitung in die Altertumswissenschaft*, ed. by ALFRED GERCKE and EDUARD NORDEN, 3rd ed., vol. 1 (1924); HERBERT HUNGER, "Griechische Paläographie," in *Geschichte der Textüberlieferung der antiken und mittelalterlichen Literatur*, vol. 1 (1961). The only reliable guide is the study of facsimiles of dated manuscripts, some of the most useful collections being: KIRSOPP and SILVA LAKE (eds.), *Dated Greek Minuscule Manuscripts to the Year 1200*, 11 vol. (1934–45); ALEXANDER TURYN, *Codices graeci Vaticani saeculis XIII et XIV scripti annorumque notis instructi* (1964); HENRI OMONT, *Facsimilés des manuscrits grecs datés . . . du IXe au XIVe siècle*, 2 vol. (1890–91); THE PALAEOGRAPHICAL SOCIETY, *Facsimiles of Manuscripts and Inscriptions*, 6 vol. (1873–1901); and THE NEW PALAEOGRAPHICAL SOCIETY, *Facsimiles of Ancient Manuscripts*, 5 vol. (1903–32).

Latin: The best short accounts in English are in BERTHOLD L. ULLMAN, *Ancient Writing and Its Influence*, new ed. (1969); and E.M. THOMPSON, *Introduction to Greek and Latin Palaeography* (1912, reprinted 1964). All Roman books and documents are cataloged (in English) in, respectively, E.A. LOWE, *Codices latini antiquiores*, 12 vol. (1934–71); and ALBERT BRUCKNER and ROBERT MARICHAL (eds.), *Chartae latinae antiquiores*, 4 vol. (1954–67, in progress). The most important monographs are JEAN MALLON, *Paléographie romaine* (1952); and several articles in E.A. LOWE, *Palaeographical Papers 1907–1965*, 2 vol. (1972).

Aramaic, Hebrew, and Arabic: G.R. DRIVER, *Semitic Writing from Pictograph to Alphabet* (1948), on the origins of Semitic writing; *Aramaic Documents of the Fifth Century BC* (1954); EUGENE TISSERANT, *Specimina Codicum Orientalium* (1914), reproductions of many Semitic pen hands; CARLO BERNHEIMER, *Paleografia Ebraica* (1924), many Ashkenazic hands; ADOLF NEUBAUER, *Facsimiles of Hebrew Manuscripts in the Bodleian Library* (1886); MOSES GASTER, *Hebrew Illuminated Bibles of the IXth and Xth Centuries . . .* (1901); RAFAEL EDELMANN (ed.), *Corpus Codicum Hebraicorum Medii Aevi* (1956), important manuscripts in Hebrew; REUBEN LEAF, *Hebrew Alphabets, 400 B.C. to Our Days* (1950), contains helpful reproductions of manuscript styles; *The Book of Jonah*, woodcuts by JACOB STEINHARDT, calligraphy by FRANZISCA BARUCH (1953); HENRI FRIEDLAENDER, *Die Entstehung meiner Hadassah-Hebräisch* (1967), on the relationship of Hebrew manuscript styles and types—also in *Typographica 16* under the title "Modern Hebrew Typefaces"; ANNEMARIE SCHIMMEL, *Islamic Calligraphy* (1970), a stimulating introduction with illustrations, including calligraphy in architecture and the decorative arts, and a useful bibliography; DAVID DIRINGER, *The Alphabet*, 3rd ed., vol. 1, pp. 210–215 (1968), a survey of the history of the Arabic script and its dissemination; NABIA ABBOTT, *The Rise of the North Arabic Script and Its Kurānic Development* (1939), a study of the origins of the Arabic script and its development in the early Islāmic period; BERNHARD MORITZ (ed.), *Arabic Palaeography* (1950), a rich collection of Arabic texts on papyrus and paper up to the 18th century AD; A.U. POPE (ed.), *A Survey of Persian Art*, vol. 2, ch. 8 (1939), deals with Arabic calligraphy in the art and architecture of Persia; V. MINORSKY, *Calligraphers and Painters: A Treatise by Qādī Ahmad* (1959), an important work (written in 1606) which illustrates cogently the Islāmic attitude toward calligraphy and calligraphers.

Chinese and Japanese: LUCY DRISCOLL and KENJI TODA, *Chinese Calligraphy*, 2nd ed. (1964); CHIANG YEE, *Chinese Calligraphy*, 3rd ed. (1973); WILLIAM WILLETTS, *Chinese Art* (1958); CH'EN CHIH-MAI, *Chinese Calligraphers and Their Art* (1966); HISAO SUGAHARA, *Japanese Ink Painting and Calligraphy . . .* (1967).

Korean: SUEHARU KATSURAGI, *Chósen Kinseki-kō* (1935), a scholarly survey of Korean epigraphy from the Three Kingdoms period to the Koryŏ dynasty that contains many discussions of calligraphic styles; EUNG-HYON KIM, "Sang-ko eui Sŏye" (Ancient Korean Calligraphy), "Koryŏ eui Sŏye" (Calligraphy of the Koryŏ Dynasty), "Yi-cho eui Sŏye" (Calligraphy of the Yi Dynasty), and "Hyondae eui Soye" (Modern Calligraphy), all in *Han'guk yesul Ch'ongnam*, ed. by the Academy of Art, Korea, Seoul (1964), the best surveys on Korean calligraphy, by a noted calligrapher; KI-SUNG KIM, *Han'guk Sŏye sa* (1966), a general survey of Korean calligraphy—some chapters are, however, not consistent and thorough in either handling or approach; YONG-YUN KIM, *Hanguk Sŏhwa Inmyŏng Sasŏ: Biographical Dictionary of Korean Artists and Calligraphers* (1959), a biographical dictionary of traditional painters as well as calligraphers up to the early 20th century (living artists are not included); SE-CH'ANG OH, *Kunyŏk Sŏhwa-jing* (1928), the fundamental biographical dictionary of traditional Korean artists compiled by an enthusiastic connoisseur and calligrapher.

(E.G.T./R.Ba./T.J.Br./Ra.N./D.An./
R.H.P.-W./C.Y./W.-Y.K.)

Calvin, John

John Calvin, a French theologian and ecclesiastical statesman, was one of the most important leaders of the Protestant Reformation of the 16th century. Theological, ecclesiastical, and political ideas that he advanced in many publications, a model church that he created and directed in the city of Geneva, and the assistance he provided to the political and intellectual leaders of several countries profoundly influenced the development of Protestantism in many parts of Europe and in North America.

By courtesy of the Museum Boymans-van Beuningen, Rotterdam

Calvin, oil painting by an anonymous master of the French school, c. 1550. In the Museum Boymans-van Beuningen, Rotterdam.

Early life and education. Calvin was born in Noyon, in Picardy, France, on July 10, 1509, the fourth son of Gérard Cauvin and Jeanne Lefranc, the daughter of a successful innkeeper. His father was a member of the town bourgeoisie and worked for the episcopal establishment as secretary to the bishop, procurator for the cathedral chapter, and in other capacities. Calvin began his education with young noblemen of the de Hangest family, relatives of the reigning bishop. He was destined for a career in the church, and two benefices (ecclesiastical foundation endowments) were assigned to him as a boy to finance his education. After he finished his elementary studies in Noyon, in 1523, he went with the de Hangest boys to Paris, where he studied the liberal arts at both the Collège de la Marche and the Collège de Montaigu, an austere and demanding institution at which the famed Dutch Humanist Erasmus, the French author Rabelais, and, at a later time, Ignatius of Loyola, founder of the Jesuit religious order, also studied. After Calvin received the master of arts degree, his father sent him on to the University of Orléans for advanced study in law under the renowned jurist Pierre de L'Estoile, and he went briefly to Bourges to follow the lectures of the famous Italian legal scholar Alciati. Calvin then returned to Paris, after his father's death in 1531. There he studied with some of the great Humanists who had recently been appointed royal lecturers, notably Guillaume Budé.

Early scholarly activities

A significant product of this second stay in Paris was Calvin's first book, a learned study of *De clementia* ("Concerning Clemency") by the Roman Stoic philosopher Seneca. Calvin's work appeared in 1532. It contained a carefully established text of Seneca's treatise of advice to the emperor Nero, together with a copious and erudite commentary. It revealed Calvin to be an accomplished Humanist on the model of Erasmus and Budé, proved that he could write Latin with elegance and force, showed that he was beginning to read and use Greek, and that he had a wide-ranging and precise command of ancient literature and history. The study also showed that Calvin had acquired a great interest in rhetorical analysis and suggested that he sided with the rhetoricians against the dialecticians in an important contemporary quarrel. He probably believed, with the rhetoricians, that the essential test of the truth of a proposition is its clarity and its ability to move men; he probably rejected the belief of the dialecticians, who held that the best measure of a proposition's truth is the ease with which it can be fitted into a coherent logical system. These skills and attitudes were to have important results in Calvin's later career as a Reformer, and they created a solid basis for friendship with other Protestant Humanist activists, including Luther's disciple Philipp Melanchthon and Theodore Beza, who was to become Calvin's successor at Geneva.

Conversion to Protestantism. Apparently a short time after the publication of the study of *De clementia*, Calvin was converted to Protestantism. He later said that the conversion was sudden but added nothing about when, where, and how it happened. It may well have been induced by Humanist friends in the circle of religious Reformers led by Jacques Lefèvre d'Étaples of France. These men were increasingly frustrated by the government's growing persecution of any religious deviations. Most of them remained Catholic, but some became Protestant. After a split among university faculty and a royal proscription of the Protestant group, Calvin left Paris, resigned his benefices (1534), and, after travel in France, settled in Basel, Switzerland, a Protestant centre, where he lived under the pseudonym Martianus Lucanius. There he devoted himself to intense study of theology, concentrating above all on the Bible, but he also studied the writings of the early Church Fathers and such contemporary Protestant theologians as Luther and Martin Bucer. Most of his knowledge of Catholic theology had been gained from two elementary medieval textbooks, Peter Lombard's *Sentences* (on theology) and Gratian's *Decretum* (on canon law). The principal result of this study was Calvin's master work, the *Institutes of the Christian Religion*, published in 1536. In its initial form it was an extended catechism, in Latin, organized in the traditional way and neatly summarizing essential Protestant doctrines. It also contained some supplementary material attacking sacraments that he viewed as false, and it outlined organizational ideas. The work quickly won a reputation for Calvin as an authoritative spokesman of Protestantism. He revised, translated, and substantially expanded the book in a number of subsequent editions. The definitive Latin edition appeared in 1559, the French in 1560. The *Institutes* became a comprehensive and systematic manual of dogmatic theology, the most influential single manual, in fact, produced during the Reformation. In its later editions it developed positions quite distinct on a number of issues not only from ideas held by radical Anabaptist (*e.g.*, Menno Simons) and Spiritualist thinkers (*e.g.*, Kaspar Schwenckfeld) but also from the teachings of many Lutheran theologians. It thus laid an ideological base for a significant new version of Protestantism.

Institutes of the Christian Religion

Even before the *Institutes* was published, Calvin left Basel for Italy. There he visited Renée de France, daughter of a former king of France and at that time duchess of Ferrara, who had Protestant sympathies and had sheltered a number of Protestant refugees at her court. She was the first of many powerful aristocrats to whom Calvin appealed personally for material support of the Reformation. In a society in which the high nobility still monopolized most military power and much of the wealth, such support was essential for the success of any reform. In tapping this source of support, Calvin displayed a political acumen that was to increase over the years. He soon resumed his travels, however, returning to Basel, then going back to France, and then finally stopping in Geneva, in the fall of 1536, on his way to Strassburg.

Participation in the Genevan reform. The stop in Geneva proved to be fateful. That city-state had just turned

Protestant. It had defied the prince-bishop who possessed both temporal and spiritual sovereignty over the city and had ousted the cathedral canons and other officials who ruled on his behalf. An elected council of local bourgeois, which had previously managed the internal affairs of the city, had assumed complete control. The bishop appealed to the powerful neighbouring duchy of Savoy, to which Genevan bishops had been allied for centuries, for help in regaining his power. The city council appealed to the powerful neighbouring republic of Bern, a source of the Swiss mercenary infantrymen who were among the best fighters in 16th-century Europe, for help in maintaining its independence. In 1528 Bern had adopted the form of Protestantism preached by Huldrych Zwingli, and it was encouraging its neighbours to follow its lead. Inflammatory preachers, notably Guillaume Farel, a former student of Lefèvre, and Pierre Viret, had stirred the Genevan population to many forms of anti-Catholic demonstration, climaxing in image-destroying riots. Consequently, Geneva turned Protestant when it revolted from its bishop. Its government proclaimed the preaching of the gospel, barred the administration of Roman Catholic sacraments, and expelled all priests and members of religious orders who were not willing to conform. But the city had still not consolidated its revolution when Calvin arrived. No settled Protestant rituals had been developed, no new ecclesiastical institutions had been founded, and little provision had been made for the ancillary social services, such as education, that 16th-century communities expected the church to provide. With no previous experience in dealing with practical problems of this kind, Calvin stepped into a considerable vacuum. He did not intend to settle in Geneva, but Farel, in a dramatic interview, persuaded him to stay, threatening him with divine vengeance if he did not use his talents where they were so desperately needed.

Early reforming activities in Geneva and Strassburg

Calvin began his career in Geneva as a public lecturer on the Bible, charged with justifying to the educated citizenry the momentous changes they had witnessed. To educate the Genevans in the Reformed faith, he wrote *Instruction in Faith* (1537). Before long he was also asked to preach sermons; and soon he was using his literary and legal skills to prepare with Farel a series of liturgical and disciplinary regulations, which many of the less austere Genevans cared for not a bit. In fact, the introduction of these regulations by Calvin and Farel proved to be premature, arousing a fear of exchanging one form of clericalism for another. The problem was not so much a cataloging of regulations on morality, which had been in the city's codes from medieval times, but rather a fear that such regulations would be enforced. In an abrupt showdown in 1538, both Farel and Calvin were forced by a newly elected city council to leave the city within three days. Farel moved on to Neuchâtel, where he spent the rest of his life directing that city's Reformation. Calvin, after some hesitation, went to Strassburg, where he became minister to a church of French refugees for a period of three years.

In Strassburg, an imperial German city whose religious establishment was now directed by the liberal Lutheran Martin Bucer, Calvin gained some very useful practical experience. He worked out a Protestant liturgy in French for his congregation, developed a workable set of institutions for running a parish, and was invited to participate in pan-German negotiations at the highest level, which were designed to reconcile Protestants and Catholics and thus reunite Christianity. He participated in religious colloquies called for this purpose in Frankfurt, Hagenau, Worms, and Regensburg (Ratisbon) during 1539–41. This gave him the opportunity to become personally acquainted with prominent Lutheran theologians, above all with Philipp Melanchthon, the chief Protestant negotiator at most of these conferences. It also gave him the opportunity to observe such irenic Catholic theologians as Cardinal Gasparo Contarini, who led the Roman delegation at Regensburg. The failure of these conferences, however, left Calvin convinced of the futility of negotiation with Catholics as an avenue to reform and reunion. During this period he published biblical (*Commentary on Romans*, 1539) and theological works (*e.g.*, *Short Treatise on the Lord's Supper*). He also married Idelette de Bure, a widow of one of his converts from Anabaptism, in 1540.

Triumphal return to Geneva. Meanwhile, Geneva was threatened with chaos. The Protestant ministers who had replaced Farel and Calvin were not able to command the respect of the citizens. Increasing pressure—coming primarily from neighbouring Savoy and from such Catholic intellectuals as Cardinal Jacopo Sadoleto, then bishop of Carpentras in southern France—was brought upon the city to return to the Church of Rome. In countering these pressures, certain Genevans appealed to Calvin in Strassburg. He prepared a *Reply to Sadoleto*, which is one of the best summaries of his theological position. A majority of Geneva's elite finally became convinced that only with Calvin's personal leadership could a Protestant establishment be maintained. Following lengthy negotiations, in which Calvin was promised considerable freedom to build a Protestant regime of the kind he wanted, he agreed to come back to Geneva. Late in 1541 Calvin returned in triumph, was installed with his new wife in a fine canon's house containing an impressive wine cellar, and was awarded a substantial salary.

The first step that Calvin took toward building a Reformed Church for Geneva, following his return, was to draft a set of ecclesiastical ordinances. They were adopted by the city council, after a number of slight amendments, and in 1561 they were redrafted by Calvin and readopted by the city. The ordinances have served as the constitution for the Church of Geneva down to the present, with only a few modifications, and have provided a model for Reformed Churches in many other communities. These ordinances established four orders of ministry for Geneva: (1) teaching doctors, (2) preaching pastors, (3) disciplining elders, and (4) deacons charged with the administration of charity. The doctors were expected to discover the true intention of God for the Christian community by scholarly study of the Bible in its original languages, Greek and Hebrew, using all the best resources of contemporary philology and theology. The pastors were expected to proclaim the Word of God from the pulpits of the city's parish churches and to administer the sacraments. The elders were expected to see to it that the general population accepted this gospel proclamation and used it as a guide for both belief and behaviour. The deacons were expected to meet the social obligations of the community by collecting and safeguarding funds earmarked for charity and by spending them to care for orphans, widows, the aged, and others who could not support themselves.

The four orders of ministry

In the beginning of Calvin's Genevan reform, he was in actuality the only doctor. Once more he delivered the regular public lectures that he had begun under Farel. The lectures were in the form of sustained commentaries on the Bible. One biblical book after another was examined verse by verse in a leisurely way, so that it took several months to gloss each book. Many of these lectures Calvin later turned into published commentaries on books of the Bible. Some were copied down by public secretaries but remained in manuscript, and only in recent times are they being prepared for publication. These lectures proved to be a considerable attraction. They interested a number of Genevans and they attracted an increasing number of religious refugees from other countries—primarily from France, but also from Italy, Germany, England, the Netherlands, Spain, and central Europe.

For some time Calvin made no attempt to institutionalize this teaching. He did assist in the revitalization of a secondary school, however, which prepared students for the theological education that he had been providing for informally. A French Humanist named Sébastien Castellion had been invited to direct the school at about the same time that Calvin was invited to return to Geneva. But when Castellion applied for the additional position of pastor, Calvin blocked the appointment, disagreeing sharply with him on the interpretation of certain biblical passages and creedal statements that Castellion explained literally and that Calvin insisted must be understood figuratively. Castellion was soon dismissed and moved to Basel, where he continued to create trouble for Calvin by attacking his intolerance in print and by criticizing his views in other ways. It was some time before Calvin could find a man of equivalent qualifications to take Castellion's place.

The spread of Calvinist doctrine

Ecclesiastical reforms. A first attempt to teach Calvinist doctrine in a systematic way was made in Lausanne, a city not far from Geneva under direct control of the Bernese state. There an academy, which had been established in 1537, began to offer linguistic and theological training on the university level for prospective Calvinist pastors. Theological controversy with the Bernese government, however, forced most of its faculty to leave in 1558 and 1559. Calvin promptly persuaded the Genevan government to fill the vacuum by creating in 1559 a new academy, which evolved into the present University of Geneva. Its first rector was Theodore Beza, a brilliant French Humanist who had studied with some of Calvin's own teachers in Orléans and in Paris and who had begun teaching in Lausanne after his conversion to Protestantism. Beza became Calvin's successor as the principal leader of non-Lutheran, or Reformed, Protestantism.

From the beginning Calvin was also a pastor. He assumed the leadership in 1542 of a corps of nine pastors, some of whom had rather dubious qualifications. In the ensuing 22 years the corps grew to 19, and almost all of its members were highly qualified. They were distributed among city parishes, the number of which varied depending on the population and the supply of pastors, and among several rural parishes belonging to Geneva. Calvin himself lived in the parish near the old cathedral church of St. Pierre and normally preached from its pulpit. Occasionally, he used the nearby parish church of the Madeleine.

The Company of Pastors

Once a week the pastors met as a body, in what came to be known as the Company of Pastors. Calvin served as its moderator, or presiding officer, until his death. This was the only official position he held in Geneva. Entrance to the Company of Pastors was basically by co-optation. When a vacancy occurred or when the city government authorized a new appointment, the company would conduct a search. A likely candidate would be assigned some Bible verses and asked to present an expository sermon on them before the company and then would be examined on the sermon and on his basic beliefs. He would be judged on the basis of competence in biblical exegesis, soundness of theological belief, and skill in speaking. Successful candidates were presented to the city council for approval. Often one or more members of the council attended the meeting of the company at which the examination was conducted. Candidates approved by both company and council were then presented to members of the parish that they were to serve, but this was only a formality.

In addition to screening candidates for the pastorate, the company, under the guidance of Calvin, made parish assignments and established the regular routine of services. It also held occasional sessions for mutual correction in which a kind of self-criticism was encouraged. Toward the end of Calvin's life the Company of Pastors handled an increasing volume of correspondence with Protestants in other countries. As moderator, Calvin often acted as spokesman for the company, particularly in its dealings with the city government. This meant that he frequently attended meetings of the city council and had an important voice in many political decisions—as a consultant rather than as an officeholder, for important offices in the Genevan government were limited to native-born citizens.

The work of the elders and Consistory

Calvin was personally involved in the work of the elders. These "policemen" of the Reformation were chosen in much the same way as all the other officials of the Genevan state, including the men who kept the accounts, maintained the city grain supply, guarded the fortifications, and sat on the municipal courts. Once a year the governing council would prepare a slate of nominees as elders, normally in consultation with Calvin and perhaps other pastors. This slate would then be presented to a general council of all voting citizens for acceptance or rejection. The same men could be elected year after year as elders, but normally there was some turnover. The elders were chosen so that they represented all of the geographic divisions into which the city was divided. Most were native-born Genevans, but toward the end of Calvin's life it became possible to elect to this position a few prominent refugees who had recently settled in the city.

Once a week the elders met with the pastors in a body called the Consistory. Its presiding officer was known as a syndic, one of the four magistrates elected to be chief executives in Geneva for the year. This body acted much like a court. To it were referred hundreds of cases of residents accused of idolatrous or heretical beliefs, of Catholic religious practices, and of misbehaviour ranging from public complaints about Calvin to serious sexual crimes. If the accused seemed penitent and if the lapse was minor, he might be merely reprimanded with a sharp scolding, often administered with considerable vehemence by Calvin. If the accused was not penitent or if the lapse was serious, he could be handed over to the city government for further investigation and punishment. The only punishment that the Consistory itself could administer was excommunication, and this was a real threat in an age when the sacraments were taken very seriously. The Consistory, however, had to fight even for this power. Few Protestant governments of the period were prepared to grant the right of excommunication to an ecclesiastical institution, and many Genevans were less than enthusiastic about the idea. It is not clear that the 1541 ecclesiastical ordinances, as amended by the city government, did in fact give the Consistory that right. Calvin insisted upon it, however, and made it an issue of confidence, threatening to leave the city again if he were forced to administer communion to any excommunicated sinner who had not been pardoned by the Consistory. After a series of sharp internal political fights on this issue, Calvin finally won his way in 1555. From then on the role of the Consistory and Calvin's power in the city were free of any effective challenge. A kind of moral "reign of terror" followed, remarkably reforming the city and creating the kind of moral austerity that later came to be labelled "Puritan."

The deacons and social work

Calvin was less personally involved in the work of the deacons. They were all associated with an institution called the Hospital-General, which coordinated all the charitable activities previously handled by a variety of Catholic foundations. This institution was not a hospital in the modern sense but rather a combination orphanage, home for the elderly, and asylum for the physically and mentally disabled, which also served as headquarters for the distribution of free bread and other forms of assistance to poor families temporally unable to support themselves. It was directed by a deacon (called the "hospitallier"), who lived in the hospital with his family and acted as its full-time administrator. He was selected by the city council whenever the position became vacant. To assist and superintend the hospitallier, the city government elected four or five more deacons, also called procurators of the hospital. They were elected once a year, in exactly the same way as the elders.

The Hospital-General had been established in 1535, before Calvin arrived in Geneva. By providing for it in his ecclesiastical ordinances he was really consecrating an existing institution. He and the other pastors were supposed to be consulted annually in the selection of nominees for procurators of the hospital, but only toward the end of his life was this legal requirement taken seriously. Calvin did, however, become quite involved in the administration of relief to the poor among the religious refugees to Geneva. He sometimes invited them into his own home upon their initial arrival in the city and helped organize, with a number of wealthy French refugees, a fund for the relief of their poor compatriots called the Bourse Française.

Theological disputes and the expansion of Reformed Protestantism. Between 1541 and 1555 much of Calvin's energy was devoted to making this ecclesiastical system work, both by winning acceptance for it from the Genevan population and by superintending its daily operation. During these same years he also faced challenges to his doctrinal authority. The most formidable of these came from Jérôme Bolsec and Michael Servetus. Bolsec was a former Catholic theologian who, in 1551, publicly attacked Calvin's doctrine of predestination, claiming that it viewed God as the author of evil. Calvin indignantly rebutted the charge, with some assistance from theologians in other cities, and Bolsec was expelled from Geneva. Servetus was a Spanish doctor who published books attacking the central Christian doctrine of the Trinity—the belief that the one God is revealed as Father, Son, and Holy Spirit. When Servetus came to Geneva in 1553, Calvin saw to it that he was arrested and convicted, with the emphatic assistance of foreign theologians, of heresy. Servetus was subsequently burned to death at the stake. In both of these cases, and in others like them, the city government strongly supported Calvin.

Calvin's final victory in Geneva over his theological opponents left him free after 1555 to devote more of his energy to the spread of Reformed Protestantism in other countries. He had already forged an alliance for this purpose with Zwinglian Protestantism, now led by Heinrich Bullinger of Zürich. That alliance had been sealed by a common confession of faith, the Consensus Tigurinus, adopted in 1549. It was further supported from 1552 on by virulent polemical exchanges on points of sacramental theology between Calvin and certain of the conservative Lutheran opponents of Zwinglianism, notably Joachim Westphal of Hamburg and Tileman Hesshusius of Heidelberg.

Attempts to win France to Reformed Protestantism

Between 1555 and 1564 most of Calvin's concern for the spread of Protestantism was directed to his native France. Under his supervision dozens of French refugees were trained as Reformed pastors, and many were given some practical training as teachers or village pastors in French Switzerland. They were then smuggled back into their native country, where their very presence was illegal until a royal edict in 1562 granted Calvinism a measure of toleration. To bind their activities together, Calvin encouraged the creation of a network of underground ecclesiastical institutions covering much of France. On the local level, congregations were established on the model of Geneva. On a regional level, representative bodies called colloquies were established, including the pastors and elders of a number of churches. Analogues to these bodies later created in other countries were the presbyteries of Scotland and America and the classes of England and the Netherlands. They constitute one of the most characteristic institutions of Calvinist Protestantism. Above the colloquies, on the provincial level, representative synods were established. To unite the entire system a national synod was created that was scheduled to meet about once a year. Its first meeting was held in 1559 in Paris, under the noses of the persecuting royal government, and it there adopted a national confession of faith and code of discipline. During Calvin's lifetime the Geneva Company of Pastors tended to act as a supreme court over this entire system, providing assistance and resolving disputes that could not be handled by the colloquies and synods.

To provide material support for this rapidly growing Reformed Church, Calvin plunged into politics. He got in touch with a number of powerful French aristocrats and urged them to patronize the burgeoning Protestant movement. The most important of these were members of the House of Bourbon, allied by blood to the French royal house, notably the head of the house, Antoine de Bourbon, king of Navarre; his wife, Jeanne d'Albret; his younger brother, Louis, first prince de Condé. Also important were the three Coligny brothers (Odet, Gaspard, and François d'Andelot) of the powerful and wealthy House of Châtillon. Though the assistance of these aristocrats provided French Calvinism with essential protection, it also involved the movement in an open challenge to the French government. That challenge led to religious war. Calvin discouraged the first steps toward war, notably the 1560 Conspiracy of Amboise, in which a group of zealous young nobles from Condé's suite tried to kidnap the young king and kill his conservative Catholic advisers. But when Condé himself mustered an army in 1562 to fight the royal government, Calvin supported him in many effective ways. He even permitted Beza to serve Condé as a consultant, propagandist, and diplomat.

Religious war

Similar kinds of support, on a more modest scale, were provided by Calvin and his colleagues in Geneva to Reformed movements in other countries. Groups of Italian, English, and Spanish refugees were welcomed to the city and permitted to establish their own local churches. Individuals from the Netherlands, many German states, Poland, and still other countries were also welcomed. When these men returned to their native countries as missionaries for Protestantism, Calvin kept in touch with them by correspondence. He also got in touch with officials in their home governments who he thought might be inclined to support Protestant evangelization, writing letters and dedicating books to them. And he did what he could to help the new Reformed Churches organize and defend themselves against attacks from other Protestant and Catholic groups. Altogether, these activities made of Geneva an important international headquarters of Reformed Protestantism. It is with some justice that the city was sometimes called a "Protestant Rome."

In the 1560s Calvin began to have serious problems with his health. More and more of his duties in both Geneva and the international Reformed movement were shared with Beza, his heir apparent, and others. He maintained a reasonably active schedule of preaching, teaching, and writing until early in 1564, the year in which he died, on May 27.

Assessment. Calvin was a rather reticent man, and consequently little is known of the more personal or relaxed sides of his character. His wife died (1549) after a relatively short marriage. He never married again, and their only child died at birth (1542). A man of great intellectual talents, with a prodigious memory, a quick mind, and a rare gift for clear and forceful expression, he became a charismatic leader who inspired hundreds of men to change their lives and run appalling risks to advance his cause. During his entire career he was sustained by the conviction that he had been called by God to reform his church. These qualities help explain the enormous impact Calvin made on Western religious history.

BIBLIOGRAPHY. A nearly definitive biography is that by EMILE DOUMERGUE, *Jean Calvin, les hommes et les choses de son temps*, 7 vol. (1899–1927); it is extremely detailed and factually precise but dubious on some points of interpretation and generally too hagiographic in tone. Another classic biography, FRANZ WILHELM KAMPSCHULTE, *Johann Calvin, seine Kirche und sein Staat in Genf*, 2 vol. (1869–99), is somewhat more critical in tone but less detailed. The most useful recent English account of Calvin's life is JOHN T. MCNEILL, *The History and Character of Calvinism* (1954). For a skillful and authoritative introduction to Calvin's thought, see FRANCOIS WENDEL, *Calvin, sources et évolution de sa pensée religieuse* (1950; Eng. trans., *Calvin: The Origin and Development of His Religious Thought*, 1963). E. WILLIAM MONTER, *Calvin's Geneva* (1967), presents a thoughtful description of the milieu in which Calvin worked. ROBERT M. KINGDON, *Geneva and the Coming of the Wars of Religion in France, 1555–1563* (1956), provides an analysis of the methods Calvin used to extend his influence to other countries. The total number of studies on Calvin is very large. ALFRED ERICHSON, *Bibliographia Calviniana* (1900, reprinted 1960); and WILHELM NIESEL, *Calvin-Bibliographie, 1901–1959* (1961), provide guides to this vast literature. Supplements to these compilations may be found in a number of surveys published in periodicals, such as PIERRE FRAENKEL *et al.*, "Petit supplément aux bibliographies calviniennes, 1901–1963," *Bibliothèque d'Humanisme et Renaissance*, 33:385–413 (1971). The best and most complete edition of Calvin's works is the *Ioannis Calvini Opera quae supersunt omnia*, 59 vol., ed. by G. BAUM, E. CUNITZ, and E. REUSS for the *Corpus Reformatorum* (1863–1900, reprinted 1964). Supplementary material may be found in the *Supplementa Calviniana* (1961–), a series of hitherto unpublished Calvin sermons; and the *Registres de la Compagnie des Pasteurs de Genève au temps de Calvin*, 2 vol., ed. by ROBERT M. KINGDON and JEAN-FRANCOIS BERGIER (1962–64), a partial record of the deliberations of the Geneva Company of Pastors from 1546 to 1564. Much of this material has been translated into English. Good recent examples include the JOHN T. MCNEILL and FORD LEWIS BATTLES edition of the *Institutes of the Christian Religion* (1960); the FORD LEWIS BATTLES and ANDRE MALAN HUGO edition of *Calvin's Commentary on Seneca's De Clementia* (1969); and the PHILIP E. HUGHES translation of *The Register of the Company of Pastors of Geneva in the Time of Calvin* (1966).

(R.M.K.)

Cambodia

Cambodia is a country located in Southeast Asia in the southwest part of the Indochinese Peninsula. Together with Laos and Vietnam, Cambodia is part of what was formerly known as Indochina. Covering a land area of 69,898 square miles (181,035 square kilometres), it is bordered on the west and northwest by Thailand, on the northeast by Laos, on the east and southeast by Vietnam, and on the southwest by the Gulf of Thailand (Gulf of Siam). With a population variously estimated between 4,500,000 and 7,000,000 people, Cambodia is an underpopulated, predominantly agricultural country with a largely underdeveloped economy.

Upheavals of the 1970s

Throughout the 1970s, Cambodia was devastated by the enlarged Second Indochinese War, civil war, and social upheavals that damaged, destroyed, or redirected much of its economy and killed hundreds of thousands of its people. In April 1975, the government of the Khmer Republic, as Cambodia was then called, collapsed under attacks by Cambodian Communist guerrilla forces that had been fighting the regime, at first with Vietnamese help, since 1970. From 1975 to 1978, Cambodia was known as Democratic Kampuchea and was governed by a pro-Chinese faction of the Cambodian Communist Party. This regime's years in power were characterized by a dramatic attempt to increase Cambodia's agricultural production by collectivizing its villages and regimenting its people. Under the regime, millions of people were moved from urban centres into rural areas, currency was abolished, and the postal system did not operate. Violent clashes along the border with Vietnam began in 1976 and developed into warfare in 1978. In January 1979 a pro-Vietnamese Communist movement, aided by Vietnamese armed forces, captured the national capital of Phnom Penh and began to administer the surrounding area as the People's Republic of Kampuchea. Remnants of the army of Democratic Kampuchea and thousands of Cambodians loyal to that government continued resistance in the northwestern region of the country. (For further history, see CAMBODIA, HISTORY OF; for an associated physical feature, see MEKONG RIVER.)

THE LANDSCAPE

Physiography. *Relief.* Cambodia's maximum extent is about 280 miles (450 kilometres) from north to south and 360 miles (580 kilometres) from east to west. The central region is a low-lying alluvial plain surrounding the Tonle Sap (Great Lake) and the beginnings of the Mekong River Delta. Extending outward from this region are transitional plains, thinly forested and with prevailing elevations no higher than several hundred feet above sea level. On the north, along the border with Thailand, the Cambodian plain abuts a sandstone escarpment that marks the southern limit of a mountain range, the Chuŏr Phnum Dângrêk. A southward-facing cliff, stretching for more than 200 miles in a west to east direction, rises abruptly from the plain to heights ranging from 600 to 1,800 feet (180 to 550 metres), forming a natural frontier boundary. East of the Mekong the transitional plains gradually merge with the eastern highlands, a region of densely forested mountains and high plateaus that extend northward and eastward into Laos and Vietnam. In southwestern Cambodia, two distinct upland blocks, comprising the Chuŏr Phnum Krâvanh (Cardamom Mountains) and the Chuŏr Phnum Dâmrei (Elephant Mountains), form another highland region that covers much of the land area between the Tonle Sap and the Gulf of Thailand. In this remote and largely uninhabited area is found Phnum Aôral (5,949 feet; 1,813 metres), Cambodia's highest peak. The southern coastal region adjoining the Gulf of Thailand is a narrow lowland strip, heavily wooded and moderately populated. It is effectively isolated from the central plain by the southwestern highlands.

Drainage. The two most dominant topographical features of Cambodia are the Mekong River and Tonle Sap. Rising in Tibet and emptying into the South China Sea, the Mekong enters Cambodia from Laos and flows broadly southward to the border with Vietnam, covering a distance inside Cambodia of approximately 315 miles. Its annual flooding during the rainy season deposits a rich alluvial sediment that accounts for the fertility of the central plain.

Tonle Sap (the Great Lake)

The Tonle Sap, joined to the Mekong by a river called the Tônlé Sab, serves as a reservoir for the Mekong. During the rainy season, from mid-May to early October, the Mekong's enormous volume of water backs up the connecting river for a distance of 65 miles and flows into the Tonle Sap lake, expanding its surface area from the dry season minimum of 1,200 square miles to a rainy season maximum of more than 3,000 square miles and increasing its maximum depth from seven feet to 35 feet. As the water level of the Mekong falls during the dry season, the process is reversed. Water drains from the Tonle Sap lake back into the Mekong, reversing its directional flow. As a result of this annual phenomenon, the Tonle Sap lake is one of the richest sources in the world of freshwater fish.

Climate. Cambodia has a climate governed by rain-bearing winds (monsoons) and characterized by two major seasons. From mid-May to early October, strong prevailing winds blow out of the southwest, bringing heavy rains and high humidity. From early November to mid-March, winds are from the northeast and are light in velocity. Cloudiness is variable, precipitation is infrequent, and humidity is low. Between these seasons the weather is transitional. Maximum temperatures are high throughout the year, ranging from the mid-90s (° F, about 35° C) in April, the warmest month, to the low 80s in January, the coldest month. Daily minimums are usually 15° to 20° F lower than maximums. Annual rainfall varies considerably throughout the country, from more than 200 inches (5,000 millimetres) on the seaward slopes of the southwestern highlands to 55 inches in the central lowland region. Between 70 and 80 percent of the annual rainfall occurs during the months of the southwest monsoon.

Vegetation and animal life. About 75 percent of Cambodia's land area is forested. The central lowland region is covered with rice paddies, fields of dry crops (such as corn [maize] or tobacco), tracts of tall grass and reeds, and thinly wooded areas. Savanna (grassy parkland) is the prevailing vegetation of the transitional plains, with grass growing to a height of five feet. In the eastern highlands the high plateaus are covered with deciduous forest and grassland. Broadleaf evergreen forests grow in the mountainous areas to the north, with trees 100 feet high emerging from thick undergrowths of vines, rattans, palms, bamboos, and assorted woody and herbaceous ground plants. In the southwestern highlands open forests of pines are found at the higher elevations, while the rain-drenched seaward slopes are blanketed with virgin rain forest growing to heights of 150 feet or more. Vegetation along the coastal strip ranges from evergreen forests to nearly impenetrable mangrove forests.

Fruit, growing wild or cultivated, includes breadfruit, jackfruit, durian, mango, mangosteen, papaya, rambutan, and bananas.

Animal life includes elephants, wild oxen, tigers, panthers and other leopards, bears, and innumerable small game. Among the more common birds are herons, cranes, grouse, pheasant, peacocks, pelicans, cormorants, egrets, and wild ducks. Four varieties of snakes are especially dangerous: the cobra, the king cobra, the banded krait, and Russell's viper.

The landscape under human settlement. Until the 1970s, Cambodia was a country of villages. Only about 10 percent of the total population lived in urban areas of 10,000 or more inhabitants; the major part of the urban population was concentrated in Phnom Penh, Cambodia's capital city, which is situated at the confluence of the Mekong, Basăk (Bassac), and Tônlé Sab rivers.

Village life

Before 1970, about 80 percent of Cambodia's people inhabited the central lowland region, where the rural village was second only to the family as the basic societal unit. The typical Cambodian village, in those days, was to a large extent autonomous and self-sufficient, made up of ethnically homogeneous people numbering fewer than 300 persons. The village (*phum*) was part of a hamlet or community (*khum*) with which it shared one or more Buddhist temples (*wat*), an elementary school, and several small shops. Cambodian villages usually developed in a linear pattern along waterways and roads; more isolated villages were rectangular or, more rarely, circular in the arrangement of their houses. Houses in Cambodia were generally built on high wooden pilings and had thatched roofs, walls of palm matting, and floors of woven bamboo strips resting on bamboo joists. More prosperous houses, while still on pilings, were built of wood, and had tile or metal roofs.

Before 1970, there were few large landowners in Cambodia; in 1975, all of them were forced off their holdings and made to work as ordinary peasants. Before collectivization in the 1970s, the typical villager owned and worked enough land to provide for his family, with a small surplus to be converted into cash for additional goods or the payment of taxes. Landholdings tended to be small in the crowded south-central regions of the country, where the least fertile soils occur. During the 1960s, the government of Prince Norodom Sihanouk was successful in colonizing frontier regions, especially in the northwest, with army veterans or needy farmers from more crowded parts of the country. These programs did not significantly alter Cambodian settlement patterns, however.

Throughout rural Cambodia, life-style was closely geared to the agricultural cycle, which was based, in large part, on family-oriented subsistence farming. Family members were awake before dawn, and the major portion of the day's work was accomplished before noon, although minor tasks were performed in the cool of the early evening. Electricity has always been rare in village areas, and country people were generally asleep soon after sunset. During the rice-growing season, all family members worked together in the fields, because the work of planting, transplanting, and harvesting must be done quickly. Without mechanical assistance, the work of more than one or two people is needed to grow enough rice to feed a family for a year. In fact, reciprocal extra-family obligations would build up within a village during the agricultural season. Festivals and marriages, celebrated by a whole village, were usually held in the off-season, after the rice had been harvested. The working day was extended by the government after 1975, and leisure time was taken up by indoctrination.

Urban areas

The urban areas of Cambodia, most of which were abandoned as an official policy in 1975, had developed, for the most part, during the first half of the 20th century as commercial and administrative centres serving their surrounding rural regions. Most of them were located at the intersections of land or river routes and were relative-

MAP INDEX

Political subdivisions

Bătdâmbâng.... 13·00n 103·00e
Kâmpóng Cham.......... 12·00n 105·30e
Kâmpóng Chhnăng...... 12·00n 104·30e
Kâmpóng Spoe. 11·30n 104·30e
Kâmpóng Thum.......... 13·00n 105·00e
Kâmpôt.......... 10·45n 104·15e
Kândal.......... 11·30n 104·50e
Kaôh Kŏng..... 11·30n 103·30e
Krâchéh........ 12·30n 106·00e
Môndól Kiri..... 12·30n 107·00e
Ŏtdâr Méanchey..... 14·05n 103·35e
Poŭthĭsăt........ 12·30n 104·00e
Preăh Vihéar... 14·00n 104·50e
Prey Vêng...... 11·30n 105·30e
Rôtânôkiri...... 13·00n 107·00e
Siĕmréab....... 14·00n 104·00e
Stœng Trêng.... 14·00n 106·15e
Svay Riĕng..... 11·15n 105·50e
Takêv.......... 11·00n 104·50e

Cities and towns

Ânlóng Vêng... 14·14n 104·05e
Bâ kêv.......... 13·42n 107·12e
Ban Tiam Piou.. 11·34n 103·08e
Battambang (Bătdâmbâng). 13·06n 103·12e
Bœng Lvéa..... 12·36n 105·34e
Boi Russey..... 12·14n 103·01e
Bok Koŭ........ 10·37n 104·03e
Bon Dak Plai... 12·58n 107·28e
Chék............ 13·48n 102·58e
Chhêb Kândal.. 13·45n 105·24e
Chŏâm Khsant.. 14·13n 104·56e
Chŏng Kal...... 13·57n 103·35e
Kâmpóng Cham, see Kompong Cham
Kâmpóng Chhnăng...... 12·15n 104·40e
Kâmpóng Saôm, see Kompong Som
Kâmpóng Spoe. 11·27n 104·32e
Kâmpóng Thum, see Kompong Thom
Kâmpóng Trâlach........ 11·54n 104·47e
Kâmpôt.......... 10·37n 104·11e
Kbal Dâmrei.... 14·03n 105·20e
Khŭm Bathéay.. 11·59n 104·57e
Kompong Cham (Kâmpóng Cham)......... 12·00n 105·27e
Kompong Som (Kâmpóng Saôm, Sihanoukville)...... 10·38n 103·30e
Kompong Thom (Kâmpóng Thum)......... 12·42n 104·52e
Krâkôr.......... 12·32n 104·12e
Kratie (Krâchéh)..... 12·29n 106·01e
Krŏng Kêb..... 10·30n 104·19e
Krŏng Khémôreăh Phumĭnt....... 11·37n 102·59e
Kruo............ 12·52n 105·55e
Léach........... 12·21n 103·46e
Lumphăt........ 13·30n 106·59e
Memon.......... 13·08n 106·40e
Mémót.......... 11·49n 106·11e
Moŭng Rœssei.. 12·46n 103·27e
Pailĭn........... 12·51n 102·36e
Paôy Pêt, see Poipet
Phnom Penh.... 11·33n 104·55e
Phnom Thbeng Meanchey..... 13·49n 104·58e
Phum Chelleut.. 14·06n 107·14e
Phumĭ Ângk Tasaôm........ 11·01n 104·41e
Phumĭ Bâ Khăm.......... 13·51n 107·21e
Phumĭ Banam.. 11·19n 105·18e
Phumĭ Béng.... 13·05n 104·18e
Phumĭ Châmbák....... 11·14n 104·49e
Phumĭ Chângho Ândêng........ 12·39n 104·35e
Phumĭ Chruŏy Slêng.......... 13·14n 105·57e
Phumĭ Chumnéap.... 11·36n 103·35e
Phumĭ Chuuk... 10·50n 104·28e
Phumĭ Dăk Dăm............ 12·20n 107·21e
Phumĭ Kâmchay Méa............ 11·35n 105·40e
Phumĭ Kâmpóng Kântuŏt........ 11·26n 104·49e
Phumĭ Kâmpóng Srâlau.......... 14·05n 105·46e
Phumĭ Kâmpŏng Trâbêk.......... 13·06n 105·14e
Phumĭ Kântuŏt Sâmroŭng...... 14·12n 104·37e
Phumĭ Kaôh Kért............ 13·47n 104·32e
Phumĭ Kaôh Kŏng........... 11·28n 103·13e
Phumĭ Khpôb... 11·02n 105·12e
Phumĭ Krêk..... 11·46n 105·56e
Phumĭ Lvéa Kraôm.......... 13·21n 102·54e
Phumĭ Moŭng.. 13·46n 103·33e
Phumĭ Narung.. 13·53n 105·34e
Phumĭ Ŏdŏngk.. 11·48n 104·45e
Phumĭ Phnum Srâlau.......... 11·03n 103·42e
Phumĭ Phsar Réam........... 10·30n 103·37e
Phumĭ Prêk Kák. 12·15n 105·32e
Phumĭ Prêk Sândêk........ 11·51n 105·22e
Phumĭ Prey Toch............ 12·54n 103·23e
Phumĭ Puŏk Chăs........... 13·26n 103·44e
Phumĭ Rôluŏs Chas............ 13·19n 104·00e
Phumĭ Sâmroûng..... 14·11n 103·31e
Phumĭ Sândăn.. 12·42n 106·01e
Phumĭ Spoe Tbong......... 12·20n 105·19e
Phumĭ Spong... 13·27n 105·34e
Phumĭ Srê Kôkir.......... 13·08n 106·04e
Phumĭ Srê Meăt........... 13·18n 107·10e
Phumĭ Srê Rônéam....... 12·16n 106·25e
Phumĭ Svay Riĕng.......... 11·05n 105·48e
Phumĭ Tbêng... 13·35n 104·55e
Phumĭ Thalabârivăt... 13·33n 105·57e
Phumĭ Thmâ Pôk............ 13·57n 103·04e
Phumĭ Tik Choŭ........... 13·36n 103·24e
Phumĭ Tnaôt.... 12·56n 104·34e
Phumĭ Trêng... 12·50n 102·54e
Phum Knol..... 12·21n 103·33e
Phum Pong..... 12·06n 103·40e
Phum Saour.... 10·55n 103·22e
Phum Ten Salavay......... 13·32n 107·26e
Poipet (Paôy Pêt)............ 13·39n 102·33e
Pônlei........... 12·26n 104·27e
Poŭthĭsăt........ 12·35n 103·55e
Prĕk Poŭthĭ...... 11·51n 105·07e
Prey Lvéa....... 11·10n 104·57e
Prey Nôb....... 10·38n 103·47e
Prey Vêng...... 11·29n 105·19e
Sala Andong Tuk............ 11·08n 103·31e
Sâmbor......... 12·46n 105·58e
Senmonorom... 12·27n 107·12e
Siĕmpang...... 14·07n 106·23e
Siem Reap (Siĕmréab).... 13·22n 103·51e
Sihanoukville, see Kompong Som
Sisŏphŏn........ 13·35n 102·59e
Skón............ 12·04n 105·04e
Snay Pôl........ 11·40n 105·13e
Snuŏl............ 12·04n 106·26e
Srê Âmbĕl...... 11·07n 103·46e
Srê Khtŭm...... 12·11n 106·54e
Steng........... 13·43n 103·34e
Stœng Tréng, see Stung Treng
Stung Drak..... 14·19n 106·47e
Stung Treng (Stœng Tréng). 13·31n 105·58e
Takêv........... 10·59n 104·47e
Tbong........... 13·21n 105·07e
Tchan Geon.... 13·54n 104·09e
Tinh-bien....... 10·36n 104·57e
Tuk Méas....... 10·41n 104·33e
Virŏcheăy....... 14·00n 106·45e

Physical features and points of interest

Angkor, Ruines d', *ruins*....... 13·25n 103·52e
Cardamones, Chaîne des, *mountains*..... 12·00n 103·15e
Chbar, *river*..... 13·22n 107·04e
Chhâk Kâmpóng Saôm, *bay*..... 10·50n 103·32e
Chhay Arêng, *river*........... 11·31n 103·25e
Chhlong, *river*... 12·15n 106·00e
Chikrêng, *river*.. 12·51n 104·14e
Dangrek, Chaîne des, *mountains*..... 14·25n 103·30e
Éléphant, Chaîne de l', *mountains*..... 11·00n 104·05e
Kaôh Rŭng Sâm Loem, *island*... 10·35n 103·28e
Kŏng, *river*..... 13·35n 106·00e
Kŏng, Kaôh, *island*......... 11·20n 103·00e
Mekong (Mékôngk), *river*........... 10·33n 105·24e
Môngkôl Bori, *river*........... 13·19n 103·24e
Phnom Aural (Phnum Aôral), *mountain*...... 12·02n 104·10e
Pôrŭng, *river*.... 12·55n 105·35e
Poŭthĭsăt, *river*.. 12·41n 104·09e
Rung, Kaoh, *island*.......... 10·35n 103·17e
San, *river*....... 13·32n 105·57e
Sângkê, *river*... 13·13n 103·41e
Sên, *river*....... 12·32n 104·28e
Srêng, *river*..... 13·21n 103·27e
Srêpôk, *river*.... 13·33n 106·16e
Staung, *river*.... 12·50n 104·19e
Thailand, Gulf of......... 10·45n 102·00e
Thâot, *river*..... 11·29n 104·57e
Tônlé Sab, *river*. 12·10n 104·40e
Tonle Sap, *lake*. 12·50n 104·00e

ly accessible to the areas they served. Phnom Penh (*phnom* means "hill"; Penh is a woman's name) was Cambodia's single metropolis before it was abandoned in 1975. Before the outbreak of war in 1970, it held some 500,000 persons; its population by 1975, then swollen with refugees, numbered some 2,000,000. Several thousand people moved back into the city in 1979, and its population was then estimated to be approximately 270,000. In 1970, Bătdâmbâng in the northwest was Cambodia's second largest city, with about 40,000 people. No other city at that time held more than 20,000.

The massive dislocations of people that characterized Cambodian history in the 1970s made it difficult to predict which, if any, of the urban centres in existence before 1970 would regain their economic and political importance. Phnom Penh will probably again become a city of 100,000 to 200,000 inhabitants. Bătdâmbâng's location in the prosperous rice-producing area of the northwest will probably ensure its resurgence as Cambodia's second largest city. Others, such as Kâmpóng Cham, Siĕmréap, and Kâmpôt, may not regain their importance or populations for some time. At any event, it is unlikely that the cities will be like those of the 1960s, with Chinese-dominated commercial centres, Vietnamese shops, and ornate, French-style administrative buildings.

PEOPLE AND POPULATION

Population size

Cambodia's first national census as an independent nation was taken in 1962. The results showed that the population totalled about 5,700,000. By mid-1979, the population was estimated by various sources to be as low as 4,500,000 or as high as 7,800,000; the maximum figure represents an annual growth rate of approximately 4 percent (statistics for Cambodia after 1970 are only estimates). In Southeast Asia, only Laos and Singapore have smaller populations than Cambodia. Overall population density is roughly 100 persons per square mile; but this figure is not especially descriptive because of the enormous losses and movements of people in the years after 1970. Because so much of the country is poorly watered and without inhabitants, the actual density in populated areas is much higher.

Ethnic and linguistic groups. Khmer (Cambodian) stock accounts for more than 90 percent of the total population. This has produced a homogeneity that is unique in Southeast Asia and has encouraged a strong sense of national identity. Before 1975, other major ethnic groups included the Chinese (350,000), Vietnamese (200,000), Cham-Malays (90,000), various tribal peoples (90,000), and Europeans, mainly French (5,000). All of these minorities, except for the ethnic Chinese and tribal peoples, were expelled from Democratic Kampuchea; many of the Chinese, in turn, sought refuge in Vietnam.

The Khmer

The Khmer are concentrated principally in the lowland regions surrounding the Mekong and Tonle Sap, on the transitional plains, and in the coastal area. They belong to the Mon-Khmer ethnolinguistic group. An end product of centuries of intricate cultural and racial blending, the Khmer descended before 200 BC into the fertile Mekong Delta from the Khorat Plateau of what is now Thailand. They were Indianized by successive waves of Indian influence and in the 8th century AD were exposed to Indo-Malayan influences and perhaps immigration from Java. This was followed by Tai migrations from the 10th to 15th centuries, by a Vietnamese migration beginning in the 17th century, and by Chinese migrations in the 18th and 19th centuries. As a result of this racial admixture, the Khmer are generally classified as Austroasiatics linked to the Veddoid, Indo-Australoid, and Mongoloid peoples. Their physical characteristics reflect their mixed background. Despite wide variations, they tend to be of short stature (the average height of a male is about five feet, three inches), robust, and muscular. Skin colour is light to brown, and hair is black. Less than 50 percent show the epicanthic fold (a fold of skin extending from the eyelid over the inner corner of the eye; it is sometimes called the mongolian fold). The typical Khmer family before 1975 consisted of a married couple and their unmarried chil-

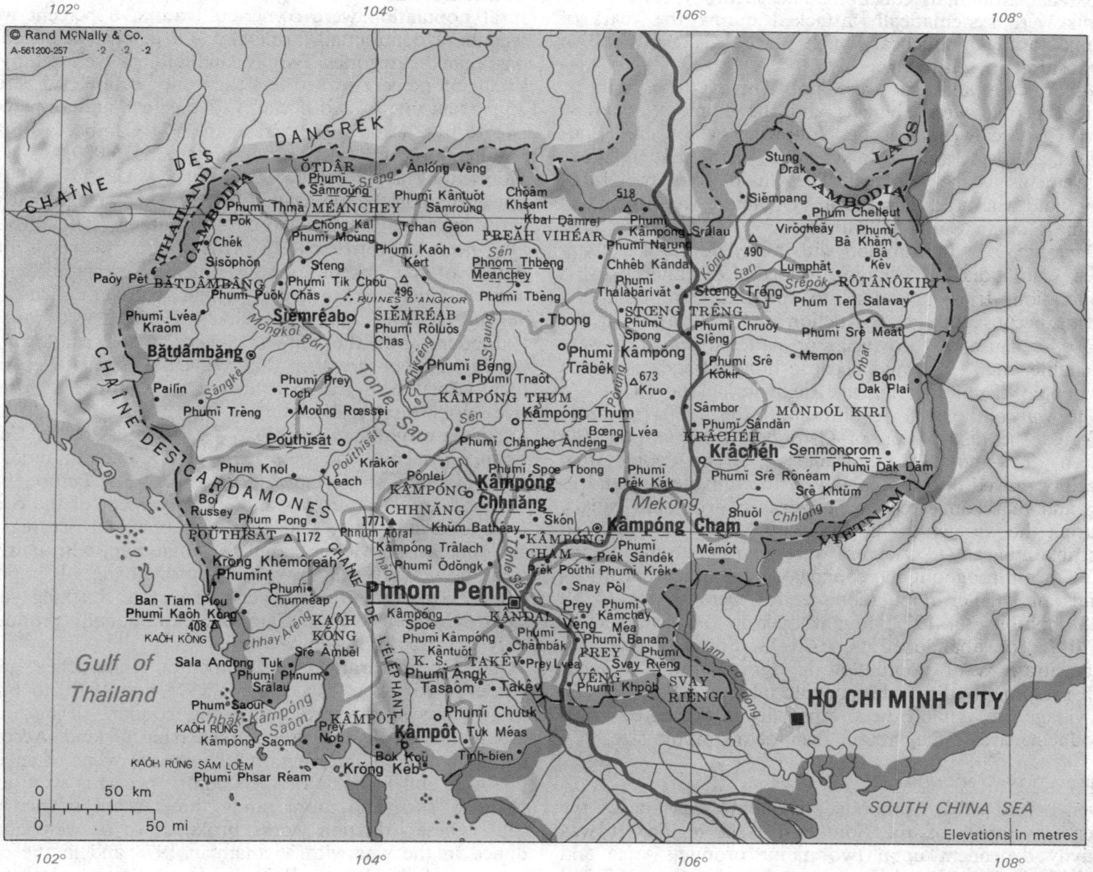

CAMBODIA

dren. Both sons and daughters usually left the parental home after marriage to establish their own households.

The ethnic minorities

Among the ethnic minorities in Cambodia before 1975, the Chinese were clearly the most important, for they controlled the country's economic life and retained a high degree of cultural distinctiveness, even though many assimilated into Khmer society through intermarriage. The Vietnamese minority occupied a somewhat lower status, and most of them fled or were repatriated to Vietnam after 1970. Centuries of mutual dislike and distrust have clouded Vietnamese-Khmer relations, and intermarriage is infrequent. The next most important minority, the Cham-Malay group known in Cambodia as Khmer Islām, also maintained a high degree of ethnic homogeneity and was discriminated against in 1975–78. By contrast, scattered evidence suggests that the tribal people of Cambodia, living originally in the forested northeast of the country, received favoured treatment during that period perhaps because the Cambodian Communists of Democratic Kampuchea had used tribal areas as guerrilla bases during the 1960s. This favouritism may also have reflected that regime's revolutionary concern for the downtrodden or forgotten inhabitants of Cambodia, for in the years before 1970, and indeed for centuries, the tribal minorities (known collectively as *phnong*, or "savages") had been mistreated by the ethnic Khmer.

Religious groups. Before 1975, the Khmer were almost universally Theravāda (Hīnāyana) Buddhists (*i.e.*, belonging to the earlier of the two great schools of Buddhism, the latter school being represented by the Mahāyāna), and Buddhism was officially recognized as the state religion. Between 1975 and 1978, Buddhist monks were made to work in the fields, like everyone else; images of Buddha from monasteries were destroyed; and temples were used as granaries and barracks. Although the social and psychological characteristics often ascribed to the Khmer—individualism, conservatism, patience, gentleness, and unconcern for material wealth—were often in the eyes of the beholder, they did represent Buddhist ideals toward which many Cambodians aspired, and Buddhist precepts permeated Cambodian education and ideology. These precepts were systematically attacked during the years of Democratic Kampuchea, which placed "superstition" in opposition to self-reliance.

Minority populations were not Theravāda Buddhists. Tribal people were animists and the ethnic Vietnamese and Chinese were eclectic, following Mahāyāna Buddhism, Taoism, and such syncretic Vietnamese religious movements as the Cao Dai. The Cham were strict Muslims, and a sizable number of Vietnamese were members of the Roman Catholic Church.

Demography. In common with many developing countries, Cambodia has a large proportion of children to its population. It is hazardous to speculate on population trends because of the destruction and dislocation of the 1970s, because no provincial or national statistics were available after 1970, and because hundreds of thousands of people of childbearing age died during the 1970s.

Population distribution

The war and social revolution in the 1970s seriously affected the distribution of Cambodia's population. Between 1975 and 1978, thousands of urban people were forcibly moved into the northwest to cultivate rice and to dig and maintain extensive networks of irrigation canals. During the war with Vietnam in 1978–79, the populated districts adjacent to Vietnam were devastated and deserted. Cities throughout the country were emptied and thousands of smaller population centres were destroyed by U.S. bombing in 1973, fought over in the civil war of 1970–75, or abandoned in 1975–78. Some of the new concentrations of population in agricultural communes will presumably disband as people take up what they can of village life, while others, especially in prosperous rice-producing areas, may retain their demographic size.

THE NATIONAL ECONOMY

Even before 1975, Cambodia's economy was one of the least developed of the Southeast Asia region. It was heavily dependent upon two major products—rice and rubber—and consequently was vulnerable to profound

Cambodia, Area and Population

	area		population	
	sq mi	sq km	1962 census	1971 estimate
Independent municipalities				
Bok Koŭ	0.4	1.1	1,000	1,000
Kâmpóng Saôm	26.3	68.2	7,000	9,000
Kêb	17.5	45.3	8,000	9,000
Phnom Penh	17.8	46.0	404,000	479,000
Provinces (*khêt*)				
Bătdâmbâng	7,407.0	19,184.2	552,000	671,000
Kâmpóng Cham	3,783.3	9,798.7	819,000	999,000
Kâmpóng Chhnăng	2,131.6	5,520.8	273,000	333,000
Kâmpóng Spœ	2,709.2	7,016.8	308,000	374,000
Kâmpóng Thum	10,657.0	27,601.6	421,000	390,000
Kâmpôt	2,302.1	5,962.4	340,000	414,000
Kândal	1,471.9	3,812.1	709,000	859,000
Kaôh Kŏng	4,309.1	11,160.6	39,000	48,000
Krâchéh	4,283.4	11,094.1	126,000	154,000
Môndól Kiri	5,516.4	14,287.6	15,000	18,000
Ŏtdar Méanchey	†	†	†	†
Poŭthisăt	4.900.4	12,692.1	182,000	219,000
Preăh Vihéar	*	*	*	*
Prêy Veng	1,885.4	4,883.2	488,000	592,000
Rôtânôkiri	4,163.0	10,782.3	49,000	60,000
Siĕmréab	6,354.0	16,456.8	312,000	380,000
Stœ̆ng Treng	4,282.6	11,092.0	35,000	42,000
Svay Riĕng	1,145.3	2,966.4	228,000	352,000
Takêv	1,375.6	3,562.7	465,000	566,000
Total Cambodia	69,897.6‡	181,035.0‡	5,729,000§‖	6,968,000

*The area and population of the new province of Preăh Vihéar are included in Kâmpóng Thum. †Area and population of the new province of Ŏtdar Méanchey are included in Siĕmréab. ‡Areas were published before the latest reorganization and include 1,158.3 sq mi (3,000 sq km) of inland water. §Final census figure. Population figures for individual municipalities and provinces are preliminary. ‖Figures do not add to total because of rounding. Source: Official government figures.

annual fluctuations caused by vagaries in rainfall and world market prices. Agriculture dominated the economy, employing about 80 percent of the population and providing more than a third of the total gross national product. Of 800,000 families residing in the rural areas, 670,000 were engaged in rice cultivation. The tradition of land ownership was strong. Approximately 80 percent of the rural population were owner-cultivators, 6 percent were tenants or contractual farmers, and 7 percent belonged to unspecified categories. Family landholdings were relatively small: 55 percent owned less than one hectare (2.5 acres), 25 percent one to two hectares (five acres), and 12 percent two to five hectares (12 acres). In 1974 Cambodia's gross national product (GNP) amounted to $570,000,000 U.S., representing a per capita income of $70 U.S. This figure, however, must be interpreted with the knowledge that the rural mass of the population was largely self-sufficient. One hectare of rice paddy provides for the needs of a family of five persons, and supplementary requirements were traditionally satisfied by fishing, cultivating fruit and vegetables, and raising livestock. Famine was rare in Cambodia, but the self-sufficiency of the rural family produced a conservatism that proved resistant to government efforts before 1975 to modernize Cambodia's primitive agricultural methods.

Sources of national income. *Agriculture.* Rice is Cambodia's principal food, its major crop, and, in times of peace, its most important export commodity. Before 1970, rice was grown on approximately 85 percent of the country's total cultivated land area. The principal rice regions surrounded the Mekong and the Tonle Sap, with cultivation particularly intensive in Bătdâmbâng, Kâmpóng Cham, Takêv, and Prey Vêng provinces. Lacking sufficient irrigation systems, Cambodia traditionally produced only one rice crop per year.

Rice production

Under the government of Democratic Kampuchea, great strides were taken, especially in 1975 and 1976, to build irrigation systems throughout the country, using mass labour and abolishing private ownership of land. According to scattered information, the results were often impressive, and in parts of the country peasants were able to grow two, and more rarely three, crops of rice per year. These irrigation works broke down or were abandoned in the war with Vietnam in 1978 and in the civil war that followed. In 1979–80, famine was widespread, and hundreds of thousands of Cambodians fled into Thailand or became dependent, inside Cambodia, on food provided by international aid.

It is unlikely that a Cambodian regime will hasten to reintroduce the massive communalization of the mid-1970s if peace is restored. For this reason, and because Cambodian agriculture is so dependent on the weather, it is worth noting the traditional patterns of planting, replanting, and harvesting a single crop. Planting normally begins in July or August, and the harvest period extends from November to January. The amount of rainfall, when there is little irrigation, determines the size and quality of the crop. Other food products include corn (maize), beans, soybeans, and sweet potatoes. The principal fruit crops, all of which are consumed locally, include oranges, bananas, and pineapple.

Traditional agriculture

Fisheries and livestock. Before the 1970s, fisheries and livestock were important components of the domestic economy. Fish in its various forms—fresh, dried, smoked, and salted—constituted the single most important source of protein in the Cambodian diet, and subsistence fishing was part of every farmer's activity. The annual freshwater catch, which included perch, carp, lungfish, and smelts, was estimated to be from 110,000 to 130,000 tons. Cattle, particularly water buffalo, were used principally as draft animals in the rice paddies and fields. Hog production amounted to 1,000,000 head per year. The efforts of the government of Democratic Kampuchea to increase the number of livestock—seriously depleted by years of war—broke down in 1978, when war and counterinsurgency again occupied the government's attention.

Mineral resources. Cambodia has few known mineral resources. Some limestone and phosphate deposits are found in Kâmpôt province, and precious stones in limited quantities are mined in Bătdâmbâng. Iron and coal traces have not justified commercial exploitation. Electrical power sources are mainly dependent upon imported oil. The construction of modest hydroelectric dams at Kirirôm and Kâmchay was halted by the war.

Industrial development. Although Cambodia's industrial development remains at a low level, successive governments until 1975 made strong efforts to build a modest industrial base suitable to the needs of the country. By the end of 1969 there were some 3,700 small plants and factories in Cambodia, the major portion of which was devoted to agricultural processing.

Management of the economy. In seeking rapid economic development, Cambodia in 1963 adopted a socialistic policy characterized by nationalization of the private banking system, establishment of a government monopoly over imports and exports, and extensive state participation in building and managing industrial enterprises. This policy proved to be unsuccessful, mainly because of defective economic planning, insufficient labour and managerial skills, and rigidly fixed agricultural prices that discouraged production incentive.

Changing development policies

The government of the Khmer Republic, in turn, supported the idea of industrialization, but was unable to accomplish much because Cambodia's cities were under siege for most of 1972–75. The regime of Democratic Kampuchea pursued a policy of self-reliance modelled on that of the People's Republic of China. This meant that existing factories were expanded and new ones were built to meet local needs for cloth, cigarettes, sheet rubber, farm machinery, fertilizer, and cement. Smaller factories were installed inside the agricultural communes, and a steel mill was planned, but not completed.

Scattered reports indicate that the People's Republic of Kampuchea hoped to restore Cambodia's modest industrial base. Its ability to do so would depend upon the availability of trained manpower, raw materials, the restoration of lines of credit with other countries, and the revival of local and international marketing and credit.

Foreign trade. Foreign trade was at a standstill in 1978, after 10,000 metric tons of latex were exported to the People's Republic of China. Imports into Cambodia after 1978 took the form of foreign aid—from China to Democratic Kampuchea, and from Vietnam and its allies to the People's Republic of Kampuchea. In 1970, the last year for which accurate statistics were available, exports totalled $39,000,000 in value and imports about $54,000,000. At that time, the bulk of Cambodia's exports, consisting almost entirely of rice, rubber, corn (maize), and other agricultural products, went to other Asian nations, while imports came mainly from Japan, the United States, and western Europe.

The effect of war on the economy. The civil war in Cambodia of 1970–75 devastated the countryside, sharply reduced foreign trade, and destroyed the nation's fragile economic infrastructure. After the Communist victory in 1975, large-scale economic policies involving the depopulation of urban areas, the construction of giant irrigation works, and the pursuit of industrial self-sufficiency met with mixed results and certainly left the people with few resources with which to fight a full-scale war against Vietnam. The port of Kâmpóng Saôm (formerly Sihanoukville) was used by both Democratic Kampuchea and the People's Republic of Kampuchea, largely to receive foreign aid. During the war of 1978–79, most of the earlier progress made in the countryside was erased.

Transportation. Before 1970, Cambodia's inland waterways and road systems constituted the main transportation routes. Each is invariably affected by the floods of the rainy season, which result in heavy silting and washouts (flash floods). Railroads ranked third in significance. Domestic shipping and civil air facilities were limited. Maritime commerce was carried out almost exclusively by foreign vessels.

The road system, which by 1970 surpassed the country's inland waterways as the principal means for moving cargo and passengers, had an overall extent of 9,300 miles. The network was originally designed by the French during the protectorate period to link the agricultural hinterland with the port of Saigon, now Ho Chi Minh City, Vietnam. Consequently the system did not serve Cambodia as a whole. Extensive land tracts in the northern, northeastern, and southwestern parts of the country were roadless. Of the total road network, about 1,600 miles were paved; other roads were surfaced with crushed stone, gravel, or laterite or were simply graded without being paved. The network contained more than 1,800 bridges of more than 20 feet in length, with average load capacities of five tons. The country's longest bridge—a ten-span structure more than 2,300 feet in length, traversing the Tônlé Sab at Phnom Penh—was destroyed in 1975.

The road system

The inland waterways have a collective extent of 1,200 miles, of which more than 90 percent are part of the Mekong and Tonle Sap systems. Phnom Penh, located about 200 miles from the mouth of the Mekong, can be reached by oceangoing vessels of less than 13-foot draft. North of Phnom Penh, the Mekong is navigable to Krâchéh for rivercraft, but rapids and winding channels in the 117-mile section between Krâchéh and the Laos border generally preclude commercial navigation.

Cambodia's single maritime port is located at Kâmpóng Saôm on the Gulf of Thailand. Completed in 1960, Kâmpóng Saôm can provide unlimited anchorage for oceangoing ships, and its main pier can accommodate four vessels of up to 15,000 tons. The port is of strategic importance to Cambodia, and considerable industrial development has taken place in the area. A modern four-lane highway links Kâmpóng Saôm with Phnom Penh.

Port at Kâmpóng Saôm

The railroad system comprises about 400 miles of single-track, metre-gauge line and is owned and operated by the Cambodian government. One line, completed prior to World War II, connects Phnom Penh with Paôy Pêt on the Thai frontier—a distance of 239 miles—and facilitates the movement of milled rice from the western provinces of Bătdâmbâng, Poŭthĭsăt, and Kâmpóng Chhnăng. The second line, completed in 1969, connects Phnom Penh with Kâmpóng Saôm, covering a distance of 168 miles through the provinces of Kândal, Takêv, and Kâmpôt.

ADMINISTRATION AND SOCIAL CONDITIONS

Administration. The People's Republic of Kampuchea, which was declared in 1979, was the fourth government in Cambodia during the 1970s. The previous governments were those of the Kingdom of Cambodia under Prince

Norodom Sihanouk, who had served as monarch, prime minister, or chief of state from 1941 to 1970; the Khmer Republic, the leaders of which, including Lon Nol, overthrew Sihanouk in March 1970; and Democratic Kampuchea, which was established in April 1975 under the leadership of Pol Pot. Each of these governments was organized in different ways; the first two, unlike the others, included elected officials, a freely elected legislature, a tenured civil service, and a system of courts. Under Democratic Kampuchea, it was difficult to determine where power really lay, although it seemed likely that after 1976 control was in the hands of the Central Committee of the Communist Party and its organization (*angkar*) in Phnom Penh.

The structure of government under the People's Republic of Kampuchea was not yet clear in 1980. Local government, as it was known under more Western-style regimes, had probably disappeared under the pressures of civil war and contending Communist ideologies. Nothing was known of the judicial system then in effect; it appeared that no judicial system functioned under Democratic Kampuchea. One peculiarity of all the regimes that followed the Kingdom of Cambodia was that each condemned to death the leaders of the preceding regime.

The armed forces. In 1979, the armed forces of Democratic Kampuchea were estimated to include 10,000 troops. No accurate statistics were available for the number of ethnic Cambodian forces loyal to the People's Republic of Kampuchea. More than 200,000 Vietnamese troops were garrisoned in Cambodia throughout 1979.

Social conditions and services. *Education.* Cambodia's educational system, as it had developed in the first 70 years of the 20th century, was another casualty of warfare and ideology. Under Democratic Kampuchea, only primary schools were open; older students attended irregularly scheduled political and technical courses, often held in the communes. The People's Republic stated its eagerness to reopen Cambodia's schools, but it was hampered by a shortage of funds, teachers, books, and students, as well as the continuing civil war. In 1970, by contrast, nearly 1,000,000 Cambodian children attended primary school on a regular basis. Another 120,000 attended secondary schools, and 10,000 or more were enrolled in colleges and universities. Education expenditures in 1970 averaged approximately 20 percent of the annual national budget.

Literacy rates

Before 1970, literacy levels in Cambodia rose slowly, but they remained below those of other Southeast Asian nations, with the exception of Laos. In 1970, it was estimated that only about 50 percent of the population aged ten and older was literate. Although Democratic Kampuchea claimed to have eliminated illiteracy in 1975–76, such an achievement seemed unlikely, given the conditions in the countryside, the absence of schools, and the government's discrimination against educated members of the "old society." Indeed, according to reports of refugees, illiterate peasants often rose to positions of power under that government.

Health. Throughout Cambodia's history, an acute shortage of medical personnel has been a major obstacle to the implementation of an effective public health program. In 1969, for example, the country had only 440 fully qualified physicians serving some 1,400 hospitals, infirmaries, dispensaries, clinics, and maternity centres, which were also staffed by paramedical personnel. The civil war of 1970–75 strained and eroded this fragile structure. Democratic Kampuchea moved medical personnel onto collective farms and, as part of its policy of self-reliance, encouraged non-Western medical practices based on the use of local herbs. Because of unsettled conditions, a lack of sanitation, and a shortage of medicine, epidemics of cholera and malaria were reported and instances of other diseases, especially those related to malnutrition, were frequent. The number of people who died of curable illnesses between 1975 and 1979 and the number of casualties of Cambodia's second civil war will never be known; an estimate of 500,000 such deaths is, perhaps, conservative.

CULTURAL LIFE AND INSTITUTIONS

Little is known of Cambodia's cultural life under the People's Republic. Before 1970, Cambodian culture and artistic expression were overshadowed by the greatness of the past. Although owing much to Indian influence, the achievements of the Khmer Empire represented original contributions to Asian civilization. The magnificent architecture and sculpture of the Angkorean period (802–1432), as seen in the restored temple complexes at Angkor Wat and Angkor Thom, marked the apex of Khmer creativity. Following the capture of Angkor by the Thai (15th century) and the crumbling of the empire, Cambodia underwent four centuries of foreign invasions, civil war, and widespread depopulation. It was not until the establishment of the French protectorate in 1863 that internal security was restored, the country's borders stabilized, and efforts undertaken to revive traditional Khmer art forms. After gaining independence from France in 1953, the Cambodian government placed particular emphasis upon accelerating that revival by establishing a national school of music, a national school of ballet and theatre, and a fine arts university. This coincided with the rapid expansion of elementary and secondary school facilities, and the emergence of education as the most important factor of social mobility in Cambodian society.

Khmer architecture

Music and dance forms. Music occupied a dominant place in Cambodian culture. It was sung and played everywhere—by children at play, adults at work, by young men and women while courting—and invariably was part of the many celebrations and festivals that took place throughout the year at Buddhist temples in the rural countryside. Instruments used in full orchestras included xylophones with wooden or metal bars, one- and two-stringed violins, wooden flutes, oboes, and drums of different sizes. The Cambodian musical scale had five tones, compared with seven in the Western scale. Orchestral music had no harmony, in the technical musical sense. The players followed the lead of one instrument, usually the xylophone, and improvised as they wished.

Dancing and drama

Dancing and drama were also popular forms of artistic expression. The Royal Ballet in Phnom Penh exemplified the classic, highly stylized dance form adapted by the Cambodians and Thai from the ancient dances of Angkor. Accompanied by an orchestra and choral narration, the dancers acted out stories and legends taken principally from Hindu epics such as the *Rāmāyaṇa*. In the countryside, folk drama and folk dances were performed at festivals and weddings by wandering troupes. The actors invariably depicted stereotyped characterizations familiar to all: the country yokel, the clumsy lover, the beautiful princess, the cruel father, and the greedy merchant. The visual arts revealed the essential conservatism of the Cambodians. Ancient themes were preferred and rarely was there an effort to improve or adapt. The principal crafts were weaving, working silver and gold, making jewelry, and the sculpture of wood and stone.

In the 1960s and early 1970s, Cambodia's traditionally conservative literature, based to a large extent on Thai literary forms, came under Western influences, as did its audience, the young, urbanized Cambodian elite. Novels, poetry, visual arts, and films came to reflect international taste. All of these forms of expression, however, were condemned as "imperialist" and "obscene" by the officials of Democratic Kampuchea. Under that regime, art was in the service of the state; revolutionary songs, however, often used traditional melodies and rhythms.

Newspapers, radio, television. Under the People's Republic of Kampuchea, one daily newspaper, *Bulletin Saporamean*, was published. Television programs, popular among the urban elite before 1975, were no longer broadcast. A national radio station broadcasts music, political programs, and news commentaries. No written works were published in Cambodia after 1975, except for political pamphlets and pictorial magazines that were intended largely for overseas consumption and often printed in China. Before 1975, Cambodia's growing number of literate citizens read approximately 60 newspapers and periodicals with a total circulation of some 600,000 copies.

Books circulated in much lower numbers. At that time, there were about 100,000 radio receivers and 30,000 television sets in the country.

PROSPECTS FOR THE FUTURE

As a small and relatively weak country surrounded by more powerful neighbours, Cambodia's prospects for survival as an independent nation will largely be determined by the support its warring factions receive from other countries and by the relations these patron countries enjoy with the rest of the world. It seems likely that Vietnam will play a prominent role in Cambodian life, just as it did in the 19th century before the arrival of the French. The role of Thailand will probably be more circumspect, while the continued patronage of anti-Vietnamese Cambodian forces by China and, to a lesser extent, the Western powers will do little to restore stability. Perhaps, as in the 19th century, Vietnam will be able to exercise effective control of Cambodia only in those areas east of the Mekong River, leaving the north and west in an anomalous state.

If peace returns to Cambodia in the early 1980s, and if foreign aid in sufficient amounts is received by its government, it is possible that steps toward the restoration of such services as education, transport, and health can be taken. Before that happens, however, it seems likely that thousands more Cambodians will die as an indirect result of the destruction of Cambodia's economy and institutions in the 1970s.

BIBLIOGRAPHY. L.P. BRIGGS, *The Ancient Khmer Empire* (1951), the most comprehensive work in English on the subject, drawn from all the major French scholars; G. COEDES, *Les États hindouisés d'Indochine et d'Indonésie*, rev. ed. (1964; Eng. trans., *The Indianized States of Southeast Asia*, 1968), a scholarly historical study of the region, useful for historical background; JEAN DELVERT, *Le Paysan cambodgien* (1961), a classic study of Cambodian geography and rural life by a French scholar who spent more than ten years in Cambodia; DAVID P. CHANDLER, *The Land and People of Cambodia* (1972), a historical treatment aimed at high school students; CLAUDE-GILLES GOUR, *Institutions constitutionnelles et politiques du Cambodge* (1965), an intensive analysis of Cambodia's constitutional institutions; FRANK M. LEBAR (ed.), *Ethnic Groups of Mainland Southeast Asia* (1964), one of the best sources of information about the numerous tribal groups inhabiting Cambodia; CHARLES MEYER (ed.), *Cambodge* (1962), a beautifully illustrated volume devoted to all aspects of life in Cambodia; JACQUES MIGOZZI, *Cambodge: Faits et problèmes de population* (1973), a detailed analysis of Cambodian demographic trends; MILTON OSBORNE, *Politics and Power in Cambodia* (1973), an analysis of Cambodia in the 1950s and 1960s; FRANCOIS PONCHAUD, *Cambodge année zéro* (1977; *Cambodia: Year Zero*, 1978), an account of Democratic Kampuchea; REMY PRUD'HOMME, *L'Economie du Cambodge* (1969), a penetrating analysis of the Cambodian economy; WILLIAM SHAWCROSS, *Sideshow: Kissinger, Nixon, and the Destruction of Cambodia* (1979), an analysis of U.S. policy toward Cambodia during the Khmer Republic period; D.J. STEINBERG *et al.*, *Cambodia: Its People, Its Society, Its Culture*, rev. ed. (1959), a compendium of information drawn from numerous published sources, somewhat outdated, but still useful; W.E. WILLMOTT, *The Chinese in Cambodia* (1967), one of the rare books devoted to the Chinese in Cambodia and their relations with the Khmer.

(L.C.O./D.P.Ch.)

Cambodia, History of

The importance of Cambodia's cultural and historical contributions to the development of mainland Southeast Asia is out of proportion to its present reduced territory and limited political power. At the height of its power (11th–13th centuries), the Khmer (Cambodian) state stretched across a vast area of the Indochinese peninsula and incorporated much of southern Vietnam, Laos, and Thailand, and the cultural influence of Cambodia on the other peoples of Southeast Asia has been enormous.

CAMBODIA BEFORE THE 9TH CENTURY AD

Knowledge of Cambodian prehistory is extremely limited. Excavations at three prehistoric sites—Samrong Sen and Longprao, in central Cambodia, and Melouprei, in northeastern Cambodia—have yielded remains from the Neolithic Age sufficient to permit only the barest reconstruction of life in the region more than 2,000 years ago. Nor is it possible to link the makers of the various artifacts that have been discovered with the succession of ethnic groups that moved through the Indochinese region as a whole in the prehistoric period, peopling both that region and the maritime areas of Southeast Asia as well.

Early inhabitants

Moving by both land and sea routes from areas to the north of Indochina, successive waves of migrants passed through the area. The original Australoid inhabitants were succeeded by Melanesians and then by Indonesians probably moving southward in two distinct phases, one by land and the other by sea. The languages spoken by these various migratory groups are increasingly seen by linguists as having had a distant common origin, whatever the later differentiations established among them. In the area of modern Cambodia, a language of the Mon-Khmer eventually became the dominant tongue after the Khmers, relative latecomers to the scene, had asserted themselves as political leaders, first in the state of Funan—centred in present southern Cambodia and the southernmost part of Vietnam—and later in the north-central Cambodian kingdom of Chenla.

The story of human activity in the area before the establishment of Funan, which Cambodian tradition ascribes to the 1st century AD, is not known in any detail. Settlements were close to lakes and rivers; the inhabitants engaged in agriculture and maintained cattle and pigs as domestic animals. They hunted with weapons that included the bow and arrow, for which arrowheads of polished stone, bone, and iron have been found. Metal cultures reached the Cambodian region well before the 1st century AD, and a site at Melouprei (now Phumĭ Mlu Prey) has revealed traces of iron and bronze casting. Close to the modern capital of Phnom Penh, the discovery of a bronze urn having close links with the Dong Son style of northern Vietnam (5th to 1st centuries BC) suggests that highly developed metalworking may have been taking place in pockets of Cambodian territory as early as the 4th century BC. Despite this evidence of growing technical capabilities, excavations at Oc Eo, Funan's major port on the southern coast of modern Vietnam along the Gulf of Thailand (Gulf of Siam), suggest that the Neolithic culture characterized by polished stone implements survived alongside the more advanced metal culture.

Funan. While future archaeological work may lead to a better understanding of Cambodian prehistory, true historical knowledge begins with the rise of Funan. From its claimed mythical beginnings in the 1st century AD until its incorporation into the successor state of Chenla in the 6th century, Funan was vitally important as a recipient of Indian culture, which shaped the political institutions, art, and general culture of later Khmer states. Always regarded by later Khmer dynasties as the state from which they sprang, Funan owed its prosperity to its position on the great east–west trade route between India and China. The name of the state is generally believed to come from a Chinese transliteration of a Khmer word *bnam* (*phnom* in modern Cambodian), meaning "hill." If correct, such a derivation is important as evidence of substantial Khmer influence over a state in which there was also a strong Indonesian ethnic and cultural presence.

Legendary origins

The national birth legend of the Funanese state tells of the arrival of a foreign Brahmin, Kaundinya, who overcame and subsequently married a local woman named Willow Leaf and set Funan upon its path to greatness. The legend is suggestive of the early influence of Indian thought and culture in the Indochinese area. Rejecting an earlier belief that large colonies of Indians settled in Southeast Asia, modern scholarship increasingly holds to a view that a relatively limited number of Indians, sometimes Buddhist traders, at other times Brahmins (high-caste Hindus), established themselves in positions of influence and propagated their more advanced knowledge of statecraft, religion, and art. A part of this view is the assumption that the existing populations of such areas as Funan were far from primitive savages and may have mastered the intricacies of wet rice cultivation.

The extent of implanted Indian influence in Funan before the middle of the 3rd century is uncertain, but a clearer picture of that period emerges from records left by two Chinese ambassadors who visited the country, *c.* AD 245. By that time Funan had extended its political power over the lower reaches of the Mekong and Tônlé Sab rivers and as far west as a section of the Malay Peninsula where trade passed from the Indian Ocean into the Gulf of Siam. This advance had taken place under the direction of King Fan Shih-man (*c.* 205–*c.* 225) and his nephew, Fan Chan (*c.* 225–*c.* 240), who took the throne as a usurper. Their successor, Fan Hsun (*c.* 240–*c.* 287), another usurper, was ruling at the time of the Chinese ambassadors' visit. The account of one of these ambassadors, K'ang T'ai, speaks of Funan as a land of walled cities whose inhabitants went unclothed through the streets but whose rulers gathered taxes in the form of precious metals, jewels, and perfumes. An Indian-based script was in use, and there were libraries and archives. The reference to the use of an Indian script is a clear indication of Indian influence, but it was not until the end of the 4th century that the full impact of Indian culture was felt in Funan.

This second "Indianization" of Funan came after a period about which there is little if any knowledge of developments within the state. Fan Chan's and Fan Hsun's reigns had seen the growth of official relationships between Funan and China and India. Relatively little is known, however, of the extent to which these official contacts were matched by a significant spread of Indian culture among the population at large. The appearance of a foreigner, Chandan, on the throne of Funan in 357 has been seen by some historians as a reinforcement of Indian influence and by others as reflecting a link with the Iranian world. Whatever may be the case, under Chandan's successors in the latter part of the 4th century and particularly in the 5th, there is a sense of Indian influence at a much wider level. Sanskrit inscriptions provide a more precise chronology of the reign of Funanese rulers and reveal that Hinduism and Mahāyāna Buddhism coexisted within the state.

Chandan's successor, according to the Chinese *History of the Liang*, was another Brahmin called Kaundinya, whose arrival in Funan was received with popular rejoicing and who instituted many reforms based on Indian models of law and administration. However mythical this Kaundinya may have been, the account of his arrival appears to capture correctly the importance of a new infusion of Indian culture. This cultural influence is abundantly apparent in the records that have survived describing the reigns of Funanese rulers during the 6th century. Funan was at the height of its power under the rule of King Kaundinya Jayavarman (d. 514).

Funan's greatest period

Excavations at the port city of Oc Eo have indicated the extent to which Funan prospered as a trading kingdom with links, indirectly, even with countries of the Mediterranean. Aerial photography has revealed a complex series of irrigation and communication canals that were established in the hinterland away from the coast. While Oc Eo may have been the most important port city, the royal capital was inland from the sea, at one time near the modern Cambodian town of Banam in Prêy Veng province and bearing the name Vyadhapura, "the city of the hunters."

From passages preserved in Chinese dynastic histories there is considerable information on the material culture of Funan in its heyday as well as insights into the state's religious life. It was a slave-owning society in which the rich decked themselves with gold and silver jewelry and wore rich brocades. The king lived in a richly constructed palace and travelled on the back of an elephant. The common people amused themselves with cock fights and contests between fighting pigs. Justice was administered through trial by ordeal. Since most buildings were constructed of wood, little is known of the style of Funanese building. A few architectural remnants at Oc Eo reinforce the evidence of Indian influence. The same initial source of inspiration was present in Funanese statuary. Sculpture from the 4th century has very obvious links with Gupta art in India. In the 6th century a distinctively Funanese art emerged in which Indian iconography was given a Cambodian form.

Hinduism was the religion of the rulers of Funan in the 5th and 6th centuries, but Buddhism was widely diffused in the kingdom also. There is evidence that Buddhism also enjoyed a measure of royal patronage. The importance of Buddhism in Funan in the 6th century was so great that a Chinese embassy visited the country between 535 and 545 to ask the ruler, Rudravarman (514–539), for Buddhist texts and teachers who could give Buddhist instruction in China.

Rudravarman was the last king of Funan to reign over an independent state. The subjugation of Funan by the rulers of the emerging state of Chenla marks a major division in Cambodian history. Although there are gaps in the history of Funan, the importance of the state is clearly apparent. It was through Funan that the initial process of Indianization took place, and it was this state which was always regarded by later Cambodians as the origin of their dynasties. Though this view was propounded in part to enhance legitimacy, it also reflected an awareness of the vital links that Funan had with its Angkorian successor state (9th–15th centuries). While the details are unclear, Funan before its absorption into Chenla already had links with the Khmers, whose base area was well to the north in the middle Mekong or Champassak area of modern Laos. There is clear evidence that Khmer princes were already associated with the Funanese ruling house and that some areas under the control of the Funanese state in the north of the kingdom were settled by Khmers.

Chenla–Funan relationship

Chenla. The first ruler claiming sovereignty over both Chenla and Funan was Bhavavarman (reigning 598), the grandson of Rudravarman of Funan, a fact which, along with his claim to power over both kingdoms, has led some authorities to suggest that the Chenla and Funan kings originally belonged to two branches of the same dynasty. Since Funan continued to send embassies to China until the beginning of the 7th century, the southern state apparently retained a degree of autonomy under Bhavavarman, whose capital was probably on the northern shore of the Cambodian Great Lake (Tonle Sap). Bhavavarman's brother, who succeeded him as Mahendravarman (*c.* 600–*c.* 611), left inscriptions that reveal considerable activity in the northeastern region of modern Cambodia around Krâchéh and Stœng Trêng. With Mahendravarman's son, Iśanavarman (*c.* 611–635), the power of the Chenla rulers over the declining state of Funan became absolute. Under Iśanavarman the power of Chenla was extended to the west as well as to the south, and good relations with the state of Champa (in present South Vietnam) were sealed by Iśanavarman's marriage to a Cham princess. Iśanavarman's capital, Iśanapura, at the modern site of Sambor Prei Kuk, near Kâmpóng Thum, is the most impressive group of pre-9th-century remains in Cambodia. A series of brick towers prefigure a number of later developments in Khmer art, and the site remained important as a centre of scholarship during the Angkorian period.

Under Iśanavarman's successors, Bhavavarman II (whose reign dates are unknown) and Jayavarman I (who reigned through most of the latter half of the 7th century), Khmer power extended throughout the Indochinese region. Yet, despite the description of Jayavarman as "glorious lion of kings" on one of his many inscriptions, the later division of the Chenla dominions into two separate regions probably began during his reign. Having expanded their power rapidly, the Chenla rulers were unable to maintain strict control over the various territories that they claimed the right to rule. Nevertheless, whatever political difficulties later sprang from the period, the 7th century was a time of continuing artistic development. Chinese accounts of court life under Iśanavarman give a picture of a rich material culture probably little different from that which had existed in Funan. Indian influence continued to be important in the art of the 7th century, and the two great Indian religions of Hinduism and Buddhism continued their coexistence. Of great significance for the future was the fact that the

Khmers, when they established their settlements in lowland Cambodia, used hydraulic techniques for agriculture that they had developed in lands further to the north. Their "captive water" technique, which damned water to be distributed by canals to less elevated regions, was later to be exploited to its full in the complex systems of Angkor.

Chenla's decline

Following Jayavarman I's death, the state of Chenla split into rival petty principalities. The history of the 8th century is obscure, but certain broad trends may be recorded. Land Chenla, the name given by the Chinese to the northern of the two divisions, apparently enjoyed a fairly stable existence with the centre of the state probably to the north of Angkor. By contrast, Water Chenla, the southern division, was an unsettled state beset by dynastic rivalries. As heir to Funan's position as an entrepot on the great east–west trade route, Water Chenla was grievously affected in the 6th and 7th centuries when traders began to bypass the Malay Peninsula, travelling to China by way of the Indonesian state of Śrivijaya in southern Sumatra. Along with the interruption of the trading link with the West, there was a sharp decline in direct cultural contact with India during the 7th century. Despite the diminution, and even elimination, of direct Indian influence, Khmer artistic achievements remained impressive until the latter half of the 8th century. And even this period of relative decline was rapidly followed by a dramatic efflorescence of Khmer artistic output, inspired by local genius rather than foreign models. This resurgence was the cultural accompaniment to the emergence of the Angkorian dynasty under the great Khmer ruler Jayavarman II (reigned *c.* 802–850), a man only distantly related to the ruling dynasties of pre-9th-century Cambodia.

THE ANGKOR PERIOD

Jayavarman II and his successors. In the latter part of the 8th century the Śailendra rulers of Java appear to have created a sphere of influence in Cambodia, and it was from Java that Jayavarman II returned to establish his kingdom about the year 800. Not the least remarkable aspect of his reign is the fact that since he left no inscriptions his achievements must be reconstructed from 11th-century inscriptions that give a clear picture of the vital importance of Jayavarman's reign. The concept of a unified Cambodian state was established, never to be forgotten by his successors, and a new state religion which established the Khmer ruler as a *devarāja* (god-king) was introduced during his reign.

On his return to Cambodia from Java, Jayavarman first established a capital at Indrapura, in modern Kâmpóng Cham province. But his subsequent three capitals were all in the region further north, close to but not actually in the area of the later Angkor complex. Strategically, the area on the east of the Great Lake was distant from the threat of external attack. The lake was a source of fish, and the plains about it were, with the application of hydraulic engineering, a great source for rice. Once Jayavarman had chosen this region as the centre for Khmer power, it remained so for most of the Angkorian era.

At his last capital of Mahendraparvata, in the Kulén hills to the east of Angkor, he took part in a Śaivite Hindu ceremony consecrating him as a *devarāja* and establishing both him and his kingdom as independent of any other power, especially that which the Javanese had claimed to exert over Cambodia. In this ceremony—perpetuated by Jayavarman's Angkorian successors—the king's sacred personality, the very essence of the kingdom, was enshrined in a sacred *liṅga* (a ritual phallic symbol) that was housed in a pyramidal structure called a temple mountain. This temple mountain was both the centre of the earthly kingdom over which the king ruled and the symbolic centre of the universe within which the kingdom existed. The details of this highly complex concept are possibly less important than the recognition that through participation in it Jayavarman and his successors saw themselves as universal rulers, subservient to no other state. The same symbolic purpose led to the establishment of the great Angkor temples, which were prefigured by those of Jayavarman's reign. In sculpture and the plastic arts, generally, the 9th century witnessed a revival and development of styles and techniques that blended Khmer traditions with those of Java and Champa.

Khmer kingship

After Jayavarman's death in 850 he was succeeded by a son, Jayavarman III (reigned 850–877), who left no significant mark upon Khmer history. The next ruler, Indravarman I, a cousin of Jayavarman III and possibly a usurper, played an important role in the development of the Angkorian state. Although his capital was not yet located on the site of the later Angkorian kings, it was at Roluos, not far distant, where Jayavarman II had founded one of his four capitals. At Roluos, Indravarman built two great stone temple mountains, Bakong and Preah Ko, which mark the beginning of Khmer classical art, the form from which the later temples developed. Even more important, however, was Indravarman's construction of a vast irrigation system that, by means of an artificial reservoir, permitted the assured exploitation of rice lands that otherwise would have remained unproductive. The later elaboration of artificial irrigation systems allowed the Khmers at Angkor to maintain a densely populated and highly centralized state in a relatively limited area. Only with such an irrigation system was it possible to feed the immense labour force necessary for the construction of the Angkor temples.

Indravarman's successor, Yaśovarman I (reigned 889–900), inherited a kingdom from his father that was at peace, and he proceeded to build solidly upon Indravarman's achievements. His new capital of Yaśodharapura, the first Khmer city in the Angkor area proper, centred on the hill Phnom Bakheng, which Yaśovarman crowned with a temple. The city complex occupied some 16 square miles; the irrigation of this area depended upon a new system, fed from a great reservoir east of the city, the so-called *baray oriental*, or eastern *baray* of modern times, which was fed from the Siĕmréab River. The power which Yaśovarman accumulated at Angkor enabled him to extend Cambodian domination over a territory as large as Funan's at that empire's height. It is uncertain whether this extension of power was the result of armed conquest or the readiness of other states to acknowledge the suzerainty of the leading power in the region. Some authorities believe that achievements attributed to Yaśovarman rightly belong to later reigns, but he was certainly a figure of great importance. He built monasteries throughout his kingdom for both Śaivites and Buddhists, and the remains of his temples, particularly that of Phnom Bakheng, show a continuing development of the Khmer genius of blending architectural construction with religious symbolism.

The 8th-century empire

The century following Yaśovarman's presumed death in 900 was one for which political records are now at a minimum. External commentary from Chinese sources vanished with the internal division of China after the fall of the T'ang dynasty. Within Cambodia itself the progress of the state must be charted through inscriptions, which provide a highly selective view of developments, and through the material evidence of temples, both royal and nonroyal in foundation. Nevertheless, close study of the extant inscriptions does permit some insight into the life of Cambodian rulers, the narrow oligarchy of priests and advisers who supervised the complex bureaucracy that presided over the daily business of the state, and even, occasionally, the activities of less elevated members of the population. Six Khmer kings ruled during the 10th century. Probably the most significant political developments of their reigns were the temporary abandonment of the Angkor capital under the usurper Jayavarman IV (reigned 928–942) and its subsequent re-establishment by Rajendravarman II (reigned 944–968). Rajendravarman's successor, Jayavarman V (968–1001), is known chiefly for his continuation of Rajendravarman's efforts to control Champa and for his promotion of scholarship and learning. In religious matters the 10th century continues to provide a record of Hindu cults coexisting with Buddhism. Although Saivism (worship of the Hindu god Śiva) was the principal royal cult, Buddhism also received its share of patronage.

Angkorian government and society. Though the Khmer monarchs were absolute rulers in theory, their power was often limited by the complex bureaucracy of the Angkorian state. The king was the final arbiter in legal matters and sometimes led his troops in battle, but much of his time was taken up with ceremonial and religious functions deemed necessary to insure the well-being of the state. If he was not a forceful personality, he might be reduced to a figurehead.

The bureaucracy

The bureaucracy was composed of learned Brahmins (members of hereditary priestly families) and military leaders who were sometimes members of the royal family. These men formed a class separate from the population at large; there is considerable evidence that their separate identity was reinforced through intermarriage. They were particularly influential in regions more distant from the capital. Although the construction of a temple mountain was the prerogative of the king alone, the great officials founded their own shrines, each supported by surrounding villages, which met the high cost of maintaining the temple and its priests. None of these shrines rivals the great royal foundations in size, but the temple of Banteay Srei, a little to the northeast of the Angkor complex, is considered by many to be the most perfect of all Khmer temples. It was built in 967 by a Brahmin, Yajñavarāha, a man of royal descent who had supervised the education of both Rajendravarman II and Jayavarman V.

Between the great officials, on the one hand, and the peasants and slaves (about whom little is known), on the other hand, there was another group, whose existence is recorded in inscriptions but whose role in the Khmer state has yet to be studied in any detail. This was a group of land-owning men who held no official position and who, unlike the priestly officials of the great foundations in provincial regions, appear to have had little contact with the capital. Their existence, and the existence of "castes" of teachers and priests who were recruited from provincial areas but who were clearly not of the elevated status of the great officials, provided some qualification to the narrow classifications into which Khmer society has frequently been divided in modern historical accounts. While the size of these intermediate groups is unknown, their existence suggests a more complex society than that which envisages a single, sharp division between the king and his officials, and the peasantry and slaves.

The 11th century. At the beginning of the 11th century one of the most energetic of the Khmer monarchs, Suryavarman I (reigned *c.* 1002–50), challenged the position of Jayavarman's legitimate successor, Udayadityavarman I, to hold the throne. A Cambodian prince, but with scant direct claim to the throne, Suryavarman had defeated Udayadityavarman by 1002, but a long civil war dragged on until he finally gained control over the whole kingdom about 1011. Although the evidence comes from chronicles of a considerably later period, Suryavarman appears to be correctly credited with the extension of Khmer power over much of modern southern Thailand and over Mekong valley regions as far north as Luang Prabang. In contrast to this activity in the west, his relations with Champa and Vietnam, to the east, seem to have been calm and stable. His long reign enabled the restoration of many of his predecessors' foundations both at Angkor itself and in other parts of the country, and the completion, notably, of the Phimeanakas and Ta Keo temples begun by Jayavarman V.

A new dynasty

Suryavarman's son, Udayadityavarman II (reigned 1050–66), carried on his father's expansionist policies. While some historians judge that this led to the Khmer state reaching its furthest limits, these policies also provide part of the explanation for the record of revolts that marked Udayadityavarman II's reign. Cham encouragement appears to have been behind a revolt in the southeast of the kingdom. And in the west the Khmers found themselves in confrontation with the newly victorious Burmese, who had conquered the Mon capital of Thaton. Other revolts within Cambodia itself are believed by some historians to have reflected resentment at the favour which the ruler showed toward Buddhism, a religion that his father had done much to promote. Despite the record of warfare and revolt during his reign, Udayadityavarman II found time to build another great *baray*, or reservoir, the western *baray*, which greatly increased the cultivable area of the region around Angkor. Udayadityavarman's successor was his brother, Harshavarman III (reigned 1066–80), who was unable to prevent a major incursion into Cambodia by a Cham army that marched to Sambhupura, a city on the Mekong near the modern town of Krâchéh, and sacked it. Harshavarman was overthrown by a usurper, who reigned as Jayavarman VI (1080–1107), but possibly never occupied the capital at Angkor. He and his successor, Dharanindravarman I (1107–13), had to contend with the opposition of members of Harshavarman's family.

From Suryavarman II to Jayavarman VII. *Suryavarman II.* This opposition was finally and forcefully crushed by Suryavarman II, one of the greatest figures in Cambodian history, who came to the throne in 1113. Reducing the kingdom of Champa to vassal status, he annexed it completely when the Cham king would not cooperate in his campaigns against the Vietnamese state further north. Suryavarman's expeditions against the Vietnamese took his armies as far north as Thanh Hoa in modern North Vietnam. The extent of his success in the Mae Nam Chao Phraya Valley is open to some doubt, but the substantial Khmer influence found in the architecture of the Thai state of Lopburi suggests an important impact on that region (present Thailand). Khmer influence also reached well down into the Malay Peninsula.

Suryavarman's empire

Suryavarman's military and political conquests are matched by the magnificence of his achievements in building the great temple complex of Angkor Wat. Completed at about the time of his death in 1150, Angkor Wat was only one of the outstanding architectural achievements of his reign. Beng Mealea, some 25 miles to the east of Angkor, and Banteay Samre on its outskirts are other magnificent examples of Khmer art and architecture.

Suryavarman blended Śaivism and Vaiṣṇavism (the cult of Viṣṇu) in his state religion. Within the inner sanctuary of Angkor Wat was a gold statue of Viṣṇu (Vishnu) mounted on the fabled winged Garuḍa, representing the deified Suryavarman as Viṣṇu. Yet once again, there was no religious exclusiveness within the Khmer state. Buddhism, even if overshadowed by the Hindu cults, continued nonetheless to have its adherents.

The first period of decline. Suryavarman's successes rested on uncertain foundations, and by the end of his reign the combined effects of an overambitious external policy and the demands that his building program placed upon the resources of the state entailed heavy costs. His repeated expeditions against the Vietnamese failed to achieve his goal of subjugating that energetic neighbouring state. A year before his death (*c.* 1150), the Chams freed themselves from Khmer domination and their strength in the immediately succeeding decades was directed toward wiping out the stigma of Khmer overlordship by attacking the Cambodian heartland. Indeed, between 1050 and the accession of Jayavarman VII in 1181, the fragility of the Khmer state after a period of greatness was demonstrated time and again. Internal rebellion was added to the challenge of the Chams to further weaken the power of the ruler. Suryavarman's immediate successor, Dharanindravarman II (1150–60), had an apparently uneventful reign, notable largely for the fact that the new king was a devotee of Buddhism rather than of Hinduism. But at his death the rightful successor, Jayavarman, was passed over and the throne was occupied by his younger brother Yaśovarman II (reigned 1160–*c.* 1166). In the space of six years Yaśovarman faced a peasant or slave revolt, which was successfully subdued, and the rebellion of an ambitious official, Tribhuvanadityavarman, which caused the king's dethronement and death. Although Jayavarman came out of exile in Champa to defend the king, he arrived after the usurpation had taken place and again retired from the scene. During Tribhuvanadityavarman's reign the resurgent Chams began their long campaign of attrition against the Khmers. Border skirmishes begun in 1167 finally culminated in the humiliating and highly successful Cham attack against the capital at Angkor in 1177. The capture

Cham attacks

Adapted from J. Buttinger, *The Smaller Dragon: A Political History of Vietnam* (1970); Praeger Publishers

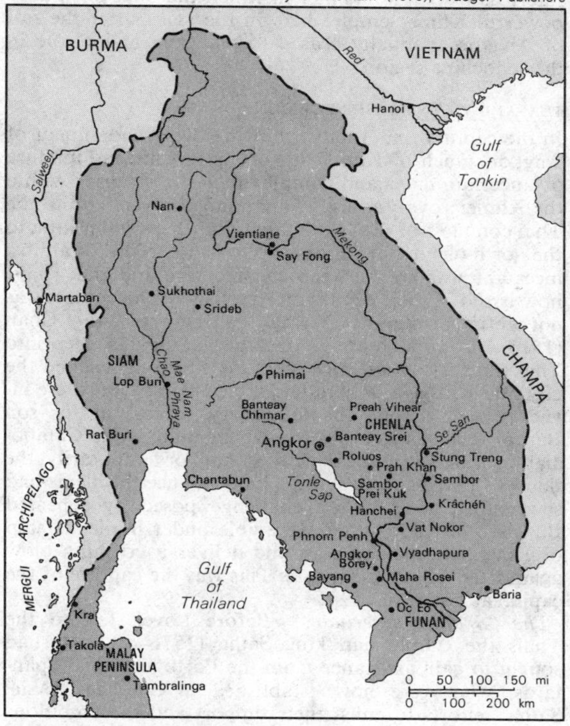

Khmer Empire, *c.* 1200.

of the capital and the death of the ruler left Cambodia in chaos.

Jayavarman VII. The accession of Jayavarman VII brought a change. This ruler ranks with Suryavarman II among the greatest of all Angkorian rulers. His energy was phenomenal: in both the success of his campaigns against the Chams and his devotion to temple construction he revivified the Khmer empire. As was the case with Suryavarman II, however, this massive outpouring of energy exacted a heavy cost. Jayavarman's policies so exhausted the state that, once his leadership had gone, no other ruler was able to maintain it in the same manner. The most active builder of all the Angkorian monarchs, he left a large number of inscriptions. To his reign belongs the great complex of Angkor Thom, which rivals Angkor Wat in magnificence.

Jayavarman was nearly 60 when, following a period of almost constant campaigning, he achieved sufficient control to assume the kingship in 1181. He repaid in full the injuries his country had suffered at the hands of the Chams. The Khmer armies laid waste to their kingdom and sacked the Cham capital of Vijaya. Through skillful use of Cham allies opposed to their own ruling family, Jayavarman prepared a campaign that finally led to the annexation of Champa, which remained under Khmer control from 1203 to 1220. Within Cambodia itself Jayavarman was unchallenged after the first year of his reign. To the west and south of Cambodia, the Chao Phraya Valley and parts of the Malay Peninsula recognized Cambodian suzerainty. An inscription near modern Vientiane, Laos, records his domination of that area.

Though Jayavarman's Buddhist adherence was to the Mahāyāna school, which had long been dominant in Cambodia, during his reign Theravāda Buddhism was introduced into Burma by the Mon monk Chapata. Among Chapata's companions was a Khmer prince who has been identified as one of Jayavarman's sons. This link with the Theravāda school foreshadowed its later patronage by the Khmer kings, which led to its supplanting the Mahāyāna school and so to a major change in the state's religion. Although modern scholarship rejects the view that the conversion of the Cambodian state to Theravāda Buddhism provides a single convincing explanation for the decline of Angkorian power, the change when it came was a profound one, not least because the Theravāda cult did not call for the construction of great temples as did both Hinduism and Mahāyāna Buddhism.

Jayavarman VII's greatest energies during his reign, as far as external policies were concerned, had been directed toward the conquest and subjugation of the Chams. Before the end of his life, however, the most formidable threat to Khmer power was developing to the west.

The Thai threat

The Thais had been filtering into the Chao Phraya Valley from well before the beginning of the 12th century. In a famous section of the Angkor Wat bas-relief, Thai mercenaries are depicted as ill-disciplined and strangely dressed men of little civilization. Thai chieftains living under Khmer rule in what was the northwestern extension of the Cambodian empire were, however, growing in power and absorbing much of the civilization of their overlords. Only 20 years after Jayavarman's death the Thais of the state of Sukhothai were powerful enough to break the shackles of foreign rule. That this should have been so emphasizes the rapid reversals that followed the end of Jayavarman's rule (*c.* 1215, possibly as late as 1219). He was the last of the great kings. Yet even if the 13th and 14th centuries were centuries of decline, they were by no means a period of eclipse, despite the repeated incursions of the Thais, which forced a temporary abandonment of Angkor before the end of the 14th century.

The final decline. After Jayavarman's death, no significant building took place at Angkor, and the Khmer empire began to contract. Control over Champa ended in 1220. In 1238 a Thai chieftain—son-in-law of Jayavarman VII—mounted a successful coup d'etat against the Khmer governor of the upper Chao Phraya region and founded the Thai state of Sukhothai. Khmer overlordship in the Malay Peninsula also disappeared after Jayavarman's death. For the greater part of the 13th century, however, Angkor remained a glittering and wealthy city, one which inspired wonder in the eyes of the Chinese traveller Chou Ta-kuan when he visited the city in 1296. The account that Chou Ta-kuan provides of Angkor at this time is both the longest and most detailed description of the Khmer capital, and despite its inaccuracies and reliance on legend it gives a remarkably vivid picture of the rich court society that continued to exist, even though the Chinese writer records the fact that Cambodia had been under attack from the Thais shortly before. Chou Ta-kuan left a picture of a bustling city in which the king still went forth in great pomp and ceremony. Whatever weakness now characterized the Khmers, Chou Ta-kuan still judged Cambodia to be the strongest of the states to the south of China. Notable among his observations was the presence in the Khmer capital of Buddhist monks of the Theravāda school. Thus, by the end of the 13th century the Cambodian state had abandoned its adherence to Hinduism and, at the court and in the capital at least, adopted Theravāda Buddhism.

Theravāda Buddhism

This change took place during the long reign of Jayavarman VIII (reigned 1243–95), probably about the middle of the century. Its causes remain a matter for some debate. The view of some of the earliest scholars of Cambodian history, that Theravāda Buddhism was a "democratic" religion that appealed to the Cambodian masses bowed down before the overwhelming exactions of their kings, has been severely qualified. The adoption and propagation of a particular religion within Angkorian society is much more likely to have been a matter for royal patronage. One intriguing suggestion is that the rulers and their advisers at Angkor were aware of the political success of the increasingly powerful Thai states to the west and attributed this to the form of Buddhism, the Theravāda school, which the Thai rulers followed. Adherence to Theravāda Buddhism was never incompatible with the pursuit of power for the Thai rulers and would not have been viewed so by those in power at Angkor. Moreover, placing importance on the population's acceptance of Buddhism seems illogical in view of the fact that their most fundamental religious adherence was to animistic cults. Viewed from a slightly different perspective, however, there may be value in considering the permeation of Theravāda Buddhism into the ranks of the general population as reflecting some readiness on the part of the people to accept a new religion that made few demands upon them—in contrast to Hinduism and Mahāyāna Buddhism, which had sapped their material and physical resources. Not only did the introduction of the new religion mean the end of temple building on the old scale, it also led to the disappearance of the use of Sanskrit; the latest Cambodian Sanskrit inscription dates from 1327. Henceforth Pāli was the sacred language.

For a short period at the beginning of the 14th century the Khmers enjoyed a respite from external threat. The great Thai ruler of Sukhothai, Ramkhamhaeng, died *c.* 1317 and his death removed the motive force that had brought Sukhothai to a position of considerable power, posing a threat to Angkor. The respite, however, was a brief one. Whereas the selection of the Angkorian region as a site for the Khmer capital in the 9th century had ensured its isolation from external threats, the ever-growing presence of the Thais in the Chao Phraya Valley meant that Angkor was in an increasingly exposed position. The king at Angkor when Chou Ta-kuan visited the city in 1296 was Indravarman III (1296–1308). His successors, the last to leave inscriptions, were Indrajayavarman (1308–27) and Jayavarman Paramesvara, who acceded to the throne in 1327 but for whom no date of death is recorded. With an absence of inscriptions and the unreliability of other records, there has been a measure of historical disagreement over developments during the 14th and 15th centuries. Recent research has challenged the previous assumption that the Thais captured Angkor in 1431, from which date the Khmers abandoned their capital. According to this new view, based on both Cambodian and Chinese sources, Angkor fell to Thai attacks in 1369 and 1389 and was on each occasion occupied by Thai forces. It was not, however, until 1444 that the final (third) great attack against Angkor took place that did, indeed, lead to its ultimate abandonment.

The fall of Angkor

The proposed new chronology, which is accompanied by evidence of considerable Thai involvement in the family rivalries of the Khmer royal house, is helpful for an assessment of why it was that Angkor was finally abandoned in such a dramatic fashion. Emphasis on the political significance of the change to Theravāda Buddhism remains important, with its overtones of a sense of crisis in Khmer national confidence. But other, more obvious, material factors were clearly involved. The record of Thai attacks against Angkor highlights the extreme fragility of the Angkorian economic system. Under pressure from the Thais, and on occasion from the Chams also, the Khmer rulers at Angkor had the greatest difficulty in maintaining the intricate hydraulic system upon which Angkor's survival depended. The reservoirs and canals needed constant attention, which was impossible under conditions of war. Damage to the system during actual attacks on the city, and the shipping off of thousands of prisoners of war, further weakened the economic base of the state. Recent analysis now discounts the view that malaria, spreading from the shattered hydraulic system, played a part in Angkor's decline. When, in a manner that became so characteristic in the years of decline after the fall of Angkor, squabbles between members of the royal family further weakened the Khmers, the stage was set for the collapse of the Angkorian empire. After the abandonment of the former imperial city in 1444, the Khmer court moved south to a site near modern Phnom Penh, and thence to Phnom Penh itself. For the remainder of Cambodian history to the present, this region was to be the centre of a contracting Khmer world.

The artistic traditions of Angkor did not immediately disappear. The expression of these traditions was no longer the mighty temples in stone but rather the more intimate art of the religious statue, and even this art form declined as political power waned more rapidly during the 17th and 18th centuries before the ever greater power of the Thais and the Vietnamese. When a French colonial presence was established in Cambodia shortly after the middle of the 19th century, it was common for the European newcomers to speak of Cambodia as having "fallen from its antique splendour." This comment accurately assessed the manner in which the once singularly powerful Khmer empire had, in the years after the fall of Angkor, gradually ceased to play any major role in the Indochina region.

THAI AND VIETNAMESE HEGEMONY

In the century and a half following the abandonment of Angkor, much of Khmer history is a confusing mixture of uncertain dates and complex dynastic rivalries within the Khmer royal family. Dominating the years up to the Thai conquest of Lovek (a later Khmer capital a little to the north of Phnom Penh) in 1594 is the record of almost incessant warfare between the Khmers and the Thais, now based in their capital of Ayutthaya. The contest was not entirely uneven. During the reign of Ang Chan (1516–66) the Khmers carried their campaign deep into Thai territory on one occasion, in 1564, but reached the city of Ayutthaya only to find it occupied by Burmese invaders. Yet despite the temporary success of his son Barom Reachea I (1566–76), which enabled the Cambodian court to reoccupy the city at Angkor temporarily, the tide was flowing against the Khmers. Once the Thais had successfully resisted the challenge posed by repeated Burmese invasions, they were able under the leadership of King Naresuen to plan and deliver a crushing blow against the Cambodian state. This was the capture of the capital at Lovek in 1594.

The "Spanish interlude." Before Lovek fell to the Thais the Cambodian king Satha (1576–*c.* 1594) had sought to gain assistance from the Portuguese and Spaniards, who were now established in Southeast Asia. Satha's efforts to enlist their support and the ambitions of both missionaries and soldiers of fortune led to one of the more curious episodes in Cambodian history. For a brief period, after the fall of Lovek, Spanish soldiers became arbiters of power within the Khmer state. A Spanish expedition arrived in Cambodia in 1596 with the intention of giving aid to King Satha. By then, however, Satha had been deposed and a usurper, Chung Prei, occupied the throne. After a series of disagreements and the sacking of the Chinese quarter of Phnom Penh by the Spanish forces, the Spaniards attacked the king in his palace at Srei Sânthôr, killing him and his son. Deciding to return to Manila after this affair, the Spaniards later changed their minds while sailing along the Vietnamese coast and marched overland to Laos, where they found one of Satha's sons and successfully installed him upon the Cambodian throne in 1597 as Barom Reachea II (1597–99). The great officials within the Cambodian court were by this time deeply resentful of the power wielded by the foreigners and were anxious to depose Barom Reachea in favour of Satha's brother, Soryopor. An incident involving one of the Spanish leaders in Phnom Penh led to a massacre of the Spanish garrison in mid-1599 and, after a period in which three princes occupied the throne, Soryopor returned to gain the throne as Barom Reachea IV (1603–18), with the assistance of a Thai army. The Spanish interlude was the last significant contact the Cambodian court had with Europeans until the onset of French colonialism in the mid-19th century. It was an exotic interregnum that had no lasting political effect but did, however, provide later historians with one of the few accounts of the Angkorian irrigation system, written by an observer who visited Angkor at a time when it had been reoccupied toward the end of the 16th century.

First European contact

Cambodia as a vassal state. Cambodian history from the accession of Barom Reachea IV until the establishment of the French Protectorate in 1863 is a sorry record of weak kings, almost always under challenge from dissident members of the royal family and forced to seek the protection of either of their stronger neighbours, Siam (Thailand) and Vietnam. Between 1603 and 1848, the date of the last Cambodian ruler to assume the throne free from French political control, no fewer than 22 monarchs uneasily occupied the throne. Several of these rulers had more than one reign, as they gave up their position either through choice or under duress, only to return when their successors either proved incapable or were themselves deposed. The details of this unstable period are less important than the record that is available of the manner in which Cambodia slowly slipped under the dual suzerainty of Siam and Vietnam. Early in the 17th century, Chey Chetta II (1618–28) successfully, if rather temporarily, declared his country's independence from Siam. In order to strengthen his position, the King sought assistance from the Nguyen lords of southern Vietnam. This fatal decision, which had involved Chey Chetta's marrying a Vietnamese princess, brought a Vietnamese demand for the right to settle Vietnamese colonists in areas of southern Vietnam, near Saigon, which until this time had been Cambodian territory. From this point onward, rival claimants for the Khmer throne sought to advance their interests through the respective support of either the Thais or the Vietnamese, at the ever-increasing cost of loss of territory or loss of power. For the Vietnamese, assistance given to Cambodian princes was followed by the extension of Vietnamese settlement into former Cambodian territories. For the Thais, the provision of aid was joined to an insistence upon Cambodia's assuming vassal status, but it did not involve the colonization of Cambodian lands.

Vietnamese expansion

That Cambodia survived at all during this bitter period was attributable in large part to the other preoccupations that weighed upon the Thais and the Vietnamese. In the middle years of the 18th century, Thai energies were largely taken up with wars against the Burmese, which led, in 1767, to the Burmese capture of Ayutthaya. Later in the same century, the Nguyen rulers of southern Vietnam were engaged in a prolonged campaign to regain power from the usurping Tay Son rebels. Yet if these facts had slowed the pace of Cambodia's decline, the situation by the end of the 18th century was nonetheless grim. Over the course of the century, all of what was to become the French colony of Cochinchina had fallen under Vietnamese control. In the west, Thai suzerainty had been firmly established over the great provinces of Bătdâmbâng and Siĕmréab. As the century drew to a close, and as the Vietnamese leader Nguyen Anh, later to reign as Gia Long, still fought to unify his country, the Thai court at Bangkok was firmly in control of the Cambodian royal family. King Ang Eng (reigned 1779–96) was actually crowned in Bangkok and was placed on the throne at the Khmer capital, Oudong, north of Phnom Penh, through the support of a Thai army. Following Ang Eng's death, Ang Chan, a minor, succeeded to the throne. He was crowned in 1806 and ruled uncertainly until 1835.

Ang Chan's reign

The reign of Ang Chan II confirmed Cambodia's dual vassalage to Siam and Vietnam. Faced with his rebellious brothers, Ang Chan gained assistance from Vietnam, while the Thais supported his brothers. The uneasy calm that was finally established, as Cambodia acknowledged both Thai and Vietnamese suzerainty, ended with Ang Chan's death. Vietnamese pressure was strong enough to ensure that a weak and powerless princess was then placed on the throne while almost total Vietnamese control was exercised over the country. Not until 1841, when Ang Duong (reigned 1848–60) returned from exile in Bangkok supported by Thai troops, were the Cambodians able to exercise even a minimal degree of independence. Because Thai support had helped him to the throne, Siam exercised a preponderant influence over Ang Duong, but he remained in tributary relations with Vietnam. As the last king to rule free from French control, Ang Duong has often been idealized in modern Cambodia. He was devoted to revitalizing the state, but his resources were desperately limited. Cambodia survived essentially because of the restraint of its neighbours, and before the end of his reign, Ang Duong's rule was troubled by internal rebellions.

FRENCH RULE

The protectorate. French control over Cambodia developed as an adjunct to French colonial involvement in Vietnam. Before his death, Ang Duong, on the urging of a French missionary, had sought to gain French assistance to regain former Cambodian lands held by the Vietnamese. He did not seek a French protectorate over his country, as many French accounts have suggested. There was no response to Ang Duong's call for help, and the French decision to advance into Cambodia came only when, with a colony implanted in Cochinchina, the French began to fear that British and Thai expansion might lead to hostile control of the Mekong River. In an almost classic use of gunboat diplomacy, the French in 1863 intimidated the Cambodian king Norodom (acceded 1860) into signing a protectorate treaty that gave France control of Cambodia's foreign affairs. When Norodom was crowned at Oudong in 1864, the French stood by as new suzerains of the weak Cambodian state.

Reign of Norodom

In the early years of the French protectorate, the European newcomers interfered little in the affairs of the Cambodian state. Indeed, French protection had distinct similarities to the part played by Cambodia's Asian suzerains in the past. At odds with his half brothers and faced with rebellion, Norodom gained rather than lost as the result of the French presence. Although he bitterly resented the French recognition of Thai control over Bătdâmbâng and Siĕmréab provinces, he might well have lost the throne if it had not been for French support. By the mid-1870s, however, French officials in Cambodia were pressing for greater control over internal affairs. Shocked by what they regarded as the profligacy and barbarity of Norodom's court and methods of government, they sought to introduce reforms. In pursuing their goals they acted with the knowledge that Norodom's half brother Prince Sisowath was ready to cooperate with them and was most ambitious to replace Norodom on the throne. Yet, despite the power that the French could exercise, their repeated efforts to change the methods of Cambodian administration foundered on the rock of Norodom's stubborn opposition to change. Exasperated by the King's intransigence, Gov. Charles Thomson of Cochinchina, who also held responsibility for the French position in Cambodia, forced Norodom in June 1884 to sign a convention virtually transforming Cambodia into a colony. The result of this action was a Cambodian rising that broke out in January 1885 and lasted for two years.

Anti-French rebellion

This rebellion was the only major anti-French movement to occur in Cambodia until after World War II. It gravely threatened the French position in the country and was finally put down only when French officials were able to persuade the King to call upon his countrymen to lay down their arms in return for some French concessions to the King's position. This was, basically, a hollow victory for Norodom. What the French had been unable to achieve in a single sweep by the convention of 1884 they proceeded to gain through piecemeal action. As Norodom's health declined and as senior Cambodian officials began to see their interests linked as much with French power as with their monarch, the way was opened for greater and greater French control over the actual business of government. In 1897 the French representative in Phnom Penh assumed the chairmanship of the Cambodian Council of Ministers, and the King's influence in government was reduced to a bare minimum. Norodom died a bitter man in 1904.

Yet Norodom's reign was not entirely one of constant loss for the Cambodian monarchy. Although the French gained political ascendancy, they ensured the survival of the Cambodian state, and, by maintaining the king in a splendour that had probably not been equalled since Angkorian times, they greatly enhanced his symbolic position within the kingdom. This fact was to be of considerable importance in the post-independence period following World War II.

King Norodom's ambitious half brother Sisowath finally did succeed to the Cambodian throne in 1904. Already in his 60s, he nonetheless continued to reign until 1927. While Sisowath held the throne, no difficulties arose between the Cambodian king and the French, nor was there any growth of nationalist activity comparable to that in Vietnam. By preserving the Cambodian monarchy, the French administration successfully prevented the development of any alternative focus for national identification. The one significant event that occurred during Sisowath's reign involved a mass peasant protest against tax and corvée (forced labour) requirements in 1916. Yet even this peasant protest was essentially peaceful, and the protesters disbanded once the King had given his assurance that royal consideration would be given to ameliorating conditions. During Sisowath's reign and that of his son and successor, Monivong (1927–41), the first notable economic developments derived from French rule took place. Red-earth lands in the east were brought under rubber cultivation, and, for the first time, there was a realization that Cambodia's economic opportunities went beyond the export of rice.

Rubber cultivation

World War II and the First Indochina War. When Monivong died in 1941, the Japanese had occupied Indochina while leaving the French administration in nominal control. In these difficult circumstances, the French governor general of Indochina, Adm. Jean Decoux, placed Prince Norodom Sihanouk on the Cambodian throne. Although some uncertainties remain about the reasons for Sihanouk's elevation, Decoux seems to have been guided by the expectation that, as a young man of 18, Sihanouk, unlike the late King Monivong's son, Prince Monireth, would be readily controlled by the French. The error of the French estimation of Sihanouk's pliability became apparent in the years after the end of the war.

The effect of the Japanese occupation on Cambodia was less profound than it was in many other Southeast Asian countries. The overthrow of the French administration throughout Indochina in March 1945 brought the opportunity for political development to Cambodia. Although Sihanouk declared his country's independence from France, he and his advisers looked forward to cooperation with the former protecting power. Others, led by Son Ngoc Thanh, who had urged opposition to the French in the 1930s and been forced into exile in 1942, urged a sharp break with France.

Re-establishment of French control

The end of World War II brought the re-establishment of French control over Cambodia. Despite abolition of Cambodia's protectorate relationship, as it became an "autonomous state within the French Union," real power remained in French hands. Yet between 1945 and Cambodia's final achievement of independence in 1953, important political developments occurred. There were more demands for full independence, and a contest developed between the King and his supporters, who wished to uphold the supremacy of the crown, and those who sought to make Parliament the predominant power.

Cambodia was ill prepared for parliamentary democracy, and the years between 1945 and 1953 were marked by factional strife. The dominant Democratic Party was frequently at odds with the King and suffered from internal dissension. The death in 1947 of its able leader, Prince Youtevong, was a blow to the party and to those who hoped for a constitutional monarchy. Outside Parliament, Son Ngoc Thanh, now a bitter opponent of Sihanouk's policies, led the dissident Khmer Issarak (Independent Cambodians), who opposed both the King and the French. With this internal disunity and with the French fighting the Vietnamese revolutionaries, the Viet Minh, throughout Indochina, Sihanouk acted. In January 1953 he dissolved Parliament, declared martial law, and left Cambodia to seek the support of world opinion for his country's independence.

INDEPENDENCE

Sihanouk finally succeeded in his personal campaign, known as the Royal Crusade, when the French granted independence on November 9, 1953. At the Geneva Conference in May of the following year, Sihanouk's representatives achieved a further triumph when his government was recognized as the sole legitimate authority within the country. This decision prevented the Viet Minh forces and the limited number of left-wing Khmers who were their allies from gaining any regional authority within the country, as happened in Laos. The King's achievements left him in a momentarily unchallengeable position; even Son Ngoc Thanh appeared ready to cooperate with Sihanouk.

Independence and the end of the First Indochina War did not, however, bring an end to political factionalism. Finding himself once again in conflict with his domestic opponents, Sihanouk took a dramatic new step. In March 1955 he abdicated in favour of his father, Norodom Suramarit, and formed a new mass political movement, the Sangkum Reastr Niyum (People's Socialist Community). Loyalty to Sihanouk and the country were the guiding principles of the Sangkum. In the elections of September 1955 it won every seat in the National Assembly. From then until his fall in March 1970, Sihanouk was the central figure in Cambodian politics, sometimes as prime minister and, after his father's death in 1960, when no new monarch was named, as chief of state. Overt political life was carefully controlled by the Prince and his advisers.

Founding of Sangkum

Before the mid-1960s, external crises posed the greatest threat to Cambodia's stability. Conscious of historical precedent, Sihanouk saw South Vietnam and Thailand as the greatest threats to Cambodia's survival, particularly as these two neighbouring states were allied with the United States, which Sihanouk distrusted. At the same time Sihanouk feared the eventual success of the Vietnamese Communists and the danger he saw in a unified Vietnam. In these circumstances he proclaimed a policy of neutrality in international affairs. Convinced, however, of U.S. involvement in plots against his state and his family in 1959 and 1960, Sihanouk finally broke relations with Washington in May 1965 and aligned Cambodia more closely with China, North Vietnam, and the National Liberation Front in South Vietnam. From 1965, in an attempt to anticipate the future, he agreed clandestinely to the use of Cambodian territory by the Vietnamese Communists.

This decision further alienated right-wing elements in Cambodian society, particularly the army officer corps. The conservative urban elite already resented the economic policies introduced in 1963 and 1964, and they saw the closer alignment with the Vietnamese Communists as potentially ruinous to their interests.

From 1966 Cambodia's internal politics developed in a complex fashion. Although Prince Sihanouk remained a revered, even semi-divine figure for most of the peasantry, he was increasingly seen as a threat by both the right and the left. Young left-wing Cambodians, many of them educated abroad, resented Sihanouk's internal policies, which did not tolerate radical dissent. The outbreak of a rural rebellion in 1967 convinced Sihanouk that the greatest danger to his regime came from the left. He increasingly bowed to pressure from the army and other conservatives to follow a policy of harsh repression against left-wing elements.

By 1969 Sihanouk's personal position had deteriorated, and conflict between the army and left-wing opponents of the Prince's regime had increased. Right-wing politicians, most notably Gen. Lon Nol and Prince Sisowath Sirik Matak, plotted to depose Sihanouk, whom they saw as the root cause of their country's problems. They enlisted the support of Sihanouk's long-time enemy Son Ngoc Thanh, who had remained a dissident throughout the 1960s at the head of the Khmer Serei (Free Cambodians), a group receiving clandestine United States assistance. The extent of U.S. involvement in this plotting against Sihanouk is a matter of controversy. There seems little doubt, however, that U.S. intelligence services were aware of developments.

Matters came to a head in March 1970 when, with Sihanouk absent in France, Lon Nol and Sirik Matak called for the evacuation of all Vietnamese Communist forces from Cambodian soil and instigated demonstrations against the North Vietnamese and National Liberation Front embassies in Phnom Penh. At the same time, Sihanouk's conservative opponents called on him to renounce his international and domestic policies. Within a week it was clear that neither the Vietnamese Communists nor Sihanouk would negotiate under threat, and on March 18, 1970, Lon Nol's faction deposed the Prince. Sihanouk took up residence in Peking, where he became the head of both a government in exile and a National United Front of Cambodia (NUFC) dedicated to overthrowing the Lon Nol regime.

Deposition of Sihanouk

Second Indochina War. Sihanouk's overthrow brought Cambodia's full involvement in the Second Indochina War, particularly after the U.S. and South Vietnamese invasion of the country on May 1, 1970. At first the Lon Nol regime confronted a largely Vietnamese military threat, but a Khmer revolutionary force slowly emerged as the principal opponent. The leaders of this newly important group included men such as Khieu Samphan, Hou Yuon, and Hu Nim, who had opposed Sihanouk's policies in the past and who had fled into the countryside before his overthrow to escape the summary justice of the Prince's security forces.

As these and other left-wing leaders emerged into prominence, Sihanouk's importance declined. Although he remained a symbol of the legitimacy of those who opposed the Lon Nol regime, Sihanouk was clearly not in charge of either the daily tactics or the long-term strategy of those fighting against the Phnom Penh forces. By 1973 he spoke publicly of his difficulties with the Cambodian revolutionaries.

Despite proclaimed policies of reform and United States military and economic aid, the Lon Nol regime never succeeded in gaining the initiative against its opponents. Gestures such as declaring Cambodia the Khmer Republic in 1970 were of little account, as the revolutionary forces pursued a strategy of attrition, choking off provincial capitals from the countryside. Following the end of the U.S. bombing of Cambodia in August 1973, the balance tilted toward the eventual success of the NUFC forces despite continuing strong U.S. aid to the Lon Nol regime. This success was finally achieved when Phnom Penh fell to the revolutionary forces on April 17, 1975.

Postwar uncertainty. Great secrecy surrounded developments after April 1975. Sihanouk returned to Phnom Penh in September 1975 as titular chief of state but resigned three months after a new constitution of Democratic Kampuchea was instituted on January 5, 1976. Amid reports by refugees of mass executions and death from disease, major political and social changes took place. Phnom Penh was forcibly evacuated and programs were instituted to reorient the country toward agricultural self-sufficiency and to remove the economic and social patterns of the prerevolutionary period. Elections for the 250-member People's Representative Assembly were held in March 1976, and in April Khieu Samphan was named head of state and Pol Pot was named premier. In 1977 the Communist Party of Kampuchea was first officially recognized as the country's governing body.

Pol Pot as premier

For a period after 1953 Cambodia appeared to occupy a unique position in Southeast Asia as Sihanouk successfully confronted both external and internal challenges. The pressures of the late 1960s ended this situation as external developments passed beyond Sihanouk's control and as political division within his country grew sharper. The onset of a savage war in 1970 brought widespread suffering and the collapse of Cambodia's economy. Those who gained control of Cambodia in April 1975 faced daunting internal problems and border clashes with Thailand and Vietnam.

BIBLIOGRAPHY

Cambodia to the end of Angkor: Much of the important material concerning Cambodian history until the fall of Angkor is in journal articles, mostly in French. Among the more valuable and readily available sources are: G. COEDES, *Les États hindouisés d'Indochine et d'Indonésie,* rev. ed. (1964; Eng. trans., *The Indianized States of Southeast Asia,* 1968), *Les Peuples de la Péninsule Indochinoise* (1962; Eng. trans., *The Making of South East Asia,* 1966), and *Pour mieux comprendre Angkor* (1943; Eng. trans., *Angkor: An Introduction,* 1963), three studies by the most distinguished French scholar of Cambodia to the end of the Angkorian period; J. BOISSELIER, *Le Cambodge* (1966), the most complete archaeological survey to the end of the Angkorian period; B.-P. GROSLIER and J. ARTHAUD, *Angkor: Hommes et pierres,* rev. ed. (1965; Eng. trans., *Angkor: Art and Civilization,* 1966), a fine pictorial study with concise text; M. GITEAU, *Les Khmers* (1965; Eng. trans., *Khmer Sculpture and the Angkor Civilization,* 1965), by a former curator of the Phnom Penh National Museum; L.P. BRIGGS, *The Ancient Khmer Empire* (1951), a detailed survey of Cambodian history to the fall of Angkor, now in need of revision; O.W. WOLTERS, "The Khmer King at Basan (1371–3) and the Restoration of the Cambodian Chronology During the Fourteenth and Fifteenth Centuries," *Asia Major,* 12:44–89 (1966), an important journal article suggesting a revision of the date of the fall of Angkor; D.G.E. HALL, *A History of South-East Asia,* 3rd ed. (1968), for a summary of Cambodian history.

Modern Cambodia: B.-P. GROSLIER, *Angkor et le Cambodge au XVIe siècle d'après les sources portugaises et espagnoles* (1958), discusses the economic basis of Angkorian times and the "Spanish interlude"; D.P. CHANDLER, *Cambodia Before the French: Politics in a Tributary Kingdom, 1794–1848* (1974), a valuable study; J. MOURA, *Le Royaume du Cambodge,* 2 vol. (1883), an early French study; A. LECLERE, *Histoire du Cambodge . . .* (1914), a monumental but flawed pioneering history; M.E. OSBORNE, *The French Presence in Cochinchina and Cambodia: Rule and Response (1859–1905)* (1969), treats the first 50 years of French rule; D.J. STEINBERG *et al., Cambodia: Its People, Its Society, Its Culture,* rev. ed. (1959), a useful but dated survey; R.M. SMITH, "Cambodia," in G.M. KAHIN (ed.), *Governments and Politics of Southeast Asia,* 2nd ed. (1964); *Cambodia's Foreign Policy* (1965), a sympathetic study of Sihanouk's policies; M. LEIFER, *Cambodia: The Search for Security* (1967), critically evaluates foreign policy issues; W.E. WILLMOTT, *The Chinese in Cambodia* (1967), a valuable study of the Chinese minority in Cambodia; M.E. OSBORNE, *Politics and Power in Cambodia: The Sihanouk Years* (1973).

(M.E.O.)

Cambrian Period

The Cambrian Period, oldest division of the Paleozoic Era, includes a time interval of about 70,000,000 years that began about 570,000,000 years ago. Precise numerical dating of events during this time is rarely possible because very few Cambrian rocks have the minerals that can be analyzed to produce such dates. The stratigraphic boundaries for the Cambrian and all younger periods are determined by the use of a relative time scale that is based on evolutionary changes in the fossil record of the common animals or plants.

The Cambrian Period is particularly important for biologists as well as geologists. It is the time of the earliest record of abundant animal life on Earth and therefore contributes valuable information to studies of evolution. The Cambrian record provides the earliest reasonably detailed data about physical and animal geography that geologists can use to build the story of the changing face of the Earth.

The name Cambrian was introduced into geologic literature in 1835 by the English geologist Adam Sedgwick. In the early 1800s, when the modern stratigraphic framework was in its formative stages, Sedgwick and Roderick Murchison undertook a study of the thick, complexly folded series of sandstones, slates, and quartzites known as the Graywacke Series that lay beneath the Devonian Old Red Sandstone in Great Britain. Sedgwick, working with the oldest rocks of this series in northern Wales, and Murchison, working with the younger rocks in southern Wales, recognized distinctive sedimentary sequences within the Graywacke Series that they proposed to call the Cambrian and Silurian systems. The times during which these systems were deposited were referred to as the Cambrian and Silurian periods. Sedgwick chose the name Cambrian because "Cambria," a latinization of the Welsh word *Cymry,* meaning "people," was popular among English writers as an ancient name for Wales. The name first appeared in its latinized form in about the 12th century in a compilation of historical and quasi-historical records of the Welsh people called *Annales Cambriae.*

Work of Sedgwick and Murchison

Shortly after 1835 the upper boundary of the Cambrian

became the subject of a bitter geological debate between Sedgwick and Murchison and their friends when further geological work established that the upper beds of Sedgwick's Cambrian and the lower beds of Murchison's Silurian were contemporaneous. The difficulty was resolved by compromise in 1879, a few years after the deaths of the principal protagonists, by introduction of the term Ordovician Period for the time of deposition of the overlapping parts of the systems.

The reference region for a system is normally the region in which the name was first applied. Because northern Wales is a region of poorly fossiliferous rocks and complex geology, it never has been a satisfactory reference for global correlation of the Cambrian System. Because of geographic proximity and similar sedimentary facies, the more richly fossiliferous and relatively undisturbed Cambrian succession of southern Scandinavia therefore has served as a reference section. The lower part of this section, however, is incomplete, and the entire section is only about 600 feet (180 metres) thick. The most complete records of Cambrian sedimentation and faunal development are in Siberia and western North America, where fossiliferous Cambrian sections exceed 6,000 feet (1,800 metres) in thickness; but neither area has become clearly established as the principal Cambrian reference area.

Cambrian rocks are important sources of many economic minerals. Ores of lead, zinc, silver, gold, and tungsten have been mined from Cambrian rocks in the Cordilleran region of western North America, the southern and central Appalachian regions of eastern United States, Sardinia, North Africa, southeastern Australia, and Tasmania. Upper Cambrian rocks of Sweden are important sources of uranium and vanadium as well as potential producers of oil from oil shales. Oil has been produced from Cambrian rocks in southern Siberia, where extensive Cambrian salt deposits also are known and from the midcontinent region of the United States. Sandstones of Cambrian age in many parts of the world are quarried as sources of silica for the glass and steel industries. Cambrian limestones are extensively quarried in many places and burned to produce agricultural lime or cement. They also are crushed for use as flux in ore smelters or quarried as slabs and blocks for use in the building industry. In many parts of the northcentral United States, Cambrian sandstones are increasingly important sources of groundwater as younger beds become exhausted through increased industrial and population demands. For additional information on the Cambrian Period, its boundaries, and its relation to other geological periods, see PRECAMBRIAN TIME; ORDOVICIAN PERIOD; and PALEOZOIC ERA, LOWER. See FOSSIL RECORD for a further discussion of life forms during Cambrian time.

CAMBRIAN ROCKS

Occurrence and distribution

Cambrian rocks occur on all continents. The most extensive and best studied areas are North America and the U.S.S.R. east of the Ural Mountains. The outcrop areas of western Europe and North Africa also have been well studied, but they are widely scattered. Cambrian rocks are known from many areas of China, but information about them is meagre. Australia is an important Cambrian area, but much of the Australian Cambrian is unstudied. Very little is known about details of the Cambrian rocks and faunas of South America, Antarctica, and New Zealand.

Most Cambrian rocks are now found in present or former mountainous regions where they have been subjected to varying degrees of folding, faulting, and in some cases metamorphism since Cambrian time. Parts of the midcontinent region of the United States, the Baltic region of northern Europe, the central Siberian plateau, and northeastern Australia are areas where Cambrian rocks have been little disturbed since they were deposited. Most of the rocks in all regions contain fossils of marine organisms or other evidence of marine origin, indicating that much of the world's surface was covered by Cambrian seas.

Sedimentary facies

The marine sediments can be grouped into three major types or facies: terrigenous (land derived), carbonate bank (shallow calcareous sediments), and deepwater deposits. Near the Cambrian land areas, the sediments were predominantly sands, silts, and clays. Many contain the distinctive marine mineral glauconite. This region of terrigenous sediments was often many tens of miles wide. Local patches of muddy carbonate sediments developed toward the seaward margins. The second principal facies is represented by limestones and dolomites, some quite pure, that accumulated to great thicknesses beyond the seaward margins of the terrigenous belt. These carbonate sediments have abundant layered structures formed by algae and many textural evidences for shallow and agitated water, such as oolites and cross-bedding, which indicate that they accumulated in areas analogous to the present-day Bahama Banks. Many Cambrian banks were more than 200 miles (320 kilometres) wide and many hundreds of miles long. The third principal facies includes thin-bedded limestones and shales, usually gray or black and containing the iron sulfide mineral pyrite. These sediments show little evidence of water agitation. In many areas, they accumulated on the seaward side of the carbonate banks and are interpreted as relatively deepwater sediments. In some restricted areas they include conglomerate beds formed of pure limestone or dolomite fragments derived from the banks. This facies is associated with marine volcanic rocks and sediments derived from local volcanic islands in some parts of the world.

In the volcanic areas Cambrian sediments are many thousands of feet thick; limestone and dolomite accumulations to thicknesses of several thousand feet are common in the regions of the carbonate banks. Similar thicknesses are also known for many areas of terrigenous sediments. Regions that, since the Cambrian, have been relatively undisturbed were subject to slow or frequently interrupted Cambrian sedimentation and thus may be represented by less than 1,000 feet (300 metres) of sediments.

CAMBRIAN LIFE

There is no Cambrian record of terrestrial or freshwater animal or plant life, and no vertebrate fossils have been found in Cambrian beds. The distribution and abundance of Cambrian organisms are related to the major marine environments represented by the principal sedimentary facies. The greatest variety of organisms lived on the margins of the carbonate banks and in the protected regions behind the banks. Most marine invertebrate phyla whose modern members have mineralized skeletons were represented in the earliest Cambrian. However, the relative abundance of these representative groups has changed significantly since Cambrian time. Only three major groups, Bryozoa, Foraminifera, and corals, each of which have well established post-Cambrian histories, are not present in Cambrian age rocks.

Invertebrate life forms

The dominant Cambrian marine invertebrates were trilobites, a major subgroup of the Arthropods that has been extinct since the end of the Paleozoic Era. Trilobites are distantly related to modern horseshoe crabs and had a similar dorsal exoskeleton divided into a head region and a tail region separated by a variable number of articulated segments. Most trilobites averaged about three inches in length, but they ranged in size from one-fourth inch (agnostids) to almost two feet (*Paradoxides*). They fed on microscopic organisms in the sea or on bottom detritus. Trilobites were abundant in all marine environments from the muddy sea floor to the sea surface. Almost 75 percent of all fossils found in Cambrian rocks are trilobites, preserved as numerous molts or parts of the dead animals.

Many other arthropod groups existed in the Cambrian seas, but they either lacked mineralized skeletons and thus were rarely preserved or they were minor elements of the Cambrian faunas. Small bivalved ostracods and the merostomes, which are close relatives of the modern horseshoe crab, are the principal nontrilobite arthropods found as fossils.

The Mollusca, the group to which modern snails and clams belong, was represented by a variety of Cambrian forms. The commonest shells of these organisms were slender, conical, and generally less than two inches long with circular or triangular cross-sections; these represented the hyolithids that became extinct at the end of the Paleozoic Era. Small, laterally compressed, cap-shaped univalve shells of the Helcionellida are also found in many Cambrian deposits. Snails with coiled shells are rare in Cambrian faunas, occurring only in younger Cambrian beds. Cephalopods with straight, chambered, conical shells, relatives of the modern *Nautilus*, are found only rarely in Late Cambrian faunas. Bivalves, with the exception of a peculiar unsymmetrical group, the Stenothecoida, that became extinct in the Middle Cambrian, are absent in Cambrian faunas. Shells of several other shapes have been assigned to the Mollusca and attest to the variety of Cambrian representatives of this phylum. Few of these groups survived the Cambrian, which seems to have been a time of unsuccessful experimentation for the Mollusca.

The Echinodermata, to which modern sea urchins and starfish belong, were represented by a variety of free-living and attached groups. Some (eocrinoids) had a cylindrical or spherical body with a stem at one end and a cluster of slender arms at the other. Others (edrioasteroids) had spherical or disk-shaped bodies without stems or arms. Most of these were relatively unsuccessful, and few survived the Cambrian. Representatives of this phylum, however, were much more abundant than the record of well-preserved specimens would suggest. They characteristically lived in areas of agitated water, and their skeletons, which are composed of many individual loosely attached plates, rarely remained intact. A large part of the calcareous sediment in many Cambrian areas is composed of disarticulated echinoderm debris.

The brachiopods, a group of bivalved animals that is very rare in modern oceans, is second in abundance and stratigraphic value to the trilobites in the Cambrian. The commonest forms were the Acrotretida—brachiopods less than three millimetres in diameter with one saucer-shaped and one conical shell composed of calcium phosphate. These are obtained, often in great numbers, from the insoluble residues of Cambrian limestones digested by dilute acetic or formic acid. They are largely unstudied but have considerable potential for stratigraphic work. Two other groups of phosphatic brachiopods occur with the Acrotretida, but they are less varied and have limited stratigraphic value. One of these, the Lingulida, is still found in modern oceans and has changed very little since the Cambrian. Calcareous shelled brachiopods are abundant in some restricted areas but generally are rare in Cambrian rocks.

During the early part of the Cambrian, a group of spongelike organisms called archaeocyathids formed crudely cylindrical or cone-shaped calcareous skeletons made up of porous inner and outer walls separated by radial partitions. The structural details were often quite elaborate. This group flourished on the carbonate banks and other areas with good water circulation, but for unknown reasons it became extinct at the end of the Early Cambrian even though the habitats remained apparently unchanged. Porifera or sponges were common in the Cambrian seas, but, like the echinoderms, they are rarely found completely preserved. Calcareous or siliceous rods that served as stiffeners within the sponge bodies are found in most Cambrian deposits.

The marine annelids were probably also abundant, as evidenced by many thoroughly burrowed Cambrian sediments. Except for rare species that formed phosphatic tubes and others that made distinctive straight or curved burrows in Cambrian sands, there is little record of their existence.

Graptolites, fragile colonial hemichordates, were rare elements of the Late Cambrian faunas and were preserved only in areas of quiet sedimentation where there were few burrowing bottom dwellers. Conodonts, small phosphatic fossils of uncertain biologic affinities, are found principally as rare elements in faunas from the areas of unrestricted access to open ocean conditions in Middle and Late Cambrian rocks.

In addition to the animal groups with mineralized skeletons that are usually found as fossils, the Cambrian seas supported a great variety of other organisms that formed important parts of the animal communities but were rarely preserved. The discovery in 1910 of a rich fauna of soft-bodied organisms in Middle Cambrian shales at Burgess Pass in the Rocky Mountains near Field, British Columbia, provided ample proof of the diversity of these Cambrian marine organisms.

The principal marine plants were algae. Blue-green algae grew in sheetlike layers that trapped fine calcareous sediment and formed laminated beds, domes, columns, or golf-ball sized spheres termed stromatolites in many of the shallow marine environments on and adjacent to the carbonate banks. Some massive calcareous structures attributed to green or red algae are also moderately common.

The origin of the Cambrian faunas

The origin and appearance of the Cambrian faunas in the geologic record constitutes a major biologic problem. The earliest Cambrian beds with skeletal remains contain several distantly related trilobite, brachiopod, mollusk, and echinoderm groups and representatives of other phyla that total about 20 distinct kinds of invertebrates. There is no indication of convergence toward a common ancestor. Slightly older sediments in Australia (Ediacara fauna) and western United States have yielded impressions of soft-bodied animals or tracks and trails indicating that a variety of invertebrates without mineralized skeletons were present at least a few million years earlier, in Precambrian time. The biologic problem is thus concerned with two major events that occurred in sequence: first, the origin of the invertebrates; and second, the origin of the conditions under which they could secrete mineralized skeletons.

An early explanation of the contrast between the Precambrian rocks that were almost barren of animal life and the Cambrian rocks bearing the rich and diversified faunas invoked a period of time called the Lipalian Interval, during which all the present land areas of the world were above sea level. Life evolved in the restricted oceans, and the record was thus not available on the present continents. When the seas inundated the continents, the already diversified Cambrian faunas came with them. The Cambrian System was believed to begin everywhere above an erosional unconformity. As knowledge increased and marine sedimentary sequences many thousands of feet thick and barren of fossils were found in continuous succession below marine beds bearing abundant Cambrian fossils, the explanation for the abrupt appearance of the Cambrian fauna based on the "lost" Lipalian Interval became untenable.

The origin of the invertebrates may have been dependent on the evolution of the earth's atmosphere. The oxygen of the atmosphere serves as a shield against ultraviolet radiation from the sun that would be lethal to life on land and in the shallow seas. Several lines of evidence indicate that the Early Precambrian atmosphere lacked oxygen and that its appearance is related to photosynthesis by marine algae, which have a geologic record almost 2,000,000,000 years older than the oldest invertebrates. The buildup of oxygen took many millions of years because much of it was consumed in the beginning by oxidation of inorganic materials in the oceans and on the land. As photosynthetic oxygen production exceeded inorganic needs, a surplus developed in the atmosphere. When this surplus reached a level sufficient to provide a shielding from solar ultraviolet radiation, conditions necessary for the evolution of the invertebrates were achieved.

Several explanations have been given for the origin of conditions permitting mineralization of invertebrate tissues, but none has been supported by convincing evidence. Two of the most plausible possibilities are that skeletons evolved as protection against some unknown predator or predators, or that skeletons became possible only after some subtle chemical change in the evolving environment created conditions in which inorganic compounds could be retained in animal tissues.

BOUNDARIES AND SUBDIVISIONS OF THE CAMBRIAN

Both biological problems discussed in the preceding section have a direct bearing on the geological problem of the lower boundary of the Cambrian System. The environmental change permitting rapid evolution and diversification of the invertebrates has been considered the significant temporal event marking the beginning of the Cambrian. It may be argued, however, that the ancient soft-bodied organisms are so unlike any Cambrian forms that they are a true Precambrian fauna; thus, the significant temporal event marking the beginning of the Cambrian would be the nearly simultaneous appearance of mineralized skeletons in many different invertebrate groups. Until a criterion for time determination is agreed upon by convention and finds general acceptance among paleontologists, the problem of worldwide identification of the beginning of the Cambrian will remain.

Within the Cambrian System, correlation of events from one region to another requires reasonably precise time criteria (see STRATIGRAPHIC BOUNDARIES). Trilobites, which were abundant, evolved rapidly throughout the period, and had preservable exoskeletons, are the principal tools used for this purpose.

Trilobite successions

In many regions of the world, empirical successions of changing trilobites have been described and subdivided into zones with characteristic assemblages of genera and species. The zones have been grouped into stages. Ideally, the stages should be worldwide subdivisions of the Cambrian System, but the major Cambrian areas have different stage sequences, and for most areas only parts of the Cambrian System have been formally divided into stages (see Table). The reason for this lack of global uniformity is that the trilobite sequences of even the major areas are not yet completely studied. In addition, as discussed below, neither the contrasts between the trilobite successions in regions of restricted environments with those in regions with unrestricted access to the open ocean nor the significance of the annihilations in the restricted regions have yet been fully appreciated.

These factors contribute to the correlation problem involving the upper boundary of the Cambrian System. When the Ordovician System was proposed, the Cambrian-Ordovician boundary was placed at the base of the Arenig Series that overlies the Tremadoc Series in northern Wales (see Table). Because of a 19th-century miscorrelation, however, upper Tremadoc beds were designated as Ordovician. Soon, the Tremadoc was regularly included in the Ordovician by almost all geologists outside Great Britain. C.D. Walcott identified the boundary between the Cambrian and Ordovician by means of the faunas in North America and correlated this with the boundary in Great Britain.

The American boundary was established in a region of restricted access to open ocean conditions and has been used as a standard in other similar regions. The British boundary was established in a region of unrestricted access to the open ocean and has been used as a standard elsewhere in those regions. Refined correlations indicated that the American boundary falls within the Tremadoc of Great Britain. The resolution of this correlation problem is still being debated.

PALEOGEOGRAPHY

The Cambrian Period was generally quiet. A few uplifts of marine areas produced short periods of erosion in small parts of the continents. Significant regions of active volcanism are recorded only in Tasmania and southeastern Australia, northwestern China, and adjacent regions

Cambrian Period

	North Africa	Great Britain	Scandinavia	U.S.S.R.	China	Korea	Australia	North America		
Upper Cambrian		Lower Tremadoc			Fengshanian			Trempealeauan	Croixan Series	Sauk Sequence
				Shidertinian				Franconian		
		Dolgelly			Changshanian	Daizan	Idamean			
		Ffestiniog				Paishan				
		Maentwrog		Tuorian	Kushanian		Mindyallan	Dresbachian		
Middle Cambrian		Menevian	*Paradoxides forchammeri*	Maya	Wenhsui				Albertan Series	
			Paradoxides paradoxissimus		Taitzu					
		Solvan	*Paradoxides oelandicus*	Amga	Tangshih					
Lower Cambrian	Issafenien			Lena	Lungwangmiao	Shihchiao			Waucoban Series	
					Tsanglangpu	Sanshih				
	Soussien			Aldan	Chingshussu	Bunsan				

of the U.S.S.R., Spain, and the extreme eastern parts of the United States. Except for these, the Cambrian Period records a slow, progressive inundation of most continental regions by the sea. By the end of the period, most of North America, Europe, and Asia and the east half of Australia were submerged beneath shallow seas. Too little is yet known about South America and Antarctica to assess the amount of submergence of these continents. Africa seems to have remained mostly above sea level.

By using organism-sediment relationships of the trilobites, a very crude picture of the major aspects of paleogeography during the Cambrian can be obtained. Among the trilobites, the Agnostida are most abundant in the areas of sedimentation farthest from the Cambrian shields, and most genera and many species have a worldwide distribution. They are most common on the seaward margins of the carbonate banks and in the sediments beyond. In some deeper water sediments beyond the banks, they are the only trilobites found. For these reasons the agnostids are believed to have lived in the surface waters of the open oceans, and the regions where they are abundant are interpreted as regions that had clear access to open ocean conditions. The regions where agnostids are rare or absent, and other trilobites with limited geographic distribution are abundant, are interpreted as regions with restricted access to open ocean conditions. These contrasting regions and their relations to major Cambrian land areas are shown in Figure 1. The boundaries between adjacent regions fluctuated during Cambrian time, but the general distribution of the regions was apparently stable. All questions of faunal provinces, migration routes, and evolutionary trends must be viewed within this context of restricted or nonrestricted access to open ocean conditions.

Faunal provinces

Throughout most of the Cambrian, four faunal provinces can be recognized in the regions of restricted environments: one included North America and perhaps South America: a second included central and southern Europe; a third included most of Siberia; and a fourth included southeastern Asia and perhaps Australia. Each of these provinces, particularly in the Middle and Late Cambrian, was characterized by its own rich variety of trilobite genera and species. In surrounding areas with apparent access to open ocean conditions, there is less differentiation into faunal provinces because the most common trilobites in these areas were the globally distributed agnostids. Associated nonagnostid trilobites indicate some differentiation into faunas typical of the Atlantic and Arctic regions on the one hand, and the Pacific and central Asiatic regions on the other.

Several times during the Cambrian, the trilobite faunas of one or more of the provinces in the restricted regions were virtually annihilated by some abrupt change in the marine environment that did not affect the sediments. Following each annihilation, the varied environmental areas within the provinces were occupied by immigrants from the surrounding open oceans. These immigrants quickly became adapted to the diverse new environments available in the restricted regions and evolved specialized forms. These forms, however, could not adapt to the next environmental crisis. The effect of these environmental crises on nontrilobite organisms is not yet clear; but abrupt changes in the sequences of brachiopods, which are second to the trilobites in abundance as Cambrian fossils, are also known and occur close to the times of the trilobite annihilations.

Most knowledge of Cambrian faunal successions has been obtained from study of the records of the restricted regions. The regions of apparent access to the open oceans are mostly in disturbed areas of complex geology and are only slowly yielding their store of Cambrian knowledge. The evidence presently available suggests that the evolutionary history of the Cambrian faunas may reflect the results of repeated attempts by most phyla to colonize the shallow regions of the seas of the world. These attempts were largely frustrated, perhaps by hostile changes in environmental factors such as temperature or solar radiation or biologic interactions that left no imprint on the sediments but which produced discontinuities in the record of shallow marine life. This conflict between colonization and environment could explain the lack of persistence during or after Cambrian time of many mollusk and echinoderm groups, as well as some Porifera and Brachiopoda and the archaeocyathids. Only toward the end of the Cambrian did many of the groups develop sufficient adaptability to become relatively persistent members of the shallow-water communities.

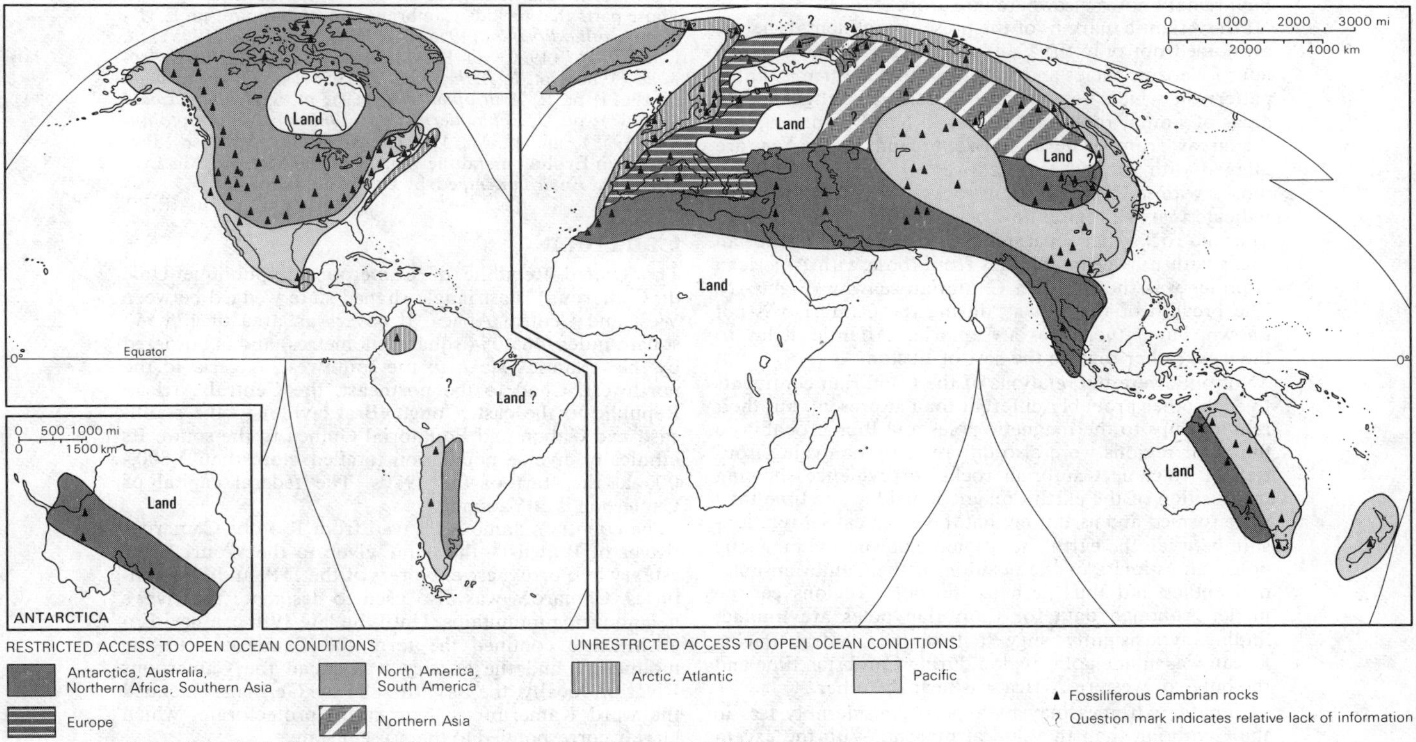

Figure 1: General paleogeography and regions of restricted and unrestricted access to open ocean conditions during Cambrian time.

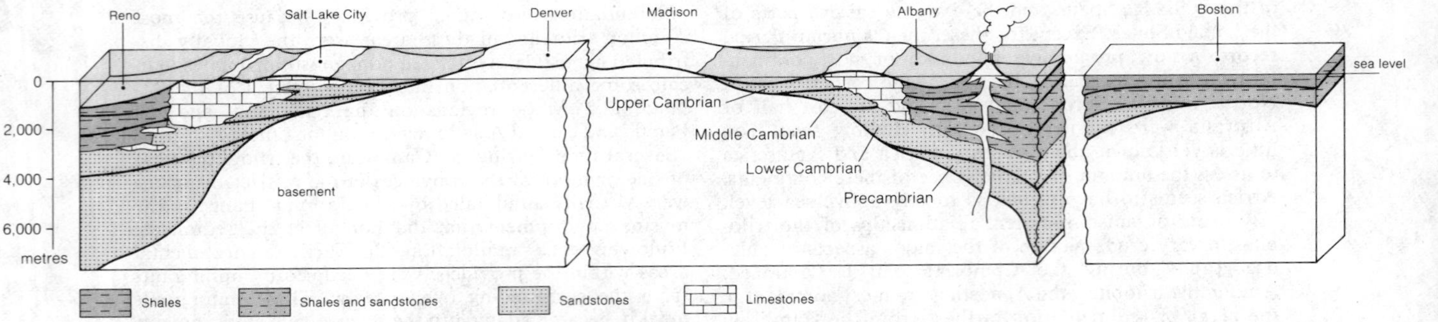

Figure 2: General relations of the principal lithofacies and biofacies regions and the problem of regional relations of Cambrian deposits of extreme eastern United States.

One additional factor complicates the Cambrian story. Increasingly strong evidence indicates that the present distribution of continents and oceans has developed during the last 100,000,000 years and that at earlier times global geography was quite different. Because this geography for the Cambrian has not yet been worked out satisfactorily, the data (Figure 1) are shown on the present geographic base. Cambrian data from the Atlantic margins of Europe and North America provide important support for the idea that the present Atlantic Ocean configuration is unlike that of the Cambrian.

Continental Drift

Along the east coast of North America near Boston, eastern New Brunswick, Nova Scotia, and eastern Newfoundland, the Lower Cambrian beds are characteristically red and include distinctive red, muddy limestones. The Middle and Upper Cambrian beds in this region are typically gray or black shales. Near the Lower-Middle Cambrian boundary is a sedimentary interval that has a very high content of manganese. This lithologic succession and almost all of the trilobites for the whole of the Cambrian can be duplicated in Great Britain exclusive of northwestern Scotland. The faunas are also typical of northwestern Europe. In Scotland, the Cambrian section includes Lower Cambrian quartzites and shales overlain by a thick succession of dolomites. The few Lower Cambrian fossils and almost all of the lithologies can be duplicated in western Newfoundland and the Appalachian region of the United States but are not known elsewhere in Europe.

If the Atlantic margins of the present continental shelves are joined not only the Cambrian facies trends but also later Paleozoic facies and structural trends form a simple pattern in which northwestern Scotland is aligned with areas of similar rocks and faunas in North America, and the areas from eastern Newfoundland to Boston are aligned with similar areas of western Europe. Furthermore, within the Cambrian rocks, the facies patterns indicate that the region now occupied by a belt of metamorphic rocks that separates the fossiliferous Cambrian rocks with European affinities from those with American affinities was the site of a Cambrian seaway (Figure 2). The breadth of the seaway during the Cambrian is not known, but if there was a Cambrian Atlantic, it lay to the west rather than to the east of Boston.

Not only were the relations of the Cambrian continents to each other probably different than at present, but their relationships to the magnetic poles and thus probably to the polar regions were also different. By analyzing iron-rich or volcanic Cambrian rocks for evidence showing the position of the earth's magnetic field at the time they were formed and assuming that there is a causal relationship between the earth's rotational axis and the magnetic poles, an estimate of the position of the Cambrian magnetic poles and thus perhaps the polar regions can be made. Although data for Cambrian poles are limited, findings consistently suggest that the central Pacific Ocean was in one polar region during Cambrian time and the bulge of western Africa was near the other.

Climatic extremes may have been considerably less in the Cambrian than they are at present. With the exception of western Europe, most Cambrian regions have significant accumulations of carbonates, which today form extensively only in the warm-temperate and tropical regions of the world. Accumulation of evaporite sequences in the Lower Cambrian of southern Siberia and parts of eastern United States is further evidence of warm to hot conditions. Although there is abundant evidence for late Precambrian glaciation, evidence for unusual cold during the Cambrian is lacking.

BIBLIOGRAPHY. Most textbooks in historical geology have chapters about the Cambrian Period. The reader who wishes more substantial summary information may turn to one or more of the following books. The references in these books will lead the serious researcher to the majority of the primary references. J. RODGERS (ed.), *El sistema Cámbrico, su paleogeografía y el problema de su base*, 20th International Geological Congress, Mexico City, is a three-volume symposium that summarizes world knowledge of the Cambrian to about 1955. Most papers in the first two volumes (1956) are in English. The third volume (1961) comprises papers in several languages. C.H. HOLLAND (ed.), *Cambrian of the New World* (1970), contains a comprehensive summary of knowledge of the Cambrian of North and South America, including the Arctic regions, through 1968. Н.Е. ЧЕРНЫШЕВА (ed.), *Кембрийская система* (1965), entirely in Russian, contains a comprehensive summary of knowledge of the Cambrian of the U.S.S.R., through 1961. T. KOBAYASHI, "The Cambrian of Eastern Asia and Other Parts of the Continent," *J. Fac. Sci. Tokyo Univ.*, sec. 2, vol. 16, pt. 3, pp. 381–534 (1967), presents an English summary of the Cambrian of southeastern Asia, through 1966. R.C. MOORE (ed.), *Treatise on Invertebrate Paleontology*, a multivolume set, includes the most recent data in English on most Cambrian fossil groups. Those parts that include Cambrian information are: pt. E, *Archaeocyatha, Porifera* (1955); pt. H, *Brachiopoda* (1965); pt. I, *Mollusca 1* (1960); pt. K, *Mollusca 3* (1964); pt. O, *Arthropoda* (1960); pt. P, *Arthropoda 2* (1955); pt. Q, *Arthropoda 3* (1961); pt. R, *Arthropoda 4* (1969); pt. S, *Echinodermata 1* (1967); pt. U, *Echinodermata 3* (1966); pt. V, *Graptolithina* (1955); and pt. W, *Miscellanea* (1962). See also "Premetazoan Evolution and the Origins of the Metazoa," in *Evolution and Environment*, ed. by E.T. DRAKE (1968).

(A.R.P.)

Cameroon

The United Republic of Cameroon (République Unie du Cameroun) is a triangle-shaped state wedged between West and Central Africa. It covers an area of 179,557 square miles (465,054 square kilometres) and is bordered by the Atlantic Ocean to the southwest, Nigeria to the northwest, Chad to the northeast, the Central African Republic to the east, Congo (Brazzaville) to the southeast, and Gabon and Equatorial Guinea to the south. Its ethnically diverse population totalled more than 5,800,000 at the start of the 1970s. The federal capital of Cameroon is at Yaoundé.

The country's name is derived from Rio dos Camaroẽs (River of Prawns)—the name given to the Wouri River estuary by Portuguese explorers of the 15th and 16th centuries. Camaroẽs was also used to designate the river's neighbouring mountains. Until the late 19th century, English usage confined the term the Cameroons to the mountains, and the estuary was called the Cameroons River or, locally, the Bay. In 1884 the Germans extended the word Kamerun to their entire protectorate, which largely corresponded to the present state.

The republic is a federation consisting of the former United Nations Trust Territory of Cameroun under

French administration in the east, which became independent in 1960, and the southern half of the former Trust Territory of Cameroon under British administration in the southwest, which voted to join Cameroon in 1961. (The northern half of British-administered Cameroon joined the Republic of Nigeria.)

Establishment of the united republic

Since unification, the Cameroonian economy has continued to display steady growth. More important, perhaps, the success of the federation has demonstrated that regions of varied colonial background can unite into larger political units. For historical aspects, see WEST AFRICA, HISTORY OF. For a related physical feature see CHAD, LAKE.

THE LANDSCAPE

The natural environment. *Relief features.* Cameroon can be divided into the four geographic regions of the south, the central, the north, and the west. The southern region extends from the Sanaga River to the southern border and from the coast eastward to the Central African Republic and Congo (Brazzaville). It consists of coastal plains that are about 25 miles wide and a densely forested plateau with an average elevation of a little less than 1,000 feet (about 300 metres).

The central region extends from the Sanaga River north to the Bénoué River. The land rises progressively to the north and includes the Adamaoua (or Adamawa, a plateau region), with elevations between 2,500 feet and 4,500 feet.

In the extreme north, the savanna plain slopes downward as it approaches the Lake Chad Basin. To the west, the relief is mountainous, the result of a volcanic rift that extends northward from the island of Fernando Po. Near the coast, the peak of volcanic Cameroon Mountain rises to the highest elevation in West Africa—13,353 feet (4,070 metres). The Monts Gotel of the Adamaoua trend from south to north, culminating in the Monts Mandara of the northwest.

Upland areas

Drainage. The rivers of Cameroon form four large drainage systems. In the south, the Sanaga, Wouri, Nyong, and Ntem rivers drain into the Atlantic Ocean. The Bénoué River and its tributary, the Mayo Kébi, flow into the Niger River Basin of Nigeria. The Logone and Chari rivers—which form part of the eastern border with Chad—drain into Lake Chad, whereas the Ngoko River joins the Sangha River and flows into the Congo River Basin.

Climate. The major factors that influence Cameroon's climate are its latitudinal extent and its relief. Lying wholly within the tropics, the country has a hot climate throughout the year; average temperatures range between 70° and 82° F (21° and 28° C), although they are lower in areas of high elevation.

The incidence of rainfall depends largely on the seasonal movements of two dominant air masses; the warm and dry tropical continental air mass is associated with dusty weather, whereas the warm and humid tropical maritime air mass brings rain-bearing winds. Rainfall decreases from south to north. Along the coast, the rainy season lasts from April to November, and the relatively dry season lasts from December to March; a transition period from March to April is marked by violent winds. The mean annual rainfall of 98 inches occurs in 150 days. In the central plateau region, rainfall decreases to 59 inches. There are four seasons—a light rainy season from May to June, a short dry season from July to October, a heavy rainy season from October to November, and a long dry season from December to May. The north, however, has only a dry season from October to May and a rainy season from June to September, with a mean annual rainfall as low as 15 inches. The wettest part of the country lies in the western highlands. Debundscha Point on Cameroon Mountain has a mean annual rainfall of about 400 inches, most of which falls from May to October.

Vegetation and animal life. The major vegetation types of West Africa are represented in Cameroon. The hot and humid south supports dense, tropical rain forests, in which hardwood evergreen trees including mahogany, ebony, obeche, dibetu, and sapelli may grow to more than 200 feet high. There are large numbers of orchids and ferns.

Mangroves grow along the coasts and the mouths of rivers. The rain forest gives place to the semi-deciduous forest of the central region, where a number of tree species shed their leaves during the dry season. North of the semi-deciduous forest, the vegetation is composed of wooded savanna with trees 10 to 60 feet high. The density of trees decreases toward the Chad Basin, where they are sparse and mainly of *Acacia* species.

Plants of the tropical rain forest

Between 4,000 and 8,000 feet, the tropical rain forest differs from that of the lowlands; the trees are smaller, are of different species, and are festooned with mosses, lichens, and other epiphytes (plants that derive their moisture and nutriments from the air and rain). Above the forest zone are drier woodland, tall grassland, or patches of mountain bamboo. Above about 7,800 feet in the interior and above about 10,000 feet on Cameroon Mountain, short grasses predominate.

The country is rich in animal life. Its dense forests are inhabited by screaming red and green monkeys, chimpanzees, and mandrills, as well as rodents, bats, and numerous birds—from tiny sunbirds to giant hawks and eagles. A few elephants survive in the forest and in the grassy woodlands where baboons and several types of antelope are the most common animals. The 656-square-mile (1,700-square-kilometre) Réserve de Waza in the north, which was originally created for the protection of giraffes and antelope, abounds in both forest and savanna animals including monkeys, baboons, lions, leopards, and birds ranging from white and gray pelicans to spotted waders.

Traditional regions and settlement. In general there is a cultural division between the north and the south. The northern savanna plateau is inhabited by Sudanic and Arab pastoralists who migrate seasonally in search of grazing land and occupy temporary dwellings, whereas the forested and hilly south is peopled by Bantu agriculturalists in permanent villages. The north is predominantly Muslim, whereas the southern peoples adhere to animism and Christianity.

Most of the large urban centres are in the south. Douala, the largest city, has a population of 250,000 and is the country's main port. The federal capital of Yaoundé, with 178,000 inhabitants, is an important communication centre. Buea, the capital of West Cameroon state, has a population of only 13,000. In the north, Garoua is a port on the Bénoué River with a population of 28,000.

PEOPLE AND POPULATION

Ethno-linguistic groups. The country has been described as a "racial crossroads" because of its more than 100 different ethnic groups. There are three main linguistic groups—the Bantu-speaking people of the south, the Sudanic-speaking people of the north, and those who speak the Bantu languages of the west.

The principal linguistic groups

The Bantus settled in the Cameroons from Equatorial Africa. The first group that invaded the country included the Makas, Ndjems, and Dualas. They were followed at the beginning of the 19th century by the Fang (Pangwe) and Bete peoples.

The Sudanic-speaking peoples in the north include the Sao, who live on the Adamaoua plateau; the Fulani; and the Kanuri. The Fulani came from the Niger Basin in two waves—in the 11th and 19th centuries; they were Muslims who converted and subjugated the Logone valley and the Mayo Kebbi and Faro areas. The third ethnic group consists mainly of small tribes, except for the 1,500,000 Bamilekes who live between the lower slopes of the Adamaoua mountains and Cameroon Mountain. Other western Bantu-speaking tribes include the Tikar who live in the Bamenda region, the Bali, the Bamum, and the Keaka.

The oldest inhabitants of the country are the pygmies, locally known as the Baguielli and Babinga, who are found within the southern forests. They have been hunters and food-gatherers for thousands of years and live in small hunting bands.

The work of European missionaries and the colonization of the country by European powers led to the introduction of European languages. During the colonial era German was the official language; it was later replaced by English and French, which have retained their official status in the unitary republic established in 1972.

Religious affiliations. More than half of the population continues to adhere to traditional beliefs. European Christian missionaries first came to Cameroon in the 19th century, and in the mid-1970s there were estimated to be about 1,500,000 Roman Catholics; older estimates indicated more than 750,000 Protestants and members of independent Christian churches. There were also about 600,000 Muslims.

Demography. In 1975 the population was estimated to number more than 6,398,000. The birth rate was about 41 per 1,000 population and the death rate about 20 per 1,000, with an annual growth rate of a little more than 2 percent. Life expectancy at birth was about 43.5 years.

The average population density for the country in 1975 was 36 persons per square mile (14 per square kilometre), but densities vary from region to region. The highest densities occur in the western mountains, where they may reach more than 700 persons per square mile (270 per square kilometre). The southeast and Adamawa (Adamaoua) Plateau are the most sparsely populated regions.

THE NATIONAL ECONOMY

Like most African countries, Cameroon has a basically agricultural economy. The economy—which is dominated by French financial institutions and banking houses—has maintained steady growth since independence in 1960. During the period of the Second (1966/67–1970/71) Plan, gross domestic product rose by 7.7 percent per year in real terms, and a remarkable 5.7 percent annually per capita; this substantial growth rate was made possible by the rapid expansion of investments and output in private industry. One of the major goals of the Third (1971/72–1975/76) Plan, however, was gradual Cameroonization of the economy. Cameroon does not suffer from a chronic trade deficit, since imports and exports are usually in reasonably good balance. The government was able to dispense with external support for its budgetary needs after 1969. Cameroon is an associate member of the European Economic Community (EEC, or Common Market) and a member of the Union Douanière et Économique de l'Afrique Central (UDEAC; Central African Customs and Economic Union) to which the Central African Republic, Gabon, and Congo (Brazzaville) also belong.

The extent and distribution of resources. In the mid-1970s there were few indications of abundant mineral wealth. The largest reserves were those of kyanite (an aluminum silicate) and bauxite at Minim-Martap and Ngaoundere on the Adamawa Plateau; the deposits, amounting to more than 1,000,000,000 tons, have a 44 percent alumina content. Another 40,000,000,000 tons

MAP INDEX

Political subdivisions

Centre-Sud	4·00n	11·30e
Est	4·00n	14·00e
Littoral	4·00n	10·00e
Nord	9·00n	13·30e
Nord-Ouest	6·30n	10·20e
Ouest	5·30n	10·30e
Sud-Ouest	5·30n	9·30e

Cities and towns

Abong Mbang	3·59n	13·10e
Afade	12·14n	14·38e
Akok	2·46n	10·18e
Akom	2·37n	10·04e
Akonolinga	3·47n	12·15e
Akouaya	6·30n	9·40e
Ambam	2·23n	11·17e
Ayos	3·54n	12·31e
Babungo	6·04n	10·26e
Bafang	5·09n	10·11e
Bafia	4·44n	11·16e
Bafoussam	5·29n	10·24e
Bagodo	6·25n	13·23e
Bakebe	5·35n	9·33e
Bali	5·53n	10·01e
Balikumbat	5·54n	10·23e
Bamenda	5·56n	10·10e
Bamendjou	5·24n	10·19e
Bangangté	5·09n	10·31e
Bangé	3·01n	15·07e
Banyo	6·45n	11·49e
Baré	5·03n	9·56e
Batouri	4·26n	14·22e
Béka	9·04n	12·53e
Bélabo	5·00n	13·20e
Bélel	7·03n	14·26e
Bengbis	3·27n	12·27e
Bérem	7·33n	13·55e
Bertoua	4·35n	13·41e
Bétaré Oya	5·36n	14·05e
Bibémi	9·19n	13·53e
Bipindi	3·05n	10·25e
Bogo	10·44n	14·36e
Boki	8·48n	13·32e
Botmakak	4·00n	10·55e
Boula–Ibi	9·34n	13·46e
Buea	4·09n	9·14e
Campo	2·22n	9·49e
Dabilda	12·46n	14·34e
Dana	10·14n	15·18e
Dang-Haoussa	5·52n	13·29e
Demsa	9·32n	13·14e
Deng Deng	5·12n	13·31e
Djaposten	3·25n	13·32e
Djohong	6·50n	14·42e
Djoum	2·40n	12·40e
Dodéo	7·29n	12·04e
Doreissou	10·33n	15·08e
Douala	4·03n	9·42e
Doumba	5·05n	14·18e
Doumé	4·14n	13·27e
Dschang	5·27n	10·04e
Dzeng	3·45n	12·00e
Ebolowa	2·54n	11·09e
Edéa	3·48n	10·08e
Elokbatindi	3·27n	10·08e
Eséka	3·39n	10·46e
Essé	4·05n	11·53e
Fonga-Tongo	5·27n	9·57e
Foumban	5·43n	10·55e
Foumbot	5·30n	10·38e
Galim	7·06n	12·29e
Garoua	9·18n	13·24e
Garoua Boulaï	5·53n	14·33e
Gouna	8·32n	13·34e
Guider	9·56n	13·57e
Kaélé	10·07n	14·27e
Kenzou	4·10n	15·02e
Kimi	6·05n	11·30e
Kombone	4·37n	9·19e
Kontcha	7·58n	12·14e
Koumban	7·43n	15·12e
Kousseri	12·05n	15·02e
Kribi	2·57n	9·55e
Kumba	4·38n	9·25e
Kumbo	6·12n	10·40e
Laro	8·17n	12·18e
Linté	5·24n	11·42e
Logone Birni	11·47n	15·06e
Lokomo	2·41n	15·19e
Lolodorf	3·14n	10·44e
Lomié	3·10n	13·37e
Loum	4·43n	9·44e
Makak	3·33n	11·02e
Makari	12·35n	14·28e
Mali	8·28n	12·35e
Mamfe	5·46n	9·17e
Mankim	5·01n	12·00e
Maroua	10·36n	14·20e
Martap	6·54n	13·03e
Matsari	5·21n	12·14e
Mayo Darlé	6·28n	11·33e
Mbalam	2·13n	13·49e
Mbalmayo	3·31n	11·30e
Mbandjouk	3·42n	10·56e
Mbanga	3·52n	10·49e
Mbanga	4·30n	9·34e
Mbonge	4·33n	9·05e
Mbor	6·24n	11·19e
Mbouda	5·38n	10·15e
Meiganga	6·31n	14·11e
Mengong	2·56n	11·25e
Mesaména	3·44n	12·50e
Mésondo	3·43n	10·28e
Meuban	2·27n	12·41e
Meyo-Centre	2·33n	11·02e
Mfou	3·43n	11·38e
Mindif	10·24n	14·26e
Mindourou	4·06n	14·34e
Minim	6·58n	12·52e
Minta	4·35n	12·48e
Mintom	2·42n	13·17e
Mislippi	10·00n	15·37e
Mokolo	10·45n	13·48e
Moloundou	2·03n	15·10e
Monatélé	4·16n	11·12e
Mora	11·03n	14·09e
Mouangko	3·39n	9·49e
Muyuka	4·17n	9·25e
Mvangane	2·38n	11·44e
Mvengué	3·17n	11·01e
Nanga-Eboko	4·41n	12·22e
Ndélélé	4·02n	14·56e
Ndikiniméki	4·46n	10·50e
Ngambé	4·14n	10·37e
Ngaoundéré	7·19n	13·35e
Ngila	4·43n	11·41e
Ngoap	4·09n	12·51e
Ngomedzap	3·15n	11·12e
Ngoulémakong	3·07n	11·25e
Ngoundi	3·54n	15·07e
Nguélémen-douka	4·23n	12·55e
Nkambe	6·38n	10·40e
Nkongsamba	4·57n	9·56e
Ntui	4·27n	11·38e
Nwa	6·30n	11·00e
Nyabéssan	2·24n	10·24e
Obala	4·10n	11·32e
Obout	3·28n	11·44e
Okola	4·01n	11·23e
Otélé	3·35n	11·15e
Ouak	7·43n	13·30e
Oveng	2·25n	12·16e
Pété	10·58n	14·30e
Poli	8·29n	13·15e
Pouss	10·51n	15·03e
Rey Bouba	8·40n	14·11e
Saa	4·22n	11·27e
Sambolabbo	7·05n	11·59e
Sangbé	6·03n	12·28e
Sangmélima	2·56n	11·59e
Somalomo	3·23n	12·44e
Tcholliré	8·24n	14·10e
Tibati	6·27n	12·38e
Tignère	7·22n	12·39e
Tiko	4·05n	9·22e
Tonga	4·58n	10·42e
Tongo	5·11n	14·00e
Torok	10·03n	14·33e
Victoria	4·01n	9·12e
Waza Garou	11·25n	14·34e
Woutchaba	5·13n	13·05e
Wum	6·23n	10·04e
Yabassi	4·28n	9·58e
Yagoua	10·20n	15·14e
Yaoundé	3·52n	11·31e
Yokadouma	3·31n	15·03e
Yoke Yokon	4·18n	9·26e
Yoko	5·32n	12·19e
Zina	11·16n	14·58e
Zoadiba	3·04n	14·02e
Zoétélé	3·15n	11·53e
Zoulabot	3·17n	14·02e

Physical features and points of interest

Adamawa Plateau	6·30n	11·10e
Bam Yanga, Ngao, *mountains*	6·42n	13·02e
Bek, *river*	2·29n	15·15e
Bénoué, *river*	9·21n	12·55e
Bénoué, Parc National de la, *national park*	8·20n	13·50e
Biafra, Bight of	2·20n	8·40e
Boubandjidah, Parc National de, *national park*	8·45n	14·45e
Boumba, *river*	2·02n	15·12e
Boumbé II, *river*	4·08n	15·08e
Cameroun, Mont, *mountain*	4·12n	9·11e
Campo, Réserve de, *wildlife refuge*	2·35n	9·57e
Chad, Lake	13·20n	14·00e
Chari, *river*	12·58n	14·31e
Cross, *river*	4·42n	8·21e
Dja, *river*	2·02n	15·12e
Dja, Réserve de, *wildlife refuge*	3·05n	13·00e
Djerem, *river*	5·20n	13·24e
Doumé, *river*	4·06n	14·34e
Faro, *river*	9·21n	13·40e
Faro, Réserve du, *wildlife refuge*	8·10n	12·35e
Gangdaba, Tchabal, *mountains*	7·44n	12·45e
Gotel, Monts, *mountains*	7·00n	11·40e
Hoséré Vokre, *mountain*	8·20n	13·15e
Kadeï, *river*	4·08n	15·08e
Kébi, Mayo, *river*	9·18n	13·33e
Kienké, *river*	2·56n	9·54e
Kim, *river*	5·28n	11·07e
Koupé, Mont, *mountain*	4·47n	9·43e
Logone, *river*	12·06n	15·02e
Lom, *river*	5·20n	13·24e
Louti, Mayo, *river*	9·38n	13·56e
Mandara, Monts, *mountains*	10·45n	13·40e
Mbabo, Tchabal, *mountain*	7·16n	12·09e
Mbakana, Montagne de, *mountain*	7·58n	15·06e
Mbakaou, Barrage de, *dam*	6·08n	12·48e
Mbam, *river*	4·24n	11·17e
Mbéré, *river*	7·45n	15·36e
Ndjim, *river*	4·38n	11·24e
Ngoko, *river*	1·40n	16·03e
Ngol-Kedju Hill	6·20n	9·45e
Noun, *river*	4·55n	11·06e
Ntem, *river*	2·15n	9·45e
Nyong, *river*	3·17n	9·54e
Sanaga, *river*	3·35n	9·38e
Sangha, *river*	1·40n	16·03e
Vina, *river*	7·45n	15·36e
Waza, Parc National de, *wildlife refuge*	11·20n	14·40e
Wouri, *river*	4·06n	9·43e
Yakounga, *mountains*	5·04n	11·19e

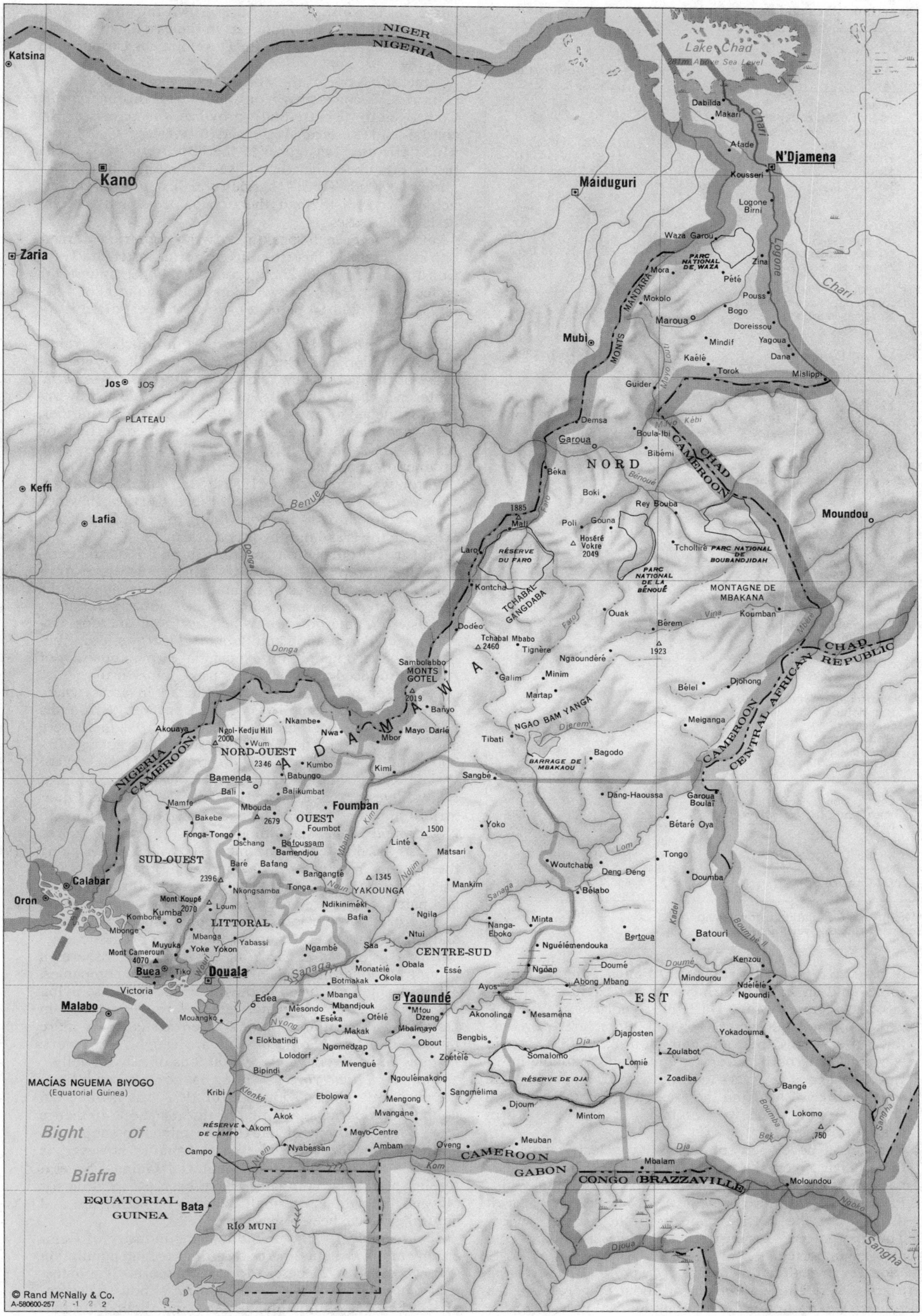

CAMEROON

Size of symbol indicates relative size of town

Elevations in metres

0 50 100 200 300 km

0 50 100 200 mi

Cameroon, Area and Population

	area		population*
	sq mi	sq km	1970 estimate
Provinces			
Centre-Sud (Centre-South)			
Departments (*départements*)			
Dja-et-Lobo	7,669	19,862	108,000
Haute-Sanaga	4,586	11,878	54,000
Kribi	4,341	11,244	60,000
Lékié	1,153	2,987	176,000
Mbam	12,717	32,936	150,000
Méfou	1,912	4,951	301,000
Ntem	6,179	16,004	119,000
Nyong-et-Kélé	2,464	6,382	75,000
Nyong-et-Mfoumou	2,385	6,178	73,000
Nyong-et-Soo	1,395	3,614	77,000
Est (East)			
Departments (*départements*)			
Boumba-Ngoko	11,735	30,394	38,000
Haut-Nyong	14,046	36,378	105,000
Kadeï	6,134	15,886	63,000
Lom-et-Djerem	10,175	26,353	63,000
Littoral (Littoral)			
Departments (*départements*)			
Mungo	1,388	3,595	206,000
Nkam	2,488	6,445	33,000
Sanaga-Maritime	3,502	9,070	121,000
Wouri	436	1,129	251,000
Nord (North)			
Departments (*départements*)			
Adamaoua	24,591	63,691	238,000
Bénoué	25,319	65,576	339,000
Diamaré	3,746	9,701	381,000
Logone-et-Chari	4,678	12,115	94,000
Margui-Wandala	2,751	7,125	337,000
Mayo-Danaï	2,048	5,305	193,000
Nord-Ouest (Northwest)†			
Departments (*départements*)			
Bui	812	2,104	118,000
Donga and Mantung	1,686	4,368	139,000
Menchum	2,401	6,218	147,000
Mezam	1,239	3,210	242,000
Momo	738	1,912	91,000
Ouest (West)			
Departments (*départements*)			
Bamboutos	447	1,157	139,000
Bamoun	2,973	7,700	184,000
Haut-Nkam	407	1,053	113,000
Ménoua	517	1,339	197,000
Mifi	457	1,183	251,000
Ndé	556	1,440	101,000
Sud-Ouest (Southwest)†			
Departments (*départements*)			
Fako	805	2,086	104,000
Manyu	3,607	9,343	127,000
Meme	3,096	8,018	143,000
Ndian	1,978	5,124	85,000
Total Cameroon	179,557	465,054	5,836,000

*De jure. †Population estimates approximate.
Source: Official government figures.

of bauxite reserves are situated at Fonga-Tongo. There is some gold in eastern Cameroon and cassiterite (a tin dioxide) occurs at Mayo Darlé in the northeast.

About 41,000,000 acres (16,000,000 hectares), or one-third of eastern Cameroon, and about 2,500,000 acres in western Cameroon are forested and yield valuable hardwood timber. The rivers and offshore ocean waters are a rich source of fish, and the grasslands support valuable herds of cattle. The wild animal life provides a firm basis for tourism.

Water-power resources

The main developed source of hydroelectric power is the Sanaga River; the power station at Edéa on the Sanaga Falls is the country's largest. The Akam-Wouri River in the west also provides hydroelectric power as it drops from the central plateau to the coastal region. Thermal power is expensive because diesel fuel and coal must be imported.

Sources of national income. *Agriculture, forestry, and fishing.* Agriculture accounts for about 80 percent of the country's export earnings and employs 90 percent of the adult population. The main subsistence crops include plantains, yams, manioc, and palm oil in the south and peanuts, millet, and manioc in the north. Most cultivation is carried out on small farms by crude methods. Some cash crops, however, are grown on large plantations owned by French interests in the east and a government agency—the Cameroon Development Corporation—in the west.

Cocoa and coffee production

Cameroon is one of the world's leading cocoa-producing countries. Cocoa is grown on small farms throughout the Centre-South (Centre-Sud) province, in parts of the coastal and western areas, and in western Cameroon. Much attention was given to the improvement of cocoa production under the second five-year plan; under "Operation 100,000 Tons," agricultural extension workers helped farmers to tend their cocoa trees and to fight pests and diseases.

Among the French-speaking African countries, Cameroon is the second largest coffee exporter, after the Ivory Coast. Eastern Cameroon produces 90 percent of the coffee crop, which is grown on an estimated total of 400,000 acres. About 64 percent of the coffee exported is robusta, the rest arabica.

Bananas are an important export product by value, but production and exports declined in the 1960s because of the lack of new markets and the loss of imperial preference in the United Kingdom in 1967. The government launched a campaign in 1965 to produce a hardier, disease-resistant banana variety. Bananas are grown on plantations in the southwest and on small farms; both production and export levels recovered in the 1970s.

Cotton was introduced in 1952 by the Compagnie Française pour le Développement des Fibres Textiles, in which the government owns the controlling interest. It is grown largely in the grasslands by private farmers.

Rubber is produced on government and domestic company plantations; the Société Africaine Forestière et Agricole owns 25,000 acres of plantations at Dizangué in the southern area of eastern Cameroon. Rubber plantations in western Cameroon are owned by the Cameroon Development Corporation and Palmol Cameroon, Ltd. Rubber is produced mainly for export, but a small quantity of rubber produced at Dizangué is used domestically.

Except for pigs, which are prohibited in areas where Islām is predominant, livestock is concentrated on the northern Adamawa Plateau. In the mid-1970s, there were about 2,500,000 cattle, 3,500,000 sheep and goats, 370,000 pigs, 96,000 donkeys, 58,000 horses, and 8,600,000 of various kinds of poultry. Domestic consumption of meat is low; livestock is exported to Nigeria, meat to Equatorial Guinea and to the Congo, and hides and skins to Nigeria and Equatorial Guinea.

Forestry

Forestry is limited to the most accessible areas along the Douala–Yaoundé railway and along the main roads. The logs are transported by water, road, and rail. Timber and palm kernels are produced for export, whereas wood for construction purposes, firewood, charcoal, kola nuts, and palm oil and kernels are produced for domestic use.

Marine fishing is carried out by individual fishermen using traditional methods as well as by large companies. The fishermen go to sea in dugout canoes and use nylon nets, whereas the companies employ trawlers based in Douala. The combined annual deep-sea catch is more than 21,000 tons. Some prawns are caught for export. Fishing in the rivers yields 50,000 tons of fish annually.

Mining and quarrying. Mining has contributed little to the economy. Gold production in 1973 was a mere 6.6 pounds (3 kilograms) and that of tin was about 40 metric tons. Small amounts of bauxite are mined to supply the aluminum smelter at Edéa; most bauxite, however, is imported from France and Equatorial Guinea. Several foreign petroleum companies have been prospecting for oil, and indications of small deposits of petroleum and natural gas have been found.

Manufacturing. The manufacturing industry of Cameroon employs about 2 percent of the working population and accounts for 25 percent of total exports. The industrial sector consists of one major heavy industrial complex—the Edéa aluminum smelter—and about 500 small and medium-sized enterprises engaged in processing, various manufacturing procedures, and the assembly of radios.

Apart from a few establishments, such as the aluminum smelter, the industrial enterprises have been operating only since the 1960s. The largest development has been in textiles, with the establishment of two factories in Douala for spinning, weaving, bleaching, dyeing, and printing cotton. In the year 1966–67 about half of the total industrial investment went into processing industries. Food-processing plants include a sugar factory at Mbandjock; palm-oil plants in Bota, Lober, Dibambari, and Edéa; a chocolate factory at Yaoundé; and flour mills at Douala.

Energy. The two power stations on the Sanaga River at Edéa have a hydroelectric capacity of 159,760 kilowatts. On the completion of a third plant, the total capacity will rise to 180,000 kilowatts.

Financial services. Cameroon is linked together with the Central African Republic, Gabon, and Congo (Brazzaville) in a monetary union (UDEAC) with a common currency, the CFA (Communauté Financière Africaine, or African Financial Community) franc. The CFA franc is convertible into any currency, but France must approve direct investment by citizens within the franc area in countries outside it, the issue and sale of foreign stocks and shares in the area, and borrowings from outside the area. France is also represented on the board of directors of the Central Bank in Yaoundé; its notes and coins are legal tender in each member state of the monetary union. Each member state has its own monetary committee, on which France is represented, and a National Credit Council. The latter body advises the respective governments on credit policy and banking organization and methods. There are seven commercial banks in Cameroon, four of which are French, two British, and one owned by the Cameroonians. Most insurance companies are French owned. There is no stock exchange.

Monetary relations with France

Foreign trade. The main exports are agricultural products and aluminum. Coffee and cocoa together accounted for almost 50 percent of the total value of exports in 1970. Aluminum accounted for 9 percent, timber 9 percent, and cotton 8 percent. There has been increasing emphasis on the importation of capital equipment and semifinished products for the growing industrial sector. Other imports include aluminum oxide, pharmaceuticals, beverages, rubber, and synthetic fabrics.

Most trade is carried on with the EEC countries, which purchased almost 70 percent of Cameroon's exports in 1970. France is the largest individual trading partner; it supplies about 50 percent of Cameroon's imports and takes about one-third of the country's exports. Trade outside the Common Market is carried out primarily with the United States and Japan.

Management of the economy. *The public and private sectors.* The government sets the guidelines in its five-year plans and attracts private capital for the development of certain sectors of the economy.

The five-year plans

The First Five Year Plan (from 1960 to 1965) laid emphasis on the expansion of educational facilities, the diversification of farm production, and selective industrialization. The objectives of the second development plan, the so-called Peasants Plan, of 1965 to 1970 emphasized rural development. It included the introduction of cooperatives as a basis for rural organization, the processing of raw materials, the choice of certain areas for integrated rural development, and the extension of the Trans-Cameroon Railway northward to Ngaoundéré. These projects were to be financed about equally from public and private funds.

The Third Five Year Plan of 1971 to 1976 is an extension of the two previous plans. The processing of local raw materials is encouraged in order to diversify the economy, to reduce urban unemployment, and to improve foreign trade.

In order to encourage private investment, the Cameroon National Federal Assembly has adopted an investment code; its objectives include stabilization of company taxes, provision of security to large businesses, and the protection of local industries from foreign competition.

Taxation. There are four different company tax systems, which offer various benefits to developing industries. Most tax revenues are derived from import and export duties.

Trade unions. There are more than 80,000 members of trade unions in the federation. Four large trade unions are recognized by the government: the Cameroon Federation of Unions (*Féderation des Syndicats du Cameroun;* FSC); the Union of Denominational Workers Organizations (*Union des Syndicats Croyants du Cameroun*); the National Teachers Union (*Syndicat National des Enseignants du Cameroun;* SNEC), and the National Federation of Private School Teachers (*Fédération Nationale des Enseignants privés du Cameroun;* FNEPCAM).

There has been industrial peace in the country since 1960. The International Labour Office (ILO) established an Inter-African Centre at Yaoundé in 1965 that provides courses for labour administration officials. Employers' associations include chambers of commerce in Douala and Yaoundé and associations for those engaged in industry and the import—export trade.

Contemporary economic problems. The main problem that Cameroon has in common with the other developing countries of Africa is the acquisition of capital to finance resource development. When foreign investment capital is scarce, the country must depend largely on moneys acquired through the sale of its products on the world market. The fluctuations in world prices of raw materials such as cocoa and coffee, however, make the future unpredictable.

TRANSPORTATION

The difficult terrain and heavy rainfall in the south have been contributory factors to the absence of an adequate transportation network linking the different regions of the country. The north has traditionally been virtually isolated from the south. Until the construction of the railway line between Mbanga and Kumba in 1965, it was difficult for products from West Cameroon to be transported to the port of Douala in East Cameroon. Transportation is more developed in some regions than in others; the best roads are in the coastal region, whereas the roads in West Cameroon are few and are often in bad condition.

Problems of transport development

The road network. There are more than 8,500 miles of roads, only about 765 miles of which are paved and most of which can be travelled only during the dry season. Douala is linked to the large population centres by roads that run through the central region, Yaoundé and Yoke Yokon, and the Adamaoua district. Two subsidiary roads from Garoua lead to Maroua and Makole. Douala is also linked by road through Bertoua and Batouri to Bangui in the Central African Republic and to Gabon via Edéa and Kribi.

Railways. The more than 500 miles of railways will increase to more than 800 miles when the Trans-Cameroon line reaches Ngaoundere from Yaoundé. The two short railway lines of metre gauge in the southwest were constructed by the Germans before World War I; they remained separated until 1955 when the Wouri Bridge made it possible for them to use a common terminus and to gain access to workshops at Bassa, just outside Douala. A 107-mile-long northern line runs from Douala to Nkongsamba and serves the coffee and banana region of East Cameroon; a line from Mbanga to Rumba was completed in the late 1960s. The Central Line runs for 191 miles between Douala and Yaoundé; it has a 24-mile branch line to Mbalmayo on the Nyong River, which serves Edéa and the cocoa-producing area.

Port facilities. The main port is Douala, on the estuary of the Wouri River. One of the best equipped ports in West Africa, it has 11 docks for cargo ships, including a wood-loading dock and a tanker dock with adjacent facilities for the unloading and storing of minerals. The fishing port above the wood-loading dock is equipped with refrigeration facilities.

Facilities at Douala

The minor ports include Kribi at the mouth of the Kienké River, which is used primarily for the shipment of logs and cocoa from the Boulon district; the ocean port of Victoria in West Cameroon, which handles only a modest amount of traffic; and the port of Tiko, on a creek leading to the Wouri estuary, which handles bananas, wood, and rubber. In the north, the river port of Garoua on the banks of the Bénoué transports goods to Nigeria; the Upper Bénoué, however, is navigable only from seven to 10 weeks in a year.

Air transport. Douala is the main international port of entry, and Yaoundé and Tiko also handle international flights. There are domestic airports at Garoua, Ngaoundéré, and Batouri, as well as numerous airfields. Air-Cameroun has scheduled domestic flights and flights to Chad.

ADMINISTRATION AND SOCIAL CONDITIONS

The structure of government. By the constitution of 1961, the states of West Cameroon and East Cameroon were linked together into a federation. Executive powers are conferred on the president, who is the head of the federal government and chief of the armed forces. The president is assisted by a vice president, who may not come from the same state as the president. They are both elected for a period of five years by direct and secret universal suffrage granted to all citizens over 21 years of age. The president appoints the federal ministers and parliamentary secretaries and may dissolve the federal legislature.

The federation of the two states

Legislative power is held by a unicameral National Federal Assembly whose members are also directly elected for five-year terms. One deputy is elected for every 80,000 inhabitants. The National Assembly shares with the president the initiative for proposing federal bills, which it adopts on a simple-majority basis.

Each of the two federal states can in law establish any institutions of its choice except those listed in the constitution as being subject to federal law; institutions restricted to the federal level include those dealing with personal liberty, law, the electoral system, national finance, and education. The head of each state government is the prime minister, who is named by the president of the republic and invested by his respective legislative assembly. In East Cameroon the legislative assembly consists of 100 representatives who are directly elected for five-year terms. The 37-member legislative assembly of West Cameroon shares its power with the 20-member Assembly of Traditional Chiefs. The prime minister of a state can be removed by a vote of nonconfidence. The president has the power to dissolve a state legislative assembly in the event of persistent disagreement between the assembly and the federal government.

The federal republic was divided into six administrative regions in 1962, and each region was placed under the authority of a federal inspector. The six units are the South Central (Centre Sud), West Cameroon (both a federal state and a regional unit), Coastal (Littoral), Northern (Nord), West (Ouest), and East (Est) regions. Each region is further divided into *départements.*

Evolution of the one-party state

In the 1950s there were no fewer than 84 political parties in East Cameroon. With the exceptions of the Union des Populations du Cameroun (UPC; Union of the Populations of Cameroon) and the Action Nationale (National Action), both of which were broadly based, the rest of the parties existed only at the tribal or regional level. In 1955 the UPC was banned by the French government; as a result a wave of terrorism broke out, especially in the Bassa Mungo, Wuri, and Bamileke districts. Political rights were restored to the party in 1960. The arrest, conviction, and imprisonment of the four principal opposition leaders in East Cameroon during 1962 left the ruling party, L'Union Camerounaise (The Cameroonian Union) as virtually the only party in the state. In 1966 the Union merged with the governing party of West Cameroon, the Kamerun National Democratic Party (KNDP), creating the Union Nationale Camerounaise (UNC; Cameroon National Union). The country is now a de facto one-party state.

Justice. A federal magistrates council, which is responsible for guaranteeing the independence of the judiciary, advises the president on the nomination of magistrates and judges and acts as a disciplinary body. The Federal High Court decides whether a bill is receivable by the National Assembly in the event of a dispute between the president and the legislature. It also settles questions of competence among the highest jurisdictions of the federated states; passes judgment on appeals with respect to the administrative actions of the federal authorities; decides whether laws passed by the states are in conformity with federal law; and settles all disputes between the states or between one of the states and the federal government.

The special High Court of Justice passes judgment on the president in case of high treason and on the vice president, the ministers of the federated states, and the state secretaries in the event of a plot against the government.

The dual system of justice

The legal system of East Cameroon consists of a supreme court, four courts of appeal, and first-instance, labour, and conciliation tribunals. It is closely modelled on the French court system. In West Cameroon, the legal system displays British influence and includes a judicial system for customary law. There is a High Court and a Magistrates' Court for state law and 70 native courts with traditional jurisdiction.

The armed forces. The armed forces include a 2,700-man army, an air force, a navy, and a civil guard. Army officers are initially trained at the École Militaire Interarmes (EMIAC) in Yaoundé and then in specialized schools in France. The first Cameroonian commander in chief of the army took office in 1965.

Apart from guaranteeing national territorial integrity, the army aids the police in the maintenance of law and order and is actively involved in the construction of roads. The navy was created in 1960 and is responsible for guarding the coasts, maritime communications, maintaining law and order in regions that are accessible to its units, and preventing illegal entry and smuggling.

The Cameroon Air Squadron was created in 1961 and is gradually being developed with the return of Cameroonians who have completed their training in France and other European countries. The National Civil Guard is an auxiliary force composed of volunteers who initially sign up for a period of one year. It was created in 1960.

Educational services. Educational services have been expanding since 1960, and the curriculum in secondary schools has been modified to make it relevant to the country's needs. About 67 percent of the children of primary school age are enrolled either in government or in Catholic or Protestant mission schools.

There were more than 150 general education secondary schools, 73 vocational schools, and 15 teacher-training schools in the early 1970s. In 1969, manual labour was made compulsory in secondary and technical schools as a means of encouraging students to take up farming on the completion of their courses instead of seeking white-collar jobs in the cities.

The Federal University of Cameroon at Yaoundé was established in 1962. There were over 2,000 students during the 1970–71 academic year, 20 percent of whom were in the schools of law and economic science. About 8 percent of the registered students were women.

Health and welfare services. The government emphasized the improvement of the nation's health facilities in the first and second five-year development plans. In 1958 there were only 12 hospitals, about 25 dispensaries, and 40 subsidiary centres; by 1967 there were approximately 85 hospitals, 340 dispensaries, and 50 elementary health centres. Between 1965 and 1970 hospitals in Yaoundé, Douala, Foumban, Garoua, and Ngaoundéré were modernized. Long-term plans call for a further expansion of dispensary and health-centre services.

In 1970, there was one doctor to every 26,000 inhabitants and one qualified male nurse for every 2,455. Nearly 70 percent of the doctors were foreign-born and were concentrated in the main cities. A Health Sciences University Centre was established at the Federal University in 1969 to train Cameroonian doctors and other medical personnel.

There is no government system of social security, and there are no pension plans or health insurance programs for workers. Most assistance is obtained through the

Housing of the Masa tribe in Mourla village, near Pouss, northern Cameroon.
Marc and Evelyne Bernheim—Rapho Guillumette

traditional kinship system. There are, however, indemnities for occupational diseases or accidents, and the Public Health Service provides free services to the poor.

Housing. The chronic housing shortage is being attacked by the government in both urban and rural areas. Housing loans may be obtained by workers through the state-owned Crédit du Cameroun. The Société de Prévoyance provides moderately priced building materials, and the Société Immobilière de Cameroun is engaged in the building of communal housing projects.

Police services. The police force consists of six regional legions, five squadrons, and a Republican Guard Legion. It is responsible for maintaining the government's authority throughout the country. It also ensures that price-control laws are enforced and traffic regulations are obeyed. The Republican Guard Legion is responsible for the safety of the president.

Social conditions. In 1970, about 2,400,000 persons were economically active, with approximately 75 percent of the labour force engaged in traditional activities such as agriculture and fishing. Unemployment was about 6 percent. In the cities, the cost of living has steadily risen since 1963. The average annual per capita income is equivalent to about $150 U.S.

Legal working hours are 48 hours per week in farming and forestry and 40 hours in industry, commerce, and the professions. Labour legislation provides for paid vacations, a minimum employment age of 14 years, the exemption of women and children from labour at night, and a minimum-wage scale.

Malaria is prevalent everywhere but in the mountainous regions, where respiratory and pulmonary diseases and dysentery are common. There are incidences of leprosy and schistosomiasis (a parasitic infestation of the bladder and intestines), as well as syphilis, sleeping sickness, and rheumatism.

Social and economic divisions in general follow ethnic lines. In the north, the Muslim pastoralists dominate, whereas the more urban south is dominated by those who have acquired Christianity and a Western education. Because of the multiplicity of tribes, precise divisions are difficult to draw.

CULTURAL LIFE

Each major ethnic group of the country has developed its own culture. The frenzied rhythms played on the drums by the people of the southern forest region contrast with the flute music of northern Cameroonians. Rich diversity is well represented in the country's art. In the Adamaoua area, the Muslim Fulani produce elaborately worked leather goods and ornate calabashes (gourds used as containers), and the Kirdi and the Matakani of the western mountains produce distinctive types of pottery. The powerful masks of the Bali, which represent elephants' heads, are used in ceremonies for the dead, and the statuettes of the Bamileke are carved in human and animal figures. The Tikar people are famous for beautifully decorated brass pipes, the Ngoutou people for two-faced masks, and the Bamum for smiling masks.

L'Institut Français d'Afrique Noir (French Institute of Black Africa) maintains a library in Douala that specializes in the sociology, ethnology, and history of Africa. Small libraries are also maintained by secondary and technical schools. Of the several museums, the Musée du Diamare et Maroua has anthropological collections relating to the Sudanese peoples and the Musée Camerounais de Douala exhibits objects of Cameroon's prehistory and natural history. Cultural institutions and organizations

Cultural organizations include the Cameroun Cultural Association, the Cameroun Cultural Society, and the Centre Fédéral Linguistique et Culturel. There are also numerous women's associations, youth movements, and sporting associations.

French is the principal language of the press, although some periodicals are printed in English and Boulon. The French *La Presse du Cameroun* is the only daily newspaper, and there is a daily government gazette of limited circulation. *The Cameroon Express* is published twice weekly. All publications are censored by the government through the Agence Camerounaise de Presse. The government owns and operates four radio stations, located at Yaoundé, Douala, Garoua, and Buea. There is no television.

PROSPECTS FOR THE FUTURE

Development has been made possible by the political stability that the republic's diverse peoples have enjoyed since independence and by the sound fiscal and monetary policies pursued by the federal government. The main problem is the regional inequalities in levels of development between the relatively isolated north and the more economically developed south and between the less developed West Cameroon and the more advanced southern section of East Cameroon. Continued stability would seem to depend largely upon the determination with which the government attempts to bridge the gap between the better developed and the poorer regions.

BIBLIOGRAPHY. DAVID E. GARDINER, *Cameroon: United Nations Challenge to French Policy* (1963); and V.T. LEVINE, *The Cameroons, from Mandate to Independence* (1964), are the best accounts of the political history of the country up to the time of reunification. Gardiner's study is limited to the former French trusteeship territory of Cameroon; LeVine traces developments in both the former French and British trusteeship territories. The realities of reunification have been examined in W.R. JOHNSON, *The Cameroon Federation: Political Integration in a Fragmentary Society* (1970); NEVILLE RUBIN, *Cameroon: An African Federation* (1971); and V.T. LEVINE, *The Cameroon Federal Republic* (1971). The MINISTRY OF INFORMATION AND TOURISM OF THE CAMEROON FEDERAL REPUBLIC, *Cameroon* (1970), is an official account of the achievements of the country since independence. K. EWUSI, *West African Economies: Some Basic Economic Problems* (1971), is an introductory study of the economies of selected West African countries, including Cameroon. H.S. BEDERMAN, *The Cameroons Development Corporation: Partner in National Growth* (1968), examines this quasi-governmental organization that manages the plantations developed in the Victoria division of West Cameroon. W.A. HANCE, *The Geography of Modern Africa*, ch. 4 (1964), gives a brief account of the geography of the country and has useful maps.

(G.Be.)

Camões, Luís de

The poet Luís Vaz de Camões was one of the few Portuguese writers to overcome the language barrier and the modern confusion of Portugal with Spain and to have a widespread influence on Western literature. He had a permanent and unparalleled impact on Portuguese literature and Brazilian literature alike not only with his epic based on Portuguese encounters in the East, *Os Lusíadas* (*The Lusiads*) but also with his posthumously published lyric poetry.

Camões, portrait miniature painted in Goa, 1581. In a private collection.
By courtesy of the Museu Nacional de Arte Antiga, Lisbon

Known biographical information. What little information there is about the man in a strict biographical sense falls into three categories: statements by his first biographers in the 17th century, a few documents unearthed in the 19th century and scant subsequent research, and very abstract allusions (some chronologically uncertain) to his own life in his works. From these rather fragile sources much irrelevant scholarship and romantic guesswork has sprung during the last four centuries.

One of Camões' countrymen and first biographers, Manuel Severim de Faria, provides a glimpse of Camões (some more-or-less authentic portraits also exist): "not too tall, strong of body and large of face, with something of a frown in his expression, long nose curved at the middle, a missing eye lost in his youth, and hair so blond as to have reddish tones; not too graceful in his manners but easygoing and witty in his conversation." Despite the lack of authentic knowledge of him, everything hints that Camões was in tune with his station in the social life of the time and with his age of imperial adventures. He never married or fathered any known children, in spite of the display of love pangs, burning eroticism, and even adolescent boasting in his works. Though the works reveal little about his life, they reveal much about his ideas, feelings, hopes, and despairs, however disguised they may be under the Petrarchan modes and tones of his time and however contrived by the dangerously repressive epoch in which he lived. Few great poets in world literature, in fact, have written so much or so obsessively about themselves as he did, even in his epic poem. Yet criticism of his work, particularly *Os Lusíadas*, has been biassed by Portuguese political pride and religious prejudice, which, stressing the national character of the epic, have served to reduce the range of Camões' thought.

Heritage and youth

It is supposed that Camões was born in Lisbon around 1524 or 1525, when Portuguese expansion in the East was at its peak. Recent research, expanding on statements of his first biographers and collating them with aristocratic genealogies, has shown him to be a member of the impoverished old aristocracy but well related to the grandees of Portugal and Spain. Vasco Pérez de Camoens, his great-great-grandfather, was a Galician gentleman who had migrated to Portugal for political reasons in the last quarter of the 14th century. A tradition that Camões studied at the University of Coimbra or that he followed any regular studies, for that matter, remains unproved, though few other European poets of that time achieved such a vast range of both classical and modern culture and philosophy. He is supposed to have been, in his youth, in territories held by the Portuguese in Morocco, but it is uncertain whether he had been exiled or whether he was there because it was simply the place for a young Portuguese aristocrat to start a military career and to qualify for royal favours. It is also assumed that his youth in Lisbon was less than subdued. King John III pardoned him in 1553, when he was under arrest for taking part in a street brawl in which a royal officer was assaulted. The pardon hints that Camões would go to India in the King's service, but none of his wanderings for nearly 17 years there has been documented. Certainly, he was there, judging from references in his works that reveal an intimate knowledge of the area's social conditions. He surely did not make his fortune there, since he complains many times about his bad luck or the injustices he met with. After his return to Portugal, in July 1572, he was granted a royal pension on account of his services in India and not merely to reward him for having published *The Lusiads*, as is commonly said. While in the East, he took part in one or two military naval expeditions and, as he alludes to it in his epic, underwent shipwreck in the Mekong Delta. His years in the East can be assumed to have been like those of thousands of Portuguese scattered at the time from Africa to Japan, whose survival and fortunes were, as he says, always hanging from Divine Providence's very thin thread. Diogo do Couto, a 16th-century historian of the Portuguese East, who never included Camões among the nobles he listed so carefully for every skirmish, did note, however, that he found "that great poet and old friend of mine" stranded in Mozambique and helped to pay his trip back to Lisbon, where Camões must have arrived in 1570. *The Lusiads* appeared in 1572, certainly in the first months of that year. It has been much debated whether his pension was enough for a decent retirement, but it seems that it was reasonable—though, according to his first biographers, Camões always spent whenever he had money in his purse. His mother, a widow, survived him and had the pension renewed in her name. Documents related to payments due and to the renewal are known, and through them the date of his death has been accepted as June 10, 1580. It is not certain that he died of anything more than premature old age brought on by illnesses and hardships; to connect his death, as some have done, with the loss of Portuguese independence in 1580, when the Portuguese and Castilian crowns became united for 60 years, is a patriotic and romantic assumption, like another legend of his faithful Javanese slave begging alms for him. Commentators have pointed out the injustice of his not having been appointed as one of the poets who, in 1578, went to North Africa to sing the praises of King Sebastian (whom Camões had promised, when dedicating the epic to him, another poem for his Moroccan deeds). But perhaps he was too ill by the time and, hence, spared the terrible fate of all the others who were caught in the military disaster in which most of the high aristocracy and the King himself lost their lives. His tombstone in the Lisbon church of Santa Ana disappeared in the great earthquake of 1755. The bones that were transferred with national and international pomp and circumstance to a glorious Gothic-revivalistic tomb at the monastery of Jerónimos in Lisbon (ordered by King Manuel I on the spot from which Vasco da Gama had sailed in 1497 on the voyage to India that Camões took as the axis of the narrative in his epic), on the occasion (1880) of the third centennial of Camões death, are certainly not his—an ironic commentary on a famous line in which Camões said that he had left his life scattered in shreds throughout the world.

Years in the East

Non-epic works. During his lifetime he did not publish any of his non-epic works, except for three complimentary pieces: an ode commending Garcia de Orta's *Colóquios dos Simples e Drogas e Coisas Medicinais da India* (1563) and a sonnet and an epistle in terza rima (an Italian form of iambic verse) offering Pero de Magalhães Gandavo's *História da Província de Santa Cruz a que vulgarmente chamamos Brazil* (1576) to a hero of the East whose family appears to have been connected with Camões in several ways. Two plays attributed to him were printed in Lisbon in 1587. His unpublished poems were first collected in 1595, though some of them had already been appearing in Spanish translations, two different versions of *The Lusiads* having been published in Spain in the year of his death. A new, expanded edition of the *Rimas* appeared in 1598. These two first editions already included many poems not by Camões, and this process of attributing inauthentic works to him continued until the end of the 19th century, with almost any poet of some distinction in Portugal and Spain after the beginning of the 16th century to the middle of the next contributing unwittingly to the growing body. A second part of the *Rimas* (1616), one more play in 1645, a third part (1668), and an immense edition of the lyric poetry (1685–88) with commentaries by Manuel de Faria e Sousa, were milestones of that pious folly that saved for later readers many pieces but reached its peak at the end of the last century (when manuscript songbooks of the 16th and 17th centuries were ransacked for the purpose) in an edition prepared by Viscount Juromenha and others prepared by a literary historian, Teófilo Braga. In the meantime, all the apocrypha were used to substantiate increasingly erudite "biographies." In the 1880s Wilhelm Storck (a German translator of the "complete" works) and the Luso-German scholar Carolina Michaelis de Vasconcellos were the first to react critically against such procedures, but it was not before the 1930s that "complete" editions started to take notice of these criticisms of authorship, never methodically furthered except in the most recent years, not to speak of the readings of many lines never corrected according to first printings or the extant manuscripts. No autograph has been discovered nor did Camões' editors ever claim to have seen anything except copies such as those in extant 16th- and 17th-century manuscript collections, not all of them duly studied and published. It must be said, however, that hundreds of the most impressive or graceful poems, like the three plays and some of the attributed prose letters, have not been subject to any suggestion of doubtful authorship, even if the authenticity of many pieces is substantiated only by the fact that no other attribution appeared since they were first printed in Camões' name. It is notable that recent research has substantially reduced his already thin Spanish output. *The Lusiads* do not offer the same textual problems, in spite of two different "first editions," one of which is thought to be "authentic" and the other pirated—the reality being that there are several small differences among copies of either one, which point only to the books having been produced much like the Shakespearian First Folio, with sheets being newly revised and composed according to demand.

Attribution of inauthentic works

Evaluation by contemporaries

Most of Camões' illustrious contemporaries have been taken to task by biographers and critics for not mentioning him in their works. But, when Camões left for the East, he was only one young poet among many. Being absent from Portugal for 17 years, he was cut off from a literary life that, by the patterns of the time, depended upon very closely knit circles in Europe. And, when he returned, many of his great contemporaries had died, and the prevailing mood of the Counter-Reformation was no longer in tune with the daring of Camões paganism, which his first biographers and critics are clearly intent on defending. Nevertheless, there are references to him by some of his contemporaries (certainly dating from his last years in Lisbon), who held him in the highest regard (notably André Falcão de Resende, Gaspar Frutuoso, and Pero de Magalhães Gandavo), and even the censor's license for his epic shows a leniency that points to strong opinion in his favour. The Italian poet Torquato Tasso's sonnet to him and the admiring quotations by the Spanish writer Baltasar Gracián in his *Agudeza y arte de ingenio* (1648) are examples of his fame, which was also noted by the Spanish dramatist Lope de Vega and poets Góngora, Milton, Goethe, the German Romantics, Byron, the Brownings, and others among his admirers, the last, but not the least, being Herman Melville.

The Lusiads. Most of this celebrity rested for long much more on the epic than on the lyric poetry, which, very much admired through the centuries, has only in the last 40 years begun to be understood as the high intellectual achievement that his own times and the 17th century had seen it to be. At the end of the 19th century, Camões was thought to be the Renaissance poet and man *par excellence*, after having been, for the European Romantics, a paragon of the adventurous genius who lives unhappy in love and dies a miser ignored by society. Today, the notion of the Renaissance proper has shrunk, and it no longer covers with its legendary luminous skies the anguish of Camões, heir to the European High Renaissance, but rather the great Mannerist frustrated by a time "out of joint" (as he called it, anticipating Shakespeare). Neither does it cover his conception of the soul of man divided among opposites and always striving to overcome them in a synthesis as much made of oppositions as the previous one nor his hunger for an ultimate freedom that only an aesthetic order could give him—either in the creation of elegant and deeply moving lyric poems or in the majestic sweep of *The Lusiads*, where Jewish and Christian traditions, paganism and Christianity, Platonism and empiricism, intellectualism and sensuality, realism and fantasy, history and literary imagination, patriotism and a universal humanist love, sad frustrations and dazzling epiphanies, the Earth with its varied civilizations and the eternal primeval sea are harmoniously fused to celebrate, much more than da Gama's voyage or Portuguese history, the impossible dream. The ten cantos of *The Lusiads* are in *octava rima* (1,102 stanzas). After an introduction, an invocation, and a dedication to King Sebastian, the action, on both the historical and the mythological levels, begins. Da Gama's ships are seen already in the Indian Ocean, sailing up the coast of East Africa, and the Olympian gods gather to discuss the fate of the expedition (favoured by Venus and attacked by Bacchus). The conclusion is a huge epiphany in which history, the voyage, and mythology are fused together. Throughout *The Lusiads*, Camões develops splendid episodes that enliven the narrative: the murder of Inês de Castro, who becomes a symbol of death for love; an impressive condemnation of the adventurous spirit by an old man when the ships are leaving Portugal; Adamastor, the giant of Classical parentage who, as the Cape of Good Hope, tells da Gama he will lie in wait to destroy the fleets coming back from India. Realistic descriptions of sensual encounters, battles, and storms and other natural phenomena transcend the thrust of Classical allusions that permeate the work, all of which make for the high-flown yet fluent style of the poem. *The Lusiads*, as well as the enormous output of lyric poems, the three plays, and the prose letters reveal an astonishing command of language and variety of styles and provide a fascinating portrait of an extraordinary man and poet. Camões felt doomed by fate to take European history to its meeting with the East (*The Lusiads* is much less an imitation of Virgil than a poem intended to be for the West what the *Aeneid* was for Rome) and to embody the ultimate loss of all human aspirations.

Camões' conception of the soul of man

Camões' thought

Camões was a Neoplatonist who believed in God as a supreme idea of love and in the pagan gods as the figures for spiritual communication with that silent idea; he was a man obsessed with erotic tensions that evoke, with no sense of sin, all the dark sides of sex; a moralist craving for honesty and human dignity, who would excuse an absolutely free license in sensual love; a Christian who saw religion as tolerance and charity and considered man to be predestined in this world but to be saved in the next or, at least, wandering in a sort of pagan paradise under the sight of God; an esoteric mind intent on building his epic on cabalistic and Christian–Pythagorean calculations and his lyric poems on despair redeemed by the contemplation of the very process of the human intelligence consuming itself in endless dialectics. He was also a proud man who could not offer his great poem to anyone but King Sebastian himself and, never bowing to anyone in his works, put many of his family or friendly connections in his epic as heroes of Portuguese history and of the Eastern Empire (himself and his shipwreck being the last exploit in the list). An adventurer in the pattern of an aristocratic society with no outlet but that Eastern Empire, a spirit so intellectualized that his spiritual yearnings refuse mystical solutions, and an overpowering personality composed of lucid reason and passionate emotions, inflexibly analyzing himself in the capturing of his own *temps perdu*, always capable of ironically looking into his own musings, and quite aware that no one would follow (in the decadent and strife-torn times that he was measuring by his chivalric ideals) his proposal of the conquest of the East as Paradise regained, Camões was all these.

MAJOR WORKS

POETRY: *Os Lusíadas* (1572; *The Lusiads*, trans. by Leonard Bacon, 1950; *The Lusiads in Sir Richard Fanshawe's Translation*, ed. and introd. by G. Bullough, 1963); *Rhythmas de Luís de Camões* (1595; *Camoens: The Lyricks*, trans. by Richard Burton, 2 vol., 1884).

PLAYS: *Anfitriões* and *Filodemo*, in *Primeira Parte dos Autos e Comedias Portuguesas Feitas por A. Prestes e por L. de C.* (1587); *El-Rei Seleuco* (first appeared in the 1644–45 ed. of Camões' works).

BIBLIOGRAPHY

Editions: The editions of Camões' works in Portuguese and other languages are in the hundreds, and his bibliography is immense. The best modern edition of *The Lusiads* is still by AUGUSTO EPIFANIO DA SILVA DIAS, *Os Lusiadas*, 2 vol. (1916–18). The best contemporary edition of the lyric works, if unsatisfactory, is ALVARO J. DA COSTA PIMPAO, *Rimas*, new ed. (1961). The first complete English translation of *The Lusiads* was by RICHARD FANSHAWE (1655), and the best modern one is by LEONARD BACON (1950). The lyric poems were often translated in the 19th century, from LORD STRANGFORD'S (1803) down to RICHARD BURTON'S (1884), the famous traveller and translator.

Biographies: A monumental modern biography is by FRIEDRICH WILHELM STORCK, *Luis' de Camoens leben* (1890; annotated Portuguese trans., *Vida e Obras de Luis de Camões*, by CAROLINA MICHAELIS DE VASCONCELLOS, 1897), in which everybody and everything in Portuguese life during the 16th century gets into the picture except Camões himself. The most prudent, shorter life (in English), though outdated, remains AUBREY F. BELL, *Luis de Camões* (1923); and the best debunking of all the biographical myths is ANTONIO SALGADO JR.'s introduction to his too eclectic edition of the *Obra Completa* (1963).

Critical studies: The numerous articles by CAROLINA MICHAELIS are still scattered in learned reviews from the 1880s to the 1920s, and with some of her other works remain the starting point of any Camonian scholarship. Other studies include: THEOPHILO BRAGA, *Camões: Época e Vida* (1907) and *Camões, a Obra Lírica e Épica* (1911); F. REBELO GONCALVES, *Dissertações Camonianas* (1937); HERNANI A. CIDADE, *Luís de Camões*, 2nd ed., 3 vol. (1952–56); CECIL M. BOWRA, *From Virgil to Milton* (1945); JORGE DE SENA, *A Poesia de Camões* (1951), *Uma Canção de Camões* (1966), *Os Sonetos de Camões* (1969), and *A Estrutura de "Os Lusíadas"* (1970); ANTONIO J. SARAIVA, *Luís de Camões* (1959); A. BARTLETT GIAMATTI, *The Earthly Paradise and the Renaissance Epic* (1966); and ROGER BISMUT, *La Lyrique de Camões* (1971).

(J.deS.)

Campanulales

Campanulales is the formal name of the bellflower order of flowering plants. The order derives its name from the diminutive of the Latin *campana*, which means "little bell," referring to the bell-shaped flowers of a number of species of the family Campanulaceae. The order includes seven families with a total of about 2,000 species. The largest and most attractive family, Campanulaceae, with about 900 species belonging to 40 genera, has received the most attention from botanists; yet the classification of the family, as well as of the order, is not quite satisfactory and many problems remain to be solved.

Scientific and horticultural importance

The main reasons for interest in the group are purely scientific, but much attention has also been paid to the great domestic importance of the large number of ornamentals in the group. Some genera—notably the best known one, *Campanula*—are very interesting with respect to problems of evolution; others show highly remarkable morphological characteristics and anatomical peculiarities. The geographical distribution of a number of groups (notably the genus *Donatia*) shows that a close affinity exists between the floras of New Zealand and South America.

GENERAL FEATURES

Most species are herbs, but shrubs and even trees up to nine metres high (*e.g.*, *Clermontia*) are also present in the order. *Campanula vidalii*, which originates from the Azores, has the growth habit of a shrubby *Sempervivum*; *i.e.*, it is adapted to dry environments and has fleshy leaves. Some giant *Lobelia* species, which may reach a height of six metres (20 feet), are characteristic of African alpine vegetation zones. They occur at altitudes between 6,500 and 14,100 feet.

The distribution of the family Campanulaceae is worldwide, but most species occur in mountainous areas of temperate regions in both hemispheres. The family Lobeliaceae inhabits tropical regions and many temperate areas of the Southern Hemisphere, with some species also distributed in temperate regions of the Northern Hemisphere. The representatives of the other families are mainly Australian. Some members of the Lobeliaceae that inhabit islands (notably the Hawaiian Islands) have a treelike or shrubby habit.

The order Campanulales is generally of slight economic importance, although one exception is the large number of ornamentals in the family Campanulaceae, particularly the genera *Wahlenbergia*, *Campanula*, and *Phyteuma*, and in the family Lobeliaceae, the genera *Lobelia* and *Downingia*.

Some members of the order, however, have a certain importance as medicinal plants. The roots of *Platycodon grandiflorum* (family Campanulaceae), known as kikyo-root, are used in China as expectorants and anti-asthmatics. The blue-flowering wild specimens, especially, contain large quantities of the active substance, platycodin (= kikyo saponin). *Scaevola koenigii* (family Goodeniaceae), a characteristic plant of the tropical beach jungle, furnishes a kind of rice paper, made by squeezing its pith flat. The fruits of *Canarina campanula*, *Clermontia macrocarpa*, and *Centropogon surinamensis* (all belonging to the family Campanulaceae) are locally eaten. *Lobelia inflata*, native to the eastern and central regions of the United States and Canada, is of medicinal importance. The plants are usually short-lived annuals with an inflated capsule. They were used by the North American Indians as an emetic and because of their tobacco-like taste were called Indian tobacco. Also known under the name Herba Lobeliae, these plants are characterized by an unusually high content of closely related alkaloids, which are derivatives of piperidine, especially of n-methyl-piperidine. The alkaloids are thought to occur only in the milky juice of the laticiferous vessels, a system of latex-bearing ducts in the stems and leaves. The best known and most active of them is lobeline, a substance characterized by its stimulating effect on respiration. Because of this property, lobeline is used to enhance the activity of certain centres of the central nervous system in cases of asphyxia in newborn infants. The action of lobeline also resembles that of nicotine to a certain extent, and based on the observation that both of these alkaloids have an additional effect, lobeline is used as a remedy against nicotine addiction. Other species of *Lobelia* also contain lobeline, especially representatives of the subgenus *Tupa*, such as *Lobelia tupa* and *Lobelia excelsa*, which occur in South America.

Medical uses of lobeline

NATURAL HISTORY

The flower. The natural history of the flowers of the family Campanulaceae is of interest, and the flowers of *Campanula* are the best known in this respect. They are provided with a nectar-secreting disk situated at the base of the style, the narrow upper part of the ovary. In most cases the disk is covered by the triangular bases of the male sex organs, or stamens, which fit closely together. The size of the flowers, their frequently blue colour, and their drooping position indicate that they are well adapted to the visit of bees. There are, however, many other insect visitors such as flies, butterflies, and moths. In nearly all species of Campanulaceae the flowers are proterandrous, which means that within an individual flower the mature pollen is always presented for dissemination before the female pollen-receiving structures, or stigmas, of the flower are receptive. The pollen is usually shed in the bud, in which the long, pollen-filled anthers form a column around the end of the style,

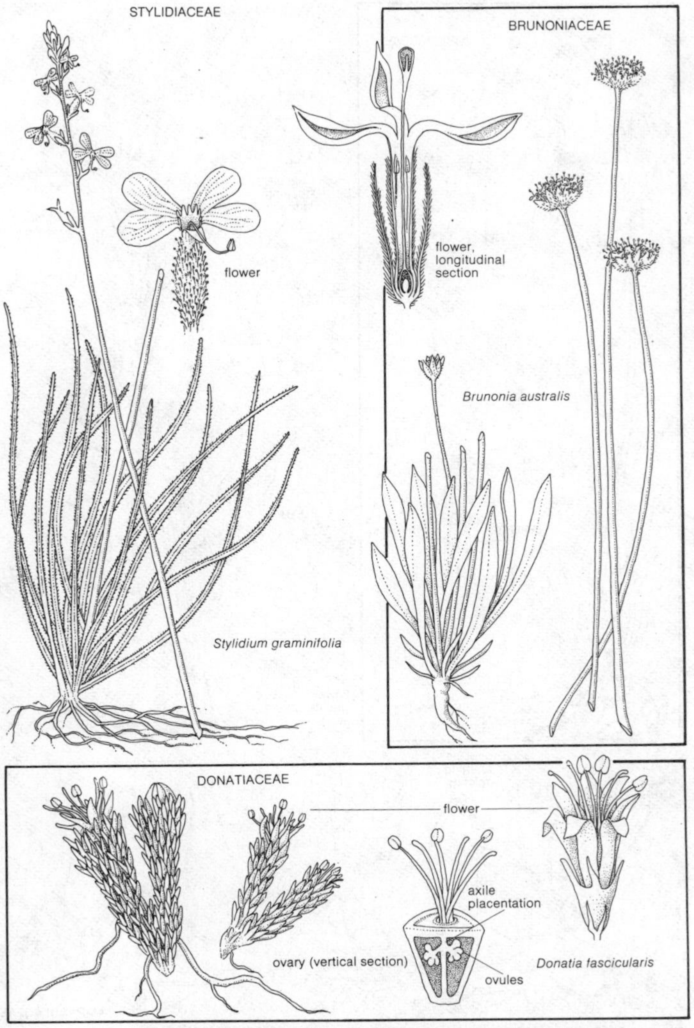

Figure 1: Representative vegetative and floral structures of three of the smaller families of the order Campanulales.
Drawing by M. Moran after Baillon from *Die naturlichen Pflanzenfamilien*

whose stigmas are closed up against one another. The style is densely covered with short, stiff hairs, which hold the pollen after it has been shed by the anthers. After the opening of the flower bud the anthers wither quickly and for some time the style acts as a pollen presenter to insects. Insects trying to get at the nectar contact the hairs of the style and carry away the pollen. The pollen-collecting hairs, each of which is formed from a single epidermal (surface) cell, invaginate at this stage into the style, which may possibly be caused by extraction of water. This implies that after some hours the style becomes denuded.

After a time the stigmas separate and expand. Usually this expansion occurs the second day after the opening of the flower, which signifies that the mature female stage has begun. The stigmas are receptive to pollen by the time they are spread. On the third or fourth day the stigmas curl back so far that they touch any pollen that may still be present on the style, thus effecting self-pollination. Self-pollination, followed by self-fertilization, does not seem to be very common, although there are self-fertile species, such as *Campanula colorata* and *C. canescens* of the Himalaya region, whose flowers may be cleistogamous—*i.e.*, they remain closed at maturity—and some populations of *Campanula rotundifolia*. In most species, however, if the pollen of a certain flower is transferred to its own receptive stigmas or those of another flower of the same plant, no fertilization is effected. The final conclusion is that, in most *Campanula* species, a considerable amount of outbreeding occurs.

Pollen presentation mechanism in *Phyteuma*

In the genus *Phyteuma* the flowers are grouped together in dense heads. The tips of the long and very thin petals cohere and form a kind of tube within which the anthers are held. The style pushes up through this tube and drives the pollen gradually out at the end where it is exposed to insects. In the final stage the style itself emerges, the stigmas expand, and the petals separate and fall back.

In the family Lobeliaceae the pollen-collecting hairs often take more or less the form of a ring, concentrated on the stigmatic branches. The anther walls and the closed stigmatic branches together form a structure that encloses the pollen. Agitation of the hairs on the top of the anthers causes the pollen grains to shake out. It is assumed that the pollen grains are no longer viable after the opening of the stigmatic branches. Some plants of the family Lobeliaceae are visited by birds for nectar. This is especially true for some species of *Clermontia*. So well adapted are both bird and flower that the birds' bills (*e.g.*, those of the Hawaiian honeycreepers) match the curvature of the tubular flowers.

The flowers of the family Goodeniaceae are also proterandrous. In *Leschenaultia formosa*, for example, before flower opening, the pollen is shed into a membranous cup surrounding the stigma. Insects rub against this cup and carry the pollen away with them, thus pollinating other flowers. The same process is also carried out in other species.

The flowers of the family Stylidiaceae are also proterandrous. The characteristic connection of the anthers and style again indicates that insect pollination is necessary. In all cases in this family, however, the pollen is presented to visiting insects while still contained within the anther lobes.

Ecology. The order Campanulales is distributed throughout the world and its members grow in very different habitats, ranging in elevation from sea level to 13,000 feet. For that reason it is impossible to give a survey of all the ecological diversity encountered in the order, but there are some general trends.

In the largest genus of the order, *Campanula*, the species show a great ecological diversity. Many, such as *C. cochleariifolia* and *C. medium*, grow on calcareous (lime-containing) soils, but some avoid such soils (viz., *C. excisa*). Some species prefer woods (*C. latifolia* and *C. trachelium*), others light woodland in more or less shady places (*C. persicifolia*), but the majority prefer sunny habitats. The Portuguese species *Campanula loeflingii* prefers sandy soils, whereas the North American *Campanula aparinoides* occurs in marshes, swamps, and bogs. Sometimes closely related species are very different in their ecological requirements: the alpine species pair *C. elatinoides* and *C. elatines* present a clear example; the first prefers dolomite, the second avoids it and all other calcareous soils as well. Most *Campanula* species, however, prefer calcareous soils.

It is remarkable that some species, such as *Campanula xylocarpa* of Czechoslovakia, which grows in rocky habitats on limestone and dolomite, never colonizes humus soils in natural habitats, even though plants growing on vertical rock walls often disseminate seeds there.

In the other large genus, *Lobelia*, many species grow in moist habitats such as ditches, marshes, and along streams. Some North American species, however, can tolerate much drier conditions; populations of *L. spicata* or *L. syphilitica*, for example, are sometimes found in open fields but mainly in areas where the soil is saturated with water.

Giant lobelias

Another very interesting group of the genus *Lobelia* consists of the giant forms, which are a characteristic element of the lower alpine and alpine mountainous regions of East Africa. They are characterized by tall, unbranched stems, numerous narrow leaves, terminal racemose (spikelike) flower clusters, large, blue or purple flowers, and large anthers, the three upper ones at the top, the two others bearded. Species of the same group occur not only in East Africa, but also in the West Indies, Brazil, and India. Five series of giant *Lobelia* species are distinguishable, conforming largely to altitudinal and precipitation zones.

In spite of the treelike habit of the giant lobelias, the

stems remain largely herbaceous (nonwoody). All giant species flower only once during their life-span. The group is thought to have evolved from some annual forest species with a branched habit and lax inflorescence (flower cluster). *Lobelia longisepala* and other species of its group are regarded as a relic of the ancestral forest forms from which the giant lobelias evolved. The dense inflorescence, the unbranched stem, and the thick, hairy leaves characteristic of the alpine species are explained as adaptations to the higher altitude and severe climate.

Seed dispersal. Knowledge concerning the seed dispersal of the various species of the order is rather limited. Usually the seeds are small. The fruits are generally capsules (only exceptionally drupes—stony-seeded fruits) and they open in various ways. The seeds are not adapted to wind dissemination and usually fall to the ground close to the mother plant. In some species, however, such as *Campanula rotundifolia*, the wind may carry the seeds up to crevices, cliffs, or walls, in which they lodge.

In the genus *Campanula* the species have capsules that open laterally. The capsules have apical pores or basal valves. Species with apical capsule pores have erect fruits, whereas those with basal valves have pendent fruits. This implies that, from the biological point of view, the pores and valves are always situated at the top position. For that reason, the seeds are shed only if the stems are moved by the wind, thus enabling the seeds to spread over some distance. In the group including the genera *Campanula*, *Legousia*, *Phyteuma*, and *Adenophora* the fruits open laterally, whereas in the genera *Wahlenbergia*, *Jasione*, and *Lightfootia* the capsules open apically. In these genera the seeds are not adapted to wind dissemination, but the wind promotes the spread to a limited extent by moving the capsule-bearing stems.

Wind-assisted release of seeds

The fruits of *Scaevola* (family Goodeniaceae) are stony-pitted fruits (drupes), their outer layers being more or less fleshy, the stone very hard, woody, or sometimes corky. Dispersal in most species is effected by fruit-eating birds. In the seashore species *Scaevola sericea* and *Scaevola plumieri*, however, the fruits float very well in seawater and retain their viability for some time. This means of dispersal accounts for their large area of distribution.

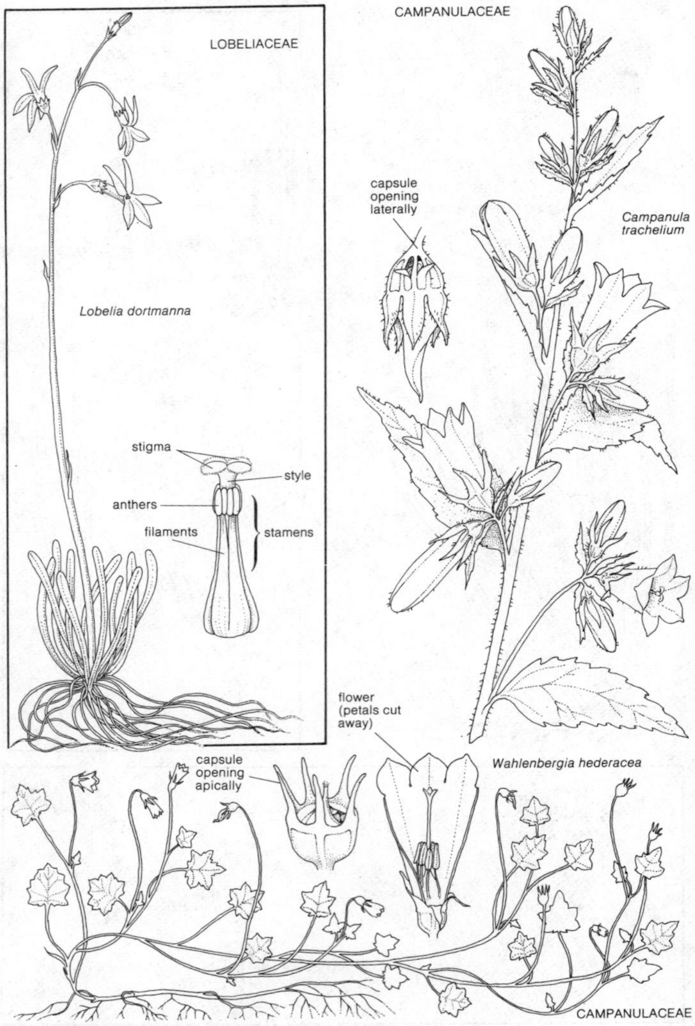

Figure 2: Representative plants and floral structures of the two largest families in the order Campanulales.
Drawing by M. Moran

FORM AND FUNCTION

Distinguishing anatomical characteristics. One of the most distinguishing anatomical characteristics of the families Campanulaceae and Lobeliaceae is the presence of laticiferous vessels, a system of ducts carrying latex and characterized by cross walls at intervals along their length. They are distributed throughout the plants. In the stems they are usually localized in the outermost portion of the vascular system (the phloem region). These laticiferous vessels are absent in the other families of the order. The family Goodeniaceae differs from the Campanulaceae and Lobeliaceae in the more complex anatomy of the cambial tissue—the region of cell division contributing to stem thickness. In the family Stylidiaceae growth in stem thickness is a result of the formation of new vascular bundles outside the primary cylinder, a situation also observed in some woody representatives of the flowering plant class Monocotyledoneae (*e.g.*, *Dracaena*, *Yucca*). The cell walls of some species of the Campanulaceae and Goodeniaceae are silicified.

With the exception of some shrubby species, most Campanulales plants are perennial herbs, surviving from year to year, but there are also some short-lived annual species that overwinter in seed form. Both of these types usually have a repeatedly branched stem. The biennial species, those that fruit and die in the second year, often have fleshy roots and a basal rosette of leaves. The leaves are always simple and lack stipules, which are small appendages at the base of the leafstalk. The leaves of the different species vary considerably in shape, from grasslike in the family Stylidiaceae to rather large in some *Campanula* species. Sometimes the basal leaves are different in form and size from those of the upper stem.

The flowers of the family Campanulaceae are sometimes solitary in the upper angles between leafstalks and the plant stem (the leaf axils) but are usually arranged in inflorescences of various shapes, including spikes, heads, and racemes, which all have a top flower. In the family Lobeliaceae the axis of the inflorescence may be branched, but the top flower is usually lacking. In both the Campanulaceae and Lobeliaceae solitary terminal flowers are sometimes found, which are thought to represent the last flower of a reduced inflorescence. The other families exhibit a variety of inflorescences ranging from solitary in Goodeniaceae to dense heads in Brunoniaceae, closely resembling those of the family Asteraceae (order Asterales).

Floral characteristics

The flowers are radially symmetrical or bilaterally symmetrical and consist in principle of five sepals, five petals, five stamens, and five carpels (ovary segments), the number of locules, or ovary chambers, varying. The number of sepals, however, may vary from three in some species of *Wahlenbergia*, to six in *Canarina*, or eight in *Michauxia*.

The corolla, or collection of petals, is bell-shaped in many species (*e.g.*, *Campanula*, *Adenophora*, *Platycodon*, and others) but in others it is deeply divided (*e.g.*, in *Phyteuma*, *Jasione*, and *Michauxia*). In *Phyteuma* the corolla lobes are united at the top but in the genus *Lobelia* the corolla is split down one side. The family Lobeliaceae has irregular corollas, but Campanulaceae has regular ones. The lips of the corolla are reversed (resupinate) in *Lobelia* by a twisting of the flower stalk. In the family Goodeniaceae the corolla is bilaterally symmetrical and usually two-lipped, whereas the irregular corolla of the family Stylidiaceae usually consists of four petals of equal size, the fifth being much smaller (*Stylidium*, *Levenhookia*). The number of stamens is usually five in the families Campanulaceae (except for some species of *Wahlenbergia*, which have three), Lobeliaceae (in which three stamens are usually longer than the other two), Goodeniaceae, Sphenocleaceae, and Brunoniaceae. The stamens number only two or three in the family Donatiaceae, however, and finally only two in the Stylidiaceae, in which they are united with the style to form a structure known as the gynostemium. The anthers are free or variously closely associated, but not fused, as in *Symphyandra* and *Jasione* (Campanulaceae) or even joined as in the Lobeliaceae. The bases of the stamen filaments are triangular and form a dome-shaped chamber over the nectar-producing disk that surrounds the ovary. This disk may be very large and glandlike in the genus *Adenophora* (Campanulaceae).

The fruits of the family Campanulaceae are usually capsules that open by apical or lateral pores or valves. In some genera (*e.g.* *Canarina*) the fruits are berries.

The same is the case in the family Lobeliaceae, in which the majority of the species have capsular fruits but some (*Pratia*, *Clermontia*) have drupaceous ones. The number of locules, or ovary chambers, varies, sometimes within the same genus (*e.g.*, three or five in *Campanula*), but is very often three in the family Campanulaceae. In the other families of the order the number of locules is often less than three. In all families there are usually numerous ovules in the ovaries. As a rule the ovules are inverted, or anatropous, and have only one integument. The endosperm formation, the development of starchy nutrient tissue for the embryo, is cellular in all families.

Some chemical characteristics. In view of the fact that the families of the Campanulales order are of little economic importance, only a few chemical investigations have been carried out. There is some information with regard to saponins, polyphenols, latex, and carbohydrates. In many species of the Campanulaceae the occurrence of inulin has been demonstrated and this substance has been used as a test for kidney function. Fructan A and fructan B are quite common, not only in the perennial species but also in the annual ones. These compounds are also found in the family Asteraceae (order Asterales), but usually they are lacking in the annual species. The accumulation of the fructans tends to corroborate the opinion that the families Campanulaceae and Asteraceae are related. Polyfructans are also present in the Lobeliaceae, but at least some members of this family differ from the Campanulaceae in the presence of alkaloids. This is an argument for separating the Campanulaceae and Lobeliaceae, which are usually united in one family.

EVOLUTION

Some authorities are of the opinion that the orders Campanulales and Polemoniales are probably derived from the Gentianales. Others, however, derive the Campanulales from the order Rubiales. Chemical and morphological characters suggest that the order Campanulales is a rather natural one, but fossil evidence is lacking, and most opinions remain speculative.

Absence of fossil evidence

On the basis of cytological, taxonomical, geographical, and geological data some authorities believe that the principle genera of the family Goodeniaceae arose in the early Tertiary Period (about 60,000,000 years ago) in Australia, the present-day species originating subsequent to the formation of distinct eastern and western floristic regions in Australia.

In the family Campanulaceae the genus *Campanula* has been most extensively studied with regard to the number of chromosomes per cell, and such studies strongly suggest that the evolution of its species ran along two separate and independent lines. A few isolated species differ in form and structure rather markedly from the other species of the genus, and it is thought by some authorities that some of them should be transferred to a number of smaller, usually monotypic (single-species) genera. *Campanula vidalli* of the Azores, for example, should be placed in the genus *Azorina*, and the North American species *Campanula americana* should be placed in the monotypic genus *Campanulastrum*. At present the genus *Campanula* contains other groups of species that are only remotely related to each other, and some of its species and species groups are undoubtedly closely related to the genera *Adenophora* and *Symphyandra*. In the eastern Mediterranean Basin and in the Caucasus the genus *Campanula* shows the greatest morphological and cytological diversity. It is thought that the genus probably originated in that area.

Studies of the North American species of the family Lobeliaceae indicate that there are four lines of speciation in that group. The earliest populations of *Lobelia* in eastern North America are thought to have been established in Tertiary times or before.

CLASSIFICATION

Annotated classification. The following classification is a recent one of wide acceptance. The order Campanulales, as defined here, includes as a family the plant group sometimes treated as a separate order in other classification systems (order Goodeniales). The family Campanulaceae is to be understood here as including the sometimes separately recognized family Pentaphragmataceae, which is a group of about 30 species found in Southeast Asia and Malaysia.

ORDER CAMPANULALES

Plants usually herbaceous, often with septate laticiferous vessels. Leaves simple and without stipules. Inflorescence racemose with a tendency to form loose heads. Flowers actinomorphic (with radial symmetry) or zygomorphic (with bilateral symmetry), generally 5-merous (with parts numbering 5 each) with a fused corolla, usually with 5 stamens in a single whorl and 2-lobed anthers variously coherent to fused. Ovary 1- to 5-locular (chambered) with many (sometimes 1) ovules in each locule. Ovules with 1 integument. Endosperm cellular. Seven families, 105 genera, about 2,000 species. Distribution worldwide.

Family Stylidiaceae

Herbs or undershrubs without milky sap. Flowers irregular. Corolla with unequal lobes, one of which is smaller or larger than the others and called a labellum. Stamens 2, united with the stigma, together forming the gynostemium. Ovary bilocular with many ovules. Fruits usually capsular. Five genera and 125 species distributed in Australia and New Zealand.

Family Goodeniaceae

Perennial herbs or small shrubs without milky sap. Flowers irregular in capitate or paniculate inflorescences. Stamens 5 and free. Ovary with 2 carpels, 2- or 2-locular with many ovules. Stigma surrounded by an indusium-like cup. Fruits drupes, capsules, or nuts. Twelve genera and 300 species distributed mainly in Australia, but also in New Zealand, South Africa, Antarctic South America, and Asia.

Family Brunoniaceae

Small perennial herbs with spoon-shaped leaves in basal rosettes. Flowers in capitate inflorescences. Corolla with 5 lobes. Stamens 5, inserted near the corolla base with 5 fused anthers. Ovary superior, 1-locular, and with 1 ovule. Style with a cupulate indusium at the base of the stigma. Fruit an indehiscent capsule. One genus and species (*Brunonia australis*) distributed in Australia and Tasmania.

Family Donatiaceae

Small herbaceous plants with linear leathery-textured leaves, densely arranged in a spiral. Flowers without stalks and solitary at the end of the stem. Calyx with 5 to 7 lobes, corolla with 5 to 10 petals. Stamens 2 or 3, free, inserted within a disk. Filaments free. Ovary inferior, with 2 or 3 locules and 2 or 3 styles, which are usually free. Stigma globose. Ovules many, placed on hanging placentas. Fruits indehiscent. One genus (*Donatia*) with two species distributed in New Zealand, Tasmania, and subantarctic South America.

Family Lobeliaceae

Annual, biennial, or perennial herbs, rarely entirely woody, often with milky juice. Flowers zygomorphic. Corolla 1- or 2-lipped of fused petals. Stamens 5, filaments free, anthers cohering into a tube around the style. Ovary inferior with 2 or 3 locules and many axile ovules. Fruits capsular or drupaceous, with many seeds. Twenty-five genera and 750 species with worldwide distribution.

Family Sphenocleaceae

Herbaceous plants with radially symmetrical flowers arranged in dense spikes that have a thick axis. Corolla lobes overlapping in the bud. Stamens inserted at the base of the corolla. Style very short without hair collectors. Ovary 2-locular with thick placentas hanging from the wall separating the locules. Capsule opening by a transverse slit. One genus and one species (*Sphenoclea zeylanica*) distributed in tropical regions.

Family Campanulaceae

Herbs, rarely small shrubs to small trees, usually with watery or milky sap. Leaves usually alternate, simple, and without stipules. Inflorescences are spikes, racemes, or capitula. Flowers regular, bisexual, usually showy. Sepals usually 5. Corolla of fused petals; tubular or bell-shaped and usually 5-merous. Stamens as many as corolla lobes, alternate with them, and inserted near the base of the corolla or on a disk. Anthers not united nor cohering. Ovary generally inferior, 2- to 10-locular with axile placentas. Ovules usually very numerous. Fruit a capsule or rarely a drupe. Forty genera with 900 species. Distribution worldwide.

Critical appraisal. Three orders, Campanulales, Calycerales, and Asterales, are often considered as separate but closely related plant groups. Many authorities, however, regard the last two orders as families (Calyceraceae and Asteraceae or Compositae), which they placed in the order Campanulales. The family Calyceraceae, however, differs from the Campanulaceae in having an undivided style and a one-locular ovary that contains only one pendulous ovule. There are some arguments in favour of placing the Asteraceae in the Campanulales order, however. The accumulation of fructans and the occurrence of derivatives of caffeic acid and triterpene saponins is a characteristic shared by both the families Campanulaceae and Asteraceae. Also, the position of the anthers, which are frequently in contact with each other in the Campanulaceae, and the usually inferior ovary, are characteristics shared by both groups. Finally the septate laticiferous vessels of the subfamily Cichorioideae of the Asteraceae and of the family Campanulaceae point in the direction of a close affinity.

Disagreements over placement of the Lobeliaceae

The position of the family Lobeliaceae is a much disputed one. The dominant genus of the Campanulaceae, *Campanula*, and the dominant one of the Lobeliaceae, *Lobelia*, differ considerably from each other, but there are so many intermediate genera that the differences become less significant as these intermediates are considered. On the other hand, as far as is known, the family Campanulaceae seems to lack alkaloids and has a much more pronounced accumulation of caffeic acid.

The family Sphenocleaceae is often united with the Campanulaceae, but it is sometimes regarded as related to the Phytolaccaceae. The pollen grains resemble those of the family Lobeliaceae, however. Combined cytological and phytochemical studies must be undertaken in order to obtain a better insight with regard to the position of this family. The same holds true for the family Donatiaceae, which is placed by some authorities near the family Saxifragaceae. This, however, does not seem justified in view of the presence of inulin, a character that the Donatiaceae share with the other families of Campanulales. Moreover, the pollen grains of the Donatiaceae are slightly similar to those of *Cyphia* (Lobeliaceae), whereas the grains in the family Saxifragaceae (*Brexia* and other genera) are different. The only resemblance between the families Donatiaceae and Stylidiaceae is the habit of *Donatia* and the species of the genus *Phyllachne*, but otherwise these families seem to be very different. There is much agreement in the various systems with regard to the inclusion of both Stylidiaceae and Goodeniaceae in the order. Only the family Brunoniaceae is treated in different ways by various authors. Earlier botanists accepted the genus *Brunonia* as constituting a separate subfamily of the Goodeniaceae. It has been raised to family rank by most recent workers, both on the basis of morphological characters and on palynological (pollen) and cytological (chromosome count) evidence.

BIBLIOGRAPHY. H.C. CROOK, *Campanulas: Their Cultivation and Classification* (1951), a nicely illustrated book, containing descriptions of many *Campanula* species (especially of horticultural value); S. SCHONLAND, "Campanulales," in A. ENGLER and K. PRANTL (eds.), *Die Natürlichen Pflanzenfamilien IV*, 5:40–84 (1894), a classic in German, now in some respects outdated but still the most complete survey available to all the genera of the order; R.C. CAROLIN, "The Structures Involved in the Presentation of Pollen to Visiting Insects in the Order Campanulales," *Proc. Linn. Soc. N.S.W.*, 85:197–207 (1960), a very clearly illustrated treatment of the pollen presentation in the bellflower order; E.A. BRUCE, "The Giant Lobelias of East Africa," *Kew Bull.*, pp. 61–88 (1934), a treatment of the remarkable giant lobelias; L. HAUMAN, "Les 'Lobelia' géants des montagnes du Congo Belge," *Mem. Inst. R. Colon. Belge, Sect. Sci. Nat. Méd. 8°*, 2:3–50 (1933), a description, with photographs, of a number of giant lobelias occurring in the Congo; R. MCVAUGH, "Studies in the Taxonomy and Distribution of the Eastern North American Species of *Lobelia*," *Rhodora*, 38:241–298, 305–329, 346–362 (1936), a historical survey of the literature of North American *Lobelia* species with keys and descriptions to 22 species, distribution maps, and a literature survey; W.M. BOWDEN, "Phylogenetic Relationships of Twenty-One Species of *Lobelia L.*, Section Lobelia," *Bull. Torrey Bot. Club*, 86:94–108 (1959), a very nice example of modern research in a group of the genus *Lobelia;* T.W.J. GADELLA, "Some Notes on the Delimitation of Genera in the Campanulaceae," *Proc. K. Ned. Akad. Wet.*, sect. C, 69:502–521 (1966), a survey of the literature pertaining to difficulties in classifying the species in the family Campanulaceae.

(T.W.J.G.)

Camping

Camping—living for a night, a weekend, a week, or more in the open with no more than a tent, motor caravan, or trailer caravan for shelter—has expanded enormously as a recreational pastime, especially since 1950, and in the 1970s counted some 60,000,000 enthusiasts, half of them in North America and most of the rest in Europe. The important difference between camping and the life of gypsies or nomads is that campers choose to camp for recreation and more and more as an escape from the pressures of a time-dominated urbanized life.

What was once regarded as a rough, back-to-nature pastime for hardy, slightly eccentric open-air lovers is now the standard holiday for vast numbers of ordinary families whose main common factor, apart from their enjoyment of camping, is the ownership of an automobile, which makes them mobile and is able to carry the modern, reasonably light but rather bulky equipment that ensures a remarkable degree of comfort in camp. The development of this fastest growing recreation in the world is, in fact, directly related to the development and growing private ownership of means of transport that are also capable of carrying camping equipment.

History of recreational camping. People camped from the earliest times, under tents of skins and leaves. The woven cloth tents of Old Testament biblical days were remarkably similar to the tents still used by the nomads of the desert areas of the Middle East. But the evolution of leisure camping is barely a hundred years old, and the great explosion of family camping began as recently as 1955.

The founder of modern camping for pleasure was Thomas Hiram Holding (1844–1930), who wrote the first book on the subject, the *Campers Handbook*, published in 1908. It is clear that, in part, his urge to camp derived from his youthful experiences in North America, for in the book he wrote:

The first *Campers Handbook*

> In the prerailway days of 1853, I crossed the prairies of America. My first experience of camping was above the wooden slope of the plateau behind Kaircock in the Mississippi when a lad of nine.
>
> There, 300 of us camped in tents and waggons . . . but it was only the beginning of a prolongation for, of course, it was a case of camping entirely across the prairies over a distance of 1,200 miles and it lasted from the Spring until August.
>
> The plains were then uninhabited save for a few wandering tribes of Indians, probably a million antelopes and possibly half a million of wary buffaloes. Soon afterwards, the gallant herd was swept away before the "railway hunger". . . .
>
> Spring and a wild and dangerous wagon trip and camp, back from Salt Lake City, up and through the Rockies, back to the States, closed the experience in that early stage. . . .
>
> In the Spring of 1877 I became the proud possessor of a canoe. The canoe led to camping and camping led to a canoe cruise in the Highlands of Scotland. . . . An account of this was published under the title, *The Cruise of the Osprey*. . . .

In 1878 another canoe and camp with several enthusiastic canoeists came off in Scotland, a full account of which, from my pen, was published by Waterlow and Co., *Watery Wanderings 'mid Western Lochs.*

Holding continued to camp throughout Great Britain and Ireland and wrote that in 1897 he was able to put into practice a long-felt urge to cycle-camp, something which only became possible when the old high-wheeled "ordinary" or penny-farthing bicycle, which, says Holding, "was practically an impossible machine with which to camp," was replaced by the safety bicycle, broadly similar to those in use today.

His trip through Ireland provided copy for another book, *Cycle and Camp* (1898), and in it he wrote of the advantages of camping:

> Who can question them? only those who have never tried it. All the horrors which outsiders fear and with which they threaten us, we neither meet nor find. In fact, they don't exist. Camping is nearly always delightful for a holiday at least, and if well managed, is pleasant and healthy, as well as cheap for a more protracted period.
>
> But it is not a lazy life—far from it.
>
> The question comes in here, perhaps, as to which kind of holiday is more beneficial—a loafing or an active one? He who would spend a holiday in sheer laziness should take luxurious lodgings or quarter himself at a fine hotel, and, next to the strain and exertion of eating, do literally nothing.
>
> To most men, however, young or middle-aged, who lead active lives and who are gifted with average energy, something less dormant is surely an advantage.
>
> The camp gives this—exercise without fatigue; fresh air night and day and sufficient excitement to create interest, and remind a man that he lives.
>
> That sounds well! Yes, and has been proved to answer when physic failed and tonics had lost their charm.

When Holding wrote of men, he should have included women, for there were women in his party in 1897. Campers use different words to describe their pastime today, but they would generally agree with the sentiments he expressed so long ago.

Camping clubs and the international federation

Holding founded the first camping club in the world, the Association of Cycle Campers, at a camping meet at Wantage, Berkshire, in August 1901. By 1907 it had merged with a number of other clubs to form the Camping Club of Great Britain and Ireland, of which it is still a flourishing part. The Camping Club published the first issue of its magazine in November 1907 and has done so continuously since that date (since 1957 under the editorship of Alan Ryalls).

Capt. Robert Falcon Scott, the famous Antarctic explorer, became the first president of the Camping Club, in 1909. On his last tragic trip to the Antarctic in 1912, he took with him a Camping Club pennon, which is presumed to have been with him when he died.

After World War I, Sir Robert Baden-Powell (founder of the Boy Scout movement) became president, and the Camping Club of Great Britain and Ireland fostered the establishment of camping organizations in a number of west European countries. In 1932, again on British initiative, steps were taken to establish the Fédération Internationale de Camping et de Caravanning (FICC), and the first international camp and congress were held in the Royal Paddocks at Hampton Court, near London, in 1933. Apart from World War II, this International Rally, as it is now called, has been held every year since, usually in different countries of western Europe, although it was held in Israel in 1964 and in Hungary in 1966, when 7,000 west European campers attended; at Woburn Abbey, England, in 1969, attendance exceeded 13,650.

Membership of the FICC includes organizations from all west European countries; from Czechoslovakia, Hungary, and Poland in eastern Europe; and from Turkey and Israel as well as from the United States, Canada, Morocco, Gibraltar, Brazil, and Japan. The FICC, through its affiliated organizations, issues an International Camping Carnet, which is a certificate that the holder is insured against third-party risks while camping anywhere in the world except mainland China. The carnet serves as an identity card, and it requires the holder to camp in a responsible way. In western Europe, except for Great Britain, it is usually presented on arrival at a campsite and may be retained until departure or until all fees are paid. On many sites a discount on fees is given to carnet holders. Lack of a carnet may lead to refusal of permission to camp, especially in the national forests of France. With a carnet, one may camp on any of the thousands of sites throughout western Europe. From 1970 onward, the FICC, in association with the Alliance International de Turismo (ATT) and the Fédération Internationale de l'Automobile (FIA), has issued a carnet common to all three organizations.

Camping and clubs in North America

In North America individuals were camping in the wilderness for recreational purposes from the early 1870s, travelling on foot, on horseback, or by canoe; but since they were, by definition, individualists, there is no record of camping organizations in the early days. A number of organizations, such as the Adirondack Mountain Club, the Appalachian Mountain Club, and the Sierra Club, have catered, in part, for campers for a very long time, but the organization of campers on a large scale is a post-World War II development.

Even now, the majority of organized campers belong to local clubs, but there are two large-scale national organizations, the National Campers and Hikers Association and the North American Family Campers Association. The NCHA has groups or chapters all over North America, and its biggest activity is its annual "campvention," a meeting of campers from all over North America, which has attracted as many as 30,000 people. The NCHA (founded 1954) affiliated to the FICC in 1960 and has been represented at every FICC International Rally and Congress since that date. The North American Family Campers Association is of more recent origin (founded 1957). It has over 50 chapters throughout the United States. The Camping Club of Canada, a national organization that affiliated to the FICC in 1953, took on a new title, the Canadian Federation of Camping and Caravanning, in 1965.

Individual camping is widely practiced in Australia and New Zealand, but organized camping facilities are relatively few. In South Africa there are several hundred campsites and a number of camping clubs. The most recently formed camping clubs are in Sri Lanka (formerly Ceylon) and the West Indies, further indications of the wide spread of recreational camping.

Organized camping. Organized camping started in the United States in 1861 with a boys camp run by Frederick William Gunn and his wife at Milford-on-the-Sound for students of the Gunnery School for Boys in Washington, D.C. Its success was immediate; it was repeated for 18 successive years and other similar camps began to develop. A private camp was established in 1876 by Joseph Trimble Rothrock and a church camp was started at Gardners Island, R.I., in 1880 by the Rev. George W. Hinckley. Camp Dudley, a YMCA camp still in existence, was founded in 1885 by Summer F. Dudley. The first girls camp was established by Luther Halsey Gulick and his wife on the Thames River, in Connecticut, in 1888.

Youth camps

The Boy Scouts of America was formed in 1910 by Ernest Thompson Seton, who had studied the movement in Great Britain and incorporated camping as a major part of the program, as emphasized by Gen. (later Sir) Robert Baden-Powell. Similar emphasis on camping was to be found in the Girl Guides (founded in Great Britain in 1910), the Campfire Girls (U.S., 1910), and the Girl Scouts (U.S., 1912; patterned after the Girl Guides). Most other organizations concerned with young people, such as the YMCA, the YWCA, the YMHA, the Boys Clubs of America, the Girls Clubs of America, and Four-H Clubs, also undertook camp development as an important part of their activity. Charles W. Eliot, former president of Harvard University, in 1912 stated that "the organized summer camp is the most significant contribution to education that America has given to the world," indicative of the importance attached to it at that time.

Camp directors had begun meeting to exchange experience and discuss common problems at the turn of the 20th century. The Camp Directors' Association was formed in 1910 and developed into the American Camping Association, a professional body that was broadened to include all those associated with organized camps. Camping standards are laid down and leadership certification is provided by it. Colleges and universities provide camping courses, and many camp leaders are recruited from these sources and from the teaching profession.

Organized camps cover a very wide variety of activities whether run by churches, youth agencies, labour organizations, municipal authorities, or privately. Many are based on a nucleus of permanent buildings but with tented sleeping accommodations. All provide supervised camping with a purpose, which may be purely educational or concerned with such activities as nature study, mountaineering, canoeing. Many teach such subjects as woodcraft and campcraft. All are designed to help those participating to develop a greater self-sufficiency while learning to live harmoniously with others of a different background.

Extent of organized camping

In Canada, the Boy Scouts and Girl Guide organizations, together with the YMCA and many churches, have long operated similar camps. So have a number of community groups and several of the provinces.

The fact that the Boy Scout movement was founded in Great Britain ensured the development of organized camping early in the 20th century, and the practice was also developed by the Girl Guides, the Boys Brigade, YMCA, YWCA, Girl Scouts, and a multiplicity of youth organizations, churches, and individual schools. The Order of Woodcraft Chivalry has organized camps for almost 50 years, and the Woodcraft Folk, an offshoot of the co-operative movement, for almost 40 years.

One of the most interesting organizations is the Forest School Camps, founded by teachers before World War II, which continue to provide a wide variety of camping vacations for children from seven to 18, all of which are designed to teach a very high degree of self-assurance, self-sufficiency, and responsibility.

The Camping Club Youth is a body of many thousands of young members of the Camping Club of Great Britain and Ireland, all of whom learn, under leaders, how to camp competently and independently. They are tested and awarded a test pennon and certificate on attaining the necessary proficiency. The CCY certificate is accepted as denoting that the owner is competent to camp without supervision in his own or other countries. It is a necessary prerequisite to camping at the FICC's International Youth Camp, held at Easter-time each year in a different European country.

Vacation camps for young people are arranged in every western European country, and they are operated on a very considerable scale in all the countries of eastern Europe, including the U.S.S.R. So are camps of the Young Pioneers, the Eastern equivalent of the Boy Scouts and Girl Guides of the West. Youth camps, which are usually arranged by schools with some state subsidy, are operated in Australia, New Zealand, South Africa, India, and Japan and are to be found in such unlikely places as Iceland and Singapore. In Israel many kibbutzim organize international work camps each year, which attract young campers from the United States and Mexico as well as from most western European countries.

Individual or family camping. It is in the area of individual or family camping that the most phenomenal growth has taken place, particularly since 1955. More and more people from all walks of life and every income group have been drawn to it as a leisure-time and vacation activity. Some find their pleasure in camping for its own sake, but far more use camping as an adjunct to travel—in their own country or abroad—to their hobbies—which vary from sightseeing and meeting different peoples and experiencing the cultures of other nations and continents—to fishing, photography, hunting, and backwooding. This growth in individual or family camping was made possible by the rapid expansion of private ownership of automobiles but also because camping manufacturers developed more and more sophisticated equipment, designed to make camping easy, comfortable, and convenient. The key development in Europe was the frame tent, a canvas cottage-like edifice of considerable proportions (up to 20 feet [six metres] square) over a strong jointed tubular metal frame, often spring-linked so that it is easy to erect. The outer tent reaches almost to the ground and is pegged by many metal pegs attached to rubber guys that are self-adjusting. There are large picture windows, often partly mosquito netted and with protective awnings. Within, there is usually a kitchen area, sometimes flameproofed; a living and eating area; and up to three separate bedrooms or inner tents, each with sewn-in groundsheet, mosquito-netted ventilation, and zippered door. There are many shapes, sizes, and colour schemes, but all are functional as well as attractive. Surprisingy, this most sophisticated of tents has never really appealed to American campers, who continue to use heavier, external-framed tents on a considerable scale.

Improved equipment and the growth of camping

Most American campers use gasoline stoves for cooking, in addition to charcoal grills and, of course, wood fires in suitable places. In Europe, almost all camp cooking is on bottled butane or propane gas stoves, which usually have two or three burners and a grill. The bottled gas is available in all European countries, the Middle East, and North Africa.

It should be noted that kerosene (called paraffin in England) is not readily available in all European countries and that alcohol (called methylated spirit in England) is very expensive in some, so that gas stoves are the most suitable. Unleaded gas, required for some stoves, is often difficult to obtain, however.

Iceboxes are used extensively both in North America and in Europe. Ice is more readily obtainable in the U.S. and Canada but is gradually becoming more readily obtainable on European campsites. On some campsites in Israel, it is possible to rent a refrigerated locker.

Polythene food and water containers, plastic dishes, nonstick cooking utensils, folding tables and chairs, air beds (air mattresses) or folding camp beds or foam mattresses, lightweight sleeping bags, and a multitude of gadgets all combine to make camping easy.

Wheel campers

Because they eliminate much of the work of family camping, the number of wheel campers has grown enormously since 1960. Some 100,000 trailer caravans are sold each year in Europe to touring caravanners and about 50,000 trailer tents, trailers that open up into a large, comfortable fully furnished tent on wheels. There is growing interest in motor caravans, small but practical caravans built into the bodies of motor vans.

In North America, wheel camping is much more sophisticated and on a much larger scale, because of the larger automobiles and cheaper gas, the bigger state and interstate highways, and the vast distances to be covered. Travel trailers are usually much longer and wider than European trailer caravans. So are the motor homes, which can be up to 35 feet (10.7 metres) long, compared with an average 15 feet (4.6 metres) in Europe. They are equipped with the main services usually found in a house—electricity, running hot and cold water, flush toilets, and waste water disposal. To cater for them, more and more North American campsites are equipped with "complete hook-ups," or connections to all the main services. Such comprehensive facilities cannot be found anywhere in Europe.

In addition to motor homes, North American campers are offered a wide variety of truck campers, or turtle backs, caravan bodies in many shapes and sizes, made to rest on a truck body but capable of being lifted off and left freestanding on a campsite while the truck is used for travelling. There is, too, a considerable variety of camping trailers or tent trailers, similar in principle to their European counterparts but again much larger and more elaborately equipped.

Surprisingly, there is a steadily growing interest in really lightweight compact tents and equipment that can be carried in pack or rucksack by those in Europe and America who choose to camp off the beaten track where they must be self-sufficient and able to carry all they need on their backs.

Pedestrian campers hitchhike their way through most countries of Europe, and cycle, scooter, and motorcycle campers are still to be found, but it is the large numbers of family campers that have led to the great development of campsites on a commercial basis.

Campsites for family campers

In Europe, particularly in France and in Scotland, there are many municipal campsites, usually transit sites adequately equipped but not suitable for long holidays. Spain is the most popular camping country, and there are vast campsites along the Costa Brava and the Mediterranean coast south of Barcelona, some capable of accommodating 15,000 campers and providing restaurants, nightclubs, supermarkets, hairdressers, doctors, and every type of amusement. The coastal areas of France and Italy have many good campsites, usually overcrowded in midsummer. Switzerland, Austria, West Germany, and the Italian lakes all attract increasing numbers of campers every year. So does Great Britain, which actually has more campsites than any other country in Europe, many of them with good facilities. Others are farm sites, with minimal facilities, that offer peace and quiet and often a superb view.

Denmark, Norway, Sweden, Finland, The Netherlands, Belgium, and Luxembourg all continue to expand their camping facilities. So does Portugal, which has a limited number of quite good sites.

It is possible to camp in the tiny countries of Andorra in the Pyrenees, Liechtenstein on the Austrian–Swiss borders, or San Marino on the Adriatic.

Iceland has few campsites but many dramatic camping possibilities, and Greece has a growing number of sites of varying standards.

In eastern Europe, Yugoslavia has many sites, those along the Adriatic coast being overcrowded in summer. Hungary has many good campsites, a number on the Danube River and most around the shores of Lake Balaton. Bulgaria has a countrywide network of sites, many along the Black Sea coast. Czechoslovakia, too, has many sites. Romania, Poland, and East Germany have some sites, and the Soviet Union makes a number of its sites available to foreign campers, though the campers must travel along predetermined routes.

There is an excellent range of motor camps in Turkey, with a variety of facilities. Israel caters well to campers. Morocco has a number of sites, often with indifferent sanitation, and there are some camping facilities in all of the North African countries.

Campsites in the United States and Canada number in the thousands, a considerable proportion of them in state and national parks, forests, and national recreation areas. Generally these sites have minimal facilities—drinking water, some sanitation, and rubbish disposal—but the beauty of their surroundings often compensates for the lack of facilities. The private campsites offer a wide variety of standards, and, though a growing number provide complete hookups, there are few North American sites to compare with the vast supersites in the popular holiday areas of Europe.

An interesting development is the franchise of a network of sites. The largest in this field organizes some 500 sites throughout the United States and Canada and guarantees a high standard of sanitation, free hot showers, laundry facilities, ice, a grocery shop, a lounge, and many other amenities, including a free reservation at the next campsite required. Camping on a dude ranch in the Rockies is an interesting experience for most campers, American or European.

One of the most interesting developments of the 1970s was intercontinental air camping—package holidays by air offered in North America, Europe, and South Africa, the package including a camping vehicle and equipment in the country chosen for the holiday.

BIBLIOGRAPHY. General manuals on camping in Europe include: A. RYALLS, *Modern Camping* (1975), and *Camping with BP: How and Where to Camp in Great Britain and Ireland* (1968); F. TINGEY, *Tackle Caravanning*, 3rd ed. (1979); N. HUNT, *Camping* (1969); and P.F. WILLIAMS, *Camping and Hill Trekking* (1969). General manuals on camping in North America include: P. CARDWELL, *America's Camping Book*, rev. ed. (1976); C. ORMOND, *Outdoorsman's Handbook* (1970); J.J. and J.L. KELLY, *Camping—Where and How* (1964); W.K. MERRILL, *All About Camping*, 2nd ed. (1964); B. RIVIERE, *Backcountry Camping* (1971); and F. STURGES (ed.), *The Camping Manual* (1967).

In addition to books, handbooks, and manuals on camp cooking, selection and use of equipment, first aid, and similar subjects, there are many specialized works on the techniques and various types of camping. Examples of these are: J.R. JOHNSON, *Advanced Camping Techniques* (1967); C. JACOBSON, *Wilderness Canoeing and Camping* (1977); E.A. SLOANE, *The New Complete Book of Bicycling* (1974), advice on touring and camping; R.C. RETHMEL, *Backpacking*, 6th ed. (1979); and C. RUTSTRUM, *Paradise Below Zero* (1968), a guide to Arctic or winter camping.

The publications most widely used by campers, however, are the guides that list the locations, facilities, fees, and other pertinent information about specific campsites. *Rand McNally European Campground Guide* provides maps and campground information in tabular form; the Camping Club of Great Britain and Ireland publishes a list of more than 2,500 campsites in the British Isles; its publication, *International Camping*, lists recommended sites throughout Europe, North Africa, and the Middle East; *Europa Camping und Caravaning* lists sites in the same areas; the Michelin guide, *Camping, Caravaning in France*, covers French sites in detail. Most of the national camping clubs list sites in their own countries, and the national tourist offices also provide site lists and maps showing their locations.

The most extensive campsite guides for North America are *Camping and Trailering*, eastern and western editions, published by the American Automobile Association; *Woodall's Campground Directory;* and *Rand McNally Campground and Trailer Park Guide.* Each state and province publishes its own list of sites, as do many of the parks, forests, and recreation areas.

(A.R.)

Camus, Albert

As novelist and playwright, moralist and political theorist, Albert Camus after World War II became the spokesman of his own generation and the mentor of the next, not only in France but also in Europe and eventually the world. His writings, which addressed themselves mainly to the isolation of man in an alien universe, the estrangement of the individual from himself, the problem of evil, and the pressing finality of death, accurately reflected the alienation and disillusionment of the postwar intellectual. Although he understood the nihilism of many of his contemporaries, Camus also argued the necessity of defending such values as truth, moderation, and justice. In his last works, before his death at the age of 46, he sketched the outlines of a liberal humanism that rejected the dogmatic aspects of both Christianity and Marxism.

Henri Cartier-Bresson—Magnum

Camus, photograph by Henri Cartier-Bresson.

Early years. Camus was born at Mondovi in Algeria on Nov. 7, 1913. Less than a year later, his father, an impoverished worker of Alsatian origin, was killed in World War I during the first battle of the Marne. His mother, of Spanish descent, worked as a charwoman to support her family. Camus and his elder brother Lucien moved with their mother to a working class district of Algiers where all three lived, together with the maternal grandmother and a paralyzed uncle, in a two-room apartment. Camus's first published collection of essays, *L'Envers et l'endroit* (1937), describes the physical setting of these early years and includes portraits of his mother, grandmother, and uncle. A second collection of essays, *Noces* (1938), contains intensely lyrical meditations on the Algerian countryside and presents natural beauty as a form of wealth that even the very poor can enjoy. Both collections contrast the fragile mortality of human beings with the enduring nature of the physical world.

Education

In 1918 Camus entered primary school and was fortunate enough to be taught by an outstanding teacher, Louis Germain, who helped him to win a scholarship to the Algiers *lycée* (high school) in 1923 (it was typical of Camus's sense of loyalty that 34 years later his speech accepting the Nobel Prize for Literature was dedicated to Germain). A period of intellectual awakening followed, accompanied by great enthusiasm for sport, especially football, swimming, and boxing. In 1930, however, the first of several severe attacks of tuberculosis put an end to his sporting career and interrupted his studies. Camus had to leave the unhealthy apartment that had been his home for 15 years, and after a short period spent with an uncle—a butcher by trade and a Voltairean by conviction—Camus decided to live on his own, supporting himself by a variety of jobs while registered as a philosophy student at the University of Algiers.

At the university, Camus was particularly influenced by one of his teachers, Jean Grenier, who helped him to develop his literary and philosophical ideas and shared his enthusiasm for football. He obtained a *diplôme d'études supérieures* in 1936 for a thesis on the relationship between Greek and Christian thought in the philosophical writings of Plotinus and St. Augustine. His candidature for the *agrégation* (a qualification that would have enabled him to take up a university career) was cut short by another attack of tuberculosis. To regain his health he went to a resort in the French Alps—his first visit to Europe—and eventually returned to Algiers via Florence, Pisa, and Genoa.

Camus's literary career. Throughout the 1930s, Camus broadened his interests. He read the French classics as well as the writers of the day—among them Gide, Montherlant, Malraux—and was a prominent figure among the young left-wing intellectuals of Algiers. For a short period in 1934–35 he was also a member of the Algerian Communist Party. In addition, he wrote, produced, adapted, and acted for the Théâtre du Travail (Workers' Theatre), later named the Théâtre de l'Équipe, which aimed to bring outstanding plays to working class audiences. He maintained a deep love of the theatre until his death. Ironically, his plays are the least admired part of his literary output, although *Le Malentendu* (*Cross Purpose*) and *Caligula*, first produced in 1944 and 1945, respectively, remain landmarks in the so-called theatre of the absurd. Two of his most enduring contributions to the theatre may well turn out to be his stage adaptations of Faulkner's *Requiem for a Nun* (*Requiem pour une nonne;* 1956) and Dostoyevsky's *Possessed* (*Les Possédés;* 1959).

Plays

In the two years before the outbreak of World War II, Camus served his apprenticeship as a journalist with *Alger-Républicain*. He fulfilled a variety of functions, including those of leader-writer, subeditor, political reporter, and book reviewer. He reviewed some of Sartre's early literary work and wrote an important series of articles analyzing social conditions among the Muslims of the Kabylie region. These articles, reprinted in abridged form in *Actuelles III* (1958), drew attention (15 years in advance) to many of the injustices that led to the outbreak of the Algerian War in 1954. Camus took his stand on humanitarian rather than politico-ideological grounds and continued to see a future role for France in Algeria while not ignoring colonialist injustices.

He enjoyed most influence as a journalist during the final years of the occupation of France and the immediate post-Liberation period. As editor of the Parisian daily *Combat*, the successor of a Resistance news sheet run largely by Camus, he maintained an independent left-wing position based on the ideals of justice and truth and the belief that all political action must have a solid moral basis. Later, the old-style expediency of both Left and Right brought increasing disillusion, and in 1947 he severed his connection with *Combat*.

Novels and philosophical works

By now Camus had become a leading literary figure. *L'Étranger* (American *The Stranger;* British *The Outsider*), a brilliant first novel begun before the war and published in 1942, is a study of 20th-century alienation with a portrait of an "outsider" condemned to death less for shooting an Arab than for the fact that he never says more than he genuinely feels and refuses to conform to society's demands. The same year saw the publication of an influential philosophical essay, *Le Mythe de Sisyphe* (*The Myth of Sisyphus*), in which Camus, with considerable sympathy, analyzed contemporary nihilism and a sense of the "absurd." He was already seeking a way of overcoming nihilism, and his second novel, *La Peste* (*The Plague;* 1947), is a richly symbolical account of the fight against an epidemic in Oran by characters whose importance lies less in the (doubtful) success with which they oppose the epidemic than in their determined assertion of human dignity and fraternity. Camus had now moved from his first main concept of the absurd to his other major idea of moral and metaphysical "rebellion." He contrasted this latter ideal with politico-historical revolution in a second long essay, *L'Homme révolté* (*The Rebel;* 1951), which provoked bitter antagonism among Marxist critics and such near-Marxist theoreticians as Jean-Paul Sartre. His other major literary works are a technically brilliant novel, *La Chute* (*The Fall;* 1956), and a collection of short stories, *L'Exil et le royaume* (*Exile and the Kingdom;* 1957). *La Chute* reveals a preoccupation with Christian symbolism and contains an ironical and witty exposure of the more complacent forms of secular humanist morality.

In 1957, at the early age of 44, Camus received the Nobel Prize for Literature. With characteristic modesty he declared that had he been a member of the awarding committee his vote would certainly have gone to André Malraux. Less than three years later, on Jan. 4, 1960, he was killed in an automobile accident.

MAJOR WORKS

NOVELS AND SHORT STORIES: *L'Étranger* (1942; English title, *The Outsider*, 1946; U.S. title, *The Stranger*, 1946); *La Peste* (1947; *The Plague*, 1948); *La Chute* (1956; *The Fall*, trans. by Justin O'Brien, 1957). Short stories collected in *L'Exil et le royaume* (1957; *Exile and the Kingdom*, trans. by J. O'Brien, 1958).

PLAYS: *Le Malentendu* (performed 1944; pub. with *Caligula*, performed 1945, in *Le Malentendu, suivi de Caligula*, 1944; *Caligula and Cross Purpose*, 1947); *L'État de siège*, (performed and pub. in 1948; *State of Siege*, trans. in *Caligula and Three Other Plays*, 1958); *Les Justes* (performed 1949, pub. 1950; *The Just Assassins*, trans. in *Caligula and Three Other Plays*, 1958). (ADAPTATIONS): *La Dévotion à la Croix* (1953, from Calderón); *Un Cas intéressant* (1955, from Dino Buzatti); *Requiem pour une nonne*, (1956, from William Faulkner); *Les Possédés* (1959, from Dostoyevsky).

ESSAYS, JOURNALISM, AND NOTEBOOKS (COLLECTIONS): *L'Envers et l'endroit* (1937), recollections of childhood and travel sketches; *Noces* (1938), four Algerian essays; *Actuelles*, 3 vol. (1950, 1953, 1958), editorials and articles written for *Combat*, 1944–45; *L'Été* (1954). (OTHER ESSAYS): *Le Mythe de Sisyphe, essai sur l'absurde* (1942, enl. and rev. ed. reprinted 1945; *The Myth of Sisyphus*, trans. by J. O'Brien, 1955), a long philosophical essay; *Lettres à un ami allemand* (1945; trans. by J. O'Brien in *Resistance, Rebellion, and Death*, 1960), four linked essays, with preface, in the form of letters written during the Occupation, the first and second previously published in the "underground" reviews, *Le Revue Libre* (1943) and *Cahiers de la Libération* (1944); *Le Minotaure ou la halte d'Oran* (written 1939, pub. 1950), poetic and satirical description of Oran, the background for *La Peste;*

L'Homme révolté (1951; *The Rebel*, 1953), a long metaphysical, historical, and political essay. (NOTEBOOKS PUBLISHED POSTHUMOUSLY): *Carnets: Mai 1935–Février 1942* (1962; *Notebooks, 1935–42*, trans. by Philip Thody, 1963); *Carnets: Janvier 1942–Mars 1951* (1964; *Notebooks, 1942–51*, trans. by P. Thody, 1965); *Carnets: Avril 1951–Décembre 1959* (1966; *Notebooks, 1951–59*, trans. by P. Thody, 1969).

BIBLIOGRAPHY. The major bibliographies of works by and about Camus are: R.F. ROEMING (ed. and comp.), *Camus: A Bibliography* (1968); and B.T. FITCH and P.C. HOY, *Essai de bibliographie des études en langue française consacrées à Albert Camus (1937–1967)* (1969). His main works are published with much excellent editorial material by ROGER QUILLIOT in two "Bibliothèque de la Pléiade" volumes: *Théâtre, récits, nouvelles* (1962), and *Essais* (1965). Collections of the author's writings in English translation are *The Collected Fiction of Albert Camus* (1961); *Resistance, Rebellion and Death* (1961); and *Lyrical and Critical* (1967). Camus's main English translators are Stuart Gilbert, Justin O'Brien, and Philip Thody. Good general studies in French include: ROGER QUILLIOT, *La Mer et les prisons*, rev. ed. (1970); J.C. BRISVILLE, *Camus* (1959); and MORVAN LEBESQUE, *Albert Camus par lui-même* (1963). Camus has been fortunate in his English and American critics. Major studies of his personality and writings are GERMAINE BRÉE, *Camus* (1959); JOHN CRUICKSHANK, *Albert Camus and the Literature of Revolt* (1959); and PHILIP THODY, *Albert Camus, 1913–1960* (1961). Two other studies offering clear expository summaries of his ideas are ADELE KING, *Camus* (1964); and P.H. RHEIN, *Albert Camus* (1969). See also EMMETT PARKER, *Albert Camus: The Artist in the Arena* (1965), an excellent analysis of Camus's political writings and ideas on artistic commitment. (J.Cr.)

Canada

The second largest country in the world in area, after the Soviet Union, but one of the most sparsely populated, Canada occupies roughly two-fifths of the North American continent. Its 3,845,274 square miles (9,959,219 square kilometres) of land and freshwater include its adjacent islands, except Greenland, a self-governing part of the Danish kingdom, and Saint-Pierre and Miquelon, parts of the French Republic. Canada is bounded on the north by the Arctic Ocean, on the east by the Atlantic Ocean, on the south by 12 states of the United States, and on the west by the Pacific Ocean and the U.S. state of Alaska. In the 1981 census the population of the 10 provinces and two territories of Canada was about 24,343,000. The national capital is Ottawa.

Because much of Canada's land is mountainous or rocky or has an Arctic climate, the developed area is probably not more than one-half of the total. Occupied farmland comprises less than 8 percent; and the productive forestland, 37 percent. Yet, its geographical position and its shape place Canada in contact with the principal powers and some of the most populous areas in the world. It not only borders the United States for a distance of 5,527 miles (8,895 kilometres), but the peninsula of southern Ontario knifes into the heart of the United States. In the north the Arctic archipelago penetrates far into the Polar Basin and brings Canada close to the Soviet Union and northern Europe. In the east the island of Newfoundland (historically considered to be Britain's oldest colony) commands the shortest crossings of the North Atlantic Ocean, while in the west the arc of the coast provides departure points for routes between North America and the Far East.

For information on related topics, see especially the article CANADA, HISTORY OF and articles on each of the provinces and territories and on MONTREAL, OTTAWA, QUEBEC (CITY), and TORONTO. See also NORTHWEST PASSAGE. The relation of Canada's land to the continent as a whole appears in NORTH AMERICA, while articles on related specific physical features include ARCTIC ISLANDS; ARCTIC OCEAN; BAFFIN BAY; BARENTS SEA; BEAUFORT SEA; COLUMBIA ICEFIELD; COLUMBIA RIVER; FRASER RIVER; FUNDY, BAY OF; GREAT LAKES; GREAT PLAINS; HUDSON BAY; MACKENZIE RIVER; NIAGARA RIVER AND FALLS; PACIFIC COAST RANGES; ROCKY MOUNTAINS; SAINT LAWRENCE, GULF OF; SAINT LAWRENCE RIVER; SAINT LAWRENCE SEAWAY; and YUKON RIVER. The history of literature in Canada is covered in LITERATURE, WESTERN. See also ICE HOCKEY.

I. The natural and human landscape

Overview of the land and settlement

In very general terms, Canada can be considered as a vast basin more than 3,220 miles in diameter. The Cordillera in the west, the Appalachians in the southeast, the mountains of northern Labrador and of Baffin Island in the northeast, and the Innuitian Mountains in the north form its high rim, while Hudson Bay, set close to the centre of the enormous platform of the Canadian Shield, occupies the basin bottom. The western rim of the basin is higher and more massive than its eastern counterpart, and pieces of the rim, notably in the far northwest and in the south, are missing. The main lines of Canadian landforms continue well into the United States, intimately linking the geography north and south of the border. Although terrain and climate always impose conditions on human activity, in Canada their influence on the patterns of human settlement and on the nation's economic development has been critical and pervasive. As a consequence, the Canadian North remains one of the least settled and least exploited parts of the world, contributing significantly to the low population density for the country as a whole.

THE NATURAL ENVIRONMENT

Physical regions. In its broad features, the land comprises eight physical regions. Almost in the centre of the country is the vast Canadian Shield. Bordering the shield are the principal lowlands: in the west, from the United States border to the Beaufort Sea, the vast interior plains; in the east, from the Great Lakes to the Atlantic, the Great Lakes–St. Lawrence lowlands; in the north, the Arctic plains and plateaus. Adjoining the plains in the far west are the high mountains and plateaus of the Canadian Cordillera, part of the backbone of the continent that extends throughout the Americas. In the southeast are the lower mountains of the Appalachian system, and in the far north are the Innuitian ranges.

Finally, where the shield is broken into by Hudson Bay and Hudson Strait, the waters are bordered by the Hudson Bay lowlands. Having recently emerged from below sea level, they are generally low, flat, and covered with ill-drained marshes, mossy (or muskeg) swamps, and bodies of standing water.

The Canadian Shield. By far the largest of Canada's physiographic regions, the Canadian Shield occupies about 49 percent of the total area of the country and is centred about Hudson Bay. It consists of ancient rocks folded by mountain-building movements and cut down by erosion until the area was reduced almost to a plain. It was warped and folded in places so that parts of it now stand much higher than others, especially around its outer edges. In the north the rim is about 7,000 feet (2,000 metres) above sea level, and fjords with walls from 2,000 to 3,000 feet high extend many miles into the mountain masses. South of Hudson Strait lie the Torngat, Kaumajet, and Kiglapait mountains, the heights of which sometimes exceed 5,000 feet. Along the north shore of the St. Lawrence River in Quebec, the shield rim is a 2,000-foot escarpment—the Laurentide Scarp. The rim is almost imperceptible in southern Ontario, but in northern Ontario it rises again to almost 1,500 feet above the north shore of Lake Superior. From Manitoba northwestward the shield edge is marked by a number of lakes, some of which, such as Lake Winnipeg, Lake Athabasca, Great Slave Lake, and Great Bear Lake, are very large.

Most of the shield itself is less than 2,000 feet above sea level. Its lack of hills of any size produces a generally monotonous landscape, but geologically recent glaciations have had a striking effect on the surface. Much of their work was erosive. By stripping off the top, weathered material, they roughened the surface into a type of rock-knob landscape, or a grained landscape, with the hollows between the knobs or the troughs between the ridges occupied by enormous numbers of lakes. In other areas the glaciers deposited till or moraine on the surface and in still others left gigantic fields of erratics and boulders. Eskers—long, narrow ridges of earth deposits—stretch across the shield, sometimes for more than 100 miles, marking the course of old, subglacial rivers. In still other places, deposits laid down by glacial lakes that have since drained away have given rise to extensive clay belts, which may be used for agriculture.

The interior plains. Taking in 18 percent of the total land area of Canada, the interior plains extend southward into the Great Plains of the United States. In the southeast is the Manitoba lowland, with an elevation of less than 1,000 feet above sea level. It includes a number of lakes, some of them very large; most of them are remnants of the huge glacial-age Lake Agassiz, which once occupied all of the lowland and adjacent areas. In the southern portion the Red River Valley is covered with clays and silts that accumulated on the floor of Lake Agassiz and today create a rich farmland. The Mackenzie lowland, in the northwest, is similar to the Manitoba lowland. It is not level throughout, but most of it is flat and covered with muskegs, swamps, and lakes sometimes interrupted by low limestone escarpments.

The Saskatchewan plain to the west of the Manitoba lowland varies in elevation from 1,500 to 2,100 feet above sea level. Its surface is varied with clay plains laid down by glacial lakes and materials deposited by the ice sheets, but its flatness makes it well suited to the use of large-scale farm machinery. Thick accumulations of moraine form occasional isolated ranges of low hills studded with kettle lakes. Undulating plains were formed by material known as glacial till spread over the bedrock by moving ice. Other common features are moraines resulting from the deposition of material, by melting glaciers, at the ice front while it was stagnant or stationary, and flat-bottomed, steep-banked stream channels, cut by the glacial meltwaters, some of which are up to four or five miles in width and 300 feet deep.

The Alberta upland, still farther to the west, is rougher and more elevated, much of it about 2,500 feet above sea level. Water and wind erosion has modified the landscape greatly since the retreat of the ice sheets. The land is deeply dissected by sharp valleys from 200 to 400 feet below the surrounding plain.

The Great Lakes–St. Lawrence lowlands. The four parts of the Great Lakes–St. Lawrence region, although much smaller than those described above, are important because of the large numbers of people living within them. The domelike Huron and Erie lowlands lie between the lakes of the same name and the Niagara Escarpment. As the ice receded from around this dome it halted periodically, and at each stage glacial meltwaters deposited sands and gravels around its edges. These deposits, known as recessional moraines, today ring the central portion of the dome. In this upland portion the glacial meltwaters also cut wide channels, or spillways. Today nearly all these spillways are occupied by streams, but they are much too small to have carved the main valley and are known as misfit streams. Beach deposits and sharp bluffs mark the former glacial shorelines of the present Great Lakes. Shallow, flat-bottomed valleys characterize the monotonously flat clay and silt plains that border the lakes in certain areas. The Ontario lowlands east of the Niagara Escarpment are made up mostly of a till plain traversed by the latitudinally extending Oak Ridges and Dummer moraines. They also include several thousand hills of glacial deposit, or drumlins.

Ottawa–St. Lawrence lowlands

The Ottawa–St. Lawrence lowlands extend east of the Ontario lowlands, from which they are separated by the Frontenac Axis, a narrow belt of ancient Precambrian rocks more than 570,000,000 years old that extends from the Canadian Shield to the Adirondack Mountains in the U.S. state of New York. These lowlands embrace the lower part of the Ottawa Valley and extend to a point some 70 miles below Quebec. The area was inundated by the Champlain Sea when seawater invaded the region as far west as the Frontenac Axis during glacial times. In the west the widest and flattest section of the lowland is pierced by outlying islands of Precambrian rocks that form conspicuous hills, and the levelness of the plain is also broken by the eight Monteregian Hills, the remains of igneous intrusions. The westernmost of these is Mont-Royal in Montreal, 763 feet (262 metres) in altitude. Anticosti Island and the Mingan islands at the mouth of the St. Lawrence form the fourth natural division of the Great Lakes–St. Lawrence region.

The Canadian Cordillera. The Cordilleran region comprises a belt of mountains some 500 miles wide that flanks the Pacific coast of Canada. Its eastern section rises abruptly from the interior plains and trends in a generally north–south direction, except in the far north, where it curves, ultimately, to run almost east–west and into the peninsula of Alaska. Three groups of mountains make up this section: the Richardson and British mountains in the extreme north are separated by the Peel Plateau from the Mackenzie and Franklin mountains, which, in turn, are separated by the Liard Plateau from the Rockies. The Rockies have at least 30 peaks over 10,000 feet high, Mt. Robson, at 12,972 feet (3,954 metres) above sea level, being the highest.

Passes through the Rockies are not numerous. The Yellowhead Pass (3,717 feet; 1,133 metres) is used by the main line of the Canadian National Railway; the Kicking Horse Pass (5,338 feet; 1,627 metres) is used by the main line of the Canadian Pacific Railway as well as the Trans-Canada Highway; and the Crowsnest Pass (4,429 feet; 1,350 metres) is also used by the Canadian Pacific Railway. Snowfields and ice fields add to the scenic attractions of the Rockies, which include five of Canada's national parks, the oldest of which, Banff, was established in 1885.

To the west the eastern ranges are bordered, for most of their length, by a sharp topographical break known as the Rocky Mountain Trench, up to 15 miles wide and several thousand feet deep. West of the trench the relief is generally lower, for plateau forms predominate; but they alternate with deep valleys and local mountain ranges.

Coast mountain scenery

Farther west still lies another belt of mountains some 50 miles wide. The mainland coast comprises the St. Elias and Coast mountains, which embrace some of the grandest and most awesome scenery in the country, including Mt. Logan—which, at 19,524 feet (5,951 metres), is the highest mountain in Canada—and several other peaks of more than 15,000 feet. All along the coast there are spectacular fjords, the steep-sided walls of which often rise above 7,000 feet. Off the coast is a lower chain of mountains that appears as a series of islands, the largest of which are Vancouver Island and the Queen Charlotte Islands. The trough that separates the insular mountains from the mainland has been drowned by the sea and forms an inside passage, an ocean-water route along the west coast.

Appalachian Canada. The Appalachian region extends from the eastern parts of Quebec province northeastward to embrace the Gaspé Peninsula, the Maritime Provinces, and the island of Newfoundland. It consists of very old folded rocks that have been eroded into low, rounded mountains that are dissected by valleys and broken by broader lowland areas developed on belts of weaker rocks. Three broad groups of highlands and uplands can be recognized. The westernmost and highest is made up of Sutton Mountains, Megantic Hills, Notre Dame Mountains, and the Shickshock Hills of Quebec. Elevations in places exceed 4,000 feet. Farther east are the Chaleur uplands and Miramichi highlands. The third and most easterly of the highland groups is made up of the St. Croix highlands, Caledonian highlands, and Nova Scotia highlands and uplands. They merge into one on the island of Newfoundland to form the Long Range, Topsail Hills, Dunamagon Highlands, and Anguille Mountains. The few lowlands of the region—the lowlands of central New Brunswick, Prince Edward Island, the Cumberland lowland, and the Magdalen Islands—generally border the Gulf of St. Lawrence.

The Arctic islands. The Innuitian region flanks the Canadian Shield to the north, extending from northernmost Ellesmere Island to Prince Patrick Island. Much of it is covered with fields of permanent ice and snow through which mountain peaks often protrude. They reach 10,000 feet in the Grantland Mountains (formerly the United States Range).

Drainage. The waters of Hudson Bay and Hudson Strait receive almost one-half of the drainage from the rivers and lakes of Canada. Not much smaller in area than the Hudson Bay Basin is the Arctic Basin, dominated by the Mackenzie, the longest river in Canada, which, with its tributaries, drains 711,000 square miles. The St. Lawrence is the largest river draining into the Atlantic Ocean. Its basin includes the Canadian portions of all of the Great Lakes, forming an inland waterway reaching 2,000 miles into the heart of the continent. The longest river that drains into the Pacific Ocean and is wholly within Canada is the Fraser, but large areas of Canada are drained by the headwaters of the Yukon and the Columbia, both of which have their lower courses in the United States.

Almost all Canadian rivers are characterized by rapids and falls, many of which have been developed for the generation of hydroelectricity. The best known example is Niagara Falls, lying on the Niagara River between Lake Erie and Lake Ontario.

Climate. Because of its great latitudinal extent, Canada experiences a variety of climates, dominated by cold winters, hot summers, and sufficient but not overabundant precipitation. Exceptions are to be found in small areas on the Pacific coast, where, due to the influence of warm ocean waters, the extremes of temperature are not great and where the presence of high mountains causes moderate to heavy precipitation on the western slopes. The same situation, though to a lesser extent, prevails on the Atlantic coast. In winter, average temperatures are below freezing everywhere but the extreme southwest.

Nearly three-quarters of Canada experiences continental climates, with very cold winters but adequate precipitation. These may be subdivided according to the warmth and length of the summer. The sub-Arctic, the coldest, covers 53 percent of Canada. Another subdivision with cool summers covers most of Canada's populous regions. The warm-summer phase, or "cornbelt" type of climate, covers only the southwestern peninsula of Ontario between Lakes Huron and Erie; its climate is similar to that of the Middle West of the United States. The remaining climatic type, similar to that of western Europe, affects the Pacific coast and is characterized by its mild winters.

Temperatures. Those parts of the country farthest from open water are the coldest, so that in the interior plains and in the North the winters are extremely cold. The lowest temperature ever recorded was −81° F (−63° C) at Snag in the Yukon. In July those parts of Canada farthest from open water are the warmest. Thus, west-coast Vancouver has an average January temperature of 37° F (3° C) and an average July temperature of 64° F (18° C), while on the Prairies Regina's temperatures vary from 2° to 67° F (−17° to 19° C). The daily range of temperature is also less on the coasts than in interior locations. The highest temperature recorded was 115° F (46° C) at Gleichen in southern Alberta.

Rainfall. Humid air masses from the Pacific cause enormous quantities of orographic (mountain-caused) rain to fall on the coast and mountain areas—Henderson Lake, on Vancouver Island, receives an average annual rainfall of 262 inches (6,650 millimetres). But the orographic effect is not the whole explanation, since southern British Columbia receives much less precipitation in summer than in winter because low-pressure, rain-producing systems move in a more northerly track in summer and seldom cross the southern part of the coast. Vancouver has an annual average precipitation of 41 inches.

Impact of the Pacific and Rockies on precipitation

In the Prairies and the North, precipitation is low. Seldom more than 15 inches a year, it is as low as two inches at Eureka on Ellesmere Island. The west-coast mountains quite effectively keep marine air out, since the dominant movement of air in Canada is from west to east. Spring and summer are wetter than winter, however, because the air is warmer and can hold more water vapour and because the melting of accumulated snow provides moisture. Thunderstorms in the Prairies reprecipitate moisture that has evaporated, thus helping to prevent water vapour from being removed from the area.

Ontario and Quebec have more rainfall than the Prairies because the air masses can pick up water vapour from the Great Lakes, Hudson Bay, the Atlantic Ocean, and the Gulf of Mexico. The average annual precipitation for Toronto is 30 inches; for Montreal, 41 inches. Since the winters are not as cold as those in the Prairies, the air is less dry, and enough snow falls to make winter precipitation equal to that in summer. The Atlantic Provinces are wetter than those of Central Canada. Yearly rainfall, most of which is cyclonic in origin, is more than 50 inches in many places and is fairly evenly distributed throughout the year. Because the weather in summer is usually cool, there are few thunderstorms, and the low Appalachian Mountains produce only a little orographic rainfall. In general, the rainfall on Canada's east coast is less than on the west coast because the prevailing wind is offshore.

Snowfall. Canada's snowfall does not follow the same pattern as rainfall. In the North and the Prairies, snowfall is light because cold air is very dry. The snow is hard and dry, falls in small amounts, and is packed down by the constant wind. The east and west coasts are areas of lighter snowfall because the ocean usually makes the air too warm for large quantities of snow to fall. The depth of snow increases inland from each coast, reaching maximums of about 240 inches in the Rocky Mountains and on the shores of the Gulf of St. Lawrence. Still farther inland, lack of moisture brings the depth of snow down again. Freezing precipitation may occur during the colder months in any part of the country, and it occasionally seriously disrupts transportation and communication in southeastern Canada.

Vegetation. The relief of the land and the climate are largely responsible for the distribution of plants. The chief plant associations are the forests, grasslands, and tundra. The forests under natural conditions once formed the cover of about 65 percent of Canada; tundra, about 20 percent; and grasslands, about 10 percent. The remaining 5 percent, either bare rock or permanent ice and snow, is devoid of vegetation. Much of the southern edge of the forests and most of the grasslands have been replaced by agriculture.

Forest zones. Three broad zones of forest occur in Canada: the eastern, the northern, and the western. The eastern forests, from the basin of the Great Lakes to the St. Lawrence Valley and the lowlands of the Maritimes, is the plant response to low plains, a relatively long growing season, and humid, temperate conditions. In the most southerly parts, the flat plains bordering Lake Erie, are remnants of a predominantly deciduous forest of oak, hickory, and chestnut, together with maple, elm, and walnut. Farther north, on the hillier morainic land of central and eastern Ontario and on the terraces overlooking the St. Lawrence, is a mixed deciduous–coniferous forest of sugar maple, beech, yellow birch, white and red pine, and hemlock. Between the hills of the Maritimes, a mixed deciduous–coniferous forest prevails.

The northern coniferous, or boreal, forest is one of the largest in the world, stretching from Newfoundland across Canada to the border of Alaska. The region has in common extensive glaciation, rather infertile and acid soils, severe winters, and a short growing season. Only a limited number of tree species do well under these circumstances. White and black spruce and white birch are common throughout the region, and balsam, poplar, and tamarack trees are also widely distributed. Species with more limited distribution are balsam fir, jack pine, and trembling aspen. Thus, the boreal forest is ideal for logging for pulpwood. Along its northern fringes the boreal forest merges with the tundra to produce a zone of forest–tundra transition. In the south, it similarly merges with the grasslands to produce a zone of aspen parkland, or forest–grassland transition, an area dotted with clumps of trees that are continuous only in the river valleys.

The western forests

The western forests of the Cordillera are very complex, as might be expected from the strong relief and the sudden change in climate within relatively short distances. The subalpine forest, of Engelmann and white spruce and lodgepole pine, is characteristic of the slopes of the Rockies from about 4,000 feet up to the timberline. The forests of the Selkirk and Purcell mountains contain Engelmann spruce at higher elevations, merging with western red cedar and western hemlock on the lower slopes. On

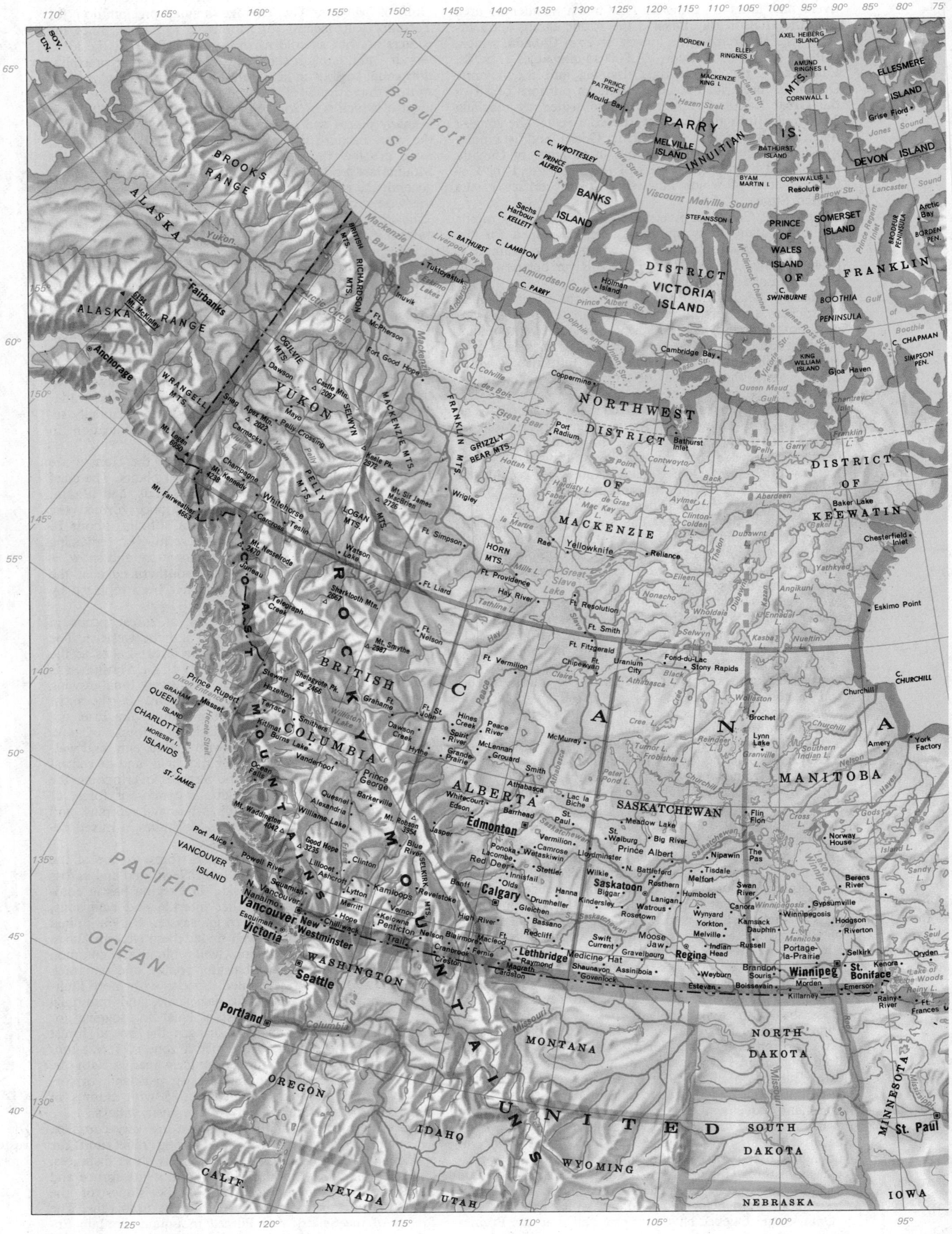

CANADA Size of symbol indicates relative size of town

Elevations in metres

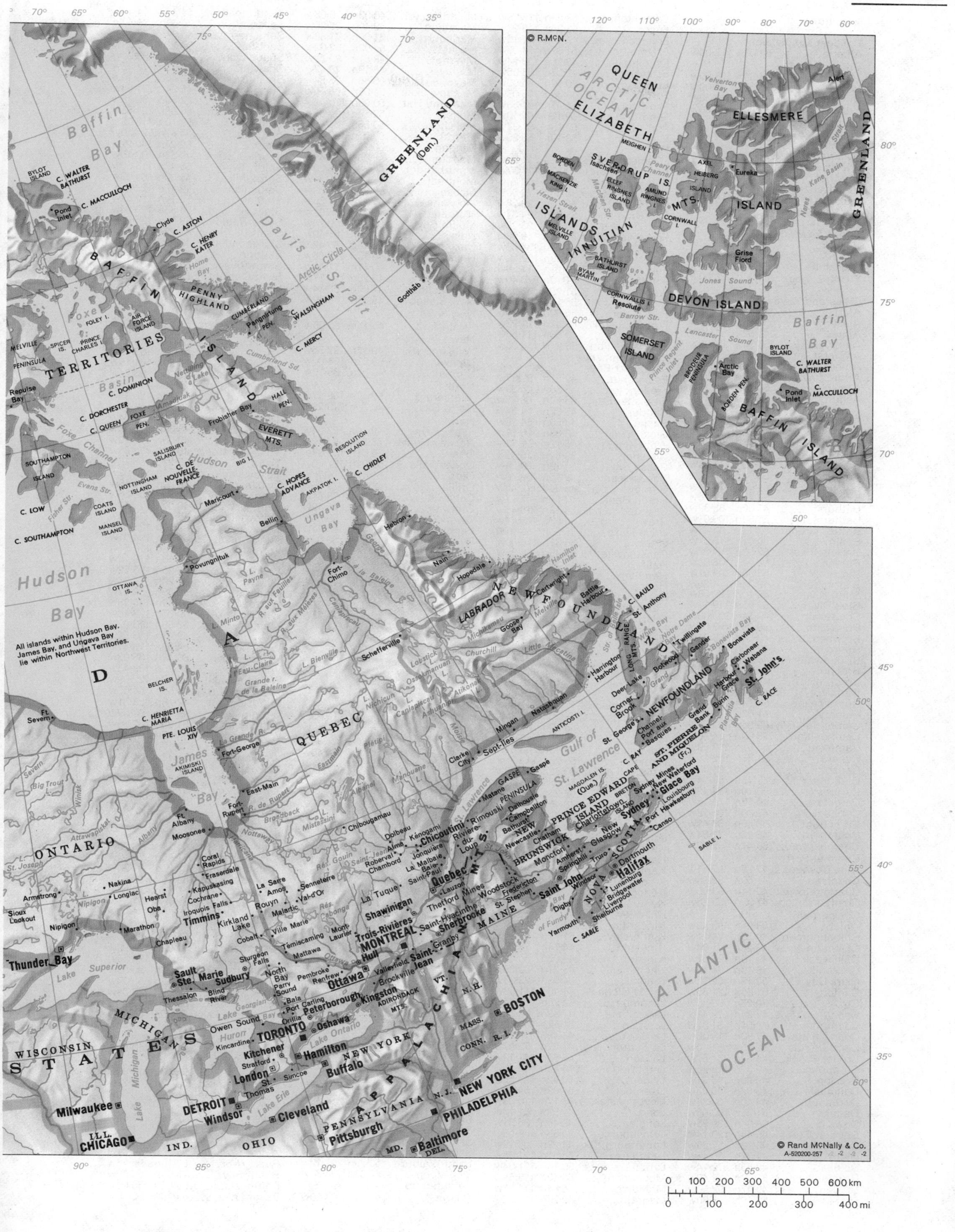
© R.McN.
QUEEN ELIZABETH ISLANDS
ARCTIC OCEAN
ELLESMERE ISLAND
GREENLAND
SVERDRUP IS.
INNUITIAN MTS.
AXEL HEIBERG ISLAND
Eureka
Alert
Grise Fiord
DEVON ISLAND
Jones Sound
Resolute
SOMERSET ISLAND
Lancaster Sound
Baffin Bay
BYLOT ISLAND
C. WALTER BATHURST
Arctic Bay
Pond Inlet
C. MACCULLOCH
BAFFIN ISLAND
MELVILLE ISLAND
BATHURST ISLAND
CORNWALLIS I.
CORNWALL I.
ELLEF RINGNES ISLAND
AMUND RINGNES I.
BORDEN PEN.
BRODEUR PENINSULA
Prince Regent Inlet
Barrow Str.
Baffin Bay
GREENLAND (Den.)
Davis Strait
Godthåb
Arctic Circle
BAFFIN ISLAND
PENNY HIGHLAND
CUMBERLAND PEN.
Pangnirtung
C. WALSINGHAM
C. MERCY
C. ASTON
C. HENRY KATER
Clyde
Home Bay
Foxe Basin
TERRITORIES
Repulse Bay
MELVILLE PENINSULA
C. DORCHESTER
C. QUEEN
C. DOMINION
FOXE PEN.
Frobisher Bay
HALL PEN.
EVERETT MTS.
RESOLUTION ISLAND
C. CHIDLEY
Foxe Channel
SOUTHAMPTON ISLAND
Hudson Strait
C. DE NOUVELLE-FRANCE
C. HOPES ADVANCE
AKPATOK I.
Maricourt
Bellin
Ungava Bay
NOTTINGHAM ISLAND
SALISBURY ISLAND
COATS ISLAND
MANSEL ISLAND
C. LOW
C. SOUTHAMPTON
Hudson Bay
OTTAWA IS.
Povungnituk
Fort-Chimo
Hebron
Nain
Hopedale
Cartwright
Battle Harbour
LABRADOR
NEWFOUNDLAND
Goose Bay
C. BAULD
St. Anthony
Schefferville
Twillingate
Gander
Bonavista
Carbonear
Wabana
St. John's
C. RACE
All islands within Hudson Bay, James Bay, and Ungava Bay lie within Northwest Territories.
BELCHER IS.
C. HENRIETTA MARIA
PTE. LOUIS XIV
Ft. Severn
QUEBEC
Fort-George
James Bay
AKIMISKI ISLAND
East-Main
Fort-Rupert
Ft. Albany
Moosonee
ONTARIO
Harrington Harbour
Natashquan
Mingan
ANTICOSTI I.
Sept-Îles
Clarke City
Gulf of St. Lawrence
Deer Lake
Corner Brook
Botwood
NEWFOUNDLAND
St. George's
Channel-Port aux Basques
Grand Bank
Burin
Harbour Grace
ST. PIERRE AND MIQUELON (Fr.)
MAGDALEN IS. (Que.)
Gaspé
GASPÉ PENINSULA
Matane
Rimouski
Chicoutimi
Jonquière
Kénogami
Dolbeau
Alma
Roberval
Chambord
La Malbaie
Chibougamau
Rivière-du-Loup
Campbellton
Dalhousie
Bathurst
NEW BRUNSWICK
Newcastle
Chatham
Moncton
PRINCE EDWARD ISLAND
Charlottetown
CAPE BRETON ISLAND
Sydney
Glace Bay
Sydney Mines
New Waterford
Louisbourg
Port Hawkesbury
Canso
SABLE I.
New Glasgow
Truro
Amherst
Springhill
NOVA SCOTIA
Dartmouth
Halifax
Lunenburg
Bridgewater
Liverpool
Shelburne
Yarmouth
Digby
Windsor
C. SABLE
Saint John
St. Stephen
Fredericton
Woodstock
MAINE
Bay of Fundy
Quebec
Lauzon
Thetford Mines
Sherbrooke
Saint-Hyacinthe
Granby
Saint-Jean
La Tuque
Shawinigan
Trois-Rivières
MONTREAL
Hull
Ottawa
Kingston
Brockville
Valleyfield
ADIRONDACK MTS.
VT.
N.H.
MASS.
BOSTON
CONN.
R.I.
NEW YORK CITY
N.J.
PHILADELPHIA
Baltimore
MD.
DEL.
PENNSYLVANIA
Pittsburgh
NEW YORK
Buffalo
Cleveland
OHIO
IND.
ILL.
CHICAGO
Milwaukee
WISCONSIN
MICHIGAN
STATES
DETROIT
Windsor
London
St. Thomas
Simcoe
Lake Erie
Stratford
Kitchener
Hamilton
TORONTO
Oshawa
Lake Ontario
Peterborough
Orillia
Owen Sound
Kincardine
Lake Huron
Georgian Bay
Parry Sound
Bala
Port Carling
Pembroke
Renfrew
North Bay
Sturgeon Falls
Sudbury
Sault Ste. Marie
Thessalon
Blind River
Lake Superior
Thunder Bay
Nipigon
Marathon
Chapleau
Sioux Lookout
Armstrong
Nakina
Longlac
Hearst
Oba
Kapuskasing
Cochrane
Iroquois Falls
Timmins
Kirkland Lake
Cobalt
Rouyn
Malartic
Val-d'Or
Amos
La Sarre
Senneterre
Ville Marie
Témiscaming
Mattawa
Mont-Laurier
Coral Rapids
Fraserdale
APPALACHIAN MTS.
ATLANTIC OCEAN
© Rand McNally & Co.
A-520200-257
0 100 200 300 400 500 600 km
0 100 200 300 400 mi

MAP INDEX

Political subdivisions

Alberta 54·00n 113·00w
British Columbia 54·00n 125·00w
Manitoba 54·00n 97·00w
New Brunswick 47·00n 66·00w
Newfoundland 52·00n 56·00w
Northwest Territories 70·00n 100·00w
Franklin, District of 72·00n 100·00w
Keewatin, District of 65·00n 95·00w
MacKenzie, District of 65·00n 115·00w
Nova Scotia 45·00n 63·00w
Ontario 51·00n 85·00w
Prince Edward Island 46·30n 63·00w
Quebec 46·50n 71·20w
Saskatchewan 54·00n 105·00w
Yukon 64·00n 135·00w

Cities and towns

Alert 82·31n 62·05w
Alexandria 52·38n 122·27w
Alma 48·32n 71·40w
Amery 56·34n 94·03w
Amherst 45·49n 64·14w
Amos 48·34n 78·07w
Arctic Bay 73·02n 85·11w
Armstrong 50·18n 89·02w
Ashcroft 50·43n 121·17w
Assiniboia 49·38n 105·59w
Athabasca 54·43n 113·17w
Baie-Saint-Paul 47·27n 70·30w
Baker Lake 64·15n 96·00w
Bala 45·01n 79·37w
Banff 51·10n 115·34w
Barkerville 53·04n 121·31w
Barrhead 54·08n 114·24w
Bassano 50·47n 112·28w
Bathurst 47·36n 65·39w
Bathurst Inlet 66·50n 108·01w
Battle Harbour 52·17n 55·35w
Bellin 60·01n 70·01w
Berens River 52·22n 97·02w
Biggar 52·04n 108·00w
Big River 53·50n 107·01w
Blairmore 49·36n 114·26w
Blind River 46·10n 82·58w
Blue River 52·05n 119·17w
Boissevain 49·14n 100·03w
Bonavista 48·39n 53·07w
Botwood 49·08n 55·21w
Brandon 49·50n 99·57w
Bridgewater 44·23n 64·31w
Brochet 57·53n 101·40w
Brockville 44·35n 75·41w
Burin 47·02n 55·10w
Burns Lake 54·14n 125·36w
Calgary 51·03n 114·05w
Cambridge Bay 69·03n 105·05w
Campbellton 48·00n 66·40w
Camrose 53·01n 112·50w
Canora 51·37n 102·26w
Canso 45·20n 61·00w
Carbonear 47·45n 53·14w
Carcross 60·10n 134·42w
Cardston 49·12n 113·18w
Carmacks 62·05n 136·18w
Cartwright 53·50n 56·45w
Chambord 48·26n 72·04w
Champagne 60·47n 136·29w
Channel-Port aux Basques 47·35n 59·11w
Chapleau 47·50n 82·24w
Charlottetown 46·14n 63·08w
Chatham 47·02n 65·28w
Chesterfield Inlet 63·21n 90·42w
Chibougamau 49·53n 74·21w
Chicoutimi 48·26n 71·04w
Chilliwack 49·10n 121·57w
Churchill 58·46n 94·10w
Clark City 50·12n 66·38w
Clinton 51·05n 121·35w
Clyde 70·25n 68·30w
Cobalt 47·24n 79·41w
Cochrane 49·04n 81·01w
Coppermine 67·50n 115·05w
Coral Rapids 50·15n 81·40w
Corner Brook 48·57n 57·57w
Cranbrook 49·31n 115·46w
Creston 49·06n 116·31w
Dalhousie 48·04n 66·23w
Dartmouth 44·40n 63·34w
Dauphin 51·09n 100·03w
Dawson 64·04n 139·25w
Dawson Creek 55·46n 120·14w
Deer Lake 49·10n 57·25w
Digby 44·37n 65·46w
Dolbeau 48·53n 72·14w
Drumheller 51·28n 112·42w
Dryden 49·47n 92·50w
East-Main 52·15n 78·30w
Edmonton 53·33n 113·28w
Edson 53·35n 116·26w
Emerson 49·00n 97·12w
Eskimo Point 61·07n 94·03w
Esquimalt 48·26n 123·24w
Estevan 49·07n 103·05w
Eureka 80·09n 86·00w
Fernie 49·30n 115·03w
Flin Flon 54·46n 101·53w
Fond-du-Lac 59·19n 107·10w
Fort Albany 52·15n 81·37w
Fort-Chimo 58·10n 68·30w
Fort Chipewyan 58·42n 111·08w
Fort Fitzgerald 59·53n 111·37w
Fort Frances 48·36n 93·24w
Fort-George 53·50n 79·00w
Fort Good Hope 66·15n 128·38w
Fort Grahame 56·38n 124·37w
Fort Liard 60·15n 123·28w
Fort Macleod 49·43n 113·25w
Fort McPherson 67·27n 134·53w
Fort Nelson 58·49n 122·39w
Fort Providence 61·21n 117·39w
Fort Resolution 61·10n 113·40w
Fort-Rupert 51·29n 78·45w
Fort Saint John 56·15n 120·51w
Fort Severn 56·00n 87·38w
Fort Simpson 61·52n 121·23w
Fort Smith 60·00n 111·53w
Fort Vermilion 58·24n 116·00w
Fort William, see Thunder Bay
Fraserdale 49·51n 81·37w
Fredericton 45·58n 66·39w
Frobisher Bay 63·44n 68·28w
Gander 48·57n 54·34w
Gaspé 48·50n 64·29w
Gjoa Haven 68·38n 95·57w
Glace Bay 46·12n 59·57w
Gleichen 50·52n 113·02w
Goose Bay 53·19n 60·24w
Govenlock 49·15n 109·48w
Granby 45·24n 72·43w
Grand Bank 47·06n 55·47w
Grande-Prairie 55·10n 118·48w
Gravelbourg 49·53n 106·34w
Grise Fiord 76·25n 83·01w
Grouard 55·31n 116·09w
Gypsumville 51·45n 98·35w
Halifax 44·39n 63·36w
Hamilton 43·15n 79·51w
Hanna 51·38n 111·54w
Harbour Grace 47·42n 53·13w
Harrington Harbour 50·30n 59·29w
Hay River 60·51n 115·40w
Hazelton 55·15n 127·40w
Hearst 49·41n 83·40w
Hebron 58·12n 62·38w
High River 50·35n 113·52w
Hines Creek 56·15n 118·36w
Hodgson 51·13n 97·34w
Holman Island 70·43n 117·43w
Hope 49·23n 121·26w
Hopedale 55·50n 60·10w
Hull 45·26n 75·43w
Humboldt 52·12n 105·07w
Hythe 55·20n 119·33w
Indian Head 50·32n 103·40w
Innisfail 52·02n 113·57w
Inuvik 68·25n 133·30w
Iroquois Falls 48·46n 80·41w
Isachsen 78·47n 103·32w
Jasper 52·53n 118·05w
Jonquière 48·25n 71·15w
Kamloops 50·40n 120·20w
Kamsack 51·34n 101·54w
Kapuskasing 49·25n 82·26w
Kelowna 49·53n 119·29w
Kénogami 48·26n 71·14w
Kenora 49·47n 94·29w
Killarney 49·12n 99·42w
Kincardine 44·11n 81·38w
Kindersley 51·27n 109·10w
Kingston 44·14n 76·30w
Kirkland Lake 48·09n 80·02w
Kitchener 43·27n 80·29w
Kitimat 54·03n 128·33w
Lac la Biche 54·46n 111·58w
Lacombe 52·28n 113·44w
La Malbaie 47·39n 70·10w
Lanigan 51·52n 105·02w
La Sarre 48·48n 79·12w
La Tuque 47·27n 72·47w
Lauzon 46·50n 71·10w
Lethbridge 49·42n 110·50w
Lillooet 50·42n 121·56w
Liverpool 44·02n 64·43w
Lloydminster 53·17n 110·00w
London 42·59n 81·14w
Longlac 49·48n 86·31w
Louisbourg 45·55n 59·58w
Lunenburg 44·23n 64·19w
Lynn Lake 56·51n 101·03w
Lytton 50·14n 121·34w
McLennan 53·42n 116·54w
McMurray 56·44n 111·23w
Magrath 49·25n 112·52w
Malartic 48·08n 78·08w
Marathon 49·46n 86·26w
Maricourt 61·36n 71·58w
Masset 54·02n 132·09w
Matane 48·51n 67·32w
Mattawa 46·19n 78·42w
Mayo 63·35n 135·54w
Meadow Lake 54·08n 108·26w
Medicine Hat 50·03n 110·40w
Melfort 52·52n 104·36w
Melville 50·55n 102·48w
Merritt 50·07n 120·47w
Mingan 50·18n 64·02w
Moncton 46·06n 64·47w
Mont-Laurier 46·33n 75·30w
Montreal 45·31n 73·34w
Moose Jaw 50·23n 105·32w
Moosonee 51·17n 80·39w
Morden 49·11n 98·05w
Mould Bay 76·14n 119·20w
Nain 57·00n 61·40w
Nakina 50·10n 86·42w
Nanaimo 49·10n 123·56w
Natashquan 50·11n 61·49w
Nelson 49·29n 117·17w
Newcastle 47·00n 65·34w
New Glasgow 45·35n 62·39w
New Waterford 46·15n 60·05w
New Westminster 49·12n 122·55w
Nipawin 53·22n 104·00w
Nipigon 49·01n 88·16w
North Battleford 52·47n 108·17w
North Bay 46·19n 79·28w
North Vancouver 49·19n 123·04w
Norway House 53·59n 97·50w
Oba 35·58n 136·04e
Ocean Falls 52·21n 127·40w
Olds 51·47n 114·06w
Orillia 44·37n 79·25w
Oshawa 43·54n 78·51w
Ottawa 45·25n 75·42w
Owen Sound 44·34n 80·56w
Pangnirtung 66·08n 65·44w
Parry Sound 45·21n 80·02w
Peace River 56·14n 117·17w
Pelly Crossing 62·50n 136·35w
Pembroke 47·49n 77·07w
Penticton 49·30n 119·35w
Peterborough 44·18n 78·19w
Pond Inlet 72·41n 78·00w
Ponoka 52·42n 113·35w
Portage-la-Prairie 49·57n 98·25w
Port Alice 50·23n 127·27w
Port Arthur, see Thunder Bay
Port Carling 45·07n 79·35w
Port Hawkesbury 45·37n 61·21w
Port Radium 66·05n 118·02w
Povungnituk 59·12n 77·51w
Powell River 49·52n 124·33w
Prince Albert 53·12n 104·46w
Prince George 54·20n 130·11w
Prince Rupert 54·19n 130·19w
Quebec 46·49n 71·13w
Quesnel 52·59n 122·30w
Rae 62·50n 116·03w
Rainy River 48·43n 94·29w
Raymond 49·27n 112·39w
Redcliff 50·05n 110·47w
Red Deer 52·16n 113·48w
Regina 50·25n 104·39w
Reliance 41·40n 109·12w
Renfrew 45·28n 76·41w
Repulse Bay 66·32n 86·15w
Resolute 74·41n 94·54w
Revelstoke 50·59n 118·12w
Rimouski 48·27n 68·32w
Riverton 50·59n 96·59w
Rivière-du-Loup 47·50n 69·32w
Roberval 48·31n 72·13w
Rosetown 51·33n 108·00w
Rosthern 52·40n 106·17w
Rouyn 48·14n 79·01w
Russell 50·47n 101·15w
Sachs Harbour 72·00n 125·00w
Saint Anthony 51·22n 55·35w
Saint Boniface 49·55n 97·06w
Saint George's 48·26n 58·29w
Saint-Hyacinthe 45·38n 72·57w
Saint-Jean 45·19n 73·16w
Saint John 45·16n 66·03w
Saint John's 47·34n 52·43w
Saint Paul 53·59n 111·17w
Saint Stephen 45·12n 67·17w
Saint Thomas 42·47n 81·12w
Saint Walburg 53·39n 109·12w
Saskatoon 52·07n 106·38w
Sault Sainte Marie 46·31n 84·20w
Schefferville 54·47n 64·49w
Selkirk 50·09n 96·52w
Senneterre 48·24n 77·14w
Sept-Îles 50·12n 66·23w
Shaunavon 49·40n 108·25w
Shawinigan 46·33n 72·45w
Shelburne 43·46n 65·19w
Sherbrooke 45·24n 71·54w
Simcoe 42·50n 80·18w
Sioux Lookout 50·06n 91·55w
Smith 55·10n 114·02w
Smithers 54·47n 127·10w
Snag 62·24n 140·22w
Souris 49·38n 100·15w
Spirit River 55·47n 118·50w
Springhill 45·39n 64·03w
Squamish 49·42n 123·09w
Stettler 52·19n 112·43w
Stewart 55·56n 129·59w
Stony Rapids 59·16n 105·50w
Stratford 43·22n 80·57w
Sturgeon Falls 46·22n 79·55w
Sudbury 46·30n 81·00w
Swan River 52·06n 101·16w
Swift Current 50·17n 107·50w
Sydney 46·09n 60·11w
Sydney Mines 46·14n 60·14w
Telegraph Creek 57·55n 131·10w
Témiscaming 46·44n 79·06w
Terrace 54·31n 128·35w
Teslin 60·09n 132·45w
The Pas 53·50n 101·15w
Thessalon 46·15n 83·34w
Thetford Mines 46·05n 71·18w
Thunder Bay 48·23n 89·15w
Timmins 48·28n 81·20w
Tisdale 52·51n 104·04w
Toronto 43·39n 79·23w
Trail 49·06n 117·42w
Trois-Rivières 46·21n 72·33w
Truro 45·22n 63·16w
Tuktoyaktuk 69·27n 133·02w
Twillingate 49·39n 54·46w
Uranium City 59·34n 108·36w
Val-d'Or 48·07n 77·47w
Valleyfield 45·15n 74·08w
Vancouver 49·16n 123·07w
Vanderhoof 54·01n 124·01w
Vermilion 53·22n 110·51w
Vernon 50·16n 119·16w
Victoria 48·25n 123·22w
Ville Marie 47·20n 79·26w
Wabana 47·38n 52·57w
Watrous 51·40n 105·28w
Watson Lake 60·07n 128·48w
Wetaskiwin 52·58n 113·22w
Weyburn 49·41n 103·52w
Whitecourt 54·09n 115·41w
Whitehorse 60·43n 135·03w
Wilkie 52·25n 108·43w
Williams Lake 52·08n 122·09w
Windsor, N.S. 44·59n 64·08w
Windsor, Ont. 42·18n 83·01w
Winnipeg 49·53n 97·09w
Winnipegosis 51·39n 99·56w
Woodstock 46·09n 67·34w
Wrigley 63·16n 123·37w
Wynyard 51·47n 104·10w
Yarmouth 43·50n 66·07w
Yellowknife 62·27n 114·21w
York Factory 57·00n 92·18w
Yorkton 51·13n 102·28w

Physical features and points of interest

Aberdeen Lake 64·27n 99·00w
Air Force Island 67·55n 74·10w
Akimiski Island 53·00n 81·20w
Akpatok Island 60·25n 68·00w
Albanel, Lake 51·09n 73·00w
Albany, *river* 52·17n 81·31w
Amadjuak Lake 65·00n 71·00w
Amund Ringnes Island 78·00n 97·00w
Amundsen Gulf 71·00n 124·00w
Anderson, *river* 69·43n 128·58w
Angikuni Lake 62·13n 99·50w
Anticosti Island 49·30n 63·00w
Apex Mountain 62·28n 138·04w
Arctic Ocean 81·00n 110·00w
Ashuanipi Lake 52·35n 66·10w
Aston, Cape 70·03n 67·23w
Athabasca, *river* 58·40n 110·50w
Athabasca, Lake 59·07n 110·00w
Atikonak Lake 52·40n 64·30w
Atlantic Ocean 40·00n 65·00w
Attawapiskat, *river* 52·18n 87·54w
Axel Heiberg Island 80·30n 92·00w
Aylmer Lake 45·50n 71·21w
Back, *river* 67·15n 95·15w
Baffin Bay 73·00n 66·00w
Baffin Island 68·00n 70·00w
Baker Lake 64·10n 95·30w

MAP INDEX (continued)

Baleine, Grande Rivière de la, *river*...........55·15n 77·45w
Baleine, Rivière à la, *river*......58·20n 67·40w
Banks Island....73·15n 121·30w
Barrow Strait...74·21n 94·10w
Bathurst, Cape..70·35n 128·00w
Bathurst Island.76·00n 100·30w
Bauld, Cape....51·38n 55·27w
Beaufort Sea...72·30n 138·00w
Belcher Islands.56·20n 79·30w
Belle Isle, Strait of........51·35n 56·30w
Bienville, Lac, *lake*...........55·05n 72·45w
Big Island......62·43n 70·43w
Big Trout Lake..44·56n 78·56w
Black Lake......59·10n 105·20w
Bois, Lac des, *lake*...........66·40n 125·15w
Bonavista Bay..48·45n 53·20w
Boothia, Gulf of.........71·00n 91·00w
Boothia Peninsula......70·30n 95·00w
Borden Island...78·30n 111·30w
Borden Peninsula......73·00n 83·00w
British Mountains.....69·20n 140·20w
Broadback, *river*...........51·20n 78·50w
Brodeur Peninsula......73·00n 88·00w
Byam Martin Island.........75·15n 104·00w
Bylot Island....73·13n 78·34w
Cabonga, Réservoir......47·25n 76·35w
Caniapiscau, Lac, *lake*......54·15n 69·50w
Caniapiscau, Rivière, *river*...57·40n 69·30w
Cape Breton Island.........46·00n 60·30w
Castle Mountain.....64·35n 135·55w
Chantrey Inlet...67·48n 96·20w
Chapman, Cape..........69·12n 88·59w
Chidley, Cape...60·25n 64·30w
Churchill, *river*, Man.-Sask.......58·47n 94·12w
Churchill, *river*, Newf.............53·30n 60·10w
Churchill, Cape.58·46n 93·12w
Claire, Lake.....58·30n 112·00w
Clinton-Colden Lake..........63·58n 107·27w
Coast Mountains.....55·00n 129·00w
Coats Island....62·30n 83·00w
Colville, Lake...67·10n 126·00w
Contwoyto Lake.65·42n 110·50w
Cornwallis Island.........75·15n 94·30w
Cornwall Island.77·40n 94·15w
Cree, *river*......59·00n 105·47w
Cree Lake.......57·30n 106·30w
Cross Lake......54·45n 97·30w
Cumberland Peninsula......66·50n 64·00w
Cumberland Sound.........65·10n 65·30w
Davis Strait.....68·00n 58·00w
Dease Strait....68·40n 108·00w
Devon Island...75·00n 87·00w
Dixon Entrance, *straits*.........54·25n 132·30w
Dolphin and Union Strait...69·05n 114·45w
Dominion, Cape..........66·13n 74·28w
Dorchester, Cape..........65·29n 77·30w
Dubawnt, *river*..64·33n 100·06w
Dubawnt Lake..63·08n 101·30w
Eastmain, *river*..52·20n 78·30w
Eau-Claire, Lac à l', *lake*...56·10n 74·30w
Eileen Lake.....62·16n 107·37w
Ellef Ringnes Island.........78·30n 104·00w
Ellesmere Island.........81·00n 80·00w
Ennadai Lake...60·53n 101·15w
Erie, Lake.......42·15n 81·00w
Eskimo Lakes...69·15n 132·17w
Evans Strait.....63·15n 82·00w
Everett Mountains......62·45n 67·12w
Faber Lake......63·56n 117·15w
Fairweather, Mount, *mountain*......58·54n 137·32w
Feuilles, Rivière aux, *river*...........58·45n 70·00w
Fisher Strait....63·15n 83·30w
Foley Island.....68·35n 75·10w
Foxe Basin......68·25n 77·00w
Foxe Channel...64·30n 80·00w
Foxe Peninsula..65·00n 76·00w
Franklin Lake...66·56n 96·03w
Franklin Mountains.....63·15n 123·30w
Fraser, *river*.....49·09n 123·12w
Frobisher Lake..56·25n 108·20w
Fundy, Bay of....45·00n 66·00w
Garry Lake......66·00n 100·00w
Gaspé Peninsula......48·30n 65·00w
George, *river*...58·30n 66·00w
Georgian Bay...45·15n 80·50w
Gods Lake.......54·45n 94·00w
Good Hope, *mountain*......51·09n 124·10w
Gouin, Réservoir.......48·35n 74·50w
Graham Island..53·50n 132·40w
Grand Lake.....49·00n 57·25w
Granville Lake...56·18n 100·30w
Gras, Lac de, *lake*...........64·30n 110·30w
Great Bear Lake..........66·00n 120·00w
Great Slave Lake..........61·30n 114·00w
Grizzly Bear Mountains.....65·22n 121·00w
Hall Peninsula..63·30n 66·00w
Hamilton Inlet...54·05n 58·30w
Hardisty Lake...64·30n 117·45w
Harricana, *river*.51·10n 79·45w
Hayes, *river*.....57·03n 92·09w
Hazen Strait....77·00n 110·00w
Hecate Strait...53·00n 131·00w
Henrietta Maria, Cape..........55·09n 82·20w
Henry Kater, Cape..........69·05n 66·44w
Home Bay.......68·45n 67·10w
Hopes Advance, Cape..........61·05n 69·35w
Horn Mountains.....62·20n 120·15w
Hottah Lake.....65·04n 118·29w
Hudson Bay.....60·00n 86·00w
Hudson Strait...62·30n 72·00w
Huron, Lake.....44·30n 82·15w
Innuitian Mountains.....77·00n 102·00w
Island Lake.....53·58n 94·47w
James Bay......51·00n 80·30w
James Ross Strait..........69·40n 95·30w
Jones Sound....76·00n 85·00w
Kane Basin, *bay*.............79·00n 70·00w
Kasba Lake.....60·18n 102·07w
Kazan, *river*.....64·02n 95·30w
Keele Peak.....63·26n 130·19w
Kellett, Cape....71·59n 125·34w
Kennedy, Mount, *mountain*......60·30n 139·00w
King William Island.........69·00n 97·30w
Kluane Lake....61·15n 138·40w
Labrador, *historic region*..54·00n 62·30w
La Grande Rivière, *river*...53·50n 79·00w
Lambton, Cape..71·05n 123·10w
Lancaster Sound.........74·13n 84·00w
Liard, *river*....61·52n 121·18w
Little Mecatina, *river*...........50·28n 59·36w
Liverpool Bay...69·45n 130·00w
Lobstick Lake...54·00n 64·50w
Logan, Mount, *mountain*......60·34n 140·24w
Logan Mountains.....61·30n 129·00w
Long Range Mountains.....50·00n 57·00w
Louis XIV, Pointe.........54·35n 79·50w
Low, Cape......63·07n 85·18w
M'Clintock Channel.....71·00n 101,00w
M'Clure Strait...74·30n 116·00w
Macculloch, Cape..........72·29n 75·06w
Mac Kay Lake...63·55n 110·25w
Mackenzie, *river*...........69·15n 134·08w
Mackenzie Bay..69·00n 136·30w
Mackenzie King Island.........77·45n 111·00w
Mackenzie Mountains.....64·00n 130·00w
Maclean Strait..78·00n 105·00w
Magdalen Islands.........47·20n 61·50w
Manitoba, Lake..51·00n 98·45w
Manouane Lake.50·40n 70·45w
Mansel Island...62·00n 79·50w
Martre, Lac la, *lake*...........63·15n 116·55w
Meighen Island.........80·00n 98·30w
Mélèzes, Rivière aux, *river*...........57·40n 69·30w
Melville, Lake...53·45n 59·30w
Melville Island..75·15n 110·00w
Melville Peninsula......68·00n 84·00w
Mercy, Cape....64·56n 63·40w
Michikamau, *lake*...........54·00n 64·00w
Mills Lake.......47·59n 123·36w
Minto, Lake.....57·15n 74·50w
Mistassini, Lake.51·15n 73·10w
Moisie, *river*.....50·13n 66·02w
Moresby Island..52·50n 131·55w
Nares Strait.....80·00n 70·00w
Nass, *river*......55·00n 129·50w
Nelson, *river*.....57·04n 92·30w
Nesselrode, Mount, *mountain*......58·58n 134·18w
Nettilling Lake..66·30n 70·40w
Newfoundland, *island*..........48·30n 56·00w
Nichicun, Lake..53·05n 71·00w
Nipigon, Lake...49·50n 88·30w
Nonacho Lake..61·42n 109·40w
North Saskatchewan, *river*...........53·15n 105·06w
Notre Dame Bay...........49·45n 55·15w
Nottaway, *river*..51·25n 79·50w
Nottingham Island..........63·20n 77·55w
Nouvelle France, Cap de, *cape*...62·27n 73·42w
Nueltin Lake....60·30n 99·30w
Ogilvie Mountains.....65·00n 139·30w
Ontario, Lake...43·40n 78·00w
Ossokmanuan Lake..........53·25n 65·00w
Ottawa, *river*....45·20n 73·58w
Ottawa Islands..59·30n 80·10w
Pacific Ocean...50·00n 130·00w
Parry, Cape.....70·08n 124·24w
Parry Islands....75·30n 106·00w
Payne, Lake.....59·30n 74·00w
Peace, *river*.....59·00n 111·25w
Peary Channel..79·40n 101·30w
Peel, *river*.......67·42n 134·32w
Pelly, *river*.......62·47n 137·19w
Pelly Lake.......65·59n 101·12w
Pelly Mountains.62·00n 133·00w
Penny Highland.......67·19n 66·20w
Peter Pond Lake..........55·55n 108·44w
Placentia Bay...47·15n 54·30w
Plétipi, Lac, *lake*.51·45n 70·08w
Point Lake......65·15n 113·04w
Prince Albert Sound.........70·25n 115·00w
Prince Alfred, Cape..........74·27n 124·40w
Prince Charles Island.........67·50n 76·00w
Prince of Wales Island.........72·40n 99·00w
Prince Patrick Island.........76·45n 119·30w
Prince Regent Inlet..........73·00n 90·30w
Queen, Cape....64·43n 78·33w
Queen Charlotte Islands.........51·30n 129·00w
Queen Elizabeth Islands.........78·00n 95·00w
Queen Maud Gulf.............68·25n 102·30w
Race, Cape......46·40n 53·10w
Rainy Lake......48·42n 93·10w
Ray, Cape......47·40n 59·18w
Reindeer Lake..57·15n 102·40w
Resolution Island.........61·30n 65·00w
Richardson Mountains.....67·55n 136·40w
Robson, Mount, *mountain*......53·07n 119·09w
Rocky Mountains.....55·00n 123·00w
Rupert, Rivière de, *river*.......51·30n 78·45w
Sable, Cape....43·25n 65·35w
Sable Island....43·55n 59·50w
Saint James, Cape..........51·56n 131·01w
Saint-Jean, Lac, *lake*......48·35n 72·00w
Saint John, *river*...........45·15n 66·04w
Saint Joseph, Lake..........51·05n 90·35w
Saint Lawrence, *river*...........49·15n 67·00w
Saint Lawrence, Gulf of........48·00n 62·00w
Salisbury Island.........63·30n 77·00w
Sandy Lake.....53·00n 93·07w
Saskatchewan, *river*...........53·12n 99·16w
Selkirk Mountains.....51·00n 117·40w
Selwyn Lake....59·55n 104·35w
Selwyn Mountains.....63·10n 130·20w
Seul, Lake......50·20n 92·30w
Severn, *river*....56·02n 87·36w
Sharktooth Mountain......58·35n 127·59w
Shelagyote Peak.........55·58n 127·12w
Simpson Peninsula.....68·34n 88·45w
Sir James Mac Brien, Mount, *mountain*......62·07n 127·41w
Slave, *river*.....61·18n 113·39w
Smythe, Mount, *mountain*......57·54n 124·53w
Somerset Island.........73·15n 93·30w
Southampton, Cape..........62·09n 83·40w
Southampton Island.........64·20n 84·40w
Southern Indian Lake..........57·10n 98·40w
South Saskatchewan, *river*...........53·15n 105·05w
Spicer Islands..68·10n 79·04w
Stefansson Island.........73·17n 106·45w
Superior, Lake..48·00n 88·00w
Sverdrup Islands.........79·00n 96·00w
Swinburne, Cape..........71·14n 98·34w
Tathlina Lake...60·32n 117·32w
Thelon, *river*....64·16n 96·05w
Turnor Lake.....56·32n 108·38w
Ungava Bay.....59·30n 67·30w
Vancouver Island.........49·45n 126·00w
Victoria Island..71·00n 114·00w
Victoria Strait...69·15n 100·30w
Viscount Melville Sound.74·10n 113·00w
Waddington, Mount, *mountain*......51·23n 125·15w
Walsingham, Cape..........66·02n 61·56w
Walter Bathurst, Cape..........73·18n 76·40w
White Bay.......50·00n 56·30w
Wholdaia Lake..60·43n 104·10w
Williston Lake...56·00n 124·00w
Winisk, *river*.....55·17n 85·05w
Winnipeg, Lake.52·00n 97·00w
Winnipegosis, Lake..........52·30n 100·00w
Wollaston Lake..58·15n 103·20w
Woods, Lake of the..........49·15n 94·45w
Wrottesley, Cape..........74·36n 121·22w
Yathkyed Lake..62·41n 98·00w
Yelverton Bay...82·20n 84·35w
Yukon, *river*.....64·45n 141·00w

drier slopes Douglas fir is common. Typical of the ranges that traverse the rather arid interior plateau is a generally open forest of aspen and yellow pine interspersed with glades of grass. Douglas fir and lodgepole pine are found on higher slopes.

The forest of the Pacific coast, where steep slopes facing rain-bearing winds produce a very high rainfall, is Canada's densest tall-timber forest. This, with the long growing season, is conducive to the growth of evergreens with very hard wood, excellent for construction lumber. Douglas fir, western hemlock, and western red cedar are the outstanding trees; they grow to great height and thickness. Alder, cottonwood, and maple are subsidiary, along with western white pine. Dense stands of immense trees, their crowns almost touching, their trunks rising to considerable heights, give a grandeur to the forest.

Grasslands. The interior parts of the Prairies, cut off by mountains or by distance from moisture-laden winds, are too dry for forest and give rise to grasslands or natural prairies. Today, the area under grass is quite small, for crops have replaced grass in all but the driest or most hilly regions. Thus, while two broad belts once existed, the tallgrass prairies in the north and the shortgrass prairies in the south, now only about half the shortgrass country remains under grass, while nearly all the tallgrass land is plowed up and lies under crops.

Tundra. Tundra is the name given to the variety of low-growing plants found in areas of permanently cold climates. The rock deserts are almost devoid of vegetation, but relatively fast-growing mosses often surround large rocks. In rock crevices such plants as the purple saxifrage survive, and the rock surfaces themselves may support lichens, some of the orange and vermilion species adding colour to the landscape. Lichen tundra is found in the drier and better drained parts. Mosses are common, and some species may dominate the landscape to such an extent that it appears snow covered. The heath and alpine tundra support dwarf, often berry-bearing shrubs, while the ground between usually is covered with a thick carpet of lichens and mosses.

Animal life. The wildlife regions of Canada correspond closely with the climatic and vegetational zones. In the Arctic the distinctive animals are the seal and the polar bear that feeds on it; the musk-ox, Barren Ground caribou, and lemming, which graze on the tundra; and the Arctic wolf and white fox that prey on them. Many species of birds find summer nesting grounds in the Arctic. The forest-tundra transition zone supports the woodland caribou; while farther south, the boreal forest proper supports nearly all the species of mammals and birds that are recognized as distinctively Canadian. These include the moose, beaver, Canada lynx, black bear, and Canada jay. In the southern, more densely populated parts of Canada, the typical large mammal is the white-tailed deer, which prefers forest borders and partially cleared areas. Smaller mammals are the gray and red squirrels, mink, and skunk, with such birds as the cardinal and, in summer, the Baltimore oriole and the catbird. The western, prairie section has a particular fauna, which includes the sharp-tailed grouse, jackrabbit, and gopher. Under the early unrestricted hunting and settlement, such species of animals and birds as the passenger pigeon and wild turkey became extinct, while others, such as the buffalo and pronghorned antelope, almost so. Such animals as the Rocky Mountain sheep, the mountain goat, and the mountain caribou roam the southern part of the western mountains.

Soils. Geology and relief, climate and vegetation are linked together and find a common expression in the soil, which can be divided into regions.

The northern groups. The thin sub-Arctic and tundra soils lie over permanently frozen ground known as permafrost. They are characterized by patterned ground in which the soil materials are sorted by the alternate freezing and thawing of the ice between the rock fragments to form circles, polygons, and stripes. In some areas, especially near the mouth of Mackenzie Delta, pingos—conical hills with a core of ice—are prevalent. The soils are usually waterlogged in early summer because of the inability of the spring meltwaters to soak into the ground. Sometimes the soil is so saturated it creeps or flows down the slopes. These soils may be dismissed for all but very limited agricultural purposes.

Forest soils. Podzols (podsols) are leached, grayish-coloured soils that extend through the forested part of the Canadian Shield and the Appalachian region. They are acid and rather infertile. Peat soils are common throughout this zone, especially in the northern part. Gray-wooded soils underlie the forested part of the interior lowlands in western Canada. They have developed under the boreal forest, where the climate is subhumid and cool.

Eastern agricultural soils. Agriculture is limited in the southerly parts of the shield and the Appalachian region, where, although soil and climatic conditions are more favourable, much of the total area is unsuitable for agriculture because of rough topography, rock outcrops, or stony soils. Many more acres could be used for agriculture, however, if economic conditions and demand for land warranted such development. Gray-brown podzolic soils extend over the low plains of the Great Lakes–St. Lawrence region. These soils are fertile and, when properly managed, produce a wide range of crops. The combination of soil, climate, and markets has given rise to an intensive agriculture and produced the highest rural population density in Canada.

Limitations on agriculture

Prairie soils. Although a large part of the Prairies is not suitable for agriculture, it contains greater reserves of potential agricultural land than any other zone. The black earths, thick surface soils rich in organic matter, are probably the most fertile soils in the country. Extending from Winnipeg to Edmonton, they lie along the subhumid margin of the Prairies, on which a lush vegetation of tallgrass once flourished. Although grain growing is important, the soils also support mixed farming. Dark brown soils, transitional between the black earths and the brown soils, have become the chief wheat-raising soils in Canada. Brown soils developed in the most arid parts of the Prairies, where the grass was short and bunchy. These soils are lower in organic matter and more alkaline than the other prairie soils, although many of them are quite productive if there is sufficient rain or they are irrigated. Stock ranching as well as crop production is of great importance in this zone.

Western mountain and coastal soils. In the Cordillera relief predominates, and the soil belts follow altitudinal zones. In the great trenches, in which there is relative aridity, brown to dark brown soils occur, with all the characteristics of the southern Prairies. Higher slopes have podzolic soils. This accounts for the considerable variety in the agriculture of the interior valleys of British Columbia. Along the Pacific coast humid brown types of soils have developed under heavy rainfall, in a long growing season under a forest of tall trees. The heavy rainfall leads to some leaching, especially on the windward slopes. The best soils are those on the alluvial deposits of the river deltas and river and coastal terraces.

TRADITIONAL REGIONS AND HUMAN SETTLEMENT

From this combination of physical elements coupled with the population distribution, popular regional terms have emerged. Thus, the Maritimes refers to the Appalachian region without the island of Newfoundland, and if Newfoundland is included, the area is referred to as the Atlantic region or the Atlantic Provinces; Quebec and Ontario are usually referred to alone but sometimes together as Central Canada; the West usually means all of the four provinces west of Ontario, but British Columbia may be referred to alone and the other three collectively as the Prairies, or Prairie Provinces; the Yukon and Northwest territories are referred to as the North.

Patterns of habitation and land use. These terms often disguise the fact that the effectively occupied part of the country, the ecumene, covers only about 10 percent of Canada and that this part is all in the south along the border with the United States. Furthermore, the ecumene is not continuous but covers the southern lowlands only. Thus, it embraces a small area around St. John's, Newfoundland; the lowlands of the Maritimes; the Great Lakes–St. Lawrence lowlands; the southern Prairies, where its width increases from less than 100 miles on the eastern Manitoba border to 600 miles on the western Alberta border; and a small area around Vancouver and Victoria, British Columbia.

Within the ecumene rural land use varies. In 1976 the proportion of farms of less than 240 acres (97 hectares) in the Atlantic Provinces ranged from 50 percent in New Brunswick to 88 percent in Newfoundland; in Quebec farms of less than 240 acres were 69 percent of the total, in British Columbia 71 percent, and in Ontario 74 percent. In the Prairies, however, more than 85 percent of the farms were larger than 240 acres.

Rural settlement patterns

The pattern of rural settlement also differs. In the Maritimes farms are spaced along the roads at irregular intervals wherever there is cultivable land. In the province of Quebec the first settlers laid off long, narrow lots from the shores of the Gulf of St. Lawrence or the St. Lawrence River into the interior. As settlement moved farther inland, roads were built parallel to the waterways, from which narrow lots extended on either side. The same pattern of land tenure is visible in many parts of the Red River Valley of Manitoba, where the early settlers were also of French origin.

In Ontario and the eastern parts of Quebec, land subdivision was made with reference to a much more definite plan. The original subdivisions were more or less square, but the grid became irregular because it was started from a number of different points, each of which used a differently oriented base. In the Prairies the grid is much more regular, partly as a result of the topography, partly because a plan for the subdivision of the whole region was laid out in advance of settlement.

The distribution of the nucleated rural settlements reflects these patterns. In the Maritimes the settlements tend to be distributed around the coast or along river valleys; in the St. Lawrence lowlands they are strung along the banks of the river; in Ontario and the Prairies, however, they are much more evenly spaced, although many of the cities of the former have developed on the shores of the Great Lakes rather than from inland centres.

Urbanized and wilderness Canada. At the beginning of the 20th century, only one-third of the people of Canada lived in urban areas, but the situation has now completely changed. By the early 1980s more than three-quarters of the population lived in communities of more than 1,000 people, and more than one-half of the total population was in the metropolitan areas of cities of 100,000 or more. Canada then had 24 such cities, easily led in size by Toronto (2,999,000), Montreal (2,828,300),and Vancouver (1,268,200). There is at least one large city in every province except Prince Edward Island, each of which functions as a major commercial centre for that province. Some of the cities are almost satellites of a larger metropolis, such as Kitchener and Hamilton with respect to Toronto.

Although rapid urbanization is a characteristic of the entire country, it is much more marked in the Great Lakes–St. Lawrence lowlands, in which more than two-thirds of Canada's urban dwellers are found. Consequently, this region's ways of life are closely related to an industrialized, sophisticated society. Yet, because the population distribution within the ecumene is far from even, no part of Canada is farther than 60 miles from an almost-deserted wilderness area, and one of the many results is an emphasis on the outdoors for recreation and relaxation. A cottage by the lakeshore or a summer home by the ocean is a tradition with many families. Camping with trailers and tents has enabled others to vary their summer locale. Winter activities have increased in recent years with improvements in transportation, and skiing especially has increased in popularity.

Proximity and impact of the outdoors

II. The people of Canada

Canadians do not form a compact, homogeneous people. They are, rather, a collection of diverse national and cultural groups. In the strictly legal sense, there was no such thing as a Canadian citizen until the Canadian Citizenship Act came into force on January 1, 1947.

MAKEUP OF THE POPULATION

National origins. The official Canadian census, which is taken decennially in years ending with the figure 1, continues to record individual origins according to the national group to which a citizen or his ancestor on the male side belonged on coming to North America. Statistics on national origins from the census of 1971 gave the following percentages for the nation as a whole: British Isles, about 45; France, about 29; other nations of Europe, about 23; Indian and Eskimo (Inuit), 1.5; Asia, 1.3; and other, 0.9.

Ethnic backgrounds

Breakdowns by province and territory, however, reveal that these proportions are far from constant. The most constant factor is the percentage of persons from the British Isles, though this varies from 98 in Newfoundland to 11 in Quebec; in Manitoba, Saskatchewan, and Alberta, these persons are exceeded in numbers by the "other-European" group. Canadians of French descent comprise 82 percent of Quebec's population but less than 3 percent of the populations of Newfoundland, of the western provinces, and of the territories. A major French cultural pattern is being created in New Brunswick, and, since early in the 20th century, French Canadians have crossed in significant numbers into Maine and other New England states of the United States. The greatest proportion of Asians lives in British Columbia, Alberta, Ontario, and Quebec. More than 100,000 Indians live in Manitoba, Ontario, Quebec, and Saskatchewan, and more than 13,000 Eskimo live in the Northwest Territories.

Assimilation. Historically, most foreign-born immigrants into Canada have felt the need to live near members of their own race, nationality, creed, or culture, but, in time, they have become assimilated into either the British-Canadian or the French-Canadian culture. Virtually all Canadians of non-British or non-French origin have chosen to identify with and become a part of the former, though by no means has this meant total abandonment of their Old World cultures, points of view, or ways of life. The rate of assimilation has varied with the national origin of the immigrant. Scandinavians and Netherlanders appear to melt quickly into Anglo-Saxon ways, Italians and Germans rather more slowly, and Poles and Ukrainians more slowly still.

The Indians and Eskimo. The earliest inhabitants of Canada came from Asia by way of the Bering Strait more than 10,000 years ago. When the European colonists began their settlements, the Indian and Eskimo popula-

Canada, Area and Population

	area*		population†	
	sq mi	sq km	1971 census	1981 census
Provinces				
Alberta	246,423	638,233	1,628,000	2,238,000
	252,908	655,029		
British Columbia	344,664	892,677	2,185,000	2,744,000
	351,640	910,745		
Manitoba	211,471	547,704	988,000	1,026,000
	250,694	649,296		
New Brunswick	27,633	71,569	635,000	696,000
	28,152	72,913		
Newfoundland	143,489	371,635	522,000	568,000
	156,629	405,667		
Nova Scotia	20,402	52,841	789,000	847,000
	21,425	55,491		
Ontario	353,953	916,734	7,703,000	8,625,000
	422,829	1,095,123		
Prince Edward Island	2,185	5,660	112,000	122,000
	2,185	5,660		
Quebec	524,193	1,357,655	6,028,000	6,438,000
	595,193	1,541,544		
Saskatchewan	220,122	570,113	926,000	968,000
	251,640	651,744		
Territories				
Northwest Territories	1,253,437	3,246,389	35,000	46,000
	1,304,902	3,379,683		
Yukon Territory	205,346	531,844	18,000	23,000
	207,076	536,324		
Total Canada	3,553,318	9,203,054	21,568,000‡	24,343,000‡
	3,845,374‡	9,959,219		

*Where two figures are given, the first is the land area and the second the total area. †De jure. ‡Figures do not add to total given because of rounding.
Source: Official government figures.

tion of Canada was probably about 220,000. In the intervening years it declined considerably before improved living conditions and medical attention caused the numbers to increase to present levels, but today the Indians are the fastest growing ethnic group, numbering more than 300,000 by 1979. They are grouped into some 570 bands and occupy or have access to more than 2,200 reserves and settlements having a total area of nearly 6,500,000 acres.

The Eskimo were never as numerous as the Indians. Their numbers were estimated at 3,700 in 1910 but increased to about 6,000 in the 1920s and to almost 19,000 by 1981. They live in scattered camps and settlements of 25 to 500 people. The resources of the far north have been too limited, however, to provide them with incomes on which they can survive except on marginal living standards. Education and training programs have been instituted to enable them to compete for employment, in particular in the industrial south.

Canadians of U.S. origin. Canadian census figures do not account for the number of Canadians whose forebears immigrated from the United States, since only origins outside North America are recorded. Migration from the United States into Canada was considerable during and after the American Revolution (1775–83), when thousands of colonists who remained loyal to the British crown, now known as United Empire Loyalists, moved north into what remained of British North America, principally into the Maritime colonies; and after 1789 many other Americans migrated into the Great Lakes lowlands to take advantage of offers of free land. It is probable that the number of people arriving from the United States in the 1780s did not exceed 50,000, but since the total population of Canada in 1790 was just over 300,000, about one-sixth of that total was certainly of U.S. origin.

Patterns of U.S.-to-Canada

This immigration introduced a new element into the population complex of British North America, for, whether they arrived with strong Loyalist views or whether they developed such views to take advantage of the land offers (the so-called late Loyalists), these people had all been exposed to the ideas of popular government and democracy that had grown up along the Atlantic seaboard. Their impact on the development of Canada was different from that of those persons who came to Canada directly from Britain. They not only influenced the British North America of their time but have implanted their ideas firmly within the Canada of today.

Linguistic and religious groups. The Canadian census defines mother tongue as the language first learned in childhood and still understood. For the entire nation, English was claimed by 61 percent in 1981 and French by 26 percent, while German, Italian, and Indian and Eskimo languages accounted for 2, 2, and 1 percent, respectively.

The percentage of persons reporting English as the mother tongue is generally greater than that of persons with origins in the British Isles, largely reflecting the fact that most persons in the category "other countries of Europe" probably will have learned English first if they were born in Canada. In British Columbia, for example, in 1981, 45 percent of the population claimed origins in the British Isles, but 82 percent claimed English as their mother tongue. In addition, a decline in the percentage claiming English does not necessarily imply an increase in French, or vice versa: in 1954–63, for example, more than 430,000 immigrants were from Italy, Germany, and The Netherlands, most of them diluting Ontario's largely English-speaking population. Few of the outstanding phenomena concerning linguistic distribution are unexpected. In Quebec, in 1981, 82 percent claimed French, but only 11 percent English, while in neighbouring Ontario the percentages were 77 English and 6 French. In the Prairie Provinces (Manitoba, Saskatchewan, and Alberta) German is the mother tongue for 7, 6, and 4 percent, respectively, and in the Northwest Territories 67 percent claim Indian and Eskimo languages.

Although some relation exists between language and religion, the relation between national origin and religion is probably the greater. About 75 percent of the population belongs to three main churches: Roman Catholic (46 percent), the United Church of Canada (17 percent), and Anglican (12 percent).

Much smaller percentages of other Protestant denominations and a number of Jewish, Greek Orthodox, and other faiths account for most of the remainder. Roman Catholicism is especially strong in Quebec (88 percent), New Brunswick (52), Prince Edward Island (46), Newfoundland (36), and the Northwest Territories (43). Lutheranism and the United Church are proportionally strong in the Prairie Provinces and Anglicanism in the territories.

DEMOGRAPHIC TRENDS

Changes in population makeup. The population composition according to origin is by no means fixed. Sometimes

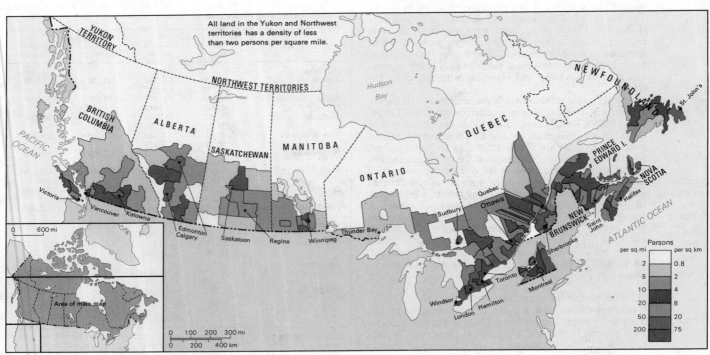

Population density of Canada.

these changes are due to direct recent migration into and out of the country, sometimes to differential birth rates among the national-origin groups. Between 1901 and 1981 the numbers of people of British Isles origin remained the largest but declined steadily as a percentage; the proportion of French origin remained constant.

The greatest change has occurred with the group that is not of French or British descent. In 1901 it made up 12 percent of the population, but by 1971 it was 27 percent. Within this group other changes have taken place. Those of German origin were long the most numerous, but by 1976 they were exceeded by Italians. Ukrainians have become the third largest non-British, non-French group.

Changes in population makeup have not occurred uniformly throughout the country, so that their regional or local impact is greater than national figures indicate. For example, though the Canadian average birth rate has declined since the 1920s, it has done so much faster in some areas than in others. Whereas Quebec at that time had a birth rate 50 percent higher than Ontario, the decline in Ontario (to 14.3 per 1,000 persons in 1981) has been less than that in Quebec (to 14.9 per 1,000), making the two provinces nearly identical.

Decline in birth and death rates

In the period 1941–79, life expectancy at birth for men rose from 63 to 70 years; for women, from 66 to 77 years. The infant mortality rate fell from 61 per 1,000 live births to 10.9. Birth rates declined gradually but steadily from 29.3 in 1921 to a low of 20.1 in 1937, rose to a postwar high of 28.9 in 1947, remained relatively stable until 1959, but since then have been declining, to reach a record low of 15.2 in 1981. The rates in most provinces followed trends very similar to the national trends, though they were highest in Newfoundland and the territories and lowest in Ontario and British Columbia.

Death rates have declined with improved sanitation and medical services. They were halved between 1851 and 1930, dropping from about 22 to 11. They declined further to a low of 7.2 in 1981, among the lowest in the world. High death rates were recorded in Prince Edward Island, Nova Scotia, and Manitoba; lows in the territories and Newfoundland.

In 1981, 23.1 percent of the population was under 15 years of age, but the number in the 0–4 age range had decreased markedly in the previous decade. Although only 9.7 percent were over 65, the figure promised to rise with the drop in birth and death rates.

As to sex distribution, the Canadian population has, until the 1970s, been characterized by an excess of males. The peak sex ratio of 113 males to 100 females was reached during the period of heavy immigration prior to World War I; after that it declined to virtual parity in 1971: 100.2. In the Prairies a high of 146 was reported in 1911, again during a period of high immigration. In 1976 females outnumbered males for the first time. In 1981 the overall sex ratio in Canada was 983 males per 1,000 females. The provinces of Alberta and Newfoundland and the territories, with rates of between 101 and 110, were the only areas in which males continued to outnumber females.

Patterns of migration. Traditionally, Canada has sought to increase its population through immigration in order to expand its domestic market, reduce per capita costs of administration, stimulate economic activity, and support a higher level of cultural development. A peak year in immigration was 1913, with 400,870 arrivals. Since World War II more than 4,600,000 immigrants have entered Canada. Of these, some 53 percent have settled in Ontario, about 21 percent in Quebec, 13 percent in the Prairie Provinces, 11 percent in British Columbia, and the remaining 2 percent in the Atlantic Provinces.

Emigration from Canada has tended to offset to some extent present and past immigration. The major outward movement has always been to the United States, and that movement, both of native-born Canadians and of Europeans who originally migrated to Canada, has attained considerable proportions at certain periods. Between 1960 and 1969, these numbers varied between 35,000 and 51,000 annually. Since 1970 the number of such emigrants has gradually decreased, and in 1979 only about 14,000 native-born Canadians entered the United States. Of these, more than half were women and children. Of the employed males, professional and technical workers formed the largest group, followed by clerical workers and craftsmen and foremen.

Shape of internal migration

During the first 20 years of the century, the notable feature of internal migration was the movement from eastern Canada to the Prairie Provinces. Although British Columbia has continued to gain from migration since 1931, much of this has been at the expense of the Prairie Provinces. Saskatchewan has had more emigration than immigration since 1941. Ontario consistently has received far more people since 1941 than the other provinces, but most of this growth has been from immigration rather than interprovincial movement. The Atlantic Provinces have lost about 275,000 persons since World War II.

Distribution of the population. The proportion of the population living in rural areas has been declining since Confederation: from 80 percent in 1871 to 46 percent in 1941, 30 percent in 1961, and 24.5 percent in 1976. The sharp drop after World War II reflected the accelerated increase in urbanization during the postwar period, particularly the growth of the large cities. In 1981, 56.1 percent of the people lived in cities of more than 100,000.

The relatively small total population is concentrated in the southern part of the country. This discontinuous ecumene covers about 463,000 square miles. In other words, 90 percent of the people live on 12 percent of the land. But the east–west belt of population along the international boundary is far from continuous. There is a marked contrast between the well-occupied humid east, with its predominance of lowlands supporting some 75 percent of the population, and the somewhat meagrely occupied drier and rougher west, which supports the remaining 25 percent. Furthermore, the major population centres of the Atlantic Provinces are separated from the St. Lawrence lowlands by the Appalachian Highlands; the densely populated Great Lakes lowlands are separated from the Ottawa–St. Lawrence plain by the Frontenac Axis; the Prairie Provinces are cut off from southern Ontario by the Canadian Shield; and the Prairie Provinces are separated from British Columbia by the Rocky Mountains. Thus, a number of population clusters are strung together like beads on a string. Between 1976 and 1981 Canada's major metropolitan areas showed widely varying growth rates: Calgary 25.7 percent, Edmonton 18.1, Saskatoon (Saskatchewan) 15.3, Oshawa (Ontario) 14.1, Vancouver 8.7, Toronto 7.0, Ottawa 3.6, and Montreal 0.9.

What is also significant about these population clusters is that each of them is nearer to a large centre in the United States than it is to a cluster within Canada. Thus, the metropolis for the Atlantic Provinces is Boston; for the Ottawa–St. Lawrence lowlands, New York City; for the Great Lakes lowlands, Buffalo, Detroit, and Chicago; for the Prairies, Minneapolis–St. Paul; and for the west coast, Seattle, Portland, and San Francisco. Thus, the influence of the United States is not simply derived from the physical presence of Americans and the descendants of Americans. It is also derived from their close proximity and the attraction of the developments within their large and nearby urban centres.

(N.L.N.)

III. The national economy

The general picture: income, output, and inflation

With a gross national product, at market prices, of more than $11,000 per capita in 1981, Canada ranked among the world's most affluent countries. The total national output increased by an average of 3 percent in the 1970s, while the population grew by 1.8 percent annually and the output per capita by about 2.9 percent. The presence of a still more affluent society in the neighbouring United States is, nevertheless, a continual irritant in Canadian society, as is the control of a significant portion of Canada's economy, through ownership or heavy financial investment, by U.S. companies. A recurrent theme of Canadian labour union demands is parity with corresponding U.S. wage rates. The practical conclusion that has tended to be drawn—at least under successive Liberal governments—is that, other things being equal, a relatively high growth rate of national income is more important in Canada than in most of its Western competitors. In the second half of the 1970s, other things were not equal, and growth potential was deliberately sacrificed in the fight against price inflation. In this struggle, Canada was fairly successful.

THE EXTENT AND DISTRIBUTION OF RESOURCES

Minerals. Canada is rich in mineral resources, and exploitation has grown rapidly since World War II. Many of Canada's mineral resources are difficult to tap because of their location under the permafrost, soil that is frozen for much of the year. By the 1970s, however, much of the thrust of Canada's economic planning and activity was directed toward developing these resources.

Canada is a leading world producer of a number of minerals and metals, with first place in nickel and zinc and great importance in asbestos, uranium, and molybdenum. It is also a major producer of petroleum and natural gas, copper, iron ore, potash, sulfur, gypsum, silver, cadmium, cobalt, magnesium, and platinum. Between 1961 and 1970 the volume of production in the mining sector rose by 75 percent, while in petroleum products it rose by almost 150 percent. During the late 1970s, however, total production levelled off. There was a considerable decline in the percentage of the total value contributed by metallics to the national economy, with a lesser decline in the relative importance of nonmetallics. Fuels, on the other hand, increased from 30 percent of the total contribution in 1970 to 57 percent by 1979.

Biological resources. In the first half of the 20th century, exploitation of Canada's abundant biological resources provided a major component of the national economy. Two elements were overwhelmingly important: agriculture and lumbering. The huge flat and fertile expanses of the prairies between the Great Lakes and the Rockies became one of the world's major grain producers, and farming in food grains remains the major land use for this enormous area.

In a rather small area (by Canadian standards) of southern Ontario between Lakes Erie and Huron, the climate makes possible the extensive growing of tobacco and fruit. The tobacco, which is important in national terms, is mostly quite high quality Virginia varieties, and in good years Canada is a significant exporter, especially to the United Kingdom.

Just under 5 percent of Canada's surface, however, is fully suitable for farming. Most of the country lies too far north, with a climate that makes farming and livestock raising economically unfeasible. This land, however, contains one of the world's largest concentrations of coniferous forest: some 1,300,000 square miles, or about one-third of the total land area, is classified as forest. The forest belt stretches across most of northern Canada. Much of this area is relatively inaccessible most of the year, but the river systems are used wherever and whenever possible to move timber out for processing in economically more hospitable areas. Canadian timber production—for lumber, pulp and paper, and other products—is among the world's highest.

Canada's fishery resources are regionally significant, both in the rivers and lakes (salmon) and in the Atlantic and Pacific oceans (especially whitefish and tuna varieties). Most of the sea fish catch comes from offshore and deep waters, close to the national coast.

Energy resources. In terms of energy resources, Canada is in a real sense the world's most richly endowed country, with great water resources, petroleum and natural gas, coal, and uranium. A severely limiting factor in the development of energy sources, however, has tended to be the cost of transmission of these resources over vast distances to widely scattered points of consumption.

Declining importance of hydroelectric power

Hydroelectric generation plays a significant though decreasing part in Canada's electric development. Although by the end of 1980 installed hydro-generating capacity was 45,400,000 kilowatts, the hydro portion of the country's generating capacity had fallen from more than 90 percent 20 years earlier to 70 percent. The undeveloped hydropower resources may exceed 60,000,000 kilowatts, but the future development of hydro power in Canada, unlike other developed Western countries, is more constrained by considerations of system load requirements and transmission costs than by the availability of water.

The contribution made by thermal energy (including nuclear power) increased by 10 percent in 1977 and 8 percent in 1978. Thermal generation is predominant in Prince Edward Island and Nova Scotia and is expected to become increasingly important in Alberta and Saskatchewan, through greater use of coal, and in Ontario and New Brunswick, through greater use of nuclear generation and coal. Projections have indicated that by 1985 the use of coal would double and of uranium nearly triple for the production of thermal energy in Canada.

Canada is a net exporter of both petroleum and natural gas and of natural uranium, and, in a geological sense, its proven resources are very large. But the development rate depends crucially on U.S. import policies; for petroleum and natural gas, the major reserves of which lie off the Arctic and Atlantic coasts, transport costs to the major markets are also a crucial factor.

SOURCES OF NATIONAL INCOME

Agriculture, forestry, and fishing. Agriculture is a major industry in Canada. Including the processing, wholesale, and retail sectors, agriculture accounts for more than 25 percent of Canada's economic activity. In 1981 the country ranked fourth as an exporter of agricultural commodities, which amounted to more than 12 percent of its export trade. This is achieved from a relatively small proportion of the labour force; less than 5 percent was classified as farmers and farm workers in 1981. Loggers and related workers made up less than 1 percent of the labour force in 1981, but the value added to the wood beyond the raw materials stage amounted to 17 percent of the value added by all goods-producing industries. Exports of wood, wood products, and paper accounted for 14 percent of the value of all commodity exports in 1980. Although the number of fishermen makes up less than 1 percent of the total labour force, Canada is one of the world's largest fish exporters.

Mining and quarrying. Exports from the mineral industry have traditionally contributed a substantial proportion, more than a third, to Canada's total merchandise exports. Historically, these mineral exports were predominantly of nonfuel materials—80 percent or more in the mid-1960s. As energy prices increased in the early 1970s, energy exports became more significant, and in 1975 they exceeded nonfuel mineral exports. Since then the value of energy exports has declined, and in 1981 they amounted to only 18 percent of the total. In addition to crude petroleum and natural gas (all of which are exported to the United States), the principal items are copper, nickel, and their products, as well as iron ore, primary iron and steel, and lead, zinc, and their products. This sector is not a major source of employment and therefore not of labour income; miners, quarrymen, and related workers make up less than 2 percent of the labour force.

Mineral exploitation and foreign investment

While the mineral industry is the largest single contributor to Canadian exports, it has been, however, a major cause of the massive capital investment that has led to the domination of Canadian industry by foreign corporations and to the crucial dependence of Canadian economic policy on U.S. economic policy. More than 60 percent of investment in the sector was from the United States in the early 1980s.

Manufacturing. The manufacturing sector in 1981 had about a 22 percent share in Canada's domestic product and labour income. Within the total of manufacturing, moreover, some large industries (particularly durable goods) have had a very rapid growth and have set the pace for other sectors in the economy. A leader is the production of motor vehicles, although in the late 1970s, as a result of weak consumer and export demand, it was overtaken by petroleum refining.

Energy. The generation and transmission of energy (excluding petroleum and natural-gas production) make up just under 4 percent of the domestic product. More than 70 percent of this is contributed by electricity, the output of which rose by an annual average of 8 percent in the

1968–78 period. In the late 1960s and early 1970s the claim of electricity production, transmission, and distribution on investment resources was relatively stable, at about 6 percent. Since 1973 the annual growth rate for electricity has fluctuated considerably and by 1978 had fallen to about 4 percent, largely because of higher prices and successful conservation measures.

Financial services. Canadian financial services have developed relatively flexibly in response to the monetary needs of the economy. To operate in Canada, a commercial bank must be individually chartered by Parliament. Most normal central-banking functions are fulfilled by the Bank of Canada, which has substantial autonomy in the determination of monetary policy. The Bank of Canada implements its monetary policies through its relations with the 11 chartered (commercial) banks, which are at the centre of the financial system and relatively highly developed. Although there are other financial institutions—credit unions, provincial savings banks, trust and mortgage-loan companies—the chartered banks remain the main financial institutions, even in some specialized activities. They are relatively free from controls on activities involving foreign exchange.

Canada has five stock exchanges, the Alberta, the Montreal, the Toronto, the Vancouver, and the Winnipeg. There is extensive interpenetration between Canadian and U.S. stock exchanges. In the bond market the role of government-sector borrowing traditionally has been dominant.

Foreign trade. Canada's economic development has been affected by foreign trade far more than that of most developed nations. Exports and imports represented, respectively, about 26 and 23 percent of Canada's gross national product in the early 1980s. This foreign trade, moreover, has grown rapidly, exports rising more than 35 percent and imports about 40 percent, as an annual average, from 1970 to 1980—the export rate rising some 20 percent faster than the growth of national output. More significant was that Canada's exports of manufactured goods over the same period rose by an annual average of 20 percent.

The late 1970s witnessed the most striking acceleration in this growth of foreign trade, both exports and imports. This dynamism was very much associated with the integration of the Canadian market into the U.S. market, particularly in automotive products. Over the five years to 1980, total Canadian exports rose by more than 120 percent, while exports to the United States rose by an even greater amount, to make up some 65 percent of total Canadian exports. Dependence on the United States was still greater in imports, however, 72 percent coming from south of the border by 1980.

Irony of trading dynamism and dependence

The dependence on trade with the United States is not just a technical matter of market shares in imports and exports. In an overall sense, the degree of export dependence means that business trends in the United States feed back directly and quickly into the Canadian business sector. Changes in consumer tastes in the United States and Canada may have disproportionate effects on Canadian producers because, to the North American consumer, it is a matter of almost no relevance whether, for example, his automobile is produced in the United States or Canada. In the second half of the 1970s, economic integration between the two countries worked very much to Canada's benefit, and through the 1970s Canada retained a small labour-cost advantage over the United States. But by 1980 higher productivity in the United States offset the lower Canadian wage rates, and Canada once again became a net importer of automotive products.

Canada also retains strong ties with traditional European trading nations and with the European Economic Community, but newly emerging trading patterns may decrease somewhat Canada's dependence on its traditional trade partners. Foremost is Canada's trading position within the Pacific rim. The growing Japanese market resulted in Japan's replacing the United Kingdom as the second largest market for Canadian exports by the mid-1970s. Exports to China increased by 72 percent from 1978 to 1980, and exports to Australia increased by 76 percent during the same period.

Canada's balance of payments remains the crucially uncertain variable in overall economic prospects. As well as the uncertain prospects for merchandise trade, there are large uncertainties about the service and capital items. One major item consists of tourist accounts, which, except for the period of Expo 67, have tended to deteriorate in recent years and have produced a widening deficit. Two other items also continue to deteriorate: interest and dividends, which represent the recurrent cost of foreign ownership of the economy.

MANAGEMENT OF THE ECONOMY

The private sector. Canada's economy is oriented aggressively to the private sector, and only a relatively small part of the goods-and-service sector—postal services, some electricity utilities, and some but not all air and railroad services—is publicly owned. Most industry is private, and agriculture is firmly private, although it is now as dependent on government protection as it is in other Western democracies. Considerable public involvement exists in the development of natural resources, but most of it is provincial rather than federal. In many cases public involvement is minor, and control rests with private investors.

The most striking feature of the Canadian goods-producing sectors is the extent of private foreign ownership, control, and influence—certainly more than 30 percent of manufacturing production in U.S.-controlled plants in the early 1980s. No other major developed economy exhibits such a degree of dependence on a neighbouring economy. Almost all major private-sector nonagricultural activities are dominated by U.S. influences: through U.S. corporate ownership of Canadian assets, through the growing dependence of Canadian producers on U.S. market trends, and through the extreme dependence of Canadian corporations on U.S. financial markets for their bond issues.

Domination of Canadian industry by U.S. capital, market

To a considerable extent and in various ways, national economic policy in the 1960s was conditioned by this growing dependence of the private sector on foreign influence. Broadly speaking, the overriding influence is a marked positive correlation between growth and foreign influence. The resumption of rapid economic growth in the first half of the 1960s, which stemmed directly from massive U.S. investment in resource-based industries (petroleum, minerals, pulp and paper) and manufacturing industries (especially automobiles), would have produced an unsustainable balance-of-payments deficit if U.S. capital had not been keen to move into Canada and if the U.S. government had not been willing to exempt Canada from successive restrictive programs to protect the U.S. balance of payments.

The most striking example of this Canadian dilemma concerns the Auto Pact. In this characteristically North American deal between government and free enterprise, the Canadian authorities traded important tariff concessions to the United States, amounting to free trade, in return for undertakings from U.S. automakers that they would increase the volume of work in their Canadian subsidiaries and associated component suppliers by more than the growth rate of the Canadian market. The results in the years 1965–70 were spectacular: Canadian exports of automotive products to the United States rose by nearly 200 percent. Although imports from the United States also rose rapidly, the trade balance in automotive products swung from a Canadian deficit in 1966 to a Canadian surplus in 1970. This growth in auto production and exports was one of the principal sources of economic dynamism in the second half of the 1960s, but the price for it was a sharply increased dependence on the United States. The federal government has attempted to check this dependence, however. In 1971 the Canada Development Corporation was established to help channel public and private savings into key privately controlled Canadian investments. The Foreign Investment Review Agency was established in 1974 to assess proposals by non-Canadians regarding acquisition of control of Canadian business enterprises or the establishment of new businesses in Canada, and the National Energy Programme, announced in 1980, aims at regaining control of the Canadian oil and gas industry from U.S. multinational companies. None of these moves seems likely to be able to substitute in volume for foreign private investment or to provide a full solution to the problems of foreign dominance of Canadian private industry.

The public sector and the role of government. By comparison with some other developed Western economies, Canadian authorities are relatively inhibited in their role in the economy. As in the United States, there is a marked political inhibition about spending public money on many social and productive sectors, though, unlike the United States, Canada does not have major military and other commitments to foreign aid or an involvement in space exploration to sustain public expenditure. Thus, through much of the 1960s, government revenues exceeded expenditures, and in 1971 the government accounts were overall in surplus by more than $2,400,000,000. This predominantly deflationary fiscal position, in fact, was deliberately pursued by the authorities in the period 1968–71 as part of a campaign against inflation.

Traditional and imposed constraints on governmental involvement

This example of classical demand management in the fight against inflation reflected the relatively limited possibilities for government intervention in the economy. First, Canadian authorities have little scope for using monetary policy: Canadian monetary developments cannot move much out of line with corresponding U.S. developments without provoking unacceptable movements of capital across the exchanges. Second, the system of federal–provincial relations reserves to the provinces such major potential areas of policy action as government procurement, public-sector wage negotiations, and price controls.

In the 1970s the federal administration continued to strengthen federal support for regions with chronic economic problems—principally the Maritime Provinces and Quebec. One thrust of this was on training and retraining programs for labour. Foreign observers judged that the policies were more successful than in most other Western countries. A second thrust was toward attracting new investment to economically backward areas by investment tax incentives and, to some extent, by governmental participation in financing. Both programs have been operating within a very unpromising context of almost historically high unemployment rates.

Taxation. Like other tax systems, Canada's has developed with its own historical peculiarities. Its most striking constraint has been the federal structure, originally established by the British North America Act of 1867, shaped since then by political tensions between Ottawa and certain provinces, and reaffirmed by the Constitution Act of 1982. Canada's federal structure gives large powers to the provinces in the area of direct taxation, although (by contrast with the United States) residual powers constitutionally lie much more clearly with the federal Parliament. Thus, federal authorities, on the one hand, have a structure of indirect taxes, and, on the other hand, in the 1950s and 1960s they came to agreements with provincial governments that balance the collection of income and corporation taxes by the central government with agreed-upon transfers to the provinces. The system remains complicated because federal–provincial cooperation varies from province to province, but the tax regime is generally uniform throughout Canada.

Federal–provincial division of taxing powers

It is difficult to characterize the Canadian taxation system in terms of its incidence between different income and social groups: it can fairly be said that it is not a particularly progressive system in the European sense of redistributing wealth, although the progressive establishment of the medicare (public medical care insurance) system and public-pension increases went a considerable way toward bringing the welfare system into line with developments in other affluent societies. One major nonwelfare preoccupation remains the taxation of foreign ownership of Canadian corporations, but, in spite of some tougher measures introduced in 1970, the fiscal regime for foreign investors remains relatively attractive.

Trade unions and employer associations. The most striking aspect of Canadian trade unionism is its international orientation, which has a crucial effect on the development of the economy. At the beginning of 1980, 3,397,000 workers, or about 33 percent of the labour force, belonged to trade unions. Of this total, two-thirds belonged to unions with international affiliations, mainly with unions in the United States.

Whether or not particular Canadian unions are closely affiliated to U.S. unions, the concept of parity with the United States seems likely to continue to echo through union bargaining. The problem about parity has been, first, that productivity levels, even in directly corresponding industries, have remained lower in Canada than in the United States and, second, that these industries remain fairly untypically high in terms of Canadian labour productivity, which sets up tensions in other sectors of the Canadian economy where parity would raise labour costs rather sharply.

POLICIES, PROBLEMS, AND PROSPECTS

Contemporary economic policies. In the early 1980s the Canadian economy was weakened by economic recession, both national and international. With decreased external and internal demand, combined with record high interest rates and inflation, the growth rate of the Canadian GDP was trending downward in comparison with the 1970s, from an annual rate of 6.4 percent in 1970 to 1 percent in 1980. In 1981 the inflation rate reached a 33-year high, with the unemployment rate climbing to 7.6 percent; a year later the unemployment rate reached 11 percent.

A number of unfavourable economic factors were responsible for this situation. High interest rates had the effect of sharply reducing the demand for housing and manufactured goods and for capital investment of all kinds, including raw materials. A policy of monetary restraint as a major weapon against inflation also contributed to the sharp increase in interest rates and a decline in the economic growth rate. Another key factor was the collapse of the energy sector, which had been such an important force in the Canadian economy during the 1970s. Revenue from taxes on the oil and gas industry was lower than expected, leaving the federal government with too little surplus to finance further development of the energy sector. Slow investment growth was also a result of the "Canadianization" program, which caused an outflow of domestic capital to purchase foreign-held interests in the oil and gas industry. The recession reduced government revenues and at the same time induced sharp increases in expenditures. The high deficit caused substantial government borrowing, and the estimated requirements in 1982 amounted to more than $17,000,000,000, compared with the $6,500,000,000 projected. The high cost of borrowing, together with the reduced level of economic activity, reduced the scope of government spending programs.

Attitudes toward inflation

In the early 1980s increased labour costs were also seen as a significant problem, with wages rising by about 12 percent annually, compared with an 8 percent increase in the consumer price index. High wages have tended to decrease Canada's competitive position in world trade. To improve the situation, high rates of investment, human resource development, industrial restructuring, and a flexible and adaptable system for the short- and long-term management of the economy were thought to be necessary.

Economic problems and prospects. Contrary to widespread impressions, Canada's geography is less a guarantee of prosperity than a continuing handicap. Recognition of its underpopulation lies behind its traditionally liberal immigration policy. With this low population density even in the south, where most of the people live, the unit cost of providing certain social and productive services—of transportation and communications—is necessarily higher than in most economically developed countries. The strategy of encouraging rapid growth in population and the labour force appeared justified to many as a long-range goal, though it created short-range policy problems in terms of absorption and employment.

The rise that has taken place in the potential output of the Canadian economy, an output that would meet the demands of the growing population for goods and services and of the growing labour force for work, has not yet been matched by a comparable rise in actual productivity. This situation was, in large measure, responsible for massive unemployment in the early 1980s. Various fiscal moves of the U.S. government in the 1980s to curb its balance-of-payments deficit further upset Canada's attempts to close the gap between potential and real productivity and threatened the favourable trade balance that it had achieved. No foreseeable political developments in Canada were likely to lose it its place as a deliberately preferred trading partner with the United States, but Ottawa's constant concern was to increase the economic advantage of its dependence on its more populous neighbour, while decreasing the attendant risks.

Disparity between potential and actual production

In aggregate economic terms Canada's per capita income and other measures of living standards are little different from other developed countries. Similar too are its problems with inflation and unemployment, although its efforts to combat these have been somewhat less successful than those of some of its trading partners. But no efforts on Canada's part can overcome the fact that the rate of recovery from economic recession depends heavily on the performance of the U.S. economy and export-led growth. Apart from that possibility the best prospects appear to lie in energy investment.

(E.I.U./N.L.N.)

TRANSPORTATION

An economical transportation system is essential to a country that, like Canada, is so largely dependent on its ability to export its large surpluses of bulky primary and manufactured goods. But the obstacles raised by the topography, the long but narrow east–west line of its main cities, and the overall patchiness of the population distribution produce unusual transportation problems.

Roads and highways. The populated sections of Canada are well supplied with highways and roads, but vast areas of the larger provinces and the territories that are sparsely settled are virtually without roads of any kind. Access to outlying settlements often is provided by roads built by logging, pulp and paper, and mining companies, although these are not generally available for public travel. The Trans-Canada Highway was opened officially in 1962, and it became possible to drive the entire length of the 4,860-mile route from St. John's, Newfoundland, to Victoria, British Columbia. Motor vehicles number more than one for every three inhabitants. Trucking as an industry has grown spectacularly since World War II.

Railways. Canada has one of the highest railway mileages per capita of any country in the world. The main railway networks, although connecting the Atlantic and Pacific coasts, are confined to the southern part of the country. Even in the west, where they extend farthest north, the transcontinental routes do not go farther north than Edmonton and Prince Rupert. North–south regional lines, however, reach Hudson Bay at Churchill, Manitoba; James Bay at Moosonee, Ontario; and central Labrador at Schefferville, Quebec.

Two great transcontinental systems operate almost all of the railway facilities in Canada. The Canadian National Railway system, a government-owned body, is the country's largest public utility. Canadian Pacific Limited is a joint-stock corporation. These systems, though highly competitive, still cooperate in many fields in which duplication of service would not be profitable. They are supplemented by a major north–south line on the west coast, the British Columbia Railway, and a number of regional independent railways.

Total track mileage has changed little since the 1930s. Since 1974, when the track in use reached 60,250 miles, there has been a gradual decline, new construction being more than offset by the abandonment of unprofitable lines. Canada also has two train subway systems, one in Toronto, with about 34 miles of track, and one in Montreal, with nearly 13 miles.

Waterways. A large proportion of goods carried in Canada, in both domestic and international trade, uses water facilities for some part of its journey. The inland shipping routes are dominated by the St. Lawrence–Great Lakes waterway, which provides navigation for vessels of 25-foot draft to the head of Lake Superior, 2,342 miles from salt water. It includes the major canals of Canada. There are seven locks between Montreal and Lake Ontario; the Welland Ship Canal bypasses the Niagara River and Niagara Falls between Lake Ontario and Lake Erie with eight locks; and the Sault Ste. Marie Canal and lock link Lake Huron and Lake Superior. These 16 locks overcome a drop of 580 feet from the head of the lakes to Montreal. The St. Lawrence Seaway accommodates all but the largest oceangoing vessels, making the upper St. Lawrence and Great Lakes area open to 80 percent of the world's maritime fleet.

St. Lawrence–Great Lakes and canal systems

Subsidiary Canadian canals or branches include the St. Peters Canal between Bras d'Or Lakes and the Atlantic Ocean in Nova Scotia; the St. Ours and Chambly canals on the Richelieu River in Quebec; the Ste. Anne, Carillon, and Grenville canals on the Ottawa River; the Rideau Canal between the Ottawa River and Lake Ontario; and the Trent and Murray canals between Lake Ontario and Georgian Bay in Ontario. The commercial value of goods carried through these canals is not great, but they are maintained to control water levels and permit the passage of small vessels and pleasure craft. The Canso Canal, completed in 1957, permits shipping to pass through the causeway connecting Cape Breton Island with the Nova Scotia mainland.

Within most of the St. Lawrence–Great Lakes system, the carriage of goods or passengers from one Canadian port to another is restricted to ships registered in Canada. Elsewhere, it is open to all Commonwealth ships.

The interchange of cargo from land to water routes and vice versa is handled at many ports on the seacoasts and along the St. Lawrence–Great Lakes waterway. Fifteen of the principal harbours are administered by the National Harbours Board, and 11 others by commissions that include municipal as well as federal appointees. In addition, there are about 300 public harbours, all of which are under the supervision of the federal Department of Transport. An overall construction program keeps Canadian harbour facilities in line with requirements. This includes aids for seaway channels, new and improved wharves and transit sheds, and additions and improvements to grain elevators and other facilities. The federal government owns and operates dry docks at Lauzon, Quebec, and Esquimalt, British Columbia, and leases one at Kingston, Ontario.

Airways. Vast distances, rugged terrain, and extreme variations in climate have shaped the development of civil aviation in Canada, and air transport is of tremendous importance. Two major airlines, Air Canada and Canadian Pacific Air Lines Limited, form the nucleus of Canada's domestic freight and passenger air service. Five major regional air carriers operate other scheduled commercial services. Some 600 small airlines operate nonscheduled services, many of them to parts of Canada that are inaccessible by other means of transportation. More than 1,580 airports and landing facilities have been established, and a network of radio aids is maintained to facilitate en route navigation and landings under instrument conditions. Weather services are provided by the Department of Transport.

Domestic and international air services

Both Air Canada and Canadian Pacific Air Lines operate international routes. In addition, in 1980 there were 37 Commonwealth and foreign air carriers licensed for internationally scheduled commercial services into Canada.

Pipelines. Pipelines are a major element in Canada's vast transportation network. Growth has been so rapid since 1950, when pipelines were a negligible factor in intercity freight traffic, that oil and gas pipelines now account for about one-fourth of intercity freight ton-miles. The world's longest oil and gas pipelines have been built to link the oil fields and gas fields of Alberta and Saskatchewan to major cities as far east as Montreal, and two major pipelines several hundred miles in length cross the Rocky Mountains and supply the lower mainland of British Columbia and the Pacific Northwest of the United States. In 1961 a 1,100-mile pipeline was completed from

Alberta to California, 400 miles of which are in Alberta and British Columbia. The oil pipeline transport industry moves crude oil through 18,000 miles of pipeline from the oil fields in Alberta, Saskatchewan, and Manitoba to the major refineries located across Canada, while the total gas pipeline length by 1979 was about 92,530 miles.

IV. Administration and social conditions

Canada is an independent federal parliamentary state, the head of which is the reigning monarch of the United Kingdom. The state was established by the British North America Act of 1867 (replaced by the Constitution Act of 1982), which united the colonies of Nova Scotia, New Brunswick, and Canada into the provinces of Nova Scotia, New Brunswick, Quebec, and Ontario. Rupert's Land and the North-Western Territory were acquired from the Hudson's Bay Company in 1869, and from them Manitoba was created and admitted to the Confederation as a province in 1870; its extent was enlarged by adding further areas from what had become the Northwest Territories, in 1881 and 1912. The colonies of British Columbia and Prince Edward Island were admitted as provinces in 1871 and 1873, respectively. In 1905 Saskatchewan and Alberta were created from what remained of the Northwest Territories and admitted to the Confederation as provinces. In 1912 the provinces of Quebec, Ontario, and Manitoba were enlarged to their present limits by adding areas from the Northwest Territories. Finally, in 1949, Newfoundland and its dependency, Labrador, joined the Confederation following a popular referendum. Yukon Territory in 1898 was separated from the Northwest Territories, the remainder of which, in 1920, was divided into three provisional districts—Mackenzie, Keewatin, and Franklin. Thus, Canada now consists of 10 provinces and two territories, all of which vary greatly in size.

STRUCTURE OF GOVERNMENT

The Constitution Act is not an exhaustive statement of the laws and rules by which Canada is governed. The constitution of Canada in its broadest sense includes other statutes of the Parliament of the United Kingdom; statutes of the Parliament of Canada relating to such matters as the succession to the throne, the demise of the crown, the governor general, the Senate, the House of Commons, electoral districts, elections, and royal style and titles; and statutes of provincial legislatures relating to provincial legislative assemblies.

Preservation of bilingualism

The preservation of both the English and French languages is safeguarded by the provision that either language may be used in all institutions (including the courts) of the Parliament and government of Canada and in all institutions of the National Assembly of Quebec, the legislature of New Brunswick, and their governments. The Constitution Act provides specific protection for fundamental rights like freedom of worship, of the press, and of assembly. It also guarantees to Quebec the right to a Roman Catholic school system under Roman Catholic control and to exclusive jurisdiction over property and civil rights, and safeguards preservation of the French system of civil law in the province.

Federal legislative and executive authority. Federal legislative authority is vested in the Parliament of Canada, which consists of the sovereign of Canada (constitutionally not the same as the sovereign of the United Kingdom although physically perhaps the same person), the Senate, and the House of Commons. The Senate has 104 members, who are appointed on a provincial basis and may hold office until they are 75 years of age. The 282 members of the House of Commons are elected by the people of Canada for maximum terms of five years.

The Constitution Act divides legislative and executive authority between Canada, on the one hand, and the several provinces, on the other. The Parliament of Canada is assigned authority over control of the armed forces, the regulation of trade and commerce, banking, credit, currency and bankruptcy, criminal law, postal services, fisheries, patents and copyrights, the census and national statistics, the raising of money by taxation, and, in the field of communication, such matters as navigation and shipping, railways, canals, and telegraphs. In addition, the federal government is endowed with a residual authority in matters beyond those specifically assigned to the provincial legislatures and including the power to make laws for the peace, order, and good government of Canada. Both the House of Commons and the Senate must pass all legislative bills before they can receive royal assent and become law. Both bodies may originate legislation, but only the House of Commons may introduce bills for the expenditure of public funds or the imposition of any tax.

The personal representative of the crown in Canada, the governor general, is appointed for a term of about five years. He exercises the executive authority of the monarch in relation to the federal government. On the recommendation of his responsible advisers, he summons, prorogues, and dissolves Parliament, assents to bills, and exercises other executive functions.

The leader of the party winning the most seats in a general election is called upon by the governor general to form a government. He becomes the prime minister and generally chooses party colleagues from among the elected members to form the Cabinet. If he wishes to have in his Cabinet someone who is not a member of the House of Commons, that person must secure a seat in the House within a short time through a by-election or receive appointment to the Senate by the governor general upon the nomination of the prime minister. Almost all Cabinet ministers are also heads of executive departments of the government, for the work of which they are responsible to the House of Commons. The Cabinet is responsible for determining all important policies of government and securing the passage of such legislation, financial measures, and administrative provisions as their supporters may approve.

Selection of ministers of the crown

The ministers of the crown, as members of the Cabinet are called, are chosen generally to represent all regions of the country and its principal cultural, religious, and social interests. Although they exercise executive power, they are collectively responsible to the House of Commons and can remain in office only so long as they retain the confidence of the House. The choice of the Canadian electorate not only determines who shall govern Canada but also, by deciding which party receives the second largest number of seats in the House, designates which of the major parties becomes the official opposition. The function of the opposition is to offer intelligent and constructive criticism of the existing government.

Provincial and territorial government. Similar political institutions and constitutional usages operate in the government of the 10 provinces as in that of the nation as a whole. In each province the sovereign is represented by a lieutenant governor appointed by the governor general in council, usually for a term of five years. The powers of the lieutenant governor in the provincial sphere are essentially the same as those of the governor general in the federal sphere.

The legislature of each province is unicameral and comprises, in addition to the lieutenant governor, a legislative assembly elected for a term of five years. The conventions of Cabinet government operate as in the federal House of Commons. The provinces have powers embracing mainly matters of local or private concern such as property and civil rights, education, civil law, provincial company charters, municipal government, hospitals, licenses, management and sale of public lands, and direct taxation within the province for provincial purposes.

Territorial administration

The vast and sparsely populated regions of northern Canada lying outside the 10 provinces—Yukon Territory and the Northwest Territories—are administered by the federal government, but they have both elected representation in the House of Commons and a measure of local self-government. The local government of Yukon Territory is composed of a commissioner appointed by the federal government, and an elected council of 16, from which an executive council is appointed. The government of the Northwest Territories is vested in a commissioner appointed by the federal government and an elected council of 22, with an executive committee composed of the commissioner, deputy commissioner, and up to five members of the elected council, who are nominated by the council. General responsibility for the administration of the Northwest Territories, for Eskimo affairs, and for the resources of both territories rests with the federal Department of Indian Affairs and Northern Development.

Federal–provincial relations. A major part of Canada's constitutional development has occurred gradually through judicial interpretation and constitutional convention and through executive and administrative coordination at the federal and provincial levels of government. Through such devices, the national and provincial legislatures have been able to retain their separate jurisdiction over different aspects of the same matter. Only in such an approach can Canada achieve an accommodation that gives fair assurances to the aspirations of the provinces without disrupting the integrated national structure of the Canadian Confederation.

The French in Canada

Of the provinces, Quebec has the most pronounced aspirations. Only there are citizens of French origin in the majority. They have overflowed into Ontario, particularly in the north and the Ottawa Valley, and into northern New Brunswick. Smaller concentrations in Nova Scotia and southern New Brunswick are descendants of those who formed the early French colony of Acadia. Elsewhere, people of French origin are scattered, although they form locally important minorities.

Their survival in Quebec as a distinctive and majority group is not hard to explain in light of the historical constitutional guarantees. They have therefore developed a culture of their own that differs in many respects from that of the rest of Canada—and, indeed, from the rest of North America. By instinct and design they have kept themselves French and Roman Catholic. The course of politics for them is not primarily material prosperity or liberty in the Anglo-Saxon sense but ethnic survival. The political consequences of this are that they tend to act as a unit in national matters and support whichever party is paying attention to their claims. It has also led, at times, to strong movements in favour of political secession of the province from the Confederation. At the national level it has also led to efforts to create a dual culture in Canada rather than simply preserve two cultures.

Thus, the Official Languages Act of 1969 declares that the English and French languages "enjoy equality of status and equal rights and privileges as to their use in all the institutions of the Parliament and Government of Canada." The significant addition is "the institutions of . . . Government of Canada," since this embraces all federal offices and organizations throughout the country. Pursuant to this act, a commissioner of official languages was appointed to ensure compliance with the intent of the act. Not only has this increased opportunities throughout the country for Canadians of French origin, but also it may increase the desire of other Canadians to speak French and interest themselves in French culture.

Local government. Since government at the municipal level falls under the jurisdiction of the provinces, there are 10 distinct systems of municipal government in Canada, as well as many variations within each system. The variations are attributable to differences in historical development and in area and population density. Thus, the legislature of each province has divided its territory into geographical areas known generally as municipalities and, more particularly, as counties, cities, towns, villages, townships, rural municipalities, or municipal districts, although the county system as understood in Britain or the United States is present only in southern Ontario and southern Quebec. The more than 4,700 incorporated municipalities and local government districts in Canada have various powers and responsibilities suited to their classification. A municipality is governed by an elected council, the head of which may be called mayor, reeve, warden, or overseer; the other members may be known as controllers, aldermen, or councillors. The responsibilities of the municipalities are generally those most closely associated with the citizens' everyday lives, well-being, and protection. The sparsely populated areas of the provinces are usually administered as territories by the provincial governments; only about one-fifth of 1 percent of Newfoundland is municipally organized, one-third of Quebec, one-tenth of Ontario, and the southern parts of the western provinces.

Justice. Canadian courts of law are independent bodies. Each province has its police, division, county, and supreme courts, with right of appeal being available throughout provincial courts and to the federal Supreme Court of Canada. At the federal level there is also an Exchequer Court, in which proceedings instituted by or against the crown may be launched and from which appeals may be made to the Supreme Court. All judges, except police magistrates and judges of the courts of probate in Nova Scotia and New Brunswick, are appointed by the governor general in council, and their salaries, allowances, and pensions are fixed and paid by the Parliament of Canada. They cease to hold office at age 75.

Legislation concerning criminal law and the procedure in criminal matters is under the jurisdiction of the Parliament of Canada. The provinces administer justice within their own boundaries, including the organization of civil and criminal codes and the establishment of procedure in civil matters.

Police and the military. The police forces of Canada are organized in three groups, the federal force, called the Royal Canadian Mounted Police (RCMP), the provincial police, and the municipal police. The RCMP—or Mounties, one of Canada's best known organizations—was established in 1873 for service in the Northwest Territories of that time. It is still the sole police force in the Yukon and Northwest territories, but it also has complete jurisdiction of the enforcement of federal statutes throughout Canada, which includes the control of narcotics. The maintenance of peace, order, and public safety and the prevention and investigation of criminal offenses and of violation of provincial laws are provincial responsibilities. Ontario and Quebec have their own provincial police forces, but all other provinces engage the services of the RCMP to perform these functions. Provincial legislation makes it mandatory for cities and towns and for villages and townships with sufficient population density and real property to furnish adequate policing for the maintenance of law and order in their communities. Most large municipalities maintain their own forces, but others engage the provincial police or the RCMP, under contract, to attend to police matters. In addition, the Canadian National Railway, Canadian Pacific Limited, and the National Harbours Board have their own police forces.

Royal Canadian Mounted Police

The control and management of all matters relating to national defense, including the armed forces, are the responsibility of the minister of national defense. The Canadian armed forces are organized on a functional basis to reflect the major commitments assigned by the government. They are formed into a National Defence Headquarters, located in Ottawa, and six major commands. Mobile Command provides military units suitably trained and equipped to support United Nations or other peacekeeping or peace-restoring operations; to provide ground forces, including tactical air support, for the protection of Canadian territory; and to maintain operational readiness of combat formations in Canada required for the support of overseas commitments. Maritime Command defends Canadian interests from assault by sea, supports the North Atlantic Treaty Organization (NATO) by assisting in conducting antisubmarine warfare, and provides any sea lift required by Mobile Command. Air Command participates in the air defense of North America, providing Canada's contribution to the North American Air Defense Command (Norad). It also provides air transport support to Canadian forces everywhere, conducts search-and-rescue operations, is responsible for maritime surveillance, and provides individual training common to more than one command.

Canadian Forces Northern Region has the responsibility for military matters in the Yukon and Northwest territories and for coordinating and supporting the activities of forces employed in the North. The Canadian Forces Communications Command provides fixed communications networks for the armed forces as well as being a national communications system for survival operations.

Canadian Forces Europe embraces the Canadian forces allocated to support NATO.

THE SOCIAL MILIEU

National attitudes in the social sphere are derived from the English poor law and of charity provided by religious institutions and voluntary agencies. These have been modified, however, by the transformation of the population from a predominantly rural–agricultural to an urban–industrial society and the social stresses engendered by two world wars, influences that have brought about the need for intervention by government. The Constitution Act assigns responsibility for charities and charitable institutions to the provinces, but it is not clear on other aspects of social welfare. The result has been a diversity of joint federal–provincial programs to meet social needs.

Standards of living. In 1982 average weekly wages and salaries were highest in construction and mining and lowest in clothing manufacture and the service occupations. By the early 1980s the Canada Labour Code provided for a minimum hourly wage of $3.50 for an eight-hour day and 40-hour week, eight general holidays with pay, and an annual vacation of two weeks with pay. Women may not be paid at a rate less than men for identical or substantially identical work, and discrimination in employment because of race, colour, religion, or national origin is prohibited. The personal income per capita is one of the highest in the world; but families who spend more than 70 percent of their income for food, clothing, and shelter are considered "poor," in a relative sense, and on this basis at least one Canadian in five suffers from poverty.

The personal income per capita varies markedly from province to province. In Ontario, Saskatchewan, and British Columbia it is higher than the national average, while the Atlantic Provinces lag behind the rest of the country. There, average incomes are only about 60 percent of those of Ontario, a disparity that has changed little in 50 years. The incidence of low incomes is also higher in the Atlantic region, but the problem of income disparity is not only a regional but also an urban one.

Health and welfare. Provincial governments bear the main responsibility for health and welfare services, administering a broad range of activities either directly or in cooperation with the municipalities, to which considerable authority often is delegated. Such activities include health insurance; general public-health services, primarily of a preventive nature; services for specific diseases or disabilities, combining prevention, treatment, and rehabilitation related to general medical and hospital care; and welfare services. The health professions and voluntary agencies and institutions supply services, initiate new activities, and stimulate better standards. The role of the federal government is primarily to provide consultative, coordinating, and financial assistance. The federal Medical Care Act (1968) provides for federal contributions to medical-care plans of participating provinces provided that such plans are comprehensive with regard to medical services, have universal coverage, are administered by a public authority, and allow portability of benefits between provinces. The federal Hospital Insurance and Diagnostic Services Act (1957) allows for federal contributions to the costs of specified hospital services and now covers 99.5 percent of the insurable population of Canada. The federal government also has responsibilities that include the administration of food-and-drug legislation (including narcotics control), quarantine, immigration and sick-mariners services, and the health and welfare of Indians, Eskimo, and past and present members of the armed forces.

Federal–provincial coordination of social activity

There are a number of social security and social assistance programs. The Canada Pension Plan provides retirement, disability, and survivors benefits. The Old Age Security Act provides a monthly pension to all persons 65 years of age or over, while the guaranteed-income supplement provides additional income for old-age pensioners. Financial aid is available under provincial or municipal auspices to persons in need and their dependents.

Housing. Although the government originally entered the field of housing in 1918, the present role of the federal government in housing stems from the National Housing Act (1954), an act to promote the construction of new houses, the repair and modernization of existing houses, and the improvement of housing and living conditions, as well as its subsequent amendments. The Central Mortgage and Housing Corporation, a crown agency, administers the act and coordinates the activities of the federal government. These activities include such matters as insured mortgage loans, direct loans for homeownership and rental housing, financial assistance for the elimination or prevention of water and soil pollution, public housing, urban renewal, and research. All provinces have complementary legislation providing for joint federal–provincial housing and land-acquisition projects, and most have special legislation with respect to housing.

Education. Under the Constitution Act, the organization and administration of public education are provincial responsibilities. The federal government is directly concerned only with the provision of education in the Yukon and Northwest territories, in Indian schools throughout Canada, for inmates of federal penitentiaries, for the families of members of the Canadian forces on military stations, and for the operation of three military colleges. In addition, it finances vocational training of adults and provides financial support to the provinces for the operating costs of postsecondary education.

Because each of the 10 provinces has the authority and responsibility for organizing its education system as it sees fit, policies and practices vary from province to province, but each has a department of education headed by a minister who is a member of the provincial Cabinet. In addition, Ontario has a Department of Colleges and Universities with a minister of its own. Most Canadian children enter an eight-grade elementary school at age six. At about 14 years of age, nearly 90 percent of those who entered grade one enter a regular four- or five-year secondary school.

Traditionally, higher education was the almost exclusive preserve of universities. Now, although universities still account for about 60 percent of full-time students, postsecondary education is conducted in a variety of other institutions without degree-granting status—regional colleges in British Columbia, institutes of technology in Alberta, institutes of applied arts and science in Saskatchewan, colleges of applied arts and technology in Ontario, and *collèges d'enseignement général et professionel* in Quebec. By 1980 there were 182 such institutions.

Canada has more than 65 degree-granting institutions. They range from institutions with a single faculty and enrollments of a few hundred to institutions with many faculties and research institutes and more than 15,000 students, such as the Université de Montréal, the University of Toronto, and the University of British Columbia.

The oldest university in Canada, Laval, in Quebec, was founded during the French regime. Universities in English-speaking Canada were established after the American Revolution. King's College, Nova Scotia (now the University of King's College); King's College, York (now the University of Toronto); and King's College, Fredericton (now the University of New Brunswick) were patterned after King's College (now Columbia University) in pre-Revolutionary New York City. Most of the other universities in pioneer days were begun by churches, but almost all have since become secular and are almost entirely financially dependent on the provincial governments. Others, particularly in the western provinces and Newfoundland, were established by provincial governments. There are no real private universities in Canada and none that is analogous to the land-grant institutions in the United States. A somewhat unusual characteristic has been the system of "affiliated colleges" linked to a "parent" degree-granting institution even though separated from it physically. English is the language of instruction at most places, French in several, and a few are bilingual.

V. Cultural life and institutions

THE ARTS AND RECREATIONS

The development of the arts in Canada today reflects a geographical and cultural pattern as well as the changes that have come to a rapidly growing and rapidly urbanizing country. The existence of two dominant cultural traditions has led to a certain diversification of artistic endeavour, a diversification encouraged further by groups of other national origins and a widely dispersed population. As there are several metropolitan centres, so there are several focal points for artistic activity.

Since 1950 economic growth has provided all Canadians with greater means for the practice and enjoyment of the arts, and the influx of immigrants from many countries has increased both the audience and the pool of available talent. Each new event in the artistic life of the country has aroused greater interest, and with it has come more substantial financial support from public and private sources. All provincial governments except Prince Edward Island provide some form of financial assistance for the arts, amateur and professional, and for cultural organizations within their borders. In 1968 New Brunswick established an office of cultural affairs; the British Columbia Cultural Fund was established in 1967; in 1962 the Ontario government set up the Council for the Arts; a similar agency was established in Quebec in 1961; and Saskatchewan has had its Arts Board since 1949. At the national level, the Canada Council was established in 1957 "to foster and promote the study and enjoyment of, and the production of works in the arts, humanities and social sciences." Its income is derived from a $50,000,000 fund with which it was endowed at its creation, an annual grant from the federal government, and private donations. Its assistance to the arts in 1978–79 amounted to nearly $42,500,000. The Canada Council also supports the Canadian National Commission for the United Nations Educational, Scientific and Cultural Organization.

Literature. The first truly Canadian literary works were written in French by explorers, missionaries, and settlers, and many of them became the inspiration of subsequent writings. Some were notable literature, such as Marc Lescarbot's *Histoire de la Nouvelle France* (1609). The years following were also marked by some works that have become classics—William Kirby's *Golden Dog* (1877), Robert W. Service's *Trail of '98*, the humorous works of Stephen Leacock, and the long series of *Jalna* novels by Mazo de la Roche. Natural and vigorous French-Canadian writing was held back by a sense of isolation, strict Roman Catholicism, a small and relatively unsophisticated reader market, and a tendency to favour academic and formal literary styles and themes. The 1940s saw the emergence of Canadian writers of the first rank. Hugh MacLennan established himself as a writer of international importance with *Barometer Rising* (1941) and *Two Solitudes* (1945), as did Thomas Raddall with *His Majesty's Yankees* (1942). Gabrielle Roy's novel *Bonheur d'Occasion* (1945) was an immediate success, and *Le Survenant* (1945), by Germaine Guèvremont, placed its author in the forefront of French-language novelists, both in Montreal and Paris. Still later came the novels of Robertson Davies and the satires of Mordecai Richler. The French-Canadian novel, long handicapped by sentimentality and stilted prose, went beyond even hard realism into the psychological realm with Marie-Claire Blais's *La Belle Bête* (1959). Since 1960 other important novelists, among them Margaret Laurence, Alice Munro, and Margaret Atwood, have emerged. Although the growth of competent novel writing was the main feature of Canada's literary scene after World War I, the period saw marked changes in the work of Canadian poets. John McCrae's *In Flanders Fields* (1919) was the only important Canadian verse related to the 1914–18 conflict, but since then E.J. Pratt, Earle Birney, Irving Layton, Anne Hébert, James Reaney, and Al Purdy, among others, have attracted widespread attention to their work.

Visual arts. The visual arts in Canada today present a scene of unprecedented activity. In some ways painting has been the most successful of all the arts in the expression of Canada's national identity in that some Canadian painting has a manner of portraying locale and atmosphere that sets it apart. Most of this specific content appeared from the first decade of the 20th century through the 1930s. Especially notable were the Group of Seven, who influenced the succeeding generation through their enthusiastic portrayals of the Canadian landscape. Today, several universities offer degree programs in fine art.

Although painting has received most of the attention in the art world of Canada, sculpture and the handicrafts have been in evidence since earliest times and only now are receiving adequate public attention. Prominent in contemporary sculpture exhibitions are stone carvings of the Eskimo people, while among the most interesting of museum-guarded sculptures are the totem-pole carvings of the Indians of the west coast.

Art collections and galleries

Along with these developments has come the establishment of art collections and art galleries. The National Gallery of Canada in Ottawa, dating from 1880, includes not only the most extensive and important collection of Canadian art in existence but also collections built up along international lines to give an indication of the origins from which Canadian tradition is developing. It also circulates exhibitions to several hundred centres in the country each year. In addition, some 20 major cities have public art galleries, and 25 arts councils and university galleries house important collections.

Music. Canadian music failed to reach beyond the borders before 1940, but the years before this prepared the way for the intense musical activity that followed World War II. Earlier developments included the music-festival movement that began in 1908 in Edmonton and now claims almost 100 units across the country. Many performers who began as amateurs in these festivals went on to achieve professional status. Some Canadian performers have become well-known internationally—among them the late pianist Glenn Gould and Metropolitan Opera performers George London and Jon Vickers.

Somewhat similarly, civic symphony orchestras have developed since 1902, when L'Orchestre Symphonique de Québec was founded. Today, most major cities have their own, particularly in the broadcast centres, where musicians can be sustained by radio and television assignments. Those of Toronto and Montreal have become fully professional and internationally recognized. In 1962 the Montreal Symphony became the first professional symphony orchestra from Canada to play in Europe.

Canadian school of composers

The years since 1940 also have seen the development of a school of Canadian composers. Providing thematic material for the new composers were assiduous collectors of early Canadian folk songs. Paralleling these developments has been an expansion in music education in the schools and universities. Today more than 30 Canadian universities have departments, schools, or faculties of music.

Choral music and choral societies are to be found in many Canadian cities and towns. Opera in Canada has benefitted from these developments. Toronto, Montreal, and Vancouver enjoy brief but regular seasons. The Toronto-based Canadian Opera Company makes extensive tours, often to remote parts of the country.

The performing arts. Ballet has been a matter of public interest only since the 1930s, but today there are three top-ranking professional companies—the Royal Winnipeg Ballet, founded in 1939, the National Ballet of Canada, founded in 1951 with headquarters in Toronto, and Les Grands Ballets Canadiens, founded in 1957 in Montreal. Les Feux-Follets, also headquartered in Montreal, is essentially a folk ensemble reflecting the founding French heritage of Quebec. The National Ballet is the largest and the most widely travelled, touring not only Canada but the United States as well.

Canada long had no professional theatre in the accepted sense, and yet from coast to coast a continuous, successful theatre movement took place under amateur auspices and involved Canadian playwrights and performers. The little theatre movement spread during the 1920s, and by 1933 the Dominion Drama Festival had come into being. A national festival, the climax of a series of regional competitive festivals, is held each year in a different city. The movement has inspired a knowledgeable and appreciative theatre audience and provided the training ground for many actors now in professional ranks.

The professional theatre developed from several year-round repertory groups such as Les Compagnons du Saint Laurent (Montreal), the New Play Society (Toronto), and Totem Theatre (Vancouver) and by a long line of summer-theatre ventures. Of these the John Holden Players (Winnipeg, Manitoba, and Bala, Ontario), Mountain Playhouse (Montreal), Straw Hat Players (Port Carling, Ontario), and the Theatre-Under-the-Stars (Vancouver) are noteworthy. In 1953 the Stratford Festival was begun in Stratford, Ontario. Shakespearean plays, as well as modern plays and concerts, are presented in three theatres during the summer season. Another celebrated summer festival is the Shaw Festival at Niagara-on-the-Lake, founded in 1964.

Influence of the Stratford Festival

The enthusiasm and excitement engendered by the success of these ventures set off a new Canadian determination to have professional theatre on a regular and nationwide scale. More than 12 spectacular new theatres have been built across the country since 1958, among them Confederation Centre in Charlottetown (Prince Edward Island), Place des Arts (Montreal), National Arts Centre (Ottawa), O'Keefe Centre and St. Lawrence Centre for the Performing Arts (Toronto), the Centennial buildings of Winnipeg and Saskatoon, the Jubilee theatres of Edmonton and Calgary, and the Queen Elizabeth Theatre in Vancouver.

Filmmaking. The impact of television on the film-production industry can be readily assessed by the fact that about three-quarters of the films produced as features, advertising, trailers, newsclips, and newsreel stories by Canada's private and governmental filmmaking agencies were for television in 1980. About 40 percent were made in French and another 10 percent in languages other than English or French. The National Film Board was established by the federal government in 1939 to produce films, filmstrips, and still photographs that reflect the life and thought of Canada and to distribute them both internally and abroad. It has earned international acclaim for the imaginativeness as well as the artistic and technical excellence of its work. During the fiscal year 1978–79, it released 381 new motion pictures, while at home and abroad its films were seen by audiences of several hundred million. It won 106 awards from film festivals around the world to bring the number of its awards to well over 1,000. In 1967 the federal government established the Canadian Film Development Corporation to foster and promote a feature-film industry through investment in productions, loans to producers, grants to filmmakers and film technicians, and advice and assistance in administrative matters.

Work of National Film Board

Sports. Several of the sports played in Canada are derived from those of the indigenous peoples or the early settlers. Lacrosse, adopted as Canada's national game at the time of Confederation, was played by Indians in all parts of the country and adopted by later immigrants. By 1867 definite rules had been established, and the game had become organized. Ice hockey is also Canadian in tradition, leadership, and playing ability. It remains Canada's most popular winter sport on outdoor and indoor rinks across the nation, and a large percentage of Canadian children learn to skate almost as soon as they can walk. The sport, in its early organizational stages at the time of Confederation, originated in Nova Scotia in 1828. Curling is a popular indoor ice sport believed to have been introduced from Scotland in 1759.

Other sports have been more strongly influenced by the recreational interests of the United States and Europe. Baseball and U.S.-style football are two examples of this. Their development in Canada owes a great deal to the influence of both radio- and television-network broadcasting. The professional Canadian league plays a football only slightly different from that of the United States, while Canadian cities have franchises in professional hockey and baseball.

PRESERVATION OF THE PAST

In 1919 the federal government established the Historic Sites and Monuments Board to advise on matters of national historic importance, with particular reference to commemoration or preservation. In the early 1980s there were 53 national historic parks. Most are military or fur-trading forts, historic buildings, or reconstructions of historic buildings; most have museums. They range from the 13,000-acre site around the reconstructed Fortress of Louisbourg, Nova Scotia, to the boyhood home of the former prime minister W.L. Mackenzie King, and a reconstructed theatre of the gold rush days in Dawson, Yukon Territory. Two are preserved Yukon riverboats. Each province has a similar policy. In the west many of the marked sites, such as Head-Smashed-In Buffalo Jump in Alberta, recall the Indian period. Several provinces have restored or reconstructed pioneer communities. British Columbia's first provincial historic park was the restored gold-mining town of Barkerville. In Ontario, Fort-Sainte-Marie, the headquarters of the Jesuit mission to the Huron Indians in the 17th century, has been restored.

Historic sites and museums

But many of the national treasures are in museums and galleries that pay special, but not exclusive, attention to Canada. Four such institutions are maintained by the federal government: the National Museum of Natural Sciences, the National Museum of Man, the National Museum of Science and Technology, and the National Gallery of Canada. All are in Ottawa, as is the Public Archives of Canada, whose purpose it is to assemble and make available source materials relating to the nation's history. Most of the provinces have similar institutions, and nearly all have a provincial museum. The Royal Ontario Museum in Toronto holds international stature. Others, such as the Saskatchewan Museum of Natural History, are newer and more concerned with provincial traditions. Some of the art galleries are municipally or privately financed and operated.

BROADCASTING

Canada's broadcasting industry ranks among the world leaders in terms of broadcasting and receiving equipment and in coverage, quality, and variety of programs. The large number of transmitters is related to the numerous services provided and the fact that the main services must be broadcast in English and French. There are two national networks for both radio and television, one in English and one in French. In addition, five regional radio programs serve the Atlantic Provinces, Quebec, Ontario, the Prairie Provinces, and the west coast, while local radio broadcasts are designed for both rural and urban audiences. Programs in other languages are provided by a number of stations for Canadians recently arrived from other parts of the world, and some radio broadcasts originate in several Indian and Eskimo languages.

Thus, the complexity of the Canadian broadcasting system stems from the vast geography of the country as well as the diverse origins and interests of the people. The proximity of the population to the United States also has its effect. From the beginning, competition from U.S. stations has been a spur to Canadian radio broadcasting, and they claim a particularly important part of the audience in Canadian cities close to the border. The same is true of television. There is no doubt, for instance, that the introduction of colour television in Canada was accelerated to meet competition from across the border.

Radio. Since the opening program from Canada's first radio station was beamed into a few Montreal homes in 1919, radio service has grown to the point that it is available, in some form, to 99 percent of all Canadians. This has been accomplished by a unique combination of private and public enterprise. In the early 1980s the publicly owned Canadian Broadcasting Corporation (CBC), a federal crown agency, maintained 64 radio stations and 393 low-power relay transmitters; in addition, some 530 privately owned stations were in operation. Many of the latter are affiliated with the CBC and help to distribute national radio services over networks operated by the CBC. The CBC operates an international service to provide information abroad. Shortwave programs are transmitted daily to Europe, Latin America, Africa, the Caribbean area, and Australasia in 11 languages—English, French, German, Spanish, Portuguese, Czech, Slovak, Russian, Ukrainian, Polish, and Hungarian. Works by Canadian composers and performances by Canadian musicians are

Combination of public–private TV

made available in a variety of categories, including classical, popular, jazz, and folk music. Dramas, talks, documentaries, and other features are included in a wide range of spoken-word transcriptions in English, French, Spanish, and Portuguese. News and special events programs are relayed upon request.

The CBC established a northern service in 1958 to meet the needs of the widely scattered population of the North. Listeners in the more remote areas are able to hear daily shortwave broadcasts of the northern service through Anik satellites. Regular broadcasts are made in Indian and Eskimo languages in addition to French and English.

Television. Canada has about 1,100 television stations, some two-thirds of which are privately operated. As with radio, many of these are affiliated with the CBC, which operates two nationwide networks, one in English and one in French. There are three major commercially operated networks—CTV, Réseau de télévision (TVA), and Global. The governments of Ontario, Quebec, and Alberta operate their own educational networks. Cable television has expanded dramatically since 1970, and by 1980 there were 562 systems in operation.

The Canadian Radio-television and Telecommunications Commission (CRTC) has regulatory power over all aspects of the broadcasting systems and federally regulated telecommunications carriers, including the establishment and authorization of networks and stations, the activities of the CBC and privately owned stations, and the relations between them. The commission is made up of nine full-time members and 10 part-time members, representative of the various regions of Canada.

CBC program policy serves a twofold purpose. In addition to fulfilling audience wants and needs, the corporation develops talent in all fields. Actors, writers, and performers are given opportunities to expand their creative talents through media that offer audiences of a size not possible in Canada through other outlets. During one recent year, some 30,000 Canadian artists, musicians, commentators, and performers of all kinds appeared on CBC radio and television.

PUBLISHING

The Canadian press: extensive, multilingual

Every weekday, some 120 daily newspapers are published in almost 5,400,000 copies. More than four-fifths appear in the afternoon. More than 100 are published in English, 12 in French, and seven in other languages. The trend in daily-newspaper publication is toward chain ownership, mainly by three large chains, one of which owned 36 papers in the early 1980s; editorial policy, however, is developed at the local level. Most newspapers have no competition in their own areas; only 14 cities have more than one paper. In addition to the dailies, about 1,000 weekly papers are published, including about 170 in French and more than 80 in foreign languages.

Behind the newspapers lie two great news-gathering organizations, the Canadian Press and the United Press International of Canada. The former, a cooperative venture formed in 1917, is owned and operated by the Canadian newspapers. United Press International of Canada serves North America, South America, Europe, and Australia with news from Canada, as well as subscribers and private broadcasting stations in Canada. Agence France-Presse maintains offices in Montreal and Ottawa, and several foreign newspapers have agencies in Ottawa to interpret Canadian news for their readers.

Daily newspapers alone contribute about 60 percent of the revenue received from Canadian periodical publications. More than 850 magazines and related publications were published in 1980, of which more than 200 were classed as trade, industry, and related publications and more than 100 as educational. But most of the general magazines that circulate in Canada are from the United States. It is believed that this competition can be met only by providing protection to Canadian publications, though many argue that to do so on a large scale would interfere with the traditional freedom of the press. Canadian book publishing suffers from the same set of circumstances, and the number of wholly Canadian book-publishing companies has declined in recent years.

BIBLIOGRAPHY. LOUIS EDMOND HAMELIN, *Canada: A Geographical Perspective* (1973), a systematic geography, written from a French-Canadian point of view; ROBERT CHRISTIE HOSIE, *Native Trees of Canada,* 8th ed. (1979), an invaluable source for the study of the predominant vegetation (well illustrated); CANADA. SURVEYS AND MAPPING BRANCH. GEOGRAPHY DIVISION, *The National Atlas of Canada,* 4th rev. ed. (1974), covering all aspects of the geography of Canada, with several hundred maps and diagrams; W. EARL GODFREY, *The Birds of Canada* (1966, reprinted 1979); NORMAN L. NICHOLSON and L.M. SEBERT, *The Maps of Canada* (1981), a guide to official Canadian maps, charts, atlases, and gazetteers, with brief accounts of their development; DIAMOND JENNESS, *The Indians of Canada,* 7th ed. (1977), the standard work on this part of Canada's aboriginal population; MASON WADE, *The French Canadians, 1760–1945,* rev. ed. (1968, reprinted 1976), a standard work on the French Canadians from the point of view of an English-speaking historian; DONALD F. PUTNAM and ROBERT G. PUTNAM, *Canada: A Regional Analysis* (1979), a comprehensive economic and geographical treatment of the various regions of Canada, rich in detail; *Encyclopedia Canadiana,* 10 vol. (1977), an invaluable reference work for all aspects of Canada; NORMAN L. NICHOLSON, *The Boundaries of the Canadian Confederation* (1979), a monograph on the evolution of the political boundaries of Canada and each of its provinces and territories; CANADA. STATISTICS CANADA, *Canada Handbook,* an annual summary of conditions and progress, with many excellent photographs and useful data—essentially a popular summary of the *Canada Year Book;* L.D. MCCANN (ed.), *Heartland and Hinterland: A Geography of Canada* (1982), a broad synthesis of the country's evolving regional geography that focusses on the heartland–hinterland paradigm as a framework for interpreting Canada's regional geographic structure; CARL F. KLINCK (ed.), *Literary History of Canada,* 3 vol., 2nd ed. (1976), a comprehensive reference on the English literary history; HELMUT KALLMANN, GILLES POTVIN, and KENNETH WINTERS (eds.), *Encyclopedia of Music in Canada* (1981), an exhaustive, thorough reference; ROBERT WEAVER and WILLIAM TOYE (eds.), *The Oxford Anthology of Canadian Literature* (1973), a dictionary-type anthology of 78 English- and French-Canadian writers.

(N.L.N.)

Canada, History of

The first inhabitants of the territories that now make up Canada were the Indians and Eskimo (Inuit). The former came from northern Asia across the Bering Strait, while the latter were part of the circumpolar dispersion of a race that lived along the edge of the Arctic ice. For the prehistory of the North American Indians, see NORTH AMERICAN PEOPLES AND CULTURES.

I. Canada to 1867

The first Europeans to reach what is now Canadian soil were Norse explorers about AD 1000, as is recorded in the Icelandic sagas and was confirmed by the archaeological discovery of a Norse site at L'Anse-aux-Meadows on the northern peninsula of Newfoundland. While the Norse made no lasting settlements, their voyages traditionally begin most general histories of Canada, largely because of their discovery of the northern route to North America.

The voyage of John Cabot

Only five years after the first voyage of Columbus, an Italian navigator, known to the English as John Cabot, sailed from Bristol in 1497 under the patronage of Henry VII of England by the northern route in an attempt to reach Cathay (China). He made a trip so expeditiously, to a landfall generally accepted as having been on the east coast of Newfoundland, that it is tempting to assume that he had the aid of local knowledge of the route and its winds, perhaps from Bristol fishermen accustomed to sailing in Iceland's waters. Cabot, however, perished in an unknown manner with a large expedition in the following year.

THE SETTLEMENT OF NEW FRANCE

Jacques Cartier. The discoverer of the great entry to Canada, the St. Lawrence River, was the Frenchman Jacques Cartier. In 1534, in a voyage conducted with great competence, he explored the Gulf of St. Lawrence and claimed its shores for the French crown. In the following year Cartier ascended the river itself and visited the sites of Stadacona (Quebec) and Hochelaga (Montreal). So favourable were his reports that the French king, anxious to challenge the claims of Spain in the New

World, decided to set up a fortified settlement. Internal and European politics delayed the enterprise until 1541, when, under the command of Sieur de Roberval, Cartier returned to Stadacona and founded Charlesbourg-Royal just above Quebec. Cartier had hoped to discover precious gems and minerals, as the Spaniards had done in Mexico and Peru. But the mineral speciments he sent home were worthless, and "false as a Canadian diamond" became a common French expression. Disappointed in his attempt to reach the mythical "Kingdom of Saguenay," the reputed source of precious metals, Cartier returned to France after a severe winter, deserting Roberval, who had arrived in Newfoundland with reinforcements. Roberval also failed, and during the century only two subsequent attempts were made at exploiting the French claim to the lands of the St. Lawrence. The French claim remained; it had only to be made good by actual occupation.

At that time overseas adventure and explorations had to earn their own expenses. The search for minerals in the St. Lawrence region having failed, there remained only two possibilities of immediate profit: the great maritime fisheries of Newfoundland and Nova Scotia and the fur trade of the adjoining lands. Indeed, the latter grew out of the former, beginning as barter between crews of fishing vessels and later becoming the object of separate trading voyages.

The monopoly of Chauvin

In 1600 the Norman entrepreneur Pierre Chauvin obtained from King Henry IV a ten years' monopoly of the fur trade in the Gulf of St. Lawrence, in return for which he was to settle 50 Frenchmen a year in the country. The monopoly was designed to exclude unauthorized traders, both foreign and French, from the area. Private traders might well garner, by being first on the spot, the furs brought down to the coast by the Indians and thus render a whole year's voyage unprofitable. But royal policy, concerned to confirm the French claim to the St. Lawrence and its approaches, knew that only permanent settlement would make good the French title against that of the Spanish, the English, and the Dutch.

Samuel de Champlain. Chauvin died in 1602 and was succeeded by the Sieur de Chaste. His geographical expert, Samuel de Champlain, was led by reports of the milder climate of Nova Scotia (Acadia) to urge that the enterprise turn to that region to form a settlement. In 1604 Champlain, under the Sieur de Monts, who had received a grant of the monopoly, led a group of settlers to Acadia. He chose as a site Dochet Island in the St. Croix River, on the present boundary between the United States and Canada. But the island proved unsuitable, and in 1605 the colony was moved across the Bay of Fundy to Port Royal (now Annapolis, Nova Scotia). The colony was to survive not only as a trading post but also as a centre of settlement. But the rugged, forested inlets of the Nova Scotian peninsula, the heavy forests of the St. John River, and the many bays and beaches of Cape Breton and Prince Edward islands made it impossible to enforce the monopoly of the fur trade against enterprising interlopers.

Foundation of Quebec

In 1608, therefore, de Monts and Champlain left Acadia and returned to the St. Lawrence. At "the place where the river narrowed" (Quebec), they built a "habitation" (*i.e.*, a fur-trading fort, or factory) to control the great river and to be the mart of its fur trade. Already in 1603 Champlain had noted that the Iroquois (or Huronian) Indians, whom Jacques Cartier had found there, had withdrawn from the St. Lawrence under pressure from the Algonkin (Algonquin) Indians of the north country and Acadia. The French now became the allies of the Algonkins in the fierce rivalry that began for control of the inland fur trade. In 1609, in accordance with this alliance, Champlain and three armed companions joined an Algonkin war party in a raid against the lands of the Mohawks, the easternmost tribe of the Iroquois Confederacy. The party ascended the Richelieu River to Lake Champlain. In an encounter with a Mohawk band, the fire arms of Champlain and his men killed some Iroquois and struck panic into the remainder. This skirmish signalled the commitment of New France to the side of the Algonkins and the Hurons (Iroquoian but hostile to the confederacy) in the century-long struggle for control of the output of furs from as far away as the western Great Lakes.

The company of de Monts and his frequent successors, to whom Champlain remained the lieutenant in New France, had the obligation to bring out settlers, as well as the exclusive right, seldom enforced, to trade in furs. Their efforts at settlement were even less successful, partly because settlement was not easy in a country of heavy forests and severe winters and partly because the fur trade had little need of settlers beyond its own employees. The company, moreover, had scant funds to bring out and establish colonists on the land. Champlain did the best he could, and he also encouraged missionaries (first the Recollects [Franciscans], then the Jesuits) to come to Quebec to convert the Indians. His greatest interest, however, lay in exploration. Already in Acadia, in 1606 and 1607, he had surveyed the coast southward and westward to Stage Harbor, only to be rebuffed by hostile Indians. Had he persisted, it is not impossible that the Hudson River, the mouth of which was discovered by the Florentine navigator Giovanni de Verrazano in French service, might have been the French entry to America rather than the St. Lawrence.

In 1613 Champlain set out from Quebec to explore the upper St. Lawrence Basin. He passed the Île de Montréal, not settled since Cartier's time but used by traders who bypassed Quebec. In order to avoid the heavy rapids of the St. Lawrence, he ascended its great tributary, the Ottawa, only to be turned back at the Île aux Allumettes by the Algonkin middlemen who were trading for the furs of the Hurons and other people further inland and who wished to retain that trade. There Champlain, however, heard of the "inland sea" (Hudson Bay), the existence of which he had divined before he could have heard of Henry Hudson's discovery of it in 1610. Undaunted, he ascended the Ottawa again in 1615, passed by the Mattawa River, Lake Nipissing, and the French River to Georgian Bay, and turned south to "Huronia" (the land of the Hurons). He wintered with the Indians and went with a Huron war party to raid an Onondaga village south of the St. Lawrence. He was slightly wounded and the party was repulsed, but Champlain had once more confirmed the alliance of the northern tribes and the Hurons against the Iroquois and, by the opening of the Ottawa route, had secured the midcontinent for the French fur trade.

Alliance against the Iroquois

The discovery of this inland, central region was perhaps Champlain's main achievement. He had no success, however, from 1616 to 1627 in maintaining the fur trade. The fault was not entirely his, for the enterprise in itself was very difficult. The coupling of trade and settlement was somewhat contradictory, and it was impossible to finance both out of annual profits, especially as the French government failed to uphold the monopoly.

The Company of New France. The French government was to supply more active support after the remarkable revival of royal power carried out by Cardinal de Richelieu in the 1620s. Richelieu sought to make French colonial policy comparable with that of England and the Netherlands, joint victors with France in the long struggle in Europe against Spain. These countries had found in the joint-stock company a means both of raising capital and enforcing trading rights. Richelieu used his power to create such a company to exploit the resources and settle the lands of New France. This was the Company of New France, commonly called the "Hundred Associates" from the number of its shareholders. It was given broad powers and wide responsibility: the monopoly of trade with all New France, Acadia as well as Canada; powers of government; the obligation to take out 400 settlers a year; and the task of keeping New France in the Roman Catholic faith.

The company was chartered, and its capital raised in 1627. The next year, however, war broke out with the English, who supported the French Protestants, or Huguenots, in their struggle against Richelieu. The war was mismanaged and inconclusive, but it gave a pretext for the Kirke brothers, English adventurers who had connections in France with Huguenot competitors of the Hundred Associates, to blockade the St. Lawrence in 1628 and to capture Quebec in 1629. For three years the fur trade was to be in the hands of the Kirkes and their French associates the brothers de Caën. It was a stunning blow to the new company and to Champlain, who was taken prisoner to England. At the same time, Acadia, already raided from Virginia in 1613, was claimed by Scotland. An attempt at settlement there was made by Sir William Alexander, to whom Nova Scotia (New Scotland) had been granted by the Scottish king James VI (after 1603, James I of England).

The Scots in Nova Scotia

It is difficult to estimate the effect of the war on the policy of the Hundred Associates. Canada and Acadia were restored by the Treaty of Saint-Germain-en-Laye in 1632, and the company retook possession in 1633. On the surface all seemed to go smoothly. In 1633 Champlain returned as governor; the government and settlement of Acadia was farmed out to the vigorous Isaac de Razilly; the Society of Jesus assumed sole responsibility for the care of souls in Canada and for the conversion of the Indians. The fur trade was resumed, and the Trois Rivières settlement was founded in 1634 to control the Saint-Maurice River. Settlement began, but the company seemed unable to recoup the losses caused by the capture of Quebec and by the disruption of five years' trade and seemed unable to make profits that would both pay dividends and provide for the costs of settlement. The company remained the proprietor of New France until 1663, providing a succession of governors and other officials, but it never succeeded in meeting its obligations to colonize. Weary of its profitless task, the company leased the fur trade to private companies and then, in 1645, to a group of Canadian residents known as the Community of Habitants. The Company of New France became merely a sort of holding company or "sleeping partner." To strengthen the government of New France in the new circumstances, a council was set up in 1647 by the King's council in France.

The character of French settlement. The fur trade was not the sole enterprise of New France. By 1645 settlers in Canada and Acadia were producing provisions for the fur traders and the annual ships. The mode of landholding, known as the seigneurial system, a modified form of feudal land law and justice, was begun. But the great partner and sometime rival of the fur trade was the missionary endeavour of the Jesuits. They had two obligations: (1) to keep New France Catholic by ministering to its people and excluding Huguenots and (2) to convert the Indians. The missionaries made the conversion of the Hurons their principal concern. Huronia, on the southeast corner of Georgian Bay, was the seat of one of the most civilized and sedentary tribes in North America. It was also the hub of the inland fur trade. To make Huronia a Christian community would create a centre of Christianity and confirm the French commercial alliance with the Hurons and their Algonkin clients. French missionaries had already visited Huronia in the mid-1620s, and in 1634 the Jesuits resumed the mission, which thrived, at least outwardly, for ten years. Its success, however, menaced the trade of the Iroquois with the Dutch in New Amsterdam, and, in 1648 and 1649, the Confederation savagely and completely devastated Huronia. Thereafter, both missionaries and traders had to follow the trading Indians farther inland across the Great Lakes and, eventually, to the Mississippi and Saskatchewan rivers.

Missionary activity

These checks to both the fur trade and the missions, at least in terms of the intentions and hopes of 1627, were the result not only of bad luck and poor management but also of the economic conditions of New France, which depended almost entirely on the fur trade for profit. Settlement was unprofitable to both the company and the colonists. Population, therefore, grew quite slowly, rising from an estimated 200 residents (*habitants*) in 1642 to perhaps 2,500 by 1663; and by no means all of these were farmers. The fur trade, however, was booming, borne up by the fashion of the beaver felt hat in Europe. The traders at Quebec, and at what after 1642 became Montreal, brought French goods to trade with the flotillas of canoes that carried the furs of the Ottawa and Great Lakes countries, which before 1648 were usually manned by Huron middlemen. This was the sole commercial enterprise of New France. The few farmers supplied Quebec, Trois Rivières, and Montreal with grain, milk, and eggs; but as yet nothing from the lands or forests of New France moved down to sea and markets abroad.

Royal control. New France, though a proprietary colony, was governed by the company, which appointed governors for Canada and Acadia, and a few dependent officers. The kings of France remained interested in the colony, both because of the vast potential wealth of the area and because the crown might have to resume the powers of government given to the Hundred Associates. Government was, in fact, very much what it would have been if the colony had been directly under the rule of the crown. The council that had been established in 1647 included the governor, the chief religious authority, the superior of the Jesuits, and the governor of Montreal. During the brief rule of the Community of Habitants, representatives (syndics) of the people of Quebec, Trois Rivières, and Montreal were consulted on local matters. This, however, was the nearest approach to anything like representative government. Government in New France, as in old, was authoritarian and paternalistic, but it was not despotic, nor was it necessarily harsh.

Nor was it always efficient, and this, with the commercial lassitude of the Hundred Associates, but most of all the assumption of power by Louis XIV and the colonial ambitions of his great finance minister, Jean-Baptiste Colbert, led to a recasting of French colonial policy and of the government of New France. Colbert entrusted commercial policy to a new Company of the West Indies. Politically, he made New France a royal province, governed much like a province of France itself. The substance of power and the immediate direction of justice, economic policy, and the militia lay in an intendant, a powerful royal official hitherto unknown in New France. Because of distance and the long winter of no communication, the governor also had a council, at first called the Sovereign Council and, later, the Superior Council, to advise him. The governor was largely a titular officer, except in his power of presiding at the council and in the conduct of relations with the Indian tribes—the most important business in a fur-trade colony. The bishop (also a member of the council) and the intendant, great powers in virtue of their offices, often quarrelled with the governor, notably the famous Comte de Frontenac, in the conduct of the colony's affairs. New France's first bishop, François de Montmorency de Laval, was installed in 1659; from 1674, he was called bishop of Quebec.

Colbert's reorganization

The general effect of Colbert's reorganization, however, was to give New France firm and rational government thereafter, strongly centralized and efficient for the times. The exception was Acadia. Torn by feuds among French rivals, claimed by England, and occupied by New Englanders eager to exploit its fishery, Acadia did not again become an effective part of New France until 1667–70.

The strength of the royal government was in inverse proportion to the weakness of a small and scattered population. Great efforts made by the first intendant, Jean Talon, did indeed bring some thousands of settlers, hundreds of them women, to New France in the 1660s and early 1670s. The population in 1666 reached 3,215; in 1676, about 8,500; thereafter, however, the population grew largely by natural increase, fortunately at a prodigious rate. Most of the population lived in the three towns (Montreal, Quebec, and Trois Rivières) and in seigneuries along the banks of the St. Lawrence between Quebec and Montreal. Scores of the men, however, went inland with the trading canoes, and some of these voyageurs remained inland permanently, marrying Indian women and fathering the Métis, or people of mixed French and Indian blood.

Intendant Jean Talon

The frontier of New France was, in brief, not a broad

front of advance but, rather, a penetration of the wilderness by the rivers. The fur trade meant dispersion of effort and resources on the Indians, with whom harmonious relations were so necessary, rather than on colonization. In general, the French allied themselves with the northern tribes against the Iroquois Confederation. The Iroquois, after destroying the Huron towns in 1648 and 1649, later subordinated all the tribes as far as Lake Michigan. The French, however, managed by repeated wars with the Iroquois to maintain their alliance and to penetrate as far inland as the Mississippi, explored as far as Arkansas by Louis Jolliet in 1672. In relations with Indians the French missionaries also played an important role, for, in addition to their religious activities, they also served as ambassadors and agents of the colony in the fur trade.

The growth of Anglo-French rivalry. In the 1660s two voyageurs, Médard Chouart des Groseilliers and Pierre Esprit Radisson, exasperated by the high cost of the long haul back to Quebec and by the heavy tax on fur pelts, fled to New England. From there they were escorted to England, where in 1668 they persuaded a group of London merchants to attempt to gain the fur trade of the midcontinent by way of Hudson Bay. This led to the formation in 1670 of the Hudson's Bay Company, a late proprietary company that was given exclusive trading rights in all the territory draining into Hudson Bay. New France now found itself caught between the Iroquois, supported by the Dutch and English, to the south, and the Hudson's Bay Company to the north. In this juncture lay one cause of the great wars of the next century. At the time, however, the French were led by Governor Frontenac's ambitions merely to maintain their inland corridor, although the French under La Salle pushed to the mouth of the Mississippi in 1682. After Frontenac's recall, they tried repeatedly to eject the English from the bay, which they also claimed. In 1686 a French expedition from Canada destroyed the English posts in James Bay (at the south end of Hudson Bay), and in the 1690s the noted Canadian commander Pierre Le Moyne d'Iberville captured all English posts in the bay but one. The French held these posts throughout Queen Anne's War (1702–13), the American phase of the War of the Spanish Succession (1701–14) in Europe. At the same time, the French were able to reduce the Iroquois to neutrality and to keep the alliance of the inland tribes. But, defeated in Europe, the French were ejected from the bay and, more important, from Acadia and a foothold in Newfoundland by the Treaty of Utrecht in 1713. New France was still held in the vise of the English to the south and north and had lost all the approaches to the St. Lawrence except Cape Breton Island.

The Treaty of Utrecht

After Queen Anne's War there followed a generation of peace during which the governors of New France built a line of fortified posts: Louisbourg on Cape Breton Island, Chambly on the Richelieu River, Carillon (Ticonderoga) on the portage from Lake George to Lake Champlain; the trading posts of Niagara, Toronto, Detroit, and Michilimackinac extended the line to the west. At the same time, French priests and military emissaries kept the Acadians and the Indian allies of New France aware of their former ties with New France. The Acadians, claiming to be "neutral," obstinately refused to take the oath of allegiance to the British crown.

For New France the early 18th century was a period of steady growth in population, settlement, and industry. French *défrichements* ("clearings") spread along the St. Lawrence between Quebec and Montreal; the iron forges at Saint-Maurice produced iron for Quebec stoves and even cannons; shipbuilding flourished. The colony nevertheless remained largely dependent on the fur trade, which, in turn, depended on keeping the west open. Access to the far west was frustrated, however, by the three Fox wars (1714–42), in which that small but obstinate tribe strove with much success to close the Wisconsin portages to French traders. Then Pierre Gaultier de Varennes, sieur de La Vérendrye, turned the flanks of the Fox and Sioux by proceeding by way of Lake Superior and the Rainy River to the Lake of the Woods and the Red and Saskatchewan River country. There he found a new region for the French fur trade and also cut into the English trade in the area of Hudson Bay and the Hayes River.

The expansion of New France in these years was challenged, however, by the outbreak of the War of the Austrian Succession in Europe in 1740. In America the war became known as King George's War (1744–48). Fighting broke out again in Acadia, on Lake Champlain, and among the English and French Indian allies in the country of the Great Lakes and the Ohio Valley. It was a confused conflict of raids and reprisals marked by only one action of major significance—the capture of Louisbourg by an expedition from New England. But the conflict revealed the need for a final struggle for the mastery of the continent. Holding the St. Lawrence Valley, the Great Lakes, and the mouth of the Mississippi, the French commanded the better strategic position in America. But the English colonies, if lacking central direction, were far wealthier and more populous. England, moreover, enjoyed the advantage at sea. In consequence, the chief outcome of King George's War was that the supply of French trade goods was cut off and replaced by cheaper and better made English goods. The loyalty of the western tribes, on which the French positions largely depended, was undermined.

King George's War

All this was perceived by Roland Michel Barrin, marquis de La Galissonière, the exceptionally able governor of New France (1747–49). He declared in a memorandum to the French court that New France must restore its position by a bold advance into the Ohio Valley, which hitherto had not really been claimed by New France or its Indian allies. His policy was adopted by his successors, and in 1749 Céleron de Blainville led an expedition down the Ohio to claim the valley for France and thereby confine English colonists and their fur trade to the east of the Alleghenies. The British colonists, from New York to Virginia, immediately felt the threat to their trade, to their expansion, and to their settlement. In 1749 the Ohio Company was formed in London with English and American support, and the fortress of Halifax in Nova Scotia was built to counter the French fort at Louisbourg, which had been restored to New France by the peace of 1748 ending King George's War. In 1753 an American expedition under young George Washington was sent to the Forks of the Ohio—the site of present-day Pittsburgh, Pennsylvania—to make good the English claim.

The French and Indian War. The French had also been active on the Ohio and had opened a line of communication from Lake Erie to the Forks. The rivals clashed on the Monongahela, and Washington was forced to surrender and retreat. This clash marked the beginning of the Anglo-French war known in America as the French and Indian War (1754–63) and in Europe as the Seven Years' War (*q.v.;* 1756–63). England resolutely supported the colonies and sought to recover the Ohio Valley by an expedition under Gen. Edward Braddock in 1755. This, too, was bloodily repulsed on the Monongahela, and both sides then reinforced their colonies with regular troops. It was to be a war for empire; how sternly it was to be fought was made clear by the expulsion of the Acadians from Nova Scotia in 1755.

Defeat of Braddock

The French in America, cut off by British blockade, fought to hold the long line from the Ohio to the Bay of Fundy, counting on the results in Europe for a victory. Britain, however, while subsidizing and aiding Prussia, its only European ally, sought victory in America and sent across the Atlantic what was, for that century, an overwhelming body of regular troops in order to stiffen the militia of the American colonies. The first victories went to the French, who captured Ft. Oswego and Ft. William Henry in 1757 and sternly repulsed the British at Fort-Carillon (Ft. Ticonderoga) in 1758. Then numbers and more skillful British generalship began to tell. In 1758 the British captured and razed Louisbourg. In 1759 Sir Jeffrey Amherst began a cautious but irresistible advance from Ft. William Henry by way of Ft. Ticonderoga to Lake Champlain. In the same year an expedition under Gen. James Wolfe sailed up the St. Lawrence and besieged Quebec, which fell to the British after the celebrated Battle of the Plains of Abraham. Sir William Johnson took Niagra, and John Bradstreet took the Forks of the Ohio. New France was caught in cruelly closing pincers. In 1760 Amherst closed in on Montreal, and New France capitulated. By the terms of the Treaty of Paris in 1763, all French North America east of the Mississippi was ceded to Britain. The Louisiana Territory, west of the river, was given to Spain. Britain and its colonies had thus eliminated France from North America.

The British victory produced three major results: (1) The danger from New France to the American colonies was ended, thus weakening their dependence on Britain. (2) The British (largely Scots with some Americans) took over and expanded the Canadian fur trade. (3) Britain now possessed a colony populated almost wholly by persons of alien descent.

CANADA UNDER BRITISH RULE, 1763–91

The Quebec Act. The governance of New France was a problem to the British government. The Royal Proclamation (October 7, 1763) made broad decisions on this and on the related matter of the territory between the Alleghenies and the Mississippi. The latter was declared to be Indian territory and was closed to settlement until the Indians there could be quieted. The French province of Canada now became the colony of Quebec, was cut off from the upper country, and provided with a royal governor with the authority to call an assembly. The assumption underlying the latter provision was that American settlers from New England and New York would move into the new colony and would outnumber the some 70,000 French habitants. Quebec, in short, was to become the traditional royal colony, with English institutions and a largely English population.

The Royal Procla-mation of 1763

This assumption proved unfounded. Few American colonists moved to Quebec, and those who did sought trade rather than land. Moreover, the summoning of an assembly, in which the French, as Roman Catholics, would be unable to sit, would place taxation and representation of the colony in the control of a small body of Protestant newcomers (perhaps 500 in all). Gen. James Murray, who had served as military governor from 1760 to 1764, was now appointed civil governor. Murray sympathized with the condition and difficulties of the French and ignored the demands of the Protestant "old subjects" for an assembly, with the result that an agitation by the old subjects led to his recall. He was replaced in 1766 by Gen. Guy Carleton, who was expected in Quebec to carry out the policy of the proclamation. Carleton, however, soon came to see that the colony was certain to be permanently French. Fearful of renewed war with France, he also envisioned Canada as returning to the role of New France as a check on the growing independence and expansion of the English colonies along the Atlantic seaboard.

Carleton returned to England to 1770 to press his new policy for Quebec on the government of Lord North. The trouble the imperial government continued to have with the colonies, together with a certain nascent liberalism among English politicians, combined to bring success to Carleton's policy. The result was the Quebec Act of 1774, by which the province of Quebec was expanded to include all the inland territory to the Ohio and the Mississippi. The new colony was given a governor and an appointed council. Roman Catholics were allowed to hold office by providing a form of oath to which they could subscribe. French was made an official language, along with English, and French civil law was restored, but with English criminal law. The Roman Catholic faith was recognized, and the church was allowed to collect the tithes of the faithful.

Political and religious toleration for the French

Toward the French Canadians the act was liberal and conciliatory; toward the American colonies it was menacing, as their strong protests gave evidence, in that it re-established to the north and west a great military power, French and Indian, despotically governed as they saw it.

The impact of the American Revolution. In any case, the act assumed the predominance of the French in Quebec. Moreover, instead of intimidating the American colonies, the act helped push the Americans to open revolt. Indeed, the first act of the American Continental Congress in 1775 was not to declare independence but to invade Canada. And the failure of that invasion ensured that north of the Rio Grande the continent would, on the recognition of American independence, be divided between the Americans and the British.

Not all American colonists had supported the cause of independence, and many had resisted it in arms. At the conclusion of hostilities, these loyalists had to make their peace with the new republic, as by far the greater part did, or go into exile. The refugees, known as United Empire Loyalists, were the object of considerable concern to the British government, which sought to compensate them for their losses and to assist them in establishing new homes. Some went to the United Kingdom, others to the British West Indies, but the majority emigrated to Nova Scotia or Canada. Nova Scotia, which to a great extent had been recently settled by American colonists, had not, except for an ineffectual rising or two, joined the revolting colonies. Overawed by British sea power and by the fortress of Halifax, Nova Scotians at first kept quiet, and later many of them even made fortunes pri-

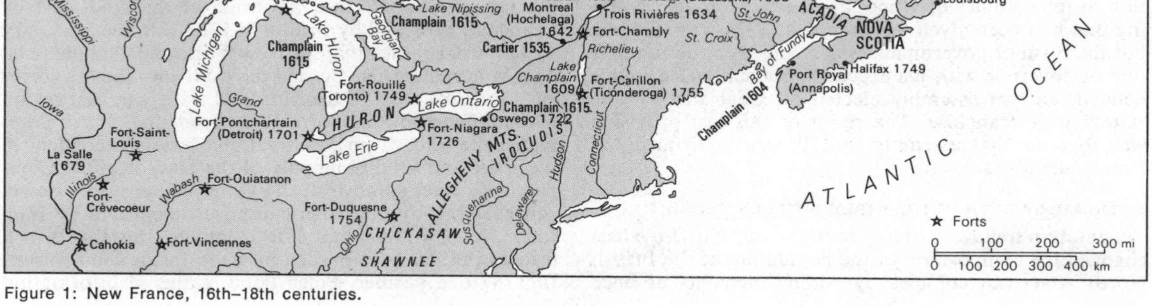

Figure 1: New France, 16th–18th centuries.

vateering against American commerce. Easily reached by sea from New York, Nova Scotia became the chief refuge of the Loyalists. Some settled in the peninsula itself, some in Cape Breton and in the separate colony of Prince Edward Island. A large number, however, settled along the St. John River, north of the Bay of Fundy. Dissatisfied with tardy government from Halifax, they promptly agitated for a government of their own, and equally promptly the new province of New Brunswick was erected for them in 1784, with its own governor and assembly.

The impact of the Loyalists on the province of Quebec was even greater, resulting also in a new province and, perhaps more important, the Constitutional Act of 1791.

The Loyalist population

The Loyalists who settled in Canada were for the most part quite different from those who went to what were soon to be called the Maritime Provinces. The latter had possessed an elite of government officials and professional men, often Loyalist regiments with their officers and men, from the long-settled seaboard areas. The Canadian Loyalists, however, were largely from upper New York, especially the Mohawk Valley country, and were almost wholly simple frontier folk and recent immigrants, driven from their homes by neighbours who often used the Revolution to dispossess them of their lands; hence, the bitter fighting along the frontier and the long Loyalist hatred in the new province for all things American.

Their coming transformed the character of the population of Quebec. That province had been given a government much like that of New France, except for the important office of intendant, and the province was in population almost wholly French, as it was in civil law. Most Loyalists simply crossed the new frontier and settled along the St. Lawrence River. They all had one desire, to hold the land granted them in simple ownership, something the civil law of Quebec did not allow. Some of them—how many is uncertain—also wanted representative government, denied by the Quebec Act. Their representations reached London and were listened to with respect, as they were, after all, from people who had lost everything fighting for the crown.

The Constitutional Act of 1791. Their appeals caused a great problem for the British government. The measures taken in the Quebec Act to conciliate the French could not in honour or policy be withdrawn. Yet the Loyalists could not be required to live under French civil and land law and without the representative assembly to which they were accustomed. One obvious answer was to divide Quebec into separate French and English provinces. The English province would have, of course, English common law and an assembly. The French province might have been left with the forms of government provided by the Quebec Act. But there had already been one revolution in America, and, by 1789, another had broken out in France. British statesmen felt that the former had occurred partly because Americans had not been granted the British constitution in its proper forms. The thing to do, therefore, was to give, not only the new province but Quebec as well, the British constitution in its entirety, or at least as far as the circumstances of small colonies might permit. The result would be, it was hoped, to assimilate the French population of Quebec to British institutions.

After a fiery debate in the British House of Commons, the Constitutional Act of 1791 gave the same constitution to the colonies of Upper and Lower Canada. Nothing that had been given the French in 1774 was revoked, but the form of government was changed to the familiar one of governor with his executive council, a legislative council, and an assembly elected on what was for the time a wide franchise. The result of this last provision was that the first assembly in 1792 had a majority of French members.

NATIONAL GROWTH IN THE EARLY 19TH CENTURY

Population trends. The coming of the Loyalists changed the composition of the population of the British North American colonies by adding elements at once American yet profoundly attached to British institutions; it also increased the population by some 6,000 in the old province of Quebec. To these were to be added the unknown numbers of "late Loyalists"—settlers, primarily land seekers, who arrived from the northern states as late as 1812. Some 80,000 came to Nova Scotia, although not all remained; of these, some 20,000 settled in what became New Brunswick, and a few hundred on Prince Edward Island.

The ethnic mixture

They added also to the growing diversity of the population of the colonies. In Newfoundland there were already the west country English and a growing number of Irish—a total of 26,505 in 1806. In Nova Scotia there were, in addition to New Englanders, Loyalists, and Yorkshiremen, the Germans of Lunenburg and the Highland Scots of Pictou county and of Cape Breton Island—in all, an estimated 65,000 in 1806, with 2,513 on Cape Breton Island. New Brunswick had a population of about 35,000 in 1806, mostly Loyalists or of Loyalist descent, but already the southern Irish, drawn by the timber trades, were beginning to appear on the rivers of the north shore. Prince Edward Island, with a population of 9,676 in 1806, had some Acadians, some Loyalists, some English, Scots, and Irish. In Upper Canada in 1806 the population numbered 70,718; in Lower it was estimated at 250,000 for the same year.

The first Canadian mosaic had taken shape as it was to remain for a century, a population of British, French, and German. The British element was to be steadily reinforced by northern English, coming by way of Liverpool, Highland and Lowland Scots, and southern and northern Irish. The result was the creation of a society in which religious liberty and a great measure of social equality were necessary for social cohesion and common effort.

Until 1815, however, the number of immigrants was small: Highlanders for Glengarry County in Upper Canada, disbanded soldiers in Lanark County south of the Ottawa River, and a straggle of Irish after the crushing of the rebellion of 1798. Nor did the numbers greatly increase after 1815; not until 1830 did the English, Scots, and Irish begin to come to the British North American colonies in great volume. Afterward, thousands came each year, until the population of Newfoundland reached 73,700 (1836); Prince Edward Island, 32,300 (1838); Nova Scotia, 202,575 (1838); New Brunswick, 156,162 (1840); Lower Canada, estimated at 716,600 (1840); and Upper Canada, 432,159 (1840). The British North American colonies had become predominantly British in population, except in Lower Canada, a fact that was to determine the course of Canadian history for the next 100 years.

The Montreal fur traders. To an important degree Canadians were becoming less American than they had been in 1783. The redivision of the continent begun by the American Revolution had been intensified by rivalry in the fur trade. As noted above, the French fur trade of Montreal had been taken over by British fur traders who conducted the trade with the aid of French experience and skill. The British supplied the capital, and the French voyageurs supplied the skill of canoemen and the knowledge of the country and the Indian. These "Montrealers" pushed the trade with great boldness southwest from Montreal, where they had persuaded the British government not to surrender the fur posts after 1783 on the ground that debts owing Loyalists had not been paid by the United States. Thus, the trade of the lands lost by France in 1763 and by Britain in 1783 was kept tributary to Montreal rather than to New York and Philadelphia. The Montrealers also pushed the trade into the far northeast. By 1784 most of the Montreal traders to that region

The North West Company

had combined in the North West Company, which dominated the trade from Montreal and seriously challenged the trade and legal monopoly of the Hudson's Bay Company. In the southwest, however, they were slowly squeezed out by the American government and by John Jacob Astor's American Fur Company. So the British traders pushed ever harder into the farthest northwest. In 1787 one partner, Peter Pond, gathered information about a great river that he was convinced flowed into the Pacific. In 1789 a young Scot, Alexander Mackenzie, followed that river, later named after him, to an outlet in the Arctic Ocean. It was a bitter disappointment, for Mackenzie had hoped to find a passage to the Pacific by which the high cost of bringing furs to Montreal could be avoided. In 1793 Mackenzie crossed what is now British Columbia to the Pacific at Bute Inlet. It was a great feat of exploration but did not lead to a route to the Pacific. That route was to be found years later, on the eve of the War of 1812 with the United States, on the Columbia River by the great geographer David Thompson, only to find that Astor's men had preceded him to the mouth of the Columbia.

The War of 1812. The War of 1812 was to a large degree caused by the Anglo-American rivalry in the fur trade. British traders and soldiers had supplied Indian tribes and afforded them moral support in their contest with the advancing American frontier. Britain had surrendered the western posts by the Jay Treaty of 1794, but the cause of the Canadian fur trade and of the Indians remained the same—the preservation of the wilderness. Certainly, apart from single ship actions and privateering, the war was fought for the conquest of Canada and its elimination as an ally of the Indian. In the end, the war was a stalemate and closed with no concession by either side. It did, however, push back the Indian frontier, increase the breach between the United States and the British North American colonies, and confirm the boundary line between Canada and the United States.

The U.S.–Canadian boundary

That boundary had been fixed in 1783, by a line running from the mouth of the St. Croix River to the "high lands" dividing Quebec from Maine; then by the mountains between the St. Lawrence and Connecticut River valleys to the 45th parallel; by that line to the St. Lawrence; then by centre line of the river and the Great Lakes and the Pigeon and Rainy rivers to the northwest angle of the Lake of the Woods. The Treaty of Ghent, 1814, confirmed this, although the location of the Maine–New Brunswick boundary remained in dispute until the Webster–Ashburton Treaty of 1842. The Rush–Bagot Agreement of 1817 limited naval armaments on the Great Lakes, while another convention in 1818 reduced the rights of American fishermen along the shores of the Atlantic colonies and made the 49th parallel the boundary from the Lake of the Woods to the Rocky Mountains. Beyond, the Oregon Territory was to be jointly occupied for a period of ten years, an occupation ended by the division of the territory, after some threat of war over the American claim to the whole, by extending the 49th parallel to the Strait of Georgia in the Oregon Treaty of 1846. Vancouver Island remained British.

The Rebellion of 1837. The colonies grew quietly but steadily after the War of 1812, aided by the development of the timber trade and shipbuilding and by increased immigration from the British Isles. The growth of population and social sophistication led to growth of a reform movement, stimulated by similar movements in Great Britain and the United States. The movement was essentially attempted to make the institutions of the colonies more popular and less the monopoly of the royal governors and the appointed and permanent councils. The rise of a middle class of professional men, especially lawyers and journalists, and the importance of religious liberty in a population so diverse in faith underlay this development. In the Maritimes, the movement proceeded peaceably and constitutionally under the leadership of forceful but moderate reformers, such as Joseph Howe of Nova Scotia. But Upper Canada, under the leadership of the irascible Scots democrat William Lyon Mackenzie, was more militant. In Lower Canada, matters became much more serious for two reasons: one was that the political division was to a great extent a national split between English and French; the other was that the wheat farming of the habitants was primitive and dependent on new lands and exhausted both the fertility and the extent of the good soils. An economic depression in 1837 intensified political grievances and burst into open rebellion. A hasty and unplanned republican rising in Lower Canada was crushed by the British regular garrison and the militia; and an even more scrambled rising in Upper Canada was put down by the militia alone.

The Union of Canada. The abortive rebellions, however, did dramatize the need to reform Canada's outmoded and constrictive constitution. The "Canadian question" became a leading issue in British politics. Lord Durham was sent out as governor general with a royal commission to enquire into the causes of the troubles.

The Durham Report (1839)

Durham's stay in Canada was brief, but his enquiry was sweeping and his recommendations trenchant. Durham perceived that the colonies had stagnated and that if they were to live side by side with the dynamic United States, they must be brought into the full stream of material progress. One political means to this end was union. Durham decided the time for the union of all the North American colonies had not yet come, but he did recommend the reunion of at least the two Canadas in order to realize the economic possibilities of the St. Lawrence Valley. In Durham's view, union would also bring the French, whom he saw as a backward people, into the progressive ways of English politics and business. Second, he adopted a proposal of certain Upper Canadian and Nova Scotian reformers for "responsible government." This would make the colonial executive responsible to the assembly and assure colonial self-government. Other than local matters would continue under imperial control.

The British government did not share Durham's confidence that such a division between local and imperial affairs could be made and refused an explicit grant of responsible government. It did, however, take measures to end the permanent tenure of members of the executive councils and ordered the governors to govern in harmony with their assembly. The government did accept the proposal to unite the Canadas, and in 1841 the united province of Canada came into being under a new and dynamic governor, Charles Poulett Thomson (later Lord Sydenham). The Union was meant to incorporate the French much like any other group into the population, but the political capacity of Louis Hippolyte Lafontaine converted the Union into a quasi-federal government in which the French remained an almost insoluble bloc. At the same time, the attempt of Sydenham to modernize the administration of Canada and govern in harmony with the assembly prepared the way for the recognition of responsible government. That was finally recognized beyond question, first in Nova Scotia, next in Canada, in 1848.

Achievement of responsible government

The British North American colonies, then, had achieved self-government by 1848; the next decade saw their laws and institutions remodelled to fit the individual needs of each colony. But for Canada at least, the time was at hand for expansion. The British repeal of the Corn Laws in 1846 had deprived the colonies of imperial protective tariffs. The Grand Trunk Railway, begun in 1853, was an attempt to draw the trade of the American Middle West down the St. Lawrence. The Reciprocity Treaty of 1854 in part replaced imperial with continental trade, but close U.S.–Canadian trade relations were dangerous in that they might end in political union with the United States, especially if the Southern states were to secede from the American Union. The only Canadian solution to Canada's difficulties was to expand into the territory of the Hudson's Bay Company in the northwest.

From 1766 to 1821 the North West Territory had been the scene of competition between the traders from Montreal and the older English monopoly. This competition had been accelerated in 1811, when Lord Selkirk had bought a controlling interest in the Hudson's Bay Company. Selkirk persuaded the company that its title to the lands of the northwest and beyond would be confirmed by planting a colony on Red River of the North. The colony, begun in 1812, lay at the juncture of the plains country, which provided pemmican to supply preserved food for the canoe brigades of the North West Company, and the forest country, where the furs were taken. The result was five years of warfare between the companies, marked by the skirmish of Seven Oaks on the Red River in 1816, in which the governor of the Red River Settlement, Robert Semple, and 20 of his men were killed by the Métis at the instigation of the North West Company. The British government had to intervene, resulting in the union of the two companies under the Hudson's Bay Company, which obtained exclusive trading rights in the northwest to the Pacific. The new company operated entirely independently of Canadian authority.

THE MOVEMENT FOR CONFEDERATION

By the 1840s, however, free trade from St. Paul on the Mississippi and renewed connection with Canada began to undermine the company's empire, and men began to ask if the fur-trade wilderness might not be capable of agricultural settlement. An affirmative answer was given by the American scientist Lorin Blodget in 1856 and by a British and a Canadian expedition in 1857–61. The northwest was worth taking, if Canada could take it, and so achieve a national destiny of its own. In 1858 an investigating committee recommended the annexation of the northwest, but the government failed either to challenge the validity of the Hudson's Bay Company's charter or to buy it out, largely because of the fears of the French Canadians. The addition of the northwest to Upper Canada was delayed until 1870, when confederation had made it possible.

Background of Confederation

That union, finally called Confederation, had been discussed for over a century and, by 1858, had become a practical possibility. A union of the Maritime colonies, with the exception of Newfoundland, was also urged by some. Nova Scotia and New Brunswick lacked both railways and a continental hinterland. An intercolonial railway from these colonies to Canada had been discussed since 1846 but was always frustrated. In Canada the great reforms necessary for self-government had been completed. Politics became sectional, and, from 1862 to 1864, a "deadlock" of parties ensued, preventing most of the necessary legislation. Even provision for an adequate militia was prevented until late 1863, despite the U.S. Civil War raging across the border. This deadlock in Canada, however, was ended by the formation of a coalition of the two main rival parties, Conservative (dependent on French support and led by George Etienne Cartier and Sir John Macdonald) and Reformer (dependent on English Upper Canada and led by George Brown). The coalition was based on a policy of Confederation.

The new government moved quickly, and, at the Charlottetown Conference (September 1, 1864), persuaded the Maritimes to postpone Maritime union and discuss Confederation. At a conference called at Quebec (October 10, 1864), an agreement was quickly reached on a general federal union; this agreement was immediately approved by the British government, which was anxious to set the colonies up on their own and to be rid of its obligation to defend them inland from Quebec. There were hitches and failures; New Brunswick voted against union in 1865, then reversed itself in 1866; Prince Edward Island refused to enter until 1873; Newfoundland also refused and did not join Canada until 1949. But the Canadas and the British government applied quiet but strong pressure on the reluctant colonies. In 1867 the four colonies of Nova Scotia, New Brunswick, and the Canadas (now the provinces of Quebec and Ontario) were united under the British North America Act as the Dominion of Canada.

That act has remained, with certain amendments, the "constitution" of Canada to the present day. The act provided constitutions, based on the British model, for the new provinces of Quebec and Ontario, confirmed the language and legal rights of the French, and above all provided for the division of power between the federal government and the provinces. The union was not, at its beginning, a truly federal one because the central government was given broad powers, not unlike those the British government had possessed over the colonies. In time, judicial interpretation and the growth of provincial rights made the union more truly federal. For the moment, however, a strong central government was needed in order to develop the northwest and the colony of British Columbia beyond and to build a railway to the Pacific that would bind the vast new territories to the original Dominion.

II. Canada from 1867 to 1920

THE DOMINION OF CANADA, 1867–1914

Purchase of Hudson's Bay Company territories

Section 146 of the British North America Act provided for the admission of Rupert's Land (the Hudson's Bay territory) to the new Dominion. The first action taken by the federal government was to buy out the title of the Hudson's Bay Company. The negotiations for this purpose, assisted by the British government, were completed in the winter of 1868–69. Canada was to pay the company £300,000 for its title, and the company was to retain 5 percent of the Fertile Belt (land fit for agricultural settlement) and designated areas around its various posts. The Canadian government passed a provisional act for the government of the Northwest Territories, sent out a survey party to begin a land survey before settlement began, and appointed as governor William McDougall of Ontario.

The first Riel rebellion. The government unwisely regarded the acquisition of the northwest as a transaction in real estate with the Hudson's Bay Company. But the company was not the only power in the territory. There was the colony of Red River, and also the Métis, who made up more than half the colony. The Métis were French in language and Catholic by faith, and they had a semimilitary, semipolitical organization of their own. They had long thought of themselves as a new nation, neither European nor Indian but both, sharing the rights of one and the title to the land of the other. And behind them were the powerful Plains tribes—Plains Cree and the Blackfoot confederacy, buffalo hunters not under the influence of the Hudson's Bay Company. Canada had taken no account of the Métis or Indians in effecting the transfer. It assumed it could take over from the company and then consider what should be done.

This policy was rendered impossible by Louis Riel, a Métis educated in Montreal, who organized resistance in Red River to a transfer to Canada without the people of the northwest having a voice in the transaction. Riel, with the support of armed Métis, seized control of Red River and forced Canada to postpone the transfer and to negotiate. The result was the creation in 1870 of the small province of Manitoba, with equality of the English and French languages and an educational system like Quebec's two systems of public, confessional schools, Roman Catholic and Protestant. The implication was that the northwest was to be open to French institutions and language, as well as English.

Addition of British Columbia

That assumption was to be thwarted, however, by the extreme smallness of the new province, which amounted to little more than the Red River Settlements, and by the Dominion's control of natural resources and of the still vast North West Territory. Riel's obstructionism did not block Canada's march to the west, and the Dominion at once opened negotiations with delegates from British Columbia. That colony consisted of Vancouver Island (organized as a colony in 1849) and the mainland to the watershed of the Rockies, the latter having first been made a separate colony in 1858, when the gold rush along the Fraser River began, and united with Vancouver Island in 1866. The chief needs of the new colony were responsible government and connection with the east. Union with Canada might afford both, and in the negotiations the chief Canadian representative, George Etienne Cartier, promised both and more—in fact, a railway was to be begun in two years and finished in ten (1881). Faced with such generosity, the Legislative Council of British Columbia could only accept. British Columbia became a Canadian province in 1871.

The transcontinental railroad. With the addition of British Columbia, Canada extended from Atlantic to Pacific. To maintain that area, however, and to ensure its independence from the United States, it was necessary to build a railway to the west coast. The effort to organize a company to undertake this enterprise, much greater than any railway yet built, was made in 1872. But Sir John Macdonald's government, charged with corruption in its dealing with the head of the new company, fell on the eve of the great depression of 1873. The railway thereafter could only be built piecemeal until Macdonald returned to power in 1878. An economically revived Canada, fortified with a new National Policy of tariff protection, incorporated the Canadian Pacific Railway in 1881, and the line was pushed ahead rapidly with government grants of land and money.

The National Policy

Even so, the railroad came to need new loans from Parliament, and its funds ran out as depression returned. Had it not been for the Riel Rebellion of 1885, which showed the need for the railway in moving troops, the last loan needed might have been refused. Despite the victory in the creation of Manitoba, many of the Métis—finding life impossible with the influx of new settlers—sold their lands and trekked westward to the Saskatchewan River. Even there, they were followed by the government land survey. The buffalo herds were vanishing, and the railway would supersede transport by boat and cart, from which many of them earned their living. The Plains Indians, alarmed by the end of the buffalo and unhappy with the treaties made with them, were also restless. The Métis again organized to claim their rights as they saw them and sent for Louis Riel, living in exile in Montana. Riel returned and a new armed resistance was formed. Canada had to rush militia to the northwest. Here the new railway, though not quite completed, proved its worth. The troops were rushed out, the rebellion was suppressed, and the railway obtained the grant that enabled it to complete its track across the Canadian Shield and the Rockies. Riel, with several associates, was tried, and despite evidence that he was of unsound mind, convicted of treason, though with a recommendation for mercy. Macdonald, as minister of justice and prime minister, refused clemency. The last spike of the Pacific railway was driven on November 7, 1885, nine days before Riel was hanged at Regina.

Canada had united its new territories with its old, but there was a fierce reaction in the French province of Quebec. Riel, who had not gained much French sympathy in 1870, was now viewed by nationalist French Canadians as a martyr to the cause of French Canadian rights. The result was the election by a narrow majority of a clerical-nationalist government in Quebec. This produced a reaction in Protestant Ontario, which, in turn, led in 1890 to the abolition of the confessional schools in Manitoba, where the Roman Catholic schools were almost wholly French speaking. French Canadians thereafter fell back on the provincial rights of Quebec to maintain the rights of French Canadians—a reaction with serious consequences for the Canadian federation.

Fall of the Conservative Party

The Conservative Party, which had lost Macdonald by death in 1891, fell from power in 1896 largely because of the Manitoba Schools Question. The Liberal Party, under the French Canadian Wilfrid Laurier, came to power by virtue of a large majority in Quebec. Canada, it seemed, was not to be governed without the support of Quebec, even though the west retained only traces (in the Northwest Territories) of French population and French rights.

The Klondike gold rush. These conflicts took place against the background of a long depression, which lasted from 1873 to 1896. With the advent of Laurier's government in 1896, prosperity returned, and with it political peace. The most exciting manifestation of the new prosperity was the Klondike gold rush of 1897. Canada had already had the great rush to the Fraser, largely made up of American miners from the mountain states. It had petered out by 1866, but prospectors continued to comb the mountains northward into British Columbia and the lands of the Yukon River beyond, both in Canada and Alaska, which the United States had purchased from Russia in 1867. In 1896 nuggets were found on Klondike Creek, a tributary of the Yukon. A rush began in 1897 and swelled in 1898, as miners and adventurers poured in, mainly from the United States. The Klondike was the last of the great placer rushes and excited a world weary of depression. The Klondike was, in fact, the most publicized of all the great rushes. Canadians, ready to exploit the newly acquired territory, and equipped with the Pacific railway, benefitted from the publicity in two ways. First, its vast, largely virgin wheatlands became known in the United States and Europe shortly after the availability of free land in the United States came to an end. Settlers from the United States and Europe as far as Russia poured into the Canadian west by the hundreds of thousands. Second, the new nation had to assert its sovereignty and institutions in far distant territories, suddenly occupied by a rush of Americans. It did so successfully, to the strengthening of its national confidence.

Other mineral finds

The Klondike, however, was not the only mineral find on the new Canadian frontiers. The beginning had been the discovery in 1883 of a great nickel bed on the route of the Pacific railway at Sudbury, Ontario. A second had occurred in the early 1890s in southern British Columbia, where great deposits of mixed base metals were found, most notably at Trail. Then, in 1903, the building of a provincially owned and operated railway northward from Toronto toward James Bay resulted in the rich silver strike at Cobalt, north of Lake Nipissing. A great wave of prospecting began that led to further silver strikes and then to the finding of gold on both sides of the Ontario–Quebec border. Suddenly, the north of those provinces, long ignored since the early days of the fur trade, became mineral empires, not to mention their resources of waterpower, wood pulp, and even agricultural land in the "clay belt" beyond the shield. The prospectors spread westward also in search of "cobalt bloom," to make the base metal stake at Flin Flon, Manitoba, in 1915, and the radium strike on Great Bear Lake in 1931. Canada had become a major mining country.

The land rush in the west. At the same time, the land rush to the prairies widened the country's agricultural base by the settlement of Manitoba and the Northwest Territories. Their population rose from 419,512 in 1901 to 1,322,709 in 1911. Manitoba had already been enlarged westward and northward in 1881. The territories, governed by a governor and appointed council since 1876, had had elected members added to the council, and began the traditional Canadian struggle, first for representative and then for responsible government. The latter, however, could only come with provincehood, and the demand arose for the creation of a province between Manitoba and the Rockies. The federal government responded after the election of 1904, and in 1905 not one but two provinces were created, Alberta and Saskatchewan. The territories were divided into roughly equal areas by the 60th parallel. A fierce political struggle arose over the question of French schools in the new provinces, and again the cause of French rights outside Quebec received a setback. Separate schools in the Canadian sense of denominational schools supported by the taxes of members of a denomination—Roman Catholics in this case—there were to be, but nothing like the dual confessional school system of Manitoba before 1890, or of Quebec. Once again the development of the west had disturbed the relations of English and French in Canada.

The Laurier era. For 15 years, Laurier's Liberal government reflected the acquiescent politics of prosperity and progress. Canada seemed at last to be entering on its own century, as the United States had done in the one just past. Nothing better exemplified the confident, easy mood of the Laurier years in Canada than the vast and extravagant railway expansion in response to the settlement of the west and the initial development of the mineral and forest wealth of the nearer, or middle, north.

Further railway construction

The Laurier government built one transcontinental railway from Quebec to a point east of Winnipeg; from there to Prince Rupert a well-subsidized Grand Trunk Railway of eastern Canada built a subsidiary line, the Grand Trunk Pacific. Not to be deterred by two transcontinental railways in a country that was yet little more than a narrow corridor from east to west, two Canadian private entrepreneurs, geniuses of their kind, William Mackenzie and D.D. Mann, built or bought the Canadian Northern bit by bit with lavish subsidies from provincial governments. By 1914 Canada had one long established coast-to-coast railway (the Canadian Pacific) and two railway lines from Montreal to the Pacific toiling to complete their tracks in the Rocky Mountains. In such a wealth of easy capital and easy prosperity, governments were not likely to be defeated.

Yet two factors—one as old as Canada, one relatively new—were to disturb the smooth current of prosperity. The former was the never quite settled place of the French in an English Canada. The question had flared up in the creation of the new provinces in the west; it now arose over participation in Britain's wars, first the South African War in 1899, then World War I. The result was the growth of a new nationalist movement among French Canadian clerics and intellectuals, who made their voices heard in a new paper, *Le Devoir*. Their spokesman, in so far as a man so independent could speak for anyone but himself, was Henri Bourassa. The second factor was the impingement of the world on a Canada intensely absorbed in its own development and its own troubles. The two were to combine to end the Laurier regime and bring Canada, still troubled, into the world at large.

Foreign relations. Canada's contacts with the world in 1900 were almost wholly through Great Britain and the United States. Indeed, Canada's formal relations with other countries were conducted only through the British Foreign Office because Canada, as a colony, had no diplomatic status.

Relations with Britain

The dependence on Great Britain raised, after 1895, the question whether Canada might be expected, on its own decision, to take some part in Britain's imperial wars. The British colonial secretary Joseph Chamberlain was anxious that the Dominion should at least be committed in principle to supporting the mother country. Laurier, at the colonial conference of 1897, remained silent on the issue; thereafter his stand was that the Canadian Parliament must decide whether or not Canada would take any action. When the South African War broke out in 1899, many English Canadians actively urged participation; but some French Canadians, led by Henri Bourassa, were actively opposed. A compromise was reached, by which Canada sent volunteers to serve under British command and with British pay. But a rift between French and English Canadians had opened over foreign policy—a rift exacerbated by trouble over schools in the northwest. Also, Britain's naval competition with Germany made Britain eager to have colonial help, preferably by contributions in money, or by the colonies' assuming their own naval defense. Again, Laurier sought a compromise. In 1910 he established a Canadian Navy, which in time of war, however, was to be placed under British command. The measure was bitterly opposed by the nationalists in Quebec, who argued that conscription in Britain's army would follow. Their clamorous opposition led to the defeat of the government candidate in a Quebec by-election, foreshadowing Laurier's fall from power in 1911. In fact, as the history of the organization of the Canadian militia reveals, Canada was preparing to fight at Britain's side.

In the last analysis, Great Britain was Canada's only ally. Relations with the United States were close and informed, but in the final analysis they were relations between states foreign to one another. There had been a long record of border disputes, the settlements of which were resented, rightly or wrongly, by Canadians. There were the perennial difficulties over fishing rights in the North Atlantic and the dispute in the 1890s over the sealing industry in the Pacific. The Fenian raids at the time of Confederation symbolized another cause of strain, the Irish-American hatred of England, and suspicion of Canada as a British colony. Matters were brought to a head in the dispute over the Alaskan Panhandle boundary. The line laid down by treaty between Great Britain and Russia had not since 1867 been marked on the ground by the United States and Canada. It became an urgent issue in 1897 with the Klondike gold rush, as the principal access to the gold fields was through the Panhandle, and the disputed territory might contain gold. Canada claimed a line that would have put the heads of major inlets in Canadian territory, and so have given it, especially the port of Vancouver, free access to the Yukon Territory. The United States claimed a boundary that would have excluded Canada from the sea. A joint commission of Americans, British, and Canadians found in favour of almost the whole of the American claim, the one British jurist voting with the three Americans. The decision was bitterly resented in Canada, the action of the British member Lord Alverstone even more than that of the Americans. In fact, Canada's case was exceedingly weak, but the combination against it of the two powers with which alone Canada dealt made the country realize it must be prepared to look out for itself. Canadian nationalism in a new sense came into being.

U.S.–Canadian friction

Two results followed. One, neither quick nor dramatic but significant, was the creation of the Department of External Affairs in 1909, in preparation for Canadian handling of its own foreign affairs. The other, encouraged by Lord Bryce, the British minister to the United States, was the cultivation of direct relations with the United States. From this followed the final settlement in 1909 of the long-vexed Atlantic fisheries issues and the creation of the Permanent Joint Commission on Boundary Waters in the same year.

Relations between Canada and the United States were assuming a new guise, and with reason. The United States was beginning to turn to Canada as an outlet for investment and as a source of raw materials, particularly minerals and newsprint. An exchange of ideas began on a new scale, particularly in the ideas of the Progressive movement, which advocated a wide range of reforms to combat the growing social evils caused by industrialism. These ideas were influential on both sides of the border, in Canada sometimes more than in the United States, as in the creation of the publicly owned and operated Ontario Hydro-Electric Power Commission in 1906. These developments, however, were abruptly upset by the Canadian election of 1911. An outburst of economic nationalism, fed to some degree at least by resentment at the Alaska boundary award, enabled the Conservative Party under Sir Robert Laird Borden to overturn the Laurier regime.

The new government was not a reactionary one—indeed, Borden had taken up some of the ideas of the Progressive movement—but it had early to deal with the heightening of diplomatic tensions in Europe. Borden did so by seeking to add monetary contributions to the Royal Navy to the maintenance of the new Canadian one, with the concurrent proposal that Canada should have a voice in Britain's imperial policy. Borden was defeated in the former by the Canadian Senate in 1913, still under Liberal control, but even so lost much of what little influence he had in French Quebec. The idea of a Canadian voice in imperial affairs was politely turned aside in England, but the idea was to survive. Thus, Canada came to the outbreak of World War I with national opinion divided and with little naval strength. Only the militia was to some degree organized and ready, by tactical training and equipment, to cooperate with the British Army.

CANADA IN WORLD WAR I

On the outbreak of World War I in August 1914, Canada might have been as divided as it had been over the South African War. But the German violation of Belgian neutrality brought instant union for participation by sending an expeditionary force of men who had volunteered for overseas service. (The Canadian Militia was for the defense of Canada only.) As a result of this unanimity, and the previous preparation of the militia, a force of 33,000 men was sent to England in October 1914. There it had to complete training, and not until the spring of 1915, at the Second Battle of Ypres, did Canadian units see action. At first they served as battalions in British formations, but the Canadian government and people were determined that Canadian units should be kept together

First Canadian mobilization

and formed into the largest formation their numbers and officers equipped for higher commands would permit. The First Division was formed in 1915, the Second in the same year, the Third and Fourth in 1916. A fifth was also organized, but it was broken up to provide reinforcements. In 1915 the Canadian Corps was formed, and its four divisions fought together in the taking of Vimy Ridge; in June 1917 Lieut. Gen. Sir Arthur Currie of Vancouver became its commander. This force not only earned an enviable record as a fighting force; it was the first authentic expression of Canada in the world. Its strength and reputation meant that Canada could not be disregarded or treated as a mere colony. The Canadian Corps won many battle honours, but its role in history was to ensure Canada that "voice" in imperial and international affairs for which Borden had asked in vain in 1912.

At home, the war effort was scarcely less impressive. Canadian foodstuffs and raw materials were of first importance in maintaining the western Allies. If the troops brought Canada into international politics, the war workers made it an industrial as well as a primary producer. But tragically, the cooperation of 1914 between English and French Canadians did not last, partly because it was not fostered, and partly because few French Canadians had the feeling for France that many English Canadians had for Britain. They were content with a limited, voluntary war effort, in which French-Canadian units had won distinction as fighting men. But the length of the war and of the casualty lists forced Canada, as it had the United Kingdom, to abandon the customary reliance on volunteers and to impose compulsory military service. French nationalist feeling had been reawakened by new troubles with respect to the use of the French language in schools in French districts in Ontario and Manitoba. French Canada, led by Laurier, opposed conscription, but was overridden by the formation of a Union government—almost wholly English in personnel—and in the wartime election of 1917. Canada had conscription, and its corps was kept up to strength; but the country was divided as it had not been since 1837.

French-Canadian opposition to war

Despite this rift at home, the entry of Canada into the world of nations went ahead. In 1917 the British government under Prime Minister Lloyd George formed an Imperial War Cabinet, of which the prime ministers of the dominions were members, to conduct the war and to plan the peace. In reality, if not yet in name, the British Commonwealth of Nations had come into being (see BRITISH EMPIRE AND COMMONWEALTH). This was recognized by Article IX of the Imperial War Cabinet in 1917, which stated that the British Empire was made up of self-governing nations as well as colonies, with India in a special position. Henceforth, it was hoped, a common policy would be worked out by government conferences in peace as well as war.

III. Canada since 1920

CANADA BETWEEN THE WARS

Commonwealth relations. Canada and the other dominion powers, however, were not content with their status within the empire. At the peace conference in 1919, they demanded separate signatures to the treaties with the defeated countries, and won at least the right to sign as members of a British Empire Panel. They also demanded and got, despite the doubts of the United States and France, membership in the newly organized League of Nations. Thus, Canada finally became a full-fledged member of the community of nations.

If independent of the United Kingdom, Canada's role was not a fortunate one, either for the League or for Canada. Membership in the League meant that Canada was now recognized in the world as an independent nation. Yet the country followed an isolationist policy. This was partly, if paradoxically, the result of its new national character. But it was mainly a consequence of its return to government by the Liberal Party, now more than ever dependent on French-Canadian support. French Canadians were themselves isolationist, and they strengthened the general disposition of Canadians to express their new national feelings by the completion of autonomy in the empire and by resuming their material development as a North American country. The idea of imperial policy made in conferences of governments had one success when Borden's successor, Prime Minister Arthur Meighen, persuaded the Imperial Conference of 1921 to accept American policy in the Pacific and allow the Anglo-Japanese Alliance, a source of some concern to the United States, to lapse. Meighen, however, was crushingly defeated in the general election late in that year by the Liberal Party, which swept Quebec and the Maritimes, and by the Progressive agrarian democrats who swept the prairies and made inroads in Ontario. The new prime minister, W.L. Mackenzie King, and his government were firmly nationalist and isolationist, as was made very clear by their prompt refusal to back the United Kingdom's policy in Turkey in 1922. This, in effect, ended the hope of a common imperial policy. Instead, there would be conference, consultation, and sharing of information, but freedom of action.

King's government had, in fact, determined on attaining complete autonomy within the Commonwealth—that is, an independent foreign policy reached in terms of Canada's interests. In this determination Canada found itself in alliance with the new Irish Free State and with the Union of South Africa. The Imperial Conference of 1923 firmly ended the hope of a common foreign policy for the Commonwealth. This was followed by Canada's signature, without that of the British Foreign Office, to the Halibut Treaty of 1923 with the United States.

A national foreign policy was not the only goal. Another was that of recognized and explicit equality of status of all members of the Commonwealth. In the Commonwealth Conference of 1926 the principle of equality of status was accepted, and a committee was set up to examine the vestiges of British sovereignty and dominion subordination and to suggest necessary changes. While the committee was at work, formal steps were taken to end the position of the governors general of the dominions as imperial officers and to make them the personal representatives of the king, appointed on the advice of dominion cabinets, not of the Imperial Cabinet. In 1931 the necessary changes to create legal equality were combined in the Statute of Westminster. This act ended all legislative supremacy of the Imperial Parliament over the dominion parliaments and made them, when they proclaimed the Act, sovereign states sharing a common crown. The Commonwealth had become a legal reality and Canada an independent nation.

The Commonwealth Conference of 1926

Canada's new independence was reflected by its establishment of its own foreign service. Canadian ministers were appointed to Washington in 1927 and to Paris and Tokyo in 1928 and 1929. (In the United Kingdom and Canada, officers called high commissioners played much the same role after 1928, although the office was to some degree political and not just diplomatic.)

Internal politics and the Great Depression. At the time, the completion of the quest for equality of status was to some degree obscured by the onset of the Great Depression, begun with the New York stock market crash in October 1929 and intensified into world depression by bank failures in Germany. Canada reacted early to the onset of depression. The Liberal Party, except for a brief interval in 1926, had been in power since 1921. In the general election of 1930, the Conservative Party, led by R.B. Bennett, succeeded in winning the election—partly because the King government had refused to give federal funds to the provinces to combat unemployment and give relief, and partly because Bennett promised to blunt the effects of the depression by protective tariffs. If the attitude of King was old-fashioned and not up to the needs of the times, so were the election promises of Bennett. The depression was so far-reaching in its effects that only drastic measures could lessen its impact and begin the process of recovery.

The Bennett government did little to increase the already high tariffs that had been in effect under the Liberals, but it did stiffen the application of customs regulations. The Conservatives also sought relief for Canadian producers by reviving an old dream of Joseph Chamberlain that the empire should have a common tariff policy. The obstacle created by Britain's policy of free trade had ended with the modification of that policy in the 1920s. Political imperialism had ended, but perhaps commercial imperialism would be revived. Prime Minister Bennett arranged an Imperial Economic Conference at Ottawa in 1932. The national interests of the representatives made agreement difficult, but all countries were desperate. The dominions badly needed the British market for their foodstuffs and other primary products, and Britain itself could not afford to ignore protected markets in the dominions. The Ottawa Agreements were a series of preferences given by Commonwealth countries to one another, to some degree at the expense of producers in other countries, particularly the United States.

The Imperial Economic Conference

The depression, however, merely intensified. Canada had known widespread unemployment in the mid-1870s and in the immediate postwar years. But an economy still predominantly agricultural had largely, if painfully, absorbed the unemployed. In 1921, however, supremacy began to pass from agriculture to industry, and from countryside to city, and the trends thereafter were rapid. The cities had now to provide for mass unemployment, and Canadian municipalities were required by law yet unfitted in financial resources to furnish welfare and relief. The municipalities had therefore to turn to the provinces for aid; the weaker provinces had to turn to the federal treasury. Thus, not only was the economy being dragged down to unexampled levels of prices and production, but the very framework of government was threatened in the poorer provinces. What happened in Newfoundland, where responsible government was replaced by administration by a commission aided with British funds, came close to happening in the prairie provinces. The brighter side of the picture was that the mining industry of Ontario and Quebec kept the revenues of those provinces comparatively good, and so the greater part of the country remained in condition to maintain the federal revenues and make possible the support of the weaker provinces. Confederation had never been more important.

Prime Minister King might refuse to aid the provinces in 1930, before the second great slump of the depression, but his successor had no such choice. Prime Minister Bennett's own remedies—stiffened protection and imperial preference—could only act slowly at best. But conditions were drastic by 1931, aggravated by unprecedented drought on the prairies. Bennett began, on entering office, to advance federal funds to the provinces for relief works. The provinces had already come to the financial aid of their municipalities, and a relief system was worked out for the unemployed. But all the means of aid that were employed ended with the giving of relief; the government still looked for recovery from the depression. The rise of parties with more fundamental solutions than relief therefore began. One was the Co-operative Commonwealth Federation, a party socialist in theory if pragmatic in fact. Another was Social Credit, a movement urging the payment of social dividends to fill the gap between the costs of production and the cost of purchase. There was even a small Fascist Party in Quebec, and a splinter group led by Paul Gouin, a Liberal rebel, which in 1936 joined with Maurice Duplessis's Conservatives to make up the Union Nationale, which became a nationalist "Quebec First" party. Disquieting findings of a Price Spreads Commission and the growing desperation of the farmers led Bennett to listen favourably to praise of the New Deal in the United States. Perhaps personally convinced, certainly politically desperate, in 1935 he had his last Parliament enact a Canadian New Deal. It quite failed to remove the resentment his government had provoked during its years of office, and the Liberals returned to power easily.

Attempts to relieve the depression

King, despite some advanced ideas in his youth, was convinced that Bennett's New Deal was unconstitutional, as indeed the courts in 1937 found nearly all of it to be. King and his government believed that the way to end the depression was to stimulate international trade. The Ottawa Agreements, of course, remained in force. Canada, however, availed itself of the United States' policy of more liberal trade agreements, and the result was what was called the Reciprocity Treaty of 1936. Reciprocity and imperial preference were reconciled. In the long run, American–Canadian trade was to grow to enormous proportions, but for the time being the depression continued, as did the drought.

The Liberal government did concern itself with the devastation wrought by the depression on government finances. In 1936 an official inquiry made by the newly created central Bank of Canada revealed that the prairie Provinces were at the end of their economic rope. A distinguished Royal Commission was set up to inquire into the allocation of revenues between the federal and provincial governments. The resulting report in fact amounted to a comprehensive study of the constitutional and financial development of government in Canada, and of how the depression had revealed its weaknesses. The federal government, with unlimited power to tax, lacked the power to spend on needed issues; the provinces possessed the necessary constitutional power but, except for Ontario, their financial resources were inadequate. The commission in 1940 recommended the assumption by the federal government of provincial debts, a scheme of federal unemployment insurance, and a reallocation of revenues between the two levels of government, on the principle that all provinces have the means to maintain a national level of governmental and social services. The first two were done, relieving the credit of the provinces and strengthening the federal government, but on the latter there was no agreement, as it involved a redistribution of income between wealthier central Canada and the Maritimes and the Prairies. At that time both Ontario and Quebec were strongly provincialist and resisted redistribution.

Growing international tension. Even domestic distress was to some degree submerged in the second half of the 1930s by the worsening outlook in international affairs. The external interests of Canada shifted from the development of the Commonwealth to the fate of the League of Nations and the first shocks of aggression in Asia and Europe. Canada was too preoccupied with its own affairs up to 1935 to take great note of Japanese aggression in Manchuria or the rise of Hitler in Europe. By that date, however, the fate of the League of Nations, clearly threatened by unprovoked aggression, drew more and more attention. Much Canadian opinion deplored the failure to stop the Italian invasion of Ethiopia or to oppose the Fascist powers in the Spanish Civil War (1936–39). The government, however, refused to take a firm line and seemed to practice a rather uncertain isolation, which became, in fact, support of the policy of appeasement. But after visiting Hitler in 1937 to inform him of the continuing cohesion of the Commonwealth, Prime Minister King let the British government know that Canada might be expected to oppose aggression in Europe. For the first time since World War I, the government began to build up the exiguous defense forces of Canada. After Hitler's occupation of Czechoslovakia late in 1938, few members of the Canadian government or of the informed public thought that there was any realistic hope of peace. Canada would again be drawn into full involvement in world affairs.

Canada's policy toward Hitler

CANADA IN WORLD WAR II

When the Parliament of Canada voted on the declaration of war against Germany on September 9, 1939, only a very few members voted in opposition. This unanimity, however, rested on two assumptions. One was that Canada's role would be, in the main, to supply raw materials and furnish training facilities; the other was dependent on the former—that conscription for overseas service would not again be necessary, or attempted, as King actually pledged. It was in a more sophisticated form the illusion of 1914, that the war would be short, and it was again to be shattered. The expulsion of the British from Europe and the fall of France in May and June of 1940 totally changed the circumstances. Canada's defenses had fallen, and it immediately concluded an agreement at Ogdensburg with the United States for the defense of North America. Moreover, Canada now stood in the forefront of the war. After England, it was for once the second most powerful of Germany's adversaries. The emphasis on supply had to give way to an emphasis on combat forces. Necessarily, the question of the allocation of manpower, including compulsory service overseas, came to the fore and was made more urgent by the Japanese attack on Pearl Harbor in December 1941. King, resolved at almost all costs to avoid a repetition of the Anglo-French cleavage, had to recognize the changed situation by holding a national plebiscite in 1942 to free him from his pledge and allow conscription if necessary. It was strongly carried in English Canada but heavily defeated in Quebec. Thereafter, compulsory service for home defense was enforced, while overseas service remained voluntary until the last year of the war. Then in 1944 unexpectedly great casualties in Normandy led to a "conscription crisis" and the ordering of 16,000 home defense men overseas. The gulf of 1917 between English and French, reopened in 1942, was deepened.

Increased Canadian involvement in the war

Even so, Canada played a greater, if less glorious, part in World War II than in World War I. This was done in three ways. The first remained supply. Canada furnished not only raw materials and foodstuffs but manufactured goods of a volume and sophistication unknown before in Canada. The industrialization of Canada was accelerated, both by investment and by increase of technology and also by government investment and control and the device of Crown corporations (autonomous government corporations). Second, the federal government of Canada developed the financial power of Canada to such an extent that Canada not only financed its own war effort without American help but even supplied money to Great Britain. Finally, Canada developed complete armed services of army, air force, and navy, through whose ranks and auxiliary services over 1,000,000 Canadians passed, not to mention those who served with the Royal Air Force.

POSTWAR CANADA

International commitments. The outcome of the war was uncertain for Canada. It had no national interest to serve except the survival of Britain and the restoration of France. The most significant outcome of the war for Canada was the relative decline of Britain and the emergence of the United States as the world's foremost economic and military power. Canada's relations with Britain remained unchanged; those with the United States became closer. The creation of the Permanent Joint Defence Board in 1940 was the greatest exercise in "continentalism" since the American invasion of 1775. Canada had moved far into the continental military system of the United States, as it had already done in the economic sphere.

Permanent Joint Defence Board

It was hoped and, indeed, assumed that this was a new continentalism, not isolationist as was the old, but international and devoted to collective security. Such was the purpose of America's wartime leaders. Canada's problem then, was not that it had fallen under the control of the United States. Its problem, rather, was to define its role in a postwar world governed by the great powers through the United Nations. Most informed Canadians welcomed the new organization, and the Canadian government took a vigorous part in its creation. But King, mindful of his own lifetime battle to remove Canada from the trammels of British imperialism, was dubious of a world to be dominated by the great powers. His advisers, for their part, wanted to find some way for Canada to play a significant role in the world. The government therefore advanced the concept of a status of "middle power," that is, a state strong economically if not militarily. Members of the United Nations should function appropriately, according to their capacities. The idea in practice meant that Canada should concern itself mainly with economic policy in world affairs and with aid to developing countries.

Similarly sensible was the Canadian decision to use its considerable knowledge of nuclear fission not for military purposes but exclusively for peaceful and economic ones. Canada, in short, wanted—as in 1918—to get back to its original peaceful character and to resume its own development, this time in the world at large.

Nevertheless, the country did not cut its armed forces to the bare bone as it had in 1919. There were two reasons for this. One was, that under the Ogdensburg Declaration it had assumed an obligation to the United States for the defense of North America. The second was that Canada planned to contribute to the peace-keeping capacity of the United Nations. Both concepts were to be tested in the Korean War of 1950.

Maintenance of armed forces

Even before that, however, a third and perhaps more powerful factor had come into play: the possibility of Soviet aggression in Europe. In 1948 this danger was felt in the Berlin crisis and in the coup d'etat in Prague that made Czechoslovakia a Communist state and brought it within the Soviet orbit. No one could be sure at that time that the Soviet move was limited and defensive. Nor was the United Nations any help, as it clearly could not coerce a power such as the Soviet Union into obedience to a collective will, if indeed such could be found. The idea of a regional agreement for the defense of western Europe against Soviet pressure or attack was therefore taken up. Devoted supporters of the United Nations in Canada as elsewhere were dismayed, for they felt that regional agreements militated against the global purposes of the general organization. The Canadian government, nevertheless, supported the United States' proposal for an alliance of North Atlantic powers. Yet Canada insisted that this alliance should not be purely military, but also political and economic. The minister of external affairs, Lester B. Pearson, pressed strongly for the adoption of that principle. It was accepted in Article 2 of the North Atlantic Treaty Organization (NATO) in 1949, sometimes referred to as the "Canadian article." The article, however, has never been made use of in any notable way. Whether that is a comment on a Canadian lack of realism, or the lack of percipience in others, it remains evidence of the outlook and intent of Canadian foreign policy, and of informed Canadian opinion at the time. Canada as a member of NATO also, for the first time in its history, assumed serious peacetime military commitments, maintaining out of its armed forces an infantry brigade and 12 air squadrons and contributing ships to the naval forces of NATO until 1969. Then a change of emphasis in foreign policy led to a reduction, much criticized by its NATO allies, of the Canadian contribution.

Just as NATO was a test of Canada's seriousness in entering world affairs, so, too, was the Korean War of 1950, which also tested the country's new relationship (since 1940) with the United States. When that country decided to assist South Korea in resisting invasion by the forces of North Korea, the question for Canadians was: Was this an endeavour to uphold the peace settlement that had divided Korea at the 38th parallel of latitude, or was it simply part of an American crusade against Communism? In the latter, few Canadians had any interest—not even French Canadians, for all their Catholic heritage. The government, as did the United Nations, decided that it was the former, and military and naval contingents from Canada served with the American forces. Canada had exerted itself to uphold a peace settlement against revision by force and was satisfied with the outcome.

The Korean War

More significant was the fact that informed Canadian opinion was already markedly diverging from the opinion of the majority of Americans on the subject of the new Communist regime in China and would have approved recognition of it as the government manifestly supported by the Chinese people. But the government, though sympathetic, thought it wise not to challenge American opinion on an issue in which no major Canadian interest was at stake. Most important, from a practical standpoint, was the economic outcome of the Korean War, which ended any possibility of a postwar depression—expected but not experienced from 1945 to 1950—and helped launch Canada on its extraordinary development in the 1950s.

U.S.–Canadian relations. The policy of the Liberal government (in power since 1935), wartime cooperation, and the close interconnections between the two economies had brought the two neighbours into a more intimate relationship than ever before. The United States, with British power and influence ended in Canada, no longer had intermittent designs on that country and had dropped the language of Manifest Destiny. Most Canadians were persuaded that the development of economic relations did not necessarily carry with them political relations that would end in annexation by the United States. The two nations, then, accepted and took one another for granted. In that development, however, there were certain dangers. Americans, including the American government, were accused by Canadians of taking Canada for granted in the sense of being unaware of and indifferent to Canadian sentiments and changes. Canadians, in turn, were apt to claim both a special standing with the United States and independence of it.

None of this was ultimately of great importance, but two new trends were to prove significant. One was the growth of "continentalism," a special relationship not provided for in the theory of national independence—except perhaps in the joint commissions, such as the Permanent Joint Commission on Boundary Waters and the Ogdensburg Declaration, in which the parties met as legal equals and in which the fundamental assumption was that both, when in agreement, would contribute a proportionate share of their population and wealth to the common undertakings. The second was the unequal rate of economic and technological development, especially after 1950. The United States, leader of the world in industrial capacity and technology, was nearing the limits, subject to strategic reserves, of its national resources. Canada, within the inner defense orbit of the United States, had many such resources undeveloped and available. The interest of the United States was, therefore, to have assured access to these resources as they were developed, largely with American capital. This, however, tended to keep Canada a primary producer and a country of relatively low employment and low income. Its national development and its hope of educational and cultural development called for the continued growth, under Canadian law and control, of its secondary industry. Yet its provinces—owners of the natural resources of the country, except for those controlled by the Northwest Territories—were driven by the need for revenue and, to satisfy the popular demand for development, were eager to alienate their resources to foreign, usually American, investors. This disparity of aim made American–Canadian relations, if much better diplomatically than in the days of territorial expansion and boundary settlements, much more subtle and complicated than ever before. Something of this lay behind Lester Pearson's warnings in the mid-1950s that henceforth those relations would be more difficult. It appeared also in the conclusion of a study prepared in 1965 by Livingstone Merchant, who was the U.S. ambassador to Canada, and A.D.P. Heeney, the Canadian ambassador to the United

The United States and Canadian resources

Adapted from R. Treharne and H. Fullard (eds.), *Muir's Historical Atlas: Ancient, Medieval and Modern,* 9th ed. (1965); George Philip & Son Ltd., London

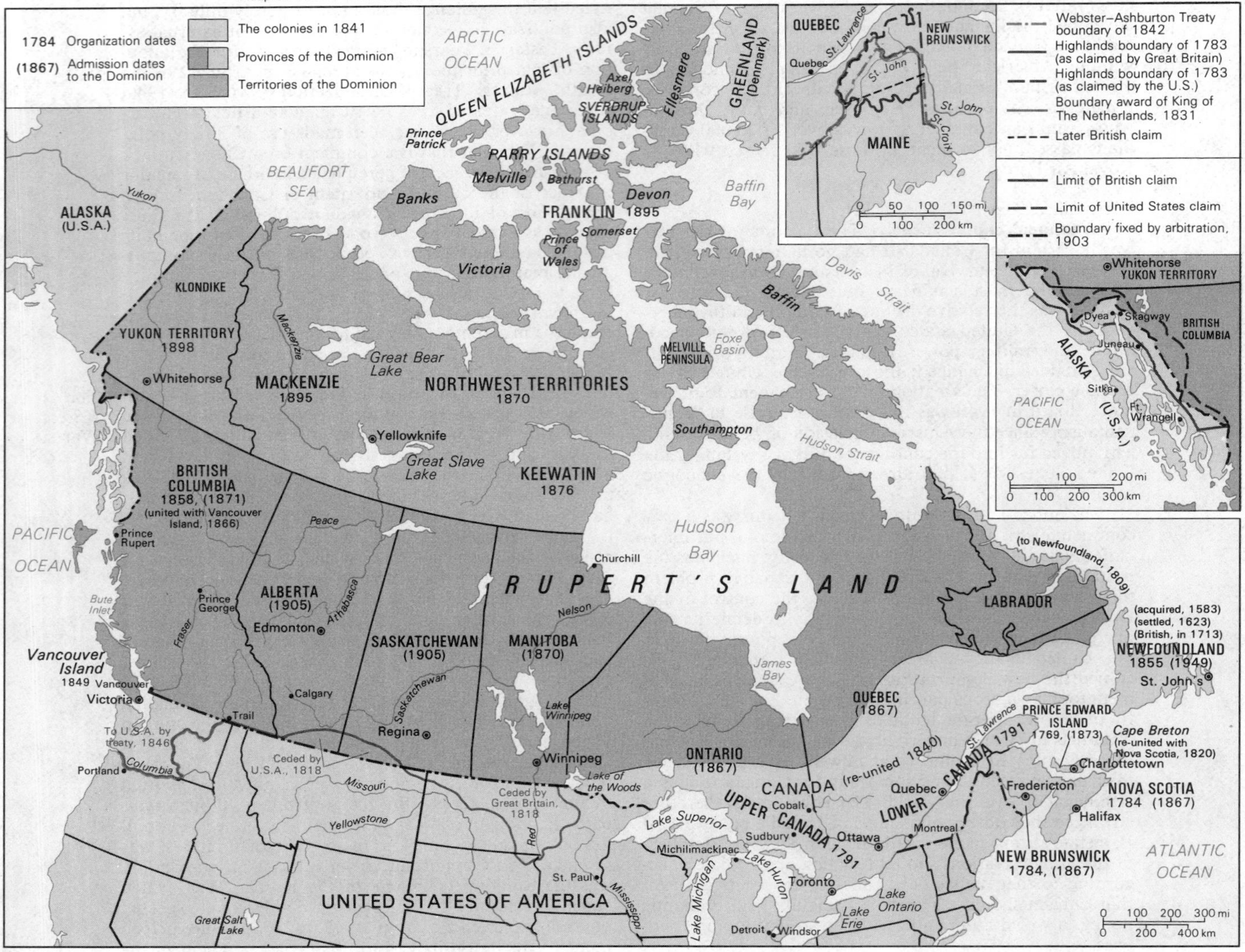

Figure 2: Territorial expansion of Canada and the evolution of provincial organization through1949.

States, that American–Canadian relations could best be handled by "the practice of quiet diplomacy"; that is, with a minimum of public discussion.

A third element of difficulty in American–Canadian relations, which became more apparent in the late 1960s and early 1970s, involved the fact that the main thrust of Canadian policy was to support the United Nations, in which Canada might evade subordination to the great powers. It did so by its peace-keeping efforts (Canadian troops served with the United Nations in Egypt after the Suez crisis of 1956 and some are still in Cyprus, and in cultivating the developing countries and those, like India, that attempted to play a neutral role between the United States and the Soviet Union in the Cold War. To do this, Canada had the advantage of being at once a materially advanced country and also a small nonimperialistic one. But Canada's special relations with the United States continued and expanded. One notable example of joint action was in the Early Warning System against surprise aerial attack, largely based in the Canadian Arctic. Another was the North American Defense Command (Norad) arrangement of 1958 for the defense of North America against aerial and missile attacks, in which elements of the Canadian Air Force were placed under American command. How could Canada be at once an influential, because uncommitted, power in the Third World, and an ally, even for limited purposes, of the United States? The opinion increased that it could not, and after the election of Pierre Elliott Trudeau as prime minister in 1968 this attitude began to affect Canadian foreign policy. Canada's contribution to NATO was reduced in 1969; Norad began to be whittled down in the Defence White Paper of 1970. At the same time, relations with the Soviet Union were improved, and in 1970 diplomatic recognition was extended to the People's Republic of China. Concurrently, however, the stress on aid to developing countries and the idea of Canada as an intermediary with the Third World were played down. The emphasis shifted to more domestic aspects of foreign policy: control of pollution in coastal waters, extension of Canadian fishing rights, and especially to confirming Canadian sovereignty in its Arctic islands and their icebound waters, a concern not much in evidence since the early years of the century. Yet in all these changes the special relationships with the United States remained unchanged, rooted in the facts of neighbourhood and common interest.

Canada's role in the United Nations

Canada and the Commonwealth. If the special ties with the United States waxed during these years, the historic ones with Great Britain waned. It cannot be said that this was willed or decided by either party. It was the outcome of the developing circumstances. The traditional ties remained—the common Crown; the parliamentary system of government; the desire for much the same kind of world; the same pragmatic, unideological temperament and outlook. Cordial relations between the two governments remained, consultation continued. Canada had, however, achieved the kind of world it wished to inhabit, with the creation of the Commonwealth; Britain, charged with the task of liquidating its empire, began to find the Commonwealth a burden and an embarrassment. Even imperial preference failed of its purpose; Canada exported more to Britain and imported more from the United States, while Britain exported less to Canada. Like relations who have moved apart, each knew it could call on the other at need, but each was going its own way with little to call them together. The British phase of Canadian history, which had begun with the great British immigration of the 1830s, seemed to have ended.

The reverse was true for the Commonwealth of Nations during the 1950s and 1960s. Canada as one of the principal creators of the Commonwealth, had a special if largely sentimental interest in it. But the Commonwealth had consisted of self-governing nations and, thus, those dependent parts of the British Empire, including India, that were not self-governing, or not wholly so, had not been members of the Commonwealth. With the rapid achievement of independence in most parts of the empire after World War II, a process of which Canadians in general approved, the new nations could choose to leave the empire entirely, or to apply for membership in the Commonwealth. Burma chose the former course, India the latter. But India had also become a republic in 1947. How could a republic be part of an association bound together by allegiance to a common Crown? Suddenly, the Commonwealth was seen as an association that might bridge the differences of race and culture in freedom as the empire had done by power. It was agreed among the members of the Commonwealth that republics could be members if they chose to accept the king as "Head" of the Commonwealth. Canadians, as members of a republican hemisphere, were perhaps particularly happy to agree, and certainly because the proposal fitted well with their desire to cultivate the widest possible associations, especially with the new and developing nations. Canada, perhaps somewhat smugly, saw a possible role for itself as an intermediary between the old and white members of the Commonwealth and the new and coloured.

Canada's relationship with the Third World

That it might, in some sense, play such a part was revealed by the Suez crisis of 1956, a great strain for the Commonwealth, as for world peace. Australia and New Zealand, for example, were disposed to sympathize with the strategic concern of the United Kingdom, while India was dismayed and angered by what it saw as an act of concerted aggression. Canada, led by Lester Pearson, was able to intervene between a wrathful and humiliated United Kingdom and a righteously angry India, and not only enable the contestants to withdraw with some saving of face but also to preserve the integrity of the Commonwealth.

The Canadian role of disinterested friend was also played in the crisis in Commonwealth affairs precipitated by the apartheid policy of the Union of South Africa. To a multiracial association such as the Commonwealth, South Africa was not only an anomaly but a reproach. Yet a basic rule of the Commonwealth was that of nonintervention in the domestic affairs of members. The issue of South Africa's racial policy came to a head in the Commonwealth Conference of 1960, at which certain members sought to have South Africa expelled. The United Kingdom, Australia, and New Zealand deplored this violation of the rule of nonintervention. Canada again tried to play the role of impartial intermediary, but when that failed, voted for expulsion. In short, Canada's Commonwealth policy was normally that of supporting the coloured members, as later in the matter of economic sanctions against the white regime in Rhodesia.

That was a defensible policy, if pursued realistically and for the purposes of mediation, and even if it led to some feeling against Canada in the United Kingdom. But in 1961 another issue was to arise at the Commonwealth Conference in Accra that raised some question of the whole future of the Commonwealth: the possible entry of the United Kingdom into the European Common Market. For it to do so would mean, if not the ending, at least the diminution of the imperial preferences, which since 1932 had given the Commonwealth a material as well as a sentimental basis. The Canadian delegates professed to be appalled by the prospect and spoke strongly against it as a betrayal of the Commonwealth. But in view of Canada's favourable economic position in trade with Britain, this attitude seemed to the British selfish and unacceptable. Britain was, in fact, not to join the market until 1971, by which time Canada, then under a Liberal government, chose merely to wish Britain well and to look out for Canadian trade with the market as best it could. But Britain's entry meant that the Commonwealth would be less and less a matter of material ties and more and more one of tradition and sentiment.

Britain and the Common Market

Ideally, perhaps, Britain might, like France, have sought to bring its Commonwealth partners into some form of economic association with the market, as it was to do with New Zealand and the African and West Indian members, heavily dependent on the British market for the sale of their primary produce. But industrialized members such as Australia and Canada, with their economic ties with the United States, had relatively little such dependency, and the members of the market were firmly opposed to their becoming even associated members. There was no hope of a special relationship in that respect. Canada must stand on its own, economically as well as diplomatically.

Franco-Canadian affairs. That Canada was regarded in Europe as being at once on its own and also an economic, if not a military, dependency of the United States was revealed by the course of Franco-Canadian relations in the 1960s. France was, of course, as much as Britain a mother country of Canada. Yet practically nothing to reveal that fact had happened since the cession of New France in 1763. Relations between France and French Canadians had been strained by the Seven Years' War. The British regime was watchful against all but private correspondence. Then the French Revolution, particularly its attack on the Roman Catholic Church, caused further friction between France and French Canadians. What influence there was was private and literary. There had been readers of the *Philosophes* in New France, and in Quebec French books and ideas were always sure of at least a small audience. Nothing was done officially and formally, however, until the 1850s when the Second Empire of Napoleon III, Catholic and expansive, took note of French Canada. Not only did the frigate "La Capricieuse" visit Quebec in 1855; in 1859 the Emperor's cousin, Prince Jérôme, visited the province incognito (under the watchful eye of the British government) and gave a sum of money for the statue on the monument to commemorate the Battle of Sainte-Foy (in which the French had defeated the British in 1760). Also in 1859, a French consul general was appointed to Quebec and a form of diplomatic relations began. But little more came of this rapprochement. French Canada's true ties abroad were with Rome, not with Paris.

The "Quiet Revolution"

All this changed a century later particularly after the "Quiet Revolution" began in the province of Quebec with the election of a Liberal government led by Jean Lesage. One result was a decisive altering of relations between French Canada and France. The former suddenly found an interest in French history, French ideas, and the place of France and the French language in the world. French-Canadian students went to universities in France, teachers were exchanged, and a liaison developed between the press of the two countries. All this the Department of External Affairs both noted and welcomed. Canada and France had exchanged ministers in 1928, but as between foreign countries.

A warming of established relations proved to be by no means enough, however, either in Quebec or in France. Perhaps the main object of the Quiet Revolution was to arouse and make flourish French culture and the French spirit in Quebec. To do so was not a matter of diplomacy, as generally practiced, or of commerce, but of cultural affairs, for which Quebec had already set up a government ministry. The urgent spirit of the new Quebec was profoundly dissatisfied with the way Ottawa dealt with such matters in the Canadian embassy in France. Quebec began to establish what might be called quasi-diplomatic relations between France and Quebec, and had constitutional grounds for thinking it might do so. The federal government could not make treaties with foreign powers on subjects coming under the jurisdiction of the provinces. Cultural affairs, Quebec claimed, were educational, a provincial matter, and therefore Ottawa could not conclude treaties in cultural matters. It followed that Quebec ought to be free to develop its own cultural relations with France and, indeed, all francophone countries. The matter was difficult, but one of concern in Quebec, and is not yet wholly resolved.

The second result arose from the personality of Pres. Charles de Gaulle of France. De Gaulle made it his particular role to restore French prestige in a world dominated by the "Anglo-Saxon" powers after World War II. De Gaulle encouraged the informal and then formal relations between the republic and Quebec. He, first of international statesmen, unless one counts the flurry of interest shown by Napoleon III, recognized Quebec for what it is, an island of French speech and culture in an Anglo-Saxon sea. His interest and those of the new nationalists of Quebec happily coincided. Moreover, de Gaulle had been rebuffed, largely because of U.S. influence, in two attempts to deal with Canada: first, in the attempt to sell French aircraft to Air Canada in 1964, and second, in an attempt to buy radium from Canada in 1965 without giving assurance that it would not be used for military purposes. De Gaulle therefore saw in Quebec an occasion to raise French prestige in the world, and in Canada a chance to separate that country from what he regarded as American domination. He visited Quebec in the summer of 1967 and received an extraordinarily emotional reception. There, in an apparently calculated move, he took the opportunity to encourage Quebec *séparatisme*, and in a speech in Montreal he created a furor by repeating the slogan of the French separatists: "Vive le Québec Libre!" ("Long Live Free Quebec!").

De Gaulle's 1967 visit

De Gaulle was gently but directly rebuked on the spot by Mayor Jean Drapeau of Montreal, his official host, and firmly by the Canadian government. His *bêtise* (foolishness), however, was possible because there was a separatist movement of growing strength in Quebec. The cause of the movement for a special status for Quebec within Confederation, or a new form of association on the basis of equality with English Canada, or complete independence as a sovereign nation, was the belief, shared by a growing number of Quebec intellectuals and labour leaders, that the economic difficulties of Quebec were caused by Confederation and could only be ended by altering, or ending, the ties with the other provinces and the central government. In part it was the outcome of the perennial desire of Québecois to have their own state, as in a sense they had from 1791 to 1841. In part it was a continuation of the minority of French-Canadian opinion that had opposed Confederation in 1867. It was also a continuation of that sense of minority grievance stimulated by the execution of Riel, given substance by the Manitoba Schools Question, and given voice in the nationalism of Jules-Paul Tardivel and Henri Bourassa.

The origins of French separatism. Yet French nationalism was much more the outcome of profound economic and sociological changes that had taken place in Quebec since about 1890. Until that time French Canadians had lived by agriculture and seasonal work in the timber trade. The middle-class French of Quebec and Montreal acted as intermediary between their humbler countrymen and the English masters of commerce and industry. The coming of hydroelectric power and the wood-pulp industry as a result of the successful national policy of protection in creating Canadian manufacturing plants in Quebec and Ontario created a labour force that brought French Canadians as workers into the cities, particularly Montreal. The rate of growth of the French-Canadian population and the lack of good workable land outside the narrow St. Lawrence and Richelieu valleys contributed to the rush to low-paying jobs in urban industries and to the growth of slums, particularly in Montreal. By 1921 Quebec was the most urbanized and industrialized of all Canadian provinces, including Ontario, and also the most populous and the wealthiest. The Quebec government, devoted to the 19th-century policy of laissez-faire, recklessly encouraged industry and did little to check its worst excesses. With few exceptions the new enterprises were owned and directed, in the English language, by English Canadians or by U.S. businesses. It was a second conquest of Quebec.

At the same time it destroyed the myths by which French Canada had survived: that of the Catholic mission to the New World, and the cult of agriculture as the basis of virtuous life. Ever more Québecois had to make their way as best they could in quite a different world, in which the old values were mockeries and the obstacles not to be overturned by the old powers of endurance.

This clash of old and new came to a head in the last years of the regime of Premier Maurice Duplessis. A Conservative who became leader of the new Union Nationale Party formed during the Great Depression, he came to power in 1936, was defeated in 1939 but returned in 1944, and remained in office until his death in 1959. Duplessis, after 1944, wielded unequalled power in Quebec. Anglo-

Canadians and U.S. businesses furnished him the money he needed for political purposes; he in return preserved a free enterprise system in the province. In the political miasma he created, all possibility of reform, all political integrity, seemed to be stifled.

Yet they were not. The fight against conscription in 1944 lifted Quebec politics out of the rut of place and favour. In 1949 the prolonged and bitter fight of the asbestos workers gave young idealists, one of them Pierre Elliott Trudeau, a chance to combine with labour in a struggle for a free society of balanced interests. Over the decade intellectuals began a searching analysis of Quebec politics and society in modern terms.

The successors of Duplessis

Duplessis' successors in office, Paul Sauvé and Antonio Barrette, initiated reforms that were limited in scope. But in the election of 1960 Jean Lesage and the Quebec Liberal Party made themselves the political vehicle of the new outlook and tried to carry out their Quiet Revolution to bring much needed reforms before demands in fact became revolutionary. They did much both to assist the power of the province against the federal government and to transform Quebec society from clerical to secular, and from 19th-century laissez-faire to positive, if not socialist, politics. Politically, indeed, they did too much to suit public opinion in the rural areas of Quebec, and the party was defeated by the Union Nationale in 1966.

In the years that followed, the extremes widened in Quebec, and the elements of opinion began to crystallize. The Liberal Party was federalist; it held that the reforms needed in Quebec could be obtained within the federal system. So, at bottom, did the Union Nationale, but, as a mainly conservative party, it had to stress the importance of remaining Québecois and of obtaining greater provincial power. To the left of the traditional parties, however, opinion ranged from a demand for a special status for Quebec to the demand for separation and independence. One active minority of Montrealers had passed far beyond the concept of constitutional reform, and in the process they broke with Trudeau and the Liberals. No social revolution (which, in their opinion, Quebec desperately needed) was possible, they believed, without independence. From their efforts came the Parti Québecois with a platform of secession from Confederation. Under René Lévesque, a former Liberal, they won 24 percent of the popular vote in the election of 1970, but the Liberals, by reason of the antiquated distribution of electoral districts, won 72 seats out of a total of 95. Constitutional reform was to be tried once more.

The growth of terrorism

Still other social revolutionaries, inspired by refugees from Algeria and by the example of the Cuban revolution, began to practice terrorism. Bombings began in 1963 and continued sporadically. This mode of action most French- and English-Canadians felt was "un-Canadian," but it illustrated both the social ills of Quebec and the ties of the French intellectuals with the world outside Canada. In October 1970, with the kidnapping of James Cross of the U.K. consular service, and Pierre Laporte, minister of labour in Quebec, who was murdered, the government of Quebec called in the federal government for help, and the War Measures Act was proclaimed. The usual civil liberties were suspended, some 500 people were arrested, and troops were moved into Quebec. Few convictions followed—except those accused of the murder of Laporte—and public opinion in Canada, including Quebec, which in the majority approved the invocation of the act, began to wonder if the action had been too drastic.

Postwar Prosperity. The rest of Canada, and even Quebec to a lesser degree, had enjoyed in the 20 years after 1950 growth and prosperity such as it had never known before. Not only did its old primary industries thrive, but Canada also entered on a new phase of industrial development. In this Canada was only moving with the greater industrial powers, especially the United States; the significance lay in it now being able to move in such company. The result was the development of electronic, aeronautic, nuclear, and chemical engineering on a great scale and the transformation of industrial Canada. Much of the growth, however, was also simple enlargement of earlier established industry, such as steel. New sources of minerals were, indeed, part of the boom of the 1950s. Not only Labrador iron but also newly discovered deposits of radium, petroleum, and natural gas gave Canada resources it had hitherto had only in comparatively small supply. Mining investment also provided an excellent example of two matters of primary importance: first, how much the greater part of Canadian economic growth had come to be financed by American capital, largely in the form of direct investment and American ownership of the plant and control of operations; and second, how foreign investment, largely American, aided by the American demand for Canadian materials, made the Canadian boom possible. Investment from abroad was, of course, eagerly sought, especially by the provincial governments, and Canada prospered both because of it and because of the resulting advanced technology and management. Growing concern over the degree of foreign control of Canadian economic life led, by 1971, to a strong movement of economic nationalism.

Ethnic minorities. Much of the new economic development took place in Canada's northlands and had some part in ending the nomadic hunting life of the forest Indians and the Eskimos of the Arctic shores and islands. This contact between the Canadian government and the Indians signalled a new dilemma that Canada faced in trying to deal equitably with its aboriginal peoples. After 1945 it was apparent that the old system of administering Indian affairs was no longer adequate. The poverty and disease common to many reserves were a reproach to Canadian policy and humanity. The health care provided was greatly improved, and in 1959 the Indian Act was amended to increase opportunities for Indian influence on decisions affecting them. The Métis, equal to whites according to the law, while in fact often treated as treaty Indians, played an important part in the growing protest. The federal government took note by granting the franchise to all Indians in 1960, and several provinces followed suit.

Improved Indian relations

Large-scale immigration after World War II challenged Canada's social structure. First displaced persons, then people leaving war-devastated Europe, and then those coming to share the prosperity of Canada in the 1950s comprised the greatest immigration Canada had known. A majority of the immigrants were from Europe, including many from southern Europe, particularly Italy, Greece, and Portugal; and almost all went into industrial cities in the east. As a whole the movement marked a new phase in the development and character of Canadian society. By 1961 Canadians of British and Irish descent had fallen to 43.8 percent and those of French descent to 30 percent, while persons of other descents had risen to 26.4 percent. Moreover, the newcomers to Quebec chose to speak English and not French and to join the English culture.

Internal politics, 1945–68. The internal politics of the years 1945–56 were quiet and complacent. Prime Minister King retired in 1948, having held that office longer than anyone in Canadian history. His successor, Louis St. Laurent, proved an admirable and amiable prime minister during a period of confidence and prosperity. A conservative revival based on the efforts of the Progressive Conservative Party (PC; formerly Conservative Party), however, led to a series of parliamentary struggles in which a government long in power was made to appear both arrogant and indifferent to public feeling and opinion, notably in a debate over the Trans-Canada Pipeline in 1956.

The Diefenbaker government

The new conservative leader, John G. Diefenbaker, an impassioned platform orator, defeated St. Laurent in 1957 to form a minority government, and then in 1958 won the greatest electoral victory in Canadian history. During Diefenbaker's term of office, however, there was a major recession. He had to face the strains of an unsuccessful British attempt to enter the European Economic Community; of relations with the United States during the Cuban missile crisis, in which Canada was not consulted and yet was expected to take part in the air defense of North America; and of a domestic struggle over the installation of nuclear warheads in Canada and their use by the Canadian NATO contingent. Internal dissension reduced the

Diefenbaker government to a minority government in 1962 and to defeat in 1963. The Liberal government of Lester Pearson that followed, however, was also a minority government and had difficulty dealing effectively with the new demands of Quebec and retaining the confidence of the country. Pearson retired in 1967 and was succeeded by Pierre Elliott Trudeau, a strong federalist, who in 1968 won a decisive victory in Canada and in Quebec.

The Trudeau years. *Domestic policies.* The signal personal influence of Prime Minister Trudeau on the political life of Canada arose from two circumstances. One was the uncertainty introduced into Canadian politics by the rise of separatist feeling in Quebec. The other was the national feeling that Canada as a whole must take its own constitution and remake it to fit the circumstances of the late 20th century. Trudeau seemed superbly equipped to deal with both. He was a strong and convinced federalist, opposed flatly to separatism. He was a constitutional lawyer, acclaimed as an expert in constitutional understanding and reform. At the same time, he was impeccably French, the answer to the need of the Liberal Party for a French leader and to that of Canada for a French champion of the federal union.

As such Trudeau was free to complete Lester Pearson's work in providing for a bilingual and bicultural Canada. To do this, his government introduced the Official Languages Bill in 1968 and issued the instructions under the resultant act, supported by all parties, which prepared the way for a bilingual federal civil service and for the encouragement of the French language and culture in Canada. (Similar encouragement was given to other ethnic cultures.) This was the foremost legislation of Trudeau's early years in office and was meant to begin a new relationship between the English and French in Canada.

Official Languages Act

Trudeau's special concern to maintain the unity of Canada and the good relations of English and French Canadians became the specialty of the Liberal Party in Quebec, both federal and provincial. Under a new leader, Robert Bourassa, the provincial Liberal Party in 1970 swept back into office. It was strongly committed to maintaining the federal system and to demonstrating the benefits of that system for Quebec. Compared with its electoral success and energetic policy of large investment and rapid economic development, the Parti Québecois seemed only a petulant minority. The Bourassa government was at the same time strongly provincial and determined to make Quebec's viewpoint known and, if possible, prevailing. Thus when the second of Trudeau's tasks taken over from Pearson, the reform of the constitution, had been, as it seemed, completed in the "Victoria charter" put before a meeting of the federal and provincial governments at Victoria, British Columbia, in 1971, Bourassa claimed a special position for Quebec. Despite agreement by all the other provinces, Quebec at the last moment withdrew its assent and the path of constitutional reform was blocked.

At the same time the Trudeau government, following a policy of heavy public expenditure initiated by Pearson (and emulated by all the provinces), entered on a program of economic growth based in the first instance on government direction and expenditure. Government revenues (and, usually, deficits) rose to unprecedented proportions of the national income. Despite this policy of governmental stimulus, the Canadian economy, which had grown and changed in the direction of industrial production, began to slow in its growth and to level off.

The failure of the U.S.-Canadian agreement on automobile manufacture (1965), which had shared the North American markets and North American skill and research of the automobile industries of the United States and Canada to give Canada a proportionate share of the market, revealed a weakness in the Canadian economy. So too perhaps did the failure to deal effectively with the difficulties created by large foreign investment, which in many cases reduced Canadian industry to the character of a branch plant industry. The Foreign Investment Review Act of 1973, if well intended, was too slight in its operation to make any real difference. The ideal of an independent Canadian industry in a politically independent Canada had not yet been attained.

As a result of the slowdown of Canadian growth, further hampered by rising costs of government and of labour—Canadian wage levels had come to equal, even exceed, those of the United States—Canadian natural resources began to resume their former position in the national economy. This was strengthened by the extending of the oil- and gas-drilling frontier to the Beaufort Sea and the Arctic Islands. Coupled with this were the construction of a pipeline from Alaska across Canada to the United States, ultimately for Canadian as well as American fuel, and the beginning exploitation of the vast oil reserves of the Alberta tar sands, which began to furnish crude oil in quantity in the fall of 1978.

Foreign affairs. In 1970 the Trudeau government issued a statement defining its foreign policy. Three major aims were presented: preservation of Canada as an independent political entity, maintenance of expanding prosperity, and constructive contribution to human needs.

In 1970–72, Canada reduced the number of its military and civilian personnel and military bases in Europe, while remaining within NATO. Canada established diplomatic relations with the People's Republic of China on October 13, 1970; ambassadors were exchanged the following year, and an exchange of consuls and most-favoured-nation trading arrangements were agreed upon in 1973. Closer relations were also sought with the Soviet Union and the European Economic Community, and Canada took a more active role in the United Nations. Canada maintained its commitment to the North American Air Defense Command (Norad), but in 1975 regional responsibility was reorganized to include only Canadian territory within Canada's jurisdiction. (In 1981 the Norad agreement was renewed for an additional five years and its name was changed to North American Aerospace Defense Command.)

Relations with China

Protection of Canada's economy led to adjustments in relations with the United States. In 1970 Canada increased the price of petroleum and natural gas sold to the United States, and in 1974 a plan to gradually reduce those sales and end them by 1982 was announced. This action was taken to protect domestic supplies of fossil fuels in the face of increasing prices of imported oil used in the eastern provinces. In 1978 Canada initiated purchases of airplanes and other military equipment to better defend its borders and fulfill its international commitments.

In accordance with the third aim of its foreign policy—to contribute to human needs—Trudeau's government pursued a policy promoting the international control of nuclear weaponry. In 1972 Canada and the United States signed the Great Lakes Water Quality Agreement to control pollution of the lakes.

Assessment. By the mid-1970s some policies of the Trudeau government were falling into confusion. The bilingual policy was found to have pushed beyond the brink of English Canada's tolerance and was hastily truncated before even the remodelling of the federal civil service was completed. The assertion of a strong federal government was shaken by the electoral victory of the Parti Québecois in Quebec's provincial elections in November 1976. The grounds of its victory were the corruption and mismanagement of the Bourassa government, but the party was committed to separation, at least in the form known as sovereignty-association. Attempts to amend the constitution had failed, apparently beyond hope of recovery.

Basic to this slow but powerful reversal of all that the prime minister had stood for was the increasing skill and power of provincial governments. A steady widening of provincial jurisdiction, especially in the field of welfare, combined with an expansion of revenues and expenditures, led to a growing sense of local importance. The provinces for the first time in 1975 spent more of the national product than the federal government did. That government had become less powerful than the provinces acting collectively. These were more and more inclined to act collectively as more and more of them came to have Conservative or opposition governments—nine of the 10 by the fall of 1978.

Growth of provincial government

Then, with startling rapidity, the failure of fundamental

policies was followed in 1978 by some failure of the policy of inflation controls and by the apparent failure of the policy of expansive expenditures. Suddenly the country was faced by the Prime Minister with major reverses of policy, enforced with large cuts in prospective expenditures. The one ongoing measure was the proposal to amend the constitution.

In a general election held on May 22, 1979, the Progressive Conservative Party won the largest number of seats, short of a majority but enough to make its leader, C. Joseph (Joe) Clark, prime minister on June 4.

(W.L.M.)

The minority Progressive Conservative government, however, proved to be ineffective; after the opposition parties joined to defeat the government's proposed budget, Clark was forced to call a general election in February 1980. The Liberal Party regained the majority and Trudeau was returned to power. He moved quickly to reorganize the federal government and restore his policies. His continued opposition to separatism was confirmed in Quebec on May 20, 1980, when the Quebec electorate rejected by referendum the opportunity, proposed by René Lévesque and the Parti Québecois, to negotiate with the rest of Canada for status as a sovereignty-association.

Trudeau's return to power

Economic planning under Trudeau centred on the petroleum industry. Petro-Canada and other Canadian firms purchased several foreign-owned oil companies in the early 1980s, and new restrictions on foreign ownership were instituted to increase Canadian ownership of the industry to 50 percent by 1990.

The Trudeau government renewed its efforts to secure for Canada possession of and authority over its own constitution. The issue centred on the British North America (BNA) Act of 1867, the major document governing Canada, which could be amended by the British Parliament on Canada's behalf but over which the Canadian Parliament had no authority. Canada's negotiations for control of its constitution were complicated by the need to adopt an amending process acceptable to the federal government as well as to the 10 provinces. On December 2, 1981, an amending process and a bill of rights were accepted, and the Canadian Parliament drafted a resolution requesting that Queen Elizabeth II ask the British Parliament to "patriate" the Act, making it the basis for Canada's own constitution. The British Parliament approved the resolution on March 25, 1982, and the Queen added her assent, thereby making Canada fully independent and designating its constitutional document the Canada Act. Canada technically remained a monarchy, and it remained a member of the Commonwealth.

(Ed.)

BIBLIOGRAPHY. W.L. MORTON, *The Kingdom of Canada*, 2nd ed. (1969), is the fullest one-volume history and the most traditional. A shorter, less conservative general history is K.W. MCNAUGHT, *The History of Canada* (1970). More intensive and interpretative are J.M.S. CARELESS (ed.), *Colonists and Canadiens, 1760–1867* (1971); and J.M.S. CARELESS and R. CRAIG BROWN (eds.), *The Canadians, 1867–1967* (1968). The development of government in Canada has received a definitive statement in J.R. MALLORY, *The Structure of Canadian Government* (1971). R. COLE HARRIS and JOHN WARKENTIN, *Canada Before Confederation* (1974), is a historical geography. A comprehensive history of the French period is GUSTAVE LANCTOT, *Histoire du Canada*, 3 vol. (1960–64; Eng. trans., *A History of Canada*, 3 vol., 1963–65). Other studies are W.J. ECCLES, *The Canadian Frontier, 1534–1760* (1969); and MASON WADE, *The French Canadians, 1760–1967*, rev. ed., 2 vol. (1968). To understand the place of the colonies that became Canada in the British Empire, the following are most useful: H.A. INNIS, *The Fur Trade in Canada*, 2nd ed. (1956), and *The Cod Fisheries*, rev. ed. (1954); and J.B. BREBNER, *New England's Outpost: Acadia Before the Conquest of Canada* (1927), and *The Neutral Yankees of Nova Scotia* (1937). HILDA M. NEATBY in *Quebec: The Revolutionary Age, 1760–1791* (1966), analyzes the factors that led to the renewed separation of Quebec from the former colonies to the south. The following works both introduce and analyze the development of the remaining British colonies to self-governing communities and their union in Confederation. W.S. MACNUTT combines in a single narrative the histories of the Atlantic provinces in *The Atlantic Provinces, the Emergence of Colonial Society, 1712–1857* (1965). FERNAND OUELLET, *Histoire économique et sociale du Québec, 1760–1850* (1966), applies with great success the demographic method of French historiography to the little known domestic development of that province. HELEN TAFT MANNING in *The Revolt of French Canada, 1800–1835* (1962), details the political conflicts of those years. G.M. CRAIG, *Upper Canada: The Formative Years, 1784–1841* (1963), traces the origins of what is now Ontario. CHESTER NEW, *Lord Durham* (1929); and CHESTER MARTIN, *Foundations of Canadian Nationhood* (1955), are the leading authorities on the achievement of self-government. For a searching critique of colonial self-government, J.E. HODGETTS, *Pioneer Public Service* (1955), should be consulted. The story of Confederation has been told in various modes by D.G. CREIGHTON, *The Road to Confederation: The Emergence of Canada, 1863–1867* (1964); W.L. MORTON, *The Critical Years: The Union of British North America, 1857–1873* (1964); PETER B. WAITE, *The Life and Times of Confederation, 1864–1867* (1961); and ROBIN W. WINKS, *Canada and the United States: The Civil War Years* (1960). An overall view and realistic interpretation of those years may be found in KENNETH BOURNE, *Britain and the Balance of Power in North America, 1815–1908* (1967). Relations with the United Kingdom and the United States are a constant in Canadian history. J.B. BREBNER, *North Atlantic Triangle* (1945), is the definitive treatment to its date of publication. EDGAR MCINNIS, *The Unguarded Frontier* (1942), tells the story of American–Canadian relations as seen at their optimum. Changes in the last generation are reflected in JAMES EAYRS, *The Art of the Possible: Government and Foreign Policy in Canada* (1961), and *Northern Approaches* (1961); and, in sombre tones, in D.G. CREIGHTON, *Canada's First Century, 1867–1967* (1970). A sober and intensive study of the fundamentals of U.S.–Canadian relations may be found in R. CRAIG BROWN, *Canada's National Policy, 1883–1900* (1964). BROWN and R.G. COOK, *Canada, 1896–1921: A Nation Transformed* (1974), is a study of the effects upon Canada of the boom that opened the 20th century and of World War I. The expansionist period is examined in DOUG OWRAM, *Promise of Eden: The Canadian Expansionist Movement and the Idea of the West, 1856–1900* (1980); and MORRIS ZASLOW, *The Opening of the Canadian North, 1870–1914* (1971). The beginnings of a critique of the Canadian mind are present in CARL BERGER, *The Sense of Power* (1970). C.P. STACEY, *Canada and the Age of Conflict, 1867–1921*, vol. 1, *A History of Canadian External Policies* (1978), is a scholarly and judicious summary of the beginnings and development of Canadian external policy to 1921. Events in French Canada since 1960 are too recent for historical treatment. A critical account of the background is found in RAMSAY COOK, *Canada and the French Canadian Question* (1966); a sensitive analysis in RICHARD JONES, *Community in Crisis: French Canadian Nationalism in Perspective* (1967); and a reasoned statement of the case for separatism in MARCEL RIOUX, *La Question du Québec* (1969; Eng. trans., *Quebec in Question*, 1971). W.L. MORTON, *The Canadian Identity*, 2nd ed. (1971), is an attempt to discover the essential fibres of Canadian nationhood.

(W.L.M.)

Canaletto

In the 18th century, the age of the grand tour, the portraiture of places (topography) reached its height; and Venice, a city unique in character and splendid in ceremony, was the centre of topographical painting. The dominating figure of the Venetian school of skilled view (*vedute*) painters was Giovanni Antonio Canal, called Canaletto. Transcending the bounds of simple topographical accuracy, Canaletto expressed in his pictures a full feeling for art, and his understanding of cloud effects, flickering contours, colour-filled shadows, and the melting textures of full daylight made him a determining influence for the landscape artists of following generations who sought to capture the light and atmosphere, as well as the facts, of their scenes.

Canaletto, who was born in Venice on October 18, 1697, was connected with a noble family whose coat of arms he occasionally used as a signature. How he came to be known as Canaletto is uncertain—perhaps the name was first used to distinguish him from his father, Bernardo Canal, a theatrical scene painter in whose studio Canaletto assisted. Canaletto is recorded as working with his father and brother in Venice from 1716 to 1719, and in Rome from 1719 to 1720, painting scenes for Alessandro Scarlatti's operas. It was in Rome that Canaletto left theatrical painting for the topographical career that was to bring him international fame so quickly, although a close connection to his theatrical work remained in his

"The Stonemason's Yard," oil on canvas by Canaletto, *c.* 1730. In the National Gallery, London. 1.238 × 1.629 m.
By courtesy of the trustees of the National Gallery, London

choice of subject matter, his use of line and wash drawings, and his theatrical perspective.

Works of the Venetian period

When he returned to Venice, he began his contact with the foreign patrons who would continue as his chief support throughout his career. Four large paintings were completed for the Prince of Liechtenstein, in or before 1723, and in 1725–26 he finished a series of pictures for Stefano Conti, a merchant from Lucca. Dated memoranda accompanying the Conti pictures suggest how busy and yet how exacting the artist was at this time. Canaletto indicates that delays in the delivery of the pictures had been due to the pressure of other commissions and his own insistence on obtaining reliable pigments and on working from nature. In his pictures of the late 1720s, such as "The Stonemason's Yard" (National Gallery, London) he combined a freedom and subtlety of manner that he was rarely to achieve again with an unrivalled imaginative and dramatic interpretation of Venetian architecture. His understanding of sunlight and shadow, cloud effects, and the play of light on buildings support the contention in his memoranda that he was working out-of-doors, which was a most unusual procedure for painters of that time.

Throughout the 1730s Canaletto was deeply absorbed in meeting foreign demands for souvenir views of Venice. Such was the pressure upon him that he ultimately was forced to work largely from drawings and even from other artists' engravings, rather than from nature. He also developed the use of the *camera ottica*, a device by which a lens threw onto a ground-glass screen the image of a view, which could be used as a basis for a drawing or painting. Finally, he developed a mechanical technique, in which ruler and compasses played a part, and architecture and figures were put into the picture according to a dexterous and effective formula. Such a vast number of views of Venice were produced during his lifetime that it is often thought that Canaletto was head of a large studio, but there is no evidence of this.

Canaletto had no serious rivals. The painter Luca Carlevaris, who may have been his initial inspiration in choosing to produce topographical pictures for a largely foreign audience, had been driven from the field; Bernardo Bellotto, Canaletto's nephew, was not yet a mature painter; and Michele Marieschi was a follower rather than a competitor. Because of this lack of rivals, Canaletto became increasingly difficult to deal with. Owen Mac Swinney, an English operatic figure and patron of Canaletto, wrote as early as 1727,

> The fellow is whimsical and varys his prices, every day: and he that has a mind to have any of his work, must not seem to be too fond of it, for he'l be ye worse treated for it, both in the price and the painting too.

The outbreak of the War of the Austrian Succession in 1740, which cut down sharply the number of visitors to Venice, seriously affected Canaletto's commissions. At this point, an early acquaintance, Joseph Smith— publisher, merchant, and later British consul in Venice— stepped into the breach. As standardized views of Venice dropped from demand, Smith seems to have encouraged Canaletto to expand his range of subjects to include Roman monuments and the area of Padua and the River Brenta. Pictures composed of more or less recognizable elements rearranged (*capriccio*) and pictures composed of almost completely imaginary architectural and scenic elements (*veduta ideata*) now began to play an increasingly important part in Canaletto's work. In 1741–44 Canaletto also made a series of 30 etchings, exceptionally skillful and sensitive, showing a command of perspective and luminosity.

Later works in England

Canaletto's international reputation served him well as the tourists became more scarce. In 1746 he went to England, where he was welcomed and remained until 1755, despite an invitation to Dresden (now in East Germany), from the Elector of Saxony. He worked mainly in London, on English views. It is notable, when considering the works executed during this period, that Canaletto— an artist 50 years of age who had evolved various conventions based on Venetian experience—was dealing with an entirely different set of atmospheric conditions and different subject matter. Occasionally, by putting English material into a Venetian framework, he achieved a masterpiece, but for the most part he fell below his own standards, and his work was lifeless and mechanical.

On his return to Venice, however, his reputation had not diminished; and at last he received official recognition—election to the Venetian Academy in 1763 and, in the same year, appointment as prior of the Collegio dei Pittori.

Canaletto died in Venice on April 20, 1768.

MAJOR WORKS

Since Canaletto executed so many paintings of views of Venice and other real and imaginary scenes, the list given here is of representative works that may be seen in public collections.

VIEWS OF VENICE: "Piazza San Marco Looking East from South of the Central Line" (Fogg Art Museum, Harvard University); "Venice: Piazza S. Marco and the Colonnade of the Procurate Nuove" (National Gallery, London); "The Piazzetta Looking North West: The Fonteghetto della Farina" (*c.* 1735–40; Museum of Fine Arts, Boston); "Scene in Venice; The Piazzetta Entrance to the Grand Canal" (*c.* 1726–28; Metropolitan Museum of Art, New York); "View in Venice" (National Gallery of Art, Washington, D.C.).

VIEWS IN ENGLAND: "Greenwich Hospital from the North Bank of the Thames" (National Maritime Museum, Greenwich, London); "Old Somerset House from the River Thames" (Minneapolis Institute of Arts, Minneapolis, Minn.); "Old Walton Bridge" (1754; Dulwich College Picture Gallery, London).

CAPRICCI AND IMAGINARY COMPOSITIONS: "Capriccio, a Tomb by the Lagoon" (Uffizi, Florence); "Capriccio, a Domed Circular Church" (Worcester Art Museum, Massachusetts).

BIBLIOGRAPHY. The most complete collections of Canaletto's paintings and drawings are held in the Royal Collections at Windsor and Buckingham Palace; see MICHAEL LEVY, *Canaletto Paintings in the Collection of Her Majesty the Queen* (1964); and K.T. PARKER, *The Drawings of Antonio Canaletto in the Collection of His Majesty the King at Windsor Castle* (1948). Other works recommended include: W.G. CONSTABLE, *Canaletto*, 2 vol. (1962), the most comprehensive biography, with catalogue raisonné and full bibliography; F.J.B. WATSON, *Canaletto*, 2nd ed. (1950), an authoritative brief account, with bibliography; BARON VON HADELN DETLEV, *The Drawings of Antonio Canal, Called Canaletto*, trans. by CAMPBELL DODGSON (1929); VITTORIO MOSCHINI, *Canaletto* (1954; Eng. trans., *Drawings by Canaletto*, 1963 and 1969), the best collection with many plates; RODOFLO PALLUCCHINI and G.F. GUARNATI, *Le Acqueforti del Canaletto* (1945), a very good work (in Italian) on the watercolours; J.G. LINKS, *Views of Venice: The Engravings by Visentini* (1971), a readable account on the etchings; and *Canaletto: Giovanni Antonio Canal, 1697–1768* (1964), an exhibition catalog from the Art Gallery of Toronto (with text by W.G. CONSTABLE)—the best introductory work for the general reader.

(W.G.C.)

Canals and Inland Waterways

Despite modern technological advances in air and ground transportation, inland waterways continue to fill a vital role and, in many areas, to grow substantially. This article traces the history of canal building from the earliest times to the present day, describes both the constructional and operational engineering techniques used, and the major inland waterways and networks throughout the world.

Transport by inland waterways may be by navigable rivers or those made navigable by canalization (dredging and bank protection) or on artificial waterways called canals. Many inland waterways are multipurpose, providing drainage, irrigation, water supply, and generation of hydroelectric power as well as navigation. The lay of the land (topography) and particularly changes in water levels require that many rivers be regulated to make them fully navigable, thus enabling vessels to proceed from one water level to another. The chief regulating method is the lock, the development of which contributed significantly to the Industrial Revolution and the development of modern industrial society.

For many types of commodities, particularly such bulk commodities as grains, coal, and ore, inland-waterway transport is still more economical than any other kind of transport. Thus, it is hardly surprising that modernized inland waterways, using the latest navigational aids and traction methods and traversing the great land masses of North America, Europe, and Asia, play an increasingly important economic role.

History

Most of the improvement of rivers and construction of artificial waterways in antiquity was for irrigation purposes. In the 7th century BC the Assyrian king Sennacherib built an 80-kilometre (50-mile) stone-lined canal 20 metres (6.6 feet) wide to bring fresh water from Bavian to Nineveh. The work, which included a stone aqueduct 300 yards (330 metres) long, was constructed in one year and three months, according to a plaque that survives on the site. Surprisingly advanced techniques were used, including a dam with sluice gates allowing regulation of the flow of the water stored. The Phoenicians, Assyrians, Sumerians, and Egyptians all constructed elaborate canal systems. The most spectacular canal of this period was probably Nahrawān, 400 feet (120 metres) wide and 200 miles (335 kilometres) long, to provide a year-round navigation channel from near Samarra to al-Kūt, using water provided by damming the unevenly flowing Tigris. Many elaborate canals are known to have been built in Babylonia. In Egypt, the Nile was dammed to control its flood waters, and an extensive system of basin irrigation was established. The Persian king Darius in the 5th century BC cut a canal from the Nile to the Red Sea. The Romans were responsible for very extensive systems of river regulation and canals in France, Italy, The Netherlands, and Great Britain for military transport. The legions in Gaul canalized one of the mouths of the Rhône to protect their overseas supply route. In the 1st century AD, the Roman consul Marcus Livius Drusus dug a canal between the Rhine and Yssel to relieve the Rhine of surplus water, and the Roman general Corbulo linked the Rhine and Meuse with a canal 23 miles long to avoid the stormy North Sea passage from Germany to the coast. Attempting to reclaim the Fens in England, the Romans connected the River Cam with the Ouse by an eight-mile canal, the Nene with the Witham by one 25 miles long, and the Witham with the Trent by the Fosse Dyke (ditch), still in use.

Use of sluice gates

Outside Europe and the Middle East, between the 3rd century BC and the 1st century AD, the Chinese built impressive canals. Outstanding were the Ling Ch'ü in Kuangsi, 90 miles long from the Han capital; Ch'ang-an (Sian) to the Huang Ho (Yellow River); and the Pien Canal in Honan. Of later canals, the most spectacular was the Grand Canal, the first 600-mile section of which was opened to navigation in 610. This waterway enabled grain to be transported from the lower Yangtze and the Huai to K'ai-feng and Lo-yang. These canals had easy gradients (changes in water levels); and at about three-mile intervals there were single gates of stone or timber abutments with vertical grooves up or down which the log closure was manually hauled by ropes to hold or release the water, thus controlling the water level. A few more elaborate gates had to be raised by windlasses. Where water level changes were too great for such simple devices, double slipways were built and vessels were hauled up the inclines.

MEDIEVAL REVIVAL

In Europe, canal building, which appears to have lapsed after the fall of the Roman Empire, was revived by commercial expansion in the 12th century. River navigation was considerably improved and artificial waterways were developed with the construction of stanches, or flash locks, in the weirs (dams) of water mills and at intervals along the waterways. Such a lock could be opened suddenly, releasing a torrent that carried a vessel over a shallow place. The commercially advanced and level Low Countries developed a system of canals using the drainage of the marshland at the mouths of the Scheldt, Meuse, and Rhine; about 85 percent of medieval transport in the region went by inland waterway.

Use of stanches

Because shipping was handicapped where barges had to be towed over the weirs with windlasses or manually, the lock and lock basin were evolved to raise boats from one level to another. Although a primitive form of lock had been in operation at Damme, on the canal from Bruges to the sea, as early as 1180, the first example of the modern pound lock, which impounded water, was probably that built at Vreeswijk, The Netherlands, in 1373, at the junction of the canal from Utrecht with the River Lek. Outer and inner gates contained a basin, the water level of which was controlled by alternatively winding up and lowering the gates. This system became widespread in the 14th century. In the 15th century, the lock-gate system was much improved with the addition of paddles to control the flow of water in and out of the lock chamber through sluices in the gates or sides of the lock.

Commercial needs soon encouraged canal construction in less ideal locations. The Stecknitz Canal, built in Germany (1391–98), ran 21 miles from Lake Möllner down to Lübeck, with a fall of 40 feet (13 metres) controlled with four stanches; the canal was later extended south to Lauenburg on the Elbe to establish a link between the Baltic and the North Sea. To deal with a fall from the summit to Lauenburg of 42 feet (13.5 metres) in 15 miles (25 kilometres), two large locks were built, each capable of holding ten small barges.

Italy, the other principal commercial region of medieval Europe, also made important contributions to waterway technology. The Naviglio Grande Canal was constructed (1179–1209) with an intake on the River Ticino, a fall of 110 feet (33 metres) in 31 miles (52 kilometres) to Abbiategrasso and Milan, the water level being controlled by sluices. To facilitate transport of marble from the quarries for the building of the Milan cathedral, the canal was linked with an old moat, and in Italy the first pound lock with mitre instead of the earlier portcullis gates was constructed to overcome difference in water level.

China may have been ahead of Europe in canal building. Between 1280 and 1293 the 700-mile northern branch of the Grand Canal was built from Huai-an to Peking. One section, crossing the Shantung foothills, was in effect the first summit-level canal, one that rises then falls, as opposed to a lateral canal, which has a continuous fall only. The Yellow River was linked with a group of lakes about 100 miles south, where the land rose 50 feet higher; and to overcome water lost through operation of the lock gates, two small rivers were partially diverted to flow into the summit level.

16TH TO 18TH CENTURIES

The development of the mitre lock, a double-leaf gate the closure of which formed an angle pointing upstream, heralded a period of extensive canal construction during the 16th and 17th centuries. The canalized rivers and ca-

The mitre lock

nals of that period foreshadowed the European network to be developed over many years.

France. In France, the Briare and Languedoc canals were built, the former linking the Loire and Seine and the latter, also known as the Canal du Midi, linking Toulouse with the Mediterranean. Both were remarkable feats of engineering. The Briare Canal (completed 1642) rose 128 feet (39 metres) to a plateau with a summit level 3.75 miles (6.2 kilometres) long and then dropped 266 feet to the Loing at Montargis. It included 40 locks, of which a unique feature was a staircase of six locks to cope with the fall of 65 feet (20 metres) on the descent from the Loing to Rogny. Construction of the 150-mile (250-kilometre) Languedoc Canal joining the Bay of Biscay and the Mediterranean via the Garonne and the Aude ran through very rugged terrain. Begun in 1666 and finished in 1681, it rose 206 feet (61 metres) in 32 miles (54 kilometres) from the Garonne at Toulouse to the summit through 26 locks, and then descended 620 feet (185 metres) through 74 locks for 115 miles (190 kilometres). Near Béziers a staircase of eight locks was built, and six miles (ten kilometres) further upstream a tunnel 180 yards (165 metres) long was constructed; three major aqueducts carried it over rivers, and numerous streams were diverted beneath it in culverts. The most notable technical achievement was a complex summit water supply that included unique diversion of flows and storage provision.

Flanders. The canal system in Flanders included one from Brussels to Willebroeck on the Rupel to shorten navigation by half, an 18½-mile (30-kilometre) canal with four locks; another of 44 miles (70 kilometres) was constructed from Bruges to Passchendaele, Nieuport, and Dunkerque and was later extended to Ostend, while Dunkerque was linked with the River Aa, at the mouth of which a large tide lock was constructed at Graveslines. The outstanding achievement in Flanders was a lock at Boesinghe on the canal from Ypres to Boesinghe beside the River Yser. The fall of 20 feet (six metres) on this four-mile (6.5-kilometre) stretch was contained by a single large lock. Side ponds with ground sluices were provided for the first time to reduce the loss of water during the lock's operation. The ponds took one-third of the water when the lock was emptied and returned it for the filling.

Germany. In Germany, the 15-mile (25-kilometre) Friedrich Wilhelm Summit Canal, completed in 1669, rose from Neuhaus on the Spree for ten feet (three metres) in two locks and from west of the summit fell 65 feet (20 metres) to Brieskow on the Oder. An extensive system of waterways in this part of Germany was finally established with the opening of the Plaue Canal in 1746, which ran from the Elbe to the Havel. The 25-mile (42-kilometre) Finow Canal along the Havel to the Liepe, a tributary of the Oder, had been built earlier but fell into decay because of flooding and neglect and was not rebuilt until 1751. In the late 17th and early 18th centuries, under the Great Elector of Brandenburg and Frederick I of Prussia, the three great rivers, the Elbe, Oder and Weser, were linked by canal for commercial and political reasons, including the bypassing of tolls charged by the numerous states and petty principalities of the Holy Roman Empire. In the Low Countries, wars, political considerations, and the rivalry between the Dutch and Belgian ports handicapped canal building. The Dutch, for example, strongly opposed a Rhine–Meuse–Scheldt canal, fearing diversion of trade to Antwerp.

The linking of the Elbe, Oder, and Weser rivers

England. The first lock was not built on an English canal until the 16th century, and the canal era proper dates from the construction of the Bridgewater Canal to carry coal from Worsley to Manchester in the 18th century by the engineer James Brindley. Opened for navigation in 1761, it was extended to the Mersey in 1776. Its success promoted a period of intense canal construction that established a network of inland waterways serving the Industrial Revolution and contributing to Britain's prosperity in the half-century preceding the railway era, which began in the mid-19th century. The Grand Trunk Canal established a cross-England route by linking the Mersey to the Trent, opened up the Midlands, and provided water transport for exports to European markets. There followed the link between the Thames and the Bristol Channel provided by the Severn Canal and the Gloucester and Berkeley Ship Canal from Sharpness on the Severn to Gloucester. Birmingham's growth and industrial prosperity were stimulated because the city became the centre of a canal system that connected London, the Bristol Channel, the Mersey, and the Humber. The Caledonian Ship Canal across Scotland, joining the chain of freshwater lakes along the line of the Great Glen, was built between 1803 and 1822.

One of the few canals to be built after the canal era was the 36-mile- (60-kilometre-) long Manchester Ship Canal, which was opened in 1894 to give oceangoing vessels access from the Mersey estuary to Manchester.

Technological development. This spate of canal construction was accompanied by technological development both in construction methods and operation. Locks, inclined planes, and lifts were developed to cope with changes in water level. At Bingley, for example, on the Leeds and Liverpool Canal, a lock staircase was built; and on the hilly areas at Ketley in Shropshire, inclined planes were constructed in 1788 to haul tugboats from one level to another. The longest plane, about 225 feet (67 metres), was on the Hobbacott Down plane of the Bude Canal in Cornwall. Vertical lifts counterweighted by water were also used; a set of seven was built on the Grand Western Canal; while at Anderton in Cheshire, a lift was later converted to electrical power and was still operating in the 20th century. The most spectacular inclined plane was built in the United States on the Morris Canal, which linked the Hudson and Delaware rivers. For a rise of 900 feet (265 metres) to the Alleghenies watershed, 22 locks were installed at the head of an inclined plane, and descending on a gradient of 1 in 10 to 1 in 12, ran down to the pound below. Barges 79 feet (22 metres) long with loads up to 30 tons were hauled up by trolleys running on rails, on which they settled as the lock emptied; the barges descended under gravity into the lower pound to float on an even keel when the water levelled off. In the reverse direction, they were hauled up by drum and cable mechanism.

19TH CENTURY

Europe. In Europe, where the canal era had also started toward the end of the 17th century and continued well into the 18th, France took the lead, integrating its national waterway system further by forging the missing links. In the north, the St. Quentin Canal, with a 3½-mile tunnel, opened in 1810, linked the North Sea and the Scheldt and Lys systems with the English Channel via the Somme, and with Paris and Le Havre via the Oise and Seine. In the interior, the Canal du Centre connected the Loire at Digoin with the Saône at Chalon and completed the first inland route from the English Channel to the Mediterranean; the Saône and Seine were linked further north to give a more direct route from Paris to Lyon; and the Rhine–Rhône Canal (Canal du Rhône au Rhin), opened in 1834, provided a direct north-to-south route; while the Canal de la Sambre à L'Oise linked the French canal system with the Belgian network via the Meuse. Toward the end of the 19th century, France embarked on the standardization of its canal system to facilitate through communication without trans-shipment. The ultimate result was a doubling of traffic between the opening of the century and World War II.

Industrial development in the early 19th century prompted Belgium to extend its inland waterways, especially to carry coal from Mons and Charleroi to Paris and northern France. Among the new canals and extensions built were the Mons-Condé and the Pommeroeut-Antoing canals, which connected the Haine and the Scheldt; the Sambre was canalized; the Willebroek Canal was extended southward with the building of the Charleroi–Brussels Canal in 1827; and somewhat later the Campine routes were opened to serve Antwerp and connect the Meuse and Scheldt. When the growth of the textile trade in Ghent created a need for better water transport, the

Ghent Ship Canal, cut through to Terneuzen, was opened in 1827, giving a shorter route to the sea. The Dutch extended their canals to serve the continental European industrial north. The Maastricht–Liège Canal was opened in 1850, enabling raw materials and steel to be transported from the Meuse and Sambre industrial areas by waterway throughout The Netherlands. In 1824 a long ship canal was built to bypass silting that obstructed navigation on the Ijsselmeer (Zuiderzee) and to enter the North Sea in the Texel Roads. Later, an even shorter ship canal was built to Ijmuiden.

Dutch canals

In Scandinavia, new canals were built to facilitate transport of timber and mineral products. In 1832 the new Göta Canal was opened, crossing the country from the Baltic to the Skagerrak and incorporating 63 locks. The political climate was less favourable for canal building in central Europe, but the Ludwig Canal, forming part of the Rhine–Main–Danube route, was opened in 1840. At the same time, steps were taken to improve river navigation generally, to provide speedier transport, and to enable a greater volume of freight to be carried. The Danube was regulated for 144 miles from Ennsmundung to Theuben, and the Franz Canal was dug in Hungary to join the Danube and Tisza. A nationwide Russian canal system connecting the Baltic and Caspian seas via the Neva and Volga rivers became navigable in 1718. A more direct route was established in 1804 with a canal between the Beresina and Dvina rivers. In the 19th century, Russia concentrated on making connections between the heads of navigation of its great rivers, the Volga, Dnepr, Don, Dvina, and Ob.

The Corinth ship canal

An outstanding engineering achievement in Greece was the cutting of a deep ship canal at sea level through the Isthmus of Corinth to connect the Aegean and Ionian seas. The Roman emperor Nero had first attempted this linking in the 1st century AD; the shafts sunk by him were reopened and sunk to their full depth. The canal, 4.8 miles (6.3 kilometres) long, 81 feet (25 metres) wide, and 27 feet (eight metres) deep in its centre section, running 280 feet (86 metres) below almost vertical rock cliffs, was opened in 1893.

United States. In the U.S., canal building began slowly; only 100 miles of canals had been built at the beginning of the 19th century; but before the end of the century over 4,000 miles were open to navigation. With wagon haulage difficult, slow, and costly for bulk commodities, water transport was the key to the opening up of the interior, but the way was barred by the Allegheny Mountains. To overcome this obstacle, it was necessary to go north by sea via the St. Lawrence River and the Great Lakes or south to the Gulf of Mexico and the Mississippi. A third possibility was the linking of the Great Lakes with the Hudson via the Mohawk Valley. The Erie Canal, 363 miles (580 kilometres) long with 82 locks from Albany on the Hudson to Buffalo on Lake Erie, was built by the state of New York from 1817 to 1825. Highly successful from the start, it opened up the Midwest prairies, the produce of which could flow eastward to New York, with manufactured goods making the return journey westward, giving New York predominance over other Atlantic seaboard ports. The Champlain Canal was opened in 1823; but not until 1843, with the completion of the Chambly Canal, was access to the St. Lawrence made possible via the Richelieu River. Meanwhile, Canada had constructed the Welland Canal linking Lakes Ontario and Erie. Opened in 1829, it met the 326-foot (98-metre) rise of the Niagara River with 40 locks, making navigation possible to Lake Michigan and Chicago. Later, the St. Mary's Falls Canal connected Lake Huron and Lake Superior. To provide a southern route around the Allegheny Mountains, the Susquehanna and Ohio rivers were linked in 1834 by a 394-mile (630-kilometre) canal between Philadelphia and Pittsburgh. A unique feature of this route was the combination of water and rail transport with a 37-mile (59-kilometre) portage by rail by five inclined planes rising 1,399 feet (413 metres) to the summit station 2,334 feet (689 metres) above sea level and then falling 1,150 feet (340 metres) to Johnstown on the far side of the mountains, where a 105-mile (170-kilometre) canal with 68 locks ran to Pittsburgh. By 1856 a series of canals linked this canal system to the Erie Canal.

The Susquehanna-Ohio Canal

Meanwhile, the Louisiana Purchase of 1803 had given the United States control of the Mississippi River, and it became the main waterway route for the movement of Midwest produce via New Orleans and the Gulf of Mexico. Developments included the Illinois–Michigan Canal, connecting the two great water systems of the continent, the Great Lakes and the Mississippi. Entering Lake Michigan at Chicago, then a mere village, the canal triggered the city's explosive growth. Several canals were constructed subsequently to link up with the Erie and Welland canals and the St. Lawrence, and a comprehensive network of inland waterways was established.

Impact of the railways. With the development of rail transport in the 19th century, canals declined as the dominant carriers of freight, particularly in the U.S. and Britain. In continental Europe the impact was less marked because the great natural rivers already linked by artificial waterways constituted an international network providing transport economically without trans-shipment; the terrain was more favourable and the canals larger and less obstructed by locks. Elsewhere, canals could not compete with rail. They were limited both in the volume carried per unit and in speed; they were too small, too slow, and fragmented; and the railways, as they became integrated into national systems, provided a far more extensive service with greater flexibility. The canals were further handicapped because they were not, for the most part, common carriers themselves but were largely dependent on intermediate carrying companies. Although transport on the canals was for some time cheaper than rail, the railways gradually overcame this advantage. To modernize and extend the waterways to enable larger boats to ply them, to reduce the number of locks that slowed down movement, and to provide a more comprehensive service, all this required capital investment on a scale that made the return problematical. The railways exploited the difficulties of the canals by drastic rate cutting that forced many canal companies to sell out to them. In Britain, in the 1840s and 1850s a third of the canals had become railway owned and many were subsequently closed down. In the U.S., half the canals were abandoned. The railways thus succeeded in eliminating their competition and obtained a near-monopoly of transport that they held until the arrival of the motor age.

The Kiel Canal. The 19th century saw the construction of three of the world's most famous canals—the Kiel, Suez, and Panama canals. The Kiel Canal carries tonnage many times that of most other canals. Frequent attempts had been made to make a route from the Baltic to the North Sea and thus to bypass the Kattegat and the dangerous Skagerrak. The Vikings had portaged ships on rollers across the ten-mile Kiel watershed, but not until 1784 was the Eider Canal constructed between the Gulf of Kiel and the Eider Lakes. A little over 100 years later, to take the largest ships, including those of the new German navy, the Kiel Canal was widened, deepened, and straightened to cut the distance from the English Channel to the Baltic by several hundred miles. Running 59 miles (95 kilometres) from locks at Brunsbüttel on the North Sea to the Haltenau locks on the Gulf of Kiel, the canal crosses easy country but has one unique engineering feature. At Rendsburg, to give clearance to the largest ships, the railway was made to spiral over the city on an ascending viaduct that crosses over itself before running on to the main span above the water.

The Suez Canal. The Isthmus of Suez so obviously provided a short sea route from the Mediterranean to the Indian Ocean and beyond as against the sea voyage around Africa that a canal had been dug in antiquity, had fallen into disuse, had been frequently restored, and finally had been blocked about the 8th century. Later there were many projects and surveys, but nothing happened until 1854 when Ferdinand de Lesseps, who had served as a French diplomat in Egypt, persuaded Saʿīd Pasha, the viceroy of Egypt, to grant a preliminary concession for construction of a new canal across the isthmus. A later report recommended a sea-level lockless canal between Suez and the Gulf of Pelusium; and the original concession was superseded by one granted in 1856 to the Suez Canal Company, an international consortium. The concession was for 99 years from the canal's opening to navigation, after which it was to revert to the Egyptian government; the canal was to be an international waterway, open at all times to all ships without discrimination. In addition to the ship canal, the company undertook to excavate a freshwater canal from the Nile at Bûlâq to Ismailia, with a branch extending to the Suez, to be available for smaller ships. Work on the ship canal lasted ten years, during which political, financial, contractual, and physical difficulties were overcome, and the canal was opened on November 17, 1869. As ultimately constructed, it was a 105-mile (169-kilometre) lockless waterway connecting the Mediterranean and the Red Sea. From its northern terminal at Port Said, the canal passes through the salt marsh area of Lake Manzala, with the freshwater canal running parallel. About 30 miles (50 kilometres) from Port Said, a seven-mile (12-kilometre) bypass built between 1949 and 1951 enables convoys to pass. At about the halfway point the canal enters Lake Timsah and passes Ismailia. Thence the waterway proceeds through the Bitter Lakes and on to Port Tawfîq, the southern terminal on the Red Sea, a few miles from the town of Suez. Since its construction, the canal has been constantly improved; originally 200 feet (60 metres) wide with a maximum depth of 24 feet (7.5 metres), it was widened in 1954 to 500 feet (150 metres) at water level and 196 feet (58 metres) at a depth of 33 feet (ten metres) with the main channel 45 feet (13 metres) deep, enabling ships of a maximum draft of 37 feet (11.3 metres) to navigate the canal.

Improvements in the Suez Canal

The canal remained open despite much political controversy. Nationalized by Egypt in 1956, it was blocked in 1967 after the Arab-Israeli War and so remained in the early 1970s.

The Panama Canal. After his success with the Suez Canal, de Lesseps was attracted to the Isthmus of Panama, where many projects had been suggested for cutting a canal to join the Atlantic and Pacific oceans and thus make unnecessary the passage around South America. De Lesseps proposed a sea-level route via Lake Nicaragua, but construction difficulties forced him to abandon this project in favour of a high-level lock canal via Panama. Further problems, especially yellow fever among the work force, halted construction after about 78,000,000 cubic yards of material had been excavated. Meanwhile, United States interest had been actively maintained, but the situation was complicated by political difficulties and questions of sovereignty. A treaty between Britain and the U.S. recognized the exclusive U.S. right to construct, regulate, and manage a canal across the isthmus; but Panama was Colombian territory, and the Colombia Senate refused ratification of a treaty with the U.S. After a revolt, a treaty was signed with independent Panama that granted the U.S. in perpetuity exclusive use, occupation, and control of the Canal Zone. (See below *Waterway Systems: Administration* for later history.)

Although preliminary work started in 1904, little real progress was made because of disputes over the type of canal that should be built; not until 1906 was the high-level lock plan finally adopted, as opposed to the previously favoured sea-level plan. Largely responsible for this decision was John F. Stevens, who became chief engineer and architect of the canal. Completed in 1914, the canal is 51.2 miles (85 kilometres) long. At its start from the large harbour area in Limon Bay on the Caribbean Sea, it rises over 80 feet (22 metres) above sea level to the Gatun Lake through the Gatun Locks and is retained at the north by these locks and dam and at the south by the Pedro Miguel Locks and Dam. The waterway then runs through the Gaillard Cut, which channels it through the Continental Divide, then between the Pedro Miguel Locks and the Miraflores Lake at an elevation of 54 feet (16 metres), ships to the Pacific Ocean being lowered by them to the Balboa Harbor entrance. The Gatun Lake, with its area of 166 square miles (450 square kilometres), is an integral part of the waterway and the principal source of its water. The minimum channel depth throughout the length of the canal is 37 feet and its width 300 feet. There are 23 angles or changes of direction between the entrances. Ships normally travel through the canal under their own power except in the locks, through which they are towed by electric locomotives.

(E.A.J.D.)

Modern waterway engineering

Waterways are subject to definite geographical and physical restrictions that influence the engineering problems of construction, maintenance, and operation.

The geographical restriction is that, unlike roads, railways, or pipelines, which are adaptable to irregular natural features, waterways are confined to moderate gradients; and where these change direction, the summit pounds (ponds) require an adequate supply of water, while valley pounds need facilities for disposal of surplus.

The primary physical restriction is that vessels cannot travel through water at speeds possible for road vehicles or railway wagons. Because transport economics are based on the Transport Unit (x tons moved y miles in 1 manhour), waterways must provide larger tonnage units than those possible on road or rail in order to be competitive.

The Transport Unit

Modern waterway engineering, therefore, is directed toward providing channels suitable for larger vessels to travel faster by reducing delays at locks or from darkness and other natural hazards. While such channels and associated works are designed to minimize annual maintenance costs, the costs of operating vessels, locks, wharves, and other waterway works can be minimized by increased mechanization.

CHARACTERISTICS OF BASIC TYPES

Fundamentally, waterways fall into three categories, each with its particular problems: natural rivers, canalized rivers, and artificial canals.

On natural rivers navigation is subjected to seasonal stoppages from frost, drought, or floods, all of which lead to channel movements and to the formation of shoals. While minimizing natural hazards, attention is primarily directed to retaining the channel in a predetermined course by stabilization of banks and bed, by elimination of side channels, and by easing major bends to obtain a channel of uniform cross section that follows the natural valley.

On canalized rivers navigation is facilitated by constructing locks that create a series of steps, the length of which depends on the natural gradient of the valley and on the rise at each lock. Associated with the locks for passing vessels, weirs and sluices are required for passing surplus water; and in modern canalizations, such as the Rhône and the Rhine, hydroelectric generation has introduced deep locks with longer artificial approach channels, which require bank protection against erosion and, in some strata, bed protection against seepage losses.

On artificial canals navigation can depart from natural river valleys and pass through hills and watersheds, crossing over valleys and streams along an artificial channel, the banks and sometimes the bed of which need protection against erosion and seepage. The route of an artificial canal can be selected to provide faster travel on long level pounds (stretches between locks), with necessary locks grouped either as a staircase with one chamber leading directly to another or as a flight with short intervening pounds. Where substantial differences of level arise or can be introduced, vertical lifts or inclined planes can be constructed. Storage reservoirs must be provided to feed the summit pound with enough water to meet lockage and evaporation losses; other reservoirs can be introduced at lower levels to meet heavier traffic movements entailing more frequent lockage operation. If supplies are insufficient to offset the losses, pumps may be needed to return water from lower to upper levels.

CHANNELS

Channel design. Natural rivers and canalized rivers away from artificial cuts need no protection against seepage and only light protection of banks against erosion. The widening or cutting off of major bends assists navigation, but wholesale straightening is undesirable because the natural sinuosity of the river, though modified, should be retained. Local widening is effected by dragline excavators cutting into the channel and dumping the material ashore either direct to form levees or to be removed elsewhere. Deepening or widening beyond the reach of shore-based excavators requires a floating plant that discharges to hopper barges for transport to a disposal point or to pipelines for pumping ashore.

Cross section of artificial canals

Artificial canals should provide a waterway with a cross-sectional area at least five, and preferably seven, times the cross-sectional area of the loaded vessel. In rock cuttings, such as those of the Corinth Canal, the waterway cross section could be rectangular, but the normal cross section is trapezoidal, with bed width three to four times and surface width six to eight times the width of the vessel, while the depth must be enough to allow the water displaced by the moving vessel to flow back under the hull.

Channel construction. The physical construction of a canal has been facilitated by the development of very large mechanical excavators. Walking draglines with 20-ton buckets such as were used on the St. Lawrence Seaway are more suitable for quarry or opencut coal workings; for general channel construction the more versatile tracked machines are preferred. Scrapers and dumper trucks with oversize pneumatic tires for fast travel over rough ground readily dispose of excavated materials to form embankments or other fill.

Water losses by percolation through bed or banks must be prevented on embankments and wherever permeable strata are encountered. While the watertight skin was originally obtained by a layer of puddled clay with protective gravel covering, other materials later became available, such as fly ash from power stations, sometimes with a cement admixture; bentonite; bituminous materials; sheet polythene; or concrete.

Bridges, aqueducts, and tunnels for waterways. Canals must frequently cross over or under roads and railways, rivers, and other canals. These crossings are made by a variety of bridges, sometimes carrying the road or railroad, sometimes carrying the canal. Most are fixed, though movable bridges are also used. On the Weaver River in England, four movable bridges, carrying main roads across the waterway, swing on pontoons.

Canals originally crossed valleys on heavy masonry structures supporting the full formation, including puddled clay lining. Cast-iron flanged and bolted troughs later provided a lighter and watertight channel; current practice uses concrete with bituminous sealing.

Canals were originally carried through hills and watersheds in small bricked tunnels through which vessels were propelled by manual haulage, by poling, or by legging—that is, by crewmen lying on their backs on the cabin and pushing with their feet against the tunnel roof. Later, tunnels were provided with towpaths.

Bank protection. On natural or canalized rivers of relatively large cross section, bank erosion can be checked by rubble roughly tipped or by natural growth such as reeds or willows.

On artificial canals of smaller dimensions, where passing vessels create a serious wash, some revetment (bank protection) is essential. Sloping banks are readily protected by close laid stone pitching, by bundles formed of interwoven willow branches, or by bituminous carpet; more permanent protection is provided by steel or concrete piles, close driven, overlapping or interlocked, and protected against impact damage by horizontal fendering above the waterline and below the waterline by roughly tipped rubble. In cuttings, the slopes are stabilized by berms (level strips) six to ten feet wide at intervals determined by the nature of the soil. On long embankments safety stop gates can minimize water losses in the event of a breach.

Towpaths. Originally provided for animal haulage, towpaths were adapted on many French canals for mechanical and electrical haulage until the general use of powered craft terminated this service in 1969. But the towpaths are still useful; in addition to providing ways for some local haulage by mechanical tractor, they provide valuable access to the canals for inspection and maintenance.

LOCKS

On canalized rivers and artificial canals, the waterway consists of a series of level steps formed by impounding barriers through which vessels pass by a navigation lock. Basically, this device consists of a rectangular chamber with fixed sides, movable ends, and facilities for filling and emptying: when a lock is filled to the level of the upper pound, the upstream gates are opened for vessels to pass; after closing the upstream gates, water is drawn out until the lock level is again even with the lower pound, and the downstream gates are opened. Filling or emptying of the chamber is effected by manually or mechanically operated sluices. In small canals these may be on the gates, but on larger canals they are on culverts incorporated in the lock structure, with openings into the chamber through the sidewalls or floor. While the sizes of the culverts and openings govern the speed of filling or emptying the chamber, the number and location of the openings determine the extent of the water disturbance in the chamber: the design must be directed toward obtaining a maximum speed of operation with minimum turbulence. The dimensions of the chamber are determined by the size of vessels using, or likely to use, the waterway. Where the traffic is dense, duplicate or multiple chambers may be required; in long chambers intermediate gates allow individual vessels to be passed.

Lock dimensions

Lock dimensions vary from the small narrow canal locks of England with chambers 72 feet (21 metres) long and seven feet (two metres) wide to the 1,500-ton capacity waterways of Europe with chambers 650 by 40 feet (190 by 12 metres). On the St. Lawrence Seaway the dimensions are approximately 800 by 80 feet (240 by 24 metres); on the Mississippi and Ohio rivers, where push-towing units are operating, the dimensions rise to 1,200 by 110 feet (360 by 33 metres).

On canalized rivers the present trend is for locks to be deeper, particularly where they form an integral part of a hydroelectric dam. On the Rhône the lock at Donzère-Mondragon has a depth of 80 feet (24 metres); in Portugal, where the Douro was being developed in the early 1970s for power and navigation, the Carrapatelo Lock has a depth of 114 feet (35 metres).

On artificial canals, where conservation of water is essential, depths do not normally exceed 20 feet (six metres): water consumption can be reduced by the provision of side pounds either adjacent to the lock, as at Bamberg on the Rhine–Main–Danube waterway, or incorporated in the lock walls, as in the (1899) Henrichenburg Lock on the Dortmund-Ems Canal.

Locks are located to provide good approach channels free from restrictions on sight or movement. Where traffic is heavy or push tows operate, adequate approach walls are needed both to accommodate vessels awaiting entry and to provide shelter from river currents while vessels move slowly into or out of the lock.

Lock gates. Movable gates must be strong enough to withstand the water pressure arising from the level difference between adjacent pounds. The most generally used are mitre gates consisting of two leaves, the combined lengths of which exceed the lock width by about 10 percent. When opened, the leaves are housed in lock wall recesses; when closed, after turning through about 60°, they meet on the lock axis in a V-shape with its point upstream. Mitre gates can be operated only after water levels on each side have been equalized.

On small canals gates may be manually operated by a lever arm extending over the lock side; on large canals hydraulic, mechanical, or electrical power is used. On the Weaver Navigations Canal in England, the hydraulic power for operating the lock gates has for 100 years been derived from the ten-foot (three-metre) head difference between the pounds.

Vertical gates, counterweighted and lifted by winch or

other gearing mounted on an overhead gantry, can operate against water pressure; as the gate leaves the sill, water enters the chamber, supplementing or replacing the culvert supply. The turbulence is more difficult to control and the overhead gantries impose restrictions on masts and other superstructure of a vessel.

The use of sector gates, which turn into recesses in the wall, depends on the physical characteristics of the site and on the traffic using the waterway; falling gates lower into recesses in the forebay; and rolling gates run on rails into deep recesses in the lock walls.

Lock equipment. Ladders recessed into the walls provide access between vessels and the lockside and are vital in case of accidents.

Bollards (mooring posts) on the lockside are used for holding vessels steady by ropes against the turbulence during lock operation; mooring hooks set in recesses in the walls provide an alternative anchorage against surging. Floating bollards are provided in deep locks; retained in wall recesses, they rise or fall with the vessel, obviating the need for continuous adjustment of the ropes. Signals, physical or visual, erected at each end of the lock indicate to approaching craft whether the lock is free for them to enter and, in the multiple-chamber locks, which chamber they should use. Control cabins, centrally situated, enable all operations of the lock gates, sluices, and signals to be carried out by one man from a push-button control panel. Telephone or radio communication between adjacent locks gives the operator advance information enabling him to have a lock prepared in anticipation of the vessel's arrival. Experiments in France in the early 1970s were directed toward the automatic passage of a vessel through a flight of locks, the various operations at each lock, once initiated, continuing automatically until the vessel left.

Communications between locks

Lock bypasses. The passage of a small pleasure boat through a deep lock is an expensive operation if it is passed alone and can be hazardous if it is passed with large barges that might surge against it. Canoes are normally brought ashore and manually moved around a lock on a portable trolley; larger pleasure craft can be transported on a cradle mechanically towed on a lockside rail track.

Water chutes have been introduced in Germany for canoes and rowboats where there are rises of 30 to 80 feet (9 to 24 metres); although more costly to install than lockside rail track, they are more popular. The canoeist, entering the approach channel, pushes a button actuating the head gates, which rise to allow the water to carry the canoe into and down the chute, where it is kept in the centre of the chute by guide vanes. For upstream passage, canoes are kept afloat by descending water but require manual towage.

Boat lifts. Vessels can be transported floating in a steel tank or caisson between adjacent pounds by a vertical lift, replacing several locks. Vertical lifts can be operated by high-pressure hydraulic rams, by submersible floats, or by geared counterweights. Hydraulic lifts with twin caissons were constructed in 1875 at Anderton, England, with a 50-foot (15-metre) lift for 60-ton vessels; in 1888 lifts were constructed at Les Fontinettes, France, for 300-ton vessels and at La Louvière, Belgium, for 400-ton vessels; in 1905 similar lifts were constructed at Peterborough and Kirkfield in Canada. Float lifts were constructed in 1899 at Henrichenburg, Germany, with a 46-foot (14-metre) lift for 600-ton vessels; in 1938 at Magdeburg, Germany, with a 60-foot (18-metre) lift for 1,000-ton vessels; and in 1962 a new lift at Henrichenburg for 1,350-ton vessels.

Counterweighted lifts were introduced in 1908 when the Anderton lift was reconstructed. Each caisson was separately counterbalanced by a series of weights and ropes with electrically driven gearing. This method was used in 1932 at Niederfinow, Germany, with a 117-foot (35-metre) lift for 1,000-ton vessels.

Inclined planes. In the 18th century, inclined planes were constructed to transport small boats on trucks between adjacent pounds, using animal power and gravity and, later, steam. A series of planes was built in the U.S. on the canal between the Delaware and Hudson rivers to transport 80-ton vessels in caissons; a similar plane for 60-ton vessels was built at Foxton, England, to bypass ten locks.

Three planes have been constructed in Europe, at Ronquières, Belgium, for 1,350-ton vessels; at St. Louis Arzviller, France, for 300-ton vessels; and at Krasnoyarsk, Russia, for 1,500-ton vessels. At Ronquières and Krasnoyarsk, vessels are carried longitudinally up relatively gentle inclines with gradients of 1 in 21 and 1 in 12, respectively, while at Arzviller the site permitted only a steep gradient of 1 in 2½, necessitating vessels being moved transversely. At Ronquières the plane rises 220 feet (66 metres) and replaces 17 locks; at Arzviller the rise is 150 feet (45 metres), and here, too, 17 locks have been replaced. At Krasnoyarsk the plane rises 330 feet (98 metres) from the downstream water level of the River Yenisei to surmount the hydroelectric dam; on top of the dam the caisson moves on to a turntable, where it is rotated through 38° before passing to a second plane running down to the water level impounded upstream of the dam.

INLAND WATERWAY CRAFT

While early navigation of natural rivers was dependent on the use of sail for upstream operation, towpaths and animal haulage were provided when rivers were canalized and artificial canals constructed. Later, mechanical haulage was developed and is still used for local movement of unpowered craft.

Tugs and barges

Steam, and later diesel, tugs improved speed of travel, particularly where lakes or estuarial lengths were encountered. Powered barges, towing one or more unpowered (dumb) barges, were introduced on rivers with adequate lock chambers; but on artificial canals double (or treble) lockage operations made this method uneconomical; and, except for local lighterage (loading, transporting, and unloading) or maintenance duties, dumb barges are little used on artificial canals.

To meet competition from road haulage, with its greater flexibility and higher speeds, water transport must find its solution in larger units, thus necessitating the enlargement of channels and locks. Consequently, the 300-ton barges operating economically early in this century have been replaced by craft as large as 1,350 tons and more.

Push tows and push tugs

In North America, transport operators grouped dumb barges into assemblies, lashing them on either side or ahead of a power unit with similar barges secured in rows ahead. These assemblies of unpowered and individually unmanned barges are known, somewhat illogically, as push tows and the power unit as a push tug. While these assemblies operate most advantageously on natural rivers, their development has justified heavy capital expenditure for enlarging lock chambers on some canalized rivers to avoid delays and increased operational costs arising from multiple lockage. In Europe, push tows normally operate with fewer than six barges, but on the Mississipi, with its deep channel and 700 miles without a lock, a push tow may aggregate 40,000 tons, an assembly of 40 barges being controlled by one 9,000-horsepower push tug, with cabins and facilities for 24-hour operation. On the Ohio River, the original 600-feet lock chambers are being lengthened to 1,200 feet (355 metres) to obviate double lockage.

Movement of push tows around bends, as on the Moselle River, is facilitated by portable power units attached to the bows and operated as required. Similar units can be attached to individual barges for transfer from push tow to wharf or vice versa; they can also be used for handling dumb barges in docks and for moving hopper barges short distances from dredger to disposal site.

WATERWAY MAINTENANCE

Inspection vessels, self-propelled and equipped with echo-sounding appliances, are necessary for regular survey of the waterway. On natural and canalized rivers, which are subject to droughts and floods, attention is particularly directed to the location of the navigable channel: transverse soundings reveal channel movements and enable marker buoys or perches to be relocated and shoals removed by dredging; longitudinal echo-sounding readings normally suffice to locate shallow lengths on artificial canals.

The dredging plant

The dredging plant is an expensive item of waterway maintenance. Bucket dredgers for major operations are supplemented by suction, or grab, dredgers for localized work; hopper barges are required for transporting dredged materials to disposal sites, which should be numerous enough to minimize the transporting period, so that the dredger remains fully operational with a minimum of hopper barges and towage units.

Bank revetment requires regular attention: special vessels are needed for carrying piling frames and light lifting tackle; other service craft are needed for concrete mixing and general duty.

Lock-gate renewal is a major maintenance item, normally planned to ensure that a predetermined number of gates are replaced annually; special vessels equipped with heavy lifting tackle are needed for transport and site handling.

Divers carry out underwater inspections and repairs; although skin diving has been developed for some operations, helmet diving is still needed for prolonged work. Both types of diving require special craft with specialized crew and equipment for servicing the divers. Salvage craft with pumps and heavy lifting tackle are used for removing obstructions from the channel or for raising sunken vessels. Tugs handle the service vessels because many are used only intermittently and thus power units are not economical. Dry docks or slipways, workshops, fitting shops, welding bays, and other special facilities, usually grouped in the vicinity of the administration offices, are part of every modern canal-maintenance system. (C.M.)

Waterway systems

ADMINISTRATION

Modern inland waterway development has been largely carried out by governments, in contrast to early canal construction, which was mainly undertaken by private enterprise. Most of the older canals were subsequently acquired by the state and are administered by them or their agencies and are subject to comprehensive regulation, frequently by independent commissions. International commissions comprising the states concerned regulate navigation on the international waterways. In the U.S., the waterways are basically a federal responsibility, with their development undertaken by the U.S. Army Corps of Engineers, but state governments and local authorities also participate in the administration of many local waterways. The Interstate Commerce Commission has responsibility for the regulation of the common carriers and requires them to publish their rates. For some major multipurpose projects, public corporations were established to undertake and administer them.

In Europe and the Soviet Union, the national networks, mainly based on navigable and canalized rivers linked by canal, were developed by the governments, who retain responsibility for finance and administration. In Britain, most canals were brought under government ownership beginning January 1, 1948, and are administered by the British Waterways Board.

European waterway regulation

Europe's main waterways have long been accepted as international waterways with navigation free to all vessels and equality of treatment of all flags guaranteed. The chief regulatory commissions are the Central Commission for the Navigation of the Rhine, the Danube Commission, and the commission for the canalized Moselle. There are also a number of bilateral agreements between states. Wars and political considerations following them have from time to time interrupted the freedom of navigation. A provisional Rhine Commission was operating in the early 1970s; a new Danube Commission was established in 1953 after the signing of the Austrian state treaty, when freedom of navigation throughout the river's length was fully restored. With the creation of a number of international organizations in Europe, a high degree of cooperation between states for the development of the inland waterways and the regulation of navigation was achieved, particularly through the United Nations Economic Commission for Europe, the European Economic Community, the Organization for Economic Cooperation and Development, and the Council of Europe.

In North America, a U.S.–Canadian International Joint Commission has functioned since 1909 with general authority over the boundary waters. The St. Lawrence Seaway is a joint Canadian and United States project, administered by the St. Lawrence Seaway Authority in Canada and the St. Lawrence Seaway Development Corporation in the United States.

The Panama Canal was originally administered under the Panama Canal Convention of 1903 by the U.S., under the supervision of the army. Panama–U.S. relations were frequently strained, and in 1964, the U.S. agreed to negotiate new treaties concerning the existing canal and construction of a new canal at sea level. Later, both countries agreed that the 1903 treaty should be replaced by a new treaty recognizing Panama's sovereignty over the Canal Zone.

The international status of the Suez Canal, constructed and administered by the Suez Canal Company, has frequently been a matter for dispute, peaceful and otherwise. Only in 1904, under an Anglo-French agreement, was the Constantinople Convention of 1888, establishing the Suez Canal as an international waterway open to all in war and peace, finally implemented. In 1956 British presence in the area ended and troops were withdrawn from the canal zone; the Egyptian government nationalized the assets of the canal company and the administration was assumed by Egypt, but the 1967 war closed the canal for an indefinite period.

MAJOR INLAND WATERWAYS AND NETWORKS

Europe. After the end of World War II, the growth of transport by inland waterway in Europe, coordinated by the various international authorities, resulted in an enlarged and integrated network brought up to a minimum common standard for craft of 1,350 tons. With the Rhine, Moselle, and their tributaries dominating the German system and providing outlets for the Dutch and Belgian systems and connecting with the French network, main improvements were concentrated on the international Rhine-Main-Danube Canal and on improving the north–south route of the Nord-Sud Canal. The latter canal leaves the Elbe about 20 miles above Hamburg and, running south, is planned to join the Mittelland Canal near Wolfsburg, Germany, in the mid-1970s, reaching a total of 71½ miles (120 kilometres) and shortening the route between Hamburg and the Ruhr by 134 miles (220 kilometres).

The Rhine–Main–Danube waterway

The Rhine–Main–Danube waterway connecting the Rhine with the Black Sea is planned to provide a route for traffic between east and west Europe through Germany by 1981, accommodating craft of 1,350 tons throughout its length. Following the River Main to Bamberg in Germany, the route proceeds by artificial waterway, including a section of the Regnitz Canal to Dietfurt, thence by the River Altmühl to below Kelheim, where it joins with the Danube, crossing the Austrian border at Jochenstein. The 43-mile (70-kilometre) Bamburg-to-Nürnberg canal section, completed in 1970, includes seven locks with a combined lift of 268 feet (80 metres). All locks are 650 feet (189 metres) long and able to accommodate vessels of 1,500 tons. Improvements of the channel of the German Danube, begun in 1965, include a pair of locks at Kachlet, just above Passau. In Austria, four pairs of locks to take 1,350-ton craft have been built and others are planned.

In 1970 the damming of the Danube at Djerdap, the Iron Gate rapids, on the border between Yugoslavia and Romania, was begun in conjunction with the improvement of navigation through these dangerous waters; it will incorporate vast hydroelectric power plants. Two locks, 1,017 feet (310 metres) long and 112 feet (34 metres) wide, with two chambers each, are being built to facilitate passage through the Iron Gates. Journey time for ships travelling from Black Sea ports upstream to Belgrade, Vienna, and central Europe will be reduced from around 100 to 15 hours by this project, and traffic is ex-

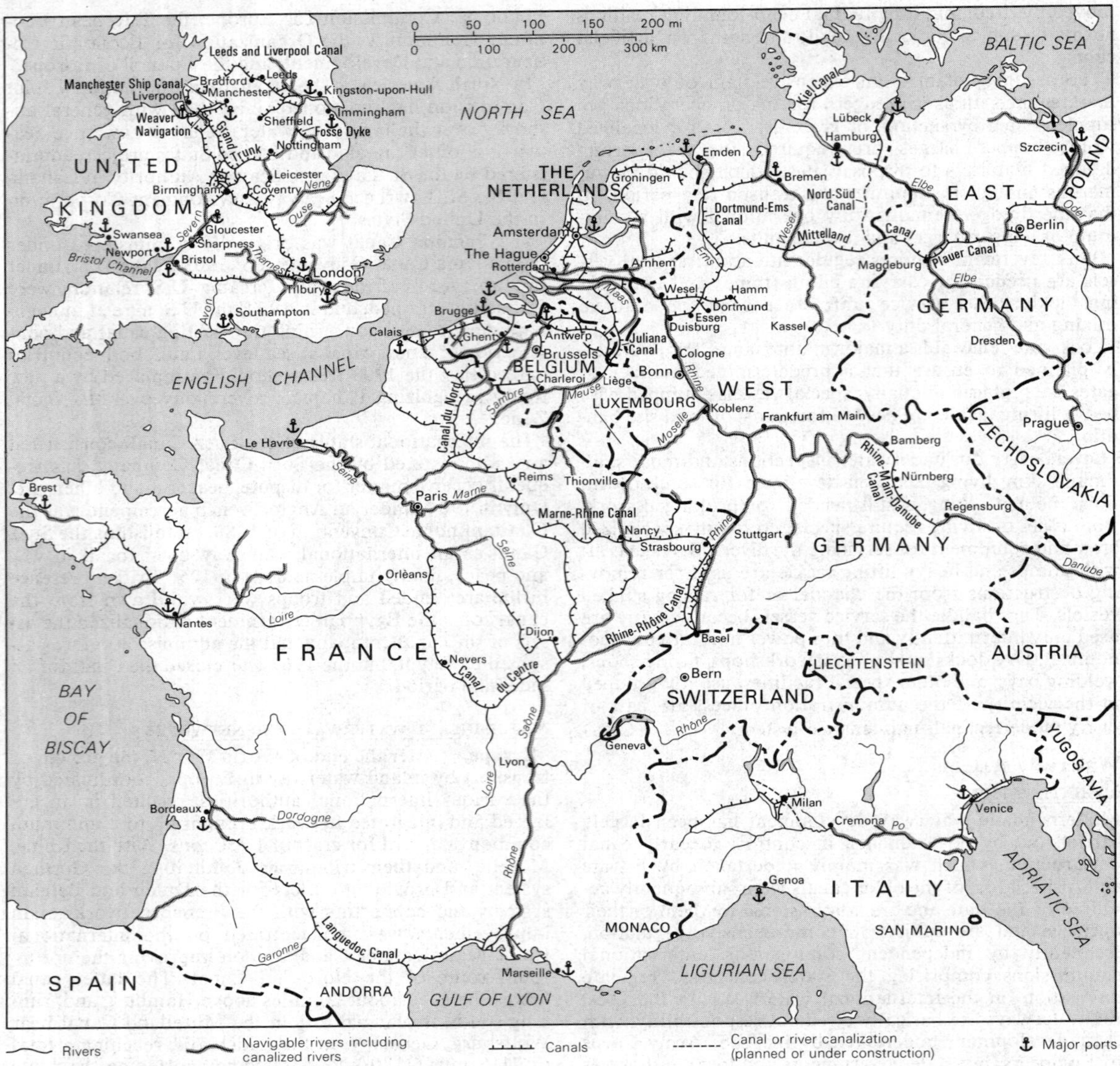

Inland waterway systems of western Europe.

pected to rise from the present 12,000,000 tons annually to 50,000,000 tons.

France's waterway network of nearly 5,000 miles is based primarily on its rivers, but many of the low-capacity canals are being raised to the 1,350-ton standard. The major development under way, in cooperation with West Germany, with completion planned for the mid-1970s, is the construction to this standard of the North Sea–Mediterranean waterway via the canalized Rhône and Rhine rivers. With four existing locks built for the Grand Canal d'Alsace, a projected lateral canal between Huningue and Strasbourg, the project was modified in 1956, and the four remaining dams were to be built on the Rhine itself and bypassed with short canals including four locks, three with two chambers each. Canalization of the Rhône started with the building of the Port of Edouard-Herriot downstream from Lyon, and work has proceeded on 12 locks and dams. Two new ports, serving Valence and Montélimar, are being constructed. Completion of the canalization is planned for 1976, when the North Sea–Mediterranean route, of which the Rhône is an essential part, will also be open. Improvements were also made on the Marne–Rhine waterway, which provides an important internal trade route connecting the Paris Basin with the industrial regions of Alsace-Lorraine. The improvements included major works on either side of the Vosges summit level, replacing 23 old locks. At Réchicourt a new lock with a lift of 32½ feet (ten metres) bypasses six locks and a winding section of the old canal; on the other side of the summit a new canal section bypasses 17 locks, which formerly required eight to 12 hours to navigate. On this section the inclined plane of Saint-Louis Arzviller deals with a difference in level of 146 feet (44 metres) with a horizontal length of 422 feet (125 metres). Two tanks each carry a 350-ton barge. Their 32 wheels run on four rails, and two sets of 14 cables connect the tanks to the two concrete counterweights. On the routes connecting the Seine with the north and east, improvements have also been made. The Canal du Nord was completed in 1965, and a bottleneck was removed on the Oise Lateral Canal with the building of two locks to accommodate through convoys to Paris.

In The Netherlands, the extensive canal system based on large natural rivers and serving the ports of Rotterdam and Amsterdam has required comparatively little modernization; but to avoid the River Maas (Meuse), between Roermond and Maastricht, the Juliana Canal was built in 1935 and improved after World War II. The Twente Canal, opened in 1936, improved communication with the industrial east. Most important of the postwar projects was the building of the Amsterdam–Rhine Canal to enhance the capital's value as a trans-shipment port for the Rhine traffic. The Noord–Hollandsch Canal from Amsterdam to Den Helder was constructed, and the Ijsselmeer was linked with the Ems estuary across the north of Holland. To shorten the distance between Rotterdam and Antwerp by 25 miles (40 kilometres), the Schelde–Rhine Canal has been built.

Italy's waterway system, based on the Po Valley, is cut off from the European network by the Alps, but it is also

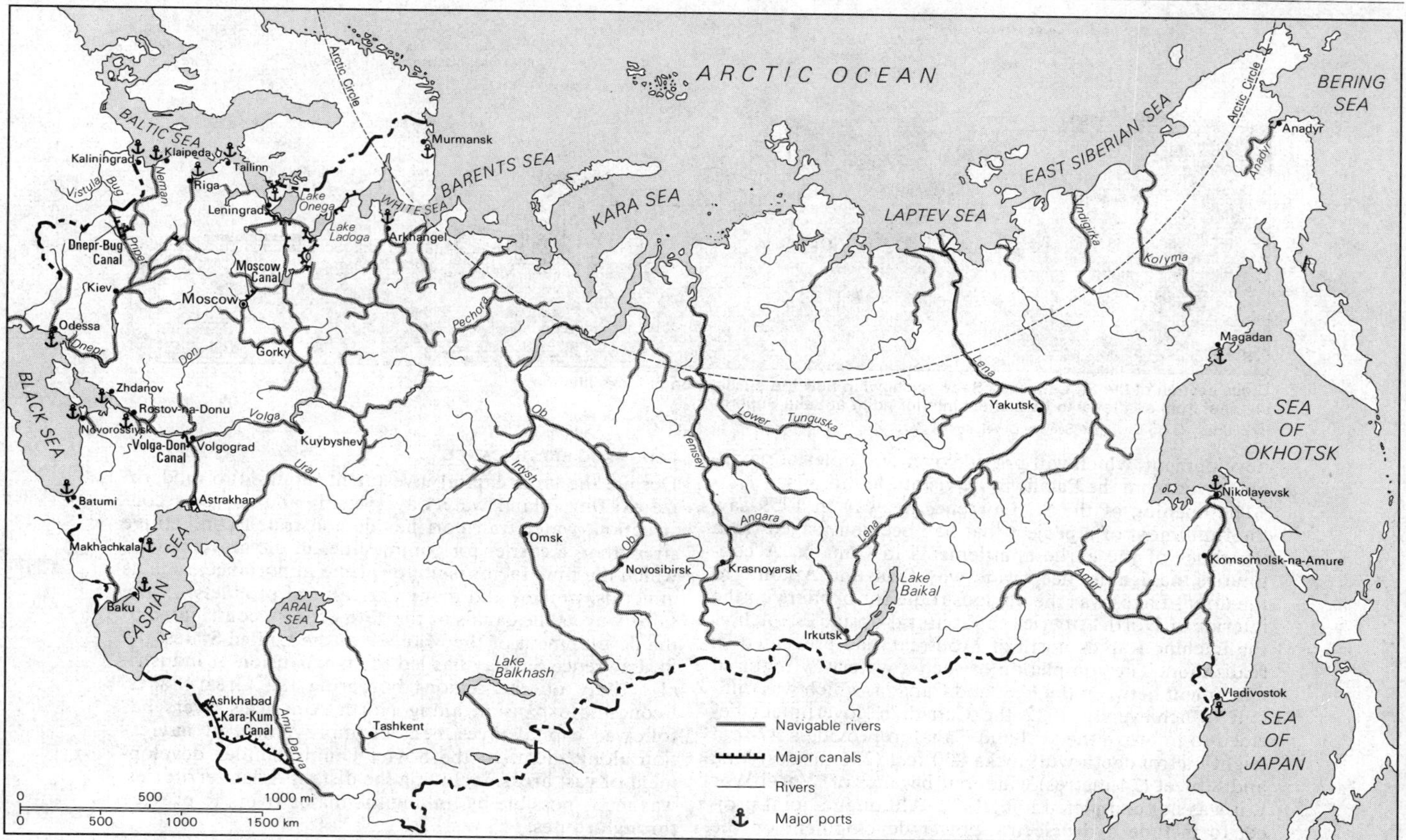

Canals and inland waterways in the Soviet Union.

being brought up to higher standards. In Scandinavia, there are two major commercial artificial waterways; the first, the Trollhätte Canal, connects the Götaälv (river) upward from Göteborg with Lake Vänern and with the Finnish lakes and connecting canals; the second, the Saimaa Canal, in southeast Finland, which carries the vast Saimaa Lake system to the sea, was being reconstructed at the time of World War II. After the Soviet-Finnish War, part was ceded to the Soviet Union; but in 1963 it was leased back to Finland, modernization continued, and the canal, with eight large locks replacing the previous 28, was reopened in 1968.

Principal Soviet links

In the Soviet Union, water navigation plays a major role in the country's economy; and after World War I its great rivers—the Dnepr, Dvina, Don, Vistula, and Volga—were linked to form an extensive network, making through navigation possible from the Baltic to both the Black Sea and the Caspian. The Black Sea and the Baltic are connected by three different systems, of which the most important is the link between the Dnepr and the Bug, a tributary of the Vistula, by way of the Pripyat and Pina rivers, a 203-kilometre canal connecting with the River Mukhavets, a tributary of the western Bug. This system is the sole wholly inland waterway connection between western Europe and the Soviet systems, giving through access to the Caspian and Black seas. When the Rhine–Danube and Oder–Danube canals are completed, a second route will be provided, via the River Berezina, a tributary of the Dnepr, the Viliya, a tributary of the Niemen, and a 21-kilometre canal through Latvia to Riga. The remaining link reaches the Baltic through Lithuania and Poland from the Dnepr by way of the Szara, a tributary of the Niemen; the Jasiolda, a tributary of the Pripyat; and a canal 54 kilometres long. Other important links in the Soviet system are the Volga–Don Canal, 101 kilometres long and completed in 1952, and the Moscow–Volga Canal, built between 1932 and 1937, which flows 128 kilometres from the Volga south to the River Moskva at Moscow. The White Sea Canal, built in 1931–33, runs from Belomorskiy on the White Sea through the canalized Vyg River across Lake Vyg and through a short canal to Pavenets at the northern end of Lake Onega, through which the waterway passes to the canalized Svir River, Lake Ladoga, and the Neva River to the southern terminal at Leningrad. The total length of the system is 140 miles (225 kilometres), reducing sea passage between Leningrad and Archangel by 2,400 miles (4,000 kilometres); through its 19 locks it rises to a maximum of 335 feet (100 metres) above sea level. Further developments in the Soviet Union are mainly in the distant Asian territories, where the Ob and Yenisei in Siberia are connected by canal, and the Karkumsky Canal has been built from Kerki on the River Amu Darya and is being continued westward to the Caspian.

North America. The United States and Canadian networks of inland waterways are based on the great navigable rivers of the continent linked by several major canals. Additionally, to reduce the hazards of navigating the Atlantic seaboard and to shorten distances, intracoastal waterways (protected routes paralleling the coast) have been developed. The total inland U.S. system, including protected coastal routes, approximates 25,000 miles (41,000 kilometres), of which well over half has a minimum depth of nine feet (three metres). The largest system is based on the Mississippi, which is navigable for about 1,800 miles from New Orleans to Minneapolis, and its vast system of tributaries. This system connects with the St. Lawrence Seaway via Lake Michigan, the Chicago Sanitary and Ship Canal, and the Illinois River and with the Atlantic coast via the New York State Barge Canal (Erie Canal) and the Hudson River. The two intracoastal waterways are the Atlantic and the Gulf, the former extending from Boston, Massachusetts, to Key West, Florida, with many sections in tidal water or in open sea. The Gulf Intracoastal Waterway comprises large sheltered channels running along the coast and intersected by many rivers giving access to ports a short distance inland. New Orleans is reached by the Tidewater Ship Canal, a more direct and safer waterway than the Mississippi Delta. The Pacific coast canals are not linked with the national network, but two major projects of importance are the Sacramento Deepwater Ship Canal and the Columbia River

Mississippi system

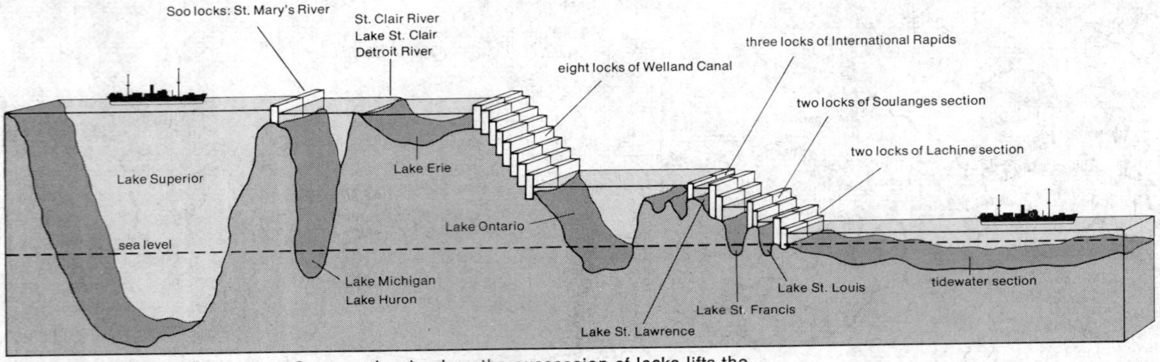

Cross section of the St. Lawrence Seaway showing how the succession of locks lifts the channel from sea level to its highest interior point at Lake Superior.
By courtesy of St. Lawrence Seaway Development Corp.

development, which will provide over 500 miles of navigable river from the Pacific to Lewiston, Idaho.

The opening of the St. Lawrence Seaway in 1959 saw the fulfillment of a project that had been envisaged from the times of the earliest settlements in Canada. A continuous, navigable, deep waterway from the Atlantic to the Great Lakes was the obvious route for opening up the interior of North America; but natural obstacles, such as the Lachine Rapids north of Montreal, had prevented its realization. The completion of such a waterway required agreement between the U.S. and Canada, which was difficult to achieve. In 1912 the Canadian government decided to improve the Welland Canal to provide a 27-foot (eight-metre) depth with locks 800 feet (236 metres) long and 80 feet (24 metres) wide; but because of World War I, it was not completed until 1932. Although a joint project to include hydroelectric power development on the International Rapids section had been provisionally agreed upon, final agreement between Canada and the U.S. was not reached until the early 1950s. The Canadian government undertook to raise the standard of the waterway to a 27-foot navigation depth between Montreal and Lake Erie, and the U.S. agreed to carry out other works, including the bypassing by canal and locks of the Barnhart Island–Cornwall generating dam at the foot of the Long Sault Rapids. This agreement enabled work on the seaway to begin in 1954. The resultant deep waterway, navigable by oceangoing ships, extends about 2,300 miles (3,830 kilometres) from the Atlantic Ocean to the head of the Great Lakes in the heart of North America.

Locks

After Montreal Harbour the first lock is the St. Lambert, which rises 15 feet (4.5 metres) to the Laprairie Basin and proceeds 8.5 miles (14 kilometres) to the second Côte Ste. Catherine Lock, which rises 30 feet (nine metres) to Lake St. Louis and bypasses the Lachine Rapids. Thereafter, the channel runs to the lower Beauharnois Lock, which rises 41 feet (12 metres) to the level of Lake St. Francis via a 13-mile (21-kilometre) canal. Thirty miles (50 kilometres) farther, the seaway crosses the international boundary to the Bertrand H. Snell Lock, with its lift of 45 feet (14 metres) to the Wiley–Dondero Canal; it then lifts another 38 feet (12 metres) by the Dwight D. Eisenhower Lock into Lake St. Lawrence. Leaving the western end of the lake, the seaway bypasses the Iroquois Control Dam and proceeds through the Thousand Islands to Lake Ontario.

Eight locks raise the water 326 feet (98 metres) over 28 miles (45 kilometres) from Lake Ontario to Lake Erie. The St. Marys Falls Canal, with a lift of about 20 feet (six metres), carries the waterway to Lake Superior, where the seaway terminates.

Indian Subcontinent. In Asia, the full potential of the rivers for navigation had not been developed by the second half of the 20th century; though the rivers constitute one of the main means of transport, there are few navigable canals and no integrated system of inland waterways. The Indus River Basin was being developed in the 1970s, however, and there were plans for international cooperation in developing inland waterway transport on the Mekong and Ganges–Brahmaputra systems.

ECONOMIC SIGNIFICANCE

Despite the large capital investment required to modernize existing inland waterway systems and for new construction, water transport has demonstrated competitive strength as a carrier for commodities in the movement of which the time factor is not of prime importance, such as minerals, timber, and many agricultural products. In the same way as the canals of the 19th century contributed to the development of the Midwest in the United States, the St. Lawrence Seaway has led to an expansion of industrial activity on the regions bordering the Great Lakes. Economic expansion along North America's rivers has followed capital investment in improvement of navigation along them. In the Soviet Union, similar development of vast areas, including the distant Asian territories, was made possible by linking the major rivers to provide through routes.

Growth of water transport tonnage

In continental Europe, the eight member countries of the Conference of European Ministers of Transport (ECMT) experienced a growth in total tons carried by inland waterways from 385,000,000 tons to 472,000,000 tons in the years 1964–68. Whereas in 1938 Germany carried 90,000,000 tons of freight on its inland waterways, by the end of the 1960s the Federal Republic of Germany alone was carrying over 230,000,000 tons a year; East Germany was carrying an additional 12,000,000 tons. Nor was this increase limited to the earlier years of the decade, as is shown by the volume of goods passing along the Rhine, which rose from 187,000,000 tons in 1963 to 265,000,000 tons in 1969. Most European countries had the same experience: the Soviet Union, which carried over its 145,000 kilometres of navigable waterways 239,500,000 tons in 1963, transported 322,700,000 tons in 1969.

It is difficult to judge the economics of water transport compared with other transport forms because of the different operating systems. On most international rivers, for example, there are no navigational charges; but on most national artificial waterways, tolls are charged. Costs of water transport are therefore mainly operating costs, which are considerably lower than the total costs of movement by other transport modes. This situation partly accounts for the fact that in the 1950s and 1960s in the U.S., costs per ton-mile stayed practically the same or fell slightly. Mergers of carrier companies and technological developments also contributed to price stability.

In West Germany it has been calculated that one horsepower could move by road 150 kilograms (330 pounds), by rail 500 kilograms (1,100 pounds), and by inland waterway 4,000 kilograms (8,800 pounds). The water-transport cost is said to be one-sixth the cost of transport by road and two-thirds the cost of transport by rail. Other transport carriers contend that such comparisons are not valid because public investment in permanent structures (*i.e.*, canals and locks) is not always taken into account, whereas for railways, private investment in right-of-way costs is reflected in carrying charges. Nor has the inland-waterway industry been without its difficulties. In Europe, for example, in the 1960s a surplus of carrying craft adversely affected the industry's profitability; but by the 1970s this problem had largely been overcome, partly by international action.

(E.A.J.D.)

BIBLIOGRAPHY. J. PHILLIPS, *A General History of Inland Navigation Foreign and Domestic,* 4th ed. (1803); A.W. SKEMPTON, "Canals and River Navigations Before 1750," in CHARLES SINGER (ed.), *History of Technology,* vol. 3, ch. 17 (1957, reprinted 1965); ROGER PILKINGTON, "Canals: Inland Waterways Outside Britain," and CHARLES HADFIELD, "Canals: Inland Waterways of the British Isles," *ibid.,* vol. 4, ch. 18 (1958, reprinted 1965); D.A. FARNIE, *East and West of Suez: The Suez Canal in History, 1854–1956* (1969); L.T.C. ROLT, *Navigable Waterways* (1969); R. CALVERT, *Inland Waterways of Europe* (1963); E.E. BENEST, *Inland Waterways of Belgium* (1960), *Inland Waterways of France,* 2nd ed. (1963, suppl. 1967), and *Inland Waterways of the Netherlands,* 2 vol. (1966–68); A. LEBED and B. YAKOVLEV, *Soviet Waterways* (1956); H.O. LOCHER (ed.), *Waterways of the United States,* 2nd rev. ed. (1963); UNITED NATIONS ECONOMIC COMMISSION FOR EUROPE, *Annual Bulletin of Transport Statistics for Europe; Annual Reports of the Conference of European Ministers of Transport; Papers Issued by the Permanent International Association of Navigation Congresses* (indexes available).

(E.A.J.D./C.M.)

Cancer

Cancer in humans is a complex of diseases characterized by uncontrolled multiplication and disorganized growth of the affected cells; it may arise in any of the body's tissues. Cancer cells infiltrate and destroy adjacent tissues, eventually gain access to the circulatory system, are transported to distant parts of the body, and ultimately destroy the host. Concomitant with their capacity for unrestrained growth, cancer cells and the tissues they constitute lose their normal appearance, as viewed through a microscope, and assume aberrant functions.

Not all abnormal growths are malignant; those that are not are referred to as benign tumours. In contrast to malignant growths, benign tumours consist of an orderly growth of cells that often are identical to or very closely resemble their normal counterparts. They are not aggressive and do not invade surrounding tissues, spread to distant sites, or kill the host. Such tumours are usually surrounded by a capsule of fibrous connective tissue.

Cancer was known in antiquity. Malignant tumours have been found in Egyptian and Pre-Columbian mummies, about 5,000 and 2,400 years old, respectively. They are documented in ancient medical writings, such as the Edwin Smith and Ebers papyruses, both written about 3,500 years ago. Cancer has also been encountered in other species, such as domestic animals, birds, reptiles, and fishes. Although growths that resemble and behave like cancer occur in invertebrates and plants, their precise equivalence to cancer in higher living forms remains to be unequivocally established.

Incidence and mortality

Statistics of cancer incidence and mortality show striking geographic differences, varying significantly from country to country; and within countries differences occur between the sexes, various ethnic groups, and various occupations. Epidemiologic analysis of such statistics continues to provide valuable clues and insights into the myriad factors that appear to be involved in the causation of cancer.

CAUSES

It is now known that cancer can be caused by a variety of factors acting either singly or in concert. These include a wide variety of chemical substances, various types of ionizing radiation, and various classes of viruses. This knowledge has accrued from a composite of epidemiologic studies of cancer in humans and from experimental studies in the laboratory. Although much is known about how cancer is caused, the precise mechanism or group of mechanisms involved continues to elude researchers.

Chemicals. Chemicals numbering in the hundreds are known to induce cancer in laboratory animals, and some of these have also been shown to be carcinogenic for humans. While it is well established that long exposure to certain chemicals gives rise to cancer in humans, it is most difficult to determine accurately what proportion of human cancer is due to such exposure. The difficulty arises from the fact that the length of time between exposure and the appearance of cancer is usually prolonged, lasting some 20–30 years; that exposure is more often than not to a variety of chemicals, so that identifying the carcinogen may be difficult, if not impossible; and that carcinogenesis, *i.e.*, the induction and development of cancer, is a process that involves many factors and many phases.

Experiments on laboratory animals have established that the majority of carcinogenic chemicals are not capable of inducing cancer in their original form. Chemical carcinogens are toxic compounds that are foreign to the host. Once they gain entrance into the body by ingestion, inhalation, or absorption, they are modified by metabolic processes in the host's tissues to forms that are less toxic and water-soluble. The modification is an attempt by the host to detoxify the foreign chemicals and eliminate them by excretion. This capacity to detoxify such substances is an adaptive property of a wide spectrum of living systems, including humans, which affords them a selective advantage to exist in a hostile environment. As in most cases, however, this protective property is not foolproof, and in the process of detoxification certain forms of the carcinogen may arise that are even more toxic and active than the parent compound. In this instance the host renders a less toxic compound into one that causes injury to its cells and may eventually cause them to become cancerous. Highly reactive forms of such chemicals interact with vital macromolecules in the host's cells, causing them to be chemically altered. It is believed that when deoxyribonucleic acid (DNA), the genetic material of cells, is so altered that its expression is accompanied by uncontrolled growth, the cell undergoes a transformation that eventually leads to the development of cancer.

DNA appears to be the most probable macromolecule whose alteration leads to cancer, because once cells become malignant their transformed behaviour is passed on to subsequent cell generations, indicating that it is a heritable change. There is a body of evidence, however, that suggests that alterations of nongenetic macromolecules capable of regulating cell growth may also be involved in the causation of cancer.

The alteration of DNA is one phase of carcinogenesis. The second phase is a prolonged one during which the genetically altered cell loses its ability to grow in a regulated fashion. During this phase the altered cell, not yet expressing its malignant potential, apparently is influenced by other factors, including noncarcinogenic chemicals; dietary components, such as fat; or substances produced by the host, such as hormones. Since this phase is prolonged and subject to manipulation, it is a major focus of contemporary cancer research; it is hoped that persons at high risk of developing cancer (presumably with cells genetically altered by a chemical, but not yet cancerous) may be treated to prevent overt cancer from developing. Certain chemical substances, such as antioxidants and vitamin A, are particularly promising in this regard.

Despite the fact that cancer is a prevalent disease in modern society, quantitative experimental evidence in animals suggests that, following the exposure of cells to a carcinogenic chemical, the ultimate development of cancer is a relatively rare event. This is no doubt due to the fact that some genetic mutations lead to the death of the affected cells, so that no cancer can develop. A second, more important, reason is no doubt due to the ability of cells to "repair" altered or damaged DNA. In this process the segments of damaged DNA are excised, and identical single strands of the required segments are synthesized; these are then spliced into the defect, reestablishing its continuity. If the synthesis has accurately copied the DNA segment as it was prior to damage, there will be no adverse effects. If, on the other hand, the repair process is defective, so that cell replication occurs before the damage is repaired, the altered DNA is copied and the damage is amplified. When such cells undergo division the genetic defect is passed on to their descendants. It is reassuring to know that repair processes appear to be uniformly present in living cells and are very efficient, rapidly repairing damaged DNA with great fidelity.

Occupational chemicals. The association of "substances" in the environment with the development of cancer was suggested in 1775 by Sir Percivall Pott, who reported the frequent occurrence of cancer of the scrotum in chimney sweeps chronically exposed to flue dusts. Pott suggested that this might be due to the prolonged exposure of scrotal skin to the dust. Since then, there have been numerous instances in which the development of cancer has been associated with specific occupations.

Numerous carcinogenic chemical hazards have been identified in a variety of industries. These include polycyclic hydrocarbons present in coal tar and its derivatives, such as pitch, tar oils, and creosote, and in products of the combustion and distillation of coal, oil, shale, lignite, and petroleum. In the past skin cancer took the lives of many long-time workers in these industries. Fumes inhaled by workers during coke-oven operations and in the fogs, mists, and sprays of various oils encountered in refineries have been associated with high incidences of lung cancer. Benzene, a product of coal-tar distillation, may affect blood-forming tissues and is suspected of being a carcinogen capable of inducing leukemia. Various metals have been implicated as carcinogens for the lung and several other body sites among copper-ore miners and smelters of nickel and cobalt ores. Beta-naphthylamine, a chemical once widely used in the manufacture of aniline dyes, has been shown to be a carcinogen for the urinary bladder.

Asbestos and lung cancer

Asbestos has been established as a carcinogen for the lung and for the mesothelium (membrane) that lines body cavities. Workers chronically exposed to dust containing asbestos fibres have an incidence of lung cancer 10 times the normal rate. (It is noteworthy that the risk of cancer is increased 90-fold in asbestos workers if they also smoke. This is an excellent example of two agents acting synergistically to induce cancer at a higher incidence and often in a shorter time than either agent does alone.) Although a serious and sustained effort has been made to monitor and reduce industrial exposure to asbestos in many countries, in some parts of the world occupational pollution remains a serious problem and is responsible for a debilitating and progressive form of lung disease (asbestosis), as well as cancer, in asbestos workers.

Environmental chemicals and pollution. The environment, which includes the atmosphere, land, seas, lakes, and rivers, reflects the activities of society. Environmental pollutants include the myriad effluents of daily living, industrial as well as naturally occurring. Among the greatest atmospheric pollutants are the gaseous and particulate emissions that range from the massive outputs of industry and motor transport, measuring millions of tons annually, to individual puffs of cigarette smoke.

Smoking and cancer

Cigarette smoke has been shown to contain numerous compounds that are known to cause cancer in experimental animals and that appear to be strongly linked to human cancer, especially cancer of the lung. In addition, tobacco smoke has been implicated in the causation of cancer of the mouth, and to a lesser extent the esophagus, pancreas, biliary system, and urinary bladder. Cigarette smoke also has been shown to contain a number of cocarcinogens, substances that appear to enhance the effect of carcinogens when they are administered concomitantly.

Increasing evidence has accrued to suggest that the release of polychlorinated hydrocarbons and certain insecticides into the environment may pose a carcinogenic hazard. Some of these compounds have enjoyed such widespread use that significant areas of land and bodies of water have been contaminated. This, coupled with the fact that such compounds, once ingested by humans, are stored in body fat and released and metabolized very slowly, has made their removal from the environment extremely important, even though it is a difficult, prolonged, and expensive undertaking.

The effect of environmental pollution can best be illustrated by describing the phenomenon of bioconcentration and its impact on the food chain. Widely used chemical substances, such as certain classes of insecticides, which metabolically degrade very slowly and are highly soluble in fat, are a case in point. After being applied on land for agricultural uses, such compounds are washed by rains into streams, rivers, and lakes, where they are ingested by microscopic life forms, which serve as food for fish that are, in turn, the major food source for larger fish and aquatic birds. Since these compounds are soluble in fat, after being ingested by an animal they are stored and concentrated in the animal's body fat. Repeated feeding eventually leads to high concentrations of the compounds in the animal's body, so that its subsequent ingestion by a larger predator, perhaps by humans, presents the predator with a significant level of the compound. This can pose a health hazard so serious that, for example, fishermen on a contaminated lake are warned not to eat the fish they catch. The magnitude of the problem is illustrated by the insecticide dichlorodiphenyl-trichloroethane (DDT), high levels of which persist in the environment and in the bodies of humans, despite the fact that its use was restricted worldwide by the early 1970s.

Food additives and cancer

Food additives are another source of environmental chemicals that has caused concern. Although these have been the object of dispute and have given rise to the "natural food" fad, there is no evidence that food additives cause human cancer. In fact, some food additives, especially those that protect foods from becoming rancid, have actually been shown to prevent chemically induced cancer in experimental animals. An additive that remains a matter of concern, however, is sodium nitrite, which is widely used to preserve processed meats. It has been shown that nitrite can react in the stomach with amines, which arise from the digestion of meat, to form nitrosamines, a group of compounds that are potent carcinogens for certain laboratory animals. These compounds are formed in such minute amounts in the stomach that some researchers doubt that they pose a significant carcinogenic hazard for humans. Similarly, the demonstration that certain compounds formed by the burning of meat are carcinogenic for animals must be placed in proper perspective. Carcinogenesis experiments in animals usually require continuous exposure to high levels of chemicals to obtain statistically valid results in their relatively short life span of a year or two; extrapolation of these results to the effect on human health should be approached most carefully.

Problems of greater importance are the naturally occurring carcinogens, which constitute an important hazard in certain environments. One of these, aflatoxin, is formed by *Aspergillus flavus*, a mold that is widely distributed and is a frequent contaminant of improperly stored nuts, grains, meals, and certain other foods. In certain areas of Africa the high incidence of liver cancer in humans appears to coincide with their ingestion of foods highly contaminated with aflatoxin. Such correlations must be interpreted conservatively, however, since these populations are also often plagued by viral hepatitis B, which also has been linked to liver cancer. In Japan and parts of China similar correlations exist, but again their interpretation must be tempered because of the presence of viral hepatitis B and other factors.

Radiation. The carcinogenic effects of ionizing radiation first became apparent at the turn of the 20th century with reports of cancer of the skin in physicians who pioneered the application of X-rays and radium to medicine. Since then it has been well established that ionizing radiations of all forms, including ultraviolet light, are carcinogenic.

Occupational radiation. Numerous examples of radiation carcinogenesis have been documented in occupational settings. Well known among these were women who developed bone cancer as a consequence of the chronic ingestion of radium salts that resulted from licking brushes to a fine point while painting luminous watch dials. Following ingestion, radium is deposited in the mineral component of bones; and the deposition of radium in the bones is sufficiently high to make them autoradiographic: that is, their image can be reproduced on X-ray film simply by placing the bones in contact with the film. Another notable example is uranium mine workers, who develop lung cancer to a significantly higher degree than the general population. The cause has been traced to the inhalation of the radioactive gas radon, released from trace amounts of radium in uranium ore.

Environmental radiation. The environment contains three major natural sources of radiation: radioactive elements in mineral deposits, ultraviolet light from the Sun, and cosmic rays. The carcinogenic potential of radioactive elements and ultraviolet light has been established, while that of highly energetic cosmic radiation remains to be documented. Clearly, chronic exposure to intense sunlight is a major cause of skin cancer in humans; incidence is high in farmers, sailors, and habitual sunbathers. Since the most effective natural screen for ultraviolet light is the natural skin pigment, melanin, individuals with large amounts of melanin—blacks, for example—are resistant to the carcinogenic effects of ultraviolet light. Fair-complexioned people, on the other hand, are quite susceptible. It is important to point out that the term skin cancer, as it is generally used, includes not only malignant tumours of the nonpigmented cells of the skin but also tumours of the pigmented cells (melanoma). Under the proper conditions ultraviolet light can cause cancer to develop in the very cells that produce the pigment that affords protection from solar radiation.

Sunlight and cancer

The environment also contains dangerous ionizing radiation from artificial sources. These include X-rays used for medical diagnosis and therapy, radioactive chemicals, radioactive elements used in atomic reactors, and radioactive fallout arising from the testing of nuclear devices. Potentially dangerous radiation also may emanate from various types of appliances that are widely used in modern homes, such as colour television sets and microwave ovens. A distance of several feet or so from such devices is generally considered to be safe, however.

Certain medical applications of X-rays, such as those used to establish the size and position of a fetus before birth and to control acne, have been largely abandoned because of the increased risk of cancer. Modern technology has greatly reduced the risk of diagnostic X-rays, however. During therapeutic X-irradiation for the treatment of cancer, great care is taken to focus radiation on the tumour and to shield the adjacent normal body tissues from undue exposure. Laboratory workers who use radioactive chemicals are careful to prevent undue exposure by contamination and to dispose of radioactive wastes properly. The cancer risk from radioactive fallout resulting from the testing of atomic devices is virtually impossible to establish with certainty because of the large geographic areas affected. In general, such exposure is not massive, and immediate effects are probably not of high significance. The absorption by growing crops and farm animals of long-lived radioactive isotopes, such as strontium, from fallout may pose a threat to humans, however, because the crops and animals are a source of food.

Viruses. Numerous viruses have been identified that can induce cancer in every major class of vertebrates, including lower vertebrates such as fish. The evidence for the viral causation of cancer in humans long remained strong but only circumstantial; it is now clear, however, that Burkitt's lymphoma, nasopharyngeal cancer, and T-cell leukemia are almost surely caused by viruses.

Oncogenic (cancer-causing) viruses are classified according to the type of nucleic acid they contain. A common feature of oncogenic viruses is that they induce malignant transformation of target cells, which, upon transplantation into suitable animal hosts, exhibit true autonomous growth, local invasion, and metastases to distant sites. Another common feature is physical integration of virus-specific genetic material in the DNA of the host cells. In the case of DNA tumour viruses, the viral genes are integrated directly, whereas with ribonucleic acid (RNA) viruses the RNA is first transcribed into DNA, which is then integrated. Furthermore, RNA tumour viruses are frequently replicated by the cells they transform, while DNA tumour viruses are not. The complexities of tumour viruses are such that progress to establish cause and effect has been quite difficult. The following viruses are strongly suspected of being oncogenic for humans.

Herpes-type viruses. A herpesvirus has been found to be closely associated with two cancers in humans: Burkitt's lymphoma, a malignant tumour of lymphatic tissue first described in children in East and Central Africa; and nasopharyngeal carcinoma, a squamous-cell carcinoma of the posterior part of the nasal cavity, which occurs in high incidence in Chinese originating from South China. Biopsies from both tumours grown in culture gave rise to cell lines in which a DNA virus of the herpes class was identified; it was named the Epstein-Barr (EB) virus. Patients with either type of cancer have high levels of antibody directed against EB virus, indicating that they have encountered the virus and responded to it. Human blood lymphocytes can be transformed in culture by EB virus, and there is experimental evidence that EB virus is also oncogenic for cottontop marmosets and owl monkeys. In addition, EB virus is considered to be the causal agent for infectious mononucleosis, a distressing but self-limited viral infection well known in North America; yet infectious mononucleosis is not followed by either Burkitt's lymphoma or nasopharyngeal carcinoma. It is not known why EB virus causes a self-limited disease in one instance and a variety of cancers in others. Evidence suggests that genetic factors may be important for development of the malignant tumour.

Burkitt's lymphoma

A second herpesvirus that is becoming increasingly suspect as a human oncogen is the herpes simplex virus type 2 (HSV-2), a close relative of the virus that causes the common fever blister. The epidemiology of squamous-cell cancer of the uterine cervix is entirely consistent with the possibility that it may be caused by an agent that is transmitted during sexual intercourse. Evidence has shown that a woman who develops a herpes infection of the cervix is at an increased risk to develop cervical cancer, and women with cervical cancer often have high titers of HSV-2 antibody. Other viruses that may be involved and are known to be transmitted by sexual contact are cytomegalovirus (CMV) and papillomavirus; both are capable of causing cell transformation in culture. The experimental application of radioactive probes of antibodies to specific viral proteins and to components of the viral genome have localized either the integrated genome or the viral antigens of HSV-2, CMV, and papillomavirus in the cells of cervical cancer in women. Although this cannot be taken as unequivocal evidence that the viruses are indeed the causal agents, it does strengthen the hypothesis that cervical cancer may have a viral basis.

Herpes simplex virus type 2 and cancer

Although the implication of virus as a cause of human cancer has been largely circumstantial, it appears that in one human cancer, thymus-derived (T-cell) leukemia–lymphoma, the evidence is quite impressive. These tumours, which appear to be localized to the southernmost island of Japan and the West Indian population in the Caribbean, have been shown by seroepidemiologic studies possibly to have an infectious basis. Furthermore, an RNA virus, human T-cell leukemia virus (HTLV), which bears no apparent relation to any of the known animal oncogenic RNA viruses, appears to be present in patients with T-cell leukemia and can be isolated from their tumour tissue with reasonable reproducibility. Finally, infection of normal blood T lymphocytes in culture by HTLV leads to their uncontrolled growth.

Infection with hepatitis B virus (HBV) is endemic in populations that also have a high incidence of liver cancer. This has led some researchers to conclude that the virus is the cause of liver cancer. As noted earlier, however, cancer is a multifactorial disease, and liver cell cancer is an excellent example. HBV infection invariably leads to the augmented growth of liver cells, which renders them exquisitely sensitive to the effects of carcinogens. Since populations plagued by a high incidence of liver cancer are also chronically exposed to numerous toxic substances, some of which are carcinogenic for the liver, it is difficult to dissect the interactions of virus and carcinogen with sufficient precision to either indict or exonerate HBV as a liver oncogen. Thus, hepatitis B virus must be considered only as a possible carcinogen. HBV may well be considered a cocarcinogen, however; it may so increase the sensitivity of liver cells to carcinogens that it decreases the latent period during which the cells undergo malignant transformation and increases the number of tumours that ultimately develop.

Oncogenes. Progress in tumour genetics and molecular

biology may lead to a clearer understanding of how cells undergo malignant transformation. As stated earlier, RNA tumour viruses invariably integrate their DNA into the host's DNA. Cells of numerous vertebrate species, including humans, have such integrated DNA in their genes. The conservation of such genes throughout so many diverse species suggests that they probably serve an important role in cells, perhaps in growth regulation. The fact that such genes are almost ubiquitous in their distribution and apparently are simply not expressed in normal cells led to the enunciation of the oncogene hypothesis, which suggests that silent (unexpressed) oncogenes, or genes capable of inducing cancer, can, upon proper stimulation, become expressed and thus cause a previously normal cell to become malignant. Oncogenes have been found in chromosome 8 in Burkitt's lymphoma cells and in a variety of other human tumours. Introduction of such oncogenes in DNA from human tumours into normal cells in culture causes the normal cells to become transformed and behave like cancer cells. Activation of an oncogene in a human tumour has been shown to be accompanied by a minor change in its chemical structure. This suggests that silent oncogenes may be activated by chemicals, radiation, and viruses, all of which are known to alter DNA and to cause cancer. The oncogene may be the common denominator through which such diverse agents act.

Genetic factors. The common cancers of humans are not generally inherited, although some families show an incidence of a particular cancer beyond expectations. Multiple cases of childhood cancer may occur in a family. When leukemia develops in one of a pair of identical twins, the other twin also develops leukemia in about 15 percent of the cases. Among fraternal twins this happens less than 1 percent of the time. Some familial tendencies have also been observed for cancer of the breast, uterus, prostate, stomach, colon–rectum, and lung, although the hereditary effect is not strong. It is possible that familial tendencies reflect common environmental relationships or an environmental factor superimposed on a genetic one.

Leukemia in twins

In studies of familial tendencies for breast cancer in England, Denmark, and the United States, an incidence two to three times that expected in the general population has been noted for close relatives of persons with the disease.

A rare cancer of the eye called retinoblastoma occurs in childhood as a result of the transmission of a single dominant gene (a dominant gene need be inherited from only one parent for the trait to become manifest).

Pheochromocytoma, a rare cancer of the adrenal gland, and carcinoma of the thyroid medulla (the inner portion of the thyroid) sometimes occur in various members of the same family. Either both tumours or only one may occur. Persons with pheochromocytoma also have an increased risk of parathyroid and other rare tumours.

Xeroderma pigmentosum, an inherited, abnormal sensitivity of the skin to ultraviolet radiation, almost always leads to skin cancers. The sensitivity is due to an inherited defect in the ability of cells to repair DNA that has been damaged by ultraviolet light.

Children with Down's syndrome, or mongolism, a disorder associated with an extra chromosome in each cell, have a much greater likelihood of developing leukemia than do other children. Persons with Fanconi's aplastic anemia (in which all types of blood cells are abnormally few and the bone marrow is not fully developed) and some other rare syndromes characterized by greatly increased chromosome breakages also have an increased risk of leukemia.

In chronic myelocytic leukemia (myelocytes are precursors of certain white blood cells), an abnormally short chromosome called the Philadelphia chromosome is a genetic marker in bone marrow cells and white blood cells of some patients. It is not known whether the cancer and chromosomal abnormality are independent events or whether one is the result of the other.

There is increasing evidence that genetic alterations are involved in the causation of cancer, and that these can be either inherited or induced and involve either a minute point in a strand of DNA or a major rearrangement of a chromosome.

Trauma and infection. Repeated trauma (injury) or irritation has been associated with some cancers. Ill-fitting dentures associated with cancer of the mouth and chronic infection of the uterine cervix associated with cervical cancer are examples. In each instance it must be remembered that injury and infection are invariably followed by healing, which involves increased local growth of host cells in the affected tissues, and such cells are quite sensitive to carcinogenic factors. There is no scientific basis to support the notion that trauma alone is a carcinogenic stimulus.

THE SPREAD OF CANCER

The ability of certain cancers to spread from their sites of origin, rendering their treatment and eradication difficult, is the major reason for the sense of hopelessness that is closely associated with them. If it were not for this ability to spread, most cancer could be successfully treated.

The spread of cancer results from either or both of two processes: cancer cells may spread by direct extension from the primary site as a consequence of growth and tumour cell movement invading the surrounding normal tissues, or they may enter the vascular system by invading lymphatics or blood vessels. In the latter process the cancer cells can be transported to sites distant from the primary site, whereas in the process of direct extension the cancer cells may remain close to the site of origin.

Direct extension. The ability of a localized focus of cancer to spread into adjacent tissues is dependent upon its interaction with surrounding adjacent tissue. Research has shown that experimental and some human cancers with a high incidence of spread contain enzymes capable of digesting elements of the surrounding normal connective tissues. This allows cancer cells to migrate through the connective tissues, which normally serve as a barrier. Once invasion by local extension has occurred, the opportunity for successful therapy is diminished. There is considerable evidence that tumour cell populations are heterogeneous and differ markedly in their ability to spread. The ability of cancer cells to digest elements of the connective tissue may be limited to a relatively small number of cells in a given tumour cell population.

Metastasis. Metastasis is the process by which cancer cells are spread to sites distant from the primary tumour. The process requires that the cancer cells enter the vascular system, which includes lymphatics, veins, and arteries. Once they are within the system, the cancer cells are transported passively to distant sites. In lymphatics they are trapped in lymph nodes, which may serve as temporary barriers. They may enter the blood vessels by extension from lymph nodes or, more rarely, by passing directly through the connective tissue sheath surrounding lymph nodes. The cancer cells are eventually entrapped in the smallest branches of blood vessels, the capillaries. Cancer cells thus trapped are the "seeds" from which larger colonies of tumour cells grow into secondary sites, called metastases.

It was once thought that the pattern of metastasis was a random process. Within certain limits, however, the patterns of metastases now appear to be tumour-specific. For example, cancer of the breast and prostate have a predilection for spreading to bone, in contrast to melanoma and kidney cancer, which lodge preferentially in the lung. It appears that the process of lodgement of cancer cells in a distant organ may be related to specific interactions (perhaps to mutual attraction) between the cancer cells and those of the organ in which they ultimately settle and resume their growth. Basic research on the nature and mechanism of such interactions may eventually lead to a better understanding of the metastatic process and may result in the development of therapeutic strategies to either limit or totally prevent the spread of cancer to distant organs. (It should be pointed out that the ultimate success of a metastatic focus to establish itself and thrive may depend on other host factors, such as cell-mediated and humoral immunity.) Since the capacity for distant metastasis appears to be a property of a small subpopulation of cancer cells within the primary tumour, prevention or control of metastases may prove to be both feasible and effective in the future.

Spread of cancer and survival. Clinical experience with the relation of the spread of cancer to patient survival is dramatically emphasized by the statistics of cancer of the colon and rectum and of the female breast. In both the colon and the rectum, cancer begins in the cells that line the inner surface of the thin-walled, sausage-like connective tissue structure of the organ. If the cancer cells are localized to and within the wall, 94 percent of patients survive five years after surgical removal of the cancer; when the cancer has spread through the wall, but has not entered the adjacent lymph nodes, five-year survival is 88 percent. On the other hand, once cancer has involved the lymph nodes, the five-year survival decreases to 55 percent. Similarly, in breast cancer in women the 10-year survival rate in the absence of nodal involvement is 72 percent, and when lymph nodes closest to the tumour are involved, 10-year survival is 66 percent. When the tumour has spread to more distant nodes, however, five-year survival decreases to only 31 percent. It is important, therefore, to diagnose cancer and begin treatment before cancer cells begin to spread.

Effects of metastasis on survival

Implications of metastasis for therapy. Just as subpopulations of cancer cells within primary tumours have varying abilities to spread by metastasis, they may also differ in response to treatment by radiation and chemotherapy. This is supported by the observation that metastases may differ significantly in their response to radiation therapy and chemotherapy, and that tumours often appear to become resistant to therapy. In both instances the different response of the cancer cells may be due to a selection process. In the first instance, the differing responses of metastases suggest a coupling of the tumour cell's sensitivity to its capacity to spread widely. In the second, the tumour's decreasing sensitivity to therapy may be due to a selection of more resistant tumour cells by virtue of therapy, in a process analogous to the appearance of bacteria resistant to a particular antibiotic during a course of treatment.

TYPES OF CANCER

Cancers are classified by pathologists based on the type of tissue in which they arise and the cell type that constitutes the tumour. This time-honoured system of classification recognizes in humans more than 150 types of cancer with different biological behaviours.

Types of tissue. The organs of the body consist of a variety of tissues, including those that line their inner surfaces (epithelia) and those that render structural support and contain their blood supply (the connective tissues). Tumours (from Latin *tumēre*, "to swell") of a given type of tissue differ from those of the normal tissues in that and other organs but may closely resemble tumours of the similar tissue in other organs or regions of the body.

Classification of cancers according to the tissue from which they evolve is by two major types: carcinoma (from Greek *korkinos*, "crab") and sarcoma (from Greek *sarkōma*, "fleshy growth"). Carcinoma, the larger category, refers to cancers of epithelial tissues, which cover the external body (the skin) and line the inner cavitary structures of organs such as the breast; the respiratory and gastrointestinal tracts; the endocrine glands, such as the pituitary, thyroid, and adrenals; and the genitourinary system, which includes the prostate, testes, ovaries, fallopian tubes, uterus, kidneys, and urinary bladder. Sarcoma refers to cancers of the various elements that constitute the connective tissues, such as fibrous tissues, muscle, blood vessels, bone, and cartilage. Rarely, a cancer is composed of both epithelial and connective tissue simultaneously and is referred to as carcinosarcoma. Leukemias, lymphomas, and other cancers of the blood-forming tissues are classified separately, although strictly speaking they can be regarded as a subset of the connective tissues. Tumours of nerve tissues, including the brain, and melanoma, a cancer of the pigmented cells of the skin, are also classified separately.

Carcinoma and sarcoma

A carcinoma of the intestine has more in common with a carcinoma of the stomach, lung, or breast than with a sarcoma of lymphoid cells of the intestine. It is on the tissue and cells of origin, not the organ of origin, that the peculiar and characteristic properties of a tumour more usually depend.

Types of cells. Tumours are also classified according to the type of cell from which they are derived. For example, skin cancer includes tumours composed of the major cellular component, squamous cells, giving rise to squamous-cell carcinoma; of the less frequent basal cells found at the base of the skin, whose tumours are referred to as basal-cell carcinomas; and of the still more rare cells that produce melanin pigment, whose malignant tumours are classified as melanomas. Cancers in different organs and individual carcinomas of the same cell type may have different doubling times (*i.e.*, the time it takes for the tumour mass to double in the number of cells or in size). Doubling times observed for lung cancer, for instance, may vary widely from case to case, with ranges from eight days for very rapidly growing tumours to more than 700 days for the more slowly growing. The doubling time is a reflection not only of the rate of tumour cell growth but also of the loss of cells through spontaneous death.

Squamous-cell and basal-cell carcinomas

In addition to the obvious problems associated with the local mechanical effects of tumours, as well as their distant spread to vital organs such as the lungs, brain, and liver, where their subsequent growth may interfere with function, tumours may also exert other potent biological effects. These tumour-associated phenomena are referred to collectively as paraneoplastic syndromes and may include a wide and bewildering variety of adverse effects, such as loss of appetite, body wasting, fatigue, stupour, coma, excessive thirst, inappropriate flushing of the skin, anemia, spontaneous bleeding, clotting, loss of motor function, dementia, and paralysis. Some of these effects have been linked to the inappropriate production and release of certain hormones by tumours, while other effects remain unexplained. The fact that some effects appear before cancer is diagnosed and disappear as soon as the tumour is removed suggests that many of the unexplained effects are probably also caused by substances released by the tumours. Such effects can be so severe and debilitating that they present a more acute clinical problem than the underlying cancers.

Paraneoplastic syndromes

Death in patients with cancer is more often than not due to a superimposed systemic complication, such as an overwhelming infection or uncontrollable hemorrhage. In certain instances death is the result of tumour invasion of contiguous tissues, leading to kidney obstruction or perforation of the gastrointestinal tract.

Sites of origin. Cancers of organs such as the brain, lung, esophagus, stomach, liver, gallbladder, pancreas, kidney, prostate, ovary, and testis grow to form firm masses and hence are referred to as solid tumours. These are contrasted with those tumours involving cells of the blood-forming organs and lymphatic systems, which are normally free and circulating and remain so when they become malignant. The most common sites in which cancers arise in adults include the skin, large intestine, lung, breast, pancreas, prostate, and uterus. Leukemia is the most common tumour of childhood. Some of the more common forms of cancer are discussed below.

The skin. Cancers of the skin are relatively common; they occur in highest incidence on the exposed skin of the head and neck of persons chronically exposed to sunlight. The most common form, about 82 percent of all cases, is that arising from basal cells in the deepest layer of the skin. The initial lesion is a small pimple-like elevation, which enlarges very slowly and after a few months forms a shiny, somewhat translucent lesion that eventually develops a small central ulcer. When the scablike surface is denuded it tends to bleed and then appears to "heal" by forming another shiny covering. Although basal-cell carcinomas grow slowly and only very rarely metastasize, they do invade locally and cause considerable destruction of adjacent tissues, which can result in disfigurement. Either ample surgical excision or radiation therapy are curative.

Squamous-cell carcinoma arises from the platelike flat cells that constitute the major cellular component of skin. The early lesion is less localized and elevated than that of basal-cell cancer. It is red and scaly and may be confused with eczema or infection. Eventually, the lesion becomes larger, elevated, and ulcerated. The behaviour of squamous-cell carcinoma differs somewhat from that of basal-cell cancer, in that the cells are not only capable of local invasion but also may metastasize to regional lymph nodes and, rarely, to more distant sites. Treatment is identical to that for basal-cell cancer.

Mortality for the Six Most Frequent Sites of Cancer (1976–77)*
(crude death rates per 100,000 population)

men		women	
site	rate	site	rate
lung	60.4	breast	26.4
colon and rectum	27.4	colon and rectum	21.2
stomach	26.8	stomach	13.7
prostate	21.2	lung	11.3
leukemia	7.3	uterus (including cervix)	10.8
oral	4.9	leukemia	4.7
all sites	223.8	all sites	144.4

*The countries on which the data are based are Australia, Austria, Canada, Chile, Denmark, France, Ireland, Israel, Japan, The Netherlands, New Zealand, Norway, Scotland, Sweden, Switzerland, the United Kingdom, the United States, and West Germany.
Source: World Health Organization, *World Health Statistics Annual*, 1979–80.

The lung. Lung cancers arise in the epithelium lining the bronchi (the branching complex of air passages), by which air passes to the lungs, or in the fine air sacs at the periphery. The most common forms arise in bronchial glandular epithelium that has been altered by long exposure to cigarette smoke to form less specialized squamous cells, which eventually evolve into squamous-cell carcinomas. Structurally, unaltered glandular epithelia of bronchi may also undergo malignant transformation to give rise to adenocarcinomas, but these tumours do not appear to be related to cigarette smoking.

Cancers of the lung tend to metastasize widely to lymph nodes in the neck and chest, to the pleura (membrane) lining the chest and lungs, and to the liver, adrenals, and bone. The average survival of persons with untreated lung cancer is about nine months after diagnosis. By the time a sign or symptom appears, spread to regional or distant lymph or to distant sites has already occurred in the majority of cases. In operable cases removal of the tumour may prolong life for a number of months. Five-year survival of patients affected with squamous-cell carcinoma of the lung is about 25 percent and for adenocarcinoma 12 percent.

The breast. Cancer of the breast is the leading cause of death from cancer in women. The incidence of and death from cancer of the breast is significantly higher in North America and northern Europe than in Asian and African countries, indicating that different populations have different risks for breast cancer. Major risk factors include menstrual and reproductive history, family history, and history of benign disease of the breast. For example, women who begin menstruation at an early age are at greater risk than those who begin later, and women who have their ovaries removed surgically before age 35 appear to be at significantly less risk than women who undergo natural menopause. Women who bear their first child before age 18 have one-third the risk of developing breast cancer of those who have their first full-term pregnancy between ages 18 and 30. Treatment is reasonably successful when it is guided by and based on knowledge of the degree of sensitivity of the tumour cells to the female hormone estrogen.

Risk factors for breast cancer

Esophagus. Cancer of the esophagus may arise at any point along the passage through which food is conveyed to the stomach, although the most frequent site is the middle third. The tumours are bulky, fungus-like growths that rapidly close the esophagus. More rarely they may spread superficially without causing obstruction. Esophageal cancers are usually poorly differentiated squamous-cell carcinomas that invade locally and metastasize rapidly to organs in the chest as well as to more distant sites. Even with the best therapy available, the cure rate is quite low. Chronic smoking and use of alcohol are considered to be major risk factors, and epidemiologic data suggests that diet and certain environmental factors may also be involved.

Stomach. Cancer of the stomach is a major cause of death from cancer worldwide. In some countries, such as the United States, the death rate from stomach cancer has decreased dramatically since the 1930s, for reasons that remain unknown. Risk factors are poorly understood, but increased rates of stomach cancer have been documented in coal miners and asbestos workers, in farmers in Japan, in nickel refinery workers in the Soviet Union, and in rubber and timber workers. The cancers are almost exclusively of the glandular epithelium lining the stomach and are adenocarcinomas. The tumours infiltrate and invade the wall of the stomach or form masses that protrude from the surface and ulcerate. These tumours tend to metastasize early and widely. Surgery is the treatment of choice but is curative only when the tumour is diagnosed and removed early. Other more rare tumours include lymphosarcomas and tumours of the smooth muscle cells of the wall. These tend to grow more slowly and as a result are more easily cured by surgical intervention.

Liver. Cancer of the liver is a disease whose incidence varies widely; in African countries such as Nigeria and Benin and among Chinese in Singapore, Taiwan, and Hawaii the incidence is high, while in the continental United States and in western Europe primary cancer of the liver is relatively rare. Environmental factors appear to play an important role; the disease is linked to infectious hepatitis B virus, to malnutrition, and to natural chemical carcinogens such as aflatoxin B_1, toxic alkaloids from plants used to brew certain native teas, and nitrosamines. Chronic alcohol abuse, which leads to cirrhosis (scarring) of the liver, is a significant risk factor, especially in the Western world, since it appears to predispose a person to the development of liver cancer. Primary cancers of the liver are carcinomas arising from liver cells, the major cellular component of liver (hepatocellular carcinomas), or, more rarely, from a minor cellular component of liver, bile duct cells (cholangiocarcinomas). Both types of carcinoma tend to spread extensively within the liver; and the hepatocellular carcinomas also grow into the veins of the liver, from which they may spread to more distant sites, such as the lungs. Cancer of the liver may be successfully treated surgically if the tumour has not spread widely within the liver or beyond it.

Pancreas. Pancreatic cancer arising from the epithelium lining the duct system is the most frequent malignant tumour of this organ. In the United States, England, Israel, and several Scandinavian countries the incidence of the disease is high; in other western and eastern European countries and Japan it is intermediate; and in southern Europe and Southeast Asia it is low. Risk factors include cigarette smoking, diabetes mellitus, and perhaps the typical Western diet, consisting of a high intake of meat and fat. Onset of the disease is insidious, so that by the time symptoms and signs such as loss of appetite and weight, jaundice, and painless enlargement of the gallbladder due to obstruction are apparent, the tumour has often already involved contiguous tissues and organs. The cancers are adenocarcinomas that metastasize early and often widely. These characteristics are responsible for the lethality of this disease, which has less than a 2-percent five-year survival rate. Despite considerable clinical research aimed at the development of new diagnostic techniques, successful results by surgical resection have been obtained only in a relatively small percentage of patients who have an early diagnosis. Cancer of the endocrine tissue in the pancreas, which secretes hormones such as insulin, can induce severe disturbances in blood-sugar levels that lead to dizziness, confusion, weakness, and loss of consciousness. These tumours are generally not aggressive and are often cured by surgery. Cancer of the acinar cells, which produce the enzymes necessary for the digestion of food, though rare, has a very poor prognosis, closely resembling that of ductal cancer.

Risk factors of pancreatic cancer

Colon and rectum. Colorectal cancer is very common in the Western world, with an equal incidence in males and females. By contrast, its incidence in Japan, many South American countries, and sub-Saharan African countries is very low. Epidemiologic studies suggest that a major risk factor may be the low fibre content and high meat protein and fat content of the Western diet. It has been observed that Japanese immigrants to the United States within a generation acquire a much higher incidence of colorectal cancer than their counterparts in Japan. Similarly, their children, and the children of other immigrant ethnic groups from countries with low incidence, have incidences for colon and rectal cancer equal to those of other Americans. This is an excellent example of the role of the environment in the causation of cancer. Numerous studies aimed at identifying the early precursor lesions seem to indicate that the majority of cases arise from certain types of preexisting polyps and that these may remain benign for many months before becoming malignant. The tumours are adenocarcinomas, and some apparently also grow very slowly, taking as long as six to eight years to reach a size of about 2.4 inches (six centimetres). The tumours are round and raised and may be ulcerated. Once the tumour has grown through the wall of the bowel, successful treatment becomes more difficult. The tumours metastasize to the liver, lung, and other distant sites. Surgery is the most favoured treatment, although chemotherapy and radiation therapy may also be used when warranted by the extent of the disease.

Kidney and bladder. Adenocarcinoma of the kidney, which arises in the epithelium lining the renal tubules, is the most common primary malignancy affecting this organ. It is more common in men than in women and appears during the fifth and sixth decades of life. Although its causes remain to be determined, a number of retrospective epidemiologic studies implicate an association with cigarette smoking. An important manifestation is blood in the urine (hematuria), which may be painless or accompanied with flank pain. Tumours are large and bulky and may occupy a large portion of the kidney. Renal adenocarcinoma spreads by direct extension to adjacent tissues, and metastasis occurs to lung and bone by way of the lymphatics and the bloodstream. Some tumours may become quite large, however, without any evidence of metastasis. The mean survival rate following surgical removal is about 35 percent. A special type of kidney cancer that occurs in infancy and early childhood is often first discovered as a mass by a parent while bathing a child. These cancers, called nephroblastoma, or Wilms' tumour, arise from abnormal embryonic tissue and involve both connective tissue and epithelial cells. They can spread both by direct invasion and by the lymphatics and the bloodstream. Early diagnosis and combined surgical removal and radiation therapy give favourable results, with a cure rate of about 80 percent.

Wilms' tumour in children

Incidence of epithelial tumour of the urinary bladder varies significantly from country to country. In the United States bladder tumours account for about 6 percent of all cancers, while in Zimbabwe, Egypt, and Iraq bladder cancer constitutes about 40 percent of all cancers. The disease is three times more frequent in men than in women. Naphthylamine and other chemicals used in the production of dyes are known to cause bladder cancer. A metabolite of the amino acid trypthophan, present in meat proteins, is also carcinogenic and may represent one of the means by which bladder cancer appears in people having no contact with the chemical industry. Chronic conditions of the bladder, such as infestation by the parasite *Schistosoma*, found in the Middle East and Africa, and developmental defects that predispose a person to the formation of bladder stones and infection are also considered high risk factors. Hematuria is the most important symptom associated with this disease. Tumours often begin as benign lesions (papillomas), which become progressively more aggressive, with a high tendency to recur, and finally assume the behaviour of malignancy. The majority are carcinomas of transitional-cell epithelium, which lines the bladder; a much smaller number are squamous-cell cancers, which arise as a consequence of the modulation of transitional epithelium to squamous epithelium by factors and mechanisms that remain obscure. The tumours can be treated successfully with early diagnosis and vigorous treatment. Once they invade the bladder wall and enter adjoining structures, however, the prognosis is poor.

Prostate. Cancer of the prostate is a common disease, but markedly low incidences are seen in Oriental populations, especially in Japan. As with other tumours, immigration from low-incidence to high-incidence countries is followed by an increased incidence in the migrant population. Although no definite etiologic factors have been established, the isolation of HSV-2 from cells of prostatic cancer and the presence and persistence of CMV virus in cultured human prostatic cells have suggested that these viruses might be involved. The fact that prostatic carcinoma is rare before the age of 50, increases in incidence in subsequent years, is not seen in castrates, and regresses following castration implicates aging and the presence of male hormone as significant factors. Cancer arises in the epithelium lining the prostatic acini and small ducts, and, more rarely, in the main ducts. The majority are adenocarcinomas that tend to infiltrate the organ stroma and break through the capsule to spread to the rectum, the base of the bladder, and eventually to more distant sites by dissemination via lymphatics and blood vessels. Metastases to the bones are quite common and, together with involvement of nerves in the pelvis, are often the cause of considerable pain. Treatments include castration, administration of the female hormone estrogen, and, as the extent of involvement may require, surgical removal, radiation therapy, and chemotherapy.

Uterus. Cancers of the uterus are relatively common and represent about 19 percent of all malignant diseases in women in the United States, as contrasted, for example, to Thailand, countries of the Far East such as Japan, and African countries, where they are relatively rare. The two major types of uterine cancer are adenocarcinoma of the lining of the uterus (endometrium) and squamous-cell carcinoma of the womb or cervix. Endometrial carcinoma has its highest incidence late in the sixth decade. The disease is associated with obesity, diabetes, hypertension, and late menopause. Etiology has not been established; there is sufficient evidence, however, to suggest that the hormone estrogen probably plays a significant role. Endometrial cancer has been induced in rabbits by sustained administration of large doses of the hormone. Endometrial cancer spreads both superficially and by invasion of the muscular wall of the uterus. Lymphatic spread occurs late. Inappropriate bleeding from the fifth decade of life onward is an important symptom that must be heeded early if treatment of the disease is to be effective. Treatment of choice is radiation therapy followed by surgical removal, and the cure rate is good. Treatment for disease that spreads beyond the uterus includes hormonal therapy with progesterone and, less frequently, chemotherapy.

Major types of uterine cancer

Squamous-cell carcinoma of the uterine cervix is a somewhat more common disease than endometrial cancer and tends to occur at a younger age, beginning as early as the third decade. A viral etiology is strongly implicated and is supported by a higher incidence of the disease in women who have had an early and active sexual history, including multiple pregnancies. Such cancers are infrequent in women who have not been pregnant and are very rare in celibate women. An early symptom of the disease is abnormal bleeding. The cancers arise in the squamous epithelium of the womb and tend to remain confined to the lining for a number of years in the in situ stage before becoming invasive. Women who have an annual examination, including a Papanicolaou (Pap) test, a painless sampling of cells from the cervix, have an improved chance of early diagnosis. Once the tumour becomes invasive, involving both direct extension and lymphatic metastasis, the prognosis becomes grave. Serious complications, such as infection and eventual failure of the kidneys as a consequence of obstruction and fistula formation, occur in late stages.

Ovary. Cancer of the ovary is the fourth most frequent cause of death from cancer in women of the highly

Incidence of cancer of the ovary

industrialized countries of the Western world. It is relatively uncommon in Far Eastern countries, especially Japan, and in less developed countries. Immigrants to Western countries show higher incidences about 20 years after their immigration, suggesting the possible role of environmental factors; no firm associations have been established, however. Many different types of ovarian cancer have been identified; they arise either in the epithelium or in connective tissue components, and very rarely in both. The most common forms are adenocarcinomas arising in the epithelium. Some of these retain their capacity to produce estrogenic hormones and, more rarely, masculinizing hormones. The tumours may be treated successfully through surgery if they are diagnosed early. Extension of the disease beyond the ovary requires more radical treatment, such as radiation therapy and chemotherapy.

Lymphoid tissue. Malignant diseases of lymphoid tissue (lymphomas) are the seventh most common cause of cancer death in the United States, and certain forms are common throughout many countries of the world. In African countries and on New Guinea, Burkitt's lymphoma is common, while in the Western countries it is relatively rare. Certain lymphomas in humans have been closely linked with viruses; other established lymphomas are linked to significant chronic exposure to ionizing radiation and to inherited immunologic deficiency or to such deficiency induced to prevent rejection of organ transplants or resulting from treatment for certain diseases. Malignancies of lymphoid tissue may arise in one or more of the organs rich in such tissue, including the lymph nodes, spleen, bone marrow, and thymus. More rarely they can arise in organs containing small amounts of such tissue, including the stomach, intestines, testis, and breast. Lymphomas are aggressive malignancies that tend to spread to distant organs and become systemic in their distribution. As with other malignant tumours, early diagnosis and aggressive treatment by radiation therapy or chemotherapy, or in many instances the two in combination, have resulted in an increasing number of cures.

Blood-forming tissues. Leukemias are a heterogeneous group of malignancies of the blood-forming (hematopoietic) tissues, which include the bone marrow, lymph nodes, and spleen. The acute form of the disease in adults is rapidly fatal, with infiltration of bone marrow and other hematopoietic tissues by the malignant cells, while the acute form in children has yielded to treatment and a number of cures are documented. The disease has a worldwide distribution, and the best established etiologic factor involves chronic exposure to ionizing radiation. Other factors that have been implicated include congenital disorders associated with increased chromosomal fragility and instability, such as Down's syndrome, Bloom's syndrome, and Fanconi's anemia; viruses; and certain chemicals and drugs. Leukemic cells tend to disseminate through the bloodstream, lodging in blood-forming and other tissues and organs. The cells proliferate to the extent that they often crowd out normal elements of the blood, so that patients afflicted with leukemia are rendered anemic by an interference with red blood cell production or from bleeding because of abnormalities of the blood-clotting mechanisms. They are rendered susceptible to infection by a diminution of the various types of white blood cells, which comprise a major defense system of the body. Treatment involves attempts to correct these complications by transfusion of normal blood and blood products, as well as the use of antibiotics to combat infection and of chemotherapeutic agents to destroy the malignant cells. Chronic, more slow-growing, and less aggressive forms of leukemia may continue for years and may respond favourably to radiation therapy, surgical removal of the spleen, and chemotherapy. In terminal cases leukemia cells either show accelerated growth or are transformed to more primitive cells that tend to disseminate widely and cause death within a few months.

(D.G.Sc.)

TREATMENT

Successful treatment of cancer requires the complete removal or destruction of all cancerous tissue. If therapy fails to remove all of the cancer cells, the disease recurs. Surgery and radiation are the most effective forms of treatment. Chemotherapy—treatment with drugs and hormones—has proved helpful in some forms of cancer. The choice of therapy is governed by the type, location, size, and extent of invasion and metastases of the cancer at the time of diagnosis, and by the general condition of the patient.

Surgery. For surgery to be curative, it must be performed before the cancer has spread into organs and tissues that cannot be safely removed. Since the late 19th century increasingly radical operations for cancer have become standard. Despite the increasing extent of these procedures, risk has been reduced by improvements in surgical techniques, anesthesiology, and preoperative and postoperative care, especially in the control of infection. Heart-lung pumps, artificial kidneys, and methods of maintaining electrolyte balance and metabolic equilibrium have permitted patients with impaired cardiovascular and kidney functions or poor general metabolism to survive cancer surgery.

Reconstructive techniques

Major advances have been made in the restoration of structures altered by cancer surgery and in the rehabilitation of people who have undergone radical surgery. Patients undergoing certain surgical procedures for cancer of the colon or rectum, for instance, can be equipped with simple devices for the elimination of solid waste. For patients with cancer of the head and neck, the use of grafting methods and of tissue flaps make it possible to apply reconstructive techniques at the time the cancer is removed.

Rehabilitation of the patient also plays an important role. Women who have extensive surgery for breast cancer are given treatment for restoration of muscle tone needed for movement of the arms. Progress has also been made in teaching new mechanisms of speech to people who have undergone surgical removal of the larynx.

In addition to saving lives by eradicating cancer, surgery also may improve the remaining months or years of life for persons whose cancers cannot be eradicated, restoring comfort and a sense of usefulness. When severe pain accompanies cancer, surgery may bring relief by severing the nerve pathways that carry the painful sensations. In addition, surgery is sometimes necessary to treat abscesses resulting from either the tumour or infection and to relieve intestinal obstructions.

Surgery is also valuable as a preventive measure in controlling cancer. It may be used to eliminate precancerous conditions in the mouth, chronic ulcers (ulcerative colitis) that may lead to cancer of the colon, and certain precancerous polyps in the colon and rectum. It may be used to remove burn scars that may lead to cancer, precancerous nodules in the thyroid gland, and certain precancerous pigmented moles.

Radiation therapy. Radiation therapy makes use of ionizing radiations—X-rays, particles (electrons, neutrons, and pi-mesons), and gamma rays—to destroy cells by impairing their capacity to divide. Although some normal cells are also killed during radiation therapy, this is minimized by careful shielding of adjacent areas.

Some cancers do not respond to radiation therapy. The differing sensitivities of various malignant tumours to irradiation are due primarily to the variations in the cells of origin of the tumours. In addition, individual cells within a tumour may have a widely different susceptibility to irradiation. In cancers composed of a variety of cells in different stages of differentiation (*e.g.*, epidermoid carcinoma), even a large dose of radiation may not affect the most differentiated cells. Poor circulation within some tumours decreases their oxygen supply, further diminishing their sensitivity to radiation.

Development of instruments that produce energy in the range of millions of electron volts has permitted extensive use of radiation therapy. Such instruments can deliver a greater radiation dose to deep-seated tumours without the serious skin reactions and discomfort often associated with lower energy X-ray beams. Large areas can be irradiated with more precise definition of the margins and alignment of the beam, less side-scatter, and therefore more protection of adjacent vital structures. The greater versatility of such equipment has made possible the development of treatment techniques involving multiple intersecting radiation beams, rotation of the patient or the radiation source, large fields of radiation shaped to the contours of particular organs, and the pinpointing of beams for cancers of the eye and the larynx. Because of their increased usefulness, instruments (linear accelerators, betatrons, and radioactive cobalt-60 teletherapy apparatus) have become standard instruments for radiation therapy of deep-seated cancers.

Chemotherapy. Chemotherapy can cure certain forms of cancer. Cancers frequently cured by drugs include choriocarcinoma, a rare, highly malignant tumour that originates in the placenta; acute leukemia of childhood; and Burkitt's lymphoma. Treatments with combinations of drugs have produced long-term, disease-free remissions in many children with acute leukemia and in persons with advanced stages of Hodgkin's disease. Some of these patients have been in remission longer than five years and may, in fact, be cured.

Multiple carcinomas of the superficial layers of the skin have been eradicated after the application of certain cancer-drug ointments to the skin. Wilms' tumour, for example, is often curable when cancer drugs are used in combination with surgery and radiation. Many other forms of cancer benefit temporarily or partially by chemotherapy. Some cancers are resistant to drugs, however.

Problems with chemotherapy

Most cancer drugs are limited in their usefulness. One problem is that only a certain proportion of cells is dividing at any one time, and most cancer drugs can destroy only that part of the cell population undergoing division. Another problem is that cancer drugs damage normal, as well as cancer, cells and tissues. In addition, some cancer cells eventually become resistant to drugs. To help overcome these difficulties, combinations of chemotherapeutic agents that act on cells in different ways have been used in various treatment programs simultaneously or in sequence. This allows cancer cells at different stages of division to be killed, causes less damage to normal cells, and diminishes the tendency of malignant cells to become resistant to a single drug.

Special measures have been developed to protect persons undergoing cancer chemotherapy from the combined effects of the drugs and the disease. Refinements in the transfusion of blood platelets permit multiple transfusions in leukemia patients with critical platelet deficiencies caused either by leukemia or drug toxicity. During periods when a patient's white blood cells are depleted, administration of antibiotics offers protection from many infections. Relatively germ-free environments, such as specially designed hospital rooms, provide sterile atmospheres to protect against fatal infection. Transfusion of type-matched white blood cells, and, more recently, transplantation of bone marrow cells from carefully matched donors, have also been of value in protecting persons with nonfunctioning bone marrows against infections.

(C.G.B./D.G.Sc.)

Experimental treatments. Since the 1970s considerable effort has been expended toward the development, control, and elimination of cancer by immunotherapy. Methods have involved the use of immunotherapeutic agents such as bacille Calmette-Guérin (BCG), a vaccine against human tuberculosis; killed suspensions of several types of bacteria; chemical products isolated from certain bacteria; and interferon, a family of proteins that inhibit the growth of viruses. All of these substances appear to stimulate the immunologic defense system. It may someday prove possible to cure cancer by manipulating the complex immunologic mechanisms of the host.

Hyperthermia

A second experimental approach involves the use of hyperthermia (high temperature). Research indicates that cancer cells are more sensitive to the killing effects of high temperature than are their normal counterparts. The success of treatment by hyperthermia appears to depend on the development of new instrumentation that will allow the application of highly localized heat to the site of a tumour.

Two developments in radiation therapy that may add significantly to its effectiveness include the use of chemicals that greatly sensitize tumour cells to the damaging effects of ionizing radiation, while not affecting normal cells, and the application of particle-beam radiation therapy, using beams of protons, helium ions, and heavy ions of such isotopes as carbon-12, neon-20, silicon-38, and argon-40. Such beams have sufficiently high energy to penetrate deeply into tissues; they do more damage to malignant cells than do the less energetic forms of ionizing radiation administered at the same dosages. Such developments may allow treatment of deep-seated tumours without significantly damaging overlying normal tissues.

(D.G.Sc.)

BIBLIOGRAPHY

Books: MARTIN D. ABELOFF (ed.), *Complications of Cancer* (1979), a text for physicians; *Cancer Risk, Assessing and Reducing the Dangers in Our Society* (1982), a report to the Office of Science and Technology by an advisory panel; NATIONAL INSTITUTES OF HEALTH, *Coping with Cancer: An Annotated Bibliography of Public, Patient and Professional Information and Education Materials* (1980); RICHARD DOLL and RICHARD PETO, *The Causes of Cancer* (1981), an epidemiologic approach toward the identification of major risk factors involved in human cancer; MARILEE I. DONOVAN (ed.), *Cancer Care: A Guide for Patient Education* (1981), written by a nurse to assist nurses; G. GIRALDO and E. BETH (eds.), *The Role of Viruses in Human Cancer*, vol. 1 (1980); I.I. KESSLER (ed.), *Cancer Control: Contemporary Views on Screening, Diagnosis and Therapy* (1980); THOMAS H. MAUGH II and JEAN L. MARX, *Seeds of Destruction: The Science Report on Cancer Research* (1975), a popular presentation; GUY R. NEWELL and NEIL M. ELLISON (eds.), *Nutrition and Cancer: Etiology and Treatment* (1981); MARVIN A. RICH and PHILIP FURMANSKI (eds.), *Biological Carcinogenesis* (1982), a general consideration of viral and chemical carcinogenesis; MICHAEL B. SHIMKEN, *Science and Cancer*, 3rd revision (1980), a general review for the layman; THOMAS SYMINGTON and R.L. CARTER (eds.), *Scientific Foundations of Oncology* (1976), an authoritative text; H.VAINIO, M. SORSA, and K. HEMMIMKI (eds.), *Occupational Cancer and Carcinogenesis* (1981); MORRIS S. ZEDECK and MARTIN LIPIN (eds.), *Inhibition of Tumor Induction and Development* (1981), a consideration of various chemical substances that inhibit the initiation and development of cancer.

Journals: *Journal of the National Cancer Institute* (monthly), published by the U.S. National Cancer Institute; *Cancer Research* (monthly), published by the American Association for Cancer Research; *Cancer* (semimonthly), published by the American Cancer Society, primarily reporting clinical research; *British Journal of Cancer* (monthly), published by the British Empire Cancer Campaign for Research; *Carcinogenesis* (monthly), a research journal; *European Journal of Cancer and Clinical Oncology* (monthly), published by the Ministry of Education of Belgium, with articles in French and English; *International Journal of Cancer* (monthly), published primarily in English by the International Union Against Cancer, with summaries in French.

(C.G.B./D.G.Sc.)

Canning, George

A British statesman who was prime minister of Great Britain for a short time during the year 1827, George Canning is chiefly remembered as foreign secretary from 1822 to 1827, when he and William Huskisson, president of the Board of Trade, taught a large portion of the Tory Party to take a more liberal view of many aspects of domestic, colonial, and foreign policy. The ablest and sincerest opponent of parliamentary reform, he nevertheless contributed largely to the creation of that independent and enlightened spirit among the younger members of the House of Commons, without which the great parliamentary Reform Act of 1832 could not have been carried without revolution.

To some, Canning seemed arrogant and contemptuous. His wit and sarcasm were remembered by all who heard or read his speeches. It was the fashion to say of him that he was no gentleman. The hatred and malignity with which he was assailed by the Tory aristocracy in 1827 showed what mountains of prejudice still existed against a prime minister born outside the governing class. In choosing Canning as prime minister, George IV found that he had to fight over again his father's battles against the pretensions of the great families to deprive the crown of its ancient right to nominate its servants.

Contemporaries said that Canning's ministry was the most popular with the middle classes that had ever been known. As member for Liverpool (1812–22), he came to recognize fully the needs of the rising commercial and industrial interests. He put his country before personal or party interests. None of the party leaders of the time had more generous notions of the obligations that he owed to his supporters. He never thought he could do too much for his friends, but he never used his influence to secure undeserved promotion for them. They, for their part, were drawn to him by bonds of intense personal devotion, and, through his disciples, such as William Huskisson and Lord Palmerston, he wielded an authority that endured beyond the grave.

Family background

Canning was born in London on April 11, 1770. His father, the eldest son of an Irish landowner, was disinherited for his marriage with a beautiful but penniless girl and died in 1771, leaving his wife and year-old son entirely destitute. The widow became an actress and the mistress of an actor, by whom she had five children. In 1783 she married another actor, by whom she had five more children, but this new connection did nothing to rescue her from discredit and misfortune. From this unsatisfactory environment, George Canning was taken away by a wealthy uncle, Stratford Canning, who raised him with his own children, one of whom was the future diplomat, Viscount Stratford de Redcliffe.

Canning was educated at Eton College and at Christ Church, Oxford. After graduating (1791), he soon decided on a political career and, in July 1792, came under the influence of the prime minister, William Pitt, who undertook to find him a seat in Parliament. He was elected for the privately controlled borough of Newtown, Isle of Wight, in July 1793 and quickly became recognized as one of the rising men on the government side of the house. Pitt further procured for him the undersecretaryship of state for foreign affairs in 1796. Though the work was "pretty hard and constant" he found time to contribute to *The Anti-Jacobin* (1797–98), a weekly paper founded to ridicule both English and French men of republican sentiment. In 1799 he left the foreign office and was appointed a commissioner of the Board of Control for the government of India. In May 1800 he was promoted to the office of joint paymaster of the forces and was made a privy councillor. A few weeks later he married an heiress, Joan Scott. By her he had four children, including Charles John, later Earl Canning and a governor general of India.

When Pitt resigned in 1801, Canning, too, left office. Disapproving of Pitt's support of the new prime minister, Henry Addington (later 1st Viscount Sidmouth), he made himself independent in 1802 by giving up the seat of Wendover, which he had represented since 1796, and purchasing election as member of Parliament for the Irish borough of Tralee. In 1803 Pitt began to turn against Addington, and Canning could then go into open opposition without forfeiting Pitt's friendship. On the formation of Pitt's last ministry in May 1804, Canning became treasurer of the navy, but his unpopularity (his biting wit made him many enemies) kept him out of the Cabinet. Much to his disgust, his colleagues resigned after Pitt's death (January 1806) because of the insecurity of their parliamentary position. When, however, in March 1807 the King called upon "the friends of Mr. Pitt" again to form a government, Canning became foreign secretary.

Foreign secretary

Actions in the Napoleonic Wars that occurred during Canning's first tenure of the foreign secretaryship included the seizure of the Danish fleet (his own brilliant planning) and the unfortunate expedition to Walcheren Island off the Scheldt River, in The Netherlands. The Peninsular War, involving British, Spanish, and French resistance to Napoleon on the Iberian Peninsula, was also begun. Holding Viscount Castlereagh, the war secretary, responsible for the disasters that overtook British arms at Corunna in Spain, and at Flushing (Vlissingen) in Holland, Canning, in 1809, insisted on his dismissal. They quarrelled and fought a duel on September 21, in which Canning was wounded in the thigh. Both had already resigned, Canning because of the nonfulfillment by the duke of Portland, William Bentinck, the dying prime minister, of his promise that Castlereagh should be removed from the War Department. Canning offered to form a government, but the King called upon his rival, Spencer Perceval, and Canning remained out of office until 1816.

Lord Liverpool, who succeeded to the premiership in 1812 on Perceval's assassination, tried hard to induce Canning to take office, but Canning refused to allow his old rival Castlereagh (who generously offered to surrender the foreign secretaryship to him and to take the inferior office of chancellor of the exchequer) to retain the leadership of the House of Commons. So Canning lost the chance of being the peacemaker of Europe in 1815, and he had further damaged his reputation in 1814 by accepting what was believed to be a rich sinecure, the post of ambassador to Portugal.

Two years later, he entered the Cabinet as president of the Board of Control. Canning, disapproving of the government's efforts to deprive George IV's queen, Caroline, of her title and position, resigned in December 1820. In the hope of improving his financial position and believing that advancement at home was blocked by the King's hostility to him, he accepted the governor generalship of Bengal in March 1822, with the additional prospect of a peerage on his return; but, before his ship was ready to sail, Castlereagh committed suicide (August 12), and George IV reluctantly acquiesced in Canning's succession to the "whole inheritance"—the foreign secretaryship and the leadership of the House of Commons. He was now the most important member of the government. Afraid of becoming too deeply involved in continental politics and disliking the great despotic sovereigns who were anxious to suppress liberal movements everywhere, he cut England adrift in 1823 from the so-called Holy Alliance engineered by the emperor Alexander I of Russia to preserve the European status quo; prevented European intervention in South America on behalf of Ferdinand VII of Spain; recognized the independence of the rebellious Spanish-American colonies; sent an army to Portugal to meet the threat of attack by Spain; gave diplomatic support to the Greeks in their struggle with the Turks for freedom; and ensured the eventual creation of an independent Greek state.

Lord Liverpool's premiership came to an end in February 1827. He had long since marked out Canning as his successor, but it was far from obvious that Canning would be the King's choice. Although since 1822 he had gained a remarkable ascendancy at Windsor Castle by the success of his foreign policy and by a judicious attention to the royal intimates there, Canning was the leading advocate of Roman Catholic emancipation, and George IV had been persuaded that the cause of the monarchy was linked with that of the Established Church and resistance to the Catholic claims. Robert Peel and the Duke of Wellington, the leading opponents of Catholic relief, knew that no government could be formed without Canning, and Canning refused to serve under another anti-Catholic premier. Finally, on April 10, he was authorized to reconstruct the ministry on the understanding that a Catholic relief bill was not to be forced on the King. Moved partly by personal animosity, partly by dislike of Canning's advocacy of Catholic emancipation, half the Cabinet refused to serve under him, and, in all, more than 40 ministers and political appointees resigned. The Whigs, however, came to his assistance, and most of the independent members of Parliament supported him with their votes. But his ministry lasted only four months; his health broke down under the strain, and he died on August 8, 1827, at Chiswick, near London, in the house of the Duke of Devonshire.

Prime minister

BIBLIOGRAPHY. The most useful biography for the general reader is SIR CHARLES PETRIE, *George Canning*, 2nd ed. (1946). Though not based on much original research, it makes good use of secondary sources. DOROTHY MARSHALL, *The Rise of George Canning* (1938), covers Canning's career to the death of Pitt. It is based on Canning's private papers formerly at Harewood House, Leeds, but now in the Leeds Public Library. However, the quotations contain many inaccuracies.

H.W.V. TEMPERLEY, *The Foreign Policy of Canning, 1822–1827* (1925), is a lengthy and valuable study based on official and private archives but perhaps too detailed for the general reader. For the specialist, there is a short study of Canning's parliamentary friends and supporters in an article by A. ASPINALL, "The Canningite Party," in *Transactions of the Royal Historical Society*, 17:177–226 (1934); and a detailed account of his premiership, based on a large quantity of new material, in A. ASPINALL, *The Formation of Canning's Ministry*, Royal Historical Society, Camden 3rd series, vol. 59 (1937). The specialist will still find useful Canning's *Speeches*, 6 vol. (1828), some corrected by himself.

(A.As.)

Canon Law

Canon law—though in its wider sense it includes precepts of divine law, natural or positive, incorporated in various canonical collections or codes—is in this article defined as that body of rules and regulations (canons) concerning the behaviour and actions of individuals and institutions within certain Christian churches (Roman Catholic, Eastern Orthodox, the independent churches of Eastern Christianity, and the Anglican Communion), which have, through proper ecclesiastical authority, defined, designated, and codified such rules. Though canon law is historically continuous from the early church to the present, it has, as a result of doctrinal and ecclesiastical schisms, developed differing, though often similar, patterns of codification and norms in the various churches that have incorporated it into their ecclesiastical frameworks. The canon law of the Eastern and Western churches was much the same in form until these two groups of churches separated in the Schism of 1054. In Eastern Christianity, however, because of doctrinal and nationalistic disputes during the 5th to 7th centuries, several church groups (especially non-Greek) separated themselves from the nominal head of Eastern Christianity, the patriarch of Constantinople, and developed their own bodies of canon law, often reflecting nationalistic concerns.

Canon law in the Western churches after 1054 developed without interruption until the Reformation of the 16th century. Though other churches of the Reformation rejected the canon law of the Roman Catholic Church, the Church of England retained the concept of canon law and developed its own type, which has acceptance in the churches of the Anglican Communion.

NATURE AND SIGNIFICANCE

A church is defined as a community founded in a unity of faith, a sacramental fellowship of all members with Christ as Lord, and a unity of government. Many scholars assert that a church cannot exist without authority—*i.e.*, binding rules and organizational structures—and that religion and law are mutually inclusive. Thus the calling of a church leader to office is regarded as important in the organizational structure and, like every other fundamental vocation in the churches that accept the validity of canon law, it is also viewed as sacramental and as linked to the priesthood—which, in turn, involves a calling to leadership in liturgy and preaching. According to Roman Catholic belief, the mission of the college of Apostles (the Apostles, presided over by St. Peter in the 1st century AD) is continued in the college of bishops, presided over by the pope. Other churches may accept this view, without at the same time accepting the authority of the pope. The validity of canon law thus rests on an acceptance of this sacramental view and of the transmitted mission of the Apostles through the bishops.

Necessity of authority

Historical and cultural importance of canon law. Canon law has functioned in different historical periods in the organization of the church's liturgy, preaching, works of charity, and other activities through which Christianity was established and spread in the Mediterranean area and beyond. Canon law, moreover, had an essential role in the transmission of ancient Greek and Roman jurisprudence and in the reception of Justinian law (Roman law as codified under the sponsorship of the Byzantine emperor Justinian in the 6th century) in Europe in the Middle Ages. Thus it is that the history of the Middle Ages, to the extent that they were dominated by ecclesiastical concerns, cannot be written without knowledge of the ecclesiastical institutions that were governed according to canon law. Medieval canon law also had a lasting influence on the law of the Protestant churches. Numerous institutions and concepts of canon law have influenced the secular law and jurisprudence in lands influenced by Protestantism: *e.g.*, marriage law; the concepts *jus in re*—*jus ad rem* (law of things); law of obligations; the doctrine of modes of property acquisition; possession; good faith in prescription; representation; wills; legal persons; the concepts of crime and punishment; the law of criminal procedure; and the law concerning proof or evidence. International law owes its very origin to canonists and theologians, and the modern idea of the state goes back to the ideas developed by medieval canonists regarding the constitution of the church. The history of the legal principles of the relation of *sacerdotium* to *imperium*—*i.e.*, of ecclesiastical to secular authority or of church to state—is a central factor in European history.

Problems in the study of canon law and its sources. Because of the discontinuity that has developed between church and state in modern times and the more exclusively spiritual and pastoral function of church organization, scholars in canon law are presently searching for a recovery of vital contact among canon law and theology, biblical exegesis (critical interpretive principles of the Bible), and church history in their contemporary forms. Canon-law scholars are also seeking a link with the empirical social sciences (*e.g.*, sociology, anthropology, and other such disciplines), which is required for insight into and control of the application of canon law. The study of the history of canon law calls not only for juridical and historical training but also for insight into contemporary theological concepts and social relationships. Many sources, such as the documents of councils and popes, are often uncritical and found only in badly organized publications, and much of the material exists only in manuscripts and archives; frequently the legal sources contain dead law (*i.e.*, law no longer held valid) and say nothing about living law. What does and does not come under canon law, what is or is not a source of canon law, which law is universal and which local, and other such questions have to be judged differently for different periods.

The function of canon law in liturgy, preaching, and social activities involves the development and maintenance of those institutions that are considered to be most serviceable for the personal life and faith of members of the church and for their vocation in the world. This function is thus concerned with a continual adaptation of canon law to the circumstances of the time as well as to personal needs.

The role and function of canon law

HISTORY

The formative period: origins to Gratian (c. 1140). The early church was not organized in any centralized structure. Over a long period of time, there developed various patriarchates (churches believed to have been founded by Apostles) and bishoprics, the leaders of which—either as monarchical bishops or as bishops with shared authority (*i.e.*, collegiality)—issued various decrees and regulatory provisions for the clergy and laity within their particular jurisdictions. After the emperor Constantine (died 337) granted tolerance to Christians within the Roman Empire, bishops from various sees (episcopal seats)—especially from the eastern part of the empire—met in councils (*e.g.*, the ecumenical Council of Nicaea, 325). Though these councils are known primarily for their consideration of doctrinal conflicts, they also ruled on practical matters (such as jurisdictional and institutional concerns), which were set down in canons. In the West, there was less imperial interference, and the bishop of Rome (the pope) gradually assumed more jurisdictional authority than his counterpart (the ecumenical patriarch of Constantinople) in the East. Throughout this period there were often conflicting canons, since there were many independently arrived at canonical collections and no centralized attempt to bring order out of the many collections until the Middle Ages.

Eastern churches. In addition to the New Testament, the writings of the Apostolic Fathers (second generation of Christian writers) and the pseudo-apostolic writings (documents attributed to but not written by the Apostles) contain the oldest descriptions of the customs existing in the East from the 2nd century until the 5th. The sources of all the others are the *Doctrina duodecim Apostolorum* (*Doctrine of the Twelve Apostles*, 2nd century?), the *Didascalia duodecim Apostolorum* (*Teaching of the Apostles*, 3rd century), and the *Traditio apostolica* (*Apostolic Tradition*), attributed to Hippolytus (a 3rd-century bishop of Rome), written in Rome *c.* AD 218 but far more widely distributed in the East. From these documents, the *Constitutiones Apostolicae* (*Apostolic Constitutions*), in which 85 *Canones Apostolicae* (*Apostolic Canons*) were included, were composed *c.* AD 400.

During the period that followed the grant of toleration referred to above, many synods held in the East legislated, among other things, various disciplinary rules, or *canones*. In addition to and in place of the law of custom, written law entered the scene. An ecumenical Council of Chalcedon (AD 451) possessed a chronological collection of the canons of earlier councils of Ancyra (314), Neocaesarea (314–325), Nicaea I (325), Antioch (341), and Gangra (343). This *Syntagma canonum* ("Body of Canons"), or *Corpus canonum orientale* ("Eastern Body of Canons"), was subsequently complemented by the canons attributed to a 4th-century council of Laodicea, Constantinople I (381), Chalcedon (451), Africa (419), Sardica (*c.* 343), Ephesus (431), 85 *Canones Apostolorum*, Constantinople (394), canonical letters of 12 Greek Fathers and of the 3rd-century Latin bishop of Carthage, Cyprian, and the *Constitutiones Apostolicae*. With the exception of the last, the Trullo (supplementary) Council of Quinisextum, or the fifth and sixth councils (692), accepted this complex, along with its own canons, as the official legal code of the Eastern churches. The canons of the second ecumenical Council of Nicaea (787) and of the two councils (861 and 879–880) under Photius, patriarch of Constantinople, were added to that.

Systematic collections and the science of canon law

The systematic collections—and there were many of them—contained either canons of councils or ecclesiastical laws (*nomoi*) of the emperors or both together (nomocanons). The first known Greek collection of canons that is preserved is the *Collectio 50 titulorum* ("Collection of 50 Titles"), after the model of the 50 titles of the work known as the *Pandecta* ("Accepted by All") composed by the patriarch Johannes Scholasticus *c.* 550. He composed from the *Novellae constitutiones* ("Novels," or "New Constitutions") of Justinian the *Collectio 87 capitulorum* ("Collection of 87 Chapters"). The *Collectio tripartita* ("Tripartite Collection"), from the end of the 6th century and composed of the entire Justinian ecclesiastical legislation, was the most widely distributed. The nomocanons were expressions of the fusion of imperial and church authority. The *Nomocanon 50 titulorum* ("Canon Law of 50 Titles") from about 580, composed of the works of Johannes Scholasticus, remained in use until the 12th century. The edition of the *Nomocanon 14 titulorum* ("Canon Law of 14 Titles") was completed in 883 and accepted in 920 as law for the entire Eastern Church.

The science of canon law was pursued together with the study of secular law, especially in the schools in Constantinople and Beirut. The *Scholia* (commentaries) on the *Basilica*, a compilation of all of imperial law from the time of Justinian, promulgated by the Byzantine emperor Leo VI (886–912), influenced the method of commenting on and teaching canon law. The best known commentators in the 12th century were Johannes Zonaras and Theodorus Balsamon. Matthaeus Blastares composed his *Syntagma alphabeticum* ("Alphabetical Arrangement"), an alphabetical manual of all imperial and church law, in 1335 from their works.

Independent churches of Eastern Christianity. The churches of Eastern Christianity that separated from the patriarchal see of Constantinople over a period of several centuries, but primarily during the 5th and 6th centuries, developed bodies of canon law that reflected their isolated and—after the Arab conquests in the 7th century—secondary social position. Among these churches are the Syrian Orthodox Church of Antioch (in Syria), the Ancient Church of the East (the Assyrians), the Armenian Apostolic Church, and the Coptic Church (in Egypt). Another independent church is the Ethiopian Orthodox Church (see also EASTERN CHRISTIANITY; INDEPENDENT CHURCHES).

Though these churches developed an extensive body of canon law throughout their histories, Western knowledge of their canon law has been very scant. In the 20th century, however, over 300 manuscripts dealing with canon law have been discovered in various isolated monasteries and ecclesiastical libraries of the Near East by Arthur Vööbus, an Estonian-American church historian. These manuscripts cover the period from the 3rd century to the 14th and deal with ecclesiastic regulations of the Syrian churches. Included among these manuscripts are the following: "The Canons of the Godly Monastery of St. Mār Mattai" (630), 26 in number, concern the jurisdiction of the metropolitan (an archbishop) over the monastery; the 22 canons of "The Canons of the Blessed Mār Gīwargī, Patriarch of Antioch and Syria, and the Holy Bishops of All Religions with Him" (785) are attempts to regulate church discipline, marriage, and ecclesiastical and social relationships with other religious communities; "The Canons of the Holy Qyriaqos, Which the Patriarch Composed and the Synod of the Saints and Bishops with Him" (794), containing 46 canons, deals with ecclesiastical and moral discipline and with liturgical, cultic, and monastic matters; "The Canons of the Holy Dionysios, the Patriarch of Antioch and Syria and of the Synod Which Was Assembled with Him" (818) contains 12 canons concerned with clergy rebellion, the standard of living of the clergy (which was poor), church property, and marriage; "The Canons Which Were Composed by the Holy Synod Which Assembled in Bēt Mār Šīlā [in the region] of Serūg, and Which Consecrated Mar Dionysios as Patriarch of Antioch, the City of God" (896), which originally contained 40 canons, though only 25 remain, deals with the election and examination of candidates for the hierarchy and clergy, the conduct of priests, marriage, pagan influences, and religious and ecclesiastical duties. These canonical collections come from the West Syrian churches. Other canonical collections of the East Syrian churches were published in the early part of the 20th century.

Western churches. From *c.* 300 until *c.* 550, canon law in Western churches had a certain unity through the acceptance of the Eastern and North African councils and the binding factor of the papal decretal law (answers of popes to questions of bishops in matters of discipline), which did not exist in the East. The African canons, like the Eastern canons at Chalcedon, were read out at the councils of Carthage and, if confirmed, included in the Acts, which contained the newly enacted canons. Thus, at the third Council of Carthage (397), the Compendium of the Council of Hippo (393) was included. The collection of the 17th Council of Carthage (419) was soon accepted in all of the East and West.

Development of canon law in Spain, Gaul, Italy, Germany, and the British Isles

In Spain the canons of Nicaea I (325) and Chalcedon (451) and also African and south Gallican canons and Roman decretals were taken over, as well as their own canons, but the later *Hispana* (Spanish collection) crowded out all earlier collections. The Council of Elvira (295–314) in Spain was the first that set up a more complete legislation, followed by Gaul in the first Council of Arles in 314. Texts from the East, Spain, and Rome, including the *Quesnelliana* (an early 6th-century canonical collection named for its publisher, the 17th-century Jansenist scholar Pasquier Quesnel), circulated there. Gennadius, a priest from Marseilles (in France), *c.* 480 wrote the *Statuta ecclesiae antiqua* ("Ancient Statutes of the Church"), principally inspired by the *Constitutiones apostolicae*. A tendency toward the unification of canon law revealed itself most clearly in Italy against the disintegrating situation that existed between the Eastern and Western churches—*i.e.*, the so-called Acacian Schism (484–518), occasioned by the patriarch Acacius of Constantinople and the emperor Zeno's neglect of the legislation of the Council of Chalcedon—and the breakup of the Western Empire soon after the fall of Rome (476), at the time of the 30-year "Gelasian renaissance," beginning during the reign of Pope Gelasius I. There also existed in Rome translations of Eastern councils: *Vetus Romana, Versio Hispana* ("Ancient Roman, Spanish Version"), *Isidoriana, versio Prisca* ("The Isidorian, Priscan Version"), and *Itala* ("Italian"). By far the most important is that of the *Liber canonum* ("Book of Canons") of the 6th-century Roman theologian Dionysius Exiguus, *c.* 500. The first two versions contain 50 *Canones apostolorum*, Greek canons, and the African canons of the 17th Council of Carthage. Dionysius Exiguus also composed a *Liber decretorum* ("Book of Decretals") from Pope Siricius to Pope Anastasius II. Together, the books form the *Corpus* ("Body") or *Codex canonum* ("Code of Canons"). The *Quesnelliana* and other Italian collections are of less importance.

Until the end of the 7th century a greater decentralization and less mutual contact occurred in the separate German kingdoms. Elements of German law found their way into Roman canon law. The *Collectio Avellana* ("Avellan Collection"), written in Rome, *c.* 555, which was a western nomocanon, the *Collectio Novariensis* ("Novarien Collection"), and the *Epitome Hispanica* ("Spanish Abridgment") entered Italy from Spain. In Africa, the first, albeit primitive, systematic collections appeared: the *Breviatio canonum* ("Abridgment of Canons") of (Fulgentius) Ferrandus, deacon of the Church of Carthage (*c.* 546), and the *Concordia canonum Cresconii* ("Harmony of the Canons of Cresconius," a 6th- or 7th-century author), a systematic compilation of the *Dionysiana*, subsequently found in different manuscripts in Gaul. Here the collections were local ones: every cathedral and monastery had its own *liber canonum*. The church of Arles, the metropolis of southern Gaul, had the *Liber auctoritatum* ("Book of Authorities"; *i.e.*, legal texts), a nomocanon of its privileges. The first systematic Gallic *Collectio Andegavetis* ("Andegavenan Collection"), from the end of the 7th century, was an attempt to unite the ancient law with the native.

In Spain, after the conversion of King Recared in 587, the church of the Visigothic kingdom became a well-knit national church with a classical provincial structure under metropolitan jurisdiction, closely linked to the crown. The national councils of Toledo preserved the unity of law and respect for the ancient law. The *Capitula* ("Chapters") of Martinus, bishop of Braga (*c.* 563), was included completely in the *Hispana* and was also copied outside Spain. The *Collectio Novariensis* was related to the *Epitome Hispanica* ("Spanish Abridgment"), the code of the hierarchy that was temporarily halted at the fourth Council of Toledo (633). The *Hispana* was recognized by popes Alexander III and Innocent III as the authentic *corpus canonum* of the Spanish church. Shortly before the *Hispana*, systematic indices (called *tabula*) were written and were subsequently expanded into *excerpta* ("excerpts") and finally into complete texts, the *Hispana systematica* ("Systematic Spanish [Code]"). After the 10th century, the *Hispana* was also called the *Isidoriana*, attributed to Isidore of Seville, a Spanish encyclopaedist and theologian, who was the author of the *Etymologiae* ("Etymologies"), a universally distributed early medieval book of doctrine.

The most disparate picture is offered by the church in the British Isles. The church there was concentrated around heavily populated monasteries, and discipline outside them was maintained by means of a new penitential practice. In place of ancient canons about public penance, the clergy and monks used *libri poenitentiales* ("penitential books"), which contained detailed catalogs of misdeeds with appropriate penances, and were a counterpart of the *Wehre* (lists of punishments) of the *Leges barbarorum* ("Laws of the Barbarians"). They were private writings without official authority and with very disparate content. From the monasteries founded in Europe by the Irish monk Columbanus and other missionaries of Anglo-Saxon background, the *libri poenitentiales* spread all over the continent, where once again new versions emerged. The *Collectio Hibernensis* ("Hibernian [or Irish] Collection"), *c.* 700, used texts from Scripture, mainly from the Old Testament, for the first time in canonical collections, and texts from the Greek and Latin early Church Fathers in addition to canons. The *Liber ex lege Moysi* ("Book from the Law of Moses"), an Irish work, drew exclusively from the Pentateuch.

The Carolingian reform

The reorganization of the Frankish church began with the Carolingian reform in the middle of the 8th century. The canon law was set down especially in the *Capitularia ecclesiastica* ("Ecclesiastical Articles") of the prince, as well as in the *Capitularia missionum* ("Mission Articles"); *i.e.*, instructions given by the prince to the bishops and abbots who visited in his name. The *Capitularia* ("Short Articles") of Charlemagne, the founder of the Holy Roman Empire, and his son, the emperor Louis the Pious, were collected in 827 by the abbot Ansegisus. Following this model the bishops composed terse *capitula*, the oldest known diocesan statutes, for their clergy. The penance books were condemned and replaced by new ones that were more closely related to tradition. The reception of the *Dionysiana* and the *Hispana* is of importance for the transmission of the text and for the Carolingian cultural renaissance. In 774 Charlemagne received from Pope Adrian I a completed *Dionysiana*, the *Dionysiana-Hadriana*, which was accepted at a national synod in Aachen in 802, but it never was adopted as an official national code. About 800 the *Hadriana* and the *Hispana* were developed into a systematic whole, the *Dacheriana* (canonical collection named for its 17th-century publisher, a French scholar, Jean-Luc d'Achéry)—the principal source of the collections before 850—which was of influence until the Gregorian reform in the 11th century.

After Louis the Pious, the central power of the prince was increasingly divided among counts and barons. German law—which linked the right to govern with land ownership, without distinction between public and private law—expressed itself in the medieval forms of the system of private churches. This northern law looked upon dioceses, churches, and monasteries—with their rights and privileges—as lucrative possessions that deserved to be confiscated, by fraudulent means if necessary.

Such situations became the occasion *c.* 850 for the massive falsifications (*i.e.*, forgeries) of the Pseudo-Isidorian collections: the *Hispana Augustodunensis* ("Spanish Collection of Autun"), the *Capitula Angilramni* ("Chapters of Angilramnus," bishop of Metz), the *Capitularia Benedicti Levitae* ("Frankish Imperial Laws of Benedict the Levite," a fictitious name), and the *Pseudo-Isidorian Decretals.* The central goal of the anonymous Frankish group of authors of these collections was to strengthen the position of the bishops and to rectify the poor condition of ecclesiastical–state affairs. This was accomplished by means of falsified and forged texts that were attributed to the esteemed authority of the old law (*i.e.*, the popes) and the Carolingian princes. They did not have much influence on the real development of canon law, although later collections drew from them abundantly. Only the Magdeburg Centuriators, authors of the *Centuries*, a 16th-century Lutheran church history, denied the genuineness of all the decretals of pseudo-Isidore; the lack of authenticity of the other three works was discovered later.

Before 1000 several collections appeared: about 882 of them in northern Italy in the *Collectio Anselmo dedicata* ("Collection Dedicated to Anselm"), a papally oriented, systematic work; in Germany in the *Libri duo de synodalibus causis et disciplinis ecclesiasticis* ("Two Books Concerning Synodical Causes and Church Discipline") of Regino, abbot of Prüm (906), a manual for the bishops for the judicial interrogation of jurymen during a visitation; and in France in the collection of Abbon, abbot of Fleury (*c.* 996), which defended the legal position of his monastery against the king and bishop. Intended as a doctrinal book for the young cleric, the Decree of Burchard—bishop of Worms (bishop 1000–25)—became the canon-law manual in the cathedral schools and in the curias (administrative bureaucracies) of bishops and abbots in Germany, France, and Italy. Burchard was a promoter of moderate imperial reform. He did not reject the system of private churches; he only rejected the misuses proceeding from it, such as simony (buying or selling church offices) and the violation of celibacy.

The Gregorian reformation

The slogans of the Gregorian reformation, initiated by Pope Gregory VII, who reigned 1073–85, were *libertas Ecclesiae* ("liberty of the church") and *puritas Ecclesiae* ("purity of the church"): freedom from the system of private churches on all levels; freedom from papal dependence on the Roman nobility and emperor; freedom from dependence of the village priest on his *senior* (the beginning of the fight against investiture); and purity from simony and from the total collapse of celibacy (which was exhibited in the practice of hereditary parishes and bishoprics). Fundamental principles of Gregorian canon law included: only canon law that is given or approved by the pope is valid; papal legates (representatives) stand above the local hierarchies and preside over synods; for possession of every ecclesiastical office, choice and appointment by church authorities is demanded, along with the exclusion of lay investiture; every form of simony makes the appointment invalid; the faithful must boycott the services of married priests. New material was sought, especially for the confirmation of papal primacy, in archives and libraries. The principal new sources were: the *Breviarium* of Cardinal Atto (*c.* 1075), the *Dictatus Papae* ("Dictates of the Pope") of Gregory VII (*c.* 1075), the *Collectio 74 titulorum*, or "Collection of 74 Titles" (1074–76), the collection of Bishop Anselm of Lucca (*c.* 1083) and that of Cardinal Deusdedit (*c.* 1085), the *Liber de vita Christiana* ("Book Concerning the Christian Life") of Bonizo, bishop of Sutri (*c.* 1090).

The investiture battle over the conflicting asserted rights of lay or ecclesiastical officials to invest a church official with the symbols of his spiritual office ended in France, England, and Germany (Concordat of Worms, 1122) in compromises. Gregorian law, which now seems too strict, had to be reconciled with the established traditions. Ivo, bishop of Chartres from 1091 to 1116, contributed to the settlement of the investiture problem by his political activities; his extended correspondence; and his three law collections, *Tripartita* ("Tripartite Collection"), *Decretum* ("Decrees"; *i.e.*, collection of decrees or canons), and *Panormia* (collections of "All the Laws"), the last two practically a fusion of Burchard's Decree with Gregorian law. The famous Prologue, written by Ivo for either the *Decretum* or the *Panormia*, indicated for the first time a method by which the bishop must handle the conflicting strict and liberal texts, with *justitia* ("justice") or *misericordia* ("mercy"). Bernold of Constance, in his little tractates, written between 1070 and 1091, listed several criteria for the reconciliation of conflicting texts: authenticity of the text; identity of the author; difference between law, counsel, and dispensation, between universal and local law, of time and place; different meanings of a word. A Liège (Belgium) canon lawyer, Alger, in his *Liber de misericordia et justitia*, or "Book Concerning Mercy and Justice" (*c.* 1105), applied Ivo's criteria to the problem of the effect of sacraments administered by heretics and persons guilty of simony. The great medieval theologian Abelard developed the method of reconciling texts that are for or against a theological position in his *Sic et non*, or "Yes and No," (1115–17). The same methods were applied by the first writers of glosses (commentaries or interpretations) at the law school in Bologna on the *Pandecta* of Justinian, which was rediscovered *c.* 1070.

The Corpus Juris Canonici (c. 1140–c. 1500). *The "Decree of Gratian."* About 1140 the monk John Gratian completed his *Concordia discordantium canonum* ("Harmony of Contradictory Laws"), later called the *Decretum Gratiani* ("Decree of Gratian"); it became not only the definitive canonical collection of the entire preceding tradition, but also a systematic application of the scholastic method (utilizing reason) to all legal material. The *Concordia* dealt with the sources of the law, ordinations, elections, simony, law of procedure, ecclesiastical property, monks, heretics, schismatics, marriage, penance, and sacraments and sacramentals. Primitive as it was, it provided a foundation for systematic compilation of the legal material by the canonists, and for the expansion of decretal law. It provided a basis for the education in canon law which began in the schools of Bologna, Paris, Orléans, Canterbury, Oxford, Padua, and elsewhere. It was accepted everywhere in the ecclesiastical administration of justice and government.

The Corpus Juris Canonici. From the time that the Gregorian reformation introduced a more centralized ecclesiastical administration, the number of appeals to Rome and the number of papal decisions mounted. New papal laws and decisions, called decretals, first added to Gratian's *Concordia*, were soon gathered into separate collections, of which the best known are the *Quinque compilationes antiquae* ("Five Ancient Compilations").

Collections of decretals

The first, the *Breviarium extravagantium* ("Compendium of Decretals Circulating Outside"; *i.e.*, not yet collected) of Bernard of Pavia, introduced a system inspired by the codification of Justinian, a division of the material into five books, briefly summarized in the phrase *judex* ("judge"), *judicium* ("trial"), *clerus* ("clergy"), *connubium* ("marriage"), *crimen* ("crime"). Each book was subdivided into titles and these in turn into *capitula*, or canons. This system was taken over by all subsequent collections of decretals. These compilations were the foremost source of the *Liber Extra* ("Book Outside"; *i.e.*, of decretals not in Gratian's Decree) or *Liber decretalium Gregorii IX* ("Book of Decretals of Gregory IX"), composed by Raymond of Peñafort, a Spanish canonist, and promulgated on September 5, 1234, as the exclusive codex for all of canon law after Gratian. On March 3, 1298, Pope Boniface VIII promulgated *Liber Sextus* ("Book Six"), composed of official collections of Innocent IV, Gregory X, and Nicholas III, and private collections and decretals of his own, as the exclusive codex for the canon law since the *Liber Extra*. The *Constitutiones Clementinae* ("Constitutions of Clement") of Pope Clement V, most of which were enacted at the Council of Vienne (1311–12), were promulgated on October 25, 1317, by Pope John XXII, but they were not an exclusive collection. The *Decretum Gratiani*, the *Liber Extra*, *Liber Sextus*, and *Constitutiones Clementinae*, with the addition of two private collections, the *Extravagantes* of John XXII and the *Extravagantes communes* ("Decretals Commonly Circulating"), were printed and published together for the first time in Paris in 1500. This entire collection soon received the name *Corpus Juris Canonici* ("Body of Canon Law").

The science of canon law was developed by the writers of glosses, the commentators on the Decree of Gratian (decretists), and the commentators on the collections of decretals (decretalists). Their notations, or glosses, were based on the system used by Gratian: next to the texts of canons parallel texts were noted, then conflicting ones, followed by a *solutio* ("solution"), again with text references. In connection with this the glosses of other canonists were also introduced. In this way the *apparatus glossarum*, continuous commentaries on the entire book, arose. The *glossa ordinaria* ("ordinary explanation") on the different parts of the *Corpus Juris Canonici* was the apparatus that was used universally in the schools. After the classical period of the glossators (12th–14th centuries), terminated by the work of a lay Italian canonist, John Andreae (*c.* 1348), followed that of the postglossators. In the absence of new legislation in the time of the Babylonian Captivity (1309–77)—named after the 6th-century-BC biblical captivity or exile of the Jews to Babylon for 70 years (traditionally)—when the papacy was situated at Avignon, France, and the Great Schism (1378–1417), when there were at least two popes reigning simultaneously, the commentaries on decretals continued, but with a larger production of special tracts; *e.g.*, regarding the laws of benefices and marriage and of *consilia* (advice about concrete legal questions).

From the Council of Trent (1545–63) to the Codex Juris Canonici (1917). *The end of decretal law.* Toward the end of the Middle Ages decretal law ceased to govern. The medieval Christian society (called the *Christianitas*) became politically and ecclesiastically divided, according to the principle of *cuius regio, illius et religio* (*i.e.*, the religion of the prince is the religion of the land). In Protestant areas the former Roman Catholic church buildings and benefices were taken over by other churches; and even in the lands that remained Catholic the churches found themselves in an isolated position as secularization forced the churches to reorganize. With the end of the medieval social system known as feudalism, canon law dealing with benefices, chapters, and monasteries, which were closely bound to the feudal structure, changed. The territorial, material, and economic character of canon law and the decentralization allied with it disappeared. The decision of the reform councils from Pisa (1409) until the fifth Lateran Council (1512–17) affected, in particular, benefices, papal reservations, taxes, and other such ecclesiastical matters. In the same period various concordats (agreements) permitted the princes to intervene in the issue of ecclesiastical benefices and property. Canon law took on a more defensive character with prohibitions regarding books, mixed marriages, participation of Catholics in Protestant worship and vice versa, education of the clergy in seminaries, and other such areas of concern.

At the Catholic reform Council of Trent (1545–63) a new foundation for the further development of canon law was expressed in the *Capita de reformatione* ("Articles Concerning Reform"), which were discussed and accepted in 10 of the 25 sessions. Papal primacy was not only dogmatically affirmed against conciliarism (the view that councils are more authoritative than the pope) but was also juridically strengthened in the conduct and implementation of the council. The central position of the bishops was recovered, over against the decentralization that had been brought about by the privileges and exemptions of chapters, monasteries, fraternities, and other corporate bodies that sprang from Germanic law, as well as caused by the rights granted to patrons. In practically all matters of reform the bishops received authority *ad instar legati S. Sedis* ("like delegates of the Holy See"). Strict demands were made for admission to ordination and offices; measures were taken against luxurious living, nepotism, and the neglect of the residence obligation; training of the clergy in seminaries was prescribed; prescriptions were given about pastoral care, schools for the young, diocesan and provincial synods, confession, and marriage; the right to benefices was purified of misuse; the formalistic law of procedure was simplified.

The Congregation of Cardinals

The council gave the duty of execution of the reform to the pope. On January 26, 1564, Pius IV confirmed the decisions, reserved to himself their interpretation and execution, and on August 2, 1564, established the Congregation of the Council for that purpose. The congregations of cardinals, which proceeded from the former permanent commissions of the *consistorium* (the assembly of the pope with the College of Cardinals), were organized by Pope Sixtus V in 1587. Since then the administrative apparatus of the Curia has consisted of congregations of cardinals together with courts and offices. This apparatus made it possible for the Latin Church to acquire a uniform canon law system that was developed in detail.

Law for the missions. The medieval church knew nothing of "missions." Expansion of the church brought with it expansion of the ordinary hierarchical episcopal structure. This was true also for the new colonies under the right of patronage of the Spanish and Portuguese kings. In the other mission areas and in the areas taken over by the Protestants, where the realization of the episcopal structure and the decretal law adopted by Trent was not possible, the organization of mission activity was taken from missionaries and religious orders and given to the Holy See. The congregation *De Propaganda Fide* ("For the Propagation of the Faith") was established for this purpose in 1622. Missionaries received their mandate from Rome; the administration was given over to apostolic vicars (bishops of territories having no ordinary hierarchy) and prefects (having episcopal powers, but not necessarily bishops) who were directly dependent on the *Propaganda*, from which they received precisely described faculties. A new uniform mission law was created, without noteworthy native influence; this sometimes led to conflict, such as the Chinese rites controversy in the 17th and 18th centuries over the compatibility of rites honouring Confucius and ancestors with Christian rites.

LATE DEVELOPMENTS IN ROMAN CATHOLIC CANON LAW

The first Vatican Council (1869–70) strengthened the central position of the papacy in the constitutional law of the church by means of its dogmatic definition of papal primacy. Disciplinary canons were not enacted at the council; but the desire expressed by many bishops that canon law be codified did have influence on the emergence and content of the code of canon law.

The Codex Juris Canonici (1917). Since the closing off of the *Corpus Juris Canonici* there had been no official or noteworthy private collection of the canon law, except for the constitutions of Benedict XIV (pope 1740–58). The material was spread out in the collections of the *Corpus Juris Canonici* and in the generally very incomplete private publications of the *acta* of popes, of general and local councils, and the various Roman congregations and legal organs, which made canon law into something unmanageable and uncertain. The need for codification was recognized even more because of the fact that since the end of the 18th century, secular law had undergone a period of great codification. Several private attempts to do this had met with little success.

Preparations for reorganization of the Code of Canon Law. On March 19, 1904, Pius X announced his intention to complete the codification, and he named a commission of 16 cardinals, of which he himself was chairman. Bishops and university faculties were asked to cooperate and to make their desires known. The schemas of the five books that were prepared in Rome—universal norms, personal law, law of things, penal law, and procedural law—were proposed in the years 1912–14 to all those who would ordinarily be summoned to an ecumenical council, and with their observations were then reworked in the cardinals' commission. The entire undertaking and all the drafts were under the papal seal of secrecy and, as a matter of fact, were not published. Meanwhile, Pius X introduced various reforms that were to a great degree the results of the commission's work. In July 1916 the preparations for the *Codex Juris Canonici* (Code of Canon Law) were completed. The code was promulgated on Pentecost Sunday, May 27, 1917, and became effective on Pentecost Sunday, May 19, 1918.

The Code of Canon Law. In contrast to all earlier official collections this code was a complete and exclusive codification of all universal church law then binding in the Latin Church. Out of fear of political difficulties, a systematic handling of public church law, especially what concerned the relations between church and state, was omitted. Its main purpose is to offer a codification of the law, and only incidentally adaptation, and so it introduces relatively little that is new legislation. The 2,414 canons are divided into five books that no longer followed the system of the collections of decretals but did follow that of the Perugian canonist Paul Lancelotti's *Institutiones juris canonici* ("Institutions of Canon Law"), Perugia, 1563, which in turn went back to the division of the 2nd-century Roman lawyer Gaius' *Institutiones: personae* ["persons"], *res* ["things"], *actiones* ["actions"], and is based on the fundamental idea of Roman law; *i.e.*, subjective right.

Areas of the Code of Canon Law

Book I, general norms, deals with the area covered by the codex, the relation between old and new law, laws, customs, the way of reckoning time, rescripts, privileges, and dispensations. Book II, about persons, deals with persons in general, corporate bodies, clerics, religious, and laity. Book III, about things, deals with sacraments and sacramentals, consecrated places and times, worship, church teachings, authority, benefices, church property, and foundations. Book IV, on processes, deals with general and special trials, beatification and canonization, and special procedures. Book V, on crimes and punishments, deals with crimes, punishments in general, special punishments, and punishments for extraordinary crimes. In some editions the sources that were used by the editors are indicated at the individual canons. Since the publication of the codex these sources belong to the history of the law. Older general and particular law, in conflict with the codex, has been given up; and, insofar as it is not in conflict with it, serves only as a means for interpreting the code. The old law of custom in conflict with the code and expressly reprobated by it is rendered null; when not reprobated and 100 years old or immemorial it can be allowed by ordinaries for pressing reasons. Acquired rights and concordats in force remain in force. With this change, an independent science of the history of canon law has become necessary, in addition to the dogmatic canonical science of canon law on the basis of the code.

Canon law after the Codex Juris Canonici. In order to ensure the unity of the codification and the law, a commission of cardinals was established on September 15, 1917, for the authentic interpretation of the new code. At the same time it was decided that the cardinals' congregations should no longer make new general decrees, but only instructions for the carrying out of the prescriptions of the code. Should a general decree appear necessary, it was determined, the commission would formulate new canons and insert them into the code. Neither of these decisions was carried out. Only two canons were altered and congregations have promulgated numerous general decrees. New papal legislation has complemented and altered the law of the code. The law on judicial procedure was extended by instructions of the Congregation for the Sacraments to the diocesan courts in cases concerning annulment of ordinations and its attached obligations and of marriages; the Congregation for Religious gave detailed prescriptions for five-year reports of pontifical religious institutes and the papal cloister for religious women; an excommunication *latae sententiae* ("of a sentence already pronounced"; *i.e.*, incurred immediately upon the commission of the offense) was imposed by the Congregation of the Council on violations of the prohibitions against business engagement for clerics and religious, and the Sacred Penitentiary reserved the excommunications of married priests most strictly to the Holy See. The *responsa* of the commission for the interpretation of the code and the documents of the Roman Curia concerning canon law are published in the order of the canons in various private collections. The Sacred Roman Rota (court) developed an extensive jurisprudence regarding marriage law: every year an official publication of the verdicts of the tenth year previous appears. The numerous commentaries on the code are principally concerned with the exegesis (critical interpretation) of the text of the canons; this is prescribed in seminaries and faculties of canon law as the basic text for instruction.

The Eastern churches in union with Rome. The principle for the Catholic Eastern churches (churches in union with the Roman Catholic Church) is that they retain their own traditions in liturgy and church order, insofar as these are not considered to be in conflict with the norms taken by Rome to be divine law. In 1929 Pius XI set up a commission of cardinals for the codification of canon law valid for all uniate churches in the East. In the following year a commission was established for the preparation of the codification and one for the collection of the sources of Eastern law, in which experts of all rites were involved. These collections were published in three series, begun respectively in 1930, 1935, and 1942.

In 1935 the preparatory commission became the Pontifical Commission for the Redaction of the *Codex Juris Canonici Orientalis* ("Body of Oriental Canon Law"). The cooperation of all Eastern ordinaries (bishops, patriarchs, and others having jurisdictions) was requested, and the drafts of the various documents were sent to them. Since then four parts have been published: in 1949, on marriage law; in 1952, on the law for monks and other religious, on ecclesiastical properties, and a title *De Verborum Significatione* ("Concerning the Meaning of Words"), a series of definitions of legal terms used in the canons; and in 1957, on constitutional law, especially of the clergy. The still incomplete codification follows the Latin code with the assimilation of the authentic interpretation and with textual corrections, and also with the insertion of the general law proper to the Eastern churches, including the Orthodox churches, regarding the patriarchs and their synods, marriage law, the law of religious, and other matters. The promulgation was made in Latin, with official translations in Greek, Slavic, Arabic, and Egyptian. The Catholic Eastern churches came under the Congregation for the Eastern Churches that was established on January 6, 1862, by Pius IX as part of the *Propaganda Fide*, and was made independent by Benedict XV on May 1, 1917, and expanded considerably by Pius XI on March 25, 1938. Roman legislation as well as the jurisdiction of a congregation of the Roman Curia was criticized as being incompatible with the traditional autonomy of the Eastern churches in legislation and administration.

VATICAN II AND POSTCONCILIAR CANON LAW

Vatican II. Fundamental to the development of canon law in the Roman Catholic Church is the second Vatican Council's (October 11, 1962–December 8, 1965) vision of the church as the people of God. In this connection the former concept of the church as *societas perfecta* (the "perfect society"), founded by Christ through the mission of the Apostles and their successors, to which one belongs through subjection to the hierarchy, is replaced by a vision of the church as a community in which all possess the sacramental mission to live and proclaim the Gospel, and all have a function in the service of the whole. The legislative and administrative functions remain related to the hierarchy, but this is much more expressly seen as a service for the religious life of the community. The idea of collegiality, resting on the recognition of the vocation received by each one from the Lord, works itself out in the relationship existing among the bishops and with the pope, of the bishops with the clergy, and of the clergy with the laity. Related to this is a tendency to co-responsibility and the democratization of the church structure. Independence has been returned to the Eastern uniate churches, and in regard to their patriarchal synods, greater autonomy is set forth for the bishops in their own dioceses and for the episcopal conferences in their territory, and also an autonomy for the laity to exercise individually and collectively the Christian Mission proper to them; viz., to bring the spirit of Christ also into the secular life of mankind. The right of clergy and laity to a share in the leadership of bishops and pope is recognized. The vision of the people of God as *sacramentum mundi*, a sign of redemption for all mankind, gave a new insight into the relationships with the Protestant churches, the other world religions, and the nonreligious atheistic and humanistic movements. In this view, freedom of religion and philosophy became the most fundamental right of man.

The church and collegiality

Postconciliar legislation. From a schematically chronological survey of the principal conciliar and postconciliar legislation a new era apparently began for canon law—*e.g.*, in 1960, establishment of the Secretariate for Promoting Christian Unity; in 1963, various faculties, previously reserved to Rome, were given to the bishops; in 1964, reorganization of the papal commission for communications media; also in 1964: establishment of the Secretariate for Non-Christians, lifting of the prohibition against cremation, and various faculties, previously reserved to Rome, given to the superiors general of religious institutes. Other legislative changes indicating a new era included several regulations that could not have been proposed with any possibility of their being accepted prior to Vatican II: *e.g.*, in 1965, pre-eminence in the College of Cardinals is given to Eastern patriarchs, after deacon and subdeacon and after the cardinals of the dioceses of the province of Rome; also in 1965, establishment of the Secretariate for Non-Believers, and the Holy Office (formerly the Inquisition) became the

Canon law after 1960

Congregation for the Doctrine of the Faith, with emphasis on the positive fostering of theological research; in 1966, greatly reduced prescriptions for fasting and abstinence were adopted, the Index of prohibited books became a moral guide instead of obligatory law, and in implementation of the conciliar degree on the episcopal office, the principle according to which ordinaries (*e.g.*, bishops) dispense from universal laws only when this is allowed by law or special faculties was replaced by the principle that ordinaries can always dispense unless it is explicitly reserved to Rome—and such reserved dispensations in question are indicated. In addition to these changes, still further canonical regulations were proposed and accepted as follows: in 1966, new regulations for mixed marriages were adopted, and norms were established for the implementation of the conciliar decrees on the office of bishops and priests, religious life, missionary activity, personal and material aid to needy churches, salaries and social insurance for priests and others in the service of the church, introduction of priests' councils and pastoral councils of priests, religious (*i.e.*, monks and nuns), and laity as advisory groups for bishops, international episcopal conferences and their mutual relationships, and other concerns. From 1967 to 1970 more changes were made in canonical regulations—*e.g.*, in 1967, total revision of the norms for indulgences, establishment in the Roman Curia of the council of laymen and the study commission, *Justitia et Pax* ("Justice and Peace"), new dispensation rights for Eastern bishops, directory for ecumenical cooperation with Christian churches, regulation of the office of diaconate, also for married men, reorganization of the Roman Curia; in 1970, a mandate to the secretary of state to discuss with the world episcopacy the question of celibacy and ordination of married men in areas that need priests, and new rules for mixed marriages.

Characteristics of the new law are: a searching for structures to allow all members of the church to have a voice in ecclesiastical decision making; decentralization and autonomy of local churches; regulations from Rome are kept to the general, with ample room for local adaptation; the giving up of the Index and the prohibition of cremation, the minimal fasting regulations and so forth, all point to the emancipation of personal religious life from laws and sanctions. In addition, new regulations are to be enacted only after extensive and open inquiry and test by experience, with possibilities for experimentation. In place of regulations of religious behaviour, canon law may be becoming an ordering of the cooperation of all members of the Roman Catholic Church for the realization of its mission in the world.

Revision of the Code of Canon Law. On January 25, 1959, John XXIII announced the revision of the church's code. On March 28, 1963, he set up a commission of cardinals for that purpose. On April 17, 1964, Paul VI named the first consultants. No publicity has been given to the commission's work, but the first episcopal synod (September 30–October 4, 1967) gave its approval to a document in which several principles for the revision were indicated (*Principia quae codicis juris canonici recognitionem dirigant*, or "Principles Which Guide the Recognition of the Code of Canon Law"): the juridical character of the code ought to be preserved and not, as some wished, be limited to a rule for faith and morals; canon law for the area of each one's personal conscience, should be maintained, but conflicts between law for conscience and public law ought to be avoided, especially in marriage and penal law; as a means to stimulate pastoral work it is recommended that the laws be expressed in a spirit of love, fairness, and humanity; no binding prescriptions are to be given where admonition and counsel suffice; pastoral workers are to be given more discretionary powers and greater freedom is to be given to bishops, especially in mission areas; laws are to be such that ample possibility is given for local adaptation, carrying through the principle of subsidiarity (*i.e.*, that nothing should be committed to higher organs that can be accomplished by individuals or lesser or subordinate bodies), however, with care to retain the unity of law and jurisdiction; regulation of administrative jurisdiction and in principle public jurisdiction; distinction of legislative, administrative, and judicial functions; limitation of punishments; and of punishments incurred immediately upon commission of the offense to very few and very serious crimes. On May 28, 1968, the commission approved the following preliminary division of the new codex:

Division of the new codex

I. Sources of the law (law and custom); the activities of government concerning the legal position of persons (dispensation, privilege, and similar matters)
II. The people of God
  A. Persons in general (duties and rights of all the faithful); legal persons (also right of association)
  B. Persons in particular or various states: clerics, laity, religious, and religious institutes
  C. Hierarchy, or church government
III. Ecclesiastical offices
  A. The teaching office
  B. Priestly office; sacraments and sacramentals, liturgy, consecrated places and times
  C. Pastoral office: administrative organs and the exercise of government in the universal and in the local church
IV. Ecclesiastical property
V. Penal law
VI. Protection of the law
  A. Civil and penal judicial procedure
  B. Administrative procedure

The schema of a *lex ecclesiae fundamentalis* ("fundamental law of the church"), a kind of constitution for the church embracing the fundamental principles of church structure for the Latin and uniate churches in the East, was sent in 1969 to the cardinals of the commission and to the members of the theological commission of the Congregation for the Doctrine of the Faith with the request that observations be submitted before December 31, 1969. A revised text was submitted to the synod of bishops in 1971 but was overwhelmingly rejected and returned to the commission for further revision.

ANGLICAN CANON LAW

The Anglican Communion embraces the Church of England and its daughter churches. Since the submission of the clergy demanded by King Henry VIII in 1534 and the Act of Supremacy in 1534, in which the Parliament recognized him as supreme head of the Church of England and which was renewed by Queen Elizabeth I, the law of the English Church rests on the supremacy of the prince or of the Parliament. It is theoretically accepted that outside the law determined by the English synods in the ancient independent national churches, only the principles of the general canon law—*jus ecclesiasticum commune* ("common ecclesiastical law")—are binding, but other norms, promulgated by popes and councils, are accepted only to the extent that they were accepted by English ecclesiastical or secular courts. For practical purposes the development of church law in the English Church is held by some canonists (usually Roman Catholic) not to be canon law but the ecclesiastical law of the state. The hierarchy has the power to ordain by virtue of the apostolic succession which was preserved—according to the Anglican view—by the consecration of Matthew Parker as archbishop of Canterbury (1559), but it does not possess legislative authority. The ecclesiastical provinces are administered by convocations of Canterbury and York, consisting of an upper house of bishops and a lower house of clergy. In 1919 a Church Assembly was established by the Enabling Act; the assembly consists of three houses (of bishops, members of the convocations, and laity) with the authority to make proposals relating to any matter concerning the Church of England—with the exception of dogmas of faith—and to present these proposals to the ecclesiastical committee of Parliament. If the committee agrees on a positive report, then the Parliament can approve or reject the proposal but not amend it; if both houses accept it, then it acquires the force of law by royal approval. Lambeth Conferences, which have been held approximately every ten years since 1867 at the London palace of the archbishop of Canterbury and which involve all Anglican bishops from all over the world, do not have legislative authority.

Ecclesiastical law of the state

Depending somewhat on Anglican canon law is the Church of South India, a union of Protestant church bodies in South Asia (the Anglican Church of India, Burma, and Ceylon; the Methodist province of South India; the South India United Church—Presbyterian, Congregationalist, and Dutch Reformed), founded in 1947. According to the constitution of the new Church of South India, at the end of an interim period of 30 years canonical reforms of that former mission area are to be anticipated.

Canon law has had a long history of development throughout the Christian era. Not a static body of laws, it reflects social, political, economic, cultural, and ecclesiastical changes that have taken place in the past two millennia. During periods of social and cultural upheaval the church has not remained unaffected by its environment. Thus, canon law may be expected to be involved in the far-reaching changes that have come to be anticipated in the modern world. (P.Hu.)

BIBLIOGRAPHY. The literature on the subject in all its branches is very elaborate, and this is particularly true of the canon law of the Roman Catholic Church. The articles "Law (Christian, Western)" and "Law (Christian, Eastern)" by A. FORTESCUE and "Law (Christian, Anglican)" by A.J. MACLEAN in *Hastings Encyclopedia of Religion and Ethics*, give concise statements of information with references for further study. For an extended study of the history of Western canon law, see A.G. CICOGNANI, *Canon Law*, authorized English version (1934). A fine discussion of legislation in the Roman Catholic Church is contained in R. METZ, *What Is Canon Law?* (1960); brief surveys of the current *Codex Juris Canonici* will be found in T.L. BOUSCAREN and A.C. ELLIS, *Canon Law: A Text and Commentary*, 4th ed. (1966); and in J.A. ABBO and J.D. HANNAN, *The Sacred Canons,* 2nd ed., 2 vol. (1960); while the post-code legislation and interpretation is collected by T.L. BOUSCAREN, *Canon Law Digest*, 4 vol. (1934–58), which is kept up-to-date by annual loose-leaf supplements. The Catholic University of America has published, under the general title of "Canon Law Studies," numerous doctoral theses dealing with particular canons. The sources used in drafting the Latin code have been published by the Vatican Press under the title *Fontes Juris Canonici*; publication of the *Fontes Juris Canonici Orientalis* was begun in 1930. ARTHUR VOOBUS, *Syrische Kanonessammlungen: Ein Beitrag zur Quellenkunde. Westsyrische Originalurkunde 1A-B* (1970–71), discusses the recently discovered canons of the West Syrian churches.

Canova, Antonio

Antonio Canova, an outstanding Neoclassical sculptor, was as important in the development of the Neoclassical style as Jacques-Louis David in painting. Canova's domination of European sculpture at the turn of the 18th century and the beginning of the 19th is reflected in countless adulations in memoirs, poems, and newspapers. "Sublime," "superb," and "marvellous" are adjectives frequently found describing Canova's work in his lifetime. Such was his contemporary fame that Catherine the Great invited him to Russia in 1794, although he declined.

Canova was born on November 1, 1757, in Possagno (Asolo), near Venice, the son of a stonemason. His father died in 1761, and the boy was reared by his grandfather, also a stonemason. Under the protection of a Venetian senator, Canova, at the age of 11, went to work with the sculptor Giuseppe Bernardi (called Torretti), who lived at Pagnano (Asolo). In the same year (1768) Bernardi moved his studio from provincial Pagnano to Venice, and Canova went with him. The boy helped his master, executed a few humble commissions on his own, and, as was customary at the time, studied classical art and drew from the nude.

In 1775 Canova set up his own studio in Venice. In 1779 he sculpted "Daedalus and Icarus," which had been commissioned by Pisani, procurator of the Venetian republic; it was Canova's first important work. Somewhat Rococo in style, the figures were considered so realistic that the sculptor was accused of making plaster casts from life models.

Canova was in Rome in 1779 and 1780, where he met the leading artists of the period, including the Scottish painter-dealer Gavin Hamilton, who directed Canova's studies toward a more profound understanding of the antique. Canova visited Naples and the ancient archaeological sites of Herculaneum, Pompeii, and Paestum. He returned briefly to Venice, but in 1781 he was again in Rome, where he was to spend most of the rest of his life. There he became an active and influential figure in the artistic life of the city and was always willing to help young artists and find them patrons.

Papal commissions

In 1783 Canova received an important commission for the tomb of Pope Clement XIV in the Roman church of Santi Apostoli. When displayed in 1787 crowds flocked to see it. That same year he was commissioned to execute a tomb in St. Peter's to Pope Clement XIII. Completed in 1792, its general treatment shows a more developed understanding of the classical aesthetic of antiquity than his monument to Clement XIV. Subsequent tombs were increasingly Neoclassical and combined restraint with sentiment, in a manner akin to the work of Canova's English contemporary, John Flaxman.

The French invasion of Rome in 1798 sent Canova northward. In Vienna he worked on a funerary monument to Maria Christina (1798–1805) in the Augustinerkirche. In 1802, at the pope's instigation, he accepted Napoleon's invitation to go to Paris, where he became court sculptor and considerably influenced French art. He spent part of 1802 in Paris working on a bust of Napoleon, and in 1806 Joseph Bonaparte commissioned an equestrian statue of Napoleon.

By courtesy of the Bundesdenkmalamt, Vienna; photograph, Eva Frodl-Kraft

Tomb of Maria Christina, marble by Antonio Canova, 1798–1805. In the Augustinerkirche, Vienna.

About 1807 he finished one of his most famous works in which he shows Napoleon's sister, Pauline Borghese, reclining almost naked on a couch as "Venus Victrix"—a fusion of classical goddess and contemporary portrait. In 1811 he completed two colossal statues of Napoleon (Brera, Milan, and Wellington Museum, London), in which the emperor is shown as a heroic classical nude. In the Napoleonic period he had also begun carving some of his most expressive and ambitious pieces, "Perseus with Medusa's Head" (1801) and the "Pugilists" (1802), both in the Vatican.

Collection of treasures for the papal state

Canova in 1805 was appointed inspector general of fine arts and antiquities of the papal state. In 1810 he was made president of the Accademia di S. Luca in Rome (a position he was to hold for life). After having visited Paris to arrange for the return of Italian art treasures plundered by the French, he went to London (1815) to give his opinion on the Elgin Marbles. The success of his mission in Paris led to the reward of the title of marquis of Ischia by the pope. While in London, the Prince Regent, later George IV, commissioned a life-size group of "Venus and Mars." Other late commissions included the Stuart monument in St. Peter's (1819), the alteration and completion of the equestrian Napoleon into Charles III of Naples (1819), and a monument of George Washington (1820; destroyed by fire in 1830), idealized in Roman costume, erected at Raleigh, North Carolina, in 1821.

Canova was also a painter. But his paintings (mostly in the Gipsoteca Canoviana at Possagno) constitute a minor part of his works and generally are poor in quality. They include a few portraits and recreations of antique paintings discovered at Herculaneum.

Canova died in Venice on October 13, 1822, and was buried at Possagno in a temple, designed by himself in imitation of the Pantheon in Rome.

MAJOR WORKS

SCULPTURE: "Eurydice" (1773; Museo Civico Correr, Venice); "Orpheus" (1776; Museo Civico Correr, Venice); "Daedalus and Icarus" (1779; Museo Civico Correr, Venice); "Apollo" (1779; Accademia, Venice); "Theseus and the Minotaur" (1781–82; Victoria and Albert Museum, London); tomb of Clement XIV (1783–87; SS. Apostoli, Rome); tomb of Clement XIII (1787–92; St. Peter's, Rome); "Cupid and Psyche" (1792; Louvre, Paris); "Monument to Angelo Emo" (1792–95; Museo Storico Navale, Venice); "Hercules and Lichas" (model 1796, marble, 1815; Galleria Nazionale d'Arte Moderna, Rome); "Perseus with Medusa's Head" (1801; Vatican, Belvedere, Rome); "Pugilists" (1802; Vatican, Belvedere, Rome); "Napoleon As First Consul" (1802; Gipsoteca Canoviana, Possagno); "Monument to Vittorio Alfieri" (1805–10; Sta. Croce, Florence); "Pauline Borghese as Venus Victrix" (1805–07; Borghese Gallery, Rome); "Dancing Girl with Her Hands on Her Hips" (1806–10; Hermitage, Leningrad); "Dancing Girl with Her Finger on Her Chin" (1806–10; Galleria Nazionale d'Arte Antica, Rome); "Venus Italica" (1812; Pitti Palace, Florence); "The Three Graces" (1813–16; Hermitage, Leningrad); "Venus and Mars" (1816–22; Buckingham Palace, London); "Theseus and the Centaur" (1819; Kunsthistorisches Museum, Vienna); "Endymion" (1819–21; Chatsworth House, Derbyshire).

BIBLIOGRAPHY. No comprehensive, up-to-date biography in English exists. The best general studies are in Italian; ELENA BASSI, *Canova* (1943); and ANTONIO MUNOZ, *Canova* (1957). ISABELLA ALBRIZZI, *Opere di Canova* (1809, and subsequent editions; Eng. trans., 1824), is still useful. Good specialized studies include: ELENA BASSI, *La Gipsoteca di Possagno: Sculture e Dipinti di Antonio Canova* (1957) and *Il Museo civico di Bassano: I disegni di Antonio Canova* (1959); and HANS OST, *Ein Skizzenbuch Antonio Canovas* (1970).

(D.I.)

Canton

The largest city of southern China, Canton lies at the head of the Chu Chiang (Pearl River) Delta, more than 90 miles inland from the South China Sea. Although the city is commonly known as Canton to Westerners—a name that derives from that of Kwangtung Province, of which it is the capital—the correct name of the city since the 3rd century AD has been Kuang-chou (Guang-zhou in the Pin-yin romanization). Because of its position at the meeting point of inland rivers and the sea, it has long been one of China's main commercial and trading centres. It has served as a doorway for foreign influence since the 3rd century AD and was the first Chinese port to be regularly visited by European traders. The city is also a historic centre of learning and, as the birthplace of the Chinese Nationalist leader Sun Yat-sen, it was the cradle of the Chinese revolution. Its 3,100,000 inhabitants are known as Cantonese and speak their own Chinese dialect. The limits of the municipality have been enlarged since 1949 to incorporate adjoining countries.

Since 1949 Canton has continued to be of great economic importance. Its harbour has been dredged, industry has been introduced, and trade has increased. The city has undergone a vast public works program and is now beautiful as well as busy. (For related articles, see HSI CHIANG [RIVER] and KWANGTUNG.)

History. The earliest known inhabitants of the Canton area were the Pai Yüeh, a Tai, or Shan, people. At the beginning of the Western Chou dynasty (*c.* 1122–771 BC), their chief built a walled town, known as Nan-wu Ch'eng, on Yüeh-hsiu Shan (Yüeh-hsiu Mountain) in the northern section of the present-day city. In 887 BC the town was taken by the mid-Yangtze kingdom of Ch'u and was known as Wu-yang Ch'eng (City of Five Goats).

Non-Chinese origins

Under the Ch'in dynasty (221–206 BC) Canton was made the capital of Nan-hai prefecture. Upon the fall of the Ch'in General Chao T'o (?–137 BC), who had been appointed to a command in 215 BC under Jen Hsiao, with whom he subdued the wild southern tribes), established an autonomous state known as Nan Yüeh, which was, however, annexed in 111 BC by the Han dynasty (206 BC–AD 220). For the next 300 years Chinese assimilation of the Yüeh people proceeded, and integration of the region into the empire took firm root.

During the four centuries from the Three Kingdoms to the founding of the T'ang dynasty (AD 220–618), when North China was overrun by "barbarian" invaders, Canton remained an integral part of the Chinese regimes based in Nanking. During this period the city grew in wealth and population; Buddhist temples were erected, and a flourishing community was maintained by Arab and Hindu traders. Peace and prosperity were further augmented under the T'ang dynasty (618–907). A mosque was built in the 7th century by Muslim traders from the Middle East. Canton's strong identification with this period is attested by the fact that the Cantonese people call themselves "the people of the T'ang" even today. An auxiliary wall and settlement were built on Yü Hill, but the city suffered considerable destruction during the civil strife at the end of the dynasty.

Under the Sung dynasty (960–1126) the increase in Canton's population and the growth of foreign trade made it necessary to enlarge the city. A second auxiliary wall and settlement were constructed on Fan Hill in the late 11th century. With the settlements on the twin hills, the city took on the name Fan-yü (hence the name of the county in which Canton is now located). Under the Southern Sung (1126–1279) Chinese seamen and traders sailed to Southeast Asia, thus opening the way for Chinese emigration abroad in subsequent ages. In the late 13th century and throughout the 14th, many Chinese families from North China moved into the Kwangtung region in the wake of the Mongol conquest. A booming economy resulted as the Yüan rulers (1279–1368) encouraged maritime trade and kept Chinese–Mongol race relations under control.

Under the Ming dynasty (1368–1644) the city underwent considerable rebuilding and expansion. In 1380 the Fan and Yü hills were razed, and the old town and the two auxiliary districts were combined into one large walled city. In 1535 an outer wall was added to incorporate the new commercial districts on the north bank of the Chu Chiang. Meanwhile, the pattern of foreign trade changed: the supremacy of the Arabs ended with the coming of the Europeans. The Portuguese sent their first embassy to Canton in the early 1500s, followed by the Dutch and the British in the 17th century.

Period of expansion

Canton came under the rule of the Ch'ing (Manchu) dynasty from 1644 to 1911. Recognizing the importance of the city, the government made it the capital of the Viceroyalty of Kwangtung and Kwangsi. The British East India Company established a "factory" (foreign traders' residences and business offices) in Canton in 1685, and annual trading operations began in 1699. Throughout the 18th century the French, Dutch, Americans, and other nationals also established trade relations with the city; the "thirteen factories" were located on the waterfront between the city walls and the western suburbs.

Trade moved without undue difficulty until friction began to mount in the 1820s. The foreigners found trade restrictions (through licensed Chinese merchants known as the Co-hong) too irksome, while the Chinese authorities refused to open normal diplomatic relations. The Chinese seized and destroyed large quantities of illegal opium brought in by the British in 1839, and in retaliation the British attacked Chinese positions in the Canton Estuary. The Opium War (1839–42) ended in humiliating defeat for China, and the city saved itself from destruction only by paying a handsome ransom.

Among its other provisions, the Treaty of Nanking (1842) with the United Kingdom opened Canton as a treaty port. In 1844 the French and the Americans obtained similar treaties. Antiforeign sentiment, however, ran high in Canton, and the city refused to open its gates until 1857. The coolie trade and the use of foreign flags to protect pirates caused a succession of crises. Another war broke out between China and Britain and France between 1856 and 1858. Canton was occupied by Anglo-French forces until 1861; and Sha-mien, to the west of the city, was made an Anglo-French concession in 1859.

Amid the woes of foreign imperialism, Canton was deeply shaken by the great antidynastic outbreak of the Taiping Rebellion (1850–64), the leader of which, Hung Hsiu-ch'üan, was born in the northern Canton suburb of Hua-hsien. Many followers of Hung formed secret societies that kept his revolutionary ideals alive even after the failure of the rebellion. For the next 50 years anti-Manchu agitation formed one of the twin forces that gripped Canton; the other was the rise of nationalism.

Canton came under the spell of its most illustrious son, Sun Yat-sen, from 1885 to 1925. Born in Chung-shan Hsien (Chung-shan County) in 1866, Sun made the city the testing ground for his campaign to overthrow the Manchu dynasty and to establish a Chinese republic. The Canton Uprising of 1911 paved the way for the success of the revolution before the end of the year. Then, Canton became the base of operations for action against the warlords between 1916 and 1925 and served as the headquarters of Sun's party, the Kuomintang. Besides completing his San Min Chu-i (Three Principles of the People), Sun reorganized the Kuomintang in 1924 to reactivate the Nationalist revolution. All manner of people flocked to Canton—the right- and left-wing members of the Kuomintang, the members of the newly formed Chinese Communist Party, and Soviet advisers. Chiang Kai-shek, Mao Tse-tung, and Chou En-lai began their careers in Canton under Sun's tutelage.

Headquarters of the Kuomintang

Chiang quickly gained power when he crushed an uprising by the Canton Merchants Volunteer Corps and defeated the disloyal local warlords (1924). With Sun's death in 1925, however, Canton was embroiled in the power struggle between the Communists and the Nationalists. Outmanoeuvring the Communists, Chiang launched the Northern Expedition in 1926, which enabled him to control southeastern China and to set up a conservative Nationalist government in Nanking in opposition to the Communists and the Kuomintang liberals. In 1927 a Communist-led coup attempted to set up a commune (or workers' government) in the city, only to be crushed by Chiang. From 1928 to 1937 Canton was officially under the control of the Nationalist government. It was, however, actually controlled by independent leaders, who levelled criticism at Chiang's dictatorship and threatened secession from Nanking. In 1937, when war against the Japanese broke out, Canton became a prime target of Japanese air raids, and in 1938 it fell to the enemy. Canton remained under Japanese occupation until 1945. The city was left in a state of economic chaos, and it was not until the Communist government took control in 1949 that Canton began a new era of peace and recovery.

The contemporary city. *Physical environment.* Canton lies within the county (*hsien*) of Fan-yü, although the municipality (*shih*) of Kuang-chou embraces the two additional northern counties of Hua and Ts'ung-hua. It is situated on the Chu Chiang, which branches off the Hsi Chiang and forms the northern border of the pear-shaped delta that is 60 miles long and about 25 miles wide. Three major rivers—the Hsi Chiang, which flows across Yunnan and Kwangsi provinces; the Pei Chiang, which forms a link with Hunan and Kiangsi provinces; and the Tung Chiang, which drains the eastern half of Kwangtung Province—converge at the delta.

The Chu Chiang Delta

Canton has three seasons. From April through October, the summer season is wet, hot, and humid; south and southwest winds are often accompanied by typhoons, which are seldom destructive. The July mean temperature is 83° F (28° C). Winter lasts from October through early February and is mild and free of snow; the January mean temperature is 56° F (13° C). The third season, from February through mid-April, is a period of transition that is marked by muggy weather. With an average annual rainfall of 64 inches, most of which falls from May to August, farmers in the surrounding country enjoy a year-round growing season.

Canton stretches along a waterfront (the Chang Ti, or Long Quay), which runs for five miles from east to west along the Chu Chiang. Both the Old City (dating back to the Ming dynasty) and the sections of Hsi-kuan to the west, Nan-kuan to the south, and Tung-kuan to the east are located on the north bank. Sha-mien is a tiny island in the river adjacent to Hsi-kuan. Since the demolition of the city walls in the 1920s, these sections have become one city. The main north–south thoroughfare of Chieh-fang Lu (Liberation Avenue) is intersected about midway by the east–west arterial road of Chung-shan Lu (Sun Yat-sen Avenue). Literally hundreds of smaller streets cut across these avenues at right angles.

On the south bank are the industrial suburbs of Ho-nan to the south and Hua-ti to the southwest and the sports grounds of Er-sha T'ou to the southeast. Another industrial section is located at Hsi-ts'un, a northwestern suburb on the Peking–Canton railroad; and due north are the delightful parks and resorts of Yüeh-hsiu Shan and Pai-yün Shan. The Hai-chu Bridge links the two banks of the river. About nine miles downriver to the east of the bridge is the outer port of Whampoa.

Transportation. Buses, pedicabs (small three-wheeled vehicles propelled by pedalling), and bicycles are the principal means of transportation in the city and its suburbs. The delta is blessed with innumerable canals and creeks; the smaller canals are used by sampans (flat-bottomed boats propelled by oars) and the larger by steamers or motor launches.

Eastfoto

Hai-chu Square in Canton overlooking the waterfront. The buildings bordering the park are exhibition halls used for trade fairs.

The city is a terminus of inland navigation. Large steamers sail regularly between Canton and Wu-chou, Kwangsi Province; and motor launches ply the multitude of rivers in the vast hinterland. Wooden boats navigate farther upstream into interior China.

Canton as transportation hub

Canton is also the focal point of coastal and ocean navigation. Since the completion of dredging and the construction of warehouses and wharf facilities in 1965, it is capable of handling ships of up to 4,000 tons, whereas similar improvements at Whampoa have made it accessible to 10,000-ton vessels.

Canton is served by three railroads—the Peking–Canton railroad, which is a national trunk line; the Canton–Kowloon line, which links the city with Hong Kong; and the Canton–San-shui line, which provides vital transport between the city and the confluence of the Hsi Chiang and the Chu Chiang. Kwangtung is the nation's most advanced province in highway development. Major arterial roads link Canton with Swatow, Mei-hsien, Chan-chiang, Hai-an, Hsin-tu (all in Kwangtung), and the Portuguese province of Macau. Canton airport is the largest in South China; it operates regular flights to major cities throughout the nation and maintains international service to North Vietnam, Burma, and Pakistan.

Demography. Canton had an estimated municipal population of 3,100,000 in 1970. With 4,000 persons per square mile, it is one of the most densely inhabited areas in China. The people speak Cantonese, a Chinese dialect with twice as many syllables as Mandarin. Some 300,000 persons lived on sampans and junks on the Chu Chiang until 1960, when they were employed in factories and their squalid homes were removed.

The earliest inhabitants, of Tai or Shan origin, were assimilated by the Chinese long ago. There are, however, small groups of Chinese Muslims (Hui) in the city. A notable demographic feature is the large number of "overseas Chinese," Cantonese who emigrated to Southeast Asia, the United States, Europe, and other parts of the world.

Living conditions. Old Canton was a crowded city of narrow streets and winding alleys. A vigorous modernization program was carried out in the 1920s and 1930s, in which the city walls were demolished, the polluted canals filled in, and the graveyards removed. In their place, wide streets were built, modern sewers introduced, arcades constructed for sidewalk shops, and a pleasant waterfront and numerous parks created. Since 1949 the Communist government has continued the modernization of the city. New housing, modern shops, and handsome government buildings are noticeable everywhere. Most of the new housing consists of buildings of three or four stories, light and well-ventilated, located along wide streets with an abundance of trees and flowers.

Expanded industrial activity

Economic life. Since 1950 there has been substantial expansion of such light industries as the manufacture of textiles, newsprint, refined sugar, processed food, jute, matches, and firecrackers. Heavy industries include the production of machinery, chemicals, iron and steel, cement, trucks, tractors, hydroelectric power, and shipbuilding. Small and medium-sized plants have also been developed for the manufacture of clocks, bicycles, cameras, sewing machines, glassware, and plastic goods. Canton is celebrated for its many handicraft products, including ivory carvings, jade objects, embroideries, sandalwood fans, porcelain ware, paper umbrellas, toys, bamboo and rattan ware, coir (coconut-fibre) matting, palm-leaf fans, and household furniture.

Canton is the centre of the trade of Kwangtung and Kwangsi and the adjacent provinces of South China. Products such as sugar, fruits (especially oranges, bananas, litchi, and pineapples), silk, timber, tea, and herbs are exported, whereas manufactured goods and industrial equipment are transshipped via Canton into the interior. Since 1957 the semi-annual Canton Fair has become an institution of world trade, and in the exhibition halls of the Hai-chu Square an Export Commodities Fair is held every spring and autumn.

Political institutions. The Canton Municipal People's Council, which is elected by the Municipal People's Congress (an elective body that is the organ of government authority in the municipality), is the executive organ of the city's government. It is composed of a mayor, deputy mayors, and some 40 council members. The council formulates policies, issues administrative orders, collects taxes, determines the budget, carries out economic plans, maintains order, and safeguards the rights of the citizens. Serving under its direction are numerous bureaus and commissions in charge of civil affairs, public security, justice, planning, finance, food taxation, industry, commerce, labour, culture, education, public health, physical culture and sports, projects of municipal construction, and public services.

The city is divided into districts (*ch'u*), each of which is administered by a district mayoralty. Under the district, there are police substations and street mayoralties. Neighbourhood associations have various functions, including mediating disputes, conducting literacy campaigns, supervising sanitation and welfare, and "weeding out bourgeois elements."

The driving force behind this governmental system is the Municipal Committee of the Chinese Communist Party. In 1959 it was estimated that the city had 60,000 party members, constituting 3 percent of the total city population and organized into 3,000 basic-level units.

Health and safety. While the people continue to lead a poor and spartan life, their houses are clean and the streets are neat and well maintained. Proper treatment of drinking water and the extermination of rodents, flies, and mosquitoes have put an end to malaria, cholera, dysentery, and bubonic plague. The Bureau of Public Health also conducts energetic campaigns for the public health education of the populace. The city has many hospitals, of which the Kwangtung Provincial People's Hospital, with 600 beds and more than 1,000 staff members, is one of the largest.

Public security is maintained by a large and efficient police department, which has branch departments and substations in all districts. The two major vices of gambling and prostitution have been effectively stamped out. As for fire control and prevention, the Canton fire department is manned by well-trained personnel who use up-to-date equipment.

Education. Canton is one of the nation's most progressive Chinese cities in regard to its educational system. In addition to a large number of kindergartens, primary schools, and middle schools, Canton has numerous institutions of higher learning. These include Sun Yat-sen University, Chinan University, South China Technical University, Canton Chinese Medical College, South China Engineering College, South China Institute of Technology, Canton Institute of Applied Chemistry, and South China Agricultural Institute.

The new educational pattern

Since the Cultural Revolution of the 1960s a new pattern of education has taken shape. The system includes five years in primary schools and four years in middle schools. All students leave middle school at 16 years of age and go directly into factories or communes to engage in physical labour for two years. Entrance to college is gained not by examination but by a "four-step system" of application by the student, selection by the worker and peasant representatives, approval by the factory or the commune, and final approval by the college or university staff. The recruitment of students has become stricter, with a noticeable drop in university enrollment. Intervention in school affairs by the army and workers' teams frequently takes place in order to "end factional strife and establish unity."

Cultural life. Canton has a large number of museums, including the Kuang-chou Museum, with exhibits of the history, industries, and the revolutionary heritage of the region; the Kwangtung Palace of Science for schoolchildren; the Sun Yat-sen Museum; and the Museum of the Peasant Institute, which commemorates Mao Tse-tung's role in the peasant revolution. There are many city and provincial libraries, the largest of which is the Chung-shan Library of Kwangtung Province, with more than 1,000,000 volumes. Equally significant are the Kwangtung Botanical Gardens and Zoological Gardens.

Canton has two daily newspapers—the *Kuang-chou jih-pao* is the official organ of the Canton Municipal Party Committee, and the *Nan-fang jih-pao* is the highest official organ published by the Kwangtung Provincial Party Committee. Influential as these papers are, it is radio broadcasting that truly affects the populace. Canton has five radio stations, three of which broadcast locally, and two of which are provincial. Every corner of the city is equipped with receiver sets, and loudspeakers blare out the day's news and the government's directives.

The vast majority of people in Canton live in austerity, but their modest existence is enlivened by laughter, buoyancy, and vitality. Much of this can be attributed to the expansion of recreational facilities since the 1950s. Public parks, gymnasiums, and sports grounds are found everywhere. Especially noteworthy are the International Sports Centre, the New Gymnasium, Kuang-chou Cultural Park, Yueh-hsiu Shan Park, Pai-yün Shan Park, Huang-hua Kang Park, and Li-chi Wan Park. The parks provide picnic grounds, resort facilities, movie theatres, drama theatres, roller-skating rinks, swimming pools, museums, and exhibition halls.

BIBLIOGRAPHY. *Nagel's Encyclopaedia-Guide to China* (1968), is useful for general reference and as a tourist guide. For geography and economic developments, see T.R. TREGEAR, *An Economic Geography of China* (1970). Handy references to the history of Canton may be found in W.C. HUNTER, *The "Fan Kwae" at Canton, Before Treaty Days, 1825–1844* (1882; 2nd ed., 1911); T'ANG LEANG-LI, *The Inner History of the Chinese Revolution* (1930); and IMMANUEL C.Y. HSU, *The Rise of Modern China* (1970). EZRA F. VOGEL, *Canton Under Communism* (1969), is a searching study of the changes in the 1950s and 1960s. *China Reconstructs* and *Far Eastern Economic Review* contain articles dealing with current developments.

(P.-c.K.)

Cantor, Georg

The German mathematician Georg Ferdinand Ludwig Philipp Cantor is remembered chiefly for founding set theory, one of the greatest achievements of 19th-century mathematics. By devising original techniques for treating the infinite in mathematics, he contributed substantially to the development of analysis and logic; and, by drawing on ideas of the infinite in the writings of ancient and medieval philosophy, he introduced new modes of thinking concerning the nature of number. His work, moreover, has had a constructive influence on the development of new curricula in basic education in mathematics.

Cantor was born of Danish parents on March 3, 1845, in St. Petersburg (now Leningrad), Russia. His artistic mother, a Roman Catholic, came from a family of musicians, and his father, a Protestant, was a prosperous merchant. When his father became ill in 1856, the family moved to Frankfurt (now in West Germany). Cantor's mathematical talents emerged prior to his fifteenth birthday while studying in private schools and at *gymnasiuma* at Darmstadt first and then at Wiesbaden; eventually, he overcame the objections of his father, who wanted him to become an engineer.

After briefly attending the University of Zürich (Switzerland), Cantor in 1863 transferred to the University of Berlin to specialize in physics, philosophy, and mathematics. There he was taught by the mathematicians Karl Theodor Weierstrass, whose specialization of analysis probably had the greatest influence on him; Ernst Eduard Kummer, in higher arithmetic; and Leopold Kronecker, the specialist on the theory of numbers who later opposed him. Following one semester at the University of Göttingen in 1866, Cantor wrote his doctoral thesis in 1867, *In re mathematica ars propendi pluris facienda est quam solvendi* ("In mathematics the art of asking questions is more valuable than solving problems"), on a question that Carl Friedrich Gauss (*q.v.*) had left unsettled in his *Disquisitiones Arithmeticae* (1801). After a brief teaching assignment in a Berlin girls' school, Cantor joined the faculty at the University of Halle, where he remained for the rest of his life, first as *Privatdozent* (lecturer, paid by fees only) in 1869, then assistant professor in 1872, and full professor in 1879.

Early work

In a series of 10 papers from 1869 to 1873, Cantor dealt first with the theory of numbers; this subject reflected his own fascination with the subject, his studies of Gauss, and the influence of Kronecker. On the suggestion of Heinrich Eduard Heine, a colleague at Halle who recognized his ability, Cantor then turned to the theory of trigonometric series (see ANALYSIS, FOURIER), in which he extended the concept of real numbers. Starting from the work on trigonometric series and on the function of a complex variable done by the German mathematician Bernhard Riemann (*q.v.*) in 1854, Cantor in 1870 showed that such a function can be represented in only one way by a trigonometric series. Consideration of the collection of numbers (points) that would not conflict with such a representation led him, first, in 1872, to define irrational numbers in terms of convergent sequences of rational numbers (quotients of integers) and then to begin his major lifework, the theory of sets and the concept of transfinite numbers.

An important exchange of letters with Richard Dedekind (*q.v.*), mathematician at the Brunswick Technical High School, who was his lifelong friend and colleague, marked the beginning of Cantor's ideas on the theory of sets (see SET THEORY). Both agreed that a set, whether finite or infinite, is a collection of objects (*e.g.*, the integers, $\{0, \pm 1, \pm 2 \ldots\}$) that share a particular property while each object retains its own individuality. But when Cantor applied the device of the one-to-one correspondence (*e.g.*, $\{a, b, c\}$ to $\{1, 2, 3\}$) to study the characteristics of sets, he quickly saw that they differed in the extent of their membership, even among infinite sets. (A set is infinite if one of its parts, or subsets, has as many objects as itself.) His method soon produced surprising results.

Set theory

In 1873 Cantor demonstrated that the rational numbers, though infinite, are countable (or denumerable) because they may be placed in a one-to-one correspondence with the natural numbers (*i.e.*, the integers, as 1, 2, 3, . . .). He showed that the set (or aggregate) of real numbers (composed of irrational and rational numbers) was infinite and uncountable. Even more paradoxically, he proved that the set of all algebraic numbers (the solutions of simple algebraic equations, as, $\sqrt{2}$ and 5) contains as many components as the set of all integers and that transcendental numbers (those that are not algebraic, as π), which are a subset of the irrationals, are uncountable and are therefore more numerous than integers, which must be conceived as infinite.

But Cantor's paper, in which he first put forward these results, was refused for publication in *Crelle's Journal* by one of its referees, Kronecker, who henceforth vehemently opposed his work. On Dedekind's intervention, however, it was published in 1874 as "Über eine Eigenschaft des Inbegriffes aller reellen algebraischen Zahlen" ("On a Characteristic Property of All Real Algebraic Numbers").

While honeymooning the same year with his bride, Vally Guttman, at Interlaken, Switzerland, Cantor met Dedekind, who gave a sympathetic hearing to his new theory. Cantor's salary was low, but the estate of his father, who died in 1863, enabled him to build a house for his wife and five children. Many of his papers were published in Sweden in the new journal *Acta Mathematica*, edited and founded by Gösta Mittag-Leffler, one of the first persons to recognize his ability.

Cantor's theory became a whole new subject of research concerning the mathematics of the infinite (*e.g.*, an endless series, as 1, 2, 3, . . ., and even more complicated sets), and his theory was heavily dependent on the device of the one-to-one correspondence. In thus developing new ways of asking questions concerning continuity and infinity, Cantor quickly became controversial. When he argued that infinite numbers had an actual existence, he drew on ancient and medieval philosophy concerning the "actual" and "potential" infinite and also on the early religious training given him by his parents. In his book on sets, *Grundlagen einer allgemeinen Mannigfaltigkeitslehre* ("Foundations of a General Theory of Aggregates"), Cantor in 1883 allied his theory with Platonic metaphysics. By contrast, Kronecker, who held that only the integers "exist" ("God made the integers, and all the rest is the work of man"), for many years heatedly rejected his reasoning and effectively blocked his appointment to the faculty at the University of Berlin.

In 1895–97 Cantor fully propounded his view of continuity and the infinite, including infinite ordinals and cardinals, in his best known work, *Beiträge zur Begründung der transfiniten Mengelehre* (published in English under the title *Contributions to the Founding of the Theory of Transfinite Numbers*, 1915). This work contains his conception of transfinite numbers, to which he was led by his demonstration that an infinite set may be placed in a one-to-one correspondence with one of its subsets. By the smallest transfinite cardinal number he meant the cardinal number of any set that can be placed in one-to-one correspondence with the positive integers. This transfinite number he referred to as aleph-null, $\aleph_0$. Larger transfinite cardinal numbers were denoted by aleph-one $\aleph_1$, aleph-two $\aleph_2$, $\cdots$, $\aleph_n$, $\cdots$. He then developed an arithmetic of transfinite numbers that was analogous to finite arithmetic. Thus, he further enriched the concept of infinity. The opposition he faced and the length of time before his ideas were fully assimilated represented in part the difficulties of mathematicians in reassessing the ancient question: "What is a number?" Cantor demonstrated that the set of points on a line possessed a higher cardinal number than $\aleph_0$. This led to the famous problem of the continuum hypothesis, namely, that there are no cardinal numbers between $\aleph_0$ and the cardinal number of the points on a line. This problem has, in the first and second halves of the 20th century, been of great interest to the mathematical world and was studied by many mathematicians, including the Czech-Austrian-American Kurt Gödel and the American Paul J. Cohen.

Transfinite numbers

Although mental illness, beginning about 1884, afflicted the last years of his life, Cantor remained actively at work. In 1897 he helped to convene in Zürich the first international congress of mathematics. Partly because he had been opposed by Kronecker, he often sympathized with young, aspiring mathematicians and sought to find ways to ensure that they would not suffer as he had because of entrenched faculty members who felt threatened by new ideas. At the turn of the century, his work was fully recognized as fundamental to the development of function theory, of analysis, and of topology. Moreover, his work stimulated further development of both the intuitionist and the formalist schools of thought in the logical foundations of mathematics. He died at the University of Halle on January 6, 1918. His work has substantially altered mathematical education in the United States and is often associated with the "new mathematics."

BIBLIOGRAPHY. *Gesammelte Abhandlungen*, ed. by ERNST ZERMELO (1932), contains the collected works of Cantor edited by an authority on set theory. For biographical information, see ERIC T. BELL, *Men of Mathematics* (1937, reprinted 1961), a well-developed history of mathematics with a full chapter on Cantor; DIRK J. STRUIK, *A Concise History of Mathematics* (1948), which discusses the principal mathematicians of the times and their influence on Cantor; and HERBERT MESCHKOWSKI, *Denkweisen grosser Mathematiker* (1961; Eng. trans., *Ways of Thought of Great Mathematicians*, 1964), which devotes a chapter to an elementary account of Cantor's theory of sets.

(Ed.)

Canute the Great, of Denmark and England

Canute (Knut or Cnut), king of England and Denmark and, after 1028, of Norway, became a power in European politics, respected by emperor and pope. Yet more remarkable than his acquisition of an empire was his development from a typical Viking to an enlightened monarch, to the surprise of contemporaries such as Fulbert, bishop of Chartres, who wrote to him: "We were amazed at your wisdom and equally at your piety." In England he was remembered chiefly as a wise ruler, but

King Canute with Aelfgifu placing a cross on the altar of Newminster Abbey, Morpeth. Angels point to Christ flanked by the Virgin and St. Peter, as the source of royal power. Drawing from the *Newminster Liber Vitae*, c. 1016–20. In the British Museum (Stowe MS. 944).

By courtesy of the trustees of the British Museum

in Scandinavia his minstrels praised his courage and military success, and the sagas his wiliness and diplomatic skill.

Neither the place nor date of Canute's birth is known. As a youth he accompanied his father, Sweyn I Forkbeard, king of Denmark, on his invasion of England in 1013. Canute was left in charge of the fleet at Gainsborough, Lincolnshire, and it was probably then that he met Aelfgifu, daughter of an ealdorman (chief officer) of Northumbria who had been murdered with King Aethelred II's connivance in 1006; she bore him two sons, Sweyn and Harold. Sweyn I Forkbeard was accepted as king of England by the end of 1013 but died in February 1014, and the English invited Aethelred to return. Canute and the men of Lindsey planned a combined expedition, but Canute deserted his allies at Easter and sailed to Denmark, putting his hostages, savagely mutilated, ashore at Sandwich. In 1015 he returned and began a long struggle with Aethelred's son Edmund II Ironside. Earl Uhtred of Northumbria submitted to Canute in 1016 and was murdered in his hall. After Aethelred died in April 1016, the English *witan* (council) elected Canute king at Southampton, but those councillors who were in London, with the citizens, elected Edmund. After several campaigns Canute won a victory at Ashingdon, Essex, on October 18, and the kingdom was then divided; but Edmund died on November 30, and Canute succeeded to the whole.

Elected king

His first actions were ruthless: he gave Englishmen's estates to reward his Danish followers; he engineered the death of Edmund's brother Eadwig; and he had some prominent Englishmen killed or outlawed. Edmund's infant sons, however, eventually reached an asylum in Hungary. Already in 1016, Canute had given the earldom of Northumbria to the Norwegian Viking Eric of Hlathir, and in 1017 he put another famous Viking chief, Thorkell the Tall, over East Anglia. Yet Canute did not rule like a foreign conqueror for long: by 1018 Englishmen were holding earldoms in Wessex and Mercia. The Danish element in his entourage steadily decreased. Thorkell was outlawed in 1021, and, during the rest of the reign, of his three most influential advisers only one was a Dane. Canute paid off most of his fleet in 1018, and the Danes and the English reached an agreement at Oxford, one authority adding "according to Edgar's law." A draft of the treaty survives, written in the style of Archbishop Wulfstan of York, who later drew up Canute's laws, mainly based on previous legislation. It is likely that it was Wulfstan who aroused in the young Canute an ambition to emulate the best of his English predecessors, especially King Edgar. Canute proved an effective ruler who brought internal peace and prosperity to the land. He became a strong supporter and a generous donor to the church, and his journey to Rome was inspired by religious as well as diplomatic motives.

Foreign relations

He needed English support against external dangers. King Aethelred's sons were in Normandy, and Canute married their mother, Emma, in 1017 to prevent her brother, Duke Richard II, from espousing their cause. English forces helped to secure Canute's position in Scandinavia in 1019, when he went to Denmark to obtain the throne on his brother's death; in 1023, when the outlawed Thorkell was causing trouble; and again in 1026, when his regent in Denmark, Ulf Jarl, the husband of his sister Estrid, joined the king of Norway and the king of Sweden in a coalition against Denmark. Though Canute was defeated at the Battle of the Holy River, Sweden, terms were made. Scandinavian sources attribute to Canute Ulf's death soon afterward. Canute fomented with bribes the unrest of Norwegian landowners against their king, Olaf II Haraldsson, and was able to drive him out in 1028. He put Norway in charge of Haakon, son of Eric of Hlathir, and, after Haakon's death, of his concubine Aelfgifu and their son Sweyn. Olaf attempted to return in 1030 but fell at Stiklestad. Aelfgifu and Sweyn became unpopular and fled to Denmark in 1035 before Canute's death.

In England, peace was broken only by Canute's expedition to Scotland in 1027, by which he secured recognition from three of the Scottish kings. English trade profited by Canute's control of the Baltic trade route. On his pilgrimage to Rome, timed for him to attend the coronation of the emperor Conrad II in 1027, he secured from the latter and other princes whom he met reductions in tolls for English traders and pilgrims. Denmark benefitted from his friendly relations with the Emperor, who surrendered Schleswig and territory north of the Eider River when negotiations were begun before Canute's death for the marriage of the Emperor's son Henry to Canute's daughter Gunhild.

Canute died on November 12, 1035. Neither his illegitimate son Harold, who ruled England until 1040, nor his legitimate son Hardecanute, who succeeded to Denmark in 1035 and to England in 1040, inherited his qualities. The English reverted to their old royal line in 1042, and Denmark passed to Sweyn II, son of Earl Ulf and Estrid.

BIBLIOGRAPHY. There is an excellent account of Canute II by FRANK M. STENTON in *Anglo-Saxon England*, 3rd ed. (1971); see also the full-scale biography by L.M. LARSON, *Canute the Great* (1912); and a recent assessment by G.N. GARMONSWAY, *Canute and His Empire* (1963). Several of the sources, *i.e.*, the Anglo-Saxon Chronicle, the skaldic verse, and the laws and charters, are translated by DOROTHY WHITELOCK in *English Historical Documents c. 500–1042* (1955); see also *Encomium Emmae reginae*, ed. by ALISTAIR CAMPBELL (1949). For Scandinavian sources that have not been translated into English, see the bibliography in Larson.

(D.W.)

Canyons, Submarine

For more than a century it has been known that there are valleys cut into the sea floor. Because most land valleys have been interpreted as the result of erosion by rivers, which lose their power to cut when they enter the sea, the origin of these marine valleys represented a puzzle. At first they were interpreted in terms of the submergence of once dry land, but that explanation became less convincing as additional data showed the wide distribution of the sea valleys. Not only did they prove to be abundant on most of the continental slopes that lead from the continental shelf to the deep ocean floor, but more recently it has been shown that they may occur at any depth.

Because the oceans could not have been lowered sufficiently to allow rivers to cut these deep valleys, other explanations were set forth. Of these, the most popular by far has been sea-floor currents. Density currents (*q.v.*) can flow down slopes wherever the ocean water becomes heavier than the surrounding water because of its sediment content; such density currents are called turbidity currents. The sediment content can be generated by water waves (*q.v.*) or by the sliding and slumping of sediments on the continental shelf and slope (*q.v.*). The American geologist Reginald Aldworth Daly suggested in 1936 that these density currents had actually cut the valleys of the sea floor. The idea gained much acceptance in the 1950s after B. Heezen and M. Ewing, of Lamont Geological Observatory, called attention to transatlantic cable breaks off the Grand Banks that accompanied the 1929 earthquake. These breaks occurred in a succession that suggested they were caused by high-speed turbidity currents that roared down the slopes with velocities of up to 60 miles an hour.

This article treats the nature and distribution of submarine canyons and considers the several mechanisms of origin that have been proposed. For additional information on sediment transport, see DENSITY CURRENTS and FLUVIAL PROCESSES. See also CONTINENTAL SHELF AND SLOPE; OCEAN BASINS; and RIVER DELTAS for relevant discussions of the physiographic locale of submarine canyons; and MARINE SEDIMENTS and RIVERS AND RIVER SYSTEMS for treatment of the sediments involved and the relation of submarine to land valleys, respectively.

TYPES OF SUBMARINE VALLEYS

Analogy to terrestrial canyons

The valleys of the sea floor are termed submarine canyons because profiles based on soundings show that many, perhaps most, of the valleys are similar to what are called canyons on land. That is, they have great relief, steep walls, and a V-shaped cross section. Once this name was applied, it was natural to apply the same name to all marine valleys. This is still a common practice, but it is no more reasonable than it would be to call all land valleys canyons. Actually, there are as many types of valleys on the sea floor as there are on land. In addition to true canyons, fault valleys (attributable to deformation of the earth's crust) are found both on the continents and on the sea bottom. Landslide valleys also occur in both environments, and these are quite different from erosion canyons, the difference being catastrophic versus gradual development. The small elongated depressions that cut alluvial fans (*q.v.*) on land can be compared with the valleys that cut the great fans of the sea floor. The U-shaped valleys that result on land from glacial erosion have their counterpart in the similar submarine valleys that cut the continental shelf off glaciated areas.

At least three types of sea-floor valleys are distinct from land types. The shallow, discontinuous valleys that cross or partly cross the continental shelves in a few areas comprise one type. A second occurs near a few large deltas, in the form of a relatively straight-sided trough that crosses the shelf and extends down the slope beyond. Finally, there are low-walled, trough-shaped valleys that wander across the deep-sea floor. None of these valley types would be called a canyon if it were exposed on land.

Because of the diversity of types, submarine valleys may most simply be discussed according to the classification above. Although all the valleys could conceivably have been formed by the same process, such as density currents, their origins were likely more diverse.

PHYSICAL CHARACTERISTICS OF CANYONS OF THE SEA FLOOR

The best known and probably the most common type of ocean-floor valley can properly be called the submarine canyon. These formations have an extraordinary resemblance to river-cut land canyons. In addition to their V-shaped cross sections, their floors slope outward as continuously as do land canyons. They have many entering tributaries that form the dendritic (branching) pattern characteristic of land canyons. Their steep walls frequently have rock outcrops, although a sediment cover is more common than in land canyons, and most of the sea canyons have similar winding courses.

Vast dimensions

The vertical dimensions of submarine canyons are surprising. Most of them have walls thousands of feet high, and the highest, in the Bahamas, rises almost three miles from the canyon floor—dwarfing, by comparison, the mile-high walls of the Grand Canyon. Some canyons have been traced for slightly more than 200 miles in length, but most extend less than 30 miles. Usually they can be traced as far as the base of the steep part of the continental slopes, often more than a mile in depth. Their width varies in the same manner as that of land valleys. A narrow gorge off La Jolla, California, is as deep as it is wide, but the more typical canyons have widths of many miles. A three-mile-deep canyon in the Bahamas, for example, is 23 miles wide at its deepest point. By comparison, the Grand Canyon is about 12 miles wide. In both cases, the average slope is small, but photographs show vertical rock walls in the Bahama Canyon, and the Grand Canyon has vertical walls interspersed with terraces and pyramidal buttes (flat-topped and steep-sided hills). The seaward gradients of the canyon floors are generally steeper than those of land canyons. The average floor slope is about 300 feet per mile, but the numerous canyons that closely approach the coastline have high gradients at their heads, sometimes as great as 45°. The gradients almost always decrease in the outer portions.

The appearance of the canyons has been ascertained in recent years both by lowering cameras to the bottom and by observation from deep-diving vehicles. The dives, which have penetrated to depths of over 7,000 feet within a canyon, have been particularly useful in describing physical features. They have indicated that vertical or even overhanging walls are commonplace, and that canyon walls often are grooved or polished as if they had been smoothed by a glacier. The floors, while generally covered with cobbles and other coarse sediment, are locally bare rock. Some have ripple-marked surfaces, which have been shown by remote camera pictures to occur at depths of more than two miles. The floors may vary considerably in gradient, ranging from a gentle slope to a steep drop-off, with the latter often occurring where boulders, fallen from the walls, have allowed sediments to build up above this obstruction.

By courtesy of (right) the Scripps Institution of Oceanography, University of California, San Diego, (left) School of Marine and Atmospheric Science, University of Miami; photograph, Robert J. Hurley

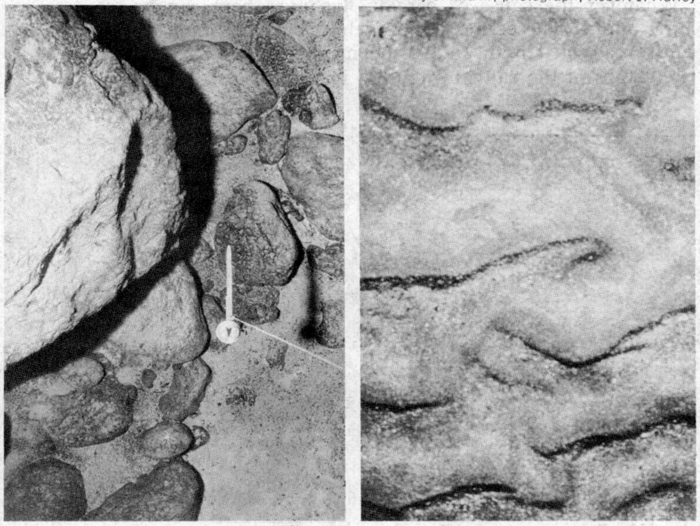

Submarine canyon floors.
(Left) Wallrock and cobbles in the Grand Bahama Canyon, at a depth of 11,560 feet. (Right) Current ripples in Mera Canyon near Tokyo Bay, at a depth of 1,673 feet.

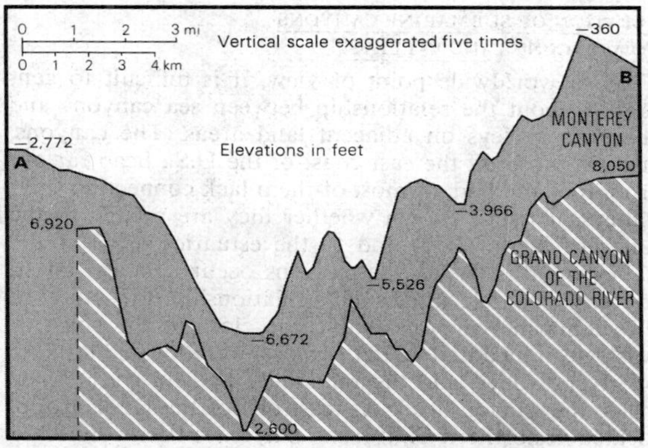

Figure 1: Profile comparison of the Grand Canyon of the Colorado River and the Monterey Canyon. The location of the Monterey Canyon profile is shown by the line A–B in Figure 3.

From F. Shepard, *The Earth Beneath the Sea*; copyright by the Johns Hopkins University Press

All of the preceding features suggest that canyons are subject to active marine processes and are by no means mere remnants of long past erosional processes. Further evidence that conditions are far from static comes from repeated soundings taken along the same ranges at the canyon heads. It has been known since the mid-20th century that the profiles sometimes undergo radical changes. Apparently depth increases very suddenly, but shoaling occurs at a more gradual pace. This sudden deepening has broken cables—notably off the Congo, where a canyon extends seaward for 120 miles. Piers and jetties built into submarine canyon heads have collapsed from the sudden removal of sediment on which they were resting.

The nature of the rocks on the canyon walls has been determined by dredging and by observation from deep-diving vehicles. Most of it has proved to be relatively soft and hence rather easily eroded, but there are some canyons that have been cut through very hard rock, even quartzite. Granite walls have been found in several places, and one vertical granite cliff was discovered in a vehicle dive to 4,150 feet off the tip of Baja California. There, both walls of the canyon were granite; in some areas only one of the walls is hard rock, whereas the other wall is relatively soft.

GEOGRAPHIC DISTRIBUTION OF SUBMARINE CANYONS

Submarine canyons are found along most continental slopes, although they have not yet been discovered around Antarctica nor along the slope into the Arctic off northern Europe and Asia, where soundings are spotty because of ice packs. Canyons are cut into the slopes off the Hawaiian Islands and possibly a few other oceanic islands. Soundings on these insular slopes are generally too incomplete to determine whether or not canyons are present. Along some slopes, canyons are as common as on typical mountain fronts, but elsewhere the slopes appear to be free from any canyons for many miles. In general, canyons are scarce wherever the upper continental slopes are very gentle, as south of Cape Hatteras and around Antarctica. A surprising concentration of canyons is found around Ceylon, the tip of Baja California, the east coast of the U.S. north of Cape Hatteras, and along the northwest coast of the Mediterranean. There appears to be little if any relationship between canyons and latitude. The Ceylon canyons and the Congo Canyon are near the Equator, but the longest and largest canyons in the world are in the Bering Sea. The oceanic slopes that are not bordered by either continents or large islands appear to lack submarine canyons, but most of these slopes are not yet sufficiently well explored to make the conclusion certain. Off New England, the oceanic slope with many canyons is separated from the land valley by a shallow bank and a deep gulf inside, but the canyons may have been cut before the inner shelf was deepened by glaciation.

Concentrations of canyons

RELATION OF SUBMARINE CANYONS TO ADJACENT LAND VALLEYS

From a worldwide point of view, it is difficult to generalize about the relationship between sea canyons and the river valleys on adjacent land areas. The canyons, such as those off the east coast of the U.S., head far out from the land and, as most of them lack connecting shelf valleys, it is not known whether they are related to the adjacent land valleys and to the estuaries (*q.v.*) at the valley mouths. When the canyons occur near the coast, it is easier to determine such a relationship. In a study of 57 submarine canyons that come close to the coast, it was determined that 46 (81 percent) were located directly off river valleys, and the remainder had no river valley inside the canyon head. At least one of the latter group, located in northern California, may have been connected with a land canyon before the faulting along the San Andreas Rift shifted the sea floor to the northeast, so that it is now located off a land cliff between canyons. Elsewhere, the shift of a stream mouth after the canyon had been cut may account for the lack of any connection, as at Cap Breton in southwest France, where the Adour River changed its course in the 15th century.

Pleistocene drainage and changes of sea level

The mouths of many streams were drowned by the relatively recent rise of sea level, which accompanied the melting of the great ice sheets of the Pleistocene Epoch (*q.v.*). The relationship of such bays to canyon heads can be compared. In a study of 77 submarine canyons, 13 were found to enter drowned valleys, 25 to lie outside broad embayments that are not clearly drowned valleys, and 39 to occur either off long straight beaches or relatively straight sea cliffs.

Another important consideration is the comparison between the type of land valley with the adjacent canyon on the sea floor. In almost all cases the characteristics of marine canyons are very different from those of land canyons, which usually have much lower gradients, much gentler side slopes, and much broader floors. The closest resemblance of land canyons to adjacent sea canyons is along the west coast of Corsica, but even there, the land valley mouths have low gradients and wide floors compared to the high gradients and narrow floors of the submarine canyon heads.

The drainage pattern of the land valleys also differs from the adjacent submarine canyons. The submarine canyons have a considerable number of tributaries at their heads, which makes them comparable to the land canyons, but in general the land valleys have more tributaries in their lower courses than do submarine canyons. An exception is the large Monterey Submarine Canyon, which has a fine display of tributaries along its entire course.

TRANSPORT OF SEDIMENT THROUGH SUBMARINE CANYONS

Streams carry large quantities of sand to the coast, and wave erosion adds to the supply. Along relatively straight coasts, like those of California, the diagonal approach of water waves (*q.v.*) causes the transport of this sediment along the shore in the direction in which the waves are approaching.

When canyon heads extend across the continental shelf to, or almost to, the coast, they have an enormous effect on sediments being carried along the coast by longshore currents. This sediment, consisting largely of sand, is carried in short jumps, in a process called saltation. Once the sediment has passed the lip of the canyon and falls on the steep sides, there is little chance for the currents, which are induced mostly by waves, to lift it clear. As it piles up on the walls, the sediment becomes unstable and slumps to the canyon floor. Repeated depth measurements across the canyons show that this process would soon fill the heads level with the surrounding shelf if there were no means of carrying the sediment down the canyon. Thus a fill of ten feet in a period of a few months is not uncommon, but ordinarily within about a year the canyon head has somehow been flushed and the sediment must have moved seaward.

Evidence of canyon flushing

The cause of canyon flushing is still somewhat uncertain. Sand flows have been observed in places along the canyon walls where the slopes have become oversteep, but these flows do not take place at slope angles of less than about 30°. There are currents that alternately move up and down the canyon floors with velocities of up to one mile an hour. Such velocity is sufficient to transport sand. The available evidence indicates that the currents moving downcanyon are the strongest. This is supported by ripple markings observed on canyon floors, most of which indicate a downcanyon movement. These ordinary currents, however, are in almost constant operation; so if they were the sole cause of canyon flushing, the long periods of canyon-head filling could not occur. Apparently, some more powerful process operates from time to time to reverse this tendency to fill. Furthermore, cobbles are transported down the canyon floors, and these relatively weak currents are certainly not the cause of their movement. Fairly substantial evidence indicates that large rocks that have fallen from the walls are eventually carried away. Instruments in the head of the canyon near the Scripps Institution of Oceanography have been lost repeatedly. Even an old car body was carried down. On one occasion, a current meter registered three knots of current before it disappeared.

It is thought that the powerful forces at work here are set into operation during large wave periods, but this is not yet confirmed. Some type of density current may be triggered by the sediment thrown into suspension by the large waves. Alternatively, the fill on the canyon floor may be transported by some type of landslide.

Whatever the cause of canyon flushing, there can be little doubt that sediment is somehow carried down the entire canyon length and is the means of building the great fans at the canyon mouths. The thickness of sedi-

From F. Shepard, *The Earth Beneath the Sea*; copyright by the Johns Hopkins University Press

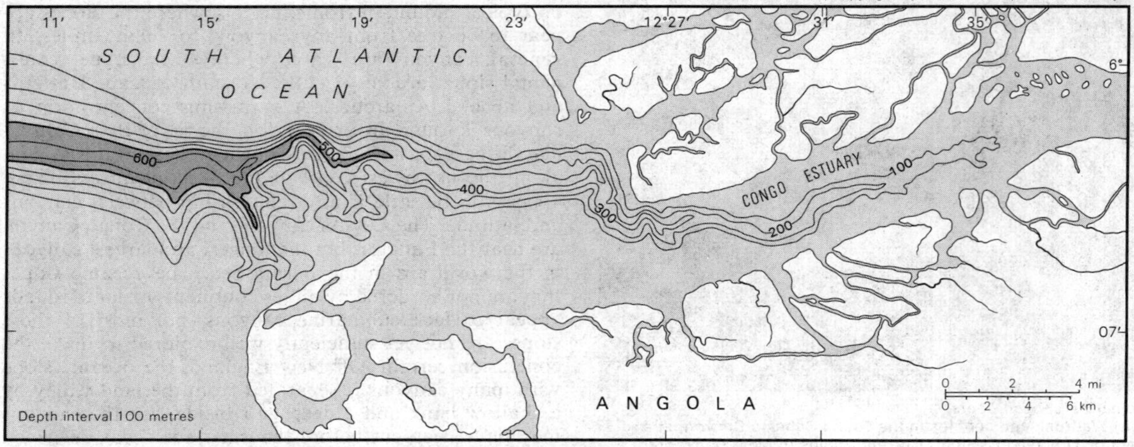

Figure 2: The topography of the Congo Canyon at the mouth of the Congo River.

Prominent land canyon directly connected to a submarine canyon along the southwest coast of Crete.

By courtesy of Scripps Institution of Oceanography, University of California, San Diego

ment in some of these fans has been measured, and its total volume far exceeds the volume that would be produced by the cutting of the canyons. This indicates that the fans are largely formed by sediment that is introduced from the land and moves down the canyon.

Presence of "fan-valleys"

One of the interesting features of the submarine fans at canyon mouths is the presence of relatively shallow valleys truncating the upper beds of the fan. These are called "fan-valleys." They differ from submarine canyons because they have relatively low walls, distributaries rather than tributaries (channels that transport water and sediment away from, not toward, the main canyon), and are usually bordered by levees, comparable to the levees on the sides of channels that cross river deltas (*q.v.*). These levees sometimes occur 100 feet or more above the channel floors, and they may rise a score of feet above the general level of the adjacent fan. They apparently result from deposition of the overflow of currents moving down the fan-valley.

Many of the fans are not cut by valleys. However, it is possible that fans can be built upward while valleys cut through them during the process. Recent evidence indicates that the fan-valley outside La Jolla Submarine Canyon has been cut by a change from depositional processes to those of erosion. The fan-valley outside Monterey Canyon has developed a meander comparable to those of rivers flowing in a flood plain.

ORIGIN OF SUBMARINE CANYONS

The discussion of the character of these canyons has provided much of the basis for the discussion of their origin. The resemblance of the canyons on the sea floor to those on land is, of course, an argument favouring a common origin. Also, the location of most known canyons off river valleys adds weight to the argument. If, however, submarine canyons are simply the submerged lower portions of land canyons, there should be a closer relationship between the submerged and the emerged portions. As A.O. Woodford has emphasized, the profiles of the land valleys show a sharp break when they are continued into the sea canyons. A sudden steepening of gradient is found, along with a decided change of character. Nor does it seem reasonable that virtually all continental margins have sunk, submerging the land canyons to extreme depths, although this explanation may account for some submarine canyons, of which those on the west coast of Corsica may well be an example. The discontinuity at the juncture between land and sea canyons could

From F. Shepard, *The Earth Beneath the Sea*; copyright by the John Hopkins University Press

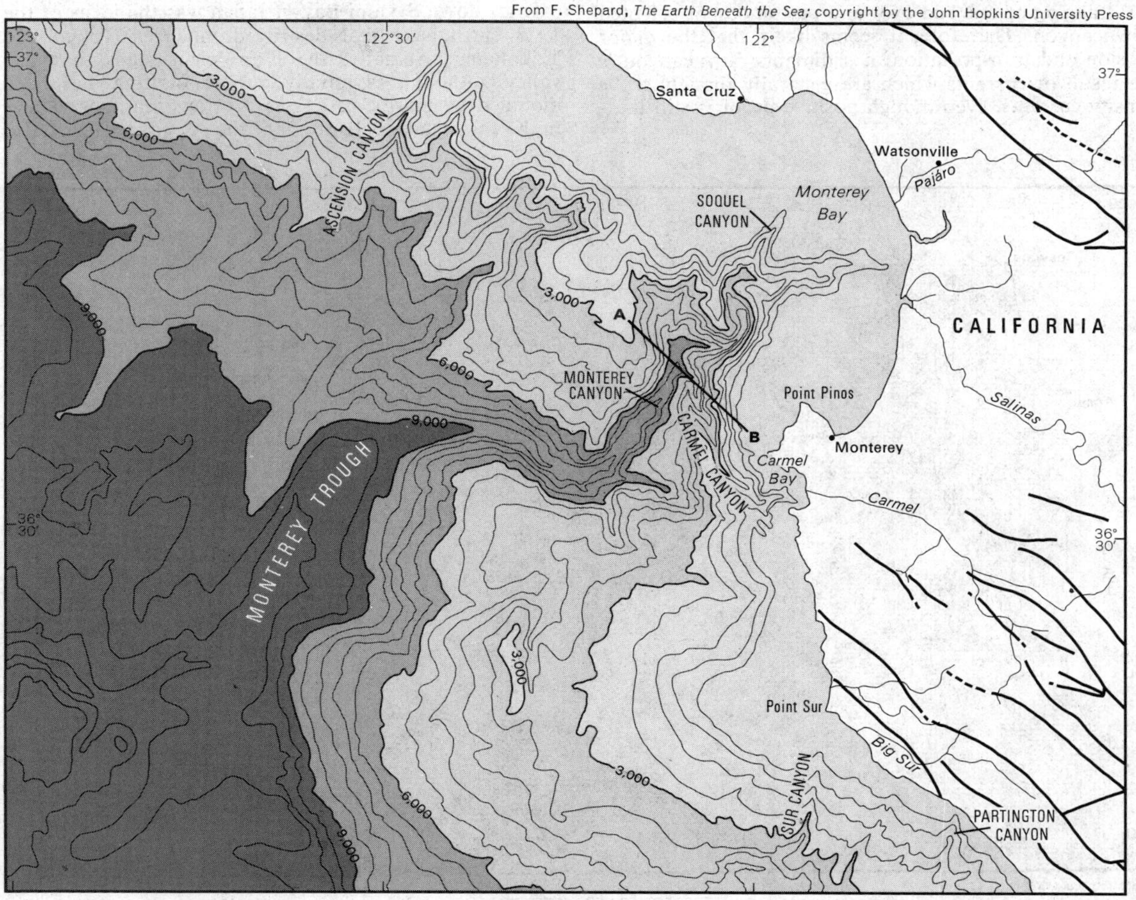

Figure 3: Ocean floor off the coast of Monterey, California. Profile along line A–B is shown in Figure 1.

be due to the delta that is built in the estuary at the mouth of the land canyon.

Importance of marine processes

Accumulating evidence indicating the importance of marine erosion in submarine canyons, and the fact that they are so different in character from the adjacent land valleys, forms convincing evidence that submarine canyons are due primarily to marine processes. In La Jolla Canyon the canyon head is being cut back towards the land at about one foot a year. If currents or other processes are capable of transporting the boulders that fall from the walls to the canyon floor, they should also be capable of eroding the canyon. Finally, the vertical or overhanging walls that occur in the canyons seem to be proof of active erosion. If these walls had been cut long ago, the action of organisms that live on them and the erosive effect of sediments sliding down from the shelf into the canyon should have greatly reduced the declivities. There must be active erosion along the canyon floors and lower walls to maintain the steep slopes.

Creeping action is occurring in the sediment at the head of La Jolla Canyon. A series of stakes driven in a line across the floor of this canyon by Robert Dill, an American marine geologist, show that the stakes in the centre move faster than those on the sides, as in a glacier. Also, an occasional major disturbance carries away all the stakes. Some stakes have been bent downcanyon because the sediment at the surface creeps forward at a faster rate than that beneath. Even in the fan-valley beyond the canyon off La Jolla, the fill shows cracks and steps that suggest a creeping movement.

On the other hand, it does not seem likely that the major transfer of sediment down the canyons, nor their cutting, are due principally to creeping action. Cores taken in the canyon floor have rather well-preserved stratification. If the sediment was creeping continuously down the canyon, this stratification would be much disturbed and would show many drag folds (bending of strata due to the dragging of one bed over and past another) oriented downcanyon. Therefore, it seems likely that the major erosion and transportation of sediments downcanyon is the result of currents which are generally thought to be density currents, even though positive proof is still lacking.

Ages of submarine canyons. Little is known about the age of the existing submarine canyons. Some geologists have thought that they were cut during low sea-level stages of the glacial period, but the huge size of the fans found beyond the canyons means that they probably have been developing for several million years. This would imply an age that antedates the glacial period. Furthermore, geologists have found many features in ancient rocks that appear to represent old submarine canyons subsequently filled with sediments. Lowered sea levels would have helped the movement of sediments onto the continental slopes because of the exposure of the shelves. Canyons certainly are forming, and there is little reason to confine their origin to the short periods when the shelves were laid bare by lowered sea level. These episodes must have been too brief for marine processes to excavate the huge gorges out of granite.

Pre-Pleistocene and present formation

The investigations of a huge canyon in the Bahamas has shown that it was probably in existence in the Pliocene, a period prior to glaciation. It is quite probable that this canyon has been forming for millions of years, while the Bahama limestone banks grew upward, keeping pace with the sinking of the sea floor. Deep wells show that Cretaceous rocks underlie the younger formations in the Bahamas at depths of 6,000 to 7,000 feet. So far as is known, these all were deposited in shallow water, whereas deep-water formations are found along the walls of the submarine canyon.

Submarine fault valleys. Blocks of the earth's crust can drop between upraised masses and can produce valleys in this way. Death Valley in California, the Jordan Valley in the Near East, and the rift valleys of Africa are examples of land valleys in earthquake belts. Most of these valleys have relatively flat floors, straight steep walls, basin depressions, developing lakes, and they lack tributaries. Using the same criteria, fault valleys can be identified on the sea floor. The valley of this type that extends down Sagami Bay in Japan was the locus of the 1923 earthquake that destroyed much of Tokyo and Yokohama. Actually, there are clear signs that this valley, although essentially due to faulting, has been modified by marine processes. Various sea-floor valleys in the earthquake belts south of the Aleutian Islands also

By courtesy of the Geological Society of America

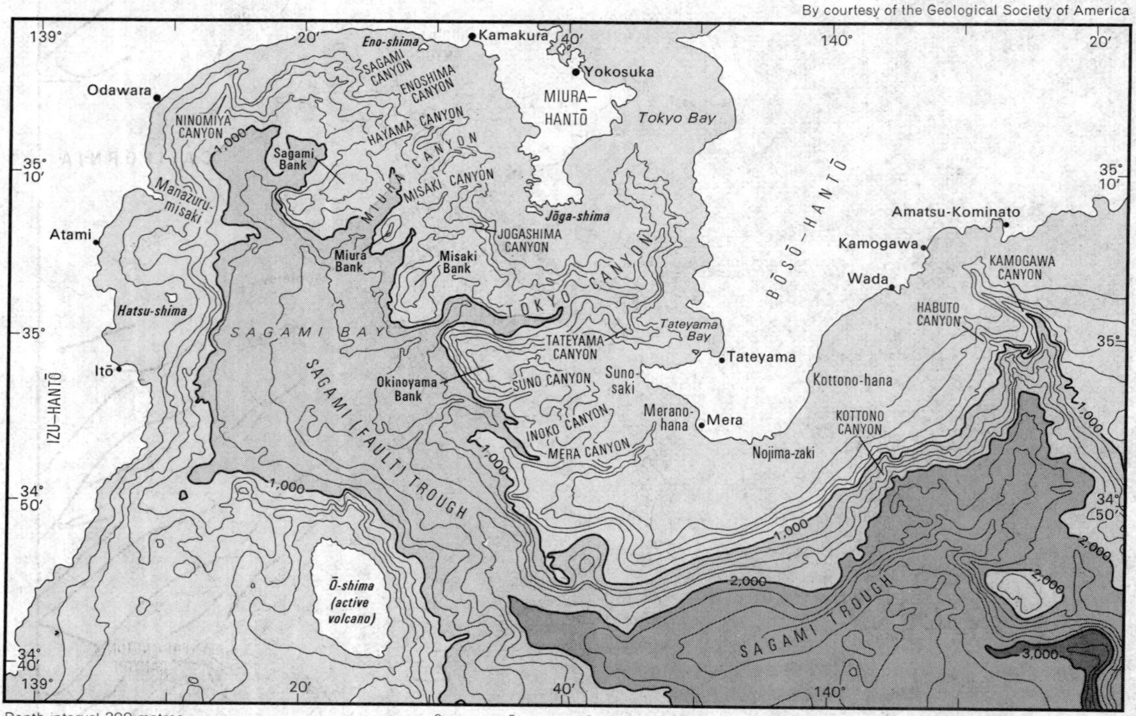

Figure 4: Underwater relief contours off the coast of east central Honshū, Japan.

appear to have the characteristics of fault valleys. Some of them are V-shaped but otherwise suggest fault origin.

Continental shelf valleys. Off New York City's harbour, the continental shelf is creased by a shallow valley that can be traced almost to its outer edge. It has walls generally less than 100 feet high, in contrast to those of the submarine canyons, which are thousands of feet high. Its floor does not slope outward continuously, like the canyons, nor are there any entering tributaries. A few other valleys of this sort are found on other continental shelves, but most of them are less continuous. One is found in the English Channel and another in the Sunda Sea between Java and Borneo. These presumably are partly filled remnants of valleys that were cut by rivers during the low stages of sea level of the glacial period.

Relation to glaciated coasts

The other type of shelf valley, termed glacial troughs or glacial channels, is found off most glaciated coasts. These are cut deeper than the river type of shelf valley and commonly have depths of at least a thousand feet. Their broad floors show deep basin depressions, and they have a considerable number of entering tributaries. Their glacial origin seems certain because many of them are continuations of glacial fjords. Notable examples are the deep Gulf of Maine, the trough in the Gulf of St. Lawrence, and the deep Strait of Juan de Fuca.

Slope gullies. Many submarine slopes have a valley with low walls that are rarely more than 100 feet high. They start and stop on the slope at various depths and have few tributaries. At their outer termini, most have hummocks suggestive of landslide origin. Such slope gullies are found in the front of several great deltas, notably those of the Mississippi, the Rhône, and the Fraser. They change position as the delta builds forward, as shown by comparing old and new surveys. They are the result of slumping of recent sediment.

Delta-front troughs. Beyond the broad deltas of the Ganges and Indus, broad-floored valleys extend across the shelf and down the adjacent floor. These valleys seem to be related to the delta building. They differ from submarine canyons in their broad trough shape, absence of entering tributaries, and relatively straight course, in contrast to the winding courses of the canyons. Outside these troughs are great fans cut by fan valleys, much the same as those outside submarine canyons.

At present, there is not sufficient information to fully understand the origin of the delta-front troughs. Apparently, sediment moves out along them, as along submarine canyons. Off the Mississippi, the head of a delta-front trough has been filled for 30 miles; but a typical trough occurs beyond that distance, and the filled portion of the trough was only discovered by borings and seismic reflection profiling across the shelf.

Role of turbidity currents

Deep-sea channels. The existence of very long channels cutting the deep-sea floor of both the Atlantic and Pacific has been well established. They are cut to depths of as much as several hundred feet below the surrounding sea floor. They have relatively flat floors that are several miles across, and, so far as is known, they slope continuously in one direction. Some of them have entering tributaries. Sediments from the channel floors include sand, indicating that strong currents are operating along them. Some of the channels extend out beyond the continental slopes, but others run essentially parallel to the base of the slopes. These channels have been attributed by Bruce C. Heezen and others to turbidity currents, but there is no clear evidence. Some valleys may represent shallow fault troughs that have been the locus of turbidity currents coming out from the continental slopes.

BIBLIOGRAPHY. Articles and books on this subject, although by prominent geologists, were written before much was known about the canyons and therefore have become seriously out-of-date. Some of these led to fruitful discussions and introduced important ideas, such as R.A. DALY, "Origin of Submarine Canyons," *Am. J. Sci.*, 31:401–420 (1936), in which the first attempt was made to explain the canyons by turbidity currents. Also, B.C. HEEZEN and M. EWING, "Turbidity Currents and Submarine Slumps, and the 1929 Grand Banks Earthquake," *Am. J. Sci.*, 250:849–873 (1952), gave the first important, although debatable, evidence of high-speed turbidity currents breaking submarine cables. H.W. MENARD, JR., "Deep-sea Channels, Topography, and Sedimentation," *Bull. Am. Ass. Petrol. Geol.*, 39:236–255 (1955), gives a complete discussion of some West Coast valleys that cross the fans near the base of the continental slopes, showing their contrast with the canyons higher up the submarine slopes. A more recent attempt to synthesize the rapidly growing information on submarine canyons is found in F.P. SHEPARD and R.F. DILL, *Submarine Canyons, and Other Sea Valleys* (1966).

(F.P.S.)

Cape of Good Hope

Cape of Good Hope, or Cape Province—officially Kaapprovinsie in the Afrikaans language—is situated on the southern extremity of the African continent and is the largest of the four provinces of the Republic of South Africa. The name Cape of Good Hope, while specifically referring to the promontory about 30 miles south of Cape Town, is officially extended to apply to the entire province. Occupying the southern and western region of the republic, the province has an area of 250,300 square miles (648,300 square kilometres), excluding the three republics, Transkei, Bophuthatswana, and Ciskei, within its borders. These republics, which were administered separately as Bantu Homelands within South Africa after 1963, were granted independent status in 1976, 1977, and 1981, respectively. The areas and populations of these republics within the borders of the province are: Transkei (16,100 square miles; population [1980], 3,037,000); Bophuthatswana (9,400 square miles; population [1980], 419,000); and Ciskei (3,200 square miles; population [1980], 636,000). Officially the province still includes an exclave of 374 square miles around Walvis Bay on the coast of South West Africa/Namibia. This territory was annexed in 1884, but since 1926 it has been administered as part of South West Africa/Namibia. In addition, 1,476 square miles of territory were transferred from Griqualand East to Natal Province in 1978.

In 1980 Cape Province had a population of 4,908,000, excluding the population of the three republics. About one-fourth of the population lives in the metropolitan area of Cape Town, the provincial capital and the legislative capital of the republic (see CAPE TOWN; for coverage of historical aspects, see SOUTHERN AFRICA, HISTORY OF; for coverage of associated physical features, see ORANGE RIVER; and VELD).

Dutch settlement

History. The first European settlement in southern Africa was located in what is now Cape Province. This was the victualling station established in 1652 by the Dutch Vereenigde Oostindische Compagnie at Table Bay, 30 miles (50 kilometres) north of the promontory that the Portuguese navigator Bartolomeu Dias had named Cabo da Boa Esperança (Cape of Good Hope) in 1488. In 1814 the Cape settlement was ceded to the British and became the Colony of the Cape of Good Hope. In 1910 the colony was constituted a province of the Union of South Africa (since 1961 the Republic of South Africa).

As the early agricultural ventures of the Dutch East India Company proved inadequate to supply the garrison and ships in transit, lands were assigned to independent settlers in 1657 and, to supplement their labour, from 1658 slaves were imported, at first from West Africa and later in larger numbers from Madagascar, Ceylon, and the East Indies. As the amount of livestock obtainable from the nomadic Khoikhoin (called Hottentots by the Dutch) to supply ships also proved insufficient, the company itself began to raise stock and later to encourage settlers to do so. At first the paucity of grazing during the summer dry season necessitated the establishment of pastoral outposts in well-watered localities in the immediate hinterland; later, however, colonial pastoralists moved inland seasonally in search of good grazing, as had the Khoikhoin.

By 1700 grain, wine, and fruit farms were scattered along the eastern foot of Table Mountain (which overlooks Table Bay) as well as along the western foot of the Hottentots-Hollandsberge and Drakenstein ranges 30 to 40 miles to the east, while pastoral farmers ranged as far as 100 miles to the north and east of Table Bay. To this encroachment the Khoikhoin offered no sustained resistance, withdrawing before the colonists or accepting service with them as shepherds, guides, and interpreters; in the smallpox epidemic of 1713 thousands died. The survivors fled, and by 1730 no tribal remnants remained within 250 miles of Table Bay. Concurrently, the growing volume of shipping and the consequent demand for livestock provided the incentive for the spread of colonial sheep farmers northeastward beyond the Roggeveldberg and Hantamsberg and eastward through the Karoo (a plateau region) until, by 1779, they were in contact and conflict with Bantu-speaking peoples along the Great Fish River.

Stock thefts and reprisals subsequently resulted in a series of frontier wars; the introduction of some 3,500 settlers by the British in 1820 between the Dutch settlers and the Africans failed to establish an effective buffer settlement, and pacification was achieved only after a series of annexations had by 1894 advanced the frontier to the Mtamvuna River, the southwestern border of the colony of Natal. All the tribal territories east of the Great Kei River were thus reduced to the status of tribal reserves under colonial administration.

The gradual northward diffusion of pastoralists across the Upper Karoo meanwhile had led to the discovery of diamonds in 1867–68 where the trail to Bechuanaland—followed for half a century by traders and missionaries—crossed the Orange River.

The diamond rush

The discovery of diamond-bearing intrusions north of the river precipitated a rush of immigrants. It also led to the annexation of Griqualand West by Cape Colony in 1871, despite conflicting claims by the Orange Free State; to the extension (between 1873 and 1884) of the small Cape Town-to-Wellington railway more than 600 miles inland to Kimberley; and to the construction of railways inland from Port Elizabeth and from the port of East London. The fortuitous discovery of diamonds was particularly timely, since the opening of the Suez Canal in 1869 threatened to bankrupt the colony. The era that followed was one of unprecedented population growth and economic activity that attracted capital from overseas. The attention paid to the potential, although then still unknown, mineral wealth of the hinterland gave impetus to expansion. Political manoeuvring culminated in 1885 in the proclamation of a British protectorate over the area extending north to 22° south latitude, and in 1895 the section south of the Molopo River, the present boundary with Botswana, was incorporated within the Cape Colony.

Natural environment. *Physiography.* Most of the province lies at an altitude of between 3,000 and 5,000 feet (900 and 1,500 metres) above sea level, occupying part of the great interior plateau of southern Africa. The edges of the plateau form conspicuous escarpments that trend southward from the Namaqua Highlands in the northwest to the Roggeveldberg in the southwest and from there eastward as the Nuweveldberge, Sneeuberg, and Stormberg mountains until the southern end of the Drakensberg escarpment is reached. These escarpments separate the plateau from a coastal zone with a varied relief in the west and from the broad basins of the Doorn Karoo and the Great Karoo plateaus to the southwest and south. Across the southern part of the province a series of sandstone ranges of equal height enclose the elongated basin of the Little Karoo, running approximately parallel to the south coast. At the western end of these ranges, a complex of similar ranges runs northward from Cape Hangklip, southeast of Cape Town, to the Bokkeveld, about 200 miles to the north. Lowlands, between the mountains and the coast, are narrow and discontinuous, apart from a strip 10 to 50 miles wide between Mossel Bay and Cape Agulhas (the southernmost tip of the African continent) and an area 20 to 60 miles wide between False Bay (immediately south of Cape Town) and St. Helena Bay (about 100 miles to the north).

Climate. Maritime influence on the climate is restricted to the coastal fringe. Over most of the province the mean annual precipitation is less than 15 inches (380 millimetres), and large areas in the northwest receive less than 5 inches. Years of drought are common. Only the southwestern and southern margins receive more than 25 inches of precipitation, mostly in the form of rain resulting from winter cyclones in the southwest, and summer rain resulting from easterly winds beyond Mossel Bay on the south coast. In the interior most of the rain is from summer thunderstorms; the occasional winter rains and the rarer snowfalls are associated with the passage of cyclones. Solar radiation is intense at all seasons, because of the latitude, the elevation, and the usually clear skies; inland mean daily maximum temperatures usually range from 65° F (18° C) in winter to 90° F (32° C) in summer. Frost occurs on more than 60 nights a year; the frostless season lasts for less than 240 days on the southern margin of the Upper Karoo. Snow occasionally mantles all the higher mountain peaks, and only the coastal zone is frost-free.

Droughts

Vegetation. The vegetation is predominantly xerophytic (adapted for growth under dry conditions). Thornbush savanna (parklike grassland) occurs in the north, while low-growing Karoo bush vegetation, typified by many species of plants adapted to semidesert conditions, occurs south of the Orange River. Desert shrub and succulents (juicy plants) are found in Namaqualand in the northwest. In the southwestern region where winter rainfall occurs, the sclerophyll bush (characterized by plants with thickened hardened foliage) is extraordinarily rich in endemic species. Indigenous forest, predominantly evergreen, is found only on the south coast between Mossel Bay and Algoa Bay and on the southern slopes of the Amatole Range, to the northeast of Algoa Bay, where rain occurs at all seasons; farther east it passes into grassland and, in the coastal zone, into xerophytic low forest and bush.

Animal life. Immense herds of springbok and other antelope, wildebeest (gnu), and zebra formerly ranged the interior, while hippopotamuses were found in all the perennial rivers, and elephant and rhinoceroses roamed the coastal zone from Natal in the east to the Olifants River in the west; lion, leopard, and other carnivores were ubiquitous. Though many local place-names recall this rich and varied animal life, today, apart from the smaller species, it has mostly disappeared. Only depleted remnants of it survive in a few scattered game reserves, in some sparsely settled areas where a few springbok still roam, and in some remote mountain areas where the rare leopard preys on the few surviving baboons. Bird life, however, remains numerous and varied. Along the coast, particularly in the west, cormorants and other sea birds abound, while inland each vegetation zone is associated with its own characteristic birds, including, in summer, great numbers of migrants from the Northern Hemisphere.

Population. The government recognizes four groups in the population: 2,191,000 Cape Coloureds (of mixed descent, principally Khoikhoin, white, and Indonesian); 1,477,000 Bantu peoples; 1,212,000 whites; and 23,000 Asians (mostly Pakistanis and Indians). About three-fourths of the population lives in the urban areas of the four largest cities: Cape Town (1,100,000), Port Elizabeth (511,000), Kimberley (136,000), and East London (112,000). Most of the province is sparsely populated. Rural population densities exceed five to the square mile only in a 15- to 50-mile-wide coastal zone from St. Helena Bay to East London and in a few irrigated areas inland, notably along the Vaal and Orange rivers.

Official languages are Afrikaans and English. Afrikaans, a derivative of Nederlands (the official name of the Dutch language), is the first language of more than half of the whites and constitutes a powerful cultural bond endowing them with a group consciousness as Afrikaners. It is also the first language of nearly 90 percent of the Coloureds; the remaining whites and Coloureds are English-speaking. Xhosa is the language of 80 percent of the Bantu peoples, Tswana (mainly in the northern interior) and Sotho of most of the remainder.

Afrikaans, English, Xhosa, and Sotho

More than half of the whites and a third of the Coloureds belong to the Nederduits Gereformeerde and allied churches (Dutch Reformed churches); about a fourth of these groups belong to Anglican or Methodist churches. Malays, constituting about 10 percent of the Coloureds, are adherents of Islām. Two thirds of the Bantu peoples are Christian, more than a fifth being Methodists and lesser numbers members of independent churches.

Administration. Legislative and administrative authority is shared between the province and the republic. While most functions are discharged by the national government, an administrator appointed by the state president and a council of 55 members chosen by the provincial white electorate direct the administration of primary and secondary schools and teacher training institutions, as well as of hospital, public health, library, and conservation services. The administrator and council regulate municipal councils and other local government bodies. The provincial administration is also responsible for the construction and maintenance of provincial roads and minor public works. Revenue is derived primarily from direct taxation, and is supplemented by annual grants from the national government.

The area east of the Great Kei River, formerly consisting of tribal territories that were given a considerable degree of local autonomy in 1894, was formed into a semiautonomous territory for Xhosa-speaking peoples within the republic in 1963. This region, Transkei, is now administered as a republic with a president and a legislative assembly of paramount chiefs, tribal chiefs, and members chosen by the Bantu electorate, with executive authority invested in a cabinet of ministers. Bophuthatswana, consisteing of an area in the north of the Cape of Good Hope, together with areas in the provinces of Transvaal and Orange Free State, was similarly constituted as a republic for Tswana-speaking peoples in 1977. It is administered by a president and an elected legislature. Ciskei adopted a republican form of government in 1981.

Social conditions. Both birth and death rates are considerably higher among Coloureds than whites. The higher Coloured death rate is attributed to high infant mortality, as well as greater incidence of diseases such as gastroenteritis, pneumonia, and tuberculosis that are associated with lower standards of living and hygiene. Life expectancy at birth ranges from 50 years among Coloured males to more than 70 years among white females. Meaningful data for the Bantu peoples, among whom registration of births and deaths is not required, are unavailable.

Free hospital services are provided for lower income groups by the administration and by charitable health services. Smallpox is no longer a hazard, but immunization against poliomyelitis is compulsory and free to all.

School attendance is compulsory for all white and Coloured children from 7 to 16 years of age. Among Bantu peoples school attendance is optional, and educational facilities for them still lag behind population growth. As late as 1970 more than half of the economically active Bantu peoples had received no formal schooling, although most urban and many rural Bantu peoples over 15 years of age were literate in at least one language. By 1980 it was estimated that three-fourths of the Bantu peoples of school age, about one-fifth of the total Bantu population, were attending school. Universities have been established for all population groups: for whites at Cape Town, Grahamstown, Port Elizabeth, and Stellenbosch; and for Coloureds and Asians at Bellville. A university for Bantu-speaking peoples is located at Fort Hare in Ciskei.

Universities

Economy. Although the economy is fairly diversified, farming remains of paramount importance. Of the economically active population one-tenth of the whites, one-fifth of the Coloureds, and nearly three-tenths of the Bantu peoples are employed in agriculture. In a normal year, of South Africa's total farm production, two-thirds of the wheat and wool, 70 percent of the alfalfa (lucerne) hay, most of the mohair, the deciduous fruit, and the grapes, and all of the wine are produced in the Cape. Sheep are raised in the Karoo and cattle in the thornveld north of the Orange River. Alfalfa, sultanas, and cotton are grown under irrigation along the Orange River near Upington; alfalfa and peanuts (groundnuts) are grown in the Harts Valley. Ostriches still graze in the Little Karoo, but alfalfa seed, hay, fruit, tobacco, wool, and mohair have long surpassed ostrich feathers in importance. In the winter rainfall region the lowlands are given over to grain cultivation, sheep raising, and dairy farming, the foothills to vineyards and orchards, and the upland basins to deciduous fruits. These activities support a lively export trade in fresh fruit, table grapes, wine, brandy, and canned goods. In the higher rainfall areas, particularly between Mossel Bay and Humansdorp on the south coast, extensive timber plantations have been established; farther east, citrus fruit is grown under irrigation in the valleys of the Gamtoos, Sundays, Great Fish, and Kat rivers. Chicory and pineapples are produced between Algoa Bay and East London.

Rich fishing grounds lying offshore from the Agulhas Bank to South West Africa/Namibia are actively exploited by South African and foreign vessels, supplying an important fish meal and canning industry.

Manufacturing industries

It is estimated that, of the economically active population, more than one-third of the whites and about one-fifth of the Coloureds and of the Bantu peoples are employed in industries, among them food processing and the manufacture of textiles, clothing, footwear, motor vehicles, tires, agricultural fertilizers, pesticides, mining explosives, and pharmaceuticals, as well as marine engineering and ship repairing.

Mineral resources are extensive, but mining employs relatively few people. Copper has been mined in Namaqualand since 1852, and diamonds in Griqualand West since 1870. Since 1928 diamonds also have been recovered in Namaqualand from deposits on coastal terraces and, more recently, from submarine deposits offshore. Blue asbestos is mined in a zone extending northward from Prieska to beyond Kuruman. Enormous reserves of manganese and high-grade iron ores also are found in Griqualand West; in 1976 a 540-mile railway was completed from Sishen to a new iron-ore-loading terminal accommodating 250,000-ton vessels at Saldanha Bay.

Transport. Harbours and public rail, road, and air transportation services are operated mainly by the South African Railways and Harbours Administration and its subsidiary, South African Airways. Ships drawing up to 40 feet can berth at Cape Town and Port Elizabeth, and ships drawing up to 35 feet at East London; there are two graving docks at Cape Town (one more than 1,000 feet long) and another at East London. Port Elizabeth has ore-loading facilities for iron and manganese, and there are grain elevators at Cape Town and East London. There are more than 5,700 miles of three-foot six-inch gauge railway track in the province as well as an extensive road network. More than 3,000 miles of modern highways link the major cities and towns; there are also more than 45,400 miles of provincial roads. South African Airways operates air services linking the port cities and Kimberley to Bloemfontein, Johannesburg, Pretoria, and Windhoek and also international services to Europe, Australia, and South America.

Cultural life and institutions. The South African Library (founded in 1818), Museum (1825), and National Gallery (1871) are located in Cape Town. There are noteworthy museums in all of the larger urban centres and numerous smaller museums in towns such as Graaff-Reinet, Swellendam, and Tulbagh that foster interest in cultural history, including the work of Cape silversmiths and other colonial artifacts. The heritage of the colonial era also is manifest in traditional country dances and folk songs and in the largely indigenous Cape Dutch architecture of many farmhouses in the western part of the province. The provincial library operates branches in most of the towns and serves rural areas with mobile libraries.

Colonial artifacts

There are several performing arts organizations, especially in Cape Town, where the city's orchestra has presented regular concerts since 1914 and the university has operated a theatre since 1931 and a ballet school since 1934. The Eoan Group, a Cape Coloured organization, fosters operatic talent through amateur productions of professional standards. Since the establishment of the Cape Performing Arts Board in 1963, government subsidies have enabled it to send touring companies to perform outside Cape Town. Since 1971 the board has staged professional ballet, operatic, and theatrical productions throughout the year in its new complex in Cape Town.

BIBLIOGRAPHY. SOUTH AFRICA, OFFICE OF CENSUS AND STATISTICS, *Official Year Book of the Union of South Africa* (annual 1918–60), detailed accounts of the history, physical geography, geology, climate, and vegetation appear in the earlier issues and of all phases of administrative and economic development in all issues; SOUTH AFRICA, DEPARTMENT OF INFORMATION, *Official Yearbook of the Republic of South Africa* (annual 1974–), a replacement for the earlier, discontinued series; SOUTH AFRICA, BUREAU OF STATISTICS, *Statistical Year Book* (annual 1964–66); and SOUTH AFRICA, DEPARTMENT OF STATISTICS (before 1970 BUREAU OF STATISTICS), *South African Statistics* (biennial 1968–), useful sources of statistical data; *Standard Encyclopaedia of Southern Africa*, 12 vol. (1970–76), a comprehensive encyclopedia; A.M. and W.J. TALBOT, *Atlas of the Union of South Africa* (1960), a graphic survey of the climate, vegetation, resources, economic development, and external trade of the Union (1910–50), presented in more than 600 maps and charts; UNIVERSITY OF STELLENBOSCH, INSTITUTE FOR CARTOGRAPHIC ANALYSIS, *Economic Atlas of South Africa* (1980), more than 130 statistical maps.

(W.J.T.)

Cape Town

The city of Cape Town, which is the legislative capital of the Republic of South Africa and the capital of Cape Province, lies at the northern end of the Cape Peninsula some 30 miles (50 kilometres) north of the Cape of Good Hope, the traditional landmark for seamen rounding the southern tip of Africa. It is located in one of the world's most beautiful natural settings for urban life. Parts of the city and its suburbs wind about the steep slopes of Table Mountain (3,563 feet, or 1,086 metres, high) and neighbouring peaks and rim the shores of Table Bay; other parts lie on the flats below the slopes or stretch southward across the flats to False Bay. Cape Town—Kaapstad in Afrikaans—is the "mother city" of South Africa. Although today it is a modern city, it was at one time an outpost at the extremity of the known world. (For further historical aspects, see SOUTHERN AFRICA, HISTORY OF.)

History. Table Bay was visited by Portuguese navigators in the 16th century; French, English, and Netherlands ships later stopped at the Cape for fresh water and provisions. Survivors of the Dutch vessel "Haerlem," wrecked in Table Bay in 1647, brought back such glowing reports of the region that the directors of the Netherlands East India Company ordered that a station to supply ships rounding the Cape be established there. In April 1652 the company's representative, Jan van Riebeeck, stepped ashore to select sites for a fort and a vegetable garden. In 1657 men began to be released from the company's employ so that they could become free burghers and farmers. Inland from Table Mountain, a second company farm was established at Newlands, and vines were planted on the slopes of Wynberg ("wine mountain").

Van Riebeeck and his senior officials formed a council of policy and constituted themselves as a court of justice. Free burghers were invited to join the court in cases involving burghers; later burgher-councillors acquired other functions. In 1681 a fire patrol was introduced, and in 1696 a burgher-watch became responsible for fire protection, the maintenance of roads and water supplies, and the preservation of order. The colony began to spread far beyond the Cape Peninsula, and the council of policy came to rely increasingly on the burgher-councillors for fact-finding and for advice on town affairs.

The importation of slaves, the introduction of political exiles from the Dutch East Indies, and miscegenation with indigenous Khoikhoin (whom the Dutch called Hottentots) increased the population, but at the beginning of the 18th century the town still consisted of only 200 houses. Its growth was accelerated by rising international tensions and growing appreciation of the strategic importance of the Cape. During the Seven Years' War (1756–63), in which the major European powers were involved, many French and British ships called at the port, which from 1773 onward was referred to by British visitors as "Cape Town." During the American Revolutionary War, which exacerbated tensions between rival European powers, a British fleet sought, in 1781, to occupy the Cape, which directors of the English East India Company described as "the Gibraltar of India." A French fleet, however, reached the Cape first, establishing a garrison there to help the Dutch to defend it. The French presence brought prosperity and gaiety to Cape Town and initiated a surge of building. A visitor in 1791 remarked, "Building here is not only a hobby, it is a passion, a contagious madness, which has infected everybody."

Garrisoned by the French

Burgher representation on the court of justice increased to six, and from 1785 onward a committee of this court, consisting of three burghers and three officials, formally advised the court of policy on urban matters. This committee acquired official status in 1793. During the French Revolutionary Wars a British force occupied the Cape in 1795. The committee, known as the burgher-senate, assumed responsibility for the town, which by then had 1,000 houses. In 1803 the colony reverted to the Netherlands. The town received its coat of arms embodying an anchor, symbolizing "good hope," and three golden rings from Van Riebeeck's personal coat of arms.

Britain reoccupied the Cape in 1806. The burgher-senate was abolished in 1828, but in 1840 Cape Town, with a population of 20,000, became a municipality divided into 12 districts, each under an elected commissioner. In 1867, the districts were reduced to six, each with three members, and the chairman became mayor. Suburban development, largely inland to the east and down the Cape Peninsula to the south, followed the radial roads and the railway line, construction of which began in 1859. The Alfred Dock opened in 1870. An influx of people followed the discovery inland of diamonds in 1870 and gold in 1886. These developments, as well as the South African War, from 1899 to 1902, between Britain and the combined forces of the Boer Republics brought about a modest industrialization in Cape Town.

Transformation into a modern city

From 1881 onward a number of separate municipalities came into being. Improved roads, the introduction of an electric tramway, and a common concern for water supplies and sewerage prompted proposals for amalgamation. It was not until 1913, however, three years after the formation of the Union of South Africa, that the town councils of Cape Town and several adjacent towns combined to form Greater Cape Town, with a total population of about 135,000.

The city and its environment. The oldest section of Cape Town lies in the area between Table Mountain, its outlying ridges known as Lion's Head, Signal Hill, and Devil's Peak, and the shores of Table Bay. Colourful neighbourhoods include the so-called Malay Quarter, on the lower slopes of Signal Hill, and an area above the Castle. The construction of the Duncan Dock between 1938 and 1945 resulted in the reclamation of 480 acres (194 hectares) from Table Bay, much of which became available for the extension of the central business district. Present-day residential suburbs stretch around the western side of Signal Hill and the mountain, northward to the adjoining municipality of Milnerton, and southward to False Bay. Industrial development largely followed the railway line eastward to the interior. In this direction lie the municipalities of Goodwood, Parow, and Bellville. The four magisterial districts of Cape, Wynberg, Bellville, and Simonstown constitute the main urbanized area of metropolitan Cape Town.

Buildings. In addition to the Castle of Good Hope, the city's oldest monument, built between 1666 and 1677, interesting buildings include the Old Supreme Court, which incorporates part of the structure of a slave lodge built in 1680. The walls of Groot Constantia, the homestead built by Gov. Simon van der Stel in the nearby Constantia Valley, date from about 1685, and the Groote Kerk ("Great Church"; 1836) incorporates a tower built in 1704. Some of the humble flat-roofed homes on the slopes of Signal Hill may date from the 18th century. One of the finest of several larger buildings remaining from that time, however, is the Koopmans-de Wet House (1701), which has furnishings from the same era; it is an annex of the Cultural History Museum.

Dutch architecture

Much of Cape Town's early architecture reflected prototypes from the Netherlands that were modified for the region. Of special interest is the local version of the gable. L.M. Thibault, a French architect who arrived in 1793, designed much that was then fashionable in building. Recent architecture reflects European and American trends, and high-rise structures are common. Planning

Cape Peninsula, showing Cape Town (centre) with Table Mountain behind. On the right of Cape Town are Lion's Head and Signal Hill.
Georg Gerster—Rapho Guillumette

of the reclaimed shore led to prolonged discussion and delay in development. A broad boulevard, the Heerengracht, now leads from the harbour to the centre of the city; in this area are situated the provincial opera house (1971) and the municipal centre (1972).

Climate. The climate is Mediterranean in type; it is locally modified by the mass of Table Mountain and by the cold Benguela Current of the South Atlantic. Temperatures average a high of 81° F (27° C) in February, and a low of 45° F (7° C) in July, but it is cooler on the mountain slopes and on the coast. Infrequent freezing occurs. On the average, rain falls on 69 days of the year, over half of it between May and August, the southern winter. The amount of fall varies with proximity to the mountain, those areas close to the slopes receiving as much as twice the precipitation of areas further away. The generally strong winds come from the northwest in winter, and vary from between southeast and southwest in summer. The southerly winds produce a cloud covering of condensed moisture over Table Mountain known as the "table cloth." Referred to as the "Cape doctor," these winds keep air pollution at a low level.

Demography. In 1970 the population of the city of Cape Town was about 722,000. This consisted of about 218,000 whites, 410,000 Coloureds (a legally defined group of mixed racial ancestry), about 10,000 Asians, and 83,000 Bantu. At the same time the population of the metropolitan area was about 1,097,000, consisting of about 379,000 whites, 599,000 Coloureds, 11,000 Asians, and 108,000 Bantu. In the metropolitan area in 1960, English was the home language of about 61 percent of the whites, Afrikaans of about 33 percent, and about 2 percent were equally at home in both languages; about 1 percent spoke German, 1 percent Netherlands, and about 0.33 percent Portuguese. Of the Coloured population, Afrikaans was the home language of 79 percent, English of 18 percent, and both languages 2 percent. The Bantu were predominantly Xosa-speaking. In 1951 about 30 percent of the whites were Anglicans, about 27 percent members of the Nederduits and allied churches, 9 percent of the Roman Catholic church, about 9 percent Methodist, and about 8 percent Jewish.

Housing. Government legislation controls the presence and employment of Bantu outside their reservations. Nearly all Bantu in Cape Town are housed in the townships of Langa, Guguletu, and Nyanga. Public utilities are affected by this policy of segregation; over three-quarters of the rush-hour bus riders are nonwhite—a circumstance which creates problems in maintaining services that are both effective and segregated.

A segregated city

The heavy influx of Coloured work-seekers from the country districts into Cape Town, coupled with the high birth rate, and the removal of Coloured people from areas of the city proclaimed by state legislation to be for white occupation, has presented the municipality with an acute housing problem. By the early 1970s more than 3,000 low-cost housing units had been built for Coloured occupancy, but almost an equal number were still required.

Government. The municipality of Cape Town functions under two main provincial ordinances—those of 1951 and of 1965. The latter brought into effect a system whereby the council delegated much of its authority to an executive committee consisting of a chairman and four members. Each of the four is chairman of a standing committee, which may make recommendations to the full council only through the executive committee. The municipal area is divided into 17 wards, with two councillors representing each ward. From 1972 onward, half the sitting councillors retired biennially. Responsibility for maintaining civil law and order rests with the state, but the municipality has its own traffic police, market constables, and beach and park control officers. There is also a municipal fire brigade.

Economic life. A petroleum refinery and chemical, fertilizer, cement, and automobile-assembly factories are situated in the metropolitan area. In the city the basic industries are connected with ship repair and maintenance, textile and clothing manufacture, food processing, and building. Cape Town is well served by department stores and supermarkets. Numbers of nationwide commercial concerns have their head offices in Cape Town, including a bank, a chain-store, and several insurance companies, one of which was founded in 1845. The result of enforced social categorization can be seen in comparative income figures. In 1960 the average income of whites was over five times that of Coloureds, and over three times that of Asiatics.

Transportation and utilities. The port of Cape Town was for long the main gateway to South Africa, handling millions of tons of cargo annually; by the early 1970s, however, most air passengers arrived at Johannesburg, and the port of Durban handled three times as much cargo as Cape Town. The port will not admit ships of more than 40-foot draft at low tide, but its repair facilities and its dry dock are of great importance to interoceanic traffic, especially when the Suez Canal is closed. Extensions to the harbour, and the first of two new basins that are planned, were under construction in the early 1970s. The D.F. Malan Airport acquired international status in 1970, when extensions were begun to accommodate the new large jet aircraft. Cape Town is the terminus of a railway network that extends northward to Rhodesia and beyond. A new railway station was opened in 1968, partly to assist with the heavy suburban passenger traffic. Two private bus companies also serve the area.

Port facilities

In 1958, a major program of freeway construction was launched, backed by the city, the provincial administration, and the central government. Two main radial freeways were developed, both leading southward to False Bay. Supplementing these were two national routes and a beltway circling the central business district.

Cape Town's water is obtained from reservoirs at Wemmershoek, 40 miles east of Cape Town; Steenbras, 30 miles southeast; and Voëlvlei, 40 miles northeast. Electricity is produced by two municipal power stations, at Table Bay and Athlone. The latter carries the major load and in the early 1970s was being expanded. Future supplies are to be purchased in bulk from the national grid of the Electricity Supply Commission, whose first nuclear power station at Melkbosstrand, on the coast 20

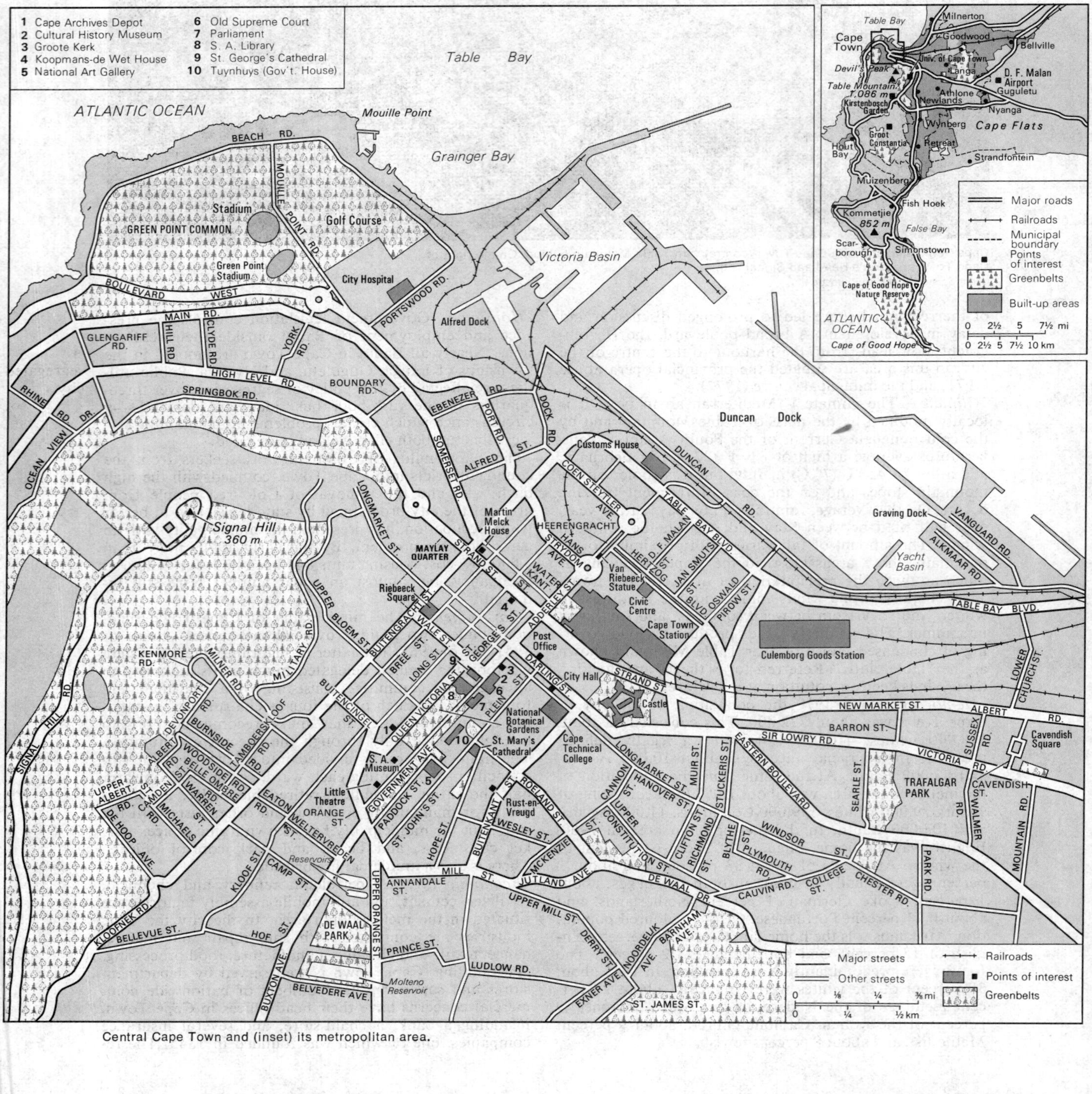

Central Cape Town and (inset) its metropolitan area.

miles north of Cape Town, was under construction in the early 1980s.

Communications. There are three daily newspapers in Cape Town, *Die Burger* in Afrikaans and the *Cape Times* and *The Argus* in English. Radio broadcasting is restricted to the state-controlled South African Broadcasting Corporation, which operates, in addition to its national English, Afrikaans, bilingual commercial, and Bantu programs, the Radio Good Hope—a commercial service that broadcasts music and news in English and Afrikaans. Television broadcasts began in 1976.

Health and welfare. The provincial administration is responsible for the main hospital services, which are virtually free to the needy. The best known of the hospitals is the Groote Schuur, where the world's first heart transplant was carried out in 1967. In suburban Bellville are the Karl Bremer and Tiervlei hospital complexes. The mental hospitals (Valkenberg and Stikland) are administered by the State Department of Health. The Cape Town municipality is responsible for infectious diseases and chest hospitals, and it maintains many treatment centres and clinics.

Social insurance measures, such as workmen's compensation, unemployment insurance, disability grants, and pensions for war veterans, the aged, and the blind, are administered by the Cape Town offices of the relevant state departments. There are also some 300 voluntary welfare associations that offer services to beneficiaries of all races and religions.

Education. The provincial administration is responsible for the schooling of whites. The South African College, founded in 1829, and Rondebosch Boys' High School are notable among the numerous government schools, and Diocesan College (founded in 1849) is notable among the private educational institutions. Schooling for Coloureds and Bantu is provided by central government departments. The Cape College for Advanced Technical Education falls under the Central Department of National Education. The University of Cape Town developed from the South African College and came formally into being in 1918. Its main buildings occupy a magnificent site on the Groote Schuur estate of Cecil Rhodes, a major historical figure in the development of South Africa's mining industry and at one time a prime minister of Cape Colony. The University of the Western Cape, for Coloureds, is situated near Bellville.

The University of Cape Town

Cultural life and recreation. The South African Library, Museum, and National Gallery occupy sites on what was once the garden of the East India Company. Adjacent is the Cape Archives Depot of the Government Archives Service. The Municipal Botanic Gardens is located in the remains of the garden; the National Botanic Gardens at Kirstenbosch are renowned. The Library of Parliament contains a notable collection of Africana, and pictures of African interest are exhibited in the Castle of Good Hope and Rusten-Vreugde. The Old Supreme Court building houses the Cultural History Museum.

The municipality of Cape Town supplies a free library service. The Cape Town Symphony Orchestra, the South African College of Music, the Cape Performing Arts Board, and the Little Theatre provide concerts, opera, ballet, and dramatic performances. Public lectures are organized by the department of extramural studies of the university.

Cape Town has more than 150 formal recreation areas, parks, and playgrounds. There are facilities for most spectator sports, from horse and motor racing to table tennis. The Green Point Stadium can accommodate 33,000. Separate recreation areas for Coloureds and for Bantu are maintained. The 90 miles of peninsula coastline abound in sites for swimming, fishing, and skin diving, and yachting has become a popular pastime. There are many scenic drives, and on the mountains are many walks and climbs. A cableway to the summit of Table Mountain provides spectacular views of Cape Town and its environs.

BIBLIOGRAPHY. No academic history of Cape Town has yet been written; the best outline available is that in J.R. SHORTEN, *Cape Town* (1963). P.W. LAIDLER, *The Growth and Government of Cape Town* (1939), is not as comprehensive as the title suggests. The most colourful descriptions of the history may be found in W.J. PICARD, *Gentleman's Walk: The Romantic Story of Cape Town's Oldest Streets, Lanes and Squares* (1968), and *Grand Parade: The Birth of Greater Cape Town 1850–1913* (1969). Commercial development is well treated by R.F.M. IMMELMAN, *Men of Good Hope* (1955), whereas the general background is sketched by A.F. HATTERSLEY in *An Illustrated Social History of South Africa* (1969). Some useful essays appear in A.H. HONIKMAN (ed.), *Cape Town: City of Good Hope* (1966). J.A. MABBUTT (ed.), *The Cape Peninsula* (1952), contains brief but valuable descriptions, whereas the geographical setting was sketched by W.J. TALBOT, "Kapstadt als Weltstadt," in J.H. SCHULTZE (ed.), *Zum Problem der Weltstadt* (1959). Vital statistical information is contained in the CAPE PROVINCIAL ADMINISTRATION, *Greater Cape Town Region, Planning Reports* (mimeographed 1967–68); in the REPUBLIC OF SOUTH AFRICA, BUREAU OF STATISTICS, *Population Census 6th September, 1960*, vol. 2, no. 1, *Report on the Metropolitan Area of Cape Town* (1966); and in DEPARTMENT OF STATISTICS, *Statistical News Release*, Pretoria, May 14, 1971, *Population Census 6 May 1970*, No. 3, Cape District, No. 4, Bellville, No. 5, Simonstown, and No. 5, Wynberg. Also valuable are annual reports by various departments of the City of Cape Town, especially that of the medical officer of health, which includes statistics of population. For town planning and traffic, see S.S. MORRIS, "South Africa's Approach to Urban Traffic and Freeways," *Traffic Quarterly*, 18:202–218 (1964); and "Cape Town: Metropolis in the Making," *Town Planning Review*, 40:102–118 (1969).

(E.A.)

Cape Verde

Cape Verde (Cabo Verde) is a republic comprising a group of islands that lie 385 miles (620 kilometres) off the west coast of Africa, between 17°30′ N and 14°30′ N, and 25°30′ W and 22°30′ W. With a total land area of 1,557 square miles (4,033 square kilometres), the population of the islands was 296,000 in 1980. Praia (population 21,500) on São Tiago is the capital.

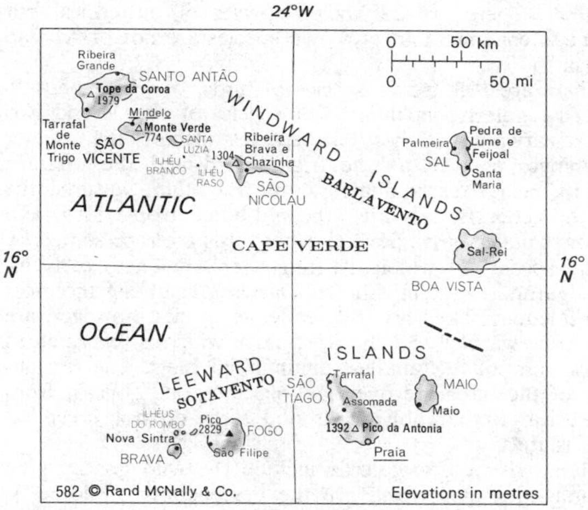

CAPE VERDE

Cape Verde is named after the westernmost cape of Africa. The country consists of 10 islands and five islets, which are divided into the Windward (Ilhas de Barlavento) and Leeward (Ilhas de Sotavento) groups. The Windward Islands consist of Santo Antão, São Vicente, Santa Luzia, São Nicolau, Boa Vista, and Sal, together with the islets of Raso and Branco. The Leeward Islands include Maio, São Tiago, Fogo, and Brava, and the three islets called the Rombos—Grande, Luís Carneiro, and Cima.

The islands of the archipelago

The largest port in the islands is Mindelo (Porto Grande) on São Vicente. Its deepwater harbour—formed by a volcanic crater with its seaward wall breached—accommodates vessels of any size and is used primarily as a fuelling station.

The landscape. *Relief.* The islands are mountainous and are volcanic in origin. Only three of them—Boa Vista, Maio, and Sal—have much level ground. Fogo (meaning "fire") is an active volcano that last erupted in

1951. Its cone rises 9,281 feet (2,829 metres) above sea level. The peak of Tope da Coroa on Santo Antão is 6,493 feet. São Tiago and São Nicolau both have mountains more than 4,200 feet high. All the islands, especially the Windwards, have been eroded by sand carried by high winds, so that the outline of the landscape appears jagged. On most of the islands the cliffs rise sheer from the sea.

Climate. Moderate, stable temperatures and extreme aridity characterize the climate. February is the coolest month, with an average temperature of 71° F (22° C), and September is the warmest, having an average of 80° F (27° C). The islands have almost no rainfall, except for a period from August through October, when an average of 0.8 inch (20 millimetres) a month is recorded. The sun, though seldom obscured by rain clouds, is sometimes blocked by a dense mist of fine sand that is brought by trade winds from the Sahara.

Vegetation. The distribution of plant life in the archipelago is strongly affected by variations in the temperature and the rainfall. Springs in the hills, replenished during the rainy season, provide water for irrigation of farms in the valleys below. On the windward slopes of the hills, the lack of rain produces desert conditions, and the sparse shrubs, already overgrazed by goats, almost disappear. The shrubs remaining in these areas are mostly thorny or bitter; some are toxic. A sea mist on the higher hills permits some agriculture. Monte Verde, the green mountain of São Vicente, is so called because aloes grow high up, and crops can be raised on a few patches of land. Salt areas on Maio and Sal have interesting xerophilous plants.

Animal life. The scarcity of water limits the number of land turtles in the archipelago, but two species of sea turtles lay their eggs on the sandy shores of the uninhabited islets. There are no venomous snakes, but there are many geckos, lizards, and several species of skinks. A species of giant skink is protected by law, but it may be extinct. There are 23 known species of butterflies, but none is endemic, and only two species are not of African origin.

Birds

There are 105 known species of birds, of which only 38 breed regularly, including four species of petrels and two of shearwaters. Other bird species include the greater flamingo, as well as the frigate bird and the buzzard (both nearly exterminated), the Egyptian vulture, the Cape Verde Islands kite, the red-billed tropic bird, and many smaller birds. Several other birds are represented by local species, of which the kingfisher, known to early investigators (including Charles Darwin), is among the most conspicuous. The only truly endemic species, however, are the cane warbler and the Raso lark, which is restricted to Raso, one of the smallest uninhabited islets. The remainder of the birds are overseas migrants, one at least from America. Remarkably, gulls and terns do not breed on the islands.

Mammals of Cape Verde include the wild goats to be found on Fogo, which are the descendants of domestic goats that were brought to the islands and managed to escape. The Senegal green monkey, found on São Tiago, was introduced to the islands from Africa. Rodents on the islands are believed to have originally escaped from visiting ships. A long-eared bat of European origin has been discovered.

People and population. *Ethnic and linguistic groups.* Of the islands' population of nearly 300,000, about 70 percent are Creoles (mulattoes) and the remainder are European and African. The population is descended, in part, from African slaves that were imported by the early Portuguese settlers to work their plantations. Others are descendants of slaves who were brought to the islands in order to be shipped across the Atlantic and were left in Cape Verde when the slave trade was abolished. Most of the principal ethnic types associated with the African continent—Arab, black, Hamitic—are in evidence among the population. European strains were introduced not only by the Portuguese but also by visiting sailors. Most of the Europeans on the islands—among whom the Portuguese predominate—live mainly in Praia on São Tiago, or in Mindelo on São Vicente. The islands farther away from these two ports are almost entirely populated by Creoles.

Apart from Portuguese, the language of the educated people of Cape Verde, the inhabitants speak a Cape Verdean Creole dialect called Crioulo. Because rough seas separate the different islands, the dialect varies from one island to another. Most of the population is officially Roman Catholic, but a flourishing Protestant mission based in São Tiago has a church and schools on most of the islands. Many animist customs and a belief in voodoo still survive, however, in the more remote and pure African villages. A Cape Verdean version of the melancholy Portuguese song and dance, the *fada*, is known locally as the *morna*.

Emigration

Demography. Since the 1940s the population has been increasing, despite a steady emigration to Brazil, Africa, Portugal, and the United States. The census taken in 1980 reported 296,000 as the total population. As a result of the Angolan war for independence (1961–75), many emigrants have returned to the islands, and others have gone to join friends and relatives in Canada, the United States, Venezuela, and Brazil, so that the 1980 census figure is only approximate. The overall density is 190 persons per square mile (73 persons per square kilometre). Praia and Mindelo are the only large towns. The remainder of the population lives in the few fertile valleys or in small fishing hamlets on the coast.

Cape Verde, Area and Population

	area		population	
	sq mi*	sq km	1970 census	1980 census*
Districts (*distritos*)				
Barlavento	861	2,230	101,800	108,000
Counties (*concelhos*)				
Boa Vista	239	620	3,500	3,400
Paúl	21	54	8,000	8,000
Porto Novo	215	558	13,700	13,300
Ribeira Grande	64	167	23,200	21,900
Sal	83	216	5,600	6,000
São Nicolau	150	388	16,300	13,600
São Vicente	88	227	31,500	41,800
Sotavento	696	1,803	170,300	188,100
Counties				
Brava	26	67	7,800	7,000
Fogo	184	476	29,600	31,100
Maio	104	269	3,500	4,100
Praia†	152	396	71,400	57,200
Santa Catarina†	93	243	31,700	41,200
Santa Cruz†	58	149	—	23,100
Tarrafal	78	203	26,300	24,500
Total Cape Verde	1,557	4,033	272,100	296,100

*Figures do not add to totals given because of rounding. †Santa Cruz was formed after the 1970 census from territory formerly belonging to Praia and Santa Catarina.
Source: Official government figures.

Almost 60 percent of the people of Cape Verde are under 20 years of age. Many of the inhabitants above this age go overseas, where they seek work as labourers in the oil fields of Venezuela or as professionals in Portuguese-speaking Brazil. These emigrants send money home to their families, and many of them return to the islands upon retirement. Some of the professionals have come back, since a new government was established in 1975.

History. The date of the islands' discovery is disputed; the Venetian captain Alvise Ca' da Mosto (Cadamosto) claimed to have visited them in 1456, but his account is not universally accepted. In 1460 the Portuguese navigators Diogo Gomes and António de Noli discovered Maio and São Tiago. In 1462 the first settlers from Portugal landed on São Tiago, subsequently founding there the oldest European city in the tropics—Ribeira Grande. With the development of transatlantic slave trade, the importance and the wealth of the islands increased. In 1532 the first bishop was consecrated, and in 1595 the first governor general was appointed. The prosperity of Ribeira Grande, however, attracted pirates, who attacked the city in 1541. The English later attacked it twice—in 1585 and 1592—the first time under the command of Sir Francis Drake. After a French attack in 1712, the city was abandoned. To protect the islands against future assaults, the fortress of São Filipe was built.

With the decline of the slave trade (which was finally abolished in 1876), and with increasing drought, the prosperity of the islands slowly vanished. In the early 1800s they experienced recurrent drought and famine as well as government corruption and maladministration. Conditions improved toward the end of the 1800s, however, as the development of internal trade and communications led to the establishment at Mindelo of a coaling station and a submarine cable station. After World War I prosperity again declined as fewer ships visited Mindelo. Only after World War II did trade again increase and relative prosperity return.

The Portuguese administration of Cape Verde was unified under a governor in 1587. The islands' status was changed in 1951 from that of a colony to an overseas province. In 1961 all citizens were given full Portuguese citizenship.

Independence

On July 5, 1975, Cape Verde Islands became an independent republic. The first president of the newly independent nation, Aristide Pereira, had been secretary general of the African Party for the Independence of Guinea and Cape Verde (PAIGC) since 1973. The island republic is a member of the Organization of African Unity and of the United Nations. A foreign policy of nonalignment has been declared.

The economy. An international airport on Sal gives work to many of that island's inhabitants. At Praia a government centre provides work, as does the bunkering trade in Mindelo.

The vast majority of Cape Verde's work force has traditionally been employed as agricultural labourers. Bananas and coffee have been the chief agricultural exports. Crops grown for local consumption include corn (maize), sugarcane, castor beans, broad beans, potatoes, and peanuts (groundnuts). Since 1969, however, a severe drought has affected the islands, causing a nearly 80 percent unemployment rate in 1975.

Salt is an important product on the islands of Sal, Maio, and Boa Vista. Volcanic rock, a pozzolana that is used in making cement, is exported. There are few other exports, and the total is not sufficient to pay for necessary imports.

Transportation. There is air service between Espargos, the international airport located on Sal, and Lisbon. Within the islands schooners and a small plane provide local service. On land there are few roads—only 471 miles; one-third of these are on São Tiago. Most of the people travel on foot.

Prospects. In the early 1980s construction began on a desalinization plant in Cape Verde. Through such methods as desalinization, it is expected that the islands' severe water shortage can be reduced or eliminated. In addition, a major goal of the islands' government is the development of a modern fishing industry, which was furthered by the building of the country's fist cold storage plant in 1981. The progress of all plans for economic advancemnt, however, depends on the amount of financial aid Cape Verde receives from the international community.

BIBLIOGRAPHY. G.R. CRONE (ed. and trans.), *The Voyages of Cadamosto and Other Documents on Western Africa in the Second Half of the Fifteenth Century* (1937, reprinted 1967), is an account by Alvise Ca' da Mosto (Cadamosto), a Venetian explorer and trader who appears to have been the first European to land on the Cape Verdes; whether he, as he claimed, or the Portuguese were the first also to discover the archipelago is discussed in the introduction to this volume. WILLIAM DAMPIER, *A New Voyage Round the World*, 3 vol. (1698–1703; various later editions and reprints), contains one of the earliest descriptions of the islands. DAVID A. and W.M. BANNERMAN, *Birds of the Atlantic Islands*, vol. 4, *A History of the Birds of the Cape Verde Islands* (1968), includes a useful general bibliography and an account of the islands' history, explorers, vegetation, birds, and butterflies. See also CAPE VERDE ISLANDS, *25 Anos de Actividade* (1951), a review of social and economic progress from 1926. For economic and demographic information prior to independence, see *Anuário Estatístico*, vol. 2, *Províncias Ultramarinas*, of the government of Portugal.

(W.M.B.)

Capital and Interest

Capital, in economics, is a word with many meanings. They all imply that capital is a "stock", in contrast with income, which is a "flow." In its broadest possible sense, capital includes the human population; nonmaterial elements such as skills, abilities, and education; land, buildings, machines, and other equipment; and all stocks of goods—finished or unfinished—in the hands of both firms and households.

In the business world the word capital usually refers to an item in the balance sheet representing that part of the net worth of an enterprise that has not been produced through the operations of the enterprise. In economics the word capital is generally confined to "real" as opposed to merely "financial" assets. Different as the two concepts may seem, they are not unrelated. If all balance sheets were consolidated in a closed economic system, all debts would be cancelled out because every debt is an asset in one balance sheet and a liability in another. What is left in the consolidated balance sheet, therefore, is a value of all the real assets of a society on one side and its total net worth on the other. This is the economist's concept of capital.

Kinds of capital

A distinction may be made between goods in the hands of firms and goods in the hands of households, and attempts have been made to confine the term capital to the former. There is also a distinction between goods that have been produced and goods that are supplied by nature; attempts have been made to confine the term capital to the former, though the distinction is hard to maintain in practice. Another important distinction is between the stock of human beings (and their abilities) and the stock of nonhuman elements. In a slave society human beings are counted as capital in the same way as livestock or machines. In a free society each person is his own slave—the value of the body and mind is not, therefore, an article of commerce and does not get into the accounting system. In strict logic human beings should continue to be regarded as part of the capital of a society; but in practice the distinction between the part of the total stock that enters into the accounting system and the part that does not is so important that many writers have excluded human beings from the capital stock.

Another distinction that has some historical importance is that between fixed and circulating capital. Fixed capital is usually defined as that which does not change its form in the course of the process of production, such as land, buildings, and machines. Circulating capital consists of raw materials, goods in process, and stocks of finished goods waiting to be sold. Either these goods must be transformed, as when wheat is ground into flour, or they must change ownership, as when a stock of goods is sold. This distinction, like many others, is not always easy to maintain. Nevertheless, it does represent a rough approach to an important problem of the relative structure of capital—that is, of the proportions in which goods of various kinds are found. The stock of real capital exhibits strong complementarities. A machine is of no use without a skilled operator and without raw materials for processing.

THE DEVELOPMENT OF CAPITAL THEORY

The classical school. Although ancient and medieval writers were interested in the ethics of interest and usury, the concept of capital did not rise to prominence in economic thought until the late 16th and early 17th centuries—the period of the classical economists Adam Smith, David Ricardo, Nassau Senior, and John Stuart Mill.

The ideas of economists about capital

Smith laid great stress on the role that was played by the accumulation of a stock of capital in facilitating the division of labour and in increasing the productivity of labour in general. He recognized clearly that accumulation proceeds from excess of production over consumption. He distinguished between productive labour, which creates objects of capital, and unproductive labour (services), the fruits of which are enjoyed immediately. His thought was strongly coloured by observation of the annual agricultural cycle. End of the harvest saw society with a given stock of grain. This stock was in the possession of the capitalists. A certain portion of it they reserved for their own consumption and for the consumption of their menial servants, the rest was used to feed "productive labourers" during the ensuing year. As a result, by the end of the next harvest the barns were full again and the stock had replaced itself, perhaps with something left over. The stock that the capitalists did not reserve for their own use was the "wages fund"—the more grain there was in the barn in October the sharper the competition of capitalists for workers, and the higher real wages would be in the year to come. The picture is a crude one, of course, and does not indicate the complexity of the relationship between stocks and flows in an industrial society. The last of the classical economists, John Stuart Mill, was forced to abandon the wages-fund theory. Nevertheless, the wages fund is a crude representation of some real but complex relationships, and the theory reappears in a more sophisticated form in later writers.

The classical economists distinguished three categories of income—wages, profit, and rent—and identified these with three factors of production—labour, capital, and land. Ricardo especially made a sharp distinction between capital as "produced means of production," and land as the "original and indestructible powers of the soil." In modern economics this distinction has become blurred.

The Austrian school. About 1870 a new school developed, sometimes called the Austrian school from the fact that many of its principal members taught in Vienna, but better perhaps called the Marginalist school. The movement itself was thoroughly international, and included such figures as William Stanley Jevons in England and León Walras in France. The so-called Austrian theory of capital is mainly based on the work of Eugen Böhm-Bawerk. His *Positive Theory of Capital* (1889) set off a controversy that has not yet subsided. In the Austrian view the economic process consisted of the embodiment of "original factors of production" in capital goods of greater or lesser length of life that then yielded value or utility as they were consumed. Between the original embodiment of the factor and the final fruition in consumption lay an interval of time known as the period of production. In an equilibrium population it can easily be shown that the total population (capital stock) equals the annual number of births or deaths (income) multiplied by the average length of life (period of production). The longer the period of production, therefore, the more capital goods there will be per unit of income. If the period of production is constant, income depends directly on the amount of capital previously accumulated. Here is the wages fund in a new form. Unfortunately, the usefulness of Böhm-Bawerk's theory is much impaired by the fact that it is confined to equilibrium states. The great problems of capital theory are dynamic in character, and comparative statics throws only a dim light on them.

Later thinking. The Marginalist school culminated in the work of three men—P.H. Wicksteed in England, Knut Wicksell in Sweden, and Irving Fisher in the United States. The last two especially gave the Austrian theory clear mathematical expression. Perhaps the greatest contribution of the Austrian theory was its recognition of the importance of the valuation problem in the relation of capital to interest. From the mere fact that physical capital produces an income stream, there is no explanation of the phenomenon of interest, for the question is why the value of a piece of physical capital should be less than the total of future values that are expected to accrue from it. The theory also makes a contribution to the problem of rational choice in situations involving waiting or maturing. The best example is that of slowly maturing goods such as wines or timber. There is a problem here of the best time to draw wine or to cut down a tree. According to the marginal theory this is at the time when the rate of net value growth of the item is just equal to the rate of interest, or the rate of return in alternative investments. Thus, if a tree or a wine is increasing in value at the rate of 7 percent per annum when the rate of interest is 6 percent it still pays to be patient and let it grow or mature. The longer it grows, however, the less the rate of value growth, and when the rate of value growth has fallen to the rate of interest, then is the time to reap the fruits of patience.

The contributions of John Maynard (Lord) Keynes to capital theory are incidental rather than fundamental. Nevertheless, the "Keynesian revolution" had an impact on this area of economic thought as on most others. It overthrew the traditional assumption of most economists that savings were automatically invested. The great contribution of Keynes, then, is the recognition that the attempt to save does not automatically result in the accumulation of capital. A decision to restrict consumption is only a decision to accumulate capital if the volume of production is constant. If abstention from consumption itself results in a diminution of production, then accumulation (production minus consumption) is correspondingly reduced.

CONTINUING PROBLEMS

Important theoretical questions

The theory of capital was not a matter of primary concern to economists in the mid-20th century, though some revival of interest occurred in the late 1950s. Nevertheless, certain problems remain of perennial interest. They may be grouped as follows.

Heterogeneous goods. First are the problems involved in measuring aggregates of goods. Real capital includes everything from screwdrivers to continuous strip-rolling mills. A single measure of total real capital can be achieved only if each item can be expressed in a common denominator such as a given monetary unit (*e.g.*, dollars, sterling, francs, etc.). The problem is particularly complicated in periods of rapid technical change when there is change not only in the relative values of items but in the nature of the list itself. Only approximate solutions can be found to this problem and no completely satisfactory measure is possible.

A related problem that has aroused considerable interest among accountants is how to value capital assets that have no fixed price. In the conventional balance sheet the value of some items is based on their cost at an earlier period than that of others. When the general level of prices is changing this means that different items are valued in monetary units of different purchasing power. The problem is particularly acute in the valuation of inventory. Under the more conventional "FIFO" (First In, First Out) system, inventory is valued at the cost (purchase price) of the latest purchases. This leads to an inflation of inventory values, and therefore of accounting profits, in time of rising prices (and a corresponding deflation under falling prices), which may be an exaggeration of the long-run position of the firm. This may be partially avoided by a competing system of valuation known as LIFO (Last In, First Out), in which inventory is valued at the purchase price of the earliest purchases. This avoids the fluctuations caused by short-run price-level changes, but it fails to record changes in real long-run values. There seems to be no completely satisfactory solution to this problem, and it is wise to recognize the fact that any single figure of capital value that purports to represent a complex, many-dimensional reality will need careful interpretation.

The accumulation process. A second problem concerns the factors that determine the rate of accumulation of capital; that is, the rate of investment. It has been seen that investment in real terms is the difference between production and consumption. The classical economist laid great stress on frugality as the principal source of capital accumulation. If production is constant it is true that the only way to increase accumulation is by the reduction of consumption. Keynes shifted the emphasis from the reduction of consumption to the increase of production, and regarded the decision to produce investment goods as the principal factor determining the rate of growth of capital. In modern theories of economic development great stress is laid on the problem of the structure of production—the relative proportions of different kinds of activity. The advocates of "balanced growth" emphasize the need for a developing country to invest in a wide range of related and cooperative enterprises, public as well as private. There is no point in building factories and machines, they say, if the educational system does not provide a labour force capable of using them. There is also, however, a case to be made for "unbalanced growth," in the sense that growth in one part of the economy frequently stimulates growth in other parts. A big investment in mining or in hydroelectric power, for example, creates strains on the whole society, which result in growth responses in the complementary sectors. The relation of inflation to economic growth and investment is an important though difficult problem. There seems to be little doubt that deflation, mainly because it shifts the distribution of income away from the profit maker toward the *rentier* and bondholder, has a deleterious effect on investment and the growth of capital. In 1932, for instance, real investment had practically ceased in the United States. It is less clear at what point inflation becomes harmful to investment. In countries where there has been long continuing inflation there seems to be some evidence that the structure of investment is distorted. Too much goes into apartment houses and factories and not enough into schools and communications.

Capital and time. A third problem in capital theory is that of the period of production and the time structure of the economic process. This cannot be solved by the simple formulas of the Austrian school. Nevertheless, the problem is a real one and there is still a need for more useful theoretical formulations of it. Decisions taken today have results extending far into the future. Similarly, the data of today's decisions are the result of decisions taken long in the past. The existing capital structure is the embodiment of past decisions and the raw material of present decisions. The incompatibility of decisions is frequently not discovered at the time they are made because of the lapse of time between the decision and its consequences. It is tempting to regard the cyclical structure of human history, whether the business cycle or the war cycle, as a process by which the consequences of bad decisions accumulate until some kind of crisis point is reached. The crisis (war or depression) redistributes power in the society and so leads to a new period of accumulating, but hidden, stress. In this process, distortion in the capital structure is of great importance.

Capital and income. A fourth problem is the relationship between the stocks and the flows of a society, or in a narrower sense the relation between capital and income. Income, like capital, is a concept capable of many definitions; a useful approach to the concept of income is to regard it as the gross addition to capital in a given period. For any economic unit, whether a firm or an individual, income may be measured by that hypothetical amount of consumption that would leave capital intact. In real terms this is practically identical with the concept of production. The total flow of income is closely related to both the quantity and structure of capital; the total real income of a society depends on the size and skills of its population, and on the nature and extent of the equipment with which they have to work. The most important single measure of economic well-being is real income per person; this is closely related to the productivity of labour, and this in turn is closely related to capital per person, especially if the results of investment in human resources, skills, and education are included in the capital stock.

INTEREST

The nature of interest

Historically, the concept of capital has been so closely bound to the concept of interest that it seems wise to take these two topics together, even though in the modern view it is capital and income rather than capital and interest that are the related concepts.

Interest as a form of income may be defined as income received as a result of the possession of contractual obligations for payment on the part of another. Interest, in other words, is income received as a result of the ownership of a bond, a promissory note, or some other instrument that represents a promise on the part of some other party to pay sums in the future. The obligations may take many forms. In the case of the perpetuity, the undertaking is to pay a certain sum each year or other interval of time for the indefinite future. A bond with a date of maturity usually involves a promise to pay a certain sum each year for a given number of years, and then a larger sum on the terminal date. A promissory note frequently consists of a promise to pay a single sum at a date some time in the future.

If $a_1, a_2, \ldots a_n$ are the sums received by the bondholder in years $1, 2 \ldots n$, and if P_o is the present value in year O, or the sum for which the bond is purchased, the rate of interest r in the whole transaction is given by the equation

$$P_o = a_1(1+r)^{-1} + a_2(1+r)^{-2} + \cdots + a_n(1+r)^{-n}.$$

There is no general solution for this equation, though in practice it can be solved easily by successive approximation, and in special cases the equation reduces to much simpler forms. In the case of a promissory note, for instance, the equation reduces to the form

$$P_o = a_n(1+r)^{-n}, \text{ or } \log(1+r) = \frac{\log a_n - \log P_o}{n}$$

where a_n is the single promised payment. In the case of a perpetuity with an annual payment of a, the formula reduces to

$$P_o = a[(1+r)^{-1} + (1+r)^{-2} + \cdots \text{ to inf.}] = \frac{a}{r}$$

whence $r = \dfrac{a}{P_o}$.

Thus if one had to pay $200 to purchase a perpetual annuity of $5 per annum, the rate of interest would be 2½ percent.

It should be observed that the dimensions of the rate of interest are those of a rate of growth. The rate of interest is not a price or ratio of exchange; it is not itself determined in the market. What is determined in the market is the price of contractual obligations or "bonds." The higher the price of a given contractual obligation, the lower the rate of interest on it. Suppose, for instance, that one has a promissory note that is a promise to pay one $100 in one year's time. If I buy this for $100 now, the rate of interest is zero; if I buy it for $95 now the rate of interest is a little over 5%; if I buy it for $90 now, the rate of interest is about 11%. The rate of interest may be defined as the gross rate of growth of capital in a contractual obligation.

A distinction is usually made between interest and profit as forms of income. In ordinary speech, profit usually refers to income derived from the ownership of aggregates or assets of all kinds organized in an enterprise. This aggregate is described by a balance sheet. In the course of the operations of the enterprise, the net worth grows, and profit is the gross growth of net worth. Stocks, as opposed to bonds, usually imply a claim on the profits of some enterprise.

THE DEVELOPMENT OF INTEREST THEORY

Interest theory since Aristotle

In ancient and medieval times the main focus of inquiry into the theory of interest was ethical, and the principal question was the moral justification of interest. On the whole, the taking of interest was regarded unfavourably by both classical and medieval writers. Aristotle regarded money as "barren" and the medieval schoolmen were hostile to usury. Nevertheless, where interest fulfilled a useful social function elaborate rationalizations were developed for it. Among the classical economists, the focus of attention shifted away from ethical justification toward the problem of mechanical equilibrium. The question then became this: Is there any equilibrium rate of interest or rate of profit in the sense that where actual rates are above or below this, forces are brought into play, tending to change them toward the equilibrium? The classical economists did not provide any clear solution for this problem. They believed that the rate of interest simply followed the rate of profit, for people would not borrow or incur contractual obligations unless they could earn something more than the cost of the borrowing by investing the proceeds in enterprises or aggregates of real capital. They believed that the growth of capital itself would tend to reduce the rate of profit because of the competition of the capitalists. This doctrine is important in the Marxian dynamics in which the struggle of capital to avoid a falling rate of profit is seen as a critical factor leading, for instance, to unemployment, foreign investment, and imperialism.

Senior and Marx. In the framework of classical economics, the work of Nassau Senior deserves mention. He raised the question whether profit or interest were "paid for" anything; that is, whether there was any identifiable contribution to the general product of society that would not be forthcoming if this form of income were not paid. He identified such a function and called it abstinence. Karl Marx denied the existence of any such function and argued that the social product must be attributed entirely to acts of labour, capital being merely the embodied labour of the past. On this view, profit and interest are the result of pure exploitation in the sense that they consist of an income derived from the power position of the capitalist and not from the performance of any service. Non-Marxist economists have generally followed Senior in finding some function in society that corresponds to these forms of income.

The Marginalists. The Marginalists generally held that profit and interest were related to the marginal productivity of the extension of the period of production. Böhm-Bawerk assumed that "roundabout" processes of production would generally be more productive than processes with shorter periods of production; he thought there was a productivity of "waiting" (to use the term of Alfred Marshall) and saw the rate of interest as an inducement to the capitalist to extend the period of production.

A low rate of interest leads to concentration on longer, more roundabout processes, and a high rate of interest on shorter, less roundabout processes. There is a limit, however, on the period of production imposed by the existing stock of accumulated capital. If one embarks on a long process with insufficient capital, he will find that he has exhausted his resources before the end of the process and before the fruits can be gathered. It is the business of the rate of interest to prevent this, and to adjust the roundaboutness of the processes used to the capital resources available. The Marginalists' theory of interest reached its clearest expression in the work of Irving Fisher. He saw an equilibrium rate of interest as determined by the interaction of two sets of forces: the impatience of consumers on the one hand, and the returns from extending the period of production on the other.

Keynes. John Maynard Keynes brought a new approach. His liquidity preference theory of interest is a short-run theory of the price of contractual obligations ("bonds"), and it is essentially an application of the general theory of market price. If people as a whole decide that they want to hold a larger proportion of their assets in the form of money, and if new money is not created to satisfy this desire, there will be a net desire to sell securities and the price of securities will fall. This is the same thing as a rise in the rate of interest. Conversely, if people want to get rid of money the price of securities will rise and the rate of interest will fall. This, then, is the theory of the "market" rate of interest, by contrast with the Marginalists' theory, which concerns itself with whether or not there is a long-run equilibrium rate of interest. The controversy, therefore, between the liquidity preference theory—which regards interest as a "bribe" to prevent people holding money rather than bonds—and the time preference theory—which regards interest as a bribe to persuade people to postpone enjoyments to the future—can be resolved by placing the former in the short run and the latter in the long run.

CONTEMPORARY QUESTIONS

Interest rates and inflation

The middle of the 20th century saw a considerable shift in the focus of concern relating to the theory of interest. Economists seemed to lose interest in the equilibrium theory, and their main concern was with the effect of rates of interest as a part of monetary policy in the control of inflation. It was recognized that the monetary authority could control the rate of interest in the short run. The controversy lay mainly between the advocates of "monetary policy" and the advocates of "fiscal policy." If inflation is regarded as a symptom of a desire on the part of a society to consume and invest more in total than its resources permit, it is clear that the problem can be attacked either by diminishing investment or by diminishing consumption. On the whole, the attack of the advocates of monetary policy is on the side of diminishing investment, through raising rates of interest and making it harder to obtain loans, though the possibility that high rates of interest may restrict consumption is not overlooked. The alternative would seem to restrict consumption by raising taxes. This has the disadvantage of being politically unpopular. The mounting concern with economic growth, however, has raised considerable doubts about the use of high rates of interest as an instrument to control inflation. There is some doubt whether high interest rates in fact restrict investment; if they do not, they are ineffective, and if they do, they may be harmful to economic growth. This is a serious dilemma for the advocates of monetary policy. On the other hand, it must be admitted that the type of fiscal policy that might be most desirable theoretically has achieved very limited public support.

The ethics of interest

The problem of the ethics of interest is still unresolved after many centuries of discussion; as long as the institution of private property is accepted, the usefulness of borrowing and lending can hardly be denied. In the long historic process of inheritance, widowhood, gain and loss, by which the distribution of the ownership of capital is determined, there is no reason to suppose that the actual ownership of capital falls into the hands of those best able to administer it. Much of the capital of an advanced society, in fact, tends to be owned by elderly widows, simply because of the greater longevity of the female. Society, therefore, needs some machinery for separating the control of capital from its ownership. Financial instruments and financial markets are the principal agency for performing this function. If all securities took the form of stocks or equities, it might be argued that contractual obligations (bonds), and therefore interest as a form of income, would not be necessary. The case for bonds and interest, however, is the case for specialization. There is a demand for many different degrees of ownership and responsibility, and interest-bearing obligations tap a market that would be hard to reach with equity securities; they are also peculiarly well adapted to the obligations of governments. The principal justification for interest and interest-bearing securities is that they provide an easy and convenient way for skilled administrators to control capital that they do not own, and for the owners of capital to relinquish its control. The price society pays for this arrangement is interest.

There remains the problem of the socially optimum rate of interest. It could be argued that there is no point in paying any higher price than one needs to, and that the rate of interest should be as low as is consistent with the performance of the function of the financial markets. This position, of course, would place all the burden of control of economic fluctuations on the fiscal system, and it is questionable whether this would be acceptable politically.

The ancient problem of "usury," in the form of the exploitation of the ignorant poor by moneylenders, is still important in many parts of the world. The remedy is the development of adequate financial institutions for the needs of all classes of people rather than the attempt to prohibit or even to limit the taking of interest. The complex structure of lending institutions in a developed society—banks, building societies, land banks, cooperative banks, credit unions, and so on—testifies to the reality of the service that the lender provides and that interest pays for. The democratization of credit—that is, the extension of the power of borrowing to all classes in society—is one of the important social movements of the 20th century.

BIBLIOGRAPHY. A standard history of interest theory up to the end of the 19th century is EUGEN VON BOHM-BAWERK, *Kapital und Kapitalzins*, 3 vol. (1884–1912; Eng. trans., *Capital and Interest*, 3 vol., 1959, reprinted 1970); for the medieval approach to interest, see GEORGE O'BRIEN, *An Essay on Mediaeval Economic Teaching* (1920, reprinted 1968). The most important writings of the classical economists are ADAM SMITH, *An Inquiry into the Nature and Causes of the Wealth of Nations* (1776); DAVID RICARDO, *Principles of Political Economy and Taxation* (1817); NASSAU W. SENIOR, *An Outline of the Science of Political Economy* (1836); and JOHN STUART MILL, *Principles of Political Economy*, 2 vol. (1848). For the Marginalist school, the great work is EUGEN VON BOHM-BAWERK, *Positive Theory of Capital* (1889), vol. 2 of *Capital and Interest*. Others include FRIEDRICH VON WIESER, *Theorie der Gesellschaftlichen Wirtschaft* (1914; Eng. trans., *Social Economics*, 1927); W.S. JEVONS, *The Theory of Political Economy*, 4th ed. (1924); LEON WALRAS, *Éléments d'économie politique pure*, 2nd ed. rev. (1889; Eng. trans., *Elements of Pure Economics*, 1954); J.B. CLARK, *The Distribution of Wealth* (1899); KNUT WICKSELL, *Über Wert, Kapital und Kente* (1893; Eng. trans., *Value, Capital and Rent*, 1954), and *Geldzins und Güterpreise* (1898; Eng. trans., *Interest and Prices*, 1936); P.H. WICKSTEED, *The Common Sense of Political Economy* (1910); IRVING FISHER, *The Nature of Capital and Income* (1906), and *The Theory of Interest As Determined by Impatience to Spend Income and Opportunity to Invest It* (1930). For Marxist theory, the beginning student should probably read the abridged Marx; that is, KARL MARX, *Capital and Other Writings*, trans. by S. TRASK (1932); a somewhat unorthodox Marxist treatment is JOAN ROBINSON, *The Accumulation of Capital* (1956); and the standard modern work is ERNEST MANDEL, *Traité d'économie marxiste*, 2 vol. (1962; Eng. trans., *Marxist Economic Theory*, 2 vol., 1968). For the Keynesian contribution, the basic texts are JOHN MAYNARD KEYNES, *Treatise on Money* (1930), and *The General Theory of Employment, Interest, and Money* (1936). A good simplified exposition of the system is L.R. KLEIN, *The Keynesian Revolution*, 2nd ed. (1966). Other works somewhat in the Marginalist tradition are F.H. KNIGHT, *Risk, Uncertainty, and Profit* (1921); F.A. HAYEK, *The Pure Theory of Capital* (1941); J.R. HICKS, *Value and Capital*, 2nd ed. (1946); GUSTAV CASSEL, *The Nature and Necessity of Interest* (1903); F.A. and V.C. LUTZ, *The Theory of Investment of the Firm* (1951); B.S. KEIRSTEAD, *Capital, Interest, and Profits* (1959); ROBERT M. SOLOW, *Capital Theory and the Rate of Return* (1963); and L.M. LACHMANN, *Capital and Its Structure* (1956). General works that may be useful are K.E. BOULDING, *Economic Analysis*, 4th ed., 2 vol. (1966); R. DORFMAN, P.A. SAMUELSON, and R.M. SOLOW, *Linear Programming and Economic Analysis*, ch. 11–12 (1958); and NICHOLAS KALDOR, *Essays on Value and Distribution*, ch. 9–10 (1960).

(K.E.Bo.)

Capparales

Capparales, the caper order of flowering plants, consists of eight families, 367 genera, and 4,000 species. The type family, Capparaceae, derives its name and importance from *kapparis*, the Greek name used by Dioscorides for *Capparis spinosa*, which is the source of capers of commerce. The genus *Capparis* is often confined to arid regions of the tropics and subtropics and includes diverse growth forms such as trees, shrubs, and stragglers. In addition to this dominant genus, the order has several other genera, which provide food and flowers to mankind. The cabbage, cauliflower, knol kohl (all three are varieties of *Brassica oleracea*), turnip (*B. rapa*), and radish (*Raphanus sativus*) are important vegetables, rich in sulfur compounds and vitamin C. The edible mustard oil is from the seeds of *Brassica juncea* and *B. campestris*. The well-known horseradish tree (*Moringa oleifera*) is cultivated for its edible roots and fruits and for ben oil, used as a lubricant for watches. The mignonette (*Reseda odorata*), stock (*Matthiola incana*), wallflower (*Cheiranthus cheiri*), and candytuft (*Iberis* species) are garden plants widely cultivated for their flowers.

The two so-called crucifixion thorns (*Koeberlinia spinosa* and *Canotia holacantha*) together constitute an interesting growth form characterized by leafless, thorny thickets found only in the southwestern deserts of North America.

GENERAL FEATURES

Diversity of habit. The members of the order exhibit diverse growth features. Some, such as *Crataeva nurvala* and *Moringa oleifera*, are small, deciduous trees, cultivated in the tropics and subtropics. Many others are armed or unarmed (*i.e.*, thorny or not) shrubs. The arms are the paired, stipular (located at the base of leafstalks), recurved thorns, as in *Capparis spinosa* (capers), *C. micrantha*, and *Apophyllum anomalum*, which are distributed in the Mediterranean region, Africa, and Australia, respectively. The arms may also consist of the tips of the branches in *Zilla myagroides* of the Nubian Desert of Africa and *Koeberlinia spinosa* and *Canotia holacantha* (crucifixion thorns) of the southwestern deserts of North America. The leaves are short-lived in many of these species. The order is also rich in stragglers (sprawling, vinelike forms), such as *Capparis sepiaria* of India, *C. cucurbitina* and *C. scortechinii* of Malaysia, and woody lianas, such as *Maerua arenaria* of India, *Roydsia parviflora* and *R. scortechinii* of Malaysia, and *Ritchiea frangrans* of tropical Africa. The Australian *Emblingia calceoliflora* is a prostrate undershrub with a hispidulous (hairy) stem. *Cleome* (bee plant) and allied genera are mostly glandular, annual (short-lived) herbs; *Isomeris arborea* (burro fat), a close ally, is a shrub in the Mexican desert. The herbaceous annuals are also represented widely by *Capsella bursa-pastoris* (shepherd's purse), the herbaceous perennials (plants that continue to grow season after season) by *Cheiranthus cheiri* (wallflower) and *Cochlearia officinalis* (scurvy grass), and the woody perennials by *Alyssum spinosum* and *Vella spinosa*, all of the above belonging to the north temperate zone. The common aquatic forms are *Rorippa palustris* (marsh cress), *Cardamine pratensis* (cuckooflower), *C. rotundifolia* (mountain watercress), *Nasturtium officinale* (watercress), and *Subularia aquatica*, which are all found in temperate regions and on tropical mountains. *Nasturtium officinale* has spreading stems that root at the nodes ("joints" of a stem) and pinnate leaves (*i.e.*, leaves with either veins or separate leaflets arranged along either side of a central axis). *Subularia aquatica* has long, narrow, centric (shieldlike) leaves; its flowers either project above water or remain submerged and then rely on self-fertilization, because they remain closed. There are tufted xerophytes (plants adapted to dry habitats) such as *Erophila verna* and *Anastatica hierochuntica* (rose of Jericho) of Europe and the Mediterranean region, which have hairy or fleshy leaves and grow on sand dunes. Saline (salty-habitat) succulents, such as *Cakile maritima* (sea rocket) and *Crambe maritima* (sea kale), are found along the Atlantic and Baltic shores and in the Mediterranean region.

Thorns

Economic importance. *Examples from the family Capparaceae.* The pickled flower buds of *Capparis spinosa* are the commercial European capers. The root bark is bitter and may be used to treat rheumatism, paralysis, toothache, and disorders of the liver and spleen. The fruits and flower buds of *C. decidua* are edible and are often preserved in salt vinegar. The flower buds are used as potherbs. The fruit is astringent and has been used to treat heart disorders. The hard, heavy wood is used to make tool handles and boat knees (a bent piece of wood used as a brace in boat construction) because it is resistant to termite attack. *C. sepiaria*, the Indian caper, is planted as a hedge. It has been used to decrease fevers and to treat skin diseases. *C. zeylanica* fruits are edible and used in curries. The root bark has been used as a sedative and is effective against cholera. *C. mitchellii* fruits are edible and are consumed in Australia and Tasmania, where they occur. *C. corymbifera* flower buds are preserved in salt vinegar and eaten. The pounded leaves and twigs of *Cadaba farinosa* are made into cakes, puddings, and cereals; as food, it is called forsa or balambe in the

Edible and useful products

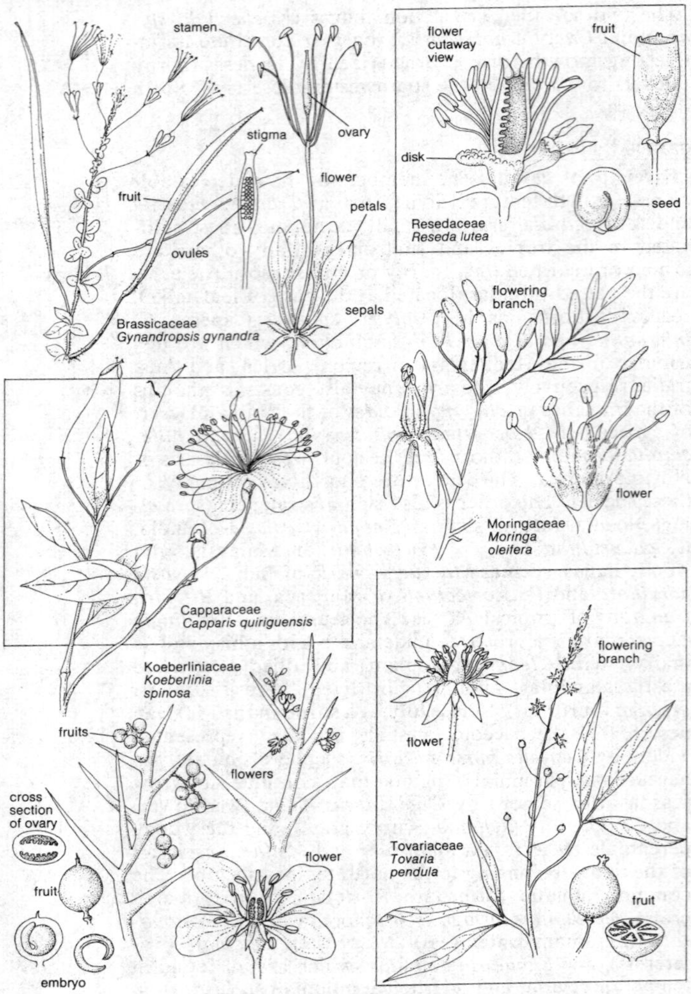

Representative plants from six of the eight families of the order Capparales.
Drawing by M. Pahl

Arabian Peninsula and tropical Africa. The leaves and seeds of *Cleome icosandra* are useful as external applications for wounds and ulcers. The seeds are also used in curries. *C. spinosa* (spiderflower) is grown as an ornamental. The ashes from the stems and leaves of *Courbonia virgate* are used as a source of salt in parts of The Sudan and Arabia.

Examples from the family Brassicaceae. *Alliaria officinalis* (garlic mustard) is used to treat gangrenous infections. *Armoracia lapathifolia* is the well-known horseradish, whose roots are used for flavouring food products. *Barbarea verna* (Belle Isle cress) is used as a vegetable. *Brassica campestris* variety *sarson* (yellow sarson, or Indian colza) provides seed oil, which is used for cooking, and oil cake, which is used as cattle feed; the tender leaves and shoots are eaten as a vegetable. *B. campestris* variety *toria* (Indian rape) has similar uses. The tender leaves and shoots of *B. hirta* (white mustard) are used as a vegetable; the seeds yield a fatty oil. *B. juncea* (Indian mustard) seed oil is used for cooking. *B. napus* (rape) leaves are used as vegetables. The seeds of *B. nigra* (black mustard) are used as a spice and condiment. *B. oleracea* variety *acephala* is the vegetable borecole, or kale. *B. oleracea* variety *botrytis* is cauliflower or broccoli, which are grown all over the world for their edible inflorescences (flower clusters). *B. oleracea* variety *capitata* is cabbage, a common vegetable. *B. oleracea* variety *gemmifera* is Brussels sprouts, a bud-bearing cabbage, the young shoots, buds, and leaves of which are edible. *B. oleracea* variety *gongylodes* is kohlrabi, or knol kohl, the short, swollen stem of which is edible. *B. pekinensis* is Chinese cabbage. *B. rapa* is the turnip. *Raphanus sativus* is the well-known radish.

Plants related to cabbage

NATURAL HISTORY

Adaptations for pollination. The perpetuation and spread of this order is facilitated by the efficient adaptation of its flowers, fruits, and seeds for pollination and dispersal. In the family Capparaceae, the pollination is by insects, which are attracted by nectar secretion, dense aggregation of the flowers, and the bright colours of the petals. Dichogamy, the maturing of the male and female organs of the same flower at different times, favours cross-pollination in many cases, as does, in *Cleome spinosa* (spiderflowers), the production of male flowers alternating with female and bisexual flowers in succession. In the family Brassicaceae, both cross- and self-pollination of the flowers occur. The twisting of stamens (male pollen-producing structures) to one side may favour cross-pollination. In such instances, however, the slightest irregularity in the movement of the visiting insect may cause self-pollination because of the close proximity of the anthers (pollen sacs) to the stigma (sticky, pollen-receiving surface of the female structure). In *Cardamine chenopodifolia* and *Subularia aquatica*, the flower remains submerged and closed (the cleistogamous condition) when the water is high. *Pringlea antiscorbutica* (Kerguelen Island cabbage) is wind-pollinated in the absence of insects suitable for its pollination. The flowers are without petals but have exerted (long, extended past the end of the flower) anthers and long, filiform (thread-like), stigmatic pollen-catching structures. In *Cardamine pratensis* (lady's smock), self-sterility favours cross-pollination. In mignonette (*Reseda odorata*) of the family Resedaceae, different parts of the flower play different functions in the process of pollination. Nectar is secreted by the large, posteriorly projected petal-like disk. The white, fringed edges of the petals, the red anthers, and the strong odour attract the insect visitors. The pistil (female structure consisting of stigma, style, and ovary), with terminal, papillose (nipple-like) stigmas, projects from the centre, and the stigmas receive the pollen carried by insect visitors. If the insects fail to visit the flowers, the stigmas, which lie directly below the anthers, eventually receive pollen from them and achieve self-pollination.

Adaptations for dispersal. The dispersal of fruits and seeds in the Capparales order is caused by a variety of agents. The wind is the chief agent of dissemination in the desert. In North African deserts, fruits and seeds are either winged or are light or hairy; a pair of wings usually surrounds the fruit in *Zilla macroptera*, and the seeds are velvety in *Cleome arabica*. In *Morettia phileana* of the Nubian Desert and *Sisymbrium altissium* (tumbling mustard) of Europe and North America, the withered plants and their inflorescences (flower clusters) are blown about, scattering the fruits and seeds. In *Anastatica hierochuntica* (rose of Jericho), of the deserts of Asia Minor and North Africa, the plants curve into balls, or "roses," in drought and are blown along by the wind until they reach a wet spot; there the balls unfold along with the valves of the fruit, dispersing the seeds. In *Biscutella californica* the fruits are edged with hairs. In *Cochlearia*, the four- to six-seeded locules (ovary chambers) are dispersed by the valves acting as wings. In *Draba verna* (whitlow grass) the thin septum of the dried fruit sends the small, light seeds away like tennis balls from a racket. The fruits of *Crataeva nurvala* and *C. macrocarpa* in Malaysia, Burma, and Indochina and the seeds of *Mathiola incana* (stock) and *Nasturtium officinale* (watercress) are dispersed by river waters. The seeds of *Cakile maritima* and *Crambe maritima* and the fruits of *Raphanus maritimus* are disseminated by sea tides. In *Nasturtium lacustre* and *Cardamine pratensis* (cuckooflower) the leaves with bulbils or adventitious buds float and develop into new plants elsewhere. Animals act as agents for the dispersal of seeds in the order Capparales through their excreta. Seeds of *Sisymbrium sophia* and *Capsella bursa-pastoris*, for example, are distributed through the excreta of cattle; fruits of *Draba alpina* and seeds of *Cardamine bellidifolia* and *Cochlearia arctica*, are dispersed in the excreta of birds; and fruits of *Draba verna* are carried in the excreta of earthworms. The seeds of Capparales

Wind-blown tumbling plants

may also be dispersed by simple adhesion to the feet of man, cattle, and the wheels of carts. The mucilaginous seeds of *Capsella bursa-pastoris* stick to the feet of gulls and those of *Cardamine* (white top), *Senebiera heleniana*, and *Lepidium perfoliatum* (peppergrass) to seashore birds.

Adaptation to environment. The propagation of plants by seeds is strongly handicapped in saline and arid conditions because of incomplete seed ripening in mother plants at times; low soil moisture; hard, nonabsorbing soil crusts; high concentrations of soluble salts; or destruction of seedlings due to various factors such as irregular rainfall, animals, wind erosion, and deposition of mud. Large seeds with large food supplies may be advantageous in establishing seedlings in spite of competition for light and moisture, eating by animals, wind erosion, and other factors. The large seeds of *Crambe maritima*, for example, send down an extensive root at an early stage of development, enabling the species to colonize adverse habitats in the early phase.

Delayed germination. Many of the desert seeds possess germination-inhibiting substances. The seeds of *Eruca boveana* and *Carrichtera annua* of the dry Mediterranean, Arabian, and Persian regions contain inhibiting factors; as much as ten to 20 centimetres (four to eight inches) of rain wash away these factors, thereby considerably improving the percentage of germination of such seeds. The fruit valves of *Sinapis alba* contain a blastokoline substance that suppresses the germination of the seeds. Some desert annuals from Arizona sprout only after a long period of ripening. *Lepidium lasiocarpum* is ready to germinate after one year and *Streptanthus arizonicus* after 26 months. The presence of inhibitors and the habit of germinating only after a long period of ripening are believed to be adaptations to the scattering of germination in time, enabling the seeds to get established at times when favourable external conditions exist. Many annuals seem to counterbalance the danger of extermination in dry habitats by profuse seed production. Even the tiniest ephemeral, such as *Erophila verna* of the Mediterranean region, sets numerous fruits and ripens large numbers of seeds.

Significance of delayed germination

Sexual versus vegetative propagation. The natural propagation of plants by seeds is observed mainly in crop plants. In ornamentals, however, the propagation is both by seeds and vegetative means.

In an environment that is favourable for growth and flowering, such as the damp woodlands of the British Isles, profuse vegetative propagation takes place as an alternative to low seed production. In *Cardamine pratensis* (lady's smock), although the plants flower profusely, because of scanty seed production, 70 percent of them reproduce vegetatively by means of buds developed at the base of the terminal leaflets. In *Dentaria bulbifera* (coralroot) the reproduction is exclusively or mainly by means of bulbils that replace the lower flowers on the inflorescence. The upper flowers rarely produce fertile seeds. The bulbils, about one millimetre in length and three in thickness, normally develop near the parent plant. Vegetative spreading is also by rhizomes, horizontal, rootlike stems. The species is restricted to certain woods in Great Britain, although many other woodlands appear to be suited for its growth. Similarly, *Nasturtium sylvestre* (wood cress) also rarely produces fertile seeds in spite of free flowering. It spreads profusely by means of prostrate stems that root at the nodes.

Ecology. Members of this order grow in varied ecological conditions. Trees, shrubs, and climbers of *Crataeva*, *Maerua*, and *Capparis* grow in tropical rain forests. In tropical deserts the undershrubs and shrubs such as *Farsetia aegyptiaca*, *Zilla myagroides*, *Capparis spinosa*, *C. decidua*, *Apophyllum anomalum*, *Koeberlinia spinosa*, and *Canotia holacantha* grow on clefts of rocks and sandy hillocks.

Plants such as *Crambe maritima*, *Cakile maritima*, and *Cochlearia anglica* grow along the seashore, enduring low concentrations of salts and the consequent physiological dryness. *Draba alpina*, *Cochlearia nudicaulis*, and *Cardamine bellidifolia* grow in Arctic regions, withstanding continuous light during summer and low temperatures and dry winds in winter. *Cochlearia fenestrata*, along with its flowers and fruits, resists low temperature without protection.

FORM AND FUNCTION

Morphological features. The order consists of herbs, shrubs, small trees, and lianas. The leaves are alternate or opposite, simple or palmately compound, and they have stipules. In *Capparis*, *Apophyllum*, *Koeberlinia*, and *Canotia*, the leafless shrubs form dense thickets either by recurved stipular spines or thorny-tipped branches.

The flowers have petals, are bisexual, and are hypogynous (*i.e.*, the sepals, petals, and stamens arise at the base of the ovary) or perigynous (sepals, petals, and stamen partly enclose the ovary), with numerous to few stamens and an ovary of two or more fused carpels. The fruit may be a fleshy berry or drupe or a dry silique, silicle, or capsule—fruits that open by one or more sutures, or lines of weakness. The seeds are curved or straight, winged or nonwinged.

Physiological features. In desert species such as *Capparis decidua* and the crucifixion thorns, spiny, leafless, green stems form thickets, and there are strongly developed taproots. *Apophyllum anomalum* of Australia is also leafless but is covered with a thick coat of plant hairs. In *Zilla spinosa* and *Ochradenus baccatus* the leaves of the rainy season are replaced by smaller, summer leaves. The seaside *Cakile maritima* and the dune-inhabiting *Cochlearia officinalis* are succulents; by storing water in their stems and leaves, the former resists high salt concentrations and the latter drought.

Dry habitat adaptations

The Arctic and Alpine *Draba alpina*, *Cochlearia nudicaulis*, *C. fenestrata*, and *Cardamine bellidifolia* have thick, small, cushion-like stems and short, leathery leaves with concealed stomata (pores).

EVOLUTION AND CLASSIFICATION

The families Capparaceae and Brassicaceae form the core of the order Capparales. They have many common vegetative and floral features and cells. Other shared features suggest that the family Capparaceae is ancestral to the Brassicaceae.

The orders Capparales and Violales are regarded by somes authorities as parallel offshoots of the order Theales. Others, however, consider the Capparales to have originated from the most primitive members of the order Violales, similar to the family Flacourtiaceae of that order.

Annotated classification.

ORDER CAPPARALES

Herbs, shrubs, small trees, and lianas; leaves alternate or opposite, simple, pinnately or palmately compound, with stipules; flowers with petals, bisexual, hypogynous or perigynous, regular or irregular; stamens numerous to few; ovary of 2 or more fused carpels with parietal placentation; fruits fleshy berries or drupes or dry dehiscent siliques, silicles, or capsules; seeds reniform (kidney-shaped) or not, or winged or nonwinged; embryo conduplicate (folded) or curved; endosperm scanty. Distribution mainly topics.

Family Capparaceae

Herbs, shrubs, climbers, and trees; leaves alternate, simple or pinnate; stipulate or not; flowers regular (radially symmetrical) and bisexual; sepals 4, overlapping; petals 4, overlapping; stamens 6 to numerous; disk annual or missing; ovary on a gynophore (a stalk), 1-celled; ovules campylotropous (turned at right angles to their stalks), with parietal placentation (*i.e.*, ovules are attached to ovary walls); stigma capitate, sessile; fruit a capsule, berry, or drupe; seeds angular or reniform (kidney-shaped); endosperm (starchy, nutrient tissue) scanty; embryo curved and folded. The family includes 42 genera and 925 species distributed in warm temperate and tropical regions of the world.

Family Brassicaceae (Cruciferae; mustard family)

Annual or perennial herbs with pungent juice; leaves alternate, without stipules; flowers bisexual, regular, sepals 4, 2 saccate (bag-shaped), imbricate (overlapping); petals 4, imbricate; stamens 6, tetradynamous (4 long and 2 short stamens); ovary 2-celled with a central partition; ovules many, in 2 series on 2 parietal placentae, or 1 or 2 erect; stigma fused or 2-lobed; fruit a silique or silicle (short or long, respectively, podlike fruits); seeds small; endosperm none;

cotyledons (seed leaves) plano-convex. There are about 373 genera and 3,200 species, cosmopolitan in distribution but centred chiefly around the Mediterranean.

Family Moringaceae

Trees; leaves deciduous, alternate, pinnate; lacking stipules; flowers bilaterally symmetrical, bisexual in panicles (many-branched clusters); sepals 5-cleft, petaloid, imbricate; petals 5; disk-lining calyx tube; stamens 5 perfect alternating with 5 to 7 sterile, antherless ones; anthers 1-locular (chambered); ovary 1-locular, parietal placentation; style (upper part of ovary) tubular; stigma truncate; fruit a capsule; seeds many, winged; endosperm none; cotyledons plano-convex; radicle (root end of embryo) short; plumule (aerial end of embryo) many-leaved. One genus with 12 species distributed from Africa to India.

Family Resedaceae

Annual and perennial herbs; leaves alternate; stipules gland-like; flowers bilaterally symmetrical, bisexual; sepals 2- to 8-lobed, imbricate; petals 6 to 8, valvate; stamens 3 to 45 on an androgynophore (a stalk supporting both male and female structures); disk strongly developed posteriorly; ovary of 2 to 7 fused carpels, 1-locular, gaping at the tip; parietal placentation; stigma sessile (*i.e.*, perched directly on the ovary —there is no style); fruit a capsule; seeds numerous, reniform; embryo curved or folded; cotyledons incumbent (*i.e.*, they lie face to face in the seed with the back of one against the hypocotyl of the embryo); endosperm absent. Six genera with 70 species distributed from Europe to Central Asia and India and in South Africa and California.

Family Koeberliniaceae

Shrubs; branches spine-tipped; leaves alternate, scalelike, deciduous; without stipules; flowers in racemes, bisexual; sepals 4 or 5, imbricate; petals 4 or 5, imbricate; stamens 5 to 10; ovary 5- to 2-locular with axile placentation; style persistent; fruit a few-seeded capsule or a berry; embryo straight or curved; endosperm scanty. Two genera with 1 species each, distributed in southwestern United States and Mexico.

Family Tovariaceae

Annuals; leaves alternate, trifoliate (of 3 leaflets); flowers bisexual, regular; sepals 8, imbricate; petals 8, imbricate; stamens 8, positioned opposite the lobes of the petals; ovary 6- to 8-locular, axile placentation; stigma sessile, 8-rayed; fruit a berry; seeds numerous, small; embryo curved; endosperm scanty. One genus with 2 species distributed in Mexico, Jamaica, and the tropical Andes.

Family Emblingiaceae

Undershrubs; leaves opposite; flowers solitary in the axils of leaves; sepals 5, the portion next to the flower axis dimidate (halved—having the appearance that ½ is missing); petals 2, connate, slipper-like, stamens 8 or 9, on an androgynophore, the 4 located away from the main flower axis fertile, the 4 or 5 next to the flower axis sterile; ovary 1, with 1 basal ovule; stigma sessile; fruit dry and indehiscent; seed flattened; embryo linear, folded together lengthwise; endosperm scanty. One genus with a single species distributed in Australia.

Family Pentadiplandraceae

Shrubs and climbers; leaves alternate; without stipules; flowers polygamous (both unisexual and bisexual flowers found on the same plant); sepals 5, valvate; petals 5, connivent (in contact) at base, imbricate; stamens 9 to 13, present in male and bisexual flowers; rudimentary ovary present in male flowers; female flowers with 10 long, slender sterile stamens; ovary superior on a short stalk, 5- to 4-locular with axile placentation; fruit a berry. One genus with 2 species in Africa.

Critical appraisal. There are many taxonomic problems in this order.

The Cleomoideae, a subfamily of the Capparaceae, closely resemble the family Brassicaceae in their herbaceous habit and capsular fruit with central partitions. Some authorities raise the Cleomoideae to the rank of family, called Cleomaceae, which is considered to be closely related and basic to the family Brassicaceae. This treatment needs support from other enquiries such as floral anatomy, embryology, and pollen morphology, however.

The resemblance and position of the family Tovariaceae with respect to the family Capparaceae could be better understood if the vascular anatomy of the axile placentation and eight-parted flower were better known.

The systematic position of the family Emblingiaceae is disputed. It shows resemblance with the families Capparaceae, Goodeniaceae, Scrophulariaceae, and Verbenaceae and Polygalaceae. More information on the floral and vegetative anatomy, embryology, and others is necessary to know the exact relationship of this group.

BIBLIOGRAPHY. L. BENSON and R.A. DARROW, *The Trees and Shrubs of the Southwestern Deserts*, 2nd ed. (1954), a treatment of the general features of plants in relation to dry habitats of Arizona, Mexico, Chile, and Argentina; N.C. FASSETT, *A Manual of Aquatic Plants* (1940), a detailed account of water plants; J.B. HARBORNE and T. SWAIN (eds.), *Perspectives in Phytochemistry* (1969), a study of chemotaxonomy and of the biosynthesis of various plant constituents; H.T. HARTMANN and D.E. KESTER, *Plant Propagation: Principles and Practices*, 2nd ed. (1968), exhaustive information on seed storage and propagation of selected annuals and herbaceous perennials used as ornamentals; P. MAHESHWARI and U. SINGH, *Dictionary of Economic Plants in India* (1965), extensive information on Indian economic plants, including an alphabetical list of plants; W.C.L. MUENSCHER, *Poisonous Plants of the United States*, rev. ed. (1951), a good account of annual weeds of the United States and Canada and the symptoms of diseases caused by them; O. POLUNIN and A. HUXLEY, *Flowers of the Mediterranean* (1965), descriptions of over 700 species with illustrations and uses covering the entire Mediterranean region; H.N. RIDLEY, *The Dispersal of Plants Throughout the World* (1930), an excellent and voluminous account of various methods of dispersal in an order; E.J. SALISBURY, *The Reproductive Capacity of Plants* (1942), information on the establishment and growth of plants with reference to their habitats, sexual versus vegetative propagation, and vegetative multiplication in relation to competition, and *Downs and Dunes: Their Plant Life and Its Environment* (1952), a good account of plants and their adaptation to the environment present on dunes and seashore.

(H.S.N.)

Caprimulgiformes

The order Caprimulgiformes includes about 100 species of soft-plumaged birds, the major groups of which are called nightjars, nighthawks, potoos, frogmouths, and owlet frogmouths. The order also includes the aberrant oilbird of South America. Most are twilight or night-flying birds. Many produce sounds that are startling, strange, or weirdly beautiful and are surrounded by an aura of mystery richly endowed to elicit interest and sometimes fear from man. The name of the type genus *Caprimulgus*, "goatsucker," derives from an ancient belief that the birds seen flitting about the goats at dusk, actually preying on the insects disturbed or attracted by the goats, were taking milk from the goats' udders, a misconception no doubt fortified by the birds' uncommonly large mouths. There is now a tendency to replace the name goatsucker with the more appropriate term nightjar, derived from the birds' voices.

The caprimulgiform birds are sparrow- to raven-sized (14–55 centimetres) birds with enormous gapes, cryptically coloured and patterned plumage, short legs and, for the most part, long wings.

All caprimulgiform birds are rather similar in general appearance, but each family has certain peculiar characteristics both in form and in habits. Their closest relatives are the owls (Strigiformes) which they resemble in many ways, but there are numerous differences between them. Many of these are internal, but among those externally apparent are the bill and feet, which are not raptorial; the flatter head with eyes placed laterally rather than in a frontal facial disk; the relatively shorter tarsi and longer tails. Closer inspection reveals differences in the number of primary feathers in the wing and usually of secondaries and tail feathers as well. The nightjars also share some features with the swifts (Apodiformes), but these seem to be more superficial and coincidental than indicative of close phylogenetic relationship. Comparison with owls

Although the true nightjars (Caprimulgidae) are amply distributed throughout the world, the other families are more restricted. The order is absent from New Zealand and some oceanic islands.

NATURAL HISTORY

The caprimulgiform birds are primarily crepuscular, their activity being largely limited to the periods of dawn and dusk, although they are also nocturnal when there is

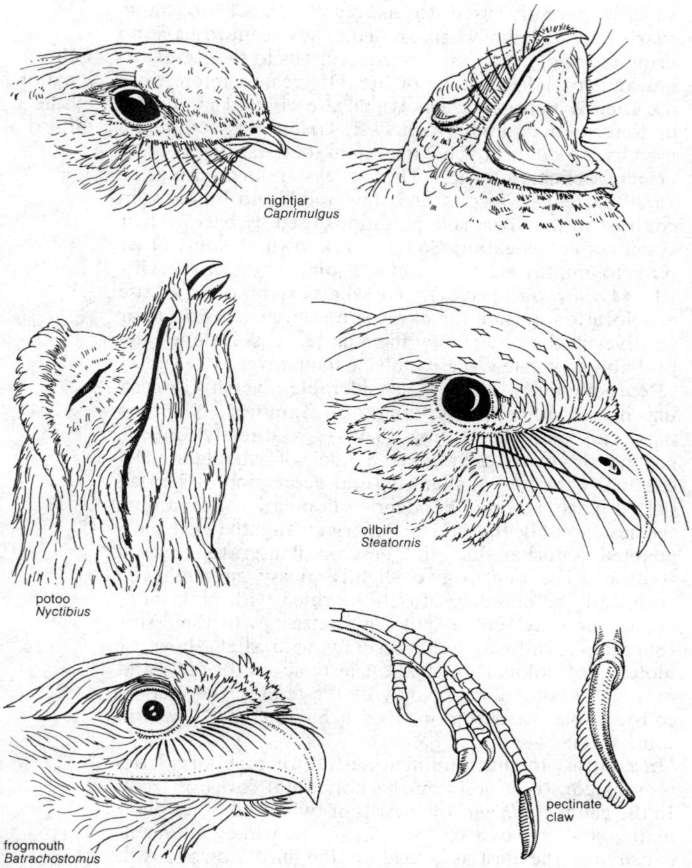

Beak and claw structure of representative Caprimulgiformes.
Drawing by E.J. Pfiffner

sufficient illumination, especially by moonlight. Some species may become active on dark, cloudy days, and a few are somewhat diurnal. Oilbirds possess a system of echolocation that permits them to fly freely in total darkness, an adaptation related to their roosting and nesting in caves, and are thus implicitly well equipped for nocturnal life. They leave their caves at dusk and return at dawn and are highly gregarious in their foraging behaviour as well as in roosting and nesting. The other members of the order are more or less solitary. Some nightjars that are migratory behave gregariously during migration and to some extent while in their "wintering" regions.

Although aerial feeders, most of the true nightjars roost on the ground, rocks, or fallen trunks, but some prefer horizontal branches of trees, in which case they usually perch lengthwise along the branch. Some ground roosters, however, will seek higher perches as singing posts or from which to forage; these are often slender branches or vines and the birds sit on them crosswise. Some species may even roost so perched. Unlike the nightjars, the frogmouths, potoos, and owlet frogmouths are arboreal. The last normally sit crosswise on a branch and fairly upright, both when active and at rest, resembling small, long-tailed owls. Potoos and frogmouths frequently sit crosswise and upright when actively foraging and also appear very owllike, although at rest they may perch quite differently. The potoos are noted for a peculiar stance, perching usually at the top of a stump, broken branch, or at a knob on an upwardly inclined limb. When alarmed in daylight they slowly flatten their plumage and stretch their bills upward in a stiff posture with the eyes nearly closed and the bill slightly open. Frogmouths adopt a similar broken-branch alarm posture.

During the day, the oilbird perches horizontally on ledges inside caves, usually on its nest. Ledges are limited and mostly occupied by nests. On its forays outside it has been observed to perch on the bare parts of tree branches. Its mien is rather hawklike, but its crouching stance, unique in some ways, is more like that of a nightjar.

Habitat. The caprimulgiform birds exploit ample food sources that are almost uniquely theirs. There are no other primarily frugivorous nocturnal birds to compete with the oilbird, its distribution being limited by the availability of suitable caves in regions providing the proper fruit for food.

Competition between species

The nightjars, by far the largest and most successful group, have no effective avian competitors for the great numbers of night-flying insects except among themselves; and the different nightjars have come to occupy almost all habitats, from semidesert to very humid regions and from sea level to 4,000 metres' altitude, with further advantage by preferring the more open areas: savannas, grasslands, and forest clearings. When woodland dwellers, they live in the more open forests or brushwood growths, and many use the woodlands only for diurnal concealment or nesting, doing most of their feeding at the edge or in clearings.

Competition between the nightjars and potoos is reduced because the latter hunt mostly from higher perches in open country or exploit the space above the great forests, a vast niche occupied by practically no other nocturnal bird.

Frogmouths and owlet frogmouths inhabit forested savannas, forest edge, second growth, and the more open forests. Thus their chief competitors are the insectivorous owls. As with the nightjars, differences in food preferences and methods of hunting minimize this competition. The hole-nesting owlet frogmouths, however, have to contend not only with owls but also many diurnal species for suitable nesting sites, and this may explain why they are apparently the least successful family in the order, as suggested by their limited distribution and paucity of numbers.

Food habits. Except for the oilbird, caprimulgiform birds are insectivorous, with some of the larger species occasionally carnivorous. Many of the nightjars and nighthawks feed in continuous hawking flight, which may be rather erratic as they pursue their prey. Others of the order make short sallies from arboreal or terrestrial perches in the manner of flycatchers, frequently taking advantage of the increased visibility afforded by roads. Many nightjars take crawling insects by swooping from arboreal perches or by running along the ground, being far more agile on their feet than is generally believed. Almost all insects are taken, but beetles predominate in the food of many species. Also important are moths, the winged forms of termites and ants, and mosquitos; even small birds are taken. There seems to be little difference between the general kinds of food items taken by the New and Old World nightjars (subfamily Caprimulginae), but the Old World species rely more on foraging in continuous flight than do most in the New World, where aerial foraging is largely limited to the nighthawks (Chordeilinae).

Potoos sally from exposed arboreal perches, sometimes fairly close to the ground, to feed on essentially the same types of insects as the nightjars. The prey items of frogmouths are mostly terrestrial. In short sallies from elevated perches, frogmouths capture large, crawling arthropods on the ground or on branches. Snails, frogs, mice, small birds, and occasionally fruit also are taken. Owlet frogmouths feed mostly on terrestrial prey, much in the manner of the frogmouths, but also sally from a perch to take flying insects.

Aberrant in so many ways, oilbirds are the only nocturnal, exclusively frugivorous birds. The fruits eaten are primarily of various trees of the palm, laurel, and bursera families and have large hard seeds. The firm, fleshy pericarp of the fruit is exceedingly rich in protein and oily fats. The fruits are swallowed whole and the seeds later regurgitated. D.W. Snow has found that oilbirds apparently possess an efficient olfactory sense, suggesting that they employ scent in locating certain of the fruit-bearing trees. The fruits of palms, however, are not aromatic and are no doubt located by sight. The actual collection of the fruit seems to depend on sight. In feeding, the birds reach out with their bills and pluck the individual fruits while hovering. When feeding on large compact bunches of fruit they sometimes cling briefly with their feet.

Males of most, if not all, nightjars have patches of white feathers that serve as signals in mating. These patches are concealed when the bird is at rest but flashed in courtship displays. Males of several species in Africa and South America develop elongated wing or tail feathers that function in courtship and are lost following the breeding season.

Drawing by E.J. Pfiffner

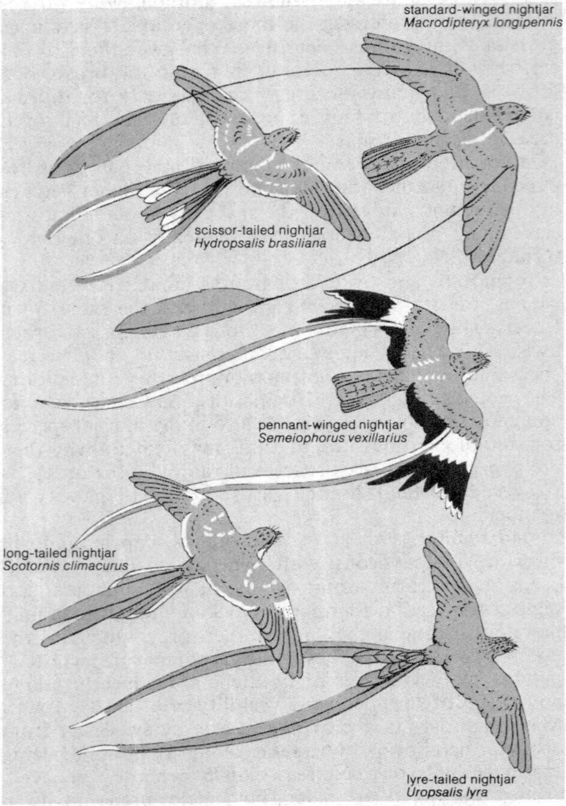

Specialized feathers in male Caprimulgiformes.

Vocalizations. The primary signals for mating and territorial purposes in most caprimulgiforms, however, are vocal and mechanical sounds. The voice is usually well developed, often having such distinctive patterns that the birds are named onomatopoeically (whippoorwill, chuck-will's-widow, etc.). The almost human lament of the common potoo (*Nyctibius griseus*) in South America has in some places earned this species the name "poor-me-one," and both it and the grotesque bawl of the great potoo (*N. grandis*) have been the source of many superstitious beliefs and legends. Frogmouths sing with various nasal booming, hooting, or croaking sounds, and the little known owlet frogmouths are reported to give owllike whistles, churring calls, and a loud hissing note. Among the true nightjars, some species produce slowly or rapidly repeated churring sounds, in some cases rather toadlike, while others produce a warbled or whistled song, not at all disagreeable. Whistled phrases may be repeated hundreds of times without a break. Many different types of calls are used in different contexts, but the primary song, different for each species, appears to be the most important mechanism for species recognition. Besides vocal sounds, many species produce mechanical sounds in displays, such as claps and whirrs of the wings. In some species the vocalizations are given primarily in flight, in others primarily when perched; still others have different calls or songs when flying than when perched.

Echolocation by the oilbird

Oilbirds produce a variety of sounds, from clucking calls, apparently used to maintain contact, to harsh snarls and screams, when excited. They seem to have no primary song, which may be superfluous to their gregarious and specialized mode of life. Of greatest interest are the rapidly pulsated clicks which are emitted in shorter or longer bursts and which D.R. Griffin has found are used by the oilbird for navigation in total darkness on the principle of echolocation. These clicks are in the range of 7,000 cycles per second and thus audible to humans, in contrast to the ultrasonic pulsations used by bats in their system of echolocation. So far as is known, the only other birds to employ echolocation are some of the cave-swiftlets (*Collocalia* species). To what extent oilbirds use echolocation outside the caves is not known. As do their relatives in the order, they have large, sensitive eyes and probably navigate visually outside their caves.

Reproduction. There is considerable diversity in nesting habits among caprimulgiform families. Nightjars make no nest, depositing their eggs directly on the ground or on the leaf-covered floor of woodland. Occasionally they use a slight natural depression or scratch out a place among the debris. Populations of a few species (notably the North American nighthawks) have adapted to urban life and nest on flat gravel-covered rooftops. The one or two slightly glossy eggs may be cryptically coloured (profusely marbled with pink, buff, brown, or gray) or be quite in contrast with their surroundings (white to buffy, usually with slight lines or blotches of colour). Incubation lasts about 19 days and may be by both adults or only by the female, there being considerable variation in this behaviour even within some species.

In contrast to the simplified nesting of nightjars, frogmouths construct nests on the horizontal forks of trees. In the genus *Podargus* the nest is of twigs and other plant matter and the two or three eggs are white; in *Batrachostomus* the nest is a pad of the birds' own down, bound and camouflaged externally with cobwebs and lichens, one white egg being laid. Both sexes are believed to incubate, the period being about 30 days. Owlet frogmouths nest mostly in hollow trees but also in tunnels in banks. They lay three or four white eggs, usually on a mat of leaves or fur. The incubation period is as yet unknown. The potoos are the most highly restricted nesters, for they must find a branch or stub with a suitable depression or crevice of just the right size to accommodate the single egg they lay. The egg is flat white, marked with brown and gray, and is incubated by both parents for 30 to 35 days.

On ledges in the caves they inhabit, the oilbirds build up a shallow nest rim of viscous, regurgitated fruit matter, which sets to a firm structure. As the accumulation of seeds raises the level inside the nest, the rim is constantly added to, so as to maintain a slight depression. The nests are used year after year and gradually grow to low mounds. Inevitably some seeds and the feces of very young nestlings contribute to the fabric of the rim. Two to four eggs are laid (white, subelliptical, slightly rough surface); both sexes incubate, the period being about 33 days.

Behaviour of the nestling

The chicks of nightjars are semiprecocial: they are down covered (buffy to brownish, plain or mottled, highly cryptic), fed by both parents, capable of opening their eyes on the first day (normally keeping them closed for several days), capable of walking on first day, and able to hop or run very well by third or fourth day. They usually run with wings raised, resembling young ducklings in gait. From the beginning chicks may solicit feeding by walking to the front of the adult, reaching up, and pecking at its bill. During the first days they are fed a regurgitated whitish viscous substance but later only partially digested insects. As early as the second day, although sometimes not until a week later, the chicks are led to different resting sites, at first only a metre or so at a time, but gradually much greater distances. Some of this moving may result from the chicks' own wanderings, for they are often restless and leave the covering adult.

In many cases both parents brood the chicks, in others

only the female does so, and rarely the male assumes the primary role. By about two weeks the young are well feathered and too large for successful brooding; they rest at first near a parent but later quite alone.

Undisturbed young birds fly voluntarily at from 22 to 28 days; disturbed young may fly much earlier. About the time they are able to fly they begin a certain amount of feeding on their own but are still largely dependent up to 40 to 50 days. When two young hatch, one of them frequently develops more slowly and most often disappears during the second week. If it survives, however, it may require up to 40 days to reach the state of voluntary flight.

The nestlings of frogmouths, potoos, and owlet frogmouths are semidependent, covered with whitish down, fed by both parents, and remain in the nest until fledged. A.F. Skutch found that a young common potoo began wandering over the boughs of the nest tree at about four weeks. This same nestling first made trial flights at 47 days and finally left the nest tree when 50 days old. Other reports indicate the nestling period of potoos to be of 40–45 days, that of frogmouth to be about 30 days. The young are brooded only during the first half of this period, by which time young potoos have attained the juvenile plumage (whitish mottled with brownish) and are already accomplished in assuming the "broken branch" posture of adults.

On the whole, the caprimulgiform birds, like most birds, breed solely or mostly at the time of maximum abundance of food supply. Oilbirds may nest to some extent throughout the year, but the maximum nesting takes place during that time of year when the greatest number of appropriate trees are fruiting. Baby oilbirds are helpless (altricial), hatched blind and virtually naked, with only a little sparse down. They have an exceedingly slow rate of development. A thicker coat of down replaces the initial one after three weeks, and the adult plumage begins to appear at five weeks, there being no special juvenile plumage. The nestlings are apparently fed semidigested fruit pulp during the first days. At about two weeks there is a gradual change to whole fruits, regurgitated by the adults into the mouths of the young. As a result of the oil-rich fruit diet, young oilbirds build up extraordinary deposits of fat, which has led to economic exploitation. The fat can be boiled down to a high quality, durable oil, suitable for cooking and lighting. For this reason oilbirds were once subject to heavy predation by their human neighbours, a practice that continues even today, on a much reduced scale because of a general trend toward protection. The fat buildup reaches its maximum at about 70 days, at which time a young oilbird may weigh half again as much as an adult. By this time the plumage is well developed but not fully grown. The weight decreases as the feathers grow, until at an age of 100–120 days the young leave the nest, flying well and looking like adults. Both parents participate in feeding and brooding, the latter ceasing after about four weeks.

Migration. A number of tropical caprimulgiforms are sedentary, but the widespread cosmopolitan nightjars exhibit all degrees of migration. These migrations may be short, even local, or quite long. Some populations of the common nighthawk (*Chordeiles minor*) of North America and the European nightjar (*Caprimulgus europaeus*) migrate south to Argentina and South Africa, respectively. Actually, transequatorial migrations in both directions occur, as birds take advantage of the general alternation of seasons, and hence of food supply, on opposite sides of the Equator.

Lowering of body temperature in torpor

Hibernation. Some nightjars are able to cope with temporary food shortages by entering into periods of torpidity, a faculty they share with some swifts, hummingbirds, and a few others. The only known instances of apparently regular, prolonged annual hibernation in these birds, however, are reported for the poorwill *Phalaenoptilus nuttallii*, a nightjar. A banded individual was found by E.C. Jaeger to hibernate in the same small hollow in a rock during several successive winters. The bird was inert, with respiration and heart rates reduced to almost immeasurable levels and body temperature about 22° C below normal. Subsequent laboratory experiments have shown that several species of nightjar have the ability to relax into a torpid state under abnormal conditions. Such an efficient means of conserving energy may be more generally possessed than is presently realized throughout a family whose habits largely limit the birds to two brief periods of feeding a day, causing them to be especially vulnerable to involuntary fasting if inclement weather should prevent feeding during those periods.

FORM AND FUNCTION

Members of this order are easily recognized by their extremely wide mouths, large eyes, short legs and small, weak feet, and, except in the oilbird, soft plumage, in which browns and grays predominate.

The size of the gape is astonishing. When the bird opens its mouth, the opening seems to span the entire head, which is nearly the case. The beak, always somewhat hooked, is large and horny in the oilbird and frogmouths but reduced to a small projection in the remaining families. In body proportions, caprimulgiforms often appear chunky on account of the fluffiness of their plumage, but their actual bodies are proportionately no stouter than most songbirds. The tail is of medium length, except in males of those species with ornamental tail features. The wings are medium to long, and rounded in most species, pointed in a few, especially the nighthawks.

The plumage of all forms presents unexcelled examples of natural camouflage. Coloured in rufescent to ochreous browns, grays, white, and black, the species are variously patterned in greatest accord with their normal surroundings during daytime rest. Those nightjars that roost inside woodlands are streaked and spotted in a way resembling fallen leaves and other detritus on the forest floor. Those that dwell on gravelly terrain are speckled or otherwise patterned. The latter often contrast rather than blend with the soil, appearing like one of the many stones scattered about. The owlet frogmouths appear as clusters of dead leaves. Potoos and frogmouths are streaked and mottled like bark so that in the daytime alarm posture they appear most effectively as dead stubs.

Red and gray colour phases

Caprimulgiform species are frequently dichromatic, having grayish and reddish phases. These appear to be randomly distributed in some cases and sex-linked in others, there being several species of nightjars in which males are more grayish, females more reddish.

Except for possible freaks, the iris colour is brown in nearly all members of the order. Yellow occurs in the irises of some potoos, and yellow, orange, and ruby in frogmouths. Contrary to some reports, oilbirds do not have blue irises nor are any nightjars known to have yellow eyes.

CLASSIFICATION

Distinguishing taxonomic characters. The most important characters used to define the caprimulgiform birds are the type of plumage, structure of the feet and legs, form and structure of the bill, palatal structure, arrangement of the pelvic muscles and flexor tendons, shape of dorsal vertebrae, meristic characters such as the number of primary and secondary feathers and rectrices, presence or absence of intestinal ceca and of an oil gland, location of syrinx, presence and type of rictal bristles, powder down patches, carotid artery relationships, and a few other anatomical details. Variations in some of these same features characterize the different subgroups.

Annotated classification. The arrangement presented is the same as that proposed by A. Wetmore (1918) in a modification of R. Ridgway (1914). The group was then considered a suborder Nycticoraciae of the order Coraciiformes. The subsequent shift to ordinal level with the name Caprimulgiformes has long been accepted.

ORDER CAPRIMULGIFORMES

Soft plumaged (except Steatornithes), cryptically patterned birds with relatively weak anisodactyle feet and very short tarsi; deeply cleft gape (except Steatornithes); pelvic muscle formula AXY (XY in Steatornithes); flexor tendons fused (synpelmous); 10 primaries; 11–13 secondaries; 10 rectrices; aftershaft small but present; 2 carotid arteries and oil gland present (except in *Podargus* and *Nyctibius*).

Suborder Steatornithes

Dorsal vertebrae opisthocoelous (concave behind); gape not exceptionally deeply cleft; rostrum movably articulated with skull; plumage firm.

Family Steatornithidae (oilbird)

No fossil record. Locally distributed in Guyana, Venezuela, Colombia, Ecuador, Peru, and Trinidad. Desmognathous palate (maxillopalatine bones fused), palatines narrow and not expanded posteriorly; large, strong bill with hard rhamphoteca (horny covering) and subterminal tooth, surrounded by long vibrissae; bronchial syrinx; 15 cervical vertebrae. One species, length 40 centimetres.

Suborder Caprimulgi

Dorsal vertebrae heterocoelous (saddle-shaped); deeply cleft gape; rostrum fixed; plumage soft.

Family Podargidae (frogmouths)

No fossil record. Confined to Australasian (except New Zealand) and southern Oriental regions (including extreme southern India). Desmognathous palate; palatines broad throughout, slightly expanded posteriorly; wide, strong bill with hard rhamphotheca; bronchial syrinx; 13 cervical vertebrae; well-developed powder down tufts on either side of rump; oil gland absent in *Podargus*, very small in *Batrachostomus;* one carotid artery (left). Twelve species, length 20–40 centimetres.

Family Nyctibiidae (potoos)

Upper Pleistocene to present. Neotropical region. Schizognathous palate (small vomers and separate maxillopalatines); palatines narrow anteriorly, greatly expanded posteriorly; small, weak bill but with prominent horny angular projection on maxillary tomium midway between tip and rictus and tomium very broad, horny, and strongly convex from that point to rictus; extremely short tarsi; toes unusually wide basally, forming a broad flattened sole; tracheobronchial syrinx; 14 cervical vertebrae; large powder down patches on sides and breast; no oil gland; one carotid artery (left). Five to 7 species, length 20–55 centimetres.

Family Aegothelidae (owlet frogmouths)

No fossil record. Australasian region (except New Zealand). Desmognathous palate; bill similar to Podargidae but shorter, weaker, and largely hidden by forehead feathering; bronchial syrinx; unique in the order in lacking ceca. Eight species; length 16–25 centimetres.

Family Caprimulgidae (nighthawks, nightjars)

Earliest probable fossil Oligocene, earliest modern fossil *Caprimulgus* in Pliocene (Europe). Worldwide in tropical and temperate zones; absent from northernmost Eurasia and America, southernmost South America, New Zealand, and some oceanic islands; subfamily Chordeilinae (nighthawks) restricted to New World. Schizognathous palate (except *Chordeiles* and perhaps other Chordeilinae); palatines narrow anteriorly, greatly expanded posteriorly; small, weak bill; well-developed rictal bristles (except *Eurostopodus* and Chordeilinae); small, weak feet; lateral toes much shorter than middle toe, fourth toe with only four phalanges (segments; five is normal for this order), middle claw with inner edge pectinated; hallux very short and directed inward; tracheobronchial syrinx; 14 cervical vertebrae. Seventy to 80 species; 14–40 centimetres (without ornamental feathers).

Critical appraisal. The major divisions of the caprimulgiform birds are clearly defined and their composition remarkably homogeneous so that there are no apparent taxonomic problems above the level of genus. The rather aberrant oilbird has some characters similar to owls, but the weight of evidence places it in this order. Studies of the egg-white proteins by C.G. Sibley show that it is clearly caprimulgiform. These investigations indicate a close relationship between the nightjars and the owls but do not support one to the swifts. Within the order the main taxonomic problems relate to re-evaluation at the generic level and clarification of species limits. These are likely to be settled only with the aid of field studies utilizing bioacoustical methods in combination with other disciplines.

BIBLIOGRAPHY. The natural history of North American nightjars is extensively discussed by A.C. BENT, "Life Histories of North American Cuckoos, Goatsuckers, Hummingbirds and Their Allies," *Bull. U.S. Natn. Mus. 176* (1940); that of European nightjars in D.A. BANNERMAN and G.E. LODGE, *The Birds of the British Isles*, vol. 4 (1955). F. HAVERSCHMIDT, *The Birds of Surinam* (1968), includes much information on the South American caprimulgiforms. J.P. CHAPIN, "Birds of the Belgian Congo, Part II," *Bull. Am. Mus. Nat. Hist.*, vol. 75 (1939), contains readable accounts of the natural history of several tropical nightjars. D.W. SNOW, "The Natural History of the Oilbird, *Steatornis caripensis*, in Trinidad, W.I." *Zoologica*, vol. 46, pp. 27–48 (1961) and vol. 47, pp. 199–222 (1962), provides an excellent and readable account of the natural history of that species. The information on nightjar hibernation is scattered among a number of short journal articles, but the reader will find interesting summaries in E.C. JAEGER, "Further Observations on the Hibernation of the Poorwill," *Condor*, vol. 51, no. 3, pp. 105–109 (1949); and J.T. MARSHALL, JR., "Hibernation in Captive Goatsuckers," *Condor*, vol. 57, no. 3, pp. 129–134 (1955). A review of the more recent work in this field is presented by G.T. AUSTIN and W.G. BRADLEY, "Additional Responses of the Poorwill to Low Temperatures," *Auk*, vol. 86, no. 4, pp. 717–725 (1969).

(P.A.S.)

Caracalla

Emperor of Rome from 211 to 217, Caracalla has often been regarded as one of the most bloodthirsty tyrants in Roman history, whose reign contributed to the decay of the Empire. His best known achievements are the Constitutio Antoniniana de Civitate, of 212, which gave Roman citizenship to almost all inhabitants of the empire and the construction in Rome of the *Thermae Antoninianae*, or Baths of Caracalla.

By courtesy of The Art Museum, Princeton University

Caracalla, marble bust, 3rd century. In the Art Museum, Princeton University.

Born at Lugdunum (Lyons), in Gaul, on April 4, 188, he was the elder son of the future emperor Lucius Septimius Severus, a North African, and Julia Domna, a Syrian. He was originally named Bassianus, after his maternal grandfather, who had been high priest of the Syrian sun-god Elagabalus. On receiving the title Caesar in 196, he assumed the name Marcus Aurelius Antoninus, because his father wanted to connect his family with the famous dynasty of the Antonines. In 198 he was given the title of Augustus, which nominally meant he had equal rank with his father. The nickname Caracalla was based on his alleged designing of a new cloak of that name. Another of his nicknames, Tarautas, was that of an ugly, insolent, and bloodthirsty gladiator whom he was thought to resemble.

The ancient sources concerning his life and character are by no means reliable. One of them, for example, recounts that as a boy he was amiable, generous, and sensitive and only later became insufferable; but the same source reports in another context that he was fierce by nature. Modern treatments emphasize Caracalla's Syrian heritage as one of the most important elements in his character, although here, too, due caution must be applied, since Eastern origin was in no way incompatible with a high degree of Romanization. Julia herself was well acquainted with Greco-Roman culture and hired excellent teachers to give her son the best education available. It is reported that he studied the Greek orators and tragedians and was able to quote long passages from the Greek playwright Euripides but also that he strongly despised education and educated people. This may have been the result of his passion for military life, which probably developed when he accompanied his father on his many military expeditions.

At the age of 14 he was married to Fulvia Plautilla, the daughter of the influential and ambitious commander of the imperial guard, Fulvius Plautianus; he is said to have hated Plautianus and played an important role in having him executed on the charge of a conspiracy against the imperial dynasty. He also exiled his own wife to an island and later killed her.

Enmity between Caracalla and Geta

A significant development was the growing rivalry between Caracalla and his younger brother Geta, a rivalry that was aggravated when Severus died during a campaign in Britain (211), and Caracalla, nearing his 23rd birthday, passed from the second to the first position in the empire. All attempts by their mother to bring about a reconciliation were in vain, and Caracalla finally killed Geta, in the arms of Julia herself, it is said. There can be no doubt about the savage brutality of Caracalla's act, but a solution that would have been at once moral and practicable was not in sight.

Caracalla next showed considerable cruelty in ordering many of Geta's friends and associates put to death. Probably in order to regain goodwill, he granted an amnesty to exiles, a move denounced as hypocritical in ancient sources, which also slander Caracalla's most famous measure, the so-called Constitutio Antoniniana de Civitate, as a device designed solely to collect more taxes.

His expeditions against the German tribes in 212/213, when he senselessly massacred an allied German force, and against the Parthians in 216–217 are ascribed by ancient sources to his love of military glory. Just before the Parthian campaign, he is said to have perpetrated a "massacre" among the population of Alexandria, probably in response to a disturbance there.

Caracalla's unpredictable behaviour is said to have prompted Macrinus, the commander of the imperial guard and his successor on the throne, to plot against him: Caracalla was assassinated at Carrhae, in Mesopotamia, at the beginning of a second campaign against the Parthians on April 8, 217.

Character

Important for the understanding of his character and behaviour is his identification with Alexander the Great. Admiration of the great Macedonian was not unusual among Roman emperors, but, in the case of Caracalla, Alexander became an obsession that proved to be ludicrous and grotesque. He adopted clothing, weapons, behaviour, travel routes, portraits, perhaps even an alleged plan to conquer the Parthian empire, all in imitation of Alexander. He assumed the surname Magnus, the Great, organized a Macedonian phalanx and an elephant division, and had himself represented as godlike on coins.

Another important trait was Caracalla's deeply rooted superstition; he followed magical practices and carefully observed all ritual obligations. He was tolerant of the Jewish and Christian faiths, but his favourite deity was the Egyptian god Sarapis, whose son or brother he pretended to be. He adopted the Egyptian practice of identifying the ruler with god and is the only Roman emperor who is portrayed as a pharaoh in a statue.

In the many portraits of him, Caracalla's head is usually shown inclined to the right, facing left—like Alexander—his look fierce, his forehead distorted by sharp wrinkles, his chin split into two halves, with curly hair, a short-cut beard and moustache, and a rather flat and blunt nose. Modern authors suggest that his features are typically North African, inherited from his father. In any event, the expression of vehemence and cruelty is obvious, and some sources say that he intentionally reinforced this impression, perhaps because it flattered his vanity to spread fear and terror. It is also said, contradictorily, that he was of small size but excelled in bodily exercises, that he shared the toils of the rank and file but also weakened his virility by a dissolute life and was not even able to bear the weight of a cuirass.

A similar inconsistency characterizes the judgments about his mental state. He was said to be mad but also sharp minded and ready witted. His predilection for gods of health, as documented by numerous dedicatory inscriptions, may support the theory of mental illness.

If Caracalla was a madman or a tyrant, the fact had no great consequences for his administration of the empire, which may or may not have been vitally influenced by Julia Domna and the great jurists who surrounded him. He was venerated by his soldiers, who forced the Senate to deify him after his death, and there is no indication that he was especially disliked among the general population. In any case, the Roman Empire at that time was still strong enough to bear a ruler who certainly lacked the qualities of an outstanding emperor.

BIBLIOGRAPHY. English translations of the ancient sources in the "Loeb Classical Library": CASSIUS DIO, *Dio's Roman History*, trans. by E. CARY, bk. 77–79; *Herodian*, trans. by C.R. WHITTAKER, bk. 3 and 4; *Scriptores Historiae Augustae*, vol. 2, trans. by D. MAGIE. The most reliable of these sources is Cassius Dio. The most detailed treatment of Caracalla's life and reign is the dissertation of D.C. MACKENZIE, *The Reign of Caracalla* (1949).

(F.P.K.)

Caracas

Caracas, capital of the Republic of Venezuela and of its federal district, is one of the most highly developed Latin American cities. From a modest city at the beginning of the 20th century, it had become the country's metropolis, with a population early in the 1970s of nearly 2,200,000 in its metropolitan area. With its new avenues, bridges, streets, and multi-storied buildings, it is a cosmopolitan business and residential centre. The city, which lies 3,025 feet (922 metres) above sea level in a valley surrounded by mountains of the central highlands, offers a series of impressive views from its numerous hilltops, to which modern construction has spread. Almost all of the valley's inhabitable area has been covered by urban growth, and the once green and peaceful valley is now an urban area, crisscrossed by automotive traffic, in which the pace of life is becoming increasingly feverish. The area of the city is 29.7 square miles, of the metropolitan area is 139 square miles, and of the federal district is 745.1 square miles.

History. A ranch was established in the valley in 1555 by Francisco Fajardo, the son of a Spanish captain and an Indian chief's daughter, and in 1561 Juan Rodríguez Suárez founded a town on the site of the ranch; but the town was soon destroyed by Indian attacks. The conquest and resettlement of the region began in 1566, and Diego de Losada is credited with the actual founding of the city in 1567. He named it Santiago de León de Caracas in honour of the apostle James, who is the patron saint of Spain; of don Pedro Ponce de León, who was the provincial governor; and of the Caracas Indians, who inhabited the region. The valley was fertile and the climate pleasant and healthy.

The colonial city

In 1578 the city was a quadrilateral formed of 24 squares centred on a plaza. The streets were straight and cobbled, and down them came rivulets of water from the hills. Three houses were made of brick, each of two floors, with straw roofs; most houses had walls of *bajareque* (cane and earth), packed earth, or adobe and roofs of straw or tile. The average house was large, with tree-filled patios and arcades and separate slave quarters and stable.

The urban area at that time was limited by the Catuche and Caroata ravines in the east and west, respectively; the Cerro El Avila on the north; and the Río Guaire on the south. Initial growth in the area was along the road to the north and then toward the south. Later, development progressed to the west and east, making necessary the construction of bridges across the ravines, and then, at the beginning of the 20th century, became more pronounced in the east. Caracas now has two urban centres:

the Old City around the main plaza (named Plaza Bolívar in 1865) and the El Recreo commercial centre located between the old city and Chacao, the area of greatest growth toward the east, where the city has expanded into the state of Miranda.

The city was sacked by English buccaneers in 1595. Its buildings were almost totally destroyed by two great earthquakes in 1755 and 1812, and, in the war of independence, it was repeatedly subjected to slaughter and pillage by both sides. In 1577 Caracas acquired its status as a provincial capital. Later, it successively became the residence of the captain general of Venezuela and, upon independence, the capital of the republic.

The contemporary city. *The city site and layout.* The site of the city is a high rift valley seven miles inland from the Caribbean Sea, to the north.

Caracas is sheltered between two mountain systems that enclose it at all cardinal points. The Cordillera del Litoral a very high mountain range, protects the north from east to west; and toward the south and east are the hills of the Serranía del Interior, the slopes of which reach as far as the valley's centre, interrupting the gentle inclines of the

Valley topography

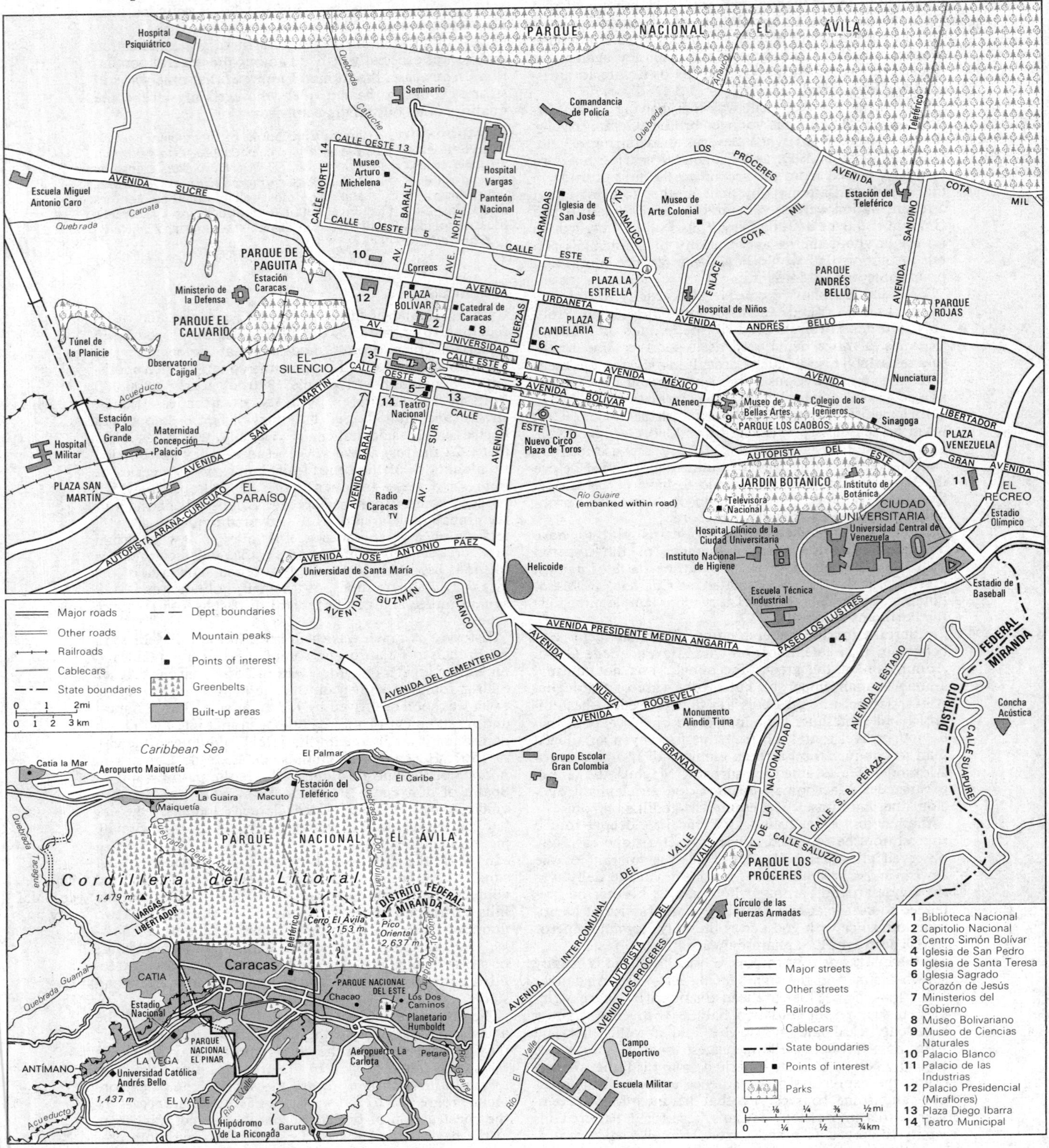

Central Caracas and (inset) its metropolitan area.

terrain that comes down from the Cordillera del Litoral. The greater part of the valley consists of hills and lowlands with occasional brief flatlands. Hill and valley interweave forming the principal valley and secondary valleys that make up the metropolitan area.

The municipal area (*i.e.*, city) extends 5.7 miles from north to south and 3.1 miles from east to west. The metropolitan area includes the municipal area, the four surrounding parishes, and five towns in the state of Miranda. It extends 9.3 miles from north to south and 17.6 miles from east to west.

Climate and environment. The decisive climatic factor is the valley's altitude. Temperatures range from 45° to 91° F (7.2° to 32.8° C), the annual mean being about 68° F (20° C). During the rainy season (May–November) the humidity is high, but during the dry season (December–April) the weather is delightful.

At the end of the 19th century and the beginning of the 20th, Caracas still retained the red roofs and blue hills evoked by its poet J.A. Pérez Bonalde. Almost all of these have now disappeared from the city. The stone streets no longer exist, and the ample houses surrounded by trees and ancient haciendas and plantations once outside the city have been replaced by rows of houses and apartment buildings.

Caracas' principal river is the Guaire, once large and important but now reduced to very small volume. Its principal affluent in the metropolitan area is the Río El Valle, and other affluents include the Quebrada Baruta and the Quebrada Anauco. These water sources are not suitable for human consumption, and the rainwater received by the catchment basin is insufficient for the population's needs.

Throughout the valley, on the numerous mountain spurs and their slopes, the abundant vegetation remains green throughout the year, irrigated by the streams and brooks flowing from the mountain ranges. This rich Caracan flora contains great variety including orchids and other tropical plants and flowers and many fruit trees and other species. The metropolitan area has 97 species of birds in its parks and gardens and is visited by migrating species from October to April, and there are many multicoloured butterfly species throughout the area all year. The valley contains fauna that abound in native species including marsupials, 30 species of bat, armadillo, sloth, mountain deer, fox, skunk, puma, and many others.

Rich plant and animal life

Pattern of growth. In 1870, the urban transformation of Caracas began under Pres. Guzmán Blanco. Under the influence of the French architectural taste of the period, many buildings in the Spanish colonial style disappeared or were modified. Bridges and avenues were built, and some streets were widened to encourage the city's growth. At the beginning of the 20th century, the first urban real-estate development, designed for the upper class, was built outside the old city and called El Paraíso. A short time later, Nueva Caracas, an urban real-estate development for the middle class, was begun in Catia, to the west.

Beginning in 1936, after the death of Gen. Juan Vicente Gómez, who had been dictator for 27 years, the country experienced a new era of prosperity. Caracas grew in population and extended its construction as far as was geographically possible. In the downtown area of the city, the El Silencio district was transformed into a middle-income complex of apartment buildings: this development was programmed in 1939, together with a Regulating Plan for Caracas. It was built between 1941 and 1945 and consisted of six blocks containing 750 residential apartments and 200 commercial locations; the first work of such magnitude in the country, the development marked the beginning of the city's modern architectural tendency.

These years marked the beginning of the city's construction fever and its urban development. The change in the appearance of Caracas was an abrupt and overwhelming one. The old city began to disappear, and the great rows of trees on the nearby haciendas gave way to modern residential developments. Numerous suburbs went up overnight on the spurs of the hills, and villas and commercial buildings were built at a feverish pace in the valley plains. In addition, there was an over-reached boom, at all levels, in the large-scale building and sale of cooperative apartment houses. Also, there progressively appeared publicly built urban housing developments controlled by the Workers' Bank.

Rapid urban development

Transportation. Caracas is linked directly by highway to several neighbouring towns and connected by a large network of heavily trafficked roads to more distant communities. La Carlota Airport links Caracas to the most important cities within Venezuela, and Maiquetía Airport, located 12 miles from Caracas on the coast, provides international connections. La Guaira and Puerto Cabello are Caracas' natural ports, through which most merchandise is imported. An aerial cablecar rises from sea level to 6,904 feet on the Cerro el Avila between La Guaira and Caracas; another goes from the city itself to

Karl Weidmann—Pix

Santa Teresa Church (lower left) and Centro Simón Bolívar in downtown Caracas.

the Avila summit. A modern highway including two long tunnels through the mountains leads to the beaches and tourist areas of the coast. Within the city a great number of buses, private automobiles, taxis, and jitneys contribute to increasing traffic congestion during rush hours. The public transportation system is deficient, but plans have been made for the construction of a subway. The city has modern avenues and several large expressways.

Demography. There were about 18,500 inhabitants in the city in 1771. The figure was 40,000 in 1800. Growth came to a halt during the war for independence between 1810 and 1830 and began to revive only toward the end of the century. The slight increase was intensified during the first decades of the 20th century. After 1930, encouraged by the country's exploitation of oil, rapid population growth began. Metropolitan Caracas' population reached the 1,000,000 mark in 1955, and the 1971 census figure approached 2,200,000. Statistics reveal that since 1936 the population of Caracas proper has increased nearly nine-fold while the city has grown six times in area, and the demand for transportation has increased eight and a half times.

Population growth

The racial elements of the Caracan population, like that of Venezuela as a whole, include the white, Indian, and black races, with white and mestizo (mixed white and Indian) predominating. The dominant religion is Roman Catholicism, but other religions are permitted, including Protestantism and Judaism. Domestic migration, intense in recent years, has created the problem of marginal slums, known as the poverty belt, surrounding Caracas. Foreign immigration is appreciable.

Housing. There were about 260,000 housing units in Caracas at the time of the 1961 census, distributed as follows: 90,000 houses and villas; 90,000 apartments; 26,000 individual rooms in rooming houses, country homes, apartments, and tenements; and 54,000 *ranchos* (poverty housing constructed with scrap materials). By 1971 there were 400,000 housing units and the number of *ranchos* had declined substantially. Since the early 1960s large blocks of uniform dwellings have gradually replaced old homes in the Spanish colonial style, of which few now remain.

Economic life. The city's growing industry includes the production of sugar, processed foods, beverages, tobacco (cigarettes), clothing, wood, paper and cardboard, graphic arts, marblework, jewelry and silversmithing, butter and vegetable oils, rubber, glass, chemical and pharmaceutical products, plastics, leather and hides, and metallurgy and naval and automotive construction. The construction industry has become the foremost urban activity, creating a parallel growth in auxiliary industries such as cement and construction materials. Caracas is the centre of both domestic and foreign commerce and supplies the domestic market with most of its industrial production. As a result of its position as the centre of private and foreign capital and of state finances, it is the principal centre of petroleum-related activities and the seat of the country's major banking houses and industrial and commercial enterprises.

Government. Caracas is the permanent site of the national government's executive, legislative, and judicial branches. Caracas itself is governed through the Liberator department of the federal district, composed of ten urban parishes and four parishes outside the urban area. Five towns in the state of Miranda (Petare, Chacao, Leoncio Martínez [Los Dos Caminos], Baruta, and El Hatillo) form an integral part of the metropolitan area. Caracas has been the seat of an archbishopric since 1804, of a bishopric since 1535.

Public utilities. The city is supplied with water by aqueducts under the control of the National Institute of Sanitary Works. The main aqueduct is the Butterfly Dam, which collects the waters of the Tuy rivers from the nearby Tuy valleys at Lagartijo.

Caracas has had electric power since 1897. There are now several thermoelectric plants in the valley, in addition to others using hydroelectric power. Gas is supplied by pipelines from two systems in the interior, Las Mercedes in Guárico and Anaco in Anzoátegui.

Health. Caracas is endowed with clinics, sanatoriums, hospitals, and rest homes for the health care of the capital's population. The principal health centre is the Clinic Hospital of University City.

Like all great cities, Caracas has a pollution problem as a result of excessive emissions from automobiles, factories, and chimneys, as well as from other contaminants produced by industrial activity and the burning of waste and rubbish collected in the city. A great deal of contaminated water collects in the lower part of the Río Guaire, complicating the problem still further. Noise, a fourth form of environmental pollution, has intensified, especially as a result of the greater number of automobiles.

Education. There are five sectors of education both public and private: primary, secondary, normal, arts and trades, and university. There are, in addition, numerous kindergartens for those under six years. The most important centre of higher education is the Central University of Venezuela (also known as the University of Caracas), established 1721. With a capacity of 30,000 students, its buildings and installations form a modern university city enclave in the centre of the valley. Other universities are Simón Bolívar, which is public and oriented toward technology, and the private universities Andrés Bello Catholic, Metropolitan, and Santa Maria. Other educational centres include the National Institute of Hygiene, the Technical Industrial School, the Gran Colombia Normal School (for girls), the Miguel Antonio Caro Normal School, and the Military Academy. Located on the highway leading to the nearby town of Los Teques is a centre of advanced scientific research. There is also a specialized institute devoted to the technical preparation of workers at all levels.

Higher education

Cultural life. Numerous cultural activities in the city include theatre, exhibitions of painting and sculpture, concerts, lectures, dance, and film. The principal cultural institutions are the academy of the language, the academies of history, medicine, political and social sciences, physical sciences and mathematics, and fine arts, as well as Writer's House, the Athenaeum of Caracas, and the Venezuelan Association of Journalists. Also in Caracas are the national library and the fine arts and the natural science museums, as well as art galleries, which have proliferated in recent years. Theatrical activity is concentrated in the municipal and national theatres, and numerous outlying theatres provide opportunities for small acting groups. The Institute of Culture and Fine Arts has developed an intense cultural program in the metropolitan area.

The media. Caracas has wide press service. The most important dailies are *El Nacional*, *El Universal*, *Ultimas Noticias*, *La Religión*, and *La Verdad*, appearing in the afternoon, and the evening papers, *El Mundo*, *Meridiano*, *El Globo*, and *Extra*. There is also an English daily, *The Daily Journal*. There are several weekly magazines, literary and cultural journals, and scientific publications. There are also four commercial television stations and one government station, as well as 28 radio stations.

Recreation. Numerous athletic stadiums are available for baseball, football, tennis, and other sports; there are also swimming pools, golf courses, a bullfighting ring, and a racetrack. The mountains and the beaches are nearby. There are public gardens and plazas, a zoo, monuments, museums, and historic buildings, churches, and avenues. The most popular parks are the Avila National Park, a forest preserve on the Cerro El Avila, Los Caobos Park, once the forest of a coffee plantation, the Central University Botanical Garden, and the Parque del Este, in La Floresta. A program for the creation of "pocket parks" out of uncultivated land in the metropolitan area has already resulted in the creation of a modern park from the old El Paraíso race track. This policy is helping in part to solve the problem of insufficient green zones within the populated area.

Sports facilities and parks

BIBLIOGRAPHY. J.A. DE ARMAS CHITTY, *Caracas, origen y trayectoria de una ciudad* (1967), on historical aspects; MARIO BRICENO PEROZO, *Documentos para la historia de la fundación* *de Caracas existentes en el Archivo General de la Nación* (1969), especially interesting for the documentary evidence it displays to clear up the debated problem of the origin of Caracas; RAMON DIAZ SANCHEZ, *Caracas Cuatricentenaria* (1966), a historical outline covering a period of 400 years; MARCO AURELIO VILA, *Monografia geográfica del Valle de Caracas* (1947), a geographic description of the Caracas Valley, also dealing with population and economic conditions; CARLOS RAUL VILLANUEVA, *Caracas en tres tiempos* (1966), an illustrated description of Caracas architecture, including colonial architecture and historic houses, by a Venezuelan architect.

(J.R.Me.)

Caravaggio

Michelangelo Merisi, called Caravaggio after his birthplace, was an early Baroque painter who was probably the most revolutionary artist of his time. Abandoning the Platonic ideal of representing human and religious experience through idealized types that had guided a century of art before him, he kept his eye firmly on man, discovering that life is always a drama and that all experience, even mystical, seems to take its first steps within the concreteness and sensuality of physical phenomena. Possessed of an intensely emotional and rebellious personality and with a thorough understanding of the significance of real events in a physical world, he became in his work a master of the dramatic moment; his paintings reveal dramatic tension drawn to the snapping point. His view of man remains unique in his period of art, however, and, although he was widely admired and his remarkable techniques imitated, he was a solitary figure in his own time.

Anderson—Alinari

"The Calling of St. Matthew," oil on canvas by Caravaggio, *c.* 1597–98. In the Contarelli Chapel, S. Luigi dei Francesci, Rome. 3.39 × 3.49 m.

Caravaggio was born September 28, 1573, in Caravaggio, a town near Milan in northern Lombardy. He was the son of Fermo Merisi, steward and architect of the Marquis of Caravaggio. Orphaned at 11, Caravaggio was apprenticed in the same year to Simone Peterzano of Milan, a painter and teacher of drawing who sometimes styled himself "the pupil of Titian" but whose painting bore little relation to that of the Venetian master. Peterzano promised to keep the boy four years and train him to work on his own. Caravaggio may have stayed on at Peterzano's studio after the four years were over, or he may have begun independent work, travelling to the art centres of Venice or Bologna.

At some time between 1588 and 1592, Caravaggio went to Rome. He was already in possession of the fundamental technical skills of painting and had acquired, with characteristic eagerness, a thorough understanding of the approach of the Lombard and Venetian painters, who opposed to idealized Florentine painting had developed a style that was nearer to representing nature and events. Travelling from Milan to Rome, the young painter must certainly have stopped at Parma, Bologna, Florence, and Assisi and seen the works of the Carracci, contemporary innovators from Bologna, and the earlier masterpieces of Masaccio and Giotto. These encounters probably influenced Caravaggio to temper with a firmer line his Milanese technique, vibrant with chromatic and atmospheric transparency, and to discipline in formal composition the passionate, almost instinctive adherence to reality that appears in his plainest and most humble subjects.

Early influences

First years in Rome. Caravaggio arrived in Rome at the beginning of the last decade of a century that had been dominated artistically by the presence of Michelangelo, held to be without equal, and dominated intellectually by the Council of Trent, which launched the energetic and exuberant period of the Counter-Reformation. Rome was a city in ferment, overflowing with visitors, among whom were artists from all over the world, like Caravaggio moved by ambition and necessity, seeking glory and fortune. Caravaggio settled into the cosmopolitan society of the Campo Marzio. This decaying neighbourhood of inns, eating houses, temporary shelter, and little picture shops in which Caravaggio came to live suited his circumstances and his temperament. He was virtually without means, and his inclinations were always toward anarchy and against tradition. In these surroundings Caravaggio began the first phase of his career in Rome.

These first five years were an anguishing period of instability and humiliation. According to his biographers, Caravaggio was "needy and stripped of everything" and moved from one unsatisfactory employment to another, working as an assistant to painters of much smaller talent. He earned his living for the most part with hackwork and never stayed more than a few months at any studio. Finally, probably in 1595, he determined to set out on his own and began to sell his pictures through a dealer, a certain Maestro Valentino, who brought Caravaggio's work to the attention of Cardinal Francesco del Monte, a prelate of great influence in the papal court. Caravaggio soon came under the protection of del Monte and was invited to receive board, lodging, and a pension in the house of the Cardinal. This patronage made possible the beginning of Caravaggio's first experience of security and prestige.

Patronage of Cardinal del Monte

Despite spiritual and material deprivations, Caravaggio had painted up to the beginning of del Monte's patronage not less than some 40 works, many of them ambitious compositions: "The Musicians," "Lute Player," "Ecstasy of St. Francis," "The Young Bacchus," "The Fortune-teller," "Rest on the Flight into Egypt," "Narcissus at the Fountain," "The Magdalene," "The Sacrifice of Isaac," and "Basket of Fruit" are the most outstanding of these early works. They form a series of astonishing pictorial inventions, which show great taste and delicacy in their craftsmanship and a sureness and felicity of expression that is in sharp contrast to the daily quality of Caravaggio's disorderly and dissipated life. These were works for private collectors. In each composition there is proof of Caravaggio's professional attitude toward painting. In particular, these early paintings proclaim his conviction that "it takes as much hard work to do flowers as a human figure" and that "the painter who is worth something can execute natural things well." In "Basket of Fruit" the fruits, painted with brilliance and vivid realism, are handsomely disposed in a straw basket, and they form a striking composition in their visual apposition.

Major Roman commissions. With these works reality won its battle with manner, but it is in the cycle of the life of St. Matthew in the Contarelli Chapel that Caravaggio's realistic naturalism first fully appears. Probably through the agency of del Monte, Caravaggio ob-

St. Matthew cycle

tained, in 1597, the commission for the decoration of the Contarelli Chapel in the church of S. Luigi dei Francesci in Rome. This commission established him, at the age of 24, as a *pictor celeberrimus*, a "renowned painter," with important protectors and clients. The task was an imposing one. The scheme called for three large paintings of scenes from the saint's life, "St. Matthew and the Angel," showing the Evangelist writing his Gospel with the assistance of an angel; "The Calling of St. Matthew," showing the moment when Christ chose Matthew as a disciple; and "The Martyrdom of St. Matthew." The execution of all three works, in which Caravaggio substituted a dramatic realism imbued with disquieting social attitudes for the illustrative formulas of the hagiographic tradition, provoked public astonishment. Perhaps Caravaggio was waiting for this test, on public view at last, to reveal the whole range of his diversity and novelty. His novelty in these works is not only one of the surface appearance of structure and subject, but it involves the artistry itself, the sense of time and the light. The first version of the canvas that was to go over the altar, "St. Matthew and the Angel," was so offensive to the canons of S. Luigi dei Francesci, who had never seen such a representation of a saint, that it had to be redone. The Evangelist has the physical features of a plowman or a common labourer. His big feet seem to stick out of the picture, brutally thrown in the face of the faithful, and his posture, legs crossed, is awkward almost to the point of vulgarity. The angel does not stand graciously by but forcefully pushes Matthew's hand over the page of a heavy book, as if he were guiding an illiterate. What the canons did not understand was that Caravaggio, in elevating this humble figure, was copying Christ, who had himself raised Matthew from the street.

The other two scenes of the St. Matthew cycle are no less disconcerting in the realism of their drama. "The Calling of St. Matthew" shows the moment at which two men and two worlds confront each other: Christ, in a burst of light, entering the room of the toll collector, and Matthew, intent on counting coins in the midst of a group of gaily dressed idlers with swords at their sides. In the glance between the two men, Matthew's world is dissolved. In "The Martyrdom of St. Matthew" the event is captured just at the moment when the executioner is forcing his victim to the ground. The scene is a public street, and, as Matthew's acolyte flies in terror, passersby glance at the act with idle unconcern. The most intriguing aspect of these narratives is that they seem to be reconstructions of visual testimony, in a scenic fiction as close as possible to the truth, as if they were being performed in thick darkness when a sudden illumination revealed them and fixed them in memory at the instant of their most intense drama.

Caravaggio's use of light

Light is the instrument of Caravaggio's pictorial revolution: it is as active and determining of the structure of the work as line and colour. A 20th-century art critic, Robert Longhi, compared the importance of Caravaggio's use of light to that of the Renaissance discovery of perspective. His light is not that of nature; it is a magical light that falls solidly from above, almost always from a point at the onlooker's shoulder, a stage light that modifies the colour scheme so that it loses affected subtleties like the iridescence of skin and becomes terse, emphatically dark in tone. The 17th-century painter Francesco Albani, said Caravaggio "ground flesh" instead of colours.

The decoration of the Contarelli Chapel was completed by 1602. Caravaggio, though not yet 30, overshadowed all his contemporaries. There was a swarm of orders for pictures, private and ecclesiastical. "The Crucifixion of St. Peter" and "The Conversion of St. Paul," "The Deposition of Christ," the "Madonna dei Palafrenieri" ("Madonna of the Serpent"), and the "Death of the Virgin" all belong to this period. Some of these paintings, done at the high point of Caravaggio's artistic maturity, provoked violent reaction. The "Madonna with Pilgrims," or "Madonna di Loreto," for the church of S. Agostino, was a scandal because of the "dirty feet and torn, filthy cap" of the two old people kneeling in the foreground. The "Death of the Virgin" was refused by the Carmelites because of the indignity of the Virgin's plebeian features, bared legs, and swollen belly like that of a drowned woman. At the advice of Rubens, the picture was bought by the Duke of Mantua in April 1607 and displayed to the community of painters at Rome for one week before removal to Mantua.

Reactions to Caravaggio's style

Culmination of mature style. Artists, men of learning, and enlightened prelates were fascinated by the subtle magic implicit in the robust and bewildering art of Caravaggio, but the negative reaction of church officials reflected the self-protective irritation of academic painters and the instinctive resistance of the more conservative clergy and much of the populace. The more brutal aspects of Caravaggio's paintings were condemned without recognition of the riddling and disquieting message Caravaggio had linked to them. It is true that Caravaggio's common people bear no relation to the graceful suppliants popular in much of Counter-Reformation art. They are plain working men, muscular, stubborn, tenacious of the only good they have: a hard life that will pass away in martyrdom, death, and poverty. The 20th-century art historian Maurizio Calvesi sees in Caravaggio's iconography an inclination away from orthodoxy. In the "Madonna of the Serpent," the Virgin is small in relation to the figure of Jesus, and while she steps on the serpent's head, it is the force of his foot pressing down on hers that crushes it. The act belongs to Jesus and not to the Virgin, immaculate symbol of the church, as tradition would have the scene. Calvesi suggests that the reason God the Father does not appear in "The Conversion of St. Paul," where he is traditionally present, is that Caravaggio's lighting is based on a principle close to the teachings of the heretic Giordano Bruno of immanent divinity, which holds that the divine participates and is inherent in nature and man.

Criticism did not cloud Caravaggio's success. His reputation and income increased, and he began to be envied. The despairing bohemian of the early Roman years had disappeared, but, although he moved in the society of cardinals and princes, the spirit was the same, still given to wrath and riot. Karel van Mander, a Dutch painter, who met him in Rome during Caravaggio's happiest period in 1602–03, wrote:

> In Italy there is a Michelangelo da Caravaggio who does wonderful things . . . He holds the works of other masters of no account . . . A mixture of grain and chaff will not stay at his work, but after two weeks will give himself over to play for a month or two, a sword at his side, a servant behind, spinning from one game to another, inclined to duels and scuffles, a hard man for company.

Problems with the law

The details of the first Roman years are unknown, but after the time of the Contarelli project Caravaggio had many encounters with the law. In 1600 he was accused of blows by a fellow painter, and the following year he wounded a soldier. In 1603 he was imprisoned on the complaint of another painter and released only through the intercession of the French ambassador. In April 1604 he was accused of throwing a plate of artichokes in the face of a waiter, and in October he was arrested for throwing stones at the Roman Guards. In May 1605 he was seized for misuse of arms, and on July 29 he had to flee Rome for a time because he had wounded a man in defense of his mistress. Within a year, on May 29, 1606, again in Rome, during a furious brawl over a disputed score in a game of tennis, Caravaggio killed one Ranuccio Tomassoni.

Flight from Rome. In terror of the consequences of his act, Caravaggio, himself wounded and feverish, fled the city and sought refuge on the nearby estate of a relative of the Marquis of Caravaggio. He then moved on to other places of hiding and eventually reached Naples, probably in early 1607. He remained at Naples for a time, painting a "Madonna of the Rosary" for the Flemish painter Louis Finson and one of his late masterpieces, "The Seven Works of Mercy," for the chapel of Monte della Misericordia. It is impossible to ignore the connection between the dark and urgent nature of this painting and what must have been his desperate state of mind. It is also the first indication of a shift in his painting style.

At the end of 1607 or the beginning of 1608, Caravaggio travelled to Malta, where he was received as a celebrated artist. He worked hard, completing several works, the most important of which was "The Beheading of St. John the Baptist" for the cathedral. In this scene of martyrdom, shadow, which in earlier paintings stood thick about the figures, is here drawn back, and the infinite space that had been evoked by the huge empty areas of the earlier compositions is replaced by a high, overhanging wall. This high wall, which reappears in later works, can be linked to a consciousness in Caravaggio's mind of condemnation to a limited space, the space between the narrow boundaries of flight and prison. On July 14, 1608, Caravaggio was received into the Order of Malta as a "Knight of Justice"; soon afterward, however, either because word of his crime had reached Malta or because of new misdeeds, he was expelled from the order and imprisoned. He escaped, however.

Flight to Sicily

Caravaggio took refuge in Sicily, landing at Syracuse in October 1608, restless and fearful of pursuit. Yet his fame accompanied him; at Syracuse he painted his late, tragic masterpiece, "The Burial of St. Lucy," for the church of Sta. Lucia. In early 1609 he fled to Messina, where he painted "The Resurrection of Lazarus" and "The Adoration of the Shepherds"; then to Palermo where he did the "Adoration with St. Francis and St. Lawrence" for the Oratorio di S. Lorenzo. The works of Caravaggio's flight, painted under the most adverse of circumstances, include some of the greatest compositions of his career. Although the structural designs are more grandly impressive than ever before, these works show a subdued tone and a delicacy of the expression of emotion that renders feeling even more intense than do the overt dramatics of his earlier paintings. The unfailing excellence of these calm, intense works is remarkable in view of the distractions that must have beset him.

His desperate flight could be ended only with the Pope's pardon, and Caravaggio may have known that there were intercessions on his behalf in Rome when he again moved north to Naples in October 1609. Bad luck pursued him, however; at the door of an inn he was attacked and wounded so badly that rumours reached Rome that the *pittore celebre* was dead. After a long convalescence he sailed in July 1610 to Port' Ercole, a Spanish possession within the Papal States. He was arrested by mistake and detained two days in prison. On his release, he discovered that the boat that was to take him to Rome had sailed, taking his belongings. Misfortune, exhaustion, and a revival of fever were at last too much for him. He collapsed on the beach in sight of the departing boat and died a few days later, on July 18, 1610, not yet 37.

MAJOR WORKS

"The Young Bacchus" (1593; Uffizi, Florence); "Boy Bitten by a Lizard" (1593; Louvre, Paris); "Boy with a Basket of Fruit" (1593; Borghese Gallery, Rome); "The Fortuneteller" ("La Zingara"; 1594; Louvre, Paris); "Rest on the Flight into Egypt" (*c.* 1590; Galleria Doria-Pamphili, Rome); "The Sacrifice of Isaac" (1594–96; Uffizi, Florence); "Lute Player" (Hermitage, Leningrad); "The Magdalene" (Galleria Doria-Pamphili, Rome); "Basket of Fruit" (1596; Pinacoteca Ambrosiana, Milan); "The Supper at Emmaus" (1596–98; National Gallery, London); "The Calling of St. Matthew" (S. Luigi dei Francesci, Rome); "St. Matthew and the Angel" (S. Luigi dei Francesci, Rome); "The Marytyrdom of St. Matthew" (1598–1601; S. Luigi dei Francesci, Rome); "The Conversion of St. Paul" (Sta. Maria del Popolo, Rome); "The Crucifixion of St. Peter" (1601; Sta. Maria del Popolo, Rome); "The Deposition of Christ" (1602–04; Vatican Museum, Rome); "Madonna with Pilgrims" ("Madonna di Loreto"; 1603–06; S. Agostino, Rome); "Madonna dei Palafrenieri" ("Madonna of the Serpent"; Borghese Gallery, Rome); "Death of the Virgin" (1605–06; Louvre, Paris); "St. Jerome" (Borghese Gallery, Rome); "Ecce Homo" (Galleria di Palazzo Rosso, Genoa); "The Supper at Emmaus" (Brera, Milan); "Madonna of the Rosary" (Kunsthistoriches Museum, Vienna); "The Seven Works of Mercy" (1607; Monte della Misericordia, Naples); "The Beheading of St. John the Baptist" (1608; Catherdral, Valletta, Malta); "Portrait of Alof de Wignacourt" (1608; Louvre, Paris); "Sleeping Cupid" (Pitti Palace, Florence); "St. John the Baptist" (Borghese Gallery, Rome); "Salome Receives the Head of St. John the Baptist" (National Gallery, London); "The Burial of St. Lucy" (1608; Sta. Lucia, Syracuse); "The Resurrection of Lazarus" (1609; Museo Nazionale, Messina); "The Adoration of the Shepherds" (1609; Museo Nazionale, Messina); "Adoration with St. Francis and St. Lawrence" (1609; Oratorio di S. Lorenzo, Palermo).

BIBLIOGRAPHY. R. LONGHI, the introduction to the catalog of the exhibition *Il Caravaggio e dei Caravaggeschi* (1951); and *Il Caravaggio* (1952), in French and Italian (with complete bibliography to date of publication), are fundamental for understanding both the man and the artist. Other important studies are: L. VENTURI, *Il Caravaggio* (1951); B. BERENSON, *Del Caravaggio, delle sue incongruenze e della sua fama* (1951; Eng. trans., *Caravaggio: His Incongruity and His Fame*, 1953); W.F. FRIEDLAENDER, *Caravaggio Studies* (1955); H. WAGNER, *Michelangelo da Caravaggio* (1958); A. BERNJOFFROY, *Le Dossier Caravage* (1959); R. JULLIAN, *Caravage* (1961), perhaps the best monograph (well documented); R.P. HINKS, *Michelangelo Merisi du Caravaggio: His Life, His Legend, and His Works* (1953); F.E. BAUMGART, *Caravaggio: Kunst und Wirklichkeit* (1955); and G. DELOGU, *Caravaggio* (1962). Important contributions concerning the problems of the Caravaggeschi may be found in the essays of D. MAHON that appeared in *Burlington Magazine* (1951, 1953, 1956) and *Art Bulletin* (1953). Among the popular monographs are: C. BARONI, *Tutta la pittura del Caravaggio*, 4th ed. (1956); S. BOTTARI, *Caravaggio* (1966); R. CAUSA, *Caravaggio*, 2 vol. (1966); and A. OTTINO DELLA CHIESA (with an introduction by R. GUTTUSO), *L'opera completa del Caravaggio* (1967), which contains the most ample iconography of the works attributed to Caravaggio by a variety of sources. S. SAMEK LUDOVICI, *Vita del Caravaggio* (1966), condenses all material on Caravaggio by the authors in his own time.

(L.Ca.)

Carbanions

Carbanions are negatively charged particles (anions or, when the sign of the charge is not specified, simply ions), in which the charge is located predominantly on carbon atoms. They are formally derived from neutral organic (carbon-containing) molecules by removal of positively charged atoms or groups of atoms, and they are important chiefly as chemical intermediates—that is, as substances used in the preparation of other substances. Important industrial products, including useful plastics, are made using carbanions.

The simplest carbanion, the methide ion (CH_3^-), is derived from the organic compound methane (CH_4) by a loss of a proton (hydrogen ion, H^+) as shown in the following chemical equation:

$$\underset{\text{methane}}{CH_4} \rightleftharpoons \underset{\text{methide ion}}{CH_3^-} + \underset{\text{proton}}{H^+}$$

in which the symbols C and H represent, respectively, carbon and hydrogen atoms; the subscripts indicate the numbers of atoms of each kind included in the molecules; the superscript plus and minus signs indicate, respectively, positive and negative charges; and the double arrows indicate that the reaction shown can proceed in either the forward or the reverse direction, a condition known as reversibility.

This equation also serves to demonstrate another definition of carbanions as the conjugate (paired) bases of carbon acids. The definition is based on the fact that the reaction shown is, in fact, an acid–base equilibrium, and that an equivalent equation can be written for the formation of every carbanion known. In addition, the definition of carbanions as bases is useful because it makes it possible to express the stability of carbanions in terms of simple acid-dissociation-equilibrium constants—numerical figures that indicate the extent to which the reaction of the type shown proceeds to the right at equilibrium. Expression of carbanion stabilities in numerical terms permits more exact comparisons than would otherwise be possible.

Carbanions as bases

Molecular structures. In discussing the structures of carbanions it is necessary to distinguish between localized and delocalized ions. In the former, the negative charge is confined largely to one carbon atom, whereas, in the latter, it is distributed over several atoms.

Localized ions. The simplest localized carbanion is the above mentioned methide ion (CH_3^-). It is isoelectronic (it has identical electron configuration) with the neutral molecule ammonia (formula NH_3, N being the chemical symbol for the nitrogen atom). Although, for reasons to be outlined below, it is difficult to determine the exact structure of isolated carbanions, the geometry of the methide ion is best represented by a pyramid with the carbon atom at the apex, a structure similar to that of the ammonia molecule. Both structures are shown below:

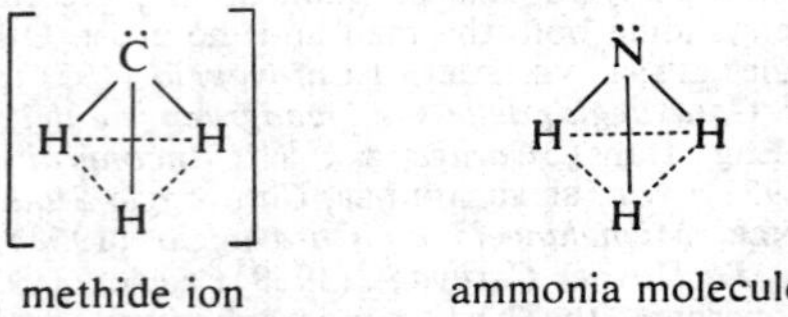

methide ion   ammonia molecule

in which the solid lines represent bonds between atoms and the dotted lines merely indicate the bases of the pyramids.

In terms of molecular orbitals—molecular orbitals being the regions that electrons occupy as they make up the bonds between atoms—this corresponds to three so-called sigma bonds (bonds symmetrical about the axis between the atoms) generated from carbon sp^3 hybrid orbitals and three hydrogen *s* orbitals, whereas the fourth sp^3 orbital is occupied by two electrons and is nonbonding—*s* and *p* orbitals being particular electron pathways associated with individual atoms, and hybridized orbitals being special combinations of the separate orbitals. A drawing of the methide ion with the various orbitals is shown below:

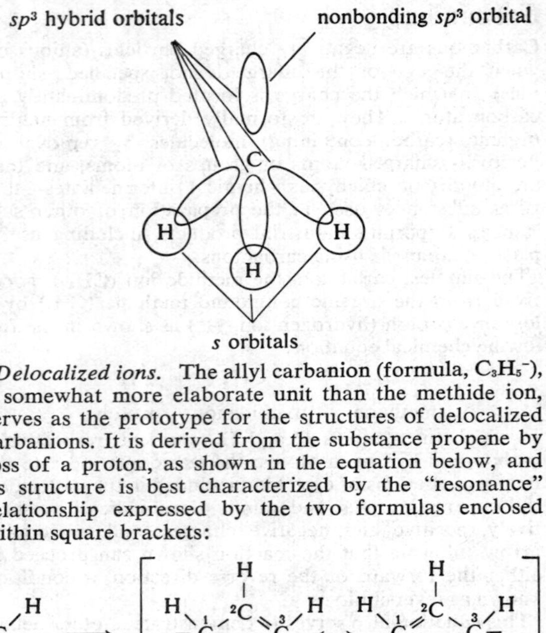

Delocalized ions. The allyl carbanion (formula, $C_3H_5^-$), a somewhat more elaborate unit than the methide ion, serves as the prototype for the structures of delocalized carbanions. It is derived from the substance propene by loss of a proton, as shown in the equation below, and its structure is best characterized by the "resonance" relationship expressed by the two formulas enclosed within square brackets:

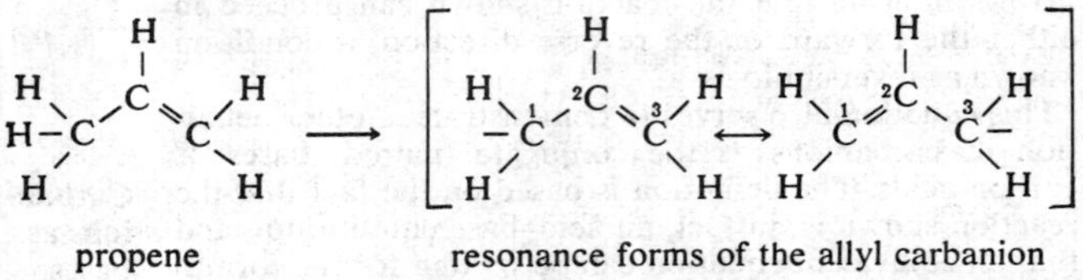

propene   resonance forms of the allyl carbanion

A substance (like the allyl carbanion), whose structural formula is expressed in terms of separate resonance forms, is considered to have a hybrid structure similar to all the resonance forms but truly expressed by none of them alone.

In molecular orbital terms, the allyl carbanion is described as a planar structure in which all three carbon atoms are sp^2 hybridized (a different form from that above) forming a sigma-bonded system, along with a pi-bonded system (pi bonds being above and below the axis of the bond) that contains four electrons in two pi orbitals, one of which is bonding and the other nonbonding. The sigma-bond and pi-bond systems of the allyl carbanion are shown below:

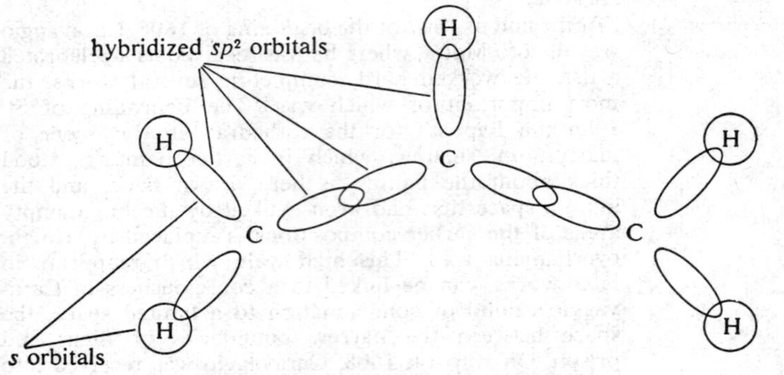

sigma-bond system of allyl carbanion

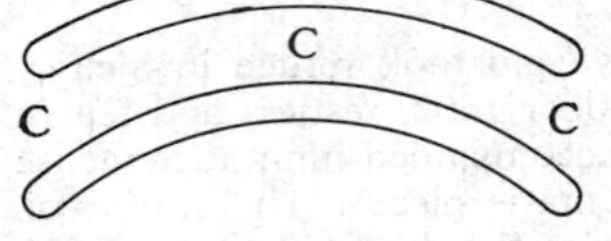

pi-bond system of allyl carbanion

Formally, the negative charge is contained in the pi system and is mainly associated with carbon atoms 1 and 3 (numbered as shown) as indicated by the resonance formalism.

An additional example of this kind of carbanion is the benzylic anion (shown below), in which the negative charge can be distributed over a much more extended pi-bond system, which includes an aromatic ring (a circle of carbon atoms joined by sigma and pi bonds). A resonance formulation of this anion is given below:

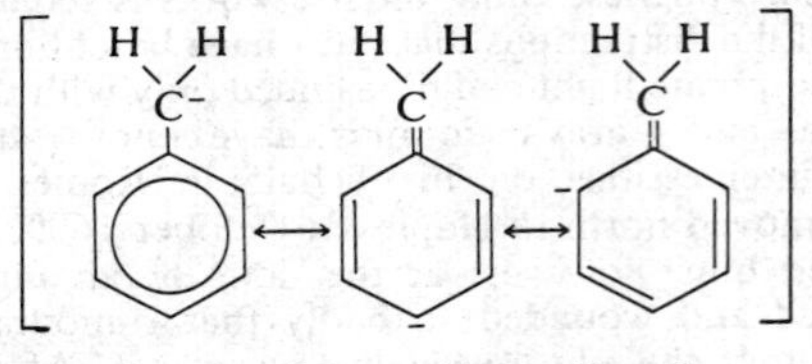

resonance forms of benzylic anion

Enolate anions

Closely related to the allyl carbanion are the enolate anions, in which one of the carbon atoms is replaced by an oxygen atom. Enolate ions are derivatives of ketones and aldehydes (compounds containing a double bond between carbon and oxygen atoms), from which they can be generated by abstraction of a proton from the carbon atom located next to the carbon of the carbonyl group. The resonance forms of an enolate ion are as shown below:

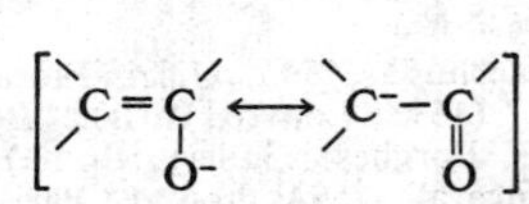

Because of the greater attraction for electrons (electronegativity) of oxygen as compared to carbon, the resonance structure with negative charge on oxygen contributes more than half to the true representation of the compound. In a typical enolate ion, in other words, the oxygen atom bears more of the negative charge than the carbon atom. As a generalization about the geometry of carbanions, it may be stated that localized carbanions are thought to have nonplanar structures, whereas delocalized ions with the negative charge residing in the pi system are most likely planar.

Ion pairs. To preserve electrical neutrality, it is mandatory that in a solution containing carbanions there must exist a corresponding cation (positive ion) for each carbanion. If the two ions of opposite charge are in close contact with each other, a covalent (nonionic) bond may form. This reaction is represented by the equilibrium that follows.

$$-\overset{|}{\underset{|}{C}}-M \rightleftharpoons -\overset{|}{\underset{|}{C^-}}M^+$$

compound with covalent bond — ion pair

in which M in most cases is a metal atom. Because for a given carbanion, the reaction of ionization is favoured by a low electron affinity of the cation, the largest carbanion character of such a compound is exhibited when the atom M is an alkali metal—lithium, sodium, potassium, cesium, and rubidium. Even in cases in which the tendency to form covalent bonds is negligible, however, the properties of free carbanions cannot always be observed. This situation arises from the fact that there is a strong electrostatic attraction (the kind of attraction that exists between positive and negative charges) between the cation and the anion, leading to the pairing of these ions of opposite charge. The resulting "tight" ion pairs can be broken up only if the interactions of the individual ions with the solvent are large enough to overcome the attraction between the ions. Therefore, only in solvents that strongly solvate at least one type of the ions can free carbanions be observed. Examples of solvents with strong tendencies to solvate the cations are ethers and dimethyl sulfoxide. In general, the energy needed to separate ion pairs is larger when the charge on the anion is localized than when it is delocalized. In fact, if the carbanion is derived from a simple alkane (compound of carbon and hydrogen, as for example the methide ion (above), no common solvent exists that provides enough solvation energy to separate the ion pairs and that is, at the same time, inert to chemical reaction with the anion. Therefore, alkyl alkali-metal compounds do not dissociate to free ions, and their properties are characteristic of the ion pairs only. Often ion pairs themselves preferentially form polymeric aggregates or ion clusters.

Preparation. Since the carbanion character is most pronounced when the associated cation is an alkali-metal ion, any preparation of organic-alkali-metal compounds is a source of carbanions. The reaction of organic halides (organic compounds containing atoms of chlorine, bromine, or iodine) with alkali metals is one of the most often used methods. This reaction can be expressed:

Reaction with alkali metals

$$\underset{\text{organic halide}}{R\text{-}X} + \underset{\text{metal atoms}}{2M} \longrightarrow \underset{\text{carbanion-metal ion pair}}{R^-M^+} + \underset{\text{metal ion-halide ion pair}}{M^+X^-}$$

in which R is an organic group; X is an atom of chlorine, bromine, or iodine; and M is an atom of an alkali metal.

The conversion of one carbanion into another is frequently useful and can be accomplished with either hydrocarbons or organic halides, as shown by the equations below:

$$\underset{\text{organic halide}}{R\text{-}X} + \underset{\text{carbanion-metal ion pair}}{R'^-M^+} \longrightarrow \underset{\text{carbanion-metal ion pair}}{R^-M^+} + \underset{\text{organic halide}}{R'\text{-}X}$$

$$\underset{\text{hydrocarbon}}{R\text{-}H} + \underset{\text{carbanion-metal ion pair}}{R'^-M^+} \longrightarrow \underset{\text{carbanion-metal ion pair}}{R^-M^+} + \underset{\text{hydrocarbon}}{R'\text{-}H}$$

in which R is any hydrocarbon group. Examples are the preparation of phenylsodium from chlorobenzene and sodium metal as in the first equation, and of phenyllithium from iodobenzene and butyllithium—as in the second equation—and the reaction of methyllithium with acetylene to give lithium acetylide—as in the third equation.

Reactions. Perhaps the most common reaction of carbanions is related to their action as carbon bases—as shown in the first equation in this article. For practical purposes, it is useful to redefine this acid–base equilibrium by the equation:

$$\underset{\text{hydrocarbon}}{-\overset{|}{\underset{|}{C}}-H} + \underset{\text{base}}{Y} \rightleftharpoons \underset{\text{carbanion}}{-\overset{|}{\underset{|}{C^-}}} + \underset{\text{conjugate acid}}{YH^+}$$

in which Y is a proton acceptor (base).

Consideration of carbanion formation in terms of such an equilibrium makes it possible to express the relative stability of the carbanion with regard to the corresponding hydrocarbon in quantitative terms—that is, to assign a numerical value to the basicity (proton-attracting power) of the carbanion. This is done, first of all, by determining an equilibrium constant for the equilibrium reaction above; the equilibrium constant is defined as the ratio of the concentrations (relative amounts) of the reaction products to the reactants or in mathematical terms

$$K_a = \frac{\left[-\overset{|}{\underset{|}{C^-}}\right]\left[YH^+\right]}{\left[-\overset{|}{\underset{|}{C}}-H\right]\left[Y\right]}$$

Equilibrium constant and acidity exponent

in which K_a is the acid equilibrium constant, and the terms in square brackets are the concentrations of the enclosed entities. For convenience equilibrium constants are frequently converted to another quantity, the acidity exponent, which is almost invariably referred to by its symbolic representation, pK_a. The pK_a is the negative logarithm of the equilibrium constant, or mathematically, $pK_a = -\log K_a$.

For a given base (Y), increasing basicity of a carbanion is reflected in a decreasing equilibrium constant (K_a) and an increasing pK_a. It is customary to express the basicity of carbanions in pK_a units defined as above for the special case in which the base (Y) is water, although for the vast majority of cases the equilibrium cannot be measured directly in aqueous solution because it is displaced too far to the left side.

Stabilizing factors

The pK_a's of most carbon acids range from approximately 15 to above 40, indicating that carbanions are much stronger bases than water (which has a pK_a of 15.7). The large variation in pK_a among the different carbon acids reflects the varying degree of internal stabilization in the corresponding carbanions. Generally, three different mechanisms of stabilizing carbanions have been recognized. The first is the already mentioned stabilization by resonance. Examples of resonance-stabilized carbanions are the allyl and benzyl carbanions, each of which has a pK_a of about 35. Particularly large resonance stabilization is encountered in the cyclopentadienyl anion (pK_a about 15), which has an aromatic pi electron system not present in the corresponding hydrocarbon, as shown below:

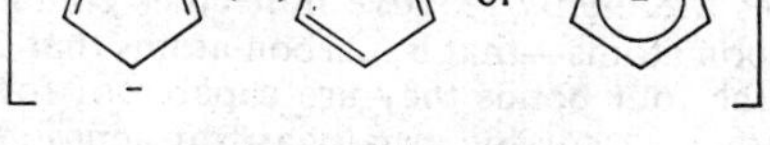

cyclopentadienyl anion

A second factor lending stability to carbanions is the inductive (electron-withdrawing) effect of neighbouring electronegative atoms. An example is provided by the comparison of the pK_a's of methane (formula, CH_4), pK_a about 40, and chloroform ($CHCl_3$), pK_a less than 25. The greater stability of the trichloromethide ion,

$$^-\overset{\overset{\displaystyle Cl}{|}}{\underset{\underset{\displaystyle Cl}{|}}{C}}-Cl$$

trichloromethide ion

which results from removal of a proton from chloroform, can be understood in terms of the inductive effect of the chlorine atoms, which reduces the free charge on carbon and distributes it to the chlorine atoms.

The third effect is based on a change in electronegativity of the carbon atom carrying the negative charge. An example of this effect is the sequence of decreasing pK_a's from ethane through ethylene to acetylene (the respective pK_a's being 42, 36, and 25). In the corresponding carbanions, shown below, the negative charge resides on carbon atoms that are, respectively, sp^3, sp^2, and sp hybridized.

$$CH_3CH_2^-, \quad H_2C{=}CH^-, \quad HC{\equiv}C^-$$

ethide carbanion — ethenide carbanion — acetylide carbanion

Since the electronegativity of the carbon increases with increasing *s*-character of the bonding (that is, in the order sp^3, sp^2, and sp) the carbanion stability follows the same trend.

Thus, it can be seen that simple alkyl carbanions have none of the effects known to stabilize carbanions, and, therefore, they should be the most basic of all carbanions. Such is indeed the case, and the pK_a's of all simple alkyl carbanions range above 40.

Carbanions in nucleophilic displacement reactions

A type of reaction that makes carbanions valuable synthetic intermediates is their ability to function as nucleophiles (positive-charge seeking groups) in displacement reactions. Methylsodium, for example, reacts with methyl bromide to give ethane, as follows:

$$CH_3^-Na^+ + CH_3Br \longrightarrow CH_3CH_3 + NaBr.$$

methylsodium — methyl bromide — ethane — sodium bromide

This reaction type is extensively used for the alkylation of ketones. In the process, the ketones are first converted into their enolate ions and then alkylated with a suitable alkyl halide, as in the example below:

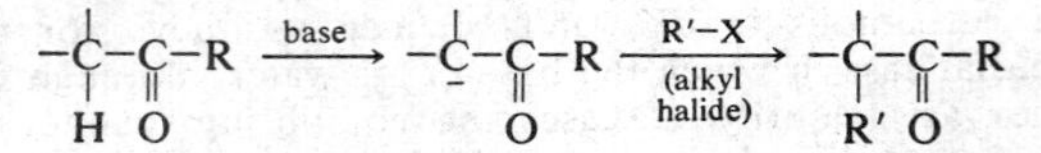

ketone — enolate ion — alkylation product

Another synthetically useful reaction is the addition of carbanions to carbonyl groups; for example, methyllithium adds to acetone to give lithium *tert*-butoxide, as shown

$$CH_3Li + H_3C{-}\overset{\overset{O}{\|}}{C}{-}CH_3 \longrightarrow H_3C{-}\underset{\underset{OLi}{|}}{\overset{\overset{CH_3}{|}}{C}}{-}CH_3.$$

methyllithium — acetone — lithium *tert*-butoxide

BIBLIOGRAPHY. A basic reference on carbanions is D.J. CRAM, *Fundamentals of Carbanion Chemistry* (1965).

(G.L.C.)

Carbenes

Carbenes are highly reactive molecules containing divalent carbon atoms—that is, carbon atoms that utilize only two of the four bonds they are capable of forming with other atoms. Occurring usually as transient intermediates during chemical reactions, they are important chiefly for what they reveal about chemical reactions and molecular structure. In addition, some chemical compounds, particularly those in which the molecules contain carbon atoms arranged in small rings, can best be prepared by the use of carbenes.

Carbenes must be clearly distinguished from compounds with multiple bonds. The simplest carbene, methylene, for example, is composed chemically of one carbon atom (indicated by the symbol C) joined to two hydrogen atoms (H) in a structure represented schematically as H – C – H. In the compound hydrogen cyanide, the carbon atom also is joined to only two atoms—in this case a hydrogen atom and a nitrogen (N) atom—and the structure of this compound is represented as H – C ≡ N. Hydrogen cyanide is not classed as a carbene, because, although the carbon atom is joined only to two other atoms, it is not divalent; all four valences of carbon are utilized in the single bond to the hydrogen atom and in the triple bond to the nitrogen atom (as represented by the three lines in the diagram between C and N). Hydrogen cyanide is, therefore, a multiply bonded compound, not a carbene.

General considerations. According to the electronic theory of bonding, bonds between atoms are formed by a sharing of electrons. In terms of this theory, then, carbenes are compounds in which only two of the four valence, or bonding, electrons of the carbon atoms are actually engaged in bonding with other atoms. By contrast, in multiply bonded compounds, such as hydrogen cyanide, all four of the valence electrons of the atoms are involved in bonds with other atoms. Because there is no excess or deficiency of electrons in the molecules of carbenes, they are substances that are electrically neutral (nonionic).

Carbenes as a class also are referred to as divalent carbon compounds or, with reference to methylene, the simplest member of the series, as methylenes. Carbenes generally are named as derivatives of carbene or methylene. For example, the substance containing a carbon atom and two chlorine (Cl) atoms, Cl–C–Cl, is known as dichlorocarbene or, less commonly, as dichloromethylene.

Early investigations of carbenes

Because of the great reactivity of carbenes, they normally have very short lifetimes, and it is not surprising, therefore, that unambiguous and direct experimental evidence of their existence has been obtained only recently. Divalent carbon compounds had been postulated, however, as long ago as 1876, when it was proposed that dichlorocarbene, Cl–C–Cl, was an intermediate in the base-catalyzed hydrolysis (decomposition brought about by water) of chloroform, (formula, $HCCl_3$). Toward the end of the 19th century, an extensive theory had been developed that postulated divalent carbon compounds as intermediates in many reactions. Later work, however, disproved many of these postulates, and, as a result, methylene was no longer put forward as a hypothetical reaction intermediate. A strong revival of carbene chemistry occurred in the 1950s after unambiguous evidence had demonstrated their existence and studies by several methods had yielded detailed information about their structures. At the same time, it became apparent that the high reactivity of carbenes was an asset to the synthetic chemist, who put them to use in the construction of molecules difficult to prepare by other means.

Electronic configuration and molecular structure. Carbenes are of interest to the theoretical chemist because the theory of chemical bonding predicts two fundamentally different electron configurations for these substances, either one of which may correspond to the ground state of the molecules (state of lower energy content) depending only on the nature of the atoms and groups attached to the divalent carbon atom. This duality arises from the fact that the two bonds of the carbene utilize only two of the four valence orbitals on carbon—orbitals being the regions occupied by the various electrons in an atom. The two valence orbitals of the carbon atom not used in bonding are available to accept the two nonbonding electrons. In general, each orbital can accommodate two electrons if their spins are paired—that is, if the angular momenta are of opposite sign. There are thus two possible distributions of the nonbonding electrons: they may be in the same orbital and have paired (opposite) spins, or they may be divided between the two available orbitals and have parallel spins. Substances with electrons having parallel (or unpaired) spins show a magnetic effect (moment). In a magnetic field this moment may be parallel, perpendicular, or antiparallel (parallel but proceeding in the reverse direction) to the direction of the field; these three possible alignments correspond to three forms of slightly different energy, and, as a result, substances with unpaired electrons can exist in all three forms and are said to be in a triplet state.

Singlet and triplet states

By contrast, substances with all electrons paired show no net magnetic moment and are referred to as singlet states. In principle, carbenes can exist in either the singlet or triplet state (depending upon whether the electrons are in the same or different orbitals, respectively).

In most organic compounds (compounds of carbon), the singlet state is more stable than the triplet state, and the normal or ground state of the molecule is of this form. In these compounds triplets occur only as excited or high-energy states. In carbenes, on the other hand, because of the two nonbonding electrons and the two vacant orbitals, it is expected on theoretical grounds that the triplet state should be of comparable stability to the singlet state and may, in fact, be the ground state.

Theoretical considerations also suggest that the carbene carbon atom and the two atoms joined to it are arranged in a "V" rather than in a linear fashion—that is, the bonds from the carbon atom to the two substituent atoms are situated at an angle that is less than 180°—in both the triplet and the singlet states. The bond angle for the singlet state, however, is predicted to be larger than that for the triplet state. These predictions are fully supported by experiments. The simplest carbene, methylene, has been shown by a technique called electron magnetic resonance spectroscopy to have a triplet ground state, in which the angle between the carbon–hydrogen bonds equals 136°. The singlet state of methylene, which can be obtained in special circumstances, has been studied by another technique, optical spectroscopy, and its bond angle has been determined to be 104°. The structures and the configurations of the nonbonding electrons of the triplet and singlet states of methylene are shown as A and B in the accompanying drawing; the loops represent

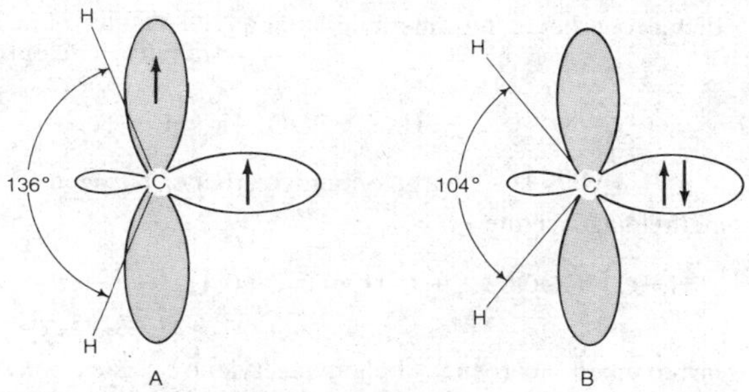

Nonbonding orbitals in the triplet (A) and singlet (B) state of methylene; the axis of the shaded orbital is perpendicular to the plane defined by the carbon atom (C), the hydrogen atoms (H), and the unshaded orbital (see text).

the orbitals not used in bonding, and the pairing and nonpairing of electron spins are indicated by antiparallel and parallel arrows, respectively. This schematic orbital representation shows both nonbonding orbitals occupied in A (the triplet state) and an empty orbital in B (singlet).

The structural features that determine whether a singlet or a triplet state corresponds to the lower energy form of the carbene molecule may be summarized by the rule that, with few exceptions, carbenes having only carbon or hydrogen atoms attached to the divalent (carbene) carbon atom have triplet ground states, whereas those with nitrogen, oxygen, and halogen substituents have singlet ground states. Examples of triplet carbenes are methylene (H–C–H), phenylmethylene (C_6H_5–C–H), diphenylmethylene (C_6H_5–C–C_6H_5) and propargylene

$$(HC \equiv C - C - H).$$

Carbenes with known singlet ground states are methoxymethylene (CH_3O–C–H), chloromethylene

$$(Cl - C - H),$$

and phenylchloromethylene (C_6H_5–C–Cl).

Formation. Because carbenes are molecules with high energy content, they must be made from high-energy precursors, or extra energy must be provided from external sources. Chemical transformations induced by light, so-called photochemical reactions, often are used to prepare carbenes, because the energy of the absorbed light is taken into the high-energy structures. Organic compounds containing a diazo group (two nitrogen atoms joined to one another and to a carbon atom by a double bond) are the most frequently used precursors of carbenes. The molecular structure of diazo compounds is

represented by the generalized formula $\begin{matrix} R \\ \diagdown \\ C = \overset{+}{N} = \overset{-}{N}, \\ \diagup \\ R' \end{matrix}$

in which R and R' represent two organic groups, which may be the same or different. On either photolysis or pyrolysis (treatment with light or heat, respectively), diazo compounds cleave to yield the corresponding carbene and a free molecule of nitrogen gas. The great stability of the nitrogen molecule constitutes the driving force of the reaction. Diazirins, which are ring, or cyclic, compounds, with a structure similar to that of the diazo compounds, undergo the same cleavage reaction and are frequently used as precursors of carbenes. The production of a carbene from either a diazo compound or a diazirin occurs as shown below:

$$\begin{matrix} R \\ \diagdown \\ C=\overset{+}{N}=\overset{-}{N} \\ \diagup \\ R' \end{matrix} \longrightarrow R-C-R' + N_2 \longleftarrow \begin{matrix} N \\ \| \\ N \end{matrix} \diagdown C \diagup \begin{matrix} R \\ \\ R' \end{matrix}$$

diazo compound   carbene nitrogen   diazirin

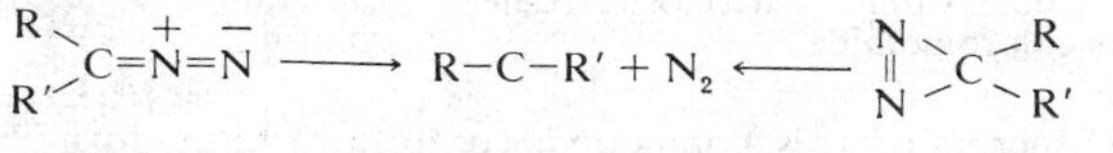

In these formulas R and R' represent organic groups (either the same or different). The alternate precursors of the carbene are here represented by the formulas on the extreme left and right; in the centre are the products—that is, the carbene and nitrogen. The arrows indicate the direction in which the chemical conversion occurs. When the photolysis of diazo compounds or diazirins is carried out at very low temperature in an unreactive solid medium, it is often possible to prevent the resulting carbene from undergoing further reaction. Measurable amounts of the carbene may persist, therefore, in the solid medium, or matrix, for a long time. For example, methylene, the most reactive carbene of all, has been generated by photolysis of diazirin in a crystalline matrix of the inert gas xenon (cooled to the boiling point of helium) in which it persisted long enough to be studied. Many other carbenes have been produced by similar matrix isolation techniques.

The photolytic decomposition of certain ketenes, substances the molecules of which contain two carbon atoms and an oxygen atom joined by double bonds,

$$\begin{matrix} \diagdown \\ C = C = O, \\ \diagup \end{matrix}$$

gives carbon monoxide and carbenes, as shown in the following equation:

$$\begin{matrix} R \\ \diagdown \\ C = C = O \\ \diagup \\ R' \end{matrix} \longrightarrow R - C - R' + CO .$$

    ketene   carbene   carbon monoxide

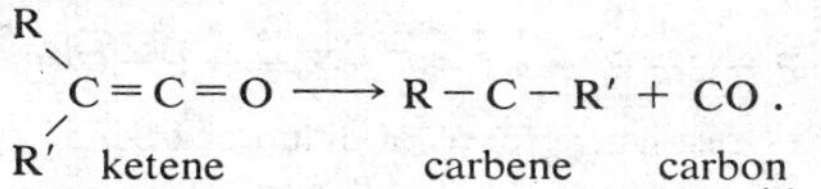

In some cases epoxides, compounds the molecules of which include three-membered oxygen-containing rings, can be cleaved photolytically into aldehydes and carbenes, as shown:

$$\begin{matrix} R \\ \diagdown \\ \diagup \\ R' \end{matrix} C \overset{O}{\diagup \diagdown} C \begin{matrix} \diagup H \\ \\ \diagdown R'' \end{matrix} \longrightarrow R-C-R' + R''-CHO$$

epoxide   carbene   aldehyde

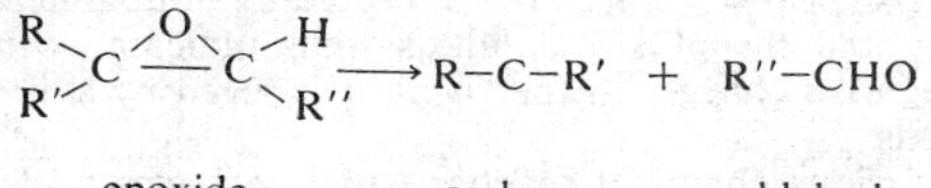

Under certain circumstances, even cyclopropanes, the molecules of which contain three-membered carbon rings, can serve as carbene precursors in photochemical reactions. For example, 1,1,2,2,-tetraphenylcyclopropane is converted to diphenylcarbene, by the reaction given below:

$$\begin{matrix} H \quad H \\ \diagdown \diagup \\ C \\ \diagup \diagdown \end{matrix}$$
$$(C_6H_5)_2C-C(C_6H_5)_2$$

1,1,2,2-tetraphenylcyclopropane

$$\longrightarrow (C_6H_5)_2C=CH_2 \; + \; C_6H_5-C-C_6H_5 .$$

1,1-diphenylethylene   diphenylcarbene

Isolation of carbenes

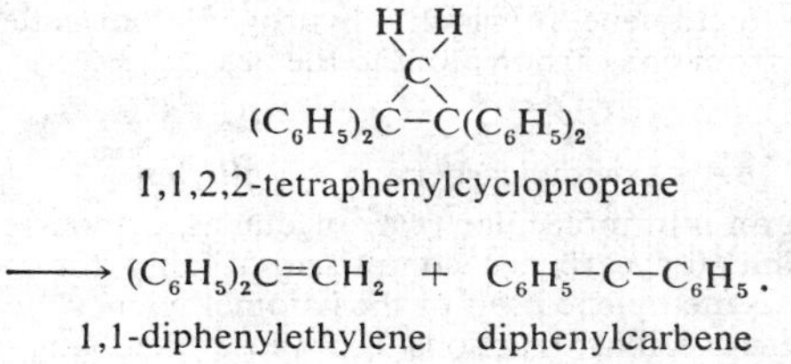

The formation of carbenes by way of electrically charged, or ionic, intermediates is exemplified by the reaction of chloroform with a strong base, potassium *tert*-butoxide.

In the first step of this reaction, a proton or hydrogen ion (H^+) is removed from the chloroform molecule in a normal acid–base reaction. The resulting potassium trichloromethide then loses potassium chloride to give dichlorocarbene, as shown:

$$Cl_3CH \; + \; KOC(CH_3)_3 \longrightarrow \overset{+}{K}\overset{-}{C}Cl_3 \; + \; HOC(CH_3)_3$$

chloroform   potassium   potassium   *t*-butyl alcohol
            tert-butoxide   trichloromethide

$$\overset{+}{K}\overset{-}{C}Cl_3 \longrightarrow Cl-C-Cl \; + \; KCl$$

potassium   dichlorocarbene   potassium
trichloromethide   chloride

Other haloforms, compounds conforming to the formula HCX_3, in which X equals an atom of chlorine, bromine, or iodine, react in an equivalent way to form the corresponding dihalocarbenes.

Organometallic compounds also can serve as precursors of carbenes. The decomposition of tribromomethylphenyl mercury to phenylmercuric bromide and dibromocarbene is an example of this reaction type.

$$C_6H_5-Hg-CBr_3 \longrightarrow C_6H_5-Hg-Br \; + \; Br-C-Br$$

tribromomethylphenyl   phenylmercuric   dibromocarbene
mercury   bromide

Reactions. Because of their unsaturated valences, carbenes are very reactive molecules. Methylene, for example, is one of the most reactive molecules known in organic chemistry, and there are few organic compounds able to resist attack by this substance. The reactivity of carbenes is somewhat reduced when stabilization results from the phenomenon known as resonance, which is said to occur when alternate electronic structures (called resonance forms) can be written for a single molecular type. The actual state of the molecule is then thought to include characteristics of all the forms and to be more stable than any of them individually. Difluorocarbene and methoxycarbene, for example, are much less reactive than methylene, presumably because the resonance forms shown in the formulas below contribute to internal stabilization.

$$F-C-F \longleftrightarrow \overset{+}{F}=\overset{-}{C}-F \longleftrightarrow F-\overset{-}{C}=\overset{+}{F}$$

resonance forms of difluorocarbene

$$CH_3O-C-H \longleftrightarrow CH_3\overset{+}{O}=\overset{-}{C}-H$$

resonance forms of methoxycarbene

In these representations, the various resonance forms of a single hybrid structure are connected by double-headed arrows, and the plus and minus signs indicate positive and negative charges, respectively, produced by shifts of electrons.

The various chemical reactions that carbenes undergo can be classified as either intramolecular or intermolecular reactions. Intramolecular reactions, or rearrangements, involve only the carbene itself and include no other outside substances; if structurally possible, they lead to stable molecules in which the carbon atom is in its normal, or tetravalent, state. An example of an intramolecular reaction is the rearrangement of methylcarbene to ethylene, in which a hydrogen atom undergoes a shift from one carbon atom to the next:

$$CH_3-C-H \longrightarrow H_2C=CH_2.$$

methylcarbene   ethylene

Such an intramolecular rearrangement, of course, is not possible for carbenes comprised of only three atoms, such as methylene itself or the halomethylenes.

Intermolecular reactions are those involving two or more separate molecules. Three important classes of intermolecular reaction of carbenes are known: dimerization, addition, and insertion reactions. Dimerization of carbenes—that is, combination of two molecules of the carbene—gives olefins, the molecular formulas of which are exactly twice that of the carbene. An example is the formation of tetramethoxyethylene from dimethoxycarbene.

$$2CH_3O-C-OCH_3 \longrightarrow (CH_3O)_2C=C(OCH_3)_2$$

dimethoxycarbene   tetramethoxyethylene

The addition of carbenes to olefins and acetylenes is a very useful reaction because it constitutes a simple way to synthesize cyclopropanes and cyclopropenes having a great variety of structures. Two examples are shown below; in one case the carbene is generated from chloroform, and in the other it is produced by photolysis of a diazo compound.

1. $$Cl_3CH + KOC(CH_3)_3 \longrightarrow Cl-C-Cl + HOC(CH_3)_3 + KCl$$

chloroform potassium   dichlorocarbene *tert*-butyl potassium
            tert-butoxide   alcohol   chloride

$$Cl-C-Cl \; + \; (CH_3)_2\,C=C(CH_3)_2 \longrightarrow \underset{(CH_3)_2C-C(CH_3)_2}{\overset{Cl\quad Cl}{\diagdown C\diagup}}$$

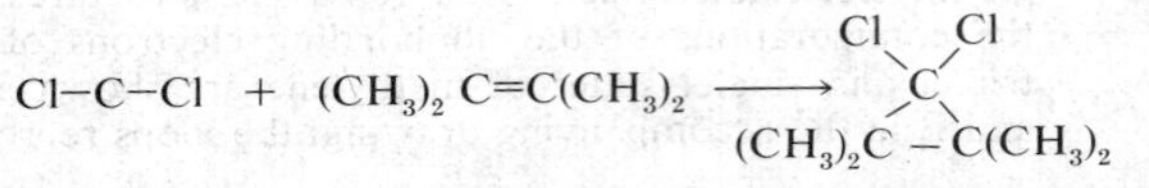

dichlorocarbene   tetramethylethylene   1,1-dichloro-2,2,3,3-
                                         tetramethylcyclopropane

2. $$\underset{COOCH_3}{\overset{|}{H-C=N_2}} \longrightarrow H-C-COOCH_3 \; + \; N_2$$

methyldiazoacetate   carboxymethylcarbene   nitrogen

$$H-C-COOCH_3 + C_6H_5-C\equiv C-C_6H_5 \longrightarrow \underset{C_6H_5-C=C-C_6H_5}{\overset{H\quad COOCH_3}{\diagdown C\diagup}}$$

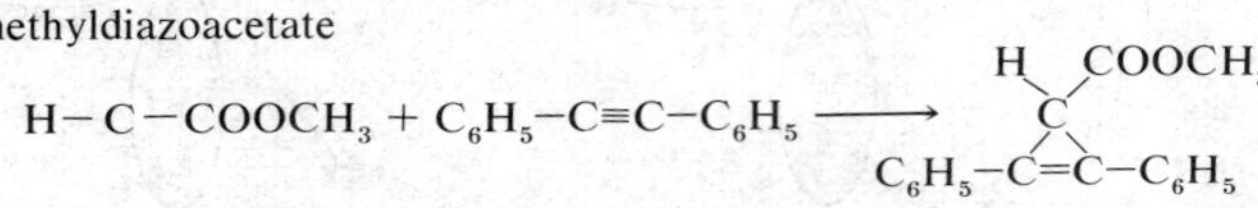

carboxymethylcarbene   diphenylacetylene   3-carboxymethyl-1,2-
                                             diphenylcyclopropene

Intramolecular versions of this type of addition reaction are also possible, as shown by the cyclization of allylcarbene generated from the corresponding diazo compound. The resulting bicyclobutane—an unusual compound, which contains a ring system with considerable strain resulting from abnormal angles between bonds—demonstrates the value of carbene reactions for the synthesis compounds difficult to obtain by other methods.

$$CH_2=CH-CH_2-C-H \longrightarrow \quad CH_2 \begin{array}{c} \overset{H}{\underset{|}{C}} \\ | \\ \underset{H}{\overset{|}{C}} \end{array} CH_2$$

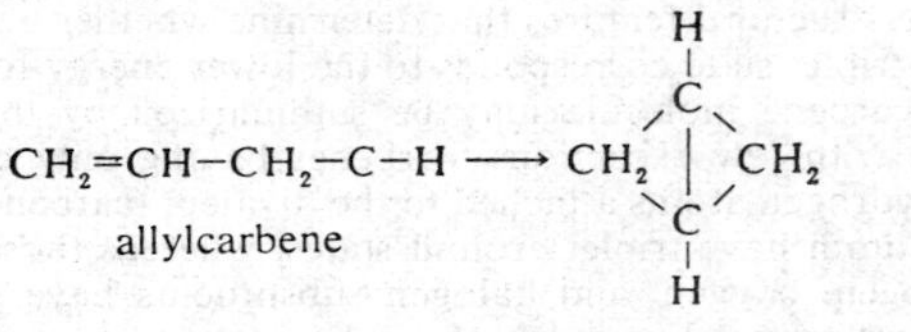

allylcarbene   bicyclobutane

The insertion reaction takes place only with the more reactive carbenes; it is defined as the insertion of a carbene into the bond between a carbon atom and an attached hydrogen atom. Methylene itself undergoes this reaction with all known types of carbon–hydrogen bonds. An example is the formation of toluene from benzene and methylene, as shown:

$$C_6H_6 \; + \; H-C-H \longrightarrow C_6H_5CH_3.$$

benzene   methylene   toluene

The less reactive carbenes; *e.g.*, difluorocarbene and methoxycarbene, do not take part in insertion reactions.

There is a substantial difference in reactivity between carbenes in the singlet and triplet states. Although both singlet and triplet carbenes undergo the same three reaction types, the triplet state is usually much less reactive. There are also differences in the mechanisms by which singlet and triplet carbenes undergo addition and insertion reactions.

Intermolecular reactions

Resonance forms

Reactivity differences between triplet and singlet states

Analytical and physical study. Because carbenes occur chiefly as intermediates in the course of chemical reactions, much of their study is conducted by kinetic methods, as the general field of investigation of rates of reaction and the factors that influence them is known. Much of the available information about the structures of carbenes has been obtained by optical spectroscopic methods —that is, by the study of light absorption patterns— which have revealed, for example, the bond lengths and angles in the various carbenes. Electron-spin resonance spectroscopy, the physical method that gives information about the angular momenta of electrons, has been especially useful in differentiating triplet from singlet states. Both optical and electron-spin resonance spectroscopy must be used in the detection of carbenes, because, generally, these substances are too reactive for analytical methods of ordinary types.

BIBLIOGRAPHY. W. KIRMSE, *Carbene Chemistry*, (1964); G.L. CLOSS, *Topics in Stereochemistry*, vol. 3 (1968).

(G.L.C.)

Carbohydrate

The term carbohydrate, which means watered carbon, represents a class of naturally occurring compounds and derivatives formed from them. In the early part of the 19th century, substances such as wood, starch, and linen were found to be composed mainly of molecules containing atoms of carbon (C), hydrogen (H), and oxygen (O), and to have the general formula $C_6H_{12}O_6$; other organic molecules with similar formulas were found to have a similar ratio of hydrogen to oxygen. The general formula $C_x(H_2O)_x$ is commonly used to represent many carbohydrates.

Carbohydrates are probably the most abundant and widespread organic substances in nature. Essential constituents of all living things, carbohydrates are formed by green plants from carbon dioxide and water during the process of photosynthesis. Carbohydrates serve organisms as energy sources and as essential structural components; in addition, part of the structure of nucleic acids, which contain genetic information, consists of carbohydrate.

GENERAL FEATURES

Basic molecular structures

Classification and nomenclature. Although a number of classification schemes have been devised for carbohydrates, the division into four major groups—monosaccharides, disaccharides, oligosaccharides, and polysaccharides—used here is among the most common. Most monosaccharides, or simple sugars, are found in grapes, other fruits, and honey. Although they can contain from three to nine carbon atoms, the most common representatives consist of five or six joined together to form a chainlike molecule. Three of the most important simple sugars, glucose—also known as dextrose, grape sugar, and corn sugar—fructose (fruit sugar), and galactose, have the same molecular formula, ($C_6H_{12}O_6$), but, because their atoms have different structural arrangements, the sugars have different characteristics; *i.e.*, they are isomers. Slight changes in structural arrangements are detectable by living things and influence the biological significance of isomeric compounds. It is known, for example, that the degree of sweetness of various sugars differs according to the arrangement of the hydroxyl groups (− OH) comprising part of the molecular structure; a direct correlation between taste and any specific structural arrangement, however, has not yet been established—that is, it is not yet possible to predict the taste of a sugar by knowing its specific structural arrangement. The energy in the chemical bonds of glucose indirectly supplies most living things with a major part of the energy necessary for them to carry on their activities. Galactose, rarely found as a simple sugar, is usually combined with other simple sugars to form larger molecules.

Two molecules of a simple sugar linked to each other form a disaccharide, or double sugar. The disaccharide sucrose, or table sugar, consists of one molecule of glucose and one molecule of fructose; sources of sucrose include sugar beets and cane sugar. Milk sugar, or lactose, and maltose are also disaccharides. Before the energy in disaccharides can be utilized by living things, the molecules must be broken down into their respective monosaccharides.

Oligosaccharides, which consist of three to six monosaccharide units, are rather infrequently found in natural sources, although a few plant derivatives have been identified.

Polysaccharides (the term means many sugars) represent most of the structural and energy-reserve carbohydrates found in nature. Large molecules that may consist of as many as 10,000 monosaccharide units linked together, polysaccharides vary considerably in size, in structural complexity, and in sugar content; several hundred distinct types have thus far been identified. Cellulose, the principal structural component of plants, is a complex polysaccharide comprised of many glucose units linked together; it is the most common polysaccharide. The starch found in plants and the glycogen found in animals also are complex glucose polysaccharides. Starch (from the old English word *stercan* meaning "to stiffen") is found mostly in seeds, roots, and stems, where it is stored as an available energy source for plants. Plant starch may be processed into such foods for man as bread, or it may be consumed directly—as are potatoes. Glycogen, which consists of branching chains of glucose molecules, is formed in the liver and muscles of higher animals and is stored as an energy source.

Names for monosaccharides

The generic nomenclature ending for the monosaccharides is -ose; thus, the term pentose (pent = five) is used for monosaccharides containing five carbon atoms, and hexose (hex = six) is used for those containing six. In addition, because the monosaccharides contain a chemically reactive group that is either an aldehydo group (H–C=O) or a keto group (R–C=O), they are frequently referred to as aldopentoses or ketopentoses or aldohexoses or ketohexoses; in the examples below, the aldehydo group is at position 1 of the aldopentose, the keto group is at position 2 of the ketohexose. Glucose is an aldohexose—*i.e.*, it contains six carbon atoms, and the chemically reactive group is an aldehydo group.

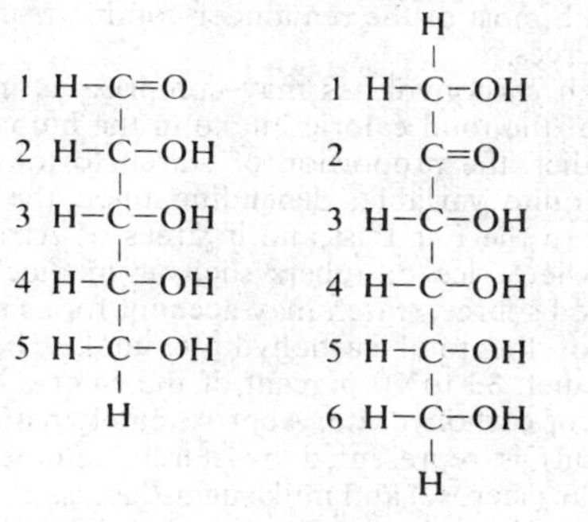

aldopentose ketohexose

Importance. The importance of carbohydrates to living things can hardly be overemphasized. The energy stores of most animals and plants are both carbohydrate and fat (lipid) in nature; carbohydrates are generally available as an immediate energy source, whereas fats act as a long-term energy resource and tend to be utilized at a slower rate. Glucose, the prevalent uncombined, or free, sugar circulating in the blood of higher animals, is essential to cell function. The proper regulation of glucose metabolism is of paramount importance to survival.

The ability of ruminants, such as cattle, sheep, and goats, to convert the polysaccharides present in grass and similar feeds into protein provides a major source of protein for man. A number of medically important antibiotics, such as streptomycin, are carbohydrate derivatives. The cellulose in plants is used to manufacture paper, wood for construction, and fabrics.

Photosynthesis

Role in the biosphere. The essential process in the biosphere, the portion of the earth in which life can occur, that has permitted the evolution of life as it now exists is the conversion by green plants of carbon dioxide from the atmosphere into carbohydrates, using light energy from the sun. This process, called photosynthesis, results in both the release of oxygen gas into the atmosphere and the transformation of light energy into the chemical energy of carbohydrates. The energy stored by plants during the formation of carbohydrates is used by animals to carry out mechanical work and to perform biosynthetic activities.

All green plants apparently photosynthesize in the same way, yielding as an immediate product the compound 3-phosphoglyceric acid; the formula, in which P represents phosphorus, is illustrated below.

$$\begin{array}{c} O \\ \| \\ C-OH \\ | \\ H-C-OH \\ | \\ H-C-PO_3H_2 \\ | \\ H \end{array}$$

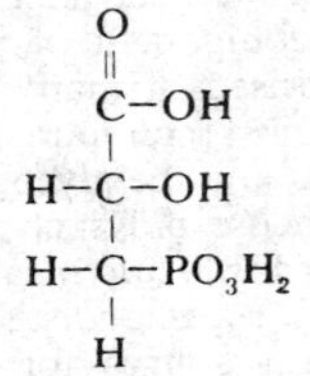

3-phosphoglyceric acid

This compound then is transformed into cell-wall components such as cellulose, varying amounts of sucrose, and starch—depending on the plant type—and a wide variety of polysaccharides, other than cellulose and starch, that function as essential structural components. For a detailed discussion of the process of photosynthesis, see PHOTOSYNTHESIS.

Role in human nutrition. The total caloric, or energy, requirement for an individual depends on age, occupation, and other factors but generally ranges between 2,000 and 4,000 calories per 24-hour period (one calorie is the amount of heat necessary to raise the temperature of 1,000 grams of water from 15° to 16° C [59° to 61° F]). Carbohydrate that can be utilized by man produces four calories per gram as opposed to nine calories per gram of fat and four per gram of protein. In areas of the world where nutrition is marginal, a high proportion (approximately one to two pounds) of an individual's daily energy requirement may be supplied by carbohydrate, with most of the remainder coming from a variety of fat sources.

Although carbohydrates may comprise as much as 80 percent of the total caloric intake in the human diet, for a given diet, the proportion of starch to total carbohydrate is quite variable, depending upon the prevailing customs. In the Far East and in areas of Africa, for example, where rice or tubers such as manioc provide a major food source, starch may account for as much as 80 percent of the total carbohydrate intake. In a typical Western diet, 33 to 50 percent of the caloric intake is in the form of carbohydrate. Approximately half (i.e., 17 to 25 percent) is represented by starch; another third by table sugar (sucrose) and milk sugar (lactose); and smaller percentages by monosaccharides such as glucose and fructose, which are common in fruits, honey, syrups, and certain vegetables such as artichokes, onions, and sugar beets. The small remainder consists of bulk, or indigestible carbohydrate, primarily the cellulosic outer covering of seeds and the stalks and leaves of vegetables.

Role in energy storage. Starches, the major plant-energy-reserve polysaccharides utilized by man, are stored in plants in the form of nearly spherical granules that vary in diameter from about three to 100 microns (about .0001 to .004 inches). Most plant starches consist of a mixture of two components, amylose and amylopectin (see diagrams following). As the diagrams show, the glucose molecules comprising amylose has a straight-chain, or linear, structure; amylopectin has a branched-chain structure and is a somewhat more compact molecule. Several thousand glucose units may be present in a single starch molecule (each –O– represents one glucose molecule).

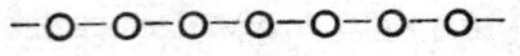

$$-O-O-O-O-O-O-O-$$

amylose

$$\begin{array}{c} -O-O-O-O-O-O-O- \\ \quad | \qquad\qquad\qquad | \\ \quad O \qquad\qquad\qquad O \\ \quad | \qquad\qquad\qquad | \\ \quad O \qquad\qquad\qquad O \\ \quad | \\ \quad O \end{array}$$

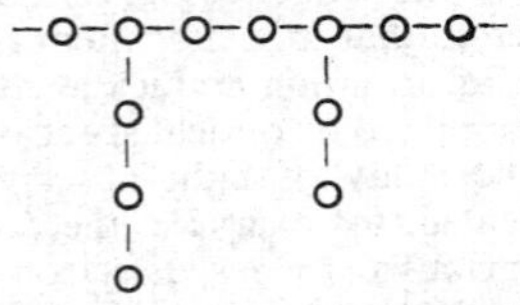

amylopectin

In addition to granules, many plants have large numbers of specialized cells, called parenchymatous cells, the principal function of which is the storage of starch; examples of plants with these cells include root vegetables and tubers. The starch content of plants varies considerably; the highest concentrations are found in seeds and in cereal grains, which contain up to 80 percent of their total carbohydrate as starch. The amylose and amylopectin components of starch occur in variable proportions; most plant species store approximately 25 percent of their starch as amylose and 75 percent as amylopectin. This proportion can be altered, however, by selective-breeding techniques, and some varieties of corn have been developed that produce up to 70 percent of their starch as amylose, which is more easily digested by man than is amylopectin.

Starch content of plants

In addition to the starches, some plants (e.g., the Jerusalem artichoke and the leaves of certain grasses, particularly rye grass) form storage polysaccharides composed of fructose units rather than glucose. Although the fructose polysaccharides can be broken down and utilized to prepare syrups, they cannot be digested by higher animals.

Starches are not formed by animals; instead, they form a closely related polysaccharide, glycogen. Virtually all vertebrate and invertebrate animal cells, as well as those of numerous fungi and protozoans, contain some glycogen; particularly high concentrations are found in the liver and muscle cells of higher animals. The overall structure of glycogen, which is a highly branched molecule consisting of glucose units, has a superficial resemblance to that of the amylopectin component of starch, although the structural details of glycogen are significantly different. Under conditions of stress or muscular activity in animals, glycogen is rapidly broken down to glucose, which is subsequently utilized as an energy source. In this manner, glycogen acts as an immediate carbohydrate reserve. Furthermore, the amount of glycogen present at any given time, especially in the liver, directly reflects an animal's nutritional state; i.e., when adequate food supplies are available, both glycogen and fat reserves increase, but when food supplies decrease or when the food intake falls below the minimum energy requirements, the glycogen reserves are depleted quite rapidly, while those of fat are used at a slower rate.

Role in plant and animal structure. Whereas starches and glycogen represent the major reserve polysaccharides of living things, most of the carbohydrate found in nature occurs as structural components in the cell walls of plants. Carbohydrates in plant cell walls generally consist of several distinct layers, one of which contains a higher concentration of cellulose than the others. The physical and chemical properties of cellulose are strikingly different from those of the amylose component of starch.

In most plants, the cell wall is about 0.5 microns thick (one micron $= 10^{-3}$ millimetre) and contains a mixture of cellulose, pentose-containing polysaccharides (pentosans), and an inert (chemically unreactive) plastic-like material called lignin. The amounts of cellulose and pentosan may vary; most plants contain between 40 and 60 percent cellulose, although higher amounts are present in the cotton fibre.

Polysaccharides also function as major structural components in animals. Chitin, which is similar to cellulose, is found in insects and other arthropods. Other complex polysaccharides predominate in the structural tissues of higher animals.

THE STRUCTURAL FEATURES OF CARBOHYDRATES

Stereoisomerism. Late 19th-century studies by the German chemist Emil Fischer showed that carbohydrates, such as fructose and glucose, with the same molecular formulas but different structural arrangements and properties (*i.e.*, isomers) can be formed by relatively simple variations of their spatial, or geometric, arrangements. This type of isomerism, called stereoisomerism, exists in all biological systems; and, among carbohydrates, the simplest example is provided by the three-carbon aldose sugar glyceraldehyde. There is no way by which the structures of the two isomers of glyceraldehyde (see the formulas, which are the so-called Fischer projection formulas commonly used to distinguish between such isomers) can be made identical, excluding breaking and reforming the linkages, or bonds, of the hydrogen (— H) and hydroxyl (— OH) groups attached to the carbon at position 2. The isomers are, in fact, mirror images akin to right and left hands; the term enantiomorphism is frequently employed for such isomerism. The chemical and physical properties of enantiomers are identical except for the property of optical rotation.

Isomers of glyceraldehyde

Optical rotation is the rotation of the plane of polarized light. Polarized light is light that has been separated into two beams that vibrate at right angles to each other; solutions of substances that rotate the plane of polarization are said to be optically active, and the degree of rotation is called the optical rotation of the solution. In the case of the isomers of glyceraldehyde, the magnitudes of the optical rotation are the same, but the direction in which the light is rotated—generally designated as plus, or *d* for dextrorotatory (to the right), or as minus, or *l* for levorotatory (to the left)—is opposite; *i.e.*, a solution of D-(*d*)-glyceraldehyde causes the plane of polarized light to rotate to the right, and a solution of L-(*l*)-glyceraldehyde rotates the plane of polarized light to the left. Fischer projection formulas for the two isomers of glyceraldehyde are given below (see *Configuration*, below, for explanation of D and L).

```
1 H—C=O            H—C=O
    |                 |
2 H—C—OH          HO—C—H
    |                 |
3 H—C—OH           H—C—OH
    |                 |
    H                 H
```

D-(*d*)-glyceraldehyde   L-(*l*)-glyceraldehyde

Configuration. Molecules, such as the isomers of glyceraldehyde—the atoms of which can have different structural arrangements—are known as asymmetrical molecules. The number of possible structural arrangements for an asymmetrical molecule depends on the number of centres of asymmetry; *i.e.*, for n (any given number of) centres of asymmetry, 2^n different isomers of a molecule are possible. An asymmetrical centre in the case of carbon is defined as a carbon atom to which four different groups are attached. In the three-carbon aldose sugar, glyceraldehyde, the asymmetrical centre is located at the central carbon atom. The four different groups attached to the atom are:

(1) H — C = O (with a bond upward from C); (2) H — ; (3) — OH; and (4) H — C — OH (with a bond upward from C and H below C).

The position of the hydroxyl group (— OH) attached to the central carbon atom—*i.e.*, whether — OH projects from the left or the right—determines whether the molecule rotates the plane of polarized light to the left or to the right. Since glyceraldehyde has one asymmetrical centre, n is one in the relationship 2^n, and there thus are two possible isomers. Sugars containing four carbon atoms have two asymmetrical centres; hence, there are four possible isomers (2^2). Similarly, sugars with five carbon atoms have three asymmetrical centres, and thus have eight isomers (2^3). Keto sugars have one less asymmetrical centre for a given number of carbon atoms than do aldehydo sugars.

A convention of nomenclature, devised in 1906 and based on the arrangement of the hydroxyl groups at the asymmetrical carbon atom in glyceraldehyde, states that the form of glyceraldehyde whose asymmetrical carbon atom has a hydroxyl group projecting to the right (see Fischer projection formulas) is designated as of the D-configuration; that form, whose asymmetrical carbon atom has a hydroxyl group projecting to the left is designated as L. All sugars that can be derived from D-glyceraldehyde—*i.e.*, hydroxyl group attached to the asymmetrical carbon atom most remote from the aldehydo or keto end of the molecule projects to the right—are said to be of the D-configuration; those sugars derived from L-glyceraldehyde are said to be of the L-configuration. See Table 1 for aldoses—*i.e.*, sugars containing an aldehydo group (H\C = O/) —of the D-configuration.

The configurational notation D or L is independent of the sign of the optical rotation of a sugar in solution. It is common, therefore, to designate both, as for example, D-(*l*)-fructose or D-(*d*)-glucose; *i.e.*, both have a D-configuration at the centre of asymmetry most remote from the aldehydo end (in glucose) or keto end (in fructose) of the molecule, but fructose rotates the plane of polarized light to the left, and glucose is dextrorotatory—hence the latter's alternative name dextrose. Although the initial assignments of configuration for the glyceraldehydes were made on purely arbitrary grounds, studies carried out nearly half a century later established them as correct in an absolute spatial sense. In biological systems, only the D or L form may be utilized.

It should be noted that when more than one asymmetrical centre is present in a molecule, as is the case with sugars containing four or more carbon atoms, a series of DL pairs exists, and they are functionally, physically, and chemically distinct; thus, although D-xylose and D-lyxose (see Table 1) both contain five carbon atoms and are of the D-configuration, the spatial arrangement of the asymmetrical centres (at carbon atoms 2, 3, and 4) is such that they are not mirror images.

DL pairs

Hemiacetal and hemiketal forms. Although optical rotation has been one of the most frequently determined characteristics of carbohydrates since its recognition in the late 19th century, the rotational behaviour of freshly prepared solutions of many sugars differs from that of solutions that have been allowed to stand. This phenomenon, termed mutarotation, is demonstrable even with apparently identical sugars and is caused by a type of stereoisomerism involving formation of an asymmetrical centre at the first carbon atom (aldehydo carbon) in aldoses and the second one (keto carbon) in ketoses.

Most pentose and hexose sugars, therefore, do not exist as linear, or open-chain, structures in solution, as indicated for the aldoses in Table 1, but instead form cyclic, or ring, structures termed hemiacetal or hemiketal forms, respectively. As illustrated for glucose and fructose, the cyclic structures are formed by the addition of the hydroxyl group (— OH) from either the fourth, fifth, or sixth carbon atom (in the diagram, the numbers 1 through 6 represent the positions of the carbon atoms) to the carbonyl group (\C = O/) at position 1 in glucose or 2 in fructose. A five-membered ring is illustrated for the ketohexose, fructose; a six-membered ring is illustrated for the aldohexose, glucose. In either case, the cyclic forms are in equilibrium with (*i.e.*, the rate of conversion from one form to another is stable) the open-chain structure—a free aldehyde if the solution contains glucose, a free ketone if the solution contains fructose; each form has a different optical rotation value. Since the various forms are in equilibrium with each other, a constant value of optical rotation is measurable; the two cyclic forms represent more than 99.9 percent of the sugar in the case of a glucose solution.

Table 1: Aldoses, up to Aldohexoses, of the D-Series

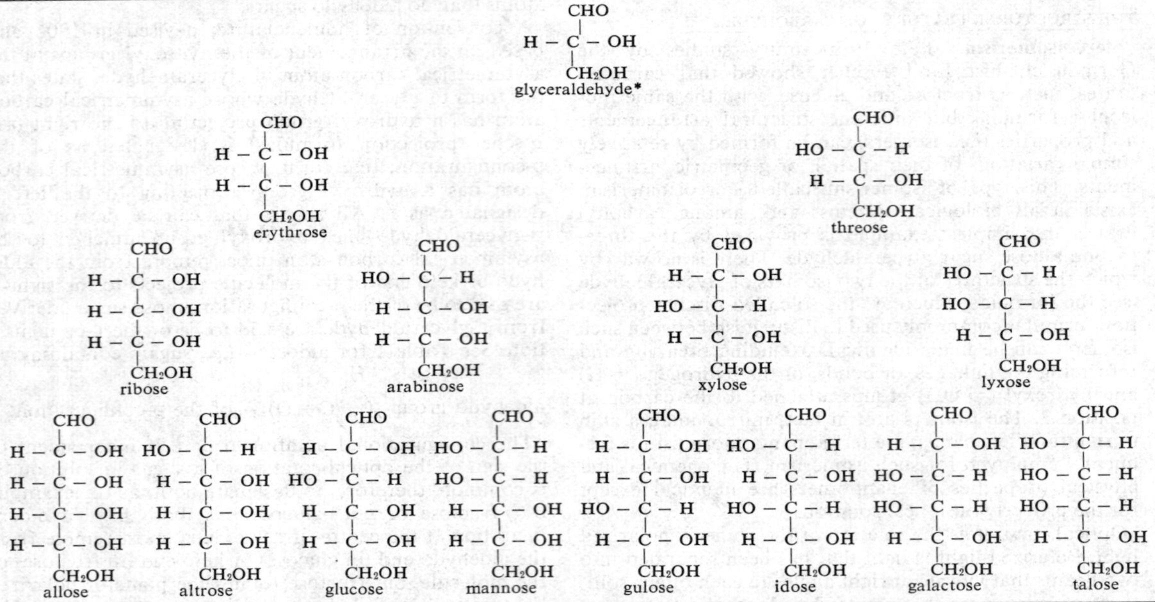
glyceraldehyde*
erythrose
threose
ribose
arabinose
xylose
lyxose
allose
altrose
glucose
mannose
gulose
idose
galactose
talose

*Aldehydo carbon (–CHO) is carbon atom 1; the remaining carbon atoms are numbered in succession. The hydroxyl groups only are shown for the asymmetrical carbon atoms. The D-configuration is derived from the asymmetrical carbon atom most remote from the aldehydo end of the molecule; *i.e.*, the hydroxyl group at carbon 3 in 4 carbon sugars; 4 in pentoses, and 5 in hexoses projects to the right. The L-series are corresponding mirror images; *i.e.*, the hydroxyl group projects to the left.

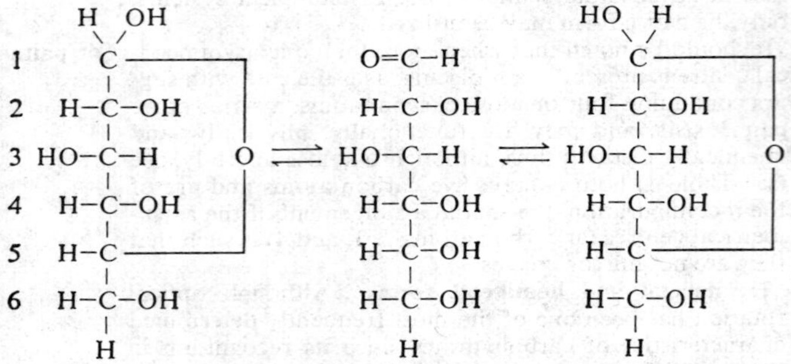

α-D-glucose (hemiacetal form) — D-glucose (linear, open-chain, or free form) — β-D-glucose (hemiacetal form)

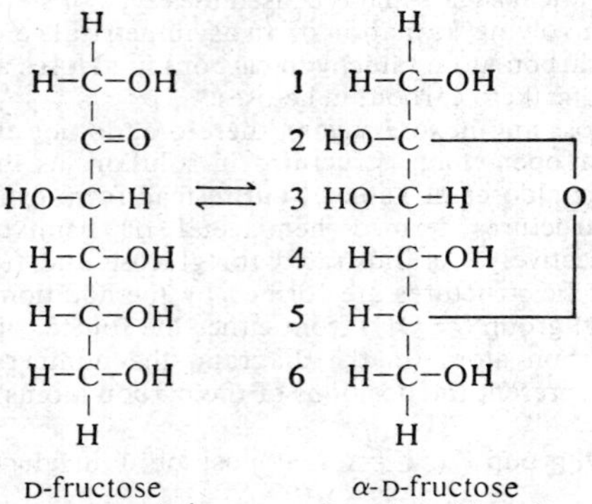

D-fructose (linear, open-chain, or free form) — α-D-fructose (hemiketal form)

Anomeric carbon atom

By definition, the carbon atom containing the aldehydo (H–C=O) or keto group (R–C=O) is termed the anomeric carbon atom; similarly, carbohydrate stereoisomers that differ in configuration only at this carbon atom are called anomers. When a cyclic hemiacetal or hemiketal structure forms, the structure with the new hydroxyl group projecting on the same side as that of the oxygen involved in forming the ring is termed the alpha anomer (see hemiacetal forms for glucose and diagram); that with the hydroxyl group projecting on the opposite side from that of the oxygen ring is termed the beta anomer (see diagram).

alpha isomer — beta isomer

The spatial arrangements of the atoms in these cyclic structures are better shown (glucose is used as an example) in the representation devised by the British organic chemist Walter Norman (later Sir Norman) Haworth about 1930; they are still in widespread use. In the formulation the asterisk indicates the position of the anomeric carbon atom; the carbon atoms, except at position 6, usually are not labelled.

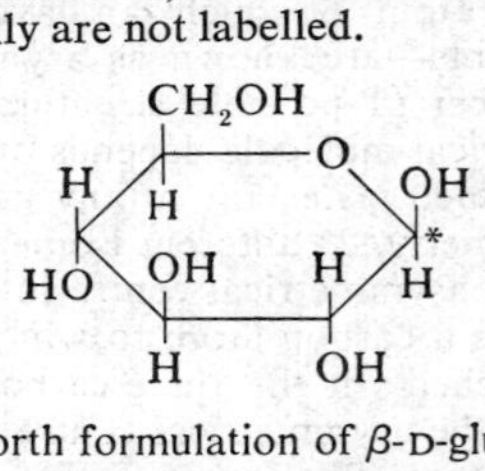

Haworth formulation of β-D-glucose

The large number of asymmetrical carbon atoms and the consequent number of possible isomers considerably complicates the structural chemistry of carbohydrates.

CLASSES OF CARBOHYDRATES

Monosaccharides. *Sources.* The most common naturally occurring monosaccharides are D-glucose, D-mannose, D-fructose, and D-galactose among the hexoses, and D-xylose and L-arabinose among the pentoses. In a special sense, D-ribose and 2-deoxy-D-ribose are ubiquitous because they form the carbohydrate component of ribonucleic acid (RNA) and deoxyribonucleic acid (DNA), respectively; these sugars are present in all cells as components of nucleic acids. Sources of some of the naturally occurring monosaccharides are listed in Table 2.

D-xylose, found in most plants in the form of a polysac-

Table 2: Some Naturally Occurring Monosaccharides

sugar	sources
L-arabinose	mesquite gum; wheat bran
D-ribose	all living cells as component of ribonucleic acid
D-xylose	corncobs; seed hulls; straw
D-ribulose	one derivative, is an intermediate in photosynthesis
2-deoxy-D-ribose	as constituent of deoxyribonucleic acid
D-galactose	lactose; agar; gum arabic; brain glycolipids
D-glucose	sucrose; cellulose; starch; glycogen
D-mannose	seeds; ivory nut
D-fructose	sucrose; artichokes; honey
L-fucose	marine algae; seaweed
L-rhamnose	poison-ivy blossom; oak bark
D-mannoheptulose	avocado
D-altroheptulose	numerous plants

charide called xylan, is prepared from corncobs, cottonseed hulls, or straw by chemical breakdown of xylan. D-galactose, a common constituent of both oligosaccharides and polysaccharides, also occurs in carbohydrate-containing lipids, called glycolipids, which are found in the brain and other nervous tissues of most animals. Galactose is generally prepared by acid hydrolysis (breakdown involving water) of lactose, which is composed of galactose and glucose. Since the biosynthesis of galactose in animals occurs through intermediate compounds derived directly from glucose, animals do not require galactose in the diet. In fact, high dietary concentrations of galactose may lead to cataract formation in the lens of the eye because galactose is readily reduced to a metabolically inactive and relatively insoluble alcohol (galactitol).

D-glucose (from the Greek word *glykys*, meaning "sweet"), the naturally occurring form, is found in fruits, honey, blood, and, under abnormal conditions, in urine. It is also a constituent of the two most common naturally found disaccharides, sucrose and lactose, as well as the exclusive structural unit of the polysaccharides cellulose, starch, and glycogen. Generally, D-glucose is prepared from either potato starch or cornstarch.

D-fructose, a ketohexose, is one of the constituents of the disaccharide sucrose and is also found in uncombined form in honey, apples, and tomatoes. Fructose, generally considered the sweetest monosaccharide, is prepared by sucrose hydrolysis and is metabolized by man.

Chemical reactions. The reactions of the monosaccharides can be conveniently subdivided into those associated with the aldehydo or keto group and those associated with the hydroxyl groups.

Reactions involving the aldehydo or keto group

The relative ease with which sugars containing a free or potentially free aldehydo or keto group can be oxidized to form products has been known for a considerable time and once was the basis for the detection of these so-called reducing sugars in a variety of sources. For many years, analyses of blood glucose and urinary glucose were carried out by a procedure involving the use of an alkaline copper compound. Because the reaction has undesirable features—extensive destruction of carbohydrate structure occurs, and the reaction is not very specific (*i.e.*, sugars other than glucose give similar results) and does not result in the formation of readily identifiable products—blood and urinary glucose now are analyzed by using the enzyme glucose oxidase, which catalyzes the oxidation of glucose to products that include hydrogen peroxide. The hydrogen peroxide then is used to oxidize a dye present in the reaction mixture; the intensity of the colour is directly proportional to the amount of glucose initially present. The enzyme, glucose oxidase, is highly specific for β-D-glucose.

In another reaction, the aldehydo group of glucose (H–C=O) reacts with alkaline iodine to form a class of compounds called aldonic acids. One important aldonic acid is ascorbic acid (vitamin C, see structure), an essential dietary component for man and guinea pigs.

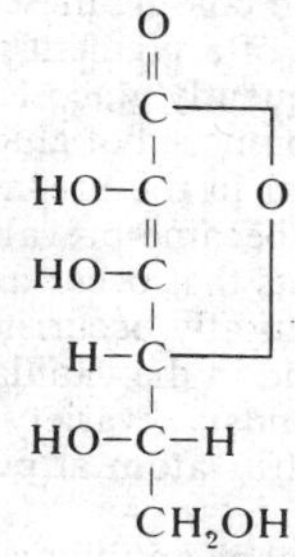

ascorbic acid, vitamin C (L-gulonolactone-2, 3-enediol)

The formation of similar acid derivatives does not occur with the keto sugars.

Either the aldehydo or the keto group of a sugar may be reduced (*i.e.*, hydrogen added) to form an alcohol; compounds formed in this way are called alditols, or sugar alcohols. The product formed as a result of the reduction of the aldehydo carbon of D-glucose is called sorbitol (D-glucitol). D-glucitol also is formed when L-sorbose is reduced. The reduction of mannose results in mannitol, that of galactose in dulcitol.

Sugar alcohols of commercial importance are sorbitol (D-glucitol), commonly used as a sweetening agent, and D-mannitol, also used as a sweetener, particularly in chewing gums, because it has a limited water solubility and remains powdery and granular on long storage.

Formation of glycosides

The hydroxyl group attached to the anomeric carbon atom (*i.e.*, the carbon containing the aldehydo or keto group) of carbohydrates in solution has unusual reactivity, and derivatives, called glycosides, can be formed; glycosides formed from glucose are called glucosides. Equilibration between the α- and β-anomers of a glycoside in solution (*i.e.*, mutarotation) cannot occur. The reaction by which a glycoside is formed (see below) involves the hydroxyl group (− OH) of the anomeric carbon atom (numbered 1) of both α and β forms of D-glucose—α and β forms of D-glucose are shown in equilibrium in the reaction sequence—and the hydroxyl group of an alcohol (methyl alcohol in the reaction sequence); methyl α-D-glucosides and β-D-glucosides are formed as products, as is water.

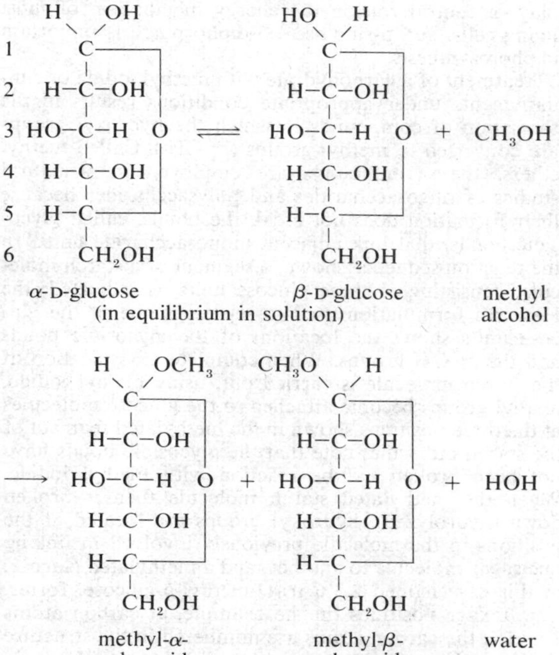

α-D-glucose, β-D-glucose (in equilibrium in solution), methyl alcohol

methyl-α-D-glucoside, methyl-β-D-glucoside, water

Among the wide variety of naturally occurring glycosides are a number of plant pigments, particularly those red, violet, and blue in colour; these pigments are found in flowers and consist of a pigment molecule attached to a sugar molecule, frequently glucose. Plant indican (from *Indigofera* species), composed of glucose and the pigment indoxyl, was important in the preparation of indigo dye before synthetic dyes became prevalent. Of a number of heart-muscle stimulants that occur as glycosides, digitalis is still used. Other naturally occurring glycosides include vanillin, which is found in the vanilla bean, and amygdalin (oil of bitter almonds); a variety of glycosides found in mustard have a sulfur atom at position 1 rather than oxygen.

A number of important antibiotics are glycosides; the best known are streptomycin and erythromycin. Glucosides—*i.e.*, glycosides formed from glucose—in which the anomeric carbon atom (at position 1) has phosphoric acid linked to it are extremely important biological compounds.

For example, α-D-glucose-1-phosphate (see formula), is an intermediate product in the biosynthesis of cellulose, starch, and glycogen; similar glycosidic phosphate derivatives of other monosaccharides participate in the formation of naturally occurring glycosides and polysaccharides.

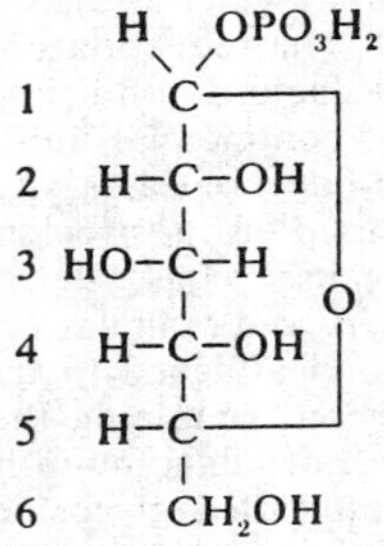

α-D-glucose-1-phosphate

The hydroxyl groups other than the one at the anomeric carbon atom can undergo a variety of reactions, several of which deserve mention. Esterification, which consists of reacting the hydroxyl groups with an appropriate acidic compound, results in the formation of a class of compounds called sugar esters. Among the common ones are the sugar acetates, in which the acid is acetic acid. Esters of phosphoric acid and sulfuric acid are important biological compounds; glucose-6-phosphate, for example, plays a central role in the energy metabolism of most living cells, and D-ribulose 1,5-diphosphate is important in photosynthesis.

Formation of methyl ethers

Treatment of a carbohydrate with methyl iodide or similar agents under appropriate conditions results in the formation of compounds in which the hydroxyl groups are converted to methyl groups (− CH_3). Called methyl ethers, these compounds are employed in structural studies of oligosaccharides and polysaccharides because their formation does not break the bonds, called glycosidic bonds, that link adjacent monosaccharide units. In the reaction sequence shown, a segment of a starch molecule, consisting of three glucose units, is indicated; the Haworth formulation used to represent one of the glucose units shows the locations of the glycosidic bonds and the − OH groups. When complete etherification of the starch molecule is carried out, using methyl iodide, methyl groups become attached to the glucose molecules at the three positions shown in the methylated segment of the starch molecule; note that the glycosidic bonds have not been broken by the reaction with methyl iodide. When the methylated starch molecule then is broken down (hydrolyzed), hydroxyl groups are located at the positions in the molecule previously involved in linking one sugar molecule to another, and a methylated glucose, in this case named 2,3,6 tri-*O*-methyl-D-glucose, forms. The linkage positions (in the example, at carbon atoms 1 and 4; the carbon atoms are numbered in the structure of the methylated glucose), which are not methylated, in a complex carbohydrate can be established by analyzing the locations (in the example, at carbon atoms 2, 3, and 6) of the methyl groups in the monosaccharides. This technique is useful in determining the structural details of polysaccharides, particularly since the various methylated sugars are easily separated by techniques involving gas chromatography, in which a moving gas stream carries a mixture through a column of a stationary liquid or solid, the components thus being resolved.

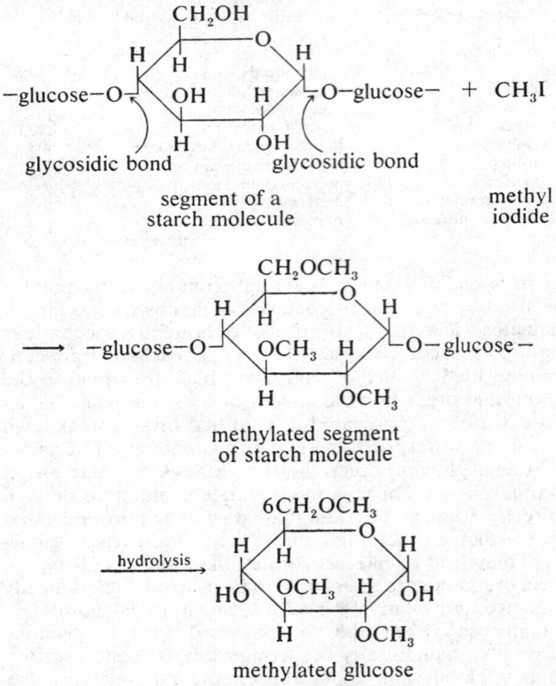

When the terminal group (CH_2OH) of a monosaccharide is oxidized chemically or biologically, a product called a uronic acid is formed. Glycosides that are derived from D-glucuronic acid (the uronic acid formed from D-glucose) and fatty substances called steroids appear in the urine of animals as normal metabolic products; in addition, foreign toxic substances are frequently converted in the liver to glucuronides before excretion in the urine. D-glucuronic acid also is a major component of connective tissue polysaccharides, and D-galacturonic acid and D-mannuronic acid, formed from D-galactose and D-mannose, respectively, are found in several plant sources.

Other compounds formed from monosaccharides include those in which one hydroxyl group, usually at the carbon at position 2 (see formulas for D-glucosamine and D-galactosamine) is replaced by an amino group (− NH_2); these compounds, called amino sugars, are widely distributed in nature. The two most important ones are glucosamine (2-amino-2-deoxy-D-glucose) and galactosamine (2-amino-2-deoxy-D-galactose).

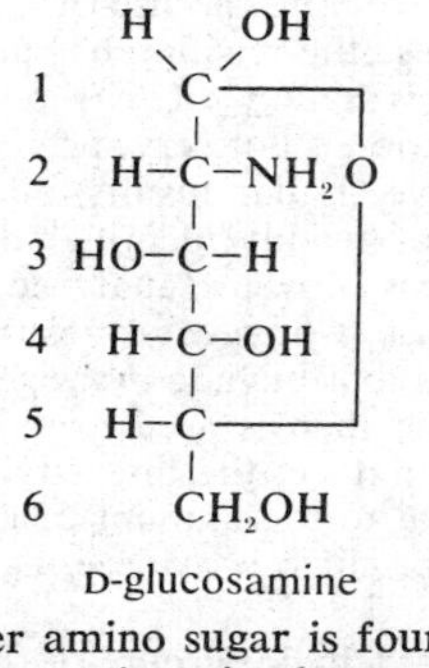

D-glucosamine

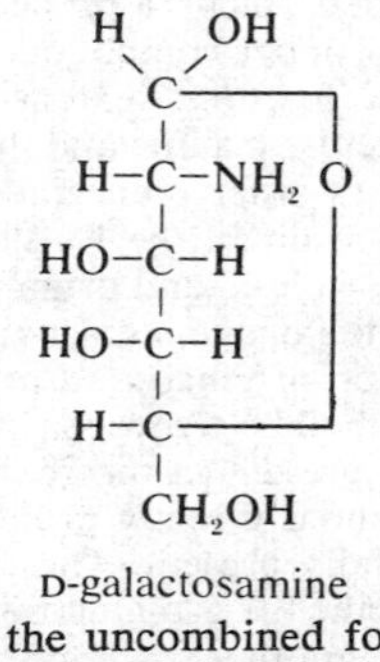

D-galactosamine

Neither amino sugar is found in the uncombined form. Both occur in animals as components of glycolipids or polysaccharides; *e.g.*, the primary structural polysaccharide (chitin) of insect outer skeletons and various blood-group substances.

In a number of naturally occurring sugars, known as

deoxy sugars, the hydroxyl group at a particular position is replaced by a hydrogen atom. By far the most important representative is 2-deoxy-D-ribose (see formula), and pentose sugar found in deoxyribonucleic acid (DNA); the hydroxyl group at the carbon atom at position 2 has been replaced by a hydrogen atom.

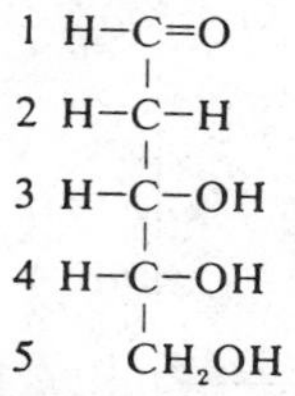

2-deoxy-D-ribose

Other naturally occurring deoxy sugars are hexoses, of which L-rhamnose (6-deoxy-L-mannose) and L-fucose (6-deoxy-L-galactose) are the most common; the latter, for example, is present in the carbohydrate portion of blood-group substances and in red-blood-cell membranes.

Disaccharides and oligosaccharides. Disaccharides are a specialized type of glycoside in which the anomeric hydroxyl group of one sugar has combined with the hydroxyl group of a second sugar with the elimination of the elements of water. Although an enormous number of disaccharide structures are possible, only a limited number are of commercial or biological significance.

Sucrose and trehalose. Sucrose, or common table sugar, has a world production amounting to well over 10,000,000 tons annually. The unusual type of linkage between the two anomeric hydroxyl groups of glucose and fructose (see formula, in which the asterisk indicates anomeric carbon atom), means that neither a free aldehydo group (on the glucose moiety) nor a free keto group (on the fructose moiety) is available to react unless the linkage between the monosaccharides is destroyed; for this reason, sucrose is known as a nonreducing sugar.

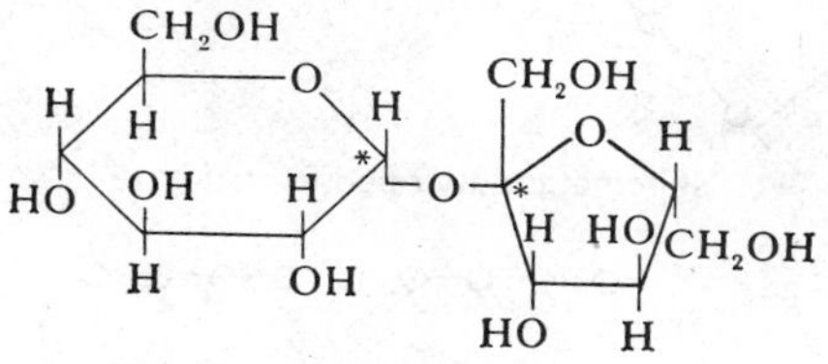

sucrose

Invert sugar

Sucrose solutions do not exhibit mutarotation, which involves formation of an asymmetrical centre at the aldehydo or keto group. If the linkage between the monosaccharides comprising sucrose is broken, the optical rotation value of sucrose changes from positive to negative; the new value reflects the composite rotation values for D-glucose, which is dextrorotatory (+ 52°), and D-fructose, which is levorotatory (− 92°). The change in the sign of optical rotation from positive to negative is the reason sucrose is sometimes called invert sugar.

The commercial preparation of sucrose takes advantage of the alkaline stability of the sugar, and a variety of impurities are removed from crude sugarcane extracts by treatment with alkali. After this step, syrup preparations are crystallized to form table sugar. Successive "crops" of sucrose crystals are "harvested," and the later ones are known as brown sugar. The residual syrupy material is called either cane final molasses or blackstrap molasses; both are used in the preparation of antibiotics, as sweetening agents, and in the production of alcohol by yeast fermentation.

Biologically, sucrose is formed following photosynthesis in plants by a reaction in which sucrose phosphate first is formed.

The disaccharide trehalose is similar in many respects to sucrose but is much less widely distributed. It is composed of two molecules of α-D-glucose and is also a nonreducing sugar. Trehalose is present in young mushrooms and in the resurrection plant (*Selaginella*); it is of considerable biological interest because it is also found in the circulating fluid (hemolymph) of many insects. Since trehalose can be converted to a glucose phosphate compound by an enzyme-catalyzed reaction that does not require energy, its function in hemolymph may be to provide an immediate energy source, a role similar to that of the carbohydrate storage forms (*i.e.*, glycogen) found in higher animals.

Lactose and maltose. Lactose is one of the sugars (sucrose is another) found most commonly in human diets throughout the world; it comprises about 5 percent or more of the milk of all mammals. Lactose consists of two aldohexoses—β-D-galactose and glucose—linked so that the aldehydo group at the anomeric carbon of glucose is free to react (see structural formula, in which the asterisk indicates position of anomeric carbon atoms); *i.e.*, lactose is a reducing sugar.

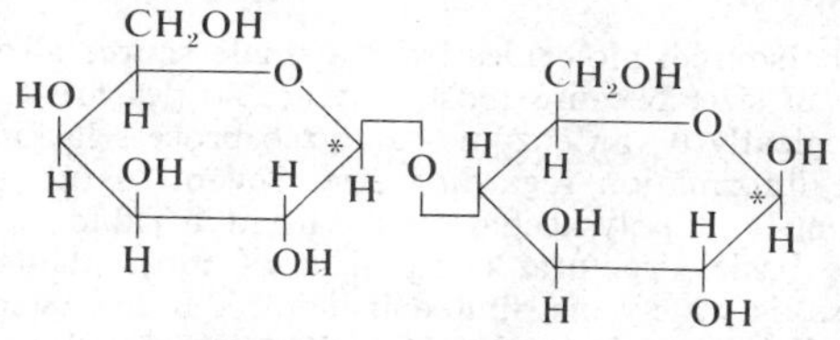

β-lactose

A variety of metabolic disorders related to lactose may occur in infants; in some cases, they are the result of a failure to metabolize properly the galactose portion of the molecule.

Importance of maltose

Although not found in uncombined form in nature, the disaccharide maltose is biologically important because it is a product of the enzymatic breakdown of starches during digestion. Maltose consists of α-D-glucose linked to a second glucose unit in such a way that maltose is a reducing sugar. Maltose, which is readily hydrolyzed to glucose and can be metabolized by animals, is employed as a sweetening agent and as a food for infants whose tolerance for lactose is limited. Table 3 lists the component sugars of, the linkage between, and the occurrence of a number of disaccharides and oligosaccharides.

Table 3: Representative Disaccharides and Oligosaccharides

common name	component sugars	linkages	sources
Cellobiose	glucose, glucose	$\beta\ 1 \rightarrow 4$†	hydrolysis of cellulose
Gentiobiose	glucose, glucose	$\beta\ 1 \rightarrow 6$	plant glycosides, amygdalin
Isomaltose	glucose, glucose	$\alpha\ 1 \rightarrow 6$	hydrolysis of glycogen, amylopectin
Raffinose*	galactose, glucose, fructose	$\alpha\ 1 \rightarrow 6$, $\alpha\ 1 \rightarrow 2$	sugarcane, beets, seeds
Stachyose*	galactose, galactose, glucose, fructose	$\alpha\ 1 \rightarrow 6$, $\alpha\ 1 \rightarrow 6$, $\alpha\ 1 \rightarrow 2$	soybeans, jasmine, twigs, lentils

*Note that raffinose and stachyose are galactosyl sucroses. †The linkage joins carbon atom 1 (in the β configuration) of one glucose molecule and carbon atom 4 of the second glucose molecule; the linkage may also be abbreviated β-1, 4.

Polysaccharides. Polysaccharides, or glycans, may be classified in a number of ways; the following scheme is frequently used. Homopolysaccharides are defined as polysaccharides formed from only one type of monosaccharide. Homopolysaccharides may be further subdivided into straight-chain and branched-chain representatives, depending upon the arrangement of the monosaccharide units. Heteropolysaccharides are defined as polysaccharides containing two or more different types of monosaccharides; they may also occur in both straight-chain and branched-chain forms. In general, extensive variation of linkage types (see Table 4) does not occur within a polysaccharide structure, nor are there many polysaccharides composed of more than three or four different monosaccharides; most contain one or two.

Homopolysaccharides. In general, homopolysaccharides have a well-defined chemical structure, although the molecular weight of an individual amylose or xylan molecule may vary within a particular range, depending

Table 4: Representative Homopolysaccharides

homopolysaccharide	sugar component	linkage	function	sources
Cellulose	glucose	β, 1 → 4	structural	throughout plant kingdom
Amylose	glucose	α, 1 → 4	food storage	starches, especially corn, potatoes, rice
Chitin	N-acetylglucosamine	β, 1 → 4	structural	insect and crustacean skeleton
Inulin	fructose	β, 2 → 1	food storage	artichokes, chicory
Xylan	xylose	β, 1 → 4	structural	all land plants
Glycogen	glucose	α, 1 → 4, 6 ← 1, α	food storage	liver and muscle cells of all animals
Amylopectin	glucose	α, 1 → 4, 6 ← 1, α	food storage	starches, especially corn, potatoes, rice
Dextran	glucose	α, 1 → 6, 4 ← 1, α	unknown	primarily bacterial
Agar*	galactose	α, 1 → 3	structural	seaweeds

*May contain sulfate groups.

on the source; molecules from a single source also may vary in size, because most polysaccharides are formed biologically by an enzyme-catalyzed process lacking genetic information regarding size. Several naturally occurring homopolysaccharides are listed in Table 4.

Cellulose and xylans

The basic structural component of most plants, cellulose, is widely distributed in nature. It has been estimated that nearly 10,000,000,000 tons of cellulose are synthesized yearly as a result of photosynthesis by higher plants. The proportion of cellulose to total carbohydrate found in plants may vary in various types of woods from 30 to 40 percent, and to more than 98 percent in the seed hair of the cotton plant. Cellulose, a large, linear molecule composed of 3,000 or more β-D-glucose molecules, is insoluble in water.

The chains of glucose units comprising cellulose molecules are frequently aligned within the cell-wall structure of a plant to form fibre-like or crystalline arrangements. This alignment permits very tight packing of the chains and promotes their structural stability but also makes structural analysis difficult. The relationships between cellulose and other polysaccharides present in the cell wall are not well established; in addition, the presence of unusual chemical linkages or nonglucose units within the cellulose structure has not yet been established with certainty.

During the preparation of cellulose, raw plant material is treated with hot alkali; this treatment removes most of the lignin, the hemicelluloses, and the mucilaginous components. The cellulose then is processed to produce papers and fibres. The high resistance of cellulose to chemical or enzymatic breakdown is important in the manufacture of paper and cloth. Cellulose also is modified chemically for other purposes; *e.g.*, compounds such as cellulose acetate are used in the plastics industry, in the production of photographic film, and in the rayon-fibre industry. Viscose rayon is produced from an ester of cellulose, and cellulose nitrate is employed in the lacquer and explosives industries.

The noteworthy biological stability of cellulose is dramatically illustrated by trees, the life-span of which may be several thousand years. Enzymes capable of breaking down cellulose are generally found only among several species of bacteria and molds. The apparent ability of termites to utilize cellulose as an energy source depends on the presence in their intestinal tracts of protozoans that can break it down. Similarly, the single-celled organisms present in the rumina of sheep and cattle are responsible for the ability of these animals to utilize the cellulose present in typical grasses and other feeds.

Xylans are almost as ubiquitous as cellulose in plant-cell walls and contain predominantly β-D-xylose units linked as in cellulose (see Table 4). Some xylans contain other sugars, such as L-arabinose, but they form branches and are not part of the main chain. Xylans are of little commercial importance.

Starch

The term starch refers to a group of plant reserve polysaccharides consisting almost exclusively of a linear component (amylose) and a branched component (amylopectin). Man's utilization of starch as an energy source depends on his ability to convert it completely to individual glucose units; the process is initiated by the action of enzymes called amylases, synthesized by the salivary glands in the mouth, and continues in the intestinal tract. The primary product of amylase action is maltose, which is hydrolyzed to two component glucose units as it is absorbed through the walls of the intestine.

A characteristic reaction of the amylose component of starch is the formation with iodine of a complex compound with a characteristic blue colour. About one iodine molecule is bound for each seven or eight glucose units, and at least five times that many glucose units are needed in an amylose chain to permit the effective development of the colour.

The amylopectin component of starch is structurally similar to glycogen in that both are composed of glucose units linked together in the same way, but the distance between branch points (see schematic diagrams, in which —O— represents one glucose unit) is greater in amylopectin than in glycogen, and the former may be thought of as occupying more space per unit weight.

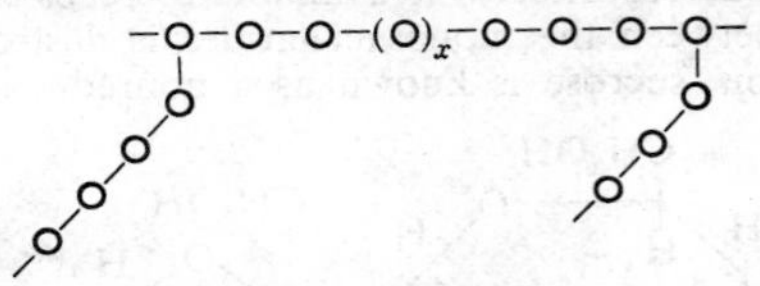

schematic amylopectin structure

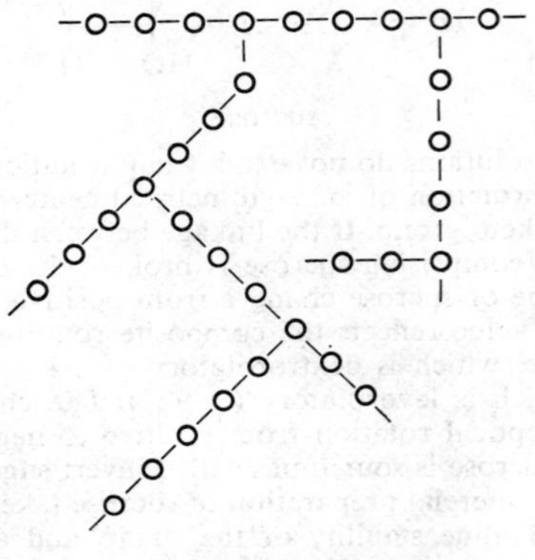

schematic glycogen structure

The applications of starches other than as foods are limited, although they are employed in adhesive manufacture; in addition, starch nitrate has some utility as an explosive.

Glycogen

Glycogen, which is found in all animal tissues, is the primary animal storage form of carbohydrate and, indirectly, of rapidly available energy. The distance between branch points in a glycogen molecule is only five or six units (see schematic diagram above), which results in a compact treelike structure. The ability of higher animals to form and break down this extensively branched structure is essential to their well-being; in conditions known as glycogen storage diseases, these activities are abnormal, and the asymmetrical glycogen molecules that are formed have severe, often fatal, consequences. Glycogen synthesis and breakdown are controlled by substances called hormones.

Large molecules—*e.g.*, pectins and agars—composed of galactose or its uronic-acid derivative (galacturonic acid) are important because they can form gels. Pectins, which are predominantly galacturonans, are produced from citrus fruit rinds; they are used commercially in the preparation of jellies and jams. Agar is widely employed in biological laboratories as a solidifying agent for growth media for micro-organisms and in the bakery industry as a gelling agent; it forms a part of the diet of people in several areas of the Far East.

Dextrans, a group of polysaccharides composed of glucose, are secreted by certain strains of bacteria as slimes. The structure of an individual dextran varies with the strain of micro-organism. Dextrans can be used as plasma expanders (substitutes for whole blood) in cases of severe shock. In addition, a dextran derivative compound is employed medically as an anticoagulant for blood.

Chitin is structurally similar to cellulose, but the repeating sugar is 2-deoxy-2-acetamido-D-glucose (*N*-acetyl-D-glucosamine, see structural formula) rather than glucose.

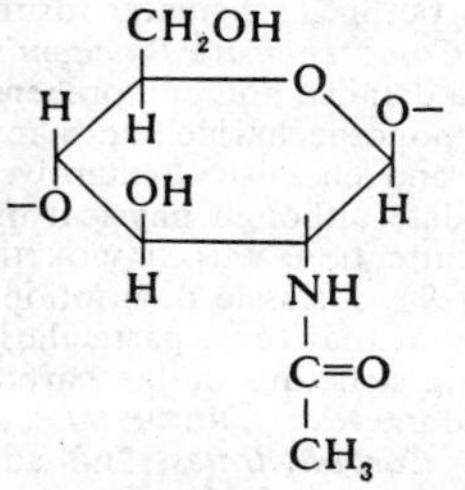

N-acetyl-D-glucosamine

Sometimes referred to as animal cellulose, chitin is the major component of the outer skeletons of insects, crustaceans, and other arthropods, as well as annelid and nematode worms, mollusks, and coelenterates. The cell walls of most fungi also are predominantly chitin, which comprises nearly 50 percent of the dry weight of some species. Since chitin is nearly as chemically inactive as cellulose and easily obtained, numerous attempts, none of which has thus far been successful, have been made to develop it commercially. The nitrogen content of the biosphere, however, is stabilized by the ability of soil micro-organisms to degrade nitrogen-containing compounds such as those found in insect skeletons; these micro-organisms convert the nitrogen in complex molecules to a form usable by plants. If such micro-organisms did not exist, much of the organic nitrogen present in natural materials would be unavailable to plants.

Heteropolysaccharides. In general, heteropolysaccharides (heteroglycans) contain two or more different monosaccharide units. Although a few representatives contain three or more different monosaccharides, most naturally occurring heteroglycans contain only two different ones and are closely associated with lipid or protein. The complex nature of these substances has made detailed structural studies extremely difficult. The major heteropolysaccharides include the connective-tissue polysaccharides, the blood-group substances, glycoproteins (combinations of carbohydrates and proteins) such as gamma globulin, and glycolipids (combinations of carbohydrates and lipids), particularly those found in the central nervous system of animals and in a wide variety of plant gums (see Table 5).

Connective tissue heteropolysaccharides

The most important heteropolysaccharides are found in the connective tissues of all animals and include a group of large molecules that vary in size, shape, and interaction with other body substances. They have a structural role, and the structures of individual connective-tissue polysaccharides are related to specific animal functions; hyaluronic acid, for example, the major component of joint fluid in animals, functions as a lubricating agent and shock absorber when stress or weight is put on a joint surface.

The connective-tissue heteropolysaccharides contain acidic groups (uronic acids or sulfate groups) and can bind both water and inorganic metal ions. They can also play a role in other physiological functions; *e.g.*, in the accumulation of calcium before bone formation. Ion-binding ability also appears to be related to the anticoagulant activity of the heteropolysaccharide heparin (see Table 5).

The size of the carbohydrate portion of glycoproteins such as gamma globulin or hen-egg albumin is usually between five and ten monosaccharide units; several such units occur in some glycoprotein molecules. The function of the carbohydrate component has not yet been established except for glycoproteins associated with cell surfaces; in this case, they appear to act as antigenic determinants—*i.e.*, they are capable of inducing the formation of specific antibodies.

PREPARATION AND ANALYSIS

In general, monosaccharides are prepared by breakdown with acids of the polysaccharides in which they occur. Because sugars usually are difficult to obtain in crystalline form, the crystallization process usually is begun by "seeding" a concentrated solution of the sugar with crystals. The techniques employed for separation of monosaccharides depend to some extent on their physical and chemical properties; chromatographic procedures are frequently used.

Oligosaccharides and polysaccharides are prepared from natural sources by techniques that take advantage of size, alkaline stability, or some combination of these and other properties of the molecule of interest. It should be noted that preparation of an oligosaccharide or polysaccharide usually results in a range of molecular sizes of the desired molecule. The purity of a carbohydrate preparation, which is frequently based on an analysis of its composition, is more easily established for monsaccharides and disaccharides than for large, insoluble molecules such as cellulose.

A variety of organic chemical analytical techniques are generally applicable to studies involving carbohydrates. Optical rotation, for example, once was frequently used to characterize carbohydrates. The ability to measure the rotation of the plane of polarized light transmitted through a solution containing a carbohydrate depends on finding a suitable solvent; water usually is used, with light at a wavelength of 589 mμ (millimicrons). Optical rota-

Optical rotation

Table 5: Representative Heteropolysaccharides

heteropolysaccharide	component sugars	functions	distribution
Hyaluronic acid	D-glucuronic acid and *N*-acetyl-D-glucosamine	lubricant, shock absorber, water binding	connective tissue, skin
Chondroitin-4-sulfate*	D-glucuronic acid and *N*-acetyl-D-galactosamine-4-*O*-sulfate	calcium accumulation, cartilage and bone formation	cartilage
Heparin*	D-glucuronic acid, *L*-iduronic acid, *N*-sulfo-D-glucosamine	anticoagulant	mast cells, blood
Gamma globulin*	*N*-acetyl-hexosamine, D-mannose, D-galactose	antibody	blood
Blood group substance*	D-glucosamine, D-galactosamine, *L*-fucose, D-galactose	blood group specificity	cell surfaces, especially red-blood cells

*Covalently linked to protein; the proportion of protein to carbohydrate in such complex molecules varies from about 10% protein in the case of chondroitin-4-sulfate to better than 95% for gamma globulin.

tion is no longer widely used to characterize monosaccharides. The magnitude and sign of the optical rotation of glycosides, however, is useful in assigning configuration (α or β) to the hydroxyl group at the anomeric centre; glycosides of the α-configuration generally have rotations of higher magnitude than do the same glycosides of the β-configuration. Optical rotation is not a completely additive property; a trisaccharide composed of three glucose residues, for example, does not have a rotation three times that of one glucose molecule. Sugar alcohols and sugar acids cannot form ring structures; their rotation values are extremely small, suggesting a relationship between ring structure and the ability of a carbohydrate to rotate the plane of polarized light. Certain types of reactions (*e.g.*, glycoside hydrolysis) can be monitored by measuring the change in optical rotation as a function of time. This technique is frequently used to examine the breakdown of disaccharides or oligosaccharides to monosaccharide units, especially if a large change in the net optical rotation may be expected, as occurs in the hydrolysis of sucrose.

A number of other optical techniques used in chemistry have been applied to the analysis of carbohydrates. Infrared spectroscopy, which is used to measure vibrational and rotational excitation of molecules, and nuclear magnetic-resonance spectroscopy, which measures the excitation of certain components of molecules in a magnetic field induced by radio-frequency radiation, are valuable, although the similarity of the functional groups (*i.e.*, the hydroxyl groups) limits use of the former technique for most sugars. Proton magnetic-resonance spectroscopy, nuclear magnetic resonance applied only to protons (H atoms), is widely employed to identify the relative spatial arrangements of individual hydrogen atoms in a molecule. When they are precisely placed, the corresponding positions of the hydroxyl groups attached to the same carbon atom can be deduced. An extension of this technique utilizes the resonance spectroscopy of carbon-13, a nonradioactive isotope of carbon, so that ring structures can be established with considerable accuracy. Both the proton and carbon magnetic resonance methods are best applied to monosaccharides; they are less valuable in studying polysaccharides because an individual hydrogen atom in a large molecule is too small for accurate detection.

The study of polysaccharide structure usually focusses on the chemical composition, the linkage between the monosaccharide units, and the size and shape of the molecule. The last two properties can be ascertained by techniques usually applied to large molecules; *e.g.*, the most accurate molecular weight method measures the sedimentation properties of the molecule in an applied gravitational field (*e.g.*, the rate at which a solid material is deposited from a state of suspension or solution in a liquid). Indications of the shape of polysaccharide molecules in solution are obtained from viscosity measurements, in which the resistance of the molecules to flow (viscosity) is equated with the end-to-end length of the molecule; the viscosity of hyaluronic acid, for example, shows a marked dependence on both concentration of the acid and the salt content of the solution, and, under conditions approximating those found in biological systems, the molecule may be thought of as occupying a great deal of space. Alternatively, the compact nature of a glycogen molecule of equal molecular weight results in its accommodation to a much smaller space.

The identification of sugars in a mixture resulting from the hydrolytic breakdown of a heteropolysaccharide is most often carried out by chromatography of the mixture on paper, silica gel, or cellulose. Ready separations can be achieved between pentoses, hexoses and, for example, deoxy sugars; closely related compounds such as D-glucose and D-galactose also can be separated using chromatographic techniques. The linkage positions in polysaccharides are usually determined using the methylation procedure described previously. The various monosaccharide methyl ethers are separated by gas–liquid chromatography.

Detailed statements about polysaccharide structure and function are limited by the statistical nature of some measurements (*e.g.*, branching frequency), the biological variability of parameters such as size and molecular weight, and incomplete information about associative interactions in living things.

BIBLIOGRAPHY. *Advances in Carbohydrate Chemistry* (published annually since 1945), multiple-authored volumes, reviewing specific areas of carbohydrate chemistry, scope now expanded to include chapters of more biological interest; F.J. BATES *et al.*, *Polarimetry, Saccarimetry and the Sugars* (1942), practical information on sucrose and other common sugars together with methods for analysis and preparation of simple derivatives, primarily of historical interest although many of the data tables provide useful reference information; E.A. DAVIDSON, *Carbohydrate Chemistry* (1967), an intermediate college-level text emphasizing stereochemistry, conformation, and modern organic reaction mechanisms as applied to carbohydrates, and including both physical and chemical methods for structural determination; S.F. DYKE, "Chemistry of Natural Products Series," vol. 5, *The Carbohydrates* (1960), an introduction to basic reactions in the carbohydrate field, written almost in outline, schematic form; M. FLORKIN and E.H. STOTZ (eds.), *Comprehensive Biochemistry*, vol. 5, *Carbohydrates* (1963), a detailed and comprehensive volume covering all aspects of monosaccharide and many areas of polysaccharide structure and chemistry, extensively referenced and reasonably up-to-date although physical methods do not receive appropriate attention; W.N. HAWORTH, *The Constitution of the Sugars* (1929), a classic description of the knowledge of sugar chemistry at that time, particularly Haworth's work in defining the ring structure of the carbohydrates—now of primarily historical interest; J. HONEYMAN, *An Introduction to the Chemistry of Carbohydrates*, 2nd ed. (1964), a short monograph on basic carbohydrate structure and reactions; and (ed.), *Recent Advances in the Chemistry of Cellulose and Starch* (1959), a thorough review of cellulose and its derivatives, primarily concerned with cellulose chemistry and industrial applications; R.J. MCILROY, *Introduction to Carbohydrate Chemistry* (1967), a short, contemporary introduction to carbohydrate chemistry recognizing the importance of stereochemistry and conformational factors; F. MICHEEL, *Chemie der Zucker und Polysaccharide*, 2nd ed. (1956), a comprehensive work, in German, on all aspects of carbohydrate chemistry; E.G.V. and E. PERCIVAL, *Structural Carbohydrate Chemistry*, 2nd ed. (1962), a standard work detailing methods of structural determination, particularly of sugar ring size and polysaccharide structure, still useful as a summary of structural methods with a heavy chemical emphasis although many modern techniques are not discussed; W. PIGMAN (ed.), *The Carbohydrates: Chemistry, Biochemistry, Physiology* (1957), a standard reference work that covers most of the classic work prior to 1957 although many of the modern developments, particularly in physical methods, stereochemistry, and reaction mechanisms are not included; W. PIGMAN and D. HORTON (eds.), *The Carbohydrates*, 2nd ed., 2 vol. of projected 4-volume work (1970), a comprehensive revision of the 1957 work cited above; J.A. RADLEY, *Starch and Its Derivatives*, 3rd ed. (1953), on industrial applications of starch and its by-products; *Specialists Periodical Report*, vol. 1, *Carbohydrate Chemistry* (1967), a detailed literature review of papers published during 1967 in all areas of carbohydrate chemistry, planned as a yearly or biennial volume and will probably be a useful reference text for active researchers in the carbohydrate field; E. OTT, H.M. SPURLIN, and M.W. GRAFFLIN (eds.), *Cellulose and Cellulose Derivatives*, 2nd rev. ed., vol. (1954–55), primarily concerned with industrial applications of cellulose and its products; M. STACEY and H. BARKER (eds.), *Carbohydrates of Living Tissues* (1962), a detailed account of the chemistry and biochemistry of polysaccharide substances, primarily those found in animal tissues; J. STANEK, M. CERNY, and J. PACAK (eds.), *The Monosaccharides* (1963); and *The Oligosaccharides* (1965), standard reference works translated from Czech, detailing structure, reaction, and properties of monosaccharides and oligosaccharides; R.L. WHISTLER and J.N. BEMILLER (eds.), *Industrial Gums, Polysaccharides and their Derivatives* (1959), on thickening agents, pectins, and plant mucilages; R.L. WHISTLER and M.L. WOLFROM (eds.), *Methods in Carbohydrate Chemistry*, 5 vol. (1962–65), a necessary reference work for research workers in the field, detailing laboratory procedures for monosaccharide and polysaccharide preparations; R.L. WHISTLER and C.L. SMART, *Polysaccharide Chemistry* (1953), a summary of chemical information on polysaccharides up to 1952, with emphasis primarily on homopolymers such as starch and cellulose since few detailed structures were known at that time.

(E.A.D.)

Carbonate Minerals

Carbonate minerals are naturally occurring substances that contain the carbonate ion CO_3^{2-} as a major structural and compositional unit. As a group, the carbonates are rather soft minerals with hardnesses between 1 and 5 on the Mohs scale (which ranges to 10 for diamond); and, with the exception of the uranyl and the alkali carbonates, they tend to be relatively insoluble in water. Because the carbonate ion reacts with the hydronium (hydrogen) ion to liberate carbon dioxide gas, the carbonates are characterized by their solubility, often with effervescence, in acids. The crystal structures of many carbonate minerals reflect the trigonal (three–fold) symmetry of the carbonate ion, which consists of a carbon atom centrally located in an equilateral triangle of oxygen atoms. The planar structure of the carbonate ion also results frequently in highly anisotropic physical properties in the carbonates, such as the high birefringence (difference between the transmission of light in different crystal directions) characteristic of many carbonate minerals.

Uses of carbonate minerals

Two common carbonates, calcite and dolomite, are among the most abundant and widely distributed minerals found on the surface of the Earth. As the principal constituents of limestones, dolostones, and marbles, these minerals have a wide variety of commercial uses and account for approximately 70 percent of all rock quarried in the United States. These materials are extensively used for building and ornamental stone, for concrete and road stone, for the production of natural and portland cements, in agriculture, and as fluxes in steel-smelting processes. In addition, calcite crystals are vital components in the manufacture of optical polarizing prisms; certain limestones are used in lithography; and natural and precipitated calcite is used in the production of candy, chewing gum, food fillers, glass, glue, pharmaceutical products (antacids, antibiotics, etc.), rubber, shoe polish, soap, toothpaste, whitewash, and many other commodities. Calcite also is used as an ore of metallic calcium and as a raw material in the manufacture of other chemical compounds of calcium. Dolomite and magnesite are used as ores, as chemical sources of magnesium, and as major sources of refractory compounds (heat–resistant substances used as furnace linings).

Other carbonate minerals are used as ores and as chemical sources of iron, manganese, zinc, lead, copper, barium, strontium, sodium, uranium, and rare-earth elements. Aragonite (pearl), malachite, rhodochrosite, smithsonite, and calcite (coral, onyx, marble) are used as gems or for other ornamental purposes (see GEMSTONES).

CLASSIFICATION

The generally accepted system of classification of minerals (*q.v.*) is based upon the principal anion (negatively charged ion) present. Subclassification within the carbonate minerals is based upon the nature of the anionic unit or upon the presence and identity of other anionic species. The subclasses within the carbonate minerals include (1) anhydrous normal carbonates, which are those minerals that contain only carbonate as an anion and no structural water; (2) hydrated normal carbonates, which are those minerals that contain only carbonate anions that do have structural water of hydration; (3) acid carbonates, which are minerals that contain the acid carbonate (bicarbonate) anion, HCO_3^-; (4) minerals containing hydroxide (OH^-) or halide (F^-, Cl^-) ions in addition to carbonate; and (5) compound carbonates or minerals that contain other anions, such as sulfate (SO_4^{2-}) or phosphate (PO_4^{3-}), in addition to carbonate. There are also some minerals that properly belong in other major classes, such as silicate or sulfate minerals. These may contain the carbonate ion as a minor anionic unit. The subclasses may further be divided into compositional types, depending upon whether single or multiple cationic (positively charged) species are present, and into isostructural groups (minerals with similar crystal structures).

The most important carbonate minerals, whether from the economic or the geologic point of view, belong to three major structural groups (calcite, dolomite, and aragonite) within the anhydrous normal carbonate class (class 1). Alkali carbonates and bicarbonates such as nahcolite, trona, thermonatrite, and natron (predominantly in classes 2 and 3), are relatively rare, and are of geologic interest because of their unusual mode of occurrence, as later described. Certain other carbonates, although geologically rare, may locally be concentrated in sufficient quantities to be economically important as minor ore minerals. Such minerals include malachite and azurite (which because of their aesthetic appeal are highly prized by mineral collectors) in class 4, lanthanite (class 2), bastnaesite and related rare-earth carbonates, and hydrozincite (all in class 4), and various uranium and uranyl carbonates such as rutherfordine (class 1), andersonite, swartzite, bayleyite, and liebigite (all in class 2). For species in each class see RELATED ENTRIES under CARBONATE MINERALS in the *Ready Reference and Index*.

CRYSTALLOGRAPHY AND CHEMICAL PROPERTIES

Calcite group. As previously noted, calcite is one of the most common and most widely distributed minerals known. It occurs in a wide variety of geological settings and frequently forms large, well-defined crystals. Calcite displays the widest variety of crystal habits of any known substance; more than 600 different crystal forms have been reported. Despite this diversity of possible forms, only a few are commonly observed. Several of the more common forms are illustrated in Figure 1. Calcite exhibits essentially perfect rhombohedral cleavage corresponding to the form r of Figure 1. Because all calcite crystals will preferentially break along these planes, virtually all crystal fragments of calcite will possess this habit.

Double refraction of calcite

The abundance and variety of large, essentially perfect crystals and the marked anisotropy (directional variation) of many of its physical properties have resulted in extensive studies of calcite throughout the history of crystallography. The phenomenon of double refraction was first observed in cleavage rhombs of calcite from Iceland and was described in detail in 1678. Further study of this phenomenon led to the discovery of polarization of light in 1808. René-Just Haüy's studies of calcite in 1781–1801 led to a theory of crystal structure and to the development of geometrical crystallography. The observed variation dependent on composition of the crystallographic and other physical properties of calcite and other members of the calcite group led to the theory of isomorphism in 1820. The crystal structure of calcite was one of the first to be determined by X-ray diffraction, being described by Sir Lawrence Bragg in 1914. Subsequently, calcite was used as a standard for X-ray wavelengths. The phenomenon of twin gliding (reorientation of a single crystal to produce twins) in crystals was not only first recognized, but was also first experimentally produced in calcite.

The crystal structure of calcite is shown in Figure 2; it is hexagonal-rhombohedral. The structure can most easily be visualized as consisting of alternating planes of calcium ions and carbonate ions, arranged with hexagonal symmetry within each plane. It is often convenient to refer to the unit cell illustrated because it corresponds to a distorted sodium chloride-type structure. This cell is referred to as the "morphological" unit cell, representing the cleavage rhombohedron (rhombohedral angle = 101° 55′) of calcite; it is not, however, a true unit cell. The directional configuration of the carbonate "triangles" alternates in successive carbonate planes, requiring a doubled c-axis component for the true unit cell.

The parallel planar arrangement of the carbonate ions accounts for the extreme anisotropy in many physical properties of calcite. The high birefringence (double refraction) of calcite arises from the fact that light vibrating parallel to the carbonate planes is propagated much more slowly than that vibrating perpendicular to the planes. This results in widely different indices and angles of refraction for light vibrating in the different directions.

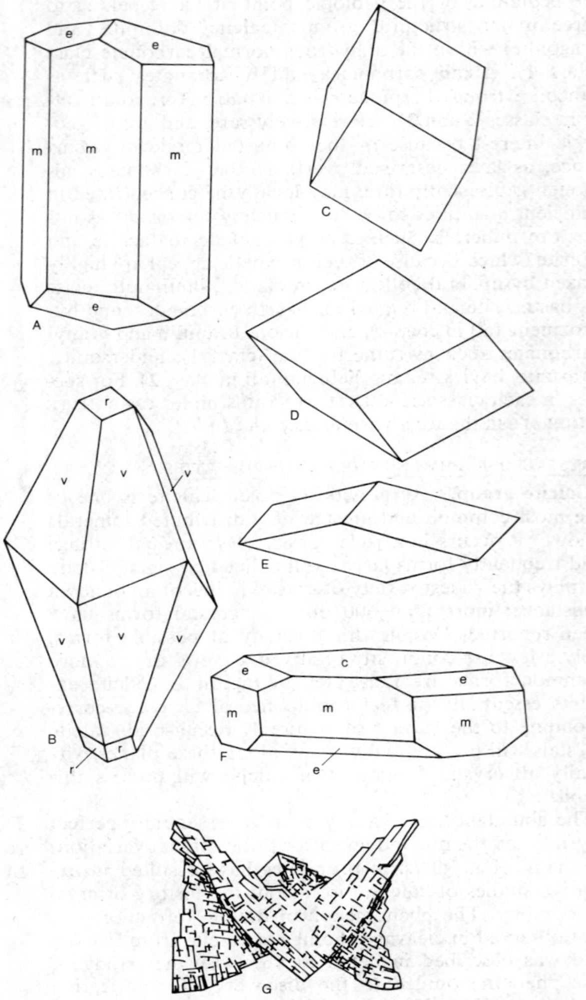

Figure 1: *Common forms of calcite and dolomite.* (A) Combined prism (faces m) and rhombohedron (faces e). (B) Combined scalenohedron (faces v) and rhombohedron (faces r). (C, D, E) Acute, basic, and flattened rhombohedra, respectively. (F) Combined pinacoid (face c), prism (faces m), and rhombohedron (faces e). (G) Saddle-shaped dolomite, formed as a distorted rhombohedron.
From E. Dana, *A Textbook of Mineralogy*, 4th ed. (1932), John Wiley & Sons, Inc.

Consequently, unpolarized light will be resolved into two plane-polarized components, refracted at different angles by the calcite crystal. This separation of totally plane-polarized light rays is utilized in the construction of optical polarizing prisms. Other anisotropic properties related to the planar carbonate configuration include thermal expansion and linear compressibility. With increasing temperature, calcite expands in a direction perpendicular to the carbonate planes but contracts in the parallel directions. This leads to a decrease in the rhombohedral angle with increasing temperature. Conversely, increasing hydrostatic pressure causes a contraction perpendicular to the carbonate planes but expansion within the planes.

From W.F. de Jong, *General Crystallography: A Brief Compendium*, Copyright © 1959; W.H. Freeman and Company

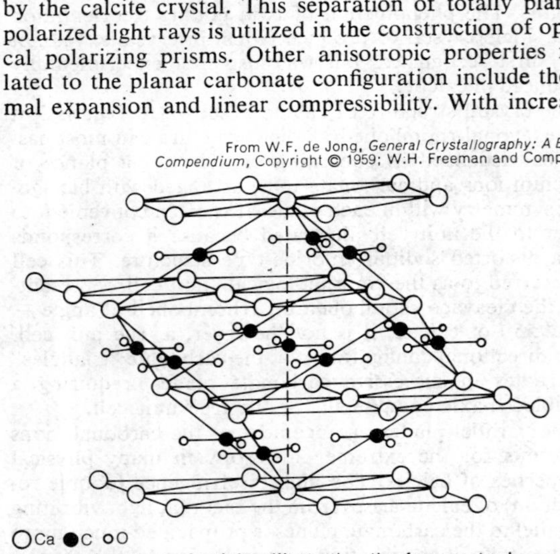

○Ca ●C ○O
Figure 2: Structure of calcite, illustrating the face-centred rhombohedron of the cleavage or morphological unit; the structure consists of alternating planes of calcium and carbonate ions, as shown.

Figure 3: Cleavage rhomb of Iceland spar showing double refraction; from Grey Cliff, Montana.
By courtesy of the Illinois State Museum; photograph, John H. Gerard—EB Inc.

Chemical composition and variability

Chemically, most natural calcite is relatively pure. Divalent (doubly charged) cations may substitute for calcium but only to a very limited extent. Small amounts of Mg^{2+}, Fe^{2+}, or Mn^{2+} commonly may replace Ca^{2+}; less commonly, Zn^{2+}, Ni^{2+}, Cu^{2+}, Co^{2+}, Sr^{2+}, Ba^{2+}, or Pb^{2+} may be found. The presence of even such small amounts of the transition metal ions Mn^{2+}, Fe^{2+}, Co^{2+}, Cu^{2+}, or Ni^{2+} may be sufficient to impart pale colours to calcite; however, strong coloration of calcite is usually caused by the presence of other finely disseminated minerals that become included during growth of the calcite crystals.

The anhydrous normal carbonates of all divalent cations smaller than calcium also crystallize with the calcite structure, forming an isostructural series. As such, the crystallographic and related physical properties of these minerals are similar to those of calcite. The variation of crystallographic parameters is given in Table 1.

Table 1: Crystallographic Parameters of Minerals of the Calcite Group

	formula	radius of cation*	crystal axes* true unit cell a_0	c_0	rhombohedral angle—true unit cell
Calcite	$CaCO_3$	1.00	4.99	17.06	46° 4′
Otavite	$CdCO_3$	0.95	4.92	16.30	47° 19′
Rhodochrosite	$MnCO_3$	0.83	4.78	15.66	47° 43′
Siderite	$FeCO_3$	0.78	4.69	15.37	47° 43′
Magnesite	$MgCO_3$	0.72	4.63	15.02	48° 11′
Smithsonite	$ZnCO_3$	0.75	4.65	15.03	48° 20′
Cobaltocalcite	$CoCO_3$	0.74	4.66	14.96	48° 33′
Gaspeite	$NiCO_3$	0.69	4.60	14.72	48° 40′

* Dimensions in angstrom units.

Of these minerals, otavite, gaspeite, and cobaltocalcite have extremely limited occurrences. Smithsonite, although not widely distributed, occasionally occurs in sufficient quantity to be mined as an ore of zinc. Magnesite, siderite, and, to a lesser extent, rhodochrosite occur in sufficient abundance and distribution to be of interest both geologically and economically. These three minerals form complete solid solution series (complete atomic substitution is possible) with one another, and minerals of intermediate composition within these series have properties proportionately intermediate between those of the pure end members. Solid solution between these minerals and calcite is limited, perhaps by the differences in ionic size between Ca^{2+} and Mg^{2+}, Fe^{2+}, or Mn^{2+}. Instead, intermediate compounds are found, forming the isostructural group dolomite, ankerite, and kutnahorite.

Dolomite group. Of all carbonate minerals, dolomite is second only to calcite in abundance, distribution, and geologic and economic importance. Compositionally, dolomite may be described as calcite with exactly half the calcium ions replaced by magnesium. Structurally, this is accomplished by the replacement of alternate planes of calcium ions in the calcite structure with planes of magnesium ions. This lowers the symmetry and more reflections appear in the X-ray diffraction pattern.

Distinction of dolomite from calcite

Dolomite commonly occurs as a massive mineral and is only rarely observed to form well-defined crystals. The forms displayed are the more common forms of calcite; the rhombohedron r of Figure 1 being most frequently encountered. Typically this form is found to possess curved faces, which, in extreme cases, result in saddle-shaped crystals, illustrated in Figure 1. When treated with cold, dilute acid, calcite effervesces briskly, whereas dolomite reacts very slowly.

As in the simple carbonates, Fe^{2+} and Mn^{2+} can substitute freely for Mg^{2+} in the dolomite structure, resulting in solid solution series. Although intermediate members are uncommon, it is likely that a complete series exists between dolomite and kutnahorite. The pure cation-ordered compound $CaFe(CO_3)_2$ never has been observed in natural or in synthetic systems; though a wide range of compositions corresponding to ferroan dolomites and ankerites may be found in natural materials. Because this solid solution series is continuous, the distinction between ankerite and ferroan dolomite is arbitrary. The name ankerite is commonly applied to those species in which at least 20 percent of the magnesium positions of dolomite are occupied by iron. The system is usually complicated by the presence of manganese and often by excess calcium. The ranges of naturally occurring compositions in the system $CaCO_3$–$MgCO_3$–$FeCO_3$ are shown in Figure 4.

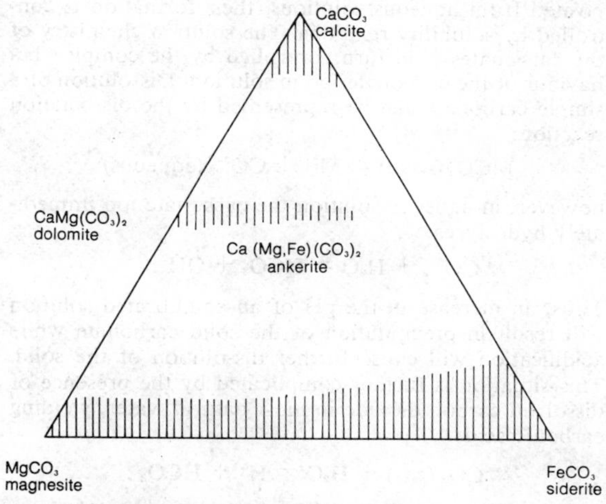

Figure 4: Naturally occurring compositions in the system $CaCO_3$–$MgCO_3$–$FeCO_3$. Shaded areas indicate the approximate compositional ranges that occur in nature.

Kutnahorite commonly contains some iron and is frequently deficient in calcium, indicating that the manganese ion is large enough to substitute in part for calcium in the dolomite structure. Dolomite and ankerite, however, are almost never deficient in calcium but frequently contain a small excess, indicating that magnesium and iron do not enter the calcium positions in dolomite, but that calcium may substitute in part for magnesium.

Crystallographic data for these minerals are given in Table 2. For purposes of comparison, calculated data for hypothetical ideal solid solutions are included. The structural change produced by cation ordering is apparent in the data for dolomite but does not cause significant change in the parameters of ankerite or kutnahorite.

Aragonite group. The third major structural group of the anhydrous normal carbonates includes aragonite, the high-pressure polymorph of $CaCO_3$ (discussed later), and the carbonates of all divalent ions larger than calcium. Aragonite, although a reasonably common mineral in modern sedimentary environments, is thermodynamically unstable with respect to calcite and, given time, it should invert to the more stable calcite structure. Accordingly, aragonite is unknown in ancient geological deposits; however, aragonitic fossil shell material as old as 450,000,000 years (Ordovician Period) has been described.

Table 2: Crystallographic Parameters of Minerals of the Dolomite Group

	formula	crystal axes*		rhombohedral angle
		a_0	c_0	
Dolomite	$CaMg(CO_3)_2$	4.81	16.01	47° 7′
Hypothetical solution†	$CaMg(CO_3)_2$	4.81	16.04	47° 4′
Ankerite	$Ca(Mg_{0.67}Fe_{0.33})(CO_3)_2$	4.82	16.10	47° 0′
Hypothetical solution†	$CaFe(CO_3)_2$	4.84	16.22	46° 52′
Kutnahorite	$CaMn(CO_3)_2$	4.88	16.36	46° 52′
Hypothetical solution†	$CaMn(CO_3)_2$	4.88	16.36	46° 52′

*Dimensions in angstrom units. †Hypothetical ideal solid solutions of the composition indicated.

Although the structure of aragonite is orthorhombic, it is related to that of calcite. The aragonite structure may also be visualized as consisting of alternating layers of calcium and of carbonate ions; however, the calcium ions form a distorted hexagonal close-packed arrangement in aragonite rather than a cubic close-packed type of array as in calcite, and each layer of carbonate ions consists of two closely spaced parallel planes containing carbonate "triangles" of opposite directional configuration. The c-axis of the orthorhombic cell is perpendicular to the calcium and the carbonate layers. The hexagonal arrangement of calcium ions within each plane results in a pseudohexagonal symmetry for the structure, which is reflected in the morphology of many twinned crystals. The variation of crystallographic parameters within the aragonite group is given in Table 3.

Structure of aragonite

Table 3: Crystallographic Parameters of Minerals of the Aragonite Group

	formula	cation radius*	crystal axes*		
			a_0	b_0	c_0
Aragonite	$CaCO_3$	1.18	4.95	7.95	5.73
Strontianite	$SrCO_3$	1.29	5.13	8.42	6.09
Cerussite	$PbCO_3$	1.33	5.17	8.48	6.13
Witherite	$BaCO_3$	1.47	5.26	8.84	6.56

*Dimensions in angstrom units.

The orthorhombic symmetry of the aragonite structure requires an optically biaxial character. The preservation of the parallel planar arrangement of the carbonate ions, however, results in a marked difference between the index of refraction perpendicular to the planes (1.530 for aragonite) and the indices parallel to the planes (1.680 and 1.685 for aragonite), thus preserving the high birefringence characteristic of the rhombohedral carbonates.

Compositional variations within the aragonite group are not systematic. A complete solid solution series appears to exist between witherite and strontianite. Compositional variations in cerussite are largely unknown; however, only limited substitution of calcium and strontium for lead is observed in natural materials. Appreciable solid solution exists between strontianite and aragonite, but the system is complicated by the metastable nature of the aragonitic materials. Substitution of Ca^{2+} in witherite is severely limited, and the intermediate compounds barytocalcite and alstonite are found. These intermediates, unlike those in the rhombohedral carbonates, bear no simple structural relationship to the isostructural end members. Substitution of cations smaller than calcium is extremely limited in all the members of the aragonite

Figure 5: (Left) Azurite (blue) and reniform masses of malachite from Zacatecas, Mexico. (Centre) Flat rhombohedral crystals of calcite from Anthony's Nose, Hudson River, N.Y. (Right) Divergent needlelike aragonite crystals from Huttenberg, Austria.
By courtesy of the (left) MacFall collection, (centre, right) Illinois State Museum; photographs, (left) Mary A. Root—EB Inc., (centre, right) John H. Gerard—EB Inc.

group. The recently discovered minerals norsethite, benstonite, and burbankite apparently are structurally related to calcite.

Other carbonate minerals. No other carbonate minerals have been investigated as extensively as those of the calcite, dolomite, and aragonite groups. Other isomorphous groups and compositional series are composed of minerals that are only of academic interest. Most other minerals of economic importance are those that have potential use as ores. Of these, the most abundant are malachite and azurite, which are among the more common minerals containing copper. The beauty of crystallized specimens of these minerals (see Figure 5) has always attracted collectors, and polished malachite has often been used as an ornamental material.

Carbonates as a source of rare-earth elements

Bastnaesite and related minerals in class 4 are among the more important sources of rare-earth elements. The chemical formulas for these minerals typically indicate only one rare-earth element, usually cerium, lanthanum, or yttrium; however, most rare-earth elements are present in solid solution. The series parisite–roentgenite–synchisite is interesting in that these minerals are intermediate, both compositionally and structurally, between bastnaesite and vaterite, a third polymorph of $CaCO_3$ that has no known stability field (conditions that govern stable occurrence).

The extremely rare uranium and uranyl carbonates rutherfordine (class 1); andersonite, swartzite, bayleyite, liebigite (all class 2); rabbittite (class 4); and schroeckingerite (class 5) have been identified as secondary minerals, forming on exposed surfaces of uranium-bearing rocks used as ores. Since most of these minerals are soluble in water, they are found only in arid regions. These minerals are characterized by bright yellow-green colour and intense fluorescence under ultraviolet radiation.

Another group of genetically related minerals are the alkali carbonates and bicarbonates, most commonly thermonatrite, natron, pirssonite, gaylussite (all class 2); trona, nahcolite (class 3); and northupite (class 4). These minerals also are characterized by relatively high solubilities in water, and typically are found in saline evaporite deposits. Such deposits occasionally are sufficiently large to permit the use of trona as an ore of sodium.

OCCURRENCE OF THE CARBONATE MINERALS

Effect of temperature, pressure, humidity, and acidity

Stability considerations. The formation of carbonate minerals in natural environments is severely limited by their breakdown, especially at elevated temperatures. Several of the hydrated carbonates are stable only in high humidity environments and readily decompose to lower hydrates or to anhydrous compounds at lower humidities. Practically all hydrated carbonates, all acid carbonates, and most carbonates containing hydroxide or halide ions decompose to anhydrous carbonates or to oxides at relatively low temperatures (less than 300° C). Accordingly, these minerals, which constitute the vast majority of species of carbonate minerals, are found only in surface or near-surface environments. The thermal stability of hydrates and hydroxycarbonates is increased somewhat by elevated water pressures; consequently, such minerals may form in low-temperature hydrothermal or metasomatic (mineral–replacement) deposits.

The anhydrous normal carbonates are the most refractory of all the carbonates, but even these minerals decompose at elevated temperatures. The stability relations are also affected by the presence of water; calcite has been found to begin melting at approximately 750° C in the presence of water at a pressure of one kilobar.

Considerations of the relative abundances of the various elements in the Earth's crust and the thermal stabilities of the various carbonates explains the ubiquitous nature of the calcium and magnesium carbonates, the relatively common occurrence of iron and manganese carbonates, and the relative rarity of all other carbonate minerals.

Because the majority of carbonate minerals are deposited from aqueous solutions, their formation is controlled by solubility relations. The solution chemistry of the carbonates is in turn controlled by the complex behaviour of the carbonate ion in solution. Dissolution of a simple carbonate can be represented by the dissociation reaction:

$$MCO_3\,(\text{solid}) = M^{2+} + CO^{2-}_3\,(\text{aqueous});$$

however, in aqueous solution the carbonate ion immediately hydrolyzes:

$$CO^{2-}_3 + H_2O = HCO_3^- + OH^-.$$

Thus, an increase in the pH of an equilibrated solution will result in precipitation of the solid carbonate while acidification will cause further dissolution of the solid. This situation is further complicated by the presence of dissolved carbon dioxide in most natural water, yielding carbonic acid:

$$CO_2\,(\text{gas}) + H_2O = H^+ + HCO_3^-.$$

Because the solubility of CO_2, forming acidic solutions, is increased by high pressures and low temperatures, these factors also increase the solubility of the solid carbonate minerals in CO_2-saturated solutions. Conversely, an increase in temperature or a decrease in pressure will cause a saturated solution to precipitate solid carbonates.

Carbonates in igneous and metamorphic rocks. Occurrences of carbonate minerals in igneous rocks are for the most part limited to the most refractory compounds: calcite, dolomite, and magnesite. Calcite frequently is found filling the cavities in amygdular basalts and occasionally is found filling huge cavities in basalt. The large, optically perfect cleavage fragments from Iceland, with which the discoveries of double refraction and of polarization of light were made, occur in this manner. In reference to the type locality, all cleavage rhombs of transparent, colourless calcite are referred to as the variety Iceland spar. Calcite and dolomite occur as primary igneous minerals in the rare but geologically important rocks kimberlite and carbonatite. Carbonatites also may include ankerite, siderite, and small amounts of the bastnaesite group of rare-earth carbonates. Certain recent carbonatite flows have crystallized carbonates containing sodium and potassium as well as calcium. Magnesite occurs as an igneous mineral in the rock-type sagvandite and has been found in some basic lava flows.

Similarly, occurrences of carbonates in metamorphic rocks (*q.v.*) consist predominantly of the refractory calcium and magnesium carbonates. Magnesite most commonly forms as an alteration product of magnesium-rich peridotites and serpentinites. Metamorphism of carbonate sediments typically results in recrystallization to form calcite or dolomite marbles, often in massive deposits such as those of the Dolomite Alps in the South Tyrol. Metamorphism of impure carbonate sediments may result in the formation of complex minerals such as spurrite and tilleyite (class 6). Increasing amounts of other minerals (especially silica or silicates) and increasing temperatures cause breakdown of the carbonates, either by chemical reaction or by simple thermal decomposition; and mineral associations with calcite and dolomite are used as indicators of the degree of metamorphism.

Carbonates in sedimentary rocks. The principal occurrences of carbonates are in sediments and sedimentary rocks (*q.v.*). Many modern marine sediments (*q.v.*) are composed largely or entirely of carbonate minerals, primarily calcite, metastable magnesian calcite, and aragonite. The vast majority of these materials are formed by the action of marine organisms. Large deposits of carbonate muds consist of the discarded exoskeletons of microscopic organisms such as Foraminifera, pteropoda, and coccolithophorida. Ancient deposits of this sort are represented by chalk, such as that forming the White Cliffs of Dover. Other carbonate accumulations of biological origin include coral reefs, such as those still active in the mid-Pacific atolls and the Great Barrier Reef of Australia, and sediments consisting of shell material from a variety of invertebrates. The mineral composition of these materials is interesting, because the highly magnesian calcites (characteristic of lower orders of organisms, particularly algae) and aragonites (typically formed by higher organisms) represent metastable forms. Most organisms secrete only one mineral (either aragonite or a calcite) that is characteristic of the species; however, the shells of certain mollusks consist of alternating layers of calcite and aragonite, and some cephalopods deposit different minerals in different parts of the skeleton (see also LIMESTONES AND DOLOMITES; ELEMENTS, PHYSIOLOGICAL CONCENTRATION OF).

Sediments and rocks of marine origin

These carbonate sediments tend to become compacted and consolidated, forming limestones. Such postdepositional changes, generally referred to as diagenesis, may involve simple cementation of shell material by further deposition of $CaCO_3$ or may involve a complete recrystallization by essentially simultaneous dissolution and redeposition, a process that may obliterate the shell outlines. Such limestones are abundant and widespread, often forming extensive deposits, and are frequently known to be precursors of extensive metamorphic deposits.

Dolomite also occurs in abundant, extensive deposits, frequently containing fossil shell material of the same sort found in limestones. These deposits constitute one of the major problems of carbonate geochemistry, for such deposits are unquestionably of sedimentary origin. Yet nowhere on Earth are similar deposits being formed today, and experimental studies have consistently failed to synthesize ordered dolomite under conditions available in natural sedimentary environments. It is generally thought that these formations were originally deposited as calcium carbonate sediments and were diagenetically converted into dolomite, perhaps by the action of magnesium-rich solutions. Such dolomitization, however, must either invoke conditions during past geologic ages that no longer exist or it must proceed so slowly that it is unobservable in modern sediments.

Dolomite in the process of formation recently has been discovered in a number of restricted localities, all characterized by the presence of hypersaline solutions. These are typically evaporite-type deposits (see EVAPORITES), which also may produce the much rarer soluble alkali carbonates and bicarbonates. The relationship between these modern dolomites and the widespread older dolomites is uncertain. It may be that the shallow epicontinental seas that are considered to have been prevalent in the past developed higher temperatures, higher salinities, and higher Mg^{++}/Ca^{++} ratios in solution than are now available in the deep oceans. These are all factors that increase the rate of dolomitization.

Carbonate in fresh water and in caves

Extensive non-marine carbonate deposits that are collectively referred to as travertine are formed from springs, rivers, lakes, and in caves. Many lake deposits result from the action of calcareous algae; but much travertine is considered to be of inorganic origin, typically precipitated from carbonate-saturated subsurface or spring water. As subsurface water, acidified by dissolved carbon dioxide, seeps through preexisting limestone strata, it dissolves calcium carbonate, often creating caverns. Occasionally vast networks of underground passages are formed, such as those of Mammoth Cave in Kentucky and the Carlsbad Caverns in New Mexico. In all probability, many other systems exist that have no surface entrances but may be revealed by sinkholes at the surface, caused by the collapse of underground chambers. During the initial stages of cave formation, the process of dissolution predominates; during later stages deposition frequently occurs as the carbonate-saturated water slowly evaporates or loses carbon dioxide (CO_2) as it enters the cavern. Such cave deposits (speleothems) include stalactites and stalagmites, flowstone, and rock-milk and are usually composed of calcite or aragonite, rarely of dolomite (see also CAVES AND CAVE SYSTEMS).

Frequently, carbonate-saturated groundwater (*q.v.*) reaches the surface, forming springs and spring-fed streams and lakes (see SPRINGS AND WELLS). As the water loses CO_2, solid carbonates are precipitated, forming travertine. These deposits may be porous and spongy or may be compact varieties, often banded due to inclusion of impurities along the "growing" surface (alabaster, Mexican onyx).

Other types of occurrence. In arid regions, such groundwater may evaporate at the surface, depositing dissolved carbonate materials as a duricrust (a hardened crust) known as calcrete. In semiarid climates, as the groundwater rises toward the surface, calcium carbonate precipitates between soil particles, cementing them together to form a deposit known as caliche. If the soil material is calcareous, the material formed by such recrystallization and cementation is called nari.

These various modes of occurrence account for the bulk of the common carbonates but not for the majority of carbonate mineral species. A number of the carbonate minerals are of exotic origin; fairchildite and buetschliite, for example, are known only from clinkers formed by fusion of wood ash in lightning-struck trees. Most carbonates are formed either by deposition from hydrothermal fluids or by metasomatic alteration of other minerals. Thus, the calcite-group minerals (calcite, magnesite, siderite, rhodochrosite, and cobaltocalcite) typically occur in relatively low-temperature hydrothermal veins; whereas smithsonite, otavite, and gaspeite occur predominantly as replacement minerals. Other carbonates occurring as primary hydrothermal minerals include witherite, strontianite, hydromagnesite, and dawsonite. The remaining carbonates, including many economically important species, usually are considered to be secondary minerals, formed either by the action of carbonated water upon metallic elements such as the sulfide minerals (*q.v.*) or by reaction between metal-bearing solutions and other carbonate deposits. Secondary carbonate minerals that typically occur in the oxidized zone of ore deposits (*q.v.*) include cerussite, malachite, azurite, bismutite, beyerite, lanthanite, zaratite, phosgenite, hydrozincite, and aurichalcite. Most sedimentary dolomite and siderite is considered to be of secondary origin, replacing original calcite or aragonite.

Carbonates in ore deposits

EXPERIMENTAL STUDIES

As new mineral species are discovered, their physical and chemical properties must be studied in sufficient detail to distinguish them from established species. Typically, such studies include the determination of the chemical composition, variations in composition, crystallographic parameters, optical characteristics, and various other physical properties such as specific gravity, hardness, colour, streak, etc. Further studies may include synthesis of the compound and the determination of the crystal structure. Virtually all of the carbonate minerals have been studied to this extent but a few (*e.g.*, kutnahorite, alstonite, huntite, shortite) have resisted attempts at synthesis, and several do not form crystals of sufficient size or perfection to allow structural analysis.

The calcium and magnesium carbonates and the other members of their isostructural groups have been the subjects of extensive investigation. The most important of these studies have been the experimental determinations of phase relations including the decomposition relations already mentioned, polymorphism, solubility studies, and phase relations among the several members of the groups. Of these studies, the most interesting and perhaps the most important are those dealing with the polymorphism of calcium carbonate and with the equilibrium phase relations in the system $CaCO_3$–$MgCO_3$.

Stability fields and their significance

Polymorphism of calcium carbonate. Calcite II is believed to have a structure similar to that of calcite, but the carbonate triangles are randomly rotated. It rapidly inverts to calcite I (normal calcite) and therefore is never observed under earth-surface conditions. Aragonite is shown to be stable only at very high pressures. Its structure is sufficiently different from that of calcite, however, so that once formed, aragonite may persist for long periods in the calcite stability field without inverting. Another polymorph, calcite III, exists at even higher pressures (above 17 kilobars at 25° C) but, like calcite II, immediately inverts to calcite I at lower pressures. Vaterite, which is known as a mineral and frequently occurs as a transient phase during laboratory precipitation of calcium carbonate, is not a stable phase in the range of pressures and temperatures thus far investigated and may be an example of a substance with no true stability field.

The equilibrium relations indicate that aragonite is stable with respect to calcite only under conditions that are rarely encountered on earth. The high pressures required for aragonite stability are met at greater depths within the earth's crust; however at these depths the temperature is considered to be sufficiently high that the stable phase must be either calcite I or calcite II. The conditions of high pressure at moderate temperatures necessary for the stable formation of aragonite occasionally may be met during metamorphism, but certainly the biogenic and inorganic sedimentary aragonites must be forming metastably, and recent experimental results indicate that some metamorphic aragonite also may form metastably within the calcite stability field.

Calcite-dolomite-magnesite equilibria. Figure 6 shows the equilibrium relationships between calcite, dolomite, and magnesite. At low temperatures, solid solution in magnesite and in dolomite is negligible and is small in calcite. The order-disorder (degree of ordering) relationship between high-temperature magnesian calcites and dolomite is not known with certainty; the dashed line separating the two fields in the diagram represents the limiting conditions under which ordering reflections appear in the X-ray patterns of dolomite. The most interesting aspect of the diagram is the implication that at lower temperatures, namely those encountered in sedimentary environments, the stable assemblages of intermediate compositions consist of mixtures of the essentially pure compounds. Thus, the magnesian calcites (often containing more than 10 mole percent magnesium) formed by many organisms are, like the aragonite formed by others, unstable under the conditions of formation. Furthermore, additional studies have shown that dolomite is the only solid carbonate that is thermodynamically stable in contact with solutions of the approximate composition of sea

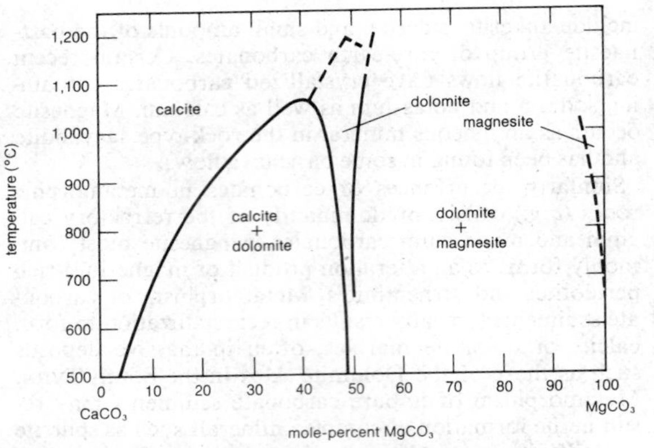

Figure 6: Phase diagram of the system $CaCO_3$–$MGCO_3$, showing the mineral species that are in equilibrium at a particular composition and temperature.
From J. Goldsmith and H. Heard, *Journal of Geology*, vol. 69 (1961); University of Chicago Press

water, which contains more magnesium than calcium. Even pure calcite is metastable when precipitated in sea water; and dolomite, the only stable phase, is almost never observed. In those instances in which dolomite is observed to be forming in hypersaline environments, it typically is calcium-rich and therefore stable only at high temperatures.

Thus the most interesting and puzzling aspects of the carbonate minerals are the frequent occurrences of metastable phases. Similar occurrences are known in other mineral groups, and the formation and persistence of metastable phases may prove to be a much more common phenomenon than is now realized.

BIBLIOGRAPHY. J.D. and E.S. DANA, *The System of Mineralogy*, 7th ed., vol. 2, rewritten and enlarged by C. PALACHE, H. BERMAN, and C. FRONDEL (1951), a classic in mineralogy that provides the most complete listing of carbonate minerals available, including descriptions, properties, occurrences, and references; W.A. DEER, R.A. HOWIE, and J. ZUSSMAN, *Rock Forming Minerals*, vol. 5, *Non-Silicates*, (1962), a modern, comprehensive treatment of the common carbonate minerals, with good bibliography; D.L. GRAF and J.E. LAMAR, "Properties of Calcium and Magnesium Carbonates and Their Bearing on Some Uses of Carbonate Rocks," *Economic Geology*, 50th Anniversary Volume, pp. 639–713 (1955), an extremely detailed review of the physical and chemical properties of the most common carbonate minerals, with extensive bibliography; J.R. GOLDSMITH, "Some Aspects of the Geochemistry of Carbonates," in P.H. ABELSON (ed.), *Researches in Geochemistry* (1959); E. INGERSON, "Problems of the Geochemistry of Sedimentary Carbonate Rocks," *Geochim. Cosmochim. Acta*, 26:815–847 (1962), reviews of the major problems of carbonate geochemistry, including both experimental and field investigations; G.V. CHILINGAR, H.J. BISSELL, and R.W. FAIRBRIDGE (eds.), *Carbonate Rocks: Origin, Occurrence and Classification* (1967), and *Carbonate Rocks: Physical and Chemical Aspects* (1967), two recent collections of review articles on natural occurrences of carbonate minerals.

(A.M.G.)

Carbon Group Elements and Their Compounds

The carbon group of five chemical elements consists of carbon (symbol C, atomic number 6), silicon (symbol Si, atomic number 14), germanium (symbol Ge, atomic number 32), tin (symbol Sn, atomic number 50), and lead (symbol Pb, atomic number 82); they comprise Group IVa in the arrangement of elements known as the periodic table (see PERIODIC LAW). Except for germanium, all of these elements are familiar in daily life either as the pure element or in the form of compounds, although, except for silicon, none is particularly plentiful in the Earth's crust. Carbon forms an almost infinite variety of compounds, in both the plant and animal kingdoms. Silicon and silicate minerals are fundamental components of the Earth's crust; silica (silicon dioxide) is sand. Tin and lead, with abundances in the crust lower than those of some so-called rare elements, are nevertheless common in everyday life. They occur in highly concentrated mineral deposits, can be obtained easily in the metallic state from those minerals, and are useful as metals and as alloys in many applications. Germanium, on the other hand, forms few characteristic minerals and is most commonly found only in small concentrations in association with the mineral zinc blende and in coals. Although germanium is indeed one of the rarer elements, it assumed importance upon recognition of its properties as a semiconductor (*i.e.*, limited ability to conduct electricity).

Carbon as an element was discovered by the first man to handle charcoal from his fire; thus, together with sulfur, iron, tin, lead, copper, mercury, silver, and gold, carbon was one of the small group of elements well known in the ancient world. Modern carbon chemistry dates from the development of coals, petroleum, and natural gas as fuels and from the elucidation of synthetic organic chemistry, both of these branches having been substantially developed since the 1800s.

Amorphous elemental silicon was first obtained in a state of purity in 1824 by the Swedish chemist Jöns Jacob Berzelius; impure silicon had already been obtained in 1811. Crystalline elemental silicon was not prepared until 1854, when it was obtained as a product of electrolysis. In the form of rock crystal, however, silicon was familiar to the predynastic Egyptians, who used it for beads and small vases; to the early Chinese; and probably to many others of the ancients. The manufacture of glass containing silica was carried out both by the Egyptians—at least as early as 1500 BC—and by the Phoenicians. Certainly, many of the naturally occurring compounds called silicates were used in various kinds of mortar for construction of dwellings by the earliest men.

Mendeleyev's prediction

Germanium is one of three elements the existence of which was predicted in 1871 by the Russian chemist Dmitry Ivanovich Mendeleyev when he first devised his periodic table. Not until 1886, however, was germanium identified as one of the elements in a newly found mineral.

The origins of tin also are lost in antiquity. Apparently, bronzes, which are copper–tin alloys, were used by man in prehistory long before pure tin metal itself was isolated. Bronzes were common in early Mesopotamia, the Indus Valley, Egypt, Crete, Israel, and Peru. Much of the tin used by the early Mediterranean peoples apparently came from the Scilly Islands and from Cornwall in the British Isles, where tin mining dates to at least 300–200 BC. Tin mines were operating in both the Inca and Aztec domains of South and Central America before the Spanish conquest.

Lead is mentioned often in early Biblical accounts. The Babylonians used the metal as plates on which to record inscriptions. The Romans used it for tablets, water pipes, coins, and even cooking utensils; indeed, as a result of the last use, lead poisoning was recognized in the time of Augustus Caesar. The compound known as white lead was apparently prepared as a decorative pigment at least as early as 200 BC. Modern developments date to the exploitation in the late 1700s of deposits in the Missouri–Kansas–Oklahoma area in the United States.

This article is divided into the following sections:

I. Comparative chemistry of the carbon group elements

The properties of the carbon elements and their compounds are best discussed by reference to their atomic structures.

ELECTRONIC STRUCTURE

The atoms of a specific element have an identical number of positive charges on the nucleus, and this number is balanced by an equal number of negatively charged electrons moving around the nucleus, attraction between electrons and nucleus overcoming repulsion among the electrons. The number of positive charges is called the atomic number of the element. In the periodic table (see the Figure) the elements are arranged sequentially in order of their atomic numbers. As the nuclei increase in size, the increasing number of electrons moving about the nucleus occupy an orderly arrangement of orbitals (regions of maximum probability for occurrence of electrons of particular characteristics) or energy levels. These are organized into concentric shells numbered from one to seven, proceeding outward from the nucleus, with an increasing number of subshells, designated by the letters *s, p, d, f* (the letters themselves being of no special significance). The number of electrons within each subshell is generally indicated by a superscript. Thus, $4s^2$ indicates the two *s* electrons in the fourth shell. Each subshell is capable of holding only a limited number of electrons, viz., 2 in an *s* subshell, 6 in a *p*, 10 in a *d*, and 14 in an *f*. The first shell (closest to the nucleus) includes only an *s* subshell, or orbital. Therefore, it can contain only two electrons. The second shell holds both *s* and *p* orbitals, or eight electrons. Shell number three can hold *s*, *p*, and *d* orbitals, for a total of 18 electrons. The atoms of the carbon group elements have in common an identical arrangement of electrons in their outermost (valence) shell. As shown in Table 1, the outermost shell of carbon has the arrangement $2s^22p^2$, and that of lead has $6s^26p^2$.

Periodic table

No outermost shell of any atom contains more than eight electrons, called an octet. The element next in the table must add an electron in a new shell, but, after one or two electrons are positioned in the outermost *s* orbital of the 4th and higher shells, the inner octet may resume accepting electrons until it has acquired its allotted maxi-

Table 1: Some Properties of Carbon Group Elements

	carbon	silicon	germanium	tin	lead
Atomic number	6	14	32	50	82
Atomic weight	12.011	28.086	72.59	118.69	207.19
Colour of element	colourless (diamond, D), black (graphite, G)	gray	white metallic	white metallic (beta, β), gray (alpha, α)	bluish-white metallic
Melting point (°C)	>3,500 (D)	1,420	937.4	231.9 (α)	327.5
Boiling point (°C)	4,827 (D)	2,355	2,830	2,270 (α)	1,744
Density Liquid (g/ml)				6.97 (231.9° C)	10.51 (400° C)
Solid	3.51 (D), 2.25 (G)	2.33 (25° C)	5.323 (25° C)	5.75 (α), 7.28 (β)	11.35 (20° C)
Oxidation states	−4, (+2), +4	−4, (+2), +4	−4, +2, +4	(−4), +2, +4	(−4), +2, +4
Electronic configuration	(He) $2s^2 2p^2$	(Ne) $3s^2 3p^2$	(Ar) $3d^{10} 4s^2 4p^2$	(Kr) $4d^{10} 5s^2 5p^2$	(Xe) $4f^{14} 5d^{10} 6s^2 6p^2$
Isotopic abundance (terrestrial, percent)	^{12}C (98.89), ^{13}C (1.11)	^{28}Si (92.21), ^{29}Si (4.70), ^{30}Si (3.09)	^{70}Ge (20.53) ^{72}Ge (27.43) ^{73}Ge (7.76) ^{74}Ge (36.54) ^{76}Ge (7.76)	^{112}Sn (0.96), ^{114}Sn (0.66), ^{115}Sn (0.35), ^{116}Sn (14.3), ^{117}Sn (7.61), ^{118}Sn (24.03), ^{119}Sn (8.58), ^{120}Sn (32.85), ^{122}Sn (4.72), ^{124}Sn (5.94)	^{204}Pb (1.48), ^{206}Pb (23.6), ^{207}Pb (22.6), ^{208}Pb (52.3)
Radioactive isotopes (mass numbers)	10, 11, 14, 15, 16	25–27, 31, 32	65–69, 71, 75, 77, 78	108–111, 113, 121, 123, 125–128	194–203, 205, 209–214
Heat of fusion (kcal/g-atom)		11.1	7.3	1.69	1.21
Heat of vaporization (kcal/g-atom)	170 (G)	71	78	61.8	42.3
Heat of sublimation (kcal/g-atom)	170	85		78	47.5
Heat capacity (cal/mole °C)	1.462 (D), 2.038 (G)	5.086 (0–100° C)	5.372	6.29 (25° C)	6.53 (15–327.5° C)
Critical temperature (°C)		about 4,920			
Critical pressure (atm)		1,450			
Electrical resistivity (microhm-cm)	1,375.0	10		11	20.648
Hardness (Mohs scale)	10 (D) 0.5–1.5 (G)	7	6	1.5–1.8	1.5
Crystal structure	cubic (D) hexagonal (G)	cubic (diamond)	cubic (diamond)	cubic (diamond, α) tetragonal (β)	close-packed, metallic
Radius					
Covalent (Å)	0.772	1.17	1.22	1.40	
Metallic (Å)			1.22	1.40	1.54
Ionic (Å)	2.60 (M^{4-}), 0.16 (M^{4+})	2.71 (M^{4-}), 0.42 (M^{4+})	2.72 (M^{4-}), 0.73 (M^{2+}), 0.53 (M^{4+})	2.94 (M^{4-}), 0.93 (M^{2+}), 0.71 (M^{4+})	1.20 (M^{2+}), 0.84 (M^{4+})
Ionization energy (kcal/g-atom)					
First	261	189	184	171	172
Second	564	378	369	339	348
Third	1,103	773	791	705	738
Fourth	1,486	1,040	1,053	941	(977)
Electronegativity					
(Sanderson)	2.47	1.74	2.31	2.02	2.01
(Pauling)	2.5	1.8	1.8	1.8	1.8

Carbon's electron structure

mum number. In the periodic table, the elements with eight electrons outermost form the group known as the noble gases (Group 0), the least reactive of the elements. The carbon group elements (Group IVa), with four electrons, occupy a middle position. Elements to the left of Group IVa have fewer than four electrons in the valence shell and tend to lose them (with their negative charges) to become positively charged ions, represented by the symbol for the element with a superscript indicating the number and sign of the charges—*e.g.*, Ca^{2+} for the calcium ion; such elements are called metals. The nonmetals (except boron) are in the groups to the right of Group IVa; each has more than four electrons in its outermost shell and tends to acquire electrons to complete its octet, forming negatively charged ions; *e.g.*, oxygen adds two electrons to its six, forming the ion O^{2-}.

Chemical reactions result from the exchange of electrons among atoms. In general, if a metal loses its few valence electrons to a nonmetal, the resulting oppositely charged ions are attracted to one another and form a bond, classified as ionic or electrovalent. Two nonmetals, neither of which can actually lose its valence electrons in chemical reaction, may nevertheless share them in pairs in such a way that what is called a covalent bond results. Metal atoms will bond to one another in a third type of bond, which releases their valence electrons in a way that allows them to conduct electricity.

All the carbon group atoms, having four valence electrons, form covalent bonds with nonmetal atoms; carbon and silicon cannot lose or gain electrons to form free ions, whereas germanium, tin, and lead do form metallic ions but only with two positive charges. Even lead, the most metallic of the carbon group atoms, cannot actually lose all four of its valence electrons, because, as each one is removed, the remainder are held more strongly by the increased positive charge. Because the distinction between covalent and electrovalent (ionic) bonds is often a matter of convenience for the chemist, and because the actual bond structure within a molecule may be quite complicated, it is often useful instead simply to count the total number of electrons an element gains or loses in bonding without regard to the nature of the bonds. This number is called the oxidation number, or oxidation state, of the element; many elements have more than one oxidation state possible, each oxidation state being found in different compounds. The oxidation state of an element is written as a Roman numeral following the name of the element in a compound—*e.g.*, lead(II) means lead in oxidation state plus two; with the chemical symbol of the element, the oxidation state may be written as a superscript, as in Pb^{II}. Covalent bonds generally are considered to be formed by interaction of the orbitals (generally, only the *s*, *p*, and *d* orbitals) in specific and varied ways. The most common are called sigma and pi bonds, written σ and π, respectively. The sigma bonds are symmetrical with respect to the axis of the bond, whereas the pi bonds are not. Examples of sigma and pi bonding as well as ionic bonding are found among the compounds of the elements of the carbon group. (For a full general discussion and further information useful to an understanding of the following sections, see CHEMICAL BONDING; CHEMICAL REACTIONS; ATOMIC STRUCTURE; and PERIODIC LAW.)

GENERAL PROPERTIES OF THE GROUP

The properties of the carbon group elements and those of their compounds are intermediate between properties associated with the elements of the adjacent boron and nitrogen groups. In all groups the metallic properties, resulting from the tendency to hold valence electrons more loosely, increase with atomic number. Within the carbon group, more than in any other, the change from nonmetallic to metallic character with increasing atomic number is particularly apparent. Carbon is a true nonmetal in every sense. Lead is a true metal. Silicon is almost completely nonmetallic; tin is almost completely metallic. Germanium is metallic in appearance and in a number of its other physical properties (see Table 1), but the properties of many of its compounds are those of derivatives of nonmetals. These changes are consequences of increase in atomic size with substantial screening of the larger nuclear charge by intervening electronic shells, as evidenced by decrease in ionization energy (see Table 1) (energy required to remove an electron) and electronegativity power to attract electrons) with increasing atomic number.

Metals and nonmetals of the group

Crystal structure. In the solid state, elemental carbon, silicon, germanium, and gray tin (defined as alpha [α] tin; see Table 1) exist as cubic crystals, based upon a three-dimensional arrangment of bonds. Each atom is covalently bonded to four neighbouring atoms in such a way that they form the corners of a tetrahedron (a solid consisting of four three-sided faces). A practical result is that no discrete small molecules of these elements, such as those formed by nitrogen, phosphorus, or arsenic, can be distinguished; instead, any solid particle or fragment of one of these elements, irrespective of size, is uniformly bonded throughout, and, therefore, the whole fragment can be considered as a giant molecule. Decreasing melting points, boiling points, and decreasing heat energies associated with fusion (melting), sublimation (change from solid to gas), and vaporization (change from liquid to gas) among these four elements, with increasing atomic number and atomic size, indicate a parallel weakening of the covalent bonds in this type of structure. The actual or probable arrangement of valence electrons is often impossible to determine, and, instead, relative energy states of the electrons, in the ground, or least energetic, state of the atom are considered. Thus, the same trend of nonmetallic toward metallic states is indicated by decreasing hardness and decreasing single-bond energy between atoms. Carbon crystallizes in two forms, as diamond and as graphite; diamond stands apart from all other elemental forms in the extreme stability of its crystal structure, whereas graphite has a layer structure. As may be expected, cleavage between layers of graphite is much easier to effect than rupture within a layer. The crystal structures of white beta (β) tin and elemental lead are clearly metallic structures. In a metal, the valence electrons are free to move from atom to atom, and they give the metal its electrical conductivity.

Uses. All the carbon group elements and many of their compounds have important uses. Carbon as diamond, for example, is the most expensive and brilliant of all the natural gemstones and also the hardest of abrasives; carbon as graphite is important as electrodes in electrochemical cells, as a lubricant, and, in microcrystalline and nearly amorphous form, as a black pigment, an adsorbent, a fuel, a filler for rubber, and in pencils. Coals are elemental carbon mixed with varying amounts of carbon compounds; coke and charcoal are nearly pure carbon. All organic compounds, such as proteins, carbohydrates, and fats, contain carbon, and all plant and animal cells consist of carbon compounds and their polymers. (Polymers are macromolecules consisting of many simple molecules bonded together in specific ways.) Carbonate minerals are important sources of various metals, such as sodium, magnesium, calcium, copper, and lead.

The almost infinite number of carbon compounds

Elemental silicon is important largely as a semiconductor. Silica (silicon dioxide) is useful as an abrasive, in the production of glass and other ceramic bodies, as an adsorbent, and as sand in mortars and concretes; and these are only a few of its applications. Both naturally occurring and synthetically produced silicates are important in ceramics, building materials, absorbents, and ion exchangers.

Applications of germanium have been limited to semiconducting devices, indicating its weak metallic nature.

Tin-plating of iron protects the latter from corrosion; tin piping and valves maintain purity in water and beverages; molten tin is the base for (float) plateglass production; and tin is a significant component of such alloys as bronzes, pewter, bearing metals, type metals, and lead-based solders. Tin exists in two oxidation states; tin(IV) oxide is useful in making ceramic bodies opaque, as a mild abrasive, and as a weighting agent for fabrics; tin(II) fluoride and tin(II) pyrophosphate are used in dentifrices. Organic tin compounds act as stabilizers in certain plastics and as wood preservatives.

Elemental lead finds extensive use. Together with the compound lead(IV) oxide and with lead–antimony or lead–calcium alloys, it is employed in common storage batteries. Type metals, bearing alloys, shot metal, and fusible alloys all contain lead. Tetraethyllead is the most important antiknock additive to motor fuels.

Electron configurations and valences. *Ionic valences.* The composition of any compound, radical, ion, complex, polymer, and so on is represented by its formula, which states the number and kinds of atoms bonded into the molecule or fragment of molecule. The formula lists the atoms by the symbols of the elements and indicates the number of atoms with subscripts following the symbols. Carbon dioxide (CO_2), for example, is a compound, the molecules of which consist of one atom of carbon and two of oxygen. Molecules of carbon monoxide (CO) contain one atom of carbon and one of oxygen. The composition of the most complicated molecule can thus be clearly stated in its formula. When a series of compounds have the same general formula, it can be expressed in general terms. All the alkanes (one of the hydrocarbon families of organic compounds), for example, have two more than twice as many hydrogen atoms as carbon atoms: CH_4, C_2H_6, C_3H_8, and so on. The general formula can therefore be written C_nH_{2n+2}. Also, if a simple molecule such as sugar, $C_6H_{12}O_6$, polymerizes (*i.e.*, links together in thousands of repeated bonds, in this case with the loss of H_2O from each such monomer), the formula of the resulting macromolecule may be written $(-C_6H_{10}O_5-)_n$, the subscript n representing any number.

The ground-state electronic configurations (see Table 1) of atoms of these carbon group elements show that each has four electrons in its outermost shells. As has been explained, if n represents the outermost shell (n being two for carbon, three for silicon, etc.), then these four electrons are represented by the symbols ns^2np^2. Such a configuration suggests the importance of referring to the relatively stable noble-gas-atom configuration preceding each element in determining the properties of the element, in particular its chemical properties. The loss of four electrons by either a carbon atom or a silicon atom to give ions having a positive charge of four (or $+4$, written C^{4+} or Si^{4+}) with the electron configurations of the preceding noble-gas atoms (see the Figure: helium and neon) is precluded by the sizable ionization energies as shown in Table 1. Ions of $+4$ charge do not exist, nor is there any evidence that carbon or silicon ions of charge $+2$ can form by the loss of only two unpaired (np, or outermost) electrons. Electron loss by atoms of the heavier elements of the family is easier, but it cannot lead to ions with noble-gas-atom configurations because of the presence of underlying (*i.e.*, d^{10}) arrangements of electrons inside the outermost shell. It is again unlikely that the $+4$ ions of germanium, tin, and lead (in symbols Ge^{4+}, Sn^{4+}, and Pb^{4+}) exist in known compounds, but it is true that the inertness of the ns^2 pair of electrons (which

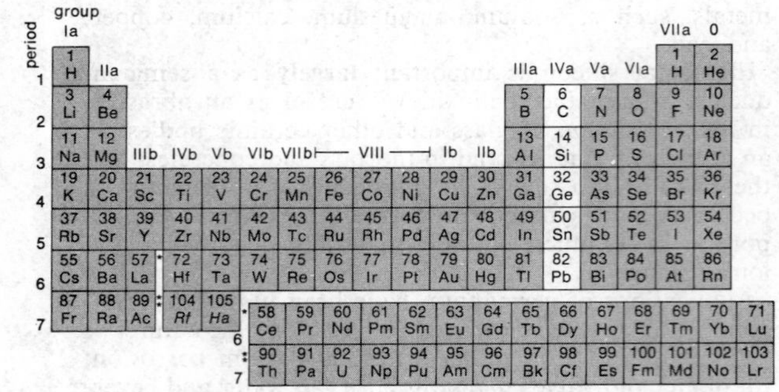

The carbon group elements in the periodic table.

are, in terms of energy states, closer to the nucleus than the np^2 pair) increases substantially with increasing atomic number in the family and thus allows the np^2 electrons to be removed separately, to form at least the ions, Sn^{2+} and Pb^{2+}. Positive two and four oxidation states can be assigned in covalent unions of each of these elements with elements that are more electronegative (*i.e.*, having greater affinity for electrons). Typical examples for the group include (1) for the +2 state: carbon monoxide (CO), silicon monoxide (SiO), germanium dichloride ($GeCl_2$), tin monoxide (SnO), and lead monoxide (PbO); and (2) for the +4 state: carbon dioxide (CO_2), carbon tetrachloride (CCl_4), silicon tetrafluoride (SiF_4), silicate(IV) ion (SiO_4^{4-}), germanium tetrabromide ($GeBr_4$), tin tetrachloride ($SnCl_4$), hexahydroxostannate(IV) ion [$Sn(OH)_6^{2-}$], and lead dioxide (PbO_2). A true negative four (−4) anion is probably limited to carbon, and it is formed only among groups of atoms constituting molecules of certain compounds in which it would be the most electronegative and smallest atom in the group. Crystals of the methanide-type carbides, of which aluminum carbide (Al_4C_3) is a typical example, undoubtedly contain C^{4-} ions. No single atom or monatomic −2 ion (*e.g.*, C^{2-}) is known for any of the elements of the family. A formal −4 state exists in some covalent unions with less electronegative elements; *e.g.*, in methane (CH_4).

Covalences. Among the covalent compounds, 4-covalent examples predominate. In each of these species, four bonds, each formed by the sharing of an electron pair with another atom, are arranged tetrahedrally (toward the four corners of a tetrahedron) about the central atom of any element in the carbon group. The ground state, or lowest energy state, of the electronic arrangement indicated by ns^2np^2 does not suggest either the existence of four bonds or their observed geometrical distribution. The excited configuration, or higher energy state, of these electrons puts one *s* electron into a *p* orbital, to give an outermost arrangement indicated by ns^1np^3. This arrangement could allow for four bonds, but it suggests that three should lie mutually at right angles to each other, with the other, the fourth one (involving the *s* orbital), essentially undirected. It is therefore assumed, to account completely for experimental observation, that the *s* and *p* orbitals combine to produce four hybrid orbitals, each with some *s* and more *p* character, which are then oriented tetrahedrally (*i.e.*, in four directions with identical angles between them) about the central atom. The sp^3 hybrid is characteristic of all 4-covalent compounds of elements of this family—*e.g.*, methane (CH_4), silicon tetrafluoride (SiF_4), germanium tetrachloride ($GeCl_4$), tin tetrabromide ($SnBr_4$), and lead tetrafluoride (PbF_4). In terms of the fact that repulsions among the four bonding pairs of electrons should most reasonably push the four bonded atoms as far apart in space as possible, the observed tetrahedral arrays are also to be expected.

Orbital explanation for bonds

Because in the electronic configuration of carbon the outer shell can hold no more than eight electrons, in one *s* and three *p* orbitals, a covalency larger than four cannot exist for the carbon atom (it has four electrons and can bond covalently only four others to complete its eight). Higher energy orbitals are potentially available for atoms of the other elements of the family because, when *n* is more than two, more complicated *d* orbitals are also possible (3*d* for silicon, 4*d* for germanium, 5*d* for tin, 6*d* for lead), and higher covalences are not then unexpected. Six-covalent combinations, with octahedral geometry (eight-sided configurations derived by six bond directions), are well known and include such species as hexafluorosilicate(IV) ion (SiF_6^{2-}), hexafluorogermanate(IV) ion (GeF_6^{2-}), hexachlorostannate(IV) ion ($SnCl_6^{2-}$) or hexahydroxostannate(IV) ion ($Sn(OH)_6^{2-}$), and hexachloroplumbate(IV) ion ($PbCl_6^{2-}$). These species are said to exemplify bonds that can be described as sp^3d^2 hybridization. Geometrically, six groups about a central species repel each other least when they are octahedrally arranged.

Covalences lower than four are exemplified by compounds such as gaseous carbon monoxide (CO) or silicon monoxide (SiO), carbon dioxide (CO_2), ethylene (C_2H_4), and similar alkene-type organic compounds; acetylene (C_2H_2) and similar alkyne-type organic compounds; germanium(II) chloride ($GeCl_2$); and tin(II) chloride ($SnCl_2$). Molecules of carbon monoxide, silicon monoxide, carbon dioxide, the alkenes, and the alkynes are commonly formulated with multiple bonds between the carbon atoms. If the electrons in the *n* shell are represented by dots around the symbol of the element, examples of multiple bonds can be shown as:

carbon monoxide	:C:::O:,
silicon monoxide	:Si:::O:,
carbon dioxide	Ö::C::Ö,
ethylene	H:C::C:H, (with H H above the carbons)
acetylene	H:C:::C:H,

the number of dots between two symbols signifying the number of electrons shared,—*i.e.*, the pairs shared—in carbon monoxide, three pairs; in silicon monoxide, three pairs; etc.

Bond formation. Described in terms of orbitals, each of these multiple bonds is believed to result from the end-on overlap of two appropriately oriented *p* orbitals to form a sigma (indicated as σ) type of single bond, plus the sidewise overlap of two or four appropriately oriented *p* orbitals to give one or two pi type (indicated as π) of additional bonds. In the ethylene molecule (C_2H_4), for example, the four electrons originally associated with each carbon atom are distributed as: (1) two shared with the *s* electrons of the two hydrogen atoms, as σ-bonds; (2) one shared with the other carbon atom through end-on overlap of singly occupied *p* orbitals as a σ-bond, and (3) one shared with the other carbon atom through sidewise overlap of singly occupied *p* orbitals at right angles to those involved in (2) as a π-bond. For the acetylene molecule (C_2H_2), the structure differs in the presence, for each carbon atom, of only one σ-bond to a hydrogen atom and two π-bonds to the other carbon atom. In the ethylene (C_2H_4) molecule, the arrangement of atoms around each carbon atom is triangular; in the acetylene molecule (C_2H_2), it is collinear (lying in the same straight line). These situations are said to exemplify sp^2 and *sp* hybridizations, respectively. The carbon dioxide molecule is a collinear species in which the central carbon atom is linked by a σ- and a π-bond to each oxygen atom. In the carbon monoxide and gaseous silicon monoxide molecules, the carbon group element is linked to the oxygen atom by one σ- and two π-bonds.

The sigma and pi bonds

The gaseous germanium dichloride ($GeCl_2$) and tin dichloride ($SnCl_2$) molecules are V-shaped entities that can be formulated electronically as

:Cl: M̈ :Cl: ,

in which M represents either germanium or tin. Although the covalence is apparently two, it is effectively three, since the unshared pair of electrons appears to occupy a position in which it and the two chlorine atoms are arranged in a planar triangle about the central M atom. The hybridization, including the unshared pair of electrons in the same sense as the bonded pairs, is effectively sp^2. In the solid state, germanium dichloride molecules ($GeCl_2$) form infinite chains through bridging by chlorine atoms.

Catenation. Carbon is unique among the elements in the almost infinite capacity of its atoms to bond to each other in long chains, a process called catenation. This characteristic reflects the strength of the bond between adjacent carbon atoms in the molecule, both in relationship to similar bonds involving other elements of the carbon family and in relationship to bonds between carbon atoms and atoms of many other elements. Only the carbon–hydrogen, carbon–fluorine, and carbon–oxygen single bonds (C–H, C–F, and C–O) are stronger than the carbon–carbon single bond (C–C), and each of these is weaker than the carbon–carbon multiple bonds (C=C or C≡C). On the other hand, the silicon–silicon single bond (Si–Si) is weaker than other single bonds involving an atom of other elements with the silicon atom. The same is undoubtedly true of the germanium–germanium and tin–tin single bonds (Ge–Ge, Sn–Sn) in relationship to single covalent bonds between atoms of these elements and atoms of other elements. Experimentally, there appears to be no practical upper limit to catenation involving carbon. This phenomenon in three dimensions produces the diamond and in two dimensions the layers in graphite. Catenation is also exhibited to a high degree by elemental silicon, germanium, and tin, but it is strictly limited in compounds of these elements; silicon may have up to 14 atoms in a chain; germanium, 9; and tin, 2 or 3 only, largely in hydrides (compounds containing hydrogen). Double and triple bonds in catenated arrangements are limited to carbon.

Silicon chains

Catenation, via single or multiple bonds or both, combined with several other factors allows carbon to form more compounds than any other element. These factors are: (1) the stability of certain carbon bonds, in particular of the C–H bond; (2) the existence of carbon in both sp^2 and sp^3 hybridizations; (3) the ability of carbon to form both chain and cyclic compounds (in which the chain of atoms is joined end to end to form a ring) based upon either carbon atoms alone or carbon atoms in combination with those of other nonmetals (*e.g.*, oxygen, sulfur, nitrogen) and either upon single- or multiple-bond arrangements; and (4) the capability of many carbon compounds to exist in isomeric forms (isomers are molecules with identical numbers of the same atoms bonded in different arrangements; such molecules have quite different properties). All but a very few carbon compounds are called organic compounds, and they are discussed in such other articles as CHEMICAL COMPOUNDS, ORGANIC; POLYMERS; ALKALOIDS; ALDEHYDES AND KETONES; and CARBOXYLIC ACIDS AND THEIR DERIVATIVES.

Atomic size. Reference has been made to some of the physical properties of the carbon group elements (Table 1). Most of the variations in properties from carbon through lead parallel increase in atomic size and are comparable with elements in the boron, nitrogen, oxygen, and fluorine groups. The general trends apparent in Table 1 are roughly those found for the adjacent boron group and nitrogen group elements (see the Figure). The significantly higher melting and boiling points of the carbon group elements reflect their tendency to exist as giant molecules, as opposed to the tendencies of elements in the adjacent families to exist as smaller, discrete molecules.

Special physical properties of carbon

As is true of the lightest element in each group of elements, the physical properties of carbon differ substantially from those of the other members of its family. To a large degree, these differences reflect the substantially higher concentration of the positive charge on the carbon nucleus relative to the size of the carbon atom. That is, the nucleus of carbon holds only six electrons in two shells and, therefore, holds them close; the nucleus of lead, on the other hand, has 82 electrons distributed in six shells. The attraction between the nucleus of lead and its outermost electrons is less than in carbon, because intervening shells in lead shield the outer electrons. Structural differences between diamond and graphite produce profound differences between them in hardness, conductivity, density, heat capacity, and other properties. Inasmuch as graphite is a unique crystalline formation among the elements, its properties should not be compared directly with those of the other elements in the family. It is interesting and worth noting here that boron nitride—a compound formed by the two elements on either side of carbon in the periodic table, with formula $(B–N)_n$, n being any number—is isoelectronic with (has the same number of electrons as) carbon–carbon molecules $(C_2)_n$ and can be prepared in both cubic and hexagonal forms that are structurally analogous, respectively, to the diamond and graphite forms. Like diamond, cubic boron nitride is extremely hard and refractory; like graphite, hexagonal boron nitride is soft and lubricating because of the ease of deformation between layers. Like graphite, hexagonal boron nitride also forms many compounds by trapping metals, nonmetals, covalent compounds, and ionic compounds between layers in its crystal lattice. These formations are called intercalation compounds.

Reactions. Certain of the more common chemical reactions of the carbon group elements are summarized in Table 2. With a given reagent, diamond is generally less reactive than graphite and, thus, requires more rigorous conditions for reaction, such as a higher temperature; the ultimate products, however, are the same. Crystalline silicon is less reactive than finely divided and, possibly, amorphous silicon. Elemental germanium resembles silicon quite closely. Tin and lead behave in general as metals and thus yield at least some ionic products in reactions that are quite different from those of the other elements. Elemental carbon is of particular importance as a

Table 2: Reactions of the Elements

key: x's—excess; NR—no reaction; g—gas; s—solid; aq.—aqueous; dil.—dilute; conc.—concentrated

reagent	product(s)				
	C	Si	Ge	Sn	Pb
F_2	CF_4	SiF_4	GeF_4	SnF_4	PbF_4
Cl_2	CCl_4	$SiCl_4$ (450° C)	$GeCl_4$	$SnCl_4$	$PbCl_4 \rightarrow PbCl_2$
Br_2	CBr_4	$SiBr_4$	$GeBr_4$	$SnBr_4$	$PbBr_4 \rightarrow PbBr_2$
I_2	CI_4	SiI_4	GeI_4	SnI_4	PbI_2
O_2	CO (x's C)	SiO (x's Si)	GeO (x's Ge, 850° C)	SnO_2	PbO (>550° C)
	CO_2 (x's O_2)	SiO_2 (x's O_2)	GeO_2 (x's O_2)		Pb_3O_4 (430° C)
S	CS_2 (>1,000° C)	SiS_2	GeS_2 (1,100° C)	SnS_2	PbS
H_2O	$CO + H_2$ (1,000° C)	$SiO_2 + H_2$			
H_3O^+ (dil. HCl, HBr, H_2SO_4, etc.)	NR	NR	NR	$Sn^{2+} + H_2$	$Pb^{2+} + H_2$
HNO_3 (hot, conc.)	CO_2 (g)	SiO_2 (s)	GeO_2 (s)	SnO_2 (s)	Pb^{2+}
NaOH (hot, aq.)	NR	$SiO_4^{4-} + H_2$	$HGeO_3^- + H_2$	$Sn(OH)_6^{2-} + H_2$	$HPbO_2^- + H_2$
HF (aq.)	NR	$H_2SiF_6 + H_2$	$H_2GeF_6 + H_2$	$SnF_2 + H_2$	$PbF_2 + H_2$
Metal oxide	metal + CO or CO_2	metal + SiO_2	—	—	—
Metals	carbides	silicides	germanides	alloys	alloys

Carbon in metallurgy

high-temperature reducing agent (a reagent that donates electrons) in metallurgical processing for metal oxides, a reaction that frees the metal. Thus to cite only a few of carbon's more important applications, carbon is used directly in the production of elemental phosphorus, arsenic, bismuth, tin, lead, zinc, and cadmium, and indirectly, as carbon monoxide, in the production of iron. Elemental silicon, in the iron–silicon alloy ferrosilicon, is also a strong reducing agent and has been used as such to liberate magnesium from its oxide.

Biological and physiological significance. The biological implications of carbon are so extensive that they can be discussed here only very briefly. All biological substances are based upon compounds in which carbon is combined with other elements, the nature of the combination determining the characteristics, function, and relative importance of the substance. To begin with the inorganic compounds of carbon, elemental carbon is nontoxic. Carbon monoxide (CO) is both more readily absorbed and more firmly bound to the hemoglobin of the blood than is oxygen and is thus, even in small concentrations, a dangerous asphyxiant. Carbon dioxide (CO_2) is an asphyxiant of significance only in relatively large concentrations; in small concentration, it stimulates breathing. Hydrogen cyanide (HCN) and its derivatives (cyanogen compounds, cyanides) are all very toxic as protoplasmic poisons through the inhibition of tissue oxidation. Carbon tetrachloride (CCl_4) and other chlorinated hydrocarbons damage the nervous system. Among organic compounds, the most toxic are derivatives that contain the halogen elements (fluorine, chlorine, bromine and iodine), sulfur, selenium, tellurium, nitrogen, phosphorus, arsenic, lead, and mercury. Most organometallic compounds are toxic, while oxygen-containing derivatives of the hydrocarbons are usually less toxic.

Elemental silicon and most silicon-containing compounds appear to be nontoxic. Indeed, human tissue often contains 6 to 90 milligrams (one milligram equals 0.001 gram) of silica (SiO_2) per 100 grams dry weight, and many plants and lower forms of life assimilate silica and use it in their structures. Inhalation of dusts containing alpha SiO_2, however, produces a serious lung disease called silicosis, common among miners, stonecutters, and ceramic workers, unless protective devices are used.

The toxicology of germanium and its compounds is poorly defined.

Elemental tin is apparently nontoxic, and quantities of tin up to 300 parts per million, as dissolved by foods packaged in tin-plated containers and cooking utensils, are not harmful. Organic tin compounds, however, commonly used as biocides and fungicides, are toxic to human beings.

Although elemental lead and difficultly soluble lead compounds are not absorbed by human tissue and are, therefore, quite innocuous, any soluble lead compound is toxic, with toxicity increasing as solubility increases. Symptoms of lead poisoning include abdominal pain and diarrhea followed by constipation, nausea, vomiting, dizziness, headache, and general weakness. Elimination of contact with a lead source is normally sufficient to effect a cure. The elimination of lead from insecticides and paint pigments and the use of respirators and other protective devices in areas of exposure have reduced lead poisoning materially. Low-level atmospheric and water pollution, stemming largely from the use of tetraethyllead, $[Pb(C_2H_5)_4]$ in motor fuels, was receiving increasing attention in the 1970s.

Tetraethyllead

General compounds. *Hydrides.* The monohydrides of the carbon group of elements, with the general formula MH_4 (in which M represents an atom of carbon, silicon, germanium, or tin), are colourless gases, the thermal stabilities of which decrease substantially with increasing molecular weight. Methane (CH_4) is stable up to relatively high temperatures; the others decompose to their elements at 450° C or below. The monohydrides are all reducing agents (donating electrons, the opposite of oxidizing agents), but methane is an effective reducing agent only at high temperatures. Monosilane (SiH_4) reduces water and many metal ions in aqueous solution. Monogermane (GeH_4) reacts similarly but less vigorously. All burn in air or oxygen. Each is a weak acid, but the acid strength increases with increasing molecular weight.

Catenated hydrides of the general formula M_nH_{2n+2} have similar properties. When M is carbon, *n* has no real upper limit, and this formulation corresponds to the huge family of saturated hydrocarbons, or alkanes. Both straight and branched chains are known, and isomerism is common. The chain may form rings (cyclization) to give compounds with the general formula C_nH_{2n}. When M is silicon, germanium, or tin, *n* is limited because of bond-energy values. Only straight-chain compounds of these elements have been described.

Unsaturated hydrides are known only for carbon; they are representative of the vast families of organic compounds called the alkenes, alkynes, and aromatics.

Halides. All possible compounds of the type MX_4 (X being any halogen element: fluorine, chlorine, bromine, iodine) are known except for the bromide and iodide of lead(IV). These compounds, which are polar covalent substances, are gases, liquids, or solids with low melting points. Each has a tetrahedral molecular geometry, reflecting sp^3 hybridization of the central atom. Each hydrolyzes, to a greater or lesser degree, either in water or in steam, to the corresponding dioxide or acid. Hydrolysis is rapid under alkaline conditions. The tetrafluorides of silicon, germanium, and tin readily attach two more fluoride ions to give hexafluoro complex anions, $[MF_6]^{2-}$. Hexachloro species are well known for tin(IV) and lead(IV).

Catenated halides of the type M_nX_{2n+2} (*e.g.*, hexachloroethane, C_2Cl_6) are well known for carbon, but only a few silicon and germanium analogues have been prepared and no tin or lead compounds. These compounds resemble the tetrahalides in their reactions.

Oxides. Each element in the carbon group forms a well-characterized monoxide with the general formula MO. Carbon monoxide is almost exclusively encountered as a gas. Both silicon and germanium monoxides are most stable in the gaseous state at very high temperatures. Condensation of these two gases to the solid state is accompanied by a reaction that results in the free element and the dioxide. Tin and lead monoxides, on the other hand, are stable solids at room temperature. Only these tin and lead compounds are sufficiently basic (alkaline) to be converted to salts by reaction with aqueous acids. Carbon monoxide is, in terms of its formula, the anhydride of formic acid, formula HCOOH (*i.e.*, if a molecule of water, H_2O, is removed from a molecule of formic acid, carbon monoxide, CO, is left), but the reverse conversion of carbon monoxide to formic acid is not easy. Tin monoxide and lead monoxide dissolve readily in alkali metal hydroxide solutions.

Dioxides

Dioxides (MO_2) are better characterized. Carbon dioxide is monomolecular and gaseous at ordinary temperatures. The other dioxides all form polymeric three-dimensional crystal lattices in which individual MO_2 groups cannot be distinguished. All of the dioxides are potential oxidizing agents, but only lead dioxide is active in this fashion. Each dioxide forms an acid by combination with water and also reacts with alkali metal hydroxides (bases) to give one or more negative ions containing oxygen; *e.g.*, carbonates, silicates, germanates. Acid strength decreases with increasing atomic number of the carbon group elements. Lead(IV) oxide (PbO_2) is unique in combining with lead(II) oxide (PbO) to give a mixed or saltlike form (Pb_3O_4)—two molecules of the latter combining with each molecule of the former.

Sulfides. Monosulfides of carbon group elements, with the general formula MS, S representing sulfur, are most characteristic of tin and lead. These compounds are precipitated from dilute acidic or alkaline solutions as brownish to black substances. They show no appreciable acidic behaviour and are soluble in strongly acidic solutions. A common mineral, lead(II) sulfide, called galena, is an industrial source of lead.

All the disulfides, general formula MS_2, are formed except lead sulfide. Again, lead(IV) is a sufficiently strong oxidizing agent to be reduced by the sulfide ion S^{2-}. Carbon disulfide (CS_2) is a low-boiling and foul-smelling liquid that yields a vapour consisting of single molecules. Silicon disulfide (SiS_2) is a polymeric solid made up of chains of the molecule held together through the sulfur atoms. Germanium disulfide (GeS_2) is a three-dimensional polymer comparable to germanium oxide. Tin disulfide (SnS_2) possesses a layer type of crystal lattice. Carbon disulfide reacts quite readily with water to form the carbonate ion. Silicon disulfide also hydrolyzes readily. Both germanium(IV) and tin(IV) sulfides resist hydrolysis and dissolve in dilute aqueous acids only with difficulty.

II. Individual carbon group elements and their compounds

CARBON AND ITS COMPOUNDS

The word carbon probably derives from the Latin *carbo*, meaning variously "coal," "charcoal," "ember." The term diamond, a corruption of the Greek word *adamas*, "the invincible," aptly describes the permanence of this crystallized form of carbon, just as graphite, the name for the other crystal form of carbon, derived from the Greek verb *graphein*, "to write," reflects its property of leaving a dark mark when rubbed on a surface. Before the discovery in 1779 that graphite when burned in air forms carbon dioxide, graphite was confused with both the metal lead and a superficially similar substance, the mineral molybdenite.

Occurrence and distribution of the element. On a weight basis, carbon is 19th in order of elemental abundance in the crust of the Earth, and there are estimated to be 3.5 times as many carbon atoms as silicon atoms in the universe. Only hydrogen, helium, oxygen, neon, and nitrogen are atomically more abundant in the cosmos than carbon. Carbon is the cosmic product of the "burning" of helium in which three helium nuclei, atomic number 4, fuse to produce a carbon nucleus, atomic number 12. In the crust of the Earth, elemental carbon is a minor component: carbon compounds (*i.e.*, carbonates of magnesium and calcium) form common minerals (*e.g.*, magnesite, dolomite, marble, or limestone). Coral and the shells of oysters and clams are primarily calcium carbonate. Carbon is widely distributed as coal and in the organic compounds that constitute petroleum, natural gas, and all plant and animal tissue. A natural sequence of chemical reactions called the carbon cycle—involving conversion of atmospheric carbon dioxide to carbohydrates by photosynthesis in plants, the consumption of these carbohydrates by animals and oxidation of them through metabolism to produce carbon dioxide and other products, and the return of carbon dioxide to the atmosphere—is one of the most important of all biological processes.

Carbon in all living tissue

Production of elemental carbon. Elemental carbon (see NATIVE ELEMENTS) is best considered in terms of its several crystalline forms—diamond, graphite, and "amorphous carbon"—since the widely different properties of these three substances require different approaches. (When an element exists in more than one crystal form, each is called an allotrope.)

Until 1955, all diamonds were obtained from natural deposits, most significant in southern Africa but occurring also in Brazil, Venezuela, British Guiana (now Republic of Guyana), and Siberia. The single known source in the United States, in Arkansas, has no commercial importance, nor is India, once historically a source of fine diamonds, a significant present-day supplier. The primary source of diamonds is a soft, bluish-coloured peridotic rock called kimberlite (after the famous deposit at Kimberley, South Africa), found in volcanic structures called pipes; but many diamonds occur in alluvial deposits presumably resulting from the weathering of primary sources. Isolated finds around the world in regions where no sources are indicated have not been uncommon. Natural deposits are worked by crushing, by gravity and flotation separations, and by removal of diamonds by their adherence to a layer of grease on a suitable table. The following products result: (1) diamond proper—distorted cubic-crystalline, gem-quality stones varying from colourless to red, pink, blue, green, and yellow; (2) bort—minute, dark crystals of abrasive but not gem quality; (3) ballas—randomly oriented crystals of abrasive quality; (4) macles—triangular, pillow-shaped crystals that are industrially useful; and (5) carbonado—mixed diamond–graphite crystallites containing other impurities.

Artificial diamonds

The successful laboratory conversion of graphite to diamond was made in 1955. The procedure involved the simultaneous use of extremely high pressure and temperature with iron as a solvent or catalyst. Subsequently, chromium, manganese, cobalt, nickel, and tantalum were substituted for iron. Synthetic diamonds are now manufactured in several countries and are being used increasingly in place of natural materials as industrial abrasives.

Graphite occurs naturally in many areas, the deposits of major importance being in the Republic of Korea, Austria, China, Mexico, Madagascar, West Germany, Sri Lanka (formerly Ceylon) and the U.S.S.R. Both surface- and deep-mining techniques are used, followed by flotation, but the major portion of commercial graphite is produced by heating petroleum coke in an electric furnace. A better crystallized form, known as pyrolytic graphite, is obtained from the decomposition of low-molecular-weight hydrocarbons by heat. Graphite fibres of considerable tensile strength are obtained by carbonizing natural and synthetic organic fibres.

Amorphous carbon, solid but not clearly crystallized, probably consists of microcrystals of graphite; it is common in commerce as coke; lampblack, or carbon black; and charcoal. These products are obtained by heating coal (to give coke), natural gas (to give blacks), or carbonaceous material of vegetable or animal origin, such as wood or bone (to give charcoal), at elevated temperatures in the presence of insufficient oxygen to allow combustion. The volatile by-products are recovered and used separately.

Structure of carbon allotropes. The crystal structure of diamond is an infinite three-dimensional array of carbon atoms, each of which forms a structure in which each of the bonds makes equal angles with its neighbours. If the ends of the bonds are connected, the structure is that of a tetrahedron, a three-sided pyramid of four faces (including the base). Every carbon atom is covalently bonded at the four corners of the tetrahedron to four other carbon atoms. The distance between carbon atoms along the bond is 1.54×10^{-8} centimetre, and this is called the single-bond length. The space lattice of the diamond can be visualized as carbon atoms in puckered hexagonal (six-sided) rings that lie roughly in one plane, the natural cleavage plane of the crystal; and these sheets of hexagonal, puckered rings are stacked in such a way that the atoms in every fourth layer lie in the same position as those in the first layer. The layer arrangement sequence is thus ABCABCA. . . . Such a crystal structure can be destroyed only by the rupture of many strong bonds: thus the extreme hardness, high sublimation temperature, the presumed extremely high melting point (extrapolated from known behaviour), and reduced chemical reactivity and insulating properties are all reasonable consequences of the crystal structure. Because of both the sense and the direction of the tetrahedral axis, four spatial orientations of carbon atoms exist, leading to two tetrahedral and two octahedral (eight-faced) forms of diamond.

The crystal structure of graphite amounts to a parallel stacking of layers of carbon atoms. Within each layer the carbon atoms lie in fused hexagonal rings that extend infinitely in two dimensions. The stacking pattern of the layers is ABABA. . .; that is, each layer separates two identically oriented layers. Within each layer the carbon–carbon bond distance is 1.42×10^{-8} centimetre, which is intermediate between the single bond and the double (1.33×10^{-8} centimetre) bond distances. All carbon-carbon bonds within a layer are the same (an observation that is interpreted in terms of complete π-bonding). The interlayer distance (3.37×10^{-8} centimetre) is sufficiently large to preclude localized bonding between the layers; the bonding between layers is probably by van der Waals interaction (*i.e.*, the result of attraction between electrons of one carbon atom and the nuclei of neighbouring atoms). Ready cleavage, as compared with diamond, and electrical conductivity are consequences of the crystal structure of graphite. Other related properties are softness and lubricity (smoothness, slipperiness). A less common form of graphite, which occurs in nature, is based upon an ABCABCA . . . stacking, in which every fourth layer is the same. The amorphous varieties of carbon are based upon microcrystalline forms of graphite.

The greater degree of compactness in the diamond structure as compared with graphite suggests that by the application of sufficient pressure on graphite it should be converted to diamond. At room temperature and atmospheric pressure, diamond is actually less stable than graphite. The rate of conversion of diamond to graphite is so slow, however, that a diamond persists in its crystal form indefinitely. As temperature rises, the rate of conversion to graphite increases substantially, and at high temperatures it becomes (thermodynamically) favorable if the pressure is sufficiently high. At the same time, however, the rate of conversion decreases as the (thermodynamic) favourability increases. Thus, graphite does not yield diamond when heated under high pressure, and it appears that direct deformation of the graphite structure to the diamond structure in the solid state is not feasible. The occurrence of diamonds in iron–magnesium silicates in the volcanic structures called pipes and in iron–nickel and iron sulfide phases in meteorites suggests that they were formed by dissolution of carbon in those compounds and subsequent crystallization from them in the molten state at temperatures and pressures favourable to diamond stability. The successful synthesis of diamond is based upon this principle.

Diamonds in meteorites

The temperature and pressure relationships of any substance can be plotted to show how, for example, the boiling point changes as pressure is changed; such graphs are called phase diagrams (see PHASE CHANGES AND EQUILIBRIA). They reveal conditions under which rearrangements in the atomic or molecular structure of a substance take place.

The crystal structure of graphite is of kind that permits the formation of many compounds, called lamellar or intercalation compounds, by penetration of molecules or ions. Graphitic oxide and graphitic fluoride are nonconducting lamellar substances not obtained in true molecular forms that can be reproduced, but their formulas do approximate, respectively, the compositions of carbon dioxide and carbon monofluoride. Graphite oxide appears to contain the groupings carbon–oxygen–carbon atoms, carbon–oxygen atoms with a double bond, and carbon–hydroxyl groups and to have the properties of the aliphatic compounds. Graphitic fluoride appears to contain one carbon–fluorine group of atoms and three carbon–carbon bonds per carbon atom. The products obtained by intercalation of the heavy alkali metals potassium, rubidium, cesium (K, Rb, and Cs), the halogens chlorine and bromine (Cl_2 and Br_2), and certain metal compounds such as aluminum chloride, iron disulfide, and molybdenum trioxide ($AlCl_3$, FeS_2, and MoO_3) conduct electric current as well as or better than graphite. In a metallic state, some of the valence electrons are free to move from atom to atom forming what is called the conduction band. At the same time, a position left vacant by an electron may be considered a positive "hole," and such holes also move about in the conduction band. The compounds just mentioned appear either to add or to remove electrons from the conduction band of graphite. Thus, in graphite treated as indicated above, the concentration either of conducting electrons or of positive holes is enhanced.

A type of chemical reaction in which one substance (an oxidizing agent) accepts electrons from another substance (a reducing agent) and is thereby reduced (while the reducing agent is oxidized) is frequently observed with carbon and its compounds. Although carbon is usually a reducing agent, under acidic conditions elemental carbon is a moderately strong oxidizing agent. The large energy of the carbon–carbon bond makes activation energy requirements for the reaction so high that direct reduction of carbon—*e.g.*, to methane (formula CH_4)—is impractical. Reduction of carbon monoxide to elemental carbon and oxidation of carbon monoxide to carbon dioxide are both feasible but impractical in solution. Under alkaline conditions, only the oxidation of formate ion (HCO_2^-) to carbonate ion (CO_3^{2-}) is a reasonable process.

Carbides. By convention, carbides are those binary compounds in which carbon has combined with elements of roughly equal or lesser electronegativity (affinity for electrons). Carbides can be classified as saltlike (saline), covalent, or interstitial. The saltlike carbides form transparent, nonconducting crystals that react with water to form the metal oxides or hydroxides and liberate hydrocarbons. The covalent carbides include the silicon compound known as Carborundum (SiC) and boron carbide (B_4C). Each of these is a refractory, extremely hard (on Mohs scale of hardness, diamond is 10, SiC is 9.15, B_4C is 9.32), and chemically inert substance, such properties being the consequence of the presence of a large number of strong bonds that must be broken. There are three crystalline forms of silicon carbide, and they have structures related to the diamond, the sphalerite, and the wurtzite arrangements of atoms, in each of which carbon and silicon atoms alternate in a tetrahedral environment. Crystals of boron carbide contain icosahedral groups of 12 boron atoms and linear carbon-atom chains of 3 atoms each. Complete covalent bonding between adjacent atoms occurs.

Carborundum

The interstitial carbides include most of the transition-metal carbides and in particular those derived from the transition metals of Groups IVb, Vb, and VIb in the periodic table. These compounds are characterized by very high melting points (3,000–4,800° C [5,400–8,600° F]), extreme hardness (on Mohs scale a hardness of 7 to 10), and chemical inertness. The crystals are formed by the entry of carbon atoms into octahedral holes in the crystal lattices of the metals. The composition by weight, or stoichiometric composition, is most commonly representable by the formula MC, in which M is the metal. Carbides formed by the metals chromium (Cr), manganese (Mn), iron (Fe), cobalt (Co), and nickel (Ni) differ in stoichiometry, as shown by the formulas Cr_3C_2, Mn_3C, Fe_3C, Co_3C, and Ni_3C, and are readily hydrolyzed by dilute acids to hydrocarbons and elemental hydrogen. Their crystals contain chains of carbon atoms in distorted metal lattices.

Halides. A number of more important physical properties of the simple halides, represented as CX_4, X being any halogen, are summarized in Table 3. The catenated halides are commonly considered simply as halogenated hydrocarbons and are better discussed in that context. Carbon tetrafluoride (CF_4) is a thermally stable, chemically unreactive gaseous compound that is obtained as the end product of the reaction of elemental fluorine with almost any carbon-containing compound. Carbon tetrachloride (CCl_4) is less stable to heat than the fluoride and quite susceptible to photochemical (light-induced) decomposition and loss of chloride ion. The tetrabromide and tetraiodide (CBr_4 and CI_4) are, respectively, yellow and red solids that undergo ready decomposition when heated. Such thermal instability is probably related both to reduced bond energies within the molecule and to the molecular structure in which large halogen atoms are crowded about the small carbon atom. That the tetrahalides of carbon hydrolyze less readily than those of silicon or germanium is caused by their containing a central atom with all its covalent bonds occupied and thus no orbitals left available for interaction with electrons from a water molecule or a hydroxide ion. No complex ions based upon the carbon tetrahalides are thus known.

Oxides. The most common and important oxides of carbon are carbon monoxide (CO) and carbon dioxide (CO_2). Carbon dioxide is the first member of a potential series of oxides with general formula C_nO_2, the *n* indicating any number of carbon atoms, while the number of

Table 3: Physical Properties of Selected Compounds
key: subl—sublimes; dec—decomposes; expl.—explodes

compound	melting point (°C)	boiling point (°C at 1 atm)	density (g/ml)
CH_4	−182.48	−164	0.415 (−164° C)
SiH_4	−185	−111.8	0.68 (−85° C)
GeH_4	−165	−88.5	1.523 (−142° C)
SnH_4	−150 (dec)	−52	
CF_4	−184	−128	3.034 (0° C)
SiF_4	−90.2	−86	1.66 (−95° C)
GeF_4	−15 (3,032 mm)	−36.5	2.46 (−36.5° C)
SnF_4	705 (subl)		4.780 (19° C)
CCl_4	−23	76.8	1.5867 (20° C)
$SiCl_4$	−70	57.57	1.483 (20° C)
$GeCl_4$	−49.5	84	1.8443 (30° C)
$SnCl_4$	−33	114.1	2.226 (1)
$PbCl_4$	−15	105 (expl.)	3.18 (0° C)
CBr_4	90–91	189.5	2.9609 (100° C)
$SiBr_4$	5.4	154	2.7715 (25° C)
$GeBr_4$	26.1	186.5	3.132 (29° C)
$SnBr_4$	31	202 (734 mm)	3.34 (35° C)
CI_4	171 (dec)		4.34 (20° C)
SiI_4	120.5	287.5	4.198
GeI_4	144	440 (dec)	
SnI_4	144.5	364.5	4.473 (0° C)
$SnCl_2$	246	652	3.95 (25° C)
$PbCl_2$	501	950	5.85
CO_2	−56.6 (5.2 atm)	−78.5 (subl)	1.56 (−79° C)
SiO_2 (quartz)	1,610	2,230	2.635
SiO_2 (cristobalite)	1,713	2,230	2.26 (25° C)
SiO_2 (tridymite)	1,703	2,230	2.26 (25° C)
GeO_2 (hexagonal)	1,115		4.228 (25° C)
GeO_2 (tetragonal)	1,086		6.239
SnO_2	1,127	1,800–1,900 (subl)	6.95
PbO_2	290 (dec)		9.375
CO	−199	−191.5	0.793 (1)
SiO	>1,702	1,880	2.13
GeO	710 (subl)		1.607
SnO	1,080 (dec)		6.446 (0° C)
PbO (litharge)	888		9.53
CS_2	−110.8	46.3	1.261 (22° C)
SiS_2	1,090 (subl)		2.02
GeS_2	>660 (subl)		2.94 (14° C)
SnS_2	600 (dec)		4.5
SnS	882	1,230	5.22 (25° C)
PbS	1,114		7.5

oxygen atoms is always two; but only one other member of the series is well characterized, namely carbon suboxide (C_3O_2). Although a substance of the formula C_5O_2 has been reported, evidence for its existence has been questioned. Resonance stabilization, meaning that the bond structure within a molecule cannot be expressed in a single mode but must be considered as an average of several possible structures, postulates for carbon dioxide the following formulations:

:Ö: :C: :Ö: ⁻:Ö:C: : :O:⁺ ⁺:O: : :C:Ö:⁻.

Resonance stabilization could be significant for species of the C_nO_2 series only where n is an odd number. Thus, C_3O_2 could be formulated as

:Ö: :C: :C: :C: :Ö: ⁺:O: : :C:C: : :C:Ö:⁻ ⁻:Ö:C: : :C:C: : :O:⁺,

but C_4O_2 or C_2O_2 could not be similarly formulated. It is significant that C_3O_2 is known, but no analogue where n is an even number has been described. An oxide with high carbon and high oxygen content, the compound $C_{12}O_9$ is also known.

The carbon monoxide molecule (CO) contains the same number of electrons as, or is isoelectronic with, the nitrogen molecule (N_2), the nitrosonium ion (NO^+), and the cyanide ion (CN^-). For each of these groups of atoms an electronic formulation containing a triple bond can be written:

⁻:C: : :O:⁺ :N: : :N: [:N: : :O:]⁺ [:C: : :N:]⁻.

The physical constants for carbon monoxide and elemental nitrogen are very nearly the same, thus reflecting structural similarities. The molecular species CO, NO^+, and CN^- resemble each other most closely in their abilities to form complexes with the same transition-metal ions (the transition metals, or elements, occupy the b groups in the periodic table and include many of the familiar metals).

Carbon monoxide as fuel

Carbon monoxide is combustible and is a significant component of fuels such as water gas and producer gas. The reaction converting carbon monoxide to carbon dioxide is represented by the equation in which *g* stands for gas (as *s* symbolizes solid and *l* liquid):

$$2CO_{(g)} + O_{2(g)} \longrightarrow 2CO_{2(g)}.$$

This reaction is characterized by a standard-enthalpy (heat-energy) change that is high enough to explain the usefulness of the gas as a fuel. Carbon monoxide is also an excellent reducing agent with metal oxides at elevated temperatures and is thus important in metallurgy for obtaining pure metals from their minerals. A typical reaction with the iron(III) oxide Fe_2O_3 is represented in the following equation:

$$Fe_2O_{3(s)} + 3CO_{(g)} \longrightarrow 2Fe_{(s)} + 3CO_{2(g)}.$$

At elevated temperatures and in the presence of a catalyst such as elemental iron, nickel, or palladium, carbon monoxide breaks up into elemental carbon and carbon dioxide according to the equation

$$2CO_{(g)} \rightleftharpoons C_{(s)} + CO_{2(g)}.$$

As the monoxide breaks up, the dioxide is also reduced by the carbon, and, at all times, the reaction is reversible —*i.e.*, taking place in both directions. As the temperature continues to increase, the percentage of carbon monoxide increases, reducing the percentage of carbon dioxide in the mixture. It is this shift that is responsible at high temperatures for the presence of carbon monoxide, often in toxic quantities, in the gaseous products of combustion when there is not an excess of oxygen to force the reaction to the right. In the presence of suitable catalysts, carbon monoxide is converted by elemental hydrogen to methanol (CH_3OH) and other organic compounds. Reaction of carbon monoxide with the halogens or sulfur gives compounds with the carbonyl group, symbolized as >C=O, in which each line represents a covalent bond. The two free bonds of the carbon atom may be bonded to hydrogen or other carbon atoms. Although the carbon monoxide molecule is weakly basic (according to the Lewis acid–base theory) it does behave as a donor to certain metal atoms to form carbonyl complexes; *e.g.*, nickel tetracarbonyl [$Ni(CO)_4$], iron pentacarbonyl [$Fe(CO)_5$], and dirhenium decacarbonyl [$Re_2(CO)_{10}$]. Carbon monoxide is obtained commercially in an admixture with hydrogen by the reduction at high temperatures of water vapour with coke.

The linear carbon dioxide molecule is isoelectronic (same number of electrons around the different nuclei) with the nitrogen(I) oxide molecule (N_2O). The physical constants of these two substances are very nearly identical. The critical constants of carbon dioxide are 31° C (87.8° F) and 73 atmospheres, which means that sufficient compression of the gas at room temperature can change it to the liquid. The triple point (at which gas, liquid, and solid phases can exist in equilibrium) is −56.6° C (−69.9° F) at 5.01 atmospheres. The high sublimation (transition from solid to gas without going through the liquid phase) pressure of the solid renders difficult the direct preparation of solid carbon dioxide, but rapid expansion of carbon dioxide gas by release of pressure above the liquid has a sufficient cooling effect to convert part of the material into solid. The white solid, known as Dry Ice, is useful as a refrigerant and is used in admixture with such liquids as acetone to maintain low temperatures in cryogenic systems.

Carbon dioxide is a comparatively weak oxidizing agent, and it does not support the combustion of carbonaceous substances, phosphorus, or sulfur. Rather, it extinguishes the combustion of such substances and is thus a highly useful fire extinguisher. Previously ignited active metals—*e.g.*, sodium, potassium, and magnesium—do burn in carbon dioxide, with the formation of oxides, carbonates, or oxalates and elemental carbon. Above 1,000° C (1,800° F), carbon dioxide dissociates appreciably to carbon monoxide and oxygen. Carbon dioxide dissolves appreciably in water to give a mildly acidic solution. The solubility is substantial in alkaline solution where both the carbonate ion (CO_3^{2-}) and hydrogen carbonate or bicarbonate ion (HCO_3^-) can form. Solid hydrogen carbonate salts are limited to the alkali metals; *e.g.*, sodium bicarbonate ($NaHCO_3$), common baking soda.

Solid carbonates are known for many metals either as natural minerals or as synthetically produced compounds. Natural calcium carbonate ($CaCO_3$) and sodium

Soda ash

carbonate (Na_2CO_3), the soda ash of commerce, are of particular industrial importance. Most carbonates have limited solubilities in water. That the carbonate and nitrate ions (NO_3^-) are isoelectronic and of similar size promotes similarities in crystal structure between certain of their salts (*e.g.*, $CaCO_3$ and $NaNO_3$). Carbonic acid (H_2CO_3) cannot be isolated as such because of its instability and ready decomposition to carbon dioxide and water. Carbon dioxide is an ultimate product of the complete reaction of carbon or organic compounds with oxygen. It is best obtained in a state of purity either by decomposing carbonates by heat, or by treating them with acids.

Carbon suboxide (C_3O_2) is a foul-smelling gas that condenses to a liquid with a boiling point of −6.8° C (19.8° F).

Sulfides. Carbon disulfied (CS_2) is an almost colourless, low-boiling liquid with a pronounced unpleasant odour. The compound has a low kindling temperature and is thus a hazardous chemical either as the liquid or the gas. With the sulfide ion it forms the thiocarbonate ion (CS_3^{2-}), and alkali and alkaline-earth metal thiocarbonates are sulfur analogues of carbonates. The arrangement of atoms in the CS_2 molecule is collinear and analogous to that in the CO_2 molecule. Resonance stabilization is important. Formation of carbon disulfide from elemental carbon and sulfur is endothermic (heat absorptive) to the extent of 22 kilocalories per mole.

Carbon oxosulfide (COS) is a toxic gaseous compound that condenses to a liquid boiling at −50.2° C (−58.4° F) and a solid melting at −138.8° C (−217.8° F). Its general properties are intermediate between those of carbon dioxide and carbon disulfide.

Nitrogen compounds. Hydrogen cyanide (HCN) is a colourless gas that condenses to a liquid boiling at 25.6° C (78.1° F) and freezing at −13.4° C (+7.9° F). The liquid has a low viscosity, measurable electrical conductivity, and a large dielectric constant (a measure of the ability to store electrical energy in an electrical field) and is thus an ionizing solvent like water. The cyanides contain the CN^- group and are either ionic, covalent, or

Cyanides

complex in nature. Cyanogen (C_2N_2) is a related compound that in alkaline solution gives both cyanides and cyanates. All cyanides are toxic. The cyanide group reacts similarly to the carbon monoxide molecule in the blood stream. Sodium cyanide is a product of the fusion of calcium cyanamide ($CaCN_2$) with carbon and sodium carbonate. Calcium cyanamide results when calcium carbide is heated with elemental nitrogen. Hydrogen cyanide is important in the synthesis of organic nitriles. The cyanides are used in extractive metallurgy and electroplating.

Nuclear properties. The notation used for the nucleus of atoms places the atomic mass as a presuperscript to the symbol of the element and the atomic number as a presubscript; thus, the isotope carbon-12 is symbolized $^{12}_{6}C$. Of the stable nuclides (Table 1), the isotope carbon-13 is of particular interest in that its nuclear spin imparts response in a device called a nuclear magnetic resonance spectrometer, which is useful when investigating the molecular structures of covalently bonded compounds containing carbon. This isotope is also useful as a label in compounds that are to be analyzed by mass spectrometry, another device that is used extensively to identify atoms and molecules. Of the unstable nuclides, only carbon-14 is of sufficiently long half-life to be important. It is formed by the interaction of neutrons, produced by cosmic radiation, with nitrogen (N) in the atmosphere in a reaction that may be written as follows (neutron is symbolized as $^{1}_{0}n$, the nitrogen atom as $^{14}_{7}N$, and a hydrogen nucleus, or proton, as $^{1}_{1}H$):

$$^{14}_{7}N + ^{1}_{0}n \longrightarrow ^{14}_{6}C + ^{1}_{1}H$$

The carbon-14 atoms from this reaction are converted to carbon dioxide by reaction with atmospheric oxygen and mixed and uniformly distributed with the carbon dioxide containing stable carbon-12. Living organisms use atmospheric carbon dioxide, whether with stable or radioactive carbon, through processes of photosynthesis and respiration, and thus their systems contain the constant ratio of carbon-12 to carbon-14 that exists in the atmosphere.

Death of an organism terminates this equilibration process; no fresh carbon dioxide is added to the dead substance. The carbon-14 present in the dead substance decays in accordance with its 5,568-year half-life, while the carbon-12 remains what it was at death. Measurement of the carbon-14 activity at a given time thus allows calculation of the time elapsed after the death of the organism. Measurement of the carbon-14 activity in a cypress beam in the tomb of the Egyptian Pharaoh Snefru, for example, established the date of the tomb as *c.* 2600 BC. Many items of archaeological significance have been dated similarly.

The nuclides carbon-12 and carbon-13 are of importance in the carbon cycle of energy creation in certain stars. The cycle can be summarized in terms of nuclear equations, the separate steps being:

$$^{12}_{6}C + ^{1}_{1}H \longrightarrow ^{13}_{7}N + \text{energy}$$
$$^{13}_{7}N \longrightarrow ^{13}_{6}C + ^{0}_{+1}e$$
$$^{13}_{6}C + ^{1}_{1}H \longrightarrow ^{14}_{7}N + \text{energy}$$
$$^{14}_{7}N + ^{1}_{1}H \longrightarrow ^{15}_{8}O + \text{energy}$$
$$^{15}_{8}O \longrightarrow ^{15}_{7}N + ^{0}_{+1}e$$
$$^{15}_{7}N + ^{1}_{1}H \longrightarrow ^{12}_{6}C + ^{4}_{2}He.$$

Summation of the equations allows the fusion process to be written as a reaction among four atoms of hydrogen to yield one atom of helium (He), two positrons ($^{0}_{+1}e$), and energy:

$$4\,^{1}_{1}H \longrightarrow ^{4}_{2}He + 2\,^{0}_{+1}e + \text{energy};$$

this equation does not show that the process uses up and regenerates the carbon-12. In a sense, carbon acts as a catalyst for this mode of converting mass to energy.

Biological implications. The biological implications of the element and its simple compounds have been discussed earlier; the most significant implications are associated with organic compounds, which are discussed in such articles as ALKALOIDS; CARBOHYDRATE; LIPID; NUCLEIC ACID; PROTEIN; STEROIDS.

Analysis. Carbon, either elemental or combined, is usually determined quantitatively by conversion to carbon dioxide gas, which can then be absorbed by other chemicals to give either a weighable product or a solution with acidic properties that can be titrated.

SILICON AND ITS COMPOUNDS

The name silicon derives from the Latin *silex* or *silicis*, meaning "flint" or "hard stone."

Occurrence and distribution of the element. On a weight basis, the abundance of silicon in the crust of the earth is exceeded only by oxygen. Estimates of the cosmic abundance of other elements often are cited in terms of the number of their atoms per 10^6 atoms of silicon. Only hydrogen, helium, oxygen, neon, nitrogen, and carbon exceed silicon in cosmic abundance. Silicon is believed to be a cosmic product of alpha-particle absorption, at a temperature of about 10^9 K, by the nuclei of carbon-12, oxygen-16, and neon-20. The energy binding the particles that form the nucleus of silicon is about 8.4 million electron volts (MeV) per nucleon (proton or neutron). Compared with the maximum of about 8.7 million electron volts for the nucleus of iron, almost twice as massive as that of silicon, this figure indicates the relative stability of the silicon nucleus. The pure element silicon is too reactive to be found in nature. In compounds, the oxi-

Silicon
minerals

dized form, as silicon dioxide and particularly as silicates, is common in the Earth's crust and is an important component of the Earth's mantle. Silicon dioxide occurs both in crystalline minerals (*e.g.*, quartz, cristobalite, tridymite) and amorphous or seemingly amorphous minerals (*e.g.*, agate, opal, chalcedony) in all land areas. The natural silicates are characterized by their abundance, wide distribution, and structural and compositional complexities. Most of the elements of the following groups in the periodic table are found in silicate minerals: groups Ia, IIa, IIIa, IIIb, IVb, Vb, VIb, VIIa. These elements are said to be lithophilic, or stone-loving. Important silicate minerals include the clays, feldspar, olivine, pyroxene, amphiboles, micas, and zeolites.

Production of elemental silicon. Elemental silicon is produced commercially by the reduction of silica (SiO_2) with coke in an electric furnace, and the impure product is then refined. Almost pure silicon is obtained by the reduction of silicon tetrachloride or trichlorosilane. For use in electronic devices, single crystals are grown by slowly withdrawing seed crystals from molten silicon.

Properties of the element. The more important physical and chemical properties of silicon have been summarized and related to the ground-state electronic configuration of the silicon atom and the position of silicon in the periodic table. Because silicon forms chains similar to those formed by carbon, silicon has been studied as a possible base element for silicon organisms. Another property resulting from the electronic structure of silicon is that it functions as an intrinsic semiconductor (see SEMICONDUCTORS AND INSULATORS, THEORY OF). Addition of an element such as boron, an atom of which can be substituted for a silicon atom in the crystal structure but which provides one less valence electron (boron is an acceptor atom) than silicon, allows silicon atoms to lose electrons to it. The positive holes created by the shift in electrons allow extrinsic semiconduction of a type referred to as positive (*p*). Addition of an element such as arsenic, an atom of which can also be substituted for a silicon atom in the crystal but which provides an extra valence electron (arsenic is a donor atom), releases its electron within the lattice. These electrons allow semiconduction of the negative (*n*) type. If *p*-silicon and *n*-silicon wafers are joined, in a manner called the *p*–*n* junction, and placed in sunlight, the absorbed energy causes

The solar
cell

electrons to move across the junction and an electric current to flow in an external circuit connecting the two wafers. Such a solar cell is a source of energy for space devices.

Unlike carbon, the only crystalline form in which silicon exists is an octahedral form based upon atoms in the diamond-type arrangement. The amorphous forms of silicon contain micro crystals of this type. The reduced bond energy in crystalline silicon renders the element lower melting, softer, and chemically more reactive than diamond.

Only the 0 and +4 oxidation states of silicon are stable in aqueous systems.

As is true with carbon, the bonds in elemental silicon are strong enough to require large energies to activate, or promote, reaction in an acidic medium, and the oxidation–reduction reactions do not appear to be reversible at ordinary temperatures. (See also SILICA MINERALS; SILICATE MINERALS.)

Silicides. A silicide is a binary compound in which silicon is combined with some less electronegative element.

Like the carbides, silicides are most commonly prepared by direct combination of the elements or by the reduction of oxides by elemental silicon, both at elevated temperatures. Roughly, but with somewhat less well-defined distinctions, silicides may be classified as ionic, covalent, or metallic. The stoichiometric compositions are widely variable; *e.g.*, MSi, MSi_2, M_2Si, M_3Si, M_5Si, M_5Si_3, and $M_{15}Si_4$ (M symbolizing specific metals). They bear little systematic relationship to the electronic configuration of the metal atom present or to its position in the periodic table. Rather, composition appears to be related to stable crystal structure, as determined by size of the atoms and by the relationships among the charges.

Crystals of metal-rich silicides (*e.g.*, M_3Si) are constructed with silicon atoms nearly or completely surrounded by metal atoms, and these solids are therefore structurally similar to the metals. On the other hand, crystals of silicon-rich silicides (*e.g.*, some MSi_2) are based upon metal atoms surrounded by silicon atoms. In other silicides, the distances between silicon atoms are close to those in crystalline elemental silicon. In terms of crystal structural type, many silicides are closer to the borides than they are to the carbides.

The calcium silicides represent several structural and chemical types, including compounds with the formulas Ca_2Si, $CaSi$, and $CaSi_2$. The latter two yield the polymers $(SiH_2)_n$ and $(SiH)_n$ when treated with aqueous acids. The metallic silicides are commonly hard, refractory substances that are used as abrasives.

Hydrides. The hydrides, called silanes, are silicon analogues of the alkanes, the hydrocarbon family of compounds with general formula C_nH_{2n+2}, and their general formula corresponds to the alkane type: Si_nH_{2n+2}. Compounds with *n* of 1 to 6 have been isolated and characterized, and there is evidence for the existence of higher members of the series. The melting points and boiling points of the lower members are comparable with those of the analogous compounds of germanium and the alkanes listed in Table 4. No cyclic or unsaturated (having more than one bond between adjacent silicon atoms) silanes are known with any degree of certainty, but solid and highly polymeric hydrides (*i.e.*, compounds composed of many hydride molecules bonded together into macromolecules) with the general formulas $(SiH_2)_n$ and $(SiH)_n$ have been described. These substances are not in any way comparable to the alkenes and alkynes (two other major carbon-compound families), and it is unlikely that any compounds with double and triple bonds between the silicon atoms exist. It is reasonable to assume, however, that either there exist linear arrangements, with the general formula $H_3Si(SiH_2)_xSiH_3$, and cyclic groups, with the general formula

Analogies
between
silicon
and
carbon

$$H_2Si \underset{(SiH_2)_y}{\overset{(SiH_2)_y}{\diagup \diagdown}} SiH_2$$

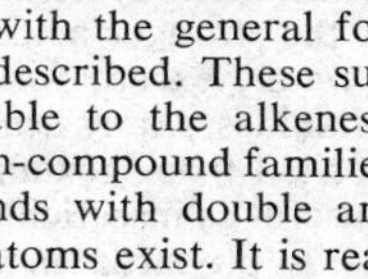

or three-dimensional networks, each based upon four-bonded and saturated (only single bonds between adjacent silicon atoms) silicon atoms. Catenation (chain forming) to give simple, single-bonded molecules is limited by bond energies; the absence of multiple bonds reflects the difficulty of overlapping *p* orbitals to form π-bonds with the larger silicon atoms.

The lower silanes are obtained as a mixture by treating magnesium silicide with aqueous hydrochloric acid, and they are separated by fractional distillation, a process that

---

Table 4: Comparison of Alkanes, Silanes, and Germanes

compound	melting point (°C)	boiling point (°C)	compound	melting point (°C)	boiling point (°C)	compound	melting point (°C)	boiling point (°C)
CH_4	−182.48	−164	SiH_4	−185	−111.8	GeH_4	−165	−88.5
C_2H_6	−183.3	−88.63	Si_2H_6	−132.5	−14.5	Ge_2H_6	−109	29
C_3H_8	−189.69	−42.07	Si_3H_8	−117.4	52.9	Ge_3H_8	−105.6	110.5
$n\text{-}C_4H_{10}$	−138.35	−0.5	$n\text{-}Si_4H_{10}$	−88.2	108.4	$n\text{-}Ge_4H_{10}$		176.9
$iso\text{-}C_4H_{10}$		−12	$iso\text{-}Si_4H_{10}$		108.4	$iso\text{-}Ge_4H_{10}$		176.9
$n\text{-}C_5H_{12}$	−129.7	36.07	$n\text{-}Si_5H_{12}$	−138		$n\text{-}Ge_5H_{12}$		234
$iso\text{-}C_5H_{12}$	−159.6	27.9	$iso\text{-}Si_5H_{12}$	−74.5		$iso\text{-}Ge_5H_{12}$		234

separates the vapours of liquids having different boiling points. The overall yields are low, in part because of reaction of silanes with aqueous solutions; and the yields of individual silanes decrease rapidly with increasing molecular weight. The lower silicon hydrides can be decomposed thermally, or in an electric discharge, to hydrogen and the higher hydrides.

The silanes burn spontaneously to silicon dioxide and water vapour on contact with oxygen. They react explosively with the lower halogens at room temperature and with the halogens yield compounds called halosilanes. The silanes do not react readily with neutral or acidic solutions but hydrolyze readily and completely with evolution of hydrogen in alkaline solutions. Many alkyl derivatives have been described.

Halides. The more important halides are the halosilanes of the type formula Si_nX_{2n+2}, X being any halogen. Compounds with *n* up to 6 and also 10 and 25 are known; all the halogens occur in the smaller molecules but only fluorine and chlorine in the larger ones. In addition, species with the general formula $(SiX_2)_n$ have been described. These compounds are large polymeric molecules that are solids at room temperature. The composition $(SiX_2)_n$ can be considered in terms of the series Si_nX_{2n+2}, in which *n* is so large in comparison with +2 that 2 is of no significance. Mixed tetrahalides comparable to carbon tetrahalides, with such formulas as SiF_3Cl and $SiFClBr_2$, are also known.

The numerical constants of the silicon tetrahalides, general formula SiX_4, are summarized in Table 3. The melting and boiling points of the catenated halides increase in general with total molecular weight, both as *n* increases for a given halogen and also in the series of the halogens from fluorine to iodine for a given *n*. Only two halides of silicon, SiF_4, and Si_2F_6, are gases at ordinary temperatures; those that are liquids are the compounds with formulas Si_3F_8, $SiCl_4$, Si_2Cl_6, Si_3Cl_8, Si_4Cl_{10}, and $SiBr_4$. The physical properties of all of these compounds are those of covalent substances.

Except for the fluorides, the silicon halides hydrolyze readily in aqueous medium to hydrous silicon dioxide and hydrohalic acid. Silicon tetrafluoride yields, in addition, a solution of the industrially useful hexafluorosilicic acid (H_2SiF_6), one of the stronger acids. The salts of this acid are soluble in water, except for those of barium, yttrium, and the lanthanides. Many heavy metals are conveniently electrodeposited from hexafluorosilicate baths. Some of its salts are useful as insecticides.

Silicon tetrafluoride is prepared in several ways; the other silicon tetrahalides are prepared by direct combination of the elements.

Oxides. Silicon dioxide and the silicates have been discussed earlier. Silicon monoxide is obtained in the gaseous state when silicon dioxide and silicon are heated *in vacuo* at 1,450° C (2,640° F). Slow cooling of silicon monoxide gas results in its condensation to a solid mixture of silicon dioxide and silicon. Rapid cooling of the monoxide, however, yields a dark-coloured, resinous, and apparently amorphous form of the compound that is hard and nonconducting and that, on reheating, reverts to silicon and silicon dioxide. The solid monoxide is used as a coating on mirrors and optical glass because it resists abrasion and tarnish.

Sulfides. Silicon disulfide, like silicon dioxide, differs markedly from its analogue, carbon disulfide. It is a colourless, fibrous, crystalline compound that reacts readily with water to form silicon dioxide and hydrogen sulfide. It is also readily converted to silicon dioxide by oxygen. In the crystal, each silicon atom is surrounded tetrahedrally by four sulfur atoms, but two of those sulfur atoms serve as a bridge between each two silicon atoms, as shown in the structural formula

Silicon–sulfur chains

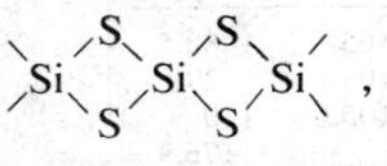

to build up a chain type of structure. Though interesting and of importance in understanding silicon chemistry, it has no practical uses.

Others. Silicon nitride (Si_3N_4), trisilylamine [$N(SiH_3)_3$], and other compounds containing silicon–nitrogen bonds are known, including organosilazanes, such as $R_3SiNHSiR_3$, $(R_3Si)_2NR$, R_3SiNHR, and $(R_2SiNH)_{3,4}$, in which R is an organic group. Complex species containing silicon are limited to the $[SiF_6]^{2-}$ ion and a few cations such as $[Si(C_6H_5)_3(2,2'\text{-dipyridyl})]^+$.

GERMANIUM AND ITS COMPOUNDS

The name germanium derives from the Latin word Germania (Germany) and was given to the element by its German discoverer, Clemens Winkler, in 1886.

Occurrence and distribution of the element. On a weight basis, germanium is a scarce but not an extremely rare element in the crust of the Earth, equalling in abundance beryllium, molybdenum, and cesium and exceeding the elements arsenic, cadmium, antimony, and mercury. In the cosmos, the atomic abundance of germanium is 50.5 (based upon $Si = 1 \times 10^6$), a value roughly equal to those for krypton and zirconium and only slightly less than that for selenium. The cosmic abundance is much less than those of a number of the heavier elements; *e.g.*, bromine, strontium, tin, barium, mercury, and lead. All of the elements of lower nuclear charge than germanium, except beryllium, boron, scandium, and gallium, are cosmically more abundant than germanium. Cosmically, germanium is believed to be one of the many elements formed by neutron absorption after the initial processes of hydrogen and helium burning and alpha-particle absorption.

Natural sources of germanium

Germanium is widely distributed in nature but is too reactive to occur free. Primary minerals include argyrodite, germanite, renierite, and canfieldite, all of them rare; only germanite and renierite have been used as commercial sources for the element. Trace quantities of germanium are found in certain zinc blendes, in sulfidic ores of copper and arsenic, and in coals, the latter possibly a consequence of the concentration of the element by plants of the Carboniferous Period in geologic history. Certain present-day plants are known to concentrate germanium. Both zinc-process concentrates and ash and flue dusts from coal-burning installations provide commercial sources of germanium.

Production of germanium. Pure germanium is obtained from these sources in a complicated process that finally yields billets or blocks, which may be purified by further refining to the quality required for the manufacture of semiconductors. Single crystals of germanium are grown in an atmosphere of nitrogen or helium from the molten material. These are then transformed into semiconductors by being doped (infused) with electron donor or acceptor atoms, either by incorporating the impurities in the melt during growth of the crystal or by diffusing the impurities into the crystal after it has been formed.

Properties of the element. The physical and chemical properties of germanium have been summarized earlier. Like silicon, germanium crystallizes in the diamond type of structure. The trend in properties noted with silicon and related to reduced bond energy continues with germanium. The electrical and semiconducting characteristics of germanium are comparable to those of silicon.

Germanium(II) compounds are well characterized as solids, and in general they are readily oxidized. Elemental germanium can be electrodeposited from many solutions and melts of its compounds. It is of interest that as little as one milligram of dissolved germanium per litre seriously interferes with the electrodeposition of zinc.

Germanides. True germanides are less well defined than the silicides. The alkali metals, M, react with germanium by direct combination to yield compounds with the general formula MGe, which yield compounds with the formula MGe_4 when heated *in vacuo* or in an inert atmosphere. Magnesium forms Mg_2Ge by direct combination, and calcium forms both Ca_2Ge and CaGe. Lanthanide compounds and actinide compounds may be classifiable as germanides. The other metallic elements, such as copper (Cu), titanium (Ti), molybdenum (Mo), palladium (Pd), iridium (Ir), and ruthenium (Ru), form combinations with germanium that are presumably more alloy-like, such as the compounds with formulas Cu_3Ge, Ti_5Ge_3, Mo_3Ge_2, Pd_5Ge_2, Ir_3Ge_4, and $RuGe_4$. Germanium does not react with carbon. Germanium and silicon are infinitely soluble in each other in both the liquid and solid states. Many metals form eutectic systems (mixtures that have a minimum melting point) with germanium.

Hydrides. The hydrides, or germanes, are comparable with their silicon analogues in most respects. They are, however, less stable to heat, less readily oxidized, and more resistant to hydrolysis under alkaline conditions than the silanes. The known germanes are all members of the saturated (containing no double bonds) series Ge_nH_{2n+2} (n being any number from 1 to 9), but physical data are known only for compounds with n up to 5. Evidences for chain branching in compounds to yield isomers (same molecular composition but different structure) have been presented. Yellowish-coloured, highly polymeric hydrides, with formulas $(GeH)_x$ and $(GeH_2)_y$, have been obtained, and, since their properties are comparable to those of the polymeric silicon hydrides, it is logical to assume that they are structurally similar. Mixed silicon–germanium hydrides are known.

The germanes react chemically very much as the silanes. Pyrolysis (decomposition through heat without presence of oxygen) results either in hydrogen and germanium or in cracking of the lower molecular weight species to those of higher molecular weight.

Halides. Well-characterized halides of germanium have been described for both oxidation states. Germanium(II) fluoride is a white, crystalline solid rapidly hydrolyzed by water; germanium(II) chloride is obtained as a white crystalline solid and is readily oxidized in air and hydrolyzed by water. Chlorine-bridged chains are present in the crystals. Germanium(II) bromide compares closely with the chloride; germanium(II) iodide is obtained as a yellow product that oxidizes easily in air.

The tetrahalides are closely comparable with their silicon analogues in both physical (Table 3) and chemical properties. The only well-characterized catenated halide is the colourless chloride Ge_2Cl_6 (melting point 40–42° C [104°–108° F]), which sublimes at room temperature.

Oxides. Germanium monoxide (GeO) and germanium dioxide (GeO_2) are, respectively, black and white solids. Germanium monoxide resists oxidation in moist air at room temperature but is converted to the dioxide at 550° C (1,020° F). It is insoluble in and unaffected by aqueous acidic and alkaline solutions. Above 700° C (1,300° F), it sublimes without decomposition. Germanium dioxide is obtained in three forms: a vitreous, or noncrystalline, glassy form; a hexagonal crystalline form; and a tetragonal crystalline form. Germanium disulfide and germanium monosulfide are, respectively, white and red to black solids.

Complexes. Complexes are formed with a variety of donor groups. In the majority of these, germanium(IV) is in an octahedral geometry (with coordination number 6). Examples include $[GeF_6]^{2-}$, $[Ge(C_2O_4)_3]^{2-}$, and $[Ge(OH)_2(On)_2]$, in which On represents 8-quinolinol.

TIN AND ITS COMPOUNDS

The symbol Sn for tin is an abbreviation of the Latin word for tin, *stannum.*

Occurrence and distribution of the element. On a weight basis, tin is a scarce but not rare element in the crust of the Earth, its abundance being of the same order of magnitude as such technically useful elements as cobalt, nickel, copper, cerium, and lead, and it is essentially equal to the abundance of nitrogen. In the cosmos, there are 1.33 atoms of tin per 1×10^6 atoms of silicon, an abundance roughly equal to that of niobium, ruthenium, neodymium, or platinum. Cosmically, tin is a product of neutron absorption. Its richness in stable isotopes is noteworthy.

The only mineral of commercial significance is cassiterite (SnO_2). No high-grade deposits are known. The major sources are alluvial deposits, averaging about 0.01 percent tin. Lode deposits, containing up to 4 percent, are found in Bolivia and Cornwall. The latter were worked at least as early as Phoenician times but are no longer of major consequence. Some 90 percent of world production comes from Malaysia, Thailand, Indonesia, Bolivia, Congo (Brazzaville), Nigeria, and China. The United States has no significant deposits. (For commerical production see TIN PRODUCTS AND PRODUCTION.)

Tin in Phoenician times

Properties of the element. The major physical and chemical properties of tin have been summarized earlier. The relationships among the allotropic modifications of tin can be represented as transformations from one crystal type to another at specific temperatures:

$$\underset{\text{(cubic-diamond crystals)}}{\text{gray or alpha } (\alpha) \text{ tin}} \xrightleftharpoons{13.2^\circ\text{ C }(55.8^\circ\text{ F})} \underset{\text{(tetragonal crystals)}}{\text{white or beta } (\beta) \text{ tin}}$$

$$\xrightleftharpoons{161^\circ\text{ C }(322^\circ\text{ F})} \underset{\text{(rhombic crystals)}}{\text{brittle tin}} .$$

(The double arrows signify that the transformation occurs in both directions, as tin is heated or as it is cooled.) Gray tin is easily crumbled, whereas white tin is malleable and ductile. The spontaneous conversion of the bright metal to a gray powder at low temperatures ("tin pest") seriously hampers the use of the metal in very cold regions. This change is rapid only below −50° C (−58° F), unless catalyzed by gray tin or tin(IV). As a consequence of internal friction, white tin emits a characteristic sound ("tin cry") when bent. Elemental tin is readily oxidized to the dipositive ion in acidic solution, but this tin(II) ion is converted to tin(IV) ion by many mild oxidizing agents, including elemental oxygen. Oxidation under alkaline conditions normally gives the tetrapositive (Sn^{4+}) state. In an alkaline medium, dipositive tin (Sn^{2+}) disproportionates readily to tetrapositive tin and the free element.

Intermetallic compounds. The compounds formed by tin with other metals are nearly all alloy-like and metallic rather than true stannides. The solid compound magnesium stannide, Mg_2Sn, is an insulator, but in the molten state it is comparable in electrical conductivity to molten tin. Although its crystal structure is like that of the ionic compound calcium fluoride (CaF_2), the crystals are not ionic. Crystals of the compounds with general formula MSn (in which M is copper, gold, iron, nickel, or platinum) have a structure in which each tin atom is surrounded by six M atoms and each M atom by six tin atoms but in different geometrical arrays.

Hydrides. The only known hydrides of tin are monostannane (SnH_4), distannane (Sn_2H_6), and the deuterated monostannes ($SnHD_3$ and SnD_4). Each of these compounds decomposes to its elements when heated—and at a lower temperature than its germanium analogue.

All of the halides of both tin(II) and tin(IV) are known. Some properties are summarized in Table 3. The fluorides are crystalline, ionic compounds, but the chlorides have covalent characteristics, and covalency increases through the bromides to the iodides.

Oxides. The monoxide of tin (SnO) is produced as a blue-black powder when the white hydroxide is dehydrated above 120° C (250° F) in the absence of air. At 550° C (1,020° F) and *in vacuo,* it changes to a red modification. Crystals of tin monoxide have layer structures in which four oxygen atoms lie in a square to one side of each tin atom. The white tin dioxide is obtained by the reaction of oxygen with the metal or the monoxide at elevated temperature, by the reaction of concentrated nitric acid with the metal, by the dehydration of the hydrous precipitate obtained by treating a tin(IV) halide solution with alkali, or by the hydrolysis of a tin(IV) halide or stannate(IV) solution.

Sulfides. Brown tin(II) sulfied (SnS) is precipitated by hydrogen sulfide from mildly acidic tin(II) chloride solution, and yellow tin(IV) sulfide (SnS_2) is precipitated from somewhat more acidic tin(IV) chloride solution. The latter is obtained as golden platelets, useful as a bronzing pigment, by direct reaction of the elements.

Complexes. Both tin(II) and tin(IV) complexes are numerous and include the species $[Sn_3(OH)_4]^{2+}$ and $[Sn(OH)_6]^{2-}$.

LEAD AND ITS COMPOUNDS

The symbol Pb for lead is an abbreviation of the Latin word for lead, *plumbum*.

Occurrence and distribution of the element. On a weight basis, lead has nearly the same abundance in the earth's crust as tin. Cosmically, there is 0.47 lead atom per 10^6 silicon atoms. The cosmic abundance is comparable with those of cesium, praseodymium, hafnium, and tungsten, each of which is regarded as a reasonably scarce element. Lead is formed both by neutron-absorption processes and the decay of radionuclides of heavier elements. Stable lead nuclides are the end products of radioactive decay in the three natural decay series: uranium (decays to lead-206), thorium (decays to lead-208), and actinium (decays to lead-207).

Although lead is not abundant, natural concentration processes have resulted in substantial deposits of commercial significance, particularly in the United States, but also in Canada, Africa, Australia, Spain, Germany, and South America. Significant deposits are found in the U.S. in the western states and the Mississippi Valley. Elemental lead is only rarely found in nature. The major minerals are galena (PbS), anglesite ($PbSO_4$), and cerussite ($PbCO_3$). (For commercial production see LEAD PRODUCTS AND PRODUCTION.)

Properties of the element. The major physical and chemical properties of lead and their relationships to electronic configuration and position in the periodic table have been summarized earlier. Only a single crystalline modification, with a close-packed metallic lattice, is known. Properties that are responsible for the many uses of elemental lead include its ductility, ease of welding, low melting point, high density, and ability to absorb gamma radiation and X-radiation. Molten lead is an excellent solvent and collector for elemental silver and gold. The structural applications of lead are limited by its low tensile and fatigue strengths and its tendency to flow even when only lightly loaded. Elemental lead can be oxidized to lead(II) ion by hydrogen ion, but the insolubility of most lead(II) salts makes lead resistant to attack by many acids. Oxidation under alkaline conditions is easier to effect and is favoured by the formation of the soluble lead(II) species. Lead(IV) oxide is among the stronger oxidizing agents in acidic solution, but it is comparatively weak in alkaline solution. The ease of oxidation of lead is enhanced by complex formation. The electrodeposition of lead is best effected from aqueous solutions containing lead(II) hexafluorosilicate(IV) and hexafluorosilicic acid.

Useful physical properties of lead

Hydrides and halides. All intermetallic compounds of lead are alloy-like with metallic properties.

The only lead(IV) hydride reported is monoplumbane (PbH_4), which is so unstable that no properties have been measured.

The lead(II) halides are all crystalline solids, the melting points of which generally decrease with increasing molecular weight (lead fluoride, 818° C [1,504° F]; lead chloride, 501° C [934° F]; lead bromide, 373° C [703° F]; lead iodide, 303° C [577° F]). The iodide is golden yellow; the others are colourless. Each is difficultly soluble in cold water. In the gaseous state, the molecules lead chloride ($PbCl_2$), lead bromide ($PbBr_2$), and lead iodide (PbI_2) have noncollinear structures.

Oxides. The oxides of lead include PbO (lead monoxide, red or yellow), Pb_2O_3 (lead sesquioxide, orange-yellow), Pb_3O_4 (red lead oxide, orange to red), and PbO_2 (lead dioxide, brownish black). The compounds Pb_2O_3 and Pb_3O_4 contain both lead(II) and lead(IV). Red PbO (with tetragonal crystal structure), called litharge, is the stable form of lead (II) oxide at room temperature. At 488° C (910° F), it transforms to the yellow modification (with rhombic crystal structure), called massicot, which has a melting point of 884° C (1,623° F) and boiling point of 1,470° C (2,680° F). Lead(II) oxide is the only stable oxide above 550° C (1,020° F), and all the other oxides lose oxygen when heated to form it. At 500° C (930° F), heating either lead(IV) oxide or lead(II) oxide in air gives Pb_3O_4 (red lead or minium), which is used extensively as a rust-inhibiting paint pigment.

The monoxides of lead are amphoteric (act as either acid or base depending on environment) and dissolve in both acidic and strongly alkaline solutions. Lead(IV) oxide is the active component of the positive plates in the rechargeable lead storage cell.

The only lead sulfide is the compound PbS, melting point 1112° C (2,034° F); both naturally occurring and synthetically produced samples vary in colour from silvery to black with a metallic lustre.

Miscellaneous compounds include the nitrate [$Pb(NO_3)_2$], which is the common, water-soluble salt; the acetate trihydrate [$Pb(C_2H_3O_2)_2 \cdot 3H_2O$], sugar of lead, which is also water soluble; the hexafluorosilicate [$(PbSiF_6) \cdot 2H_2O$], also water soluble; a basic carbonate [$2PbCO_3 \cdot Pb(OH)]_2$, white lead, the classic, universally used white paint pigment; the chromates, chrome yellow ($PbCrO_4$) and chrome red ($PbCrO_4 \cdot PbO$), both important as pigments in rust-inhibiting paints; and the sulfate ($PbSO_4$), which is difficultly soluble in water.

Lead(II) complexes are common; lead(IV) complexes are largely limited to the species $[PbCl_6]^{2-}$ and $[Pb(OH)_6]^{2-}$.

Nuclear properties. Of the radionuclides of lead, the following appear as members of the three natural decay series: (1) thorium series: lead-212; (2) uranium series: lead-214 and lead-210; (3) actinium series: lead-211. The atomic weight of natural lead varies from source to source, depending on its origin by heavier element decay.

BIBLIOGRAPHY. *Gmelins Handbuch der Anorganischen Chemie*, 8th ed., System-Number: 14-Carbon (1967–70), 15-Silicon (1958–59), 45-Germanium (1956–58), and 47-Lead (1969), each a comprehensive critical summary of all available information; C.A. HAMPEL (ed.), *The Encyclopedia of the Chemical Elements* (1968), see articles on "Carbon," pp. 106–115; "Germanium," pp. 237–244, "Lead," pp. 357–367; "Silicon," pp. 634–647; "Tin," pp. 722–732, each article a short but comprehensive account of occurrence, recovery, properties, and more significant compounds; T. MOELLER, *Inorganic Chemistry*, ch. 16 (1952), comprehensive coverage of the group in systematic fashion, with many literature citations; A. STANDEN (ed.), *Kirk-Othmer Encylopedia of Chemical Technology*, 2nd ed. (1964–69), see articles on "Carbon," 4: 70–510; "Germanium," 10:519–527; "Lead," 12:207–282; "Silicon," 18:46–268; "Tin," 20:273–327.

(T.Mo.)

Carboniferous Period, Lower

The Carboniferous Period is the time interval between 345,000,000 and 280,000,000 years ago. It therefore comprises approximately 65,000,000 years of the Paleozoic Era, between the earlier Devonian Period (*q.v.*) and the later Permian Period (*q.v.*). It is divided into two parts, the Lower and Upper Carboniferous, which in North America are more often referred to under the names Mississippian and Pennsylvanian.

The Carboniferous System was defined by W.D. Conybeare and J. Phillips in 1822 in England and Wales as a class of rocks that

> . . . will contain not only the great coal deposit itself, but those of the limestone and sandstone also on which it reposes; which, though entitled to the character of distinct formations, are yet so intimately connected with the above, both geographically and geologically, that it is impossible to separate their consideration.

The name refers to the rich deposits in these strata.

The most characteristic biological feature of the Carboniferous is the development of terrestrial fauna. Until the beginning of the Carboniferous, water was the only realm of animal life, and the land was only sparsely inhabited by small plants. With the onset of Carboniferous time, a fauna began to develop on the land that grew ever richer in the course of the succeeding geological periods and moved toward its present complexity. The first dense plant cover on land and the first trees, some reaching heights of up to 30 metres (100 feet), appeared. Favourable geographic and climatic conditions gave rise to immense swamp forests and bogs, from which coal deposits were created. The lush vegetation was accompanied by the first insects and reptiles. Because crawling amphibians inhabited the swamp forests, the Carboniferous is sometimes termed the Amphibian Age.

Lower Carboniferous Time Designations in Europe, the Soviet Union, and North America

Western Europe		U.S.S.R.		North America	
Silesian	Namurian	Middle Carboniferous		Pennsylvanian	
		Lower Carboniferous	Namurian	Mississippian	Chesterian
Dinantian	Viséan		Viséan		Meramecian
	Tournaisian		Tournaisian		Osagian
					Kinderhookian

The term Lower Carboniferous denotes different periods of time in Europe, North America, and the Soviet Union. In Europe the time span treated by this article is termed the Dinantian; in North America the Mississippian; and in the Soviet Union it is simply called Lower Carboniferous. The lower limits of these three designations are approximately contemporaneous, but their upper limits differ (see Table). To the Dinantian is assigned about 25,000,000 years, constituting more than one-third of Carboniferous time. Because the investigation and systematization of the Carboniferous began in western Europe, by convention the Lower Carboniferous is internationally understood to mean the Dinantian. (For further treatment of these intervals, see below *Stratigraphic correlations.*)

Boundaries of Dinantian

The boundaries of the Dinantian are defined by the first appearance of certain molluskan species: its lower limit is based on the occurrence of the cephalopod *Gattendorfia subinvoluta* and its upper limit by that of the cephalopod *Eumorphoceras (Edmooroceras) tornquisti*. The localities in which these index species are commonly found are in Germany in the case of the lower limit and in England and Ireland in the case of the upper.

Lower Carboniferous rocks are primarily derived from marine sediments. Igneous and metamorphic rocks are much less common than sedimentary rocks and are nowhere dominant. The Lower Carboniferous sedimentary rocks contrast with those of most other geological ages by the strong predominance of two basic rock types, which are found in almost all occurrences of Lower Carboniferous strata. These are limestones rich in fossils and clastic rocks.

The noteworthy mineral fuel deposit that is characteristic of the Lower Carboniferous is coal, which is mined in Spitsbergen, the Scottish Midland Valley, and the European part of the Soviet Union. In the United States there are large deposits of petroleum as well as coal in the Lower Carboniferous rocks. Lower Carboniferous limestones are quarried on all the continents. In Scotland the oil shales have limited importance. Economically important ore deposits are not a prominent feature of the Lower Carboniferous. Near coal fields some iron ores of sedimentary origin occur; these are only locally important and were mined mainly in the 19th century.

This article treats the rocks, life, and environments of Lower Carboniferous time. Similar information on subsequent geological history is contained in the article CARBONIFEROUS PERIOD, UPPER. See also COALS and PETROLEUM for information on mineral fuels that formed during the Carboniferous, and CYCLOTHEMS for treatment of the rhythmic sedimentation so characteristic of Carboniferous deposits and coal measures.

LOWER CARBONIFEROUS ROCKS

Lower Carboniferous formations are scarce in the Southern Hemisphere. Marine conditions prevailed only intermittently in parts of South America and Australia. Terrestrial sediments are known at some localities in these regions. Lower Carboniferous rocks are primarily known over wide expanses of the Northern Hemisphere. The sea covered large parts of the present continents and extended far across the continental shields, upon which its deposits have been preserved in their original, near horizontal position.

Deposits on shield areas and in geosynclines

The continental shields were covered by shallow shelf seas in which limestones, several hundred metres in thickness, were formed. In most cases they are rich in fossils. Similar sediments were deposited over regions consisting of Lower Paleozoic rocks. The limestone sediments, which are often in the form of reefs or reef rubble, are called carboniferous limestones (Kohlenkalk) because of their connection to sediments rich in carbon: they underlie coal-bearing sediments or coal seams are embedded in them.

The largest of these Lower Carboniferous shelf regions is in North America; a smaller one is in eastern Europe. In both areas they occur on the continental shields. In North America the Lower Carboniferous shelf sea extended approximately from the Appalachians to the Rocky Mountains, in eastern Europe approximately from Poland to the Urals.

In contrast to the stable shelf regions, unstable, rapidly sinking basins also were sites of sediment deposition. Enormous masses of debris collected in these basins, and after they had been filled, mountains were later created by folding and uplift.

The extensive, deep ocean basins (geosynclines), from which high mountains subsequently arose during the Mesozoic Era are also identifiable in the Lower Carboniferous. The Tethys Geosyncline can be followed from the Mediterranean region through Turkey, Iran, and the Himalayas to Southeast Asia. The Cordilleran Geosyncline, the other principal oceanic trough, followed the north-south orientation of the coasts of North and South America.

Mountains arose from smaller geosynclines during the Upper Carboniferous. The Appalachian Geosyncline in Lower Carboniferous time already was restricted by earlier mountain-building processes. The northern part of this depression, which is preserved in Nova Scotia and New Brunswick, was sufficiently filled with sediments to have become dry land. This is attested by strata that contain freshwater fossils. Farther to the southwest, in Pennsylvania, this condition was not reached until Upper Carboniferous time. Circumstances in central Europe were quite similar at this time. A developing mountain range, extending from France to eastern Germany, supplied coarse debris to subsidence areas in which the coal bogs of the Upper Carboniferous were subsequently created. In the direction of the more stable shelf regions to the west (Belgium, Great Britain, Ireland) and to the east (Poland, Soviet Union), the coarser clastic sediments grade into the predominantly chalky series of the shelf sea.

Limestones, along with lime-rich clay rocks and sandstones, are surely the most widely distributed rocks of the Lower Carboniferous. They were formed almost exclusively in the shelf seas on the margins of the continental shields or over areas solidified before the Carboniferous Period. In many places—*e.g.,* in the European part of the Soviet Union—such series contain economically important coal strata. Less widely distributed, but usually of greater thickness, are the graywackes, sandstones, and clay rocks of the geosynclines.

Coal-bearing strata

Terrestrial deposits are rare in the Lower Carboniferous. Sandy formations are found in South America and Australia, and coal-bearing strata occur in some locations, mostly as forerunners of the Upper Carboniferous coal-bearing series. They appear in the more stable shelf regions (Belgium, Scotland, European part of the Soviet Union) and in the orogenic regions of Nova Scotia and New Brunswick.

The limestone strata in the stable regions and the predominance of clastic rocks such as shales and sandstones in the orogenic regions are the distinctive characteristics of Lower Carboniferous deposits. The thickness of the limestone series is more uniform that that of the sandy sediments of the orogenic facies. In the Northern Hemisphere the limestone is mostly between 500 and 1,000 metres (1,640 and 3,280 feet) thick. The marine series of North America and Great Britain are about 1,000 metres (3,280 feet) thick, the coal-bearing series of the Moscow Basin about 250 metres (820 feet), and that of the Donetz Basin, in which coal also occurs, more than 1,000 metres (3,280 feet) thick. Marine and nonmarine deposits alternate rhythmically in these coal-bearing strata.

Even over short horizontal distances, the clastic facies vary greatly in thickness. Because these deposits represent debris of local origin they can vary greatly over short distances. In central Europe such deposits are up to 2,000 metres (6,560 feet) thick (Czechoslovakia, Germany); when a less abundant supply of sediment is available, an entire series of strata may be as thin as 500 metres (1,640 feet).

Intrusive and extrusive igneous rocks are of local to regional importance in the Lower Carboniferous. They occur in the geosynclines, on the shelf (Kazakhstan), and in nonmarine areas (Scottish Midland Valley, Eastern Siberia).

Metamorphic rocks from the Dinantian are known principally from the high mountains that originated from the great Cordilleran Geosyncline and from the Eurasian Tethys Geosyncline in Mesozoic or Cenozoic time. Knowledge of these rocks is limited, as they are altered by the high pressures and temperatures of folding and mountain formation. The formation of new minerals and mechanical deformation of the rocks have often altered beyond recognition or destroyed the fossils that would have aided the determination of the age of the rocks.

LOWER CARBONIFEROUS LIFE

The Lower Carboniferous is characterized principally, and especially as compared to that of all older geological formations, by the abundance and variety of its plants. These plants are excellently preserved in the coal-bearing strata. During the course of the Devonian, plants had indeed spread over large areas of the land surface (before this there had been only water plants); but in the Lower Carboniferous, because of particularly favourable climatic conditions, plant coverage was very dense. Trees appeared for the first time, grew to considerable heights, and developed woody trunks.

The Psilophytales, which had constituted a considerable portion of the pre-Carboniferous flora, died out in the Carboniferous. The "coal forests" of the Lower Carboniferous consisted of Lycopodiales, lower vascular plants whose trunks reached heights of 30 metres. High-growing trees with woody trunks also were found among the Articulata, but these also constituted the "reeds" in the vicinity of the coal bogs and in moist locations, including coastal areas. For this reason Articulata are also known from marine deposits, particularly of the detritus facies, although less well preserved.

A very notable advance in terms of evolutionary history was the appearance of the first seed plants (Pteridospermales or Cicadoficiles). Gymnospermae also appeared for the first time, as trees.

Among the algae (thallophytes), only those that precipitate lime are of geological significance. Sea algae existed in great quantity, sometimes forming reefs, and these became part of the limestone facies of the shelf regions.

General character of animal life

In the animal world, the great changes were afoot that led to the fauna of Mesozoic time. In the Carboniferous, animal life followed the plants onto the land. Crossopterygii-like amphibians appeared, inhabiting the swamp-forests; some were more than five metres long.

Of great importance for the history of life on Earth was the first appearance of the Goniatitidae (belonging to the Mollusca) at the lower border of the Carboniferous: these spiral-shelled animals, related to the cuttlefish of the present day, are among the decisive guide fossils for the determination of the age of strata from the beginning of the Carboniferous to the end of the Mesozoic.

In the rest of the animal world no fundamental changes were to be observed. Because of the wide distribution of favourable conditions for Lower Carboniferous life (in the shelf seas large areas were covered with shallow water rich in nutrients and oxygen), a number of animal groups expanded into a great multiplicity of forms. Among the single-celled animals this was true of the Foraminifera; among the Echinodermata, it applied to the crinoids and blastoids, which appear particularly on the North American midcontinent shelf as rock-forming agents. Among the mollusks, snails and mussels were richly developed. Surprisingly, the Brachiopoda declined in number of forms; this group inhabited the same environments as the Mollusca. Whereas they had been present in extraordinary variety in the pre-Carboniferous systems, they were represented by far fewer forms in the Carboniferous. Only the small systematic group of the Productoidea expanded in the Carboniferous; almost all other groups were impoverished. Not until the middle of the Mesozoic did the Brachiopoda again experience something of a heyday before contracting again to the few species that survive today.

In the series containing coal beds in the northeastern United States, in Scotland, and in the European part of the Soviet Union, brackish water and lacustrine (lake-dwelling) organisms were rather widely distributed and numerous for the first time in the Earth's history. The fauna consisted predominantly of mussels, which resembled in structure the brackish-water mussels of today.

The marine fauna known from the Lower Carboniferous constituted a very uniform group. The occurrences on what are now separate continents indicate that the more or less contemporaneous fauna often consists of dissimilar species; endemic species also occur. But at the same time a considerable number of genera are found throughout the world. There were as yet no faunal or floral provinces, which first began to develop in the Upper Carboniferous and which are so clearly delineated today. This uniformity is the more astonishing because similar fauna inhabited regions of dissimilar climate.

The Lower Carboniferous formations of North America, Europe (including Spitsbergen), and North Africa originated in the vicinity of the Equator, in tropical and subtropical climates. In these regions, coal beds are found that were formed in tropical or subtropical swamp forests and bogs during Carboniferous time. On the other hand, the similar marine fauna of eastern Australia must have developed in a significantly colder climate, for in the Upper Carboniferous there appear throughout the southern part of Australia traces of glaciation; this is also true in South Africa and South America.

Marine invertebrate faunas

The fauna contained in limestones, which formed in the shelf regions at the periphery of the continental shields or over substrata consolidated in pre-carboniferous time, consist mainly of benthonic organisms—those living on the ocean floor. Particularly richly developed in these facies are the calcareous algae, which also formed reefs: the Stromatopora, Tabulata, Coralla, and Bryozoa. A variety of forms developed in the Foraminifera, in the productid brachiopods and in the snails and mussels. The trilobites of these facies have not yet been thoroughly studied; the Phillipsiidae and Brachymetopus seem to predominate. Among the Echinodermata, the crinoids and blastoids of the North American midcontinent shelf are well known for their variety and good preservation.

The much poorer fauna of the predominantly clastic facies, which developed in the deeper seas of the orogenic regions, consisted mainly of swimming and floating types of life. The seawater at greater depths was so poorly supplied with oxygen that for the most part only a few specialized species, such as primitive burrowing animals, could live there. With the exception of these, the ocean floor was little inhabited. Cephalopods, relatives of the present-day cuttlefish, are particularly characteristic of these facies, which are also called Culm Facies. Mussels that lived attached to floating seaweed masses, swimming trilobites, and conodonts (*q.v.*) were numerous and widely distributed.

The two types of fauna, the benthonic of the shelf seas and the nektonic-planktonic of the deeper basins, hardly ever occurred together in the same region. The boundaries between shelf and basin are extraordinarily sharp. The compositions of the rocks and of the fauna change almost in a hairbreadth and as far as is known scarcely ever blend. Because the ages of rocks are determined with the aid of the fossils that they contain, there was great difficulty in finding time relationships between the shelf deposits and the basin deposits. The discovery and study of distinctive microfossils, particularly the foraminifera and conodonts, ultimately made this possible.

STRATIGRAPHIC CORRELATION

Upper and lower boundaries and boundary problems

The limits of the Dinantian (see table) have been defined bindingly at international conferences of experts. Because the stratigraphy of the Lower Carboniferous was first developed in western Europe and because the geological relationships there seemed favourable, the type sections are located in western Europe. The type section for the lower boundary is in West Germany and that for the upper boundary is in England and Ireland. The definition of the upper limit is not questioned but that of the lower limit is in dispute. The disagreement is on questions of principle; in the series of strata the disputed interval seldom amounts to more than 60 metres (192 feet).

In North America the Lower Carboniferous is called the Mississippian, because strata of this age are extensively exposed in the Mississippi Valley and have been known and studied for many years. The lower limit of the Mississippian coincides with the lower limit of the Dinantian, but the Mississippian extends higher, including in its upper part strata, which, according to international terminology, belong to the Namurian Series in the Upper Carboniferous (the Silesian).

The different locations of the boundaries between Lower and Upper Carboniferous in North America, western Europe, and the Soviet Union is due primarily to historical reasons. Formerly, the boundaries between geological units were set at surfaces of discontinuity, at distinct changes of rock type, or at changes in the attitude of bedding. The boundary between the Upper and Lower Carboniferous in North America and western Europe was set at the base of the principal coal formation. In North America, with the exception of the Lower Carboniferous beds in Nova Scotia and New Brunswick, the age of this stratum was younger than in the "classical" region of western Europe (Belgium). Furthermore, in North America this change of facies is associated with an evident hiatus or gap in the series of strata, an elevation of a broad region above sea level, and mild folding. A hiatus in the series of strata also is found over a wide area in the Soviet Union.

Within the Lower Carboniferous, shelf facies sedimentation is often discontinuous. This applies particularly to the North American midcontinent shelf and presumably to the Soviet Union as well. Such gaps in the strata make the determination of series difficult because the succession is interrupted. The shoreline and bottom of the sea that covered North America and the European part of the Soviet Union was very sensitive to movements of the sea floor or alterations of the sea level because of its shallow character. Small local uplifts were sufficient to cause the formation of sea-floor rises or islands, and small local subsidences caused great distinctions between somewhat deeper basins and the shallower areas. Also, of course, the position of the shorelines changed, and this produced shifts in the boundary between marine and nonmarine sediments.

In the upper part of the Mississippian, shallow-water formations become more frequent and are interbedded with more widely distributed clastic sediments. This suggests an increase in the energy of the environment with respect to erosion and transportation of sediment. The tectonic phase that uplifted and mildly folded large parts of the North American sedimentation realm began at this time. In the Pennsylvanian, a completely new geological situation began.

Weak tectonic movements occurred in Europe at this time. In western Europe, the Dinantian strata were not folded until the Upper Carboniferous or later.

The Asiatic Dinantian is scarcely folded at the edge of the continental shield. Metamorphic remains of Lower Carboniferous strata are known from the Himalayas, but the exact time of the folding and alteration is not certain.

In eastern Australia the Carboniferous strata proceed without any break from the Devonian. The transitional strata are without fossils, however, and thus the position of the boundary cannot be established precisely. The upper boundary of the Dinantian also cannot be determined. In the upper part of the Lower Carboniferous, the sediments in the New England Geosyncline become successively more coarse grained, and the latest sediments, from approximately the end of the Namurian, show signs of terrestrial origin.

LOWER CARBONIFEROUS PALEOGEOGRAPHY

When the contemporaneity of Lower Carboniferous rocks is established it is possible to map the distribution of land and sea at this time in the past; however, terrestrial deposits are less often preserved than marine deposits because they tend to be removed by erosion. Their location and boundaries can only be inferred from some erosional remnants. It must be remembered that over large areas of the Earth's surface the Lower Carboniferous marine formations also have undergone erosion or have been masked by younger sediments. Finally, there are other areas of the Earth that are still really unknown geologically. Reconstructions of the distribution of land and sea in Lower Carboniferous time must, therefore, be understood as being to a large degree hypothetical.

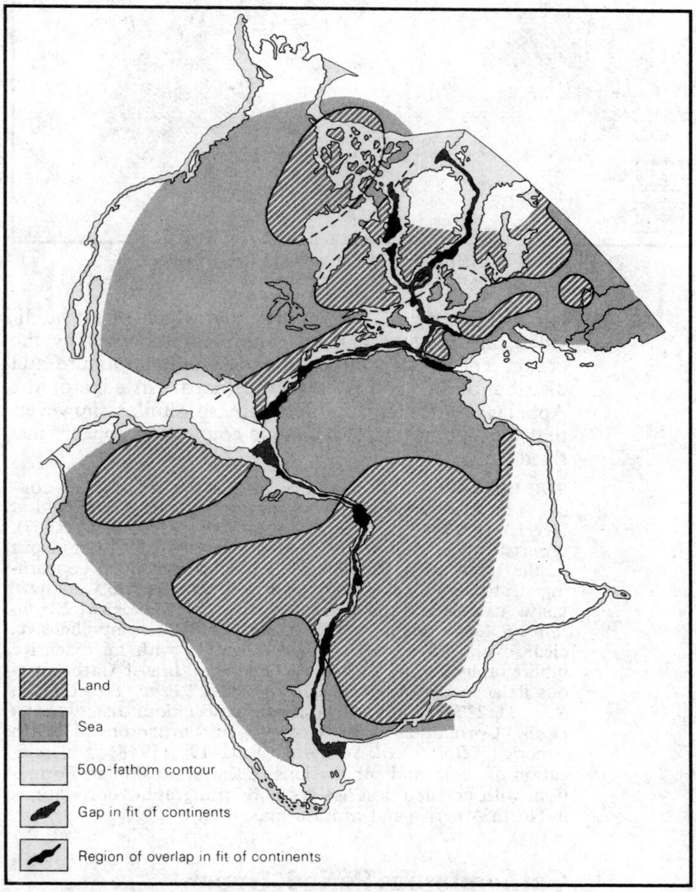

Figure 1: Distribution of land and sea bordering on the Atlantic Ocean in Lower Carboniferous time, plotted on a predrift reconstruction of continents. The fit is at the 500-fathom contour.

Figures 1 and 2 show the present conception of Lower Carboniferous paleogeography. The maps show the greatest extent of the sea during this period. In the course of time, the sea retreated more and more, particularly from the southern continents.

Figure 1 shows the continents bordering upon the Atlantic in their probable relative positions in the Lower Carboniferous. The connection across the Atlantic is difficult to demonstrate. The continuity of the upland ridge from the Appalachians to Bohemia is uncertain. The upland ridge need not be assumed to be a continuous moun-

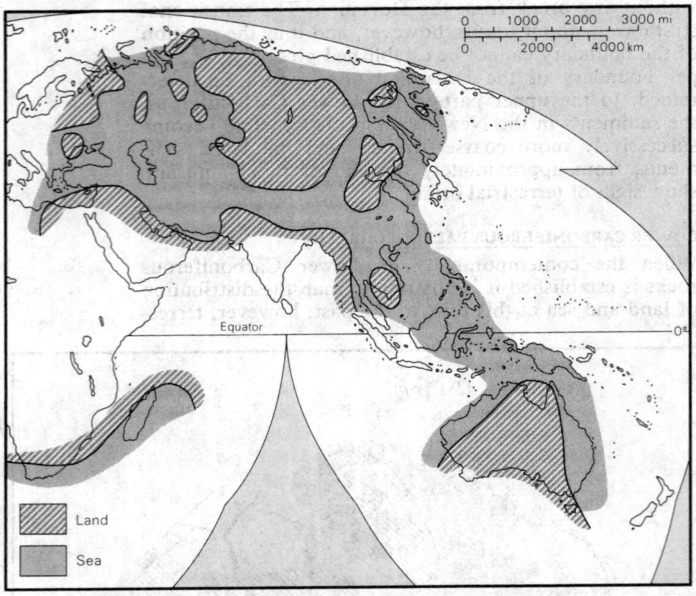

Figure 2: Distribution of land and sea in the Eastern Hemisphere during Lower Carboniferous time.

tain range but rather an uplift zone, which might be divided into sections and in some places covered by the ocean. The geological development and the nature and distribution of the fossils on the (northern) edge of the Appalachian-Bohemian uplift are so similar, however, that the assumption of a genetic connection appears justified.

BIBLIOGRAPHY. Proceedings of the INTERNATIONAL CONGRESS ON STRATIGRAPHY AND CARBONIFEROUS GEOLOGY, held at Heerlen (1927, 1935, 1958); Paris (1963); and Sheffield (1967), reports, official statements, and discussions of Commissions of the International Union of Geological Sciences, concerning stratigraphy, palynology, and coal petrology; D.A. BROWN, K.S.W. CAMPBELL, and K.A.W. CROOK, *The Geological Evolution of Australia and New Zealand* (1968), a comprehensive, clear overlook of the geological history, with an extensive bibliography through 1965; T.N. GEORGE, "Lower Carboniferous Palaeogeography of the British Isles," *Proc. Yorks. Geol. Soc.*, 31:227–318 (1958), a classic description; J.M. WELLER *et al.*, "Correlation of the Mississippian Formations of North America," *Bull. Geol. Soc. Am.* 59:91–196 (1948), a classification of rocks and subdivisions of the Mississippian Formation, with detailed descriptions and stratigraphic correlations in North America and with Europe.

(E.P.)

Carboniferous Period, Upper

Definition and general nature of the record

The name Carboniferous is derived from coal-bearing strata in the type areas of England and Wales that form the upper part of the sequence described as "Carboniferous" by the British geologists William Conybeare and William Phillips in 1822. The Carboniferous is part of the Paleozoic Era of Earth history, which occurred from 225,000,000 to 570,000,000 years ago. The Upper Carboniferous refers to the rocks deposited during the time interval from about 315,000,000 to 280,000,000 years ago. It roughly coincides in time, and usage, with the Pennsylvanian Period, a name that is particularly applied to the time of formation of rocks of the same age in North America (see further GEOLOGICAL TIME SCALE). Boundaries of this system of rocks have been established by the International Congress of Carboniferous Stratigraphy and Geology. The base, or lowermost strata, of the Upper Carboniferous is defined by the first occurrence of the cephalopod species *Eumorphoceras (Edmooroceras) tornquisti*. There is no generally accepted definition of the upper limit. A variety of changes of floral and faunal assemblages occur and are useful in restricted regions, but are probably not strictly synchronous.

In Europe, North America, Australia, and to a much lesser extent North Africa, the Upper Carboniferous and overlying Permian strata contain a huge volume of coals—the greatest such concentration in the Earth's history. This can be related to the great Variscan (Hercynian) orogenic (mountain-building) episode that, in Carboniferous time, created new mountain chains flanked by deep sedimentary basins. Late in Carboniferous time, sediments from these new mountains had filled the associated basins, producing large flat areas near sea level and similar areas within some of the mountain-belt zones. These developments coincided with an explosive evolution of land plants and, following plant decomposition, with enormous accumulations of peat, especially in the equatorial regions during Late Carboniferous time. The peats were subsequently compressed and petrified, and thus became coals.

The southern continents were still united as the single landmass called Gondwana (see below) during Carboniferous time. This supercontinent was glaciated, and fossil moraines and tillites—ice-transported sedimentary deposits of clay, silt, sand, and gravel—are widespread in the southern continents today. There the Carboniferous and Permian strata are continuous in character, and the Northern Hemisphere's index fossils are lacking. It is often convenient to regard the "Permo-Carboniferous" of the southern continents as a single rock system.

Deposits of epicontinental (shallow) seas are preserved in the southern midcontinent region of North America, on the Russian Platform, and in eastern Asia. They include large volumes of fossiliferous limestone. The areas receiving shallow-water, calcareous sediment were, however, much restricted compared with pre-Upper Carboniferous sites of marine deposition.

Deposits of economic significance

The most significant economic deposits of the Upper Carboniferous are coals. An estimated 3×10^{12} metric tons, the major part of the Earth's coal reserves, occurs in Carboniferous strata and, to some extent, in Permian deposits. The process by which peat becomes coal frees large quantities of natural gas, and this can migrate into any suitably porous rocks that are available. This relationship, with Upper Carboniferous coals serving as the gas source, has been proved to hold for gas fields in The Netherlands, Germany, and the North Sea. Upper Carboniferous sandstones in Oklahoma and Montana are important reservoirs of oil.

Occurrences of metallic ores in Europe, Asia, and Australia are related to large granite masses that were emplaced in the folded rocks that formed during the Late Carboniferous or Early Permian mountain-building episodes. Metal-bearing solutions deposited gold, silver, lead, copper, tin, zinc, tungsten, bismuth, and other metals. Only the tin ores of Southeast Asia are still economically important on a world scale however. But it should be remembered that the European ore fields in Cornwall (England), Germany, France, and Spain stimulated the development of the classical mining techniques, and from this geology emerged as a science.

This article treats the rocks, life forms, and paleogeography of the Upper Carboniferous. For additional information on prior and subsequent geological time intervals, see CARBONIFEROUS PERIOD, LOWER; PERMIAN PERIOD. See also EARTH, GEOLOGICAL HISTORY OF and PALEOZOIC ERA, UPPER for the relation of Upper Carboniferous events to Earth history in general. Further detail on life forms is presented in the article FOSSIL RECORD, and aspects of the correlation of sedimentary rocks and the elucidation of ancient environments are covered in the articles STRATIGRAPHIC BOUNDARIES; SEDIMENTARY FACIES; and PALEOGEOGRAPHY.

UPPER CARBONIFEROUS ROCKS

Gondwana and continental drift

Geographic framework. The geography during the Upper Carboniferous Period was very different from that of the present. The continental masses that exist today were arranged in two great supercontinents. The Gondwana supercontinent comprised South America, Africa, Antarctica, Australia, and India south of the Himalayas. The present shapes of these fit almost perfectly (eastern South America to West Africa, South Australia to Antarctica, Western Australia to eastern India), and much geological and geophysical evidence supports the con-

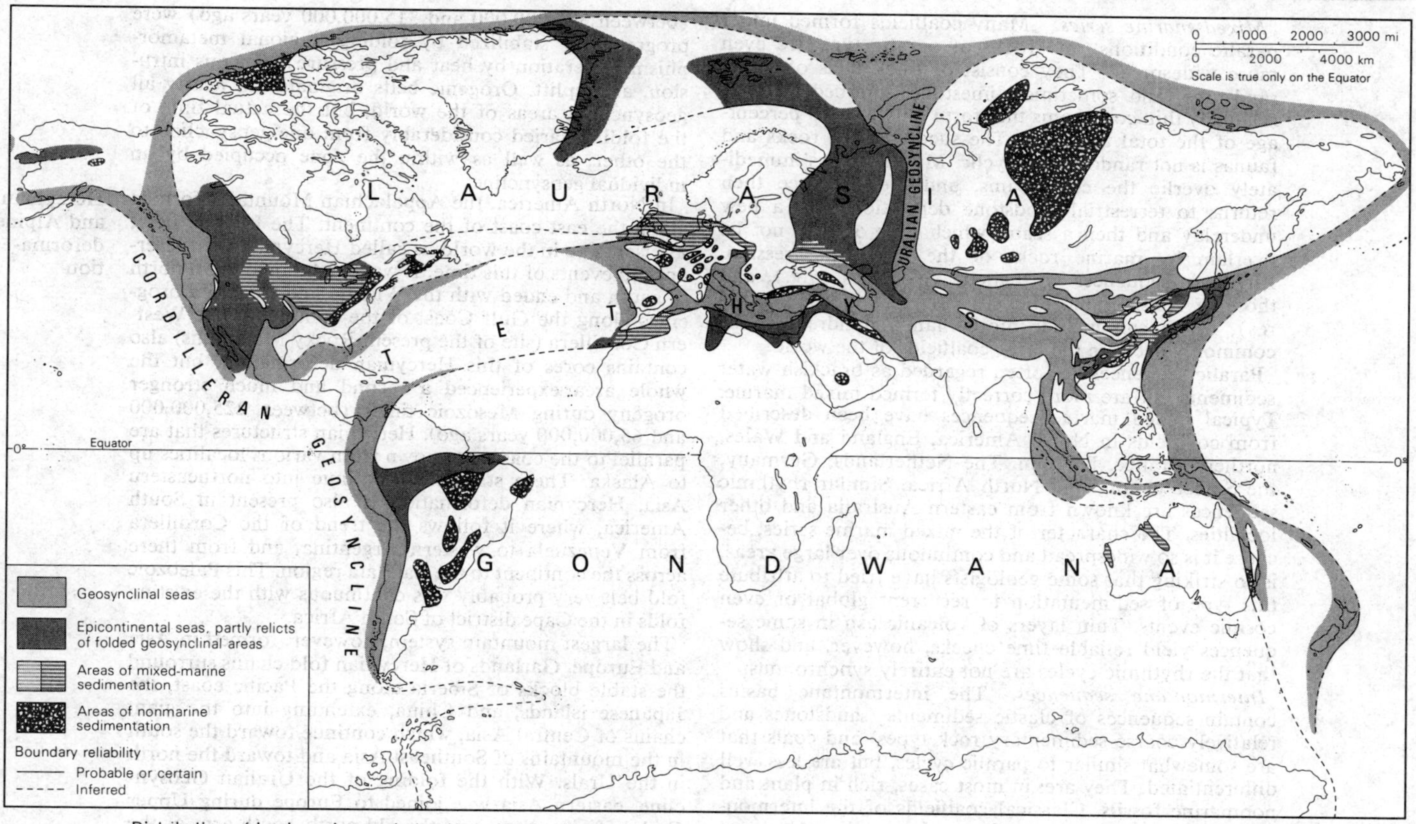

Distribution of lands and seas during Upper Carboniferous time.

cept that they did once fit together. No record of oceanic geography can, therefore, be expected to occur within this mass. It was a continental shield (stable continental nucleus) overlapped by the seas only peripherally, at its margins. Similarly, North America, Greenland, and western Europe were united. The position held by Asia relative to Europe is not certain. Asia appears to have been subject to rifting (separation) along north-south lines. An oceanic area still existed along the site of the Urals during Late Carboniferous time.

The Gondwana supercontinent centred on the South Pole. The North Pole was situated in the northern Pacific Ocean area, close to Siberia. The great ocean, called Tethys, which intervened between the two supercontinents, occupied equatorial latitudes. Tethys extended in an east-west direction from China to Spain and into the Caribbean. This major oceanic area of Carboniferous time later suffered reduction as the continents drifted and the sediments in this seaway were folded and uplifted to form new mountain chains.

Within this general geographical framework the Upper Carboniferous sediments accumulated as epicontinental deposits (marginal deposits in shallow areas) or as the fill received by basins flanking the major supercontinental blocs. Many of the Upper Carboniferous rocks originated in a system of basins that extended from western South America to southern Africa, and thence, probably, to western Antarctica and eastern Australia, thus girdling Gondwana. Branches of Tethys extended into central and western Europe and probably also into the site of the present Appalachian Mountains. Adjacent continental platforms (*e.g.*, the Russian Platform and a large part of North Africa) were covered by shallow areas.

The northern continents, like the southern, consisted of the one mass flanked by oceanic basins. But it is obvious that an elongate basin feature along the site of the Urals effected a connection of Tethys and the Arctic. The northern supercontinent (the so-called Laurasia) was thus divided into a western shield (comprising parts of Canada, Newfoundland, Greenland, northern Britain, Scandinavia, and the Baltic region) and an eastern shield (the Siberian platforms).

Sedimentary rocks. The Upper Carboniferous rocks for the most part document sedimentation in basins bordering the continents or on the stable platforms. The rapid crustal movements of Late Carboniferous time permitted local accumulation of great thickness of sediment. The basin sediments are of graywacke character (a type of sandstone with a clay-rich matrix; see further GRAYWACKES) where deepwater situations existed, or, where the deliveries of sediment outdid the ability of crustal subsidence to accommodate them, the upper surface of the sedimentary pile would remain close to sea level, resulting in a mixed, marine-nonmarine (paralic) sedimentary succession. Many of the mixed marine series grade landward into deltaic deposits and into dominantly marine sediments seaward. An example is found in the western slope of the Appalachians. The thin veneers of epicontinental marine sediments formed on the stable platforms consist predominantly of limestones and sandstones.

Implications of relief

Graywackes. The Upper Carboniferous graywackes owe their character to the availability of bold relief at the time of their formation. Material derived from uplifted welts (narrow, geosynclinal folds) was deposited rapidly in deltaic flats and on narrow shelves bordering the subsiding basins. Where these piles of sediment locally exceeded the natural angle of rest or stability in the face of gravitational forces on slopes, the unconsolidated material on the continental shelves would collapse, be transformed into a relatively high density suspension, and would travel into the basins as high-velocity turbidity currents, a variety of density currents, in which the density results from large quantities of sediment carried in suspension. The resulting basin deposits are poorly sorted. They consist of angular grains of quartz, feldspar, and mica, together with fragments of previously existing igneous, metamorphic, or sedimentary rock. They may also include mud pebbles. Individual graywacke beds have a distinct grading, with a continuous decrease of grain size from bottom to top. Intervening between graywacke beds are fine-grained shales that represent slow, permanent, background sedimentation of the basin.

Mixed marine series. Many coalfields formed under paralic conditions, and rocks of paralic type are even more widespread. They consist of thick beds of shale, sandstone, and sometimes limestone, interbedded with relatively thin coal seams that form only a small percentage of the total thickness. The succession of rocks and faunas is not random, but cyclic. Marine shales immediately overlie the coal seams, and the sequence then returns to terrestrial sandstone deposition with a new underclay and then a seam, which may or may not be overlain by marine rocks of the next transgression. Rhythmic sequences are called cyclothems (*q.v.*), and those of considerable thickness (several thousand metres), which can include more than a hundred seams, commonly occur in the large coalfields of the world.

Paralic sequences are often regarded as brackish water sediments but are more correctly termed mixed marine. Typical mixed marine sequences have been described from coalfields in North America, England and Wales, northern France, Belgium, The Netherlands, Germany, the Soviet Union, and North Africa. Similar rhythmic sequences are known from eastern Australia and other localities. The character of the mixed marine series, because it is so widespread and continuous over large areas, is so striking that some geologists have tried to attribute this type of sedimentation to recurrent global or even cosmic events. Thin layers of volcanic ash in some sequences yield reliable time checks, however, and show that the rhythmic cycles are not entirely synchronous.

Intermontane sequences. The intermontane basins contain sequences of clastic sediments (sandstones and relatively coarse sedimentary rock types) and coals that are somewhat similar to paralic cycles, but are less well differentiated. They are, in most cases, rich in plant and nonmarine fossils. Classical coalfields of the intermontane type occur in the northeasterly trending Variscan fold belt in western Europe and along the east coast of North America (in the Rhode Island and Acadian basins).

Limestones. Deposition of fossiliferous limestones occurred on continental shelves, if they were relatively stable, and generally in epicontinental or shallow sea areas. The calcareous sequences often show evidence of discontinuous sedimentation, with reworking (erosion and redeposition), interbedded conglomerates, and times of nondeposition. Shallow-water fossils are abundant in some areas. They include calcareous algae, large fusulinids—wheat-grain-like foraminiferans, and brachiopods. Echinoderms are rare by comparison with the Lower Carboniferous limestones.

Shallow-water limestones are found in the midwestern United States, on the Russian Platform, and in China and Southeast Asia. In some places limestones are interbedded with mixed marine sequences, as in the Donets Basin in the Soviet Union and in parts of England.

Evaporites and terrestrial sediments. In equatorial latitudes, the deposition of evaporites (sedimentary rocks formed by precipitation of salts from saline waters) under arid conditions began in the Upper Carboniferous but, generally, reached its maximum within the Permian. In the basins of North Dakota–Montana and southeast Utah–southwest Colorado of the United States, crustal movements during Pennsylvanian time produced conditions that favoured the accumulation of salts (of Upper Carboniferous and later age) in isolated basins.

Terrestrial sediments were deposited near the newly formed mountain chains, mostly as alluvial fans, fan-shaped accumulations of gravel, sand, and silt deposited by streams draining mountain basins. They grade into deltaic and mixed marine sediments toward the open sea.

A different type of terrestrial sediment formed in polar areas. Some conglomerates and sandstones and tillites of the great Permo-Carboniferous glaciation are locally regarded as Carboniferous. No definite proof exists, however, because guide fossils are lacking.

Igneous and metamorphic rocks. Rapid crustal development occurred during the Upper Carboniferous Period. The zones of the crust that had undergone geosynclinal development (subsidence and filling with sediment) during the Devonian and Lower Carboniferous periods (between 395,000,000 and 315,000,000 years ago) were progressively stabilized by folding, regional metamorphism (alteration by heat and pressure), igneous intrusion, and uplift. Orogenic belts originated in nearly all geosynclinal areas of the world, but the actual time of the folding varied considerably from one geosyncline to the other, as well as within the zone occupied by an individual geosyncline.

Hercynian and Alpine deformation

In North America, the Appalachian Mountains formed along the east coast of the continent. The folding, here, as elsewhere in the world, is called Hercynian with reference to events of this time. It was gradational from north to south and ended with the Wichita and Ouachita orogenies along the Gulf Coast of the continent. The Western Cordillera (site of the present Rocky Mountains) also contains cores of this Hercynian deformation, but the whole area experienced a second and much stronger orogeny during Mesozoic times (between 225,000,000 and 65,000,000 years ago). Hercynian structures that are parallel to the coast are known from various localities up to Alaska. These structures continue into northeastern Asia. Hercynian deformation is also present in South America, where it follows the trend of the Cordillera from Venezuela to western Argentina, and from there across the continent to the La Plata region. This Paleozoic fold belt very probably was continuous with the existing folds in the Cape district of South Africa.

The largest mountain system, however, formed in Asia and Europe. Garlands of Hercynian fold chains surround the stable blocks of Siberia along the Pacific coast, the Japanese islands, and China, extending into the giant chains of Central Asia, which continue toward the south in the mountains of Southeast Asia and toward the north in the Urals. With the folding of the Uralian Geosyncline, eastern Asia was joined to Europe during Upper Carboniferous time, and the old north–south arm of the ocean was closed.

South of the Urals the Hercynian chains continue through the Hindu Kush and Elburz mountains into Turkey. The tectonic structures of central and western Europe are greatly complicated by a large number of local arches, by rapidly changing degrees of deformation, and metamorphism.

Most of the Asian and European mountain belts were produced by the great Alpine orogeny of Tertiary age (between 65,000,000 and 2,500,000 years ago), which affected even larger areas than the Hercynian and produced greater deformation, but which in general followed the grain of the Hercynian orogeny. The Alpine orogeny complicated certain of the Hercynian structures by folding and metamorphosing the rocks a second time. Another system of mountains was formed by folding and uplift along the eastern coast of Australia and in New Zealand. This continued to Antarctica and was probably connected to the South American Cordillera (site of the present Andes Mountains).

The Hercynian orogeny was accompanied by the typical cycle of volcanism during initial geosynclinal activity (mostly submarine effusions) and post-orogenetic intrusion of igenous rocks that may result in the emplacement of enormous granitic plutons. Regional metamorphism may accompany these intrusions. In Upper Carboniferous time most of the geosynclinal volcanism was already over. Important volcanic rocks are known only from the western geosyncline of North America and from China, Japan, and Kashmir. Granitic intrusions and metamorphism are widespread, but the exact age relations are not easily determined, especially in areas affected by later diastrophism. Absolute age determinations by radiometric methods are important for identifying Hercynian granites and metamorphic rocks.

UPPER CARBONIFEROUS LIFE

Life forms and their distinctive character

Many of the Upper Carboniferous life forms represent a stable continuation of previously established groups. This was the case with such marine invertebrate groups as corals (especially the tabulates), brachiopods, lamellibranchs, gastropods, nautiloids, orthoceratids, and crinoids. Limulids achieved their characteristic form.

Evolutionary trends and index fossils. Protozoans appeared for the first time in relatively large forms, up to 15 millimetres (0.6 inch) long. These fusulinids were abundant and widely distributed. Often they contributed a large part of the content of limestones. A group of coiled decapods, the goniatites, developed steadily (thus providing for a suite of useful guide fossils), and, toward the end of Carboniferous time, forms transitional to the Mesozoic ammonites appeared.

Active sharklike fishes dominated the seas. There was rapid development of the ancestors of modern fishes, the paleoniscids. Large amphibians inhabited the coal swamps. Prominent among them were the plump labyrinthodonts and the slender leptospondyls. The first reptiles appeared in Late Carboniferous time. The greatest advances occurred among the plants. Algae formed much of the bulk of certain limestones because reef-building corals were essentially absent. Enormous swamps covering vast areas had well-developed associations of lycopsids, ferns, articulates, and cordaites. Their height was comparable to that of modern trees. Minor species of climbing or submerged habits were also present. Mosses were not important in this association.

The groups that combine wide distribution and rapid changes of form are utilized as guide, or index, fossils for correlation purposes. The preferred Upper Carboniferous groups are the goniatites of the open seas, the fusulinid foraminiferids of the shelf seas, and the higher plants on land. Each of these groups is restricted to its own environment, and it is, therefore, difficult to match the three schemes of indices. Recently, conodonts (small, toothlike, enigmatic fossils) also have revealed themselves to be useful index fossils, and they occur in abundance in open sea and epicontinental marine sediments as well as in marine transgression portions of the paralic succession of sediments.

Goniatites, fusulinids, and fossil plants

The suite of goniatites has the genera *Eumorphoceras*, *Homoceras*, *Reticuloceras*, *Gastrioceras*, *Anthracoceras*, and *Schistoceras*. The Carboniferous–Permian boundary may be set at the first appearance of *Properrinites*.

The fusulinid sequence begins in the Lower Carboniferous with *Millerella* and continues with *Profusulinella*, *Fusulinella*, *Fusulina*, and *Triticites*. *Pseudoschwagerina* marks the beginning of the Permian. These forms are identified by internal characteristics that must be examined in thin sections.

Fossil plants also are difficult to deal with, in this case because it is usual to find only parts of plant fronds, stems, and rhizomes. Individual parts were given names before the composition of the whole plant was known. The taxonomy of fossil plants is, therefore, complex. Also, plants are subject to local climatic controls, such as humidity. An observed change in fossil-plant associations may have been caused by ecological factors. The proliferative organs such as spores, on the other hand, are distributed freely by the wind and can be found fossilized in rocks that contain no larger plant material—for example, in marine shales. The importance of spores as guide fossils is rapidly increasing.

Faunal realms and migrations. No distinct faunal realms can be recognized at present. Plants break down into local regimes in Late Carboniferous times, presumably because of climatic deterioration. There are artificial sources of confusion in this matter. Paleontologists, if they neglect work done in other countries, may create "nomenclatorial" provinces (see correlation chart: plant zonation). Problems of this kind are known and their solution requires much time and effort.

STRATIGRAPHIC CORRELATION

Boundary and correlation problems. In the type areas in Europe a notable change of facies (rock type and associated environmental factors) occurs within the Carboniferous. Marine limestones change to black shales, siltstones, and graywackes. The separation of Lower and Upper Carboniferous is based on this change. The lowermost unit of the Upper Carboniferous is named Namurian after the type area in the Namur Basin of Belgium. The facies change, it is now known, is not strictly isochronous (*e.g.*, the sedimentary formations involved are not precisely of the same age—they are not time correlative) within Europe. Furthermore, it is known that the boundary defined in Belgium does not correspond with the Mississippian–Pennsylvanian boundary in North America—this is set later in time. The major change of facies is not in evidence in eastern Europe. Soviet geologists favour a three-fold subdivision of the Carboniferous and recognize a "Middle Carboniferous" that is roughly equivalent to the Lower and Middle Pennsylvanian.

The upper limit of the Carboniferous is not clearly defined. The Late Carboniferous was a time of drastic tectonic and climatic change. Nowhere is there a continuous record of Carboniferous to Permian pelagic (deepwater) sedimentation. Many local definitions of the Permo–Carboniferous boundary exist, but it is unlikely that the various definitions employed in intermontane basins and shallow marine areas will be found to match one another.

The major stratigraphical subdivisions of the Upper Carboniferous are shown on the correlation chart. In regions with continental and mixed-marine sediments, correlation is based on lithological evidence, and the boundaries are drawn at coal seams, layers of volcanic ash, or the beginnings of major sedimentary cycles. The correlation is controlled by the paleontological evidence available from interbedded marine or plant-bearing deposits. In marine areas with no widely effective, contemporaneous changes of sedimentary conditions, the stratigraphical subdivisions depend directly on the evidence of fossils. There is much work still to be done in improving intercontinental correlations of the units.

Mississippian-Pennsylvanian boundary

Unconformities and gaps in the record. The effect of an unconformity (discontinuous sedimentation) is best illustrated by the case of the pre-Pennsylvanian break in the midcontinent area of the United States. The boundary between the Mississippian and Pennsylvanian periods is placed at the surface of unconformity. The base of the Pennsylvanian is not everywhere of the same age, however, because of local accidents of renewal of deposition after the uplift and the erosion that produced the discontinuity.

Until recent years it was thought that orogenic events were catastrophic, concentrated in short passages of time, and worldwide in their effect. It is now generally accepted that deformation and uplift in orogenic zones is an evolutionary process that may occupy an interval as long as a geological period or more. Unconformities, therefore, can no longer be assumed to record widespread contemporaneous events.

Gaps between Lower and Upper Carboniferous rocks exist in many parts of the world. The Carboniferous of the Himalayas and Southeast Asia down to Burma, for instance, is reported to include such a break. It is not unlikely that the unconformity on that regional scale will later be resolved into a number of local and individual breaks, as has happened in areas now intensively surveyed, such as the southeastern United States. Countless local breaks are known in areas of epicontinental, shallow-water sedimentation. In such cases (there are many examples in the American midcontinent), the Upper Carboniferous record is reduced to thin occurrences of heterogeneous and discontinuously developed sedimentary rocks.

UPPER CARBONIFEROUS CLIMATES

Floral indication of climatic change

A remarkable differentiation of climate begins within the Upper Carboniferous Period as indicated by the development of circumpolar floral assemblages (the southern, or Gondwana, and northern, or Angara, types), which contrast with the more equatorial floras. This differentiation increased during the Upper Carboniferous and resulted in a broad equatorial zone with arid conditions, reddish-coloured and other desert deposits, and evaporites, while at the same time the greater part of Australia, the eastern part of South America, Africa south of the present Equator, India, and Antarctica were covered by a polar ice cap. Little is known about the north pole of these times. Some indications of a cold, arid climate have recently been reported from evidence in the Upper Carboniferous

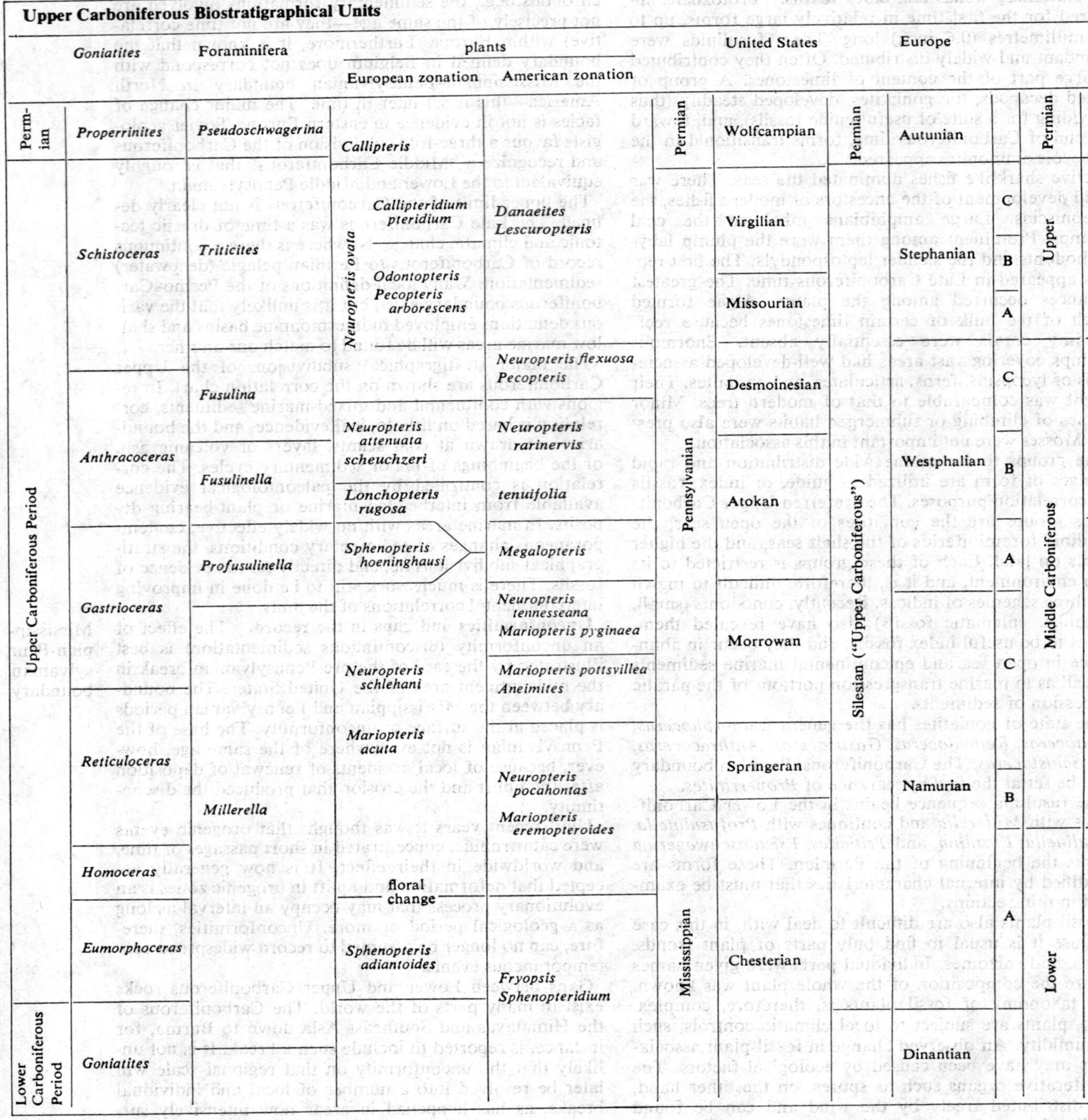

Upper Carboniferous Biostratigraphical Units
Goniatites
Foraminifera
plants
European zonation
American zonation
United States
Europe
Russia
Perm-ian
Properrinites
Pseudoschwagerina
Callipteris
Permian
Wolfcampian
Permian
Autunian
Permian
Asselian
Callipteridium pteridium
Danaeites
Lescuropteris
Virgilian
C
Schistoceras
Triticites
Neuropteris ovata
Stephanian
B
Upper
Uralian
Odontopteris
Pecopteris arborescens
Missourian
A
Neuropteris flexuosa
Pecopteris
C
Fusulina
Desmoinesian
Neuropteris attenuata
Neuropteris rarinervis
Moscovian
Anthracoceras
scheuchzeri
Westphalian
B
Fusulinella
Lonchopteris rugosa
tenuifolia
Atokan
Upper Carboniferous Period
Sphenopteris hoeninghausi
Megalopteris
Pennsylvanian
Profusulinella
A
Gastrioceras
Neuropteris tennesseana
Mariopteris pyginaea
Morrowan
Neuropteris schlehani
Mariopteris pottsvillea
Aneimites
C
Bashkirian
Silesian ("Upper Carboniferous")
Middle Carboniferous
Mariopteris acuta
Reticuloceras
Neuropteris pocahontas
Springeran
Namurian
B
Millerella
Mariopteris eremopteroides
Homoceras
floral change
A
Eumorphoceras
Sphenopteris adiantoides
Chesterian
Lower
Serpuchovian
Fryopsis
Sphenopteridium
Mississippian
Lower Carboniferous Period
Goniatites
Dinantian

rocks of east Siberia. The maximum climatic differentiation occurred in the Permian Period.

The reason for this worldwide change of climate is not well understood. It was, however, preceded by a rapid shift of the magnetic poles and by extensive modifications of the configuration of the continents and oceans resulting from the worldwide Hercynian orogeny. The process of evolution of the Earth's crust may, therefore, have been the most effective cause of climatic and biological evolution during Upper Carboniferous time.

BIBLIOGRAPHY. Comprehensive books and monographs on the distribution and regional aspects of Upper Carboniferous formations include: G.M. BENNISON and A.E. WRIGHT, *The Geological History of the British Isles* (1969); D.A. BROWN, K.S.W. CAMPBELL, and K.A.W. CROOK, *The Geological Evolution of Australia and New Zealand* (1968); T.H. CLARK and C.W. STEARN, *The Geological Evolution of North America* (1960); R. FURON, *Géologie de l'Afrique*, 3rd ed. rev. (1968); S.H. HAUGHTON, *Geological History of Southern Africa* (1969); M. MINATO *et al.* (eds.), *The Geologic Development of the Japanese Islands* (1965); D.H. RAYNER, *The Stratigraphy of the British Isles* (1967); M.G. RUTTEN, *The Geology of Western Europe* (1969); and H.R. WANLESS, "Marine and Non-Marine Facies of the Upper Carboniferous of North America," *6th Congr. Int. Stratigr. Géol. Carbonifère, Compte Rendu*, 1: 293–336 (1969). Periodical reports on Carboniferous stratigraphy and geology are presented in *Congrès International de Stratigraphie et de Géologie du Carbonifère, Compte Rendu* (Heerlen, 1927, 1935, 1958; Paris, 1963; Sheffield, 1967; Krefeld, 1971).

Books presenting information on the background of Upper Carboniferous history that are of general interest include: A.L. DU TOIT, *Our Wandering Continents: An Hypothesis of Continental Drifting* (1937); B. KUMMEL, *History of the Earth* (1961); M. SCHWARZBACH, *Das Klima der Vorzeit*, 2nd ed. (1961); and A. WEGENER, *Die Entstehung der Kontinente und Ozeane*, 3rd ed. (1922; Eng. trans., *The Origin of Continents and Oceans*, 1924).

(D.M.)

Carbonium Ions

Carbonium ions are carbon-containing molecules with positive charges (cations). Certain carbonium ions can be prepared in such a way that they are stable enough for study; more frequently, however, they are only short-lived transient forms (intermediates) occurring in the course of chemical reactions.

Carbonium ions are, in fact, one of the most common classes of intermediates in organic reactions, and knowledge of the structures and properties of these substances is fundamental to the understanding of the reactions in which they occur. Many of these reactions are of great synthetic, biochemical or industrial importance.

Discovery of carbonium ions as intermediates

The first carbonium ions (called triarylmethyl compounds) were observed in 1901, and their saltlike character was discerned shortly afterward. It was not until 21 years later, however, that the German chemist Hans Meerwein concluded that a neutral product (isobornyl chloride) was formed from a neutral reactant (camphene hydrochloride) by rearrangement involving a carbonium ion intermediate. This was the first conceptualization of a carbonium ion as an intermediate in an organic rearrangement reaction. The idea was generalized by the U.S. chemist Frank Clifford Whitmore from 1932 onward and placed on a firm experimental basis by the English chemists Sir Christopher Ingold and E.D. Hughes, beginning in the late 1920s. Although a great deal had been surmised about carbonium ions by indirect methods in the meantime, it was only after 1960 that general methods for the formation of stable, long-lived carbonium ions became available.

Classical and nonclassical carbonium ions

Classification. Two distinct classes of carbonium ions have come to be recognized. The first are the "classical" carbonium ions, which contain a trivalent instead of the usual quadrivalent carbon atom centre. The carbon atom is in an sp^2 state of hybridization—that is, the three bonding electrons of the carbon atom (the electrons in the outermost electron shell of the atom) occupy orbitals, or pathways, within the shell that are alike, each formed by the combination (hybridization) of three ordinary orbitals, one denoted *s* and two, *p*. All three orbitals lie in one plane; thus, the cationic centre of the molecule formed by bonding the carbon atom with three other atoms or groups tends to be planar. Since in most compounds the carbon atom centre has four pairs of bonding electrons, the carbonium ion is electron deficient; hence it carries a positive charge. The parent for these ions is the carbenium ion, or methyl cation, with the formula CH_3^+ (C being the chemical symbol for a carbon atom and H the symbol for hydrogen, with the subscript indicating the number of atoms in the structure and the plus sign the positive charge). Schematically, this structure is as shown below (the solid lines representing bonds between atoms):

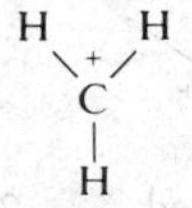

carbenium ion
(methyl cation)

The second class of carbonium ions includes the pentacoordinated, or "nonclassical," carbonium ions, which have three single bonds, each joining the carbon atom to one other atom, and a triangular two-electron, three-centre bond—that is, a bond that connects three atoms, rather than the usual two, with a single electron pair. Such units are positively charged because they include an extra atomic nucleus, and the carbon atom generally maintains tetrahedral geometry; that is, the attached groups form the corners of a tetrahedron with the carbon atom at the centre, as in the parent structure for these ions, the methonium ion, CH_5^+, in which the dotted lines represent a three-centre bond:

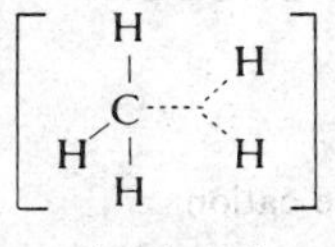

methonium ion

It has been proposed that the term carbocation be used for all types of carbonium ions, with the name carbenium ion being used for the trivalent types and the name carbonium ion being reserved solely for the pentacoordinated substances. As of the early 1970s, however, this usage had not been generally adopted.

It is frequently possible to distinguish between these two types of carbonium ions experimentally, as, for example, by the use of certain instrumental methods—nuclear magnetic-resonance spectroscopy, which gives information about atomic nuclei; infrared and Raman spectroscopy, which are based on light absorption; and, more recently, X-ray-induced electron-emission spectroscopy, which gives information about bond energies.

Preparation and stability. Several methods are known for the generation of carbonium ions. They may all, however, be classified in one of the following categories: (1) heterolytic (unsymmetrical) cleavage of the two-electron bond between a carbon atom and an attached group; (2) electron removal from a neutral organic compound; (3) addition of a proton, or other cation, to an unsaturated system; and (4) protonation, or alkylation (addition of an alkyl, or hydrocarbon, group), of a carbon–carbon or carbon–hydrogen single bond. Since carbonium ions are positively charged species, they are most readily formed in relatively polar solvents (solvents consisting of molecules with unsymmetrical distribution of electrons), which help disperse their charges or the charges on the accompanying negatively charged ions throughout the medium. Commonly used solvents include methanol, aqueous acetone, acetic acid, and trifluoroacetic acid.

Effects of solvent on carbonium-ion stability

The fate of a carbonium ion produced by one of these methods is determined essentially by two factors: (1) the nature of the medium in which the ion is generated and (2) the inherent stability of the ion itself. Carbonium ions are generally produced in solvents in which they react rapidly with the solvent or with an available nucleophilic agent (a substance attracted to positively charged entities). Since, under these conditions, carbonium ions have only a fleeting existence, indirect methods must be used for their study. The commonly used methods are kinetics (measurements of rates of reaction), chemical analysis of the product formed by reaction of the carbonium ion (particularly, determination of spatial arrangements of atoms in a molecule), and isotopic labelling (that is, the use of radioactive isotopes to identify particular atoms).

Recently, "superacid" solvents (solvents of low nucleophilicity) have been found that do not react with many carbocations. These solvents are hydrogen fluoride–antimony pentafluoride and fluorosulfuric acid–antimony pentafluoride with sulfur dioxide or sulfuryl chloride fluoride also present. In these solvents, the lifetime of many carbonium ions is sufficient to allow their direct observation. Modern instrumental methods have been particularly useful in this regard. The most widely used and the most important instrumental method has been nuclear magnetic-resonance spectroscopy, which gives information concerning the magnetic environment of the various nuclei in the carbonium ion as well as information about the charge distribution within the ion. Other spectroscopic methods that have been employed are X-ray crystallography; infrared, ultraviolet, and mass spectroscopy; and X-ray-induced photoelectron spectroscopy.

Effects of structure on carbonium-ion stability

The stability of carbonium ions depends upon various electronic and steric (spatial) factors. Among the electronic factors are inductive effects (the simple attraction of electrons by positive centres), conjugation (interaction with electrons from double bonds), hyperconjugation (interaction with electrons from carbon–hydrogen or carbon–carbon bonds), and aromaticity (interaction with electrons from cyclic, electron-rich systems). The steric factors to be considered are strain (distortion of bonds for spatial reasons), deviations from planarity (for the sp^2 carbonium centre atom), and nonbonding interactions (influences between atoms not joined to one another by chemical bonds). It is the interplay of these factors that determines the stability of a particular carbonium ion.

Tertiary carbonium ions, for example, are generally more stable than secondary carbonium ions, which, in turn, are more stable than primary ones. In tertiary carbonium ions, the sp^2 carbon is bonded to three alkyl groups; in secondary carbonium ions, the sp^2 carbon atom is bonded to two alkyl groups and one hydrogen atom; in primary carbonium ions, the sp^2 carbon is bonded to either one alkyl group and two hydrogen atoms or, in the case of the methyl cation, three hydrogen atoms. Examples of each are shown below.

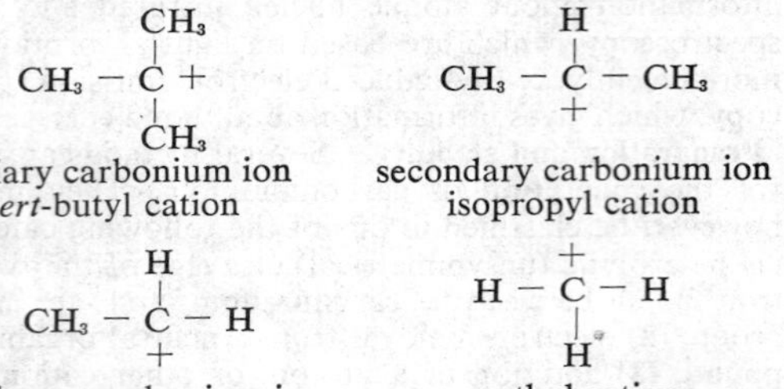

tertiary carbonium ion *tert*-butyl cation — secondary carbonium ion isopropyl cation — primary carbonium ion ethyl cation — methyl cation

This relative order of stability is explained on the basis of the ability of an alkyl group to disperse the charge on the sp^2 carbon atom by hyperconjugation (an effect that overcomes the destabilizing inductive effect of the alkyl group).

Benzyl cations are more stable than most primary cations because the benzyl ions are stabilized by resonance —that is, the delocalized electrons in the aromatic ring make possible a distribution of the positive charge among the carbon atoms so the cation can exist in many forms, all of which contribute to the overall structure. Resonance forms of the benzyl cation are shown below:

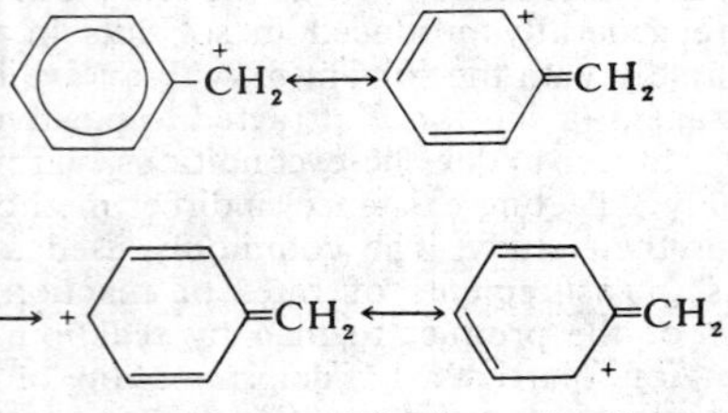

resonance forms of the benzyl cation

In these structures the benzene ring is indicated by a hexagon, each corner of which is considered to be a carbon atom (the attached hydrogens not being shown). The form with a circle in the hexagon represents structures with alternating double and single bonds in the ring; the other forms are those in which charges appear at various locations in the ring.

Reaction with nucleophiles

Reactions. Since carbonium ions are electron-deficient entities, they react with any electron-donor molecules, which are also referred to as nucleophiles. There are three types of nucleophiles; *n*-bases, pi bases, and sigma bases, in which *n*, pi, and sigma refer to the bonding state of the donor-electron pair in the nucleophile—that is, nonbonded, pi-bonded, and sigma-bonded, respectively. (Sigma bonds are ordinary covalent bonds between atoms and pi bonds are the special bonds that occur in unsaturated and aromatic systems.) The nucleophile may be either external or internal (that is, constituting a portion of the cation itself). In the latter case, rearrangement may occur. Examples of the various possible reaction types are shown below:

1. Reaction with external *n*-base: acid-catalyzed hydration (addition of water) of isobutylene. In this reaction, there is an unshared (nonbonded) electron pair on the oxygen atom of the water molecule:

$$(CH_3)_2C{=}CH_2 + H^+ \longrightarrow (CH_3)_3C^+$$

isobutylene — proton — *tert*-butyl cation

$$\xrightarrow{H_2O} (CH_3)_3C\overset{+}{O}H_2 \longrightarrow (CH_3)_3COH$$

water — *tert*-butyl alcohol

2. Reaction with external base: alkylation of benzene using isopropyl chloride (Friedel–Crafts reaction). Benzene acts as the donor molecule, with the donated electrons coming from the pi-bonded system of the benzene ring:

$$CH_3\overset{Cl}{\overset{|}{C}}HCH_3 \xrightarrow{AlCl_3} CH_3\overset{+}{C}HCH_3$$

isopropyl chloride — aluminum chloride — isopropyl cation

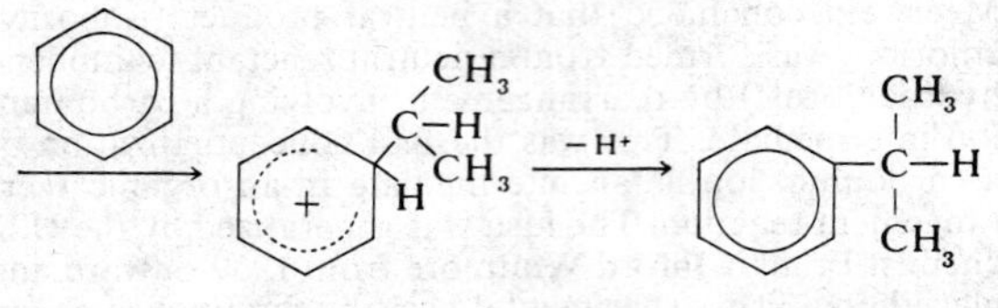

benzene — proton — cumene

In the above equation, the partial circle with the plus charge in the hexagon stands for those forms of the cation in which the positive charge is distributed around the ring (as in the benzyl cation, pictured above).

3. Reaction with external sigma base: hydride transfer reaction in which the donor electron pair comes from the carbon–hydrogen sigma bond in isobutane:

$$(CH_3)_3CCH_2\overset{+}{C}(CH_3)_2 + HC(CH_3)_3$$

isooctyl cation — isobutane

$$\longrightarrow (CH_3)_3CCH_2CH(CH_3)_2 + \overset{+}{C}(CH_3)_3$$

isooctane — *tert*-butyl cation

4. Reaction with internal *n*-base: cyclization reaction, with nonbonded electron pair on an oxygen atom serving as donor:

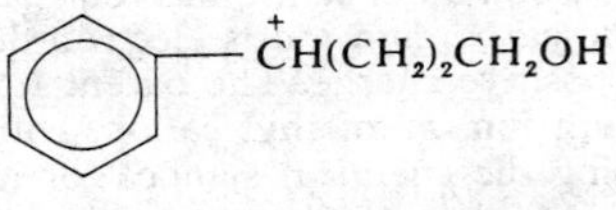

benzyl-type cation

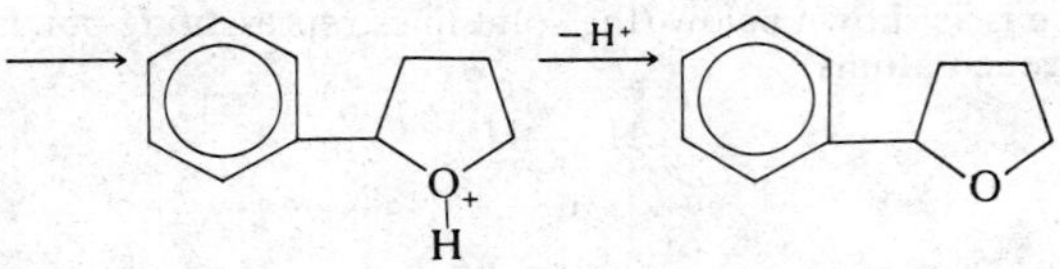

oxygen-protonated 2-phenyltetrahydrofuran — 2-phenyltetrahydrofuran

5. Reaction with internal pi base: acid-catalyzed cyclization to form β-ionone, with the donor electrons coming from the pi electrons of the unsaturated system:

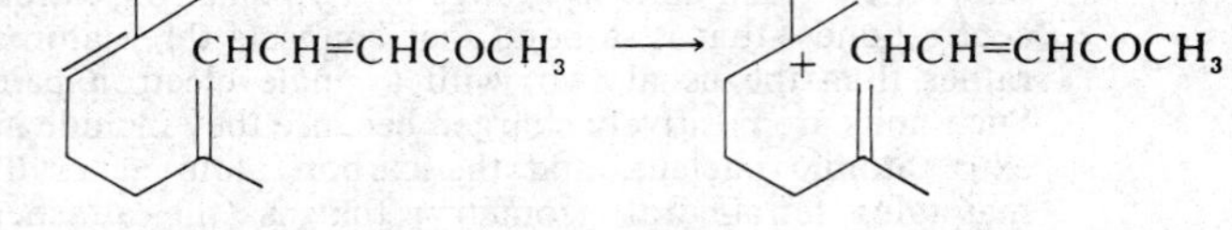

pseudoionone — intermediate cation

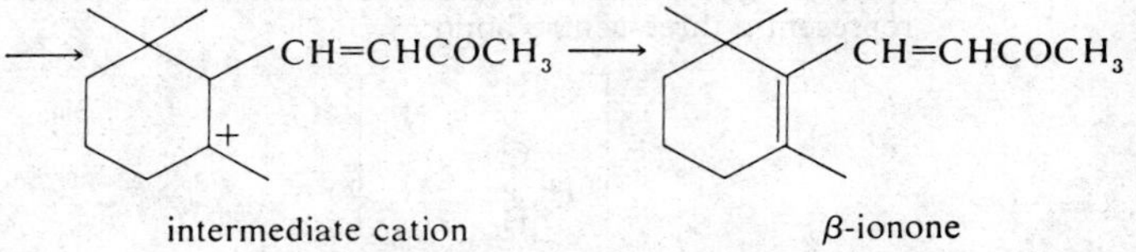

intermediate cation — β-ionone

6. Reaction with internal sigma base: acid-catalyzed rearrangement of neopentyl alcohol, the electron pair coming from an internal carbon–carbon sigma bond:

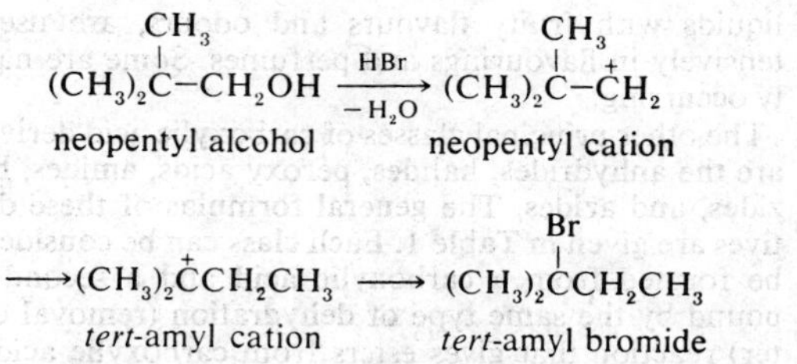

$$(CH_3)_2\overset{CH_3}{\underset{|}{C}}-CH_2OH \xrightarrow[-H_2O]{HBr} (CH_3)_2\overset{CH_3}{\underset{|}{C}}-\overset{+}{C}H_2$$

neopentyl alcohol → neopentyl cation

$$\longrightarrow (CH_3)_2\overset{+}{C}CH_2CH_3 \longrightarrow (CH_3)_2\overset{Br}{\overset{|}{C}}CH_2CH_3$$

tert-amyl cation → *tert*-amyl bromide

Each of these reaction types is widely employed in synthetic organic reactions, and the many acid-catalyzed hydrocarbon transformation reactions are fundamental in petroleum chemistry and in vital bio-organic processes. An important process in the manufacture of high-octane gasoline, for example, consists of the acid-catalyzed isomerization of straight-chain hydrocarbons to branched-chain hydrocarbons. One example of the significance of carbonium ions in bio-organic processes may be found in the biological synthesis of the important material cholesterol from a precursor, squalene, by way of another compound, lanosterol. In this transformation, acid-catalyzed rearrangements—reaction type 6. above—occur repeatedly, as shown in the sequence below:

Carbonium ions in biological syntheses

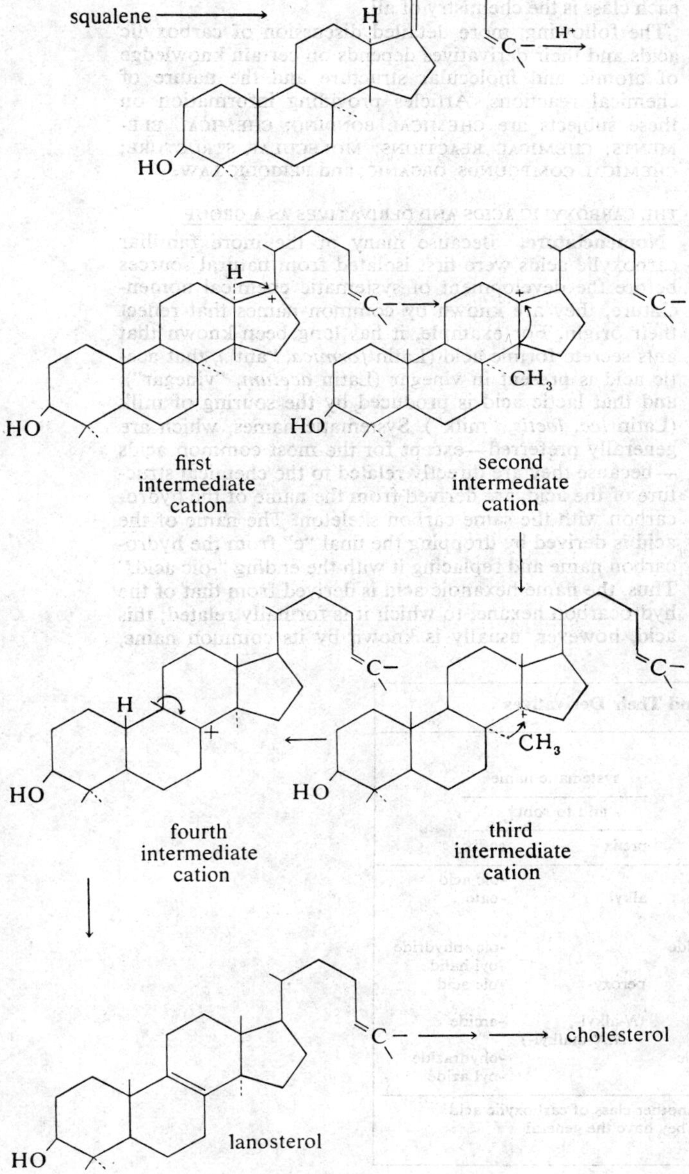

BIBLIOGRAPHY. D. BETHELL and V. GOLD, *Carbonium Ions* (1967), is an excellent introduction to most aspects of carbonium-ion chemistry; includes an extensive bibliography. G.A. OLAH and P.V.R. SCHLEYER (eds.), *Carbonium Ions*, 4 vol. (1968), is a review of particular aspects of carbonium-ion chemistry, with individual chapters written by active researchers in the field. The initial chapter is a historical review of carbonium ions and a summary of major trends. G.A. OLAH, "Stable Carbonium Ions in Solution," *Science*, 168:1298–1311 (1970), summarizes much of the work concerning the direct observation of carbonium ions as stable, long-lived species.

(G.A.O./P.R.Cd.)

Carboxylic Acids and Their Derivatives

The carboxylic acids and their derivatives are organic chemical compounds, either prepared synthetically or found naturally in fats, vinegar, milk products, and fruit juices and flavours. They are used as solvents and in the preparation of other chemical compounds that are employed in the production of plastics, dyes, pharmaceuticals, and a large number of other products.

THE CARBOXYL GROUP

The molecules of the carboxylic acids contain a particular arrangement of carbon, oxygen, and hydrogen atoms, called a carboxyl group. It is this group that is responsible for the characteristic chemical behaviour of the carboxylic acids. In the carboxyl group, a carbon atom (designated by the symbol C) is joined to two oxygen atoms (symbol O), one of which also is joined to a hydrogen atom (H). In chemical symbols, this structure of the carboxyl group is written $-\overset{O}{\overset{\|}{C}}-O-H$, in which each line represents one chemical bond between the atoms. As indicated by this structure, the hydrogen atom forms only one bond (or, in chemical terminology, has a valence of 1); oxygen forms two bonds (valence, 2) and carbon four (valence, 4). In order to apportion the bonds properly, one of the oxygen atoms must be attached to the carbon by two bonds or, as it is commonly called, a double bond. The carbon atom has one unused bond left over after the carboxyl group is formed (as indicated by the line in front of the carbon symbol in the diagram above), and this bond must be used if the molecular structure is to be completed.

The simplest way that this can be done is to add a hydrogen atom, giving the simplest possible carboxylic acid, formic acid, the structure of which may be written $H-\overset{O}{\overset{\|}{C}}-O-H$, or in shorter form as HCOOH or HCO_2H. Formic acid is used as a disinfectant and as an acidifying agent in textile and paper manufacturing.

Alternatively, a carbon atom bearing three hydrogen atoms—*i.e.*, a methyl group—may be joined to the carbon of the carboxyl group to give acetic acid, with the structure $H-\overset{H}{\underset{H}{\overset{|}{\underset{|}{C}}}}-\overset{O}{\overset{\|}{C}}-O-H$ or CH_3COOH. A dilute form of acetic acid is commonly known as vinegar.

The structures of many other carboxylic acids may be made by joining other atoms to the methyl carbon in place of the hydrogen atoms. Such structures consist of chains of carbon atoms joined to one another in linear sequences, with side branches formed of other short chains and rings made when the chain doubles back and rejoins itself; each such structure represents the molecule of a different carboxylic acid. Often, for convenience, the symbol R is used to represent a general and unspecified arrangement of carbon and hydrogen atoms (a hydrocarbon unit) and the formula RCOOH is used as a general representation for all carboxylic acids.

The derivatives of the carboxylic acids all have molecular structures that contain variants of the carboxyl group. In general, these conform to the pattern $R-\overset{O}{\overset{\|}{C}}-Z$, in which R has the same meaning as above and Z is some atom other than carbon or hydrogen (*i.e.*, a heteroatom), usually oxygen, nitrogen, or a halogen (*i.e.*, one of the group of elements including fluorine, chlorine, bromine, and iodine). Often hydrogen (or other) atoms must be attached to the heteroatom to complete its valence bonds, and in these cases the Z represents a group of atoms. The carboxylic acids themselves conform to the general formula $R-\overset{O}{\overset{\|}{C}}-Z$, the Z in this case being the hydroxyl, or $-OH$, group.

Esters

Probably the most familiar class of carboxylic acid derivatives is the family of compounds known as esters. In esters, the heteroatom is oxygen, and a hydrocarbon unit is joined to it. In the methyl esters (the simplest of the family), the hydrocarbon unit joined to the oxygen atom is simply a methyl ($-CH_3$) group. Perhaps the most important ester of commerce is ethyl acetate, in which an ethyl ($-C_2H_5$) group is attached to the oxygen atom. Ethyl acetate is an ester of acetic acid, CH_3COOH. Its structural formula is $CH_3COOC_2H_5$. Ethyl acetate is used as a solvent, a flavouring and perfume ingredient, and a chemical intermediate (substance converted to other chemical compounds).

Esters can be formed from carboxylic acids by reaction with other organic compounds called alcohols under conditions that remove a molecule of water from the two constituents. This process is indicated in the following equation, which represents the chemical reaction that occurs:

$$\underset{\text{carboxylic acid}}{R-\overset{O}{\overset{\|}{C}}-O-H}+\underset{\text{alcohol}}{H-O-R}$$

$$\rightleftharpoons \underset{\text{ester}}{R-\overset{O}{\overset{\|}{C}}-O-R'}+\underset{\text{water}}{H-O-H}.$$

In this equation, as in other chemical equations, the structural formulas of the starting materials are written to the left of the arrow and the products to the right. The double arrows indicate that the chemical reaction proceeding from left to right may be reversed, the products reacting to produce the reactants. In the structural formulas, written as above, the letters represent atoms of the various elements and the lines represent bonds between the atoms. Also, as above, R represents an unspecified hydrocarbon unit and R′ a second hydrocarbon unit, which may be the same as the first or may be different from it. As the general formula for esters, RCOOR′, suggests, this family of compounds is large, since both the R and R′ groups can be varied to include a great many kinds of hydrocarbon structures, as well as units with heteroatoms of various kinds substituted in them. Many simple esters, liquids with fruity flavours and odours, are used extensively in flavourings and perfumes. Some are naturally occurring.

Other derivatives

The other principal classes of carboxylic acid derivatives are the anhydrides, halides, peroxy acids, amides, hydrazides, and azides. The general formulas of these derivatives are given in Table 1. Each class can be considered to be formed from a carboxylic acid and a second compound by the same type of dehydration (removal of water) reaction that gives esters from carboxylic acids and alcohols. The second molecule that reacts with a carboxylic acid to give the derivative in each case is as follows: anhydride, a second molecule of carboxylic acid; halide, a halogen acid; peroxy acid, hydrogen peroxide; amide, an amine; hydrazide, hydrazine; and azide, hydrazoic acid. The preparation of the various derivatives, in actual practice, may not follow this idealized scheme since more convenient methods of synthesis have been worked out. Amides (particularly proteins) and esters are the most important carboxylic acid derivatives found in nature. Many of these derivatives, however, are synthesized for important industrial uses.

Typically, the carboxylic acids themselves are readily converted to the various classes of derivatives, and the derivatives in most cases can be converted into one another. Thus, the carboxylic acids and their derivatives comprise a family of closely related and readily interconvertible compounds. In many ways, the chemistry of each class is the chemistry of all.

The following, more detailed discussion of carboxylic acids and their derivatives depends on certain knowledge of atomic and molecular structure and the nature of chemical reactions. Articles providing information on these subjects are CHEMICAL BONDING; CHEMICAL ELEMENTS; CHEMICAL REACTIONS; MOLECULAR STRUCTURE; CHEMICAL COMPOUNDS, ORGANIC; and PERIODIC LAW.

THE CARBOXYLIC ACIDS AND DERIVATIVES AS A GROUP

Nomenclature. Because many of the more familiar carboxylic acids were first isolated from natural sources before the development of systematic chemical nomenclature, they are known by common names that reflect their origin. For example, it has long been known that ants secrete formic acid (Latin *formica*, "ant"), that acetic acid is present in vinegar (Latin *acetum*, "vinegar"), and that lactic acid is produced by the souring of milk (Latin *lac*, *lactis*, "milk"). Systematic names, which are generally preferred—except for the most common acids—because they are directly related to the chemical structure of the acid, are derived from the name of the hydrocarbon with the same carbon skeleton. The name of the acid is derived by dropping the final "e" from the hydrocarbon name and replacing it with the ending "-oic acid." Thus, the name hexanoic acid is derived from that of the hydrocarbon hexane, to which it is formally related; this acid, however, usually is known by its common name,

Table 1: Formulas and Nomenclature of Carboxylic Acids and Their Derivatives

class	formula: $R-\overset{O}{\overset{\|}{C}}-Z$. Z=	common name: add to root* prefix	common name: add to root* suffix	systematic name: add to root† prefix	systematic name: add to root† suffix
Carboxylic acid	$-OH$		-ic acid		-oic acid
Ester	$-OR'$	alkyl	-ate	alkyl	-oate
Anhydride	$-O\overset{O}{\overset{\|}{C}}R$		-ic anhydride		-oic anhydride
Acyl halide	$-Cl$ ($-Br$)		-yl halide		-oyl halide
Peroxy acid	$-OOH$	peroxy- (or per-)	-ic acid	peroxy-	-oic acid
Amide‡ (substituted amide)	$-NH_2$ ($-NHR$, $-NR_2$)	(*N*-alkyl-, *N,N*-dialkyl-)	-amide	(*N*-alkyl-, *N,N*-dialkyl-)	-amide
Hydrazide	$-NHNH_2$		-ohydrazide		-ohydrazide
Azide	$-N_3$		-yl azide		-oyl azide

**E.g.*, acet-, propion-, etc. †*E.g.*, ethan-, propan-, etc. ‡Nitriles, another class of carboxylic acid derivative, may be considered to be dehydration products of amides. They have the general formula $R-C\equiv N$ and are named -onitrile.

caproic acid (Latin *caper*, *capri*, "goat"). Systematic and common names of straight-chain saturated acids are given in Table 2.

Table 2: Straight-chain Saturated Acids and Their Methyl Esters

chain length	systematic name	common name	acid		methyl ester	
			melting point (°C)	boiling point* (°C)	melting point (°C)	boiling point* (°C)
1	methanoic	formic	8.4	101	−99.0	32
2	ethanoic	acetic	16.6	118	−98.1	57
3	propanoic	propionic	−20.8	141	−87.5	80
4	butanoic	butyric	− 4.3	164	−84.8	102
5	pentanoic	valeric	−33.8	186	−80.7	127
6	hexanoic	caproic	−2.0	205	−11.0	151
7	heptanoic	enanthic	−7.5	223	−55.7	172
8	octanoic	caprylic	16.5	239	−40.0	193
9	nonanoic	pelargonic	12.2	255	−34.3	214
10	decanoic	capric	31.5	270	−18	224
11	undecanoic	—	28.6	280	−11.3	250
12	dodecanoic	lauric	44.0	131^1	5.2	262
13	tridecanoic	—	44.5	140^1	6.5	90^1
14	tetradecanoic	myristic	58.0	149^1	19.1	114^1
15	pentadecanoic	—	53.5	158^1	18.5	154
16	hexadecanoic	palmitic	62.9	167^1	30.0	148^2
17	heptadecanoic	margaric	62.5	175^1	29.7	148^1
18	octadecanoic	stearic	71.5	184^1	39.1	156^1
19	nonadecanoic	—	69.4	—	38.5	191^4
20	eicosanoic	arachidic	77.0	204^1	46.4	188^2
21	heneicosanoic	—	75.2	—	—	207^4
22	docosanoic	behenic	80.0	—	54.0	206^2
23	tricosanoic	—	79.6	—	53.9	—
24	tetracosanoic	lignoceric	84.2	—	57.4	222^2
25	pentacosanoic	—	83.5	—	59.5	—
26	hexacosanoic	cerotic	88.5	—	63.5	237^2
27	heptacosanoic	—	87.6	—	64.6	—
28	octacosanoic	montanic	90.4	—	67.5	—
29	nonacosanoic	—	90.4	—	68.8	—
30	triacontanoic	melissic	93.6	—	71.5	—

*Boiling point at 760 millimetres unless at one, two, or four millimetres as indicated by superscript.

Naming of derivatives

Methods of naming carboxylic acid derivatives vary. Suffixes or prefixes are used, or both, as indicated in Table 1, to indicate the type of derivative; the root of the acid's name gives the acid from which the compound is derived. As an example, in the naming of esters, the alcohol portion of the ester is given first, as a radical or partial molecule—such as ethyl from ethyl alcohol—followed by the root of the acid name—as acet- from acetic acid—followed by the suffix -ate. The ester formed from ethyl alcohol and acetic acid, then, is called ethyl acetate. When the systematic name of the acid (-oic) is employed, the ending used is -oate. The systematic name of ethyl acetate is ethyl ethanoate.

Classification. Carboxylic acids and their derivatives are classified in different ways, depending on the purpose of the classification. Many of the acids with straight carbon chains, particularly those with even numbers of carbon atoms, are constituents of fats and are commonly classed together as fatty acids. Generally the carboxylic acids are classed as aliphatic (a term that means an ordinary hydrocarbon chain) if the rest of the molecule (other than the carboxylic acid group) is aliphatic. The fatty acids, by this definition, are aliphatic; aliphatic acids frequently are classified further as saturated or unsaturated depending upon whether or not they contain unsaturation—that is, multiple bonds (double or triple) between the atoms of the carbon chain. When the carboxyl group is directly attached to an aromatic system—*e.g.*, a benzene ring—a carboxylic acid is, however, classed as an aromatic acid. Benzoic acid is the parent compound of the aromatic acids. Acetylsalicylic acid, or aspirin, the best known aromatic carboxylic acid, is derived from benzoic acid. The structural formulas of benzoic acid and acetylsalicylic acid are:

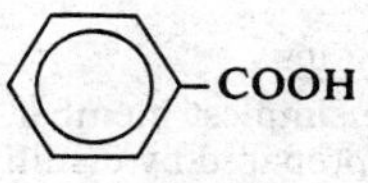

benzoic acid

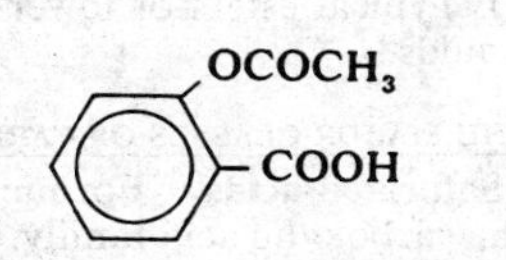

acetylsalicylic acid (aspirin)

in which the hexagon containing a circle represents a benzene ring (that is, a circular structure of six carbon atoms each of which has one hydrogen atom attached to it).

Carboxylic acids are often categorized by the extra functional groups their molecules carry. Dicarboxylic and tricarboxylic acids are common. Carboxylic acids are classed as halo, keto, hydroxy, or amino acids when a halogen atom or a carbonyl, hydroxyl, or amino group is also part of the molecule.

Classification of derivatives

Generally carboxylic acid derivatives are placed in the same classes as the acids from which they are derived. Thus, aliphatic, aromatic, and various substituted esters, amides, and other derivatives are known. Exceptions occur when the acid-derived group makes up a relatively small part of the molecule. The derivative is then considered to be another type of substance altogether, modified by addition of the carboxylate grouping. Thus acetylsalicylic acid usually is considered a derivative of salicylic acid, not an ester of acetic acid.

Natural occurrence. Carboxylic acids occur widely in nature. In addition to acetic and formic acids, which are found in the free state, many of the fatty acids—straight-chain acids, saturated and unsaturated—occur as fats; that is, as esters of the trihydric alcohol glycerol (the term trihydric meaning that there are three hydroxyl or alcohol groups in each molecule of the substance). The structural formula of glycerol and a generalized formula of a fat derived from glycerol by the formation of ester bonds with three fatty acids are as follows:

$$\begin{array}{ll} CH_2OH & CH_2OCOR \\ | & | \\ CHOH & CHOCOR' \\ | & | \\ CH_2OH & CH_2OCOR'' \end{array}$$

glycerol — fat (R,R′, R″ = fatty acid side chains, saturated and unsaturated)

Fatty acids occur also as esters and amides of long-chain alcohols and amines. Free fatty acids are readily obtained from these sources by hydrolysis—cleavage of the ester or amide bond with addition of a single molecule of water. The free acids, however, are almost invariably obtained from such sources in the form of mixtures that are very complex and difficult to separate.

Substituted carboxylic acids also are found extensively in natural materials. Lactic acid occurs in sour-milk products and citric acid in fruits. These, other hydroxy acids, and many keto acids, are important metabolic products and exist in most living cells. Amino acids are constituents of proteins, from which they can be secured by hydrolysis. Halogen-substituted acids also occur, as do polycarboxylic acids and a number of aromatic acids.

With the exception of esters and amides, few carboxylic acid derivatives appear in natural products. Esters, with their fruity and fragrant odours, are common constituents of plant flavours and essences. The carboxylic acids and their derivatives are all readily available by synthetic procedures (see below), often of such simplicity that even naturally occurring substances are prepared synthetically rather than isolated from natural sources.

General chemical and physical properties. The carboxyl group, in a sense, is a special form of the carbonyl group, the doubly bonded carbon–oxygen function characteristic of aldehydes and ketones. Structural representations of the carbonyl group and the generalized formulas of aldehydes, ketones, and carboxylic acids (and derivatives) are all given here for purposes of comparison:

$$\overset{O}{\overset{\|}{-C-}} \qquad R-\overset{O}{\overset{\|}{C}}-H \qquad R-\overset{O}{\overset{\|}{C}}-R' \qquad R-\overset{O}{\overset{\|}{C}}-Z$$

carbonyl group — aldehyde — ketone — carboxylic acid and derivatives

In the molecules of aldehydes and ketones, the carbonyl group is attached directly to carbon or hydrogen atoms, neither of which exerts a major influence on the chemical behaviour of that carbonyl group. In the carboxylic acids and their derivatives, however, the carbonyl carbon is joined directly to an atom with one or more pairs of electrons over and above those employed in the bond with the carbon atom. These so-called unshared pairs of electrons are able to interact with the electrons of the carbonyl group, thereby greatly modifying the chemical properties of that group and of the heteroatom as well. The nature of this interaction usually is represented in terms of the following diagrams:

$$\overset{\overset{\cdots}{\overset{\cdot\cdot}{O}}}{\underset{}{R-C-Z}} \longleftrightarrow \overset{\overset{-}{\overset{\cdot\cdot}{O}}}{\underset{}{R-C=Z}} \cdot^+$$

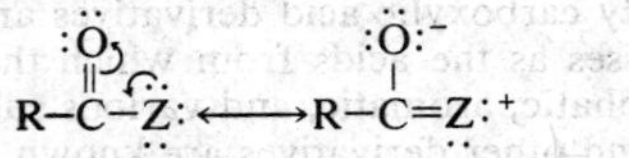

In these diagrams the dots represent single electrons, situated in pairs; the curved arrows indicate a tendency for the electron pairs, or the bonds (which are equivalent to pairs of electrons), to migrate as shown; and the plus and minus signs stand for local electric charges brought about by the movement of the electrons. The double-headed arrow between the two representations implies that the complete structure of the molecule is a resonance hybrid of these two structures—that is to say, that the molecular structure incorporates aspects of both forms but duplicates neither. When such resonance forms exist for a molecule it is said to be stabilized by resonance. In this case, the most important feature of the electronic interaction represented by the resonance forms is that it gives this modified carbonyl group new chemical properties of its own, which justify classifying the group as a new and unique structure; *i.e.*, a carboxyl group.

As the name indicates, the chief characteristic of carboxylic acids is their acidity. As a class the carboxylic acids are more acidic than most other organic compounds containing hydroxyl ($-OH$) groups, but they are generally much weaker acids than the familiar mineral acids, such as nitric, sulfuric, and hydrochloric acids. The acidity of the carboxyl group results from the loss of a proton or hydrogen ion (that is, a hydrogen atom bearing a positive charge, as indicated by the symbol H^+), leaving behind a carboxylate anion—a negatively charged unit derived from the carboxyl group.

The carboxylate anion, like the carboxyl group, exists as resonance hybrid (see above) of several forms, two of which are shown below for each structure:

$$\left[\overset{O}{\underset{}{R-C-O-H}} \leftrightarrow \overset{O^-}{\underset{+}{R-C=O-H}} \right] \longrightarrow \left[\overset{O}{\underset{}{R-C-O^-}} \leftrightarrow \overset{O^-}{\underset{}{R-C=O}} \right] + H^+.$$

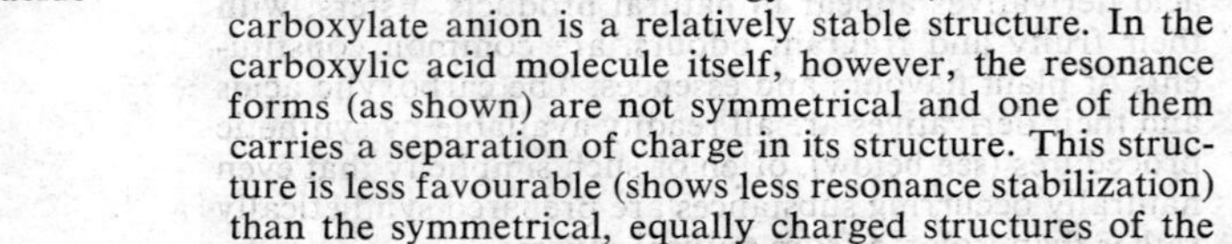

carboxylic acid   carboxylate anion

The basis for acidity of carboxylic acids

It is significant that the two resonance forms shown for the carboxylate anion are symmetrical and both carry a negative charge (as shown by the minus signs on the symbols for the oxygen atoms); this situation, which produces a structure of low energy content, means that the carboxylate anion is a relatively stable structure. In the carboxylic acid molecule itself, however, the resonance forms (as shown) are not symmetrical and one of them carries a separation of charge in its structure. This structure is less favourable (shows less resonance stabilization) than the symmetrical, equally charged structures of the carboxylate anion. As a result of this disparity in resonance stabilization, the carboxylic acid readily gives up a proton—acts as an acid—to produce the anion, which is favoured by its extra resonance energy.

The nature of the R group of the carboxylic acid has an effect on the acidity of the carboxyl group by making it more or less easy for the proton to depart. Generally speaking, electron-attracting groups increase acidity by withdrawing electrons from the vicinity of the proton, thereby facilitating its departure; the opposite is true of electron-repelling groups. In many of the carboxylic acid derivatives, the carboxyl group has been modified, with the result that the proton in question is no longer present, and such substances are not acidic.

Chemical properties

The chemical reactions undergone by the carboxylic acids and their derivatives can be put into two broad categories. The first is a nucleophilic (positive-charge-seeking) reaction directed at the carbonyl carbon atom. The overall effect of this type of reaction is the displacement of one group, Z, which is capable of carrying a negative charge by another, Z'. The reaction is customarily represented by the following equation:

$$\overset{O}{\underset{}{R-C-Z}} + Z' \longrightarrow \overset{O}{\underset{}{R-C-Z'}} + Z^-.$$

The reaction proceeds, however, by way of attack on the carbonyl carbon as shown in the representation below:

$$\overset{O}{\underset{Z'^-}{R-C-Z}} \longrightarrow \left[\overset{O^-}{\underset{Z'}{R-C-Z}} \right] \longrightarrow \overset{O}{\underset{}{R-C-Z'}} + Z^-$$

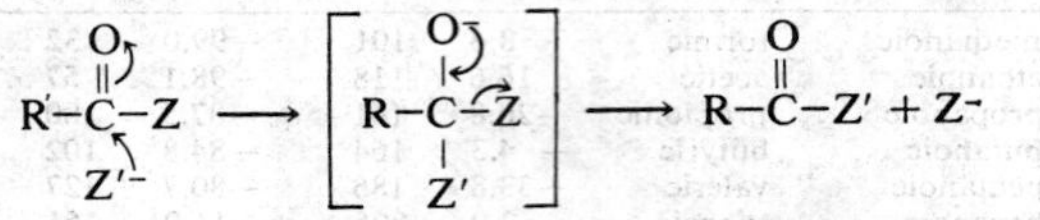

in which the movement of electron pairs (or bonds) is indicated by curved arrows and the structure enclosed within brackets is an intermediate substance that is not isolated. It is by reactions of this type that carboxylic acid derivatives are interconverted, one variety being readily prepared from another under the proper chemical conditions.

Secondly, carboxyl compounds undergo the sort of reaction undergone by typical carbonyl compounds (aldehydes and ketones), in which the substituents are introduced into the so-called alpha position (the carbon atom adjacent to the carbonyl or, in this case, carboxyl group). Such reactions proceed by way of an intermediate resonance-stabilized anion (an anion being a negatively charged unit), which subsequently reacts with a positively charged unit. The latter is incorporated into the final structure. The reaction occurs as shown in the following equation:

$$\overset{O}{\underset{}{RCH_2CZ}} \xrightarrow{\text{base}} \overset{O}{\underset{}{R\bar{C}H-CZ}} \longleftrightarrow \overset{O^-}{\underset{}{RCH=CZ}} \xrightarrow{R'^+} \overset{O}{\underset{}{RCHR'CZ}}.$$

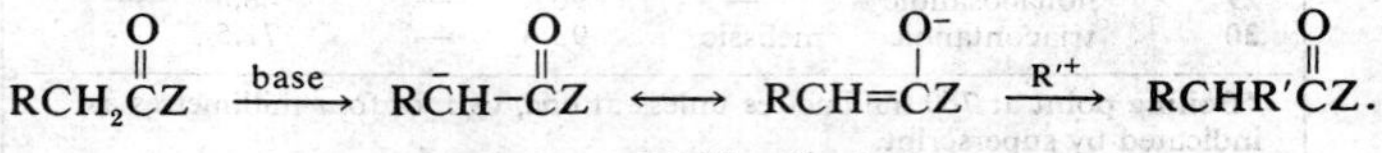

resonance-stabilized anion

Esters resemble carbonyl compounds more than the carboxylic acids—or the other derivatives—do, and, as a result, esters are more prone to undergo substitution reactions in this category.

Physical properties

The members of the carboxylic acid family with low molecular weight are liquids with boiling points appreciably higher than those of hydrocarbons of comparable molecular weight (see Table 2). This is because of extensive hydrogen-bond formation, a type of secondary association between molecules, which makes the acids behave as dimers (two molecules held together as one):

$$R-C\overset{\overset{}{O\cdots H-O}}{\underset{O-H\cdots O}{}}C-R.$$

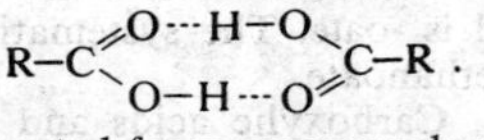

As would be expected from compounds whose molecules contain hydroxyl groups, the lower members of the series are extremely water-soluble—the hydroxyl group ($-OH$) being structurally similar to the water molecule (HOH) and therefore prone to solubility in it. This property diminishes as the non-carboxylic acid portion of the molecules increases in size, and acids containing nine or more carbon atoms are insoluble. Because of their solubility and acidity, members of the series containing few carbon atoms—such as acetic acid, found in vinegar—have a sour taste. The carboxylic acids with one to three carbons have sharp odours, whereas those with four to eight carbons have rank, disagreeable odours. Rancid butter and strong cheese contain the latter carboxylic acids.

Many carboxylic acid derivatives are less associated (that is, their molecules are held together less strongly) than the free acids. This is especially true of the esters and halides, whose boiling points are much lower than those of the acids from which they are derived (see Table 2). Typical esters of lower molecular weight are volatile liquids.

THE MAJOR CLASSES OF CARBOXYLIC ACIDS

Saturated acids. Formic acid, the simplest member of the carboxylic acid family, was first prepared by distilling ants with water. The stinging nettle owes its irritating quality to the formic acid content of the juice. On a commercial scale, the acid is prepared by adding carbon monoxide under pressure to hot sodium hydroxide. The free acid is liberated by careful reaction with sulfuric acid. The series of reaction is shown below:

$$CO \xrightarrow{\text{NaOH}} HCOONa \xrightarrow{\text{H}_2\text{SO}_4} HCOOH$$

in which the symbols NaOH and H_2SO_4 written above the arrows indicate that the successive reactions occur in the presence of sodium hydroxide and sulfuric acid, respectively. In addition to its acidic properties, formic acid shows pronounced reducing activity (reduction being the chemical opposite of oxidation), a quality not shared by other carboxylic acids. The reducing action stems from the fact that formic acid is in a sense an aldehyde as well as an acid, as shown in the following structural formulas:

$$\overset{O}{\overset{\|}{HCOH}} \qquad \overset{O}{\overset{\|}{HCR}} \qquad \overset{O}{\overset{\|}{RCOH}}.$$

formic acid · · · · · aldehyde · · · · · carboxylic acid

Formic and acetic acids

Acetic acid, the next higher homologue—that is, the compound with one more carbon atom in its molecule—can be produced by oxidation of ethyl alcohol and is present as a dilute solution in vinegar, where it is formed by bacterial oxidation of dilute alcoholic liquors. Acetic acid may also be isolated from the liquid called pyroligneous acid, which is formed by the destructive distillation of wood. The most important commercial preparation of acetic acid involves the catalytic atmospheric oxidation of acetaldehyde, itself prepared from acetylene. These reactions are shown below:

$$CH \equiv CH \xrightarrow[\text{HgSO}_4]{\text{dilute H}_2\text{SO}_4} CH_3CHO$$

$$\xrightarrow[\text{Mn(CH}_3\text{COO)}_2]{\text{air}} CH_3COOH.$$

Acetic acid is extensively employed in the preparation of metal salts and in the form of acetyl chloride or acetic anhydride in the production of esters and amides. Aspirin, the acetic ester of salicylic acid, is a good example of a commercially important ester prepared from acetic acid. Acetic acid is also recognized as an important substance in the biosynthesis of many biologically important materials. In this case it chiefly appears as an acetyl group bound to coenzyme A—*i.e.*, a molecule necessary for the action of certain enzymes. Acetyl-S-coenzyme A takes part in the biological production of fatty acids, many aromatic compounds, and isoprenoids and steroids. The natural fatty acids have an even number of carbon atoms in their molecules because they are produced from acetyl-S-coenzyme A, which adds carbon atoms to the molecules two at a time.

With increasing numbers of carbon atoms per molecule, the carboxylic acids have increasing possibilities for alternate arrangements of the atoms within the molecules (isomerism), and many branched-chain acids, both natural and synthetic, are known. The straight-chain compounds are, nevertheless, more common, especially those with even numbers of carbon atoms in the chain, and these make up the great percentage of the fatty acid content of common fats.

Carboxylic acids and their derivatives

The lower fatty acids (with four to ten carbon atoms) occur mainly in milk fats and a few seed fats. Cow's milk contains 10 percent (on a molecular-weight basis) of butyric acid (a four-carbon acid) with smaller amounts of the acids containing six, eight, ten, and 12 carbon atoms; sheep's-milk and goat's-milk fats contain these same acids, with capric (containing ten carbon atoms) in greatest amount (up to 10 percent). Capric acid also is a major component (60 percent) in the seed fat of the elm, and caprylic and capric acids (each 5–10 percent) accompany the higher proportion of lauric acid (12 carbon atoms) in coconut oil and, to a lesser extent, in palm-kernel oil. Lauric acid and myristic acid (14 carbon atoms) occur extensively in seed fats of the Lauraceae (laurel family) and Myristicaceae (nutmeg family) respectively. Lauric acid, for example, can be obtained from cinnamon oil (80–90 percent), coconut oil (45–50 percent), or palm-kernel oil

(45–55 percent) and myristic acid from nutmeg butter (60–75 percent) or from the more readily available coconut and palm-kernel oils (15–18 percent). Palmitic acid (16 carbon atoms), the most widely occurring of the saturated acids, is present in almost every fat examined. Useful sources include cottonseed oil (22–28 percent), palm oil (35–40 percent), and Chinese vegetable tallow (60–70 percent).

Palmitic and stearic acids

Stearic acid (18 carbon atoms) is less common than palmitic acid. It occurs in most vegetable fats but is a major component in only a few, such as cocoa butter (35 percent). It is present in most animal fats but attains major proportions only in the tallows of ruminants (30 percent). Stearic acid is conveniently obtained by hydrogenation of readily accessible unsaturated fats.

Still higher fatty acids are less common but occur in a few seed fats or in some waxes as esters of long-chain alcohols. Acids with odd numbers of carbon atoms in their chains are even rarer, but modern methods of investigation have revealed their presence, often as trace components, in many fats. Acids with hydrocarbon chains containing short branches (side chains of carbon atoms) or rings (circular sequences of carbon atoms) also are uncommon. Those that are found include a series of acids with one or more methyl groups in various positions along the chain, as well as acids with cyclopropane groups. Many branched-chain acids have been synthesized.

Unsaturated acids. Although most of the important unsaturated acids (acids with multiple bonds) are long-chain compounds obtained from fats, some shorter chain acids, such as acrylic, crotonic, methacrylic, and the isomeric angelic and tiglic acids, are also important. The formulas of these acids are shown below:

$$CH_2 = CHCOOH \qquad \text{acrylic acid}$$

$$CH_3CH = CHCOOH \qquad \text{crotonic acid}$$

$$CH_2 = C(CH_3)COOH \qquad \text{methacrylic acid}$$

$$\underset{H}{\overset{H_3C}{\diagdown}} C = C \underset{CH_3}{\overset{COOH}{\diagup}} \qquad \text{angelic acid}$$

$$\underset{H}{\overset{H_3C}{\diagdown}} C = C \underset{COOH}{\overset{CH_3}{\diagup}} \qquad \text{tiglic acid}$$

Acrylic acid, employed as its methyl ester in the production of polymers known as acrylates, is prepared on a large scale from acetylene, carbon monoxide, and water in the presence of a nickel catalyst, as well as by hydrolysis of the substance acrylonitrile ($CH_2 = CHCN$), an even more important monomer.

Acrylic acid polymers

Methacrylic acid, in the form of its methyl ester, is also used as a monomer, furnishing Perspex or Plexiglas when polymerized. Crotonic acid exists in *cis* and *trans* forms, which differ in the arrangement of substituents about the double bond. Only the *trans* isomer occurs naturally, in croton oil. Angelic and tiglic acids also are a pair of *cis* and *trans* isomers, both of which occur naturally.

Natural unsaturated acids number more than 200 and are subdivided into three groups: (1) acids with only one unsaturated centre; (2) conjugated (conjugation being an alternation of single and double bonds), polyunsaturated acids; (3) multiply unsaturated, or polyunsaturated, acids that are nonconjugated.

Apart from two acetylenic (triple-bonded) acids, tariric and stearolic, the natural monounsaturated acids are olefinic (double bonded) and almost entirely *cis* isomers.

Mono-unsaturated acids

Oleic acid, with 18 carbon atoms and a double bond between the ninth and tenth carbon atoms in the chain, is the most common of all fatty acids and the prototype for all monoolefinic acids:

$$CH_3(CH_2)_7CH = CH(CH_2)_7COOH \qquad \text{oleic acid.}$$

More than 90 monoenoic acids, containing ten to 30 carbon atoms, have been identified in lipid sources. Nature appears to have a preference for certain chain lengths, es-

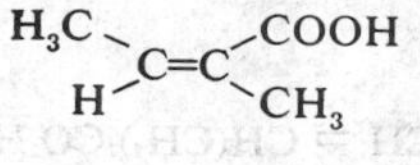

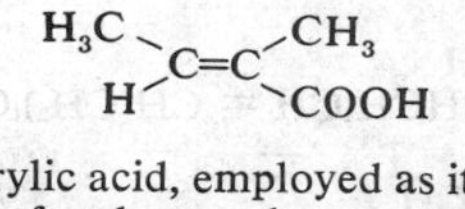

pecially those of 16 and 18 carbons, and for particular positions for the unsaturation, especially between C_9 and C_{10}. These circumstances are a natural consequence of the enzymatic oxygen-dependent desaturation process whereby double bonds are most commonly introduced into fatty acids between carbons 9 and 10, and of the readiness by which natural acids undergo chain elongation by one or more two-carbon units at the carboxyl end of the molecule. In addition to these natural acids, many isomers that do not occur in nature have been synthesized.

The monounsaturated acids show the properties expected of olefins, in addition to those of carboxylic acids. As acids, they form salts, are reduced to primary alcohols, and are converted directly or indirectly to the various types of acyl compounds listed in Table 1. As unsaturated compounds they undergo hydrogenation (that is, the addition of hydrogen to the multiple bond) with hydrogen and a catalyst or with hydrazine; hydroxylation (introduction of hydroxyl groups) with potassium permanganate, osmium tetroxide, performic acid, or peracetic acid; and halogenation (introduction of halogen atoms) with chlorine or bromine or with iodine monochloride. Vigorous oxidation by potassium permanganate or ozone leads to breaks in the carbon chains (chain fission). Atmospheric oxidation first gives unsaturated hydroperoxides (molecules containing two joined oxygen atoms), followed by a variety of secondary reaction products. Among these are volatile short-chain compounds (aldehydes and other substances) responsible for both the acceptable and unacceptable flavours that develop in fat-containing foods.

Polyunsaturated acids

Over 90 nonconjugated, polyunsaturated acids occur naturally. Most are acids with 16, 18, 20, or 22 carbons and two to four double bonds, although more highly unsaturated members are also known. Unsaturation is almost entirely *cis* in the compounds and usually is methylene interrupted; *i.e.*, with successive double bonds separated by single methylene ($-CH_2-$) groups. These structural features are clearly apparent in linoleic acid, linolenic acid, and arachidonic acid, the most important members of this class, the structures of which are shown below:

linoleic acid
$$CH_3(CH_2)_4CH = CHCH_2CH = CH(CH_2)_7CO_2H$$
linolenic acid
$$CH_3CH_2CH = CHCH_2CH$$
$$= CHCH_2CH = CH(CH_2)_7CO_2H$$
arachidonic acid
$$CH_3(CH_2)_4CH = CHCH_2CH$$
$$= CHCH_2CH = CHCH_2CH = CH(CH_2)_3CO_2H.$$

Interest in acids of this type has increased since the recognition that some of them, called essential fatty acids, are required for the maintenance of normal animal growth, reproduction, and permeability of the skin. The particular requirement is for methylene-interrupted polyolefinic acids, with unsaturation beginning at the sixth carbon from the methyl end of the chain.

Arachidonic acid is the most effective of the fatty acids for meeting the essential fatty acid requirements. Many authorities consider it likely that essential fatty acids are converted to other compounds before fulfilling their as yet unknown biological function.

Of possible significance in this regard is the discovery of a series of compounds called prostaglandins, which cause certain muscles to contract and lower the blood pressure. These compounds are produced in vivo from essential fatty acids such as arachidonic:

$$CH_3(CH_2)_4(CH=CHCH_2)_4(CH_2)_2CO_2H \longrightarrow$$
arachidonic acid

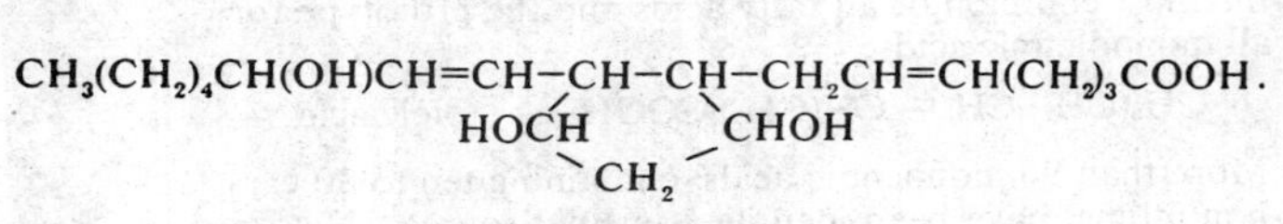

$$CH_3(CH_2)_4CH(OH)CH=CH-CH-CH-CH_2CH=CH(CH_2)_3COOH.$$
$$HOCH \qquad CHOH$$
$$CH_2$$
(a prostaglandin)

Conjugated polyunsaturated acids are much less common. About 40 are known to occur naturally, almost all of them being 18-carbon acids of plant origin. The best known is eleostearic acid from tung oil.

Substituted acids. Carboxylic acids, particularly those with long hydrocarbon chains, may contain one or more other groups, such as halo, hydroxy, alkoxy, epoxy, or keto groups. The several functional groups usually operate independently, and most substituted acids show only those properties that would be expected from the two functional groups. Sometimes, however, the two functional groups interact to give new properties.

Halogen-substituted acids

Acids substituted with chlorine in the alpha position are prepared by the reaction of chlorine or sulfuryl chloride on an acyl chloride or on the acid itself under reaction conditions that produce an acyl chloride. For example:

$$RCH_2COCl \xrightarrow{Cl_2, I_2} RCHClCOCl \xrightarrow{H_2O} RCHClCOOH$$

$$RCH_2COOH \xrightarrow{Cl, P} [RCH_2COCl]$$
$$\longrightarrow RCHClCOCl \xrightarrow{H_2O} RCHClCOOH$$

$$RCH_2COOH \xrightarrow[SOCl_2]{SO_2Cl_2} [RCH_2COCl]$$
$$\longrightarrow RCHClCOCl \xrightarrow{H_2O} RCHClCOOH.$$

The corresponding bromo acids are prepared by reactions with bromine and phosphorus, phosphorus trihalide, or thionyl chloride:

$$RCH_2COOH \xrightarrow{Br_2, P} [RCH_2COBr]$$

$$\longrightarrow RCHBrCOBr \xrightarrow[R'OH]{H_2O} \begin{array}{l} RCHBrCOOH \\ RCHBrCOOR' \end{array}$$

Iodo acids are best prepared by halogen exchange between potassium iodide and the chloro acid or bromo acid.

Acids substituted with halogen in other positions are produced by standard procedures for preparing alkyl halides, such as the addition of halogen acid to a double bond, or by the conversion of a hydroxyl group to halogen. Examples are:

$$RCH=CHCOOH \xrightarrow{HBr} RCHBrCH_2CO_2H$$

$$RCH(OH)(CH_2)_4COOH$$
$$\xrightarrow{SOCl_2} [RCHCl(CH_2)_4COCl] \xrightarrow{H_2O} RCHCl(CH_2)_4COOH$$

The reactions of halogen-substituted acids and other acyl derivatives include dehydrohalogenation, nucleophilic substitution, and the formation of certain organometallic derivatives:

$$CH_2BrCH_2(CH_2)_nCOOH \xrightarrow{pyridine} CH_2=CH(CH_2)_nCOOH$$

$$RCHBrCOOH \xrightarrow[\text{of } Z^-]{HZ \text{ or source}} RCHZCOOH$$
$$(Z=-NH_2, -OH, -CN, \text{ etc.})$$

$$RCHBrCOOCH_3 \xrightarrow{Zn} RCH(ZnBr)COOCH_3$$
$$\xrightarrow{R'CHO} R'CH(OH)CH(R)COOCH_3 \xrightarrow[\text{hydrolysis}]{-H_2O} R'CH=C(R)COOH.$$

The presence of the carboxyl group influences the reactions of the 2-, 3-, and 4-halo acids so that each of these furnishes a different type of product when it reacts with alkalies:

$$RCHBrCOOH \xrightarrow{NaOH} RCH(OH)COOH \qquad \text{(2-hydroxy acid)}$$

$$RCHBrCH_2COOH \xrightarrow{NaOH} RCH=CHCOOH \quad (\alpha, \beta\text{-unsaturated acid})$$

$$RCHBrCH_2CH_2COOH \xrightarrow{NaOH} \begin{array}{c} CH_2-CH_2 \\ | \quad\quad | \\ RCH \quad CO \\ \backslash O / \end{array} \quad \text{(}\gamma\text{-lactone)}$$

Among the few naturally occurring halo acids is fluoro-acetic acid, a highly toxic compound that occurs as the potassium salt in the African shrub *Dichapetalum cymosum*. Compounds that undergo degradation in vivo to fluoroacetic acid are also highly toxic, and 18-fluorooleic acid, for example, is the poisonous principle in certain unusual seeds.

Hydroxy and amino acids

Hydroxy acids can be prepared from the appropriate carboxylic acid intermediates by standard methods of preparing hydroxy compounds, or from the appropriate hydroxy compounds by methods for producing carboxylic acids. Some of the more important general methods include (1) the hydrolysis of halo acids, (2) the hydrolysis of cyanohydrins, (3) the reaction with α-bromo esters in the presence of zinc, and (4) the reduction of keto esters or half esters of dibasic acids:

(1) $RCH_2COOH \xrightarrow{Br_2, P} RCHBrCOOH \xrightarrow{NaOH(aq)} RCH(OH)COOH$

(2)
$$RCHO \xrightarrow{HCN} RCH(OH)CN \xrightarrow{hydrolysis} RCH(OH)COOH$$
$$RCH=CH_2 \xrightarrow{HOCl} RCH(OH)CH_2Cl$$
$$\xrightarrow{KCN} RCH(OH)CH_2CN \xrightarrow{hydrolysis} RCH(OH)CH_2COOH$$

(3) $RCHO \xrightarrow{BrCH_2COOC_2H_5} RCH(OH)CH_2COOH$

(4)
$$RCO(CH_2)_nCOOCH_3 \xrightarrow[\text{hydrolysis}]{NaBH_4;} RCH(OH)[CH_2]_nCOOH$$
$$HOOC(CH_2)_nCOOCH_3 \xrightarrow{SOCl_2} ClCO(CH_2)_nCOOCH_3$$
$$\xrightarrow[\text{hydrolysis}]{NaBH_4;} HOCH_2(CH_2)_nCOOH$$

The 2-, 3-, 4-, and 5-hydroxy carboxylic acids differ in their behaviour on heating and give, respectively, a lactide, α, β-unsaturated acid, a γ-lactone, and a δ-lactone:

$$2RCH(OH)COOH \longrightarrow \begin{array}{c} RCH \quad CO \\ | \qquad | \\ OC \quad CHR \\ \end{array}$$

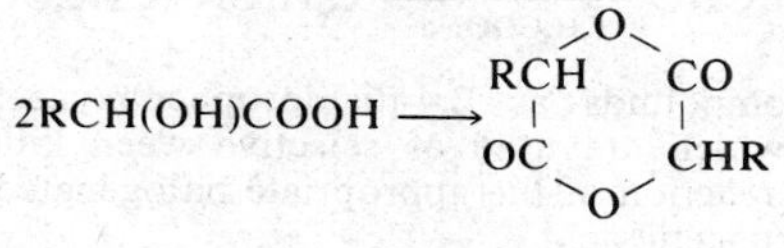

lactide

$$RCH(OH)CH_2COOH \longrightarrow RCH=CHCOOH$$

α, β-unsaturated acid

$$RCH(OH)(CH_2)_nCOOH \longrightarrow RCH(CH_2)_nC=O.$$

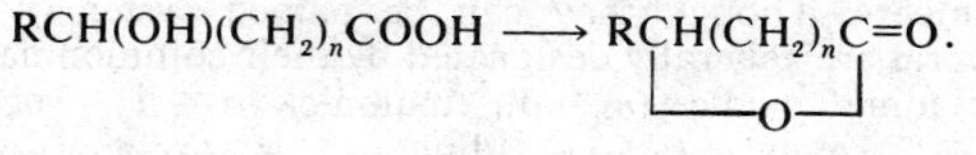

lactone

There are many naturally occurring hydroxy acids, including glycolic, lactic, and ricinoleic:

$$HOCH_2COOH \qquad\qquad CH_3CH(OH)COOH$$

glycolic acid $\qquad\qquad\qquad$ lactic acid

$$CH_3(CH_2)_5CH(OH)CH_2CH=CH(CH_2)_7COOH$$

ricinoleic acid

Ricinoleic is the major acid present in castor oil and provides a source of other useful chemicals prepared on an industrial scale. These include the diene glycerides resulting on dehydration of castor oil, as well as the products of pyrolysis—heptanal and 10-undecenoic acid—and alkali fusion—2-octanone, 2-octanol, 10-hydroxy-decanoic acid, and sebacic acid.

The α-amino acids, $RCH(NH_2)COOH$, are of great importance since they are the monomeric units that make up the peptides and proteins. Twenty different amino acids commonly occur in these materials.

Keto acids

Carboxylic acids that also carry carbonyl groups (aldehydes or ketones) usually can be prepared by oxidation of the corresponding hydroxy acids. The β-keto compounds (in the form of their esters) are of considerable importance and are prepared by special condensation procedures.

Among the more important shorter chain acids bearing extra carbonyl groups are glyoxylic acid ($OHCCOOH$), pyruvic acid ($CH_3COCOOH$), levulinic acid ($CH_3COCH_2CH_2COOH$), and especially acetoacetic acid (CH_3COCH_2COOH).

Ethyl acetoacetate and most β-keto esters exhibit tautomerism—that is, the esters exist as equilibrium mixtures of two compounds and exhibit the properties of both. The keto form, which preponderates in most cases, contains a normal carbonyl group; the other form, called the enol form, bears an alcoholic group attached directly to one of the carbons of a double bond. The enol form is usually present in small amounts, but it can be detected by its reactions. As the enol form is consumed in a reaction, more is generated from the keto form by re-establishment of the equilibrium:

$$CH_3COCH_2COOC_2H_5 \rightleftharpoons CH_3\overset{OH}{\underset{}{C}}=CHCOOC_2H_5.$$

keto form $\qquad\qquad$ enol form

Typical reactions of the keto form include reactions with hydrogen cyanide and with hydroxylamine to give cyanohydrins and oximes respectively. On the other hand, reaction with diazomethane to give an *O*-methyl ether and with ferric chloride to yield a coloured complex are considered to be typical of the enolic form.

Of major importance chemically (because it is the basis for many chemical reactions) is the fact that the methylene ($-CH_2-$) group of a β-keto ester, which is flanked by two electron-withdrawing groups ($-CO-$ and $-COOC_2H_5$), can give up one of its protons to a strong base to yield a resonance-stabilized carbanion. Intermediates of this type react readily with alkyl and acyl halides to give alkylated or acylated derivatives of the original β-keto ester, as follows:

$$CH_3COCH_2COOC_2H_5$$
$$\xrightarrow{\bar{O}C_2H_5} CH_3CO\bar{C}HCOOC_2H_5 \longleftrightarrow CH_3\overset{O^-}{\underset{}{C}}=CHCOOC_2H_5$$

resonance-stabilized carbanion

$$\underset{RX}{\swarrow} \qquad\qquad \underset{RCOX}{\searrow}$$

$$CH_3COCHRCOOC_2H_5 \qquad\qquad CH_3COCH(COR)COOC_2H_5$$

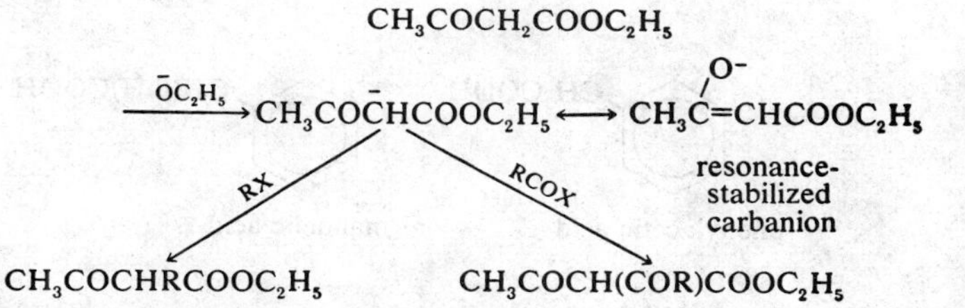

The monoalkylated and monoacylated compounds formulated in the above sequence also contain a second hydrogen atom, which can be replaced by a second alkyl or acyl group, not necessarily the same as the first. These alkylated or acylated derivatives yield valuable products after hydrolysis, a reaction that can follow two different courses:

1. Under mild conditions—*i.e.*, with dilute acid or alkali—the ester function is hydrolyzed in the usual way, but the β-keto acid so formed is unstable and decarboxylates readily to give a ketone:

$$CH_3COCH_2COOC_2H_5 \longrightarrow CH_3COCHRCOOC_2H_5$$

ethyl acetoacetate $\qquad$ mono-alkylated derivative

$$\longrightarrow CH_3COCHRCOOH \longrightarrow CH_3COCH_2R.$$

free acid $\qquad\qquad\qquad$ ketone

Reactions of this type are used to prepare monosubstituted and disubstituted derivatives of acetone (CH_3COCH_2R and CH_3COCHR_2) or 1,3-diketones (CH_3COCH_2COR).

2. With stronger alkali, the molecule is attacked at both carbonyl groups to produce acetic acid and alkylated derivatives of that substance, as in the following examples:

$$CH_3COCH_2COOC_2H_5 \begin{cases} \nearrow CH_3COCHRCOOC_2H_5 \\ \longrightarrow CH_3COOH + RCH_2COOH \\ \searrow CH_3COCR_2COOC_2H_5 \\ \longrightarrow CH_3COOH + R_2CHCOOH. \end{cases}$$

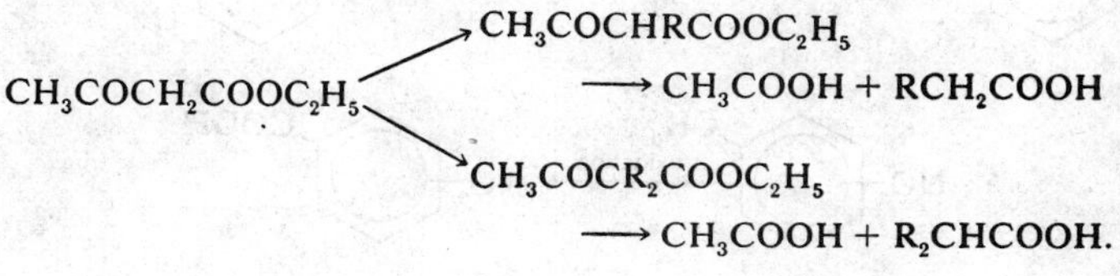

The polyfunctional nature of ethyl acetoacetate and related β-keto esters makes them valuable intermediates in the preparation of many heterocyclic compounds.

Aromatic acids. In addition to the typical reactions undergone by the carboxyl group, aromatic acids also enter into the electrophilic substitution reactions commonly displayed by aromatic compounds.

Reaction of aromatic carboxylic acids

A carboxyl group directly attached to an aromatic ring exerts a deactivating influence and directs substituents to one of the two *meta* positions in the ring (that is, not to the adjacent carbon but the one next to that). Nitration of benzoic acid, for example, requires moderately vigorous conditions and gives first *m*-nitrobenzoic acid and then 3,5-dinitrobenzoic acid.

The simplest and best known aromatic acid is benzoic acid; this compound may be considered to be the parent of a wide range of substituted benzoic acids. Those acids in which the carboxyl group is part of an aliphatic side chain and not directly attached to the aromatic ring, such as phenylacetic, mandelic, and cinnamic acids, often are not classed as aromatic acids. Many polybasic acids, such as the isomeric phthalic acids, are commercially important. The most important aromatic acids are:

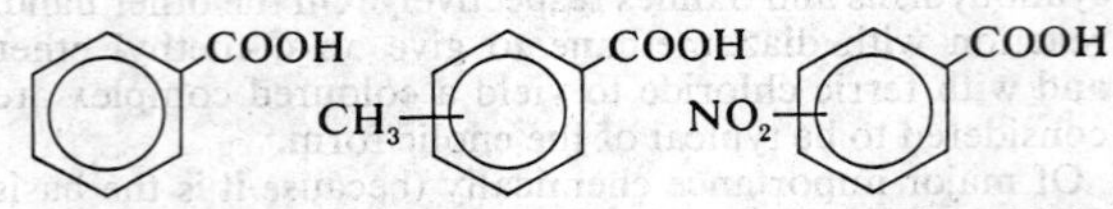

benzoic acid toluic acids* nitrobenzoic acids*

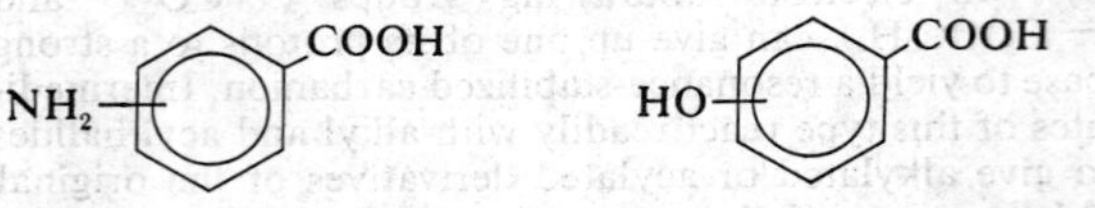

aminobenzoic acids* hydroxybenzoic acids*

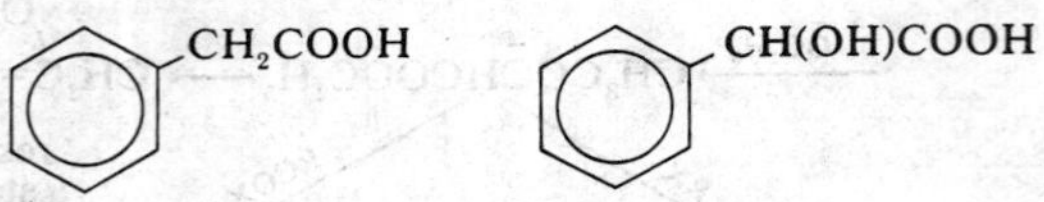

phenylacetic acid mandelic acid

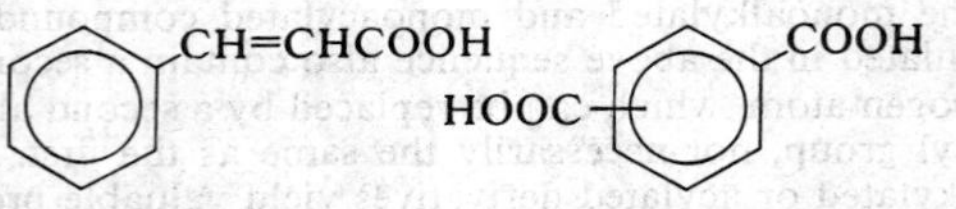

cinnamic acid phthalic acids*

*These are convenient representations of the three isomeric acids (*ortho*-, *meta*-, and *para*-), which differ in the relative positions of attachment of the two groups on the ring.

Aromatic carboxylic acids, like their aliphatic counterparts, can be prepared by hydrolysis of nitriles or by the addition of carbon dioxide to organometallic compounds, usually derived from the appropriate halide; also, they often are obtained from aromatic hydrocarbons by oxidation. The aromatic ring is so resistant to oxidation that it remains intact while carbon-linked side chains are degraded to carboxyl groups. Certain noncarbon constituents such as nitro and halo groups survive this treatment, so that nitrotoluenes or halotoluenes may be oxidized to nitrobenzoic or halobenzoic acids:

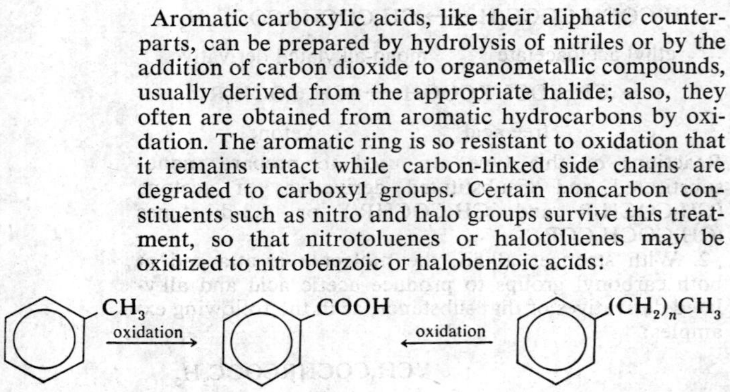

Benzoic acid

Benzoic acid has been known for centuries, having been first obtained from gum benzoin, a resin extracted from an Indonesian tree. The well-known aromatic hydrocarbon benzene can be prepared by decarboxylation of benzoic acid. By standard procedures benzoic acid can be converted to the usual range of acyl derivatives, including benzoyl chloride, benzoate esters, and benzamides. The acid also enters into several aromatic substitution processes, although certain of the substituted benzoic acids are prepared preferably by alternative routes. Several of these substituted acids, such as salicylic acid (*o*-hydroxybenzoic) and anthranilic acid (*o*-aminobenzoic), are of considerable commercial importance. The latter, which is used as an intermediate in the preparation of many dyes, is generally prepared from phthalimide, itself a derivative of the dibasic acid phthalic acid. Salicylic acid is manufactured chiefly by the reaction of sodium phenolate (C_6H_5ONa) with carbon dioxide under pressure at 120°–140° C. Derivatives of salicylic acid, especially phenyl salicylate, acetylsalicylic acid (aspirin), and 4-aminosalicylic acid are used medicinally.

Phthalic acids

The phthalic acids are prepared by oxidation of appropriate aromatic hydrocarbons. The *ortho* isomer (in which the substituents are on adjacent positions on the ring) readily forms an anhydride. The *para* isomer (in which the substituents are located directly across from one another on the ring), which is also known as terephthalic acid, is used with dihydric alcohols to produce polymers, such as Terylene, which is a linear polymer that is made by the condensation of terephthalic acid and ethylene glycol.

Cinnamic acid, one of the more important acids in which the carboxylic group is not directly attached to the aromatic ring, is prepared from benzaldehyde by several condensation procedures, one of which is carried out as follows:

$$C_6H_5CHO \xrightarrow[CH_3COONa]{(CH_3CO)_2O} C_6H_5CH{=}CHCOOH.$$

Such compounds as 2,4-dichlorophenoxyacetic acid (2,4-D), which are used as selective weed killers, are made by reaction of the appropriate halogenated phenol and chloroacetic acid.

Polycarboxylic acids. The most common dicarboxylic acids belong to the series of compounds with carboxyl groups at both ends of a hydrocarbon chain; that is, compounds with the general structural formula $HOOC(CH_2)_nCOOH$, in which n can be any of many numbers. Though they can be named systematically, several are generally designated by their common names, including oxalic ($n = 0$), malonic ($n = 1$), succinic ($n = 2$), glutaric ($n = 3$), adipic ($n = 4$), azelaic ($n = 7$), and sebacic ($n = 8$) acids.

Oxalic acid, a common natural product, is readily obtained by oxidation of table sugar, or other carbohydrates, or by heating sodium formate. Oxalyl chloride (ClCOCOCl) is a useful reagent for preparing acyl halides from other carboxylic acids.

Malonic acid

Malonic acid and its more important ethyl ester are usually prepared from acetic acid by the following synthetic sequences:

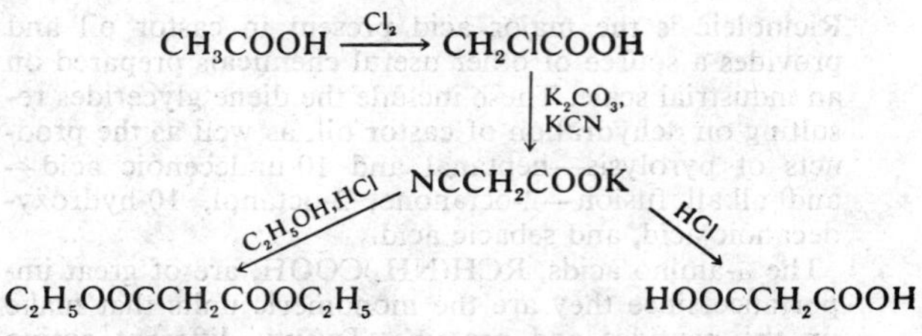

The importance of diethyl malonate is that, like ethyl acetoacetate, it readily forms a resonance-stabilized carbanion, which readily can be alkylated and, by way of the corresponding free acid, decarboxylated. Diethyl malonate, therefore, can be used to prepare monosubstituted and disubstituted derivatives of acetic acid, as in the following example:

$$CH_2(COOC_2H_5)_2 \xrightarrow[C_3H_7I]{NaOC_2H_5,} C_3H_7CH(COOC_2H_5)_2$$

$$\xrightarrow[C_2H_5I]{NaOC_2H_5,} \underset{C_2H_5}{\overset{C_3H_7}{C}}(COOC_2H_5)_2 \xrightarrow{hydrolysis}$$

$$\underset{C_2H_5}{\overset{C_3H_7}{C}}(COOH)_2 \xrightarrow{heat} \underset{C_2H_5}{\overset{C_3H_7}{C}}HCOOH$$

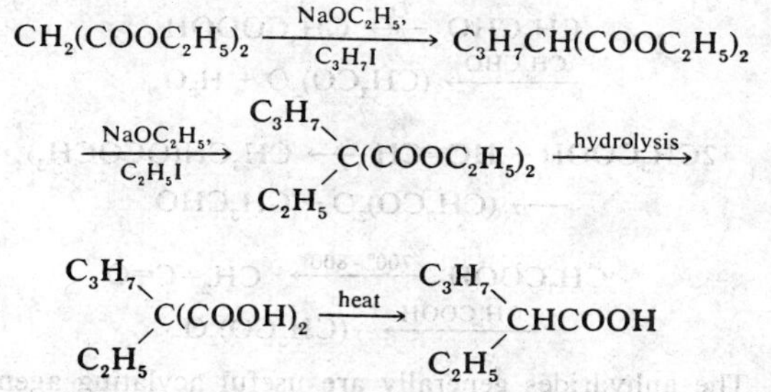

Succinic and glutaric acids differ from the other members of this series in that they readily give cyclic anhydrides (see below *Anhydrides*) when heated. Oxalic and malonic acids fail to form cyclic anhydrides, and the members of the series above glutaric usually give linear polymeric anhydrides:

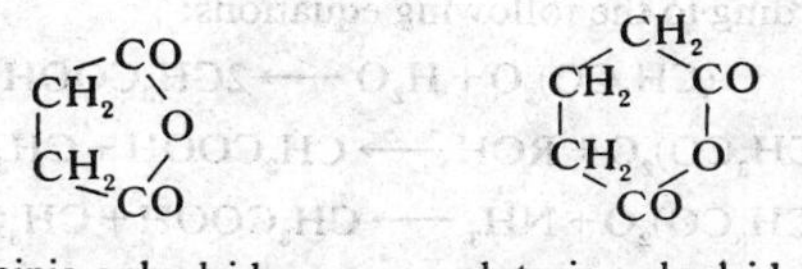

succinic anhydride   glutaric anhydride

Dibasic acids with six or more carbon atoms undergo cyclization reactions of various kinds. The examples given below show the production of a cyclic ketone, cyclopentanone, from the calcium salt of adipic acid and of an α-hydroxyketone (or acyloin) from a 16-carbon dicarboxylic acid ester:

$$\begin{matrix} CH_2CH_2COO \\ | \\ CH_2CH_2COO \end{matrix} Ca \xrightarrow{heat} \begin{matrix} CH_2CH_2 \\ | \\ CH_2CH_2 \end{matrix} CO + CaCO_3$$

$$\begin{matrix} COOC_2H_5 \\ | \\ (CH_2)_{14} \\ | \\ COOC_2H_5 \end{matrix} \xrightarrow[xylene]{sodium,} (CH_2)_{14} \begin{matrix} CO \\ | \\ CHOH \end{matrix}$$

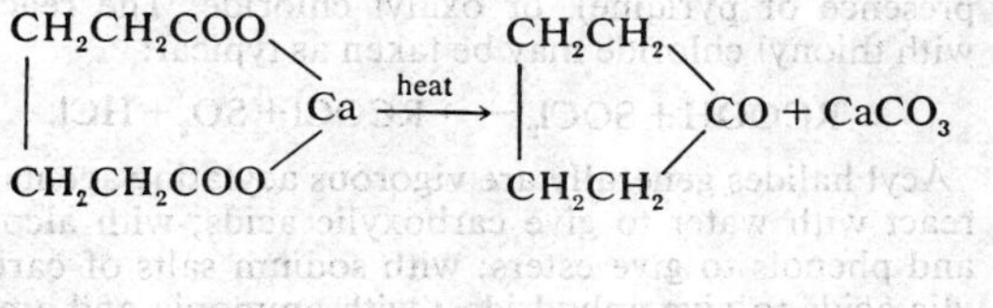

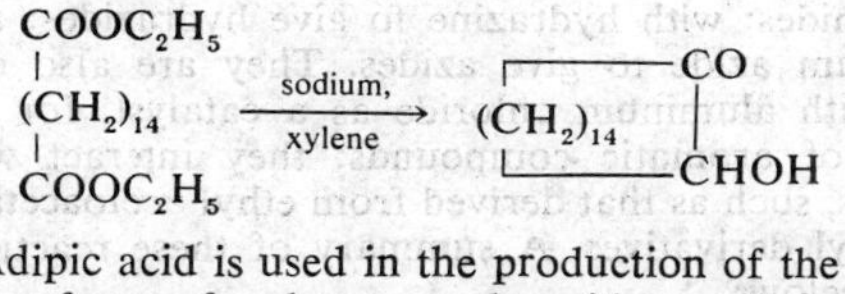

Adipic acid is used in the production of the most common form of nylon—a polyamide made from that dibasic acid and 1,6-hexanediamine. Maleic and fumaric acids are isomeric unsaturated dibasic acids. Malic acid, tartaric acid, and citric acid are important hydroxy-polycarboxylic acids of natural origin:

$$HOOCCH(OH)CH_2COOH$$

malic acid

$$HOOCCH(OH)CH(OH)COOH$$

tartaric acid

$$\begin{matrix} CH_2COOH \\ | \\ HO\text{--}C\text{--}COOH \\ | \\ CH_2COOH \end{matrix}$$

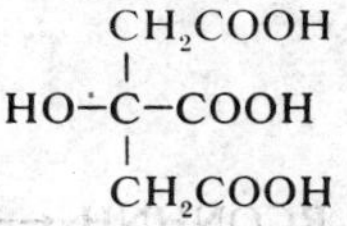

citric acid

THE CARBOXYLIC ACID DERIVATIVES

Esters. Formally, an ester with the structure RCOOR′ may be thought to be derived from a carboxylic acid of structure RCOOH, by replacement of hydrogen, − H, by an alkyl group, − R′, but the nature of the esterification process is such that it is more appropriate to describe the change as the replacement of the hydroxyl group, − OH, by an alkoxy group, − OR′. It is established experimentally in most esterification procedures that the alkoxy oxygen atom in an ester does, in fact, come from the alcohol—that is, that it remains attached to the R′ group.

Esterification Esters are prepared most often by interaction of an acid and an alcohol in the presence of a catalyst, but other useful procedures also are available. The reversible reaction between alcohols and carboxylic acids is shown by the following equation:

$$RCOOH + R'OH \rightleftharpoons RCOOR' + H_2O.$$

Because the equilibrium is attained only slowly, it is usual to add a catalyst, such as hydrogen chloride or sulfuric

acid, and to arrange the experimental conditions so that the equilibrium is shifted to the right. This shift is generally achieved by removal of water by distillation or by adding a large excess of one of the reactants. Hydroxy acids in which the hydroxyl group is three or four carbons from the carboxyl group undergo intramolecular reaction to give cyclic esters known as lactones:

$$RCH(OH)CH_2CH_2COOH \longrightarrow \begin{matrix} CH_2\text{--}CH_2 \\ | \quad\quad | \\ RCH \quad CO \\ \diagdown O \diagup \end{matrix}$$

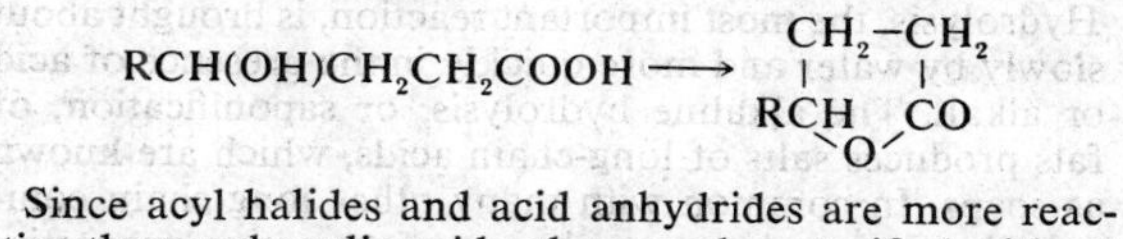

Since acyl halides and acid anhydrides are more reactive than carboxylic acids, they can be esterified without the use of acidic catalysts. This method is especially useful for preparing the half esters of dibasic acids from their cyclic anhydrides and for producing the esters of phenols, which cannot be obtained directly from the acids:

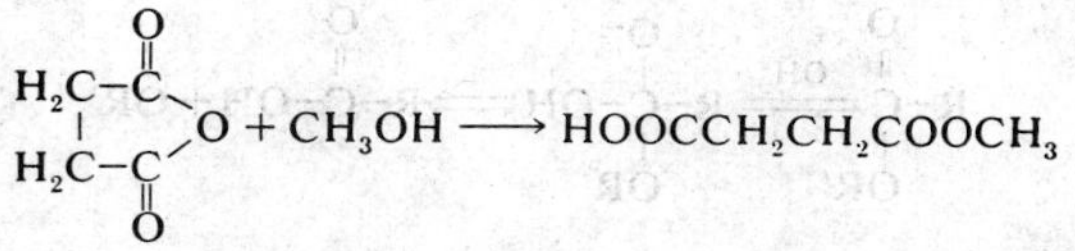

$$\begin{matrix} H_2C\text{--}C \\ | \quad\quad \\ H_2C\text{--}C \end{matrix} O + CH_3OH \longrightarrow HOOCCH_2CH_2COOCH_3$$

succinic anhydride   methyl hydrogen succinate

$$CH_3COCl + C_6H_5OH \longrightarrow CH_3COOC_6H_5 + HCl.$$

acetyl chloride   phenol   phenyl acetate

The salts of carboxylic acids react with alkyl halides to form esters. The silver salts are most commonly employed for this purpose, but sodium salts may be used when the alkyl halide is a reactive one, p-nitrobenzyl bromide, for example:

$$p\text{-}NO_2C_6H_4CH_2Br + NaOOCCH_3$$

$$\longrightarrow p\text{-}NO_2C_6H_4CH_2OCOCH_3.$$

p-nitrobenzyl acetate

Methyl esters are conveniently obtained by reaction of carboxylic acids with diazomethane in ether solution:

$$RCOOH + CH_2N_2 \longrightarrow RCOOCH_3 + N_2.$$

Since esterification is a catalytic, reversible process, one ester can be prepared from another by reaction with an alcohol (alcoholysis), with an acid (acidolysis), or with a second ester (transesterification) in the presence of a suitable acidic or basic catalyst:

alcoholysis

$$\begin{matrix} CH_2OCOR \\ | \\ CHOCOR \\ | \\ CH_2OCOR \end{matrix} + 3CH_3OH \xrightarrow{CH_3ONa} 3RCOOCH_3 + \begin{matrix} CH_2OH \\ | \\ CHOH \\ | \\ CH_2OH \end{matrix}$$

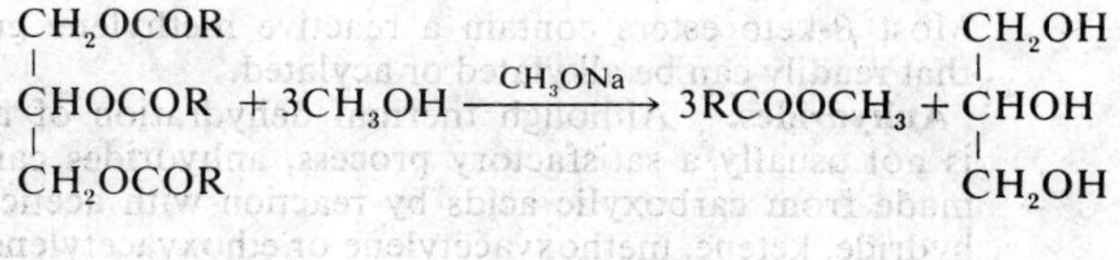

acidolysis

$$RCOOR' + (NO_2)_2C_6H_3COOH$$

3,5-dinitrobenzoic acid

$$\xrightarrow{H_2SO_4} RCOOH + (NO_2)_2C_6H_3COOR'$$

transesterification

$$RCOOCH_3 + CH_3COOCH=CH_2$$

vinyl acetate

$$\xrightarrow{H_2SO_4} RCOOCH=CH_2 + CH_3COOCH_3$$

Esters are neutral compounds. The esters of long-chain acids occur naturally as waxes (esters of long-chain alcohols), as glycerides or fats (esters of glycerol), and as phosphoglycerides (esters of glycerophosphoric acid). Esters can be converted to amides by reaction with ammonia, to hydrazides by reaction with hydrazine, and to

Reactions of esters

acids by hydrolysis. They are not converted easily to acid chlorides or anhydrides:

$$RCOOCH_3 + NH_3 \longrightarrow RCONH_2 + CH_3OH$$

$$RCOOCH_3 + N_2H_4 \longrightarrow RCONHNH_2 + CH_3OH$$

$$RCOOCH_3 + NaOH \longrightarrow RCOONa + CH_3OH.$$

Hydrolysis, the most important reaction, is brought about slowly by water and more quickly in the presence of acid or alkali. The alkaline hydrolysis, or saponification, of fats produces salts of long-chain acids, which are known as soaps. In common with many other long-chain compounds, these substances show surface-active properties and have long been used as cleansing agents. The enzyme-catalyzed hydrolysis of esters is important in the metabolism of lipids.

The mechanism of alkaline hydrolysis of esters is as follows:

$$R-\overset{\overset{\displaystyle O}{\|}}{\underset{\underset{\displaystyle OR'}{|}}{C}} \overset{OH^-}{\rightleftharpoons} R-\overset{\overset{\displaystyle O^-}{|}}{\underset{\underset{\displaystyle OR'}{|}}{C}}-OH \rightleftharpoons R-\overset{\overset{\displaystyle O}{\|}}{C}-OH + \bar{O}R'$$

$$\longrightarrow R-\overset{\overset{\displaystyle O}{\|}}{C}-O^- + R'OH.$$

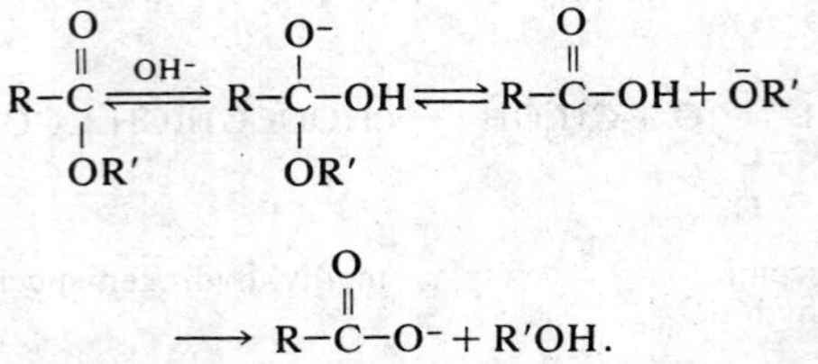

With sodium in an inert solvent, esters give acyloins (α-hydroxy ketones). Esters can be reduced to primary alcohols (RCH_2OH) by several methods, either catalytically with hydrogen and copper oxide–chromium oxide ($300°$ C and 250 atmospheres pressure), or chemically by reaction with sodium and alcohol or lithium aluminum hydride or diborane.

As is true of other carbonyl compounds, most esters undergo self-condensation in the presence of a base. The reaction involves the formation of a resonance-stabilized carbanion and reaction of this material with a second molecule of ester to give, finally, a β-keto ester. The best known example of this reaction is the preparation of ethyl acetoacetate from ethyl acetate:

$$CH_3COOC_2H_5 \overset{NaOC_2H_5}{\rightleftharpoons} CH_2\overset{\overset{\displaystyle O}{\|}}{\underset{\underset{\displaystyle OC_2H_5}{}}{C}} \longleftrightarrow CH_2=\overset{\overset{\displaystyle O^-}{|}}{\underset{\underset{\displaystyle OC_2H_5}{}}{C}} \overset{CH_3COOC_2H_5}{\rightleftharpoons}$$

$$CH_3\overset{\overset{\displaystyle O^-}{|}}{\underset{\underset{\displaystyle OC_2H_5}{|}}{C}}CH_2COOC_2H_5 \rightleftharpoons CH_3COCH_2COOC_2H_5.$$

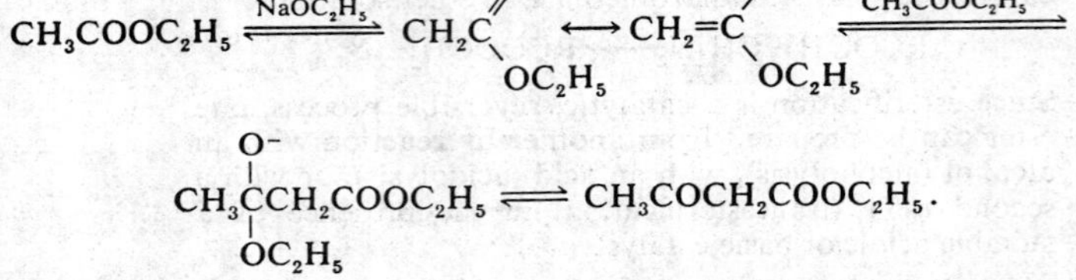

ethyl acetoacetate

Most β-keto esters contain a reactive methylene group that readily can be alkylated or acylated.

Anhydrides. Although thermal dehydration of acids is not usually a satisfactory process, anhydrides can be made from carboxylic acids by reaction with acetic anhydride, ketene, methoxyacetylene or ethoxyacetylene, or isopropenyl acetate:

$$2RCOOH + 2CH_2{=}C{=}O$$

ketene

$$\longrightarrow 2RCOOCOCH_3 \longrightarrow (RCO)_2O + (CH_3CO)_2O$$

mixed anhydride

$$2RCOOH + HC \equiv COR' \longrightarrow (RCO)_2O + CH_3COOR'.$$

From acyl halides, anhydrides can be produced by reaction with the appropriate acid salt ($RCOCl + RCOONa \rightarrow (RCO)_2O + NaCl$). Acyl halides also react with carboxylic acid and pyridine or with acetic anhydride to produce anhydrides.

Acetic anhydride   Acetic anhydride, $(CH_3CO)_2O$, is of sufficient commercial importance to be prepared industrially by atmospheric oxidation of acetaldehyde in the presence of a metal acetate, as well as from acetic acid by reaction with acetylene or ketene:

$$CH_3CHO \overset{O_2}{\longrightarrow} CH_3COOOH$$

$$\overset{CH_3CHO}{\longrightarrow} (CH_3CO)_2O + H_2O$$

$$2CH_3COOH + HC \equiv CH \longrightarrow CH_3CH(OCOCH_3)_2$$

$$\longrightarrow (CH_3CO)_2O + CH_3CHO$$

$$CH_3COOH \overset{700°-800°}{\longrightarrow} CH_2{=}C{=}O$$

$$\overset{CH_3COOH}{\longrightarrow} (CH_3CO)_2O.$$

The anhydrides generally are useful acylating agents, being more reactive for this purpose than acids or esters, but less so than acyl halides. They react with water to give carboxylic acids, with alcohols or phenols to give esters, and with ammonia and amines to give amides. Acetic anhydride, a widely used acetylating agent, for example, reacts with water, an alcohol, and ammonia, according to the following equations:

$$(CH_3CO)_2O + H_2O \longrightarrow 2CH_3COOH$$

$$(CH_3CO)_2O + ROH \longrightarrow CH_3COOH + CH_3COOR$$

$$(CH_3CO)_2O + NH_3 \longrightarrow CH_3COOH + CH_3CONH_2.$$

Anhydrides can also be used to acylate aromatic compounds in the presence of aluminum chloride.

Halides.   The acyl halides, of which the chlorides are the best known, are among the most reactive of acyl compounds. They are easily made from carboxylic acids or their salts by reaction with phosphorus pentachloride, phosphorus trichloride, thionyl chloride (usually in the presence of pyridine), or oxalyl chloride. The reaction with thionyl chloride may be taken as typical:

$$RCOOH + SOCl_2 \longrightarrow RCOCl + SO_2 + HCl.$$

Acyl halides generally are vigorous acylating agents and react with water to give carboxylic acids; with alcohols and phenols to give esters; with sodium salts of carboxylic acids to give anhydrides; with ammonia and amines to give amides; with hydrazine to give hydrazides; and with sodium azide to give azides. They are also employed, with aluminum chloride as a catalyst, for the acylation of aromatic compounds; they interact with carbanions, such as that derived from ethyl acetoacetate, to give acyl derivatives. A summary of these reactions is shown below:

Reactions of acyl halides

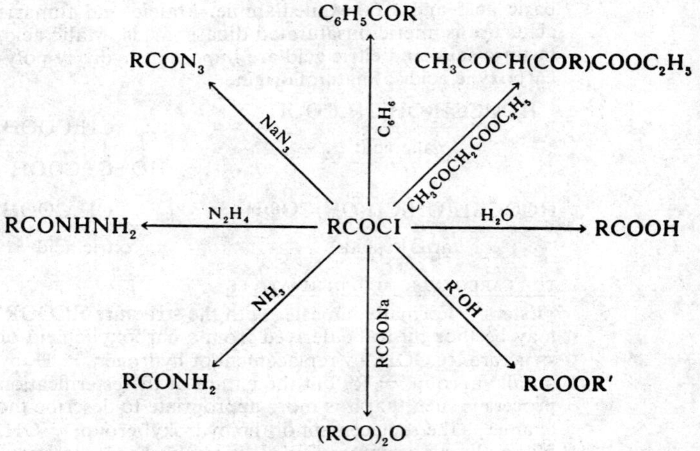

Acyl chlorides furnish ketones with organometallic compounds, especially those of zinc and of cadmium. They also are reduced to (1) aldehydes, by reaction with hydrogen, using a catalyst; or (2) alcohols, with lithium aluminum hydride or sodium borohydride. Aldehydes also can be prepared from acyl halides by way of N,N-dialkylamides, which are reduced with lithium aluminum hydride only to the aldehyde stage:

$$RCH_2OH \overset{LiAlH_4}{\longleftarrow} RCOCl \overset{R_2'NH}{\longrightarrow} RCONR_2' \overset{LiAlH_4}{\longrightarrow} RCHO.$$

alcohol   acyl chloride N,N-dialkylamide   aldehyde

Peroxy acids. The peroxy acids, or peracids as they are sometimes called, may be considered as monoacyl derivatives of hydrogen peroxide. They are important oxidizing agents and are prepared from carboxylic acids and hydrogen peroxide in the presence of acidic catalysts (usually sulfuric acid or methanesulfonic acid) or from acid anhydrides and hydrogen peroxide. It is not always necessary to isolate the peracid, and mixtures of carboxylic acid and hydrogen peroxide may be employed as oxidizing agents.

Peracetic acid is manufactured by the atmospheric oxidation of acetaldehyde.

Reactions of peracids As oxidizing agents, the peracids are used (1) to prepare epoxides and 1,2-diols from alkenes; (2) to convert ketones to esters; and (3) to oxidize amines to amine oxides, nitroso compounds, or nitro compounds. Epoxides result when alkenes are treated with aromatic peracids, such as peroxybenzoic or monoperoxyphthalic acid, or with aliphatic peracids in a buffered solution. Without a buffer the reaction mixture containing the aliphatic acid is so acidic that the epoxide ring is cleaved to give the 1,2-diol:

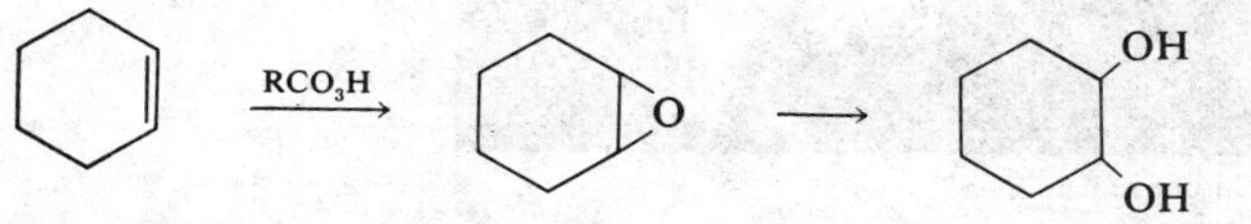

cyclohexene   epoxycyclohexane   cyclohexane-1,2-diol

The aliphatic peracids most widely used are peroxyformic, peroxyacetic, and peroxytrifluoroacetic.

Nitrogen-containing derivatives. *Nitriles.* Nitriles, or cyanides, with the general structure $RC \equiv N$, are made (1) from alkyl halides (or sulfates) by reaction with sodium or potassium cyanide, (2) from acids by dehydration of the corresponding amides, or (3) from aldehydes by dehydration of the aldoximes. These reactions are shown below:

$$RX \longrightarrow RCN$$

$$RCOOH \longrightarrow RCONH_2 \longrightarrow RCN$$

$$RCHO \longrightarrow RCH = NOH \longrightarrow RCN.$$

Reactions of nitriles Nitriles can be hydrolyzed to amides and to acids, or they can be converted directly to esters. They are reduced easily to primary amines; but reaction occurs via imines and, under suitable conditions, reduction can be halted at this stage, with the imine being hydrolyzed subsequently to an aldehyde:

$$RCOOR' \xleftarrow{R'OH,H^+} RCN \xrightarrow{hydrolysis} RCONH_2 \xrightarrow{hydrolysis} RCOOH$$

$$RCH_2NH_2 \xleftarrow{LiAlH_4} RCN \xrightarrow[(C_2H_5)_2O]{SnCl_2,HCl,} RCH=NH \xrightarrow{H_2O} RCHO.$$

Nitriles share with esters the ability to undergo base-catalyzed self-condensation, one molecule acting as a nitrile and the second as a source of carbanion. Dinitriles undergo internal condensation and are used to prepare cyclic compounds in this way:

$$(CH_2)_n \overset{CH_2CN}{\underset{CN}{\Big|}} \xrightarrow[(C_2H_5)_2O]{C_6H_5NLiC_2H_5} (CH_2)_n \overset{CHLiCN}{\underset{CN}{\Big|}}$$

$$\longrightarrow (CH_2)_n \overset{CHCN}{\underset{C=NLi}{\Big|}} \xrightarrow[decarboxylation]{hydrolysis} (CH_2)_n \overset{CH_2}{\underset{CO}{\Big|}}$$

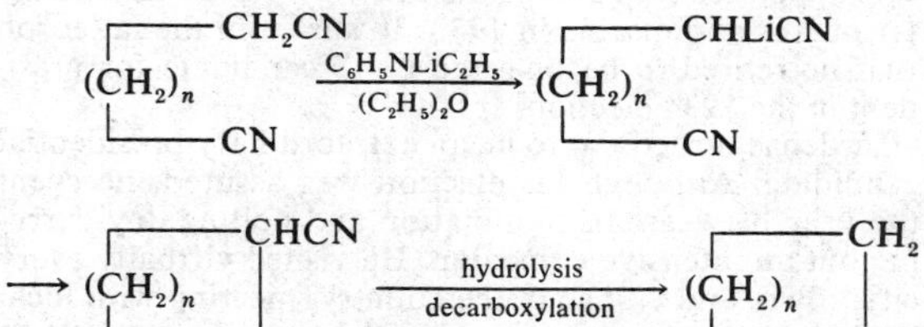

Amides. The preparation of amides from acyl halides or anhydrides (or sometimes esters) is generally accomplished by reaction with ammonia or with a primary or secondary amine. Amides also are the products of the partial hydrolysis of nitriles, and they can be obtained directly from carboxylic acids by reaction with urea, sulfamide (in the presence of pyridine), thiourea, or hexamethylphosphoramide.

Reactions of amides Amides are hydrolyzed by acid or alkali to carboxylic acids, and they are dehydrated readily to nitriles. Amides are normally reduced to amines, but *N,N*-dialkylated amides give aldehydes. With bromine and alkali, amides are degraded to amines with one less carbon atom, as follows:

$$RCONH_2 \xrightarrow{Br_2,NaOH} [RCONHBr] \longrightarrow [RNCO] \longrightarrow RNH_2 + CO_2.$$

Urea (NH_2CONH_2) is an amide present in mammalian urine and is the form in which many animals excrete waste nitrogen.

Hydrazides and azides. Hydrazides ($RCONHNH_2$) may be considered formally to be derived from carboxylic acids and hydrazine, and acyl azides ($RCON_3$) are analogous to the acyl chlorides, the azide (N_3) group having replaced a chlorine (Cl) atom. In actual practice, the hydrazides and azides are prepared from acyl halides by reaction with hydrazine and sodium azide, respectively. Nitrous acid converts hydrazides to azides:

$$RCOCl \begin{cases} \xrightarrow{N_2H_4} RCONHNH_2 \\ \xrightarrow{NaN_3} RCON_3 \end{cases} \xrightarrow{HNO_2}$$

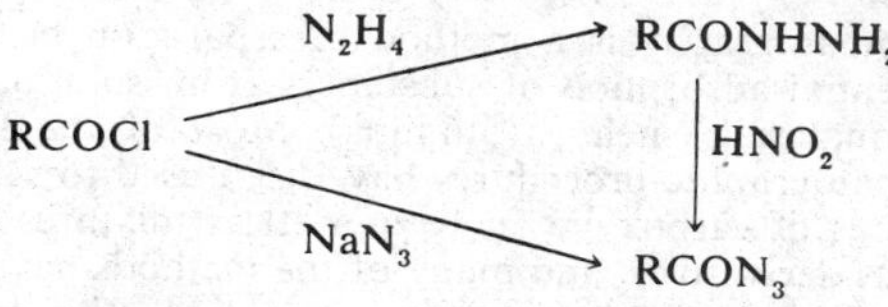

THE IDENTIFICATION AND ANALYSIS OF CARBOXYLIC ACIDS AND DERIVATIVES

In the qualitative analysis of organic compounds, carboxylic acids are recognized by their solubility in aqueous alkali and by their ability to liberate carbon dioxide from bicarbonate solutions. When treated with potassium hydroxide and hydroxylamine, esters give hydroxamic acids, which are easily recognized by the deep red or purple colours they give with ferric salts.

Infrared spectra of carboxyl compounds All acyl compounds have distinctive bands in their infrared spectra (particular patterns of light absorption, instrumentally determined). The absorption is believed to result from energy taken up by certain carbonyl stretching motions in the molecules. The exact frequency of this absorption depends on the molecular environment of the carbonyl group, and it is sometimes possible to distinguish the various types of carbonyls by the frequency of the infrared absorption (see Table 3). A double

Table 3: Characteristic Infrared Absorption Bands of Selected Classes of Carbonyl Compounds

class	infrared absorption frequency, C=O stretching (cm^{-1})
Anhydrides	1850–1740*
Acyl halides	1815–1750
Esters	1750–1710
Aldehydes	1740–1680
Ketones	1725–1660
Carboxylic acids	1720–1660
Amides	1680–1630

*Two peaks, about 60 cm^{-1} apart.

bond, or an aromatic system in the alpha position with reference to the carbonyl group, causes the absorption in each case to appear at the lower end of the range.

Carboxylic acids can be characterized by the preparation of a wide range of solid derivatives. Among the most commonly employed are the

amides	($RCONH_2$),
anilides	($RCONHC_6H_5$),
p-toluidides	($RCONHC_6H_4CH_3$),
p-nitrobenzyl esters	($RCOOCH_2C_6H_4NO_2$),
S-benzylthiuronium salts	$[RCOO(\overset{-}{N}H_2)_2C\overset{+}{S}CH_2C_6H_5]$,
p-bromophenacyl esters	($RCOOCH_2COC_6H_4Br$),
and hydrazides	($RCONHNH_2$).

Esters and other acyl derivatives usually furnish these compounds after hydrolysis to the acid; or, in some cases, they are converted directly to the compound without production of the free acid.

The reaction of carboxylic acids and esters with alkali is the basis of several procedures for the quantitative estimation of these groups. Acids react quickly at room temperature and can be titrated directly in aqueous or alcoholic solution. Alternatively, they can be treated with excess of alkali, the excess being titrated with standard acid solution. Esters usually react with hot alkali, and the normal procedure for their quantitative determination is heating with excess alkali and titration of the surplus. This procedure is the basis of the standard method for determining the saponification (hydrolysis) equivalent, or saponification value, of fats. Carboxylic acids can also be quantitatively estimated by determination of (1) the methane liberated during reaction with methylmagnesium iodide or (2) the water formed during esterification.

Chromatography of carboxyl compounds

Chromatography is a method of separation based on differential adsorption of substances from solution by a solid material (such as alumina). Most of the known chromatographic procedures have been used to separate mixtures of carboxylic acids, as well as mixtures of the various derivatives, and many of the methods have been adapted for qualitative or quantitative identification or both. Indeed many useful developments in chromatography have come about from the need to analyze the mixed amino acids resulting from protein hydrolysis and the mixed fatty acids produced by lipid hydrolysis.

The most important analytical procedure for esters is the form of chromatography known as gas–liquid chromatography. By the use of an appropriate stationary phase, and long capillary columns when necessary, even closely related esters can be separated and quantitatively analyzed. In difficult cases this technique may have to be allied with other separation procedures.

Limited information about the carboxyl group (and other acyl groups) is obtainable by nuclear magnetic resonance spectroscopy, an instrumental technique that gives information about the magnetic properties of atomic nuclei. Although this method may not reveal much about the carboxyl group, it may provide considerable useful information about the remainder of the molecule. Mass spectrometry, the separation of substances on the basis of their respective masses, is an increasingly important tool in the recognition of complex compounds containing carboxyl and other acyl groups, especially those derived from lipids and other natural sources. Fragmentation of the molecule during the mass spectrometry procedure frequently gives valuable information about the molecular structure of the compound or compounds under investigation. Esters, particularly methyl esters, have been more extensively used in mass spectrographic studies than the acids themselves or the other derivatives.

BIBLIOGRAPHY. A modern comprehensive treatise dealing with all classes of organic compounds is E.H. RODD (ed.), *Chemistry of Carbon Compounds*, 2nd ed. by S. COFFEY (1965). Volume 1, parts C and D are particularly relevant to this article. Several monographs devoted exclusively to carboxylic acids and their derivatives are: S. PATAI (ed.), *The Chemistry of Carboxylic Acids and Esters* (1969); and F.D. GUNSTONE, *An Introduction to the Chemistry and Biochemistry of Fatty Acids and Their Glycerides*, 2nd ed. (1968). Additional material may be found in selected chapters in the following review series: R.T. HOLMAN (ed.), *Progress in the Chemistry of Fats and Other Lipids;* R. PAOLETTI and D. KRITCHEVSKY (eds.), *Advances in Lipid Research;* and F.D. GUNSTONE (ed.), *Topics in Lipid Chemistry*.

(F.D.G.)

Cárdenas, Lázaro

Lázaro Cárdenas, during his six-year term as president of Mexico (1934–40), did more than any other president to carry out the Mexican Revolution's promises of land reform, strong organized labour, mass education, and government control of the economy. His administration ended one phase of the revolution started by Francisco Madero in 1910 and opened another.

Cárdenas, born on May 21, 1895, in Jiquilpan, in the state of Michoacán, was largely of Indian descent. After

Archivo Casasola, Mexico City

Cárdenas.

a rudimentary education, he received his first job in a local branch of the Public Revenue Office.

Revolutionary activities

In January 1913 Pres. Francisco Madero, who had led the struggle to overthrow the long dictatorship of Porfirio Díaz, was taken prisoner and assassinated by the orders of the rebellious Gen. Victoriano Huerta, who now seized control of the government. Huerta's repressive military dictatorship provoked civil war almost immediately, and Venustiano Carranza headed the new revolutionary forces. At the age of 18, Cárdenas joined a branch of the revolutionary army led by one of Carranza's principal lieutenants, Gen. Álvaro Obregón, and within a year he had risen to the rank of captain. In 1923 he was appointed general, the highest rank in the Mexican Army, and continued to participate in military campaigns until 1929.

Like most of the revolutionary military leaders, Gen. Lázaro Cárdenas was also active politically, and in 1928, at the age of 33, he was elected governor of his native state of Michoacán. He served in that position for a full term, until 1932. Cárdenas also played an important role in forming a nationwide party to reinforce the revolutionary regime. Under the leadership of former president Plutarco Elías Calles, in office from 1924 to 1928, the Partido Nacional Revolucionario (PNR) was launched in 1929; and in the following year, Governor Cárdenas was chosen to be the party's new chairman. Cárdenas worked hard to transform the PNR from a loose federation of state parties, each led by a military-political caudillo ("boss"), into a truly national party and a major element of stability in the revolutionary regime. After his retirement as governor of Michoacán, Cárdenas was appointed minister of the interior in 1931 and minister of war and marine in 1933. It was from the latter job that he retired to become the PNR's candidate for president in the 1934 election.

Cárdenas turned out to be an extraordinary presidential candidate. Although his election was assured, he spent the year between his nomination and polling day carrying out an intensive campaign. He visited virtually every city, town, and village in the country, meeting with local leaders and ordinary citizens, and building up an extensive personal following in all parts of the country. During this campaign, he made clear his intention to carry out PNR's six-year plan of social and economic reform.

Reforms during presidency

Once elected president, General Cárdenas moved cautiously at first. The army, the civil administration, and much of the political structure of the regime remained under the control of former president Calles, who had wielded vast influence while in power. During his first year in office, President Cárdenas spent much of his time establishing his own influence in these branches of the administration. Finally, he felt strong enough to have Calles sent into exile in the United States.

As president, Cárdenas carried out a wide range of reforms. Under the agrarian reform program, he distributed more land than all of his predecessors put together, with the result that by the end of his administration about half of the country's cultivated land was in the hands of previously landless farmers. He also extended the services of government banks so that the peasants who had received land under the reform could borrow money. In an effort to provide a political base for the land redistribution program, he organized all of its beneficiaries in a new National Peasant Confederation (Confederación Nacional Campesina, CNC). This was but one more step in strengthening the general political structure of his new regime. Another major step in this direction was taken early in 1936 when most of the country's dispersed central labour groups were organized into the Confederación de Trabajadores de México (CTM), which, for the next generation, continued to represent at least half of the country's organized workers.

Cárdenas also reorganized the government party. In 1938 a national convention restructured the party and renamed it the Partido de la Revolución Mexicana (PRM). Whereas in the past only government employees and aspiring politicians were members of the party, the new organizational scheme allowed mass groups to join the PRM directly. Four "sectors" of the party were established: labour, peasant, "popular," and "military." Most national labour groups were affiliated with the first; the CNC constituted the second; a variety of middle-class groups made up the third; and the armed forces were incorporated into the last. In the next administration the military sector was suppressed, and since then the military role in Mexican politics has been reduced considerably.

The Cárdenas administration was most famous abroad for its efforts to expropriate foreign-owned industries and place them under Mexican control. In 1937 the government expropriated the nation's principal railways, and in March 1938 President Cárdenas signed a decree nationalizing the country's oil industry. After short-lived experiments of putting both of these industries under the control of their workers' unions, they were placed under autonomous public corporations, which were to function more or less like any other large private industry.

When his term in office came to an end, President Cárdenas presided over the election of his successor, Gen. Manuel Ávila Camacho. He intended to withdraw from active political life. With the outbreak of World War II, however, in which Mexico became an active participant early in 1942, Cárdenas returned to public office. He served as minister of national defense from 1943 to 1945, and in the last year of his term he was made commander in chief of the Mexican Army. He retired once again late in 1945.

Political influence after retirement

For the following 16 years, he held no public office. In 1961, however, when Pres. Adolfo López Mateos gave each living former president of Mexico an important position in the national administration, Cárdenas became the executive member of the Comisión del Río Balsas, which ran one of the country's major regional electrification and development agencies, in the state of Guerrero. His sharply diminished responsibilities notwithstanding, he remained a major figure in national politics. He became the symbol of the left in the government party, renamed Partido Revolucionario Institucional in 1946. He remained the major supporter of the cooperative type of agrarian reform, and the chief opponent of the United States' economic and political influence in Mexico. Cárdenas never withdrew from the government party, although he continued to support alternative political organizations. In the early 1960s he sponsored a rival group to the CNC, the Independent National Peasant Confederation (Confederación Nacional Campesina Independiente, CNCI), and patronized—but never joined—a left-wing political coalition, the National Liberation Movement.

In the years following his retirement as minister of national defense, Cárdenas maintained a strongly anti-United States position also in international affairs, which won him the Stalin Peace Prize in 1955. After the victory of the Castro Revolution, he became the most forceful ally of the Cuban revolutionaries in Mexico. Basically, however, Cárdenas' political influence had substantially declined during the last years of his life. Nevertheless he remained a highly controversial figure and a rallying point for those who were critical of the policies of succeeding administrations. In the last half decade of his life, Cárdenas spoke out on public affairs only less and less frequently, spending most of his time at his estate in Jiquilpan, Michoacán. Cárdenas died on October 19, 1970.

BIBLIOGRAPHY. Several books have been written in English about Lázaro Cárdenas and his administration, during and after his period in power. These include NATHANIEL and SYLVIA WEYL, *The Reconquest of Mexico: The Years of Lázaro Cárdenas* (1939); EVELYN WAUGH, *Mexico: An Object Lesson* (British title, *Robbery Under Law: The Mexican Object-Lesson*, 1939); WILLIAM CAMERON TOWNSEND, *Lázaro Cárdenas: Mexican Democrat* (1952); HENRY A. PHILLIPS, *New Designs for Old Mexico* (1939); and J.H. PLENN, *Mexico Marches* (1939). Aspects of the Cárdenas administration have been dealt with in various sources. Organized labour is handled in JOE C. ASHBY, *Organized Labor and the Mexican Revolution Under Lázaro Cárdenas* (1967). Agrarian reform under Cárdenas is treated in CLARENCE O. SENIOR, *Land Reform and Democracy* (1958). Mexican industrialization during and after the Cárdenas period is dealt with in SANFORD A. MOSK, *Industrial Revolution in Mexico* (1950); and FRANK TANNENBAUM, *Mexico: The Struggle for Peace and Bread* (1950). The oil problem was discussed by DONALD R. RICHBERG, an attorney for the expropriated oil companies, in *The Mexican Oil Seizure* (1939); as well as in ROSCOE B. GAITHER, *Expropriation in Mexico: The Facts and the Law* (1940); and WENDELL C. GORDON, *The Expropriation of Foreign Owned Property in Mexico* (1941). Political matters are dealt with in ROBERT E. SCOTT, *Mexican Government in Transition*, rev. ed. (1964); KARL M. SCMITT, *Communism in Mexico* (1965); and ERNST HALPERIN, *Communism in Mexico* (1963).

(R.J.Al.)

Cardiovascular System, Human

The cardiovascular system is a closed tubular system in which blood, propelled by a muscular heart, flows through vessels to and from all parts of the body. Two circuits, one that is called pulmonary and the other systemic, consist of arterial, capillary, and venous components.

The primary function of the heart is to serve as a muscular pump propelling blood into and through vessels to and from all parts of the body. The arteries, which receive this blood at high pressure and velocity and conduct it throughout the body, are thickly walled with elastic fibrous tissue and a wrapping of muscle cells. The arterial tree—the branching system of arteries—terminates in short, narrow, muscular vessels called arterioles, from which blood enters simple endothelial tubes (*i.e.*, tubes formed of endothelial, or lining, cells) known as capillaries. These microscopically thin capillaries are permeable to vital cellular nutrients and waste products and serve as both distributing and receiving points for nutrients and wastes. From the capillaries, the blood, now depleted of oxygen and burdened with waste products, moving more slowly and under low pressure, enters small vessels called venules, which converge to form veins, ultimately guiding the blood on its way back to the heart.

HEART

Description. *Shape and location.* The human adult heart is normally slightly larger than a clenched fist with average dimensions of 5 × 3½ × 2½ inches (about 13 × 9 × 6 centimetres) and weighing approximately 300 grams (10.5 ounces). It is cone shaped in appearance, with the broad base directed upward and to the right and the apex pointing downward and to the left. It is located in the chest (thoracic) cavity behind the breastbone, or sternum, in front of the windpipe, or trachea, the esophagus, and the descending aorta, between the lungs and above the diaphragm, which is the muscular partition between the chest and abdominal cavities. About two-thirds of the heart lies to the left of the midline.

Fibrous pericardium

Pericardium. The heart is suspended in its own special membranous sac, the pericardium. The strong outer portion of the sac, or fibrous pericardium, is firmly attached to the diaphragm below, the mediastinal pleura on the side, and the sternum in front and gradually blends with the coverings of the superior vena cava and the pulmonary (lung) arteries and veins leading to and from the heart. (The space between the two lungs, the mediastinum, is bordered by the mediastinal pleura, a continuation of the membrane lining the chest. The superior vena cava is the principal channel for venous blood from the chest, the arms, the neck, and the head.)

Smooth, serous (moisture-exuding) membrane lines the fibrous pericardium, then bends back and covers the heart (Figure 1). The portion of membrane lining the fibrous pericardium is known as the parietal serous membrane, that covering the heart as the visceral serous layer, or the epicardium.

The two layers of serous membrane are normally separated only by ten to 15 millilitres (0.6 to 0.9 cubic inch) of pericardial fluid, which is secreted by the serous membranes. The slight space created by the separation is called the pericardial cavity. The pericardial fluid lubricates the two membranes with every beat of the heart as their surfaces glide over each other. Fluid is filtered into the pericardial space through both the visceral and parietal peritoneum.

From S. Jacob and C. Francone, *Structure and Function in Man* (1970); W.B. Saunders Co.

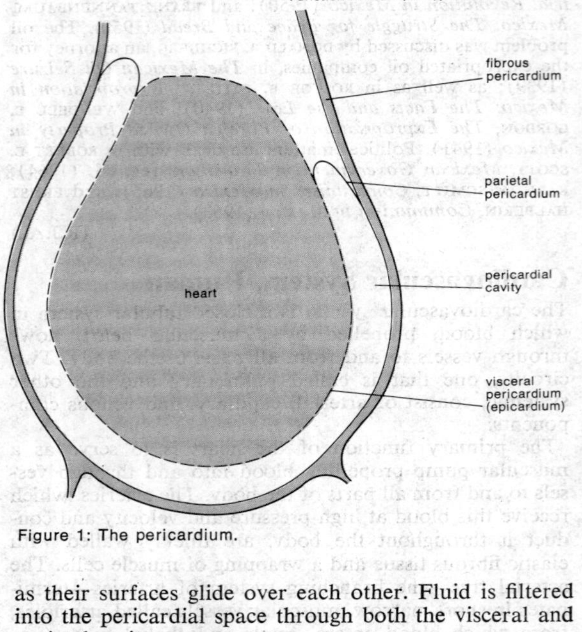

Figure 1: The pericardium.

Chambers of the heart. The heart is divided by septa, or partitions, into right and left halves, and each half is subdivided into two chambers. The upper chambers, the atria, are separated by a partition known as the interatrial septum; the lower chambers, the ventricles, are separated by the interventricular septum (Figure 2). The atria serve as receiving chambers for blood from the various parts of the body and pump blood into the ventricles. The ventricles, in turn, pump blood to the lungs and to the remainder of the body.

The right atrium, or right superior portion of the heart, is a thin-walled chamber receiving blood from all tissues except the lungs. Three veins empty into the right atrium, the superior and inferior venae cavae, bringing blood from the upper and lower portions of the body, respectively, and the coronary sinus, draining blood from the heart itself. Blood flows from the right atrium to the right ventricle.

The right ventricle, the right inferior portion of the heart, is the chamber from which the pulmonary artery carries blood to the lungs.

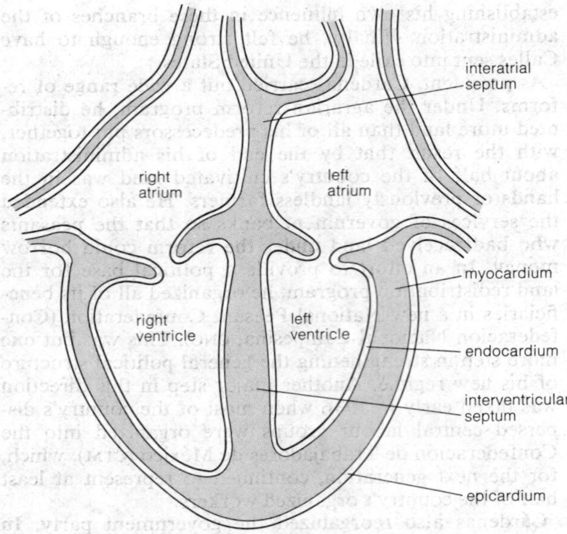

Figure 2: The walls and chambers of the heart.
From S. Jacob and C. Francone, *Structure and Function in Man* (1970); W.B. Saunders Co.

The left atrium, the left superior portion of the heart, is slightly smaller than the right atrium and has a thicker wall. The left atrium receives the four pulmonary veins, which bring oxygenated blood from the lungs. Blood flows from the left atrium into the left ventricle.

The left ventricle, the left inferior portion of the heart, has walls three times as thick as those of the right ventricle. Blood is forced from this chamber through the aorta to all parts of the body except the lungs.

External surface of the heart. Shallow grooves called the interventricular sulci, containing blood vessels, mark the separation between ventricles on the front and back surfaces of the heart. There are two grooves on the external surface of the heart. One, the atrioventricular groove, is along the line where the right atrium and the right ventricle meet; it contains a branch of the coronary artery (the coronary arteries deliver blood to the heart muscle). The other, the anterior interventricular sulcus, runs along the line between the right and left ventricles and contains a branch of the left coronary artery.

On the posterior side of the heart surface, a groove called the posterior longitudinal sulcus marks the division between the right and left ventricles; it contains another branch of the coronary artery. A fourth groove, between the left atrium and ventricle, holds the coronary sinus, a channel for venous blood.

Origin and development. In the embryo, formation of the heart begins in the pharyngeal, or throat, region. The first visible indication of the embryonic heart occurs in the undifferentiated mesoderm, the middle of the three primary layers in the embryo, as a thickening of invading cells. An endocardial (lining) tube of flattened

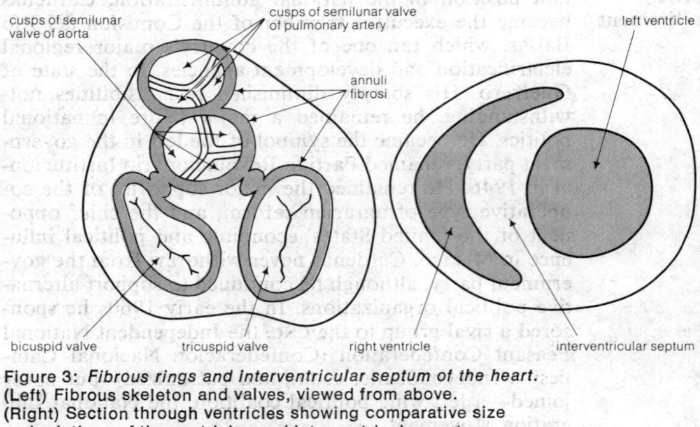

Figure 3: *Fibrous rings and interventricular septum of the heart.* (Left) Fibrous skeleton and valves, viewed from above. (Right) Section through ventricles showing comparative size and relations of the ventricles and interventricular septum.

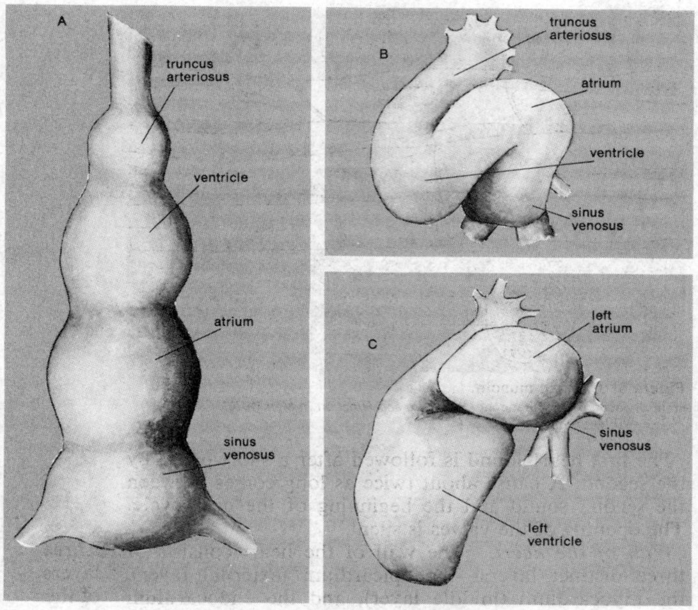

Figure 4: *Stages in embryonic development of the heart.*
(A) Primitive heart tube. (B) Beginnings of flexion.
(C) Complete flexion with separation of chambers.
From S. Jacob and C. Francone, *Structure and Function in Man* (1970); W.B. Saunders Co.

cells subsequently forms and continues to differentiate until a young tube with forked anterior and posterior ends arises. As differentiation and growth progress, this primitive tube begins to fold upon itself, and constrictions along its length produce four primary chambers. These are called, from posterior to anterior, the sinus venosus, atrium, ventricle, and truncus arteriosus (Figure 4). The characteristic bending of the tube causes the ventricle to swing first to the right and then behind the atrium, the truncus coming to lie between the sideways dilations of the atrium. It is during this stage of development and growth that the first pulsations of heart activity begin.

Four primary chambers in embryo

Endocardial cushions (local thickenings of the endocardium, or heart lining) "pinch" the single opening between the atrium and the ventricle into two portions, thereby forming two openings. These cushions are also responsible for the formation of the two atrioventricular valves (the valves between atria and ventricles), which regulate the direction of blood flow through the heart.

The atrium becomes separated into right and left halves first by a primary partition with a perforation and later by a secondary partition, which, too, has a large opening, called the foramen ovale, in its lower part. Even though the two openings do not quite coincide in position, blood still passes through, from the right atrium to the left. At birth, increased blood pressure in the left atrium forces the primary partition against the secondary one, so that the two openings are blocked and the atria are completely separated. The two partitions eventually fuse.

The ventricle becomes partially divided into two chambers by an indentation of myocardium (heart muscle) at its tip. This developing partition is largely muscular and is supplemented by membranous connective tissue that develops in conjunction with the subdivision of the truncus arteriosus by a spiral partition into two channels, one for systemic and one for pulmonary circulation (the aorta and the pulmonary artery, respectively). The greater portion of blood passing through the right side of the heart in the fetus is returned to the systemic circulation by the ductus arteriosus, a vessel connecting the pulmonary artery and the aorta. At birth this duct becomes closed by a violent contraction of its muscular wall. Thereafter the blood in the right side of the heart is driven through the pulmonary arteries to the lungs for oxygenation and returned to the left side of the heart for ejection into the systemic circulation.

A distinct median furrow at the apex of the ventricles marks the external subdivision of the ventricle into right and left chambers.

Hearts in lower animals

Hearts in lower animals are found in forms corresponding closely to the various stages described in human embryonic development. Fish have a primitive heart, four chambers in series (the sinus venosus, atrium, ventricle, and truncus arteriosus) with some folding. Valves are present between all chambers, and contraction occurs in all chambers except the truncus. The heart receives deoxygenated blood at the rear and pumps it forward for aeration in the gills.

The heart becomes more specialized when associated with the use of lungs for oxygenation of the blood, bringing about partial or complete anatomic separation of chambers within the heart, which is associated with the separate return of oxygenated and deoxygenated blood. In amphibians the atrium is at least partially subdivided into two chambers. The left chamber receives blood directly from the lungs, while the right receives venous blood. The ventricle is undivided, but the pulmonary and systemic streams are kept reasonably well separated by ridges and pockets in the ventricular wall. Atrioventricular valves, with fibrous cords called chordae tendineae, prevent the backflow of blood, as do valves in the pulmonary vessels.

From S. Jacob and C. Francone, *Structure and Function in Man* (1970); W.B. Saunders Co.

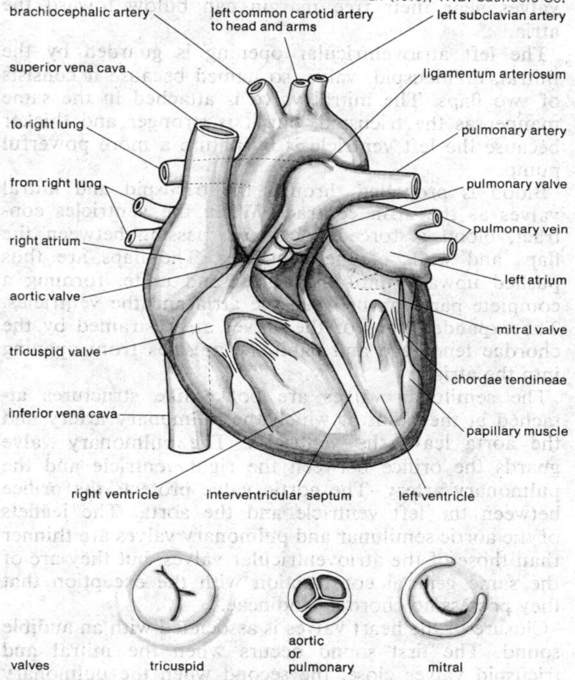

Figure 5: Schematic "transparent" drawing of the heart showing the relations of the various heart valves.

The muscular walls of the hearts of both fish and amphibians are sufficiently irrigated by the blood within the heart so that there exists no need for an additional separate system of vessels that serve the heart muscle itself. Reptiles, however, representing a step up the evolutionary scale, possess two coronary arteries branching from the right aortic trunk, and the reptilian heart has four chambers. The atrium is completely divided into right and left chambers, but the ventricle remains only partially divided by a septum, or partition. As a result, some mixing of the venous and systemic blood occurs. The truncus arteriosus has become subdivided by a spiral partition into a pulmonary trunk and two aortic trunks.

In birds and mammals, four completely separate heart cavities are formed. Venous blood flows through the right atrium and ventricle through the pulmonary arteries to the lungs; then it flows back to the left atrium via pulmonary veins, then to the left ventricle, and then, by way of the aorta, into the systemic circulation. With the complete separation of the ventricles, the thickness of the muscular wall of the left ventricle becomes greater than that of the right.

Structure and function. *Valves of the heart.* To prevent backflow of blood, the heart is equipped with special valves that permit the blood to flow in only one direction (Figure 5). There are two types of valves located in the heart: the atrioventricular valves (tricuspid and mitral) and the semilunar valves (pulmonary and aortic).

The atrioventricular valves are thin, leaflike structures located between the atria and the ventricles. The right atrioventricular opening is guarded by the tricuspid valve, so called because it consists of three irregularly shaped cusps, or flaps.

The leaflets consist essentially of folds of endocardium (heart lining) reinforced with a flat sheet of dense connective tissue. At the base of the leaflets, the middle supporting flat plate becomes continuous with that of the dense connective tissue of the ridge surrounding the openings.

Chordae tendineae and papillary muscles

Tendinous cords of dense tissue (chordae tendineae) covered by thin endocardium extend from the nipple-like papillary muscles to connect with the ventricular surface of the middle supporting layer of each leaflet. The chordae tendineae and the papillary muscles from which they arise limit the extent to which the portions of the valves near their free margin can billow toward the atria.

The left atrioventricular opening is guarded by the mitral, or bicuspid, valve, so named because it consists of two flaps. The mitral valve is attached in the same manner as the tricuspid, but it is stronger and thicker because the left ventricle is by nature a more powerful pump.

Blood is propelled through the tricuspid and mitral valves as the atria contract. When the ventricles contract, blood is forced backward, passing between the flaps and walls of the ventricles. The flaps are thus pushed upward until they meet and unite, forming a complete partition between the atria and the ventricles. The expanded flaps of the valves are restrained by the chordae tendineae and papillary muscles from opening into the atria.

The semilunar valves are pocket-like structures attached at the point at which the pulmonary artery and the aorta leave the ventricles. The pulmonary valve guards the orifice between the right ventricle and the pulmonary artery. The aortic valve protects the orifice between the left ventricle and the aorta. The leaflets of the aortic semilunar and pulmonary valves are thinner than those of the atrioventricular valves, but they are of the same general construction with the exception that they possess no chordae tendineae.

Closure of the heart valves is associated with an audible sound. The first sound occurs when the mitral and tricuspid valves close, the second when the pulmonary and aortic semilunar valves close. These characteristic heart sounds have been found to be caused by the vibration of the walls of the heart and major vessels around the heart. The first heart sound, or "lubb," is heard when the ventricles contract, causing a sudden backflow of blood that closes the valves and causes them to bulge back. The elasticity of the valves then causes the blood to bounce backward into each respective ventricle. This effect sets the walls of the ventricles into vibration, and the vibrations travel away from the valves. When the vibrations reach the chest wall where the wall is in contact with the heart, sound waves are created that can be heard with the aid of a stethoscope.

The second heart sound results from vibrations set up in the walls of the pulmonary artery, the aorta, and, to a lesser extent, the ventricles as the blood reverberates back and forth between the walls of the arteries and the valves after the pulmonary and aortic semilunar valves suddenly close. These vibrations are then heard as the "dupp" sound as the chest wall transforms the vibrations into sound waves.

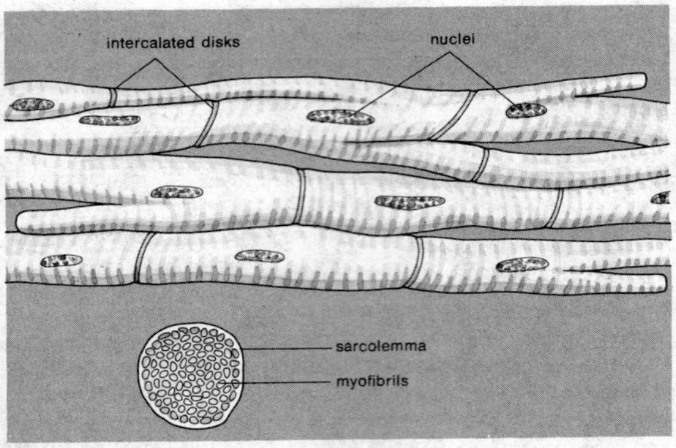

Figure 6: Cardiac muscle.
From S. Jacob and C. Francone, *Structure and Function in Man* (1970); W.B. Saunders Co.

The first heart sound is followed after a short pause by the second. A pause about twice as long comes between the second sound and the beginning of the next cycle. The opening of the valves is silent.

Three layers of the heart wall

Wall of the heart. The wall of the heart consists of three distinct layers—the epicardium (external layer), the myocardium (middle layer), and the endocardium (inner layer). Coronary vessels supplying arterial blood to the heart penetrate the epicardium before entering the myocardium. This outer layer, or visceral pericardium, consists of a surface of flattened epithelial (covering) cells resting upon connective tissue.

The myocardium consists of interlacing bundles of cardiac muscle fibres (Figure 6) possessing the appearance of striated muscle (striped skeletal muscle) with intermittent dark plates crossing the fibres, but these highly specialized fibres differ fundamentally from those of skeletal muscle in the arrangement of nuclei and in the smaller calibre of the individual fibre. The nuclei are oval in appearance and situated along the central axis of the fibre, which may range in size from 12 to 21 microns in diameter (there are about 25,000 microns in one inch). Each fibre consists of a bundle of smaller fibres, called myofibrils, each of which passes through the full length of the fibre and is covered by an external limiting membrane known as the sarcolemma.

The individual cardiac muscle cells are striped crosswise throughout, with alternating dark bands that are opaque to light and with light bands that permit the passage of light. Prominent plates of condensed dark bands called intercalated disks, crossing the muscle fibre at uneven intervals, are perhaps the most conspicuous feature unique to cardiac muscle.

It is the myocardial layer that causes the heart to contract; the bundles of the muscle fibres are so arranged as to result in a wringing type of movement that efficiently squeezes blood from the heart with each beat. The thickness of the myocardium varies according to the pressure generated to move blood to its destination.

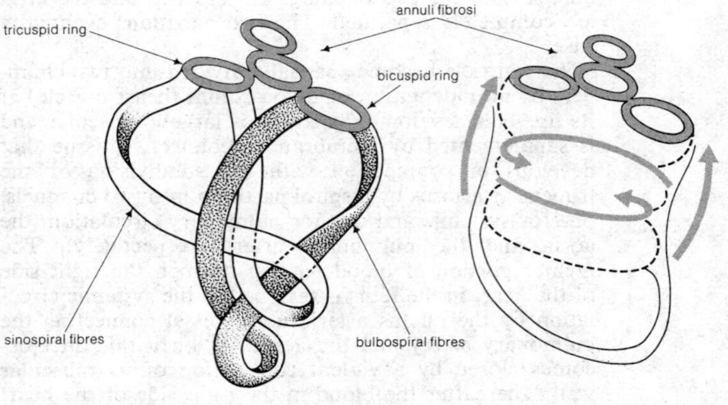

Figure 7: *The myocardium of the ventricles.*
(Left) Spiral muscles of ventricles. (Right) Dotted lines indicate changes in shape of heart due to contraction of ventricular muscle (arrows).

The myocardium of the left ventricle, which must drive blood out into the systemic circulation, is, therefore, thickest; the myocardium of the right ventricle, which propels blood to the lungs, is moderately thickened, while the atrial walls are relatively thin.

Forming the inner surface of the myocardial wall is a thin lining called the endocardium. This layer lines the cavities of the heart, covers the valves and small muscles associated with opening and closing of the valves, and is continuous with the lining membrane of the large blood vessels.

Blood supply to the heart. Because of the presence of the watertight lining of the heart (the endocardium) and the thickness of its muscular walls, the heart cannot depend for oxygen and nourishment on the blood contained in its chambers but must possess a vascular (vessel) system of its own. Two coronary arteries branch from the aorta as it leaves the heart and curl back across the chambers of the heart, sending twigs through the muscular walls. These coronary vessels are "end arteries"; that is, they follow their own course and have few cross connections with other nearby branches.

Branches of the coronary arteries

The left coronary artery remains intact for a short distance and then branches into two main arteries. One of these, the anterior descending coronary artery, supplies the front of the heart, particularly the left ventricle; the other, the left circumflex branch, supplies the left ventricle and the left atrium. The right coronary artery provides blood for the right side of the heart and the lower posterior portion of the left ventricle. Venous blood is returned to the heart through veins called cardiac veins that empty into a channel known as the coronary sinus, which then delivers the blood to the right atrium.

Heartbeat. *Regulation of heartbeat.* Proper functioning of the heart necessitates the presence of several unique characteristics. One quality is the inherent rhythmicity of cardiac muscle; no nerves are located within the heart itself, and no outside regulatory mechanisms are necessary to stimulate the muscle to contract rhythmically. That the heartbeat originates in the cardiac muscle can be substantiated by observing cardiac development in the embryo; cardiac pulsations begin before adequate development of nerve fibres. In addition, it can be demonstrated in the laboratory that even fragments of cardiac muscle in tissue culture continue to contract rhythmically. Furthermore, there is no gradation in degree of contraction of the muscle fibres of the heart, as would be expected if they were primarily under nervous control.

The mere possession of this intrinsic ability is not sufficient, however, to enable the heart to function efficiently. Proper function requires coordination, which is maintained by an elaborate conducting system within the heart that consists primarily of two relatively large masses of tissue, or nodes, from which impulses originate; of nerve-like conduits for the transmission of impulses; and of terminal portions of branches of the conduits at the inner surface of the ventricles.

From S. Jacob and C. Francone, *Structure and Function in Man* (1970); W.B. Saunders Co.

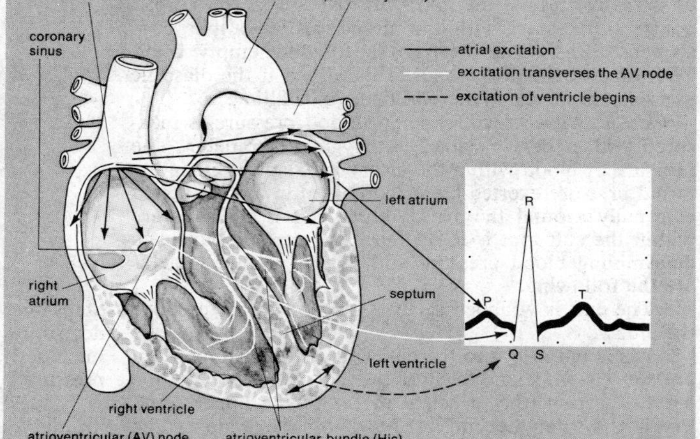

Figure 8: Conducting system of the heart showing source of electrical impulses produced on electrocardiogram.

A basic understanding of the method by which an impulse is transmitted is essential before the conduction system that exists within the heart can be properly understood.

Electrical potentials exist across membranes of essentially all cells of the body—that is, there is an electric tension created, generally by an excess number of negative ions immediately inside the cell membrane and an equal number of excess positive ions on the outside of the membrane, also known as a resting potential. (Ions are atoms or groups of atoms in solution that carry positive or negative electrical charges.) Further, some cells, such as nerve and muscle cells, have the additional distinction of being "excitable"—*i.e.*, capable of conducting impulses along their membranes.

Any factor that suddenly increases the permeability of the cell membrane and allows positive ions to flow through the membrane to the inside, while negative ions flow to the outside, is likely to bring about a sequence of rapid changes in the membrane potential, lasting only a fraction of a second. This change is followed by the return of the membrane potential to its resting value. This sequence of changes in potential is called an action potential and is responsible for the initiation of impulses transmitted, in the case of the heart, along the muscle fibres and the special conducting tissue fibres. Electrical stimulation, application of chemicals, mechanical damage, heat, and cold are among the various factors that can bring about a change in the state of a cell membrane, momentarily disturbing its normal resting state and creating an action potential.

The action potential occurs in two separate stages called depolarization and repolarization.

Depolarization and repolarization

During the process of depolarization, the normal negative potential inside the muscle fibre is lost, and the membrane potential actually reverses, or becomes slightly positive inside and negative outside the membrane. This process of depolarization proceeds as a wave along the length of the muscle fibres. It lasts only a fraction of a second before the positive ions begin to resume their original position on the outside of the membrane, necessary before another impulse can pass. This process is termed repolarization. An action potential is necessary to generate each depolarization wave.

The sinoatrial node (Figure 8) possesses the ability to generate an action potential spontaneously. This highly important structure is a small strip of specialized muscle located in the posterior wall of the right atrium, immediately beneath the point of entry of the superior vena cava. As an action potential is generated in the sinoatrial node, the impulse immediately spreads through the atrial muscle in the form of a ripple pattern similar to the pattern of waves generated when a stone is thrown into a pool of water.

A few specialized fibres possess the responsibility of subsequently relaying this potential, or impulse, to the atrioventricular node, located in the lower part of the right rear atrial wall. To permit sufficient time for complete contraction of the atria before subsequent simultaneous contraction of the ventricles, the impulse is delayed slightly in its passage through the atrioventricular node. The fibres that leave this node constitute the Purkinje system. These fibres pass between the atrioventricular valves and lead into the interventricular septum, where bundles of fibres in right and left branches project downward beneath the endocardium on either side of the septum. They then curve around the tip of the ventricles and back toward the atria along the side walls. These fibres terminate in the ventricular muscle, and depolarization in the muscle fibres is initiated.

Conducting system of the heart. Both the atrioventricular node, with an intrinsic beat of 40–60 beats per minute, and the Purkinje fibres, with an intrinsic beat of 15–40 beats per minute, are self-stimulating and capable of rhythmic contraction, but at a rate slower than that of the sinoatrial node, which possesses an intrinsic capacity to beat 72 times per minute. Therefore, since recovery time is faster in the sinoatrial node, it controls the rate of the heartbeat, serving as the primary pacemaker. The atrioventricular node, with its 40-60 beats per minute, is termed the secondary pacemaker.

Effect of ions on heart function. Potassium, sodium, and calcium have a marked influence on transmission of action potential within cardiac muscle. In addition, calcium-ion concentration is important in the contractile process. The concentration of ions in extracellular fluids (those outside the cells) also affects cardiac function to a degree.

Excess potassium and excess calcium

Excess potassium ions in extracellular fluid slow the heart rate and cause the heart to dilate and become flaccid (flabby). There is general weakness of cardiac muscle. This weakening of the strength of contraction is caused by a decreased resting membrane potential with resulting decrease in the intensity of the action potential.

Calcium ions in excess produce just the opposite effect; the heart goes into spastic contraction. There is, however, little danger of the presence of excess calcium ions within the extracellular fluid in cardiac muscle, for excess calcium is precipitated as salts in the body tissues before a dangerous level is reached in the heart.

A depressed cardiac function occurs when sodium ions are present in excess. These ions interfere with the effectiveness of calcium in bringing about normal muscular contraction.

Presumably because of an increased permeability of muscle membrane to ions, temperature may also affect heart function. An increased heart rate occurs as temperature increases, and, conversely, heart rate decreases with decreased temperature.

Electrocardiogram. As an impulse travels along the cardiac muscle fibres, an electric current is generated by the flowing ions. This current spreads into the fluids around the heart, and a minute portion actually flows to the surface of the body. An electrocardiogram is a record of this electrical activity (Figure 8) as measured by a device called a galvanometer. Leads (*i.e.*, wires to the galvanometer) are placed on the surface of the body at various points, depending on the type of information desired. An electrocardiogram thus has the prime function of assessing the ability of the heart to transmit the cardiac impulse. Each portion of the cardiac cycle produces a different electrical impulse, causing the characteristic deflections of an electrocardiographic recording needle. The deflections, or waves, on the recording apparatus are, in order, the P, QRS complex, and T waves. As a wave of depolarization passes over the atria, the impulse is recorded as the P wave. As it continues on through the ventricles, it is registered as the QRS complex. The T wave is caused by currents generated as the ventricles recover from the state of depolarization. This repolarization process occurs in the muscle of the ventricles about 0.25 second after depolarization. There are, therefore, both depolarization and repolarization waves represented in the electrocardiogram.

The atria repolarize at the same time that the ventricles depolarize. The atrial repolarization wave is, however, obscured by the larger QRS wave.

Nervous control of the heart. Nervous control of the heart is maintained by the parasympathetic fibres in the vagus nerve (parasympathetic) and by the sympathetic nerves. The vagus nerve is the cardiac inhibitor, and the sympathetic nerves are the cardiac excitors. Stimulation of the vagus nerve depresses impulse formation and atrial contractility and thereby reduces cardiac output and slows the rate of the heart. Parasympathetic stimulation can also produce varying degrees of heart block in diseases of the heart. (In heart block the atria and the ventricles beat independently.) Stimulation of the sympathetic nerves increases contractility of both atria and ventricles.

Diastole and systole

The cardiac cycle is defined as that time from the end of one heart contraction to the end of the subsequent contraction and consists of a period of relaxation called diastole followed by a period of contraction called systole. During the entire cycle, pressure is maintained in the arteries; however, this pressure varies during the two stages, the normal diastolic pressure being 80 millimetres of mercury and the normal systolic pressure being 120 millimetres of mercury.

Blood-pressure regulation. Variation in blood pressure may depend on several regulating mechanisms. Arterioles represent the main resistance to blood flow. Blood pressure can, therefore, only be maintained if resistance in these arterioles falls each time cardiac output increases. The nerves that control the action of the small muscle fibres of the vessels maintain resistance at a level sufficient for satisfactorily high arterial blood pressure by constricting the channel, or lumen, of the arteriole. During dilation of the vessel pressure is decreased. Arterial pressure is also affected by the chemical composition of the blood. A decreased oxygen or increased carbon dioxide tension (pressure) causes a reflex elevation of blood pressure. Respiratory activity is, therefore, an important regulator of arterial pressure.

The renin–angiotensin system provides hormonal control of blood pressure. Decreased blood flow to the kidney, changes in posture, or blockage of one or both renal (kidney) arteries may lead to increased production of the enzyme renin by the kidney. This substance causes development in the circulating blood of the substance angiotensin II, which causes blood vessels to contract, with resultant increase in blood pressure.

Receptors in great veins, in the aortic arch (the bend in the aorta above the heart), and the carotid sinus are sensitive to changes in blood pressure as blood is forced from the ventricles. These receptors, known as pressoreceptors, function as an aid in modifying shifts in pressure. When the receptors are stimulated by a rise in arterial pressure, which distends the arterial wall, they have an inhibiting effect on the heart, causing it to beat more slowly and with less force. At the same time there is a decrease in the contraction of the blood vessels. A fall in pressure, on the other hand, causes increased sympathetic and decreased parasympathetic stimulation, with resultant increased heart rate and also a subsequent constriction of the blood vessels.

Force of cardiac contraction. The force of the heartbeat depends on the initial length of the heart muscle fibres, the length of the pause in diastole, the oxygen supply, and the integrity and mass of the heart muscle, or myocardium. The greater the initial length of the muscle fibres in the heart, the more forceful will be the contraction. Artificially increasing venous return of blood to the heart distends the heart and intensifies the force of the beat. The greater inflow is handled by an increased output of the heart, without a change in its rate. When the ventricle does not completely fill (for example, after loss of blood), the force of the heartbeat is reduced. When the venous inflow during diastole is increased, as in muscular exercise, the beats become more forceful. If, as a result of excessive filling, the fibres are overstretched, a weak contraction results, with diminished cardiac output; consequently, the heart does not adequately empty itself. The force of the heart is also diminished if the diastolic phase is too short and there is inadequate filling.

Blood-pressure measurement. Blood pressure is measured with a device called a sphygmomanometer. The pressure of blood within the artery is balanced by an external pressure exerted by air contained in a cuff applied externally around the arm. Actually, it is the pressure within the cuff that is measured. The steps employed in determining blood pressure with a sphygmomanometer are the following:

Steps in determining blood pressure

1. The cuff is wrapped securely around the arm above the elbow.

2. Air is pumped into the cuff with a rubber bulb until pressure is sufficient to stop the flow of blood in the brachial artery (the principal artery of the upper arm). Pressure within the cuff is shown on the scale of the sphygmomanometer.

3. The observer places a stethoscope over the brachial artery just below the elbow and gradually releases the

air from within the cuff. The decreased air pressure permits the blood to flow, filling the artery below the cuff. Faint tapping sounds corresponding to the heartbeat are heard. When the sound is first noted, the air pressure within the cuff is recorded on the scale. This pressure is equal to the systolic blood pressure.

4. As the air in the cuff is further released, the sounds become progressively louder, until the sounds change in quality from loud to soft and finally disappear. At the point at which the sounds change from loud to soft, the instrument reading corresponds directly to the diastolic pressure.

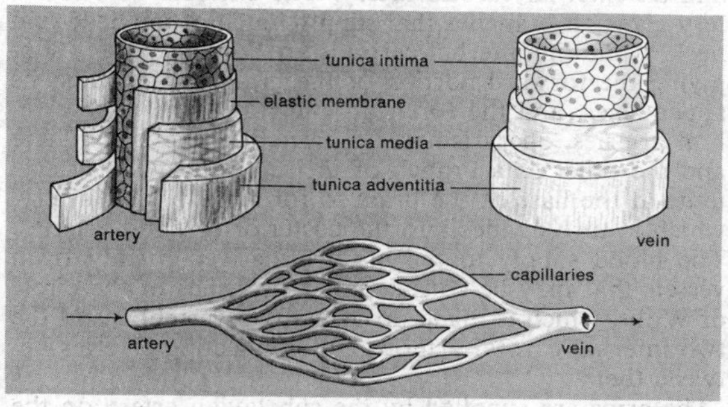

Figure 9: Component parts of arteries and veins.
From S. Jacob and C. Francone, *Structure and Function in Man* (1970); W.B. Saunders Co.

The American Heart Association recommends that, when a large disparity exists between the level at which the sound becomes dull or muffled and the point at which the sound completely disappears, the level at which the sound completely disappears should also be recorded as diastolic blood pressure. If the two levels are identical, only one level is recorded.

BLOOD VESSELS

Because of the need for the early development of a transport system within the developing embryo, the organs of the vascular system are among the first to appear and to assume their functional role. In fact, this system is established in its basic form by the fourth week of embryonic life.

At approximately the 18th day of gestation, cells begin to group together between the outer skin (ectoderm) and the inner skin (endoderm) of the embryo. These cells soon become rearranged so that the more peripheral ones join to form a continuous flattened sheet enclosing more centrally placed cells; these cells remain suspended in a fluid medium as primitive blood cells. The tubes then expand and unite to form a network; the primitive blood vessels thus appear.

Structure. The blood vessels consist of a closed system of tubes functioning to transport blood to all parts of the body and back to the heart. As in any biological system, structure and function of the vessels are so closely related that one cannot be discussed without the other's being taken into account.

Arteries function to transport to the various body tissues blood under high pressure that is exerted by the pumping action of the heart. The heart forces blood into these elastic tubes, which recoil, sending blood on in pulsating waves. It is, therefore, imperative that the vessels possess strong, elastic walls to ensure fast, efficient blood flow to the tissues.

Three layers of the artery wall

The wall of an artery consists of three layers, the innermost consisting of an inner surface of smooth endothelium and an outer surface of elastic tissues: the two form the tunica intima. The tunica media, or middle coat, is thicker in arteries, particularly in the large arteries, and consists of smooth muscle cells intermingled with elastic fibres. The muscle-cell and elastic fibres circle the vessel. In larger vessels the tunica media is composed primarily of elastic fibres. As arteries become smaller, the number of elastic fibres decreases while the number of smooth muscle fibres increases. The outer layer, the tunica adventitia, is the strongest of the three layers. It is composed of collagenous and elastic fibres. (Collagen is a connective-tissue protein.) The tunica adventitia provides a limiting barrier, protecting the vessel from overexpansion (Figure 9). Also characteristic of this layer is the presence of small blood vessels called the vasa vasorum that supply the walls of larger arteries and veins; the inner and middle layers are nourished by diffusion from the blood as it is transported. The thicker, more elastic wall of arteries enables them to expand with the pulse and to regain their original size.

The transition from artery to arteriole is a gradual one, marked by a progressive thinning of the vessel wall and a decrease in the size of the lumen, or passageway. The tunica intima is still present as a lining covered by a layer of thin, longitudinal fibres. A single layer of circular or spiral, smooth muscle fibres now comprises the tunica media, and the tunica adventitia consists of connective-tissue elements.

Being the last small branches of the arterial system, arterioles must act as control valves through which blood is released into the capillaries. The strong muscular wall of arterioles is capable of completely closing the passageway or permitting it to expand to several times its normal size, thereby vastly altering blood flow to the capillaries. Blood flow is by this device directed to tissues that require it most.

As the arterioles become smaller in size, the three coats become less and less definite, the smallest arterioles consisting of little more than endothelium, or lining, surrounded by a layer of smooth muscle.

The microscopic capillary tubules consist of a single layer of endothelium, a continuation of the innermost lining cells of arteries and veins.

As the capillaries converge, small venules are formed whose function it is to collect blood from the capillary beds (*i.e.*, the networks of capillaries). The venules consist of an endothelial tube supported by a small amount of collagenous tissue and, in the larger venules, by a few smooth muscle fibres as well. As venules continue to increase in size, they begin to exhibit the wall structure that is a characteristic of the arteries, although they are much thinner.

In veins, which function to conduct blood from the peripheral tissues to the heart, an endothelial lining is surrounded by the tunica media, which contains less muscle and elastic tissue than is found in the arterial wall. The outermost layer, tunica adventitia, is composed chiefly of connective tissue. Blood pressure in these vessels is extremely low as compared with that in the arterial system, and blood must exit at an even lower pressure. This creates a need for a special mechanism to keep blood moving on its return to the heart.

Venous valves

To achieve this, many veins possess a unique system of valves. These valves, formed by semilunar folds in the tunica intima, are present in pairs and serve to direct the flow of blood to the heart, particularly in an upward direction. As blood flows toward the heart, the flaps of the valves flatten against the wall of the vein; they then billow out to block the opening as the pressure of the blood and surrounding tissues fills the valve pocket. These valves are more abundant in the veins of the extremities than in any other parts of the body.

The veins are more distensible than arteries, and their walls are so constructed as to enable them to expand or contract. A major function of their contractility appears to be to decrease the capacity of the cardiovascular system by constriction of the peripheral vessels in response to the heart's inability to pump sufficient blood.

Veins tend to follow a course parallel to that of arteries but are present in greater number. Their channels are larger than those of arteries, and the walls are thinner. Seventy-nine percent of the blood volume is in the systemic circulation, and 59 percent is normally present in the veins.

Pulmonary circulation. The pulmonary circuit comprises the right ventricle, the exiting pulmonary artery and its branches, the arterioles, capillaries, and venules of the lungs, and the pulmonary veins that empty into the left atrium.

The pulmonary trunk, the common stem of the pulmonary arteries, arises from the upper surface of the right ventricle and extends some four to five centimetres (1.6 to two inches) beyond this origin before dividing into the right and left pulmonary arteries, which supply the lungs. Three semilunar valves guard the opening between the right ventricle and the pulmonary trunk. The trunk is relatively thin walled for an artery, having walls approximately twice the thickness of the vena cava and one-third that of the aorta. The right and left pulmonary arteries are short but possess a relatively large diameter. The walls are distensible; the vessels are able, therefore, to accommodate the stroke volume of the right ventricle, which is a necessary function equal to that of the left ventricle.

Pulmonary arteries and their branchings

The pulmonary trunk passes diagonally upward to the left across the route of the aorta. Between the fifth and sixth thoracic vertebrae (at about the level of the bottom of the breastbone), the trunk divides into two branches—the right and left pulmonary arteries—which enter the lungs. After entering the lungs, the branches go through a process of subdivision, the final branches being capillaries. Capillaries surrounding the air sacs (alveoli) of the lungs pick up oxygen and release carbon dioxide. The capillaries carrying oxygenated blood join larger and larger vessels until they reach the pulmonary veins, which carry oxygenated blood from the lungs to the left atrium of the heart.

Arteries. *The aorta and its principal branches.* The aorta is the largest vessel in the systemic circuit, arising from the left ventricle. For the sake of convenience, it is commonly divided into the ascending aorta, the arch of the aorta, and the descending aorta; the latter may be further subdivided into the thoracic and the abdominal aorta.

Originating from the ascending portion of the aorta are the right and left coronary arteries, which serve the heart. Branching from the arch of the aorta are three large arteries named, in order of origin from the heart, the innominate, the left common carotid, and the left subclavian. These three branches serve to supply the head, neck, and arms. As the innominate (sometimes referred to as the brachiocephalic) artery travels upward toward the clavicle, or collarbone, it divides into the right common carotid and right subclavian arteries. The two common carotid arteries, one branching from the innominate and the other directly from the aorta, then extend in a parallel fashion on either side of the neck to the top of the thyroid cartilage (the principal cartilage in the voice box, or larynx), where they divide, each to become an internal and an external carotid artery. The external carotid artery gives off branches that supply much of the head and neck, while the internal carotids are responsible for supplying the forward portion of the brain, the eye and its appendages, and the forehead and nose. The two vertebral arteries, one arising as a branch of the innominate and the other as a branch of the left subclavian artery, unite at the base of the brain to form the basilar artery, which in turn divides into the posterior cerebral arteries. The blood supply to the brain is derived mainly from vessels that may be considered as branches of the circle of Willis, which is made up of the two vertebral and the two internal carotid arteries and connecting arteries between them.

The arms are supplied by the subclavian artery on the left and by the continuation of the innominate on the right. At approximately the border of the first rib, both of these vessels become known as the axillary artery; this, in turn, becomes the brachial artery as it passes down the upper arm. At about the level of the elbow, the brachial artery divides into two terminal branches, the radial and ulnar arteries, the radial passing downward on the distal (thumb) side of the forearm, the ulnar on the medial side. Interconnections (anastomoses) between the two, with branches at the level of the palm, supply the hand and wrist.

From S. Jacob and C. Francone, *Structure and Function in Man* (1970); W.B. Saunders Co.

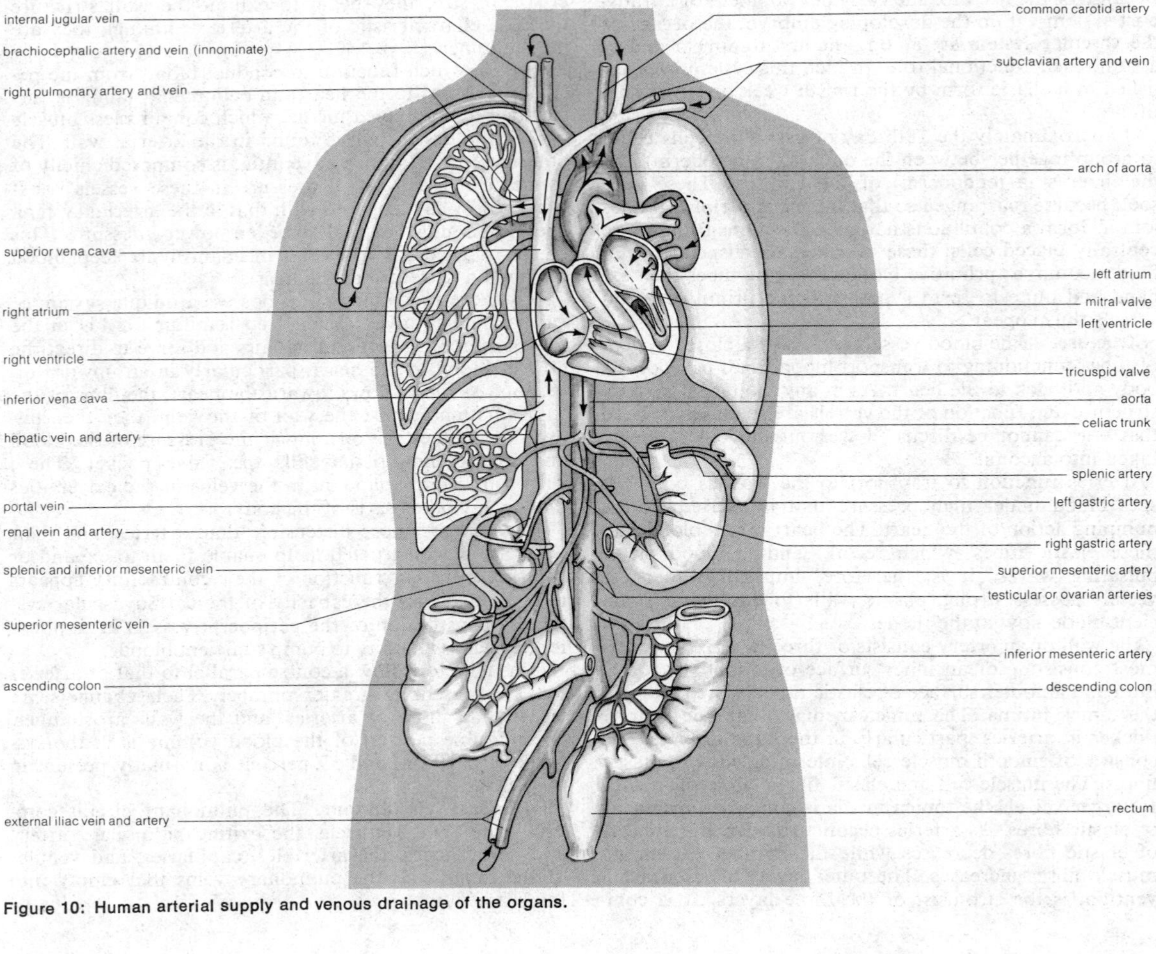

Figure 10: Human arterial supply and venous drainage of the organs.

Thoracic aorta

The thoracic (chest) portion of the descending aorta gives off branches (Figure 10) that supply the viscera (visceral branches) and the walls surrounding the thoracic cavity (parietal branches). The visceral branches provide blood for the pericardium, lungs, bronchi, lymph nodes, and esophagus. The parietal vessels supply the intercostal muscles (the muscles between the ribs) and the muscles of the thoracic wall; they supply blood to the membrane covering the lungs and lining the thoracic cavity, the spinal cord, the vertebral column, and a portion of the diaphragm.

As the aorta descends through the diaphragm, it becomes known as the abdominal aorta and again gives off both visceral and parietal branches. Visceral vessels include the celiac, superior mesenteric, and inferior mesenteric, which are unpaired, and the renal and testicular or ovarian, which are paired. The celiac artery arises from the aorta a short distance below the diaphragm and almost immediately divides into the left gastric artery, serving part of the stomach and esophagus; the hepatic artery, which primarily serves the liver; and the splenic artery, which supplies the stomach, pancreas, and spleen.

The superior mesenteric artery arises from the abdominal aorta just below the celiac artery. Its branches supply the small intestine and part of the large intestine. Arising several centimetres above the termination of the aorta is the inferior mesenteric artery, which branches to supply the lower part of the colon. The renal arteries pass to the kidneys. The testicular or ovarian arteries supply the testes in the male and the ovaries in the female, respectively.

Parietal branches of the abdominal aorta include the inferior phrenic, serving the suprarenal (adrenal) glands, the lumbar, and the middle sacral arteries. The lumbar arteries are arranged in four pairs and supply the muscles of the abdominal wall, the skin, the lumbar vertebrae, the spinal cord, and the meninges, or spinal-cord coverings.

The abdominal aorta terminates by dividing into two common iliac arteries, each of which descends laterally and gives rise to external and internal branches. The right and left external iliac arteries are direct continuations of the common iliacs and become known as the femoral arteries after passing through the inguinal region, giving off branches that supply structures of the abdomen and lower extremities. At a point just above the knee, the femoral artery continues as the popliteal artery; from this arise the posterior and anterior tibial arteries. The posterior tibial artery is a direct continuation of the popliteal, passing down the lower leg to supply structures of the posterior portion of the leg and foot. Arising from the posterior tibial artery a short distance below the knee is the peroneal artery; this gives off branches that nourish the lower leg muscles and the fibula (the smaller of the two bones in the lower leg) and terminates in the foot. The anterior tibial artery passes down the lower leg to the ankle, where it becomes the dorsalis pedis artery, which supplies the foot.

Pulse. An impulse can be felt over an artery that lies near the surface of the skin. The impulse results from alternate expansion and contraction of the arterial wall because of the beating of the heart. When the heart ejects blood into the aorta, the blood's impact on the elastic walls creates a pressure wave that continues along the arteries. This impact is the pulse. All arteries have a pulse, but it is most easily felt at points where the vessel approaches the surface of the body. The pulse is readily distinguished at the following locations: (1) at the point in the wrist where the radial artery approaches the surface; (2) at the side of the lower jaw where the external maxillary (facial) artery crosses it; (3) at the temple above and to the outer side of the eye, where the temporal artery is near the surface; (4) on the side of the neck, from the carotid artery; (5) on the inner side of the biceps, from the brachial artery; (6) in the groin, from the femoral artery; (7) behind the knee, from the popliteal artery; (8) on the upper side of the foot, from the dorsalis pedis artery.

Where pulse can be distinguished

The radial artery is most commonly used to check the pulse. Several fingers are placed on the artery close to the wrist joint. More than one fingertip is preferable because of the large, sensitive surface available to feel the pulse wave. While the pulse is being checked, certain data are recorded, including the number of beats per minute, the force and strength of the beat, and the tension offered by the artery to the finger. Normally, the interval between beats is of equal length. Irregularity occurs when there is abnormal heart rhythm.

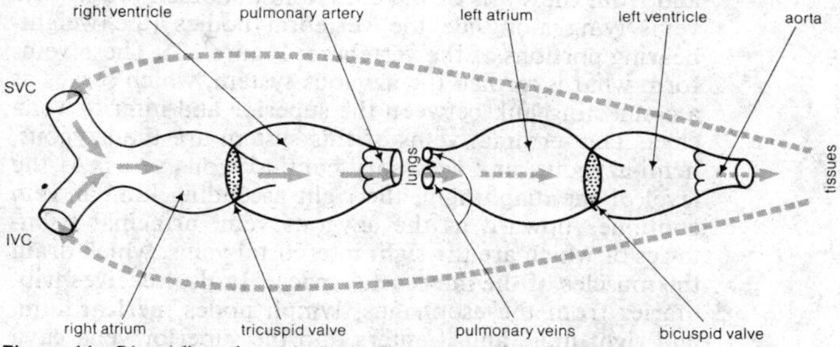

Figure 11: *Blood flow through the heart, lungs, and tissues of the body.*
Pulmonary circulation is indicated by solid arrows; systemic circulation by dashed arrows. SVC is superior vena cava; IVC is inferior vena cava.

Veins. Venules collect blood from the capillaries and the blood channels known as sinusoids and unite to form progressively larger veins that terminate as the great veins, or venae cavae. In the extremities there are superficial and deep veins; the superficial lie just under the skin and drain the skin and superficial fasciae (sheets of fibrous tissue), while the deep veins accompany the principal arteries of the extremities and are similarly named. Interconnections between the superficial and the deep veins are frequent.

Venous blood enters the right atrium from three sources: the heart muscle by way of the coronary sinus; the upper body by way of the superior vena cava; and the lower body by way of the inferior vena cava.

Superior vena cava and its tributaries. Tributaries from the head and neck, the arms, and part of the chest unite to form the superior vena cava. Venous channels called venous sinuses lie between the two layers of the dura mater, the outer covering of the brain; they possess no valves. Venous drainage of the brain is effected by these sinuses and communicating vessels. The internal jugular vein is a continuation of this system downward through the neck; it receives blood from parts of the face, neck, and brain. At approximately the level of the collarbone, each unites with the subclavian vein of that side to form the innominate veins.

The external jugular vein is formed by the union of its tributaries near the angle of the lower jaw, or mandible. It drains some of the structures of the head and neck and pours its contents along with the subclavian into the innominate vein of the same side.

All of the veins of the arm are tributaries of the subclavian vein of that side. They are found in both superficial and deep locations and possess valves. Most of the deep veins are arranged in pairs with cross connections between them.

Superficial and deep veins of the arm

Venous drainage of the hand is accomplished superficially by small anastomosing (interconnecting) veins that unite to form the cephalic vein, coursing up the radial (thumb) side of the forearm, and the basilic vein, running up the ulnar side of the forearm and receiving blood from the hand, forearm, and arm. The deep veins of the forearm include the radial veins, continuations of deep anastomosing veins of the hand and wrist, and the ulnar veins, both veins following the course of the associated artery. The radial and ulnar veins converge at the elbow to form the brachial vein; this, in turn, unites with the basilic vein at the level of the shoulder to produce the axillary vein. At the outer border of the first rib, the axillary vein becomes the subclavian vein, the terminal point of the venous system characteristic of the upper extremity.

The subclavian, external jugular, and internal jugular veins all converge to form the innominate vein. The right and left innominate veins terminate in the superior vena cava, which opens into the upper posterior portion of the right atrium.

In addition to the innominate veins, the superior vena cava receives blood from the azygous vein and small veins from the mediastinum (the region between the two lungs) and the pericardium. Most of the blood from the back and from the walls of the chest and abdomen drains into veins lying alongside the vertebral bodies (the weight-bearing portions of the vertebrae; Figure 12). These veins form what is termed the azygous system, which serves as a connecting link between the superior and inferior vena cava. The terminal veins of this system are the azygous, hemi-azygous, and accessory hemi-azygous veins. At the level of the diaphragm, the right ascending lumbar vein continues upward as the azygous vein, principal tributaries of which are the right intercostal veins, which drain the muscles of the intercostal spaces. It also receives tributaries from the esophagus, lymph nodes, pericardium, and right lung, and it enters into the superior vena cava at about the level of the fourth thoracic vertebra.

The left side of the azygous system varies greatly among individuals. Usually the hemi-azygous vein arises just below the diaphragm as a continuation of the left ascending lumbar vein and terminates in the azygous vein. Tributaries of the hemi-azygous drain the intercostal muscles, the esophagus, and a portion of the mediastinum. The accessory hemi-azygous usually extends downward as a continuation of the vein of the fourth intercostal space, receiving tributaries from the left intercostal spaces and the left bronchus. It empties into the azygous vein slightly above the entrance of the hemi-azygous.

Inferior vena cava and its tributaries. The inferior vena cava is a large, valveless, venous trunk that receives blood from the legs, the back, and the walls and contents of the abdomen and pelvis.

The foot is drained primarily by the dorsal venous arch, which crosses the top of the feet not far from the base of the toes. The arch is connected with veins that drain the

From S. Jacob and C. Francone, *Structure and Function in Man* (1970); W.B. Saunders Co.

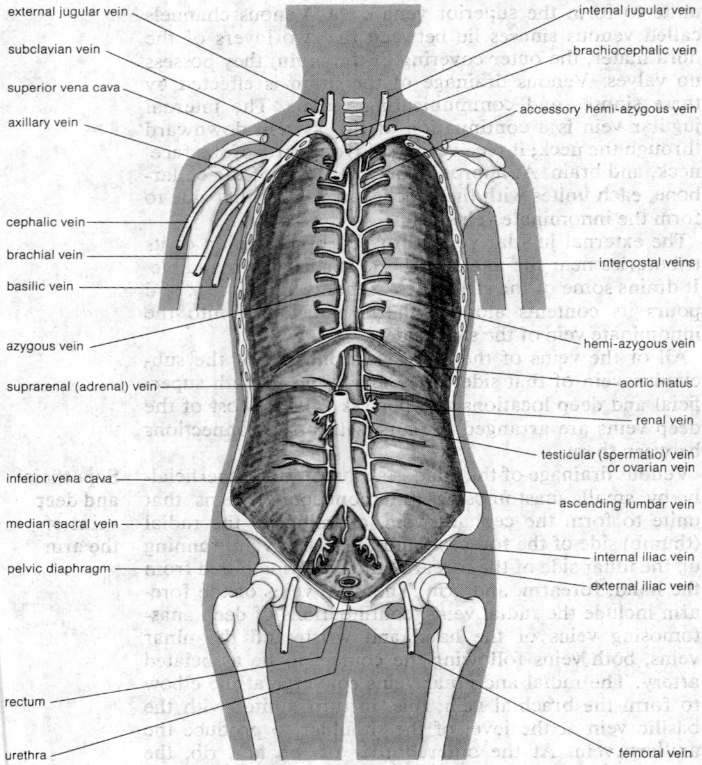

Figure 12: Vena cava and tributaries.

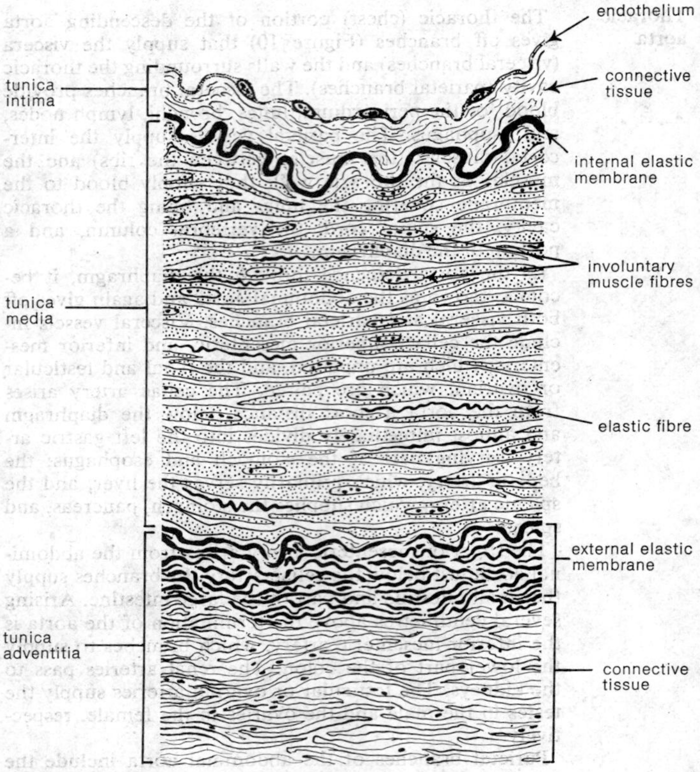

Figure 13: Transverse section of an artery.
From W. Bloom and D. Fawcett, *Textbook of Histology*, 9th ed.; W.B. Saunders Company

Superficial veins of the leg

sole. Superficially the lower leg is drained by the large and small saphenous veins, which are continuations of the dorsal venous arch. The small saphenous vein extends up the back of the lower leg to terminate usually in the popliteal vein. There is some interconnection with deep veins and with the great saphenous vein. The latter vein, the longest in the body, extends from the dorsal venous arch up the inside of the lower leg and thigh, receiving venous branches from the knee and thigh area and terminating in the femoral vein.

Most blood from the lower extremity returns by way of the deep veins. These include the femoral and popliteal veins and the veins accompanying the anterior and posterior tibial and peroneal arteries. The anterior and posterior tibial veins originate in the foot and join at the level of the knee to form the popliteal vein; the latter becomes the femoral vein as it continues its extension through the thigh.

At the level of the inguinal ligament (which is at the anterior, diagonal border between the trunk and the thigh), the femoral vein becomes known as the external iliac vein; the latter unites with the internal iliac vein to form the common iliac vein. The internal iliac vein drains the pelvic walls, viscera, external genitalia, buttocks, and a portion of the thigh. Through the paired common iliac veins, the legs and most of the pelvis are drained. The two common iliacs then unite at a level above the coccyx (the bottommost bone in the spine) to become the inferior vena cava. As it courses upward through the abdomen, the inferior vena cava receives blood from the common iliacs and from the lumbar, renal, suprarenal, and hepatic veins before emptying into the right atrium.

The pairs of lumbar veins (which drain blood from the loins and abdominal walls) are united on each side by a vertical connecting vein, the ascending lumbar vein; the right ascending lumbar vein continues as the azygous and the left as the hemi-azygous. These veins usually enter separately into the inferior vena cava.

Renal veins lie in front of the corresponding renal artery; the right renal vein receives tributaries exclusively from the kidney, while the left receives blood from a number of other organs as well. The right suprarenal vein terminates directly in the inferior vena cava as does the right phrenic, above the gonadal vein. Two or three short hepatic trunks empty into the inferior vena cava as it passes through the diaphragm.

Portal system. The portal system may be described as a specialized portion of the systemic circulatory system. It is unique in that blood from the spleen, stomach, pancreas, and intestine first passes through the liver before it goes to the heart. Blood flowing to the liver comes from the hepatic artery (20 percent) and the portal vein (80 percent); blood leaving the liver flows through the hepatic vein and then empties into the inferior vena cava. The hepatic arterial blood supplies oxygen requirements for the liver. Blood from the abdominal viscera, particularly the intestinal tract, passes into the portal vein and then into the liver. Substances in the portal blood are processed by the liver (see LIVER, HUMAN).

Hepatic artery and portal vein

Venous pulmonary system. From the pulmonary capillaries, in which blood takes on oxygen and gives up carbon dioxide, the oxygenated blood is collected first into venules and then into progressively larger veins; it finally flows through four pulmonary veins, two from the hilum of each lung. (The hilum is the point of entry on each lung for the bronchus, blood vessels, and nerves.) These veins then pass to the left atrium, where their contents are poured into the heart.

Capillaries. The vast network of some 10,000,000,000 microscopic capillaries functions to provide a method whereby fluids, nutrients, and wastes are exchanged between the blood and the tissues. Even though microscopic in size, the largest capillary being approximately 0.2 millimetre in diameter (about the width of the tip of a pin), the great network of capillaries serves as a reservoir normally containing about one-sixth of the total circulating blood volume. The number of capillaries in active tissue, such as muscle, liver, kidney, and lungs, is greater than the number in tendon or ligament, for example; the cornea of the eye, epidermis, and hyaline cartilage (semitransparent cartilage such as is found in joints) are devoid of capillaries.

The interconnecting network of capillaries into which the arterioles empty is characterized not only by microscopic size but also by extremely thin walls only one cell in thickness. The vessels are simply tubular continuations of the inner lining cells of the larger vessels, normally uniform in size, usually three to four endothelial cells in circumference, except toward the venous terminations, where they become slightly wider, four to six cells in circumference. A thin membrane, called a basement membrane, surrounds these cells and serves to maintain the integrity of the vessel.

A single capillary unit consists of a branching and interconnecting (anastomosing) network of vessels, each averaging 0.5 to one millimetre (0.02 to 0.04 inch) in length. The wall of the capillary is extremely thin and acts as a semipermeable membrane allowing substances having small molecules, such as oxygen, carbon dioxide, water, and glucose, to pass through the membrane. Oxygen and nutritive material pass into the tissues through the wall at the arteriolar end of the capillary unit; carbon dioxide and waste products move through the membrane into the vessel at the venous end of the capillary bed.

Constriction and dilation of the arterioles is primarily responsible for regulating the flow of blood into the capillaries. Muscular gatekeepers, or sphincters, in the capillary unit itself, however, serve to direct the flow to those areas in greatest need.

Two routes through capillary wall

There are two modes of transport across the cellular membrane of the capillary wall. Substances soluble in the lipid (fatty) membrane of the capillary cells can pass directly through these membranes by a process of diffusion. Other substances needed by the tissues and soluble in water but completely insoluble in the lipid membrane pass through minute water-filled passageways, or pores, in the membranes, by a process called ultrafiltration. Only $1/_{1,000}$ of the surface area of capillaries is represented by these pores.

Fetal circulation. The circulatory system of the fetus differs from that of the adult, since the lungs and alimentary canal of the fetus are nonfunctional. These differences disappear at birth or shortly thereafter.

Oxygenated blood is carried from the placenta to the fetus by the umbilical vein. It then passes to the inferior vena cava of the fetus by way of a vessel called the ductus venosus. From the inferior vena cava, the blood enters the right atrium, then passes through the foramen ovale into the left atrium; from there it moves into the left ventricle and out the aorta, which pumps the oxygenated blood to the head and upper extremities. Blood from the upper extremities returns via the superior vena cava into the right atrium, where it is largely deflected into the right ventricle.

From the right ventricle, a portion of the blood flows into the pulmonary artery to the lungs. The largest fraction flows through an opening, the ductus arteriosus, into the aorta. It enters the aorta beyond the point at which the blood of the head leaves. Some of the blood supplies the lower portion of the body. The remainder returns to the placenta via the umbilical arteries, which branch off from the internal iliac arteries.

The changes that take place at birth and that permit routing of the blood through the pulmonary system instead of the umbilical vessels have been touched upon above in the section on the origin and development of the heart.

TECHNIQUES OF EVALUATING THE HEART AND VASCULAR SYSTEM

Certain diagnostic techniques with respect to the heart require an exact knowledge of the anatomy of the circulatory system.

Right-heart catheterization. Right-heart catheterization is performed by insertion of a catheter (a long tube) into the cubital vein (at the bend of the elbow), the saphenous vein (in the inner thigh), or the femoral vein (at the groin). The catheter, which is opaque to X-ray, is advanced into the right atrium, right ventricle, and pulmonary artery while the surgeon is guided by X-ray views. This procedure makes it possible to measure pressure and oxygen saturation in the right heart chamber itself, so that abnormalities in the valves of the right side of the heart can be diagnosed.

Left-heart catheterization. Left-heart catheterization is accomplished by introducing a catheter into the brachial or femoral artery (in the upper arm and thigh, respectively) and advancing it through the aorta across the aortic valve and into the left ventricle. Mitral and aortic valvular defects and myocardial disease can be evaluated by this technique.

Angiocardiography. X-ray outlines of the cardiac chambers and great vessels (the large vessels opening directly into the heart) are provided by rapidly injecting X-ray-opaque material through an arm vein or through a catheter threaded into the right or left side of the heart. This procedure is followed by a series of rapid exposures to X-ray (angiocardiography) or to X-ray movies, called cineangiography. Angiocardiography permits direct visualization of the cardiac chambers and great vessels. By outlining abnormal circulatory pathways, it provides one of the best methods of detecting the site and extent of congenital abnormalities of the heart. It can also be used to study arteries and veins.

BIBLIOGRAPHY. S.W. JACOB and C. FRANCONE, *Structure and Function in Man*, 2nd ed. (1970), with exceptionally fine illustrations; and C.R. ANTHONY and N.J. KOTTHOFF, *Textbook of Anatomy and Physiology*, 8th ed. (1971), two good basic anatomy and physiology texts; J. KERNICKI, B.L. BULLOCK, and J. MATHEWS, *Cardiovascular Nursing* (1971), a good basic anatomical reference; A.A. LUISADA, *Development and Structure of the Cardiovascular System* (1961), a comprehensive and detailed study of the entire cardiovascular system and its development; A.C. GUYTON, *Basic Human Physiology: Normal Function and Mechanisms of Disease* (1971), an excellent technical description of the physiology of cardiac muscle, heart function, and hemodynamics; E.F. ADOLPH, "The Heart's Pacemaker," *Scient. Am.*, 216:32–37 (1967), a good account of the development and functioning of sinoatrial node in man and other animals.

(S.W.J.)

Cardiovascular System Diseases and Disorders

The cardiovascular system, by which the blood is circulated, consists of the heart and the blood vessels. There are two subsystems of vessels in the system: (1) those that carry oxygenated blood out from the heart to the bodily tissues and bring back to the heart the blood laden with carbon dioxide and low in oxygen, and (2) those that convey blood to the lungs and from the lungs back to the heart. The first of these subsystems makes up the systemic circulation; the second, the pulmonary circulation. The vessels conveying blood from the heart to the tissues are, in descending order of size, the arteries, arterioles, and capillaries; those returning blood to the heart from the tissues are, in ascending order, capillaries, venules, and veins.

Each side of the heart is a pump, and each has two chambers, an upper chamber (atrium) and a lower chamber (ventricle). Blood low in oxygen and high in carbon dioxide enters the right atrium through two large veins, the venae cavae. From the right atrium the blood passes into the right ventricle, which pumps it through the pulmonary artery to the lungs. There it receives oxygen and loses carbon dioxide. From the lungs the blood returns to the left atrium through the pulmonary vein. It then passes into the left ventricle, which pumps it out into the systemic circulation through the aorta. The heart muscle (myocardium) is supplied with oxygenated blood through the coronary arteries (see also CARDIOVASCULAR SYSTEM, HUMAN; RESPIRATION, HUMAN).

Significance. Diseases of the heart and blood vessels constitute one of the major health problems of modern man. Because life depends on the function of the heart, the stopping of its activity has been a major criterion of death for centuries. Thus, the heart is involved in all death, but this does not account for its prominence in causing death. To some degree, as medical science advances, more and more people are saved from other illnesses, only to die from one of the unsolved and uncontrolled disorders of the cardiovascular system. Whether the rising incidence of heart disease represents an actual increase in disease or only a redefinition related to the eradication of other diseases cannot now be answered. Fortunately, some forms of cardiovascular diseases are receding as causes of death, and there is hope that continued research and preventive measures may provide even greater benefits.

History. Heart disease as such was not recognized by primitive man, but he did appreciate the beating heart and its relationship to death. Sudden death, now usually attributed to heart disease, was recognized as early as the 5th century BC by the Greek physician Hippocrates, and noted to be more common in the obese. The role of disease in affecting the heart itself did not become apparent until examination of the body after death became acceptable in the 17th century. Gradually, the involvement of the heart valves, the blood vessels, and the heart muscle itself was observed and categorized in an orderly fashion. The recognition of the manifestations of heart failure came later, as did the ability to diagnose heart ailments by physical examination through the techniques of percussion (thumping), auscultation (listening) with the stethoscope, and other means. Not until early in the 20th century did the clinical determination of arterial blood pressure and the use of X-rays for diagnosis become widespread.

Early knowledge of heart disease

In 1912 James Bryan Herrick, a Chicago physician, first described in clinical terms what he called coronary thrombosis (he was describing symptoms actually caused by myocardial infarction; see below). Angina pectoris (described and discussed in a later section) had been recorded centuries earlier. Cardiovascular surgery in the modern sense began in the 1930s, and open-heart surgery in the 1950s.

Incidence. The exact incidence of heart disease in the world population is difficult to ascertain, because complete and adequate public health figures for either prevalence or deaths are not available. In the more highly developed countries of the world, such as the United States, Great Britain, and most European countries, arteriosclerotic heart disease (heart disease resulting from thickening and hardening of the artery walls; see below) constitutes by far the most predominant form and is increasing in incidence. Whether this represents a true increase in the incidence of the disease itself or merely reflects the eradication of other diseases cannot yet be answered. In other areas, such as the countries of Equatorial Africa, arteriosclerotic heart disease is far less common; other forms of heart disease, however, are frequently reported as the cause of death. In the Orient and islands of the Pacific, hypertensive cardiovascular disease, disease involving high blood pressure, constitutes a major health hazard.

Consideration of the diseases and disorders of the heart, the pericardium (the membranous sac enclosing the heart), and the vessels that open directly into the heart makes up the first major division of this article. A section on surgical treatment of the heart is also included in this division. The remainder of the article is concerned with the diseases of the rest of the blood vessels.

The heart and the great vessels

CONGENITAL HEART DISEASE

The heart's complicated evolution during embryologic development from a long tubular structure into an organ with four chambers and many vessels presents the opportunity for many different types of congenital defects to occur. Congenital heart disease is one of the important varieties of cardiovascular system diseases, although its frequency is less than that of some forms of acquired heart disease. Congenital disturbances are varied and involve almost all components of the heart and great vessels. At times, the incompletely developed cardiovascular system is incapable of sustaining life and the infant is stillborn.

Classification with respect to cyanosis

Those systems that are compatible with life have been classified into the cyanotic and the noncyanotic varieties. In the cyanotic variety, the body turns blue. The blue colour may result from the presence of a shunt that bypasses the normal circulation and delivers venous (deoxygenated) blood into the arterial circulation. Cyanosis (manifested by the dusky blue appearance of the skin) may also occur in congenital heart disease in which there is inadequacy of blood flow, or in disease of the pulmonary vascular bed that prevents adequate oxygenation of the arterial blood. The last of these forms of cyanosis usually comes later in life and is not considered a part of the cyanotic group of disturbances at birth. Some congenital anomalies may exist and those having them may have a full life expectancy. Many can be corrected by surgery.

A classification of the many types of recognized abnormalities follows.

Abnormalities of individual chambers of the heart. Abnormalities of the heart chambers may be serious, and even incompatible with life. They are often found combined with other defects. The group includes incomplete development of the right ventricle; infundibular stenosis of the right ventricle (narrowing of the right ventricle in the area from which blood flows into the pulmonary artery); the presence of an accessory left atrial chamber; and subaortic stenosis, a narrowing of the left ventricle near the valve that opens into the aorta.

Abnormalities of the atrial septum. The atrial septum is the wall between the two atria, the upper chambers of the heart. Defects in the septum are one of the more important congenital malformations. During normal intrauterine life, the blood passes through the atrial septum via an aperture called the foramen ovale. This aperture normally closes at the time of birth, but may remain open and, in effect, is a form of atrial septal defect. Other forms of atrial septal defect may persist into adult life. Some are small; others are large, with almost no septum remaining and with significant effects on the circulation of the blood. An atrial septal defect is a noncyanotic type of congenital heart disease; it may occur in later life as a result of complications. Septal defects, unless they are major, are compatible with a long life. In the presence of a major defect there is shunting of blood from the left side of the heart to the right, and the blood flow in the pulmonary circulation may greatly increase. This condition places an added burden on the right side of the heart and may result in high blood pressure in the pulmonary artery. If this pressure persists, disease of the pulmonary vascular system may follow, and interference with the oxygenation of blood may occur, causing cyanosis to occur later in life.

Abnormalities of the ventricular septum. Small defects in the interventricular septum, the partition that separates the lower chambers of the heart, are common and are compatible with long life. They often create loud murmurs, but unless the defect is sizable, no significant changes in the blood circulation occur. If the defect is sizable, a significant amount of blood is shunted from the left ventricle to the right and a circulatory situation similar to that in the large atrial septal defect occurs. In the most severe form there is, in effect, a common ventricle, with mixing of arterial and venous blood. An additional hazard in septal defect, moreover, is that it increases the possibility of bacterial endocarditis, inflammation of the heart lining as a result of bacterial infection.

The tetralogy of Fallot

A septal defect is often combined with other congenital defects. The most widely known of these is the tetralogy of Fallot, named after the French physician, Étienne Louis Arthur Fallot, who first described it. In this condition (1) a ventricular septal defect is combined with (2) pulmonary stenosis, the narrowing of the opening into the pulmonary artery, with (3) the opening into the aorta more to the right than normal, and (4) with right ventricular hypertrophy—a thickening of the muscle of the right ventricle, thus completing the tetralogy. The pulmonary stenosis causes venous blood to be shunted from the right to the left side of the heart, whence it is pumped out into the systemic circulation. This defect of the cyanotic type is the most common form of cyanotic congenital heart disease compatible with survival beyond infancy; approximately three-fourths of the cyanotic persons over ten years of age have this defect or a variant of it. The prominent features besides cyanosis are difficulty in breathing on exertion, retarded growth, an abnormally high level of red blood cells, and a characteristic easing of respiration by squatting. It is the classic type of defect treated surgically by the so-called blue-baby operations.

Abnormal origins of arteries. Abnormal points of origin of arteries, such as transposition of the origin of the aorta and that of the pulmonary artery, are serious defects causing cyanotic disease. In other instances, both the aorta and the pulmonary artery originate from the right ventricle, and there is a ventricular septum defect; this combination of defects presents a severe form of cyanotic heart disease. Some palliation may be possible by surgery.

Abnormalities of valves. A heart valve may be abnormal or completely absent. Some valve defects are minor and not important except as a possible site for the development of bacterial endocarditis. Others are more severe and may result in circulatory impairment such as that which occurs in acquired valve disease. Treatment is surgical.

Abnormalities of the myocardium (the heart muscle). Several types of heart muscle abnormality may occur. Hypertrophy (enlargement) is present in almost all heart disease, because enlargement is the compensatory mechanism for the heart that is failing to provide an adequate circulation to the rest of the body organs. Hypertrophy of the myocardium is not in itself bad, but it indicates some type of cardiac (heart) disease. Glycogen storage diseases and congenital tumours of the myocardium are extremely rare problems associated with the heart muscle. (In the glycogen storage diseases abnormal amounts of the carbohydrate glycogen build up in the tissues because enzyme defects prevent its normal breakdown into lactic acid. Treatment is largely by regulation of the diet.) Congenital tumours may be surgically removed but are often so extensive that surgery is not helpful.

Abnormalities of the endocardium. Abnormalities of the endocardium, the membrane lining the heart, may be present, although they are rare. The abnormalities include fibroelastosis, a disease in which the endocardium becomes a thick fibrous coat, causing interference with the normal contraction of the heart. Endocardial cords that support the heart valve structure may also thicken, become fibrous, and interfere with the normal heart valve function. There is no known treatment for these rare abnormalities.

Thickening of the endocardium

Abnormalities of the pericardium. Abnormalities of the pericardium, the membraneous sac containing the heart, may be congenital. The most frequent abnormality, absence of the pericardium, however, is without functional significance.

Abnormalities of the coronary arteries. Various abnormalities are found in the coronary arteries, the blood vessels supplying oxygen to the heart muscle itself. One is the significant reduction in size or the absence of one or more of the three main vessels, a condition leading to failure of sufficient oxygen to reach sections of heart muscle, with consequent death of these tissues (see below *Myocardial infarction*). The coronary arteries may arise abnormally from a pulmonary artery rather than from the aorta, causing unoxygenated rather than oxygenated blood to flow through (perfuse) the heart muscle. Congenital weak spots may be present in the coronary arteries, which thus become susceptible to rupture. The coronary sinus, the common vein that collects blood that has perfused the heart muscle, may be unusually enlarged or absent. Finally, abnormal openings may be present between the coronary arteries and the coronary sinus or a chamber of the heart. Remarkably, most of the congenital abnormalities of the coronary arteries cause no symptoms and may well be associated with long life. Rarely, surgery is employed to correct a coronary-artery abnormality.

Abnormalities of the aorta. Abnormalities of the aorta, the major blood vessel arising directly from the left ventricle of the heart and supplying blood to the systemic circulation, may also occur on a congenital basis. The early part of the aorta, the ascending aorta, may be stenotic (that is, unusually narrowed), usually as a result of a defect in the wall of the aorta itself or of the presence of fibrous tissue that narrows the valve. There may be an opening between the aorta and the pulmonary arteries that did not close at the appropriate time during embryologic development of the cardiovascular system; this defect is called a truncus arteriosus. The aortic arch, the curving portion of the aorta immediately above the heart, may have several congenital defects. It may be incompletely developed embryologically, or there may be an opening, known as a patent ductus arteriosus, at this point between the aorta and the pulmonary artery. This opening between the two vessels is necessary during uterine life, but normally closes at the time of birth and the clamping of the umbilical cord. Coarctation of the aorta, a deformity of the aortic wall resulting in severe narrowing of the blood vessel, may also occur. Any of the congenital abnormalities of the aorta may be present for a long time before being identified, and almost all are surgically correctable.

Stenosis of the ascending aorta

Anomalous pulmonary venous return. Of the abnormalities of the pulmonary veins, the most common is the anomalous pulmonary venous return. In this condition, the pulmonary veins normally draining oxygenated blood from one or more lobes of the lung to the left side of the heart abnormally return to the right side of the heart. Occasionally an arteriovenous fistula may occur, an abnormal opening between the pulmonary artery and the pulmonary vein. These abnormalities frequently cause no significant cardiac disease by themselves, but they are frequently associated with other congenital abnormalities. Surgical correction is occasionally employed.

Abnormalities of the venae cavae. The most common abnormalities of the venae cavae, the major veins returning venous blood to the right side of the heart, are a persistent left superior vena cava (normally there is but one superior vena cava, opening into the right side of the heart), and an abnormal termination of the vena cava. If these cause significant symptoms, surgical correction is possible.

ACQUIRED HEART DISEASE

The coronary arteries and the heart. The blood vessels supplying the muscle of the heart are called the coronary arteries and veins. Disease involving the coronary arteries may result from several possible causes, arteriosclerosis being by far the most common. Because arteriosclerosis and the other processes involving the coronary arteries produce an inadequacy of blood flow (ischemia), the term ischemic heart disease has been used virtually synonymously to indicate that the clinical manifestations are due to the lack of blood flow to the heart.

Arteriosclerotic heart disease.. Arteriosclerosis is a disease in which lesions known as atheromas develop in the arterial wall and undergo a sequence of changes that may lead to "hardening of the arteries" and, eventually, to arterial obstruction. The atheromas are characterized by localized thickening of the blood vessel wall with variable deposits of lipid (fatty) material. This thickening and deposition result in a deterioration of the normal structures of the wall, so that formation of scar tissue (fibrosis); deposits of calcium salts; tortuosity (*i.e.*, a twisting or turning of the vessel); and, later, bleeding under the inner coat (intima) of the vessel, obstruction, and clot formation may occur. Such vascular lesions may be widespread in the body, but severe lesions are more likely to be found in the coronary vessels. The development of vascular disease of this type is so common with advancing age that it has been thought by many to be a part of the aging process itself. Modern medical opinion, however, describes it as a disease that begins as an abnormal metabolic process of the vascular wall and leads to the various types of blood vessel deformity that, in the case of the coronary arteries, in turn leads to interference with the blood supply to the heart muscle (ischemia) and to the group of symptoms associated with ischemia.

Whether arteriosclerosis is a part of aging

The cause of coronary arteriosclerosis is not clear, but it undoubtedly does not spring from a single cause. A wide variety of studies of causes has been carried out, some demonstrating that ischemic heart disease is much more frequently found in the temperate zones of the world, and that in relatively advanced and affluent cultures it is much more common in men than in women, although the incidence in women rises appreciably after the menopause. A number of additional notable correlations have been made. The disease is more common in those countries in which the diet is substantial and high in animal fat. It has been demonstrated that the lipid content of the blood is altered with a notably high level of cholesterol in persons from these areas. (Cholesterol is a substance present in all animal fat and prominent in the lipid material in the atheromas.) It has similarly been noted that there is a substantially increased hazard of developing the clinical manifestations of coronary artery disease in those individuals with a history of heavy cigarette smoking and in those with arterial hypertension (high blood pressure). Additional, but less well documented, positive correlates include excessive weight, a sedentary rather than an active existence, and, in certain circumstances, a life of unusual stress. Certain racial groups, such as Jewish populations, appear to be more susceptible to the disorder, and it is less common in the black races, except when arterial hypertension is present. In general, the medical profession feels that these factors contribute to the rapidity of the development of the disease, but that they are not primarily causative.

Asymptomatic coronary artery disease. Considerable coronary artery disease may be present without symptoms, particularly in the male. Autopsy studies conducted on U.S. soldiers who died of battle wounds in Korea and Vietnam (average age of 24 years) indicated an appreciable degree of coronary artery disease in a majority of them. In an older population group, the incidence would undoubtedly be much higher and the involvement more severe. It is suspected that as high as 40 percent of all myocardial infarctions (death of sections of heart muscle) fail to cause symptoms and that the affected person is not aware of them. The conventional diagnostic tools of the physician are unable to detect the presence of coronary artery disease unless there has been some element of muscular involvement that generally, but not always, causes changes in the electrocardiogram, a tracing reflecting the electric current produced when the heart muscle is contracted. Special coronary X-rays give a reasonably exact picture of the coronary blood vessel pattern, but do not indicate the small nonobstructive lesions that may be the forerunner of more serious involvement. The procedure for making coronary X-rays is complicated, moreover, and somewhat hazardous, and it is not applied on a widespread basis in persons who do not have symptoms. No entirely satisfactory method of evaluating the presence and degree of coronary artery disease in a person who has no symptoms is available.

Angina pectoris. Angina pectoris, resulting from severe underlying coronary artery disease or, much less commonly, from other types of impairment of coronary flow, is characterized by paroxysms of deep seated, aching pain beneath the breastbone and in the region over the heart and stomach. These paroxysms are usually distinctive in character, location, and radiation, and are generally induced by walking, other physical exercise, or emotional stress. The pain is characteristically an oppressive type, often associated with a sense of strangulation or anxiety. Affected persons often use a clenched fist to describe the sense of heaviness and constriction, and some deny that it is a "pain." The discomfort may spread from the chest, particularly in the leftward direction, down the left arm and up into the left side of the jaw. On rare occasions, pain may be noted only in the more peripheral areas. Persons affected often attribute the discomfort to indigestion, and, at times, similar discomfort can be caused by spasm of the esophagus and by other disorders. The characteristic pattern of anginal pain, its occurrence upon physical exertion, especially in cold weather, and its relief by nitroglycerin form a pattern that is usually quickly identified by the physician. At times the pain may occur while a person is at rest, particularly when he is under emotional stress, but it may occur at night while he is lying quietly in bed.

Characteristics of angina pectoris

Physical examination may reveal no abnormalities. The electrocardiogram may show transient changes; but, more often than not, there is no distinctive alteration in the electrocardiographic pattern while the affected person is resting. The use of coronary X-rays has demonstrated that persons with angina pectoris usually have widespread involvement of the coronary arteries, with obstruction of two or more of the major vessels. On occasion, a physician may elect to have the patient exercise while his electrocardiogram is being recorded to bring out abnormalities that may make the diagnosis more certain.

Treatment of angina pectoris includes a change in the affected person's pattern of exercise and activity. The drug nitroglycerin usually provides remarkably effective immediate relief from the pain. Other drugs, often less effective, may provide long-term diminution of the symptoms.

Myocardial infarction (heart attack). A syndrome (symptom complex) of prolonged, severe chest pain was first described in the medical literature in 1912 by James Bryan Herrick, as noted above. He attributed the syndrome to coronary thrombosis, the development of a clot in a major blood vessel serving the heart. Although aspects of this common disease had been described earlier, it remained for Herrick to put the information together in a concise and direct fashion. As a result of Herrick's convincing description, the disorder was termed coronary thrombosis or coronary occlusion (blockage of a coronary artery). Later evidence indicated, however, that, although arteriosclerosis of the coronary arteries is by far the most common cause of the disorder, the manifestations are in reality the result of the death of an area of heart muscle (infarction).

The term myocardial infarction, therefore, is more appropriate. Indeed, it has been demonstrated that a coronary thrombosis in the true sense is not present in many such patients. The more general and less specific term heart attack may, thus, be more desirable because of these difficulties in describing the causation of the disease entity.

Characteristics of myocardial infarction

Myocardial infarction occurs as a result of arteriosclerosis of the coronary arteries and is characterized pathologically by cellular death (necrosis) of a segment of the heart muscle. Generally, it involves an area in the forward wall of the heart related to the blood distribution of the anterior descending coronary artery, although in other instances, the posterior wall or the septum (partition) of the ventricle is involved. The exact immediate cause of the myocardial infarction is not clearly understood. Coronary thrombosis is present in a majority of the hearts examined at autopsy and undoubtedly plays an important role in some cases. In others, changes in metabolic demands of the heart muscle in the presence of a restricted blood flow may be enough to cause death of ischemic cells.

The outstanding clinical feature is pain, similar in many respects to that of angina pectoris. The important difference is that the pain lasts for a much longer period, at least half an hour, and usually for several hours and perhaps for days. The pain is often described as "crushing," "compressing," "like a vise," and is associated with some difficulty in breathing. As with angina pectoris, the pain may radiate to the left arm or up the neck into the jaws or head. There is occasional nausea, vomiting, and weakness. The affected person frequently is pale, and he may perspire profusely. On the other hand, most of these symptoms may be absent, and the occurrence of an infarction can then be detected only by laboratory means. The physical examination at the time of the painful episode may not provide the physician with positive evidence that an infarction has occurred. Laboratory studies may show an elevation of the white-blood-cell count in the blood or a rise in the enzyme content of the blood, indicating leakage from damaged heart muscle cells. The electrocardiogram in many instances shows distinct and characteristic abnormalities, but the electrocardiographic abnormalities may be less characteristic or totally absent.

Physical signs of infarction

In most persons who experience an acute myocardial infarction, the circulation remains adequate, and only by subtle evidence such as rales (abnormal respiratory sounds) in the lungs or a gallop rhythm of the heart beat may the evidence of some minor degree of heart failure be detected. In a relatively small percent of cases, the state of shock occurs, with pallor, coolness of the hands and feet, low blood pressure, and rapid heart action. In these cases, myocardial infarction is highly lethal, with survival rates of only 20–40 percent, in contrast to the current survival rate in many hospitals of 70–80 percent. Mortality is also related to age, for the process is more lethal in the elderly. Another cause of death is sudden arrhythmia, or irregularity, of heart action, which constitutes one of the situations in which death comes suddenly. In a small number of persons there may be death from heart rupture caused by thromboembolism (obstruction caused by a clot that has broken loose from its site of formation). In some individuals, the damage caused by the infarction may interfere with functioning of the mitral valve, the valve between the left upper and lower chambers, and result in a form of valvular heart disease, or it may cause a rupture of the interventricular septum, the partition between the left and right ventricles, with the development of a ventricular septal defect, such as is seen in some forms of congenital heart disease.

In the modern treatment of acute myocardial infarction, the affected person is admitted to a hospital coronary-care unit, where the use of appropriate electronic devices for monitoring heart rhythm and detecting abnormalities enables an experienced nursing staff to reduce the possibility of sudden death. Drugs are used to control arrhythmias and to strengthen myocardial function.

Convalescence from an acute myocardial infarction may last several weeks to several months, allowing time for scar tissue to form in the area of an infarction and a gradual return to activity. Although some persons may have residual evidence of heart failure or other cardiac malfunction, the majority of individuals may return to an active life after a period of weeks and are not in any way invalided by the process. They do, however, have an increased potential for subsequent myocardial infarction.

Sudden death. The term "sudden death" as used in medicine is not explicit and may be used to describe death that is almost instantaneous or in which rapidly fatal disease processes may occupy as much as two or three days. In heart disease both may occur, but the term characteristically refers to relatively instantaneous death, similar to turning off a light switch. This type of demise is frequent in coronary artery disease and constitutes one of the major hazards of this disease. Sudden death from coronary artery disease occurs so frequently that less than half of the persons who die from heart attacks each year in the United States survive long enough to reach the hospital.

Relatively instantaneous sudden death is usually related to an arrhythmia of the heart, with either total mechanical and electrical standstill of the heart or ventricular fibrillation (an uncontrolled and uncoordinated twitching of the ventricle muscle), with total mechanical inadequacy of the heart and erratic and ineffective electrical activity. Sudden death may occur without any previous manifestations of coronary artery disease. It may occur in the course of angina pectoris and causes about one half of the deaths due to acute myocardial infarction in hospitalized patients, although this number is decreasing with the more widespread use of coronary-care units. A reduced supply of blood to the heart undoubtedly is the precipitating factor, but there does not have to be acute myocardial infarction. In a vast majority of persons who have died almost instantaneously, no infarction was present, but there was widespread coronary artery disease. In rare instances, sudden death occurs without a major degree of coronary artery disease. The use of closed chest cardiopulmonary massage (massage of heart and lungs without making an opening in the chest wall), coupled with electrical defibrillation (the use of electrical shocks), if applied within a few minutes of the sudden death episode, may resuscitate a person and provide a possibility of long-term survival. In coronary-care units where the facilities and trained personnel are immediately available, the percentage of successful resuscitations is high. In general hospitals where resuscitation teams have been established, the percentage is less satisfactory. Sudden death outside the hospital is, of course, a more difficult problem, but mobile coronary-care units responding as emergency ambulances to the site of a sudden death were on trial in the 1970s. Effective resuscitation depends upon the prompt arrival of the unit. The use of drugs and other means to prevent the onset of sudden death has been relatively successful in the coronary-care unit, except in situations in which the disease has been present for a long period of time.

Resuscitation after apparent death

Arteriosclerotic heart disease with congestive failure. The ischemic process of arteriosclerotic heart disease may render the heart less effective as a pump, and the constellation of findings indicating congestive failure occurs (see below). Congestive heart failure may be present for a number of years and may be treated with good symptomatic relief. It may be caused by impaired function of the mitral valve or by a ventricular septal defect resulting from myocardial infarction. These difficulties can be treated surgically with relief of congestive failure, but, unfortunately, this treatment is afforded only to a minority of the persons with heart failure resulting from arteriosclerotic heart disease.

In the past, the diagnosis of arteriosclerotic heart disease was often used loosely for a large group of persons who had unexplained congestive heart failure. As medical knowledge advanced, however, more specific diagnoses became applicable, so that the number of patients in the category is diminishing.

Treatment of coronary artery disease. The specific treatment of angina pectoris and myocardial infarction has already been discussed. Attempts to prolong life and diminish the likelihood of an additional or recurrent myocardial infarction are commonly undertaken on a long-term basis. Primary prevention, relating to measures taken to prevent even the first clinical manifestation of coronary artery disease, has as yet shown limited measurable success. Although a number of correlates have been noted, there is not yet unequivocal proof that changing one's mode of life will result in greater life expectancy. In persons whose hypertension is successfully treated, however, there appears to be excellent evidence that the incidence of clinical manifestations of coronary artery disease will be retarded and that life expectancy will be extended. There is also some evidence, although much less convincing, to indicate that the cessation of cigarette smoking, the reduction of blood cholesterol levels, and other similar factors may result in greater life expectancy. Substantiation of such evidence requires large-scale studies involving many persons, including controlled observations on a group of untreated persons.

Relief of high blood pressure

Other disease of the coronary arteries. Although coronary artery disease is by far most frequently caused by arteriosclerosis, there are many types of inflammation of the blood vessels that may rarely cause obstructive lesions of the coronary vessels. In persons with cardiovascular syphilis, the disease process may involve the mouth of the coronary vessels as they leave the aorta and cause obstruction to blood flow. On rare occasions, clots arising from some other part of the body may enter the coronary vessels and cause acute obstruction and clinical manifestations.

Rheumatic heart disease. Rheumatic heart disease results from inflammation of the heart lining, heart muscle, and pericardium occurring in the course of acute rheumatic fever, an infection with *Streptococcus pyogenes* organisms. The disease includes those later developments that persist after the acute process has subsided, and may result in damage to a valve, which may in turn lead to heart failure.

Rheumatic fever is poorly understood. The disease process occurs days or weeks following the initial streptococcal infection. Later infections may bring recurrences of the rheumatic fever that damage the heart. Immunologic processes (reactions to a foreign protein) are thought to be responsible for the response that damages the heart and particularly the heart valves. Rapid and effective treatment or prevention of streptococcal infections stops the acute process.

Many other factors of a geographic, economic, and climatic nature influence the incidence of rheumatic fever, but are not primarily causative. Rheumatic fever is becoming less common in the second half of the 20th century. With better control of streptococcal infections, there is indication of a sharp decline, with only one-fifth as many deaths as occurred in the 1930s and only one-half as many deaths as occurred in the 1960s. It is currently estimated, however, that about 1,000,000 people in the United States have rheumatic heart disease of one form or another.

It is thought that the basic pathologic lesion involves inflammatory changes in the collagen, the main supportive protein of the connective tissue. There is also inflammation of the heart lining (the endocardium) and the pericardium, the sac containing the heart. Only a relatively small percentage of deaths occur in the acute phase, with evidence of overwhelming inflammation associated with acute heart failure. There may be a disturbance of the conduction system of the heart and involvement of other tissues of the body, particularly the joints. About one half of the persons found to have late rheumatic valvular disease give some indication that they have had acute rheumatic fever.

Major effect of rheumatic fever

The major toll of rheumatic fever is in the deformity of the heart valves created by the initial attack or by frequently repeated attacks of the acute illness. Although there may be valve involvement in the acute stages, it usually requires several years before valve defects become manifest as the cause of heart malfunction. The valve most frequently affected is the mitral valve, less commonly the aortic valve, and least common of all, the pulmonic and tricuspid valves. These valves are, respectively, the valve between the left atrium and left ventricle; the valve at the opening into the aorta; the valve at the opening into the pulmonary artery; and the valve between the right upper and lower chambers. The lesion may cause either insufficiency of the valve, preventing it from operating in a normal fashion, or stenosis (narrowing) of the valve, preventing a normal flow of blood and adding to the burden of the heart.

Mitral valve involvement is the most common effect of rheumatic fever. The presence of mitral involvement is indicated by symptoms of heart failure, with shortness of breath and edema (abnormal accumulations of fluid in the bodily tissues). Heart murmurs are reasonably accurate signposts for specific valvular diagnoses. A murmur during the diastolic, or resting, phase of the heart, when blood normally flows through the mitral valve to fill the ventricle, generally indicates the presence of mitral stenosis. On the other hand, a murmur during the systole, or contraction, of the left ventricle, indicates an abnormal flow of blood back through the mitral valve into the left atrium (mitral insufficiency). When this latter condition is present, each beat of the heart must pump enough blood to supply the body as well as the wasted reflux into the pulmonary vascular system. This additional work load causes dilation and enlargement of the ventricle and leads to the development of congestive heart failure.

In addition to the clinical findings, X-rays of the heart and electrocardiographic findings may give evidence of the presence of mitral-valve disease. The passage of a long flexible tube or catheter through the venous or arterial system into the heart allows for pressure measurements and blood flow determinations that more specifically verify the clinical impression of mitral-valve disease. The injection of radiopaque contrast material into the blood stream (angiocardiography) to outline the blood-containing part of the heart in X-rays as the contrast material passes through makes possible the diagnosis of valvular defects, hypertrophy, and dilation, as well as any abnormal shunts or paths of blood flow.

Involvement of the aortic valve is also common, and again there may be evidence of stenosis or insufficiency. The presence of aortic stenosis may lead to a marked hypertrophy (enlargement) of the left ventricle of the heart. Involvement of either the tricuspid or pulmonic valve occurs in a similar fashion. In many persons with rheumatic valvular disease, more than one valve is involved. The specific type of valve involved influences the clinical picture of congestive failure (see the section on congestive failure).

Surgical treatment of heart valves

For many years the only therapy available for rheumatic heart disease was the treatment of the resultant heart failure by digitalis and other drugs. As the result of the spectacular development of cardiovascular surgery since the mid-1940s, it is now possible to treat many valve defects by surgery and by the installation of artificial replacement valves.

The heart, the pulmonary artery, and the aorta. *Pulmonary heart disease (cor pulmonale).* An obstruction to blood flow through the network of vessels in the lungs develops in various types of lung disease. Impingement on blood flow in this integral part of the total path of blood flow through the body impairs the total circulation and places a particular burden on the right side of the heart, which normally pumps against a low-pressure load with little impedance to blood flow. Pulmonary-artery pressures are low compared to those in the aorta.

Pulmonary heart disease may be divided into acute and chronic forms. The classic form of acute pulmonary heart disease (acute cor pulmonale) occurs when there is sudden obstruction to the pulmonary blood-flow pattern, as occurs with a massive embolus—a blood clot that has broken loose from its point of formation. This impairs blood flow through the lungs, causes additional reflex changes that add to the heart's burden, and creates an acute form of high blood pressure in the pulmonary arteries, with dilation and failure of the right ventricle. The right ventricle's pumping ability is acutely depressed, and, therefore, the amount of blood available for the left side of the heart is equally restricted, so that systemic circulatory failure occurs. Respiratory symptoms are not prominent, and the disorder in its early stages is not accompanied by edema in the lung. The clinical picture in the more severe form is one of shock, with cold, pale, and clammy skin, low arterial pressure, and high pulse rate. The heart may be acutely dilated. The electrocardiogram may show the characteristic changes of acute right ventricular strain. In some instances, surgical removal of the obstruction may be life-saving. In others, the disorder may become less severe, but if recurrent, a more chronic form of cor pulmonale may develop.

In chronic cor pulmonale the causative factors may be either a form of pulmonary disease, such as emphysema (abnormal distension of the lungs with air), which obstructs flow through the pulmonary circulation, multiple blood clots in the vessels of the lung, or pulmonary vascular disease. The net result is a form of heart failure based primarily on obstruction to flow through the pulmonary blood vessels. Pulmonary arterial hypertension is common to most all of these forms. In many there may be cyanosis, with evidence that the arterial blood is not saturated with oxygen. The manifestations of heart failure are present, particularly when there is edema, except that shortness of breath as it is seen in ordinary congestive failure is not prominent, since the pulmonary blood vessels are not congested.

The right side of the heart is enlarged, the valve sounds from the pulmonic valve are loud, and there is electrocardiographic evidence of chronic strain on the right side of the heart. This condition is a form of chronic heart disease that is difficult for the physician to control and that may last for many years.

Hypertensive heart disease. Arterial hypertension (high blood pressure) is a disease in which the regulation of blood pressure is abnormal, resulting in the chronic maintenance of a higher-than-normal arterial pressure.

Types of hypertension

Transient elevations of blood pressure occur in the normal individual, but in the hypertensive individual the blood pressure, although still rising and falling in various circumstances, maintains a level that is on the average higher than normal. The disorder may result from one of several possible causes. In certain structural abnormalities of the aorta, such as coarctation, in which the artery's middle coat is deformed, with resultant narrowing of the channel, arterial pressure in the upper half of the body is abnormally high, as it is also in some tumours of the adrenal glands and, rarely, of other organs. Hypertension results also in a number of types of chronic renal (kidney) diseases. All these types of hypertension collectively, however, form only a relatively small percentage of the clinical occurrences of high blood pressure. A majority of occurrences, in which the cause is not obvious, are termed essential hypertension. Regardless of the cause, but in some ways coloured by it, the effects on the cardiovascular system are similar. The impact on the vascular system varies from person to person. In some persons, for unknown reasons, the body withstands the abnormal elevation of blood pressure with minimum change in the heart and blood vessels. In other situations, blood vessel damage is early and severe, coupled with serious deterioration of heart function. In general, the rule is that the higher the blood pressure, the higher the degree of cardiovascular damages, although there are many exceptions. In certain persons, a vicious and damaging form of hypertension occurs, often called malignant hypertension, which results in small blood vessel damage throughout the body, but particularly affecting the heart, brain, and kidneys. Persons with hypertensive disease have an increased susceptibility to atherosclerosis (a lesion of large and medium-sized arteries, with deposits in the intima—the inner coat—of yellowish plaques containing cholesterol, other lipid material, and cells that absorb fat) of the coronary arteries, thus making it difficult to separate the cardiac manifestations from those caused by hypertension, per se. Hypertensive persons, therefore, may eventually have congestive heart failure following enlargement of the heart caused by chronic increase in arterial pressure. In addition, they may suffer the effects of a decline in blood supply to the heart because of coronary artery disease and the classic manifestations of coronary arteriosclerosis, such as angina pectoris or death of a portion of heart muscle, myocardial infarction. There is clear evidence that treatment of hypertension with antihypertensive drugs reduces the likelihood that the heart will be affected, and it improves the condition of those who have a chronically elevated arterial pressure. Hypertensive cardiovascular disease may also become manifest through defects in the vessels supplying the brain, leading to stroke or other abnormalities of the brain. Furthermore, hypertensive cardiovascular manifestations may be complicated by the development of kidney failure and resultant abnormal retention of fluid in the tissues, adding to the problems of congestive heart failure.

Syphilis of the heart and aorta. Syphilis, a disease caused by infection with a micro-organism, *Treponema pallidum*, in its early phases becomes widespread in the human body. At this time, there may be transient inflammation of the heart muscle, but usually with little or no impairment of the circulation. In the late stages of the disease, there may be syphilitic involvement of the heart, confined almost purely to the aorta and aortic valve. A particularly severe form of aortic insufficiency may develop, with subsequent dilation and enlargement of the heart and, eventually, heart failure. The disease process often involves the base of the aorta and the blood flow through the openings into the coronary vessels from the aorta, causing impairment of the coronary circulation, with resultant angina pectoris and, on rare occasions, myocardial infarction, the death of portions of heart muscle.

Aneurysms of the aorta

The syphilitic process may also involve the wall of the aorta, resulting in the loss of the elastic properties, in dilation, and, at times, in the formation of aneurysms of the aorta. (An aneurysm is a bulging of the vessel wall at a point of weakness.) The aneurysms may become large and interfere with blood flow through the tributaries of the aorta in the involved area. They may be the source of pain and eventually may rupture, causing sudden death from loss of blood into the thoracic cavity. Syphilis of the aorta was common in the past, but with the advent of more modern control mechanisms, plus effective early treatment with the use of penicillin, the disorder has become much less common. The rise in the incidence of syphilis and other venereal diseases in the late 1960s and early 1970s has not yet involved an increased incidence of the late complications. These can be effectively avoided by early antisyphilitic treatment.

Other diseases of aorta and pulmonary arteries. Arteriosclerosis may involve the aorta and its major branches. Indeed, it seems to be an almost inevitable process with increasing age, but the rate of development and the extent of involvement vary greatly. The process may merely limit the elasticity of the aorta and allow for some dilation and tortuosity as age advances. In more severe instances, there may be a major degree of dilation or localized formation of aneurysms, generally in the abdominal portion of the aorta. These aneurysms may result in pain and may occasionally rupture, causing sudden death. The arteriosclerotic process may impair the flow of blood to the tributaries of the aorta and lead to a variety of ischemic states—*i.e.*, result in various types of damage that come from an insufficient supply of blood. This condition is particularly notable when the renal vessels are involved, creating a state of renal ischemia, occasionally creating hypertension, and possibly terminating in renal failure.

Medial necrosis is a lesion of the aorta in which the media, the middle coat of the artery, deteriorates and, in association with arteriosclerosis and often hypertension, may lead to a dissecting aneurysm. In a dissecting aneurysm a rupture in the intima, the innermost coat of the artery, permits blood to enter the wall of the aorta, causing separation of the layers of the wall. Obstruction to tributaries may occur, which is usually associated with severe chest pain. In many instances, there is a secondary rupture of the exterior wall, which may lead to fatal internal bleeding. Inflammation of the aortic wall may occur as an isolated process.

Deposition of calcium salts in the aorta wall may occur as a part of the arteriosclerotic process or of other disease involvement, such as syphilis. The pulmonary artery may be the seat of similar disease processes, but it is less frequently involved by syphilis. In certain conditions, such as congenital heart disease, blood clots (thrombi) may form in the pulmonary artery, and these may break loose. Blood clots in the lungs (pulmonary emboli) may arise from this and other sources in the systemic venous circulation. These fragments of clot may be small, causing no detectable manifestations, or large, causing obstruction of either the total pulmonary arterial flow (see the section on cor pulmonale, above) or of flow to an area of lung.

Blood clots in the lungs

Other diseases of endocardium and valves. Bacterial endocarditis, a disease in which bacterial or fungus infection becomes established on the surface of a heart valve or, less commonly, in a blood vessel wall or in the endocardium (lining) of the heart, usually occurs where there has been some previous lesion, either congenital or acquired. Most frequently, the location is at the line of closure of the valve. The disease may be acute and severe, or may be a more chronic situation, often referred to as subacute bacterial endocarditis. It may erode the valve structure, or it may be of an inflammatory nature, producing nodules with the ulcerative surface of active infection. Because the bacteria are imbedded in the lesion, the normal body defenses contained in the blood have difficulty entering into play; for this reason, certain types of bacterial endocarditis become more chronic and more slowly progressing. The effects of the lesion are complex, relating to the presence of a bacterial infection in the body, local damage to the valve, and systemic damage caused by fragments of blood clot breaking off and travelling through the blood stream to distant organs, causing infarctions or abscesses, a type of kidney disease, or other small areas of bleeding and necrosis in the skin, eyes, and other parts of the body. Before the advent of antibiotic therapy, bacterial endocarditis was almost always a fatal disease. Many affected persons can now be successfully treated, given the best conditions, although the mortality rate still remains relatively high. Inflammation of the heart lining, endocarditis not caused by infection, may occur in some illnesses, but it does not result in formation and breaking loose of blood clots.

In the course of rheumatoid arthritis, a chronic inflammation of the joints of unknown cause, a type of valvular damage has been recognized. It is different from that caused by rheumatic fever but leads to valvular insufficiency and stenosis (narrowing) in much the same fashion and is particularly likely to attack the aortic valve. The tendencies toward heart failure and toward impairment of heart function are the same as in rheumatic valvular disease.

In a variety of cardiovascular disorders, the heart becomes dilated and the blood flow inside the atrial and ventricular cavities may become sluggish. These conditions render the heart more susceptible to the formation of blood clots on the wall of the heart (mural thrombi). They are particularly likely to occur in the presence of atrial fibrillation, a disturbance in heart rhythm that causes ineffective contractions of the atrium. When mural thrombi occur, the local lesion is of little consequence unless it reaches great magnitude. The major hazard to the affected person is the fragmentation of the thrombus to form detached clots (emboli) in the peripheral circulation.

Other diseases of the myocardium. There has been increasing recognition of a type of heart disease characterized as primary myocardial disease. The disorders, called cardiomyopathies, directly affect the muscular tissue of the heart, resulting in heart disease and heart muscle failure. The process may be related to a disseminated disorder that involves the entire body.

The cardiomyopathies may cause no symptoms, and may be detected only by evidence of an enlarged heart and disturbances in cardiac conduction mechanisms detected on electrocardiography. In other instances, extensive involvement may lead to heart failure. Some cases may be chronic, with exacerbations and remissions over a period of years. Cardiomyopathies constitute a major segment of heart disease in the temperate climates. In some instances, therapy aimed at the underlying disease will produce what is in effect a cure, as in myxedema or thyrotoxicosis, conditions caused, respectively, by underactivity and overactivity of the thyroid gland. In most other instances, no specific remedies are available.

Cardiomyopathies

Infections, such as acute rheumatic fever, early stages of syphilis, and several viral infections, may cause any of a number of types of myocarditis. Myocarditis may also occur as a manifestation of a generalized hypersensitivity (allergic or immunologic) reaction throughout the body.

A large number of cardiomyopathies are apparently not related to an infectious process, but are not well understood. A number of these are congenital and many cause enlargement of the heart. About one-third of these diseases are familial, and some of these are transmitted as a non-sex-linked autosomal dominant trait (*i.e.*, a person may be affected if he inherits the tendency from one parent). They are particularly common in the black races. A number of metabolic diseases associated with endocrine disorders may also cause cardiomyopathies. Other metabolic disorders that may contribute to cardiomyopathy include beriberi, caused by a nutritional deficiency; cobalt poisoning in heavy beer drinkers; or a form of cardiomyopathy in chronic alcoholics. There are also rare cardiomyopathies caused by drugs.

The heart may be affected by any of a considerable number of collagen diseases. Collagen is the principal connective-tissue protein, and collagen diseases are diseases of the connective tissues. They include diseases primarily of the joints (*e.g.*, rheumatoid arthritis); primarily of the skin (*e.g.*, scleroderma); and systemic disease (*e.g.*, systemic lupus erythematosus).

The collagen diseases

Diseases of the pericardium. The pericardium is the membranous sac that encloses the heart. Pericardial disease may occur as an isolated process or as a subordinate and clinically unsuspected manifestation of a disease elsewhere in the body. Acute pericarditis—inflammation of the pericardium—may result from invasion of the pericardium by one of a number of agents (viral, fungal, protozoal, or tuberculous in nature); as a manifestation of certain connective tissue and allergic diseases; or as a result of chemical or metabolic disturbances. Cancer and injury to the pericardium are also potential hazards.

Pain is the most common symptom in acute pericarditis, although pericarditis may occur without pain. A characteristic sound, called friction rub, aids in the diagnosis of pericarditis. There are also characteristic electrocardiographic findings. Acute pericarditis may be accompanied by an outpouring of fluid into the pericardial sac. The presence of pericardial fluid in excessive amounts may enlarge the silhouette of the heart in X-rays but not impair its function. If the fluid accumulates rapidly or in great amounts, however, or if the pericardium is diseased so that it does not expand, the heart is compressed, a state called pericardial tamponade. There is interference with the heart's ability to fill with blood and reduction of cardiac output. In its more severe form, cardiac tamponade causes a shocklike state that may be lethal. Removal of the fluid is lifesaving in an emergency and aids in the identification of the cause.

Impairment of cardiac function is present in chronic constrictive pericarditis, caused by scar tissue in the pericardium that restricts the activity of the ventricles. In many instances, the cause of this type of disorder is not known, but in some it is the result of tuberculosis and other specific infections. It is treated most effectively by surgery. Tumours that either arise directly from the pericardium or are secondary growths from other sources may impair cardiac function and cause pericardial effusion (escape of fluid into the pericardium).

Disturbances in rhythm and conduction. The heart's rhythmical beat is initiated and regulated from centres within the organ. The primary pacemaker, the sinoatrial node, is a small mass of specialized muscle cells located at the juncture of the upper vena cava and the right atrium. Electrical impulses are emitted by this group of cells. The excitation spreads through the two atria and, by way of a band of fibres called the bundle of His, into the ventricles. The bundle of His, named for the German anatomist Wilhelm His, Jr., who described it in 1893, has its beginning in a small mass of cells, the atrioventricular node, located beneath the lining of the right atrium. Normally initiated heart rhythm, originating in the sinoatrial node, is called sinus rhythm.

Normal variations in heart beat

Under stimulation from the central nervous system and other metabolic factors, heart rate may normally rise and fall, with a slight variation, in part related to respiratory activity. In young individuals in excellent physical condition, the resting heart rate may fall as low as 40 to 50 beats per minute, and, under stressful psychologic stimulation, the heart rate may rise to as high as 200 beats per minute. These situations are to be differentiated from pathologic variations in heart rate. Sinus bradycardia (a slow sinus rhythm with a rate below 60, caused by disturbance of the sinoatrial node) or tachycardia (excessive rapidity in the action of the heart with a pulse rate of above 100 beats per minute) without abnormality in mechanism may occur in a wide variety of disease states, and either is merely symptomatic of the underlying disease.

Extra beats arising from the atrium, the nodal tissues, or the ventricle are not in themselves abnormal, although beats arising from the ventricle are more often associated with organic heart disease. Occasional extra systoles (contractions) occur in many normal individuals. In cardiovascular disease they are much more common. They do not interfere with normal cardiovascular function if infrequent. It has been noted that continued psychologic stress, excessive smoking, and drinking of large amounts of tea and coffee enhance the tendencies for premature contractions of the atria. Premature contractions of the ventricles are more ominous, especially those that occur after exercise. They have been found to be associated with coronary artery disease in a large percentage of instances. If frequent enough, they may be the harbinger of more serious ventricular arrhythmias.

Abnormalities in the rhythm of atrial contractions include atrial tachycardia (swift heartbeat), atrial flutter, and atrial fibrillation (see below). As noted earlier, atrial tachycardia may be a manifestation of underlying disease such as thyrotoxicosis or may be merely a matter of stressful stimulation in a normal individual. Some individuals have characteristic episodes of paroxysmal atrial tachycardia of varying frequency and duration, with a rapid onset and termination. Ordinarily the episodes occur in the absence of any other heart abnormality. Occasionally, especially when the episodes are prolonged or when they occur in the presence of organic cardiovascular disease, they may be accompanied by evidence of heart failure or, in rare instances, of the shock state.

Atrial flutter

Atrial flutter represents a form of tachycardia associated with very rapid atrial activity. The atrial activity is regular, but the conduction of the impulses to the ventricle may be delayed and impaired so that only one of two, three, or four impulses excite ventricular activity. This disorder is most often, but not always, seen in persons with organic heart disease.

Atrial fibrillation is another form of atrial tachycardia, in which there is wildly erratic and ineffective atrial contraction. The ventricular response is also erratic, so that the pulse is irregular without a basic underlying rhythm. This disorder is seen most frequently in persons with organic heart disease, such as rheumatic heart disease with mitral involvement and thyrotoxicosis, but also occurs in normal individuals, often on a paroxysmal basis. It renders the atrium ineffective, and therefore the contribution of this chamber to the normal pumping of blood is negated. This condition may be of no real functional importance in the normal heart, but may have a significant detrimental effect in the failing heart. The circulation functions reasonably well, although, in the case of severe mitral stenosis, a rapid heart action is not well tolerated because of the limited speed of ventricular filling through a small mitral opening. A complication of atrial fibrillation is the development of blood clots within the walls of the fibrillating atria. Because these clots may eventually fragment and pass into the circulation, atrial fibrillation is a condition that should be treated if possible. The abnormal rhythm may be slowed by digitalis or terminated by the use of electrical shocks (electrical defibrillation).

Atrioventricular node mechanisms. Normally, the impulse for ventricular contraction arises from a focus in the atria, passes through a conduction system that slightly delays progression, and then excites ventricular activity. This mechanism may not operate properly in various pathologic states. In some instances, more rapidly firing (*i.e.*, impulse-emitting) tissue in the atrioventricular node may initiate the ventricular activity, supplanting the normal atrial focus and resulting in tachycardia, called nodal tachycardia because of the part played by the atrioventricular node. More frequently, the abnormal mechanism is one of delay or obstruction in progression of the impulse, creating "heart block," a lack of synchronization between atria and ventricles; there may be varying degrees of severity. In first-degree heart block, there is merely a short delay over the normal conduction time from the atrium to the ventricle. This condition does not result in clinical manifestation but is detected electrocardiographically by a longer than normal period of time between the P wave, which is associated with atrial activity, and the QRS complex, which is associated with ventricular excitation.

Three degrees of heart block

In a more severe (second-degree) form, the impulse may travel relatively normally through the conduction system, but some beats are blocked. Alternate beats may be blocked, resulting in what is known as a two-to-one heart block, or the ratio may be three-to-one, four-to-one, etc. The degree of blockage may be influenced by stimulation from outside the heart, such as from the carotid sinus or the central nervous system, and is dependent in part on drug action. (The carotid arteries are the principal arteries to the head. The carotid sinus, located at the fork where the common carotid divides into the external and internal carotid arteries, is an important centre for monitoring and regulating blood pressure.)

The conduction system below the atrioventricular node divides into two major branches, to the two ventricles, and, therefore, blockage of either of these is termed right or left bundle branch block. This condition again is primarily determined by an electrocardiographic diagnosis and is most frequently associated with organic heart disease, although it may occur rarely in normal individuals.

A final major form of heart block, complete heart block, is characterized by total dissociation of atrial activity and ventricular activity. In this situation, atrial activity usually continues at a normal or higher than normal rate. Independently the ventricle establishes its own rate, usually slower than normal, but in some instances within the normal range. If the latter is the case, the difficulty is without major consequence on the circulation. More frequently, however, it is at a slower rate, and there may be some resultant inadequacy of the circulation. This condition is usually associated with forms of organic heart disease, and the slowness of the rate may precipitate congestive heart failure or other manifestations. It may be treated by the use of drugs or electrical pacemakers to increase the rate of ventricular activity. At times, the degree of heart block or its occurrence may be variable and erratic. This condition may result in considerable pauses in left-ventricular depolarization and contraction, the basic mechanism that precipitates the Adams-Stokes syndrome, which leads to occasional episodes of unconsciousness. (The syndrome is named for the Irish physicians Robert Adams and William Stokes, whose descriptions of the disease are celebrated.)

Ventricular arrhythmias. The ventricle may respond regularly or erratically to atrial or nodal (atrioventricular) disturbances of rhythm. In addition, it is subject to other intrinsic forms of abnormal rhythm. In the course of severe heart disease, such as coronary artery disease, ventricular tachycardia (fast beating of the ventricles) may occur. The beat is regular, but may be so rapid that it interferes with normal cardiac filling and ejection, and, therefore, results in either congestive failure, if prolonged, or in the development of a shock state, if severe and acute. Ventricular tachycardia is perhaps most important because it may be the forerunner of ventricular fibrillation, in which, as in atrial fibrillation, the contractions are widely erratic and ineffective, so that essentially ventricular fibrillation is a form of ventricular standstill with respect to the movement of blood. Unless stopped within seconds or minutes, it is lethal. The recognition of the forerunners of ventricular tachycardia has been the basis for the success of modern coronary-care units. It is treatable either by drugs or, more frequently, by the use of external electrical defibrillation, the application of electrical shocks.

Ventricular tachycardia and fibrillation

Some of the major recognized forms of arrhythmia have been presented. There are many special variants on this pattern, but even with the most complex electrocardiographic studies, some arrhythmias defy explanation.

Congestive heart failure. Congestive heart failure, a syndrome resulting from disease that has caused the heart to be inadequate as a pump, is characterized by manifestations distant from the heart, predominantly related to salt and water retention in the tissues. It may vary from the most minimal symptoms to sudden pulmonary edema (abnormal accumulation of fluid in the lungs) or to a rapidly lethal shocklike state. Chronic states of varying severity may last years. The symptoms relate predominately to secondary manifestations resulting from retention of fluid and vascular congestion throughout the body, rather than to the direct effect of lessened blood flow. In most instances, congestive failure results from a diseased heart, although on occasion the burden of other systemic diseases may exceed the capacity of the previously adequate heart and produce the condition. A physiologic characteristic of the normal heart is its ability to meet the fluctuating demands of the body for blood flow. The diseased heart may no longer be able to respond in this way. This failure may be the result of severe and acute damage, such as an acute myocardial infarction, or of chronic and lesser impairment, such as scarring of a valve in the course of a long-standing rheumatic heart disease.

The possible causes of the underlying heart disease are numerous. In the United States, the largest percentage of persons with congestive heart failure have manifestations of coronary artery disease that has interfered with the blood supply to the heart muscle and resulted in failure of the heart as a pump. Other common causes are rheumatic valvular disease, hypertensive vascular disease with involvement of the heart, or one of the multitudinous but less common types of primary disease of the myocardium. Regardless of the cause, the common denominator leading to heart failure is altered function of the heart muscle, with lessened ability to pump blood. In many sophisticated studies, clear-cut disturbances in the mechanics of heart muscle contraction have been demonstrated.

The presence of cardiac failure becomes apparent largely by signs and symptoms not directly related to the heart. With early and untreated heart failure, the person with congestive heart failure usually has a normal salt and water intake, but his ability to regulate and promptly excrete excess sodium and water is impaired. The nature of this impairment is not entirely clear.

Salt and water accumulate in the body as extracellular fluid that manifests itself as clinically detectable edema. If the person is active and in the upright position, the fluid may gather particularly about the ankles and legs. If he is in bed, it may be in the back overlying the sacrum. If the left ventricle is particularly affected by the heart disease, there is marked congestion of the vessels in the lungs, with respiratory symptoms. In heart failure, there may also be low blood sodium levels.

The pulmonary circuit (the blood vessels in the lungs) usually becomes congested in heart failure, because heart diseases most frequently affect the left ventricle in one way or another. If disease impedes the left ventricle's pumping of blood out into the systemic circulation, the left side of the heart is unable to receive the normal flow of oxygenated blood from the lungs, there is consequent back pressure, and blood accumulates in the lung's blood vessels. If this congestion of the pulmonary vessels occurs, it lessens the amount of space available in the lungs for air, and tends to stiffen the lungs. Finally, pulmonary capillary pressure may reach the point at which fluid flows into the tissues outside the vessels, a condition called pulmonary edema. These phenomena account for the frequency of difficulty in breathing, inability to breathe except in an upright position, attacks of respiratory distress without apparent cause during sleep at night (paroxysmal nocturnal dyspnea), and other respiratory symptoms in congestive heart failure.

Effect on the lungs

A person affected rarely speaks of symptoms that can be directly related to the inadequacy of cardiac output. In severe and chronic heart failure, there may be a general deterioration of the body with a form of general ill health and malnutrition that simulates that seen in cancer. There is rarely evidence that blood flow is insufficient to provide adequate tissue function except in the shock state that occurs in acute and severe heart failure, in which there is acute inadequacy of flow to some critical tissues. Although heart failure may occur in certain circumstances, such as severe anemia, in which there is a high cardiac output, in general, heart failure occurs when the cardiac output is reduced from the normal value for the particular person. The inadequacy of the heart may not be constant but may occur, especially in early heart failure, only under the stress of exercise.

Incipient heart failure. Persons in the early stages of heart failure may have no circulatory impairment, although the heart may be dilated or enlarged. Such persons may eventually be unable to respond to stressful situations that demand a high cardiac output. Difficulty in breathing may occur during exertion, but usually edema is not present.

The degrees of heart failure

Mild to moderate congestive heart failure. The person with mild to moderate congestive heart failure may have a heart that has an adequate pumping function for the demands at rest, but that is unable to meet circulatory needs under stress. Such a person may experience difficulty in breathing during exertion and other early manifestations of heart failure, and these symptoms may even be present to a limited degree at rest. In those situations affecting primarily the left ventricle, episodes of paroxysmal nocturnal dyspnea indicating temporary inadequacy of the left ventricle may be present. There may be mild edema of the ankles at the end of the day. The manifestations are not severe or grossly disabling. As the condition becomes more severe, increasing frequency of difficulty in breathing (dyspnea) and greater amounts of edema may be present.

Severe congestive heart failure. Heart failure may become totally disabling, with severe respiratory distress and inability to lie flat and to exercise. Gross edema including abnormal amounts of fluid in the abdomen (ascites) and in the chest cavity (hydrothorax) are present. When such circumstances are prolonged, general body deterioration may develop, with various secondary effects, such as appetite loss or diarrhea.

Cardiogenic shock. A degree of heart failure from mild to severe may occur after acute and severe cardiac damage, such as an acute myocardial infarction. In some instances, this condition may progress to a shock-like state, with such classic manifestations as low blood pressure, a rapid, thready (thin) pulse, and pallor, a condition known as cardiogenic shock. It may or may not be accompanied by respiratory symptoms or evidence of edema. No edema from congestion in the peripheral vessels develops if the condition is of short duration, but acute pulmonary edema may be experienced.

Pulmonary edema. Acute pulmonary edema developing in the course of heart failure may be severe, occasionally even fatal. It occurs particularly in such situations as arterial hypertension and aortic valve disease. Peripheral edema may or may not be present. This combination of events is often called left heart failure.

Right heart failure. In heart disease affecting primarily the right side of the heart, such as cor pulmonale or disease of the tricuspid valve, between the right atrium and right ventricle, the effect on respiration may be less, and there is greater evidence of edema, congestion of the liver, and high pressure in the veins. Although actually the circulation as a whole is failing, those factors that produce manifestations in the lungs are not prominent. (J.V.W.)

SURGICAL TREATMENT OF THE HEART

The heart-lung machine. The heart-lung machine serves as a temporary substitute for a patient's heart and lungs during the course of open-heart surgery. The patient's blood is pumped through it for artificial introduction of oxygen and removal of carbon dioxide. Before its first successful application to operations on the human heart in the early 1950s, all heart operations had to be done either by the sense of touch or with the heart open to view but with the patient's whole body held to a subnormal temperature (hypothermia).

The latter procedure was feasible only for very brief periods (less than ten minutes). An open-heart operation with the aid of the heart-lung machine may last for an hour or more.

The first heart-lung machine (pump oxygenator) resembled only slightly the complicated apparatus currently used for correction of cardiac defects. With this machine the blood bypasses the heart and lungs (cardiopulmonary bypass) so that the surgeon has an unobstructed view of the operative field. Cardiopulmonary bypass (Figure 1) is accomplished by use of large drainage tubes (catheters) inserted in the superior and inferior venae cavae, the large veins that return the blood from the systemic circulation to the right upper chamber of the heart. The deoxygenated blood returning to the heart from the upper and lower portions of the body enters these tubes, and by gravity drainage flows into a collecting reservoir on the heart-lung machine. Blood then flows into an oxygenator, the lung component of the machine, where it is exposed to an oxygen-containing gas mixture or oxygen alone. In this manner, oxygen is introduced into the blood and carbon dioxide is removed in sufficient quantities to make the blood leaving the oxygenator similar to that normally returning to the heart from the lungs. From the oxygenator, blood is pumped back to the body and returned to the arterial tree through a cannula (small

The oxygenator

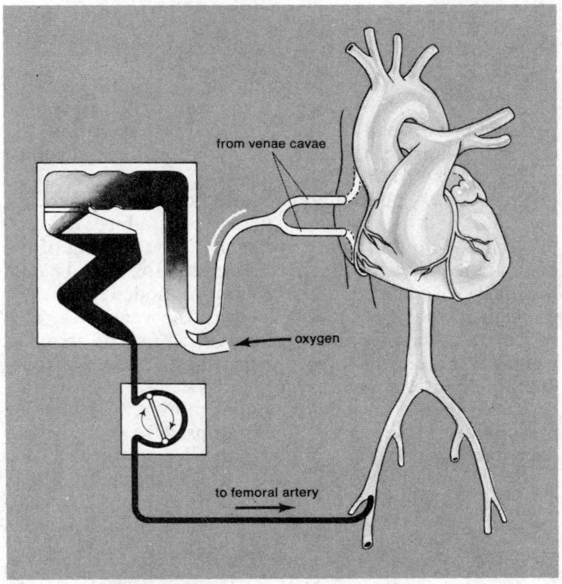

Figure 1: Cardiopulmonary bypass. At left wastes are removed from the blood and oxygen added (see text).

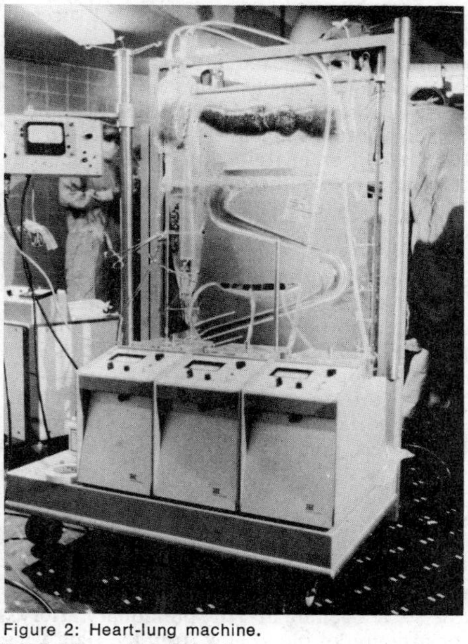

Figure 2: Heart-lung machine.
M.E. DeBakey and E.B. Diethrich

tube) introduced in a major systemic artery, such as the femoral (groin) artery. Oxygenated blood then flows to the vital organs, such as the brain, kidneys, and liver. Meanwhile, the heart may be opened and the corrective operation performed. A small quantity of blood, which may be present in the bronchial circulation, is returned to the heart-lung machine through a separate pump section.

The assemblage and sterilization of the components of the heart-lung machine are essential considerations, because the blood comes in contact with the apparatus outside of the body. Many heart-lung machines have totally disposable tubing and plastic bubble oxygenators (Figure 2), which make it possible for each patient to have new tubing and oxygenators. Even the latest models, however, have limitations on the duration of bypassing the patient's blood.

Most cardiac operations can be performed in less than one hour, but occasionally longer periods of cardiopulmonary bypass are required. In these circumstances, there is a tendency for the blood to be damaged by destruction of its red blood cells and denaturation (modification) of its proteins.

Administration of an anticoagulant (heparin) prevents clotting of the blood while it is circulating in the heart-lung machine. Upon completion of the operation, the patient is given a coagulant (protamine) so that the normal coagulation properties of the blood are restored. Researchers in the 1970s were working on development of pump-oxygenators that will provide longer periods of partial, as well as total, support of the circulation (see below *Artificial heart*).

Congenital cardiac defects. Cardiac defects are congenital (present at birth) or acquired (developing later in life). A number of congenital cardiac defects were surgically corrected long before the heart-lung machine became available.

Patent ductus arteriosus. During fetal life and the early days after birth, a channel (the ductus arteriosus) exists between the pulmonary artery and the first segment of the descending thoracic aorta. Before birth, blood flows from the right ventricle, out the pulmonary artery, and across the ductus arteriosus to the aorta. The function of this ductus is to shunt blood away from the lungs, because the process of oxygen-carbon dioxide gaseous exchange is initiated only at the time of birth. Normally, the ductus closes spontaneously within the first few weeks after birth. If it remains open, a variety of symptoms may occur, including those resulting from severe cardiac failure.

Treatment for patent ductus arteriosus is ligation (tying

off) of the ductus, an operation first performed successfully in 1938.

Coarctation of the aorta. Coarctation of the aorta, a constriction of the aorta usually found in the same region of the aorta as patent ductus arteriosus, is a common congenital defect. It often reduces the blood flow to the abdominal and pelvic organs and to the legs. The opposite effect occurs above the coarctation—the blood pressure may be greatly elevated, and symptoms of hypertension may be manifested.

In 1945 Robert E. Gross and Charles Hufnagel performed the first successful operations for coarctation of the aorta in the United States. In most infants and adolescents the constricted portion of the aorta is cut out and the two normal ends are sewed together. In adults it is often necessary to bridge the defect with a Dacron graft or to use a bypass graft. In the latter case, a Dacron tube is attached to the aorta above and below the narrowed segment. The blood is, thus, able to bypass the defect to reach the organs below the defect and the lower limbs. Both of these techniques restore satisfactory blood supply to structures in the lower part of the body and relieve the high blood pressure in the arms.

Pulmonary valvular stenosis. The most common congenital defect of the valves is a narrowing of the pulmonary valve (the valve opening into the pulmonary artery), resulting in obstruction of blood flow from the right ventricle to the lungs. In this condition, the valve leaflets, usually pliable and delicate, are fused in a conelike fashion. Blood is expelled from the right ventricle across the narrow valve with great force, so that often the pulmonary artery beyond the diseased valve is dilated. Shortness of breath on exertion is the most common symptom in those affected. The original surgical treatment consisted in inserting a special dilating instrument through the apex of the right ventricle and through the valve. Today, except in very young infants with severe heart failure, the valvular stricture is corrected under direct vision with use of the heart-lung machine.

Effects of stenosis of the pulmonary valve

Atrial and ventricular septal defects. "Holes in the heart," or abnormal openings between the right and left chambers of the heart, are common congenital cardiac anomalies. The upper chambers of the heart (the atria) are separated by a partition called the interatrial septum, and the lower chambers (the ventricles) by the interventricular septum. During embryonic development the tissues of the heart normally fuse to form intact membranes (septa) between these chambers, so that blood is directed from the right atrium and ventricle through the pulmonary circulation to the left atrium and ventricle and out the aorta into the systemic circulation. Failure of the tissues to form complete septa results in an opening between the chambers that permits the abnormal mixing of blood from the right and left sides of the heart. This admixture of blood can cause cyanosis, which is typical when the pressure in the right side of the heart exceeds the pressure in the left side (see below *Tetralogy of Fallot*).

Interatrial and interventricular septal defects may be closed surgically with the patient's circulation supported by the heart-lung machine. If the defect is small, the tissues on either side of it can be sewed together. A patch of Dacron material must be sutured over larger defects to close the opening and redirect the flow of blood in the normal direction.

Tetralogy of Fallot. Of the congenital cardiac anomalies that cause cyanosis, the tetralogy of Fallot, described earlier, is the most common. The first attempt to treat children affected with it was an operation to relieve cyanosis introduced in 1945. This procedure made it possible for many critically ill infants to live to an age when the heart-lung machine could be used, and the complex defects could be surgically repaired under direct vision. The results of surgical treatment of patients with tetralogy of Fallot have been excellent. The operation represents an important chapter in the history of surgical correction of congenital cardiac anomalies.

Acquired heart defects. *Valvular disease.* Among the diseases that can affect the heart after birth, rheumatic fever is one of the most serious. It has a predilection for the two major valves of the heart, the aortic and mitral. Although the bacteria responsible for rheumatic fever invade the blood stream and attack these valves during childhood or adolescence, the destructive effects are usually not apparent until young adulthood or even later in life. Normal function of the aortic and mitral valves may be altered because they are too tight (stenotic) or too loose (insufficient). In the stenotic valve, the flow of blood past the valve is obstructed; the result is increased pressures and damage to the heart. When the valve is insufficient, leakage of blood back into the ventricles places increased stress on the heart with resultant cardiac failure.

Destroyed heart valves can be replaced with artificial valves (prostheses) made of stainless steel, Dacron, or other special materials (Figure 3). The heart-lung machine is used during these operations, in which one, two, or even three cardiac valves may be removed and replaced with the appropriate artificial valve. In the 1970s cardiac researchers were investigating the use of some substitute for the heart valve other than the artificial valve. The use of both homograft valves (valves obtained from human beings after death) and heterograft valves (valves secured from other animals) was being investigated. One of the advantages of such valves is the absence of clotting, which occurs occasionally with use of artificial valves. The long-term durability of the homograft and heterograft valves, however, had not yet been determined.

M.E. DeBakey and E.B. Diethrich

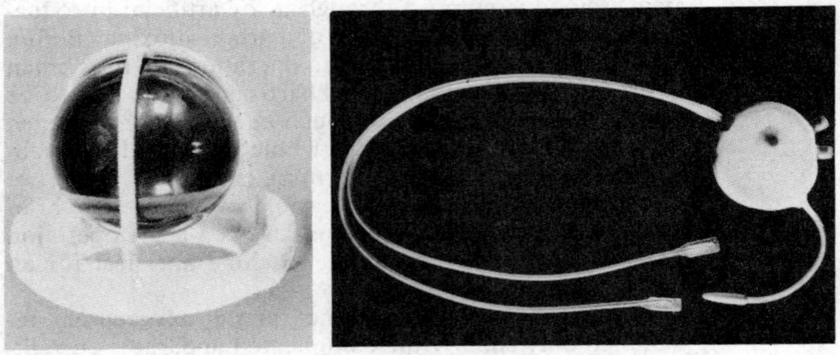

Figure 3: *Implanted devices.*
(Left) Artificial heart valve replaces destroyed natural valve.
(Right) Pacemaker stimulates regular heart beat.

Substitutes for damaged valves

Chronic constrictive pericarditis. Another inflammatory process, chronic constrictive pericarditis, can affect the surface of the heart and the sac (pericardium) surrounding it. The pericardium becomes thickened and fibrotic, and over a period of time constricts the heart so that the normal filling of the ventricles during the resting phase of the cardiac cycle is limited. This condition in turn reduces the output of the heart and eventually affects all the organ systems, including the brain, liver, and kidneys. Treatment is surgical removal of the thickened pericardium around the heart, which permits normal filling and expansion of the ventricles and restores adequate cardiac output to the vital organs.

Heart block. A common acquired disease of the heart, the cause of which is poorly understood, affects the conduction system that controls the rhythmic beating of the heart. Normally, the electrical stimulus for each beat of the heart originates in the sinoatrial node and passes through special conduction fibres to the ventricles. This process accounts for the regular cardiac rate of about 72 beats per minute in most persons. If the electrical conduction is interrupted, heart block occurs, and the rate is slowed to as low as 30 beats per minute, and in some persons until the heart actually stops. Use of a cardiac pacemaker artificially stimulates the heart to beat at any predetermined rate and, thus, corrects the heart block. Two types of implantable pacemakers are used for treatment of permanent heart block. In one model, electrodes are attached to the surface of the heart and the battery is buried beneath the soft tissues of the abdominal wall (Figure 3). In the other model, electrodes are passed through a vein in the neck directly into the heart, and a

Two types of pacemakers

battery is implanted beneath the skin of the armpit or the forward chest wall. Several types of battery units (pulse generators) are available, depending on the type of electrical stimulus desired for the individual patient. These batteries, like any other, must be changed periodically.

Heart arrest. Cessation of the heart beat, in addition to occurring in heart block, may occur in numerous other circumstances and require emergency treatment. Until the early 1960s, when the heart stopped (cardiac arrest) the chest was opened, frequently with a pen knife or any other available instrument, and the heart was massaged with the hands until beating was resumed. A new technique (closed cardiac massage) has been developed whereby pressure is applied to the breastbone (sternum) directly over the heart. The sternum is compressed intermittently about 60 times a minute while the lungs are expanded with oxygen. Persons may be kept alive with normal blood pressure and circulation for hours by this method. So effective is closed cardiac massage that many laymen are trained in its use for emergency support of the circulation.

Heart wounds. Heart wounds are caused by blunt or penetrating instruments. Rapid deceleration, often experienced in automobile accidents, is a common cause of injury to the heart muscle, resulting in bruising and even disruption of a valve or the ventricular septum. Both bullet and stab wounds account for many patients treated in the emergency clinics of major hospitals. Prompt diagnosis and effective surgical treatment, usually consisting of control of bleeding by sewing the heart muscle at the point of entry of the foreign object, have resulted in a high rate of successful treatment of these persons.

Coronary arterial disease. The most important acquired disease of the heart is hardening (atherosclerosis) of the coronary arteries. More than 600,000 persons in the United States die each year of this disease, and countless others suffer from one or more of its complications. The basic problem in coronary atherosclerosis is narrowing of one or more of the coronary arteries, which reduces the blood flow to the heart muscle and produces severe pain in the chest (angina pectoris). If the blood supply is reduced below a critical level, the artery may become blocked by a blood clot (coronary thrombosis) and the person has a heart attack (myocardial infarction).

Provision of new blood supply to the heart

Operations have been devised to bring a new blood supply into the heart when the coronary arteries become narrowed by atherosclerosis. One of the earliest and still occasionally performed operations is myocardial revascularization. In this operation, an artery beneath the breastbone (sternum) is dissected free and then is implanted into the heart muscle. One or more of these arteries can be implanted, depending on the extent of arterial disease.

Another technique is to use a vein removed from the leg as a bypass around the diseased portion (Figure 4). The vein is attached to the aorta above as it leaves the left ventricle. The other end of the vein is then sutured directly to any one of the coronary arteries. Large quantities of blood can be delivered to the heart muscle by this direct form of myocardial revascularization.

The latest advance in coronary arterial surgery is the carbon dioxide endarterectomy operation. Carbon dioxide, which in the bloodstream is readily absorbed and does not cause blockage of the small vessels, is injected directly into the obstructed coronary artery. The gas tends to loosen the inner atheromatous core from the outer adventitial wall of the artery. The atheromatous core is then totally removed, and blood flow is restored through the artery. The heart-lung machine is used to support the circulation during most operations on the coronary arteries.

Heart transplantation. If the heart muscle has been damaged beyond surgical repair, heart transplantation may be performed. The diseased heart is removed and the donor's heart is sewed in position. More than 173 human heart transplantations have been performed since the initial operation in Cape Town, South Africa, December 3, 1967. Several patients have lived more than three

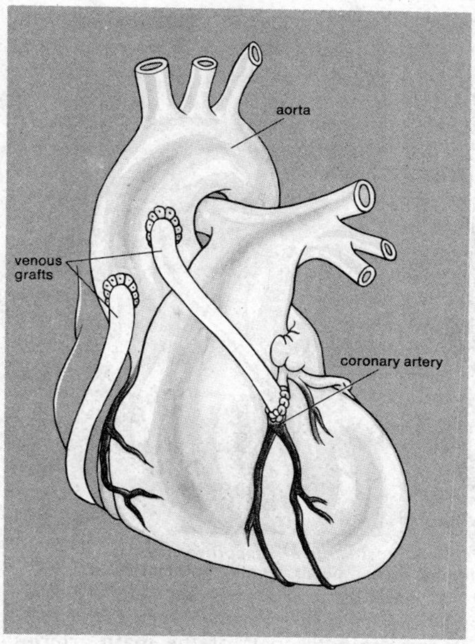

Figure 4: Restoration of blood supply to heart muscle. The vessels shown in white are venous grafts leading from the aorta to coronary vessels (see text).

years after heart transplantation. It is hoped that results will improve as more is learned about tissue matching and recognition and control of tissue rejection.

Artificial heart. Many scientists are directing their efforts toward development of an artificial heart. The heart-lung machine effectively supports the circulation for a few hours; if it is used for longer periods, the blood is damaged by the pumping and oxygenation. Current research is directed toward development of pumps and oxygenators that can be used for partial or total support of the circulation for long periods without damage to the blood.

Partial cardiac assistors have been used successfully to aid the heart after operation until it has had sufficient time to recover. One of these is the left ventricular bypass pump (Figure 5). It reduces the work load of the heart, because blood is removed from the left atrium of the heart and pumped back to the body through the axillary artery. No oxygenator is required, because the lungs are not bypassed.

A totally implantable mechanical heart is the ultimate goal of scientists working on the artificial heart, but many problems must be solved before a completely satisfactory mechanical heart becomes available. One of the newest experimental models (Figure 5) replaces both the atria and ventricles but requires external power to activate the pump. Ultimately, both the pumping chamber and the driving mechanism will be implanted within the body to enable the patient to move about freely and carry on normal activities. (M.E.DeB./E.B.D.)

The blood vessels

DISEASES OF THE ARTERIES

There are many types of arterial disease. Some are generalized and affect arteries through the body, although often there is variation in the degree they are affected. Others are localized. These diseases are frequently divided into those that result in arterial occlusion (blockage) and those that are nonocclusive in their manifestations.

Occlusive disease. *Arteriosclerosis.* The various types of arteriosclerosis are by far the most common occlusive diseases of the arterial system. It is a major cause of death in one form or another. Arteriosclerosis of the coronary arteries has already been discussed. Arteriosclerotic lesions of the cerebral vessels may lead to formation of blood clots and stroke.

Medial (Mönckeberg's) arteriosclerosis is the condition

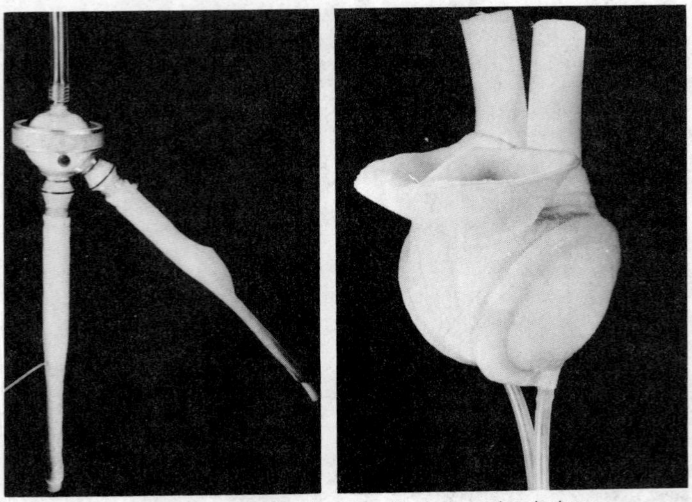

Figure 5: *Surgical and post-surgical supportive devices.* (Left) Left ventricular bypass pump. (Right) Artificial heart.
M.E. DeBakey and E.B Diethrich

affecting the media (middle coat) of the main arteries. There are deposits of calcium salts in the media, but in general the channel (lumen) is not blocked. This disease is quite common and may contribute to the other major form of widespread arteriosclerosis, atherosclerosis obliterans, in which there is complete obliteration of the vessel channel.

Intermittent claudication

The classic manifestation of arteriosclerosis affecting the legs is called intermittent claudication (intermittent lameness), which results from inadequate blood flow to the muscles involved in walking. In such individuals a cramplike discomfort associated with a limp occurs in the calf of the leg on exercise and is relieved by rest. The vascular disease may lead to changes in the extremities caused by reduced blood supply. These may be manifest as ulcerated areas and eventually gangrene, and most frequently involve the lower extremities. The lack of adequate blood flow renders the extremities susceptible to infection, and, therefore, the manifestations of reduced blood supply (ischemia) are frequently combined with those of infection. There is no specific therapy available.

Thromboangiitis obliterans (Buerger's disease). Thromboangiitis obliterans is a disease of an inflammatory nature, poorly understood, which involves the arteries of the extremities, although other vessels, including those of the heart, may be involved. It is thought to be a disease of hypersensitivity, and the persons who are afflicted with it are often heavy cigarette smokers. It almost exclusively affects men of any race between the ages of 17 and 45 years. The symptoms are similar to those of arteriosclerosis of the peripheral vessels, with intermittent claudication, later pain during periods of rest, and eventually gangrene. An inflammation of the veins, phlebitis, occurs in almost 50 percent of those affected.

Polyarteritis nodosa. Polyarteritis nodosa, also called periarteritis nodosa and essential polyangiitis, is an uncommon disease of unknown cause; hypersensitivity may play an important role. It is more common in males and may occur at any age. Small arteries and veins in various parts of the body are affected, producing effects as a result of occlusion or bleeding or a combination of the two. The course may be rapid, involving only weeks or months, or it may be highly prolonged. The involvement of the blood vessels may affect blood flow to the skin, the gastrointestinal tract, the kidneys, and the heart. There are associated symptoms of arthritis, and involvement of almost all organs has been noted. There is an associated fever in most instances, an increase in the number of leukocytes in the blood, and evidence of inflammation. No recognized specific mode of therapy is available.

Effects of polyarteritis nodosa

Arteritis. Arteritis is an inflammation in localized segments of arteries. One particularly notable type is cranial arteritis (temporal arteritis), a disease of variable duration and unknown cause that is accompanied by fever and involves the temporal and occasionally other arteries of the skull. In general, older persons are affected. Excision of the involved artery may be carried out, but the general symptoms may remain.

Ergotism. Ergotism results from the excessive ingestion of ergot (a fungus that grows on rye and other cereals), and its derivatives. There is evidence of lack of blood flow and eventual gangrene in the small peripheral arteries, particularly in the legs, the nose, and the ears. Treatment includes use of measures to improve the circulation.

Hypertensive vascular disease. Severe arterial hypertension may result in a variety of lesions in the arteries of affected persons. It is a contributing factor to the development of the arterial diseases already described and to cerebral arterial disease in particular. The small arteries of the kidney may be involved, leading to kidney failure. In addition, a variety of lesions may occur in small arteries throughout the body. Measures that may be used to combat hypertension include administration of antihypertensive drugs and restriction of dietary sodium chloride.

Arterial thrombosis. Arterial thrombosis, the formation of blood clots in arteries, may occur in either a normal or a diseased vessel. More frequently, however, it is related to injury, either by physical means or by X-rays or local infection. Such alterations in the blood as an abnormally high level of red blood cells may predispose to thrombosis, and any situation such as heart failure or local vessel disease may be a predisposing factor because of the diminished blood flow. The clots may be removed by surgery or a channel may open through them while the patient is under therapy with anticoagulant drugs. The clots may, however, lead to gangrene and necessitate amputation of an extremity.

Frostbite. Frostbite may occur after exposure to subfreezing temperature momentarily or to less severe temperature for a longer period. It occurs more readily if blood vessels are diseased. Several degrees of frostbite produce thrombosis of the arteries and arterioles and also may involve veins. Symptoms may vary from a mild stage of reddening to gangrene and eventual loss of the extremity.

Types of embolus

Arterial embolism. An embolus, a foreign or abnormal particle circulating in the blood, may block a vessel too small to permit further passage. The sources of emboli include blood clots from the chambers of the diseased or abnormally functioning heart. Fat emboli may occur after fracture of bones and discharge of fatty marrow. Air emboli may be suspected after major injury, especially when large veins are opened during accidents or during vascular surgery of the neck or chest cavity. Bacterial emboli occur in bacterial endocarditis and occasionally in other infections. Cancers may produce minute emboli of tumour cells. Fungus growth or foreign materials, such as fragments of bullets, may become emboli. These emboli may cause transient local symptoms from diminished blood flow and may result in death of tissue. Treatment may include anticoagulant therapy and surgical removal of the clot.

Nonocclusive disease. *Aneurysm and dissecting aneurysm.* Certain disease processes, notably arteriosclerosis and syphilis, may cause damage to the wall of the aorta and large vessels so that they become dilated and, at times, form large bulges (aneurysms). These may produce pain and disturbances to blood flow in tributary vessels; they may rupture, leading to fatal internal bleeding. Treatment is surgical removal of the defective section of the artery and its replacement with a fabric tube. In general, syphilitic involvement occurs predominantly in the thoracic (chest part of the) aorta, whereas arteriosclerotic involvement is more likely to occur in the abdominal part of the aorta and in peripheral vessels. A smaller, more localized form of aneurysm may occur at the site of bacterial infections in the vessel wall. Dissecting aneurysms occur as the result of deterioration of the medial layer of the large vessels, primarily the aorta. A splitting of the arterial wall caused by a rupture of the lining (intima)

Dissecting aneurysm

and escape of blood under high pressure into the middle layer (media) in the presence of arterial high blood pressure causes sudden enlargement of the vessel. Such dissection often causes obstruction to blood flow, particularly to the tributaries of the aorta, and may lead to secondary lethal hemorrhage from the vessel into the chest or other body cavities. The aortic valve is at times involved in such a lesion, or there may be hemorrhage into the pericardial cavity, causing compression of the heart (pericardial tamponade). When there is a dissecting aneurysm, drugs may be given to lower arterial pressure and ultimately lessen the stresses on the arterial wall, or surgery may be resorted to.

Arteriovenous fistula. A penetrating injury such as that caused by a bullet or a sharp instrument may result in an opening between an artery and its immediately adjacent vein (an arteriovenous fistula). Large amounts of blood may be shunted from the artery to the vein. Arteriovenous fistulas are particularly common in war time as a result of shell fragments and other types of injury involving the arms and legs. They may also occur as a complication of surgery. Others are congenital in origin. The physician may hear a loud murmur caused by the turbulent flow of blood from the artery to the vein. Enlargement of the heart and all of the manifestations of congestive heart failure may occur if the amount of blood shunted is large. In the area around the site of the arteriovenous fistula, the blood vessels become dilated and bacterial infection of the artery lining may develop. A cure can usually be achieved by surgery, although in some situations the remaining arterial flow may be impaired. A special kind of arteriovenous fistula occurs from the pulmonary artery to the pulmonary vein. Here the situation is complicated by the fact that unoxygenated venous blood is being shunted into a vessel normally containing oxygenated blood. Cyanosis results, and produces a stimulation for formation of red blood cells, leading to a form of secondary polycythemia, abnormally high red-blood-cell level. Arteriovenous fistulas are treated by surgery.

Physical injuries. Physical injuries to arteries may lead to damage of the vascular wall, with consequent formation of blood clots and blockage. On other occasions, a form of inflammation may develop that may lead to rupture and may be the source of emboli in the peripheral arteries. Sudden disastrous external stress such as in severe automobile accidents, airplane crashes, and underwater explosions may cause death through rupture of the major arteries, such as the aorta, rupture of the heart valves, or rupture of the heart itself.

Radiation injuries. X-ray, radium, and other radioactive substances in large dosages have marked effects on the vascular system. Initial reactions are inflammatory, and secondary changes caused by scarring and retractions may occur, which in turn lead to vascular occlusion (obstruction). The effects may be progressive for a period of years and are, at times, complicated by the development of cancer.

Raynaud's phenomenon and Raynaud's disease

Functional disease. *Vasoconstriction.* Raynaud's phenomenon is said to occur when the extremities, including occasionally even the ears, nose, or cheeks, become pale, cyanotic, and numb under the influence of cold or emotion. Pain is also present at times. On cessation of the stimulus redness develops and there is a tingling or burning sensation lasting some minutes. This sequence of events is apparently caused by the excessive constriction of the small arteries and arterioles of the fingers upon stimuli that ordinarily cause only a minor degree of vasoconstriction (constriction of blood vessels). Raynaud's disease, which is initially manifested by this phenomenon, is a disease in which there is spasmodic contraction of the blood vessels, usually beginning in early adulthood and affecting women about three times as often as men. The limb involvement is usually symmetrical (on both sides), and may lead to gangrene. Attacks may subside after return to a warm environment or release from tension.

The symptoms associated with Raynaud's disease may occur in people without other evidence of organic disease, especially in cold and moist climates. It may result from the operation of pneumatic hammers, or may occur in individuals with various disorders such as a cervical rib, a supernumerary (extra useless) rib arising from a neck vertebra. It may appear as a complication of arteriosclerosis, thromboangiitis obliterans, and syphilitic aortitis. Various substances, such as nicotine, arsenic, ergot, and lead, have occasionally been blamed. Therapy includes treatment of the primary condition and avoidance of the precipitating cause.

Acrocyanosis is a similar condition, characterized by episodes of coldness and cyanosis of the hands and feet. It is often associated with profuse sweating and, at times, with local edema. It is a form of local sensitivity to cold, and is frequently seen in mentally or emotionally disturbed people or in those with neurocirculatory asthenia (a symptom-complex in which there is breathlessness, giddiness, and a sense of fatigue, pain in the chest over the heart, and palpitation, a fast and forcible heart beat of which the affected person is conscious). Reassurance and avoidance of cold help to eliminate attacks.

Cause and relief of erythermalgia

Vasodilation. Erythermalgia (erythromelalgia) is an uncommon condition in which the extremities, especially the palms of the hands and the soles of the feet, are red, hot, painful, and often somewhat swollen. Dilation of the blood vessels (vasodilation) is the underlying factor. The condition is relieved by elevation of the extremity and cooling. Usually it occurs in middle and later life and is chronic in the primary form; it may occur as a secondary manifestation of underlying vascular disease. It may also occur as a manifestation of an abnormally high red-blood-cell level and, occasionally, as the result of injury or a variety of other disorders.

DISEASES OF THE VEINS

Organic disease. In thrombophlebitis there is thrombosis (clot formation) in the veins and a variable amount of inflammatory reaction in the vessel wall. In some instances, the inflammatory reaction is predominant and thrombosis is secondary. In other instances, thrombosis appears before reaction in the vein wall. Embolization—breaking loose of a blood clot—is most likely to occur during this period, although it may occur at any stage of the disease. A form of the disease in which little or no inflammatory reaction or pain develops is called phlebothrombosis. Thrombophlebitis most frequently involves the veins of the legs. It may occur without apparent cause and tends to recur. At times, it occurs as a result of local injury, either from a penetrating wound or from an external blow without a break in the skin. It may occur as a result of severe muscular effort or strain and in the course of infectious diseases, thromboangiitis obliterans, and a wide range of underlying diseases. Thrombophlebitis may develop in various parts of the body if there is cancer, especially cancer of the pancreas. The presence of varicose veins (see below) in the legs causes a tendency to the development of thrombophlebitis. Treatment includes bed rest and anticoagulant therapy.

Pulmonary embolism may occur in bedridden persons as a result of a clot from a thrombophlebitic lesion, or it may occur in an apparently healthy individual. If the embolus is small, it may not have any effect on the systemic circulation. With larger pulmonary emboli, there may be massive bleeding from the lungs and the development of a large area of pulmonary infarction, resulting in sudden death. Getting up and walking soon after an operation or after congestive heart failure is the best method for avoiding pulmonary embolism. Anticoagulant therapy is useful both as prevention and as therapy after the condition has developed. Surgical removal of a massive pulmonary clot has, on rare occasions, been spectacularly successful.

Varicose veins

Varicose veins are permanently tortuous (twisted) and enlarged. The medium and large veins, especially in the legs, are most likely to be affected. The condition may occur without obvious cause or as a result of postural changes, occupation, congenital anomaly, or localized causes of increased venous pressure. The veins may be near the surface and easily seen or they may be hidden and unrecognized. Without complication, they rarely cause symptoms, but they may become the site of thrombophlebitis with inflammatory changes and the production of emboli in the peripheral circulation. The veins may rupture on occasion, with bleeding into the surrounding tissues. Varicose veins may occur around the rectum and anus, producing hemorrhoids. If they occur within the scrotal sac in the region of the testes, they are called varicocele. In all forms of varicose veins, the walls of the veins become hardened, and a certain amount of inflammation develops through the years. Dilated veins in the legs may be supported by appropriate elastic-type stockings or bandages, or they may be treated by surgery.

Functional disease. Direct mechanical injury or an infection or other disease process in the neighbouring tissues may produce spasms in the veins (venospasms). Local venospasm is usually of relatively minor significance because of the adequacy of alternate pathways for the blood. If venospasm is widespread, however, involving an entire extremity, or the veins in the lungs, it may impair blood flow and therefore be of greater significance.

DISEASES OF THE CAPILLARIES

The capillaries are the smallest blood vessels. Through their thin walls oxygen and nutrients pass to the tissue cells, in exchange for carbon dioxide and other products of cellular activity. Despite the small size and thin walls of the capillaries, the blood pressures may be quite high as, for instance, in the legs of a person in a motionless, upright position. In certain disease states, there is increased fragility of the capillary wall, with resultant hemorrhages into the tissues. These hemorrhages are referred to as petechiae when small or, if large, may become a large area of discoloration of the skin. Vitamin C deficiency and a variety of blood disorders may be associated with increased capillary fragility. Small petechial hemorrhages occur in bacterial endocarditis and certain other infectious processes. In some instances, petechiae are caused by minute emboli; in others, they appear to be directly related to capillary fragility itself. Treatment is of the underlying disorder.

Capillary fragility

The capillaries are freely permeable to water and small molecules but ordinarily are not highly permeable to proteins and other materials. In some pathologic situations, such as in certain allergic states (*e.g.*, hives) or because of local injury as in burns, there may be local areas of permeability, with escape of fluid high in protein into the surrounding tissues. If the disease affects the entire body, a significant amount of plasma (the blood minus its cells) leaks into the nonvascular spaces, with resultant loss in blood volume. Again, treatment is of the underlying disorder.

HEMODYNAMIC DISORDERS

Hypertension. Hypertension has been discussed in the sections on hypertensive heart disease and on hypertensive vascular disease.

Hypotension. Moderate hypotension (low blood pressure) may occur in persons who are weak and enfeebled, but more often does not represent a diseased state. Indeed, life insurance figures demonstrate that the life expectancy of people with such a condition is greater than average. Hypotension of a severe degree may develop in heart failure, after hemorrhage, in overwhelming infections, and in a variety of circumstances that lead to the development of the clinical picture of shock. In shock, the circulation is inadequate, blood pressure is low, heart rate is rapid, and irreversible tissue damage from insufficient blood supply may occur if the condition is not terminated. (For a discussion of the treatment of shock, see SHOCK, PHYSIOLOGICAL.) Transient hypotension may occur as a normal reaction in certain forms of syncope (see below), but is not necessarily associated with organic disease.

Syncope. Syncope is the sudden loss of consciousness associated with a transient disorganization of circulatory function, as differentiated from other brief losses of consciousness associated with abnormal central nervous system activities, as in certain forms of epilepsy. Syncope may be related to a transient cessation of circulatory activity as in the Adams-Stokes attacks described earlier. Other forms of syncope occur as a result of lowered blood pressure upon assumption of an upright position, a condition often called orthostatic hypotension. In some individuals, disease of the autonomic nervous system prevents appropriate postural adjustments for the upright stance. The disorder may be caused by vascular or central nervous system involvement of the autonomic system. In other instances, postural hypotension may occur as a result of inadequate blood volume, of taking various drugs that affect the nervous control of the circulation, and from a wide variety of other causes. Transient hypotension also may result from hypersensitivity of the carotid sinus. The most common kind of syncope is ordinary fainting. Some individuals are more susceptible than others. Blood loss, exhaustion, the presence of other illness, and psychologic factors may contribute to a tendency to faint. An affected person is usually in the upright position, becomes weak, pale, and sweaty, and may have nausea. The heart rate at this time is usually relatively rapid, but with the abrupt onset of syncope, the heart rate falls often to below the normal level and the person collapses as if he were dead. There is usually a rapid recovery without complications. (J.V.W.)

BIBLIOGRAPHY. The standard English texts of cardiology are: C.K. FRIEDBERG, *Diseases of the Heart*, 3rd ed. (1966); P.H. WOOD, *Diseases of the Heart and Circulation*, 3rd ed. rev. (1968); and J.W. HURST and R.B. LOGUE, *The Heart, Arteries, and Veins*, 2nd ed. (1970). A.L. BLAKESLEE and J. STAMLER, *Your Heart Has Nine Lives: Nine Steps to Heart Health* (1963), is a popular account of the so-called risk factors in coronary artery disease. See also F.A. WILLIUS and T.J. DRY, *A History of the Heart and Circulation* (1948); and G.E. BURCH and T. WINSOR, *A Primer of Electrocardiography*, 5th ed. (1966), a relatively nontechnical volume.

Other recommended works include: R.A. KILDUFFE and M.E. DEBAKEY, *The Blood Bank and the Technique and Therapeutics of Transfusions* (1942); G.W. BEEBE and M.E. DEBAKEY, *Battle Casualties* (1952); D.C. ELKIN and M.E. DEBAKEY (eds.), *Vascular Surgery in World War II* (1955); *Christopher's Minor Surgery*, 8th ed. by A. OCHSNER and M.E. DEBAKEY (1959); M.E. DEBAKEY and B.M. COHEN, *Buerger's Disease: A Follow-Up Study of World War II Army Cases* (1963); and the annual publication *Year Book of Surgery*.

(J.V.W./M.E.DeB./E.B.D.)

Cards and Card Games

For centuries one of man's principal social and intellectual diversions, cards and card games, fit every degree of skill, from the simplest children's games to advanced games requiring inferential reasoning of a high order, psychology, and speculation. Card games remain popular despite the proliferation of other forms of entertainment, and cards are also used for education, divination, and conjuring.

In most games the cards are dealt out face downward and are subsequently played with the object of capturing other cards or acquiring varying combinations of cards, according to the game being played. Modern cards are divided into four suits—spades, hearts, diamonds, and clubs—with 13 cards in each suit. The set of 52 cards together is known variously as the pack or the deck, the term used in Shakespeare's day. Two jokers, bearing the image of a medieval court jester, are usually included with the standard 52-card deck, although they are not always used in play. Millions of decks are sold annually throughout the world.

This article first traces the history of cards, then studies the general principles of different kinds of games. A brief guide to the vast literature on the subject is included. For more information on specific games, see BRIDGE; CRIBBAGE; POKER; and RUMMY GAMES; see also RELATED ENTRIES under CARDS AND CARD GAMES in the *Ready Reference and Index*.

PLAYING CARDS

Origins. Though where and when cards originated is uncertain, China seems the most likely place, and the 7th

Two round ivory cards, the *avatāra* (top) and ten of Paraśurāma, painted in miniature technique. Probably from Deccan, India, 18th century.

By courtesy of the Deutsches Spielkarten Museum, Bielefeld, Germany

to the 10th century the earliest probable time. An Indian origin has been suggested by the resemblance of symbols on some early European decks to the ring, sword, cup, and baton classically depicted in the four hands of Hindu statues. Yet another theory is that both cards and chess are derived from ancient divinatory procedures used by primitive peoples.

Nor is it known how cards were introduced to Europe. Some early decks had symbols resembling the Chinese markings and may have been taken back by a Venetian, possibly Niccolò Polo or his more famous son Marco, during travels to and from China in the latter half of the 13th century. Another speculation is that cards may have been brought from Arabia by the Gypsies, but the Gypsies did not reach western Europe in appreciable numbers until after cards had become firmly established. If an Arab origin is to be sought, the Saracen invasion of Sicily or the Moorish conquest of Spain could provide a link. The Spanish word for cards, which is *naipes*, and an earlier Italian word, which is *naibi*, are probably of Arab origin.

Cards in Europe

There are references to cards in Italy from 1299, in Spain, from as early as 1371, the Low Countries, from 1379, and in Germany from 1380. A French manuscript of the early 14th century contains a reference to cards, and in 1392 the registers of the Chambre des Comptes of Charles VI recorded the purchase of three games of cards "in gold and diverse colours." In England by 1465 the use of cards was well enough established for manufacturers to petition for protection against imports.

Cards may have first reached America with Columbus; they became firmly established with the arrival of the English, French, and Dutch colonists; after which they gradually became known and were played throughout the world.

Among many notable collections of historic playing cards are those of the British Museum; that of the United States Playing Card Company, presented to the Cincinnati Art Museum; as well as that of the Morgan Library, New York; and that of the Bibliothèque Nationale, Paris.

The Tarot deck. One type of deck appears to be indigenous to Italy—the Tarot or picture cards, as distinct from the number cards of the East. Called *attutti* ("trumps") or *naibes* and numbered consecutively from 1 to 21, they allegorically represent material forces, virtues, and vices, with the addition of a card unnumbered or numbered 0 or 22, the Fool—precursor of the modern joker. It is probable that the Venetians were the first to add 56 numeral cards to the Tarot deck, thus producing the 78-card deck still used in some parts of the world.

In comparison to the Tarot deck, the numeral cards were divided into four suits (cups, coins, swords, and cudgels), each containing a king, queen, knight, page or valet, along with cards numbered from 1 to 10.

The 22 Tarots could be used for fortune-telling and simple games, the full deck for the earliest form of a game called Tarocchi (German Tarok, French Tarot) that is still played in central Europe. The full deck, too, was and still is used for fortune-telling, for which it provides more scope than other decks. When so used, the Tarots are known as the greater or major arcana, and the 56 suit cards as the lesser or minor arcana, since in interpretation the Tarots exercise a controlling influence over the suit cards. Each suit is attributed with an overall character and each card with a more specific meaning. Thus, hearts may represent the aristocracy, ecclesiastics, and politicians, also pleasure and happy marriage, whereas the seven of hearts may indicate broken promises, disappointment, and betrayal. The Tarots themselves, after many changes, now show pictures of various conventionalized personages and objects to which are attached meanings. For example, the Fool represents Everyman on the path of life, which is folly. In telling a fortune, the cards are interpreted according to the meanings assigned to them, modified by the combination of one card with others, when drawn or dealt, and by the seer's assessment of the client.

Fortune telling with cards

The French scholar Count de Gébelin in *Le Jeu des Tarots* (1781) attempted to trace Tarot cards to an Egyptian origin embodying an ancient philosophical system. His work inspired a Parisian wigmaker named Alliette, who redesigned the old Tarot cards described

By courtesy of (left) the Deutsches Spielkarten Museum, Bielefeld, Germany, (right) the Victoria and Albert Museum, London; photograph, C.H. Cannings

(Left) Tarot XVI from a Marseilles pack of 1750. Lightning is shattering the battlements of the tower, tumbling a man and woman to earth. (Right) Tarot card showing death wearing a cardinal's hat and mantelletta. Attributed to Antonio Cicognara, *c.* 1500.

by the Count and enjoyed enormous success at court with his divinations. In the 1970s Tarot decks were being used in about 60 countries, their revival attributable in part to renewed interest in the occult and in Eastern philosophies, especially among the young.

Development of modern cards. The 52-card French deck, now standard throughout the world, evolved from the numbered cards of the Tarot deck. The deck, in usual descending order of rank, consists of an ace, king, queen, jack (formerly knave), and nine numerals (10 to 2) in each of four suits. A German deck of 32 cards and a Spanish deck of 40 also evolved, but modern games requiring a short deck are usually played by removing cards from a standard deck.

Suits

The suits had different names and often different symbols in the various countries. The English adopted the French symbols but gave them different names; the French (*pique*, "pike") looked like a spade to the English; the French (*carreau*, "square") became the English diamond, and the French (*trèfle*, "trefoil") became the English club. The traditional suit designations are shown in the Table. The spread of games such as Whist and Piquet, and later Contract Bridge, made the 52-card deck current among card players throughout the world.

Traditional Suit Designations

English	French	German	Spanish	Italian
spade	pique	Grün ("leaf")	espada	spada ("sword")
heart	coeur	Herz	copa ("cup")	coppa ("cup")
diamond	carreau	Schelle ("bell")	oro ("gold")	denaro ("money")
club	trefle	Eichel ("acorn")	basto	bastone ("rod")

Card manufacture. The making of cards has been closely linked with the development of printing. The earliest cards were hand-painted, but it would appear that German production in the 15th century almost certainly was so large as to mean that wood-block printing must have been employed. German cardmakers may, in fact, have been the first wood-block engravers in Europe.

The great diversity of early decks gradually lessened, influenced by 15th century French exporters, whose simple designs became widely popular. Modern variations of those designs may be found primarily in the design of the court cards (kings, queen, and jacks); those in English decks for instance, show figures dressed in the style of Henry VII. The traditional superstition of gamblers and the more modern tendency to preserve fragments of the past have tended to prevent change, including official attempts in some countries to provide proletarian substitutes for the court cards.

Manufacture of cards

Cards were manufactured by laborious methods until 1832, when Thomas de la Rue was granted letters patent by William IV of England for production by typographical processes. The standard modern card measures about 2½ × 3½ inches (6 × 9 centimetres) and is double-headed to aid recognition, with indices at two opposite corners. The backs are printed with identical designs or pictures and frequently are used for advertising.

A full deck, including two jokers, is printed on pasteboard consisting of two sheets gummed together with black paste to ensure opaqueness. The spades and clubs normally are printed in black, the hearts and diamonds in red. Each card is stamped out with a die and simultaneously given a knife edge; sometimes the edges are lacquered. Almost invariably the manufacturer's seal is affixed to the wrapped deck.

Many novel ideas have been tried in connection with cards, such as the addition of a fifth suit or the use outdoors of metal cards played onto a magnetized board. Braille cards enable blind players, especially in tournament play, to compete with sighted opponents on almost equal terms.

Taxation. Governments have often found cards to be a useful source of revenue. In 1615 James I of England granted letters patent for a duty on imports, and in 1628 Charles I taxed manufacturers at a rate gradually increased to the considerable sum of half-a-crown per pack. After 1765, the tax paid was shown in the design of the ace of spades, printed officially by the commissioner of stamps. The heavy impost caused a boom in second-hand sales and a traffic in forged aces of spades, but since 1862 the tax has been moderate. In some countries, however, manufacture is a state monopoly. The high taxes imposed in Austria led to the printing of oversized cards, which were trimmed and cleaned when their edges became soiled, and encouraged the invention in the 1930s of playing cards printed on plastic, which far outlasted those printed on pasteboard.

Cards and society. Card games catering to social and competitive inclinations have proved vastly more important than other uses of cards. It is frequently suggested that one prime ingredient of their success is that such games allow women to compete with men on equal terms and in mixed society.

Cards have been popular with all classes, despite spo-

By courtesy of the Deutsches Spielkarten Museum, Bielefeld, Germany

(Left) The knave (jack) of diamonds, depicted in woodcut as a foot soldier, from a French "Portrait de Rouen" deck, 1540. (Centre) Two of bells from a German deck, Dresden, 1848. The bells are equivalent to diamonds, acorns to clubs, and leaves to spades. Hearts are the same in English and German decks. (Right) The king of spades from a pack made by Hardy of London, 1800. Modern international packs are based on this design, traceable to the 15-century Norman variety of French playing cards.

radic attempts by monarchs, nobles, and governments to discourage their use by stringent laws. When cards were first introduced into Europe, some of the clergy condemned them; others dismissed them as harmless. Some cards bore religious texts, and religious foundations derived funds from their sale. Puritans called them the "Devil's Picture Book" or "Devil's Tickets" and held that the Second Commandment was violated by the court cards. By many it was considered a sin to have them in the house, and in early Puritan settlements in America cardplayers frequently were punished.

Laws forbidding card playing

Both governments and churches condemned card playing in later years when gaming fever became widespread, bringing with it reckless wagering and a cruelly strict code of honour. Quarrels led to duels and to many causes célèbres, including the Tranby Croft Baccarat Scandal of 1890, a libel suit over charges of cheating, which, because it involved royalty, rocked Victorian England. In modern times the social and intellectual prestige of games such as Bridge, and the fact that the attention of gamblers was engaged by other means of speculation, led to an abatement of objections to card playing.

Education. From earliest times, cards have been used for instruction in diverse subjects. A cardinal, for example, used playing cards, each bearing a full-length figure with a description below, to instruct the young Louis XIV in the names of the kings and queens of France, geography, and Greek myths. Heraldry was also a popular subject for instruction by cards. Today there are many games, played mainly by children, based on the assembly of sets of pictures, while other decks—printed with the letters of the alphabet—are used for word games by adults as well as children.

Conjuring and sleight of hand. The use of playing cards to perform "magical" tricks was no doubt originally connected with their use in fortune-telling, perhaps to impress the client with the powers of the seer. The rise of gaming led to cardsharping, in which cards were marked surreptitiously and then dealt or played unfairly; today unscrupulous operators can cheat the gullible with such ruses as the "three-card trick," similar to the shell game, in which a victim is led to think that he can successfully keep his eye on a card, usually a queen, in face of the operator's attempt to shuffle the cards. Card tricks are more innocently employed in the repertoire of the professional stage magician, while the clearly defined patterns of playing cards are also used for transmission in psychic experiments, both serious and lighthearted.

CARD GAMES

Early games. Card games are probably coeval with cards themselves and may have been invented by the Chinese when they began shuffling paper money into various combinations. The Chinese are thought to have played both for and with this money, and in China today the general term for playing cards means paper tickets.

Early playing cards proper were mostly numeral cards. In China they were used for games in which the higher cards captured the lower or in which they were formed into winning combinations. Those two principles are still the basis for the two great families of card games.

Circular cards from India are said to have been used on chess boards in a game of pure skill, from which games of chance evolved, but no book gives any account of them. A Persian game, As Nas, has also been called a link in the development of modern games.

Development of modern card games. The number of possible games is practically unlimited, and a vast number of them have been devised. All depend either upon the concept of rank or that of cards in combinations. Some are designed for a specified number of players, a popular number being four; others may be played by any reasonable number. In most games a player's cards are known only to himself until exposed in conformity with the rules.

Games based on rank. In these games each card may defeat or be defeated by other cards when played to a trick. A trick consists of a card from each participant, usually played in clockwise rotation, although in games of Spanish origin, such as Ombre, the cards are played and dealt anticlockwise. Each trick is taken by the highest ranking card of the suit led. Often a trump suit, determined by the rules of the game, may predominate; in this case, any card of that suit may capture any card of the other suits. Except for the trump suit, suits have no order of precedence in the capture of tricks but may have relative values in other matters, such as scoring.

Trump

One of the earliest games of this type was an English game called Triumph, popular in the 16th and 17th centuries, although it seems likely that similar French and Spanish games preceded it. A three-handed Spanish game, Ombre, then became very fashionable, and this, in turn, was followed by a still-enduring family of games of which Loo in England and Spoil Five in Ireland had by the 18th century become "national" games, while in the 19th century Écarté in France, Napoleon in England, and Euchre in the United States achieved similar status, the last seriously rivalling Bridge at the end of the century. In all of these the player receives five cards, a card is turned to fix the trump suit, and the object is to win a specified number of tricks. Even more significant, in terms of the evolution of card games, is that the player's ability to value his cards is vital. Thus, in Napoleon the player assesses his hand with a view to bidding, or declaring, whether he is prepared to win two, three, four or five tricks. The highest caller plays his cards against the combined attempts of the others to defeat him. Players found the challenge of assessing the mathematical relationship between their own cards, those of the other players, and any undealt cards so appealing that the idea of a declared contract, or covenant to take a certain number of tricks resulting from competitive bidding, became a prominent feature in a host of other games, such as Boston, Vint, and Plafond. The very popular German game of Skat incorporates the same idea, each player bidding his hand in competition with the others but with a wide range of options.

Bidding games

In terms of the actual battle for tricks, however, it appears that no game was as satisfying as Whist. By employing the partnership principle of two against two, Whist catered to propensities for both cooperation and opposition, and it also involved the limitless permutations of the complete deck. The combination of the competitive bidding of other games with Whist produced modern Contract Bridge.

Games based on combinations. In this family, which is of older lineage, the object is to acquire combinations of cards that have a prescribed scoring value, a principle seen in ancient Chinese Domino games. The popular example today is Poker. Poker developed from a long line of European games of which the first may have been Primero, a Spanish game that the antiquary Joseph Strutt in *Sports and Pastimes of the People of England* (1801) believed to be the most ancient of the card games played in England. According to Shakespeare, Primero was played by Henry VIII on the night Queen Elizabeth was born. From Primero came the still popular English game of Brag, which was referred to as Brag or Pocher (Ger. *pochen*, "to knock"). It is similar to Poker in that: (1) it is based on groups of cards in sequence or of the same rank, and the best hand, determined by arbitrary rules, wins; (2) players can bet on their chances; (3) if the highest bet is unchallenged, the hands are not exposed; (4) bluffing is therefore an important element. Modern Poker, which first emerged in the United States in the early 19th century, became popular by virtue of its superior opportunities for calculation and psychology.

Poker games

The other widely popular game based on grouping, or melding, cards in combinations is Rummy and its countless variations. Instead of each deal ranking as a separate event as in Poker, play is continuous. Scoring follows the principle that cards not melded (grouped) into scoring combinations when a critical point is reached are counted as penalty cards. One game of this family, Conquian, or Cooncan, entered the United States from Mexico in the early 1900s. In 1949 Canasta, invented in Latin America, spread rapidly to North America and Europe.

Rummy games

Games of both rank and combination. Trick play and melding have often been combined, notably in Piquet, which has a courtly terminology that is derived from a lengthy association with aristocrats and with serious gamesters, especially in France. For centuries Piquet reigned as the king of games for two players, although it is now little played. The object is to score points first by melding and then by capturing tricks, so in the early stages a player tries to acquire cards with both objectives in mind. The game Bezique is based on a similar idea but is played with two or more packs and is a test of memory. Games of this type include the Pinochle group, highly popular in the United States in its four-handed versions.

The old English game of Cribbage appears to have evolved separately. Although it involves melding and trick play, they are performed differently than in the other games.

The Solitaire or Patience games. There are at least 350 variations of games that can be played by one person. They are played with either one or two decks. The game usually begins by setting out certain key cards and trying to build the remaining cards upon them in a prescribed order. The disadvantage of most Solitaire games is that success or failure depends largely on the chance initial arrangement of the cards. Some, however, especially those of the two-deck variety, require an appreciable amount of skill.

Children's and party games. Games for children are necessarily simple, because they must appeal to all age groups and are seldom played in a serious manner. Children enjoy such games because it is possible for them to compete with adults with a chance of winning. Most of these games can be played by almost any number of people, and many games accentuate the element of suspense by giving each player three lives, after which the player is out. Some games introduce actions, as in Slapjack, in which the player who first slaps a jack when it appears takes all the cards that have accumulated in a common pile. Some are educational, such as Casino, which is a popular children's game because it gives practice in elementary arithmetic, and can also be played at a more advanced level by older children and adults. Other popular games in this category are Old Maid and Beggar-My-Neighbour.

Older children quickly learn to outshine most adults in such games as Concentration (Memory, Pelmanism) in which, on each turn, the player faces two cards from a complete deck laid out face down. If a pair is formed, the player keeps them; if not, they are returned to their places, again face down. The winner is the player who collects the most cards.

Casino games. The most widely played casino card games in Europe are Baccarat Banque, its more popular variant Chemin de fer or "Chemmy," and Trente et Quarante; in the United States the single most popular casino card game is Blackjack (Twenty-one). All are derived from 15th- and 16th-century European games, and all are simple to play. The underlying principle is to assemble cards whose value does not exceed a specified number—nine in Baccarat, 21 in Blackjack—and to bet on the probability of the player or the bank being successful.

BIBLIOGRAPHY. C.P. HARGRAVE, *A History of Playing Cards and a Bibliography of Cards and Gaming* (1930, reprinted 1966), a comprehensive, well-illustrated text tracing the history of the worldwide manufacture of playing cards; ROGER TILLEY, *A History of Playing Cards* (1973), a history that includes legends and myths surrounding cards; H. PHILLIPS and B.C. WESTALL, *The Complete Book of Card Games* (1939), a reference work that includes some of the older games not found in more recent books; H. PHILLIPS, *The Popular Book of Card Games*, new ed. (1972), rules and tactical advice for the popular modern card games and for some lesser known games; R.L. FREY, *According to Hoyle*, rev. and enl. ed. (1970), text covering a brief history, rules, and suggested strategy for more than 200 of the most popular card, board, and dice games; C.H. GOREN, *Goren's Hoyle Encyclopedia of Games* (1961), a work that is similar to Frey's in character and content.

(C.H.Go.)

Caribbean Cultures

The large islands of Cuba, Hispaniola, Jamaica and Puerto Rico and the smaller islands of the Lesser Antilles stretch from near Florida, in the United States, to the Venezuelan coast of South America. These islands form the heartland of Caribbean cultures; but the Bahamas and Bermuda, northward in the Atlantic, as well as Guyana, Suriname, and French Guiana, on the South American mainland, and Belize (British Honduras), in Central America, are also considered integral parts of the culture area.

Of the 30,000,000 people who live in the Caribbean, nearly one-half of them live in Cuba and Haiti. The remainder are divided into more than 50 distinct geographical, political, and cultural entities ranging in size from Guyana (83,000 square miles [210,000 square kilometres] but only 884,000 people) to such minuscule island nations as Barbados (166 square miles), whose population of 249,000, or 1,500 per square mile (579 per square kilometre) is one of the densest in the world. All of the islands together cover only 90,560 square miles, roughly the size of the island of Great Britain, and Cuba makes up almost half of this total area, with 42,827 square miles.

Languages spoken in the region are diverse and include Spanish; Papiamento, a Spanish Creole spoken in Curaçao and Aruba; English; Sranan (Taki-Taki), or the English Creole of Suriname; French; at least three distinct dialects of French Creole; Dutch; Hindi-Urdu; and Chinese. Although the aboriginal languages are extinct in the islands, in Belize the language known as Island Carib has been kept alive by the so-called Black Caribs, who were forcibly transported there from St. Vincent in 1797, and Mayan, Tupi-Guarani, and other Indian languages are spoken in the mainland countries. Politically the range is equally great, from Cuba's experiment with Socialism, through military and civilian dictatorships, parliamentary democracies, Puerto Rico's internally independent Commonwealth, and Britain's "special relationship" with the associated state of St. Kitts-Nevis, to three integral *départements* of France (Martinique, Guadeloupe, and French Guiana), a state of Venezuela, and a considerable number of dependencies.

In spite of the wide divergencies in size, ancestry, language, history, population density, and political organization, the countries of the Caribbean share a common culture, the result of their somewhat parallel experiences as plantation colonies populated by African and Asian labourers dominated by distant European economic and political powers. Cut off from their homelands and in most cases unable to attain the schooling that would have given them entrée into the European ruling class, the Caribbean peoples made a virtue of necessity by combining the disparate elements of their past and of their new environment to produce a truly new cultural manifestation that is best called Creole culture. From Portuguese *crioulo*, meaning "locally raised," Creole (Spanish *criollo*) has come to describe the local culture and people of mixed foreign origin. In the same way, linguists use the term to describe languages that have evolved from pidgins used by speakers of mutually unintelligible languages and that have become the first language of the local people. In the Caribbean the French, Spanish, and English Creoles are a blend of these languages with African and aboriginal Indian languages and with each other. In the same way, Creole culture takes pride in its lively cultural scene, with frequent dances, parties, and festivals culminating in carnival, the marvelously diverse foods and drinks, the beauty and generosity of the people of mixed ancestry, and the easygoing but frenetic quality of interpersonal relationships. Today, "real Creoles" may be of any ancestry and class but must be devoted to the local culture in all of its unlikely juxtapositions, and must not look to the institutions and gadgetry of industrially more complex societies.

Creole culture

Social organization. *Stratification.* Caribbean societies may be considered to be stratified both vertically by ancestry and horizontally by class. For instance, in Trinidad, possibly the most complex of all Caribbean societies, blacks and mixed Creoles can each be further subdivided on the basis of Catholicism or Protestantism, with a third division for similarly African-derived people who migrated in recent times from nearby islands, such as Barbados and St. Vincent. Other vertical divisions exist for Hindu, Muslim, and Christian East Indians, foreign-born and locally born whites, the Chinese, Portuguese, and Lebanese merchant communities, Venezuelan immigrants, and several others. Each of these communities has at least a few representatives at the top of the social pyramid and sharply differing percentages of their members at each step farther down the social scale. North American teaching volunteers serving rural areas might, for instance, be the lowest class foreign-born whites, while proportionally more members of each succeeding group are farther down the social scale, with the rural dark Creole plantation labourers and Hindu cane cutters in the largest numbers on the lowest rungs of the scale. As a result, the Trinidadian middle and upper classes are truly international in ancestry, education, and outlook, while the rural proletariat is equally divided between the uneducated and impoverished blacks and East Indians.

In other areas the components are quite different; there are additionally, for instance, the Javanese and American Indians in Suriname, the Latin Catholic mestizos in Belize, and the 11 percent local "Conchy Joe" whites of distant British origin in The Bahamas. But the patterns of stratification remain similar from country to country with a largely foreign-educated governmental, business, professional, and landed elite; a relatively small middle class consisting of local traders, landed proprietors, and small businessmen; and a large lower class made up of landless rural and urban labourers, the underemployed, and the unemployed.

Family and resident patterns. The origins of West Indian family organization have been the subject of considerable controversy among scholars. Although lifelong monogamous unions on the European model and Hindu and Muslim polygynous marriages can be found in the Caribbean, the most common pattern is serial monogamy, wherein each person has two or more mates one after the other in the course of a lifetime. In this context legal or church marriage is rare and is considered a validation of social position rather than as a statement of cohabitation. Sexual activity usually begins early for both sexes, and illegitimate birth carries no stigma when the overwhelming majority of the population is illegitimate, legally at least, if not functionally. West Indians do frown on conception resulting from casual sexual contact, but a family-sanctioned nonlegal union of a duration of even a few weeks gives any resulting children a type of local legitimacy not recognized in official statistics. Young girls welcome children as proof of their attractiveness and fertility, and young men are willing to claim their offspring and contribute to their support as proof of their virility. A number of wealthy men support 50 or more children by many mates, and a few claim to have fathered even more. Because women can earn income as domestics and raise food in kitchen gardens while the market for men's unskilled labour is seasonal and uncertain, many households become "matrifocal," centring around an older woman and her daughters and grandchildren but with no permanent male members. Because such families resemble those of female members of African polygynous marriages and the serial monogamy resembles standard West African marital patterns, the American anthropologist, Melville J. Herskovits has postulated an African origin for Caribbean family structure. Other authorities have seen these marital types as resulting from slavery wherein the men had been deprived of control over their wives and children. Although the controversy has never been completely resolved, this family system works as well as any in ordering human relations and in caring for offspring, and it may be worth noting that in recent years American and European mating patterns have conformed more and more to those of the islands.

Serial monogamy

West Indian family structure sometimes finds physical expression in the yard, tenement, or barracks, all terms for multiple housing units inhabited by members of a family. Although many West Indian families in rural and urban environments live in individual privately owned or rented houses set on owned or leased lots, a significant number of city dwellers live in clusters of small jerry-built houses around a common yard or in teeming multistoried rental buildings. The residents are largely blood relatives and their mates, as well as close friends, the children of rural relatives, adopted children, and an occasional crippled, demented, or aged person who has no other place to go. The yard is a cooperative enterprise, supported by those who are working and operated by those who are not. The latter do the cooking and what cleaning and laundry may be necessary and care for the children. Residents are expected to contribute whatever they can, and a person who holds back his salary when working finds little hospitality when unemployed. But if he is pleasant and cooperative and contributes food and cash and judiciously offers gifts when he is working, he can always find food and shelter in the years to come, so that his contributions might be considered a West Indian form of unemployment and retirement insurance. In this context ties of love and mutual need supersede ties of blood, and it is quite common for a young man to give a substantial portion of his income to the old woman, no kin of his, who fed him when he first left the bush and came to town. Such cooperative enterprises are, of course, a common resort of the very poor in many societies. The clearing and preparing of fields, seeding, weeding, harvesting, pulling in large fishnets, house building, and many other activities are organized in this way. Young men are recruited for the work with promises of food, rum, and prestige, plus firm social pressure, and these otherwise exhausting chores are transformed into social events, with special songs and drum rhythms for each task. (Although family organizations in Africa and Asia were badly disrupted by the experiences of slavery and indenture, it is notable that small communities of runaway slaves, or "maroons," established isolated villages, some of which still exist today, and supported themselves by subsistence agriculture. These sometimes maintained the old ways of life.)

Cooperative enterprise

Economic patterns. Soon after emancipation, which took place in 1834 in British territories but not until 1886 in Cuba, the new freedmen did their best to break away from plantation labour and obtain farmlands through purchase, renting, or sharecropping, or simply by squatting on unused lands or deserted plantations. In a few cases, church groups organized cooperative efforts to purchase and divide former sugar estates into family farms, but all too often, especially on the smaller islands, the former slaves had no choice but to stay on the plantations as low-paid wage labourers. In Guyana, Trinidad, and, to a lesser extent, in other areas, the former slaves soon found themselves in competition for the available jobs and land with Chinese, Portuguese, East Indian, and even African indentured labour. As a result of the interplay of these factors with geography, each country developed differently. Some islands, such as Barbados, St. Kitts, Antigua, and Martinique, produce sugar on huge foreign owned or locally owned private plantations, while in others, such as Grenada, St. Vincent, Guadeloupe, and St. Lucia, new plantation crops such as bananas and long-staple cotton have been introduced, and peasant crops such as nutmegs, arrowroot, cocoa, coconuts, pineapples, and citrus fruit earn income for small landowners. Cuba has nationalized its sugar estates, not without considerable cost in output per year, and most of the other governments hold substantial percentages of arable land as well as stock in banana estates, bauxite mines and processing plants, oil wells and refineries, and other large-scale agriculture and industry.

Religious beliefs and arts. Virtually all Caribbean people except the East Indian Hindus and Muslims are members of at least one Christian sect, with Catholicism strongest in the Spanish- and French-speaking areas and Protestantism in the English-speaking areas. But, as they do with so many other borrowed parts of their culture, the West Indians give new content to these alien forms. Alongside virtually every major sect of Christianity, West

Blend of religious sects and beliefs in magic

African cults such as Shango, from Nigeria, and Rada, from (Benin) Dahomey, have persisted in many areas, and the much-publicized Haitian voodoo represents an amalgam of Christian and African beliefs and practices. Charismatic leaders frequently organize distinctive local variants of Christianity, such as the Baptist sects that are graphically termed "Shouters" or "Jumpers," or attempt to reproduce the rituals of Islām, the Ethiopian Coptic Church, or Judaism. Although most people are entirely devoted to their own sect, many others continue to search for a faith that is more suitable to their own needs and desires. It is quite common for a High Church Anglican to consult an African magic practitioner, or obeahman, in search of knowledge of the future, cures for spiritual illnesses and insanity, or protection against the magical machinations of enemies. In Puerto Rico a European spiritualist cult has taken root as orthodox Roman Catholicism increasingly divorces itself from magic practices beyond prayer. Because of the wide choice of sects that are available to the people and the virtually universal belief in at least the possibility of magic, Caribbean peoples have retained religious concerns at the centre of their consciousness.

African and European traditions have intermingled in a particularly spectacular way to produce the music and carnival arts of the Caribbean. Witty and allusive calypso songs, written and sung by professionals, precede the Trinidad carnival, with its huge bands of masked and costumed dancers "jumping up" to music made by beating on tuned steel oil drums. The steel "pan" is made of an upturned oil drum, the flat surface of which has been hammered and incised to make as few as three or as many as 20 convex areas, each tuned differently. These unique musical instruments, typical of the Caribbean in their creative use of discarded alien objects, can be played solo, in unison, or in complicated musical arrangements giving the effect of a giant theatre organ. Some Afro-Cuban music, such as the rumba "La Cumparsita," also deriving from carnival, has long been an established genre of popular music throughout the world; and in spite of the present overwhelming concern with economic problems, the music remains one of Cuba's most influential ambassadors. Every other area can claim musical or dance forms of international renown—Jamaica's *mentos*, Martinique's beguine, Haiti's merengue, Puerto Rico's *plenas*, Bahamian "Junkanoo," Bermudian Gombey, and the distinctive music of Suriname and Curaçao. Probably no area of comparable size and population on Earth has so many qualified musicians and performers. The other arts have also grown lively in recent years, producing distinguished painters such as Wilfredo Lam, of Cuba, novelists such as Edgar Mittelhölzer, of Guyana, Pierre Marcelin and Jacques Roumain, of Haiti, V.S. Naipaul, of Trinidad, and George Lamming, of Barbados, and poets such as Nicolás Guillén, of Cuba, and Derek Walcott, of St. Lucia. Aimé Césaire is a noted Martiniquais poet, politician, and political philosopher of Negritude.

Tradition and current social change. Throughout a long and cruel history of slavery, colonialism, and exploitation, the peoples of the Caribbean have had to learn to be realistic and adaptable. They learned what they could from the planter aristocrats and *petit blancs* (poor whites) and kept what they could of their African heritage in music, lore, religion, and values. In spite of the innate poverty and isolation of their far-flung rocky islands and infertile tropical lands, they have slowly developed a distinctive and piquant culture, a unique and highly successful blend of many lands and ages plus a great deal of local creation. After Ethiopia, Haiti is the oldest black nation on Earth, and political independence has come to most of the other areas in the past generation. Ties with the former colonizing powers remain close, and their continuing aid is crucial in supporting the fledgling independent governments. More and more, the leaders of the new nations are coming to recognize the similarity of their problems and aspirations with those of Asia, Africa, and South America.

Problems of inequality

In the present postcolonial world of parliamentary democracies, the Caribbean system of stratification has resulted in political power devolving to the representatives of the majority, usually the blacks in most Caribbean nations, but with economic power left in the hands of foreign investors or local elites. A few families in Martinique, for instance, control most of the productive land, a situation that goes far to explain the strong Communist Party in that French *département*. Even in the original "Black Republic" of Haiti, the relatively light-skinned descendants of the planters control the wealth while the black professionals and army control the government, and the poor blacks eke out a precarious living on their worked-out and eroded hill farms. As a result of these glaring and ever increasing inequalities, the Caribbean nations, whether newly independent or long established, are experiencing increasing revolutionary ferment and governmental instability in the unenviable pattern of South America. Proponents of effective change, such as Juan Bosch in the Dominican Republic, do not remain long in office, being all too often overthrown by military and business interests in defense of their privilege. With little to attract foreign investment on the scale necessary for industrialization and former opportunities for emigration now limited to those trained professionals whom these countries can least afford to lose, the outlook for just and stable governments and equitable distribution of the available resources appears unpromising to most authorities in the Caribbean. Under these circumstances, the graceful and sanguine Creole culture gives meaning to otherwise difficult lives.

BIBLIOGRAPHY. LAMBROS COMITAS, *Carribbeana 1900–1965: A Topical Bibliography* (1968), is the best of the recent bibliographical sources on the area; and the most recent issue of the *Yearbook of the West Indies and the Countries of the Caribbean* is useful for up-to-date facts and statistics. For scholarly studies of particular islands or communities, see MELVILLE J. HERSKOVITS' classic ethnographies, *Life in a Haitian Valley* (1937, reprinted 1971), and *Trinidad Village* (1947, reprinted 1964); and DOUGLAS TAYLOR, *The Black Carib of British Honduras* (1951); for a psychological approach, EDITH CLARKE, *My Mother Who Fathered Me* (1957); and EDWIN A. WEINSTEIN, *Cultural Aspects of Delusion: A Psychiatric Study of the Virgin Islands* (1962); for a full-length analysis of a political crisis, A.W. SINGHAM, *The Hero and the Crowd in a Colonial Polity* (1968); and for a fascinating historical economic study, RICHARD PARES, *A West-India Fortune* (1950). M.G. SMITH, *The Plural Society in the British West Indies* (1965), is a careful theoretical study of the special nature of Caribbean social organization; DAVID LOWENTHAL, *West Indian Societies* (1972), is a brilliant comparative analysis; HYMAN RODMAN, *Lower-Class Families: The Culture of Poverty in Negro Trinidad* (1971); GEORGE L. BECKFORD, *Persistent Poverty: Underdevelopment in Plantation Regions of the Third World* (1972); and IVAR OXAAL, *Race and Revolutionary Consciousness: A Report on the 1970 Black Power Revolt in Trinidad* (1971), are complementary reports on current conditions in a single country. For contrasting but competent travel books on the Caribbean area by a Briton and an American, see MARY SLATER, *The Caribbean Islands* (1968); and BRADLEY SMITH, *Escape to the West Indies* (1956); and for a masterpiece of travel literature, PATRICK LEIGH FERMOR, *The Traveller's Tree* (1950). For *belles lettres* by Caribbean scholars, see PHILIP M. SHERLOCK, *West Indies* (1966); and KENNETH RAMCHAND, *The West Indian Novel and Its Background* (1970).

(D.J.C.)

Caribbean Sea

The Caribbean Sea is a suboceanic basin, approximately 1,020,000 square miles (2,640,000 square kilometres) in extent lying between 9° to 22° N and 89° to 60° W. To the south, it is bounded by the coasts of Venezuela, Colombia, and Panama; to the west, by Costa Rica, Nicaragua, Honduras, Guatemala, Belize (British Honduras), and the Yucatán Peninsula of Mexico; to the north, by the Greater Antillean islands of Cuba, Hispaniola, Jamaica, and Puerto Rico; and to the east by the Lesser Antillean chain, composed of the island arc, that extends from the Virgin Islands in the northeast to Trinidad, off the Venezuelan coast, in the southeast. Within the boundaries of the Caribbean itself, Jamaica, to the south of Cuba, is the largest of a number of islands. (For articles on localized aspects of the region, see PANAMA CANAL, as well as articles on individual Caribbean countries. For articles on associated physical features, see ATLANTIC OCEAN, and MEXICO, GULF OF. For historical aspects, see article CENTRAL AMERICAN STATES, HISTORY OF.)

Together with the Gulf of Mexico, the Caribbean Sea has been erroneously termed the American Mediterranean—due to the fact that, like the Mediterranean, it is located between two continental land masses. In both hydrography and climate, however, the Caribbean does not resemble the Mediterranean. The preferred oceanographic term for the Caribbean is the Antillean–Caribbean Sea, which, together with the Gulf of Mexico, forms the Central American Sea. The Caribbean's greatest known depth is Cayman Trench (Bartlett Deep) between Cuba and Jamaica, at approximately 25,216 feet below sea level.

Climate. The climate of the Caribbean is generally tropical, but there are great local variations, depending on mountain altitude, water currents, and the trade winds. Rainfall varies from 350 inches a year in parts of Dominica, to only 10 inches a year on the island of Bonaire off the coast of Venezuela. The northeast trade winds dominate the region with an average velocity of 10 to 20 miles per hour. Tropical storms reaching a hurricane velocity of more than 75 miles per hour are seasonally common in the northern Caribbean as well as in the Gulf of Mexico; they are almost non-existent in the far south. The hurricane season is from June to November, but hurricanes occur most frequently in September. The yearly average is about eight such storms a year. The Caribbean has fewer hurricanes than either the Western Pacific (where these storms are called typhoons) or the Gulf of Mexico. Most hurricanes formed in the Caribbean follow the arclike path of the trade winds into the Gulf of Mexico, although the exact path of any hurricane appears unpredictable. In 1963 Hurricane Flora caused the loss of over 7,000 lives and $528,000,000 of damage in the Caribbean alone. Such storms have also been a major cause of crop failure in the region.

Tropical storms

Physiography and submarine morphology. The Caribbean Sea is divided into five submarine basins, roughly elliptical in shape, which are separated from one another by submerged ridges and rises. These are the Yucatán, Cayman, Colombian, Venezuelan, and Grenada basins. The northernmost of these, the Yucatán Basin, is separated from the Gulf of Mexico by the Yucatán Channel, which runs between Cuba and the Yucatán Peninsula, and has a sill depth of only 5,250 feet. Cayman Basin, to the south, is partially separated from the Yucatan Basin by Cayman Ridge, an incomplete fingerlike ridge that extends from the southern part of Cuba toward Guatemala, rising above the surface at one point to form Cayman Island. Jamaica Ridge, a wide triangular ridge with a sill depth of about 4,000 feet, extends from Honduras to Hispaniola, bearing the island of Jamaica, and separating the Cayman Basin from the Colombian Basin. The Colombian Basin is partly separated from the Venezuelan Basin by the Beata Ridge. The two basins are connected by the submerged Aruba Gap at depths of over 13,000 feet. The Aves Ridge, incomplete at its southern extremity, separates the Venezuelan Basin from the small Grenada Basin, which is bounded to the east by the Antillean arc of islands.

Subsurface water enters the Caribbean Sea across two sills. These sills are located below the Anegada Passage, which runs between the Virgin Islands and the Lesser Antilles, and the Windward Passage, which runs between Cuba and Hispaniola. The sill depth of Anegada Passage is between 6,400 to 7,700 feet (1,950 to 2,350 metres); the sill depth of the Windward Passage is from 5,250 to 5,350 feet (1,600 to 1,625 metres).

Hydrography and currents. North Atlantic Deep Water enters the Caribbean beneath the Windward Passage and is characterized by an oxygen maximum of six millilitres per litre, and a salinity of just under 35 parts per thousand. From there it divides to fill the Yucatan, Cayman, and Colombian Basins at depths near 6,500 feet. This Caribbean Bottom Water also enters the Venezuelan Basin, thus introducing high oxygen water at depths of between 5,900 and 9,800 feet. Subantarctic Intermediate Water (*i.e.*, water differing in several characteristics from the surface and bottom layers of water that it separates) enters the Caribbean below the Anegada Passage at depths of between 1,600 to 3,300 feet. Above this water, the subtropical undercurrent and surface water both enter. The shallow sill depths of the Antillean arc block the entry of Antarctic Bottom Water, so

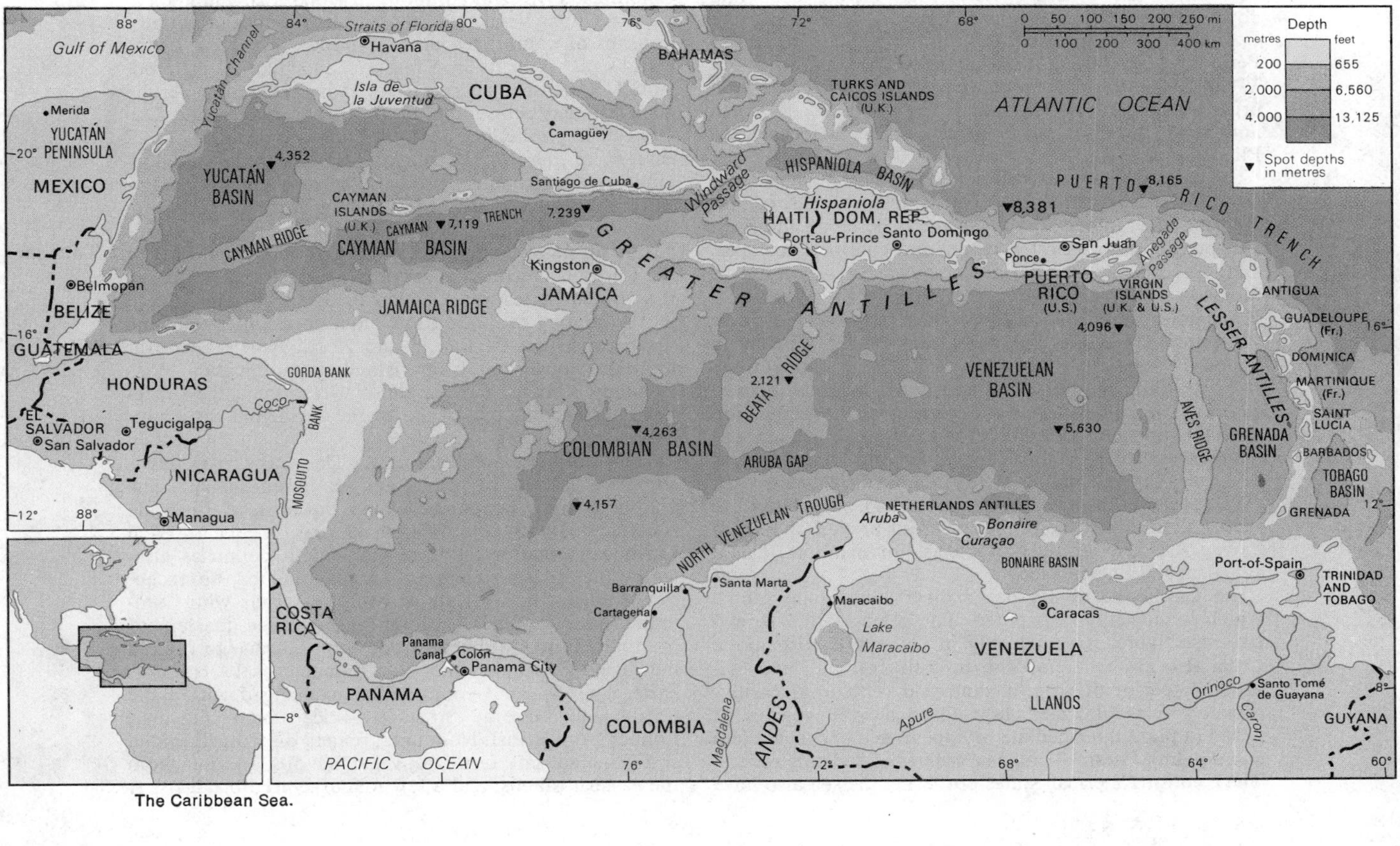

The Caribbean Sea.

that the bottom temperature of the Caribbean Sea is close to 4° C (39° F), as compared with the Atlantic bottom temperature of less than 2° C (36° F).

Surface currents

Surface currents, bearing both high- and low-salinity water depending on the source, enter the Caribbean mainly through the channels and passages of the southern Antilles. These waters are then forced by the trade winds through the narrow Yucatán Channel into the Gulf of Mexico. The wind-driven surface water piles up in the Yucatán Basin and the Gulf of Mexico, where it results in a higher average sea level than in the Atlantic, forming a hydrostatic head that is believed to constitute the main driving force of the Gulf Stream. Of the 26,000,000 cubic metres of water passing through the Yucatán Channel each second, only 6,000,000 represent the deeper Subantarctic Intermediate Water. The remainder is the surface water that passed over the Antillean arc at depths of less than 2,600 feet.

Geology. The geologic age of the Caribbean is not known with certainty. As part of the Central American Sea, it is presumed to have been connected with the Mediterranean during Paleozoic times (from about 225,000,000 to about 570,000,000 years ago) and then gradually to have separated from it as the Atlantic Ocean was formed. The ancient sediments overlying the sea floor of the Caribbean, as well as of the Gulf of Mexico, are called the Carib beds. They are about one kilometre (0.62 of a mile) in thickness, with the upper strata representing sediments from the Mesozoic–Cenozoic Era, and the lower strata presumably representing sediments of the Paleozoic–Mesozoic Era. Three phases of sedimentation have been identified. During the first phase the basin was free of deformation, as it also was during the second phase, when the Carib beds were deposited. The Central American Sea had apparently become separated from the Atlantic before the end of the first phase. Near the end of the second phase, gentle warping and faulting occurred, forming the Aves and the Beata Ridges. Forces producing the Panamanian isthmus and the Antillean arc were vertical, resulting in no ultimate horizontal movement. The Carib beds tend to arch in the middle of the basins and to dip as land masses are approached. The younger Cenozoic beds (formed during the last 65,000,000 years) are generally horizontal, having been laid down after the deformations occurred. Connections were established with the Pacific Ocean during the Cretaceous Period (which lasted from about 65,000,000 to about 136,000,000 years ago) but were broken when the land bridges that permitted mammals to cross between North and South America were formed in the Miocene and Pliocene epochs.

The existing Cenozoic sediment cover of the seabed consists of red clay in the deep basins and trenches, of globigerina ooze (a calcareous marine deposit) on the rises, and pteropod ooze on the ridges and continental slopes. Clay minerals appear to have been washed down by the Amazon or Orinoco rivers, as well as by the Magdalena River in Colombia. Coral reefs fringe most of the islands.

Vegetation. While the vegetation of the Caribbean region is generally tropical, variations in topography, soils, rainfall, humidity, and soil nutrients have made it diverse. The porous limestone terraces of the islands are generally nutrient poor. Near the seashore, black and red mangroves form dense forests around lagoons and estuaries. Coconut palms typify the sandy vegetation of the littoral. On the dry side of each island, succulents and cactus plants are common. Rain forests prevail on islands having sufficient altitude—such as, for example, Cuba, Jamaica, and Puerto Rico.

The Caribbean region has a diversity of land fauna, which is unevenly distributed. The solenodon, a shrew-like insectivore, is found only in Cuba and Hispaniola. Cuba also has an atelopidid (brightly coloured and poisonous) species of frog, a xanthusid (nocturnal carnivorous) species of lizard, as well as a relict species of cycad (a plant intermediate in appearance between a jem and a palm). Puerto Rico has a species of endemic rodent. The Central American states bordering the sea also have a great diversity of land plants and animals. The three-toed sloth, cats, marsupials, and monkeys abound in the forests, as also do snakes and other reptiles not usually found on the islands. Both the Central American region and the Antillean islands are on the routes of birds migrating to or from North America, so that large seasonal variations occur in the bird populations. Parrots, parakeets, and toucans are typical resident Caribbean birds, while the frigate bird also is seen frequently.

Shallow-water fauna

The shallow-water marine fauna and flora of the Caribbean are far more homogenous than are those of the land. Marine life in the shallows centres around the submerged fringing coral reefs, which attract assemblages of fishes and other forms of marine life. The marine biota as a whole represents a survival—a relict of the warm seas of the Cretaceous Period. Coral reef growth throughout the Antillean region is favoured by uniformly warm temperatures, clear water, and little change in salinity. Submerged fields of turtle grass are found there. Sea turtles of several species, the sea cow, and the Manta (devilfish) ray are also characteristic of the region. The spiny lobster is harvested throughout the Caribbean, being sold mainly in the markets of North America.

Fishes of commerce are the sardine from Yucatan, and the tuna fish. Among common game fish are the bonefishes of the Bahamian reefs, barracuda, dolphin, marlin, and wahoo.

Economic resources. The economic resources of the Caribbean countries are poor. Such industrialization as exists is restricted to one or two countries. Coffee-producing countries include Colombia, El Salvador, Guatemala, Costa Rica, Nicaragua, Honduras, Dominican Republic, Haiti, Cuba, Venezuela, and Trinidad and Tobago. Banana-exporting countries include Honduras, Costa Rica, Panama, Colombia, Martinique, Jamaica, Guatemala, and Guadeloupe; most other Caribbean countries are minor producers. Sugar is exported by Cuba, the Dominican Republic, Jamaica, Colombia, Trinidad and Tobago, Guadeloupe, Barbados, Venezuela, and other countries. These three products between them account for 28 to 72 percent of the total exports of each individual country in the region with the exception of Venezuela. Among the minerals mined are gold in Nicaragua and Colombia; silver and antimony in Honduras; and manganese in Cuba. Venezuela, the richest Caribbean country in terms of natural resources, produces 8 percent of the world's oil. With its iron reserves and hydroelectric potential, it also has prospects for industrialization. Aruba and Trinidad refine and export oil. Jamaica, the Dominican Republic, and Haiti are the sources of about 22 percent of the world's bauxite. Jamaica and the Dominican Republic also produce gypsum. Fish and agricultural products are mostly used for domestic consumption. Much farming is on a subsistence basis.

Tourism

Tourism has become an increasingly important part of the Caribbean economy, serving the huge populations of the United States and Canada to the north, and Brazil and Argentina to the south. Communications by air and sea between the Caribbean and North America are far more developed than is interisland communication. With its sunny climate, and recreational resources, the Caribbean has become one of the world's principal winter vacation resort areas.

Trade and communications. The Caribbean has a complex pattern of trade and communications. The volume of trade per capita is high, but most of this trade is conducted with countries outside the Caribbean. Each Caribbean country tends to trade with countries elsewhere that share a common language. Cuba, an exception, trades with a variety of countries, trade with Communist bloc countries accounting for three-quarters of the total. Intra-Caribbean trade is small, due to limited industrial resources and the monocultural economic pattern. Goods and commodities exchanged within the Caribbean economy are few—rice from Guyana; lumber from British Honduras; refined oil from Trinidad and Curaçao; salt, fertilizer, vegetable oils, and fats from the eastern islands; and a few manufactured products. A lack of capital and limited natural resources discourage industrial development. Markets for most Caribbean products are in the United States and Canada, which import bananas, sugar, coffee, bauxite, rum, and oil. All of the Atlantic–Pacific shipping using the Panama Canal passes through the Caribbean.

It is anticipated that emergent local nationalisms will lessen prospects for future unions or federations that could foster diversification and industrialization. A continuation of the monocultural economic pattern appears likely for some time to come. Tourism is likely to continue to increase and to result in better prices for local produce, as well as in a strengthening of island economies. Measures to protect such natural resources as unpolluted water, beaches and sand will, however, be necessary if the island countries are to continue to benefit from them.

BIBLIOGRAPHY. A. COLLIER, "The American Mediterranean," in R.C. WEST (ed.), *The Handbook of Middle American Indians*, vol. 1, pp. 122–142 (1964), a good summary on early Caribbean populations and hydrography; G.E. DUNN and B.I. MILLER, *Atlantic Hurricanes* (1960), frequency distribution of hurricanes plotted regionally by season; G. WUST, "On the Stratification and the Circulation in the Cold Water Sphere of the Antillean-Caribbean Basins," *Deep-Sea Research*, 10:165–187 (1963), an extensive compilation of existing hydrographic data and an excellent synopsis of circulation patterns into and in the Caribbean; J. EWING, M. TALWANI, and M. EWING, *Sediment Distribution in the Caribbean Sea*, Fourth Caribbean Geological Conference, Trinidad, pp. 317–323 (1965), continuous seismic profiles suggest the history of Caribbean basins and other major features; A. EYRE, *A New Geography of the Caribbean* (1962), a reasonably contemporary synopsis of economic growth and political structure in the Caribbean countries; D. PERKINS, *The United States and the Caribbean*, rev. ed. (1967), international acts and laws relating to Caribbean economic growth.

(R.J.Me.)

Caricature, Cartoon, and Comic Strip

Caricature, cartoon (in the satirical sense), and comic strips (including comic books) are related forms. Historically, they arose in the order given, but they all have flourished together. All use the same artistic mediums of drawing and printmaking; caricature and the element of satire is usually present in each.

DEFINITION OF TERMS

Caricature. Caricature is the distorted presentation of a person, type, or action. Commonly, a salient feature is seized upon and exaggerated, or features of animals, birds, or vegetables are substituted for parts of the human being, or analogy is made to animal actions. Generally, one thinks of caricature as being a line drawing and meant for publication to people to whom the original is known; the personal trait is usually present.

Origin of the word caricature

The word caricature derives from the Italian verb *caricare* ("to load," "to surcharge" as with exaggerated detail) and seems to have been used first by Mosini in *Diverse Figure* (1646). The 17th-century sculptor-architect, Gian Lorenzo Bernini, who was a skilled caricaturist, seems to have introduced the word *caricatura* into France when he went there in 1665. There is perhaps, in the choice of the verb *caricare* as a source for the noun, some influence from the idea of *carattere* (Italian: "character") or even from *cara* (Spanish: "face"). At any rate, the face is the point of departure for most caricatures. It is conceivable that underlying the series of overlapping profiles with varieties of extraordinary noses and chins and brows which Leonardo da Vinci and Albrecht Dürer drew independently about 1500 was an observation not only of contemporary human types but of the fact that the heads of rulers on coins and medals, when worn with age, often became ridiculous. A latter-day case is the penny showing Queen Victoria, whose coiffure began to look like an elephant's head when the coin was well worn down.

Caricature, after its spread as idea and practice from Italy and France to Britain in the 18th century, became rather a broad term. In the late 19th century, Gilbert and Sullivan, the English creators of comic operettas, spoke of one of their subheroines as having "a caricature of a face." Perhaps, therefore, it is not surprising that, although cartoons as they are now known developed gradually out of a caricature from the 15th century, cartoon is a 19th-century word.

Satirical deformations and comic analogies in sculpture, the drama, and vase painting are older than purely graphic caricature. The ancient Egyptians represented men as animals; Greek comedy had by-products in burlesqued figures on vases and in terra-cotta statuettes; Romanesque and Gothic sculptors made fun of human failings in stone capitals and wood miserere seat carvings all through the Middle Ages. The marginal flourishes of illuminated manuscripts contain grotesque faces and occasional exaggerated scenes from daily life, or references to the morality plays which have the same relationship to those plays as Greek clay representations have to the stage. All such works verged upon caricature in the narrow personal sense; some were caricature in a broad sense. In the generations since caricature became a clearly defined idea, there have been occasional examples in painting and sculpture alongside the more usual drawing for reproduction.

Cartoon. A cartoon originally was and still is a drawing, a full-size pattern for execution in painting, tapestry, mosaic, or other form. The cartoon was the final stage in the series of drawn preparations for painting in traditional Renaissance studio practice. In the early 1840s, when that studio practice was rapidly decaying, cartoon rather suddenly acquired a new meaning: that of pictorial parody, almost invariably a multiple-reproduced drawing, which by the devices of caricature, analogy, and ludicrous juxtaposition sharpens the public view of a contemporary event, folkway, or political or social trend. It is normally humorous but may be positively savage. Just as the personal caricature was for an audience which knew the original, so the cartoon was and is based on wide acquaintance with the subject. It serves as a capsule version of editorial opinion when it makes political satire, and it is a running commentary on social change, sometimes intended as a corrective to social inertia (for animated cartoons, see ANIMATION). (W.Am.)

Comic strip and comic book. The comic strip consists of a series of adjacent drawn images, usually arranged horizontally, that are designed to be read as a narrative or a chronological sequence. The story is usually original in this form. Words may be introduced within or near each image; they may also be dispensed with altogether. Words should never functionally dominate the image, which then would become merely illustration to a text. The comic strip is essentially a mass-medium, printed in a magazine, newspaper, or book. A comic book is a bound collection of strips, telling a single story or various different stories. Most of the better newspaper strips eventually appear in book form.

Misleading use of "comics"

The word comic in connection with these strips is used only in the English language. Although now firmly established, it is misleading, for the early (pre-19th-century) strip was seldom comic either in form or content, and a large proportion of contemporary strips are in no sense primarily humorous. The terms comics and comic strip became established around 1900 in the United States, when all strips were indeed comic. The French term is *bande dessinée* (*i.e.*, "drawn strip," or BD for short). The older German term is *Bildergeschichte* or *Bilderstreifen* ("picture story," "picture strip"), but the Germans now tend to employ the English word. In Italy the term is *fumetto* (meaning literally "little puff of smoke," after the balloon within which most modern strips enclose verbal dialogue). (D.M.Ke.)

ORIGINS OF CARICATURE AND CARTOON

Individual satire. Caricature was a product of the Renaissance and Reformation emphasis on the importance of the individual. If a man was seen officially as an emperor, he was seen unofficially to have feet of clay or to be wearing no clothes. From about the first third of the 16th century the emphasis on decorum was so strong in Italy and spread so fast northward and westward, reinforced by a still more solemn decorum from Spain, that it produced a reaction. Desiderius Erasmus' *In Praise of Folly* was both a Renaissance effort at satire and a carry-over of medieval mockeries; the marginal drawings made in one copy of it by early 16th-century members of the German-Swiss Holbein family are neither caricature nor cartoon in the modern sense, but they are in the same stream of subjective comment on objective observation as the series of exaggerated profiles drawn by Leonardo da Vinci and Albrecht Dürer. In the 16th century the work of the Flemish painter Pieter Brueghel is full of near caricature, as in the familiar drawing of an artist who is troubled at his easel by a nosy peering connoisseur behind his shoulder. In the work of Brueghel and that of his contemporary the Dutch painter Hieronymus Bosch, there are witty and sometimes horrendous dislocations of parts of the body, combinations of human anatomy with fishes, birds, animals, and windmills, and exaggeration of obese or emaciated physical types that are likewise near cartoons.

Staatliche Museen Preussischer Kulturbesitz, Kupferstichkabinett Berlin (West)

"Two Fabulous Animals," pen and brown ink drawing by Hieronymus Bosch (c. 1450–c. 1516). In the Staatliche Museen Preussischer Kulturbesitz, Kupferstichkabinett, Berlin. 16.3 × 11.7 cm.

Yet true caricature in the sense of the satirical portrait of an individual is almost impossible to identify before the work of a late 16th-century Bolognese painter, Agostino Carracci. The first caricatures of persons whose names are still known today are by Bernini.

Social satire. The less personal and caricature-like features of the modern cartoon developed slowly through the 16th century and up to the last third of the 17th. In part consciously based on Bosch and Brueghel, in part an autonomous protest against the Renaissance belief in order, symmetry, and fixed canons of beauty, there rose a European family of grotesqueries with sources as mixed as its appearance. Its only visible overall characteristic might be said to be that it reacted, from the depth of old folkways, against the novelty of the Renaissance, the New World, and the various hierarchies. Echoes of the dark Gothic forests mixed with fantastic reports of travel (some of them not really new but rehashed from Marco Polo) and with travesties of the Renaissance ornament of such works as Raphael's decorations for the loggias of the Vatican Palace. One result was the double images of faces and landscape or of human figures built of books, fish, or pots and pans by the 16th-century Italian painter Giuseppe Arcimboldo. In a slightly different area lay two types of pictorial comedy. The first type was the conscious satire by professional printmakers, illustrating such works as the *Ship of Fools* (1494), an allegory by the German poet Sebastian Brant, or issued as independent prints. Some of them were tendentious to the point of libel (such were Lucas Cranach's attacks on the papacy, inspired by Martin Luther); others were merely mockery, such as the 16th-century German painter Hans Beham's satirical view of mercenary soldiers and their camp followers. The second type was the unconscious pictorial comedy by comparatively untutored practitioners of woodcut or etching, hastily made and issued as newspaper extras might be issued now. These works were the ancestors of 18th- and 19th-century broadsides.

Development of the modern cartoon

If caricature deals with the individual and with what makes him individual, cartoons may be said to deal with groups and with their corporate characteristics; both are connected with the Renaissance love of classification and categorizing. Up to the time, in the mid-17th century, when both caricature and cartoon jelled in forms which answer to the modern definition, caricature had been prepared on the whole by knowledgeable artists; and cartoons had been prepared (though often with the assistance of professional artists) at a somewhat lower level. Thereafter, cartoons (in the modern sense of the term) came to be created in response not merely to artistic impulses but to the same sorting-out impulses that were creating the modern state and its society, its science, and its religion. Besides the sublime–ridiculous and the artist–layman dualisms in this field, there is a sort of class dualism that is a result of historical factors rather than of general human disposition. The history of caricature and cartoon is intimately connected with the history of the way in which one class has looked at another. Dürer looked down on the heavy-bodied man whom he called farmerish; yet within two generations Brueghel was draw-

Class distinctions in caricature

By courtesy of Gripsholm Castle, Sweden

"John Calvin," oil caricature by Giuseppe Arcimboldo, 1566. In Gripsholm Castle, Sweden. 64 × 51 cm.

ing peasants in a sympathetic manner. A 16th-century Swiss engraver, Jost Amman, treated trades and professions dispassionately, as did the 17th-century French engraver Abraham Bosse, although Bosse did create some lampoons on unpopular types and callings. Jacques Callot, an early 17th-century French etcher, satirized dandies, beggars, and all classes between, and he even made the generally detested gypsies (who were not yet romantic) almost sympathetic.

A rather comfortable social climate developed in the 17th century: the wars of religion had quieted in France and the Low Countries, though civil war occupied Britain in the middle of the century. But by the time the Restoration had quieted Britain, a general European threat appeared in the form of Louis XIV. Against his absolutism and against his influence through agents in Britain and the Netherlands, the first modern cartoon campaign was made. It was modern in that it was on a large scale—cartoons were published on a fairly regular serial basis, much like that of the modern daily newspaper's editorial cartoon (though the newspaper was still in the letter-and-gazette stage); and it was based on a fairly large and general acquaintance with the persons satirized if not always with the literary analogies used. The cartoons, which as yet made no particular use of personal caricature (that was still on a friendly studio footing), were prints made in Holland by a group of artists of whom Romeyn de Hooghe was the chief, and they were sold cheap. There had been Dutch political cartoons before, but they were laborious and appeared irregularly. The Dutch–English connection in the person of William III, the continuing threat of Louis XIV, and a succession of shattering events in various spheres stimulated a vast production of cartoons from the 1680s on.

Separation of cartoon and caricature

As the cartoon spread—along with its almost indispensable element, caricature—it began to divide; and although the periodical carrying cartoons was not to appear regularly until the third quarter of the 18th century, nor the true comic periodical until early in the 19th century, the divisions were real enough to follow from that time.

PERSONAL AND POLITICAL SATIRE (PURE CARICATURE)

18th century. About 1740 the English printmaker Arthur Pond published together 25 caricatures after original drawings by a number of artists. This collection must have been effective in spreading the idea and the word, for it was an excellent publication. Pier Leone Ghezzi, one of the artists included, was probably the first professional caricaturist, for he made a living with his pen portraits of Romans and visitors to Rome, many of which he engraved. He was a minor master in comparison to his contemporary the Venetian artist Giovanni Battista Tiepolo, yet the caricatures by the latter, delightful though they are, appear to deal with types or at least with anonymous individuals rather than with nameable ones. Tiepolo's pen-and-wash drawings were a small side issue in his enormous production, and they were not engraved or otherwise multiplied in his lifetime. Both artists had an eye for ungainly legs and posture and for odd clothing and the obvious features of the face.

On the heels of Pond's reproductions came the handbill-like personal caricatures circulated from time to time. Apparently begun in the 1760s by the Englishman George Townshend (later Marquess Townshend), these were comic portraits with punning titles or accessories, intended by disingenuous means to avoid being outright libellous. A flood of imitations followed, and it was not long before Townshend's cards became comic illustrations in magazines such as *The London Magazine*, the *Political Register*, and the *Town and Country Magazine*.

Early 19th century. *Great Britain.* Thomas Rowlandson created the comic images of a great many public characters in his day: royal dukes, actresses, auctioneers, hack writers of Grub Street. He was the perfect professional to carry on what the amateur Townshend had begun. Like Tiepolo, he was able to make the person and the costume assume a homogeneously ludicrous or pathetic–bathetic look, with factitious coiffures, wildly

Rowlandson's comic images

"Marquis Spada," pen and ink drawing by Pier Leone Ghezzi (1674–1755). In the Allen R. Hite Art Institute, University of Louisville, Kentucky. 20.3 × 29.2 cm.
By courtesy of the Allen R. Hite Art Institute, University of Louisville, gift of Janos Scholz, 1953

frogged uniforms, enormous bosoms and bottoms, and the dejected attitudes of trailing handkerchiefs.

Rowlandson's contemporary James Gillray was less of an artist and more of a professional cartoonist in the modern sense. Coming from the theatre to the political scene, he brought a highly dramatic sense of situation and analogy, but he was peculiarly violent and often scurrilous or scatological. His greatest talent was with patterns and ornaments of costume, which he would allow to take on a luxuriant life of their own. The Swiss-born English painter and teacher Henry Fuseli, though hardly a professional caricaturist, stood halfway between the painted Italianate caricature groups of Sir Joshua Reynolds, an academic English painter, and the Rowlandson–Gillray drawings and etchings; he had something of Gillray's theatrical manner, but his satirical drawings were more often sensual than scatological.

France. The French painter and engraver Philibert-Louis Debucourt might have equalled Rowlandson if he had not been so occupied with the intricacies of colour prints; but he produced a few superb cartoons of the Paris of his day, full of caricatures of fashionable personages.

The whole Napoleonic period gave rise to such passion that, besides the British caricaturists of "Boney," a school of French caricature was generated, the effect of which was to come after the Restoration. Two members of an older generation, Louis-Léopold Boilly and Jean-Baptiste Isabey, really began the work. Boilly, starting where Debucourt left off, satirized the modes and manners of the French. He was not in the direct sense a political caricaturist but frequently used satirical portraits.

Isabey was primarily a portrait painter, but he was in contact with all the great continental political personalities of the first half of the 19th century, and he caricatured many of them privately. Most of the caricatures were not published, but they had an effect among artists, as did the satirical prints of Francisco de Goya.

The tendency of the Restoration to suppress Napoleonic enthusiasms provided another rich ground for cartoon as political complaint. As soon as the first stage was over (in

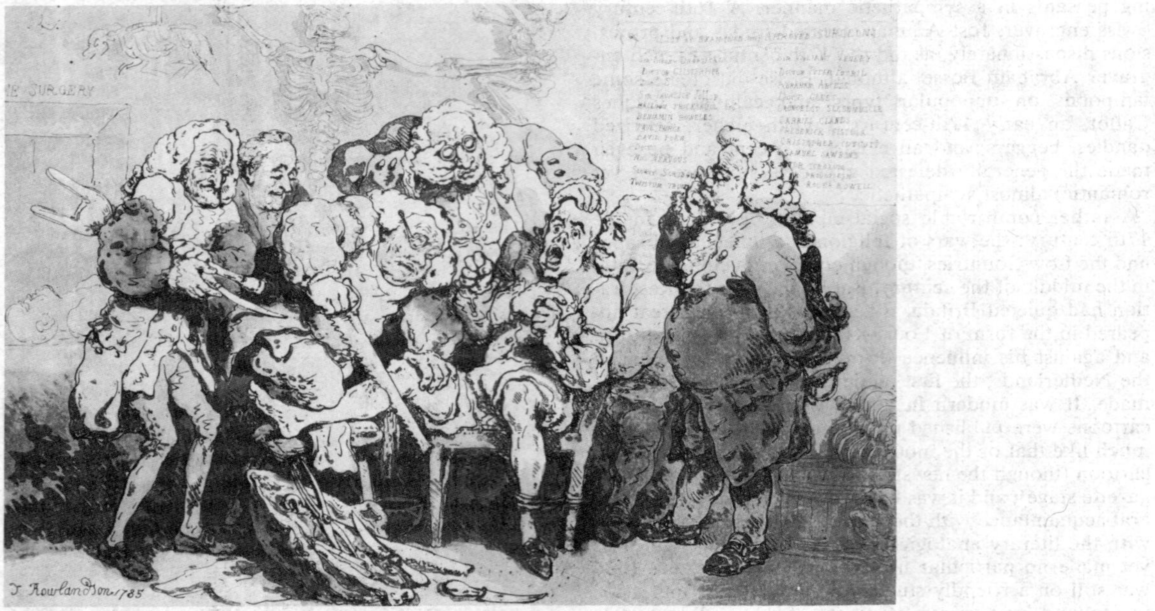

"Amputation," hand-coloured etching by Thomas Rowlandson, 1785. 24.4 × 13¾ cm.
By courtesy of The Metropolitan Museum of Art, New York, Elisha Wittelsey Fund, 1959

The cartoon as political complaint

1830), a change of administration was accompanied by the appearance of Charles Philipon's periodical *La Caricature*, the first great vehicle of Honoré Daumier, Henri Monnier, Grandville, and others. The presiding genius had great politico-legal skill and knew exactly how far he and his artists could go. The famous likening of Louis Philippe to a pear, which was both a visual and a verbal pun, was not the least of *La Caricature's* successes. Daumier's colossal gifts included personal caricature, though in his later life he dealt almost entirely in more general social satire. In the early '30s he created for Philipon "Le Ventre legislatif" ("The Legislative Belly"), at once a political indictment, a rogue's gallery of caricatures, and a monumental composition; not to mention a long series of more detailed single antiportraits. Daumier's composite sociopolitical villain, Robert Macaire, and Monnier's Joseph Prudhomme, the sum of bourgeois pettiness, served as butts of satire when censorship caught up with directly personal caricature in Philipon's three or more overlapping papers.

Middle 19th century. *Great Britain*. The specifically cartoon-bearing journal was by this time an established fact. The *Monthly Sheet of Caricatures* had begun publication in London in 1830, lithographed like Philipon's journals. In these and other ventures, the publisher Thomas McLean issued hundreds of political caricatures during a great formative period of modern legislation; his artist, Robert Seymour, was in the Gillray line rather than the later one of John Doyle, who also worked for McLean. John Doyle's son Richard became one of the masters of the mid-century British school of subtler cartooning. The younger Doyle was one of the initial staff of *Punch* when Henry Mayhew started it in 1841.

First caricaturists of *Punch*

Punch began as a fiercely democratic weekly which applied to the young Queen Victoria and her growing family, as a matter of course, the same savage treatment that had been given by caricaturists of the previous hundred years to the Hanoverians. *Punch* was born (1841) in the years when the new Westminster Palace (Houses of Parliament) was under construction. Prince Albert and his team of artistic advisers, wishing to revive fresco painting as a means of decorating the vast wall spaces of the new buildings, opened a competition. When the cartoons (in the original sense of the word) of the proposed compositions were exhibited, it was evident that many of the painters were unfamiliar with work on so heroic a scale, and some of their designs were ludicrous. *Punch* was quick to satirize them in a series of "*Punch*'s Cartoons." One of the reasons for "*Punch*'s Cartoons" on the Westminster hall exhibition was that the unpopular foreign Prince Albert had fomented the competition. But *Punch* was not so much merely antiroyal as it was antihumbug (the novelist W.M. Thackeray, after all, was another of the staff). Though its first few years were marked by some of the worst puns in a punning age, it not only kept up, with its fairly small fixed staff, a remarkable fire of lampoon but soon developed the weekly full-page political cartoon, certainly one of the chief ancestors of the modern editorial cartoon. Nineteenth-century British and general European politics might be briefly comprehended in a few dozen of these. The most famous is probably still that farewell to Otto von Bismarck, "Dropping the Pilot," by Sir John Tenniel.

The woodcut technique used for many decades in *Punch* caused the cartoons on the political page, the largest in scale of the cartoons, to be almost invariably dull in surface. The speed required of the divided-labour teams which produced the cuts from the artists' drawings did not allow for subtleties.

Other countries. The earliest really impressive makers of personal caricature and political cartoon in the United States were David Claypoole Johnston and Thomas Nast. Nast first made his name with American Civil War cartoons in *Harper's Weekly*, which like *Punch* used the woodcut process with an elaborate division of labour in the back shop for the rapid reproduction of cartoons.

The middle and late century produced in Italy the brilliant political caricaturist Virginio, who was to the rise of Italian nationalism what Nast had been to the North in the American Civil War; he worked for *Il Fischietto* of Turin. In 1848 *Kladderadatsch* started in Berlin. Munich had *Fliegende Blätter* and *Punsch*. *Punsch* was more political than the others, which were long-lived comic weeklies in the social-comment style. Schleich's *Punsch* cartoons were a running Bavarian comment on Prussianism.

Nast's personal satire

Late 19th century. *The United States*. In the boom days of the 1870s, Thomas Nast became a master of personal satire; his long practice in dealing with the professional wood engravers gave him at last a style and scale that triumphed over finicky crosshatching and gave full effect to his ruinous attacks on William Marcy "Boss" Tweed and other grafters; he was one of the most fertile of symbol makers outside the personal field and is probably the creator of the donkey of the Democratic Party as well as of the Tammany Hall tiger of the New York Democratic organization.

In 1876 *Puck* was founded. It was soon to develop new artists, notably Joseph Keppler and Bernhard Gillam. They worked in a lithographic style of considerable artis-

"Who Stole the People's Money?—Do Tell. 'Twas Him," by Thomas Nast (1840–1902).
Harper & Row, New York

tic competence, without the force of Nast or the effortless flow of Daumier, but with plenty of clever analogies and with an understanding of the sort of likeness required in caricature.

England. *Punch* meanwhile had settled into its richest period, with Sir John Tenniel and Harry Furniss as political cartoonists. *Vanity Fair* (from 1868) offered some competition, especially at first with its regular coloured lithographic antiportraits. These were signed "Ape" (Carlo Pellegrini) and "Spy" (Leslie Ward, later knighted); they kept up a steady supply of big-headed comic figures against an almost invariably blank background. They also kept up the old device of never quite naming the subject in so many words, but as they were directed at a public which was "in the know," this was part of the fun. These colour caricatures were much loved, and were often framed and hung on private walls. Max Beerbohm (knighted in 1939) devoted himself largely to social and literary satire but almost always on a basis of personal caricature. His deceptively understated outlines and pallid washes, the latter used as local colour for the sake of the overall design, were the perfect means for parodying the good taste of the *fin de siècle.* His symbols for the writers G.K. Chesterton, G.B. Shaw, Joseph Conrad, and W. Somerset Maugham have become almost the standard views of those writers.

Technical developments. Toward the end of the century there was a rebirth of personal satire which accompanied new techniques of reproduction and perfected enrichments of such older techniques as colour lithography. Photomechanical reproduction, especially after the development of halftone, allowed direct reproduction of the artist's drawing without personal interpretation by wood engravers or other technicians. Colour lithography, which had been either limp or turgid on the whole, found a new life. The caricaturists who had been able to draw directly on the stone, as Daumier did, had always had more freedom and better control over results than those who worked with pen and paper; now the latter could depend upon themselves and a photomechanical process.

Influence of photomechanical reproduction

France. Henri de Toulouse-Lautrec produced large-scale posters and, earlier, polychrome lithographs for the Parisian publication *Le Rire* (from 1894) and for independent distribution. He created a new style of informal composition, somewhat influenced by Japanese prints, with bright clear colour, broad, rather casual outlines drawn largely with the brush, a trick of making tone by means of spatter, and a wit which saw through ugliness to a new sort of eloquence. His view of Oscar Wilde was economical and devastating, and his caricatures of theatre and music-hall personalities are unmatched. Another French artist, Caran d'Ache (Emmanuel Poiré), worked on a smaller scale with pen and brush and was one of the most effective continental commentators on the South African War.

Germany. The artists of the Munich satirical publication *Simplicissimus* (from 1896) were all somewhat influenced by Toulouse-Lautrec in their use of white space, spatters, and often random outline; they all commented on those features of German life which were most disliked outside Germany—the didactic professor, the tourist, and the military dandy. Their caricatures in the last field were very thinly veiled; Eduard Thöny, one of this group, was especially popular for the way he conveyed the upper-class boorishness of Prussian officers.

20th century. *The United States.* Charles Dana Gibson was a virtuoso of the pen, using the manner of *Punch*'s Phil May as a point of departure. He used the pen as he pleased, sometimes in a direct descriptive manner, sometimes with colouristic suggestion, sometimes almost anti-graphically. Though he helped to create the caricature types of Theodore Roosevelt and Woodrow Wilson, he was more a social than a personal caricaturist. He is mentioned chiefly because he introduced American physical types called Gibson girls and Gibson men.

Role of *The Masses*

A position much like that of *Simplicissimus* was occupied in the years 1911–17 by *The Masses* of New York, which had an editorial policy based on old-fashioned socialist idealism. It was served by a remarkable group of artists whose fine drawing made their often sharp propaganda for reform tolerable in quarters where they might not otherwise have gotten a hearing. John French Sloan, George Bellows, Boardman Robinson, and Art Young were as likely to deal in general social terms as in personal ones, for by this time personal, particularly political, caricature was tending to move into the newspaper editorial cartoon or the pages of theatrical or sporting news.

Photomechanical reproduction not only allowed greater freedom for comic artists; it made possible the daily newspaper cartoon and later the syndicated editorial cartoon and the comic strip. From about the same time as the new generation of weeklies there was a rise in the use, the autographic character, and the influence of pictorial journalism. John T. McCutcheon of the *Chicago Tribune*, though he used a rather dry and old-fashioned pen technique, was able to range over a world that included politics, the "good old days," the mores of the moment, and sports. His cartoon world, like that of *The Masses*, was almost entirely urban, but he was one of the first of a generally imperturbable type of American cartoonist, whose view is amused rather than aroused. His career ran from before Theodore Roosevelt to after Franklin D. Roosevelt's time. In his line of succession stood such men as Edwin Marcus and S.J. Woolf in the *New York Times*, Oscar Cesare of *The Sun*, Herbert Block ("Herblock") of the *Washington Post*, Daniel Fitzpatrick of the *St. Louis Post-Dispatch*, Rollin Kirby of the *New York World-Telegram*, Bill Mauldin of the *Chicago Sun-Times*, John Fischetti of the *Chicago Daily News*, and others too numerous to list.

Dominance of David Low

England and the Continent. The outstanding political commentator of the first half of the 20th century was David Low, a New Zealander, who worked for the *Sydney Bulletin* before going to Britain. Low was perhaps the best all-round man in the field of caricature since Daumier. His brush drawing was of an Oriental economy, his invention of analogy gleeful without being really outside the classic British educated tradition, and his hatred reserved for a few needful occasions. Like many before him, he employed hackneyed devices (*e.g.*, the heads of a pack of British politicians on dogs' bodies) but by slyness of expression always managed an original twist. There was almost no one in the political field to touch Low except for the Dutchman Louis Raemaekers during World War I, and Raemaekers was bitter where Low was dry and crisp, with footnotes of rumbling laughter. Jean-Jacques Sennep (pen name of J.-J.-C. Pennès) of the Paris *Le Figaro* and Fritz Meinhard of the *Stuttgarter Zeitung* were important French and German caricaturists of the 20th century.

COMEDIES OF MANNERS (THE CARTOON)

Types and groups, rather than politics and the politician or any nameable individuals, are the concern of the co-

"Tricks or Treaties," by Herbert Block.
"Tricks or Treaties,"—from *Straight Herblock* (Simon & Schuster, 1964)

median of manners. He may love mankind for its imperfections or set out to seek improvement, but his method will be much the same. He does not need, as the political cartoonist does, to set up allegories and analogies or to write names on labels, but he may sometimes sharpen his comment by treating human beings as animals (monkeys and apes for obvious reasons have long been the favourites, along with dogs and birds). If the personal caricature is an antiportrait, the cartoon on human foibles is often a sort of anti-sumptuary law or a countergrammar which says, "The exceptions are more fun than the rules."

16th to 18th century. Brueghel and Callot were certainly comedians of manners. Brueghel's picturizing of Flemish proverbs, themselves often comments on foibles, and his prints of the Seven Deadly Sins with satirical examples filling the backgrounds combine a bit of moralizing with the delighted empathy of a participant. Callot is slightly more detached, possibly because of his more conscious style and because he was himself the printmaker (Brueghel drew for professional engravers and woodcutters); but in the catalogs of byplay in his panoramic scenes of fairs and in his trick of making the beggar wear his rags handsomely, he is always balancing and measuring.

Parallel to two-dimensional comment in this vein ran the theatre, notably the commedia dell'arte, puppet theatre, and the performances of the jester and clown. Both appeared in the late 17th and early 18th centuries in the rather courtly comic drawings of the Frenchman Claude Gillot, Antoine Watteau's predecessor. These are not really comedies of manners, for the clowns are used as if they were monkeys aping human ways at a remove toward greater elegance rather than toward apishness. They point the way to a good many 18th-century practices: Gillot and Watteau both made decorations which included monkeys (singerie) just as François Boucher and later artists were to use pseudo-Chinese scenes (chinoiserie) occasionally as ways of commenting on contemporary European life.

Hogarth's cartoons of manners

It is with William Hogarth that the cartoon of manners reached great stature. His series "Marriage à la Mode," "A Rake's Progress," "A Harlot's Progress," the "Four Stages of Cruelty," and the unfinished "Industrious and Idle Apprentices" were loaded with observation not only of human beings but of objects and their ecology, as if he were using his own proliferation of comic images in protest against waste of time, talents, life, and pride. Hogarth, like Sir Joshua Reynolds after him, even painted comic subjects, but he kept to social satire and avoided personal caricature. His pictures of depravity and ferocity are hard to beat, but he could put an expression of by no means unholy delight on a wicked face. In the "Laughing Audience" he gave a full measure of laughter. Hogarth's engravings ran to very large editions and were recut and reissued and then copied at reduced scale for books of the *Complete Works*.

19th century. *Spain.* Francisco de Goya is hard to place in the historical development of the comedy of manners. His "Caprichos" (1796–98), etchings prepared

By courtesy of The Metropolitan Museum of Art, New York, Harris Brisbane Dick Fund, 1932

"Marriage à-la-Mode: Breakfast Scene," engraving by William Hogarth, 1745. 35.2 × 43.8 cm.

"Actualities No. 190; Des dames d'un demi-monde mais n'ayant pas de demi-jupes" ("Demi-mondaines with more than demi-skirts"), lithograph by Honoré Daumier, 1855. 19.7 × 25.7 cm.
Courtesy of the Fogg Art Museum, Harvard University

by some of the most simple and trenchant brush drawings ever made, appeared in the last years of the 18th century and can be called comedies of manners only insofar as they are related to folk sayings and the bittersweet Spanish folk wisdom. Thus, they stand in the line of Bosch and Brueghel, so many of whose paintings were in Habsburg collections in Madrid. The "Proverbios" of 1813–19 are even more monumental transfigurations of various states of the human condition. Like the "Caprichos," they used the caricaturist's means for irony and satire, but there was little of the comic left in them and none at all in the "Desastres de la guerra" (1810–14, "Disasters of War"), which used the Peninsular phase of the Napoleonic Wars as a point of departure. They are closer to universality than even Callot's similarly inspired series and are searching comments on more stages of cruelty than Hogarth covered. In them, Goya was really a political cartoonist using no names; yet he was hardly a public cartoonist in the normal sense because censorship and other factors allowed only a very small circulation of his later work until a sizable edition was printed a generation after his death. The earlier work, which contains elements of comedy, did get abroad and had influence in France and England probably before Goya's death. Artistically, if not politically, his work would have had the same powerful effect whenever "discovered" or circulated.

The folk wisdom of Goya

France. "Paul Gavarni" (Sulpice-Guillaume Chevalier) was more purely a comedian of manners than Daumier, although he was no less perceptive and no less sympathetic with the *petit parisien.* He had a grace derived from his apprenticeship in fashion illustration that produced enchanting jokes on young people in love, dandies, and the theatre and circus. He worked late in life for the *Illustrated London News,* as did Constantin Guys, the French foreign correspondent who reported the Crimean War to the British. Guys, a prolific draftsman who always kept a comic touch, was peculiarly subtle in reporting the great but contrived elegance of Napoleon III's court. He helped both British and French to see themselves as others saw them. "Grandville" (J.I.I. Gérard) was a comic artist on *La Caricature* whose work recalls some of the complicated inventions of Arcimboldo.

Daumier was, of course, the great master of social comedy with or without political content. His series of affectionate if disenchanted comments on married life, the theatre, the courts, concierges, musicians, painters, bluestockings, bathhouses, and children constitute as full a report on Paris in his time as Rembrandt's drawings were for 17th-century Amsterdam. The words were often important, especially when Daumier was indicating in his text the unspoken thoughts of his characters (thus anticipating the 20th-century cartoon in which a thought or vision is indicated as a balloon with cloud-scalloped edges and a picture rather than words inside). His often untidy line and knowingly casual accents of tone produced (at will) sensations of chill weather, of ecstasies of gluttony, of juvenile pride, or of legal craftiness.

England. Rowlandson, as noted earlier, was a political caricaturist part of the time, but above all he was a lampooner of ludicrous and excessive behaviour. He created almost unaided a gallery of types missed by Hogarth, many of which persist in British life—the antiquarian, the old maid, the harried foreign servant, the pleasantly blowzy barmaid, the decent old parson. He was by no means as bawdy as he is supposed to have been, but he liked to push action, like appearance, to an extreme. His Dr. Syntax may be called an ancestor of comic strips.

George Cruikshank carried Rowlandson's methods almost beyond extremes in his youth. He used superfantastic costume and sometimes that device of enormous heads which some 17th-century caricaturists used and which is still used by sports-page cartoonists and comic advertising artists.

The longest continuing habit and tradition of humorous comment on the passing world has been made by the English humour magazine *Punch.* Though it began in puns and peevishness, it warmed up during the 19th century with John Leech, Charles Keene, George du Maurier, and in the 20th century with George Belcher, "Fougasse" (Kenneth Bird), H.M. Bateman, Nicolas Bentley, E.H. Shepard, and Osbert Lancaster. Leech was in a sense the pictorial equivalent of Thackeray (Thackeray was an excellent comic draftsman but better at getting the feel of past time with a comic flavour than at considering his contemporaries other than in words). Leech and Keene belong to the era of wood-engraved reproduction; when one sees their original drawings and manuscript captions or dialogue, it is apparent that something was lost in detail and finesse of line but nothing in sense of comedy, in the affectionate tone. The enormous self-confidence of the optimistic Victorians, expressed at first through the violent or bumptious Regency manner of the young George Cruikshank, was tempered by the staff-meeting or meeting-of-minds conduct of *Punch.* The "manners" part of the phrase "comedy of manners" became subjective as well as objective. *Punch* became an upper-class weekly and continued as such for three or four generations, reflecting the large knowledge of all classes which it was possible for its staff to offer its readers, and the large delight of the upper class in seeing its own foibles and those of its servants, tradesmen, lame ducks, and "climbers" exposed. The swing of a crinoline by Leech and the curl of a cabdriver's hat brim by Keene were perfect selective imitation, themselves almost inimitable; the crinoline and the hat are gone with those who knew how to wear them, but the picture in *Punch* remains.

Humorists of *Punch*

Photomechanical reproduction came in during du Maurier's day but hardly affected his generation of artists. Phil May's pen was better served by the camera and the zinc block than Leech's had been by end-grain boxwood and gravers, but the general language was the same. With the generation of George Belcher there was a great change. His own crumbly charcoal or crayon strokes were perfectly adapted to the new process—indeed it was mutual—as were the fat blacks of the Frenchman Jean-Louis Forain and the mid-20th-century cobwebs of Rowland Emett. Fougasse's highly personal little curly stick men, drawn perhaps with a signwriter's pen, could be reproduced by almost any method, but the sharp lines and solid black areas of Bateman (deriving ultimately from Aubrey Beardsley's decorative style) and the thick–thin pen strokes of Shepard (more in the Keene tradition) were well served by modern processes. Shepard was more truly an illustrator than a cartoonist, but Bateman's towering humours and bulging-eyed apoplectic businessmen were in the direct line from Edward Lear to such frantic American cartoonists as Virgil Partch.

Edward Lear practiced as a comic draftsman an economy and geniality that are hard to improve upon, but like Daumier he supposed that his own best gifts lay in an-

"That reminds me, dear—did you remember the sandwiches?" by Fougasse (Kenneth Bird).

Contributions of Edward Lear

other field. Humour had been brought into satire by Hogarth; a truly funny style of drawing was brought into cartooning by Lear. Hitherto, standard drawing techniques had been applied to grotesque shapes and comic situations, but Lear's line went wandering off into a sort of joke on calligraphy. Furthermore, he travelled into areas of fantasy previously barely hinted at.

Aubrey Beardsley used a caricaturist's methods, but little of his work, except perhaps the illustrations to *The Rape of the Lock*, was actually caricature or cartoon. If some of Cranach's prints can be called illustrated libels, some of Beardsley's can be called illustrated yearnings by unfrocked lechers. They are important because their combination of large white spaces, clear lines, and solid or slightly irritated blacks could be reproduced successfully in a choice of dimensions and thus laid down a discipline for illustration, commercial art, and the comic strip.

20th century. The whole tenor of pictorial comedy was shifted by World War I and by the boom times thereafter. Some previously forbidden subjects became admissible. Political caricature during and after the war was excessively partisan, while the cartoons about the war itself tended to alleviate the pain of the struggle. Bruce Bairnsfather's Old Bill and his colleagues in Britain got through it by joking. After it was over, the public for comic publications was greatly enlarged; while the newly rich were standard butts for cartoonists catering to all classes, they were themselves buying comic weeklies.

In the United States the usually monthly comic magazines of universities and colleges had a sudden flowering, to such an extent that an anthology for their cartoons called *College Humor* was published for several years in the 1920s and '30s. The tendency of previously serious weeklies to use small cartoons here and there or to insert a funny page somewhere, created not only new markets for cartoonists but also a temporary decline in the purely humorous magazines, and *Punch, Life*, and *Judge* had difficulty surviving the Depression of the 1930s. The title of *Puck* had already passed to a newspaper chain which used it for a Sunday supplement, and the title of *Life* eventually passed to a periodical of different character. *Simplicissimus* never quite rose between wars to its pre-1914 stature; the effort which went into Dada and Surrealist publications in Germany and France in the '20s, when art itself became an object of social satire, meant a loss to other comic publications. Meanwhile, the public in general gradually became aware of modern art, and its presumed incomprehensibility became almost as routine a subject by 1940 as mothers-in-law or freshly painted park benches.

In the United States an older generation of humorists somewhat of the upper-class *Punch* style lingered briefly after World War I. Of such were Oliver Herford, whose *Alphabet of Celebrities* and other comic verses with pictures were published as small books; Peter Newell, whose highly original *Slant Book, Hole Book*, etc., had a sharp eye to late prewar costume, and Gelett Burgess, whose *Goops* for children were spaghetti-like little figures whose behaviour illustrated a moral.

But to these was now added a new generation of sophisticated but slightly flashier performers, many of them with theatrical connections, many at first employed by the fashion magazine *Vanity Fair* and later by the *New Yorker* (beginning in 1925); Ralph Barton, who did superb roués; Rea Irvin of the thin trembly line, poached eyes, and almost oriental splendour; Gluyas Williams and Ellison Hoover, who satirized business, industrial labour, and other subjects not well-known to the *Punch* tradition; and Alfred Frueh, whose caricatures of theatre people recalled Toulouse-Lautrec. The Depression of the 1930s brought forward a few artists with a genius for social protest, few of whom had any real sense of comedy because tragedy was not to them, as it had been to Daumier, the other side of the same coin. In the United States the Communist *Daily Worker* had the services of William Gropper, a distinguished lithographer and editorial cartoonist who was sometimes able to capture something of the humorous tone of the prewar *The Masses*. And it gradually became known that in the Soviet Union a comic magazine called *Krokodil* was allowed to gibe at the ways of its brothers and even occasionally of its masters.

Cartoons of the Depression years

The two most interesting features of cartoon and caricature in the first half of the 20th century were the rises of the one-line joke and the pictorial joke without words, and the enormous diversity of styles of drawing. The *New Yorker* was probably the inventor or reinventor of the one-line joke and certainly its chief fomenter. Five-decker dialogues with headings were swept away even from *Punch*, and there was a greater unity of words with picture, paralleling the tendency toward tabloid newspapers with large photographic halftones and very pithy text. The joke without words, often in two or more frames, was the extreme of economy of language. One result of this change was that the comedy-of-manners cartoon must convey its comment entirely through costume, setting, and (to a lesser extent) situation, and the emphasis thus tended to fall more on comic situation than on plays on words, class differences, or marked action. The *New Yorker* and magazines whose cartoons had been influenced by it aimed at a sophisticated audience. The *New Yorker* itself, while enjoying in its maturity a position equivalent to that of *Punch* in the 1880s, aimed its advertising and much of its writing at upper-income classes, but its cartoons were aimed at the classes described as highbrow and upper-middle-brow. Such features of the old-fashioned British-style upper class as servants were always treated by *New Yorker* cartoonists (notably Mary Petty) as necessarily comic fossils of an old order and hence in, rather than out of, that old upper class. Whole new areas of social-comedy subject matter arose in this

"For heaven's sake, can't you do anything right?" by Charles Addams.

magazine: the life of the Jewish community, the fauna of bars, the managerial class and its flavour, the lighter side of the well-kept woman, commercialized sports, and the imagined life of colonies or races of antisocial beings.

The diversity of styles of drawing reflected the influence of Postimpressionist art quite as much as did the use of modern art as a subject for jokes. The great draftsmen who were on the edges of Impressionism (such as Toulouse-Lautrec) had much influence on caricature and cartoon; while the same photomechanical reproduction that advanced the latter communicated modern painting to a vast public. The loose, almost deliberately ugly method of the Expressionists got into some of the single-cartoon commentators to such an extent that their shorthand was sometimes difficult for those who did not read them daily. The meandering willful line of the 20th-century Swiss painter Paul Klee certainly influenced Saul Steinberg; the Cubists' studies in African sculpture were echoed in cartoons by Miguel Covarrubias and Virgil Partch; the "classical" period of Pablo Picasso in Richard Taylor and others; the curving economical line of Henri Matisse (oddly enough) in Richard Decker. Occasionally, cartoonists parodied one another: Oliver Herford once presented Gibson girls as paper dolls without expression; Al Capp in the comic strip "Li'l Abner" parodied "Dick Tracy" and "Mary Worth." *Mad* magazine parodied everybody: style, subject, everything from politics to pornography.

The cartoon of predicament or situation

The comic strip having taken over the comic presentation of events almost completely, especially since the rise of the one-line joke or picture caption, the modern cartoon became one largely of situation or of predicament that was stated without a solution's being worked out or suggested. The mother of a side-show circus family, confronted with more than she can manage, simply says that after all she has only three hands; a young girl is in ecstasies over a sunset, while behind her a bearded artist-stereotype says, "Too much purple." Meanwhile, the longer sort of comic anecdote retreated to a purely oral–aural life or to the bound volume of jokes, where it sometimes had a vignette-like illustration.

The cartoon of situation was certainly not new, but it predominated in the first half of the 20th century. A Daumier lithograph showing a very fat woman in a crinoline climbing into an omnibus bore no dialogue, but simply the caption, "A mere nothing, and the bus is full." This was a cartoon of predicament. There has tended to be a cluster of these situation subjects: the desert island no larger than a hearthrug, the man who meets a woman walking and imagines her naked (in a scalloped balloon), the flying carpet with novel chauffeur or passenger, the picture gallery with mutual reaction between work of art and viewer, the psychoanalyst's couch, the big-game hunter's trophy room. If the situation was clear, not even one line of joke was required. Such cartoons had a sort of family connection with the earliest caricatures, but they were not merely anti-portraits of types, they were portraits with accessories that created the predicament. So were the tiny single woodcut figures that were inserted as pictorial puns into the text pages of *Punch* in the 1840s. But the latter-day predicament may be highly complicated; in the hands of such a cartoonist as George Price, whose split pen line built up tattered edifices of dowdiness, or Rowland Emett, whose fantastic locomotives and wispy codgers were half infernal and half heavenly, the comedy came from an accumulation of frustrating but ludicrous detail. Frustration, that renowned companion of modern life, was dissolved by laughter. Even the presumably invincible American businessman was often represented in cartoons in frustrating situations, often briskly indicated by the graphic lines on the charts in his office (Whitney Darrow excelled in this genre). André François, who worked for both French and British papers, was a master of the rapidly sketched situation; so was "Anton" of *Punch* (a man and a woman jointly using the name), who kept up the tradition of satire through clothes, being particularly good at pseudo-Edwardian nattiness. Herb Stansbury's "Smart Chart," a one-frame comic for the

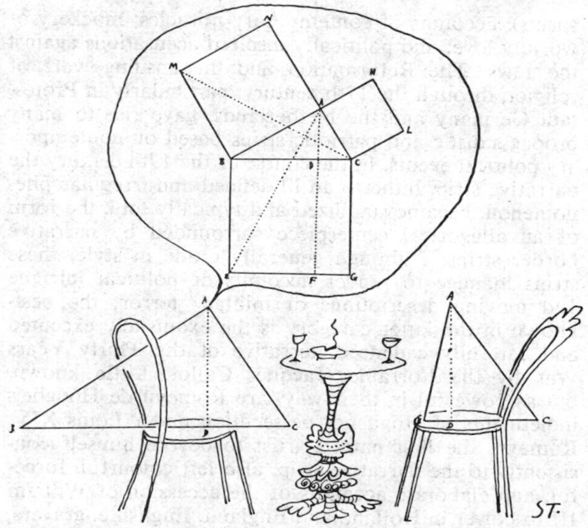

Captionless cartoon by Saul Steinberg.

financial page, satirized stock market graphs. In the drawings of the Romanian-born Saul Steinberg there was almost a parody of the cartoon of situation, for his lines doubled back on themselves and bit their own tails: the hand was indicated as drawing the portrait of which it was a part, or the frustrating details positively engulfed the subject (a wicker chair taken over entirely by its curlicues; tattooing extended beyond the tattooed man; the woman with a lozenge-shaped face, on her lap a baby whose lozenge-shaped face is one-quarter of the larger lozenge).

Unique style of Steinberg

Yet there were also extraordinarily simple performances; the unassuming little people of Jean Effel (François Lejeune) moved gently through the trials of Adam and Eve; Jacques Faizant's bad children produced hilarious effects by conveying their concentration in a few lines; Otto Soglow's stenographic vocabulary of forms for human bodies (perhaps slightly indebted to Burgess' *Goops*) was so graphic that it could be used in minuscule dimensions with perfect legibility. On the other hand, Peter Arno's large-scale and heavy outlines, despite simple straightforward design, made his beaky and bosomy figures almost jump off the page (for many years one of his near-bawdy cartoons almost invariably occupied a position in the *New Yorker* on the full page immediately after "The Talk of the Town," which suggested that the political cartoon of *Punch* was being ridiculed). Ronald Searle, after a long British career of making spiky and raffish pseudo-Edwardians and fiendish schoolgirls, had a success as an artist for American advertising. A pair of delightful opposite numbers were W. Heath Robinson and the slightly later Rube Goldberg, who on both sides of the Atlantic created wild half-anthropomorphic parodies of intricate machinery. During World War II, Bill Mauldin's disenchanted soldiers were proper descendants of Bairnsfather's. (W.Am.)

COMIC STRIPS AND COMIC BOOKS

Early strips. The comic strip, defined as a mass medium, cannot reasonably be said to exist before the invention of printing. In the early period two principal forms may be observed: the series of small images printed on a single piece of paper (narrative strip proper), and the series composed of several sheets of paper, with one image per page, which when displayed on the wall of a house formed a narrative frieze or picture story. From the outset two basic groups of themes emerge: political morality and private morality.

Early German woodcuts

Surviving pre-1550 strips, most of which are German woodcuts, deal with such subjects as the lives of saints (subdivided in the manner of late medieval painted altarpieces, an arrangement that may be considered a decisive factor on the compartmentalization layout of broadsheets); accounts of contemporary miracles; mockery of worldly love; and politically inspired accusations against the Jews. The Reformation and the ensuing wars of religion through the 17th century, particularly in Protestant Germany and the Netherlands, gave rise to many propagandistic and patriotic strips based on contemporary political events. In the course of the 17th century the narrative strip, hitherto an ill-defined and irregular phenomenon, became stabilized and typically took the form of an allegorical centerpiece surrounded by narrative border strips. Although generally crude in style, these strips manage to render accounts of political intrigue and moving descriptions of military terror; the best-known in the latter category is the exquisitely executed and carefully cadenced narrative of the Thirty Years War by the Lorrainer Jacques Callot. Little known, but as powerful in their way, are Romeyn de Hooghe's indictments of Huguenot persecution under Louis XIV. Romeyn, the first named artist to devote himself consistently to the narrative strip, also left colourful, forceful, and elaborate accounts of the accession of William III to power in Holland and England. English engravers, inspired by the Dutch example and led by Francis Barlow, retailed the complex political events of the period in the form of playing cards, which were often sold in uncut broadsheets.

The earliest strips concerning private morality are German and recount particularly atrocious forms of murder and their public punishment, the emphasis shifting progressively from the latter (in the 16th century) to the former (in the 18th century). The crime strip eventually developed into the more or less exaggerated and romanticized life of the famous brigand, which is the precursor of the modern detective strip. Narratives based on a wider spectrum of ideally immoral behaviour took as their point of departure illustrations for the parable of the Prodigal Son, woodcut versions of which, independent of the biblical text, were first produced by Cornelius Teunissen of Amsterdam. The riotous living of the Prodigal, enriched with elements from illustrations for the Seven Deadly Sins and the Ten Commandments, was distilled in various Italian lives of harlots and rakes, the most comprehensive and drastic of which are mid-17th century Venetian. A generation later, the Bolognese artist G.M. Mitelli was giving his narrative and semi-narrative satires almost caricatural moral emphasis. German artists in the 17th century specialized in satirically exposing the tyranny of shrewish wives and proposing violent remedies. The Dutch at this time produced frankly farcical strips of very primitive design, made expressly for children. By mid-18th century the Russians, too, were making satirical strips.

Hogarth's picture stories

The various social and moral themes that had been crudely treated in different countries and at different times were the raw material for the English artist William Hogarth, who raised the anonymous broadsheet picture story to an aesthetic level which rarely has been surpassed. With a social insight both broad and deep, with an unrivalled sense of satirical counterpoint and topicality of reference, and with exceptional physiognomic finesse, Hogarth dealt with types from all classes of society. His narrative richness is entirely visual, for he dispensed with all the broadsheet paraphernalia of caption–balloon–legend–commentary, permitting only such inscriptions as can be introduced naturalistically into the scene. Hogarth's moral attitude was also new: he depicted the follies and the punishment of his protagonists with a measure of sympathy, reserving the full fire of his satire for those who exploit them. Among Hogarth's many followers, two stand out: the German Daniel Chodowiecki, who reduced the Hogarthian picture story within the compass of almanac illustrations, and the Englishman James Northcote, who tried to combine Hogarthian realism with a Neoclassical sentimentality ("Diligence and Dissipation," 1796).

It was the introduction into the broadsheet of the essentially comic mechanism of caricature that established the "comic strip" as basically comic in both form and content. The major exponents of the caricatural strip during the "Great Age" of English caricature around 1800 were minor artists such as Henry Bunbury, George Woodward, and notably Richard Newton, who in his brief career combined elements of Hogarthian satire with the grotesque exaggerations of Rowlandson and Gillray. Economy of line, instantaneousness of comic effect, and visual and verbal wit now became the hallmark of the strip. With the story concentrated on a single page, backgrounds and narrative incident were minimized in favour of striking facial expressions and silhouetted poses.

Rodolphe Töpffer

19th century. The heir to the experiments of the English caricaturists, and the father of the comic strip in its modern sense, was Rodolphe Töpffer, a schoolmaster of Geneva, whose life spanned roughly the first half of the 19th century. Exempt from the personal–political preoccupations of the English caricaturists, Töpffer created a species of absurdist anti-heroes who struggled desperately, fruitlessly, and farcically against the caprices of fate, nature, and an irrational, mechanistic society. The stories (lithographed in little oblong albums containing up to 100 pages) are purposefully purposeless, flow with calculated non sequiturs, and make digression a narrative principle. The pace is sustained by another revolution in draftsmanship, for Töpffer discovered how to turn systematic doodling to account, how to exploit the accident, and how to vary physiognomies experimentally. By abandoning the academic concept of anatomical, three-dimensional drawing, he showed how to render movement for movement's sake. Töpffer's strips are also morally mobile: the normal relationship between cause and effect or crime and punishment, which had underpinned all the older stories, disintegrated.

The Töpfferian mode was introduced into the new French satirical periodical journalism by various minor artists. By entering the regular newspaper press, the old broadsheet cartoon exchanged independence for security, and became, for better or worse, subject to editorial control. Cham (pseudonym of Amédée de Noé) published several albums modelled on Töpffer in the 1840s, before settling for a style nearer to that of Daumier. The photographer Nadar, among others, flirted intermittently

"Profanation of the Host by Jews at Passau 1477." German broadsheet, *c.* 1490.

Und schon ist er auf der Brücke,
Kracks! die Brücke bricht in Stücke;

Grad als dieses vorgekommen,
Kommt ein Gänsepaar geschwommen,
Welches Böck in Todeshast
Krampfhaft bei den Beinen faßt.

Wieder tönt es: „Meck, meck, meck!"
Plumps! da ist der Schneider weg!

Beide Gänse in der Hand,
Flattert er auf trocknes Land. —

"Max und Moritz" by Wilhelm Busch.

with the new mode, rendering style and story line more realistic and therefore heavier. Léonce Petit, who had Töpffer's lightness of touch but not his imaginative flair, specialized in rustic farce. A special place is occupied by the illustrator Gustave Doré, who developed a new method owing relatively little to Töpffer (shown in, *e.g.*, *Histoire de la Sainte Russie*, 1854). This was the illustrated chronicle in which a startling hodgepodge of picturesque effects was arranged casually or with deliberate incongruity into a loose chronological sequence.

The contribution of English 19th-century artists is as yet undetermined. George Cruikshank, Cham visiting England in 1847, and thereafter T.H. Nicholson produced Töpfferian variations. Du Maurier around 1869–70 executed some curious animal metamorphoses and wordless gag stories. Among dozens of artists who later tried the comic strip, one may tentatively single out J.F. Sullivan, whose working-class types are drawn in a style that may owe something to Wilhelm Busch and W.G. Baxter, whose Ally Sloper, a proletarian loafer, appeared in *Ally Sloper's Half Holiday* (1884–1923).

Dominance of Wilhelm Busch

The dominant figure of the late 19th century is the German Wilhelm Busch, whose immense popularity in his own day has survived into the late 20th century. At first in periodicals, then in separately published albums, Busch quickly established himself as the first fully professional and truly popular comic-strip artist, appealing to educated and simple, young and old alike. Not being bound to journals, he could, like Töpffer, develop much longer stories than his French contemporaries, whose strips rarely exceeded 50 or so scenes running over three successive issues of a magazine. His graphic and narrative line appears more controlled, more predictable than that of Töpffer; it is comic in an earthier and more rational way. He revived the tradition of realistic social satire, although only two of his stories (*Helen* and *St. Anthony*) have a simply definable satiric butt (religious hypocrisy). Busch appears as a man obsessed with the farcical situation and its potential for physical violence. Happiness appears to lie in the avoidance of the petty annoyances of life and in the repression of instinctual behaviour. His cautionary tales of naughty children and animals may be regarded, on one level, as sophisticated parodies of the didactic juvenile literature of Germany and, on another, as condemnations of the childish sadism that is assumed to lie in everyone. On yet another level, all his work can be viewed as essays on the vulnerability of human dignity. His best known characters, the infant pranksters Max and Moritz, have spawned innumerable progeny down to our own day. Busch's graphic inventiveness was tremendous: his use of patterns of oscillation to represent movement and new conventional signs to express shock, pain, and other emotions constitute a vocabulary that has served the humorous strip cartoonist down to our own times. The rolling rhythm of Busch's graphic line has its counterpart in his facile comic verse, which is both independent and complementary. Variation in the amount of this verse accompanying each picture plays an essential part in the pace of the narrative.

The only German follower of Busch worthy of the name was Adolf Oberländer, a sharp observer of human behaviour. The heir to Busch in France was Caran d'Ache (pseudonym of Emmanuel Poiré), who in supplements to *Le Figaro* in the later 1880s drew the first strips to appear in a general-interest daily newspaper rather than in a weekly satirical magazine of relatively restricted readership. Always witty in a purely graphic sense, he frequently dispensed with captions altogether. In this respect, as in his technique of motif accumulation —his manner of letting a motif or movement snowball or crescendo ad absurdum—he taught much to later cartoonists, especially to H.M. Bateman in the 1920s.

The influence of Busch on the development of the American newspaper strip was decisive; but European children's illustrated literature derived more from *Imagerie d'Épinal* and from the comic-strip artist Christophe. Throughout the 19th century the common people in France and The Netherlands, especially in rural areas, had subsisted on *Imagerie d'Épinal*, single broadsheets emanating from the town of Épinal, France, and hawked about the countryside. They covered, often in narrative form, such topics of folk interest as religious stories, patriotic histories, and fairy tales. The severe and simple didactic plates had a more or less realistic social emphasis. Some *Imagerie d'Épinal* are comic in content, although not always comic in style, relating, for instance, the folly of certain traditional social stereotypes or satirical characters from folklore and literature like Tyl Eulenspiegel and Baron Munchhausen. It was Christophe (pseudonym of Georges Colomb) who raised this type of popular imagery to the level of the intelligent, urban child, first in the children's periodical, then in various albums published separately. These were originally designed, like Töpffer's, for the children of his own household and the pupils of his school. Christophe's gentle mockery of such types as the naïve bourgeois and the

Influence of the *Imagerie d'Épinal*

"Krazy Kat," by George Herriman.
Reprinted through the courtesy of Grosset & Dunlap, Inc. Copyright © 1969 by King Features Syndicate, Inc., Nostalgia Press, Inc., and Grosset & Dunlap, Inc.

absent-minded professor is now implanted in French folklore. Christophe established a format for English and French children's comics which survived down to World War II, whereby the text is excluded from the image instead of being incorporated in the balloons of American usage.

First newspaper strips

20th century. *United States.* The modern newspaper strip was born in the heat of rivalry between giants of the American press. In January 1894 a comic strip filled, for the first time, a full-colour page of Joseph Pulitzer's newspaper the *New York World;* in October 1896 the publisher William Randolph Hearst announced in his rival paper the *Morning Journal* the first regular weekly full-colour comic supplement. This supplement ran to eight pages and included the "Yellow Kid" of Richard Outcault, whom Hearst had enticed away from the *New York World.* The "Yellow Kid" was the first continuous comic character in the U.S. Outcault established earthy, strictly urban farce as the keynote of the early American strip, which thereafter grew in sophistication and sentimentality. The "Yellow Kid" also standardized the speech balloon, which had fallen largely into disuse since the 17th century and its occasional appearance in the English caricatural strip around 1800. In 1897 Rudolph Dirks, at the instigation of Hearst, who had enjoyed the work of Wilhelm Busch as a child, worked up a strip based on "Max und Moritz," called the "Katzenjammer Kids," which proved an instant success. It had, for the first time, the fully developed form of the newspaper strip; *i.e.*, it used balloons, had a continuous cast of characters, and was divided into small regular panels (dispensing with the full panoramic scenes in which the "Yellow Kid" had appeared). The spread of comics to other newspapers was rapid and was aided by the development of newspaper syndication. The aesthetically outstanding strip of the early years was Winsor McCay's "Little Nemo in Slumberland" (first appearance 1906), which created a dreamworld at once gentle, exciting, and humorous. The strip was executed in fairy-tale illustration style, with a conscious display of colouristic effects.

The daily strip in black and white, indispensable to all major newspapers since 1915, was inaugurated in 1904 in the Chicago *American* with Claire Briggs' "A. Piker Clerk," in which a character gave tips on horse races. Harry C. "Bud" Fisher's "Mr. A. Mutt" (later "Mutt and Jeff") appeared in 1907. Initially a tip sheet, it soon became a general-interest comic.

Establishment of subject categories

During the years 1907–20 most of the major categories of American comics were established, including the first aviation, ethnic-character, and career-girl strips. The most important gag strip was George McManus' "Bringing up Father," dating from 1913. It was the first American strip to achieve international fame. Outstanding among the family-saga or domestic-problem strips that burgeoned during the '20s was Frank King's "Gasoline Alley," which dated from 1919. It strove for realism rather than farcical effects, and had a strict continuity (as opposed to the daily gag), during which, moreover, characters actually grew older. The first career-girl strip (Martin V. Branner's "Winnie Winkle") appeared in 1920. It was followed by the fashion-conscious "Tillie the Toiler" in 1921 by Russ Westover. Another major group of the '20s were fantastic, satirical, and parodistic. Elzie Crisler Segar's "Popeye" (first appearance 1919) still depended upon slapstick, but George Herriman's "Krazy Kat" (1911–44) created a tender world of poetry, at once surreal and humorous. Drawn with the greatest of graphic economy, the absurd interrelationships of a tiny cast of characters (basically three) were presented using the thinnest imaginable plot line. "Krazy Kat" was the first newspaper strip anywhere to be aimed at relatively intellectual adults.

During the '30s the comics page expanded both in quantity of strips and in range of subject matter. Several of the strips created then have survived for more than 40 years. One of these, Chic Young's domestic comedy strip "Blondie" (first appearance 1930), has achieved unparalleled international renown.

A new category of immense significance emerged: the continuous-action adventure strip. This category took many forms: domestic and detective drama, science and space fiction, and, by 1938, war and supermen strips. The earliest adventure strip was "Tarzan" (first appearance 1929) whose creator Harold Foster broke completely with the prevailing caricatural style, adopted cinematic techniques, and sought picturesque, documentary realism. No less concerned with classic aesthetic effects was Alex Raymond, first master of the exotic space strip ("Flash Gordon," first appearance 1933). An aggressively cinematic, adventure strip, meticulously researched, was evolved by Milton Caniff in his "Terry and the Pirates," which appeared in 1934. Caricatural simplifications and grim forms of humour were introduced into the genre by Chester Gould's "Dick Tracy" (first appearance 1931), the detective strip par excellence, which is laced with science-fiction gadgetry and bizarre eroticism. Truly satirical forms of exaggeration returned to the strip with Al Capp's "Li'l Abner" (first appearance 1934).

The comic book

The demand for adventure stories spawned a new and highly lucrative vehicle for the comic strip: the cheap, staple-bound comic book. The first true comic books were marketed in 1933 as give-away advertising premiums. These had a 7½- by 10¼-inch (19- by 26-centimetre) page size, a format that has continued. By 1935 such titles as *Famous Funnies*, *Tip Top Comics*, *King Comics*, at first chiefly reprints of newspaper strips, then with original stories, were selling in large quantities. Specialization soon set in: *Detective Comics* (1937) and *Action Comics* (1938). "Superman," which appeared first in *Action Comics*, was the creation of Jerry Siegel (scenario or text) and Joe Shuster (art); it was soon syndicated and transposed to other media. The "Superman" formula of the hero who transcends all physical and social laws to punish the wicked, was widely imitated. The animated cartoon characters of Walt Disney, aimed at younger children, took root in the comic book.

World War II hastened the development of strips and comic books dealing with war and crime, the latter finding a new and avid readership among American soldiers stationed abroad. Being outside the control of newspaper editors, the comic book became increasingly violent and gruesome. The sadism of the American comic became proverbial; the "comic" became equated by Europeans with the "horror comic," and voices of educators were raised against it on both sides of the Atlantic. United States Congressional investigations in 1951 and 1954 blamed rising juvenile deliquency on the pernicious influence of the comic book. The industry responded by

"Dick Tracy," by Chester Gould.
Reprinted through the courtesy of the Chicago Tribune–New York News Syndicate, Inc.

instituting systems of self-censorship, administered by several organizations; the more vicious-looking material was restrained, but, in Europe, some U.S. adventure strips continued to be criticized for their pursuit of violence and for their racist, militarist, and fascist tendencies.

Perhaps as a reaction, there was a parallel, postwar development in newspaper strips devoted to sentimental domestic drama—such as "Rex Morgan, M.D.," "Mary Worth," and "The Heart of Juliet Jones"—and simple-looking, but subtly conceived gag strips—such as "Beetle Bailey," the incorrigible draftee, and "Dennis the Menace," a sophisticated Katzenjammer. "Pogo" (first appearance 1946) by Walt Kelly was generally considered the most humorous and most cerebral. Drawn in a style reminiscent of Walt Disney, the strip transcended Disney's moral simplism, presenting a highly nuanced world populated with an almost Dickensian multitude of comic characters. "Pogo" exuded a tender, nostalgic air, perpetually ruffled by the breezes of sociopolitical allusion. Kelly's dialogue was also much admired, particularly since it appeared at a time when the comic strip was widely criticized for verbal poverty.

Literate strips of the 1950s

The literate strip with philosophical, psychological, and sociological overtones was the principal innovation of the later 1950s. Most successful in this group was Charles Schulz's "Peanuts" (first appearance 1950), a strip in which all the characters were children, dispensing with the adult foil. Of comparable psychological finesse, and imbued with truly satirical flashes, was Johnny Hart's "B.C." (first appearance 1958) and "Wizard of Id" in collaboration with Brant Parker (first appearance 1964), which had prehistoric and medieval settings, respectively. The major strip of political satire, "Feiffer" by Jules Feiffer (first appearance 1956), appeared weekly and was not run on the comics page but on editorial pages of the more liberal or "left" papers. In this strip the dialogue was more important than the drawings, which were deliberately repetitive; the content played upon the logic-twisting rhetoric of politicians and the neurotic relationships between social competitors and lovers.

The most significant innovation since about 1965 has been in the parodistic, erotic, and surrealistic comic. This type emerged in opposition to the newspaper comic strip, in protest as it were against the mass media's saturation with conservative, bourgeois values. Parody and burlesque of the newspaper strip was pioneered by *Mad* magazine (first published in 1952). The erotic, laced with parody, found a home in the liberal periodical press ("Little Annie Fannie" in *Playboy* in 1962 and "Phoebe Zeitgeist" in *Evergreen Review* in 1968). Comic books satirizing a cultural underworld "liberated" by sex and drugs became popular, particularly among college students. These comics were pioneered in San Francisco by Robert Crumb, Rick Griffin, and S. Clay Wilson. The major drug-oriented strip, Gilbert Shelton's "Fabulous Furry Freak Brothers," was in 1970 reaching 100,000 persons weekly in the *Los Angeles Free Press*.

Europe. The first recurrent British comic characters, after Ally Sloper appeared in 1884, were Tom Brown's tramps "Weary Willie and Tired Tim." The strip was sponsored in 1896 by the publisher Alfred Harmsworth and was originally intended for the newly literate and semi-literate masses, but it developed into children's fare.

Strips for young children in Great Britain

Distinctive British contributions were the magazine of strips designed for pre-literate children (*Tiger Tim's Weekly*, first published in 1920, and *Playbox*, which first appeared in 1925); the picture paper based on film comedy (*Film Fun, Kinema Comic*); and the multitude of children's magazines containing both articles and comic strips. The first strip for young children to appear in an adult newspaper was "Rupert, the Adventures of a Little Lost Teddy Bear," created by Mary Tourtel for the *Daily Express* in 1920. The text is fitted in below the balloonless pictures, in order to facilitate reading aloud by adults. The first British adult newspaper strip and after *Krazy Kat* the first daily strip anywhere designed exclusively for adults was the witty "Pop" by John Millar Watt, which first appeared in 1921. "Pop," together with Reginald Smythe's "Andy Capp" (first printed in 1957), were among the very few European strips to be exported to the United States. A notably original strip was Norman Pett's "Jane," published first in the *Daily Mirror* in 1932. It used an artful striptease theme and had great popularity with servicemen during World War II. The mildly satirical strip was pioneered in 1949 in the *Daily Express* by "Flook," a continuing narrative of various kinds of adventure (drawn by Wally Fawkes and written since 1958 by George Melly), and by Frank Dickens' "Bristow," a daily gag strip set in a business office. The outright satirical and political strip flowered in the new satirical magazines such as *Private Eye* (first published in 1961).

Comics in France and Italy

In France, Jean-Pierre Pinchon's "Bécassine" (first appearance 1905), modelled on Christophe, depicted the humorous adventures of a stupid but well-intentioned Breton servant; Louis Forton's "Bande des pieds-nickelés" (first appearance 1908), although ostensibly for

Reprinted courtesy Publishers—Hall Syndicate. © Walt Kelly

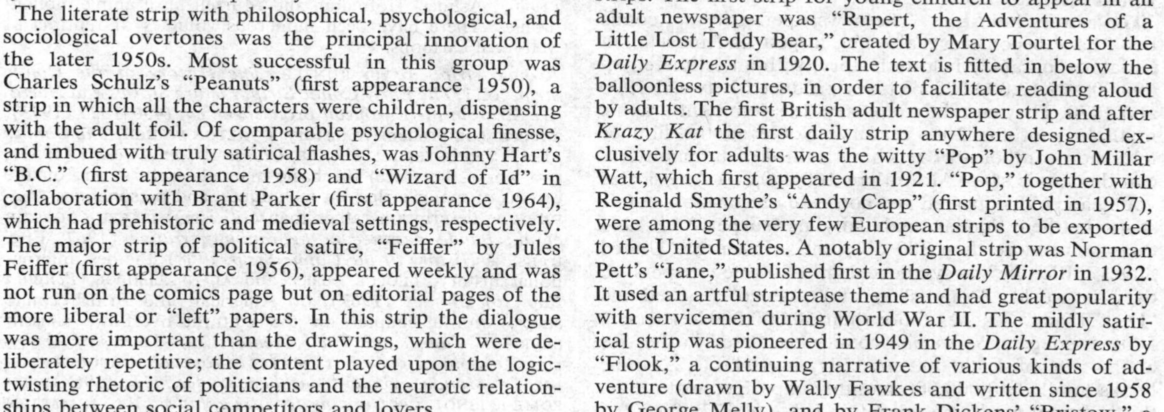

"Pogo," by Walt Kelly.

children, had political touches and a mocking tone that appealed to adults as well. The first European strip to be fully developed in the American sense (notably as regards the use of balloons) was Alain de Saint-Ogan's "Zig et Puce" (first appearance 1925), which also was published in an adult newspaper. France had no daily comic strip until 1934. There and in Italy, even more than in England, the market was smothered in the 1930s and '40s by American imports and imitations. An outstanding and hardy domestic product was "Tintin," created by the Belgian Hergé (pseudonym of Georges Rémi), a realistically conceived and relatively didactic adventure strip with a kind of Boy Scout hero. The immense popularity of "Tintin" has (since about 1964) been challenged by a warrior of ancient Gaul called "Astérix," the work of the writer (and comic-strip theorist) René Goscinny and the artist Albert Uderzo. "Astérix," besides being simply humorous and adventurous, indulges in sophisticated puns, witty anachronisms, and satirical flashes. The albums are produced in beautiful, accurately printed colour.

Colour, previously distorted and cheapened on the coarse newsprint of weekend papers and children's magazines, at last began to change the whole aesthetic character of the picture story—and improve it beyond recognition. In the 1960s Italian and French strips for adults by such artists as Guy Peellaert ("Jodelle"), Guido Crepax ("Valentina"), and Nicholas Devil ("Saga de Xam") paved the way for a new era in the comic strip, in which aesthetic expression aligned itself with contemporary art movements such as Pop, Op, and psychedelic art and availed itself of the most advanced printing techniques. The influence worked both ways. American art, particularly the Pop movement, was profoundly affected from about 1963 by comic-strip imagery. In Europe, where leading film makers admitted their debt to the comics, it was predicted that film, graphic art, and the comic strip would fuse into a new medium.

The comics industry. The newspaper strip and comic book have become arguably the largest and most influential iconographic field in history, with an estimated 8,000,000 to 12,000,000 pictures produced between 1900 and 1970. They certainly represent the dominant graphic mythology of the 20th century. Not even the film or television can boast of reaching a third of humanity, as can the comic strip. More than 100,000,000 Americans, young and old, educated and not, read one or more comic strips in their Sunday and daily newspapers. In 1963 there were more than 300 different strips in the United States. "Blondie" is syndicated in 1,200 newspapers all over the world, "Peanuts" in 1,000; "Pogo" reached and "Dick Tracy" reaches more than 50,000,000 readers in 500 newspapers. *Superman* comics circulated in the '50s at the rate of 1,500,000 monthly; in 1943 U.S. comic books totalled 18,000,000 monthly copies, constituting a third of total magazine sales, to a value of $72,000,000.

Dissemination of comics

Not surprisingly, reader participation has reached extraordinary heights; readers truly laugh and suffer with their favourite characters. Chic Young received 400,000 suggestions for a name for Blondie's new baby.

Perhaps in no other form of art has the creator become to such an extent prisoner of his creation, to which he may be locked for his lifetime and which becomes in a real sense independent of his own existence, for the successful strip will almost always be continued by other artists if the original creator should die or lose interest in it. The newspaper strip is also in fief to the syndicates, publishers, and editors who regard it primarily as a circulation booster. It must not offend any conceivable readership or commercial-interest group and therefore must observe strict, conservative codes of morality and decorum. This explains the extent to which the newspaper strip generally has avoided controversial issues of the day. Often enough, a new strip has been conceived by a newspaper proprietor and his art editor according to a pretested formula based on sociological surveys. Regular, efficient production is guaranteed by assembly-line methods: the adventure or soap-opera strip may pass through at least six stages and six different pairs of hands: scenario writing, blocking out, drawing of figures, drawing of background, lettering, colouring, copy editing, etc. Once printed on a crowded page containing up to 20 others, the strip may be "killed" aesthetically; and the small scale, the rigid format, and cheap printing put severe limits on the artist's graphic freedom. It was against such restrictions that the American underground comic and the European *bande dessinée pour adultes* ("adult strip") struck out. (D.M.Ke.)

BIBLIOGRAPHY

Caricature and cartoon: British Museum, Department of Prints and Drawings, *Catalogue of Political and Personal Satires*, from 1320 to date of compilation by FREDERIC G. STEPHENS and MARY D. GEORGE, 11 vol. (1870–1954); MARY D. GEORGE, *English Political Caricature*, 2 vol. (1959); "CHAMPFLEURY" (JULES FLEURY), *Histoire de la caricature* (1865) and three expanded subdivisions of this work for the ancient world, the Middle Ages, and the Renaissance; MARION H. SPIELMANN, *The History of Punch* (1895, reprinted 1969); EDUARD FUCHS, *Die Karikatur der europäischen Völker vom Altertum bis zur Neuzeit* (1901), a rather Marxian view; CHARLES R. ASHBEE, *Caricature* (1928); ERNST H.J. GOMBRICH and ERNST KRIS, *Caricature* (1940), which goes to the psychological root of the matter, and "The Principles of Caricature," in ERNST KRIS, *Psychoanalytic Explorations in Art*, pp. 189–203 (1952); WERNER HOFMANN, *Die Karikatur von Leonardo bis Picasso* (1956; Eng. trans., *Caricature from Leonardo to Picasso*, 1957), a purely European view; WILLIAM MURRELL, *A History of American Graphic Humor*, 2 vol. (1934–38, reprinted 1967); ALLAN NEVINS and FRANK WEITENKAMPF, *A Century of Political Cartoons: Caricature in the United States from 1800 to 1900* (1944); DAVID LOW, *A Cartoon History of Our Times* (1939, many reprints); JAMES PARTON, *Caricature and Other Comic Art in All Times and Many Lands* (1969); WILLIAM G. ROGERS, *Mightier Than the Sword: Cartoon, Caricature, Social Comment* (1969); THOMAS WRIGHT, *A History of Caricature and Grotesque in Literature and Art* (1968); RALPH E. SHIKES, *The Indignant Eye: The Artist As Social Critic in Prints and Drawings from the Fifteenth Century to Picasso* (1969); BEVIS HILLIER, *Cartoons and Caricatures* (1970). Ashbee, Hofmann, and Murrell have ample bibliographies. There have been numerous volumes of reprints of well-liked cartoons.

Comic strip: DAVID KUNZLE, *The History of the Comic Strip*, vol. 1, *The Early Comic Strip: Picture Stories and Narrative Strips in the European Broadsheet, ca. 1450–1826* (1973), a recent comprehensive history; COULTON WAUGH, *The Comics* (1947); and STEPHEN BECKER, *Comic Art in America* (1959), two works that form the basic manual—both strong on the origins of major strips, on techniques, and personalities (picturesque description rather than criticism); PIERRE COUPERIE et al., *Bande dessinée et figuration narrative* (1967; Eng. trans., *A History of the Comic Strip*, 1968), the best international history; GEORGE PERRY and ALAN ALDRIDGE, *Penguin Book of Comics* (1967), on American and British comic strips, with a chapter on the cultural overflow; MARTIN SHERIDAN, *Comics and Their Creators: Life Stories of American Cartoonists*, rev. ed. (1944). (*European*): JACQUES MARNY, *Le Monde étonnant des bandes dessinées* (1968); JEROME PEIGNOT, *Les Copains de votre enfance* (1963); MARTEN TOONDER, *Beknopte Striptologie zijnde een poging tot verheldering bij de bestudering van de oudste verhaalvorm die de mensheid kent* (1962), includes a bibliography of Dutch strips; OSCAR MASOTTA, *La historieta en el mundo moderno* (1970), with bibliography; ENRIQUE LIPSZYC, *La historieta mundial* (1958). (*Anthologies*): JACQUES STERNBERG, MICHEL CAEN, and JACQUES LOB, *Les Chefs d'Oeuvre de la bande dessinée* (1967), international, includes some little known examples; JULES FEIFFER, *The Great Comic Book Heroes* (1965), American only; LUIS GASCA, *Los comics en España* (1969). (*Technique*): ROBERT BENAYOUN, *Le Ballon dans la bande dessinée, vroom, tchac, zowie* (1968); MANFRED WELKE, *Die Sprache der Comics* (1958), highly analytical; FRANCIS LACASSIN, *Pour un neuvième art, la bande dessinée* (1971). (*Sociology*): DAVID MANNING WHITE and ROBERT H. ABEL (eds.), *The Funnies: An American Idiom* (1963), articles by critics, creators, and scholars, including sociological statistics of readership and comics content, a comprehensive bibliography of articles in professional, specialized, and general periodicals, and of theses and special studies; FREDERIC WERTHAM, *Seduction of the Innocent* (1954, reprinted 1971), on the theory that the horror comic has contributed to juvenile delinquency; ARIEL DORFMAN and ARMAND MATTELART, *Para leer al Pato Donald* (1972), the Donald Duck comic viewed in Latin America as imperialist, capitalist propaganda.

(W.Am./D.M.Ke.)

Carlyle, Thomas

Scottish essayist and historian, Thomas Carlyle became one of a select group of sages whom the serious-minded Victorian public read avidly, discussed endlessly, and revered deeply. Whether his subject was historical, political or economic, religious or biographical, his aim was always to be a prophet; and though it is possible to challenge his merits as a writer, few would doubt his historical importance.

By courtesy of the National Portrait Gallery, London

Carlyle, oil painting by G.F. Watts, 1877.
In the National Portrait Gallery, London.

Early life. Carlyle was born at Ecclefechan, Annandale, in southern Scotland on December 4, 1795. The second son of James Carlyle, Thomas was the eldest child of his second marriage. James Carlyle was a mason by trade and, later, a small farmer, a man of profound Calvinist convictions whose character and way of life had a profound and lasting influence on his son. Carlyle was equally devoted to his mother as well as to his eight brothers and sisters, and his strong affection for his family never diminished.

Calvinist background

After attending the village school at Ecclefechan, Thomas was sent in 1805 to Annan Academy, where he apparently suffered from bullying, and later to University of Edinburgh (1809), where he read widely but followed no precise line of study. His father had intended him to enter the ministry, but Thomas became increasingly doubtful of his vocation. He had an aptitude for mathematics, and in 1814 he obtained a mathematical teaching post at Annan. In 1816 he went to another school, at Kirkcaldy, where the Scottish preacher and mystic Edward Irving was teaching. He became one of the few men to whom Carlyle gave complete admiration and affection. "But for Irving," Carlyle commented sometime later, "I had never known what communion of man with man means." Their friendship continued even after Irving moved to London in 1822 where he became famous as a preacher.

The next years were hard for Carlyle. Teaching did not suit him and he abandoned it. In December 1819 he returned to Edinburgh University to study law, and there he spent three miserable years, lonely, unable to feel certain of any meaning in life, and eventually abandoning the idea of entering the ministry. He did a little coaching and journalism, was poor and isolated, and was conscious of intense spiritual struggles. About 1821 he experienced a kind of conversion, which he described some years later in fictionalized account in *Sartor Resartus*, whose salient feature was that it was negative—hatred of the devil, not love of God, being the dominating idea. Though it may be doubted whether everything was really experienced as he described it, this violence is certainly characteristic of Carlyle's tortured and defiant spirit. In those lean years he began his serious study of German, which always remained the literature he most admired and enjoyed. For Goethe, especially, he had the greatest reverence, and he published a translation of *Wilhelm Meister's Apprenticeship* in 1824. Meanwhile, he led a nomadic life, holding several brief tutorships at Edinburgh, Dunkeld, and elsewhere.

Marriage. On October 17, 1826, Carlyle married Jane Welsh, an intelligent, attractive, and somewhat temperamental daughter of a well-to-do doctor in Haddington. Miss Welsh had been one of Irving's pupils, and she and Carlyle had known one another for five years. The hesitations and financial worries that beset them are recorded in their letters. It is interesting that Carlyle, usually so imperious, often adopted a weak, pleading tone to his future wife during the time of courtship, though this did not prevent him from being a masterful, difficult, and irritable husband; and, in spite of their strong mutual affection, their marriage was full of quarrels and misunderstandings. Those who knew him best believed Carlyle to be impotent.

In the early years of their marriage the Carlyles lived mostly at Craigenputtock, Dumfriesshire, and Carlyle contributed to the *Edinburgh Review* and worked on *Sartor Resartus*. Though this book eventually achieved great popular success, he had at first much difficulty in finding a publisher for it. Written with mingled bitterness and humour, it is a fantastic hotchpotch of autobiography and German philosophy. Its main theme is that the intellectual forms in which men's deepest convictions have been cast are dead and that new ones must be found to fit the time but that the intellectual content of this new religious system is elusive. Its author speaks of "embodying the Divine Spirit of religion in a new Mythus, in a new vehicle and vesture," but he never says very clearly what the new vesture is to be.

Sartor Resartus

London. In 1834, after failing to obtain several posts he had desired, Carlyle moved to London with his wife and settled in Cheyne Row. Though he had not earned anything by his writings for more than a year and was fearful of the day when his savings would be exhausted, he refused to compromise but began an ambitious historical work, *The French Revolution*. The story of how the partially completed manuscript was lent to J.S. Mill and accidentally burned is well known. After the accident Carlyle wrote to Mill in a generous, almost gay, tone, which is truly remarkable when Carlyle's ambition, his complete dependence upon a successful literary career, his poverty, the months of wasted work, and his habitual melancholy and irritability are considered. The truth seems to be that he could bear grand and terrible trials more easily than petty annoyances. His habitual, frustrated melancholy arose, in part, from the fact that his misfortunes were not serious enough to match his tragic view of life; and he sought relief in intensive historical research, choosing subjects in which divine drama, lacking in his own life, seemed most evident. His book on the French Revolution is perhaps his greatest achievement. After the loss of the manuscript he worked furiously at rewriting it. It was finished early in 1837 and soon won both serious acclaim and popular success, besides bringing him many invitations to lecture, thus solving his financial difficulties.

Greatest achievement

True to his idea of history as a "Divine Scripture," Carlyle saw the French Revolution as an inevitable judgment upon the folly and selfishness of the monarchy and nobility. This simple idea was backed with an immense mass of well-documented detail and, at times, a memorable skill in sketching character. The following extract is characteristic of the contorted, fiery, and doom-laden prose, which is alternately colloquial, humorous, and grim:

> . . . an august Assembly spread its pavilion; curtained by the dark infinite of discords; founded on the wavering bottomless of the Abyss; and keeps continual hubbub. Time is around it, and Eternity, and the Inane; and it does what it can, what is given it to do (part 2, book 3, ch. 3).

Though many readers were thrilled by the drama of the narrative, it is not surprising that they were puzzled by Carlyle's prophetic harangues and their relevance to the contemporary situation.

In *Chartism* (1840) he appeared as a bitter opponent of conventional economic theory, but the radical-progressive and the reactionary elements were curiously blurred and mingled. With the publication of *On Heroes, Hero-Worship, and the Heroic in History* (1841) his reverence for strength, particularly when combined with the conviction of a God-given mission, began to emerge. He discussed the hero as divinity (pagan myths), as prophet (Muḥammad), as poet (Dante and Shakespeare), as priest (Luther and Knox), as man of letters (Johnson and Burns), and as king (Cromwell and Napoleon). It is perhaps in his treatment of poets that Carlyle shows to the best advantage. Perverse though he could be, he was never at the mercy of fashion; and he saw much more, particularly in Dante, than others did. Two years later this idea of the hero was elaborated in *Past and Present*, which strove "to penetrate . . . into a somewhat remote century . . . in hope of perhaps illustrating our own poor century thereby." He contrasts the wise and strong rule of a medieval abbot with the muddled softness and chaos of the 19th century, pronouncing in favour of the former, in spite of the fact that he had rejected dogmatic Christianity and had a special aversion to the Roman Catholic Church.

The hero

It was natural that Carlyle should turn to Cromwell as the greatest English example of his ideal man and should produce the bulky *Oliver Cromwell's Letters and Speeches. With Elucidations* in 1845. His next important work was *Latter-Day Pamphlets* (1850), in which the savage side of his nature was particularly prominent. In the essay on model prisons, for instance, he tried to persuade the public that the most brutal and useless sections of the population were being coddled in the new prisons of the 19th century. Though incapable of lying, Carlyle was completely unreliable as an observer, since he invariably saw what he had decided in advance that he ought to see.

In 1857 he embarked on a massive study of another of his heroes, Frederick the Great, and the *History of Friedrich II of Prussia, Called Frederick the Great* appeared between 1858 and 65. Something of his political attitude at this time can be gathered from a letter written in April 1855 to the exiled Russian revolutionary A.I. Herzen, in which he says "I never had, and have now (if it were possible) less than ever, the least hope in 'Universal Suffrage' under any of its modifications" and refers to "the sheer Anarchy (as I reckon it sadly to be) which is got by 'Parliamentary eloquence,' Free Press, and counting of heads" (quoted from E.H. Carr, *The Romantic Exiles*).

Unfortunately, Carlyle was never able to respect ordinary men. Here, perhaps, rather than in any historical doubts about the veracity of the gospels, was the core of his quarrel with Christianity—it set too much value on the weak and sinful. His fierceness of spirit was composed of two elements, a serious Calvinistic desire to denounce evil and a habitual nervous ill temper, for which he often reproached himself but which he never managed to defeat.

Last years. In 1865 he was offered the rectorship of Edinburgh University. The speech that he delivered at his installation in April 1866 was not very remarkable in itself but its tone of high moral exhortation made it an immediate success. It was published in 1866 under the title *On the Choice of Books*. Soon after his triumph in Edinburgh, Mrs. Carlyle died suddenly in London. She was buried in Haddington and an epitaph by her husband was placed in the church. Carlyle never completely recovered from her death. He lived another 15 years, weary, bored, and a partial recluse. A few public causes gained his support: he was active in the defense of Governor E.J. Eyre of Jamaica, who was dismissed for his severity in putting down a Negro uprising in 1865. Carlyle commended him for "saving the West Indies and hanging one incendiary mulatto, well worth gallows, if I can judge." He was excited by the Franco-German War (1870–71), saying "Germany ought to be President of Europe," but such enthusiastic moments soon faded. In these last years he wrote little. His history *The Early Kings of Norway: Also an Essay on the Portraits of John Knox* came out in 1875, and *Reminiscences* was published in 1881. Later he edited his wife's letters, which appeared in 1883 under the title *Letters and Memorials of Jane Welsh Carlyle, Prepared for Publication by Thomas Carlyle*. Carlyle died in London on Feb. 5, 1881, and although Westminster Abbey was offered for burial, he was buried, according to his wish, beside his parents at Ecclefechan.

Rector of Edinburgh University

Carlyle's contribution. It is perhaps difficult to be fair to Carlyle. Those who do not accept him as an inspired prophet find he makes intolerable claims on his readers' patience and on their emotional energy. A sentence, a paragraph can be pithy, but a whole book, on the other hand, is always repetitive and diffuse, and he was invariably biassed.

Though he was a man of many words and wide learning, his religious sense, intense in its way, played always round two grand and simple ideas that many religions have in common: the terror of God's glory and the immortality of the soul. The whole of his life and writings can be seen as an attempt to secularize, to reclothe the Calvinist insights without mitigating them. In the effort to preserve religion while discarding its doctrines, he has affinities with several famous Victorians, particularly Matthew Arnold. But whereas Arnold, working from a moderate Anglican basis, attempted to turn Christianity into sweetness and light, Carlyle preserved to the full and even increased the fierceness, the momentous drama, the seriousness of Calvinism. The idea of the elect and the reprobate, even though transferred into moral and secular terms, was an ever-present reality to him. For an infallible Bible he substituted an infallible History, what he called "the true epic poem and universal Divine Scripture, whose plenary inspiration no man out of Bedlam or in it shall bring in question." He stirred the conscience of his century; he helped thousands to see their experience in a historical and spiritual context and thus to find new meaning in a monotonous existence; and in an age of prolonged physical toil, he inspired thousands with belief in the dignity of their work.

MAJOR WORKS

HISTORY: *The French Revolution*, 3 vol., 1837; *On Heroes, Hero-Worship, and the Heroic in History*, 1841; *Oliver Cromwell's Letters and Speeches. With Elucidations*, 2 vol., 1845; *The History of Friedrich II of Prussia, Called Frederick the Great*, 6 vol., 1858–65; *The Early Kings of Norway: Also an Essay on the Portraits of John Knox*, 1875.

BIOGRAPHY AND CRITICISM: *The Life of Friedrich Schiller*, 1825; *Critical and Miscellaneous Essays*, 4 vol., 1838; *The Life of John Sterling*, 1851; *On the Choice of Books*, 1866 (inaugural address at his installation as rector of Edinburgh University).

SOCIOLOGY: *Sartor Resartus: The Life and Opinions of Herr Teufelsdröckh*, 1836; *Chartism*, 1840; *Past and Present*, 1843; *Latter-Day Pamphlets*, 1850; *Last Words of Thomas Carlyle on Trades-Unions, Promoterism and the Signs of the Times*, 1882.

BIBLIOGRAPHY

Bibliographies: I.W. DYER, *A Bibliography of Thomas Carlyle's Writings and Ana* (1928); C. MOORE, "Thomas Carlyle: A Critical Bibliography" in C.W. and L.H. HOUTCHENS (eds.), *English Romantic Poets and Essayists*, rev. ed. (1966); the *New Cambridge Bibliography of English Literature*, vol. 3 ed. by G. WATSON (1969).

Collections of manuscripts: About 70 percent of the manuscript letters of Carlyle and Jane Welsh Carlyle are in the National Library of Scotland, Edinburgh. Other public institutions with considerable collections of letters include the Victoria and Albert Museum, London; the John Rylands Library, Manchester; Harvard University; Yale University; the Henry E. Huntingdon Library, San Marino, California; and the New York Public Library. For Carlyle's collections, see W.C. LANE, *The Carlyle Collection: A Catalogue of Books on Oliver Cromwell and Frederick the Great, Bequeathed by Thomas Carlyle to Harvard College Library* (1888); M.E. WEAD, *A Catalogue of the Dr. Samuel A. Jones Carlyle Collection* (1919).

Major collected editions and selections: The fullest collected works is the Centenary Edition by H.D. TRAILL, 30 vol.

(1896–99). Selections include: *The Carlyle Anthology*, ed. by E. BARRETT (1876); *The Best of Carlyle*, ed. by T.O. GLENCROSS (1923); *Carlyle: An Anthology*, ed. by G.M. TREVELYAN (1953); *Selected Works, Reminiscences and Letters of Carlyle*, ed. by J. SYMONS (1955); and *Selections from Carlyle*, ed. by A.M.D. HUGHES (1957).

Biographies: J.A. FROUDE, *Thomas Carlyle*, 4 vol. (1882–84), is not only the best life of Carlyle but one of the greatest of English biographies, combining the attitude of an intelligent disciple with penetrating observation and remorseless moral criticism. See also Froude's, *My Relations With Carlyle* (1903), his private account of the writing of the biography, voicing his suspicions that sexual impotence may have been responsible for troubles in Carlyle's marriage. Froude also edited two autobiographical pieces, *T. Carlyle: Reminiscences* (1881), which gives a vivid picture of Carlyle's father and wife, among others; and *Letters and Memorials of Jane Welsh Carlyle: Prepared by T. Carlyle*, 2 vol. (1883), which gives full documentary evidence about Jane's life and character and conveys in notes and comments Carlyle's intense remorse for his shortcomings as a husband. Principal critical works include BASIL WILLEY, *Nineteenth Century Studies* (1949), which places Carlyle judiciously in relation to Samuel Taylor Coleridge, Matthew Arnold, and other leading thinkers; and JOHN HOLLOWAY, *The Victorian Sage* (1953), which provides an admirable account of the philosophical and rhetorical aspects of Carlyle's persuasive methods.

(A.O.J.C.)

Carnap, Rudolf

Rudolf Carnap was one of the originators and eventually the leading figure of the Logical Positivist school of thought. A highly creative and original thinker, he made important contributions to logic, the philosophy of science, and the theory of probability and inductive inference. His many writings, most of which are quite technical, reflect his thorough mathematical and scientific training and pervasive concern for clarity and rigour.

By courtesy of the University of California, Los Angeles

Carnap, 1960.

Education and military service

Early life. Carnap was born on May 18, 1891, at Ronsdorf in northwestern Germany. From 1910 to 1914 he studied mathematics, physics, and philosophy at the universities of Jena and Freiburg im Breisgau. At Jena he attended the lectures of Gottlob Frege, now widely acknowledged as the greatest logician of the 19th century, whose ideas exerted a deep influence on Carnap.

After serving in World War I, Carnap earned his doctorate in 1921 at Jena with a dissertation on the concept of space. He argued that the conflicts among the various theories of space then held by scholars resulted from the fact that those theories actually dealt with quite different subjects; he called them, respectively, formal space, physical space, and intuitive space, and exhibited their principal characteristics and their fundamental differences.

For several years afterward Carnap was engaged in private research in logic and the foundations of physics and wrote a number of essays on problems of space, time, and causality, as well as a textbook in symbolic, or mathematical, logic (*Abriss der Logistik*, 1929; a considerably different later German version appeared in English translation: *Introduction to Symbolic Logic and its Applications*, 1958).

Participation in the Vienna Circle

Career in Vienna and Prague. In 1926 Moritz Schlick, the founder of the Vienna Circle—a small group of philosophers, mathematicians, and other scholars who met regularly to discuss philosophical issues—invited Carnap to join the faculty of the University of Vienna, where he soon became an influential member of the Circle. Out of their discussions developed the initial ideas of Logical Positivism, or Logical Empiricism. This school of thought shared its basic Empiricist orientation with David Hume, a Scottish Empiricist, and Ernst Mach, an Austrian physicist and philosopher. Its leading members, informed and inspired by the methods and theories of contemporary mathematics and science, sought to develop a "scientific world view" by bringing to philosophical inquiry the precision and rigour of the exact sciences. As one means to this end, Carnap made extensive use of the concepts and techniques of symbolic logic in preference to the analytic devices of traditional logic, which are limited and often entirely inadequate.

Carnap and his associates established close connections with like-minded scholars in other countries, among them a group of Empiricists that had formed in Berlin under the leadership of Hans Reichenbach, an eminent philosopher of science. With Reichenbach, Carnap founded a periodical, *Erkenntnis* (1930–40), as a forum for the new "scientific philosophy."

The basic thesis of Empiricism, in a familiar but quite vague formulation, is that all of man's concepts and beliefs concerning the world ultimately derive from his immediate experience. In some of his most important writings, Carnap sought, in effect, to give this idea a clear and precise interpretation. Setting aside, as a psychological rather than a philosophical problem, the question of how human beings arrive at their ideas about the world, he proceeded to construe Empiricism as a systematic–logical thesis about the evidential grounding of empirical knowledge. To this end, he gave the issue a characteristically linguistic turn by asking how the terms and sentences that, in scientific or in everyday language, serve to express assertions about the world are related to those terms and sentences by which the data of immediate experience can be described. The Empiricist thesis, as construed and defended by Carnap, then asserts that the terms and sentences of the first kind are "reducible" to those of the second kind in a clearly specifiable sense. Carnap's conception of the relevant sense of reducibility, which he always stated in precise logical terms, was initially rather narrow but gradually became more liberal.

First works

In his first great work, *Der logische Aufbau der Welt* (1928; Eng. trans.—with a smaller work—*The Logical Structure of the World: Pseudoproblems in Philosophy*, 1967), Carnap developed, with unprecedented rigour, a version of the Empiricist reducibility thesis according to which all terms suited to describe actual or possible empirical facts are fully definable by terms referring exclusively to aspects of immediate experience, so that all empirical statements are fully translatable into statements about immediate experiences.

Prompted by discussions with his associates in Vienna, however, Carnap soon began to develop a more liberal version of Empiricism, which he elaborated while he was professor of natural philosophy at the German University in Prague (1931–35); he eventually presented it in full detail in his important essay "Testability and Meaning" (*Philosophy of Science*, vol. 3 [1936] and 4 [1937]). Here, Carnap argued that the terms of empirical science are not, indeed, all fully definable in purely experiential terms but can at least be partly so defined by means of "reduction sentences," which are a logically much refined version of operational definitions, and by virtue of which an empirical statement implies various consequences in the form of "observation sentences," whose truth can be checked by direct observation and which thus permit an experiential test of the given statement. Carnap stressed that usually such tests cannot provide strict proof or disproof but only more or less strong "confirmation" for an empirical statement.

Sentences that do not thus yield observational implications and therefore cannot possibly be tested and confirmed by observational findings were said to be empirically meaningless. By reference to this testability criterion of empirical significance, Carnap and other Logical Empiricists rejected various doctrines of speculative metaphysics and of theology, not as being false but as making no significant assertions at all.

Carnap argued that the observational statements by reference to which empirical statements can be tested may be construed as sentences describing directly and publicly observable aspects of physical objects, such as the needle of a measuring instrument turning to a particular point on the scale or a subject in a psychological test showing a change in pulse rate. All such sentences, he noted, can be formulated in terms that are part of the vocabulary of physics. This was the basic idea of his "physicalism," according to which all terms and statements of empirical science—from the physical to the social and historical disciplines—can be reduced to terms and statements in the language of physics.

In later writings, Carnap liberalized his conception of reducibility and of empirical significance even further so as to give a more adequate account of the relation between scientific theories and scientific evidence.

Career in the United States. By the time "Testability and Meaning" appeared in print, Carnap had moved to the United States, mainly because of the growing threat of German National Socialism. From 1936 to 1952 he served on the faculty of the University of Chicago. During the 1940–41 school year, Carnap was a visiting professor at Harvard University and was a very active participant in a discussion group that included Bertrand Russell, Alfred Tarski, and W.V.O. Quine.

Founding of the *International Encyclopedia of Unified Science*

Soon after going to Chicago, Carnap joined with the sociologist Otto Neurath, a former fellow member of the Vienna Circle, and with an academic colleague, the Pragmatist philosopher Charles W. Morris, in founding the *International Encyclopedia of Unified Science*, which was published, beginning in 1938, as a series of monographs on general problems in the philosophy of science and on philosophical issues concerning mathematics or particular branches of empirical science.

Since his Vienna years, Carnap had been much concerned also with problems in logic and in the philosophy of language. He held that philosophical perplexities often arise from a misunderstanding or misuse of language and that the way to resolve them is by "logical analysis of language." On this point, he agreed with the "ordinary language" school of Analytic Philosophy, which had its origins in England. He differed from it, however, in insisting that more technical issues—*e.g.*, those in the philosophy of science or of mathematics—cannot be adequately dealt with by considerations of ordinary linguistic usage but require clarification by reference to artificially constructed languages that are formulated in logical symbolism and that have their structure and interpretation precisely specified by so-called syntactic and semantic rules. Carnap developed these ideas and the theoretical apparatus for their implementation in a series of works, including *Logische Syntax der Sprache* (1934; *The Logical Syntax of Language*, 1937; 2nd ed., 1959) and *Meaning and Necessity* (1947; 2nd enlarged ed., 1956).

Carnap's interest in artificial languages included advocacy of international auxiliary languages such as Esperanto and Interlingua to facilitate scholarly communication and to further international understanding.

Analyticity, induction, and rational decision

One idea in logic and the theory of knowledge that occupied much of Carnap's attention was that of analyticity. In contrast to the 19th-century radical Empiricism of John Stuart Mill, Carnap and other Logical Empiricists held that the statements of logic and mathematics, unlike those of empirical science, are analytic—*i.e.*, true solely by virtue of the meanings of their constituent terms—and that they can therefore be established a priori (without any empirical test). Carnap repeatedly returned to the task of formulating a precise characterization and theory of analyticity. His ideas were met with skepticism by some, however—among them Quine, who argued that the notion of analytic truth is inherently obscure and the attempt to delimit a class of statements that are true a priori should be abandoned as misguided.

From about 1945 onward, Carnap turned his efforts increasingly to problems of inductive reasoning and of rational belief and decision. His principal aim was to construct a formal system of inductive logic; its central concept, corresponding to that of deductive implication, would be that of probabilistic implication—or, more precisely, a concept representing the degree of rational credibility or of probability that a given body of evidence may be said to confer upon a proposed hypothesis. Carnap presented a rigorous theory of this kind in his *Logical Foundations of Probability* (1950).

Carnap spent the years from 1952 to 1954 at the Institute for Advanced Study in Princeton, where he continued his work in probability theory. Subsequently, he accepted a professorship at the University of California at Los Angeles.

During those years and indeed until his death in Santa Monica, California, on September 14, 1970, Carnap was occupied principally with modifications and considerable extensions of his inductive logic.

BIBLIOGRAPHY. NORMAN M. MARTIN's article on Carnap in the *Encyclopedia of Philosophy*, vol. 2 (1967), gives a lucid survey of Carnap's work and the development of his ideas with extensive bibliography. An especially valuable source is *The Philosophy of Rudolf Carnap*, ed. by P.A. SCHILPP (1963). It includes a far-ranging intellectual autobiography, 26 critical essays by other philosophers on aspects of Carnap's work, his replies to these essays, and a complete bibliography of his publications through 1961. Included in ROGER C. BUCK and ROBERT S. COHEN (eds.), *Boston Studies in the Philosophy of Science*, vol. 8 (1971), are 13 pieces in homage to Carnap; they convey a vivid idea of his qualities as a man, a teacher, and a thinker.

(C.G.H.)

Carnivora

The order Carnivora includes ten families of living mammals: Canidae (dogs, wolves, jackals, and foxes), Ursidae (bears), Procyonidae (raccoons), Mustelidae (skunks, mink, weasels, badgers, and otters), Viverridae (civets and mongooses), Hyaenidae (hyenas), Felidae (cats), Otariidae (eared seals), Odobenidae (walrus), and Phocidae (earless seals). The term carnivore is frequently applied by mammalogists to members of this order and is employed in that sense in the present article. In a more general sense, a carnivore is any animal (or even, occasionally, a plant) that eats the flesh of other animals, as opposed to a "herbivore," which eats plants. Although the Carnivora are basically meat eaters, a substantial number, especially among bears and procyonids, feed extensively on vegetable material.

This article is divided into the following sections:

I. General features

IMPORTANCE OF CARNIVORA

There is probably no other group of animals more familiar to man than mammals belonging to the order Carnivora. The more popular domesticated pets of man, the dog and the cat, are both derived from wild members of this order. The majority of luxurious natural furs (ermine, mink, sable, otter) worn by women of fashion, as well as the furs of utility used by primitive man, come from members of the Carnivora. Many of the animals that attract the largest crowds at circuses and zoos are members of this order. Most of the large, dangerous carnivores are the objects of hunters, who wish to obtain a trophy grizzly bear, polar bear, or tiger. The man stranded in the wild fears the wolf, dhole, bear, tiger, leopard, or jaguar, virtually the only predators capable of injuring him. The stockman is concerned about possible depredations upon his herd by nature's large predators.

The carnivores, the meat eaters, form the apex of the pyramid of life, the food pyramid, and thus are basic to the existence of a "balance of nature" in a world unmolested by man. In today's world, man's world, this precarious balance was first upset by the extermination of many carnivores. Formerly considered undesirable because of their predation on game animals, carnivores are now recognized as necessary elements in natural systems. Far from depressing game numbers, carnivores improve the stability of game populations by keeping numbers within the carrying capacity of the food supply. As a result, individual animals are better fed and less subject to disease. Many of these predators dig dens and provide burrows in which other forms of wildlife can take refuge. Those carnivores best known for their burrow building are the badgers and the skunks. Digging results in the mixing of soils and the reduction of the runoff of water during rains.

Intelligence and training

Carnivores rank high on the scale of intelligence among mammals. The large size of the brain, compared to that of the animal, is an indication of their superior mental powers. For this reason, these animals are among the easiest to train for entertainment purposes, as pets, or as hunting companions. Their highly developed sense of smell supplements the sharper vision of man. Dogs are the most common carnivores trained for hunting, but the cheetah, caracal, and ferret have also been used to some extent. In China the otter is trained to drive fish under a large net, which is then dropped and pulled in. Carnivores, dependent for survival upon their ability to prey upon living animals in a variety of situations, have evolved a relatively high degree of learning ability (see LEARNING, ANIMAL).

Carnivorous mammals tend to establish territories, areas defended against others of the same species; herbivorous ones, which eat vegetation, are less apt to do so. Territories are often exclusive, defended by the residents against other animals of their own kind. Such areas may sometimes be marked by secretions produced by anal or scent glands.

There is a wide range of social patterns among carnivores. Some (bears, raccoon, red and gray foxes, genets, most cats, and most mustelids) are strictly solitary, except during the breeding season. Some remain paired throughout the year (black-backed jackal and lesser panda) or occasionally hunt in pairs (gray fox, crab-eating fox, and kinkajou). Other carnivores, such as the wolf, African hunting dog, dhole, and coatimundi, normally hunt in packs or bands. Still others form sedentary colonies during the breeding season (sea lions, fur seals, and elephant seals), during a somewhat larger part of the year (sea otters), or all year round (meerkats).

FORM AND FUNCTION

The smallest living member of the Carnivora is the least weasel (*Mustela nivalis*), which weighs about two ounces. The largest terrestrial form is the Alaskan grizzly (*Ursus arctos*), weighing up to 780 kilograms (1700 pounds). The largest aquatic form is the elephant seal (*Mirounga leonina*), which may weigh 3,630 kilograms (four tons). Most carnivores weigh between four and eight kilograms (9–18 pounds).

Most members of the order are terrestrial. Some, such as the sea otter, river otter, and polar bear, spend most of their lives in water. The pinnipeds, or seals, are more aquatic than other members of the order. Aquatic or semi-aquatic forms tend to have body specializations such as a streamlined body and webbed feet for this mode of life.

Dentition

Carnivores, like other mammals, have a number of different kinds of teeth: incisors in front, followed by canines, premolars, and molars in the rear. Most carnivores, especially those that feed exclusively on meat, have carnassial, or shearing, teeth that function in slicing meat and cutting tough sinews. The carnassials are usually formed by the fourth upper premolar and the first lower molar, working one against the other with a scissorlike action. Cats, hyenas, and weasels, all highly carnivorous, have well-developed carnassials; while the bear and procyonids, which tend to be omnivorous (eating both plants and animals) and the seals, which eat fish or marine invertebrates, have little or no modification of these teeth for shearing. The teeth behind the carnassials tend to be lost or reduced in size in highly carnivorous species. Most members of the order have six prominent incisors on both the upper and lower jaw, two canines on each jaw, six to eight premolars, and four molars above and four to six molars below. Incisors are adapted for nipping off flesh. The outer-most incisors are usually larger than the inner ones. The strong canines are usually large, pointed, and adapted to aid in the stabbing of prey. The premolars always have sharply pointed cusps, and in some forms (*e.g.*, seals) all the cheek teeth (premolars and molars) have this shape. Except for the carnassials, molars tend to be flat teeth utilized for crushing. Terrestrial carnivores that depend largely on meat, such as weasels, cats, and hyenas, tend to have fewer teeth (30–34), the flat molars having been lost. Omnivorous carnivores, such as raccoon and bear, have more teeth (40–42). Seals have fewer teeth than terrestrial carnivores. In addition, seals exhibit little stability in the numbers of teeth; for example, a walrus may have from 18 to 24 teeth.

Several features of the skull are characteristic of the order Carnivora. The articulating surfaces (condyles) on the lower jaw are transverse, their axis at right angles to that of the head, forming a half-cylindrical hinge that allows the jaw to move only in a vertical plane but with considerable strength. The clavicles (collarbones) are either reduced or absent entirely and, if present, are usually embedded in muscles without articulation with other bones. This allows for a greater flexibility in the shoulder area and prevents breakage of the clavicles when the animal springs on its prey.

The brain is large in relation to the weight of the body and contains complex convolutions characteristic of highly intelligent animals. The stomach is simple, and a blind pouch (cecum) attached to the intestine is usually reduced or absent. Since animal tissues are in general simpler to digest than plant tissues, the carnivore's dependence on a diet with a high proportion of meat has led to less-complex compartmentalization of the stomach and a decrease in the length and folding (surface area) of the intestine. The teats are located on the abdomen along two primitive lines (milk ridges), a characteristic of mammals that lie down when nursing.

DISTRIBUTION AND ABUNDANCE

Carnivores are found worldwide. Terrestrial forms are absent from most oceanic islands, though the coastlines are usually visited by seals (pinnipeds). Except for the dingo (which probably was introduced by aboriginal man), Australia has no native terrestrial members of the Carnivora. Man has taken his pets, as well as a number of wild species, to most islands. For example, a large population of the red fox now inhabits Australia, having been introduced there by fox hunters.

Since carnivores are large and depend on meat, there must be fewer carnivores in the environment than those animals that form their diet. The maintenance of established territories limits the number of predators to the carrying capacity of prey populations. In general, carnivores have a population density of approximately one per square mile. By comparison, omnivorous mammals average about 20 per square mile, and herbivorous rodents attain densities of up to 100,000 per square mile at peak population. Existing at relatively low densities, carnivores are vulnerable to prey, population fluctuations, habitat disturbance, and predation by man. In some cases the mobility and adaptability of carnivores has enabled species to shift ecological roles and survive the changes brought about by human activities; in other instances less-flexible species have become extinct.

World carnivore population

The world population of aquatic carnivores (pinnipeds) has been estimated to be between 13,000,000 and 27,000,000 animals. Estimates of the total numbers of terrestrial carnivores have not been made. The yearly sale of furs indicates a harvest of at least 6,000,000 pelts of wild carnivores; this is equalled only by the number of mink raised and harvested on fur farms (approximately 8,000,000 annually in the mid-1960s). There are probably around 50,000,000 to 60,000,000 terrestrial members of the Carnivora present today. Some species (many cats, pandas, and bear, some seals) are becoming quite rare and near extinction.

Figure 1: Representative carnivores: Procyonidae, Ursidae, Canidae.
Drawing by R. Keane; Indian dhole based on Zoological Society of London photograph

II. Survey of carnivore families

DOGS AND ALLIES (FAMILY CANIDAE)

Natural history. Canids are basically meat eaters, although some vegetable matter is taken. The gray or timber wolf (*Canis lupus*), the African hunting dog (*Lycaon pictus*), and the dhole, or wild dog of India (*Cuon alpinus*), are strictly carnivorous. The various foxes and jackals, coyotes, and the raccoon dog eat whatever food is abundant—small mammals, birds, insects, crustaceans, mollusks, fruits, or berries. The canids that are strictly carnivorous tend to hunt in packs; those that are omnivorous tend to be solitary in their hunting habits. Since the carnivorous forms depend primarily on one or a few prey species, they usually follow the moving herds of caribou or antelope, on which they feed, or move into areas where the prey species are more numerous. African hunting dogs are extremely social, always hunting in packs so intricately organized that some researchers doubt that an individual dog could survive alone. The varied diet of the omnivore reduces the necessity for organized attack on the prey species and for extensive movement.

Canids have the ability to endure a continuous chase pattern with exceptional stamina but are not capable of great bursts of speed. Their senses of smell and hearing are highly developed. Smell is used largely to track prey, and hearing to warn of impending danger. Smell is also used in association with the demarcation of territory, which tends to be outlined by frequent urination at established scent posts. Sight is less well developed, but movement is noted quickly. Canids are highly intelligent, can be trained easily, and form a basis for such sayings of man as "sly as a fox." From a behavioural standpoint wild canids are cunning or crafty, even vicious or treacherous by human standards, but usually cowardly or furtive unless running in a pack.

Reproductive behaviour of canids

Canids give birth in a den in the ground, in a hollow log or tree, in a hidden brushy area, among boulders, or in a crevice of rock. The African hunting dog often dens in old diggings of the aardvark. Usually one litter of from four to six young is produced each year after a gestation period of from 51 to 80 days, depending on the species. The Arctic fox, *Alopex lagopus*, may produce two litters in a season. Most breeding takes place late in the winter, the young being born in middle or late spring. Canids living in the northern regions breed a month or so later than those in the southern regions. Carnivorous animals tend to produce young soon after the peak in the prey reproduction, a time of abundant food availability. Thus the timing of the breeding season and the duration of the gestation period must be coordinated with the season of available food in order that the young be produced when the most food is available for their rapid growth. The eyes of the young usually open in about two weeks, and they nurse for from four to six weeks. Canids of the smaller species can begin production of their own young when only one year old, but the larger forms, such as the wolf, reach sexual maturity at two or three years of age.

Canids are basically adapted to running and do so on their toes (a mode of walking or running called digitigrade). They live in a variety of habitats but generally tend to be animals of the open or grassland areas where their prey species are more abundant. Only the rare bush dog (*Speothos venaticus*) confines itself to forested areas. The red fox (*Vulpes vulpes*) tends to be an animal of the forest edge, and the gray fox (*Urocyon cinereoargenteus*) an animal inhabiting wooded areas. Thus, in North America, where both forms exist, these foxes live in slightly different niches. Although basically terrestrial in habits, the gray fox is not averse to climbing trees. The raccoon dog (*Nyctereutes procyonoides*) often lives in tree hollows if the entrance is close to the ground. The family Canidae is worldwide, being absent only from New Zealand, Antarctica, and most oceanic islands. The Arctic fox is found farther north than any other strictly terrestrial mammal. Every major habitat has some type of canid, from the Arctic tundra, through the desert and grassland, to the tropical forest.

Canid communication

Canids communicate with a variety of sounds. The vocal repertoire, most highly developed in social species, includes howls, yelps, snarls, barks, and growls. These sounds are frequently associated with specialized visual signals involving movements of the ears and tail, raising of certain areas of the fur, and baring of the teeth. Within the social group or pack there is a complex dominance hierarchy, involving age levels, pair bonds, physical condition, and sexual state. Vocal and visual signals serve to minimize aggressive interactions, such as quarrels over food, that might prove injurious to the group as a whole and to the individual members. In solitary species vocalizations serve to advertise the territory, to ward off aggressors, and to communicate with the mate and young.

Importance to man. The domestic dog (*Canis familiaris*) is undoubtedly the canid of the greatest importance economically. Numerous humans are actually employed in raising, selling, doctoring, grooming, training, or providing and manufacturing food for "man's best friend." Dogs probably were the first wild animals to be domesticated; they have been found associated with Neolithic sites dating back some 8,000 years. (For information on domestic dogs, see DOG.)

Some canids are important to the fur trade. At one time a mutant form of the red fox, called the "silver fox," formed a significant part of the fur-farming industry, with a breeding pair bringing as high as $40,000. The raccoon dog is still raised in some regions of the Soviet Union. The more important canids whose fur is utilized are the raccoon dog, red fox, grey fox, Arctic fox, and timber wolf. Coyotes, kit and swift foxes (*Vulpes macrotis* and *V. velox*), jackals (*Canis aureus*, *C. adustus*, *C. mesomelas*), Corsac fox (*Vulpes corsac*), hoary fox (*Vulpes cana*), dhole, South African silver fox (*Vulpes chama*), Cape fox (*Octocyon megalotis*), maned wolf (*Chrysocyon brachyurus*), crab-eating fox (*Cerdocyon thous*), and the South American foxes (*Dusicyon* species) are occasionally used by the fur trade. Other canids, especially the red fox, are hunted for sport. Some hunters call or lure foxes up to them by using an imitation of the sound of an injured rabbit to attract the attention of the fox.

Canids also are basically important as a natural control over rodent populations. Livestock is occasionally endangered when not properly protected from the forays of wild canids. Individual foxes learn where an easy meal is located, if the farmer does not have his chickens properly housed. In many cases all individuals of the species are condemned because of the damaging activity of a few. Proper selective control of those individuals actually doing the damage is the only sane conservation practice. Some species also form important natural reservoirs for parasites, causing a number of diseases, especially the virus producing rabies. Not many canids are utilized by man for food, but the American Indian once regarded dog meat as a delicacy to be eaten on special occasions.

Form and function. Canids have unspecialized incisor teeth, and large fanglike canines used to kill their prey by slashing. The premolars are narrow and sharp and the carnassials well developed; the molars form broad surfaces that can crush substantial bones. Most canids have the basic dental formula of terrestrial carnivores, with a total of 42 teeth.

Distinguishing physical features of canids

The possession of a long face or muzzle is characteristic of wild canids. All have a relatively long and obviously bushy tail. The ears are pointed, held erect, and often quite large in desert species. As well as functioning for sound detection, these large ears are believed to act as heat regulators, allowing a greater amount of heat to be dissipated in hot climates. Arctic foxes tend to have small ears, providing less loss of heat in a region where heat conservation is important to survival. Most canids have relatively long legs (especially long in the maned wolf, *Chrysocyon brachyurus*, of South America). The long legs and digitigrade gait are special adaptations for ease of running. Canids have four well-developed toes, plus a dew claw (reduced hind toe) on the front foot (except in the African hunting dog, which lacks the dew claw), and four toes on the rear foot. Each toe is capped by a blunt, nonretractile claw (*i.e.*, with no sheath into which it can be withdrawn). The short claws are not adapted for use as a weapon but do aid the animal during the digging of a den or during pursuit of small prey animals in their burrows. Scent glands are often present at the base of the tail. Most canids have a uniform coloration, although there are some contrasting colours on the gray fox, a raccoon-like mask on the raccoon dog, a blotching of black, yellow, and white colours on the African hunting dog, and a lighter coloured belly in most canids.

BEARS (FAMILY URSIDAE)

Natural history. Members of the Ursidae, except for the carnivorous polar bear (*Ursus maritimus*), are omnivorous, consuming many items that seem small for an animal the size of a bear. Ants, bees, seeds of trees, roots of the skunk-cabbage, nuts, berries, insect larvae such as grubs, and even the dainty dog-toothed violet are eaten. Many bears relish honey, and the sun bear (*Helarctos malayanus*) is sometimes called the "honey bear" because of its preference for this food. Meat items taken by bears include rodents, fish, deer, pigs, and lambs. Grizzlies and Alaskan brown bears (North American subspecies of the widespread *Ursus arctos*) are known for their skillful fishing abilities during the spawning runs of the salmon. The polar bear feeds almost exclusively on seals and is the most carnivorous of all bears, but little vegetation grows within its range, so the carnivorous habit is dictated by the Arctic environment. The sloth bear (*Melursus ursinus*) delights especially in raiding and destroying termite nests, sucking up termites and larvae with its funnel-like lips. Bamboo shoots form the major food of the giant panda (*Ailuropoda melanoleuca*), which has a special bone formation of the forefoot that functions as a sixth digit, opposable to the other five and thus useful in handling bamboo.

Moving slowly about, bears seem to be sluggish and oblivious to much that is going on around them, but once disturbed their reactions may be violent and highly unpredictable. Although clumsy in appearance, a grizzly can move surprisingly fast, even through dense cover that would seriously impede a man or a horse. Their senses of sight and hearing are poorly developed, and most hunting is done by the sense of smell. Thus the smell of bacon kept in camp is an invitation to a bear in search of food. Bears, like many of their canid relatives, are solitary, except during the mating season.

Bears tend to congregate during the mating season and then pair off and mate in seclusion. Males play no role in raising the young, leaving the female soon after mating. The gestation period may vary, the fertilized egg remaining dormant in the uterus (delayed implantation), insuring the birth of young when food is abundant. Ursids breed only once a year. With a breeding season usually in late spring or early summer, and delayed implantation, most young are born in January or February when the female is in the winter den. Newborn grizzlies weigh about one pound and are about nine inches long from the tip of the nose to the tip of the short tail. The Himalayan brown bear (a race of *U. arctos*) have their young later (in April and May) than the North American populations, but the polar bear has the greatest variation of any bear population in the dates when young are born (January to April). Twins are most common in bears, but up to five young may be produced. The cubs nurse for about two months and stay with the female until the next breeding (about a year and a half after birth). Most young, however, can get along on their own when about six months old. Bears reach breeding condition at three and one-half to four years of age, males usually a few months later than females. Litters are produced every second year after the initial litter.

Winter sleep of bears

Most bears eat large amounts of food before entering a den for a period of deep sleep during the winter. The polar bear digs a den in the snow. Grizzlies build large mounds of dirt in front of their dens. Bears are not true hibernators, since they lack the physiological characteristics (lower heart rate, body temperatures, breathing rate, and blood pressure) exhibited by those animals that do hibernate. A true hibernator is slow to be awakened from its deep sleep, and those who believe bears hibernate need only kick a sleeping bear to become convinced to the contrary. Bears usually are quiet, but they do growl at times when feeding or when being challenged by another bear.

Ursids do not roam over great distances even though they are rather large carnivores. Black bears (*Ursus americanus*) tend to stay within an area of about 14 square miles, grizzlies within an area 10 miles in diameter, or about 80 square miles. A grizzly marks the boundary of its territory each spring by rubbing trees, scratching bark, or even biting large pieces from the trunks of trees. All bears, except the grizzly, Eurasian brown, and probably the polar bear, climb trees. Bears inhabit forested areas and areas that have a minimum of disturbance by man. At one time the grizzly was an animal of the plains and was one of the mammals reported by Lewis and Clark in their journey through eastern Montana in 1804. Polar bears have been noted in the open sea 40 miles from the nearest shore and on ice 200 miles from the nearest land.

Ursids are largely animals of north temperate regions, being found farther north than any other mammal (only the Arctic fox is found as far north on land). Most of the southern continents, Central and South America, Africa, and Australia, lack bears. The bear that formerly occurred in the Atlas Mountains of Morocco (*Ursus crowtheri*) became extinct in the early 19th century. The spectacled bear (*Tremarctos ornatus*) of the Andes is the southernmost form.

Importance to man. If taken when young, the grizzly can be tamed quite easily and is not uncommon in circus acts. Unfortunately, man has come to picture the bear as being quite tame and harmless, with the result that the bear is viewed without the respect that this potentially dangerous creature deserves. The grizzly is the most dangerous of the bears to man, of the most interest economically because of the damage that it can do to livestock, and of the most interest to the big-game hunter as a prized trophy. Some ursids, such as the Asiatic black bear (*Selenarctos thibetanus*), destroy fruits. At times the North American black bear does considerable damage to fruit crops and to corn fields when the corn is in the milk stage, pulling the stalks into a pile from as far as the bear can reach.

Use of bear pelts

The pelts of bears have been used for a number of purposes. Perhaps most popular has been the bearskin rug. Skins also have been used for lap rugs or sledge rugs, hats for the English Guard regiments, trimmings of coats, and for muffs. Skins of the rare giant panda commanded a high price in the early 1900s, but this animal apparently is close to extinction today. Black bears are prized as a food source in China, as is the flesh of the polar bear in the far north. The liver of the polar bear, however, is highly poisonous, due to high levels of vitamin A. The teeth and claws of bears have been favourite ornaments with the Indians and Eskimos for years, and the fat furnishes the "bear grease" of commerce.

Form and function. The teeth of the omnivorous bears are unspecialized. The first three premolars are usually either missing or extremely small. The carnassials are poorly developed, and the molars have broad, flat crowns. Except for variability as to the presence of premolars, the ursid dental formula is that of the Carnivora generally. The sloth bear lacks one pair of upper incisors. The jaw of the bear is controlled at the hinge by a powerful set of muscles.

Bears have an elongate skull that is especially heavy in the back portion. These plantigrade animals (plantigrades walk on the sole and heel of the foot) are powerful in build and have relatively short, massive legs with five toes on each foot. The toes end in enlarged, nonretractile claws that are especially well developed in the sloth bear and to some extent in the grizzly. The claws on the front feet are usually better developed than those on the rear and are especially adapted for digging out marmots or other small rodents. Bears, however, seldom use the claws to construct burrows. They generally have naked soles, but those of the polar bear are covered with hair, enabling the animal to walk on ice with a firm footing. In swimming, the polar bear uses only its front limbs, an aquatic adaptation found in no other four-legged mammal. Bears lack a clavicle but have a baculum (penis bone). Their lips, which are not attached to the gums, are protrusible and mobile. Ursids have a short (7 to 13 centimetres), stubby tail and are the largest living terrestrial members of the Carnivora. The Alaskan grizzly may weigh as much as 780 kilograms (1,700 pounds), and the smallest bear, the sun bear, weighs approximately 27 kilograms (60 pounds). In most species the two sexes are about the same size, but the male tends to be larger in the grizzly and polar bear. Bears of the genus *Ursus* tend to be of a uniform colour, ranging from white to brown, blue gray, and black. Unlike the majority of carnivores, ursids are often black or mostly black. The North American black bear occurs in a number of colour variants or phases; in addition to the typical black phase, there is a tan-brown phase (called the cinnamon bear) and a bluish-black phase (called the glacier bear). The spectacled bear and the several specialized Asian bears are black with white or tan markings. The giant panda is strikingly black and white, and the remaining genera largely black, with areas of white or orange on the chest, neck, or face. The fur is coarse, long, and shaggy in most northern forms.

RACCOONS AND ALLIES (FAMILY PROCYONIDAE)

Natural history. The family Procyonidae includes raccoons, coatis or coatimundis, olingos, and the ringtailed cat, kinkajou, and lesser panda. Procyonids, like bears, are omnivorous, eating numerous types of insects, crayfish, crabs, fishes, amphibians, reptiles, birds, small mammals, and a variety of fruits, nuts, roots, and young plants. A characteristic of most omnivorous animals is that they take whatever foods are available, varying their food habits with the season, the locality, and the abundance or population levels of the food items from one year to the next. The ringtailed cat (*Bassariscus astutus*) tends to be more carnivorous than the raccoon (*Procyon lotor*). The lesser panda (*Ailurus fulgens*) is the most vegetarian of the group.

The various senses of procyonids do not seem to be especially well developed, but the raccoons and lesser panda appear to be above average in intelligence and are often described as being cunning. Raccoons are well known for their insatiable curiosity and ability to use their "hands" in performing feats such as opening doors and getting into mischief when kept as pets. This curiosity of raccoons is well known by trappers, who have used bright objects placed on the treadle of a trap to attract them. The sense of touch probably is of the greatest importance to the raccoon in its food-gathering activities. Most procyonids, except perhaps the coatis (*Nasua* species), are more active in the twilight and evening hours than in the daylight. Procyonids tend to be solitary, although families often move and feed as a group. Coatis travel in bands, some individuals moving through the trees as others follow on the ground. Olingos (*Bassaricyon* species) also move about in small bands. All procyonids are arboreal and move around in trees with agility. On the ground, the raccoon resembles a small bear as it ambles along.

Figure 2: Representative carnivores: Mustelidae.
Drawing by R. Keane; striped skunk based on E. P.Walker, *Mammals of the World*

Procyonid breeding habits

Procyonids breed in late winter or early spring. During copulation, the female raccoon makes sharp rattling cries. After a gestation period of about two months (for the raccoons 54 to 66 days, for lesser panda 90 days), two to six young are produced. One litter a year is usual. Young raccoons "twitter" like young birds when disturbed in the nest, and the young of other procyonids also produce high-pitched calls. Most adult procyonids produce a variety of snarls, growls, whines, screams, and barks. Most of these calls have little carrying power. Young raccoons are dependent on the female for the first ten weeks but may nurse until approximately 20 weeks of age (ringtails to about four months) and may stay in the family group into winter. Being mainly arboreal, young procyonids are born in tree dens. Raccoons use old buildings or dens in the ground if tree dens are scarce. Ringtails use crevices in rocks.

Except for the lesser panda, which is found in the southeastern Himalayas of Asia at elevations from 6,500 to 12,000 feet, procyonids are found naturally only in the New World. They are largely mammals of the lower elevations of temperate and tropical regions, in areas well supplied with water and trees. Raccoons have been introduced successfully into many parts of Europe (Germany, White Russia, the Ukraine) and Asia (Lake Balkhash, Siberia).

Importance to man. The raccoon is the only procyonid of major economic significance. Raccoon hunting is a sport of substantial importance in the United States, and in some parts of the United States many people own dogs trained to hunt raccoons. The coatimundi also is hunted with dogs and its flesh is also eaten. Meat of the raccoon is in more demand as food than that of any other carnivore. The meat is roasted, fried, stewed, barbecued, fricasseed, and made into patties. The "coonskin" cap has become part of American legend. The fur of the raccoon is one of the staple items of the fur trade in the United States today, as it has been over many of the past 100 years. Also used are the furs of the ringtailed cat, kinkajou (*Potos flavus*), and the lesser panda.

Raccoons at times do damage to fields of corn and to abandoned buildings, which they frequently inhabit when natural dens are scarce. In certain regions, raccoons become a problem to nesting waterfowl, especially wood ducks and goldeneye, which, like the raccoons, raise their young in hollow trees.

Most procyonids make interesting pets. Raccoons, kinkajous, and coatis are frequently sold as house pets, but their inquisitive nature and climbing ability make them troublesome if allowed to run loose indoors.

Form and function. The unspecialized teeth of procyonids are adapted for an omnivorous diet. The elongate canines are oblong in cross section, and the premolars are small, narrow, and pointed. As in bears, the carnassials are poorly developed and the molars are broad. Procyonids have the basic dental formula of the Carnivora, except that there is one less lower molar.

Procyonids are plantigrade or semiplantigrade, with legs of moderate length and five flexible toes with nonretractile or (in the ringtail cat and lesser panda) semiretractile claws. The tail is well developed (20 to 70 centimetres long), bushy, and in all forms except the kinkajou ringed by light and dark bands. In the kinkajou, it is prehensile, gripping a branch like a fifth limb. The anal scent glands of the kinkajou and lesser panda produce a musky odour when the animal becomes excited. The snout is extremely flexible in the coati and somewhat movable in other procyonids. The members of this family are medium in size, ranging from 0.8 to 22 kilograms in weight (the record weight of a raccoon is 66 pounds, 6 ounces). There is no difference in size between males and females. In coloration the procyonids range from gray or brown to the rich, reddish brown of the lesser panda.

MUSTELIDS (FAMILY MUSTELIDAE)

Natural history. The family Mustelidae contains a variety of animals unmatched by any other family in the Carnivora except the civets (Viverridae). The family includes the weasels, ferrets, mink, marten, fisher, skunks, wolverine, otters, badgers, and a number of less well-known animals, a total of about 70 species in 25 genera. The weasels, mink, and polecats (*Mustela* species) are fierce predators, feeding exclusively on small mammals and birds, hunting and trailing their prey with a keen sense of smell. At times, bird eggs, salamanders, snakes, and insects are taken. The smallest mustelid, the least weasel (*M. nivalis*), consumes a third to half its body weight per day, killing the prey by biting at the base of the skull. Weasels often store food in underground caches. The Asiatic polecat (*M. eversmanni*) and the North American black-footed ferret (*M. nigripes*) feed almost exclusively on the animals whose colonies they inhabit, the polecat on marmots and ground squirrels, the ferret on prairie dogs. Both of these animals occasionally feed on insects. Mink (*M. vison* and *M. lutreola*) feed largely on aquatic animals (muskrats, crayfish, mollusks, and fish) as well as on organisms inhabiting the banks of bodies of water.

Feeding habits of mustelids

The fisher (*Martes pennanti*) feeds mainly on mammals, but a few nuts, birds and eggs, fish, and seeds are taken. This animal is noted for its ability to kill and eat porcupines. Small terrestrial mammals make up over 90 percent of the food of the American marten (*M. americana*). The Eurasian pine marten (*M. martes*) and the stone or beech marten (*M. foina*) feed largely on small mammals but in the autumn may turn to wild berries and fruit. The yellow-throated marten (*M. flavigula*) of Asia is one of the largest martens and feeds on the young of larger mammals such as musk deer, wild boars, roe deer, spotted deer, and raccoon dogs, as well as on squirrels, rabbits, and the smaller rodents. These large mustelids also take a variety of other food items: mollusks, grasshoppers, spawning fish, birds and their eggs, cedar nuts, grapes, and berries.

Badgers are quite variable in their diet. About 50 percent of the diet of the American badger (*Taxidea taxus*) is composed of ground squirrels, which are captured in their burrows. Badgers can dig with remarkable speed and can overtake the rodent when the latter has taken refuge in a blind tunnel. The remainder of their food is made up of small rodents, rabbits, birds and their eggs, snakes, turtle eggs, and insects. Insects, in fact, form a staple food of the young badger. The Eurasian badger (*Meles meles*) and the ferret badgers (*Melogale* species) are more omnivorous than the American badger and prefer insects (especially bees) and their larvae (grubs). Earthworms, mollusks, crustaceans, frogs, lizards, birds, eggs, as well as vegetable matter, such as berries, nuts, grains, fruits, bulbs, and green vegetation, are also taken. Ratels or honey badgers (*Mellivora capensis*) eat small mammals, lizards and snakes, insects, fruit, and especially honey. An interesting association exists between the African honeyguide (a piciform bird) and the honey badger. When the bird finds honey it gives a special call, which attracts the badger. The latter breaks open the hive with its long, sharp claws, exposing enough honey for both bird and mammal. If the bird does not succeed initially in attracting a honey badger, it seeks one out and, using the "honey" call, which the badger recognizes, leads it to the bee tree.

Skunks (*Mephitis, Spilogale, Conepatus*) are omnivorous mustelids, with small mammals forming an important part of the diet. Skunks may be becoming scarce in some parts of North America due to poisons gradually accumulated through extensive feeding on insects poisoned in agricultural control programs.

Otter feed largely on the invertebrates and vertebrates (especially fish) found in their aquatic environment. The oriental small-clawed otter (*Aonyx cinerea*) and the clawless otter (*Aonyx capensis*) feed to a greater extent on invertebrates (clams, snails, crabs) than do the river otter (*Lutra* species). *Lutra canadensis* at times take large numbers of crayfish. The African small-clawed otter (*Aonyx* species) are believed to feed on small mammals, the eggs of birds, and amphibians more than on fish. The sea otter (*Enhydra lutris*) is perhaps known best for its habit of breaking open sea urchins and clams on a rock held on its chest while it floats on its back. Seaweed, cuttlefish, and small fishes also are eaten.

Sharp senses of mustelids

Smell apparently is the most important sense to mustelids hunting on land. Black-footed ferrets have been noted to stop repeatedly and sniff the air while hunting. Hearing is also well developed and seems to be utilized as a means of detecting danger. Sight is less developed and, in the ferret at least, of little importance beyond about 300 feet. Of most importance to otters, living in an aquatic environment, is an acute sense of touch, through their very sensitive whiskers, which they use as an aid to guide them through the water. Most mustelids are silent, seldom making more than a squeak, whistle, or bark. Many will snarl or growl when annoyed. The giant otter (*Pteronura brasiliensis*) of South America is perhaps the most vocal, with its high-pitched whistle. Yellow-throated martens give a harsh cry when excited and often chuckle in a low tone.

Almost all mustelids are active both day and night, although most of their activity is nocturnal. Only the Old World badgers (*Meles meles*), ferret badgers (*Melogale* species), spotted skunks (*Spilogale* species), and hog-nosed skunks (*Conepatus* species) seem to be almost strictly nocturnal. The giant otter and sea otter seem to be more diurnal than other mustelids.

Except when travelling with young in a family group, most adult mustelids are solitary in habits. Sea otters seem to be more or less gregarious, as are Old World badgers. Badgers build a labyrinth of underground passages that some call "badger cities," because of the extent of the burrows and number of badgers that inhabit them. Female skunks (*Mephitis* species) often den together in large groups during the winter. Grisons (*Galictis* species) and yellow-throated martens often travel in groups of five or six individuals. Tayras (*Eira barbara*) and ratels tend to travel in pairs.

Since a great variation exists in the habits of mustelids, a great diversity would be expected in the habitats in which they live. Most mustelids, however, are terrestrial, living in forested or brushy areas. Many species can survive in a variety of habitats, from forest to desert. Some, like the marten and fisher, are strongly arboreal. Others, like the otter, are largely aquatic. The New World skunks and the North African spotted weasel (*Poecilictis libyca*) tend to inhabit areas farmed by man. The ferrets, American badger, and Eurasian polecats live mainly in grassland or semi-arid areas. Wolverines live in the more northern areas of taiga and forested tundras.

The locomotion of mustelids also varies. Most small mustelids scamper across the ground, making intermittent bounds as they move along. The larger forms sometimes lumber slowly. During their travels, mustelids tend to stop, sit up on their haunches, and look over the area. Some are extremely agile in trees; others are excellent swimmers.

Delayed implantation is perhaps more characteristic of the mustelids than any other group of the Carnivora. Members of the genus *Mustela* have gestation periods (determined from the date of fertilization) ranging from as much as 220 to 337 days (long-tailed weasel, *M. longicauda*) or as little as 36–42 days (ferrets). In the genus *Martes* the period is highly variable, between 220 and 297 days. The gestation period of badgers (*Taxidea, Mellivora, Meles*) ranges from six to eight months and that of otter from eight months to a little more than a year. Skunks (*Mephitis* species) do not have delayed implantation and apparently have the least variation in the period of gestation (62 to 72 days). Mink (*Mustela vison*) usually produce young in 45 to 50 days, with extremes from 38 to 76 days. On mink ranches, the later in the year that mink are bred, the shorter the gestation period.

Mustelid reproduction

The breeding season usually is in the late winter or early spring (mink, skunks, polecats, otters) or in the summer (weasels, marten, wolverine, sables, European and American badgers). Some mustelids breed at almost any time of the year (least weasel, river and sea otters). Those with exceptionally long gestation periods breed soon after the litter is born or in the following year. Some forms have two litters a year (striped skunk, least weasel, ratel), but in most only one litter is produced. Average litter size varies from one young in the sea otter to between 8 and 12 young (up to 18) in the Asiatic polecat. Most mustelids have between three and five young in a litter. The young of mustelids are born in ground dens, in rock crevices, under the roots of trees, under haystacks or buildings, or in hollow trees (the pine and American martens). The young of most species are weaned when between six and ten weeks of age, but young river otters nurse for about four months. Wolverine young are allowed to remain with the female for two years before establishing their own territories. In most species, however, the family disperses near the end of the summer or early fall. Mustelids are found worldwide, except for most oceanic islands, Australia, and Madagascar. Introductions have been made on some of the larger islands, such as New Zealand. Mustelids, like bears, generally are more abundant in the more northern continents.

Importance to man. Of all mammalian families, the Mustelidae contains the greatest variety of valuable mammals utilized by the fur trade. Fur coats that command the highest prices are usually those made from these luxuriant furbearers, especially mink, ermine (short-tailed weasel), and sable (a name applied by the fur trade to several species of *Martes*, especially the Eurasian *M. zibellina*, but also the American *M. americana*). Excellent skins are produced by the marten, fisher, skunk, and otter. In fact, the durability of all furs, including those from other mammalian orders, is based on the river otter, which has been given the top rank of 100. Pelts of the ermine and sea otter have been the furs of royalty for hundreds of years. More than $100,000,000 worth of ranch-mink skins alone are produced yearly, and some breeds (like the Kojah mink) brought $2,700 per skin in the late 1960s. During the 18th and 19th centuries a collar made from the sea otter was regarded by some as the highest of status symbols, equivalent to owning a Rolls Royce or private yacht today. In 1968, at the first sale of sea-otter skins in 55 years, the better quality skins brought $2,300 apiece.

The pelt of the wolverine is prized highly by the Eskimos and others in Arctic areas because, when used for the lining of a parka, it can be cleared of frost from breath by a sweep of the hand. Moisture does not freeze to wolverine hair as it does to other furs. Badger hair has been utilized in the past to manufacture shaving brushes. Hair from the tails of many species is in high demand for paint brushes. Among the Chinese, the tail of the kolinsky or China mink (*Mustela sibirica*) is used for making delicate paint and artists brushes and is in more demand than is the rest of the pelt. The tails are removed from the skins and sold by the pound. Hairs from the tail of the sable also make excellent brushes, since the taper of the individual hairs causes the brush to form a sharp point when wet (see also FURS).

Importance in the food chain

Being largely carnivorous, the mustelids form an important link in the biological food chain. Rodents are kept at a reasonable level by this natural control. The spotted skunk, ferret badger, long-tailed weasel, Patagonian weasel, zorille (*Ictonyx striatus*), and sometimes the striped skunk (*Mephitis mephitis*) have been encouraged to live in or near the habitations of man because of their ability to keep the rodent and pest insect populations under control. Systematic destruction of these valuable predators can be a costly mistake to farmers.

Being carnivorous, mustelids sometimes become pests, especially around poultry—particularly when the poultry farmer is lax in his sanitation. Weasels, marbled polecats, and striped skunks are the common offenders. Considerable exaggeration of the prowess and deliberate maliciousness of the wolverine exists in literature. The behaviour of this animal has led many trappers to regard it as a true "demon of the north." A wolverine travels a trapline because it learns that a ready source of food is being held captive. In many cases the wolverine will follow the trapline back to the trapper's cabin and ransack the area in its search for food. The largest of the mustelids (around 25 pounds), this animal can do extensive damage.

Those mustelids that are proficient diggers (*e.g.*, badgers) sometimes become a hazard to horses (and riders), which stumble when stepping into a burrow. Other mustelids, such as the North American skunk, tend to be one of the more common wild mammals that serve as a reservoir for rabies. Meat of the Malayan stink badger (*Mydaus javanensis*), and sometimes the skunk (*Mephitis mephitis*), is eaten in some areas of the world. The obnoxious scent glands of mustelids discourage man from eating most of these animals, however. On the other hand, the scent from these glands was used in the past as a base for perfumes. Grisons and the ferret (*Mustela putorius*) have been trained by man to enter the burrows of other animals and drive them out; the grison to flush chinchillas, and the ferret, rabbits and rats. In China Oriental clawed otter and river otter are trained to catch fish or to chase them under nets which are then dropped, securing the catch. In some areas the bones or various parts of the tayra, African striped weasel, Malayan stink badger, hog-nosed skunks, and the African small-clawed otter are believed to possess medicinal value.

Form and function. Being highly carnivorous, mustelids have well-developed carnassials and a reduced number of premolar and molar teeth, the total number of teeth being between 30 and 38 (average, 34). With such a reduction in tooth number, the facial area of these animals is shortened. In the wolverine and American badger the bone of the lower jaw has a projection, the postglenoid process, that curves over the jaw articulation (glenoid fossa), resulting in a condition in which the mandible can be locked in place.

Mustelids are either digitigrade or plantigrade, and they have five toes on each foot. Most mustelids have short legs and many tend to have an elongate, slender body. They are quiet, agile, and graceful in their movements. There is a great variation in the tails of mustelids: flattened and elongate in the otter; stubby in the stink badgers; short in some of the weasels and badgers, long and thin in other weasels; long and bushy in marten; and especially elongate, with long hairs, in the skunks. The ears are small and rounded. Colours are usually brown or black. Some weasels change colour, becoming white in the winter, thus protecting the animal or, perhaps more probably, hiding it from its prey and making capture easier. Such white weasels are called ermine in the fur trade. Most mustelids have well-developed anal scent glands. The skunks, zorille, and the marbled polecat (*Vormela peregusna*), and to some extent the stink badger and ratel, can forcibly eject the vile-smelling material as a spray or fluid. All mustelids that possess powerful, controllable scent glands (except the stink badger) are marked in obvious contrasting colours, usually black and white. Such a striking colour combination may serve as a warning to potential predators, minimizing the likelihood that the animal will be attacked. After a single encounter with an adult mustelid, a predator avoids all animals so marked, including the less formidable young of the mustelid.

Repellent scent of mustelids

The smallest member of the Carnivora, the least weasel, belongs to the family Mustelidae and weighs 30 to 70 grams (1 to 2.5 ounces). The largest mustelid is the sea otter, which may weigh 41 kilograms (90 pounds). In most mustelids the males are larger than the females.

CIVETS AND ALLIES (FAMILY VIVERRIDAE)

Natural history. Viverrids are more numerous than the mustelids in terms of living genera (about 36) and species (about 75).

They are largely omnivorous in food habits, eating a variety of small mammals, birds, reptiles, eggs of birds and reptiles, amphibians, fishes, crustaceans, insects and their grubs, and earthworms, as well as vegetation such as fruits, nuts, bulbs or roots, and other plant material. A few, such as the palm civets (*Nandinia*, *Arctogalidia*, *Paradoxurus*, *Macrogalidia*), tend to be mostly vegetarian but at times take small mammals, birds, and insects. The binturong (*Arctictis binturong*), the largest member of the family, feeds mainly on fruit, although carrion is sometimes eaten. Although the suricates or slender-tailed meerkats (*Suricata suricatta*) tend toward an omnivorous diet, bulbous roots constitute most of their food. Approximately half of the genera of viverrids are composed of species that tend to be more carnivorous than herbivorous; the remaining genera are truly omnivorous. Some species tend to feed on one type of food: the ruddy mongoose (*Herpestes smithi*) on large snails, the Indian mongoose (*H. edwardsi*) on carrion remaining from the feasts of the large predators, the water mongoose (*Atilax paludinosus*) on crocodile eggs, the striped-necked mongoose (*H. vitticollis*) and the Congo water civet (*Osbornictis piscivora*) on fish. The banded palm civet (*Hemigalus derbyanus*) and Owston's civet are sometimes known to eat significant amounts of earthworms.

A number of viverrids (*Herpestes*, *Atilax*, *Mungos*, *Helogale*) are noted for their peculiar habit of opening eggs, as well as other food items with hard shells (crabs, mollusks, nuts). The animal stands on its hindlegs and hits the egg against the ground. Sometimes it carries the egg to a rock and, standing with its back to the rock, throws the egg between its legs and against the rock until the shell is broken. (Early reports of this behaviour met with skepticism but have been verified by other observers.) The Madagascar narrow-striped mongoose (*Mungotictis lineatus*) exhibits the same behaviour but lies on its side and uses all four feet to toss the egg. Viverrids are per-

Figure 3: Representative carnivores: Viverridae, Felidae, Hyaenidae.
Drawing by R. Keane

Viverrids as snake-killers

haps best known for their ability to kill poisonous snakes, especially cobras, which are slow in striking and apparently unable to strike when at close quarters. The mongoose can dart within the outer striking range of the snake and grab and break the lower jaw. The mongoose is much less successful against a viper such as a rattlesnake, which has a very rapid strike and return to the pre-strike defensive position. The white-tailed mongoose (*Ichneumia albicauda*) has the unusual habit of feeding on the tree hyrax, which it follows and kills in the tops of trees.

Viverrids are highly variable in hunting and social behaviour. Some species are solitary; others hunt in groups, ranging from a single pair to a family group or a wandering band of more than 20 individuals. Two species, the meerkats (*Suricata suricatta* and *Cynictis penicillata*), live in colonies. Colonial organization is unusual for animals that are largely carnivorous but is found also in the European badger. An interesting relationship exists between the type of association and the time of day that viverrids are active. The viverrids that travel singly or hunt in pairs comprise the majority of species, and all are nocturnal. All those viverrids that hunt in bands or live in colonies are diurnal. The only exceptions are the mongooses of the genus *Herpestes*, which may hunt singly or in bands and may be either nocturnal or diurnal depending on the species involved.

The senses for seeing, hearing, and smelling are well developed in viverrids. Predatory birds apparently are recognized almost instantly and at considerable distances. Viverrids, like mustelids, tend to be silent, but such sounds as purring, grunting, chirping, low-pitched coughing, growling, hissing, whining, twittering, and barking have been described. More elaborate or complex "language" usually is found in gregarious forms. Specific warning or danger cries, signifying the approach of either a ground or aerial predator, are known in the social meerkats. The noisiest viverrid, however, is the nocturnal, arboreal binturong, which growls, hisses, and, at times, howls loudly. Also extremely noisy are the cusimanses (*Crossarchus* species), which travel in large groups grunting, chattering, and twittering.

Viverrid habitats

Most viverrids are terrestrial, but at least ten genera have forms that inhabit trees to a considerable extent. Mostly arboreal are the African palm civet (*Nandinia binotata*), the small-toothed palm civet (*Arctogalidia trivirgata*), the musang (*Paradoxurus* species), the masked palm civet (*Paguma larvata*), the binturong, the fossa (*Cryptoprocta ferox*), and the slender mongoose (*Herpestes sanguineus*). The linsangs (*Prionodon* species), although spending some time on the ground, are good climbers and live in the hollows of trees. Palm civets (subfamily Paradoxurinae), a few other civets, and genets also spend considerable time in trees. Mongooses, however, seldom climb and are unable to move about easily in trees. This inability is evident when they descend from trees. An efficient well-adapted climber comes down a tree head first. Of the mongooses, only the slender mongoose, and perhaps the Indian gray mongoose, have been observed descending head first. All other mongooses back down. Although most viverrids can swim if need be, three genera have semi-aquatic members: the Congo water civet, the African civet (*Viverra civetta*), and at least three species of mongooses of the genus *Herpestes* (*H. brachyurus*, *H. urva*, and *H. vitticollis*). The otter civet (*Cynogale bennetti*) has slightly webbed feet and is aquatic. An even more aquatic viverrid, or at least more agile one, is the water mongoose, which dives and swims like an otter, although, unlike the otter, its feet are not webbed.

Some mongooses exhibit curious antics to attract their prey. The white-tailed mongoose may dance outside of chicken pens and bite off the heads of chickens that curiously stick their heads through the netting. The banded mongoose is said to stand upright and fall over on its side, using such antics to attract curious guinea fowl close enough for capture. An interesting habit found in the meerkat plays a role in heat regulation. The belly of this animal has little hair, much less than the back. In the winter or during cold weather, the meerkat basks in the sun, standing on its hind feet with the ventral surface directed toward the heat source. When the temperatures are high, the animal seeks out cool surfaces, on which it lies on its stomach. It may even dig out an area to expose the cool subsurface layers of earth before lying down.

The fossa walks on the soles of its feet and thus is plantigrade or semiplantigrade, but most other viverrids walk on their toes (digitigrade).

Information concerning reproduction in viverrids is sketchy. In most species studied there are two litters a year (usually one in spring and one in fall), although breeding can occur throughout the year. The gestation period is usually between 49 and 64 days, but in various mongooses of the genus *Herpestes* it ranges from 32 to 49 days. Most litters consist of three or four young, but the black-legged mongooses (*Bdeogale* species) may have only a single young. Most female viverrids have two pairs of abdominal nipples, thus perhaps restricting the litter size to four, but some females of the genus *Herpestes* have three pairs. The young are born in burrows, in a nest of grass on the ground, or in hollow trees.

Viverrids are found in the Old World tropics and subtropics, throughout Africa, southern Asia, Madagascar, and southeastern Europe. Only the genet (*Genetta genetta*) occurs naturally in Europe. Although restricted to southern France and Spain today, it was at one time found as far north and east as Belgium and Germany. Various mongooses (*Herpestes* species) have been introduced into the West Indies, Hawaii, and New Zealand, as well as Italy and Yugoslavia. Viverrids are most abundant in Southeast Asia (India and the Malay Peninsula). In habits and habitat they fill the niches of the mustelids and procyonids found more abundantly in the northern regions or in the New World. Viverrids are the only members of the Carnivora to reach Madagascar, where they have flourished and undergone adaptive radiation. About a sixth of the known genera of viverrids are restricted in distribution to this large island.

Importance to man. Probably of most significance economically is the musk, called civet, produced by the anal gland in members of the viverrid group known as "civet cats." Civet is a yellowish substance with the consistency of butter and is of great importance as a base for perfumes. It is produced by the anal scent glands and stored in a sac near the genital region. The Oriental and African civets (*Viverra* species) and the lesser Oriental civet, or rasse (*Viverricula indica*), are kept in captivity so that this musky secretion can be collected several times weekly. The secretion is obtained by scraping the sac with a wooden spatula. As much as four grams of civet can be obtained in one week. Long, narrow cages are used to prevent the animal from turning and biting while the secretion is being collected.

Viverrids as the source of musk

This musk has been in great demand for many years and has commanded high prices. Civet is used as a base for perfume extracts, and in India the product of the lesser Oriental civet has been used to flavour tobacco. In some areas, parts from viverrids (the binturong and the linsang, *Poiana richardsoni*) are believed to have various medicinal values.

The only civets of value to the fur trade are certain members of the subfamily Viverrinae. Of these, the large Indian, or "Chinese," civet (*Viverra zibetha*) is the only one to be utilized for fur to any great extent. Fur of the small Indian civet and the genet is used for trimming clothing. Some members of tribes in Madagascar use the tails of civets for ornamentation. The meat of both the large and small Indian civets has been described as delicious.

The genet, white-tailed mongoose, and fossa often become pests in areas where poultry is raised. Most viverrids are efficient rat catchers, and some, such as the binturong, suricate, cusimanse, and certain mongooses, are domesticated because of their affectionate nature and their ability to eliminate mice, rats, and cockroaches from the residence of the owner. In some areas, Greece and southern Italy for example, genets have been kept as house pets, and this animal may have been the "cat" of the ancient Greeks. In other areas, the binturong is tamed to follow its master like a dog.

Form and function. Viverrids have from 36 to 42 teeth. The canines are slender and elongate and the carnassials well developed.

Viverrids have short legs with five toes on each foot, except for the meerkats; *Suricata* has four toes on each foot and *Cynictis* four on the hindfoot. The pollex ("thumb") and hallux ("big toe") are functionless and do not touch the ground. Each toe is capped with semiretractile claws that are more retractile in digitigrade species than in those that are semiplantigrade. Most viverrids have a long, slim body and a long, bushy tail. Except for some marsupials, the binturong is the only Old World mammal with a prehensile tail. The elongate head ends in a pointed, foxlike muzzle. Coloration in the civets can be quite variable in pattern, from uniform to spotted, blotched, or striped, and ranges from black and gray through various shades of brown to rufous and yellow. The stripes may run longitudinally (*Mungotictis*, *Galidictis*) or vertically (*Mungos*, *Chrotogale*, *Hemigalus*). Some forms of civets (especially *Bdeogale*, *Ichneumia*) have black legs.

Viverrids range in size from the dwarf mongoose (*Helogale parvula*) with a weight of about 500 grams (about one pound) and a total length of 300 millimetres (12 inches) to the binturong with a weight of up to 14,000 grams (about 30 pounds) and a length of 1,800 millimetres (72 inches).

HYENAS (FAMILY HYAENIDAE)

Natural history. Hyenas form a relatively homogeneous family that includes two basic types: the true hyenas (two species of *Hyaena* and one of *Crocuta*) and the aardwolf (*Proteles cristatus*). Hyenas are noted for their scavenger feeding and bone-crushing habits, although they do hunt live animals. Their food consists largely of the remains of artiodactyls, such as the antelope, left by the large cats. Vultures and jackals often feed on such kills after the cats and before the hyenas move in. The spotted hyena (*Crocuta crocuta*) eats large amounts of bone and skin, seeming to prefer them to meat. These, of course, are the remains after the predator has had its fill. Spotted hyenas hunt in aggressive packs and at times attack and kill larger animals, even as large as a young rhino. If the animal attacked puts up a fight, the hyenas stop the attack and move away. In addition to carrion, brown hyenas (*Hyaena brunnea*) feed on small mammals, young or newborn larger mammals, reptiles, eggs, insects, fruits, and berries. In coastal areas they may feed on dead crabs, whales, and other sea life washed up on shore. The brown hyena is less apt to attack living animals than is the spotted hyena. The striped hyena (*Hyaena hyaena*) has food habits similar to those of the brown hyena. The aardwolf feeds almost exclusively on termites but eats a few other insects, such as beetles. A large quantity of soil and grass is usually eaten accidentally while feeding at termite mounds.

Feeding habits of hyenas

Since carrion produces a distinctive odour, hyenas depend on the sense of smell to a great degree. Most of their food probably is located by this sense alone, sight and hearing being less important. Sight is poorly developed in hyenas.

The well-known howl of the "laughing hyena" is the call of the spotted hyena. The other species are not as noisy.

In areas undisturbed by man, hyenas hunt during the day. Members of this family inhabit open areas of plains and brushland but at times may be found in open forested areas. Hyenas form packs and are tireless trotters and runners, at times wandering great distances.

Spotted hyenas breed during the dry months, from April to July; the aardwolf breeds from October to November. The gestation period is approximately three months (95 to 110 days in the spotted hyena). Hyenas usually have three or four young. Dens may be located in abandoned burrows, caves, dense brushy areas, or among rocks. Some hyenas use the burrows of the aardvark for nesting spots, as does the African hunting dog.

The Hyaenidae have a distribution similar to, but more restricted than, that of the viverrids. They are found throughout Africa and from southern Asia east to eastern India.

Importance to man. The scavenger habits of most of the members of the Hyaenidae make them of considerable benefit to the ecosystem as a whole and often directly to man. They perform the service of eliminating the remnants left by the large predators and thus fit into a niche unused by most mammals. In some parts of Africa, hyenas are allowed to roam the villages, cleaning up garbage. In some areas people place their dead out in the open to be removed by these inexpensive "natural undertakers."

Hyenas at times will attack and kill livestock and sometimes people, usually sleeping persons or young children. Being cowardly, they seldom fight if the individual puts up any type of defense. When hungry, they may raid camps and carry off various items made of leather. In attacking large livestock or antelope, they usually approach from the rear and kill their prey by tearing open the abdomen.

Form and function. Hyenas have a total of 34 teeth, fewer than the generalized number found in other carnivores. The aardwolf has fewer upper and lower premolars and molars, resulting in from 28 to 32 teeth. The incisors are unspecialized in all members of the Hyaenidae, with the third incisor being the largest. The canines are well-developed, sharp, and elongate. Premolars of hyenas have well-developed crowns, useful in bone crushing, and tend to be conical. In the aardwolf the premolars are small, widely spaced, and, along with the small molars, tend to be vestigial. The lack of development of the cheek teeth is related to its insect-food diet, which does not require a powerful dentition. The molars of the hyenas are large and powerful, aiding in bone crushing, as do the jaws, the most powerful found in any mammal of comparable size. The head tends to be massive, with a broad muzzle, not long-nosed as in the canids or short-faced as in the cats. Anal glands are present in most forms and are well developed in the aardwolf, which can eject an obnoxious fluid when threatened.

All hyenas have a characteristic stance. The front legs are longer than the hindlegs, causing the back to slope conspicuously from a high point at the shoulders to a low point at the hindquarters. Hyenas walk on their toes and run well. There are four toes on each foot, capped by blunt, nonretractile claws. *Proteles* has five toes on the front foot. Most members of the family have a well-developed mane on the neck, which may extend down the midline of the back. This mane often is more noticeable in the young hyenas, although well developed in all age classes of the aardwolf. All have large, rounded ears. These animals are grayish or brownish in colour, marked with spots (*Crocuta*), stripes (*Proteles, Hyaena hyaena*), or uniform with bars on the legs (*Hyaena brunnea*). The tail is medium in size, bushy at the base, and pointed at the end.

CATS (FAMILY FELIDAE)

Natural history. Almost all cats are strictly carnivorous and feed on small mammals and birds or on the larger herbivorous artiodactyls like deer and various types of antelope. The fishing cat (*Felis viverrina*) feeds largely on fishes and clams or snails and thus fits into a slightly different niche from that of most cats. The flat-headed cat (*Felis planiceps*) is the only felid known to feed to any extent on vegetation, with fruit and items like sweet potatoes being preferred when available. The large cats sometimes drag the kill into a tree or place it under a bush after the initial gorging. Cats live on a feast-or-famine routine, gorging themselves when a kill is made and then fasting several days between kills.

Cats have good senses of sight and hearing. Long, sensitive whiskers on the face aid the cat during the stalking of the prey by brushing against any obstacle in a path and enabling the cat to avoid making excessive noise as it stalks its prey. The easiest, most open path can be followed through vegetation, even at night. Smell apparently is not as well developed as in some other carnivores, such as the dogs. Cats are nocturnal in habits. The cheetah is an exception to this rule, hunting predominantly by day. Their large eyes are especially adapted for seeing at night, when the amount of light is low. The cat stalks its prey to a point as close as allowed by available cover, then closes the final distance by a leap or a short dash. A chase may ensue, with the predator relying on superior speed and reflexes to overtake the dodging prey, which often has greater endurance. Although the endurance of most felids is sufficient for a chase of only a few hundred metres at most, the cheetah may pursue its prey for much greater distances, up to about 5,500 metres (about three miles). If overtaken, the prey is thrown down and dispatched with a deep bite, usually in the neck. Almost all hunting by these animals is done alone and quietly. The major exception to the solitary habit is the lion (*Leo leo*), in which the group, or pride, may number as many as 30 individuals. Cheetahs sometimes are found travelling in small groups but stalk and chase their prey individually.

Hunting method of cats

The gestation period of most smaller cats is approximately two months (50 to 68 days), and that of the large cats is three or three and a half months (88 to 113 days). Two or three kittens make up the usual litter. The jaguar (*Leo onca*) tends to have only one kitten. The domestic cat (*Felis catus*) sometimes has more than six kittens. Female cats may have from four to eight nipples. The breeding season usually is in the late winter or early spring. In smaller species those females that have early litters may produce a second litter in late summer or early fall. Some cats are capable of breeding at any time during the year (lion, tiger, and leopard). The size of the animal does not seem to determine the litter size, number of litters, or the time of the breeding season. In the larger cats, however, the age of initial breeding is greater; the females may be three or four years of age and males as much as five or six years old. Smaller cats may breed when less than a year old. Most litters are born in places seldom disturbed by man, such as in a rocky cavern, under a fallen tree, or in a dense thicket. The serval (*Felis serval*) uses an old porcupine or aardvark burrow. In most species the male does not aid in the care and raising of the young, and in fact, the female may have to guard against his attacks on the kittens. The male jaguar and ocelot (*Felis pardalis*) do help in raising the young.

Vocalizations of cats

Cats are noted for their purring when apparently content and for their snarling, howling, or spitting when in conflict with another member of their kind. The larger forms, especially the lion, often roar, growl, or shriek. Usually, however, cats are silent. Many cats have "clawing trees," upon which they leave the marks of their claws as they stand and drag their front feet downward with the claws extended. House cats are well known for this habit, and an owner may supply an artificial tree to save damage to furniture. Whether such behaviour is for the purpose of cleaning or sharpening the claws is debatable, but the behaviour is innate; kittens raised in isolation soon begin to claw objects. Other characteristics of cats are the constant movement of the tail when stalking, the habit of washing the face, and the habit of digging a hole in which to bury the fecal material and urine.

Almost every area on earth has some type of native cat. Australia is the only continental area that has no native felids, though the family also is absent from Madagascar and a number of oceanic islands. Cats are found in most habitats, from the forest to the desert, although they are typically animals of wooded environments. Many are in danger of extinction because of their incompatability with the activities of man or because of their combined value to zoos and the fur trade.

Importance to man. The cat, like the dog, was originally taken into the home of man as a pet. Unlike the dog, the cat has not been trained to hunt or to serve as a guardian. Cats may perform the function of "mouse catcher" in those areas where mice become a problem, but most urban house cats do not have the opportunity to perform this unless garbage and trash are allowed to accumulate. On farms, where storage of grain is common and rodents become numerous, cats help to hold their numbers in check. (For information on domestic cats, see CAT).

The fur of cats is sometimes in great demand, especially when high fashion calls for "fun furs," those with contrasting colours involving spots or stripes of the type found on the pelts of many cats. The demand is such that numerous kinds of cats are in danger of becoming extinct. In some regions of the world, catskins have been in great demand for many years. In parts of Africa the royal furs are usually those of a cat, as those in Eurasia are from the ermine or the sea otter. Chiefs and other high dignitaries of some native tribes use the pelt of the serval as a sleeveless cloak thrown over the shoulders.

Man-eaters

The larger cats are strong, fierce, and extremely dangerous when hungry. Should one of these animals learn that the flesh of man is edible, it must be eliminated. In many, if not most, cases the "man-eater" is an old cat no longer able to kill native wild prey. Although tigers and leopards are most famous for man-eating activities, lions and jaguars also may become dangerous. The American lion or puma (*Felis concolor*) tends to avoid contact with man and most records of its attacking man, except when cornered, are questionable. Similarly, if a large cat learns that a ready meal is available in the form of fenced or domesticated livestock, the rancher will have problems until the predator is eliminated. As in the case of the man-eater, the problem is caused by one animal and not all the individuals should be condemned.

Cats are intelligent and can be trained. Many kinds of cats can be tamed as pets, but some, especially the larger species, really can never be trusted when they become older or when they are sexually active. Most wild animals, to be trustworthy, must be fed by bottle before their eyes open, in which case the cat apparently will regard the human as its actual mother. The domestic cat, when liberated in the wild or allowed to roam in the field, may become a more serious and damaging predator on wildlife than the native predators in the region.

Form and function. Cats have a reduced number of premolar and molar teeth; the typical dental formula includes only 30 teeth. The incisors are small and chisel-like and the canines long and pointed. The premolars are sharp, and occasionally an upper premolar may be lacking. The lower molar is elongate and sharp, the upper molar rudimentary. Because of the reduction in the number and size of the cheek teeth, a space remains between the canines and premolars in all cats except the cheetah. Felids form the most carnivorous group in the order, and the highly developed carnassial teeth reflect this specialized food habit. There is little if any specialization in the teeth for grinding or chewing. The strong masseter (chewing) muscles of the jaw restrict the amount of lateral movement and primarily permit vertical movements of the jaw, for holding the prey in a viselike grip and for slicing off pieces of meat with the carnassials. Thus meat is cut off and swallowed in relatively unchewed chunks that are broken down by strong enzymes and acids in the digestive tract. Cats use the rasplike tongue to remove the flesh from the bone.

Because of the reduction in the number of teeth, cats have a short face and a rounded, compact head. The ears tend to be short or, in some forms, tufted with hair. Most forms, except the lynxes (*Felis lynx*, *Felis rufa*), have an elongate tail that comprises about a third of the total length. The agility of a cat is evident in its anatomy. The clavicle, or collarbone, is much reduced in size. It does not connect with other bones but is buried in the muscles of the shoulder region. This type of construction allows the animal to spring on its prey without danger of a supporting or connecting structure, like the clavicle, being broken. The hindlegs are well developed, with powerful muscles that propel the animal in its spring toward or onto the prey animal. In addition to the power of the hindlegs, the animal uses strong back muscles to straighten the spinal column and provide extra force in springing and running. Most of the skin covering the body of the cat is loose, allowing for even more freedom of movement as well as providing some protection during a fight.

Anatomical basis of feline agility

The legs of the jaguarundi (*Felis yagouaroundi*) are rather short, and those of the cheetah elongate. All cats, except the cheetah, have retractile claws. Such claws can be drawn back into a sheath when the animal is walking, rendering the footsteps noiseless and keeping the claws sharp; or they can be extended as an aid in pulling down and holding the prey when the animal is attacking or in protecting the cat when attacked. The sharp, strongly curved claws are also utilized when the cat climbs trees. There are five toes on the front foot and four on the rear. The first toe and its pad on the front foot are raised so that only four toes register in a track.

Cats are usually some tone of brown in colour. Some, like the American mountain lion and jaguarundi, are uniform in coloration, but most are marked with spots, stripes, or rosettes. The young of the mountain lion are spotted, which may indicate a spotted ancestor. Characteristic of all cats is a dark stripe extending laterally from the external corner of the eye. This stripe tends to exaggerate the expression on the animal's face toward one of meanness but probably serves to conceal the face by breaking the roundness of the eyes. Many of the colour patterns are repeated again and again in the different species of cats, from the largest to the smallest. Several species have black or nearly black colour phases mixed into normally coloured populations. The only cat with a well-developed mane or long hair on the back and chest, or both, is the male African lion, which is also the only terrestrial member of the order Carnivora that shows obvious sexual dimorphism. In many felids the male is larger than the female, but this sexual difference is not easy to distinguish, because the difference in size is slight.

WALRUS AND SEALS (FAMILIES OTARIIDAE, ODOBENIDAE, AND PHOCIDAE)

Natural history. Members of the families Otariidae (eared seals), Odobenidae (walrus), and Phocidae (earless seals), commonly called pinnipeds, are strictly carnivorous and mostly marine. A few venture up freshwater rivers, and two forms (*Pusa* species) are landlocked on inland lakes. In actuality, pinnipeds are amphibious, being aquatic as to food habits but terrestrial for mating, bearing young, and resting. The diet of pinnipeds consists mainly of fishes, cuttlefishes, octopuses, and crustaceans. Most of the fishes fed upon by seals are those which school. A few pinnipeds are specialized for feeding on krill (macroscopic pelagic plankton, primarily small shrimplike euphausians). Seals known to feed largely on krill are the ringed seal (*Pusa hispida*), harp seal (*Pagophilus groenlandicus*), and the crabeater seal (*Lobodon carcinophagus*); all take fishes, as well. The crabeater seal is misnamed, as it is not known to feed on crabs. Some seals, such as the leopard seal (*Hydrurga leptonyx*), are quite predatory, feeding on penguins, other birds that land on water, and other seals. The Australian sea lion (*Neophoca cinerea*) feeds largely on penguins. Such predators take advantage of the surface light at night and probably feed by visual discrimination from below. The bearded seal (*Erignathus barbatus*) and walrus (*Odobenus rosmarus*) are bottom feeders, taking largely sessile organisms such as mollusks. The walrus occasionally feeds on small whales, narwhals, and seals.

Pinniped feeding

Generally, the senses of hearing and smell are poorly developed in the pinnipeds, although smell is fair in the phocids. Both the ears and the nostrils are closed when the animal is underwater. Sight is good and is adapted for use underwater and at night. All pinnipeds have well-developed facial whiskers and a well-developed system of nerves in the facial area. Seals probably have an excellent sense of touch in the whiskers, which aids in locating their prey or warns the animal of a possible collision with a submerged object. Young walrus have such well-developed whiskers that these appear as a brushlike mustache. The walrus and bearded seal utilize these whiskers to filtre food organisms found on the bottom and as a tactile organ. Phocid seals have patches of elongate hairs above the inside corners of the eyes. There is no evidence that seals use echolocation (reflected pulses of sound) in their movements or food-seeking activities, as has sometimes been postulated.

Pinnipeds may be solitary at certain times of the year but are usually gregarious, much more so than terrestrial carnivores. During the breeding season more than a million individuals may congregate on an island. Each male sets up a territory and gathers as many females as he can. The territory is maintained by frequent loud vocalization, a threat stance with neck outstretched, rushing at an approaching rival, and possibly through the use of olfactory odours thought to be produced in the mouth. Although the term harem is usually used to describe the large number of females in the territory of a male, this concept is misleading, since the females can move from one group

Territoriality in pinnipeds

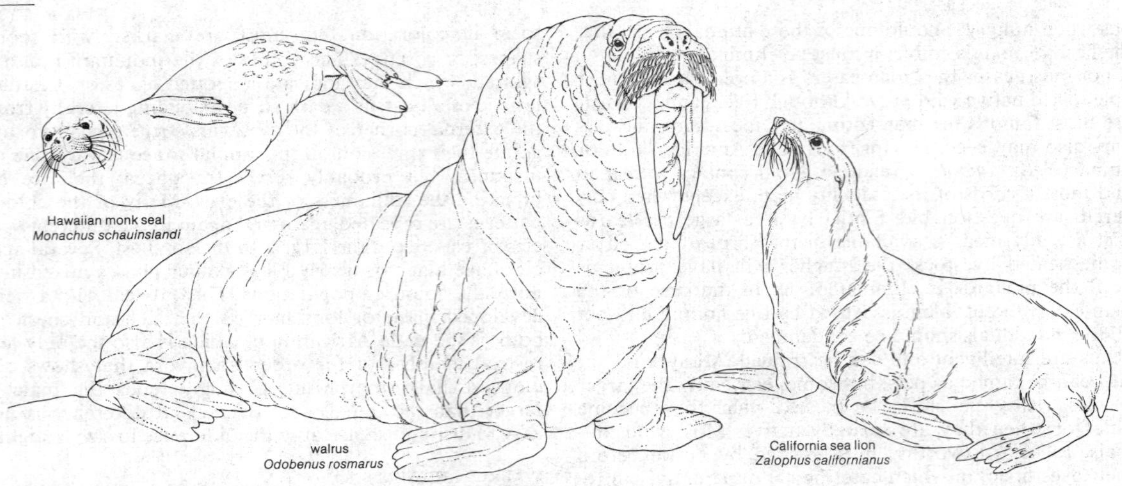

Figure 4: Representative carnivores: Pinnipedia.
Drawing by R. Keane; Hawaiian monk seal based on San Diego Zoological Garden photograph

to another. The groups are a result of the females staying clear of the males as the latter patrol their territories. Once the territory is established the male remains to protect it, going as long as two months without eating (sea lions and fur seals). Eared seals (the otarids) and walrus tend to gather harems, while the earless seals (the phocids) are mostly monogamous (one male, one female) in their breeding activities. The gathering of harems forces the mating activity to be terrestrial rather than aquatic. In many, if not most, of the northern species of seals the breeding season is restricted in many ways by the environment. In most areas only four months exist with a climate favourable for the production of young.

Pinnipeds have a fairly long gestation period, ranging from eight months in the leopard seal to 12 months in fur seals and sea lions. Breeding often takes place soon after the birth of the young (five days in the fur seal) or, as in the leopard seal, four months after the young are born. Copulation is usually on land, but some phocids mate in the water. Most seals, except the walrus and perhaps the crabeater seals, exhibit delayed implantation in embryonic development. The young are born on land or on ice. Usually there is but one young born, although most females have two pairs of mammary glands (some phocids have one pair). The mother goes out to sea to feed soon after the young is born. Since she must search to find her young when she returns, there has probably been a selection against the production of more than one young, at least in highly gregarious forms, for the time spent searching for the second pup would be at the expense of the first. It is evolutionarily better to produce one vigorous offspring than two weak ones. Nursing usually takes place on land. At birth the newborn pup can travel on land and swim, although young otarids are several weeks old before they develop enough blubber to keep them floating and insulated against the cold water. The young of the earless seals nurse for only three to six weeks, and the females remain near the young throughout this period. Pinniped milk is low in water content and high in fat. Such high fat content results in the rapid growth of the young, but perhaps of more importance is the low water content, of benefit to the mother in a habitat where water conservation is so important.

Female pinnipeds are sexually mature when two to eight years of age, usually at the age of three or four years. Males, at least in the polygamous species (those which gather a "harem"), may not be allowed to mate for several years after reaching sexual maturity. In these species the younger males are driven by the old males to a bachelor group located outside of the breeding group and restricted to a given area. After the breeding season, pinnipeds are largely pelagic (open-sea dwellers), travelling long distances either singly or in small groups.

A number of animals prey on seals: large sharks, killer whales, polar bears, and other seals, such as the leopard seal and walrus. Seals, especially the young, spend a good deal of time playing. They resemble the river otter in this regard.

Pinnipeds produce a number of different types of sounds. Barking by male seals may be related to social dominance and territorial defense, as the polygamous species are extremely vocal and the monogamous forms extremely quiet. The "barking" of the circus seal (the California sea lion, *Zalophus californianus*) is familiar to most people. The study of underwater communication in seals is difficult and in its infancy, but a variety of sounds have been recorded. These sounds may play a role in navigation, social behaviour, and foraging. Seals also roar or bellow, honk, chirp, bleat, grunt, or cough.

Seal barking

These aquatic, carnivorous animals are found throughout most of the coastal regions of the world. They are especially abundant in the cold polar waters. The walrus and phocids are well distributed throughout the northern coastal and ice-front areas. The otarids do not extend as far north, southern Alaska and Kamchatka being the most northern points, and are absent from the mid-Atlantic and North Atlantic Ocean areas. Pinnipeds are absent from the region of the Indian Ocean, southern Asia and northern Australia, the coastal regions of Central America and northern South America, and most of the coastline of central Africa. A few seals are landlocked on the Caspian Sea (*Pusa caspica*) and Lake Baikal (*Pusa sibirica*), where they subsist mainly on fish.

Importance to man. The seal is of significant importance to the survival of the Eskimos and other inhabitants of the north, who use almost every part of the animal: the meat is eaten; bones used for implements; tendons for sewing; hides for leather to make footwear, boats, shelters, bags, clothing, and ornaments; and the oil and fat for fuel, lubrication, and tanning. The ivory tusks of the walrus are carved into statues and knife handles. Seals also are taken commercially for their oil, for meat that can be used for food or fertilizer and for their hides that are used as leather.

A few seals are of importance to the fur trade. Of special interest are the true fur seals, *Callorhinus ursinus* in the northern regions of the Pacific Ocean and *Arctocephalus* species in the southern regions off the coasts of South America, Africa, and Australia. Most of the species utilized by the fur trade are members of the family Otariidae, which have dense underfur. The young of members of the Odobenidae and Phocidae have an insulating coat of short, dense, woollike hair at birth. Skins of these young animals are of some interest to the fur trade but are used mostly for novelties. Adult phocids have skins with stiff hair; the underfur is reduced to the point that the hide appears naked. However, some of the extremely striking phocids were in demand for furs in the late 1960s.

California sea lions are trained to entertain at circuses

and zoos. Some seals become pests to commercial fisheries and may gather during salmon or herring runs, sometimes being killed in large numbers by fisherman.

Form and function. Basically, the difference in the tooth pattern of pinnipeds, in comparison to the dentition of terrestrial carnivores, reflects an adaptation toward grasping and tearing rather than chewing. Thus there is less variation in the form of the different teeth (commonly said to be homodont, or "similar teeth"), and there tends to be a reduction in the number of teeth. There are, generally, two or three pairs of upper incisors and one or two pairs of lowers. There is a pair of conical canines that form elongate tusks in the walrus. The premolars and molars are conical and so similar that they are difficult to differentiate and are usually referred to as postcanines. There are no carnassial teeth. Usually there are ten postcanine teeth each in the upper and lower jaws, but the exact number can vary so greatly, even within one species, that the total number of teeth may range from 26 to 38. In the walrus the tooth number is reduced even further, the usual number being two upper incisors, no lower incisors, four canines, and twelve postcanines, a total of only 18 teeth. This number is variable, with some individuals having as many as 24 teeth. Weddell's seals have canines and incisors adapted for cutting holes in the ice so that areas are available for breathing when the water freezes over. The upper incisors extend forward and contact the ice before the canines.

Adaptations for aquatic life

Pinnipeds have a number of aquatic adaptations that separate them from the terrestrial carnivores. The body is streamlined, allowing the animal to pass through the water with the least amount of friction. External ears are reduced or absent, also aiding in making the pattern of the body more streamlined. Adaptive features of the skull include an overlapping of the bones, a feature even more exaggerated in the whales, and a flattening of the head, an advantage during diving. The neck is thickened by increased musculature but is more flexible (at least in the eared seals) than in the terrestrial carnivores, allowing the animal to capture its prey in the water with greater ease. In most pinnipeds the face is short, with the cranial part of the skull longer than the facial region. The eyes are large, located forward, close together, and imbedded in a cushion of fat. The iris of the eye is contracted when out of water, dilated and almost circular when diving. This type of eye can accommodate rapidly when the animal moves from dim to bright light. The ears and nostrils can be closed while diving. The pelvic girdle is more nearly parallel to the vertebral column than in terrestrial forms. Such a change in the location of the pelvis enables the hindlimbs to be held in more of a trailing position and to be more efficient in propulsion through the water. The limbs are enclosed within the body skin to or beyond the elbows and knees. This enclosure also streamlines and results in a more efficient passage through the water. The extremities of the limbs are flattened to form paddles used to steer or propel the animal through its environment. Each paddle contains five toes, extending from bones in the palm and sole (metapodials), elongated to increase the surface area of the paddles. The first digit on both forefeet and hindfeet is more elongate than the other four. The tail is short and rudimentary, a condition approached by the sea otter but quite unlike the paddle-like tail of the freshwater otter. Mammary teats and external reproductive organs are so constructed that they can be withdrawn beneath the skin to aid in preserving the smooth outline of the body. The skin, adapted to a water environment, is tough and thick and contains a thick layer of subcutaneous fat or blubber. The blubber provides a source of energy that can be used during lactation or at times of fasting. Such fasting is characteristic of pinnipeds. This layer also provides the animal with more buoyancy, so that sinking in the water is less apt to occur. In addition, the blubber insulates the body so that the body temperature remains nearly constant. A pinniped living in cold water may be exposed to a surface temperature of about 0° C and yet have a body temperature of 37° C, requiring an efficient system of heat production and insulation. In warm waters, and especially in warm air, the animal cannot get rid of excess body heat rapidly enough to prevent overheating. The flippers, so useful for swimming, can be used on land as radiators to get rid of excess body heat. One of the most obvious behavioural features of a colony of seals on land is the waving or extension of the naked flippers.

Physiological adaptations for diving

There are a number of physiological adaptations to life in the sea. Being air breathers, seals must be able to carry as much oxygen as possible with them in diving and to conserve what they do take. This adjustment is obtained by the increased volume of blood (very large for an animal their size) and the decreased rate in the use of oxygen by the body (decreased metabolism). The heart rate decreases in the elephant seal from about 85 beats per minute when the animal is on the surface to approximately 12 per minute during a dive. This drop in heartbeat rate conserves oxygen in terms of the amount being carried in the blood. There cannot, however, be a decrease in the amount of oxygen being carried to some parts of the body. The heart and brain, for example, must have a constant and sufficient supply, or the cells in these organs will be damaged. This problem is alleviated by closing down the small arteries in the tail and flippers, while the larger arteries to the head and brain remain unchanged. The muscles function without free oxygen during submergence; the energy is obtained by partly breaking down the blood sugars and without expending the limited supply of oxygen. Most dives last less than 15 minutes, and upon return to the surface there is a greater exchange of oxygen and carbon dioxide than is found in terrestrial mammals. The amount of tidal air in one respiratory cycle may be as much as 90 percent, compared to 20 percent in man. Most dives are deep vertical dives rather than extensive horizontal dives because of the problems of orientation toward the breathing hole in the ice when horizontal directions are taken. Since there is no exchange of gases with the environment while submerged, seals have the additional problem of an accumulation of carbon dioxide. They seem to be less sensitive than terrestrial animals to increased amounts of this gas. The body temperature is lowered, a result of the decreased rate of metabolism. Seals are also adapted to withstand the great pressures during their dives. Weddell's seal (*Leptonychotes weddelli*), for example, dives as deep as 1,100 feet, more than four times the distance that man can go in a diving suit. The longest known dive by a Weddell's seal lasted 43 minutes and 20 seconds (to 350 metres), with one elderly bull reaching a depth of 600 metres (2,000 feet) but remaining down a shorter time. Exactly how these animals can accomplish such feats is unknown. The anatomy of the seal reveals part of the answer. Many structures in the body are built to yield to such pressures, not to resist them. Some of these adaptations are smaller lungs; elimination of most air from the lungs before the dive; a thorax that permits the lungs to collapse; incomplete rings of cartilage in trachea, permitting complete collapse; driving air out of the middle ear by partly filling the ear cavity with blood; and redistribution of blood in general. The phocids are more efficient divers than the otarids, and, of the phocids, those living in the Antarctic dive the deepest.

The clavicle or collarbone is absent, allowing more flexibility in the shoulder. The kidneys, unlike those of most mammals, are composed of numerous lobes resembling a bunch of grapes, a condition also found in the terrestrial bear and otter.

Members of the families Otariidae and Odobenidae can walk on their limbs when on land. Phocids must move by undulations of the body as the limbs cannot be turned in a position to support the body. This does not mean that the phocids are helpless on land; the crabeater seal, a phocid, is probably the fastest moving seal on land, being difficult for even a running man to catch.

III. Evolution and paleontology

Opinion is divided as to whether the order Carnivora arose from the ancient creodonts or had a separate and independent origin from the order Insectivora. Most paleontologists now favour the latter view. The Cretaceous insectivore *Procerberus* seems to be morphologically close to the most primitive carnivores (miacids), the creodonts, and the primitive hoofed mammals (ungulates). *Procerberus* was an unspecialized rat-sized predator. The order seems to be a separate and distinct line that includes the modern Fissipedia (terrestrial forms) as well as Pinnipedia (marine and aquatic forms), while also including the more ancient and extinct family Miacidae.

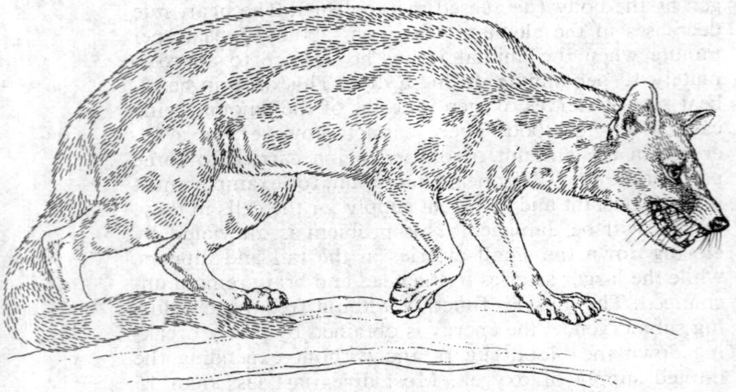

Figure 5: Early Eocene carnivore, *Hesperocyon*, an ancestor of the dogs.

The extinct Miacids

Although not much is known about them, the miacids were probably arboreal forest dwellers of the tropics. Animals from this type of habitat are rarely preserved as fossils, which accounts for our incomplete knowledge of the group. These primitive carnivores may have resembled our modern weasels, with elongate bodies, short limbs, and long tails. Miacids possessed several creodont features, such as an unossified tympanic bulla (a large bubble of bone or cartilage surrounding the internal ear) and lack of fusion of the carpal (wrist) bones. Miacids differed from the creodonts in having a larger brain capacity, toe sections that were not grooved, and well-developed carnassial teeth. The carnassials, as in modern carnivores, involved the fourth upper premolar and first lower molar.

In the late Eocene and early Oligocene these primitive miacids underwent an adaptive radiation; *i.e.*, they produced diverse lines that seem to have been the beginnings of the present-day families of the Carnivora. The changes needed to convert a miacid into a modern terrestrial carnivore are minor: fusion of the separate bones of the carpus and ossification of the tympanic bulla. Carnivores that began to resemble the modern weasels, dogs, and civets were in evidence in the Oligocene, but these early carnivores were still quite similar to each other and had not differentiated to the extent of representing different families.

Two major lines within the Carnivora were distinct by the late Eocene. One, the Feloidea (or Aeluroidea), today contains cats, viverrids, and hyenas; the other, the Arctoidea (or Canoidea), contains the mustelids, dogs, bears, and raccoons. Some fossils are intermediate between the two lines, but most show definite relationships to one or the other.

Feloids had the tympanic bulla made up of an external (tympanic) and an internal (endotympanic) bone, each being a separate ossification. In many forms the claws were retractile. The transition between the miacids and viverrids (civets) was so gradual that some authorities have placed the miacids in the family Viverridae. Because of the similarities to the miacids, the viverrids are considered to form the basal stock of the feloid line. Hyenas appear to be a more recent line, having evolved from the viverrids in the early Miocene. *Ictitherium*, a mid-Miocene viverrid, had characteristics intermediate between the viverrids and hyenas, but apparently was more like the "true" hyenas. Other fossil viverrids also showed similarities to the hyenas. Although the cats seem to have evolved "suddenly," the resemblance of certain catlike viverrids (such as the Oligocene *Stenoplesictis* and the modern *Cryptoprocta* of Madagascar) to the recognized felids is regarded by some authorities as indicating the close relationship of the felids to the viverrids. In the late Eocene and early Oligocene, the felids were quite distinct, with a number of highly specialized cats already present. Of particular interest are the sabre-toothed cats such as *Hoplophoneus* and the false sabre-tooth *Dinictis*, which had large upper canines fitting into a flange on the lower jaw. The Pleistocene *Smilodon*, a more recent genus, is probably the best-known sabre-toothed cat. The genus *Felis* dates back to the early Pliocene, by which time its members had features similar to those of the modern cat.

In contrast to the feloids, the arctoids almost never had retractile claws; the tympanic bulla was made up of the tympanic bone alone; and there was a canal below the bulla, through which the carotid artery passed, supplying blood to the brain. Some of the earlier miacids are difficult to separate from the mustelids, which were distinct as early as the late Eocene. They probably were one of the first arctoid lines to differentiate. By the close of the Miocene, several general types of mustelids were evident: the weasels, badgers, skunks, and otters. Another ancient arctoid line included the dogs. Oligocene canids, represented by the genera *Cynodictis* and *Hesperocyon*, resembled elongate, short-legged weasels and civets. Both genera, although considered to be primitive dogs, were generalized enough to be ancestral to many carnivores. Genera that were more typically canid appeared in the early Oligocene. These were running animals, with four well-developed toes and reduced hindtoes (hallux and pollex), each ending in a blunt claw. More than 50 genera of doglike forms are known, but the main line of evolution seems to have passed through forms like *Temnocyon* (upper Oligocene) and *Cynodesmus* (lower Miocene) to the modern genera *Canis* (first seen in the lower Pliocene deposits), *Vulpes* (perhaps in the upper Miocene), and *Urocyon* (Pleistocene). Two lines of extinct canids are the hyena-like dogs and the bear dogs, neither of which has any relationship to the living hyenas or bears. Because of the close relationships of the bears, dogs, and raccoons, various taxonomists have disagreed on the placement of intermediate genera. For example, *Dinocyon*, *Hemicyon*, and *Cephalogale* were once considered to have been canids but are now placed with the bears and regarded as perhaps part of the ancestral lineage that diverged from the canid line in the late Oligocene or early Miocene. *Phlaocyon* and *Aletocyon* were once considered to be primitive procyonids because of their teeth, but the skull and ear structures are more reminiscent of the dogs. A recent form, the giant panda (*Ailuropoda*), considered by some to be a bear and by others to be a procyonid, probably diverged from primitive ursid stock when the ancestor of the bear and raccoon lines still had features common to both. Procyonids (raccoons) are poorly represented in the fossil record, perhaps because of their arboreal habits. They appear to have diverged from the canid line in the late Oligocene.

The preponderance of carnivorous and carrion-eating fishes and mammals in the open sea, along with the buoyant characteristics of the bodies of the pinnipeds, results in the almost immediate destruction of any seal that dies. Dead pinnipeds seldom settle intact and become buried (the first steps toward becoming a fossil) and so are poorly represented in the fossil record. Relationships must be inferred through studies of recent forms. Although there is no fossil record of pinnipeds prior to the Miocene, it is probable that the ancestors of the pinnipeds evolved during the adaptive radiation of the miacids in the Eocene.

Evolution of pinnipeds

There are two rather distinct evolutionary lines in the animals called pinnipeds. One includes the two rather closely related families Otariidae and Odobenidae. This line may have become distinct in the early Miocene or late Oligocene, evolving from a form closely related to the canid ancestor of the bears. The other line

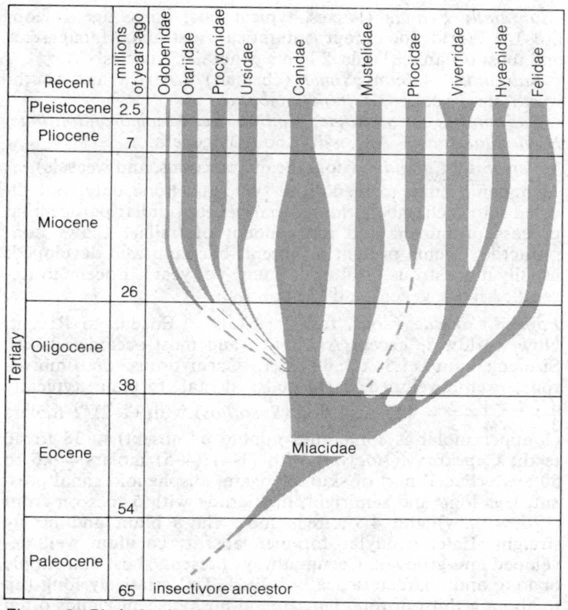

Figure 6: Phyletic dendrogram of Carnivora.

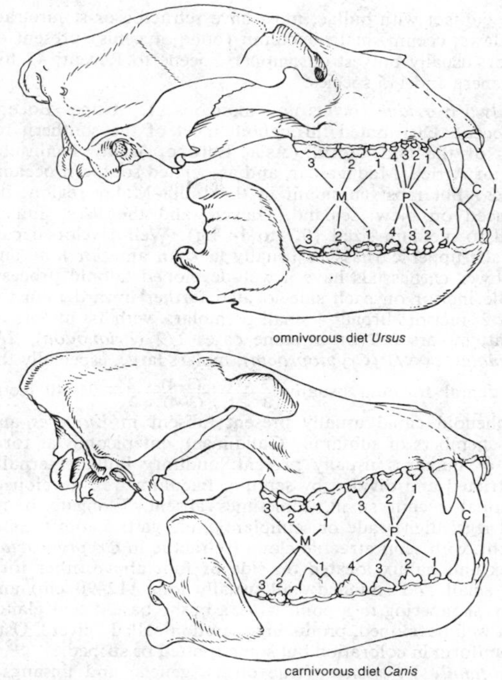

Figure 7: Tooth patterns in omnivorous and carnivorous members of Carnivora. Side view of lower mandible and cranium.

led to the modern phocids, which are quite different from the otarid–odobenid group. Their affinity to any other group of the Carnivora has not been shown, although the mustelids have more frequently been suggested as related to the phocids than any other group. *Semantor*, an aquatic carnivore from the lower Pliocene, was once considered to belong to a separate pinniped family, but is now considered a mustelid. The separation of the phocid and otarid–odobenid lines must have occurred at an extremely early date, if the two lines ever had a common pinniped ancestor. Some paleontologists postulate a separation in the early Miocene or late Oligocene. Possibly the two lines never evolved from a single aquatic group but had separate origins within the miacids, sometime in the late or even mid-Eocene. Or perhaps the otarids stemmed from an ancestral ursid type in the early Oligocene. Such an early separation, or lack of any real ancestral association, could have produced the dissimilarity of the two types of pinnipeds, as well as the difficulty in associating the phocids with any other family of the Carnivora.

IV. Classification

DISTINGUISHING TAXONOMIC FEATURES

If one groups the seals with the terrestrial carnivores, the number of characteristics common to all members of the order Carnivora is small.

The characteristics used to separate the Carnivora from other mammalian orders and to define the subdivisions of the Carnivora are primarily structural. Of great importance are certain features of the skull (the type of jaw articulation and the shape of the paroccipital process), of the feet (the number of toes, lack of opposability of the hindtoe, type of claws, and fusion of the scaphoid and lunar bones), and of the teeth (both the overall tooth pattern and the shape of the individual tooth). The dentition is especially important in determining the relationships of fossil forms. Also useful in the taxonomy of modern carnivores are the convolutions (irregular ridges) around the lateral or sylvian fissure of the brain, the relative weights of the adrenal and thyroid glands, the type of uterus and placenta, and the position of the nipples.

ANNOTATED CLASSIFICATION

Although the terrestrial and marine carnivores are grouped together in the following classification, many authors separate them into two orders. In this article the split is indicated by erecting two suborders, the Fissipedia and Pinnipedia, based largely on the degree of specialization undergone by the members as they evolved and adapted to radically different environments. Basically the taxonomy presented combines the classifications by G.G. Simpson and A.S. Romer, North American paleontologists.

Numerical dental formulas are used below to indicate the number of each type of tooth in the right or left half of the upper and lower jaws and the total number of teeth in the mouth. 4 tooth types are indicated in the following manner:

$$\frac{\text{Upper jaw: incisors . canines . premolars . molars}}{\text{Lower jaw: incisors . canines . premolars . molars}} = \text{total number of teeth}$$

ORDER CARNIVORA

Medium- to large-sized terrestrial or aquatic meat eaters distributed worldwide; composed of 10 extant families, about 115 living genera, and 274 living species.

Suborder Fissipedia

Terrestrial (except otters and polar bear); usually 3 pairs of incisors above and below, adapted for biting off flesh; premolars vary in number from the usual 4 on each half of each jaw (4/4) to 4 above and 2 below (4/2); molars vary from 2/3 to 1/2; carnassial teeth well developed and formed by the 4th upper premolar and 1st lower molar; usual dental formula: $\frac{3 \,.\, 1 \,.\, 4 \,.\, 2}{3 \,.\, 1 \,.\, 4 \,.\, 3} = 42$ teeth; all-inclusive dental formula: $\frac{3 \,.\, 1 \,.\, (2\text{–}4) \,.\, (1\text{–}4)}{(2\text{–}3) \,.\, 1 \,.\, (1\text{–}4) \,.\, (1\text{–}5)} = 28\text{–}50$ teeth; facial part of skull usually elongate; tympanic bullae large; alisphenoid canal (a perforation in the skull for a branch of the carotid artery) usually present; lacrimal duct present; pelvis at distinct angle from vertebral column; femur (thigh bone) straight, moderately slender, with small head; fibula (minor lower bone of hindlimb) much smaller than tibia (shinbone); 1st metatarsal and bones of phalanges with epiphyses only at proximal ends; metapodials never elongate; vertebrae with interlocking processes; external ears (pinnae) well developed; large intestine short (6 to 8 times length of body in dog); kidneys simple, not lobulate except in otters and young bears.

Superfamily Miacoidea

All extinct generalized carnivores with carnassial teeth. Middle Paleocene to upper Eocene. There is one family, Miacidae, about 13 genera.

Superfamily Feloidea (cats, civets, and hyenas)

Tympanic bullae divided, composed of external tympanic and internal endotympanic bones; paroccipital process in close contact with bullae; most have retractile or semiretractile claws; cecum small; baculum (bone of penis) present or absent; usually polyestrous; upper Eocene to Recent; 42 living genera and 115 species.

Family Viverridae (civets and mongooses). Upper Eocene to Recent. Distributed throughout most of the southern regions of the Old World (Asia, Europe, Malay Peninsula, most of Africa, Madagascar, and associated southern oceanic islands) but most abundant in the India–Malay region; introduced on New Zealand, Hawaii, and the West Indies. Small to medium sized (0.7 to 14 kg). Well-developed carnassials; upper carnassials usually lack an anterior lobe and the lower carnassials have a well-developed talonid process; middle incisor on each side located farther inward than the outer 2; incisors broad; 4 small premolars, with 1st minute or absent; molars 2/2 or in some cases 1/2 (*Prionodon*), 2/1 (*Salanoia*), or 1/1 (*Cryptoprocta*); molars large, especially the 1st; dental formula usually $\frac{3\ .\ 1\ .\ (3\text{–}4)\ .\ 2}{3\ .\ 1\ .\ (3\text{–}4)\ .\ 2}$ = 36–40 teeth. Alisphenoid canal usually present (absent in *Eupleres* and most members of subfamily Galidiinae); entepicondylar foramen of humerus usually present; auditory bulla externally constricted and divided by septum. Baculum well developed. Intestinal cecum small, sometimes absent. Elongate body, short legs; digitigrade or semiplantigrade gait; 5 toes usually present, with semiretractile claws (retractile in *Cryptoprocta*); pollex and hallux located on side of foot above other toes. Ears small and rounded; tail usually long (12–90 cm) and bushy or tapering to a point from a bushy base. Scent glands often well developed, producing secretion called "civet." Usually uniform in coloration but some spotted or striped.

Subfamily Viverrinae (true civets, genets, and linsangs). Mainly African; approximately 7 living genera and 15 species.

Subfamily Paradoxurinae (palm civets). Mainly Asian, 6 living genera and 8 species.

Subfamily Hemigalinae (banded palm civets, web-footed civets). Asia or Madagascar, 5 living genera and 7 species.

Subfamily Galidiinae (striped and ring-tailed mongooses). Restricted to Madagascar, 4 living genera and 7 species.

Subfamily Herpestinae (true mongooses and meerkats). All African, 13 living genera and approximately 37 species.

Subfamily Cryptoproctinae (fossa). Monotypic. *Cryptoprocta ferox*, found only in Madagascar.

Subfamily Stenoplesictinae. Fossil. Upper Oligocene to middle Miocene of Europe.

Family Hyaenidae (hyenas and aardwolves). Middle Miocene to Recent. Found today throughout most of Africa and southern Asia (Turkey to eastern India). Medium-sized (10 to 80 kg) carrion feeders; teeth specialized for crushing bones; incisors unspecialized, outer (3rd) larger than other 2; canines powerful; premolars strong and conical; molars strong and large; carnassials well developed (hyenas); long, slender canines in aardwolf (*Proteles*) with small and widely spaced premolars, small molars, and no development of carnassials. Dental formula $\frac{3\ .\ 1\ .\ 4\ .\ 1}{3\ .\ 1\ .\ 3\ .\ 1}$ = 34 teeth for hyenas; premolars 3/(2–1), molars 1/(1–2) = 28–32 for aardwolf. Alisphenoid canal absent; auditory bullae partially divided by a rudimentary septum in hyenas, divided in aardwolf; front legs longer than rear legs; digitigrade; 4 toes (5 on forefoot in aardwolf); claws blunt and nonretractile; entepicondylar foramen absent; baculum absent; more thoracic vertebrae (15) than any other feloid: tail of medium length (20 to 33 cm) and bushy. Preanal scent glands absent. Cecum 15 to 23 cm long. Short mane usually present. Ears large and rounded.

Subfamily Protelinae (aardwolf). African. 1 species. *Proteles cristatus.*

Subfamily Hyaeninae (hyenas). Africa and southwest Asia; 2 living genera, 3 species.

Subfamily Ictitheriinae. Fossil. Miocene–Pliocene. 1 Old World genus.

Family Felidae (cats). Upper Eocene to Recent. Now worldwide except for Antarctica, Australia, Madagascar, and some oceanic islands. Size medium to large (2.5 to 275 kg). Highly carnivorous; well-developed carnassials. Total number of teeth reduced from primitive carnivore condition; dental formula typically $\frac{3\ .\ 1\ .\ 3\ .\ 1}{3\ .\ 1\ .\ 2\ .\ 1}$ = 30 teeth; alisphenoid canal absent; auditory bullae not constricted externally; posterior palatine foramina on maxillopalatine suture instead of on maxilla. Elongate body with relatively short legs; digitigrade; 5 toes on front, 4 on rear feet, capped with sharp, curved, retractile claws. Entepicondylar foramen present; baculum absent or vestigial; cecum small; tail short (lynx) to long (up to a third of total length). Preanal scent glands absent; tongue covered with horny papillae.

Subfamily Felinae (lynxes, typical cats, lions, tigers, leopards). Worldwide except Antarctica, Australia, Madagascar, and most oceanic islands. 2 living genera, 35 species.

Subfamily Acinonychinae (cheetah). Africa and southwest Asia. 1 species, *Acinonyx jubatus.*

Subfamilies Proailurinae, Nimravinae, Machairondontinae, Hyainailourinae. All fossil. About 39 genera.

Superfamily Canoidea (dogs, bears, raccoons, and weasels)

Tympanic bulla formed from tympanic bone only; not divided into 2 chambers; long canal beneath bulla; paroccipital process prominent and independent of bullae. Claws nonretractile. Cecum present or absent; baculum well developed; usually monestrous (1 litter of young per year). Eocene to Recent; 53 living genera and 133 species.

Family Canidae (dogs, foxes, jackals). Eocene to Recent. Now worldwide except Antarctica and most oceanic islands. Size medium (1.5 to 80 kg). Carnivorous or omnivorous; well-developed carnassials; dental formula typically $\frac{3\ .\ 1\ .\ 4\ .\ 2}{3\ .\ 1\ .\ 4\ .\ 3}$ = 42; bush dog (*Speothos*) with (1–2)/2 molars (1 upper molar is sometimes minute or absent) = 38 to 40 teeth; Cape fox (*Otocyon*) with (3–4)/(4–5) molars = 46 to 50 teeth. Facial part of skull elongate; alisphenoid canal present; legs long and semirigid; digitigrade with 5 toes on front (1 dew claw) and 4 on rear foot; claws blunt and nearly straight. Entepicondylar foramen absent; baculum well developed and grooved. Cecum always present, short and simple or long and characteristically folded. Tail relatively long (up to about a third of total length) and bushy; scent glands often on dorsal part of base of tail. Ears pointed, erect, and large.

Subfamily Caninae (dogs, jackals, and foxes). Worldwide except Antarctica and most oceanic islands; dingo probably introduced on Australia in prehistoric times; wild dogs of New Guinea probably derived from domestic dogs. 11 living genera and approximately 37 species.

Subfamily Simocyoninae (dhole, hunting dog, bush dog). Asia, Africa south of the Sahara, and northern South America. 3 living monotypic genera: *Cuon alpinus, Lycaon pictus, Speothos venaticus.*

Subfamily Otocyoninae (big-eared fox). Eastern and southern Africa; monotypic, *Otocyon megalotis.*

Subfamilies Amphicynodontinae, Amphicyoninae, Borophaginae. Fossil only. Total genera about 34.

Family Ursidae (bear and giant panda). Middle Oligocene to Recent. Restricted to larger land masses of world, ice floes of Arctic, and in South America to Andes; bear of Atlas Mountains of northwest Africa now extinct. Size medium to large (27 to 780 kg); usually omnivorous; carnassials poorly developed; dental formula variable, but typically $\frac{3\ .\ 1\ .\ 4\ .\ 2}{3\ .\ 1\ .\ 4\ .\ 3}$ = 42 teeth. Skull elongate; alisphenoid canal present. Legs short, large, and powerful; plantigrade; 5 toes on each foot, capped by elongate, powerful, nonretractile claws. Entepicondylar foramen of humerus usually absent; lacrimal bone of skull, clavicle, and cecum absent; tail short, practically absent; ears small and rounded; lips mobile and free from gum. 6 genera and 8 living species.

Family Procyonidae (raccoons, coatis, lesser panda). Upper Eocene (probably) to Recent. Fossils through Pleistocene in Europe. Except for the lesser panda (*Ailurus*) of the southeastern Himalaya region of Asia, family is restricted to northern South America, Central America, and southern North America. Size medium (0.8 to 22 kg); omnivorous; carnassials poorly developed; dental formula usually $\frac{3\ .\ 1\ .\ 4\ .\ 2}{3\ .\ 1\ .\ 4\ .\ 2}$ = 40, with some variation in number of premolars (kinkajou 3/3, lesser panda 3/4); alisphenoid canal absent except in *Ailurus;* legs of medium length; semiplantigrade to plantigrade; 5 flexible toes on each foot capped by nonretractile or semiretractile claws; entepicondylar foramen sometimes present; baculum well developed and, except for *Ailurus*, bilobed and hooked at distal end; cecum absent; clavicle vestigial; tail long (20 to 70 cm), often ringed, prehensile in *Potos;* ears small to medium in size and rounded. 7 living genera and approximately 14 species.

Family Mustelidae (weasels, badgers, skunks, otters). Eocene to Recent. Now worldwide except Madagascar, Australia, and most oceanic islands; introduced into New Zealand; more common in Northern Hemisphere. Size from smallest of carnivores (35 gm) to medium; mainly carnivorous; carnassials usually well developed; dental formula usually $\frac{3\ .\ 1\ .\ 3\ .\ 1}{3\ .\ 1\ .\ 3\ .\ 2}$ = 34 teeth but may range from 30 to 38 teeth, with variation in incisors (3/2 in sea otter), molars (1/1 in ratel and African striped weasel), but especially premolars (2/3 in the African striped weasel, 4/2 in the river otter, 4/4 in American badger); alisphenoid canal absent; legs short in relation to elongate body; plantigrade to digitigrade; 5 toes on each foot, capped with nonretractile claws; entepicondylar foramen present or absent; tail usually long (up to 1/3 of total length); ears small and rounded; anal scent glands well developed.

Subfamily Mustelinae (weasels and Old World polecats). Subfamily with widest distribution and most kinds. There are 11 genera and 33 recent species.

Subfamily Mellivorinae (ratel or honey badger). African and southern Asia. There is 1 species, *Mellivora capensis.*

Subfamily Melinae (badgers). North America, Europe, Asia, with most forms found in Southeast Asia. There are 6 genera and 8 recent species.

Subfamily Mephitinae (skunks). New World only. There are 3 living genera and 11 species.

Subfamily Lutrinae (otters). Worldwide. There are 5 living genera and 19 species.

Subfamily Leptarctinae. Fossil. Miocene and Pliocene. New World. 3 genera.

Suborder Pinnipedia

Aquatic; teeth nearly homodont (uniform) and adapted for grasping and tearing, not chewing; 2 pairs of incisors below; postcanines (premolars and molars) similar, never more than 2-rooted, and usually 5 on each jaw (varies from 3 to 7); carnassials absent; usual dental formula $\frac{3 \cdot 1 \cdot 5 \text{ (postcanines)}}{2 \cdot 1 \cdot 5 \text{ (postcanines)}}$ = 34 teeth; all inclusive dental formula $\frac{1\text{–}3 \cdot 1 \cdot (3\text{–}7)}{0\text{–}2 \cdot 1 \cdot (3\text{–}6)} = 18\text{–}38$ teeth; cranial part of skull longer in proportion to facial part than in most fissipeds; face profusely innervated by extremely large trigeminal nerve; brain more spherical and with greater development of convolutions than fissipeds. Tympanic bullae small in some; alisphenoid canal present or absent; lacrimal duct absent; basioccipital and sphenoid relatively large as compared with fissipeds; pelvis small and nearly parallel to vertebral column; femur broad, flattened, with globular head on short neck; fibula almost as large as tibia; metatarsals and all bones of phalanges with epiphyses at both ends of shaft; metapodials elongate; 5 well-developed digits on each limb; 1 digit on manus and 1st and 5th digits of pes usually longer than other digits; feet fully webbed; nails small to absent; baculum massive. Fusiform-shaped body; external ears (pinnae) reduced or absent; tail short or vestigial (5 to 20 cm long) with 8 to 15 caudal vertebrae. Intestine long; cecum short; kidneys lobulate. Thick layer of subcutaneous fat (blubber). One large, precocial young.

Family Otariidae (eared seals). Lower Miocene to Recent. Coastlines of Pacific, South Atlantic, and Indian oceans. Hindlimbs useful for support on land; nails well developed on middle 3 digits, rudimentary on outer ones. Small external pinnae of ears. 2 pairs of lower incisors; upper incisors of 1st pair notched transversely; usually 20 to 22 postcanine teeth; dental formula $\frac{3 \cdot 1 \cdot 4 \cdot (1\text{–}3)}{2 \cdot 1 \cdot 4 \cdot 1} = 34$ to 38 teeth. Males are 2 to 4 times as large as females (males 120 to 1,000 kg; females 60 to 270 kg); testes suspended in distinct external scrotum; small but distinct tail; obvious neck; skin whitish or light gray.

Subfamily Otariinae (sea lions). Coastal regions of northern and eastern Pacific Ocean, southern Australia and southwestern New Zealand; coastal regions off eastern coast of South America. There are 4 living genera and 5 species.

Subfamily Arctocephalinae (Pacific and southern fur seals). Southern coastal areas of all southern continents; north Pacific region. There are 2 living genera, 7 species.

Family Odobenidae (walrus). Upper Miocene to Recent. Circumpolar holarctic distribution, seldom south of about 58° north latitude. Hindlimbs useful for support on land. External pinnae absent; postorbital process absent; alisphenoid canal present. Lower incisors absent in adult; upper canines of both sexes form tusks; usually 12 postcanine teeth; dental formula $\frac{(1\text{–}2) \cdot 1 \cdot (3\text{–}4) \cdot 0}{0 \cdot 1 \cdot (3\text{–}4) \cdot 0} = 18\text{–}24$ teeth; males larger (up to 1,270 kg) than females (up to 860 kg). Testes abdominal (internal). No free tail. Skin whitish or light gray. Monotypic, *Odobenus rosmarus.*

Family Phocidae (earless seals). Middle Miocene of Europe and North America; Pliocene of Asia; lower Pleistocene of Africa; Recent along northern and southern coastal areas, sporadic in tropical and southern regions. Hindlimbs useless on land (cannot be placed forward under body); nails equally well developed on all digits; external pinnae absent; postorbital process rudimentary or absent; alisphenoid canal absent; 2 to 4 lower incisors; usually 16 to 20 postcanine teeth; dental formula $\frac{(3\text{–}2) \cdot 1 \cdot 4 \cdot (0\text{–}2)}{(1\text{–}2) \cdot 1 \cdot 4 \cdot (0\text{–}2)} = 26$ to 36 teeth; males may be much larger than females (elephant seal, hooded seal), slightly larger (some members of subfamily Phocinae), equal in size (some Phocinae and some Monachinae), or females may be larger than males (some Monachinae); olfactory apparatus reduced; testes abdominal; stubby tail; no visible neck; skin brown or black.

Subfamily Phocinae (northern seals). Northern temperate to Arctic waters; 7 living genera and 9 species.

Subfamily Monachinae (southern seals). Tropical and Southern Hemisphere waters; 6 living genera and 9 species.

CRITICAL APPRAISAL

The taxonomy of the major categories of major groups placed in the Carnivora has been in a state of flux for at least 100 years, and these categories do not seem to be stabilizing, even today. Most mammalogists at present regard the seals and terrestrial carnivores as belonging to different orders, the Pinnipedia and Carnivora. There are, in reality, only a few features common to the seals and their terrestrial relatives because of the extensive and numerous adaptations the aquatic forms have undergone to make them efficient carnivores of the sea. Mammalogists who have studied seals intensively now realize that there is no anatomical structure unmodified by the extensive aquatic adaptations; every organ and tissue examined has been found to be different in some way from its counterpart in terrestrial forms. In many, if not most, ways there is more difference between seals and terrestrial carnivores than between the bats and the insectivores, and few mammalogists would place the bats and insectivores in the same order. Other mammalogists, tending toward conservative taxonomy, feel the relationship of the terrestrial and aquatic carnivores can be best expressed by retaining them in two suborders, the Fissipedia and Pinnipedia, of the single order Carnivora. The conservative attitude is retained in this article.

Of the ten living families recognized in the Carnivora, two have separated from their lines most recently and are most easily associated with other existing families: the Odobenidae with the Otariidae and the Hyaenidae with the Viverridae. The family Procyonidae has perhaps the greatest number of taxonomic problems. It appears to be a collection of primitive forms whose relationships are not yet clear. Most of the living genera have at one time been placed in distinct families or subfamilies (Nasuidae, Bassariscidae, Ailuridae, Bassaricyonidae, Procyoninae, Potosinae). In most other families there are also genera sufficiently different from other members of their family that they have been given separate families (the canids *Lycaon* and *Otocyon;* the giant panda *Ailuropoda;* the otters; the viverrid fossa *Cryproprocta;* and the aardwolf *Proteles*).

The arrangement of the ten families into two distinct superfamilies, Canoidea and Feloidea (or Aeluroidea), appears to be a natural arrangement dating back to the works of W.H. Flower and H. Winge in the late 1800s. In the Canoidea, as revealed by studies in comparative anatomy and the fossil record, the families Canidae, Ursidae, and Procyonidae seem to be most closely related. Also placed in the Canoidea is the family Mustelidae, although some of the more primitive members show resemblances to the primitive viverrids as well as the canids. In the Feloidea, the families Viverridae and Hyaenidae seem most closely related, the Felidae being the most aberrant.

Those families that contain rather diverse lines have been subdivided into subfamilies; the number of subfamilies in each family indicating the amount of evolutionary divergence that has occurred. The groups that have probably been distinct the greatest length of time have the most subfamilies; the Viverridae with six and the Mustelidae with five. Within the viverrids some of the subfamilies are distinct, a few less distinct. Most distinct are the subfamilies Herpestinae and Cryptoproctinae. The Cryptoproctinae seems to be an ancient group with the genus *Cryptoprocta* retaining characteristics of the felids as well as the viverrids, so much so that some taxonomists, have placed *Cryptoprocta* in the felids, although most mammalogists regard them to be more similar to the viverrids. The remaining four subfamilies have been combined and split in a number of ways. Usually retained, along with the two above subfamilies, are the subfamilies Viverrinae and Galidiinae. Each of the five mustelid subfamilies seems to be distinct from the others. Some authorities feel that the skunks and badgers may be close enough to place them in the same subfamily. Of the five subfamilies, the most diverse is the Mustelinae with 11 distinct genera.

What much of the discussion above means, in terms of critical taxonomic appraisal, is that a system of classification is in some ways an artificial system set up for the convenience of man. Ideally, the system reflects real evolutionary relationships, but these must be inferred from a scanty fossil record and from comparisons of modern species. Since there are differences of opinion among specialists as to which taxonomic characters should be given the most weight, there are certain to be alternate classifications, the acceptability of which depends on new information continually being discovered. Just as the animals have evolved, so does the taxonomic system.

BIBLIOGRAPHY. For general information on the biology of the carnivores, see E.P. WALKER *et al.*, *Mammals of the World*, 3 vol. (1964), in which each genus is described and illustrated, along with a brief summation of its biology. The taxonomy of carnivores is discussed in G.G. SIMPSON, "Principles of Classification and a Classification of Mammals," *Bull. Am. Mus. Nat. Hist.*, vol. 85 (1945), a classic work on classification, followed by most recent mammalogists; and H.J. STAINS, "Carnivores and Pinnipeds," in S. ANDERSON and J.K. JONES, JR. (eds.), *Recent Mammals of the World: A Synopsis of Families* (1967). F.E. BEDDARD, *Mammalia* (1902), is a definitive early work on mammalian anatomy. The paleontology of the Carnivora is summarized in two works by A.S. ROMER: *Vertebrate Paleontology*, 3rd ed. (1966), basic to an understanding of fossil forms, and *Notes and Comments on Vertebrate Paleontology* (1968), containing additional information not found in the general text. Books devoted to particular subgroups of the carnivores include: A. DENIS, *Cats of the World* (1964), an excellent summary of the status of all members of the Felidae; C.J. HARRIS, *Otters* (1968), a fine summary of the status of the otters of the world; H.E. HINTON and A.M.S. DUNN, *Mongooses: Their Natural History and Behavior* (1967), which contains much interesting information difficult to find, except in scattered literature; R.J. HARRISON *et al.* (eds.), *The Behavior and Physiology of Pinnipeds* (1968), an excellent summation of recent knowledge of these aquatic carnivores; and V.B. SCHEFFER, *Seals, Sea Lions, and Walruses: A Review of the Pinnipedia* (1958), a major work on the taxonomy of the Pinnipedia.

(H.J.S.)

Carnot, Lazare

Lazare Carnot, the French military engineer and politician known to French history as "the Organizer of Victory" for his role in the Revolutionary Wars of the early 1790s, was born at Nolay in Burgundy on May 13, 1753, the son of a lawyer. Carnot studied at the Collège d'Autun and subsequently at the small seminary in the same town. After attending the artillery and engineering preparatory school in Paris from 1769 to 1771, he graduated from the Mézières school of engineering, in January 1773, with the rank of lieutenant. Thus he began the life of a garrison officer, going from one provincial town to another, moving in literary circles wherever he was stationed. In 1780 he was admitted to a distinguished literary society and in 1784 became known for a eulogy of Sébastian Le Prestre de Vauban, the French military engineer, which received an award from the Dijon Academy. In 1787 he was elected a member of the Arras Academy, the director of which at that time was Robespierre, who was to be a leading figure in the Revolution.

When the Revolution broke out in 1789, Carnot was still a captain, a rank he had received in 1784. In 1791 he was elected deputy from Pas-de-Calais to the Legislative Assembly. As a member of the diplomatic and public education committees, Carnot did not distinguish himself; but on August 11, 1792, the day after the attack on the royal palace of the Tuileries in Paris, he was sent to the Army of the Rhine to report what had occurred.

Lazare Carnot, lithograph by Ambroise Tardieu (1788–1841), after an engraving by C.A. Forestier.
By courtesy of the Bibliotheque Nationale, Paris

In September 1792, Carnot was elected representative from Pas-de-Calais to the National Convention—the assembly elected under the influence of the fall of the monarchy—and at the end of the month was sent, with two other representatives, on a mission to Bayonne to organize the defense against a possible attack from Spain.

Since he was absent from Paris until the beginning of January 1793, Carnot did not take part in debates accompanying Louis XVI's trial. He did, however, take part in the decisive votes, in which he voted against an appeal to the people and in favour of the King's death. He thus indicated that he had been won over to the position of the Jacobins—the radicals—even though by temperament and inclination he was a man of the independents of the centre.

As a member of the Committee of War, Carnot was assigned to the Committee for General Defense, a predecessor of the Committee of Public Safety, which was to act as the executive branch throughout the republic. In this capacity Carnot presented various reports to the Convention, particularly one on March 9, 1793, which resulted in the dispatch of 82 representatives into the provincial *départements* to expedite the conscription of 300,000 men. Carnot himself was sent into the *départements* of the Nord and of Pas-de-Calais and at the end of March to the Army of the North. He remained with the Army of the North until August 1793, establishing his mastery in military operations as well as in the command of men. He reorganized the army, re-established discipline, and took part, musket in hand, in the attack and capture of Furnes.

On August 14, 1793, the Convention appointed Carnot a member of the Committee of Public Safety. Shortly after, he set out again for the Army of the North, while the enemy besieged Maubeuge. This mission ended in the victory of Wattignies on October 16, 1793 and in the raising of the siege of Maubeuge. Once again Carnot, at the side of the generals, led the attack and entered the recaptured town alongside them. At the end of the month, he resumed his seat on the Committee of Public Safety.

From then on, Carnot devoted himself to the immense task of the Committee, concentrating on the conduct of military operations, although he did not entirely divorce himself from general policy. From the very start Carnot demanded that the ancient tactic of line combat be abandoned, advocating instead attack by masses concentrated at decisive points; eventually his views were adopted by the entire Committee. Carnot took a dominant part in the development of campaign plans, which were discussed by the entire Committee; Robespierre and Saint-Just, one of Robespierre's chief aides, concerned themselves particularly with strategy.

Beginning in May 1794, dissensions arose within the

Committee of Public Safety between Carnot and Robespierre and Saint-Just, all of whom were of equally authoritarian and unyielding temperament. Carnot, basically a conservative, did not approve of the egalitarian aims of the social policy of Robespierre and his followers. If he did not play a decisive role during the coup of 9 Thermidor, year II (July 27, 1794), which overthrew Robespierre and marked the end of the Reign of Terror, Carnot must at least have approved of the fall of Robespierre.

Subsequently, however, Carnot's role began to diminish. He continued to occupy himself with directing military operations for another few months, but he soon had to defend himself against attacks by the executors of the Thermidorian coup, aimed without distinction against all former members of the Committee of Public Safety. Thus, in March 1795, in an attempt to dissociate himself from his former colleagues, he claimed that each of them was responsible only for the duty with which he was charged and that the signatures to decrees regarded as reprehensible were only a formality. Yet Carnot did not succeed in silencing the charges. In May 1795, when an obscure deputy demanded the arrest of all the members of the former committees and named Carnot, he was saved by another deputy who shouted "He organized the victory."

Carnot was elected to the Directory, the French government from 1795 to 1799, the executive branch of which consisted of five directors; and he became even more conservative than before. When the elections of the spring of 1797 brought in a royalist majority, Carnot bowed to the results, so that during the coup d'état of 18 Fructidor, year V (September 4, 1797), which quashed the elections, he had to flee in order to escape arrest. He crossed into Germany and settled in Nürnberg.

After the coup d'état of 18 Brumaire, year VII (November 9, 1799), which brought Napoleon Bonaparte to power as first consul of France, Carnot returned. He was minister of war for a few months in 1800 but resigned. Appointed in 1802 a member of the Tribunat, a body chosen by the Senate to debate legislation, he fought the authoritarian development of the consular regime, opposed the institution of the Legion of Honour, voted against bestowing on Napoleon the consulate for life, and courageously opposed the establishment of the Empire under Napoleon. He continued, however, to hold a seat on the Tribunat until that assembly was suppressed in 1807, when he withdrew from public life.

Return under Napoleon

The allied invasion of 1814 forced him out of retirement. Napoleon appointed him governor of the town of Antwerp, where he remained until after the fall of the Empire. Carnot sided with the Restoration under Louis XVIII, but in July 1814 he published his *Mémoire au roi en juillet 1814*, in which he denounced the excesses of the reaction under the Bourbon king. During the Hundred Days, when Napoleon attempted to reestablish his power, Carnot served as minister of the interior, and after Napoleon's defeat at Waterloo, Carnot encouraged him to resist, but in vain. The Second Restoration marked the end of Carnot's political career.

In July 1815, Carnot was exiled from France. He left Paris in October and settled at Warsaw in January 1816. In August 1816, Carnot left Warsaw for Magdeburg, where he died on August 2, 1823.

Assessment

The Third Republic, eager to acquire ancestors, exalted Carnot's memory, consecrating him as "the Organizer of Victory." When his grandson, Sadi Carnot, was president of the republic, the ashes of Lazare Carnot were placed in the Panthéon in Paris. Carnot was indeed "the Organizer of Victory" but only in collaboration with the other members of the Committee of Public Safety, with whom he shared responsibility for the Terror as well. For although the Committee of Public Safety was able to raise, equip, arm, and feed 14 armies and lead them to victory, it succeeded only by means of a mass levy, mass requisitions, and nationalization of military production—measures based on the revolutionary government's use of force, that is, an authority relying on the Terror. The characterization of Carnot as "the Organizer of Victory" is a legend created by the victors of the Thermidor coup, who, holding those vanquished in the coup responsible for the Terror, surrounded the survivors with all the brilliance of the victory.

BIBLIOGRAPHY. P.F. TISSOT, *Mémoires historiques et militaires sur Carnot, rédigés d'après ses manuscrits, sa correspondance inédité et ses écrits* (1824). The greater part of these *Mémoires* were drafted by Carnot himself; the rest were collected from his notes, writings, and papers. MARCEL REINHARD, *Le Grand Carnot*, vol. 1, *De L'Ingénieur au conventionnel, 1753–1792* (1950), vol. 2, *L'Organisateur de la victoire, 1792–1823* (1952), the best biography of Carnot currently available, gives a favourable interpretation of its subject. An English-language treatment may be found in R.R. PALMER, *Twelve Who Ruled* (1958).

(Al.S.)

Carnot, Sadi

Sadi Carnot, French army engineer and physicist, is remembered chiefly for his study of the so-called heat cycle, which greatly contributed to the modern science of thermodynamics. In 1824 he examined the basic problems of the operation of the steam engine: the amount of heat supplied as compared with the work produced, the maximum amount of work that can be produced, the suitability of water as the best medium of power. He identified the ideal conditions in which mechanical energy is produced from heat in a steam engine and in heat engines in general. In spite of his intentions, Carnot's work had no practical effect on the design of engines, but its greatest impact was on pure science, particularly on the study of the thermal properties of matter.

By courtesy of the Bibliotheque Nationale, Paris

Sadi Carnot, engraving after a painting by A. Bailly, 1813.

Early years

Born in Paris on June 1, 1796, Carnot was named for a medieval Persian poet and philosopher, Saʿdī of Shīrāz, whose writings were then enjoying a minor vogue in Paris. His father, Lazare Carnot, was a member of the five-man Directory that governed France between the Revolution and the rise of Napoleon. In this period of unrest, the family suffered many changes of fortune. His father fled into exile a few months after Sadi's birth; three years later he returned to be appointed Napoleon's minister of war but was soon forced to retire. A writer on mathematics and mechanics as well as military and political matters, the elder Carnot now had the leisure to direct his son's early education.

Sadi entered the École Polytechnique in 1812, an institution providing an exceptionally fine education, with a faculty of famous scientists aware of the latest developments in physics and chemistry, which they based on a rigorous mathematics. By the time Sadi graduated in 1814, Napoleon's empire was being rolled back, and European armies were invading France. Soon Paris itself was besieged, and the students, Sadi among them, fought a skirmish on the outskirts of the city.

During Napoleon's brief return to power in 1815, Lazare Carnot was minister of the interior, but, following the Emperor's final abdication, he fled to Germany, never to return to France.

Army career

Sadi remained an army officer for most of his life, despite disputes about his seniority, denial of promotion, and the refusal to employ him in the job for which he had been trained. In 1819 he transferred to the recently formed General Staff but quickly retired on half pay, living in Paris on call for army duty. Friends described him as reserved, almost taciturn, but insatiably curious about music, science, and technical processes.

The mature, creative period of his life now began. Sadi attended public lectures on physics and chemistry provided for workingmen. He was also inspired by long discussions with the prominent physicist and successful industrialist Nicolas Clément-Desormes, whose theories he further clarified by his insight and ability to generalize.

The problem occupying Carnot was how to design good steam engines. Steam power already had many uses—draining water from mines, excavating ports and rivers, forging iron, grinding grain, and spinning and weaving cloth—but it was inefficient. The import into France of advanced engines after the war with Britain showed Carnot how far French design had fallen behind. It irked him particularly that the British had progressed so far through the genius of a few engineers who lacked formal scientific education. British engineers had also accumulated and published reliable data about the efficiency of many types of engines under actual running conditions; and they vigorously argued the merits of low- and high-pressure engines, and of single-cylinder and multicylinder engines.

Work on the heat cycle

Convinced that France's inadequate utilization of steam was a factor in its downfall, Carnot began to write a nontechnical work on the efficiency of steam engines. Other workers before him had examined the question of improving the efficiency of steam engines by comparing the expansion and compression of steam with the production of work and consumption of fuel. In his book, *Reflections on the Motive Power of Fire*, published in 1824, Carnot tackled the essence of the process, not concerning himself as others had done with its mechanical details.

He saw that, in a steam engine, motive power is produced when heat "drops" from the higher temperature of the boiler to the lower temperature of the condenser, just as water, when falling, provides power in a waterwheel. He worked within the framework of the caloric theory of heat, assuming that heat was a gas which could be neither created nor destroyed. Though the assumption was incorrect and Carnot himself had doubts about it even while he was writing, many of his results were nevertheless true, notably the prediction that the efficiency of an idealized engine depends only on the temperature of its hottest and coldest parts and not on the substance (steam or any other fluid) which drives the mechanism.

Although formally presented to the Academy of Sciences and given an excellent review in the press, the work was completely ignored until 1834, when Émile Clapeyron, a railroad engineer, quoted and extended Carnot's results. Several factors might account for this; the number of copies printed was limited and the dissemination of scientific literature was slower, and such a work was hardly expected to come from France when the leadership in steam technology had been centred in England for a century. Eventually Carnot's views were incorporated by the thermodynamic theory as it was developed by Rudolf Clausius in Germany (1850) and William Thomson (later Lord Kelvin) in Britain (1851).

Little is known of Carnot's subsequent activities. In 1828 he described himself as a "constructor of steam engines, in Paris." When the Revolution of 1830 in France seemed to promise a more liberal regime, there was a suggestion that Carnot be given a government position, but nothing came of it. He was also interested in improving public education. When absolutist monarchy was restored, he returned to scientific work, which he continued until his death on August 24, 1832, in the cholera epidemic in Paris.

BIBLIOGRAPHY. E. MENDOZA (ed.), *Reflections on the Motive Power of Fire, by Sadi Carnot, and Other Papers . . .* (1960), contains translations of Carnot's memoir and two important articles by E. CLAPEYRON and R. CLAUSIUS. The introduction gives biographical details of Carnot's life and a technical discussion of the physics background of his work. The primary source of Carnot's biography is *Réflexions sur la puissance motrice du feu et sur les machines propres à développer cette puissance* (1878), which includes a biography by his brother, HIPPOLYTE CARNOT. A few more fragments are included in E. MENDOZA, "Contributions to the Study of Sadi Carnot and His Work," *Arch. Int. Hist. Sci.*, 12:377–396 (1959). The engineering background is discussed from a technical point of view in two papers: MILTON KERKER, "Sadi Carnot and the Steam Engine Engineers," *Isis*, 51:257–270 (1960); and ROBERT FOX, "Watt's Expansive Principle in the Work of Sadi Carnot and Nicolas Clément," *Notes Rec. R. Soc. Lond.*, 24:233–253 (1969).

(E.M.)

Carpathian Mountains

The Carpathians are a young European mountain chain forming the eastward continuation of the Alps. From the Danube Gap, near Bratislava, Czechoslovakia, they swing in a wide arc, some 900 miles (1,450 kilometres) long to near Orşova, Romania, at the portion of the Danube Valley called the Iron Gate. These are the conventional boundaries of these arcuate ranges, although, in fact, certain structural units of the Carpathians extend southward across the Danube at both sites mentioned. The true geological limits of the Carpathians are, in the west, the Vienna Basin and the structural hollow of the Leitha Gate in Austria and, to the south, the structural depression of the Timok River in Yugoslavia. To the northwest, north, northeast, and south, the geological structures of the Carpathians are surrounded by the sub-Carpathian structural depression separating the range from other basic geological elements of Europe, such as the old Bohemian Massif and the East European Platform. Within the arc formed by the Carpathians are found the depressed Pannonian Basin, composed of the Little and the Great Hungarian Plain, and also the relatively lower mountain and hill zone of Transdanubia, which separates these two plains. Thus defined, the Carpathians cover some 80,000 square miles (200,000 square kilometres).

Although a counterpart of the Alps, the Carpathians differ considerably from them. Their structure is less compact, and they are split up into a number of mountain blocks separated by basins. The highest peaks, Mt. Gerlach in the Carpathians (8,711 feet [2,655 metres]) and Mont Blanc in the Alps (15,771 feet [4,807 metres]), differ greatly in altitude, and in average elevation the Carpathian mountain chains are also very much lower than those of the Alps. Structural elements also differ. The sandstone–shale band known as flysch, which flanks the northern margin of the Alps in a narrow strip, widens considerably in the Carpathians, forming the main component of their central zone, whereas the limestone rocks that form a wide band in the Alps are of secondary importance in the Carpathians. On the other hand, crystalline and metamorphic (heat-altered) rocks, which represent powerfully developed chains in the central part of the Alps, appear in the Carpathians as isolated blocks of smaller size surrounded by depressed areas. In addition to these features, the Carpathians contain a rugged chain of volcanic rocks.

Similar differences can be observed in the relief of these two mountain systems, notably in the way that the destructive processes of erosion have occurred. The relief forms of the Alps today result for the most part from the glaciations of the last Ice Age. These affected practically all mountain valleys and gave them their specific relief character. In the Carpathians glaciation affected only the highest peaks, and the relief forms of today have been shaped by the action of running water.

HISTORY OF SCIENTIFIC STUDY

Many nationalities are in contact with each other in the Carpathians, and this has had its effect on the develop-

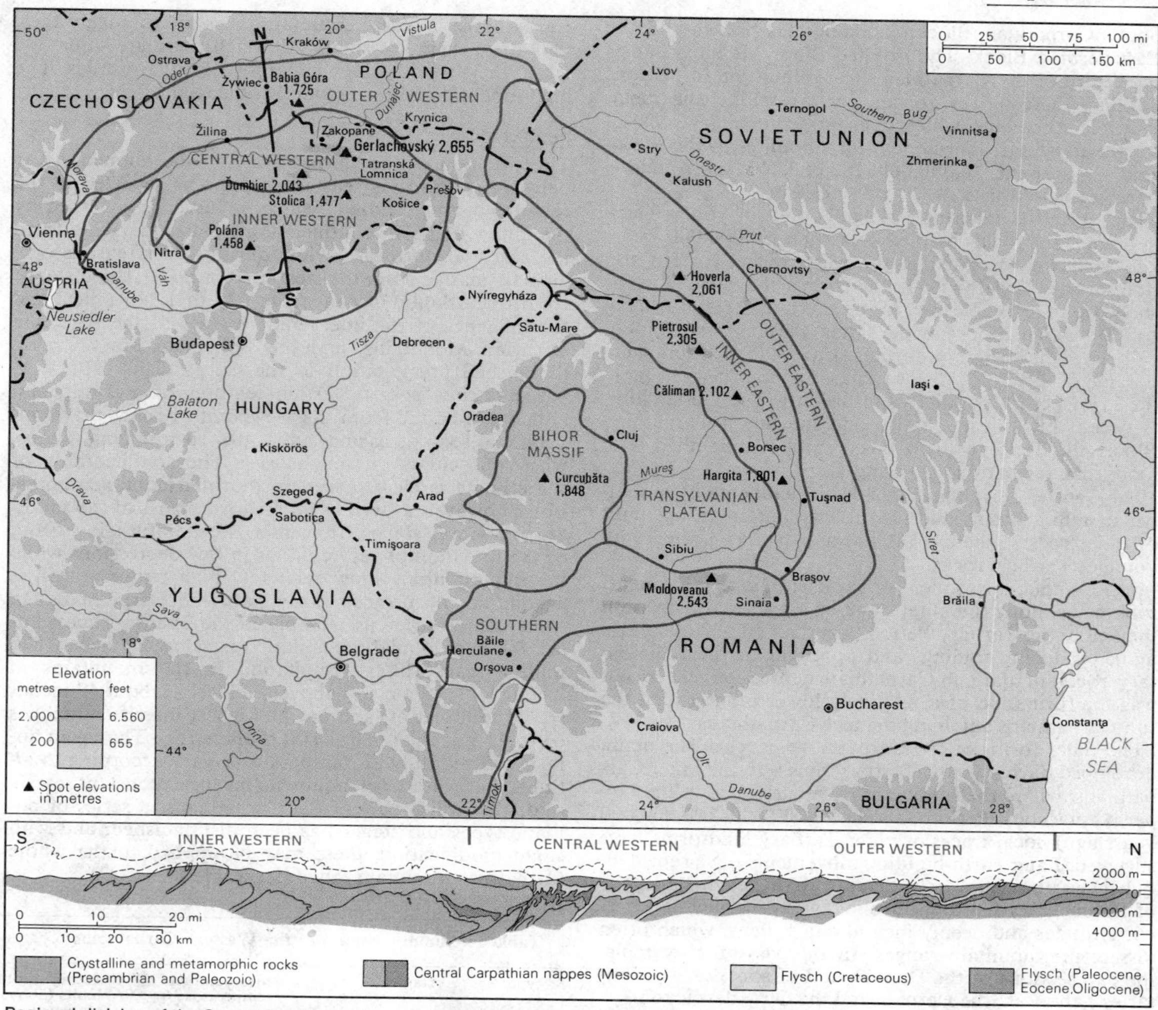

Regional division of the Carpathian Mountains and a geological cross section of the Western Carpathians. The location of the cross section is shown by the line N-S on the map.

ment of scientific research in the region. From the end of the 18th century until World War I, most of the Carpathians were within the boundaries of Austria-Hungary; and throughout this long period the Carpathians were readily accessible to all scientists of this multinational empire, the work of Polish scientists, together with that of Germans and Hungarians, being most noteworthy. In the late 19th century the Austrian general staff published the first comprehensive topographic map of the region. A century later, each of the countries whose territory covered part of the Carpathians—Czechoslovakia, Poland, Romania, Hungary, and the Soviet Union—had at hand new topographic maps drawn to a scale of 1:50,000 and 1:200,000—compiled on the basis of a coordinated geodetic system and in a mutually correlated sheet pattern.

Mapping

As for geological maps, the first paper dealing with the geology of the Carpathians as a whole was published in 1815. Today, each of the Carpathian countries has its own general geological maps, and there is also abundant regional geological literature. In 1922 the International Geological Congress created an association of Carpathian geologists, which met every three years thereafter. Regional research in physical geography is also well advanced, and in 1963 a geomorphological committee for the Carpathians and the Balkans was established.

Research is somewhat less advanced in climatology and biogeography, although a number of papers began to appear in the second half of the 20th century. In human geography much attention has been given to the problems of pastoral life and associated population movements. By 1970 no synthetic survey of the economic geography of the whole Carpathians had appeared as economic problems were being studied separately in each of the countries involved. Indeed, the only comprehensive geographic account of the Carpathians as a whole remains that published in 1895 by the Polish geographer Antoni Rehman.

Studies in human geography

By the 1970s the Carpathians had become the object of research by a number of scientific centres in the countries involved, with the geographic institutes of the several national academies of sciences and the geographic and natural history institutes of various universities playing a leading role. National geological institutes and institutes of hydrology and meteorology also amassed a considerable body of information.

STRUCTURE AND RELIEF

The Carpathians extend in a geological system of parallel structural ranges. The Outer Carpathians—whose rocks are composed of flysch—run from near Vienna, through Moravia, along the Polish-Czechoslovak frontier, and through the Western Ukraine into Romania, ending in an abrupt bend of the Carpathian arc north of Bucharest. In this segment of the mountains, a number of large structural units of nappe character (vast masses of rock thrust and folded over each other) may be distinguished. In the eastern part of the outer Carpathians, this fringe is formed by the Skole Nappe, and in the western part it is formed by the Silesian Nappe, both of which are split by the longitudinal central Carpathian depression. Overthrust on the Silesian Nappe is the Magura Nappe, the counterparts of which in the east are the Čorna Hora and the Tarcău nappes.

The Inner Carpathians consist of a number of separate blocks. In the west lies the Central Slovakian Block; in the southeast lie the East Carpathian Block and the

South Carpathian Block, including the Banat and the East Serbian Block. The isolated Bihor Massif occupies the centre of the Carpathian arc. Among the formations building these blocks are ancient crystalline and metamorphic cores onto which younger sedimentary rocks—for the most part limestones and dolomites of the Mesozoic Era (about 70,000,000–185,000,000 years ago)—have been overthrust.

The third and innermost range is built of young Tertiary volcanic rocks formed less than 50,000,000 years ago, differing in extent in the western and eastern sections of the Carpathians. In the former they extend in the shape of an arc enclosing, to the south and east, the Central Slovakian Block; in the latter, they run in a practically straight line from northwest to southeast, following the line of a tectonic dislocation, or zone of shattering in the earth's crust, parallel with this part of the mountains. Between this volcanic range and the South Carpathian Block, the Transylvanian Basin spreads out, filled with loose rock formations of young Tertiary age.

The Central Slovakian Block is dismembered by a number of minor basins into separate mountain groups built of older rocks, whereas the basins have been filled with younger Tertiary rocks.

In Romania, orogenic, or earth-building, movements took place along the outer flank of the Carpathians until the end of the Tertiary Period (less than 10,000,000 years ago), producing foldings and upheaval of the sedimentary rocks of the sub-Carpathian depression; the result was the formation of a relatively lower range called the sub-Carpathians adjoining the true Carpathians.

Relief forms

The relief forms of the Carpathians have, in the main, developed during young Tertiary times. In the inner Carpathians, where the folding movements ended in the Upper Cretaceous Period (about 70,000,000–100,000,000 years ago), local traces of older Tertiary landforms have survived. Later earth-building movements have repeatedly heaved up this folded mountain chain, leaving a legacy of fragmentary flat-topped relief forms situated at different altitudes and deeply incised gap valleys, which often dissect the mountain ranges. In this way, for example, the gap sections of the Danube and of some of its tributaries—the Váh, the Hernad, and the Olt—developed.

The last Ice Age affected only the highest parts of the Carpathians, and glaciers were never more than a few miles long, with a maximum of up to 9 miles (14 kilometres) in the Tatras, where the line of eternal snow ran at 5,000 feet above sea level.

HYDROLOGY

The water runoff from the Carpathians escapes for the most part into the Black Sea. The great curve of the mountain chain abuts in the south upon the Danube; in the east it is flanked by a tributary of the Danube, the Prut River, and farther on by the Dnestr River tributary to the Black Sea. Only the northern slope of the Carpathians, mostly in Poland but partly in Czechoslovakia, is linked to the Baltic Sea by the drainage basins of the Vistula and (in part) Oder rivers. Thus, some 90 percent of the surface of the Carpathians drains to the Black Sea and only about 10 percent to the Baltic. Larger rivers originating in the Carpathians include the Vistula and the Dnestr and the following Danube tributaries: Váh, Tisa, Olt, Seret, Prut. The Carpathian rivers are characterized by a rain–snow regime; high-water periods occur in the spring (March–April) and in summer (June–July), with the latter usually more powerful. Often these floods

Flood peril

assume catastrophic dimensions caused by the poor ground retention of the rainfall. There has been an urgent need for the construction of storage basins, work on which was initiated on a large scale in the decades following World War II. None of the contemporary Carpathian storage basins are of great size. Among the largest are a basin in the Bistrita Valley in Romania, dam 416 feet high, capacity about 35,320,000,000 cubic feet; a basin in the San Valley in Poland, dam 262 feet high, capacity 17,660,000,000 cubic feet; and a basin in the Orava Valley in Czechoslovakia of 12,362,000,000-cubic-foot capacity. Altogether there are some 50 storage basins in the Carpathians. Natural mountain lakes are relatively rare, and all of them are small. Although there are some 200 lakes, their total surface is barely 1.5 square miles. The high-mountain lakes are mainly of glacial origin.

CLIMATE

The situation of the Carpathians, on the boundary line between western and eastern Europe, is reflected in the features of their climate, which in winter is governed by the inflow of polar–continental air masses arriving from the east and northeast, while during other seasons oceanic air masses from the west predominate. The distance from the Atlantic Ocean (from 620 to 1,240 miles) and the influence of the intervening masses of the Alps, the Dinarian Mountains, and the Bohemian Massif cause diminished precipitation in the Carpathians. The Carpathians thus possess certain features of a continental climate, although from the viewpoint of relief they constitute a sort of island amid the surrounding plains, where the climate is much drier. The continentality of the climate is clearly seen in the intermontane depressions, however, as well as on the lower parts of the southern mountain slopes. In winter, temperature inversion, or the retention of very cold air in low depressions while the mountaintops show relatively high temperatures, is a common occurrence throughout the Carpathians. In some depressed areas, notably in the Transylvanian Basin, the total annual precipitation is below 24 inches (600 millimetres), while precipitation in the mountains at 2,600 feet (800 metres) above sea level is about 47 inches (1,200 millimetres) and on the highest massifs it reaches 63 to 71 inches (1,600–1,800 millimetres). The mean annual and monthly air temperatures vary according to altitude above sea level, but by no means at constant rates.

For the Polish part of the Carpathians, a series of climatic types and stages has been distinguished; and with slight modification, these may be applied to the whole Carpathian mountain range (see Table 1).

Table 1: Climatic Stages of the Western Carpathians

type	stage	mean annual temperature		average altitude limits (above sea level)	
		°F	°C	ft	m
Nival	cold	25	−4	8,710	2,655
Nival-pluvial	temperate cold	28	−2	6,070	1,850 (1,670)*
	very cool	32	0	5,080	1,550 (1,400)*
	cool	36	2	3,600	1,100
Pluvial-nival	temperate cool	39	4	2,300	700
	temperate warm	43	6	820	250
	mountain foreland	46	8	under 820	under 250

*The figures in parentheses refer to the Outer Carpathians.

VEGETATION AND ANIMAL LIFE

Different vegetation stages may also be distinguished for the various altitudinal zones of the Carpathians. These are given in detail in Table 2. The alpine stage is characterized by high mountain pastures, the subalpine by dwarf-pine growth, the upper forest stage by spruce, and the lower forest stage by beech. The foreland stage is noted for oaks and elms. The natural vegetation stages are matched by stages of economic land use: the foreland by rye and potato growing, the lower forest stage by oats and potato growing (up to 3,280 feet), and the upper forest stage and the subalpine stages by pastoral life.

The plant life of the Carpathians contains many unique species, especially in the southeastern part of the mountains where the effect of Quaternary climatic cooling was less marked. Forests have been best preserved in the eastern part of the Carpathians, and here the animal life includes bears, wolves, lynx, deer, boars, and, in the highest parts (in the Tatras), chamois and marmots.

REGIONAL DIVISIONS

Taking into consideration surface relief, geological structure, climate, and vegetation as noted above, regional divisions of the Carpathians may be discerned.

Table 2: Vegetation Stages of the Carpathians
(feet [metres])

stages	Western Carpathians		Eastern Carpathians	Southern Carpathians
	Outer	Inner		
Nival	—	up to 8,710 (2,655)	—	—
Alpine	up to 5,660 (1,725)	up to 7,200 (2,200)	up to 6,600 (2,000)	up to 8,344 (2,544)
Subalpine	up to 5,480 (1,670)	up to 5,900 (1,800)	up to 6,070 (1,850)	up to 7,200 (2,200)
Upper forest	up to 4,600 (1,400)	up to 5,080 (1,550)	up to 5,080 (1,550)	up to 5,900 (1,800)
Lower forest	up to 3,770 (1,150)	up to 4,100 (1,250)	up to 4,100 (1,250)	up to 4,900 (1,500)
Foreland	up to 1,800 (550)	up to 2,300 (700)	up to 2,000 (600)	up to 2,800 (850)

Generally speaking, the Carpathians have been divided into the Western and the Eastern Carpathians, the latter also called—probably more accurately—the Southeastern Carpathians. There are marked differences between these parts. The Western Carpathians show a clearly marked zoning in geological structure and relief forms, and the highest elevations occur in the central part of this province, in the Tatras and the Lower Tatras. The geological structure of the inner part of the Western Carpathians is marked by a break running from the east and the south along a line of dislocation in the earth's crust. Along this line, masses of volcanic rocks have been piled up surrounding the Central Western Carpathian Block in a wide arc, with its convex side turned eastward. The boundary between the Western and the Southeastern Carpathians occurs at the narrowest part of the mountain range, marked by the valley of the River San to the north, the Łupków Pass (2,100 feet) and the Laborec Valley to the south. Here the Carpathians are only some 75–80 miles wide, while in the west they are 170 miles and in the east as much as 220–250 miles across.

The Southeastern Carpathians are formed by a triangular block of mountains surrounding a basin. The three mountain formations concerned differ in origin and structure. The Eastern Carpathians, running in a northwest to southeast direction, include the flysch band, which represents the continuation of the Outer Western Carpathians, and also an inner band of crystalline and volcanic rocks. In contrast, the Southern Carpathians, running in an east–northeast to west–southwest direction, consist, in the main, of metamorphic rocks. The Bihor (Apuseni) Massif is also of metamorphic rock but is covered with older sediments.

The extent of these Carpathian regions and their subdivisions are as given in Table 3. The Outer Western Carpathians are generally of low altitude; the highest elevation is Babia Góra (5,658 feet [1,725 metres]) in the Beskid Range, straddling the borders of Poland and Czechoslovakia. On the Polish side, a national park has been established. A considerable part of the Outer Western Carpathians lacks a truly mountainous landscape and rather resembles a hilly plateau elevated to 1,300–1,600 feet above sea level.

Table 3: Subdivisions of the Carpathians

	approximate area	
	sq km	sq mi
Western Carpathians	68,000	26,000
Outer Western Carpathians	27,500	10,500
Central Western Carpathians	15,500	6,000
Inner Western Carpathians	25,000	9,500
Southeastern Carpathians	131,000	50,500
Outer Eastern Carpathians	35,500	13,500
Inner Eastern Carpathians	21,250	8,000
Southern Carpathians	28,250	11,000
Transylvanian Plateau	28,500	11,000
Bihor Massif (Apuseni Mountains)	17,500	7,000

The Central Western Carpathians consist of a series of isolated mountain ranges separated by structural depressions. Highest among them are the Tatras (Gerlach, 8,711 feet [2,655 metres]), exhibiting a typical high-mountain glacial relief with ice-scoured (cirque) lakes and waterfalls. This highest Carpathian massif is built of crystalline (granite) and metamorphic rocks, but the northern part contains, upthrust from the south, several series of limestone rocks with associated karst, or water-incised, relief forms. On both the Polish and Slovakian side national parks have been established. South of the Tatras, separated by the Liptov and Spiš basins, run the parallel Lower Tatras, similar in geological structure but lower (Ďumbier Peak, 6,703 feet [2,043 metres]) and with a less conspicuous glacial relief. Along the boundary line between the Outer and the Central Western Carpathians extends a narrow strip of klippen (limestone) rocks, which, north of the Tatras, has developed into the small but very picturesque Pieniny mountain group. Here, a narrow and sharply winding gap valley has been incised by the Dunajec River, a tributary of the Vistula.

The Tatras

The Inner Western Carpathians are lower and more broken. The principal mountain groups here are the Slovak Ore Mountains (Slovenské Rudohorie), with Stolica (4,846 feet [1,477 metres]) as the highest peak; they are built of metamorphic rocks and of sedimentaries of the Paleozoic Era more than 250,000,000 years old. Also found here are tableland areas of Mesozoic limestones, about 150,000,000 years old, which contain such large caves as the Domica-Aggtelek Cave on the Slovak–Hungarian boundary, which is 13 miles long. Mountain groups of volcanic origin are important in this part of the Carpathians; the largest among them is Polána, 4,783 feet (1,458 metres).

Compared with the Outer Western Carpathians, the Outer Eastern Carpathians, which are their continuation, are higher and show a more compact banded structure. The highest mountain group is Czarnohora (Čorna Hora) on the Ukrainian side, with Hoverla (6,762 feet [2,061 metres]) as the highest peak. The Inner Eastern Carpathians attain their highest altitude in the Rodnei Mountains in Romania; they are built of crystalline rocks and reach a peak in Pietrosul (7,562 feet [2,305 metres]). In this range, some 248 miles long, extinct volcanoes have, to some extent, kept their original conical shape. The highest peaks of these mountains are Călimăn (6,896 feet [2,102 metres]) and Hargita (5,909 feet [1,801 metres]). Fringing the true Eastern Carpathians runs a rather narrow zone called the sub-Carpathians which is made up of folded young Tertiary rocks superimposed on the sub-Carpathian structural depression.

The Southern Carpathians culminate in the Făgăraş Mountains (highest point Moldoveanu, 8,343 feet [2,543 metres]), which show Alpine-type relief forms. The western part of the Southern Carpathians, that is, the Banat Mountains and the mountains of east Serbia (which, at the Iron Gate, are split apart by the gap valley of the Danube), do not exceed an altitude of 5,000 feet.

The Bihor Massif (the Apuseni Mountains), which occupies an isolated position inside the Carpathian arc, features widespread flat summit plains bordered by narrow, deep-cut valleys. The highest peak is Curcubăta (6,063 feet [1,848 metres]).

Finally, mention should be made of the Transylvanian Plateau. This is made up of poorly resistant young Tertiary rocks and characterized by a forestless hilly landscape with elevations of 1,500 to 2,300 feet above sea level; the valleys are cut to depths of 325 and 650 feet.

HUMAN GEOGRAPHY

The Carpathians are inhabited by some 13,000,000–14,000,000 people and have an average population density of about 180 per square mile. The distribution of this population depends on natural land features and on socio-economic conditions; hence it is very much diversified. In the valleys between the mountains, and again on the northern slopes of the Western Carpathians, the population density locally exceeds 520 per square mile, while close by practically uninhabited mountain massifs are to be found. On the whole, the Southeastern Carpathians are less densely settled than the Western Carpathians, but here also marked aggregations of people occur in the valleys.

Nationalities

The western slope of the Western Carpathians is inhabited by Czechs, the northern slope by Poles, the entire central part of the Western Carpathians by Slovaks, and the southern portion by Hungarians. The northern part of the Eastern Carpathians, both its outer and inner sectors, is occupied by Ukrainians; but south of 47° latitude, a Romanian population predominates. Inside the arc of the Eastern Carpathians, and also partly on the Transylvanian Plateau, lives a compact island of Hungarian population, also some remnants of German colonists dating back from the Middle Ages. Finally, the southwestern margin of the Carpathians, beyond the Danube gap, is occupied by Serbs. Generally speaking, the greater part of the Western Carpathians and the northern part of the Eastern Carpathians is inhabited by a Slav population, and the southern part of both these Carpathian provinces, with the exception of the mountains of east Serbia, by Romanians and Hungarians.

In the 13th and 14th centuries Romanian shepherds, wandering with their flocks, moved along the Carpathians into what is today Ukrainian, Slovakian, and Polish territory, and traces of this penetration have survived in geographic nomenclature and in economic methods and also in types of buildings, garments, and customs, although by the second half of the 20th century many of the latter were gradually disappearing. In general outlines, but by no means in detail, the diversity in nationality coincides with today's pattern of the political boundaries.

Economic development

From an economic point of view, the Carpathians are a region of agriculture and forestry, with industry in an early stage of development. Agriculture flourishes on the Transylvanian Plateau, in intramontane basins, and on lower parts of the mountains, up to some 3,000 feet elevation. On the northern slope rye, oats, and potatoes predominate; on the southern slopes maize, sugar beets, grapes, and tobacco are grown. Above 3,000 feet elevation forestry and pastoral life are the rule. Natural gas, found mainly on the Transylvanian Plateau, is important among natural resources. Oil is also significant; the richest deposits lie in the Romanian sub-Carpathians, with an annual production by the 1970s of 12,000,000–14,000,000 tons. Brown coal is found in low-lying areas of the Western Carpathians in Czechoslovakia and Hungary, and some bituminous coal is mined in the Romanian Southern Carpathians. Also noteworthy are the rock salt beds of the Transylvanian Plateau, the Romanian sub-Carpathians, and the base of the Polish Carpathians, and the potassium salts found at the base of the Ukrainian Carpathians. Iron ores, ores of non-iron metals, and gold and silver ores were intensively mined in the Middle Ages in the Bihor Massif and in the Slovakian Western Carpathians, but today all these deposits are of minor importance.

Larger industrial centres are Bratislava, the capital of the Slovak Republic, with a 1970 census population of 283,539 and a thriving machinery and a petro-chemical industry; and Košice, the principal town of eastern Slovakia, with a population of 145,027 and a modern steel mill. Prominent in Romania are Cluj, which, with some 170,000 people, is the principal town of the Transylvanian Plateau, concentrating on machinery making and chemical and food products; Braşov, situated in a basin near the boundary between the Western and Southern Carpathians, a town of over 140,000 people where machine production predominates; and Sibiu, about 100,000 in population, lying between the Transylvanian Plateau and the Southern Carpathians. In none of the remaining towns, however, did the population exceed 50,000 by the early 1970s.

TRANSPORT

The historical legacy

The railway network of the Carpathians came into existence in the latter half of the 19th century and the beginning of the 20th, at a time when most of the mountains were in Austria-Hungary. In this period the nodal point was Budapest, situated in the centre of the Carpathian arc. The principal railway lines were laid out radially from Budapest across the various mountain passes and were tied in with the important longitudinal west–east railway track running along the northern flank of the Carpathians—the link between Vienna (by way of Ostrava, Kraków, and Lvov)—with Chernovtsy, which then was also situated in Austria. This northern trunk line had its continuation in the sub-Carpathian Romanian railway line running toward Bucharest, and, farther on, by way of Craiova to Orşova, which, in turn, was linked by a Hungarian railway section with Budapest and thus with Vienna also. After the Austro-Hungarian Empire had collapsed, this system lost much of its economic and strategic importance. Within its boundaries the new state of Czechoslovakia started to build longitudinal west–east railway lines. For Romania, on the other hand, which had been allotted Carpathian Transylvania, the previously neglected lines became highly important. To some extent, a change in this pattern came about after World War II, when the northern part of the Eastern Carpathians and Trans-Carpathian Ukraine became part of the Soviet Union. The railway lines crossing this part of the Carpathians became arteries linking the Soviet Union, Czechoslovakia, and Hungary. Although the lines between Poland and Slovakia lost most of their importance in passenger and freight transport, truck routes, utilizing the Dukla (1,640 feet [500 metres]), Jablonka, and other passes, became significant in freight traffic between Poland and the countries south of the Carpathians.

The Ukrainian Carpathians are crossed by railway lines utilizing the Užok Pass (2,916 feet [889 metres]) and the Lavochne and Woronienka passes, while in the Romanian Carpathians the railways run through passes at Ghimeş, Oituz, Predeal (3,390 feet [1,033 metres])—the gap valley of the river Olt—and by the low pass of "Porta Orientalis."

By the early 1970s the most important Carpathian railway lines had been electrified, although the Budapest–Vienna line was electrified before World War II.

TOURISM

The Carpathians play an important role in fulfilling the needs of tourism and recreation, especially for the people of Poland, Czechoslovakia, Hungary, and Romania. By the 1970s, international tourist travel was less developed, although there were a number of regions and sites attractive to visitors from abroad. Most important among these were Zakopane, a centre of sport activities, tourism, and recreation, situated in Poland north of the Tatras. On the Slovak side of the Tatras, a similar role is played by a number of localities, notably Tatranská Lomnica, Smokovec, and Štrbské Pleso. Based on a tourist travel agreement between both countries, passes valid for both sides facilitate access by citizens of both countries to the entire Tatra Massif. In Romania the outstanding centre for winter sport and tourism is Sinaia, situated in the Prahova Valley, at the dividing line between the Eastern and Southern Carpathians.

The Carpathians are noted for their abundance of watering places with mineral springs of high therapeutic value. Among the best known Carpathian health resorts, which are also of international repute, are Krynica in Poland, Piešt'any in Czechoslovakia, and Borsec, Băile Herculane, and Tuşnad in Romania.

BIBLIOGRAPHY. SLOVAK AND POLISH ACADEMIES OF SCIENCES, GEOGRAPHICAL INS 'TUTES, *Geomorphological Problems of Carpathians*, 2 vol. (1965–66), reports of two international conferences dealing with the results of geomorphological research work done in the Carpathian countries; EMMANUEL DE MARTONNE, *L'Europe Centrale: Géographie Uni-*

verselle, vol. 4 (1930), a classical study of regional geography, including authoritative descriptions of the Romanian Carpathians; FERDINAND PAX, *Grundzüge der Pflanzenverbreitung in den Karpathen*, 2 vol., in *Die Vegetation der Erde* (1898–1908), an old publication, but valuable for the description of the plant distribution it contains for all of the Carpathians; MARTON PECSI and BELA SARFALVI, *Geography of Hungary* (Eng. trans. 1964), a compact, well-written outline of Hungary's physical and economic geography; M.R. SHACKLETON, *Europe: A Regional Geography*, 7th ed. (1964), the most popular handbook on the regional geography of Europe; ch. 28 deals with the Carpathians.

(J.A.K.)

Carpentaria, Gulf of

The Gulf of Carpentaria is a shallow, rectangular embayment of some 120,000 square miles (310,800 square kilometres) on the northeast coast of Australia. During the 1960s and early 1970s, following centuries of existence as a vast but unimportant backwater, the gulf suddenly became of international significance with exploitation of its aluminum, manganese, and prawn (shrimp) resources; its shore-living population increased from a mere handful to some thousands, and revolution was taking place in the communications with Australia and the world.

The gulf floor is made up of the continental shelf common to Australia and New Guinea. The greatest water depth (230 feet [70 metres]) is found in the northeast of the gulf, although, in the same region, a ridge with water depths of less than ten metres extends across Torres Strait, separating the floor of the gulf from the Coral Sea of the Pacific Ocean. To the northwest, a ridge extending northward from Wessel Island, with water depths of less than 182 feet (55 metres), separates the floor of the gulf from that of the Banda Basin of the Arafura Sea. The gulf-floor gradient is very low; north of 21° S latitude the great western plains of Queensland drain north or northwestward, across the shore and well out into the gulf, in a very gentle fall of only one foot per mile. As the plains approach the sea, they merge into a belt of salt flats, which reach their widest extent—some 20 miles (32 kilometres) across—just west of the Flinders River. About 20 rivers drain into the gulf; they wind profusely in their lower courses and have extensive deltas.

Boundaries

Historical and scientific associations. The eastern side of the gulf was first explored by the Dutch, between 1605 and 1628, and the southern and western coasts were discovered by the explorer Abel Tasman in 1644. The gulf was named after Pieter Carpenter, who visited the area in 1628. The first chart was prepared by Matthew Flinders in 1802, and supplementary data were added by Captain J.L. Stokes in HMS "Beagle" in 1841. In the later stages of the 20th century, there was remarkable activity in the exploration of the bauxite and manganese deposits on the shores and islands of the gulf, and also of its prawn resources. A search for petroleum had not achieved success by the early 1970s. The Royal Australian Navy hydrographic survey ship HMAS "Moresby" completed a detailed survey of the gulf in 1969.

Geological background. The gulf lies on the northern, central, and western half of the Carpentaria Basin—itself a northern subbasin of the Great Artesian Basin—of the Mesozoic Era (about 200,000,000 years ago). The Mesozoic sedimentary rocks, which lie on a basement of very old Precambrian rocks, are some 5,000 feet (1,500 metres) thick. They are made up of rock layers of both terrestrial and marine origin and thicken gradually toward the middle of the gulf. A substantial period of uplift and erosion followed the withdrawal of the sea at the beginning of the Upper Cretaceous Period, about 130,000,000 years ago, and the 1,968 feet (600 metres) of sediments subsequently deposited are again terrestrial. These later rock layers, about 50,000,000 years old, have, at least on the shores of the gulf, given rise to layers of bauxite up to 33 feet (10 metres) thick. Overlying these deposits, on the Wellesley and Sir Edward Pellew islands, are beds of sandstone that may represent a higher stand of sea level than that of today. The latest sediments below the waters of the gulf are at most 15 feet (4.5 metres) thick. A white clay is found solely in the western portion, but there and elsewhere layers of a younger, dark-gray to chocolate-coloured clay and fine silt are overlain by a green marine mud. The latter may have been deposited since the rise in sea level at the end of the Pleistocene Epoch, which initiated the gulf as a marine feature.

The huge manganese deposits, which, by the 1970s, were being developed by Broken Hill Proprietary Limited on Groote Eylandt, in the west of the gulf, appear to have been formed along an irregular shoreline of an ancestral gulf. Equally vast bauxite deposits also were being exploited at Weipa, on the Cape York Peninsula, and at Gove Peninsula, in Arnhem Land.

Mineral deposits

Hydrology and water composition. The salt pans of the southeastern gulf shores are the result of complexly interacting factors. In the extreme north, the tides are resolved into one normal and one very small tide each day; farther south the small tide diminishes until, around two-thirds of the Queensland shores, there is in effect only one tide a day, with a rise for most of the year of from four to six feet. In summer there are three very important changes; the monsoonal rains come (between December and March, with a 40-inch fall at the coast), the winds change from southeasterly offshore to northwesterly onshore, and the tidal amplitude increases to an average of 18 feet. With these conditions of very flat land drainage, monsoonal rain, onshore piling up of the sea by wind, and magnified amplitude of the tide, the salt pan area is submerged by the sea, and behind it the land area is submerged by the drainage water backing up the blocked estuaries. The junction of saltwater and freshwater floods is marked by the transition from bare salt pan to vegetated plains.

The composition of the waters of the gulf, at any one time, is governed by the relative proportions of three major water masses. The first mass is of low salinity, low nitrate and phosphate content, and relatively high temperature (79° F [26° C]). It is formed during summer monsoonal conditions off the western coast of New Guinea, to the north. By March and April this drifts into the northern gulf region but is driven back out again by August by the southeast trade winds. The second water mass is of high salinity, low nitrate and phosphate content, and high temperature (77.9° F [25.5° C]). This originates in the Coral Sea, to the east, and moves through the Torres Strait into the gulf after May. Spreading south along the eastern side, it evaporates and cools, displacing the first mass and mixing with it as it spreads westward. The third mass is of medium salinity, but high nitrate and phosphate content, and is made up of relatively cooler water (68°–72° F [20°–22° C]), with oxygen saturation less than 50 percent. This derives from the northwest, specifically from the subsurface (330–495 feet [100–150 metres]) waters of the Banda Sea, but during its spreading eastward increases considerably in nutrient content, while decreasing in oxygen. Upwelling of the water at the surface of the gulf probably occurs only in restricted areas, where the shelf depth is less than about 16 feet.

Marine life and resource development. By the early 1970s, prawn fishing had developed rapidly. Processing is done in specially equipped ships and, on shore, at Karumba Groote Eylandt and Thursday Island. Banana prawns are the major catch. Because of their habit of coming together in large schools known as prawn boils, in which the bottom mud is churned up, banana prawns can be easily located from the air or by echo sounders. Catches have fluctuated during the few years of operation, and the scientific work necessary before the industry can be regulated is now being done by the Council for Scientific and Industrial Research, Department of Fisheries and Oceanography.

As a result of these important economic developments, settlement increased on the shores and islands surrounding the gulf, and a start was made in improving the transport and communication links with the rest of Australia and with the world economy (see also QUEENSLAND).

BIBLIOGRAPHY. N.A. MEYERS, "Carpentaria Basin," *Rep. Geol. Surv. Qd.*, 34:1–36 (1969); C.V.G. PHIPPS, "Gulf of

Carpentaria," in R.W. FAIRBRIDGE (ed.), *Encyclopedia of Oceanography*, pp. 316–324 (1966); H.J. NEWTON, "Petroleum Possibilities of the Gulf of Carpentaria," *A.P.E.A. Journal*, pp. 32–37 (1964).

(D.Hi.)

Carpentry

Carpentry is the art and trade of cutting, working, and joining timber. This term includes both structural timberwork in framing and items such as doors, windows, and staircases. The working of wood in buildings is an ancient craft and still comprises one of the most important activities in construction work.

In the past, when buildings were often wholly constructed of timber framing, the carpenter played a considerable part in building construction; along with the mason he was the principal building worker. The scope of the carpenter's work has altered, however, with the passage of time. Increasing use of concrete and steel construction, especially for floors and roofs, means that the carpenter plays a smaller part in making the framework of buildings, except for houses and small structures. On the other hand, in the construction of temporary formwork and shuttering for concrete building, the carpenter's work has greatly increased.

Wood (see also WOOD AND WOOD PRODUCTS), being a natural material, is not uniform in quality. Furthermore, whereas most building materials are subject to slight and fairly predictable changes in form caused by moisture and heat, timber, because of the large quantity of natural moisture present after its conversion into wood, is particularly vulnerable in this respect. Thus, the jointing and framing of wooden members in building work must be done carefully in anticipation of considerable and variable movements that may follow either absorption or loss of moisture.

Nature of wood

Because wood is widely distributed throughout the world, it has been used as a building material for centuries; many of the tools and techniques of carpentry, perfected after the Middle Ages, have changed little since that time. On the other hand, world supplies of wood are shrinking, and the increasing cost of obtaining, finishing, and distributing timber has brought continuing revision in traditional practices. Further, because much traditional construction wastes wood, engineering calculation has supplanted empirical and rule-of-thumb methods. Stress grading of timber and mechanical joints (*i.e.*, grading materials in terms of the stresses they are capable of withstanding; see MATERIALS TESTING) and the development of laminated timbers such as plywood have also simplified and lowered the cost of carpentry.

CARPENTERS' TOOLS

Nonpowered hand tools. Many of the nonpowered hand tools have been used in virtually the same form for centuries by carpenters, modified only by the improvement modern steel can give to cutting edges (see also HAND TOOLS).

Planes. Used for smoothing rough surfaces and for reducing wood to size, planes are made of wood or iron (the blade is steel) in a wide variety of sizes. Special plow, or grooving, planes are used for forming channels and grooves; a wide variety of planes was used for cutting special moldings in the past, but this work is now done entirely by machine, and special hand planes are used only to repair existing work.

Saws. Handsaws cut wood either with or across the grain. Tenon and dovetail saws are used for fine, accurate work, whereas the bow saw, keyhole saw, and pad saw cut curved surfaces or are used to form holes.

Chisels. For removing surplus wood or cutting special shapes, a wide variety of chisels is available. Although most chisels have flat blades, the gouge, with a semicircular blade, is used to hollow out rounded grooves.

Other nonpowered hand tools. Hammers, mallets, screwdrivers, bradawls, gimlets, pincers, and pliers are small tools used for making holes, fixing screws, and for driving and extracting nails. There exists also a large group of tools utilized to set out work and check it for truth and alignment. Included are the trisquare, for testing the right angle between adjacent surfaces; the bevel, for testing angles other than right angles and for marking lines inclined to the surface of the material; and gauges, for marking lines parallel to the surfaces of materials.

Powered hand tools. The principal advantage of powered hand tools is portability. Many tasks that would be cumbersome or time-consuming if performed on the site with ordinary hand tools or inconvenient to move to a workshop can be quickly and economically carried out with powered hand tools.

Electric hand drills. Probably the most versatile of all powered hand tools, the electric hand drill can be used for all kinds of drilling and forms a power unit that can be fitted to perform other tasks, such as sanding, polishing, rebating (cutting grooves), and molding. Most drills can be fitted to a bench so that work can be taken to them.

Portable saws. Circular in shape, these tools are powered handsaws. Their chief use is for making straight cuts, ripping (cutting with the grain), and crosscutting against the grain of wood at any angle. The portable saw has advantages not only on the job but also in the workshop, where it takes up less space than the fixed bench saw. Portable saws are equipped with a device called a fence to enable parallel cuts to be made. In the interests of both safety and accuracy, the wood is held securely during cutting. For circular and internal cutting the narrow-bladed jigsaw is used.

The router. Used for recessing, grooving, molding, and general shaping, the router can be used freehand or fixed with a jig, which controls the timber. The router works at very high speed and cuts the fibres cleanly, either with or against the grain. A high-speed circular tool of this kind requires careful control, however, to prevent drifting.

Fixed power tools. Fixed woodworking machines have sped up output and reduced costs. Automated machines linked in series permit continuous operation for the reduction of large lumber to manufactured components. They are also used to produce furniture.

Automated power tools

Circular bench saw. The vertical circular saw is mounted on a frame in a flat metal table. The blade runs in a slot in the table and is used for general cutting purposes, such as sawing planks and small scantlings (pieces of lumber used in frameworks), and for ripping, edging, and crosscutting. A fence mounted parallel to the saw is adjusted to keep the wood at the correct distance from the saw. Held against the fence and fed toward the revolving saw, the wood is kept under pressure until the cut is complete. A riving knife behind the saw keeps the cut open during sawing.

Band saw. Sometimes known as the band resaw, this device performs a wide variety of tasks in cutting lumber. Instead of a circular saw, the band saw employs a continuous flexible steel blade that passes over two pulleys placed one above the other. The diameter of the pulleys varies: for heavy work it is likely to be not less than 36 inches (90 centimetres) and may be 42 or 48 inches (105 or 120 centimetres) for exceptionally heavy work. The saw blade varies in width up to about one and one-half inches (38 millimetres) for the 36-inch pulley and up to two and one-half inches for the heaviest saws. The saw passes through a slot in a steel table about three by three feet (one by one metre) and is hand-fed.

Surface planer and thicknesser. Used to reduce timber to parallel thickness and to plane its surfaces, this device usually operates in one of two ways. Fixed-knife planing follows the principle of the hand plane, except that the wood is passed over the knife. Cutter-block, or rotary, planing is accomplished by passing the wood over a revolving block into which a number of cutters have been fixed.

Mortising machines. A mortise is a cavity, usually rectangular in shape, cut into a piece of timber to receive a tenon, or projection, from another piece of wood, to make a joint. The hollow mortise chisel consists of a hollow square chisel with the four sides sharpened at the cutting edge. An auger, or screw-shaped boring tool, re-

The mortise

volves through the length of the chisel and cuts away all but the corners of the mortise; these are removed by the sharp edges of the chisel. Another mortising machine is the chain cutter, in which the cutters are the links of an endless chain that is brought down onto the material and removes the wood from the mortise in a circular motion. Many machines are equipped for both methods and are operated by a hand lever.

Molding machines. To make trim and molding, sections of wood are passed over blades that cut out unwanted material. Such machines often employ more than one cutter for complicated molding, and thus, most have more than one set of cutter blocks. A spindle molder is used to form moldings on both straight and curved members and for such processes as planing, edging, and recessing. Dovetailing can also be carried out on spindle machines.

Sanders. The finishing of planed surfaces to high standards is done by sanding machines using sandpaper that revolves on a drum, belt, or disk over the surface to be smoothed.

JOINING

Types of joints. The object of a carpentry joint is to fix two pieces of wood together as strongly and unobtrusively as possible. There are a large number of joints in use; long experience with wood as a building material and with certain types of joints has tended to produce accepted patterns for the most commonly used items (see Figure 1). Practically all are based on handwork, for with few exceptions machine-made joints follow the traditional patterns. For their strength, most joints rely upon a combination of mechanical fit and glue, though some are solely dependent upon wedging or pinning and a few on gluing alone.

A joint is made in a thick portion of a member and should be easy to fabricate. If the joint relies on glue, the areas available for gluing are made as extensive as possible. If used out of doors, the joint is designed to resist dampness. Junctions are made as unobtrusive as possible so that, if shrinkage occurs because of moisture, the gap is not easily seen. Allowance is made for movement and tightening of the joint. For the sake of economy, joints are also designed to avoid wasting wood and to minimize the number of operations required for fabrication and assembly. Animal glue, applied hot, is widely used, but, because animal glue is brittle and is not waterproof, glues made of either casein or synthetic resins have been developed for greater strength and weather resistance.

Mortise and tenon joint. Used to join a horizontal with the vertical member of a frame, the mortise and tenon is one of the most common type of joints (see Figure 1A–C). A rectangular projection (tenon), usually a third of the total thickness of the member, is fitted into a rectangular cavity (the mortise) cut out of the other member, so there is enough timber at the top and bottom to enable wedges to be driven in to tighten the joint. A pin, dowel, or bolt may be used to secure the joint (Figure 1D). Where the vertical member (stile) does not continue past the horizontal member (rail) as in the top and bottom members of a doorframe, the tenon must be "haunched" (Figure 1A) to leave enough timber at the top of the stile for wedging. In cabinetwork and highly finished joinery, foxtail wedging, in which the end of the mortise is expanded to prevent withdrawal, may be used (Figure 1A). Here the wedging is "secret," or hidden; it is expensive and requires considerable skill in assembly, for, once the joint is made, it cannot be taken apart.

The tenon

In thick sections, as in heavy doors and frames, tenons are often doubled; in wide members, twin tenons may also be used. The principle is the same as for a single tenon, but the reduction in the size of the tenons offers more opportunities for wedging and less danger of twisting due to shrinkage. An alternative form of mortise and tenon, the dowelled joint (Figure 1E), is commonly used in factory made joinery and mass-produced fittings, such as built-in cabinets for houses.

Other types of joints. The dovetail joint (Figure 1F, G) is used to join two flat members together at right angles, as in drawer construction or at the corners of a bookcase. It may be cut by hand or machine. The rebated joint (Figure 1H) is easily made but not very strong. It is suitable for light construction: wooden boxes, for receiving the backing to fittings, and in small drawers. The housed joint (Figure 1I) is widely used in furniture and fitment construction; for example, to make the shelves in a bookcase. It is not mechanically strong, but it conceals the end grain of the housed member and provides support for light loads. For joining flat boards to form tabletops or similar large areas, edge-to-edge or butt joints are often used. These rely solely on the adhesion of the glue; to make the joint stronger, tongue (loose) or tongue-and-groove boards are used.

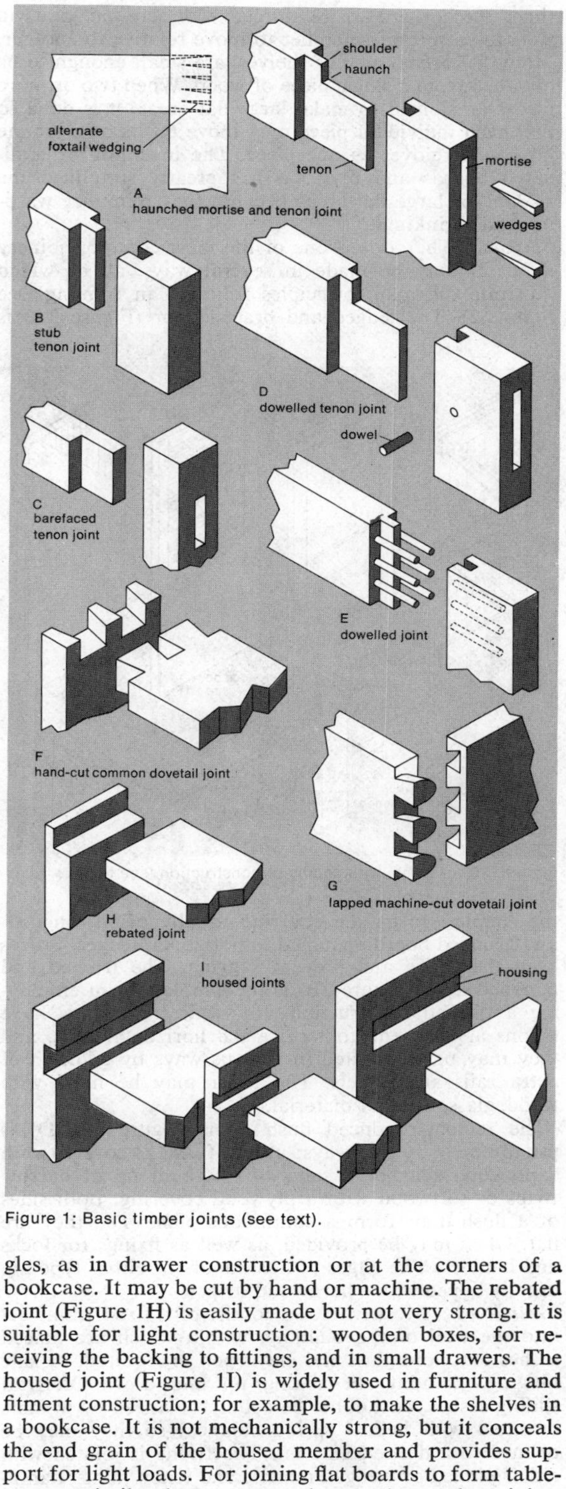

Figure 1: Basic timber joints (see text).

Preparation and assembly. A strong permanent framework must possess individual members of necessary strength joined together so that the inherent disadvantages of wood are minimized. Design is further complicated by the fact that, for the sake of stability, most frameworks are composed of many small members, each of which must be joined.

The frame and flat areas

In making a framework such as a door or a shelf, both the frame and the flat areas are considered. Four pieces of wood are joined to make a frame so that it will remain square with as little shrinkage as possible. Sometimes the corners are reinforced with screwed joints in slots to permit one member to move relative to another. Many flat areas, such as shelves, are small enough to be obtained from a single piece of wood. When two or more pieces are joined to make large flat areas, it is done so that each individual piece may move on its own, or the large area moves as one piece. The invention of laminated boards and plywood has greatly simplified the making of large flat areas because they minimize warping and shrinking.

Doors. The door is one of the most common joinery items. It may be made in several ways, all of which illustrate the main principles followed in framing (see Figure 2). The ledged and braced door (Figure 2A) is

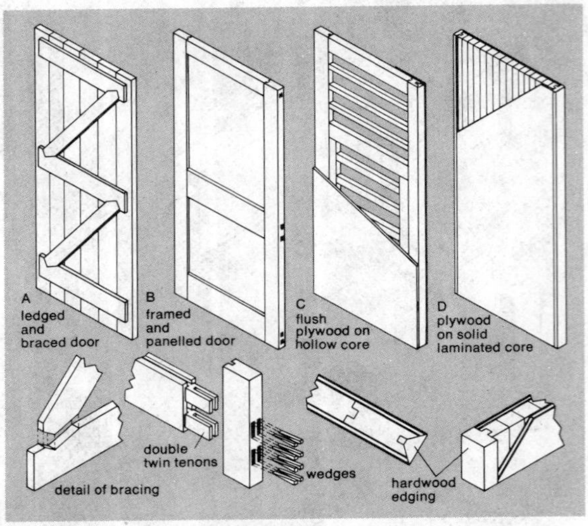

Figure 2: Door types, with details of construction (see text).

the simplest form, the covering usually being tongued-and-grooved boarding nailed to horizontal ledges. Braces keep the shape and prevent sagging. The framed and panelled door (Figure 2B) is the simplest form employing a framed construction. Its vertical members have tenons at each end to receive the horizontal rails, and they may be elaborated in various ways by addition of extra rails and panels. The latter may be filled with wood, glass, or other material.

The factory-produced flush door (Figure 2C, D) is usually made in two ways: a light frame is covered with a plywood skin, or a solid core is built up of narrow strips of softwood with a plywood covering. Both sides of a flush door form a continuous plane; *i.e.*, they are flat. Glass may be provided, as well as fixings for locks and handles. The edges of flush doors of either type are usually lipped with a hardwood strip.

Windows. Most windows consist of a fixed frame set into the wall of the building, within which are placed sashes that hold glass and may open as required, by side hinging, pivoting, or sliding up and down. Vertical sliding sashes must either be counterbalanced by weights or fitted with helical spring balances so they may be opened to a desired amount. The frame is jointed with either pinned or wedged mortise and tenon joints; damp-resistant glues are also employed. The usual fixing for the opening sash is by side hanging, but pivot hanging may be used, and the sash is then hinged at either side at its centre and can rotate horizontally. Windows are particularly vulnerable to changes in weather conditions because they are usually exposed to considerable variation in temperature and moisture on either face. Thus, weather checks (groove-shaped cuttings) are incorporated in the bottom rails of sashes and beneath sills to keep them from warping.

Staircases. Whether simple or elaborate, staircase design illustrates the principles of framing, especially in the precautions taken to resist the inevitable movement that occurs in the framing from the load and movement of persons ascending and descending. Steps are placed between strings, which are members inclined to the angle of the stairs that carry the main weight of the flight. The strings are framed into newel posts, vertical members of which also support a handrail. Each step consists of a tread (the horizontal member) and a riser (the vertical member). The horizontal distance travelled is known technically as the going and the vertical distance the rise. The string is trenched to receive the treads and risers, which are secured and tightened in the trenches by long wedges driven from the underside during assembly of the staircase. The wedging ensures that the treads and risers are securely held in the parallel strings. The risers are also housed into the treads and further secured by means of glued blocks in the angle between tread and riser. The handrail, spanning the newel posts, is supported on balusters, which may be of square or turned sections. Flush or panelled balustrades are also used.

OTHER CARPENTRY FUNCTIONS

Framing of buildings. The principal task of the carpenter at the building site is to cut and fix the timbers with such jointing as is necessary. Joints are made in different ways according to the use to which they are to be put and the stresses they must resist. Though specially designed timber connectors have replaced nails, especially in roof framing, wire nailing is still widely employed.

Platform and balloon framing. Timber-framed buildings are of two main types: platform (or Western) framing (Figure 3) and balloon framing. In platform

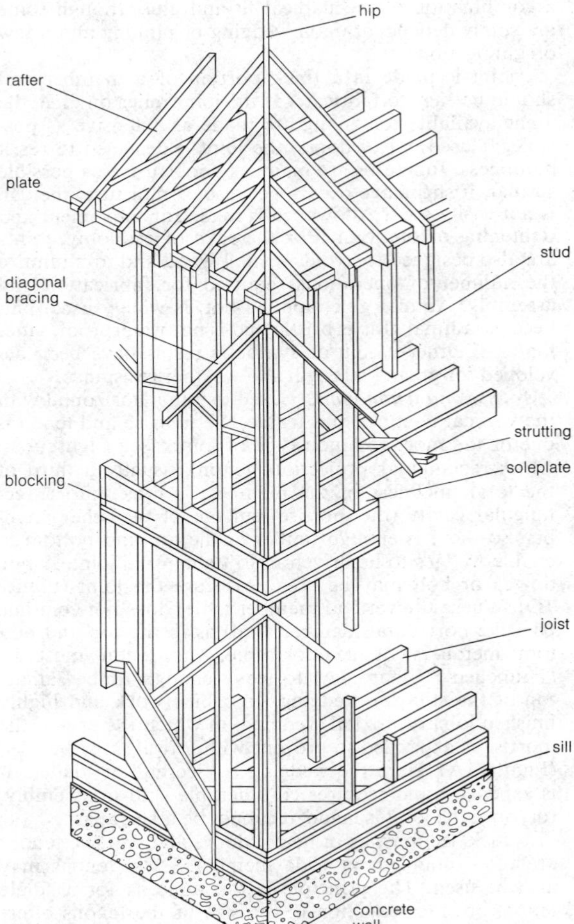

Figure 3: Western (platform) framing.

framing, floors are framed separately, story by story, then raised into place. Such construction provides fire stops for walls and partitions at each floor level. Each finished floor provides a working platform for construction of the next. In balloon framing, by contrast, the studs (vertical members) extend the full height of the building (usually two stories) from foundation plate to rafter plate.

The roof. The traditional pitched roof with various coverings (tiles, slates, shingles) still remains the most common method of covering small buildings. The framework for the roof is influenced in its design both by the weight and type of covering used and by the space covered. The weight of the roof covering is transmitted to the common rafters, key members in the design of the framing. Common rafters, usually placed about 16 inches (40 centimetres) apart from the eaves to the ridge of the roof, are generally timber of small cross section, either two by three or two by four inches (50 by 75 or 50 by 100 millimetres). In small roofs only the common rafter may be required, but as the length of the rafter increases it is necessary to provide support to prevent sagging. If suitable support can be found (on the cross wall or above partitions, for example), a support (purlin), running horizontally and at right angles to the rafters, is introduced at the midpoint of the rafter span. Light ceiling joists are also required; these span from wall to wall and are secured to the feet of the rafters.

The truss

Where no walls or partitions are available to give support to purlins or where a large clear span is required (as in a hall, for example), it is necessary to use a truss, which is an independent framed unit spanning from wall to wall on which the purlins can be carried. Traditional trusses use a large amount of timber and in consequence are very heavy. For these reasons, they are rarely used today, having been displaced by timber that is graded with respect to its ability to withstand given measured stresses. In consequence, much smaller members are now being used. Standard designs have been developed for various spans and slopes; the trussed rafter roof and the trussed purlin roof have entirely displaced the older and heavier trusses. By using specially laminated and formed beams and portal frames, it is possible to construct timber roofs of virtually any span. Such work, however, is outside the scope of what is normally understood by the term carpentry.

Timber-joisted upper floors. This familiar construction is used for light loads and small spans and, like the suspended ground floor, mainly for buildings of domestic scale and in conjunction with load-bearing brick walls. Joists (see Figure 3) are usually spaced 16 inches (40 centimetres) apart, and depth is selected according to the span, the joists being two inches (five centimetres) in thickness. Three-inch- (75-millimetre-) thick joists are used to carry extra loads. The joists are covered with hardwood or softwood planks and lined underneath with plaster, boarding, or other suitable finish. An ordinary timber floor of this type with three-fourths inch (19 millimetres) of plaster forming the ceiling is rated as fire-resisting for one-half hour. A longer fire-resistance rating, such as the two hours normally demanded for public buildings, will require a concrete floor of some kind. Published tables of joist sizes related both to span and spacing exist; these offer some economy in the amount of timber used. Alternatively, the floor may be designed in accordance with normal engineering practice for its special conditions and loadings. As the depth of a joist increases (with the span), cost of timber rises; it is not generally economical to increase the depth of timber joists over about nine inches (225 millimetres).

Joist sizes

If a span requires more than nine inches depth and will be covered with a timber-joisted floor, it is necessary to introduce an intermediate support in the form of a strengthened steel beam, thus reducing the size of the common joists. Herringbone strutting (bridging) is used to steady the joists against lateral movement whenever the length of the joist exceeds 50 times the thickness.

The joists in upper floors constructed of timber may be supported at the wall by means of pressed steel hangers, spiked to or notched over timber plates. Joists may also be built into the brickwork, in which case it is customary to rest them on a steel strip. Because upper floors are not normally ventilated, built-in timber is treated with a suitable preservative. Where chimneys pass through timber floors, a trimmed opening is formed to keep timber a safe distance from the flues.

Pipes and conduits. For convenience, water and gas pipes and electrical conduits are often run through the first floor; braces may be provided between the joists to support them. Wherever possible, pipes and conduits run parallel with the joists. If it becomes necessary to carry them through a joist, this is generally accomplished by boring through the centre of the joist.

Framed partitions. Framed timber partitions for subdivision of rooms have been in use for centuries, especially in houses. Partitions traditionally consisted of oak posts secured at the foot and head and plastered on both sides. This arrangement is still used today, except that the framing is normally of softer timber.

Usually constructed of light members, the timber frame consists of uprights or studs fixed by spiking, screwing, or mortise joints to headplates and soleplates. Intermediate horizontal members, called noggings, are also inserted for stiffening, for special fixings such as baseboards, or for carrying cupboards or fittings.

Determined by the nature of the job and by the dimensions of the covering to be used, spacing between the studs is likely to be about 18 inches (45 centimetres). In addition to lath and plaster or plasterboard covering, insulating fibreboards, plywood, hardboards, veneered boards, or plastic-impregnated sheeting may be used.

Siding materials

A number of materials are available for exterior wall covering (siding) of timber-framed buildings. The chief categories include wood, laid either horizontally or vertically; wood shingles and tiles; and plywood panels especially treated for external use. Fibreboard, hardboard, and particle board, usually covered with a laminated vinyl surface coating for protection and decoration, can also be employed.

Constructing concrete forms. Formwork is the term applied to all wooden molds used for the casting of concrete; its construction is a specialized branch of carpentry. Work may range from simple house slabs or walls to complicated structures such as reinforced-concrete framing for high-rise buildings, dams, silos, and engineering projects. Formwork must be designed to give adequate support to the weight not only of the concrete but also of the men placing it and the load of hand or mechanical ramming. In addition, formwork must be designed so that it can be erected, taken down, and if necessary reused during the progress of the work. The broad surfaces of forms are usually either plywood sheets or timber boards. These are kept apart the required distance by ties and stiffened by vertical members (studs or walings). Because forms must withstand considerable pressure from the wet concrete, adequate stiffening and bracing are essential to prevent distortion. For special work, formwork is erected on site, which is an expensive process because of the building time involved and because only a small proportion can easily be reused.

Standardized formwork

Today, modular panels of standard size are built and reused as much as possible from one site to another. When constructing formwork for horizontal concrete beams, it is customary to arrange the formwork so that the panels at the sides can be removed without disturbing those supporting the underside. This is done because it is safe to remove the side members as soon as the concrete has set (a matter of a day or two). The entire beam, however, is not ready to support considerable weight for several weeks. The formwork for a long lintel (horizontal member above an opening) is similar in principle to that used for beams.

Building custom-made furniture. Many buildings today, particularly houses, have cabinets and furniture built in. These are generally supplied by specialist firms and delivered complete for installation by the carpenter on the job. The largest area of this special equipment is certainly in the kitchen. Extensive ranges of factory-made cabinets are available, which usually comprise base units with work tops and wall cupboards for general storage but include housings for built-in ovens and sinks. In bedrooms, wardrobes, chests of drawers, and other storage fitments are increasingly found. The principal materials used for making these fittings are blockboard or plywood on lighter timber framing.

Finishing woodwork. The surface of wood is treated for protection and decoration (see also PAINTS, VARNISHES, AND ALLIED PRODUCTS). Traditionally, for both external and internal finishes, the two main treatments have been staining and polishing or painting with oil paint. Staining and polishing tend to increase the inherent interest of the wood itself by emphasizing the natural colour and grain pattern; this is often enhanced by the use of coloured stains. Oil paint, being opaque, disguises the character of the wood but enables a wide variety of colour to be used on wooden fittings and trim. In recent years the range of possible wood-surface treatments has increased considerably to include an extensive range of sealants and treatments, such as sandblasting. Most modern surface finishes, usually polyurethane sealers, are clear and are intended not only to protect but also to bring out the grain, structure, and colour of the wood. Prefinished plywoods are increasingly employed for internal panelling; these boards are faced with veneers of birch, walnut, oak, mahogany, and other woods having decorative grains, prefinished by sanding and staining to colour, then heat-treated with a vinyl sealer. After filling with a synthetic resin filler, the boards are further treated with thermosetting epoxy or synthetic polymer lacquer and again heat cured. In this way a highly polished and very durable finish is produced. It is also possible to simulate the grain of expensive veneers by photographic methods and by a synthetic polymer coating cured by heat treatment to make this available on cheaper boards.

Staining wood

Timbering and centring. The carpenter is frequently called upon to erect temporary timberwork for the assistance of other construction tradesmen. Examples of such work include timbering for demolition and excavation work and centring for the construction of arches and vaults in brick or stone.

Excavation. Where trenches are excavated on a building site for foundations, drains, or basements, it is usually necessary to support the sides of the excavation by timbering to prevent collapse of the earth and to safeguard those working below. The arrangement and the amount of timberwork required depends on various factors—the depth, the condition of the ground, and the width of the trench. Vertical boards called poling boards, which may be spaced at intervals in firm ground or set closely butted if the ground is loose or waterlogged, are set in contact with the earth. The poling boards are held in place by horizontal timbers called walings, and struts are then driven tight between the walings across the trench.

Arches. For simple brick arches of a flat, segmental, or cambered outline, the centre is formed by cutting a piece of wood to the required curvature; when made in this way the centre is called a turning piece. It is supported in the opening on props with folding wedges that allow not only easy adjustment but also the removal of the centre after the arch has been completed. For wider arches the centre is constructed with two or more ribs set parallel to each other.

The main consideration in the design and construction of a centre is that it shall remain rigid and not alter in shape during the building of the arch. The tendency, especially in wide arches, is that, as the building of the arch proceeds, the weight of the superimposed masonry tends to compress the centre at the haunches (sides) and, in so doing, forces down the crown (top). The reverse tendency is experienced when the weight is put on the crown as the arch nears completion.

ECONOMIC IMPACT

The tendency in the construction industry of the early 1970s was to concentrate an increasing amount of carpenter's work in the manufacture of large components in the workshop and factory and the erection of these items on site by means of mechanical plant, particularly cranes. Though factory manufacture is customary for components such as doors, windows, staircases, and roof trusses, this is being extended to the production of large-scale floor and wall panels. Though there are a number of reasons for this development, the most important single factor is probably the desire to reduce site labour. The ease of assembly and the rapid enclosure of the building against inclement weather speeds up erection time. Improved thermal and sound insulation can be achieved, and the total weight of timber construction, being far less than that of brick, masonry, or concrete, gives a consequent saving on foundation costs or, alternatively, makes it possible to use sites where the ground conditions would not otherwise be satisfactory.

Factory-produced building components

BIBLIOGRAPHY. The published books on carpentry and woodworking practice are, for the most part, written for the practicing designer or manufacturer, and therefore tend to assume some professional acquaintance with the subject. In most cases, however, they are readily understood by the layman because they are usually well illustrated and describe processes in stages with both practical hints and descriptions as well as the underlying theory. Among informative, well-illustrated works explaining basic skills and processes are C.H. HAYWARD, *Carpentry for Beginners* (1960), *Woodwork Joints* (1949), and *Tools for Woodwork* (1963); L.P. MCDONNELL, *Hand Woodworking Tools* (1962); and F. HILTON, *Craft Technology for Carpenters and Joiners* (1968). Definitive texts on English and American practice include W.E. DURBAHN and E.W. SUNDBERG, *Fundamentals of Carpentry*, vol. 2, *Practical Construction*, 4th ed. rev. (1969), a comprehensive statement of American construction practice with extensive practical hints and illustrations; a useful supplement to this book is N.L. BURBANK and O. SHAFTEL, *House Construction Details*, 5th ed. (1959). J. EASTWICK-FIELD and J. STILLMAN, *Design and Practice of Joinery*, 3rd rev. ed. (1966), though written from the point of view of the architect and designer of woodwork, is also an informative and instructive book on woodwork for the general reader, with clear illustrations. D.W. EGELSTAFF and D. HARRIS, *A Designer's Approach to Woodwork* (1970), also sets out to explain the underlying principles in the design and manufacture of woodwork.

For the advanced student of carpentry, there are a number of comprehensive works to cover the whole field of practice and to illustrate current methods of construction of timber details in building. These include R. BAYLISS, *Carpentry and Joinery*, 2nd ed., 3 vol. (1969); A.B. EMARY, *Advanced Carpentry and Joinery for Craftsmen* (1967); C.H. GRONEMAN and E.R. GLAZENER, *Technical Woodworking* (1966); F. HILTON, *Advanced Carpentry and Joinery*, 2nd ed. (1969); and F. KEELING, *Carpentry and Joinery: Advanced Examples*, 2nd ed. (1963).

Two books intended for the student of architecture and building that are well illustrated in detail are W.B. MCKAY, *Carpentry*, 4th ed. (1969), and *Joinery*, 2nd ed. (1965).

For information on woodworking machinery, see F.L. DUNSMORE, *The Technique of Woodworking Machinery*, 2 vol. (1965), a comprehensive manual of machine practice. H.J. FULKER, *Foundations of Machine Woodworking* (1965); and T. HESP, *Principles of Woodcutting Machinists' Work*, 2nd ed. (1965), are smaller books dealing with essentially practical points for the craftsman. Light machinery and portable tools are covered in C.H. HAYWARD, *Light Machines for Woodwork* (1963); and L.P. MCDONNELL, *Portable Power Tools* (1962).

(A.Re.)

Carpini, Giovanni da Pian del

Giovanni da Pian del Carpini, a Franciscan friar, was the first noteworthy European traveller in the Mongol Empire and also the author of the earliest important Western work on Central Asia.

Born in Umbria (*c.* 1180), probably at Piano della Magione (formerly Pian di Carpini) near Perugia, Carpini was a contemporary and disciple of St. Francis of Assisi. By 1220 he was a member of the Franciscan order and subsequently became a leading Franciscan teacher in northern Europe; he held successively the offices of custos ("warden") in Saxony and of minister ("subordinate officer") in Germany and afterward in Spain (perhaps also in Barbary and Cologne). He was in Cologne at the time of the great Mongol invasion of eastern Europe and of the disastrous Battle of Liegnitz (April 9, 1241).

Fear of the Mongols had not abated when four years later Pope Innocent IV dispatched the first formal Catholic mission to them, partly to protest against their invasion of Christian territory and partly to gain reliable information about their numbers and their plans; there may also have been the hope of alliance with a power that might be invaluable against Islām. At the head of the mission, the pope placed Friar Giovanni, then already more than 60 years of age.

Mission to the Mongol Empire

On Easter day, 1245, Carpini set out. He was accompanied by Stephen of Bohemia, another friar, who was subsequently to be left behind at Kiev. After seeking counsel of Wenceslaus, king of Bohemia, the friars were joined at Breslau (now Wrocław) by Benedict the Pole, another Franciscan appointed to act as interpreter. The mission entered the Mongol posts at Kanev and thereafter crossed the Dnepr, the Don, and the Volga. On the Volga stood the *ordu*, or "camp," of Batu, the supreme commander on the western frontiers of the Mongol Empire and the conqueror of eastern Europe. Carpini and his companions, with their presents, had to pass between two fires before being presented to Batu at the beginning of April 1246. Batu ordered them to proceed to the court of the supreme khan in Mongolia, and accordingly, on Easter day, April 8, 1246, they began the second and more formidable part of their journey. Their bodies were tightly bandaged to enable them to endure the excessive fatigue of their great ride through Central Asia. Their route was across the Ural (Yaik) River and north of the Caspian Sea and the Aral Sea to the Syr Darya (Jaxartes) and the Muslim cities, which then stood on its banks, then along the shores of the Dzungarian lakes and thence to the imperial camp of Sira Ordu (*i.e.*, the "yellow pavilion") near Karakorum and the Orkhon River. They reached their destination on July 22, after a ride of about 3,000 miles in just over 106 days.

On arriving at Sira Ordu, the Franciscans found that the interregnum that had followed the death of Ögödei, the supreme khan or imperial ruler, had ended. His eldest son, Güyük (Kuyuk), had been designated to the throne; his formal election in a great *kuriltai*, or general assembly of shamans, was witnessed by the friars along with more than 3,000 envoys and deputies from all parts of the Mongol Empire. On August 24 they were present at the formal enthronement at the nearby camp of the "Golden" Ordu and were presented to the supreme khan. They were detained until November and were then dismissed with a letter for the pope; this letter, written in Mongol, Arabic, and Latin, was little more than a brief imperious assertion of the khan's role as the scourge of God. The friars suffered greatly on their long winter journey homeward and not until June 9, 1247, did they reach Kiev, where they were welcomed by the Slavic Christians as risen from the dead. Subsequently they delivered the khan's letter and made their report to the pope, who was still at Lyons.

Major work

Immediately after his return, Carpini recorded his observations in a large work variously styled in the manuscripts extant as *Historia Mongalorum quos nos Tartaros appellamus* and *Liber Tartarorum*, or *Tatarorum*. He divided his treatise into eight chapters on the country of the Mongols, their climate, customs, religion, character, history, policy and tactics, and on the best way of resisting them; in a ninth chapter he described the regions traversed. He added four name lists: of the peoples conquered by the Mongols, of those who had successfully to his time (1245–47) remained unconquered, of the Mongol princes, and of witnesses to the truth of his *Historia*, including several merchants trading in Kiev. His *Historia* discredited the many fables concerning the Mongols current in Western Christendom. Its account of Mongol customs and history is probably the best treatment of the subject by any medieval Christian writer, and only on geographical and personal detail is it inferior to one written a few years later by the papal envoy to the Mongols William of Rubruquis, or Rubrouck. Carpini's companion, Benedict the Pole, also left a brief account of the mission, taken down from his dictation. Not long after his return, Carpini was installed as archbishop of Antivari in Dalmatia and was sent as legate to Louis IX. He died on August 1, 1252.

For a long time the *Historia* was only partially known through an abstract in the great compendium of Vincent of Beauvais (*Speculum historiale*), made a generation after Carpini's own and first printed in 1473. R. Hakluyt (1598) and P. Bergeron (1634) published portions of the text, but the complete work was not printed until 1839: M.A.P. d'Avezac (ed.) in *Recueil de voyages et de mémoires*, vol. 4, Geographical Society of Paris.

BIBLIOGRAPHY. C.R. BEAZLEY (ed.), *The Texts and Versions of John de Plano Carpini . . .* (1903, reprinted 1967), remains a standard work. Carpini's possible connection with the *Tartar Relation*, "an independent primary source on the Carpini Mission to Central Asia in 1245–47," is discussed in R.A. SKELTON, T.E. MARSTON, and G.D. PAINTER, *The Vinland Map and the Tartar Relation* (1965). Other useful works are *Fra Giovanni da Pian di Carpine nel vii centenario della sua morte, 1252–1952* (1952); CHRISTOPHER DAWSON (ed.), *The Mongol Missions* (1955); and F. RISCH (ed. and trans.), *Johann de Plano Carpini: Geschichte der Mongolen* (1930).

(E.M.J.C.)

Carracci

In late 16th-century Italy, three painters of the Carracci family were a major influence in diverting the course of art from the excesses and exaggerations of Mannerism toward a return to the strength and style of the masters of the High Renaissance. The Mannerist style was marked by a certain distortion in dealing with figures that was sometimes bizarre and by an emphasis on virtuosity for its own sake. Much of the influence of the Carracci was exercised through the academy they established in 1582 in their native Bologna, in which many of the leading artists of the next generation were trained. Their influence was felt long and far afield; on 17th-century art in Flanders, particularly through the active admiration of Rubens; and, through the policy of the French Academy in Rome, on young French artists until the end of the 18th century. In addition, each of the three Carracci—the brothers Agostino and Annibale and their cousin Lodovico—developed a distinctive artistic personality in his own right. Annibale was the truest artist of the three and the greatest; Agostino, the most cerebral, was a natural court painter; whereas Lodovico, the eldest and the leader of the family at first, conveyed a deep feeling of religious mystery in his early paintings. All three were also graphic artists of importance.

Births and backgrounds

The Carracci were born in Bologna, in modest circumstances: Agostino, born in 1557 (baptized August 16), and his brother Annibale, born November 3, 1560, were tailor's sons; and their cousin Lodovico, who was born in 1555 (baptized April 21), was the son of a butcher. Early in their careers, Annibale would paint "The Butcher's Shop," and also a smaller version of that subject, to remind the socially ambitious Agostino of their humble origins.

Lodovico in Bologna became the pupil of a fashionable painter, Prospero Fontana. Later he went to Florence and then to Parma; and he visited Venice with the intention of working under a great master, Jacopo Tintoretto. Mannerist influences persisted less in the styles of the two younger Carracci, although Agostino was influenced by a Flemish Mannerist painter, Denis Calvaert, who established an academy in Bologna that was a forerunner of the Carracci's. The precocious talents of the two brothers were developed in tours of northern Italy, their visits to Venice and Parma (1580s) being of special significance. Agostino was first to imbibe 16th-century Venetian art, notably that of Tintoretto and Paolo Veronese, both still active then; and his "Adoration of the Shepherds" for Sta. Maria della Pioggia (1584) demonstrates this influence. Annibale is reported to have lodged in Venice with Jacopo Bassano, by whose style of painting he was for a time affected. Annibale may be credited with the rediscovery of an early 16th-century genius, Correggio, who had been effectively forgotten outside Parma for a generation; Annibale's "Baptism of Christ" for S. Gregorio, Bologna (1585), is a brilliant tribute to this Parmese master.

Lodovico surpassed both his cousins in the mystery of

"Flight into Egypt," oil on canvas by Annibale Carracci, *c.* 1604. In the Galleria Doria-Pamphili, Rome. 1.2 m × 2.3 m.
Anderson—Alinari

his earlier devotional works, such as "The Vision of St. Anthony of Padua," and in the aristocratic sentiment of his portraits. His first signed and dated painting, the altarpiece for the Bargellini family (1588), demonstrates his peculiar sensibility in figure composition and, in particular, his justly praised rendering of hands. Of the three Carracci, he alone really comprehended the tender feelings conveyed by the deeply religious art of the Urbino master Federico Barocci, and he alone mastered the poetry of night. The illumination and characterization of his "Madonna and Child with St. Francis, St. Joseph and Donors" (1591) was to be a formative experience for the youthful Guercino, one of the most important painters of the next generation; and the treatment of landscape in his early works, inducing mood rather than locality, was to be of importance for Bartolomé Esteban Murillo, the most popular Spanish painter of the Counter-reformation. Lodovico's imaginative approach to religious sentiment in his "Martyrdom of S. Angelo" anticipates another Spanish painter, Francisco de Zurbarán.

Lodovico's sensibility in figure composition

For more than 20 years Lodovico was to lead the Carracci's school, the Accademia degli Incamminati. As an informal and progressive institution, it proved to be the most attractive centre of modern art in Italy and a training ground for many distinguished artists who sought, more or less consciously, to free themselves of Mannerism. They include Guido Reni, ultimately Lodovico's successor in Bologna, Francesco Albani, Domenichino, and Alessandro Algardi.

Early in their careers, each of the Carracci, by painting a monumental altarpiece for an Emilian church, evinced a distinctive claim to individual consideration. Annibale's "Enthroned Madonna with St. Matthew" (1588) for S. Prospero, Reggio, glowing with Venetian colours, manifests two persistent characteristics of his genius combined: the noble, classicizing strain in the angel seated in the foreground, which is reminiscent of Correggio, and the genial and bucolic in the simulated stone enrichment of the Madonna's plinth, a swag of fruits, and a harpy. These last elements, although painted in tones of grey, convey sensations of warmth and colour that would radiate from his later successes—the decorations of palace rooms. Lodovico's "Preaching of the Baptist" (1592), in S. Gerolamo della Certosa, Bologna, hung opposite Agostino's almost contemporaneous masterpiece, "The Communion of St. Jerome," which was to inspire further masterpieces on similar themes by Domenichino in Rome and by Rubens in Antwerp.

The three Carracci worked in concert on frescoes in three noble houses in Bologna—two friezes in Palazzo Fava (1584), a frieze in Palazzo Magnani (modern, Palazzo Salem) (1588–92), and decorations in Palazzo Sampieri (1593–94). The "Story of Jason" in the first of these palaces is their earliest public work of that kind. In the great salon of Palazzo Magnani, the cycle of scenes from the "Story of Romulus" initiates for European painting ordered and airy landscape as a principal subject; it was designed by Annibale, who was by this time the leading master in this exceptionally talented family. In the subsequent evolution of heroic landscape in Rome, Domenichino and Nicolas Poussin were to become Annibale's heirs. His lunette-shaped paintings, set high on the walls of the chapel of the Palazzo Aldobrandini, especially the "Flight into Egypt" and the "Entombment" (1604), are of supreme beauty and consequence.

Annibale's ascendancy

In the summer of 1595, leaving his stupendous "St. Roch Giving Arms" for Reggio to be finished by Lodovico, Annibale obeyed the summons south of the rich young cardinal Odoardo Farnese. Cardinal Farnese was determined to decorate with fresco and stucco some rooms on the principal floor of the palace that he had inherited, the most splendid in Rome. In Rome the 35-year-old painter turned eagerly to the study of Michelangelo, Raphael, and ancient Greek and Roman art in order to invest with sonority and grandeur the style he had formed in the artistic centres of North Italy.

Having decorated the Camerino (study) in Palazzo Farnese, Annibale was joined (1597) by Agostino in the chief enterprise of his career—painting the frescoes of the coved ceiling of the Galleria (1597–1603/4) with love fables from Ovid. This decoration, interweaving various illusions of reality in a way that was more complex even than Raphael's famous paintings in the Vatican Loggia, was a triumph of classicism tempered with humanity. Surprisingly, in view of its pagan and erotic subjects, it was acceptable from the first to churchmen as well as laymen. The biographer Bellori described the theme as "human love governed by celestial love." It quickly became and remained a virtually indispensable study for painters until well into the 18th century—the Roman equivalent to what Masaccio's frescoes in the Brancacci Chapel in Florence had meant to the 16th century. A long succession of visitors to Rome made copies of it, and Annibale's prolific preparatory drawings for it became collector's items from the second decade of the 17th century. It was to be an especially rich feeding ground for the Baroque imaginations of Rubens, Bernini, and many others. Bernini called it the best secular decoration in Rome since Raphael; and he expressed his disgust that the largest commission available in the metropolis, the decoration of the Sala Clementina in the Vatican, had not been entrusted to Annibale.

Influence of Galleria frescoes

Annibale's long and highly concentrated efforts had been dismally underpaid by Cardinal Farnese, and he never fully recovered from the ingratitude of his patron. By the summer of 1605 he had quit the Farnese palace forever. His team of loyal young assistants in Rome, which included Albani and Domenichino, could not rally him thereafter to complete any major undertaking unaided. It required a full year of their efforts to induce him to bring a "Nativity" for the Duke of Modena beyond the design stage.

Agostino Carracci had parted company with Annibale in 1600, leaving him to finish the Galleria, in order to work for Odoardo Farnese's brother Ranuccio in Parma. Agostino had already painted at least two portraits of Duke Ranuccio; and he was by nature more apt than either his brother or his cousin to be a court painter. He was proud also of his skill in both music and letters, being aware of the prestige to be gained thereby. In the Duke's service, he died at Parma on February 23, 1602, without completing his own major endeavour in fresco, the decoration with mythologies of a small room in the Palazzo del Giardino.

After Agostino's death, the Duke sent his most promising Parmese pupils, Lanfranco and Sisto Badalocchio, to complete their education by assisting Annibale in Rome. Misinterpretation of the oration delivered in Bologna by Lucio Faberio, secretary of the academy, at Agostino's funeral occasioned the long-continuing legend that the Carracci advocated an eclectic program of copying elements of the style of various masters. Their brilliant renewal of art was made possible by frequent observation of nature, study and revision of poses from life, and boldness of scale in drawing figures with chalk. Such procedures enabled them to profit by the visual knowledge they had gained through drawing and making prints of the works of past masters.

Lodovico published in 1604 an elegant print of the Madonna, but copper engraving was scarcely as important an activity for him as it was for Agostino, who had begun his artistic training as an engraver. Engraving formed a major part of his total output from 1580, when he engraved a "Christ and the Samaritan." The circulation of his prints after Barocci, after Tintoretto—*e.g.*, the large "Calvary" (1589)—and after Titian was of outstanding significance. Annibale's prints of "The Holy Family" (1590) and "Jupiter and Antiope" (Venus and Satyr"; 1592) were evidently appreciated by Rembrandt; and his two engravings on silver, the "Christ of Caprarola" (1598) and the "Drunken Silenus" (for the Farnese dish), rank among the most beautiful and influential designs of their period. As late as 1606 Annibale was able to produce the superb, and justly famous, engraving on copper, "La Madonna della Scodella." He was responsible also, at a much more mundane level, for recording the everyday look of the various tradesmen in his native city by a series of prints, published as the "Arti di Bologna." His gift of humorous perception, exercised in the streets and inns and studios, made him the first caricaturist of note. But that gift was scarcely used in the intermittent production of his last four years of melancholic sickness in Rome. He was smitten in 1605 with a kind of paralysis, which caused temporary amnesia and even loss of speech. Yet he continued to make dutiful efforts to attend meetings of the Academy of St. Luke, the artists' academy, as well as to guide the training and practice of his considerable workshop. In 1607 Albani failed as his chief assistant in frescoing the Herrera Chapel of S. Giacomo degli Spagnuoli; the next year, Annibale made it plain that his mantle was to fall on Domenichino, whose "St. Andrew" fresco in S. Gregorio Magno he preferred to Reni's. On July 15, 1609, Annibale died in Rome. For a decade thereafter, Lodovico remained active in Bologna. There he painted a succession of altarpieces in an increasingly grandiose and heavily mannered style until his own death on November 3, 1619, after painting his "St. Bernard Saving Carpi." Although his hugest undertaking was in the choir and presbytery of Piacenza Cathedral (1606–09), his finest achievement was in his own city of Bologna: it was his illustrations in the cloister of S. Michele in Bosco to the story of St. Benedict, founder of the Olivetan Order, which he frescoed during the summers of 1604 and 1605. This work shows how admirably he had profited by study of the great Venetian and Parmese masters of the 16th century, as well as Raphael and Michelangelo. Its significance in his production corresponds to that of the Galleria Farnese in Annibale's.

Annibale's last four years

Alinari

Annibale Carracci, self-portrait; in the Uffizi, Florence.

MAJOR WORKS

LODOVICO CARRACCI: "St. Francis Adoring the Crucifix" (1583–84; Capitoline Museum, Rome); "Portrait of a Youth" (*c.* 1583; Capitoline Museum, Rome); "Mystical Marriage of a Saint" (*c.* 1583; Beretta Collection, Bologna); "The Baptism of Christ" (*c.* 1583; Alte Pinakothek, Munich); "The Annunciation" (*c.* 1585; Pinacoteca Nazionale, Bologna); "The Vision of St. Anthony of Padua" (*c.* 1585; Rijksmuseum, Amsterdam); "The Conversion of St. Paul" (*c.* 1587–88; Pinacoteca Nazionale, Bologna); "Madonna dei Bargellini" (1588; Pinacoteca Nazionale, Bologna); "History of Rome" (fresco, 1588–92; Palazzo Salem, Bologna); "Madonna and Child with St. Francis, St. Joseph and Donors" (1591; Pinacoteca Civica e Galleria d'Arte Moderna, Cento, Italy); "Supper in the House of Simon" (1592; Pinacoteca Nazionale, Bologna); "The Martyrdom of St. Ursula" (1592; Pinacoteca Nazionale, Bologna); "The Preaching of the Baptist" (1592; Pinacoteca Nazionale, Bologna); "Flora" (1592–93; Galleria e Museo Estense, Modena); "La Dea Opi" (1592–93; Galleria e Museo Estense, Modena); "Martyrdom of S. Angelo (*c.* 1598; Pinacoteca Nazionale, Bologna); "The Martyrdom of St. Ursula" (1600; SS. Nicola e Domenico, Imola); "The Assumption" (1601; Corpus Domini, Bologna); "The Divine Providence" (*c.* 1604–05; Capitoline Museum, Rome); "Apostles at the Tomb of the Virgin" (1606–09; Galleria Nazionale, Parma); "Funeral of the Virgin" (1606–09; Galleria Nazionale, Parma); "St. Peter Repenting" (1617; S. Pietro, Bologna).

ANNIBALE CARRACCI: "The Crucifixion and Saints" (1583; Sta. Maria della Carità, Bologna); "The Butcher's Shop" (*c.* 1583; Christ Church, Oxford); "The Baptism of Christ" (1585; S. Gregorio, Bologna); "The Triumph of Truth" (1585; Hamptom Court Palace, Middlesex); "Deposition" (1585; Galleria Nazionale, Parma); "The Assumption" (1587; Gemäldegalerie, Dresden); "Self-Portrait and Portrait of the Father and Nephew Antonio" (1587–88; Brera, Milan); "Enthroned Madonna with St. Matthew" (1588; Gemäldegalerie, Dresden); "St. Roch Giving Alms" (1588–95; Gemäldegalerie, Dresden); "Madonna with SS. Luke and Catherine" (1592; Louvre, Paris); "The Assumption of the Virgin" (1592; Pinacoteca Nazionale, Bologna); "Christ at the Tomb" (1593; Louvre, Paris); "Hercules at the Crossroad" (1595; Museo e Gallerie Nazionali di Capodimonte, Naples); frescoes (1597 to 1603–04; Palazzo Farnese, Rome); "The Assumption" (1600–01; Sta. Maria del Popolo, Rome); "Christ Appearing to St. Peter on the Appian Way" ("Domine, Quo Vadis?"; *c.* 1601; National Gallery, London); "Pietà" (*c.* 1603; Kunsthistorisches Museum, Vienna); "The Dead Christ Mourned" ("The Three Maries"; *c.* 1603; National Gallery, London); "Martyrdom of St. Stephen" (*c.* 1604; Louvre, Paris); "Flight into Egypt" (*c.* 1604; Galleria Doria-Pamphili, Rome); "Entombment" (*c.* 1604; Galleria Doria-Pamphili, Rome); "Christ and the Samaritan at the Well" (*c.* 1604–05; Kunsthistorisches Museum, Vienna); "Pietà" (*c.* 1607; Louvre, Paris).

AGOSTINO CARRACCI: "Communion of St. Francis" (1582–83; Dulwich College Picture Gallery, London); "Bacchus and Ariadne" (1584–85; Pinacoteca Nazionale, Bologna); "Adoration of the Shepherds" (1584; Sta. Maria Della Pioggia); "Madonna with Child and Saints" (1586; Galleria Nazionale, Parma); "The Communion of St. Jerome" (1591–93; Pinacoteca Nazionale, Bologna); "Assumption of the Virgin" (1591–93; Pinacoteca Nazionale, Bologna); "Pluto" (1592; Galleria e Museo Estense, Modena); "Christ and the Adultress" (*c.* 1594; Brera, Milan); "Portrait of Giovanna Parolini-

Guicciardini" (1598; Staatliche Museen Preussischer Kulturbesitz, Berlin).

BIBLIOGRAPHY. The earliest considerable source from the first quarter of the 17th century, but then unpublished, is GIULIO MANCINI, *Considerazioni sulla pittura*, ed. by ADRIANA MARUCCHI and LUIGI SALERNO, 2 vol. (1956–57). The earliest published lives of the Carracci, on which all subsequent accounts depend, are in G.P. BELLORI, *Le vite de pittori . . .* (1672); and C.C. MALVASIA, *Felsina Pittrice*, 2 vol. (1678). HEINRICH BODMER, *Ludovico Carracci* (1939), is the first modern monograph (in German) on this artist. DENIS MAHON, *Studies in Seicento Art and Theory* (1947, reprinted 1971), contains the most brilliant critical rehabilitation of the Carracci. FRANCESCO ARCANGELI, "Sugli inizi dei Carracci," *Paragone*, 7:17–48 (1956), deals imaginatively with this special problem. The *Catalogo critico della mostra dei Carracci* (1956), with complete bibliography to that date, established a massive basis for fresh investigations. MICHAEL JAFFE, "Some Drawings by Annibale, and by Agostino Carracci," *Paragone*, 7:12–16 (1956), drew further attention to the problems raised by the drawing section of the 1956 exhibition. See also L. DURRAND, *Les Estampes composant le lascivie du graveur Agostino Carracci* (1957). DENNIS MAHON, "Afterthoughts of the Carracci Exhibition," *Gazette des Beaux-Arts*, 49:193–207 (1957), is a significant addendum by one of the scholars chiefly responsible for the exhibition the previous year. J.R. MARTIN, *The Farnese Gallery* (1965), is a richly illustrated book, devoted to the principal enterprise of Annibale, and especially to its iconography. DONALD POSNER, *Annibale Carracci*, 2 vol. (1971), is the first full-scale treatment of Bellori's hero since Bellori.

(Ml.J.)

Carriage of Goods, Law of

Until the development of railroads, the most prominent mode of transport was by water. Overland transportation of goods was relatively slow, costly, and perilous. For this reason, the law governing carriage of goods by sea developed much earlier than that governing inland transportation. The preclassical Greek city-states had well-developed laws dealing with the carriage of goods by sea, along with specialized commercial courts to settle disputes among carriers, shippers, and consignees. The sea laws of the island of Rhodes achieved such prominence that a part of them was carried, many centuries later, into the legislation of Justinian.

In Roman law the contract of carriage did not achieve the status of a distinct contractual form; jurisconsults (legal advisers) dealt with it in the framework of the contractual forms known to them, such as deposit and hire of services or of goods. There was special regulation only insofar as the responsibility of the carrier was concerned: shipowners (*nautae*), along with innkeepers and stable keepers, were liable without fault for destruction of or damage to the goods of passengers. Nevertheless, they could be relieved of responsibility by proving that the loss was attributable to irresistible force.

Early developments in common law

In English common law the principles applying to the relationship between the carrier and his customers go back to a time when neither railways nor canals existed. Whether influenced by Roman law or derived quite independently, early English decisions imposed on carriers the obligation not only to carry goods but to carry them safely and to deliver them intact to the owner or his agent. The carrier was always liable for the loss of the goods and also liable for any damage to the goods, unless he could prove that the loss or damage had resulted from an excepted cause. This duty of the carrier to deliver the goods safely was considered to exist quite apart from any contract. It was imposed upon him by the law because he had been put in possession of another's goods. In legal language, this meant that the carrier was considered to be a bailee, who, in certain circumstances, was liable to the bailor if he failed to deliver the goods intact. This law of bailment developed in England long before the law of contract. The contractual element of bailment was not stressed until after the 17th century. Today, in common-law countries, the rights and liabilities of shippers, consignees, and carriers are in the large majority of cases based on a contract of carriage, whether express or tacit. The mere fact that, in the ordinary course of his business, a carrier accepts goods for carriage and delivery implies the making of a contract of carriage. The right of the carrier to claim the freight depends on this contract, and this contract is also the foundation of his duty to carry the goods to their destination. But there remain vestiges of bailment in the law of carriage of goods. Thus, the owner of the goods, though not a party to the contract of carriage between the shipper and the carrier, may sue the carrier for loss of or damage to his goods.

Early developments in civil law

In civil-law countries, the contract of carriage first achieved distinct form in the early 19th century. The French Civil Code of 1804, following the Romanist tradition, still dealt with the contract of carriage as a species of the contract for the hire of services and further subjected carriers to the same obligations as depositaries; but the French Commercial Code of 1807 established a special legal regime for professional carriers, making the contract of carriage a distinct contractual form. Subsequent civil and commercial legislation in civil-law countries gave expression to the same idea. Today, in the civil-law world, the contract of carriage may be regarded as a variation of the contract for the hire of services, namely, a contract whereby one of the parties engages to do something for the other party in consideration of a price agreed upon between them. Specifically, the contract of carriage of goods may be defined as the contract whereby a professional carrier engages to carry goods in accordance with a determined mode of transport and within a reasonable time, with the understanding that the carriage of the goods is the principal object of the contract.

In France and in a great number of countries following the French system, a contract of carriage requires the presence of three indispensable elements: carriage, control of the operation by the carrier, and a professional carrier. If any of these elements is missing, the contract is one for the hire of services rather than a special contract of carriage. The classification of a contract as a contract of carriage involves significant legal consequences. Exculpatory clauses in a contract of carriage are ordinarily null and void; receipt of the goods by the consignee and payment of the freight without protest within a designated period of time exclude all actions against the carrier; actions that may be brought against the carrier are subject to a short period of limitation, that is, one year; the carrier has a privilege, which corresponds to a common-law lien, on the things carried for the payment of the freight; and, finally, either party to a contract of carriage may demand that experts determine the condition of the things carried or intended to be carried.

LIABILITIES OF CARRIERS FOR PUBLIC HIRE

Common carriers

In English and American law, common carriers are distinguished from other carriers. A common carrier is one who holds himself out as being ready to carry goods for the public at large for hire or reward. In England carriers of goods by land that are not classified as common carriers are termed private carriers; carriers of goods by sea or by inland water that are not classified as common carriers may be public carriers, namely, professional carriers who do not hold themselves out as ready to serve the general public or persons who carry goods incidentally to their main business or for one consignor only. In the United States distinction is made among common carriers, contract carriers, and private carriers. A person who engages to carry the goods of particular individuals rather than of the general public is a contract carrier; a person who carries his own goods is a private carrier. Both a common carrier and a contract carrier are engaged in transportation as a business. The basic difference between them is that a common carrier holds himself out to the general public to engage in transportation, whereas a contract carrier does not hold himself out to serve the general public. The exact boundary between common carriage and contract carriage is not always clear.

A person may be a common carrier, although he limits the kinds of goods that he is ready to carry for the public, the mode of transport, or the route over which he is prepared to carry. He is a common carrier only to the extent that he holds himself out as ready to carry goods for the public. It is indispensable for the classification of a person as common carrier that he accepts reward for the carriage and that his principal undertaking is the carriage of goods. Ancillary carriage for purposes of warehousing does not make one a common carrier. Unless the law provides otherwise, a carrier may cease at any time to be a common carrier by giving notice that he is no longer ready to carry goods for the public at large.

The distinction between common carriers and carriers that are not classified as common carriers, such as private carriers or contract carriers, involves significant legal consequences in the light of both common law and legislation. Common carriers are everywhere subject to strict economic regulation. Thus, a common carrier is forbidden in the United States to charge unreasonably high rates or to engage in unjust discrimination, whereas a contract carrier may charge rates as high as he pleases and may discriminate among his customers, provided that none of his discriminatory rates in motor and domestic water transportation is unreasonably low. In both England and the United States, a common carrier must serve everyone who makes a lawful request for the services he offers, but a private or contract carrier may select his customers; a common carrier is liable for any loss or damage to the goods during carriage, unless the damage or loss is attributable to certain excepted causes, whereas a contract carrier or private carrier is only liable for damage or loss through his negligence; contractual clauses relieving the carrier from liability may have different effects depending on the status of the carrier as common carrier or private carrier; and, finally, the common carrier has a common-law lien on the goods, whereas other carriers may have none in the absence of contractual provision or may have a less extensive lien than that of the common carrier.

The civil-law counterpart of the common carrier

The concept of common carrier has no exact equivalent in civil-law systems. But, if one looks to substance rather than form or terminology, one may conclude that the concept of public carrier in civil-law systems is a functional equivalent of the concept of common carrier. A public carrier is a professional carrier of goods or passengers; he is distinguished from a private carrier who either carries his own goods exclusively or carries goods incidentally to his other business. Generally, the scope of private carriage is narrowly defined so that most carriage operations fall under the rubric of public carriage; this ensures maximum application of rules designed to safeguard the public interest in the carriage of goods. Public carriers, like common carriers in common-law countries, are subject to strict economic regulation and are under the supervision and control of administrative agencies. When a public carrier is also a professional merchant, normally an individual or a private corporation, he assumes all the duties, obligations, and liabilities attaching to merchants under applicable commercial codes or special legislation. Like a common carrier, a public carrier must accept the goods lawfully delivered to him for carriage, either because he is held to a permanent offer made to the public or because he is under obligation to carry by virtue of public legislation or administrative regulations. Unlike common carriers, public carriers are not liable for loss or damage to the goods without fault; this difference is more apparent than real, because carriers in civil-law systems are presumed to be liable, unless they prove that the loss or damage occurred without their fault.

Duties to carry. Common carriers and public carriers are under duty to carry goods lawfully delivered to them for carriage. The duty to carry does not prevent carriers from refusing to transport goods that they do not purport to carry generally. Carriers may indeed restrict the commodities that they will carry. Further, everywhere, carriers may refuse to carry dangerous goods, improperly packed goods, and goods that they are unable to carry on account of size, legal prohibition, or lack of facilities.

Liability for safety of the goods. Everywhere, carriers incur a measure of liability for the safety of the goods. In common-law countries carriers are liable for any damage or for the loss of the goods that are in their possession as carriers, unless they prove that the damage or loss is attributable to certain excepted causes. The excepted causes at common law include acts of God, acts of enemies of the crown, fault of the shipper, inherent vices of the goods, and fraud of the shipper. In maritime carriage perils of the sea and particularly jettison are added to the list of excepted causes. All these terms have technical meanings. An act of God is an operation of natural forces so unexpected that no human foresight or skill may be reasonably expected to anticipate it. Acts of enemies of the crown are acts of enemy soldiers in time of war or acts of rebels against the crown in civil war; violent acts of strikers or rioters are not an excepted cause. Fault of the shipper as an excepted cause is any negligent act or omission that has caused damage or loss—for example, faulty packing. Inherent vice is some default or defect latent in the thing itself, which, by its development, tends to the injury or destruction of the thing carried. Fraud of the shipper is an untrue statement as to the nature or value of the goods. And jettison in maritime transport is an intentional sacrifice of goods to preserve the safety of the ship and cargo.

Excepted causes of loss

When goods are damaged or lost as a result of an excepted cause, the carrier is still liable if he has contributed to the loss by his negligence or intentional misconduct. In this case, however, the burden of proof of the carrier's fault rests on the plaintiff.

In civil-law countries the carrier under a contract of carriage is ordinarily bound as a warrantor for any damage to or loss of the goods carried, unless he proves that the damage or loss has resulted from irresistible force (*force majeure*), the inherent vice of the goods, or from the fault of the shipper or of the consignee. This contractual liability of the carrier under the general law is frequently modified by special legislation or by international conventions. In addition to his contractual liability, the carrier may, of course, incur liabilities that arise without contract. The carrier's contractual liability is often termed an "obligation of result," because the carrier, or a warrantor, is bound to make full restitution, unless he manages to exculpate himself in part or in whole.

Limitations of liability. In the absence of contrary legislation or decisions, carriers in common-law jurisdictions have been traditionally free to exclude or limit their liabilities by contract. In civil-law jurisdictions, as a rule, contractual clauses tending to limit liability for negligence or for willful misconduct have been considered null and void. Today, in most countries, municipal legislation and international conventions ordinarily limit the liability of certain carriers to a specified amount per weight, package, or unit of the goods carried. In this way, the liability of certain carriers has largely become standardized, at least in international carriage of goods. Parties are free to stipulate that the carrier shall be liable in excess of any statutory limitation, but clauses designed to reduce the liability of the carrier below statutory limits are ordinarily null and void. Statutory limitations cover both direct and indirect losses incurred by shippers or consignees. In most legal systems, the benefit of statutory limitation of liability is unavailable if the goods have been delivered to the wrong person or if the carrier is guilty of intentional misconduct or gross negligence.

International conventions limiting liability

The liability of a maritime carrier for loss or damage to goods carried under a bill of lading is limited in most countries to a specified amount per package or unit by application of the provisions of the Brussels Convention of 1924 or by municipal legislation containing rules similar to those of the convention. The liability of air carriers for loss or damage to goods carried in international trade is almost everywhere controlled by the provisions of the Warsaw Convention of 1929, as amended by the Hague Protocol of 1955. Air carriage in domestic trade is subject either to the rules of the international convention or to municipal legislation patterned after the model of the convention. In most countries the liability of railroad carriers is limited by legislation or administrative regulations that regularly become part of the contract of carriage. International carriage of goods by railroad is largely subject to the various Berne Conventions, the first of which was adopted in 1890. Most European nations, including Great Britain, Northern Ireland, and Communist countries with the exception of the U.S.S.R., have adhered to these conventions.

SCOPE OF THE LAW

The law of carriage of goods covers a variety of matters.

Goods in transit

Delay and misdelivery. In all legal systems, carriers incur liability for delay in delivering the goods to the consignee. Statutes, international conventions, administrative regulations, or even contractual agreements may fix the period of transportation with reference to the applicable means of carriage and determine the consequences of the delay. Under the law of contracts, failure of the carrier to deliver the goods within the prescribed period of time will be treated as a breach of contract.

In common-law jurisdictions, if the delay is caused by a deviation, the carrier is ordinarily answerable for damages. A deviation takes place when the carrier leaves the route that he has expressly or impliedly agreed to follow or when he goes past his destination. In civil-law jurisdictions carriers are not bound to follow any particular route in the absence of special legislation or contractual agreement. Thus, a deviation from the normal route does not itself constitute a fault of the carrier; if the deviation causes a delay, the carrier will be liable only if he is at fault.

Like delay, misdelivery engages the responsibility of the carrier. Misdelivery is the delivery of the goods by the carrier to the wrong person or to the wrong place.

Diversion and reconsignment; stoppage in transit. The terms diversion and reconsignment are used interchangeably to refer to a change in the destination or billing of a shipment before or after it reaches its original destination. Reconsignment is of considerable importance to the commercial world, because goods may be shipped from a distant source of supply toward a certain destination and then diverted to the most favourable market. Carriers are generally permitted to make a charge for the exercise of a diversion or reconsignment privilege. The number of diversions is generally limited in order to prevent the use of means of transport as places of storage.

The owner of the goods may, in all legal systems, change the carrier's instructions as to the place of destination or as to the person entitled to take delivery. The carrier must comply with this order, provided that he has satisfied himself that the person designating a new place of delivery or a new recipient is the owner of the goods at the time the order is given. In civil-law jurisdictions the person in possession of the title of transport, be it a bill of lading or other document, is ordinarily entitled to change the destination of the goods. This rule has been largely followed in international conventions, including the Warsaw Convention of 1929. At common law, in the absence of other provision, the consignee is regarded as the owner of the goods while they are in transit; therefore, it is ordinarily the consignee who is entitled to change the destination of the shipment.

Stoppage in transit is technically the right of an unpaid seller of goods to change their destination before they are delivered to the consignee. The seller has this right by virtue of directly applicable legislation even if he has not reserved the ownership of the goods in his transaction with the buyer. Indicatively, the British Sale of Goods Act of 1893, which codified the common-law rules, declares that the unpaid vendor may resume possession of the goods as long as they are in the course of transit and may retain them until payment or tender of the price. There are analogous provisions in civil-law jurisdiction.

Dangerous goods. Dangerous goods are those that, from their nature, are liable to cause damage to persons, to means of transport, or to other goods. In all legal systems, the carriage of dangerous goods has given rise to distinct problems and to the development of special rules.

In civil-law countries legislation or administrative regulations define categories of goods considered to be dangerous and either exclude their shipment by public carriers or determine the conditions under which they may be shipped. In common-law jurisdictions the shipper is liable to the carrier for all damage caused by dangerous goods delivered for shipment, unless he has declared the dangerous nature of the goods at the time of delivery, and the carrier has accepted them with knowledge of their nature.

Carriage by two or more carriers. Goods frequently reach their destination after they have passed through the hands of two or more carriers. This may happen when the shipper has contracted with several carriers, when the shipper has authorized one of the carriers to act as his agent with other carriers, or when the carrier, without authority, delivers the goods to another carrier.

If the carrier, without authority, delivers the goods to another carrier, he is liable to the shipper for any misdelivery by the second carrier and for any loss or damage suffered by the owner of the goods while the goods were in the possession of the second carrier. This means that the carrier cannot relieve himself from liability by performing the contract through the services of an agent. Moreover, delivery of the goods to another carrier may be a breach of contract by virtue of an implied or express condition that the carriage shall be effected by the vehicles of the carrier. Such a condition is implied in maritime transports.

The carrier's assurance of payment

Carrier's liens. The law strives everywhere to secure payment of the freight to a carrier who has carried the goods to their destination. In common-law jurisdictions the carrier may have to this effect a common-law lien, a statutory lien, or even a contractual lien. In civil-law jurisdictions the carrier has, ordinarily, a privilege on the things carried.

A common carrier in common-law jurisdictions has a common-law lien under which he is entitled to retain possession of the goods until earned freight is paid to him. The carrier is not entitled to sell the goods or to use them; parties, however, may agree that the carrier shall have an active lien, namely, that he shall have the right to sell the goods. Thus, in maritime carriage in the United States, the shipowner is clearly entitled to seize and sell the goods carried by him in case of nonpayment of the freight. Parties may agree that the carrier shall have no lien at all or that he shall have a general lien on the goods carried, namely, a lien covering debts other than the pending freight. After the lien is exercised, the carrier has the rights and duties of a bailee. He may thus be liable for loss or damage occasioned by his negligence, and he may be entitled to recover expenses that were reasonably necessary for the preservation of the goods.

Carriers in civil-law jurisdictions ordinarily have a privilege on the goods carried by them for the payment of the freight and of incidental expenses. In France and in systems following the French model, this privilege is available only to professional carriers who carry goods by contract of carriage. The civil-law privilege differs from a common-law lien in that it confers on the carrier power and authority to sell the goods for the satisfaction of his claims. The privilege covers the whole shipment as determined by the documents of transport and is extinguished upon delivery of the goods to the consignee. Quite apart from the privilege, the carrier in civil-law jurisdictions may be entitled, under the general law of obligations, to refuse delivery of the goods until payment of the freight; moreover, he may secure payment of the freight by a variety of contractual arrangements.

The carrier's role as a warehouseman and bailee. In all legal systems, the peculiar liabilities imposed on carriers extend only for the duration of the carriage, that is, from the time the goods are delivered to the carrier for shipment until the carrier has taken all reasonable steps to deliver them to the consignee. This means that the carrier is not under his liability as a carrier for the whole time during which the goods may be in his possession. Indeed, goods may be delivered to a carrier for safekeeping before the carriage begins or after it terminates in accordance with the terms of a special contract that may qualify as bailment in common-law jurisdictions and as a deposit in civil-law countries. Further, goods may be in the possession of the carrier because the consignee has unjustifiedly refused to take delivery, in which case the carrier may occupy the position of an involuntary bailee or depositary.

Goods not in transit

Generally, a carrier who is in possession of the goods before the beginning or after the end of the carriage is a warehouseman, and he is liable accordingly. In common-law jurisdictions the liability of a warehouseman is that of an ordinary bailee. In most cases a bailee, namely, a person entrusted with the goods of another, is not liable for the loss of or damage to the goods in his possession, unless the prejudice was caused by his intentional misconduct or negligence. In civil-law jurisdictions, if the parties agree that the carrier shall be in possession of the goods as a warehouseman before the beginning or after the end of the carriage, they form in effect a contract of deposit for reward, which is distinguishable from a contract of carriage. The elements of the contract of deposit and the rights and liabilities of the parties are dealt with in civil codes; exoneration clauses are valid under the conditions of the general law, and the period of limitation of actions is longer than one year. The depositary for reward is generally liable for intentional misconduct and negligence.

Measure of damages. Damages for the breach or nonperformance of a contract of carriage ordinarily are determined by application of the general rules of the law of contracts. Exceptional provisions applicable in case of breach of a contract of carriage are rare; they are mostly encountered in international conventions.

Bills of lading. Many shipments are made under bills of lading, issued by the carrier to the shipper upon delivery of the goods for shipment. The shipper is entitled to demand issuance of a bill of lading, unless his right is excluded by the contract of carriage. The bill of lading is, in the first place, an acknowledgment by a carrier that he has received the goods for shipment. Secondly, the bill of lading is either a contract of carriage or evidence of a contract of carriage. Thirdly, if the bill of lading is negotiable, as usually happens in carriage by sea, it controls possession of the goods and is one of the indispensable documents in financing the movement of commodities and merchandise throughout the world.

The bill of lading usually states the quantity, weight, measurements, and other pertinent information concerning the goods shipped. It frequently contains the statement that the goods have been shipped in apparent good order and condition. In this case, the carrier is not allowed to contradict the statement as to defects that were reasonably ascertainable at the time of delivery against an endorsee of the bill who relied on the statement. The bill of lading may be signed by the master or by a broker as agent of the carrier. As a receipt, the bill of lading is prima facie evidence that the goods have been delivered to the carrier; the burden of proof of nondelivery thus rests on the carrier.

In some jurisdictions the bill of lading is regarded as the contract of carriage itself. In other jurisdictions it is regarded merely as evidence of the contract of carriage; hence, oral testimony may be admissible to vary the terms of the contract evidenced by the bill of lading. When goods are shipped under a charter party or other document and a bill of lading is issued to cover the same goods, the bill of lading may ordinarily be regarded as a mere receipt. The terms of the contract are embodied in the charter party or other document, unless the parties intended to vary the terms of the agreement by the issuance of a bill of lading. A bill of lading that has been endorsed is ordinarily considered to contain the terms of the contract between the carrier and the endorsee.

Negotiable bills

At common law, a bill of lading functions as a semi-negotiable instrument. Delivery of the bill of lading to a transferee for valuable consideration transfers the ownership of the goods to the transferee, but the transferee cannot acquire a better title than that of the transferor. Under statutes, however, and under international conventions, bills of lading are in all legal systems fully negotiable instruments, unless they show on their face that they are not negotiable. When a bill of lading is negotiable, it confers a privileged status on the good faith purchaser, known as the holder in due course. A carrier who has issued a nonnegotiable bill of lading normally discharges his duty by delivering the goods to the named consignee; the consignee need not produce the bill or even be in possession of it. But a carrier who has issued a negotiable bill of lading will be discharged only by delivery to the holder of the bill, because, in a way, the goods are locked up in the bill of lading. The carrier who delivers goods without the bill of lading remains liable in common-law jurisdictions to anyone who has purchased the bill for value and in good faith, before or after the improper delivery. In civil-law jurisdictions, in case of an improper delivery, the carrier may remain liable to the endorsee of the bill of lading, even if the endorsee is himself not the legal owner of the bill but merely a finder or a thief.

Freight or forwarding agents. Shippers frequently engage the services of freight or forwarding agents, namely, persons who undertake for a reward to have the goods carried and delivered at their destination. The services of these persons are ordinarily engaged when the carriage of the goods involves successive carriers or use of successive means of transport.

A forwarding agent makes contracts of carriage for his principal. He may be a carrier or he may be merely a forwarding agent. When a carrier enters into a contract with the shipper by which he undertakes to carry goods in circumstances that involve an obligation on his part to hand over the goods to another carrier, he may be regarded as acting to some extent in the capacity of a forwarding agent. Conversely, when a forwarding agent carries the goods himself, he is to that extent a carrier and incurs the liabilities of a carrier.

Responsibilities of forwarding agents

In common-law jurisdictions a forwarding agent who is not a carrier is not responsible for what happens to the goods once they are handed over to a carrier with whom the forwarding agent has made a contract for his principal. By his transaction with the carrier, the forwarding agent establishes a direct contractual relationship between his principal and the carrier. Under the principles of the law of agency, the forwarding agent is under obligation toward his principal to conclude the contract on the usual terms. He is under no obligations, in the absence of an express contractual provision, to insure the goods. If, exceptionally, a forwarding agent acts as a carrier throughout the journey and uses other carriers on his own account, he is liable to the owner for any loss or damage to the goods during carriage. The extent of his liability depends on whether he is a common carrier or a contract carrier. If he is a common carrier, his liability to the owner of the goods may be heavier than the liabilities he can enforce against the carriers he has engaged.

In civil-law jurisdictions forwarding agents are clearly distinguished from carriers, and the contracts they make are clearly distinguishable from contracts of carriage. The profession of a forwarding agent, however, is not exclusive; thus, most frequently, carriers qualify as forwarding agents and vice versa. A forwarding agent has ordinarily a privilege on the goods under his control that is much broader and more effective than the privilege of the carrier. He has, in the absence of contrary contractual provision, freedom of choice of the means of transport and of particular carriers. His main obligation is to have the goods carried to their destination and delivered to the consignee. In the discharge of this obligation, he is generally entitled to engage the services of another forwarding agent. The forwarding agent is liable to his principal for any violation of his obligations resulting from negligence or intentional misconduct. He is relieved from liability if he proves that the loss or damage was occasioned by irresistible force. The liability of the forwarding agent for negligence may be excluded by contractual stipulations but not his liability for grave fault and intentional misconduct. A forwarding agent is considered as a carrier to the extent that he carries the goods himself, and to that extent he incurs the liabilities of a carrier. In contrast with the rule in common-law jurisdictions, the forwarding agent in civil-law countries is fully responsible for loss or damage suffered by the goods in the hands of carriers that the forwarding agent has engaged for the performance of the contract with his principal, unless the services of the particular carrier were requested by the principal. The liability of the forwarding agent does not exceed that of the carrier he has engaged, and, if the carrier is exonerated by virtue of an excepted cause, so is the forwarding agent.

Mixed-carrier transportation. The expression mixed-carrier transportation refers to situations in which goods are carried to their final destination by two or more means of transport, such as road and sea or rail, sea, and air. There are at least two possibilities. The successive carriers may have no common juridical link, as when the shipper has contracted with each carrier independently or when the shipper has contracted with a forwarding agent. In these cases, each carrier is subject to his own regime and has his own rights and duties toward the shipper or forwarding agent. A second possibility is that the successive carriers may be bound by a common juridical link toward the shipper or owner of the goods by virtue of directly applicable legal or contractual provisions or by virtue of the fact that the goods travel under a single document of transport, as a through bill of lading. In these cases, municipal laws in civil-law jurisdictions tend toward the irreconcilable aims of subjecting each carrier to his own regime and, at the same time, holding all carriers solidarily liable. In domestic carriage in common-law jurisdictions, the liability of each carrier is ordinarily determined by application of the rules governing carriage by two or more carriers.

The through bill of lading

Mixed-carrier transportation in international commerce under a through bill of lading or similar document has been dealt with in international conventions. A through bill of lading covers carriage of goods by two or more successive carriers or by two or more means of transport. It is issued by the first carrier and constitutes a single title to the goods. Under a purely maritime through bill of lading, successive carriers are equally bound, unless the contrary has been stipulated. Solutions differ, however, when carriage is effected by two or more means of transport. Under the Berne Railroad Conventions for the carriage of goods, carriage by rail and sea may be subject to the rules governing railroad carriage at the option of the contracting states, unless reservation has been made by them for application of certain rules of maritime law to the portion of sea carriage. Since these conventions may be entirely inapplicable to the portion of sea carriage, interested carriers and international organizations have concluded agreements for a uniform, legal regime of rail and sea carriage. In fact, accords have been concluded among United States and Canadian railway and ocean-shipping companies for application of the rules of the Brussels Convention of 1924 to goods carried under through bills of lading by rail and sea. The rules of the Warsaw Convention for carriage of goods by air apply always to the portion of air carriage and to that portion only, but the International Air Transport Association and the International Union of Railways have concluded agreements for carriage by rail and air under a single document. Only the Geneva Convention of 1956 has undertaken to establish rules applicable to all means of transport under a single document. The convention provides, however, that, if damage has been incurred in a portion of the journey other than road carriage, the carrier shall be subject to his proper law. This convention may conflict with the Berne Conventions and does conflict with the Warsaw Convention to the extent that carriage by air is subjected to the Brussels rather than the Warsaw Convention.

Transportation by official carrier. In the Western world, the transport of goods is divided between public and private enterprise. The basis of the legal relationship between a carrier and his customer is the same whether the carrier is a public corporation, a local authority, or a private corporation or individual. The law of carriage of goods governs the rights and duties of the shipper, carrier, and consignee.

PRINCIPAL LEGISLATIVE APPROACHES

In all legal systems the law of carriage has been influenced by the idea that carriers enjoy a factual monopoly. The services that a customer may demand and the remuneration that a carrier may exact are generally regulated by legislation or administrative regulations. The growth of competition among carriers and means of transport in the Western world has led to a reduction in the scope of municipal legislation in a number of countries, but international conventions and administrative regulations have proliferated. The right to carry on a transport business is still everywhere regulated through elaborate licensing systems, and the operations of transport are subject to continuous supervision and control by appropriate agencies. The legal relation between the carrier and his customer is affected by this intervention of the public authorities, and public as well as private laws form the body of the law of carriage.

U.S. and British regulatory laws

Roads, railways, and inland waterways. Since the 19th century, legislation has been enacted in most countries to safeguard the public interest in the movement of goods by road, railway, and inland waterway. In the United States a decisive step toward regulation of transportation was taken with the Act to Regulate Commerce of 1887. This act was made applicable to all common carriers by railroads engaged in interstate or foreign commerce and to common carriers transporting goods in part by railroad and in part by inland water when both were used under a common control, management, or arrangement for a continuous carriage. The act created the Interstate Commerce Commission, which today has wide powers to hear complaints against carriers concerning alleged violations of law, to investigate matters in dispute, to order carriers to cease and desist from unlawful practices, and to determine the amount of damages suffered as a result of violations. The commission also possesses rate-making power.

Since the time the 1887 act was adopted, new forms of transport have arisen, and older ones have been improved. The Interstate Commerce Commission now has jurisdiction over railroads, pipelines, motor carriers, and certain carriers by water. Other federal agencies that have been charged with regulation of transportation are the Civil Aeronautics Board and the Federal Maritime Commission.

In England the Carriers Act of 1830 was the first legislative intervention in the field of carriage of goods. The act originally applied to all common carriers by land, including both road and railway carriage. The Railways Act of 1921, however, made special provisions with regard to the railways, and the Transport Act of 1962 enacted that the Railways Board shall not be regarded as a common carrier. Consequently, carriage by railways is now regulated by the contract between the Railway Board and the shipper or other contracting party, as laid down in the Book of the Rules of British Railways. The Carriers Act has never been applicable to private carriers and to common carriers by sea or by inland waterway. If part of the carriage is by sea or inland water and part by road, the act applies to the land part only.

The Berne Conventions

For many decades the law governing the international carriage of goods by railway has been codified in a number of international conventions. These are frequently referred to as the Berne Conventions. The first international convention concerning the carriage of goods by rail was concluded in Berne in 1890 and came into operation in 1893; after World War I it was replaced by a new convention concluded in 1924, which was again amended by a convention signed in Rome in 1933. This in turn was replaced after World War II by the Berne Convention of 1952. A new convention was signed in Berne in 1961 and came into operation in 1965. The conventions apply whenever goods have been consigned under a through consignment note for carriage over the territories of at least two of the contracting states and on certain specified lines. They regulate mostly the form and conditions of the contract of carriage; its performance, including delivery and payment of the charges; its modifications; the liability of the carrier for delay, loss, or damage; and the enforcement of the contract by actions. Further, the conventions establish the obligation of the railways to carry goods and the rights and obligations of the various railway authorities of the contracting states. Most contracting states have incorporated into their municipal laws rules similar to those of the conventions for the regulation of the domestic carriage of goods by railway.

The Treaty of Rome of March 25, 1957, which created the European Economic Community, contains a number of provisions concerning matters of transport. Members of the Community are specifically bound to develop a common policy in matters of transport. The provisions of the treaty have been largely implemented by a number of international agreements. Since all members of the Common Market are members of the Berne Conventions, the mandate for uniformity of rules governing carriage of goods has been largely achieved as to carriage by railway.

Conflicts of laws

Sea carriage. Until the emergence of modern national states, the law governing maritime commerce had been largely uniform in the Western world. In the 18th and 19th centuries, however, legislative enactments and judicial decisions in pursuit of narrowly conceived national interests gradually displaced in various countries the venerable and uniform law of the sea and gave rise to sharp conflicts of laws. The movement of goods from country to country was thus hampered at a time when advancing technology and the spreading Industrial Revolution were about to lead to an expansion of maritime commerce on a world scale. Beginning with the last decades of the 19th century, it has become increasingly apparent that these conflicts of laws might be overcome by means of international conventions. The law of merchant shipping was quite naturally one of the first branches of private law to attract attention for possible international regulation.

The movement for uniformity culminated in the signing in 1924 of the International Convention for the Unification of Certain Rules of Law Relating to Bills of Lading. The convention was merely intended to unify certain rules of law relating to bills of lading and only with regard to damages occurring to hull cargo other than live animals. All bills of lading covered by the convention are subject to certain standard clauses defining the risks assumed by the carrier, which are absolute and cannot be altered by contrary agreement, and the immunities the carrier can enjoy, unless the parties agree otherwise. In general, clauses relieving the carrier from liability for negligence in loading, handling, stowing, keeping, carrying, and discharging the goods or that diminish his obligation to furnish a seaworthy vessel are declared null and void. The carrier, however, is relieved from liability for negligence in navigation or in the management of the vessel and from the absolute warranty of seaworthiness. The convention was originally intended to apply to all bills of lading issued in any one of the contracting states.

Most maritime nations, including the U.S.S.R., have ratified or adhered to the convention, and others, such as Greece and Indonesia, have enacted domestic legislation incorporating the rules agreed upon in Brussels. Some adhering nations, including Germany, Belgium, Turkey, and The Netherlands, have incorporated the rules of the convention into their commercial codes. Others, including the United States, Japan, Great Britain, and most members of the British Commonwealth, have enacted the rules in the form of special statutes known as Carriage of Goods by Sea Acts. Still others, including France, Italy, Egypt, and Switzerland, have given the convention itself the force of law and in addition have enacted domestic legislation modelled on the convention. The substantive standards governing bills of lading in maritime carriage have become largely uniform in most of the civilized world.

Carriage by air. The Warsaw Convention of 1929, as amended by the Hague Protocol of 1955, exemplifies still another legislative approach to problems raised by the carriage of goods. It constitutes a major step toward international unification of the rules governing carriage of goods by air. The convention applies to international carriage of persons, luggage, and goods for reward, as well as to gratuitous carriage performed by an air-transport undertaking. It applies whether the aircraft is owned by private persons or by public bodies; but, as to aircraft owned by a state directly, application of the convention may be excluded by appropriate reservation. According to the convention, there is an international carriage when the points of departure and destination are located within different contracting states or within the same contracting state but stopping has been agreed upon in another state, even if that state is not a member of the convention. The convention applies during the time the goods are in the charge of the carrier in any aircraft, airfield, or other facility. It does not apply when goods are carried by a land, sea, or inland-water carrier. Most nations, including the United States, Great Britain, and the U.S.S.R., are members of the convention. Only a few nations in South and Central America and in the Middle East have remained outside the convention. Although the convention applies to international carriage only, a great number of contracting states, including France and Great Britain, have made its rules applicable to domestic carriage of goods as well.

The Warsaw Convention

The air carrier is liable under the convention for delay and for the loss of or damage to the goods, provided that the occurrence that caused the prejudice took place during the carriage by air. The carrier is relieved from liability if he proves that he had taken all the necessary measures to avoid the damage or that it was impossible for him to take such measures. Unlike carriers by land and by water, the air carrier is not bound to prove the actual cause of the damage and that the damage was not attributable to his fault. If the cause of the damage remains unknown, there is no recovery. Contractual provisions tending to relieve the carrier from liability are null and void, except those concerning limitation of liability for loss or damage attributed to the inherent vice of the goods. Provisions tending to increase the liability of the carrier, however, are valid.

The convention contains provisions as to the jurisdiction of courts in case action is brought against the carrier and establishes a two-year period of limitation for the bringing of actions. No provision is made for liability of the carrier in case of deviation, for a carrier's lien, or for stoppage in transit, as this term is understood at common law. Accordingly, these matters are governed by the municipal law of the contracting states.

Other international agreements. The international movement of goods may be regulated in certain countries by international agreements other than the Berne Conventions, the Brussels Convention of 1924, or the Warsaw Convention of 1929. The Communist countries in eastern Europe, including the U.S.S.R., have established a uniform regime for the movement of goods by railway that is comparable to that of the Berne Conventions. Since these nations, with the exception of the U.S.S.R., belong to the Berne Conventions as well, it is possible that conflicts may arise as to the scope of application of each convention.

Other agreements in the field include the Geneva Convention of 1956 for the carriage of goods by road. The convention became operative in 1961, and its original membership includes France, Austria, Italy, The Netherlands, and Yugoslavia. It applies to international carriage of goods by road for reward, with the exception of certain items, such as mail. Carriage is international if it involves two countries, one of which is a member of the convention. An original feature of the Geneva Convention is that it covers mixed-carrier transportation. It applies for the whole journey, even if the road vehicle has been carried, without being unloaded, by another means of transport, unless there is proof that the damage occurred in a portion of the journey other than that of carriage by road.

BIBLIOGRAPHY. General works on transportation law include D. PHILIP LOCKLIN, *Economics of Transportation,* 6th ed. (1966); J.H. TEDROW, *Regulation of Transportation,* 6th ed. (1964); WILLIAM L. GROSSMAN, *Fundamentals of Transportation* (1959); FRANK M. CUSHMAN, *Manual of Transportation Law* (1951); and I.L. SHARFMAN, *The Interstate Commerce Commission,* 5 vol. (1931, reprinted 1969). Works dealing with the carriage of goods in general are HENRY N. LONGLEY, *Common Carriage of Cargo* (1967); JOHN MCKNIGHT MILLER, *Freight Loss and Damage Claims,* 3rd ed. (1967). Comprehensive works dealing with carriage of goods by a variety of means of transport are JASPER G. RIDLEY, *The Law of the Carriage of Goods by Land, Sea and Air,* 2nd ed. (1965); R. RODIERE, *Manuel de transports terrestres et aériens* (1969) and *Droit des transports,* 3 vol. (1953–62); PAUL SCAPEL, *Traité théorique et pratique sur les transports par mer, terre, eau-air et fer* (1958). On mixed carrier transportation, see GEORGES O. ROBERT-TISSOT, *Le Connaissement direct* (1957); on carriage of goods by road, rail, and inland water: OTTO KAHN-FREUND, *The Law of Carriage by Inland Transport,* 4th ed. (1965); EDGAR WATKINS, *Shippers and Carriers,* 5th ed., 2 vol. (1962); ALAN LESLIE, *The Law of Transport by Railway,* 2nd ed. (1928); on carriage of goods by sea: W. PAYNE, *Carriage of Goods by Sea,* 8th ed. (1968); W.E. ASTLE, *Shipowners' Cargo Liabilities and Immunities,* 3rd ed. (1967); THOMAS EDWARD SCRUTTON, *Charterparties and Bills of Lading,* 17th ed. (1964); LEON LAVERGNE, *Les Transports par mer,* 3rd ed. (1968); and on carriage of goods by air: H. TARNER, *Air Cargo* (1967); ROBERT M. KANE and ALLAN D. VOSE, *Air Transportation* (1967); BIN CHENG, *The Law of International Air Transport* (1962); JACOB W.F. SUNBERG, *Air Charter* (1961); KURT GRONFORS, *Air Charter and the Warsaw Convention* (1956).

(A.N.Y.)

Carroll, Lewis

An English mathematician and logician, whose real name was Charles Lutwidge Dodgson, Lewis Carroll is the author of two outstanding children's books, *Alice's Adventures in Wonderland* and *Through the Looking-Glass,* which are among the most quoted books in English and are almost alone of their kind in being read and enjoyed as much by adults as by children. They and a pendant, a narrative poem called *The Hunting of the Snark,* carry the art of "nonsense literature" to its highest levels.

By courtesy of the Gernsheim Collection, the University of Texas at Austin

Lewis Carroll, shown holding a camera lens; photograph by Oscar G. Rejlander, 1863.

Charles Dodgson was the eldest son and third child in a family of seven girls and four boys born to Frances Jane Lutwidge, the wife of the Rev. Charles Dodgson. He was born on January 27, 1832, in the old parsonage at Daresbury, Cheshire. His father was perpetual curate there from 1827 until 1843, when he became rector of Croft in Yorkshire—a post he held for the rest of his life (though later he became also archdeacon of Richmond and a canon of Ripon Cathedral).

Daresbury, in the mid-19th century, was a small country village isolated from the industrial development that was beginning to spread over southern Lancashire. The Dodgson children had few friends outside the family but, like many other families in similar circumstances, found little difficulty in entertaining themselves. Charles from the first showed a great aptitude for inventing games to amuse them. With the move to Croft when he was 12 came the beginning of the "Rectory Magazines," manuscript compilations to which all the family were supposed to contribute. In fact, Charles wrote nearly all of those that survive, beginning with *Useful and Instructive Poetry* (1845; published 1954) and following with *The Rectory Magazine* (c. 1850, mostly unpublished), *The Rectory Umbrella* (1850–53), and *Mischmasch* (1853–62; published with *The Rectory Umbrella* in 1932). All are interesting, but only the last two contain items worthy of comparison with the mature works of Lewis Carroll.

Meanwhile, young Dodgson attended Richmond School, Yorkshire (1844–45), and then proceeded to Rugby School (1846–50). He disliked his four years at public school, principally because of his innate shyness, although he was also subjected to a certain amount of bullying; he also endured several illnesses, one of which left him deaf in one ear. After Rugby he spent a further year being tutored by his father, during which time he matriculated at Christ Church, Oxford (May 23, 1850). He went into residence as an undergraduate there on January 24, 1851.

Academic career

Dodgson's academic career was all that could be desired. He excelled in his mathematical and classical studies in 1852; on the strength of his performance in examinations, he was nominated to a studentship (called a scholarship in other colleges). In 1854 he gained a first in mathematical Finals—coming out at the head of the class—and proceeded to a bachelor of arts degree in December of the same year. He was made a "Master of the House" and a senior student (called a fellow in other colleges) the following year and was appointed lecturer in mathematics (the equivalent of today's tutor), a post that he held until he resigned it in 1881. He held his studentship until the end of his life.

As was the case with all fellowships at that time, the studentship at Christ Church was dependent upon his remaining unmarried, and, by the terms of this particular endowment, proceeding to holy orders. Dodgson was ordained a deacon in the Church of England on December 22, 1861. Had he gone on to become a priest he could have married and would then have been appointed to a parish by the college. But he felt himself unsuited for parish work and, though he considered the possibility of marriage, decided that he was perfectly content to remain a bachelor.

Dodgson's child friends

Dodgson's association with children grew naturally enough out of his position as an eldest son with eight younger brothers and sisters. He also suffered from a bad stammer (which he never wholly overcame, although he was able to preach with considerable success in later life) and, like many others who suffer from the disability, found that he was able to speak naturally and easily to children. It is therefore not surprising that he should begin to entertain the children of Henry George Liddell, dean of Christ Church. Alice Liddell and her sisters Lorina and Edith were not, of course, the first of Dodgson's child friends. They had been preceded or were overlapped by the children of the writer George MacDonald, the sons of the poet Alfred, Lord Tennyson, and various other chance acquaintances. But the Liddell children undoubtedly held an especially high place in his affections—partly because they were the only children in Christ Church, since only heads of houses were free both to marry and to continue in residence.

Properly chaperoned by their governess, Miss Prickett (nicknamed "Pricks"—"one of the thorny kind," and so the prototype of the Red Queen in *Through the Looking-Glass*), the three little girls paid many visits to the young mathematics lecturer in his college rooms. As Alice remembered in 1932, they

> used to sit on the big sofa on each side of him, while he told us stories, illustrating them by pencil or ink drawings as he went along. . . . He seemed to have an endless store of these fantastical tales, which he made up as he told them, drawing

busily on a large sheet of paper all the time. They were not always entirely new. Sometimes they were new versions of old stories; sometimes they started on the old basis, but grew into new tales owing to the frequent interruptions which opened up fresh and undreamed-of possibilities.

On July 4, 1862, Dodgson and his friend Robinson Duckworth, fellow of Trinity, rowed the three children up the Thames from Oxford to Godstow, picnicked on the bank, and returned to Christ Church late in the evening: "On which occasion," wrote Dodgson in his diary, "I told them the fairy-tale of *Alice's Adventures Underground*, which I undertook to write out for Alice." Much of the story was based on a picnic a couple of weeks earlier when they had all been caught in the rain; for some reason, this inspired Dodgson to tell so much better a story than usual that both Duckworth and Alice noticed the difference, and Alice went so far as to cry, when they parted at the door of the deanery, "Oh, Mr. Dodgson, I wish you would write out Alice's adventures for me!" Dodgson himself recollected in 1887

how, in a desperate attempt to strike out some new line of fairy-lore, I had sent my heroine straight down a rabbit-hole, to begin with, without the least idea what was to happen afterwards.

The first version of *Alice*

Dodgson was able to write down the story more or less as told and added to it several extra adventures that had been told on other occasions. He illustrated it with his own crude but distinctive drawings and gave the finished product to Alice Liddell, with no thought of hearing of it again. But the novelist Henry Kingsley, while visiting the deanery, chanced to pick it up from the drawing-room table, read it, and urged Mrs. Liddell to persuade the author to publish it. Dodgson, honestly surprised, consulted his friend George MacDonald, author of some of the best children's stories of the period. MacDonald took it home to be read to his children, and his son Greville, aged six, declared that he "wished there were 60,000 volumes of it."

Accordingly, Dodgson revised it for publication. He cut out the more particular references to the previous picnic (they may be found in the facsimile of the original manuscript, later published by him as *Alice's Adventures Underground* in 1886) and added some additional stories, told to the Liddells at other times, to make up a volume of the desired length. At Duckworth's suggestion he got an introduction to John Tenniel, the *Punch* magazine cartoonist, whom he commissioned to make illustrations to his specification. The book was published as *Alice's Adventures in Wonderland* in 1865. (The first edition was withdrawn because of bad printing, and only about 21 copies survive—one of the rarest books of the 19th century—and the reprint was ready for publication by Christmas of the same year, though dated 1866.)

The book was a slow but steadily increasing success, and by the following year Dodgson was already considering a sequel to it, based on further stories told to the Liddells. The result was *Through the Looking-Glass and What Alice Found There* (dated 1872; actually published December 1871), a work as good—or better—than its predecessor.

By the time of Dodgson's death, *Alice* (taking the two volumes as a single artistic triumph) had become the most popular children's book in England: by the time of his centenary in 1932 it was one of the most popular and perhaps the most famous in the world.

There is no answer to the mystery of *Alice*'s success. Many explanations have been suggested, but, like the Mad Hatter's riddle ("The riddle, as originally invented, had no answer at all"), they are no more than afterthoughts. The book is not an allegory; it has no hidden meaning or message, either religious, political, or psychological, as some have tried to prove; and its only undertones are some touches of gentle satire—on education for the children's special benefit and on familiar university types, whom the Liddells may or may not have recognized. Various attempts have been made to solve the "riddle of Lewis Carroll" himself; these include the efforts to prove that his friendships with little girls were some sort of subconscious substitute for a married life, that he showed symptoms of jealousy when his favourites came to tell him that they were engaged to be married, that he contemplated marriage with some of them—notably with Alice Liddell. But there is little or no evidence to back up such theorizing. He in fact dropped the acquaintance of Alice Liddell when she was 12, as he did with most of his young friends. In the case of the Liddells, his friendship with the younger children, Rhoda and Violet, was cut short at the time of his skits on some of Dean Liddell's Christ Church "reforms." For besides children's stories, Dodgson also produced humorous pamphlets on university affairs, which still make good reading. The best of these were collected by him as *Notes by an Oxford Chiel* (1874).

Photographic portraits

Besides writing for them, Dodgson is also to be remembered as a fine photographer of children and of adults as well (notable portraits of the actress Ellen Terry, the poet Alfred, Lord Tennyson, the poet-painter Dante Gabriel Rossetti, and many others survive and have been often reproduced). Dodgson had an early ambition to be an artist: failing in this, he turned to photography. He photographed children in every possible costume and situation, finally making nude studies of them. But in 1880 Dodgson abandoned his hobby altogether, feeling that it was taking up too much time that might be better spent. Suggestions that this sudden decision was reached because of an impurity of motive for his nude studies have been made, but again without any evidence.

Before he had told the original tale of *Alice's Adventures*, Dodgson had, in fact, published a number of humorous items in verse and prose and a few inferior serious poems. The earliest of these appeared anonymously; but in March 1856, a poem called "Solitude" was published over the pseudonym Lewis Carroll. Dodgson arrived at this pen name by taking his own names Charles Lutwidge, translating them into Latin as Carolus Ludovicus, then reversing and retranslating them into English. He used the name afterward for all his nonacademic works. As Charles L. Dodgson, he was the author of a fair number of books on mathematics, none of enduring importance, although *Euclid and His Modern Rivals* (1879) is of some historical interest.

His humorous and other verses were collected in 1869 as *Phantasmagoria and Other Poems* and later separated (with additions) as *Rhyme? and Reason?* (1883) and *Three Sunsets and Other Poems* (published posthumously, 1898). The 1883 volume also contained *The Hunting of the Snark* (first published 1876), a narrative nonsense poem that is rivalled only by the best of Edward Lear. Dodgson died at Guildford, Surrey, on January 14, 1898.

Later in life, Dodgson had attempted a return to the *Alice* vein but only produced *Sylvie and Bruno* (1889) and its second volume *Sylvie and Bruno Concluded* (1893), which has been described aptly as "one of the most interesting failures in English literature." This elaborate combination of fairy-tale, social novel, and collection of ethical discussions is unduly neglected and ridiculed. It presents the truest available portrait of the man. *Alice*, the perfect creation of the logical and mathematical mind applied to the pure and unadulterated amusement of children, was struck out of him as if by chance; while making full use of his specialized knowledge, it transcends his weaknesses and remains unique.

MAJOR WORKS

CHILDREN'S BOOKS: *Alice's Adventures in Wonderland* (1865); *Through the Looking-Glass and What Alice Found There* (1872).

VERSE: *Phantasmagoria and Other Poems* (1869); *The Hunting of the Snark* (1876); *Rhyme? and Reason?* (1883); *The Collected Verse* (1929).

MATHEMATICAL BOOKS: *A Syllabus of Plane Algebraical Geometry* (1860); *Euclid and His Modern Rivals* (1879); *Curiosa Mathematica* (1888–93).

OTHER WORKS: *Sylvie and Bruno*, 2 vol. (1889–93), novel.

BIBLIOGRAPHY. The primary sources are *The Life and Letters of Lewis Carroll*, by his nephew STUART DODGSON COLLINGWOOD (1898); *The Diaries of Lewis Carroll*, 2 vol., ed. and augmented by ROGER LANCELYN GREEN (1953); and *The Letters of Lewis Carroll*, ed. by MORTON N. COHEN and ROGER

LANCELYN GREEN (1973). The best of recent biographies is DEREK HUDSON, *Lewis Carroll* (1954); and the fullest is FLORENCE BECKER LENNON'S, published in 1945 as *Victoria Through the Looking-Glass*, and in a revised edition in 1962 as *The Life of Lewis Carroll*. Other studies of importance include HELMUT GERNSHEIM, *Lewis Carroll: Photographer* (1949); ALEXANDER L. TAYLOR, *The White Knight: A Study of C.L. Dodgson* (1952); ROGER LANCELYN GREEN'S "Bodley Head Monograph," *Lewis Carroll* (1960); and JEAN GATTEGNO, *Lewis Carroll* (1970), in French.

For bibliography, see *The Lewis Carroll Handbook*, by S.H. WILLIAMS and FALCONER MADAN (1931 and rev. by ROGER LANCELYN GREEN in 1962); and for collections of his works, the so-called *Complete Works of Lewis Carroll*, ed. by ALEXANDER WOOLLCOTT (1937); and the fuller, but still not complete, *The Works of Lewis Carroll*, ed. by ROGER LANCELYN GREEN (1965). For special editions of the two *Alice* books, see *The Annotated Alice*, ed. by MARTIN GARDNER (1960); and *Alice*, in the "Oxford English Novels Series," ed. by ROGER LANCELYN GREEN (1971). The manuscript of *Alice's Adventures Underground*, originally given to Alice Liddell, is now in the British Museum; so also are the surviving volumes of his *Diary*. No other major work seems to be extant in manuscript, but the four family magazines and miscellaneous juvenalia and mathematical and logical items are scattered among various collections, mainly in the United States.

(R.L.G.)

Cartesianism

In its broadest sense, Cartesianism is a set of philosophical traditions and scientific attitudes derived from the writings of René Descartes (1596–1650), the father of modern philosophy. The primary doctrine of Cartesianism is the division of reality between mind, the essence of which is thinking, and matter, the essence of which is extension in three dimensions. The ideas of these two substances, plus that of God, whose essence is necessary existence, are innate. Careful examination of these ideas provides a complete Rationalistic metaphysics, or theory of the ultimate nature of Being. The division between mind and matter gives rise, however, to two serious problems in Cartesian metaphysics: how can active, unextended mind interact with passive, extended body? and how can mind contact and thus know matter when the two substances are essentially unlike one another? The various lines of Cartesian philosophy are developed from different answers to these questions.

Descartes's *cogito* and mechanism

Nature of Cartesianism. Descartes is best known for his *cogito:* "I think, therefore I am." This indubitable proposition was the intuitive result of a course of methodic doubt in which the supposed truths of tradition, the senses, and reason were subjected to skeptical attack with the precise goal of refuting Skepticism. The search for certainty in both philosophy and science thus rested on a psychologistic foundation. Ideas—or propositions—that are as clear and distinct as the *cogito* were used to prove the existence of God, to establish the reality of the external world, and to elaborate the sciences of mind and matter.

Descartes denied the intelligibility of Scholastic (medieval Aristotelian philosophical) explanations of physical phenomena that depend on the effects of occult forces and powers, such as those attributing the white colour of objects to an activating quality of whiteness. He also was opposed to any notion of action over a distance, and so denied the existence of a vacuum. Thus, the Cartesians not only opposed the Aristotelians but also the Atomism of Pierre Gassendi, a French Epicurean, and the mitigated Skepticism of the New Scientists—the leaders of the 17th-century scientific revolution—who were satisfied with probabilities.

The present article, however, is concerned not with the philosophy of Descartes (*q.v.*) but with that of his followers.

Cartesian physiologists and physicists followed Descartes by explaining the behaviour of both living and inanimate bodies exclusively in terms of contiguous parts of corpuscular matter in motion. All bodies operate according to mechanistic principles, and all animal bodies —including those of men—are machines. Thus, Cartesianism provided a rationale for experimentation in physics, for vivisection in physiology, and for intensive psychological speculation about man—for man alone in the animal kingdom was said to possess a self-conscious mind in control of a living body.

The first Cartesians were physicists and physicians who applied Descartes's principles to the working out of mechanistic explanations. In Holland, this endeavour led to such vicious disputes as that between the Cartesian physician Regius (Henri de Roy) and the Aristotelian Gisbertus Voetius, a Reformed theologian. In France, the lectures of the Empiricist Pierre-Sylvain Régis on Cartesian physics attracted such attention that Louis XIV forbade them on the ground that civil disturbance could arise from any such general criticism of traditional authority. Throughout Europe, the question of animal machines was debated in a large popular literature; and in England, one of the most widely read expositions of Isaac Newton's physics was a translation of the French dualist Jacques Rohault's treatise on Cartesian physics corrected and annotated with footnotes by the Newtonian moralist Samuel Clarke.

Historical development of Cartesianism. Cartesianism has Neoplatonic roots in the psychologistic philosophy of St. Augustine, who prefigured the aforementioned *cogito*, and in the views of the mathematical physicist Galileo, who made the crucial distinction between the real, quantitative properties of bodies—the so-called primary qualities, such as size, shape, and position—and the sensible properties—the so-called secondary qualities, such as colour, taste, and odour, said to exist only in the perceiving mind. The movement began as a well-orchestrated development. Descartes's philosophical method, and particularly his discoveries in mathematics and his approach in physiology, had been current many years before the publication of his *Meditations* (1641), which was arranged by one of his champions, the influential Rev. Marin Mersenne, to be a century-shaking event. This work was accompanied by seven sets of objections by such distinguished critics as the Materialist Thomas Hobbes, Pierre Gassendi, the Jansenist theologian Antoine Arnauld, and Mersenne himself. These objections, which, together with Descartes's replies, are five times as long as the *Meditations*, set the stage for most further Cartesian controversies. Cartesian writings, letters, and controversies continued to be published long after the master's death.

Malebranche and occasionalism

Mind–matter dualism. The most important philosophical work stemming directly from Descartes's writings is that of Nicolas Malebranche, known as an occasionalist because he held that on the occasion of every perception and motion each such event occurs by God's action. Malebranche denied, however, that he was a Cartesian on several grounds: Descartes taught that the mind is better known than the body, whereas Malebranche claimed (like the Scottish Skeptic David Hume after him) that introspection provides no direct contact with the mind. Descartes also believed that ideas—both notions and sensations—are caused by bodily actions on the mind exerted through the mediation of the pineal gland, near the middle of the brain. Malebranche, on the other hand, being convinced of the objection—urged against the Cartesians most insistently by the Skeptical chaplain Simon Foucher—that Cartesian mind and matter cannot interact, developed a system of occasionalism. This is the view—suggested by Descartes and adopted also in part by Arnold Geulincx, a Flemish convert to Calvinism, and by Géraud de Cordemoy, a Parisian historian and philosopher—that mind and body do not interact but that, on every occasion of their appearing to interact, God causes the appropriate responses in both mind and body. If causal interaction is ruled out, however, so also is the possibility of the mind's knowing bodily properties directly. Because external objects are known for Cartesians only mediately by way of ideas, the Skeptical problem arises of how one can know that ideas are true of their objects. Indeed, Descartes himself raised the spectre of a demon that might cause one to have such ideas even in the absence of an external world. To this last, Malebranche said tersely that the existence of the material world is assured by the first chapter of Genesis.

As for the truth of ideas, Malebranche offered the Platonic view that all ideas actually reside in the mind of God: on the proper occasions, God illuminates these ideas for human observation; thus we see all things in God and rest assured in his goodness.

Orthodox Cartesians followed Malebranche's lead in accepting the dualism of mind and body, but, unlike Malebranche, they continued to insist on the interaction between the two. Régis gave a typical answer to the problem by saying simply that God could make it so, even if the philosopher cannot understand how—a ploy that was taken by his critics as an abdication of philosophy in favour of mysticism. A similar answer was given to the question of how mind could know matter. Accepting Foucher's analysis that the mental representation of an object depends on a resemblance between idea and object and his criticism charging that Cartesian mental ideas cannot resemble material objects, Rohault spoke for orthodox Cartesians in saying that it is simply the nature of ideas to represent their objects: God has made it so that mental ideas represent material objects; thus, no resemblance between the two or any further explanation is necessary.

Applications in religion

Though Thomistic philosophers (followers of St. Thomas Aquinas) had said that the soul or mind is the form of the human body, all Cartesian philosophers emphatically denied this formulation, presenting man as a compound substance formed by the union of mind and body. Beyond the problems of interaction discussed above, this raised the problem of the ultimate nature of man. The French physician Louis de la Forge and several other Cartesians came to the logical conclusion that at death the mind is completely severed from all knowledge of individual bodies; sensations are but confused ideas issuing from this union and are available neither in memory nor in experience when that union is broken. What the soul knows of matter after death is, in this view, only the general disposition of intelligible extension—*e.g.*, the axioms and theorems of solid geometry. Like the notion that animals are mere machines, however, the Cartesian conclusion that the sensible manifestations of this life will be neither continued nor remembered in the next was quite generally unpopular in the 17th century.

Though Descartes explicitly denied any concern with theology, he did offer physical explanations of the Christian doctrine of transubstantiation. It was Rohault, however, who gave the clearest exposition of the mechanistic view that, in the miracle of the Eucharist, the bread and wine are replaced point by point with the flesh and blood of Christ. In the Cartesian view, sensations are produced merely by the configurations of material objects in motion against the sense organs. Flesh and blood, if organized in the configurations of bread and wine, would cause one to have sensations of bread and wine. In this explanation, Thomistic substantial forms that persist despite the absence of underlying substances are unnecessary. Nevertheless, the church was not pleased with this and other Cartesian attacks upon Thomistic-Aristotelian dogma and so banned Descartes's works and forbade the teaching of Cartesianism.

Cartesianism was popularized in England by Antoine Le Grand, a French Franciscan. Though, like Rohault and Régis, he was primarily interested in physics, he attempted to provide expositions of the complete Cartesian philosophy. In response to critics who said that the essence of mind cannot be thinking because it is sometimes thoughtless, he taught, for example, that the mind is always thinking, even when in deep sleep, though these thoughts are not often remembered.

Mechanistic physics. As an example of the mechanistic Cartesian explanations given by Le Grand and others, that of light and colour is typically ingenious. Light was said to consist of tiny globes of highly elastic, subtle matter. In proportion to the speed and spin of the globes, the light is seen in various colours. Moreover, they bounce like tennis balls exactly along lines consistent with mathematical optics. On a grand scale, the entire physical universe consists. in this view, of a plenum of matter of differing degrees of subtlety, whirling at different speeds in vortices as great as that in which the planets sweep around the sun or as small as those of single globes of light. God set this great system going by imparting to it a given quantity of motion that is maintained through all transformations within the universe. The conservation of motion is thus the key to Cartesian-Rationalistic physics: Cartesians recognized the need for experimentation but believed that, if the speeds or amounts of motion and the positions of all portions of matter in the universe were once described for any given time, then simple deductions with reference to the laws of motion would lead to the description of their positions and configurations for any other time. Obviously, only the great mathematical physicist, God, is in a position to make these calculations. The primary cause in this universe is God; secondary causes may not be entirely understood, but they can be adequately described as bumpings among bodies. Thus, whereas Cartesian Rationalism in philosophy depends on the clarity and distinctness of the innate ideas of God, mind, and matter, Cartesian-Rationalistic physics depends on simple mechanistic laws operating in a material world where the quantity of motion is constant.

Vortices and motion

Deterministic ethics. Descartes's moral precepts consisted mostly of prudent advice to adhere to the laws and customs of one's country, station, and religion. Geulincx, however, developed a strict Cartesian ethics based on the deterministic will of God. Although a man can do only what God wills, he is free to accept this willingly or unwillingly. For Geulincx, virtue consists in the humble, diligent, and obedient acceptance of the justice of God's will in the light of reason; sin and evil result from man's egotistic (and futile) stand against God. Human freedom and happiness reside not in action but in the understanding of necessity. Cartesian ethics is thus as deterministic as Cartesian physics.

As a total system, traditional Cartesian philosophy and science were more or less refuted by the end of the 17th century. Cartesian-Rationalistic physics was exceeded in ingenuity and explanatory power by more skeptical empirical physicists. But more than that, Descartes's laws of motion proved to be just wrong, and even Cartesians were forced to admit that the principle of the conservation of motion must be replaced by the Newtonian conservation of energy. The Cartesian metaphysical system was doomed by its failure to solve the problems of its dualism. On more popular grounds, Cartesianism was ridiculed because of its doctrine that animals are machines. And finally, neither theologians nor laymen were satisfied with Cartesian claims to have faith in the doctrines of the church, in the face of the fact that the Cartesian system seemed to deny some of them.

Influence of Cartesianism. Thus, Cartesianism proper should probably be viewed as having flourished only through the time of Régis, who published his *Système* in 1690. Benedict de Spinoza, however, an important secular Jewish Rationalist, is also, on occasion, classed as a Cartesian. Spinoza studied Descartes carefully, concluding that mind and matter cannot interact. His solution was to elevate God to the level of the only existing substance, from which mind and matter emanate as distinct attributes that are parallel in every respect but do not interact. Like Malebranche, Spinoza did not explain how mind and matter can interact but only why they appear to interact. In this broader Cartesian context, another Rationalist, Gottfried Wilhelm Leibniz, also a scientist and diplomat, likewise gave a parallelistic answer. Though the Leibnizian monads, or psychic units of reality, are self-complete and do not interact, each has a pre-established harmony with all the others so that the appearance of interaction is maintained. The Materialist Thomas Hobbes solved the problem by doing away with mind, saying that it is merely an epiphenomenal manifestation of interacting material objects. The phenomentalist George Berkeley, on the other hand, did away with matter, saying that material objects are simply constructions out of the mind's ideas. All of these single-substance systems—Spinoza's God, Leibniz' monads,

Monistic and parallelistic systems

Hobbes' matter, and Berkeley's mind—were developed as major solutions to the problems posed by the Cartesian dualism of mind and matter.

The influence of the distinction between primary and secondary qualities has also been significant. Thus, Galilean–Cartesian–Newtonian science, on the one hand, described primary properties almost exclusively, as does contemporary physics, whereas George Berkeley's phenomenalism, on the other hand, assimilated primary properties to secondary ones. Moreover, the Humean distinction between fact and value issued in part from the exaltation of what is mathematically objective over that which is merely emotional and subjective; and in contemporary philosophy, the primary- and secondary-property distinction is the ground of sense-datum philosophy. In contemporary metaphysics, this distinction returns once again with the *cogito* in the Phenomenology of the German philosopher Edmund Husserl and the Existentialism of the French philosopher and dramatist Jean-Paul Sartre.

Descartes also stands at the base of modern mathematics through his invention of analytic geometry, which laid essential ground for the discovery of the calculus by Leibniz and Newton. Cartesian method was brilliantly elaborated by the Jansenists (followers of the Dutch Catholic predestinarian theologian Cornelius Jansen) Antoine Arnauld and Pierre Nicole in works on logic and grammar that are fundamental to the science of linguistics. Even in ethics, Descartes's prudentialism prefigures the abstracted conservativism of the modern scientific community.

Contemporary significance of Cartesianism. Despite the early demise of the Cartesian system, Descartes's influence has been so broad and pervasive that philosophers in the West can all be said to be Cartesians, just as they are all Greeks, in the sense that, even when they are utterly opposed to Cartesianism, the stances they assume are responses to issues originally posed by Descartes. Descartes's skeptical method and his mathematics helped to underpin the New Science; his methods of analysis and conventional morality have formed Western man's modern consciousness; and his intense desire to master mind and matter is strongly reflected in contemporary thought.

Objections and rejoinders

Two major objections to Cartesianism survive in importance today. As Arnauld was the first to point out, Descartes's proof of the existence of God and thus of the external world is circular: the existence of God is first proved because the idea of God is seen to be clear and distinct; but an undeceiving God's existence is necessary to assure the philosopher of the indubitability of the criterion of clarity and distinctness. One answer to this charge, however, is that the truth that God exists is neither deduced nor dependent on any criterion but is, like the *cogito*, understood in a nondiscursive intuitive moment upon presentation of the idea.

Of more contemporary ferment is the question of the dualism of mind and matter, which most contemporary philosophers deny. Neutral monist positions, holding that the world and man can be described as material or mental depending upon one's interest, were developed by such philosophers as the distinguished logician Bertrand Russell and the U.S. Pragmatist William James; and the American John Dewey and Gilbert Ryle, an outstanding British Analytical philosopher, have made attacks on the dualism based on Pragmatic and behaviouristic principles that stress behavioural responses rather than introspective consciousness. All of these criticisms stem basically from the tradition of British Empiricism. From traditional Thomistic–Aristotelian and Rationalistic backgrounds, similar criticisms have been made by the two foremost medievalists, the French philosophers Étienne Gilson and Jacques Maritain.

The strongest defenders of the dualism of mind and matter continue to be physiologists. Those like the Australian Sir John C. Eccles and Wilfred E. Le Gros Clark, an English primatologist, who have looked deeply into the structure of the brain, sometimes view the mind as an entity existing on a plane other than the material. Their work is related to the widely discussed issue of whether machines can think.

A most important recent revival of Cartesian Rationalism has been made by the U.S. linguist Noam Chomsky. In discussing underlying principles that are basic to all languages, Chomsky argues that human beings can utilize principles that are not learned. Because both the principles and the capacity to use them can be said to be innate ideas, the mind might then be compared to a preprogrammed computer with creative capacities—a view that presents in contemporary form the old Cartesian questions: how can machines think? That is, how can computers be self-conscious? Does the existence of innate ideas prove the existence of God? That is, who—if anyone—programmed the computer?

BIBLIOGRAPHY

Works in English: For sources on René Descartes himself, see the bibliography for the article DESCARTES, RENE. For a guide to the critical literature, much of which is in other languages, see the indispensable work of GREGOR SEBBA, *Bibliographia Cartesiana: A Critical Guide to the Descartes Literature, 1800–1960* (1964). The best background studies for Cartesianism are found in EDWIN ARTHUR BURTT, *The Metaphysical Foundations of Modern Physical Science*, rev. ed. (1954); and RICHARD H. POPKIN, *The History of Scepticism from Erasmus to Descartes* (1960). See J.S. SPINK, *French Free-Thought from Gassendi to Voltaire* (1960), for a general view. Classic studies of Cartesians are found in A.G.A. BALZ, *Cartesian Studies* (1951). RICHARD A. WATSON, *The Downfall of Cartesianism, 1673–1712* (1966), shows the failures of Cartesianism as a complete metaphysical system. Perhaps the best general study of Cartesianism in the broadest sense is NORMAN KEMP SMITH, *Studies in the Cartesian Philosophy* (1902, reprinted 1962), which covers the failure of Rationalism from Descartes through Kant. LEONORA COHEN ROSENFIELD, *From Beast-Machine to Man-Machine*, new and enl. ed. (1968), poses most readably the question whether animals have souls and shows Descartes's important influence on modern physiology. NOAM CHOMSKY, *Cartesian Linguistics* (1966), combines historical exposition with the important claim that Cartesian Rationalism is the best general guide to the study of the language-originating mind of man. An overall study of reactions against Cartesian metaphysics is brilliantly presented by ARTHUR ONCKEN LOVEJOY, *The Revolt Against Dualism* (1930). Finally, GILBERT RYLE, *The Concept of Mind* (1949), uses a critique of Cartesian dualism as a springboard for the presentation of doctrines of contemporary linguistic philosophy and philosophy of mind.

Sources in other languages: JOSEF BOHATEC, *Die cartesianische Scholastik in der Philosophie und reformierte Dogmatik des 17. Jahrhunderts* (1912); FRANCISQUE BOUILLIER, *Histoire de la philosophie cartésienne*, 3rd ed. (1868), a standard source, though somewhat unreliable; E.J. DIJKSTERHUIS *et al.*, *Descartes et le cartésianisme hollandais* (1950); ETIENNE GILSON, *Études sur le rôle de la pensée médiévale dans la formation du système cartésien* (1930); GEORGES MONCHAMP, *Histoire du cartésianisme en Belgique* (1886); PAUL MOUY, *Le Développement de la physique cartésienne, 1646–1712* (1934), for Cartesianism in physics; JOSEPH PROST, *Essai sur l'atomisme et l'occasionalisme dans la philosophie cartésienne* (1907); M.PH. DAMIRON, *Essai sur l'histoire de la philosophie en France, au XVIIe siècle* (1846); GASTON SORTAIS, *Le Cartésianisme chez les jésuites francais au XVIIe et au XVIIIe siècle* (1929) and *La Philosophie moderne depuis Bacon jusqu'à Leibniz* (1920).

(R.A.W.)

Cartier, Jacques

The French mariner Jacques Cartier was among the first to explore the coastline of North America west of the Grand Banks fishing grounds and within the Gulf of St. Lawrence. He appears also to have voyaged to Brazil.

Cartier was born at Saint-Malo in 1491. When King Francis I of France decided in 1534 to send an expedition to explore the northern lands in the hope of discovering gold, spices, and a passage to Asia, Cartier received the commission.

First two voyages

Cartier sailed from Saint-Malo on April 20, 1534, with two ships and 61 men; he explored the Gulf of St. Lawrence as far as Anticosti Island, then seized two Indians at Gaspé and sailed back to France. His report piqued the curiosity of Francis I sufficiently for him to send Cartier back the following year, with three ships and

110 men, to explore further. Guided by the two Indians he had brought back, he sailed up the St. Lawrence as far as Quebec and established a base near an Iroquois village. In September he proceeded with a small party as far as the island of Montreal, where navigation was barred by rapids. He was warmly welcomed by the resident Iroquois, but he spent only a few hours among them before returning to winter at his base. He had, however, learned from the Indians that two rivers led farther west to lands where gold, silver, copper, and spices abounded.

The severity of the winter came as a terrible shock, Quebec being farther south than Paris and no Europeans since the Vikings having wintered that far north on the American continent. Scurvy claimed 25 of Cartier's men. To make matters worse, the explorers earned the enmity of the Iroquois. Thus, in May, as soon as the river was free of ice, they treacherously seized some of the Iroquois chiefs and sailed for France. Cartier was able to report only that great riches lay farther in the interior and that a great river, said to be 800 leagues (about 2,000 miles [3,200 kilometres]) long, possibly led to Asia.

War in Europe prevented Francis I from sending another expedition until 1541. This time, to secure French title against the counterclaims of Spain, he commissioned a nobleman, Jean-François de La Rocque de Roberval, to establish a colony in the lands discovered by Cartier, who was appointed Roberval's subaltern. Cartier sailed first, arriving at Quebec on August 23; Roberval was delayed until the following year. Cartier again visited Montreal, but as before he remained only a few hours and failed to go even the few miles necessary to get beyond the rapids. The subsequent maps based on the knowledge he provided fail to indicate that he had reached a large island at the confluence of the Ottawa and St. Lawrence rivers.

Third voyage

The winter at his new base above Quebec proved as severe as the earlier one. Cartier appears to have been unable to maintain discipline among his men, and their actions again aroused the hostility of the local Indians. But what were thought to be gold and diamonds were found in abundance. In the spring, not waiting for Roberval to arrive with the main body of colonists, Cartier abandoned the base and sailed for France. En route he stopped at Newfoundland where he encountered Roberval, who ordered him back to Quebec. Cartier, however, stole away during the night and continued back to France. There, his gold and diamonds were found to be dross. Roberval enjoyed no better success. After one winter he abandoned the plan to found a colony and returned to France. The disappointment at these meagre results was very great. Not for more than half a century did France again show interest in these new lands.

Cartier received no new commissions from the crown. He apparently spent his remaining years attending to his business affairs at his estate near Saint-Malo, where he died on September 1, 1557. His claim to fame rests on his exploration of the St. Lawrence River to the height of navigation. Yet his failure to proceed any farther (when it would have been easy to do so), his treacherous dealings with the Iroquois, and his leaving Roberval in the lurch, detract somewhat from his stature.

BIBLIOGRAPHY. The journals of Cartier's voyages, in original and translation, were edited by H.P. BIGGAR, *The Voyages of Jacques Cartier* (1924), as was *A Collection of Documents Relating to Jacques Cartier and the Sieur de Roberval* (1930). BERNARD G. HOFFMAN, *Cabot to Cartier* (1961), critically examines the source material. The best account of Cartier's voyages is in MARCEL TRUDEL, *Histoire de la Nouvelle-France: Les vaines tentatives 1524–1603* (1963). Briefer accounts, in English, are contained in J.B. BREBNER, *The Explorers of North America* (1933); and W.J. ECCLES, *The Canadian Frontier, 1534–1760* (1969).

(W.J.E.)

Cartier-Bresson, Henri

The works of the photographer Henri Cartier-Bresson are among the photographic images of the 20th century that linger most persistently: fat picnickers on the banks of the Marne; children of Spain playing in Civil War ruins; a grinning eunuch in Peking. Further, such images helped establish photojournalism as an art form. Cartier-Bresson took things as they came. He had an antipathy for arranged photographs and contrived settings and would not tamper with the image. But his photographs are more than random views of the world. No matter how spontaneous or automatic they were in the moment of making, they depended upon a richly nurtured intuition and a highly selective eye.

Jean Marquis—Magnum

Cartier-Bresson.

Henri Cartier-Bresson was born on August 22, 1908, at Chanteloup, not far from Paris, where he attended school. In 1927–28 he studied in Paris with André Lhote, an artist and critic associated with the Cubist movement. Lhote implanted in him a lifelong interest in painting, a crucial factor in the education of his vision. In 1929 Cartier-Bresson went to Cambridge, where he studied literature and painting.

As a boy, Cartier-Bresson had been initiated into the mysteries of the simple "Brownie" snapshot camera. But his first serious concern with the medium occurred in about 1930, after seeing the work of two major 20th-century photographers, Eugène Atget and Man Ray. Making use of a small allowance, he travelled in Africa in 1931, where he lived in the bush, recording his experiences with a miniature camera. There, he contracted blackwater fever, necessitating his return to France. The portability of a small camera and the ease with which one could record instantaneous impressions must have struck a sympathetic chord, and in 1933 he purchased his first 35-millimetre Leica. The use of this type of camera was particularly relevant to Cartier-Bresson. It lent itself not only to spontaneity but to anonymity as well. So much did Cartier-Bresson wish to remain a silent, and even unseen, witness, that he covered the bright chromium parts of his camera with black tape to render it less visible, and he sometimes hid the camera under a handkerchief. The man was similarly reticent about his life and work.

Preference for the 35-millimetre camera

In more than 40 years as a photographer, Cartier-Bresson wandered continually around the world. But there was nothing compulsive about his travels, and he explicitly expressed a desire to move slowly, to "live on proper terms" in each country, to take his time, so that he became totally immersed in the environment.

In 1937, the year of his marriage to Mlle. Ratna Mohini, Cartier-Bresson produced a documentary film, his first, on medical aid in the Spanish Civil War. The date also marked his first reportage photographs made for newspapers and magazines. His enthusiasm for film making was further gratified when, from 1936 to 1939, he worked as an assistant to the film director Jean Renoir in the production of *Une Partie de campagne* ("Picnic") and *La Règle du jeu* (*The Rules of the Game*). As a photographer he felt indebted to the great films he saw as a youth. They taught him, he said, to choose precisely the expressive moment, the telling viewpoint. The importance he gave to sequential images in still photography may be attributed to his preoccupation with film.

In 1940, during World War II, Cartier-Bresson was taken prisoner by the Germans. He escaped in 1943 and the following year participated in a French underground photographic unit assigned to record the German occupation and retreat. In 1945 he made a film for the U.S. Office of War Information, *Le Retour*, which dealt with the return to France of released prisoners of war and deportees.

Though Cartier-Bresson's photographs had been exhibited in 1933 in the prestigious Julien Levy Gallery in New York City, a more important tribute was paid to him in 1947, when a one-man exhibition was held in that city's Museum of Modern Art.

The same year, Cartier-Bresson, in partnership with the U.S. photographer Robert Capa and others, founded the cooperative photo agency known as Magnum Photos. The organization offered periodicals global coverage by some of the most talented photojournalists of the time. Under the aegis of Magnum, Cartier-Bresson concentrated more than ever on reportage photography. The following three years found him in India, China, Indonesia, and Egypt. This material and more, taken in the 1950s in Europe, formed the subjects of several books published between 1952 and 1955. Such publications helped considerably to establish Cartier-Bresson's reputation as a master of his craft. One of them, and perhaps the best known, *Images à la sauvette* (*The Decisive Moment*), contains what is probably Cartier-Bresson's most comprehensive and important statement on the meaning, technique, and utility of photography. The title refers to a central idea in his work—the decisive moment—the elusive instant when, with brilliant clarity, the appearance of the subject reveals in its essence the significance of the event of which it is a part, the most telling organization of forms.

Books and exhibitions

He was singularly honoured by his own country in 1955, when a retrospective exhibition of 400 of his photographs was held in the Musée des Arts Décoratifs, Paris, and was then displayed in Europe, the United States, and Japan before the photographs were finally deposited in the Bibliothèque Nationale in Paris.

In the mid-1960s Cartier-Bresson continued to live in Paris and to make frequent trips abroad. In 1963 he was photographing in Cuba; in 1963–64 he was in Mexico, and in 1965, India. The French film maker Louis Malle recalled that, during the student revolt in Paris, in May 1968, Cartier-Bresson was there with his 35-millimetre camera, but despite the explosive activities, he took photographs at the rate of about four per hour.

In recent years Cartier-Bresson diverted most of his interest to making motion pictures. He believed that still photography and its use in pictorial magazines was, to a large extent, being superseded by television. On principle, he always avoided developing his own prints, convinced that the technical exigencies of photography were a harmful distraction. Similarly, he directed the shooting of films and did not wield the camera himself. With this medium, however, he was no longer able to work unobtrusively by himself.

His Leica—his notebook, as he called it—accompanied him wherever he went, and, consistent with his training as a painter, he always carried a small sketch pad. There was for Cartier-Bresson a kind of social implication in the camera. To his mind, photography provided a means, in an increasingly synthetic epoch, for preserving the real and humane world.

BIBLIOGRAPHY. Collections of Cartier-Bresson's work may be found in the Bibliothèque Nationale, Paris; the Museum of Modern Art, New York; and the George Eastman House, Rochester. A useful bibliography and several perceptive essays are included in LINCOLN KIRSTEIN and BEAUMONT NEWHALL, *The Photographs of Henri Cartier-Bresson* (1947). In more recent editions the bibliographies have been deleted. A selected bibliography appears in NATHAN LYONS (ed.), *Photographers on Photography* (1966), where also the complete text of Cartier-Bresson's essay in his *Decisive Moment* (1952) is reproduced. No complete biography of Cartier-Bresson exists. The present literature deals mainly with the character of his work. BEAUMONT NEWHALL, "The Instant Vision of Henri Cartier-Bresson," *Camera*, 34:485–489 (1955), is a valuable discussion of the photographer's equipment and manner of working. See also CARTIER-BRESSON's work, *The World of Henri Cartier-Bresson* (1968).

(A.Sc.)

Carver, George Washington

A distinguished agricultural chemist and experimenter, George Washington Carver became a public benefactor of the entire American South and a black hero of popular history whose name has been appropriated by almost as many black schools, lodges, clubs, movie theatres, banks, and insurance companies as that of the famous educator Booker T. Washington. Adjusting himself to what he considered a transient racial situation in the South, Carver attempted to prepare rural Negroes for full citizenship rights by teaching them how to become skilled farmers and useful citizens. He dedicated his life to making Tuskegee Institute, Tuskegee, Alabama, an instrument of ministry to the needs of these people, and, in the process, he became an outstanding teacher, artist, humanitarian, and prophet.

Early life and education. Carver was born near Diamond Grove, Missouri, early in the 1860s, the son of a slave woman owned by Moses Carver. During the Civil War, slave owners found it difficult to hold slaves in the border state of Missouri, and Moses Carver, therefore, sent his slaves, including the young child and his mother, to Arkansas. After the Civil War, Moses Carver learned that all his former slaves had disappeared except for a child named George who had become ill with whooping cough. Frail and sick, the motherless child was returned to his former master's home and nursed back to health. The boy had a delicate sense of colour and form and learned to draw; later in life he was to devote considerable time to painting flowers, plants, and landscapes. He also became well-known among the blacks as a singer and organist. Though the Carvers told him he was no longer a slave, he remained on their plantation until he was about ten or 12 years old, when he left to acquire an education. He spent some time wandering about, working with his hands and developing his keen interest in plants and animals.

By both books and experience, George acquired a fragmentary education. Throughout his adolescence he was a stranger in a strange land, doing whatever work came to hand in order to subsist. The diversity of Carver's talents, later demonstrated in his scientific work, was forecast in these early years of wandering, when he supported himself by varied occupations that included general household worker, hotel cook, laundryman, farm labourer, and homesteader. In his late 20s, he managed to obtain a high school education in Minneapolis, Kansas, by working as a farmhand. After a university in Kansas refused to admit him because he was black, Carver matriculated at Simpson College, Indianola, Iowa, where he studied piano and art, subsequently transferring to Iowa State Agricultural College, where he received a degree in agricultural science in 1894 and a master of science degree in 1896.

Tuskegee Institute. Drawn to Tuskegee Institute because he believed its industrial type of education would help solve the race problem, Carver left Iowa for Alabama in the fall of 1896 to head the school's newly organized department of agriculture. He had learned of Booker T. Washington's efforts at Tuskegee to achieve the best interests of the black man through education rather than by political agitation and had been deeply moved by the educator's speeches, which tended to stress conciliation, compromise, and economic development for the black man. Despite many offers elsewhere, Carver remained at Tuskegee because he believed in its destiny as an institution for black people.

Influence of Booker T. Washington

After becoming the Institute's director of agricultural research in 1896, he devoted his life to research projects aimed primarily at helping Southern agriculture. During his early years as an administrator, he spent most of his time demonstrating ways in which the Southern farmer could improve his economic situation. As an administrator Carver was unable to get along with his colleagues. He clashed not only with other members of the Tuskegee administration and faculty but even with Washington. He was, furthermore, unable to keep his department financially solvent. Nonetheless, his great ability and rare talents in other fields were unquestioned, and he was praised for his capacity as a teacher, lecturer, and experimenter, as well as for his unusual ability to demonstrate the use of various foods and their preservation. By 1910, however, Booker T. Washington had relieved him of his administrative duties, and Carver was able to devote most of his time to research.

Development of products from peanut and soybean

Products he derived from such soil-enriching crops as the peanut and the soybean helped to revolutionize the economy of the South by liberating it from excessive dependence on cotton, which depleted the soil. Peanuts and soybeans, since they belong to the legume family, could restore nitrogen to the soil and provide proteins essential for better health for farmers. When he arrived at Tuskegee in 1896, the peanut had not even been recognized as a crop. Within the next half century it became one of the six leading crops throughout the U.S., and in the South, the second cash crop (after cotton) by 1940. In 1942 the U.S. government allotted 5,000,000 acres of peanuts to farmers. Carver's research program ultimately developed 300 derivative products from peanuts—among them cheese, milk, coffee, flour, ink, dyes, plastics, wood stains, soap, linoleum, medicinal oils, and cosmetics—and 118 from sweet potatoes, including flour, vinegar, molasses, rubber, ink, a synthetic rubber, and postage stamp glue. He also succeeded in making synthetic marble from wood pulp. His exhibits were displayed throughout the South.

Among Carver's many honours were his election as a fellow of the London Royal Society for the Encouragement of Arts, Manufactures, and Commerce in 1916 and his receipt of the Spingarn Medal in 1923. Late in his career, Carver declined an invitation to work for Thomas A. Edison at a salary of over $100,000 a year. Presidents Calvin Coolidge and Franklin Roosevelt visited him, and his friends included Henry A. Wallace, a vice president under Franklin Roosevelt, Henry Ford, and Mahatma Gandhi. Foreign governments requested his counsel on agricultural matters: Joseph Stalin, for example, in 1931 invited him to Russia to superintend cotton plantations in southern Russia and to make a tour of the U.S.S.R., but Carver refused.

Reputation. Many scientists and some blacks were critical of Carver. Scientists thought of him more as a concoctionist than as a contributor to scientific knowledge and regarded with suspicion his reference to God as a collaborator in the laboratory. Though only a few blacks envied Carver's success, many were critical of his humility and regarded him as subservient—an Uncle Tom. Finally, this small, mild, soft-spoken, innately modest man, eccentric in dress and mannerism, who attempted to live up to Christian teachings, seemed unbelievable because he gave the impression that he disregarded the conventional pleasures and rewards of this life.

These qualities endeared Carver to many whites, who were almost invariably pleased by his humble demeanour and his quiet role in attending strictly to his work in self-imposed segregation at Tuskegee. As a result of his accommodation to the mores of the South, whites came to reward him with a sort of patronizing adulation. While he worked in the Deep South until his death at Tuskegee on January 5, 1943, people approached Carver as if he were part saint, part scientist, and part performing bear. The pattern of race relations at that time tended to distort the real significance of the contribution of black scientists and scholars, and Carver became increasingly a symbol of the intellectual achievements of Negroes. He fulfilled the white man's conception of the Negro, and he played a convenient role in "interracial politics." Accordingly, Carver's public image was built into that of an intellectual giant. His great desire in later life, nevertheless, was simply to serve humanity; and his work, which began for the sake of the poorest of the Negro sharecroppers, paved the way for a better life for the entire South. His efforts brought about a significant advance in agricultural training in an era when agriculture was the largest single occupation of Americans, and he extended Tuskegee's influence throughout the South by encouraging improved farm methods, diversification, and conservation.

Role as symbol to his race

BIBLIOGRAPHY. RACKHAM HOLT, *George Washington Carver: An American Biography*, rev. ed. (1963), although impressionistic, is still the most useful for adult readers. LAWRENCE ELLIOTT, *George Washington Carver: The Man Who Overcame* (1966), largely superficial and uncritical, emphasizes Carver's career during the 1920s and 1930s. ARNA WENDELL BONTEMPS, *The Story of George Washington Carver* (1954), is addressed to a juvenile audience, written with restraint and sensitivity. The George Washington Carver Papers and the Robert Russa Moton Papers are located at the Tuskegee Institute in Alabama. The Booker T. Washington Papers, located in the Library of Congress, are rich in Carver material from 1896 to 1915.

(J.L.Ki.)

Caryophyllales

The order Caryophyllales includes a wide variety of dicotyledonous plants (plants whose embryos have two leaves), ranging from attractive garden subjects and vegetables to bizarre succulent plants that resemble stones. The garden plants include carnations, pinks, four-o'clocks, amaranths, portulacas, and Madeira vines. Vegetables in the order include beet, spinach, rhubarb, and buckwheat. The carpetweed family (Aizoaceae) includes ice plants, sea figs, and living stones. Some authorities include the cacti (as the family Cactaceae) in this order as well; however, in view of evidence to the contrary and because the cacti are of such general interest, they are dealt with separately (see CACTALES).

General features. The name of the order is derived from that of the pink family, Caryophyllaceae, which was based upon a pre-Linnaean genus, *Caryophyllus*. The number of species in the order has been estimated between 6,500 and 8,500, depending upon the interpretation of the order; *i.e.*, which families are included in it and particularly whether the cactus family (Cactaceae) and the buckwheat family (Polygonaceae) are included. In this treatment of the order, the Cactaceae are excluded and the Polygonaceae are included.

The Caryophyllales include mostly herbs, but various families have shrubs, vines, and trees. On the whole, the order is not noted for the size attained by its members. Commonly, the species are most prevalent in moist temperate or tropical environments, but many members of the goosefoot family (Chenopodiaceae) are restricted to salty, alkaline soil. In some salt tolerant species, the leaves are succulent (fleshy). Leaf succulence is also common in the family Aizoaceae and remarkably so in its numerous South African members.

Ecological patterns

Natural history. The most striking single ecological feature in the order is the dominance of the Chenopodiaceae in alkaline situations and the prominence of succulent Aizoaceae in the deserts of southern Africa. The other members of the order occur in any of several types of vegetation, but in general none is conspicuous. Even the Aizoaceae in the southern African deserts are not conspicuous except when they are in flower.

Characteristic geographical distribution patterns occur in individual families, but none is typical of the order as a whole. The poke family (Phytolaccaceae) and the Madeira-vine family (Basellaceae) include plants primarily of the American tropics. The amaranth family (Amaranthaceae) is most highly developed in tropical America and tropical Africa. The four-o'clock family (Nyctaginaceae) is common throughout the tropics but occurs also in the warmer temperate regions. The carpetweed family (Aizoaceae) occurs over most of the Earth, but its chief centre of distribution is in desert and temperate latitudes of southern Africa. The Caryophyllaceae (pink family),

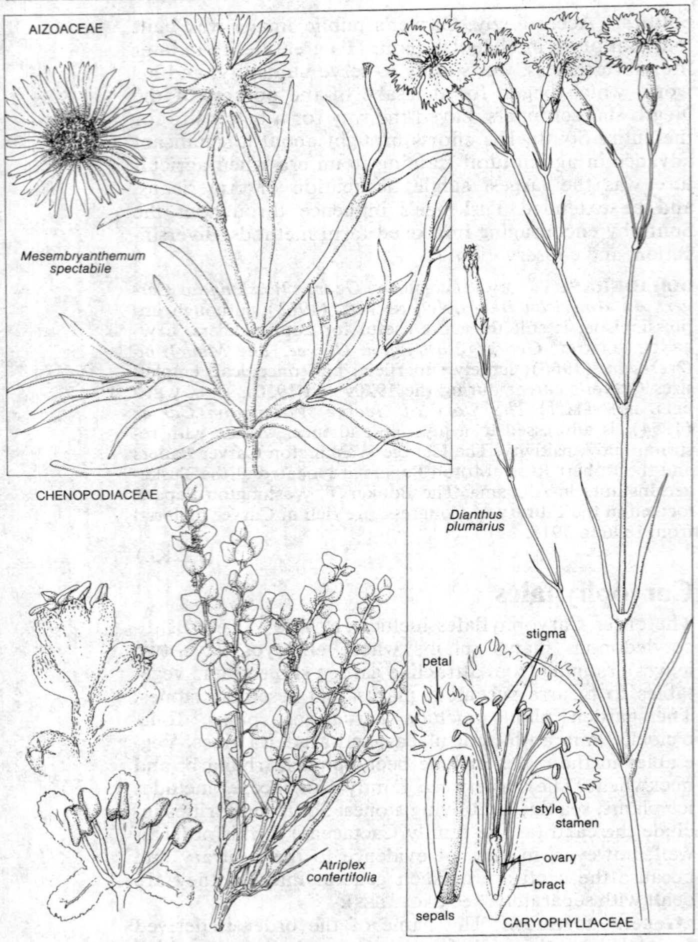

Figure 1: Representative plants from the three largest families of the pink order.
Drawing by M. Pahl

the Portulacaceae (portulaca family), and the Polygonaceae (buckwheat family) are characteristic of temperate regions. The goosefoot family (Chenopodiaceae) occurs throughout the world, but its greatest development is in salty or alkaline areas, particularly those of coastal salt marshes and deserts.

Form and function. *Vegetative characteristics.* The external vegetative characteristics of the plants in the Caryophyllales vary greatly; no specific feature can be singled out as indicative of the group. Certain tendencies are noteworthy but not distinguishing. Only rarely do the leaf bases bear stipules (leaflike tabs). Succulents occur in the Aizoaceae and in the Didiereaceae (a small Madagascan family), as well as in some of the Portulacaceae, Chenopodiaceae, Basellaceae, and Phytolaccaceae. Absence of stipules is almost a distinguishing characteristic of the order, but the presence of succulent tissues is not.

Two internal vegetative features characterize many members of the Caryophyllales. Eight of the families have some members in which conductive tissues (xylem and phloem) are produced from generative tissue called cambium at various depths inside the stem or the root, rather than only at the position of this tissue in most other plants. This produces additional cambial layers, as readily seen in a cross section of a beet root. Despite the commonness of this feature, it has not been proved to occur in all members of the order.

Pigments

The second internal feature is the chemical uniqueness of pigmentation in many of the Caryophyllales. In most flowering plants colours ranging from nearly red to nearly blue (*i.e.*, from violet to purple) are dependent upon the presence of chemical compounds called anthocyanins; colours ranging from yellow to reddish orange are dependent upon compounds called anthoxanthins. A distinct but parallel series of pigments occurs only in a large number of Caryophyllales and the cacti. These substances, known as betalains, include betacyanins, which produce colours from near red to near blue, and betaxanthins, which produce colours in the yellow to reddish-orange series. The presence of betacyanins especially, rather than anthocyanins, is presumed to be of taxonomic significance. Betacyanins have been found in many of the Caryophyllales but not in any members of the family Caryophyllaceae or the Molluginoideae (a group sometimes considered to be a separate family but included here as a subfamily in the Aizoaceae). Their presence also in the cacti is an indication of the relationship of these plants to the Caryophyllales and has led some authorities to include the cacti in this order.

Drawing by M. Pahl

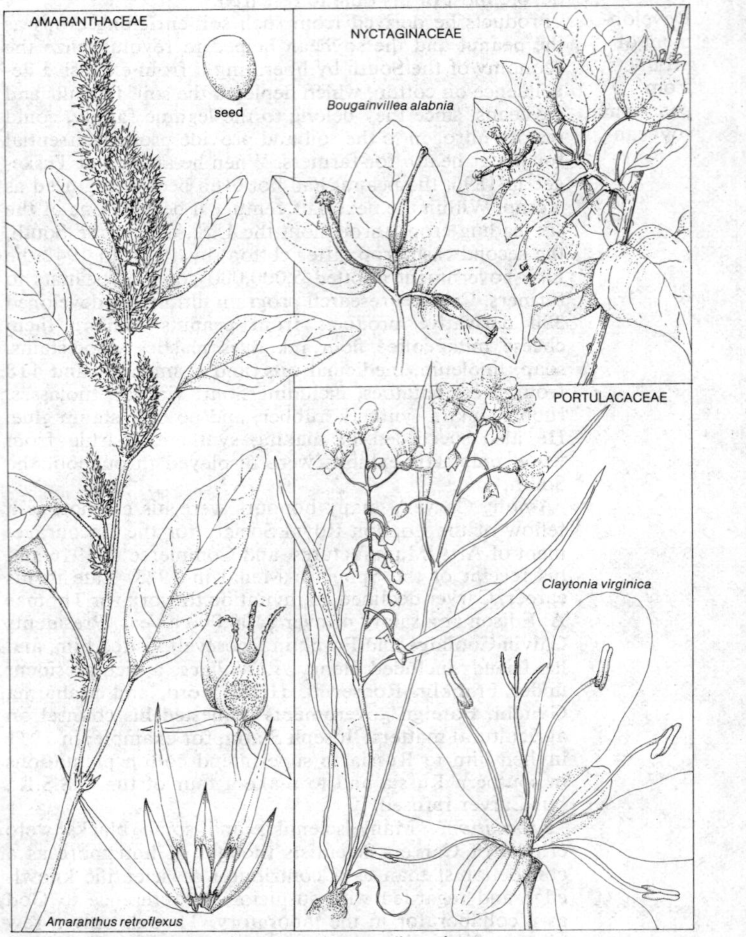

Figure 2: Representative plants from three medium-sized families of the pink order.

Reproductive characteristics. Throughout most of the order, the flowers have true sepals (modified petallike structures) but no true petals (*i.e.*, not embryologically derived from petal primordia). Some families that display what appear to be petals (Portulacaceae, Nyctaginaceae) are thought to have greatly modified sepals, in which case the sepallike appendages are then interpreted as bracts (specialized leaves subtending flowers). The Caryophyllaceae, however, apparently have true petals developed by the usual means; that is, through modification of individual stamens (the male parts of a flower) or portions of them. This is the only family in the order that, so far as has been determined, has ordinary petals.

In most members of the order, the stamens are in one or two series (concentric circles around the central axis of the flower) or sometimes in three series of three; in some cases, however, as in many of the Aizoaceae, there are numerous stamens.

The carpels (specialized leaves each forming all or part of a pistil, the female part of the flower) are united and commonly enclose a single seed chamber, but there may be three to 12, one for each carpel. Usually, there are as many styles—extensions above a plant ovary bearing stigmas, structures that receive pollen grains at their tips—as carpels, and they are not united. The structure and positioning of the ovule in most members of the Caryophyllales differ from the common type in the flowering plants in being curved or coiled in a special way. The ovule is surrounded by two coverings (integuments), the inner being longer than the outer. The embryo lies toward the outside of the ovule, surrounding the food-storage tissue, which usually is not formed from a nutritive tissue (endosperm) during fertilization, as in most flowering plants. Commonly, most of the food is stored in the perisperm. The features of the ovules, embryos, and seeds are similar to those of the cacti, which further strengthens the case for a relationship of the two groups.

The placenta (the tissue that bears the ovules) in many Caryophyllales is either basal and low or forms a column arising from the base of the ovary. This type of placenta is rare in other orders of flowering plants. It does occur in the Primulales, probably indicating some relationship of these two orders.

Evolution and classification. *Evolution.* As is true of most other chiefly herbaceous orders of flowering plants, the Caryophyllales have left virtually no fossil record. Any evidence, therefore, of phylogeny must come primarily from a consideration of the living members of the order. The origin of the Caryophyllales, in consequence, is largely a matter of speculation. The order was presumably derived from the ancestral complex of the buttercup order (Ranales), but the present relationship of these orders is not close, and the lines of origin of the Caryophyllales are obscure.

Distinguishing taxonomic features. Consideration for inclusion in the order rests primarily upon such matters as absence of stipules (basal appendages of leafstalks), an unusual arrangement of cambial tissue, and the wide occurrence in the order of betalains, a unique class of pigment compounds. Disposition into families is based chiefly upon floral features such as numbers of parts and position of the ovary with regard to the floral envelope. Of taxonomic significance also are the number and position of ovules and the type of fruit.

Annotated classification.

ORDER CARYOPHYLLALES

Dicotyledonous plants; herbs, less frequently shrubs, rarely vines or trees. Flowers typically perfect (with male and female parts) but usually lacking true petals (except in the Caryophyllaceae and in some Aizoaceae). Betalain pigments occurring in most families. There are 10 to 16 families (depending on the authority); with more than 300 genera and between 6,500 and 8,500 species (an accurate figure is not possible because of the differences in interpretation of taxa by different authorities). Distribution is worldwide, with a concentration of species in the tropics and subtropics.

Family Phytolaccaceae (pokes)

Herbs, shrubs, trees, or rarely woody vines. Leaves simple, entire (with a continuous margin), alternate; stipules lacking or much reduced. Flowers commonly bisexual (but the plants sometimes monoecious), almost always radially symmetrical, hypogynous (borne under the ovary); epigynous (seemingly upon the ovary) in *Agdestis;* often arranged in racemes (stalked flower clusters with lowest flowers blooming first) or cymes (flower clusters with the terminal, or central, flower opening first); sepals (modified petallike structures) 4–5, persisting after flowering; no petals. Stamens (male parts of flowers) mostly 3–10, sometimes more, commonly in 1 or 2 series; carpels (specialized leaves each forming all or part of a pistil, the female part of the flower) 1–15 but usually 5–12. Ovary single, divided into chambers according to the number of carpels; placentation axile (ovules borne at or near the centre of the ovary) unless there is a single carpel; ovules solitary in the carpels. Fruit dry or fleshy, an achene (small, with tight, firm wall, or pericarp), utricle (bladderlike), berry, or drupe (stone fruit), the carpels separating at maturity. About 15 or 20 genera and 100 to 150 species; includes *Phytolacca* (the pokes). Centre of distribution is tropical America.

Family Aizoaceae (carpetweeds)

Herbs or small shrubs. Leaves simple, often succulent, opposite, but rarely appearing to be in whorls; stipules rarely present. Flowers bisexual, radially symmetrical; sepals 5–8, united; true petals absent, but with numerous staminodia (sterile stamens) resembling petals. Stamens 5 or numerous. Carpels 3–20, the ovary commonly with as many chambers, the styles (prolongations of plant ovaries bearing stigmas, which receive pollen grains at their tips) separate; placenta usually axile, ovules numerous. Fruit usually a dry capsule but sometimes leathery or berrylike. The number of genera and species described is great and dubious, having been subdivided beyond recognition, because members of the family (especially of the Ficoideae) are popular in horticulture. About 1,500 to 3,000 species is an estimate; includes *Mesembryanthemum* (ice plants) and *Lithops* (living stones). Chief distributional centre in southern Africa, where there is a special abundance of Ficoideae.

Family Nyctaginaceae

Herbs, shrubs, or trees. Leaves simple, entire, usually opposite; stipules lacking. Flowers usually bisexual, rarely otherwise, radially symmetrical, hypogynous or sometimes perigynous (or capable of being interpreted as perigynous); single flowers or flower clusters often surrounded by a calyxlike involucre of 2 to 5 leaflike or highly coloured bracts; sepals 5, often united and elongated, appearing as a corolla (or petals); stamens commonly 5 but sometimes 1 to 3. Carpel 1; ovule solitary. Fruit dry, an achene, commonly enclosed in the hardened persistent lower part of the calyx (the sepals as a group). From 25 to 30 genera with 200 or 300 species, includes *Mirabilis* (four-o'clocks) and *Bougainvillea.* Distributional centre is the tropics and warm regions of the world.

Family Polygonaceae

Herbs, shrubs, or trees, but rarely vines. Leaves simple, alternate; stipules usually present and sheathing the stem. Flowers nearly always bisexual, radially symmetrical, arranged in panicles, spikes, heads, or cymes; sepals 3–6, usually in 2 series of 3; petals usually 3. Stamens in 2 or 3 series of 3. Ovary 1-chambered; 1 ovule, basal. Fruit dry, usually a 3-angled achene. About 30 genera with perhaps 800 species; includes *Polygonum*, *Fagopyrum* (buckwheat) and *Rheum* (rhubarb). Chief distributional centre is the temperate region.

Family Chenopodiaceae

Herbs or shrubs, rarely small trees. Stems and leaves usually scurfy with drying external cells forming white scales. Leaves simple, sometimes succulent or scalelike, nearly always alternate; stipules absent. Flowers nearly always bisexual but sometimes staminate and pistillate and on the same plant, nearly always radially symmetrical; sepals ordinarily 5 but sometimes absent; petals absent. Stamens usually 5. Carpels commonly 2 but sometimes 3; styles commonly 2; ovary with a single chamber and a single ovule. Fruit dry at maturity, an achene or a utricle; embryo curved or coiled. About 100 genera and about 1,500 species; includes *Beta* (beets), *Spinacia* (spinach), and *Kochia.* Found particularly in alkaline habitats in North and South America, the Middle East, southern Africa, and Australia.

Family Amaranthaceae (amaranths)

Commonly herbs, rarely shrubs, trees, or vines. Leaves simple, commonly entire, either alternate or opposite; stipules absent. Flowers usually bisexual, radially symmetrical, commonly subtended by membranous bracts that persist in fruit; sepals usually 5, membranous, dry and persistent in fruit; petals absent. Stamens usually 5, the anthers (pollen-bearing structures) sometimes with only 2 (instead of the usual 4) pollen chambers. Carpels 2, rarely 3–5; ovary with a single chamber and a single basal ovule. Fruit a utricle, nutlet, or capsule, rarely a drupe or berry. From 50 to 60 genera and 500 to 800 species; include *Amaranthus* and *Celosia* (cockscomb). Centred in the American and African tropics.

Family Portulacaceae (portulacas)

Herbs, rarely small shrubs. Leaves simple, often more or less succulent, alternate or opposite, commonly forming basal rosettes; stipules commonly present and threadlike. Flowers bisexual, radially symmetrical, hypogynous or epigynous; apparent "sepals" (probably bracts) 2, petallike sepals 2–6; true petals absent. Stamens usually 5, opposite the sepals; carpels usually 2 but sometimes 3; ovary with a single chamber with several to numerous ovules; basal placentation. Fruit dry, usually splitting lengthwise, but sometimes opening by a terminal lid. Perhaps 15 genera and 250 species; includes *Portulaca* (rose moss) and *Lewisia* (bitterroot). Geographical centres are Pacific North America and southern South America.

Family Basellaceae

Herbaceous, perennial, somewhat woody vines, sometimes more or less succulent. Leaves simple, sometimes succulent, alternate; stipules absent. Flowers bisexual, radially symmetrical, hypogynous, arranged in cymes, racemes, or panicles;

sepallike bracts in a pair resembling a calyx; petallike sepals commonly 5, usually coloured and persistent at fruiting time; true petals absent. Stamens 5. Carpels 3; ovary with a single chamber and only 1 ovule. Fruit fleshy, a drupe; embryo forming a circle or a spiral. Five genera consisting of about 15 to 25 species; includes *Boussingaultia* (Madeira vine). Centred in the New World tropics.

Family Caryophyllaceae (pinks)

Herbs, but stems often woody at the bases. Leaves simple, usually opposite; stipules absent. Flowers bisexual, radially symmetrical, hypogynous, in complex (or simple) inflorescences; sepals 5 (rarely 4); petals 5 (rarely 4), separate. Stamens 3–10; ovary commonly 1-chambered but 2–5 chambered or partly so in the subfamily Sileneae; ovules usually numerous. Fruit dry, a capsule. About 75 genera and perhaps 2,000 species; includes *Dianthus* (pinks and carnations), *Lychnis* (campions), *Gypsophila* (baby's breath), and *Saponaria* (soapwort, or bouncing Bet). Of almost worldwide occurrence in temperate regions.

Family Didiereaceae (didiereas)

Trees with soft wood and with spines. Leaves simple, alternate; stipules absent. Flowers unisexual (plants dioecious), radially symmetrical, hypogynous; sepals petaloid; doubtful true petals 2. Stamens 8–10, basally somewhat united. Carpels 2; ovary with only 1 of the 3 chambers developing; ovules solitary, erect. Fruit 3-sided. Three genera native to Madagascar. This family is of uncertain relationships.

Critical appraisal. In some classifications six additional families are included as follows (their disposition in this article follows in parentheses): Gyrostemonaceae (Phytolaccaceae), Bataceae (Phytolaccaceae), Molluginaceae (Aizoaceae), Tetragoniaceae (Aizoaceae), Halophytaceae (Chenopodiaceae), and Hectorellaceae (Portulacaceae). The Polygonaceae are separated by some as the order Polygonales. The families Batidaceae and Thelygonaceae are sometimes grouped with the Caryophyllales but may be separated under orders of their own. The proposed alliance of the cacti with certain succulent members of the Aizoaceae (subfamily Ficoideae) is based on similarity of pollen grains, the presence of betacyanins, and distinctive common features of the ovules and embryos. The differences that serve to separate the cacti are dealt with in the article CACTALES.

BIBLIOGRAPHY. General reference works that list sources bearing on a specific member of the order include; L. BENSON, *Plant Classification* (1957); A. CRONQUIST, *The Evolution and Classification of Flowering Plants* (1968); G.H.M. LAWRENCE, *Taxonomy of Vascular Plants* (1951); and A. TAKHTAJAN, *Flowering Plants: Origin and Dispersal* (1969; Eng. trans. from the 2nd Russian ed., 1961).

Specific works on constituent families include: P.C. STANDLEY, "Chenopodiaceae," *N. Am. Flora*, 21:1–93 (1916); A.C. JOSHI, "Contribution to the Anatomy of the Chenopodiaceae and Amaranthaceae," *J. Indian Bot. Soc.*, 10:213–265 (1931); F. PAX and K. HOFFMAN, "Aizoaceae," in A. ENGLER and K. PRANTL, *Die natürlichen Pflanzenfamilien*, 16c:179–233 (1934); P.A. RYDBERG, "Portulacaceae," *N. Am. Flora*, 21: 279–336 (1932); and B. MAGUIRE, "Studies in the Caryophyllaceae," *Bull. Torrey Bot. Club*, 73:326 (1946).

(L.Be.)

Casablanca

Casablanca (or White House; Arabic, ad-Dār al-Bayḍā'; colloquial Arabic, Dar el-Beida) has been so called since the 16th century because most of its houses are white. It is the largest and most important port and city in Morocco. By 1960 it had become the fourth largest city in the Arab world after Cairo, Alexandria and Baghdad. It is situated on the Atlantic coast of Morocco. In 1971 its population numbered about 1,500,000.

History. The origin of the town is not known. A Berber village called Anfa stood on the present-day site in the 12th century; it became a pirates' base for harrying Christian ships, and in consequence of this the village was captured and destroyed by the Portuguese in 1468. One of the most fashionable districts of Casablanca is now named Anfa.

The Portuguese returned to the area in 1515, this time with the intention of settling. They built a new town called Casa Branca (White House) in Portuguese, but it had to be abandoned in 1755 after a devastating earthquake. The ʿAlawī sultan Sīdī Muhammad ibn ʿAbd Allāh rebuilt the town in the late 18th century. The Moroccans were not interested in overseas trade, however, and left the use of its then insignificant harbour to Spanish merchants, who named it Casablanca and began to settle there. Other European traders arrived; the French after a time outnumbered other European settlers, and the name Maison Blanche became as common as Casablanca.

The French interregnum

Rioting broke out in the town in 1907, when the Moroccan Shawia tribes claimed that their cemetery had been desecrated by European construction workers in the port area. Eight Europeans were killed during the clashes, and this incident led to intervention by French troops and the killing of several thousand Moroccans. In the early years of the French protectorate over Morocco (1912–56), the French resident general, Marshal Louis-Hubert-Gonzalve Lyautey, embarked on a policy of expansion and development to make Casablanca the chief port of Morocco. Since then, the growth and development of the city have been continuous and rapid. During World War II the city was the seat of an Anglo-United States summit conference in 1943. In 1961 a conference at Casablanca, presided over by King Muḥammad V of Morocco, founded the Casablanca group of African states.

The contemporary city. Casablanca extends for 12 miles along the coast and for more than five miles inland. Its site is fairly flat, rising slowly inland at the rate of 50 to 100 feet every mile. In the extreme west is the Anfa Ridge, a ridge of dunes about 200 feet high that stretches obliquely along the coast toward Cap el-Hank, immediately northwest of the city. The underlying rocks of the area are mainly hard metamorphic types (formed by heat and pressure), such as schist (a coarse-grained rock) and quartzite. The surface is covered by recent sedimentary limestones and sandstones. To the west the lower parts of the surface are covered by reddish limestone, gray sand, or black silt. To the northeast the hard underlying rocks appear almost bare. Such surface differences probably influenced the planning of the town. The western section has been developed as a modern residential district, while an industrial area has been established in the northeast. The coast is mostly rocky and directly receives the shock of the ocean's strong surf. The hinterland consists of pastoral and poorly cultivated areas, in which the Shawia tribes still follow traditional methods of agriculture.

The medina

The man-made port of Casablanca has 16,000 feet of deepwater quays and is protected from the sea by a breakwater; it handles about three-quarters of Morocco's import and export trade. It is also a port of call for many cruise ships from western Europe; Boulevard Hansali, which leads to the port, is lined with shops for tourists. Inland from the docks and the harbour is the old medina, the original Arab town. Still enclosed in parts by its original rampart walls, it is a maze of narrow streets and whitewashed brick or stone houses. In a semicircle outside the walls of the medina is the town built by the French. Avenues radiating from Muḥammad V Square are intersected by ring roads that reach to the coast on either side of the harbour. Muḥammad V Square, near the gateway of the old medina, and United Nations Square are the business and administrative centres of the town, where banks, hotels, and large modern shops are located. Farther south, overlooking the gardens of the Park of the Arab League, is the white Cathedral of the Sacré Coeur. West of the park and stretching toward the coast are the gardens and villas of residential districts, such as Anfa.

Beyond this French-built town, the new medina has been built—an immense area of 200,000 inhabitants.

Climate. The climate is pleasant most of the year, with monthly average temperatures varying between 54° F (12° C) in January and 73° F (23° C) in August. Daily and seasonal ranges of temperature are small. The average annual rainfall is about 16 inches. Rain may fall in any month, though it is scarce in summer.

Humidity is high the year around. The combination of humidity and high temperatures in summer can create rather oppressive weather. Gales and strong winds are frequent in winter. Fog often forms in the fall.

Residential section of Casablanca, near the city's harbour.
Ewing Galloway

Transport. As the town expanded, transport problems increased. People living in the suburbs and in the new medina were obliged to travel long distances to the central business district. Improvements were made, however, and communications within the city, as well as between Casablanca and other cities, are now generally easy and comfortable; buses are the principal means of public transport. Good roads join Casablanca with Rabat, Marrakech, Fès, Meknès, and other places; the best of these is the 55-mile highway to Rabat, the political capital of Morocco. There is also a railway line that runs northeastward to Rabat, Meknès, and Fès, after which it crosses the border into Algeria and Tunisia. There are two international airports, the Casablanca-Anfa to the southwest and the Casablanca-Nouaceur to the east of the city.

Population. At the 1971 census the population was 1,500,000. At the 1960 census the population of Casablanca was 965,000, comprising about 779,000 Moroccan Muslims, 72,000 Moroccan Jews, and 114,000 foreigners, mainly French and Spanish. The rate of population growth since the beginning of the 20th century has been about 6 percent annually. The total was 20,000 in 1907, 89,000 in 1920, 257,000 in 1936, and 680,000 in 1952. The million mark was passed in the 1960s. The exceptionally high rate of growth, which is in contrast to much lower rates in other Moroccan towns, has been caused by the immigration of Europeans and Moroccan Jews from other parts of the country, by the arrival of Europeans and other foreigners from abroad, and by an influx of Moroccan Muslims from rural areas.

The number of foreigners and Moroccan Jews in Casablanca in the 1960s and early 1970s remained approximately constant though many left the country, because others moved in from other parts of Morocco to take their place. Many used the town as a temporary place of residence before leaving the country. Moroccan immigrants are mainly poor Muslims who are attracted to the town by its prosperity and its industrialization. Their numbers have always been greater than the available employment vacancies, and many have, in consequence, remained unemployed for long periods. The influx of these immigrants has created a large poor community whose numbers have increased rapidly. They live in shantytowns known as *bidonvilles* ("tin-can towns"), which have spread rapidly on the outskirts of the city.

The *bidonvilles*

Housing. In the earlier years of the 20th century, Casablanca was divided into districts according to the wealth and nationality of the inhabitants. As a result of the continuous exodus of Europeans and Jews, however, the districts previously occupied by them—such as the fashionable Anfa and Le Polo quarters—are now for the most part inhabited by well-to-do Moroccan Muslims. In contrast, the *bidonvilles* clearly indicate the extreme poverty of a large section of the population. The more prosperous and industrialized the town becomes, the greater the influx of poor immigrants, and the greater the expansion of the *bidonvilles.* To check this tendency, a scheme for building large blocks of working-class flats in the new medina was started in 1944; although many such blocks have since been built, the *bidonvilles* nevertheless still constitute a serious social problem.

Architectural features. Most buildings in the modern districts of Casablanca follow the architectural style of Le Corbusier, the French-trained Swiss architect. They are supported by slender pillars and have large white walls and large windows protected from the sun by concrete screens; the radical modernization of the city has not, however, obliterated the traditional characteristics of the old medina with its ancient houses and narrow streets. There is a great mosque, built in the late 1700s. In the centre of the town, as already mentioned, is the large, busy Muḥammad V Square; from the square the palm-lined Boulevard Hansali leads down to the docks.

Economic life. The rapid commercial progress of Casablanca, especially the growth of its port, has established it as the economic capital of Morocco. It accounts for more than half of the bank transactions and industrial production of Morocco and possesses more than half of the country's industrial labour force. Casablanca's industries include textiles, electronics, leather works, food canning, and the production of beer, spirits, and soft drinks. Its industrial area has expanded very rapidly in the northeast in the direction of Fedala, which until 1960 was a separate suburb but has since become an integral part of the town. Fishing is important in coastal waters, where a fairly wide continental shelf provides a good fishing ground. The catch includes soles, red mullet, turbot, sea eels, crabs, and shrimps.

Government and services. Casablanca is administered as an urban prefecture; it is headed by a governor, appointed by the king and assisted by a secretary general. Police and fire services are each controlled from a central headquarters. In 1971 Casablanca had 24 medical clinics and about 225 doctors.

Education and cultural life. Casablanca has Arab and French schools at different educational levels. There are also various cultural and utilitarian institutes, such as the Goethe-Institut, the Municipal College of Fine Arts, the Municipal Library, a prehistory society, an institute of fishing, and an horticultural society.

Three daily French newspapers appear in Casablanca; there are also 16 periodicals. A television station was opened in 1962.

Recreation. Casablanca is Morocco's principal centre for entertainment and recreation. Along the seafront are a number of pleasant beaches, the most popular of which are Kon Tiki, Miami, Tahiti, and the Lido. There are several parks, including the Park of the Arab League, and attractive promenades along the seafront. Casablanca has cinemas, a modern municipal theatre, and a variety of hotels, restaurants, sporting clubs, and nightclubs.

BIBLIOGRAPHY. A. ADAM, *Casablanca: Essai sur la transformation de la société Marocaine au contact de l'Occident*, 2 vol. (1968), an illustrated and detailed geographical work; H. AWAD, "Morocco's Expanding Towns," *Geogrl. J.*, 130: 49–64 (1964), a useful introduction to the urban geography of Morocco, with special attention given to growth in population and area; F. BESSON, "Le Port de Casablanca," *Notes Marocaines*, 16:57–59 (1961), a detailed study of the development and functions of the port; R. BRYANS, *Morocco* (1965), an interesting tourist's account, including descriptions and other important information; D. OGRIZEK (ed.), *L'Afrique du Nord* (1952; Eng. trans., *North Africa*, 1955), brief descriptions of many North African towns accompanied by coloured sketches and pictures.

(A.elA.T.S.)

Casimir III the Great, of Poland

The only one of the long line of Piast dynasts (who ruled Poland from its beginnings until 1370) to be dignified by the epithet "the Great," Casimir III (Polish Kazimierz Wielki) was king of Poland from 1333 to 1370. Although the epithet was given to him a century after his reign by the chronicler Jan Długosz to distinguish him from Casimir IV, it has survived among historians and in national legend because it expresses the sentiment that this peaceful ruler, "peasant king," and skilful diplomat, has more claim to greatness than Poland's many conquerors and warriors.

By courtesy of Panstwowe Zbiory Sztuki na Wawelu, Krakow

Casimir III, sarcophagus figure, after 1370. In Wawel Cathedral, Kraków.

Casimir was the second king of the reunited and resuscitated Poland that for nearly two centuries had been split up into numerous small principalities. His father, Władysław I, who had succeeded in reuniting Great Poland and Little Poland, renewed the long-forgotten kingship with his coronation in Cracow in 1320. Casimir continued the work of his father, adding two large and important regions (Red Russia and Masovia) to the country and making it a solid and respected partner among the other 14th-century powers in central Europe. In addition, he provided the country with a well-organized government, codified its unwritten law, and founded its first university (Cracow 1364). By all this he so strengthened feelings of popular unity that after his death (although he left no legal heir) there were no attempts at restoring the former duchies and principalities. Casimir was born on April 30, 1310. His mother was Jadwiga, daughter of Bolesław the Pious (Pobożny) of Great Poland. After the death of his elder brother in 1312, Casimir was regarded as heir and was prepared for the kingship by Jarosław, later archbishop of Gniezno and Casimir's counsellor. Of his three sisters, one, Elizabeth, who in 1320 married King Charles Robert of Hungary, figured prominently in his foreign and dynastic policy.

Dynastic alliances. In 1325 Casimir married Aldona Ona, the pagan daughter of Gediminas (Giedymin), duke of Lithuania. Baptized before the wedding, Aldona brought with her thousands of Polish prisoners of war (one chronicle tells of 24,000) as a sign of reconciliation between Poland and the then still heathen Lithuania. The marriage seems to have been unhappy, and the Queen died in 1339 leaving no sons. Two years later Casimir married a German princess, Adelhaid of Hesse, but this marriage proved barren, and Adelhaid was sent home in 1356. A third marriage in 1365 with the Silesian princess Hedwig of Glogau-Sagan still brought no legal heir. The question of a successor was, therefore, one of Casimir's main problems. He finally designated as his heir his nephew, Louis of Hungary. Since Louis had no sons either, Casimir named as his second choice Casimir of western Pomerania, a son of his eldest daughter. The act strengthened the position of the nobility whose consent had to be obtained by the granting of privileges.

Casimir's heirless marriages

The marriages of his daughters and grandchildren further strengthened Casimir's foreign support. His second daughter was married to Louis of Brandenburg (1345); the third was betrothed to Wenzel, son of the Holy Roman Emperor Charles IV (1369), and the emperor himself married first a grandniece and, later, a granddaughter of Casimir. The king thus had relatives in several important contemporary dynasties: the Wittelsbachs, the Anjous, the Luxemburgs, and the Lithuanians (later known as the Jagiellons). Casimir also had many mistresses, about whom little is known; the most famous of them, the beautiful Jewess, Esther, may have been invented by the chroniclers to explain the King's notable friendliness toward the Jews.

Foreign policy. Casimir's foreign policy reflected his own character: prudent, cool, obstinate, and self-controlled. He preferred diplomacy to war, though he did not entirely refrain from the latter, as evidenced by a series of forced occupations of foreign territory, notably Red Russia, in 1340 and 1349. At the beginning of Casimir's reign Poland was beset by several difficulties: the King of Bohemia claimed the Polish crown; the German knights of the Teutonic Order disputed East Pomerania; and the country lacked powerful allies. By a series of treaties concluded with Hungary, Bohemia, and the Teutonic Order between 1335 and 1348, Casimir obtained a strong ally in Hungary and dropped his claims to Silesia and East Pomerania (claims that would in any case have been difficult to realize). The Bohemian king, in exchange, dropped his claims to Poland; and the Order withdrew from the territories of Kujawy and Dobrzyn, which it had occupied. Having his western frontier secure, Casimir was now able to occupy the former duchies of Halič and Vladimir (Red Russia) and to unite them step-by-step (though never completely) to Poland. As a result of this carefully planned policy, the Masovian princes, long anxious to preserve their independence, declared themselves Casimir's vassals (1351–53); even in the West some German nobles preferred Casimir's to Brandenburg's lordship.

By 1370 Casimir, under different titles, had increased his territory to about 90,000 square miles (233,000 square kilometres) from about 50,000 at his accession. More important than these territorial gains, some of which were lost after Casimir's death, was the growth of the King's prestige throughout Europe. A congress held

The congress of Cracow

in Cracow in 1364 was attended by the kings of Hungary, Bohemia, Denmark, and Cyprus, as well as a great number of other princes. Casimir, who 30 years previously had been a humble petitioner at the Congress of Visegrád in Hungary, was now asked to arbitrate a quarrel between the Emperor and Louis of Hungary.

Domestic achievements. Domestically, Casimir encouraged economic activity and attempted to unite the country under one prince, one law, and one currency. He founded several new towns—two of them named Kazimierz after himself—and gave them, together with already existing towns, the so-called Magdeburg Law, the privilege of self-government. Casimir built more than 50 castles, fostered church building, and embellished the royal castle at Cracow. A special court was established in Cracow to arbitrate in all quarrels and to administer the law codified in the *Liber juris Teutonici* ("Book of Teutonic Law"). The former privileges of the Jews were confirmed and improved. Though Casimir was able to inaugurate his principle of one law in Little Poland and Great Poland, Masovia and Red Russia kept their own nonwritten law. Wishing to educate native lawyers and administrators, he founded the University of Cracow in 1364, which, however, flourished for only a few years before his death in a hunting accident in 1370.

Since little is known of Casimir's sympathies, personal interests, thoughts, and feelings, he must be judged on his deeds, which characterize him as an especially good, wise, and, to a degree, even modern ruler. He was a sober administrator but not a hero; a man who earned the respect of his contemporaries and posterity but was, perhaps, too cool, too aloof, and too faultless to obtain great sympathy.

BIBLIOGRAPHY. O. HALECKI, "Casimir the Great, 1333–70," in *The Cambridge History of Poland*, vol. 1, pp. 167–187 (1950).

(G.K.S.R.)

Casimir IV of Poland

Casimir IV, grand duke of Lithuania (1440–92) and king of Poland (1447–92), was neither a great warrior and builder nor a man of lively cultural interests. Nevertheless, he succeeded by his skillful and patient policy in securing for his lands a period of peaceful evolution and in making his dynasty one of the foremost in Europe, which, by the end of his life, occupied no fewer than four thrones. During his reign, the Grand Duchy of Lithuania was the most important power in eastern Europe; its frontiers in the northeast extended to within 100 miles of Moscow, and in the south it approached the shores of the Black Sea. At the same time, the kingdom of Poland defeated its old enemy, the Teutonic Order, in the Thirteen Years' War and obtained sovereignty over eastern Pomerania and, by that, the control of the mouth of the Vistula River.

Casimir was born on November 30, 1427, the second son of Władysław II Jagiełło and his fourth wife, Zofja Holszańska. His father was already over 75 at Casimir's birth, and his brother Władysław III, three years his senior, was expected to become king before his majority. Casimir was thus the second in succession to the throne, and, after Władysław had succeeded his father in 1434, he became the legal heir. Strangely, little was done for his education; he was never taught Latin, nor was he trained for the responsibilities of office, despite the fact he was the only brother of the sovereign. Yet the necessity of taking office was thrust upon him in 1440, when the grand duke of Lithuania, Sigismund, was murdered. The boy was sent to Wilna to act as governor for his brother, but he was proclaimed grand duke in a coup d'état by the leading boyars (nobles), who evidently hoped to use him as a convenient tool.

Grand duke of Lithuania

The coup practically severed the ties between Lithuania and Poland, but these were restored after Władysław III's death in the Battle of Varna against the Turks (November 10, 1444). The Poles, having to elect a new king, had no other candidate but Casimir. The young man, despite his lack of experience, knew how to wield his new power. He acted to preserve the hereditary rule of

Casimir IV, sarcophagus figure by Veit Stoss, 1492–93. In Wawel Cathedral, Kraków.
By courtesy of Panstwowe Zbiory Sztuki na Wawelu, Krakow

the dynasty in Lithuania with no connection with Poland other than the common monarchy; and when he was finally crowned king of Poland (June 25, 1447), he had succeeded in affirming his right to live in Lithuania and choose his counsellors freely. Considering his deeds and policy (no personal utterances of his are recorded), it may be inferred that he regarded himself more as the head of a dynasty than as the elected king of Poland. His policy, therefore, is partly family policy, and in cases of conflict between dynasty and state the former had priority. His marriage to Elizabeth of Habsburg in 1454 had clear political aims; as the daughter of Albert II of Habsburg, Elizabeth had claims to Bohemia and Hungary. In fact, this first connection between the Habsburgs and the Jagiellons was a happy one; because of her six sons and seven daughters (born between 1456 and 1483) Elizabeth was called the "mother of Jagiellons." Casimir did everything he could to provide his children with advantageous marriages. In this he was more than successful: the eldest son, Władysław, became king of Bohemia (1471) and of Hungary (1490); three others were his successors on the thrones of Lithuania and Poland; one became an archbishop and, later, a cardinal. Five of his daughters were married to German princes, as a result of which the Polish name Casimir became a familiar one among German dynasties. When he died June 7, 1492, he left a dynasty renowned among the courts of Europe.

Because of his neglected education, Casimir seems to have been personally narrow, preferring hunting in Lithuania to court life in Cracow; he often absented himself from the Polish capital for more than a year at a time. On the other hand, he evidently had a strong feeling of his dignity and was able to show it distinctly. His tombstone in Cracow Cathedral, carved by the Nürnburg sculptor Veit Stoss, who for many years lived in Cracow, vividly portrays Casimir's simplicity, energy, perseverance, and dignity mingled with pride.

Foreign policy

In foreign policy, Casimir had few far-reaching plans or great ambitions. He neither organized a crusade against the Turks as his brother had done, nor did he build up an efficient defense system against the aggressions of the Grand Duchy of Moscow. He failed also to support Moscow's enemies and contented himself with the favourable treaty of 1449, which, however, did little to prepare Lithuania for the attacks that were to begin in 1486. Thus, a number of Russian princes, vassals of Lithuania, went over to the Muscovite Grand Duke after 1486 because they had obtained no protection from Casimir. When, in 1484, two important harbours on the Black Sea, Kilia and Akkerman—previously under Lithuania's protection—were captured by the Turks, Casimir made little attempt to recover them. Although these territorial losses at the end of his reign did not seriously threaten Lithuania, they did weaken its former dominant position in eastern Europe.

Similarly, in Poland the King showed little initiative in foreign policy. When the Prussians, however, revolted in 1454 against their overlord, the Teutonic Order, and placed themselves under the protection of Casimir, he was aware that this was a unique opportunity to destroy the power of the Order and incorporated the whole of Prussia by the act of March 6, 1454. When, as a result, war broke out and Polish troops were severely defeated near Konitz (September 18, 1454), it was mainly the King's perseverance and stubbornness that led to the final success in the second Treaty of Toruń (Thorn; October 19, 1466). Though the Order retained a part of its former territory and "Royal Prussia" was not formally incorporated but only united with the kingdom while preserving its own diet and administration, this treaty was Casimir's most important foreign policy success. Thus, in spite of his own sympathies, his reign was more successful for Poland than for his beloved Lithuania.

Domestic policy

In domestic affairs Casimir was relatively passive but anxious to preserve the prerogatives of the crown, notably his right to nominate bishops. In the question of territories in dispute between his two states (Volhynia and Podolia) he was not impartial but favoured Lithuania. During the war against the Order he was forced to grant the Polish nobility substantial concessions by the Privilege (statute) of Nieszawa (November 1454); these, however, became important only after his death, and royal power was not greatly diminished during his lifetime. Casimir governed his realm mostly by counsellors of his own choice after the death of the almost all-powerful bishop of Cracow, Zbigniew Oleśnicki, in 1455.

Casimir was neither a splendid ruler nor a good and wise administrator, but a mistrusting, cautious, and sober head of a large family who regarded Lithuania as his personal estate; he enjoyed authority, and his reign was remembered as being both successful and peaceful.

BIBLIOGRAPHY. A biography in English does not exist. See A. BRUCE BOSWELL, "Jagiello's Successors," and F. PAPEE, "Imperial Expansion and the Supremacy of the Gentry, 1466–1506," in *The Cambridge History of Poland*, vol. 1, pp. 232–272 (1950), for a discussion of Casimir and his reign.

(G.K.S.R.)

Caspian Sea

The world's greatest inland sea, the Caspian Sea lies beyond the Caucasian mountain peaks at Europe's southeasternmost extremity and dominates the huge, flat expanses of western Central Asia. Its name derives from the ancient Kaspi peoples, who once lived in Transcaucasia to the west; among its other historical names, Khazarsk and Khvalynsk derive from former peoples of the region, while Girkansk stems from Girkanos, "the country of the wolves." Its elongated shape sprawls for nearly 750 miles (1,200 kilometres) from north to south, although its average width is only 200 miles (320 kilometres). It currently covers an area of 143,000 square miles (371,000 square kilometres)—larger than Japan—while its surface lies some 93.5 feet below ocean level. The maximum depth, toward the south, is 3,360 feet. Except for its southern shores, which lie at the foot of the giant Elburz Mountains of Iran six-sevenths of the Caspian coast runs through Soviet territory.

It is often stated that the Caspian is the greatest salt lake in the world, but this is not absolutely correct, as scientific studies have shown that, until geologically quite recent times, it was linked, via the Sea of Azov, the Black Sea, and the Mediterranean, to the world ocean. This factor has molded strongly all aspects of its physical geography. The Caspian is of exceptional scientific interest, because its history, particularly in respect to former fluctuations in both area and depth, offers clues to the complex geological and climatic evolution of the region. Man-made changes, notably those resulting from the construction of dams, reservoirs, and canals on the im-

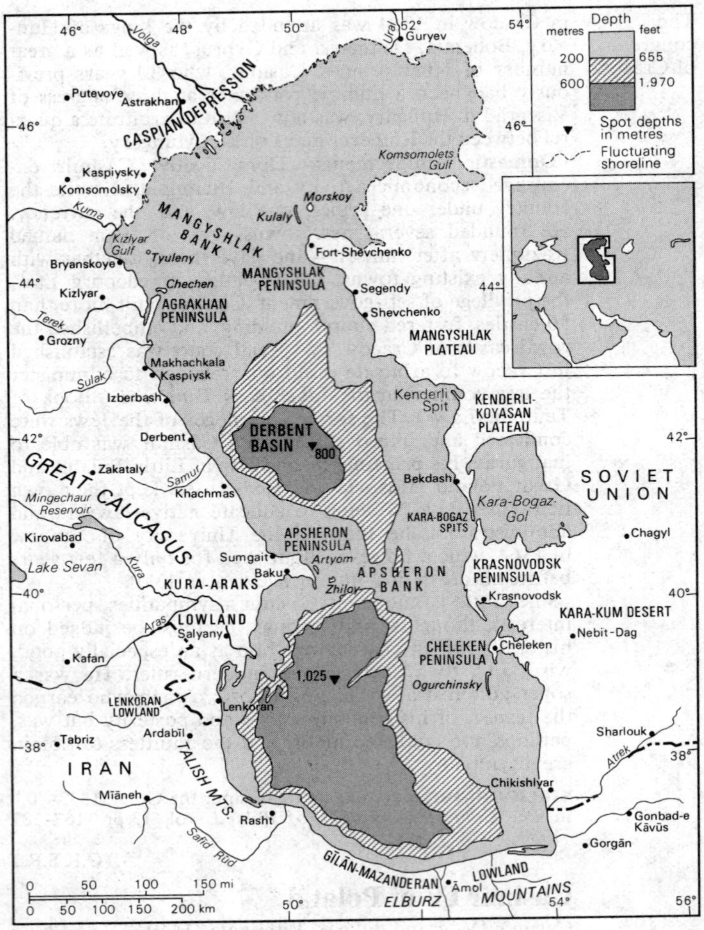

The Caspian Sea.

mense Volga River system (which drains into the Caspian from the north), have had their own effect on the contemporary hydrological balance. The Caspian is also of great importance in the transportation networks of the region and in the production of petroleum and gas. It is anticipated that the use of its splendid sandy beaches for health and recreation resorts will increase considerably in the future. (For related physical features, see CAUCASUS MOUNTAINS; VOLGA RIVER; and ELBURZ MOUNTAINS; for human geography, see the articles RUSSIAN SOVIET FEDERATED SOCIALIST REPUBLIC; KAZAKH SOVIET SOCIALIST REPUBLIC; TURKMEN SOVIET SOCIALIST REPUBLIC AZERBAIJAN SOVIET SOCIALIST REPUBLIC.)

Importance of sea-level fluctuations

Topography. The Caspian possesses as many as 50 islands, mostly small. Chechen, in the northwest, is the largest, followed by Artyom, Zhiloy, Tyuleny, Morskoy, Kulaly, and Ogurchinsky. The basin, as a whole, is usually divided into the North, Middle, and South Caspian, using relief and, in part, hydrological characteristics as the basis.

Shoreline features. The shores of the North Caspian are low and reflect the great accumulation of alluvial material washed down by the Ural, Terek, Sulak, and, above all, the Volga rivers, the deltas of which are extensively developed. The western shore of the Middle Caspian is hilly. The foothills of the Great Caucasus loom close but are separated from the coast by a narrow marine plain. The Apsheron Peninsula, on which the city of Baku is sited, thrusts out into the sea here, while, just to its south, the floodplain of the Kura and Araks rivers forms the Kura–Araks Lowland. The southwestern and South Caspian shores are formed of the sediments of the Lenkoran and Gīlān-Mazanderan lowlands, with the high peaks of the Talish and Elburz mountains rearing up close inland. The eastern shore of the South Caspian is also low and is formed by sediments resulting from wave action; it is broken sharply by the low, hilly Cheleken and Krasnovodsk peninsulas. For the most part, the eastern shore of the Middle Caspian is precipitous, with the sea destroying the margin of the limestone plateau of Mangyshlak and Kenderli–Koyasan. A most important feature of this area is the Kara-Bogaz-Gol, the Caspian's largest, split off from the main body of water by the Kara-Bogaz barrier spits; the Krasnovodsk and Kenderli spits are similar in type.

The major rivers—the Volga, Ural, and Terek—empty into the North Caspian, with their combined annual flow accounting for 88 percent of all river water entering the sea. The Sulak, Samur, Kura, and a number of smaller rivers flow in on the western littoral, contributing about 7 percent of the flow, and the remainder comes in from the rivers of the Iranian shore. The eastern littoral is notable for a complete lack of permanent streams.

The three main topographic divisions

Submarine features. The North Caspian, with an area of 30,000 square miles, is the shallowest portion of the sea, with an average depth of 13 to 20 feet, reaching a maximum of 66 along the boundary with the Middle Caspian. The bottom is formed of a monotonously rippling sedimentary plain, broken only by a line of southern bars and shoals—some of which provide foundations for Tyuleny, Kulaly, and Zhemchuzhny islands—reflecting underlying structural rises. Beyond this belt, known as the Mangyshlak Bank, the Middle Caspian, 53,000 square miles in area, forms an irregular depression with an abrupt western slope and a gentler eastern gradient. The shallowest portion—a shelf with depths up to 330–460 feet—extends along both shores, with the westernmost slope furrowed by submerged landslips and canyons. The remains of ancient river valleys have been discovered on the gentler northern slope; the bottom of the depression is formed of a plain that deepens to the west. The Apsheron Bank, a belt of shoals and islands rising from submerged elevations of older rocks, marks the transition to the South Caspian, a depression covering about one-third of the sea. This is fringed by a shelf that is narrow to the west and south but widening to the east. A series of submerged ridges breaks up the relief to the north, but otherwise the bottom of the depression is a flat plain, with the maximum depth of 3,360 feet.

Geological origins. The relief of the Caspian Sea reflects its complex geological structure. The northern portion forms a peripheral section of the North Caspian tectonic depression, a vast downwarp in the Earth's surface that is itself part of the great ancient structural block known as the Russian Platform. The Mangyshlak Bank links the mountainous peninsula of the same name to the east with underlying western shore structures; all the rocks concerned reflect an outlying structural uplift of the Hercynian mountain-building movement, which occurred some 290,000,000 years ago. The bottom of the Middle Caspian is very complex. To the west, the submarine shelf is part of the sagging edge of the Great Caucasus Geosyncline, while the submerged Turan Platform on the east swells up in the feature known as the Kara-Bogaz swell. The Apsheron Peninsula regions bear the impress of the Alpine mountain-building and folding period (dating from some 10,000,000–26,000,000 years ago), which created the Caucasian ranges, as do the folded structures of the western South Caspian depression. The entire South Caspian, in fact, has as its base a suboceanic-type basalt crustal structure, although this is overlain in the south by huge accumulations of sedimentary layers many miles thick. The great age thus indicated for the area has led geologists to postulate that this is the remnant of the geologically ancient Tethys Sea. Similarly, the North Caspian Sea bottom is also very old, dating back to Precambrian times, or at least 570,000,000 years ago. The bottom of the North and Middle Caspian has a continental-type crustal structure. It has been suggested that the Middle Caspian depression results from a sagging at the edge of these ancient structures that occurred in Late Paleozoic times, about 250,000,000 years ago; the border between the Middle and South Caspian is, in fact, still experiencing folding activity.

Until the upper Miocene, about 12,000,000 years ago, the sea basin of the Caspian was connected closely to the Black Sea, through the structural depression known as the Manych Trench. This link was broken after an upper-Miocene elevation, and the Caspian became an enclosed body of water, with oceanic submarine characteristics preserved today only in the Southern Caspian. The connection with the ocean was re-established in the upper Pliocene, about 2,500,000 years ago, and it is possible that there was also a link northward across the expansive Russian plain to the Barents Sea of the Arctic.

Pre-Miocene link with the Black Sea

In the ensuing Quaternary times, great glaciers advanced and retreated across the Russian plain, and the Caspian Sea itself—in successive phases known as Bakin, Khazar, and Khvalyn—alternately shrank and swelled out. This process left a legacy in the form of peripheral terraces, marking old shorelines, and can also be traced in the recent underlying sedimentary layers.

The Caspian Sea bottom is now coated with young sediments, finely grained in the shallow north but with shell deposits and oolitic sand—reflecting the high lime content of the Caspian waters—widespread in other coastal areas. Lime also affects the composition of the much deeper bottom layers.

Climate. The North Caspian lies in a moderately continental climatic zone, while all the Middle (and most of the South) Caspian lies in the moderately hot belt. The southwest is touched by subtropical influences, and this remarkable variety is completed by the desert climate prevailing on the eastern shores. Atmospheric circulation is dominated in winter by the cold, clear air of the Asiatic anticyclone, while in summer spurs of the Azores high-pressure and the South Asian low-pressure centres are influential. Complicating factors are the cyclonic disturbances rippling in from the west and the effect of the Great Caucasian ranges. As a result of these factors, northwesterlies (32 percent of occurrences) and southeasterlies (36 percent) dominate circulation patterns. Savage storms are associated with northerly and southeasterly winds.

Summer air temperatures are quite evenly distributed (average July–August figures: 75°–79° F [24°–26° C], with an absolute maximum of 111° F [44° C] on the sun-baked eastern shore), but winter temperatures range from 14° F (−10° C) in the north to 50° F (10° C) in the south. Average annual rainfall varies from 67 inches to eight inches over the sea. Most falls in winter and spring. Evaporation from the sea surface is very high, reaching 40 inches a year. Ice formation afflicts the North Caspian, which usually freezes completely by January, and in very cold years floating ice comes as far south as the Apsheron Peninsula region.

Fluctuations in water level. Short-term wind-induced fluctuations in the sea level can rise to up to seven feet, though such rises average about two feet. Seiches (rises induced by barometric pressure changes) can cause similar fluctuations. Tidal changes are but a few inches, and seasonal rises induced by high spring water in the rivers are not much more.

One of the more fascinating aspects of the study of the Caspian, however, is the reconstruction of long-term fluctuations over the centuries from archaeological, geographical, and historical evidence. It seems the Caspian reached a level of 72 feet below sea level about 4,000 to 6,000 years ago and again early in the 19th century AD. A still lower level held from the 7th to the 11th centuries, while the lowering that took place between 1929 and 1957 stemmed from the effects of climatic change resulting in lesser river influx and increased evaporation amplified by reservoir construction on the Volga, and from river water consumption for irrigation and industry. The flow of water into the Kara-Bogaz-Gol, now about 12 feet lower than the Caspian, has also had an effect. By the early 1970s, the water level was very close to the −93.5 feet level, reflecting a balance between input (rainfall, river inflow, subterranean upwelling) and consumption (evaporation, flow into the Kara-Bogaz-Gol, human usage) that gave the latter a slight edge and hence a projected annual lowering of the level by three inches. If, however, the north-flowing Vychegda and Pechora were diverted into the Volga, it would seem that the pres-

Recent attempts to preserve the sea level

ent level could at least be maintained (and increased, under favourable climatic conditions) until the year 2000. Soviet planners have given serious attention to such an ambitious project.

Hydrology and life forms. In summer, the average sea-water temperature is 75°–79° F (24°–26° C), with the south a little warmer. There are, however, significant winter contrasts, from 37°–45° F (3°–7° C) in the north to 46°–52° F (8°–11° C) in the south. Upwellings of deep water at the eastern littoral—a result of prevailing-wind activity—can also bring a marked drop in summer temperature. Salinity in the Caspian is about 1.27 percent on average, but this conceals a variation from a mere 0.1 percent near the Volga outlet to a high of 32 percent in the Kara-Bogaz-Gol, where intense evaporation occurs. Caspian waters differ from those of the ocean in their high sulphate, calcium, and magnesium carbonate content and—as a result of river inflow—low chloride content.

Water mass circulation occurs, basically, in a north to south movement along the western shore, with a complex pattern developing further south, where there are several subsidiary movements. Currents can be speeded up where they coincide with strong winds, and the sea surface is often ruffled by wave action, with the maximum storm waves being observed near the Apsheron Peninsula.

There are about 850 animal and more than 500 plant species in the Caspian—a relatively low figure. Animal life has been affected greatly by changes in salinity. It includes, among the fish, sturgeons, herring, pike, perch, and sprat; several mollusks; and a variety of other organisms including sponges. Some 15 species of Arctic (*e.g.*, the Caspian seal) and Mediterranean types complement the basic fauna. Perch are important among freshwater fish varieties. Some organisms have migrated to the Caspian quite recently: barnacles, crabs, and clams, for example, have been transported by sea vessels; grey mullets have been deliberately introduced by man.

The human imprint. The Caspian was long famous for its sturgeon catch, but this has been reduced greatly in recent years, as a result of the decline in sea level, and the connected drying up of the most favourable places for spawning. The seal industry is, however, being developed in northern regions. Oil and gas have now become the region's most important resources, following extensive geological surveys in the 1940s and 1950s. Seabed oil is extracted from derricks and artificial islands, most of which are concentrated off the shores of the Azerbaijan S.S.R., supplying half that republic's total oil extraction volume. The extraction of such minerals as sodium sulphate from the Kara-Bogaz-Gol is also of considerable economic importance. Finally, the Caspian is of major importance for transportation in the region: petroleum, wood, grain, cotton, rice, and sulphate are the basic goods carried, while Astrakhan, Baku, Makhachkala, Krasnovodsk, and Shevchenko are the most important ports. They are also connected by regular passenger runs, while railway stock is transported direct, without unloading, on the Baku–Krasnovdsk run.

The future of the Caspian will depend on the success of measures to maintain the present sea level, on restoration and development of fishing resources, on further oil and gas exploitation, and on the creation of a large chemical complex at Kara-Bogaz-Gol. Further transportation developments will require, as a necessity, new port facilities and new ferries. The hitherto largely deserted eastern shores will benefit from development associated with oil extraction, and an extensive development of the fine shores of the sea as health and recreation resorts figures largely in Soviet long-term plans for the area.

(A.N.K./O.K.L.)

Caste Systems

Caste systems are moral systems that differentiate and rank the whole population of a society in corporate units (castes) generally defined by descent, marriage, and occupation. Elaborately differentiated and ranked caste systems have developed especially in the regional societies of India and among adjacent Hindu and related populations in the territories of modern Pakistan, Bangladesh, Nepal, and Sri Lanka (Ceylon) over the past 2,000 years. Simpler caste systems have developed elsewhere. The nature, history, and variety of these systems, their significance for general understanding of human society and for particular understanding of South Asian society and religion are the subjects of this article.

CASTE SYSTEMS IN GENERAL

So intricate are the connections of caste systems in South Asia with regional systems of ideas regarding such matters as genetics, physiology, kinship, ethics, and cosmogony that they have been equated by some scholars with the whole culture of Hinduism and declared to be unique phenomena inseparable from it. Caste systems are found, however, in combination with other religions and cultures in South Asia and elsewhere. Their features as a general type may be compared with other systems of social class or stratification. (See SOCIAL DIFFERENTIATION AND STRATIFICATION.)

Caste systems compared to other systems of social stratification

Caste systems resemble racial stratification in their biological concern with differences of birth and marriage; they resemble stratified plural societies in their presumption of profound differences in group behaviour; they depart from both in conceiving of themselves simultaneously as unitary societies that are culturally integrated. Unlike racially or culturally plural societies, where prior intractable difference among groups is taken as a moral reason for the divided constitution of the society, established caste systems may differentiate into further, new units or they may reassemble their units into one.

Caste systems resemble the much more widespread systems of social and economic classes in containing ranks that tend to be culturally marked, occupationally linked, hereditary, and endogamous (marrying within a group). They differ from such systems in having as their ranked units not only individual persons and families but also larger corporate groups. Corporate caste units differ from social classes in being necessarily defined—rather than incidentally distinguished—by occupation, descent, and marriage. Castes have no other necessary cultural markings, although classes, being assemblages of persons on the basis of their attributes, necessarily do. The ranking of corporate units in caste systems creates an illusion of individual immobility (a feature sometimes taken as typical of caste systems); yet rates of individual rise and fall are not known to differ between class systems and caste systems, as the types are here defined.

Caste systems are comparatively rare among large-scale moral systems in making the differentiation and interrelations of corporate groups into major concerns; but in this they are at one with a large and diverse category of small-scale societies. The sharings and exchanges by which caste systems reckon the boundaries, alliances, and ranks of their corporate units have much in common with widespread forms of marriage and parent–child relationships, gift giving and tribute, ritual, sports competitions, communication networks, and dominance in animal as well as human societies. But caste systems are unique in their ways of combining these features—in having biological and behavioral schemes for differentiating and ranking occupational and ethnic units according to the determined way they relate to each other in sharings and exchanges. They have proven uniquely capable, in each of the regional societies of South Asia, of relating hundreds of units in dozens of higher and lower ranks and of generating new societal forms through combinations and transformations of existing schemes.

FOREIGN CONCEPTIONS OF SOUTH ASIAN CASTE SYSTEMS

For about two centuries, the explanation and analysis of South Asian caste systems have been matters of interest and controversy among foreign observers, who have brought with them assumptions and sensitivities peculiar to their own respective societies and times.

No visitor of ancient or medieval times seems to have felt that rank, corporateness, heredity, and endogamy among the occupational and ethnic groups of India were worthy of special mention. The Portuguese seafarers who traded mainly on the west coast of India in the 16th and 17th centuries described groups they called *castas* (from which derive the English and French words *caste*), meaning "species" or "breeds" of animals or plants and "tribes," "races," "clans," or "lineages" among men. Only in the 18th century did the distinction that is now made between unranked tribes and ranked castes begin to be drawn clearly in the usage of the French and English.

Consideration of the thoroughgoing inequality and exclusiveness of the castes, as well as the peculiar occupational division of labour prescribed for them, generally produced a sense of shock in Western missionaries and officials of the turbulent 19th and 20th centuries. Attempts were made to explain the castes as an imagined rational legislation by some unknown past authority, as a self-serving invention by the system's top-ranking priestly castes, or (after Charles Darwin) as the unplanned evolution of successively higher castes through the growth of superior technological specialization.

Attempts by Western observers to explain castes

The insufficiency of these—or, indeed, of any—simple conjectures for explaining the origins of these apparently irrational systems strengthened a trend toward more complex historical speculation. Castes were seen as heirs of the Indo-European language family's common traditions of private kin-group ritual by Émile Senart, a late-19th-century Sanskrit scholar. In 1891 H.H. Risley, a British Indian census commissioner, reported that proportionally wider noses correlate with lower caste rank and also with a geographic gradation from northern to southern India; this suggested a hypothesis of repeated invasion from Central Asia and from the north to the south by longer nosed racial elements. Other official British Indian research stressed separate surveys of the physical traits and customs of each of the thousands of castes and tribes. Compendious reports of such surveys reinforced a conception of Indian society as a geographical accident and a political composite. Many authors speculated on historical factors favouring the development of the Indian caste systems—such factors as diffusions of primitive customs, ancient movements of peoples, and the mutually distancing adaptations of allegedly alien peoples to each other—and these speculations were compiled in a list of 15 factors by J.H. Hutton, census commissioner and ethnologist, at the end of the British regime in 1946.

What was missing from these atomistic historical analyses was any conception of a caste system as an integrated whole. Such conceptions were provided in nationalistic political contexts in the late 19th and early 20th centuries. Max Weber, a German sociologist, emphasized the connections of caste with Hindu religion as part of his larger effort to reveal why the West had progressed more rapidly than Asia. Skeptical toward Hindu religious explanations, the French sociologist Célestin Bouglé in 1908 postulated, from descriptions of the relations of the castes, an underlying set of social structural "ideas"—hereditary specialization, rank, and mutual repulsion concerned with purity and impurity—governing the whole system. Hutton held that social differentiation in caste systems requires an assumption of a once widespread preliterate philosophy concerning the powers of bodily and other substances and the dangers of magical contagion. The British social anthropologist A.M. Hocart, combining observations in Sri Lanka (Ceylon) and Polynesia with Vedic (early Indian-language) texts, saw caste systems as organizations for royal rituals of worship. In 1952 M.N. Srinivas, an Indian anthropologist working in southern India, attempted to derive both the unity and the ranks of Indian caste systems from the imitation by diverse groups of the customs of the highest Hindu castes, a process that he called "sanskritization."

Western social values reflected in explanations

Western comparative social theorists have generally placed caste systems not in a unique religious ideological or structural category by themselves but at the end of a theoretical series of types beyond medieval and ancient Europe and furthest from the equalitarian, competitive tendencies of the modern West in matters of social differentiation and social stratification. The enclosure of individuals in culturally diverse ranked ethnic groups (castes) was seen as poles away from a culturally homogenizing and individualizing modern society. The multiplicity of the castes and their apparent social distance and segregation from each other through endogamy and restrictions on contact seemed to exceed in stringency any but the most extreme differentiations (*e.g.*, Black and white in the U.S.) among ethnic groups of a single society in the West. Castes were also commonly regarded in Western comparative perspective simultaneously as social-status groups and as economic classes. They were considered rigidly closed classes, permitting recruitment of individuals into caste membership only by birth, not by achievement. Caste systems were further mistakenly thought to allow vertical mobility only through movement by the whole corporate unit, not through individual or familial movement. They were seen as guaranteeing the virtual immobility of groups, as well, owing either to the preponderant power of the conservative high-caste elite or to the strength of cultural consensus and traditional sacred sanctions or to both.

Although comparative sociology thus attempted to look at South Asian caste systems as extreme instances of presumed universal features of human society and implied a view of them as social systems rather than as accidental collections of ideas and peoples, its typifications of these systems remained sociocentric, reflecting modern Western society's assumptions about essential elements and processes, while reversing some cherished Western values. It did not attempt to base its understanding closely upon the cognitive assumptions actually prevalent in South Asia. For understanding of this sort, one must examine certain Indian social concepts that are known first from Vedic texts from 1000 BC. These are maintained to the present by the predominant Hindu population and are widely shared among persons of all religions residing in South Asia.

CASTE SYSTEMS IN SOUTH ASIA

Indian social concepts. *Substance and code in the relationships among castes.* The organization of South Asian society is premised on the ancient and continuing cultural assumption that all living beings are differentiated into genera, or classes, each of which is thought to possess a defining coded substance. One of the commonest words for genus in most Indian languages, *jāti*, is derived from an Indo-European verbal root meaning "genesis," "origin," or "birth." It is applied to any species of living things, including gods and humans. Among humans, *jāti* can designate a distinct sex, a race, a caste, or a tribe; a family, a lineage, or a clan; an ethnic group, a regional population, the followers of an occupation or a religion, or a nation.

Jāti

Every human genus (and therefore every caste) is thought to have as the shared or corporate property of its members a particular substance (*e.g.*, *śarīra*, "body," *rakta*, "blood") embodying its code for conduct (*dharma*). Each caste's inborn code enjoins it to maintain its substance and morality, its particular occupation, and its correct exchanges with other castes. Indian thought does not separate "nature" and "morality" or "law," so that castes are, in Western terms, at once "natural" and "moral" units of society. These units make up a single order, one that is profoundly particularized.

The persons of each caste are believed to transmit the particles of substance that are peculiar to their caste from one generation to the next through a series of natural and moral acts extending from birth to marriage. The male and female sexes, like castes, are thought to be composed of nonequivalent, complementarily coded bodily substances; the reproductive essence of each, variously conceptualized but often identified with semen and uterine blood, is required to make the child complete from birth in his caste's particular nature. Acts that wrongly mix bodily substances, such as improper procreation, are thought to alter the embodied morality of the caste and its offspring. Each caste must therefore be concerned with regulating marriage.

Castes are related to each other externally not by

hereditarily shared substance but by exchange of nonhereditary substances. Each caste is involved through its existence and its means of subsistence in transformations and exchanges of transformed natural substances. Of these substances, a caste's own bodily substances (*e.g.*, hair, blood, semen, and feces) and food (which is seen as becoming transformed into human bodily substance) are considered capable of creating, expressing, or altering relationships of rank and solidarity between it and other castes. The substances derived from each caste's pursuit of its occupation are also major media, along with services, of intercaste exchange. Each caste is thought to maintain or alter its moral standing (that is, its rank with respect to other castes), its hereditary substance, and its natural code according to the way that it receives or refuses to receive bodily substances, consumes or refuses to consume food, and gives or refuses to give services in exchanges with particular other castes.

Varṇa categories in the Vedic sacrifice. A conception of Indian society in terms of genus (*varṇa*, here synonymous with *jāti*) appeared first in the Ṛgveda, the oldest collection of Vedic priestly hymns, composed in Punjab about 1200–1000 BC. The Vedic people of that time saw themselves as members of a single "genus of respectable men" (*ārya-varṇa*), "the humans" (*manuṣa*). Their code enjoined them to offer sacrifice (*yajña*) to members of another genus of beings, the Vedic gods (*devas*); it also enjoined them to smite and enslave their enemies, "the nonhumans" (*dasyu-varṇa*), who were naturally and morally fit for service.

The conception of society as containing more than two *varṇa*s appeared only after 1000 BC, when descendants of these early Aryans began to settle in the upper Ganges region and built a more complex society containing towns and the beginnings of states. It appeared then in the increasingly elaborate body of Vedic sacred texts and ultimately reached its culmination in the classical moral code book (*Dharma-śāstra*) of the Manu school (*c.* 200 BC–AD 200).

Division of Puruṣa into specialized *varṇa*s

The whole later Vedic society continued to think of itself as sharing one original natural substance, conceived as the body of Puruṣa, the original code man. The division of Puruṣa by the gods into distinct specialized *varṇas* mythically inaugurated the Vedic sacrifice. Henceforth, only those who had the substance of Puruṣa in their bodies were to follow the code of exchanges required by the sacrifice.

Sacrifice was seen as fundamental for upholding the natural and moral order of the cosmos. It required exchanges between the two specialized genera, gods and men. Gods, the beings who wield divine power (*brahman*), were seen as the ultimate source of bodily existence and well-being; men were the givers of the food that the gods needed to sustain themselves. Mutual exchange of food through the sacrifice thus created solidarity between gods and men.

Exchange in the sacrifice also created a ranked relationship between gods and men. Only pure food was fed to gods by men, while gods, after they had eaten, returned only their leavings for men to eat. These same asymmetrical events that created rank—that elevated the gods and lowered men—were conversely interpreted as expressions of rank previously established. Thus, men regarded their own food leavings as contaminated by saliva and therefore as impure and valueless to others but considered the leavings of the gods as transvalued—pure and incomparably valuable precisely because they were filled with the divine natural substance that brought human well-being.

Rank in this ancient South Asian moral order was thought of as being based less upon established possessions than upon generosity. Gods were of higher rank than men not so much because they possessed the attribute of divine power as because they were incomparably generous in bestowing that power on men. Men were of lower rank because they could not return this gift. They could give the gods the most valued foods, but they could not equal the value of the divine power contained in the gods' gift to men.

The same relationship existed among the specialized natural genera within the society of men—between the "once-born" and the genera of the "twice-born" (*dvi-jāti*), those who became divinized humans through a second, ritual birth. The once-born, called Śūdra (Servant), was not to hear the sacred Vedic words or to sacrifice directly or to receive the gods' leavings. He was instead to exchange with the twice-born in the same way that the twice-born, to whom the term *ārya* was exclusively applied, exchanged with the gods. Born of the lowest part of Puruṣa, the feet, the Śūdra followed a code enjoining him to serve the twice-born in exchange for maintenance. He could symbolize his ranked relationship, as was done in the sacrifice, by feeding pure food to his human superiors and eating their leavings in return. His service was a form of worship but an inferior one that properly brought only the divine gift of maintenance in return. Because the Śūdra was defined as being unable to return even this gift of maintenance, his moral rank was considered to be lower than the rank of the twice-born.

The twice-born was the divine human genus of Aryans, whose males came to share the divine sounds of the Veda through a second, divine birth and initiation into Vedic study and sacrifice. Their code also required married male householders to exchange gifts among themselves. The wife and children of a twice-born householder were forbidden, as was the Śūdra, from hearing Vedic sounds and from carrying on the sacrifice. But women and children were conceived as sharing the effects of those duties through having bodily substance in common with their household head.

The three types of twice-born persons

The code book enjoining sacrifice and exchange also defined three specialized genera of people within the twice-born genus. The substance of each of these had its distinctive ranked origin and inherent ranked powers, and the code for conduct of each was specialized. The Brāhmaṇa, born from the highest part of Puruṣa, his mouth, possessed godly power (*brahman*): he was to teach the Vedas, perform sacrifices for the Kṣatriya and Vaiśya, and accept gifts from them in exchange. The Kṣatriya, born from the arms of Puruṣa, possessed royal power (*kṣatra*): he was to fight enemies, give gifts and food to the Brāhmaṇa, and protect the Vaiśya; in exchange, he received a share in the leavings of the sacrifice from the Brāhmaṇa and wealth from the Vaiśya. The Vaiśya, born from the thighs of Puruṣa, possessed productive power (*viś*): he was to produce wealth for the Brāhmaṇa and the Kṣatriya through agriculture, commerce, and animal herding, and was to give a share of it as taxes to the Kṣatriya in exchange for protection.

Each superior genus is considered divine in relation to each inferior genus. The moral ranks of the genera were gauged in *varṇa* theory also by the values assigned to the different things they gave each other. Since the wealth given by the Vaiśya to the Kṣatriya was considered less valuable than the divine protection received in exchange, the Vaiśya ranked below the Kṣatriya. The Brāhmaṇa acting as representative of the whole society, fed the gods through the sacrifice and was first to eat their leavings, to take their power. In comparison to the Kṣatriya and the Vaiśya, he was therefore a "god on earth." Because the gifts and food given by the Kṣatriya and the Vaiśya to the Brāhmaṇa were considered to be less in value than the remainder of the sacrificial leavings that he gave to them, he was thought to have a higher rank than they. Beneath all three was the Śūdra, with his offering of mere labour, benefitting by the activities of all.

The four *varṇa*s of Vedic theory may have had a waning existence in parts of northern India when the theory was first being formulated, between 1000 and 300 BC. But the authors of the classical moral code books in the centuries following (*c.* 200 BC–AD 200) were concerned with reconciling this theory with the multitude of specialized *jātis* of uncertain *varṇa* that they actually saw about them. They explained the existence of non-Vedic *jāti*s by a theory of miscegenation: the *jāti*s were offspring of improper mixing and remixing among descendants of the four pure Vedic *varṇa*s. The numerous *jāti* units, their varied codes for conduct, and many ranks were all seen in the Vedic scheme itself as responses to the requirements of particular places, times, and genera of persons. The four *varṇa*s together with the sacrifice from which they were thought to spring were seen as the universal, eternal, and logically complete scheme for upholding nature and morality.

Hindu worship and the castes. The Vedic scheme continues to the present as a template, generating systematic conceptions of the local, everchanging castes (*jāti*s) and their exchanges in the closely connected scheme of Hindu image worship, called *pūjā* (literally, "respect"). Evidences of the proliferous systems of castes connected with image worship appeared gradually after AD 500.

Complex systems of castes required by Hindu image worship

The Hindu gods to be worshipped are related among themselves, like men, by shared and exchanged natural substance. They have not merely abstract qualities and representations like the Vedic gods, but also particular lifelike images, biographies, bodily functions, and specialized relations to men. They are attached by particular codes of worship to particular occasions, communities, and genera of persons. The occasions for their worship are times of bodily events in their own or their worshippers' lives—births, weddings, deaths, and the routines of such things as the daily bath or meals—and in the natural cycles of the Sun, Moon, Earth, and other planets, whose heat and cold, dark and light, wet and dry, etc., are seen as bodily states affecting human beings.

The codes of Hindu worship require the existence of complex local communities of castes. Worship cannot proceed without a priest to bring the living substance of the god into the image, made by an image maker. The priest must utter formulas (*mantras*) that activate this divine life substance and other formulas that have the power to transform the ordinary materials of worship into sublime offerings. The priest must be a male of the highest, most godlike caste available—ideally a Brahmin skilled by heredity in the maintenance of ritual boundaries between substances, and empowered to transform them.

To sponsor the worship there must be a local worshipper of means, typically a ruler or man of wealth, who can by gifts entreat a priest to mediate with the god. There must be specialists of appropriate castes—*e.g.*, temple keeper, garland maker, cook, sweet maker, singer, musician, dancer—to feed, attend, and entertain the god. Before the worshipper can approach the god, he must prepare himself and his caste to be as godlike as possible and must remove as much as possible from his person and his caste any insulting, transmissible bodily substance. He does so through bathing and through engaging the services practiced by other castes, such as those who do the work of barber, washerman, midwife, funeral priest, leatherworker, scavenger, or sweeper. These castes are by their intimate receivings of bodily substance rendered subordinate to the worshipper, as a child's receiving of bodily substance renders him subordinate to his parents. Each caste contributes in its particular way to the worship, directly or indirectly, and each then receives in return and in order of rank a share, either in the transvalued leavings of the god's food (called *prasāda*, "favour") or in the leavings of those who do receive a share.

Hindu worship thus greatly ramifies the specialities assigned to the four *varṇa*s and invites specialization by caste. One effect of such worship is a ranking of all participating castes by a pattern of exchanges in which natural substances and services go up and divinely transvalued substances containing divine benefits go down. Another effect is the establishment of a solidarity of substance among all the castes.

Varieties of caste systems. Caste groups range in size from hundreds up to millions, with their estimated median population lying between 5,000 and 15,000. Such populations are likely to be spread over dozens or hundreds of villages and cities and over hundreds of miles of territory. Thus, few castes ever meet as wholes in one place. Nevertheless, the universality of concern for a caste's substance and code and for its rank (which can be altered for all by the conduct of a single member) guarantees at least an informal, diffuse organization of authority within each caste. Recruitment of allies or a shift to a larger context of competition may lead a caste to fuse with groups otherwise treated as separate categories.

In the eyes of others, a caste is most often categorized in an occupational role. Each caste in fact owns a set of related occupations among which its members may choose according to their particular economic situation. Thus, for example, each of the "royal," traditionally warrior, castes (called Rājput) includes landlords, cultivating tenants, and landless labourers, as well as princes and soldiers. Least specialized are some of the tribal *jāti*s in the hills and forests of central India, who traditionally do for themselves all work except metal-working and the literate professions. About one-third of all the South Asian population is in castes for whom some aspect of agriculture is the main traditional occupation. Another third, traditionally specialized by caste in nonagricultural work, in fact earns most of its living in agriculture.

Local communities and class

Settlements of fewer than 1,000 persons have contained most of the predominantly rural population of South Asia up to the 20th century. These settlements have commonly comprised members of from five to 20 castes—the number varying according to the density of the particular region and the wealth of the local population. Contact among persons of different castes is typically close and frequent in villages, being required by economic division of labour and by the forms of ceremony. Persons are readily identified by one another as members of known castes and the import of their actions accurately assessed. On the average, villagers agree with each other by majorities of 90 percent or more concerning the ranks of eight out of any 12 local castes.

Apart from their belonging to castes, the households of most villages are organized in economic and political systems that concentrate power in the hands of a landed or commercial minority. Membership in the local ruling class rarely corresponds closely with the membership of any local caste group: individuals, households, and families may rise or fall in their economic resources and influence, apart from the ranks of their castes. Local caste groups often differ greatly in their members' aggregate or average wealth and influence. Castes that have no other economic resources must serve and defer in ritual ways to those with power in order to subsist. Rank is traded in order to eat. Thus, the actual distribution of politico-economic power within a community can effect a rearrangement of the order of ranks among the castes.

The rankings of castes in villages are alterable but are not quickly altered, locally supported as they usually are by politico-economic interests, restrained by complex multilateral exchanges, and remembered by minds accustomed to a hereditary order. The mild but ubiquitous inclination of castes to improve their ranks can be estimated from the finding that the average villager believes the correct rank of his own caste to be about half a rank higher than what nonmembers of his caste are willing to concede. Efforts by rural caste groups to depart from the locally accepted line of precedence are numerous, even if moderate and slow to take effect. That castes' local ranks do change is known from case histories and from the differences in the same castes' ranks that occur from place to place.

The caste systems of rural people, as they are believed to have existed at the beginning of British rule in 1858 and as they continue to some degree into the present, can be divided into five major regions of South Asia.

Caste systems in southern India and Sri Lanka (Ceylon). Dravidian-speaking south India is characterized by a proliferation of castes, consistent with regional concern for the integrity of female bodily substance. Except in the matrilineal castes (in which membership is gained through the mother) of Kerala, both parents are thought of as contributing caste code to their offspring. Marriages outside Kerala are uniformly made within the caste. Endogamous castes here tend to become very small and close, to divide into numerous smaller circles by the preferred repetition of reciprocal, protective marriages among cousins and other known kin. Distinctions between castes are more often marked by visible attributes. Only whole, uncooked foods, such as betel leaf and nut, are much exchanged beyond the caste and household.

The relatively small spread of each caste leaves it available to be ranked consistently by its members' exchanges with other castes in just a few nearby localities; there is little danger of conflict over precedence through comparisons with possibly inconsistent rankings of the same castes in any remote villages or kingdoms. At the same time, local communities are the largest and most complex in South Asia, averaging ten to 15 local caste groups in the southeast and 15 to 20 in the southwest.

The stability of rice agriculture and government in the lowlands of southern India have also favoured a formal administration of land tenure from the state down to the cultivator (*raiyatvāri* tenure), operating either through hereditary local officials whose castes (*e.g.*, the Nāyar) have been or become regarded as the high castes or through land-endowed temples administered by Brahmins. Dynasties have had long durations, and conquests by other than neighbouring kingdoms have been few. One result has been a frequently close identification of land-tenure positions with certain castes and a closer correlation than elsewhere between castes' ranks and their powers. Brāhmaṇa caste groups have in some areas taken the positions of rulers. Another result of these conditions has been the formal social organization of the whole village community on caste lines for the several purposes of legal administration, occupation, and ritual.

Rankings of local castes in 20 or more grades are encountered in Kerala. An extreme etiquette of formal speech, clothing, gesture, and distancing among the castes is required there. On the other hand, repetition of the sets of priestly and pollution-removing (*e.g.*, barber, washerman) castes for patrons at three or four ranks and marriage of women above their caste (intercaste hypergamy) integrate the many castes into single, ranked schemes. The central role of Hindu temples in focussing the services and ranks of castes continues from Kerala up the western coast of Mysore and also down to Sri Lanka (Ceylon), especially in its Kandyan highland region. In much of Sri Lanka (Ceylon), however, the small village settlements have few castes, favouring their Buddhist caste system.

The caste systems of villages in Tamilnadu and Andhra Pradesh are less centrally structured and somewhat less elaborately ranked than in Kerala. Local communities contain fewer castes, castes whose wealth and power are less closely correlated with their ranks and whose residences are divided into hamlets with separate caste-linked temples. In some districts castes are organized in competing sets—*e.g.*, castes of the "right hand" versus those of the "left hand"—reflecting rivalries between ruling castes, between indigenous and immigrant castes, or between agriculturalists on the one hand and traders and artisans on the other.

Castes in the northern plains

Caste systems in the northern plains of India. The region of the later Aryan settlement in eastern Punjab and in the upper Ganges Valley (in Uttar Pradesh) and of the plains in the north Indian area where Indo-Aryan languages continue to be spoken today (Bihār, West Bengal, and Gujarāt) are generally densely populated with moderately sized villages having caste systems somewhat less elaborate than those in southeastern India. Each settlement averages about 500 persons belonging to ten castes, nine of which are Hindu and one is Muslim.

Centralization and formal organization are slight. Villages in the northern parts generally have no temple at all; those of Gujarāt generally have many private temples but none that can bring all the castes of a locality together in a ranked order of worship; those of Bihār and West Bengal that have centralized worship, organized by a local landlord, are few. The intercaste organization in the villages of the northern plains, both for worship and for control of land and conflict, tends to be based upon a plurality of landed households, mostly of the higher castes. Each household conducts its separate worship, and each separately employs specialist members of five to 15 castes. Such specialists serve by heredity on fixed rates of annual payment either in land or crop shares.

The main occasions for proving the ranks of the castes, beyond the regularly rendered services and payments, are household-sponsored feasts. Intercaste feasts in this region use a class of perfected (*pakkā*) cooked foods that are based on clarified butter, need not be served hot, and are therefore thought to be not so open to combination with bodily substance. Such feasts are offered to representatives of every caste in the village, and the resulting acceptances and rejections of food make public show of each caste's relative standing.

Local rankings of the castes in most of the northern plains are less isolated and more subject to contravention by rankings occurring elsewhere, primarily as a result of the very wide range of marriage. Except in Bengal, clan terms of kinship are used locally among persons of all castes, and locally born women must marry outside their localities. Caste by caste, linear rankings of local castes become impossible. Nevertheless, high local agreement occurs on blocks of castes; about three-quarters of the possible ranks are distinguishable.

Some castes of the northernmost plains, with some higher castes of the central region and all castes of the western region, hold that their natural code is transmitted by the father alone. Many of these marry hypergamously, linking higher with lower clans and castes. Castes here tend to have larger spreads and the largest regional populations.

The small kingdoms and pockets of Hindu and Buddhist settlement on the Himalayan slopes of northern South Asia differ greatly from the plains and among themselves in their environments. Many villages here are composed of only one, two, or three castes or tribes and thus have a very simple division of labour. These villages may be quite isolated settlements, practicing close reciprocal marriages.

The more densely populated Himalayan areas, such as the valley of Nepal, were strongly Hinduized by Rājput and Brāhmaṇa immigrants, increasingly so after the Muslim conquests of the plains. Nepal contains dozens of Buddhist and Hindu castes that are elaborately graded and linked, both by position in the state and sometimes by intercaste hypergamous marriages. Both parents are believed to transmit caste-coded substance, and offspring of mixed marriages are assigned to third castes having ranks between those of their two parents' castes.

Caste systems in central India

Caste systems in central India. The central Hindu region extending from Rājasthān in the north through Madhya Pradesh to Mahārāshtra on the south and Orissa on the east is characterized by relatively sparse rural population that tends to be concentrated in villages of moderately large size—500 to 700. The average number of castes present in these villages is less than in the northern plains, for in each state and locality two or three out of a few very large clusters of castes preponderate.

Within the central zone, the regions of Rājasthān, Kutch, Kāthiāwār, and much of Madhya Pradesh contain large desert or hilly areas that can be exploited fully only by herders and semimigratory farmers. Where permanent villages exist, they organize hereditary intercaste services by household. But wide and flexible networks of organization are advantageous within the castes of these mobile farmers. They are essential for the controlling castes of Rājput and other warriors and among the numerous small Hindu and Jaina (a religion founded in India in the 6th century BC) trading castes of the region. Such networks are structured for these higher castes not by close caste councils such as those that prevail in southern India but rather by the rulers' deep and widespread corporate lineages and clans (recorded for them by genealogist castes), by belief in exclusively male transmission of caste code, and by broad rules of marriage like those found in the northern plains. Within such rules, alliances may be sought and broken. Equipped with such effective structures for mutual aid in an otherwise famine-prone environment, cultivating (Rājput), herding (Gūjar, Ahīr), and merchant (Mārwāri) castes of the dry lands have spread into the neighbouring plains, often as predatory forces in politics and commerce. At the same time, the nondominant castes of Rājasthān, although widely dispersed, follow an opposite strategy of reciprocating, caste-endogamous marriage (inside the caste) that tends to consolidate rather than expand their scarce resources.

South of Rājasthān and north of Mahārāshtra is the fertile plateau of Mālwa, a crossroads of trade, migrations, and routes of conquest in all directions. Villages here, like villages in parts of southeastern India, are often divided between two sets of castes: on the one hand, those who eat meat, worship the Hindu goddesses, and follow the Rājput and local Brāhmaṇa codes and, on the other hand, those who are vegetarian, worship the Hindu god Viṣṇu, follow the Vaiśya code, and are often immigrant castes.

Farther south in the central zone is Mahārāshtra. The Mahārāshtrian village makes public feasting an important focus of intercaste relationships, although restricting feasting to the feeding of kinsmen and traditional servants; it also separates its lowest castes (*e.g.*, Mahār) from the others in a distinct residential hamlet, regards its specialist castes as serving the village as a whole, and organizes all its castes around one or more temples. What distinguishes and moderates intercaste relations in the Mahārāshtrian village is the strongly communitarian nature of village institutions: the village runs its affairs by decision of a village council that includes representatives of all castes and typically makes its main temple into a community centre. It shares some of these features with villages in adjacent sections of western Andhra Pradesh (Telingana or Telengana) and northwestern Mysore.

On the wide eastern and southern margins of the central zone and through its heart in the hills of the west and on both sides of the Narmada River Valley are forested areas inhabited largely by hundreds of tribal peoples—endogamous ethnic groups that have distinct moral systems, that trade their products in peasant markets, but that engage little if at all in the exchanges related to worship that would make them part of any neighbouring Hindu moral system of ranked groups. Non-Hindu tribes are also numerous in Assam and in the North East Frontier Agency (*e.g.*, Nāga). Many Hindu castes derive from such tribes.

Caste systems in Bangladesh and Pakistan

Caste systems in Bangladesh. The densely populated floodplain of the Ganges and Brahmaputra rivers differs radically from northern India in the ecology of its human settlement. A conception of the stable village of locally exchanging castes does not exist. Instead, the scattered households, loosely linked in shifting affiliation with the stronger leaders among them, seek to fill their needs for caste-specialized products through resort to cash exchanges at rotating markets. What specialized services and goods are not traded at markets are brought door-to-door by waterborne artisans and merchants. Even agricultural labourers are often itinerant and indistinguishable from mobile fishermen; only domestic service is generally rendered on long-term local contracts.

The rural population of this socially fluid region is also for the most part relatively undifferentiated by caste and even by kinship groupings of any considerable depth. Localities for miles may be inhabited by a single genus of Muslim cultivators: specialized Hindu castes concentrate themselves apart or cluster at the rare permanent markets and centres of land administration. Thus, neither the human materials nor the institutions of domestic or community worship are present to encourage any elaborate rankings of castes. Indeed, the region is not known to have been Hindu in any large degree or for any appreciable time. Its older past was Buddhist in regime; it came at last under the rule of a Hindu dynasty only a century before its conversion to Islām began in the 13th century. Both Buddhist and Islāmic treatments of caste are congenial to the peculiarities of the region.

Caste systems in Pakistan. Like Bangladesh, the provinces of Pakistan—the desert of Baluchistan, the hills of the Northwest Frontier Province and Kashmir, and the plains of Sind and West Punjab—passed from a Buddhist to an Islāmic regime without elaborate development of caste ranking in the Hindu style. Here, again, the ecology of much of the region does not permit the coresidence of many ethnic groups. Neither the mobile herdsmen of the desert and hills nor the cultivators in tiny hamlets on the Indus Plain can assemble many castes to construct complex local systems. Exchanges among the castes of these areas take place more often in towns and for cash at market rates.

Where villages are larger and richer, as in West Punjab, they have attracted members of numerous castelike lineages, or clans, and have become more than equal in ethnic complexity to villages of Hindu eastern Punjab. But here conditions of instability—like those noted for Rājasthān and Mālwa in the central region of India—play a part, for both West Punjab and the Northwest Frontier Province have been shattered socially by repeated tribal incursions. Parts of the same tribes and lineages have taken widely varying ranks, according to their political fortunes in different localities. Although marriage is spatially closer than in south India, tribal and lineal names are spread over great distances and tend to confound ranks based on local exchanges. Fewer than one-third of the possible ranks are therefore found to be distinguished among castes in villages and towns of this region.

Caste systems outside South Asia

South Asian caste systems overseas. Caste systems have been carried by South Asians to other continents but are found there only in drastically reduced versions.

Traders and settlers from India established elite cultures of Vedic, then Buddhist religion in many parts of Southeast Asia during the early centuries of the Christian Era, but only on the small Hindu island of Bali are traces of a caste society known to have survived beyond the advent of Islām. In Bali, the four Vedic *varṇa*s are employed as a ranked classification of patrilineal titles (those handed down through the father's line of descent) held by generally endogamous (sometimes hypergamously related) lineages. Higher titleholders are more likely to marry nonlocally. They often receive elaborate verbal deference from lowers. They may refuse cooked food from lowers to assert superiority without believing that food transfers alone can alter rank. Apart from some specialization in worship, Balinese caste titles in practice designate claims to rank, rather than major occupational groupings.

The millions of South Asians who went as labourers to Africa, Malaya, Fiji, Trinidad, Surinam, and Guyana in the 19th and 20th centuries proved unable to carry complex caste systems with them. The regional heterogeneity of those who migrated permanently made their caste identities and their codes of exchange mutually unintelligible. Original caste names have been changed, and identities of code and substance are everywhere merged by marriage into composite regional or linguistic and religious castes. Such a composite Hindu caste is commonly further divided by a single distinction into a priestly and nonpriestly caste. Only those overseas traders (in Burma, Malaya, or East Africa) who return periodically to their home regions are able to adhere to their original codes of marriage and caste identity. Nowhere abroad have modern South Asians set up local communities having a caste division of labour in work or worship, again excepting the Brāhmaṇa role among Hindus.

Caste systems in cities. Caste systems are also modified by the conditions of city life. Like overseas migrants, urban residents in South Asian cities of all regions and since ancient times have had to cope with the difficulty of identifying and ordering great numbers of regionally heterogeneous castes. They have attracted and supported specialized groups little known in rural areas. They have also had to cope with largeness of scale, with recognizing the castes of thousands of mobile individuals. Their larger populations within each caste have furthermore tended to segregate themselves in self-sufficient enclaves, each with its own internal division of labour and its separate cult or sect. Finally, their intercaste exchanges have always tended to be mediated more by shifting power and prices in the marketplace than by corporate group codes.

Specialized mercantile, administrative, and military camp cities of the northern and western regions have seen these tendencies carried furthest, also suffering frequent depopulation and relocation with changes in their specific functions. Certain more permanent royal and religious cities, especially in the south, have seen these tendencies counteracted most fully by centralized exchanges at palace or temple among formal representatives of the various castes. Royal regulation of service, payment, residence, and consumption according to caste rank and unilateral arbitration of disputes over rank also reduced the urban potentialities of anonymity and disorder.

Caste and the religions related to Hinduism. Belonging to a caste is thought by South Asians of the indigenous religions to raise difficulties for the perfection of a person's "soul," his unique natural code (*ātman*). Yet a person cannot exist embodied in the natural order without belonging by birth to one of that order's natural genera and without being subject to its inborn generic code.

Religious attempts to find liberation from caste

Vedic liberation and caste. In the Vedic view, the soul is contained in two kinds of body: a gross body that is abandoned at death and a subtle body that clings to the soul. The gross body belongs to a natural genus, while the subtle body does not; yet, being still a unit in the natural order, the subtle body must go on to be reborn sooner or later within a gross body belonging to some natural genus. The moral actions (*karman*) of a person in following the code of his genus affect the quality of his natural substance; and this determines where in the ranked order of natural genera his soul will be reborn—among plants, animals, demons, gods, or in the same or some other caste of humans.

Further Vedic views stress not the unknowable ultimate rebirth of the soul but its long continuity in its original birth as a heaven-dwelling spiritual ancestor, fed by offerings from corporeal descendants, or as a dissatisfied terrestrial ghost, troubling living persons. These and still other Vedic views continue in the beliefs of some Hindu castes, along with popular theories of this-worldly punishment and reward for moral actions.

Liberation (*mokṣa*) from the endless flux (*saṃsāra*) of birth and rebirth—often called transmigration—is the highest goal of the Vedic religion. Liberation means absorption of the individual code or soul into Brahman, the divine, perfect substance that is the ultimate source of the natural and moral order. This goal is attainable only by a male of twice-born genus who has followed the sacrificial code through the three life stages of student, householder, and forest dweller. Only he is to enter the fourth, or ascetic (*sannyāsi*), stage by abandoning the sacrifice and performing his own funeral. As an ascetic, he is morally dead and thus need have no more concern for his caste nor it for him. He is to own nothing and give nothing to others but is to beg from others of any caste a minimum of food. Thus abasing himself, the ascetic reverses his former high rank. Through knowledge and meditation and aided by such austerities, he strives to obtain control over the relationship of his soul and body in order to effect their complete separation. At his second, natural death, if he has achieved control, his soul is thought to attain perfect liberation from the caste-bound natural order.

Hindu sects and caste. Later, in Hinduism, liberation is thought to be attained through the individual's participation in one of the numerous Śaiva, Vaiṣṇava, or Śākta "sects." Each sect is both a divine and a human moral order thought to have a code above and beyond the natural and moral codes that are inborn in the ranked human genera. Each sectarian order consists of three kinds of persons—gods, preceptors (gurus), and devotees. Persons of any caste or sex are thought eligible to participate. They are related within the sect not by their previous particular natures but by manipulations of divinely coded substance.

In some sects, liberation is attained by assembling these persons more closely. By means of direct personal devotion (*bhakti*) to a chosen supreme deity, devotees are believed to attain a permanent relationship of superior love (*parā-bhakti*) equivalent or superior to liberation. By accepting or eating substances, especially food leavings transvalued by preceptor and deity, the devotees bind themselves to the god and to each other as members of his divine family, overriding the ranks of their castes as they are ordinarily maintained through image worship.

In other sects, those called Tantric, liberation is attained by reversal. By means of secret words and prescribed collective ritual acts directly contrary to ordinary moral codes—*e.g.*, eating meat, drinking wine, having promiscuous sexual intercourse—a person is thought to destroy the bonds that normally link him to the lower human order. He is thereby thought to attain a superior liberated state (*parā-mukti*) while still in human form.

Liṅgāyats and Sikhs. The Liṅgāyat community of Mysore arose within Hinduism in opposition to Jaina and Brāhmaṇa domination during the 12th century; the Sikh community of the Punjab arose as a synthesis of Islām and Hinduism during the 16th century. Both religious communities make radical revisions by manipulating together the mutually immanent, nondual constituents of the Hindu systems that are seen either as encoded substances or embodied codes. Liṅgāyats and Sikhs both believe that they become a divine human genus when they are given initiation (*dīkṣā*) into the making of natural sacred sounds by their teachers (gurus). The Liṅgāyats believe that they become human incarnations of their supreme god, Śiva. Being divine, they reason that their bodily substances at birth, death, or menstruation no longer pollute, as do those of ordinary Hindus. The Sikhs believe that through initiation they incorporate their teachers, who are believed to be perfect and divine, even though human. Both Sikhs and Liṅgāyats believe that they attain liberation while still belonging to their many original castes. These castes are thought to continue as a simply human, therefore lower, order. Ranks of castes in these orders, as among Muslims, are expressed in upward transfer of daughters in marriage.

The higher divine order within both of these communities consists of the categories of teachers, priests, and disciples. These categories are also conceived to be both moral and natural. Any person of any caste or sex who comes to possess the sacred natural sounds of the Liṅgāyats or Sikhs may become a Liṅgāyat or Sikh disciple; and any Liṅgāyat or Sikh may in theory become a priest or teacher. In fact, it tends to happen that members of the higher castes are more likely to become teachers or priests, and members of the lowest castes are liable to be regarded as inferior disciples and therefore excluded in some ways. What distinguishes these communities from their Hindu neighbours, despite such discrimination, is their members' mutual sharing and exchange of transvalued substances. Thus, Liṅgāyat disciples and gurus mutually regard each other as gods, drinking the dirt of each other's feet, while Sikhs of all castes drink nectar from a common bowl and take food reciprocally.

Caste systems among non-Hindus in South Asia. Other major religious communities in South Asia share with Vedic and Hindu peoples some basic assumptions regarding the particularity of human genera, the unity of substance and code, and most of the meanings of exchanges. Unlike Hinduism, however, both indigenous Buddhism and the foreign religions are at pains to distinguish human from divine substance and the inferior order of castes from another order of superior morality.

Buddhist conception of a universal moral code

Buddhism and caste. The Buddha and his followers advocated a universal moral code transcending all particular codes. By this code, each person should honour the Buddha and his followers with gifts and should be personally nonviolent, moderate, generous, and self-denying in emulation of the Buddha. Living by this code, any person eventually escapes both from the social order and from the world of nature. He attains a superior non-natural state called Nirvāṇa.

Buddhism relegates the natural Vedic *varṇas* to a lower moral order and distinguishes from it a higher moral order conceived as containing three new categories—householders, king, and monks. Householders of all castes, rather than only Vaiśyas and Śūdras, are seen as the providers of food, wealth, and service. The king and his officials are to be chosen from among the most qualified persons rather than from among Kṣatriyas only. The highest teachers of morality, the Buddhist monks, are to be chosen by personal qualifications, rather than being hereditary Brāhmaṇas.

Ranks among these social categories are conceived in Buddhist thought as emerging from exchanges like the Vedic exchanges. The Buddhist exchanges differ, however, in being conceived as contractual or voluntary in origin, rather than inherent in any genus. Householders owe taxes to the king as a reward for his godlike gifts of protection and charity. Both king and householders make gifts to the propertyless monks; monks should accept these regardless of the nature of the gift or the donor's sex or caste but should return no food substance, not even leavings, to their benefactors. Instead, monks are to return only the supreme gift—instruction in the words of the Buddha regarding knowledge of nature and regarding the code leading to liberation of the soul from the natural order.

The Buddhist conception of society prevailed among peoples on the trade-oriented peripheries of South Asia (the Himalayan borderland, the present Bengal-Bihār, Pakistan, and Sri Lanka [Ceylon]) and in scattered urban areas until the 8th to 13th centuries, when it was supplanted in most areas by Hinduism or Islam. Only in Sri Lanka did a Buddhist society survive along with castes until the British period. There, many gods and ranked systems of 20 or more natural castes are found, much as in Hindu South Asia. Above is the distinctive higher moral order of Buddhism, consisting of the Buddha and several orders of monks, the state, and householders, all concerned with the goal of personal spiritual liberation. In the modern Buddhist democracy of Sri Lanka, natural castes tend to lose their moral significance as units of exchange and rank, while the state's legislation is seen as "returning" the society more and more to the remade social order conceived by the Buddha.

Jainism and caste. Jainism arose at the same time and in the same region (Bihār) as Buddhism, and, like Buddhism, it conceives of certain householders and ascetics—not castes—as the social units of a transcendent moral order. It differs from Buddhism in that it does not present an alternative conception capable of embracing the whole of society. The Jaina code for conduct is more extreme than that of Buddhism, requiring adherence to a rule of thoroughgoing nonviolence. In theory, persons of any *varṇa* or *jāti* may become Jainas; but virtually all occupations, with exceptions such as banking and commerce, are considered to be violent. Hence, most adherents have been members of castes of merchants. Hundreds of small Jaina castes are now found in western India (Gujarāt, Mahārāshtra, Rājasthān).

Islām and caste. Islām was introduced into South Asia by merchants, conquering armies, and missionary Ṣūfīs (Muslim mystics). It became established by the 13th and 14th centuries and became the predominant religion in Pakistan and Bangladesh, where the Buddhist pattern of social organization had predominated. Like the Buddhists, Muslims of South Asia conceive of society as containing a lower and a higher moral order. The lower moral order consists of ranked genera—caste brotherhoods (*berādarīs*) thought to be related by the shared natural substance of blood.

Muslim conception of a lower and a higher moral order

The moral ranks of these rural blood brotherhoods in Pakistan are often based on a reputation for past violence and on the local, hypergamous exchange of women. A brotherhood should take care of its own women; hence, the brotherhood that gives women to another is thought to be morally deficient and to rank lower. In the northern plains of India, where Muslim castes live among Hindu majorities, their moral ranks are more likely to be based on food exchanges. In Muslim-majority communities, however, the public donation of cooked food shows a brotherhood's piety and raises its rank, although the receiving of such donations is not considered to lower its rank.

The moral order of blood brotherhoods, or castes, is felt by Muslims to be transcended by a number of purely social, contractual brotherhoods whose members are supposed to behave toward each other as if they were related by blood even though they are not. The largest purely social brotherhood in the higher moral order is a religious one and consists of those persons who worship Allāh and submit to the Islāmic code for conduct enshrined in the Qur'ān. The single Islāmic deity is said to be the source of the natural and moral order but to transcend it himself. Men depend on him for their bodily existence and salvation, but he does not depend on them, not even for food. Muslims offer up their total submission, but no material goods. However, exchanges of food are made among Muslims on ritual occasions to express the equality and solidarity of the members of a social brotherhood, and also to express the differences of rank in the higher social order. By reciting the sounds of the Qur'ān, eating substances animated by the words of saints, and venerating the remains of dead saints and of the Prophet (Muḥammad) himself, the worshipper becomes more like the saint or the Prophet. Servants of a landholder or followers of a village headman—also brotherhoods in the Muslim moral order—express their subordination by taking ordinary cooked food from him.

The relative ranks of these purely religious and social roles in the higher moral order usually coincide with the relative caste ranks of their occupants in the lower moral order. Persons who occupy the higher roles of saint, pious Muslim, and landholder are usually members of the higher castes, and persons who occupy the lower roles of casual Muslim and servant are usually members of the lower castes. Yet Muslims are quite clear that, when there is a discrepancy between the two, the role occupied by a person in the higher moral order takes precedence. As a result, there is a persistent strain in Muslim communities to bring the caste membership of a person into accord with the role he occupies in the higher Islāmic moral order.

Judaism and Christianity and caste. Other religions accommodate what are seen in South Asia as natural castes. Thus, in Bombay there are Jews of white, black, and recent immigrant descent; in Cochin, besides white and black, there are Jews of slave-mixed descent. Christian converts of many centuries marry and eat within their respective original castes or adopted sects, especially in south India. Adaptations in the higher moral spheres of these religions are much like those made within Buddhism and Islām.

Legal and political roles of caste. *During the pre-British period.* By Hindu conception, castes are categories essential to defining morality (*dharma*, sometimes translated "law"), but not to the calculations of political or economic advantage (*artha*) that all men make as individuals. Morality is conceived to be as highly particularized as nature. Its stratified principles are partly compiled in the moral code books, but its full contents include the varied and innumerable unwritten moral codes (*ācāra*) that are thought to inhere in particular corporate units of each specified kind—lineages (*kula*), castes, or localized communities (*deśa*). If individuals or groups of different castes compete for the same advantages or ends, their competition is not necessarily a matter of moral concern. However, one point of contact between self-interested behaviour and morality is elaborately considered by Hindu legalists: the office of the king. It is the moral duty of the ruler (properly a Kṣatriya) to use force (*daṇḍa*) so as to establish the moral order, especially in order to maintain the rank and separation of the castes, so that their internal self-government and their proper exchanges may continue.

Content of Hindu moral law

All rules, rewards, and punishments among the castes are systematically unequal. Lower castes are customarily prohibited not only from participating in higher worship but also from such acts as touching the higher castes' water, wells, utensils, clothing, persons, or food and from trespassing on their furniture, buildings, roadways, light, sight, and air. Such acts of trespass, along with many more crimes, are scaled from more to less consequential, as the castes involved are ranged from high to low. Done at the command of a person of higher caste to a person of lower caste, such acts are thought to be privileged or acceptable, but, done on the lower's initiative, they cause insult or "pollution" to the higher and deserve graded retaliation or punishment.

During the British period. British administration took an interest in the Vedic moral code books as statements of abstract principle but followed their own views of law as essentially above nature and as unconnected with particular categories of men. As part of a policy of nonintervention in religious and social matters, they declined to play explicitly either the Hindu ruler's role of enforcing caste distinctions or the reformer's role of abolishing them. Local officials were generally as unsympathetic to reform as were local communities, so that, in effect, local caste codes of exchange tended to be supported. At the same time, other governmental measures and widened communications unintentionally encouraged an intensification of internal caste organization. Military units were recruited on a caste basis. The caste membership of individuals was registered in censuses and published in composite totals, and competitive claims by about one-fifth of the castes to affiliation with Vedic *varṇa*s were stimulated by court applications of Hindu personal law.

Limited reforms of the political relationships among castes were undertaken after 1919 in connection with the widening of political franchise. These reforms included reserved legislative seats and benefits in education and employment favouring the lowest ("Scheduled"; *i.e.*, officially listed) and very low ("Backward") castes and tribes. Such reforms underlined the separateness of caste groups and rewarded political allegiance to them and to the imperial government awarding the new advantages. Certain larger castes or merged clusters of similar castes also became politicized, forming associations to press for advantages in the widened arena of governmental competition. In all regions, effective organization for gaining power required less narrowly based political alliances, factions, and parties that could incorporate members of many castes.

Effects of the Indian independence movement

Such political changes during the later British era, along with the British exclusion of religion from governmental concern, stimulated leaders of the independence movement to try to reshape the Hindu social system, seen as a whole made up of particular natural genera, into a structure suited to the winning and the running of a nation of united citizens. B.G. Tilak in Mahārāshtra in the 1890s mobilized urban ceremonies of communal worship in which representatives of all Hindu castes and neighbourhoods offered prayers for political salvation to the Vedic and regional god Gaṇapati. Mahatma Gandhi, Tilak's pupil and the architect of India's freedom, in the 1930s urged a return from the multiplicity of *jāti*s and secular individualism to a neo-Vedic system of four *varṇa*s and stages of personal life (*varṇāśrama-dharma*). This was to be a system emphasizing the mutual responsibility of each to all, one in which men would affiliate themselves with *varṇa*s (interpreted as organically related socioeconomic classes) according to the way they reshaped their bodily natures by following codes of vegetarian and nonalcoholic diet, fasting, sexual abstinence, and public service. Gandhi's hope was to abolish the category of the lowest, sub-Śūdra castes—whose members he labelled Harijans (Offspring of God)—by reversing their former position in the code of exchanges. Harijans were made to serve cooked food to workers of the higher castes, while these in turn swept the garbage from the Harijans' streets. Harijans entered previously forbidden temples of southern India under Gandhi's leadership. Ultimately, as the reformers hoped, the many previous grades in worship tended to become reduced for all persons to the minimal two grades of priest and worshipper, if not to a single grade. The wide popular appeal of these and similar programs of revival and reform must be ascribed to their speaking initially in the caste idiom of substance and code. Their successes led to the strengthening and activation of still larger regional and religious castes, such as Hindus, Muslims, and Dravidian nationalists, which sometimes clashed with others in subsequent competition for power.

A still more innovative and prominent change in caste thinking, devised first in 19th-century Bengal, declares the land substance of India to be the nourishing mother of all her people, Hindu and Muslim, high caste and low. Mother India's code for conduct enjoins unity on all residents in her service and defense. This universalizing scheme spread officially through the nationalist movement to the new nations of India and Bangladesh.

Modernizing tendencies in caste thinking

Since 1947. The independent governments of South Asia have moved vigorously to modify caste conduct through legislative action. Most consistent with earlier Buddhist and Islāmic roles was Pakistan's declaration to be an Islāmic state having transcendent law and therefore having no need to recognize the natural castes.

A secular legislative Indian approach to conduct is seen in the Hindu code laws of the 1950s. These replace the particularistic Vedic moral code books by a uniform code taking no account of *varṇa*. They also abolish caste endogamy as a requisite for valid marriage. The legislative approach is seen fully in the Indian constitution of 1950, authored chiefly by B.R. Ambedkar, leader of a party of the lowest castes. The constitution rests on the notion that government must regulate individuals directly and not through autonomous corporate castes. It abolishes caste "untouchability" (now to be legally defined by courts), and forbids any other restriction on public facilities arising out of caste membership. Subsequent legislation against caste restrictions has proven generally influential at the urban temple or the crossroad coffeeshop but not at the village well. Ambedkar advised his followers to renounce Hinduism in favor of Islām or Buddhism, which he saw as providing casteless social systems.

Many modern South Asians consider caste-reform actions by government as necessary and desirable but regard the distribution of economic resources among castes as the most crucial problem. South Asian Marxists go further in their economic program, yet less far in their program for action, holding that castes are secondary and need not be a subject of policy; Marxists expect that castes will disappear by general intermarriage once the only real forces—the antagonisms of the economic classes—are resolved by revolution. The overall official Indian position on caste systems by the 1970s was a compromise: natural ethnic groups are relegated to a lower order that is devoid of legality, and provision of

UPI Compix

An "untouchable" woman sweeping the street in Jaipur, Rājasthān. The Indian constitution now abolishes caste "untouchability."

comprehensive moral, economic, and political codes is a function reserved to the processes of the transcendent national state.

The ideas of South Asian citizens as to what caste systems are and should be vary widely among the positions sketched. Practice also differs. Thus, norms of caste endogamy appear generally to have stiffened, while marriages outside of certain small urban groups of high caste nevertheless may exceed 20 percent. Traditional caste occupations are followed by an overall minority that grows less each year, but these occupations are often replaced by similar substitutes. The forms of Hindu worship are subject to constant innovation, but worship itself—ranked exchange between the genera of men and gods—is not abandoned. Where prevailing opinion is conservative, as in most rural localities, caste codes of exchange may continue to be observed publicly although individuals violate them privately; where opinion follows the official position, as it often does in cities, ranked exchanges among the castes may be confused or transcended publicly but maintained by conservative families in the domestic sphere. Most individuals move among social compartments that differently organize the enduring linkage between substance and code.

CASTE SYSTEMS IN OTHER SOCIETIES

Caste systems need not be thought of as unique to South Asia or to its emigrants. Rudimentary caste systems have appeared elsewhere to the extent that similar situations, structures, and cultural concepts were present.

Situations of encroachment between alien ethnic groups have generally been productive of simple, short-lived caste systems like that of Aryans and Dasyus in northern India in early Vedic times. Many a society has opposed itself as a superior whole to a despised immigrant population of traders, artisans, or Gypsies but usually without developing systematic conceptions or mutual consensus regarding ranks. Many a society has incorporated but ranked separately, then in time assimilated a caste of foreign conquerors (*e.g.*, Peru), slaves (*e.g.*, Brazil), or noncitizens (*e.g.*, imperial Rome). Occasionally, a society such as Mexico, with its duality of European and Indian cultures, has preserved contrasting ethnic styles of life long after rank, descent, and marriage have ceased to insulate the onetime castes from each other socially.

A relatively small number of ethnically heterogeneous, expanding societies—certain medieval African tribal kingdoms and some recent European colonial states such as the United States, Rhodesia, and the Republic of South Africa—have used political means to perpetuate the ranks, occupations, and biological relationships of two to four ethnic categories. The legality of the black and white caste systems in the United States did not endure two centuries, and the moral future of other recently legislated colour-caste systems is in question, but there is no doubt that ritualized composite tribal kingdoms such as Mali and Rwanda in Africa did maintain simple caste systems with moral authority for some five centuries.

Castes have rarely developed out of a single society's classes. In East Asia, several homogeneous societies sharing Buddhist ideas regarding the bodily pollution of death (Tibet, Korea, Japan) have generated internally their own local fractions of morally abhorred specialists, originally leatherworkers. These occupationally outcaste persons constitute small, scattered populations, separated in marriage and descent from the local majorities, although not thought of as ethnic or corporate units. In the lower Mississippi Valley of North America, the Natchez and Chitimacha tribes developed internal caste systems tied to hereditary offices in village war and temple cults while absorbing alien ethnic groups as the lowest of four ranks. The relative success of the Natchez in developing an internal caste system may be attributed to their facing, like the later Aryans, sharply defined alien ethnic units with an internal moral system of sharing and exchange.

BIBLIOGRAPHY

Caste systems in general: L. DUMONT, *Homo Hierarchicus* (1966; Eng. trans. 1970), description, history, and theories of the Hindu caste system in contrast to Western philosophies, with comprehensive bibliography up to 1962; J. SILVERBERG (ed.), *Social Mobility in the Caste System in India* (1968), corrects Western stereotypes.

Foreign concepts of South Asian caste: The most complete review is in Dumont (above). Important classical statements are those of C. BOUGLE, *Essais sur le régime des castes* (1908; Eng. trans., *Essays on the Caste System*, 1971); A.M. HOCART, *Les Castes* (1938; Eng. trans., *Caste: A Comparative Study*, 1950); J.H. HUTTON, *Caste in India*, 4th ed. (1963); and MAX WEBER, *Hinduismus und Buddhismus* in vol. 2 of *Gesammelte Aufsätze zur Religionssoziologie* (1921; Eng. trans., *The Religion of India: The Sociology of Hinduism and Buddhism*, 1958). D.M. SCHNEIDER, *American Kinship* (1968), provides the theoretical approach used here; it was first applied to an Indian caste by S. Barnett.

Caste systems in South Asia: P.V. KANE, *History of Dharmáśāstra*, 5 vol. (1930–62), an encyclopaedic digest of Vedic codes; G.S. GHURYE, *Caste and Race in India*, 5th ed. rev. (1969), historical interpretation of social developments; the *Census of India* (1881–1971), statistics and descriptions; D.G. MANDELBAUM, *Society in India*, 2 vol. (1970), summary of recent field studies with bibliography; M. MARRIOTT, *Caste Ranking and Community Structure in Five Regions of India and Pakistan* (1960), ecological comparisons and bibliography of older descriptive works.

Caste systems in other societies: G. DEVOS and H. WAGATSUMA, *Japan's Invisible Race: Caste in Culture and Personality* (1966); J.R. SWANTON, *Indian Tribes of the Lower Mississippi Valley and Adjacent Coast of the Gulf of Mexico*, Bull. Bur. Am. Ethnol. 43 (1911); A. TUDEN and L. PLOTNICOV (eds.) *Social Stratification in Africa* (1970).

Legal and political roles of caste: A. BOPEGAMAGE and P.V. VEERARAGHAVAN, *Status Images in Changing India* (1967); D.E. SMITH (ed.), *South Asian Politics and Religion* (1966); M.N. SRINIVAS, *Social Change in Modern India* (1966).

(Mc.M./R.B.I.)

Castlereagh, Viscount

As British foreign secretary from 1812 to 1822, Robert Stewart, better known as Viscount Castlereagh, guided the Grand Alliance that defeated Napoleon and played a major part in the peace conference at Vienna that redrew the map of Europe after the Napoleonic Wars. In Britain, during his lifetime, he enjoyed a reputation for reaction and was distrusted as an associate of continental despots. Modern historians, however, are more likely to consider him one of the more forward-looking statesmen of his time. He certainly acted as a moderating force at Vienna and did much to develop diplomacy by conferences and the idea of the concert of Europe. Born Robert Stewart in Dublin on June 18, 1769, to a prominent Anglo-Irish family, from 1796 to 1821 he was known by the courtesy title of Viscount Castlereagh, and on his father's death became the 2nd marquess of Londonderry. Educated at Armagh and St. John's College, Cambridge, he was elected to the Irish parliament of 1790 as an independent member. In 1794 he married Emily Anne Hobart, a beautiful if slightly eccentric woman to whom he remained devotedly attached throughout their long and childless marriage. From March 1798 he served as acting chief secretary to his relative Earl Camden, then lord lieutenant of Ireland. In November 1798 he was formally appointed to that office by Camden's successor, Lord Cornwallis.

Chief secretary for Ireland

Castlereagh's tenure as chief secretary coincided with the two most important events of Irish history in the late 18th century: the 1798 rebellion and the union with Great Britain. While taking severe and successful measures to quell the revolt in 1798, Castlereagh shared the view of Cornwallis that a policy of clemency was essential to end the disturbances. The threat of French invasion and the 1798 rebellion convinced Castlereagh of the need for a parliamentary union with Britain. The passage of the Act of Union through the Dublin parliament in June 1800 provided the first great demonstration of Castlereagh's abilities as he singlehandedly forced the measure in the Irish Commons against bitter Protestant opposition. He believed that the union with Britain must be accompanied by the political emancipation of Roman Catholics. When, in February 1801, Pitt failed to obtain George III's consent to emancipation, Cornwallis and Castlereagh at once sent in their resignations.

Castlereagh, painting by Sir Thomas Lawrence (1769–1830). In the National Portrait Gallery, London.
By courtesy of the National Portrait Gallery, London

Though out of office after May 1801, Castlereagh continued to advise Henry Addington's ministry on Irish questions, and in July 1802 he was appointed president of the Board of Control responsible for Indian affairs. His energy and intellectual powers gained him an immediate influence in the Cabinet, and after Pitt's return as prime minister (May 1804), he also became in July 1805 secretary of state for war. His first important task, the dispatch of a British expeditionary force to Hanover, was rendered ineffectual by Napoleon's victory at Austerlitz (December 1805); but the move convinced Castlereagh of the strategic value of the British Army in continental warfare. On Pitt's death in January 1806 he left office and became the chief opposition spokesman on foreign and military affairs. He returned to the War Department in the Duke of Portland's ministry in 1807, and showed his determination to engage in major warfare against a continent now completely dominated by Napoleon. The adoption in 1808 of his plan for reorganizing the regular, reserve, and militia forces provided the country with adequate home defenses and a larger and more efficient army for overseas operations. When the Spanish revolt against Napoleon broke out the same year, it was decided at once to send a major expedition to the peninsula. Castlereagh was influential in securing the command for Sir Arthur Wellesley (later duke of Wellington) in 1809. In 1809 a British expedition sent by Castlereagh against Napoleon's naval base at Antwerp was allowed to waste away of disease on the island of Walcheren. The disaster was in no way Castlereagh's fault, but it brought to a head the long-standing divisions and intrigues in the Cabinet. Since March 1809, George Canning, the foreign secretary, had been pressing for a change of policy, and even before the Walcheren expedition he had secured secret agreement to the replacement of Castlereagh by the marquess Wellesley. When Castlereagh learned of the ignominious position in which Canning had placed him, he challenged him to a duel that was fought September 21. Canning was slightly wounded and both men later resigned office. Castlereagh remained out of office for the next two and a half years.

Duel with Canning

In 1812 he rejoined the government as secretary for foreign affairs, and after Prime Minister Perceval's assassination in May he became leader of the House of Commons. British foreign policy then passed for a decade under unified control. Castlereagh's first task was to hold together the shaky and distrustful elements in the general European opposition to Napoleon; but as the end of the war drew near he worked increasingly to obtain preliminary agreement among the allies for the resettlement of Europe. In talks in Châtillon in 1814, he secured acceptance in principle of his plans for a peace settlement under the control of the great powers. By the Treaty of Chaumont (March 1814), he obtained provision for allied cooperation for 20 years after the war. On the fall of Napoleon the Treaty of Paris (May 1814) secured immediate British requirements (the restoration of the Bourbon monarchy and the separation of the Low Countries as an independent kingdom), and set Castlereagh free to play a commanding and mediatory role at the peace conference at Vienna. His main European objectives were to prevent the aggrandizement of Russia and to strengthen the weak central European areas of Germany and Italy. He and Metternich, the Austrian minister for foreign affairs, dominated the inner negotiations, though it was Castlereagh who took the lead in resisting the territorial demands of Russia and Prussia. The final settlement, with some compromises, was a practical embodiment of his principle of the "just equilibrium."

Castlereagh also attached fundamental importance to regular consultation by the great powers on matters of common concern; and the peace treaty contained specific provision for periodic meetings of the contracting parties. Though the practice of holding such meetings became known as the "congress system," Castlereagh's aim was to make possible diplomacy by conference rather than to establish any system to preserve the status quo in Europe or interfere in the internal developments of other nations. The distinction became increasingly apparent in the remaining seven years of his career. The Congress of Aix-la-Chapelle in 1818 readmitted France to the concert of powers. Castlereagh firmly resisted, however, a Russian attempt to institute a league of European powers to guarantee the existing order under sanction of military force. When the liberal movement in Germany after 1818 and the revolutions in Spain and in the Kingdom of the Two Sicilies in 1820 brought Austria and Russia closer together, he refused to treat their meeting at Troppau in October 1820 as a full European congress; and after the Congress of Laibach (1821) he openly repudiated the Troppau principle of intervention and coercion. His classic state paper of May 1820 emphasized the difference between the despotic states of eastern Europe and the constitutional structures of Britain and France, and made it clear that the British government could only act on the expediency of any given issue and within the limits of its parliamentary system. With the emergence in 1821 of the questions of Greek independence and the fate of the Spanish colonies, however, British political and commercial interests became directly affected and Castlereagh decided to attend in person the Congress of Verona in 1822. The instructions he drew up for himself showed plainly that he would not sanction forcible interference in either Greece or Spain, and that Britain would ultimately be prepared to recognize de facto governments resulting from successful revolutions. It is clear that Castlereagh was preparing for that detachment of Britain from the reactionary policy of the continental powers that was accomplished after his death.

This development was largely hidden from the British public by the personal nature of Castlereagh's diplomacy and his aloofness from public opinion. His apparent involvement with the eastern autocracies was disliked at home, and his role as spokesman for the government in the violent domestic politics of the postwar era kept him in a position of unpopular prominence. As leader of the House of Commons he was identified with the repressive policies of the years 1815–19, and with the cabinet's unsuccessful introduction in 1820 of a bill to dissolve George IV's marriage with Queen Caroline. He was savagely attacked by such liberal romantics as Lord Byron, Thomas Moore, and Shelley. After the abortive Thistlewood plot to assassinate the Cabinet in 1820, he always carried pistols in self-defense, and during the trial of Queen Caroline he was obliged to take up his residence in the Foreign Office for greater safety. The burden imposed on him by the royal divorce affair of 1820, in addition to his duties at the Foreign Office and in the House of Commons, probably hastened his final collapse. In 1821 he showed signs of abnormal suspiciousness, which by 1822 became outright paranoia. He was, or thought he was, being blackmailed on charges of homosexual acts, and on August 12, 1822, he committed suicide shortly before he was due to set out for Verona.

BIBLIOGRAPHY. H. MONTGOMERY HYDE, *The Rise of Castlereagh* (1933), is a fine account of Castlereagh. The *Memoirs and Correspondence of Viscount Castlereagh, Second Marquess of Londonderry*, ed. by CHARLES VANE, 12 vol. (1850–53), correspondence from Castlereagh to members of his family, provides source documents for historians.

(Ed.)

Castro, Fidel

Fidel Castro Ruz led the Cuban revolution to power in 1959 and has headed the Cuban government ever since—the first and only Communist regime in the Western Hemisphere. His international influence grew in the late 1970s after he dispatched tens of thousands of combat troops to fight in Africa.

Elliott Erwitt—Magnum

Castro, 1964.

He was born near the village of Birán, in the Mayarí municipality of Oriente province, the easternmost in Cuba, on August 13, 1926. His father, Angel Castro y Argiz, an immigrant from Galicia in northwest Spain, had seven children, two by his first wife. While still married to her, he had five more illegitimate children from his cook, Lina Ruz González. Fidel was the second of these; Raúl, later to become, too, a major figure in Cuban affairs, was the youngest. Fidel's father cultivated sugarcane and some other crops. Although the Mayarí region was poor, Angel Castro was financially well off, though not a very wealthy man, in an area long dominated by the United Fruit Company.

Parents

Fidel Castro attended Roman Catholic boarding schools in Santiago, the capital city of Oriente province, and later attended the country's leading Jesuit-run boarding school, Belén, in the city of Havana. He graduated from the School of Law of the University of Havana after five years. Although he probably began reading Marxist works at the university, he did not become a Communist until the late 1950s.

His main activity at the university—where organized violent gangs sought to advance a mixture of romantic goals, political aims, and personal careers—was politics. In a minor way he participated in an attempted invasion of the Dominican Republic organized in Cuba in 1947 and in urban riots that broke out in Bogotá, Colombia, in April 1948. He was charged with the assassination of another prominent student leader, but the charge was never proved.

In October 1948 Castro married Mirta Díaz-Balart, over the objections of her family, and his only son, also named Fidel, was born in September 1949. He and his wife were divorced in 1955.

Castro became a member of the Cuban People's Party (called Ortodoxos) in 1947 and was their candidate for a seat in the House of Representatives (from a city of Havana district) in the elections scheduled for 1952. On March 10, 1952, however, the former Cuban president, General Fulgencio Batista, overthrew the government of Pres. Carlos Prío Socarrás and cancelled the elections.

Fidel Castro began to organize a revolution early in 1953. On July 26 he led a small group against the Moncada military barracks in the city of Santiago, but it failed and Castro himself was arrested. A subsequently edited version of his self-defense at his trial was to become his major statement during the 1950s. Known by its concluding words, "History Will Absolve Me" (*La Historia Me Absolverá*), the document attacked the anticonstitutional, repressive, and corrupt practices of the Batista government, calling for political and civil liberties. He also called for a land reform and other rural improvement programs along with programs for industrialization, the partial sharing of profits between shareholders and workers, and a pledge not to introduce new taxes.

"History Will Absolve Me"

As the need to build up a large coalition to overthrow the Batista government became more evident, his statements became less specific: the more sweeping reforms were no longer mentioned, and some, such as the expropriation of foreign-owned public utilities, were explicitly repudiated. Many of these views were changed drastically after he came into power.

Upon his release from prison in 1955, Castro went to Mexico to organize the next step in the revolution, heading an organization called the 26th of July Movement. On December 2, 1956, he led a group that landed in Oriente province, Cuba, aboard the yacht "Granma." Meeting initial setbacks, Castro, his brother Raúl, Ernesto (Che) Guevara, and a few others retreated into the Sierra Maestra of southwestern Oriente province to wage guerrilla warfare against the demoralized, ill-equipped, and badly led armed forces of Batista. Independently of Castro, many other efforts were made to overthrow the Batista government, but none of these others succeeded. As internal political support waned and military defeats multiplied, Batista fled the country on December 31, 1958.

Fidel Castro has always remained the commander in chief of the Cuban armed forces. In February 1959 he became prime minister and thus head of the Cuban government. In December 1976 he became also president of the State Council of the Cuban National Assembly, while continuing as head of the government. He is also the chief executive officer, called the secretary general, of the Communist Party of Cuba (Partido Comunista de Cuba, with which Castro's movement was merged in 1961)—the only political party operating legally in Cuba under the constitution of 1976. He is also a member of the party's principal organ, the Political Bureau (Politburo), and of the Central Committee.

Fidel Castro's political style has emphasized active engagement and self-discipline. Moderately tall, athletic, and bearded, he believes that individuals can overcome most obstacles if they have the will to do so and that revolution, at home and abroad, is the important mission worth pursuing. As he said, "The duty of every revolutionary is to make the revolution."

He is a man of extraordinary personal energy, keen intelligence, and a very fine political sense in domestic affairs and foreign policy. He is a spellbinding orator who can speak often and at great length. He has had the support of many, but he also provoked revolt and exile among hundreds of thousands of Cubans (many of whom left for the U.S.). He aligned his government with the Soviet Union in 1960 and in 1961 announced that he was a Marxist-Leninist.

His policies have been far reaching. His government has vastly expanded educational opportunities and institutions. It has redistributed economic wealth, income, and access to health facilities. All education and health services in Cuba are free of charge. Every citizen is guaranteed employment and also has the obligation to work. The Cuban economy under the Castro regime, however, has barely kept up with population growth and has become inefficient in many respects. The government owns most of the means of production.

Cuban economy

Castro's government has also established authoritarian political rule. There is no political competition among parties; no national elections were held until 1976, and then only local government officials were directly elected. All mass media are controlled by the government and express its views. The government reserves for itself wide powers to deal with opponents. Power is concentrated in a very centralized bureaucracy—notwithstanding some trends toward decentralization in the late 1970s—headed by Castro, which plans for the economy and the society. Most of Castro's associates in the party's Political Bureau and in the State Council have been with him since the fight in the 1950s against Batista. His brother Raúl, minister of the armed forces, ranks second to him in all government and party posts.

Fidel Castro's government on gaining power took over property owned by U.S.-based enterprises in 1959 and 1960. By the early 1960s, all economic ties between Cuba and the United States were broken, and the U.S. government was equipping thousands of Cuban exiles to overthrow Castro's government; their landing at the Bay of Pigs in April 1961, however, failed. Castro's close alliance with the Soviet Union has provided Cuba with economic subsidies and military support against the United States.

In 1962 the Soviet Union stationed ballistic missiles in Cuba, and the world came close to nuclear war. The crisis ended when the Soviet Union agreed to withdraw its nuclear weapons from Cuba in exchange for a pledge that the U.S. would no longer seek to overthrow the Cuban government. Nevertheless, operatives of the U.S. Central Intelligence Agency continued for some time to plot to assassinate Castro.

Support for revolution abroad

Castro has supported violent revolution abroad, especially in Venezuela, Bolivia, and Guatemala in the 1960s. In 1975 the Cuban government (with Soviet support) decided to enter the Angolan civil war on the side of the Popular Movement for the Liberation of Angola that won the war. Again with Soviet support in 1978, the Cuban government assisted Ethiopia in defeating an invasion by Somalia. Fidel Castro's government entered the 1980s with as many combat troops—about 40,000—posted abroad (relative to Cuba's population) as the U.S. had in Vietnam at the height of the war.

BIBLIOGRAPHY. ROLANDO E. BONACHEA and NELSON P. VALDES (eds.), *Revolutionary Struggle, 1947–1958*, vol. 1 of *Selected Works of Fidel Castro* (1972), includes most of Castro's statements for those years, along with a biographical introductory essay; JORGE I. DOMINGUEZ, *Cuba: Order and Revolution* (1978), analysis of Cuban politics before and after the revolution, with special attention to postrevolutionary political institutions, decisions, and participation; EDWARD GONZALEZ, *Cuba Under Castro, The Limits of Charisma* (1974), analysis of Cuban politics, mostly since the revolution, with special attention to the role of Castro; LEE LOCKWOOD, *Castro's Cuba, Cuba's Fidel* (1969), long and wide-ranging interview of Fidel Castro conducted in mid-1960s, with many good photographs; FRANK MANKIEWICZ and KIRBY JONES, *With Fidel* (1975), long interview with Castro conducted in early 1970s, with a focus on politics and relations with the U.S.; HUGH THOMAS, *Cuba: The Pursuit of Freedom* (1971; British title *Cuba; or, Pursuit of Freedom*), monumental history of Cuba from the late 18th century to the early 1960s; U.S. CONGRESS, SENATE SELECT COMMITTEE TO STUDY GOVERNMENTAL OPERATIONS WITH RESPECT TO INTELLIGENCE ACTIVITIES, "Alleged Assassination Plots Involving Foreign Leaders," *An Interim Report*, 94th Congress, 1st Session (1975).

(J.I.D.)

Casuariiformes

The order Casuariiformes includes two families of large flightless birds: Dromaiidae for the emu (*Dromaius novaehollandiae*), found only in Australia; and Casuariidae for three species of cassowaries (*Casuarius*), restricted to northern Australia, New Guinea, and nearby islands. Of the two groups, the emu is far better known, both biologically and popularly, being exhibited in zoos around the world.

The emu was first discovered by European explorers in 1788, more than a century after the first cassowaries had been seen by Europeans; in 1697 a Dutch navigator, Willem de Vlamingh, had seen the emu's footprints in western Australia and had attributed them to a "Kasuarius." Cassowaries first became known to Europeans in the 17th century—there was a published reference to a "Casoaris" in 1658—when the Portuguese and Dutch colonized the East Indies. Both names, emu and cassowary, were originally applied to cassowaries; the emu was known as the New Holland or New South Wales cassowary until the early 19th century, when the name emu was gradually transferred to it. By the late 19th century about 11 species of cassowaries were recognized, but greater understanding of variation within species has reduced the number to three: the double-wattled, or Australian, cassowary (*Casuarius casuarius*), the single-wattled, or one-wattled, cassowary (*C. unappendiculatus*), and the dwarf, or Bennett's, cassowary (*C. bennetti*).

Importance to man. The emu and cassowaries are important foods for the indigenous peoples of New Guinea and Australia; the flesh of the thigh muscles resembles beef. In New Guinea cassowaries are captured as chicks and held in enclosures until large enough to eat. The feathers are used for personal adornment. In Australia cassowary feathers formerly were used for the notorious *kurdaitcha* shoes, or "shoes of silence," worn by Aboriginal executioners on nocturnal missions of tribal vengeance or punishment. During World War I members of Australian cavalry regiments wore tufts of emu plumes on their slouch hats.

Since the time of European settlement in southeastern Australia, the emu has become much less abundant, and three island forms have been exterminated by hunting. In Western Australia, however, the bird has remained common and has become a pest in the wheat-farming areas, breaking fences and trampling and eating crops. In 1932 members of an army machine-gun unit were employed in a campaign against a concentration of emus, estimated to be about 20,000, in the vicinity of the wheat-belt centre of Campion.

The Emu War in Australia

The outcome of this bizarre Emu War, as it was called, has been summarized by the ornithologist D.L. Serventy as follows:

> . . . the machine-gunners' dreams of point blank fire into serried masses of Emus were soon dissipated. The Emu command had evidently ordered guerrilla tactics, and its unwieldy army soon split up into innumerable small units that made use of the military equipment uneconomic. A crestfallen field force therefore withdrew from the combat area after about a month.

Yearly kills of emus in Western Australia for bounty payments vary from 5,000 to nearly 40,000 birds; but the birds remain plentiful, and small parties may be seen within 15 or 20 kilometres of Perth, the capital of the state.

Natural history. *Reproduction.* Throughout its climatically varied range the emu is a winter breeder; egg laying begins at the end of April. The nest is a flattened bed of bark, grasses, and leaves near a tree or bush and is so situated that the sitting bird (always the male) has a good view of its surroundings. Despite their size, nests are extremely difficult to find. The large green eggs, with granulated shells, average about 130 millimetres (slightly over five inches) in length and 87 millimetres (3.4 inches) in width and weigh 450 to 800 grams (16 to 28 ounces). They are laid at intervals of about four days, and the male starts incubation when the hen has laid five to nine. The normal clutch size is eight, nine, or 10 eggs, with large clutches up to 16. In exceptionally good seasons as many as 20 eggs may be laid, in poor seasons as few as four or five. Incubation varies from about 58 to 61 days, during which the male seldom leaves the nest, even to feed.

Eggs

The newly hatched chicks, which are concealingly streaked with black, are brooded by the male for two or three days before they begin to move around in his company. Normally two years are required to reach maturity. In the nonbreeding season the groups coalesce into flocks, which may undergo local movements or more extensive migrations. Marking with leg bands has proved that individual emus may travel hundreds of kilometres.

Far less precise data are available on the annual cycle of the cassowaries. According to several observers, the

Emu and cassowary.
Drawing by R. Keane

eggs are laid in winter and are incubated by the male for 49–52 days. The eggs are paler green than those of the emu and there are fewer in the clutch, which varies from three to eight. Maturity may not be reached until the second or third year. Cassowaries are not gregarious in the nonbreeding season but live as pairs or family parties.

Ecology. Cassowaries are more pugnacious and aggressive than the emu. They are essentially creatures of the tropical rain forests, where they are very difficult to observe. Their diet is mainly fruit. Emus, on the other hand, live under a wide variety of environmental conditions, from dense temperate forest to open plains and arid scrub country. They often exhibit a curious inquisitiveness toward the activities of man and may be lured to close range by various devices, such as the waving of objects in the air, a habit that was utilized by the Australian Aborigines in hunting them. Though basically vegetarian, subsisting on fruits, seeds, and vegetation of all kinds, emus will also take insects, including caterpillars and grasshoppers, when they occur in great numbers.

The emu and cassowaries swim well and are fast runners. The emu is capable of a stride of nearly three metres (ten feet) and can keep up with an automobile travelling up to 40–50 kilometres (about 25–30 miles) per hour.

Vocalizations. Both sexes of the emu are reported to utter resonant drumming notes and guttural grunting calls, under varying conditions. Less is known about the calls of cassowaries, but scattered accounts indicate that they are similar to those of the emu.

Size and weight of emus

Form and function. Next to the ostrich (*Struthio camelus*), the emu is the largest and heaviest of living birds; large individuals stand between 1.5 and 1.8 metres (five and six feet) high and weigh up to 55 kilograms (120 pounds), although most are well below that weight. Females are slightly larger, averaging about 40 kilograms (90 pounds) while the males average about 36 kilograms (80 pounds). The sexes are alike in colour; the plumage is sombre, brown, or brownish black, and the naked skin on the head and neck is blue. All three species of cassowaries are black and, except for the dwarf cassowary, have fleshy pendulous wattles of red, orange, or yellow on the head and neck. The head is crowned with a horny casque or helmet, believed by some authorities to protect the bird from injury by branches during rapid movements in the forest. The plumage of casuariiforms is loose and hairlike due to the lack of barbules, the secondary branches that interlock to form the flat vane in the feathers of most birds. There are no feathers differentiated as tail feathers, but cassowaries have five quills of the wing modified into hollow, unbranched spines.

As with many running birds, casuariiforms have only three toes, the hindtoe having been lost. The inner toe of cassowaries is armed with an elongated, dagger-like claw, making the foot a formidable weapon in kicking.

The casuariiform skeleton is similar to that of the other large flightless birds (ratites) in the reduction of the wing elements and of the keel on the sternum (breastbone) and in the enlargement of the leg elements. Vestigial clavicles (collarbones) remain in the shoulder girdle, but the humerus (upper "arm" bone) is much reduced, being shorter than the combined forewing and manus ("hand"). The manus has a single digit, now believed to be the third, which bears a long claw.

The pattern of bones in the palate, an important diagnostic feature in the taxonomy of ratites, is of the palaeognathous or dromaeognathous type (common to all ratites), in which the vomer bones of the skull extend back to separate the palatines. The casuariiforms have the simplest form of this palate type, with large vomers and short palatines.

Evolution and classification. *Paleontology.* No fossil remains of casuariform birds have been found outside of the Australian region, and most of those recorded are from the Pleistocene, with one doubtfully from the Pliocene (about 4,000,000 years ago). The latter, although definitely a member of the emu assemblage, showed features linking it with the cassowaries. Despite the absence of fossil material, the order must have had a long evolution during the Tertiary Period (the last 65,000,000 years). The relationship of the Casuariiformes with the other orders of large flightless birds—the rheas (Rheiformes), ostriches (Struthioniformes), kiwis and moas (Dinornithiformes), and elephant birds (Aepyornithiformes), formerly grouped in a distinct subclass of birds, the Ratitae—is uncertain, but the Casuariiformes appears to be the most primitive of the living orders. The upper Pleistocene of Australia has produced several fossil species of emus assigned to the modern genus *Dromaius* and dating from as much as 100,000 years ago. Other Pleistocene finds from Australia have been placed in a separate family, Dromornithidae. These include *Dromornis*, known only from leg bones, and the gigantic *Genyornis newtoni*, almost the entire skeleton of which is known. The only known fossil cassowary is a species from Pleistocene cave deposits in the Wellington Valley, New South Wales, Australia, which resembles closely, and is probably identical with, the dwarf cassowary (*Casuarius bennetti*), now restricted to New Guinea and nearby islands. The distribution of the Casuariidae has evidently shrunk in recent millennia; the only species on the Australian mainland is the double-wattled cassowary (*C. casuarius*), restricted to New Guinea and the Cape York Peninsula of northern Queensland.

Relationship to other flightless birds

Classification. The following classification of the order is universally accepted.

ORDER CASUARIIFORMES

Large graviportal (ponderous) flightless birds with 3 toes. Other physical features described in *Form and Function*, above. Monogamous. Eggs green in colour.

Family Casuariidae (cassowaries)

Beak laterally compressed. Prominent horny casque on mesethmoid, nasal, and frontal bones of the skull. Coracoid bone of the shoulder much shorter than in emu. Bony union (symphysis) between various posterior elements of the pelvis may be present or absent. Femur not pneumatized by air sac system. Cervical vertebrae 18 or 19. Wing with 5 quills modified as long hollow spines. Pendulous coloured wattles on throat and neck (except in dwarf cassowary). Three species.

Family Dromaiidae (alternatively Dromiceiidae; emu)

Beak flattened dorsoventrally. Head not casqued. Pubic symphysis lacking. Femur pneumatic. Trachea with an aperture in front, leading to an inflatable neck sac. Pendulous wattles absent. Fossil record limited to the Pleistocene of Australia and nearby islands. One Recent species.

Family Dromornithidae
Fossil only; Pleistocene of Australia; 2 genera, 2 species.

BIBLIOGRAPHY. D. FLEAY, "Nesting of the Emu," *Emu*, 35: 202–210 (1936), presents observations of this species in captivity. D.W. GAUKROGER, "The Emu at Home," *Emu*, 25:53–57 (1925), describes the nesting habits in the wild. A.L. RAND and E.T. GILLIARD, *Handbook of New Guinea Birds* (1967), is a summary of the biology and classification of cassowaries; and D.L. SERVENTY and H.M. WHITTELL, *Birds of Western Australia*, 4th ed. (1967), a summary of emu habits and statistics of kills. H.L. WHITE, "Notes on the Cassowary (*Casuarius australis* Wall)," *Emu* 12:172–178 (1913), presents field observations on habits and nesting in Queensland, with illustrations.

(D.L.Se.)

Cat

All cats are grouped in the family Felidae. From the largest, the tiger, to the smallest, the house cat, felids are characterized by supple, low-slung bodies, finely molded heads, long tails that aid in balance, and specialized teeth and claws that adapt them admirably to a life of active hunting. The family of cats belongs to the order Carnivora, the "flesh-eaters"; for an account of the family and its relationships, see CARNIVORA.

This article discusses domestic cats (*Felis catus*), which possess the features of their wild relatives in being basically carnivorous, remarkably agile and powerful, and finely coordinated in movement. It is noteworthy that the ancestors of man's other common household pet, the dog (and most of his other domestic animals as well), were social animals that lived together in packs in which there was subordination to a leader. The dog has readily transferred its allegiance from pack leader to human master. The cat, however, has not yielded as readily to subjugation. Consequently, the house cat is able to revert to complete self-reliance more quickly and more successfully than most other domestic animals.

ORIGIN AND HISTORY

The "cat pattern," established very early in the evolution of modern mammals, was a successful one: early cats were already typical in form at a time when the ancestors of most other modern mammalian types were scarcely recognizable. They first appeared in the early Pliocene Epoch, approximately 7,000,000 years ago, and they have continued with remarkably little change into modern times.

Domestication. Although its origin is hidden in antiquity, the domestic cat has a history that dates nearly 3,500 years to ancient Egypt. There are no authentic records of domestication earlier than 1500 BC, but it may have taken place sooner. Although the cat was proclaimed a sacred animal in the 5th and 6th dynasties (about 2500–2200 BC), it had not necessarily been domesticated at that time. It is probable that the Egyptians domesticated the cat because they realized its value in protecting granaries from rodents. Their affection and respect for this predator led to the development of religious cat cults and temple worship of cats.

Cats have long been known to other cultures. Wall tiles in Crete dating from 1600 BC depict hunting cats. Evidence from art and literature indicates that the domestic cat was present in Greece from the 5th century BC and in China from 500 BC. In India cats were mentioned in Sanskrit writings around 100 BC, while the Arabs and the Japanese were not introduced to the cat until about AD 600. The earliest record of cats in Great Britain dates back to about AD 936 when Howel Dda, prince of south central Wales, enacted laws for their protection. The first domestic cats in the United States date from around 1750.

Ancestry of breeds

Even though all cats are similar in appearance, it is difficult to trace the ancestry of individual breeds. Since tabby-like markings appear in the drawings and mummies of ancient Egyptian cats, present-day tabbies may be descendants of the sacred cats of Egypt. The Abyssinian also resembles pictures and statues of Egyptian cats. The Persian, whose colouring is often the same as that of mixed breeds (although the length of hair and the body conformation are distinctive), was probably crossed at various times with other breeds; the tailless, or Manx cat, may be derived from another species or may be a mutation. The ancestry of Persian and Siamese cats may well be distinct from other domestic breeds, representing a domestication of some Oriental wild cat (the ancestor of the Egyptian cat is believed to have come from Africa). In fact, nothing is known of the ancestry of the Siamese types, and there is no living species of Oriental cat that would serve as ancestor.

Associations with man. The cat has long played a role in religion and witchcraft. In the Bible "cat" is mentioned only in the apocryphal Letter of Jeremiah (Bar. 6:21). The cat figured prominently in the religion of Egypt, the Norse countries, and various parts of the Orient. The Egyptians had a cat-headed goddess named Bast, whose chief seat of worship was the city of Bubastis. Thousands of cat mummies have been discovered in Egypt, and there were even mouse mummies, presumably to provide food for the cats. More often, however, the cat has been associated with sorcery and witchcraft, and the superstitions regarding cats, common in all countries, are innumerable. Superstitions often took extremely vicious forms, and throughout the ages cats have been more cruelly mistreated than perhaps any other animal. Black

By courtesy of (left) the trustees of the British Museum, (centre left) the Vatican Museums; photographs, (center right) Holmes Lebel, (right) Gisele Freund

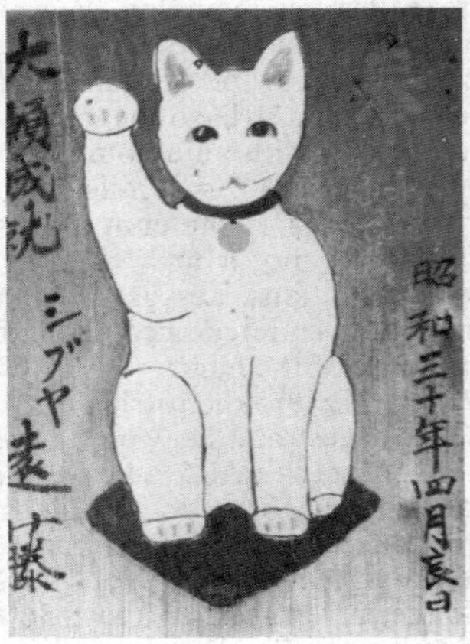

The antiquity and cult of the cat.
(Left) Mummified Egyptian cat of the Roman period. (Centre left) Roman mosaic, *c.* AD 76–138, depicting a cat killing a chicken. (Centre right) Japanese temple cat from Go-To-Ku-Ji Temple in Tokyo; the raised paw symbolizes ability to attract luck. (Right) Mexican "Judas Cat" constructed of papier mache inset with firecrackers; in a contemporary Holy Saturday custom, believed to derive from Spain, the figures are burned in effigy of enemies.

cats in particular have long been regarded as having occult powers and as being the familiars of witches. Cat lovers are called "ailurophiles"; persons in whom cats inspire fear are termed "ailurophobes."

The cat is a familiar figure in nursery rhymes and stories. The legend of Dick Whittington and his cat is a particular favourite. The writers Théophile Gautier and Charles Baudelaire have paid it homage and, in the 20th century, Rudyard Kipling, Colette, and T.S. Eliot wrote of cats. The influence of the cat also appears most clearly in everyday language where its many-sided character is crystallized in proverbs and sayings.

CATS AS PETS

The cat is of ever-increasing economic importance. There are businesses that manufacture and sell only cat foods or cat accessories, veterinarians who treat only cats, hospitals that cater to sick cats, cemeteries that bury cats, and special boarding places or kennels that keep cats.

Increasing popularity

The popularity of the cat continuously grows, especially that of pedigreed breeds. The cat's independent personality, combined with its grace, cleanliness, and subtle signs of affection, are traits that have wide appeal. Typically, cats are creatures of habit; they are inquisitive, but not adventurous, and are easily upset by sudden changes of routine. The ideal household cat has been raised in a clean home, kept away from unhealthy animals, separated from its mother between the ages of two and four months, and inoculated against common infectious cat diseases. The problems of discipline and training may be complicated in a household containing two cats of the same age. A year-old cat, however, may accept a new kitten, other than its own, and teach it, in turn, the disciplines that it has been taught.

A good disposition and overall good health are important criteria for any pet. Disposition varies only slightly between male and female cats. There are, however, distinct differences in intelligence and disposition between the alley cat (or mixed breed) and the pedigree. The mixed breed is a heterogeneous breed of unknown lineage; therefore, its temperament and disposition are difficult to assess. By chance the mixed breed may prove a happier, healthier, and more robust pet than a pedigree. On the other hand, the behaviour and vigour of the direct ancestors of pedigreed cats are indicative of the characteristics the offspring will possess as adults.

GENERAL FEATURES AND SPECIAL ADAPTATIONS

The average weight of the household cat varies from six to ten pounds, although among nonpedigreed cats weights up to 28 pounds are not uncommon. Average lengths are 28 inches for males and 20 inches for females. In keeping with a carnivorous habit, the cat has a simple gut; the small intestine is only about three times the length of the body.

The skin of the cat, composed of dermis and epidermis, regenerates and fights off infection very quickly. Tiny erector muscles, attached to all hair follicles, enable the cat to bristle all over. Thus, although the cat is a relatively small animal, it can frighten enemies by arching its back, bristling, and hissing.

Coordination and musculature. Cats are among the most highly specialized of the flesh-eating mammals. Their brains are large and well developed. Cats are digitigrade; *i.e.*, they walk on their toes. Interestingly, the cat, unlike the dog and horse, walks or runs by moving first the front and back legs on one side, then the front and back legs on the other side. Only the camel and the giraffe move in a similar way. The cat's body has great elasticity. The vertebrae of the spinal column are held together by muscles, rather than by ligaments as in man, so the cat can elongate or contract its back, curve it upwards, or oscillate it along the vertebral line. The construction of the shoulder joints permits the cat to turn its foreleg in almost any direction. Cats are powerfully built animals; these animals are so well coordinated that they almost invariably land on their feet if they should happen either to fall or be dropped.

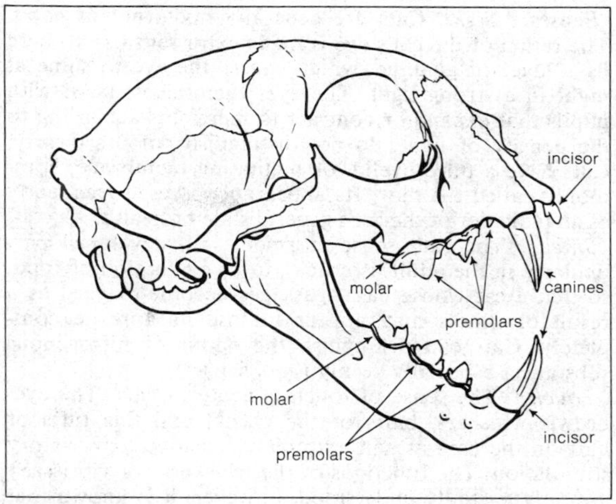

Figure 1: Skull of cat.

Teeth. One of the most characteristic and specialized features of the cat is its teeth (Figure 1). They are adapted to three functions: stabbing (canines), anchoring (canines), and cutting (molars). Cats have no flat-crowned crushing teeth and therefore cannot chew their food; instead, they cut it up. Other than the canines and molars, the teeth are more or less nonfunctional; most of the cheek teeth do not even meet when the mouth is closed. The dental formula in all cats, for either side of both upper and lower jaws, is: incisors 3/3, canines 1/1, premolars 3/2, molars 1/1. The total number of teeth is 16 in the upper jaw and 14 in the lower. Primary or milk teeth number 24; these are replaced by the permanent teeth at about five months in the domestic cat. Each half of the jaw is hinged to the skull by a transverse roller that fits tightly into a trough on the underside of the skull—making grinding movements impossible even if the cat had teeth suitable for grinding.

Retraction of claws

Claws. Another special adaptation is the cat's strong, sharp claws. There is a remarkable mechanism for retracting the claws when they are not in use (Figure 2). The claw is retracted or extended by pivoting the end bone of the toe (which bears the claw) over the tip of the next bone. The action that unsheathes the claws also spreads the toes widely, making the foot more than twice as broad as it normally is and converting it into a truly formidable weapon. This claw-sheathing mechanism is present in all species of the cat family except the cheetah. Although there are no nerve endings in the nail itself, blood capillaries are present in the inner part.

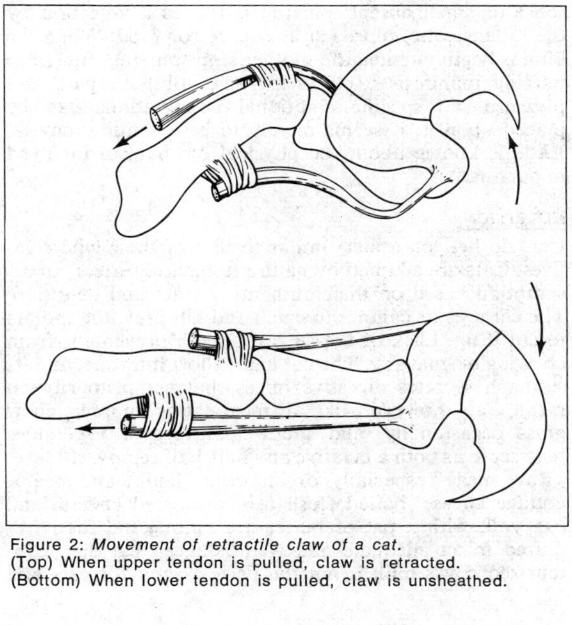

Figure 2: *Movement of retractile claw of a cat.*
(Top) When upper tendon is pulled, claw is retracted.
(Bottom) When lower tendon is pulled, claw is unsheathed.

Senses. *Sight.* Cats are generally nocturnal in habit. The retina of the cat's eye is made extra sensitive to light by a layer of guanine, which causes the eye to shine at night in a strong light. The eyes themselves, large with pupils that expand or contract to mere slits according to the density of light, do not distinguish colours clearly. Cats have a third eyelid, or nictitating membrane, commonly called the haw. Its appearance is used frequently as an indicator of the cat's general state of health.

Smell. The cat's sense of smell, well developed particularly in the adult, is crucial to its evaluation of food, so that a cat whose nasal passages become clogged as a result of illness may appear to lose its appetite completely. Cats can distinguish the odour of nitrogenous substances especially keenly (*e.g.*, fish).

Touch. The sense of touch is acute in cats. The eyebrows, whiskers, hairs of the cheek, and fine tufts of hair on the ears are all extremely sensitive to vibratory stimulation. The functions of the whiskers (or vibrissae) are only partially understood; however, it is known that if they are cut off, the cat is temporarily incapacitated. The toes and paws, as well as the tip of the nose, are also very sensitive to touch.

Hearing. Cats also have an acute sense of hearing. Their ears contain almost 30 muscles (compared with 6 in man); as a result they can turn them many times more quickly in the direction of a sound than can a dog. The ears of cats, although receptive to ultrasonic frequencies up to 25,000 vibrations per second, are slightly inferior to those of dogs, which register 35,000 vibrations per second.

Behaviour. *Grooming and tail-wagging.* The tongue of all cats, which has a patch of sharp, backward-directed spines near the tip, has the appearance and feel of a coarse file; the spines help the cat to lap up liquids and also to groom itself. The disposition to cleanliness is well established in cats; they groom themselves with their rasplike tongues and preen at length, especially after meals. Another peculiarity of behaviour is the nervous tail-wagging common to all cats, from the lion to the house cat; it is believed to be learned from the mother and is associated with early play, a prelude to adult habits of predation.

Purring. While lions and other big cats roar, the domestic cats and other *Felis* species purr. Purring has been described as a low, continuous, rattling hum and has been interpreted as an expression of pleasure or contentment. It has nothing to do with the true voice of the animal; the vibration frequency is far lower than that of the vocal chords. Purring in domestic cats appears to be introduced to the kittens by the mother, who uses it as a means of calling the young to nurse. At birth the kitten's eyes are closed, the ears undeveloped, and the sense of smell absent; purring is felt as a vibration by the kittens, who approach its source for food. When the kittens begin nursing, the mother stops purring. But since purring manifests itself in extremes of both pain and pleasure, no specific emotional connotations can be placed upon it; it seems merely to be a homing device. Little is known about the physical mechanism involved in purring.

NUTRITION

Cats do best on a diet similar to that of their wild relatives. Cats are adapted by nature to be flesh eaters, an assumption based on their alimentary tract and dentition. The cat uses its canines to catch and kill prey, the molars to cut it up. Lack of flat-surfaced teeth prevents it from chewing or gnawing. The cat has a short intestine, and its stomach secretes digestive juices that act primarily on meat. Cats, however, like all meat-eating animals, chew grass occasionally, and small quantities of vegetables may serve as both a laxative and hair-ball remover.

Raw meat (especially organ meat, lamb, and beef), cottage cheese, boiled fresh fish, processed cheese, and egg yolk with a pat of butter are among the foods required in an adequate and well-balanced cat diet. Pasteurized cow's milk is not the perfect food for cats and sometimes causes gastric disturbances difficult to remedy. In addition, many other foods important in human nutrition are unacceptable in the cat diet, including most cooked foods, egg whites, liver, pork kidney, horsemeat, vegetables, spicy cold cuts, cereals, ice cream, and sweets.

Polyunsaturates such as corn oil, peanut oil, or safflower oil are important dietary supplements, not only for their nutritive value but also because they act as lubricants to prevent constipation and eliminate hair balls. These oils have been known to arrest formation of kidney stones (*i.e.*, urinary calculi) in cats. On the other hand, mineral oil or preparations with a petroleum base can cause severe harm to cats if given routinely to eliminate hair balls.

REPRODUCTION

As a rule, domestic cats reach reproductive age between 7 and 12 months. A breeding female (called a queen) can be in heat or estrus as many as five times a year. During these periods, which last about five days, she "calls," or caterwauls intermittently. The gestation period for cats varies but averages 63–65 days, and the birth usually lasts about two hours. The birth is often known as kittening, and the kittens are known as a litter. The average litter numbers four; however, the Abyssinian usually has fewer, the Siamese more.

Each kitten is born in a separate amniotic sac that is generally broken open at the moment of birth. If it is not, the mother breaks it. She also severs the umbilical cord and eats the placenta (in many cases this stimulates lactation). The kittens are born blind, deaf, and helpless, as are many other carnivores; their senses only begin to function 10 or 12 days after birth. Soon after birth the mother licks her kittens; this action not only cleans them, but also helps stimulate their circulation. Kittens at birth lack distinction and beauty. Their markings are highly deceptive, and many do not acquire their characteristic markings and colour for weeks. For example, Siamese kittens are white at birth, while Blue Persians have tabby markings and Black Persians are brown.

Characteristics of newborn

A cat by nature is capable of bearing up to three litters every year. Obviously, regulation of the cat population cannot be left to nature alone, and relatively safe and simple operations, known as spaying, neutering, or altering, are desirable from a practical viewpoint. Cats that roam unsupervised may live eight or nine years; those supervised and cared for live an average of 14–15 years.

DISEASES AND PARASITES

Until relatively recently little research was concerned directly with cat diseases, their symptoms, or clinical cures. For many years cat treatments were simply extensions of those given dogs. Now, however, cat disorders of the skin, the eyes, the ears, the various systems (circulatory, respiratory, urinary, digestive, nervous, skeletal), and the blood, as well as contagious cat diseases, and external and internal parasites are studied, so that appropriate preventions and treatments can be developed.

Symptoms

Many cats suffer and die because their ailments become serious before their general conditions change sufficiently to reveal symptoms of illness. On the other hand, many symptoms used in diagnosing cat ailments are not definitive for given disorders. For example, signs of possible illness include general symptoms such as a dull coat, lack of appetite, and listlessness. Diarrhea may be a result of serious illness or simply a reflection of a change in diet. Tearing of the eyes may indicate conjunctivitis or a cold, especially when accompanied by sneezing. Since however, sneezing is the cat's only mechanism for blowing its nose, not all sneezing indicates a problem. Open sores, usually at the base of the ear, around the mouth, or on the toes, can point to a ringworm infection or to a fight with another animal.

Cats are attacked by several kinds of external and internal parasites. External parasites are most generally found in kittens, although they occur in adults. The most frequent parasites are fleas, but lice, ticks, and ear mites also occur. Internal parasites include roundworms, tapeworms, and protozoan coccidia. Modern veterinary medicine has made all of these easy to control.

Panleucopenia, often called feline distemper, is the most well-known viral disease in cats. Highly contagious and infectious, with a high mortality rate, it is seen most often in young cats. Vaccines are effective protective measures. Feline pneumonitis, also caused by a virus, has become a common infectious disease of cats. The course of the disease is protracted, and there is no permanent immunization. Vaccines for pneumonitis have an effectiveness of from six to eight months. Rabies is less of a problem with cats than with dogs.

GENETICS

Cats have never been bred for economic purposes; their matings are extremely difficult to control unless the animals are completely confined. There has been relatively little scientific breeding of cats, and the facts of inheritance in these animals are not well known.

Cats are genetically far less plastic than dogs and therefore have not offered the same opportunities to breeders. The size differences between breeds in the domestic dog have no parallel in the domestic cat, nor has anything even remotely approaching the wide range of head shapes and body proportions in different breeds of dogs ever appeared among the cats. In cats the differences between one breed and another are largely differences in colour and texture of the coat. The basic classification is into long-haired and short-haired cats.

Colour. The commonest basic coat colours in non-pedigreed cats are black, yellow, white, and various combinations and dilutions of these colours, such as tabby or striped. Solid white is dominant to all other colours. The mode of inheritance of black is imperfectly understood; the possibility that it is sex-linked is widely accepted. Tortoiseshell, a piebald pattern of black, yellow, and white that results from crossing black and yellow, appears to be sex-linked in some way, for tortoiseshells are born only rarely and are sterile (there is, however, no monetary value for them).

Dominance of white

Siamese dilution, the typical coloration of Siamese cats, has been described as a case of imperfect albinism and has been compared to the Himalayan pattern in rabbits. Its heredity is not well understood. There are also dilutions of the other ordinary colours: blue is dilute black and cream is dilute yellow. White spotting also occurs and is dominant to uniform or self colour.

Other characters. The long-haired coat of the Persian (the usage Angora is archaic) appears to be a simple unit character. It is recessive to short hair. Eye colour is known to be inherited, but its mode of inheritance is not thoroughly understood. Blue eye colour seems to be associated with dilution in coat colour; blue-eyed white cats are usually deaf, a fact commented on by Charles Darwin. Asymmetry of eye colour is known to be inherited. Polydactylism, the presence of extra toes, is inherited and behaves as a dominant to the normal condition. It seems to be due to a single gene. The extra toes occur on the inner or thumb side of the foot.

BREEDS

Recognized show breeds and the characteristics valued most highly by show judges include those listed below.

Longhair division. These are the Persian cats. The perfect type should be cobby—low on the legs, deep in the chest, the head round and massive, eyes large and round, the coat long all over the body. The acceptable colour standards are:

White. Pure white, no coloured hairs; eyes deep blue or deep orange.

Black. Dense coal black from roots to tips of hair; eyes copper or deep orange.

Blue. One level shade of blue gray without shading from nose to tip of tail; eyes brilliant copper or deep orange.

Red. Deep, rich, clear, red orange without shading, marking, or ticking; eyes brilliant copper or deep orange.

Cream. One level shade of cream; eyes brilliant copper or deep orange.

Chinchilla (silver). The undercoat pure white, the coat on back, flanks, head, and tail tipped with black to give the characteristic "sparkling silver" appearance; eyes green; rims of eyes, lips, and nose outlined with black; centre of nose brick red.

Shaded Silver. Pure, unmarked silver; shades gradually down the sides, face, and tail, from dark on the ridge to white on chin, chest, belly, and under the tail; eyes green; rims of eyes, lips, and nose outlined with black, centre of nose brick red.

Smoke. Black, with white undercoat and black points and mask, light silver frill and ear tufts; eyes brilliant copper or deep orange.

Brown Tabby. Ground colour any shade of true brown affording good contrast with markings of dense black with clearly defined and broad pencillings; legs evenly barred, the "bracelets" coming up high to meet the body markings; tail barred; barring on neck and chest, like chains or "necklaces"; head barred with distinct "spectacles" on cheeks; eyes copper.

Silver Tabby. Pale clear silver with broad, dense black markings to conform in pattern to those described for brown tabby; eyes green or hazel.

Blue Tabby. Ground colour pale bluish ivory with fawn overtones; markings deep blue in pattern described for brown tabbies; eyes copper.

Red Tabby. Ground colour red orange, with markings as for brown tabby but in darker red; eyes copper or deep orange.

Tortoiseshell. Black, orange, and cream, the colours bright and well broken; half the nose black, half orange, known as the "blaze"; eyes copper or deep orange.

Calico. Three colours—black, red orange, and cream—well distributed, clearly patched and interspersed with white; white blaze desirable; eyes brilliant deep orange or copper.

Blue Cream. The two colours—blue and cream—bright and well defined, divided and broken into patches; eyes brilliant copper or deep orange.

Shell Cameo. The undercoat pale cream, the coat on the back, flanks, head, and tail tipped with red orange; eyes gold or copper.

Shaded Cameo. Pure, unmarked red orange, with gradual shading down the sides, face, and tail from dark on the ridge to whitish cream on the chin, chest, and stomach; eyes gold or copper.

Smoke Cameo. Deep reddish beige with white or cream undercoat; eyes gold or copper.

Tabby Cameo. Pale cream broken with well-defined reddish or beige tabby markings; eyes gold or copper.

Himalayan. Colour and points same as for Siamese (see below); eyes blue; correctly called a colour-point Persian or a Persian with Siamese marking, not long-haired Siamese.

Shorthair division. *Siamese.* A sleek, smooth coat; straight tail; and eyes that are not crossed; points (face mask, ears, feet, and tail) all the same colour; eyes vivid deep blue. The acceptable colours are:

Seal point: even, pale fawn to cream, shading gradually to a lighter colour on the chest and belly; deep seal-brown points.

Blue point: bluish white, shading gradually to oyster white on the chest and belly; points of definite blue, giving strong contrast.

Chocolate point: ivory all over; milk-chocolate-brown points.

Lilac point: even glacial white without shading; points frosty gray with pinkish tone.

Abyssinian. Larger than Siamese, with regal, alert posture; ruddy brown ticked with shades of darker brown or black; inside of forelegs and belly should harmonize with the main colour (preference is given to orange brown or burnt sienna); lip and chin lightest in colour, off-white or cream; eyes hazel, gold, or green.

Burmese. The ideal Burmese would be of medium size and rich sable-brown colour, with the head rounder than in the Siamese; profile should show visible nose break; fine, glossy, satinlike coat; eyes yellow to gold.

Russian Blue. Bright blue gray even throughout and free from tabby markings and shadings; thick coat, different from that of any other breed of cat; eyes green.

Manx. Completely tailless with decided hollow at the end of the backbone, double coat, back legs to be longer than front giving characteristic hopping gait; all colours of Manx are recognized, including ticked and mackerel tabbies and parti-coloured.

Rex. One of the newly recognized breeds, it has a wavy coat, like Persian lamb to the touch; all coat colours and eye colours acceptable.

Domestic Shorthair. While the domestic shorthairs seen in shows may resemble ordinary mixed breeds, the breeding of the show type is as exacting as for other breeds; recognized in all Persian colours.

BREEDERS' ASSOCIATIONS AND CAT SHOWS

Innumerable societies and associations have been formed to foster interest in cats and to set standards for the recognized breeds. Unrelated organizations, promoting various breeds, have also set up breed standards. None of these organizations has absolute power and occasionally standards conflict.

Cat shows are held annually in many large cities. Shows usually are divided into at least three parts: all breed, shorthair specialty, and longhair specialty. Each shorthaired or long-haired cat may compete in the all-breed and in the appropriate specialty show. Almost any healthy cat may be entered in a show, since often there are classes for kittens, altered cats, and household pets, as well as for pedigreed animals.

In general, an adult, pedigreed, show cat begins its career as a novice, at the age of eight months or older, when it may win its first blue ribbon for its particular breed and colour. It is not thereafter eligible for novice and must compete in the open class. Novice and open classes compete for the winners' ribbons, which designate championship points. Champions, having acquired sufficient ribbons, compete for grand championship status. "Finals" awards are made to best novice, open, etc., in show and "Best Cat in Show" is selected from these finalists.

BIBLIOGRAPHY

General works: AMERICAN SOCIETY FOR THE PREVENTION OF CRUELTY TO ANIMALS, *Official ASPCA Encyclopedia of Cat Health and Care* (1964); DORIS BRYANT, *Pet Cats: Their Care and Handling* (1963); DOROTHY BEVILL CHAMPION, *Everybody's Cat Book* (1909); ANN CURRAH (ed.), *The Cat Compendium* (1969); MILAN GREER, *The Fabulous Feline* (1961); FERNAND MERY, *Le Chat, se vie, son histoire, sa magie* (1966; Eng. trans., *The Life, History, and Magic of the Cat*, 1967); PERCY M. SODERBERG, *Pedigree Cats, Their Varieties, Breeding and Exhibition* (1958); LEON F. WHITNEY, *The Complete Book of Cat Care* (1953).

Technical references: FRANK BLOOM, *Pathology of the Dog and Cat* (1954); EARL J. CATCOTT (ed.), *Feline Medicine and Surgery* 1964); MELLON INSTITUTE OF INDUSTRIAL RESEARCH, *Nutritional Data*, 5th ed. (1962); A.C. JUDE, *Cat Genetics* (1955); HANS KALMUS, *Genetics*, 2nd ed. (1964); *Modern Veterinary Practice*, vol. 46, no. 5, Red Book Edition (April 1965); JACOB REIGHARD and HERBERT S. JENNINGS, *Anatomy of the Cat*, 3rd ed. by RUSH ELLIOTT (1961); O.H. SIEGMUND (ed.), *The Merck Veterinary Manual*, 3rd ed. (1967); periodicals such as *Modern Veterinary Practice* (13/year) and the *Journal of the American Veterinary Medical Association* (semimonthly).

(Ed.)

Catalysis

The transformations that occur among atoms and molecules (or molecular fragments), bringing about new arrangements or alignments of the atoms within the larger structures, are known as chemical reactions. The rates of such reactions—that is, the velocities at which they occur—depend upon a number of factors, including the chemical nature of the reacting species and the external conditions to which they are exposed. A particular phenomenon associated with the rates of chemical reactions that is of great theoretical and practical interest is catalysis. This phenomenon is the acceleration of chemical reactions by substances not consumed in the reactions themselves—substances that have come to be called catalysts. The study of catalysis is of interest theoretically because of what it reveals about the fundamental nature of chemical reactions; in practice, the study of catalysis is important because many industrial processes depend upon catalysts for their success. Finally, the peculiar phenomenon of life would hardly be possible without the biological catalysts termed enzymes.

HISTORY

The term catalysis (from the Greek *kata-*, "down," and *lyein*, "loosen") was first employed by the great Swedish chemist Jöns Jacob Berzelius in 1835 to correlate a group of observations made by other chemists in the late 18th and early 19th centuries. These included: the enhanced conversion of starch to sugar by acids first observed by Gustav Kirchhoff; Sir Humphry Davy's observations that platinum hastens the combustion of a variety of gases; the discovery of the stability of hydrogen peroxide in acid solution but its decomposition in the presence of alkali and such metals as manganese, silver, platinum, and gold; and the observation that the oxidation of alcohol to acetic acid is accomplished in the presence of finely divided platinum. The agents promoting these various reactions were termed catalysts, and Berzelius postulated a special, unknown catalytic force operating in such processes.

In 1834 the English scientist Michael Faraday had examined the power of a platinum plate to accomplish the recombination of gaseous hydrogen and oxygen, the products of electrolysis of water, and the retardation of that recombination by the presence of other gases, such as ethylene and carbon monoxide. Faraday maintained that the essential for activity was a perfectly clean metallic surface (at which the retarding gases could compete with the reacting gases and so suppress activity), a concept that would later be shown to be generally important in catalysis.

Early applications of catalysis

Many of the primitive technical arts involved unconscious applications of catalysis. The fermentation of wine to acetic acid, the manufacture of soap from fats and alkalies, and the formation of ether from alcohol and sulfuric acid—all catalytic reactions—were well-known in man's early history. Sulfuric acid prepared by firing mixtures of sulfur and nitre (sodium nitrate) was an early forerunner of the lead chamber process of sulfuric acid manufacture, in which sulfur dioxide oxidation was accelerated by the addition of oxides of nitrogen. (A mechanism for the latter process was suggested by Sir Humphry Davy in 1812 on the basis of experiments carried out by others.)

In 1850 the concept of a velocity of reaction was developed during studies of hydrolysis, or inversion, of cane sugar. The term inversion refers to the change in rotation undergone by monochromatic light when it is passed through the reaction system, a parameter that is easily measured, facilitating study of the reaction. It was found that the rate of inversion was, at any moment, proportional to the amount of cane sugar undergoing transformation and that the rate was accelerated by the presence of acids. (Later it was shown that the rate of inversion was directly proportional to the strength of the acid.) This work was, in part, the precursor of later studies of reaction velocity and the accelerating influence of higher temperature on that velocity by J.H. van't Hoff, Svante Arrhenius, and Wilhelm Ostwald, all of whom played leading roles in the developing science of physical chemistry. Ostwald's work on reaction velocities led him in the 1890s to define catalysts as substances that change the velocity of a given chemical reaction without modification of the energy factors of the reaction.

This statement of Ostwald was a memorable advance since it implied that catalysts do not change the position of equilibrium in a reaction (equilibrium being that point at which the conversion of reactants to products is equalled by the reconversion of products to reactants). In 1877 Georges Lemoine had shown that the decomposition of hydriodic acid to hydrogen and iodine reached the same equilibrium point at 350° C, 19 percent, whether the reaction was carried out rapidly in the presence of platinum sponge or slowly in the gas phase. This observation has an important consequence: a catalyst for the forward process in a reaction is also a catalyst for the reverse reaction. P-E-M. Berthelot, the distinguished French chemist, had confirmed this observation in 1879 with liquid systems when he found that the reaction of organic acids and alcohols, called esterification, is catalyzed by the presence of small amounts of a strong inorganic acid, just as is the reverse process—the hydrolysis of esters (the reaction between an ester and water).

Industrial applications

The application of catalysts to industrial processes was undertaken deliberately in the 19th century. P. Phillips, an English chemist, patented the use of platinum to oxidize sulfur dioxide to sulfur trioxide with air. His process was employed for a time but was abandoned due to loss of activity by the platinum catalyst. Subsequently poisons in the reactants were found to be responsible, and the process became a technical success at the turn of the 20th century. In 1871, an industrial process was developed for the oxidation of hydrochloric acid to chlorine in the presence of cupric salts impregnated in clay brick. The chlorine obtained was employed in the manufacture of bleaching powder (a dry substance that releases chlorine on treatment with acid) by reaction with lime. Again, in this reaction, it was observed that the same equilibrium was reached in both directions. Furthermore, it was found that the lower the temperature, the greater the equilibrium content of chlorine; a working temperature of 450° C produced the maximum amount of chlorine in a convenient time. Toward the close of the 19th century, the classical studies of the eminent French chemist Paul Sabatier on the interaction of hydrogen with a wide variety of organic compounds were carried out using various metal catalysts; this research led to the technical development of a German patent for the hydrogenation of liquid unsaturated fats to solid saturated fats with nickel catalysts. The development of three important German catalytic processes had great impact on the industrial scene at the end of the 19th century and in the early decades of the 20th. One was the so-called contact process for producing sulfuric acid catalytically from the sulfur dioxide produced by smelting operations. Another was the catalytic method for the synthetic production of the valuable dyestuff indigo. The third was the catalytic combination of nitrogen and hydrogen for the production of ammonia—that is, the Haber process for nitrogen fixation—developed by the German chemist, Fritz Haber.

HOMOGENEOUS CATALYSIS

When the catalyst and the reacting substances are present together in a single state of matter, usually as a gas or a liquid, it is customary to classify these as cases of homogeneous catalysis. Oxides of nitrogen serve as catalysts for the oxidation of sulfur dioxide in the lead-chamber process for producing sulfuric acid, an instance of homogeneous catalysis in which the catalyst and reactants are gases. Traces of water vapour catalyze some gas reactions; for example, the interaction of carbon monoxide and oxygen, which proceeds only slowly in dry conditions. Sulfuric acid used as a catalyst for the formation of diethyl ether from ethyl alcohol is an example of homogeneous catalysis in the liquid phase (when the products, water and ether, are continuously removed by distillation); by this method, considerable quantities of alcohol can be converted to ether with a single charge of sulfuric acid. The inversion of cane sugar and the hydrolysis of esters by acid solutions (see above) also are examples of homogeneous catalysis in the liquid phase.

The oxidation of sodium sulfite solutions by dissolved oxygen is greatly accelerated by minute traces of copper ions in the homogeneous liquid system. This system is of especial interest since it has been shown that the process is a chain reaction—that is, it is characterized by a succession of repeating reactions, proceeding to the same end point. In this case many thousands of molecules of sodium sulfite can be oxidized to sulfate if the initial activation process is produced by absorption of a limited number of quanta (discrete energy measures) of light. The best example of a light-initiated chain reaction is the photo-combination of hydrogen (H_2) and chlorine (Cl_2); as many as 1,000,000 molecules of hydrogen chloride can be formed by absorption of a single light quantum (designated $h\nu$). Here the sequence of reaction is

(1) $Cl_2 + h\nu \rightarrow 2Cl\cdot$

(2) $Cl\cdot + H_2 \rightarrow HCl + H\cdot$

(3) $H\cdot + Cl_2 \rightarrow HCl + Cl\cdot$

with reactions (2) and (3) repeated over and over again. It is of interest to note that such chain reactions can be retarded by the presence of negative catalysts, more commonly termed inhibitors. These are materials that slow down the overall reaction by shortening the reaction chains, generally by entering into a non-chain reaction with one of the chemical components that maintain the chain. A wide variety of substances, including alcohols, sugars, and phenols, has been found to act as inhibitors of the oxidation of sulfite solutions.

Basic mechanisms of homogeneous catalysis

A generalized treatment of homogeneous catalysis by acids and bases was given by the Danish physical chemist J.N. Brønsted in 1924 on the basis of his concept of acids and bases. According to the Brønsted theory an acid is a molecule that can furnish a proton, whereas a base is a molecule that takes up a proton. On this assumption, the range of acids includes such varied materials as bisulfate ion, HSO_4^-; acetic acid, CH_3COOH; water, H_2O; hydronium ion, H_3O^+; ammonium ion, NH_4^+; and the corresponding bases are sulfate ion, SO_4^{2-}; acetate ion, CH_3COO^-; hydroxide ion, OH^-; water H_2O; and ammonia, NH_3 (these substances accept protons to yield the listed acids). Brønsted studied a number of acid- and base-catalyzed reactions, including: (1) the acid-catalyzed hydrolysis of an ester, ethyl orthoacetate; (2) the basic catalysis of nitramide decomposition ($H_2N{-}NO_2 \rightarrow H_2O + N_2O$); and (3) the acid–base catalysis of the conversion (mutarotation) of glucose to a closely related form. In each case he observed a linear relationship (indicating a direct connection) between the catalytic velocities of the reaction and the logarithm of the acid or base strength of the solution.

Based in part on the ideas of Brønsted, a general scheme for a change of a substance A to another substance B catalyzed by a material C can be formulated thus:

(1) $$A + C \underset{k_2}{\overset{k_1}{\rightleftharpoons}} Z$$

(2) $$Z \xrightarrow{k_3} B + C$$

The designation Z refers to an intermediate stage, which is formed with a velocity indicated by k_1; Z can disappear either to reform $A + C$, with a velocity k_2, or it can decompose by path (2), with velocity k_3, to give the product B and regenerate the catalyst C. If k_3 is much greater than k_2 the intermediate Z is used up almost as quickly as it is formed. The product will then be formed at a rate governed by the expression $k_1[A][C]$, in which the square brackets indicate concentrations of reactant and catalyst. If k_2 is much larger than k_3, however, the velocity-determining process is the decomposition of Z, the rate of formation of the product being represented by the expression $k_3[Z]$, in which $[Z]$ is the concentration of the intermediate. Examples of both types of change have been studied.

In certain instances two or more catalysts present at the same time produce effects greater than either would produce alone. It is then customary to speak of promoter action. Thus, iron ions in solution fortify the action of copper ions in catalyzing a reaction between hydrogen peroxide and iodine. It is assumed that each catalyst activates only one of the reactants.

The most important modern examples of homogeneous catalyses are found in the petrochemical industry. The oxo reaction is one such process; in this process carbon monoxide and hydrogen are added to olefins (unsaturated hydrocarbons) at around 150° C and 200 atmospheres of pressure to form aldehydes and alcohols, oxygen-containing organic compounds. A cobalt carbonyl catalyst $Co_2(CO)_8$ is employed; this hydrocarbon-soluble catalyst is believed to activate hydrogen by formation of $HCo(CO)_4$, which then reacts with the olefin. This reaction has led to a number of studies of organometallic chemistry. Copper, silver, and mercury cations (positively charged ions) and permanganate anions (negative ions) also are known to act as homogeneous catalysts for hydrogen activation. Palladium chloride is employed industrially in the catalytic oxidation of ethylene to acetaldehyde in the presence of cupric chloride. The palladium is presumed to be repeatedly converted from the salt to the free metal, the function of the cupric chloride being to participate in the re-formation of the palladium salt from the metal.

Homogeneous catalysis of industrial importance

Phosphoric, sulfuric, sulfonic, and hydrobromic acids are important agents in the industrial processes of isomerization, polymerization, hydration, and dehydration, as well as in the classical esterification reactions. Free radicals (molecular fragments bearing unpaired electrons) that are generated by the decomposition of peroxides or metal alkyls also initiate homogeneous catalytic processes.

The chemistry of organic isocyanates R–N=C=O (in which R equals an alkyl or aryl group) in the presence of water and alcohols has become in the second half of the 20th century a major concern of industry, especially in the manufacture of polyurethane foams. Bases, especially amines, together with organometallic salts of tin, are the important catalysts industrially employed in these reactions. Solid dimers and trimers (polymers with two and three monomers) are produced under certain conditions, but linear polymerization yields

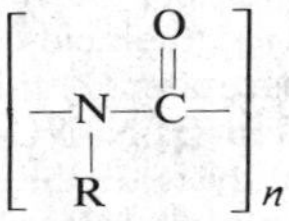

in which R is normally an aromatic group, usually phenyl (C_6H_5–) or tolyl ($CH_3C_6H_4$–). Reaction of these polymers with water or with polyhydroxy alcohols yields carbamic acids, which decompose with liberation of carbon dioxide gas to form the desired foams. When gas formation and polymer growth are suitably matched, foams with strength and other favourable qualities are achieved.

HETEROGENEOUS CATALYSIS

Many catalytic processes are known in which the catalyst and the reactants are not present in the same phase—that is, state of matter. These are known as heterogeneous catalytic reactions. They include reactions between gases or liquids or both at the surface of a solid catalyst. Since the surface is the place at which the reaction occurs, it generally is prepared in ways that produce large surface areas per unit of catalyst; finely divided metals, metal gauzes, metals incorporated into supporting matrices, and metallic films have all been used in modern heterogeneous catalysis. The metals themselves are used or they are converted to oxides, sulfides, or halides.

With solid catalysts, the reactants are chemisorbed (a portmanteau term for chemically adsorbed) by the catalyst. A catalyst is chosen that releases the products formed as readily as possible; otherwise the products remain on the catalyst surface and act as poisons to the process. Chemisorption can occur over a wide temperature range, the most effective temperature for adsorption depending on the nature of the catalyst. Thus, hydrogen is chemisorbed readily by many metals even at liquid air temperatures (below −180° C). With a series of hydrogenation–dehydrogenation catalysts—*e.g.*, zinc oxide–chromic oxide ($ZnO–Cr_2O_3$)—chemisorption of hydrogen often occurs above room temperature. Nitrogen is chemisorbed on synthetic ammonia-iron catalyst rapidly in the region above 400° C. It has been shown that iron films chemisorb nitrogen even at liquid air temperatures, with additional chemisorption found above room temperatures. It follows from such considerations that whereas physical adsorptions, which parallel the ease of liquefaction of the adsorbed substance, occur spontaneously, chemisorption, which involves the making and breaking of chemical bonds, often requires activation energies (energy needed to initiate reactions) as do uncatalyzed chemical processes. To be efficient catalytically, a process must involve energies of activation for all the steps involved that, at their maxima, are less than those required for the uncatalyzed reaction. This situation is illustrated graphically in the Figure, for a hypothetical reaction, which can occur by either an uncatalyzed or a catalyzed route. Two

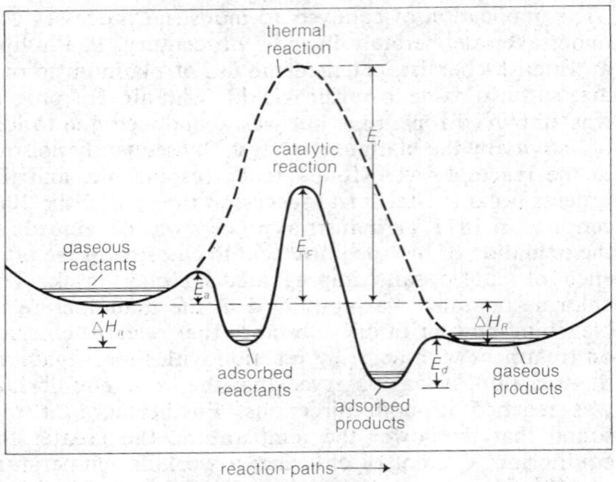

Energy profiles for catalytic and thermal (noncatalytic) reactions in the gaseous phase: E_c is activation energy for catalytic reaction; E_t is activation energy for thermal reaction; E_a is activation energy of adsorption of gaseous reactants; E_d is activation energy of desorption of gaseous products; ΔH_a is heat of chemisorption of reactants; ΔH_R is heat of overall reaction.

competing proposals have been made concerning the mechanism of catalytic reactions at surfaces, and it has not been possible to choose between them. Originally, Irving Langmuir, the American physical chemist, proposed chemisorption of both reacting species at the surface, followed by interaction between adjacent species and evaporation of the products. An alternative proposal involves interaction between an impinging molecule and species already adsorbed on the surface. Subsequent developments have suggested various modes of attachment of the adsorbed and adsorbing species.

Basic mechanisms of heterogeneous catalysis

A major advance in the science of surface catalysis was the development of a method for determining the surface area of catalysts (and other materials) by measuring the multimolecular adsorption of nitrogen at liquid nitrogen temperatures or the adsorption of other gases close to their boiling points. It then became possible to calculate a quantity, designated V_m, which represents the volume of gas necessary to form a monolayer on the accessible surface; furthermore, the area of the surface can be determined from the known dimensions of the adsorbed molecules. It has also been found possible to titrate (measure quantitatively) the area of surfaces by chemisorption of gases.

When measurements of surface areas became possible, it was seen at once that many constituents present in minor quantities in the main catalyst material—and known as promoters—could act by extending the effective surface area of the catalyst. It also was shown, however, that a promoter might produce an increase in the quality of the surface for the given reaction. Acting in a reverse direction are minor constituents of the reacting system or unwanted products of the reaction, which by preferential adsorption on the reaction sites and resistance to removal give rise to poisons for the process.

Much can be learned about mechanisms of surface processes by studying the behaviour of isotopic species of the reactants and products on the catalyst. An example of such use concerns the technically important synthesis of ammonia from its elements, the well-known Haber process on promoted-iron catalysts. The synthesis of ammonia involves three types of bonds, hydrogen–hydrogen, nitrogen–hydrogen, and nitrogen–nitrogen, all of which can be studied using isotopes of hydrogen and nitrogen. The first of these can be examined on the reduced-iron catalyst by following the progress of the reaction $H_2 + D_2 \rightarrow 2HD$ (in which D equals the deuterium atom, an isotope of hydrogen) on the surface. The reaction is found to occur rapidly even at liquid air temperatures. Nitrogen–hydrogen bond activation can be studied by following the reaction $NH_3 + ND_3 \rightarrow NH_2D + NHD_2$. This proceeds steadily at room temperatures. The reaction involving only N–N bonds, however, studied by following the process $^{14}N_2 + {}^{15}N_2 \rightarrow 2{}^{14}N{-}{}^{15}N$ (in which ^{14}N and ^{15}N are stable isotopes of nitrogen), is shown to proceed only at the higher temperatures of ammonia synthesis, around 400° C. From these data one concludes that the activation of the nitrogen molecules is the slow step (the process that limits the overall reaction) in ammonia synthesis. This conclusion is confirmed by measurement of rate of adsorption of nitrogen on the iron catalysts. Other, similar isotopic studies have yielded valuable information on the reactions of hydrocarbons, using deuterium and carbon-14 as the isotopic tracers.

Catalysis in stereoregular polymerization

The importance of the concept of adsorption of reactants on the surface of catalysts has been greatly increased by the development of stereoregular polymerization processes—that is, methods that yield polymers whose molecules have definite three-dimensional patterns. Such processes were developed independently by the German chemist Karl Ziegler and the Italian Giulio Natta. An example is the polymerization of propylene with a titanium trichloride–alkyl aluminum catalyst. In the case of a generalized ethylenic compound, $CH_2{=}CHR$, stereoregular polymerization may yield three different arrangements of the polymer; an isotactic polymer, a syndiotactic polymer, and an atactic polymer. These have the following arrangements of their molecular chains:

(1)
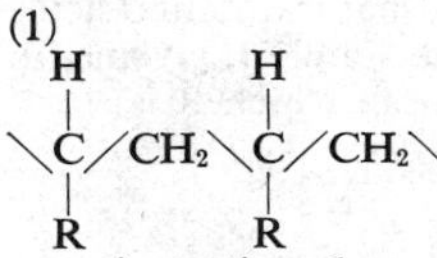
isotactic polymer

(2)
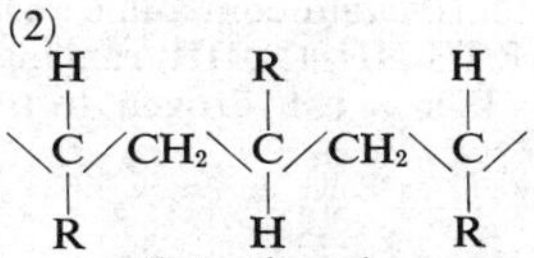
syndiotactic polymer

(3)
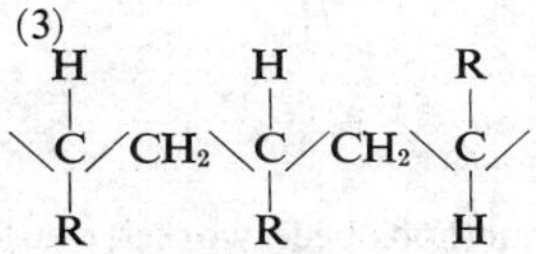
atactic polymer

In the isotactic polymer the monomer units have added head-to-tail, to give a series of C–R tertiary bonds with the same configuration in space; in the syndiotactic polymer, the tertiary carbon atoms in the chain have alternate (dextro and levo) spatial configurations; and in the atactic polymer there is no regularity in the distribution of steric configurations of the asymmetric carbon atoms. The various forms differ in their physical properties. Isotactic polypropylene has a density of 0.92 g/cm^3 and a melting point of 165° C, whereas an atactic polymer has a smaller density, 0.85 g/cm^3, and a melting point of −35° C. The more regular isotactic polymer is denser and has a higher melting point than the atactic product because of its greater tendency to crystallize (in spite of the fact that the substituent R may be quite large, hindering crystal formation). Stereoregular polymerization suggests a stereoregulated adsorption at the active centres of the catalyst. In the case of polypropylene, the catalytic centres have been identified by electron micrographs as α-$TiCl_3$ surfaces, which cover only a small fraction of the total surface area, whereas the β-$TiCl_3$ surfaces, which are more abundant, appear to be covered with polymer. The difference between the α- and β-surfaces lies in the random (α) and linear (β) arrangements of Ti^{3+} sites in the two surfaces.

Since the Ziegler–Natta studies, other stereoregulating catalysts have been investigated, notably oxides of chromium, vanadium, molybdenum, and tungsten on silica–alumina or other supports. Other cationic, anionic, and free-radical catalysts are known to produce stereoregulated polymerization. Stereoregular polymerization of dienes has undergone industrial development with the polymerization of isoprene to synthetic natural rubber.

Catalytically active centres

The nature of the active centres in catalytic material is further demonstrated by the enhancement of the catalytic activity of relatively inactive materials when they are subjected to intense radiation. Silica gel bombarded by gamma rays from cobalt-60 turns purplish in colour and becomes capable of inducing the reaction $H_2 + D_2 \rightarrow 2HD$ at liquid nitrogen temperatures. The colour centres, which are positive "holes" (deficiencies) trapped in the vicinity of an oxygen ion next to an aluminum impurity, are bleached *in vacuo* above 200° C and are destroyed by hydrogen even at room temperature.

The properties of dilute concentrations of platinum metals in oxide matrices, such as silica and alumina, as well as on carbon carriers have been studied by Soviet and American scientists. Such catalysts have technical significance in processes for the reforming of gasoline. In such catalysts—containing about 0.5 percent by weight of platinum or palladium—the degree of dispersion of the metal (that is, the ratio of the number of surface metal atoms to the total number present) is close to one. By contrast, on platinum foil the dispersion is only about 4×10^{-3}. The titration and adsorption procedures with hydrogen and oxygen (see above) are employed to evaluate these dispersions.

From these studies it becomes clear that there are two types of behaviour resulting from dispersion. For numerous catalytic processes, ranging from hydrogen–deuterium exchange to the hydrogenation of benzene and the hydrogenolysis of cyclopentane, the reactions are independent of dispersion in the critical region—with catalyst particle size of 50Å or less. Such structure-insensitive processes have been termed facile reactions. On the other hand, there are reactions, such as the isomerization of neopentane to isopentane and simultaneous cracking of the latter to isobutane and methane on platinum–alumina catalysts, where the selectivity for isomerization varies by a factor of 100 for the various catalysts studied (when the hydrogen–neopentane ratio is 10). Thus, the same 1 percent platinum-on-carbon catalyst showed a selectivity ratio of isomerization to hydrogenolysis of 2.5 when the catalyst was reduced in hydrogen at 500° C and a selectivity ratio of 13 when the catalyst was fired *in vacuo* at 900° C (the percentage dispersion remaining at 35 percent in both cases). Such structure-sensitive catalytic reactions have been called demanding reactions. The gain in selectivity appears to be due largely to a reduction in the rate of hydrogenolysis. Since other studies have shown that heating *in vacuo* to 900° tends to develop certain (111) facets of the metal, it is thought that the increase in selectivity is due to a more abundant triadsorption of neopentane on the samples fired at high temperature. It has been shown that a crystallite of platinum about 20Å in size has unusual surfaces not present in a regular octahedral crystallite of similar size. A number of sites where an adsorbed molecule could be surrounded by five platinum nearest neighbours were found on the crystallite with the unusual surface.

Electronic factors in heterogeneous catalysis

An alternative approach to the problem of surface catalysis involves the consideration of electronic factors in catalyst and reactants. Many catalytic materials are semiconductors. It is thought that these can form a variety of bonds with reactants depending on the free lattice electrons and the "holes" (deficiencies) in the catalyst lattice. Chemisorbed particles react in ways that are dependent on the form of attachment to the surface and that vary with the extent of coverage of the surface as well as with the available supply of electrons and holes. The surface behaves as would free radicals that are introduced directly into the reacting species, dependent on the electrochemical properties of the surface and the bulk of the semiconductor material. Such considerations have led to the determination of the character of the catalyst as a semiconductor and of the adsorbate as an electrochemical species, whether it is composed of positive or negative ions or free atoms or radicals. Catalytic activity also has been explored as a function of the d-band character —that is, the number of electrons in d orbitals, or pathways, in the atoms of the catalyst materials.

During the period from 1940 to 1970 various instrumental techniques were developed to explore the structure of catalytic materials and the character of the adsorbed species, even during the reaction itself. Among these techniques are electron microscopy, field emission microscopy, electron microprobe methods, magnetic measurements, infrared spectroscopy, Mössbauer spectroscopy, measurements of heats of immersion, flash desorption procedures, low energy electron diffraction studies, and nuclear magnetic resonance and electron spin resonance techniques.

Polyfunctional heterogeneous catalysis

The term polyfunctional heterogeneous catalysis is applied to a group of catalysts in which more than one component of the surface is active in the processes under study. One example of a bifunctional heterogeneous catalyst is the catalyst of metal (platinum or nickel) deposited on a silica–alumina "acidic" base. Such dual functional catalysts are involved in the interconversions of saturated hydrocarbons (paraffins) and unsaturated hydrocarbons (olefins), and normal (straight-chain) and iso (branched-chain) hydrocarbons, as well as in the splitting (cracking) of the hydrocarbon molecules. The interrelations involved are as follows:

$$n\text{-paraffin} \underset{X_2}{\overset{X_1}{\rightleftharpoons}} n\text{-olefin} \underset{Y_2}{\overset{Y_1}{\rightleftharpoons}} \text{iso-olefin} \underset{X_2}{\overset{X_1}{\rightleftharpoons}} \text{isoparaffin}$$

Cracked paraffins (by hydrogenolysis)   Cracked paraffins (by hydrocracking)   Cracked paraffins (by hydrogenolysis)

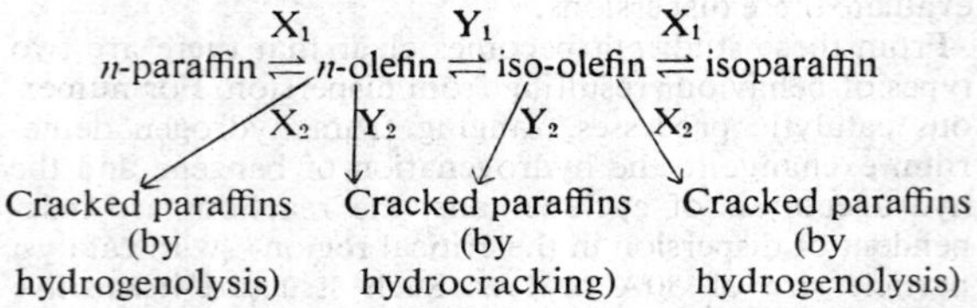

in which X_1 and X_2 are metal-catalyzed processes and Y_1 and Y_2 are acid-catalyzed processes. Operating conditions can be altered to maximize the hydrocracking reactions relative to hydrogenolysis.

A variety of catalysts with "acidic" sites has been found to be active in the dehydration of alcohols and (as above) in the cracking and isomerization of hydrocarbons. Among these are: silica, obtained by calcination (heating) of silica gel; high purity alumina, prepared by the calcining of specially prepared aluminum hydroxide; and silica–alumina mixtures. The catalytic sites have been found to have varying degrees of acidity; their exact nature is still under discussion as well as their characterization in terms of the atomic architecture of the solid catalyst. In the case of silica–alumina, the sites are ascribed to the presence of trivalent aluminum ions Al^{3+}, in a matrix of quadrivalent silicon ions, Si^{4+}, which gives rise to charge differences in the neighbourhood of the aluminum ions. These acidic sites can be poisoned by ammonia and by amines, a finding that confirms their acidic nature. When these catalysts are treated with alkalies their catalytic character is greatly modified. On the other hand, treatment with halogens, especially fluorine or chlorine, enhances the acidic properties of these oxide materials.

Zeolites

Zeolites are naturally occurring crystalline aluminosilicates having a porous structure and containing cations, generally of the alkali or alkaline earth metals. The cations can be exchanged reversibly with other metal ions without destroying the aluminosilicate structure. Because the zeolites rapidly adsorb certain molecules and exclude others, they have been given the name of molecular sieves. The adsorption characteristics of natural and synthetic zeolites have been studied since the 1930s. Manufactured zeolites, some of which have structures not found in nature, are employed as dehydrating agents but also may be used for the production of catalytic materials by exchange with cationic elements or by impregnation of

metal salt solutions into the pores of the zeolite; a large number of zeolitic catalysts have been developed.

Electron donor–acceptor complexes

A class of compounds termed electron donor–acceptor complexes also has been studied for its catalytic activity. The class may be exemplified by a complex between metallic sodium (the donor) and anthracene, $C_{14}H_{10}$, a tricyclic hydrocarbon (the acceptor). The complex can be visualized as an anthracene anion and a sodium cation. Such complexes can exchange the hydrogen of the anion with molecular hydrogen that has been brought into contact with the complex. A complex represented by ZH (in which Z represents all of the molecule except for the exchangeable hydrogen) could undergo exchange with deuterium, as follows: $ZH + D_2 \rightarrow ZD + HD$. It could also take part in corresponding exchanges with hydrocarbons or bring about hydrogenation of hydrocarbons. Among other electron-acceptor catalysts are the metal phthalocyanines (compounds related to certain biological catalysts) and activated charcoal. Some donor–acceptor complexes synthesize ammonia from nitrogen–hydrogen mixtures. This reaction represents a close approach to the activity of biological and bacterial catalysts.

BIOLOGICAL CATALYSTS: THE ENZYMES

Enzymes are substances found in biological systems that are catalysts for specific biochemical processes. Although earlier discoveries of enzymes had been made, a significant confirmation of their importance in living systems was found in 1897 by the German chemist Eduard Buchner, who showed that the filtered cell-free liquor from crushed yeast cells could bring about the conversion of sugar to carbon dioxide. Since that time more than 1,000 enzymes have been recognized, each specific to a particular chemical reaction occurring in living systems. More than 100 of these have been isolated in relatively pure form, including a number of crystallized enzymes. The first enzymes to be crystallized were urease, isolated from the jack bean and crystallized in 1926 by James Batcheller Sumner, and pepsin, crystallized in 1930 by John Howard Northrop, both men being American biochemists. These purified materials were shown to be proteins, chain compounds of about 20 natural amino acids $RCH(NH_2)COOH$, ranging from the simplest, glycine, in which R is hydrogen, to tryptophan, in which R is

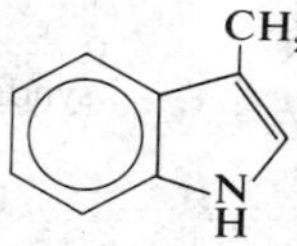

Not only have methods been worked out for determining the amino acids, found in an enzyme, but also the sequence of amino acids in an enzyme can be elucidated by a method developed by the English biochemist Frederick Sanger in determining the structure of the protein hormone, insulin. The first enzyme to have its complete amino acid sequence determined in this way was the enzyme bovine pancreatic ribonuclease, which has 124 amino acids in its chain and has a molecular weight of about 14000; the enzyme catalyzes the degradation of ribonucleic acid, a substance active in protein synthesis in living cells. In January 1969, the synthesis of this same enzyme was reported from two different laboratories. The activity of an enzyme depends upon a three-dimensional, or tertiary, structure, but this, in turn, appears to depend solely upon the linear sequence of amino acids. The success of a synthesis of an enzyme can be unequivocally checked by test of its enzymatic activity.

Enzyme reactivity

Enzymes are extremely reactive, as can be shown with a very simple reaction, the splitting of hydrogen peroxide to form water and oxygen, brought about by colloidal metals and by the enzyme catalase. It has been found that one molecule of the latter will cause several million molecules of peroxide to decompose per minute, a rate comparable to that obtained with the best colloidal preparations. This speed of catalase decomposition is probably a maximum for enzymes. Slower acting enzymes normally react at speeds of hundreds of reactions per minute. The rate of reaction is often expressed by an equation developed by L. Michaelis and M.L. Menten of the form:

$$\text{Rate} = \frac{V[S]}{K + [S]}$$

in which V and K are constants for the particular enzymatic process, K being termed the Michaelis constant, and $[S]$ is the concentration of the reactant undergoing change. At low concentrations of S the rate is $V[S]/K$ or proportional to the substrate concentration [S], whereas at high substrate concentrations the $[S]$ terms cancel out and the reaction is essentially independent of the substrate concentration.

A second characteristic of enzymes is their extreme specificity. It has been suggested that each biochemical process has its own specific enzyme. The biochemical processes induced by enzymes fall into broad classifications, such as hydrolysis, decomposition (or "splitting"), synthesis, hydrogenation–dehydrogenation; as with catalysts in general, enzymes are active for both forward and reverse reactions.

Like the laboratory catalysts, enzymes frequently have activators—coenzymes, which may be prosthetic groups (firmly bound to the enzyme itself) and inorganic ions. Adenosine triphosphate, ATP, is an important coenzyme participating in energy-producing processes and passage across cell membranes. Coenzymes often contain vitamins as parts of their structure. Calcium and magnesium ions are important enzyme activators. As with catalysts there are many substances that inhibit, or poison, enzymes. Cyanide ion is a potent inhibitor in many enzymic processes, as are such substances as nerve gases and insecticides.

BIBLIOGRAPHY. P. SABATIER, *La Catalyse en chimie organique* (1913; Eng. trans., *Catalysis in Organic Chemistry*, 1922), a classic work written by a Nobel prize winner; E.K. RIDEAL and H.S. TAYLOR, *Catalysis in Theory and Practice*, 2nd ed. (1926), an account of the state of the subject during World War I and the rapid advances in theory that occurred shorty after; P.H. EMMETT (ed.), *Catalysis*, 7 vol., (1954–60), a monumental treatment of the subject, both theory and practice, contributed by a group of international experts in the field; W.G. FRANKENBURG *et al.* (eds.), *Advances in Catalysis and Related Subjects*, 20 vol. (1948–70), a record of the year-to-year advances in the field as reported by international authorities; G.A. MILLS, *Catalysis*, vol. 4, *Encyclopedia of Chemical Technology*, 2nd ed., pp. 534–586 (1964), a detailed record of the chemistry and chemical technology of catalysis, written especially from the point of view of a research scientist associated with the petroleum industry.

(H.S.Ta.)

Catherine II the Great, of Russia

As Empress of Russia Catherine II continued the work of her predecessor, Peter the Great: Peter gave Russia "a window on Europe," and Catherine opened wide the doors; Peter forced Europe to recognize the existence of a strong and independent Russia, and Catherine established Russia as a great European power; Peter destroyed ancient Russian culture in order to introduce Western culture, and Catherine laid the groundwork for a national culture influenced by Europe yet truly Russian. The woman who earned the name Catherine the Great correctly appraised her role in Russian history when she erected a statue of Peter the Great, bearing the inscription "Petro Primo Catharina Secunda" (Peter first, Catherine second).

The names of Peter and Catherine are forever linked in the minds of most Russians, even Soviet Russians. Peter inspires a deeper respect, yet Russians continue to admire Catherine, the German, the usurper and profligate, and regard her as a source of national pride. Non-Russian opinion of Catherine is less favourable. Because Russia under her rule grew strong enough to threaten the other great powers, and because she was in fact a harsh and unscrupulous ruler, she figured in the Western imagination as the incarnation of the immense, backward, yet

Catherine II the Great, portrait by A. Roslin (1718–1793). In the collection of Mrs. Merriweather Post, Hillwood, Washington, D.C.
By courtesy of Mrs. Merriweather Post, Hillwood, Washington, D.C.

forbidding country she ruled. One of Catherine's principal glories is to have been a woman who, just as Elizabeth I of England and Queen Victoria gave their names to periods of history, became synonymous with a decisive epoch in the development of her country.

Origins and early experience. Sophie Friederike Auguste von Anhalt-Zerbst was born in Stettin on May 2 (April 21, old style), 1729, the daughter of an obscure German prince, Christian August von Anhalt-Zerbst, but she was related through her mother to the dukes of Holstein. At the age of 14 she was chosen to be the wife of Karl Ulrich, duke of Holstein-Gottorp, grandson of Peter the Great and heir to the throne of Russia as the Grand Duke Peter. In 1744 Catherine arrived in Russia, assumed the title of Grand Duchess Catherine Alekseyevna, and married her young cousin the following year. The marriage was a complete failure; the following 18 years were filled with deception, humiliation, and disappointment for her.

Marriage in Russia

Russia at the time was ruled by Peter the Great's daughter, the empress Elizabeth, whose 20-year reign greatly stabilized the monarchy. Devoted to much pleasure and luxury and greatly desirous of giving her court the brilliancy of a European court, Elizabeth prepared the way for Catherine.

Catherine, however, would not have become empress if her husband had been at all normal. He was extremely neurotic, rebellious, obstinate, perhaps impotent, nearly alcoholic, and, most seriously, a fanatical worshiper of Frederick II of Prussia, the foe of the empress Elizabeth. Catherine, by contrast, was clearheaded and ambitious. Her intelligence, flexibility of character, and love of Russia gained her much support.

She was humiliated, bored, and regarded with suspicion while at court, but she found comfort in reading extensively and in preparing herself for her future role as sovereign. Although a woman of little beauty, Catherine possessed considerable charm, a lively intelligence, and extraordinary energy. During her husband's lifetime alone, she had at least three lovers; if her hints are to be believed, none of her three children, not even the heir apparent Paul, was fathered by her husband. Her true passion, however, was ambition; since Peter was incapable of ruling, she saw quite early the possibility of eliminating him and governing Russia herself.

The empress Elizabeth died on January 5, 1762 (December 25, 1761, old style), while Russia, allied with Austria and France, was engaged in the Seven Years' War against Prussia. Shortly after Elizabeth's death, Peter, now emperor, ended Russia's participation in the war and concluded an alliance with Frederick II of Prussia. He made no attempt to hide his hatred of Russia and his love of his native Germany; discrediting himself endlessly by his foolish actions, he also prepared to rid himself of his wife. Catherine had only to strike: she had the support of the army, especially the regiments at St. Petersburg, where her lover, Grigory Orlov, was stationed; the court; and public opinion in both capitals (Moscow and St. Petersburg). She was also supported by the "enlightened" elements of aristocratic society, since she was known for her liberal opinions and admired as one of the most cultivated persons in Russia. On July 9 (June 28, old style), 1762, she led the regiments that had rallied to her cause into St. Petersburg and had herself proclaimed empress and autocrat in the Kazan Cathedral. Peter III abdicated and was assassinated eight days later. Although Catherine probably did not order the murder of Peter, it was committed by her supporters, and public opinion held her responsible. In September 1762, she was crowned with great ceremony in Moscow, the ancient capital of the tsars, and began a reign that was to span 34 years as empress of Russia under the title of Catherine II.

Coronation as empress

Early years as empress. Despite Catherine's personal weaknesses, she was above all a ruler. Truly dedicated to her adopted country, she intended to make Russia a prosperous and powerful state. Since her early days in Russia she had dreamed of establishing a reign of order and justice, of spreading education, creating a court to rival Versailles, and developing a national culture that would be more than an imitation of French models. Her projects obviously were too numerous to carry out, even if she could have given her full attention to them.

Her most pressing practical problem, however, was to replenish the state treasury, which was empty when Elizabeth died; this she did in 1762 by secularizing the property of the clergy, who owned one-third of the land and serfs in Russia. The Russian clergy was reduced to a group of state-paid functionaries, losing what little power had been left to it by the reforms of Peter the Great. Since her coup d'etat and Peter's suspicious death demanded both discretion and stability in her dealings with other nations, she continued to preserve friendly relations with Prussia, Russia's old enemy, as well as with the country's traditional allies, France and Austria. In 1764 she resolved the problem of Poland, a kingdom lacking definite boundaries and coveted by three neighbouring powers, by installing one of her old lovers, Stanisław Poniatowski, a weak man entirely devoted to her, as king of Poland.

Attempts at reform

Her attempts at reform, however, were less than satisfying. A disciple of the English and French liberal philosophers, she saw very quickly that the reforms advocated by Montesquieu or Jean-Jacques Rousseau, which were difficult enough to put into practice in Europe, did not at all correspond to the realities of an anarchic and backward Russia. In 1767 she convened a commission composed of delegates from all the provinces and from all social classes (except the serfs) for the purpose of ascertaining the true wishes of her people and framing a constitution. The debates went on for months and came to nothing. Catherine's Instruction to the commission was a draft of a constitution and a code of laws. It was considered too liberal for publication in France and remained a dead letter in Russia.

Frustrated in her attempts at reform, Catherine seized the pretext of war with Turkey in 1768 to change her policy; henceforth, emphasis would be placed above all on national grandeur. Since the reign of Peter the Great, the Ottoman Empire had been the traditional enemy of Russia; inevitably, the war fired the patriotism and zeal of Catherine's subjects. Although the naval victory at Çeşme in 1770 brought military glory to the Empress, Turkey had not yet been defeated and continued fighting. At that point, Russia encountered unforeseen difficulties.

Revolt of 1773

First, a terrible plague broke out in Moscow; along with the hardships imposed by the war, it created a climate of disaffection and popular agitation. In 1773 Yemelyan Pugachov, a former officer of the Don Cossacks, pretending to be the dead emperor Peter III, incited the greatest uprising of Russian history prior to the revolution of 1917. Starting in the Ural region, the movement spread rapidly through the vast southeastern provinces, and in June 1774 Pugachov's Cossack troops prepared to march on Moscow. At this point, the war with Turkey ended in a Russian victory, and Catherine sent her crack troops to crush the rebellion. Defeated and captured, Pugachov was beheaded in 1775, but the terror and chaos he inspired were not soon forgotten. Catherine now realized that for her the people were more to be feared than pitied, and that, rather than freeing them, she must tighten their bonds.

Before her accession to power, Catherine had planned to emancipate the serfs, on whom the economy of Russia, which was 95 percent agricultural, was based. The serf was the property of the master, and the fortune of a noble was evaluated not in lands but in the "souls" he owned. When confronted with the realities of power, however, Catherine saw very quickly that emancipation of the serfs would never be tolerated by the owners, whom she depended upon for support, and who would throw the country into disorder once they lost their own means of support. Reconciling herself to an unavoidable evil without much difficulty, Catherine turned her attention to organizing and strengthening a system that she herself had condemned as inhuman. She imposed serfdom on the Ukrainians who had until then been free. By distributing the so-called crown lands to her favourites and ministers, she worsened the lot of the peasants, who had enjoyed a certain autonomy. At the end of her reign, there was scarcely a free peasant left in Russia, and, because of more systematized control, the condition of the serf was worse than it had been before Catherine's rule.

Thus, 95 percent of the Russian people did not in any way benefit directly from the achievements of Catherine's reign. Rather, their forced labour financed the immense expenditures required for her ever-growing economic, military, and cultural projects. In these undertakings, at least, she proved herself to be a good administrator and could claim that the blood and sweat of the people had not been wasted.

Influence of Potemkin. In 1774, the year of Russia's defeat of Turkey, Grigory Potemkin, who had distinguished himself in the war, became Catherine's lover, and a brilliant career began for this official of the minor nobility, whose intelligence and abilities were equalled only by his ambition. He was to be the only one of Catherine's favourites to play an extensive political role. Ordinarily, the Empress did not mix business and pleasure; her ministers were almost always selected for their abilities. In Potemkin she found an extraordinary man whom she could love and respect, and with whom she could share her power. As minister he had unlimited powers, even after the end of their liaison, which lasted only two years. Potemkin must be given part of the credit for the somewhat extravagant splendour of Catherine's reign. He had a conception of grandeur that escaped the rather pedestrian German princess, and he understood the effect it produced on the people. A great dreamer, he was avid for territories to conquer and provinces to populate; an experienced diplomat with a knowledge of Russia that Catherine had not yet acquired and as audacious as Catherine was methodical, Potemkin was treated as an equal by the Empress up to the time of his death in 1791. They complemented and understood each other, and the ambitious minister expressed his respect for his sovereign through complete devotion to her interests.

Potemkin's role in the expansion of Russia

The annexation of the Crimea from the Turks in 1783 was Potemkin's work. Through that annexation and the acquisition of the territories of the Crimean khanate, which extended from the Caucasus Mountains to the Bug River in southwestern Russia, Russia held the north shore of the Black Sea and was in a position to threaten the existence of the Ottoman Empire and to establish a foothold in the Mediterranean. Catherine also sought to renew the alliance with Austria, Turkey's neighbour and enemy, and renounced the alliance with Prussia and England, who were alarmed by Russian ambitions. Yet, during Catherine's reign, the country did not become involved in a European war, because the Empress scrupulously adhered to the territorial agreements she had concluded with several western European nations.

Catherine's glorification reached its climax in a voyage to the Crimea arranged by Potemkin in 1787. In a festive Arabian Nights atmosphere, the Empress crossed the country to take possession of her new provinces; the Emperor of Austria, the King of Poland, and innumerable diplomats came to honour her and to enjoy the splendours of what became known as "Cleopatra's fleet," because Catherine and her court travelled partly by water. She dedicated new towns bearing her name and announced that she ultimately intended to proceed to Constantinople.

Effect of the French Revolution. Catherine, like all the crowned heads of Europe, felt seriously threatened by the French Revolution. The divine right of royalty and the aristocracy was being questioned, and Catherine, although a "friend of the Enlightenment," had no intention of relinquishing her own privileges: "I am an aristocrat, it is my profession." In 1790 the writer, A.N. Radishchev, who attempted to publish a work openly critical of the abuses of serfdom, was tried, condemned to death, then pardoned and exiled. Ironically, the sentiments Radishchev expressed were very similar to Catherine's Instruction of 1767. Next, Poland, encouraged by the example of France, began agitating for a liberal constitution. In 1792, under the pretext of forestalling the threat of revolution, Catherine sent in troops and the next year annexed most of the western Ukraine, with Prussia helping itself to large territories of western Poland. After the national uprising led by Tadeusz Kościuszko in 1794, Catherine wiped Poland off the map of Europe by dividing it between Russia, Prussia, and Austria in 1795.

Division of Poland

Catherine's last years were darkened by the execution of Louis XVI, the advance of the revolutionary armies, and the spread of radical ideas. The Empress realized, moreover, that she had no suitable successor. She considered her son Paul an incompetent and unbalanced man; her grandson Alexander was too young yet to rule. On November 17 (November 6, old style), 1796, Catherine died of a stroke in St. Petersburg.

Assessment. At the end of Catherine's reign, Russia had expanded westward and southward over an area of more than 200,000 square miles, and the Russian rulers' ancient dream of access to the Bosporus Strait (connecting the Black Sea with the Aegean) had become an attainable goal. At the end of her reign Catherine claimed that she had reorganized 29 provinces under her administrative reform plan. An uninhibited spender, she invested funds in many projects. Over a hundred new towns were built; old ones were expanded and renovated. As commodities were plentiful, trade expanded and communications developed. These achievements, together with the glory of military victories and the fame of a brilliant court, to which the greatest minds of Europe were drawn, have won her a distinguished place in history.

Catherine's critics acknowledge her energy and administrative ability but point out that the achievements of her reign were as much due to her associates and to the unaided, historical development of Russian society as to the merits of the Empress. And when they judge Catherine the woman, they treat her severely.

Private life

Her private life was admittedly not exemplary. She had young lovers up to the time of her unexpected death at the age of 67. After the end of her liaison with Potemkin, who perhaps was her morganatic husband, the official favourite changed at least a dozen times; she chose handsome and insignificant young men, who were only, as one of them himself said, "kept girls." Although in reality devoted to power above all else, she dreamed endlessly of the joys of a shared love, but her position isolated her. She did not love her son Paul, the legitimate heir, whose throne she occupied. On the other hand, she adored her grandsons, particularly the eldest, Alexander, whom she wished to succeed her. In her friendships she was loyal and generous and usually showed mercy toward her enemies.

Yet it cannot be denied that she was also egotistical, pretentious, and extremely domineering, above all a woman of action, capable of being ruthless when her own interest or that of the state was at stake. As she grew older she also became extremely vain, for which there was some excuse; the most distinguished minds of Europe heaped flatteries on her that even she ultimately found exaggerated.

A friend of Voltaire and Diderot, she carried on an extensive correspondence with most of the important personages of her time. She was a patron of literature and a promoter of Russian culture; she herself wrote, established literary reviews, encouraged the sciences, and founded schools. Her interests and enthusiasms ranged from construction projects to lawmaking and the collection of art objects; she touched on everything, not always happily but always passionately. She was a woman of elemental energy and intellectual curiosity, desiring to create as well as to control.

BIBLIOGRAPHY

Contemporary sources: Mémoires de Catherine II, ed. by DOMINIQUE MAROGER (1953; Eng. trans., 1955), is of great importance for the history of Catherine's beginnings and for an analysis of her character. This edition is not complete but it constitutes a choice made among the various versions of the autobiography begun by Catherine; all versions stop very near to the date of her accession to power. Equally important are the *Correspondance* of Catherine II with Voltaire (published in various editions of the complete works of Voltaire, as well as in the Evdokimov edition of the complete works of Catherine II, 1893); the *Correspondance avec le Baron F.M. Grimm (1774–1796)*, Grot edition (1878), is interesting for its autobiographical character; Grimm was Catherine's confidant. See also *Lettres d'amour de Catherine II à Potemkine*, Georges Oudard edition (1934), unfortunately edited without chronological order.

Works about Catherine II and her reign: V.A. BILBASSOV, *Geschichte Katharina II*, 3 vol. (1891–93; also published in French as *Histoire de Catherine II*, 1900), is the most important work written about Catherine II, with quotations from many documents of the period; the last volume was banned in Russia under the tsarist regime. IAN GREY, *Catherine the Great: Autocrat and Empress of All Russia* (1961), a remarkable work, is a penetrating analysis of Catherine's character and notably of her relationships with Potemkin. OLGA WORMSER, *Catherine II* (1957), is particularly interesting for its analysis of the social and cultural situation in Russia (in French). Z. OLDENBOURG, *Catherine de Russie* (1964), is a work devoted primarily to the first half of Catherine's life (also in French).

(Z.O.)

Catherine de Médicis

As queen mother, Catherine de Médicis was the most prominent—though not the most powerful—figure in the history of France for 30 years from the death of her husband, Henry II, in July 1559 to her own in January 1589. Though still highly controversial, she nevertheless provides the principal element of continuity through seven of the eight so-called Wars of Religion that occurred within these years. Her contribution should be seen in terms of her incessant struggle for the security of France against the traditional enemy Spain, and against the breakdown of royal authority in the face of centrifugal forces that embraced and exploited the politico-religious conflicts released by the Reformation.

Catherine was born in Florence on April 13, 1519, to Lorenzo de'Medici, duke of Urbino, and Madeleine de la Tour d'Auvergne, a Bourbon princess related to many of the French nobility. Orphaned within days, Catherine was highly educated, trained, and disciplined by nuns in Florence and Rome and married in 1533 by her uncle, Pope Clement VII, to Henry, duc d'Orleans, who succeeded his father, Francis I, in April 1547. Artistic, energetic, and extroverted, as well as discreet, courageous, and gay, Catherine was greatly esteemed at the dazzling court of Francis I, from which she derived both her political attitudes and her passion for building. Of the chateaus she designed herself–including the Tuileries–Chenonceaux was her unfinished masterpiece.

In spite of Henry's abiding attachment to his mistress Diane de Poitiers, Catherine's marriage was not unsuccessful and, after 10 anxious years, she bore him 10 children, of whom four boys and three girls survived. She herself supervised their education. Thus occupied,

Catherine de Médicis, portrait by an unknown artist, 1561. In the Bibliothèque Nationale, Paris.
Giraudon

Regency

Catherine lived privately though she was appointed regent in 1552 during Henry's absence at the seige of Metz. Her ability and eloquence were acclaimed after the Spanish victory of Saint-Quentin in Picardy in 1557, possibly the origin of her perpetual fear of Spain, which remained, through changing circumstances, the touchstone of her judgments. It is essential to understand this in order to discern the coherence of her career.

Catherine's first great political crisis came in July 1559 upon the accidental death of Henry II, a traumatic bereavement from which it is doubtful if she ever recovered. Under her son, Francis II, power was retained by the Guise brothers. Thus began her lifelong struggle —explicit in her correspondence—with these extremists who, supported by Spain and the papacy, sought to dominate the crown and extinguish its independence in the commingled interests of European Catholicism and personal aggrandizement. It is also necessary to understand this political struggle of the Catholic crown with its own ultramontane extremists and to perceive its fluctuations in changing circumstances, in order to realize the fundamental consistency of Catherine's career. Her essentially moderate influence was first perceptible during the Conspiracy of Amboise (March 1560) an instance of tumultuous petitioning by the Protestant ("Huguenot") gentry, primarily against Guisard persecution in the name of the King. Her merciful Edict of Amboise (March 1560) was followed in May by that of Romorantin, which distinguished heresy from sedition, thereby detaching faith from allegiance.

Catherine's second great political crisis came with the premature death on December 5, 1560, of Francis II, whose royal authority the Guises had monopolized. Catherine succeeded in obtaining the regency for Charles IX, with Antoine de Bourbon, king of Navarre and first prince of the blood, as lieutenant general, to whom the Protestants vainly looked for leadership. The 10 years from 1560 to 1570 were, politically, the most important of Catherine's life. They witnessed the first three civil wars and her desperate struggle against the Catholic extremists for the independence of the crown, the maintenence of peace, and the enforcement of limited toleration. In 1561, with the support of the distinguished chancellor Michel de L'Hospital, she began by trying to propitiate the leaders of both religious factions, to effect reforms and economies by unassailably traditional methods, and to settle the religious conflict. Religious reconciliation was the conveners' purpose of the Colloquy of Poissys (September–November 1561). Catherine appointed a mixed commission of moderates that devised two formulas of consummate ambiguity, by which they hoped to resolve the basic, Eucharist controversy. Possibly Catherine's most concrete achievement was the Edict of January 1562, which followed the failure of reconciliation. This afforded the Calvinists licensed coexistence with specific safeguards. Unlike the proposals of Poissy, the edict was law, which the Protestants accepted and the Catholics rejected. This rejection was one basic element in the outbreak of civil war in 1562 in which—as she had predicted—Catherine fell, politically, into the clutches of the extremists, because the Catholic crown might protect its Protestants subjects in law, but could not defend them in arms. Thence-forth the problem of religion was one of power, public order, and administration.

Outbreak of civil war

Catherine ended the first civil war in March 1563 by the Edict of Amboise, an attenuated version of the Edict of January. In August 1563 she declared the King of age in the *Parlement* of Rouen and, from April 1564 to January 1566, conducted him on a marathon itinerary round France. Its principal purpose was to execute the edict and, through a meeting at Bayonne in June 1565, to seek to strengthen peaceful relations between the crown and Spain and to negotiate for Charles's marriage to Elizabeth of Austria. During 1564–68, Catherine was unable, for complex reasons, to withstand the cardinal de Lorraine, statesman of the Guises, who largely provoked the second and third civil wars. She quickly terminated the second (September 1567–March 1568) with the Peace of Longjumeau, a renewal of Amboise. But she was unable to avert its revocation (August 1568), which heralded the third civil war. She was not primarily responsible for the more far-reaching Treaty of Saint-Germain (August 1570), but she succeeded in disgracing the Guises.

For the next two years Catherine's policy was one of peace and general reconciliation. This she envisaged in terms of the marriage of her daughter Marguerite to the young Protestant leader, Henry of Navarre, (later Henry IV of France) and alliance with England through the marriage of her son Henri duc d'Anjou, or, failing him, his younger brother Francis duc d'Alençon, to Queen Elizabeth. The complexity of Catherine's position during these years cannot be briefly explained. To some extent she was eclipsed by Louis of Nassau and a group of Flemish exiles and youthful Protestants who surrounded the King and urged him to make war upon Spain in the Netherlands, which Catherine inevitably resisted. The issue of war or peace in the Netherlands was closely linked with the Massacre of St. Bartholomew's Day in Paris on August 23–24, 1572. Upon this occasion, following an abortive attempt against the life of the admiral Gaspard de Coligny, he and a number of his principal lieutenants, together with several thousand Huguenots, were killed. Catherine traditionally has been blamed for these events, which have therefore fashioned the interpretation not only of her subsequent, but frequently also of her previous, career, resulting in the familiar myth of the wicked Italian queen. There are two principal reasons for this. First, after some hesitation and inconsistency, the King assumed the responsibility by a declaration of August 26 in the *Parlement* of Paris, and "the crown" has been taken to mean Catherine. The second reason for the traditional inculpation of Catherine is the work of the pamphleteers and the polemical nature of the historiography of the event. It is impossible to establish the origin of the assault upon Coligny but, as a member of the court—the royal family and the council—Catherine was among those who appear to have authorized not the massacre itself, but the death of the admiral and his principal followers. This and the subsequent royal declaration of August 26 are both explained by the danger of the situation after the unsuccessful assault upon Coligny—in which the infuriated Huguenots allegedly threatened the court with extinction and the kingdom with war.

After the Massacre of St. Bartholomew's Day, Catherine was more concerned with the election of Anjou to the throne of Poland (May 1573) than the prosecution of the fourth civil war. Upon the death of Charles IX a year later, she assumed the regency with the support of the *Parlement* until the return from Poland of Henry in August. Catherine placed high hopes in her favourite, Henry, for the regeneration of France, for which she longed, but not without simultaneous misgivings, knowing his weakness of character and his previous subjection to the Catholics. For these reasons Catherine neither sought to dominate Henry nor to rule in his place but rather suffered him to exploit her and strove with unremitting pains to supply his deficiencies. Until the death of Alençon in 1584, much of her attention was devoted to restraining his dangerous ambitions, which again threatened to involve France in hostilities with Spain. After the Treaty of Joinville (December 1584) between the Guises and Spain, at Henry's bidding, Catherine, though gravely ill, returned to this dual threat. But after three months of continuous effort, in order to avert a public breach between the crown and the Guises, she was obliged, by the Treaty of Nemours (July 1585) to commit the King to making war against the Huguenots. Having failed with the Guises, the crown turned to Navarre, the Protestant leader who, as heir presumptive, had an interest in the preservation of the throne. In July 1586 Catherine undertook the arduous journey to see him at Saint-Brice near Cognac. But there was nothing to which Navarre could safely commit himself. Thus, despite the heroic efforts of Catherine's old age, France was sinking into chaos when she died at Blois on January 5, 1589, eight months before the murder of Henry III. Nevertheless, her ultimate achievement was to have saved the kingdom just long enough to ensure the succession of the Bourbon Henry IV, by whom the royal authority was restored.

BIBLIOGRAPHY. H. DE LA FERRIERE and BAGUENAULT DE PUCHESSE, *Lettres de Catherine de Médicis*, 10 vol. (1880–1909), with valuable introductions; LUCIEN ROMIER, *Le Royaume de Catherine de Médicis*, 2nd ed., 2 vol. (1922), for background analysis; N.M. SUTHERLAND, *The Massacre of St. Bartholomew and the European Conflict 1559–1572* (1972), distinguishes the role of Catherine from that of the King and the cardinal of Lorraine; PAUL VAN DYKE, *Catherine de Médicis*, 2 vol. (1922), an old-fashioned account of Catherine's life and times.

(N.M.Su.)

Catullus

Gaius Valerius Catullus, generally considered to have been the greatest lyric poet of ancient Rome, created from his intense capacity for love and hate a poetry that has few equals in its powers of direct emotional expression. His love lyrics have inspired poets of succeeding ages; but it is, above all, the self-revelatory quality in his work that speaks so strongly to his readers in the 20th century.

Life. *The facts.* No ancient biography of Catullus survives. A few facts can be pieced together from external sources, in the works of his contemporaries or of later writers, supplemented by inferences drawn from his poems, some of which are certain, some only possible. The unembroidered, certain facts are scanty. Catullus was alive 55–54 BC on the evidence of four of his poems and died young according to the poet Ovid—at the age of 30 as stated by St. Jerome (writing about the end of the 4th century), who nevertheless dated his life erroneously 87–57 BC. Catullus was thus a contemporary of the statesmen Cicero, Pompey, and Caesar, who are variously addressed by him in his poems. He preceded the poets of the immediately succeeding age of the emperor Augustus, among whom Horace, Sextus Propertius, Tibullus, and Ovid name him as a poet whose work is familiar to them. On his own evidence and that of Jerome, he was born at Verona in northern Italy and was therefore a native of Cisalpine Gaul (Gaul this Side of the Alps); he owned property at Sirmio, the modern Sirmione, on Lake Garda, though he preferred to live in Rome and owned a villa near the Roman suburb of Tibur, in an unfashionable neighbourhood. According to an anecdote in the Roman biographer Suetonius' *Life of Julius Caesar*, Catullus' father was Caesar's friend and host, but the son nevertheless lampooned not only the future dictator but also his son-in-law Pompey and his agent and military engineer Mamurra with a scurrility that Caesar admitted was personally damaging and would leave its mark on history; the receipt of an apology was followed by an invitation to dinner "the same day," and Caesar's relations with the father continued uninterrupted. (Suetonius cites the episode as an example of Caesar's clemency.)

Lampoon of Julius Caesar

Catullus' poetry reports one event, externally datable to *c.* 57–56 BC, a journey to Bithynia in Asia Minor in the retinue of Gaius Memmius, the Roman governor of the province, from which he returned to Sirmio. It also records two emotional crises, the death of a brother whose grave he visited in the Troad, also in Asia Minor, and an intense and unhappy love affair, portrayed variously in 25 poems, with a woman who was married and whom he names "Lesbia," a pseudonym (Ovid states) for Clodia, according to the 2nd-century writer Apuleius. His poems also record, directly or indirectly, a homosexual affair with a youth named Juventius.

Conjecture. Such are the stated facts. The conjectural possibilities to be gleaned mostly from the internal evidence of Catullus' poetry extend a little further. It is accepted that Catullus was born *c.* 84 BC and that he died *c.* 54 BC. His father's hospitality to Caesar may have been exercised in Cisalpine Gaul when Caesar was governor of the province, but equally well at Rome—Suetonius does not indicate time or place. Catullus' Roman villa may have been heavily mortgaged (depending on the choice of manuscript reading of one poem). A yacht retired from active service and celebrated in an iambic poem may have been his own, built in Bithynia, in northwestern Asia Minor, and therefore available to convey him on his way home to Sirmio after his tour of duty. His fellow poet Cinna may have accompanied him to Bithynia. For the governor Memmius, himself a litterateur (to whom the Roman philosophic poet Lucretius dedicated his poem on the nature of things, *De rerum natura*), such company might be congenial, and it is possible to speculate that Cinna was on board the yacht. The brother's grave could have been visited en route to or from Bithynia.

The poet's Clodia may have been a patrician, one of the three Clodia sisters of Cicero's foe Publius Clodius Pulcher, all three the subject of scandalous rumour, according to Plutarch. If so, she was most probably the one who married the aristocrat Metellus Celer (consul 60 BC, died 59 BC), who in 62 was governor of Cisalpine Gaul. It may have been at that time that the youthful poet first met her and possibly fell under her spell. She is accorded a vivid if unflattering portrait in Cicero's *Pro Caelio*, in which the orator had occasion to blacken her character in order to defend his client against Clodia's charge that as her lover after her husband's death he had tried to poison her. The client was Marcus Caelius Rufus, conceivably the Rufus reproached by Catullus in poem LXXVII as a trusted friend who had destroyed his happiness (but if so, the Caelius of poem C is a different person). This identification of Clodia, suggested by an Italian scholar of the 16th century, has found support in some uncertain inferences from the Lesbia poems: the poet's mistress besides being married perhaps moved in society, enjoyed fashionable amusements, was cultivated and witty, and was licentious enough to justify Cicero's attack. On the other hand, the poet twice appears to have included the protection of his own rank among the gifts he had laid at her feet.

The poetry. *Textual examination.* A consideration of the text of Catullus' poems and of its arrangement is of unusual interest. Its survival has been as precarious as his biography is brief. Not being part of the school syllabus, from roughly the end of the 2nd century to the end of the 12th century, it passed out of circulation. Knowledge of it depends on a single manuscript discovered *c.* 1300, copied twice, and then lost. Of the two copies, one in turn was copied twice, and then it was lost. From the three survivors—in the Bodleian Library at Oxford, the Bibliothèque Nationale in Paris, and the Vatican Library in Rome—scholars have been able to reconstruct the lost "archetype." Incorrect transcription in the preceding centuries (some 14 instances are beyond repair), however, has invited frequent and often uncertain emendation. Depending on whether one poem is divided or not, 113 or 114 poems survive. In the printed total of 116, numbers XVIII to XX were inserted by early editors without proof that they were written by Catullus. In 14 instances gaps are visible (eight of these of one or more lines), and in possibly six poems fragments of lost

Discovery of Catullus' poetry

poems have been left attached to existing ones. Ancient citations indicate the existence of at least five more poems. The surviving body of work is therefore mutilated and incomplete and (in contrast to the *Odes* of Horace) cannot in its present published form represent the intentions of either author or executors, despite the elegant dedication to the historian Cornelius Nepos that heads it. With these qualifications, it permits the reconstruction of a poetic personality and art unique in Latin letters.

The collection is headed by 57 "short poems," ranging in length between five and 25 lines (number X, an exception, has 34) in assorted metres, of which, however, 51 are either hendecasyllabic—that is, having a verse line of 11 syllables (40 such)—or iambic—basically of alternate short and long syllables (11). These rhythms, though tightly structured, can be characterized as occasional or conversational. There follow eight "longer poems," ranging from 48 lines to 408 (number LXV, of 24 lines, is prefatory to number LXVI) in four different metres. The collection is completed by 48 "epigrams" written in the elegiac distich, or pair of verse lines, and extending between two and 12 lines, a limit exceeded only by two poems, one of 26 lines and the other of 16.

Content, style, and influence. This mechanical arrangement, by indirectly recognizing the poet's metrical virtuosity and proposing three kinds of composition, justly calls attention to a versatility disproportionate to the slim size of the extant work. The occasional-verse metres and the elegiac distich had been introduced into Latin before his day. Traditionally both forms, as practiced by Greek writers after the 4th century BC and their Roman imitators, had served for inscriptions and dedications and as verse of light occasions, satirical comment, and elegant sentiment. Catullus and his contemporaries continued this tradition; but in some 37 instances the poet uniquely converts these verse forms to serve as vehicles of feelings and observations expressed with such beauty and wit, on the one hand, or such passion, on the other, as to rank him, in modern terms, among the masters of the European lyric—the peer of Sappho and Shelley, of Burns and Heine—but exhibiting a degree of complexity and contradiction that the centuries-later Romantic temperament would scarcely have understood. The conversational rhythms in particular, as he managed them for lyric purposes, achieved an immediacy that no other classic poet can rival.

Influence on the Augustans

In his longer poems Catullus produced studies that deeply influenced the writers and poets of the Augustan Age: two charming marriage hymns; one frenzied cult hymn of emasculation; one romantic narrative in hexameters (lines of six feet) on the marriage of Peleus with the sea goddess Thetis; and four elegiac pieces, consisting of an epistle introducing a translation of an elegant conceit by the Alexandrian poet Callimachus, followed by a pasquinade, or scurrilous conversation between the poet and a door (of poor quality, perhaps a youthful effort), and lastly a soliloquy (unless indeed this be two poems) addressed to a friend and cast in the form of an encomium, or poem of praise. The Augustan poet Virgil is content to imitate Catullus without naming him, even going so far, in the *Aeneid*, as thrice to borrow whole lines from him. Horace both imitated Catullus and criticized him. Tibullus, Propertius, Ovid, and later Martial both imitate and affectionately commemorate him.

In his lifetime, Catullus was a poet's poet, addressing himself to fellow craftsmen (*docti*, or scholarly poets), especially to his friend Licinius Calvus, who is often posthumously commemorated along with him. It is now fashionable to identify this coterie as the *poetae novi*, or "Neoterics" (the modern term for these new poets), who preferred the learned allusiveness and mannered and meticulous art of the Alexandrian poets to the grander but archaic fashion of Ennius, the father of Roman poetry. The school was criticized by Cicero and by Horace, who names Calvus and Catullus. To the degree that Catullus shared such conceptions of what might be called poetic scholarship, he is to be numbered in the company of Gerard Manley Hopkins, T.S. Eliot, and Ezra Pound rather than with the Romantics.

For the general reader, the 25 Lesbia poems are likely to remain the most memorable, recording as they do a love that could register ecstacy and despair and all the divided emotions that intervene. Two of them with unusual metre recall Sappho, the poetess of the Aegean island of Lesbos, as also does his use of the pseudonym Lesbia. As read today, these two seem to evoke the first moment of adoring love (number LI, a poem that actually paraphrases its Sapphic model) and the last bitterness of disillusionment (number XI). On the other hand, the poems of invective, which spare neither Julius Caesar nor otherwise unknown personalities, male and female, may not have received the critical attention some of them deserve. Their quality is uneven, ranging from the high-spirited to the tedious, from the lapidary to the laboured, but their satiric humour is often effective, and their obscenity reflects a serious literary convention that the poet himself defends. Between these two poles of private feeling lies a handful of transcendent and unforgettable compositions: the lament at his brother's grave; the salute to Sirmio his beloved retreat; the exchange of vows between Acme and Septimius; his elegy for the wife of Calvus; and even that vivid mime of a moment's conversation in a leisured day, in which the gay insouciance of a few young persons of fashion, the poet included, going about their affairs in the last days of the Roman Republic, is caught and preserved for posterity.

MAJOR WORKS

Catullus' 116 extant poems may be classified under the headings lyric, epithalamium, miniature epic, elegy, and epigram. They were mostly written between 61 and 54 BC, but cannot be dated exactly.

Apart from V, VII, VIII, XI, LVIII, and LXXVI, which, with many others, are all devoted to the theme of Lesbia, Catullus' mistress, whether in delight, sorrow, or anger, special mention may perhaps be made of XXX, to a false friend; of XXXI, on his home at Sirmio; and of CI, on his brother's death.

BIBLIOGRAPHY. The original Oxford text by ROBINSON ELLIS (1904) has been superseded by that of R.A.B. MYNORS (1958), whose *Praefatio* succinctly explains the procedures essential for reconstruction of the text and summarizes the history of the first printed Renaissance editions. This text may be supplemented by the German edition of MAURITIUS SCHUSTER (1949; rev. with additional bibliography by W. EISENHUT, 1958); and by the French Budé text of GEORGES LAFAYE (1922; 3rd ed. rev. by M. DUCHEMIN, 1949).

Commentaries: The second edition of ROBINSON ELLIS (1889) remains a classic despite its age. The American text and commentary of E.T. MERRILL (1893, reprinted 1951) was for a long time the only unabridged edition available in English; it is now joined by KENNETH QUINN, *Catullus: The Poems, Edited with Commentary* (1970). The otherwise exhaustive edition of C.J. FORDYCE (1961) omits certain poems of significant critical interest, either literary or biographical. The German commentary of WILHELM KROLL (1923, reprinted 1968) is a standard and complete work. That in Italian by M.L. DE GUBERNATIS, 2nd ed. (1933, reprinted 1953), stresses literary interpretation.

General: Estimates of Catullus' poetry and its place in Latin letters are offered by A.L. WHEELER, *Catullus and the Traditions of Ancient Poetry* (1934, reprinted 1964), who gives special attention to the longer poems; by E.A. HAVELOCK, *The Lyric Genius of Catullus* (1939, reprinted 1967), who sees the secret of the poet's significance in the short poems; and by KENNETH QUINN, *The Catullan Revolution*, 2nd rev. ed. (1969), who stresses the poet's place within the Roman tradition; as does DAVID O. ROSS, JR., *Style and Tradition in Catullus* (1969). The biographical approach to the poems, initiated over 100 years ago (SCHWABE, *Quaestiones Catullianae*, 1862), pervasive in Merrill's commentary and criticized by Havelock (pp. 73–86), has been revived by T.P. WISEMAN, *Catullan Questions* (1969).

Translations: These, unabridged, responding to a new tolerance of the obscene in literature, have recently proliferated. Aside from the Loeb Library edition (text and translation by F.W. CORNISH, 1912), versions in a more contemporary style include the following: F.O. COPLEY, *Complete Poetry of Catullus* (1957); R.A. SWANSON, *Odi et Amo: Complete Poetry* (1959); PETER WHIGHAM, *Poems of Catullus* (1966); and RENEY MYERS and ROBERT J. ORMSBY, *Catullus: The Complete Poems for American Readers* (1970).

(E.A.Ha.)

Caucasian Languages

The term Caucasian languages as used here includes groups of languages indigenous to the Caucasus region, between the Black and Caspian seas within the Soviet Union; it excludes the Indo-European (Armenian, Ossetic, Talysh, Kurdish, Tat) and Turkic languages (Azerbaijan, Kumyk, Noghay, Karachay, Balkar) and some other languages of the area, all of which were introduced to the Caucasus in historical times. The Caucasian languages are also referred to as Paleocaucasian and Ibero-Caucasian languages.

The Caucasian languages are found in the territory north and south of the main Caucasian mountain range; their number varies, according to different classifications, from 30 to 40. The concentration of so many languages in such a small territory is indeed remarkable. There are more than 5,000,000 speakers of Caucasian languages; their language communities range in size from only a few hundred people to large national groups of millions.

Three Caucasian language groups

The Caucasian languages fall into three typologically well-defined language families: the Northwest Caucasian, or Abkhazo-Adyghian, languages; the Northeast Caucasian, or Nakho-Dagestanian, languages; and the South Caucasian, or Kartvelian, languages (also called Iberian). From the typological point of view, the Northwest and Northeast Caucasian groups present opposite structural types, with South Caucasian holding an intermediary position.

The exact genetic relationships of the Caucasian languages are still unclear on many points, not only in regard to interrelationships of the three major groups but also to some internal groupings. Although the genetic relationships between Northwest and Northeast Caucasian seem probable, the interrelationships of North and South Caucasian are as yet uncertain because of the absence of any regular sound correspondences between them. At the present stage of comparative Caucasian linguistics, North Caucasian and South Caucasian must be viewed as separate language families.

The theories relating Caucasian with such languages as Basque and the non-Indo-European and non-Semitic languages of the ancient Near East also lack sufficient evidence and must be considered as inconclusive.

SOUTH CAUCASIAN (KARTVELIAN) LANGUAGES

Languages of the group. The Kartvelian (South Caucasian) language family comprises Georgian, Mingrelian (Megrelian), Laz (or Chan), and Svan. The speakers of these languages constitute the Georgian nation and number 3,245,000 (according to the 1970 census).

Georgian. Georgian (self-designation: *kartuli ena*), used as the language of literature and instruction, is the state language of the Georgian Soviet Socialist Republic. It is common to all speakers of the Kartvelian languages within the Georgian S.S.R. Beyond the Georgian republic, Georgian is spoken in the adjacent regions of the Azerbaijan S.S.R. and northeast Turkey. There are also 14 villages of Georgian speakers in the province of Isfahan, Iran.

The designation Georgian that is used in the European languages was coined during the Crusades; it is based on Persian *gorji* (Georgian), from which the Russian *gruzin* was also derived. The Greek term *íbēres* (Georgians) is connected with an Old Iranian name for Georgia.

The dialects of Georgian fall into two groups—East and West Georgian—divided by the Suram Mountains. These exhibit only slight differences.

Georgian literary tradition

Among the Caucasian languages, only Georgian has an ancient literary tradition, which dates back to the 5th century AD, when the oldest datable monuments were inscribed in an original script. This old Georgian script must have been derived from a local variety of Aramaic with influences—in regard to the order of the alphabet and the shape of some characters—from the Greek alphabet. The modern Georgian writing system is based on the round-form cursive, developed from the angular book script of the 9th century; the latter was a direct descendant of the old Georgian script. The Georgian writing system accurately reflects the distinctive sounds of the language.

During the Old Georgian period (from the 5th to the 11th century), original and translated literary monuments were produced, among them the Georgian translation of the Bible. The conventions of the New Georgian literary language, ultimately established in the middle of the 19th century on the basis of an East Georgian dialect, originated in the secular literature of the 12th century. New Georgian differs structurally in many respects from Old Georgian, but the old language is still comprehensible to the Georgians of today. Until the beginning of the 19th century, Old Georgian was still in use in religious services and theological writings.

Mingrelian. The Mingrelian language (self-designation: *margaluri nina*) is spoken in the territory north of the Rioni River and west of the Tskhenis-Tskali and along the Black Sea coast from the mouth of the Rioni up to the city of Ochamchire. The language is unwritten.

Laz. The Laz language (self-designation: *lazuri nena*) is spoken along the Black Sea coast from the Chorokh River (Georgian S.S.R.) to south of Pazar (Atina) in Turkish territory. The language is unwritten, Georgian being used as the literary language in the Georgian S.S.R. and Turkish in Turkey. In view of the structural closeness between Mingrelian and Laz, they are sometimes considered as dialects of a single language.

Svan. The Svan language (self-designation: *lušnu nin*), also unwritten, is located south of Mt. Elbrus, in the high valleys of the upper Tskhenis-Tskali and its tributary Kheledula and in the valleys of the upper Ingur. There are four fairly distinct dialects: Upper and Lower Bal in the Ingur region, and Lashkh and Lentekh in the Tskhenis-Tskali region.

Linguistic characteristics. Correspondences between sounds and meanings in words and word elements provide a basis for considering the Kartvelian languages as being closely related and descended from a common ancestral language (a protolanguage).

Vowel differences in Kartvelian

Phonology. The sound system of the Kartvelian languages is relatively uniform, with only the vowel systems exhibiting considerable differences. Apart from the five cardinal vowels *a*, *e*, *i*, *o*, *u*, which exist in all the Kartvelian languages, the Svan dialects show several additional vowels: the front (or palatalized) vowels, *ä*, *ö*, *ü*, and a high central vowel, *ə* (as the *a* in English "sofa"). All these vowels also have distinct lengthened counterparts, thus giving a total of 18 distinctive vowels in some dialects of Svan. Vowel length is not distinctive in the other Kartvelian languages.

Within the Kartvelian consonant system the stops and affricates have voiced, voiceless, and glottalized varieties. (Stops are produced by complete but momentary stoppage of the breath stream some place in the vocal tract; affricates are sounds begun as stops but released with local friction, such as the *ch* sounds in "church." Voiced sounds are made with vibrating vocal cords; in voiceless sounds, the vocal cords do not vibrate; glottalized consonants, indicated in phonetic transcription by dots below or above certain letters, are pronounced with an accompanying closure of the glottis (the space between the vocal cords). Fricative sounds (*e.g.*, *s*, *z*, *v*), which are characterized by local friction, have only voiced and voiceless types.

Although most word roots begin with one or two consonants, instances of long consonant clusters in word-initial position occur quite frequently, especially in Georgian, in which such clusters may comprise up to six consonants; *e.g.*, Georgian *prckvna* "peeling," *msxverpli* "sacrifice," *brʒola* "fighting."

Grammatical characteristics. The Kartvelian languages exhibit a developed system of word inflection (*e.g.*, the use of endings, such as English "dish, dishes" or "walk, walks, walked") and derivation (word formation). Derivation is characterized by compounding, the combination of words to form new words, as well as by affixation, the addition of prefixes and suffixes; *e.g.*, Georgian *kartvel-i* "Georgian," *sa-kartvel-o* "Georgia"; Mingrelian *žir-i* "two," *ma-žir-a* "second."

The verb system distinguishes the categories of person,

number (singular and plural, with differentiation of inclusive and exclusive plural in Svan), tense, aspect, mood, voice, causative, and version (the latter defines the subject–object relations). These categories are expressed mainly by the use of prefixes and suffixes, as well as by internal inflection (changes within the verb stem), which is frequently a redundant grammatical feature.

Multi-personal verbs

The system of verb conjugation is multipersonal; that is, the verb forms can indicate the person of the subject (the agent) and of the direct or indirect object by the use of special prefixes. (The subject of the 3rd person is marked by endings in Georgian and Mingrelo-Laz and by a lack of ending in Svan.) An example is Georgian *m-çer-s* "he writes to me," *m-xaṭav-s* "he paints me," in which *m* denotes the 1st person as object and *s* marks the 3rd person as subject. The finite verb forms fall into three series of tenses: the present tense, the aorist (indicating occurrence, usually past, without reference to completion, duration, or repetition), and the perfect or resultative (denoting an action in the past not witnessed by the speaker).

There is a developed system of preverbs, elements preceding the verb stem and attached to it, with local meaning indicating location of the action in space, as well as its direction (especially in Mingrelian and Laz). Simple preverbs are combined into complex ones. The preverbs are also used to mark the aspect (nature of the action indicated by the verb, with reference to its beginning, duration, completion), which is used for the formation of future and aorist forms; *e.g.*, Georgian *çer-s* "he writes" versus *da-çer-s* "he will write" and *da-çer-a* "he wrote."

The nominal (noun, pronoun, adjective) system is distinguished by less structural complexity than the verb system and has cases varying in number from six to 11. The six cases common to all the Kartvelian languages are: nominative, marking subject of the intransitive verb; ergative (see below), modified in Mingrelian and Laz; genitive, marking possession; dative, marking indirect objects; ablative–instrumental, expressing relations of separation and source and means or agency; and adverbial, expressing goal of the action—*e.g.*, "to make it." There are also some secondary local cases (in New Georgian, Mingrelian) that indicate location and direction toward the object as well as from the object (rendered in English by such prepositions as "in," "on," "to," "from," and so on). The nominal system does not distinguish gender, which is absent even in pronouns, and there are no special articles (such as English "a," "the").

Ergative sentence constructions

A basic feature of Kartvelian syntax is the ergative construction of the sentence. The subject of a transitive verb (the agent) is marked by a special agentive, or ergative, case, while the case of the direct object is the same as that of the subject with intransitive verbs, traditionally called the nominative case; *e.g.*, Georgian *ḳac-i* (nominative) *midis* and Svan *māre* (nominative) *esγri*, "the, or a, man goes" but Georgian *ḳac-ma* (ergative) *moḳla datv-i* (nominative) and Svan *mārēm* (ergative) *adgär däšdw* (nominative) "the, or a, man killed the, or a, bear." A specific feature of the Georgian and Svan ergative construction is its restriction to the aorist series. In the present-tense series the subject (agent) of transitive as well as intransitive verbs is put into the same nominative case, and the direct object is in the dative; *e.g.*, Georgian *ḳac-ma* (ergative) *moḳla datv-i* (nominative) "the man killed a bear" (aorist), but *ḳac-i* (nominative) *ḳlavs datv-s* (dative) "the, or a, man kills the, or a, bear" (present tense). In Mingrelian the ergative case in *k* extends in the aorist series to the constructions with intransitive verbs and results in a formation of two distinct subject cases. In Laz, conversely, the case in *k* extends to the constructions with transitive verbs in the present-tense series.

Vocabulary. The genetic closeness of the Kartvelian languages is evidenced by a large number of structural correspondences and of common lexical (vocabulary) and grammatical items. Though the Kartvelian languages abound in ancient loanwords from Iranian, Greek, Arabic, Turkish, and other languages, it is nevertheless possible to single out the basic vocabulary and grammatical elements of original Caucasian origin, which exhibit a system of regular sound correspondences. The common Kartvelian vocabulary comprises the kinship terms, names of animals, birds, trees, and plants, the parts of the body, as well as different human activities, qualities, and states. The words for the numerals from one to ten and the word for hundred are also original common Kartvelian terms.

Proto-Kartvelian. A comparative study of the Kartvelian languages enables specialists to outline the general structure of the parent language, called Proto-Kartvelian, which yielded the known Kartvelian, or South Caucasian, languages. One of the most characteristic features of the Proto-Kartvelian language is the functional vowel alternation, or ablaut; different forms of a word root or word element appear either with a vowel (*e, *a, *o), called full grade, or without a vowel, called zero grade. (An asterisk [*] indicates that the following form is not attested but has been reconstructed as a hypothetical ancestral form.) In a sequence of word elements (called morphemes) only one element may occur in full grade, the others being in either zero or reduced grade forms (*i.e.*, in a form with **i*). To a word root with a full-grade vowel, for example, a suffix in zero may be added, and vice versa: **der-ḳ-* (intransitive) "stoop, recline" and **dr-eḳ-* (transitive) "bend." When a full-grade ending is added to these stems, the preceding full-grade element is shifted to zero or a reduced grade; *e.g.*, **der-ḳ-* plus the ending **-a* becomes **dr-k-a*. In such patterns the lengthened grade, a long vowel, may also appear.

Ablaut in Proto-Kartvelian

These ablaut patterns, strikingly parallel to those of the Indo-European languages, and other linguistic features may have arisen in Proto-Kartvelian as a result of contacts with Indo-European at a comparatively early date. Such contacts between Kartvelian and Indo-European are further evidenced by a number of Indo-European loanwords in Proto-Kartvelian, such as Proto-Kartvelian **ṭep* "warm" (compare Indo-European **tep* "warm"), Proto-Kartvelian **mḳerd* "breast" (compare Indo-European **k̂erd* "heart"), and others.

In Mingrelo-Laz the ancient ablaut patterns were eliminated and new forms were set up with a stable, non-interchanging vowel in each word element. The ancient ablauting models were better preserved in Georgian and especially in Svan, in which new ablauting patterns, in addition to the old structures, were established.

The pronominal system of Proto-Kartvelian is characterized by the category of inclusive–exclusive (*i.e.*, there are two forms of the pronoun "we," one including the hearer, and the other excluding him), which survived in Svan but has been lost in other languages of the family. Along with it, Svan has preserved a certain number of archaic structural features of the Proto-Kartvelian epoch, setting it apart from Georgian and Mingrelo-Laz, which share a number of common lexical and grammatical innovations. Svan must have been separated fairly early from the rest of Proto-Kartvelian, which later yielded the Mingrelo-Laz and Georgian languages. (Th.V.G.)

NORTH CAUCASIAN LANGUAGES

The North Caucasian languages are divided into two groups: Abkhazo-Adyghian, or the Northwest Caucasian, languages, and Nakho-Dagestanian, or the Northeast Caucasian languages.

Abkhazo-Adyghian languages. The Abkhazo-Adyghian group consists of the Abkhaz, Abaza, Adyghian, Kabardian (Circassian), and Ubykh languages. Abkhaz, with about 80,000 speakers, is spoken in the Abkhazian A.S.S.R. (in the South Caucasus, Georgian S.S.R.). The other languages are spread over the western part of the northern Caucasus. Abazians (25,000) live in the Karachay-Cirassian Autonomous Oblast; Adyghians (100,000), in the Adyghe Autonomous Oblast; Kabardians or Kabardino-Circassians (about 320,000) dwell mainly in the Kabardino-Balkar A.S.S.R. Both Adyghians and Kabardians call themselves *adəge*. The Ubykh language was formerly found to the north of the area where Abkhaz is spoken, in the vicinity of Tuapse. In 1864 Ubykhians as well as a substantial part of the Abkhaz- and Adyghe-speaking population migrated to Turkey, where before long they lost their native tongue. In the early 1970s Ubykh was spoken by about 20 people living near the Sea of Marmara. The total number of people speaking Abkhazo-Adyghian languages is 530,000 (in the U.S.S.R.). Many Circassians speaking Abkhazo-Adyghian languages live in the countries of the Near East—Turkey, Jordan, and Iraq.

All Abkhazo-Adyghian languages, with the exception of Ubykh, are written. From the dialectological point of view, the Abkhazo-Adyghian languages are not widely differentiated, the differences being mainly of phonetic character. In Abkhaz two dialects are distinguished; Adyghian and Kabardian differentiate four dialects each. Abkhaz and Abaza are very close to each other and are considered by some scholars to be dialects of the same language. The same kind of affinity exists between Adyghian and Kabardian. Ubykh occupies an intermediate position between the Abkhaz-Abaza and Adyghe-Kabardian languages.

Phonology. A characteristic feature of the sound system of the Abkhazo-Adyghian languages is a rather limited number of distinctive vowels—*a* and *ə* (pronounced as the *a* in English "sofa"). Some scholars consider it possible to posit only one vowel, which, depending on the position, can be realized in different ways: *a, ə, i, o, e.* On the other hand, the languages are notable for a great diversity in their consonant systems. The number of consonants distinguished reaches about 70 (in the Abkhaz and Adyghian languages) or even 80 (Ubykh). Along with the consonants that occur in all the Caucasian languages, the Abkhazo-Adyghian languages are characterized by different sets of labialized consonants (formed by rounding the lips), strong (hard or tense) consonants, half-hushing consonants, and velarized consonants (formed with the back of the tongue approaching the soft palate).

Few vowels, very numerous consonants

Grammatical characteristics. The grammatical characteristics of the Abkhazo-Adyghian languages include an extremely simple noun system and a relatively complicated system of verb conjugation. There are no grammatical cases in Abkhaz and Abaza, and in the other languages only two principal cases occur: a direct case (nominative) and an oblique case, combining the functions of ergative, genitive, dative, and instrumental. In nouns, possession is expressed by means of pronominal prefixes; *e.g.,* Abkhaz *sarra s-č:ə* "my horse" (literally: "I my-horse"), *wara u-č:ə* "your horse" (pertaining to a man), *bara b-č:ə* "your horse" (pertaining to a woman), and so forth. (The symbol *:* indicates that the preceding consonant is a strong consonant.)

The Abkhaz and Abaza languages distinguish the grammatical classes of person and thing (the latter class includes all nouns denoting nonhuman objects). The class of person also differentiates between the subclasses of man and woman.

The verb in the Abkhazo-Adyghian languages has a pronounced polysynthetic character; that is, various words combine to form a composite word that expresses a complete statement or sentence. The most important verbal categories are expressed by prefixes, although suffixes also form tenses and moods. The principal verb categories are: dynamic versus static, transitivity, person, number, class, tense, mood, negation, causative, version, and potentiality. "Dynamic versus static" is a verb form expressing action versus state of being; "version" is a verb category denoting for whom the action is intended (compare Georgian *v-c̣er* "I write," but *v-u-c̣er* "I write for him"); "potentiality" is a category expressing the possibility of an action (*e.g.,* Abkhaz *s-zə-ωuam* "I cannot write"). The verb is multipersonal and can denote up to four persons.

Adverbial relationships (such as "where," "when," "how") are expressed by prefixes following the personal markers. On the whole, the verb forms appear as a long string of word elements expressing the above mentioned categories; *e.g.,* Abkhaz *i-u-z-d-aa-sə-r-g-an* "that (thing)-you (a man)-for-them-hither-I shall make-bring" (*i.e.,* "I shall make them bring that for you"). In a sequence of prefixes, up to nine morphemes are possible.

The simple sentence has three constructions: indefinite, nominative, and ergative (in Abkhaz and Abaza only indefinite). An indefinite construction has the subject in the indefinite case (*i.e.,* not marked with a special suffix); a nominative construction has the subject in the nominative case. The same personal markers, depending on their arrangement, can denote both the subject and various objects: *e.g.,* Abkhaz, *wara sara u-s-šweiṭ* "I kill you (a man)," *sara wara s-u-šweiṭ* "you (a man) kill me."

Three sentence types

Nakho-Dagestanian languages. The Nakho-Dagestanian group consists of the Nakh and Dagestanian languages. Some investigators subdivide the Nakho-Dagestanian languages into two independent groups: Central Caucasian languages (Nakh) and East Caucasian languages (Dagestan), although the great proximity of these groups, and their equal remoteness from the Abkhazo-Adyghian languages, may justify regarding them as a common group of languages.

The Nakh languages consist of Chechen (613,000 speakers), Ingush (158,000), and Bats (or Tsova-Tushian, about 3,000 speakers). The Chechens and Ingushes live in the Chechen-Ingush A.S.S.R.; the Bats dwell in the village Zemo-Alvani in the Akhmeta district of the Georgian S.S.R. Both Chechen and Ingush, which are fairly close to one another, are written. The Bats language is unwritten; Georgian is used as the literary language for Bats speakers, and they consider Georgian as their mother tongue.

The Dagestan languages are numerous. The following groups can be distinguished:

Groups of Dagestan languages

1. The Avaro-Ando-Dido languages: These occupy the central and western part of Dagestan and part of the Zakataly region of the Azerbaijan S.S.R. The member languages are the Avar language; the Andi subgroup of languages, including Andian, Botlikh, Godoberi, Chamalal, Bagulal, Tindi, Karata, and Akhvakh; and the Dido subgroup, including Dido, or Tsez, Khvarshi, Hinukh, Bezhta, and Hunzib, or Kapucha.

The Avaro–Ando–Dido language with the most speakers (about 400,000) is Avar, a written language. All Andi–Dido languages are unwritten, and most of them are spoken by about 3,000 to 5,000 people each. From ancient times the Andi–Dido nationalities used the Avar languages for intertribal communication. Avar is still widely known and spoken among them. The Andi languages are phonetically and grammatically very close to each other. The same affinity is observed among the Dido languages, to the effect that Hinukh is considered by some specialists as a dialect of Dido, while Bezhta and Hunzib are viewed as two dialects of the same language. In respect to dialectology, the majority of Avaro–Ando–Dido languages are widely differentiated.

2. The Lakk-Dargwa languages: Lakk (or Lakh, with 86,000 speakers) and Dargwa (or Khjurkili, with 231,000) are spoken in the central part of Dagestan. Both are written languages. The Lakk language is quite homogeneous with regard to its dialects; Dargwa, however, possesses several diversified dialects—sometimes considered as separate languages (*e.g.,* Kubachi). Some view Lakk and Dargwa as independent language groups.

3. The Lezgian languages: This group includes Lezgi (Lezghi), or Kuri (with 200,000 speakers in the Dagestan A.S.S.R. and about 100,000 in the Azerbaijan S.S.R.); Tabasaran (55,000); Agul (about 9,000); Rutul (about 12,000); Tsakhur (about 11,000); Archi (1,000); Kryz (or Dzkek, about 6,000); Budukh (1,000); Khinalug (about 1,000); and Udi (about 4,000). The majority of Lezgi languages are found in Dagestan occupying its southern part, but some of them (Kryz, Budukh, Khinalug, Udi, partly Tsakhur) are spoken in Azerbaijan; and one village of Udi speakers is located in Georgia. It must be noted that in Azerbaijan, as well as earlier in Russia, all Dagestanians—including Avars—called themselves Lezginians. Among the Lezgian languages, Lezgi and Tabasaran are written. The inclusion of Archi in this group gives rise to some doubt, and it has also been noted that the Khinalug language stands out from the Lezgian group in many respects. The Udi language is supposed to be one of the languages of ancient Caucasian Albania.

Phonology. The sound systems of the Nakho-Dagestanian languages are diverse. There are up to five vowels (*a, e, i, o, u*); in some languages *o* is only now becoming an independent distinctive unit. Along with these cardinal vowels, in a number of languages there are also long and nasalized vowels (the Andi languages), pharyngealized vowels (in Udi), and labialized vowels (in Dido). In the Nakh languages (Chechen) the vowel system is fairly intricate, the number of distinctive vowels amounting to 30 (including diphthongs and triphthongs).

Nakh and Dagestanian consonants

The consonant systems of the Nakh languages are relatively simple, coinciding, on the whole, with those of the South Caucasian languages (apart from a number of pharyngeal consonants characteristic of all the Nakh languages and a lateral sound peculiar to Bats). The opposition of strong and weak voiceless consonants is typical of the majority of the Dagestanian languages. This contrast has been lost in a number of languages and dialects; *e.g.*, in the Dido languages, in some dialects of Avar. The labialized clusters *kw, qw, sw*, and so on are widespread. In the Avaro-Ando-Dido languages and in Archi there are fricative and affricate lateral sounds (*i.e.*, different types of *l*), with the maximum possible number being six (in Akhvakh).

All the Caucasian languages have a series of stops of three types—voiced, voiceless aspirated, and glottalized (*i.e.*, pronounced, respectively, with vibrating vocal cords; with vocal cords not vibrating but with an accompanying audible puff of breath; and with accompanying closure of the glottis [space between the vocal cords]). In some languages strong and weak consonants also contrast. Usually, in the languages with a strongly developed vowel system, the system of consonants is comparatively simple (*e.g.*, Chechen, Ingush, Dido), and vice versa (*e.g.*, Avar, Lakk, and Dargwa have complicated consonantisms and relatively simple vowel systems).

Grammatical characteristics. There are several common structural features in morphology (word structure), the most characteristic being the existence of the grammatical category of classes (eight classes in Bats; six in Chechen and Andi; five in Chamalal; four in Lakk; three in Avar; two in Tabasaran).

In a number of languages (Lezgi, Udi), noun differentiation by classes has disappeared. The class of "thing" is distinguished from the "person" class, which can be differentiated into the subclasses of man and woman. Compare, for example, Avar *emen w-ačana hani-w-e* "father has come here" (in which *w* is equivalent to the marker of the class of man), *ebel j-ačana hani-j-e* "mother has come here" (in which *j* is equivalent to the marker of the class of woman), and *ču* (*kaɣat*) *b-ačana hani-b-e* "a horse (a letter) has come here" (in which *b* is equivalent to the marker of the class of thing). In the plural there are usually fewer grammatical classes denoted.

Nouns have many cases, both in singular and in plural; there are cardinal cases (nominative, ergative, genitive, dative) and local cases that denote the location of a thing ("on," "in," "near," "under"), with a specification of movement ("where," "which way," "from where," "over what"). The ergative case, the case of the real subject of transitive verbs, is present in all the Nakho-Dagestanian languages. Nouns have different stem forms in the nominative and the oblique (non-nominative) cases; *e.g.*, Avar *gamač* "a stone" (nominative), *ganč-i-c:a* (ergative), and *ganč-i-da* "on the stone." In pronouns the category of inclusive–exclusive is distinguished; *e.g.*, Avar *nil'* "we with you," *niž* "we without you."

The class of the noun in the nominative case (*i.e.*, in the case of the subject of intransitive verbs and of the direct object of transitive verbs) is reflected in the verb; *e.g.*, Avar: *was* (nominative, class I) *w-ačana* "the boy has come," *jas* (nominative, class II) *j-ačana* "the girl has come."

In the Lezgi language, a characteristic structural feature is agglutination, the combination of various elements of distinct meaning into a single word. A typical feature of Nakho-Dagestanian syntax is the presence of the ergative construction of the sentence (the subject of transitive verbs is put in the ergative case and the real object in the nominative case). Complex sentences are usually formed with participial and adverbial–participial construction; *e.g.*, Avar *haniwe wačaraw či dir wac: wugo* "the man who arrived here is my brother" (literally, "the here arrived man my brother is").

Vocabulary, writing, and alphabets. The original vocabulary of the North Caucasian languages has been fairly well preserved in the modern languages, although there is a substantial number of words borrowed from Arabic (through Islām), the Turkic languages, and Persian. There are also loanwords from the neighbouring languages (Georgian, Ossetic). Russian has played a major part since the late 19th century and is currently the main source for new words, especially technical terminology.

Sources of loanwords

The written languages of the area are the state languages. Newspapers, magazines, and books, as well as radio and television programs, use the local languages, and children in primary schools are taught in their mother tongue.

The alphabets of the North Caucasian written languages (Abkhaz, Abaza, Adyghe, Kabardian, Chechen, Ingush, Avar, Lakk, Dargwa, Lezgi, Tabasaran) are based on the Cyrillic alphabet, which was introduced for these languages in 1936–38 (in Abkhaz, from 1954). Previously, from 1928, the modified Latin alphabet was used; it superseded the Arabic script, which was adapted to the local languages in the Soviet period, at a time when a number of North Caucasian languages became literary languages.

Some written attempts had been made earlier. In the 18th century an insignificant number of monuments were created (with the use of Arabic writing) in Lakk and Avar. Stone crosses with Old Georgian–Avar bilingual inscriptions, dating from not later than the 14th century AD, have been preserved in central Dagestan. (T.E.G.)

BIBLIOGRAPHY

General works of reference: G. DEETERS, *Armenisch und kaukasische Sprachen* (1963), a general survey and a combined presentation of the structure of the Caucasian languages according to the most characteristic features of phonology, morphology, and syntax, with an extensive bibliography; G.A. KLIMOV, *Die kaukasischen Sprachen* (1969; orig. pub. in Russian, 1965), a brief exposition of the history and structures of the Caucasian languages, with a general characterization of each group, including an extensive bibliography; A.H. KUIPERS, "Caucasian," in THOMAS A. SEBEOK (ed.), *Current Trends in Linguistics*, vol. 1, *Soviet and East European Linguistics*, pp. 315–344 (1963), a useful brief survey of Caucasian linguistics, with a selected bibliography; A. DIRR, *Einführung in das Studium der kaukasischen Sprachen* (1928), contains a survey of the structure of individual Caucasian languages and their interrelationships; "Yazyki Narodov SSSR," IV. *Iberijsko-Kavkazskie jazyki* (1967), a brief exposition of the structures of all the Caucasian languages, with a selected bibliography.

South Caucasian languages: The following is a selection of the more important special works on the South Caucasian languages: G. DEETERS, *Das kharthwelische Verbum: Vergleichende Darstellung des Verbalbaus der südkaukasischen Sprachen* (1930), a comprehensive comparative study of the verb structure of the Kartvelian languages; A.S. CHIKOBAVA, *Drevnejšaja struktura imennyx osnov v kartvel'skix jazykax* (1942; in Georgian, with a Russian and French summary), a comparative analysis of the ancient structure of nominal stems in the Kartvelian languages, with an interpretation of certain prefixes as the ancient classmarkers; K.H. SCHMIDT, *Studien zur Rekonstruktion des Lautstandes der südkaukasischen Grundsprache* (1962), a detailed analysis of sound correspondences with a reconstruction of the Proto-Kartvelian phonemic system; T.V. GAMKRELIDZE and G.I. MACHAVARIANI, *Sistema sonantov i ablaut v kartvel'skikh iazykakh* (1965; in Georgian with a Russian summary), a detailed comparative analysis of the Kartvelian phonological and morphophonological system, with a reconstruction of resonants and ablaut alternations in Proto-Kartvelian and their typological evaluation. For the grammars of the individual languages see A.G. SHANIDZE, *Osnovy gruzinskoj grammatiki*, vol. 1 (1953), a most comprehensive exposition (in Georgian) of the structure of modern Georgian; and H. VOGT, *Grammaire de la langue géorgienne*, rev. ed. (1971). An account of the Georgian sound system is given in G. AXVLEDIANI, *Osnovy obščej fonetiki* (1949, in Georgian). For a detailed descriptive analysis of the Svan verb system according to dialects, see

V.T. TOPURIA, *Svanskij jazyk*, vol. 1, *Glagol* (1931; 2nd ed., 1967), in Georgian, with a Russian summary. Much useful information about Georgian and the history of Georgian (Kartvelian) studies is contained in S.V. DZIDZIGURI, *The Georgian Language* (Eng. trans. 1968). A useful practical guide to Georgian is K. TSCHENKELI, *Einführung in die georgische Sprache*, vol. 1, *Theoretischer Teil*, vol. 2, *Praktischer Teil* (1958).

North Caucasian languages: P.K. USLAR, *Etnografija Kavkaza. Jazykoznanie*, 6 vol. (1887–96), contains descriptive grammars of the individual North Caucasian languages; A. TSCHIKOBAVA, "Die ibero-kaukasischen Gebirgssprachen und der heutige Stand ihrer Erforschung in Georgien," *Acta Orientalia Academiae Scientiarum Hungaricae*, 9:109–161 (1959), a brief survey of the North Caucasian languages, containing an extensive bibliography; N. TRUBETZKOY, "Nordkaukasische Wortgleichungen," *Wiener Zeitschrift für die Kunde des Morgenlandes*, vol. 37, no. 1–2 (1930), establishes sets of sound correspondences between the West and East Caucasian languages and deals with the history of their consonantism; G. DUMEZIL, *Études comparatives sur les langues caucasiennes du nord-ouest (morphologie)* (1932), a comparative analysis of the grammatical structure of the Abkhazo-Adyghian languages; A.H. KUIPERS, *Phoneme and morpheme in Kabardian (Eastern Adyghe)* (1960), a detailed analysis of the phonemic structure of morphemes in Kabardian with a typological comparison with other linguistic systems; W.S. ALLEN, "Structure and System in the Abaza Verbal Complex," *Transactions of the Philological Society of London*, pp. 127–176 (1956), a comprehensive analysis of the verb structure in Abaza; A. SOMMERFELT, "Études comparatives sur le caucasique du nord-ouest, *Norsk Tidsskrift for Sprogvidenskap*, vol. 7 and 9 (1934–38), a comparative study of the sound system of the Nakh languages; E.A. BOKAREV, *Vvedenie v sravnitel'no-istoričeskoe izučenie dagestanskix jazykov* (1961), a comparative study of the vocalism and consonantism of the languages of Dagestan; T.E. GUDAVA, *Konsonantizm andijskix jazykov* (1964), a reconstruction of the original consonant system of the Avaro-Ando-Dido languages.

(Th.V.G./T.E.G.)

Caucasus Mountains

The great historic barrier of the Caucasus Mountains rears up across the wide isthmus separating the Black and Caspian seas, at that extreme southern portion of the European section of the Soviet Union where Europe and Asia converge. If the ranges are placed in Europe, then Mt. Elbrus, at 18,510 feet (5,642 metres) their highest peak, is also the highest point in Europe; but the environment of the whole region is so subject to Asian influences that there is a good case for assigning the Caucasus to western Asia. Traditionally, the watershed of the Great Caucasus Range (Bolshoy Kavkaz), the backbone of the system, is regarded as part of the line dividing the continents.

The name Caucasus is a Latinized form of "Kaukasos," which the ancient Greek geographers and historians used, and the Russian "Kavkaz" is of the same origin. The ultimate derivation is thought to be from "Kaz-kaz," the Hittite name for a people living on the southern shore of the Black Sea. This ancient nomenclature reflects the historical importance of the region: the Greeks made the mysterious range the scene of the mythical sufferings of Prometheus, and the Argonauts sought the Golden Fleece in the land of Colchis, nestling against the range on the Black Sea coast. The ranges also filtered cultures of the ascendant civilizations of the Near Eastern "fertile crescent" through to the north, besides nurturing their own distinctive societies. The peoples of the region have exhibited an extraordinary variety since early times: the Colchians, for example, as described by the 5th-century-BC Greek historian Herodotus, were black skinned, and the subsequent centuries witnessed successive waves of peoples migrating across Eurasia, adding to, and being molded by, the Caucasian cultural heritage. Not surprisingly, a larger quantity of different languages is spoken in Caucasia than in any other area of similar size in the world.

The ethnic and linguistic heritage

Caucasia is defined as the region including not only the soaring mountain ranges of the Caucasus proper but also the country immediately north and south of them. The northern country is called Ciscaucasia (Predkavkaz; *i.e.*, Hither Caucasia); the southern is Transcaucasia (Zakavkaz, or Farther Caucasia). The whole region, which has an area of 170,000 square miles (440,000 square kilometres), is nevertheless predominantly mountainous. It extends from the lowlands of the Kuma and Manych basins southward to the political frontiers separating the Soviet Union from Turkey and from Iran and so comprises the southernmost divisions of the Russian S.F.S.R. (including Dagestan), the Georgian S.S.R., the Armenian S.S.R., and Soviet Azerbaijan, besides several minor administrative units constituted on an ethnic basis. For related information on the human geography of the area, see the articles AZERBAIJAN SOVIET SOCIALIST REPUBLIC; ARMENIAN SOVIET SOCIALIST REPUBLIC; and GEORGIAN SOVIET SOCIALIST REPUBLIC; also the article RUSSIAN SOVIET FEDERATED SOCIALIST REPUBLIC; for linguistic information, see CAUCASIAN LANGUAGES; see also URARTU AND ARMENIA, HISTORY OF.

THE NATURAL ENVIRONMENT

Relief and geological structure. The Great Caucasus extends for approximately 750 miles southeastward across the Caucasus from the Taman Peninsula (Tamansky Poluostrov) thrusting between the Black Sea and its northern extension, the Sea of Azov, to the Apsheron Peninsula (Apsheronsky Poluostrov), which juts into the Caspian past the oil-rich port of Baku. The vast plains and uplifted areas of Ciscaucasia stretch from its northern foothills to the Kuma-Manych depression lying southwest of the huge Caspian delta of the Volga. Western Ciscaucasia consists largely of plains: from the lowland north of the Kuban River, the delta of which adjoins the broad, low ridges of the Taman Peninsula, a plain slopes gradually southward up to the foothills of the mountains. Central Ciscaucasia comprises not only the Stavropol Highland (Stavropolskaya Vozvyshennost), mainly characterized by tablelands of limestone or sandstone and by deep valleys, but also the Mineralnye Vody-Pyatigorsk zone to the southeast (where Mt. Beshtau rises to 4,593 feet [1,400 metres] from a surrounding plateau) and, still farther southeastward, beyond the middle Terek River, the highlands backing the Terek and the Sunzha, with the Alkhan Churt Valley between them. Eastern Ciscaucasia is lowland traversed by the lower Terek and, to the north beyond the sands of the vast Nogay Steppe, by the Kuma. Both rivers flow into the Caspian.

The northern slopes of the Great Caucasus are not as steep as the southern. The middle of the system is comparatively narrow, but its western and eastern ends have widths of 100 miles or more. The watershed and a lateral range to the north of it, which together constitute the axis of the system, contain, in addition to Mt. Elbrus itself, such magnificent lofty peaks as Mt. Dombay-Ulgen, 13,274 feet (4,046 metres), in the western sector; Mts. Shkhara, Dykhtau, and Kazbek, all well over 16,000 feet, in the central sector; and Mts. Tebulos-Mta and Bazar-Dyuzi, both over 14,000 feet, in the east. Spurs tonguing north and south from the main axis in places reach heights approaching 10,000 feet.

The Great and Little Caucasus

South of the Great Caucasus, on the Black Sea coast, lies the alluvial plain of Kolkhida (ancient Colchis). On the Caspian side, in the basin of the Kura River, plains and such uplands as the long Shirak Steppe (Shirakskaya Step) succeed one another till the level falls sharply into an extensive depression, in the centre of which the Kura receives its major right-bank tributary, the Araks. To the northeast, the hills of southeastern Kobystan separate the Kura-Araks Lowland (Kura-Araksinskaya Nizmennost) from the Apsheron Peninsula. From the extreme southeast of the Kura-Araks Lowland, the narrow Lenkoran Lowland (Lenkoranskaya Nizmennost) extends southward between the Caspian Sea and the Talysh Mountains, which reach heights exceeding 8,000 feet.

West of the Kura-Araks Lowland rises the Little Caucasus, which is continued southward by the Dzhavakhet mountain range and the Armenian Highland, the latter straddling the Soviet–Turkish frontier. East of Lake Sevan, the highest peaks rise to 12,000 feet or more, while Mt. Aragats (Alagez), west of the lake, rises an-

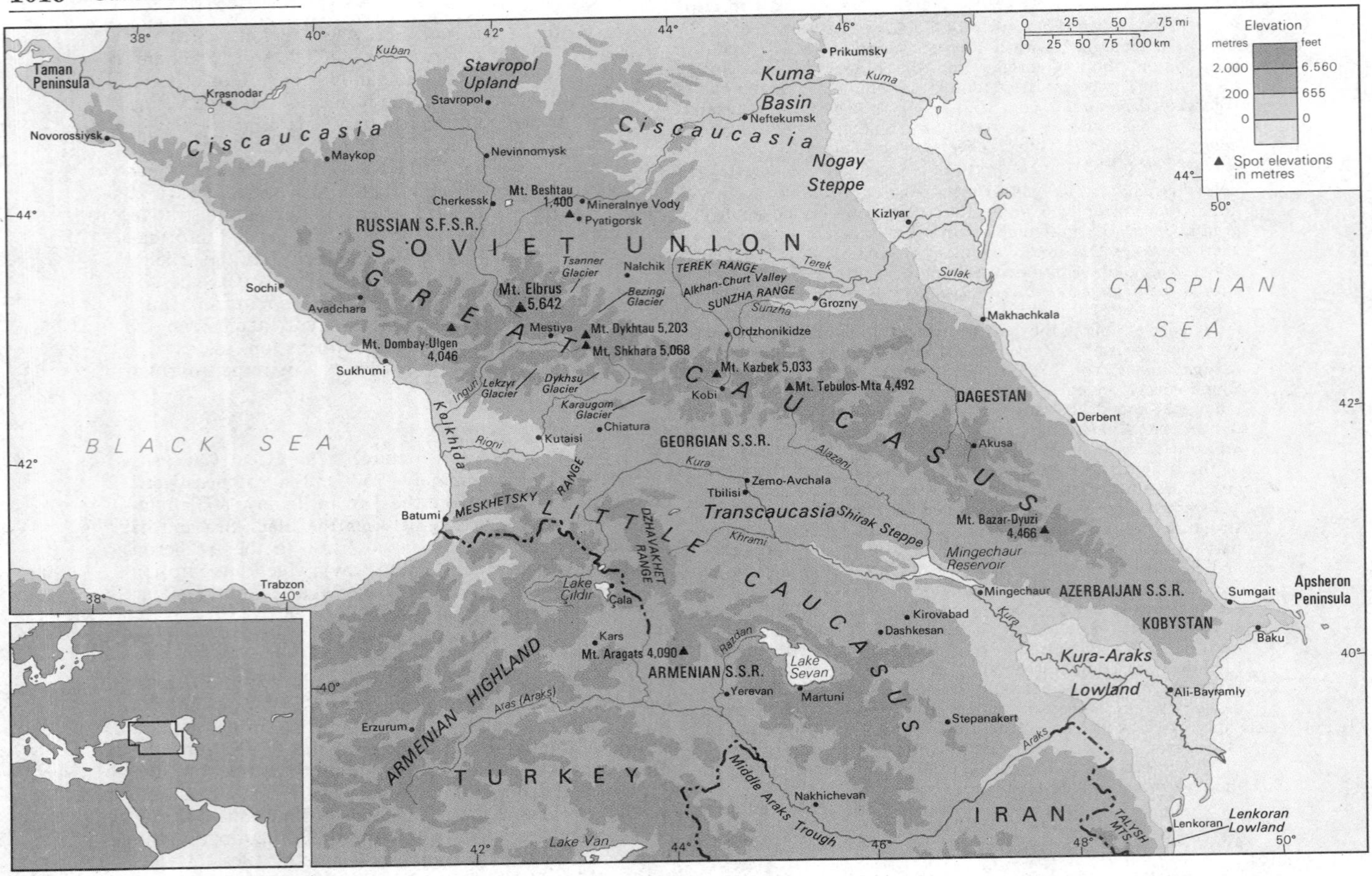

The Caucasus Mountains.

other 1,000 feet. From their western sources in the Armenian Highland, the Kura and the Araks both flow round the Little Caucasus, the one north of it, the other south, before their confluence in the east.

The greater part of Caucasia originated in the vast structural downwarp in the earth's crust known as the Alpine Geosyncline, dating from about 25,000,000 years ago, and thus reflects the mountain-building movement that produced the younger mountains of Europe. Northern and central Ciscaucasia has a platform-like construction, with a foundation of folded structures dating from Hercynian times, about 345,000,000 years ago. Southwestern and southeastern Ciscaucasia lie on the margins of the vast downfold in the earth's surface that rose later in the Alpine mountain-building movement, with the collapse deepest on the lower courses of the Kuban and Terek rivers. The surface of Ciscaucasia is composed essentially of Tertiary and Quaternary rocks less than 65,000,000 years old; on the Stavropol Highland there are layers of various ages in folded, platform-like structures.

Structurally the Great Caucasus represents a great upfold, or anticline, thrown up at the margin of the Alpine Geosyncline about 25,000,000 years ago and subsequently altered by fresh cycles of erosion and uplift. Hard, crystalline, heat-altered rocks such as schists, gneisses, and granites, of pre-Jurassic origin (more than 190,000,000 years old), have been exposed at the core of the western sector, while somewhat softer, clayey schists and sandstones of Lower and Middle Jurassic origin have emerged in the east. The spurs of the Great Caucasus are composed of younger limestones, sandstones, and marls.

Kolkhida and the Kura-Araks Lowland are both structural depressions linked to the Alpine Geosyncline; the former is related to the formation of the Black Sea, the latter to that of the Caspian. In Kolkhida, the overall surface of Quaternary deposits laid down less than 25,000,000 years ago is broken, at the foot of the mountains, by the emergence of slightly earlier sedimentary rocks. Late Tertiary and Quaternary rock also underlies the Kura-Araks Lowland.

The structures of the Little Caucasus, of the Talish Mountains, and of the Dzhavakhet–Armenian ranges likewise reflect folds uplifted from the Alpine Geosyncline. While the western sector of the Little Caucasus and the Talish are formed chiefly of deposits of Tertiary Age (about 50,000,000 years ago) laid down in the great former downwarp of the geosyncline, the intervening eastern sector of the Little Caucasus consists, north of Lake Sevan, of layers of Jurassic and Cretaceous sedimentary and intruded volcanic rock, which are at least twice as old. Volcanism and the intrusion of heat-altered rock have everywhere played a great role: the folded base of the Dzhavakhet Range and of the Armenian Highland is masked by debris from eruptions of Tertiary–Quaternary date. Much older rocks emerge largely between the middle course of the Araks and the latitude of Lake Sevan.

Mineral resources. The geologically recent rock layers around the Great Caucasus, notably in the Kura-Araks Lowland and beneath the Caspian Sea, contain oil-bearing deposits. These also occur, together with fuel gases, among the earlier rocks of Ciscaucasia, while, in Dagestan, oil, fuel gas, and coal deposits are found. Metallic ores are associated with magmatic rocks thrust up from deep in the crust: magnetite iron occurs near Dashkesan, in Azerbaijan; copper and molybdenum are found in several parts of the Transcaucasian upland; several metallic ores lie in the Great Caucasus; and manganese is found near Chiatura, in Georgia. Building materials include the cement marls of Novorossiysk south of the Taman Peninsula and the rose-coloured tufas of Aragats. The mineral-water springs of the Caucasus are known throughout the Soviet Union.

Climate. Standing on the border between the temperate and subtropical climatic zones, the Great Caucasus accentuates the difference between them by impeding the movement of cold air masses from the north into Transcaucasia and, conversely, that of warm air masses into Ciscaucasia from the south. Thus average January temperatures, which range from between 23° and 28° F (−5° and −2° C) in Ciscaucasia, are between 40° and 43° F (4.5° and 6° C) in Kolkhida and between 34° and 38° F (1° and 3.3° C) in eastern Transcaucasia. In summer, when differences of temperature between north and south are small, there is a more noticeable contrast between the west (average temperatures 73°–79° F [23°–26° C]), with its maritime climate, and the continental east (77°–84° F [25°–29° C]).

Temperature ranges

Ciscaucasia has a moderately continental steppe climate in the west and a more continental, drier, semidesert one in the east. In Transcaucasia, Kolkhida has a humid, subtropical climate with mild winters and an annual rainfall of 47 to 71 inches (1,200 to 1,800 millimetres); as does the Lenkoran Lowland but with a dry season at the start of the summer; the Kura-Araks Lowland has a dry subtropical climate, an annual rainfall of eight to 16 inches (200 to 400 millimetres), but lower in the east, and mild winters and hot summers, which favour the cultivation of cotton; and the Middle Araks Trough in the Armenian Highland has a climate like that of the lowland downstream, but not so warm.

In the Great Caucasus, temperatures naturally fall, and agricultural seasons become shorter, as altitude rises; more rain falls on the mountain slopes than on the neighbouring plains. From the altitude of approximately 6,500 feet, a westerly air current prevails, strengthening maritime influences: average air temperatures reach 18° F (−8° C) in January and 55° F (13° C) in August. As the Great Caucasus stands at an angle to the westerly air currents, the heaviest precipitation, reaching a maximum of no less than 160 inches (4,000 millimetres), accumulates on the south-southwest-facing slopes. Higher up, a cold climate with severe humidity prevails, and perennial snow shrouds the highest crests. In the northern Black Sea coast region, the climate is Mediterranean, with humid winters and dry summers.

The slopes of the Little Caucasus facing toward those of the Great Caucasus have a climate similar to that of the latter at corresponding altitudes, with rainfall concentrated in the west. On the slopes of the Talysh Mountains, the climate is humid, with yearly precipitation up to 68 inches (1,700 millimetres). The Armenian Highland has a climate more continental than that of the Great Caucasus at corresponding altitudes (at 6,500 feet the average temperature 10° F [−12° C] in January, 64° F [18° C] in July). Snow cover lasts for four or five months. Annual precipitation averages 20 inches (500 millimetres), with a spring maximum. The climate of the upland steppe plateaus is moderately cold and continental, whereas that of the heights is more humid and Alpine, with cool summers and cold, prolonged winters.

Rivers and lakes. The Kura (with its tributary the Araks), the Sulak, the Terek, and the Kuma rivers flow into the Caspian Sea, the Rioni and the Inguri, into the Black Sea; and the Kuban, into the Sea of Azov. In the warm season, when snow and ice begin to melt, rivers of the Great Caucasus and some of those of the Little may be in flood for six months; and other Transcaucasian rivers are characterized by spring flooding. The rivers of the southern slope of the Great Caucasus generally have summer floods also. The rivers of Ciscaucasia, except those flowing from the Great Caucasus, flood in spring and freeze in winter but become very shallow and sometimes even dry up in summer, while the Stavropol area is artificially irrigated from the Kuban River. In the eastern and central Caucasus, brief storm flooding occurs. The soluble limestone spurs of the Great Caucasus have karst-type rivers that intermittently plunge beneath the earth.

Flood perils

The lower reaches of the Kura, of the Kuban, and of the Rioni are navigable. Water from many of the rivers serves to irrigate the arid zone of Ciscaucasia, the Kura-Araks Lowland, and the lands around the Middle Araks. Hydroelectric stations have been built on the Kura at Mingechaur and at Zemo-Avchala, near Tbilisi; on the Khrami (a right-bank tributary of the Kura); on the Rioni; and on several rivers of the Great Caucasus.

Ozero Sevan in the Transcaucasian Range is the largest lake of Caucasia. Its overflow, draining into the Razdan tributary of the Araks, is exploited for hydroelectricity by a chain of stations and also for the irrigation of the south of the Armenian S.S.R. The high parts of the Little Caucasus contain numerous small lakes, while saltwater lakes occur in the arid regions of northeastern Caucasia.

Glaciers. The Great Caucasus has 2,200 glaciers, occupying 1.36 percent of its total area. About 70 percent of them occur on the northern face, with a concentration in the centre. The largest, notably Dykhsu, Bezingi, and Karaugom, on the northern face, and Lekzyr and Tsanner, in Svanetian Georgia, are often eight miles or so long. The desolate flanks of Mt. Elbrus are streaked by many glaciers.

Plant and animal life. In western and central Ciscaucasia, steppe vegetation used to prevail on the rich black soils but has now largely been plowed up. Forest-steppe vegetation, with oaks and beeches, is found on the higher ground of the Stavropol Highland, around Pyatigorsk, in the west sector of the Sunzha Range (Sunzhensky Khrebet), and at the foot of the Great Caucasus. Eastern Ciscaucasia is semidesert, with grasses and sagebrush (*Artemisia*) on chestnut soils and saltworts where the soil is salty. *Artemisia*, saltworts, and ephemeral species on gray soils characterize the arid Kura-Araks Lowland; and similar vegetation occurs in the Middle Araks Trough. In Kolkhida and in the Lenkoran Lowland, subtropical broad-leaved forest has given way before the advances of agriculture.

In the mountains themselves, at altitudes between 2,000 and 3,000 feet, arboreal brushwood predominates. On the Black Sea slopes of the Great Caucasus and in the mountainous hinterland of Kolkhida, there are mixed forests—beech, oak, hornbeam, chestnut, and alder—with evergreen undergrowth and lianas on red and on yellow soils. In the Talysh Mountains, forests of chestnut-leaf oak and *Parrotia persica* flourish on yellow soils likewise. On the heights backing the Kura-Araks Lowland, there are xerophytic (adapted to a limited water supply) leaf-bearing forests and brushwood on brown soils. On the northern face of the Great Caucasus, oak forests and secondary brushwood occur.

In the next zone, at altitudes up to 6,500 feet, both the Great and the Little Caucasus sustain forests of oak and hornbeam and of beech on brown soils; but these trees are superseded at the higher levels by Caucasian elm and Nordmann fir in the west and in the southwest and sometimes by pine farther east. Feather grass and needlegrass cover the black soil of the steppes on the lava plateaus and plains of the Armenian sector. Steppes and meadow steppes are widespread also among the mountains of Dagestan.

Above 6,500 feet in the Great Caucasus and in the Transcaucasian Range, mountain-meadow vegetation covers three belts, sub-Alpine, Alpine, and subnivean, up to the lonely zone of glaciers and perpetual snow—which begins at about 10,000 feet.

The animal life of the Great and of the Little Caucasus includes certain indigenous species—the West Caucasian and the Dagestanian bison, or tur, the Caucasian black grouse, and the Caucasian pheasant, or ular—and even indigenous genera, such as the long-clawed mole-vole (*Prometheomys schaposchnikowi*). It also includes chamois, red deer, bear, lynx, and fox. Ciscaucasia's fauna is connected both with eastern Europe's and with Central Asia's; and the latter connection is also evident in the Kura-Araks Lowland, which has the Persian gazelle (*Gazella subgutturosa*), the long-eared hedgehog, the jerboa, and the reed cat (*Felis chaus*). The fauna of the Talish Mountains, which includes leopard and porcupine, is related to that of more southerly territories, while that of the Armenian Highland is related to that of Anatolia, with the ground squirrel, or suslik (*Citellus*), and the mountain jerboa (*Allactaga williamsi*). (N.A.G.)

Indigenous animals

THE HUMAN IMPRINT

The people. According to the Soviet census of 1970, the total population of Caucasia amounts to 22,800,000.

Of this total, 12,300,000 live in Transcaucasia and 10,-500,000 in the north. About half of the people live in towns, notably 1,261,000 in Baku, 889,000 in Tbilisi, 767,000 in Yerevan, 465,000 in Krasnodar, 341,000 in Grozny, and 236,000 in Ordzhonikidze. The rural population is unevenly distributed. The most densely populated area is on the Black Sea coast; the Rioni Valley and several smaller valleys in Transcaucasia are intensively cultivated; and the foothills of the mountains also have a considerable density of population. The Alpine regions of the Caucasus and the arid steppes and lowlands of the Caspian littoral are sparsely populated.

Caucasia has long played a major role as a link between Europe and Asia, and through it the culture of ancient Mesopotamia spread northward. Indigenous cultures also arose; in particular, Caucasia was one of the most ancient centres of bronze working from the first half of the 2nd millennium BC. Autochthonous peoples of the Caucasus are mentioned by Herodotus and by later writers such as Strabo. In the centuries between pre-Classical antiquity and the 14th century AD, Caucasia underwent successive invasions by various peoples, including Scythians, Alans, Huns, Khazars, Arabs, Seljuk Turks, and Mongols; and contacts were also maintained with the Mediterranean world. All this history has left its imprint on the culture of the Caucasian peoples: Near Eastern and Middle Eastern influences, in particular, disseminated Iranian languages on the one hand and Islāmic and Christian religion on the other. The later history, beginning with a long period of rivalry between Ottoman Turkey and Iran, is marked by the advance of Russian culture, which penetrated farther and farther into Caucasia from the 16th century onward. Throughout this process, individual ethnic groups, under pressure from stronger neighbours, took refuge in the ravines of the mountain ranges to preserve themselves in isolation.

Ethnic succession

More than 50 different peoples inhabit Caucasia. Russians and Ukrainians, who constitute more than 80 percent of the total population of Ciscaucasia, speak Slavic languages of the Indo-European family. The Armenians also speak an Indo-European language, but one that stands by itself. The Ossetes, the Kurds, the Tats, and the Talysh speak Indo-European languages of the Iranian branch. The majority of the peoples, however, speak tongues that are sometimes tentatively classed together as belonging to a Caucasian language "family," although not all the languages in this "family" are genetically related to one another. The most important Caucasian language is Georgian, spoken by a nation into which numerous tribes have long been amalgamated. Georgian and its many dialects belong to the Kartvelian group of Caucasian, the other groups being the Adyghian and Abkhazian, the Nakhian, and the Dagestani. Adyghian and Abkhazian comprise the languages of Kabarda, of the Adygei, and of the Cherkes, or Circassians (all three of them closely related), as well as those of the Abaza and of the Abkhaz (who have both been strongly influenced by the neighbouring Georgians); Nakhian comprises Shishan (Chechen) and Ingush; and the Dagestani group of the "family" is chiefly represented by the languages of the Lezgian, of the Tabasaran, of the Dargante, and of the Laki peoples, together with those of the 15 minor nationalities collectively described as Avarian. The Dagestani group of "Caucasian" languages is of course quite distinct from the Turkic languages spoken in Dagestan, namely those of the Kumyk and of the Nogay. Other Turkic languages of Caucasia include Karachay and Balkar—besides the extensive Azerbaijani. If Caucasia is the world's best stocked linguistic museum, Dagestan is Caucasia's.

High up in the Caucasus, the people can only raise cattle, grow some mountain crops, and pursue a few domestic crafts. On the plains and on the foothills, viticulture is traditional. The Soviet governments promote heavy or light industry wherever practicable. (S.I.B.)

Mapping and climbing. Modern cartographic studies of the region were begun by Russian scientists in Ciscaucasia about 1815, and some medium-scale maps were drawn up in 1862. Large-scale maps began to appear in 1866; and a survey of the heights of the Great Caucasus, from 1881, provided the basis for the study of its glaciation. The first ascent of Mt. Elbrus was achieved in 1829 by a Kabard mountaineer, Killar Khashirov, who reached the eastern peak; the higher western peak was first climbed in 1874 by four Englishmen. Another Englishman, Douglas Freshfield, made a useful exploration later in the 19th century; but contemporary geographers rely chiefly on Russian research and on the works of indigenous experts.

Prospects. The exploitation of Caucasia's natural resources can be further integrated. Mining and, in particular, hydroelectric development could produce greater yields. The same is true of agriculture, not only in irrigable areas but also higher up. Similarly, forestry and stock raising could be improved, without exhausting the woods and pastures. The tourist trade could be increased if the sanatoriums, spas, and sports centres (for skiers and mountaineers) had better facilities and were made more accessible.

BIBLIOGRAPHY. Н.А. ГВОЗДЕЦКИЙ, *Кавказ* (1963), discusses the wealth and diversity of the nature of the Caucasus; special attention is given to the economic value of the natural resources. D.W. FRESHFIELD, *Exploration of the Caucasus*, 2 vol. (1896–1902), is the classic work of the famous English alpinist about his investigations of the alpine Caucasus.

(N.A.G.)

Cavendish, Henry

One of the leading physicists and chemists of the 18th and early 19th centuries, Henry Cavendish achieved a breadth of interest, originality, and lasting significance in his work that makes him the peer of the major men of science. His contributions fall into five partially overlapping categories: chemical researches, the discovery of the composition of water, electrical researches, researches on heat, and studies in meteorology and dynamics. Cavendish was born in Nice on October 10, 1731, a descendant of two great families, with the duke of Devonshire and the duke of Kent as his grandfathers. His mother died two years later, after giving birth to his brother Frederick. In 1742 he entered the Hackney seminary near London and during 1749–53, he was at Peterhouse College at the University of Cambridge, but he did not take a degree, possibly because he balked at the required declaration of adherence to the Church of England. After a tour of the Continent, he lived in London with his father until the latter's death in 1783. It was during this period that he carried out all of his electrical, and most of his chemical, researches, starting as an assistant to his father, whose own experimental skill was remarkable enough to draw the praise of Benjamin Franklin. Father and son lived in relatively modest circumstances at first, but when Henry Cavendish was 40 he became a millionaire through the inheritance of a fortune that made him, according to Jean-Baptiste Biot, a contemporary French scientist, "the richest of all learned men, and very likely also the most learned of all the rich."

Riches and intellect

His wealth made little difference to his style of living. As before, most of his expenditures went for scientific apparatus and books; in time he accumulated a large library, which he then made available to other scientists. To the outside world he appeared to be a shabby, eccentric man who spoke little and then only hesitantly in a shrill, thin voice. One aspect of his shyness is revealed in an incident later adapted by Aldous Huxley and ascribed to a character in the novel *Point Counter Point* (1928). It occurred when his banker called on Cavendish to suggest the investment of a portion of his funds and was ungraciously told by Cavendish never to plague him again about the growing balance: "If it is any trouble to you, I will take it out of your hands!" Except at meetings of fellow scientists, he almost never appeared in public and was so pronounced a misogynist that he communicated with his housekeeper by daily notes and ordered all female domestics to keep out of his sight. Not only did he not marry, he apparently never formed a sympathetic attachment with any person outside of his family. The costume he usually wore consisted of a

Cavendish, drawing by William Alexander (1767–1816). In the British Museum.

By courtesy of the trustees of the British Museum; photograph, J.R. Freeman & Co. Ltd.

faded, crumpled violet suit of an earlier time, with a high collar and frilled cuffs, and a three-cornered hat. Even among fellow scientists he was so taciturn as to lead Lord Brougham, who knew him, to remark that he

> probably uttered fewer words in the course of his life than any man who ever lived to fourscore years, not at all excepting the monks of La Trappe.

Cavendish's scientific intellect was of a calibre that appears rarely. For all that, he lacked popular acclaim. In part this lack was the result of his own disdain for public reputation, although he did accept such honours as being made Fellow of the Royal Society (1760) and being elected one of the eight foreign associates of the Institut de France (1803). Though he did write for publication, beginning with a three-part paper on the preparation of various gases in 1766, he also completed many researches without publishing the details and sometimes baffled contemporaries by using the results of his own unpublished work in papers describing subsequent work.

Experiments with gases

Experiments on gases form the bulk of his chemical researches. In addition to being among the first to recognize hydrogen, which he called inflammable air, as a separate substance, and performing ingenious experiments with carbon dioxide, then called fixed air, he noted that a small residue remained when air was decomposed into oxygen and nitrogen; this finding was crucial in the discovery of argon and other inert gases more than a century later. He also made other contributions to chemical theory and anticipated later scientists in unpublished experiments with arsenic acid.

Cavendish's experiments on air, described in 1784–85, led to the discovery that water is not an element but a compound and to the discovery of nitric acid. Joseph Priestley, an English scientist, had noted that when a mixture of hydrogen and air is exploded by means of an electric spark—a method that had been proposed a few years before—the walls of the vessel are covered with moisture, a fact that Priestley disregarded. By a careful repetition of Priestley's experiment, Cavendish concluded that this moisture was mainly water. An analogous conclusion was reached at about the same time by James Watt, the Scottish engineer, and communicated to Priestley and to the Royal Society. The great controversy that ensued over priority of discovery was complicated by the fact that authors of papers, and editors, too, had the right to interpolate additions between the reading of the paper and its publication, and that during this particular interval the Royal Society elected a new secretary who had previously assisted Cavendish in some of his experiments. Much of the earliest biography of Cavendish by George Wilson (1851) is taken up with this controversy over who had discovered the fact that when hydrogen burned in air, water was formed. The principals themselves resolved their differences amicably after Watt was made Fellow of the Royal Society in 1785.

The electrical researches of Cavendish were equally remarkable and, had they been published, would alone have brought him fame. Cavendish discovered for himself that the force between a pair of electrical charges is inverse to the square of the distance between them, a basic law of electrostatics subsequently established by a French physicist, C.A. Coulomb, and known by his name as Coulomb's law. Cavendish anticipated Michael Faraday in demonstrating that the capacity of a condenser depends on the substance inserted between its plates. He freely used the concept of potential (then called degree of electrification, from the practice of measuring it by noting the angle formed between the two gold leaves of an electrometer when they become charged and repel one another), well known in mathematics but not previously used in connection with electrical experiments, in developing the idea that all points on the surface of a good conductor are at the same potential with respect to a common reference, the earth. This concept, first made explicit by Cavendish, was of paramount importance for the further development of electrical theory. Finally, in a series of experiments on various conductors, he discovered that the potential across them was directly proportional to the current through them, thus anticipating the law enunciated by George Simon Ohm, a German physicist, in 1827. The last finding was the more remarkable since Cavendish had no means of measuring current and managed only by turning his own body into a meter, estimating the strength of the current by grasping the ends of the electrodes with his hands and noting whether he could feel the shock in his fingers, up to his wrists, or all the way up to the elbows. All these researches were subsequently repeated, after the discovery of his notebooks and manuscripts over a century later, by the great Scottish mathematical physicist, James Clerk Maxwell, who devoted the last five years of his life to the task and published an annotated version of the electrical papers of Cavendish in 1879.

Cavendish's researches on heat likewise remained largely unpublished during his lifetime. They anticipated later work by a Scottish chemist, Joseph Black, and there is some evidence that Cavendish deliberately delayed publication of this work so as not to appear to be competing with Black.

Not all of his work was in pure science. He also interested himself in meteorology and other applied sciences. On one occasion, he served as member of a committee charged with the practical task of devising the best method of protecting a powder magazine at Purfleet from lightning; on another, he helped to investigate the physical properties of gold alloys, in response to the government's concern over the loss of gold in coins, owing to wear.

The Cavendish experiment

His last research, performed when he was nearly 70, was the very difficult and exacting job, known as the Cavendish experiment, of deducing the density of the earth from measurements made by means of an intricate apparatus involving a highly sensitive torsional balance—a horizontal rod suspended from its center by a thin wire or fibre that resists a twist. A British physicist, John Henry Poynting, who later developed an analogous method employing a common balance, said in his book *The Earth* (1913) that Cavendish made his experiment "in a manner so admirable that it marks the beginning of a new era in the measurement of small forces."

An English physicist and physiologist, Thomas Young, in the *Supplement to the Encyclopædia Britannica* (1815–24), said that Cavendish, after his election to the Royal Society in 1760, continued for almost fifty years to contribute to the *Philosophical Transactions* some of the most interesting and important papers that have ever appeared in that collection, expressed in language which affords a model of concise simplicity and unaffected modesty, and exhibiting a precision of experimental demonstration commensurate to the judicious selection of the methods of research and to the accuracy of the argumentative induction; and which have been considered by some of the most enlightened historians, as having been no less instrumental in promoting the further progress of chemical discovery, by banishing the vague manner of observing and reasoning that had too long prevailed, than by immediately extending the bounds of human knowledge with respect to the very important facts which are first made public in these communications . . . . Such were the diversified labours of a philosopher, who possessed a clearness of comprehension and an acuteness of reasoning which had been the lot of very few of his predecessors since the days of Newton.

Cavendish died in his 78th year after what was very likely his first illness and was buried in what is now Derby Cathedral, England. He left his considerable fortune to his relatives, most of it to Lord George Cavendish, the son of his first cousin. He left nothing to science, an omission that the Cavendish family repaired in 1871 by endowing the Cavendish Laboratory in Cambridge University where, under a succession of brilliant directors, much of the development of modern physics took place.

BIBLIOGRAPHY. A *Life* by GEORGE WILSON was published in 1851. The previously unpublished *Electrical Researches*, edited and partially repeated by J.C. MAXWELL, came out in 1879. In 1921, a two-volume edition of previously published papers, together with some of the unpublished experiments, appeared as *The Scientific Papers of the Honourable Henry Cavendish, F.R.S.;* vol. 1 (rev. by SIR JOSEPH LARMOR), contains the electrical researches, and vol. 2 (ed. by SIR THOMAS EDWARD THORPE, with additions by CHARLES CHREE and others), the chemical and dynamical work. More recent biographies include: W.R. AYKROYD, *Three Philosophers* (1935); and A.J. BERRY, *Henry Cavendish: His Life and Scientific Work* (1960).

Among articles dealing with specific aspects of the work of Cavendish are: C. SUSSKIND, "Henry Cavendish, Electrician," *J. Franklin Inst.*, 249:181–188 (1950), which emphasizes his contributions to electrical theory; and R. MCCORMMACH, "Henry Cavendish: A Study of Rational Empiricism in Eighteenth-Century Natural Philosophy," *Isis*, 60:243–306 (1969), which traces his descent from Newton. This theme is elaborated in the same author's entry on Cavendish in *Dictionary of Scientific Biography*, vol. 3 (1971), which also contains an extensive bibliography of original and secondary works.

(Ch.S.)

Caves and Cave Systems

Definitions

Caves are natural cavities in the ground, including all subterranean voids except mines and tunnels fashioned by man. According to this definition, small cavities in rocks buried deep in the earth, natural conduits filled with water, and shallow rock overhangs commonly described as grottos or rockshelters also are caves. Although the term cave is sometimes restricted to air-filled, subterranean galleries and chambers penetrating to total darkness and passable to man, it is used in the broad sense in this article. The related word cavern is commonly used in the plural interchangeably with cave, as in Carlsbad Caverns, New Mexico. A cavern is a chamber-like, underground cavity; hence a cave composed of a number of chambers is properly described as a series of caverns.

Likewise, a cave system can be an assemblage of caverns interconnected by smaller passageways. Although sometimes applied to a cluster of neighbouring caves, whether connected or not, some form of channel-like communication is required during their evolution to permit at least water or air to interchange; this justifies their union as a system. One cannot pass underground among all of the caves comprising the nearly 250 kilometres of explored passageway underlying Mammoth Cave National Park, Kentucky, yet at some time they have been hydraulically interconnected and share a common origin as the Mammoth Cave system.

The study of caves and cave systems is called speleology. Like oceanography, it is the science of an environment, involving a variety of disciplines applied specifically to the explanation of subterranean phenomena. Branches of speleology include cave geology, cave hydrology, cave anthropology, and cave biology, or biospeleology. In addition, the study of karst, landscape resulting from solution processes underground, is an important facet of speleological research.

Though some solution caves have been accidentally opened through mining, most known caves possess natural entrances (Figure 1). These range in size from narrow squeeze-ways to broad gaping holes like the entrance to Carlsbad Caverns. Entranceways may extend horizontally or gently descend (even ascend) toward the interior; others are vertical chasms attaining depths of several hundred metres, demanding mountaineering equipment for descent. Cave interiors can be as varied

By courtesy of (centre) the French Government Tourist Office; photographs, (left) A. Kaplan, (right) M. Woodbridge-Williams

Figure 1: *Entranceways to caves.*
(Left) Thunder Spring, a karst spring in Mauve limestone, Grand Canyon, Arizona. (Centre) Entrance of the Padirac Cave in the Causses of southern France. (Right) Sea caves at La Jolla, California.

as their portals. In some, long horizontal galleries on different levels are interconnected by vertical pits, and huge chambers are separated by long, tight crawlways, admitting only the most persevering explorers. Lower regions of caves commonly contain streams, waterfalls, and lakes, enabling cave proprietors to provide boat trips for their visitors. Scuba divers have discovered unforeseen galleries of cave systems by diving beneath underwater barriers in cave lakes. Mirrored in the cave waters and decorating most of the largest limestone caves is a variety of cave deposits that transform otherwise bare rock walls and mud banks into enchanting stone forests of stalactites, stalagmites, and crystals.

Distribution of caves

Caves of one kind or another can be found in most countries of the world (Figure 2). Solution caves, penetrating deep underground and richly decorated with carbonate deposits, are the best known and can be found in most areas underlain by rocks soluble in natural waters. These rocks include limestone, marble, dolomite, gypsum, and salt. Limestones in the Ozark and Appalachian mountains of the United States are literally riddled with caves, many of which have been developed into showplaces for visitors. In desert areas of the southwestern United States one finds caves dissolved during former wet climates, whereas beneath the glaciers and snowfields of the Canadian Rockies, caves are just beginning to form from the meltwater.

Europe is famed for its highly ornate solution caves that range from Belgium, France, and Spain eastward through the Alps to the Karst of Yugoslavia, where cave formation has occurred on a grand scale. Many European caves have yielded priceless remains of early man and anthropoids, as have cave sites in southern Africa. Caves in rock salt occur in Bulgaria and the U.S.S.R., whose steppes and mountains contain gypsum and limestone caves as well. Solution caves are plentiful in southern China, Southeast Asia, and the larger islands of the southwest Pacific including Australia and New Zealand. Even Antarctica is represented by crevasses and ice caverns deep beneath its glaciers.

Volcanic caves accompany lava fields around the world. Their distribution correlates with areas of present and former volcanism, notably the circum-Pacific volcanic belt linking the Andes, western North America, and Alaska with the volcanoes of Japan and the South Seas.

Theories of cave origin

Speleology is one of the youngest sciences. The exploration of caves gained little headway until the 18th century because of superstitions which were defied only occasionally by ambitious miners in quest of ore.

Early writers on cave origin attributed the unexplored abysses to earthquake and volcanism. During the Age of Enlightenment, about the mid-18th century, scholarly curiosity stimulated the excavations of European caverns for their fossil remains; with it came an appreciation for the role of underground water in forming voids in limestone and depositing carbonates. At first, underground streams were believed to carve their tunnels by mechanical erosion. Even within the present century, some authors attributed vaulted chambers and cylindrical tunnels to mechanical corrasion by powerful eddies of torrential water. The important role of solution, however, became accepted gradually. Controversy then reigned over the manner in which it acted. Scholars studying alpine caves containing high gradient streams tended to view all caves as the product of descending underground rivers. Those working in the lowlands and in integrated cave systems, however, witnessed solution acting within a continuous underground reservoir, whose upper boundary they called the karst water table. Some confined solution to a zone just below this level; others, basing their argument on the discovery of cavities at depth in mines and drill holes, felt that circulating ground water generated caverns at considerable depth. There is, no doubt, some truth in all the theories, depending on the geologic setting and stage of development of a particular cave. A truly comprehensive theory of cave origin in soluble rocks must at least explain the several lines of evidence. This will be later discussed under the heading *Origin of caves and cave systems.*

Caves have made a major contribution to the welfare of man in the form of shelter. The greater part of our present knowledge of man's origins has come from artifacts and skeletal material found within caves. Discoveries of remains in the Sterkfontein and other African caves suggest that man originated on that continent. More highly developed species appear in caves in China. Neanderthal man, an early type, was first discovered in a German cave and since has turned up in many other European sites. Cro-Magnon man, succeeding *Homo neandertalensis,* left as his memorial some remarkable paintings depicting man and contemporary animals. These occur in sites such as the caves of Altamira, Spain, and Lascaux, France. Since Paleolithic time, man has continued to utilize caves as temples, fortresses, and sanctuaries as well as shelter. No remains of such antiquity have been found in American caves, but evidence of the presence of early man is accumulating. Sandia Cave, New Mexico, Danger Cave, Utah, and caves in Oregon and Nevada contain remains

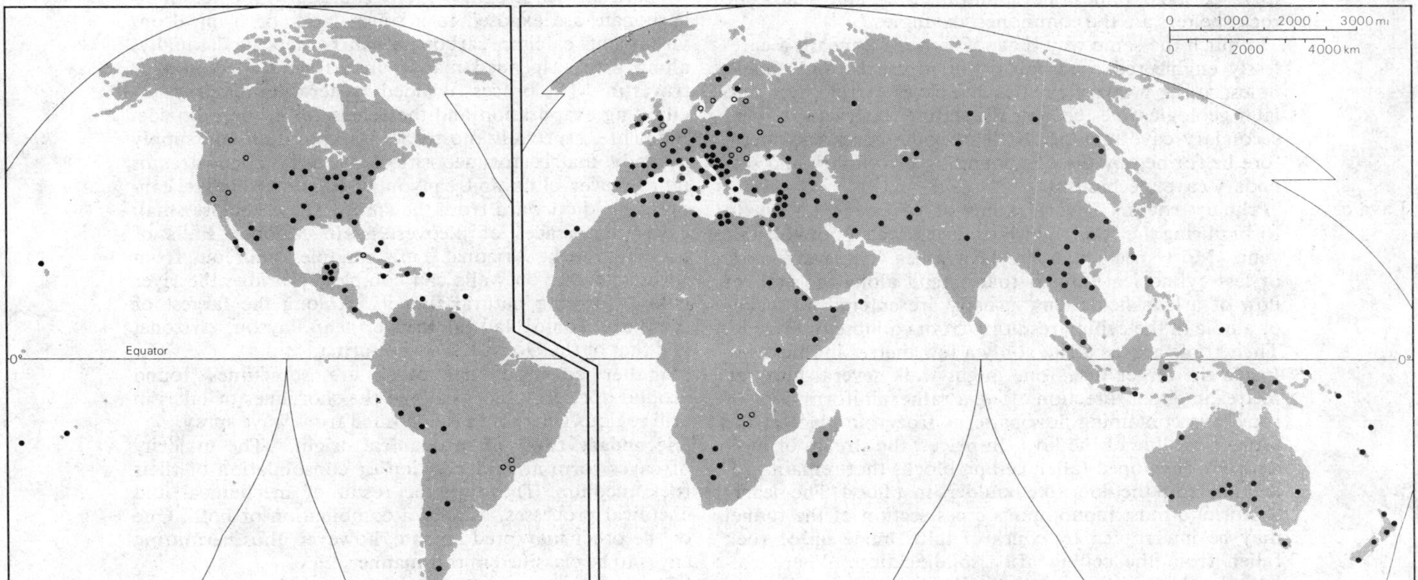

Figure 2: World distribution of exposed and buried limestone karsts.

and artifacts that extend the presence of man beyond 10,000 years in North America.

Caves play an important role in man's present-day environment but in ways other than the providing of shelter. Much of the world's surface is underlain by caves and solution conduits that divert runoff into underground streams. In most of these areas, underground water is scarce except where wells intercept these channels or where springs discharge. The questions of where to drill for water in karst terrain and how to prevent contamination of underground streams undergoing little or no filtration demand an understanding of the origin of caves and karst drainage. Subsidence and collapse of structures and roads, as well as leakage and failure of reservoirs built on soluble terrain, compound the problem.

Life in caves

Caves have been more influential on the development of animals than they have on man. The deep interiors of caves provide an environment of total darkness and relatively constant climate, to which many forms of animal life, as well as plants and micro-organisms, have adapted. Species have evolved that lack eyes and pigment in adulthood, properties not needed for survival underground. The European cave salamander, *Proteus anguinus,* and the cave fish *Amblyopsis spelaea,* from Mammoth Cave, Kentucky, are the best known troglobites or cave dwellers. Many other cave-adapted creatures are represented among the spiders, insects, and lower orders.

Although no mammal species spend their entire lives underground, many do nest, hibernate, or roost in the protective, constant cave environment. Some mice, wood rats, and particularly bats spend much of their lives underground. The many puzzling questions that arise concerning the evolution of cave life, its ecology, and habits comprise the subject matter of the biospeleologist. Several caves have been equipped to serve him as natural laboratories for the observation and investigation of cave life, among them the Laboratoire Souterraine de Moulis, at Moulis, France, and the Ozark Underground Laboratory, near Branson, Missouri.

ORIGIN OF CAVES AND CAVE SYSTEMS

Caves originate in a variety of ways, which fall conveniently into two major groups, depending on their relationship in time with the host rock. Primary caves form during the time when the host rock is being laid down or solidifying. The cavities in lava that result from the cooling of magma around pockets of gases are an example. Secondary caves develop after consolidation of the host rock—in some cases, after the passage of several geologic periods. Limestone solution caves and sandstone rock shelters are the commonest examples.

In much the same way that soft ground beneath a carelessly engineered road can result in cracks and chuckholes, so the primary cavities and caves carried over into later geologic times become the setting for fracturing and secondary cave making. At least some caves can therefore be formed by the compounding of primary and secondary cave mechanisms.

Lava caves

Primary caves. Several kinds of caves are known to form during the cooling of lava discharged from volcanic vents. Most spectacular are lava tubes. These are more or less cylindrical tunnels that extend along the path of flow of a lava field. They usually are entered by means of a hole in the ceiling resulting from collapse or erosion. Their roofs are, as a rule, only a few metres in thickness. Inside the larger tubes one might walk several hundred metres in either direction along a rather uniform floor of ropy lava containing flow patterns frozen in place at the time of cooling of the lava. In places, the stream of molten rock enveloped fallen ceiling blocks that remain protruding from the floor like boulders in a flood. The nearly uniform, almost monotonous cross section of the tunnel may be interrupted by cones of talus made up of rock fallen from the ceiling after solidification. Where collapse has broken through to the surface, one may have to climb outside and re-enter beyond the blockage in order to proceed. Tubes not blocked by collapse terminate in a pinch-out, where ceiling and floor meet.

Although most lava tubes consist of a single, unbranching tunnel, some, like Catacombs Cave in Lava Beds National Monument, California, divide at intervals to form interlacing side passages that either end in rockfall or rejoin the main channel. Nearby Crystal Cave contains several levels, representing cave making in successive lava flows, one atop the other, and at different times. Breakthrough of their roofs permits one to pass vertically among them.

Lava tubes are conventionally explained as the result of cooling and solidification of the surface of a lava flow, accompanied by the draining of the still molten interior to leave the characteristic cylindrical void. The solidified lava streams that form the floors of most lava tubes demonstrate that such draining did indeed occur as the magma cooled. Hot gasses, however, also played an important role in providing the pressure necessary to sustain the ceiling as it solidified. Evidence of these fluid pressures is seen in the high domed ceilings of some caves; where their pressure exceeded the competence of the roof, the gases broke forth to the outside, forming crater-like vents (see also IGNEOUS ROCKS, EXTRUSIVE; VOLCANOES).

Lava tubes are embellished by a variety of dripping and flowing lava structures, notably stalactite-like lava pendants resulting from drippage of the cooling ceiling or remelting by hot gasses. In lava tubes in temperate and cold regions, ice accumulates from the settling of cold air and evaporation, producing "skating rink" floors, overhung with a translucent decor of icicles, and ice crystals and draperies. Coloration of the rock by mineral stains contribute to the beauty and interest of many lava tubes.

Lava tube systems occur throughout the lava fields of northwestern United States and in almost all lava flows around the world that have not suffered excessive erosion. The longest known is Cueva de los Verdes (6.1 kilometres) on the Canary Islands. Iceland, Japan, Mexico, Kenya, and Hawaii all contain noteworthy examples of lava tubes.

Coral and tufa caves

With the progressive expanding and uniting of colonies of coral in shallow, warm waters, submarine voids remain between the lacy or bulbous walls of the living reef. Where shorelines have risen or sea level fallen, these coral caves have been exposed to wave action and surface weathering, both of which tend to enlarge or obliterate the voids and their features. Where reefs have been deeply buried by later sediments, the cavernous reef rock has formed reservoirs of ground-water and petroleum that are prime targets for exploration drilling.

Where surface streams heavily charged with calcium bicarbonate are exposed to a warm, arid, or tropical environment, calcium carbonate can be deposited rapidly, along with suspended matter, in a form called tufa or travertine. The process is aided by aeration in spray, facilitating evaporation and the release of carbon dioxide. Plant life, especially mosses, aid evaporation and supply a ready matrix for deposition. As tufa-laden streams plunge over cliffs and canyon walls, umbrellalike canopies build outward from the spray. These enclose small caves in terraces of alcoves, as in Mooney Falls of Havasu Creek, Arizona. Tufa canopies built out from springs in canyon walls can completely bridge the river below, forming natural tunnels. Among the largest of these are Tonto Natural Bridge, near Payson, Arizona, and that of the Gokteik Gorge, Burma.

Smaller constructional caves are sometimes found around hot spring deposits and the shorelines of lakes in arid regions where tufa is deposited from wave spray.

Secondary caves of mechanical origin. The majority of caves form after deposition or consolidation of their rock medium. They are the result of mechanical and chemical processes, usually a combination of both. One or the other may predominate, however, thus permitting caves to be classified in this manner.

Fissures in rock are produced by tectonic disturbances, such as earthquakes, intrusions, and rock folding at depth, and also by surface disturbances, namely local subsidence, rock creep, and shearing by moving ice of glaciers. Some fissures remain empty and dry to considerable depths, others fill with ice and snow, and still others carry streams that eventually may erode them into gorges.

Where the walls of open fissures converge or overhang, they form, in effect, caves. Great vertical cracks in limestone and sandstone beds of the Colorado Plateau at Wupatki National Monument, Arizona, have been explored to a depth of 200 metres, deep beyond the reach of daylight. Similar fissure caves occurring in deep gorges form parts of Ausable Chasm, New York, and the Canyon of Olhadibie in the French Pyrenees.

Landslides sometimes roof vertical fissures with boulders, as in Pinnacles National Monument, California. In colder regions such roofs are frequently composed of snow and ice; and in glaciers, treacherous crevasses walled entirely by ice result from shear within the moving ice mass. Finally, caves occur between the blocks of talus or boulders dumped by glaciers or landslides commonly along the base of high cliffs. The Indian Caves of Yosemite National Park, California, are an example.

Shoreline and water-worn caves

The mechanical action of water along the shores of streams, lakes, and oceans plays a major role in the generation of strandline caves. Sea caves or marine grottoes form where a sea cliff, either containing incompetent rock at tide level or weakened by fracturing, is exposed to wave action. Quarrying takes place through grinding by contained particles that range from sand to boulders (corrasion) and by hydrodynamic pressure changes within the waves that pry cliff blocks loose (see also WATER WAVES; COASTAL FEATURES).

Chemical processes and the boring of organisms also aid in excavating sea caves. Some found high above sea level contain marine shells, which indicates that the land has risen relative to sea level. On the other hand, some marine grottoes contain underwater stalactites; these features that form in air-filled caves provide evidence that the shoreline has been submerged.

Sea caves are found along most of the world's more rugged coastlines. Most famous are the Blue Grotto on Capri, Italy, and Fingal's Cave on the Island of Staffa, the Hebrides, both in basalt; and La Jolla sea caves near San Diego, California, in marine shale and sandstone.

Caves also form by wave action along the shoreline cliffs of inland seas and lakes. These lacustrine caves have been utilized by man throughout his development as fishing camps and shelter. Their floor deposits contain valuable clues to man's history and origins, including the famed Dead Sea Scrolls, discovered in a cave along an elevated shoreline in Jordan.

Streams and rivers also are effective in quarrying caves in their banks, using as tools the contained silt, sand, and gravel, particularly during flood stages. Gigantic meander cuts, such as Redwall Cavern in Marble Gorge of the Colorado River and the massive sandstone alcoves in which Pueblo Indians erected their famed cliff dwellings, were formed mainly in this way. Rainbow Bridge, in southeastern Utah, resulted when such a meander cut completely through a spur in the canyon wall. Small caves also are generated in riverbeds and banks in the form of circular potholes. Caves also form beneath the ice of glaciers in ways similar to those of streams.

Weathering cavities and ice caves

Innumerable honeycomb-like cavities, small caves, and rock-shelters result from exposure of rock faces to the elements. Weak zones in the rock are attacked and excavated by rain, wind-driven sand, and alternating freezing and thawing, hydration and drying. Spring sapping by water seeping through cracks aids in the quarrying process as do plants growing from the rock or tree roots wedging apart its blocks. Although weathering cavities form in all kinds of rock, they are particularly prevalent in sandstone terrain, where expansive, picturesque alcoves decorate cliffs and prominences, providing dwelling sites, fortresses, and settings for temples.

Where weathering (*q.v.*) attacks two sides of a narrow ridge, a breakthrough joins the two cavities, leaving a rock window or natural arch. Arches National Park, Utah, is famed for its variety of sandstone arches.

Although ice is regarded as a rock by geologists, caves formed therein result more from melting than from mechanical processes. Glacier crevasses that result from fracture are an exception. Meltwater flowing beneath glaciers sculptures intricate labyrinths within and along the base of the ice. Similarly, in snowfields streams and wind currents create translucent blue-tinted tunnels whose scalloped semicircular walls become glazed with ice.

Secondary caves formed by solution. The most extensive and best known caves and cave systems of the world principally result from chemical dissolution of a soluble, weakened host rock (Figure 3). These include the vast underground showplaces like Carlsbad Caverns and Mammoth Cave, which are renowned for their ornamentation and magnitude. The solution process that creates these great voids is highly complex in detail but elementary in principle. Just as a block of rock salt will dissolve away along its faces when subjected to rainfall, all rocks dissolve in certain natural acids. They dissolve not only on their exposed outer surfaces but also on their interiors, where fractures and partings permit solvent to circulate. Rocks other than salt that are particularly soluble in natural solvents are limestone, dolomite, gypsum, and anhydrite. Caves formed in these media, although preconditioned by fracturing and abetted by weathering and mechanical erosion, enlarge predominantly by chemical solution.

The formation of caves can be illustrated by the solution of limestone host rock, composed mainly of calcium carbonate ($CaCO_3$). In naturally occurring carbonic acid (H_2CO_3), made up of carbon dioxide and water, the following equilibrium condition will prevail:

$$H_2CO_3 \rightleftharpoons H_2O + CO_2.$$

The water and carbonic acid dissociate to form acids, and the bicarbonate ion also dissociates according to:

$$H_2O \rightleftharpoons H^+ + OH^-, \; H_2CO_3 \rightleftharpoons H^+ + HCO_3^-, \; HCO_3^- \rightleftharpoons H^+ + CO_3^=.$$

The released acid reacts with the limestone, which dissociates as follows:

$$CaCO_3 \rightleftharpoons Ca^{++} + CO_3.$$

These ions in equilibrium with the other ions yield calcium bicarbonate in solution, effectively giving the result:

$$CaCO_3 + CO_2 + H_2O \rightleftharpoons Ca(HCO_3)_2.$$

The forward reaction summarizes the dissolution of limestone; the reverse, the precipitation of calcium carbonate, usually in the mineral form calcite, from which many varieties of speleothems or cave deposits are constructed.

Natural waters not in dynamic equilibrium according to the above ionic equations can dissolve limestone and create a cave. The rates of reaction and solubility are dependent on temperature, pressure, concentration of added salts, pH, and total carbon dioxide in solution. In general, the less saturated the water and the more frequently it exchanges, the more rapidly solution proceeds. Thus, a swiftly moving fluid, particularly if accompanied by turbulence, permits rapid washing of limestone walls with fresh solvent.

Calcium carbonate is only slightly soluble in pure water, but where the water contains carbon dioxide, the resulting calcium bicarbonate can attain concentrations up to 1,600 parts per million (ppm), depending on the partial pressure of the carbon dioxide (CO_2). Along the ground surface, water in equilibrium with carbon dioxide dissolves only small amounts of calcium carbonate (63 ppm measured), but within air trapped in soil, amounts up to 400 ppm have been recorded. Thus, water trickling through soil tends to dissolve an underlying limestone mass quite readily. If descending waters penetrate the cracks of limestone to emerge into an air-filled chamber, a new environment of temperature and partial pressure affects the constitution of the fluid. If the partial pressure of CO_2 within the chamber is less than that in the cracks and soil, then CO_2 is released from the water. If saturation results from this release, calcium carbonate precipitates, giving rise to stalactites, draperies, or other speleo-

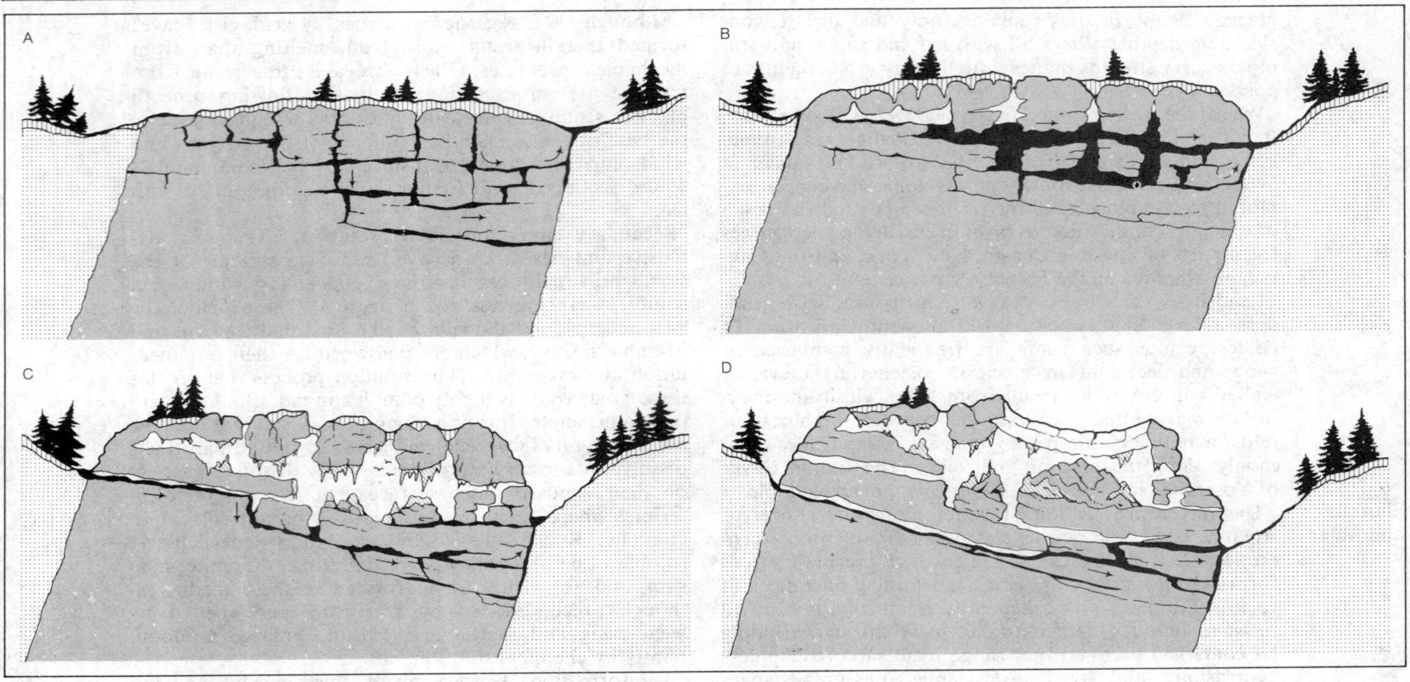

Figure 3: *Evolution of a limestone cave system.*
(A) Fracture pattern conducts surface drainage toward discharge in a subriver spring along contact with nonsoluble terrain. (B) Low resistance paths enlarge by solution into trunk channels causing water levels to fall and sinkholes to form on the surface. (C) Deepening stream on the right drains upper portions of cave, inducing local collapse, while carbonate deposits form from trickling water; surface stream on the left has been pirated to the underground system. (D) Surface erosion and stoping from below result in extensive collapse of the cave roof, while solution continues along deeper fracture paths.

thems. Furthermore, under ambient, above-freezing conditions, an increase in temperature lowers the CO_2 concentration of water; therefore, trickling winter drainage entering a warm underground chamber may release CO_2, tending to deposit calcite. Reversal of these conditions may redissolve calcite deposited during the previous winter or during an earlier climatic episode. This will leave a characteristic lacework of corroded speleothems; eventually these may be obliterated completely.

As solvent waters penetrate underground, partially or totally filling cave conduits, they become increasingly concentrated unless diluted by tributary sources along the way. In many cave systems, underground streams discharge as springs long before saturation is attained; in others they become fully saturated, to the point of depositing calcite along the channel walls, just as scale forms in metal pipes. With dilution by an incoming, less saturated stream, increased solution can take place downstream from the juncture. Paradoxically, the mingling of two or more saturated streams can result in an undersaturated mixture capable of further solution under certain conditions. This recently discovered phenomenon is called mixture-solution and is believed to be a possible explanation of cavern generation beyond the penetration distance or limit of undersaturation of a single cave stream.

Other naturally occurring acids, such as sulfuric and organic acids, also attack limestone; and corresponding equilibrium equations can be written for their reactions. Dolomite, $CaMg(CO_3)_2$, behaves similarly to limestone. Gypsum ($CaSO_4 \cdot 2H_2O$) often derives from the hydration of anhydrite ($CaSO_4$), a mineral deposited in shallow saturated seas and lakes. Anhydrite expands in contact with water so that its alteration to more soluble gypsum is accompanied by fracturing that facilitates attack by ground water. Gypsum is much more soluble in natural waters than is limestone, hence gypsum caves form rather rapidly. Other evaporites, especially rock salt (NaCl) are still more soluble, so that caves evolve rapidly in salt beds, but these have a relatively short life span because surficial erosion proceeds at a commensurate rate.

The role of fracturing

In granular rocks such as sandstone, surface runoff from precipitation trickles downward through the rock pores until it meets the zone of saturation, namely, a more or less continuous reservoir of groundwater whose upper boundary is commonly called the water table. Within this reservoir, groundwater (*q.v.*) migrates through the pores as a unified body. In dense limestones, on the other hand, the bulk of the underground water movement takes place through rock partings and openings; only a relatively small amount of water moves through the pores. With localization of flow along fractures, these partings then enlarge by solution to accommodate additional fluid. The fracture patterns of the host rock, therefore, become the scaffold along which a developing cave system grows.

Two kinds of fractures are important in cave making: joints, along which no slippage has occurred; and faults, whose walls have moved parallel to one another. Faults accompanied by considerable open fracturing and brecciation (crushing of rock) form highly permeable zones for the passage of dissolving waters. Hence, they are responsible for some of the largest cave systems.

Surface drainage and groundwater

Most limestone cave systems are dissolved by meteoric waters draining downward and laterally away from a collecting area of the ground surface toward springs and discharge zones in valleys or beneath the sea. Surface water penetrates underground through fractures in outcrops or soil-covered limestone, conducting it vertically downward, dissolving and enlarging the feeder cracks along the way. Surface runoff thus has little chance to flow along the ground and collect as streams that normally would carve surface drainage paths along the topographic gradient, as on sandstone and other nonsoluble terrains. In limestone, the "valleys" instead are vertical and represent the initial stage in the development of a typical solution landscape called karst.

Drainage cannot continue, however, to proceed downward unless it encounters a through path to a discharge point. If permeability permits, the waters will find a route to a discharge zone at lower elevation in a valley or perhaps on the sea floor. Because the solution rate increases with gap width, tight fractures are not more likely to pass water and enlarge than is the rock itself. Thus, solution channels must originate along at least partially open fractures or along openings already present in the rock, such as primary caves formed in earlier geologic time. If the network is short and relatively open, dissolving may continue throughout; otherwise, initial solution may be confined to the upper supply zone of undersaturated water or to the discharge zone of higher velocity flow. In time these zones may enlarge and unite. Meanwhile, the geometry of the primitive solution network is determined by the fracture path and geologic structure.

With the widening of interstices, accompanied by accelerated solution, the pattern of underground water movement alters, channelling flow along the lower resistance paths of shorter conduits with larger diameters. These develop into underground drainage trunks at the expense of the longer, tighter routes. So long as recharge and discharge keep pace, the connecting system remains water filled. If blockage of the discharge route occurs, the entire system up to the surface can be impounded, spilling over across the collecting surface and clogging its lower paths with sediments. If, on the other hand, discharge gains over recharge, upper portions of the system fill with air, permitting the formation of a chain of underground lakes that become standpipes of the system, with perhaps interconnecting free-flowing streams and waterfalls. With progressive enlargement of feeder channels, collapse, or surface erosion, portals may develop that make the partially drained cave accessible to man.

In general, continuous faults give rise to long, linear solution passages, as typified by New River Cave, Virginia. The extent of passage ramification, in these cases, depends on the degree of subsidiary fracturing accompanying the fault. In contrast, joint sets that parallel the axis of an anticline or arched fold enlarge along with associated bedding plane faults to construct a reticulated maze of cavern passages of which the elaborate labyrinth of Anvil Cave, Georgia, is a classic example. Most caves, however, form along less regular patterns of faults and joints, expressing the diversity of geologic events that preceded cave making.

In regions of high relief, the steep hydraulic gradient between uplands and canyon discharge points favours solution along steeply inclined fractures, producing cave systems made up of vertical fissures, pits, and underground canyons. In gentler terrain, horizontal lineaments provide the shortest paths to discharge points and, hence, favour formation of more or less horizontal cave passages related to valley levels.

A stream originating in upland, nonsoluble terrain is subject to diversion into underground channels where it crosses karst rock. Subterranean piracy (diversion) may conduct the stream only a short distance underground, to re-emerge at the downstream terminus of the limestone. In other cases it is known to abduct the stream away from its regular watershed, beneath surface divides, even passing beneath other valleys, to emerge as springs in neighbouring or distant drainage basins. The resurgences of such "lost rivers" are identified and correlated by means of radioactive and dye tracers committed to the water where it disappears from the surface. Many of the large springs of Missouri, Arkansas, and Arizona are believed to derive their water from karst sinks many kilometres distant.

THE EVOLUTION AND DEMISE OF CAVES AND CAVE SYSTEMS

The development of an open, air-filled cave from a system of fractures and primitive solution tubes has been described above as a more or less continuous process which involves progressive solution, enlargement, partial draining, and gradual lowering of water stands within the system. Mountain building, canyon cutting, and changes in climate, however, can dramatically alter the course of events underground. If, for example, a limestone block containing a solution network is uplifted, canyons on the surface become incised, valleys are deepened, and underlying fractures are exposed and become new routes for draining of the cave waters. The previously submerged cave thus will be left hanging high and dry in the canyon walls. Rapid dissection by the Colorado River and its tributaries in Grand Canyon, induced by uplift of the surrounding plateau, has drained numerous caverns and cave springs that discharge as waterfalls down the limestone cliffs. An episodic course of events brought on by uplift in that manner is called the two-cycle theory of cave development, as advanced by William M. Davis to illustrate the cave-making process. The theory has been augmented by J. Harlen Bretz, who describes the earlier, submerged phase of enlargement as phreatic and the subsequent air-filled phase as vadose.

Regional uplift

The two-cycle process may be likened to that of a valley reservoir or lake that is filling with sediment carried down by streams from the hills. Should uplift of the land cause headward erosion to the retaining dam, the lake could drain and its emptied basin undergo a new phase of stream dissection. Some cave systems undoubtedly experience just such a course of events; others, however, must be interpreted as the product of continuous subterranean processes through time. Solution, draining, and gravity stream flow, resulting in a chain of underground lakes that are connected by streams and filled tubes, with local water levels determined by intervening resistance paths, seem probable in many instances. Upper regions of such caves may be completely drained and dry, while the nether regions remain completely submerged.

The action of cave draining and opening can be reversed through either increased precipitation, subsidence of the host rock, or damming of valleys. Landslides, glacial moraines, and artificial dams can result in the flooding and silting of cave systems. Numerous caverns in the Tennessee Valley are no longer accessible since partly or totally submerged by man-made reservoirs.

Subaerial processes

Portions of a newly drained cave are subjected to a variety of subaerial processes that tend either to enlarge or to reduce the volume of the void. Flowing water, whether in the form of gentle rivulets collecting from ceiling drippage or large surface streams and storm water, corrades and dissolves the limestone walls and excavates or deposits sediments. Boulders and gravels dumped underground by subsiding torrents attest to the great volume of material carried through alpine caves during spring runoff and in times of glacial retreat. The Nakimu Caves of Glacier National Park, British Columbia, contain giant potholes scoured in the marble floors by rubble borne on glacial meltwater.

The deposition of calcite and related minerals in the form of subaerial speleothems commences with the draining of the cave, provided that water trickling downward is saturated when it encounters the cave air. Stalactites, stalagmites, draperies, flowstone, and many other familiar cave structures coat the rock walls and cave fill, in effect decreasing the volume of the void. Under conditions particularly favourable to deposition, passages can become completely blocked by barriers of calcite. The main tourist route of Cueva de Cacahuamilpa, Mexico, terminates in this way.

Rockfall and subsidence effect profound modification of cave form. Unstable ceiling blocks eventually give way, either through solution of their binding joints, earthquake, or through loss of buoyancy upon draining of the cave. Progressive stoping (material removal) in this manner can transform an originally flat ceiling into an arched vault whose ultimately stable shape coincides with the tension dome prescribed by stress patterns within the rock. The rubble accumulating beneath the vault forms huge mounds of talus that frequently block passages, divert subterranean streams, or bring about impounding. The 41-metre high Monument Mountain in Wyandotte Cave, Indiana, formed in this manner beneath an expanding vaulted ceiling. Most of the largest underground chambers, such as the Big Room in Carlsbad Caverns, New Mexico, exhibit vaulted ceilings and talus mounds brought about by ancient rockfall. Solution and flushing by streams aid in reducing the volume of debris that collects as a result of the breakdown process.

In caverns near the surface, underground material removal often breaks through the roof, which, in turn, produces a collapse sink or collapse doline that serves as a portal to the cave. Most large, near-surface caverns contain collapse openings of this sort. The underlying talus cones usually contain the remains of animals that have had the misfortune of accidentally plunging into the cave from the surface.

The walls of caverns can open in a different manner, with excavation proceeding from without. This occurs when streams cut laterally into their banks and intercept a cavern or sever cave passages as they deepen and extend their valleys. With further downcutting by the stream, cave portals are left perched in the walls, where they have served as the retreat and dwelling places of primitive man throughout his development.

The opening of caves to the atmosphere in these and other ways initiates the destruction of their passages through progressive collapse, weathering, and erosion. With denudation of the terrain and encroachment of valleys, additional portions of the cave galleries become revealed. Natural arches and tunnels stand for a while between collapse zones; in time, these too give way, leaving only a trench and perhaps fragments of speleothems to mark the site of the former cavern passage. These cave vestiges may become buried beneath later sediments to become "fossilized" in the geologic record

CAVE FEATURES

The dissolving of caves under submerged and subaerial conditions sculptures the rock walls with forms characteristic of solution and flow processes. Continuous and discrete structures forming in this way can be interpreted to determine the manner of origin of cave passages. Such excavated structures or forms are called speleogens and include ceiling and wall pockets, floor slots, and vertical shafts.

Features formed by solution. Uniform solution, wherein removal of rock proceeds equally at all points along its walls, is approximated in submerged portions of many caves where flow patterns are rather random. The future shapes of an initial structure, such as a block of limestone subjected to uniform solution (Figure 4), can be predicted through mathematical analysis and results in the following rule: successive cross sections of the rock are described by the paths of a hypothetical circle rolled inside the rock but kept in contact with the outline of the structure. The interior envelope described by the rolling circle (in three dimensions, a sphere) represents the rock boundary at some future time determined by the radius of the circle. Thus a planar wall retreats parallel to itself. Two walls making a projecting angular corner retreat parallel to themselves, preserving the sharp corner. The inside corner, on the other hand, rounds, because the imagined circle pivots at the apex, describing an arc. Filamentary tubes expand radially in concentric cross sections. The future sculpture of any irregular cave walls can be determined in this manner, as demonstrated by the hand specimen of marble shown in Figure 5, that was dissolved in a nearly uniform acid bath in the laboratory. In nature, the effects are borne out by the characteristic solution relief of irregular ceiling and wall pockets separated by cuspate ridges found in most formerly submerged caverns.

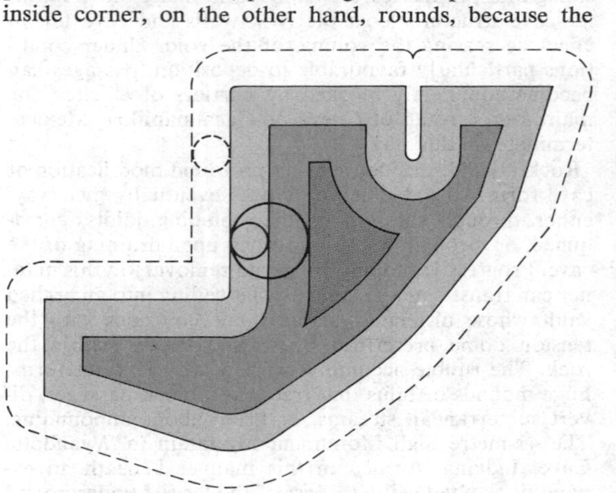

Figure 4: Hand specimen of marble subjected to uniform solution. Successive cross sections are described by rolling a circle along the outline from within. The outer dashed outline would result from uniform deposition around the specimen, as described by rolling the dashed circle around the outside.

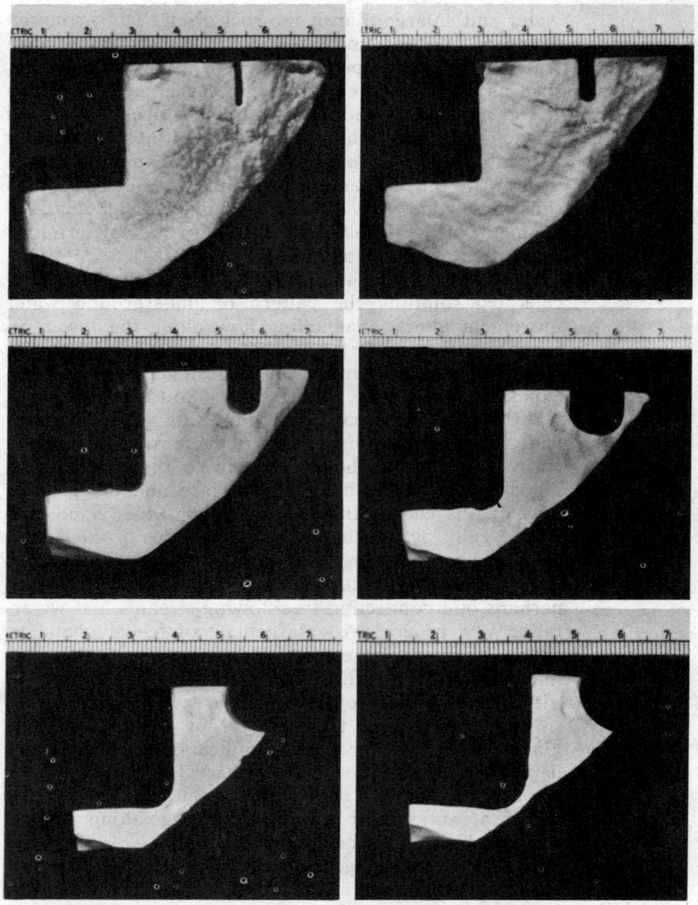

Figure 5: Successive stages of solution of a hand specimen of Yule marble dissolved in a weak nitric acid bath. Experiment demonstrates the preservation of projecting corners and the rounding of inside corners.
From G. Mowat, *Cave Notes*, vol. 4, no. 6 (1962)

Particular speleogens that indicate former episodes of submerged, uniform solution include dissolved fallen ceiling blocks whose projecting corners have been preserved, the rounded inside corners remaining in the ceiling, angular pillars resulting from the recession of vertical joint sets, and circular-cylindrical solution tubes formed radially from the line of intersection of two joints.

Other speleogens originate from conditions of nonuniform solution. A stepwise solution gradient consisting of uniform solution beneath a constant water level, above which dissolving has ceased, produces truncated ceilings called water-level planes, which usually can be related to a spillover point elsewhere in the cave. These features are extremely valuable in establishing former underground water levels. Unequal directional dissolving takes place where silting accompanies solution, because the veneer of sediments accumulating on positive slopes less than their critical angle of repose discourages further retreat of the underlying rock. The resulting planes of repose exhibit a constant slope and can be found at various heights. When they form in conjunction with water-level planes, continuous overhanging grooves ring cave chambers, indicating solution in a turbid cave lake.

Figure 6: *Interiors of caves.*
(Left) The Cypress Swamp, Lehman Caves National Monument, Nevada, showing the standing pool of a river, stalactites, stalagmites, and columns. (Right) Old Mill Cave, Virginia, with stalactites and short stalagmites.
By courtesy of (left) Western Speleological Institute; photographs, (left) George Mowat, (right) J.F. Quinlan

Boxwork, scallops, and speleothems

Boxwork, as illustrated from Wind Cave, South Dakota, is composed of projecting fragile veins of minerals less soluble than the wall rock, proving that quiet solution with virtually no accompanying corrasion has taken place. Scallops, by way of contrast, are parabolic ripples dissolved in limestone walls from eddies in definite currents. Where they appear on ceilings, they show that the passage was once completely filled with water flowing in the direction indicated by their concave arcs. Free-surface streams incising both downward and laterally excavate slots in passage floors and meander niches in wall rock. Trickling and dripping water produces still other forms. The most spectacular of these are the vertical shafts corroded by water from overlying granular caprock, falling down vertical cracks into a lower drainage channel. Vertical shafts more than 100 metres in height are encountered in caves in eastern United States and Mexico, proving a great challenge to explorers. Excellent examples can be seen in the region called the Ruins of Karnak in Mammoth Cave, Kentucky.

The deposition of calcite and other cave minerals from aqueous solution builds forms that are characteristic of the underlying rock structures, flow patterns, chemistry, and deposition rate. The resulting structures are termed speleothems and comprise the feature attractions of many well-known caves. Speleothems can form under water as well as in air.

Features formed by deposition. Uniform deposition, analogous to uniform solution, takes place within pools of saturated water. Clusters of delicate dogtooth spar crystals and amorphous crusts of calcite and other minerals coat the walls in bulbous masses. The cross section of these crusts is described in a way similar to that of uniform solution; that is, by rolling a circle along the original wall, but in this case within the fluid, rather than the rock. The crust assumes the shape of the envelope of the moving circle, with the result that projecting sharp corners become rounded, whereas inside corners remain as sharp hollow cusps. Mammillary crusts formed in this way cover walls of some caves to a thickness of several metres.

Along the surfaces of pools, where carbon dioxide is released directly to the cave air, undersaturated water can locally saturate and deposit a crusted strand of calcite, ringing projections in patterns resembling lily pads. Where pools spill over, aeration aids deposition, and natural dams elevate themselves through the accretion of calcite. These are genetically akin to the rimstone dams of tufa that form in surface streams. In very quiet pools, fragile rafts of calcite, which resemble ice, and calcite "bubbles" float upon the surface.

Irregular knobby growths of calcite, appropriately named cave coral, form within cave pools, as well as in the air, where films of moisture deposit. Flowing films of water moving down positive-sloping walls, build up layers of flowstone, usually white or translucent but locally stained by minerals carried by the water. Films descending over-hanging walls and ceilings collect along the steepest gradients, irregular ridges, and prominences, from which they deposit outward and downward wavy curtains of calcite, often stained by colourful bands of mineral matter. These beautiful speleothems, called draperies, adorn numerous caves.

Stalactites and stalagmites

Water entering a cave chamber through ceiling cracks can deposit at its point of emergence when conditions favour deposition. A stalactite commences growing in this manner from a delicate film of calcite covering the hanging water drop. As it falls, the film is broken except along a ring of attachment. Subsequent drops build successive rings in the form of a cylinder resembling a soda straw, typically six millimetres in diameter, through which the descending water must pass. All true stalactites begin in this manner and contain a central canal. The falling drops splatter as they hit the floor, where a bulbous upward building mass, a stalagmite, forms from the spray and spilled water. Given sufficient time, the stalactite and stalagmite may meet to form a column. Changing conditions, however, can bring about blockage of the stalactite, or it may redissolve or shatter in an earthquake.

Stalactites can thicken radially either from water exuding outward through the walls of the tube or from the flowing of ceiling moisture down the outside. A conical or tapered stalactite, much more rigid than the original soda straw, results. The massive stalactites and columns typical of the Big Room in Carlsbad Caverns formed in the manner described, though over long periods of time and varieties of conditions.

Helictites resemble soda-straw stalactites because they are cylindrical and pass water through a central canal. They differ in that they grow from walls and floors, as well as ceilings, in winding, contorted patterns that seem to defy gravity. They are fed through small openings in the rock, but at so slow a rate that the drops evaporate at the tips of the structure rather than fall to the floor. The forces of surface tension and the crystal habit of calcite exceed that of gravity and determine a direction of growth substantially independent of the latter. Helictites of both aragonite and calcite decorate several well-known caves, notably Skyline Caverns, Virginia, and Caverns of Sonora, Texas.

Cave flowers grow from the base rather than the tip, exuding from the cave walls and curling back like squeezed toothpaste. Gypsum flowers up to 25 centimetres long can be seen in portions of Mammoth Cave.

Shields, sometimes called palettes, are believed to form from water seepage from cracks. Ridges of calcite are deposited on both walls of a crack, and these ridges grow

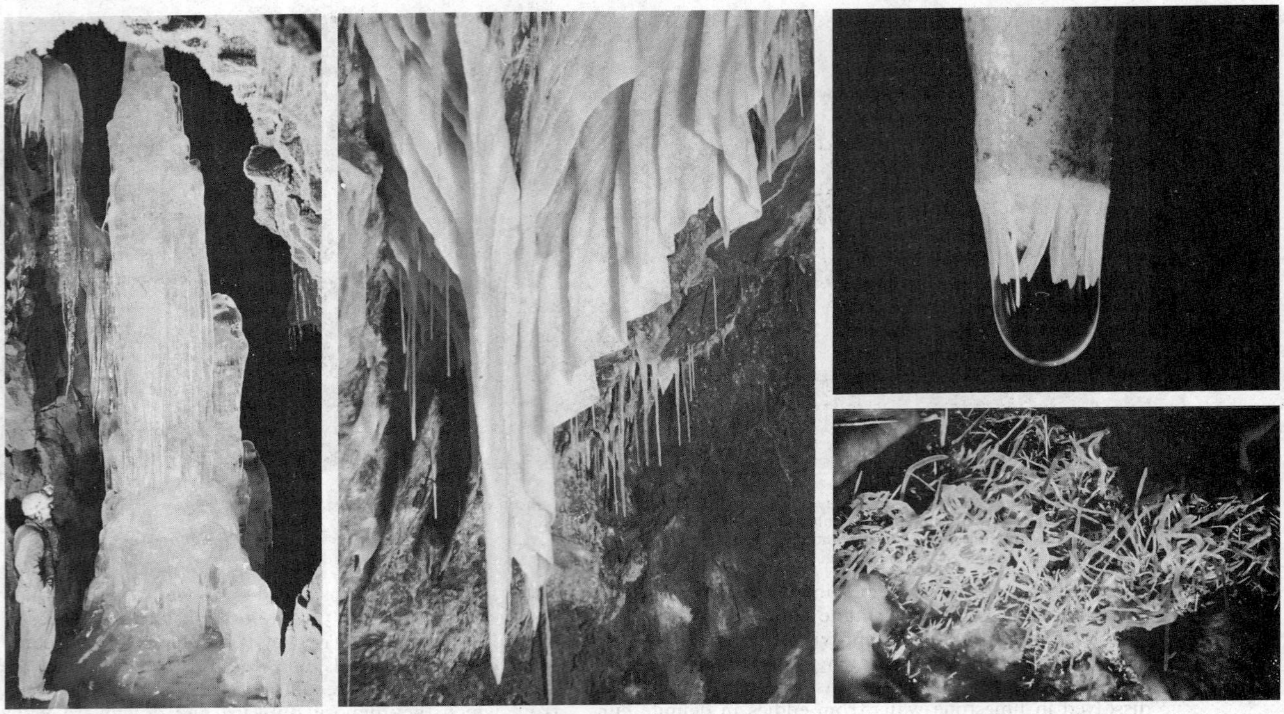

Figure 7: *Cave features.*
(Left) Ice column over 30 feet high in Crystal Ice Cave, American Falls, Idaho. (Centre) Travertine drapery, Haughton's Cave, California. (Top right) Drop of mineral-enriched water suspended from the growth tip of a tubular stalactite, Steinamwasser, West Germany. (Bottom right) Helictites, twiglike growths of calcium carbonate, Lost Soldier Cave, California.
By courtesy of (centre, bottom right) Western Speleological Institute; photographs, (left) James L. Papadakis, (centre, bottom right) George Mowat, (top right) Lou R. Goodman

radially outward as parallel plates, or disks, separated by a thin parting, the extension of the original crack, through which seepage continues. The shield expands in its plane toward an ever more circular form. When water supply exceeds evaporation, overflow descends from the rim, building draperies. Shields of several metres in diameter are feature attractions at Lehman Caves National Monument, Nevada, and Grand Caverns, Virginia.

A speleothem seldom seen except in newly discovered caves forms in floor depressions where saturated water drips with such vigour that a coherent stalagmite cannot form. Gravel and sometimes fragments of bone contained in the pocket become coated at the same time that agitation polishes and rounds them. These concretions, approaching in form spheres, are known as cave pearls and owe their scarcity to their unattached condition and the collecting instinct of cave visitors.

Numerous attempts have been made to date stalactites and other speleothems based on a measured rate of growth, such as the rate of lengthening of a stalactite over a period of several years. Most of these age estimates, though not necessarily unreasonable, assume constant rates of accretion over the centuries. Many documented cases of alternating depositing and resolution of calcite, as well as extreme variations in flow rate within stalactites, invalidate this method of age dating. Greater success is being experienced by the recent application of radiocarbon and other isotope methods to the dating of chemical constitutents of speleothems.

Cave ice and sedimentation. Wherever frigid winter air settles into downward leading caverns, or where moisture freezes by evaporation in currents of cold air, a variety of underground ice formations can arise.

Alpine ice cave systems

Although splendid examples of caves containing permanent ice can be found in the lava tubes of northwestern United States, none begin to match in magnitude or grandeur the limestone ice cave systems of the Alps. Most renowned is the Eisriesenwelt (Ice Giant World) in Austria, a labyrinthine wind tunnel whose frozen landscape of underground cascades and draperies extends through more than 40 kilometres of passage.

Some cave sediments originate underground from solution of the rock walls, but others are carried in from the outside. During the early phases of cave excavation, when solution is expanding a network of small cracks into conduits, particles of clay contained within the limestone fall out as residues. Those that do not discharge with the fluid collect in low points of the system, tending to discourage further solution downward. Larger rock fragments, bones, and shells also are released from the rock by solution and these accumulate amid the fill. Oxidized residues derived from surface weathering of limestone wash into the cave through feeder cracks and constitute dense deposits of clay in some caves.

The air-filled phase of cave evolution is characterized by a greater variety of sediments than the submerged phase. Perennial streams diverted into underground channels bring in silt, sand, and cobbles of upland rocks. Floods can wash in debris as large as boulders, sometimes even trees, blocking passages and filling entire caves. Rockfall from ceiling failure forms rubble heaps mingling with fluvial deposits and residues. Breccia working downward through surface fissures contributes its own characteristic rubble. Open portals permit windblown material to circulate within the cave, from which layers of aeolian sand, glacial dust, and volcanic ash settle on cave floors and in underground pools. Incorporated pollen and the ash from known volcanic eruptions aid in dating these strata. Most animal remains, such as bones, guano, and debris, accumulate during the subaerial phase.

KARST TOPOGRAPHY

The presence of solution channels and caves in a rock permit surface runoff to drain directly underground instead of forming dendritic valleys. As a result, characteristic solution features evolve to comprise what is called karst terrain, or simply karst. Its prototype is the Karst of the Dinaric Alps, Yugoslavia, where caves and solution landscape have formed on a grand scale.

Temperate karst. Drainage trickling through soil and into the small vertical cracks that feed underlying caves enlarges cracks with the aid of weathering. Jagged pinnacles called orgeln and karren form as residual rock masses between the cracks, beneath soil, and on exposed rock, respectively. Amid them occur solution depressions (dolines) and openings (ponors) that connect with caves below.

"Lost rivers" and waterfalls

Streams entering karst may disappear through open sinks, or swallow holes, and may reappear elsewhere in a spring called a karst rise or resurgence, usually at the lower boundary of the soluble rock. In the Indiana limestones, karst windows resulting from collapse provide glimpses of the "lost rivers" in their course between sink and rise. Downstream from the rises in warm, dry climates, precipitating carbonates build up rimstone dams, waterfalls, and tufa caves from the saturated karst waters.

The karst landscape just described is typical of the Mediterranean and other temperate lands. It can come about wherever fractured soluble rocks reach the surface and rainfall is plentiful. The landscape can assume the countenance of rugged rock badlands of gaping holes and crags (barren karst) or rolling meadows and forests (covered karst), depending on geographic factors such as precipitation, relief, and forestation. Barren karst is typical of Alpine limestones of Europe as well as the mountains of western North America. Covered karst is found in lowlands of Europe and central United States (notably Mammoth Cave National Park) but is also well developed in the high plateaus of northern Arizona and Utah.

Tropical karst. In the tropics, karst formation proceeds at a high rate, aided by heavy rainfall and abundant amounts of organic acids in the soil. In the uplands, the jungle-covered, pocketed terrain of giant sinkholes is given the name cockpit country. As this very irregular surface lowers toward sea level, surface planation encroaches upon the residual rock that protrudes in high mounds and pinnacles called mogotes, forming a tower karst. Tropical karst landscapes have been frequently described from Jamaica, Puerto Rico, Cuba, Southeast Asia, and Java.

Floridian karst. Flat-lying limestones near sea level in warm climates develop a peculiar kind of karst composed of large solution conduits of low gradient, through which ground water slowly makes its way from distant hills to discharge as offshore submarine springs of fresh water. In the Yucatan Peninsula of Mexico, bottle-like collapse sinkholes called cenotes lead down to the subterranean streams, where drowned archaeological remains of Mayan civilization have attracted anthropologist-divers. The Ocala limestone plain of Florida contains similar features, some of which discharge on land as large springs.

BIBLIOGRAPHY. The literature on caves and cave systems is vast. Because much research originated in the Balkans, valuable information is contained in books and journals of lesser known Slavic languages. The following references represent only a sampling of the world literature on this subject but will lead the reader to additional books and articles on particular aspects.

General discussions on cave origin and speleology include: C.H.D. CULLINGFORD (ed.), *British Caving: An Introduction to Speleology* (1953); E. MARTEL, *Les Abîmes* (1894); G.W. MOORE and G. NICHOLAS, *Speleology: The Study of Caves* (1964); H. TRIMMEL, *Höhlenkunde*, (1968); and F. TROMBE, *Traite de Spéléologie* (1952).

More specific treatments of cave origin and fauna can be found in: V. BAILEY, *Cave Life of Kentucky, Mainly in the Mammoth Cave Region* (1933); T.C. BARR, "Caves of Tennessee," *Bull. Tenn. Div. Geol. 64* (1961); M. BOULE and H. VALLOIS, *Fossil Men* (1957); J.H.BRETZ, "Vadose and Phreatic Features of Limestone Caverns," *J. Geol.*, 50:675–811 (1942); W.E. DAVIES, "Caverns of West Virginia," *W. Va. Geol. Surv. Rep. 19* (1949); W.M. DAVIS, "Origin of Limestone Caverns," *Bull. Geol. Soc. Am.*, 41:475–628 (1930); and A. LANGE, "Introductory Notes on the Changing Geometry of Cave Structures," *Cave Stud.*, 11:69–90 (1959).

Among the many important works on karst are: J. CVIJIC, "Das Karstphänomen," *Geogr. Abh.*, 5:217–330 (1893); S.N. DICKEN, "Kentucky Karst Landscapes," *J. Geol.*, 43:708–728 (1935); N.A. GVOZDETSKY, *Karst*, in Russian (1954); and O. LEHMANN, *Die Hydrographie des Karstes* (1932).

Popular accounts on cave exploration include: N. CASTERET, *Darkness Under the Earth* (1955); G. DE LAVOUR, *Caves and Cave Diving* (1958); H. KUHN, *On the Track of Prehistoric Man* (1955); C.E. MOHR and H.N. SLOANE (eds.), *Celebrated American Caves* (1955).

The largest source of information on this subject is found in periodicals. Some of the most prominent in the English language, devoted exclusively to speleology, are: *Caves and Karst*, formerly *Cave Notes* (1959–); *National Speleological Society Bulletin* (1941–); and *Studies in Speleology* (1964–).

(A.L.L.)

Cavour, Count

Camillo Benso, conte di Cavour, Piedmontese statesman largely responsible for uniting Italy under the House of Savoy and first prime minister of the Kingdom of Italy, was born at Turin on August 10, 1810, the second son of Michele Benso, marchese di Cavour, and Adele di Sellon. The Cavours were an ancient family that had served the House of Savoy as soldiers and government officials since the 16th century. Genevan by birth and Calvinist by religion, his mother brought into the Cavour family the influence of Geneva, a city open to all the political, religious, and social movements of the period.

Alinari—Anderson

Cavour, oil painting by Francesco Hayez (1791–1882). In the Pinacoteca de Brera, Milan.

Years of growth. The French Revolution imperilled the fortunes of the Cavours because of their close ties with the *ancien régime;* but the energy of the marchese Michele re-established the family in an eminent position in Napoleonic society. Camillo even had as godparents Prince Camillo Borghese—after whom he was named—and Pauline Bonaparte, the Prince's wife and the favourite sister of Napoleon.

The restoration of the House of Savoy in Piedmont-Sardinia caused yet another crisis for the Cavour family, which had compromised itself by its prominent association with the Napoleonic regime: but the marchese Michele succeeded in establishing a lasting friendship with the future king of Piedmont-Sardinia, the hereditary prince Charles Albert of Carignano, when the prince was suspected and deserted by both legitimists and liberals as a result of his equivocal participation in the constitutionalist military coup of 1821. Thus, his father was able to enroll the lively and domineering Camillo at the age of ten at the Military Academy of Turin. As the younger son who could not hope for the economic and social position that would fall to his elder brother, Camillo saw a brilliant career open up before him under the protection of the court. Yet Camillo had to endure the academy's harsh discipline, inspired by 18th-century regulations, from 1820 to 1826, when he obtained a commission as lieutenant in the corps of engineers.

Education

During those six years that, forever after, he remembered as the worst period of his life, his liveliness and youthful intolerance, always disconcerting to those close to him, increased. His acts of open insubordination made life difficult for him and for his superiors, who—from the commanding officer of the academy down—were bound by ties of friendship to his family. The rigours of military discipline strengthened rather than weakened his pride and the consciousness of his own superiority, as well as the ambition to assert this superiority. He soon distinguished himself in mathematics and history, while making little progress in Latin and literary subjects in general. In those years, political ideas began to fascinate him; echoes of the constitutionalist Piedmontese revolution of 1821 reached the academy, provoking in some of its members a flash of liberal and national spirit that was, however, immediately extinguished. Among his family, Camillo heard the great issues of the day being discussed: the internal politics of France under the restored Bourbons; the revolt against Turkish repression in Greece; the liberal Decembrist rising in Russia in 1825. He showed his sympathy, in his usual enthusiastic manner, with the liberals and with personalities such as Benjamin Franklin and Santorre di Santarosa, the famous ill-fated leader of the 1821 revolution in Piedmont, who was also a distant relative. One close friendship at the academy seems to have had a particular influence on his political views. The cadet Baron Severino Cassio, three years older than Camillo, was the first purely Italian person to whom he attached himself with real affection. Until that time all his affections had centred on his parents and relatives, who constituted a privileged cosmopolitan group that by then was completely committed to the ideas of the restoration.

Friendship with Severino Cassio

Severino Cassio, suspected of republicanism, imbued Camillo with patriotic ideas. Later, on leaving the academy, Cassio was also suspected of Socialism. The Cavour family, greatly disturbed by their son's association with a cadet holding such compromising political views, ordered Camillo to terminate it—not without provoking his indignation and bitterness. This interference of the family was dictated by expediency, for in July 1824 the marchese Michele had obtained for Camillo the appointment as personal page to Charles Albert. The fees for the academy would henceforth be paid by the court, but, above all, the appointment held the promise of a splendid future for the new page of the king-to-be. The person who showed least enthusiasm was Camillo himself, who publicly displayed his resentment at having to wear the red page-boy's uniform—he called it a "livery"—fit for court lackeys. This demonstration caused a scandal and confirmed the growing suspicions about the rebellious disposition of the young count Cavour. An even greater scandal, however, took place when Camillo, after obtaining his commission, appeared publicly for the last time as a page and expressed his satisfaction at "finally doffing that lobster's livery." The phrase referred to Charles Albert, who banished Camillo from court and—vainly—tried to persuade King Charles Felix to strip Camillo of his commission. The episode created an irreparable break between Camillo and the hereditary prince and for about 20 years made it impossible for Cavour to take any part in official political life.

Military career and foreign travel. His military career began in the engineers. He was first stationed in Turin, then in various frontier posts, where fortifications were being constructed; yet, wherever he was, Cavour remained dissatisfied. He tried to find compensation in gambling and in philandering; in fact, he never gave up these distractions until his death. In 1830 he was sent to Genoa, where he met Anna Giustiniani Schiaffino. Three years older than he, a beautiful and passionate woman, she espoused ultrademocratic and republican ideas, and her salon was frequented by many members of the Carbonari, the secret revolutionary society whose guiding force then was Giuseppe Mazzini, who was to become the key figure in the risorgimento, the movement for the unification of Italy. Cavour and Mazzini may well have met at that time. Cavour's fervent radicalism was inspired by his love for Anna Schiaffino and by his renewed friendship with Severino Cassio, now a fellow officer in the engineers at Genoa.

Early radicalism

The French revolution of July 1830, which overthrew the last Bourbon, Charles X, and installed Louis-Philippe, "the citizen king," also played a great part in strengthening Cavour's revolutionary ardour. Under the direction of Severino Cassio, he studied English in order to follow more easily the newspapers reporting political events in Europe. On hearing of the fall of Charles X, he was unable to restrain his enthusiasm—going so far as to cry "Long live the Republic!" in the officers' quarters. Cavour's state of exaltation did not, however, endure for long. His affection for Anna Giustiniani waned quickly, causing the suicide of the sensitive woman, and his republican ideas were for a time relegated to a place among his cherished memories of a youthful enthusiasm. Yet he had already made his choice in those years—the choice of liberty and progress as opposed to obscurantism, the choice of reason and civilization as opposed to ignorance. Influenced by the liberal ideas of the French writers Benjamin Constant and François Guizot, Cavour's adversaries remained those of his childhood: paternalistic absolutism; legitimist reactionaries representing the landed interests, the aristocracy, and the clergy; and the union of throne and altar. Of necessity this attitude pitted him consciously against the caste to which he belonged.

The influence of the events in France on the temperamental Cavour once again aroused official suspicions, and this time he was subjected to police surveillance. As usual, his father's intervention helped to avert more serious consequences; in this case he was simply transferred to a remote mountain fort. It had become obvious, however, that he could no longer remain in the army. When the threat of war caused by the revolutionary upheavals of 1830–31 in Italy and elsewhere had passed, he handed in his resignation, in November 1831. He went to live in his father's palace at Turin, though still opposing, often violently, the political views of his family, with whom he was forced to live. His father found him a sort of occupation: he was appointed mayor of a village south of Turin and also became the administrator of extensive holdings in the vicinity belonging to his uncles.

Although these modest occupations served to fill his time and to insulate him from his family, they aggravated his despondency by demonstrating the contrast between what he considered his true worth and the conditions to which he had been reduced. Only a few years before, he had believed that one day he could be prime minister of the kingdom of Italy. His condition embittered him, often plunged him into despair, and, impulsive and excitable as he was, brought him to the brink of suicide. Only his amorous intrigues succeeded to some extent in providing a distraction, although nothing equalled his overwhelming political passion. Frequent visits to the French Embassy at Turin—where two young diplomats soon became good friends of his—allowed him to satisfy his thirst for news and discussions about the liberal regime in the France of Louis-Philippe, for it was now his desperate hope that Piedmont might be blessed with a similar government. Social interests began to absorb him: the problems of poverty and of prisoner education became the subjects of his researches. In 1834 he wrote a memoir on poverty in Piedmont, which was published the following year in London in the *Report from His Majesty's Commissioners for inquiring into the Administration and practical Operation of the Poor Laws.* A second pamphlet on the history of the Poor Laws in England was edited and published by Cavour in 1835 at Turin.

Writings

During those years he was at last able to make his first long-awaited visit to Paris and London, thus widening his knowledge of Europe. In addition to his frequent visits to his relatives in Geneva and his correspondence with them as well as with others of his cosmopolitan acquaintances, he now came to know the two greatest and most advanced Western capitals—both ruled by constitutional and liberal regimes (however much they differed in character) and both attempting to effect the boldest economic and social changes. His journey was an exhausting combination of study and worldly pleasure, though even on social occasions he managed to study political and social problems. In the salons he met the most important personalities of the epoch and talked with them about these problems. He personally knew, or listened to the speeches of such French statesmen as Guizot, the duc de Broglie; and Adolphe Thiers; the English statesmen Sir Robert Peel and Lord John Russell; the English chemist Michael Faraday; and the French historian Alexis de Tocqueville. He took a feverishly active interest in the parliamentary life of England and France; he attended university lectures and visited factories, railways, ports, hospitals, schools, and prisons. The experience he acquired in the two Western capitals and in Geneva set him firmly on the path he had already instinctively chosen: always to follow the "golden mean." He was repelled equally by the revolutionaries who wished to destroy society through terror in order to construct a better one without realizing that their methods would defile human dignity, and by the reactionaries, who, in blindly opposing all progress, eventually provoked revolutionary uprisings. Rejecting all extremes, he wanted above all to be a good European. Yet Cavour always remained a patriot. When his worth and his great ambition were acknowledged in France and one of his friends invited him to abandon the small, petty, and wretched Piedmont of Charles Albert for a brilliant career in France, Cavour rejected the invitation.

Revolution and reform, 1848–49. In 1835, after his return from his travels, he began to engage in a fruitful series of enterprises that helped him to become a leading agriculturalist, an expert financier, and a dynamic industrialist. He chose activities that would not attract the attention of the police but would at the same time satisfy his longing for action and profit. Starting as a lowly cadet with few resources, he was to accumulate, before beginning his career as minister and then prime minister, a considerable fortune; but this fortune was in fact to decrease rather than increase during the ten years in which he occupied the most important posts in his country. He also achieved a certain reputation with his writing. Even without directly facing the question of Italy's future political structure, all his writings proclaimed social or economic principles that could in no way be reconciled with the prevailing conditions in Italy. Above all, the economic measures and the construction of railroads proposed by Cavour would have transformed the Italy of that period beyond recognition.

Financier and industrialist

Gradually, as the year 1848 drew near and the first gusts of the great revolutionary storm of that year could be felt, Cavour's interest in politics began once more to dominate all others. This is shown by the chronological sequence of his writings. His transition to politics was completed when King Charles Albert decided to embark on measures of reform and to concede a certain amount of freedom to the press. Cavour took advantage of this to found the newspaper *Il Risorgimento*, which soon became the champion of increasingly drastic reforms and eventually also of the constitution that Cavour insisted must be the pillar supporting every type of reform.

Cavour now entered the final and culminating phase of his life. From 1848 to 1861, the year of his death, he made himself a part of political events in Piedmont, Italy, and Europe—often aiming to divert these events imperceptibly from their natural course toward ends he felt were better, sometimes being violently dragged into their vortex and almost overwhelmed by them, but finally dominating them by means of his accomplished political and diplomatic talents.

His life was now inextricably involved with one of the most glorious chapters in the history of Europe, a period that witnessed, through a series of continual crises and wars, both the birth of Italy as a new nation, free and independent, and the emergence of prospects for the liberation and creation of other nations. After taking a leading part in persuading Charles Albert to grant a liberal constitution, Cavour used *Il Risorgimento* to propagate the idea of an immediate war with Austria (which still ruled Lombardy and Venetia) as a historical necessity. Once elected a member of Parliament in June 1848, however, he assumed an intermediate position between the conservatives and the revolutionaries, thus calling forth the enmity of both left and right.

Internal and foreign policy, 1850–58. The war against Austria was undertaken, but developments went against the Piedmontese. This prompted Cavour to offer his services as a volunteer until, on being elected a deputy in the third Legislature (July 1848), he began to fight for the approval of a peace treaty with Austria, although the extremists of the left wanted to continue a war that was, in effect, already lost. The intelligence and expertise he displayed in the debates on financial and military questions gained him a prominent place among the deputies of the majority that supported the right-wing government of Massimo d'Azeglio. In October 1850, he was offered the post of minister of agriculture and soon became the most active and influential member of the Cabinet. His advancement was helped by the fact that d'Azeglio, a man of artistic and literary rather than political bent, was glad to leave everything to Cavour, who was not only an expert in political and administrative problems but tackled them with enthusiasm despite their apparent tediousness. Through a series of treaties with France, Belgium, and England, Cavour attempted to bring about the greatest possible amount of free trade. He also sought to form a network of economic interests with the great powers to pave the way for a political alliance against Austria. His appointment as minister of finance in 1850 was evidence of his growing ambitions. His politics seemed too daring and liberal to the extreme conservatives of his own party, who began to oppose him, and he was compelled to assume leadership of the moderates. The latter favoured cautious reforms and found support among the opposition deputies of the centre left.

Minister of finance

Cavour now sought to create an alliance between the centre right and the centre left that would form a new majority with greater ability to move toward a policy of secularization and modernization in Piedmont. The alliance, called the *connubio* ("marriage"), brought about the resignation of d'Azeglio, whose parliamentary standing had been completely destroyed. After vain attempts to restore an effective d'Azeglio ministry, Victor Emanuel II, who had succeeded his father Charles Albert in 1849, resigned himself to entrusting the formation of a government to Cavour, who from that time (November 4, 1852) until his death was his country's acknowledged political leader. Piedmont's swift political, financial, economic, and military progress made it a model for the Italian states and provided a foretaste of what all of Italy could become if it were liberated from Austrian domination and from inept local governments.

The European drama into which Cavour was drawn against his will began in 1854 with the Crimean War (1853–56), which saw France and England allied against Russia in order to defend the integrity of the Turkish territory threatened by Russia's determination to open the Dardanelles for passage from the Black Sea to the Mediterranean. Since the English and French had no common frontiers with Russia, they had to fight an expensive war with little possibility of rapid success in the far-distant Crimea unless they could induce Austria to join them. Urged by the allies to enter the war on their side, the Austrian emperor refused because the Piedmontese threat forced him to keep his troops in the Po Valley. London and Paris thereupon put pressure on Turin to join them against Russia in order to invalidate Vienna's pretext for preserving its neutrality. Victor Emanuel immediately pledged his help to the French and English representatives. Cavour, whose ministers voted against the Crimean venture, was on the point of being dismissed by the King if he rejected the alliance or of being forced to resign by his colleagues if he accepted it. Accepting the alliance with customary boldness and self-confidence, he averted dismissal by the King and embarked upon war. The turning point of the war came with the Anglo-French-Sardinian victory that persuaded Austria to cast aside its neutrality and, by means of an ultimatum, force Russia to make peace.

With some difficulty, Cavour secured the participation of the small power of Piedmont in the peace negotiations at the Congress of Paris (1856), at which the greatest European powers were represented. Fully aware that these negotiations were not likely to yield any gains for Piedmont that would justify the Crimean adventure in Italian eyes, he tried to send Massimo d'Azeglio to Paris as his country's representative. When d'Azeglio refused, Cavour was forced to assume the responsibility for what was regarded as an inevitable diplomatic failure. But his special abilities focussed European attention on his performance at the congress. By supporting Napoleon III's undeclared yet obvious intention to intervene militarily in Italy in the near future and by taking advantage of the general animosity toward Austria, which had joined the allies in the Crimean War only when victory over Russia was assured, Cavour succeeded in proposing the discussion of the Italian problem on the grounds that it was one that threatened European peace. In his view, peace was threatened by Austrian enchroachment, papal misgovernment in Central Italy, and the autocratic rule of the Spanish Bourbons in southern Italy. Thus, for the first time, the Italian question was presented for diplomatic consideration in a manner favouring the liberation of the peninsula. The difficulty was to persuade the two great powers, France and England, to persevere in their support of an anti-Austrian policy on the part of Piedmont. England, however, was not prepared to weaken Austria, which was needed to maintain a political balance against both France and Russia. In France, too, a strong faction consisting of many influential personages of the Second Empire—including the Empress herself—desired a policy of peace with Austria and with the pope, in order to strengthen the new dynasty.

Congress of Paris

In Paris, Cavour had occasion to meet and appraise the stature of Europe's most capable diplomats and to examine the reasons behind the policies of the great powers. He knew full well that it was illusory to hope for the disinterested assistance of Europe in the Italian cause; nevertheless, with his tireless energy and unlimited capacity to take advantage of the most adverse situations, he finally succeeded in winning Napoleon III over to his side. His trump card was the proposition to re-establish France as the leading power on the Continent by an expedition into Italy that would replace Austrian domination of the Peninsula with French rule. Cavour knew that times were changing and that once the flame of national feeling was kindled in Italy, it would no longer be possible to extinguish it. He received unexpected help from the Italian Republicans by their attempt, led by Felice Orsini, on the lives of Napoleon III and the empress Eugenie, a plot which almost succeeded. The attempted assassinations seemed to confirm what Cavour had maintained for a long time—that Italy was a powder magazine, which, if suitable precautions were not taken, would cause a major explosion throughout the Continent.

Meeting with Napoleon III at Plombières

The war of 1859. At a secret meeting at Plombières in July 1858, Napoleon III and Cavour agreed to provoke a European war against Austria in the following year. At the first suspicions of a secret agreement, the European powers—especially England—began a campaign to prevent the French and Piedmontese from carrying out their intentions, a campaign so intense that Cavour saw himself being dragged toward the brink of personal and national catastrophe. In vain he had persuaded a reluctant Victor Emmanuel II to permit the marriage of his young daughter Maria Clotilde of Savoy to Napoleon's middle-aged cousin Prince Jérôme. In vain he had accepted, between January and April 1859, all of Napoleon's conditions—even the most humiliating ones—in order not to appear as the aggressor against Austria but as the injured party, thus providing the *casus bellis* that Napoleon III required to persuade France to accept the war and Europe to remain neutral. All these efforts seemed to have been wasted when an order from Paris commanded Cavour in April to demobilize the troops and dismiss the volunteers. According to several historians and biographers, he was on the point of committing suicide. He was saved by an incredible blunder on the part of Austria, which sent an ultimatum threatening war unless Piedmont disarmed at once. The Franco-Piedmontese alliance accordingly came into force, and this time, Austria's superior military power was counterbalanced by the French contribution. Franco-Piedmontese victories followed one after another until Napoleon signed an armistice with Emperor Francis Joseph I at Villafranca in July 1859.

The war had unleashed revolutionary movements in Tuscany, in the duchies of Modena and Parma, and in the papal states between the Po and the Apennines, from Bologna to Cattolica; the ducal rulers had been expelled, as had the papal legates. The armistice seemed to call everything into question, except for Victor Emmanuel's acquisition of Lombardy, which was a minimal gain compared with Cavour's dreams of liberating Italy from the Alps to the Adriatic. At Villafranca, Cavour vented his rage and frustration on the King and resigned his office. Victor Emmanuel, who for some time had found it difficult to tolerate his prime minister, accepted his resignation.

Cavour's character had always shown a strongly contradictory combination of two elements: a calculating logic, capable of rapidly absorbing and evaluating the complexities of political reality, and an extreme, almost irrational, irrascibility (which at Villafranca endangered the results of the most sophisticated political reasoning). Contrary to his usual perception, he realized only later the advantages to be derived from the armistice. The revolutionary landslide in Italy could no longer be checked, nor could the French emperor withdraw from his position as protector of Italian self-determination. After being returned to power by the reluctant King in January 1860, Cavour worked for the annexation of the central duchies that had formerly belonged to the ancient rulers of Piedmont; he was able to do this only by ceding Savoy and Nice to France. This action, while alarming England, tied the hands of Napoleon, who henceforward had to accept the fact that, as an accomplice, he could oppose Turin's policy of annexation only within certain limits.

Return to power

Unification of Italy. The surrender of Nice to France vastly sharpened the conflict between Cavour and Giuseppe Garibaldi, for Nice was the popular hero's birthplace. The surrender of Piedmont's Alpine bulwark could be compensated for only by territorial expansion into Central Italy (at the pope's expense) and into the Kingdom of the Two Sicilies. But Cavour, by now the black sheep of European diplomacy for having disturbed its tranquillity too often, was not in a position to take the initiative, even though England now favoured his policy.

It was Garibaldi who resolved the stalemate caused by Cavour's enforced inactivity. Sailing with his famous Thousand to Sicily, he destroyed Bourbon rule there and in the south. The daring diplomacy of Piedmont and Cavour seemed momentarily to be eclipsed by the military exploits of the red-shirted hero, but more important, there now appeared the first outlines of rivalry between a moderate, monarchist Italy and a revolutionary, republican Italy. The danger of a rupture was averted by the good sense and magnanimity of Garibaldi and by a diplomatic strategem of Cavour. Cavour, taking up his stance before Europe as the defender of law and order against revolutionary excesses, and before Napoleon as the defender of the last strip of papal territory against attack by Garibaldi, sent an army under Victor Emmanuel across Marche and Umbria in order to check the "hero of the two worlds" and to weld the two Italies into one united kingdom.

There still remained the problem of establishing a capital. Turin had to be ruled out because of its location at the extreme northwest corner of the country. Cavour felt that only Rome could be the capital of the new state; but that meant he had to face the most complex problem of his life—that of the position to be assigned to the pope, the head of Catholicism, once Rome had become the capital of Italy.

He turned once more to the political and religious convictions that had developed since his youth through the lively discussions held in Geneva with his relatives and through his meetings with brilliant minds in Paris and London. Cavour wholeheartedly accepted the concept of the separation of church and state, according to the ideas formulated above all in Geneva. In his negotiations with the papacy he became a passionate supporter of the idea. He maintained that the liberty of the church was to be the fulcrum of the renewal of the world, even though this involved the renunciation of its temporal power and the surrender of Rome to the Italian nation. An entirely spiritual church and papacy, he asserted, would revive mankind. Pius IX's answer to these proposals was negative; but while Cavour was still vigorously promoting his formula of "a free church in a free state," he fell seriously ill and died on June 6, 1861, after having formed a nation in ten years of impassioned and restless activity.

BIBLIOGRAPHY. P. MATTER, *Cavour et l'unité italienne*, 3 vol. (1922–27), is the most complete biography in existence today. A.J. WHITE, *The Early Life and Letters of Cavour, 1810–1848* (1925) and *The Political Life and Letters of Cavour, 1848–1861* (1930), are the best documented works available in English. W. ROSCOE THAYER, *The Life and Times of Cavour*, 2 vol. (1911), with a full bibliography, is at times somewhat sketchy. H. VON TREITSCHKE, *Cavour* (1869, reprinted 1939), depicts Cavour as an exponent of *Realpolitik*. R. ROMEO, *Cavour e il suo tempo*, vol. 1 (1969), promises, when completed, to be the definitive work on Cavour. DENIS MACK SMITH, *Cavour and Garibaldi, 1860: A Study in Political Conflict* (1954), is strongly adverse to Cavour.

(U.M.)

Cayley, Arthur

Arthur Cayley ranks high among 19th-century mathematicians for his analytical power and the originality of the concepts he pioneered. He played a great part in founding the modern British school of pure mathematics.

Cayley was born at Richmond, in Surrey, on August 16, 1821, during a periodic visit of his talented merchant family to England from Russia, where his father was engaged in trade. Cayley's remarkable mathematical ability became apparent by his skill as a child in doing complex calculations for amusement. On the advice of school authorities, his father, who had by then settled in England, enrolled him in May 1839 at Trinity College, University of Cambridge, where he mastered several languages—Greek, French, German, and Italian—and distinguished himself in mathematics.

By courtesy of The Master and Fellows of Trinity College, Cambridge, England

Cayley, oil painting by W.H. Longmaid, 1884. In the collection of Trinity College, University of Cambridge, England.

Following his graduation in 1842, he obtained a three-year appointment at Trinity, which allowed him to begin work on the problems in mathematics that occupied his attention for the next 50 years. During this extremely productive period, he also began a lifelong interest in mountaineering, painting, and travel. Because no positions in mathematics were open to him when his term ended in 1845, he entered Lincoln's Inn, London, to prepare for a legal career. Admitted to the bar in 1849, Cayley earned just enough by practicing law during the next 14 years to allow him to pursue his real interest in mathematics. During this time, Cayley wrote his brilliant mathematical papers. In 1850 he met James Joseph Sylvester, a fellow lawyer and mathematician; and the two henceforth spent much time in enthusiastic collaboration.

Cayley's work treated nearly every subject of pure mathematics. The concept that the order of points formed by intersecting lines is always invariant, regardless of spatial transformations, is an application of the theory of algebraic invariance, which he originated and developed with encouragement from Sylvester. This concept is of importance in working out space–time relationships in physics. Cayley's development of *n*-dimensional geometry is also significant in conceptualizing four dimensions (space–time) in relativity and in going beyond the dependence on points and lines as elements by which geometric space is constructed. Cayley also developed the algebra of matrices, which are arrays of numbers in rows and columns, in which the order and direction of multiplication determines the quantitative result. This tool was used by the German physicist Werner Heisenberg in 1925 for his work in quantum mechanics. Cayley also prepared the way for the idea that Euclidean and non-Euclidean geometries are special cases of the same kind of geometry. He did this by devising a means of uniting projective geometry, which is dependent on invariant properties of figures, and metrical geometry, which is dependent on sizes of angles and lengths of lines. He also prepared two British Association for the Advancement of Science reports (1857, 1862) on theoretical dynamics and on the Moon's mean motion.

Development of *n*-dimensional geometry

Cayley practiced law until 1863, when he was elected to the new Sadlerian chair of pure mathematics at Cambridge. He married Susan Moline the same year. From the time of his arrival at Cambridge until his death he constantly engaged in mathematical investigation. He was also influential in assisting women to be admitted as students for the first time. His lectures at Cambridge attracted very few students; among them, however, was A.R. Forsyth, who succeeded him in the Sadlerian chair, and who, by introducing the new theory of functions that had been making progress in France and Germany, helped to bring English mathematics back into the mainstream of European trends.

In 1881–82 Cayley lectured at Johns Hopkins University in Baltimore on Abelian functions—a means of combining numbers such that the result of mathematical treatment is independent of the order. At Johns Hopkins he again met his friend Sylvester, who had become professor there in 1876. Cayley's more than 900 mathematical notes and papers were published in Cambridge in 1889–98 in 14 volumes of his *The Collected Mathematical Papers*.

Honours

Cayley was the recipient of nearly every academic distinction that can be conferred upon an eminent man of science: honorary degrees from Oxford, Dublin, Edinburgh, Göttingen, Heidelberg, Leiden, and Bologna; and election as fellow or foreign corresponding member of the French National Institute, and of the academies in Berlin, Göttingen, St. Petersburg, Milan, Rome, Leiden, Uppsala, and Budapest; and recipient of the Copley Medal in 1883 from the Royal Society of London. At various times he was president of the Cambridge Philosophical Society, of the London Mathematical Society, and of the Royal Astronomical Society.

He died at Cambridge on January 26, 1895.

BIBLIOGRAPHY. The basic biography is by A.R. FORSYTH in the *Proc. R. Soc.*, 58:1–43 (1895), and is reprinted, with slight changes, in vol. 8 of *The Collected Mathematical Papers of Arthur Cayley*, 13 vol. (1889–97). For other biographical studies, see GANESH PRASAD, *Some Great Mathematicians of the Nineteenth Century*, vol. 2, ch. 1 (1934); ALEXANDER MACFARLANE, *Lectures on Ten British Mathematicians of the Nineteenth Century*, pp. 64–77 (1916); and E.T. BELL, *Men of Mathematics* (1937, reprinted 1961).

Ceará

Ceará, a primarily agricultural state (*estado*) in northeastern Brazil, is bounded on the north by the Atlantic Ocean, on the east by the Atlantic and the states of Rio Grande do Norte and Paraíba, on the south by the state of Pernambuco, and on the west by the state of Piauí. It covers an area of 57,149 square miles (148,016 square kilometres), and its population in the early 1970s was nearly 4,500,000—about 40 percent of it urban. The capital, Fortaleza, is the principal cultural, commercial, and seaboard shipping centre, with a population of over 520,000. Other principal towns are Juazeiro do Norte, Sobral, Crato, Iguatu, and Crateus. The seaboard, the mountains and mesas, and the backlands are the main regional settings of the state. Each has a population reflecting different ways of life: the *jangadeiro*, or raftsman, living near the seashore and engaged in fishing; the *vaqueiro*, or cowboy, employed on the farms and ranches; and the *morador*, or subsistence farmer, along the littoral and upcountry.

Physical features

The state lies partly upon the northeast slope of the great Brazilian Highlands and partly upon the sandy coastal plain. Its surface is a succession of great terraces, facing north and northeast, formed by the erosion of an ancient sandstone plateau; the terraces are seamed by watercourses, and their valleys are broken by hills and ranges of highlands. The sandy coastal plain is nearly bare of vegetation; behind it is an elevated region with sandy soil that is amenable to cultivation and produces fruit, cotton, and many tropical products. The soil of the backlands is thin and porous.

The long dry season turns this part of the country into a barren wasteland, or *sertão*, relieved by vegetation only along riverbanks and on mountains; spiny, stunted groves of *caatinga*, or scrub forest, the trees of which lose all their leaves in the dry season and turn gray, are typical.

Ceará is semi-arid, precipitation ranging from 63 inches (1,600 millimetres) on the seaboard and in the mountains to 16 inches (406 millimetres) in the backlands; regardless of the amount, it is almost wholly concentrated in the three months of March, April, and May, so that there is a long dry period during which all rivers and streams eventually become dry beds. Although in some years the rains may fall torrentially for days on end, occasionally they may fail altogether. Severe droughts cause famine and pestilence, economic disruption, and migrations of rural peoples; a drought and accompanying plague in 1877 took 57,000 lives. Average temperatures year-round range from 79° to 82° F (26° to 28° C) but may peak to 86° or 90° F (30° or 32° C) in the backlands during the dry season, thus aggravating the aridity. The problem of drought, however, is only partly a result of the workings of nature. Man himself, by stripping away the cover of natural vegetation and subjecting the land to intensive and careless use, has destroyed much of the soil's capacity to retain moisture.

Economy

Like other states of the Northeast, Ceará was settled as a "captaincy," or fiefdom, of the Portuguese crown, its economy in the 18th century centring on sugar plantations worked by Negro slaves. Slavery, indeed, persisted in Brazil until the late 19th century; Ceará in 1884 became the first state to free all its slaves. As early as the 18th century cattle were introduced to the *sertões*, and in the 19th century long-staple cotton was planted and thrived. Today Ceará is the third largest producer of cotton in Brazil (after São Paulo and Paraná), with about 350,000 tons annually. With more than 2,000,000 head of cattle, it has the third largest herd in the Northeast (after Bahia and Maranhão). Sugarcane, though now less important, is still grown, largely for manufacturing brown sugar and spirits; other commercial crops include cashew nuts, cassava, carnauba wax, oiticica oil, fruits, and vegetables. Cotton and other commercial crops and cattle are grown on the great estates, which include sharecroppers, whereas the large population of smallholders are restricted to the hard life of subsistence farming. Generally, the possibilities of improving agriculture and the lives of farmers are limited by climatic conditions, lack of capital, and antiquated technology.

Though the federal government has fostered the building of numerous dams, there has been no comparable development of irrigation networks. Rural life remains primitive.

There are indications of mineral resources in the state, but prospecting and research have not proceeded far enough to establish their economic potential. Gypsum and limestone are being produced, however, and the possibilities for future production of iron, copper, manganese, and graphite seem encouraging.

The cities of Ceará have developed as centres for collecting, processing, and marketing the regional products, particularly cotton. Trade has been accompanied by inchoate industrial activity, involving the production of textiles, food, chemicals, and pharmaceuticals. Fortaleza is not only the commercial and metropolitan centre of the state but also the seat of its administrative life, with the governor and the state assembly at its head. The capital city is also the site of the Federal University of Ceará.

BIBLIOGRAPHY. FORTALEZA, BRAZIL, UNIVERSIDADE DO CEARA, INSTITUTO DE PESQUISAS ECONOMICAS, *Diagnóstico Sócio-Econômico do Ceará*, 2 vol. (1964), an important document on the state (in Portuguese) that covers physiographic aspects and the demographic, economic, and social evolution; AMELIA A. NOGUEIRA MOREIRA, *Nordeste Brasileiro e Tentativas de Desenvolvimento* (1969), a study of development plans for Northeast Brazil, written in Portuguese but with an abstract in English.

(A.A.N.M.)

Cecil, William, Lord Burghley

William Cecil, Lord Burghley, has enjoyed fame as a great Elizabethan statesman and a master of Renaissance statecraft. Elizabeth I's trust in him made his a persistent if not always decisive voice in her counsels for nearly 40 years. His talents as a diplomat, politician, and administrator won him high office and a peerage.

By courtesy of the National Portrait Gallery, London

Cecil, oil painting on panel attributed to M. Gheeraerts. In the National Portrait Gallery, London.

Early life. William was born on September 13, 1520, at Bourne, Lincolnshire. His grandfather David left the Welsh border to follow Henry Tudor to victory at Bosworth in 1485. His rewards established him at Stamford, and by service to the Tudors and marriage to local heiresses David and his son, Richard, acquired wealth, office, and the status of gentry. Richard educated his only son, William, at schools in Grantham and Stamford. In childhood William served as a page of the robes at court, where his father was a groom of the wardrobe. In 1535 he entered St. John's College, Cambridge, where he studied classics under the versatile Humanist John Cheke and came under Protestant influence. At the age of 20 he fell in love with Cheke's sister, Mary; family disapproval of his unambitious attachment may have precipitated William's move in 1541 to Gray's Inn, London, to study law. William married Mary later in 1541; but she died in 1543, leaving him a son, Thomas.

In 1542, for defending royal policy, William was rewarded by Henry VIII with a place in the Court of Common Pleas. A year later he first entered Parliament. Through his second marriage, to the learned and pious Mildred Cooke in 1545, he joined an influential Protestant circle at court; it included his father-in-law, Sir Anthony Cooke, his former brother-in-law, John Cheke, the future protector, Edward Seymour (Lord Hertford and duke of Somerset), and the queen consort Catherine Parr, for whom Cecil edited a devotional tract. When Edward VI succeeded, Cecil joined the protector Somerset's household, accompanied him on a Scottish campaign of 1547, and became his master of requests and, in 1548, his secretary. On Somerset's first fall from power, in 1549, Cecil was briefly imprisoned in the Tower of London. By acting as go-between for Somerset and his rival, John Dudley, earl of Warwick, Cecil regained favour and became in 1550 a councillor and one of the two secretaries to the king, alongside William Petre. After Somerset's final fall, in 1551, Cecil was knighted by the victorious Warwick, who assumed the dukedom of Northumberland. Cecil was committed to Northumberland; but, when the Duke proposed to alter the succession, Cecil, though fearing for his life and contemplating flight, sided with the judges in opposition. He capitulated to Northumberland only on royal command. Ever loyal to the Tudors, Cecil deserted Northumberland after Edward VI's death. He approached the triumphant Mary Tudor as representative of the council, winning her approval as "a very honest man."

Influential friends at court

As junior secretary, Cecil had had little scope under Edward VI. He shared neither the social idealism nor the iconoclastic urge of the more extreme reformists at court. He did share in the spoils of a corrupt government; but he established himself as an able bureaucrat, a moderate with a sense of legal propriety, and, like his ally the archbishop of Canterbury Thomas Cranmer, a gradualist in religious reform. Yet, although offered employment on Mary's accession, he, unlike most of his colleagues, withdrew from the Catholic court. His concept of a subject's duty persuaded him to conform outwardly as a Catholic, while remaining inwardly Protestant, to serve in local government, and to undertake two missions, his only visits to the Continent. In Parliament in 1555 he incurred suspicion by defending the property rights of exiles and by entertaining disaffected members; but he was acquitted. He lay low and cultivated Elizabeth Tudor, for whom he had acted as surveyor since 1550.

Career under Elizabeth I. On Elizabeth's accession, in 1558, Cecil was appointed her sole secretary. His first major diplomatic achievement was to persuade a reluctant queen to intervene in Scotland and conclude the Treaty of Edinburgh (1560), which removed French forces from Scotland. His gift for compromise facilitated the church settlement in 1559; his financial sense, the recoinage in 1561. Elizabeth's flirtation with John Dudley's son Robert, however, weakened Cecil's position. Despite threats of resignation and opposition to Robert Dudley, Cecil retained Elizabeth's trust and was rewarded with the lucrative mastership of the Court of Wards in 1561.

Rivalry with Robert Dudley

Decision on the succession was necessary to settle policies. While Cecil intrigued to thwart Dudley, he sympathized with Protestant efforts in Parliament to make Elizabeth marry. He resisted Mary Stuart's claims to succeed but recommended the Habsburg suitor, the archduke Charles. Dudley, capturing the initiative, backed an ill-fated expedition to France to aid the Huguenots, which ended the Treaty of Troyes, became a councillor, and in 1564 became earl of Leicester. On the defensive, Cecil restored the balance by introducing Thomas Howard, 4th duke of Norfolk, into the council. But the consequences of Mary Stuart's marriage to Lord Darnley in 1565 worked to Cecil's disadvantage; Cecil's hopes of drawing England and Scotland together were threatened. While Elizabeth prevaricated with Parliament in 1567 over the succession, Mary Stuart, with an heir, James, was attracting an English following.

Mary Stuart's flight to England in 1568 embarrassed Cecil; although it opened diplomatic opportunities in Scotland, it led to Norfolk's plan to marry the widowed Queen of Scots. Norfolk opposed Cecil over Mary's fate, over secret aid to the Huguenots, and over policy toward Spain. Resenting the threat of the Duke of Alba's Spanish army in the Netherlands, Cecil nearly precipitated war in December 1568 by instigating the seizure of ships carrying bullion to Alba, who retaliated by closing Antwerp to English trade. Leicester joined Norfolk, and they prepared to oust Cecil; but they faltered before the Queen's support for her secretary. A consequence of Norfolk's opposition was an avowedly Catholic rebellion of the northern earls in 1569; but again Cecil survived to punish the rebels.

His challengers defeated, Cecil was created a peer, 1st Baron Burghley, in 1571, and in 1572 he became a knight of the Garter and lord treasurer; he now shared royal favour on equal terms with Leicester. Meanwhile, the papal bull of 1570, deposing Elizabeth, confirmed Cecil in his defense of the Elizabethan church, in which he cooperated with his nominee, Archbishop Matthew Parker. The intrigue called the Ridolfi Plot, a planned Spanish invasion of England to put Mary Stuart on the throne, led to Norfolk's execution in 1572 and discredited Mary Stuart and the pro-Spanish interest. Burghley's rebuff to Spain was underlined by the Treaty of Blois with France in 1572. Neither French influence in the Netherlands nor the St. Bartholomew's Day Massacre (1572) deterred Burghley from the French alliance; but he also soothed Spain, and the embargo on trade with Antwerp was lifted. In Scotland he settled the regency; but he failed to persuade the Scots to try and depose their queen, who remained a focus of Catholic intrigue in her English prison.

In the 1570s Leicester, supported by Francis Walsingham, who became a secretary in 1573, courted Puritan support; agitated for aid to William of Orange, Protestant leader of the rebels in the Netherlands; and favoured negotiations with France. Burghley, restraining the French and trying to avoid open commitment to the rebels, pursued a policy that, in advocating nominal Spanish suzerainty over a Netherlands enjoying its traditional liberties, ignored Philip II's obvious intentions. Failing to gain a settlement in 1576, Burghley finally joined Leicester in urging Elizabeth to act an behalf of Orange. Rather than fight openly, Elizabeth tried to utilize French influence in the Netherlands by marriage negotiations with the Duke of Anjou. Burghley accepted royal policy, but Puritan opposition prevented a definite conclusion to the Anjou affair.

Support of William of Orange

Burghley's moderation in politics and church reform was overtaken by Puritan extremists who, in Parliament and in the church under the patronage of aristocrats such as Leicester, attacked episcopacy, advocated presbyterianism, and urged anti-Catholic measures. Although his hopes for moderate reform collapsed when his chosen archbishop, Edmund Grindal, was made powerless following a quarrel with the Queen, Burghley could not afford to weaken the Puritan militants against aggressive Catholicism. A Jesuit mission and papal intervention in Ireland in 1580 roused Burghley to anti-Catholic action and to alarm over the intentions of Catholic Spain. The assassination of William of Orange in 1584 and the knowledge of a planned French landing at Arundel led Burghley to take measures to protect the Queen's life and to incline toward war against Spain. His hesitation over the costs of war and the peace feelers he extended to Alessandro Farnese, the 3rd duke of Parma, the Spanish commander in the Netherlands, created ill will with Leicester. But by 1585 Burghley supported Leicester's expedition to the Netherlands and Sir Francis Drake's voyage to the Caribbean. In 1586, on Walsingham's revelation of the Babington plot—a plan by Anthony Babington, once page to Mary Stuart, to assassinate Elizabeth

—Burghley pressed to ensure the trial of Mary Stuart and her execution in 1587. His initiative put him in brief disgrace with the diplomatically outraged Elizabeth. Under the growing threat of the Spanish Armada in 1587, Burghley parleyed with Parma, courted Henry of Navarre and James VI of Scotland, and kept a sharp eye on the Irish and English Catholics. His diplomatic, military, naval, and financial preparations proved just adequate in 1588 to defeat the Armada. He exploited victory with propaganda, and his fame as principal councillor of Elizabeth spread through Europe.

After the failure of the Armada, Leicester died (1588), but Burghley survived to preside over the politics of a new generation. He strove to contain the new royal favourite, the Earl of Essex, and to recreate a stable balance of faction. But Essex's desire to dominate drove the Queen to counter him by giving patronage to Burghley. Burghley coached his son Robert, born in 1563, for the secretaryship, which he obtained for him in 1596; Robert had taken over its responsibilities after Walsingham's death in 1590. Despite ill health, Burghley remained active, performing his official duties, writing memorandums, and dealing with suits. But he devised no new policies to check declining prosperity. Instead, he intensified a program of retrenchment and pressed the Commons for grants. His attitude toward Puritans and sectaries hardened after pamphlets, secretly printed and signed by "Martin Marprelate," ridiculed the bishops (1588–90). In foreign affairs he supported campaigns waged against Spain in France and the Netherlands and naval expeditions by Drake and Essex. But finally he urged peace with Spain, fearing a Franco-Spanish settlement and the strain of prolonged war. In the midst of negotiations and still in office, Burghley died in his house in the Strand on August 4, 1598.

Policies during his last years

Assessment. As a statesman Burghley saw that his duty was to give the Queen his best advice and then to carry out whatever policy seemed expedient to her. His loyalty in this task won Elizabeth's confidence. A master of discretion, Burghley as a royal servant assumed an official mask and learned "to walk invisible." His contribution to policy making was his intuitive appreciation of the national interest, which he strove to convey to the Queen. The inspiration of the "common cause" of European Protestantism did not lead him to subordinate insular national interests; he reduced the ideological ends of international Protestantism to the more practical aims of secular patriotism. Preferring diplomacy to war on practical grounds, he exploited informal contacts, rebels, and factions among foreign enemies. In economic affairs he tried to maintain England's security by conventional statecraft. In agriculture and industry he encouraged self-sufficiency; in commerce, those trades that amassed bullion. His pragmatism as an administrator usually overcame any tendency as an intellectual and lawyer to indulge in balanced appreciations and legalistic argument rather than in action.

When there was a threat to England's independence he acted boldly. His Treaty of Edinburgh (1560) closed England's "postern gate" to France and drew Protestant Scotland to England. His opportunist seizure of Alba's treasure broke English dependence on Spain and Antwerp, leading temporarily to greater flexibility in diplomacy and commerce. His removal of Mary Stuart, the Catholic pretender, secured the Protestant succession. His preparations enabled England to survive the Armada. But he failed to induce Elizabeth to marry or to reform her church; and his policy over the Netherlands was unrealistic and in the end led to open conflict with Spain. Often Burghley was frustrated by the equivocations of the Queen, but he came to accept her good fortune as the care of Providence for Protestant England.

Burghley's recommendation was his diligence and competence in handling the administration. No eager innovator, he fought corruption and made the existing system work. His patronage in church and state enabled him to harness the clergy, the gentry, and the nobility to the tasks of administration. His attendance in council and Parliament was constant, and he understood how to manage both. He directed censorship, propaganda, and an intelligence network at home and abroad.

Administrative diligence and competence

As lord treasurer he maintained solvency until the overwhelming war expenditure of the late 1580s. Convinced of the damaging political and constitutional effects of heavy taxation on the Queen's relations with her people and on Parliment, he pursued retrenchment and economy rather than expansion of revenues. Through financial control of the royal household and of the military and naval establishments, he increased their efficiency. In the conciliar and departmental courts he gained a reputation for probity as a judge. His handling of royal finance and justice was scrupulous. His personal fortune derived from the unofficial opportunities for profit that attached to office in the 16th century; but in exploiting fees and gifts Burghley was careful not to go beyond the limits of contemporary public morality. He presided over one of the least oppressive and most efficient administrations in 16th-century Europe.

Elizabeth's determination to rule through faction forced Burghley to protect his interests by maintaining a following. But he was a reluctant faction leader, because his real aim was to find an acceptable official policy and to manipulate the balance of faction rather than to dominate too obviously as an overmighty minister. Despite the impressive portraits of him, Burghley, although he had dignity, was not an imperious or heroic personality. He practiced patience and persistence, argued, and induced. His reputation for wisdom won him respect and influence. His caution, pessimism, awareness of limited national resources, and bureaucratic professionalism brought him into opposition with the optimistic belligerence and courtly amateurism of Leicester and then of Essex. Minimizing personal antagonisms and avoiding violence, Burghley helped to civilize Elizabethan politics and to preserve the domestic peace. Only once, in 1569, did he lose control of the faction balance, but even then he was not isolated from the Queen. His realization of the central position of the monarch in the constitution and in society gave him security and a focus for his sense of the national interest. Responsible to the crown alone, he understood that neither council nor Parliament nor faction provided an alternative basis for legal power.

Loyalty to the crown

For him there could be no divided loyalties even in the name of religion. Burghley did not allow that obedience to a pope or to a Puritan Providence might override allegiance to the sovereign and supreme governor. His patriotism, loyalty to the Tudors, and religious convictions were fused into one by his belief that church and state were but two aspects of one body politic. In his eyes Protestantism was the guarantee of England's independence, which, in its turn, ensured the survival of Protestantism in Europe. He defended the Church of England and upheld its middle way between Catholicism and Calvinism. He could permit only one public practice of religion.

Burghley tolerated variety in private beliefs, provided that it caused no political disturbance. He demanded outward conformity and punished recusants, sectaries, and separatists. His sympathy for the Puritan movement extended to its emphasis upon pious private conduct, evangelical preaching, and antipopery but not to its attack upon established ecclesiastical government. Because the papal bull of 1570 allowed Catholics to withdraw allegiance from the Queen, he treated activist Catholics as political offenders and had such men as the Jesuit Edmund Campion executed for treason.

To Calvinists and Catholics who assumed the separation of church and state, Burghley's unitary concept of church and state appeared as Politique, and his concentration upon the political implications of dissent seemed to be Machiavellian. Burghley answered such charges in *The Execution of Justice in England* (1583). He justified himself in intellectual argument, and his theological learning was respected by theologians.

Burghley was modest about his learning. He was trained in common law and was conversant with Roman law. Expert in Greek and Latin, he possessed a knowledge of French, Italian, and Spanish. His library, rich in manuscripts and maps, reflected his wide acquaintance with Renaissance learning. Among his interests was genealogy, history, topography, and cartography. He was knowledgeable in mathematics and cosmography and about the skills of artisans and men of mechanical trades. If his patronage of music and vernacular drama and poetry was minimal, he did encourage his favoured studies.

As chancellor of the University of Cambridge from 1559, he influenced discipline rather than the curriculum, but he made his household a resort of scholars and an educational centre for the Queen's wards and the young aristocracy. His intellectual interests, like his italic handwriting, were formed in the advanced humanist circle of John Cheke. His artistic eclecticism, developed under Somerset and Northumberland, was revealed in his personal planning for his three houses—Burghley House at Stamford, Cecil House in the Strand, and Theobalds in Hertfordshire; their decoration, furnishings, collections of pictures, coins, and "things of workmanship," and their gardens, supervised by the botanist John Gerard, won universal admiration. Burghley made a creative contribution to the Elizabethan architectural achievement.

Home and family life

Burghley's home life was disciplined by the pious routine of Bible reading and prayer and enlivened by the hospitality that he extended to friends and suitors. He entertained the Queen some dozen times. At his gates was charity for the poor. He was considered a good landlord. Belief in hierarchical society made him study to live like a lord, to cultivate his family tree, and to indulge in the ostentation expected of his rank. But his Puritan conscience made him thrifty in management and frugal in personal living. He did not allow ambition to ruin him. In his conduct was emerging the ideal of a gentleman whose personal virtues of humility, moderation, and moral rectitude were coming to count for as much as the traditional standards of aristocratic behaviour.

In his family life the early deaths of his first wife and of his daughters Anne and Elizabeth, the youthful escapades of his son Thomas, the unhappy marriage of Anne to Edward de Vere, 17th earl of Oxford, and the physical frailty of Robert were Burghley's personal griefs and anxieties. Gout from his youth and deafness in old age were his afflictions. But he enjoyed the adoration of his mother until 1588 and the spiritual support of his accomplished and high-minded second wife, Mildred, until 1589. In moments of relaxation his favoured pastime was reading or learned discourse at table. He loved horses and dogs. He practiced archery, went hunting, and trotted through his gardens on his mule. As a dynast he could rejoice in having married his family among the nobility. Late in life he delighted in his grandchildren—and had the satisfaction of endowing two dynasties—Thomas became earl of Exeter with his seat at Burghley House; Robert was made earl of Salisbury, installed first at Theobalds and then at Hatfield House. Burghley's descendants still reside in the houses once occupied by his sons. Burghley's remains lie in his canopied tomb, probably designed by Cornelius Cure, in St. Martin's Church, Stamford.

Burghley has always been a controversial figure. The hostility of his Catholic victims, foreign ambassadors, disappointed suitors, and rivals started a critical tradition that was perpetuated by Catholic historians. The favourable treatment of Lord Burghley by Protestant historians was begun by Francis Bacon and William Camden. Inevitably, religious partisanship affected Burghley's reputation as a statesman and as a man. The estimates of his responsibility for policy have depended on the roles in government assigned by historians to the Queen and to his colleagues. The assessments of his professional competence have emerged from studies of Elizabethan administration, finance, faction politics, and diplomacy. The lineaments of Burghley's public role and of his characteristics as a man of his time are becoming clearer, but the depths of his individuality remain difficult to probe.

BIBLIOGRAPHY. The main sources for Burghley's life are the Hatfield Manuscripts at Hatfield House, the Lansdowne Manuscripts at the British Museum Library and the State Papers at the Public Record Office. The most useful biography is B.W. BECKINGSALE, *Burghley: Tudor Statesman, 1520–1598* (1967). CONYERS READ, *Mr. Secretary Cecil and Queen Elizabeth* (1955) and *Lord Burghley and Queen Elizabeth* (1960), provide a detailed survey, especially of diplomacy. On Cecil in faction politics to 1572, see W.T. MACCAFFREY, *The Shaping of the Elizabethan Regime* (1968); on Burghley in administration, see J. HURSTFIELD, *The Queen's Wards: Wardship and Marriage Under Elizabeth I* (1958); and A.G.R. SMITH, "The Secretariats of the Cecils, Circa 1580–1612," *English Historical Review*, 83:481–504 (1968). On his parliamentary activities, see J.E. NEALE, *Elizabeth I and Her Parliaments*, 2 vol. (1953–57, reprinted 1966); on his family origins, see A.L. ROWSE, "Alltyrynys and the Cecils," *English Historical Review*, 75:54–76 (1960). On his artistic patronage, see J. SUMMERSON, "The Building of Theobalds, 1564–1585," *Archaeologia*, 97:107–126 (1959); J.A. VAN DORSTEN, "Mr. Secretary Cecil, Patron of Letters," *English Studies*, 50:545–553 (1969); and ROY C. STRONG, *Tudor and Jacobean Portraits* (1969).

(B.W.B.)

Celastrales

The Celastrales is a moderately sized order of flowering plants composed of 12 families containing about 147 genera and 2,000 species. The four major families (Celastraceae, the staff-tree family; Aquifoliaceae, the holly family; Hippocrateaceae, the Hippocratea family; and Icacinaceae, the Icacina family) contain well over 90 percent of the total genera and species. The holly family, the best known in the order, is widely cultivated and economically important as an ornamental.

General features. *Distribution.* The families of the order Celastrales are primarily tropical and subtropical; only the Celastraceae and the Aquifoliaceae occur to any degree in the temperate zones. The larger families have a broad distribution in their climatic range; the smaller have relatively limited ranges.

Size range and diversity of structure. Most members of the order are either trees or shrubs; a few occur as herbs. The family Hippocrateaceae is somewhat unusual within the order in that it is composed primarily of woody vines, but shrubs and slender trees also occur within this family. Members of the family Celastraceae often are characterized by a scandent mode of growth—climbing or twining in other vegetation without the aid of tendrils. *Celastrus scandens*, the American bittersweet, is a familiar native shrub of the northeastern United States that exhibits this mode of growth, often reaching with long whiplike shoots to the tops of tall trees. The family Stackhousiaceae is unique within the order because all of its members are herbs.

Economic importance. The economic importance of this order can be attributed primarily to one genus in the family Aquifoliaceae—the genus *Ilex*, which is composed of species of the well-known holly. The use of the holly plant dates back many centuries. European pagans brought holly sprays into their homes, offering them to the fairy people of the forests as refuges from the harsh winter weather. During the Saturnalia, the Roman winter festival, branches of holly were exchanged as tokens of friendship. The earliest Roman Christians apparently used holly as a decoration at the Christmas season. Despite its past and present association with holy seasons, however, the root of the term holly is *holen* (*holegn*), an old English word meaning holly; holly has no etymological connection with the word holy.

Place of holly plants in history

Holly now is grown commercially for use as Christmas decorations. The red berries and shiny green foliage make it an ideal decoration, and, as it is an evergreen, it possesses excellent lasting qualities. Hollies are also cultivated extensively as ornamentals, and numerous horticultural varieties have been bred. The attributes that give this group such ornamental appeal include hardiness, long life, beauty of form and colour, considerable variation in berry colour (there are red-, black-, and yellow-berried varieties), and variation in leaf form. In addition, hollies can be adapted to a wide range of uses—as accent trees, driveway plantings, hedges, foundation plantings, bonsai, topiary, and even as ground covers.

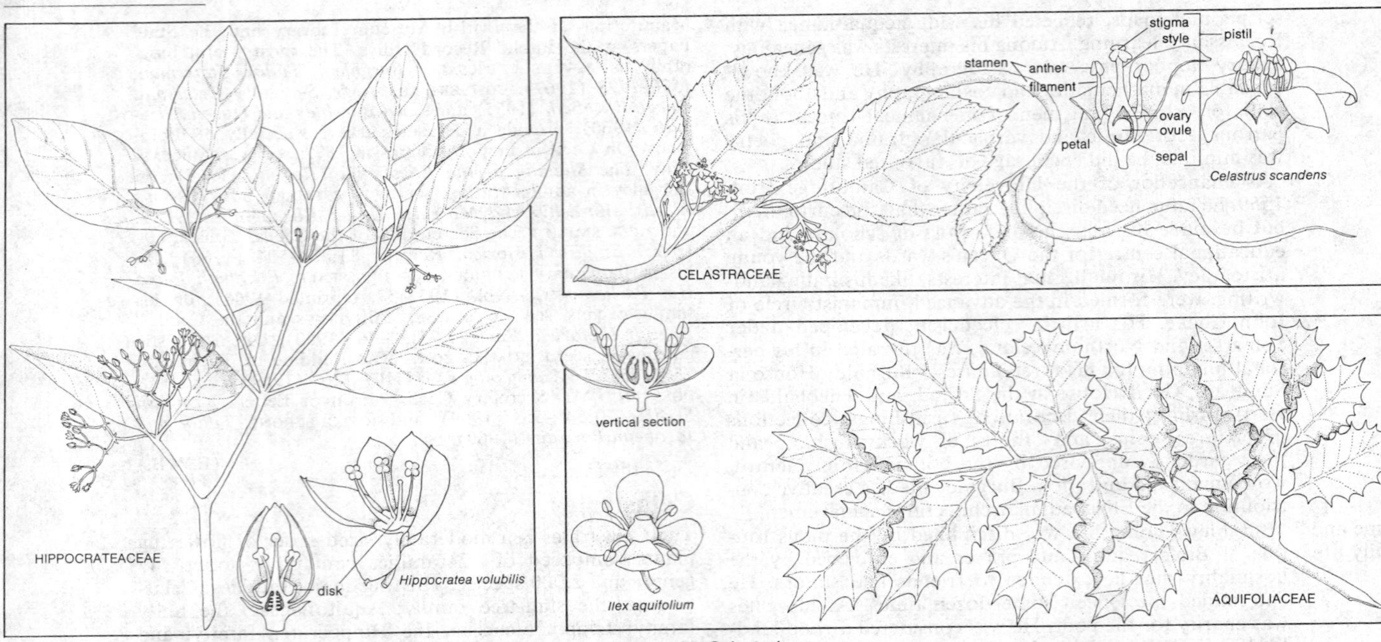

Representative plants from three of the largest families of the order Celastrales.
Drawing by M. Moran

Holly also has other important economic values. It has been used for centuries as a hot drink, in the same manner as tea or coffee. Spanish explorers in 1542 commented on the use of yaupon holly (*Ilex vomitoria*) as a ceremonial and medicinal drink of the coastal Indians of the southeastern United States. In South America, particularly in Brazil, Paraguay, and Argentina, a drink called *yerba maté* enjoys a wide popularity; it is made from a native holly, *Ilex paraguariensis*. The best *yerba maté* is made from wild trees, although they are also cultivated for this purpose. The leaves are dried, ideally first in the sun and then over wood fires, after which they are steeped in hot water as in tea making. The active ingredient is the stimulant caffeine, whose content in the leaves approximates that of tea leaves.

The wood of holly, particularly that of the American holly (*Ilex opaca*), is also of some commercial importance. Small ornamental objects, inlay, and extremely fine furniture are made of its wood. The honey of holly has an extremely delicate flavour.

Although hollies are the commercially dominant group in the order Celastrales, several other plants also have economic value. A few members of the family Icacinaceae are raised domestically as garden ornamentals. In the family Celastraceae, the American and the oriental bittersweet are grown as ornamentals and are noted for their brightly coloured fruits. Several other members of the Celastraceae are also grown as ornamentals; particularly *Euonymus* species. In the Soviet Union two species of this genus, *E. verrucosus* and *E. europaeus*, are cultivated as sources of gutta-percha, a resinous, rubberlike substance that is used principally as an electric insulator and in temporary fillings for teeth.

Natural history. *Specialized reproductive systems.* The order Celastrales does not possess any unique feature that clearly delineates it from other orders; rather, it is classified on the basis of a number of unifying morphological characters. There are, however, within some families in the order, two particularly relevant features. The first is the frequent occurrence of a nectar-producing disk of tissue either to the inside or to the outside of the whorl of stamens (male reproductive structures) in the flower. This disk, which is a reduced whorl of stamens, serves as a means of attracting pollinators, such as bees, to the flower.

Multiple embryos in seeds

The second feature is the presence of polyembryony (more than one embryo in a seed) in some members of the family Celastraceae, especially in the genus *Euonymus* and in *Celastrus scandens* (American bittersweet). The polyembryony is a somatic type—the extra embryos developing from vegetative cells rather than from sex cells—known as adventitious embryony, in which the adventive, or extra, embryo originates from the inner integument, or covering, of the egg-containing body (ovule). A relatively uncommon phenomenon, polyembryony most frequently occurs in species of plants that are native to warm temperate or tropical climates. Further research may well reveal other examples of polyembryony within the order.

Ecology. Beyond a general adaption to tropical and subtropical climates, the order Celastrales possesses no unusual ecological characteristics and no particular adaptations to special habitats or modes of life. A few families within the order, however, have some interesting ecological characteristics. The family Celastraceae often shows a scandent mode of growth, enabling shrubby plants to attain a considerable height by climbing and twining up neighbouring trees. The family Hippocrateaceae often includes woody vines that can also reach considerable heights. Three families exhibit an adaptation to xerophytic (hot and dry, often arid) conditions: the Stackhousiaceae to a limited degree, the Geissolomataceae, and the Salvadoraceae. Species of the family Salvadoraceae are often adapted to very salty coastal regions; such habitats require considerable morphological and physiological modifications for survival.

Form and function. The Celastrales is an order of primarily woody plants, usually shrubs or trees but occasionally vines or herbs. The leaves are consistently simple throughout the order and can be either alternate or opposite in arrangement. The flowers are usually perfect (both sexes in one flower) but are sometimes unisexual. They typically have only one cycle of stamens alternating with the petals and frequently a nectar-producing disk inside or outside the whorl of stamens. Several types of fruits occur within the order, but they all characteristically have only one or two ovules per locule (compartment within the fruit).

Evolution. *Fossil record.* Three families—the Aquifoliaceae, the Celastraceae, and the Icacinaceae—are reasonably well documented in the fossil record. The Wilcox flora of the early part of the Eocene Epoch (38,000,000 to 54,000,000 years ago), found in about 130 localities in the southeastern United States, has many records of the Celastraceae, as does the Paleocene (54,000,000 to 65,000,000 years ago) flora of northeastern France. The London Clay flora, also Eocene, has members of the Icacinaceae, and the Aquifoliaceae and Celastraceae are well recorded in the boreal (northern) flora of the Tertiary (beginning 65,000,000 years ago) and in the excellent amber fossils of the late Eocene Baltic flora.

The genus *Celastrus,* in the family Celastraceae, is of particular interest because fossil members are well represented in many localities. In strata from the Cretaceous (about 125,000,000 years ago) fossil records from such disparate places as the northeastern region of China, Greenland, and Alaska have been found. The majority of records for this genus are from the central European floras of the Eocene and Miocene (7,000,000 to 26,000,000 years ago), from the Wilcox flora localities, and from the western United States.

Phylogeny. The phylogenetic (evolutionary) relationships of this order are not clear. The fossil record has not yet yielded much definitive information, and there is disagreement among the leading authorities; according to one of them, the order Celastrales is thought to be closely related to the Saxifragales—apparently derived from the common ancestors of some families within that order. The orders Oleales, Santalales, and Elaeagnales appear to share a common origin with the Celastrales; they are also particularly closely associated with three Celastrales families: Icacinaceae, Aquifoliaceae, and Salvadoraceae.

Classification. *Distinguishing taxonomic features.* The families have several common features: simple leaves; stamens alternating with the petals, with the exception of the Corynocarpaceae, a family of somewhat doubtful affinities; and usually one to two ovules in a locule. In addition, the nectar-producing disk is an important diagnostic character for seven of the families—the Celastraceae, Hippocrateaceae, Siphonodontaceae, Goupiaceae, Corynocarpaceae, Aextoxicaceae, and occasionally the Icacinaceae. The absence of the disk separates the Aquifoliaceae from the families most closely related to it. If the disk is present, its position inside or outside the whorl of stamens is of importance in further delineating families. Among the major criteria for delineating families within the order are: the presence or absence of stipules (leaflike appendages at the bases of leafstalks); the type of inflorescence, or arrangement of flowers; the presence of the lianous, or climbing, habit; the polygamodioecious state (male and female flowers on different plants but with a few flowers of the opposite sex or a few bisexual flowers on all plants at flowering time); the structure of the gynoecium (female parts); the curvature of the ovule; and seed characteristics.

Presence of the nectar-producing disk

Annotated classification. The order Celastrales is given here in accordance with one modern taxonomic authority. Most present-day taxonomists would agree that the following families should be classified together: Aquifoliaceae, Celastraceae, Hippocrateaceae, Siphonodontaceae, Stackhousiaceae, Salvadoraceae, Icacinaceae, and Geissolomataceae. The family Phellineaceae is sometimes included within the Aquifoliaceae but is considered here as a separate family on several characteristics: its valvate petals (those that touch at the edges), its inflorescence, the position of the ovules, the wood anatomy, and the pollen-grain morphology.

The relationships of the families Goupiaceae and Corynocarpaceae are not completely clear; in both cases the presence of the disk offers support for including them in this order. Taxonomic research could cause their status to be revised in the future, however. The family Aextoxicaceae has an even more uncertain position, but it does exhibit the following characteristics of the order: simple leaves, a nectar-secreting disk, and two ovules per locule.

The following descriptions give a wide range of characters which, taken as a whole, serve to delineate each family. Anomalous members also exist within most families of flowering plants, so that a familial description can be only a general one to which most members of that family adhere.

ORDER CELASTRALES

Woody plants: shrubs, trees, or vines; occasionally herbs. Leaves simple, alternate or opposite. Flowers usually bisexual, occasionally unisexual; hypogynous to perigynous (attachment of other floral parts either beneath the ovary or around it but not above it). Petals separate from each other. Stamens in a single cycle alternating with the petals; often a nectar-secreting disk of tissue inside or outside the whorl of stamens. Ovules typically 1 or 2 in a locule (compartment of an ovary or fruit). Twelve families, 147 genera, 2,000 species. Distribution pantropical and subtropical, with centres of distribution in Southeast Asia and South America.

Family Aquifoliaceae (holly family)

Trees or shrubs, typically with leathery alternate (rarely opposite) leaves. Flowers bisexual or unisexual. If unisexual then dioecious (sexes on different plants) or polygamodioecious (a few bisexual flowers or flowers of the opposite sex on all plants at flowering time). Flowers symmetrical, small and greenish, 1 to a few in small close clusters or cymes (more or less flat-topped flower cluster with central flowers opening first) located in axils. Sepals 3 to 6, joined basally and overlapping. Petals 4 or 5, free or only somewhat joined basally and overlapping, with point of attachment under the ovary (superior ovary). Stamens 4 or 5, distinct, alternating with the petals and sometimes fused with them. Nectar-secreting disk absent. Female flowers usually with anther-bearing staminodes (sterile stamens); male flowers usually with a rudimentary pistil (female structure). Pistil 1, style (elongated upper part of pistil) short or absent, stigma (pollen-receiving region at tip of style) lobed or capitate. Ovary with 3 to many locules. Ovules 1 or 2 per locule, hanging downward and anatropous (the opening near the point of attachment to placenta); placenta located at the centre of the ovary; fruit a berry; seeds with small straight embryo and copious endosperm (nutrient tissue for developing embryo). Three genera, 300 species, approximately 295 of which are in the genus *Ilex* (holly). Major centre of distribution is in Central and South America, with a secondary distribution in Asia. *Nemopanthus,* a genus of northeastern North America; *Byronia* a genus of Polynesia and Australia.

Family Icacinaceae (Icacina family)

Trees or shrubs, often vines, rarely herbs. Leaves leathery, simple, usually alternate. Flowers bisexual (occasionally unisexual through abortion), symmetrical, usually in panicles (many-branched inflorescences with stalked flowers). Sepals 4 or 5, small. Petals 4 or 5, usually free, meeting at their edges without overlapping. Stamens 4 or 5, distinct, alternating with the petals. Nectar-secreting disk rarely present. Pistil 1, ovary superior, with 3 to 5 carpels (structural segments), one locule each. Ovules 2 per locule, hanging from top of locule, anatropous. Style 1, usually with 3 stigmas. Fruit usually a drupe or occasionally a samara (indehiscent, winged fruit). Seeds with straight or curved embryo; endosperm typically absent. Fifty-eight genera and 400 species distributed throughout the tropics but more abundant in the Southern Hemisphere than in the Northern Hemisphere.

Family Celastraceae (staff-tree family)

Usually smooth-surfaced trees or shrubs, often twining (but rarely vines). Leaves simple, opposite or alternate, deciduous or persistent. Inflorescences axillary or terminal or flowers solitary or clustered in leaf axils. Flowers small, symmetrical, bisexual or unisexual on same or different plants (if on different plants, then polygamodioecious). Sepals 4 or 5, small, joined half their length or more, usually overlapping. Petals 4 or 5, small, free, usually overlapping and inserted under the disk. Stamens 4 or 5 (rarely 8 to 10), distinct, alternating with petals, inserted on or under disk. Usually a conspicuous nectar-secreting disk between the stamens. Ovary superior or with other floral parts arising from around ovary; carpels 2 to 5 (rudimentary in male flowers); stigma 1, style single and short or lacking. Ovules 2 (rarely 1 or 4 to 6), erect and anatropous. Fruit a capsule, drupe, berry, or samara. Seeds characteristically with a conspicuous brightly coloured, pulpy outer covering. Endosperm usually present. Fifty-five genera and 850 species, widely distributed throughout the world except for Arctic regions.

Family Hippocrateaceae (Hippocratea family)

Woody vines, shrubs, or slender trees; frequently with latex (milky sap) ducts in all parts of the plant. Leaves simple, opposite (occasionally alternate). Flowers bisexual, symmetrical, usually small, with bracts (leaflike structures located just below flowers), often with abundant mucilaginous fibres. Sepals 5, free, overlapping, persistent. Petals 5 free, overlapping or touching at edges. Stamens 3 (rarely 2, 4, or 5), inserted in the disk. Disk in a usually continuous ring forming pockets; pistil 1; ovary superior, sometimes joined to disk and concealed by it; locules 3 (rarely 5); carpels 3; style short and 3-parted (occasionally absent); stigmas usually 3. Ovules 2 to 14 per locule, anatropous. Fruit a schizocarp (dry fruit that splits into two halves), berry, or unusual capsule—3-locular and deeply 3-parted with a large flattened segment containing seeds. Seeds compressed or, if in capsule, then winged from base. Twenty-one genera and 400 species, with a main centre of distribution in South America and a minor one in Africa.

Family Phellineaceae

Trees or shrubs. Leaves simple, alternate, persistent, and membranous or leathery. Inflorescence a solitary raceme (simple, elongated cluster with stalked flowers) in axils of leaves. Flowers dioecious. Sepals minute or lacking. Petals 4 to 6, free, meeting at edges without overlapping. Stamens 4 to 6, free, reduced staminodes present in female flowers. Ovary with 1 pistil, 2 to 5 locules, and 1 ovule per locule. Ovules weakly campylotropous (curved by uneven growth, with axis nearly at right angles to stalk of ovule) or hemitropous (partly campylotropous). Fruit a drupe. Seeds with copious endosperm. One genus (*Phelline*) and 10 species, endemic (restricted) to New Caledonia.

Family Stackhousiaceae

Annual or perennial herbs, somewhat xerophytic, with rhizomes (underground stems). Leaves simple, entire. Flowers bisexual, symmetrical, with bracts, in simple, unbranched, elongated spikes. Sepals 5, overlapping. Petals 5, arising from around the ovary, possessing long claws joined in their middle portions, lobes of petals overlapping. Stamens 5, 3 long and 2 short. Pistil with 2 to 5 free or joined styles. Ovary with 2 to 5 carpels and 2 to 5 locules. Ovules 1 per carpel, erect, anatropous. Fruit a schizocarp with 2 to 5 parts, each with 1 seed. Endosperm present. Three genera (*Stackhousia*, *Macgregoria*, and *Tripterococcia*) and 27 species, distributed in Australia, Tasmania, New Zealand, and the Philippines.

Family Salvadoraceae

Trees, shrubs, or scramblers, occasionally spiny. Entire plant usually of an olive-gray colour. Leaves opposite, entire. Flowers bisexual or polygamodioecious. Sepals 2 to 4, overlapping or meeting at the edges. Petals 4 or 5, overlapping or contorted, and usually with teeth or glands on the inner side. Anthers 4 or 5, alternating with the petals, free or arising from the petals and occasionally with the filaments connected into a tube. Ovary superior consisting of 2 carpels, each with 1 or 2 locules containing 1 or 2 erect ovules. Style short and usually 2-cleft. Fruit a 1-seeded berry or drupe. Endosperm absent. Three genera and 12 species, distributed in the hot and dry regions of Africa, Madagascar, and Asia (also often along salty coasts).

Family Siphonodontaceae

Trees or climbing shrubs. Leaves simple, entire, alternate. Sepals 5; petals 5; stamens 5. Ovary superior, usually of 10 united carpels. Floral structure unique: each locule partitioned horizontally into two parts; upper ovule ascending from partition, lower hanging; the whole embedded in a disk having a central channel lined with five grooves or stigmatic lines that end in 5 tufts (serving as stigmas) and filled by a column resembling a style and barely reaching the opening of the disk; stamens bent and pressed to the disk so that anthers form a 5-rayed star at the top of the disk. Large fruit pear-shaped to globose, usually with 20 radiating bony pyrenes (single seeds with a hard outer covering). Embryo with large cotyledons (seed leaves) in bony endosperm. One genus (*Siphonodon*) and 5 species distributed from Southeast Asia to Australia.

Family Geissolomataceae

Small, xerophytic shrubs. Leaves simple, opposite, entire, evergreen; stipules present. Flowers bisexual, symmetrical, solitary in leaf axils, subtended by 6 persistent bracts. Sepals 4, resembling petals, overlapping, persistent. Petals absent. Stamens 8, free, 4 opposite the sepals and 4 alternating with the sepals. Ovary superior; styles 4, tapering from base to apex, free at base but coherent above (touching adhesively but not actually fused); carpels 4; locules 4, ovules 2 per locule, hanging. Fruit a capsule. One genus and 1 species (*Geissoloma marginata*) endemic to South Africa.

Family Goupiaceae

Trees or shrubs. Leaves simple, entire, alternate, with stipules; with 3 main veins extending the length of the leaf and with transverse veins. Flowers bisexual, symmetrical, stalked in false umbels (flat-topped inflorescence that mature from the margin inward). Sepals 5, overlapping, small. Petals 5, awl-shaped, meeting at the edges and rolled inward; yellow with red base; the top one-third strongly inflexed in the bud and remaining curved upon opening. Stamens 5 arising from edge of cup-shaped disk. Pistil with 5 short, free styles. Ovary superior, with 5 carpels and many ascending ovules. Fruit a globose drupelike berry, small, hard, with 2 or 3 locules and many seeds. Fleshy endosperm present. One genus (*Goupia*) and 3 species distributed in South America.

Family Aextoxicaceae

Large trees. Leaves simple, opposite or nearly so, nearly entire (smooth-margined), lepidote (with small scurfy scales on the surface). Inflorescences in axils of leaves, lepidote, in racemes. Flowers symmetrical, unisexual, enveloped in bud by bracts. Sepals 5, overlapping. Petals 5, overlapping, broadly clawed with a thick midvein and spreading at the apex. Female flower also with 5 broadly linear, fleshy staminodes. Stamens 5, alternating with 5 disk glands. Pistil lepidote with recurved, 2-cleft style. Ovary superior, with 2 carpels and 2 hanging ovules in only 1 locule. Fruit a small, dry drupe. Seed with mottled endosperm. One genus and 1 species (*Aextoxican punctatum*) endemic to Chile.

Family Corynocarpaceae

Trees or shrubs. Leaves simple, entire, alternate, lacking stipules. Inflorescence a terminal panicle. Sepals 5, overlapping. Petals 5, overlapping, joined to the base of the whorl of sepals. Stamens 5, opposite petals and epipetalous (arising from the petals); alternating with 5 petallike staminodes. Disk of 5 large glands opposite staminodes. Pistil with 1 or 2 free styles. Ovary superior with 1 or 2 carpels; 1 fertile locule with one hanging ovule, 1 sterile locule. Fruit a drupe, globose, fleshy. Endosperm absent. One genus (*Corynocarpus*) and 5 species with centre of distribution in the southwest Pacific.

Critical appraisal. Many taxonomic questions are yet to be resolved in this order. Some present-day taxonomists would consider various other families to be part of the Celastrales and would exclude some that are discussed here. Most authorities agree, however, that there is a solid core of distinct families that definitely belong in the Celastrales: Aquifoliaceae, Icacinaceae, Celastraceae, and Hippocrateaceae. The Geissolomataceae, Stackhousiaceae, Salvadoraceae, and Siphonodontaceae are accepted to a lesser degree as being definite members of the order, but some taxonomists would place them elsewhere. The members of the family Phellineaceae clearly belong in the Celastrales, but the one genus of the family (*Phelline*) often is considered as part of the Aquifoliaceae and not as comprising a separate family. The remaining three small families of the order—Goupiaceae, Aextoxicaceae, and Corynocarpaceae—generally are considered to have rather unclear relationships. Their placement in the Celastrales can be contested on the basis of present knowledge, but the problem cannot be resolved until more information is gathered both about these families and about the groups to which they appear to have affinities.

Other taxonomic schemes

BIBLIOGRAPHY. H. HAROLD HUME, *Hollies* (1953), a well-written, authoritative, and interesting book giving considerable background information on hollies in general, as well as detailed information about particular species and varieties; *American Horticultural Magazine* (Fall 1970), a special issue devoted entirely to hollies with well-written and extremely interesting articles on almost every aspect of the genus, from folklore and legends to holly propagation and varieties of hollies now commercially available; E. BERKELEY, "Morphological Studies in the Celastraceae," *J. Elisha Mitchell Scient. Soc.*, 69:185–208 (1953), a detailed anatomical floral study investigating the relationships of several genera within the family, fairly difficult for the non-botanist; R.A. HOWARD, "Studies of the Icacinaceae, I. Preliminary Taxonomic Notes," *J. Arnold Arbor.*, 21:461–489 (1940), a discussion of the historical taxonomic problems in the family Icacinaceae, and an interesting preliminary report on the nature of the research to be done to resolve these problems; I.W. BAILEY and R.A. HOWARD, "The Comparative Morphology of the Icacinaceae," 4 pt., *ibid.*, 22:125–568 (1941), an excellent, thorough study of several morphological structures, clarifying trends of specialization and relationships of genera within the family—requires a botanical background.

(E.C.Du.)

Celibacy

Though the term celibacy refers simply to the state of being unmarried, it is usually used in connection with the celibate individual's role as a religious official, specialist, or devotee. Not all persons in a religious vocation, or calling, who happen to be unmarried are technically celibate; the term celibate applies only to those for whom the unmarried state is the result of a sacred vow or act of renunciation or of a belief that it is preferable for a person because of his religious position or his degree of religious seriousness.

Celibacy has existed in some form or another throughout man's religious history and has appeared in virtually all the major religious traditions of the world. A distinction, however, could be made between those traditions in which celibacy has had a great and continuing prestige and is considered to be the preferred state of most spiritual leaders (*e.g.*, Hinduism, Buddhism, Taoism, Roman Catholicism, and Eastern Orthodoxy) and those in which it is only an occasional and often suspect deviation from a norm that gives marriage greater honour, for spiritual leaders as well as for the laity (*e.g.*, Judaism, Islām, Confucianism, and Protestantism).

Wherever celibacy has appeared, it has generally accompanied an emphasis that views the religious life as essentially different or even alienated from the normal structures of society and the normal drives of human nature. On the other hand, the religious style that disparages celibacy gives priority to the role of religion as employing and sanctifying the "natural" states of life: sexuality, family, and work. While the religions that encourage celibacy in leaders and devotees may not neglect the sanctification of the natural states, they stress the importance of certain symbols of separation, even of polarization, between the life of the person who has a sacred vocation and that of the ordinary man. They emphasize the difference between the religious and the natural life.

FUNCTIONS OF CELIBACY

Symbolism of celibacy

The basic function of celibacy is to establish a symbol of the sacred or holy within the life of an individual and make him its living, objective image. The priest or monk is to have the internal wholeness and self-sufficiency of God, of Christ, of the Buddha, or of other sacred beings. He is to be spiritually hermaphroditic, not needing the other sex for completeness, because he is an image in the world of men of the sacred, the ultimate reality which is beyond external needs. The celibate also demonstrates before men an utter dependency on the sacred.

Ritual purification. More specifically, however, celibacy functions in the history of religion as a means of ritual purification. In archaic religion (the religions of early and primitive cultures), the whole area of sexuality is commonly pervaded by negative taboo. Women in menstruation are to be avoided; sexual activity is forbidden before the hunt, war, or religious ceremonial. Celibacy serves as a permanent extension of this sort of preparedness for sacred and special activity. The celibate priest also serves as a pure *representative* of the community; he is viewed by the community as it would like to be seen by the gods.

Institutional control. A celibate class is created when the permanent celibate state becomes "routinized" into a regular, necessary qualification for those performing sacred activities. Some celibates have simply made a total withdrawal (*e.g.*, the "holy man," the hermit) and do not exercise sacerdotal powers. But if celibacy is a necessary qualification for priesthood, as in traditional Buddhism and Roman Catholicism, then it may functionally serve to demarcate and perpetuate a special group that possesses greater or lesser control of religious institutions. Ideally, it releases this group for more than ordinary expenditures of time and energy on behalf of their purposes.

Moral or spiritual advancement. At the same time, within the celibate community, celibacy is taught with the view that it contributes to the moral or spiritual advancement of individuals. According to such teachings, those in the married state can attain a positive balance of good over bad in their lives, and hence a favourable judgment on the last day or a desirable reincarnation. Nevertheless, the life of exemplary supernatural perfection, and of those advanced mystical states that give one a direct experience of the spiritual absolute, is held to be compatible only with the celibate state.

Other functions. Celibacy also functions as an example within a society, constantly suggesting the possibility of a life directed to more than natural ends; in other words, that continence is possible and the marital state a relative rather than an absolute end.

TYPES OF CELIBACY

Sacerdotal. Parallel to the diverse functions that celibacy plays in the religious life of man is a diversity of types. One type is sacerdotal celibacy, the celibacy of priests and priestesses. A priest may be defined as one who, as a mediator, performs the sacred function of communicating through rites the needs of the people to heaven and the sacred power and presence from heaven to the congregation. His function is objective. Its efficacy is assured if the priest knows and does the proper rite and has the proper qualifications of ordination and, perhaps, of ritual purity, regardless of whether he is particularly moral or fervent. Celibacy, if required for the priesthood, would be such an objective mark of special state and ritual purity. Celibacy probably is derived from taboos that regarded sexual power as a rival to religious power, and the sexuality of the opposite sex as a polluting factor, especially in sacred or crisis situations.

Monastic. Another type of celibacy is the monastic. While the monk may (or may not) also be a priest, his main motive will be moral and spiritual advancement, not the ritual purity required for sacerdotal rites. To this end the interior freedom, the opportunity for asceticism and meditation, and perhaps the "new family" of the religious community, all contribute to a sense of separation from the ordinary that releases the monk for religious growth. Types of monasticism range from the solitary—the hermit in the woods or desert, the anchorite living in isolation in a church or monastery—through the cenobite living a stabilized monastic life in community, to the mendicant ascetic who, either alone or with a band of friars, wanders from place to place gathering alms. In any case, the celibate state is viewed as an inseparable part of his way of life.

Anchorites, cenobites, and mendicants

Institutional (nonsacerdotal). Mention must be made also of states of institutional celibacy for women. Very frequently this life has no connection with sacerdotalism and is rather designed to aid spiritual advancement. Virginity and celibacy are considered to be assets in the attainment of spiritual goals. Generally, institutional female celibates are nuns in residential cloisters, although occasional solitaries, like the anchoress (lady hermit) Dame Julian of Norwich (14th–15th century) may be noted. Orders of nuns often perform important social service functions and in traditional societies may provide refuges for orphans, widows, and other women without family support.

Individual (noninstitutional, nonsacerdotal). Individual noninstitutional and nonsacerdotal religious celibacy is normally the state of the lay celibate or the occasional clergyman in a faith not requiring celibacy, who makes a vow to remain unmarried out of devotion or to allow the performance of some special religious service. Often these persons make their commitments in connection with a special relationship to a monastic order, as in the case of Catholic oblates (a lay person who unites with a religious order) or devout Buddhist laymen. Sometimes, as often obtains with high-caste Hindus, private vows of this type may be taken late in life, after an individual has been married and a householder. Even in these cases, however, the vow of celibacy is made in the presence of another: the abbott of the order or one's guru (spiritual guide).

Other types. There may also be cases of what might be called spontaneous or unofficial celibacy, especially in faiths in which the celibate state has no regularized standing. An individual may find his religious enthusiasm so all-consuming or his vocation so demanding that marriage can find no place in his life, and it is thereby consciously or unconsciously rejected for religious reasons. A good example of this type was John Chapman, "Johnny Appleseed," the Protestant mystic and wanderer of the American frontier. Islāmic mysticism also offers examples of this type.

CELIBACY IN THE RELIGIONS OF THE WORLD

Primitive religions. Among primitive peoples, the celibate state is chiefly connected with shamans and ritual purity. The shaman is an ecstatic who speaks to and from the gods or spirits on behalf of the people. Not all shamans are unmarried. But because the shaman has undergone a profound initiatory experience and has had a quite

The shaman

extraordinary calling, the prototype of the celibate may be found among his ranks. Some shamans, for example in the Goldi tribe of Siberia, "marry" initiatory female spirits at the time of their call. In other cultures, such as in that of ancient Japan, the female shaman was often the spouse of the god of whom she was the medium. Other shamans have been transvestite or homosexual. Priests also have been celibate in some archaic societies; *e.g.*, among the Aztec.

Ancient peoples and civilizations. With the rise of the great civilizations of antiquity, celibacy emerged in various contexts. The requirements for the famous Vestal Virgins of Rome, celibate for at least the thirty years of their service, indicate that celibacy had some place in a very ancient stratum of Roman religion. As classical civilization developed, two types of religious styles involving masculine celibacy appeared, that of the ascetic philosopher and that of the priest of the mystery religions. The Pythagoreans, perhaps influenced by the mysteries of Orpheus, are an excellent example of the former. Pythagoras himself established a small community at Croton in southern Italy (*c.* 529 BC). The community life was one of study, vegetarianism, and sexual restraint or abstinence. Later philosophers, including the well-traveled Neo-Pythagorean Apollonius of Tyana (1st century AD), under the influence of this tradition believed that celibacy would be conducive to the detachment and equilibrium required by the philosopher's calling. The Stoic philosopher Epictetus (born *c.* AD 50) taught that the ideal teacher would be unmarried and that his task required a calm freedom from family care. As a celibate teacher, the philosopher would make a far greater contribution to the world than that of bringing into being a few more children, and the single state could justifiably be substituted for the latter duty (*Discourses*, III, 22).

Priests of the mystery religions

A different mood was set by the celibate priests of the mysteries. Celibacy was especially characteristic of priest-devotees of the Great Mother cults. The Syrian goddess, for example, was described by Apuleius as being served by eunuchs who, in their zeal, would dance and lacerate their bodies with knives before her image. In contrast, the well-organized priesthood of the religion of Isis represented serene sacerdotalism. Sexual abstinence was an absolute requirement of those who celebrated her holy mysteries. Tertullian (the 2nd-century Christian rigorist) held up their continence as a reproachful example to Christians. He likewise noted that the sect of the Mithraists had "their virgins and their continents."

Similarly, the increasing number of cults—*e.g.*, Manichaeans (Iranian-based religion flourishing in the 3rd to 5th century that upheld the dualism of spirit and matter), Gnostics (early Christian heretics who believed that matter was evil and spirit good), and Hermeticists (Hellenistic believers in the occult and astrology)—influenced by the Platonic and Neoplatonic quest for the One through contemplation, esoteric knowledge, or theurgy (the art of influencing gods), typically had an inner or esoteric circle requiring strict continence. Thus, almost all important religious movements in the classical world show a strong drift in the direction of continence as an ideal and set the stage for Christian celibacy and monasticism.

Religions of the East. *Hinduism.* The ideal of the celibate state is also important in religions of the East. In Hinduism, celibacy is divorced from the priesthood, which is hereditary. Prominent, however, among the religious personages of India are the *sādhus*, "holy men," who live a life free of possessions and family obligation. They may be *sannyāsins*, devotees of Śiva (Shiva); *bairāgis*, devotees of Viṣṇu (Vishnu); or *yogins*, practitioners of yogic techniques. The *sādhus* have no organization or corporate discipline. Many *sādhus*, male and female, become celibates after marriage or widowhood; others early in life. The *sādhu* is one who has left the type of life ruled by the order of *dharma* (cosmic and societal law; *i.e.*, of caste, family, money, state, and all their responsibilities and privileges) in order to seek *mokṣa* (final liberation). Worldly involvements are believed to increase one's activities and distractions and hence militate against attainment of a life of controlled equilibrium or devotional ecstasy that is the goal of the spiritual techniques. Certain schools of yoga teach continence so that sexual energy may be redirected toward the opening of psychic and enlightenment centres in the body.

The *arhat*

Buddhism. Buddhism began as a celibate order in India dedicated to the attainment of the *arhat* state, which is one of enlightenment. The *arhat* is a person who has attained enlightenment, also called the nirvanic consciousness, through the control of the passions and the withdrawal of the senses from attachment to external objects. Buddhism has both monks and nuns. As Buddhism became a world religion, certain variations arose: in Southeast Asia, most young men spent only a year in the order; in Tibet, Tantric monks were married; in Japan, the large Jōdo Shinshū denomination dispensed with the celibacy ideal altogether. At its core, however, Buddhism is a faith that teaches that all suffering is caused by particularized attachment to objects perceived by the senses, and that this desire is overcome best by meditative states of consciousness. Thus the image of the detached monk, an emulator of the Buddha himself who gave full priority to the meditative task of analysis and self-transcendence, remains at the centre of the Buddhist road to salvation.

Jainism. The Jain religion arose in India about the same time as Buddhism. Its monastic groups were marked by an even greater austerity than that of Buddhism. Those of the Digambara school go about entirely naked after being fully initiated. All Jain monks are to avoid even looking at women, for, according to a Jain source, "they are to monks what a cat is to a chicken" (S.B. Deo, *History of Jaina Monachism*, p. 208).

Other religions of the East. Chinese Taoism has moastics and independent celibate adepts. Originally the tradition was probably derived from shamanism, but now the Taoist monasticism and priesthood is modelled on the Buddhist. Shintō in Japan has no monks or celibate priesthood; it has embraced shamanesses "married" to the shrine god and celibate priestesses in major shrines, especially in premodern times.

Ṣūfism

Religions of the West. *Islām.* Celibacy was not part of the original practices of Islām. But after the faith of Muḥammad had conquered vast stretches of the world, mystical movements, particularly Ṣūfism (Islāmic mysticism), arose and sometimes produced celibates. Islāmic celibacy was a matter of personal spiritual advancement or enthusiasm rather than of sacerdotal purity or institutional control, and most of the famous saints were married. In various places, bands or fraternities of Ṣūfī mystics, such as the dervishes, developed out of a need for rigorous training or practice. Celibacy was exceptional even among members of these mystical orders, however, except for the Bektāshīyah of Turkey and Albania, which had a celibate wing. Religious celibacy, together with the traditional practice of Ṣūfī mysticism, seems to be on the decline in the Islāmic world today.

Judaism. Celibacy has had little part in normative Judaism. The creation accounts in Genesis 1 and 2 in the Old Testament present the marriage relationship as a good and natural one. "Any Jew who has no wife is no man," said Rabbi Eleazar (3rd century AD). The single, dramatic exception in the Old Testament is that of the prophet Jeremiah.

There were, however, prescribed periods of sexual abstinence in connection with rituals and sacrifices, and while engaging in holy wars.

Celibacy does appear, however, in sectarian Judaism in post-Old Testament times. Some members of the Essene sect, as described by Pliny, Philo, and Josephus, rejected marriage. The Qumrān community near the Dead Sea apparently was Essene, but there is some uncertainty as to just what part celibacy played in its life. One manuscript makes a note of women and children in the Qumrān community; however, a holy war was believed to be imminent; and to be ready for this apocalyptic conflict, ritual purity, including sexual abstinence, was necessary.

Christianity. Celibacy first appears in Christianity out of similar apocalyptic expectations. It was believed among the original Christians that the present age was ending and that the Kingdom of God was at hand, and that in the new age there would be no marriage, since all would be like angels. Some of the followers of Jesus gave up family life in order to devote themselves to proclaiming the Kingdom. St. Paul commended celibacy but insisted that he, like the other Apostles, had the right to be married if he so desired.

In the subapostolic period (late 1st and early 2nd centuries), discussion and practice of celibacy varied. Some took the extreme view that all Christians should renounce marriage. Middle positions were developed to defend marriage in opposition to Encratic (heretical ascetic) and Gnostic (heretical ascetic or libertarian) views that the flesh and all matter were evil and to defend celibacy in opposition to the widespread sexual license and chaos of the times. Many writers held that marriage was good, but that celibacy was better.

As time passed and expectations of the consummation of history dimmed, a belief that sexual intercourse was defiling and incompatible with holiness emerged as the dominant motivation for the practice of celibacy. Some persons dedicated themselves to lifelong virginity. Others, already married when converted, separated from their spouses from the time of their Baptisms or practiced continence within marriage; some became celibate after being widowed. The pre-Christian idea that sexual activity was particularly wrong for those who officiated at the altar was assimilated by Christians, and it became the custom for ordained men to give up sexual relations with their wives, but there was no uniformity on the matter. The regional Council of Elvira in Spain (*c.* AD 306), decreed that all priests and bishops, married or not, should abstain from sexual relations. On the other hand, the ecumenical Council of Nicaea (AD 325) declined to make such a prohibition. The council condemned the practice in which supposedly celibate priests kept a "subintroduced woman" in their households in order to test and prove their moral strength.

Beginnings of clerical celibacy

The position of the Eastern churches was made clear by the time of the decrees of the Council in Trullo in Constantinople in 691. Bishops must be celibate, but ordained priests, deacons, and subdeacons could continue already-established marriages.

In the West, a series of popes and regional councils in the 4th and 5th centuries confirmed the general position taken at Elvira requiring clergy in various places to be celibate or, if married, continent.

The social chaos caused by the breakup of the Roman Empire had the effect of extending the practice of celibacy among the laity. Lay persons fleeing the cities to live as hermits or to form monastic communities sought safety as well as purity.

In the 10th and 11th centuries a crisis in the practice of clerical celibacy resulted from the decline of the Carolingian Empire and the Norse (Viking) invasions. Churches were destroyed, church lands secularized, and many priests married or lived in concubinage. Not only the practice but also the principles of clerical celibacy were challenged. Popes and councils reacted strongly with reassertions of the traditional law.

The first and second Lateran Councils (1123 and 1139) put an end to the legality of theoretically continent clerical marriages. They declared priestly orders an impediment to valid marriage and vice versa. This is still the official position of the Roman Catholic Church, although occasionally exceptions are made.

The churches of the Reformation (Lutheran, Anglican, Reformed, and others) discontinued the requirement of clerical celibacy. Lay celibacy was also discontinued, but about 1845 monastic orders began to reappear in the Church of England. About the time of World War II, small Protestant monastic groups (*e.g.*, Taizé community) were founded on the continent of Europe.

Debates on clerical celibacy

In connection with the second Vatican Council (1962–65) clerical celibacy has once again become a cause of ferment in the Roman Church. The council permitted a married diaconate. Subsequent to the council, the number of priests seeking to leave the priesthood and marry has vastly increased.

A substantial number of European and American Catholics began to urge that celibacy be made optional for priests. The National Association for Pastoral Renewal was formed in St. Louis and New York, 1966–67, to work toward this change. A survey carried out by the association revealed that 62 percent of lower echelon American priests favoured optional celibacy.

Pope Paul VI, however, issued an encyclical, *Sacerdotalis Caelibatus* (June 23, 1967), reaffirming the traditional law on celibacy. The pope and those who are in agreement with his position tend, in their defense of the present practice, to pass over the antisexual writings of early centuries and to return to the New Testament texts. Thus, in this view, for the sake of Christ and the coming Kingdom of Heaven, the priest must be totally available and free of domestic responsibilities; he must witness by his way of life to the transcendent reality that fills and grips him.

In general those who urge change indicate that they hold celibacy in high regard and want it to continue both among laity and some priests. Making it voluntary should, they believe, actually enrich and strengthen it. They refer to New Testament practice of freedom in this area, and they also point out that in present practice many men are not motivated by the exalted New Testament reasons when they take on celibacy. To insist that the two vocations of celibacy and priesthood must necessarily coexist in the same person at the same time, they claim, is arbitrary and is contradicted by centuries of Orthodox and Protestant experience.

The Roman Catholic law of clerical celibacy is of ecclesiastical origin; it is not considered by either side to be infallible or divine, and thus theoretically it can be changed. The issue may thus be seen in large measure as a crisis of authority.

BIBLIOGRAPHY. S.B. DEO, *History of Jaina Monachism From Inscriptions and Literature* (1956), a standard study of monasticism and celibacy in the Jain tradition; S. DUTT, *Early Buddhist Monachism, 600 B.C.–100 B.C.* (1924); MIRCEA ELIADE, *Le chamanisme et les techniques archaïques de l'extase* (1951; Eng. trans., *Shamanism: Archaic Techniques of Ecstasy*, rev. ed., 1964), a standard work on the way of life of the shaman; G.S. GHURYE, *Indian Sādhus* (1953); F.C. GRANT (ed.), *Hellenistic Religions: The Age of Syncretism* (1953), original sources for mystery cults and Neoplatonism; H.C. LEA, *History of Sacerdotal Celibacy in the Christian Church* (1957, orig. pub. 1867); G. VAN DER LEEUW, *Phänomenologie der Religion* (1933; Eng. trans., *Religion in Essence and Manifestation*, 2 vol., with new appendices, 1963), useful for general phenomenological categories; E.C.F.A. SCHILLEBEECKX, *Het ambts—celibaat in de branding* (1965; Eng. trans., *Celibacy*, 1968), a standard contemporary study of the history and current position of the Roman Catholic Church; W. STARK, *Sociology of Religion*, vol. 4, *Types of Religious Man* (1969); D.T. SUZUKI, *The Training of the Zen Buddhist Monk* (1934); G.H. FREIN (ed.), *Celibacy: The Necessary Option* (1968), a useful collection of symposium papers from a reformist Roman Catholic perspective; M. THURIAN, *Mariage et célibat* (1955; Eng. trans., 1959), the view of a contemporary French Protestant monastic; H. WELCH, *The Practice of Chinese Buddhism, 1900–1950* (1967), an excellent study of contemporary Chinese monasticism.

(R.S.E.)

Cell and Cell Division

Cells are the units of life; they survive and conserve their kind by reproduction. The distinction between the two main designs of cells, procaryotic and eucaryotic, is that between life-forms that appeared on the Earth 3,000,000,000 years ago and relative newcomers that date back no more than 2,000,000,000 years.

In the following discussion of the designs and workings of cells, molecules are distinguished from the structures and mechanisms in which they participate. The interpretation of life processes as chemical processes has answered some of the most important biological questions. The answers to others involve considerations of the ways in which molecules are organized because, ultimately, it is the organization of molecules that is responsible for the coordination of activities in the cell.

This article is divided into the following major sections:

I. The designs of cells

Two basic cell designs

Two quite distinct designs of cells are recognized. One, the procaryotic plan, is found in all bacteria and blue-green algae. The second, the eucaryotic plan, occurs in the true algae, the fungi, the protozoans, and the cells of multicellular plants and animals. The same principles of reproduction, inheritance, molecular composition, and metabolism apply to both kinds of cells; the differences between them are dealt with below (see below *Procaryotic and eucaryotic cells*).

THE CELL AS A MOLECULAR SYSTEM

The same kinds of molecules are found in all types of living cells. The following is a catalog and evaluation of the important classes of molecules found in cells.

Macromolecules in cells. Macromolecules can be defined arbitrarily as molecules of molecular weight greater than 10,000 daltons (10,000 times the weight of a hydrogen atom). They are characteristic of living things and are not found in nature except as components or products of organisms. In all cases, the molecules are polymers; *i.e.*, they consist of chains of smaller units called monomers. Much of biochemistry is a description of two processes: the synthesis of monomers and the polymerization, or joining, of monomers to form macromolecules. Each of the kinds of macromolecules—proteins, nucleic acids, or polysaccharides—is assembled from one class of monomers. Proteins are polymers of amino acids, molecules characterized by the presence of a nitrogen-containing amine group, NH_2, attached to the carbon atom adjacent to the organic carboxyl acid group, COOH. Nucleic acids are polymers of units known as nucleotides, each of which is composed of a specific sugar molecule (deoxyribose or ribose), a molecule of phosphoric acid, and a molecule of one of four organic bases (adenine, guanine, cytosine, or thymine). Polysaccharides are polymers of carbohydrates, which are molecules composed of carbon, hydrogen, and oxygen atoms. In the cell, these polymers are generally heteropolymers; *i.e.*, the monomers that comprise them belong to the same chemical class (*e.g.*, amino acids in proteins), but they are not all identical in structure—there are about 20 different amino acids. The term sequence refers to the order in which the different monomers of one class appear in the polymer.

Nucleic acids and genetic conservation. Deoxyribonucleic acid (DNA) is literally the substance of heredity; it carries the essence, or character, of an organism from generation to generation. DNA is a heteropolymer of four types of monomers, called deoxyribonucleotides because they contain deoxyribose. The inherited character of every organism is encoded in the sequences of these four nucleotides; thus the ultimate basis of reproduction lies in the exact replication of these sequences. The basis of evolution involves occasional modification of them.

Another group of nucleic acids, ribonucleic acids (RNA), consists of sequences of four types of monomers called ribonucleotides because they contain ribose. RNA's that can copy sequences of deoxyribonucleotides in DNA are called messenger RNA's or MRNA's; they function in the expression of the genetic code contained in the DNA. The most immediate expression of the genetic code is the synthesis of proteins (see NUCLEIC ACID; GENE).

The roles of proteins. Proteins are heteropolymers of about 20 kinds of amino acids. The functioning of a protein depends on its structure; the three levels of structural complexity that are recognized are primary, secondary, and tertiary. The primary structure of proteins is described by the sequences of the amino acids, which are polymerized in chains. The terms secondary and tertiary structure are used to describe the coiling of the polypeptide chains into helices (secondary structure) and the further folding of the helices into three-dimensional shapes, the conformations and surface features of which are important for the biological activities of the proteins (tertiary structure). The conformation of protein molecules is important because their activities involve the way in which they "fit" with other molecules; the two molecules must fit together very exactly because any distortion in the conformation affects the functioning of the protein molecule.

Several distinct roles of proteins can be recognized in the operations of the cell; for example, catalysis, transport, structure, and regulation (all treated below) are some of the principal functional processes in which proteins are important.

The chemical reactions in the cell are catalyzed (*i.e.*, assisted so that the rate of reaction is increased) by enzymes, and all enzymes are proteins. Each kind of reaction is catalyzed by a different enzyme. It is estimated that as many as several thousand different enzymes are contained in certain cells.

Certain proteins are found in the cell membranes, where they function as transport proteins. Each transport protein recognizes a specific molecule, combines with it, and carries it across the membrane into the cell.

Structural proteins

Proteins are responsible for the properties of cells—their form, structure, and movements. The existence of a class of structural proteins is recognized, although less is known about them than is known about enzymes. Such proteins are present in cells in large amounts because they build massive structures rather than serve catalytic functions.

Procaryotic cells contain a class of proteins called repressors, which are agents of genetic regulation. They function as genetic valves by combining with specific genes to turn off their activity. In eucaryotic cells, protein components of chromosomes are thought to serve similar functions, although the case is far less clear (see PROTEIN; ENZYME).

The role of polysaccharides. The polysaccharides, polymers of various sugars, are prominent in functions that occur at the outer face of the cell but have few functions inside the cell. Bacterial cells are encased in cell walls the most prominent components of which are polysaccharides; frequently they are associated with proteins and lipids. The walls surrounding plant cells are composed of cellulose, a polymer of the sugar glucose. Animal cells do not have walls, but an important compound of their outer face is a polysaccharide containing sialic acid (see CARBOHYDRATE).

Small molecules in the cell. An inventory of the small molecules of cells, those smaller than macromolecules, would be immense. Those groups—lipids, nucleotides, porphyrins, and water—that are central to the concept of the cell as a molecular system are described below.

Lipids. The term lipid lumps together a variety of fatty molecules that are insoluble in water but soluble in organic solvents (*e.g.*, ether); lipids comprise about 10 to 20 percent of the dry weight of a typical cell and are major components of all cell membranes. They constitute about 50 percent of the material of cell membranes and account for a number of their important properties. Functionally, layers of lipids are effective in separating water regions from one another (*e.g.*, cell interiors from their environments) in such a way that their components do not mix freely (see LIPID; MEMBRANE, BIOLOGICAL).

Nucleotides. Nucleotides, the monomeric units of nucleic acids, contain a nitrogenous base; a sugar, generally either ribose or deoxyribose; and one or more phosphate groups. It is remarkable that one type of molecule plays such a variety of roles. In the respiration of all cells, for example, certain of the key compounds involved are nucleotides combined with proteins. In most chemical reactions of all cells in which a transfer of energy occurs, the nucleotide adenosine triphosphate (ATP) is involved.

The cyclic adenosine monophosphate (cyclic AMP or cAMP) molecule is a nucleotide that functions as a major communicator molecule in cells. In both procaryotic and eucaryotic organisms it has been shown that cells respond to various stimuli (*e.g.*, hormones, events at junctions between nerves, substances that induce enzyme synthesis in bacteria) by producing cyclic AMP, which then plays an essential part in turning on the necessary activity (*e.g.*, enzyme synthesis; see METABOLISM).

Porphyrin derivatives. Porphyrins are widely distributed in plant and animal cells. Certain porphyrin derivatives, the cytochromes, are essential for oxidative processes, especially in cells that utilize oxygen. Other porphyrin derivatives, the chlorophylls, are responsible for the utilization of light energy in photosynthesis.

Water. Water, the simplest and most abundant of all the molecules, is also the most mysterious. Cells contain 70 to 80 percent water. If the water content of a cell falls much below about 50 percent, life processes stop, sometimes irreversibly. Cell chemistry involves the study of reactions in aqueous solutions. But much of the water in cells is not ordinary water; rather it is structured in shells surrounding macromolecules, especially proteins. In fact, it has been suggested that most of the water in cells is structured and that the reactions of aqueous solutions in test tubes are not synonymous with the chemistry of the living cell.

The unique role of water in cells

CELL MORPHOLOGY—FORM AND STRUCTURE

It is possible to make generalizations about the structure of eucaryotic cells because all are built of a relatively small number of similar structural elements; each kind of cell thus can be considered as a variant of a basic plan.

Sizes and shapes of cells. All eucaryotic cells can be thought of as spheres with diameters ranging from about ten to 100 microns (1 micron = 0.001 millimetre [0.0004 inch]). Few are smaller. Larger ones can be considered as specialized cases—cells that contain many nuclei can be regarded as several cells sharing the same skin (*e.g.*, giant amoebas and slime molds); cells that include an exceptionally large amount of storage material (*e.g.*, eggs); cells in which a large part of the volume is occupied by vacuoles (cavities) rather than by active cytoplasm (*e.g.*, many specialized cells of plants).

Most cells are not actually spherical in shape but can be converted to spheres. The deviation from the spherical form depends on supporting structures. In animal cells, for example, the supporting structure, sometimes called the cytoskeleton, is an internal one; it contains fibrous elements, of which the most prominent is the microtubule system (see below *Microtubules*). Many animal cells, which assume a flat shape by adhering to a solid surface, assume a spherical form when they are detached from the surfaces. The shapes of many protozoans are determined by an external rigid covering, or pellicle. Plant cells are encased in cellulose walls of definite shapes. There are many other kinds of cell walls—*e.g.*, the siliceous walls of diatoms. Plant cells and other cells contained in cell walls form spherical bodies called protoplasts when the walls are removed.

Morphological elements—parts of cells. *The cell membrane.* The cell membrane, or plasma membrane, is the boundary between the external environment and the internal environment; it can be defined functionally as the barrier to the free passage of molecules. Structurally, it is recognized as a layer 60 to 100 angstroms (one angstrom = 0.0001 micron) thick and is thus visible only with the electron microscope. It has a trilayered appearance after treatment by certain electron microscopic techniques. Because the appearance of the surface membrane is much the same in all kinds of cells—procaryotic and eucaryotic—and similar to that of internal membranes of eucaryotic cells, the term unit membrane is widely used. It should be made clear, however, that the term is morphological and that the chemistry and functions of various unit membranes differ greatly.

Chemically, all unit membranes consist of lipid and protein, the protein representing 50 to 75 percent of the material. The major classes of lipids prominent in most membranes are the phospholipids and cholesterols, which are present in varying proportions. Proteins found at the outer surface of membranes differ from those found at the inner surface. Those at the outer surface include prominent amounts of glycoproteins—*i.e.*, proteins combined with polysaccharides; in animal cells, the conspicuous carbohydrate component is sialic acid. Less is known about the proteins of the inner membrane face, but it is thought that they are not glycoproteins. In the case of the mammalian red blood cell, the best studied membrane, the number of structural proteins is not extremely large, there being perhaps three major kinds and five or six smaller components.

Chemical composition of membranes

Physically, the outstanding characteristic of cell membranes is their extremely high electrical resistance, in the range of 1,000 to 10,000 ohms per square centimetre. This resistance is consistent with the presence of a continuous layer of lipid, which has only a few channels for the passage of ions (charged particles). The negative charge at the surface of cell membranes is attributed to the negatively charged sialic acid groups in the glycoproteins of the outer layer.

There is no accepted molecular model of a cell membrane at present. A classical "sandwich" model, in which a continuous inner layer of lipids two molecules thick is sandwiched between two layers of protein, has served very well to account for many properties of membranes. Its validity is questionable, however, in view of evidence from the freeze-fracture method of electron microscopy, in which the membrane appears to be peelable into two layers with particles dispersed between them. It has been proposed that the membrane consists of particles of both lipids and proteins rather than a distinct double layer of lipids and outer and inner layers of proteins (see MEMBRANE, BIOLOGICAL).

Extracellular coats. Many, if not all, animal cells have structures that lie outside the cell membrane as it has been defined above. A common feature is that of hairlike projections, which give the cell a fuzzy appearance. At the places where cells come together, as in tissues, layers of a cement-like substance are laid down outside the cell membrane. These surface layers play an extremely important part in the attachment of cells to solid surfaces and to each other. Since freely suspended cells can be obtained from tissues or from cells growing on surfaces by treating them either with a protein-digesting enzyme, with a reagent that removes calcium ions, or both, it seems probable that the extracellular coats are composed of proteins—in some cases they have been identified as glycoproteins—the adhesive properties of which depend on calcium ions.

Intracellular membrane system. The intracellular membrane system of eucaryotic cells consists of structures inside the cell membrane that are bounded by unit membranes. Membranes are employed in a variety of functions to sequester some of the material of the cell. The endoplasmic reticulum, for example, is a complex network of sacs, sometimes flattened, that are enclosed by unit membranes. The Golgi apparatus is a stack of very flattened vesicles (dictyosomes); the vesicles are one to two microns in diameter and have an inner space 100 to 200 angstrom units thick. The lysosomes, little round vesicles about 0.5 micron in diameter, contain a variety of digestive enzymes.

Mitochondria. Mitochondria are typically sausage-shaped particles about 0.5 to one micron wide and five to ten microns long; they are surrounded by an outer unit membrane that is separated by about 70 angstroms from an inner membrane. The outer membrane is comparable to other cell membranes in that it controls the passage of material into and out of the mitochondrion and governs its internal environment. The inner membrane is the site of the respiratory functions that make the mitochondrion the so-called powerhouse of the cell.

The study of mitochondria has focussed on the enzymes and on their relation to mitochondrial structure. The membranes consist of about 30 percent lipids; a considerable proportion of the proteins are thought to be enzymes involved in respiration and the phosphorylation—the addition of phosphate groups—of ATP.

Mitochondrial activities

Mitochondrial membranes not only contain the respiratory enzymes but are also active in controlling the inward and outward passage of ions, especially those of calcium, and molecules. Further, they may be active in a "contractile" way; *i.e.*, expansions and contractions of the mitochondrial surfaces are correlated with decreasing and increasing respiratory activity. In general, mitochondria provide the best examples within the cell of correlations between structure and activity.

The mitochondrion has a degree of autonomy that makes it quite unlike the other components of cells. It contains DNA in the form of a "chromosome" resembling that of a procaryotic cell; this chromosome carries the genes for some of the enzymes found in mitochondria. Thus the mitochondrion can synthesize some of its own proteins and can reproduce itself. In one respect the mitochondrion is a part of the eucaryotic cell; in another, it is an independent organism.

Ribosomes. Ribosomes are particles about 200 angstrom units in diameter consisting of about 40 percent protein and 60 percent RNA. Very numerous in a cell, they may account for 40 to 60 percent of its total RNA. In typical eucaryotic cells, ribosomes may occur both as free particles and as particles attached to the membranes of the endoplasmic reticulum.

Ribosomes are so small that it has not yet been possible to determine fine details of their structure, even with the electron microscope; it is known, however, that they are composed of two subunits, one larger and different in shape from the other. Although they are usually described as macromolecules, their chemistry in fact is quite complex; they contain 20 or more different kinds of proteins.

Microtubules. To account for the forms of cells and for certain processes such as cell division, the existence of fibrillar elements was long postulated; their existence was proved in the late 1950s using the electron microscope. The discovery of microtubules provided an explanation for many problems of cell structure.

Microtubules are about 200 angstroms in diameter; their length ranges from ten to hundreds of microns; and they have the appearance of straight, unbranched tubes. The tubules appear as cylindrical arrays of filaments about 35 to 40 angstroms in diameter; typically there are 12 or 13 such apparent filaments. The filaments are rows of particles about 35 to 40 angstroms in diameter; this diameter corresponds to that of a protein molecule of 50,000 to 100,000 molecular weight.

Chemically, the microtubules are composed of protein molecules, each with a molecular weight of about 100,000; the protein molecules in turn consist of two subunits of slightly different structure, each with a molecular weight of about 50,000. The proteins of microtubules combine with the drug colchicine, a characteristic that is often used to identify existing microtubules or to prevent the formation of new ones; both are important in establishing relationships between microtubules and various cell functions.

The microtubules often provide the structural frame for cell shapes. The shapes of many cells—for example, cells such as the protozoan *Actinosphaerium*, the surface of which is extended in long spikes—are the result of the disposition of microtubules; the cells revert to a spherical form if the microtubules are broken down. The structure of cilia and flagella, short and stiff or long and whiplike organs of locomotion, respectively, is accounted for by an arrangement of microtubules.

Microfilaments. Only in the late 1960s were microfilaments perceived as a universal element of cell structure—one especially involved in the motility of cells. Microfilaments, about 40 to 50 angstroms in diameter and of indefinite length, are composed of a protein with general properties similar to actin, the protein of the thin filaments of muscle, which was intensively studied long before it was realized that such filaments are universal components of eucaryotic cells.

Functional aspects of microfilaments

Microfilaments are involved in many kinds of cell motility; the evidence showing the equivalence of the thin actin filaments of all kinds of muscle and microfilaments is quite strong. Microfilaments are associated with cytoplasmic streaming movements in plant and animal cells, with amoeboid movement, and with the "ruffling" movements so characteristic of the surfaces of animal cells when grown in culture. Microfilaments have not been found, however, in association with flagella, cilia, or the mitotic apparatus (*i.e.*, the spindle-shaped structure evident in cells during cell division). Microfilaments are the supporting structures of microvilli, fingerlike outward extensions covering many kinds of cells, and the inward cuplike extensions of many cell surfaces when they take up large molecules and particles by the processes of pinocytosis and phagocytosis—intaking of water drops or solid particles at the membrane surface of the cell.

The nuclear envelope. In all eucaryotic cells, the chromosomes are contained within a nuclear envelope during at least a large part of the cell cycle; this interval, called interphase, is the period between cell divisions. In most single-celled eucaryotes (fungi, protozoans, and algae) the chromosomes are encased by the nuclear envelope at all times; in cells of multicellular plants and animals, the nuclear envelope breaks down during mitosis (cell division).

The nuclear envelope has a characteristic structure, consisting of two unit membranes separated by about 200 angstroms. The membranes appear to be perforated by pores, which are about 500 angstroms in diameter and which occupy 10 to 20 percent of the cell surface. It has not yet been established with certainty whether these pores actually are open passages between the nucleus and cytoplasm. Although they can always be seen under the electron microscope, other kinds of evidence suggest that the nuclear envelope is sometimes open and sometimes closed to the passage of ions, molecules, and particles.

In any case, the pores are not regarded as mere perforations; rather, they are quite elaborate structures, called annuli, that persist after the rest of the membrane has been destroyed experimentally. Moreover, there is now good evidence that the annuli are the sites at which chromosome threads attach to the nuclear surface, and they

Opposite page: Figure 1: *Generalized animal and plant cells and some of their component structures.*
(A) Freeze-etch preparation of cell showing (NE) nuclear envelope with its (NP) nuclear pores (magnified about 5,200 ×). (B) Cell nucleus showing darkly stained (Nu) nucleolus, (Nm) nucleoplasm, and (NE) nuclear envelope (magnified about 13,300 ×). (C) Giant (polytene) chromosome of fruitfly (*Drosophila*) showing dark-staining (Ch) chromomeres that in many cases correspond to the locations of single genes (magnified about 47,000 ×). (D left) Centriole (magnified about 148,000 ×) and (D right) interpretative drawing showing (MT) microtubule triplets and encircling bands of (Mm) macromolecules. (E left) Endoplasmic reticulum (magnified about 40,000 ×) and (E right) interpretative drawing showing (Ri) ribosomes covering (MS) membrane sheets. (F left, F centre) Mitochondrion in two longitudinal sections at right angles to one another (magnified about 24,000 × and 47,000 × respectively) and (F right) interpretative drawing showing (OM) outer membrane, (IM) inner membrane, (Cr) cristae, and (Ma) matrix. (G left) Chloroplast (magnified about 7,700 ×) and (G right) interpretative drawing showing (Gr) grana and (Ig) intergrana. (H) Plant cell wall showing (CW) cellulose wall material, (ML) middle lamella, and (Pd) plasmadesmata (magnified about 21,000 ×). (I) A microtubule bundle in the cytoplasm (magnified about 15,000 ×). (J) Ribosomes in whorls attached to the exterior of the endoplasmic reticulum, seen here in longitudinal section (magnified about 9,000 ×). (K left) Golgi apparatus (magnified about 47,000 ×) and (K right) interpretative drawing showing (Ve) vesicles and (PL) parallel lamellae or flattened membrane sacs.

By courtesy of Harry T. Horner, Jr., and James P. Braselton, Department of Bota ny and Plant Pathology, Iowa State University, Ames, (B,K left) Eldon H. Newcomb, (C) Harvey A. Bender, (D left) Etienne de Harven, (E left) Melvin Weinstock, (F left) Keith R. Porter, (F centre) Humberto Fernandez-Moran, the University of Chicago, (G left) L.K. Shumway, Genetics and Botany, Washington State University, Pullman, (H) Harry T. Horner, Jr., Department of Botany and Plant Pathology, Iowa State University, Ames, (I) Richard D. Allen, (J) H.T. Bonnett, Jr., and E.H. Newcomb; (D right) From the book *Cells: Their Structure and Function* by E.H. Mercer, Copyright © 1962 by the American Museum of Natural History, Copyright © 1961 and 1965 by E.H. Mercer. Reprinted by permission of Doubleday & Company, Inc. (E right, K right, generalized animal cell) after *Biology Today* (© 1972); Communications Research Machines, Inc., (F right, G right, generalized plant cell) after Payson Stevens from *Biology Today* (© 1972); Communications Research Machines, Inc.

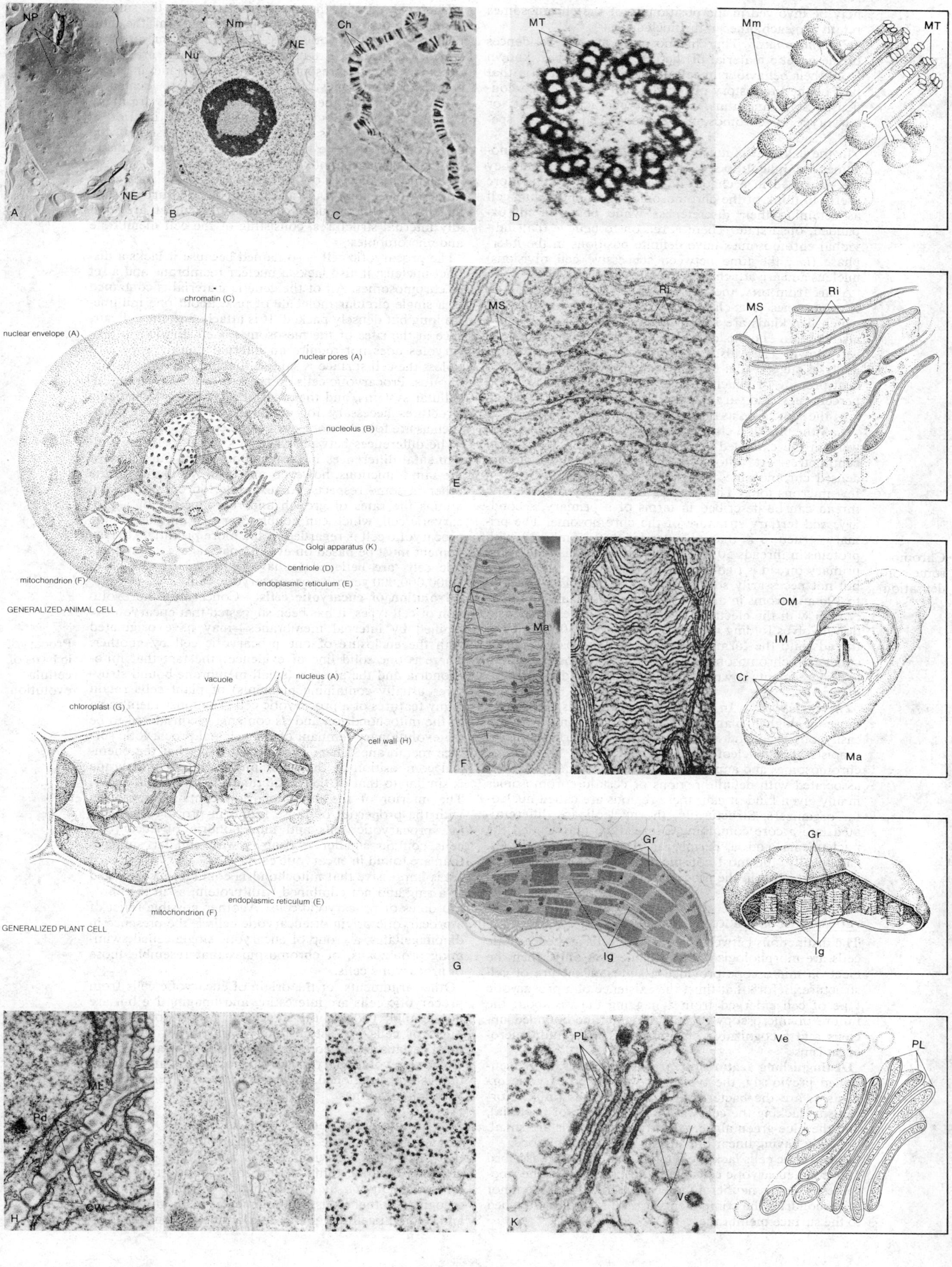
NP
NE
A
Nm
Nu
NE
B
Ch
C
MT
D
Mm
MT
chromatin (C)
nuclear envelope (A)
nuclear pores (A)
nucleolus (B)
Golgi apparatus (K)
centriole (D)
endoplasmic reticulum (E)
mitochondrion (F)
GENERALIZED ANIMAL CELL
Ri
MS
E
MS
Ri
vacuole
nucleus (A)
chloroplast (G)
cell wall (H)
mitochondrion (F)
endoplasmic reticulum (E)
GENERALIZED PLANT CELL
Cr
Ma
F
OM
IM
Cr
Ma
Gr
Ig
G
Gr
Ig
ML
Pd
CW
H
PL
Ve
K
Ve
PL

may be involved in the positioning of the chromosomes relative to each other in the nucleus.

Chromosomes. The chromosomes are the residences of the genetic material of the cell. They are best known from their behaviour in cell division because it is in that part of the life history of the cell that they are in a condensed state and thus visible. A characteristic set, or karyotype, of chromosomes is recognized for each species.

In the cell that is not dividing, the individual chromosomes are difficult to see, although it is not true that they are dispersed in a chaotic tangle of threads. It is more useful to think of the chromosomes in a nondividing cell as retaining their discreteness while being in an expanded, open state. There is reason to believe that individual chromosomes have definite positions in the interphase (*i.e.*, the time between successive cell divisions) nucleus and are attached to the nuclear membrane.

Apart from DNA, the most characteristic constituent of chromosomes is a class of proteins called histones, of which five kinds are found in most cells. Chromosomes also contain "nonhistone proteins," about which little is yet known. They also contain RNA. The few published analyses suggest that chromosomes contain 60 to 70 percent protein, of which half or more is histone; 15 to 30 percent DNA; and varying amounts of RNA, most of which is of the same kind as the RNA of ribosomes.

If all the DNA of a chromosome of a plant or animal cell were in the extended form, it would extend for several centimetres. At mitosis (cell division), the fully condensed chromosomes are thick elongated bodies only a few microns long. The packing of the very long genetic thread can be described in terms of a primary, secondary, and tertiary structure of the chromosome. The primary structure is that of extended DNA combined with proteins in threads 50 to 100 angstroms in diameter. The primary thread is tightly packed, perhaps by tight coiling but not necessarily so, to form thick threads about 200 to 300 angstroms in diameter. Such threads are commonly seen with the electron microscope. Further condensation involves folding or coiling the 200- to 300-angstrom threads into the forms recognized in the observation of condensed chromosomes with the light microscope; there is disagreement, however, as to whether folding or coiling occurs.

Chromosome condensation

The nucleolus. In many eucaryotic cells, especially those of higher plants and animals, the nucleoli are easily observed and were noted by the earliest microscopists. The nucleoli are best understood as parts of chromosomes and appendages to chromosomes. They are associated with definite regions of certain chromosomes in any given kind of cell; these regions are called nucleolus organizers. Structurally, the nucleoli are differentiated into a core containing a threadlike mass called the nucleonema and a peripheral zone full of particles. Chemically, the most conspicuous nucleolar constituent is RNA, which is in the process of being converted to ribosomal RNA.

PROCARYOTIC AND EUCARYOTIC CELLS

The distinctions between procaryotic cells and eucaryotic cells are morphological and became firm only when the electron microscope provided a sufficient picture of cell structure. Before that time, the existence of a procaryotic type of cell emerged from a nagging unease about the failure of microscopy to find a membrane-bounded nucleus and recognizable chromosomes in certain microorganisms.

Distinguishing features of procaryotic cells. As mentioned previously, the typical groups of procaryotic organisms are the bacteria, the mycoplasmas (minute organisms lacking the cell walls characteristic of bacteria), and the blue-green algae. All procaryotic cells are small, typically having linear dimensions below ten microns.

Procaryotic cells lack the internal components described above for eucaryotic cells, with the exception of the ribosomes. There is neither an internal membrane system nor mitochondria; the components are built into or attached to the surface membrane.

When viewed with the electron microscope, the surface membrane does not differ appreciably from the unit membrane of eucaryotic cells. Masses called mesosomes, which are inrolled extensions of the surface, are sometimes visible. The respiratory enzymes found in mitochondrial membranes of eucaryotic cells are located in the surface membranes of procaryotic cells, as are many of the other enzymes normally found in the interior of eucaryotic cells. It is of evolutionary interest that the cells considered to be the most primitive have so many components packed into a single membrane.

The motile flagella of procaryotic cells are molecular threads that extend outward from the cell surface. The flagella and cilia of eucaryotic cells, in contrast, are actually internal structures, consisting of the cell membrane and microtubules.

The procaryotic cell is so named because it lacks a distinct nucleus; it also lacks a nuclear membrane and a set of chromosomes. All of the genetic material is contained in a single circular molecule of DNA, about one millimetre long but densely packed. It is attached to the cell surface at the sites of the mesosomes. Cell division in procaryotes does not require an internal mitotic apparatus unless the cell surface is said to function as a mitotic apparatus. Procaryotic cells do not associate to form multicellular systems, and they lack the cytoplasmic bridging structures necessary for communication between cells, such as are found among eucaryotic cells.

The differences between the two kinds of cells are fundamental differences in design. Both carry out many of the same functions, however, and each is superior to the other in some respects; for example, no eucaryotic cell attains the rates of growth and reproduction of a procaryotic cell, which can double every 20 minutes. If the procaryotic cell is regarded as the more primitive, the argument must be based on evolutionary age; *i.e.*, procaryotic cells are believed to have appeared on the earth 1,000,000,000 years before eucaryotic cells.

Evolution of eucaryotic cells. Concerning the evolution of cell types, it has been suggested that eucaryotes—typified by internal membranes—may have originated with the enclosure of one procaryotic cell by another. There is one solid line of evidence: the fact that mitochondria and the plastids (small membrane-bound structures usually containing pigments) of plant cells retain many features of a procaryotic cell. The inner membrane of the mitochondrion and its contents is considered to be the evolutionary remnant of the original procaryotic surface membrane. There is some evidence that the chemical composition of the inner mitochondrial membrane is similar to that of the membranes of procaryotic cells. The interior of the mitochondrion contains ribosomes with the properties of those found in procaryotic cells; *i.e.*, procaryotic cells and mitochondria of eucaryotic cells contain smaller ribosomes with smaller subunits than are found in eucaryotic cells.

Procaryotic basis of cellular evolution

It is impressive that mitochondria contain DNA arranged in a ring and not combined with protein, as in the chromosomes of procaryotic cells. Another possible relict of a procaryotic origin of eucaryotic cells is the presence in dinoflagellates, a group of eucaryotic single-celled swimming protozoans, of chromosomes that resemble those of procaryotic cells.

Other arguments for the origin of eucaryotic cells from procaryotic cells are interesting and imaginative but are not factual. In fact, the molecular aspects of the two kinds of cells are astonishingly similar, but the structural designs are different in almost all important aspects. Common evolutionary origin of procaryotes and eucaryotes is not questioned, only the point of divergence between the two lines.

II. Functional aspects of cells in life

Contemplation of the living cell leads to the recognition that it exhibits behaviour and is a wiggling, streaming, growing, dividing thing capable of adapting to extraordinary conditions by responding to various stimuli. It recognizes other cells, communicates with other cells, and, in multicellular plants and animals, transforms itself according to genetic directions from the organism of which it is a part.

THE INTERNAL ENVIRONMENT AND THE CELL MATRIX

The conceptual image of the cell has passed between two extremes. On the one hand there has long existed the idea of a "protoplasm," implying the existence of a unique complex of matter—in effect, a supermolecule, in which are embodied the properties of life. At the other extreme is the idea that the cell is a "bag" containing a water solution of molecules or a bag containing a suspension of particles, such as mitochondria, ribosomes, and others, in an aqueous solution variously called the "soluble fraction" or cytosol.

If the latter image is considered, the nature of the internal environment can be described as follows. The cell water would contain a fair amount of macromolecular material; since about 50 percent of the proteins are soluble by conventional criteria, the cell water would be about a 10 percent solution of free macromolecules. From the analyses of the whole cell, it can be calculated that the internal environment would contain 0.1 to 0.2 molar—moles per litre of solution; each mole contains about 6.024×10^{23} atoms, ions, or molecules—potassium ions (K^+), 0.02 to 0.05 molar sodium ions (Na^+), 0.01 to 0.05 molar magnesium ions (Mg^{++}), and about 0.001 to 0.0001 molar calcium ions (Ca^{++}). There are some chloride ions (Cl^-), some sulfate ions (SO_4^-), and some phosphate ions (PO_4^{3-}); but most of the negatively charged ions (anions) would be organic acids. The pH (acidity, a measure of the hydrogen ion concentration) would be 6.9 to 7.2 (7 is neutral, lower numbers are acidic, higher ones basic). Some of these figures are misleading in one important way; for example, because much of the internal calcium is sequestered within internal membranes, the concentration prevailing throughout the cell is far lower than that measured by whole-cell analysis. In fact, the concept of "compartments" dominates much thought about the cell; figures such as the averages given above, therefore, do not necessarily reveal anything about the local environment in the living cell.

When the idea of a "protoplasm" was more prevalent than now, it was supposed that the matrix of the cell must have a characteristic structure. The physical properties of that structure were thought to be capable of definition by study of intracellular viscosity. If the matrix of the cell were an aqueous solution containing various proteins and ions, the viscosity should not be much greater than that of water; yet early work showed that the viscosity of "protoplasm" is highly variable; that, in different states of activity, the cell substance can behave as a watery fluid or as a fairly rigid substance (gel). Modern techniques have provided more substantial information about the cellular matrix; its viscosity has been found to be rather high—about 20 times that of water. The mechanical properties of the whole cell contents (called visco-elastic properties) have also been studied: the movement in a magnetic field of a small iron ball introduced into the cell and its recoil after the field has been removed reveal that the cell contents do have a relatively high viscosity—about 100 times that of water. The viscosity can be even higher; for example, the contents of a sea urchin egg become a very viscous gel at the time of fertilization. These results have led to the belief that there may be an as yet unexplored level of cell structure, indeed a structured matrix.

Mechanical properties of cell contents

The contents of the cell are variable; for example, internal membranes appear and disappear readily, as do microtubules. The molecular principle by which the formation of such structures is described is called the assembly principle. It is postulated that the cell contains a pool of free-floating molecules, which, under suitable circumstances, fall together spontaneously to form a structure. A conceivable alternative is that the molecules are not free-floating but already assembled and need only to assume the correct geometric order; in this case, the formation of a structure would be a transfiguration rather than an assembly. Such latent structure would be part of the underlying structure of the cell and thus would not be observed by present microscopic methods.

LIVING MEMBRANES

The surface membrane accounts for fundamental properties of the cell, the interior of which is never in equilibrium with the environment; in fact, an immediate sign of the death of a cell is the penetration of molecules that could not enter the living cell. If a nontoxic dye that does not penetrate living cells is added to a population of cells, for example, the number of cells that become coloured is the number of dead cells.

Membranes as barriers. The passive permeability properties of cells—their ability to take up certain substances without the expenditure of energy—have been well studied. The penetration of water is retarded, compared with free diffusion, as would be expected of a lipid layer; on the other hand, molecules soluble in lipids penetrate readily, independently of their size. Molecules soluble in water but insoluble in lipids, however, penetrate only if they are small; a molecular weight of about 100 is about the upper limit. Salts do not penetrate the membrane, which may be permeable to positively or negatively charged ions but not to both. These properties are exploited practically, as in the design of drugs that will enter cells or of blood plasma additives that will not.

Membranes and transport. The cell is not at the mercy of the passive properties of the membranes, however; it regulates the passage of molecules by the mechanism of active transport, employing a specific transport protein for each kind of molecule pumped into or out of the cell (see MEMBRANE, BIOLOGICAL). One important discovery of recent years has been that transport proteins (*e.g.*, sodium-potassium ATPase) may also be enzymes (biological catalysts) that split ATP (adenosine triphosphate); since the inside of cells is high in potassium but low in sodium and their environment is high in sodium but low in potassium, the cell must pump potassium inward and sodium outward.

Membranes and endocytosis. Most eucaryotic cells take up not only molecules but droplets of liquid (pinocytosis) and solid particles (phagocytosis); collectively these processes are termed endocytosis. During endocytosis, the cell membrane bends itself into a cup or channel, surrounding the droplet or particle; this piece of membrane is pinched off, forming a vacuole, which then passes to the cell interior. This process enables molecules and particles too large to pass through the membrane to enter the cell. The contents of the vacuole, however, cannot be used by the cell until the enclosing membrane has been broken down. The vacuole becomes a digestive vacuole, or phagosome, by fusion with lysosomes, particles that carry digestive enzymes.

Lysosomes

The lysosomes contain enzymes within their membranes that can digest such large molecules as proteins, nucleic acids, lipids, and carbohydrates; in fact, these enzymes destroy the cell if set free. Accordingly lysosomes are sometimes called "suicide bags." Within the digestive vacuoles (phagosomes), the enzymes of the lysosomes break down the material taken in by endocytosis, setting the products free for use by the cell. The used digestive vacuole may then pass to the cell surface, fuse with it, and eject undigested material outward.

Membranes and export. The internal membrane system often serves as a channel between the cell and the outer world. The endoplasmic reticulum, which often is associated with ribosomes, takes up proteins that are to be delivered to the outside. Proteins are made on the ribosomes, pass into the cavities of the endoplasmic reticulum, and are passed to the surface in vacuoles that fuse with the surface membrane. The Golgi apparatus plays a similar role but is thought to specialize in the formation and export of the polysaccharide-containing proteins that are important components of the outer coats of the cell. Cells that are very specialized for the movement of water and solutes into and out of organisms—such as cells of the gills of fish—undergo extensive development of internal vacuoles that sequester the water and ions on one side of the cell and carry them to the other for ejection.

Membranes have been imaginatively described as undergoing movements such as bending, engulfing, fusing, pinching off, and migrating. Some of these processes, such as fusion, can be understood in terms of the physical properties of membranes themselves; others involve different intracellular mechanisms. Extensions of the cell surface in fingerlike processes called microvilli, which increase the surface area of a cell, are supported by microfilaments inside the microvilli. Similarly, the formation of the vacuole during endocytosis depends on microfilaments, as does the active ruffling, wavelike motions of cell surfaces. The projection of the surface membrane to form a cilium of flagellum, the length of which can be greater than the diameter of the cell, is supported by microtubules.

Membranes and the generation of electricity. The generation of electric currents by cells depends on the properties of the surface membrane. There is a bioelectric potential—a voltage drop caused by biological processes —across the cell surface, typically about 0.06 volt (60 millivolts), with the inside of the cell negative. This potential depends on the concentration differences of ions across the surface and sometimes on the active pumping of ions. Electric potentials occur in all cells studied thus far, although their biological importance is recognized in only a few cases. The properties of membranes have been extensively developed in nerve cells, making possible the conduction of nerve impulses.

Responses to stimuli. Responses to stimuli involve changes of state in cells, and such responses are purposeful in the sense that they serve survival in some way; for example, it was proposed some decades ago that one of the first responses to a stimulus is the release of calcium ions (Ca^{++}) within the cell. In the case of muscle, it is now known that most of the calcium ions within a muscle cell are sequestered in the internal membrane system (sarcoplasmic reticulum) that surrounds the contractile fibrils. The concentration of calcium ions near the fibrils of a resting muscle is very low; when the muscle cell is stimulated, the sarcoplasmic reticulum releases calcium ions to the fibrils. The ions are required for the activity of the enzyme (calcium-sensitive ATPase) that catalyzes the breakdown of ATP during the contraction of the fibrils. Relaxation involves the rapid pumping of calcium ions back into the sarcoplasmic reticulum.

Reception of stimuli by cells

The initial reception of the stimulus is also a membrane event. It is signalled by a wave of depolarization—a change of the electrical potential across the cell surface —that reflects an increase in the penetrability of sodium ions followed by an active pumping out of sodium ions (see MUSCLE CONTRACTION; NERVE IMPULSE).

INTERPLAY OF NUCLEUS AND CYTOPLASM

Overall function of the nucleus. In the eucaryotic cell, most of the genetic information resides in the nucleus. Because the existence of the nucleus was recognized from the early days of microscopy, there were many speculations as to its functions. One basic experiment was to remove the nucleus and to observe the enucleated cell; invariably the cell lived more or less normally for a while and then died. If a nucleus was restored in time, the cell revived. The main function of the nucleus is to make gene products called messenger RNA (mRNA), which pass into the cytoplasm and there direct the synthesis of new proteins. The cytoplasm of a cell deprived of its nucleus survives for a while because it can function with existing proteins until they have to be replaced. Some mRNA molecules remain active for extended periods of time (hours or days) in some eucaryotic cells, although this is not the case in procaryotic cells. In such eucaryotic cells, therefore, the proteins can be replaced until the mRNA no longer functions, and the cell can live for days or weeks—but not indefinitely—without a nucleus.

Most of the many enzymes in the nucleus are found in even larger amounts in the cytoplasm. The nucleus is, however, the main site for a relatively few enzymes concerned with such processes as the making of the nucleotides of which the nucleic acids are composed; the replication of DNA; the transcription of DNA into RNA; and the regulation of these processes. The proteins associated with DNA (histones) are formed in the cytoplasm.

Exchange between nucleus and cytoplasm. Among the substances shuttled between nucleus and cytoplasm are proteins. Although it has been established that certain proteins pass back and forth through the nuclear membrane, their function is not clear. It has long been inferred, but could not be proved, that nucleus-cytoplasm interaction is a two-way process and that the cytoplasm does more than transfer raw materials and ATP into the nucleus for purposes of synthesis. Now the problem has been studied by using certain viruses (Sendai viruses) that change cell membranes so that adjacent cells fuse; as a result, their nuclei share a common cytoplasm. The fusion of a growing cell (the nucleus of which is making RNA) with a nongrowing cell (the nucleus of which is not making RNA) will turn on RNA synthesis in the latter. It has been shown that signals to or between nuclei can pass through the cytoplasm. Apparently, some of the signals are not very specific, since the same results are obtained when cells from quite unrelated organisms are fused. The molecular nature of the signal has not yet been established.

The effect of the cytoplasm on the nucleus can be summarized by the following generalization: whenever several nuclei share the same cytoplasm, their activities tend to become synchronized.

CELLS IN SOCIETIES

The organism level of cellular organization

The evolution of multicellular life, as it occurs in higher plants and animals, requires the extension of the cell concept to include means by which cells can combine, communicate, contribute to the survival of the collective society, and respond to the regulatory actions of the organism as a whole. The organism as a whole is a society of cells, all of which possess the same genes. In the society different cells acquire different structures and functions in a process called differentiation; in each kind of cell, some genes are active, others not. The life-span of the organism is limited, so that most of the cells ultimately die; but the organism is propagated in kind by reproduction through germ cells, ova (eggs) and spermatozoa, which initiate the development of succeeding generations of the same kind of organism. Some diseases—of which cancer is an example—can be described as the escape of cells from the rule of the organism.

Individuality of cells. The idealized cell, as so far described, is very much insulated from other cells. It can maintain its own internal environment; it can proceed on its own timetable, its processes not in synchrony with those of its neighbours; and it can be different morphologically and functionally from neighbouring cells. Although fusion of membranes within the cell is common, cells normally do not fuse to other cells, probably because of some property, perhaps involving the polysaccharides, of the outer surfaces of membranes.

Cells in culture. Cells can be taken out of organisms and grown as individual cells in culture. One observation noted from isolating cells in this way is that many that do not divide when in the organism do divide when grown as individuals in cultures. Equally impressive is the fact that the cells quickly—after a few generations of cell division—lose their distinctive structures and revert to a few general types. Specialized animal cells, for example, revert to elongated, spindle-shaped cells called fibroblasts; or to bricklike epithelioid forms (*i.e.*, that resemble the cells of cavity linings such as the inside of the mouth). It has been observed, however, that the fibroblastic form is maintained by microtubules and can be converted to an epithelioid form by the action of the microtubule-attacking drug colchicine. In studies of the biochemical rather than the morphological characteristics, it has been found that the distinctive synthetic abilities of cells within the original organism are often lost; *e.g.*, cells cultured from mammary glands no longer make the milk-producing enzymes, but cells derived from the retina of the eye may retain the ability to make pigments. Such evidence demonstrates the rule of the organism over the character of cells.

When cells derived from multicellular organisms are cultured for many generations, they undergo a kind of evolution. The chromosome set (karyotype) tends to change; *i.e.*, the numbers and kinds of chromosomes are no longer the same as in the original organism. Certain karyotypes, presumably those best adapted to life independent of the organism, survive in culture and become cell lines, which are populations of cells capable of indefinite propagation. In some cases it is possible to maintain diploid cell lines—that is, cells that maintain the original chromosome set. Such lines tend to die out after a certain number of generations, however—about 50 in some cases. It is as if aging is built into body cells (but not germ cells) and is overcome when cells are grown in culture by modifications of the chromosome set.

Cell cultures are now a widely used tool in research on the cellular problems of higher organisms, especially mammals—differentiation, effects of the environment, cancer, immunity, and especially heredity are studied (see TISSUE CULTURE).

Cell junctions. Cells in the organism are not walled off from each other. In many groupings of cells in tissues, cell junctions can be detected by a physical method or by electron-microscopic observation. The physical method draws on the fact that cell membranes have a very high electrical resistance. If two unjoined cells are placed side by side, an electrode is put inside each, and an electrical potential imposed, there is an extremely high resistance to the passage of current across the two membranes. The electrical resistance between two cells in a tissue—in fact among all the cells of a tissue—however, may be quite low. Some low-resistance channel therefore exists at the apposed membranes; such channels are called junctions, and cells joined by them are said to be electrically coupled. The structure of cell junctions has been studied extensively. Cell membranes, even in a densely packed tissue such as epithelium, normally do not touch each other but are separated by about 150–200 angstroms of intercellular space. This space contains the extracellular cementing material, which is rich in polysaccharides. At the site of junctions, the membranes come very close and, in some cases, may even appear to fuse in rather elaborate structures called desmosomes. In other cases, the two membranes may seem to be held together by cross-connections in a configuration called a septate junction. The exact nature of the substances that pass across the junctions has not yet been established, although it is known that they permit the passage of ions and small molecules.

Structural features of cell junctions

The ability to form junctions is a general property of membranes of cells that normally live in an organism. Cells grown in culture will also form junctions if their numbers become so great that they are pressed against each other. Moreover, junctions may be formed in culture between cells of quite different kinds; such cells would not be joined in an organism.

Recognition and association among cells. Cells in tissues may be experimentally separated from each other in various ways: by procedures that dissolve the intercellular cements; by the use of proteolytic—protein-attacking—enzymes; and by the removal of calcium ions from the environment. Remarkably, cells in tissues can reassociate when returned to a normal medium. Such experiments are most successful when cells from embryos are used. In such cases not only do the cells join but they organize themselves—outside the organism—into excellent facsimiles of normal tissue organization. If two kinds of cells are used (*e.g.*, kidney cells and retinal cells) they sort out to form groupings resembling the two original tissues. If the same kind of cells, but from different species, are mixed, they form a tissue consisting of a mixture of cells of the two species; that is, they organize according to the functional kind of cells they are, not according to the species from which they came.

Some research has been done on the molecules that guide such recognition and association. The molecules are proteins, probably those of the outer coats of cells.

III. The cell cycle—growth and division

Cells have short lives as individuals, but they reproduce. The cell cycle—doubling of a cell in size by growth, then division into two cells, which double in size and divide—guarantees survival of the species if, during division, the daughter cells obtain a set of genes identical to those of the mother cell.

CELL GROWTH

Doubling. During interphase, the period from the "birth" of a cell to the time when it divides, a cell duplicates itself. Experimentally, the doubling may be followed as an increase in volume, mass, or protein content.

The duplication process, or doubling, is relatively exact; careful measurements have shown that the cell stops growing when its mass is twice that at birth with a variation of only about 10 to 15 percent. (Exceptions are micro-organisms grown in very rich conditions; they may divide before they have doubled.) Cells that will not divide again sometimes grow to be more than twice their birth size.

Attention has been devoted to the growth curves (*i.e.*, plots or graphs) of cells as they double; such curves reveal whether growth is linear, exponential (*i.e.*, an accelerating growth rate), or follows some other path. The genetic functions of the growth period involve the read-out of the genes—the conversion of the information contained in a gene to a chemical structure—that results in the synthesis of enzymes. It is known that some genes are read out continuously during the period of growth; others are read out in a specific sequence. An increase in the rate of growth depends on the production of enzymes involved in protein synthesis; if production increases continuously, the growth rate increases continuously. Both linear and exponential growth curves—and some that show sudden changes in the rate of growth—have been found in different cells.

Explanation of growth rates in cells

Genetic replication. Cell division is the equipartition of replicated (doubled) chromosomes, but the replication process (*i.e.*, duplication of chromosomes) takes place in anticipation of division. After the replication of chromosomes begins, it goes to completion, and the cell is committed to divide. The chromosomes of differentiated cells that never divide do not replicate. The replication of chromosomes is measured experimentally as the appearance of "new" DNA, detectable by using radioactive isotopes of substances that are incorporated in the new DNA.

In the typical eucaryotic cell (*i.e.*, in most plant and animal cells) the period of chromosome replication is a so-called *S* period, which takes place about the middle of interphase (the phase of growth between successive cell divisions). The period of interphase preceding the *S* period is generally called *G1*, and the period from the end of the *S* period until the onset of mitosis is called *G2*. The whole of interphase is longer than the period of division; typical schedules of the cell cycle, using the *S* period as the reference point, are shown in the Table. Cells of

Typical Schedules of the Cell Cycle

phase	duration (in hours)	
	in a mouse fibroblast	in a bean root cell
G1	6	10
S	8	7
G2	5	6
Mitosis	1	1

plants and animals require about 12 to 24 hours to complete their cycle, and the replication of the chromosomes generally takes several hours. Within a species, there can be great uniformity of the duration of the *S* phase from cell to cell. The *G1* period, which is not yet completely understood, is the most variable; it must include processes that decide the future division of the cell; if the transition from *G1* to *S* takes place, the cell is committed to divide.

Many unicellular eucaryotes double in a few hours; many procaryotes, however, double in less than an hour. In procaryotes there is no *G1* or *G2;* chromosome replication occupies the whole of interphase. Some kinds of eucaryotic cells, such as many kinds of eggs in the early stages of division (cleavage) or in plasmodial slime molds, have no *G1; S* begins at the end of division and may require only ten to 15 minutes. In animal tissues, some cells remain in *G2* for a long time but enter mitosis immediately upon injury to the tissue. Thus these "*G2* populations" represent an immediate reserve of cells ready to divide for healing processes, without the need to wait for cells to go through the full 24-hour cycle.

Replication of chromosomes

The typical long *S* period involves chromosomal replication, which occurs according to a specific program. Although the DNA in an individual chromosome is physically continuous, it is not continuous for the purposes of replication; instead there are replicating units, regions of the DNA at which replication can be initiated and proceed. A reasonable estimate of the number of replicating units in the chromosomes of a plant or an animal is about 1,000. Replication begins earlier in some chromosomes than in others; however, some chromosomes—the sex chromosomes, for example—typically replicate later than the others. On a given chromosome, different replicating units replicate in a definite order, not necessarily in sequence from one end of the chromosome to the other. In summary, the *S* period is a time during which the replicating units complete the program—each makes one copy of itself. At the end of the *S* period there are two sets of chromosomes, which will become visible after the *G2* events have been completed.

By courtesy of D.T. Hughes, The Chester Beatty Research Institute, London

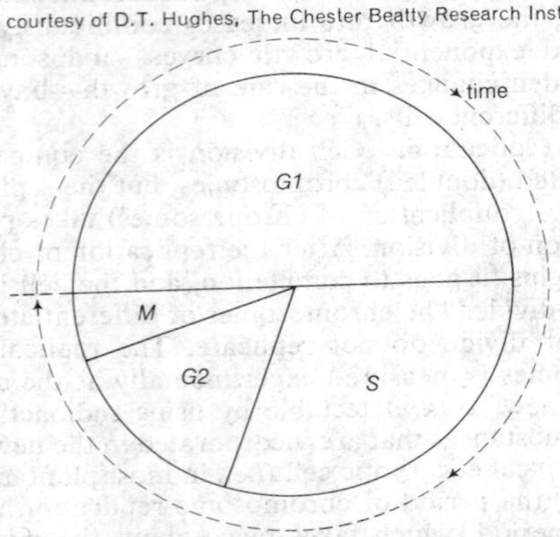

Figure 2: The time course of the cell cycle, showing the relative amount of time a cell spends in each of the phases of growth and division. *M*, time of mitosis; *G1*, interval between end of mitosis and onset of DNA synthesis; *S*, DNA synthetic phase; *G2*, phase between DNA doubling and onset of next mitosis (see text).

When cells whose chromosomes have different durations for the *S* period are fused, both nuclei enter *S* at the same time but need not complete it at the same time. This is because the initiation of the *S* period is a distinct event of the cell; the completion of *S* is determined by the chromosomes.

Preparations for mitosis. Certain events of interphase involve preparations for division; the distinction is meaningful since such events need not take place in cells that grow but will not divide. One of the obvious preparations is the replication of the chromosomes. Another is the replication of the centrioles, bodies that (in animal cells and some others) determine the poles to which the chromosomes will move. The mitotic apparatus, a spindle-shaped structure in the cytoplasm, consists of proteins; the best known are those forming the microtubules of the mitotic spindle. Evidence indicates that a cell will not enter division if the synthesis of proteins is interrupted during interphase, even if the interruption occurs shortly before division. It has also been established that microtubule proteins are synthesized before division.

MITOSIS

Mitosis in eucaryotic cells can be defined as the separation of sister chromosomes to the opposite poles of the mitotic apparatus. Procaryotic cells have no mitotic apparatus unless special devices in the cell membrane, not yet discovered, move chromosomes; it will be recalled that the chromosomes are attached to the membrane at sites called mesosomes (see above *Distinguishing features of procaryotic cells*). Apparently, growth of the membrane between the attachment points of sister chromosomes moves them apart. Separation of chromosomes is part of growth in procaryotic cells; the eucaryotic cell ceases to grow during mitosis.

The typical mitosis sequence of a eucaryotic cell can be displayed in a diagram (see Figure 3). The major events are the chromosome cycle and the alignment and deployment of the chromosomes by the mitotic apparatus in the cytoplasm. The nuclear membrane breaks down when the chromosomes are engaged by the mitotic apparatus. Chromosomes make attachments to the poles in such a way that each sister chromosome is attached to a different pole. The attachments, seen as spindle fibres, appear to draw the sister chromosomes to opposite poles. At the end, the chromosomes are no longer condensed, and a new nuclear membrane forms around each group of chromosomes. Then the cell divides in two.

Variations in the pattern of mitosis

Observation of more primitive and smaller eucaryotic cells using electron microscopy has resulted in the recognition that this generalized pattern of mitosis applies mainly to multicellular plants and animals. In many unicellular eucaryotic cells, the nuclear membrane does not break down. In cases in which the mitotic apparatus is inside the nucleus, elongation of microtubules results in elongation of the nucleus, which pinches in two after the chromosomes have separated. In other unicellular forms (*e.g.*, the flagellated protozoan *Barbalunympha*, found in termites and related forms), a spindle forms in the cytoplasm but the nuclear membrane does not break down. The spindle fibres connect to the chromosomes at the nuclear membrane, separating them as the spindle elongates. In the unusual case of the dinoflagellate protozoans, in which the chromosomes resemble those of procaryotic cells, the spindles consist of bundles of microtubules that run through "tunnels" in the nucleus and attach to the chromosomes, which remain inside the nuclear membrane. In most of the following discussion, mitosis is treated as it is seen in multicellular plants and animals.

Special structures in mitosis. *Centrioles.* Centrioles are bodies that define the poles of mitosis in animal cells, some plant cells, and some lower forms; they are not seen as such in the cells of higher plants. Poles can be identified by the presence of visible particles whose behaviour reveals something about important mitotic events. Even though visible centrioles are lacking in plant cells, there are no good reasons to propose different mechanisms of mitosis. It may be assumed that the true pole is some part of the centriole that can be recognized and that an equivalent body will eventually be found in cells in which the poles are apparently not marked by particles. The idea of the poles themselves is unambiguous: they determine the axes of the spindle and of the spindle fibres, and they are the points toward which chromosomes separate. The cell usually divides in a plane midway between the poles and at right angles to the axis connecting them.

The animal centriole has a well-defined structure; typically, it is a cylinder about 0.5 micron long or longer and 0.5 micron in diameter; the centriole can be resolved into nine groups of short microtubules arranged as cylinders. Each group consists of three microtubules, each of which is slightly different in length. Particles may be arrayed around the centriole. The kinetosomes, which organize the microtubules of cilia and flagella at cell surfaces, are similar in structure and derive from centrioles.

In yeasts, definite centrioles with a different morphology from that of the animal centriole are found. Some flagellate protozoans have structures that have been called centrioles by virtue of their functions.

The centrioles are regarded as self-replicating bodies. Even though there is as yet no good evidence that they contain DNA, it is significant that they can be seen to reproduce during the *S* period of the cell. The centriole does not divide, but a daughter centriole, a procentriole, grows out from one end—almost always at right angles to the axis of the mother centriole. This generative form of reproduction suggests that somewhere in the centriole is a seed that replicates to produce a daughter, which can then organize another centriole. In most cases centrioles occur as pairs, a mother and a daughter at right angles to each other. The mitotic poles are normally observed as such pairs, but it is known that each member of the pair, given time to separate, can form a pole.

Kinetochores. The kinetochores, also called centromeres, are regions of condensed chromosomes that attach to spindle fibres and thus to the poles. Their positions on the chromosomes are so well defined that the shapes of chromosomes are accounted for by the positions of the kinetochores, which act as bending points or constrictions. If a chromosome loses the part containing the kinetochore, as can occur after radiation, it cannot attach to the mitotic apparatus and will be ejected and lost at mitosis.

When viewed with the electron microscope, kinetochores appear as a region denser than the rest of the chromosome, sometimes layered, at the points of attachment of the microtubules of the mitotic spindle. The kinetochores as structures have been seen only in condensed mitotic chromosomes. Evidence indicates that they are attached to the nuclear membrane before it breaks down.

Chromosome behaviour at the beginning of mitosis

The chromosome cycle. In mitosis, the tertiary or highly condensed structure of chromosomes develops. In light microscopy, thin, long threads that define the early prophase stage of mitosis become resolvable, and they soon became shorter and thicker. There is increasing evidence that the chromosomes occupy definite positions in relation to each other: the kinetochores are near the nuclear membrane; the ends of the chromosome arms attach at early prophase to form a chain of chromosomes; and homologous chromosomes—chromosomes of the same kind but from different parents—are next to each other. The condensation does not depend on the mitotic apparatus; it goes to completion even in the presence of colchicine, which prevents the formation of a mitotic apparatus. The condensation proceeds past the time of the breakdown of the nuclear membrane and even past metaphase (the stage of mitosis at which all the chromosomes are aligned on the plane of cell division); maximum condensation is seen at anaphase (the stage of mitosis when the chromosomes are separated and are approaching the poles of the mitotic apparatus).

It is known that condensation is a distinct event, elicited by a specific cytoplasmic signal. Mitosis can be delayed by small doses of irradiation, and it has been proved that the delay is accounted for by a delay in the onset of prophase condensation of the chromosomes; whatever invokes condensation is sensitive to radiation. If a cell in mitosis, with condensed chromosomes, is fused with a cell in any other phase of the cell cycle, the chromosomes of the latter cell condense. If these chromosomes happen to be in the *S* period of interphase, they condense in fragments, as though the chromosome were not physically continuous during its replication period.

Early stages of the formation of the mitotic apparatus. Even as the chromosomes are condensing within the still-intact nuclear membrane, the mitotic apparatus may begin to assemble and to form poles. In the light microscope the assembly may be seen as the formation of a clear zone near or around the nucleus. The clarity of the developing mitotic apparatus is significant; as its constituents are assembling in a dense mass, larger particles of the cytoplasm, such as mitochondria, are ejected. The focus of the assembly is seen to be the centriole—more accurately, the two centrioles, each consisting of a fully grown centriole and a procentriole growing at right angles from it. The material being assembled consists of a matrix of densely packed vesicles, which sometimes extend radially from the centrioles, and microtubules, which radiate from the centrioles. In many cases, in both plants and animals, the developing mitotic apparatus polarizes even before the breakdown of the nuclear membrane, and it can be determined where the chromosomes will go even before they are committed. There are even cases in which the early spindle passes right through the still-intact nucleus, which has the conformation of a doughnut.

The cell is thus polarized for mitosis, and the direction of movement of the chromosomes is determined, as is the plane of cell division. The two poles, each defined by a pair of centrioles in the animal cell, are connected by the spindle, which contains bundles of microtubules running from pole to pole. Although the pole-to-pole microtubules are described as "continuous," evidence indicates that they consist of tubules coming from the two poles and joining at overlapping ends. It is not known how the poles move apart; perhaps they are "pushed" apart by the growth of the microtubules between them. The separation of poles has not yet received serious study.

Engagement of chromosomes and metakinesis. The breakdown of the nuclear membrane is another important mitotic event that has not yet been studied intensively. The kinetochores are engaged to the poles by spindle fibres composed of microtubules (chromosome-to-pole fibres). Other parts of the chromosomes do not make connections to the poles, and kinetochores still function if chromosome arms are lost. The connections, if broken, are remade. If a chromosome is pulled away from the forming mitotic apparatus and its connections severed,

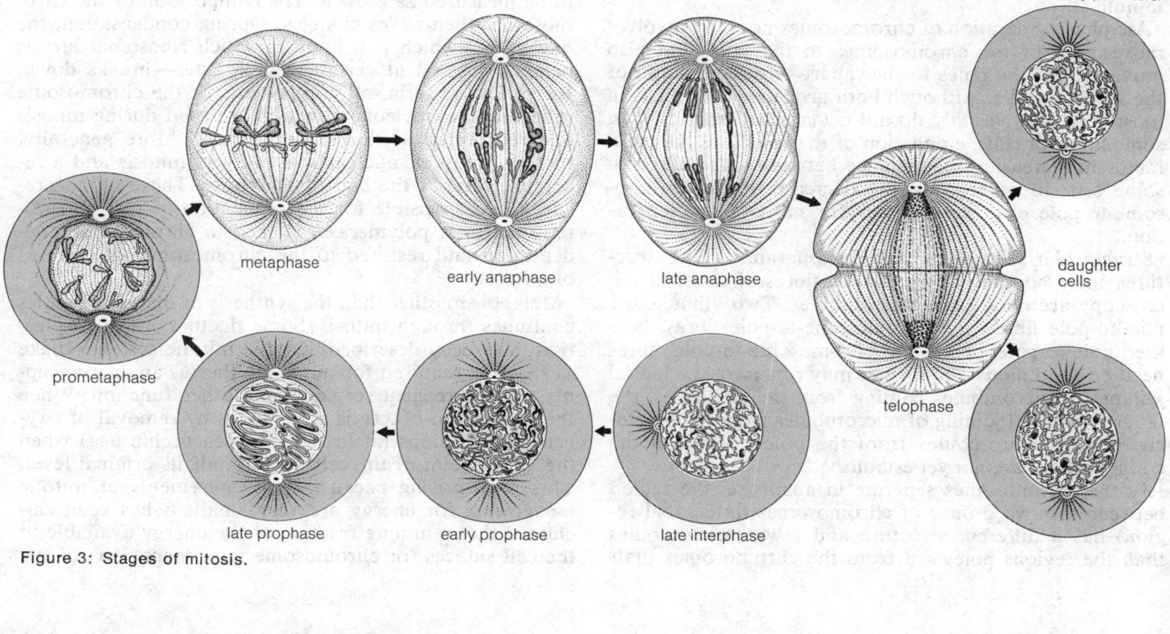

Figure 3: Stages of mitosis.

the connections reform, and the chromosome is moved back into position.

Determination of the direction of chromosome migration

The great mystery of the engagement of the chromosomes is the exclusion principle, according to which sister chromosomes must attach to different poles; there are almost no exceptions. It is as if both sister chromosomes and sister poles could join in no other way.

In some kinds of cells, the engagement of the chromosomes to the mitotic apparatus is not simply a question of attachment of kinetochores to poles. In the cells of craneflies, for example, the microtubules running from pole to pole pass right through the chromosomes, which appear to be threaded by the continuous spindle fibres rather than attached to the ends of chromosome-to-pole fibres.

Once the connections are made, the chromosomes begin to move in the process called metakinesis, the termination of which is the disposition of the chromosomes in a plane midway between the poles; this forms the equatorial plate or metaphase plate of the cell. Whatever the path followed by a chromosome, its movement is accounted for by the movement of the kinetochore. The process requires a mitotic apparatus and, in that sense, is executed by mechanisms similar to those that later move the chromosomes to the poles. However the movement is generated, it is best describable as the attainment of an equilibrium in which the chromosomes lie on the equator because the force imposed from the two poles is equal. More difficult to explain is the fact that individual chromosomes in the metaphase plate can have definite positions relative to each other, the same in every cell. Sometimes the smaller chromosomes are closest to the central axis, the larger on the circumference of the plate. In other cases, such as plant cells with large chromosomes, the kinetochores are arrayed around the circumference of the equatorial plate with the arms of the chromosomes dangling outside the spindle.

The duration of metaphase is the time during which the chromosomes lie on a metaphase plate (oscillating a bit back and forth across the equator) before they begin to separate toward the poles.

Anaphase movement. The separation of sister chromosomes is an event in that it involves a definite signal or process, all of the sister pairs separating at the same time. If fragments of chromosomes lie outside the mitotic apparatus, as occurs in radiation-damaged cells, they also split at the same time; the event thus is broadcast through the whole cell.

Anaphase movement, the actual separation of sister chromosomes to the poles, is regular in that chromosomes of a set usually move at nearly the same speed. The speed is not related to the size of the chromosomes; in fact, the speeds of anaphase movement are remarkably similar in many kinds of cells—about one micron per minute.

Anaphase separation of chromosomes not only involves movements of the chromosomes to the poles but also movement of the poles further apart—*i.e.*, elongation of the whole spindle. Although both processes take place in most cells, they usually do not occur simultaneously. In some kinds of cells, elongation of the spindle is the main factor in increasing the distance between sister chromosome sets; in other cells, the decrease of the chromosome-to-pole distance accounts for most of the separation.

Structural aspects of the mitotic apparatus. The structures corresponding to the spindle fibres of classical microscopy are bundles of microtubules. Two kinds exist: pole-to-pole fibres and chromosome-to-pole fibres. Neither pole-to-pole fibres nor chromosome-to-pole fibres need be continuous; the former may represent the lateral joining of microtubules coming from the two poles, the latter the lateral joining of microtubules from the kinetochore with microtubules from the poles, although the configurations are not yet established.

As the chromosomes separate in anaphase, the region between the two groups of chromosomes (interzonal region) has a different structure and fewer microtubules than the regions poleward from the chromosomes (half spindles). Between chromosomes and poles, the matrix in which the microtubules lie is a dense mass of vesicles, excluding mitochondria and larger particles. The structure of the microtubules does not change during anaphase—they may grow shorter or longer but not thicker or thinner.

Mechanisms of chromosome movement. Most earlier theories of chromosome movement—those that invoked electrical or magnetic attractions, jet propulsion, tactoid bodies (spindle-shaped colloidal particles), autonomous migration of chromosomes, and others—have been discarded in their original form. Current theories are devoted to microtubules and appeal to contractile mechanisms, following the visual indications that spindle fibres grow longer and shorter. One view is that the fibres (microtubules) are in a dynamic state of assembly and disassembly, in equilibrium with a pool of unassembled molecular units. The shortening of a microtubule would be explained by a return of some of its molecules to the pool, a "degrowth," so to speak. The elongation of a microtubule would be explained by the insertion of molecules from the pool; the inherent structure of a microtubule would demand that such growth could be only an elongation.

An explanation of microtubule shortening

Another more recent view draws on the sliding filament mechanism of contraction that has been successful in explaining muscle contraction. In such a mechanism, two filaments slide past each other; shortening is seen as increasing overlap. In muscle the sliding depends on structural bridges between parallel filaments. Such bridges have been observed between microtubules of the mitotic apparatus. If microtubules from kinetochores slide toward the poles along microtubules from the poles, the span of the overlap should increase, and the number of tubules seen in cross sections of the poleward halves of the spindle should increase; data suggest that this occurs.

Descriptively, the exactness of chromosome separation does depend on the shortening of the distance between chromosomes and poles, although it is achieved in some cells by the lengthening of the distance. Several theories deal with these changes in terms of microtubules. It has been asked, however, if it is possible that the behaviour of the microtubules represents the guidance system without necessarily being the motor.

Metabolic aspects of mitosis. In eucaryotic cells, growth stops during mitosis; in procaryotic cells, there is no interruption of growth during the cell cycle. The arrest of growth in the eucaryotic cell is associated with the condensation of the chromosomes. In early prophase, however, there is still RNA synthesis on the chromosomes; and DNA synthesis for repair, but not for replication, is observed. During mitosis, a residual synthesis of proteins occurs; it may be important but is not massive enough to be measured as growth. The composition of the chromosomes themselves changes. During condensation, the nucleolus—which is a body in which ribosomal RNA is being processed at certain genetic sites—breaks down. By various criteria, all components of the chromosome reflecting the nucleolar function are shed during mitosis and recaptured at the end of mitosis. More generally, there is a loss of nuclear RNA early in mitosis and a recapture of it at the end of anaphase. The enzyme presumably responsible for the replication of DNA (a chromosomal DNA polymerase) is shed in chromosome condensation and restored to the chromosomes at the end of mitosis.

Metabolism other than the synthesis of macromolecules continues through mitosis. Some fluctuations of respiration have been described, but the mitotic cell can make ATP. ATP is required for mitosis, either as an energy supply or as a reagent serving some other function. When the production of ATP is arrested, as by removal of oxygen, mitosis stops (at least in the sea urchin egg) when the ATP content of the cell falls to half its original level. This is surprising because the requirements of mitotic movements for energy are very small; it has been calculated that a minute fraction of the energy available to the cell suffices for chromosome movement. Part of the requirement is not for movement but for the maintenance of structure; that is, if the ATP level falls too low, the mitotic apparatus disorients and perhaps disassembles. The mitotic apparatus thus is a dynamic structure, requiring ATP to hold together.

Telophase—restoration of nuclei. After chromosomes have completed their poleward movement, they decondense and surround themselves with a nuclear membrane. The telophase process is best described by considering a rather atypical case in which it is rapid and foreshortened. In many cleaving egg cells, for example, each chromosome begins to decondense as soon as it reaches the pole. As the chromosome reaches the pole, it surrounds itself with a double membrane with pores, a typical nuclear membrane. Early in the process the nuclear membrane can be seen forming in patches over a chromosome before it covers it entirely. Such a process of forming karyomeres, or individual membranes around each chromosome, is possible in any cell if a given chromosome is far from the others; each chromosome can lay down nuclear membrane. In the egg cell, the karyomeres fuse, so that all the chromosomes are finally contained within a common nuclear membrane. In more typical cases, the chromosomes decondense more slowly, and the group is surrounded by a nuclear membrane. If the chromosomes are associated with the "pores," it can be imagined that the chromosomes are the sites of formation of these annuli, which in turn determine the pattern of assembly of the two membranes.

Reformation of the nuclear membrane

The other remarkable event of telophase is the recapture of nuclear constituents that were lost in prophase. Not only do the nucleoli reconstitute, but they regain some of the molecules that were lost earlier. Generally, RNA that was lost from the mother nucleus is recaptured by the daughter nuclei. It is a puzzle how they return to the nucleus if these molecules were scattered through the cell.

Cytokinesis—division of the cell body. Superficially, the division of typical animal cells is seen as a pinching of a sphere into two spheres by constriction in the plane of the mitotic apparatus. The obvious hypothesis, that there is in fact a contractile ring around the belly of the dividing cell, was advocated through a period when other alternatives were prominent. The subjective impression was confirmed objectively only when, with electron microscopy, microfilaments were identified; more recently, the drug cytochalasin has become available to intervene in the functions of microfilaments. In fact, there is a contractile ring of microfilaments underlying the surface of dividing cells at the equator, and cytochalasin prevents the division of the cell body. The mechanism of cell division in animal cells thus becomes part of the more general problem of cell movements involving microfilaments. The ring of microfilaments, however, forms only around the equator defined by the poles of the mitotic apparatus; therefore it must be determined by these poles. It is not known if this determination is an event that takes place sometime earlier in mitosis. Beyond a certain point (metaphase or early anaphase), the mitotic apparatus may be removed and the cell will still divide in its now-predestined plane. Experiments support the idea that some determinant of the formation of the division furrow passes from the poles to the surface; even fragments of cells containing a piece of the surface so determined will constrict.

Cell division in plants

Plant cells, confined in cell walls, do not divide by constriction; new membranes form across the equatorial plane of the mitotic spindle. The movement of microtubules toward the equator after chromosome separation has been completed is prominent and must be an important part of the process of building partitions between the sister nuclei. The other conspicuous part of the process, one that is also seen in animal cells, is the aggregation of internal membrane components (or vesicles) along the equatorial plane. These gather and fuse to make the two membranes separating the sister cells. In plant cells, the plane of division can be predetermined; there are cases in which, after the nuclei have been displaced in a cell, it will divide along the somehow-established plane to produce one cell with two nuclei and another without a nucleus. From the standpoint of the plant, true cell division as the partitioning of each nucleus within a separate cell membrane is only the first step. The next is the laying down of a phragmoplast, a surface layer that will develop into a cellulose wall.

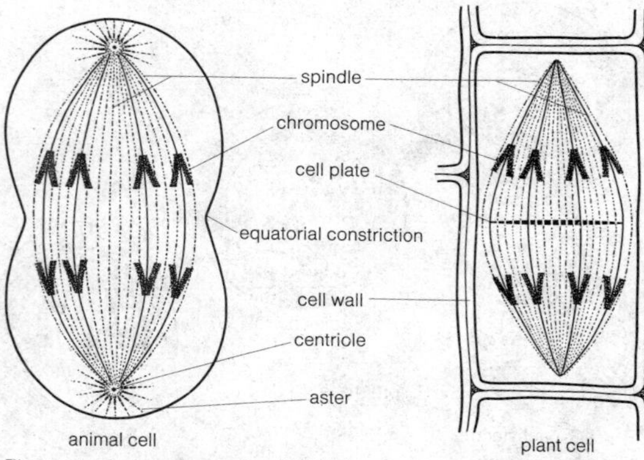

Figure 4: Comparison of cell division in a generalized animal cell and a generalized plant cell.

From Biological Sciences Curriculum Study, *Biological Science: An Inquiry into Life*, 2nd ed. (1968); Harcourt Brace Jovanovich

In procaryotic cells, cell division is less rigidly linked to the procaryotic equivalent of mitosis. It has been shown that certain cells incapable of replicating their chromosomes will nevertheless divide, producing some cells lacking DNA entirely; despite the absence of DNA, the coordination between chromosome separation and cell division in normal procaryotic cells assures that daughter chromosomes will be segregated into daughter cells.

MEIOSIS

The events and significance of meiosis. The meaning of meiosis, cell division that produces daughter cells with half the number of chromosomes of the parent cells, relates not to the everyday life of the cell but to genetics and evolution. As a process that involves halving of the chromosome number, its events differ in important respects from those of the somatic cell cycle; in addition, the homology of chromosomes (*i.e.*, their similarities and origins) becomes important. The diploid or double set of chromosomes in ordinary cells consists of two haploid or single sets, one from each parent; the members of each pair (homologues) are identical in appearance and contain the same kinds of genes in allelic, or different, forms. The pairing of the homologous chromosomes in the preliminary prophase of meiosis divides the number of chromosomes in half; a pair of homologues behaves as one chromosome. Each homologue has replicated before the pairing; after pairing, the chromosomes are bivalents, structures consisting of two parts (homologues), each of which is a pair of sister chromosome strands. With the number of chromosomes now reduced by pairing, the cell undergoes two divisions. The first meiotic division separates the homologues; the daughter cells receive half the number of chromosomes characteristic of the organism, and the two are not genetically identical. Each kind of chromosome is represented in this haploid set, however. Because the separation of homologues is random, each daughter cell can have any permutation of chromosomes of maternal or paternal origin. The second meiotic division merely separates the already-doubled sister chromosomes. The genetic recombination—literally the random sorting of maternal and paternal genes in one chromosome set—is enhanced by the fact that crossing over—the homologues exchanging pieces of chromosomes—between paired maternal and paternal chromosomes had taken place at the time of pairing. Thus the combination at fertilization of male and female germ cells, each having an haploid set of chromosomes, assures that individuals of successive generations of sexually reproducing organisms will have the same chromosome complement: one haploid set from each parent. From an evolutionary standpoint (otherwise there would be no real significance to sexual reproduction), it

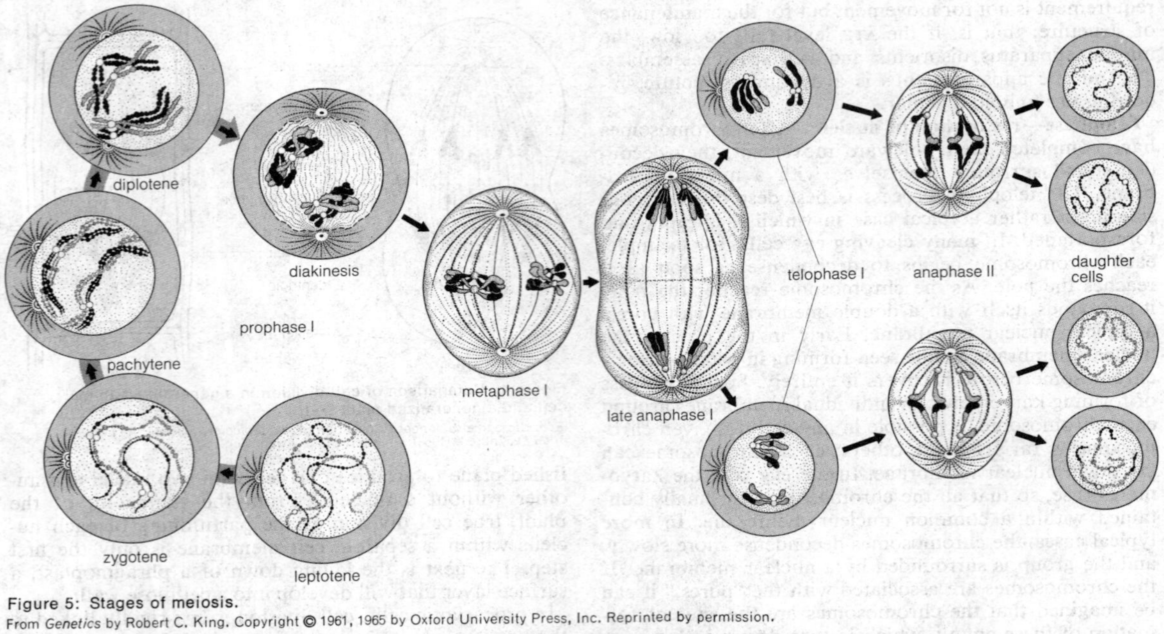

Figure 5: Stages of meiosis.
From *Genetics* by Robert C. King. Copyright © 1961, 1965 by Oxford University Press, Inc. Reprinted by permission.

assures that all possible combinations and recombinations of genes can be realized.

Differences between meiosis and mitosis. Meiosis differs from mitosis in a few important respects. There is no pairing of homologous chromosomes in mitosis, but evidence indicates that they are in propinquity even in ordinary cells. Somatograms, pictures that describe the arrangements of mitotic chromosomes in mitotic prophase, show that all the chromosomes are attached end-to-end in a chain and that homologues are attached to each other. It has been shown that homologues lie side by side in metaphase plates. If these findings are general, the problem is not so much how homologues find each other but how they pair so closely and exactly. Homologous genetic regions come together and can be exchanged by crossing over. At least a structural basis has been found; chromosomes pairing in the zygotene stage (one of the stages of the meiotic prophase) do not merely lie side by side; they are firmly joined by a structure, the synaptinemal complex, which is not seen in mitotic prophase. Overall, the synaptinemal complex is a ribbon-like structure about 1500 to 2000 angstroms wide running between the opposing faces of the homologous chromosomes. It resolves into a central element running down the middle of the space between the chromosomes, with dense lateral elements along the faces of the chromosomes and fibres running across the space.

Structural basis of meiotic chromosome pairing

The orientation of kinetochores in meiotic chromosomes differs in an instructive way from that in mitosis. In mitosis, in which the sister chromosomes will move in opposite directions, the kinetochores lie on opposite sides of the pair, facing in opposite directions. In the first meiotic division, which separates homologues but moves sister chromosome units to the same pole, the sister kinetochores lie side by side in the four-part chromosome, facing in the same direction.

A great deal of attention has been devoted to DNA synthesis in meiosis because it was theoretically attractive to attribute crossing over to events that took place during the replication of chromosomes and correspondingly difficult to imagine how condensed chromosomes could break at several places, exchange pieces, and rejoin. Nevertheless, most of the DNA is replicated before meiotic prophase, and crossing over does seem to be a process of breaking and rejoining segments of condensed chromosomes. It is known that a small amount of DNA is synthesized during meiotic prophase, long after the *S* period, during which most of the chromosomal material is replicated in anticipation of meiosis. The relation between this delayed replication and the singularities of meiosis is not known. It is also a fact that the histone content of chromosomes changes during meiosis; in the preparations for ordinary mitosis the increase in histone parallels the increase in DNA, and the ratio of the two remains constant.

Although these special features of chromosomes in meiosis are known, there are no known fundamental differences in the spindle apparatus or in the mechanisms of chromosome separation. There are a few singularities in the behaviour of the meiotic spindle; for example, in many animals the ovum is arrested in the metaphase of the first meiotic division and does not proceed further through meiosis until it is fertilized. Such long and stable metaphases are not known in mitosis.

BIBLIOGRAPHY. The current perspectives of cell science are made accessible to the general reader in three recent textbooks: E.J. AMBROSE and DOROTHY M. EASTY, *Cell Biology* (1970); E.D.P. DE ROBERTIS, W.W. NOWINSKI, and F.A. SAER, *Cell Biology*, 5th ed. (1970); and ARIEL G. LOEWY and PHILIP SIEKEVITZ, *Cell Structure and Function*, 2nd ed. (1969). These volumes supply the introductory chemical background in graphic form. The first two are more complete on morphological and genetic aspects of the subject, while the last work stresses the molecular basis of cell functions. A larger text by H. ROTHSTEIN, *General Physiology: The Cellular and Molecular Basis* (1971), treats the physiological ramifications of cell biology more completely, and traces the history of the major discoveries in a successful way. A thorough presentation of the cell as a molecular system is found in E.J. DUPRAW, *Cell and Molecular Biology* (1968).

The reader interested in the historical development of cell biology will find that some of the classics are much more than archives; rather, they record the recurrence of certain constant themes, enriched in each cycle. The outlook on the cell at the turn of the century may be recaptured in MAX VERWORN, *Allgemeine Physiologie*, 2nd ed. (1897; Eng. trans., *General Physiology*, 1899). The brilliance of classical microscopy and especially the excitement about the revelation of the chromosome is recaptured in E.B. WILSON, *The Cell in Development and Heredity*, 3rd ed. (1925). Two important texts trace the development of the study of cell function in the 20th century: W.M. BAYLISS, *Principles of General Physiology*, 4th ed. (1924); and L.V. HEILBRUNN, *An Outline of General Physiology*, 3rd ed. (1952). J. BRACHET and A.E. MIRSKY (eds.), *The Cell*, 5 vol. (1959–61), is the major treatise and most of the contents are still valuable to the contemporary reader. Volume 3 includes a monograph by D. MAZIA on "Mitosis and the Physiology of Cell Division," which can serve as a starting point for the literature on cell division.

A few monographs for the reader who would extend his reading on matters stressed in the present article include: A.B. NOVIKOFF and E. HOLTZMAN, *Cells and Organelles* (1970), an outstandingly lucid and beautifully illustrated summary of the present knowledge of cell structure, with emphasis on animal cells and tissues; E.J. DUPRAW, *DNA and Chromosomes* (1970), which treats problems of nuclei and chromosomes in depth in a concise way; and A.L. LEHNINGER, *Bioenergetics* (1965), an excellent source of information on the energetic problems of the cell and the complexities of mitochondria. The series *Protoplasmatologia*, which is published in the form of monographs at irregular intervals, has now accumulated useful summaries of a considerable variety of topics in cell biology.

Up-to-date summaries of most of the topics covered in this article may be found by scanning the following annual review publications: *The International Review of Cytology*, *Annual Review of Biochemistry*, *Annual Review of Physiology*, and *Annual Review of Genetics*.

The rate of progress of cell studies is so rapid that the student or general reader, as well as the specialist, will have occasion to consult the research journals for information more recent than that contained in reviews and monographs. Major advances are reported in summary form in *Nature* and in *Science* (both issued weekly). Reports of exceptional significance often appear in the *Proceedings of the National Academy of Sciences*. Most of the primary literature of the field is published in the following journals, which are available in most biological and medical libraries: *Caryologia* (Italy); *Chromosoma* and *Zeitschrift für Zellforschung* (Germany); *Experimental Cell Research* (international); *Journal of Cell Biology*, *Journal of Cellular Physiology*, and *Journal of General Physiology* (United States); *Journal of Cell Science* and *Journal of Molecular Biology* (United Kingdom); *Journal de Microscopie* (France); *The Nucleus* (India); *Tsitologiya* (U.S.S.R.); and *Protoplasmatologia* (Austria).

Cellini, Benvenuto

The fame of Florentine goldsmith and sculptor Benvenuto Cellini is due more to his record of his own life than it is to his work as an artist. First printed in Italy in 1728, Cellini's autobiography was translated into English (1771), German (1796), and French (1822) and, launched on the tide of the Romantic movement, gained immediate popularity. Dictated to a secretary, it is composed in colloquial language with no literary artifice and gives a firsthand account of the writer's experience in the Rome of Clement VII, the France of Francis I, and the Florence of Cosimo de' Medici. Despite its manifest exaggerations and its often boastful tone, it is a human document of surprising frankness and incomparable authenticity and thanks to it Cellini's character is more intimately known than that of any other figure of his time.

As an artist, however, Cellini was not only a craftsman of surpassing taste and skill but a sculptor of great significance, enjoying a position of importance both in France and in Florence, where he executed all but one of his large-scale works. He declared in his "Treatise on Sculpture" (*Tratto della scultura*) that he "always had a desire to do some great works in marble," and the tone of frustration and disappointment that runs through his autobiography is due in the main to the failure of his contemporaries to supply scope for his transcendent gifts. His "Perseus" (1545–54) is perhaps the greatest statue produced in Florence by any member of the generation after Michelangelo's, and the scene of "Perseus Rescuing Andromeda" originally in its base (now in the Bargello, Florence) leaves no doubt of his talent as an artist in relief.

Cellini was born in Florence on November 1, 1500. Resisting the efforts of his father to train him as a musician, he was apprenticed as a metalworker in the studio of the Florentine goldsmith Andrea di Sandro Marcone. Banished to Siena as a result of a brawl in 1516, he returned to Florence during 1517–19 and then moved to Rome. Prosecuted for fighting in Florence in 1523 and condemned to death, he fled again to Rome, where he worked for the bishop of Salamanca, Sigismondo Chigi, and Pope Clement VII. Cellini participated in the defense of Rome in 1527, during which, by his own account, he shot the constable of Bourbon as well as the Prince of Orange.

Early career

After the sack of Rome he returned to Florence and in 1528 worked in Mantua, making a seal for Cardinal Gonzaga (Episcopal Archives of the City of Mantua). Moving back to Rome in 1529, he was appointed *maestro delle stampe* ("stamp master") at the papal mint and in 1530–31 executed a celebrated morse (clasp) for Clement VII. Like so many of Cellini's works in precious metals, this was melted down, but its design is recorded in three 18th-century drawings in the British Museum, London. The only survivors of the many works he prepared for the Pope are two medals made in 1534 (Uffizi, Florence).

Guilty of killing a rival goldsmith, Cellini was absolved by Pope Paul III; but in the following year, having wounded a notary, he fled from Rome and settled in Florence, where he executed a number of coins for Alessandro de' Medici (now in the Cabinet of Coins, France). After a further year in Rome, he paid a brief visit to France, where he was received by Francis I, a portrait medal of whom (1538; Bargello, Florence) is the sole relic of the journey. On his return to Rome in 1537, he

Alinari

"Perseus," bronze sculpture by Benvenuto Cellini, 1545–54. In the Loggia dei Lanzi, Florence, Italy. Height 3.2 m.

was accused of embezzlement and imprisoned. He escaped, was once more imprisoned, and was finally released in 1539 at the insistence of Cardinal d'Este of Ferrara, for whom he executed a seal (*c.* 1540; original lost; lead impression in Lyon). Again invited to France by Francis I, he arrived at Fontainebleau in 1540, carrying with him an unfinished saltcellar, which he completed in gold for the King in 1540. This, Cellini's only fully authenticated work in precious metal (Kunsthistorisches Museum, Vienna), is the supreme example of the Renaissance goldsmith's work. In 1542 Cellini was granted letters of naturalization by the King and in 1544 received a royal commission for 12 silver candlesticks decorated with figures from mythology. The design of one of these, representing Juno, is recorded in a drawing in the Louvre, Paris. Also in 1543–44 he modelled and cast a large bronze lunette of the Nymph of Fontainebleau for the entrance to the palace (Louvre). For a projected fountain at Fontainebleau he prepared a model in 1543 for a colossal figure of Mars (lost).

Later years in Florence and Venice

In 1545 Cellini left Paris precipitately and returned to Florence, where he was welcomed by Cosimo de' Medici and entrusted with the commissions for his best known sculpture, the bronze "Perseus" in Florence's Loggia dei Lanzi, where it still stands, and for a colossal bust of the Grand Duke of Tuscany (Bargello, Florence). Fleeing to Venice in 1546 to escape charges of immorality, Cellini completed the bust by 1548. In the same period he restored an antique torso from Palestrina as "Ganymede" (1546–47; Uffizi, Florence) and carved his marble figures of "Apollo" and "Hyacinth" (1546) and of "Narcissus" (1546–47); all three works are now in the Bargello in Florence, as is a small relief of a greyhound made as a trial cast for the "Perseus" (1545). A bronze bust of a banker and patron of the arts, Bindo Altoviti (*c.* 1550; Isabella Stewart Gardner Museum, Boston), was executed by Cellini in Florence, probably in 1550. After the unveiling of the "Perseus" (1554), he began work on a marble crucifix originally destined for his own tomb in the Florentine church of SS. Annunziata; this is now in the church of the royal monastery of the Escorial (Spain). The "Escorial Crucifix" (1556) exemplifies the superiority of Cellini's art to the works of his rivals Bartolommeo Ammanati and Baccio Bandinelli. Two designs for the seal of the Academy of Florence (British Museum and Graphische Sammlung, Munich) date from 1563. His autobiography was begun in 1558 and completed in 1562; and in 1565 he began work on his important treatises dealing with goldsmiths' work and sculpture, the *Trattato dell'oreficeria* and the *Trattato della scultura.* Cellini died in Florence on February 13, 1571.

BIBLIOGRAPHY. The best Italian edition of Cellini's autobiography is that of ORAZIO BACCI, *Vita di Benvenuto Cellini* (1901); the standard Eng. trans. is by JOHN A. SYMONDS (2 vol., 1888; reprinted with notes and bibliography as *The Life of Benvenuto Cellini Written by Himself*, 1949 and 1968). On Cellini's works see EUGENE PLON, *Benvenuto Cellini, orfèvre, médailleur, sculpteur*, 2 vol. (1883); and ETTORE CAMESASCA, *Tutta l'opera del Cellini* (1955). For the *Trattati* see CARLO MILANESI, *I Trattati dell'oreficeria e della scultura di Benvenuto Cellini* (1857); C.R. ASHBEE, *The Treatises of Benvenuto Cellini on Goldsmithing and Sculpture* (1898, reprinted 1967); and JOHN POPE-HENNESSY, *An Introduction to Italian Sculpture* (1963).

(J.W.P.-H.)

Cell Theory and Classification

The cell theory is not as much a theory in the conventional sense as it is a statement of fact: life is manifest only through the functioning of intact cells, never in their absence. A cell and even some of its isolated parts are capable of growth and reproduction as a result of the assimilation of substances drawn from the environment; but an intact cell is the simplest structure that displays all of the characteristics of life. The similarity of structure and function in all cells, although modified by evolution to produce the great diversity that occurs in living things, results from the fact that the molecules and processes responsible for energy manipulation, growth, and reproduction are basically similar in all cell types. The differences among the cells of plants, animals, and microorganisms mostly represent specialized features that permit a cell to adapt to a particular way of life.

This article is divided into the following sections:

The features of cells mentioned in this article are described in greater detail in the article CELL AND CELL DIVISION.

THE CELL THEORY

Historical background. The history of the cell theory is a history of the actual observation of cells, because early prediction and speculation about the nature of the cell were generally unsuccessful. The decisive event that allowed the observation of cells was the invention of the microscope in the 17th century, after which interest in the new invisible world was stimulated. Robert Hooke, who described cork and other plant tissues in 1665, introduced the term cell because the cellulose walls of dead cork cells reminded him of the blocks of cells occupied by the monks of that period. Even after the publication in 1672 of excellent pictures of plant tissues, no significance was attached to the contents within the cell walls. The magnifying powers of the microscope and the inadequacy of techniques for preparing cells for observation precluded a study of the intimate details of the cell contents. The inspired amateur of early microscopy Antonie van Leeuwenhoek, beginning in 1673, discovered blood cells, spermatozoa, and a lively world of "animalcules." A new world of unicellular organisms was opened up. Such discoveries extended the known variety of living things but did not bring insight into their basic uniformity. Moreover, when Leeuwenhoek observed the swarming of his animalcules but failed to observe their division, he could only reinforce the idea that they arose spontaneously.

The role of microscopy

The cell theory was not formulated for nearly 200 years after the introduction of microscopy. Explanations for this delay range from the poor quality of the microscopes to the persistence of ancient ideas concerning the definition of a fundamental living unit. Historians of this period have chronicled many observations of cells, but apparently none of the observers was able to assert forcefully that cells were the units of biological structure and function.

Three critical discoveries made during the 1830s, when improved microscopes with suitable lenses, higher powers of magnification without aberration, and more satisfactory illumination became available, were decisive events in the early development of the cell theory. First, the nucleus was observed by Robert Brown in 1833 as a constant component of plant cells. Soon nuclei were also observed and recognized as such in some animal cells, even though they were not surrounded by the cellulose walls found in plants. Last, a living substance called protoplasm was recognized within cells, its vitality made evident by its active streaming, or flowing, movements, especially in plant cells. After these three discoveries, cells, previously considered as mere pores in plant tissue, could no longer be thought of as empty, because they contained living material.

Two German biologists, Theodore Schwann and Matthias Schleiden, clearly stated in 1839 that cells are the "elementary particles of organisms" in both plants and animals and recognized that some organisms are unicellular and others multicellular. This statement was made in 1839 in a book by Schwann entitled *Microscopic Researches into the Accordance in the Structure and Growth of Animals and Plants.* Schleiden's contributions on plants, which had appeared in 1838, were acknowledged by Schwann as the basis for his comparison of animal and plant structure.

Schleiden and Schwann's descriptive statements concerning the cellular basis of biological structure are straightforward and acceptable to modern thought. They recognized the common features of cells to be membrane, nucleus, and cell body and described them in comparisons of various animal and plant tissues. A statement by Schleiden pointed toward the future direction of cell studies:

> Each cell leads a double life: an independent one, pertaining to its own development alone; and another incidental, insofar as it has become an integral part of a plant. It is, however, easy to perceive that the vital process of the individual cells must form the first, absolutely indispensable fundamental basis, both as regards vegetable physiology and comparative physiology in general; and therefore, in the very first instance, this question especially presents itself: how does this peculiar little organism, the cell, originate?

Historians point out, however, that Schwann and Schleiden were not alone in contributing to this great generalization of natural science—strong intimations of the cell theory occur in the work of their predecessors. Recognizing that the basic problem was the origin of cells, these early investigators invented a hypothesis of "free cell formation," according to which cells developed *de novo* out of an unformed substance, a "cytoblastema," by a sequence of events in which first the nucleolus develops, then the nucleus, the cell body, and finally the cell membrane. The best physical model of the generation of formed bodies then available was crystallization, and their theory was inspired by that model. In retrospect, the hypothesis of free cell formation would not seem to have been justified, however, since cell division, a feature not characteristic of crystallization processes, had frequently been observed by earlier microscopists, especially among single-celled organisms. Even though cell division was observed repeatedly in the following decades, the theory of free cell formation lingered throughout most of the 19th century; however, it came to be thought of more and more as a possible exception to the general principle of the reproduction of cells by division. The principle of division of cells was affirmed in 1855 by a German biologist of great prestige: Rudolph Virchow asserted that "omnis cellula e cellula" ("all cells come from cells"); but doubt remained.

The hypothesis of "free cell formation"

The inherently complex events of cell division prevented a quick resolution of the complete sequence of changes that occur during the process. First, it was noted that a cell with a nucleus divides into two cells, each having a nucleus; hence, it was concluded that the nucleus must divide, and direct division of nuclei was duly described by some. Better techniques served to create perplexity, because it was found that, during cell division, the nucleus as such disappears. Moreover, at the time of division, dimly discerned masses, now recognized as chromosomes, were seen to appear temporarily. Observations in the 1870s culminated in the highly accurate description and interpretation of cell division (mitosis) by Walther Flemming in 1882. His advanced techniques of fixing and staining cells enabled him to see that cell reproduction involves the transmission of chromosomes from the parent to daughter cells by the process of mitosis and that the division of the cell body is the terminal event of that reproduction.

The discovery that the number of chromosomes remains constant from one generation to the next resulted in the full description of the process of meiosis. The description of meiosis combined with the observation that fertilization is fundamentally the union of maternal and paternal sets of chromosomes culminated in the understanding of the physical basis of reproduction and heredity. Meiosis and fertilization are therefore complementary events in the life cycle of organisms: meiosis halves the number of chromosomes in the formation of spores (plants) or gametes (animals), while fertilization restores the number through the union of gametes. By the 1890s "life" in all of its manifestations could be thought of as an expression of cells.

Protoplasm as the living substance of the cell

The protoplasm concept. As the concept that the cell is the elementary particle of life developed during the 19th century, it was paralleled by the "protoplasm" concept—the idea that the protoplasm within the cell is responsible for life. Protoplasm had been defined in 1835 as the ground substance of living material and hence responsible for all living processes. That life is an activity of an elementary particle, the cell, can be contrasted with the view that it is the expression of a living complex substance—even a supermolecule—called a protoplasm. The protoplasm concept was supported by observations of the streaming movements of the apparently slimy contents of living cells.

Advocates of the protoplasm concept implied that cells were either fragments or containers of protoplasm. This interpretation threw doubt on the existence of a cell membrane as a defining characteristic of cells; its supposed absence from some cells was considered to be a refutation of the cell theory. The doubt, though unproductive, was justified, since the existence of the cell membrane, which lies below the limits of resolution of the light microscope, was based on indirect evidence and was experimentally demonstrated only after the introduction of advanced techniques such as electron microscopy. The weakness of the protoplasm concept was its inability to account for the origin of formed structures within the cell, especially the nucleus. The existence of a nucleus in all cells could be denied as long as microscopic techniques were incapable of demonstrating one in all cells, and the importance of the nucleus could be ignored until the discovery of the chromosomal basis of reproduction was established.

In retrospect, those who stressed the protoplasm concept and those who stressed the cell theory converged. The preoccupation with protoplasm resulted from research on intact living cells and provided much information about cells. Advocates of the protoplasm concept, suspicious and often contemptuous of information obtained from dead and stained cells, discovered most of the basic information on the physical properties—mechanical, optical, electrical, and contractile properties—of the living cell. It was also a matter of concern that observed structures might not be actual cell components but extraneous changes caused by experimental techniques (artifacts); as a result, the development of important methods for studying cell components was delayed. An assessment of the usefulness of the concept is difficult. It was not wholly false; on the one hand, it encouraged the study of the chemical and mechanical properties of cell contents, but it also generated a resistance, evident as late as the 1930s, to the realization that very large molecules (macromolecules) could be cellular constituents.

As the cell has become fractionated into its component parts, protoplasm, as a term, no longer has meaning in a modern sense. The word protoplasm is still used, however, in describing the phenomenon of protoplasmic streaming—the phenomenon from which the protoplasm concept originally emerged.

Evolution of the cell theory. Appreciation of the cell as the unit of life has accrued from important sources other than microscopy; perhaps the most important is microbiology. Even though the small size of micro-organisms prohibited much observation of their detailed structure until the advent of electron microscopy, they could be grown easily and rapidly. Thus it was that the studies of microbes by Louis Pasteur, published in 1861, helped to establish the principle of biogenesis, namely, that organisms arise only by the reproduction of other organisms. Fundamental ideas regarding the metabolic attributes of cells—that is, their ability to transform simple nutritional substances into cell substance and utilizable energy—came from microbiology. Pasteur perhaps overplayed the relation between catalysis and the living state of cells in considering enzymatic action to be an attribute of the living cell rather than of the catalytic molecules (enzymes) contained in the cell; it is a fact, however, that much of cell chemistry is enzyme chemistry—and that enzymes are one defining attribute of cells. The techniques of microbiology eventually opened the way for microbial genetics, which, in turn, provided the means for solving the fundamental problems of molecular biology that were inaccessible at first to direct attack by biochemical methods.

The role of microbiology

The science of molecular biology would be most capable of overthrowing the cell theory if the latter were an exaggerated generalization. On the contrary, molecular biology has become the foundation of cell science, for it has demonstrated not only that basic processes such as the genetic code and protein synthesis are similar in all living systems but also that they are referrable to the same cell components in living things—*e.g.*, chromosomes, ribosomes, and membranes.

In the overlapping histories of cell biology and medicine, two events are especially important. One, the identification in 1827 by Karl Ernst von Baer of the ovum (unfertilized egg) as a cell, was important considering the many ways it often differs from other cells; von Baer not only laid the foundations for reproductive biology but also provided important evidence for the cell theory at a critical time. The second important event was the promotion in 1855 of the concept of "cellular pathology" by Rudolph Virchow. His idea that human diseases are diseases of cells and can be identified and understood as such gave the cell theory an authority not easily undermined by deficiencies in the theory.

Although biochemistry might have made considerable progress without the cell theory, each influenced the other almost from the start. When it was established that most biochemical phenomena are shared by all cells, the cell could be defined by its metabolism as well as by its structure. Cytochemistry, or histochemistry, made a brilliant start in 1869, when a Swiss biochemist, Friedrich Miescher, postulated that the nucleus must have a characteristic chemistry and then went on to discover the nucleic acids, which have since been shown to be the crucial molecules of inheritance and metabolism.

Critique of the cell theory. The cell theory has been subject to remarkably little debate. Disputes have arisen about the validity of various generalizations—whether all cells possess membranes and nuclei; whether cells can reproduce other than by mitosis; and whether chromosomes are the bearers of heredity. And at times the cell has moved into the background when the existence of more fundamental living units in cells has been postulated; indeed, the first crystallization of a virus, in 1935, pointed to the existence of molecules endowed with life. But none of these doubts or findings questioned the validity of the cell theory as a general statement.

Inadequacies of the cell theory

Nevertheless, several difficulties requiring a broadened view of the cell theory may be mentioned. The existence of syncytial forms of life (*i.e.*, many nuclei sharing the same cytoplasm) certainly detracts from the precision of the cell theory; in certain giant plant cells (*e.g.*, the common pond plant *Nitella*), for example, many nuclei share the same cytoplasm. The so-called acellular slime molds are living masses of indefinite size and contain many nuclei. In animals, such important tissues as skeletal muscle are syncytial in nature; all such apparent acellular organisms, however, arise from cells, either by the absence of division of the cell body following nuclear division or by the fusion of cells. These are thus special cases in which individual nuclei are not separated from each other by cell membranes but are contained within a common membrane.

A seemingly more serious extension of the cell theory is required by the existence of unicellular organisms, especially certain protozoans, which show remarkable complexity as free-living organisms. They have well-differentiated structures for the capture and digestion of food, for coordinated movement, for reception of stimuli, and for purposeful behaviour of the kind usually associated with multicellular animals. All this complexity results from the remarkable flexibility of the cell membrane in producing a variety of subcellular organelles. Such organisms express the potential of the cell for internal differentiation; modern techniques (*e.g.*, electron microscopy) sustain this opinion by revealing that these complex protozoans have the same structural elements—microtubules, microfilaments, membranes, centrioles—as are responsible for differentiation in plant and animal cells.

The most serious difficulty of the cell theory is that it cannot explain the development and unity of the multicellular organism; a cell is not necessarily an independently functioning unit. A plant or an animal is not merely a congeries of individual cells; fortunately, however, the controversy centring on the individuality and separateness of cells has ended. Cell biology of the 1960s and 1970s focussed on the interactions and communications between cells, as well as on the analysis of the single cell; and the exchanges of materials between cells, contact phenomena, and cell junctions have all become important aspects in the study of the cell (see CELL AND CELL DIVISION). The influence of the environment on the cell has aways been important; now it has been recognized that one very important part of the environment of a cell is other cells—recognition, association, and cooperation between cells have become observational and experimental questions.

The importance to cells of other cells

The cell theory thus is not so comprehensive as to eliminate the concept of the organism as a whole. But the study of a particular organism requires the investigation of cells as both individuals and groups. The cancer problem is an example: a plant or animal governs the division of its own cells; the right cells must divide, be differentiated, and then integrated into the proper organ system at the right time and place. Breakdown results in a variety of abnormalities, one of which is cancer. When the cell biologist studies the problem of the regulation of cell division, his ultimate objective is to understand the effect of the whole organism on an individual cell.

CLASSIFICATION OF CELLS

A taxonomy of cells does not play a large part in modern biological thought. In the preceding section, convincing evidence of the fundamental similarities among cells was presented. It can be plausibly argued, in fact, that all cells that have ever existed have had a common origin. Cells are classified by types for purposes of discourse and to study the diversification and specialization of common designs.

General features. *Cells and viruses.* Viruses are small masses of material that can enter and reproduce in cells. They are organisms only in a limited sense—whatever can survive and reproduce itself indefinitely possesses the most essential attribute of an organism. The propagation of a virus requires the internal environment of a complete cell, including its biochemical machinery. A nonviral organism, however, can reproduce in a nonliving external environment, from which it draws only simple nutrients and energy sources while maintaining its own internal environment; it possesses the biochemical machinery for transforming the matter it captures into living matter.

Viruses are not merely pieces of nucleic acid and may be rather complex. Complexity is expressed in the protein coat, which contains and thus protects the genetic material before it enters a cell (infectious phase). In the infectious phase the virus does not reproduce. The structure of the complete infectious virus (*e.g.*, the bacteriophages that infect bacteria) thus is concerned both with the survival of the virus outside a cell and with the mechanisms by which it enters the cell. The virus loses the protein coat upon entry into a cell, after which the genetic material of the virus reproduces, using materials made by the host cell. The virus leaves the host cell surrounded by the protein coat; the characteristics of these proteins are determined by genes in the virus, but the proteins are made within the host. It might be supposed that viruses are the ultimate parasites—"naked genes," as they were once designated—which have discarded all the other attributes of complete cells. But the idea is difficult to sustain, since the genetic material of so many viruses is RNA, whereas that of true cells is DNA.

Procaryotic and eucaryotic cells. Cells can be placed in one of two groups on the basis of whether or not they have a membrane-bound nucleus; those with a membrane-bound nucleus are called eucaryotic cells, and those lacking this structure but containing nuclear material are called procaryotic cells. As recently as 1941 the difference could be expressed only in negative terms: the failure to find certain features (*e.g.*, a distinct nucleus surrounded by a nuclear membrane) of a "typical" cell in certain micro-organisms (procaryotes). Detection of the numerous distinctions that exist between procaryotic and eucaryotic cells depends on techniques that were not available before the 1950s. These distinctions are elaborated upon in CELL AND CELL DIVISION.

Most procaryotic cells, such as bacteria and blue-green algae, appear to have very little internal structure when viewed through the light microscope. Simple eucaryotes, such as the yeasts and many unicellular algae, have more complex internal structure than the procaryotes but live under conditions similar to those of the procaryotes, drawing upon the same simple nutrients and energy sources.

After the discovery of the differences between procaryotes and eucaryotes, impressive similarities between simple eucaryotic organisms (*e.g.*, yeasts) and the eucaryotic cells of higher organisms were found—a yeast cell is probably more similar to a mammalian cell than it is to a bacterial cell. It has been of value to examine the differences between simple eucaryotes and the always eucaryotic cells of higher organisms. Unicellularity and multicellularity are important because the multicellularity found in higher organisms is accompanied by definite capabilities for differentiation. Differentiation in turn depends on communications between cells; such communication is not seen in unicellular organisms. In addition, the chemistry of the chromosomes of multicellular plants and animals differs from that of unicellular organisms; those of the former always contain proteins called histones, which apparently are not found in a number of simple eucaryotic organisms.

Unicellularity and multicellularity

The mechanisms of mitosis also differ. In the typical mitosis that occurs in plant and animal cells, the nuclear membrane breaks down; in some unicellular eucaryotes, mitosis takes place within the nucleus. In both cases, however, chromosome movements depend on structures called microtubules, which are not seen in procaryotic cells. Finally, it is suspected that the mechanisms of genetic regulation—the determination of which genes are active in a given cell at a given time—may differ in cells of multicellular and unicellular eucaryotes. It would seem that this is likely, since, in the case of multicellular eucaryotes, cells with the same genes must differentiate into many types, so that complex control mechanisms are essential; in the case of unicellular eucaryotes, such differentiation does not occur; hence, elaborate controls are not necessary.

Tissues: a functional classification of cells. The tissue concept preceded the cell theory. As developed in the early 19th century, the theory of tissues proposed that the organs known to gross anatomy could be analyzed in terms of tissues. The tissue was said to be defined by a characteristic structure and texture, and membranes and "vessels" were emphasized rather than fluids. Tissues were said to represent the level of organization intermediate between unorganized matter and the functional organ; *i.e.*, the existence of cells was not anticipated. When the cell theory was expressed, tissues were redescribed in terms of cells.

Modification of the definition of a tissue

The study of tissues, the science of histology, is a well-developed discipline in both plant and animal science. In the following section, comments are limited to representative cell types in order to illustrate the ways in which the basic design of eucaryotic cells has been modified to serve the specialized functions of tissues and organs.

Animal tissues. *Absorptive cells.* In animals, layers of cells covering an organ (epithelia) may serve the function of exchanging material between the environment and the body fluids of the organism, as well as having a supportive role to play. A common modification of this cell type is the fingerlike projections of the cell membrane, called microvilli, which increase the total area of the absorptive surface. Another modification may occur at the cell surface, so that specific transport processes are located on the outer surface or inner surface of the membranes or, in some instances, within the mosaic structure of the membrane itself. In many cases, such as in the cells of gills that transport salts into or out of the blood and body fluids of aquatic animals, the internal membrane system is conspicuous as pockets called vesicles, in which the substances being transported are sequestered. The cells forming an absorptive surface are very often united at cell junctions.

Secretory cells. Well-developed in glandular tissues, secretory cells are adapted to synthesize molecules not used by the cells themselves but exported from them. Outstanding is their extensively developed internal membrane system, the components of which include the endoplasmic reticulum and the Golgi apparatus, both of which are present in all eucaryotic cells. The accumulation of secretory products may be massive, often occurring as secretory droplets.

Nerve cells. In nerve cells (neurons), most cellular functions occur in a cell body containing the nucleus. The specialized function of the neuron—conduction of impulses—is performed by extensions of the cell body: short dendrites, at which chemical or electrical transmissions from other neurons are received, and very long axons, which conduct impulses to other neurons, muscles, or glands. Biosynthesis occurs in the cytoplasm of the cell body. The axon contains many small filaments called neurofilaments and small tubes called neurotubules along its length; materials synthesized in the cell body may be transported along these structures to the end of the axon. The ends of the axons may be highly differentiated as bulbous structures at the surfaces of which vesicles of substances, made in the cell body and transported down the axon, are secreted when impulses arrive. These secretions stimulate the next neuron in the nerve circuit or some effector cell, such as a muscle.

An extreme example of cell differentiation is the Schwann cell. It develops extensive surface membranes and wraps itself around the membrane of the neuron, providing an insulating sheath (called the myelin sheath).

Sensory cells. Sensory cells, which transduce stimuli such as light, touch, and the "tastes" of chemicals so that they set off impulses in adjacent neurons, show unexpected adaptations of typical cells. In cells adapted to respond to mechanical stimuli (touch or bending, for example), the receptor is provided with a modified hairlike projection (cilium). More remarkably, animal evolution has produced photoceptors (rods and cones), which also contain an array of membranes in which the light-receiving pigments are incorporated. Although receptive processes, in which the energy in stimuli is received, are fairly well understood, much less is known about the way in which the receptor cell triggers an impulse in an adjoining neuron.

Muscle cells. Muscle cells, though specialized, have been derived from a typical cell. Contractility is a function of arrays of filaments, which, in the case of skeletal and heart muscle, are collected into bundles called myofibrils. In smooth muscle, the filaments are not associated so definitely into bundles. All kinds of muscle contain thin filaments composed of the protein actin. Heart and skeletal muscle contain arrays of thick filaments, which are composed of the protein myosin and spaced at regular intervals along the thin filaments, accounting for the striated appearance of the cells. Smooth muscles also contain myosin but not in the form of thick filaments. The modified internal membrane system of a muscle cell, called a sarcoplasmic reticulum, sometimes has many vesicles; in skeletal muscle it consists of an array of sacs investing the myofibrils. The surface membrane of skeletal muscle is highly and regularly involuted to "connect" the surface with the contractile fibrils, thus conducting the effects of stimuli to the vicinity of the contractile elements. Skeletal and smooth muscles consist of very large cells containing many nuclei and produced by the fusion of single cells to form a syncytium. Heart muscle is composed of single cells, richly provided with cell junctions in order that their contraction can be coordinated as the beat of the whole tissue. The consistency between the general design of the eucaryotic cell and the extreme specialization of muscle is an example of the interpretive power possible with the cell theory.

Types of muscle

Cells in supporting tissues. Although, in a histological survey, connective tissue, bone, and cartilage deserve a detailed treatment, only the features common to these very different tissues are noted below. The cells comprising them show no great structural deviation from that of a typical cell, but they are specialized for large-scale production of the protein collagen and, in bone, for the laying down of mineral crystals of definite structure. The role of certain cells in providing the body with supporting structures is a fundamental expression of the differentiation of animal cells; a comparable expression is even more important in plants (see below *Cells and tissues of higher plants*).

Circulating cells. The red blood cells of mammals may be considered the ultimate simplification (or degeneracy) of cells or the best example of the adaptive subordination of the cell to the requirements of the organism as a whole. They have, in their final state of differentiation, neither nuclei (and thus cannot divide) nor the other components typical of eucaryotic cells and can be regarded as bags containing a concentrated solution of the iron-containing protein hemoglobin, which carries oxygen and carbon dioxide. On the other hand, their membranes are highly developed to control the internal environment in which the hemoglobin is dissolved. The regulatory devices in the membranes of red blood cells enable them to pick up a maximum load of oxygen in the lung and release it with great efficiency in the tissues.

White blood cells (leucocytes) utilize the capacity of many cells to engulf and digest particles, including bacteria and the debris of injured tissue (phagocytosis). The production of antibodies in the immune response is the result of the cooperation of specialized cells derived from certain white cells called lymphocytes (*i.e.*, macrophages and plasma cells). None of these types of leucocytes is organized into tissues; since their structures resemble that of a typical eucaryotic cell, these cells give no clues to the several important and specialized functions they perform in the animal.

Reproductive cells: gametes. Although the gametes—ovum and spermatozoon—contribute an equal set of genes to the new individual, the contribution of each to the success of the reproductive process is quite different. The ovum of an animal is adapted to meet the nutritional requirements of the early developmental stages of the embryo. It is always a large cell because it contains sufficient cytoplasmic substance for the development of a self-sufficient embryo. Some of the substance, which is packaged in yolk particles, contains cell components; typically, an ovum contains sufficient quantities of components for many cells. Thus, the ovum need not grow as it divides—as the nuclei divide, the cytoplasm subdivides until the ovum consists of a large number of normal-sized cells. Perhaps a remarkable adaptation of the ovum involves fertilization: the cell surface is specialized to receive and engulf sperm at the time of fertilization and to reject all but one sperm. By contrast, spermatozoa are motile cells that contain very little cytoplasm, have a short life, and cannot divide. Typically, a spermatozoon has a small head and a long motile tail (flagellum), but many variations occur. The head contains the nucleus and a complex structure, the acrosome, which is responsible for the attachment of the spermatozoon to the surface of the egg.

Cellulose walls and vacuoles

Cells and tissues of higher plants. *The plant cell.* The outstanding features of plant cells, as compared with animal cells, are the rigid cellulose walls external to the cell membranes and the cavities (vacuoles) within the cell. Both cellulose walls and vacuoles are intimately involved in the life of the plant and constitute the main reference points for the diversification of plant cells.

Because the cellulose walls provide mechanical support, there is no need for an internal skeleton or an external shell. At the cellular level, cell walls permit cells to function in an environment dilute with regard to salts and other molecules. The tendency for water to enter the cell is translated into a pressure by the cells against the walls, a turgor that contributes to the rigidity of the plant. In fact, plants wilt in the environments required by animal cells.

The internal vacuoles of plant cells—typically a single vacuole surrounded by a membane, or tonoplast—may occupy most of the volume of the cell; the cytoplasm is a thin layer immediately beneath the cell membrane. The vacuoles are filled with an aqueous solution consisting mostly of small molecules, such as organic acids and pigments; some very large molecules (macromolecules); and, often, metabolic end products in the form of crystals. Growth in plants is, to a large extent, an increase in the size of the vacuoles without a corresponding increase in other cytoplasmic structures and often occurs by an increase in cell length with little increase in width. Thus, the control of cell elongation by the lengthwise deposition of cellulose walls, with a corresponding expansion of the vacuoles, is a major difference between plant cells and animal cells. Remarkable regulatory substances, notably the auxins, control these processes.

The most conspicuous structures found only in plant cells are chloroplasts, the sites of photosynthesis (*q.v.*). These structures are bounded by double membranes; the inner one is modified to form stacks of flattened vesicles, which contain chlorophyll, other photosynthetic pigments, and photosynthetic enzymes. The chloroplasts contain deoxyribonucleic acid (DNA) and, as semi-independent, self-reproducing parts of plant cells, behave much as does another component, mitochondria, of all eucaryotic cells. In fact, the similarities between chloroplasts and mitochondria exemplify the unities of cellular organization. Their structures have uncertain origins in the evolution of cells, but both perform the same fundamental process: the mobilization of energy for the cell by the synthesis of the energy-rich compound adenosine triphosphate (ATP). The chloroplasts convert the energy of light into energy-rich ATP and use the ATP to convert carbon to specific organic substances. In turn, mitochondria oxidize carbon-containing compounds, thereby recovering the ATP energy stored in them.

Remarkably few other structures in the cytoplasm of plant and animal cells differ, and the nuclei of the two are similar. The components of plant cells that deposit cellulose on the cell surface are called dictyosomes; their structure resembles other membrane-bound structures found in cells (*e.g.*, the Golgi apparatus); the dictyosomes, which are stacks of flattened vesicles, apparently concentrate the compounds from which cellulose is formed and deposit them on the outer surface of the cell.

Intercellular channels of communication in plants

Cytoplasmic connections between plant cells are common. Called plasmodesmata, they are thin bridges of cytoplasm (containing few or no components) covered by the cell membrane, which is thus continuous from one cell to the next, and pass through very small holes in the cellulose wall. It has not yet been established whether or not these intercellular channels of communication have different significance in animals and in plants, because the study of intercellular junctions between animal cells—quite different in structure from plasmodesmata—is a comparatively new one.

Another characteristic of plant cells, apart from photosynthesis and the incorporation of cellulose into the cell wall, is the production of a great variety of useful end products, such as oils, resins, pigments, drugs, latexes, and tannins, as well as substances incorporated into perfumes and flavourings. Noncellulose components of cell walls, such as pectins and lignins, also are used by man. Production of such substances requires elaborate synthetic mechanisms that are not found in animal cells.

Differentiation of plant cells, though simple to describe, is less easy to explain. It begins with cell divisions, which produce not identical daughter cells but cells the different destinies of which are recognizable at the time of division. In higher plants, cells capable of division are usually concentrated in tissues called apical or lateral meristems, such as are found at root and shoot tips and at the outer edge of woody plants beneath the bark. When meristematic cells divide, one daughter cell remains a meristematic cell, and the other differentiates; *i.e.*, it elongates, and a vacuole develops. In some cases of differentiation, the plane of division determines the properties of the daughter cell: a long cell may divide crosswide into two short cells, lengthwise to form two thin cells, or unequally to produce one large and one small daughter cell. As mentioned, the main expressions of further differentiation are not modifications of basic cell structure but modifications of the cell wall and the vacuole.

Diversity of plant cells

Cell types. Despite concern with the classification of plant cells, tissues, and tissue systems, there is as yet no agreement as to how they should be classified. The difficulty for the botanist in classifying plant cells lies in the extreme modifications of the typical cell structure.

At one extreme are cells that are no longer alive; in this case, arrangements of the cell walls serve the plant in important ways. Examples of nonliving plant cells include the phellem (cork) cells, which provide mechanical protection and insulation; fibre cells of various kinds, which provide mechanical support; and cells of the vascular tissues, which conduct water and nutrients in the plant. It is remarkable that living cells lacking striking internal peculiarities associate with each other at the right place and time, grow by the formation of walls made of cellulose and other molecules (lignins of wood, for example), and then cease to live as cells while they serve the organism.

At the other extreme, the meristem cells at the tips of roots and the apexes of shoots are a major source of new cells in the plant. Initials are cells that divide to produce one cell that retains the properties of an initial and another that differentiates; thus, a small population of initials can be the long-term source of cells for extensive growth and differentiation. Daughter cells that differentiate may divide several times. Structurally, the initials of meristems are typical eucaryotic cells, except for their cellulose walls. The counterpart in animals to these cells, which remain capable indefinitely of generating and regenerating complex tissues and organs, are those found in the blood- and skin-forming areas of the body.

Between the extremes of the meristematic cell and the nonliving plant cell are many types, the walls and vacuoles of which are specialized. Although the epidermal cells of leaves, for example, contain a nucleus and cytoplasm, their main specialization is the elaboration of a waxy outer cover (cuticle) that is impervious to water. In contrast, the mesophyll cells of leaves, which contain chloroplasts and carry out photosynthesis, make cellulose walls that are especially permeable to water and gases—a striking adaptive contrast to the epidermal cells, the thick walls and cuticle of which are a barrier to water and gases. Some epidermal cells secrete substances responsible for the tastes and odours of plants; as in secretory cells of animals, the internal membrane system is well developed. Epidermal cells of flowers concentrate pigments in their vacuoles.

The most active organs of the higher plant are the stomata, which open and close to adjust the movement of gases and water vapour into and out of the leaf. The opening is controlled by two curved, sausage-shaped guard cells; they change the aperture by changing their shape. The changes of shape result from changes in the water content of the cells and are not the result of any active contractile process.

Summary. The bases for the differentiation and hence the classification of animal and plant cells are quite different. In the case of animal cells, diversity results from modification of the internal structural components of the typical cell. In the case of plant cells, modifications of internal structure are not as important as differences in cell walls and vacuoles. Even in extreme cases, however, the fundamental unity of the cell concept is upheld. All plant and animal cells result from reproduction and differentiation of cells that are rather similar in both groups. Each structure within a living animal cell has its counterpart in a living plant cell. Each structure within plant cells, with the possible exception of the chloroplasts, has its counterpart in animal cells. Differences result from the elaboration of one or another part of a cell. Even the production of cellulose walls in plant cells is similar to the production of surface coats in animal cells. The important difference is that cellulose, a large molecule containing the sugar glucose, which is found in all cells, has special mechanical properties. Since many types of plant cells do not carry out photosynthesis, the presence or absence of chloroplasts is not a very good criterion for distinguishing a plant cell from an animal cell, although it is a most important distinction between a plant and an animal.

BIBLIOGRAPHY

Cell theory: The historical setting of the cell theory is found in the exposition by FRANCOIS JACOB, *La Logique du vivant* (1970). In a work demanding little technical background, Jacob describes historical changes in attitudes toward the nature of life, views that prevailed before the advent of theories on the cell and evolution, and the contemporary outlook that would resolve the major problems in terms of molecular biology. As a comprehensive reference work, E. NORDENSKIOLD, *The History of Biology* (1935), has not been superseded. An important series of articles on cell theory is J.R. BAKER, "The Cell Theory: A Restatement, History and Critique," *Q. Jl. Microsc. Sci.*, vol. 89 (1948), vol. 90 (1949), and vol. 93 (1952). ARTHUR HUGHES, *The History of Cytology* (1959), is a vivid and thoughtful account of that large part of the history and criticism of cell biology involved with observations using light microscopy. Hughes' book was published at the time when the major advances in electron microscopy had only begun. An evaluation of the precursors of the cell theory, somewhat downgrading the contribution of Schwann and Schleiden, is given by E.G. CONKLIN in a collective work *The Cell and Protoplasm* (1940). The original work of Schwann and Schleiden was published in English translation under the title of *Microscopical Researches into the Accordance in the Structure and Growth of the Animals and Plants* (1847). The German text of Schwann's work, *Mikroskopische Untersuchungen über die Übereinstimmung in der Struktur und dem Wachstum der Tiere und Pflanzen*, was reprinted in 1910. A culminating event in the history of the subject, the elucidation of mitosis, is described in the publications of W. FLEMMING. The original papers, "Beiträge zur Kenntniss der Zelle und ihrer Lebenserscheinungen" ("Contributions to the Knowledge of the Cell and Its Vital Processes"), were published in the journal, *Archiv für mikroskopische Anatomie*, vol. 16 (1878) and vol. 18 (1880). An English translation of the second and definitive article appeared in the *Journal of Cell Biology*, vol. 25 (1965). In his book *Zellsubstanz, Kern- und Zelltheilung* (1882), Flemming summarized a great deal of what was known about the cell at that time and the historical development of the field. All the further developments of classical cell biology are summarized in E.B. WILSON, *The Cell in Development and Heredity*, 3rd ed. (1924), which, still being read and useful, defies the usual implications of the term "classical." MAX VERWORN, *Allegemeine Physiologie*, 2nd ed. (1897; Eng. trans., *General Physiology*, 1899), marks a turning point in which the cell theory became a major force in physiology as well as in microscopic anatomy. The protoplasm concept is developed from different standpoints in L.V. HEILBRUNN, *The Colloid Chemistry of Protoplasm* (1928); and in W. SEIFRIZ, *Protoplasm* (1936). A critique of the protoplasm concept (asserting its downfall) is found in G. HARDIN, "Meaninglessness of the Word Protoplasm," *Scient. Mon.*, 182:112–120 (1956).

Cell classification: A collection of papers on "Prokaryotic and Eukaryotic Cells" was published in 1970 as number 20 of the *Symposia of the Society for General Microbiology*. In this volume, an essay by R.Y. STANIER on "Some Aspects of the Biology of Cells and Their Possible Evolutionary Significance" summarizes the problems of the designs of cells in an incisive way. The divergence of cells from a common type for particular functions is dealt with in *The General Physiology of Cell Specialization*, ed. by D. MAZIA and A. TYLER (1963). Books on microbial anatomy, protozoology, animal histology, and plant histology are easily accessible sources of information on the varieties of cells. Unfortunately, no work compares all the cell types in all the varieties of organisms in a comprehensive way. In the present article, the classes of animal cells have been drawn largely from A.B. NOVIKOFF and E. HOLTZMANN, *Cells and Organelles* (1970), which is outstanding with regard to clarity, concision, and illustrations. The information on plant cells has been drawn from K. ESAU, *Plant Anatomy*, 2nd ed. (1965); E.M. GIFFORD, "Plant Anatomy," in PETER GRAY (ed.), *Encyclopedia of the Biological Sciences*, 2nd ed. (1970); and M.C. LEDBETTER and K.R. PORTER, *Introduction to the Fine Structure of Plant Cells* (1970).

Modern treatises on the cell: JEAN BRACHET and A.E. MIRSKY (eds.), *The Cell*, 6 vol. (1959–64); D.W. FAWCETT, *An Atlas of Fine Structure* (1966); A. LIMA-DE-FARCIA (ed.), *Handbook of Molecular Cytology* (1969); LAWRENCE PICKEN, *The Organization of Cells and Other Organisms* (1960); HERBERT STERN and D.L. NANNEY, *The Biology of Cells* (1965); S.L. WOLFE, *Biology of the Cell* (1972).

Celtic Languages

The Celtic languages form one branch of the Indo-European language family, having in common certain sound shifts and vocabulary items. On both geographical and chronological grounds, the languages fall into two divisions, usually known as Continental Celtic and Insular Celtic.

Continental Celtic. Continental Celtic is the generic name for the languages spoken by the people known to classical writers as Keltoi and Galatae; at various times during a period of roughly 1,000 years (approximately 500 BC–AD 500), they occupied an area that stretched from Gaul to Iberia in the south and Galatia in the east.

Evidence for Continental Celtic

The great bulk of evidence for Continental Celtic consists of the names of persons, tribes, and places recorded by Greek and Latin writers. Only in Gaul and in northern Italy are inscriptions found, and the interpretation of these is in most cases doubtful. Given the nature of the evidence, knowledge for these languages is confined largely to the sound system and a small part of the vocabulary, and no certain conclusions can be reached as to their historical development or the differences between them.

Insular Celtic. Insular Celtic refers to the Celtic languages of the British Isles, together with Breton (spoken in Brittany, France). As the name Breton implies, it is an importation from Britain and is not a Continental Celtic dialect. Although there is some scanty evidence from classical sources—mainly place-names—and a small body of inscriptions in the Latin and ogham alphabets from the end of the 4th to the 8th centuries AD, the main source of information on the early stages of these languages is manuscripts written from the 7th century onward in Irish and somewhat later in the British languages.

The Insular languages fall into two groups—Irish and British. Irish (often called Goidelic, from Old Irish *Goídel* "Irishman," or Gaelic, from *Gael*, the modern form of the same word) was the only language spoken in Ireland in the 5th century, the time when historical knowledge of that island begins. The two other members of this group, Scottish Gaelic and Manx, arose from Irish colonizations that began about that time. There were also important Irish-speaking colonies in Wales, but no trace of their language survives apart from a few inscriptions.

British (often called Brythonic, from Welsh Brython "Briton") had almost the same degree of influence on the island of Britain and the Isle of Man. Inscriptions and personal names surviving from Scotland show clearly that there was a non-Indo-European language spoken there, usually called Pictish, which was later replaced by British. There were undoubtedly dialectal differences within the island, but the existing dialects arose from the fragmentation of British by the Irish invasions of Man and what is now Scotland and by the English invasions that began in what is now southern England and finally reached Scotland. Scotland has ever since been partitioned linguistically between English (or "Scots") and Irish (or "Erse"—the Scots form of "Irish" —or "Gaelic"). A British dialect, now labelled **Cumbric,** lingered on in the western borderlands between England and Scotland until perhaps the 10th century, but almost nothing is known about it. In what is now Wales, British survived as the dominant language until a century or so ago; it is now known as Welsh. Another pocket of British speech survived in Cornwall until the end of the 18th century.

Re-establishment of Celtic on the European mainland

It was from this area that emigrants in the 5th and 6th centuries AD had brought Celtic once more to the European mainland by establishing a colony in northwestern France, still called Brittany. It is just possible that there were some traces of the Continental Celtic language (*i.e.*, Gaulish) at that time in this remote area, although Breton is too similar to Cornish (an Insular Celtic tongue) to suggest any serious influence from Gaulish.

HISTORICAL DEVELOPMENT

Common Celtic. The reconstruction of Common Celtic (or Proto-Celtic)—the parent language that yielded the various tongues of Continental Celtic and Insular Celtic—is of necessity very tentative. Whereas Continental Celtic offers plenty of evidence for phonology (the sound system), its records are too scanty to help much with the grammar (morphology or syntax), for which the best available evidence is Old Irish, the most archaic of the Insular languages. The records provide a picture of a language of the same type as Latin or Common Germanic; that is, one that still maintains a considerable part of the structure of the ancestral Indo-European language and has not lost final or medial syllables. Its vowel system differs only slightly from that reconstructed for Indo-European by the French linguist Antoine Meillet. Differences include the occurrence of Celtic *$\bar{\imath}$ for Indo-European *$\bar{e}$ (*e.g.*, Gaulish *rix* and Irish *rí*, "king"; compare Latin *rex*) and *$\bar{a}$ in place of *$\bar{o}$. (An asterisk [*] before a letter or word indicates that the sound or word is not attested but is a hypothetical, reconstructed form.)

The consonantal system, too, is conservative, although there are some striking features. Among them are the loss of **p* (*e.g.*, Irish *athair* "father"; *cf.* Latin *pater*) and the falling together of the aspirated and unaspirated voiced stops assumed for Indo-European. (A stop is a consonant made with complete momentary stoppage of the breath stream some place in the vocal tract; voiced stops are those produced with the vocal cords vibrating, such as *b*, *d*, *g*. An aspirated sound is accompanied by a puff of breath, often written as an *h*, as in *bh*, *dh*, *gh;* an unaspirated consonant lacks this accompanying puff of breath.) Thus, Old Irish *dán* "what is given" corresponds to Latin *donum* "gift" (from Indo-European **d*), but Old Irish *de-naid* "sucks" corresponds to Latin *fe-* in *fe-mina*, *fe-llare* (from Indo-European **dh*). This loss of distinctive aspiration occurs with three out of the four voiced stops, a situation close to that of Slavic.

Other considerations, however, show that Celtic belongs to the so-called southern group of the European branch of Indo-European languages, or in another classification, to the same centum group as Latin, whereas Slavic belongs to the satem group. (The centum and satem divisions of Indo-European languages are made according to the treatment of certain sounds, called palatals, that existed in the ancestral Indo-European language.)

Correspondence of Celtic *p* and *q*

The loss of **p* in Celtic was very early; only the place-name Hercynia, preserved in Greek, shows that, in initial position, it became an *h* sound before disappearing. In most of the known Celtic languages, a new *p* sound has arisen as a reflex of the Indo-European *k^w sound. Thus there is Gaulish *pempe*, Welsh *pimp* "five," compared to Old Irish *cóic* and Latin *quinque* "five." The Irish evidence shows that *k^wenk^we must be reconstructed as the form in Common Celtic. The terms P-Celtic and Q-Celtic are sometimes used to describe assumed divisions of Common Celtic; to use one sound shift to distinguish dialects is, however, hardly justified, and the classification will not be used in this article.

The morphology (structure) of nouns and adjectives shows no striking changes from Indo-European. The Irish verb, however, exhibits a remarkable archaism not found in any other recorded Indo-European language. It has recently been demonstrated that the so-called primary and secondary endings of the Indo-European verb, as in the 3rd person singular endings *-(*e*)*t* and -(*e*)*ti*, both occurred in the same tense. The forms with *-*i* were used when the verb had absolute initial position; those without it were used in the normal verbal position at the end of the sentence. This is reflected in the Old Irish forms *beirith* (from **bereti*) "he bears" and *ní beir* (from **beret*) "he does not bear." It cannot be stated with certainty that Continental Celtic had preserved such forms. The Continental Celtic dialects show a few cases of sentences—admittedly imperfectly understood—in which the verb appears to be placed after the subject and before the object, as in modern western European languages. The history of Insular Celtic, however, shows a gradual shift from the older final position of the verb to the initial position, a position that has now become regular in all of the languages.

Relationships and ancient contacts of Celtic. The question of the relationship of Common Celtic to the other Indo-European languages remains open. For some time, it was held that Celtic stood in an especially close relation to the Italic branch; some scholars even spoke of a period when an Italo-Celtic "nation" existed, toward the end of the 2nd millennium BC. The existence of a *q–p* relationship (see above) inside Italic too (*e.g.*, Latin *quattuor* "four," but Oscan *petora*) was thought by some to support this view. Much of this argument is, however, based on accidental resemblances (*e.g.*, the Irish future tense in *f-* and the Latin future in *b-*) or on formations such as the deponent and passive verb forms ending in *-r*, which at one time were known mainly in Italic and Celtic but have since been found in the Hittite and Tocharian languages as well. The undeniable common features between Celtic and Italic, such as the superlative endings of adjectives (Latin *-issimus;* Celtic **-samos*, **-isamos*), are hardly sufficient to justify the assumption of a special relationship, and the whole concept of an Italo-Celtic unity has been powerfully criticized by the linguists Carl J.S. Marstrander and Calvert Watkins.

The original home of the Celts cannot be located precisely, but, on the whole, the evidence points to the eastern part of central Europe. There is more evidence for their contacts with other Indo-European peoples. One group of Celts, at least, found themselves neighbours of the Germanic peoples and were often confused with them by classical writers. It can be inferred that the Celts had attained a higher standard of social organization than the Germanic peoples from the existence of words such as Gothic *reiki* and *andbahts* (modern German *Reich*, *Amt*), apparently borrowed from Celtic **rīgion* "kingdom" and **ambactos* "officer." To the Greeks and Romans, on the other hand, the Celts were inferior in culture; Celtic words in Greek are restricted to those describing Celtic institutions, such as *bardoi* "poets." The borrowings from Celtic into Latin, which derive mainly from the period before the expansion of Roman power, belong to a few restricted categories, such as war (*lancea* "lance"), transport (*carrus* "baggage wagon" and *carpentum* "light carriage"), and agricultural products (*cervesia* "beer"). When the Romans finally conquered Gaul and imposed their language, a number of Celtic words came into Latin, but the Celtic terms were mainly concerned with rural life. These are more common in French dialects than in standard French, which preserves a mere handful, such as *mouton* "sheep," *ruche* "beehive," and *arpent* "land measure."

Contacts with the Greeks and Romans

Early records of Celtic. *Continental Celtic.* Celtic died out very quickly in eastern Europe. In its farthest outpost in Asia Minor, it may be assumed that the *Letter of Paul to the Galatians* was addressed to a people whose culture was already Greek but whose Celtic origins are clear from names preserved by classical authors; *e.g.*, Drunemeton "the very sacred place," formed from two distinctively Celtic elements. When commenting on that Letter, St. Jerome (died AD 419/420) said that the Galatians still spoke a language almost the same as that of the people of Trier. As he had been in both places, his evidence cannot be dismissed offhand, and it may be that a few speakers of Celtic still existed in both areas. Since St. Jerome did not claim to know any Celtic dialect, however, his statement cannot be accepted with certainty. Speaking generally, the history of Continental Celtic comes to an end as that of Insular Celtic begins.

Insular Celtic. The earliest evidence for Insular Celtic consists, like that for Continental Celtic, mainly of names recorded by Greek and Latin authors. In the case of Ireland, these were entirely by hearsay, and many of the Irish place-names recorded by Ptolemy in the 2nd century AD have not yet been identified. From perhaps the 4th century, ogham inscriptions (see ALPHABETS) are found in Ireland, consisting almost entirely of personal names. From the 5th century onward, British names in Latin inscriptions are recorded in Wales, as well as Irish names in both Latin and ogham alphabets in areas of Irish settlement. These scanty records are of value above all in establishing that, up to very nearly the time at which written documents become available, British and Irish had remained similar in structure to Gaulish. Thus, in Britain is found the genitive (possessive form) Catotigirni, which in Old Welsh gives Cattegirn, and in Ireland the genitive Dovatuci exists, which in Old Irish gives Dubthaich. These changes—loss of final syllables and connecting vowels, weakening of consonants between vowels, and so on—are very similar to what was happening to Latin in France at the same time; *e.g.*, Latin *avicellus* and *aqua* finally became *oiseau* and *eau*. There is no satisfactory explanation of why these profound changes should have occurred at this time, nor can the period at which they occurred be fixed precisely, for the engravers of the inscriptions clearly went on using traditional forms long after the sound had changed.

LINGUISTIC CHARACTERISTICS OF THE INSULAR CELTIC TONGUES

The new languages, the only forms of Celtic that are known thoroughly, present a considerable number of unusual features, some of them unknown to other Indo-European languages. Some scholars have argued that these features may have resulted from the presence of a large non-Celtic substratum in the British Isles. Because it is hardly likely that the Celtic invasions of those islands began much before 500 BC or that the invaders exterminated the existing inhabitants, such a possibility cannot be denied. On the other hand, some features once thought to be exotic, such as the initial position of the verb in the sentence, have been convincingly demonstrated to be organic developments from Indo-European. Others, such as the system of counting by 20s, are clearly innovations, but this system is shared by English ("three score and ten"), French (*quatre-vingts* "80"), and Danish, in all of which it is also an innovation, as well as Basque, in which it appears to be old.

Possible influences of substratum languages

Phonological characteristics. The most remarkable phonological feature of Insular Celtic is the development of a double series of consonants in which strongly articulated consonants are distinguished from their weak counterparts. The two series were originally merely phonetic variants, with the strong variety occurring in absolute initial position and in certain consonant clusters and the weak elsewhere. Later, however, the two series became independent, or phonological. In the languages as they first appear in writing, considerable changes have taken place in the phonetic forms of the two series. Both in Irish and in Welsh, Cornish, and Breton, the opposition (contrast) of strong:weak in the voiced stops has been replaced by stop:spirant (*e.g.*, *b:v*). (A spirant, such as *v*, *f*, *s*, is produced with local friction and without complete stoppage of the breath stream.) Irish has the same system for the unvoiced stops (*e.g.*, *t:th*), but Welsh, Cornish, and Breton have voicing in this instance (*e.g.*, voiceless *t*:voiced *d*). These changes by themselves are not very different from the weakening of consonants between vowels that occurs in other western European languages (compare Welsh *pader* "prayer," a loanword from Latin *pater* "father," with Spanish *padre* "father," deriving from Latin *patrem*), but, in Insular Celtic, they occurred not only inside the word but also inside the phrase, so that the initial consonant of a word preceded by another word ending in a vowel was weakened. When the final syllables were lost in the evolution to the modern languages, these variations remained, and a system of initial mutations (changes) was thus set up. If, for example, a Goidelic nominative form **sindos kattos koilos* "the thin cat" is reconstructed, this will give Old Irish *in catt coel* after the loss of final syllables, but the genitive **sindī kattī koilī* "of the thin cat" will give *in chaitt choíl* with changed initial consonants. The same sort of change occurred in one Italian dialect: in Tuscan, there occur *porta* "door," *la forta* "the door," *tre pporte* "three doors," from Latin *porta, illa porta, tres portae*. In both cases, consonant weakening has spread from word to sentence; there is a common development, but it cannot be claimed that it is distinctively Celtic.

Grammatical characteristics. Another feature of Insular Celtic is its lack of the infinitive form of the verb found in most other Indo-European languages—*e.g.*, English "to do," "to call." The equivalent is the verbal noun, which is a noun closely linked to the verb, though not necessarily derived from the same stem. Being a noun, it can have a following noun in the genitive case, which, in the older languages at least, is subjective or objective according to whether the verb with which it is linked is intransitive or transitive. Thus, from the Old Irish sentence *téit in ben* "the woman goes," the verbal noun phrase *techt inna mná* "the coming of the woman" can be derived, whereas from *marbaid in mnaí* "he kills the woman" can be formed *marbad inna mná (lais)* "the killing of the woman (by him)." Among many other functions of the verbal noun is its use, when preceded by the appropriate preposition, with the substantive verb to provide a tense with continuous meaning. Thus, to *téit in ben* there is a parallel *a-tá in ben oc techt* "the woman is at going" (= "the woman is going"), and to *marbaid in mnaí* corresponds *a-tá oc marbad inna mná* "he is killing the woman." The close resemblance of this system to that of modern English, in which it is a comparatively recent development, has been variously explained as the working of a substratum or, more recently, in terms of areal (regional) development.

Verbal nouns

MODERN LANGUAGES OF THE FAMILY

The discussion of the individual languages that follows divides them into the two main groups, beginning with Irish, which is the oldest attested.

Irish. The history of Irish may be divided into four periods: that of the ogham inscriptions, probably AD 300–500; Old Irish, 600–900; Middle Irish, 900–1200; and Modern Irish, 1200 to the present. This division is necessarily arbitrary, and archaizing tendencies confuse the situation, especially during the period 1200–1600, when a highly standardized literary norm was dominant. After 1600, the modern dialects, among them Scottish Gaelic and Manx, begin to appear in writing.

The Latin alphabet was introduced into Ireland by British missionaries in the 5th century and soon began to be used for writing Irish. By the middle of the 6th century, the process of putting into literary form the rich oral tradition of the native learned class was certainly well advanced. The problems of interpreting the early writings are complicated by the fact that the orthography was based on that of Latin, but with a British pronunciation; *e.g.*, Latin *pater* was read as *pader*, the form of the loanword in Modern Welsh, and Old Irish *Pátric* was read as *Pádraig* (as it is spelled in Modern Irish). No new letters were evolved; the weak (less forceful) consonants were distinguished only in instances in which there were Latin spellings that could be utilized (*e.g.*, strong *ll*:weak *l*, strong *rr*:weak *r*, *nn:n*, *c:ch*, *t:th*) or with the help of the *punctum delens* (*s:ṡ*, *f:ḟ*), a dot that shows that the sound is not pronounced. As a result, many ambiguities remain: *ní beir* can mean either "he does not carry" or "he does not carry it," according to whether the *b-* is read as a *b* sound or a *v* sound. Nor was the Latin alphabet capable of dealing with the new system of consonant quality that appears in Irish alone among the Celtic languages. Thus, from the Celtic nominative singular and plural forms *bardos*, *bardī* developed Welsh *bardd*, plural *beirdd*, with a vowel alternation like that of English "mouse, mice." In Irish, the forms are *bard, baird;* the *-i-* of *baird* is purely graphic, serving to indicate that the following consonants are both palatalized. (Palatalized consonants are those in which the pronunciation is modified by raising the tongue toward the hard palate.) This palatalization had been purely phonetic as long as the *-ī* that caused it survived, but in Old Irish the palatalization became independent, so that each consonant of Common Celtic evolved into four distinct consonants (*i.e.*, phonemes); for example, from original Common Celtic *b* are derived a *b* sound and a palatalized *b* sound, and a *v* sound and a palatalized *v* sound.

Development of palatalized consonants

Apart from these phonetic developments, Old Irish is striking chiefly for the extraordinary proliferation of particles that appear before the verb and are used in forming compound verbs. For example, the Latin word *suffio* "I fumigate" is translated as *fo-timmdiriut*, composed of *fo* "under," *to* "to," *imb-* "around," *di* "from," and the stem *reth-* "run," with vowel and consonant changes appropriate to the 1st person singular present tense. Such forms, combined with a system of infixed accusative and dative pronouns (*i.e.*, pronouns inserted within a word) and syntactical accent shifts, produced a verbal system almost as complicated as that of Basque, though transparently Indo-European in origin. This system began to break down during the Old Irish period; the process was no doubt accelerated by the Viking raids that began at the end of the 8th century and that disrupted the monastic system, the guardian of the literary norm of Old Irish. Popular forms broke through in the Middle Irish period, though always mixed with archaizing forms; the backward-looking Irish scribes were never content to write down their own vernacular. During the 12th century, many ecclesiastical synods were held with the object of bringing the organization of the Irish Church more closely into line with that of western Europe, and the Anglo-Norman invasion took place in the latter part of the same century. It may have been these far-reaching changes that inspired the Irish literati to undertake a new standardization of their language. From the beginning of the 13th century, there is a rigidly fixed norm, often called Classical Modern Irish, which, for over four centuries, was used as the exclusive literary medium in Ireland and in Gaelic-speaking Scotland (there is no evidence for the Isle of Man).

The Scandinavians were first contained and then absorbed; they contributed a small number of loanwords to Irish, mainly in the field of navigation but also in that of urban life, for they were the first to establish towns in Ireland, though only on the coast. The Anglo-Normans were a more serious problem. After almost complete success in the early period, however, they became largely Gaelicized in custom and language outside the towns they had founded. They contributed a large number of loanwords to Irish in the fields of warfare, architecture, and administration, though many of these were comparatively short-lived. When English took over from Anglo-Norman as the language of administration and English colonies began to be planted in Ireland, English loanwords began to come into Irish. Few of these, however, were recognized in the literary language, and only from the evidence of the modern dialects has it become clear that they were quite numerous.

It was not until the beginning of the 17th century that the English power was finally consolidated in Ireland, first by military conquest and later by the planting of English-speaking colonists on a much larger scale than before. From this time onward, the decline of Irish began, with Irish becoming the language of an oppressed people. With no schools to teach the literary language nor any native nobility to support the literati who used it, the dialects appeared for the first time and began to be written in the paper manuscripts that constituted almost the only form of publishing available to those using Irish. By the beginning of the 19th century, it is probable that the population was almost equally divided between Irish speakers, mainly in the western half, and English speakers, mainly in the eastern half. The real imbalance lay in the fact that many of the Irish speakers were bilingual, whereas few of the English speakers were. The first census to record language use was taken in 1851, after the great famine that had struck the western areas with exceptional severity. By this time, the total number of Irish speakers was 1,524,286 (23 percent of the population), but only 319,602 spoke Irish exclusively. The decline of Irish has continued to the present day, in spite of a revival campaign initiated by the Gaelic League in 1893 and made part of official policy after the establishment of the Irish Free State in 1921.

The decline of Irish

Since then, Irish has been recognized as the first official language of the state; it is a compulsory subject in all of the schools and is a requirement for civil service and some other posts. There are probably more people able to read Irish—perhaps 300,000—than there ever were before. From 1945 onward, a standard written language has evolved, and there is a small but flourishing literary movement. Nearly all of the readers of Irish are English speakers by upbringing, however, and not many of them would claim that Irish had become their main language. In the western areas in which Irish was the traditional speech, there are now fewer than 50,000 people to whom it is a mother tongue, and all but a handful of these have a more or less adequate command of English.

Scottish Gaelic. Some aspects of the modern Scottish Gaelic dialects show that they preserve features lost in the language of Ireland during the Old Irish period; such archaism is characteristic of "colonial" languages. The innovations are, however, more striking than the archaisms. Most remarkable is the loss of the voicing feature (*i.e.*, the vibration of the vocal cords) in the stops. All of the stopped consonants are unvoiced, and the original voiceless stops have become strongly aspirated; for example, the equivalent of Irish *bog* "soft" is [pok], *p* being the voiceless counterpart of *b*, and that of *cat* "cat" is [k^haht], the superscript ^{h} after *k* indicating the aspirated quality. (The brackets indicate that the symbols printed within them are phonetic rather than orthographic.)

Scottish Gaelic was planted on British soil, and the verbal system has been remolded on the lines of the British language, which originally had no future tense. As in Modern Welsh, the inherited present tense has largely future meaning, and present time is mainly expressed by the present-tense form of the substantive verb and the preposition *a(ig)* with the verbal noun. (In Insular Celtic, there are two verbs for "to be," a substantive verb with the meaning, roughly, "to exist," and a linking verb such as "is" in "John is a boy" or "sky is blue.") Thus, from Old Irish *téit in ben* "the woman goes" is derived Scottish Gaelic *théid a' bhean* "the woman will go," and from Old Irish *a-tá in ben oc techt* "the woman is going" results the Scottish Gaelic form *thà an bhean a' dol* "the woman goes" or "the woman is going."

It is only from the 17th century onward that the development of Scottish Gaelic can be studied, for, up until then, Classical Modern Irish was the literary norm. Indeed, the first book to be printed in Irish was a translation of the Calvinist *Book of Common Order*, published in Edinburgh in 1567, and the Scottish Reformers used the Irish Bible for some time, until it became clear that it was too foreign for the people to understand. A native Scottish standard emerged gradually during the 17th century, as poets ignorant of the Irish norm began to compose in their native dialects. It was not until the 18th century that the orthography became more or less fixed, and, until recent reforms in Ireland, the divergencies between the written languages were comparatively small. It is clear, however, that Scottish Gaelic must now be regarded as a separate language, though the differences between it and Irish are no greater than those between standard German and the Swiss dialects.

Scottish Gaelic as a separate language from Irish

Scottish Gaelic was confronted by northern dialects of English (Scots) from the very beginning; these rapidly penetrated into the east of the country, especially in the area centred on Edinburgh, the capital. The so-called Highland Line, marking the boundary between the two languages, has been steadily receding to the west since medieval times. By 1901, there were 230,806 speakers of the language, including 28,106 who spoke Scottish Gaelic exclusively; 106,466 persons, including nearly all of the monolingual Scottish Gaelic people, lived in the two counties of Inverness and Ross. The decline has continued steadily, and, even in those two counties, Gaelic is rapidly disappearing from the mainland, though it is holding its ground well in the Hebrides. Scottish Gaelic speakers in the 1961 census numbered 80,978, which shows that the state of Scottish Gaelic survival is in many ways less serious than that of Irish. Because the majority of Gaelic speakers are Protestants who are accustomed to reading the Bible and using the vernacular in their religious services, literacy in Gaelic has been widespread. Furthermore, however low the census figures may be, they give an accurate picture of the number of those to whom Gaelic is a mother tongue because the number of English speakers who have acquired it is negligible. It must be admitted, however, that the recent literary revival finds its audience among the displaced Gaelic speakers of Edinburgh and Glasgow rather than in the Hebrides, where Gaelic is still confined to the home and English is the language of culture. In addition, the Canadian census of 1961 recorded 3,702 Gaelic speakers in Nova Scotia.

Manx. The history of the Isle of Man is imperfectly known. It was first inhabited by British speakers, then colonized from Ireland, and later became part of the Scandinavian Lordship of the Isles until 1266, when the King of Norway ceded both Man and the Hebrides to Scotland. From then on, it became involved in the wars between England and Scotland until 1346, when it passed finally to England. Though an Irish dialect survived as the speech of the majority of the people, these circumstances were not propitious for literary contacts with Ireland, and Manx was apparently not written until the Welsh bishop John Phillips translated the Anglican *Book of Common Prayer* in 1610, using an orthography based on that of English. This orthography makes Manx difficult to understand for readers of Irish and Scottish Gaelic, to whom it is of considerable interest because it represents a dialect entirely free of literary influences. The orthography soon became fixed, and a far-reaching series of later phonetic changes made the written form a highly inaccurate representation of the final stages of the language. Phonologically, it has more in common with the eastern dialects of Irish than with Scottish Gaelic, but its morphology and syntax are much more like those of Scottish Gaelic, probably because of the common British substratum. Its tense system is similar to that of Scottish Gaelic and Welsh, and its use of periphrastic verb forms (*i.e.*, longer forms with several elements) with the auxiliary meaning "to do" goes further than either of these, especially in its final stages.

In the beginning of the 18th century, English was still not understood by most of the people, but during the 19th century the decline of Manx was rapid, and the census of 1901 showed only 4,419 speakers of the language, all bilingual. Twenty years later, the language had ceased to be used as a normal means of communication, but, until recently, investigators have been able to find old people capable of giving useful information.

Extinction of Manx in the early 20th century

British languages. Britain was thoroughly romanized, and it is clear that the British language itself had been much affected by Latin; on the level of vocabulary, such an everyday word as Welsh *pysg* "fish," for example, derives from Latin *piscis*. The vowel system lost independent vowel quantity, the length of vowels becoming determined by the structure of the syllable, a situation that also occurred when the later Latin developed into Romance. Even after the collapse of Roman rule, Latin retained the same prestige among British Christians that it had in the rest of the Western Empire. The Irish monks introduced to the British speakers the custom of writing down the vernacular language at about the end of the 8th century; they adapted the clumsy Irish orthography for that purpose. At this period, the British dialects were very close to one another and can hardly be classed as separate languages, though they soon began to diverge. Like Old Irish, they had lost their final syllables and had undergone many other changes from the state shown by the inscriptions. Notably, the languages show only the merest traces of the declension of the noun, although the verb preserves a full inflectional system (that is, it has a full series of endings). It is clear that no future tense existed in early British, though the separate languages were later to fill this gap by various means.

Welsh. Welsh is the earliest and best attested of the British languages. Although the material is fragmentary until the 12th century, the course of the language can be traced from the end of the 8th century. The earliest evidence may represent the spoken language fairly accurately, but a poetic tradition was soon established, and by the 12th century there was a clear divergence between the archaizing verse and a modernizing prose. The latter was characterized by a predominance of periphrastic verbal-noun constructions at the expense of forms of the finite verb. By this time, too, the forms corresponding to other Celtic and Indo-European present-tense forms had largely acquired future meaning; *e.g.*, Welsh *nid â* "he will not go" (future) contrasts with Irish *ní aig* "he does not drive" (present). The gap thus left was filled, as in Scottish Gaelic and Manx, by a construction involving the substantive verb and the verbal noun; *e.g.*, *y mae'r wraig yn myned* "the woman goes" or "the woman is going" is composed of the verb *mae* "is" and the verbal noun *myned* "going."

By the 14th century, prose and verse styles became more similar, the prose being less colloquial and the verse less archaic. This marks the beginning of modern literary Welsh, which was finally fixed by the Bible translation of 1588. Modern literary Welsh developed at a time when Welsh national identity was beginning to be seriously threatened by the close relations with England that followed on the accession of the Welshman Henry Tudor (Henry VII) to the English throne in 1485. Welsh was being written less and less, and the spoken language was being penetrated by English words. In 1536, the Act of Union deprived Welsh of its official status. By the beginning of the 18th century, the position of the Welsh language had fallen very low, though it was still the vernacular of the vast majority of the people. It was saved by the Methodist revival of the 18th century, which established schools everywhere to teach the people how to read the Welsh Bible and which brought the Bible itself, together with Welsh religious books, into almost every home. The literary language rejected most of the English loanwords that had come into the popular speech, and, by the 19th century, a highly literate Wales was equipped with reading material of every kind in the Welsh language. Meanwhile, however, the popular speech diverged further from the fixed literary norm, which was never spoken except in the pulpit or on the platform. Modern Wales has a literary language that no mother speaks to her child and widely differing dialects that appear in print only to represent dialogue in stories and novels.

Effect of the 18th-century Methodist revival on Welsh

The Industrial Revolution of the 19th century first undermined the dominance of Welsh in Wales: English-speaking workers were brought into the mines and factories in such numbers that they could not be absorbed linguistically. By 1901 English speakers outnumbered Welsh speakers for the first time. Out of a population of 2,012,876, only 929,824 were reported as Welsh-speaking, though 280,985 people spoke Welsh alone. By 1961 the number of Welsh speakers had dropped to 656,002, representing just under 25 percent of an increased population. Most of rural Wales, however, is still Welsh speaking, and recent years have seen a great improvement in the official status of Welsh and a considerable increase in its use in the schools; it is certainly the most firmly rooted of the modern languages of Celtic origin.

In addition, there are still about 8,000 Welsh speakers in parts of Patagonia, Argentina, which was colonized by Welsh settlers in 1865. These people maintain cultural contacts with the homeland but are all bilingual in Welsh and Spanish and seem fated to final assimilation.

Breton. Breton disappeared from sight after the early period, and no literary texts are available until the 15th century. These, mainly mystery plays and similar religious material, are written in a standardized language that is by now completely differentiated from Welsh and, to a lesser degree, from Cornish. The divergence between Breton and Cornish is largely a matter of the English loanwords in Cornish and the French loanwords in Breton. The present tense was retained in its original function, whereas a future and conditional were formed from the present and past subjunctive, respectively. Later, the Breton dialects became written and showed considerable divergencies in this form. Not until the 1920s was an attempt at standardization made, and even then it was necessary to adopt two norms. One was called KLT, from the initials of the Breton names of the dioceses of Cornouaille, Léon, and Tréguier, the dialects of which agree with Welsh and Cornish in having the stress accent on the next to the last syllable. The other norm was the dialect of Vannes in the south, which has the stress accent on the final syllable and many other distinctive features, at least some of which can be explained by its close contacts with French. More recently, two norms have been evolved to cover all four dialects; one of these is used by most writers, whereas the other is officially recognized by the universities of Brest and Rennes, in both of which Breton is taught.

Breton dialect norms

Up until recently, Breton was the common language of the people in Cornouaille, Léon, Tréguier, and Vannes, within the boundaries of the *départements* of Côtes-du-Nord, Finistère, and Morbihan. Breton may still have more speakers than Welsh, but this is quite uncertain because no language statistics exist for France. There is, however, general agreement that very few children today are being brought up speaking Breton. This is at least partly the result of French official policy, which in effect excludes the language from primary and secondary schools, though the poor economic opportunities in Brittany also play a part. The literary movement is, therefore, confined to an intelligentsia of perhaps not much more than 10,000 people, many of whom live outside Brittany. The overwhelming mass of the remainder of Breton speakers are literate only in French, and chances for the survival of Breton seem very poor.

Cornish. Like Breton, Cornish had no literary texts before the 15th century. Those that exist are mainly mystery plays, some of which are almost literal translations from English. Cornish is much closer in structure to Breton than to Welsh, but it has also been heavily influenced by English. At the beginning of the 18th century, there were still a number of areas in which Cornish was spoken, but it died out as a means of communication by the end of the century.

BIBLIOGRAPHY. H. LEWIS and H. PEDERSEN, *A Concise Comparative Celtic Grammar* (1937), is the most recent survey of the entire field. The early history of the British group is discussed in detail by K.H. JACKSON, *Language and History in Early Britain* (1953); for the later history of Welsh and Breton, J. MORRIS JONES, *A Welsh Grammar* (1913), and F. GOURVIL, *Langue et littérature bretonnes* (1952), give useful information. R. THURNEYSEN, *Grammar of Old Irish*, rev. ed. (1946), is a classic among linguistic handbooks; for the later development of Irish, T.F. O'RAHILLY, *Irish Dialects Past and Present* (1932), is full of information and contains chapters on Scottish Gaelic and Manx. B.O CUIV (ed.), *A View of the Irish Language* (1969), containing 12 essays by various hands, maps, and illustrations; and D. GREENE, *The Irish Language* (1966), are directed to the general reader rather than to the linguist. The relevant sections of GLANVILLE PRICE, *The Present Position of Minority Languages in Western Europe* (1969), give full bibliographies of works dealing with the political and social status of the surviving Celtic languages.

(D.Gr.)

Celtic Religion

The Celts, an Indo-European people who were at the height of their power numerically and geographically in 4th-century-BC Europe, have left no literature on the Continent. The literature of the insular Celts (Irish and Welsh), however, though late in time, imparts valuable information about their religion in the myths that have been preserved. Celtic religion, presided over by the Druids (the priestly order), presents beliefs in various nature deities and certain ceremonies and practices that are similar to those in Indian religion. The insular Celts and the people of India also shared certain similarities of language and culture, thus indicating an ancient common heritage.

SOURCES

For information about the Celts of the Continent scholars depended upon what Greek and Roman historians have reported, often at second hand. Another important source of information is found in Celtic sculpture and inscriptions. The Greek and Latin historians seem to have derived their information from a single source, namely, the historical works of Poseidonius, a Stoic philosopher of the late Roman Republican period. The most important witnesses dependent upon Poseidonius are Strabo, Diodorus Siculus, and Julius Caesar. The sculpture dates almost entirely from the Gallo-Roman period.

Greek, Roman and Celtic sources

Julius Caesar stated in *The Gallic War* that in Gaul Mercury was the most honoured of all the gods and that many images of him were to be found. Mercury was regarded as the inventor of all the arts, the patron of travellers and of merchants, and the most powerful god in matters of commerce and gain. After him the Gauls honoured Apollo, Mars, Jupiter, and Minerva. Of these gods they held almost the same opinions as other peoples did: Apollo drives away diseases, Minerva promotes handicrafts, Jupiter rules the heavens, and Mars controls wars. Caesar distinguished five separate gods among the Gauls, but he cited them only by their Roman names; however, his statement may well have been based upon deliberate inquiry.

As for the inscriptions, they are in a few instances associated with effigies of a god, such as on the famous Paris "altar" and the altar at Sarrebourg, and from them the Celtic gods Cernunnos, Esus, Sucellus, and Taruos Trigaranus can be recognized. Esus and Sucellus, and the god with the wheel, Taranis, can be identified elsewhere, but the images of most of the sculptures are not positively identifiable. The 1st century AD Latin poet Lucan, in a passage of his *Pharsalia* describing various Gaulish tribes, named three of the Celtic gods—Teutates, Esus, and Taranis—and stated that they were appeased by human sacrifice. An early commentator on Lucan's work identified Teutates with Mars, Esus with Mercury, and Taranis with Jupiter, and thus later scholars have a working hypothesis from which to start their inquiries.

MYTHOLOGY

The Celtic pantheon

Pre-Roman gods. The Celtic pantheon is difficult to construct, since some 400 names of Celtic gods are known and of these more than 300 occur only once and are apparently names of minor local deities. Caesar distinguished five gods, and names of three more gods were supplied later by Lucan. Besides these there are the names of two gods that occur more often than any others, Belenus (20 times) and Grannus (19 times), both later identified with Apollo. Moreover, three others have been mentioned already, as well-known from sculpture: Cernunnos, the god with the horns of a stag; Sucellus, the god with the mallet; and Taruos Trigaranus, the bull with three cranes. One god, perhaps the greatest of all, survived in Irish mythology as Lug Lámfota, Lug of the Long Hand. On the Continent he is known directly from three dedications, two of them in plural form; but his name is widespread in the place name Lug(u)dunum, which has given the modern Lyon, Loudun, and Laon in France, Leiden in The Netherlands, and Legnica in Poland. Most of the goddesses appear only in association with one or other of the gods. Sucellus has for consort Nantosuelta; Luxovius, a god of healing and patron of the baths at Luxeuil, has Brixia; Borvo, another god of healing, has Damona. Rosmerta, a goddess of plenty, appears with Mercury and chiefly in eastern Gaul. The most interesting goddess is Epona, the mare goddess, whose name occurs 26 times and whose cult seems to have been known all over the Celtic world. Epona is often represented as mounted on a mare, and she was the patroness of the cavalry and of travellers on horseback, and of mares and foals. Her image was often used to adorn the stables.

Most notable, however, among female deities are the mother goddesses, of whom there are many effigies. In Gaul the mother goddess was worshipped in triple form under the title Matres or Matronae. The dedicatory texts that survive are in Latin, and the figures are either represented with baskets of fruit, or with horns of plenty, or with children in their laps. (Matrona was the name of the River Marne, which was also thought to be a goddess.)

Gallo-Roman gods. The 20th-century French scholar Paul-Marie Duval distinguished two periods in the history of the worship of the Gaulish gods: the early period ending in the middle of the 1st century AD and the later period of Roman Gaul, when much syncretism (accretion and coalescence) between Celtic and Roman gods had taken place and the effigies of old Gaulish gods appeared under Roman names.

The great god of the Celts was the one Caesar called Mercury, the god of all the arts, but his Gaulish name is not given. In the later period, under the name Mercury, he appeared in 440 inscriptions and 350 sculptures, which are still extant, and thus he is the most richly documented of all the gods. In Ireland he was called Lug of the Long Hand, and the name Lugus appears in three dedicatory texts on the Continent: one in Switzerland at Avenches, where the form is Lugoues; one at Asma (Tarragona), where the form is Lugouibus, in a dedication by the guild of cobblers; and one at Peñalba de Villestar, where the form is Luguei. He was apparently sometimes thought of as a triple god. In Ireland Lug was called *samildánach* ("possessed of many talents"), which is in agreement with Caesar's account of Mercury, and his regular epithet was *lámfota.* A very ancient cult of the God with the Long Hand, who appears in rock-carvings in Sweden, was also known in the Caucasus, and one of the Swedish effigies is known to this day as "the Cobbler," echoing the dedication of Asma. In the Welsh tale *Math fab Mathonwy* the hero is called Lleu Llaw Gyffes ("Lug of the Dexterous Hand"), and in one episode he appears disguised as a shoemaker. Plainly there was a myth about Lugus as patron of cobblers, and he was also known as the dexterous god, patron of the arts. His Irish epithet connects him with the ancient God of the Long Hand, and a similar epithet *pṛthu-pāṇi* ("of the large hand") is applied in India to the Vedic Savitṛ, god of the sun. The web of tradition is difficult to disentangle, but Lugus emerges as a great god, whose name was for some reason rare on the Continent as the name of a god but familiar in Ireland. In Ireland his feast, Lugnasad, was on August 1, the date of the harvest festival, and it has survived to the present as "Garland Sunday." The identification of Esus with Mercury is probably not exclusive; the god to whom Caesar referred as Mercury probably was Lugus.

Lug of the Long Hand

Taranis, whose name was noted by Lucan, was later identified with Jupiter; *taran* means "thunder" in Welsh. He may be identified as the god of the sky and of thunder, and his symbol was the wheel. Though some have identified Sucellus with him, this is doubtful. The symbol of Sucellus is the mallet, depicted in more than 20 effigies. Henri Hubert has suggested that Sucellus might be the patron of brewers.

Teutates, later identified with Mars (Mars Toutatis), bears a name that is derived from the reconstructed word *teuta* ("tribe, people") and could mean "(god) of the tribe," and that may have been in origin a common noun. In Irish sagas the common form of oath is: "I swear by the god by whom my tribe swears," suggesting that each tribe had its own tutelary god whose proper name was subject to a tabu. Lucan stated that victims sacrificed to these gods were killed by being plunged headfirst into a vat. Such a scene is presented on the Cauldron of Gundestrup, now in the National Museum at Copenhagen. Teutates was probably the tribal god and also the god of war.

Esus, the third of Lucan's triad, is a mysterious figure. His name is on the Paris "altar," where he is depicted in the act of cutting a tree and in the company of a bull with three cranes on his back under the legend Taruos Trigaranos. A similar scene is presented on the altar at Trier, and it probably portrays a lost myth. The bull figures in Irish mythology, too, but no Irish tradition helps to explain the character of Esus. Because of the lack of a written literature the myth involving Esus is not known.

The horned god Cernunnos

Another mysterious deity is the horned god Cernunnos, who appears on the Gundestrup Cauldron in the yoga posture, with the horns of a stag, and surrounded by animals, including the Serpent with a Ram's Head, who is elsewhere associated with Teutates. Here Cernunnos strongly resembles the Indian god Śiva Paśupati ("lord of animals") on a seal from Mohenjo-daro now in the Delhi

(Left) Gundestrup Cauldron, from Gundestrup, Himmerland, Denmark, 2nd–3rd century. (Right) Interior of the cauldron showing Cernunnos as "lord of the animals." In the Danish National Museum, Copenhagen.

By courtesy of the Danish National Museum, Copenhagen

Museum. He is also portrayed and named on the Paris "altar," again in the yoga posture, and with the horns of a stag. Cernunnos and Taruos Trigaranus are animal deities, the Stag and the Bull, and there was probably a serpent god as well. In Britain the Horned God is widely attested. In Ireland the bull god survives in shadowy form in the great *Táin Bó Cuailnge*, and Donn, the Brown Bull of Cooley, and the White-Horned Bull seem to be supernatural beings. They appear at the end of a series of transmigrations in which two fairy swineherds change themselves into stags, champions, spectres, dragons, and worms; and as worms they are taken from sacred springs by two cows at their drink and are reborn as the two great bulls of Ireland.

Belenus and Grannus were both later identified with Apollo. Belenus may have been a god of the sun. His name echoes the Irish Beltine ("fire of Bel"), name of the summer festival, May 1. Grannus was a god of healing. Borvo was another healing deity, and several thermal springs had local patrons. The cult of a god of healing under various names could lie behind Caesar's mention of Apollo. Another god that is worthy of mention is Ogmios, the god of eloquence, who was described by Lucian as the god who was represented as Hercules, because the Celts believed that eloquence was more powerful than strength.

British and Irish Celtic gods. Insular tradition provides the names of other gods common to Ireland and Wales, but their Gaulish names are not known. Goibniu is the smith among the Irish gods, and his Welsh name is Gofannon. Manannán (Welsh Manawydan) is the god of the sea, and Nuadu of the Silver Arm (Welsh Lludd of the Silver Arm) is a god who is portrayed in a dedication that occurs on a monument in Gloucestershire and shows him equipped as a fisherman. He is probably the ancestor of the Fisher King in the Quest of the Holy Grail in Arthurian romance. In Ireland Nuadu preceded Lug as king of the gods, and Lug was succeeded by the Dagda, "the Good God."

Triple deities

Lugus was sometimes thought of in the plural, and the Matres were adored in triple form. There are as many as 32 images of a three-headed god extant on the Continent, and some have been found in Britain and in Ireland. On a stela at Reims, Mercury has three faces, but the Three-Headed God is more often anonymous. In Ireland several deities appear in threes, notably the Three Gods of Danann, from whom Lug received his weapons. There are three Brigits: a goddess of poetry, a goddess of healing, and a goddess of smithcraft. There are three Machas and three goddesses of battle: Morrígan, Badb, and Nemain. The trio Mac Cuill, Mac Cécht, and Mac Gréine are husbands of three goddesses of Ireland, Banba, Fótla, and Ériu. Brigit ("the exalted one") appears in Britain as Brigantia and was perhaps the tutelary goddess of Brigantes, although her name does not occur in Gaul. She has been identified with Caesar's "Minerva" and would then be an important Gaulish and Insular Celtic goddess.

Wells, rivers, and sacred trees were objects of devotion and had patron gods or goddesses. There was a sanctuary of the Dea Sequana at the source of the Seine and one of the Dea Matrona near the source of the Marne. The Yonne (Icaunis) and the Saône (Souconna) rivers were also viewed as divine. In Ireland the Boyne (derived from *bōuvindā*, "cow finder") and the Shannon rivers also were regarded as goddesses. Of the trees of the forest, the beech, the oak, and the yew were revered in Gaul, and in Ireland there were many sacred trees. There is a word *bile* ("sacred tree") that occurs in the place name Moville (*Mag Bile*, "plain of sacred trees") in Ireland, and the place name Billom (from the reconstructed word *Biliomagus*) in France.

BELIEFS, PRACTICES, AND INSTITUTIONS

Beliefs. Little is known about the religious beliefs of the Celts of Gaul. They believed in a life after death, for they buried food, weapons, and ornaments with the dead. The Druids, the early Celtic priesthood, taught the doctrine of transmigration of souls and discussed the nature and power of the gods. The Irish believed in an Otherworld, imagined sometimes as underground and sometimes as in islands beyond the sea. These two notions, it has been suggested, arose from the cult of a sun god, who arose at dawn out of sea or earth and returned there at night. The Otherworld was variously called "the Land of the Living," "Delightful Plain," "Land of the Young" and was believed to be a country where there was no sickness, old age, or death, where happiness lasted forever, and a hundred years was as one day. It was similar to the Elysium of the Greeks and may have belonged to ancient Indo-European tradition. In Celtic eschatology (pertaining to the end of history), as noted in Irish vision or voyage tales, a beautiful girl approaches the hero and sings to him of this happy land. He follows her, and they sail away in a boat of glass and are seen no more; or else he returns after a short time to find that all his companions are dead, for he has really been away for hundreds of years. Sometimes the hero sets out on a quest, and a magic mist descends upon him. He finds himself before a palace and enters to find a warrior and a beautiful girl who make him welcome. The warrior may be Manannán, or Lug himself may be the one who receives him, and after strange adventures the hero returns successfully. These Irish tales, some of which date from the 8th century, are infused with the magic quality that is found 400 years later in the Arthurian romances. Something of this quality is preserved, too, in the Welsh story of Branwen, daughter of Llyr, which ends with the survivors of the great battle feasting in the presence of the severed head of Bran the Blessed, having forgotten all their suffering and sorrow. But this "delightful plain" was not accessible to all. Donn, god of the dead and ancestor of all the Irish, reigned over Tech Duinn, which was imagined as on or under Bull Island off the Beare Peninsula, and to him all men returned except the happy few.

Life after death

Practices and institutions. Though there was a full pantheon of gods and probably a rich mythology among the Celts, many local deities, and some whose cult was widespread, no detailed account of individual gods is possible. Even the Irish gods have little personality, and of Irish pagan rites practically nothing is known. Human sacrifice was practiced in Gaul: Cicero, Caesar, Suetonius, and Lucan all refer to it, and the elder Pliny says that it occurred in Britain too. It was forbidden under Tiberius and Claudius. There is some evidence that human sacrifice was known in Ireland and was forbidden by St. Patrick, who apparently also reproached the Irish for worshipping the sun; and if the God with the Long Hand was a sun god, then Lug may have been originally the god of the sun. There is no clear evidence, however, of sun worship in Ireland.

Sacrifice

Druids. The priests who served the Celtic gods and presided over the sacrifice were the Druids. The name means "knowing the oaktree" (*dru-vid-*) and may derive from Druidic ritual, which seems in the early period to have been performed in the forest. Caesar stated that the Druids avoided manual labour and paid no taxes, so that many were attracted by these privileges to join the order. They learned great numbers of verses by heart, and some studied for as much as 20 years: they thought it wrong to commit their learning to writing but used the Greek alphabet for other purposes.

Shrines. As far as is known, the Celts had no temples before the Gallo-Roman period, and their ceremonies were performed in forest sanctuaries. In the Gallo-Roman period pagan temples were erected, and many of them have been discovered by archaeologists in Britain as well as in Gaul.

Divination. There were also seers (*vates,* Greek *manteis*) who had various means of divination and could foretell the future by watching the flight of birds or observing the animals slain in sacrifice. On important occasions a human victim was stabbed in the midriff, and from the manner of his fall, the twitching of his limbs, and the flow of blood they could foresee events. The Irish word for seer is *fáith* and both men and women practiced divination. One of the rites was called "bull-sleep" (*tarb-ḟeis*) and involved the slaughter of a bull. Its flesh was boiled, and the seer bathed in the broth and ate the meat and then slept, and in his sleep he saw the future king of Tara.

Festivals. Irish sources provide important information about Celtic religious festivals. The year was divided into two periods of six months by the feasts of Beltine (May 1) and Samain (November 1), and each of these periods was equally divided by the feasts of Imbolc (February 1), and Lugnasad (August 1). Samain was, in Ireland at least, the great feast of the year. The word was thought to mean "end of summer" (*sam,* "summer," *fuin,* "end"), but it may mean "assembly," for Beltine is also called *Cetšamain* ("First Samain"). Imbolc has been compared by the French scholar J. Vendryes to the Roman lustrations and apparently was a feast of purification for the farmers. It was sometimes called *oímelc* ("sheep milk") with reference to the lambing season. Beltine ("Fire of Bel") was the summer festival, and there is a tradition that on that day the Druids drove cattle between two fires as a protection against disease. Lugnasad was the feast of the great god Lug Lámḟota, presumably a harvest festival when the Fair of Tailtiu was held.

Beltine and Samain

One rite practiced in Ireland down to the Middle Ages deserves mention because it closely resembles the Hindu ritual of the horse sacrifice (*aśvamedha*) and is therefore probably of Indo-European date. The Welsh ecclesiastical writer Giraldus Cambrensis (died *c.* 1223) described a ritual practiced in one of the northern kingdoms of Ireland that involved the sacrifice of a mare at the inauguration of the king. The king went through a symbolic union with the victim and then bathed in the broth of its flesh and drank thereof. Through this ritual the king sought fertility for himself and his kingdom. A just king brought prosperity to the kingdom. If he was unjust, a curse fell upon the land.

Sovereignty was regarded in Ireland as a goddess whom the king must wed in order to ensure the welfare of his people. The notion may have been a development from the primitive idea of marriage of a tribal god to a goddess of the earth, or of water, as a source of fertility.

Art and iconography. Two of the most interesting examples of the religious art of the Celts are the mysterious Cauldron of Gundestrup and the Paris "altar" now preserved at the Musée de Cluny (France). The cauldron is the most curious object of all. Its date and provenance are unknown. Though it was found at Gundestrup in Jutland, it is believed to have been brought there as plunder and to have come originally from the territory of the Scordisci on the middle Danube. It may belong to the 1st century BC, but another opinion is that it came from eastern Gaul and is as late as the 4th century AD. Another strange monument, apparently of religious significance, is the Monster of Noves, which perhaps portrays a bear god. The human form must at least sometimes have been represented in sculpture in Gaul before the Roman conquest, for there are a few headless figures from Roquepertuse that may be as early as the 3rd century BC. Most of the religious sculpture of the Celts, however, is Gallo-Roman. The highest achievement of Celtic art lies in the purely imaginative decoration of metalwork on helmets and shields, on mirrors and collars and coins, or of stone monuments such as the pillar at St. Goar.

The Gundestrup Cauldron

CONCLUSION

At the present stage of scholarship, the picture of Celtic religion is necessarily vague and confused. It is possible to suggest probable functions for some of the many gods and goddesses and to sense a rich mythology that, so far, is only dimly visible. Esus and the horned god Cernunnos remain enigmas. There was a cult of wells and rivers and a cult of trees with marked specialization of the oak. The king was sacred and was closely concerned with fertility and with the prosperity of his people. This much is known, and there remains the hope that more may be learned about the religion of the Celts from a closer study of insular Celtic sources.

BIBLIOGRAPHY. J. RHYS, *Lectures on the Origin and Growth of Religion as Illustrated by Celtic Heathendom*, 2nd ed. (1897), the classic work in English, now out-of-date; J. VENDRYES, *Les religions des Celtes, des Germains et des anciens Slavs* (1948), the best general account of the subject; J. ZWICKER (ed.), *Fontes Historiae Religionis Celticae 1* (1934), a collection of excerpts from Greek and Latin authors; W. DINAN (ed.), *Monumenta Historica Celtica 1* (1911), a collection of passages from Greek and Roman histories; P.-M. DUVAL, *Les dieux de la Gaule* (1957), very useful account of the Gaulish gods; J. MACNEILL, *Celtic Religion* (n.d.), brief outline for an overview of the subject; T.F. O'RAHILLY, *Early Irish History and Mythology* (1946), massive learning based on a great wealth of material, including some very fanciful conclusions; J. RAFTERY (ed.), *The Celts* (1964), a collection of popular lectures; M.-L. SJOESTEDT-JONVAL, *Gods and Heroes of the Celts* (1949), a general survey of Celtic religion, with emphasis on mythology; P. MACCANA, *Celtic Mythology* (1970), the most recent and best book on Celtic mythology, with the best collection of photos.

(M.D.)

Celts, Ancient

The Celts were the first prehistoric people to rise from anonymity in the European territories north of the Alps. Until the middle of the first millennium BC nothing was known of them by the civilized Mediterranean world. For the Greeks they were *Keltoi;* the Romans called them Gauls. At the time when these Celts had become the predominant people in the barbarian world they were settled throughout a great part of Europe, extending from Ireland and Britain to the Balkans, and even as far as Anatolia. They were a numerous people of considerable political and military significance. Their creative activity completed the prehistoric development of Europe; by the 4th century BC Greek writers ranked the Celts, together with the Scythians and the Persians, among the most numerous "barbarian" peoples of the then known world. Although they never formed a unified ethnic group or a great empire and were split into many tribes with differ-

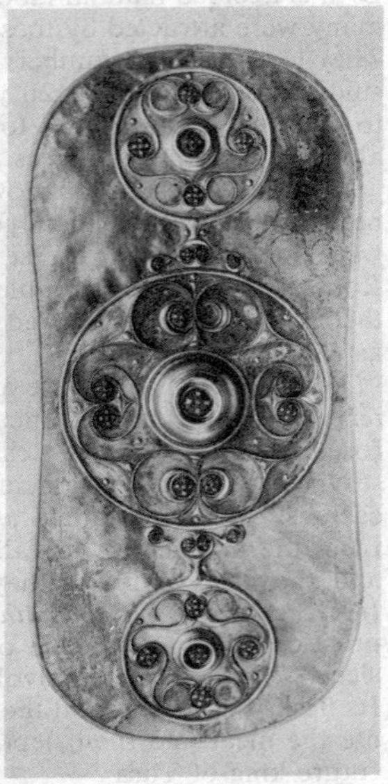

Artifacts of celtic cultures.
(Top left) Pottery vessel, Hallstatt culture 7th–6th century BC. In the Württembergisches Landesmuseum, Stuttgart, West Germany. Height 14 cm. (Top right) Bronze warrior, Hallstatt culture, 6th–5th century BC. In the Naturhistorisches Museum, Vienna. Height 7.9 cm. (Bottom left) Bronze flagon decorated with coral, La Tène culture, late 5th century BC. In the British Museum. Height 38.8 cm. (Bottom centre) Back view of a mirror, La Tène culture, early 1st century BC. In the British Museum. Height 35 cm. (Bottom right) Bronze enamelled shield, La Tène culture, early 1st century BC. In the British Museum. Height 77.5 cm.

By courtesy of (top left) the Wurttembergisches Landesmuseum, Stuttgart, (top right) the Naturhistorisches Museum, Vienna, (bottom left, bottom centre, bottom right) the trustees of the British Museum

ent dialects, they became an important factor in the development of a specifically European civilization.

HISTORY

From the 5th century BC on, the Celts became well known throughout the contemporary world, and their culture at the time of the zenith of their power (5th–1st centuries BC) has been exhaustively studied by archaeologists. Called the La Tène culture after a Swiss archaeological site on Lake Neuchâtel, it represented the second Early Iron Age and followed chronologically upon the Hallstatt Age (see below). But the history of the Celts before the 5th century remains very uncertain.

Early Celtic settlements. Archaeological investigation strongly suggests that the area in which the historical Celtic tribes developed comprised part of present-day France, southern Germany, and adjacent territory reaching as far as southern and central Bohemia. It is possible to trace their origins as far back as the Bronze Age Tumulus culture, which reached its high point about 1200 BC. Various cultural components were unified in the succeeding Urnfield culture (12th–8th centuries BC; "tumulus" and "urnfield" refer to the burial customs of these cultures). This was followed by the Hallstatt Period (7th–6th centuries; named after the burial ground near Hallstatt in the Salzkammergut in upper Austria). During that time other peoples known to history made their appearance in Europe: the Illyrians in the southeast and the Germans in the north.

From the Urnfield period on, archaeological evidence of the Celtic confederation northwest of the Alps is increasingly noteworthy, producing, in the later Urnfield stage, a fresh phase of Tumulus burials, some of these being located in areas where Celtic power later became predominant.

Burial grounds of the Hallstatt period comprise chamber graves containing four-wheeled wagons, splendidly decorative yokes and harness fittings, and a large amount of pottery and other artifacts, which indicate a complex burial ceremony. Such elaborate burials, found in Bohemia, throughout southern Germany, and in northeastern France, would appear to be those of chieftains or members of a leading oligarchy. To this period there may also be ascribed the first known fortified castles of western central Europe. The fortified hill residence at Heuneburg on the Danube, dating from the late Hallstatt period, was rebuilt at least five times. One phase shows a mature building technique including the use of brick

Burial finds

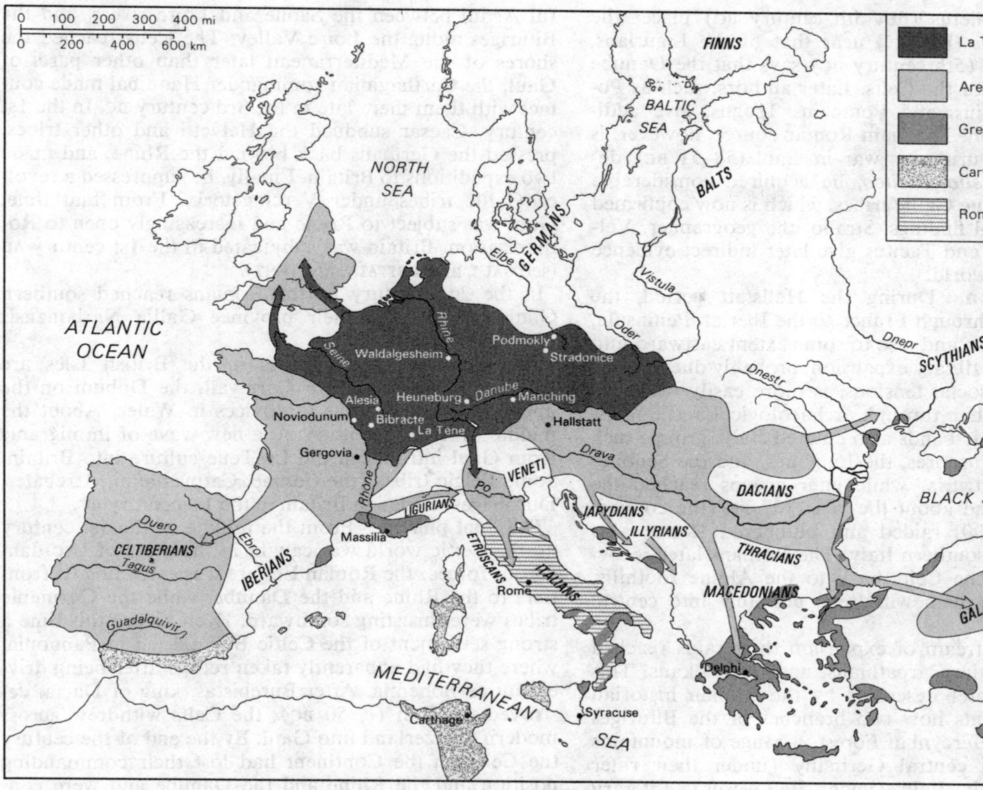

The Celtic migrations.
From Grossen Historischen Weltatlas, vol. I, *Vorgeschichte und Altertum* (1963); Bayerischer Schulbuch-Verlag, Munich

masonry in towerlike bastions, a Mediterranean characteristic quite alien to the region. Adjacent to Heuneburg is a group of chieftains' barrows, one of which, Hohmichele, has wood-lined chambers and wall draperies and contains a four-wheeled wagon, gold decorations, and jewelry. It is clear that imports from the south, such as amphorae of wine or Greek Black Figure pottery, were common. A fortified hill site on Mt. Lassois near Châtillon-sur-Seine, France, in which Greek pottery was found, was built at the junction of long-distance trade routes. A bronze vessel, also of Greek manufacture, was found in the neighbouring grave of a Celtic princess.

The wealth of the Celtic princes seems to have been very great, some of the barrows (mound graves) being particularly richly furnished for their size. That at Apremont (Haute-Saône), with an average diameter of 70 metres, contained a wagon, gold objects, a crown, brooches, and a vessel. The grave at Pflugfelden near Ludwigsburg (Württemberg) was the burial of a man in a splendid robe and a golden crown; the hilt of his dagger was inlaid with amber. By the 6th century the wealth of the ruling Celtic groups was well established and they were able to import Etruscan wares, the merchants of Massilia (Marseille) acting as distributing agents.

The unusual concentration of early Hallstatt chieftains' burials on the upper Danube and on the upper Rhine as far north as the Neckar River lasts only to the beginning of the 5th century. At that time the Celts were preparing armed raids into the remaining parts of Europe. Thereafter, rich burials are found farther northwest, on the middle Rhine or on the Saar and Moselle rivers. The number and the richness of the burials steadily increased, including two graves at Schwarzenbach that contain two beaked flagons, a vessel in a gold openwork casing, and various gold ornaments showing mask motifs. Other sumptuous burials were at Bad Dürkheim in the Rhineland-Palatinate (including a complete set of table dishes), at Reinheim near Saarbrücken (including a bronze mirror), and a celebrated double grave at Waldalgesheim (Hunsrück), where the jewelry shows the maturation of a new art style (La Tène).

The La Tène culture. Artifacts from this culture, which developed in the 5th century BC, are found in the barrows of the middle Rhine and of Champagne in France. From the second half of the century at the latest native Celtic craftsmen were adapting southern models and developing their own style with increasing confidence. The geometric patterns found in ornament of the Hallstatt period give place to zoomorphic and floral designs, supplemented by human-head motifs or masks.

A remarkable genre of the style are the bronze-mask brooches, adorned with human and animal masks varying from lifelike to fantastic portrayal. Such brooches have been found at Panenský Týnec near Louny (animal mask) and near Manětín-Hrádek in the Plzeň region (imaginative human likeness) in Czechoslovakia and at Parsberg and Oberwittighausen in Germany.

These early La Tène pieces, typical of the second half of the 5th century BC, are still much influenced by southern models. The mature La Tène style, also called the Waldalgesheim style, dates from the second half of the 4th century, and its products are found in chieftains' graves throughout Europe. In the 3rd century the use of jewelry extended to all social classes, and craftsmen became more numerous, no longer working exclusively in the entourage of the rulers. While elaborately linked bracelets and brooches became common ornaments, the skill of leading craftsmen was adapted to ornamenting swords, scabbards, and helmets for the aristocracy.

The development of Celtic art in Britain was quite individual in character. Local workshops and "schools" were established, in which the native craftsmen combined technical skill with a freshness of conception. When the Celtic art of the Continent had passed its zenith, that of Britain continued to flourish, producing a variety of beautiful artifacts, such as gold and silver jewelry, swords and scabbards, shields inlaid with enamel, and bronze mirrors.

Literary Sources. The archaeological evidence for the close relationship of the Celts with the south is borne out by contemporary literature, which shows that the Celts were known to the Greeks as early as the 5th century.

Hecataeus of Miletus (6th–5th century BC) places the land of the Celts (Keltikē) near that of the Ligurians, while Herodotus (5th century BC) says that the Danube rises in the land of the Celts. Later authors, such as Polybius, Poseidonius, and Pompeius Trogus, give additional information. The main Roman source, however, is Julius Caesar. During his war in Gaul (58–51 BC), described in *De bello Gallico*, he acquired considerable knowledge of some Gallic tribes, which is now confirmed by archaeological findings. Strabo, the geographer, Velleius Paterculus, and Tacitus give later indirect evidence about the Celtic world.

Caesar and the Celts

Celtic expansion. During the Hallstatt period, the Celts expanded through France to the Iberian Peninsula, to the British Isles, and also to some extent eastward into central Europe. Military expansion, probably due to overpopulation and social tensions, is more easily traced in literary sources than through archaeological and linguistic evidence. Celtic bands also entered Italy, groups such as the Boii, the Insubres, the Lingones, and the Senones first attacking Etruria, while later groups reached the Adriatic coast and about the year 387 BC (the conventional date is 390) raided and plundered Rome, also penetrating into southern Italy. The Romans later recovered and drove the Celts back to the Alpine foothills, whence some of them withdrew, probably into central Europe.

In the second stream of expansion their raids reached central Europe, the Carpathians, and the Balkans. This expansion was later described by the Roman historian Livy, who recounts how two branches of the Bituriges settled near the Hercynian Forest, a range of mountains of southern and central Germany (under their ruler Sigovesus) and in Italy (under Bellovesus). Literary sources suggest that the Celts reached the Carpathians in the 4th century, later moving into present-day Bulgaria, Romania, Thrace, and Macedonia; they raided the shrine at Delphi, Greece, in 279. One group reached Anatolia, where they settled and gave their name to Galatia. In the 3rd century Celts were serving as mercenaries in Greece, Anatolia, and Egypt.

Military cemeteries

The archaeological remains of the Celtic military occupation of central Europe are their so-called flat (*i.e.*, imperceptible) cemeteries, containing mainly inhumation burials, although cremation burials became more common later. They have been dated between the 4th and the early 1st centuries BC. A striking concentration of these burial grounds extends from the Krušné Mountains, through Bohemia, Moravia, and Austria, to the Carpathian region, including also part of Slovakia and Transylvania. To the north it covered part of Polish Silesia, in the vicinity of Wrocław. These burials show many features common to the La Tène culture and also to the more Western Celtic art forms. Some of the cemeteries are military, containing burials of men with their weapons, the condition of some of the skeletons showing that death occurred in battle. The counterparts of these military graves were elaborate graves of women furnished with jewelry and bronze and glass ornaments. There are also simple graves containing no artifacts at all.

Invasions by the Cimbri and Teutones. An important dividing line in the history of the Celts was the incursion of the Germanic Cimbri. Their assault was repulsed by the Boii about 113 BC, somewhere in the neighbourhood of Bohemia. They then attacked the Scordisci near Belgrade, and later, in association with the Teutones, they attacked several Celtic tribes in the west, penetrating as far as Aquitania in Gaul. Although the Cimbri were defeated by the Romans in the Po Valley at the end of the 2nd century, their incursion into Celtic territory foreshadowed later invasions.

Gaul and Britain. In the 1st century BC Gaius Julius Caesar described Gaul as having three regions, inhabited respectively by the Galli (Gauls, present central France), the Aquitani (southwestern France), and the Belgae in the north. The Gauls comprised many tribes: the Helvetii in present-day Switzerland, the Sequani and Lingones farther west, the Arverni in Auvergne, the powerful Aedui between the Saône and Loire rivers, and the Bituriges along the Loire Valley. The Celts reached the shores of the Mediterranean later than other parts of Gaul; the Carthaginian commander Hannibal made contact with them there late in the 3rd century BC. In the 1st century, Caesar subdued the Helvetii and other tribes, pressed the Germans back beyond the Rhine, and made two expeditions to Britain. Finally, he suppressed a revolt of Gallic tribes under Vercingetorix. From that time, Gaul was subject to Rome and increasingly open to Romanization. Britain was subjugated in the 1st century AD (see GAUL and BRITAIN, ANCIENT).

In the 2nd century BC the Romans reached southern Gaul and founded their province Gallia Narbonensis (Provence).

The names of many tribes in the British Isles are known: the Dumnonii in Cornwall, the Dobuni on the upper Thames, and the Ordovices in Wales. About the middle of the 3rd century BC a new wave of immigrants from Gaul introduced the La Tène culture into Britain. Some Belgic tribes (the Cantae, Catuvellauni, Atrebates, Durotriges) settled in Britain in the 1st century BC.

The final phases. From the middle of the 1st century BC the Celtic world was caught in the press of two dangerous forces: the Roman Empire was extending its frontiers to the Rhine and the Danube, while the Germanic tribes were thrusting southward. Even before this time a strong settlement of the Celtic Boii existed in Pannonia, where they had apparently taken refuge after being driven out of Bohemia. After Burebistas, king of Dacia, destroyed the Boii (*c.* 50 BC), the Celts withdrew across modern Switzerland into Gaul. By the end of the century the Celts on the Continent had lost their commanding position and the Rhine and the Danube and were confined to the frontier between the Roman and Germanic worlds.

The Celtic tradition survived most strongly in Britain and Ireland, where its art was still flourishing at the beginning of the Christian Era. Several of its elements were revived in the neo-Celtic art forms of the 7th to 9th centuries AD (see BRITAIN AND IRELAND, HISTORY OF).

CELTIC SOCIETY

In the eyes of Greeks and Romans, the Celts were remarkable for their height, muscularity, and fair colouring. These were characteristics of the warrior class rather than of the whole population, and skeletal remains point to considerable variations in stature and head form. Strabo describes them as a people who love war and adventure, pleasure and feasts. Information on Celtic institutions is available from various classical authors and from ancient Irish literature. A striking feature, even as early as the La Tène period, is the large number of tribes competing for dominance. Kingship was common among some tribes in the La Tène period. Some kings, however, were elected, and the power of the aristocracy tended to increase, their rule predominating in Gaul in Caesar's time. In Ireland, by customary law, the social system was threefold; king, warrior aristocracy, and freemen farmers. In the later period in the western Celtic world, the strength of the aristocracy was increased and the freedom of common people was diminished by the widespread introduction of clientism, a system by which lesser men placed themselves under obligation to a powerful lord from whom they received protection. As in other Indo-European systems, the family was patriarchal and kinship was recognized by agnatic descent (from a common male ancestor). Landownership was vested in the family, which was also responsible for many social obligations. The household was of the "archaic-joint" type, consisting of a man with his wives, children, and grandchildren. The status of women seems to have varied considerably according to rank and the prosperity of the community.

Druids

The Druids, who were occupied with magico-religious duties, were recruited from families of the warrior class but ranked higher. They offered sacrifices and were responsible for the education of the young nobles, and the sacred oak groves were under their protection. Druidism, still flourishing at the beginning of the Roman occupation of Celtic areas, strongly resisted Romanization and was thus particularly marked out for deliberate suppression. It survived longest in Ireland, where the Romans did not penetrate. Caesar describes the Celtic sacred sites, woods with sacred trees and groves (*loci consecrati*). There is no evidence that they had temples in his time, but these were built later, in the Gallo-Roman period. Cult sites have been found, however, in several places in central and western Europe. An example is at Libenice near Kolín in Bohemia, excavated in 1959, which had a stone slab for sacrifices. In the centre of the cult area a woman was found buried, with typical La Tène ornaments. Cauldrons connected with the cults spread as far as northern Europe, and splendid examples have been found in silver at Gundestrup and at Brå in East Jutland. It is difficult to generalize about Celtic religion and mythology, because each tribe seems to have had its own cults and local deities. There is no firm distinction between gods and heroes; the names of some deities (*e.g.*, Taranis, Teutates, Esus, Lug) antedate the Romanization of Gaul, but later they sometimes became associated with Roman gods. Divine or semidivine pairs and trinities also occurred.

The basic economy of the Celts was mixed farming, and, except in times of unrest, single farmsteads were usual. All kinds of grain were cultivated, also flax, hemp, beetroot, and several other kinds of vegetables. The grain was stored in special pits or silos deep in the ground or in large jars. Owing to the wide variations in terrain and climate, cattle raising was more important than cereal cultivation in some regions. The prevalence of oak forests encouraged the breeding of pigs, and boar hunts were a popular sport. The wool of Celtic sheep was well known in Rome. Later, Gaul supplied the Roman armies on the Rhine with horses.

Trousers, perhaps an Eastern innovation, were worn by men of the Cisalpine Gaulish tribes from at least the 3rd century BC and are attested in the 1st century BC in Transalpine Gaul, but a belted tunic, or shirt, with a cloak seems to have been the most widespread form of male dress. Women wore a single long garment with a cloak. Coarse linen as well as wool was employed, and bright colours were popular. According to Poseidonius the food of the Celts consisted of bread and meat, either boiled or roasted. Beer, home brewed from barley, was the most common drink; the upper classes also used wine imported from the south. The Celts were hospitable, fond of feasting, drinking, and quarrelling, and incapable of prolonged concerted action. At feasts bards sang the praises of those present, accompanying the song with a lyrelike instrument. The Celts greatly prized music and many forms of oral literary composition.

Hill forts. The earliest Celts had fortified strongholds or chieftains' residences; hill forts (*oppida*), with a considerable concentration of population and production, were constructed from the second half of the 2nd century BC, partly as a result of Germanic pressures. A belt of flourishing hill forts existed in Caesar's time, but his victory led to their decline in Gaul, although many in central Europe were occupied until the end of the last century BC.

The hill forts varied in construction and size. Bibracte, the centre of the Aedui, about 2,625 feet (800 metres) above sea level and covering an area of about 333 acres, is the most thoroughly excavated hill fort in France. Alesia covered an area of 240 acres, Gergovia (Clermont) 185 acres, Noviodunum about 99 acres. The *oppidum* of the Vindelici tribe at Manching near Ingolstadt, Bavaria, is in the process of excavation. It covers an area of 939 acres and is the easternmost known hill fort with walls built in the Gallic style described by Caesar. The hill fort at Kelheim, Bavaria, is still larger, while Heidengraben, north of Urach in Württemberg, comprises a whole series of fortified sites on an area of more than six square miles. Six *oppida* are known in Bohemia, the most notable, in Stradonice near Beroun, having the richest finds and covering an area of about 203 acres.

Coinage. Celtic prosperity and widespread trade necessitated the minting of coins, the first that were produced by barbarians in Gaul and central Europe. The Celtic coinage is of gold and silver, coins of other metals being much rarer. Ultimately derived from Macedonian-Greek exemplars, they first appear in the second half of the 2nd century BC. Later the Celts minted a coinage of their own design (horse and rider, human figure, etc.). In central Europe at the turn of the 2nd and 1st centuries gold coins appeared bearing the picture of a boar or coiled dragon, and in the first half of the 1st century two kinds of sunk-panel gold coins appeared: the so-called rainbow drops (*guttae iridis*), attributed to the Vindelici tribe, and shell staters marked with crescent signs. Coarse forms with indistinct pictures were a part of the celebrated hoards, each of about 5,000 coins, found in Podmokly near Zbiroh in the Rokycany region of southwest Bohemia. Later on, silver coins came increasingly into circulation. One of them, the latest Celtic coin found in central Europe, dating from the second half of the 1st century BC and strongly influenced by the Roman denarius, is commonly called a Biatec, after one of the issuing chieftains. Most of the hoards of this coin were discovered in the Bratislava region of Slovakia.

BIBLIOGRAPHY. JAN FILIP, *Celtic Civilization and Its Heritage*, trans. by R.F. SAMSOUR (1962), a summary of research and study done in various parts of Europe, and *Kelten in Mitteleuropa* (1956), on the historical significance of the archaeological findings in central Europe; C.F. FOX, *Pattern and Purpose* (1958), an important work surveying early Celtic art in Britain; F.R. HODSON, *The La Tène Cemetery at Münsingen-Rain* (1968), on major Celtic cemeteries in Switzerland, particularly that of Münsingen-Rain, establishing an improved basis for comparing the chronology of continental cultures with those of the British Isles; PAUL JACOBSTHAL, *Early Celtic Art*, 2 vol. (1944), a basic work on the origin and development of Celtic art; S. PIGGOTT, *The Druids* (1968), a general study of the place of Druids in Celtic society, and "The Celtic World and Its Aftermath," *Ancient Europe*, ch. 6 (1968), an illustrated text that gives an outline of the development of Celtic culture in Europe; T.G.E. POWELL, *The Celts* (1958), a basic work emphasizing Celtic culture in Britain and Ireland; M.L. SJOESTEDT–JONVAL, *Gods and Heroes of the Celts*, trans. by M. DILLON (1949); A. ROSS, *Pagan Celtic Britain* (1967), studies in later Celtic iconography in Britain; A. GRENIER, *Les Gaulois* (1945), comprehensive study of the Celts in Gaul; G. RIEK, *Der Hohmichele* (1962), a study of the late Hallstatt grave excavated in the surroundings at Heuneburg, Germany; H. HUBERT, *Les Celtes depuis l'époque de La Tène et la civilisation celtique*, rev. ed. (1950); R. JOFFROY, *Le Trésor de Vix* (1962), a report on the famous grave at Vix containing rich furnishings, imported objects, and gold jewelry; A. RYBOVÁ and B. SOUDSKY, *Libenice: Sanctuaire celtique en Bohême centrale* (1962), a study of a recently found cult site containing a stone stele and the grave of a woman with La Tène burial furnishings.

(J.F.)

Cement

The word cement is used to define adhesive substances. It is derived from the Latin *caementum*, which meant stone chippings such as were used in Roman mortar, not the binding material itself. In its general sense it covers a wide variety of binding materials used for many different purposes, but more commonly it implies the binding materials used in building and civil engineering construction. These constructional cements, which will set and harden under water, are often called hydraulic cements. The most important of these is portland cement. Others are the slag-containing cements and high alumina cement. This article covers constructional cements. Adhesive cements are covered under ADHESIVES.

Cements are finely ground powders that, when mixed with water, set to a hard mass. Setting and hardening result from the hydration of the cement compounds, giving submicroscopic crystals or a gel-like material with a high surface area. Cements may be used alone (*i.e.*, "neat," as grouting materials), but the normal use is in mortar and concrete in which the cement is mixed with inert material known as aggregate. Mortar is cement mixed with sand or crushed stone less than 3⁄16 inch (4.8 millimetres) in size. Concrete is a mixture of cement, sand or other fine aggregate, and a coarse aggregate that for most purposes is up to ¾ or 1 inch (1.9–2.5 centimetres) in size but that may also be as large as 6 inches (15 centimetres) for concrete placed in large masses, as in dams. Mortars are used for binding bricks, blocks, and stone in walls or as surface renderings. Concrete is used for a large variety of constructional purposes (see CONCRETE). Mixtures of soil and portland cement are used as a base for roads. Portland cement also is used in the manufacture of asbestos cement sheets, pipes, tanks, and other goods. The products are made in a factory and supplied ready for installation in a building.

Because concrete is the most widely used of all construction materials today, the manufacture of cement is widespread. The consumption of cement per capita ranges from several hundred kilograms in industrialized countries to 20 kilograms or less in developing countries (see Table 1).

Table 1: Cement Production and Consumption

	production (1970) (000 metric tons)	consumption (1966) (kg per capita)
Continents		
North America	88,000	334
South America	23,000	102
Western Europe	177,000	416
Eastern Europe	135,000	296
Africa	18,000	47
Asia	123,000	46
Countries		
U.S.	69,000	329
Canada	7,000	398
Argentina	5,000	149
Brazil	9,000	72
Mexico	7,000	113
France	29,000	456
West Germany	38,000	557
Italy	33,000	425
U.K.	17,000	306
U.S.S.R.	95,000	336
Japan	57,000	361
India	14,000	22
Australia	5,000	319
World total	571,000	137

HISTORY OF CEMENT

The origin of hydraulic cements goes back to classical Greece and Rome. The materials used were lime and a volcanic ash that slowly reacted with it in the presence of water to form a hard mass. This formed the cementing material of the Roman mortars and concretes of 2,000 years ago and of subsequent construction work in western Europe. Portland cement is a successor to hydraulic lime first developed by John Smeaton in 1756 when he was called in to erect the Eddystone Lighthouse off the coast of Devon, England. The next development, about 1800 in England and France, was a material obtained by burning nodules of clayey limestone and later in the U.S. of what was called "cement rock." These materials belong to a class known as natural cement, allied to portland cement but more lightly burned and not of controlled composition. The invention of portland cement usually is attributed to Joseph Aspdin of Leeds, Yorkshire, who in 1824 took out a patent for a material produced from a synthetic mixture of limestone and clay. He called the product portland cement because of a fancied resemblance of the material, when set, to portland stone, a limestone used for building in England. Aspdin's product may well have been too lightly burned to be a true portland cement, and the real prototype was perhaps that produced by Isaac Charles Johnson in southeast England about 1850. The manufacture of portland cement rapidly spread to other European countries and, about 1870, to the U.S.

Portland cement

RAW MATERIALS

Portland cement consists of compounds of lime mixed with silica, alumina, and iron oxide. The lime is obtained from a calcareous raw material and the other oxides from an argillaceous (clayey) material, the two mixed in the required proportions. Additional raw materials such as sand, iron oxide, and bauxite may be used in smaller quantities to get the desired composition. The commonest calcareous raw materials are limestone and chalk; but others, such as coral or shell deposits, are also used. Clays, shales, slates, and estuarine muds are the common argillaceous raw materials. Marl, a compact calcareous clay, and cement rock contain both the calcareous and argillaceous components in proportions that sometimes approximate cement compositions. Another raw material is blast-furnace slag, which consists mainly of lime, silica, and alumina and is mixed with a calcareous material of high lime content. Kaolin, which contains little iron oxide, is used as the argillaceous component for white portland cement. Industrial wastes, such as fly ash and calcium carbonate from chemical manufacture, are other possible raw materials; but their use is small compared with that of the natural materials. The magnesia content of raw materials must be low because the permissible limit in portland cement is 4 to 5 percent. Other impurities in raw materials that must be strictly limited are fluorine compounds, phosphates, metal oxides and sulfides, and excessive alkalies.

Blast-furnace slag

Another essential raw material is gypsum, some 5 percent of which is added to the burned cement clinker during grinding to control the setting time of the cement. Portland cement also can be made in a combined process with sulfuric acid using calcium sulfate or anhydrite in place of calcium carbonate. The sulfur dioxide produced in the flue gases on burning is converted to sulfuric acid by normal processes.

The percentage compositions of some typical raw materials used for the manufacture of portland cement are shown in Table 2. Raw materials are extracted by quarrying in the case of hard rocks such as limestones, slates, and some shales, with the aid of blasting when necessary. Some deposits are mined. Softer rocks such as chalk and clay can be dug directly by excavators. The excavated materials are transported to the crushing plant by trucks, railway freight cars, conveyor belts, or ropeways, or in a wet state or slurry by pipeline. In regions where limestones of sufficiently high lime content are not available, some process of beneficiation can be used. Froth flotation will remove excess silica or alumina and so upgrade the limestone, but it is costly and used only when unavoidable.

Table 2: Raw Materials Used in the Manufacture of Portland Cement
(percentage composition)

raw material	lime	silica	alumina	iron oxide	magnesia	loss on ignition
Limestone	52	3	1	0.5	0.5	42
Chalk	54	1	0.5	0.2	0.3	43
Cement rock	43	11	3	1	2	36
Clay	1	57	16	7	1	14
Slag	42	34	15	1	4	0

Froth flotation

MANUFACTURE

There are four stages in the manufacture of portland cement: (1) crushing and grinding the raw materials; (2) blending the materials in the correct proportions; (3) burning the prepared mix in a kiln; and (4) grinding the burned product known as cement clinker together with some 5 percent of gypsum (to control the time of set of the cement). The three processes of manufacture are known as the wet, dry, and semidry processes and are so termed when the raw materials are ground wet and fed to the kiln as a slurry, ground dry and fed as a dry powder, or ground dry and then moistened to form nodules that are fed to the kiln.

Crushing and grinding of raw materials. All except soft materials are first crushed, often in two stages, and then ground, usually in rotating, cylindrical ball, or tube

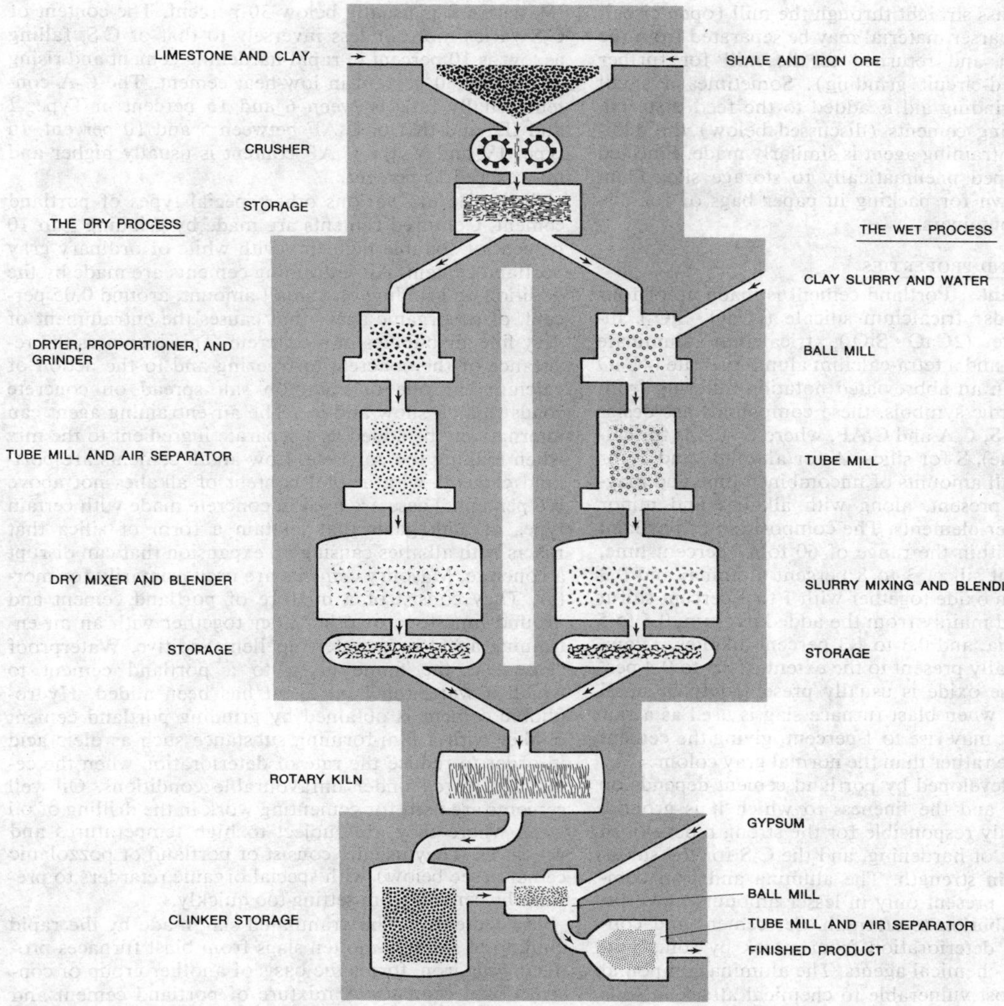

Cement-making process, dry and wet methods.
Drawing by D. Meighan

mills containing a charge of steel grinding balls. This grinding is done wet or dry according to the process in use, but for dry grinding the raw materials may need first to be dried in cylindrical, rotary dryers. Soft materials are broken down by vigorous stirring with water in wash-mills, producing a fine slurry, which is passed through screens to remove oversize particles.

Blending. A first approximation of the required chemical composition is obtained by selective quarrying and control of the raw material fed to the crushing and grinding plant. The finer control is obtained by drawing ground material from two or more silos containing raw mixes differing slightly in composition in the dry process and from slurry tanks in the wet process. Thorough mixing of the raw materials in the silos in the dry process is ensured by agitation and vigorous circulation induced by compressed air. In the wet process, the slurry tanks are stirred by mechanical means and/or compressed air. The slurry, which contains 35 to 45 percent water, is sometimes filtered, reducing the water content to 20 to 30 percent; and the filter cake is then fed to the kiln. This reduces the fuel consumption for burning.

Burning. The earliest kilns in which cement was burned in batches were bottle kilns, followed by chamber kilns and then continuous shaft kilns. The shaft kiln in a modernized form is still used in some countries, but the dominant means of burning is the rotary kiln. These kilns —up to 200 metres (660 feet) long and 7 metres (23 feet) in diameter in wet process plants but shorter for the dry process—consist of a steel, cylindrical shell lined with refractory materials. They rotate slowly on an axis that is inclined a few degrees to the horizontal. The raw material feed, introduced at the upper end, moves slowly down the kiln to the lower or firing end. The fuel for firing may be pulverized coal, oil, or natural gas injected through a pipe. The temperature at the burning end ranges from 1,300° to 1,500° C (about 2,400° to 2,700° F), according to the raw materials being burned. Some form of heat exchanger is commonly incorporated at the back end of the kiln to increase heat transfer to the incoming raw materials and so reduce the heat lost in the waste gases. The burned product emerges from the kiln as small nodules of clinker that pass into coolers where incoming air is heated and the product cooled. In the semidry process, the raw materials in the form of nodules, containing 10 to 15 percent water, are fed onto a travelling chain grate before passing to a shorter rotary kiln. Hot gases coming from the kiln are sucked through the raw nodules on the grate, preheating the nodules.

Rotary kilns

Dust emission from cement kilns can be a serious nuisance; and in populated areas it is usual and often compulsory to fit cyclone arrestors, bag-filter systems, or electrostatic dust precipitators between the kiln exit and the chimney stack.

Modern cement plants are equipped with elaborate instrumentation for the control of the burning process. Raw materials in some plants are sampled automatically, and a computer calculates and controls the raw mix composition. The largest rotary kilns have outputs up to 3,000 tons per day. The clinker may be immediately ground to cement or stored in stockpiles for later use.

Grinding. The clinker and the required amount of gypsum are ground to a fine powder in horizontal mills similar to those used for grinding the raw materials. The material may pass straight through the mill (open-circuit grinding), or coarser material may be separated from the ground product and returned to the mill for further grinding (closed-circuit grinding). Sometimes a small amount of a grinding aid is added to the feed material. For air-entraining cements (discussed below) the addition of an air-entraining agent is similarly made. Finished cement is pumped pneumatically to storage silos from which it is drawn for packing in paper bags or for dispatch in bulk containers.

Closed-circuit grinding

COMPOSITION AND PROPERTIES

Portland cement. Portland cement is made up of four main compounds: tricalcium silicate ($3CaO \cdot SiO_2$), dicalcium silicate ($2CaO \cdot SiO_2$), tricalcium aluminate ($3CaO \cdot Al_2O_3$), and a tetra-calcium aluminoferrite ($4CaO \cdot Al_2O_3Fe_2O_3$). In an abbreviated notation differing from the normal atomic symbols, these compounds are designated as C_3S, C_2S, C_3A and C_4AF, where C stands for calcium oxide (lime), S for silica, A for alumina, and F for iron oxide. Small amounts of uncombined lime and magnesia also are present, along with alkalies and minor amounts of other elements. The composition of portland cements falls within the range of 60 to 67 percent lime, 19 to 25 percent silica, 3 to 8 percent alumina, and 0.3 to 6 percent iron oxide together with 1 to 3 percent sulfur trioxide, derived mainly from the added gypsum, 0.5 to 5 percent magnesia, and 0.3 to 1.3 percent alkalies. Titanium oxide is usually present to the extent of 0.1 to 0.4 percent. Manganese oxide is usually present only in small amounts except when blast-furnace slag is used as a raw material; then it may rise to 1 percent, giving the cement a brownish tinge rather than the normal gray colour.

The strength developed by portland cement depends on its composition and the fineness to which it is ground. The C_3S is mainly responsible for the strength developed in the first week of hardening, and the C_2S for the subsequent increase in strength. The alumina and iron compounds that are present only in lesser amounts make little direct contribution to strength. Set cement and concrete can suffer deterioration from attack by some natural or artificial chemical agents. The alumina compound (C_3A) is the most vulnerable to chemical attack in soils containing sulfate salts or in seawater, while the iron compound (C_4AF) and the two calcium silicates are more resistant. Calcium hydroxide is released during the hydration of the calcium silicates, and this is also vulnerable to attack. Cement liberates heat when it hydrates; and consequently concrete placed in large masses, as in dams, can cause the temperature inside the mass to rise up to 40° C (72° F) above the outside temperature. Subsequent cooling can be a cause of cracking. The highest heat of hydration is shown by C_3A, followed in descending order by C_3S, C_4AF, and C_2S.

Resistance to chemical attack

Five types of portland cement are standardized in the U.S.: ordinary (Type I), modified (Type II), high-early-strength (Type III), low-heat (Type IV), and sulfate-resisting (Type V). In other countries Type II is omitted, and Type III is called rapid-hardening. Type V is known in some European countries as Ferrari cement. Typical compositions are shown in Table 3. These various types are differentiated both by requirements as to their composition and by various tests. Thus in Type V, the content of C_3A is limited to 3.5 to 5 percent in different countries, and in Type IV to a slightly higher value. The content of C_3S ranges from about 40 to 65 percent except for Type IV, where it is usually below 30 percent. The content of C_2S varies more or less inversely to that of C_3S, falling as low as 10 percent in rapid-hardening cement and rising as high as 60 percent in low-heat cement. The C_3A content usually falls between 6 and 15 percent in Types I and III, and that of C_4AF between 5 and 10 percent. In types IV and V, the C_4AF content is usually higher and may exceed 15 percent.

Table 3: Typical Percentage Compositions of Portland Cement

type of portland cement	lime	silica	alumina	iron oxide	magnesia	alkalies	sulfur trioxide
Ordinary	64	21	6	3	2	1	2
Modified	63	22	4	3	2	1	2
High-early-strength	65	20	6	3	2	1	2.5
Low heat	61	25	4	3	2	1	2
Sulfate-resisting	64	23	3	4	2	1	2

There also are various other special types of portland cement. Coloured cements are made by grinding 5 to 10 percent of suitable pigments with white or ordinary gray portland cement. Air-entraining cements are made by the addition on grinding of a small amount, around 0.05 percent, of an organic agent that causes the entrainment of very fine air bubbles in a concrete. This increases the resistance of the concrete to freezing and to the action of calcium chloride or common salt spread on concrete roads to melt snow and ice. The air-entraining agent can alternatively be added as a separate ingredient to the mix when making the concrete. Low-alkali cements are portland cements with a total content of alkalies not above 0.6 percent. These are used in concrete made with certain types of aggregates that contain a form of silica that reacts with alkalies causing an expansion that can disrupt a concrete. Masonry cements are used primarily for mortar. They consist of a mixture of portland cement and ground limestone or other filler together with an air-entraining agent or a water-repellent additive. Waterproof cement is the name given to a portland cement to which a water-repellent agent has been added. Hydrophobic cement is obtained by grinding portland cement clinker with a film-forming substance such as oleic acid in order to reduce the rate of deterioration when the cement is stored under unfavourable conditions. Oil-well cements are used for cementing work in the drilling of oil wells where they are subject to high temperatures and pressures. They usually consist of portland or pozzolanic cement (see below) with special organic retarders to prevent the cement from setting too quickly.

Slag cements. The granulated slag made by the rapid chilling of suitable molten slags from blast furnaces producing pig iron, forms the basis of another group of constructional cements. A mixture of portland cement and granulated slag, containing up to 65 percent slag, is known in the English-speaking countries as portland blast-furnace (slag) cement. The German *Eisenportlandzement* and *Hochofenzement* contain up to 40 and 85 percent slag, respectively. Mixtures in other proportions are found in French-speaking countries under such names as *Ciment Portland de Fer*, *Ciment métallurgique mixte*, *Ciment de haut fourneau*, and *Ciment de liatier au clinker*. Properties of these slag cements are broadly similar to those of portland cement, but they have a lower lime content and a higher silica and alumina content. Those with the higher slag content have an increased resistance to chemical attack.

Slag mixtures

Another type of slag-containing cement is a supersulfated cement consisting of granulated slag mixed with 10 to 15 percent hard burned gypsum or anhydrite (natural anhydrous calcium sulfate) and a few percent of portland cement. The strength properties of supersulfated cement are similar to those of portland cement, but it has an increased resistance to many forms of chemical attack. Pozzolanic cements are mixtures of portland cement and a pozzolanic material that may be either natural or artificial. The natural pozzolanas are mainly materials of volcanic origin but include some diatomaceous earths. Artificial materials include fly ash, burned clays, and shales. Pozzolanas are materials that, though not cementitious in themselves, contain silica (and alumina) in a reactive form able to combine with lime in the presence of water to form compounds with cementitious properties. Mixtures of lime and pozzolana were used by Roman engineers 2,000 years ago and still find some application but largely have been superseded by the modern pozzolanic cement. Hydration of the portland cement fraction releases the lime required to combine with the pozzolana.

High alumina cement. High alumina cement is a rapid-hardening cement made by fusing at 1,500° to 1,600° C a mixture of bauxite and limestone in a reverberatory or electric furnace or in a rotary kiln. It also can be made by sintering at about 1,250° C. Suitable bauxites contain 50 to 60 percent alumina, up to 25 percent iron oxide, not more than 5 percent silica, and 10 to 30 percent water of hydration. The limestone must contain only small amounts of silica and magnesia. The cement contains 35 to 40 percent lime, 40 to 50 percent alumina, up to 15 percent iron oxides, and preferably not more than about 6 percent silica. The principal cementing compound is calcium aluminate ($CaO \cdot Al_2O_3$). This cement gains a high proportion of its ultimate strength in 24 hours and has a high resistance to chemical attack. It also is used in refractory concretes for furnaces. A white form of the cement, containing minimal proportions of iron oxide and silica, has outstanding refractory properties.

Refractory properties

Expanding and nonshrinking cements. Expanding and nonshrinking cements expand slightly on hydration, thus offsetting the small contraction that occurs when freshly made concrete dries for the first time. Expanding cements were first produced in France about 1945, but their present manufacture is confined to the U.S. and the U.S.S.R. The U.S. type is a mixture of portland cement and an expansive agent made by clinkering a mix of chalk, bauxite, and gypsum.

Other cements. Gypsum plasters are used for plastering, the manufacture of plaster boards and slabs, and in one form of floor-surfacing material. These gypsum cements are mainly produced by heating natural gypsum ($CaSO_4 \cdot 2H_2O$) and dehydrating it to give calcium sulfate hemihydrate ($CaSO_4 \cdot \frac{1}{2}H_2O$) or anhydrous calcium sulfate. Gypsum and anhydrite obtained as by-products in chemical manufacture also are used as raw materials. The hemihydrate (plaster of paris) sets within a few minutes on mixing with water; for building purposes a retarding agent, normally keratin, a protein, is added. The anhydrous calcium sulfate plasters are slower setting, and often another sulfate salt is added in small amount as an accelerator. Flooring plaster, originally known by its German title of *Estrich Gips,* is of the anhydrous type.

Magnesium oxychloride (Sorel cement) is the cementing agent in magnesite flooring. This is made from a mixture of lightly burned magnesia, magnesium chloride solution, and an inert filler. Magnesium oxysulfate is similarly used as a binder in some wood-wool slabs.

Epoxy resin cements

Plastics cements find a use in construction as binding materials. Epoxy resin cements are used as a jointing material between structural units, as binders for the repair of concrete, and in protective surface coatings. Polyester and some other resins are similarly used. Synthetic polymer emulsions such as polyvinyl acetate and acrylic resins, natural rubber latex, and bituminous emulsions find use as additives to concrete mixes for flooring, jointing, and lining where special properties are required.

There are many other materials—protein glues, vegetable gums, rubber solutions and emulsions, and synthetic resins solutions and emulsions—that are used as adhesives in thin films; but these are not classed as constructional cements.

Cement testing. Various tests to which cements must conform are laid down in national cement specifications to control the fineness, soundness, setting time, strength, and chemical composition. Fineness was long controlled by sieve tests, but more sophisticated methods are now largely used. The most common method, used both for control of the grinding process and for testing the finished cement, measures the surface area per unit weight of the cement by a determination of the rate of passage of air through a bed of the cement. Other methods depend on measuring the particle size distribution by the rate of sedimentation of the cement in kerosene or by elutriation (separation) in an air stream. After it has set, a cement must not undergo any appreciable expansion, which could disrupt a mortar or concrete. This property of soundness is tested by subjecting the set cement to boiling in water or to high-pressure steam. Unsoundness can arise from the presence in the cement of too much free magnesia or hard-burned free lime. The setting and hardening of a cement is a continuous process, but two points are distinguished for test purposes. The initial setting time is the interval between the mixing of the cement with water and the time when the mix has lost plasticity, stiffening to a certain degree. It marks roughly the end of the period when the wet mix can be molded into shape. The final setting time is the point at which the set cement has acquired a sufficient firmness to resist a certain defined pressure. Most specifications require an initial minimum setting time at ordinary temperatures of about 45 minutes and a final setting time no more than 10 to 12 hours.

The tests that measure the rate at which a cement develops strength are usually made on a mortar commonly composed of one part cement to three parts sand, by weight, mixed with a defined quantity of water. Tensile tests on briquettes, shaped like a figure eight thickened at the centre, were formerly used but have been replaced or supplemented by compressive tests on cubical specimens or transverse tests on prisms. The American Society for Testing and Materials (ASTM), Philadelphia, specification requires tensile tests on a 1:3 cement-sand mortar and compressive tests on a 1:2.75 mortar. The British Standards Institution (BSI), London, gives as alternatives a compressive test on a 1:3 mortar or on a concrete specimen. An international method issued by the International Standards Organization (ISO) requires a transverse test on a 1:3 cement-sand mortar prism, followed by a compressive test on the two halves of the prism that remain after it has been broken in bending. Many European countries have adopted this method. In all these tests the size grading of the sand, and usually its source, is specified.

Tensile and compressive strength

In the testing of most cements a minimum strength at 3 and 7 days and sometimes 28 days is specified, but for rapid-hardening portland cement a test at one day also is sometimes required. For high alumina cement, tests are required at one and three days. Strength requirements laid down in different countries are not directly comparable because of the differences in test methods. In actual construction, to check the strength of a concrete, compressive tests are made on cylinders or cubes made from the concrete being placed.

BIBLIOGRAPHY. A.C. DAVIS, *A Hundred Years of Portland Cement, 1824–1924* (1924), R.W. LESLEY, *History of the Portland Cement Industry in the U.S.A.* (1924), historical accounts; F. KEIL, *Hochofenschlacke,* 2nd rev. ed. (1963), on the properties and uses of slag in cements as an aggregate and for slag-wool; F.M. LEA, *The Chemistry of Cement and Concrete,* 3rd ed. (1970), on the chemistry and physics of all types of constructional cements, aggregates, and concretes; T.D. ROBSON, *High-Alumina Cements and Concretes* (1962), an account of the manufacture, properties, and uses of high alumina cement; H.F.W. TAYLOR (ed.), *The Chemistry of Cements* (1964), a review of the science of cements and experimental techniques used for investigation.

(F.M.L.)

Cenozoic Era

The history of the earth is divided into three parts in accord with the fossil evidence of organic evolution: the Paleozoic Era (225,000,000 to 570,000,000 years ago) is the "ancient age" of animals, the Mesozoic Era (65,000,000 to 225,000,000 years ago) is the "middle age," and the Cenozoic Era (the last 65,000,000 years) is the "new age" of animals; the latter is subdivided into the Tertiary and Quaternary (the last 2,500,000 years) periods.

Characteristics of Cenozoic time

The Cenozoic Era is distinguished by mammals and angiosperm plants, and because Cenozoic sediments tend to be unconsolidated and only slightly altered, they frequently are richly fossiliferous. The modern characteristics of continents and seas, and of life as it exists today, became evident during Cenozoic time. Evidence favouring continental drift indicates that present continental positions and climatic zones were established during the Cenozoic. The rise and evolution of mammals (including man) as the dominant terrestrial animal group is, however, one of the most fascinating aspects of Cenozoic history.

The Mesozoic/Cenozoic time boundary (about 65,000,000 years ago) is characterized by the reduction or extermination of many groups of organisms that were prominent in Upper Cretaceous faunas. Most impressive is the disappearance of many orders of reptiles and invertebrates. Complete stratigraphic sections show the evolution of planktonic (floating and swimming) foraminifers during Cenozoic time; the highly evolved globotruncanas of the Upper Cretaceous disappear and are succeeded by a zone of primitive globigerinas at the base of the Tertiary. At the end of the Tertiary Period (about 2,500,000 years ago), climatic deterioration affected the distribution of organisms and vital, robust life forms spread widely, as more delicate organisms either died out or retreated to equatorial regions.

This article presents an overview of earth history during Cenozoic time. For greater detail on the relevant time intervals, see TERTIARY PERIOD; PLEISTOCENE EPOCH; HOLOCENE EPOCH. See also FOSSIL RECORD and MAMMALIA for further information on the principal animal groups of Cenozoic time and STRATIGRAPHIC BOUNDARIES for discussion of the Mesozoic-Cenozoic and wholly Cenozoic boundaries.

CENOZOIC STRATIGRAPHY

Tertiary and Quaternary periods

Subdivision of Cenozoic time. By international agreement the Cenozoic is divided into the Tertiary and Quaternary periods. The Tertiary is subdivided as follows:

subdivision	epoch	duration (000,000 years)
Younger Tertiary or Neogene	Pliocene	4.5
	Miocene	19.0
Older Tertiary or Paleogene	Oligocene	12.0
	Eocene	16.0
	Paleocene	11.0

The epochs of the Tertiary are further subdivided into stages, although this subdivision has always been open to much discussion. Subdivision into biozones, based upon the evolution of planktonic Foraminifera, is preferable to the classical subdivision. Similarly, subdivision of the Quaternary can be based upon the glacial record; the preglacial, glacial, and postglacial (Holocene) stages generally can be distinguished within the Quaternary record. Correlation of the preglacial in northwestern Europe, the Mediterranean region, and North America is as follows:

Northwestern Europe	Mediterranean	North America
Waal warm period Eburon cold period	Siciliano	Rexroad
Tegelen warm period Bruggen cold period	Calabriano	Blanco

The Quaternary also is subdivided into the Holocene Epoch (also termed Recent, Alluvium, or Postglacial), which comprises approximately the last 10,000 years, and the Pleistocene Epoch (Diluvium, or Glacial Age, are sometimes used synonymously), which comprises approximately the last 2,500,000 years.

Alternation between periods of glacial advance and retreat permits subdivision of the Pleistocene Epoch. Classical regions are the southern limit of glaciated areas in Europe and North America and the Alpine region of central Europe. The subdivisions that are generally used in the respective regions and their assumed correlations are as follows:

Subdivisions and Assumed Correlations of the Pleistocene Epoch

North Germany	Alps	North America
Weichsel Ice Age	Würm Ice Age	Wisconsin Ice Age
Ehm Warm Period	Riss/Würm Interglacial	Sangamon Interglacial
Saale Ice Age	Riss Ice Age	Illinoian Ice Age
Holstein Warm Period	Mindel/Riss Interglacial	Yarmouth Interglacial
Elster Ice Age	Mindel Ice Age	Kansan Ice Age
Cromer Warm Period	Günz/Mindel Interglacial	Aftonian Interglacial
Weybourne Ice Age	Günz Ice Age	Nebraskan Ice Age

Tectonic-volcanic phases

The Tertiary Period was a time of major crustal movements (tectonic changes), the most important of which was the Alpine mountain building that began in Mesozoic time. The Tertiary tectonic phases gave rise to the big mountain chains of today (*e.g.*, Cordilleran, Andes, Alps, Caucasus, Himalayas) and are largely responsible for the present form and appearance of these chains. Worldwide volcanic activity was associated with this tectonism and created the present volcanic regions of the world. Intrusions of Pacific-type granites, basaltic eruptions on a gigantic scale, and regional deposition of volcanic rocks occurred. The volcanic belt from Greenland across Iceland to Scotland, the basalts of the Columbia and Colorado plateaus in North America, and the Deccan Trap of India, which cover areas as large as 100,000 square kilometres (40,000 square miles) in great thickness, are especially remarkable. Volcanic activity and crustal movement continued in the Quaternary, and although much of this movement was truly tectonic in origin, isostatic movements (adjustment toward equilibrium) also occurred, caused by the melting of large ice sheets; thicknesses of several kilometres of Pleistocene ice depressed entire continental blocks, and slow glacial rebound of the land followed its removal during the Holocene Epoch.

Tectonic phases during the Cenozoic Era and their relation to subdivisions of Cenozoic time are as follows:

Cretaceous/Tertiary boundary	Laramic phase
Upper Eocene/Lower Oligocene boundary	Pyrenean phase
Oligocene/Miocene boundary	Savic phase
Middle to Upper Miocene	Styrian phase
Pliocene	Rhodanic phase
Tertiary/Quaternary boundary	Wallachian phase

General characteristics of sediments. Marine sediments of Paleogene age are widely distributed in regions that were tectonically stable; marginal deposits (marine and nonmarine) also cover considerable areas. Highly fossiliferous limestones or calcareous sandstones predominate and these marine sediments are interbedded with river and lake deposits.

The subdivision of epicontinental strata (sediments deposited in stable areas in relatively shallow water) can be based upon changes of facies (lateral gradations of sediment type), cyclic repetition of marine transgressions, and freshwater influences. Many classical localities for Paleogene stages are within the epicontinental strata of western Europe, where they are best developed in the Paris Basin and in Belgium. Paleogene sediments of geosynclinal facies are characterized by flysch deposits consisting of a repeated succession of turbidites (sandstones deposited by density currents) and marly layers at great depths; tracks and burrows of animals are characteristic fossils.

Due to mountain building, the advance of nappes (great overturned folds), and the narrowing of the geosynclines, the original area of deposition of flyschlike rocks is not preserved, and paleogeographical reconstruction of Paleogene environments is rather difficult.

Neogene sediments generally are less consolidated and disturbed than those of the Paleogene; marls, clays, and gravels predominate and *Lithothamnium*-limestones characterize the marginal facies. These unconsolidated rocks are termed molasse, and molasse zones follow geosynclinal axes that form the foreland of the Alps and Carpathians. Continental (nonmarine) sediments are widely distributed over the surface of the old continental shields in North and South America, Siberia, and Central Asia, and sands, gravels, and clays attain considerable thickness in areas of downfaulting or warping. Vertebrates are the most important fossils in these deposits of lacustrine and fluvial origin, and important mammal discoveries have been made in the interior continental basins of North America.

Deposition of continental sediments

During the Cenozoic, sea level attained its present altitude, and the area of the continents covered by marine strata progressively diminished. During Quaternary time the deposition of continental sediments predominated. The low-lying parts of the continents are almost completely covered by Pleistocene or Holocene deposits and, following the change of climatic conditions, sediments in northern regions were characterized by loess (wind derived sediments) and glacial deposits. In the south, in the region of present savannas and deserts, the sediments suggest that the climate was wetter than at present; clastic sediments of fluvial origin (river sands and gravels) represent the Pleistocene over wide areas of the earth.

Other characteristics of sedimentation include the increased rate of deposition in deep-sea areas during the Pleistocene because of an increased supply of materials of glacial, fluviatile, or eolian origin. In addition, the circumpolar belts of glacial-marine deposits and of diatom ooze advanced toward lower latitudes, especially during glacial ages, thus narrowing the equatorial zone of Globigerina-ooze.

Distribution of Tertiary rocks. *Europe.* In western Europe, Paleogene epicontinental facies with rich and typical faunas are present in the Paris Basin, in Belgium, and in Great Britain. They also are present in northern Germany and Denmark. In central and southern Europe flysch-type deposits of Paleogene age exist within the young mountain chains (Pyrenees, Alps, Carpathians, Dinarids, and others). A richly fossiliferous calcareous facies extends across southeastern Europe (Crimea) to the Caucasus.

The Neogene of Europe exhibits a differentiation of faunal provinces (regions characterized by distinctive plant or animal assemblages), and in the north the Neogene sequence of the northwestern European region can be clearly defined. Northern faunal elements distinguish it from the Atlantic-Mediterranean region, and it is possible that a land bridge between Great Britain and Iceland existed at this time. Continental deposits with considerable soft coal were formed in central Europe, and marine sequences of the Atlantic region were developed in Brittany and Aquitaine. In southern Spain a connection between the Atlantic and Mediterranean Region temporarily existed.

The Mediterranean sequence includes richly fossiliferous strata, especially in the Po region, where the Pliocene begins with a transgressive fauna and connections existed from the eastern Mediterranean to the Indo-Pacific regions.

The molasse zone accompanying the Alpine Arc is mostly Neogene in age, whereas the area east of the Alps to the Aral Sea is covered by Neogene sediments that contain characteristic faunas.

Asia. Epicontinental facies of Paleogene age extend east of the Urals in a northerly direction, separating Siberia from Europe and, farther south, Paleogene rocks exist in the Tarim Basin. Continental Neogene deposits cover large areas in Siberia and Mongolia.

Following the axial direction of young mountain chains, the Paleogene (mainly Eocene) occurs in Anatolia and Iran. Through Baluchistan and the Punjab it extends into the Himalayas, where it may underlie alpine type nappes; across the Middle East—in Syria, Iraq, and the Arabian Peninsula—calcareous facies of Paleogene age are distributed; Neogene rocks are limited to regions near the coast. Tertiary sediments also exist in Assam and Burma, Indonesia, the Philippines, Taiwan, and on Honshu and West Hokkaido in Japan. West of Kamchatka, a marine embayment from the Pacific region extends far into eastern Siberia.

Australia, New Guinea, and the islands of the southwestern Pacific. Tertiary rocks occur in Western Australia only within a narrow zone along the coast. In the south they are present in the Eucla, Adelaide, Murray-Southwest-Victoria, and Gippsland embayments, and marine Tertiary surrounds Mesozoic cores in several basins on New Zealand.

In western and central New Guinea, the Tertiary is represented by foraminiferal-calcareous Eocene facies, and in the east a geosynclinal-abyssal (deepwater) facies is present. In the southwest Pacific region, the outer Melanesian Zone comprises the Solomon Islands, New Hebrides, Fiji, and Tonga, each of which contains Tertiary rocks; the interior Melanesian Zone comprises southeastern New Guinea and New Caledonia.

North America. Marine sediments of Tertiary age in North America exist only along continental margins. They are developed along the Pacific coast in western Washington, western Oregon, California, and the southern region of Vancouver. On the Atlantic coast, Tertiary rocks extend from New Jersey in the north, across Maryland, Virginia, the Carolinas, and Georgia, south to Florida. Tertiary sediments are perhaps best represented along the Gulf Coast, however, where they extend from Florida to the east coast of Mexico and down to Yucatan; the Mississippi embayment extends far into the continent. Sediments of the Gulf Coast are, of course, closely related to the Caribbean faunal province. Tertiary faunas of the West Coast are rather distinctive and are known as the Californian faunal province, being quite different from the West-Atlantic Province along the East Coast. The deposits in the interior of the continent contain mammalian faunas and are of great importance because they show that Central North America was a mammalian evolutionary centre during the entire Tertiary.

The Central America land bridge

Central and South America. Central America is important as a land bridge that made possible the migration of mammals during Cretaceous-Tertiary time, although North and South America were separated during most of the Tertiary, and only certain faunal elements could enter South America. It was not until the close of the Pliocene Epoch that the Panama land bridge became passable for mammals, although marine connections permitted exchange of faunal elements between the Atlantic and the Pacific. Eocene and Miocene sediments exist at several localities in Central America and the West Indies, whereas marine sediments of Neogene age in South America are limited to coastal regions despite their relatively great extent in comparison to the size of the subcontinent. In the north (Trinidad, Venezuela, Colombia), they are closely connected with the Caribbean faunal province. Separated by large continental areas, marine Tertiary occurs again in the south, in the La Plata Basin, Patagonia, and Tierra del Fuego; but in central South America only lacustrine and other nonmarine sediments are known.

A seaway across the Sahara

Africa. During Upper Cretaceous time (Maastrichtian) a great marine transgression occurred and the Mediterranean was connected with the Gulf of Guinea across the Sahara. Eocene sediments also reflect a time of transgression, and an incomplete sequence in the east and flysch facies in the west characterize the Upper Eocene. Neogene deposits are transgressive upon the margins of the continent. In South Africa, the Tertiary is represented primarily by the continental series of the Kalahari System. Richly fossiliferous sediments of the Eocene in Egypt are of great interest because they contain large nummulites (distinctive, shallow-water Foraminifera that occur in calcareous facies) and because materials for the construction of the pyramids were obtained from these rocks.

CENOZOIC LIFE

Flora. The cenophytic flora appeared in the Middle Cretaceous and became dominant in the Tertiary. It largely replaced the gymnosperms, the dominant forms of the Mesozoic, although during the warm epoch of the Eocene the floral distribution on earth was similar to that of the Upper Cretaceous. The Tertiary-Holocene flora of angiosperms originated in the Arctic region and spread steadily southward; Eocene floras from Greenland and Alaska reached the middle latitudes of North America and Eurasia during the Miocene.

With the retreat of floral belts southward, the trends of mountain ranges became an important ecological factor. In most of Eurasia the ranges trend east–west, and most of the Tertiary plants therefore died out and could not return after Pleistocene time. In America and southeast Asia, however, mountain ranges extend north-south and in warmer periods the floras could return to the north. The similarity of European Tertiary floras to those now existing in Mexico, California, or South China is explained by this fact.

Calcareous algae belonging to the Dasycladaceae were predominant in Mesozoic seas and persisted into the Tertiary, but they are unimportant compared to the Corallinaceae or Nullipora (*Lithothamnium*, *Melobesia*), whereas Characeae are widely distributed in freshwaters. The nannoplankton (very small, floating marine organisms) of the Tertiary are distinguished from that of the Cretaceous by the appearance of discoasterids.

The decrease of temperatures during the Quaternary established the modern zones of vegetation. Tundra, characteristic of Arctic latitudes, and mosses and polar willows covered much of central Europe at the southern limit of glaciation, and the limit of forests also retreated toward the south. Interglacial periods show conditions similar to former ones (see CLIMATIC CHANGE).

Evolution of the Foraminifera

Lower animals. In the Tertiary, as in older strata, fossils come from marine sediments. Many genera and species of Mesozoic Foraminifera persisted into Tertiary time, although the majority of benthonic Foraminifera showed a tendency to evolve new forms that accelerated in the younger Paleocene, especially among the Rotaliacea, which evolved large forms with a complicated structure. The trend reached its maximum in the Middle Eocene, although contrary to the peak of foraminiferal evolution in the Upper Paleozoic, large and complicated Foraminifera appeared in several phylogenetic groups in the Tertiary. The most widely known are the nummulites, which are paralleled only by the vertebrates with respect to their intensive evolution.

In the older Paleocene "pillar-bearing rotalids" are widely distributed and the discocyclines appear, reaching their peak in the Eocene and disappearing in the Upper Eocene. Several genera of the Nummulitidae evolved giant forms. Nummulites in the restricted sense appeared as small forms in the Upper Paleocene and reached their optimum size in the Middle Eocene, with tests (shells) as large as 200 millimetres in diameter or more. In the Upper Eocene small or very small forms with a diameter of two to five millimetres again predominate, and in Europe they disappear in the Upper Oligocene. Evolutionary sequences of larger Foraminifera also appear in the Neogene; the most important of these for stratigraphic purposes are miogypsins and lepidocyclines.

Benthonic foraminifers evolved numerous new forms during the Cenozoic. Most important for stratigraphic correlation is the evolution of the plankton, because their worldwide distribution provides a base for intercontinental correlation. The *Globigerina*-range in the oldest Paleocene (Danian) is followed by the evolution of the Paleogene plankton with *Globorotalia* and *Truncorotalia.* During the Oligocene the variety of forms is much reduced, and only primitive globigerinas persist. The characteristic genus *Globigerinoides* appeared in the Miocene; *Praeorbulina* and *Orbulina* appeared in the Middle Miocene. The Miocene-Pliocene boundary is based upon species of *Globorotalia.*

Evolution of other invertebrate groups

Corals did not evolve to any great extent in the Tertiary, but their distribution changed because of a decrease of water temperatures. Mollusks, especially gastropods and bivalves, are among the most important fossils of the Cenozoic; many genera and species evolved among the Cenogastropods, among which siphonostomous forms are especially noteworthy.

Evolution of landsnails also was marked. Only a few species are known from the Cretaceous, but during the Tertiary several groups evolved distinctive genera and species, especially the *Pupillacea*, *Clausiliacea*, and *Heliacea.* During the Quaternary, heat-loving species disappeared from the northern continents, and robust forms spread over Eurasia and North America.

The rising of young mountain chains in Neogene time separated the northern part of the Tethys Geosyncline from the oceans in central Europe, southeastern Europe, and central Asia. During the Miocene and Pliocene, this led to the evolution of molluscan faunas with some extremely specialized types. This is an excellent example of the results of isolation of which few parallels can be provided within the history of life.

At the end of the Pliocene, temperature lowering caused species of the northwest European province to migrate into the Mediterranean province and this "advance of northern guests," together with a retreat of more delicate species, is taken as a criterion for the beginning of the Pleistocene and the onset of glacial conditions.

The evolution of the arthropods in the Tertiary appears to show a trend toward their present importance, and although terrestrial invertebrates can be fossilized only under very favourable conditions (for example, in amber), it appears that during the younger Paleogene many species were similar to those living today.

Ostracodes occupy a special place among the arthropods because they are abundant in the fossil record and show a strong trend toward evolution of different and distinctive forms in the Tertiary.

Among Bryozoa, cheilostomate forms dominate in the Tertiary. The number of brachiopod species is strongly reduced compared with the Cretaceous; some groups were forced down to lower bathymetric levels, and banks of *Terebratula* are relatively frequent. Remains of echinoderms are not rare in the Tertiary and echinoids occur frequently, especially irregular and burrowing forms. Most of the groups dominant during the Paleozoic and Mesozoic lose their importance, however.

Vertebrates. At the Cretaceous/Tertiary boundary the highly specialized reptiles of the Mesozoic disappeared, although turtles, crocodiles, snakes, and lizards continued. Several Mesozoic groups of fishes died out, whereas others existed as rare relics (crossopterygians); teleost diversity increased. Among amphibians, frogs and toads showed progressive evolution. Bird fossils are rare, but it seems that in the Paleogene most of the living groups already had evolved.

Evolution of mammalian faunas

The evolution of the mammals is the most important biologic phenomenon of the Tertiary. During the Mesozoic, small, primitive mammals spread all over the earth, and most of them became extinct during the Mesozoic, although a few relics persist in Australia. Generally speaking, only the stem groups of marsupials (pouched mammals) and placental mammals survived the end of the Mesozoic.

The isolation of Australia throughout the Tertiary led to a separate evolution of marsupials, with many forms adapting to different conditions; however, autochthonous (originating within) placental mammals do not exist in Australia. During the Paleocene, specialized groups evolved out of the primitive placentals, and, together with marsupials, they reached South America, which then lost its direct connection with the other continents until the Pliocene. Contrary to the Australian example, the marsupials did not evolve to the same extent, although the primitive placentals evolved many specialized forms, some of which still exist.

In the Old World and in North America, the mammalian fauna of the Paleocene was replaced in the Lower Eocene by increasingly progressive and differentiated forms; such forms as rodents, carnivores, hoofed animals, and primates became predominant. Some evolutionary branches returned to the sea; seals and whales are prominent examples.

During the Paleogene, the carnivores are represented by creodonts (*Arctocyon*, *Hyaenodon*, and others) whose dentition is not as specialized as is that of the more modern carnivores of the Oligo-Miocene (*Amphicyon*, *Hemicyon*, *Felis*).

Herbivorous ungulates evolved multicusped molars, broad and high-crowned, with their dentine and enamel folded into narrow ridges that enabled the tooth to deal with tough grasses. Swift-running ungulates reduced their number of toes, and the evolutionary line of horses leads from four-toed forms (*Hyracotherium*) to three-toed ones (*Miohippus*, *Merychippus*). *Hipparion* of the Lower Pliocene ran only on the middle toe, a trend continued by the Pleistocene genus *Equus.*

At the beginning of the Neogene, mastodonts migrated from Africa to Europe and later to Asia and America. They also showed specialization of their dentition, particularly with respect to size of tusks. In the Middle Miocene the cervids had primitive antlers (single-ended), which became more and more complicated as evolution progressed. The largest mammals that ever lived on land (Baluchitherium) existed in the Paleogene.

At the beginning of the Pleistocene, modern mammalian faunas consisting of *Equus*, *Elephas*, *Ursus*, and others spread over the Eurasian continent, and these faunas are useful for defining the boundary between Tertiary and Quaternary. During the Quaternary, the modern mammalian species appeared, probably as a result of adaptation to swiftly changing climatic conditions. Robust forms inhabited the polar regions, more delicate forms retreated into warmer regions, and glacial relics remained in high mountains and other isolated territories.

Evolution of Hominids. Manlike forms appeared at the beginning of the Quaternary, and even the oldest remains show that upright posture and modern limb proportions had been developed. The earliest remains are known from East Africa, South Africa, and Indonesia, together with associated implements. The brain increased in size, dentition became weaker, face profiles became steeper. *Homo erectus* in Europe and Asia developed the "hand-ax cultures" of the older Paleolithic, and *Homo neanderthalensis* perfected these stone tools. In the Würm glacial time, *Homo sapiens* appeared; cave paintings in France and Spain show his artistic achievements. Mesolithic and Neolithic man devised settlement and agriculture, and civilization commenced.

BIBLIOGRAPHY. R. BRINCKMANN, *Geologic Evolution of Europe*, 2nd rev. ed., pp. 114–150 (1969; pub. orig. in German, 1956), on the historical geology of the Cenozoic of Europe; M. GIGNOUX, *Géologie stratigraphique*, 4th ed. (1950; Eng. trans., *Stratigraphic Geology*, pp. 467–664, 1955), on the Cenozoic history of Europe and North Africa, somewhat dated; S.H. HAUGHTON, *The Stratigraphic History of Africa South of the Sahara*, pp. 305–348 (1963), an overview of African Cenozoic history; M. KAY and E.H. COLBERT, *Stratigraphy and Life History*, pp. 501–630 (1965), an excellent summary of the Cenozoic of North America; B. KUMMEL, *History of the Earth: An Introduction to Historical Geology*, pp. 348–505 (1961), a readable account of Cenozoic geology and life history of the world; A. PAPP, *Handbuch der stratigraphischen Geologie*, vol. 3, *Tertiär: Grundzüge regionaler Stratigraphie* (1959), a description of the Tertiary stratigraphy with regard to the methodical principles of the intercontinental correlation.

(A.P.)

Censorship

To censor is to judge and criticize, to count and calculate, and to prohibit and suppress. The function or office of censorship in a political, religious, or social community is to proclaim common ends and values for the community, draw up programs of action, adherence, and ideology to achieve them, establish devices and agencies to enforce them, and enumerate crimes and sins, errors and obscenities, heresies and treasons by which they are endangered. The history of censorship is therefore part of the history of learning (the construction of encyclopaedias of true knowledge and factual information to supplant ignorance, misinformation, and superstition), of education (the development of liberal arts to correct distorted or bad education), of political institutions (the establishment of democracy to replace despotism and imperialism), of religious beliefs (the adjustment of old doctrines to new prophecies, the propagation of beliefs to new believers, the reformation of practices to new circumstances), and of the arts (the renaissances, revolutions, or changes of style in opposition to academic, imitative, and sterile art).

Some form of censorship has appeared in all communities, small and large, in all parts of the world, at all stages of history. The operation of censorship, like the operation of civil law, religious commandments, and social customs, is by sanction, negation, prohibition, and restriction. The problems of censorship today reflect changes in communication (and misrepresentation and secrecy), in community (and prejudice and tension), in belief (and skepticism and commitment), and in knowledge (and ignorance and misconception). New extensions of rights and of freedom of thought and expression have been achieved, and unprecedented devices of intimidation, repression, and suppression have been constructed. A review of what has been censored in the past and of the methods of censorship and the reasons advanced in its defense and promotion may clarify present problems.

ANCIENT CENSORSHIP

Dynasties, learning, and history in China. In ancient China, Tao (the Way or the Law) was the way of ordering one's life and the world; it was the moral and political law expounded in philosophy and institutionalized in the state. Philosophers studied the ways of past dynasties to find guidance in the great Tao or great Community; rulers protected the law of their dynasties from criticism and opposition by destroying the records of the dynasties they supplanted. The teachings of Confucius (*c.* 551–479 BC) were one of the "100 schools" that flourished in his time. He lamented the lack of documents by which to study the learned men of earlier dynasties, since such study was the only source of wisdom. The philosophy of Confucianists was a philosophy of humanity—love of men and understanding of men. Among their opponents were the Legalists, who advocated power and control as the goals of life. On the command of the first Chinese emperor, Shih Huang Ti, the Legalists prepared the first of the long line of Chinese encyclopaedias about 220 BC. This encyclopaedia, "The Mirror for the Emperor," provided an authoritative ideological foundation for the Ch'in dynasty (221–206 BC). Shih Huang Ti built the Great Wall and burned books to protect his realm from opposition. In 213 he ordered the destruction of all books except those in medicine, pharmacy, divination, agriculture, and arboriculture. Five hundred scholars were executed and thousands were banished. The *Analects* of Confucius was among the books burned. The punishment for failure to burn proscribed books within 30 days was branding and condemnation to forced labour.

Destruction of opposition in China

Empires, religions, and ways of life in India. In ancient India, Dharma (the Law) was found in the sacred literature of the Hindus and was expounded by philosophical and religious commentators as universal law—divine and moral, transcendental and human. Dharma was the basis for distinguishing classes or functions in society and stages or ways of life. There were four classes, or *varṇas* (colours): Brahmins (priests and thinkers), Kṣatriyas (rulers and warriors), Vaiśyas (farmers, artisans, and merchants), and Śūdras (laborers, unskilled workers, and slaves). There were four stages of life: austere life as a student, married life as a householder, a life of meditation and penance as a hermit, and a life of homeless wandering as an old man. Two unorthodox sects, Jainism and Buddhism, departed from the Veda and from gods, priests, and rites to interpret Dharma in terms of the actions of saintly men.

The Aryan invasions, which began about 1500 BC, subjugated the earlier inhabitants of India and introduced Indo-Iranian religious and cultural ideas in the Vedas. The unification of India reached its widest extent in the Mauryan Empire under Aśoka, a Buddhist, who, in the 3rd century BC, after a bloody war, abandoned conquest by war for conquest by Dharma. Aśoka proclaimed that Dharma applied to all sects in his empire—Brahmins, Ājīvikas, Jains, and "other sects as well as Buddhists"—and to all peoples of the world—such as the kings of Syria, Egypt, and Macedonia. But he also drew up a canon of texts for Buddhists, and to eliminate sectarianism he called the third Council of Buddhists about 247–246 BC, which made the Theravāda school orthodox and expelled many heretics. Missionaries were sent to Ceylon, Burma, Thailand, and Cambodia to preach the orthodox version, where it continues to this day, while the Buddhist sects of China and Japan grew out of the Mahayana tradition. The fate of religion and philosophy in India and China illustrate two kinds of censorship: one a cultural, sectarian censorship resulting in the disappearance of books and studies; the other a dynastic, official censorship resulting in their destruction and outlawing.

Imposition of conformity in India

The people and the Law of God in Israel. In ancient Israel, Moses had led his people from bondage to a God-promised land, where they were to live under a law received from God. The Torah (the Law) was considered unchanging, and in times of crisis "the book of the law of Moses which the Lord had given to Israel" was consulted. Since at each consultation a prophet is needed to explain the Law's meaning, the formulation and interpretation of the Law varied with circumstances and with prophets. The development and preservation of Israel depended on a double censorship, one by which the written book of the Law was preserved intact and uncontaminated, and another by which the secret art of interpretation was transmitted orally. The interpretation of the Law guided the people and helped Israel in its wars against its enemies. After the fall of Jerusalem (586 BC), however, the problems of the preservation of the canon and the continuity of the oral tradition took a new turn during the Babylonian Captivity. A hierarchical government prepared the way for the Sanhedrin (the supreme rabbinic court), and priestly legislation laid the foundations of rabbinic interpretation. Judaism was Hellenized under the Hellenistic kings of Egypt and Syria, and in 168 BC the Seleucid king Antiochus IV Epiphanes established the worship of Olympian Zeus (merged with the Syrian god Baal), burned the Torah, and condemned those who possessed the book, or followed the Law, to death.

Preservation of a people in Israel

The interpretation of the divine Law transmitted in the Torah provided the means both of distinguishing the Jews from other peoples and of adjusting Judaism to other cultures. The methods of interpretation evolved in controversies which, in the Hellenistic period, resulted in the formation of sects—*e.g.*, the Pharisees, the Sadducees, and the Essenes. In Hellenized Alexandria, a Greek translation of the Old Testament, the Septuagint, was prepared for Jews who knew no Hebrew or Aramaic. The canon of the Old Testament was extended in the Septuagint to include the Law, the Prophets, the Hagiographa, and the Apocrypha; and Philo of Alexandria (died after AD 40) used the analogical methods of Greek literary criticism and Neoplatonic dialectic to interpret the books of the Old Testament. Christians later learned the method from Philo and applied it to the New Testament. As Tao had been used to establish the rule of a dynasty and Dharma to relate peoples, Torah was used to preserve the uniqueness of a people.

War, politics, and education in Greece. The Greeks came into existence by the assimilation of a succession of invading peoples and achieved unity by resisting invasion by the Persian Empire in the early part of the 5th century BC. Victory over the Persians did not lay the ground for a continuing unity of the Greeks: Themistocles, the Athenian, and Pausanias, the Spartan, who had been outstanding in contributing to the victory, were judged guilty of treason, un-Hellenic activities, and Persian sympathies; and Athens and Sparta signed a treaty under which they carried on a cold war that developed into the Peloponnesian War (431–404 BC). The avowed purpose of both sides in that war was to free the Greeks. Censorship appeared in education and in politics. According to Plutarch in *The Ancient Customs of the Spartans*, the Spartans learned to read and write for purely practical reasons, and all other educational influences—books and treatises as well as learned men—were banned. The arts and philosophy flourished in democratic Athens, but many artists and philosophers, among them Aeschylus, Euripides, Phidias, Socrates, and Aristotle, were exiled, imprisoned, executed, or took flight. Aeschylus was accused of violating the secrecy of the Eleusinian Mysteries.

Greek dimensions of censorship

Greek philosophers framed the theoretic arguments that have been used for centuries in support of freedom and of censorship, and Greek lawgivers distinguished the practical reasons that have become standard grounds for censorship. Plato would have banished poets because, he claimed, they lied about gods, heroes, and men and thus impeded the formation of virtue in the individual citizen and justice in the state; and he opposed rhetoricians and naturalistic scientists because, he charged, they deceived in communication or erred in inquiry. Later censors have been able to think of no reasons for banning books or other forms of expression other than the four accusations levelled against Socrates: (1) impiety; (2) corrupting the morals of the young; (3) popularizing science that might lead to skepticism or disbelief; and (4) deceiving by trickery and making the weaker argument stronger. The Greeks condemned such discourse and teaching because they endangered the state, and Socrates himself justified the judgment against him, in the *Crito*, as essential to the preservation of the laws of Athens.

The Hellenistic kingdoms, after 323 BC, established libraries, two of which—those at Alexandria and Pergamum—laid the foundation of Western culture and censorship. The Hellenistic libraries were not formed by collecting books but by making them. The texts of the books had to be established, frequently from scattered fragments, as in the case of Homer; the authors had to be identified and distinguished from other authors of the same name or of similar works, and their works had to be verified; sequences, synchronisms, and classifications had to be established, and empirical sciences had to be developed for these purposes. The Hellenistic libraries marked the beginning of two forms of censorship. The work of editors and the classification of great books influenced the content as well as the interpretation of the books, for the choice and the compilation of the editor fixed the texts of the classics that have survived. The works of other authors not chosen and edited did not survive, sometimes to the regret of later scholars. The concentration of books in large numbers encouraged and facilitated a second form of censorship—the burning and pillaging of books. There are many accounts (which are significant as accounts even when they are inaccurate factually) of the burning, in several stages, of part or all of the library at Alexandria, from the siege of Julius Caesar in 47 BC to its destruction by Christians in AD 391 and by Muslims in 642. In the latter two instances, it was alleged that pagan literature presented a danger to the Old and New Testaments or the Qur'ān.

Law, morals, and monotheism in Rome. The office of censor was established in Rome in 443 BC. Taking the census, *i.e.*, counting and classifying the inhabitants of Rome, included regulation of their morals, violations of which might result in a citizen being deprived of status and functions. The mechanism of censorship in Greece was judicial trial; in Rome it was executive judgment in which the informer or delator played an important part in protecting the native virtue of Rome from treason and immorality. After the accession of Augustus, imperial censorship was directed to extirpating treason and curbing immorality. Treason included allusion, statement, and criticism. A drama that attacked Agamemnon, the semimythical commander of the Greeks against Troy, and a history that presented as the last of the Romans Brutus and Cassius, the assassins of Julius Caesar, uncle of Augustus, were condemned, as well as statements interpreted as being critical of the government. Philosophers and rhetoricians were twice banished by law, and the political rights of actors were curtailed by edicts of the censors. Immorality often took the form of adultery, which provided lucrative opportunities for informing. Even during the republic, when Rome came into contact with the culture of Greece, Cato the Elder, also known as Cato the Censor, a statesman and ardent advocate of the Third Punic War, remembered for his reiterated proclamation, "Carthage must be destroyed," opposed the spread in the 2nd century BC of Greek arts and pedantry as dangers to the ancient virtues of Rome, whereas Scipio Aemilianus, who also served as censor later in the same century, formed a group of philosophers, historians, poets, and statesmen (the Scipionic Circle) who looked to Greece as a source of Roman culture. When Rome abandoned its policy of maintaining the freedom and independence of the Hellenistic kingdoms, the admission of citizens into the new provinces was made a censorial act. The emperor Augustus purged the Senate in the 1st century BC as an exercise of censorial powers.

The Roman censor

The persecution of the Jews and the Christians during

the first three centuries of the Roman Empire arose from a conflict of laws and of books. The laws of Rome tolerated all gods, but the Jews and the Christians refused to place their one God in a pantheon and they refused to perform civic duties (including service in the army or attendance at civic functions, games, and the theatre) that required sacrifice to idols. Christians, Jews, and later Muslims (who recognized their affinity in opposition to heathens as three peoples of the Books) developed different patterns of censorship to interpret divine law. They interpreted their three Books—the Old Testament, the New Testament, and the Qu'rān—as formulations of the law of Moses, but each tradition included in its censorship interpretations made in the other two traditions; and in all three traditions the controversy concerning whether pagan arts and sciences, Greek philosophy and Roman law, should be prohibited or should be used to interpret sacred writings continued unabated and unresolved. Despite prohibitions, pagan philosophy, science, and literature were preserved to the present only by the labour and erudition of medieval scribes, translators, and commentators. Each tradition faced the problem of drawing up a canon of authentic sacred books and lists of heretical schismatic, and erroneous books.

Law and tradition in Judaism. The destruction of Jerusalem and of the Temple by the Romans in AD 70 raised grave problems in the interpretation of the Torah, since much of the Law centred on the Temple and its ritual. The Torah was reinterpreted and reformulated in the Palestinian Talmud by rabbis who fled to Babylonia. The Talmud consists of two parts, the Mishna or "Repetition," a codification begun before the destruction of the Temple, and the Gemara or "Completion," a commentary on the Mishna. The Torah is not limited to the Ten Commandments, or to the laws of Deuteronomy; the Talmud itself is Torah. The law is formulated in dialectical exposition and defense in the *Halakha;* its moral implications and precepts are presented narratively and are made accessible to all in the stories of the *Haggada.* It is universal law, but it separates Jews from other peoples, including the Romans. One book of the Talmud is devoted to idolatry and to the problems Jews faced in an empire of idolators. Jews were persecuted with Christians, and Roman officials sometimes did not distinguish between them. In the 4th century, Christianity became the religion of the empire, and Christian officials persecuted Jews.

Law, doctrines, and institutions in Christianity. During the period of persecution, the Christian Apologists argued that Christian law was not a danger to the law of Rome; in AD 313 the Edict of Milan gave Christians equality with other religious groups in the empire. According to the Christians, the New Testament was a continuation of the Old Testament, a fulfillment of the prophecies of the Old Testament in the teaching of Jesus. The creed was the statement of the facts that established that continuity. The Nicene Creed was formulated at the first ecumenical Council at Nicaea, called by the Roman emperor Constantine in AD 325, and the decisions of councils and of the Church Fathers were put on a level of authority only after the Old and New Testaments for the interpretation of law and doctrine. The ecumenical councils did not succeed in unifying the empire or the church. The empire was divided into two empires in 363, and the last ecumenical council recognized by the Greek Church was the second Council of Nicaea in 787. The church was divided by the schism of East and West in 1054. From the first, Latin Christians constructed ecclesiastical institutions, like the councils and the curia, for the statement and interpretation of laws and doctrines, while the Greek Christians formed theological systems and adapted the dialectical, analogical method of Philo of Alexandria in the interpretation of Christian and pagan doctrines. The canon of Holy Scripture proclaimed officially by Pope Damasus I in 382, by Pope Gelasius I in 496, and by Pope Hormisdas in 520 was based on earlier compilations, and later compilations were sometimes ascribed to an earlier author. Thus, the *Apostolic Constitutions*, probably written in the 4th century but ascribed to a companion of the Apostles, contains a list of falsely ascribed and apocryphal books of Scripture and also a prohibition of all gentile books on the ground that the "law of God" (the Bible) includes all genres of literature—history, sophistry, poesy, and law. The *Gelasian Decretal* contains five lists, of which the second is a canon of Holy Scripture and the fifth a Decretal of "Books to be Accepted and Books not to be Accepted." The rejected books were branded apocryphal or heretical. The Roman canon of the Old Testament differs from the Jewish by including the works classified by the Jews as Apocrypha; the Greek canon contains some but not all of those works. The Protestants later returned to the Jewish Canon, but the longer canon was then reaffirmed by the Council of Trent for the Roman Catholics.

The development of a church canon

Law and learning in Islām. The Qu'rān is a revelation of eternal law by returning to the law of Abraham undistorted by human prophecies, institutions, or speculations. The interpretation of the law is a science and is to be expounded in the context of other sciences. Three sciences were of particular importance for the interpretation of law in Muslim encyclopaedias: political science, which treats law under ideal conditions following Plato; legal science, which treats actual laws in existing states; and the *kalām*, which is a speculative science of religion and government. The great rift in Muslim interpretations of the science of law was over the possibility of the science of *kalām*.

The *kalām* of Islām

All three monotheistic religious traditions made use of pagan arts and sciences in interpreting the law, but a kind of unconscious cultural censorship determined their selection of what to use and what to omit. The Jews used Neoplatonic dialectic and Hellenistic literary criticism; the Latin Christians used Roman law and Ciceronian rhetoric and philosophy; the Greek Christians used Greek speculative philosophy and literature; the Muslims used the whole body of Greek sciences. Contact with Muslim speculation on the *kalām* turned Jewish theologians to the consideration of philosophical questions, and translations of arabic medical works into Latin in the 11th century and of arabic works on mathematics, astronomy, the organization of the sciences, and Aristotle in the 12th century were the beginning of scientific inquiry in western Europe. Many of the new translations from Arabic, Greek, and Hebrew and many of the works in philosophy and science stimulated by them were prohibited by ecclesiastic, academic, and political authorities, but they slowly became the basis of education, inquiry, and culture.

MEDIEVAL AND RENAISSANCE CENSORSHIP

Doctrinal and academic censorship in the Middle Ages. Translations brought Jewish, Christian, and Muslim monotheistic cultures into contact. Paradoxically, Christian theologians and philosophers of the 13th century knew and discussed Jewish and Muslim positions more fully and soundly than philosophers have communicated across cultures at any time since, but Christian inquisitors burned the Talmud in the 13th century, and the 12th-century Latin translation of the Qur'ān made by Peter the Venerable (abbot of Cluny) was later prohibited.

The 12th century was a period of the cultivation and development of the liberal arts in an atmosphere of tolerance and curiosity. John of Salisbury castigated the arrogance of the illiterate masses and set forth maxims to guide reading of the potentially harmful as well as the potentially helpful books. He argued that all writings should be read, but although the wise man "does not shun fables, stories, or spectacles in general," the Fathers condemned the evil careers of actors and mimes. Theodoric of Chartres, who made an enormous collection of the liberal arts in the *Heptateuchon* and encouraged his students to study Arabic and to translate Arabic science, was summoned before a council to answer for the theological consequences of his cosmological system.

The liberal 12th and restrictive 13th centuries

The introduction of the new sciences into programs of education encountered problems of censorship, as is often the case in framing a new program for a public institution. The Council of Paris in 1210 prohibited the teaching, publicly or privately, of Aristotle's works on natural philosophy and of commentaries on them. The statutes of the newly founded University of Paris in 1215 authorized the teaching of Aristotle's logic but prohibited his books on metaphysics, physics, and natural science, as well as expositions of them, together with the books of three heretics. The prohibitions were repeated during the course of the century, but the statutes also set requirements for degrees which included knowledge of Aristotle's scientific and metaphysical doctrines. The medieval European universities, in the same paradoxical fashion, laid the foundations of academic freedom and freedom of thought and expression, but the faculties of the universities met periodically to condemn or expurgate the writings of their colleagues. The record of this censorship, or judgment, fills the three large volumes of the *Collection of Judgments Which Have Been Proscribed and Noted in the Church from the Beginning of the Twelfth Century After the Incarnation of the Word to the Year 1632 as well as the Censorial Judgments of the Outstanding Academies, Among Others Paris and Oxford and Louvain and Douai in Belgium and Other Colleges of Theology Among the Germans, Italians, Spaniards, Poles, Hungarians, and Lorrainians.* After the proscriptions against the works of Aristotle had been lifted, controversies continued concerning doctrines derived from or attributed to Aristotle. In 1277 the Bishop of Paris condemned 219 errors and was echoed in less than two weeks by the Archbishop of Canterbury. The errors included positions set forth by the Arabic and Persian philosophers Averroës and Avicenna and also some of Thomas Aquinas. Teaching was controlled, not only by prohibition of errors, but also by regulations placed on booksellers or "stationers" (stationarii) who were authorized under oath by the university.

Effects of Humanism

Corrective and preventive censorship in the Renaissance and Reformation: the Index. The rebirth of letters, the reformation of religion, and the development of printing brought about changes in the methods of censorship. Censorship of books before publication was differentiated from prohibition of uncensored books after publication. Ecclesiastical and secular censorships were separated by the establishment of official bodies of clerical and governmental censors. Prohibition of distribution, possession, and reading of books was guided by the publication of catalogs and indexes.

The humanists of the Renaissance transformed the liberal arts by applying them to the study of ancient literature, art, and oratory. They ended the medieval cultural censorship of ancient literature and imposed a censorship on medieval letters of their own, which continued to be effective until the 19th century. During the Renaissance, programs of study arranged according to the subject matters that were treated in the new learning and handbooks of factual information concerning those subject matters were both called encyclopaedias.

The theologians of the Reformation transformed theology by returning to the study of the Bible and the Church Fathers. Medieval theological theses were refuted as heresies by Protestant theologians, and Protestant innovations were in turn refuted as new heresies. The word controversy became a technical term, and new lists of banned books and new rules for judging books and statements were produced by the controversies. Pope Innocent VIII late in the 15th century decreed that all books be submitted for examination and permission before being issued for general reading. The regulation was repeated at the Lateran Council in 1515 and was formulated as one of the rules for judging books drawn up at the Council of Trent in 1563. In the condemnation of the heresies of Luther by the faculties of theology of Cologne and Louvain in 1519 and of Paris in 1521, the propositions enumerated for censure were often accompanied by detailed lists of books that affirmed the error. In 1520 Pope Leo X anathematized the doctrines and books of Luther; and Luther, in response, burned the bull of the pope. In 1543 the University of Paris published a list of 65 books condemned or accepted with qualification, which included unauthorized translations of the Bible and works by Luther, Calvin, Rabelais, and Erasmus. Four "catalogs" of books, in Latin and in French, censored by the faculty from 1544 to 1551, fill 23 folio columns. In 1559 Pope Paul IV used the word "index" in the title of his Index of Forbidden Books; and in 1564 the Index of the Council of Trent appeared, prefaced by ten general rules for the control of literature elaborated at the council.

The Index

The first rule provided that all books condemned prior to 1515 and not mentioned in the Index were still condemned. The second was concerned with the judgment of heresiarchs, including the Protestant reformers; and the third and fourth with editions and translations of Scripture. The fifth set down conditions by which books edited by heretics may be permitted or emended, and the sixth stated regulations concerning books of controversy between Roman Catholics and heretics. The seventh treated lascivious or obscene subjects that might corrupt morals. The eighth provided that books of which the principal argument is good but which occasionally tend to heresy or impiety, divination, or superstition may be allowed after they have been corrected by Roman Catholic theologians under the authority of the General Inquisition. The ninth prohibited books of magic and superstition, and the tenth set up conditions for the examination and licensing of books before publication and for the inspection of printing houses and bookshops.

The Congregation of the Index was established in 1571 to publish new editions of the Index and to pronounce on works referred to it. The governments of various nations promulgated laws and appointed officials to regulate the printing and distribution of books. In France the number of printing houses and bookshops permitted in each city was established by law. Like regulations were extended to newspapers and theatres.

Dynastic patterns of censorship in India and China. In India and China, as in Europe and the Near East, periods of imperial unification alternated with periods of dynastic rivalry and foreign subjugation, and a diversity of sects and philosophies alternately interpreted a common eternal law in tolerant coexistence or fought for dominance to the exclusion of other interpretations of the law and the truth. Two forms of censorship evolved, one in India, one in China, both distinct from the forms of censorship developed in the Western monotheistic religions based on tradition, creed, or science.

Censorship in imperial China and India

Missionaries took the Theravāda or Pāli canon of Buddhism from India to Ceylon, Burma, and Thailand during the empire of Aśoka. Beginning in AD 67, Indian and Chinese scholars took the Mahayana or Sanskrit canon to China and Tibet, and eventually to Japan. Buddhism was still flourishing in India in the 4th century. In the 11th century, monks fled with manuscripts to Tibet. From the 8th to the 15th century, India suffered three successive invasions from Arabia. The Mughal Empire reached its widest extent in the 16th century under Akbar, who returned to the ideal of a united, pluralistic India. In the 18th century, Akbar's grandson, Aurangzeb, reversed Akbar's policy of tolerance.

The Chinese empire was unified in the Sung period, during the 10th century. Confucianism had triumphed, and the "Emperor's Mirror from the Era of Greatest Peace," completed in 983, was compiled as a collection of the whole scientific and literary knowledge available at the time. At the beginning of the 15th century, a vast encyclopaedia, the "Great Handbook of the Era of Eternal Joy," in 11,000 volumes, was assembled. Like the "Emperor's Mirror," it was a collection of all Chinese writings, but it included unorthodox Buddhist and Taoist as well as Confucian works. In the 18th century the Manchu emperor Ch'ien-lung undertook to reduce the "Great Handbook" to manageable size by purging it of unorthodox and seditious books. The results included a new encyclopaedia, an imperial catalog—now indispensable in scholarly work—and two indexes, one of meritorious books, the other of banned books.

The three great empires that unified India without ideological censorship or subjugation of minorities under a Buddhist, a Hindu, and a Muslim emperor were followed by imperial, censorial, and social suppression; and the modern introduction of Western forms of censorship under the British rule led to an independence that separated India into two parts that practiced two forms of censorship, one Muslim scientific, the other Hindu legal. The succession of dynasties that unified China prepared larger and more inclusive, or smaller and more orthodox, encyclopaedias, and China achieved independence of the Manchu emperors and Western powers, first with a Western form of freedom of thought and expression, modulated by administrative and judicial censorship, and then with a Western form of Marxist censorship that reiterates the Legalist ideology of the first encyclopaedia and the first empire: the ideas of force and control, a bamboo curtain rather than a Great Wall, and the hundred flowers rather than the hundred schools.

MODERN CENSORSHIP

Controversies and interpretations in the West in the 17th and 18th centuries. Since the Roman Catholic Indexes denounced the doctrines of the Protestant Reformation as heresies, Protestants for their part analyzed the Indexes as instruments of repression of truth and faith and as promulgations of error and superstition. The Indexes were recommended and used as lists of books to be acquired and studied. Indexes appeared in great numbers, periodically, and in all parts of Europe. They encountered opposition not only because of religious differences, but also because of jurisdictional rivalry. Paolo Sarpi, whose *History of the Council of Trent*, published in 1619, is a chief source of information concerning deliverations and debates in the preparation of the Tridentine Index, advocated in his controversy with Pope Paul V regulation by the state of the temporal powers of the church. He advised his countrymen in Venice not to yield to Roman authorities but to preserve their own right to ban pernicious books, and he argued that the Expurgatorial Index made it impossible to ascertain whether a book presented the author's views or those of the Curia.

It is difficult to reconstruct the early stages of the controversy concerning the Index since arguments against the Index were themselves prohibited and destroyed, and the Index Expurgatorius was at first secret and not given general circulation. The nature, methods, and subjects of controversy were, however, given classical statement by Cardinal Robert Bellarmine, who worked on the Clementine edition of the Vulgate to reduce the inaccuracies of the previous edition of the official translation of the Bible and a friend and adviser of Galileo and one of the examiners of Galileo's works prior to his trial and condemnation, in his *Disputations on Controversies of Faith against the Heretics of the Time* in three volumes from 1586 to 1593 during the early disputes concerning the Tridentine Index of 1584. During the 17th century many replies to Protestant critics of the Index appeared. Jakob Gretser, a Jesuit, wrote *On the Law and Morality of Prohibiting, Expurging, and Abolishing Heretical and Harmful Books* in 1603. Another Jesuit, Théophile Raynaud, differentiated four kinds of books in his *Erotemata on Bad and Good Books and on the Justice and Injustice of Incapacitating Them* in 1653. Some books, he said, are bad and harmful—books of heretics and atheists, books of magic and superstition, and obscene books. Some books are bad but not harmful—polytheistic, Islāmic, rabbinic, and Talmudic books, and some heretical books. Some are not bad but are harmful—some because of the fragility of the reader, some, like books on alchemy, because the practice is dubious, and some because the argument is inane. Some are neither bad nor harmful—books that might stir up disorders, anonymous and pseudonymous books, and books that present new doctrines.

Patterns of censorship established in the West in the Renaissance were modified with the development of new methods of publication, new organizations of religious doctrine, new institutions of nation states, new encyclopaedias of arts and learning, and new modes of communication. The reasons that were advanced to justify censorship were similar to those given by the Greeks: impiety, treason, immorality, and heretical or treasonable science. In the 16th century the emphasis was on heresy and subversion; in the 19th century it shifted to morality and science. Philosophical speculations in the 17th century concerning freedom prepared the way for the formulation of the French and American bills of rights in the 18th century, both of which included provisions for freedom of speech and of the press. The 17th-century Dutch philosopher Spinoza argued, in the *Tractatus Theologico-Politicus*, that the bases of morals, religion, and politics are distinct, and that not only may freedom of thought and speech be granted without prejudice to piety and public peace but they may not be withheld without endangering piety and public peace. The English political philosopher John Locke argued, in his first *Letter Concerning Toleration* (1689), that the commonwealth is constituted for civil interests which do not include the salvation of souls and that toleration of differences is an essential part of Christianity.

Movements for toleration

During the Middle Ages, the universities had assumed the function of judging books. Their judgments had been enforced by ecclesiastical decreta and governmental proclamations. With the introduction of printing, prepublication censorship assumed a new importance. It could be used to control an edition rather than single manuscripts, and agencies of ecclesiastical approbation and governmental registry were formed to authorize the issue of books marked with imprimaturs and licenses. Secular was separated from ecclesiastical censorship in different ways in different countries as the Reformation proceeded. The universities continued to supply experts to serve as members of boards of censors, but the faculties lost their function of preparing corporate judgments of books and doctrines. The task of censoring was broken into parts by the separation of kinds of errors—such as heresy, treason, and obscenity—and kinds of subject matter—such as drama, literature, and science.

The mode of licensing

Licensing was applied in the control of the theatre before it was applied to books. In the Middle Ages, authorization was needed to play in the cathedral or in adjacent courtyards or streets. In France players were prohibited by act of Parlement or were required to secure permits from civil authorities in the 14th and 15th centuries. In 1609, authorization was required for comedies and farces, but the absence of designated licensing agencies left the possibility of conflicts of judgments—as in the case of Molière's *Tartuffe*, which was authorized by the king, prohibited by the Parlement, and placed on the Index by the archbishop. In 1706 special censors were appointed for the theatre, 35 years before the institution of censors for printed works.

In England the official who had authorized the production of spectacles in the Middle Ages had been the Master of Revels or the Lord of Misrule. In 1559 Queen Elizabeth I established a licensing system designed to prohibit plays that presented matters of religion or government not suited for treatment before general audiences. The revenue derived from licensing fees provided a motive for extending the functions of the Master of the Revels after 1623, until all stage plays were prohibited under the Puritan Commonwealth in 1647 and theatres were demolished. With the restoration of the Stuart dynasty in 1660, the licensing of plays was re-established with an emphasis on the control of plays dangerous to religion and morality. In 1698 Jeremy Collier, a nonjuring clergyman and conversationalist, published *Short View of the Immorality and Profaneness of the English Stage*. Many dramatists acknowledge the truth of his allegations, and criticisms, including John Dryden, from whom they elicited a confession of fault and a declaration of repentance. The function of restraining or preventing immorality on the stage reverted to the Lord Chancellor of his majesty's household, and in 1737 the Playhouse Bill conferred the statutory power of licensing plays on that official. In the history of English censorship, the original permissive rule of holiday revelry or misrule was successively modified by the misrule of graft, of puritanical suppression, and of fear of the masses, who might be corrupted and roused to sedition against religious or political authority.

Printing began in France in 1470 when three German printers set up their presses in the Sorbonne on the invitation of the university under the medieval provision of sworn bookdealers (*libraires jurées*). The number of bookdealers and publishers was limited by law, first in Paris, then in all the cities of France. In 1470 the number of printing houses for Paris was four; by 1704 it was 36. Though bookshops and printing houses were searched, and clandestine presses were prohibited, such clandestine organizations for the distribution of manuscripts and books continued to flourish. Books were published with false names of publishers and false places and dates of publication, and prohibited books were smuggled across borders. In 1530 Francis I set up a board of censors, consisting of magistrates selected by Parlement and divines selected by the Sorbonne, and the list of prohibited and permitted books was published by the authority of Parlement and the guild of bookdealer-publishers. In 1563 Charles IX prohibited the publication of books without the permission of the king. In the 18th century, censors were appointed for their competence in different fields: of the 79 censors in 1742, 35 were for belles lettres, ten for theology, ten for jurisprudence, ten for medicine, natural history, and chemistry, and eight for mathematics.

Printing was introduced into England in 1476. Patents were issued by the King's Stationer under Henry VII after 1485, and Henry VIII issued catalogs in 1526 and 1529 prohibiting the publication of works of the Protestant heretics. The Privy Council administered censorship from 1538 until it was transferred to the Company of Stationers, which was incorporated in 1556. Prepublication censorship came to an end in 1695 when the Licensing Act was not renewed, in part because of corrupt practices of the Company of Stationers in licensing. The abolition of prepublication censorship was later described by the English historian Thomas Macaulay as a greater contribution to liberty and civilization than either the Magna Carta or the Bill of Rights.

During the 18th century, fear of disorder "across the waters" (first the agitations of the Jacobite rivals to the English throne and later the turmoil of the French Revolution) and of the enemy within (first the religious dissenters, then the seditious critics such as John Wilkes) led Samuel Johnson and David Hume to view the problem of censorship as one of achieving a balance between the danger of unbounded liberty and the danger of bounding it. Morality, obscenity, and libel changed their effective meanings as the audiences affected by the press increased in size, age, and diversity. Restraints on libel were designed to protect reputations. Even after the lapse of the Licensing Act in 1695, seditious, blasphemous, obscene, and defamatory publications were still punishable at common law, but defamation led primarily to actions for *scandalum magnatum* ("scandal directed at the great"). With the spread of communication and democracy, all men acquired reputations; the crime of "obscene libel" took its place beside "seditious libel."

In France, prepublication censorship continued in the 18th century under a code, promulgated for Paris in 1723 and extended to all France by decree in 1744, administered by the chancellor of France. The character of censorship and of resistance to it varied with the policy of the administration of the publishing industry. Writers of prominence and authority presented numerous and well-reasoned arguments against censorship. Important works by Montesquieu, Voltaire, Rousseau, and many of their contemporaries were published in Switzerland, Holland, or England and circulated clandestinely in France; and the small city of Trévoux, north of Lyons, became a publishing centre for works like the *Journal de Trévoux* and the *Dictionnaire de Trévoux*, published by the Jesuits there because they could not publish in Paris. The prospectus and the first two volumes of the French *Encyclopédie* were attacked for plagarism and irreligion, both in the *Journal* and the new edition of the *Dictionnaire*. On the other hand, during the administration of Chrétien de Malesherbes as director of the *librairie* (that is, head of press censorship) from 1750 to 1763, quarrels of authors, theologians, and booksellers and enforcement of judgments of competent censors proceeded so judiciously that Voltaire called Malesherbes the "minister of literature." Malesherbes was succeeded in 1763, however, by the lieutenant general of the police in Paris.

"Positive" censorship: developing culture

Censorship may be the enforcement of judgments based on power, passion, corruption, or prejudice—political, popular, elite, or sectarian. It may also be based on scholarship and the use of critical methods in the interest of advancing a taste for literature, art, learning, and science. Adrien Baillet, librarian of the advocate general of Lamoignon, found time during the labours of preparing an index of that excellent library to write *Judgments of Scholars Concerning the Principal Works of Authors*. In the first volume, *On Books in General*, he argued for the liberty of authors to write and the liberty of readers to judge. But the art of judging is difficult, and one needs a knowledge of how to judge in order to gain access to the knowledge in books. After examining 14 prejudices, such as the prejudice for the ancients, which influence the judgment of books, information is presented concerning publishers and critiques. The successive volumes provide the reader with further information concerning fields and authors in which he can make his own judgments.

Judgments and regulations in the West in the 19th and 20th centuries. In Revolutionary France, the "free communication of thoughts and opinions" was exercised within the repressive limits imposed by the Reign of Terror and the guillotine. The theatre was never freed from the requirements of licensing. Prepublication censorship was established, and censors were appointed in 1822. Each subsequent change of regime and republic made provision for the licensing of books and plays—within the formula of freedom of writing and printing and in conformity with laws guarding against abuse of the freedom. These regulations were extended to motion pictures after 1912 and later to radio and television.

The evolution of censorship followed a different pattern in 19th-century England. Political censorship was coloured from 1792 to 1832 by the fearful example of what was happening in France and the mounting tension in Ireland. Publication of seditious writings ("seditious libel") or utterance of seditious speech ("seditious words") was a crime at common law. Libel law was liberalized in the Libel Act of 1792 by referring decision concerning whether or not a publication or a statement is seditious to juries. Tom Paine's *Rights of Man* was condemned in 1792. Treason trials against members of the early workers' education and trade-union movement took place in 1794. Membership in societies which take mutinous oaths or engage in seditious activities was prohibited in a series of acts culminating in the Seditious Meeting Act of 1817. Efforts were made to control the radical press as well as radical organizations and meetings. The Reform Bill of 1832 removed many of the causes of complaint and attenuated restrictions on the freedom of the press.

A Society for the Suppression of Vice was established in England in 1802, and Thomas Bowdler issued his "bowdlerized" version of Shakespeare in 1818. Control of the circulation of obscene books extended to bookdealers and lending libraries who found it prudent to refuse to stock a book questioned by clientele, except on demand. The question of freedom and control was a subject of philosophic differences among writers. The philosopher Herbert Spencer argued against governmental restraint of freedom of speech in his *Social Statics* (1851), and the philosopher John Stuart Mill sought to establish the case for absolute freedom of expression in *On Liberty* (1859).

The Obscene Publications Bill was passed in England in 1857. Few prosecutions were brought against serious works of literature in the 20th century, in part because publishers guided themselves prudently by earlier conceptions of obscenity; although D.H. Lawrence's *The Rainbow* was banned in 1915, publication of his *Lady Chatterley's Lover* was not even attempted in England until after passage of the more liberal Obscene Publications Act of 1959. This act differed from the Obscene

Publications Act of 1857 by making statutory provision for the acquittal of works whose publication would be in the interest of literature, science, or learning. A bill to amend the blasphemy laws, which would have removed blasphemous libel from the calendar of crimes, was introduced in the House of Commons in 1930 but dropped. A succession of laws clarified the legal meanings of libel, obscenity, pornography, blasphemy, sedition, and malicious misrepresentation, reducing the incidence of legal repression and removing the danger of a return to censorship. But extralegal pressures and indirect governmental actions continued to restrain the circulation of newspapers, magazines, and books; and censorship continued in drama, motion pictures, radio, and television, and in the self-censorship of publishers and writers.

Liberalization of censorship

The history of censorship in the United States has reflected the diverse censorships of the countries from which the colonists came and the diverse injustices and intolerances from which they fled. The fugitives from repression did not establish freedom of speech and communication in their new communities. The Massachusetts Bay Colony was a censorial theocracy. By law, every Quaker book was burned by the public executioner and its possessor fined ten pounds per book, half of the fine to be paid to the informer. A president of Harvard University said, "I look upon unbounded Toleration as the first born of all abominations." Roger Williams fled into the wilderness to found Rhode Island and to establish freedom of religion and speech. The middle colonies were more humane, and Quakers in Pennsylvania and Delaware tolerated other religions but not infidels and non-Christians. Maryland, and later Louisiana, gave evidence of French respect for and deviation from the Index. Sir William Berkeley, colonial governor of Virginia, thanked God in 1671 that Virginia did not have free schools or printing, "for learning has brought Disobedience and Heresy and Sects into the world and Printing has divulged them and libels against government." The publisher John Peter Zenger was charged in 1734 with "scandalous, virulent, false and seditious reflections" in articles published in the *New York Weekly-Journal*. The jury decided in Zenger's favour on the basis of the truth of the alleged libellous statements, contrary to English procedures, and made a step in advancing the freedom of the press from judicial censorship.

In common law, the publication of such writings or pictures as are of a blasphemous, treasonable, seditious, or obscene character constitutes libel. A libel upon a person is a tort, and the truth of the libel, or the fact that it is a privileged communication, or a fair comment on public acts of public men, is a defense in civil action. A libel on the government or the state is a crime, and in criminal prosecutions the truth of libel is not a defense at common law.

The first amendment to the U.S. Constitution in 1791, by which Congress can make no law abridging freedom of speech or press, has been interpreted as prohibiting prepublication censorship. The control of newspapers and books has taken the form of administrative acts of banning or impeding the distribution of books and printed matter, or nongovermental pressures (such as might be exerted by a local parent–teacher association or chamber of commerce, for example) on booksellers and libraries, and judicial reviews of such actions.

Classified information in government

All four age-old grounds for censorship have been used in those governmental and nongovernmental acts of censorship and in their defense in court when their legality has been questioned. (1) Sedition has occupied a prominent place in such actions from the Alien and Sedition Act of 1798 against "false, scandalous, and malicious writing or writings against the government of the United States," through the restrictions put on the press during wars and immediately after their cessation, to the limitation of access to "classified" information, on the ground that its publication might endanger national safety or diplomatic negotiations or military policy, and to the "credibility gap" caused by the difference between statements of policy released for publication and actions undertaken in the administration of policy. Philosophers such as Francis Bacon have distinguished two methods of communication, the method of disclosure and the enigmatical method, the method of teaching and the method of concealment, which are applied to the secrets and mysteries of religion, policy, and philosophy. The controversy concerning the publication of the *Pentagon Papers* is one more stage in the struggle between censorship and the right to information. Freedom of speech and the press was an issue in the advancement of labour organizations, and free-speech fights were prominent in radical organizations and activities such as those of the Industrial Workers of the World (IWW) in the early 20th century. (2) Impiety and blasphemy functioned as motivations in organized movements for decency in literature, the theatre, and the motion pictures. (3) Obscenity continued to be the subject of legislation to define and prohibit pornography or to regulate its flow through action to be undertaken by the customs or postal services. The importation of obscene literature was prohibited under the Tariff Act of 1842 and its distribution by the mails prohibited by the Comstock Law of 1873. (4) Censorship of science was effected primarily in education, as, for example, in the banning in certain states of the teaching of Darwin's evolutionary theory. The choice of textbooks for public schools has profound effects on the content and orientation of education.

Throughout the world the fundamental force and the basic processes of censorship are being modified, as they have been in the past, by changes in communication, knowledge, and law. As in the past, censorship reflects the movements of peoples and their oppositions, the interplay and the suppressions of cultures, and the cultural perspectives, which have transformed what has been accepted and which have been modified by what has been rejected. Today, two fundamentally opposed frameworks of censorship still operate, but under profoundly altered conditions. In Russia prepublication censorship modelled on the French system was abolished in 1905. Under Communism, the Soviet Union provides no freedom of speech or of the press to enemies of Socialism. The government press has made selected classics widely available, but in the name of protecting Socialism, a great deal of literature and science has been prohibited. A flourishing clandestine circulation of literature has developed, along with sources of publication abroad. In Great Britain and the United States in the absence of prepublication censorship, the struggle against censorship has pressed for a series of judicial decisions that have removed some restrictions and prohibitions. In the wake of these decisions and in response to reactions against established values, all four of the ancient and perennial arguments for censorship—immorality, sedition, treasonable science, and impiety—have undergone paradoxical reversals, moderated only by vestigial limitations defended in the name of the young or of the public good. Obscene words have appeared in print and have been used on the stage and in motion pictures without restraint for the protection of morality, and erotic acts have been portrayed in all three media, though with some lingering concern to repress "hard-core pornography." But such material has not been permitted on radio and television. There is no reliable or scientific knowledge of the psychological or moral effects of the portrayal of violence or sexual acts, but it is unlikely that such lack of knowledge will weaken the conviction of many that it corrupts the young. The control of sedition and treason by banning radical literature, which was in process of attenuation, is rendered even more difficult by the "new radicalism" which the youth evoke against established institutions in general and against established law and order for the advancement of human rights and the removal of newly recognized injustices, the establishment of peace, and the protection of the environment. Large scale science depends on the "establishment" and comes under attack as an instrument for prolonging warfare and extending inequality; and a warfare has been detected between two or three cultures, science and the humanities with the social sciences mediating or enlarging the oppositions. Heresies are no longer proscribed because impiety and blasphemy are as much

Censorship under Communist and Western governments

matters of indifference as obscenity, and ecumenical cooperation of religions is in part an effort to revive a recognition of the "relevance" of religion.

Future of censorship

Censorship in its preventive and prohibitive forms continues, but there is hope that the positive side of censorship will assume a new importance. Statements of opposed ideologies are more easily available and an increased interest in understanding them would contribute to peace and cooperation among diverse political and economic systems. The availability of great books in paperback editions could lay the foundations of a world culture in which the arts and sciences contribute to the appreciation of values across cultural and subject-matter lines. The eternal law governing the movements of things, thoughts, aspirations, and arts reappears from time to time, despite the obscurities which have been thrown over it by the dogmatisms and skepticisms of religion, politics, science, and culture.

The positive form of censorship depends on the availability of information, art, and ideas; on the individual's alert and well-grounded interest in considering, appreciating, and understanding them; on circumstances that stimulate their expression and production; and on confidence in the possibility of sympathy and understanding as restraints on prejudice and discrimination, so making the pursuit of common interests and values possible. The old censorships will continue and will provide stimulation for the new censorship, if it emerges, for it will not be a new imposition but a new actualization of equality of opportunity for self-realization and for education in common values.

BIBLIOGRAPHY. In antiquity censorship was advocated by philosophers, debated by orators, institutionalized by statesmen and jurists, and practiced by conquerors of cities and upholders of traditions; see EDWARD A. PARSONS, *The Alexandrian Library, Glory of the Hellenic World: Its Rise, Antiquities, and Destructions* (1952).

The ancient monotheistic religions, the religions of the "books," like the ancient libraries, prepared lists, or canons, or indexes of genuine and spurious books; or, in the case of religious indexes, authentic, apocryphal, and banned books. For the development of the canons and indexes, see HEINRICH DENZINGER and ADOLFUS SCHONMETZER, *Enchiridion Symbolorum, Definitionum et Declarationum de Rebus Fidei et Morum*, 33rd ed. (1965; Eng. trans. of 30th ed., *The Sources of Catholic Dogma*, 1957); and, for an interpretation of the effect of ecclesiastical censorship, GEORGE H. PUTNAM, *The Censorship of the Church of Rome and Its Influence upon the Production and Distribution of Literature*, 2 vol. (1906). After the 16th century science joined philosophy and theology as sources of error to inquisition and censorship: ANDREW D. WHITE, *A History of the Warfare of Science with Theology in Christendom* (1896); GEORGE G. COULTON, *Inquisition and Liberty* (1938); and JOSEPH M. PERNICONE, *The Ecclesiastical Prohibition of Books* (1932).

In the West censorship was applied to literature and the stage from the time of the Greeks. See JOHN MCCORMICK and MAIRI MACINNES (eds.), *Versions of Censorship* (1962); ALEC CRAIG, *The Banned Books of England and Other Countries: A Study of the Conception of Literary Obscenity* (1962); ANNE L. HAIGHT, *Banned Books*, 2nd ed. (1955); W.M. DANIELS (ed.), *The Censorship of Books* (1954); EDWARD DE GRAZIA, *Censorship Landmarks* (1969); H. MONTGOMERY HYDE, *A History of Pornography* (1964); and ELMER E. SMEAD, *Freedom of Speech by Radio and Television* (1959). See also IRA H. CARMEN, *Movies, Censorship and the Law* (1966).

Political censorship, likewise, has taken different forms in different times and cultures: LEONARD W. LEVY, *Legacy of Suppression: Freedom of Speech and Press in Early American History* (1960); ROBERT B. DOWNS (ed.), *The First Freedom: Liberty and Justice in the World of Books and Reading* (1960); HAROLD L. CROSS, *The People's Right to Know* (1953); JAMES R. WIGGINS, *Freedom or Secrecy*, rev. ed. (1964); RALPH E. MCCOY, *Freedom of the Press: An Annotated Bibliography* (1968); JACK NELSON and GENE ROBERTS, JR., *The Censors and the Schools* (1963); HAROLD SWAYZE, *Political Control of Literature in the USSR, 1946–1959* (1962); PETER COLEMAN, *Obscenity, Blasphemy, Sedition: Censorship in Australia* (1962); and LIN YUT'ANG, *A History of the Press and Public Opinion in China* (1936).

Problems of censorship—of repression, suppression, and control—are treated, more and more, as problems of fundamental human rights and freedoms: MILTON R. KONVITZ, *Fundamental Liberties of a Free People* (1957); HARRY STREET, *Freedom, the Individual and the Law* (1963); DERRICK SINGTON, *Freedom of Communication* (1963); and RICHARD MCKEON, ROBERT K. MERTON, and WALTER GELLHORN, *The Freedom to Read* (1957).

(R.McK.)

Central Africa, History of

In this article, the area designated Central Africa includes what is now the Central African Republic, Gabon, Congo (Brazzaville), and Zaire (former Democratic Republic of the Congo).

The article is divided into the following sections:

I. Developments to the 19th century

EARLY INHABITANTS

Development of toolmaking

The evolution of man in Central Africa is closely associated with the development of the skill of toolmaking and with climatic factors. Most of Central Africa consists of woodland and grass savanna, and it would seem that the reasons this environment gave rise to stone and pebble toolmaking are at least in part cradled in economic and social necessity.

The long dry season of the savanna combined with climatic deterioration to induce the small and very defenseless hominids to develop ways of supplementing their sources of vegetable foods; this, according to some theories, is the reason for the resort to eating the flesh of such small animals as could be caught, and this demanded the development of some sharp cutting tool. Such a tool was necessary in order, for example, to open the skin of an antelope and could at the same time be used to point sticks for digging and even for attack and defense. Detailed knowledge of the development of prehistoric cultural patterns depends heavily on the unique evolutionary sequence laid bare by the British archaeologists L.S.B. Leakey and Mary Leakey in the Olduvai Gorge in northern Tanganyika, outside Central Africa; but inductive reasoning provides substantial evidence that toolmaking spread through most of Central Africa (and, indeed, through western Europe and certain other parts of the world) to form the Acheulian, or hand-ax, industry. The latter term is derived from the most common type of tool, a small, hand-held, biface ax made by chipping a stone core to form a cutting edge.

During the Acheulian industry there took place a population movement into hitherto uninhabited areas, while Acheulian man developed larger and more varied stone tools. At the very end of Acheulian times, some 50,000 years ago, man in Central Africa first became a regular user of fire, probably as a response to the climate becoming cooler and wetter. This, in turn, assisted population increase in areas that previously had been only sparsely populated, and a more sophisticated stone industry, the Sangoan, became dominant throughout most of Central Africa. In the words of the British archaeologist J. Desmond Clark,

> For the first time Man now began to occupy caves and rock shelters as regular homes, for, with his control of fire, these provided safe and more comfortable living-quarters. Furthermore, because of the regulation of the seasonal movements of the bands and the use of efficient carrying devices [both of which can be deduced from African Early Stone Age sites], he could now afford to stay in one place for much

longer. . . . Increase in the size of the band, more permanent residence, and ability to live in a greater variety of habitats, previously unfavourable, must have been the inevitable concomitant of increasing technical skill and mental ability.

From about 35,000 BC, Middle Stone Age cultures began to evolve from the Sangoan; and in the Congo forests, which comprise much of Central Africa, its local variant is known as the Lupemban culture, a culture characterized by many types of ax and magnificent lanceolate knives. It is in this period that *Homo sapiens* evolved by natural selection from earlier hominoid types with an accompanying appearance of religious beliefs, manifested in careful burial of the dead, and of an aesthetic sense, shown by the use of paint and ornamentation.

Evolution of *Homo sapiens*

The Middle Stone Age lasted until 10,000–8000 BC; and during its last period (as during the so-called Makalian period—*c.* 5500–2500 BC) a wetter and cooler climate, which improved water supplies and made possible a southward extension of Mediterranean flora, led to north–south contacts between Mediterranean and Negroid peoples. These contacts resulted, for example, in the appearance of tanged projectile heads in the Congo, while the later of the two wet phases gave a new significance to waterside habitats, and rivers and lakes were exploited for their food resources as never before.

This later Stone Age also witnessed such further technical advances as the bow and arrow, the discovery and use of poison, and barbed fish spears, and probably the beginnings in some areas of primitive cultivation. Also evident is the emergence of distinctive culture variants, with those on plateaus differing from those in the forests. Around the beginning of the Christian Era a development of critical importance took place—stone tools began to be replaced by metal, possibly accompanied by the introduction of Asian food plants. This, in turn, made possible the spread of Negroid and Bantu culture in Central Africa and beyond, a theme that dominates the study of Central Africa during the next 1,000–1,500 years.

In the study of the early stages of Bantu expansion the linguistic evidence predominates. From a lexical comparison of about 50 common words in Western Sudanic and Bantu languages, the American scholar Joseph H. Greenberg concluded that Bantu languages belonged to the Western Sudanic family but that they did not even form a distinctive subgroup within this family; rather, they formed part of a subgroup that also included most of the languages spoken in east central Nigeria and the Cameroons. From this, Greenberg concluded that, when the speakers of the Western Sudanic languages began to move southward from the savanna into the forest belt, those at the eastern end of the line of advance, not being stopped by the sea, continued southward and eastward into the Congo Basin and thence fanned out to occupy what is now Bantu Africa. To this theory another U.S. anthropologist, G.P. Murdock, added an important condition of this expansion—that these Western Sudanic peoples had received Southeast Asian food plants, which had made their way to the far-western coast after entering Africa through the lowlands of Ethiopia. A linguistic contribution of equal or greater importance with Greenberg's was that of Malcolm Guthrie of Great Britain, whose thorough and wide-ranging approach was through the study of cognates in different Bantu languages; he was able to construct some 2,300 sets of cognates with items from some 200 Bantu languages. From this, Guthrie inferred that all the cognates in a given set evolved from a "general root" in some ancestor language; of such general roots he discovered more than 500 distributed over the Bantu area as a whole. The important historical application of this linguistic research was that it could easily be used to plot the movements of peoples from an original core by simply counting the number of general roots present in each language, expressing them as a percentage of all general roots, and plotting the percentages on a map. The percentages range from about 15 to about 55, with the cluster at the higher end taken as the location of the Proto-Bantu language. That location was "in the bush country to the south of the equatorial forest midway between the two coasts."

Guthrie's study of Bantu languages

In more recent work, the British historian Roland Oliver built on the research of Guthrie and found no necessary contradiction between Guthrie and Greenberg. Greenberg's thesis is a perfectly possible explanation of the movement southward and eastward, while Guthrie's accounts for the first main population increase and the directions and intensity of its expansion. Oliver also did more. He plotted the percentages of general roots on a map and showed that

> the highest percentages form a cluster on the map, in the shape of a long, flat ellipse, with its main axis running east and west, roughly from the mouth of the Congo to the mouth of the Rovuma, with its centre in the Luba country of northern Katanga. . . . On present evidence the explosive nucleus at the heart of the whole system would seem to have been, again and again, the Luba-speaking peoples of the Katanga.

Oliver drew attention to the fact that Guthrie's "long, flat ellipse," with its average rainfall and intersecting rivers, is comparable with what the new arrivals would have known in their original habitat north of the forest barrier. He suggested, on limited evidence, that the important means of their ability to thrust southward was their mastery of iron making, with all the improvement in tools, woodwork, and weapons that this implies, and pointed to the significance of the practice of iron smelting in the Nok culture north of the Benue by about 250 BC. Oliver reasoned that the likely significance of Southeast Asian food plants is in connection with a third stage of the expansion (tentatively dated as during the second half of the 1st millennium AD), not all of which was in Central Africa, for this northward and southward expansion was in the areas of higher rainfall where the Southeast Asian food plants, especially the banana, are known to have played a vital role.

The evidence thus far is linguistic, but Oliver rightly invoked archaeological evidence from the important burial ground of the 8th and 9th centuries AD on the shores of Lake Kisale in the heart of the Luba country. This as yet scarcely worked site, in its sheer size and in the quality and quantity of its grave goods, bespeaks a society of considerable wealth and technical skill.

Traditional and archaeological evidence may help to establish the chronology; much archaeological research remains to be done in Central Africa, but there is substantial agreement that the most promising hypothesis for the Bantu expansion, the dominant movement in Central African history in the first millennium and a half of the present era, is on the lines set out by Greenberg, Guthrie, and Oliver.

CENTRAL AFRICA, 14TH–19TH CENTURIES

The Bantu states. As noted above, the Luba country of North Katanga constituted the heartland of the Bantu expansion. It is therefore appropriate to begin a study of this 400- to 500-year period of Central African history with the emergence of Luba culture and Luba states and then to follow the emergence of the various Lunda states that themselves owed so much to Luba culture, noting also such cultures—only less important, though their territorial sway was more restricted—as those of the Lower Kasai and as the Bolia to the north of Lake Léopold II. Of comparable importance to the Luba and Lunda cultures was the Congo kingdom of the Atlantic coast; because the Congo was the scene of an important early European attempt to disseminate Western culture in Africa, a good deal of attention is devoted to this experiment. The section concludes with some study of the impact on the rest of Central Africa of European influences.

The Luba kingdom. According to tradition, the first Luba state made its appearance during the 16th century. At that time, the whole country between Lake Tanganyika and the Kasai was largely divided into small chiefdoms, and Luba history began with the appearance in central northern Katanga of a powerful warrior, Kongolo, who, after subjecting a number of small chiefdoms, set up his capital near Lake Boya. There he was joined by a hunter, Ilunga Mbili, and his following; but after a

The beginning of Luba history

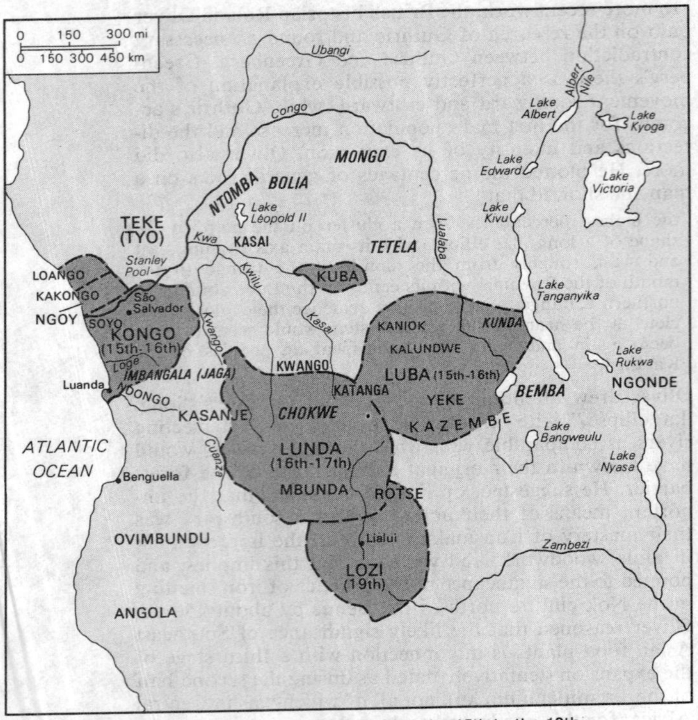

Bantu states of Central Africa from the 15th to the 19th century.
From J. Fage, *An Atlas of African History;* Edward Arnold (Publishers) Ltd.

period of amity Ilunga returned whence he came as a result of a quarrel. Shortly afterward a son, Ilunga Kalala, was born to Kongolo's half sister (Ilunga Mbili's wife); when he grew up, Ilunga Kalala showed great prowess at war and helped Kongolo to extend the area of his kingdom to the west. Jealous of Ilunga Kalala's success, Kongolo sought to kill him, whereupon Ilunga Kalala returned to his father's homeland, where he recruited an army with which he defeated Kongolo, brought the first Luba empire to an end, and established the second. Organized in patrilineal lines, with one or several of such lines forming a village and several villages a chiefdom and with each chief in the line of either Ilunga Kalala or Kongolo, the Luba state pyramid culminated in the king. In an important sense the king was the motive force of the state, because he drew his authority not merely from the fact of belonging to one of the two original lineage lines but also from the divine right to rule, which direct descent from the previous king conferred. Three other states—Kaniok, Kalundwe, and Kikonja—became established as Luba kingdoms during the same period.

The Lunda kingdoms. The Luba kingdoms proper never attained really large dimensions, but Luba influence was paramount in the transformation of the original Lunda kingdom, situated southwest of Luba territory. According to Lunda tradition, a member of the Luba royal house, Cibinda Ilunga, married a princess of the Lunda country and became its king. In the third generation the name of the king gave birth to what was thenceforth the dynastic title of the Lunda monarch, the Mwata Yamvo; and by the close of the 17th century the Lunda state had so far grown as to be bounded, approximately, by the Kasai in the north and south and by the Kwilu River in the west. The political structure of the Lunda kingdom is the key both to its rapid expansion and to the ability of Lunda bands, using the same methods, to set up their own loosely associated satellites in a wide arc from west to east of their homeland. The administrative structure was hierarchical and lineage based, as with the Luba, but in addition, in the words of the Belgian-American scholar Jan Vansina (*Kingdoms of the Savanna;* University of Wisconsin Press, 1966),

Lunda political structure

> the whole political structure rested on the twin mechanisms of positional succession and perpetual kinship. A successor inherited not only an office but also the personal status of the deceased, including his name and kinship relationships.

This meant that the political structure was not bound to the real descent structure and, no less importantly, that Lunda political institutions could be adopted by peoples subjected by Lunda bands without the necessity of great changes in their social structure. Because the Lunda expansion was primarily an affair of small groups gaining recognition by force of arms where the formidable reputation of the Lunda did not suffice, it is evident that there could not have been tight political control, quite apart from the centrifugal tendency implicit in the departure of Lunda bands from the homeland. The Lunda's success was due, at one level of explanation, to their acceptance of the need to secure the assent of the subjected; at another it was due to their technique of government. To quote Vansina again:

> The crucial event in the earlier history of Central Africa has been not the creation of a Luba kingdom by Kongolo and Kalala Ilunga, but the introduction of Luba principles of government into Lunda land under Cibinda Ilunga and their transformation by the Lunda. The new political pattern, which evolved around 1600 in the Lunda capital, could be taken over by any culture. Its diffusion was to condition until 1850 the history and the general cultural evolution of a huge area. . . . It was not the military might of the Lunda which was responsible for the upheavals: it was the superiority and the adaptability of their pattern of government, and the adventurous spirit of the *conquistadores,* who spread it wide and far. And this diffusion was facilitated by the simple fact that this was an open savanna where no natural boundaries could stem the flow.

Lunda influence thus spread in a wide arc from the Kwango in the west to southeastern Katanga. Lunda adventurers brought about the submission of the formidable Imbangala (Jaga) state in Angola, to the west of the Kwango, in the early 17th century. In that same century the Lunda expanded into the more northerly part of the Kwango Basin, and by the end of that century they had established themselves on the plateau of Northern Rhodesia and in southeastern Katanga. In the 18th century the Lunda kingdom, the heartland, expanded southward so that it took in the sources of the Zambezi; between 1750 and 1850, as the outcome of an expansion begun in the early 18th century, the Lunda kingdom of Kazembe, in south central Katanga, was the most extensive and the strongest of all the Lunda states. In the same period the Lozi kingdom in the valley of the Upper Zambezi, although less powerful, also bore its tribute, in both the literal and metaphorical senses, to the Lunda genius.

The Mongo people. But Lunda influence did not permeate everywhere in Central Africa. To the north and west of the Luba, pressing up to the inside of the vast inverted U described by the Congo River, were the Mongo, an ethnic group characterized by the possession of a segmentary political structure based on a grouping, the *etuka,* comprising some half dozen lineages. Only in certain parts of the Mongo cluster—notably in the west and among the Tetela of the east—did the political structure include an area larger than the village or small group of villages.

An important development among the western Mongo was the concept of divine kingship, which was brought westward to the region of Lake Léopold II by the Bolia, perhaps in the 14th century, and diffused by them among other western Mongo, namely the Ntomba group and the Sengele. The western Mongo bordered on the Lower Kasai group of peoples to their west and south. In the 14th century this Kasai group—apart from the Teke (Tyo), who had possibly also developed a form of kingship similar to that of the Congo kingdom (see below, *The Congo kingdom*)—had an unsophisticated two-level chieftaincy system. The village headman was the eldest male member of the senior patrilineal line, while the district chief was the senior member of a single patrilineage. The Teke constituted the largest of these Lower Kasai states: their territory was bounded, downstream and upstream of Stanley Pool, by the Congo River until their border cut across to Mushie on the Kwa, back to

Bolobo on the Congo River, and then described a wide arc in Congo (Brazzaville) to rejoin the Congo west of Stanley Pool. It appears that the most striking developments in the centuries after the 14th are a limited diffusion among the Lower Kasai group of the Bolia concept of divine kingship and the appearance of a variety of political systems, most notably the Kuba, with a sophisticated system of checks and counterbalances of royal authority. Developments of a different kind resulted from the European intrusion into the Congo kingdom and Angola (see below).

Concept of divine kingship

The Congo kingdom. Other than that their earlier history was a part of the Bantu expansion, nothing certain is known about the pre-14th-century history of the Congo people. Sometime in the 14th century, however, the son of a petty chief in the region of Boma, on the north bank of the Congo River, crossed south of the river with a small following, conquered the Kimbundu (Ambundu) people living there, and made himself master of that whole plateau, which included the site of the future São Salvador do Congo. The invaders intermarried with the local people and rapidly either subdued the surrounding area or incorporated existing kingdoms. By some time in the 15th century the core of the Congo (Kongo) kingdom thus included the provinces of Nsundi, Mpangu, Mbata, Mpemba, Soyo, and Mbamba; additionally, territories between the Loge and Cuanza rivers on the southern marches, because they sent intermittent tribute to the Congo king, or *mani* Kongo, can more equivocally be included within the kingdom.

In the kingdom of the Congo the basic political unit was the village, presided over by a chief whose office was hereditary in a core matrilineage. Above the village was the district and above the district, the province, the governor of which, together with many of the district heads, was usually appointed by the king. All these officials were titleholders and constituted a self-aware aristocracy. The kingship itself was not hereditary, the monarch being chosen, by a kind of electoral college, from the male members of every line of descent from the founder of the kingdom or, after 1540, from Affonso I. Such a state structure could command an income from taxation and labour service. Tribute was in raffia cloth, ivory, hides, and slaves, and there was also a shell currency, over which the king had absolute control.

An important weakness in this sophisticated political structure was the lack of clear rules for the succession to the throne, and its effects became ever more serious as the number of eligible candidates increased with time. Factions developed years before the likely death of a reigning monarch, while the very existence of separate provinces was potentially divisive. The Congo kingdom, though with increasing difficulty, survived nearly two centuries of considerable Portuguese influence, an influence that brought it some benefits as well as much harm; but interaction of outside intervention with the two above-mentioned institutional weaknesses were important reasons for the decline and fall of the Congo kingdom.

Weakness in the Congo political structure

Portuguese contacts. In 1483 the Portuguese navigator Diogo Cam (Cão), in quest of a passage linking the Atlantic to the Indian Ocean, stumbled upon the Congo Estuary and so first brought that great river within the ken of Europe. Cam sent an embassy to the King of the Congo; but, believing its members to have been forcibly detained and wanting to return to Portugal himself, Cam took with him some Congolese hostages against the return of his own men when he should make a second voyage to the Congo. The Congolese hostages were evidently well treated in Portugal and returned full of praise for Christianity and things European; powerful though their testimony was, the appeal of the newly revealed European culture to the Congolese generally was enhanced because it was borne to them in ships issuing out of the sea, which was traditionally the domain of the sacred. Entirely credible was the Congolese king's request to John II of Portugal, spelled out by a contemporary Portuguese chronicler:

> he asked him in his grace and required him in the name of God to accord him without delay that which with so much love and devotion he had invited him to receive, the Holy Water of Baptism.

To this was joined a request for Portuguese artisans to instruct the Congolese, while other Congolese youths were sent to Portugal to learn to read and write and to become Christians.

Portuguese missionaries. A considerable Portuguese missionary effort resulted. The King of Portugal responded to the original request with an expedition despatched in 1491. The missionaries were Portuguese secular clergy and found early triumphs in the baptism of the Governor of Soyo and subsequently of the King of Congo himself, who took the European name of John I, and of most of the nobility. John's successor, Affonso I (ruled 1506–43), was a completely serious and devoted convert who worked hard to further the conversion of his kingdom. According to a tradition recorded by J. Cuvelier, Belgian missionary and historian in 1946, Affonso called all his nobles together and told them:

> Cease to honour fetishes, to believe in amulets, now that we have seen the Cross of the Son of God. . . . Whoever honours them will be condemned to death.

But even Affonso's considerable efforts were vitiated by the inability of Portugal to supply enough priests, and too many of those who came were either unsuited or succumbed to the climate. After the triumphs of the initial period, which ended with Affonso's death, the most fruitful missionary work was probably that of the Italian and Spanish Capuchins, who, for two centuries after 1645, bore their witness of poverty, austerity, and devotion, though from the beginning of the 18th century in declining numbers and with declining effect.

Interestingly, at the very beginning of the 18th century the Congo witnessed a prophet movement—Antonianism, the name of a politico-religious sect centring on a young Congolese woman, Kimpa Vita, who took the name Saint Anthony. This movement, though it attested the tension between old beliefs and the new faith, no less showed that Christianity had significantly entered into the life of the Congo. (It was also a most interesting forerunner of a not dissimilar movement in 20th-century Congo land, see Kimbanguism under *Belgium's Congo policies* below.) All in all, there is credibility in a Capuchin missionary's assessment of 1710:

> It is true that the Congolese, and much more those who were at San Salvador, embraced the holy faith completely and lovingly. They had a true knowledge of it and became true Christians. However, in the provinces, the peasants were subsequently baptised always in too great numbers, but never had the true knowledge of the faith. They never abandoned their pagan customs. . . . That being said, I would say that Christianity in the Congo is at present a true Christianity, catholic and Roman, but much weakened by ignorance, war and superstition.

But, by the end of the 18th century and certainly in the 19th century, the missionary presence was slight, and corruptions of Christianity were widespread.

The original hopes, shared by Portuguese and Congolese alike, of a rapid and authentic Christianization of the Congo kingdom were only very partially realized. But the reasons for this are only partly noted above. Portuguese political involvement and, above all, economic exploitation of the kingdom combined with the interplay of African politics to cause the breakup of the Congo kingdom and in so doing to confirm the verdict of failure on this experiment in acculturation.

Failure of acculturation

Portuguese involvement. A quarter of a century after Affonso's death the warlike Jaga of Angola fell upon the Congo kingdom with such effect that the Congolese king had to take refuge on an island in the Congo Estuary. In this extremity he appealed to Portugal for help, and in 1571 an army appeared from the Portuguese Atlantic colony of São Tomé and, after arduous campaigning and profiting from the moral effect rather than the destructive power of the harquebus (a portable firearm), drove the Jaga from the land. This was the most striking intervention in support of the Congo kingdom that Portugal ever made, and it helped the Congo to endure for another century. But long before this intervention the main weight of the Portuguese presence, other than the missionary, had been harmful. It was not so much that, at least as early as 1512, the Portuguese crown made it abundantly clear that it expected payment for its services to the Congo (although these payments were to include slaves, as well as ivory and copper, a limited and controlled development of this slave trade would not necessarily have done widespread harm); it was rather that the Portuguese crown proved unable to control the Portuguese who went to the Congo, and what the king of Portugal was unable to do the king of the Congo had little hope of achieving. Coinciding as the period of Portuguese involvement did with the rise of the slave trade to São Tomé and across the Atlantic, the great hope of the resident Portuguese was to grow rich on the profits of slave trading, an activity in which a faction of them were commonly abetted by the governor of São Tomé. The most that the Congolese authorities could do, and that not always successfully, was to prevent the enslavement of their own subjects; but a continuing slave trade was possible only if there was continual skirmishing on the frontiers. The problem was compounded by all the possibilities of intrigue that the political structure of the kingdom presented. The autonomous tendencies of the provinces and the bitter rivalries that attended the succession gave abundant opportunity to the slave traders, thus eroding the power of the king, while provincial governors often became virtually independent and the common people periodically suffered greatly from oppression.

Rise of the slave trade

Specifically, by 1556 the Portuguese in São Tomé had opened a direct trade with the loosely attached Ndongo peoples on the southern borders of the kingdom, and in 1560 Portugal ceased to defend the Congo king's monopoly rights in that area (indeed, Portugal soon established its own colony of Angola). Before this, in 1550, the governor of São Tomé and some newly arrived Jesuits backed a rival claimant to the throne, though the plot was defeated. In the 17th century, matters became worse. From at least 1600, Soyo became virtually independent, using its maritime position and the resulting wealth to conclude its own agreements with both Portuguese and Dutch. Soyo openly proclaimed its independence in 1641, by which time there was also frequent trouble in and with the other provinces. The substantial end of the original kingdom came with the Portuguese defeat at the Battle of Ambuíla in 1665, over whether the allegiance of the duke of Wandu was to be to the Congo or the Portuguese colony of Angola, and over the possession of the mines in the area. The enforced abandonment of São Salvador between 1678 and 1703 made the decline of the Congo kingdom clear. By 1795 only about 100 people lived in 22 huts scattered among the imposing ruins of São Salvador's churches.

After Ambuíla the peoples of the Congo still recognized the king but accorded him no significant authority. Effective power was now in a series of chiefdoms, but it was not simply that the top levels of the pyramid of government had been removed, leaving the lower levels functioning in the same way as before. Rather, the whole basis of political power in the Congo region had changed, and it had changed because of the slave trade. The men who gained effective power in Soyo, south of the Congo River, or in Kakongo, Ngoy, and Vili (Loango)—kingdoms north of the Congo River—were those who built up their own bands of domestic slaves and used their strength to supply slaves from the interior to the Europeans on the coast. The political offices that counted were those that dealt with the European slave traders (*e.g.*, the harbour governor, or *mafuk*). Just as the slave trade had been an important cause of the decline of the unitary Congo kingdom, so it both determined the political structure of the chiefdoms that remained and led to such further fragmentation that by the end of the 19th century there was usually no political unit larger than the village.

Changes in the basis of political power

But the effects of the European demand for slaves and of the introduction of guns—which were among the most coveted of the goods the Europeans gave in exchange and the means by which those possessing them raided ever more widely for slaves—were not restricted to the Atlantic coast. The Teke, in the Stanley Pool region, received slaves from up the river and passed them on by a variety of routes to points along the coast from Luanda in the south to Loango in the north. So important was this monopoly that in the 19th century the upriver Bangi (Bobangi) frequently challenged it. Similarly, the Imbangala of the kingdom of Kasanje raided in the Kwango, but most of their trade was probably with the Portuguese in Angola. Nor was this the limit of the effect of the European demand for slaves and the complementary introduction of European goods into Central Africa. From the late 17th century onward, trade routes extended even farther inland, with the Lunda states of the interior sometimes directly participating in long-distance trade but in any event consciously profiting from it. For example, from the late 17th century the Imbangala organized an important trade route back to the capital of the Lunda kingdom, whence, after 1740, the route was extended to Kazembe, where it connected with trade routes from the east coast. The rise of the Lunda states is integrally connected with their use of the guns that reached them along the trade routes from the mid-17th century onward and with the profit they drew from slave raiding and slave trading (as well as with the political structure noted above).

In the mid-19th century, changes came in the Lunda-dominated interior. This was not because of a decline in the importance of the slave trade—when the Atlantic trade ended in the 1860s, slaves were still bought by the coastal peoples and used to produce wealth in exchange for European manufactures, and from about 1840 the Arab slave trade from the east coast became ever more important—but as a result of internal convulsions in the Lunda states. The Chokwe, whose homeland was some 50 miles southeast of Kasanje, were a Lunda people almost unheard of before 1850, but in the next half century they overthrew existing authorities in the Kasai and as far eastward as western Katanga; the Lozi kingdom fell to Rotse invaders from the south; the Yeke, originating in the Nyamwezi country far to the northeast, conquered most of Kazembe and dominated southern Katanga up to the right bank of the Lualaba; by the early 1890s the Arabs from the east coast dominated the country from the upper Lomami almost to Lisala on the Congo River and raided beyond it. But, before this new pattern could settle down, a new and yet more powerful force appeared—the Europeans who were now engaged in establishing formal colonial rule.

Changes in the Lunda-dominated interior

Unifying influences. It would be wrong to exaggerate the extent to which Central Africa between the 14th and 19th centuries was a unity. But a number of factors of different kinds did impose their own unities. This was the first great area of the Bantu expansion; some degree of political unity or, at any rate, association was given by the Lunda expansion, while kingship was widespread. There was much similarity in religion, material culture, economic life, and social organization, and matrilinearity was common; trade routes made possible the spread of maize (corn) and manioc throughout virtually the whole area from their Congo and Angola points of introduction in the late 16th and 17th centuries, respectively. Above all, the slave trade gave its own sombre unity to the area. Indeed, Vansina, who has made a uniquely valuable contribution to the history of Central Africa, concludes his own study of the kingdoms of the savanna with the judgment that

> the interaction between the growing slave trade and the normal evolution of the political systems explains most of the history of the kingdoms in Central Africa from 1500 to 1900.

II. From the 19th century to the present

EUROPEAN PENETRATION IN THE 19TH CENTURY

The previous sections have demonstrated that Central Africa had a history of its own in the precolonial era, albeit a history profoundly influenced by the export slave trade, by firearms, and by trade goods. In the 19th century, however, actual European penetration of the region became more important. Up until the last quarter of the century, that penetration was almost exclusively the work of European explorers, and it is their work that marked the transition between the period when Central Africa, though profoundly influenced by Europe, was autonomous and the era of colonial rule.

European exploration. The 19th-century British explorer-missionary David Livingstone was not the first to explore Central Africa, and indeed he was only peripherally concerned with that part of the continent; but his achievements inspired other explorers, who made more direct contribution to the knowledge of the region, and the felt need to carry relief to him led directly to the major journeys of exploration in Central Africa.

Livingstone's explorations. Livingstone's first journey, begun from his South African mission-station base, was designed to blaze a path northward for the Christianity that it was his passion to propagate. "It appeared very plain," he said,

> that no mission could succeed unless we could get a well-watered country having a passage to the sea either to the East or the West coast. This is a project I am almost afraid to meet but nothing else will do.

Meet the project he did, and his most significant discovery was the course of the Upper Zambezi. This he followed northward until he crossed the divide into the Congo Basin and, after many hardships and much danger, came to the Atlantic Ocean at Luanda.

Significance of Livingstone's explorations

There was a twofold significance in these early explorations of Livingstone, spanning the years 1851–56. In geographical terms he confirmed the hypothesis of Sir Roderick Murchison, president of the Royal Geographical Society, that, in Livingstone's own words,

> the peculiar form of the continent was then ascertained to be an elevated plateau, somewhat depressed in the centre, and with fissures in the sides by which the rivers escaped to the sea.

Moreover, he revealed the border areas of south central Africa to be often fertile, well watered, and well forested. Additionally, the devastation by slave raiders of parts of the Zambezi and southern Congo Basin that he witnessed attested that here was no possibility of simple missionary advance but rather a need for commerce to join with the Christian missionary to extirpate the slave trade. Linked to this and stemming also from the simple fascination of the geographer for search and discovery was a growing conviction of the importance of navigable waterways for the extension of civilization. Only with the beginning of his last journey, in 1866, was Livingstone's work again directly significant for the exploration of Central Africa—in the intervening decade his work had centred on the Middle and Lower Zambezi and on Lake Nyasa. Now his major concern, the quest for the source of the Nile involved him in much exploration in the Lake Tanganyika–Lake Bangweulu–Lualaba River area in order to prove his theory that the Lualaba was the Nile's ultimate source.

Livingstone died in May 1873, 18 months after his famed meeting with the explorer-journalist Henry Morton Stanley, probably uncertain whether in the Lualaba he had discovered the true source of the Congo or of the Nile. But the very impression that his missionary zeal, his devotion to Africa, and his geographical discoveries had made in Britain inspired others to carry on his work. Although one of the two expeditions sent to carry succour to Livingstone itself got no farther than São Salvador when its leader, Lieut. W.J. Grandy, died, the expedition under Lieut. V.L. Cameron, which approached from the east coast, had considerably greater success. Cameron concluded that "the Lualaba had nothing whatever to do with the Nile, but was, in very truth, the main stream of the mysterious Congo." But beyond Nyangwe, in the Manyema country some 200 miles west of Lake Tanganyika, Cameron felt unable to take the obvious course of navigating down the mighty Congo to the Atlantic. This was because he could have obtained the necessary canoes only by seizing slaves with which to pay for them, a refusal entirely consonant with the general conduct of an explorer who was in this respect in the Livingstone tradition. Instead, availing himself of an offer by Tippu Tib, the Arab potentate of the interior, to escort him southward through rich and unexplored country, Cameron entered upon a march to the Atlantic well to the south of the Congo River, which took him through such rich territory as Katanga; he finally reached the sea at Benguella in November 1875. An interesting portent of Cameron's journey was his signing of numerous treaties with African chiefs along his route aimed at securing for his country a species of colonial authority. But the old tradition of noninvolvement in so unpromising an area, as tropical Africa was still thought to be in official circles, was strong enough to secure the rejection of Cameron's treaties by the British government.

Stanley's expedition of 1874–77. Stanley's great transcontinental expedition of 1874–77, financed by the London *Daily Telegraph* and the *New York Herald* and designed to complete Livingstone's work, began with exploration in the Lakes region and an attempt to resolve most outstanding problems concerning the sources of the Nile. But his ultimate objective was to follow the course of the Lualaba and prove conclusively that it emptied into the Atlantic. Equipped with a sectional boat, the "Lady Alice," Stanley took to the water somewhat below Nyangwe and added canoes to his fleet. Soon afterward, when the local people refused to sell the expedition food, Stanley allowed his men to seize it. In addition to major attacks on his expedition, stemming possibly from the unrest into which the country had been cast by the ravages of Arab slave traders, Stanley had to manhandle the boats around the cataracts above present-day Kisangani. Only with the rounding of the greatest of these, which he proudly called Stanley Falls, at the site of the future city long called Stanleyville, did the expedition enter upon what proved to be more than 1,000 miles of navigable waterway. Only below Stanley Pool, the site of what are now Kinshasa and Brazzaville, was the river's course again broken by cataracts. These imposed an overland haul on Stanley until he reached the Congo Estuary at Boma, after a coast to coast journey lasting two years and nine months.

Stanley's attempt to follow the course of the Lualaba

Exploration of the interior. The same series of cataracts that constituted Stanley's last great obstacle had also caused the failure of the first attempt to penetrate up the Congo from the Atlantic. This was the British government's expedition of 1816, led by Capt. J.H. Tuckey. It was then widely believed that the Congo, whose massive outlet was known, was in fact the Niger, which was, from knowledge of its upper reaches, already known to be a major river. Tuckey bestowed on the Congo the highest compliment an Englishman can bestow, namely that "the scenery was beautiful, and not inferior to any on the banks of the Thames," but his own death and the decimation of his expedition by fever shed no light on the course of the river. Nor did a later explorer, Adolf Bastian, penetrate beyond the lower-river region in his expedition of 1858. In the period 1850–65, however, a number of explorers began to penetrate inland from the coast of the French colony of Gabon. The most important contributions were those of Lieutenant Commander Aymes, who led a naval expedition in 1867, and Paul du Chaillu, who reached one of the headstreams of the Ogowe, travelled through southern Gabon, and explored some of the shorter rivers to the north and south of the Ogowe.

Exploration farther into the interior of Gabon was the work of P.S. de Brazza of France in the later 1870s and the 1880s, but by that epoch exploration was positively associated with the founding of colonies, a process that, in Central Africa, had begun in the aftermath of Stanley's transcontinental journey. Stanley himself had developed the hope that the vast lands rendered accessible by the great river he had followed could be opened up to the beneficient operation, as he saw it, of European commerce and humanity. "I had hoped," he wrote in his journal,

> to have inspired Englishmen with something of my own belief in the future of the Congo. I delivered addresses after

dinner speeches, and in private have spoken earnestly to try and rouse them to adopt early means to secure the Congo basin for England.

But, just as Cameron's words had fallen on stony ground in official circles, so did Stanley's in the commercial world to which he primarily addressed them. Disappointed, he was receptive to the invitation of Leopold II of Belgium to undertake a great work for him in Africa, and with Stanley's acceptance began the new stage in African exploration—the closer association of exploration with the foundation and consolidation of colonies.

Colonization

The African enterprises of Leopold II. As sovereign of a small European state that scarcely provided him with sufficient outlet for his energies and enthusiasms, Leopold turned to overseas enterprise as a field for his drive and ambition. Impelled by the conviction that colonial rule, if carried out on the model of the Dutch East Indies, could be both profitable to Belgium and advantageous to the colonized, he also saw colonial achievements as likely to redound to the credit of the dynasty. Leopold realized early on that inward-looking Belgium was unready for colonial expansion; he therefore made numerous bids on his own account to acquire territory in parts of the world ranging from Sarawak to Argentina. All were unsuccessful, but he lit on a different approach in 1876, when, taking advantage of the prevalent enthusiasm for African exploration, he convened a geographical conference at Brussels and saw it accept his proposal for the opening up of Central Africa by the establishment of a chain of rest houses and scientific stations spanning the continent. Little had come of this when Leopold, alone among kings and statesmen, saw the opportunity given by Stanley's revelation of the Congo as a superb route into the interior, subject only to the rounding of the cataracts on the lower river. For the opening up of the Congo, Leopold formed the Association Internationale du Congo and selected as his chief agent Stanley, whose task included further exploration, the establishment of stations, and the blazing of a permanent portage route around the cataracts and the preliminary reconnaissance for the constitution of a railway to link Stanley Pool with the estuary. In the five years 1879–84 Stanley kept up the searing pace of his earlier expeditions and, in addition to making such discoveries as Lake Tumba and Lake Léopold II, established a chain of stations on the river itself. During this period and in the years immediately following, other explorers—often with Leopold's backing and sometimes, indeed, employees of the association—made further significant discoveries. Most notable were the German explorer Hermann von Wissman's three journeys, with the Kasai River system as his main focus and achievement; the penetration up the Ubangi of Alphonse Van Gele, an agent of the Congo State; and the varied work on a number of the Congo's tributaries of the English Baptist missionary George Grenfell. The conclusion of the heroic age of exploration in Central Africa came with Stanley's forcing of a passage over the Congo–Nile divide in 1887–88 and with a mission of exclusively political inspiration, namely the Frenchman Col. J.B. Marchand's great march from Libreville to the Upper Nile at Fashoda in 1897–98.

In the Stanley Pool region, Stanley entered into serious rivalry with the Frenchman de Brazza. This naval lieutenant had reached the pool from the Gabon coast and in this and other journeys undertaken after 1875 laid the basis of the French colony of Moyen-Congo. This rivalry was but a major instance of the political dimension that exploration now possessed and also pointed up the fragility, in terms of international law, of Leopold's Association Internationale. Leopold was aware of the vulnerability of his work now that the powers of Europe were beginning to display some interest in tropical Africa. To meet this and by masterly diplomacy, Leopold played a major part in defeating an Anglo-Portuguese attempt to establish Portuguese sovereignty (with important safeguards for free trade) over the Congo mouth, his lifeline, and obtained both French and United States recognition of his association—all in 1884. He completed the task of acquiring recognition by a series of bilateral agreements with the powers, conducted on the sidelines of the Berlin West Africa Conference of 1884–85, and thereby emerged as sovereign in his own right (*i.e.*, not as king of Belgium) of the Etat Indépendant du Congo (Congo Free State).

An important key to understanding Leopold's creation in the quarter century of its life is its sheer size—the Congo state was some 80 times the size of Belgium—and this combined with Leopold's undisciplined imagination, passion for further expansion, and lack of interest in good administration to give the state its special characteristics. Leopold was fascinated by the Nile, and from the first days of the Congo state's life he began to plan for expansion toward Egypt. Despite these immense African commitments, Leopold maintained his quest for rule or concessions in other parts of the world. From Mongolia to the Canary Islands, from Eritrea to Siberia, he sought lodgments. Well might Stanley complain, as early as 1885, of the "enormous voracity to swallow a million of square miles with a gullet tnat will not take a herring."

The resources for these large enterprises in Africa were inadequate. The Berlin Act, a product of the Berlin West Africa Conference, in creating a Free Trade Zone straddling Central Africa and including the Congo state, had stipulated that there should be no import duties. And, though he was a wealthy man in his own right, Leopold could not sustain the expense of adequately financing his African estate. He was saved by a burgeoning demand for wild rubber following on the development of rubber tires. From 1891 onward, by unusually rigorous application of the principle that all vacant lands belong to the state, by decreeing that taxes could be levied in labour or in kind, by premiums to administrative officers, and sometimes by the making over of whole areas to concessionaire companies, an ever larger tribute of the precious rubber was exacted. Abuses were numerous. In 1899, for instance, a state official told a British consular officer of his method of rubber collection in the Ubangi region. He would arrive at a village, whereupon the inhabitants invariably bolted; his soldiers then started looting and after this attacked the inhabitants and seized some of their women as hostages. The ransom demanded was a couple of goats apiece and the required amount of wild rubber. In this way the official went from village to village until he had obtained his quota of rubber. Nor was this the worst, for on numerous occasions brutality passed over into atrocity. From 1904 onward the earlier, isolated voices of protest were gathered into a chorus of denunciation, a chorus that questioned Leopold's right to continue as ruler of by far the largest colony in Central Africa.

THE CENTRAL AFRICAN COLONIES

The Belgian Congo and its northern periphery. The rubber atrocities were the beginning of the end for Leopold and the Congo Free State; they engendered a public clamour for reform that could not be withstood. The report of the British consul Roger Casement on a journey of investigation through certain of the rubber areas, published in 1904, inspired the Congo Reform Campaign, and such was its pressure that the British government, with the support of the United States government and against the background of mounting protest in Belgium itself, eventually demanded that Belgium take over the Congo. In international law the Congo Free State had no standing; Belgium, however, had its due place in the comity of nations and could be held accountable by the larger European powers in a way that was impossible with the Congo state. Belgians, too, came to see that it was almost a matter of national honour to remedy the evils for which its king was responsible, with the result that a vote to annex the Congo followed Leopold's reluctant yielding to the diplomatic pressure that demanded he give up his private colony and at a time not of his choosing.

Belgian acquisition of the Congo

In an important sense, therefore, Belgium was a reluctant colonial power, a nation that had assumed charge of an empire out of a sense of national obligation and that had no habits of imperial rule to draw upon. But Belgium was also a nation that owed its sure, if modest, stature in the world to the commercial and industrial achievements of its people. It thus naturally hoped that the development of the Congo's resources might yield a profit. Alongside these considerations and assumptions was the belief that Europe had a civilizing and Christianizing mission in Africa, a task that, in the Congo, should as far as possible be entrusted to Catholic missions (Belgium was predominantly a Catholic country). Also influencing Belgium's conduct in the Congo was the extreme pragmatism and distrust of theorizing that seems to be a characteristic of Belgians. These then, rather than any defined national purpose, were the determinants of Belgian policy in the Congo.

Belgium's Congo policies. In the early years of Belgian rule, attention was primarily given to preventing the recurrence of the kind of abuses that had marred the Free State and to fulfilling the various demands of World War I (1914–18). During the interwar years (1918–39), however, the Belgians developed the ad hoc responses of their first decade of rule into more considered policies. World War II (1939–45) had important repercussions in the Belgian Congo, but it was not actually a turning point, because most of the policies of the 1920s lasted into the 1950s and some even to independence, 1960. The new minister of the colonies, Louis Franck (appointed 1918), quickly realized the disarray into which native administration had fallen. He saw a fragmentation of both the administration and Congolese society because of the recognition of a large number of *chefferies*, or chiefdoms, and it was especially clear that many of these *chefferies*, numbering more than 6,000 in 1917, either differed from traditional groupings or were groupings under a chief who possessed no traditional authority. Franck stated that

> the *chefferies* are too small, many chiefs lack all authority. The means of obtaining obedience formerly possessed by the chief have disappeared. The time is not far distant when, if we are not careful, in many regions, the collapse of indigenous authority will be complete.

Franck's solution was to restructure the native administration. The legislative basis was two decrees, of 1926 on Tribunaux Indigènes, and of 1933 on Circonscriptions Indigènes, but the reform process actually preceded the decrees in several areas. In essence the reforms amalgamated *chefferies* that had been wrongly constituted or that were too small to be viable into new administrative entities called *secteurs*. The chiefs of the dissolved *chefferies* would become members of the *secteur* council, and the most suitable one would be made chief of the *secteur*. The administrative authority of this chief would be increased, while the *secteur*'s viability would be built up by the location at its headquarters of a school and a dispensary and of a native tribunal that would administer customary law in civil and criminal matters and that, by express authorization, might also try statutory offenses.

The creation of *secteurs*

The new *secteurs* were to be launched carefully and tactfully so that the chiefs and people would not see them as just imposed groupings. This sometimes happened, but many busy administrators had neither the time nor the insight to carry out such a delicate and difficult task. Africans with experience of European ways—*e.g.*, former clerks or noncommissioned officers—were all too often appointed chiefs; their understanding of European ways made them valuable to the administrators, but their lack of position in traditional society gave such appointments a clear balance of disadvantage. The native policies beginning in the 1920s seemed, in their application, more concerned about regulating traditional life than about restructuring local government to satisfy the people. The world depression forced the accentuation of this tendency by administrative economies of 1933. A reduction in the number of administrative officers left those remaining without enough time for the thorough investigation that was to precede the creation of *secteurs* and put them under greater pressure to find chiefs who would serve as mouthpieces of the administration.

Implicit in the too frequent nomination of acquiescent chiefs was a positive concern to intervene in traditional life. This was an important characteristic of the Belgian presence in the Congo, and its effects were particularly important because the population was relatively small—perhaps 9,000,000 at the beginning of Belgian rule and about 13,000,000 in 1960. An even more overt type of intervention in traditional life, however, was that of large European companies—especially mining and plantation firms. The Congo's rich mineral deposits, especially in Katanga, had been a lure since the early 1900s, and with the mining of copper and other minerals, mining townships developed involving great demands for labour. By the 1920s this created a serious population imbalance in a number of districts, and the administration tried to restrict recruitment. Real change, however, began in 1925 when the Union Minière du Haut Katanga (an extensive Belgian mining company in Katanga) initiated the stabilized-labour policy, whose aim was to form a permanent work force that would necessarily be more efficient. To obtain workers for a minimum of three years, conditions and amenities were improved, and, above all, the workmen were encouraged to bring along their wives and families. This new policy was so successful that by the 1950s enough workers were voluntarily renewing contracts to allow the Union Minière to recruit new workmen almost entirely from the families of older ones. Other large companies followed suit, and pleasant communities adjoining mines or plantations became common features.

Stabilized-labour policy

The motives for the stabilized-labour policy were economic, but it resulted in a significant achievement in controlled acculturation. Considerable evidence, not least in increasing readiness to re-engage, indicates that it met a real need of the African confronted with a new work situation and with new and more complex relationships resulting from the departure from tribal life. Other Congolese, too, were subject to European influences. The peasants remaining in villages were increasingly subject to European intervention. There was a conviction imbued by the depression and voiced by Leopold III, on a tour of the Congo as heir apparent, that there was too much emphasis on mineral extraction and too little on peasant agriculture. As a result a policy of compulsory crop production to encourage peasant agriculture was taken seriously beginning in 1933. During World War II the need to increase the supply of primary agricultural produce by every possible means made compulsion even more onerous. Even after the war, a scheme (the *paysannat indigène*) to resettle peasants under conditions in which production for market could yield them a good living, though its intentions were beneficial, involved major intervention. Pressures in the bush were an important reason for drift to the towns.

Administration and economic enterprise by Europeans were two overt agencies of change. Less obvious but more fundamental change came because of the Christian missions and their schools. Assessment of their impact is difficult because of a wide variation in the degree and mode of acceptance of Christianity and Western education; many Africans who did not seriously accept the new became dissatisfied with the old. There were natural tensions between Western, Christian individualism and the more corporate African life; between a culture that distinguished between the natural and supernatural and one that did not; between a culture with technological sophistication and one with inferior technology. An indication of the cultural stress was the emergence in the 1920s of prophet movements—especially of Kimbanguism, named for Simon Kimbangu, its founder—which protested what were felt to be the inadequacies of both traditional religion and Christianity and which developed some kind of synthesis of them.

Cultural stress during the colonial period

The changes stemming from the Belgian presence were most apparent and least controlled in the towns. There, Africans were involved in a variety of different relationships—with Europeans and with other Africans. An African man was more likely to marry a woman from another tribe so that the marriage became much more an individual compact than a traditional alliance between two groups. A town dweller's friendships, especially if he became educated, were no longer confined to members of his own tribe. He was more aware of European political, technological, and cultural dominance and, if he progressed up the educational ladder, would himself enter the colonizer's culture. And the number of town dwellers was growing. By the end of 1958 nearly a quarter of the Congolese population, a relatively high proportion, lived away from the bush.

Congolese nationalism. It was in the towns, too, that Congolese nationalism was born in the years following World War II. This was because it was in the towns that a Congolese usually entered the colonizer's culture, but, as Bronislaw Malinowski pointed out 30 years ago, the entry itself was usually partial and frustrating; the colonial situation denied an African adopting European ways full admission into European culture. In commerce, in politics, in the drawing room, in the police or army, there was eventually a barrier that could not be crossed without the colonizer yielding up power. Naturally, the better educated Congolese became more aware of this barrier, and it was this class—called *évolués*, in French-speaking Africa—that formed the vanguard of the nationalist movement.

After the war the Belgians tried to satisfy this class by giving it a special status. Originally a small but growing number of *évolués* was, by a process termed immatriculation, to achieve the same legal status as Europeans. But the *évolués* themselves apparently expected the new status to apply to nearly all their number, while the actual scope of immatriculation was greatly whittled down, making it hardly worth coveting. The *évolués*, therefore, felt a double disappointment. Although there are substantial indications of a continuing *évolué* attachment to Belgian culture and rule, from the mid-1950s there was a transition to political activity in order to obtain personal and national emancipation.

Political activity of the 1950s

External influences and forces were important in the nationalist movement's launching and development and, indeed, in determining Belgium's response to it. In 1955 a Belgian academic, A.J. van Bilsen, called for Congolese independence in 30 years. He apparently named such a period in order to be heard by a nation whose pragmatism and whose distrust of the long view had kept it from realizing that African nationalism had become a fact of life. The nationalist movement grew rapidly during the next five years. Some parties evolved out of ethnic cultural associations, most notably the Abako (Alliance des Ba-Kongo) Party. Many others made implicit or explicit ethnic appeals; with the lack of developed national feeling, and with the pillars of the colonial universe shaking and a need for an alternative seat of authority, the natural recourse was to the ethnic group. Some regional parties emerged, however, either because they had only partly reached their professed goal of becoming national parties or because several tribes united in resistance to other tribes they believed were dominating them. An example of the latter was Conakat (Confédération des Associations Tribales du Katanga).

Against all odds, two serious national parties developed. The most significant was the Mouvement National Congolais, led by Patrice Lumumba, which gained meaningful support in four of the six Congo provinces. Its success was apparently a result of Lumumba's charisma and his flair for forming profitable tactical alliances with smaller ethnic parties.

Party rivalries

Serious party rivalries began in 1957–58 and quickly increased as parties felt the need to outbid their rivals. An economic recession in the late 1950s brought unemployment and gave the parties new opportunities. External events, such as Charles de Gaulle's visit to nearby Brazzaville in 1958 and his offer to the French Congo of either complete independence or autonomy within the French Community, had a considerable influence. Meanwhile, nationalist movements elsewhere in Africa were gathering pace, and the Brussels government must have seen that Britain and France, the two major colonial powers, were not resisting them seriously. Moreover, the United States, the major power in the North Atlantic Treaty Organization, could still allow itself the luxury of anticolonial statements. By mid-1959 Belgium's colonial administration had begun to lose control in a few regions, and at the Brussels Round Table Conference in January 1960 Belgium agreed to Congolese independence beginning that June 30.

Belgium did in 1960 only what the major colonial powers had earlier decided to do. It undoubtedly reasoned that the Belgian companies' economic interests, the Belgian planters' livelihood, and the missionaries' and teachers' labours would be assured after independence because the Congolese could not manage without them. It must be said, however, that Belgium left the Congo ill-prepared for independence. Because Belgium failed to think ahead it also failed to prepare Congolese to take over authority by neglecting to give them a significant growing share in it under Belgian rule. Nevertheless, Belgium did give the Congo a number of valuable things, especially in the fields of economic development and welfare, in extensive missionary work, and in a massive program of primary education. Although too many Belgian nationals continued to exhibit a racial arrogance, by 1960 even the virtuous actions of a colonial power could gain no credit.

The French colonies. To the north of the Belgian Congo lay three French colonies—Gabon, Moyen-Congo, and Oubangui-Chari—which, with Chad, constituted Afrique Équatoriale Française (AEF). The three territories together were little more than half the size of the Belgian Congo, and their combined populations probably never amounted to as much as one-half of the Congo's. AEF is commonly compared with the larger French colonial federation of Afrique Occidentale Française (AOF; comprised of Senegal, Mauritania, the French Sudan, Upper Volta, Niger, French Guinea, the Ivory Coast, and Dahomey), which inspired it. In both there was centralization on the *gouvernement-général* at Brazzaville and Dakar, respectively; both were fields for working out the same colonial policies, and both witnessed marked fluctuations in policy aims and methods. The decisive difference was that AEF was always the poor relation.

France had come to possess the AEF area with little positive purpose, and various administrative arrangements were followed in the early years of French rule. The AEF federation was set up in 1908—the same year that the Belgian Congo proper was established. But there had been further similarities. From 1898 onward most of what was then termed French Congo had been parcelled out to concessionaries on the model, seemingly, of the Congo Free State. Similar abuses resulted from the methods used to acquire rubber and ivory, and eventually this led in 1905 to de Brazza's recall from retirement so that he might report on the problem. Significantly, local officials obstructed de Brazza's investigation, but enough of his strongly critical report was published to bring improvement in the so-called Clementel reforms of 1906 (de Brazza himself died at Dakar on the way home). Steadily, the area leased out to concessionaries was cut down to a fraction of its former size, and tighter control was enforced on fewer companies—again, the parallel with Belgian policy after 1908 is striking. But abuses continued and were again brought before French public opinion by writers such as René Maran in *Batouala* (1921) and André Gide in *Voyage au Congo* (1927). Clearly, abuses by concessionaire companies were still being condoned or echoed by administrators. The resulting outcry led to the colonial ministry refusing to extend or renew existing leases.

Parallels with the Belgian Congo

Underlying these abuses was the poverty of the whole area, accentuated by an absence of communications, apart from rivers. French national pride refused to accept the permanent use of the Belgian Congo railway between the Lower Congo and Stanley Pool, but work on the alternative, a new railway from Pointe Noire to Brazzaville, commenced in 1924, only made abuses worse for a time. This was because the absence of sufficient local labour forced the use of conscripted labour from the interior parts of the federation, and insufficient attention to diet and housing led to probably 15,000–20,000 deaths in the construction camps. In the long run, however, the Congo–Ocean Railway brought major benefits by giving the federation a good link, joined as it was by the river route up to Bangui, with the outside world.

(R.T.An.)

Little assimilation ever took place in the AEF, but in the forest regions of Gabon and Moyen-Congo some centralized administrative control was introduced and a hierarchy of village and cantonal chiefs was set up without recognized traditional authority. In other parts of the federation, such as eastern Oubangui, "indirect rule" through traditional rulers continued for lack of an alternative. Administrative problems were compounded by the low calibre and insufficient number of French administrators.

AEF prominence and prosperity

If the AEF was little regarded by Frenchmen before World War II, it leaped into prominence in 1940 under the leadership of Félix Éboué, the West Indian governor of Chad, and became the main centre of Free French support in Africa. The consequent involvement in the war brought muted prosperity, and Éboué became governor general in 1941. He furthered the role of the *évolués* in preparing for self-government before he died in 1944. The postwar years saw notable economic and political advance. In 1946 the foundation by France of FIDES (Fonds d'Investissement et de Développement Économique et Social) introduced an era of modest metropolitan investment and of increased economic activity, which resulted in turn in expansion of health services and education. At the political level, the constitution of the Fourth Republic and the French Union, promulgated in the same year, created federal and territorial assemblies in the AEF whose members included elected Africans.

The constitutional changes of 1946 gave political experience to Africans and stressed the importance of the territories at the expense of the federation. The *loi cadre* of 1956 gave self-government to the territories, and two years later they became members of the new French community as the Republic of Gabon, the Congo Republic (soon to be better known as Congo [Brazzaville]), the Central African Republic, and the Republic of Chad.

(R.T.An./Ed.)

THE REPUBLICS

In 1960 the European powers decided to withdraw from formal colonial occupation of West and Central Africa rather than face the military cost of challenging national aspirations to independence. They hoped to cobble together instant parliamentary regimes that would inherit French and Belgian institutions, but the colonial tradition of authoritarian rule backed by military force was too deeply entrenched, and power generally passed rapidly to military and paramilitary organizations. The military governments adopted a variety of outward political forms—"Marxist" in the Congo, dictatorial and "imperial" in the Central African Republic (CAR), "authentic" and presidential in the Democratic Republic of the Congo, or Congo (Kinshasa; renamed Republic of Zaire in 1971). But the economic realities of continued neocolonial partnership with Europe were little affected by ideological and political debate. Even the revolutionary changes brought by urban unrest in the Congo and rural rebellion in Zaire were never allowed to break the links, though foreign troops had to be flown in on several occasions in the 1960s and '70s to defend the interests of France, Belgium, and the United States. France was particularly successful in maintaining control over the ex-colonial currency and aid programs and benefitted from significant discoveries of oil in Gabon and the Congo. It also extended its influence into Zaire, which remained heavily dependent on the export of copper and highly vulnerable to world price fluctuations. The only nonextractive industry to play an important role in exports was coffee, mainly from Zaire and the CAR. Elsewhere, rural production was neglected, and all governments suffered from a major drift of population to the towns despite inadequate employment opportunities.

(Ed.)

Republic of Zaire. The road to autocracy saw certain differences. Congo (Kinshasa) enjoyed an even moderately tranquil independence for less than a week. Starting on July 5, 1960, there was a mutiny of the Force Publique, the combined army and gendarmerie. Exaggerated reports of counteraction by Belgian metropolitan troops at Matadi led to escalation and to a panic in the country; most Belgians and many other Europeans fled as reports of the killing of Europeans flooded in, and the inexperienced government of Prime Minister Patrice Lumumba was, understandably, unequal to the occasion.

Mutiny of the Force Publique

United Nations intervention. United Nations intervention began in mid-July, desired by the Congolese government as a means of getting Belgian troops out and by member states as a means of preventing both anarchy and the escalation of the situation. Because its military contingents remained in Congo (Kinshasa) for four years, the United Nations necessarily became a force in Congolese politics. Because there were no real precedents for the role it must fulfill, once it departed from a posture of nonintervention in the affairs of a member state, its actions were controversial in the view of some member nations and of factions in the Congo. Agreement in the United Nations on policy could be obtained only by refuge in ambiguities, which it was left to the secretary generals, Dag Hammarsjköld and his successor, U Thant, to resolve. Particularly controversial was its action or, as some thought, inaction over Katanga (now Shaba) province, which had seceded from Congo (Kinshasa) on July 11, 1960. The secession, aided by Belgian officers and civilians, of the wealthiest of the Congo's provinces was a major problem for the government in Léopoldville (renamed Kinshasa in 1966); the apparent role of Katanga's prime minister, Moise Tshombe, as a puppet of Belgian mining interests gave the secession a broader significance. In fact, however, the Katanga government, though dependent for its survival on Belgian aid, was no one's puppet. This did not, however, prevent its collapse when the United Nations took the offensive at the end of 1962.

Meanwhile, secessionist attempts, accompanied by intertribal warfare, in northeastern Congo and in South Kasai, had also been ended. But the dismissal of Lumumba by Pres. Joseph Kasavubu in September 1960, a military coup presided over by Col. Joseph-Désiré Mobutu, and five months' rule by a college of commissioners set up by Mobutu, indicated a fundamental political instability that was only apparently ended by Prime Minister Cyrille Adoula, whose three-year government began in August 1961. More dramatically, Patrice Lumumba, who after his dismissal had fallen into the hands of the college of commissioners, was murdered in Katanga.

(R.T.An./Ed.)

Rebellion. After a period of increasing difficulty in financing the UN Congo peacekeeping operation, it came to an end in mid-1964. No sooner had the last UN troops left the Congo in 1964 than the country again erupted into rebellion, especially in the Kwilu region and the eastern and northeastern parts of the country. Enjoying some external aid, the rebels for a time carried all before them and at one time denied to the central government control of about half the country. In a major political reversal Tshombe was recalled to power in July 1964 as prime minister of the central government. Rebel power in Stanleyville (now Kisangani) was ended by the combined attack of a force of European mercenaries, raised by Tshombe, and of a force of Belgian paratroopers dropped over the city in November 1964. The presence of a few good units of the Congolese army and the bravery of its commander, General Mobutu, combined with the mercenaries' sophisticated weapons and ruthlessness and with Belgian and U.S. logistical support, were enough to drive into forest fastnesses a rebellion whose leadership became increasingly divided.

Tshombe in power again

Mobutu's regime. Division among the leadership was not, however, a prerogative of the rebels. In the autumn of 1965 General Mobutu overthrew Tshombe. As president of the republic he steered a relatively successful course between the radicalism of the educated young and a moderation necessary to attract overseas capital.

Major features of Mobutu's rule were the establishment of internal political stability, the expansion of the economy, and an active program to foster nationalism. The rebellion in Katanga was ended in 1967. In that year a new constitution establishing a strong federal government was accepted by a referendum in which women voted for the first time. In the national elections of 1970, Mobutu was reelected to the presidency. All members of the legislature ran unopposed as members of the one political party, the Mouvement Populaire de la Révolution (MPR), which held its first congress in 1972.

In foreign affairs Mobutu worked to improve international investment and to increase trade with his country's African neighbours. Economic ties with the West were strengthened, and in 1972 full diplomatic relations with China were established. As president of one of the states bordering white-controlled southern Africa, Mobutu allowed guerrillas fighting the Portuguese regime in Angola during the 1970s to take refuge in his nation.

The economy continued to depend upon mining, especially of copper. In 1967 the Union Minière, the largest of all Congo companies, was nationalized amid charges of mismanagement; terms of compensation were agreed upon in 1969. The mines are managed by the state agency Générale des Carrières et des Mines du Zaire (Gécamines). A major hydroelectric project was begun on the Congo River at Inga in 1969; the first stage was inaugurated in 1972, and the final unit (Inga 1) was put into service at the end of 1974. By the late 1970s work was under way on the Inga 2 project. Rising unemployment and low copper prices led in 1973 to nationalization of foreign-owned agricultural land and of controlling interest in foreign-owned mining companies. A second wave of nationalization two years later included all industry, the building trades, and distribution services. In 1976, however, more than half of the companies were restored to the private sector.

Nationalized mines

Nationalization was paralleled by a political campaign to promote nationalism. It began when the country's name was changed to the Republic of Zaire on October 27, 1971. Place-names throughout the country were also changed. A nationality law of 1972 required the taking of Zairian names by all citizens, including President Mobutu, who changed his name to Mobutu Sese Seko.

For 10 years Mobutu was reasonably successful in using copper revenue to maintain his personal authority and satisfy the aspirations of the large administrative middle class. By 1977, however, his balancing act became more difficult, rural areas became restive again, exiles aspired to return for a share of power and prosperity, and the copper province of Shaba (formerly Katanga) contemplated a renewed bid for autonomy. In both 1977 and 1978 the president had to call for foreign, especially French, military intervention to retain power. The military crisis was paralleled by a financial one as U.S. and other bankers invested huge, ill-secured sums in maintaining a regime that was peculiarly hospitable to foreign capital but unable to provide the personnel or infrastructure for real developmental growth.

The Central African Republic. In the years before independence, Barthélémy Boganda dominated the politics of Oubangui-Chari. His party was the Mouvement d'Évolution Sociale de l'Afrique Noire (MESAN), and by 1957 it controlled the territorial assembly. Boganda himself became president of the grand council of Afrique Équatoriale Française (AEF) in June 1957 and sought to create and lead into independence a united Central African state as the heir to the old AEF. This proposal foundered because of the opposition of the principal politician in Moyen-Congo, Fulbert Youlou; and Boganda's death in 1959 left no successor of comparable stamp. David Dacko, the man chosen by MESAN to lead, believed in an organic conception of the state with the party becoming a mass movement, but he never succeeded in ending corruption in the civil service or even keeping it within bounds. His problems were compounded by a near-stagnant and extremely poor economy, and a move to make all civil servants refund 10 percent of their salaries failed.

In 1965 Dacko was overthrown by the army, which ushered in an era of cruel and arbitrary government led by Jean-Bédel Bokassa, who became president for life in 1972 and "emperor" in 1976. The dictatorship only disturbed French diamond and uranium interests when accusation of high-level political bribery in Paris began to circulate. The French government decided in 1979 to remove Bokassa and restore Dacko as their client ruler. Their choice, however, was neither popular nor acceptable to the army, and Dacko was replaced in 1981 by a new military ruler, Gen. André Kolingba, who was better able to balance domestic politics with the realities of French economic control.

The People's Republic of the Congo. The former French colony Moyen-Congo also came under military rule, but it was by a more complex route in which ethnic rivalries played a more evident role. At the time of independence there were two main parties—the Mouvement Socialist Africain (MSA) and the Union Démocratique de Défense des Intérêts Africains (UDDIA). Formally, the former, led by Jacques Opangault, was in the Socialist tradition, and the latter, led by Fulbert Youlou, was in that of the Christian Democrats. The Mboshi and other peoples of the north constituted the main strength of MSA, and the Kongo (Bakongo) of the south, with their Vili allies of the coast, formed the backbone of UDDIA. A crisis developed at the territorial assembly in November 1958, when a vote switch between the finely balanced parties gave Youlou the right to form a government. But there were immediate rioting and deaths in Pointe-Noire, a coastal enclave of MSA strength, followed by much more serious intertribal rioting at Brazzaville in February 1959. Youlou, however, was elected premier and president in November 1959. In August 1963 an attempt to curb the opposition and trade unions led to arrests of union leaders, a general strike in Brazzaville, Pointe-Noire, and Dolisie, the forcible liberation of the arrested leaders, and the resignation of Youlou.

Ethnic rivalries

For the next five years the Congo (Brazzaville) was ruled under a partly presidential, partly parliamentary contitution; and, although Pres. Alphonse Massamba-Débat was a moderate politician, there was a marked shift toward Marxist radicalism, seen notably in the formation of the Mouvement National de la Révolution (MNR) and of its militant youth wing.

The President's dismissal of a conspicuously pro-Chinese prime minister in January 1968 and Massamba-Débat's own apparent ineffectiveness led to a disturbed year until the army commander in chief, Maj. Marien Ngouabi, seized power in August, becoming head of state in 1969. That year the new regime adopted the name of People's Republic of the Congo and the form and trappings of a Marxist state, combined with presidential–one-party rule, but political groupings within the country remained obscure.

During the 1970s Congo politics precariously balanced the factors of regional rivalry, ideological purity, and economic dependency. Violent changes of political personnel were frequent; President Ngouabi was assassinated and Gen. Joachim Yhombi-Opango took the presidency in 1977, and Col. Denis Sassou-Nguesso was inaugurated in 1979. The search for an appropriate Marxist model was pursued against a background of stagnating agricultural and forestry production and a rise in petroleum exports. France remained the largest trade and aid partner, but the United States, the Soviet Union, West Germany, China, Brazil, and Cuba were all involved in development.

The Gabon Republic. Of all the former AEF territories, Gabon was the least enamoured of interterritorial collaboration. It felt itself the loser from the construction of the Congo–Ocean Railway and as the paymaster, from its own buoyant economy, of other members of the federation. Of its close relations with France, on the other hand, stemming from a contact more than a century old, there was never much doubt. Three further important features of Gabon were its considerable economic resources, its relatively small population, and its ethnic (Fang) homogeneity. The considerable and ever-growing prosperity of a state well-endowed with natural resources evidently eased its emergence as an independent nation. Until his death in 1967, the dominant figure in Gabon politics was Léon

Relations with France

M'ba, who had been elected president in February 1961. Friction with his main rival, Jean-Hilaire Aubame, and opposition to M'ba's moves toward a one-party state led to a rising in February 1964 in which the army and Aubame seized power. Within three days M'ba was restored, as a result of intervention by French troops in response to a plea by the vice president. In March 1967 the opposition was forbidden to participate in elections, and in March 1968 the Bloc Démocratique Gabonais was renamed the Parti Démocratique Gabonais and was declared the sole political party, a move that Aubame supported.

Upon the death of M'ba, the presidency passed to Albert-Bernard Bongo (forename changed to Omar in 1973). He successfully administered the country's prospering economy and its apparently stable political structure. Gabon became an important producer of petroleum; unaffected by the international oil crisis of 1974, it acquired full membership in the Organization of Petroleum Exporting Countries (OPEC) the following year. In 1976 Gabon announced its withdrawal from the Organisation Commune Africaine, Malgache et Mauricienne (OCAM). In 1974 construction of a trans-Gabon railway was begun to provide access to interior mineral deposits and aid in the development of the lumber industry. A 115-mile stretch from Owendo to Ndjolé was completed in 1979.

BIBLIOGRAPHY

General: A comprehensive survey of Central Africa is DAVID BIRMINGHAM and PHYLLIS M. MARTIN (eds.), *History of Central Africa*, 2 vol. (1983), which covers the later Iron Age, the trading states, the colonial experience, and the first 20 years of republican independence. ROLAND OLIVER and BRIAN M. FAGAN, "The Emergence of Bantu Africa," in the *Cambridge History of Africa*, vol. 2 (1978), discusses the Bantuization of the region; DAVID BIRMINGHAM, *Central Africa to 1870* (1981), discusses the precolonial experience in three essays reprinted from the *Cambridge History*. See also PIERRE DE MARET, "New Survey of Archaeological Research and Dates for West-Central Africa," *Journal of African History*, 23:1–15 (1982); and the essays collected in FRANCIS VAN NOTEN (ed.), *The Archaeology of Central Africa* (1982), which survey the Iron Age researches of the late 1970s.

The kingdoms: JOSEPH C. MILLER, *Kings and Kinsmen: Early Mbundu States in Angola* (1976), is a pioneering study based on oral and documentary evidence; THOMAS Q. REEFE, *The Rainbow and the Kings: A History of the Luba Empire to 1891* (1981), is a reassessment of Luba history in southern Zaire; JAN VANSINA, *The Tio Kingdom of the Middle Congo:1880–1892* (1973), and *The Children of Woot: A History of the Kuba Peoples* (1978), are both works that transform the basic perception of history in the forest–savanna margin of Central Africa; PHYLLIS M. MARTIN, *The External Trade of the Loango Coast, 1576–1870* (1972), reassesses the impact of European trade in the Atlantic coast; ROBERT W. HARMS, *River of Wealth, River of Sorrows: The Central Zaire Basin in the Era of the Slave and Ivory Trade, 1500–1891* (1981), presents a new social and economic history of the Central African heartland.

Colonial rule: The conquest by King Leopold of the Belgians is surveyed in RUTH M. SLADE, *King Leopold's Congo* (1962, reprinted 1974); and in LEWIS H. GANN and PETER DUIGNAN, *The Rulers of Belgian Africa: 1870–1914* (1978). The fall of Leopold is portrayed in W. ROGER LOUIS and JEAN STENGERS (eds.), *E.D. Morel's History of the Congo Reform Movement* (1968). The later history of Belgian rule is chronicled by ROGER ANSTEY, *King Leopold's Legacy: The Congo Under Belgian Rule, 1908–1960* (1966); J. STENGERS, "La Belgique et le Congo, politique coloniale et décolonisation," in *Histoire de la Belgique contemporaine: 1914–1970* (1975); and MICHEL MERLIER, *Le Congo, de la colonisation belge à l'indépendance* (1962). A valuable economic study is JEAN P. PEEMANS, "Capital Accumulation in the Congo under Colonialism: The Role of the State," in P. DUIGNAN and L.H. GANN, *Colonialism in Africa*, 4:165–212 (1975). Peemans also wrote a monograph on colonial economic history in French, *Diffusion du progrès économique et convergence des prix: le cas Congo-Belgique, 1900–1960* (1968). CHARLES PERRINGS, *Black Mineworkers in Central Africa* (1979), is partly concerned with Katanga (Shaba) province. A major colonial history of French Equatorial Africa is CATHERINE COQUERY-VIDROVITCH, *Le Congo au temps des grandes compagnies concessionnaires 1898–1930* (1972). Historical information can also be gleaned from GILLES SAUTTER, *De l'Atlantique au fleuve Congo: une géographie du sous-peuplement* (1966). See also JEAN SURET-CANALE, *French Colonialism in Tropical Africa: 1900–1945* (1971; originally published in French, 1958); and PIERRE KALCK, *The Central African Republic* (1971; originally published in French, 1971). PIERRE-PHILIPPE REY, *Colonialisme, néo-colonialisme et transition au capitalisme: exemple du Comilog au Congo-Brazzaville* (1971); and BRIAN WEINSTEIN, *Gabon: Nation-Building on the Ogooué* (1966), are useful studies. JOHN A. BALLARD surveys "Four Equatorial States" in GWENDOLEN M. CARTER (ed.), *National Unity and Regionalism in Eight African States* (1966). The best known literary classics on the region are ANDRÉ GIDE, *Travels in the Congo* (1927, reissued 1962; originally published in French); and GRAHAM GREENE, *A Burnt-Out Case* (1961; reissued 1982).

Liberation and independence: The literature on Zaire's decolonization is extensive. Major works include HERBERT F. WEISS, *Political Protest in the Congo* (1967); CRAWFORD YOUNG, *Politics in the Congo: Decolonization and Independence* (1965); and RENÉ LEMARCHAND, *Political Awakening in the Belgian Congo* (1964). Important personal perceptions are given in CONOR CRUISE O'BRIEN, *To Katanga and Back: A UN Case History* (1963); V.S. NAIPAUL, *A Bend in the River* (1979), a novel; and PATRICE LUMUMBA, *Congo, My Country* (1962). A vivid documentary record of the 1960s rebellions is BENOÎT VERHAEGEN, *Rébellions au Congo*, 2 vol. (1966–69). A more recent collection of essays is Guy Gran (ed.), *Zaire: The Political Economy of Underdevelopment* (1979). A concise comparative survey of the first 20 years of independence is CRAWFORD YOUNG, "The Northern Republics, 1960–1980," in BIRMINGHAM and MARTIN, *History of Central Africa*. A standard reference is VIRGINIA M. THOMPSON and RICHARD ADLOFF, *The Emerging States of French Equatorial Africa* (1960). Important events are recorded each year in *Africa Contemporary Record: Annual Survey and Documents*. ELIKIA MBOKOLO examines the end of French colonialism in "French Colonial Policy in Equatorial Africa in the 1940s and 1950s" in PROSSER GIFFORD and WILLIAM ROGER LOUIS (eds.), *The Transfer of Power in Africa: Decolonization, 1940–1960* (1982). Two works on the Congo are HUGUES BERTRAND, *Le Congo* (1975); and RENÉ GAUZE, *The Politics of Congo-Brazzaville* (1973).

(Ed.)

Central African Republic

The Central African Republic (République Centrafricaine) is an independent state located in the centre of the African continent. It has an area of more than 240,000 square miles (620,000 square kilometres) and is bordered by Chad to the north, The Sudan to the east, the Congo and Zaire to the south, and Cameroon to the west. It is thinly populated. In 1968 the government estimated the population to be about 2,256,000, but later UN estimates were about 600,000 persons lower. A census conducted in 1975 reported a population of 2,088,000. In 1981 the population was estimated to be almost 2,400,000. The capital, Bangui, is situated on the southern boundary, which is formed by the Ubangi (Oubangui) River, a tributary of the Congo.

The country has long suffered from isolation and lack of economic development. Upon independence from France in 1960, agriculture was at a subsistence level; there was a chronic trade deficit and a grave lack of funds and trained personnel, so that the country remained almost wholly dependent upon France. By the early 1980s production of cotton and peanuts (groundnuts) had grown substantially, though coffee had fallen off somewhat; and educational and health facilities had been expanded; important mineral deposits had been located.

For historical aspects, see CENTRAL AFRICA, HISTORY OF.

The landscape. *The natural environment.* The republic occupies a vast rolling plateau that rises to between 2,000 and 2,500 feet (610 and 760 metres) above sea level and forms the watershed between the Lake Chad and Congo River basins. In the north the rivers flow into the Bahr (river) Aouk, a tributary of the Chari River. In the south the rivers join the Ubangi River. For associated physical features, see CHAD, LAKE; CONGO RIVER.

Topography

The vast central plains rise gradually to the Chaîne des Mongos (4,593 feet [1,400 metres]) to the northeast and to the Massif du Tondou in the east and southeast. In the west, the Monts Karre (4,000 feet) form a high granite range that declines eastward into sandstone plateaus, dissected by the Lobaye and Nana rivers. Spurs run into the area of Bouar and Baboua, where great round boulders give a chaotic aspect to the landscape.

In the east, gneisses (coarse-grained rocks in which bands containing granular minerals alternate with bands containing schistose minerals) and quartzites predominate. Surfaced with sandstone and occasional granitic knolls, a vast plain gradually climbs from the valley of the Mbomou River to the crest of the Congo–Nile watershed. The rock formations that interrupt the monotony of the landscape reach a height of 3,900 feet (1,200 metres) at Djebel Abourassein.

In the north, in the region of Ndélé and Ouanda Djallé, rock formations caused by the erosion of sandstone cover a metamorphic and quartzite base. The most important mountains are those of the Dar Challa range, which rise to 4,423 feet (1,348 metres) at Mt. Tinga.

In the southeast, an ancient layer of quartzites is covered by horizontal layers of sandstone. This territory forms a plain that gradually climbs toward the crest of the Congo Basin; rivers often cut deep into its landscape. The granite massif (mountainous mass) of ranges surrounding M'Poko and Libby, north of Bangui, forms a zone of hills that traverses the surrounding plain.

The climate is tropical. The Central African Republic lies in a transitional climatic zone between those of the sub-Saharan to the north and the equatorial to the south. In the southern region, the climate is hot and humid; the highlands are cooler and experience more frequent thunderstorms.

During the wet season (from March to October or November) heavy rainstorms occur almost daily and are frequently accompanied by thunderstorms. Early morning fog is also typical. Maximum annual rainfall occurs during August and September, especially in the upper Ubangi region (71 inches) and in the Karre highlands (59 inches). During this season of southwest monsoon (rain-bearing) winds, the temperature ranges between 66° and 86° F (19 and 30° C).

The dry season—brought by the northeast trade winds, or harmattan—generally begins in October and ends in February or March. The air is dry, and temperatures range between 64 and 104° F (18° and 40° C); it is warm during the day and considerably cooler at night. The skies are clear and seldom cloudy, although some dry fog can be observed. Sand or dust storms also occur in the extreme north.

The country lies largely in the savanna (grassy parkland) zone of Africa. While the north is treeless, dense rain forests follow the southern rivers and stretch far into the savanna country. Bush fires in the dry season are a constant threat to the republic's 7,500,000 acres of timberland, which is densest in the Lobaye and Upper Sangha regions.

Animal life

There is a great variety of wild animals. In the dense forests are gorillas, chimpanzees, monkeys, and giant squirrels, while the savanna regions are inhabited by a variety of deer and antelope, buffalo, elephants, and hyenas. Along the rivers, abundant with fish such as Tilapia (an African freshwater food fish), hippopotamuses, crocodiles, and rhinoceroses are to be found. A rich and varied birdlife—in addition to many varieties of snakes, bats. and insects, including many butterflies and moths—

MAP INDEX

Political subdivisions
Bamingui-
Bangoran....... 7·50n 20·15e
Basse-Kotto..... 5·00n 21·30e
Haute-Kotto..... 7·00n 23·00e
Haute-Sangha... 4·30n 16·00e
Haut-Mbomou... 6·00n 26·00e
Kemo-Gribingui . 7·00n 19·00e
Lobaye.......... 4·00n 18·00e
Mbomou......... 5·00n 23·30e
Nana Nambere... 6·00n 16·00e
Ombella-Mpoko.. 5·00n 18·00e
Ouaka........... 6·00n 21·00e
Ouham.......... 7·00n 18·00e
Ouham-Pendé... 7·00n 16·00e
Vakaga..........10·00n 22·30e

Cities and towns
Abba............ 5·20n 15·11e
Adelaye......... 7·07n 22·49e
Alindao......... 5·02n 21·13e
Ancien Goubéré. 5·51n 26·46e
Andjeguéré...... 6·41n 21·03e
Baboua.......... 5·48n 14·49e
Bade............ 6·41n 17·07e
Baïna Bondio.... 5·10n 16·33e
Bakala.......... 3·46n 17·33e
Bakala.......... 6·11n 20·22e
Bakouma........ 5·42n 22·47e
Balakété........ 6·56n 19·54e
Bambari......... 5·45n 20·40e
Bamingui........ 7·34n 20·11e
Bangassou...... 4·44n 22·49e
Bangbari........ 5·12n 22·21e
Bangui.......... 4·22n 18·35e
Bania........... 4·00n 16·07e
Baoro........... 5·40n 15·58e
Batangafo....... 7·18n 18·18e
Batibla......... 5·56n 21·09e
Bayanga......... 2·53n 16·19e
Béle-Kété....... 6·01n 17·26e
Bélézé.......... 3·51n 16·19e
Benima.......... 5·26n 23·54e
Berbérati........ 4·16n 15·47e
Bianga.......... 4·51n 20·25e
Bigéné.......... 3·25n 15·38e
Bimbo........... 4·18n 18·33e
Birao...........10·17n 22·47e
Boali............ 4·48n 18·07e
Bocaranga....... 6·59n 15·39e
Boda............ 4·19n 17·28e
Bodanga Dawili.. 5·33n 16·45e
Bodoupa......... 5·43n 17·36e
Bogangolo....... 5·34n 18·15e
Bogoin.......... 5·10n 18·26e
Bolaï I.......... 4·20n 17·21e
Bossangoa....... 6·29n 17·27e
Bossembélé..... 5·16n 17·39e
Bossemtele II.... 5·41n 16·38e
Bouala.......... 6·23n 15·37e
Bouar........... 5·57n 15·36e
Bouca........... 6·30n 18·17e
Boulouba........ 6·49n 22·15e
Bouméntana..... 6·59n 16·56e
Bouraéré........ 4·44n 17·25e
Boykétté........ 5·28n 20·50e
Bozoum......... 6·19n 16·23e
Bria............ 6·32n 21·59e
Carnot.......... 4·56n 15·52e
Damara......... 4·58n 18·42e
Dekoa.......... 6·19n 19·04e
Délimbé........ 9·53n 22·37e
Dembia......... 5·07n 24·25e
Denguiro........ 5·38n 23·02e
Djema.......... 6·03n 25·19e
Djouho Battinga. 6·38n 20·34e
Dobane......... 6·24n 24·42e
Doumdégué..... 7·29n 18·58e
Fodé............ 5·29n 23·18e
Fort-Crampel.... 6·59n 19·11e
Fort de Possel... 5·01n 19·15e
Fort-Sibut....... 5·44n 19·05e
Gadzi........... 4·47n 16·42e
Gambo.......... 4·39n 22·16e
Gamboula....... 4·08n 15·09e
Garba........... 9·12n 20·30e
Golongoso....... 9·00n 19·09e
Gordil........... 9·44n 21·35e
Gréfodé......... 5·43n 21·33e
Grima........... 3·59n 17·06e
Grimari......... 5·44n 20·03e
Grivai Pamia..... 7·03n 19·26e
Guita Koulouba.. 5·56n 23·19e
Hyrra Banda..... 5·57n 22·04e
Ippy............ 6·15n 21·12e
Kabo........... 7·39n 18·37e
Kaboro......... 6·59n 17·33e
Kaka........... 6·01n 26·30e
Kambakota...... 7·10n 17·54e
Kazanga........ 5·10n 23·06e
Kembé......... 4·36n 21·54e
Kongbo......... 4·44n 21·23e
Koropele........ 4·44n 17·11e
Kouango........ 4·58n 19·59e
Kouki........... 7·10n 17·18e
Koumbal........ 9·26n 22·39e
Koundé......... 6·07n 14·38e
Les Moroubas.... 6·11n 20·13e
Limassa......... 4·14n 22·02e
Mambéllé....... 3·51n 16·42e
Mangoupa....... 5·53n 24·40e
Marali.......... 6·01n 18·24e
Marcounda...... 7·37n 16·59e
Mayaka......... 5·17n 16·52e
Mbaïki.......... 3·53n 18·00e
Mbala.......... 7·48n 20·51e
Mboula......... 4·27n 16·29e
Mbrés.......... 6·40n 19·48e
Mélé........... 9·46n 21·33e
Miaméré........ 8·52n 19·50e
Mingala......... 5·06n 21·49e
Mobaye......... 4·19n 21·11e
Mongoumba..... 3·38n 18·36e
Mopoï.......... 5·08n 26·55e
Mouka......... 7·16n 21·52e
Mpoko......... 4·22n 18·34e
Nao............ 4·35n 15·09e
Ndélé.......... 8·24n 20·39e
Ngadza......... 5·10n 20·12e
Ngolo.......... 9·56n 22·16e
Ngotto......... 4·00n 17·21e
Nguiroungou.... 6·27n 22·37e
Niem........... 6·12n 15·14e
Nola........... 3·32n 16·04e
Obo............ 5·24n 26·30e
Ouadda........ 8·04n 22·24e
Ouamiri........ 6·12n 20·45e
Ouanda Djallé... 8·54n 22·48e
Ouandago....... 7·13n 18·50e
Ouango......... 4·19n 22·33e
Ouomba........ 4·53n 19·04e
Paoua.......... 7·15n 16·26e
Rafaï........... 4·58n 23·56e
Saba........... 7·50n 17·49e
Salo............ 3·12n 16·07e
Sarki........... 6·53n 15·19e
Satema......... 4·18n 21·42e
Sido............ 8·13n 18·43e
Soboko......... 6·49n 24·50e
Taley........... 6·40n 16·23e
Tiroungoulou.... 9·34n 22·09e
Voulou......... 8·33n 22·36e
Yakotoko....... 5·20n 25·20e
Yalinga......... 6·31n 23·15e
Yaloke......... 5·19n 17·05e
Yao Malikidza.... 5·19n 19·36e
Zaorosongou.... 5·02n 16·13e
Zemio.......... 5·02n 25·08e
Zinga.......... 3·43n 18·35e
Zouginindja...... 5·24n 21·40e

Physical features and points of interest
Abourassein, Djebel, *mountain*....... 8·39n 24·14e
André Félix, Parc National, *national park*.... 9·25n 23·20e
Aouk, Bahr, *river*. 8·51n 18·53e
Aoukalé, *river*.... 9·26n 20·50e
Baba, *river*....... 6·25n 17·07e
Badé, *river*....... 4·26n 18·16e
Bakalé, Kaga, *mountains*...... 7·21n 20·29e
Bamingui, *river*.. 8·33n 19·05e
Bamingui Bangoran, Parc National du, *national park*.... 8·00n 19·40e
Bangoran, *river*.. 8·42n 19·06e
Bongo Mountains, see Mongos, Chaîne des
Bongou, *river*.... 6·42n 22·04e
Boulou, *river*..... 6·45n 24·15e
Boumbé I, *river*.. 4·04n 15·23e
Boumbé II, *river*.. 4·08n 15·08e
Chinko, *river*..... 5·40n 24·21e
Dar Challa, *mountain range*. 8·58n 23·28e
Dji, *river*......... 6·47n 22·14e
Goangoa, *river*... 5·48n 25·09e
Gounda, *river*.... 9·25n 20·57e
Gribingui, *river*... 8·33n 19·05e
Kadei, *river*...... 3·31n 16·05e
Karre, Monts, *mountains*...... 6·33n 15·40e
Kerre, *river*...... 5·19n 25·40e
Kobou, *river*..... 6·13n 23·19e
Koddo, *river*..... 7·05n 19·10e
Kotto, *river*...... 4·14n 22·02e
Kotto Falls, *waterfalls*....... 4·45n 21·45e
Koukourou, *river*. 7·32n 19·42e
Koumbala, *river*.. 9·14n 20·42e
Koumou, *mountain*....... 9·34n 23·38e
Lobaye, *river*..... 3·41n 18·35e
Loto, *river*....... 6·49n 24·14e
Mambéré, *river*... 3·31n 16·03e
Manovo, *river*.... 9·12n 20·29e
Mbaéré, *river*.... 3·47n 17·31e
Mbali, Kaga, *mountains*...... 7·14n 21·30e
Mbali Lim, *river*.. 4·26n 18·20e
Mbari, *river*...... 4·34n 22·43e
Mbomou, *river*... 4·08n 22·26e
Mongos, Chaîne des, *mountains*.. 8·40n 22·25e
Nana, *river*....... 5·00n 15·50e
Nana Barya, *river*............ 7·59n 17·43e
Ngaya, *mountain*. 9·18n 23·28e
Ngouo, Mont, *mountain*....... 7·55n 24·38e
Ouada, Djebel, *mountain*....... 8·56n 23·26e
Ouaka, *river*...... 4·59n 19·56e
Ouandjia, *river*... 9·35n 21·43e
Ouarra, *river*..... 5·05n 24·26e
Oubangui, *river*.. 3·28n 18·39e
Ouham, *river*..... 7·59n 17·43e
Oulou, *river*...... 9·48n 21·32e
Pama, *river*...... 4·23n 18·27e
Pipi, *river*....... 7·27n 22·48e
Saint-Floris, Parc National de, *national park*.... 9·40n 21·35e
Sangha, *river*.... 2·15n 16·10e
Tinga, *mountain* . 9·21n 23·38e
Tomi, *river*....... 5·07n 19·19e
Tondou, Massif du, *mountains*.. 7·50n 23·45e
Ubangui, see Oubangui
Vakaga, *river*.... 9·48n 21·32e
Vovodo, *river*..... 4·50n 23·53e
Yadé Mountains, see Karre, Monts

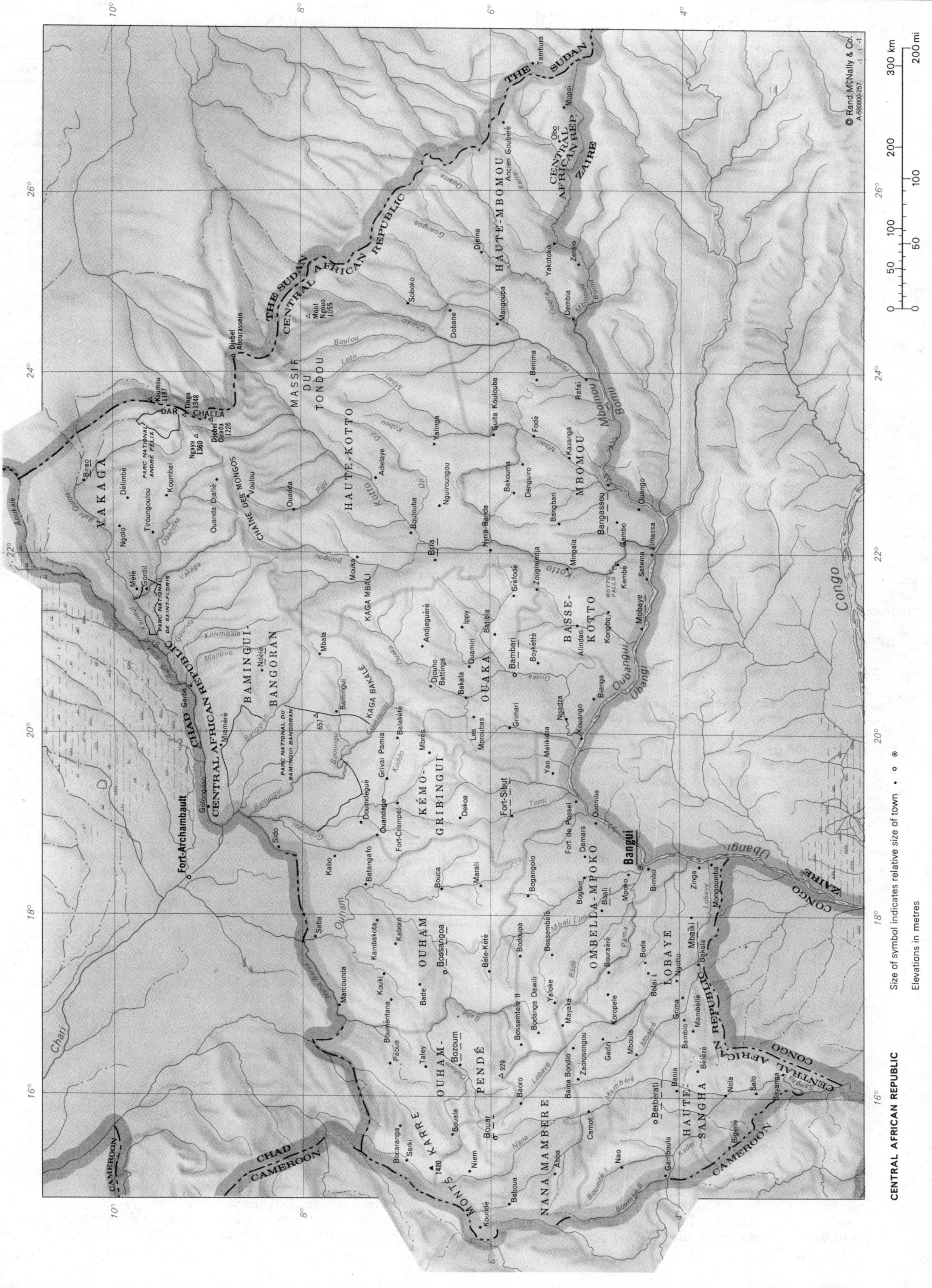
CENTRAL AFRICAN REPUBLIC
Size of symbol indicates relative size of town
Elevations in metres
© Rand McNally & Co.
A-580800-257
0 50 100 200 300 km
0 50 100 200 mi
CHAD
CAMEROON
THE SUDAN
ZAIRE
CONGO
CENTRAL AFRICAN REPUBLIC
VAKAGA
HAUTE-KOTTO
HAUTE-MBOMOU
MBOMOU
BASSE-KOTTO
OUAKA
BAMINGUI-BANGORAN
KÉMO-GRIBINGUI
OUHAM
OUHAM-PENDÉ
NANA MAMBÉRÉ
OMBELLA-MPOKO
LOBAYE
HAUTE-SANGHA
MASSIF DU TONDOU
CHAINE DES MONGOS
KAGA BAKALE
KAGA MBALI
MONTS KARRE
PARC NATIONAL ANDRÉ FÉLIX
PARC NATIONAL DE SAINT-FLORIS
PARC NATIONAL DU BAMINGUI BANGORAN
KOTTO FALLS
Bangui
Fort-Archambault
Birao
Ndélé
Bambari
Bangassou
Bria
Bouar
Berbérati
Bossangoa
Bozoum
Fort-Sibut
Fort-Crampel
Obo
Zémio
Rafaï
Ouadda
Mobaye
Kouango
Damara
Boali
Mbaïki
Nola
Carnot
Baboua
Bocaranga
Paoua
Batangafo
Kabo
Mbrès
Dekoa
Grimari
Ippy
Alindao
Kembé
Satéma
Ouango
Dembia
Djema
Yalinga
Ouanda Djallé
Congo
Ubangi
Oubangui
Mbomou
Bomu
Kotto
Chari
Ouham
Lobaye
Mambéré
Sangha
Kadéi
Ouaka
Vakaga
Bamingui
Djebel Abourassein
Mont Ngaoui 1055
Ngaya 1360
Kounou 1187
Tinga 1348
Djebel Ouada 1226
DAR CHALLA
1420
929
657

makes the territory zoologically one of the most interesting in Africa.

The landscape under human settlement. About 75 per cent of the total population is rural. The main purpose of the country's agrarian reform program (known as "Operation Bokassa") is to alter the organizational structure of the peasant communities so as to raise production and the standard of living. This is to be achieved partly by the creation of large state farms in the form of cooperative-type agricultural centres (one now exists). This policy, however, has met with opposition from the traditional village farmer, whose land and hunting rights are threatened.

Tribal traditions in the savanna country assign men to the tasks of fighting, hunting, and fishing, and it is often considered dishonourable for a male from the age of 15 years upward to till the land. Cultivation is the work of women, who grow a little manioc and a few banana trees around their huts; in the savanna lands peanuts are grown for family consumption.

In the early 1970s the largest urban area was the capital city of Bangui (population 238,000) on the Ubangi River. Other towns were Berbérati (40,000), Bossangoa (36,000) and Bouar (29,000), in the west; Bambari (31,000) and Bria (25,000), in the central plains; and Bangassou (28,000) and Mbaïki (18,000), on the Ubangi.

Central African Republic, Area and Population

	area		population	
	sq mi	sq km	1959–60 census	1968 estimate
Prefectures				
Bamingui-Bangoran	22,471	58,200	19,000	28,000
Basse-Kotto	6,795	17,600	113,000	183,000
Haute-Kotto	33,456	86,650	19,000	44,000
Haute-Sangha	17,127	44,360	83,000	235,000
Haut-Mbomou	21,440	55,530	22,000	54,000
Kémo-Gribingui	14,367	37,210	92,000	134,000
Lobaye	9,459	24,500	72,000	150,000
Mbomou	23,513	60,900	82,000	127,000
Nana-Mambere	10,270	26,600	92,000	199,000
Ombella-Mpoko*	12,528	32,447	130,000	397,000
Ouaka	19,220	49,780	128,000	191,000
Ouham	19,402	50,250	182,000	263,000
Ouham-Pendé	12,394	32,100	144,000	232,000
Vakaga	17,934	46,450	12,000	18,000
Total Central African Republic	240,377†	622,577	1,227,000‡§	2,256,000§

*Including Commune de Bangui. †Converted area figures do not add to total given because of rounding. ‡Including 38,000 nomadic and semi-nomadic tribesmen. §Figures do not add to total given because of rounding. Source: Official government figures.

People and population. The national language, Sango, is a lingua franca, although it has many dialects. A written form is used in mission publications and schools. The official written language is French, which is taught in the schools. Other tribal languages, such as Zande, are also spoken. There is no written history nor does a strong oral tradition prevail.

The east and northeast are thinly populated. Only along limited zones of the Ubangi River and along the Chad border are rural population concentrations found.

Origin of the population

Almost all of the inhabitants of the country trace their origin to settlements established in the 19th century. These came into existence when populations fled from Arab and European slave traders operating between the Nile and the Atlantic: the Baya, for example, arrived between 1805 and 1830 from the north and the Banda between 1830 and 1890 from the Anglo-Egyptian Sudan. These people found asylum in an almost desert-like country, which, since the end of the 18th century, had been depopulated by the slave trade. Therefore, they did not have to fight against an indigenous population. Despite ethnic differences in the population, there was a considerable degree of unity, and tribalism constituted no problem. Since independence, however, a different situation has emerged. In the role of traders and fishermen, the Mbaka, Yakoma, Banziri, and Buraka tribes had served other groups as middlemen, thus providing the colonial administration with an indigenous infrastructure. In the early 1970s, with few exceptions, most leading political figures belonged to these Ubangi region tribes, and other tribes, far more numerous, were beginning to resent this situation.

The Ubangi (a general name for the riverine peoples, numbering about 150,000) live along the shores of the Ubangi River and in Mbomou prefecture; they include the Buraka, the Azande (who number almost 20,000 in the republic but who have 1,000,000 kinsmen in Zaire and The Sudan; they are related linguistically to the 30,000 members of the Ubangi group called Nzakara), the Yakoma, the Sango, the Banziri, and the Mbaka. The Banda (336,000) live in the highlands in the centrally located triangle between Bria, Bambari, and Fort-Sibut; some of their settlements also stretch into Zaire and The Sudan. The Mandja (260,000), who live mainly around Fort-Sibut, are mixed with the Baya (300,000), especially in the southwestern square between the towns of Bouar, Bossangoa, Boda, and Berbérati. The Sara (85,000) are spread along the northern border; their settlements stretch into Chad as far as Fort-Archambault. The Fertit (30,000) live in the northeast. The Mbum (73,000) reach as far as Chad and Cameroon; the majority live a poor and isolated existence in the northeast. The Pygmies (10,000), a remnant of the original population, inhabit the southwestern rain forest. In the 1920s some 15,000 nomadic Bororo-Fulani (Bororo-Peul) settled around Bouar and Bambari; in the early 1970s they were still basically a nomadic people, about 90 percent of whom were cattle herders. The European minority, largely French, numbers about 9,000, and most live in Bangui.

Animism is practiced by 60 percent of the population. Of about 145,000 Christians, the majority are Roman Catholics and the remainder Protestants. There is a small Muslim community in the north.

Since 1955 and especially since 1965, political refugees from the southern Sudan have entered the republic. Numbering about 24,000 in 1971, most were resettled in Haut-Mbomou prefecture with the aid of the United Nations and other international organizations. Some 3,700 refugees from Zaire were considered as being permanent settlers.

The population is unevenly and generally thinly distributed. The annual birth rate was 46 per 1,000 population, the death rate 25 per 1,000, and the infant mortality rate 190 per 1,000 births. About 42 percent of the population was under 15 years of age, and the annual rate of population growth was 2.1 percent.

The national economy. The Central African Republic is a member of the Communauté Financière Africaine (CFA; African Financial Community); the currency is the CFA franc. The country is an active member of the Union Douanière Économique de l'Afrique Centrale (UDEAC; Central African Customs and Economic Union), the Organisation Commune Africaine, Malgache, et Mauricienne (OCAMM; Afro-Malagasy and Mauritius Joint Organization), and other African and international organizations. It is also an associate member of the European Economic Community (EEC).

Mineral deposits

Natural resources. Diamond deposits are located north of Bria, west of Bangui, and near Berbérati. About 8,000 tons of uranium deposits were discovered near Bakouma in 1969; there are also reserves of lignite (brown coal) and peat and coal in the same area, and about 700,000 tons of iron ore have been located near Bogoin. Other known mineral reserves include mercury at Baboua, limestone at Fatuma and Bangui, chalk at Bobossa, manganese at Bour-N'Gam, and copper at N'Gade.

The country's forests represent substantial wealth in such hardwoods as mahogany, obeche (with soft white to pale yellow wood), and limba (a straight-grained wood from a tall whitish-trunked tree). The coal deposits are a potential source of thermal power, and the country's waterfalls, especially Kotto Falls on the Kotto River, a tributary of the Ubangi in the eastern part of the country, constitute a source of hydroelectric power.

Sources of national income. Most agricultural activity is on the subsistence level. Crops grown for domestic consumption include corn, rice, manioc, sorghum, plantain, and sweet potatoes. About one-tenth of the peanuts and one-sixth of the sesame grown are for commercial use. The main cash crops are cotton, grown in the Karre highlands and around Bambari, and coffee, raised particularly in the southwest.

Livestock includes 470,000 head of cattle and 580,000 sheep and goats. Sleeping sickness, caused by the deadly tsetse fly, is a serious threat to cattle throughout the country, and most meat for Bangui is imported from Chad or The Sudan.

Agricultural production has been increased through the development program known as "Operation Bokassa." The agronomical institute (Institut d'Études Agronomiques d'Afrique Centrale) in Wakombo assists in crop diversification; new crops include oil palms, cacao, pepper, rubber, tobacco, and jute. The purchase, processing, and sale of all cotton is a monopoly of the Central African Cotton Union, in which the government owns a controlling interest, in Bangui.

Forestry was little developed in the early 1970s. Commercial rights over 889,000 acres of forests were granted to 12 French and other European companies in 1969.

Diamonds are the most important export product. They represented over 40 percent of the total value of exports in 1970; the diamond industry is the largest in the country, employing about 45,000 people. Uranium mining was expected to begin in 1972 or 1973, with an anticipated yield of 500 to 700 tons of ore annually, which is to be refined at Bakouma. Mining is to be carried out under the auspices of the Compagnie des Mines d'Uranium de Bakouma (Bakouma Uranium Mines Company) in which the government has an interest of 20 percent, the United States Atomic Energy Commission 40 percent, and the French Uranium Corporation 40 percent.

Manufacturing, concentrated in Bangui, was still in the infant stage in the early 1970s and employed 20,000 Africans and 1,500 expatriates. Small factories produce cotton textiles, processed food, soap, and beer; there are also assembly plants for motor bicycles and radios. There is a dairy products plant at Sarki, and a refrigerated slaughterhouse is to be built at Bangui.

Electric power is produced by hydroelectric power stations at Boali, Bouar, Mbaïki, and by a thermal station at Bangui. Total production in 1970 was 45,727,000 kilowatt-hours. Construction was scheduled to begin in 1972 on a diesel power station in Bangui and a hydroelectric station at Kotto Falls. The Banque Centrale des États de l'Afrique Équatorial et du Cameroun (Central Bank of the Equatorial States and Cameroon) is the main bank. Others include the Banque Nationale de Développement de la République Centrafricaine (National Development Bank of the Central African Republic), the Union Bancaire en Afrique Centrale (Banking Union of Central Africa), and the Banque Internationale pour l'Afrique Occidentale (International Bank for West Africa).

Tourism is based on big-game hunting and fishing. The scenery and waterfalls are also attractions, as are the two national parks—Saint-Floris and André Félix. There are also several nature reserves. Safaris are expensive, however, and few tourist accommodations are available, except for luxury hotels in Bangui.

Balance of trade

There is an unfavourable balance of trade. The main export commodities are diamonds, coffee, cotton, wood, and tobacco, which are sold to France, Israel, Italy, and the United Kingdom. The chief imports are automobiles, petroleum products, cotton textiles, and machinery, which are bought mainly from France, West Germany, the United States, The Netherlands, and Italy.

Management of the economy. While the government's economic emphasis is on Socialism, the economy is primarily dependent upon foreign investments and foreign aid. Private investment is negligible, and public government funding has difficulty in finding its priorities. The principal sources of foreign loans and aid are the United Nations, the EEC, the International Development Association (IDA), France, the United States, West Germany, China, and the Soviet Union.

Taxes are levied on property and income. The rural population tends to be taxed more heavily than the urban. All imports, except those from other UDEAC countries (Cameroon, Chad, the Congo, and Gabon), are taxed. Since many items of daily use must be imported, the country has one of the highest cost of living indexes in Africa.

The General Union of Central African Workers (UGTC) is the only labour union. Created in 1964, it had some 55,000 members in the early 1970s; its president is also president of the republic. A central office of social security administers the labour laws and regulations.

Transport and communications. The transport system is controlled by the fact that the Central African Republic is a landlocked country 900 miles from the Atlantic Ocean. The road network was once said to be the best of all the French colonial territories, but the construction and upkeep of the much deteriorated internal road system now consume vast amounts of foreign aid. About one-third of the road system consists of all-weather roads, of which fewer than 50 miles are paved. The main roads run from Bangui through Bossangoa to Fort-Lamy (capital of Chad) and from Bangui, via Bambari, to Tambura in The Sudan.

Inland waterways

There are no railroads in the republic, and waterways are the main means of communication and commerce. The most used is the 370-mile stretch of the Ubangi River between Ouango and Ouadda, which is navigable for ten months of the year (*i.e.*, except in the dry season). The usefulness of this stretch is greatly diminished by its being cut off north of Bangui by 31 miles of rocks and rapids. The Ubangi is again navigable the year round from Bangui to Brazzaville, Congo; from there, goods are shipped by rail through the Congo to the Atlantic port of Pointe-Noire. A number of the Ubangi's tributaries, such as the Lobaye and Sangha rivers are seasonally navigable, but many of them flow through sparsely inhabited regions that are untouched by external trade.

Bangui is the chief port. It has been gradually improved since the mid-1950s and has about 1,000 feet of quays, which handle about 264,000 tons of cargo annually. The port of Salo on the Sangha River is also important, and a port for the evacuation of timber is being constructed upstream from Salo at Nola.

There is an international jet airport at M'Poko, near Bangui. Nine other all-weather airports are capable of taking DC-4 aircraft; 15 are open to DC-3s and 13 to light planes depending on weather conditions. The two local air companies are the privately owned Air Centrafrique and Air Bangui, which both operate regular internal services. Outside Bangui there is no telephone service, but radio contact is maintained with population centres.

Administration and social conditions. *The government.* Since the coup d'etat of 1966, the constitution has been abrogated and the National Assembly dissolved. The president rules by decree, and frequent changes in ministers and ministries have taken place. The president is also prime minister and heads a number of the ministries, including the Ministry of National Defense. Under presidential command, power is held by the National Gendarmerie, the Republican Guard, the river navy, the army (3,000 men, scheduled to be doubled), and the small air force, which consists of about 20 planes. All government officials must take a four-month military training course.

Administratively, the country is divided into 14 prefectures, 46 subprefectures, and four administrative control ports, established within subprefectures. Beneath the subprefecture level are mayors or burgomasters, who are also chairmen of local representative councils.

There is no expression of political opposition in the capital and no focus for concerted action for whatever discontent there may be in the provinces. The execution of the minister of health in 1969 effectively silenced any expression of independent action. In the early 1970s the only political party, the Mouvement d'Évolution Sociale de l'Afrique Noir (MESAN), was headed by the president.

Judiciary

Besides the Supreme Court, a court of appeals, and a criminal court, there are several lower tribunals and a military tribunal. Judges are appointed by the president. The judicial system is loosely based on that of the French. There are traditional courts on the local (subprefecture) level. Disorders sometimes bring prison sentences of between five and ten years.

Social conditions. In the early 1970s between 70 and 80 percent of the population was illiterate. Over 170,000 children were receiving primary education in 2,700 primary schools; 7,200 students obtained a secondary education at 25 secondary schools and two teacher-training institutes; and some 800 attended a secondary technical school. There is also a school of administration, a technical college, the Agricultural College (École Territoriale d'Agriculture) in Grimari, and the agronomical institute in Wakombo. Higher education is available at the Jean-Bédel Bokassa Université de Bangui, which offers courses in law, science, and medicine. Of the university students who study abroad, a high proportion go to France. A trade school is to be established in Bangui for use of the members of the UDEAC.

Health and welfare

In the early 1970s the Bangui hospital was the main health facility, but there were also 36 hospitals on the prefecture level, 36 maternity clinics, about 100 dispensaries, and 200 first-aid posts. All but two of the country's 40 to 50 doctors were expatriates. Sleeping sickness, leprosy, and tuberculosis were rampant. A national institute for the training of public health personnel was established in 1968. Welfare benefits include maternity and child-care allowances.

Cultural life and institutions. Traditional tribal life in the countryside persists, and the stress on tourism is likely to increase the government's attention to the preservation of this cultural heritage. The Musée Ethnologique in Bangui contains exhibits of traditional musical instruments, implements of warfare, and village architecture, hunting tools, pottery, and religious objects. Written histories of the various tribes do not, however, exist.

The press is centred in Bangui. *Bangui La So*, published in French, is one of the two daily newspapers. Government publications include a weekly information bulletin and the *Journal Officiel de la République Centrafricaine* (published twice a month). Newspapers from France and Zaire are available in the capital, but all foreign news publications are censored by the government.

Radio Bangui (Radiodiffusion Nationale Centrafricaine) is owned and operated by the government. It broadcasts programs in French, English, and Sango to most population centres. A television station was being constructed in Bangui in the early 1970s.

Prospects for the future. In the early 1970s the lack of cash in the treasury seriously threatened the republic's economic and political stability. General Bokassa was making a determined effort to maintain good diplomatic relations with a large number of countries in order to overcome this handicap—for example, by possibly obtaining substantial support for the five-year development plan announced in 1971. This plan stressed agriculture, tourism, and forestry. The officially sponsored policy of "Centrafricanization" (replacing expatriate personnel with nationals) had shown few results in the private sector because of the lack of capital and trained manpower. Thus, most development projects were still in the hands of foreign companies that repatriated their earnings rather than investing them in the republic. Under the tense political atmosphere, economic recovery appeared uncertain. Meanwhile, the absence of a parliament prevented the airing of subjects of potential dispute between the political haves and have-nots.

BIBLIOGRAPHY. A good historical survey of the country's development is VIRGINIA THOMPSON and RICHARD ADLOFF, *The Emerging States of French Equatorial Africa* (1960). JOACHIM DE DREUX-BREGE, *Le Problème du regroupement en Afrique Équatoriale* (1968), treats historical development in the wider context of Equatorial Africa as a whole. For reliable and accurate information on current political, social, and economic developments, see the *Africa Research Bulletin: Political, Social and Cultural Series*, and *Economic, Financial and Technical Series*. The German journal *International Afrika Forum* performs a similar critical function. *Jeune Afrique*, supplement no. 423 (1970), provides a somewhat popularized but rather complete survey and description of industry, agriculture, and tourism. Statistical sources vary in their reliability because no official statistics have been released since *Annuaire Statistique de la République Centrafricaine* (1962). "L'Afrique d'expression française et Madagascar," *Europe/France Outremer* (June 1970) is, however, a relatively trustworthy source, although the figures may be somewhat inflated in an attempt to justify European and U.S. economic aid. Projected aid is described in *Development Plans for the CAR* published by the UNITED NATIONS DEVELOPMENT PROGRAM. There is a relatively large literature available on the refugee situation, including reports from the *United Nations High Commissioner for Refugees* (Geneva) and the *Commission on Interchurch Aid, Refugees and World Service* (World Council of Churches, Geneva); while more specifically, the CHURCH WORLD SERVICE, *M'Boki: A Style of Diakonia* (1969); and UNHCR, *The Promise of M'Boki* (March 1969), outline program aims and objectives of voluntary agencies. On cultural life and institutions there are few scholarly or other works.

(J.v.H.)

Central American and Northern Andean Cultures

The Central American and Northern Andean culture area comprises most of Central America (south from Guatemala) and the northern coast of South America (including the northern drainage of the Orinoco River); the West Indies are also customarily included. Although the area has meaning in terms of the distribution of indigenous cultures and languages, it does not coincide with any named region in a geographic sense, nor does it coincide with contemporary national political boundaries.

The area is situated entirely within the tropics, and the seasons are marked more by differences in precipitation than in temperature. Lowlands tend to be hot, but elevation tempers the climate on some of the islands and along the mountain ranges that run through Central America, Colombia, and Venezuela. Areas of heavy rainfall support dense forest, whereas a few dry regions support little more than sparse grass.

NATIVE PEOPLES

In archaeological terms, this area is of strategic significance for various reasons. First, as the relatively narrow corridor between the northern and southern continental land masses, Central America is a promising area in the search for remains of the ancient culture of the palaeo-Indians, of a generalized Mongoloid stock, who moved into South America at least 10,000 years ago. Second, an exceptionally rich and diverse variety of local cultures had evolved in the area by 500 BC. Third, between AD 1000 and 1500 the area was intermediate between the major centres of high civilization in Mexico and Peru.

In this region, unlike much of Latin America, most native cultures did not long survive the arrival of the Europeans, and there is controversy among anthropologists over whether many of the indigenous groups may, by reference to such criteria as language, patterns of beliefs and behaviour, or political affiliation, be justifiably designated tribes. Map 1 illustrates the approximate distribution of about 30 of the best known "tribes" in 1492; nearly 200 "tribes" were reported in early Spanish documents, but descriptions of most are sporadic and imprecise.

Native languages spoken in the area at the time of European conquest were many and varied. Although some historical and structural linkages can be traced with other groups in North and South America, individual languages reflect millennia of relative isolation (see SOUTH AMERICAN INDIAN LANGUAGES; MESO-AMERICAN INDIAN LANGUAGES).

PRE-COLUMBIAN CULTURE PATTERNS

Accounts of the indigenous cultures are fragmentary and based largely on occasional reports by missionaries, explorers, and soldiers. In some instances, widespread and apparently important cultures are represented by little more than archaeological evidence, but it is possible to

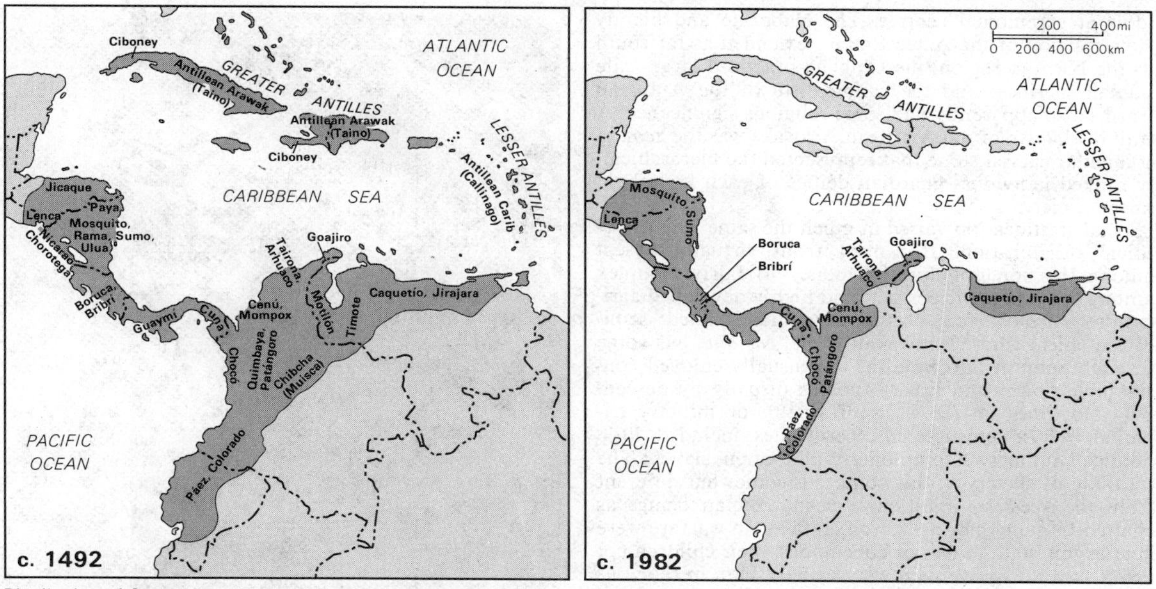

Distribution of Central American and Northern Andean cultures.

note a series of characteristic patterns and variations on those patterns that recur in the area.

Economic practices

With respect to basic subsistence, for example, intensive horticulture by the slash-and-burn (swidden) method was general. A variety of crops, including manioc, maize, sweet potato, bean, and others, were staples in various regions. Numerous other vegetables, as well as tropical fruits and sometimes cotton, were also grown in some areas. This form of horticulture was far more efficient than is popularly believed and produced abundant food without enormous or constant effort. In the cultures of this region, unlike many of those in the Amazon Basin, such intensive farming was usually done by the men. Improvements on the basic slash-and-burn pattern have been rare throughout the world, but in this area they included irrigation, and even occasional terracing, by the Antillean Arawak, Arhuaco, Chibcha, Jirajara, Páez, and Timote, all of whom showed evidence of other cultural elaborations as well. In contrast with such highly developed groups, a few cultures were based more on hunting or fishing than on even simple farming; among those were the Antillean Carib, Chocó, Ciboney, and Motilón.

The form and scale of communities tended to be closely linked to economic activities. Those groups, for example, whose subsistence base was fishing or gathering had the smallest houses and most dispersed settlement patterns in the area. Similarly, the largest and most permanent buildings, as well as the most densely populated villages, occurred among those tribes that had the most intensive and varied food production, including some with highly developed agriculture. The warring expansionist groups, such as the Chibcha and Guaymí, even built palisades around their larger towns, many of which included palaces and temples. Ball courts and large ceremonial plazas were constructed only among the Antillean Arawak, who were unusual in having communities with as many as 3,000 people.

Arts and crafts

The high degree of regional variation in crafts is probably related to the small scale of political organization, in which regional chiefdoms predominated. The hammock apparently originated in this area and was widespread; little other furniture was used. Houses varied considerably in size and shape, although virtually all had palm-thatched roofs and walls of thatch or adobe. A wide variety of baskets was made, usually by women; bark cloth was made in those few regions where loom weaving was unknown. Clothing was simple, usually comprising no more than a breechclout for men and a short skirt for women, and few remains of textiles have survived. Most of the Indians adorned their bodies richly, however, with painted designs, tattooing, and a wide variety of jewelry and feathered ornaments.

Nearly all of the peoples in the area made at least some pottery, and a few of the mainland groups produced exceptionally abundant, fine, and varied ceramics. Excellent in their own right, some of these wares reflect styles, media, and techniques from both the Andean and the Mexican centres of high civilization. The same few groups—notably the Chibcha, Chorotega, Guaymí, and Nicarao—carved jade and other stones and worked copper, gold, and several alloys with an unusual combination of technical skill, imagination, and aesthetic sensitivity. Abundant ornaments were made of metal and of precious and semiprecious stones, both for adornment and for interment in the graves of distinguished men, but few utilitarian tools are known.

Overland transportation was by foot, and widespread trade was carried on throughout much of the area without the benefit of either draft or pack animals. Dugout canoes, often of considerable size, provided transportation from island to island and along rivers.

Outposts of the sophisticated and warlike Aztec Empire extended as far south as the region inhabited by the Nicarao, where military and commercial operations linked what is now Costa Rica with Mexico. In the south the Colorado and Páez peoples of the northern Andes similarly faced the frontier of an empire—that of the Incas—and carried on trade with the centre of high civilization in what is now Peru. The Chibcha proper (also called Muisca) comprised several feudal states, among whom war and tribute were commonplace, and their fine manufactures of gold, copper, and pottery became widespread through extensive trade. Not only were there regular markets but in some regions even a standard of exchange (namely cacao) was recognized.

The majority of the cultures of this region, however, were small chiefdoms, in which a single village or a small group of nearby communities was led by a chief whose semidivine position was inherited through the maternal line of descent. Such men were powerful within limited regions, but widespread confederations of such chiefdoms were rare, and warfare among them was typical in some areas. The Antillean Caribs, for example, had been encroaching on the peaceful Antillean Arawaks just prior to the arrival of the Europeans, taking both territory and captives. In general, it was the cultures with more highly developed agriculture that had the greatest degree of political integration, whereas those with the simplest subsistence economies rarely had any organization beyond the local community.

Religious practices

Shamanism for curing and sorcery, as well as popular worship of natural phenomena, was widespread. In areas of relatively dense population there were full-time religious practitioners who maintained temples dedicated to idols at ceremonial centres. The elaborate and bloody state religion of the Aztec Empire extended as far south as the Nicarao region; the Chibcha practiced large-scale human sacrifice; and the cannibalism of the Antillean Caribs also apparently had some religious significance. A trait distinctive of the Antillean Arawaks was the *zemi*, a triangular carved stone that represented the hierarchically ranked individual guardian deities of each household in the society.

Social stratification varied in much the same way as political organization. It ranged from virtually absent among the nonagricultural Ciboney to fairly complex among the warring tribes that had highly developed agriculture. At most, four classes were differentiated: semidivine chiefs whose Arawakan name, *cacique*, has come through Spanish into English, who usually enjoyed considerable power and luxury; nobles (usually by descent but sometimes on the basis of wealth or military exploits), whose prestige and perquisites included little political authority; commoners; and often slaves. The meaning of slavery in this context is somewhat different from the Western tradition of using human beings as chattel. In many instances, women taken in warfare were kept as low status wives or concubines, their children not being slaves. Captive men were usually slain in religious sacrifice, as human trophies, or for cannibalism.

The idea that a man should have many wives was widespread, especially among chiefs and nobles, and descent was often reckoned through the maternal line, but there is no firm basis for popular accounts of female-dominated societies that were given by some early writers. An unusual outcome of the pattern of marriage with prisoners was the use of Arawak as "the language of women" in Carib society, illustrating how a vanquished people can change the customs of their conquerors.

Cuna Indian woman, Archipiélago de las Mulatas, Panama.
Dan Slaby

EUROPEAN CONTACT AND ITS AFTERMATH

The coming of Europeans resulted in the downfall of most of the cultures of the Central American and Northern Andean region. Few of the chiefdoms survived beyond the 17th century, and none exists in similar form today. Many of the cultures summarily described above are now extinct, including all of those in the West Indies and most of those in Central America. Vestiges of some cultures remain, significantly transformed, in a few areas remote from cities and roads.

Although this was the area first explored by the Spaniards, it was soon surpassed in importance by Mexico and Peru, both of which were rich in minerals and had large native populations accustomed to paying tribute in wealth and labour. Shallow sources of gold in the Antilles were quickly exhausted, and neither Central America nor the northern coast of South America offered much of interest to the conquistadors. None of the peoples of the region worked effectively under the Spaniards.

Disintegration of indigenous cultures

One striking feature that characterizes the history of contact with European culture in virtually every one of these instances is the disintegration or impoverishment of the indigenous culture. Whereas many observers might have expected new and increasing elaborations in those cultures that survived, the opposite has occurred. Agriculture is less varied and less productive; pottery and weaving are practiced less and are less sophisticated, and metallurgy has disappeared. Communities are generally smaller now than they were four centuries ago, and even regional political integration is lacking. The temples, warfare, and class stratification characteristic of many chiefdoms are gone, and, with few exceptions, the contemporary peoples try to avoid contact with others.

Although there had been warfare, trade, and other kinds of intercultural contact in pre-Columbian times, the impact of the Spanish conquest was different in kind as well as in scale, involving as it did not only unprecedented military power but also a wholly new economic system and a deliberate policy of reshaping Indian life to conform to European ideals.

One need not believe literally in the "black legend" about Spanish cruelty toward the Indians to understand the rapid depopulation of the West Indies. Newly introduced diseases took a heavy toll among the natives during the early years of contact, as did forced labour at unaccustomed tasks. Survivors often fled to the forested mainland coasts that were scorned as useless by the Europeans. Others quickly lost their cultural and racial identity as a result of mixture with Negroes who had been imported from Africa as slaves. Some of the mixed populations remained in the islands while others sought refuge from the Europeans on the coasts. Noteworthy among this latter group are the Black Caribs (descendants of Carib Indians and Africans, also called Bush Negroes), who went to British Honduras and Guyana.

There are, however, a few exceptions to the general pattern of extinction or isolation. The Cuna of Panama, for example, have become largely Hispanicized, but their colourful dress makes them an asset in terms of the tourist trade, unlike the similarly acculturated Lenca of Honduras. As early as 1550, the Goajiro of northeastern Colombia had virtually abandoned their pre-Columbian slash-and-burn horticulture in favour of an economic pattern previously unknown in the New World—the herding of goats and cattle. Small nomadic bands, based on ties of kinship, travel constantly to find pasturage within their limited and arid territories, which are the subject of frequent feuds. The hot, humid Mosquito Coast of eastern Honduras and Nicaragua was long used as a base by English loggers, buccaneers, and others who sought to undercut Spain's commercial and political dominance throughout the Caribbean, and the Jicaque, Mosquito, Paya, and Sumo Indians, as well as many free and runaway Negroes, collaborated with them. However, these peoples have again been relegated to a position that is economically and politically marginal.

During the 20th century the remaining cultures have resisted modernization to a degree unusual among Indians of the Americas. As pressures on their refuge areas mount, however, it is not clear whether they will adapt or become extinct.

BIBLIOGRAPHY. The most comprehensive work is still JULIAN H. STEWARD (ed.), *Handbook of South American Indians*, vol. 4, *The Circum-Caribbean Tribes* (1948). JULIAN H. STEWARD and LOUIS C. FARON, *Native Peoples of South America* (1959), provides a convenient summary and relates the peoples of the area to their neighbours. On the prehistoric and early historic periods, useful articles appear in GORDON F. EKHOLM and GORDON R. WILLEY (eds.), *Handbook of Middle American Indians*, vol. 4, *Archaeological Frontiers and External Connections* (1966).

(D.B.H.)

Central American States, History of the

The independent states of Central America are Belize (formerly the crown colony of British Honduras), Guatemala, Honduras, El Salvador, Nicaragua, Costa Rica, and Panama. With the exception of Belize, the states enjoyed a brief period of federation in the 1820s and 1830s, after they gained independence from Spain and separated from Mexico. Since the 1840s, however, except for a few unsuccessful attempts at unification, their histories have been separate. Because of its location between the Atlantic and Pacific oceans, Central America has been important since the 16th century as a potential link between the two oceans. Indeed, both Panama and Nicaragua were considered for the interoceanic canal that was finally built across the Isthmus of Panama early in the 20th century.

The Maya Indians developed a flourishing civilization in Honduras, in Guatemala, and at Chiapas and the Yucatán Peninsula of Mexico before the Spanish conquest in the early 16th century (see MESO-AMERICAN CIVILIZATION, HISTORY OF). Today, descendants of the Maya still live in parts of Central America and Mexico.

Spain ruled the Central American region for about 300 years, contending with English, French, and Dutch interests in the Caribbean. The danger of Caribbean invasion forced most Spanish settlements to develop away from the Caribbean coasts. Among the Spanish cities were León and Granada in Nicaragua, Guatemala City, and Panama City and Portobelo in Panama. The British attempted to settle several regions in Central America; successful settlements included those at British Honduras and along the Mosquito Coast, but only British Honduras remained in British hands until independence in 1981.

British and U.S. commercial interests in Central America conflicted in the mid-19th century and were settled by the Clayton–Bulwer Treaty of 1850, which prevented either nation from controlling any region in Central America and guaranteed the neutrality of any route that might be built. The United States built railroads in Panama, Costa Rica, El Salvador, and Guatemala, which aided the development of banana plantations and the production of coffee and also brought large profits to U.S. businessmen. In 1901 the United States and Great Britain signed the Hay–Pauncefote Treaty, which allowed the United States to build the Panama Canal.

THE UNITED PROVINCES OF CENTRAL AMERICA

Independence from Spain. Central American political, military, religious, and university leaders proclaimed independence at Guatemala City in 1821, and the cities in El Salvador, Honduras, Nicaragua, and Costa Rica agreed with the decision. On September 15, 1821, the Spanish captain general of the *Audiencia* of Guatemala became the head of a new independent Central America. The Central American conservatives, however, preferred annexation to the new Mexican empire of Agustín de Iturbide. Despite liberal opposition, conservative leaders in Guatemala City decided on the annexation to Mexico on January 5, 1822, believing that the new nation needed the protection of Mexico to survive. Salvadorans, under Manuel José Arce and the priest José Matías Delgado, resisted the annexation and found sympathizers among Central American republican liberals, including those of Guatemala City. A Mexican army led by Gen. Vicente Filisola reached Guatemala City, where it reorganized the government and then invaded San Salvador, which resisted for several months before its defenses were broken.

Under attack from republicans in Mexico, Iturbide's empire fell in 1823, a triumph for Mexican and Central American liberals. Filisola then convoked a congress in Guatemala City, according to a provision of the 1821 declaration of independence.

The Central American congress

Federation. The congress prepared a decree of absolute independence from Mexico, Spain, or any other nation (July 1). It adopted a republican form of government, appointed an executive triumvirate, and demanded Filisola's departure. Filisola persuaded Chiapas to remain with Mexico, although its southern part, Soconusco, continued under Guatemalan jurisdiction until 1842. The congress designated itself the National Constituent Assembly of the United Provinces of Central America and formed a federal system, with the states of Guatemala, El Salvador, Honduras, Nicaragua, and Costa Rica as its members.

During the next year the assembly made a series of institutional changes and revisions of public finance and suppressed monopoly and privilege. Indians were freed of tributes. Slavery was abolished (April 24, 1824), and many slaves fled to the new republic from British Honduras. A constitution was drawn up, and general elections were held in 1825. The Liberals gained enough strength in the federal congress to elect their candidate, Manuel José Arce, as the federation's first president. The Conservative candidate was José Cecilio del Valle.

Arce had problems finding qualified people to fill the executive offices of the government and in asserting his authority. Another problem developed because the central government was located in Guatemala City, which had not been placed under federal jurisdiction, and Juan Barrundia, the governor of the state of Guatemala, also remained in the city. Meanwhile, the congress appointed a French officer, Nicolás Raoul, as an adviser to its commission of defense. Raoul, however, refused to recognize Arce as the general in chief. Repeated differences forced Arce to order the capture of Raoul and the arrest of Barrundia. The vice governor of Guatemala, Dr. Cirilo Flores, left the city and moved to Quezaltenango, where he decided to make armed resistance against Arce. But local opinion in Quezaltenango, led by Conservatives, turned against Flores, who was murdered by a mob.

Great ideological differences had developed between Arce and his own Liberal Party. The federal congress now refused to approve any more of the President's decrees, whereupon Arce assumed dictatorial powers and ordered that an extraordinary congress be elected to meet at Cojutepeque, in El Salvador. Meanwhile, he prepared to fight the Liberals of San Salvador, who were the leaders of the opposition. He won a victory over Salvadoran forces at the Battle of Arrazola, near Guatemala City, but the Liberals continued in open rebellion.

Morazán's liberation of San Salvador

Conservatives then controlled Guatemala City and supported the federation, identified with Arce. While San Salvador resisted a federal siege, Francisco Morazán led an army from Honduras to rescue the city (1829). When part of the federal army left San Salvador to meet Morazán's forces, Salvadorans broke the siege. Morazán defeated the federal forces at the Battle of Chalco and arrived in San Salvador as a liberator. Then, reinforced by Salvadoran troops and officers, he marched toward Guatemala City. Arce resigned his office. The Guatemalan Liberals welcomed Morazán, and the Conservatives signed a capitulation, giving up all resistance. When Morazán's followers allegedly found a secret cache of military supplies at the cathedral of Archbishop Casaus y Torres, the conditions of the capitulation were disregarded. Arce and the leading Conservatives were arrested and forced to leave the country, as was the archbishop. José F. Barrundia, brother of the former Guatemalan governor, became provisional president of the federation.

The leadership of Francisco Morazán. Morazán gained the presidency in the 1830 elections and tried to restore peace to the republic. But he faced a Conservative uprising in Honduras and political unrest and economic difficulties in El Salvador, which was still the leader among the provinces. Morazán tried, with little success, to bring all the factions together. Meanwhile, Arce led a two-pronged invasion of Central America—one force from Cuba, the other from Mexico. Because these forces were weak, Morazán and Raoul overcame the invasion.

In the 1834 elections the Conservatives chose José Cecilio del Valle to oppose Morazán. Valle won the election, but he died of natural causes a few days before congress could confirm the results. Thus, Morazán remained in office and set out to institute a radical program—a balance between the states and the federal government. He moved the government to San Salvador. The congress issued constitutional reforms—accepted only by Nicaragua and Costa Rica—that strengthened the federal executive at the expense of the states.

In 1837 Guatemala, under the leadership of Gov. Mariano Gálvez, instituted a new penal code, based on that of Louisiana, which included jury trials and other reforms. But the new code faced opposition among the state's illiterate peasants and Indians. Gálvez finally ordered its suspension for political reasons. An embittered public debate developed between Barrundia and Gálvez. The Liberal Party in Guatemala, already split, lost prestige. At the same time, a cholera epidemic had killed hundreds of Guatemalan peasants, particularly in the eastern provinces, which were the centre of unrest. The government tried to isolate the region and impose an effective quarantine. A powerful popular movement took shape, led by a barely literate but charismatic mestizo, Rafael Carrera, who gained the help of the lower clergy, the support of the Conservatives, and the sympathy of Barrundia's followers, who saw a peasant rebellion as a useful tool to fight Gálvez. Gálvez assumed dictatorial powers and imposed martial law. But Carrera, aided by the popular discontent and by the Conservatives and the church, both fighting for their survival, defeated Gálvez' forces in January 1838 and captured Guatemala City. Gálvez resigned, and Carrera was acclaimed a hero by Liberals and Conservatives.

The rise of Rafael Carrera

End of the federation. Western Guatemala then demanded recognition from Guatemala City as a separate state—Los Altos, with its capital at Quezaltenango. The state legislature referred the matter to the federal Congress, which accepted Los Altos as the federation's sixth state. The Congress passed a resolution in May 1838 that permitted each state to leave the federation. By April 1839 only El Salvador remained loyal. Meanwhile, although Morazán's term had expired in February, no elections had been held to name a successor, and Carrera seized control of the state of Guatemala and assumed dictatorial powers. Early in 1840 Morazán invaded Guatemala, hoping to restore the Liberal government. On March 18 his army assaulted Guatemala City; Carrera had purposely abandoned the city, and Morazán captured it easily. Carrera then surrounded Morazán's army and inflicted a disastrous defeat. Morazán returned to San Salvador. He resigned his office and left for Panama and, later, Peru. Two years later he gained control of the Costa Rican government, but he was executed during an insurrection there (September 15, 1842).

(Ed.)

NATIONAL HISTORIES OF THE CENTRAL AMERICAN STATES

Guatemala. The origin of the name Guatemala is certainly Indian, but its derivation and meaning are undetermined. Some hold that the original form was Quauhtemallan (which indicates an Aztec rather than a Mayan origin), meaning "land of trees," and others hold that its origin was Guhatezmalha, meaning "mountain of vomiting water," referring no doubt to the so-called volcano of water that destroyed Ciudad Vieja (Santiago), the first permanent Spanish capital of the captaincy general.

The colonial period. Under the Spaniards the capital was eventually established at Antigua; it achieved a certain magnificence, and the major towns acquired some aspects of Spanish culture, but the outlying areas were only lightly affected. When Antigua was razed by an earthquake in 1773, the capital was moved by royal order to the site of modern Guatemala City.

The colony developed no great degree of economic prosperity. The cultivation for export of agricultural staples, principally cacao and indigo, by Indian or African slave labour was the major economic activity, exclusive of production for subsistence. Commerce, however, was never extensive; a satisfactory port was never developed, internal transportation was difficult, and pirates harassed the coasts and preyed on shipping.

The postcolonial period. Following independence from Spain (1821) and Mexico (1823), Guatemala was the political centre of the United Provinces of Central America. The principal factor in the collapse of the federation was the backcountry uprising in Guatemala led by Rafael Carrera, who established himself as the military arbiter of the state (1838) and, from the executive's chair or from behind it, controlled policy until his death in 1865. Elections were dispensed with in 1854, when the presidency was conferred upon him for life.

Rafael Carrera

Carrera, with Conservative support, returned Guatemala to a regime similar to that of the colonial period. He restored the church to its position of privilege and power and catered to the aristocracy. He followed a nationalistic policy, and in March 1847 he formally declared Guatemala an independent and sovereign nation. In 1859 he made a treaty with Great Britain defining the status and boundaries of British Honduras, an issue that remains alive despite Belize's independent status.

In 1871 a revolution headed by Miguel García Granados and Justo Rufino Barrios overthrew Gen. Vicente Gerna, Carrera's Conservative successor in office, and introduced a period of Liberal ascendancy that extended almost unbroken to 1944. After a brief period in the presidency, García Granados ceded to Barrios (1873), known as the Reformer because of the sweeping changes he introduced.

With the approval of the assembly, Barrios broke the power of the local aristocracy; brought the church under civil control and confiscated its properties; instituted lay education; promulgated a new constitution (1876); fostered the construction of roads, railways, and telegraph lines; encouraged development by private initiative of Guatemala's resources; and opened the country to foreign capital. He stimulated the cultivation of coffee to replace the declining trade in cochineal and enacted legislation designed to assure producers of a ready supply of labour. He was an ardent exponent of the idea of Central American union, and, when persuasion failed to produce the ends he desired, he invaded El Salvador and lost his life at the Battle of Chalchuapa (1885) in an attempt to accomplish them by force.

After the death of Barrios, Manuel Lisandro Barillas occupied the presidency. He was succeeded by José María Reina Barrios, a nephew of the Reformer, who was elected in 1892 and assassinated in 1898. Manuel Estrada Cabrera then became provisional president, regularized his status by an election, and by repeated reelections maintained himself in power until leaders of the opposition Unionist Party, with the cooperation of some of his former adherents, forced him from office by having the assembly declare him insane (1920).

Manuel Estrada Cabrera

During his long tenure in power, Estrada Cabrera fostered economic development and progress along the lines established by Barrios. He encouraged improvements in agriculture, made concessions to the United Fruit Company (owned by U.S. businessmen), continued to build roads, supported railroad construction, and had the satisfaction of seeing the completion of the railroad to the Atlantic. Health conditions were improved, and education, especially in practical fields, was stimulated. Estrada Cabrera's political policies were less admirable, however. He persecuted political opponents, disregarded individual rights and liberties, muzzled the press, and summarily disposed of his enemies.

After the fall of Estrada Cabrera, the presidency was held by Carlos Herrera, Gen. José M. Orellana, Lázaro Chacón, Baudilio Palma, Gen. Manuel Orellana, and José María Reina Andrade, for periods ranging from a few days to nearly a full six-year term. In 1931 Jorge Ubico was elected president and began the fourth of Guatemala's extended dictatorships.

Contemporary period. Ubico stressed economic development and, in particular, the improvement and diversification of agriculture and the construction of roads. He balanced the national budget and transformed a deficit into a surplus. His paternalistic policies toward the Indians established him as their patron, although his vagrancy law (1934) made workers, especially Indians, liable to periods of forced labour at critical seasons. During his motorcycle tours of the country or in his office, he listened to their complaints and dispensed immediate "justice." This relationship deluded Ubico, called Tata (Father), into stating that Guatemala no longer had an Indian problem. Education, which had received considerable emphasis under preceding Liberal regimes, was of but slight interest to Ubico. He closed several institutions of secondary level

Jorge Ubico

outside the capital, allowed teachers' salaries to remain at low levels, and required teachers and students to march in his parades and festivals.

Ubico's administration dramatized the degree to which Liberal thought had lost its idealism and was concerned principally with material progress. The new socioeconomic groups found no stimulation and no hope in the dreary materialism and military repression that had come to characterize Liberal regimes, and these potential sources of opposition were brought together by the increasing disregard shown for individual rights and liberties. Discontent was increased by economic dislocation during World War II. Ubico was thought to admire the totalitarian dictators, but in December 1941 his government declared war on Japan, Germany, and Italy.

A general strike forced Ubico to resign in June 1944. Labour was allowed to organize, political parties were formed, and a presidential electoral campaign was begun in which Juan José Arévalo soon emerged as the most popular candidate. Gen. Federico Ponce Vaides, head of the interim government, was deposed on October 20, 1944, during an uprising headed by students and teachers, workers, and younger elements of the military forces. A revolutionary junta presided over the drafting of a new constitution, the electoral campaign, and, in March 1945, the inauguration of Arévalo.

Juan José Arévalo

The Arévalo administration attempted to consolidate the social revolution implicit in the October uprising. A favourable labour code was enacted, and a social security system that promised progressive extension of benefits was inaugurated. Arévalo also pressed the Belize issue with Great Britain, subjected foreign enterprises to regulation, and attempted to guarantee Guatemalan labourers a larger share of the benefits produced by their toil. Thus, the Arévalo regime transferred political power from the military forces to a popular group, of which organized labour was the most important element.

Lack of leadership from the rank and file allowed Guatemalan Communists to organize the labour movement and use it for their own ends. Arévalo was not friendly to their activities, but his nationalistic bent gave them opportunity to establish themselves as his most enthusiastic and reliable supporters. Thus they secured a degree of toleration that permitted them to operate.

The most likely candidates to succeed Arévalo were Francisco Arana and Jacobo Arbenz. Arana was assassinated in 1949. Arbenz became the official candidate, was elected—with Communist support—over Gen. Miguel Ydígoras Fuentes, and assumed office in March 1951. Arbenz made agrarian reform the central project of his administration. With strong Communist support, the National Congress passed a measure providing for the expropriation of unused portions of landholdings in excess of a specified acreage and for the distribution of the land among landless peasants.

The growth of Communist influence in Guatemala became the most troublesome issue of the Arbenz regime. Internal opposition to the trend was eventually stifled by increasingly terroristic means, but exiles and foreign recruits, headed by Col. Carlos Castillo Armas and assisted by the U.S. Central Intelligence Agency (CIA), planned outside the country to overthrow the government. When the invasion began, military officers informed Arbenz that the army would not fight in his defense and forced him to resign (June 1954).

The rise of Castillo Armas

Castillo Armas emerged from a military junta as provisional president, and a plebiscite regularized his status. He attempted to extirpate Communist influence, moderate social reforms, and restore the confidence of foreign investment capital, but he was assassinated in July 1957. After two temporary governments and an election nullified by the congress, Ydígoras Fuentes was declared elected to the presidency and took office March 2, 1958. In March 1963 a coup led by the defense minister, Enrique Peralta Azurdia, removed Ydígoras. As provisional president, Peralta cancelled the election, promising to hold one later. The frustration, during these regimes, of the social reforms promised by the revolution of 1944 made restive elements of the population increasingly receptive to counsels of resistance and even of violence.

An orderly election on March 6, 1966, gave Julio César Méndez Montenegro, a law professor and the candidate of the moderately left wing Partido Revolucionario (PR; Revolutionary Party), an unexpectedly large plurality of votes over the candidate of the military regime but not the absolute majority required for election. Congress elected him, but the understanding with the military officers that had to be reached before a civilian government could take office undermined his authority. Hopes for reform, therefore, were largely frustrated, and the energies of the administration were consumed in attempts to control increasing violence. Rural guerrillas were substantially eliminated by military and paramilitary operations such as those conducted by Col. Carlos Arana Osorio, but urban guerrilla and terrorist activity worsened.

Arana Osorio, the "law-and-order" candidate, won the election of 1970. His major activity was "pacification" of the country by the extermination of "habitual criminals" and leftist guerrillas. Assassination of opposition leaders of the democratic left, however, gave rise to the conviction that Arana was attempting to eliminate all opponents of his regime, whether left, right, or centre. The victims of his pacification program numbered in the thousands.

Carlos Arana Osorio

With dissent eliminated or hushed, the country experienced a period of relative quiet and unaccustomed personal liberty. As the election of 1974 approached, optimists could find in the trend of events some reason to hope that a new basis had been laid for reform. The coalition of opposition parties chose Gen. Efraín Ríos Montt, a leading officer of the progressive wing of the military forces, to contend with Gen. Kjell Laugerud García, a nonpolitical military officer, named as the official candidate by the coalition of rightist parties.

When returns showed Ríos Montt winning an absolute majority, which constituted election, the government abruptly suspended election reports, brazenly manipulated the results, and finally announced that Laugerud García had won a plurality of votes. The government-controlled National Congress promptly elected him. Laugerud thus took office under circumstances that made him the protégé of Arana and deprived him of any moral force. He faced problems of inflation, a series of volcanic eruptions (October 1974), and division and consequent weakening of his principal political support, the Movimiento de Liberación Nacional (MLN; National Liberation Movement). He met a recrudescence of violence and terror with the same repressive measures that Arana had applied. (In February 1978 Amnesty International reported that since 1966 Guatemalan government "death squads" had killed more than 20,000 persons.)

The pattern of electoral manipulation set in 1974 persisted in subsequent elections. Gen. Fernando Romeo Lucas García, declared the winner in 1978 after another suspect count, presided over a regime that essentially continued that of Laugerud. Both administrations confronted the nation's problems with resources greatly reduced in consequence of natural calamity. The devastating earthquake of February 1976 left such numbers dead, injured, and homeless as to be labelled the greatest natural disaster ever recorded in Central America.

Earthquake of 1976

A major factor in both administrations was the discovery of oil and incipient production of petroleum from a deposit in northern Guatemala. Because the deposit was thought to extend across British Honduras to the continental shelf, resolution of persistent, conflicting boundary and territorial claims was sought. On March 11, 1981, Guatemala, Great Britain, and British Honduras reached preliminary agreement, but a final settlement was not reached, and, in September 1981, Great Britain granted independence to Belize over Guatemala's protest.

The discovery of oil was also thought by some to be the reason behind government violence in the largely Indian departments of the north. The devastation and wholesale massacres that occurred there and the thousands of Indians driven as refugees into Mexico suggested, at least to some, that the members of the administration were making "counterinsurgency" a device for clearing indigenous claimants from petroleum lands that others might then appropriate. Certainly, Indians were driven in unprecedented numbers into the guerrilla movements, thereby giving the movements a new, ominous quality.

In the elections of March 1982, the government coalition candidate, Gen. Angel Aníbal Guevara, was declared elected. On March 23, however, young army officers seized the government and installed a junta headed by General Ríos Montt, who had been denied the presidency in 1974.

Ríos Montt

Ríos Montt, who dissolved the junta and declared himself sole ruler on June 9, moved promptly to purge the public service of miscreants, to rout corruption, and to disband the notorious death squads. His major task was to end the guerrilla war, but the amelioration of conditions that gave root to dissidence, obviously a work of time and patience, made small progress for want of material resources, appropriate agencies, and qualified personnel. The campaign against the rebels was resumed with new intensity and precision at the expiration of an offer of amnesty on July 1, 1982.

Disillusionment with the regime quickly began to erode the support of early backers. When the Council of State was established on September 15, 1982, the four political parties that originally backed the coup refused to participate, and neither the direction nor the future of the regime was entirely clear.

(W.J.Gr.)

Honduras. In the 1570s a silver strike in the highlands brought a rush of prospectors to Honduras, resulting in the rise of an important population centre at Tegucigalpa. The Caribbean coastal area became a rendezvous for the buccaneers who preyed on Spanish commerce. Later the region, with its rich logwood and mahogany forests, attracted the British, who by the late 18th century controlled the Mosquito Coast from the Río San Juan in Nicaragua to Belize, as well as the Bay Islands offshore.

Francisco Morazán

Early history. Independence from Spain came after 1821. Francisco Morazán, elected to head the United Provinces of Central America in 1830, was a Liberal whose influence on his native Honduras and on the confederation derived from a principal goal of liberalism, to curtail the traditional power and privileges of the church and clergy. Honduras declared its absolute independence on November 5, 1838. The pro-church Conservatives in Honduras took control under Francisco Ferrera, who was inaugurated as the first constitutional president on January 1, 1841.

Domination by the Conservatives lasted until the 1870s, and the church was restored to its former position. In 1861 the Honduran government signed a concordat with the Holy See. After 1871 the ascendancy of Justo Rufino Barrios in Guatemala influenced a return to liberalism in Honduras, where Marco Aurelio Soto, a Liberal, assumed the presidency (1876). A new constitution (1880) sought to undo the work of the Conservatives. Five years later, when Barrios was killed in an attempt to revive the old Central American union by force, Liberals in Honduras and elsewhere proved to be nationalists first and blocked this attempt at domination by Guatemala. Liberals of this generation were positivist and devoted to material progress as the way to achieve humanitarian ideals. Ramón Rosa was their exemplar in Honduras.

20th century. In the first decade of the 20th century, the "strong man" in Nicaragua, José Santos Zelaya, put Miguel Dávila into the Honduran presidency. This led in 1911 and 1912 to something more serious than periodic revolutions. The U.S. president, William Howard Taft, sent marines to protect U.S. banana investments, which by this time had grown considerably, with three companies exploiting this Honduran product. All three made large capital outlays in the form of improved port facilities, railroads, workers' settlements, and similar developments in the northern plantation area and the lowland region along the Caribbean coast.

Carías Andino

In 1918 Honduras declared war on Germany but took no active part in World War I. Political upheavals continued after the war. In 1932, after years of unrest, another "strong man," Gen. Tiburcio Carías Andino, was elected president and remained in office until 1949. Honduras declared war on Japan, Germany, and Italy in December 1941. Lack of shipping brought much economic distress during the war; export surpluses of bananas, coconuts, and copra piled up, leading to widespread unemployment and consequent unrest. But the government was able to maintain itself, and it promulgated some beneficial reforms. The United Fruit Company increased wages for its employees and inaugurated several new enterprises. Carías survived a revolution in 1947, but two years later the combination of two rival parties proved his undoing.

Development policies under Juan Manuel Gálvez (1949–54), Julio Lozano Díaz (1954–56), and Ramón Villeda Morales (1957–63) brought some modernization to the transportation system and to labour legislation. The International Court of Justice awarded the large area north of the Río Coco, which had been disputed by Nicaragua, to Honduras in 1960. In 1963 Villeda Morales was deposed by a military coup led by Col. Osvaldo López Arellano, who declared himself head of state and regularized his regime in 1965. In the summer of 1969 occurred the Soccer War with El Salvador, triggered indeed by a soccer game but caused by severe economic and demographic problems (see below *El Salvador: War with Honduras*). Though brief, the war dampened hopes for economic and political integration of Central America.

After 1963 Honduras was ruled by military governments, except for the civilian administrations of Ramón Ernesto Cruz (1971–72) and Roberto Suazo Córdova (beginning in 1982). Cruz's election resulted from the Soccer War, which Honduras had lost militarily. But López Arellano, as chief of the armed forces, retained real power, and in December 1972 he removed Cruz from office. Pressured toward modernizing reforms by younger military officers, López Arellano astonished many by announcing, in January 1974, a reform program that included land redistribution. His program had little success, however.

López Arellano was discredited and forced to resign in 1975 because of an international bribery scandal; he was replaced by Col. Juan Alberto Melgar Castro (1975–78). Honduras prospered under Melgar. High earnings from the elevated world coffee market during those years were particularly helpful because coffee production was widely dispersed through the country. His administration was weakened, however, by a series of scandals and political embarrassments.

Gen. Policarpo Paz García, who attained power through a bloodless military coup in late 1978, pledged to continue Melgar's policies, but he soon faced harder times. Central America entered a cycle of violence with the revolution in Nicaragua that overthrew Anastasio Somoza Debayle in the summer of 1979 and the revolution in El Salvador that was under way in 1980. Honduras appeared to be an island of stability as Nicaragua, El Salvador, and Guatemala experienced the extreme consequences of guerrilla warfare and Costa Rica verged on bankruptcy. By September 1982, however, it became clear that Honduras was not immune to these regional disturbances. Government corruption and military involvement in the Salvadoran and Nicaraguan border zones brought terrorist bomb blasts in Tegucigalpa and the capture by guerrillas of the entire chamber of commerce of San Pedro Sula. As a military buildup, financed by the United States, continued, the stability of Honduras was clearly in question.

(W.M.Cl.)

Sonsonate and San Salvador

El Salvador. The provinces of Sonsonate and San Salvador developed separately under the Spaniards. Sonsonate, the smaller of the two, remained wealthier until the cocoa trade declined under competition from Ecuador. San Salvador grew more slowly, with dependence upon stock raising, general agriculture, and the manufacture of indigo, but eventually became more important. Its territory included the city of San Miguel, the town of San Vicente, and Cihuatehuacán (Santa Ana), an Indian centre that grew to be next in size to the city of San Salvador. By the late 18th century both provinces contained large mestizo populations with some admixture of an African strain, and important Indian villages such as Ahuachapán, Chalchuapa, Zacatecoluca, Cojutepeque, Suchitoto, and Usulután had become less Indian in their customs.

Independence. San Salvador played an active role in the evolution of Central American affairs from 1811 to 1840. The first isthmian defiance of Spain occurred there in 1811, inspired by the deeds of a priest, Miguel Hidalgo, in Mexico. Another priest, José Matías Delgado, led the movement in company with his nephew Manuel José Arce, but the attempt failed, as did another in 1814. When the regime in Guatemala declared independence from Spain in 1821, subject to the approval of a Central American congress, San Salvador refused the proposed incorporation into Mexico. San Salvador (including Sonsonate) became a state in the United Provinces of Central America in 1823; Arce was the union's first president, and the federal capital was moved to San Salvador in 1834. The union ended when Francisco Morazán, its second president, left San Salvador in 1840.

The Republic of El Salvador received its name (Spanish: The Saviour) on January 30, 1841, though only provisionally so until 1856. For 45 years Conservatives (heirs of the opposition to Morazán) struggled with Liberals (proponents of renewed union) for control. Agitation quieted somewhat during the administrations of Francisco Dueñas (1863–71) and Rafael Zaldívar (1876–85), when coffee, introduced as a crop in 1840, became a sizable export.

Coffee became all-important to the economy of the republic from 1885 to 1931, as international conflicts became less frequent and the presidential succession more regular. The relative absence of confusion did not encourage democracy; all power remained in the hands of the wealthy, as each president chose his own successor, at times even a close relative. The coffee plantations, however, flourished; British and North American companies built a national system of railroads; the port for La Unión developed; and El Salvador enjoyed peace.

Military dictatorships. An attempt to move toward democracy resulted in military intervention when Pío Romero Bosque (president 1927–31) decided not to pick his successor. Arturo Araújo, chosen by the legislature after winning only a plurality of the vote, soon found himself deposed. Gen. Maximiliano Hernández Martínez, who maintained an authoritarian regime from 1931 to 1944, established a new coinage system, organized a national bank, completed the Inter-American Highway across the country, and extended state control over the export of coffee. He also followed a ruthless policy toward his critics, resorting to mass executions of protesters. Although considered pro-Axis at the outset of World War II, he later declared war on the Axis powers.

Elections followed a fierce revolt that brought the resignation of Hernández Martínez. Salvador Castaneda Castro, who won, served as president from 1945 until a military junta deposed him in 1948. From this junta arose the Partido Revolucionario de Unificación Democrática (PRUD; Revolutionary Party of Democratic Unification), which dominated the republic under Maj. Oscar Osorio (1950–56) and Lieut. Col. José María Lemus (1956–60). During this period cotton became a second significant export crop. Very low standards of living, however, prevailed for the masses of underpaid workers, both urban and rural. When Lemus stifled the opposition in elections, so that PRUD ran the nation alone, and resorted to severe repression of the demonstrations against him, he was removed by force in October 1960. In three months a second junta seized control, and the new Partido de Conciliación Nacional (PCN; National Conciliation Party) replaced PRUD as the ruling force in the nation. Under its auspices, Lieut. Col. Julio Adalberto Rivera (1962–67) and Col. Fidel Sánchez Hernández (1967–72) held the presidency. Rivera set a minimum wage for agricultural labour (though at a very low figure) and encouraged fair elections. Business prospered during his term, as many new industries appeared. The Partido Demócrata Cristiano (PDC; Christian Democratic Party) arose as a serious opposition group.

Military junta

War with Honduras. Unemployment and the scarcity of farming land in overpopulated El Salvador led some 300,000 of its people to migrate to Honduras in the 1950s and 1960s. Arriving without legal permits and occupying unassigned acres, the migrants found themselves in difficulty when a Honduran agrarian reform, enacted in 1962 but not executed till 1969, made no provision for them. About 15,000 of them returned to El Salvador with stories of physical mistreatment. Their arrival coincided with a great surge of emotion in both countries, stemming from a three-game soccer series; hence the ensuing conflict is often labelled the Soccer War (Guerra de Fútbol).

The Soccer War

Each side complained to the Organization of American States (OAS) of atrocities allegedly committed by the other. While the OAS investigated, however, El Salvador opened hostilities (July 14, 1969), dropping bombs on Honduran airports and penetrating Honduran territory. Honduran planes reciprocated the bombing, but Honduran troops maintained a defensive role. The OAS demanded and finally received (July 29) an agreement from El Salvador to withdraw unconditionally. At the same time, the OAS granted assurances to migrants from either side.

For 11 years after the war, attempts at peace talks foundered repeatedly. Honduras refused to make concessions until a clear boundary could be determined. In October 1976 both sides accepted the services of a mediator, and a peace treaty was signed in October 1980. In the meantime, the Salvadoran economy suffered from the loss of trade with Honduras, Nicaragua, and Costa Rica.

Civil war. Harsher economic conditions led to widespread unhappiness with the increasingly arbitrary and repressive regime. The PCN again won the presidency in 1972, with Col. Arturo Armando Molina. Many observers believed, however, that in a fair count the PDC candidate, José Napoleón Duarte, would have triumphed. Duarte then gave his support to a coup and found himself exiled when it miscarried. In 1973 left-wing activist groups formed to protest the situation. They began their programs with bombings, moving on to kidnapping and murder. A right-wing terrorist group adopted similar tactics.

President Molina in 1974 announced a new minimum agricultural wage. In 1976 he obtained consent for an agrarian reform affecting the properties of 250 large landowners. At the same time, his army raided illegal peasant associations, killing many peasants in the process. In this manner, the regime fell afoul of the church, many of whose priests had encouraged the associations.

The old El Salvador had not disappeared completely. Its coffee and cotton remained in demand, and its material progress found renewed support in the development of geothermal energy near Ahuachapán. But Molina faced a sullen people by the end of his term.

The PCN won the presidency again in 1977, with Gen. Carlos Humberto Romero as its candidate. There was a mass protest of fraud. Right-wing terrorists murdered two Jesuits who had acted in behalf of the peasants and threatened the entire Jesuit order with extinction, though Romero, after his inauguration (July 1), provided some protection for the churchmen. After the PCN swept the elections of 1978, the opposition again having withdrawn, the army killed at least 29 persons during demonstrations against economic conditions. Archbishop Oscar Romero, who said that outbursts of popular violence would not end so long as the authorities were guilty of institutionalized violence, became the government's most formidable opponent. He was assassinated, possibly by right-wing factions, on March 24, 1980.

Archbishop Oscar Romero

In January 1979 the Inter-American Commission on Human Rights accused the Romero government of torturing and murdering political opponents. Other human rights organizations also charged the government with violations of human rights. Guerrilla violence, from both left and right, reached extreme proportions.

(F.D.P./Ed.)

Romero was ousted on October 15, 1979, and a military junta, led by Col. Jaime Abdul Guitérrez and Col. Adolfo Majano, was installed. Despite a program of agrarian reform, nationalization of the banks, a declared commitment to human rights, and economic and military assistance by the United States, the junta failed to control the situation. The violence grew throughout 1980. On December 3, three U.S. nuns and a lay worker were murdered; they were among the 22,000 persons to lose their lives to political violence in a single year.

José Napoleón Duarte, then a civilian member of the junta, was sworn in as president on December 13, 1980. The junta was supported by the military forces, some right-wing factions, and the United States. The economy and the political situation worsened, however, with 13,000 persons killed in 1981. On March 28, 1982, elections for the Constituent Assembly resulted in an unstable coalition of rightist political parties, including the PDC and PCN. Duarte was forced to resign, and Alvaro Mangaña Borjo, a banker and economist, was sworn in as president in the face of unabated political strife and civil war.

(Ed.)

Nicaragua. The name Nicaragua is derived from that of Nicarao, an important Indian chief of the region. Under Spanish rule, the cities of Granada and León took precedence, Granada as a centre of trade, León of agriculture. The town of Rivas and the Indian villages of Managua and Masaya also grew in importance. Persons of African descent, coming from the West Indies, inhabited the east coast, where the few permanent settlements included Bluefields. Late in the 17th century, Great Britain formed an "alliance" with the Mosquito tribe, and, after some English persons settled there, the Mosquito Coast for a time (1740–86) became a British dependency.

Independence. In 1811, inspired by struggles in Mexico and El Salvador, revolutionaries deposed the governing intendant of Nicaragua. León, however, soon returned to the royalist cause, and Granada bore the brunt of the punishment for disobedience, causing ill feeling between the two regions. In 1821 León rejected and Granada approved the Guatemalan declaration of independence from Spain. Both accepted union with Mexico (1822–23), but they fought one another until 1826, when Nicaragua took up its role in the United Provinces of Central America. Dissension remained lively until 1838, when Nicaragua seceded from the federation, and subsequently continued as part of the general isthmian struggle between Liberals and Conservatives.

Foreign intervention. After the withdrawal of Spain, relations between the "king" of the Mosquito Coast and the British government strengthened, until again there were English officials in Bluefields. In 1848 they seized the small Caribbean port of San Juan del Norte, changing its name to Greytown. The discovery of gold in California in that year attracted attention to the strategic position of Nicaragua for interocean traffic, and four years later Cornelius Vanderbilt's Accessory Transit Company began moving passengers by steamship and carriage between Greytown and the Pacific. In 1856 William Walker, a filibuster from Tennessee who had been invited to assist the Liberals in warfare (1855), made himself president of the country, but he was routed a year later by the joint efforts of the five Central American republics and the transit company.

William Walker

Tomás Martínez (president 1857–67) was the first in a line of Conservative presidents who ruled until 1893 and who brought Nicaragua relative peace but little democracy. As a compromise between Granada and León, Managua was made the capital in 1857. A railroad connected Managua to Corinto, a new port on the Pacific. In 1860 a treaty with Great Britain provided for the reincorporation of the east coast with the rest of the nation but as an autonomous reservation. It was not until the Liberal presidency (1893–1909) of José Santos Zelaya that complete jurisdiction over the Mosquito region was established.

The decision of the United States to locate its interocean canal in Panama rather than Nicaragua brought strained relations between the United States and the Zelaya regime. In 1909 two U.S. citizens who had participated in an uprising against Zelaya were executed, and U.S. Marines landed at Bluefields. Though Zelaya resigned, the United States refused to recognize his successor, José Madriz (1909–10), and prevented government occupation of Bluefields, the revolutionary headquarters. Further civil war led to the presidency of a Conservative, Adolfo Díaz (1911–17), for whom the U.S. Marines intervened directly in 1912. A 100-man guard at the U.S. embassy symbolized that country's support also for the Conservative president Emiliano Chamorro (1917–21) and his uncle and successor, Diego Manuel Chamorro (1921–23). The Bryan–Chamorro Treaty of 1916 gave the United States exclusive canal privileges in Nicaragua and the right to establish naval bases on the Gulf of Fonseca and the Corn Islands. Withdrawal of the marine guard led quickly to a new crisis (1925), with Emiliano Chamorro in rebellion against a new regime. Díaz returned as a compromise president (1926–28), reinforced in 1927 by 2,000 U.S. Marines. The Liberal leaders Juan Bautista Sacasa, José María Moncada, and César Augusto Sandino rose in rebellion, but after six months Sacasa and Moncada made peace and subsequent elections under U.S. auspices brought the presidency to both of them (Moncada, 1928–33, and Sacasa, 1933–36). Sandino, however, fought on as long as the marines remained in the country.

U.S. intervention

The Somoza years. The marines withdrew upon the inauguration of Sacasa, and Sandino submitted to his government. A Nicaraguan National Guard (Guardia Nacional), commanded by Gen. Anastasio Somoza García (married to a niece of Sacasa), became responsible for maintaining order in the country. In 1934 Somoza gave his assent to the murder of Sandino by officers of the guard. Somoza then deposed Sacasa, and, with the support of both Liberal and Conservative factions, became president on January 1, 1937.

Somoza (known as Tacho) controlled Nicaragua for the next two decades. A revised constitution gave him a new eight-year term (1939–47) and increased the powers of the presidency. In 1947 Leonardo Argüello succeeded to the office, but Somoza removed him within a month and the congress designated a temporary president. Still another constitution was promulgated, under which Víctor Manuel Román y Reyes, an uncle of Somoza, became president. As a gesture to Emiliano Chamorro, another constitution was passed that guaranteed the opposition a minority voice in the congress. On the death of Román y Reyes in 1950, Somoza reassumed the presidency and defeated Chamorro for a six-year term beginning in 1951.

A small gold-mining industry, developed in the 1930s, yielded Nicaragua's first sizable export commodity, and cooperation with the United States during World War II brought more material benefits. An air of prosperity developed after the war, but Somoza family holdings bound the economy together, while the people at large benefitted little from the rise in national income.

On September 21, 1956, a day after the Partido Liberal Nacionalista de Nicaragua (PLN; Nationalist Liberal Party of Nicaragua), his own creation, nominated Somoza García for another term, a young man named Rigoberto López Pérez shot the President, and Tacho died eight days later. Congress at once gave Luis Somoza Debayle his father's position, and in February 1957 he was elected to his own term (1957–63) against a contrived opposition. Somoza Debayle ruled more gently than his father had. In foreign affairs, he accepted a settlement in favour of Honduras of a long-standing border dispute between the two countries (1960) and cooperated with the United States in the Bay of Pigs Invasion of Cuba (1961). In 1962 a Marxist, Carlos Fonseca Amador, founded the guerrilla Frente Sandinista de Liberación Nacional (Sandinist National Liberation Front, called Sandinistas) in opposition to the regime, naming it for César Augusto Sandino.

Assassination of Tacho

As time for the election of 1963 approached, the Partido Conservador Tradicionalista (Traditionalist Conservative Party) and the Partido Liberal Independiente (Independent Liberal Party) proposed that it be supervised by neutral observers. Somoza Debayle (who had previously decided not to run for reelection) refused, and the two parties in consequence declined to nominate candidates. René Schick Gutiérrez, the PLN candidate and a close friend of the Somozas, thus easily won the presidency. The national economy was prospering, though the basic poverty of the masses remained relatively unchanged. Lorenzo Guerrero Gutiérrez became president for one year upon the death of Schick in office. Luis Somoza Debayle died in 1967, and in that year his younger brother, Anastasio Somoza Debayle (called Tachito), defeated the Traditionalist Conservative Fernando Agüero Rocha for the next five-year term. In 1970 the Bryan–

Chamorro Treaty was abrogated.

On May 1, 1972, constitutionally unable to succeed himself, Somoza relinquished the presidency to a triumvirate (composed of Agüero and two leaders of Somoza's own party). On December 23, however, an earthquake shook the city of Managua, leaving 6,000 persons dead and 300,000 homeless. Somoza (commanding the National Guard) again took charge as the head of a National Emergency Committee. Agüero, who protested, found himself replaced (March 1, 1973) on the triumvirate by a more compliant Conservative, Edmundo Paguaga Irías. In March 1974 a new constitution (the country's 10th) made it possible for Somoza to be reelected president, and on December 1 he again assumed the office.

Managua earthquake

Before the end of the year, two genuine opposition groups attracted wide attention—the Sandinistas and the organization founded by Pedro Joaquín Chamorro, editor and publisher of *La Prensa* of Managua, and called the Unión Democrática de Liberación (Udel; Democratic Union of Liberation). Many noncombatants were the victims of atrocities in clashes between Sandinistas and the National Guard. Fonseca and two other Sandinista leaders died in battle in 1976, and the remaining band declared itself in favour of democratic elections, seeking friends where it could find them. A group called Los Doce (The Twelve) sought an anti-Somoza alliance to include Udel, the Sandinistas, and other organizations. Assassins murdered Pedro Joaquín Chamorro on January 10, 1978, and a general strike and violence followed. On August 22 the Sandinistas occupied the national palace, holding more than 1,000 hostages for two days and winning most of their demands. Though the National Guard regained partial control, the insurrection spread, with another general strike and Sandinistas seizing and holding more and more cities. Somoza declared a state of siege on June 6, 1979, but the rebels continued to gain ground. By late June Managua itself was under siege, and on July 17 Somoza resigned, ending the long years of Somoza rule in Nicaragua.

(F.D.P./Ed.)

The Sandinista regime. With the end of the civil war, the new government inherited a devastated country. About 500,000 persons were homeless, more than 30,000 had been killed, and the economy was in ruins. In July 1979 the Sandinistas appointed a five-member Government Junta of National Reconstruction and a 47-member Council of State, the latter to act as an interim national assembly. In 1981 the junta was reduced to three members and the council increased to 51.

In 1979–80 the government expropriated the property held by Anastasio Somoza Debayle, members of his government, and their supporters. Local banks and insurance companies and mineral and forest resources were nationalized, and the import and export of foodstuffs were placed under government control. The Statutes on Rights and Guarantees, which acted as the country's new constitution, assured basic individual rights and freedoms. The government disclaimed any responsibility for the assassination of Somoza on September 17, 1980, in Asunción, Paraguay.

As the Sandinistas struggled with domestic reconstruction, they met with tense foreign relations. In 1981 Nicaragua accused the United States of harbouring Nicaraguan exiles training to invade their home country. The United States, in turn, accused Nicaragua of delivering arms to leftist guerrillas fighting against the government of El Salvador. In April the United States suspended economic aid to Nicaragua, an act that seemed to threaten economic recovery, and in October border tensions flared up between Nicaragua and Honduras. Although the Sandinista government retained ties with the West, its relations with Cuba and other Communist-bloc nations seemed to indicate an increased leaning toward the left.

(Ed.)

Costa Rica. The name Costa Rica, or Rich Coast, probably reflected Columbus' belief in the presence of gold in the region he discovered in 1502. Because of the resistance of the Indians and the mismanagement of several attempts at conquest, Costa Rica did not fall under Spanish control until the 1570s. The colony was never rich, and most Costa Ricans, or "Ticos," were peasants or small farmers, largely ignored by the Spanish crown because of the region's lack of mineral wealth. For three centuries these conditions changed little; a middle-class handful of merchants and more successful farmers emerged, but in Costa Rica the differences between these groups and the poorest peasants were much smaller than they were elsewhere in the Spanish colonies.

Independence. When Mexico declared its independence from Spain in 1821, Costa Rica, with other parts of Central America, joined the short-lived Mexican Empire. In 1823 Costa Rica helped create the United Provinces of Central America but, disenchanted with the strife in the other four states of the federation, severed its ties in 1838. Already a pattern of isolationism had been formed, and in the many attempts to revive the federation the Costa Ricans have invariably shown little interest.

Costa Rica's first influx of foreign capital was brought by agriculture; from the 1840s a constant stream of oxcarts carried coffee from the Meseta Central to Pacific ports and ships bound for Europe. This trade brought British investment. Farmers with even small acreage could derive an adequate if simple existence, and the ground was laid for a society that demanded schools and roads from its government and found political participation necessary to achieve these goals.

The coffee trade

Costa Rica's policy of isolationism did not completely save it from foreign troubles. In 1825 the province of Guanacaste seceded from Nicaragua and joined Costa Rica, an issue contended until the boundary treaty of 1896. Sharing the Río San Juan with Nicaragua, Costa Rica also shared some of the canal and filibustering fevers that nearly destroyed its neighbour.

Material progress came to Costa Rica during the era of Gen. Tomás Guardia, who dominated the nation from 1870 until 1882. His government curtailed liberty and increased the debt, but it also brought increases in coffee and sugar exports as well as widespread construction of schools. A new constitution, adopted in 1871, remained in effect until 1949. The emphasis on agricultural exports strained transportation, and, with mainly British funds, Costa Rica sought to link the Meseta Central with the seaports by railway. The chief promoter was an American, Minor C. Keith, who made a fortune with the opening of his rail line between Cartago and Limón. With vast land grants, Keith then entered the banana business. By the late 19th century bananas were beginning to rival coffee as the chief source of Costa Rican foreign exchange, especially after Keith's investments were merged with others to form the United Fruit Company in 1899.

Tomás Guardia

The last decades of the century were also marked by a gradual decline in Roman Catholic Church activity in secular affairs. The Jesuits were expelled for a few years, cemeteries were secularized, and public education was expanded. In 1886 free public education became compulsory; normal schools, a museum, and a national library were founded. Though the government continued to support the church, the constitution of 1871 provided for religious toleration. Strengthening the tradition of democracy for which Costa Rica is famed throughout Latin America was the victory in 1890 of Pres. José Joaquín Rodríguez in what is considered the first entirely free and honest election in all of Central America.

20th century. When Nicaragua, in the Bryan–Chamorro Treaty of 1916, gave the United States permission to use the Río San Juan (the border between Nicaragua and Costa Rica) as part of an interoceanic canal route, Costa Rica protested that its rights were being ignored. The claim was brought before the Central American Court of Justice, which ruled that Nicaragua had violated Costa Rican claims to the river; Nicaragua refused to accept the decision and withdrew from the court, a major factor in the court's death a year later.

Costa Rica's boundary with Panama (originally with Colombia) was in dispute. Arbitration awards by France and the United States in 1900 and 1914, respectively, had been generally favourable to Costa Rica and were rejected by Panama. In 1921 Costa Rica attempted forcible occu-

Boundary dispute with Panama

pation of this area (on the Pacific coast) but was diverted by the intervention of the United States. Panama then evacuated the region, but relations between the two small states were not reestablished until 1928. In 1941 the governments finally reached an accord over the boundary.

When Costa Rica held an election under direct suffrage for the first time in 1913, no candidate won a majority, and the Legislative Assembly chose Alfredo González Flores as president. Gen. Federico Tinoco Granados, disgruntled over reforms proposed by González, in 1917 led one of the nation's few revolutions. Tinoco's despotic behaviour soon cost him his popularity. His administration was also impeded by the refusal of the U.S. government to recognize his regime, and revolts and the threat of U.S. intervention caused him to resign in 1919.

This experiment in dictatorship was not repeated, and Costa Rica continued its tradition of democratic elections, nonmilitary rulers, and orderly government. A literacy test for voters was adopted in 1920 and the secret ballot in 1925. On December 8, 1941, the day after Japan attacked Pearl Harbor, the Costa Rican legislature declared war on Japan (even before the United States did) and on December 11 extended the declaration to Germany and Italy.

Costa Rica's most serious political crisis since 1917 came in 1948. A faction containing some alleged Communists tried to prevent the seating of President-elect Otilio Ulate. José Figueres, a Socialist landowner, put down the rebellion and turned the government over to Ulate. A new constitution, promulgated in 1949, prohibited the establishment or maintenance of an army, and the army was replaced by the Civil Guard (Guardia Civil). Elected in his own right in 1953, Figueres nationalized the banks and threatened the holdings of the United Fruit Company and several utility corporations. In 1955 he repelled an invasion by exiles residing in Nicaragua, and the election of Mario Echandi Jiménez in 1958 brought an end to threats of uprisings. Figueres was elected again in 1970, having meanwhile established his Partido de Liberación Nacional (PLN; National Liberation Party) as the dominant group in the Legislative Assembly.

In 1974 Daniel Oduber succeeded Figueres as president. Although both belonged to the PLN, they soon fell out over Figueres' ties to the U.S. financier Robert Vesco, who had found refuge in Costa Rica from an indictment on conspiracy charges in New York. Vesco left Costa Rica in 1978. The splintering of the PLN made possible the presidential victory of Rodrigo Carazo Odio in 1978.

More serious than shifting political alliances were the diplomatic and economic problems faced by the Carazo government. When rebellion broke out against the Somoza regime in Nicaragua, thousands fled to Costa Rica. After the overthrow of that regime in 1979, the Costa Rican tradition of political hospitality was further strained by the arrival of new waves of fugitives escaping from civil war or civil-rights abuses in the other states of Central America. Many refugees were deported for taking advantage of the exile and using Costa Rica as a military base.

Economic problems

Even more enduring were economic troubles. Inflation rates fluctuated sharply, and unemployment rose. Hospital, dock, banana, and railroad workers received small raises after disruptive strikes. Economic growth slowed to near zero when the price of oil became so high that almost the entire coffee crop was needed to pay for that single import. Many years of easy credit, excessive government spending, and unfavourable trade balances brought the nation to the brink of economic ruin. Carazo and the bankers failed to reach agreement and left the problem for the new president, Luis Alberto Monge Álvarez of the PLN, who took office in 1982. In return for extending Costa Rica's debts, the International Monetary Fund and the World Bank insisted that Monge impose severe austerity measures, including devaluation of the colón, budget and tax cuts, and suspension of some subsidies. President Monge—with years of experience as a labour organizer, legislator, cabinet member, and ambassador—announced a 100-day plan based on a "Back to the Land" movement, austerity, self-reliance, and less dependence on foreign purchases. In late 1982 he could report to his nation's 2,500,000 people the completion of vast new hydroelectric projects planned to reduce the need for imported oil.

(T.L.K.)

Panama. Panama was an important part of Spain's commercial system, and Portobelo (on the Caribbean coast) was the centre of Spain's commerce in the New World until the British admiral Edward Vernon stormed it in 1739. Nine years later the port's great annual fair was discontinued. Political subordination paralleled economic decline, and in 1751 the isthmus was demoted to a dependency of Santa Fe de Bogotá, Colombia.

Union with Colombia. Panama proclaimed its independence from Spain in 1821, but after a few months it voluntarily joined the Colombian union. For a time Panama enjoyed considerable local autonomy, but in 1843, under a new constitution, the executive power was greatly strengthened, and provincial governors were appointed. The building of the Panama Railroad was negotiated in 1845, and a convention with the United States guaranteed that country the neutrality of, and free transit across, the isthmus. The discovery of gold in California in 1848 provided the incentive for building the railroad, which upon completion in 1855 encouraged the canal planners. In 1880 Ferdinand de Lesseps began construction of an interoceanic canal, but his company collapsed in 1889. The United States became interested in the canal project in the 1890s, and, after it had extinguished English and French interests, Colombia, which was desperately in need of money, agreed in the Hay–Herran Treaty of 1903 to the transfer to the United States of a canal strip. The Colombian Senate, however, rejected the treaty.

Trans-isthmian canal plans

Oppressed by Colombian requisitions of property and impressment of men, and confident of help from the United States, Panama proclaimed its independence on November 3, 1903. Colombian forces, landed to crush the rebellion, were rendered ineffective by the trickery of officials of the Panama Railroad Company, and reinforcements from Colombia were deterred by the presence of U.S. naval forces. According to the terms of the Hay–Bunau-Varilla Treaty of November 18, 1903, the United States gained from Panama, in perpetuity, the exclusive use, occupation, and control of the Panama Canal Zone. Formal acquisition took place on May 4, 1904, and the canal was opened on August 15, 1914.

The Republic of Panama. On February 13, 1904, a constitution was adopted that contained a provision authorizing U.S. intervention in times of disorder and that provided for a centralized government headed by a president who had the authority to appoint and dismiss provincial governors. (This arrangement was altered in 1917 and 1919 to allow popular election of the president, vice president, and governors.) The constitutional convention of 1904 unanimously elected Manuel Amador Guerrero as the first president. Subsequent elections were tumultuous, and in 1908, 1912, and 1918 U.S. military forces intervened to preserve order.

The political life of the republic remained stormy, and there were many internal upheavals. In June 1940 Arnulfo Arias Madrid was elected president and promptly changed the constitution to extend the length of his term and to expand his power. Before the outbreak of World War II the United States requested sites, outside the Canal Zone, for landing fields, roads, antiaircraft batteries, and warning stations. Arias, who was pro-Fascist, demanded compensation in the form of cash, cancellation of certain debts, and the transfer to Panama of several railroad, sewer, and power properties. He was removed from office in October 1941, and Ricardo Adolfo de la Guardia succeeded to the presidency. After the attack on Pearl Harbor (December 7, 1941), Panama followed the United States into the war and transferred the defense sites.

During and after the war the United States returned 98 defense sites to Panama, and the two countries engaged in long negotiations on the remaining 36. Agreement was reached, but the Panamanian National Assembly, influenced by the threat of mob violence, rejected the proposals, and the sites were abandoned in 1947.

The year 1951 was chaotic. In January the former president (1941–45) Ricardo de la Guardia returned from exile, and the balance of power between his followers and those of Arias (president again from 1949) was seen to be held by José Remón, head of the national police force. Early in May a run on the government-supported savings bank brought the arrest of de la Guardia and others. On May 10 Remón turned against Arias, who was overthrown, and on May 11 the vice president, Alcibíades Arosemena, assumed the presidency. In the election of May 11, 1952, Remón won a decisive victory, but he was assassinated on January 2, 1955. The year 1955 was notable for the flow of capital into Panama. Work on the Inter-American Highway and on local roads was promoted by a loan from the World Bank. In 1957 the Panama Refining Company and the Panama Refining and Petrochemical Company began investing in two refining establishments.

Disorders in 1958–59

Student riots led to the imposition of a state of siege in the spring of 1958. Caches of arms were seized, and there were riots and charges of subversion. Disorders occurred in each of the first four months of 1959, and Independence Day produced a march, by men said to have been students, into the Canal Zone to raise the Panamanian flag there. The police turned them back.

In the presidential elections of 1960, Roberto F. Chiari emerged as the victor. Despite a national debt of about $83,000,000 and a budget deficit of some $10,000,000, he plunged into a vast program of slum clearance, housing, hospital construction, and health service. The plans for aiding the poor found a champion in Arnulfo Arias Madrid, who was defeated in a close contest for the presidency in 1964 by Marco A. Robles.

Under Robles the economy of Panama was uneven. Riots in January 1964 reduced the income from the Canal Zone and frightened away foreign capital. Unemployment was a serious problem, and agricultural progress continued to be retarded. Tax reforms distributed the burden of taxation more equitably. Restlessness among the populace, however, occasionally broke into open rioting, which Robles suppressed with the National Guard (Guardia Nacional). Particularly severe were disorders in March and May 1968, when Arias, again a candidate for the presidency and in control of the National Assembly, unsuccessfully attempted to bring about the impeachment of the President. Once again Arias won, and once again (after only 11 days) he was removed from office, this time by the National Guard. The guard took control of the government on October 11 and the next day formed a ruling junta that instituted censorship of the press, television, and radio; suspended other constitutional guarantees; and dissolved the National Assembly.

Emergence of Torrijos

By degrees, Col. Omar Torrijos Herrera emerged as leader of the coup. In 1972 the assembly gave him full executive powers for a period of six years. He established a facade of popular government and by a spectacular public works program transformed the appearance of much of Panama City. The costs of this and other building programs plunged the country into a heavy debt and by 1977 threatened an economic crisis.

In mid-1978 Torrijos' triumph over the Panama Canal treaties (see below) seemed to promise economic improvement. On August 6 Panamanians elected a National Assembly to choose a new president. Torrijos withdrew as a candidate and as chief of state, but he retained his position as head of the National Guard. Aristides Royo was chosen president and sworn in on October 11 (the 10th anniversary of the coup).

(A.R.W.)

Despite the transfer of the Panama Canal to Panama, the early 1980s saw no respite from the country's economic and political woes. Inflation, unemployment, and the national debt continued to grow, while income from the canal was at expected levels. Torrijos was killed in a plane crash on July 31, 1981. He was succeeded as commander of the National Guard by Florençio Flórez Aguilar, who was replaced by Rúben Darío Paredes del Río in early 1982. Royo resigned from the presidency that July, and Ricardo de la Espriella was sworn to the post.

(Ed.)

Relations with the United States. Throughout the years of Panama's independent existence, treaty relations with the United States have been subjected to several major changes, the results, for the most part, of economic stress and national pride. By the agreements of 1936, the United States yielded the right of land seizure for canal purposes and the obligation to defend Panama. The worldwide depression of the 1930s prompted an increase in the canal annuity and an expansion of trade opportunities. Eighteen years later, U.S. Pres. Dwight D. Eisenhower and Remón again raised the annuity and decreased U.S. landholdings, opening the door for Panamanians to build roads across the isthmus and to manage sanitation.

In 1958 President de la Guardia expressed the desire for equal status for the Spanish language and Panamanian flag in the Canal Zone. That year the U.S. Congress appropriated $19,000,000 for a bridge across the canal, and an instrument of transfer was signed that conveyed to Panama real estate valued at about $25,000,000. The disorders in 1958–59, with the demands to fly the Panamanian flag in the Canal Zone, led to recognition by President Eisenhower that titular sovereignty over the zone resided with Panama and to the display of the flags of both nations at specified places in the zone.

On January 9, 1964, U.S. and Panamanian schoolboys engaged in a scuffle over flying their flags over Balboa High School. Several thousand persons turned the melee into a riot that cost the lives of about 20 persons and brought injuries to scores of others; many buildings and automobiles were burned. Panama blamed the Americans, severed relations, and demanded reparations. The United States, in turn, rejected the accusations and charged Panama with inciting the riot and withholding police protection. Later an International Commission of Jurists (with a minor exception) upheld the U.S. contentions.

Treaties of 1967

Negotiations between the United States and Panama during the first part of the Robles administration led to three new treaties, signed in June 1967. The first abrogated the accord of 1903, reduced the size of the Canal Zone, and provided for joint operation of the canal. The second continued the responsibility of the United States for the Canal Zone's defense, and the third provided for a possible sea-level canal, built by and at the cost of the United States but administered jointly with Panama. These proposals aroused objections from many affected quarters, and they remained unratified.

On September 1, 1970, Torrijos formally notified the United States of his rejection of the agreements of 1967, but seven months later he moved to resume negotiations. Panama succeeded to one of the two American seats on the Security Council of the United Nations, and its delegate in March 1973 introduced a resolution urging the fulfillment of Panama's aspirations for sovereignty over the isthmus and continued negotiation under the auspices of the United Nations. The delegate from the United States vetoed the resolution. The Panamanians continued to press their cause in negotiations that resulted in a set of principles (1974) to serve as guidelines for a new treaty; one of these was that U.S. control over canal and zone would be limited in duration.

The reaction to the proposed ultimate transfer in the U.S. Congress in 1974 and 1975 was hostile. Torrijos possessed several methods of pressure with which to respond. If there was not a peaceful settlement, he declared, then there would be violence, and this produced in the U.S. government the desired spectre of guerrilla war. To further agitate the nerves of the opposition, Torrijos contrived to have officers of the National Guard inspect Soviet weapons in Cuba, and with a considerable entourage he paid a visit to Fidel Castro in January 1976.

Treaties of 1977

The U.S. presidential elections of 1976 held up the treaty conversations, but after the election of Jimmy Carter progress was rapid. On August 10, 1977, agreement was announced, and Carter and Torrijos signed the documents on September 7. The new basic treaty provided for gradual transfer of the operations of the canal to Panamanians, accomplished on April 1, 1982; phasing out of U.S. military bases; and step-by-step reversion of lands and waters used in the management of the canal. Similarly, Panama was to assume jurisdiction over the zone—including police, courts, and teachers—by degrees. A second pact promised an open and neutral canal in peace and war. The transfer was to be completed by 2000, but in ratifying the treaties in 1978 the U.S. Senate attached reservations that extended U.S. rights to defend the canal beyond that date and to maintain limited rights of intervention. Panama approved the treaties in a national plebiscite in October 1977, and the U.S. Congress passed legislation to implement the treaties on September 26, 1979. The treaties went into effect on October 1, 1979. (A.R.W./Ed.)

Belize. Belize (Spanish, Belice) was formerly called British Honduras. The current name is thought to derive from the Spanish pronunciation of Wallace, after Peter Wallace, a Scottish buccaneer who is said to have begun a settlement at the mouth of the Belize River, fronting on the Gulf of Honduras of the Caribbean Sea, about 1638. It is also possible, however, that the name could be traced to any of several Mayan words. Although the coast had been inhabited in centuries past by Maya Indians, Wallace and other British buccaneer–logwood cutters found it to be uninhabited and inhospitable. The enclaves that they founded along the coast signaled the beginning of British occupation and exploitation. Spain always regarded these adventurers as interlopers.

By treaties signed in 1763, 1783, and 1786, Spain granted to British subjects the privilege of exploiting logwood within specified boundaries but retained sovereignty over the area. The British called the establishment a settlement, to distinguish it from a colony. No formal government existed within the settlement, but its affairs were conducted by a Public Meeting and elected magistrates. The crown in 1786 appointed a superintendent, who built up royal authority at the expense of the local institutions. An Executive Council replaced the magistrates in 1840, and a Legislative Assembly was created in 1854.

The settlers earned their livelihoods largely by exploiting forest products. They first cut logwood and then turned to mahogany, employing African slaves in far-ranging, virtually independent logging crews. Early in the 19th century, mercantile interests built up a flourishing transit trade with neighbouring Spanish Central America, and this continued after the Spanish colonies attained independence in the 1820s.

Expansion of British woodcutting operations beyond treaty limits, defeat by the Bay settlers of a military expedition from Yucatán sent to expel them (1798), and claims asserted by the Central American successor states to all former Spanish interests in the area provided the basis for widely disparate views on the status of Britain in Belize. The United Provinces of Central America first challenged the British occupation, then Guatemala continued the controversy, and from time to time Mexico also asserted claim to a part of the region.

Boundary dispute with Guatemala

Great Britain and Guatemala appeared to have settled their differences in 1859 by a treaty that defined boundaries for Belize. The final article of the treaty, however, bound the parties to establish "the easiest communication" between Guatemala and Belize. The signatories disagreed on the intent of the treaty, and the communication link was not built. Guatemala insisted that the entire treaty was thus invalidated and its claims reinstated.

The nature of the settlement changed notably during the second and third quarters of the 19th century. When slavery was abolished in all British dependencies in the 1830s, the relative freedom of the logging operations made easy the transition from slave to free labour. The Caste War (or War of the Races) in Yucatán between 1847 and 1853 added some 6,000 refugee Spanish-speaking residents in northern Belize to the existing population of indigenous Maya Indians, Black Caribs, black freedmen, descendants of Europeans, and people of mixed descent. Finally, after the treaty (1859) with Guatemala, Belize became the British colony of British Honduras in 1862 and a crown colony in 1871. It remained subordinate to Jamaica until 1884, when it acquired a separate government.

The old economy based on forest products and transit trade decayed after the mid-19th century; there were promising developments in the cultivation of bananas, sugar, and citrus fruits, but underpopulation and prevailing patterns of land tenure impeded attainment of hoped-for levels of production.

After 1954 British Honduras was led through several stages of self-government to the verge of independence by George Price and his People's United Party (PUP). Unrelenting Guatemalan hostility, however, halted the process until anticipation of a regional oil boom prompted settlement. Accordingly, in March 1981 Guatemala, Great Britain, and British Honduras signed a preliminary agreement that essentially guaranteed British Honduras independence and peaceful coexistence with Guatemala. It assured Guatemala of access to the open sea from its north coast and free transit by roads and pipelines across British Honduras to free deepwater ports. When opposition in both affected countries prevented execution of these measures, Great Britain, on September 21, 1981, granted British Honduras its independence as Belize.

Belize was admitted to the United Nations, but a rule that bars admission of states involved in territorial dispute with a member delayed membership in the Organization of American States and denied Belize the protection of the Rio mutual defense pact. A British force of 1,600 remained on duty in the country, but the uncertainty of the force's tenure and of the source and nature of any replacement caused Price's government grave concern.

The strategic situation of Belize has made it the focus of sharp rivalry for influence among regional and more distant states. Sparse population, a struggling economy, bitter rivalries among political parties and factional divisions within them, the inchoate state of its national institutions, and the uncertainty of its defense capabilities continue to make Belize particularly vulnerable to meddling. (W.J.Gr.)

BIBLIOGRAPHY. The early works of JOHN L. STEPHENS, *Incidents of Travel in Central America, Chiapas and Yucatán*, 2 vol. (1841); EPHRAIM G. SQUIER, *Travels in Central America, Particularly in Nicaragua*, 2 vol. (1853), and *Notes on Central America, Particularly the States of Honduras and San Salvador* (1855); and HUBERT H. BANCROFT, *History of Central America*, 3 vol. (1882–87), remain important sources of information on the subject. Extensive bibliographies may be consulted in MARIO RODRÍGUEZ and VINCENT C. PELOSO, *A Guide for the Study of Culture in Central America* (1968); and CHARLES C. GRIFFIN (ed.), *Latin America: A Guide to the Historical Literature* (1971). MURDO J. MACLEOD, *Spanish Central America: A Socioeconomic History, 1520–1720* (1973), provides numerous insights into colonial Central American life and development. Modern and contemporary interpretations include the standard work, RALPH LEE WOODWARD, JR., *Central America, a Nation Divided* (1976); DANA G. MUNRO, *The Five Republics of Central America* (1918, reprinted 1967); FRANKLIN D. PARKER, *The Central American Republics* (1964, reprinted 1981); MARIO RODRÍGUEZ, *Central America* (1965), with an appendix of suggested readings, and *The Cádiz Experiment in Central America, 1808 to 1826* (1978), a penetrating examination of the independence epoch; and WILLIAM L. SHERMAN, *Forced Native Labor in Sixteenth-Century Central America* (1979), a massive study of Indian servitude. On the United Provinces of Central America (Central American Federation), see THOMAS L. KARNES, *The Failure of Union: Central America, 1824–1975* (1976); and ROBERT S. SMITH, "Financing the Central American Federation, 1821–1838," *Hispanic American Historical Review*, 43:483–510 (1963). On the British role in Central America, see TROY S. FLOYD, *The Anglo-Spanish Struggle for Mosquitia* (1967); WILLIAM J. GRIFFITH, *Empires in the Wilderness* (1965); ROBERT A. HUMPHREYS, *The Diplomatic History of British Honduras* (1961, reprinted 1981); ROBERT A. NAYLOR, "The British Role in Central America Prior to the Clayton-Bulwer Treaty of 1850," *Hispanic American Historical Review*, 40:361–382 (1960); DAVID A.G. WADDELL, *British Honduras: A Historical and Contemporary Survey* (1961, reprinted 1981); WAYNE M. CLEGERN, *British Honduras: Colonial Dead End, 1859–1900* (1967); O. NIGEL BOLLAND, *The Formation of a Colonial Society: Belize, from Conquest to Crown Colony* (1977); WILLIAM D. SETZEKORN, *Formerly British Honduras: A Profile of the New Nation of Belize*, rev. ed. (1981), a wide-ranging collection of information, lore, and comment gathered in anticipation of independence; RALPH LEE WOODWARD, *Belize* (1980), a bibliography; and CEDRIC H. GRANT, *The Making of Modern Belize* (1976), a discussion of 20th-century events. On the U.S. role in Central America, see CHARLES D. KEPNER and JAY HENRY SOOTHILL, *The Banana Empire: A Case Study of Economic Imperialism* (1935, reissued 1967); THOMAS L. KARNES, *Tropical Enterprise: The Standard Fruit and Steam-*

ship Company in Latin America (1978); DAVID MCCULLOUGH, *The Path Between the Seas: The Creation of the Panama Canal, 1870–1914* (1977); DANA G. MUNRO, *Intervention and Dollar Diplomacy in the Caribbean, 1900–1921* (1964); ERNESTO J. CASTILLERO REYES, *Historia de Panamá*, 7th ed. (1962); and the UNITED STATES DEPARTMENT OF STATE, *Foreign Relations of the United States* (annual), which includes information on both domestic history and international relations. STEPHEN C. SCHLESINGER and STEPHEN KINZER, *Bitter Fruit: The Untold Story of the American Coup in Guatemala* (1982); and RICHARD H. IMMERMAN, *The CIA in Guatemala: The Foreign Policy of Intervention* (1982), are both studies of the U.S. role in the overthrow of Jacobo Arbenz. Representative monographs include JOHN H. ADLER *et al.*, *Public Finance and Economic Development in Guatemala* (1952, reissued 1970); KENNETH J. GRIEB, *Guatemalan Caudillo: The Regime of Jorge Ubico, Guatemala, 1931–1944* (1979); DAVID MCCREERY, *Development and the State in Reforma Guatemala* (1982), a study of the regime of Justo Rufino Barrios; INTERNATIONAL BANK FOR RECONSTRUCTION AND DEVELOPMENT, *The Economic Development of Nicaragua* (1953); RICHARD MILLETT, *Guardians of the Dynasty: A History of the U.S. Created Guardia Nacional de Nicaragua and the Somoza Family* (1977); NEILL MACAULEY, *The Sandino Affair* (1967); CHARLES D. AMERINGER, *Don Pepe* (1978); STACY MAY *et al.*, *Costa Rica: A Study in Economic Development* (1952); JOHN P. BELL, *Crisis in Costa Rica: The 1948 Revolution* (1971); ROBERT S. CHAMBERLAIN, *The Conquest and Colonization of Honduras, 1502–1550* (1953, reprinted 1966); LUIS MARIÑAS OTERO, *Honduras* (1963), a history; PAUL THEROUX, *The Mosquito Coast: A Novel* (1981); THOMAS P. ANDERSON, *The War of the Dispossessed: Honduras and El Salvador, 1969* (1981); STEPHEN WEBRE, *José Napoleón Duarte and the Christian Democratic Party in Salvadoran Politics, 1960–1972* (1979); DAVID A. HOWARTH, *Panama: Four Hundred Years of Dreams and Cruelty* (U.K. title, *The Golden Isthmus*, both 1966), a popular history; JOHN and MAVIS BIESANZ, *The People of Panama* (1955); ALEX PÉREZ-VENERO, *Before the Five Frontiers: Panama from 1821–1903* (1978), a survey of the period between Spanish rule and separation from Colombia; and DIANE DE GRAFFEN-REID and PHILIP WHEATON (eds.), *Panama: Sovereignty for a Land Divided* (1976), a statement against U.S. presence in Panama.

Central Asian Cultures

Central Asia comprises the inland part of Asia, farthest removed from the world oceans, in the midst of the greatest landmass on Earth. Because of its geographic location, prevailing winds, and drainage, it is a zone of great aridity, extending from the Caspian Sea in the west to northwestern China and Mongolia in the east, and from southern Siberia in the north to northern Iran and Afghanistan in the south. Throughout the region rainfall never exceeds 12 inches (300 millimetres) in an average year, far too little to grow grain; parts of Central Asia receive less than 4 inches of rain per year. The exception is near mountain ranges, where there is higher rainfall and a more rapid change from one climatic and ecological zone to the next. The prevailing winds blow from west to east, losing their moisture before reaching the inland parts of Asia. Consequently, all agriculture requires artificial irrigation.

Natural zones

There are four major natural, or ecological, zones of Central Asia: steppe, steppe–desert, desert, and mountain. Only recently and in a minor way have human beings disturbed the ecological processes in the area. These ecological zones run in broad bands from east to west across Eurasia. The northernmost zone is the steppe, a belt of grassland covering Mongolia and northern Kazakhstan and extending into southern Siberia and eastern Europe. The terrain is flat, almost featureless, with few rivers and mountains. The grass cover is denser toward and within the European parts, where there is somewhat more rainfall; in eastern Kazakhstan the grass cover thins out, becoming the dry steppe. Mongolia is a high-altitude steppe, averaging about a mile above sea level; Kazakhstan is low-altitude steppe, lying at sea level. Steppe–desert (semidesert), too, is grassland, drier than the steppe, lying at low altitude and not extending into Europe or Siberia. There the grass cover is thinner than in the steppe, with patches bare of plant cover increasing in size and number toward the south. It is likewise flat terrain with few watercourses and no mountains. In the desert grasses give way to dry vegetation. There lie the innermost parts of Asia, south of the steppe and steppe–desert farthest from the moisture-bearing winds and the seas, with most intensive water evaporation. The Central Asian deserts are vast, spreading from the Red Sands (Kyzylkum) of Turkmenistan to the Black Sands (Kara-Kum) of southern Kazakhstan, to Sinkiang, and to the Gobi. The mountain zone lies in the southeast of Soviet Central Asia, the Pamirs rising to nearly five miles as part of the highest mountain systems in the world.

Cereal grasses, including forms of wheat, are native to the region, being found wild even at present. They were domesticated by the early farmers and have been continuously grown since. Other crops, such as rice and cotton, are historically recent imports. The grasses of the steppe and steppe–desert provide good livestock fodder. Animals native to the steppe include the wild horse and wild cattle, the camel, and the wild goat. The wild yak is native to the mountains of Tibet and Mongolia, and other mountain fauna include wild sheep and goats. All these animals, when domesticated, play roles in the herding economy and are raised for food, trade, and transport.

The few rivers are shallow, narrow, and shifting and many are dry in summer. They flow only inland, some into the Caspian, Aral, Balkhash, and lesser lakes of the region; others lose themselves in the sands of the desert. They are of limited usefulness for transport and navigation, but they irrigate bands of fields along the rivers.

Transportation is chiefly overland, hence the importance of the domesticated animals. The historical significance of Central Asia to the world was that it served in the manner of a great inland sea, connecting China, India, Iran, and Europe by means of camel, ass, and horse caravans that moved goods and peoples, permitted military invasions, and spread technology, religions, ideas, and science through and across its breadth.

The vegetation and fauna of the arid zone made possible two indigenous economic specializations. First, irrigation agriculture developed near the valleys of the Amu Darya, Syrdarya, Ili, and Zeravshan rivers and in such mountain valleys as the Fergana. Second, specialization in pastoralism occurred in the steppe and steppe–desert belts where grasses and water provide sustenance for livestock. Herding communities near the deserts take their flocks there in the spring when the desert briefly flowers. The agricultural and pastoral economies were mutually supportive, each being dependent on the products of the other.

The peasants lived in permanent settled villages, in houses of sun-dried brick. The herding families lived in tents of felt stretched over lattice frames that they could collapse and pack into carts as they moved from pasture to pasture. Their communities were always mobile, each family having a camel or two to pull the family cart, its tent, and possessions; horses to transport goods and carry the herdsmen to, from, and around the pastures; mares and cows for breeding and milking; sheep and goats for milk and wool. The herders owned many sheep and goats but only small numbers of the other stock.

Languages

The languages of the region are members of the Altaic and Indo-European families. The Altaic family comprises three major divisions, two of which, Turkic and Mongol, are represented in Central Asia and neighbouring parts of Siberia and China. The Turkic speakers include Kazakhs, Kirgiz, Uzbeks, Kara-Kalpaks, and Turkmens. The Mongol speakers include the Khalkhas of Mongolia, Buryats of southern Siberia, Kalmyks of the Volga, and several groups in the neighbouring provinces of China (*e.g.*, Daghur and Monguor). The Indo-European speakers are the Tadzhiks, speaking an Iranian language; in ancient times Central Asia was inhabited by a number of other Iranian-speaking groups (Scythians, Massagetai, Parthians). Central Asia has in recent centuries received new migrants speaking Russian and Ukrainian.

The Turkic, Mongol, and Iranian speakers of Central Asia were encountered in antiquity, and modern peoples in the region are their descendants, mixed together with the later immigrants, invaders, settlers, and resettlers.

TRADITIONAL CULTURE PATTERNS

Continental setting. The historical period in Central Asia began about 500 BC with the rise of the traditional cultures. These cultures flourished about AD 500 down to the 20th century, when the region was absorbed in the great revolutionary movements emanating from Russia and China.

Pastoral culture patterns

The cultural pattern of the herdsmen grew rapidly, and, according to Chinese reports, these peoples by the 3rd century BC had already formed the herding communities that they now have. The Chinese reported that their country "is the back of a horse," meaning that the communities were nomadic.

The herding village community moved as a single unit across pastoral tracks that they owned and defended, for if others used their tracks their own herds would die for lack of grass or water on the way from pasture to pasture. Herds and men spread out in the summer pasture, gathering in closely during the winter encampment. The herdsmen defended the herds from predacious beasts, such as wolves and snow leopards, and helped the herds to forage beneath the snow. They helped the mares to foal, the cows to calve, and the lambs and kids to find the teats of their mothers beneath the woolly undercoats. The herds provided food (mainly milk, rarely meat) and materials for clothing and housing. The pastoralists were traditionally nomadic; that is, they moved about in small communities together with their herds in fixed annual round, from winter camp to spring and summer pastures, and back to the winter camp. The Kazakhs, Kirgiz, Turkmens, Uzbeks, and Karakalpaks raised herds of horses, cattle, sheep, goats, camels, and asses; the Mongols raised all of these except the ass; in the east, the Mongols of Mongolia also raised the yak.

The cultural pattern of the Central Asian irrigation-cultivators differed little from that of the great agricultural civilizations neighbouring them in China, Iran, India, and the Near East. Water was scarce, and thus life depended on careful maintenance of the soil and water systems by village communities that collectively coordinated their labour and managed their resources. The result was an ability to support great populations in dense concentrations, ranging up to hundreds of persons per square mile. Harnessed to the needs of their livestock, the pastoral peoples stood in sharp contrast: they spread out thinly over the landscape, their average density being no more than two or three people per square mile.

Irrigation required a collective and planned effort and a peaceful inner regime so that the peasants could work together. War disturbed these efforts both by preventing peaceful labours and by drawing the peasants away to military defense and attack. When wars came, the irrigation channels deteriorated, and civilizations raised upon them disappeared rapidly.

The Tadzhiks had an old tradition of agriculture in Central Asia; the Turks, their neighbours, originally herdsmen, gradually developed an agricultural wing to their village economies. Over centuries agriculture became increasingly important among the Uzbeks, somewhat less so among the Turkmens, Kazakhs, and Kirgiz. The agricultural peoples grew grain (rice and wheat), cotton, and vegetables and raised fowl. Central Asia, together with Iran and Sinkiang, is still a world centre of melon growing; many fruits and nuts such as the peach, pistachio, and almond originated there.

Exchange systems

Mongols and Turks became highly specialized herders and undertook little or no agriculture. They traded for most of their agricultural needs with farmers who were likewise specialized. The Mongols traded with the northern Chinese, who spared no land for pasture; and the Turks traded with the neighbouring cultivators, some of whom were Turks, some Chinese, and some Iranian (Tadzhiks, Persians). Neighbouring Chinese, Iranians, and the farmers of Central Asia similarly depended on the herders for pastoral products, being bound together in great institutional networks of economic exchange, their products distributed in the bazaars and caravan trade and collected and offered as political tribute—actions of great economic significance. Marriage ceremonies also were occasions for ritual presentations and gifts in localized exchanges. The great institutional networks embraced the entire Asian continent, as well as parts of Europe and North Africa during the period of the nomadic empires in the Middle Ages. The most highly specialized relation was that of the Mongols and the Chinese; the former monopolized the herding, the latter the farming of east Asia. Their symbiotic system was not a smoothly working mechanism; it broke down frequently, accompanied by wars and unrest among the great economic wings and civilizations.

Social organization. The Central Asian Turks and Mongols had the same kinship system, founded upon the principle of common descent reckoned patrilineally, from father to son. The founding father and his son or sons formed a kin-village community, together with their wives, children, more distant collateral kin, dependents, and clients. The villages were maintained by the direct male descendants over a number of generations, forming new ones as the population grew and the need for land increased. Families related by descent and marriage lived in a common household, raised the crops or herds together, and maintained a common economy. Several such great families, whose founders were related as brothers or close cousins, formed a village. Each family owned stock and land in common; the agricultural village was the unit of management of the cultivated land and the irrigation channels; the nomads' village was the unit of range (pasture, camp, and track) management.

Marriage rules

A son brought his wife to the paternal household; the daughter joined that of her husband and his father. Marriage with several wives was practiced, but it was costly and rare. In arranging marriages, elders would trace ancestry back to the sixth generation and even further. In theory, a marriage was permitted only if a common male ancestor existed beyond the sixth generation. This restriction meant that a marriage partner could be found not only out of the village, but out of the neighbouring villages or districts, because these villages were generally composed of kinsmen descended from a common male ancestor only four or five generations removed. The kin-community clusters formed a local district and had a number of economic functions, managing the pastoral range land, maintaining local resources and pasture tracks, and fending off incursions. They also provided troops of horse to the imperial armies when levies of men were made.

The village of the sedentary agricultural peoples of Central Asia was likewise composed of patrilineal extended families, but the long lineage organization of the herdsmen was not found there. Marriage outside the peasant village community was nevertheless required; the husband took his wife to the father's household; and the daughter left the family into which she was born to join that of the husband, under the patriarch, his father. The peasant villages were bound to the political system of the Oriental empires, which centred on the great cities.

Political organization. At the base of the Mongol empire of Genghis Khan, which flourished in the 13th and 14th centuries, stood the nomadic kin communities that were clustered in groups, tracing descent through the male line from a common male ancestor and living on a common territory. These descent groups formed a clan ruled by a chief. The clan chief was a relative in the father's line of every member of the clan. He was a minor nobleman and the senior member of the highest line traced back according to the principle of primogeniture to the founding ancestor. The differentiation into aristocracy and commoners began at this point. The clans were grouped into clan confederations, and these in turn into principalities, with the nobility becoming ever grander. At the peak stood the emperor, who was related in theory to every Mongol in the first to twentieth degree or even higher. He was, however, also surrounded by courtiers and retainers, warriors who respected neither kinship nor grandeur in carrying out the imperial commands. The Mongol empire ruled briefly over most of Asia and eastern Europe when the strength of the herding peoples prevailed over the agricultural empires whose leadership was broken down. Life in the villages below went on as before.

The peasant villages were linked in local exchange systems with the herding communities; the empires of herdsmen and agriculturists were linked in great, continent-wide exchange institutions. When these institutions of trade, tribute collection, and exchange broke down, one side would sweep in and conquer the other. Thus Genghis Khan and his dynasty prevailed during the 13th century. China then was using its soldiers to maintain internal order and could not keep the nomads out. The horsemen came to trade, but instead they took the agricultural produce they wanted and retained the stock they had intended to exchange. The nomad chief returned from the encounter doubly enriched, and this attracted further braves to his standard. The increased wealth and armed might enabled him to extend his conquests further. The pattern on different scales and with some variations in products is encountered again in the west of Asia, between Kazakhs, Uzbeks, Tadzhiks, Turkmens, and Iranians.

Relationship between the city and peasantry. The agricultural principalities centred on the great cities of Central Asia, such as Samarkand, Bukhara, and Khiva, all known for their magnificence. Their wealth was based on the labour of the peasantry. At times their hegemony embraced the surrounding pastoral peoples; at times the pastoral dynasties swept in and conquered the city-based empires. The cities usually tempered and civilized the nomad conquerors, so that after a few years their dynasties were no different from any other.

City centres

The cities were the centres of rulership over the agricultural domains, at times over those of the pastoralists as well, alternating between dynasts of one or the other provenience. The cities served as the centres of trade and exchange between the products of the herdsmen and the soil cultivators; also, they served as the centres for the great transcontinental exchange between China, India, and the West; hence their wealth. They were also local manufacturing centres, particularly of the sumptuary ware of the courts: the jewels, silks, brocades, rugs, tiles, and metalwork that were the wonder of the world. The separation between town and countryside was not so pronounced as in the modern day, and the opposition between peasants and townsmen was not so deep as that found, for instance, in European history. The peasants engaged in manufacture and in cottage industries such as spinning and weaving. The nomads worked in leather, felt, and other pastoral products. All brought their goods to the bazaars and caravanseries of the cities for trade. The cities were also international trade centres, typically for the medieval Silk Road linking China and the Mediterranean across Central Asia. Gardens and orchards were cultivated by the urban populations within and immediately without the city walls. During the 14th to 16th centuries there were no greater centres for astronomy, mathematics, medicine, history, theological doctrine, metaphysical speculation, and poetry.

The great Oriental monarchies were built around the urban centres. Land was cultivated by the peasantry living in the village communities. The monarchs taxed the peasants heavily, but solely to maintain themselves, their court, and their army. Nothing was spent on the health, education, or welfare of the subjects. The only other enterprise in which the monarchic power and the peasantry interacted occurred when the central power mobilized the peasantry to clean the irrigation canals.

Religions of Central Asia. The religious leaders of the Turks and Mongols were shamans. The shaman is a figure who induces a state of trance in himself, wherein he believes that he communicates with the spirits of the supernatural world. He then performs rites of divination and makes oracular pronouncements about the outcome of a hunt or of battles; and he dispels the evil spirits that cause disease and bring misfortune to men and beasts. As the Turks and Mongols came into increasing contact with the great civilizations of Asia, their shamanist practices and beliefs became intermingled with those of the great world religions, particularly Buddhism and Islām. Buddhism, originating in India, became implanted in Tibet and then in Mongolia. It gained influence among the Mongols as their relations to the Chinese and Tibetans were intensified and diminished when the contacts faded. The Mongols were converted in some degree to Buddhism in the 13th and 14th centuries; its role among them retreated in the 15th and 16th centuries; but they were converted again in the 1590s, and its influence remains among them today.

Buddhism and Islām

The forms of Buddhism are many. The Mongolian form is that of Tibet, founded on the existence on earth of the perpetual reincarnation of the Buddha. The Dalai Lama is the "Living Buddha," the head of the cult. His chief officers are manifestations on earth of the lesser members of the Buddhist pantheon, who intercede on behalf of the salvation of the devout. The entire cult centres on a system of monasteries governed by abbots and staffed by monks who perform the rituals of the faith and in turn are supported by its followers. It is now a state church in the Mongolian People's Republic.

Islām came to western and Central Asia within a few decades of the Hegira or Flight of Muḥammed (supposedly in AD 622). It has been the traditional religion of the Turks and Tadzhiks for more than 1,200 years. Most of the Muslims are Sunnī, as opposed to the Shīʿites of Iran and to the Ismāʿīlīs, a sect represented by a few small tribes in the mountains of Tadzhikistan, but more importantly in Afghanistan and Pakistan. The tradition of Islām was rigidly followed in the cities and sedentary villages of central Asia and more liberally or freely observed in the nomadic communities. Women went veiled in the cities, less so in the villages, and not at all in pastoral encampments. The doctrine was fully debated in the cities, but superficially, if at all, among the peasants and herdsmen; there were many mullahs, or clerics, in the cities, but few in the villages, and fewer still among the nomads. The great urban mosques and *ʿulamā*'s (religious colleges) were centres not only of prayer but also of learning—primarily theology and, to some extent, philosophy and of the sciences.

The religious systems of Buddhism and Islām involved Central Asia in a great set of institutions and institutional relations that bound the area to similar institutions of east and south Asia (in the case of Buddhism) and to the Near East (in the case of Islām). These institutional networks of the Buddhist monasteries and of the Islāmic mosques and religious foundations (*waqf*) and orders (brotherhoods of monks and preachers) traced out paths across the entire continent similar to the economic and political networks of institutions. In addition to religious conversions of entire countries and transfer of cults and belief systems from one part of the world to another, the widespread movement of people, ideas, world views, science, and technology resulted. Whole populations were brought from the Middle East to Central Asia in the wake of the Islāmic conquest and conversion. Primitive peoples in the refuge areas of the mountains and the Arctic were brought into contact with the literate civilizations to the south, east, and west. And the great literate civilizations were brought into contact with one another, Central Asia serving as the zone of contact. The means for bringing this active contact was not any vague process of diffusion; instead, it was the network of trade routes, the institutions of political rulership, and those of the world religious systems.

THE CULTURES TODAY

The Turks and Mongols of Central Asia are all parts of the Soviet Union and of the Peoples' Republics of China and Mongolia. The traditional ways of life have been radically changed by the revolutionary processes of the 20th century. Since the 1920s, millions of Russians and other peoples from different parts of the U.S.S.R. have been settled in Central Asia, continuing a process begun in the 19th century. The surviving remnants of older regimes, such as the emirate of Bukhara and the Khanate of Khiva, have been replaced by the Soviet political system. As a consequence, the profound divergencies and symbiosis between cultivators and pastoralists have been virtually eradicated. The two great cultural wings have been caught in a single institutional system emanating from the Soviet regime.

Modern agriculture

Central Asian agriculture continues to require artificial irrigation, and the same crops are raised: the cereal grains (wheat, rice), cotton (of improved sorts), vegetables, hemp and other fibres, fruits and melons. The agricultural production of Soviet Central Asia today, however, is carried on not by the family or the village but by a system of state and collective farms. Tractors and trucks have advanced the mechanization of agriculture. The agricultural population still lives in villages of sundried brick, but electric power is everywhere. The pastoral practices of Central Asia and Mongolia have been rationalized. The herds now consist of great flocks or herds of one type of animal, instead of mixed combinations as of old, because the family no longer maintains the old pastoral practices; teams of herders are now employed. The family used to need animals in a definite proportion; now the herding family lives in a settled village and the herders go off to ranges with the animals for pasturing (transhumance). They no longer live in tents but in the same kinds of houses and villages as the tillers of the soil.

The Islāmic faith is much restricted, the number of colleges and mosques reduced, and the brotherhoods and foundations absolutely banned. The Buddhist monastic system is sharply reduced in Mongolia: at one time, it is guessed, the monasteries included one-third of all the males of the country; today there are only two major monasteries, numbering together but a few score monks. Religious proselytization is restricted throughout the region.

Soviet Central Asia is organized into the union republics of Uzbekistan, Tadzhikistan, Kirgizia, and Turkmenia; Karakalpakskaya is a part of Uzbekistan, each republic bearing the name of one of the major peoples of the region. Kazakhstan is included with these republics in the ethnographic accounts. Russians form the majority of the population of Kazakhstan, and they are second in number to the native people in each of the other republics. The Russian migration into the area has accompanied a vast effort, begun in the 1930s, to collectivize the agriculture and the herding according to the Soviet pattern, and to nationalize all the land for farming and herding and all the manufacturing and mining industry. The cities have been built up along modern lines, and transportation has been modernized. The Russian population has been closely associated with the new developments, as well as with the Soviet administration. The capitals and other cities of the region are at once administrative centres of the Soviet system and centres of industry, trade, education, the arts, and public entertainment. The natural resources of Central Asia are intensively exploited, including oil, iron ore, coal, and nonferrous metals. Railroads and airfields have replaced the caravans of old.

Mongolia has been developed on the pattern of the Soviet system; the Mongolian People's Republic is a member of several economic and political blocs of nations in which the U.S.S.R. is the dominant power. There are 1,200,000 people in Mongolia, whose capital, Ulaanbaatar, the administrative, industrial, and cultural centre of the country, includes one quarter of the total population of the country.

The ancient lineage and clan systems have been entirely forgotten. The genealogies are no longer kept up because their function in social organization, marriage, and military and economic activities is no longer applicable in modern Central Asia. The great extended families, under a patriarch's dominion, have been replaced by the new forms of the family, small in size and composed of parents and their children. The father of the family is typically a wage earner in a factory or state farm. The children now go to school in the Soviet educational system, rather than, as before, in the schools run by the Islāmic or Buddhist clergy. Modern technology is being introduced throughout the region, and modern medical, educational and welfare practices have been instituted. The desire of parents to have many children in order to have someone to take care of them in old age is no longer a deeply felt social incentive; medical practices have reduced infant mortality so that the need to have many children in the hopes that a few would survive to care for the parents has likewise been reduced as a social force in child breeding. These trends hold equally for pastoralists and cultivators, for the old differences in institutional organization between them have been eradicated by the broad trends of modernization and collectivization.

BIBLIOGRAPHY. General surveys of the peoples and culture of Soviet Central Asia may be found in LAWRENCE KRADER, *Peoples of Central Asia*, 3rd ed. (1971); and in GEOFFREY WHEELER, *The Peoples of Soviet Central Asia* (1966). General histories of Mongolia and of Soviet Central Asia have been prepared by CHARLES R. BAWDEN, *The Modern History of Mongolia* (1968), and GEOFFREY WHEELER, *The Modern History of Soviet Central Asia* (1964). The cultural background of the Turks and Mongol pastoralists are given in LAWRENCE KRADER, "The Cultural and Historical Position of the Mongols," *Asia Major*, 3:169–183 (1952); "Feudalism and the Tatar Polity of the Middle Ages," *Comparative Studies in Society and History*, 1:76–99 (1958); and "Pastoralism," *International Encyclopedia of the Social Sciences*, vol. 11, pp. 453–461 (1968). See also Т.А. Жданко (ed.), *Материалы к историко-этнографическому атласу Средней Азии и Казахстана* (1961). W.F. ALBRIGHT, *From the Stone Age to Christianity*, 2nd ed. (1957), contains an attack on the notion of geographic determination of Central Asian history and culture. FRANCOIS BERNIER, *Voyages de François Bernier*, 2 vol. (1699; Eng. trans., *Travels in the Mogul Empire A.D. 1656–1668*, rev. ed., 1891), is an early report on Oriental despotism. K.A. WITTFOGEL, *Oriental Despotism* (1957, reprinted 1963), is a recent statement of the same subject. J.A. BOYLE (trans. and ed.), *History of the World Conqueror*, 2 vol. (1958), is the medieval account of Genghis Khan by 'Ala-ad-Din 'Ata-Malik Juvaini. The *Central Asian Review* (3/year), is a periodical surveying current developments.

(L.Kr.)

Central Asian Peoples, Arts of

The term Central Asia has no specific boundaries in a geographical context, but cultural historians generally apply it to the territory bordered on the north by Siberia in the Soviet Union and on the south by Iran, Pakistan, Bangladesh (formerly East Pakistan), and India. This area comprises the present Soviet republics of Kazakstan, Turkmenistan, Uzbekistan, Kirgiziya, and Tadzhikistan and portions of the Sinkiang Uighur Autonomous Region of China—the populations of which are largely of Turkic stock—and the kingdom of Afghanistan. For the purposes of this article, the term is further extended to include as well Siberia and the Soviet Arctic lands and, in the south and east, the Altaic regions of Mongolia, Manchuria (Northeast Provinces), and Tibet and the Himalayan kingdoms of Nepal, Bhutan, and Sikkim.

This immense tract of land—with its highly varied topography and climate and its diversity of ethnic and linguistic backgrounds—encouraged the development of greatly varied artistic styles and traditions among the inhabitants of widely separated regions. These differences were magnified by the emergence of dissimilar religions, which in turn encouraged the formation of distinctive schools or traditions of art. Further artistic variances can be attributed to cultural time lag, for comparable stages of artistic development were not reached simultaneously throughout the area.

The arts that developed across Central Asia often fed or were fed by those of adjoining cultural regions or by such supraregional influences as Islām. Although reference will be made to such cross-cultural interactions wherever appropriate, more detailed information on these other areas may be found in such articles as ISLAMIC PEOPLES, ARTS OF; and SOUTH ASIAN PEOPLES, ARTS OF and in separate articles on the specific arts of East Asia, especially the sections on China. (T.T.R.)

This article is divided into the following major sections:

The study of Central Asian music

III. Performing arts: dance and theatre
- Shamanic ritual
- Buddhist ritual
- Folk dance

IV. Visual arts
- Prehistoric cultures
- Nomadic cultures
- Parthia
- The kingdoms of western Turkistan and Afghanistan
- Kushan
- Eastern Turkistan
- Arctic regions
- Himalayan cultures of Nepal and Tibet

I. Literature

Of the relatively few Central Asian languages that have developed written literatures, the most important are Turkic, Tibetan, and Mongol. (For a treatment of the Central Asian languages, see ALTAIC LANGUAGES; PALEO-SIBERIAN LANGUAGES; SINO-TIBETAN LANGUAGES.) This article will deal with Tibetan and Mongolian literatures from their inception to the 20th century and with Turkic literature from its inception to the 11th century, when the Muslim invasion introduced a period of Islāmic culture. Subsequent Turkic literature is treated in the Turkish literature section of ISLAMIC PEOPLES, ARTS OF, which also treats Central Asian literatures written in Arabic and Persian. (For literature in Chinese, written in Central Asia, see the article LITERATURE, EAST ASIAN.)

TURKISH LITERATURE

The purely Turkish period in the history of Turkish literatures came before the conversion of the Turks to Islām and covers approximately the 8th century to the 11th AD. The oldest literary legacy of the pre-Islāmic period is to be found in the Orhon inscriptions, discovered in the valley of the Orhon, northern Mongolia, in 1889 and deciphered in 1893 by the Danish philologist Vilhelm Thomsen. The inscriptions are on two large monuments, erected in 732 and 735 in honour of the Turkish prince Kül and his brother Bilge Kagan and are carved in a script used also for inscriptions found in Mongolia, Siberia, and western Turkistan and called by Thomsen "Turkish runes." They relate in epic and forceful language the origins of the Turks, the golden age of their history, their subjugation by the Chinese, and their liberation by Bilge Kagan. The polished style suggests considerable earlier development of the language. Excavations in Chinese Turkistan have brought to light important specimens of writings of the Uighur Turks from the 9th century to the 11th. Maḥmūd Kāshgarī's comprehensive dictionary (1071?) contains specimens of old Turkish poetry in the typical form of quatrains (*dörtlük*), representing all the principal genres: epic, pastoral, didactic, lyric, and elegiac. (F.I.)

"Turkish runes"

TIBETAN LITERATURE

Tibetan was developed as a literary language from the 7th century onward as a result of earlier cultural contacts with neighbouring Buddhist countries, namely, the small states of the Takla Makan, especially Khotan (Ho-t'ien) and the ancient kingdoms of northwestern India (modern Gilgit, Kashmir, and Kulu) and Nepal. Scripts of Indian origin were in use in these countries, so the Tibetans also adapted an Indian script to suit their own very different language. By far the greater number of the works produced between the 7th century and the 13th are skillfully methodical translations of Buddhist works, largely from Sanskrit, on which Indian scholars and Tibetan translators worked side by side. In order to translate them, the Tibetans had to create an entirely new (and therefore artificial) vocabulary of religious and philosophical terms, mainly by ingenious compounding of simple terms available in their own language. Apart from some religious terms in daily use, this vocabulary remains a specialized scholarly language. An indigenous literature was also produced: annals and chronicles, sets of spells and prognostications, legendary and liturgical works, all representing the remains of ancient oral traditions. Large collections of such manuscript fragments, all earlier than the 11th century, were discovered early in the 20th century in the Cave of the Thousand Buddhas near Tun-huang (at the eastern side of the Takla Makan).

Indigenous literature of Tibet

The quasi-official work of translating authorized Indian Buddhist texts, which continued for six centuries, gave incentive to the Bon-pos (the followers of the pre-Buddhist religion of Tibet) to collect and write down their own early traditions; but in so doing they adopted many Buddhist ideas and, inevitably, used the new vocabulary. The followers of the earliest Buddhist traditions to enter Tibet (the rNying-ma-pa, or "The Old Order") also committed their teachings to writing; and, conversely, these are interspersed with pre-Buddhist traditions.

The official Tibetan Buddhist canon was closed in the 13th century; it consisted of two parts, the *Kanjur* ("translated word," teachings or reputed teachings of the Buddhas themselves) and the *Tanjur* ("translated treatises," mainly commentaries by Indian teachers). By this time, however, there already existed some orthodox Buddhist works of Tibetan origin (for example, *Mi-la ras-pa* and *sGam-po-pa*); and from the 13th century onward, under the impetus given by the prolixity of religious houses and orders, there were produced such lengthy and numerous collections of historical and biographical works, treatises and commentaries, liturgy and religious drama that Tibetan literature must be one of the most extensive in the world. Just as in the European Middle Ages there was little secular literature worth the name, so there is none in Tibetan except for a great epic (*Rgal-po Ge-sar dgra-'dul gyi rtogs-pa brjod-pa*, "The Great Deeds of King Gesar, Destroyer of Enemies") that recounts the exploits of the king and magic hero Gesar. This work grew through the centuries, assimilating whatever material pleased the fancy of the bards.

Secular literature

After the craft of printing from incised wood blocks was introduced from China, possibly in the 14th century, certain monasteries became famous printing houses. This form of printing continued until the Chinese invasion in 1959. Manuscripts and block-printed books are always of elongated shape, thus imitating the form of ancient Indian palm-leaf manuscripts. There are considerable collections in some European libraries—London, Paris, and Rome—but few translations are available because of the small number of scholars of Tibet.

Despite the phonetic changes in the spoken dialects since the script was fixed, the Tibetans have never changed their system of writing. Thus, once the literary language and the various types of script have been mastered, the reader has immediate access to all literature of the 7th to the 20th century, though changes in style and vocabulary have left many obscurities in the earliest works. Since there is no modern style of writing, the 20th-century colloquial language can be written only in the traditional medium (as though, for example, one had to write modern Italian with Latin spellings and grammatical forms); the Tibetans themselves compose even personal letters in a conventional literary style. (D.L.S.)

MONGOLIAN LITERATURE

Mongolian literature begins with the *Secret History of the Mongols*, an Imperial chronicle dealing with the life and times of Genghis Khan and his successors, written about 1240. *Üligers*, orally transmitted epic stories in verse, form the bulk of native literary expression. Highly stylized, they relate adventures of legendary heroes and villains. In spite of their great length (sometimes more than 20,000 lines), they are recited from memory by bards. Like the other epics, such as the Greek *Iliad* and the Roman *Aeneid*, they are genuine artistic creations. The verses alliterate in couplets or quatrains, are seven or eight syllables long, and are characterized by parallelism. Besides Genghis Khan, the epic stories tell of heroes such as Erintsen Mergen, Engke Bolod Khan, and Geser Khan (the last of Tibetan origin). The villain of the epics is the many-headed monster, the *manggus*, whom the hero always defeats.

Historical chronicles represent another important form of indigenous literature. Usually beginning with the creation of the world from primordial elements, they attempt to link the Indian and Tibetan rulers with the house of Genghis Khan. Such are the *Altan tobchi* ("The Golden Button"), composed about 1655 and giving a world history down to Ligdan Khan (1604–34); another *Altan tobchi* (written about 100 years later); and the *Erdeni-yin tobchi* ("The Jeweled Button"), written in 1662 by Saghang Sechen.

Mongolian historical chronicles

Mongolian written literature was profoundly influenced by the introduction of Buddhism around the end of the 1500s. Earlier surviving written works (on stone or paper) are mostly official documents; and no oral epics were written down until the late 1880s. The advent of Buddhism evoked translations of its sacred writings and related works. A Buddhist canonical collection, the *Kanjur* (comprising the *sūtras* and *vinaya* of the *Tripiṭaka*), was translated and printed in 1635 in 108 volumes; the *Tanjur*, containing canonical commentary and noncanonical works in its 225 volumes, followed in 1741. Two especially well-known sermons (*sūtras*) of Buddha are the *Altan gerel* ("Golden Beam") and the *Chagan lingqua* ("White Lotus"), or, as they are known in Sanskrit, *Suvarṇaprabhāsa* and *Saddharmapuṇḍarīka*. None of these works, however, is indigenous.

Religious but nondogmatic birth stories (called in Sanskrit *Jātaka*) deal with Buddha's meritorious deeds, and, like the parables of Christianity, illustrate religious truths. Best known is the *Üliger-ün dalai* ("The Sea of Stories"). Translations of other Indian fables are the *Siddhi Kür* ("Tales of the Vampire") and the *Bigarmijid* ("Saga of King Vikramāditya").

In the 18th and 19th centuries Chinese traders brought from China many Mongolian translations of Chinese novels of enchantment and romance, including the *San Kuo chih yen-i* (*Romance of the Three Kingdoms*) and others.

20th-century literature

In the early 20th century T. Zhamtsarano, a Russian-educated Buriat writer and intellectual, founded the short-lived Mongolian newspaper *Shine toli* ("The New Mirror"). He also translated the works of some Western authors, such as Edgar Allan Poe, Jules Verne, and H.G. Wells.

After a Soviet state was established in Mongolia in the early 1920s, the power and influence of the Tibetan Buddhist church declined, and with it the literature it sponsored. There began to arise a revolutionary and Socialist literature serving the people according to the current beliefs of the Communist Party. Popular themes were social criticism of the feudal past, with its exploitation of the people, and exemplary tales that showed new Socialist values and educated readers to overcome the resistance of reactionary forces. Mongolian reliance on and gratitude for the fraternal Soviet Union and its assistance is an ever-present undercurrent. The rise of a system of schooling, extending to the university level, has enabled many young Mongolian writers, poets, artists, and actors to achieve, within limits, a self-expression never before available to them. Leading 20th-century modern writers are Dashdorjiyn Natsagorj, Ts. Damdinsürün, D. Sengee, S. Erdene, and others. (J.R.Kr.)

II. Music

Music in Central Asia flowered along centuries-old caravan routes linking the Near East with China and India via Turkistan, the vast region extending from the Caspian Sea to Sinkiang province in China. Musical instruments diffused from one region to another, and many of the musical styles still display foreign influence. The variety of musical styles ranges from the systematically organized classical music of Turkistan, to the notated religious chants of Tibet, to the highly varied folk music styles of the region's numerous ethnic groups. The main thrust of this examination of Central Asian music will be on the traditions and styles first of Afghanistan and the sedentary population of Turkistan, then of the Turkic nomads, the Mongols, and the Siberian peoples, and, finally, of the Himalayan peoples in Tibet, Bhutan, Nepal, and Sikkim.

AFGHANISTAN AND THE SEDENTARY POPULATION OF TURKISTAN

This region of Central Asia includes Afghanistan, present-day Uzbek Soviet Socialist Republic (Uzbekistan) and Tadzhik S.S.R. (Tadzhikistan), and the oases of eastern (Chinese) Turkistan. The region lies within the Persian cultural area, and in the arts and in language the Persian imprint has endured over many centuries. In music the links with Persia appear most clearly in terminology and instruments. Islām, another Near Eastern heritage, predominates in this region and results in a generally low social status of musicians and musical performance—a situation generally not found in other regions of Central Asia.

The area includes two main streams of musical practice: folk music in a broad range of styles, often closely linked to specific ethnic groups; and the more exclusive, cosmopolitan, classical music, derived from the medieval court music of Bukhara, Samarkand, and other urban centres of Transoxania (modern Uzbek S.S.R., Tadzhik S.S.R., and Turkmen S.S.R). A third stream is now in the process of formation: popular music disseminated through the mass media.

Folk music. Generally characterized by a scarcity of musicians and musical instruments, folk music of this region is predominantly a matter of solo playing and singing, small ensembles, and a complete lack of musical notation or codified musical theory. In their general types, the musical instruments are closely related to those of Persia and the Near East, but specific forms and playing styles are purely local. Thus, there are numerous variants of the Persian long-necked lute, with names derived from the Persian *tanbūr* or *dūtār;* small spike fiddles, in which the neck skewers the body, forming a spike at the base; various block or fipple flutes, with air ducts like that of the Western recorder; transverse (horizontally held) flutes; oboes; metal jew's harps; and two basic drum types, a single-headed vase-shaped drum of pottery or wood and a large single-headed frame drum, or tambourine—all instrumental types widely diffused in the Near East.

Musical instruments

Stylistically, the music relates to that of both the Near East and the surrounding nomadic Turkic peoples of Central Asia. Songs are completely monophonic (*i.e.*, consisting only of a line of melody), but instrumental music often includes two-part polyphony (music in more than one voice, or part). The polyphony may take the form of a drone (sustained note) with a melody played above it. Or it may be organum style; *i.e.*, the second part playing the same melody as the first but at a higher or lower pitch. Most common are parallel fourths or fifths (a fourth encompasses four notes of a Western major or minor scale; a fifth, five). In structure, much of the music is based on small forms, frequently binary, or two-section, and ternary, or three-section. Small musical units may be repeated many times and varied slightly at each appearance. The recurrence of melodic phrases and an emphasis on marked rhythms is common and is related to the frequent role of music as dance accompaniment. Thus in the following example, a dance tune from Afghan Turkistan, sections A and B are similar in their overall melodic structure, and also in the small units of three or four notes on which they are built. The se-

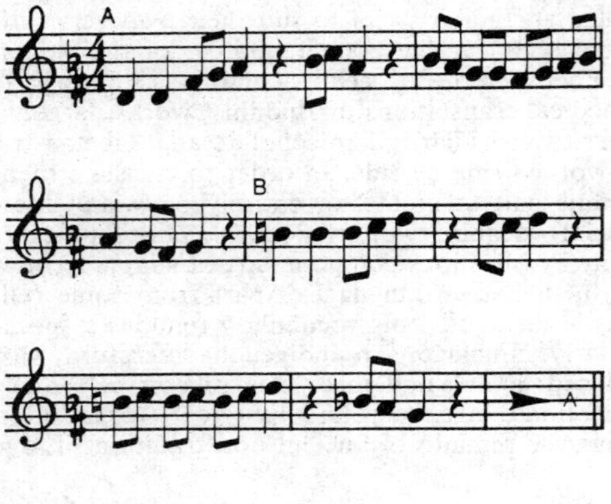

quence ABAB, etc. is repeated throughout the dance. Vocal music may have greater rhythmic flexibility and melodic range, but in form it is almost always subordinated to the structure of the song text. Quatrains such as the *rubai* and *charbaitai* are the most prominent village verse forms, with the exception of the *lundai*, a couplet used by the nomadic Pashtuns of Afghanistan. In the urban oases, couplet forms based on the classical Persian *ghazal*, a lyric poem of 6 to 15 couplets, are more common.

Attitudes toward music

The generally negative attitude of Islām toward music has led in Afghanistan to strictures against musical performance and to extremely low social status for musicians. Music is heard mainly in male-dominated public teahouses or at private celebrations such as weddings and circumcisions. Women may have their own musical genres within their enclosures; in this context the strong tradition of women's music in the Fergana Valley of the Uzbek S.S.R. is noteworthy.

Within this general picture there is enormous diversity. The Uzbeks (a Turkic people) and Tadzhiks (an Iranian group), who live side by side across northern Afghanistan and southern Turkistan, tend to share many musical traits and instruments. In contrast, most groups, such as the Pashtuns, Ḥazāra, and Baluchi of Afghanistan and Pakistan or, in the extreme, the isolated mountain peoples of Nūrestān in Afghanistan and of the Pamirs in the Tadzhik S.S.R. and Afghanistan, have maintained distinctive musical styles and, in some cases, unique musical instruments. The Nūrestāni *vaji*, an arched harp (having a bow-shaped body with no forepillar), is a striking case of the possible survival of an instrument type on the margins of a now disintegrated culture area; there are no other harp traditions today between the Caucasus and Burma, although iconographic evidence indicates that in ancient times harps were widespread in Central Asia, the Near East, and India. The music of the Ḥazāra includes vocal effects produced by striking the throat while singing, causing a break in the sound, and Baluchi music also features a broken-voice style.

Classical music. In contrast to the folk music styles just described, the court-derived classical style of Bukhara and Samarkand represents a highly systematic, theoretically grounded, cosmopolitan musical tradition. Lying along the medieval silk route, the Turkistani oases were open to musical cross-currents. Today's musical roots may reach back to the period in which urban Central Asian music was in vogue at T'ang dynasty courts in China (618–907). The movement of musical instruments across the caravan trail from the Near East to China via Central Asia is well documented since early times. Over the centuries, town musicians evolved an urban style patronized by the local courts, notably under Timur (Tamerlane) and his descendants (*c.* 1350–1500) in Herāt (now in Afghanistan) and Samarkand. The degree of musical eclecticism characteristic of the era is illustrated by a court historian's description of the festivities of Timur's son:

Medieval court music

> Golden-tongued singers and sweet-sounding musicians played and sang to motives [melodic figures] in Persian style, to Arab melodies according to Turkish practice and with Mongol voices, following Chinese laws of singing and Altai meters.

By the 17th century the court style had been codified into sets of nonimprovised suites of instrumental and vocal pieces using poetic texts in classical Persian and local court Turkish (Chaghatai). In Bukhara this collection of suites was known as the *Shashmaqām*, or six *maqām*s (suites), with each *maqām* (an Arabic term, but changed in meaning) set in one of the classical Persian musical modes. (The Persian modes are melodic frameworks, each with a given scale, typical melodic figures, and accepted emotional content.) Regional courts and large towns developed their own sets of *maqām*s, performed in unison by an orchestra and a male chorus.

Areas of Turkistan under Soviet rule since about 1920 have undergone far-reaching modification of traditional music practice, although the older styles such as the *Shashmaqām* are also maintained. Changes include the reconstruction of local instruments to fit the Western musical scale of 12 equally spaced half steps, establishment of music schools and conservatories, creation of orchestras of folk instruments, introduction of vocal polyphony and the writing of works in Western forms (symphonies, operas, chamber music) by native and European Soviet composers. In Afghanistan, musical change has begun on a national basis since the 1950s under the influence of Radio Afghanistan, which broadcasts principally popular styles based on Pashtun folk music and songs of the Indian film industry.

20th-century changes in music practice

TURKIC NOMADS, MONGOLS, AND SIBERIAN PEOPLES

This region includes primarily the great open spaces of Central Asia, from the Turkmen desert in the southwest to the Kazakh steppes, Mongol plains, and from the Gobi to the vast Sub-Arctic Siberian evergreen forests, or taiga, and tundra, or Arctic plains, stretching to the Pacific. The considerable mobility and often close linguistic affinity of the peoples in the area led to substantial interchange of musical terms and instruments, and to common social functions of music relating to the traditional tribal social structure of most of the groups of this region.

Social role of music. Three basic functions of music are common throughout most of the region: music as ritual, with magical connotations (shamanism), music as tribal record, aiding group solidarity (epic recitation), and music as entertainment (itinerant performers, festivals). Music is the medium of the shaman, or priest-medicine man, as he performs his role as mediator between the seen, or men, and the unseen, the spirits that inhabit the spheres above and below the earth. Traditional shamanistic séances were creative, impassioned musico-dramatic scenes produced by a single performer, the shaman. Not only is music the shaman's aid in inducing the trance that enables him to contact spirits, but in Siberia his drum (a very large tambourine) may be considered a steed for the trip to other worlds. Thus great attention is given to each stage of drum construction, from selecting the wood of certain trees to the painting of symbolically charged designs on the drumhead. The metal hangings, sometimes including bells, on the shaman's costume also play a musical role. Among the Kirgiz and Kazakhs and until recently among the Turkmens, a fiddle with horsehair strings and bow performs the same function as the Siberian drum. Metal ringlets are attached to the head of the fiddle, and a niche is hollowed there for a mirror to catch the reflections of spirits. Shamans' horsehair fiddles can even be found among townspeople of northern Afghanistan. The occurrence of shamanism has sharply declined in Soviet portions of Central Asia.

The shaman's music

Epic recitation, which may serve as tribal history, also has magical overtones. Among Turks, the same term (*bakhshi*) may be used for both shamans and bards, and both may be called to their trade by spirits to undergo a difficult period of initiation. Storytellers use a fiddle or lute as accompaniment, and tales may run through several nights of exhaustive performance; one Kirgiz bard is known to recite 300,000 verses of the *Manas*, the major Kirgiz epic. Such marathon performances are facilitated by the use of stereotyped melodic motives—standard short melodic figures—often invented by the individual performer. Local epic traditions vary widely in dramatization; *i.e.*, the proportion of dialogue, monologue, and narrative.

The third area-wide musical function, entertainment, takes many forms. One common diversion is the singing contest, in which rival minstrels compete in wit and virtuosity. Such trials of skill are most notable among the Kirgiz, Kazakhs, and Mongols. The contests follow strict rules of versification, musicality, and procedure. Often the loser must pay a forfeit to the victor, who receives acclaim from the audience and gifts from wealthy patrons; a singer's reputation may be made or broken in a single afternoon. Frequently a contestant will vilify the clan championed by the opposing singer and laud his own faction. In Siberia another type of entertainment

The singing contest

is the widespread practice of bear festivals at specific times of the year, during which a bear is killed and his head displayed, to the accompaniment of music, dance, and games.

Instrumental and vocal styles. Across the region the principal instrument types are lutes, with two or three strings, the necks either fretted or fretless; fiddles, largely horsehair fiddles; flutes, mostly open at both ends and either end-blown or side-blown; and jews' harps, either metal or, often in Siberia, wooden. Few percussion instruments are found, except for the shaman's magic drum. Considerable instrumental polyphony is played on lutes and fiddles, particularly among the Turkic peoples. Vocal polyphony may occur in special ways: singers among the Mongols and Tuvins (a Siberian people northwest of Mongolia) can produce two parts while singing solo, as in the example below, by strongly reinforcing

upper partials (overtones) while singing a very deep fundamental pitch. West of the Urals, Bashkirs may hum a basic pitch while playing solo flute pieces, and certain Siberian peoples may sing choral overlapping responsorial songs (in which group and soloist alternate, one beginning slightly before the other finishes).

The vast geographic stretch of the region produces musical links to neighbouring areas as well as highly distinctive local styles. The Turkmens live in Afghanistan and Iran as well as Turkistan and manifest some Persian influence in musical terms and instruments, yet they possess unique vocal and instrumental styles. Particularly striking is their series of guttural sounds serving as vocal ornaments. The Kirgiz and Kazakhs, closely related musically, maintain ties to Mongol and northern styles (*e.g.*, of the Bashkir and Tatar peoples, west of the Urals) as well as to Turkistan. Nevertheless, their relaxed voice quality, musical scales, and distinctive instrumental polyphony set them off. Noteworthy here is the versatile polyphonic style of the three-stringed Kirgiz *komuz* lute, based on extensive development of short melodies called kernel tunes. In the *komuz* piece shown below, the kernel tune is stated in the first two measures and is varied and developed as the piece progresses. Another Kirgiz-Kazakh specialty is programmatic music, in which instrumentalists tell specific stories without words, through musical images alone.

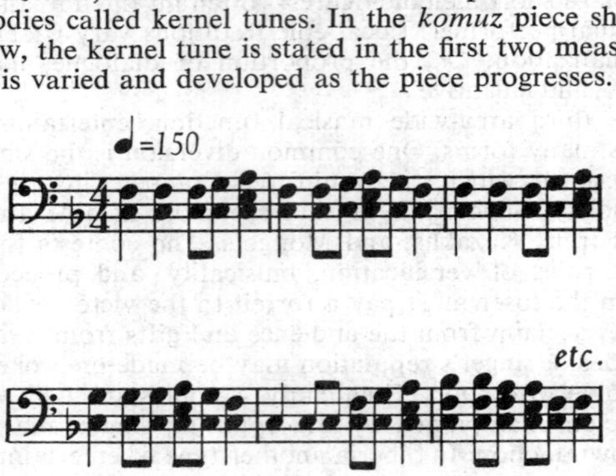

Mongolian and Siberian music

The Mongols display links to both Chinese and Tibetan music. Chinese influence is apparent in the use of certain instruments (*e.g.*, some flutes and fiddles) and perhaps in the structure of melodies; Tibetan impact occurs in the religious music and musical instruments of Tibetan Buddhism, introduced in the 16th century. Mongolian music also has its own distinctive profile, sporadically documented since the 13th-century *Secret History of the Mongols*, the first written Mongolian chronicle. Of interest is the fact that Arghūn Khān, Mongol ruler of Persia, sent a musician as emissary to Philip IV the Fair of France in 1289. Because of the focal position of Mongolia at the heart of Central Asia, some Mongol epic melodies have spread westward as far as the Kalmuks on the Volga River, and eastward to the Ainu of Sakhalin Island, north of Japan. Mongol songs may be either quick and marked rhythmically or drawn-out in free rhythm, with extensive melodic ornamentation. The Mongol horsehair fiddle accompanies a singer with simultaneous variations on the melody, a technique called heterophony.

Siberian music includes a broad spectrum of styles over a huge geographic expanse. Many unique traditions occur, such as the bridgeless, often rectangular zithers of the Khants and Mansi, Ugrian peoples along the Ob River; farther east, the solo flute-and-voice polyphony of the Tuvins and Bashkirs; and the rapid, compact songs with nonsense syllables of the Gilyaks, Chukots, and other peoples of the Far Eastern Amur River region and Pacific coast. At that northeastern shore of Siberia there is a carryover of musical style to the Ainu of northeastern Japan and possible musical ties between the Eskimos of Asia and of North America. Other links beyond Central Asia may exist at the far western end of Siberia, for example, to the music of Lapland in the Scandinavian Arctic; or the relation of tunes of certain peoples of the Volga River region, such as the Mari or Cheremis, with old Hungarian folk songs.

Outside the few written Mongol references to music, the only approach to discovery of the stylistic history of this region of Central Asia is through fragmentary information about musical instrument types. Perhaps the most remarkable instrument finds were made at Pazyryk in south central Siberia, where Soviet archaeologists found wooden objects which possibly form pieces of a harp and an artifact resembling a vase-shaped drum, both dating from the 5th century BC.

THE HIMALAYAN PEOPLES

This region, including Tibet, Sikkim, Bhutan, and Nepal, occupies an important middle ground between India and China, and its central position is reflected in the local music cultures. Of utmost importance for musical life was the introduction of Buddhism from India via Turkistan, beginning in the 7th century AD. Music became an integral part of the official creed of Tibetan Buddhism, and the considerable cultural influence of Tibet spread Tibetan religious music to the nearby areas of Nepal, Sikkim, and Bhutan and, much later, to Mongolia.

Tibetan music. Tibetan religious music is the only Central Asian repertoire that has a long history of written notation. This notation, for liturgical chant, consists of neumes; *i.e.*, symbols representing melodic contour rather than precise pitch, similar to the earliest music writing of medieval Europe. Also distinctive is the metaphysical aspect of Tibetan Buddhist music, related to Indian philosophy. Each instrument of the monastery orchestra, as well as the drawn-out tones of chant, is believed to represent an externalized form of the *mantras*, or sounds inherent in the human body, accessible otherwise only through steadfast meditation. For the monks, such music is a basic aid to devotion and prayer. Musical styles vary somewhat among the sects of Tibetan Buddhism, but the basic approach and instruments are the same.

The monastery instruments typify the crossroads position of Tibet. Some, such as the large cymbals, stem from China, while others (the majority), such as the conch-shell trumpet and handbells, can be traced to Indian influence and are found as instruments of Buddhist worship as far away as Japan. Still other instruments, such as the large oboe and the ten-foot metal trumpet, are perhaps Near Eastern in origin. One wind instrument, the short trumpet made from a human leg bone, seems to be of purely local invention. Similarly, the structure of the music seems basically Tibetan. It is founded on a principle of greatly prolonged dense, deep sounds, such as unison long and short trumpets with oboe, or the seemingly endless bass chant of groups of monks, whose long, drawn-out notes are punctuated by sharp, extended bursts of percussion. Each monk is said to be able to sing two or even three notes simultaneously.

Festival dramas

Much of this music emerges from monasteries only at festival time, when the great *cham* dramas, which may last several days, are performed for the public's entertainment and edification. These plays, which generally show the triumph of Buddhism over Bon, the earlier shamanistic religion of Tibet, may involve hundreds of musicians in the guise of masked dancers with drums, backed by a large temple orchestra. Other types of public music also abound, such as secular, perhaps Chinese-related historical plays with an alternation of dialogue and songs with orchestral accompaniment. There is also a strong tradition of folk dance, which may include songs sung by mixed antiphonal choirs (*i.e.*, two alternating groups of singers). Minstrels ply their trade along the caravan routes and play instruments perhaps more related to general Central Asian traditions than to the Indian and Chinese background of religious music.

The music of Nepal, Bhutan, and Sikkim. Little is presently known about the music of Nepal, Bhutan, and Sikkim. Minstrels play a major role in the musical life of Nepal, where under Indian influence musicians are classified according to caste, and each group features specific instruments and repertoire. There appears to be a great deal of both Indian-related and indigenous folk music in the three Himalayan kingdoms. Varieties of lute, such as the long-necked *damyan* of Nepal and its Sikkimese relative, may be linked to a similar instrument of the Pamir Mountains; while a Sikkimese flute having an outside air duct (in contrast to the inside duct of a Western recorder) seems to be a unique instrument. The Sherpas of Nepal and other Tibetan-related populations of the Himalayas, along with the thousands of Tibetan refugees now living in the area, maintain the traditions of Tibetan Buddhist religious music. The *mani-rimdu* dance-drama of the Sherpas, a variant of *cham*, is a good case in point.

THE STUDY OF CENTRAL ASIAN MUSIC

In the West, the study of Central Asian music has until recently been restricted largely to travellers' accounts and analyses of small samples of music. By far the bulk of collection and study of Central Asian music of Turkistan and Siberia lies in the domain of Soviet scholars, who instituted systematic fieldwork as early as the 1920s; this literature remains largely inaccessible to the non-Russian reader. Mongol music was the subject of sporadic but intensive fieldwork by Scandinavian researchers in the 1920s and early 1930s, so that some of the traditional music culture was documented before Mongol society underwent the changes brought by war and the advent of socialism. Tibetan music has attracted increasing attention since the late 1950s, when large numbers of Tibetan refugees poured into the Himalayan kingdoms and northern sectors of India, thus making Tibetan music more accessible to outside observation. Afghanistan has been the object of intensive musical investigation only since the mid-1960s. Thus, outside Soviet contributions, Central Asia remains a lightly researched although quite fertile area of musical investigation. (M.S.S.)

III. Performing arts: dance and theatre

The performing arts have played an important role in the spiritual and social life of Central Asia, where they evolved as didactic art forms within a religious context. Performance, therefore, occurs in conjunction with some religious or special event. There are two main types of performance which predominate throughout Tibet, Nepal, Sikkim, Bhutan, Mongolia, and parts of Asian U.S.S.R.: those related to shamanism and those derived from Buddhism. The performing arts of the Turkic peoples of Afghanistan and Turkistan are different from these because of the influence of the Islāmic religion and are discussed in the article ISLAMIC PEOPLES, ARTS OF. The Hindu influence found in Nepalese theatre and dance is treated in the article SOUTH ASIAN PEOPLES, ARTS OF.

Although primarily intended to serve the overt purposes of religion, dance and theatre in Central Asia are performing arts with covert aesthetic values. Vocal and physical expressions of appreciation by an audience attending a performance depend on the graceful and rhythmic execution of hand gestures, body movements, and footwork. Aesthetic values are best expressed in the elaborate and artistic costumes, masks, and makeup, coupled with effective though crude stage effects and props.

Use of music in dance and theatre

Musical instruments play an important role in the performance of Central Asian dance and theatre. Usually a drum, but in some cases a string instrument, is used by the shaman to induce the ecstatic trance during which he symbolically journeys to the heavens or to the netherworld when playing the role of a psychopomp, or conductor of souls. Performances of the Buddhist monastic dance, known as 'Cham (dance), and the Buddhist morality plays, called *a-che-lha-mo* (Older Sister Goddess), were accompanied by a variety of instruments, especially drums and horns. The word is, like *'cham*, Tibetan. There were large and small drums, short horns with fingering holes, and long horns, particularly the *dung-chen* (great conch shell) made of brass and extending many feet. The *dung-chen* with a deep haunting wail accentuates the macabre that is so much a part of *'cham*. The Tibetan guitar *sgra-synan* (pleasant sound) is a stringed instrument used almost exclusively by Himalayan peoples for folk song and dance.

Perhaps because of the subjectivism of their religions, it was not the custom among the peoples of Central Asia to carry out objective studies of elements in their cultures, and, therefore, no indigenous evaluation of their dance and theatre is available. Although a few manuals for the performance of shamanic rituals, music, and the *'cham* do exist, as do scripts for the *a-che-lha-mo*, much of the history and traditional staging of these forms of theatre and dance was handed down by oral tradition.

SHAMANIC RITUAL

Teachings that spirits are responsible for unexplainable phenomena, such as disease and death, and that these spirits can be controlled by an individual with special powers, such as a shaman, evolved in many primitive societies throughout the world, including those of the nomadic peoples of Central Asia. The roles of the shaman include oracle, healer, sacrificer, and psychopomp, and each role calls for the performance of specific rituals. The earliest form of theatre and dance in Central Asia, these rituals developed into an often complex genre of the performing arts. The horse-sacrifice ceremony among the Altaic peoples of east Central Asia, for example, embraces a full range of dramatic elements despite the fact that like all shamanic ritual it is essentially a one-man performance. The ceremony, which lasts two to three days, is one in which the shaman undertakes a journey to the heavens. After having set the stage, the shaman symbolically releases the soul of a real horse and then, astride a goose-shaped device, he chases the soul of the horse, all the while imitating the noises of the goose and the horse. Capturing the soul of the horse, the shaman, with help from the audience, then kills the real horse, and the flesh is prepared. The next evening, the shaman offers pieces of the horse meat to the spirits, and, amid loud drumming and chanting, symbolically goes to the heavens on the soul of the horse while ascending a notched pole. As he ascends through the higher and higher heavenly

Altaic horse-sacrifice ceremony

planes, the shaman communicates to the audience important information, such as predictions about the success of the coming harvest and about epidemics and misfortunes that threaten and how to avoid them through sacrifices. The ceremony is followed by merrymaking and drinking.

Shamanism maintains that the soul of one who dies a heroic or violent death ascends to the heavens, but that the soul of one who dies from disease, which is caused by an evil spirit, must go to the underworld. The part of a psychopomp, or conductor of souls to the netherworld, was, therefore, another role commonly played by the shaman. The shaman guides the soul to its destination while narrating details of its journey to his audience. In some cultures, such as that of the Lolo, or Yi, in the mountains of southwestern China, the souls of all the dead are led in this manner to the underworld; while in others, such as that of the Tungus, a subarctic forest people of eastern Siberia, the shaman is only called upon to act as psychopomp if the soul of the deceased continues to haunt his residence.

The shaman also serves as the repository of tribal folklore and beliefs. Through dance and dialogue, he instructs the audience in the traditional teachings of their ancestors, and by passing his knowledge and techniques down to his successor, those teachings remain intact for future generations.

Rituals for curing the sick, guiding the soul of the dead to the netherworld, invoking a deity, or visiting the heavens are performed by the shaman in a state of trance induced by frenetic dancing to the music of a drum or a string instrument. Elaborate, symbolic costumes and ritual objects used in the ceremony provide a dramatic and mystic spectacle. The expectations of the audience are directly connected with the purpose of the shamanic performance; but whether it is the hope that the patient would be cured or that the oracular communication be auspicious, those attending the shamanic performance do so with the expectation that it will be an entertaining religious experience.

Regional variations in costumes

Before the introduction of Buddhism in shamanic Central Asia, there were no centres for the performing arts in the usual sense of the word. Each shaman performed his dramatic arts at his own residence or environs as the occasion demanded. He had his own ritual costumes and paraphernalia, which displayed regional variations, particularly in ornamentation. The representation of animals and birds is common, and metallic objects, which are thought to possess a soul and do not rust, are also important. For example, the costume of a Siberian Yakut shaman must have from 30 to 50 pounds (15 to 25 kilograms) of iron to be efficacious, while a Siberian Buryat shaman, except for an iron casque, or helmet, wears mostly furs. The metal ornaments represent such diverse things as the internal organs, bones, a woman's breasts, the sun or the moon; but the object common to all shamans is a metal mirror, in which the shaman can see the souls of the dead. Regardless of the variations in dress, the purpose and performance of the rituals remain essentially the same, whether carried out by a Buddhist monk among the Sherpas of Nepal, or by a true shaman among the Siberian Yakut.

By courtesy of the trustees of the British Museum; photograph, J.R. Freeman & Co. Ltd.

Tungus shaman, detail of an engraving from Witsen's *Noord en Oost Tartarye*, 1785.

Oracle priest of Tibet in a trance.
Paul Popper (Popperfoto) Ltd.

The shamanic rituals of the steppe and desert peoples have analogies among the dramatic arts of the Himalayan kingdoms, where, because of the tolerance of local beliefs and rituals, many shamanic practices were adopted into Tibetan Buddhism. For example, the State Oracle of Tibet, a monk whose oracular powers were exercised on behalf of the government and the monastic system, was regarded as a high ranking ecclesiastic, yet his ritualistic performances were no different than those of shamanic mediums throughout Central Asia. The adaptation of the psychopompic role of the shaman into Tibetan Buddhism resulted in the recitation of the *Tibetan Book of the Dead* to an effigy of the corpse. This book describes in detail the frightening apparitions the deceased encounters day after day while in the forty-nine-day interval between death and rebirth, and its reading is analagous to the shaman's narration of his journey to the underworld.

BUDDHIST RITUAL

Buddhist Monastic Dance. The second major genre of the performing arts to develop in Central Asia was 'Cham, the ritualistic dance performed in Buddhist monasteries. The origins of *'cham* may well be an older form of shamanic ceremonial dance in Tibet, but centuries of evolution within a Buddhist dominated society led to the recasting of the roles and theme of the dance in keeping with Buddhist dogma. *'Cham,* which was introduced along with Tibetan Buddhism into Mongolia and parts of the southern Asian U.S.S.R. in the 16th century, became the main form of religious entertainment in eastern Central Asia.

Origins of *'cham*

The origins of *'cham* lie in Tibet's dim past, long before the introduction of Buddhism. Initially, it was performed as a ritual to drive out evil spirits and to appease the guardian spirits by means of human and animal sacrifices, thus assuring an auspicious and prosperous new

(Left) *'Cham* performance during the New Year celebrations at the Potala, Lhasa, Tibet.
(Right) *'Cham* dancer representing the Spirit of Barren Mountain, near Gangtok, Tibet.
(Left) Paul Popper (Popperfoto) Ltd., (right) EB Inc.

year. According to Tibetan tradition, the ancient shamanic dance was adapted as a Buddhist one by Padmasambhava, the Indian tantric teacher who introduced Buddhism into Tibet in the 8th century AD. He is said to have interpreted the dance as symbolizing the victory of Buddhism over the shamanism of Tibet, and, since blood sacrifices are abhorrent to a Buddhist, these were simulated by clever techniques using effigies and red-coloured substances.

Sectarianism developed in Tibetan Buddhism in the 11th century, primarily as a reaction to the unreformed teachings of Padmasambhava and his followers; nevertheless, each of the sects retained the monastic dance as part of their religious repertoire. The reformed Yellow Hat sect changed the time for its performance from the birthday of Padmasambhava to the end of the official year, which would coincide with the lunar month from the middle of January to the middle of February.

The acceptance and spread of Buddhism led to the eventual establishment of monastic communities throughout eastern Central Asia. These monasteries became fixed centres for the performance of 'Cham. Every monastery of adequate size and monastic population maintained its own masks, costumes, props, and musical instruments. In spite of regional and sectarian variations, the performance of *'cham* remains basically the same. The stage is set outdoors in the courtyard of the monastery called the *'cham-ra* (dance enclosure). With the exception of high lamas and members of the nobility who sat on special seats, the audience stood or sat around on the edge of the dance floor or ground. The musicans with horns and drums take their places, usually under a cloth canopy. Then, accompanied by music, the various dancers emerge from a building or from behind a stage curtain and perform. The first to appear are dancers wearing wide-brimmed black hats, topped with a simulated human skull. The costume of these dancers has led to the performance being referred to in some Western works as the Black-hat devil dance. Although of shamanic origin, the costume of the black-hat dancers is said by the Buddhists to represent the black disguise worn by Dpal-gyi-rdo-rje, a 9th-century Tibetan monk who assassinated the fanatic anti-Buddhist king, Glang-dar-ma.

Black-hat dancers

The black-hat dancers are followed by a variety of performers, including those wearing monstrous masks representing a host of evil spirits that harass mankind, those costumed as skeletons and wearing skull masks, and those representing Indian teachers of Buddhism. There are also masked dancers representing the tutelary deities of Buddhism, and the most impressive of all is the Chos-kyi-rgyal-po (King of the Religion), who wears a mask fashioned after the head of a bull, which is emblematic of the aspect of the deity that vanquishes the Lord of the Dead. It is this dancer who dismembers an effigy of a corpse and scatters the parts in a simulation of the sacrificial and expulsional elements of the ancient shamanic dance rituals.

The dance is not all macabre. Comic relief is provided by a dancer wearing a mask with an expression of stupidity. This buffoon represents Ho-shang, the Chinese monk, who was defeated in an 8th-century debate on the merits of Indian versus Chinese Buddhism. Ho-shang is represented in the 'Cham of the Sherpas of Nepal by a dancer wearing a mask portraying a balding, bearded old man, called Mi-tshe-ring (Long-life Man), who delights the audience by his farcical antics and pratfalls.

The whole of the 'Cham performance, which takes two or three days, is a visual presentation of the fear of demons and monstrous creatures and the way in which Buddhism serves to alleviate that fear. The audience is reassured that the good forces of religion have neutralized the evil powers of demonic spirits, and so the new year will be a prosperous one. This religious dance is performed on varying scales of grandeur in monasteries throughout the Buddhist cultures of Central Asia, but the most magnificent of all is its performance in Lhasa for the Dalai Lama, the ruler of Tibet.

Buddhist morality plays. The last performing-arts genre to develop in Central Asia was the Buddhist morality play, called *a-che-lha-mo*. The plays are based on the lives of legendary and historical figures, and through costume and masks the ethnic origin and ethical character of the players are revealed. Folktales, as well as historical and Buddhist canonical literature, are sources for the stories presented in *a-che-lha-mo*. Most plays are about mythical heroes who prove that Buddhism and its virtues conquer all evil in the end; but there are those that tell the story of historical personages.

Origins of *a-che-lha-mo*

Although traditions among the Central Asian peoples are vague about the development of shamanic rituals and *'cham*, they are clear about the origin of *a-che-lha-mo* and even point out the historical creators of the art. Some scholars regard the plays as derivatives of Indian theatre, but Tibetan tradition claims that the first performance of a morality play was produced by Thang-stong rgyal-po, a famous bridge builder of the 15th century.

One story is of some Tibetans who were building a bridge and found that what they assembled during the day, demons dismantled at night. Thang-stong rgyal-po, a holy man well versed in the capricious ways of demons, advised the Tibetans to stage a play to divert the attention of the evil spirits. Thus, they were able to complete the bridge. This story would seem to indicate that the primary purpose of the play was to entertain, but another story states that Thang-stong rgyal-po realized that religious teachings would have a greater influence on the people if they were dramatized, so he developed the morality play to serve this purpose. Regardless of his intent, *a-che-lha-mo* evolved as didactic entertainment, and Thang-stong rgyal-po is regarded by the Tibetans as its patron saint.

From primitive beginnings, the morality plays developed into a popular performing art, complete with stylized costumes and masks, complex scenarios and effective staging. The scripts are written in a dialogue song style called *rnam-thar*. There are at least nine traditional plays in the Tibetan repertoire.

Mythical and historical plays

The most common type of *a-che-lha-mo* is the drama based on legend and mythology which often reflects a strong influence of Indian theatrical tradition. An example is the play *'Das-log Snang-sa. 'Das-log* means to return (*log*) from the beyond (*'das*) and is used in Tibetan to refer to anyone who was believed to be dead and then returns to life and relates all that was witnessed in the netherworld. The story, *'Das-log Snang-sa*, is about a virtuous woman named Snang-sa who was unjustly accused of adultery and beaten to death by her jealous sister-in-law. When Snang-sa was led before the fierce Lord of the Dead (*gshin-rje*), he found that she was pure of heart and mind, and he allowed her to return to life. Once home again, her husband and relatives began to mistreat her, so she became a nun. The play ends with Snang-sa flying away from the convent roof and disappearing like a rainbow in the sky.

Another type of *a-che-lha-mo* is the plays based on the lives of Tibetan holy men or pious kings. *Rgya-bza' Bal-bza'* ("Chinese-wife, Nepalese-wife"), for example, tells the story of king Srong-btsan sgam-po (died AD 649) and his two Buddhist wives: Wen-ch'eng, a Chinese princess, and Bhrikuti, a princess from Nepal. These three historical figures are believed by faithful Tibetans to have been incarnations of Buddhist deities, and their story is very popular with the audience.

The performance of a play may take more than a day. Narrative recitation is used to set scenes, delineate character, and give continuity to the songs that tell the main story. Comic sketches or dances are performed between the acts. Each character in a play has a distinctive costume or mask. Usually Tibetan male characters and the heroes wear no mask, while virtuous female characters wear flat, teardrop-shaped masks, particularly the serpentine deities. Three-dimensional masks are worn by evil foreigners, demons, and witches, and masks that cover the entire head are used to portray animals. Like the *'cham*, the morality play is performed outdoors, with the audience, except for the specially seated lamas and nobles, standing or sitting on the ground around the performing area.

The morality plays are performed for profit by groups consisting of lay men and women, and some have Buddhist monks or nuns as members. These troupes are generally associated with a given locale, such as a village or a monastery; however, they often travel to give performances on special occasions, transporting their wardrobe and stage props with them. In time, four of the most popular troupes were required by the Tibetan government to perform plays at the summer palace of the Dalai Lama. These performances were obligatory as a kind of taxation. There are still several of the *a-che-lha-mo* troupes to be found among the Tibetan refugees in Nepal and India, where their performances are in popular demand.

The *a-che-lha-mo* did not spread from Tibet into other parts of Central Asia until the 19th century. According to tradition, the Monoglian lama Noyan Hutuqtu (1803–56) studied *a-che-lha-mo* as performed in the Kokonor (Tsinghai) region of northeastern Tibet and then introduced his own adaptations of it at Tulgatu-yin keyid, his own monastery near the village of Saynshand, in Mongolia. For the first time, in 1832, he produced a repertoire of four plays, and their performance required 17 full days. The four plays were based on the textual biographies of the historical Buddha, the Indian Buddhist Teacher Atīśa, the revered Tibetan hermit-poet Mi-la Ras-pa, and the fabulous "Moon-cuckoo" (*Saran-u Kökügen-ü Namtar*), a mystical story of a pious prince who became a cuckoo bird living in the forest.

Mongolian plays of Noyan Hutuqtu

Noyan Hutuqtu's productions differed from the usual performance of *a-che-lha-mo* in certain respects. His repertoire did not include any of the plays traditional in Tibet. His actors, unlike those of *a-che-lha-mo*, wore no masks; instead they painted their faces, a makeup technique associated with Chinese opera. Whereas *a-che-lha-mo* is usually performed outdoors in the Himalayan regions, Noyan Hutuqtu had a special theatre constructed near his monastery. It was a three-sided, two-storied, mud-brick building with two stage floors; thus, two scenes could be performed at the same time. The upper stage represented the sky, the lower one the earth. There were stage exits on both sides and trap doors in the floor.

The first Mongolian actors were called *schabi*, or disciples, of the lama Noyan Hutuqtu. These men and women formed a regular troupe and were invited all over Mongolia to perform.

FOLK DANCE

Among the peoples of Central Asia, folk dancing occurs as a form of entertainment at social occasions, such as festivals, weddings, and other celebrations, and private parties. Often impromptu, folk dances are sometimes performed without the accompaniment of musical instruments, and the performers rely on singing and footwork to maintain the rhythm.

Formalized folk dance does not appear to have evolved among nomadic peoples of the steppe and desert regions, but such dances did develop among the sedentary agriculturists, particularly in the Himalayan regions, where troupes of amateur performers were formed for local entertainment. Some dances were performed by a group of men and women forming a circle; in others, facing each other in lines. The dance steps and body movement were done according to a stylized routine, and the rhythmic beat was accented by a measured stamp of the foot. (T.V.W.)

IV. Visual arts

The immense tract of Central Asia, with its varied topography and climate, encouraged the development of different artistic styles and traditions among the inhabitants of its widely separated sections. These differences were increased by the growth of dissimilar religions, which encouraged the formation of distinct schools of art. Further artistic variance can be attributed to cultural time lag, for comparable stages of artistic development were not reached simultaneously throughout this vast territory. In this article, the diverse and complicated subject of Central Asian art is divided into the following sections: prehistoric; nomadic cultures; Parthian kingdoms of western Turkistan and Afghanistan; Kushan; eastern Turkistan; Arctic regions; and the Himalayan cultures of Nepal and Tibet.

PREHISTORIC CULTURES

Paleolithic cultures. The earliest artifacts discovered in the Central Asian region were found in Siberia and western Turkistan and are from around the 13th millennium BC. During the millennia that followed, migrants entered the region from various directions, regardless of the geographical obstacles they encountered. As a result, some of their artifacts correspond with those produced at a similar stage of development in more western areas; some finds from the northeastern part of Soviet Turkistan, for example, are related to certain objects made in Iran and Mesopotamia, and those from northwestern Central Asia are linked to eastern and central Europe by means of the Volga River and of Kazakhstan.

The Paleolithic (Old Stone Age) sites of western Turkistan are mainly concentrated in the Lake Baikal area. A cave in the Baysuntau Range containing the body of a Neanderthal boy aged about nine had been so carefully prepared that it is evident that the people who made his grave believed in an afterlife. The site of Malta, 50 miles (80 kilometres) to the southeast of Irkutsk, and that of Buret, 80 miles (130 kilometres) to the north, are noted for their mammoth-tusk figurines of nude women. They resemble Paleolithic statuettes of Europe and the Near

East and probably served as fertility symbols or as representations of the great goddess, whose cult was widespread. Some of these figurines depict elegant, slender women, others heavy, corpulent ones. Of five found at Buret, one is unusual in that it is of a clothed woman wearing a one-piece trouser suit with a hood attached to it comparable to those still worn by present-day Eskimos. In recent years Paleolithic sites have been discovered south of Samarkand, and rock paintings have been found at Zaraut Say (Zaraut Stream) in the Babatag Range, 50 miles east of Termez, and in the Shakty Caves in the Pamirs. Executed in red ochre, they depict hunting scenes. Those in the Shakty Cave are the older and include a man disguised as a bird and other men wearing skins and shooting at wild oxen with bows and arrows.

Fertility images and rock painting

The invention of the bow is ascribed to the 10th millennium BC, the Mesolithic Period. Man's artistic development during this period is attested by a pottery fragment of a most expressive woman's face dating from the 3rd millennium BC and recovered from the site of Vosnessenovka in western Siberia.

By courtesy of the Siberian Department, Academy of Science of the U.S.S.R., Novosibirsk

Pottery fragment with a woman's face from Voskresenovka, Siberia, 3rd millennium BC. In the Siberian Department, Academy of Science of the U.S.S.R., Novosibirsk. 15 cm × 13 cm.

Neolithic and Metal Age cultures. Numerous Neolithic sites have been discovered in Asiatic U.S.S.R., and the number of Bronze Age sites is even higher. The majority have been found on the middle reaches of the Yenisey River, especially in the Minusinsk Basin, where metallurgy developed early. They testify to the existence of three main, basically successive, yet often overlapping cultures: the Afanasevskaya, Andronovo, and Karasuk, so-called after the three villages near which each culture was identified.

Afanasevskaya burials

A cemetery to the southwest of Krasnoyarsk, on the slopes of the Afanasevskaya Mountains, contained 80 burials dating from the 2nd millennium BC. The earlier ones were flat and marked by stone circles symbolizing the sun god; the later ones took the form of barrows, or large mounds of earth, but were also encircled by similar stone slabs. The earlier graves contained elongated, spherical pottery vessels with pointed bases decorated with herringbone patterns. In the later graves this type of ware was superseded by flat-bottomed pots usually associated with sedentary pastoralist cultures. The graves also contained numerous stone and bone objects. Although copper objects were rare, they heralded the dawn of a new cultural period, the Metal Age.

The Andronovo culture succeeded the Afanasevskaya in the 2nd and 1st millennia BC. Although found to the southwest of Krasnoyarsk, it is more frequently encountered in western Siberia and Kazakhstan. The settlement and cemetery of Alekseevskoe (present Tenlyk), some 400 miles (600 kilometres) south of Sverdlovsk, is especially important, because its earth houses were designed for permanent habitation. Their roofs rested on logs, and each dwelling had a central hearth used for heating purposes with side hearths intended for cooking. Bronze objects were numerous, and workshops existed for working copper. The metal probably came from mines in the Minusinsk Basin, Kazakhstan, and the western Altai Mountains, the latter having been worked as early as the 14th century BC.

Houses of Andronovo culture

Dating from about 1200 to about 70 BC—the dawn of the Iron and historical age—the Karasuk culture was located in the Minusinsk Basin, on the Yenisey River and on the upper reaches of the Ob River. Its creators must have been in touch with East Asia, for certain bronze objects, notably elbow-shaped knives, are related to those used between the 14th and 11th centuries BC in China during the Shang period. Stone pillars topped either with ram's heads, stylized animal forms, or human figures have also been discovered. Dzheytun, northwest of Ashkhabad, in what is called the Kyzylkum desert, is the oldest known agricultural settlement in Central Asia. It possessed a thriving Neolithic flint industry.

Annau, six miles (ten kilometres) southeast of Ashkhabad, and Namazga-Tepe, situated in the same region and occupying an area of some 145 acres (60 hectares), are important Bronze Age sites. The pottery vessels recovered from Namazga-Tepe are decorated with painted plant and animal motifs showing affinities with contemporary pottery wares from the Near East. Figurines of dogs and sheep were numerous, and a model of a house has also been found. At Karatepe, also near Ashkhabad, an agricultural society produced fine pottery from the 3rd millennium BC, but it reached its fullest development in the 2nd millenium BC in a series of vessels decorated with particularly spirited animal designs.

Pottery in the Ashkhabad region

The main Neolithic and Bronze Age cultures produced several distinctive offshoots, which began to emerge by the early Iron Age. In Chorasmia, the Neolithic culture discovered at Dzhan-Bas-Kala is known as the Kelteminar and that of the Bronze Age, as represented by the Chorasmian level of Kokcha III, as the Tazabagyab. The Neolithic Hissar culture of southern Tadzhikistan spread across northeastern Central Asia into the Semirechiye, or foothills of the Tien Shan, while in Siberia the Bronze Age Karasuk culture was replaced in the 8th century BC by the Tagar culture. The latter endured until the 2nd century BC, producing an art of animal motifs related to that of the Scythians of southern European Russia.

The Bronze Age culture on Fergana's western border is associated with settlers living in large houses grouped to form settlements of considerable size. Some of the inhabitants worked in copper mines at the time when potters of the Chust Bronze Age culture of the Fergana Valley were producing fine-quality tableware, as well as cruder pottery articles. The best Chust pottery was very thin, covered with a red slip (liquid clay) and decorated after glazing with black triangular and scroll designs.

NOMADIC CULTURES

During the 1st millennium BC and the 1st centuries of the Christian Era, certain nomadic tribes affected the course of Central Asia's artistic history. Cyrus II the Great, the ancient Persian king who founded the Achaemenid Empire, was killed by the nomadic Massagetae when campaigning in eastern Iran in 530 BC. At the time, the Śaka tribe was pasturing its herds in the Pamirs, central Tien Shan, and in the Amu Darya Delta. Their gold belt buckles, jewelry, and harness decorations display sheep, griffins, and other animal designs that are similar in style to those used by the Scythians, a nomadic people living in the Kuban Basin of the Caucasus region and the western section of the Eurasian plain during the greater part of the 1st millennium BC. When considered together with objects of a like nature recovered from the frozen burial sites of the western Altai Mountains, it becomes evident that many of the Central Asian tribesmen commonly shared the traditions and culture that were once associated only with the Scythians.

Altaic tribes. Because of a freak climatic freeze, some of the Altaic burials, notably those of the 5th century BC at Pazyryk and neighbouring sites, such as Katanda, Shibe, and Tuekt, were isolated from external climatic variations by a protective layer of ice that conserved the organic substances buried in them. At Pazyryk these included the bodies of horses and an embalmed man whose

By courtesy of the State Hermitage Museum, Leningrad

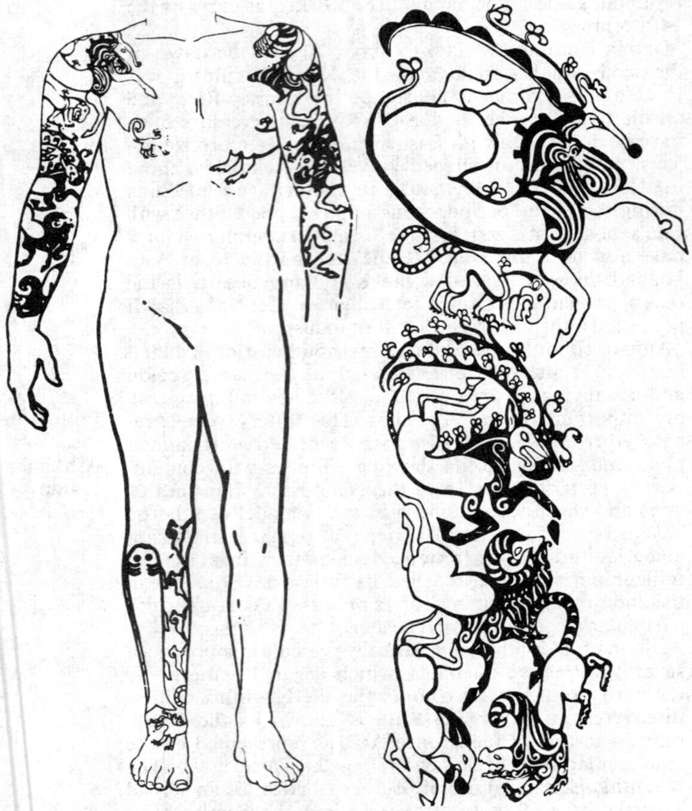

Tattooed designs on the male body found in Kurgan II, Pazyryk, 4th century BC. (Right) Detail from the right shoulder and right arm. In the Hermitage, Leningrad.

The Pazyryk burial site

body was covered with tattoos of Scythian animal motifs. The remarkable textiles recovered from the Pazyryk burials include the oldest woollen knotted-pile carpet known, the oldest embroidered Chinese silk, and two pieces of woven Persian fabric (Hermitage Museum, Leningrad). Red and ochre predominate in the carpet, the main design of which is of riders, stags, and griffins. Many of the Pazyryk felt hangings, saddlecloths, and cushions were covered with elaborate designs executed in appliqué feltwork, dyed furs, and embroidery. Of exceptional interest are those with animal and human figural compositions, the most notable of which are the repeat design of an investiture scene on a felt hanging and that of a semihuman, semibird creature on another (both in the Hermitage Museum, Leningrad). Clothing, whether of felt, leather, or fur, was also lavishly ornamented. Horse reins either had animal designs cut out on them or were studded with wooden ones covered in gold foil. Their tail sheaths were ornamented, as were their headpieces and breastpieces. Some horses were provided with leather or felt masks made to resemble animals, with stag antlers or rams' horns often incorporated in them. Many of the trappings took the form of iron, bronze, and gilt wood animal motifs either applied or suspended from them; and bits had animal-shaped terminal ornaments. Altaic animals frequently display muscles delineated with dot and comma markings, a formal convention that may have derived from appliqué needlework. Although such markings are sometimes included in Assyrian, Achaemenid, and even Urartian animal representations of the ancient Near East, they seldom appear on those of purely Scythian origin. Roundels containing a dot serve the same purpose on the stag and other animal renderings executed by contemporary Śaka metalworkers. Animal processions of the Assyro-Achaemenid type also appealed to many Central Asian tribesmen and are featured in their arts.

Altaic decorative motifs

Certain geometric designs and sun symbols, such as the circle and rosette, recur at Pazyryk but are completely outnumbered by animal motifs. Such specifically Scythian features as zoomorphic junctures—*i.e.*, the addition of a part of one animal to the body of another—are rarer in the Altaic region than in southern Russia. The stag and its relatives, however, figure as prominently in Altaic as in Scythian art. Combat scenes between carnivores and herbivores that occur quite often in Scythian art are exceedingly numerous in Pazyryk work; but, whereas the Scythians show the victim passively accepting its fate, as on 5th-century BC gold triangular plaques from the so-called Seven Brothers burial in the Kuban, the Pazyryk beasts are locked in such bitter fights that the victim's hindquarters become inverted.

Siberian tribes. In the virtually contemporary metalwork of Siberian nomads, single animals of the cat family, such as panthers, carry the Altaic tendency of exaggeration further by twisting their bodies into a circle. In slightly later Siberian plaques, subtle openwork is used, a feature rarely present in Altaic or Scythian objects but frequently encountered in the more rounded versions of the animal style produced in the Ordos region of China, perhaps by Hunnish craftsmen, between the 4th century BC and the 2nd century AD. In the latter part of the 1st millennium BC, Siberian metalworkers adorned many of their gold and bronze plaques with artificial gems made of glass, as well as with jewelled inlays. They produced belt buckles shaped like the letter *B*. Two such gold buckles (Hermitage Museum, Leningrad) are of particular interest because of their figural content. It has been suggested that they illustrate some ancient Central Asian epics, for one depicts a hunting scene and the other a warrior lying under a tree with his head resting on a woman's lap, while a servant holds their two horses. These subjects, possible forerunners of certain episodes in the *Shāh-nāmeh* ("Book of Kings," a work by the 10th century Persian poet Firdausi giving an account of ancient Iranian history), are thought to complement those on a series of openwork plaques, some of them of Ordos origin, on which either two dismounted riders are shown fighting while their horses stand passively on either side or two horses are seen locked in battle, pursuing their masters' quarrel (Hermitage Museum, Leningrad).

Mongolian Huns. In the 4th century BC the Huns started to migrate westward from the Ordos region. By the 3rd century BC, they had reached the Transbaikalia and had begun to enter Mongolia, which soon became the centre of their empire. Numerous mounds mark their progress. Those in the Zidzha Valley lie in the same latitude as the Pazyryk mounds and were subjected to similar conditions of freezing temperatures, which helped to preserve their contents. The richest of the excavated burial sites, however, are those of Noin Ula, to the north of Ulaanbaatar, on the Selenge River. Like those at Pazyryk, they included horse burials. The furnishings of one tomb were especially lavish. The prince for whom it was made must have been in contact with China, for his coffin was apparently made for him there, as were certain of his possessions buried with him (among them, a lacquer cup inscribed with the name of its Chinese maker and dated September 5, AD 13, now in the Hermitage Museum, Leningrad). His horse trappings (Hermitage Museum, Leningrad) are as elaborately decorated as many of those discovered at Pazyryk. His saddle was covered with leather threaded with black and red wool clipped to resemble velvet. The magnificent textiles in his tomb included a woven wool rug lined with thin leather (Hermitage Museum, Leningrad); the centre of the rug depicts a combat, of Scytho-Altaic character, between a griffin and an elk, executed in purple, brown, and white felt appliqué work. The animals' bodies are outlined in cord and embroidered. The design on another textile is embroidered in the form of a tiger skin with a head at each end. The animal's splayed-out body is formed of

Chinese influences in the Noin Ula burials

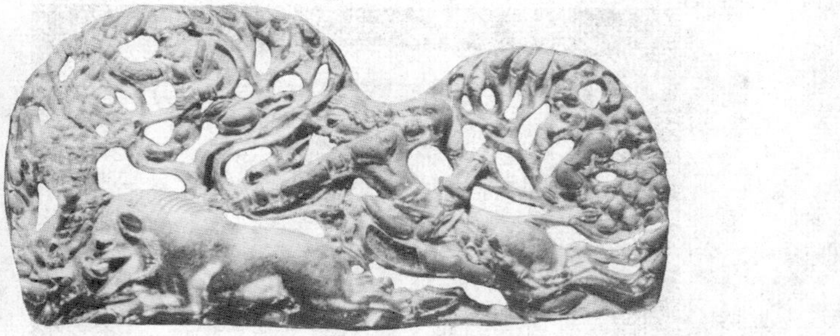

Metalwork of Siberian nomadic tribes.
(Left) Openwork bronze plaque from the Ordos region, showing two men fighting with their horses standing by; 3rd century BC. In the Victoria and Albert Museum, London. 6.5 cm × 12.8 cm. (Right) Gold B-shaped belt buckle from Siberia showing a mounted hunter chasing a wild boar; 1st century BC—1st century AD. In the Hermitage, Leningrad.
By courtesy of (left) the Victoria and Albert Museum, London, and (right) the State Hermitage Museum, Leningrad

black and white embroidered stripes. Other textiles are of Greco-Bactrian and Parthian origin. In some of the Parthian fragments, Central Asian and Sāsānian Persian influences prevail over Hellenistic ones.

By courtesy of the State Hermitage Museum, Leningrad

Fragment of a large rug from Noin Ula showing a griffin attacking an elk, 1st century AD onward. The woven woolen rug was mounted on fine leather and then purple, brown, and white felt was appliqued onto the rug over a cord binding after which it was embroidered. In the Hermitage, Leningrad.

Tashtyk tribe. On the Yenisey River, the Bronze Age Tagar culture was replaced by the Tashtyk culture, dating from the 1st to the 4th century AD. The physical appearance of the Tashtyk people has been preserved by a series of masks, some of them modelled; others, casts taken from the dead. They were painted with the features rendered in blue, red, and green against a yellow ground. Spirals disposed on the foreheads, temples, and cheeks of many of these masks probably represent tattoos. In many cases pearl necklaces worn by the women are also included. Although the animal motifs of the Tashtyks remained strongly Scytho-Altaic in style, the community was so much influenced by China that even its architecture was affected. Just south of Abakan, a large house made of beaten clay in the Chinese style has been discovered. Its roof had been covered with Chinese tiles, some of which carry inscriptions of the Han dynasty.

Painted masks

Thames and Hudson, Ltd.

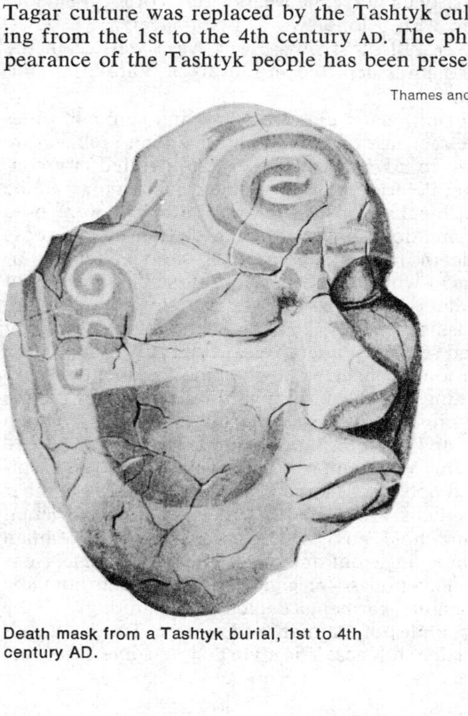

Death mask from a Tashtyk burial, 1st to 4th century AD.

PARTHIA

The Parthian Empire came into being in Khorāsān during the reign of Seleucus I, 358–281 BC, following the absorption by the Parthians of Parni (Dahae) tribesmen. The caravans traversing their territory brought them wealth and ideas from abroad. The figural art of the Hellenistic world made an especially strong impression on them. The finest Parthian objects come from Old Nisa, a town situated on the edge of the Karakoram Range, some 11 miles (18 kilometres) south of Ashkhabad in Tadzhikistan, close to the later town of New Nisa. Old Nisa was founded around 171 BC by Mithradates I to serve as a royal Parthian residence and necropolis, as well as the kingdom's capital. It contained several fine temples and an impressive palace built around a vast central hall, the roof of which was upheld by wooden supports set in stone bases—a practice followed in the town's larger houses. Lifesize clay statues of men and women stood between these supports. The royal treasuries contained many valuables, including silver and silver gilt statuettes of local Parthian deities and of Greek gods, bronze and iron weapons, burnished and painted pottery, glass, and cast bronze animals, such as griffins. The most significant of these treasures, however, is a series of ivory horn-shaped drinking vessels, or rhytons. Some are embellished with paste inlays and precious stones, other have a carved frieze or band encircling their open ends. One rhyton (Hermitage Museum, Leningrad) has a frieze of a procession that includes a Greek god. Conceived in the purest Hellenistic style, the frieze contrasts sharply with the rhyton's horned, lion–griffin-shaped terminal ornamentation, which is admirably modelled in the round, in accordance with the Scytho-Altaic tradition.

THE KINGDOMS OF WESTERN TURKISTAN AND AFGHANISTAN

Skill in irrigation, with the resulting expansion in agriculture, encouraged urbanism and the growth of states, changes that coincided with the rise of nomadism. While the nomadic cattle and horse breeders took over the steppelands, the culturally distinct states of Sogdiana (part of Uzbekistan and much of Tadzhikistan), Fergana (the greater part of Uzbekistan), Chorasmia (the Tashkent region), and Bactria (mainly Afghanistan) were established. At times independent, at other times reduced to vassaldom, the first three states were centred on rivers —Sogdiana around the Zeravshan and Kashkadarya, Fergana on the lower Syrdarya, and Chorasmia on the Amu

Detail of an ivory rhyton from Nisa, 2nd century. The frieze shows a procession that includes a Greek god. In the Hermitage, Leningrad.

By courtesy of the State Hermitage Museum, Leningrad; photograph, Josephine Powell, Rome

Darya's basin. (The earliest references to these states are to be found in the Avesta, the principal scriptural work of the Zoroastrian religion, and in the inscription cut by order of the Persian king Darius I (reigned 522–486 BC) on the face of the rock of Bīsitūn in the Kermanshah province of Iran.) Bactria extended from the Syrdarya to the Hindu Kush (southern Tadzhikistan and Afghanistan) and is rich in unexplored mounds. Excavations at Balkh show that its first inhabitants settled there when others were doing so at Afrasiab (Samarkand) and Merv.

The political and economic changes that developed in the 4th century BC, following the Macedonian Greek king Alexander the Great's conquest of these states and their incorporation in the Seleucid Empire, and the conquests made, in turn, by the Parthians, Arabs, Turks, and Mongols are reflected in the regions' arts. The city of Alexandria-Kapisu (Begrām), founded by Alexander the Great, became the clearing house for India's western trade. India's religious beliefs, especially Buddhism, and the scriptural style that evolved in Gandhāra (an area situated between the Qondūz and Indus rivers in the Lower Kābul Valley of northwestern Pakistan) and Mathurā (in the Punjab [Pañjāb] region of northwestern India) followed along the trade routes and reached not only Bactria but, at times, also Kashmir, Tibet, China, and even the remote oasis towns of the Tarim Basin in Sinkiang. At the same time, Seleucid support resulted in the introduction of Greco-Roman art forms into Bactria, Kapisu, Taxila (Rāwalpindi), Gandhāra, Mathurā, and, after thirty years, even into Seistan.

Sogdiana. Sogdiana, with its capital of Afrasiab, was already noted for the sophistication and number of its towns when Alexander the Great conquered it in 328 BC and opened it up to Greek soldiers and administrators, and eventually to Roman traders. The Sogdians resented being governed by Alexander's successors, the Greek kings of the Seleucid dynasty. It is difficult to establish their relationship with their Seleucid suzerains and still more so with the later Kushans, but there is ample evidence to show that neither group of conquerors hindered the rise in both Sogdiana and Chorasmia of a local feudal nobility and class of rich farmers.

Pottery sculpture

A considerable amount of secular and religious pottery sculpture dating from the early Christian Era to the Arab invasion of the 8th century has been found at Afrasiab. The more interesting examples consist of statuettes of clothed women, some of them representing Zoroastrian deities such as Anahita. They have foreshortened bodies and large heads with a withdrawn expression on their faces and wear tiaras, hats, or hoods sewn to their cloaks. When the cloaks are sleeveless, they are worn over straight, long-sleeved robes instead of draped garments. All of the figures hold a piece of fruit, a symbol of fertility. Third-to-fourth-century statuettes from the fortified town of Tali Barsu, to the south of Samarkand, depict Syavush, the god of annual death and spring rebirth, as a musician. Statuettes of women flutists, riders, animals, and the Iranian semihuman-semianimal demi-god Shah Gopat have also been discovered there. In the 7th and 8th centuries, sculpture, whether in clay or alabaster, was highly developed at Pyanjikent, a site some 40 miles (60 kilometres) east of Samarkand, where Indian influence was often felt.

The earliest of Turkistan's mural paintings have been found in its eastern section. Those at Niy date from the 2nd century AD; those at Miran, from the 3rd. The inspiration in both stemmed from Rome, whereas Buddhism provided the impulses for the slightly later murals at Bāmiān and Kizil. In the eastern zone the paintings were designed as backgrounds to sculpture, and, as in western Turkistan, they were executed in tempera. Some very high quality murals recently discovered in western Turkistan are dated slightly later. The oldest ones, which are extremely fragmentary, are from the Varakhsha, a princely residence to the northeast of Bukhara, now lying in the desert; they date from the 3rd to the 4th century AD. Murals discovered at the beginning of the 20th century at Samarkand, which are almost contemporary with those at Varakhsha, have been lost. The importance of these murals is wholly eclipsed by the slightly later works discovered recently in Sogdiana, such as the 7th-century works at Varakhsha. Some of the rooms in the main apartments of the Varakhsha Palace (which consisted of several detached buildings) are decorated with high-relief alabaster stucco panels and carved woodwork, as well as with paintings. Benches are inserted into the walls of one room, the area above them divided into two registers, or horizontal rows, both painted red. In the upper register was a procession of animals, little of which survives, and, in the lower, splendidly attired hunters seated on elephants pursued spirited leopards and creatures of the griffin family.

Mural paintings at Varakhsha

Some 200 miles (300 kilometres) east of Samarkand, in a once fertile, now desert tract of land, the ruins of the great feudal castle of Mug survive. Among the objects excavated there was part of a wooden shield with the painted figure of a rider (Hermitage Museum, Leningrad), which foreshadows a type commonly found in Islāmic Persian book illumination. Mounted on a splendidly caparisoned horse, he wears a tunic of local cut and is equipped with a long sword, two daggers, two bows, and a quiver full of arrows. He is wasp waisted in the manner of figures depicted in murals of Varakhsha and Pyanjikent.

At Pyanjikent, a site close to Mug, and some 40 miles (60 kilometres) east of Samarkand, Sogdian architecture can be seen to advantage. The desert-engulfed city contained several large temples built of rectangular adobe bricks and blocks of beaten clay. The bricks were used for vaults and domes, while the flat sections of the roofs were made of rafters supported by wooden pillars or piers, some of which had been set in stone bases. Many of the more important houses were two storied. A square room measuring 26 by 26 feet (eight metres by eight metres) had served as a temple sanctuary. Although, in a series of rooms connected to it, some fragmentary religious paintings survived, the paintings in another temple are better preserved. They depict the death, the Sogdian burial rite, and the rebirth of a youthful Syavush. Over 50 figures of this vast composition survive, some representing Sogdian noblemen, some a group of Turks. A number of the Sogdians are seated crosslegged in the oriental manner and hold gold and silver vessels of Sāsānian shape in three fingers of one hand. The men's single, close fitting Sogdian tunics—elegant versions of the nomadic dress—resemble garments depicted in paintings of the Buddhist temples of Bāmiān and eastern Turkistan, notably at Kizil and Kuca. The style and, in some cases, the

Temple architecture and decoration at Pyanjikent

subject matter of these Sogdian scenes must have influenced the illuminators of such Islāmic Persian works as the Shāh-nāmeh. Another set of murals is unusual in that it is executed in high relief and then coloured. It shows human beings, sea monsters, and fish, with the waves of the sea rendered in lower relief than the figures. Yet another mural depicts a feast against a black background; a king and several priests sit crosslegged under a canopy; a woman harpist, some musicians and dice players, and a procession of elephants complete the scene. By placing light figures against dark or vivid backgrounds, Sogdian artists evolved a distinct form of perspective.

A study of the religious paintings shows that Central Asian Zoroastrianism retained elements from the earlier indigenous cult of the sun and moon. Some of the scenes in the secular works are linked in their subject matter (but not their style) to a small group of older Siberian gold and bronze *B*-shaped buckles and to the Siberian and Ordos plaques that are thought to illustrate local epics. Other secular scenes give full expression to Sogdian interest in the splendour of contemporary court life and prowess in hunting and warfare. The love of overall decoration and of animal motifs is as prevalent as in nomadic art. Details incorporated in Sogdian paintings proclaim the eclecticism of the society they depict and for which they were created. Sāsānian influence from Persia is seen in crowns trimmed with ribbons, veils, and bells; in the styling and trimming of hair and beards; and in many of their vessel shapes. The helmets worn by the warriors in the Pyanjikent libation scene resemble those depicted in the murals of eastern Turkistan. The clothes follow local fashions, and certain horse trappings display disks the shapes of which recall nomadic types.

Sāsānian motifs in Sogdian textiles

Sogdian textiles are known to have been in great demand among their neighbours. Sāsānian motifs must have reached Sogdian weavers by way of imports from Persia, indirectly routed through Parthia, and also from Zoroastrians seeking protection in Sogdiana from Persian persecution. These motifs often figure both on surviving textiles and on those recorded in the paintings. The murals at Varakhsha, for example, include motifs taken from textiles; and a 5th-century mural from Balalyk Tepe displays the head of a tusked, boarlike animal set in a roundel that is almost identical to that on a Sāsānian fabric found at Astana in eastern Turkistan.

Between the 5th and 7th centuries, the Sogdians made dried-brick caskets shaped like rectangular rooms to contain ossuaries, or urns for the bones of the dead. The sides and lids of the ossuaries were decorated. The ornamentation on an ossuary from Bia Naiman (Hermitage Museum, Leningrad) has so many points in common with the decorations on a series of silver vessels that were, until recently, assigned to Bactria that the latter have come to be accepted as Sogdian. Several ewers have niches containing nude women rendered in a markedly Indian style, thereby recalling many a carved ivory plaque from Begrām. Very similar niches adorn the Bia Naiman ossuary, but these contain crowned figures. In both cases the niches owe their form to Western influence, but those on the ossuary are formed of columns surmounted by capitals upholding pearl-studded arches, while on the ewers the Central Asian rosette replaces the capitals and the pearls.

Sculpture, both in relief and in the round, was widely produced in Sogdiana. Much of the earlier work takes the form of panels or friezes made of alabaster, stucco, and, occasionally, wood. Rosettes, roundels, disks, and vegetation provide the chief motifs. Audience chambers and large reception rooms often contained statues in the round. Even the statues attached to the wall had the appearance of being worked in the round. The earliest wooden caryatids, or columns in human form, are found in western Turkistan at Pyanjikent. The caryatids in the form of women have their hair elaborately dressed, and, although nude at the waist, they wear boleros, as well as close fitting, heavily trimmed skirts and splendid necklaces of Indian appearance. Once again, these figures recall those on Begrām's ivory plaques and Buddhist statuettes of the 1st to 5th centuries.

Sogdian art from Pyanjikent.
(Left) Charred wooden caryatid, 7th century. In the Hermitage, Leningrad. (Right) A harpist, fragment of a mural in a private house, 7th–8th century. In the Hermitage, Leningrad.
By courtesy of the State Hermitage Museum, Leningrad; photograph, (left) Josephine Powell, Rome

Fergana and Chorasmia. Fergana produced much pottery of quality, but, as yet, there have been no finds of comparable importance to those in Sogdiana. Its arts appear to have paralleled the developments in the more prosperous, more heavily populated, and more highly urbanized state of Chorasmia. Chorasmia's defensive architecture was particularly notable. Its great citadels and palaces were enclosed by two lines of walls strengthened by massive towers that were fitted with lookout posts and firing slits and topped by archers' galleries. Chorasmian entrance gates were labyrinthine in plan. Many of these splendid buildings have disappeared be-

Citadels and palaces

By courtesy of the trustees of the British Museum

Chorasmian architecture.
(Left) Bronze relief of a citadel or palace from Toprakkale and (right) bronze model of a defensive tower, 8th–7th century BC, from Toprakkale. In the British Museum. (Left) 28 cm × 36 cm; (right) height 16.5 cm.

neath the desert's encroaching sands. Recently excavated, Toprak kala, near Termez, is thought to have served not only as a citadel but perhaps as Chorasmia's capital until about the 7th century. Defended by stout walls, the palace of sun-dried bricks was equipped with three lookout towers. The ground floor of this two storied building acted as a foundation for the living rooms and storerooms above. Many of the rooms were adorned with sculpture: its most impressive room, the Hall of Kings, had niches fitted with grills ranged along the tops of its walls to hold statues of Chorasmia's rulers and notables; the Alabaster Hall contained many sculptures executed both in the round and in relief; a Hall of Victories contained statues of kings seated in the presence of a goddess of victory; statues of warriors carrying shields adorned the Warriors' Hall. All of the Chorasmian figural works are so lifelike that it is evident that portraiture had reached a high state of development by the 3rd and 4th centuries AD. Surviving decorations in the fortified manorhouse of Teshik Kala display the palmette, rosette, lotus, and ace-of-spade motifs that the Seljuqs later carried westward to Anatolia and beyond in the 11th and 12th centuries.

Bactria. The most Hellenized of these states in western Turkistan and Afghanistan was Bactria. Its fine coinage, for example, was distinctly Hellenistic in style, and Bactrian silversmiths were often influenced as much by Roman as Greek Hellenistic metalwork. Alexander the Great annexed Kābul to Bactria and founded Alexandra-Kapisu, a city astride the Indian caravan route, to serve as the province's capital. The multiracialism of Kapisu's population is reflected in the origins of the objects found there. Imports included articles from India, China, and the Greco-Roman world, especially from Syria. Artistic conventions characteristic of all these countries blended with the local Central Asian ones, with the Indian conventions predominating, to create Bactria's own distinctive style in sculpture, whether in alabaster, stone, ivory, or wood. Its mural paintings are wholly Buddhist in content, but they often contain features that link them to Fundukistan in India and the Sāsānian Persian world.

Importance of the decorative arts in Bactria

The decorative arts were highly developed in Bactria. Many of their sun-dried-brick houses were large enough to include several reception rooms, which contained many luxurious decorative objects. Potters remained attached to animal forms derived from nomadic art. The large production of votive statuettes, especially representations of Anahita and Syavush, may be partly attributed to the belief that Zoroaster was born in Balkh. This tradition was also evident at Merv until the Arab Invasion of Central Asia. The Bactrians mastered the technique of working metals at an early date. A 4th-century-BC lion-griffin (British Museum) in cast bronze is descended from a Scytho-Altaic prototype and so, too, is a pair of slightly earlier gold armlets (British Museum, London), originally embellished with inlay, from the Oxus Treasure. A series of silver dishes (Hermitage, Leningrad) from the end of the 1st millenium BC are, on the other hand, decorated with scenes drawn from the tragedies of the Greek dramatist Euripides and Greco-Roman mythology rendered in a markedly Hellenized style. Other silver dishes employ Indian motifs such as elephants. By the 8th century, these diverse ornamental motifs had fused, as on a silver-gilt bowl (Hermitage, Leningrad), dated between the 5th and 8th centuries AD, into a Kushan style that may well have provided the basis for Persia's later Rey figural pottery style.

By courtesy of the trustees of the British Museum

Bactrian lion-griffin, cast bronze, 4th century AD. In the British Museum. Height 24.9 cm.

KUSHAN

The Kushans replaced the Greeks in Bactria around 130 BC. They are thought to have been of Yüeh-chih stock with a strong admixture of Hephtalites, Asiani, Śaka, and Tokharian. One branch of this group migrated to the Tarim Basin and founded a short-lived empire, while the other, under the name of Kushan, gained control of Central Asia. Capturing a section of the great trade route leading from India and China to the west, the Kushans derived much of their revenue from the transit dues they exacted from the caravans crossing their territory, which often were carrying supplies of Chinese gold, silver, and nickel from the Tarim oasis towns to the Seleucid Persians. Around 106 BC, the first caravan to carry silk from China direct to Persia passed through territory that had belonged to the Seleucids but was now divided between the Kushans and Parthians.

Kushan art reached its fullest development in the 2nd century AD, when the great king Kaniṣka is believed to have reigned. A magnificent, almost lifesize, now headless sculpture of Kaniṣka (Archaeological Museum, Mathurā) shows him wearing an elegant version of nomadic dress. His kingdom extended from Central Asia to include Gandhāra and Mathurā, where the Seleucids had so firmly established Hellenistic art that Western influence continued to maintain its hold even in the reign of the first members of India's Gupta dynasty. When Mahāyāna Buddhism reached Gandhāra during the 4th and 5th centuries AD, its sculptors turned to the Hellenistic world as a matter of course for a visual conception of Buddha and quickly evolved several Hellenistic versions. In the popular Apollo version Budda is long faced, long nosed and has wavy hair. This type survived into the 5th century and penetrated as far as Kashmir and Turkistan.

The Gandhāra and Mathurā styles of Buddhist sculpture

A school of religious sculpture equal in importance to that of Gandhāra developed almost simultaneously at Mathurā. Its earliest Buddhist images are virtually contemporary with the earliest ones produced in Gandhāra but, in Mathurā, Indian influences predominate. The portrayal of Buddha in the Mathurān style is softer yet more direct. The features are more Eastern; eyebrows extend in a continuous, sinous line; hair is straight; the earlobes are elongated; and an enigmatic smile replaces the withdrawn expression of the Hellenized Buddhas of Gandhāra. While the sculptors of Mathurā used a red sandstone, the Gandhārans worked in limestone or a local gray schist. They generally chose the latter for the small, uniform-sized panels with which they faced their *stūpa*s and *vishana*s, carving them with scenes of Buddha's life. On the panels, the story unfolds from left to right, each scene being framed either within trees, leaves, or Corinthian columns sometimes linked by arches. These religious narratives often include furniture and details drawn from contemporary life. The figures, which use gestures of Indian origin to convey emotion, display racial characteristics that range from Indo-European to Mongolian. Many figures are presented in the frontal position favoured by Parthian artists, while others appear three-quarter face, as in Hellenistic art. Some wear Hellenistic robes and headdresses such as those worn in Palmyra, an ancient city in Syria. The Gandhāran style of sculpture was no longer produced after this area was invaded by the White Huns, in the 6th century.

Mathurān and Gandhāran sculpture.
(Left) Indian-style colossal head of Buddha from Mathurā, red sandstone, Mathurā, 1st century AD. In the Archaeological Museum, Mathurā, India. Height 57 cm. (Centre) Birth of Buddha, limestone relief showing Hellenistic influence, Gandhāra, 1st–2nd century AD. In The Art Institute of Chicago. 27.4 cm × 50 cm. (Right) Apollo version head of Buddha from Gandhāra, grey schist, 2nd–3rd century AD. In the British Museum. Height 38.1 cm.
By courtesy of (left) the Archaeological Museum, Mathura, India; (centre) the Art Institute of Chicago, S.M. Nickerson Collection; and (right) the trustees of the British Museum

Central Afghanistan is rich in Kushan sites. Āteshkadeh-ye Sorkh Kowtal, situated in the Qondūz Valley, close to the Kābul-Mazār-e Sharīf road, is dated by an inscription to the time of Kaniṣka's reign. Architecture was highly developed there. The town was protected by a double row of walls that ascended the hill on which it stood. The most impressive site within the wall was occupied by a dynastic fire temple, built to an Achaemenid plan in large blocks of well-dressed stone and approached by an imposing staircase. Within, columns topped by Corinthian capitals supported the roof. Numerous sculptures had originally adorned the interior, those worked with floral and animal motifs conforming to the Gandhāran tradition, while figural works followed Scytho-Parthian and, to some extent, Hellenistic traditions.

Buddhist art at Bāmiān

The Buddhist art of central Afghanistan is admirably represented at Bāmiān, where Mani, the Iranian founder of the Manichaean religion, probably lived and encouraged the growth of a religious pictorial art in the 3rd century AD. At both the eastern and western approaches to Bāmiān, a huge statue of Buddha as ruler of the world was cut into the face of the rock. The smaller statue measures 120 feet (about 40 metres) and dates from soon after the town's foundation in the 4th century AD; the other measures 170 feet (50 metres) and dates from the 5th century. In their commanding monumentality, both statues reflect the influence of the Mathurān image of King Kaniṣka and the portrait sculpture of Sāsānian kings and Parthian notables. Traces of painting showing Sāsānian and Indian influences survive in the rock-hewn niche behind the earlier Buddha.

Regardless of Manichaean influence, Sāsānian elements prevailed at Bāmiān between the 4th and 6th centuries. At Dūktar-e Nowshirvān, near Bāmiān, a 4th-century painting of a Sāsānian king flanked by attendants survives. The murals in Bāmiān's 5th-century temple of Kakrak include one of a deified king of Sāsānian appearance, while others display the figure of Buddha set within a circle and wearing a costume of the Sāsānian type. Sāsānian motifs of paired birds and griffins placed in medalions or pearl circlets are common. In the murals at Imgur-Enlil, Buddha wears a close-fitting tunic resembling that worn by the Sāsānian king depicted on the rock carvings of Ṭāq-e Bostān. The traces of Hellenism, which are also evident in these wall paintings, began to disappear by the 5th century, when Sāsānian influence gradually gave way to the Gupta style of India.

Stemming from Gupta art is the practice adopted at Bāmiān between the 5th and 6th centuries of painting in the dome of a sanctuary a Buddha within a circle or hexagon. Gradually, these circles and hexagons became symbols of the heavenly Buddha. Many developed into rosettes and eight pointed stars—motifs that were retained in the 10th and 11th centuries by the Islāmic Seljuqs, who carried them to Persia and Asia Minor. As Gupta influence increased, sculpture gained in importance. A new style had evolved by the 8th to 9th centuries, but it did not penetrate into western Turkistan,

By courtesy of the Afghan Information Bureau, London

Colossal Buddha carved from the rock at Bāmiān, Afghanistan, 5th century. Height 51.8 m.

Buddha in a mandorla preaching, a painting from the dome of a cave shrine at Bāmiān, Afghanistan, 5th–6th century.
Josephine Powell, Rome

where the Arab conquerors religiously opposed figural art. In the 9th century many Buddhists left Kashgaria, and Islām gained ground. Figural sculpture was forced underground and was primarily produced by secret shamanistic cults of an indigenous Central Asian origin. Although figural art was never to flourish in western Turkistan as gloriously as it had prior to the Arab invasion, there was a revival under the Mongols in the form of book illuminations.

EASTERN TURKISTAN

Uighurs. The figural arts found new patrons in eastern Turkistan among the Turkic Uighurs, who while living in T'ang dynasty China had been influenced by Manichaean figurative art. The overthrow in China in 846 AD of Buddhism by Confucianism forced the Buddhist Uighurs to migrate to eastern Turkistan. Gradually, they gained control over the Tien Shan region, Turfan, and the northeastern section of the Tarim Basin. The Turkic Uighurs especially favoured portraiture. In the 7th and 8th centuries Uighur artists already had acquired great proficiency in rendering likenesses in a style heavily influenced by Chinese portraiture of the T'ang period. These portraits were painted on silk and often inscribed with the sitter's name.

Portraiture of the Turkic Uighurs

Khitans. The figural style is believed to have been transmitted to the Mongols by the Khitans when the latter were living on the middle reaches of the Yenisey. The wealth of the Khitan princes is reflected in the furnishings of burial mounds discovered at Kopeni, some 200 miles (300 kilometres) to the south of Krasnoyarsk. Dating from the 7th to 8th centuries, these mounds were similar in type to those constructed by the nomads of the 1st millennium BC. One of the richest graves contained four gold jugs set on a silver dish and a number of gold, silver, and bronze ornaments (Hermitage Museum, Leningrad). Two of the jugs, although undecorated, carry Orkhon inscriptions on their bases. Two others are covered with delicate relief representations of birds and fish surrounded by flowers and vegetation, executed in a style influenced by Islāmic art. A Scytho-Altaic hunting motif of riders pursuing a tiger, a deer, and a panther appears on a bronze ornamental object.

Turkic tribes had been massing in Central Asia from about the 5th century AD. In the 6th century the Kul Tepe and Bilge Khan tribes established a state of their own in the Orkhon Valley. The inscriptions that they carved on the valley's rocks are of considerable historical importance. In the 7th century the Turkic Oğuz people were so numerous that they constituted 24 tribes. The Sāmānids, Ghaznavids, Ghūrids, and Seljuqs were of Oğuz extraction.

Sāmānids. The Sāmānids centred their kingdom in Khorāsān. In the 9th century, under the leadership of Esmāʿil, they ruled over Transoxiana and eastern Persia from their capital of Bukhara. Esmāʿil's *türbe*, or mausoleum, the oldest Islāmic monument surviving in Bukhara, reproduces the form of the Zoroastrian *chanar taq*, or fire temple. In Sāmānid and Seljuqid hands, the *türbe* generally took the form of a small circular or octagonal building, roofed with a turret shaped like the point of a pencil. Mounted on a solid or single vaulted substructure, its single chamber had a domed ceiling and a mihrab, or niche indicating the direction of Mecca. In the more elaborate *türbe*s, the single door was framed with bands of geometric decoration, and the turret was sometimes ribbed.

Türbe construction

Ghaznavids and Ghūrids. Alptegin, a slave of Turkic origin at the Sāmānid court, escaped in 962 AD to Kābul, where he rapidly gained control of the town. He transferred his headquarters to Ghazna in central Afghanistan and established his dynasty there. Few Ghaznavid works of art have survived, but the admirably proportioned and

Josephine Powell, Rome

One of the two mortuary towers at Ghazni, Afghanistan, 10th–11th century.

decorated mortuary towers at Ghazna are architectural achievements of great splendour. Still finer is the minaret of Jām, a Ghūrid structure of the 11th century. Standing alone in a desolate region, it escaped discovery until 1957. It is conjectured that the minaret may mark the position of the lost Ghūrid capital of Fīrūzkūh.

Seljuqs. The art of the Seljuqs, who founded kingdoms in Persia, eastern Byzantium, Syria, and Iraq, eclipsed that of the Sāmānids, Ghūrids, and Ghaznavids. They were great architectural patrons and constructed numerous mosques, madrasah (Islāmic religious schools), hospitals, orphanages, baths, caravanserais, bridges, and *türbe*s notable for their decorative masonry, elaborately ornamented portals, and use of Kūfic script as an architectural decorative device. The Seljuqs also attained a high standard in their decorative arts, especially metalwork, wood carving, and pottery. The Mongols, who terminated the Seljuq period, adopted certain Seljuqid artistic conventions, particularly the use of ornamented portals and glazed-tile paneling.

Mongols. Genghis Khan (died 1227), the renowned Mongol conqueror, sacked and destroyed Bukhara in 1224, sparing only the 12th-century Kalyan tower, which was used for throwing criminals to their death. The 14th-century Turkic conqueror Timur, however, endowed Samarkand with new glory by building a series of religious monuments widely renowned for their splendour and decorative use of glazed tiles. In the 16th century, Bābur, prince of Fergana, coveted Samarkand. Failing to capture it, he chose Kābul as his headquarters for his conquest of India. His tomb there (he died in 1540) is the only visible testimony to the years he spent in the city.

Emirate of Bukhara. Although fine-quality pottery decorated with animal, bird, and figural designs was being made in New Nisa in the 15th century, the artistic revival of the Mongol period that Timur had launched in western Turkistan had died out by the 16th century, when the emirate of Bukhara, incorporating much of Sogdiana, was established. Except for gold-thread embroidery and carpet making, in most of Central Asia the visual arts largely stagnated. In Mongolia the conversion of the Buryats to Lamaism in the 18th century brought into their tradition of ornamentation such Tibetan motifs as the lotus, dragon, and lion.

Russian-Soviet period. In 1882 the emirate of Bukhara was incorporated as a Russian state. This political act had little cultural effect, and European art remained unknown to Central Asians. Traditional indigenous architecture of baked or unbaked brick construction was revived in the 18th century. Carved doors and screens were again produced. Old styles of Islāmic script were combined with arabesques to adorn metalwork. Zoomorphic junctures persisted in the animal designs created by metalworkers and potters alike, although the ornaments worn by nomadic women had become so stylized as to have lost all resemblance to the ancient animal motifs from which they were descended. Openwork remained a feature of much of the jewelry, notably of the necklaces formed of small openwork plaques linked by rings or chains.

Revival of traditional architecture and decoration

Following the Russian Revolution, a new phase of art began in the Soviet-controlled regions of Central Asia. Although the Soviet authorities took steps to maintain the existing carpet and textile industries, they encouraged the inclusion of genre scenes and native animals and vegetation. They also founded schools to train artists in the traditions of European art. Pictorial arts are naturalistic in style, conforming with the principles of social realism as defined by the Soviet authorities. The first Buryat-Mongolian Turkmen painter to achieve distinction in this style was Tsyrenzhap Sampilov.

ARCTIC REGIONS

In the arctic zone of Central Asia, the prehistoric age extends from the 3rd millennium BC to the arrival of Europeans around AD 1800. Knowledge of the region's arts is still very limited, for it is wholly dependent upon the sculptures produced by Eskimos living on the shores and in the hinterland of Siberia and the Bering Strait. These sculptures are mostly in walrus tusk, though wood and reindeer horn examples also exist. The majority are small in size and worked in the round to form terminal ornaments for utilitarian or ceremonial objects or statuettes. The latter are not provided with bases and thus must have been designed to be carried about. Many of the implements are decorated with incised patterns formed chiefly of lines and dots. As in all early arts, the statuettes and terminal ornaments are largely concerned with hunting or the magical practices of shamanism. The earliest and finest statuettes are assigned to the Okvik culture, which some scholars date to the pre-Christian era, others to its early centuries. Okvik art is concerned primarily with the representation of the human figure, differing in that respect from the contemporary or slightly later Old Bering Sea culture, where interest largely centres on animals, such as reindeer, elks, bears, and seals.

Okvik sculpture

Works of the Okvik and later Arctic schools often depict women, sometimes in the nude, sometimes clothed. The nude figures seldom include more of the arms than shoulder stumps. Their bodies are short and flat, their heads large, pear-shaped, and carefully worked, as are hands when included. The faces are carved and are sometimes incised with lines, probably denoting tattooing. The so-called Okvik Madonna (University of Alaska Museum, College) is perhaps the most expressive of these statuettes.

By courtesy of the University of Alaska Museum, Fairbanks

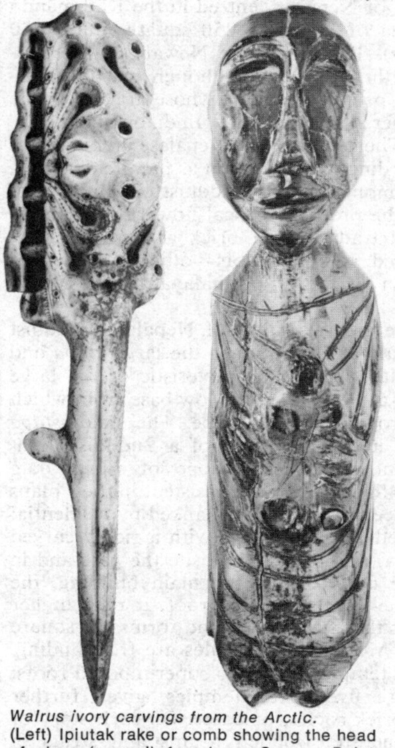

Walrus ivory carvings from the Arctic.
(Left) Ipiutak rake or comb showing the head of a bear (or seal), found near Spencer Point, near the western tip of the Seward Peninsula in northeastern Alaska, 1st–6th century AD. Length 26 cm. (Right) The Okvik Madonna, found on an island off the southeastern coast of St. Lawrence Island in the Bering Sea, 1st–5th century AD. Height 17.1 cm. In the University of Alaska Museum, College.

Some Okvik animal designs are particularly interesting because of certain stylistic details that point to a relationship with works of the Scytho-Siberian school. Reindeer are so frequently depicted that the discovery at Pazyryk of a horse's mask in the form of a reindeer's head led to the suggestion that the mask was a survival from a reindeer cult acquired by the Altaians from a northern people such as the Eskimo. That theory has been discounted, yet some Okvik works are undoubtedly related to certain slightly older examples of Siberian metalwork. Thus, the heads of some terminal ornaments bear a close resemblance to those of certain Siberian works. The lozenge-shaped muscles that appear on Eskimo carvings amid lines intended to portray the animal's skeleton are very similar to those of the Pazyryk dot and comma markings. In late- or post-Okvik times certain specifically Eskimo objects, such as masks, were decorated with stylized animal heads executed in relief and accompanied by bosses that recall the Altaic, especially those that reflect Chinese influence. Compositions such as that on an unidentifiable object (possibly a rake or comb) in the University of Alaska Museum, which includes as its central motif the head of a bear resting on its forepaws and flanked by griffins, display a marked affinity with west Siberian ones.

In the 17th century, climatic changes led, in the 19th century, to contacts with the outer world and brought the traditional Eskimo school of sculpture to an abrupt end. When, toward the end of the century, art started to revive, it did so under European influence, eventually developing a greater concern for aesthetic than religious considerations. The new style retained much of the directness of approach and formal conventions of the traditional style, but, in addition, there was a greater emphasis on naturalism. Group scenes, too, became popular, as did animal and bird compositions. There has been an extensive production of small sculptures, chiefly of fish, bird, or animal forms, in the 20th century. (T.T.R.)

HIMALAYAN CULTURES OF NEPAL AND TIBET

Nepal. The art of Nepal is centred in the Kāthmāndu Valley, in an area of less than 250 square miles (650 square kilometres). The artists are Newars, or Mongoloids, different ethnically from, though partly intermingled with, the peoples of India, whose art they made their own—whether its themes were Hindu or Buddhist.

Architecture. There is only one Nepalese architectural style, varied according to its function as private dwelling, palace, Buddhist monastery, or Buddhist or Hindu temple. The style is the protracted local flowering of an Indian architectural tradition—of brick and wood architecture with tiered, sloping roofs—other varieties of which are found in the western Himalayas and in Kerala in the southwest.

Essentially, there are two kinds of Nepalese Buddhist shrine, or *stūpa* (also called *caitya*): the large *stūpa* and the small, monolithic *stūpa*. Characteristic of the large *stūpa* like the one at Bodnath is the low base from which it rises and its crowning dome-shape. The small *stūpa* was generally set in the courtyard of a Buddhist monastery. The extant monasteries, none of which date earlier than the 14th century, are consistent in their plans and structures. A central courtyard flanked by residential buildings is entered through a gate with a richly carved tympanum (torana) and porch. Opposite the gate and in the centre of the courtyard is the main building, the *stūpa;* with its one- to three-tiered roof, it rises higher than the buildings that surround it and forms the square of the courtyard. Most Hindu temples are freestanding. The more ancient temples have two superimposed roofs; the later ones are five-roofed temples, given further height by tiered brick socles, or bases. On each story of the towerlike structure, wooden beams and struts (a structural piece designed to resist pressure in the direction of its length) support a widely projected slanting roof, the struts ascending diagonally from the central structure to the edge of the tiled roof. The majestically tapered, ascending profile of the structure, with its strong contrast of light playing on the roofs and masses of shade looming below, is peculiar to Nepal. Rich in textures and colours, the temples are embellished with carved and painted struts, carved doorframes and window frames, and embossed, gilded copper sheets. Like the pantheon on the stone temples of India, the pantheon of Nepal is laid out mainly on the exterior of the temple—in contrast to Tibet, where it is displayed on the interior of the temple.

Buddhist monasteries

Sculpture and painting. Combinations of Hindu and Buddhist iconography came about easily, though there is something facile about them, a smoothness found also in the form of the Nepalese images, which lack the surging dynamism of Indian form. Characteristic of the Nepalese transformation of Indian styles is a loss of depth but a gain in grace. Suavity of line, temperance of modelling, tonal clarity of vivid, contrasting colours raise Nepalese works far above the merely derivative. An indigenous physiognomy, too, modifies the physical formulas for sculpture laid down in India.

While Nepalese sculpture is known to exist from the 2nd century BC (terra-cotta plaques, a stone *bodhisattva*, and a Buddha image), it was in the 5th to the 7th centuries BC that stone sculpture in Nepal came into its own. Viṣṇu Vikrānta (the three strides of Viṣṇu), dated AD 467, and 6th-century panels illustrating the Kumārasambhava ("Birth of the War-God," an epic by the 5th-century Indian poet and dramatist Kālidāsa) are masterworks of narrative relief and dramatic mythical composition. On the more intimate level of daily life, sculpture takes the form of the many fountains that adorn watering places (*pranali*) of Nepal. Water spouts forth from *makara* (Hindu water monster with the body of a crocodile and the head of an elephant) snouts sheathed in gilt copper into reservoirs laid out with architectural dignity. As far as present knowledge goes, Newari sculpture was dominated from the 8th century into the 18th by gilt-copper images. In their glowing splendour, the gilt, sometimes jewel-encrusted images embody the Buddhist quality of compassion that leads to enlightenment.

Painting. Painting in Nepal is known from the 11th century on palm leaves and wooden bookcovers of manuscripts, some of them hardly distinguishable, at first, from the Bengali prototypes. The Nepalese style, less nervous, more conscious of the beautiful line and clear, compartmental order of the surface, is fully developed in scrolls, or *prabhas* (most of them, vertical), on cotton known from the 13th century. These scrolls are of two kinds: one consists of arrays of religious images with a large figure of the main deity in their midst; the other consists of a *maṇḍala*, the Hindu and Buddhist symbol of the universe—a circle enclosing a square with the deities disposed within. Narrative panels or sections in the margins of both types of scroll soften the rigour of the composition. While this Nepalese hieratic, or sacerdotal, style was at its peak, a narrative style developed in manuscript illuminations such as the

Kinds of Nepalese *prabha* painting

(Left) Larry Reynolds; (right) Josephine Powell, Rome

Nepalese Architecture.
(Left) Bodnath *stūpa*, near Kāthmāndu, *c.* 13th century. (Right) Temples on Durbar Square, Lalitpur.

A rider on an elephant attacked by two leopards, Sogdianan fresco from Varaksha, possibly 7th–8th century AD. In the Hermitage, Leningrad. Height about 1.2 m.

Art of Turkistan and Afghanistan

Griffin armlet from the Oxus Treasure, Achaemenid period (559–330 BC). In the British Museum.

A female donor, fragment of a wall painting from Bezeklik in Eastern Turkistan. In the Museum für Indische Kunst, Staatliche Museen Preussischer Kulturbesitz, West Berlin.

Yakshi (River Goddess), ivory carving from Bagrām, Afghanistan. In the Kābul Museum, Afghanistan. Height 46 cm.

Plate 1: By courtesy of (top) the Hermitage, Leningrad, (bottom left) the Museum fur Indische Kunst, Staatliche Museen, Berlin, (centre) the trustees of the British Museum, (bottom right) the Kabul Museum, Afghanistan; photographs, (top and bottom right) Josephine Powell, Rome, (centre) EB Inc.

Taleju Bhavani Temple door facade, Bhaktapur, Nepal, 17th century.

Reliquary casket of gilt bronze from the monastery dPal-l'or c'os-de in Gyangtse, southern Tibet, 16th century. In the Rijksmuseum voor Volkenkunde, Leiden, The Netherlands. Height 35 cm.

Art of Tibet and Nepal

Hayagrīva, *thang-ka* from Tibet, early 19th century. In the Rijksmuseum voor Volkenkunde, Leiden, The Netherlands.

Ratnasambhava, the Dhyāni Buddha of the south, surrounded by the eight *mahābodhisattvas*, Nepalese painting.

Plate 2: By courtesy of (top right and bottom right) the Rijksmuseum voor Volkenkunde, Leiden, The Netherlands, (top left) from M. Singh, *Himalayan Art* (UNESCO, 1968); photographs, (top left) Madanjeet Singh, (bottom left) Holle Verlag

Detail of the Rathayātrā Scroll, Nepalese, 1617. In the Prince of Wales Museum of Western India, Bombay. Height 64.2 cm, width (entire scroll) 252.7 cm.
By courtesy of the Prince of Wales Museum of Western India, Bombay

Hitopadeśa (1594; Kāthmāndu) and horizontal scroll paintings such as the Rathayātrā Scroll (1617; Cambridge). Its planar intricacies reveal a new and vital aspect of Nepalese painting, an immediacy of emotion and action of its protagonists, the figures of which are placed on an opaque, velvety ground. The colours of these book illustrations and scrolls retain the strength and depth of those of the hieratic scrolls, which continued to be painted into the 17th century. The influence of the more realistic Indian, Rajasthani paintings, from the latter part of the 17th century, finally overwhelmed the hieratic style. Its disappearance was further hastened by a wave of Chinese-influenced Tibetan painting. (S.Kh.)

Tibet. Tibetan art comprises ancient pre-Buddhist decorative and domestic crafts and the all-prevading religious art that was gradually introduced from the 8th century onward from surrounding Buddhist countries and developed subsequently as recognizably distinct Tibetan imagery, sculpture, and decorative architectural motifs. In all its forms Tibetan art has remained subservient to special lay or religious intentions and has never become an art pursued for aesthetic ends alone. The religious art is primarily didactic and symbolic; the lay art, decorative. Therefore, while lay art may be easily appreciated, to understand the significance of the religious art requires knowledge of Tibetan religion and religious symbolism. Since the destruction of Tibetan cultural traditions by Chinese-trained Communists from 1959 onward, a greater interest has arisen in the West in the surviving Tibetan *objets d'art* preserved in museums and private collections.

Up to the 9th century AD, Tibet was open to cultural influence from Central Asia, especially Khotān, and from China. For two centuries, up to the collapse of the old Tibetan kingdom in 842, the Tibetans controlled the whole Takla Makan and the important trade routes from the Middle East to China. Stone carving and metalwork were certainly practiced in the pre-Buddhist period, and Persian, Indian, and Chinese influences, all received through Central Asia, have been noted.

The introduction of Buddhism from the 8th century onward led to the arrival in Tibet of Buddhist craftsmen from Central Asia and later from Nepal and northwest India, all of which were then Buddhist lands. Some cast images from this first Buddhist period may survive in Lhasa. After 842, central Tibet dissolved into political chaos for over 100 years, and from the 10th century onward the cultural initiative passed to a line of kings in western Tibet. For temple decorations, such as wood carving of doorways and posts, decorative painting on ceilings and woodwork, temple frescoes, and terra-cotta and stucco images, they drew heavily on the cultural resources of pre-Islāmic Kashmir. Surviving monasteries and temples, with their magnificent contents, were made known to the Western world in the 1930s. With the establishment of religious hegemonies in central Tibet from the 11th century onward, cultural contacts with Nepal and the Buddhist centres in the main Ganges Valley flourished as never before. Conversely, cultural contacts with China dwindled for several centuries, at least in central and southern Tibet. From this time until the 20th century, Tibetan religious art and Nepalese Buddhist art remained a single unified tradition. Meanwhile, eastern Tibet, where the ancient pre-Buddhist crafts of metalwork had never died out, began to develop religious styles under the influence of craftsmen from central Tibet. From that time, the spread of Tibetan culture and art became coterminous with the spread of Tibetan religion; and, thus, from the 13th century onward, when Tibetan lamas began to convert the Mongols, Mongolian religious art developed as a branch of Tibetan art. Through the Mongols, China began to extend its political influence over Tibet, and this led to a steady increase in Chinese cultural influence, especially in the east. From 1721, when the Chinese emperors became the suzerains of Tibet, Chinese influence was felt much more strongly throughout central as well as eastern Tibet, and Tibetan religious paintings and especially domestic decoration reveal distinct Chinese features.

Chinese cultural influence

Decorative arts. In the main temple (*fo-khang*) of Lhasa there is a pre-Buddhist silver jug with a long neck surmounted by a horse's head; and there are textual references to all kinds of articles made of gold: a large golden goose holding seven gallons of wine, a wine vase, a miniature city decorated with gold lions, and golden bowls. Gold animals are mentioned as decorating the camp of King Ral-pa-can when a Chinese envoy visited him in 821. These early Tibetan skills lived on through the Buddhist period. Tibetan metalworkers have excelled in producing fine things for ritual and domestic use: ritual lamps, vases, bowls, bells, prayer wheels, decorated trumpets and horns, for the temples, and, for home use, ornamented teapots, jars, bowls, ladles, and especially

By courtesy of the American Museum of Natural History, New York

Bronze statuette of Yamāntaka, the ferocious form of the Tibetan deity of wisdom, Mañjuśrī, who waged war against Yama, king of hell; Tibetan. in the American Museum of Natural History, New York.

beautiful stands, often in silver or gold, to hold porcelain teacups, capped by finely worked lids of precious metals. Hand-woven rugs of magnificent Central Asian and Chinese designs, always adapted to Tibetan preferences, cover low seats, and tables and cabinets of carved and painted wood were commonplace in prosperous homes.

Sculpture. From the 7th to 9th centuries there survive pre-Buddhist carved-stone pillars decorated with Chinese, Central Asian, and Indian motifs and also a stone lion showing traces of Persian influence.

Metal casting

The art of casting images in bronze and other metals entered Tibet from Nepal and India. Having first followed foreign models, the Tibetans gradually developed their own styles and began to depict their own lamas and teachers as well as the vast pantheon of buddhas, gods, and goddesses inherited from India, each distinguished iconographically by posture, hand gestures, and accoutrements. (Of lesser divinities and especially of lamas, the identification is often difficult. It is rare that an image is named in an inscription and even rarer to find a date. Because of the extremely conservative nature of Tibetan art, correct dating within several centuries is often impossible.) Images of vast size, rising up through two or three stories, are quite often seen in Tibetan temples, and their construction and dedication is considered a work of vast religious merit.

Since images are mainly cast or molded, carving is restricted to decorative motifs, especially on wooden pillars and roof beams. Wood carving and terra-cotta, particularly in western and southern Tibet, were common. Papier-mâché, elaborately painted, was also used for the masks of divinities, especially for those worn in monastic dances. This use presumably originated in Kashmir.

Painting: frescoes and temple banners. Temple interiors are usually covered with frescoes and often hung with painted banners (*thang-ka*). For the preparation of the latter, a taut cotton cloth is impregnated with a mixture of chalk and glue, rubbed smooth by some suitable object; for example, a flat polished stone. A religious painter trained in the tradition draws in the outline, often using printed designs for the main figures. There is no scope for originality so far as the iconographic details of divinities are concerned, and, thus, such painting is a highly skilled craft. For decorative details—for example, flowers, cloud effects, rocks, and groups of devotees—there is wider scope. The tradition of fresco painting and temple banners certainly goes back to that of the great Buddhist monasteries of northwest India and the Ganges Valley, but these Indian origins of the 9th to 12th centuries are now entirely lost. The Indian Buddhist paintings of Ajanta are of a much earlier period (up to the 6th century AD), thus predating the great increase in the Buddhist pantheon and in occult symbolism typical of the later Indian Buddhism received by the Tibetans. Central Asian styles certainly reached central Tibet well before the 9th century, but, after that date, it was India and Nepal that

Influence of Indian Buddhist painting

Tibetan painting of Lcang-skya Rol-pa'i rdo-rje. The Saint carries a book, one of the attributes of his patron, Tsong-kha-pa, founder of the Yellow Hat sect of Tibetan Buddhism. Chinese influence is shown by the architecture of the monasteries. In a private collection.
By courtesy of O. Burchard, Berlin

were to have lasting influences on the development of Tibetan art. In more recent times, especially from the 18th century onward, Chinese influence became noticeable in the details of paintings, particularly in the freer but still balanced arrangement of the main figures and the use of Chinese-style landscapes as subsidiary decoration. With the disappearance of Buddhism from Central Asia and India from the 12th century onward, Tibetan art developed as a style exclusive to the Tibetans, the Newari Buddhists of the Nepal Valley, and the Tibetan converts of Mongolia.

Decorative architectural motifs. For temples, monasteries, and official residences such as the Potala Palace

Paul Popper (Popperfoto) Ltd.

The Potala Palace, Lhasa, Tibet, 17th century.

of the Dali Lama in Lhasa, the Tibetans used their own solid indigenous styles but embellished these with Indian, Nepalese, and (very much later) Chinese motifs. Tiered, ornamented temple roofs are originally of Indian origin, as received through Nepal and later through China. The magnificent interior carving is of Indian and Nepalese inspiration. (D.L.S.)

BIBLIOGRAPHY

Literature: (*Turkish literature*): *Philologiae Turcicae Fundamenta*, vol. 2 (1965), a collection of monographs on literatures of Turkish-speaking peoples—see ALESSIO BOMBACI, "The Turkic Literatures: Notes on the History and Style"; also his *Letteratura turca* (1969), an important survey with several chapters on Central Asian Turkish literature; JANOS ECKMANN, *Chagatay Manual* (1966), mainly a grammar containing selections of Central Asian literary texts and a vocabulary; TALAT TEKIN, *A Grammar of Orkhon Turkic* (1968), an excellent introduction to the language and literature of the Central Asian Turks before Islām; SIR GERARD CLAUSON, *An Etymological Dictionary of Pre-13th Century Turkish* (1972) and *Turkish and Monogolian Studies* (1962); and the *Handbuch der Orientalistik*, vol. 5 (1963), three important studies of the arts of the Central Asian peoples; E. DENISON ROSS, "The Tonyukuk Inscription," *Bulletin of the School of Oriental Studies* (London University), vol. 6 (1930), English translation of one of the oldest Turkish inscriptions. (*Tibetan literature*): JACQUES BACOT, *Grammaire du tibétain littéraire*, 2 vol., 2nd ed. (1954), HEINRICH A. JASCHKE, *A Tibetan-English Dictionary*, rev. ed., with English-Tibetan vocabulary (1949); and *A Short Practical Grammar of the Tibetan Language* (1865, reprinted 1954); JOSEF KOLMAS, "Tibetan Literature in China," *Archiv Orientální*, 30:638–644 (1962); EBERHARDT RICHTER, *Grundlagen der Phonetik des Lhasa-Dialektes* (1964); GEORGES DE ROERICH, "Le Parler de l'Amdo," *Serie Orientale Roma*, vol. 18 (1958); HANS N. VON KOERBER, *Morphology of the Tibetan Language* (1936); TURRELL V. WYLIE, "A Standard System of Tibetan Transcription," *Harvard Journal of Asiatic Studies*, 22:261–267 (1959). (*Mongolian literature*): RICHARD P. LISTER, *The Secret History of Genghis Khan* (1969), a retelling of the ancient chronicle of Genghis' life and successors; CHARLES R. BAWDEN, *The Mongol Chronicle Altan Tobči* (1955), a translation with notes of a major native historical work incorporating folk elements; THE MONGOLIA SOCIETY, *Mongolian Folktales, Stories, and Proverbs in English Translation* (1967), a small collection of typical old tales; TS. ZHAMTSARANO, *The Mongol Chronicles of the Seventeenth Century*, trans. by RUDOLF LOEWENTHAL (1955), a description of five major historical chronicles; WALTHER HEISSIG, "Mongolische Literature," in *Altaistik*, vol. 5 of the *Handbuch der Orientalistik*, pp. 227–274 (1964), the best overall general sketch; LUDMILLA K. GERASIMOVICH, *History of Modern Mongolian Literature, 1921–1964* (Eng. trans. 1970), a careful survey of the modern decades and writers.

Music: RICHARD A. WATERMAN *et al.*, "Bibliography of Asiatic Musics," 13th installment, *Notes of the Music Library Association*, 8:100–118 (1950); MARK SLOBIN, "Zentralasien," in *Die Musik in Geschichte und Gegenwart*, vol. 14 (1968), see sect. 1, "Afghanistan and the Sedentary Population of Turkestan"; and Record notes for "Afghanistan," vol. 1–4, series *Anthology of the World's Music*, include photographs, musical illustrations; H.G. FARMER, "Turkestani Music," *Grove's Dictionary of Music and Musicians*, 5th ed., vol. 8, pp. 610–612 (1954), historical background and general information; A. HUTH, "Instruments of East Turkestan," *ibid.*, pp. 608–610, historical background; JOHANNA SPECTOR, "Musical Tradition and Innovation," in EDWARD ALLWORTH (ed.), *Central Asia: A Century of Russian Rule*, pp. 434–484 (1967), detailed information on Turkestani music, with emphasis on the court tradition, including excellent illustrations and charts. (*Music of the Turkic Nomads, Mongolia, and Siberia*): ERNST EMSHEIMER *et al.*, *The Music of the Mongols* (1943, reprinted 1971), the classic work; MARK SLOBIN, *Kirgiz Instrumental Music* (1969), detailed study of one Central Asian tradition. (*Music of the Himalayan Peoples*): P. CROSSLEY-HOLLAND, "Tibetan Music," *Grove's Dictionary of Music and Musicians*, vol. 8, pp. 456–464, a thorough basic survey; LUTHER G. JERSTAD, *Mani-rimdu: Sherpa Dance-Drama* (1969), a thorough account of a specific Himalayan tradition.

Dance and theatre: MIRCEA ELIADE, *Le Chamanisme et les techniques archaïques de l'extase* (1951; 2nd ed., 1968; Eng. trans., *Shamanism: Archaic Techniques of Ecstasy*, rev. ed., 1964), a classic study of the rituals, costumes, and symbolisms of shamanic performances; LUTHER G. JERSTAD (*op. cit.*), an analytical and descriptive study of *'cham* as performed in the Tengpoche monastery of northern Nepal. Materials and translations of some morality plays have been published by MARION H. DUNCAN in his *Harvest Festival Dramas of Tibet* (1955) and *More Harvest Festival Dramas of Tibet* (1967); and a study of the "Moon-cuckoo" play of the Mongols has been published in Japanese by HIDEHIRO OKADA. Information on the performing arts may be found scattered in various other publications, but it is usually descriptive in nature and deals with only one genre. As yet no scholar has carried out a comprehensive analytical study of the origins and interrelations of dance and theatre in Central Asian regions.

Visual arts: ALEKSANDR BELENITSKY, *Central Asia* (Eng. trans. 1969), a short general survey of the area and its art; M.P. GRIAZNOV and A.P. BULGAKOV, *L'Art ancien de l'Altai* (1958), a helpful introduction to the subject (in Russian and French); BASIL GRAY, *Buddhist Cave Paintings at Tun-huang* (1959), a scholarly study; RENE GROUSSET, *L'Empire des steppes: Attila, Gengis-Khan, Tamerlan*, 4th ed. (1960; Eng. trans., *The Empire of the Steppes: A History of Central Asia*, 1970) and *De la Grèce à la Chine* (1948), especially useful historical surveys; ORMONDE M. DALTON, *The Treasure of the Oxus*, 3rd ed. (1964), a specialized and authoritative survey of this collection of objects; RICHARD N. FRYE, *The Heritage of Persia* (1962), a helpful widely embracing survey of the Persian culture; BRUNO DAGENS, MARC LE BERRE, and DANIEL SCHLUMBERGER, *Monuments préislamiques d'Afghanistan* (1964), an aid to understanding Kushan art; KARL JETTMAR, *Die frühen Steppenvölker* (1964; Eng. trans., *Art of the Steppes*, 1967), a useful survey of nomadic animal art; ALBERT VON LE COQ, *Auf Hellas Spuren in Ostturkistan* (1926; Eng. trans., *Buried Treasures of Chinese Turkestan*, 1928), of great importance for the work in this area; SERGEI RUDENKO, *Frozen Tombs of Siberia: The Pazyryk Burials of Iron Age Horsemen* (1970; orig. pub. in Russian, 1953), indispensable to the student of Altaia nomads; TAMARA TALBOT RICE, *The Ancient Arts of Central Asia* (1965), a useful introduction to the subject; W.W. TARN, *The Greeks in Bactria and India* (1938), still an indispensable work; DAVID L. SNELLGROVE and HUGH E. RICHARDSON, *A Cultural History of Tibet* (1968), a general work that helps to place the various expressions of Tibetan art in an historical context—the index may be consulted for carving, metalwork, painting, and carpets; GIUSEPPE TUCCI, *Tibetan Painted Scrolls*, 3 vol. (1949), the classic work on Tibetan religious painting; and *Indo-Tibetica*, 4 vol. (1932–41), a basic work (in Italian) for anyone seriously interested in Tibetan art, consisting largely of photographic plates, unobtainable elsewhere, and records of Tucci's early researches into Tibetan art history; GEORGE ROERICH, *Tibetan Paintings* (1925), a useful introductory work containing 17 plates and detailed description; WALTER EUGENE CLARK (ed.), *Two Lamaistic Pantheons*, 2 vol. (1937, reprinted in 1 vol., 1965), a detailed study of two sets of metal cast images useful for iconographic identifications; ALICE GETTY, *The Gods of Northern Buddhism*, 2nd ed. (1928, reprinted 1962), an old but useful work that relates the main Tibetan Buddhas and divinities to their corresponding forms in Indian, Chinese, and Japanese tradition; B.B. BHATTACHARYYA, *The Indian Buddhist Iconography*, 2nd ed. rev. (1958), an indispensable introduction; STELLA KRAMRISCH, *The Art of Nepal* (1964), the first stylistic history; PRATAPADITYA PAL, *Vaiṣṇava Iconology in Nepal* (1970), an important contribution to the structure of meaning in the images of Visnu; DAVID L. SNELLGROVE, "Shrines and Temples of Nepal," *Arts Asiatiques*, 8:3–10, 93–120 (1961); an introductory survey; D. BARRETT, "The Buddhist Art of Tibet and Nepal," *Oriental Art* (1957), chronological study.

(T.T.R./M.S.S./T.V.W./S.Kh./D.L.S./J.R.Kr./F.I.)

Centrifuge

A centrifuge is any device that applies a sustained centrifugal force; that is, a force due to rotation. Effectively, it substitutes a similar, stronger, force for that of gravity. Every centrifuge contains a spinning vessel; there are many configurations, depending on use. A perforated rotating drum in a laundry that throws off excess water from clothes is a type of centrifuge. A similar type is used in industry to separate fluids from solid matter after crushing. Another application is separating fine suspensions of solid or liquid material; *e.g.*, a cream separator.

GENERAL PRINCIPLES OF CENTRIFUGATION

The fact that a force tending in an exterior direction occurred whenever a mass changed its direction was certainly known to primitive man, but the exact nature and significance of the force were only formulated by Sir Isaac Newton in the 17th century.

As Newton showed in his laws of motion, a freely moving body tends to travel in a straight line and if directed along a curved path by some restraining force (for example, a string) exerts a force of its own against the string. Further, the strength of this latter force can be increased by increasing either (1) the speed of rotation (2) the mass of the body, or (3) the radius, or distance of the body from the centre of the curve. Increasing either the mass or the radius increases the centrifugal force proportionally, but increasing the speed of rotation increases it in proportion to the square of the speed; that is, an increase in speed of ten times, say from 10 to 100 revolutions per minute, increases the centrifugal force by a factor of 100. Centrifugal force is expressed by the basic relation $F = mv^2/R = 4\pi^2 mn^2 R$; F is the centrifugal force, m the mass, R the radius, v the speed, and n the number of revolutions per second.

Centrifugal force is expressed as a multiple of g, the symbol for normal gravitational force (strictly speaking, the acceleration due to gravity). Centrifugal fields of over 1,000,000,000 g have been produced in the laboratory.

The widest use of centrifuges at the present time is for the concentration and purification of materials in suspension or dissolved in fluids.

Speed of migration

Suspended particles more dense than the suspending liquid tend to migrate toward the periphery, while those less dense move toward the centre. The rapidity with which the migration proceeds is dependent on the intensity of the centrifugal field, the difference between the density of the particle and that of the suspending liquid, the viscosity of the liquid, the size and shape of the particle, and to some extent the concentration of the particles and the degree to which they are electrically charged. The net motivating force exerted on the particle is the difference between the centrifugal field acting on it and the opposing buoyancy of the liquid. All other things being equal for two particles, one with a diameter ten times that of the other will require only one one-hundredth as much average centrifugal field to move a given distance in a given time as the smaller.

From the foregoing discussion, it is clear that a practically complete separation of the suspending medium and the suspended particles can be produced if the centrifugation is allowed to continue until all particles have collected against the outer wall of the spinning vessel or centrifuge. It should also be noted that a partial separation of two groups of suspended particles of different size can be effected by allowing centrifugation to continue only long enough for all of the larger particles to be completely packed into the sediment, since then many of the small particles will still be suspended in the fluid. If separation of the larger as well as the smaller particles is desired, the surface fluid can be drawn off and the sediment resuspended in some suitable liquid and subsequently centrifuged again to effect further separation.

TYPES OF CENTRIFUGES AND THEIR APPLICATIONS

Centrifuges may be classified in three general categories depending upon whether the spinning centrifuge bowl that contains the material to be separated has a solid wall, a perforated wall, or some combination of the two. Also, they may be characterized according to whether the material is treated in a continuous flow process, a batch process, or a combination of the above processes. The common notation used for centrifuges employed in industry has not been standardized, and often essentially the same type of centrifuge, when used in different industries, is known by different names, which sometimes leads to confusion. In this article, a few clear-cut individual types will be described in order to illustrate the wide application of the centrifuge in research and industry.

Bottle centrifuges. A bottle centrifuge is a batch-type separator primarily used for research, testing, or control. The separation takes place in test tube or "bottle-type" containers, which are symmetrically mounted on a vertical shaft. The shaft is usually driven by an electric motor, gas turbine, or a hand-driven gear train located above or below the rotor. The rotating parts are mounted on resilient supports so that they can partially seek their own axis of rotation and so that excessive vibrations are damped. Usually, the bottles are supported by high strength metal containers in such a way that their axis is perpendicular to the axis of rotation. The machine is designed so that a breakage of a bottle will not cause the rotating parts to become sufficiently unbalanced to damage the centrifuge or injure the operator. The sedimentation takes place in a radial direction and in some bottle centrifuges the test tubes or bottles are inclined at an angle of about 37° to the axis of rotation in order to reduce the distance that the material must settle. In such cases, when the material reaches the inclined wall of the test tube it slides down and collects on the bottom and hence is not forced to settle the whole length of the bottle. The bottles are usually sealed to prevent evaporation and the rotating parts are surrounded by a chamber strong enough to contain the rotor in case of an explosion. Radial temperature variations, if large enough, will produce convection, which in turn produces remixing.

Uses of bottle centrifuges

Bottle centrifuges are standard equipment for most biological, chemical, or medical laboratories. They are used to separate solid materials in suspension or to clarify liquids when precipitation will not take place in a reasonable time in the gravitational field g. In most commercial bottle centrifuges the centrifugal field may be varied from a few g's up to tens of thousands. Commercial uses of the bottle centrifuge include tests for the butter-fat content of milk, determination of the sediment in crude mineral and vegetable oils, and clinical tests of various kinds.

Tubular centrifuges. The tubular centrifuge is used primarily for the continuous separation of liquids from liquids, or of very fine particles from liquids, although in some cases it is used as a batch-type centrifuge. In general, it is used when higher centrifugal fields are required for separation. The rotating bowl consists of a long hollow tube (length many times its diameter) mounted at one or both ends in damper bearings as shown schematically in Figure 1. These damper bearings are necessary because such a long tubular body, if given a large disturbance, will tend to turn over. Furthermore, a long tube spun at high speeds may pass through speeds at which it vibrates. These are known as critical speeds. At speeds removed from the critical, the rotor spins comparatively smoothly. Except in special cases, tubular centrifuges are designed to spin below the first critical speed of the tube. For continuous separation the feed or material to be centrifuged enters at one end near the axis and is removed in two streams containing the separated material. In many cases the separation is not complete and the separated

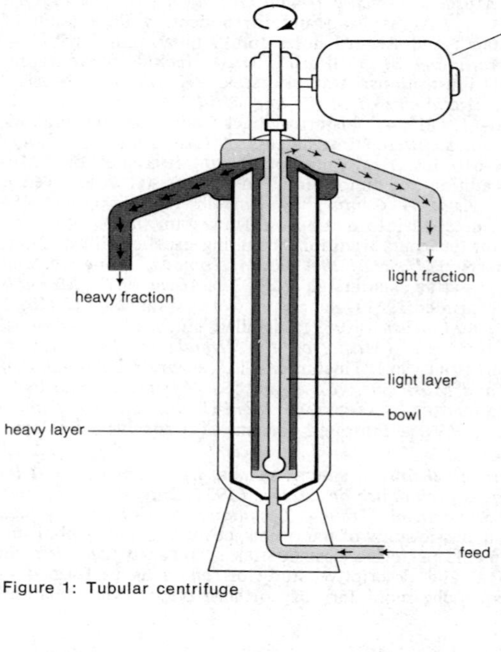

Figure 1: Tubular centrifuge

fractions must be passed through the machine several times. Many different designs for the internal structure of the tube are employed, but in general radial vanes are used to bring the feed material up to speed and to slow down the separated streams before they are discharged. Great care must be taken to prevent the internal structure of the tubular rotor from producing imbalance or from developing its own critical vibrations. The centrifuge is driven by a high-speed motor or an air or steam turbine. The sedimentation takes place as the fluid flows from one end of the tube to the other. When the heavy material consists of very fine particles or molecules and the concentration is very low, the solid material is usually allowed to deposit on the wall. In this case the machine is operated as a batch centrifuge.

The tubular centrifuge is finding an increasing number of applications because of the high centrifugal fields that may be used (10^5 g near the periphery in some cases). A few typical uses are as follows: (1) the purification of vaccines (uncentrifuged vaccines contain a large amount of nonessential and harmful material); (2) purification of lubricating and industrial oils; (3) clarification and purification of food products such as essential oils, extracts, and fruit juices; (4) separation of immiscible liquids that cannot be separated by gravity.

Disk-type centrifuge. The disk-type centrifuge consists of a stack of thin disks in the shape of cones. The sedimentation takes place in the radial direction in the space between adjacent cones. This greatly reduces the settling distance and hence increases the rate at which the material is separated. The angle of the cones is designed so that upon reaching the inside surface of the cone the heavier material slides down along its surface in a manner that is similar to that of the 37° fixed-angle bottle centrifuge.

The disk-type centrifuge usually operates continuously. The material to be processed enters in one stream and is separated into two purified streams. These centrifuges are used primarily for the separation of liquids in which the solid or immiscible components occur in relatively low concentrations. The familiar cream separator, widely used in the dairy industry and on farms for separating cream from milk, is a typical example of this type of centrifuge. They also are used for the purification of fuel oil, the reclamation of used motor oil, and the removal of soap stock in the refining of vegetable oils.

Basket centrifuges. Basket centrifuges are often called centrifugal filters or clarifiers. They have a perforated wall and cylindrical tubular rotor. In many cases the outer wall consists of a fine mesh screen or a series of screens with the finer mesh screens supported by the heavier coarse screen, which in turn is supported by the bowl. The liquid passes through the screen, and the particles too large to pass through the screens are deposited. Though in most cases the centrifuge must be stopped for discharge, in some types it may be discharged at full or reduced speed. The size and design of the basket centrifuge are dictated by its intended use, but usually the bowl is shorter than its diameter. The basket centrifuge is employed in the manufacture of cane sugar, in the home and in laundries for the rapid drying of clothes, and in the washing and drying of many kinds of crystals and fibrous materials, etc.

In the case of tubular-, disk-, and basket-type centrifuges that are employed in manufacturing processes, operation with high efficiency and low cost is critical.

Continuous and batch operation

This usually requires the continuous operation of the centrifuge since the batch process requires extra labour, increased power, and is time-consuming. As a result, many ingenious methods have been devised for unloading the sediment collected in the bowl while the machine is operating at full speed and without disturbing the sedimentation continuously taking place in the centrifuge.

Vacuum-type centrifuges. In the centrifuges described above, the rotor spins in air or some other gas at atmospheric pressure. The gaseous friction on a spinning rotor increases at a relatively high rate so that the power required to drive the rotor also increases rapidly. As a result, the temperature of the rotor rises until heat convection and conduction to the walls balances the heat generated. For high-speed rotors in air at atmospheric pressure this temperature may exceed the boiling point of water. Since the rotor surface near the periphery moves faster than near the axis a thermal gradient or variation in temperature through the rotor wall is established along the radius with the periphery at a higher temperature than the axis. This arises not only from gaseous friction but from the direction of the air or gas circulation around the rotor. As shown previously, small radial temperature gradients are effective in producing convection within the centrifuge. These convection currents cause remixing and disturb sedimentation. Convection-free sedimentation has been obtained in a high-speed oil-driven centrifuge by surrounding the rotor with hydrogen at about 10 torr (1 torr = 1 millimetre of mercury). At 660 revolutions per second the temperature of the rotor was only 1.5° C above that of the walls. Convection-free centrifuges have been called ultracentrifuges.

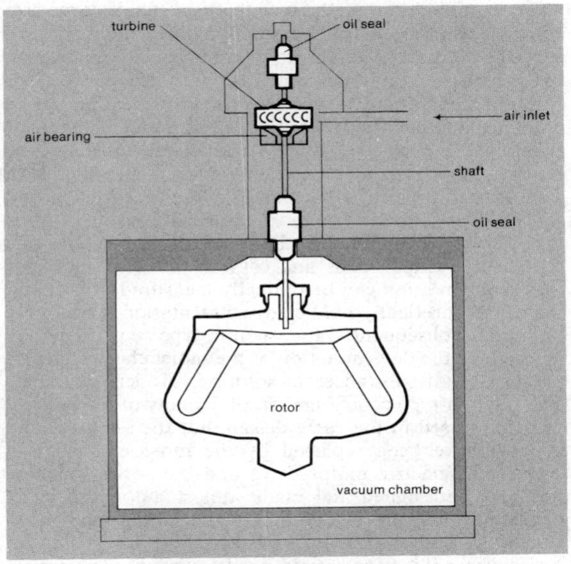

Figure 2: Air-driven, vacuum-type ultracentrifuge.

The gaseous friction on a rotor decreases with decreasing pressure and becomes negligible at pressures routinely produced by mechanical and diffusion pumps. Consequently, a centrifuge rotor spinning in a vacuum should be convection free and, therefore, ultracentrifuge at any speed, provided a negligible amount of heat is conducted to the rotor by the shaft on which it spins. This was accomplished in 1934. Figure 2 shows a schematic diagram of one of the early vacuum-type ultracentrifuges. The centrifuge rotor located inside the vacuum chamber is connected to the air-supported, air-driven turbine by a vertical, small-diameter, flexible steel shaft. The rotating members are supported by an air bearing and are spun by air impinging upon the turbine. The air pressure surrounding the rotor is very small (less than 10^{-6} torr) so that the air friction on the rotor is negligible even at the highest peripheral speeds possible. Also, the diameter of the shaft is small (0.1 inch), which reduces friction in the lower oil seal and heat conduction to the rotor. Constant temperature of the lower oil seal is maintained by circulating oil at the same temperature as the thermostated metal vacuum chamber. This chamber is heavy enough to contain the rotor should it explode. Consequently, the temperature of the rotor is held constant at the known value of the surrounding chamber and hence is free of thermal gradients. The comparatively long flexible shaft allows the rotor to seek its own preferred axis of rotation and consequently to spin smoothly without the need of precise dynamic balancing. It is, however, always desirable to have a good dynamic balance even with a flexible shaft. In practice the maximum rotational speed is set only by the mechanical strength of the rotor.

The combination of high-centrifugal field, large-size rotor, lack of need for tedious dynamic balancing, absence of thermal gradients, low power requirements, etc., makes the vacuum-type centrifuge an ideal convection-free ultracentrifuge. A typical rotor is 18 centimetres in diameter and carries 300 millilitres of liquid in a centrifugal field of over 300,000 g. Practically all substances of importance in medicine and biology and all other substances with molecular weights of 50 daltons (one dalton is 1.66×10^{-24} grams) or more are easily purified in this type of bottle centrifuge. If the rotor is replaced with one with sector-shaped cells and crystal quartz windows so that sedimentation can be optically measured, it is found that the theoretically predicted sedimentation is routinely obtained. Consequently, the vacuum-type centrifuge may be used for the determination of the molecular weights of practically all substances in solution. Modern commercial vacuum-type centrifuges employ many of the general principles used in the early design, but the air drive and support have been replaced by the more efficient and convenient electric motor drive and the entire machine has been redesigned and made almost automatic in its operation. The present commercial vacuum-type ultracentrifuge has become an indispensable tool in laboratories where it is necessary to purify substances of importance in biochemistry, biophysics, biology, and medicine.

Molecular weight

The ultracentrifuge can be used in two principal ways for determining the molecular weights of various proteins. The first consists in carrying out the sedimentation in a centrifugal field high enough to produce a relatively sharp sedimentation boundary; *i.e.*, the boundary between the sedimenting molecules and the pure solvent. The rate at which this boundary moves out along the radius toward the periphery is then measured and the value of the molecular weight is calculated. This is called the rate of sedimentation method. The second method consists in centrifuging the material until equilibrium is established in the centrifuge cell; *i.e.*, until the rate at which the material settles out is balanced by back diffusion. If the concentration in the centrifuge cell is then determined (usually through optical observation) at various radial distances, the value of the molecular weight (M) can be calculated.

Although the equilibrium method of measuring M is much more reliable than the rate of sedimentation method, the latter has a wider use because of the comparatively long time (days) required for the equilibrium measurements and the stringent requirements of speed and temperature controls.

Vacuum-type tubular centrifuges are finding a most important use in the purification of many biological materials that cannot easily be separated in other ways. They have been used both as continuous-flow and as density-gradient centrifuges. The density-gradient centrifuge consists in setting up a radial density variation or gradient in the tubular centrifuge with slowly sedimenting nonreactive smaller molecules such as sucrose or calcium chloride. If then the density of the substance to be purified falls within the range of the artificial density gradient, it will collect in a thin cylindrical surface at a definite radius. If more than one substance is in the solution, each of the substances will collect at a radius determined by its particle density. Various devices have been used to harvest the separated material after it has collected on the cylindrical surfaces. A density-gradient centrifuge method of purifying vaccines has recently been used on a commercial scale. This timely and important development will probably be used to purify most vaccines and many other biomedical materials.

The ideal centrifuge

An ideal centrifuge would be one in which the rotor is free to spin about "its own axis" and hence would not require accurate balancing. Also, the rotor should not be limited in size or weight. It should spin in a vacuum on a friction-free bearing and when desired, attain speeds limited only by the strength of the material. It should not have a shaft that will conduct heat to the rotor during operation. It should be free of speed fluctuations and it should be readily accessible so that the sedimentation taking place in the centrifuge can be observed optically or otherwise. Starting in 1937, workers at the University of Virginia developed a magnetically supported ultracentrifuge, which essentially meets these specifications. Figure 3 is a schematic diagram of a method of magnetically supporting a rotor inside a vacuum chamber. The axial core of the rotor is made of steel or other ferromagnetic material. When sufficient electrical current is passed through the solenoid, the rotor is pulled upward by the solenoid and would strike the top of the vacuum chamber if it were not for the operation of the support servo circuit. As the rotor rises the impedance of the small sensing coil is changed in such a way that the servo circuit reduces the current through the solenoid. When the rotor starts falling, the current through the solenoid is increased, and effective damping in the servo circuit prevents vertical oscillations. In this way the rotor is held very precisely at the desired vertical position in the vacuum chamber. The only measurable friction on the rotor is that due to the residual air in the vacuum chamber. When this pressure is reduced to 10^{-7} torr, which is not difficult with a diffusion pump, a 30-pound ultracentrifuge rotor will lose less than one revolution per second per day when spinning at 800 revolutions per second, or roughly 10^{-8} of its speed per second.

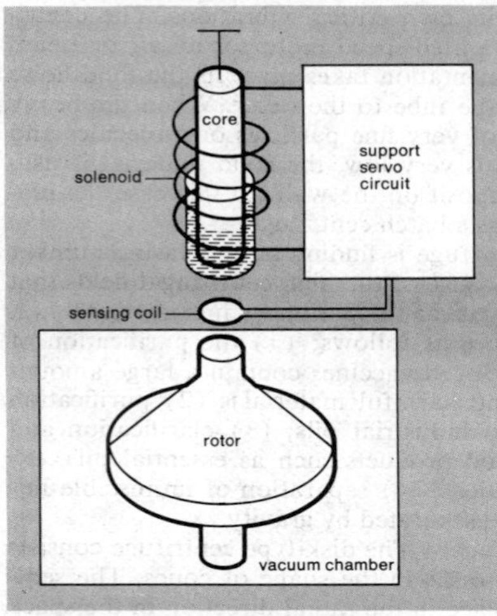

Figure 3: Magnetically suspended rotor.

The rotor may be driven to operating speed in a number of ways but usually it is spun up to speed with a motor outside and below the vacuum chamber. The thin flexible drive shaft passes through a vacuum oil gland in the bottom of the chamber. When the desired operating speed is attained the shaft is pulled downward and disconnected from the rotor and the rotor is allowed to coast freely during the sedimentation process. When the measurements have been completed the shaft is reconnected to the rotor and the rotor decelerated to rest. Since the rotor coasts during the measurements, troublesome speed fluctuations are eliminated. Also, the very slow deceleration of the rotor allows the sedimentation to reach equilibrium faster than if the rotor speed was absolutely constant. A second method of driving the rotor consists in mounting nonelectrical conducting permanent magnets on the bottom of the rotor in such a way that they can be driven by a rotating synchronous magnetic field surrounding the rotor. With care in design, negligible heating is produced in the rotor during the period of acceleration and deceleration. Much less heat is, of course, produced during the long sedimentation period when the speed is automatically held at the desired value to one part in 10^5.

The size of the rotor in Figure 3 may be varied over large ranges. Their weights have been varied from 10^{-9} to over 10^2 pounds. Rotor speeds of 1.5×10^6 revolutions per second and centrifugal fields of over $10^9 g$ have been obtained. The method has been used accurately to measure the tensile strength of materials both in bulk and in thin sheets. It has also been used to determine the absolute value of adhesion of one substance to another, and for spinning rapidly rotating, constant-speed mirrors.

Gas separation by centrifuge

When a gas is subjected to a centrifugal field a radial pressure gradient is immediately established. Consequently, a mixture of any two gases with different molecular weights may be separated in a centrifuge with the lighter gas being concentrated on the axis. In 1919 after it was pointed out that it should be possible to separate the isotopes of an element by centrifuging, a number of attempts were made to obtain separation but were all unsuccessful, probably due to convection and remixing in the centrifuge. In 1937 the isotopes of chlorine were separated with a vacuum-type ultracentrifuge. An evaporative centrifuge method was used in which the material to be separated is admitted to the rotor and condensed on the periphery with the rotor stationary. The rotor is then driven to operating speed and the lighter material pumped out through the hollow shaft while the heavier material remains in the centrifuge to be collected later. While the separation obtained was in excellent agreement with the theory, the method is a batch operation and not efficient except for small-scale separations. The centrifuge should be spun as rapidly as possible and should be as long as possible. Also, the centrifuge method is suited to the separation of the heavier isotopes as well as the lighter ones, since it depends upon the differences in the masses rather than on their absolute values.

It will be surmised from the above discussion that the tubular vacuum-type centrifuge is perhaps the best-suited type for the isotope or gas separation problem. As a result, the need for the purification of the isotope of uranium-235 in considerable quantity has stimulated the development of long high-speed centrifuges. During World War II centrifuge tubes of various lengths were used with uranium hexafluoride gas to test the method both in the U.S. and in Germany. In the U.S. a centrifuge tube 11.33 feet (345.5 centimetres) long and 7.35 inches (18.66 centimetres) inside diameter was used in some of the experiments. A number of different flow patterns inside the tubular centrifuge were tested. It has been shown both experimentally and theoretically that a countercurrent flow method produces the largest amount of separative work when properly used. In the countercurrent method the gas or vapour flows in two continuous cylindrical concentric streams along the length of the spinning tube. One stream flows from top to bottom along the periphery, and the other from bottom to top near the axis. The centrifugal and diffusive action between the two flowing streams concentrates the lighter isotope in the axial stream and the heavier one in the peripheral stream. This produces a buildup of material with the lighter isotope enriched at the top and the heavier isotope at the bottom of the spinning tube. The materials are drawn off at any desired rate, one from the top, the other from the bottom. The two axial concentric streams are found to be stable over considerable distances along the tube so that long tubes may be used. It is easy to see roughly why this is true in a hollow tubular centrifuge. If, for example, a small quantity of the gas in the peripheral stream moves inward along the radius, its angular velocity is increased like a figure skater going into a spin, since angular momentum is conserved. This in turn increases the centrifugal effect and the gas moves back outward. Furthermore, the pressure gradient is large so that the element of gas moving inward expands and cools, which also tends to move it back toward its original radial position.

Since World War II the technique of gaseous centrifuging has been further developed and extended. Workers in Germany and in The Netherlands have reported considerable success with the method. A remarkably simple vacuum-type gas centrifuge that is especially adapted to uranium isotope separation has been devised. According to reports in 1970 a centrifuge plant was being planned in Europe for the purpose of commercially producing reactor grade uranium-235 for use in nuclear power plants.

Uranium-235 for power plants

It is clear that current improvements in the ratio of strength to density of rotor materials and in machine design and control should greatly increase the potential of the centrifuge for isotope separation and the general purification of gases.

BIBLIOGRAPHY. J.W. BEAMS, "High Speed Rotation," *Physics Today* 12:20–27 (1959), a review article on modern research in centrifuging; T. SVEDBERG and K.O. PEDERSEN, *The Ultracentrifuge* (1940), a treatise on sedimentation in centrifuges, 1924–40; H.K. SCHACHMAN, *Ultracentrifugation in Biochemistry* (1959), an authoritative review of more recent work on sedimentation in the centrifuge; A.C. LAVANCHY, F.W. KEITH, JR., and J.W. BEAMS, "Centrifugal Separation," *Kirk-Othmer Encyclopedia of Chemical Technology*, 2nd ed., vol. 4, pp. 558–710 (1964), on modern centrifuges and their application to industrial processes; *Proceedings of the 2nd International Conference on the Peaceful Uses of Atomic Energy*, vol. 4 (1958), a review of research on isotope separation by gas centrifuging carried out in the United States, Germany, and The Netherlands before 1958; K. COHEN, *Theory of Isotope Separation* (1951), on the theory of isotope separation in the centrifuge; M. BENEDICT and T.H. PIGFORD, *Nuclear Chemical Engineering* (1957), a discussion of the problem of centrifugal gas separation.

(J.W.B.)

Cephalochordata

The Cephalochordata, a subphylum of the phylum Chordata, are small, eel-like animals (*e.g.*, amphioxus, or lancelet) up to eight centimetres (about three inches) long. About 23 species—all living—are known. Exclusively marine, cephalochordates usually live in an area of the seabed consisting of fairly coarse shell gravel.

Cephalochordates are distributed throughout tropical and subtropical shallow seas where suitable bottom conditions exist. They also occur in the waters of many temperate areas, and some have been observed as far north as the coastal waters of Norway. Although they are known to occur at depths of 100 fathoms (600 feet [about 180 metres]), cephalochordates are usually found at depths of less than 50 fathoms. Some species are very widespread; others are restricted in distribution. The group apparently originated in the Indo-West Pacific, the majority of species being found there. The presence of cephalochordates usually indicates clean water with a minimum rate of flow. The filtering activity of large numbers of the organisms actually helps to maintain cleaner conditions. *Branchiostoma caribaeum* occurs in concentrations as great as 5,000 per square metre (500 per square foot).

Biological significance

Cephalochordates are of particular interest because they exhibit chordate features in a most primitive form. The biological significance of amphioxus arises from its structure, which is clearly related to that of vertebrates, despite the fact that it lacks a true head and backbone. Any theory concerning the origin of the entire class Vertebrata—and thus man's own origin—rests heavily on the nature of amphioxus, even though this animal, as a living form, may or may not have changed since its origin. Amphioxus is particularly abundant in certain coastal waters of China. The animal is so abundant that a commercial amphioxus fishery has long been established there.

Natural history. *Reproduction and life cycle.* Cephalochordates are dioecious; *i.e.*, the sexes are normally separate but with no external differences. The development of both male and female gonads in the same individual (apparent hermaphroditism) has occasionally been observed. In temperate waters, there is one breeding season per year, in the tropics two or more. No special mating behaviour is known. The gonads develop singly or in pairs in successive body regions corresponding with separate myotomes, or sections of muscle, in the region between the mouth and the atriopore, an opening about two-thirds of the way back on the ventral (lower) side. In the genus *Branchiostoma* a row of gonads develops on both sides of the body; in the genus *Asymmetron* gonads develop only along the right side. Each gonad is a separate sac projecting into the atrial cavity, a chamber surrounding the pharynx. Eggs or sperm, released by rupture of the gonad wall, pass out through the atriopore into the water, where fertilization occurs.

The rate of growth and development is related to the temperature. About 48 hours after fertilization, the egg develops into a larval stage with a single gill slit. As the larva grows, additional gill slits develop, the number varying from about 12 to 35, according to the species. The larval form, similar in general appearance to the adult, is planktonic, or drifting, in habit. Larvae eventually assume the vertical migration pattern well-known in planktonic animals. When the larva is between three and 11 millimetres (0.1 and 0.4 inch) in size, depending on the species, a change in body form (metamorphosis) occurs. The larva becomes more symmetrical—for example, the mouth, in most cases, opens on the ventral midline instead of on the left side. Secondary gill bars develop, the gut grows, and the endostyle, a ventral groove, develops. After metamorphosis, the larva settles to the bottom and adopts the life of the adult.

If, during the normal vertical migrations, a larva drifts into water so deep that it cannot reach the bottom, growth probably continues, thus giving the larva more time in which to find a suitable area in which to live. In such circumstances the larva grows to a larger than normal size.

Burrowing

Behaviour and ecology. Normally, the adult lives buried, usually in rather coarse shell gravel but sometimes in sand or sandy mud. Burrowing is very rapid, either forward or backward; both the shape of the body, which is pointed at both ends, and the tough cuticle (rough body covering) facilitate the burrowing movements. The feeding position is nearly vertical, with the anterior end up and about a quarter of the body length projecting above the bottom. A water current drawn into the buccal cavity passes out through the gill slits into the atrium. Food particles are filtered off in the process. When not feeding, the animal is usually withdrawn completely into the substrate, but at night it is not uncommon for the animals to rise and swim near the bottom. Cephalochordates are not normally very reactive to changes in the intensity of light, but a sudden change of light immediately provokes swimming, burrowing, or both. They are very sensitive to touch, particularly anteriorly, and the lightest touch induces withdrawal into the gravel or rapid swimming. Swimming is not continuous but consists of short bursts of activity at intervals. There is no buoyancy mechanism, and in water of normal salinity the animal sinks rapidly to the bottom after activity ceases.

Form and function. *Structural features.* All species of cephalochordates are generally similar in body structure. Maximum length is about 80 millimetres (three inches), but tropical species are usually much shorter. The name of the best known species, *Branchiostoma lanceolatum*, refers to its lanceolate, or spearlike, shape. The body, somewhat flattened sideways, is covered by a tough, iridescent cuticle. The muscles of the body wall are divided into myotomes, which usually number between 50 and 85, depending on the species. The myotomes of the two sides do not develop in parallel but are staggered. When the animal swims forward, contractions begin at the anterior myotome; the myotome immediately posterior then contracts, and so on down the body. Bending of the body is effected by myotome contractions to provide forward motion.

The notochord

The notochord is a hydrostatic (*i.e.*, supported by internal fluid pressure) structure; its rigidity is variable and controlled by the nervous system and by contraction of notochordal muscle. A dorsal fin along the back continues around the tail and becomes a ventral fin. In some species this continuous median fin is expanded at the tail to form a distinct caudal fin. Dorsal and ventral fins are supported by fin chambers. No paired fins are present, but folds along the edge of the ventral side, the metapleures, could be the homologues of the lateral, or side, fin folds of ancestral fish.

There is no true differentiation of a head in cephalochordates, but a slight swelling at the anterior end of the dorsal hollow nerve cord forms a cerebral vesicle. A pigment spot is prominent at its anterior end. There are seg-

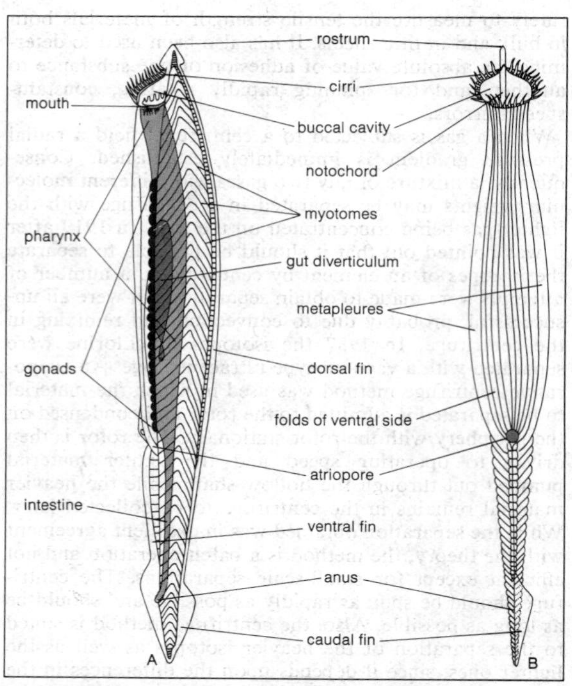

Amphioxus (*Branchiostoma lanceolatum*). (A) left lateral and (B) ventral views.
From P. Grasse, *Traite de Zoologie*, vol. 11 (1948); Masson & Cie, Paris

mental dorsal and ventral nerve roots, but these do not join to form mixed nerves as in higher chordates.

The circulatory system is typically chordate, with forward blood flow along the ventral side and backward flow along the dorsal side. There is no differentiated heart. The colourless blood contains no respiratory pigment but includes cells known as lymphocytes.

Feeding and digestion. Cephalochordates are filter feeders and require a large surface area for the extraction of particles. The mouth is covered by an oral hood, the edges of which form the buccal cirri. When feeding, the cirri overlap to form a primary coarse filter to keep out large particles. The inflowing current originates from the beating of cilia on the gill bars. The gill bars form the so-called branchial basket, which has a cartilaginous support but can be contracted by muscles. The feeding current passes in through the buccal cirri and through the tentacles of the velum, a structure surrounding the actual mouth. After following a rather complicated path, the water enters the pharynx, passes out through the gill basket into the atrium, and out of the body through the atriopore. Particulate matter is trapped by a mucus lining of the gill basket. Part of this mucus originates from the endostyle, which is located along the floor of the pharynx. The path followed by the mucus-enmeshed food particles is quite involved; basically, however, the particles move up the sides of the pharynx, are collected in the epipharyngeal groove, and then pass into the gut and into its diverticulum.

Enzymes and phagocytosis

Digestion appears to occur mainly in an area of the gut whose walls are more opaque than are those of the rest of the gut. Digestive enzymes include protease, lipase, and amylase. In larval forms a part of this area known as the iliocolonic ring contains a bright-green fluorescent pigment. Phagocytosis (*i.e.*, the engulfing of food particles by cells) and digestion within cells occur, both of which features are nonchordate in character.

Excretory and biochemical features. Perhaps the feature most atypical of chordates is the excretory system, the basic unit of which is a nephridium. Each primary gill bar has a corresponding nephridium; thus, there are about 200 nephridia in one individual. All of these structures are situated above the pharynx, and the main excretory canal from them opens into the atrium.

The endostyle, an important structure of the Cephalochordata, is also found in the Hemichordata, Tunicata, and, in modified form, in lamprey larvae. It is the homologue of the vertebrate thyroid gland, and, although it is not certain that iodinated tyrosine molecules (an active product of the vertebrate thyroid secretion) function as regulatory substances (hormones) in cephalochordates, such molecules are produced in the cephalochordate pharynx, almost certainly in the endostyle. It is significant that the endostyle develops at the time of larval metamorphosis and that the metamorphosis of axolotls, a type of salamander, is accelerated by implants of cephalochordate endostyle.

Classification. *Distinguishing taxonomic features.* No positively identified fossil cephalochordate has yet been found. The classification of the group, then, is based entirely on the characters of living species. The dorsal hollow nerve cord, the branchial apertures, and the well developed notochord extending almost to the anterior tip are all present in both larva and adult, clearly indicating that they are chordates. Affinities between the Cephalochordata and the subphylum Vertebrata can be shown with the Cyclostomata; for example, the so-called ammocoete larva of the lamprey, a cyclostome, is similar to the cephalochordates in its endostyle and thyroid gland.

Annotated classification.

SUBPHYLUM CEPHALOCHORDATA

Small, fish-like, and free-swimming; all chordate and many vertebrate features; complex system of blood vessels; excretion by means of nephridia; sexes separate (dioecious); about 23 species; occur throughout tropical and subtropical shallow seas, some temperate regions.

Family Branchiostomidae

One genus, *Branchiostoma*, and about 15 species; double row of gonads along body wall; metapleural folds (located laterally along ventral side) symmetrical.

Family Asymmetrontidae

One genus, *Asymmetron*, and about 8 species; 1 row of gonads along the right side only; metapleural folds asymmetrical; right fold merges with the ventral fin.

Critical appraisal. The general taxonomy of the Cephalochordata is simple and accepted by modern workers, but specific identification is not always positive, especially with immature animals. Various families and genera have been erected in the past, but are not now generally accepted, as are the two families given above. A small point for debate is that there is some justification for the inclusion of a second genus, *Epigonichthys*, within the Asymmetrontidae specifically for the New Zealand lancelet *E. hectori*. This species retains the larval sinistral (*i.e.*, on the left side) mouth at maturity.

BIBLIOGRAPHY. E.J.W. BARRINGTON, *The Biology of Hemichordata and Protochordata* (1965), a more advanced text incorporating recent research; T.G. CHIN, "Studies on the Biology of the Amoy amphioxus *Branchiostoma belcheri* Gray," *Philipp. J. Sci.*, 75:369–424 (1941), a comprehensive study of a single species; E.G. CONKLIN, "The Embryology of *Amphioxus*," *J. Morph.*, 54:69–118 (1932), a classic of embryology; E.S. GOODRICH, "On the Structure of the Excretory Organs of Amphioxus," *Q. Jl. Microsc. Sci.*, 45:493–501 (1902) and 54:185–205 (1909), still the authoritative work on the excretory system; J.E. WEBB, "The Ecology of Lagos Lagoon. III. The Life History of *Branchiostoma nigeriense* Webb," *Phil. Trans. R. Soc.*, Series B, 241:335–353 (1958), a specialized ecological study of one species; J.H. WICKSTEAD, "On the Status of the 'Amphioxides' Larva," *J. Linn. Soc. (Zoology)*, 45:201–207 (1964), a review of the taxonomic position of this anomalous animal; A. WILLEY, *Amphioxus and the Ancestry of the Vertebrates* (1894), an early but very good comprehensive account; J.Z. YOUNG, *The Life of Vertebrates*, 2nd ed. (1962), a good general account for students.

(Jo.W.)

Cephalopoda

Cephalopoda is a small class of highly organized exclusively marine mollusks with about 130 known living genera and 650 species, of which the octopus, squid, and cuttlefish are familiar representatives. The extinct forms outnumber the living, the class having attained great diversity in late Paleozoic and Mesozoic times. Of the extinct cephalopods, the ammonites and belemnites are the best-known examples.

GENERAL FEATURES AND IMPORTANCE TO MAN

The cephalopods agree with the rest of the Mollusca in general structure and appear to have the closest affinity with the Gastropoda. The best-known feature of the Cephalopoda is the possession of tentacles, 8 or 10 in most forms, but about 90 in *Nautilus*. Except for the nautilus, all extant members of the class show great reduction of the characteristic molluscan shell.

Cephalopods range greatly in size. The giant squids (*Architeuthis* species) are the largest living invertebrates, *A. dux* attaining a length of more than 20 metres (60 feet), including the extended tentacles. The smallest cephalopod is the squid *Idiosepius*, rarely an inch in length. The average octopus usually has arms no longer than 30 centimetres (12 inches) and rarely longer than a metre (39 inches). Specimens with arm spans of up to nine metres (30 feet) have been reported. The shell of the fossil ammonite *Pachydiscus seppenradensis* from the Cretaceous measures 205 centimetres (6 feet 8 inches) in diameter; it is considered to have been the largest shelled mollusk. Though not as abundant as in earlier times, the Cephalopoda are still a major group of marine animals.

Cephalopods occur in large numbers and form one of the greatest potential food resources of the oceans. They are eaten in many parts of the world but have never been accepted as part of the general diet in North America or northern Europe. They also are indirectly important to man since they furnish a large part of the diet of the sperm whale and smaller whales and seals.

Commercial landings of cephalopods

Japan leads in the cephalopod production, landing about 600,000 tons of squid annually. Korea is second, with 117,000 tons of squid; China produces 80,000 tons of cuttlefish alone, but accurate statistics are unavailable. The United States produces about 10,000 tons, while Newfoundland alone produces about 11,000 tons in good years. Nearly 2,000,000 tons are produced annually throughout the world.

Cephalopods are taken in many ways, the squids usually by trawls, purse nets, jigs, or traps. Octopuses are taken in fish traps, in earthen pots strung together, or else by hooking or spearing them and by trawling. They may be eaten fresh, sun-dried, or canned in olive oil.

NATURAL HISTORY

Life cycle. The eggs of most cephalopods are enclosed within a capsule that may be gelatinous and transparent (*Octopus* and squids of the genus *Loligo*) or opaque and leathery (cuttlefish). Little is known about the eggs of oceanic species. The eggs of most coastal species are laid inshore and are attached singly or in clusters, primarily to bottom objects. Parental care is exhibited only by octopuses, in which the female broods over the eggs, and in the paper nautilus (*Argonauta*), in which the eggs are carried in a special shell secreted by the female. In most others the eggs are left uncared for. Squids that attach their eggs to the bottom engulf them in a gelatinous mass that protects them from fungus and deters predators. Cuttlefish squirt their eggs with ink to hide the otherwise white egg case.

All cephalopod eggs are provided with a remarkable amount of yolk, unlike that in the rest of the Mollusca, so that segmentation is incomplete and restricted to one end of the egg. The embryo is localized at this end. The mouth in early development is not surrounded by the arm rudiments; these arise as outgrowths of the lateral and posterior edges of the primordial embryonic area. They pass forward during latter development until they reach and encircle the mouth. The funnel arises as a paired outgrowth of the same area, a condition that is retained in *Nautilus;* in all others the two portions fuse together in the median line.

The embryo of cuttlefish (*Sepia*), squid (*Loligo*), and octopus (*Octopus*) is provided with a yolk sac. In certain presumably archaic Teuthoidea there is less yolk, and the yolk sac is practically absent. There is, nevertheless, no certain indication in the development of any known cephalopod of those larval phases that characterize the development of other mollusks.

Incubation is variable, but in *Octopus* young hatch in

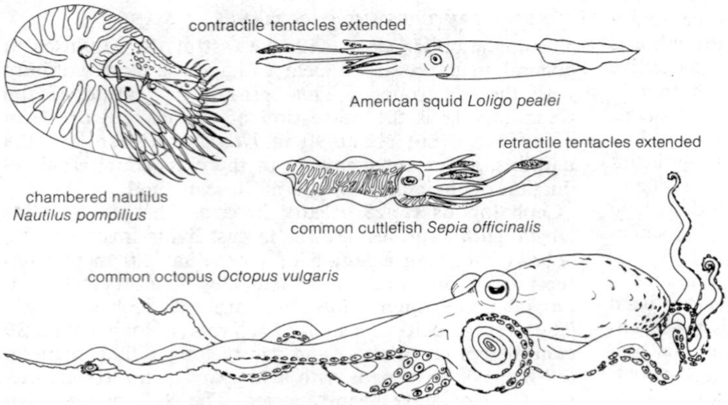

Figure 1: Body plans of typical Cephalopoda.

about 50 days and in *Loligo* in about 40 days. At hatching, the animal may closely resemble the adult or may go through a larval stage, differing widely from the adult, and spend a considerable time in the plankton as part of the drifting life. The larvae of many cephalopods were described as distinct genera before their larval status was discovered, and the generic names are still used for certain distinctive larval forms. In octopods with small eggs (*e.g.*, *Octopus vulgaris*) the larvae are planktonic, spending several weeks in the plankton; the "*Macrotritopus*" stage of *Scaeurgus* may greatly prolong its larval life until a favourable bottom is found. In octopods with large eggs (*Octopus briareus*) the young resemble the adult and immediately assume a bottom life.

In the order Sepioidea (cuttlefish and bottle-tailed squid) the young closely resemble the adults and are only briefly planktonic. In the Teuthoidea (squids), especially the Oegopsida, the larvae differ widely from the adult and the larval period is quite long.

Life span

Little is known about the life span of cephalopods. Studies have shown that in *Octopus joubini* raised from the egg in aquariums, sexual maturity and spawning were reached in five months; in a loliginid squid (*Sepioteuthis sepioidea*), likewise raised from the egg, sexual maturity and full growth were also attained in five months. It thus appears that the smaller inshore species may have a life span of no more than one year, or exceptionally, two or three. Nothing is known of the life span of the large oceanic squid, but it is presumed that giants like *Architeuthis* attain their bulk only after a period of years. In the smaller octopus and squid observational data indicate that many of the males die after mating and females after the first major spawning.

Behaviour. Cephalopods are unique among the invertebrates in the degree of cephalization and cerebralization exhibited. The uniting of the major ganglionic centres of the central nervous system constitutes a brain of considerable complexity. Studies undertaken at the Zoological Station in Naples by J.Z. Young, M.J. Wells, and others have demonstrated that *Octopus* is capable of learning and considerable intelligence. Most of the research has been concentrated on octopuses because they can be maintained in aquariums. A few investigations have been conducted on cuttlefish, but squids have not been investigated, largely because of the inability of experimenters to maintain them in confinement. It is expected that the behaviour of these two groups (squid and octopus) would be considerably different because of their different modes of life.

Laboratory behavioural studies have dealt mainly with learning processes and have centred around food acceptance, reward and punishment, maze work, and shape discrimination. By means of surgical techniques it has been possible to determine the various locomotor centres of the brain of *Octopus* and transmission and receiving pathways.

Less research of a detailed nature has been concerned with colour change. A wide range of colours may be exhibited. Most cephalopods possess colour pigment cells (chromatophores) and reflecting cells (iridocytes) in the skin. The chromatophores are expanded by nerves controlled by the brain and the colours exposed (brown, black, red, yellow, or orange red), each species usually possessing three pigments. Colours and colour patterns are exhibited according to specific behavioural conditions; *e.g.*, attack on prey, camouflage, rest, and alarm or defense. Alarm patterns are the most readily recognized, consisting of strong contrasting light and dark areas, bars and peripheral dark outlines, or sudden displays of spots.

Other behavioural patterns are found in changes in skin sculpture: the erection of branched or straplike papillae and curling of the arms. These often are attempts at concealment or camouflage imitating bottom type (sand, seaweed, etc.).

Discharge of ink

The ink of cephalopods is used as both defense and escape mechanisms. In *Octopus* under attack by a moray eel the cloud of ink seems to paralyze for some time the eel's senses of sight and smell. The ink cloud may also be used as a screen behind which the octopus escapes. In squids the ink is ejected as a cigar-shaped object about the size of the squid itself, the ink coagulating in the water. With this "dummy" left behind, the squid contracts its chromatophores, becomes nearly transparent, and speeds away.

Many cephalopods (but not *Nautilus* and *Octopus*) possess special light organs (photophores), which emit cold light or bioluminescence. Light is produced by the enzymatic reaction of luciferin and luciferase or, in bottle-tailed squids (sepiolids), indirectly, through cultures of luminescent bacteria. Photophores distributed over the body are employed at night or in the mid-depths in mating play, recognition of the sexes, aid in schooling, attracting prey, defense, and camouflage. The light organs of the squid *Histioteuthis* are highly complicated, consisting of reflector, light source, directive muscles, lens, diaphragm, window and colour screens.

Octopus, squid, and cuttlefish display considerable skill and cunning in hunting, stalking patiently, or luring prey within reach of their arms or tentacles. Both cuttlefish and octopus use the tips of their arms as wormlike lures to attract small fishes, and octopus has been reported to thrust stones between the valves of clams to prevent their closing. This has not been verified by later observers, but such intelligence is not beyond belief.

Locomotion. Cephalopods move by crawling, swimming, or jet propulsion, mainly the latter. The mantle, which has a passive role in the majority of mollusks, in cephalopods has become involved in locomotion, having almost entirely lost its rigid shell and become highly muscular. Its expansion and contraction produce a locomotory water current by drawing water into the mantle cavity and expelling it through the funnel. The rapid ejection of this jet of water enables the animal to execute quick backward and forward movements.

Jet propulsion

Water is drawn into the mantle cavity by the relaxation of the circular muscles and resultant expansion of the mantle. It enters around the neck region or aperture of the mantle and through the funnel in some species. In the oceanic squid the system is more efficient, with a valve that prevents water from entering through the funnel. When the mantle is contracted the aperture is closed by locking mechanisms and contraction of the anterior ring muscle, and the water is forced out through the funnel. This mobile organ is constructed similarly to a jet nozzle and may be turned in any direction, giving great flexibility of motion to the animal.

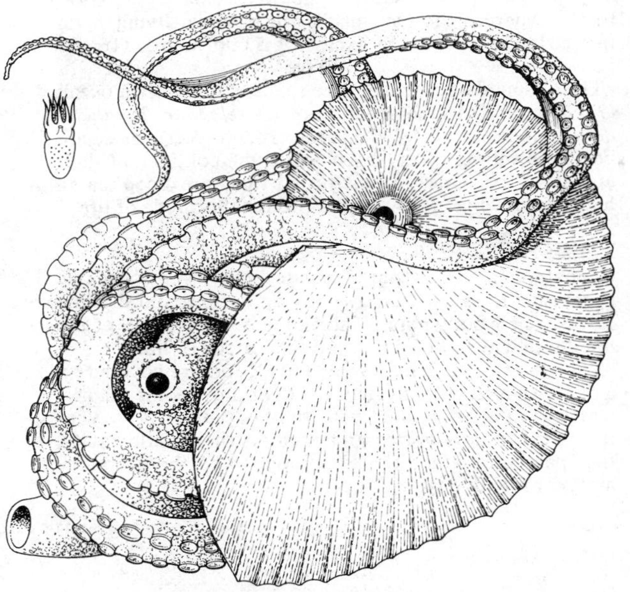

Figure 2: *Paper nautilus (Argonauta).*
(Upper left) Male about 16 millimetres (⅝ inch) in longest dimension; female about 150 millimetres (6 inches) from tip of siphon to outer curve of shell.

Squids also possess terminal or lateral fins used in slow movement or hovering. Locomotion is by the rapid undulation of the outer edges of the fins. Movement downward or upward is aided by lateral expansions (swimming keels) on the outer surface of the third pair of arms. Some squids (*Onychoteuthis, Thysanoteuthis*) are able to "fly" for several hundred feet, driven into the air by powerful thrusts from their jets and gliding on their expanded fins and arm keels. When the squid jets rapidly through the water, the fins are often curled tightly around the mantle. Cuttlefish, because of the large cuttlebone, are less active animals and spend most of their life lying on or hovering slightly above the bottom. Both jet and fins are used, the latter more frequently.

The benthic octopods are bottom crawlers, gliding about the bottom and in and out of crannies with amazing agility through the use of their eight arms and suckers. Because of the extraordinary flexibility of the body, they are able to pass through openings hardly larger than the diameter of one eye. When disturbed, octopods swim rapidly by jet propulsion. Mass swimming migrations have been reported.

The finned octopods and the bottle-tailed squids have paddle-shaped fins that are probably most useful for balancing and slow hovering movements. The female paper nautilus (*Argonauta*) propels herself by jet propulsion while encased in her paper-thin shell. The true *Nautilus* is a less active swimmer, partly due to the funnel, which is composed of two flaps instead of a single fused tube.

The active swimmers and most bottom dwellers apparently possess no hydrostatic organ. The cuttlefish, however, which swims or hovers above the bottom or rests on the bottom, adjusts its buoyancy through the amount of gases contained in the porous cuttlebone. *Nautilus*, which swims slowly above the bottom or in midwater, accomplishes this similarly, adjusting the gases in the chambered shell. Inactive oceanic squid such as some cranchiids concentrate light ions in their body chamber, while others, such as *Bathyteuthis*, concentrate light oils in the fatty cells at the posterior end of the mantle.

Reproduction. The sexes are usually separate in the Cephalopoda. Sexual dimorphism is common but is usually expressed in slight differences of size and in the proportions of various parts. In the paper nautilus (Figure 2) and the blanket octopus (*Tremoctopus*), the males are not only different in appearance but are much smaller than the females; they exhibit one of the greatest size discrepancies in the animal kingdom.

The female reproductive system is simple, consisting of posterior gonads and paired oviducts. Nidamental glands exist in species that lay eggs encased in heavy capsules.

In males, the reproductive system contains a series of chambers or sacs along the course of the vas deferens, which produce long tubes (spermatophores) to contain the spermatozoa. The final sac (Needham's organ) is also used for storage of spermatophores. The spermatophores are complicated, containing sperm reservoir, mid-part, horn, cap, and a delicate triggering mechanism for bursting the tube. Since spermatophores vary from species to species, they are important taxonomic characters.

During courtship, the male deposits spermatophores in the female, either within the mantle cavity or on a pad below the mouth, by means of a specially modified arm, the hectocotylus. The hectocotylized arm of *Octopus* bears a deep groove on one side, ending in a spoonlike terminal organ. In *Argonauta* and *Tremoctopus* the arm is highly modified and in mating is autotomized and left within the mantle cavity of the female. In the squids a much larger section of the arm may be modified; often the suckers are degenerate and the distal half of the arm bears rows of slender papillae, although special pouches and flaps may often be found. The modified arm of *Nautilus* is termed the spadix.

Little is known about the mating habits of most cephalopods. In the common octopus the male and female remain some distance apart while the male caresses the female with the tip of the hectocotylized arm. The male then inserts the tip of the arm into the mantle cavity of the female, where it remains for over an hour, during which time the sperm bundles travel down the spermatophoral groove of the arm. In the cuttlefish (*Sepia*) according to L. Tinbergen, the pair swims side by side, the male indulging in some "love play" with its arms. Eventually, mating takes place by the pair intertwining their arms and remaining together while the spermatophores are placed on the inner side of the female's mouth membrane. In loliginid squids a somewhat similar type of mating occurs except that it takes place en masse in schools of thousands of individuals.

Eggs are laid shortly after mating. In loliginids they are fertilized as they are ejected and before being fixed in the egg capsule. In the octopods, they may be fertilized as they pass through oviductal glands near the end of the oviduct. In cuttlefish, the eggs are fertilized before the heavy capsule is formed. Egg laying in octopods is accomplished by the female individually fixing the eggs singly or in festoons by a short stalk or thread (see Figure 3). In loliginids the eggs often form immense mops, the result of the communal spawning of perhaps hundreds of individuals. Spawning of oceanic squids has not been observed. The number of eggs laid during a spawning period varies greatly; it may range from only a few dozen in octopuses with large eggs to over 100,000 in the common octopus, laid over a period of about two weeks. In cuttlefish the number of eggs is smaller, about 200 to 300 being laid in a season. In loliginids several thousand eggs may be laid by a single female, and the egg mop of the European common squid, resulting from the efforts of many individuals, may contain more than 40,000 eggs.

Numbers of eggs produced

Ecology. The Cephalopoda are exclusively marine animals. There are numerous littoral species, but few have been reported from even slightly brackish water except for the squid *Lolliguncula brevis*, which occurs along the Florida coast in several areas having a salinity of 15–17 parts per thousand (about half that of the open ocean). Cephalopods are excluded from the Baltic Sea by lower salinities but have been found in areas of the Suez Canal where salinities are higher than in the oceans. There is some evidence that in parts of the open sea that differ

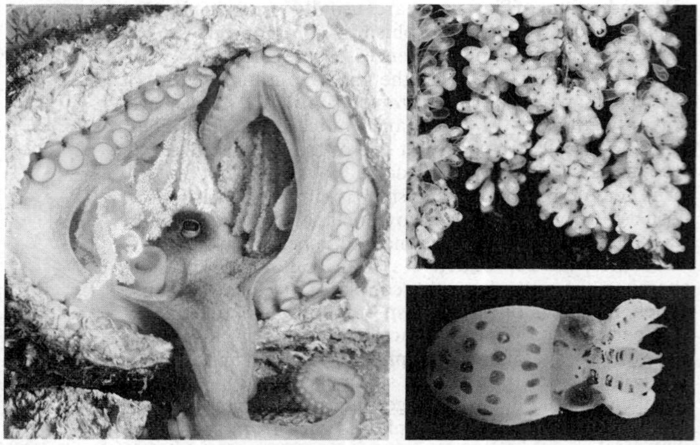

Figure 3: *Common octopus (Octopus vulgaris).*
(Left) The female remains in her lair guarding her eggs until they hatch. She continually washes the eggs in a fresh stream of water to increase aeration and keep them free of parasites. (Top right) Actual size of egg cluster. Fifty thousand eggs may be produced in a two-week period. (Bottom right) Underside of larva (magnified 5 ×) showing pigment spots. At this stage the arms are relatively undeveloped; the young swim freely with the current rather than "walk" on the ocean floor.
(Left, top ri ght) Marineland of Florida, (bottom right) Douglas P. Wilson

only slightly in salinity there may be a varying cephalopod fauna. G.E. Pickford has found that the vertical distribution of young in *Vampyromorpha* is governed by water density, and according to C.F.E. Roper a similar situation exists in the squid *Bathyteuthis.*

The majority of Coleoidea are carnivorous and live principally on crustaceans and small fishes. An interesting food cycle has been shown for the squid *Illex*, in which the adults feed upon young mackerel and the adult mackerel feed upon young squid. Squid also are cannibalistic. *Octopus* feeds upon bivalve mollusks and on decapod crustaceans, sometimes causing severe losses to the lobster industry. The smaller oceanic squid probably feed primarily upon small fish, copepods, heteropods and caridean shrimp. The Cirrata, which have reduced musculature and radula, indicating a loss of activity and of masticatory power, probably feed on bottom debris or minute plankton.

The Cephalopoda are fed upon by many marine mammals, large fish, and sea birds. The stomachs of sperm whales often contain whole and fragmentary squids, from small to giant species.

The nineteenth-century French naturalist Alcide d'Orbigny asserted that the Cephalopoda are in general sociable, and this statement is certainly true of *Nautilus*, which are found together in droves. Some authorities, studying the Mediterranean forms, have concluded that only certain pelagic cephalopods are gregarious (*Todarodes, Ocythoe*). Schools of the large oceanic squid *Thysanoteuthis rhombis* have been reported at Madeira. Although there is no proof that numbers constitute gregariousness, octopus colonies have been reported.

The breeding season has a marked effect on the local distribution of certain Cephalopoda. The common cuttlefish comes into shallow water in the spring and summer to breed, and similar migrations have been observed in some squids (*Loligo, Alloteuthis*).

The geographical distribution of cephalopods is incompletely known. In general, the open ocean pelagic and bathypelagic forms are cosmopolitan in warm and temperate waters (*Onychoteuthis banksi, Cranchia scabra*). Others may be limited by genera to particular oceans or to continental waters. Even some species of bathypelagic habitat are limited to one ocean. The Octopoda, as a result of their bottom-dwelling habits, show stronger restrictions in their distribution, but *Octopus vulgaris* and *O. macropus*, both species with planktonic larvae, have gained worldwide distribution. In general, the pelagic and planktonic cephalopods conform in their distribution to other pelagic animals.

The vertical distribution is also incompletely known. *Nautilus* moves vertically through the water, living near the bottom, and has been obtained at a depth of about 550 metres (1,800 feet). It is fished in the Philippines, however, when it comes into shallow water. Of the cuttlefishes, the Sepiidae are littoral, whereas the Sepiolidae dwell on or near the bottom, down to considerable depths. Among the squids, the Myopsida are coastal forms, whereas the Oegopsida are oceanic, living from the surface to depths in excess of 5,000 metres (16,400 feet).

The Octopoda occur from the surface of the open ocean (*Tremoctopus*) to the ocean floor (*Pareledone, Benthele-done*) in excess of 4,500 metres (14,700 feet); most are bottom-dwelling forms restricted to the continental shelf and its slope. One group, the Cirrata, are deep-sea in habitat, showing many adaptations for this mode of life.

FORM AND FUNCTION

Cephalopods vary from elongate, streamlined oceanic organisms to saccular, slow-moving bottom and drifting forms. Their body plan is indicative in many ways of the habitat in which they dwell and their mode of life.

The viscera of a generalized cephalopod are covered by a dome-shaped or elongated sheath of muscle, the mantle, which is in close contact with the body anteriorly. Ventrally, the mantle is free and encloses the mantle cavity, the space into which the gills project and the excretory and reproductive systems open.

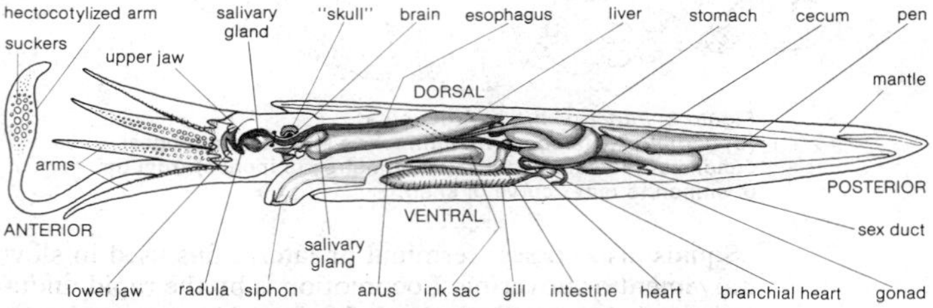

Figure 4: Internal structure of squid (*Loligo*); left side of body and five arms removed.

Number of arms and tentacles

Anterior to the mantle is the head-foot, which bears a ventral muscular tube, the funnel. Surrounding the mouth there are eight long, prehensile arms, provided with suckers in octopuses and argonauts (order Octopoda), or eight arms and two tentacles, equipped with horny ringed suckers bearing teeth or hooks in squids and cuttlefishes (orders Sepioidea and Teuthoidea). The primitive *Nautilus* has about 90 small suckerless tentacles.

The fossil nautiloids and ammonites (represented today only by *Nautilus*) were primitive, less-specialized forms, probably leading a rather inactive sluggish life. The modern octopuses, squids, and cuttlefishes have acquired an active, vigorous life that has led to marked departures in structure and function from the type represented by *Nautilus*. Modern forms are divided into three basic life styles: the ancestral sluggish life in the great depths of the sea, a floating life in the midwaters; and a more active, aggressive existence near the surface. The nautiloids and ammonites were probably shallow-water animals living near the bottom and, like the slow-moving *Nautilus*, relied for protection on a calcareous external shell.

All cephalopods have an internal cartilaginous covering of the main ganglia of the nervous system. In all except ammonites and nautiloids it constitutes a cranium. Various other skeletal supports are found at the base of the fins, and in the "neck," gills, and arms.

The alimentary system consists of a buccal mass with a pair of jaws (mandibles) and a rasping tongue (radula), esophagus, salivary glands, stomach, cecum, liver, and intestine. In the Octopoda the esophagus may be expanded to form a crop, while in the deep-sea Cirrata the radula may be degenerate or lacking. Except in *Nautilus* and certain deep-sea Octopoda there is an intestinal pouch or ink sac located near the anus. This secretes a dark fluid, the sepia or ink, which can be forcibly ejected.

All members of the Coleoidea (octopuses, squids, and

cuttlefishes) possess a closed circulatory system of blood vessels; in *Nautilus* it is partly lacunar (*i.e.*, made up of minute spaces). The blood contains a blue respiratory pigment, hemocyanin (a copper compound), dissolved in the plasma. There are three hearts, one systemic and two branchial, one at the base of each gill. The rhythmical contractions and expansions of the mantle cause a circulation of water over the gills where gas exchange takes place between the sea water and blood. The feather-like gills, consisting of a central axis with a row of lamellae on either side, are suspended freely in the mantle cavity.

The excretion of nitrogenous wastes is carried out exclusively by the kidneys. There are four kidneys in *Nautilus* and two in the coleoids.

Nervous system and sense organs

The central nervous system is highly developed, the major ganglionic centres being concentrated in the head. In some of the cuttlefishes (Sepioidea) the cerebral centres are subdivided for specialization, with the pedal ganglia divided into brachial and epipodal elements that innervate the arms and funnel respectively. In certain squids the mantle is innervated by giant paired dorsal axons, the largest nerve fibres known. Much of the present knowledge of mechanisms of nerve impulse conduction has come from the study of these giant axons. The sense organs of the cephalopods are eyes, rhinophores (olfactory organs), statocysts (organs of equilibrium), and tactile organs. In *Nautilus* the eyes are open pits without lenses. In the Coleoidea the eyes are complex and approach those of vertebrates in efficiency.

EVOLUTION AND PALEONTOLOGY

The first cephalopods were probably provided with a simple, caplike shell. With elongation of the shell and the formation of septa or partitions, the nautiloid shell could be formed (Early Cambrian). The primitive elongate shell of *Orthoceras* would become unmanageable and coiling would result, as in the Gastropoda.

The Ammonoidea are usually considered to have evolved from Devonian straight-shelled forms (*Bactrites*) with certain nautiloid traits. Coiled ammonites appeared in the Late Devonian (*Goniatites*).The subclass became extinct in the Cretaceous.

From *Guide to Fossil Invertebrates;* by permission of the trustees of the British Museum (Natural History)

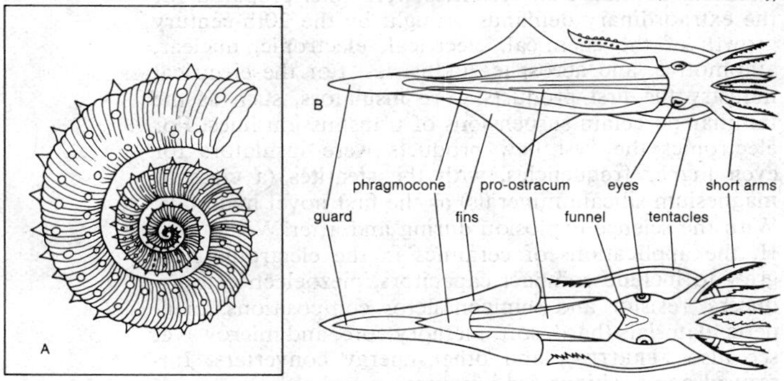

Figure 5: *Examples of fossil cephalopods.*
(A) Partially coiled Cretaceous ammonites. (B) Restoration of two belemnites.

Modern cephalopods possess an internal and partly degenerate shell, straight except in *Spirula*. The state of the shell in modern forms is due to the progressive overgrowth of it by the mantle, probably accompanying the acquirement of an active swimming life. The first evidence of the modification of the shell is in *Aulococeras* in the Triassic. The belemnites, with their modified, internal shell gave rise to *Spirula* (coiled shell), to cuttlefish (calcified phragmoconal septa, forming a thick shell), and to the squids (only the pro-ostracum as a horny "pen"). These forms appeared in the Jurassic and were probably derived from belemnite-like ancestors.

In the Octopoda the shell persists as cartilaginous stylets or fin supports. *Palaeoctopus newboldi*, from the Cretaceous of Syria, the oldest known octopod, was already too advanced to provide a clue to the derivation of the Octopoda. The Vampyromorpha are considered to be a possible connecting link between the Teuthoidea and the Octopoda.

CLASSIFICATION

Distinguishing taxonomic features. In fossil cephalopods reliance is placed upon shell details (general shape, type of coiling, external sculpture, and sutures). In living forms, except for the Sepioidea, the shell is strongly degenerate or missing and the characters used consist of details of the soft parts: presence or absence of an eyelid, tentacles retractile or contractile or both, shape and size of fins, number of arms, number of sucker rows, presence or absence of teeth and hooks on arm and tentacular suckers, radular dentition, structure of funnel organ, and spermatophores.

Annotated classification. The following classification has gained considerable acceptance among modern specialists.

CLASS CEPHALOPODA

Mollusks in which typical molluscan foot surrounds head and forms arms and tentacles. Mantle surrounds mantle cavity and is part of locomotory system; central nervous system highly developed, forming true brain encased in cartilaginous cranium; mouth contains pair of parrot-like jaws (or beak); body usually somewhat streamlined. Eyes highly developed, most closely resemble those of vertebrates. About 650 living species.

Subclass Nautiloidea (Nautiloids)

Cambrian to present; now living only in the Indo-Pacific region, particularly East Indies. External coiled or straight chambered shell present, chambers connected by median siphuncle; smooth septa; sutures simple, little or no external sculpture; tentacles suckerless, adhesive; living and supposedly fossil forms with 4 gills; funnel formed of 2 nonfused flaps. About 6 living species, in genus *Nautilus*.

†**Subclass Ammonoidea** (Ammonites)

Devonian to Cretaceous; fossils only. External, coiled or straight chambered shell with marginal siphuncle, last chamber protected by single horny plate or 2 calcareous plates; septa wrinkled; complex sutures; external sculpture.

Subclass Coleoidea (octopuses, squids, belemnites, cuttlefishes)

Triassic to present. Shell internal, reduced, vestigial or lacking; 2 sets of gills; 8 or 10 arms, having suckers or hooks.

†*Order Belemnoidea* (belemnites)

Triassic to Tertiary; fossils only. Shell consisting of solid rostrum, small chambered phragmocone and anterior, broad pro-ostracum; 6 to 10 arms bearing hooks in 1 or 2 rows. Total length 5–210 cm.

Order Sepioidea (cuttlefishes and bottle-tailed squid)

Tertiary to present. Worldwide with family exceptions. Shell coiled and chambered (Spirulidae), straight with vestigial chambering (Sepiidae), vestigial, or lacking; eyes covered; 8 sucker-bearing arms and 2 retractile tentacles. Total length 2.5–90 cm.

Order Teuthoidea (squids)

Tertiary to present. Worldwide. Shell thin, horny gladius; 8 arms, 2 tentacles, which are contractile only. Total length 1.5 to at least 1800 cm. (0.75 in to 60+ ft).

Suborder Myopsida. Eye covered by skin; neritic, inshore animals.

Suborder Oegopsida. Eye open to water, completely surrounded by free eyelid; open ocean animals living from the surface down to at least 3,000 metres.

Order Vampyromorpha

Present. Worldwide. Purplish-black gelatinous animals with 1 or 2 pairs of paddle-shaped fins at various stages of growth; 8 arms and 2 small retractile filaments not homologous with tentacles; deep web between the arms. One species.

Order Octopoda (octopuses)

Cretaceous to present. Worldwide. Shell lacking or vestigial, secondary shell or egg case in female argonautids, fins absent or present, body generally saccular, with 8 mobile, highly contractile sucker bearing arms. Total length 5–540 cm (2 in–18 ft); arm spread to about 900 cm (30 ft).

Suborder Palaeoctopoda (finned octopod). Cretaceous, some living.

Suborder Cirrata. Recent. Soft-bodied, deep-webbed forms with cirrate arms, and small to large paddle-shaped fins. Primarily deep sea. Sometimes called Cirromorpha.

Suborder Incirrata. Present. Compact, saccular to round bodied, finless forms with muscular, contractile arms. Pelagic to deep-sea and shallow waters. Somewhat secretive.

Critical appraisal. The elucidation of higher classification of the cephalopods is fraught with difficulties. Early specialists divided the living cephalopods into Octopoda and Decapoda without relation to their internal structure; these were both placed in the Dibranchia, in contrast to all fossil forms, which were considered as Tetrabranchia because *Nautilus* has four gills rather than two. This unnatural classification, accepted by d'Orbigny in 1838, was gradually modified through the efforts of A. Naef and G. Grimpe and later workers to the form given above. Phylogenetic linkages are still highly theoretical, but with X-ray techniques that reveal soft parts in fossils, and with new paleontological finds the unfolding of the evolutionary history is in sight.

BIBLIOGRAPHY

General treatises: P. PELSENEER, "Mollusca," in E.R. LANKESTER (ed.), *Treatise on Zoology* (1906), the only general technical treatment of the cephalopods in English; F.W. LANE, *Kingdom of the Octopus* (1957), an excellent general popular work with an extensive bibliography.

Systematics and distribution: G. PFEFFER, "Cephalopoden," in *Ergebnisse der Plankton-Exp.*, vol. 2F (1912), the only full systematic treatment of the Oegopsid squid of the world—old but useful; G.C. ROBSON, *A Monograph of Recent Cephalopoda*, 2 vol. (1929–32), descriptions of all known octopods to 1931; W. ADAM and W.J. REES, "A Review of the Cephalopod Family Sepiidae," *Sci. Rep. John Murray Exped. 1933–34* (1966), a discussion of the systematics, distribution, and relationships of the cuttlefishes of the world—an invaluable work; N. VOSS, *Bull. Mar. Sci.*, vol. 19, no. 4 (1969), a comprehensive monograph on the deep sea squid family Histioteuthidae; G.E. PICKFORD, *Dana Rep.*, no. 29 and 32 (1946, 1949), two volumes on the external morphology and distribution of the Vampyromorpha; G.L. VOSS, "A Review of the Cephalopods of the Gulf of Mexico," *Bull. Mar. Sci. Gulf Caribb.*, 6:85–178 (1956); S.S. BERRY, "A Review of the Cephalopods of Western North America," *Bull. Bur. Fish., Wash.*, vol. 30 (1910); M. SASAKI, "A Monograph of the Dibranchiate Cephalopods of the Japanese and Adjacent Waters," *J. Coll. Agric. Sapporo*, suppl. (1929), an extensive monograph in English of the Japanese cephalopods; I.I. AKIMUSHKIN, *Cephalopods of the Seas of the U.S.S.R.* (1965; orig. pub. in Russian, 1963) a monograph; M.R. CLARK, "A Review of the Systematics and Ecology of Oceanic Squids," *Adv. Mar. Biol.*, 4:91–300 (1966).

(G.L.V.)

Ceramics, Industrial

Industrial ceramics comprise all industrially used solid materials that are neither metallic nor organic. This definition expands the scope of ceramics far beyond the clay-based bodies of the potter and traditional industrial ceramics, as well as beyond the sand-dominated formulas of the glassmaker. In physical structure ceramics may be polycrystalline, glass, combinations of multicrystals with glassy phases, or single crystals. The universal properties of ceramics that account for their enduring utility include: mechanical strength in spite of brittleness; chemical durability (at both normal and elevated temperatures) against deteriorating effects of oxygen, water liquid or vapour, acids, bases, and salts at all concentrations, and organic solvents; hardness, contributing to resistance against erosion; and the ability to be decorated in a wide range of colours, textures, and designs.

Universal properties of ceramics

This article deals primarily with the raw-materials, manufacturing processes, and glazing techniques for industrial ceramics. Industrial ceramics products include glass; cement; structural clay products; refractories (high-temperature materials); abrasives; whitewares; porcelain enamels or ceramic-metal systems; ceramic mineral preparations; and newer technical products such as electronic and nuclear ceramics, carbon, graphite, diamonds, and ceramic composites. For information on glass, see GLASS PRODUCTS AND PRODUCTION. Cement is covered in the articles CEMENT and CONCRETE. The article BRICK AND TILE PRODUCTION describes structural clay products. For information on abrasives, see ABRASIVES.

In addition to the primary producers of glasses, cements, and multicrystalline ceramics, there are numerous industries that rework the primary materials into subassemblies, components, or systems that have strategic and economic importance. Often these products, such as computers, electric lamps, or television picture tubes, could not exist were it not for their ceramic constituents, yet the cost of the ceramic materials is small compared to the component and system values.

Functionally, ceramics technology draws upon the knowledge and skills of the pertinent sciences (physics, chemistry, rheology) and the design arts and the process capabilities of engineering to convert starting materials into new chemical and mineral compositions, with controlled microstructures (or, more broadly, character), dimensions, properties, and behaviour.

Separation of the ceramics and glass industries

Though the glass and the ceramics industries share in common most raw materials, many unit operations and processes and the same underlying sciences, they have throughout the world generally developed as two separate industries. This division has arisen because of competition for some markets, as well as because of differences in the technologies. The same is true of the industries based on cement. In the following text, then, industrial ceramics derived by compacting particulates and subsequent heat treatment will be differentiated from the products of the glass and cement industries, in which the materials are first heated and then formed.

A new class of ceramic materials has been developed by first forming the material as a glass and then reheating to precipitate crystal phases with 50 percent or less residual glassy phase. These "glass ceramics" (known by a variety of other names in each country) can be made to approximate many traditional particulate-formed and sintered (heated but not melted to give coherence) ceramics in chemical and mineral composition; because there are fewer inherent restrictions on control over microstructure, these materials can have superior properties, such as improved resistance to heat shock.

History. Industrial ceramics may be said to have begun with the first barter of the potter's ware. Through ancient times and the Middle Ages, the techniques for making clayware continued to advance, and, with the coming of the industrial and scientific revolutions, the industries were ready to supply the scientist with porcelain for chemical experimentation and manufacturing and also to supply an increased demand for containers, tableware, sanitary ware, and construction materials.

Makers of industrial ceramics were thus prepared for the extraordinary demands brought by the 20th-century growth of the chemical, electrical, electronic, nuclear, automotive, and aerospace industries. For the electrical industry the first products were insulators, such as the familiar porcelain suspensions of transmission lines. For electronics the first new products were insulators for even higher frequencies, with the steatites (a class of magnesium silicate minerals) as the first novel materials. With the science explosion during and after World War II, the applications of ceramics in the electronic field grew to include compact capacitors, piezoelectric transducers, resistor and semiconductor compositions, magnetic materials (hard, soft, memory core, and microwave; see also FERRITES), and other energy converters. Improved compositions for automotive and aviation spark plugs led to high alumina (aluminum oxide) ceramics that have been applied to many mechanical, wear, and electronic uses, including even lamps. Nuclear reactors use ceramics for moderators and controls and the ceramic forms of nuclear fuels (uranium and plutonium) in fuel rods. Strong, hermetic seals of alumina and other ceramics to metals are vital in many applications.

Particle bonding and packing. The forming of ceramics involves particle technology, including size reduction (comminution), measurement, and separation; blending and packing of particles; surface chemistry and physics; rheology, or the flow of more or less plastic materials under pressure; and bonding of particles. Other sciences contribute to the understanding and control of heat treatment.

Ceramics came into being because of the useful rheological properties of the clay–water system, with its capability of being shaped, whether as a paste or as a fluid suspension or as a damp, crumbly powder. Modern industrial ceramics often replace clay with organic or inorganic additives to make the raw material easier to form and to provide strength before firing (final heating). Clay-based ceramics undergo both chemical–mineralogical and physical changes during heat treatment to form new phases, including a glassy phase that often constitutes the bond between the grains in the new microstructure. Such heat treatment involves sintering in the presence of a liquid phase. The complex series of occurrences accompanying heat treatments include gas evolution, oxidation, valence changes, chemical reactions, phase transformations, melting, shrinkage, and still other chemical and physical changes. The trend with modern ceramics technology is to simplify such changes by establishing the chemical and mineral changes before forming. Maximum density is sought in the forming batch, and compaction is achieved by applying the principles of particle packing. Then heat treatment brings about sintering in the solid state with a minimum of shrinkage; gas evolution; and attendant flaws, such as warping, cracking, or the formation of unwanted pores.

Changes induced by heat treatment

Many significant ceramic products, such as thermal insulation and filters for liquids and gases, require controlled porosity, both in terms of percent by volume and in pore diameters and distributions. In fact, texture comprises the prime distinction between refractories, whitewares, and electronic and glass-ceramics that may otherwise be identical in chemical and mineral compositions.

Processing of raw materials. Raw materials for industrial ceramics were originally derived from specific locations around the world where geological processes had prepared ore bodies of sufficient chemical purity and appropriate particle sizes and rheological characteristics for each specific product. Examples of this include the English china and ball clays for better grades of porcelain, the Grossalmerode clay that for centuries was considered essential for pots for melting glass, the Vallendar clay of the porcelain enameller, and the Manchurian talcs deemed superior for the early steatites.

Only with the increasing knowledge about the chemical and physical characterization of these materials and their transformations during processing was it possible to replace these geologically prepared, strategic materials, first with beneficiated minerals (minerals that have been concentrated by removing unwanted materials) and then with chemically prepared compounds. Economically, the natural minerals, more or less beneficiated, still are lowest in cost and remain the largest tonnage used in most established ceramic products. Even with the more specialized technical ceramic products, the ceramist at first tended to retain a pinch of his favourite clay in the formula. Completely synthesized ceramics are still a relatively small proportion of total output, though significant in strategic and monetary value.

With the depletion of the geologically prepared resources and with the possible savings in processing costs through faster firing rates and higher yields, synthesized raw materials are becoming acceptable substitutes for natural minerals. Many of the newer ceramics demand raw materials that either never existed in natural minerals or did not exist in useful ore concentrations. One example of the latter kind is silicon carbide. A current classification of materials used in the manufacture of ceramic products includes over 500 items.

Ceramic raw materials are classified functionally as aggregates, plasticizers, binders, fluxes, and modifiers (chemical, thermal, physical, electrical, colour). Traditional ceramic materials were largely derived from the elements most common in the earth's crust: oxygen, silicon, aluminum, iron, and so forth, but modern ceramics draw upon nearly every element. Although oxides remain most common, other useful compounds include carbides, nitrides, borides, sulfides, and fluorides.

Mining, crushing, grinding, milling, beneficiation, and mixing of the standard materials for ceramics are similar to the operations in other chemical and engineering industries. Clays going into common bricks, sewer pipe, or stoneware may be processed directly as dug out of the ground, though even here blending, aging, and tempering for uniform distribution of water are practiced. Such impure clays are workable because they contain fillers and fluxes associated with the clay minerals. For whitewares, the clays are washed and purified by settling out some impurities and floating off others. Silicas are purified by washing and separating unwanted minerals by gravity and by magnetic and electrostatic means. Feldspars are increasingly beneficiated by froth flotation, a process in which a frothing agent is added to separate the desired material from impurities. Blending from stockpiles is utilized to maintain constancy of chemical composition.

Use of impure clays

Raw materials for the newer ceramics are generally prepared by chemical reactions involving precipitation, filtering, calcination (firing at high temperature), solid-state reactions, melting, and even vapour formation, as well as other sophisticated methods. Freeze drying has been under intensive development as a means for providing a very fine-particled, free-flowing powder feed. Spray drying has become a widely used technique for removing process water at the raw material preparation plants and in mixed batches at the ceramic-processing factory.

Much of the art of the ceramic technologist has always lain in the compounding of raw materials into batches. The formulas, traditionally jealously guarded secrets, involve selection of the raw materials that confer the desired working characteristics and responses to heat treatment, yielding the sought-for character and properties. The clays must be selected and apportioned among the kaolins and ball clays for workability, fusibility, fired colour, and other requirements. The silicas, likewise, must meet criteria of chemical purity and particle size distribution. The fluxing ingredient is selected from one or more feldspars, nepheline syenites, Cornwall stone, bone ash, fritted (finely divided) glasses, and other candidates. The considerations include balance between sodium and potassium oxides, content of iron oxides and other unwanted impurities, and particle size distribution and behaviour during heat treatment. With the burgeoning of technical ceramics no longer requiring or permitting clays and traditional fluxes, the skill of the batch formulator has become dependent on his awareness of the functions and behaviour of organic aids.

Forming processes. Clay-based bodies utilize the plasticity of clay–water mixtures to permit easy shaping of the ware, in most cases accompanied by expulsion of air and densification. Forming processes are adapted to the dimensional requirements. The four principal processes are plastic forming, slip casting, pressing, and fusion casting.

Plastic forming. This is the oldest technique and can be visualized from offhand molding, coiling, and throwing on a wheel. In jiggering, the topside of the piece (dinner plate or bowl) is shaped by throwing a wad of body (forming batch of suitable consistency) on a gypsum plaster mold mounted on a rotating spindle; the bottom surface is formed by pressing a contoured pattern against the exposed face of the body. In plastic extrusion a stiff paste is forced through a die of the desired shape and cross section in a continuous column, which can then be cut to length. The body may be prepared separately or may be processed in a continuous apparatus that mixes the raw materials and water (pug mill), passes the mix through a vacuum chamber to remove air and thereby improve plasticity, and then forces it through the die. Structural clay products, such as brick and sewer pipe, are normally formed by this technique. Plastic formed bodies generally contain 15 to 25 percent of water by weight.

Slip casting. This process utilizes a fluid suspension of the body with controlled pH (acidity or alkalinity), specific gravity, water content, and additives for deflocculation (prevention of the small particles from combining into larger aggregates) called the slip. The deflocculants (for example, a few tenths of a percent each of sodium carbonate and a sodium silicate) confer the same fluidity at about 25 percent water as would require 100 percent water in their absence. Lower water means lower drying shrinkage and consequently lessened tendency to warp and crack and better dimensional control. The slip is poured into a plaster of paris mold that withdraws enough water from the adjacent suspension to build a layer of solid body. After the desired wall thickness has been attained, excess slip is poured off. Vacuum, pressure, or centrifugal forces are sometimes used in conjunction with slip casting.

Slip casting applications

The slip casting technique is applied to many clay-free, nonplastic particulate materials. By deflocculation of the finer particles, a high-solids-content suspension can be prepared. Either alkaline or acid slips can be prepared at a pH where like electrical charges transferred to the particles cause them to repel each other. Similarly, nonclay bodies can be extruded or die pressed by using organic additives as plasticizers, binders, and lubricants. Like water, these additives are transient constituents, being expelled during the firing operation.

Pressing. Pressing forms a shape or a blank by compacting a free-flowing powder mixture in a die until the particles are bonded strongly enough to permit removal from the die and handling before heat treatment. Water content varies from 5 to 15 percent for clay down to as low as zero for bodies utilizing organic binders. In addition to the complexity of shapes (including holes) that can be formed, dry pressing has the advantage that the low water content results in less drying shrinkage. Pressing is carried out in rigid steel or carbide dies with equipment of increasing sophistication for controlling the rate and uniformity of load application, air expulsion, and ejection from the die. Flexible dies of rubbery polymers are also used for isostatic (uniform pressure) pressing, permitting more uniform density throughout a piece. Plastic bodies are being pressed by procedures that permit simultaneous forming and water removal, thus lessening shrinkage and increasing strength. The steam evolved in warm pressing acts as a parting agent to facilitate removal from the mold. Hot pressing is carried out in molds, usually made of graphite, that can be sufficiently heated by induction or radiation to bring about simultaneous shaping, densification, and in some cases chemical reactions. The resultant body can be of full density (pore free), of the same dimensions as the mold (no drying or firing shrinkage), and completely matured (fired). The chief barrier to wider use of this process has been the short life and high cost of the molds.

Fusion casting. In this process the batch is heated all the way up to melting temperatures and then shaped by casting into a mold, usually made from sand, corresponding to the casting of metals in foundries. So far, it has been largely limited to making large blocks of refractories for glass and metal melting furnaces. Other kinds of forming from melts and from vapours are being used for making ceramics, both in single crystal and in multicrystalline structures.

Heat treatment. Formed ware is generally passed through a drying oven to remove the liquid water carefully without introducing cracking or warping. The basis for the operation is to maintain initially a high humidity, so that the movement of water through the cross section is uniform. Dryers are usually based on heated air, but infrared and dielectric (radio-frequency) heating are being applied.

The goal of subsequent heating (firing) is to obtain cycles of time–temperature–atmosphere that are accurately reproducible. Again the rate of temperature increase must be carefully controlled to avoid spalling (chipping), cracking, warping, nonuniformity within a piece, and nonreproducibility from piece to piece and from day to day. Not only must dimensions be kept within tolerances, but colour and other pertinent physical properties must be maintained within acceptable limits.

Heat treating equipment

Equipment for heat treatment has undergone a considerable advance; the intermittent kilns of the potteries have been superseded by continuous tunnel kilns, and the means for transporting the ware through the cycle is undergoing active innovation.

Regardless of kiln design, there are four basic elements common to all heat treatments: (1) the source of the heat, (2) the containment of the heat, (3) the containment of the ware, and (4) the instrumentation for control of temperature and atmosphere.

Heat sources include combustion of fossil fuels and the passage of electrical current through metallic alloys or ceramics, such as silicon carbide. Induction and arc heating are not common in the ceramics industries, but very-high-frequency induction (radio frequencies in the megahertz range) finds special uses, as have other new sources of heat, such as electron beam, ion beam, and solar and arc imaging.

Containment of heat involves furnace design, including choice of refractories (furnace linings). The availability of refractory materials useful to ever-higher temperatures has been paralleled by advances in insulating refractories, cement-bonded materials that can be cast into the desired shapes, and high-temperature fibres. Lighter weight materials have made faster heating and cooling cycles possible and have contributed to lower fuel or power consumption.

Containment of ware has also moved in the direction of better heat economy and faster cycles with materials of higher thermal conductivity, higher service temperatures, less creep and deformation, and less reaction with the ware.

The use of instrumentation has also advanced rapidly with the innovations in program controllers and analysis of atmospheres. Computer-controlled firing is being evaluated.

Glazes and enamels. Glazes and porcelain enamels provide a meeting ground for glass technology and particulate ceramic technology. Glazes are generally used for reasons of appearance but can be designed to improve other properties, such as strength and imperviousness, and to improve smoothness, thus making cleaning easier and improving resistance to electrical tracking (development of paths over the surface along which electrical current can flow).

Glaze formulation

Traditionally, glazes were the province of the ceramic technologist and were frequently synthesized from raw materials at the site on the matured ware during a special gloss firing. Now formulation of glazes has become a specialty of supplier companies that melt glaze, enamel, and bonding formulas and quench them to glassy frits (finely divided material) by rapid cooling in water or passing through steel rollers. Coating slips (suspensions) comprised of milled frits, opacifiers, bonding clays, and various modifiers are applied to the ceramic or metal base by spraying, dipping, or flowing. With ceramic bodies the maturing of the glaze may take place in a single firing with the maturing of the body. With porcelain enamels a carefully cleaned metal surface is coated from a slip (or more rarely by dry dusting), and the glass coating is matured by a rapid heating and cooling requiring only about five minutes at peak temperature.

BIBLIOGRAPHY. ERNST ROSENTHAL, *Pottery and Ceramics* (1949), is a good introduction to the manufacture, properties, and uses of clay-based wares; M. CHANDLER, *Ceramics in the Modern World* (1968), extends the treatment, while F. and S.S. SINGER, *Industrial Ceramics* (1963), goes into more technical detail. For the individual product categories, selected references include F.H. NORTON, *Fine Ceramics* (1970), for a well-illustrated coverage of whitewares, and the same author's *Refractories*, 4th ed. (1968), remains the outstanding text for high-temperature materials. V.V. VARGIN, *Technology of Enamels* (1968; orig. pub. in Russian, 1965), is the most current treatment of porcelain enamelling, though A.I. ANDREWS, *Porcelain Enamels*, 2nd ed. (1961), is still authoritative. B.E. WAYE, *Introduction to Technical Ceramics* (1967); and E.C. HENRY, *Electronic Ceramics* (1969), are brief, informative treatments on newer ceramic products. To supplement a basic text such as W.E. WORRALL, *Raw Materials* (1964), current data on raw materials and processing appear each year in special issues of the trade journals *Ceramic Industry* for January (also see the annual *Ceramic Data Book*) and *Ceramic Age* for July. W.D. KINGERY's misleadingly named *Introduction to Ceramics* (1960), marked the transition from teaching of ceramics by separate industries to consideration of the principles underlying the full scope of ceramics as a broad class of materials. Symposia such as R.M. FULRATH and J.A. PASK (eds.), *Ceramic Microstructures* (1968), have brought together the producers of ceramics and those who are using them in specific, often extreme environments.

(A.G.P.)

Cereals and Other Starch Products

Starch, a carbohydrate stored in most plants, is a major constituent of the average human diet, providing a low-cost energy source with good keeping qualities. Cereals are high in starch, which may be used in pure or flour form. Starches are also obtained from such root sources as potatoes and from the pith of tropical palm trees. Various starches are used commercially in food processing and in the manufacture of laundering preparations, paper, textiles, adhesives, explosives, and cosmetics.

Cereals, or grains, are members of the grass family cultivated primarily for their starchy seeds (technically, dry fruits), which are used for human food, livestock feed, and as a source of industrial starch. Wheat, rice, maize (called corn in the U.S.), rye, oats, barley, sorghum, and some of the millets are common cereals.

This article is divided into the following sections:

I. Origin and development of cereals

Cereals were among the first plants to be domesticated, having been grown long before the beginning of recorded history. Each of the world's great civilizations has depended upon cereals as a major food source. When ancient man learned to grow cereals, he was able to produce more than enough food for his own immediate needs, thus making possible settled communities.

Early man lived precariously by hunting and fishing and by eating edible roots, wild fruits, and wild grains. The early hunter required 10 to 15 square miles of land to feed himself, an area that when cultivated can provide food for 5,000 people. Thus a major turning point occurred when man learned that certain parts of food plants, saved from one season to another and put into the ground at appropriate times, produced many new plants similar to the original. Archaeological evidence indicates that early ancestors of cultivated wheat existed in the very early Stone Age (Early Paleolithic); crude milling implements have been found dating back 75,000 years. The earliest actual remains of grain date from about 5000 BC, toward the close of the Neolithic Period. Basic crops of Neolithic agriculture in the Near East were primitive husked wheats, wild einkorn (*Triticum boeotichum*) and wild emmer wheat (*T. dicoccides*), the latter regarded as the ancestor of cultivated emmer (*T. dicoccum*). Einkorn probably appeared earlier than emmer wheat, but the cultivated variety of emmer was widely distributed. Production of both einkorn and emmer decreased in the Bronze Age, with the greater use of barley (*Hordeum vulgare*). The main centres of cultivated barley were probably the northeast portion of Africa, including the mountainous districts of Ethiopia, and Southeast Asia. Barleys originated from *Hordeum spontaneum*. Rice is another primary crop, domesticated from a wild type. Secondary crops, originating as weeds in the primary crops, include oats and rye.

Einkorn and emmer

Maize, or corn (*Zea mays*), was cultivated in America before the first Europeans arrived, and little is known of its early history. Rice, now comprising some 25 species, was cultivated in Southeast Asia as early as 3000 BC. Rice growing (paddy cultivation) normally requires either irrigation or swamp conditions. There is no evidence of rice cultivation in the ancient Near East; it is not represented on Egyptian tombs and is not mentioned in the Bible.

Cereal grains were originally crushed between two stones and made into crude cakes. Remains of a kind of cake made from coarsely ground grain have been found in explorations of the Swiss lake dwellings (*c.* 3500 BC). Cereals were probably used primarily as human food by early communities but may also have been used as feed for wild cattle caught and kept as a reserve food supply.

By about 3000 BC all of the major cereals had been brought under cultivation; not a single new major crop has been introduced since.

NOMENCLATURE AND CLASSIFICATION

This article treats the major cereals, wheat, rice, barley, rye, oats, maize, sorghum, millet, and buckwheat; important starchy foods consumed in certain countries instead of cereals, including potatoes and cassava; and soybeans, legumes widely used in the bakery industry. Wheat species will be treated in detail, other cereals in a more general way throughout the article.

Wheat: varieties and characteristics. The three principal types of wheat used in modern food production are *Triticum vulgare* (or *aestivum*), *T. durum*, and *T. compactum*. *Triticum vulgare* provides the bulk of the wheat used to produce flour for bread making and for cakes and biscuits (cookies). It can be grown under a wide range of climatic conditions and soils. Although the yield varies with climate and other factors, it is cultivated from the southernmost regions of America almost to the Arctic and at elevations from sea level to over 10,000 feet. *T. durum*, longer and narrower in shape than *T. vulgare*, is mainly ground into semolina (purified middlings) instead of flour. Durum semolina is generally the best type for the production of pasta foods. *T. compactum* is more suitable for confectionery and biscuits than for other purposes and is decreasing in importance.

The wheat grain, the raw material of flour production and the seed planted to produce new plants, consists of three major portions: (1) the embryo or germ (including its sheaf, the scutellum) that produces the new plant; (2) the starchy endosperm, which serves as food for the germinating seed and forms the raw material of flour manufacture; and (3) various covering layers protecting the grain. Although proportions vary, other cereal grains follow the same general pattern. Average wheat grain composition is approximately 85 percent endosperm, 13 percent husk, 2 percent embryo.

Wheat grain composition

Characteristic variations of the different types of wheat are important agricultural considerations. Hard wheats include the strong wheats of Canada (Manitoba) and the similar hard red spring (HRS) wheats of the United States. They yield excellent bread-making flour because of their high quantity of protein (approximately 12–15 percent), mainly in the form of gluten. Soft wheats, the major wheats grown in the United Kingdom, most of Europe, and Australia, result in flour producing less attractive bread than that achieved from strong wheats. The loaves are generally smaller, and the crumb has a less pleasing structure. Soft wheats, however, possess excellent characteristics for the production of flour used in cake and biscuit manufacture.

Wheats intermediate in character include the hard red winters (HRW) of the central U.S. and wheat from Argentina. There are important differences between spring and winter varieties. Spring wheats, planted in the early spring, grow quickly and are normally harvested in late summer or early autumn. Winter wheats are planted in the autumn and harvested in late spring or early summer. Both spring and winter wheats are grown in different regions of the U.S. and the Soviet Union. Winter varieties can be grown only where the winters are sufficiently mild. Where winters are severe, as in Canada, spring types are usually cultivated, and the preferred varieties mature early, allowing harvesting before frost.

In baking and confectionery manufacture the terms strong and weak indicate flour from hard and soft wheats. The term strength is used to describe the type of flour, strong flours being preferred for bread manufacture and weak flours for cakes and biscuits. Strong flours are high in protein content, and their gluten has a pleasing elasticity; weak flours are low in protein, and their weak, flowy gluten produces a soft, flowy dough.

Wheat breeders regularly produce new varieties, not

Table 1: Yield of Wheat per Acre in Various Countries (bushels)

	1934–38 (average)	1949–53 (average)	1954	1956	1958	1960	1962	1964	1966	1968	1970	1972
Argentina	14.5	17.3	20.9	19.6	19.1	16.4	21.6	27.3	17.8	14.6	18.6	24.0
Australia	11.9	17.3	15.8	17.1	20.7	20.3	19.0	20.6	22.4	20.2	17.1	13.4
Canada	10.5	20.7	13.7	25.2	18.0	21.1	21.1	20.2	27.9	22.2	26.6	25.0
France	23.2	28.1	35.0	30.8	30.9	37.6	45.8	46.9	42.1	54.4	51.1	68.1
Germany, West	32.8	40.5	38.9	45.0	42.1	52.9	51.8	53.5	48.5	62.9	56.3	60.4
Italy	21.9	24.4	22.7	26.5	29.5	22.2	31.1	29.0	32.7	33.3	34.6	36.7
Netherlands, The	45.0	56.1	53.6	53.3	53.9	69.8	67.5	70.0	60.1	65.8	66.3	64.0
Soviet Union	13.8	14.4	12.9	16.2	17.1	15.8	15.5	16.3	21.4	20.7	21.4	21.8
Spain	14.2	12.6	16.6	14.5	15.5	12.3	16.9	14.3	17.3	19.9	16.0	18.9
Tunisia	7.6	8.5	6.8	6.4	6.1	4.8	7.1	6.3	6.1	8.6	7.9	13.1
U.K.	34.4	41.7	42.3	46.3	45.8	53.1	60.1	63.1	57.0	52.8	61.4	62.8
U.S.	12.9	16.5	18.1	20.2	27.2	26.2	15.1	25.8	26.3	28.6	31.1	32.7

only to combat disease but also to satisfy changing market demands. Many varieties of wheat do not retain their popularity, and often those popular in one decade are replaced in the next. New varieties of barley have also been developed, but there have been few varieties of rice.

Distribution and production: acreage and yield. There are considerable differences in yield per acre between the soft wheat grown in the U.K. and many parts of Europe and the hard wheats grown in the U.S. and Canada. A yield of as much as 50–60 bushels per acre is not uncommon in the U.K., but the strong wheats of North America yield only around 25 bushels per acre (an average bushel of wheat is about 60 pounds, or 27 kilograms). Table 1 illustrates wheat yield differences. The figures for individual countries show interesting variations. For example, in the U.K., during the period 1949–53, the average yield in bushels per acre was 41.7, but in later years it rose to well over 50. The highest figure recorded was 73.9 bushels in 1971 for The Netherlands (not included in table because year was odd-numbered). The yields in Canada and the U.S. from 1950 to 1970 varied around 17 to 31, but the tendency was toward an increase. In the Soviet Union the yield per acre has increased but is still on the low side; the yields in Asia, including China, remain poor.

Table 2 gives statistics on world wheat production. These figures show how much the harvest can vary from year to year and also the trend for the total wheat yield and production to increase.

CEREALS AND CEREAL PRODUCTS IN THE HUMAN DIET

Cereals and population

The world population is increasing at the rate of 75,000,000 persons a year. Of the present world population (around 3,850,000,000), half lives in Asia and three-quarters in developing countries. In these areas cereals play the leading dietary role. Thus it is of major significance that world production of wheat and some other cereals (see Table 3) has risen considerably owing to improved varieties, better resistance to disease, and higher yields per acre due to scientific application of fertilizers; but the demand for a sufficient supply of food, and for a more nutritious food, continues.

Nutrients. Foodstuffs consist of many types of nutrients, including carbohydrate, protein, fat, mineral matter, and vitamins. Carbohydrates (starches and sugars), proteins, and fats all provide energy. Their values are measured in calories, the heat unit required to raise the temperature of one gram of water from 15° to 16° C.

The heat-producing values, in calories, of the main food constituents (per gram) are carbohydrates 3.7, proteins 4.1, fat 9.3, and alcohol 7. Based on the percentage of the various food constituents contained, the values of some common foods, expressed as calories per pound, show the following comparison between cereals and non-cereals: white bread 1,037; wholemeal bread 1,012; rump steak 2,006; bacon (back) 2,696; chicken 360; hen eggs (in shell) 659; apples 196; butter 3,503; and cheese (full cream) 2,011.

Table 3: World Cereal Acreage, Production, and Yield (1972, including China)

cereal	acre-age*	produc-tion*	average yield (bushels/acre)
Wheat	30.6	27.3	24.2
Maize (corn)	15.5	23.6	41.4
Rice, paddy	18.8	23.2	33.5
Barley	12.2	11.9	26.7
Oats	4.5	4.0	24.4
Other	18.5	10.0	14.6

*Percent of world total, by weight.

On the whole, the carbohydrate-rich cereals compare favourably with the protein-rich foods in energy value; in addition they are significantly less expensive to produce. Therefore most of the world's diets are arranged to meet main calorie requirements from the cheaper carbohydrate foods, and the proteins are used primarily to provide essential amino acids. Individual calorie requirements depend upon age, sex, and the amount of physical work being carried out. A man performing heavy work may require as many as 4,500 calories daily, while 2,400 will suffice for sedentary workers. Children require from 800 to 2,250 calories. The average figure often taken for the population as a whole is 2,400.

Protein consumption is of major importance in diets; insufficient protein intake ranks second to general insufficiency of food as a cause of malnutrition. Proteins are

Table 2: Wheat Area and Production

	wheat area (000 acres)				wheat production (000,000 bushels)			
	average 1948–52	average 1961–65	average 1966–70	average 1971–72	average 1948–52	average 1961–65	average 1966–70	average 1971–72
Europe, excluding Soviet Union	69,237	70,611	69,377	68,777	1,512.4	2,180.7	2,543.8	3,004.3
Soviet Union	105,350	164,629	165,993	151,398	1,313.9	2,359.2	3,314.0	3,390.7
North America	94,551	75,559	76,025	69,366	1,635.4	1,778.6	2,049.9	2,112.7
Latin America	18,654	20,218	21,224	20,674	292.4	427.4	416.1	447.2
Asia, excluding China	65,968	93,951	100,007	111,926	785.6	1,237.5	1,541.8	2,066.1
China	56,956	62,173	67,926	70,676	584.7	816.9	1,030.9	1,231.0
Africa	14,256	17,117	20,118	21,828	168.1	232.6	263.3	342.9
Oceania	11,542	16,816	22,161	18,164	194.7	311.2	406.5	291.6
World	428,203*	521,074	542,827	532,807	6,288.7*	9,343.5	11,566.1	12,886.5

*Regional totals and world totals obtained separately.

made up of combinations of 26 amino acids, of which 8 are essential to the human diet: valine, leucine, isoleucine, threonine, methionine, phenylalanine, lysine, and trytophan. Protein from vegetable sources, with the exception of soybean, normally does not provide sufficient essential amino acids and is especially deficient in lysine. Such protein is described as having limited biological value. Although ideally only about half of the protein in the diet should come from vegetable sources, this is not possible in the developing countries, where animal protein sources are limited. Cereal products generally contribute a large proportion of the vegetable protein, in addition to their carbohydrate content. The soybean is an important source of protein in many countries.

Nutritional significance of cereals. Cereals are largely consumed as bread and to a lesser extent as cakes, biscuits, and breakfast foods. They are also consumed in other forms in some countries. There has been controversy as to the relative merits of white bread and bread made from flour of much longer extraction, which is darker in colour. Whiter flour consists of about 72 percent of the grain but contains little of the germ, or embryo, and of the outer coverings (bran). Since the B vitamins are concentrated mainly in the scutellum (covering of the germ), and to a lesser extent in the bran, the vitamin B content of white flour, unless artificially enriched, is much less than that of brown flour, particularly in vitamin B_1. Because the whole meal normally has a higher vitamin content than white flour, arguments have been advanced against excluding the vitamin-rich portions of the grain in flour produced for bread making. In most developed countries, the public prefers white flour and bread. It may be argued that there is no serious disadvantage if humans consume white flour, as opposed to darker flour, since the discarded portion is fed to animals, producing animal food for the human diet. Man does not digest brown flour and bread as easily and as fully as he does the white variety.

Role of the B vitamins

The relative value of the two types of bread became less important when vitamin B_1 was synthesized and could be manufactured and added to white flour. The chemically synthesized vitamins are identical with those occurring naturally and have the same biological activity. White flour is often routinely fortified with vitamins so that the vitamin content is similar to that of the darker flours.

Treatment by chemicals to improve baking quality is distinct from flour enrichment (see *Composition and Grade*). Table 4 gives the Joint Food and Agriculture Organization/World Health Organization Expert Committees' recommendations on flour treatment.

In the U.K. the law requires enrichment of each 100 grams of flour to reach minimum standards of 0.24 milligram B_1, 1.60 mg nicotinic acid or nicotinamide, and 1.65 mg iron. Bread-making flours are also fortified by the addition of calcium in the form of calcium carbonate, so that each 100 grams of white flour contains not less than 235 mg, or more than 390 mg of "chalk." Table 5 compares the composition of flour of various extractions.

In the U.K., where an attempt was made at one time to standardize flour on an 80 percent extraction, a committee studied the relative merits of the darker 80 percent extraction flour (milled to contain as much germ rich in B vitamins as possible) and fortified (or enriched) white flour (around 72 percent extraction) and concluded that the differences between low-extraction flour enriched as specified and 80% extraction flour would not significantly affect the health of the population.

Table 4: Recommended List of Flour-Treatment Agents

	maximum treatment level (mg/kg)
Ascorbic acid	200
Azodicarbonamide	45
Benzoyl peroxide	40 75 for special purposes*
Chlorine dioxide	30 75 for special purposes*
Potassium bromate	20 75 for special purposes*

*E.g., for certain biscuit flours.

Nutrients in bread

Many of the important nutrients in the diet are contributed by bread, the main form in which cereals are consumed. Besides providing close to 17% of the calories required, fortified bread provides 17%–18% of the total protein in the diet, 16% of the calcium, 20% of the vitamin B_1, and 19% of the nicotinic acid. Taking all cereal products, these percentages are much higher. Although the protein is not ideal in biological quality because of its rather low lysine content, it is possible (now that pure synthetic lysine is available) that this situation could be remedied. In developed countries with good mixed diets, this may not be necessary. In developing countries, where the population lives largely on cereals, compulsory lysine enrichment may be of value. Where maize (exceptionally low in lysine) is a staple flour, another method has become practical: the cultivation of maize with a higher than usual lysine content.

Table 6 illustrates the value of bread in the diet compared with other principal foodstuffs.

Based on cost, enriched bread in some countries is a comparatively inexpensive source of calories, protein, iron, vitamin B_1, nicotinic acid, and calcium in the diet. Cereal consumption varies enormously in different countries, and the more developed a country becomes, the lower is the amount consumed, because more of the attractive and expensive foods become available. In less developed countries, however, the bulk of the diet consists of cereals, and such diets are frequently insufficient in protein and carbohydrates. In the U.S.S.R. the diet is adequate in calories, but over half of the calorific value is supplied by flour and other cereals. In contrast, in the U.S., less than 25 percent of the calories in the diet come from flour, cereal products, and potatoes. Most western European countries fall somewhere between.

Other cereals are similar to wheat in nutritive value, containing mainly carbohydrates and some protein of

Table 5: Composition of Flour of Various Extractions*
(per 100 g)

	patent flour (about 50% extraction)	straight run (about 72% extraction)	straight run (enriched)	75% extraction	80% extraction (10½ oz per sack *creta praeparata*†)	85% extraction (10½ oz per sack *creta praeparata*†)	wholemeal (95%–100%)
Protein (g)	10.0	11.0	11.0	11.2	11.4	11.6	12.0
Available iron (mg)	0.9	1.0	3.0	1.1	1.8	2.2	2.7
Available calcium (mg)	15.0	18.0	22.0	22.0	57.0	50.0	negative
Vitamin B_1 (mg)	0.08	0.11	0.50	0.15	0.26	0.31	0.40
Nicotinic acid (mg)	0.70	0.72	4.0	0.77	1.20	1.60	6.0
Riboflavine (mg)	0.03	0.035	0.30	0.04	0.05	0.07	0.12
Pantothenic acid (mg)	0.4	0.6	0.6	0.75	0.9	1.1	1.5
Pyridoxine (mg)	0.1	0.15	0.15	0.2	0.25	0.3	0.5
Biotin (mg)	0.0005	—	—	—	—	—	0.007

*With the long-extraction flours, there has sometimes been no enrichment with calcium; sometimes there has been an addition of 7 oz per sack and sometimes 14 oz per sack. For the purpose of this table the middle figure has been used. †*Creta praeparata:* official British Pharmacopoeia name for prepared chalk . . . the form in which calcium is added to flour (14 oz per 280-lb sack).

Table 6: Comparative Value of Bread in the Diet
(percent)

	energy value	protein	calcium	iron	vitamin B_1	nicotinic acid
Milk, cream, and cheese	12.7	23.1	60.8	3.8	13.1	3.7
Vegetables	7.2	8.8	5.9	17.0	21.3	17.9
Bread	16.6	19.4	15.7	20.4	22.1	18.7
Meat	15.3	26.1	2.1	28.1	24.5	39.3
Fruit	2.0	1.0	1.6	4.0	3.3	2.8
Cereal foods other than bread	15.0	10.1	8.1	13.4	10.6	9.8
Sugar and preserves	12.4	—	0.3	0.9	—	0.1
Fats	14.4	0.2	0.3	0.6	—	0.4
Eggs	1.9	5.1	2.0	6.7	3.3	0.2
Fish	0.9	4.7	1.7	2.0	0.9	3.7

rather limited biological value. The nature of a protein is largely determined by its amino acids. Table 7 indicates the chief amino acids in various cereals. Although the distribution of the amino acids in these cereals is somewhat similar, the total amount of protein varies, with wheat usually containing 11 to 14 percent protein, and other cereals around 8 to 10 percent.

Wheat protein

The output of cereals is steadily growing. Overall, about 70 percent of the total crop goes for human consumption in the form of flour products, about 10 percent is returned to the soil as seed, and the remainder is divided among livestock feed, industrial uses, and waste. These proportions vary greatly among different countries; in the U.K., for example, half of the tonnage produced may go for livestock feed. Despite steadily increasing production, which has resulted in large stocks, or "carryovers," in the wheat-exporting countries, there remains a shortage. A critical problem is the loss resulting from insect damage to crops and from the various forms of spoilage occurring during storage.

II. Cereal production

CULTIVATION

The cultivation of cereals varies widely in different countries and depends partly upon the degree of development existing. The condition and purity of the seed is receiving increasing attention. Other factors include the nature of the soil, the amount of rainfall, and the techniques applied to promote growth. In illustrating production problems, this article will use wheat as the example; the procedures for other cereals are similar. Exceptions for rice and other cereals will be treated later.

Wheat can be cultivated over a wide range of soils and can be successfully grown over large portions of the world, ranging in altitude from sea level to over 10,000 feet. Annual rainfall of 10 inches (254 millimetres) is generally considered the minimum, and the soil should be sufficiently fertile. (Barley can be grown in soil less fertile than that required for wheat.) Soil benefits from a good humus content (partially decayed organic matter), and chemical fertilizers are also helpful.

Table 7: Amino Acid Content of Cereal Grains
(g amino acid/16g nitrogen)

amino acid	wheat	barley	rye	oats	rice	maize	sorghum
Arginine	4.3	5.0	5.0	6.6	7.7	5.0	4.7
Cystine	2.1	2.1	1.8	1.8	1.1	2.1	—
Histidine	2.1	1.9	2.1	1.9	2.3	2.4	3.3
Isoleucine	3.8	3.8	3.9	4.6	3.9	4.0	4.7
Leucine	6.4	6.9	6.1	7.0	8.0	12.0	14.3
Lysine	2.7	3.4	3.7	3.7	3.7	3.0	2.9
Methionine	1.6	1.4	1.6	1.4	2.4	2.1	1.6
Phenylalanine	4.6	5.0	4.6	5.0	5.2	5.0	4.3
Threonine	2.9	3.7	3.6	3.4	4.1	4.2	3.8
Tryptophan	1.3	1.4	1.3	1.3	1.4	0.8	0.7
Tyrosine	3.2	3.5	4.2	3.8	3.3	3.8	2.7
Valine	4.3	5.0	5.0	5.4	5.7	5.6	6.0
Alanine	3.4	4.5	—	5.1	6.0	9.9	—
Aspartic acid	5.0	5.9	—	4.2	10.4	12.3	—
Glutamic acid	27.7	20.5	19.7	18.4	20.4	15.4	21.9
Glycine	3.8	4.3	—	4.2	5.0	3.0	—
Proline	10.1	9.3	—	5.8	4.6	8.3	—
Serine	4.8	3.7	3.8	3.4	5.2	4.2	—

Importance of seed purity

Purity of the seed is important. The seed wheat (or other cereal seeds) must be true to its particular variety and as free as possible from foreign seeds. Seeds are frequently cleaned to avoid contamination by other seed crops. Modern cleaning methods employ such devices as oscillating sieves or revolving cylinders. Seed obtained with a combine harvester is often unsuited for use as seed wheat without preliminary treatment. Spring and winter varieties exist for both wheat and barley. Winter varieties generally produce better crops. Winter wheat should form a good root system, and the plant should begin to form new shoots before the cold weather sets in; winter wheat is likely to have more tillers than spring wheat.

The rate of sowing varies from 20 pounds per acre upward. Depth of sowing, usually one to three inches (2.5 to 7.5 centimetres), can be less in certain areas.

Breeding. Wheat and other cereals are self-fertilized. The pollen carried by the stamen of a given flower impregnates the pistil (stigma and ovary) of the same flower, enabling the variety to breed true. Wheat flowers are grouped in spikelets, each bearing from two to nine flowers, or florets. To produce new varieties by cross-fertilization, the cereal breeder artificially transfers the stamen from one variety to the flower of another before self-fertilization takes place. The production of a sufficient supply of the new type of seeds for sowing is time-consuming and expensive, but it allows new varieties to be evolved, retaining the desirable characteristics from each parent. For example, especially in the U.K. and Australia, varieties of the wheat that yield well often produce flour of poor baking quality; proper selection of parent plants permits new varieties to be produced that yield well and still possess good baking qualities.

Other reasons for developing new varieties include resistance to rust (fungus; see below) and other diseases, resistance to drought, and development of stronger and shorter straw to make harvesting easier.

Seedbed preparation. Various types of plowing machinery and other implements are employed to render the soil more suitable for seed wheat planting. The equipment used depends upon such factors as the climate, the nature of the ground, and the rainfall. Tillage is the process of preparing soil for cultivation purposes. The practices used and the implements employed vary considerably. Serious soil erosion may require special procedures to maintain clods and plant residues in the soil.

Tillage

In North America it is normal practice to grow wheat on the same ground for as long as sufficiently clean crops are produced, but eventually the ground must rest fallow for a year. The moisture of the land at the time of sowing is an important factor. The ancient procedure of growing legumes occasionally to improve the soil is still common in Europe, though less so in North America. Fertilization of the ground is useful to increase the crop yield, but it does not generally increase the protein content of the crop. In the large collective state farms of the Soviet Union, huge harrows set with spikes or teeth are employed, as well as the disk cultivating plow set with disks that break up the soil; the scarifier, a machine that pulverizes the soil, is popular in Australia.

Practices also differ between the semi-arid and subhumid climates.

Plant protection. Winter crops are frequently disturbed by frost, and the ground must then be rolled in the spring to consolidate the soil around the roots. If soil has become crusted by heavy rains followed by surface drying, the crop is usually harrowed in the spring to aerate the soil and kill young weeds. Although all of the required mineral nutrients may be added to the soil at the time of sowing, sometimes only part of the nitrogenous fertilizers are added at that time, and the remainder is applied to the growing crop in the form of a top dressing. In the cultivation of spring wheat all of the fertilizer is usually added before or at sowing time, but sometimes a small portion is reserved for later.

Weeds. Weeds present difficulties, as they compete with cereal crops for water, light, and mineral nutrients. The infestation of annual seeds planted in a field may cause many weeds in that field for successive years. Charlock or wild mustard, wild oats, crouch grass, and other common weeds are disseminated by wind, water, and birds.

Insects. In addition to weeds, wheat and other cereals are seriously affected by insects.

Grasshoppers and locusts cause immense damage. Spraying from airplanes with chemicals such as gamma BHC, Dieldrin, Chlordane, or Toxaphene is effective; on small farms grasshopper control is often accomplished by weed killers such as MCPA (2-methyl-4-chlorophenoxyacetic acid) and 2,4-D (2,4-dichlorophenoxyacetic acid).

The eggs of wireworms are laid in the soil, and the larvae live underground for some years, feeding on the roots and stems of the young plants (particularly slow-growing plants). To combat such damage, chemical seed dressing is used together with nitrogenous fertilizers. Other measures use such chemicals as gamma BHC (Lindane) or Dieldrin.

Aphids attack many plants, and the wheat aphid, or "greenbug," causes damage throughout the world. Preventive action includes preparing a good seedbed, sufficient fertilization, and early sowing.

The wheat stem sawfly (*Cephus cinctus*) is found in many parts of the world. Infested wheat shows fallen straw filled with a fine sawdust material harbouring brown-headed larvae that pass the winter in the base of the wheat straw; the wasplike adult insect emerges around June. The females thrust their eggs into the upper plant tissues, and the larvae feed within the stem toward the base until the stem collapses. Varieties of Manitoba wheat such as Rescue and Chinook are reasonably resistant to the pest, and thorough plowing in of the infested stubble is generally effective. Certain crops, such as brome grass, attract this pest and may be grown on the borders of wheat crops to distract the pests away from the wheat. The hessian fly (*Mayetiola,* or *Phytophaga, destructor*), resembling the mosquito, attacks the stems of wheat, barley, and rye. Late wheat usually escapes damage from this pest.

Many wheats in central Europe and the Middle East have shown evidence of attacks from the wheat bug (*Weizen-wanze,* or *blé punaisé*). The two main varieties are the *Aelia* and the *Eurygaster.* The eggs are laid in the spring, and the new generation appears in the summer. When the wheat is harvested, the bugs leave the stubble field and migrate to nearby foliage for the winter. To thrive and multiply, wheat bugs require sun, warmth, and absence of pronounced dampness.

Gluten damage

The wheat bugs puncture the grain and introduce by means of their saliva an enzyme that profoundly modifies the nature of the gluten. The puncture mark can be seen on the grain, usually surrounded by a yellow patch, and sometimes the grain is shrivelled. The main damage comes from attacks on the grain just before maturity. Although the insects leave, the damaged grain remains normal in size and remains in the wheat mixture sent to the mill.

The gluten of flour produced from infected wheat rapidly loses its cohesion upon standing in water, eventually disintegrating completely. Strong wheats resist wheat-bug attack better than soft, weak wheats do. There is little change in strong baking flours if only 1 percent of the grains are affected; in flour from soft wheats, the damage with even 1 percent to 2 percent of the grains affected can make the baking quality unacceptable. Countries in which the crop is affected by this pest include the Soviet Union, Romania, Hungary, Greece, and Morocco.

Fungus diseases. In the fungus group known as rust, the chief damage is caused by black rust (*Puccinia graminis*). Because this fungus spends part of its life on cereals, and part on the barberry bush, these bushes are often eradicated near wheat fields as a preventive measure. Black rust causes cereal plants to lose their green colour and turn yellow. The grain produced is small, shrivelled, and has a low weight per bushel. New wheats, more resistant to rust, are being introduced.

In many countries wheat is attacked by smut. Stinking smut (or bunt) is fairly common in the United Kingdom. Malformed grains are produced, filled with black spores that spread over noninfected grain and give off a "fishy" smell.

Ergot (*Claviceps purpurea*) is a fungus more often attacking rye than wheat. It forms a dark purple mass, larger than the grain, containing 30 percent fatty material and the alkaloid ergotoxine, which has a profound pharmacological effect on the human and animal body and can produce abortion. Much of this fungus is likely to be removed in the mill screen room, and the clean grain sent on to the mill should contain not more than 0.04 percent of this fungus and preferably less.

Harvesting. In the developed countries, harvesting of wheat and often other cereals is done principally by the combine harvester, though in the developing countries the ancient scythe, sickle, and flail are still widely used.

The McCormick reaper

The mechanical ancestor of today's large combines was the McCormick reaper, introduced in 1831 and followed by self-raking reapers that delivered the cut grain in bunches on the ground to be bound by hand. In 1843 a "stripper" was brought out in Australia that removed the wheat heads from the plants and threshed them in a single operation. Threshing machines were powered first by men or animals, often using treadmills, later by steam and internal-combustion engines. The modern combine harvester, originally introduced in California about 1875, came into wide use in the U.S. in the 1920s and 1930s and in the U.K. in the 1940s. In 1940 the self-propelled combine was introduced. The combine cuts the standing grain, threshes out the grain from the straw and chaff, cleans the grain, and discharges it into bags or grain reservoirs. Other crops can also be worked by adaptations of the machine, and the reduction in harvesting time and labour is striking; in 1829 harvesting one acre of wheat required 14 man-hours, while the modern combine requires less than 30 minutes. In the early part of the 19th century harvesting a bushel of wheat required three man-hours' work; today it takes five minutes.

For satisfactory results, crops should not be too damp and should be reasonably ripe. If the grain contains over 14 percent moisture, as often happens in the U.K. and other European countries, it must be dried after harvesting under controlled conditions to avoid damage to the gluten. Rice can be combine-harvested, but because of its high moisture content (approaching 20 percent) it must be immediately dried.

Grading. Wheat is an important commodity in international commerce, and many attempts have been made to ensure reliability in grading. In North America excellent grading allows the buyer to ascertain the type and standard of wheat he acquires. Canada has statutory grades for most of its wheats. For wheat moving overseas from the terminal positions, standard export samples are used in grading.

Flour from an inferior grade is not automatically weaker than the top grade.

In the U.S. much of the wheat is officially graded, notably the hard spring and the hard winter wheats. Grading also takes place in Argentina and Australia, although it is not usually as precise as in North America. In many countries there is little commercial grading of wheat, and the buyer relies on his own testing and assessments of wheat arrivals. In Australia, "fair average quality" (FAQ) indicates wheat not obviously unsatisfactory visually but takes no account of the baking strength and the character of the flour yielded. In recent years, however, considerable improvement in grading has taken place, especially when hard strong varieties are sold, as in the case of special high-protein Australian wheat from northwest New South Wales and from Queensland.

In the U.K., there is no official wheat or barley grading as in North America. Barley is bought on appearance or by named variety. This is largely true in much of Europe, although the U.S.S.R. has introduced a grading system for wheat covering red spring, durum, white spring, red winter, and white winter, with special subclasses based on factors such as vitreousness, colour, and weight.

Storage. Cereal storage has been of concern from the earliest times; references are made to it in the Bible. Harvest variations from season to season produced carry-over requiring storage, a problem that grew with increasing populations and developing commerce. The diary of Samuel Pepys (1633–1703) records the destruction of the wheat storehouses in the Great Fire of London (1666) and mentions the existence of these storehouses from the reign of Henry VIII (1491–1547). With modern international cereal trade, huge silos are now found at the main points of export and at the docks of importing countries. In the major exporting countries silos at the country elevators feed the terminal silos; inefficient storage at any of these points makes the cereals highly vulnerable to insects and rodent attack. In certain regions, such as India, losses have amounted to 40 percent of the crop.

Grain respiration

A constant danger also lies in the respiration of the grain. If the moisture content of grain is low (10–12 percent), a rise in temperature resulting from respiration is unlikely; but if the bulk is large and the moisture content high (over 16 percent), the heat may not be dissipated, causing the temperature to rise and further increase the rate of respiration. Consequently, cereal stocks are turned over to ventilate the grain and to keep the temperature low. The problem also occurs in the holds of ships; much litigation has resulted from the arrival of hot and damaged cargoes.

Molds and fungi are other sources of spoilage that have received extensive study in recent years. Cleaning processes remove as much as possible of external molds before storage, but in hot countries, particularly, the problem remains serious. Under primitive conditions the habits and development of communities depended largely on their skill in storing grain.

Heat is also frequently a cause of loss of weight, loss in milling value, and loss in food value through its provision of a favourable environment for such insects as the grain weevil (*Sitophilus granarius*), the rice and maize weevils (*S. oryzae*), the lesser grain borer (*Rhyzopertha dominica*), and the angoumois grain moth (*Sitotroga cerealella*). These are all endosperm borers. Among the grain germ eaters are the rust-red grain beetle (*Cryptolestes ferrugineus*), the saw-toothed grain beetle (*Oryzaephilus surinamensis*), the khapra beetle (*Trogoderma granarium*), and the warehouse moth (*Ephestra elutella*).

Secondary pests include the mill pest known as the Mediterranean flour moth (*Anagasta kuehniella*), the confused flour beetle (*Tribolium confusum*), the rust-red flour beetle (*T. castaneum*), the flat grain beetle (*Cryptolestes pusillus*), the broad-horned flour beetle (*Gnathocerus cornutus*), the cadelle beetle (*Tenebroides mauritanicus*), and a number of miscellaneous insects, including the yellow mealworm (*Tenebrio molitor*), the Australian spider beetle, and the biscuit beetle. Of the mites that invade mills, storehouses and bakeries, the commonest is the flour mite (*Tyroglyphus farinae*).

Good housekeeping, with special attention to sacks and bags and their regular cleaning and disinfecting, contributes to insect control. Frequently used insecticides include inert dusts, Pyrethrum (and synergists), gamma BHC. Other contact insecticides or fumigation may be required. The common fumigator is hydrogen cyanide, but methyl bromide and ethylene oxide have been recommended.

In Canada most of the older elevators hold 20,000 to 30,000 bushels of grain, but some hold as much as 100,000 bushels. A new Canadian elevator system at Port Cartier on the St. Lawrence River is designed for the berthing of supertankers; licensed storage capacity of this installation is 10,500,000 bushels. Unloading of lake vessels can be carried out at 88,000 bushels an hour; the two shipping belts each have maximum capacities of 50,000 bushels an hour.

In the U.S. storage facilities are similar, though the proportion of wheat exported is not as great as in Canada. Many interior terminals in the U.S. handle large amounts of grain received directly from farmers.

Storage methods in Australia have improved considerably in recent years, with increasing attention given to country storing and the modernization of terminal elevators. There has been a change from bag to bulk handling; 95 percent of the grain was bulk handled by the end of the 1960s. Huge terminal elevators operate in Sydney and Newcastle.

In Argentina large terminal elevators deal with a major export trade, but grading is not as reliable as that in North America. Argentine ports receive the wheat grown in their respective areas, which gives buyers some guidance on grade and type. Considerable quantities of maize are also exported from Argentina, with precautions taken to ensure reasonably low moisture content to prevent deterioration of cargoes in shipment.

Tilbury Grain Terminal

Handling of grain received in Europe from overseas is a large operation. The Tilbury Grain Terminal in London is a good example of modern grain handling. Capable of servicing bulk carriers of up to 65,000 tons, at a maximum rate of 2,000 tons an hour, the terminal not only feeds adjacent mills but offers a deepwater outlet for transshipment to both rail and road. Two marine leg (dockside) elevators each have a discharge rate of 1,000 tons an hour. Normal silo capacity of 105,000 tons can be extended to 240,000 tons. The silos are 127 feet high and individual bin capacities range from 60 to 900 tons.

PROCESSING AND UTILIZATION

Milling. Cereal processing is complex. The principal procedure is milling; that is, the grinding of the grain so that it can be easily cooked and rendered into an attractive foodstuff. Cereals are not usually eaten raw, but different kinds of milling (dry and wet) are employed, depending on the cereal itself and on the eating customs of the consumer. Wheat may be crushed with grinding stones or similar devices or by modern automated systems employing steel cylinders, followed by air purification and numerous sievings to separate the endosperm from the outer coverings and the germ.

Maize is often milled by wet processes, but dry milling is also practiced, especially in the developing countries. Maize, with its high germ, or embryo, content is inclined to respire more during storage and, unless precautions are taken, may increase in temperature on incorrect storage. Most other cereals are ground in the dry state.

Some cereal grains are polished, removing most of the bran and germ and leaving the endosperm.

Uses. *Human food.* Cereals are used for both human and animal food and as an industrial raw material. Although milled white flour is largely used for bread production, especially in industrialized countries, the grain may be converted to food in other ways. In India the major part of the grain is not ground into flour in roller mills but is roughly ground in small crushing mills into a meal called *atta.* This meal is cooked into flat cakes known as *chapatis.*

Animal feed. Cereals are important components of animal feeds; the modern farmer either uses balanced rations or attempts to balance the animal diet himself. The cereals mainly used are wheat and such wheat by-products as the outer coverings separated in the preparation of white flour (bran and the more floury middlings), maize, barley, sorghum, rye, and oats. These are supplemented by protein foods and green fodders.

Animal foods require proper balance between the cereals (carbohydrates) and the more proteinous foods, and they must also contain suitable amounts of necessary minerals, vitamins, and other nutrients. The compounded ration for a milking cow generally contains about 50–80 percent of cereals, consisting of wheat by-products, flaked or ground maize, barley, sorghum, wheat, and oats. Requirements for most balanced rations for pigs and poultry are similar. Maize is especially useful in high-energy feeds either as meal or as the flaked and partly gelatinized product; barley is desirable for fattening, and oats help provide a better balanced cereal for livestock.

Without cereals for use in farm animal foods, the available supply of the animal protein required in the human diet would be greatly reduced.

Industrial uses. The relatively minor use of cereals in nonfood products includes the cellulose in the straw of cereals by the paper industry, flour for manufacturing sticking pastes and industrial alcohol, and wheat gluten for core binders in the casting of metal. Rice chaff is often used as fuel in Asia, and oats have been used for the preparation of the chemical furfural.

MARKETING AND TRADE

Cereals account for over 70 percent of the world's harvested area, and they provide over 50 percent of the food energy supply. Approximately four-fifths of the total wheat produced is used where it is grown, but the remaining one-fifth, a considerable quantity, enters into international trade. Conditions vary widely from year to year, and it may occur that a normally exporting country will at times require importation of grain, especially of wheat.

Production cost varies in different countries, and it is sometimes necessary to provide protection for domestic cereal producers, especially to cover the possibility of a large world "carryover" in the exporting countries, causing prices to fall. Permanent protection, or financial assistance, is administered in various ways to growers in both the wheat-importing and wheat-exporting countries. The economics of cereal production is complicated by the occasional vast surpluses produced and exported by the large wheat-growing countries. This surplus wheat is usually in potential competition with the domestic producer, and governments must consider production costs, selling prices, and other factors.

Carryover

In the developed countries cereal production is increasingly concentrated in large farm operations and in specific areas. In the U.K., for example, the Minimum Import Price Scheme was instituted to reduce instability in the domestic cereal market, caused by low priced imports, and to reduce the need for large government subsidy payments to domestic producers to fulfill price guarantees. By mutual consent with the cereal-exporting countries, a minimum price was set, and levies were to be imposed on the imported consignments if their price on entry dropped below the agreed minimum. When the U.K. joined the European Economic Community (EEC) in 1973, complicated trade agreements had to be negotiated.

Prices may be largely guaranteed by a managed market, coupled with import controls, or there may be a relatively free market with guarantees to the grower effected by deficiency payments, a form of subsidy.

EEC price supports

In the EEC, prices are maintained largely by official support, in the form of "intervention buying," when market prices approach or reach a predetermined level. Grain acquired by intervention is subsequently resold at subsidized prices on world markets or wheat may be denatured for animal feeding. The cost of subsidizing the sale of stocks on world markets or of denaturing for sale as animal feedstuff is met by EEC funds contributed by member states.

Although cereal consumption tends to decrease in the developed countries, there is a continuous demand for more grain in the less developed countries, and international trade in cereals will probably continue to grow with the growing world population.

The main wheat-exporting countries are the U.S., Canada, Australia, U.S.S.R., Argentina, and France; the main importing countries are the U.K., China, West Germany, India, Japan, Brazil, and a number of smaller countries. The U.K., for example, may import as much as 4,500,000 tons of wheat a year, as well as large quantities of maize. The volume of exports and imports is influenced by the extent of the carryover, or unsold portion of the previous year's crop, but the international wheat trade often amounts to as much as 50,000,000 metric tons annually. China, although an importer, is the second largest producer of wheat (after the U.S.S.R.), illustrating the needs of an increasing population and improved food standards.

Most of the international trade in cereals follows the same pattern, mainly wheat for human consumption and secondarily maize and similar cereals for animal feedstuffs. Storage facilities and highly developed transportation systems have made wheat and other grains available for export throughout the year, with movement and trade no longer concentrated in immediate postharvest periods.

Soon after World War I, especially around the 1930s, some international coordination in the wheat trade was considered necessary to assure stability and fair treatment for both the exporting countries and the farmers in the importing countries. Although conferences were held, progress was delayed by World War II. In 1945 the United Nations, through its Food and Agriculture Organization (FAO) acted to increase coordination, an action that became the basis of the formation of the World Bank, with capital subscribed by member countries. The International Monetary Fund was established in 1946 with the objective of helping to stabilize exchange rates. The General Agreement on Tariffs and Trade (GATT) in 1948 was followed by the International Wheat Agreement accepted by bulk exporters and importers; similar agreements were made in 1953, 1956, 1959, and 1962. These agreements, specifying guaranteed purchases by importers, balancing lists of guaranteed sales by exporters, and maximum and minimum prices, contributed to stabilization of wheat prices.

III. Products

WHEAT FLOUR

The milling of wheat into flour for the production of bread, cakes, biscuits, and other edible products is a huge industry. Cereal grains are complex, consisting of many distinctive parts. The objective of milling is separation of the floury edible endosperm from the various branny outer coverings and elimination of the germ, or embryo. Because wheats vary in chemical composition, flour composition also varies. Table 8 shows the approximate composition of wheat and white flour.

Table 8: Composition of Wheat and White Flour
(percent)

	wheat	flour
Moisture	9–18	13.0–15.5
Starch	60–68	65–70
Protein	8–15	8–13
Cellulose (fibre)	2.0–2.5	trace–0.2
Fat	1.5–2.0	0.8–1.5
Sugars	2–3	1.5–2.0
Mineral matter	1.5–2.0	0.3–0.6

Although some important changes have occurred in flour milling, basic milling procedure during the past 100 years has employed the gradual reduction process as described below.

Milling. In modern milling considerable attention is given to preliminary screening and cleaning of the wheat or blend of wheats to exclude foreign seed and other impurities. The wheat is dampened and washed if it is too dry for subsequent efficient grinding, or if it is too damp it is gently dried to avoid damaging the physical state of the protein present, mainly in the form of the elastic substance gluten.

Gradual reduction process

The first step in grinding for the gradual reduction process is performed between steel cylinders, with grooved surfaces, working at differential speeds. The wheat is directed between the first "break" or set of rolls and is partially torn open. There is little actual grinding at this stage. The "chop," the resulting product leaving the rolls, is sieved, and three main separations are made: some of the endosperm, reduced to flour called "first break flour"; a fair amount of the coarse nodules of floury substances from the endosperm, called semolina; and relatively large pieces of the grain with much of the endosperm still adhering to the branny outsides. These largish portions of the wheat are fed to the second break roll. The broad objective of this gradual reduction process is the release, by means of the various sets of break rolls, of sufficient inner endosperm of the grain, in the form of semolina, so that the various semolinas from four or five break rolls can be separated by suitable sieving and the branny impurities can be removed by air purifiers and other devices. The cleaned semolinas are reduced to fine flour by grinding between smooth steel rolls, called reduction rolls. The flour produced in the reduction rolls is then sieved out. There are usually four or five more reduction rolls and some "scratch" rolls to scrape the last particles of flour from branny stocks. Since the various sieving and purification processes free more and more endosperm in the form of flour, flour is obtained from a whole series of processing operations. The flour is sieved out after each reduction roll, but no attempt is made to reduce to flour all of the semolina going to a particular reduction roll. Some of the endosperm remains in the form of finer semolina and is again fed to another reduction roll. Each reduction roll tends to reduce more of the semolina to flour and to flatten bran particles and thus facilitate the sieving out of the branny fractions. The sieving plant generally employs machines called plansifters, and the air purifiers also produce a whole series of floury stocks.

Modern flour processing consists of a complicated series of rolls, sieves, and purifiers. Approximately 72 percent of the grain finally enters the flour sack.

The sacked flour may consist of 20 or more streams of flour of various states of purity and freedom from branny specks. By selection of the various flour streams it is possible to make flour of various grades. Improvements in milling techniques, use of newer types of grinding machinery in the milling system, speeding up of rolls, and improved skills have all resulted in flour produced by employing the fundamentals of the gradual reduction process but with simplified and shorter milling systems. Much less roll surface is now required than was needed as recently as the 1940s.

Patent flour

The purest flour, selected from the purest flour streams released in the mill, is often called patent flour. It has very low mineral (or ash) content and is remarkably free from traces of branny specks and other impurities. The bulk of the approximately 72 percent released is suited to most bread-making purposes, but special varieties are needed for some confectionery purposes. These varieties may have to be especially fine for production of specialized cakes, called high-ratio cakes, that are especially light and have good keeping qualities.

In many countries the flour for bread production is submitted to chemical treatments to improve the baking quality.

In modern processing, regrinding of the flour, and subsequent separation into divisions by air treatment, has enabled the processors to manufacture flour of varying protein content from any one wheat or grist of wheats.

Composition and grade. As seen above in Table 8, flour consists of moisture, proteins (mainly in gluten form), a small proportion of fat or lipids, carbohydrates (mainly starch, with a small amount of sugar), a trace of fibre, mineral matter (higher amounts in whole meal), and various vitamins. Composition varies among the types of flour, semolinas, middlings, and bran.

For bread making it is usually advantageous to have the highest protein content possible (depending on the nature of the wheat used), but for most other baked products, such as biscuits (cookies) and cakes, high protein content is rarely required. Gluten can easily be washed out of flour by allowing a dough made of the flour and water to stand in water a short time, followed by careful washing of the dough in a gentle stream of water, removing the starch and leaving the gluten. For good bread-making characteristics, the gluten should be semielastic, not too stiff and unyielding but not soft and flowy, although a flowy quality is required for biscuit (cookie) manufacture.

Gluten

The gluten, always containing a small amount of adhering starch, is essentially hydrated protein. With careful drying it will retain its elasticity when again mixed with water and can be used to increase the protein content of specialized high-protein breads.

Sometimes locally grown wheat, often low in protein, may be the only type available for flour for bread making. This situation exists in parts of France, Australia, and South Africa. The use of modern procedures and adjustment of baking techniques, however, allow production of satisfactory bread. In the United Kingdom, millers prefer a blend of wheat, much of it imported, but modern baking procedures have allowed incorporation of a larger proportion of the weak English wheat than was previously feasible.

Treatment of flour. Use of "improvers," or oxidizing substances, enhances the baking quality of flour, allowing production of better and larger loaves. Relatively small amounts are required, generally a few parts per million. Although such improvers and the bleaching agents used to rectify excessive yellowness in flour are permitted in most countries, the processes are not universal. Improvers include bromates, chlorine dioxide (in gaseous form), and azodicarbonamide.

The most popular bleacher used is benzoyl peroxide (see Table 4).

Grade. The grade of flour is based on freedom from branny particles. Chemical testing methods are employed to check general quality and particularly grade and purity. Since the ash (mineral content) of the pure branny coverings of the wheat grain is much greater than that of the pure endosperm, considerable emphasis is placed upon use of the ash test to determine grade. Bakers will generally pay higher prices for pure flour of low ash content, as the flour is brighter and lighter in colour. Darker flours may have ash content of 0.7 percent to 0.8 percent or higher.

A widely employed modern method for testing flour colour is based on the reflectance of light from the flour in paste form. This method requires less than a minute; the indirect ash test requires approximately one to two hours (see also BAKING AND BAKERY PRODUCTS).

NONWHEAT CEREAL PRODUCTS

Barley. Most of the barley grown in the world is used for animal feed, but a special pure barley is the source of malt for beer production.

Barley can be cultivated on poorer soil and at lower temperatures than wheat, and world production has increased considerably in recent years. In the 1860s slightly over 1,000,000 acres were harvested in the U.S.; by the 1960s acreage had passed 10,000,000. Yield per acre in the 1860s was around 22 to 25 bushels, with total production of 23,000,000 to 30,000,000 bushels; in the late 1960s the yield reached 41 bushels per acre, with total production over 393,000,000 bushels. In the U.K. the 1935–39 barley crop was well under 1,000,000 metric tons; in 1964 it had reached nearly 8,000,000 metric tons, equalling the amount produced in France and in Argentina. World figures for the year 1971 suggest a world crop (excluding China but including the Soviet Union) of about 127,000,000 metric tons.

An important characteristic in barley is "winterhardiness," which involves the ability to modify or withstand many types of stresses and particularly that of frost.

Barley is subject to many of the diseases and pests that affect wheat. Although used principally in animal feed and malt production, barley is also used in the manufacture of vinegar, malt extract, some milk-type beverages, and in certain breakfast foods. Barley is also used in flaked form in some sections of the brewing industry, and pearl barley (skins removed by emery friction) is used in various cooked foods.

The use of barley in animal feed is increasing; it has been a basic ingredient of pig foods for years and is increasingly used for cattle feed. Its use in poultry foods has decreased because of its lower starch equivalent when compared with wheat or maize, thus providing a lower energy ration, unsuitable in modern poultry production. Barley vitamin content is similar to that of wheat.

Maize (corn) and sorghum. These grains are sometimes called "coarse grains." Maize, or corn, a cereal cultivated in most warm areas of the world, has many varieties. The U.S., the principal producer of maize, cultivates two main commercial types, *Zea indurata* (flint corn) and *Zea indentata* (dent corn). The plant grows to a height of up to ten feet or more. The maize kernel is large for a cereal, with a high embryo content, and maize oil extracted from the germ is commercially valuable. The microscopic appearance of the starch is distinctive, and the principal protein in ordinary maize is the prolamin zein, constituting half of the total protein. On hydrolysis zein yields very little tryptophan or lysine, making it low in biological value. The proteins of maize, like those of most cereals other than wheat, do not provide an elastic gluten.

Flint and dent corn

World production of maize averages about 250,000,000 metric tons annually, with the U.S. providing almost 42 percent of the total.

Much of the maize is wet processed to produce corn flour, widely used in cooking. Maize, dry milled as grits or as meal or turned into flaked maize with some of its starch partially gelatinized, is a popular component in compounded animal feed stuffs. In dry milled form it is also the basis of human food throughout large areas of Africa and South America. Its nutritive value is limited by its low lysine content. Much recent research has involved development of a maize with higher lysine content. Mutants have been produced containing much less zein but possessing protein with higher than normal lysine and tryptophan contents, sometimes increased as high as 50 percent. These maizes, called Opaque-2 and Floury-2, possess certain drawbacks. They are generally lower in yield than dent hybrids, are subject to more kernel damage when combine harvested, and may be more difficult to process. Nevertheless, these new hybrid maizes are expected to become widely cultivated, and the principles involved in their production may also be applied to sorghum, wheat, and rice. Maize is popular for use in breakfast foods.

Sorghum, also called milo, is of smaller size than maize but is generally the same type of cereal, with similar appearance. Its numerous types are mainly used for animal feeding. It is grown extensively in the U.S., Pakistan, central India, Africa, and China. Annual world production averages around 44,000,000 metric tons. In the sorghum endosperm, the proteins soluble in hot 60 percent alcohol, called kafirin, constitute the major portion of the protein. Milo germ oil is similar to maize germ oil; its major fatty acids are palmitic, stearic, and particularly oleic, and linoleic. Milo is commercially graded in the U.S. In waxy varieties, the starch is principally in the form of amylopectin, with very little amylose. Such starches possess special viscosity characteristics.

The vitamin content of maize and sorghum generally approximates that of wheat, but these cereals have lower nicotinic acid contents.

Oats. Oats belong to the botanical genus *Avena*, including many types, the principal being *A. sativa*, *A. sterilis*, and *A. strigosa*. Oats are widely grown in most countries but are not suitable for Mediterranean climates. Annual world production is about 53,000,000 metric tons. Oats are often grown on farms as feed for the farm's livestock. They are well balanced chemically, with fairly high fat content, and are particularly suitable for feeding horses and sheep.

Although a large portion of the world's oat production is used for animal feed, oatmeal is a popular human food in many countries. Thin-skinned grains, fairly rich in protein and not too starchy, are selected. Preliminary cleaning is essential for human consumption. The oats are then kilned (roasted). Thin-husked oats yield 60 percent oatmeal; varieties with thick husks yield only 50 percent.

Rapid development of rancidity is a serious problem in oats and oat products. The free fatty acid content must be controlled because formation of these acids tends to produce a soapy taste resulting from the activity of the enzyme lipase. A few minutes of steam treatment normally destroys the lipase activity in the grain.

Rye. Rye, which has been known for some 2,000 years, ranks second to wheat as a bread flour. World production is around 30,000,000 to 35,000,000 metric tons, the main producers being Germany, Poland, the U.S.S.R., and other eastern European countries. The popularity of true rye bread is decreasing, and a similar bread, retaining some of the original characteristics, is now made from a rye and wheat blend. The protein of European rye tends to be low and does not yield gluten in the same way as does wheat. Rye bread, closer grained and heavier than wheat bread, is aerated by the use of a leaven (sour dough) rather than yeast. The grain is susceptible to attack by the parasitic fungus ergot (*Claviceps purpurea*).

Rice. Cultivated rice is known botanically as *Oryza sativa*, comprising some 25 species. The importance of this cereal to certain parts of the world may be seen from the fact that in Sanskrit there exists, besides the usual word for rice, another term signifying "Sustainer of the Human Race."

Rice is the staple food for millions in Southeast Asia, almost equal to wheat in importance among the world's cereal crops. The bulk of the crop is produced in relatively small quantities by large numbers of producers who are bound by customs and tradition but are shrewd, hardworking, and resistant to change. The term paddy is applied to both the land on which the plant is grown and to the unhusked seed. Over 90 percent of the world's rice is grown in Asia, principally in China, India, Pakistan, and Southeast Asia, with small amounts grown in Japan and the Philippines. The conversion of paddy to milled rice varies from about 62 percent to 72 percent. Rice is also cultivated in parts of Europe, North and South America, and in Australia.

As stated, most of the world's rice is produced in relatively small quantities by primitive methods. The bulk of the rice cultivated in Asia is grown under water in flooded fields. Successful production depends upon adequate irrigation, including construction of dams and waterwheels, and on the quality of the soil. Long periods of sunshine are essential. Although the bulk of the rice produced is consumed by the inhabitants of the areas in which it is grown, Burma, Thailand, Laos, Vietnam, and Cambodia are normally exporters.

Table 9 indicates the extent of world rice production.

Table 9: World Area and Production of Paddy

continents and countries	area (000 acres)		production (000 metric tons)			
	average 1948–52	1970	paddy		estimated rice equivalent	
			average 1948–52	1970	average 1948–52	1961–62
Asia (including India, Pakistan, Indonesia, Burma, Japan, Philippines, Thailand, etc.)	171,937	223,863	97,600	180,103	63,096	89,329
Mainland China	66,243		58,188	100,000	37,822	55,250
Europe	766	976	1,320	1,912	871	1,049
U.S.S.R.	336	816	202	1,200	133	158
Africa	6,867	9,516	3,460	7,455	2,194	2,684
North and Central America	2,816	3,631	2,520	5,372	1,703	2,418
South America	5,903	13,920	4,120	10,514	2,678	4,537
World total	254,410	334,899	164,600	306,817	106,990	157,430

Measured against China, the largest producer, India's rice production is about 60 percent, Pakistan's 20, and that of Thailand and Burma together 10–15. Rice yields vary considerably, ranging from 600 to 3,500 pounds per acre. Adequate irrigation, which means inundation of the fields to a depth of several inches during the greater part of the growing season, is a basic requirement.

Dry land paddy production, with harvesting by modern mechanical means, is limited to a few areas, and it produces only a fraction of the total world crop.

As with other cereals, weeds, especially wild red rice, are a constant problem. The commonest pests include plant bugs, stem borers, worms, and grasshoppers. The crop, often harvested with a sickle, is frequently dried in earth or concrete pits. Threshing is often carried out by trampling or with crude implements. Only in a few rice-growing regions are more modern procedures used in harvesting.

Manpower requirements for crops vary enormously, but over 400 man-hours per acre are required in small holdings in Asia, where labour is cheap.

Rice paddy soils

In Asia the paddy is cultivated in three main types of soil, including clays with a firm bottom within a few inches of the surface; silts and soft clays with soft bottoms becoming hard on drying; and peats and "mucks" containing peat, provided the depth of the peat is not excessive. Fields must be drained and dried before harvesting. When combine harvesters or binder threshers are employed, the grain must be dried to about 14 percent moisture so that no deterioration takes place in storage. When reaper binders are used, the crop is "shocked" in certain ways so that grain is protected from rain. Artificial fertilizers have had little success in Asia.

Milling methods used in most of Asia are primitive, but large mills operate in Japan and some other areas. Hulling of the paddy is usually accomplished by pestle and mortar worked by hand, foot, or water power. Improvements are slowly taking place. The yield of milled rice is dependent on the size and shape of the grain, the degree of ripeness, and the extent of exposure to the sun. Some large mills, producing 500 to 1,000 tons of paddy daily, have specialized hulling plants with consequent smaller losses from broken grain. They generally employ modern milling techniques and rely upon controlled drying plants instead of on sun drying.

The weight of the husk is around 20 percent of the weight of the paddy, and there are losses of about 5 percent from dirt, dead grains, and other impurities. Approximately 74 percent of the paddy is available as rice and rice by-products. The yield from milling and subsequent emery polishings includes about 50 percent whole rice, 17 percent broken rice, 10 percent bran, and 3 percent meal. Rice grains have a series of thin coats that can be removed or partially removed in the process of pearling and whitening.

About 60 percent of the Indian rice is parboiled. In the parboiling process the paddy is steeped in hot water, subjected to low-pressure steam heating, then dried and milled as usual. Parboiling makes more rice available from the paddy, and more nutrients (largely vitamin B_1) are transferred from the outer coverings to the endosperm, improving the nutritive value of the finished product. Parboiled rice may contain two to four times as much thiamine (vitamin B_1) and niacin as milled raw rice, and losses in cooking may also be reduced.

Alcoholic drinks, such as sake in Japan and *wang-tsin* in China, are made from rice with the aid of fungi. The hull or husk of paddy, of little value as animal feed because of a high silicon content that is harmful to digestive and respiratory organs, is used mainly as fuel. Table 10 illustrates the composition of husked and milled rice and also indicates losses in milling and polishing.

Nutrition value

The lysine content of rice is low. As rice is not a complete food, and the majority of Asians live largely on rice, it is important that loss of nutrients in processing and cooking should be minimal. Lightly milled rice has about 0.7 milligram of vitamin B_1 per 1,000 nonfatty calories, and the more costly highly milled product has only 0.18 milligram of B_1 on the same basis. For adequate nutrition, vitamin B_1 in the daily diet on this basis should be 0.5–0.6 milligram. The amount of fat-soluble vitamins in rice is negligible.

In some countries rice is enriched by addition of synthetic vitamins. According to U.S. standards for enriched rice, each pound must contain 2–4 milligrams of thiamine (B_1), 1.2–2.4 milligrams of riboflavine, 16–32 milligrams of niacin, and 13–26 milligrams of iron. In enriched rice the loss of water-soluble vitamins in cooking is much reduced because enrichment is applied to about one grain in 200, and these enriched grains are protected by a collodion covering. In ordinary rice, especially when open cookers are employed or excessive water is used, nutrient losses can be high.

Millet. This term is applied to a variety of small seeds originally cultivated by the ancient Egyptians, Greeks, and Romans and still part of the human diet in China, Japan, and India, though in Western countries it is used mainly for birdseed. The genus is termed *Panicum*. The small seed is normally about two millimetres long and nearly two millimetres broad. The term *proso* is one of several alternative names. Japanese barnyard millet is a well-known variety. Millet is not a major cereal; around 21,000,000 short tons are grown annually.

PRODUCTS FROM OTHER STARCH-YIELDING PLANTS

Cassava. Cassava, often called manioc, is not a cereal but a tuber; however, it replaces cereals in certain countries, supplying the carbohydrate content of the diet. The botanical name is *Manihot esculenta*, and the plant is native to South America, especially Brazil. It is now grown in Indonesia, Malaysia, the Philippines, Thailand, and parts of Africa. A valuable source of starch, cassava is familiar in many developed countries in a granular form known as tapioca.

Tapioca

Easily cultivated and curiously immune to most food-crop pests, cassava is a staple crop in several areas of Latin America. The actual tubers may weigh up to 30 pounds. Some tubers may be bitter and contain dangerously large amounts of prussic acid.

Table 11 compares the nutrients in cassava roots with those in potatoes (also a tuber) and rice. Dry milling of cassava is rarely practiced because it yields a product inferior to wet-processed starch in which the tubers are crushed or rasped with water and the starch is permitted to settle. Wet starch is dried to a point where it can be crumbled by pressing it through metal plates (or sieves). This crumbled material is subjected to a rotary motion, sometimes carried out on canvas cloth fastened to cradle-shaped frames or tumbled in revolving steam-jacketed cylinders so that the particles assume a round pellet form and are partially gelatinized as they dry. Sun drying is employed in both homes and small mills.

Table 10: Composition of Rice—Husked and Polished
(percent)

	husked			milled			losses on milling and polishing		
	Platt	Kik and Williams	Rosedale	Platt	Kik and Williams	Rosedale	Platt	Kik and Williams	Rosedale
Fat	2.45	2.0	2.23	0.37	0.3	0.4	84.9	84.6	86.5
Crude fibre	0.88	1.0	0.6	0.16	0.2	0.4	81.8	79.1	33.3
Ash	1.22	1.9	1.19	0.36	0.4	0.9	70.5	78.5	24.1
Protein	8.9	8.9	9.54	8.15	7.6	6.7	6.0	11.4	29.4
Carbohydrates	86.67	77.0	86.34	90.79	79.0	91.4	4.7	6.5	5.5

Table 11: Comparison of Nutrients in Cassava Roots with Those in Other Foods

	moisture (percent)	calories per 100 g	proteins (percent)	fat (percent)	carbohydrates (percent)	ash (percent)	fibre (percent)
Cassava tubers (peeled)	65	127	0.8–1.0	0.2–0.5	32	0.3–0.5	0.8
Tapioca flour	15	307	0.5–0.7	0.2	85	0.3	0.5
Potatoes	77	89	2.1	0.1	20	1.0	0.7
Potato flour	15	331	—	0.3	82	0.3	0.4
Husked rice	15	347	8.0	2.5	73	1.5	0.7–1.0

Many tapioca factories and mills are equipped with modern raspers, special shaking or rotating sieves, and settling tanks of various types; but some fermentation takes place, and small rural mills can often be identified by the smell of butyric acid. In larger mills, centrifuges are replacing the settling tanks.

For its various industrial uses, the tuber usually goes under its alternative name, manioc. It is used in the textile industries, explosives manufacture, leather tanning, and production of glues and dextrins and alcohol.

Fresh cassava leaves are rich in protein, calcium, and vitamins A and C. Their prussic acid level must be reduced to safe limits by boiling; the duration of boiling depends on the variety. Cassava leaves are a popular vegetable in Africa, and the tuber is also used in meal for animal feed.

Soybean. Soybean (*Glycine max*) is not a cereal but a legume; because of its widespread use in the baking industry, it may appropriately be dealt with here. Soybean provides protein of high biological value. Although Asia is its original source, the U.S. is currently the major producer, providing in the early 1970s over 1,000,000,000 bushels out of a total world production of 1,500,000,000 bushels.

U.S. annual production of soybean meal is about 17,600,000 long tons, with oil production of about 3,500,000 long tons. Total U.S. soybean production is over 30,000,000 long tons, and nearly 8,000,000 tons are exported.

The valuable oil of the soybean, widely used in industry, is extracted either by solvents or by expellers. The amino acid distribution of soy protein is more like that found in animal protein than the protein from most vegetable sources; for example, lysine comprises about 5.5 percent. The oil content includes useful amounts of phosphorus; the phosphatide content of soy flour is about 2 percent and is a mixture of lecithin and cephalin. The low carbohydrate content exists mainly as sugars. Table 12 shows the chemical composition of soybeans on a moisture-free basis; the amino acid composition of soy protein is given in Table 13.

Table 12: Chemical Composition of Soybeans on a Moisture-Free Basis
(percent)

component	based on 10 varieties in 5 crop years		
	lowest	highest	average
Ash	3.67	5.90	4.99
Oil crude	14.95	22.90	19.63
Crude fibre	4.34	7.60	5.52
Crude protein (N × 6.25)	36.62	53.19	42.78
Sugar (total as sucrose)	2.70	11.97	7.97
Phosphorus	0.42	0.82	0.66
Potassium	1.29	2.17	1.67
Calcium	0.16	0.47	0.275

Although soybeans are a good source of thiamine, much of this may be lost in processing. Average vitamin contents of soybean (as micrograms per gram) are as follows: thiamine 12; riboflavin 3.5; nicotinic acid 23; pyridoxine 8; pantothenic acid 15; and biotin 0.7.

The bulk of the soybean produced in the U.S. is used for animal feed; the Asian crop goes principally for human diet.

Soybean milk

Soybean milk is produced and used in the fresh state in China and as a condensed milk in Japan. In these preparations, certain anti-nutritive factors (antitrypsin and soyin) are largely removed. In the Western world most soy products are treated chemically or by heat to remove these anti-nutritive factors along with the unpopular beany taste. Such processing affects the enzymic activity.

Soybean is milled to produce soy flour. The flour is often used in a proportion of less than 1 percent in bakery operations. It stiffens doughs and helps to maintain crumb softness. Unprocessed soy flour, because of its lipoxidase enzyme system, is employed with high-speed mixing to bleach the flour in a dough.

In addition to their use in bread, soy products are used in confectionery, biscuits, macaroni, infant and invalid foods, ice cream, chocolate, sausages, sauces, lemon curd, mayonnaise, meat and fish pastes, certain diabetic foods, and in such nonfood products as paint, paper, textiles, and plastics.

A recent development is the isolation of the soybean proteins for use as emulsifiers and binders in meat products and substitutes. Enzyme-modified proteins provide useful egg-albumen supplement for whipped products.

Table 13: Amino Acid Composition of Soy Protein
(calculated to 16 percent nitrogen)

	percent
Arginine	5.8
Histidine	2.3
Lysine	5.4
Tyrosine	4.1
Tryptophan	1.2
Phenylalanine	5.7
Cystine	0.9
Methionine	2.0
Threonine	4.0
Leucine	6.6
Isoleucine	4.7
Valine	4.2
Glutamic acid	21.0
Aspartic acid	8.8

Buckwheat. Botanically, buckwheat is not a cereal but the fruit of *Fagopyrum esculentum*. Its name is probably derived from its resemblance to beechnut. Believed to have originated in China, the plant grows to a height of two to three feet or more and thrives best in cool, moist climates, although it does not easily tolerate frost. It can be grown on a wide range of soils, and a crop can be obtained within 10–12 weeks of sowing. The seed is dark brown in colour and often triangular in shape. It contains about 60 percent carbohydrate, 10 percent protein, and 15 percent fibre. A white flour can be obtained from the seeds (buckwheat cakes and pancakes are popular in certain areas), and buckwheat meal is also used in animal feed. The whole seed may be fed to poultry and game birds. There is some medical interest in buckwheat as a source of rutin, possibly effective in treatment of increased capillary fragility associated with hypertension (high blood pressure) in man.

OTHER CEREAL AND STARCH PRODUCTS

Flour by-products. Flour by-products, derived from the outer coverings of the wheat grain separated in extraction of the flour from the grain, consist of bran (coarse or fine according to the state of subdivision and how much adhering endosperm is attached) and the finer, more floury outer coverings called "middlings." The composition of such products may vary considerably, depending on the wheats used and the amount of endosperm present. Table 14 gives the general composition

Table 14: Approximate Analyses of Wheat By-Products (Offal) on Dry Basis
(percent)

	protein	fat	carbo-hydrates	fibre	ash
Bran	15.5	4.5	61.5	12.25	6.25
Pollards	16.6	5.5	64.0	8.9	5.0
Coarse middlings	19.0	5.8	65.0	6.0	4.2
Fine middlings	18.0	3.9	73.1	2.2	2.8

of these by-products, mainly used in livestock feed.

Cereals in bakery products. The water-absorption power of the flour employed is a critical factor affecting bread yield. Strong proteinous flours absorb more water than weak flours in producing a dough of correct consistency. The percentage of "damaged" starch in the flour is also an important factor. In making a dough of correct consistency, the amount of water that can be used depends on that taken up by the flour constituents. Approximately one gram of protein will absorb one gram of water, but one gram of ordinary undamaged starch will absorb only about 0.4 gram of water. All flour contains some of its starch in a "damaged" form (resulting from the mechanical action during milling), and the percentage may vary from 5 to 12 percent of the flour. One gram of damaged starch will take up two grams of water, which makes damaged starch an asset in commercial bread-making operations. There is, of course, an upper limit to the useful amount of damaged starch, and if there is much sprouted grain (rich in α-amylase) in the grist too much damaged starch is particularly dangerous.

Role of damaged starch

Increasing attention is being given to the regulation and control of this flour characteristic.

Modern baking operations require knowledge of the various enzymes in the flour (such as the α- and β-amylase) that affect the starch portion and of other enzymes producing physical change in the protein (gluten) portion of the dough. The amount of α-amylase is an important factor acting on the damaged starch and producing more sugar for the yeast to ferment toward the end of the fermentation stage, after the yeast has used the small amount of sugar originally in the flour. Additional sugar is sometimes added at the dough-making stage to ensure an ample supply throughout the fermentation process. Some baking operations employ malts (containing α- and β-amylase and certain sugars). Much depends on the nature and soundness of the wheats from which the flour has been made. Fungal enzymes, products rich in α-amylase produced by growing certain mold strains, are useful in many circumstances. Such enzymes possess a lower "thermal-destruction point" than cereal α-amylase and are destroyed early in the baking process before the mass of starch is gelatinized and rendered attackable. Marked changes in bread making have taken place since it has ceased to be necessary to ferment for several hours to achieve the essential ripeness in the dough before baking.

In the manufacture of biscuits (cookies), many different types of flour are used. Most biscuits require soft, weak flours (see also BAKING AND BAKERY PRODUCTS).

Commercial starches. Starch has been used for many centuries. An Egyptian papyrus paper dating from 3500 BC was apparently treated with a starch adhesive. The major starch sources are tubers, such as potatoes and cassava, and cereals. Current starch production is considerable. Among the major producing areas, the European countries use both domestic wheat and potatoes and imported maize as the raw material; the U.S. uses maize and such similar cereals as sorghum; and in South America the cassava plant is the major raw material.

Separated from tubers and cereals, starch is used for conversion into various sugars, and half of the world's separated starch is processed into glucose. Starch is also processed for use in adhesives manufacture. In the food industry starch is used as a thickener in the preparation of cornstarch puddings, custards, sauces, cream soups, and gravies. Starch from tubers and cereals provides the carbohydrate of the human diet.

Large quantities of starch and its derivatives are used in the paper and textile industries.

Potato farina

In Germany, The Netherlands, Poland, and a number of other countries, the extraction of the starch from potatoes (sometimes called farina) is a major industry. Some factories produce over 300 tons daily. Processing involves continuous and automatic cleaning of the potatoes, thorough disintegration in raspers or hammer mills, and separation of the fibres from the pulp by centrifugal (rotary) sieves. The resulting starch "milk" contains starch in suspension and soluble potato solids in solution. The starch is separated and washed free from the solubles, the water is removed by centrifugal action, and the damp starch is dried. The flash type of dryer, using hot air, is widely employed for starches derived from both tubers and cereals. Sulfurous acid is generally introduced into the process to prevent the development of various micro-organisms.

Potato flour is also produced in Germany and other countries, slices of cleaned potatoes being dried, ground, and sieved.

Starch granules from various plants as seen under the microscope differ widely in type, size, and shape. Some exhibit a dark spot, or hilum, around which the granule has grown. The hilum is often useful in identifying a starch. The character of the granules influences the ease with which the particular starch can be separated. Maize has a granule of fairly regular shape, simplifying the extraction of the starch. Wheat and barley both have a number of large roundish granules, comprising the bulk of the starch, which can be separated easily in centrifuges, but they also have a proportion of very small granules that cannot easily be collected by such means and can cause serious effluent problems.

In Germany a "potato sago" is produced. The starch cake obtained from the potatoes is crumbled to produce reasonably uniform-sized particles that are rounded by tumbling or similar operations, heated to gelatinize the outside layers of the starch, and then dried.

Potatoes were employed in baking to make the barm, or leaven, before compressed distiller's yeast was available, and they have also been used to supplement limited supplies of wheat flour. The potatoes are cleaned, boiled until soft but not mushy, and mixed, in a proportion of 2 to 3 percent, in the dough.

Modern, ready-to-use, dried and powdered mashed potatoes are popular consumer products.

Cassava and tapioca starches are sometimes partially gelatinized by vacuum drying. Protein impurities are low in commercial starches of potato, sago, and tapioca but as high as 0.2 percent in wheat starch and higher in corn flour.

Maize is wet milled to produce corn flour, or cornstarch, desirable for cooking because it forms a paste that sets with a "short" texture and separates from molds more cleanly than do the gels produced by such starches as potato, tapioca, and arrowroot, which are "long," or elastic. In wet milling, the grains are first dry-cleaned so that other cereals and some of the impurities are removed, then steeped in warm water containing sulfur dioxide. This process softens the grains, and the outer skin and the germ are rendered removable. The maize is coarsely ground in "degerminating mills," and the slurry is further wet-ground and sieved to remove all the germ and complete the separation of the starch.

The germ, rich in oil, is eventually dried, and the oil is expelled by pressure, providing an excellent edible oil for culinary use, often replacing olive oil. Corn oil is used for salad oil, margarine, and shortening and for such nonfood items as soap.

The pure starch, held in suspension, was formerly collected by gravity as it flowed down tables, but in modern practice the starch suspension is thickened by the elimination of water by means of machines, and the starch is finally separated by the use of centrifuges. The starch is readily dried without gelatinization taking place.

Corn flour

There is a regular demand for a good grade of corn flour, or cornstarch. Roller-milled maize is still produced for human consumption in Africa and elsewhere.

In the U.S. some maize grits are used by brewers, but the bulk of the maize grown is used for animal feed as meal, grits, or in partially gelatinized flake form.

Starch forms. The bulk of the starch produced is in an air-dry state as a microgranular powder, but there are other important varieties, including pearl, crystal, and pregelatinized forms.

The pearl form of starch is illustrated by sago, starch derived from the pith of several kinds of palm trees in the West Indies. Sago palms include *Sagus rumphii* and *S. farinifera*, but *S. laevas* produces most of the export material. The pith obtained from the trees yields a milky starch suspension. After purification, the starch settles out. The moist starch is semidried and converted into pearl sago. The sieved pearls are roasted in shallow metal pans, which partially gelatinizes and dries them.

Rice starch, largely used in laundry work, is normally prepared from broken white rice. The broken grains are steeped for several hours in a caustic-soda solution, and the alkali is finally washed away with water. The softened grains are ground with more caustic-soda solution, and the resulting mass is settled or submitted to centrifugation in a drum. The starch layer is agitated with water (often with 0.25 percent formaldehyde solution added), and the resulting starch liquor is dewatered, washed on a continuous rotary vacuum filter, resuspended in water, and finally dewatered in a perforated basket centrifuge to around 35 percent moisture. In modern processing it is usual to roll out a thick layer of moist starch, which is then slowly dried and falls to pieces as crystals.

Industrial starches

When a starch suspension in water is passed over hot rollers, the starch is gelatinized and dried simultaneously. This pregelatinized starch, unlike raw starch, swells in cold water but does not reconstitute to as thick a paste as starch boiled in water. The pregelatinized starch, ground to a powder, has a number of important industrial applications. Added to pulp in paper production it helps bind the fibres together; added to sand in the foundry it helps form molds; it is used in making wallpaper paste, to help cool drills, and for many other purposes. Industrial starches are derived from wheat in Australia, the U.K., and Germany; from potatoes in Germany; and from maize in the U.S. and southern Europe.

The various cereals and tubers produce starches that vary in size, shape, and appearance and possess varying characteristics. Cornstarch is valuable in cooking, rice starch in laundering, and arrowroot tuber starch is popular in toiletries. Wheat starch, a by-product of gluten production, can be heated and moistened to form a paste used chiefly for industrial purposes.

Starch composition. Starch consists of two components: amylose and amylopectin. The relative proportion of these two components varies, and they react differently to enzymatic attack. The enzyme β-amylase (maltogenic) attacks the straight chain amylose but is unable to attack most of the branch chain amylopectin. If only β-amylase is present, maltose is produced, together with a residue of the amylopectin portion, or dextrin of high molecular weight. When α-amylase (dextrinogenic) attacks starch, gummy dextrins of low molecular weight are formed and can produce a sticky crumb in bread.

In bread making there is only limited time for such enzymic attacks on the starch, and only the "attackable" or "damaged" granules can produce the fermentable sugar for the dough. The β-amylase has little effect on viscosity. The viscosity of gelatinized starch is markedly reduced by α-amylase, however, and is therefore valuable in syrup and dextrose manufacture.

The gelatinization of starch that occurs in hot water is an important characteristic, and the viscous pastes formed are influenced by the treatment the starch has received in its preliminary separation from the cereal or tuber. Chemicals affect degree and speed of gelatinization and the nature and viscosity of the pastes formed.

In certain cereals, particularly in special maizes, the starch consists almost entirely of amylopectin, and the term waxy is applied to such cereals. They are useful for their unusual physical properties and viscosities. They possess outstanding paste clarity, high water-binding capacity, and resistance to gel formation and retrogradation; they are helpful in production of salad dressings, sauces, and pie fillings and in some canned goods; they are useful because of resistance to irreversible gel formation and syneresis on freezing and especially for many products stored in the frozen state.

Processing. The carbohydrate starch is rarely consumed in the raw state and in cooking is always gelatinized to some degree. For industrial purposes, starches are submitted to many processes. Starch is often partially or almost wholly gelatinized or may be converted by heat or chemical treatment into dextrins for use in adhesive pastes, with the starch assuming a completely new form. Other treatments increase solubility, and hydrolysis with acids produces completely new products, including a variety of sugars.

Starch may be converted into sugars by the use of acids, and the sugars may be marketed as starch syrup, glucose syrup, or corn syrup; as glucose; and as commercial dextrose. Such sugars are useful in confectionery production.

Starch hydroxyl groups can take up metal ions yielding starchates, highly reactive with organic acids, anhydrides, chlorides, epoxides, etc., that produce commercially valuable products. Ethylene and propylene oxides are used to produce ethoxy or propoxy derivatives possessing special characteristics that give clear gels, solutions, or films widely used in the paper and textile industries. With chloracetic acid, or similar acids, completely soluble methyl or other carboxy acids having high viscosity and clarity, useful in textile printing, are formed.

The viscosities of these derivatives can be controlled by oxidizing the original starch before making the derivative or by treatment with various chemical agents that cross-link adjacent starch chains via the hydroxyl groups in the glucose units. Only a low degree of substitution, oxidation, or hydrolysis is usually required to exert a marked change in the physical properties of starches.

Other uses of starch include production of ethyl alcohol by fermentation procedures and production of acetone and other products. Indeed, it is impossible to record all the hundreds of uses of starch in the science-based industries.

Alimentary pastes. Alimentary pastes include such products as macaroni, spaghetti, vermicelli, and noodles. Such products are often called pastas. Italy is regarded as the place of origin of macaroni products, and annual consumption in that country is as high as 30–35 kilograms per person. Annual consumption is about 6.3 kilograms in France, 3.7 in the U.S., and only 0.4 kilogram in the U.K. Pasta is manufactured in a wide variety of sizes and shapes, the commonest being long, narrow strands. The most slender type of strand, vermicelli, sometimes called *capelli d'angeli* ("angel's hair") in Italy, has a diameter ranging from 0.5 to 0.8 millimetre and is normally cut into lengths of about 250 millimetre and twisted into curls. Short-cut vermicelli (15–40 millimetres) is easy to manufacture and to dry. Spaghetti has a diameter of about 1.5–2.5 millimetres and is usually straight. Noodles are solid ribbons, about 0.8 millimetre thick, and in a variety of widths. Macaroni is the commonest type of alimentary paste; it is hollow and has a greater thickness than the others. It can be shaped in a variety of forms, such as long, short, large, small tubes, etc.

Annual consumption of pastas

Macaroni is now commercially produced in large factories in Italy, North and South America, and other regions. Drying of the extruded paste is an important process, previously accomplished in Italy by sun drying.

Semolina, not flour, is the form of cereal used, and various plain macaroni products are made by combining the correct form of semolina, from durum wheat, with water. Richer alimentary pastes are made with the addition of eggs in fresh, dried, or frozen form, and egg noodles are popular. In low-income families, alimentary pastes often provide the bulk of the calories in the diet. Macaroni products supply about 3,500 calories per kilogram and, although not themselves good sources of vitamins, are commonly cooked and consumed with butter, oil, cheese, and other items containing the needed vitamins.

The use of hard durum semolina contributes to good quality in macaroni and other alimentary-paste products. The special mills involved use many breaks, and only a few reduction rolls, to produce as much clean semolina as possible. An efficient mill employing appropriate purifiers can produce as much as 65 percent semolina (together with a little flour). Before continuous processes for pasta production were introduced, a coarse semolina was valued. In modern production, semolina is dusted and freed from flour, and regularity in size is considered important for water absorption. Very fine semolina is not popular, and the preferred semolina usually has a moisture content of around 13 percent with less than 0.8 percent ash. Freedom from bran is desired to avoid the appearance of specks. The gluten in the semolina should be reasonably strong but not as elastic as that required for bread making.

In the early factories, batch mixing of semolina and water was followed by extrusion of the resulting paste through presses containing dies. In modern practice, the bulk of alimentary pastes is made by continuous processes.

The basic procedure for most macaroni products consists of adding water to a semolina made from suitable wheat to produce, in a short time, a plastic homogeneous mass of about 30 percent moisture. This mixture is extruded through special dies, under pressure, producing the desired size and shape, and is then dried. There are many types of continuous paste processes adapted to the specific types of paste wanted and to the manufacturer's requirements. In the earlier days of the cottage industry, long-cut products such as spaghetti were spread evenly by hand on wooden dowels about an inch thick and over 50 inches long, and the filled sticks were then placed on racks for sun drying. "Short" cut products were often scattered on wire mesh trays.

Automatic processing

In modern automatic processing the objective is to dry the extruded product, containing 31 percent moisture, to a hard product of about 12 percent moisture, decreasing the possibility of the goods being affected by the growth of molds and yeast. If moisture is removed too rapidly, the dried product may tend to "check" or split. If moisture is removed too slowly, souring or mold growth may occur. Proper drying is therefore ensured by adjusting air circulation, temperature, and humidity. Drying procedures differ for long and short macaroni. In the continuous process, after a first hour in which a crust is formed to protect against mold infection, slow drying is practiced.

Cooking tests are used to ensure that the final product is satisfactory. Considerable research has been carried out to control factors tending to destroy the desirable yellow colour. Destruction of the colouring matter, a xanthophyll, can occur in mixing due to excessive lipoxidase. Certain types of durum wheat may possess a high degree of lipoxidase activity, and it is difficult to control or check this action. The addition of ascorbic acid has been suggested as a means to decrease the destruction of the semolina pigments in processing.

In the U.S., alimentary-paste goods, described as noodles, egg spaghetti, or egg macaroni, must contain 5.5 percent of the solids of egg in the final product. The eggs can be used in the form of frozen yolks, dried yolks, frozen whole eggs, dried whole eggs, or fresh whole eggs or yolks. Spray dried egg yolks of good quality are now available.

Alimentary pastes are also used in the production of soup, puddings and sweets, and a variety of other food products.

Malt. Beer is produced in many countries, and barley is the main cereal employed. Until recently brewers have been unable to utilize the carbohydrate of barley directly. Instead, malt was produced by allowing the grains to sprout, changing the starches and proteins into more soluble forms of sugars and amino acids.

Modern techniques offer the possibility of brewing beer direct from barley, employing industrial enzymes. Such methods are not yet established commercial practice, and their success will depend primarily on the acceptability of the resulting flavour and character to both the brewing industry and the public. Partial substitution of wheat flour for malted barley has also been introduced.

In countries with damp climates, the barley used in beer making is dried in kilns or rotating drums, but in modern practice these devices are being replaced by newer types of driers. In the vertical type, the grain falls through heated air, and in the horizontal type air is blown through a moving band of barley. Safe storage of barley in bulk requires drying to 14 percent, and preferably 12 percent, moisture. The dried barley is then screened to remove awns (slender bristles), half corns, very thin corns, and weeds. The grain is usually stored for at least four weeks to overcome its natural dormancy and render it suitable for uniform germination.

The basis of the malting process is modification of the grain (morphological and histological changes) and degradation of the proteins and starch in the barley into more soluble substances by formation and liberation of certain change-producing enzymes.

The basic process is simple, but problems arise from the fact that the maltster produces various kinds of malt, each uniform and consistent in character, from a highly variable natural raw material. Some barleys germinate unevenly because of sensitivity to excess water, and this condition can be overcome by allowing the grain to take up about 30 percent moisture, arranging for growth to commence in the absence of free water and then completing the steeping process to the 45 percent or so of moisture required for malting. Certain additives are sometimes used in malting to reduce production costs and allow better control of the quality of the finished product. Minute quantities of gibberellic acid can stimulate the barley enzymes, shortening germination time. Potassium bromate may be used to restrict respiration and rootlet formation and to increase the malt yield. All malting techniques require control of temperature, atmospheric humidity, and grain moisture during the germination phase of the process.

Malt extract

Considerable attention is given to evaluation of the finished malt for brewing purposes, but techniques vary in the different countries. The most important analytical measurement is that of "extract," which gives a measure of the brewing value of a malt since it controls the quantity of beer of a given strength that can be produced from a standard weight of malt. Malt colour must be measured accurately since it strongly influences the colour of beer. The nitrogen or protein content is also considered since this factor is associated with beer hazes.

The quality of malt is largely dependent on the quality of barley employed. Analytical studies are often made on the barley to determine protein content, germination capacity, and potential extract. Great care is exercised in the selection of barley for malting, certain barley varieties being considered more suitable for malting than others.

In major brewing countries, beer production requires hundreds of thousands of tons of ordinary malt annually. In addition, a whole series of special malts are also used in brewing. There is a demand for coloured malts produced by roasting, imparting special colours and flavours to beer. Enzymic malt is made by subjecting germinating barley to an anaerobic phase (absence of oxygen) just prior to kilning (drying), and this malt is used to adjust acidity.

Malt is used in substantial quantities in the distilled liquor (*q.v.*) industry, with some 150,000 tons of barley used annually for this purpose in Scotland. The type of malt required is somewhat different from that used by the brewer, as the distiller wants a malt in which as much as possible of the starch has been converted into simple sugars, providing a maximum amount of fermentation material.

Apart from beer and liquor production, malt is used in some breakfast cereals and for the production of vinegar and malt extract, the latter useful because of its enzymic properties. Malted milk beverages are made by adding milk preparations to malt extract powder. Malt extract is used in desizing textiles, in making dextrin adhesives, in the baking industry, and in laundries for the removal of starch from woven fabrics, although industrial enzymes are replacing malt in some of these processes. Malt extracts normally have to meet pharmacopaeia specifications (see also BREWING).

Breakfast cereals and snack foods. The modern packaged breakfast-food industry owes its beginnings to an American religious sect, the Seventh-day Adventists, who wished to avoid consumption of animal foods. In the 1860s they organized the Western Health Reform Institute in Battle Creek, Michigan, later renamed the Battle Creek Sanitarium. James Jackson of Dansville, New York, produced a cereal food by baking wholemeal dough in thin sheets, breaking and regrinding into small chunks, rebaking and regrinding. J.H. Kellogg of Battle Creek made biscuits about one-half inch thick from a dough mixture of wheatmeal, oatmeal, and corn meal. The dough was baked until fairly dry and turning brown, and the product was ground and packed. A patient at the sanitarium, C.W. Post, saw the possibilities in such a product entirely apart from the original conception of healthfulness and started a business. Kellogg's brother, W.H. Kellogg, did likewise, and the breakfast-food industry was launched, soon achieving mass sales of cereal products in flake, granule, shred, and puffed forms, with flavour obtained by roasting and the addition of sugar.

Kellogg and Post

Some breakfast cereals require cooking; others are packaged ready-to-eat. Roasted and rolled oatmeal, eaten as porridge, requires brief boiling. Cooking time of these processed cereals has been greatly reduced, and various "instant" forms are available.

Although cooked oatmeal porridge was formerly a standard breakfast food, the ready-to-eat cereals of various types are now the favourite breakfast-cereal foods.

The middlings produced in flour milling, essentially small pieces of endosperm free from bran and germ, are sold as farina and often consumed as a breakfast food in the U.S. Farina is usually enriched with vitamins and minerals and may be flavoured. To reduce cooking time, 0.25 percent disodium phosphate may be added; some products require only one minute of boiling before serving.

Ready-to-eat-cereals. These cereals are available in a variety of forms and are normally consumed with milk and sometimes sugar. Flaked and toasted varieties are the most popular. During processing the starch is gelatinized, halting enzymic reactions and thus ensuring product stability and good shelf life. The sugar content is dextrinized and caramelized by a roasting process. Roasting also ensures attractive crispness resulting from moisture reduction.

Wheat and rice flakes are manufactured, but most flaked breakfast foods are made from maize (corn), usually of the yellow type, broken down into grits and cooked under pressure with flavouring syrup consisting of sugar, nondiastatic malt, and other ingredients. Cooking is often accomplished in slowly rotating retorts at around 18 pounds steam pressure.

After leaving the cooker, the lumps (containing about 33 percent water) are broken down by revolving reels and sent to driers. These are usually large tubes extending vertically, through several stories, with the wet product entering the top and encountering a current of hot air (150° F). Other types of driers consist of horizontal rotating cylinders with steam-heated pipes running horizontally. The drying process reduces moisture to about 20 percent, and the product is transferred to tempering bins for up to 24 hours, to even moisture distribution.

The product is next flaked by passing it between large steel cylinders (180–200 revolutions per minute), with the rolls cooled by internal water circulation. The cooked and rather soft flakes then proceed to rotating toasting ovens (normally gas fired), where the flakes tumble through perforated drums. This treatment requires two to three minutes at 550° F (228° C). The product is dehydrated, toasted, and slightly blistered. After toasting, it is cooled by circulating air, and at this stage enrichment by sprays may be carried out.

The manufacture of wheat flakes is similar to that of corn flakes. Special machinery separates the individual grains so that they can be flaked and finally toasted.

Shredded wheat, differing from other breakfast foods, is made from whole grains with the germ and bran retained and no flavour added. In its final form it is in tablets composed of shreds of cooked and toasted wheat. The wheat is cleaned and then boiled in water, often at atmospheric pressure. The grains reach a moisture content of 55 to 60 percent and require preliminary drying to around 50 percent. They are then placed in bins to condition them. The shredding process consists of passing the cooked and partially dried wheat to the shredding rolls (six to eight inches in diameter and as wide as the finished tablet). On one pair of the rolls is a series of about 20 shallow corrugations running around the periphery; the surface of the other roll is smooth. The soft wheat is forced into the rolls under pressure and is cut into long shreds falling to a conveyor in such a way as to obtain superimposed shreds. These layers are cut into tablets by knives, and the tablets are transferred to baking pans. The pans pass to a revolving oven, with a baking temperature of approximately 500° F. After 10–15 minutes, the outside of the product is dry and toasted, while the interior is still damp. The tablet is transferred either to another hot air oven or to a different section of the same oven, where it is dried at 250° F for an additional 30 minutes and then cooled and packed.

Granular types are made by very different processes from the others. The first step is production of a stiff dough from wheat, malted barley flour, salt, dry yeast, and water. After mixing, fermentation proceeds for about five hours. The dough is then formed into large loaves and transferred directly to the oven. Baking requires about two hours at 400° F (205° C). The baked loaves are fragmented and the product is thoroughly dried. Grinding by corrugated rolls follows, and the product is sieved to standard size. Very fine pieces are added to subsequent dough batches.

Early in the 20th century, an American patent was taken out for the preparation of puffed wheat and rice. Puffed oats and maize are now also produced. The principle of the puffing process is heating the cereal, and sometimes other vegetable products, in a pressure chamber to a pressure of 100 to 200 pounds per square inch, then instantaneously releasing this pressure by suddenly opening the chamber, or puffing gun. Expansion of the water vapour occurs when the pressure is suddenly released, blowing up the grains or cereal pellets to several times their original size (8-fold to 16-fold for wheat, 6-fold to 8-fold for rice). The final product is toasted to a moisture content of about 3 percent to achieve desired crispness. In processing wheat, a preliminary step may be applied to free the grain from much of its bran coatings.

The puffing gun

Rice is usually parboiled, pearled, and cooked with sugar syrup, dried to about 25 to 30 percent moisture in rotating louvre driers, binned, and toasted and puffed. In puffing of mixed cereal products it is necessary to start with a stiff dough containing sugar, salt, and sometimes oil, and this mixture is then cooked. The dough is pelleted by extrusion through dies and dried to attain a suitable condition for the final puffing process.

Enrichment of breakfast cereals with minerals, and especially with vitamins, is now common practice. In many of the manufacturing processes employed in breakfast-food production, considerable vitamin destruction occurs. The various heat treatments involved may destroy 90 percent of the original B_1 content of the cereal, especially in flaked and puffed products. On the other hand, a proportion of the somewhat harmful phytic acid in cereals, interfering with absorption by the body of calcium, is also destroyed; and enrichment of the products with vitamin B_1, and sometimes other components of the Vitamin B complex, is not difficult to perform after the various cooking operations have been completed.

Ready-to-eat snack foods. In addition to potato crisps, or chips, pretzels, and popcorn, new types have recently been developed. Cereals are usually the base, and special attention is given to texture and flavour. Baked snacks can usually be produced in bakeries using special extrusion equipment. Crackers are produced especially for hors d'oeuvres, and potato crisps are flavoured with cheese, onions, and other ingredients. Partially puffed varieties are popular, but great care is required to ensure crispness and flavour; and the final process usually involves drying, frying, puffing, or toasting. Oil and seasoned oils are often ingredients, and packaging is an important factor in marketing successful snacks.

Bakery products can be cooked and frozen for fast reconstitution and have good shelf life. A variety of starch products is produced using milo starch. Attention has been given to the ratios of amylose and amylopectin; the waxy-type (amylopectin) starches promote puffing and produce attractive light, but fragile, products.

There is also some demand for especially prepared breadcrumbs.

Sweeteners. Various types of sweeteners are made directly from starch. Glucose products made by starch conversion differ in composition and in sweetness according to whether conversion is effected by acid or by enzymes. Enzyme-produced glucose is higher in dextrose and maltose content than acid-produced glucose, which normally is higher in dextrin. Sucrose is a more powerful sweetening agent than dextrose, but glucose syrup made by enzymic treatment usually has twice the sweetening power of that produced by acid action.

In the production of starch separated by the wet milling of maize, one stream is normally used to produce starch, and the other stream is converted into corn syrup by heating the starch slurry in pressure tanks with acid or enzymes and following with refining processes. If the process of hydrolyzing starch is completed, the resulting product is glucose. Often the treatment is not carried to completion, and a series of dextrins and reversion products is produced. If full conversion is required, the treatment usually employs acids to liquefy, followed by saccharifying enzymes to complete the change to dextrose. Modern syrups and crystalline dextrose are made by continuous processes. The degree of conversion of the starch into the sugar dextrose is expressed as D.E. (dextrose equivalents), and confectionery syrups have a D.E. of around 36 to 55, while the fuller conversion of products with D.E. of 96 to 99 can be made for the production of almost pure glucose or dextrose, used in many food products (see also SUGAR PRODUCTION).

Sweeteners in the form of syrups are largely used in cake and confectionery products and also, especially in the U.S., in bread manufacture. U.S. bread is distinctly sweeter than normal European bread because of the fats and sweeteners used, and the loaves are larger per unit of weight than in the U.K. and most European countries.

In the U.S. the baking industry uses more than one-half of the dextrose and 10 percent of the corn syrup produced. Cookies (biscuits) and breakfast foods are also large users of sweeteners. The U.S. baking industry currently uses some 1,600,000 tons of sweeteners, of which 13 percent is dextrose and 6 percent corn syrup. Confectioners in Europe also used syrups of many types but not as widely as in the U.S.

BIBLIOGRAPHY. The composition, technology, and uses of the various cereals are treated in: D.W. KENT-JONES and A.J. AMOS, *Modern Cereal Chemistry*, 6th ed. (1967), a comprehensive work covering the chemistry of cereals and of breakfast foods and compounded animal feeding stuffs, with chapters on nutrition and analysis of cereals; N.L. KENT, *Technology of Cereals, with Special Reference to Wheat* (1966), a short, concise survey of the technology of cereals including useful world crop statistics, chemical composition, milling, and baking; S. MATZ (ed.), *The Chemistry and Technology of Cereals as Food and Feed* (1959), a discussion of the uses of cereals in foodstuffs and the technology involved; various articles of interest appear in the periodical *Cereal Chemistry* (bimonthly).

Works treating specific cereals include: R.F. PETERSON, *Wheat: Botany, Cultivation, and Utilization* (1965), with chapters on morphology, physiology, cytology and genetics, origin and history, varieties, distribution, diseases, husbandry, storage, chemical composition of various wheat types, and surveys on utilization and trade; I. HLYNKA (ed.), *Wheat Chemistry and Technology* (1964), chapters by various experts on production and utilization of wheat, quality criteria, microscopic structures, principles of milling, chemical components of wheat and flour, dough proteins, end products, soft wheat flours, and bread production; UNITED STATES DEPARTMENT OF AGRICULTURE, "Barley," *U.S. Agriculture Handbook No. 338* (1968), covers the origin of barley, its culture and production in the U.S., insect pests and diseases, breeding new varieties, genetics, and winter hardiness; A.H. COOK, *Barley and Malt* (1962), surveys the use of barley malts in brewing; D.H. GRIST, *Rice*, 4th ed. (1965), discusses the origin of the plant, characteristics, varieties and classification, paddy production, mechanics of cultivation, weeds, diseases, milling, nutritional value, parboiling, and enrichment. A detailed treatment of starch is available in J.A. RADLEY, *Starch and Its Derivatives*, 3rd ed. rev., 2 vol. (1953–54; 4th ed., vol. 1, 1968), a widely accepted textbook, treating the structure of starch, the manufacturing of starch and starch products, industrial applications, and examination of starches. Flour production is treated by J.F. LOCKWOOD, *Flour Milling* (1945), a standard work on modern flour milling; and L. SMITH, *Flour Milling Technology*, 3rd rev. ed. (1945), a useful survey of the technology of flour milling and the problems facing flour millers throughout the world. E.M. WIDDOWSON and R.A. MCCANCE, "Studies on the Nutritive Value of Bread and on the Effect of Variations in the Extraction Rate of Flour on the Growth of Undernourished Children," *Medical Research Council Special Series Report No. 287* (1954), tells of a nutritional study based on tests carried out in 1947 and 1948 on children in German orphanages to determine the effects of diets using breads made from flours of varying extractions. C. HUMMEL, *Macaroni Products*, 2nd ed. (1966), covers the manufacture of macaroni products, including ingredients, batch and continuous processes, drying, quality, storing, and packaging.

(D.W.K.-J.)

Cerebrospinal Fluid

In the vertebrate embryo the central nervous system is formed as a hollow tube with a canal extending its entire length. In later life the canal remains open in the brain stem but narrows considerably in the spinal cord. In each of the two cerebral hemispheres of the brain (see NERVOUS SYSTEM, HUMAN) the canal widens into cavities called ventricles. The cerebrospinal fluid (CSF) fills these ventricles and the canal within the brainstem. It also surrounds and bathes the spinal cord and the brain, acting as a lubricant and a mechanical barrier against shock. The fluid flows slowly from the ventricles, the principal site of formation; down through the canal of the brainstem; and ultimately out into the tissue spaces surrounding the central nervous system.

It is a clear and colourless liquid of low specific gravity. Like the blood it is slightly alkaline in reaction, hav-

Table 1: Comparison of Normal Cerebrospinal Fluid and Blood Plasma Average Values

	cerebrospinal fluid	blood plasma
Calcium	2.4 mEq/1	5.2 mEq/1
Carbon dioxide tension	46 mm Hg	40 mm Hg
Chloride	124 mEq/1	100 mEq/1
Bicarbonate	22 mEq/1	22 mEq/1
Glucose	50–80 mg/100 ml	70–110 mg/100 ml
Lactate	1.7 mEq/1	1.7 mEq/1
Lipids, total	1.25 mg/100 ml	876 mg/100 ml
Cholesterol	0.4 mg/100 ml	180 mg/100 ml
Cholesterol esters	0.3 mg/100 ml	126 mg/100 ml
Magnesium	2.6 mEq/1	1.8 mEq/1
Nonprotein nitrogen	19 mg/100 ml	27 mg/100 ml
Ammonia	6 μg/100 ml	56 μg/100 ml
Creatinine	1.1 mg/100 ml	1.6 mg/100 ml
Urea	14 mg/100 ml	14 mg/100 ml
Uric acid	0.24 mg/100 ml	4 mg/100 ml
Phosphorus	1.6 mg/100 ml	4 mg/100 ml
Potassium	3 mEq/1	4.5 mEq/1
Protein, total	15–45 mg/100 ml	7,000 mg/100 ml
Prealbumin	5%	0 (?)
Albumin	50%	56%
Globulin, total	45%	44%
Alpha globulin	15%	14.5%
Beta globulin	19%	12%
Gamma globulin	11%	17.5%
Sodium	142 mEq/1	137 mEq/1

ing a pH of 7.3–7.4. It is about 99 percent water and has an average freezing point of 0.57° C. The fluid normally has less than five leukocytes (mononuclears or possibly lymphocytes) per cubic millimetre and no red blood cells. The relationship of the various chemical constituents of the cerebrospinal fluid to that of blood plasma is shown (Table 1).

Functions of CSF. The cerebrospinal fluid's many functions are chiefly mechanical. It bathes brain and spinal cord and helps to bear the weight of the brain. It lubricates the surfaces between brain and spinal cord, on the one hand, and the bones that encase them, on the other. The fluid is a buffer that distributes the force of a blow on the head. It helps to keep intracranial pressures relatively constant; its volume decreases to compensate for increased arterial pulsations or greater volume of blood or brain tissue and increases to compensate for a decrease in these factors, as in degeneration or atrophy of the brain. By means of the cerebrospinal fluid, substances are removed from the tissues of brain and spinal cord and carried into the blood stream, and the fluid may possibly act also in the reverse direction. Materials carried away by the fluid include metabolic waste products, antibodies, abnormal chemical constituents, and pathologic products of disease. It helps to circulate drugs administered in therapy. It does not carry enough nutritional substances to be of much help in the normal metabolism of nervous tissue.

During certain diseases that affect the meninges or the central nervous system or both, the cerebrospinal fluid may change significantly in physical characteristics, cytological constituents, and chemical contents; and there may be microbiologic and serologic alterations in the fluid. Careful examination of the cerebrospinal fluid in such a situation may be very useful in differential diagnosis. Table 2 illustrates the changes in the profile of the cerebrospinal fluid in the differentiation of certain diseases of the meninges and the central nervous system.

Formation and re-absorption of CSF. Although there are still differing views concerning the mechanisms of the formation of cerebrospinal fluid, the general belief is that the fluid originates largely by filtration across the membranes that line the spaces containing the fluid (the ependyma of both the choroid plexuses and the ventricles, as well as the arachnoid) but also by active secretion of substances such as protein and sodium.

From the cerebrospinal spaces the fluid enters into the venous system. It was formerly held that the greater part of the fluid is absorbed through the arachnoid villi or pacchionian granulations and passes into the dural sinuses and thence into the venous blood. Probably, however, much of the fluid is absorbed into the veins from the spaces around the spinal roots and cranial nerves and from the perivenous spaces. Some may also be absorbed through the ventricular ependyma and, in a reverse direction, through the choroid plexus and some, by osmosis, directly into the pial veins on the brain surface and into the capillaries of the pia arachnoid.

"Circulation" of CSF. Unlike the blood, the cerebrospinal fluid is not given energy for circulation by an organ like the heart; but there is a definite movement of the fluid from the lateral ventricles down into the third and fourth ventricles, the basal cisterns, and the subarachnoid space; and there is constant circulation in the sense that

Table 2: Cerebrospinal Fluid in Differential Diagnosis

condition or disease	initial pressure (mm CSF)	spinal subarachnoid block	appearance	cells (per mm³)	protein (mg/100 ml)	glucose (mg/100 ml)	chlorides as NaCl (mg/100 ml)	colloidal gold curve	comments
Normal	70–150	absent	clear colourless	0–5 mononuclear	15–45	50–80	700–750	0000000	
Infections on the central nervous system and meninges									
Acute purulent meningitis	200–600	absent	cloudy to purulent	500–20,000 mainly polymorphonuclear	100–1,000	10–20 mg or less	575–700	variable	organisms may be found by direct stain or culture
Tuberculous meningitis	200–500	absent	opalescent to faint yellow	100–500 mainly lymphocytes	60–700	15 mg or less	525–675	variable	tubercle bacilli may be found by stain or guinea pig inoculation
Cryptococcus meningitis	200–400	absent	slightly opalescent	100–500 mainly lymphocytes	50–300	30–40 mg or less	normal or slightly decreased	variable	yeasts may be found with India ink stain or special culture
Syphilitic meningitis	150–300	absent	clear to slightly opalescent	300–2,000 mononuclear	50–400	normal or slightly decreased	normal or slightly decreased	first or midzone	serologic tests usually positive
Parenchymatous central nervous system syphilis	normal	absent	clear	10–50 mononuclear	50–100	normal	normal	first or midzone	serologic tests usually positive except in late treated tabes
Viral meningitis and encephalitis	100–250	absent	clear	25–250 polymorphonuclear early; later lymphocytes	40–80	normal (occasionally more)	normal	normal or non-specific	occasionally virus may be found
Acute anterior poliomyelitis	normal	absent	clear	50–250 mainly mononuclear	40–100	normal	650–750	variable	polymorphonuclear cells may be found in preparalytic stage; gradual rise in protein
Brain abscess	200–800	absent	clear colourless	30–100 mainly mononuclear	40–200	normal	normal	variable	polymorphonuclear cells present early, before encapsulation
Miscellaneous meningeal and nervous system diseases									
Carcinomatous meningitis	150–400	absent	clear to opalescent	100–500 mainly mononuclear	40–200	moderately decreased	normal	variable	cancer cells may be found in stained sediment
Brain tumour	150–500	absent	clear to yellow	usually normal, may be up to 50–100	20–150	normal	normal	variable	pleocytosis usually indicates tumour near ventricles or meninges
Spinal cord tumour	normal or decreased	partial or complete	clear to yellow	usually normal	50–5,000	normal	normal	first or midzone	with complete block may be marked increase in protein
"Guillain-Barre syndrome"	normal	absent	clear to yellow	normal	50–1,000	normal	normal	variable	often marked increase in protein without associated pleocytosis
Subarachnoid or ventricular hemorrhage	150–400	absent	bloody yellow	crenated red blood cells	50–500	normal	normal	variable	fluid grossly bloody; supernatant yellow
Multiple sclerosis	normal	absent	clear colourless	5-50 mononuclear	40–70	normal	normal	first zone in 20%; variable in 40%	

the fluid is being continuously secreted and absorbed. There is clinical evidence that obstruction of one opening, the foramen of Monro, between one lateral ventricle and the third ventricle will cause hydrocephalus on one side, with enlargement of that ventricle, and that obstruction of the Sylvian aqueduct will cause hydrocephalus on both sides, involving the third and both lateral ventricles. The forces that bring about the flow of the cerebrospinal fluid and affect its rate include the arterial pulsations within the choroid plexus, respiration, the increase in venous pressure brought about by thoracic and abdominal movements, movements of the head and body and changes in their position, and filtration and secretion pressures.

The normal adult has from about 100 to 150 millilitres cerebrospinal fluid. This fluid is replaced every six to eight hours or three or four times a day. Abnormally large volume is caused either by excessive formation or deficient absorption.

Lumbar puncture. In lumbar puncture a needle is inserted into the subarachnoid space in the lumbar region, and a little cerebrospinal fluid is withdrawn for use in diagnosis. In most cases the cerebrospinal fluid pressure is also measured and the flow of the fluid investigated. The interspace between the third and fourth lumbar vertebrae is chosen for the site of the puncture because at this level the spinous processes are farthest apart and because, in the adult, this point is below the level of the lower end of the spinal cord.

After clear fluid has been obtained, the pressure is determined, ordinarily by means of the Ayer water manometer. Pressures from 70 to 150 millimetres (of cerebrospinal fluid) are normal. If the pressure is within the normal range and there is no other contra-indication, such as suspected intracranial disease, the Queckenstedt test is done. This is a test of the response of spinal fluid pressure to constriction of the jugular veins in the neck and release of the constriction. Normally the pressure rises rapidly and falls with equal rapidity. A slow, incomplete rise and fall or no response whatever is a positive Queckenstedt reaction and indicates a partial or complete spinal subarachnoid block. The Ayala index, computed by dividing the final pressure by the initial pressure and multiplying by the amount of fluid removed (at least ten millilitres must be removed if the test is to be reliable), helps in differentiating between an expanding intracranial lesion and other causes of pressure within the cranium. A quotient of 5.5 to 6.5 is normal. A swift drop in pressure and a quotient of less than 5 are indications of a small fluid reservoir and point to the possible presence of brain tumour or abscess, obstructive hydrocephalus, or a spinal subarachnoid block. A large reservoir is indicated by a value of more than 7, and nonobstructive hydrocephalus or cerebral atrophy is suspected. Lumbar puncture is contra-indicated by infections in or near the puncture site, by systemic infections (except when meningitis is suspected), and by symptoms or signs of increased intracranial pressure (unless diagnostic gains outweigh potential dangers). If the contra-indications mentioned are taken into account aftereffects of lumbar puncture are usually negligible. Postpuncture headache, the most frequent sequel, occurs in 15–30 percent of patients. It usually is mild and lasts only a day or two. The occasional severe headache may incapacitate for a week or longer; it is often accompanied by neck stiffness, is aggravated by movement, and is lessened or relieved by lying down. Current studies tend to indicate that postpuncture headache may occur less frequently if a needle of very narrow gauge is used.

Contra-indications against lumbar puncture

BIBLIOGRAPHY. D. BOWSHER, *Cerebrospinal Fluid Dynamics in Health and Disease* (1960), a detailed study of the pressure relationships and hydrodynamics of cerebrospinal fluid in both normal and diseased states; H. DAVSON, *Physiology of Ocular and Cerebrospinal Fluids* (1956), a review of the functions and biochemistry of cerebrospinal fluid as well as of ocular fluids; R.N. DEJONG, *The Neurologic Examination*, 3rd ed. (1967), a textbook dealing with the anatomic and physiologic basis of the neurologic examination with separate chapters on cerebrospinal fluid circulation and syndromes, spinal puncture, examination of the cerebrospinal fluid, and related examinations and procedures; R.A. FISHMAN, "Cerebrospinal Fluid," in A.B. BAKER (ed.), *Clinical Neurology*, 2nd ed., vol. 1 (1962), an authoritative discussion on the physiology and composition of spinal fluid and various spinal fluid syndromes; S. LUPS and A.M.F.H. HAAN, *The Cerebrospinal Fluid* (1954), a well-recognized textbook by Dutch investigators on the functions and anatomy of cerebrospinal fluid; H.H. MERRITT and F. FREMONT-SMITH, *Cerebrospinal Fluid* (1937), although now somewhat out-of-date, remains the classic reference book; J.W. MILLEN and D.H.M. WOOLLAM, *The Anatomy of the Cerebrospinal Fluid* (1962), a comprehensive discussion of the morphologic aspects of cerebrospinal fluid by current British investigators; W.W. TOURTELLOTTE *et al.*, *Post-Lumbar Puncture Headaches* (1964), a detailed critical analysis of the various theories regarding post lumbar puncture headache and methods for their prevention and treatment.

(R.N.DeJ.)

Ceremonial and Ritualistic Objects

Throughout the history of religions and cultures, objects used in cults, rituals, and sacred ceremonies have almost always been of both utilitarian and symbolic nature. Ceremonial and ritualistic objects have been utilized as a means for establishing or maintaining communication between the sacred (the transcendent, or supernatural, realm) and the profane (the realm of time, space, and cause and effect). On occasion, such objects have been used to compel the sacred (or divine) realm to act or react in a way that is favourable to the participants of the ceremonies or to the persons or activities with which such rituals are concerned or to prevent the transcendent realm from harming or endangering them. These objects thus can be mediatory devices to contact the divine world, as, for example, the drums of shamans (religious personages with healing and psychic-transformation powers). Conversely, they can be mediatory devices used by a god or other supernatural being to relate to man in the profane realm. They may also be used to ensure that a chief or sovereign of a tribe or nation achieves, and is recognized to have, the status of divinity in cultic or community ceremonies. Of such a nature may be phallic cult statues bearing the name of a king associated with that of the Hindu god Śiva, in areas under Indian influence (such as in ancient Vietnam, Cambodia, and Indonesia, where the lingam was worshipped under a double name: Indrés vara [Indra king of the gods, plus Īśvara, Lord—a name of Śiva]), or the Buddhist "body of glory" statues in Cambodia dating from the end of the 7th century. The religious dance masks of many societies, including those used in ancient Tibet and in Buddhist sects of Japan, may, to some extent, also belong to this class.

VARIETIES OF CEREMONIAL AND RITUALISTIC OBJECTS

Because such objects vary as much in nature as they do in form and material, they are difficult to evaluate. If limited strictly to religious practices, an inventory of ceremonial and ritualistic objects remains incomplete, because these objects have played significant roles on solemn secular occasions, such as consecrations, enthronements, and coronations, which may be closely linked to the divine order, as in Hindu-, Buddhist-, and Christian-influenced cultures.

Icons and symbols. Constituting a most significant category of cult objects are representations of a deity. Though such representations are often depicted in the form of statues and images (icons) of divine or sacred beings, they may also be either figurative or symbolic, the meanings often being equivalent. In Tantrism (a Hindu and Buddhist esoteric, magical, and philosophical belief system centred on devotion to natural energy), for example, the sacred Sanskrit syllable Om—which is a transcendent word charged with cosmological (order-of-the-universe) symbolism—is identified with the feminine counterpart of the god. In its written form, particularly on Tibetan banners (*thang-ka*), the word Om (often corresponding with the feminine counterpart—Tārā—of the patron of Tibet) is considered to be eminently sacred, even more so, in some instances, than an anthropomorphic (human-form) divine effigy.

Religious statues and images

Statues and painted images occur most frequently in religious iconography, as noted above. These are often viewed as the permanent embodiments of the deities they represent, whether they are located in sacred places of religious communities, such as temples, shrines, or chapels, or on domestic altars, which contain statues or icons of the divinities of prosperity and fertility, mother goddesses, household gods, saints, relics, the tablet of the ancestors in ancient China, and other similar domestic cult objects. Many household cult objects are made from clay or terra-cotta and are sometimes multicoloured. The material of which major cult objects are composed is often explicitly defined and assumes a certain importance. If the statue is fashioned in wood, the choice of the wood (acacia, sandal, or any other) is symbolically important because it is considered auspicious. By the same token, the choice of stone is likewise important, depending on the region. If metal is chosen, it is one that is deemed precious (*e.g.*, golden statues bring prosperity). In the case of bronze statues and other cult objects, the composition is carefully defined and often corresponds to alloys to which symbolic values are attached. In addition to a proper and distinct form and material, the technique of fabricating and the procedural patterns of composing such objects are controlled by traditional rules that have become established rituals in many religions—sophisticated, folk, and primitive. In the production of statues in human or animal form, the last procedure is often the "opening the eyes" (*i.e.*, the painting of the eyes of a statue of a deity or inserting gold in them by an officiating priest during the installation of the statue [*pratiṣṭhā*] in the sanctuary, along with the reciting of appropriate prayers that make the statue "living" and "real"), particularly in Brahmanic India and Chinese-influenced areas (see also SYMBOLISM AND ICONOGRAPHY, RELIGIOUS).

Religious dress and vestments. The practice of wearing special garments for conducting rites, participating in worship, or even witnessing such ceremonies is very unevenly distributed, and the conceptions associated with this practice are highly varied and complex. The shamans of the Buryats, Yakuts, Altaic Turks, and other Asian peoples wear a ritual costume with a cloak made to look like a bird, with fringes symbolizing plumes; according to their beliefs, this costume magically transforms the wearer into a real bird that will fly to the sacred realm and back to the profane world. In many cases, however, worship requires no special costume, and the monastic or sacerdotal vestment of the officiant or priest may be without adornment, as in Theravāda (Way of the Elders) Buddhism. Sometimes the garment used in religious rites is merely more sumptuous in material or colour than that used in everyday wear. Occasionally, additional objects of liturgical or ritual significance are added to the costumes normally used in religious ceremonies. Certain types of headgear (which are primarily symbols of dignity), such as papal and episcopal mitres of Christian ecclesiastical officials or the "helmets" of the Tibetan Mahāyāna Buddhist monastery dignitaries, are used only on solemn religious ceremonies. In the various Christian churches, especially the Orthodox, Roman Catholic, Anglican, and Lutheran, both the colours and the components of sacerdotal vestments for celebrating worship rites are specifically defined according to the holiday or liturgical season. Garments, under certain circumstances, are even used to clothe cult statues in lands under the influence of both Western and Eastern religions—*e.g.*, in Czechoslovakia, Poland, Spain, and France and in India (see also RELIGIOUS DRESS AND VESTMENTS).

Forms and symbolic conceptions of religious dress

Instruments for worship and religious ceremonies. The types and varieties of instruments used in worship and religious ceremonies are almost innumerable. The role they play in ritual occasions may be as containers and sacred furniture, as objects with properties necessary for worship, and as "mediatory" objects, through which a magical or mystical connection is believed to be made between the human and divine worlds. There are also the materials used in bloody or nonbloody sacrifices.

Amulets and talismans. Amulets (charms) have been used for protection in all ages and in all types of human societies; they persist even today in industrial societies, in which they are mass-produced by the most modern methods (*e.g.*, mustard seeds encased in plastic to be worn as necklaces reminding the wearer of Jesus' words about the growth of the Kingdom of Heaven). The purpose of most amulets is not so much religious as it is for protection against danger, sickness, and bad luck (*e.g.*, the "mystical eye" of the ancient Egyptians or the "Hand of Fatima" of Muslims). The same is true of talismans, which offer the additional advantage of conferring supernatural power on other people, even on the deity, from a distance. Dancers' masks and jewels, such as earrings, bracelets, necklaces, and belts, may be classified with amulets. Such objects are individually worshipped in order to gain their goodwill among some Hindus in India and among the Pueblo and Navajo Indians of North America (see also MAGIC).

TYPES OF SACRED SETTINGS FOR CEREMONIAL AND RITUALISTIC OBJECTS

Places of worship and sacrifice. Throughout man's history, there is evidence that he worshipped at natural sites as well as at sites constructed for ritualistic purposes. In the protohistory and perhaps the prehistory of most ancient civilizations, people venerated trees, stones, bodies of water, and other natural objects, which gradually became the objects of established cults and which often were included, in some form, as aspects of later official ritual. Initially, the objects of this frequently occurring process were sacred trees considered to be the habitats of spirits or gods, such as in Vedic, Brahmanic, and Buddhist India or pre-Islāmic Arabia; sacred stones, such as fragments of meteorites, menhirs (upright stones), and rocks—such as the celebrated Kaʿbah, the black stone of Mecca; flowing waters, natural lakes, and sacred and purifying rivers, such as the Ganges; crossroads and junctions, such as the *tīrtha* (river fords and, by extension, sacred spots) in India; and other such objects or places of nature. According to Hesiod, an 8th-century-BC Greek writer, such objects of nature were venerated in the popular piety of the rustic people of Greece in his times.

Importance of the natural elements

The association on the same site of four natural elements (mountain, tree, stone, and water) is supposed to constitute a sacred whole (a quarternity of perfection), a sacred landscape or "geography" similar to the world of the gods. Such sites, in many civilizations, were the initial points of departure for pilgrimages or for the establishment of places of worship. In some instances the natural sacred places were gradually adapted for religious use (*e.g.*, the oracle at Delphi, in Greece), but in others the earlier natural sites were artificially recreated by using man-made symbolic equivalents. An artificial or natural hill, such as a barrow, mound, or acropolis (elevated citadel), often served as a base for the temple, but in many instances the temple itself has been an architectural representation of the mountain, as were the *bamot* ("high places," usually constructed with stones) of the ancient Hebrews, the ziggurats (tower temples) of the ancient Babylonians, and the pyramidal temples of Cambodia, Java, and pre-Columbian Mexico. A branchless tree has often been transformed into a cultic object: a sacrificial post, such as the Vedic *yūpa;* the central pole of a nomadic tent in Siberia and Central Asia, the *yurt*, or initiation hut; or a parasol shaft (*chattrāvalī*) in the Buddhist *stūpa*s (reliquary buildings) and the Japanese and Chinese pagodas. If represented in stone, the tree evolved into a column gnomon (a perpendicular shaft), such as the Buddhist *lāṭ*, the sacred pillar (*matzeva*) of the ancient Hebrews, or the obelisk of pre-Hellenistic Egypt (before the 4th century BC, especially from the 3rd millennium to the early 1st millennium BC). Stone, transformed into an altar, has been used either to support or seat the image or symbol of the deity, or to receive sacrifices, burnt offerings, plant offerings, or aromatic perfumes. Water, because to it is generally ascribed a power that is purifying or even curative or miraculous, almost always plays an important role in or near sacred places. The whole assemblage of actual or symbolic mountains, trees, stone, and water is usually arranged architecturally within an enclosed space. An example of this arrangement is the typical Christian church, with its raised chancel (the mountain), the cross or crucifix (the tree), the altar (usually stone, but sometimes wood), and the baptismal font or tank (water).

This widespread scheme is almost everywhere bound up with a cosmology (theory of the universe) that establishes a symbolic identity between the divine world and the temple. This identity holds true in all stages of culture; *e.g.*, the sacred sites of the Algonquin, Sioux, and Blackfoot North American Indian tribes; the *templum* (temple) of the Etruscans in ancient Italy; the temple of Bel at Palmyra (in Syria); the Mithraic crypts centring on devotion to the Iranian god Mithra throughout the Roman Empire; the *kiva* (a circular, partly underground ceremonial room) of the Pueblo villages; the Temple of Heaven at Peking and that at Hue (Vietnam); the Buddhist *stūpa;* and Brahmanic, Buddhist, and Mexican mountain temples. The cosmic character of the Israelite king Solomon's Temple, of the 10th century BC, constructed on Mt. Moriah in Jerusalem, was not given such an interpretation, however, until Hellenistic times (3rd century BC–3rd century AD), as in the writings of Philo of Alexandria and Josephus. That of the Muslim mosques is very subdued, although the Kaʿbah of Mecca, which contains the black stone, is believed by Muslims to be the centre of the cosmos. The cosmological scheme has been applied to Christian basilicas and churches—with square floor plans, an overarching dome, and symbolic ornamentation—from as far back as the 6th and 7th centuries.

Sacred furniture and related objects. Whatever its size and form, a sacred area is usually delimited by an enclosure, such as a simple fence around sacred trees or Buddhist *stūpa*s or high walls with immense gates around temples. The sacred space may comprise multiple enclosures, such as that of huge sacred structures—such as the temple of Śrīraṅgam in southeastern India, which has seven concentric enclosures. The dominant idea in delimiting the holy place is to protect the sacred element and its mystery. Access to the sanctuary is often hidden by grills or screens: the veil of the Jewish Temple in ancient Jerusalem, which separated the holy area (or *hekhal*) from the Holy of Holies (or *devir*); or the Eastern Orthodox *ikonostasis* (image screen), which hides the chancel from the view of the faithful except on certain ritual occasions when it is opened to them. Hindu sanctuaries also are concealed by hangings. In Roman Catholic, Lutheran, and Anglican churches, the chancel has usually been separated from the nave by a railing, before which the faithful kneel to receive the eucharistic (communion) meal.

Objects hiding access to sanctuaries

In Indo-European civilizations the essential element of the sacred furniture is the altar, the site of which varies according to the cult and period under consideration. Tables for sacrifice, burnt offerings, and offerings of plants or perfume have sometimes been placed outside the temple, as at the Temple of Solomon in Jerusalem and in temples of ancient Egypt. In early Christian cults, a single altar was placed in the chancel. Later, about the 6th century, the number of altars was increased, with one in each chapel of the larger church building.

The most sacred furnishings of temples are those most closely related to altars, such as the Jewish ark of the Law, or *aron ha-qodesh*, in the synagogues, which is made in the image of Moses' ark of the Covenant, and the tabernacle (the receptacle containing the consecrated bread and wine) of Roman Catholic and Eastern Orthodox churches. The ark, which is portable, is a kind of chest (*aron*) with a cover (*kapporet*), and the tabernacle, made of wood, metal, or stone, is a locked chest. On the fire altars of Zoroastrianism (a religion founded by the Iranian prophet Zoroaster in the 7th century BC) is a sacred metal urn (*ātash-dān*), containing the eternal fire, ashes, and aromatic substances.

When temples or other major sanctuaries are also places for assembly and common prayer, as, for example, Muslim mosques and Catholic and Protestant churches, pulpits are provided. They may be integral parts of the masonry, of the anterior screen of the chancel—as are ambos (raised platforms), or wooden furnishings fixed to the walls, like the formerly mobile *minbar* (domed boxes in mosques). In Manichaeism (a dualistic religion founded by the Persian prophet Mani in the 3rd century AD), the Bēma Feast was centred on the exaltation of a reconstructed pulpit (Bēma), which symbolically represented the rostrum from which Mani spread his teachings. Another important element of sacred furniture is the lectern, on which is placed one or more sacred books (from which one of the officiants reads aloud) or a collection of hymns and religious chants intoned by a cantor in monasteries or other religious structures.

Use of pulpits and lecterns

Permanent lighting is also required in certain cults. This has encouraged the creation of supports or vessels for inflammable materials, the most characteristic of which are the seven-branched candelabrum of the Jerusalem Temple, the Easter candle holder of Roman Catholicism, the sanctuary lights of Roman Catholicism that signal the presence of the Eucharist in the tabernacle, lights suspended before icons in Orthodox rituals, glass or perforated-metal lamps in mosques, and spherical lanterns adorned with an eye, which represents the universal monad (one), of Vietnamese Cao Daism (a syncretistic religion combining Roman Catholicism and Buddhism).

Protective devices and markers of sacredness. Other objects, such as fans, flyswatters, parasols, and standards—analogous to the symbols of royalty—often complete the permanent furnishings of sacred places. In addition to their utilitarian role, they are endowed with a sacred character; fans used in Brahmanic and Buddhist cults may be compared to the *flabella* ("fans") in the Roman Catholic and Orthodox churches. They are waved before the iconostasis during the Eucharist in the divine liturgy of the Eastern Orthodox Church, and they also are placed on either side of the papal chair in solemn processions. The parasol, or umbrella, is generally a symbol of the vault of heaven, as in India and China; the domes of *stupa*s are often surmounted by parasols (*chattra*s). In its symbolic and protective role the umbrella can be compared to the *baldachin* (canopy) in many of its forms. Whether it covers the altar, the statue or symbol of a deity, or even the imperial throne—as in Zoroastrian Iran during the Sāsānian period (3rd–7th centuries) and Orthodox Byzantium (during the 4th–15th centuries)—the *baldachin*'s celestial symbolic ornamentation is generally explicit, and its cosmic character is apparent. The standard (*dhvaja*), in the Brahmanic cults, takes on the appearance of a high column (*dhvajastambha*) erected in front of temples; it is surmounted by a divine effigy, most often that of the sacred steed, or *vāhana*, of the god. Simultaneously a signal (because of its height) and a protective device, it first receives the homage of pilgrims. The poles adorned with flags erected before the pylons of the temples of ancient Egypt may also have had such a double character.

The symbolic character of parasols, canopies, and standards

FORMS OF CEREMONIAL AND RITUALISTIC OBJECTS ACCORDING TO THEIR FUNCTIONS

Summoning, mediating, and expelling devices. In the form of magic or sacred words, singing, and music, sound plays or has played an important role in the worship of most religions. The same is true of light and of aromatic substances, such as oils, perfumes, and incense. The importance of these elements has brought about the creation or adoption of specific objects with functions that often serve converging purposes in worship. In most cases they are used to draw the attention of the deity, to establish a connection with it, and to exorcise forces that are evil or harmful to the god and to men. Because of the need to attract the deity's attention, the sound-producing instruments are usually percussive or shrill, rather than melodic, and drums, gongs, cymbals, bells, conches, and sistra (timbrils, or rattles) are the most common forms.

Sound devices. Summoning devices are played either alone, as objects to accompany prayers or litanies, as in Tantric Buddhism, or as instruments in a temple orchestra. Their size and form and the materials used to make them vary according to locale. Generally viewed as sacred, they are often worshipped, as in West Africa, Malaysia, and Burma, and partake of divine attributes, as in Brahmanism, Mahāyāna (Greater Vehicle, or northern) Buddhism, and Tantrism. Drums vary most greatly in both size and form. The two-skinned *ḍamaru* (drum) of Śivism (devotion to the Hindu god Śiva) and Tantrism, which is shaped like an hourglass, with striking balls, is believed to be effective in communicating with the divine world. Gongs usually are suspended metallic disks, with or without a central protuberance. The gongs of ancient and contemporary China, however, are of varied form, with cutout designs, and may be made of resonant stone or of jade. Cymbals are very widespread and were used in the Hellenistic mystery (salvatory) religions, such as those of Dionysus (a god of wine) and the Eleusinian mysteries (centred on devotion to Demeter, a seasonal-renewal goddess). They were the only instruments played in the Temple of Jerusalem, where they were known as *metziltayim* or *tzeltzelim*. The sistrum, used in pre-Hellenistic Egypt in the worship of the goddesses Isis and Hathor and in Rome and Phoenicia, as well as among the Hebrews, is composed of a handle and frame with transverse metal rods and mobile disks. Producing a sharp ringing sound, it was regarded as particularly sacred and was carried to the temple by women of high rank. There are countless types of bells; the Indian *ghaṇṭā*, or Tibetan *dril-bu*, a metal handbell with a handle shaken during prayers in order to attract beneficent spirits and to frighten away evil ones, is used particularly during Brahmanic and Mahāyāna Buddhist ceremonies.

In this category of objects, the shaman's drum of the Buryats, Yakuts, Altaic Turks, and Eskimos is composed of a skin stretched over a circular or oval frame provided with a handle; it is struck with a curved beater. It plays the same magical role as the *ghaṇṭā*, but it also serves as a mode of ascending to the realm of the sacred for the shaman. The bull-roarer—a flat, elongated piece of wood, ivory, reindeer antler, or other material—used in primitive religions of Australia, equatorial Africa, western North America, Colombia, Brazil, and Sumatra, and the similar rhombus of the Hellenistic mystery religions, was propelled and whirled by a thin strap. Its humming sound and trajectory gave it the dual character of a summons to the divine world and a link with the celestial regions.

Lighting devices. In comparison with sound, which in worship usually presents a coercive character, lighting and fire, whether permanent or occasional, generally signify a sacred or spiritual presence, an offering, prayer, intercession, or purification. They are often viewed as sacred or even of divine origin, if not directly identified with the deity, as in the Zoroastrian fire altars. Their supports and containers can be made of either durable or perishable materials, depending on the ritual or ceremonial requirements. Torches have been used throughout history: in ancient Assyria and Babylonia they were used to carry a newly consecrated fire from torch to torch throughout the city three times a month; in ancient Rome they were sometimes placed in a hollow clay or metal shaft; and in the ancient Hebraic religion a lamp (*ner*) filled with sacred oil was used in the worship of the god Yahweh. In the Roman Catholic Church, from about the 10th century on, wax candles have been used, with bronze or copper candle holders—the forms of which changed according to style. Two of them were placed on the altar for the mass, and two others were carried by acolytes (light bearers). The Easter (Paschal) candle, made of beeswax around a wood core, had a candle holder appropriate to its size. At Westminster, in England, during the 14th century, a *candela rotunda* ("round candle") was the centre of a "festival of lights" during the feast of the purification of the Virgin Mary (February 2), also called Candlemas Day.

The use of torches

Festivals of lights have been and still are common throughout the world, especially among the Jews, who celebrate Ḥanukka, the Feast of Dedication of the Temple. In India and in Indian-influenced countries (particularly Thailand), the festival of lights (Dīpāvālī or Dīvālī) is celebrated by the Vaiṣṇava Hindus (devotees of the god Viṣṇu) in October–November, at the end of the monsoon season. It is practiced on other religious occasions by the Jaina (followers of the Indian reformer Mahāvīra, of the 6th century BC), Thais, and Tibetans, who celebrate it in December. The lamps, which are lit everywhere (*e.g.*, in temples, in houses, and at crossroads), are also set afloat on streams, rivers, and lakes. Some lamps are made of glass—like the votive lights of Roman Catholicism—with a wick dipped in a vegetable oil, usually coconut; some are made of clay; and others are made of rice paste with a central hollow filled with ritual clarified butter, or ghee (*ghī*), or are cut out of a plant stalk in the shape of a bark or raft. The Jaina use earthen saucers containing either wicks immersed in coconut oil or pieces of lighted camphor. Another form of this festival was known in Thailand, where three earthen pots, containing rice, seeds, beans, and an oil-soaked wick, were placed at the top of three poles opposite the temple entrance, and the fire was kept burning for three days.

The "cordons of light" placed around the sacred places of Buddhism during great festivals, such as at Bodh Gayā, in India, for the Buddhajayantī (the commemoration of the Buddha's 2,500th birthday) in 1958, are composed of thousands of small brass lamps in the form of footed cups filled with ghee, in which a cotton wick is soaked.

Incense and other smoke devices. The use of incense or the fumes of aromatic substances is especially widespread in the great religions of the world and has many symbolic meanings. It may signify purification, symbolize prayer (as among the Hebrews), or be an offering that rises to the celestial or sacred realm. Bronze incense burners were cast very early, as exemplified by such objects from the Chou period (*c.* 1122–221 BC). Their forms were often inspired by cosmological themes. In early Taoist ritual the fumes and odours of incense burners of varying size produced a mystic exaltation and contributed to well-being. Under the T'ang dynasty (AD 618–907), perforated golden vessels with handles were carried in the hand to accompany a votive offering. In Japan the censer (*kōdan*)—a vessel with a perforated cover and carried by chains—was used in both Buddhist and Shintō rituals. In pre-Hellenistic Egypt and among ancient Jews, incense was burned in golden bowls, which sometimes had handles, and also in cauldrons placed on or beside the altar or outside the temple. In pre-Columbian Mexico and Peru, incense burners were made of terra-cotta and sometimes of gold. Censers of precious metal provided with chains for hanging have been used since the 4th century in Christian churches, and the rite of swinging the censer is practiced in many rituals, both Christian and others.

Symbolism of incense and other aromatic substances

Expelling and other protective devices. Several of the objects already described serve as protection against evil or demonic spirits. Of such a nature are the *ghaṇṭā* and *dril-bu*, the shaman's drum, the lamps of the Indian Dīpāvālī, and the burning of incense, which has also been practiced in ancient Greece, pre-Columbian America, Morocco, and many other regions. The possession of a large number of the same form of a protective object often is believed to be effective; this is the reason for the large number of bells (*ghaṇṭāmālā*) suspended on lattices on the handrail of the balustrade (*vedikā*) around the *stūpa*s of ancient India; even today, small bells are hung from the roofs of Buddhist pagodas in Sino-Japanese regions. Like the small bells seen on the roofs of Romanian country dwellings until the beginning of the 20th century, these bells have a clapper provided with a feather or plaquette that enables the wind to ring them continually. Perhaps the most effective protective object, however, is the "diamond thunderbolt" (Sanskrit *vajra;* Tibetan *phur-bu*, or *rdo-rje*) of Mahāyāna Buddhism, Tantrism, and Lamaism (a Tibetan form of Buddhism and folk religion). Well-known in early Buddhism as an instrument held in the hand, the *vajra* is handled in the middle and has, at one or both ends, four curved points that meet at the tips. Of varying size, they are usually made of gilded or ungilded bronze. The Tantric *vajra* is also associated with the *ghaṇṭā* (*vajra-ghaṇṭā*), for which it forms a handle. A symbol of the indestructible force of religion, it is believed to be able to drive away all manifestations of evil. Although they are perishable, gunshots and firecrackers are viewed as protective and expelling devices, as in China and Cambodia (where soldiers, in the early 1970s, fired ammunition at a lunar eclipse to drive away the dragon they believed was devouring the moon).

Representational objects. In many religions, the god or divine order is represented among men by objects, which may be regarded simply as the god's material form on earth or may be totally identified with the god and endowed with his powers. In pre-Hellenistic Egypt the god was believed to be present in his statue, and elsewhere the statue frequently was believed to contain the god.

Statues of divine beings and sacred masks

Figures. Statues of human or animal figures are the most explicit of the objects representing the divine order. In most iconic (image-using) religions the gods are generally anthropomorphic, half man, half animal (as in Egypt and India) or often entirely animal. In most cases the statues conform to an ideal physical type that is symbolic and conventional. The formulation of the ideal is governed by precise aesthetic and iconometric (ritual image proportion) rules, as well as by iconographic (image-representation) requirements, as in Egypt, Greece, and India. All such standards and requirements guarantee conformity to the divine model and, therefore, the effective presence of the god in his statue. Typical in this regard are the sculptured animals of the Hindu pantheon, such as elephants, lions, horses, bulls, and birds, which—erected at sacred places in India and other Hindu-influenced countries—serve as ever-ready sacred mounts (*vāhana*) for the journeys of the corresponding gods.

The masks representing beneficent and maleficent sacred or holy forces in religious dances—particularly in Buddhist monasteries of Nepal, Tibet, and Japan and in the majority of primitive societies—constitute another category of sacred representational objects. They are usually worshipped just as statues are worshipped.

Certain customs incorporating representational figures have been widespread since prehistoric times and appear to be more related to magic than to religion. One example of this type of practice is a custom observed in primitive or prehistoric societies—the incorporation of a skull in an anthropomorphic statue in order to emphasize its divine, sacred, or magical character. To some extent, a similar use of a skull, human bones, a mummified corpse, or a skeleton appears in Christian churches in the veneration of relics.

Plants and plant representations. In all civilizations, plants and trees have been viewed as sacred. Generally, the tree is either a god's habitat or the god himself and is worshipped. Such was the case, for example, in early Indian Buddhism. Trees may also be associated with the divine order because of some incident and subsequently venerated, as was the bodhi tree, under which the Buddha received his Enlightenment. Fences or even open-air temples, the form adopted for the early Bodh Gayā Buddhist temples, are built around such trees. Innumerable cases of sacred or divine trees and their painted or sculptured representations are found throughout written religious tradition and in the ethnological data. The branches of trees such as the palm, olive, and laurel are often associated with the gods; such branches may crown the god or be included among his attributes. Many are used in worship, as are the branches of the *bilva* (wood-apple tree) among the adepts of Śiva, and the *tulasī* (basil), symbol of Lakṣmī (Hindu goddess of prosperity and Viṣṇu's wife) and sacred plant of the Vaiṣṇavites.

Plants as symbols of life and immortality

As symbols of life and immortality, plants such as the vine of the Greco-Roman and the Christian world and the *haoma* (a trance-inducing or intoxicating plant) of pre-Islāmic Iran are planted near tombs or represented on funerary steles, tombstones, and sarcophagi. Two similar and related rites involving plants, the *haoma*, noted in the Avesta (ancient Zoroastrian scriptures), and the *soma*, noted in the Vedas (ancient Hindu scriptures), pertain to the ritual production of exalted beverages presumed to confer immortality. The ritualistic objects for this ceremony included a stone-slab altar, a basin for water, a small pot and a larger one for pouring the water, a mortar and pestle for grinding the plants, a cup into which the juice drips and a filter or strainer for decanting it, and cups for consuming the beverage obtained. In many sacrifices, branches or leaves of sacred plants, such as the *kuśa* plant (a sacred grass used as fodder) of the Vedic sacrifice and the Brahmanic *pūjā* (ritual), are used in rituals such as the Zoroastrian sprinkling (*bareshnum*), or Great Purification, rite, in which the notion of fertility and prosperity is combined with their sacred characters (see also ANIMALS AND PLANTS IN MYTH AND LEGEND; PURIFICATION RITES).

Use of banners and shields

Other representational objects. The staves of martial banners or standards are often surmounted by the figure of a god, which is frequently in its animal form. Such effigies, used by the Indo-Iranians, the Romans, the Germanic tribes, the Celts, and other ancient peoples, were probably meant to ensure the presence of the god among the armies. From the 4th century on, Byzantine armies placed the *labarum* (a cross bearing the Greek letters XP, signifying Christ) on their standards. Shields, such as the Greek *gorgonōtos* ("gorgon-headed"), were also often decorated with sacred figures, emblems, and symbolic themes, particularly in post-Gupta (4th-century) India, as seen in the 6th-century findings from the frescoes of Ajantā. In the Mycenaean civilization (15th–12th centuries BC) of ancient Greece, shields were worshipped in front of the temple, and at Knossos (in Crete) votive offerings were made of clay and ivory in the form of shields. The famous *ancilia* ("figure of eight" shields) of Rome were kept by the Fratres Arvales (a college of priests) and used by the Salii (Leapers), or warrior-priests, for their semiannual dances (in March and October) honouring the god Mars.

Relics. Relics of saints, founders of religions, and other religious personages, which are often objects of worship or veneration, generally consist of all or part of the skeleton (such as the skull, hand, finger, foot, or tooth), a piece or lock of hair, a fingernail, or garments or fragments of clothing. Such veneration is nearly universal, as is the production of reliquaries, or shrines that contain relics. The size, form, and materials of reliquaries vary greatly and often depend on the nature of the relic being exhibited. They may be fixed but are generally portable so that they can be carried in processions or on pilgrimages. Wood, bone, ivory, quartz, glass, semiprecious stones, and metals such as gold, silver, bronze, and copper are frequently used materials, and chasing (embossing), enamelwork, and precious stones often ornament reliquaries. They vary considerably in form; like the Tibetan reliquaries, or *ga'u*, they may be constructed on a small scale to look like churches, chapels, towers, *stūpa*s, or sarcophagi, but sometimes they assume the form of the relic, such as in the form of anthropomorphic statues, busts, hands, feet, and other forms. Occasionally, as in Tantrism and Tibetan Lamaism, the bones of holy persons are used to make ritual musical instruments—flutes, horns (*rkang-gling*), and drums (*ḍamaru*)—or objects such as the ritual scoop made of a skull cup (*thod-khrag*) and a long iron handle encrusted with silver.

In many Asiatic regions, however, human relics are replaced by copies of sacred texts introduced into statues of bronze, as in Tibet and Yunnan (China), or of stucco, as in Afghanistan (Haḍḍa, an archeological site near Jālālābād excavated since 1928) in about the 4th–6th centuries.

Other ritual objects. *Objects used in prayer and meditation.* In many religions the practice of prayer requires the use of certain objects, among which rosaries (strings of beads) and chaplets (circular strings of beads) occupy an important place in the popular piety of various religions. They are widespread in Hinduism, Buddhism,

Multiple gateways and enclosures delimit the sacred area of the temple of Srīrangam, India.

Protecting the mystery by creating a sacred space

Jewish ark of the Law, functioning as sacred furniture, encloses and protects the Torah. Wooden ark from Modena, Italy, 1505. In the Musée de Cluny, Paris.

Muslim prayer rug, protective object associated with prayer, symbolizes the sacred area of the mosque. Silk and wool rug from Turkey, 17th century. In the Staatsbibliothek, Berlin.

Torii marks the entry to the sacred space around a Shintō shrine, Hakone-yama, Japan.

Plate 1: By courtesy of (top) UNESCO, (right) Staatsbibliothek, Berlin; photographs, (top) G. Kruysen, (centre left) Eddy Van der Veen, (bottom left) Ray Manley—Shostal

Tibetan skull cup, 18th century. In the Museum of Fine Arts, Boston.

Chimú ceremonial knife from Peru, repoussé gold. In the Art Institute of Chicago.

Byzantine chalice, agate. In St. Mark's, Venice.

Objects used in the enactment of rituals

Throne-altar, Kaṭrā Buddha, sandstone stele from India, 2nd century. In the Archaeological Museum, Mathura, India.

Ryoo being performed at Itsukushima-jinja, Japan. The dancer's mask becomes a representation of holy forces and, as such, is an object of worship.

Plate 2: By courtesy of (top left) The Art Institute of Chicago, (top right) the Museum of Fine Arts, Boston, John Gardner Coolidge Collection; photographs, (centre) SCALA, N.Y., (bottom left) Otsuka Kogei-sha Co., Tokyo, (bottom right) Holle Bildarchiv, Baden-Baden

Plate 3: By courtesy of (top centre) the Historical Museum, Stockholm © A.T.A. Stockholm; photographs, (top left) Holle Bildarchiv, Baden-Baden, (top right) FISA, (centre, bottom) Shostal, (centre) W. Kaufman, (bottom) C. Reyes

Tree element transformed into the parasol shaft or chattravati of the Buddhist religion. Stone shaft in the Mohrā Morādu *stupa,* Taxila near Rāwalpindi, Pakistan.

Symbolic equivalents of the natural elements

Water element brought into the Christian totality in the sacrament of Baptism, performed at baptismal fonts. Stone font from Tingstäde Church, Ostergötland, Sweden, 12th century. In the Historical Museum, Stockholm.

Tree element symbolized by Christians as the cross. Crucifix, polychromed wood, 12th century. In the Museo de Bellas Artes de Cataluña, Barcelona.

Stone element transformed into an altar by the Minoan culture, palace at Mália, Crete.

Mountain element represented by the Mayan culture in pyramidal stone temples. Temple of Inscriptions, Palenque, Mexico.

Summoning, mediating, and expelling devices

Dorje and bell, bronze, Tibetan, 19th century. In the Newark Museum, New Jersey.

Tripod incense burner, bronze, Chinese, late Chou dynasty. In the Metropolitan Museum of Art, New York City.

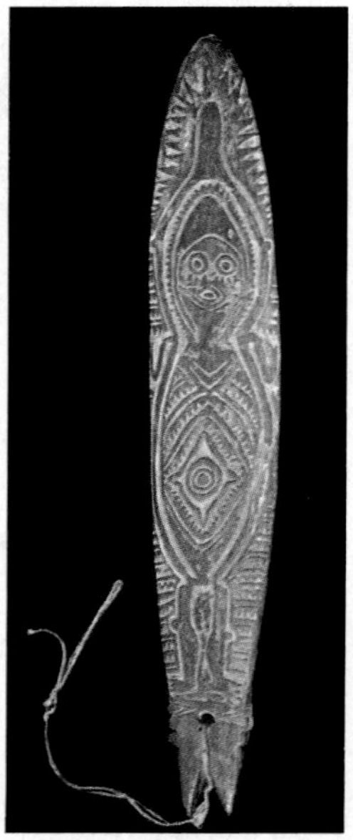

Bull-roarer from the Gulf of Papua, New Guinea, early 20th century. In the Field Museum of Natural History, Chicago.

Shaman's drum, Lapland, wood and painted hide. In the Nationalmuseet, Copenhagen.

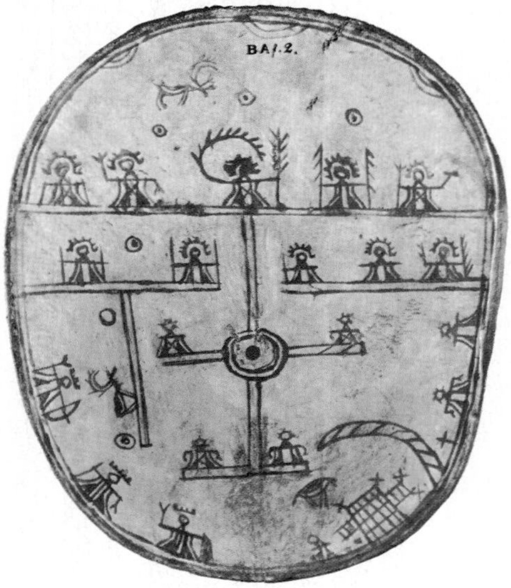

Hanukka *menora*, silver with enamel medallions, by Johann Adam Boller, early 18th century, Frankfurt am Main, West Germany. In the Jewish Museum, New York City.

Plate 4: By courtesy of (top left) The Newark Museum, New Jersey, Shelton Collection, (top right) the Metropolitan Museum of Art, New York, Rogers Fund, 1947, (centre left) the Field Museum of Natural History, Chicago, Captain Fuller Collection, (bottom left) Ethnographical Department, Nationalmuseet, Copenhagen, (bottom right) The Jewish Museum, New York City

Islām, Roman Catholicism, Eastern Orthodoxy, and Judaism, although they are not found in Shintō. Brahmanic and Buddhist rosaries have 108 beads, made of *tulasī*, or basil (in Vaiṣṇavism), of lotus seeds or small bones (in Śaivism), or of small disks of human bone (in Lamaism). In China, rosaries are composed of coloured beads. Elsewhere, their number varies; the rosary of Japanese Buddhism has 112 wooden beads, that of Islām has 99 amber beads, and that of the Christian world—and of the well-to-do Jaina—has 150 beads made of various materials, such as wood, pearl, mother-of-pearl, precious or semiprecious stones, gold, and silver. The beads of Brahmanic and Buddhist rosaries are usually strung continuously, except in Japan, where cords—which may or may not have beads on them—are tied to the principal cord in several combinations. The Christian rosary is divided into "decades" (tens) with intercalations, and in many cases the rosary has a "head" composed of a larger bead, several other beads, and a Christian cross.

Use of rosaries and chaplets

There are several other objects pertaining to prayer—in addition to the rosary, which is principally a mnemotechnic (memory-technique) device. One example is the Lamaist prayer wheel (*'khor-lo*), which varies widely in size. It is a cylinder, generally of chased metal, rotating on an axis and containing prayers inscribed on strips of paper, fabric, or parchment. Weighted by two balls suspended externally on small cords, the prayer wheels are set in motion when a hand rotates a handle extending from the axis or when the prayer wheels are aligned along a common axis. Some are driven by hydraulic power and others even by electrical power. There is some evidence of the use of prayer wheels among other peoples, such as the Japanese, the ancient Celts and Bretons, the ancient Greeks, and the ancient Egyptians. The idea of permanent prayer through the agency of objects is found in the candles lit in churches, in the perpetually burning lamps (*chōmyōtō*) of Buddhist Japan, and in Tibetan prayer flags, with sacred formulas painted on them, which wave in the wind around temples, houses, and villages. The phylacteries (*tefillin*) worn by traditional Jews during weekday morning prayers consist of two leather cases bound by leather straps to the forehead and left forearm; they contain parchment citations from the Pentateuch enjoining this as a reminder of God's commandments. An amuletic function has been attributed to them, but this is disputed. Among protective objects associated with prayer are Muslim prayer rugs, the rectangular shape of which symbolizes the sacred area of the mosque, and the fringe-trimmed prayer shawl (*ṭallit*) worn by devout Jews during synagogue services.

Permanent prayer by means of ritualistic objects

Related to prayer and meditation are sacred and magical diagrams. Typical examples are the *yantra*s (two- or three-dimensional meditation apparatus, often geometrical or anthropomorphic in form) and *maṇḍala*s (symbols of the cosmos in the form of circles, squares, or rectangles) of Brahmanism, Tantric Buddhism, and Lamaism and found in India, Nepal, Tibet, China, Korea, and Japan. Derived from sacred syllables (*mantra*s) or from geometric designs endowed with mystical and cosmological symbolism, they are executed on sand, on the ground with coloured powders, and on durable materials. They may be made on stones, engraved on plates of copper, silver, or some other metal, or drawn and painted on skins, linen, silk, or hempen cloth. Like statues, they are consecrated by the rite of "initiation of breath," *prāṇapratiṣṭhā* (see also PRAYER).

Objects used in purification rites. Large numbers of purification rites are performed universally on widely varying occasions, both in private life, from conception to death, and in religious ceremonies. Such rites employ materials that include water, dust, or dry sand (in Islām); water and henna, a reddish-brown dye (in Islām); oil, incense, balm, and natron, a salt (in ancient Egyptian religion); ale (*öl*) or wine (in post-15th-century Germanic religion); salt (in Shintō); bread, sugar, spices, and animal blood (in ancient Greek and Scandinavian religions); paper, used in the Shintō *gohei*, a white paper "whip" that is shaken; ashes, among the Brahmans; and other materials. Water, fire, and light play especially important roles in purification rites. Objects used in such rites include water vessels of various shapes and sizes used for ablutions; jugs and vats containing ale or wine; terra-cotta or glass containers used for balms and perfumes; incense burners, cauldrons, and censers for fumigation; containers used in Confucian rituals, which include a basin (*chin-lei*) for pure water, another small basin (*huan-po*), and seven goblets (*chio*) for the sacrificial wine; and ewers and basins of gold, silver, or copper used in purifying the hands and feet, as in pre-Hellenistic Egypt, or for ritual sprinklings.

Forms of objects in purification rites

The wearing of new clothes that have not yet been washed is also a purification rite, practiced, for example, in the spring of the year (October–November) in Brahmanic India, where it is associated with the festival of lights, the Dīpāvālī.

Purification may also be attained through mortification and penance, practices that were especially common in medieval Christianity and in Judaism. Methods included the wearing of hair shirts or sackcloth, wearing haircloth undergarments and belts bristling with spikes next to the skin, and flagellating oneself with a scourge made of leather straps or lashing oneself with a whip, such as the *sraoshō-karana* of Persia (see also PURIFICATION RITES).

Objects used in rites of passage. Most of the objects noted above have played or still play a role in rites of passage. Such objects play a secondary role in all such rites, which include rites of initiation, marriage, and death.

Objects of initiation and ordination rites

Circumcision in pre-Hellenistic Egypt and among the Hebrews, Muslims, Ethiopians, and certain primitive peoples was and is performed with a flint-blade knife, with some other kind of sharp knife, perhaps of metal, with a razor, or (as in Africa) with a pair of scissors. Among the Zulus and other African tribes, bull-roarers were launched on such an occasion of initiation. In the Brahmanism, Zoroastrianism, and Parsiism of the Indo-Iranian world, a sacred cord (Pahlavi *kuṣṭī;* Sanskrit *yajñopavīta*) is the mark of initiation; in Iran and among the Parsis (Zoroastrians in India), the *kuṣṭī* is wound around the torso, and in India the *yajñopavīta* is passed diagonally from shoulder to waist. Among the Parsis, including the women, the cord is made of strands of lamb's wool or of goat's or camel's hair, and in India the material varies according to caste and may be cotton, hemp, or wool. In addition, the Zoroastrians and Parsis wear a sacred shirt (*sudra*) made of two pieces of white cambric stitched together. For ordination, a shawl, a cotton veil (*padān*) to cover the nose and mouth, and a mace are added; the Brahmanic (Vedic) initiate also receives a tall staff and a black antelope skin. In Sikhism (an Indian religion combining Hindu and Muslim elements, founded by Gurū Nānak in the 16th century), initiations of novices formerly included drinking water into which sugar had been mixed with the blade of a dagger (*khaṇḍā*).

In the initiation of Buddhist monks, the tonsure (cutting the hair of the head) is performed with a razor with a handle, and each initiate receives three red or yellow garments, a belt, a bowl for alms (*pātra*), a filter or ewer (*kuṇḍikā*), an alms-collector's staff (*khakkara*), a needle, a toothpick, and a fan. Japanese Tantric monks are initiated when they are past 50 years of age, at which time they are baptized (*abhiṣeka*) by having water from five *kuṇḍikā* poured on their heads and receive, in addition to the objects listed above, a *vajra* ("thunderbolt"), a wheel (*cakra*), and a conch (*śaṅkha*). The principal objects involved in the initiation of Christian priests and monks are the tonsure and sacerdotal vestments. The Buryat shaman receives, in addition to his magical cloak and drum, a four-legged chest (*shiré*) decorated with lunar and solar symbols.

Objects related to rites of marriage

The religious character of marriage is not universal. Objects involved in the ceremonies of betrothal and marriage include jars (*loutrophoroi*) for the water of the prenuptial bath of ancient Greece; metal rings placed on the ring finger of the betrothed or married couple among Hebrews, Zoroastrians and Parsis, and persons in classical Rome and in both Eastern and Western Christianity; the bridal veil, orange (*flammeum*) in Rome and white in the Christian and Slavic worlds; the bride's crown, made first of marjoram and verbena and later of myrtle and orange blossoms in Rome and of various materials in the Christian and Slavic worlds; and the crown held above the heads of the bridal couple in Eastern Orthodox marriage ceremonies. In Roman and Slavic marriage rites a tunic or shirt was used, and in Hindu rites a yellow wool bracelet (*kautukasūtra*) is tied around the wrist of the betrothed girl by her mother.

The marriage ceremony sometimes takes place under a marriage pavilion or canopy, as among the ancient Etruscans of Italy. The Hebrews first used a closed tent (*ḥuppa*) and later a silk or tapestry canopy to symbolize the nuptial chamber. Hindus and Parsis use a tent or pavilion (*pandāl*), in which the bridal couple are initially separated by a curtain. Among the Sikhs, a paper parasol (*agast*) is rotated continually over the head of the bridegroom.

In some areas, particularly in contemporary Hindu India, a swing (*dolā*) is set up under the *pandāl*, on which the couple seat themselves after the official ceremony. The seesaw here symbolizes prosperity, love, and the union between earth and sky. The *aiōra* ("swing") used in the ancient Athenian Dionysiac festival, the swings of the spring festivals at Puri (Orissa) and in Thailand, also have similar symbolic connotations. During the winter solstice, a Vedic sacrifice (*hotṛ*) is performed on the swing (*preṅkha*).

Objects related to funeral rites

Except for Brahmanic and Buddhist ritual suicides by drowning, which require neither ceremony nor funeral apparatus, there are three methods of disposing of dead human bodies: cremation, stripping of the flesh, and inhumation, performed with or without embalming. These methods have coexisted and still coexist throughout the world. The preparation of the corpse often depends on the method adopted, which, in turn, governs the objects and instruments used. In Japanese sects, particularly in the Shingon and other Buddhist sects, a razor (made of gold in the Jōdo sects) is used for an actual or simulated tonsure of the head of the deceased. A mirror, used in magic to detect evil spirits, figured in the judgment of souls in ancient China. A copper mirror was placed under the head of the dead of pre-Hellenistic Egypt; one of bronze was placed near the head in Buddhist Japan. In Vedic and Brahmanic India, thin pieces of gold were used to close the facial and bodily orifices, and pieces of jade served the same purpose in ancient China. Mortuary masks made of gold, bronze, hard stone, many-coloured terra-cotta, and other materials were used at Mycenae, in pre-Hellenistic and later in Coptic (early Christian) Egypt, in Peru, and elsewhere to cover the face and sometimes the chest. Elsewhere, a cloth covering the face or a shroud, which often was red, was considered sufficient. Pieces of money to pay for the passage from this world to the next were placed in the mouth of corpses in ancient Mycenae, Greece, and Rome and in a pouch in Japan.

Corpses have been borne to funeral sites by various means. Among primitive peoples and in Tibet, they are carried on the back or in the arms, and among the Jews, Muslims, Parsis, Slavs, and Hindus they are carried on biers, which are sometimes richly decorated and are either put in a tomb or destroyed. In modern Western countries, the funeral chariots of Rome and elsewhere have been transformed into motor hearses, while the contemporary Chinese and Vietnamese use carts that have been specially fitted out. Funeral boats were used in pre-Hellenistic Egypt, in ancient Scandinavia, and in the Pacific islands; Venetians of Italy still use gondolas for funeral rites. The sledge was used in the Kurgans of southern Russia.

Cremation practices and objects

When cremated, the corpse is often burned with its bier. In the Buddhist world, as, for example, in Cambodia and Thailand, it is burned in a wood and paper coffin made in the form of a sacred animal, with a cloth canopy surmounting the pyre. If the ashes are dispersed after cremation, as in India, they are collected in a cinerary urn. The form and composition of such urns have varied considerably, being made of terra-cotta, stone, porphyry, alabaster, bronze, silver, gold, ceramic ware, and other materials. The urn is placed in the grave, as in ancient Assyria and elsewhere, on a bronze or terra-cotta support (usually an armchair) and lowered into a large jug, as among the Etruscans, or in the niches of the cineraria (places containing ashes of cremated bodies), columbaria (vaults containing urns of cremated bodies), or catacombs, as in Etruria (in Italy), Greece, and Rome. Among the Zapotec of Mexico, the ceramic urn was placed in the niches of cells, the *mogotes*, made beneath hills set aside for the purpose, a practice also observed by the Mosquito Indians of Nicaragua. In Buddhist countries the urn is often displayed on the domestic altar, and in Tibet the imperfectly calcined bones are ground up and mixed with clay and the mixture is molded into the form of a votive offering (*tsha-tsha*), which is placed in the niches of the funeral *stūpa* (*mchod-rten*). In ancient India the terra-cotta "feminine" urns had a pair of "breasts" formed by two bowls stuck onto the bulge of the urn.

Stripping the flesh of the corpse generally does not require the use of specific objects, since it is the work of vultures or sometimes of pigs, dogs, or other animals. The Parsis, however, build "towers of silence" (*dakhma*) for the purpose, to which they accompany the deceased with a pot containing fire.

Use of coffins, burial boats, and sarcophagi

Bodies have been and still are sometimes buried without coffins, as in Rome, where they were put into pit tombs. Among primitive and prehistoric peoples, ancient Egyptians, and the people of the Harappā civilization (*c.* 2500–1700 BC) of the Indus, the corpse was wrapped in a mat made of plant fibres. Coffins are sometimes carved or painted, and the crudest ones—such as those used by ancient Romans and primitive peoples—are made from hollowed-out tree trunks. Some coffins are modelled according to the human form, such as the colourful wooden coffins of pre-Hellenistic Egypt or the Chinese coffins covered with jade mosaic of the 2nd-century-BC Han dynasty. The majority, however, are oblong and made of wood; in ancient Greece, coffins were made of cypress. Tibetan coffins (*ro-sgam*) and Japanese Buddhist and Shintō coffins, however, are cubical, with the corpse placed in a sitting or crouching position. Among certain coastal peoples—*e.g.*, the Vikings—the deceased is either buried in his boat or put out to sea and cremated with it. Sarcophagi—used in many civilizations—were made of various materials; terra-cotta in Etruria, Greece, southern India prior to the 2nd century BC, and Japan; wood and stone in Japan; and marble in late Rome and in the Christian world. They are often richly decorated with symbolic or allegorical carvings and are frequently very colourful. In ancient Egypt the viscera were placed separately in canopic (burial) jars. The Etrurians also used such jars, the covers of which were decorated with the portrait of the deceased.

From prehistoric times, the deceased was accompanied by ordinary objects placed either in the coffin or in the grave itself, the most common of which were drinking cups, pitchers, cups or vessels for solid food, weapons, tools and ornaments, and jewelry. Ancient Chinese collections of funerary objects of high quality have been exhumed, but the most complete outfitting of the dead was that of the Egyptian tombs, which is completed by scenes painted or carved on the interior walls of the rooms of the tomb. Funeral models of houses, wells, farms, herds, and armies were used in the Han (206 BC–AD 220), T'ang (618–907), and Ming (1368–1644) periods of China as well as in ancient Egypt. Figurines representing the deceased were included among Egyptian funerary objects, along with figurines representing his retinue; in China the retinue figurines included dancers, musicians, and soldiers (*ming-ch'i*). The models were probably substitutes for the servants who formerly had been sacrificed in the royal tomb. For a long time the Chinese figurines were made of ceramic decorated in many colours, but in more recent periods (*i.e.*, after the revolution of 1911 and during the 19th century) they were straw effigies.

Some of the individual objects used in funeral rites include situlae, Roman and Egyptian bronze libation jars with a handle on the tops; Indian Brahmanic terra-cotta jars with perforated bases, which are broken after their use in the aqueous purification of the pyre; and cages containing birds (Buddhist Japan), sometimes eagles (ancient Rome), released near the tomb after burial. There are also the objects used in postmortem rites, such as the tablet of the ancestors (Japanese *ihai*) in China, Japan, and Vietnam and the miniature straw boat, flat-bottomed and with a curved prow, which is set afloat with a bit of candle and food during the Japanese Shintō festival of lights (Bon Matsuri), returning the spirit of the ancestor to the land of souls after three days' visit (see also PASSAGE RITES).

Sacrificial sites

Objects used in sacrifices and in sacred meals. The most elementary type of site in which a sacrifice is performed is simply a massive rock or a hilltop, with no accoutrements. Menhirs (*e.g.*, the Hebrew *matzeva*, a conical stele rubbed with oil at the top), megaliths, and sacrificial posts (*e.g.*, the Vedic *yūpa*)—which are widespread throughout the primitive world—are also quite rudimentary. Altars, properly speaking, are set up either on sacrificial sites or in temples and may be either hollowed out in the earth or raised or constructed. Both of these categories are unknown in Africa and South America, where sacrifices are made on the ground or on a bed of sand. The first category includes the *vedi* ("altar") of Vedic rites, trenches, pits, and ditches dug in the earth. Some of the hollowed-out sites are used for a sacrificial fire and some for collecting victims' blood, as in Greece, pre-Sāsānid Iran, and pre-Islāmic Arabia. The altar is most often a table with one, three, four, or more legs. The top may be smooth, or it may be provided with drains for blood and liquid libations or with dishes to hold solid offerings, such as the firstfruits—*e.g.*, the *kernoi* (small sacrificial pots) of the pre-Hellenic Aegean civilization.

The altar may be round or oblong or may imitate other forms, such as the Indian Vedic altar, which was made in the form of a bird with spread wings. Altars are usually fixed in place and are made of various materials: clay (pre-Columbian religions of Central America); terra-cotta (*kernos*) and stucco-covered sun-baked bricks (religions of ancient Greece); fired bricks (Vedism in ancient India); wood (Buddhism and Shintō of Japan, primitive religions of Polynesia, and Christianity in Western and Nestorian—an Eastern independent church—churches until the 10th or 11th century); wood plated with metals, such as bronze and gold (the religions of the Hebrews and Byzantine Christians); and metals, such as iron (Germanic religion), bronze (ancient Near Eastern religions), and gold (5th- and 6th-century Byzantine Christianity). Most commonly, however, altars are made of stone slabs resting horizontally on legs, columns, or lateral supports, although the pre-Sāsānid Iranian slab altar (*ādōshi*) rested on a pedestal. The Christian altar is square or oblong; that used in Greek hero worship was rectangular, as was the altar of pre-Hellenistic Egypt, which was made of alabaster. Some altars, such as the marble Altar of the Earth at Peking, are cubical, and others, such as the Altar of Heaven at Peking and ancient Phoenician altars, are cylindrical. Occasionally, as in Greece, they are hollow and contain the ashes of burnt offerings. The Roman Catholic altar is required to contain a stone, no matter what the predominant material may be.

A throne may be a special form of altar and may be either a true piece of furniture fashioned in wood or metal or a seat carved out in rock. It also may surmount a stele, as in northern Vietnam and Bali.

Equipment for sacrifices

Sacrificial weapons, like the utensils, vary according to the nature of the sacrifice. The most common weapon is the knife, which is used to slit the throat of the human or animal victim, a practice observed, for example, by Semites, Muslims, and ancient Greeks. Sometimes the knife is cast into the sea after use. An ax involved in the Athenian Bouphonia ("Ox-Slaughtering Festival") was carried to the tribunal of the Prytaneum (the town hall, containing a community altar or hearth), inspected, and then submerged in the same way. Sometimes a poniard or dagger was used, such as in the Mithraic sacrifice of a bull; a ritual knife (*khaḍga*) shaped like a sickle, with the outer edge forming the cutting edge, is used in the sacrifice of black goats to Kālī (a Hindu goddess who is the consort of Śiva) in Calcutta. In the great imperial sacrifice of the horse (*aśvamedha*)of Vedic India, a gold-ornamented knife was used to sacrifice the horse, but knives of copper and iron were used for other animals. In the sacrificial rites of contemporary primitive peoples, a sword, which varies in size and form, generally is used. In ancient Iran the victim was slaughtered with a log or pestle. In all sacrificial rites, it should be noted that a flow of blood is always necessary, even when the victim is clubbed.

Sacrificial victims are also very frequently burned or else are cooked for a communal meal. Vessels for holding and maintaining the sacrificial fire may be used in such situations. Two such vessels have been well described in religious literature: the Vedic Indian vessel (*ukhā*) made of earth and fired in a pit on the sacrificial grounds and the urn (*ātash-dān*) of pre-Sāsānid Iranian fire altars. Sometimes the ashes were collected in cauldrons (the ancient Hebrews), and occasionally the viscera were placed separately in a gourd (Africa) or on a tray (pre-Hellenistic Egypt and contemporary Africa). When intoxicating beverages—such as the Avestan Iranian *haoma* and the Vedic Indian *soma*—are made at the same time as the sacrifice, the inventory of ritual objects necessarily includes the stones for pressing the plants, a wooden vat, a filter, and a libation cup at the fire.

Types of objects in libation rites

Three types of objects used in ablution and libation rites may be distinguished. First are the containers for storing liquids, such as water, fermented liquor, wine, and blood. A second type includes utensils—*e.g.*, spoons and ladles—used for drawing off liquids, which are fashioned out of pieces of wood of different, although ritualistically defined, varieties. The third type comprises the containers used directly for ablutions, libations, and oblations—*e.g.*, the ewers of Sumer, Egypt, and Vedic India; gold, silver, copper, or iron *pātra* of the Vedic and Brahmanic world; Hebrew goblets; cups of various forms, such as the Vedic and Tantric skull cup; the phial (bowl) and patera (shallow libation dish) of the Roman and early Christian worlds, made of gold, chased and engraved metal, semiprecious stones, or glass; the Australian bark *pitchi*; and the ciborium (covered container for the consecrated bread) and chalice (cup containing the consecrated wine) of Roman Catholic, Anglican, and Lutheran worship. The cup of the chalice must be made of gold, silver, or vermeil (gilded silver, bronze, or copper).

Other objects pertaining to sacrifice

The sickle for harvesting plants, a winnowing basket for preparing grain offerings, a reed broom for cleaning the sacrificial area, the scoop for collecting ashes used in Vedic India and by the Hebrews (who made it of gold or bronze), and baskets for presenting offerings of fruit or cakes are among the many other objects used in sacrificial rites. In order to consecrate such offerings, a priest of ancient Egypt touched them with a sceptre (*kherep*).

Ornaments used in sacrificial rites are of many different types. The adornment of the victim before sacrifice may take the form of gilding the horns, as in ancient Greece, or putting a necklace or garland of flowers on it. The priest may wear a breastplate, as in Egypt, Etruria, and Jerusalem, or a gold ornament—*e.g.*, the Vedic Indian *nikṣa*—around his neck. Divine statues also may be adorned with jewels, diadems, tiaras, and garments consisting of goldworked covers, a practice still observed in southern India, or with ceremonial apparel, a Christian practice observed in the veneration of saints, particularly in Czechoslovakia (Prague), Poland, and France (Brittany). Altars are permanently or occasionally decorated with incense burners, candelabra, and vases of flowers. Artificial flowers have been used on altars in Japan since the 7th century.

Finally, many sacrifices are accompanied by music, which may be viewed either as a protective measure or as an offering of sound. The musical instruments used in worship do not necessarily assume any special form, but they are often played by the priests themselves, as among Hindus, Tibetan Tantrists, and Hebrews, or are reserved for the accompaniment of particular rites. The silver trumpets of the Hebrews and the conches of Indian-influenced countries are used in this way.

Objects used in temple, state, and private ceremonies. A large number of ordinary objects produced especially for the god have been used in the daily worship of divine statues. The most complete and best described rites were those practiced in ancient Assyria and Egypt and those still observed in the Vaiṣṇavite temples of southeastern India. Such objects are identical in form to those ordinarily used by men, although the materials may vary: earthenware jars for "pure" water; table service, which may include plates, trays, bowls, cups, and pitchers; clothing; pots and flasks for salves and perfumes; jewels, ornaments, flower garlands, and metal mirrors; thrones and platforms; a swing; palanquins (enclosed litters), processional chariots, and boats for the god's journeys outside the temple; musical instruments, such as drums of all sizes, lutes, clarinets, and conches; and parasols, fans, flyswatters, standards, and oriflammes (banners).

The principal ceremony that pertains to the state is the coronation of the king or emperor. In addition to the pomp displayed on such occasions, the most significant objects generally are the containers used in baptizing or anointing the king, such as the sacred conches or antelope horns used for the lustral water in Indian-influenced countries and the Holy Ampulla (flask) for consecration oil, used particularly in France; the throne, which is the essential object of the ceremony in almost all civilizations; and the crown, the sceptre, the hand of justice, and the globe of the Byzantine, Iranian, and Western worlds.

Domestic rites were observed daily in ancient Rome, Brahmanic India, the Buddhist world, China, Japan, and other areas, as they still are in many places. The objects involved in such ceremonies are the same as those used in temple worship. Permanent altars, which are often placed near the entrance, contain statues, the tablets of the ancestors, and offerings of flowers, incense, fruits, and lights.

CONCLUSION

Ceremonial and ritual objects in past times have held and still hold, in many cases, a very important place in the civilizations of the world. From prehistoric times, they have played an integral part in the evolution of the various civilizations on two levels: (1) on the level of rites and rituals practiced in everyday life and (2) on the level of the more solemn and rare cultic and communal rites. From a merely functional standpoint, such objects serve sacred or symbolic purposes; their construction, forms, dimensions, and styles have been, from earliest times, codified. Some have been so closely associated with the divine or the sacred that they have been considered either a symbolic manifestation of the deity or an actual manifestation of the deity itself. In general, however, they lose in the course of time this particularistic characteristic. In this process, they generally survive only in a formal sense, and thus henceforth are devoid of any sacred power.

BIBLIOGRAPHY

General Works: JAMES HASTINGS (ed.), *Encyclopaedia of Religion and Ethics*, 13 vol. (1908–26, reprinted 1955), is the most complete source, although it is already outdated. See also the *Histoire générale des religions*, 2nd ed., 2 vol. (1960); *Symbolisme cosmique et monuments religieux*, 2 vol. (1953), texts and illustrations from an exhibit at the Musée Guimet, Paris; and *Le Symbolisme cosmique des monuments religieux* (1957), the proceedings of an international conference of the Istituto per il Medio ed Estremo-Oriente, Rome.

The Ancient period: CHARLES V. DAREMBERG and EDMOND SAGLIO (eds.), *Dictionnaire des antiquités grecques et romaines . . .*, 5 vol. (1877–1919), complemented by the work of PIERRE LAVEDAN, *Dictionnaire illustré de la mythologie et des antiquités grecques et romaines* (1931). MIRCEA ELIADE, *Le Mythe de l'éternel retour*, 5th ed. (1949; Eng. trans., *The Myth of the Eternal Return*, rev. ed., 1965).

The Holy Place: JEANNINE AUBOYER, *Introduction à l'étude de l'art de l'Inde* (1965), is a basic work. For the principal components of the Holy Place, see JAMES FERGUSSON, *Tree and Serpent Worship*, 2nd ed. (1873), which uses Indian facts as a base but makes many comparisons with data from antiquity. This work is complemented by ODETTE VIENNOT, *Le Culte de l'arbre dans l'Inde ancienne* (1954). JEANNINE AUBOYER, *Le Trône et son symbolisme dans l'Inde ancienne* (1949), makes many references to the role and to the morphology of the throne (royal and/or divine) in the different ancient and modern civilizations. D.R. SHASTRI, *Origin and Development of the Rituals of Ancestor Worship in India* (1963), is helpful. JEAN PRZYLUSKI, "Le Symbolisme du pilier de Sarnath," in *Mélanges d'Orientalisme*, vol. 2 (1932), deals with the gnomon and the cosmic pivot. See also LEOPOLD M. CADIERE, *Croyances et pratiques religieuses des Annamites dans les environs de Hue:* vol. 1, *Le Culte des arbres* (1918) and vol. 2, *Le Culte des pierres* (1919).

Architectural symbolism: GEORGE COEDES, *Pour mieux comprendre Angkor*, rev. 2nd ed. (1947; Eng. trans., *Angkor: An Introduction*, 1963), contains pertinent information in the chapters on temples and tombs and on architectural symbolism. ROLF A. STEIN, "Architecture et pensée religieuse en Extrême-Orient," *Arts Asiatiques*, 4:163–186 (1957), deals with tents used in Central Asia, especially Siberia and Rupestral temples, with their particular arrangements.

Icons and ritual symbols: See J.N. BANERJEA, *The Development of Hindu Iconography*, 2nd ed. (1956), particularly ch. 2, "The Antiquity of Image-Worship in India," ch. 5, "Deities and Their Emblems on Early Indian Seals," and 8, "Canons of Iconometry"; also GEORGE COEDES (*op. cit.*), ch. 3; and PIERRE FRANCASTEL (ed.), *Emblèmes, totems, blasons* (1964), an exhibition catalog of the Musée Guimet.

Cultic and ritual objects: HENRIETTE DEMOULIN-BERNARD, *Masques . . . exposés dans l'annexe du Musée Guimet en décembre 1959* (1965); for Judaism, see JAMES HASTINGS, *A Dictionary of the Bible*, rev. ed. (1963); for Christianity, *Historia Religionum*, vol. 1, *Religions of the Past* (1969); and OSCAR CULLMANN, *Urchristentum und Gottesdienst*, 2nd ed. (1950; Eng. trans., *Early Christian Worship*, 1953); for Hinduism, *The Cultural Heritage of India*, vol. 1, *Vedic Rituals*, rev. ed. (1958); and PAUL E. DUMONT, *L'Aśvamedha: description du sacrifice solennel du cheval dans le culte védique* (1927); for Buddhism, *Hôbôgirin: Dictionnaire encyclopédique du Bouddhisme . . .*, 4 vol. to date (1937–67); and GEORGE P. MALALASEKERA (ed.), *Encyclopaedia of Buddhism*, 2 vol. to date (1961–68); for the Indian world, JAN GONDA, *Die Religionen Indiens*, 3 vol. (1960–64); for Indonesia, WALDEMAR STOEHR and PIET ZOETMULDER, *Die Religionen Indonesiens* (1965; French trans., 1968); for the Islāmic world, the *Encyclopaedia of Islam*, 5 vol. (1908–38; new ed., 1960–); for Tibet, ROBERT B. EKVALL, *Religious Observances in Tibet* (1964); HELMUT HOFFMANN, *Symbolik der tibetischen Religionen und des Schamanismus* (1967); ROLF A. STEIN, *La Civilisation tibétaine* (1962); and TURRELL WYLIE, "Apropos of Tibetan Religious Observances," *Journal of the American Oriental Society*, 86:39–45 (1966); and for Japan, WILLIAM G. ASHTON, *Shinto* (1905).

(J.Au.)

Cervantes, Miguel de

Miguel de Cervantes Saavedra was the outstanding genius and supreme innovator of Spanish literature. His *Don Quixote*, after the Bible the world's most widely translated book, is considered both the first and, by many, still the greatest of modern novels. A playwright and poet as well as a novelist, he was also the inventor of the psychological short story in Spain. His influence on the English novel—Fielding, Sterne, Smollett—was profound. His 68 years span the era of Spain's greatness and incipient decline. From the long record of struggle and achievement in the face of consistently hostile circumstance, he emerges as one of the noblest characters in his country's story.

He was born, the second son and fourth of seven children of Rodrigo de Cervantes and Leonor de Cortinas, at Alcalá de Henares, some 20 miles east of Madrid, which since 1510 had been the seat of Spain's second great university. His birthdate is not recorded, but the choice of name—Michael—suggests Michaelmas, September 29; he was baptized on October 9, 1547. Rodrigo's father had made a career in the law, serving as magistrate in various parts of Spain; but Rodrigo led the more precarious existence of an itinerant apothecary-surgeon. Known to have been in Valladolid in 1552–53, where he was imprisoned for debt, he moved his family to Madrid when Philip II established that still-small town as his capital in 1561. Miguel thus lost his chance of a university education; in its place he had early contracted a passion for reading, so that, as he tells, he would pick up scraps of

Cervantes, oil painting by Juan de Jaurigui, 1600. In the Real Academia Española, Madrid.
By courtesy of the Real Academia Espanola, Madrid; photograph, Dominguez Ramos

First literary interests

paper in the street to read. The self-educated man, later to become one of the best read and most intellectually curious Spaniards of his day, was already in the making; and in Madrid he had his chance of further schooling.

In 1569 Cervantes published his first known work in a volume of exequies to Philip's third wife, Elizabeth of Valois, the beautiful French princess whose early death on October 3, 1568, had plunged the nation into mourning. The editor, Juan López de Hoyos, Latin scholar and schoolmaster, included an elegy by Cervantes "composed in the name of the whole school" and twice referred to him as "my beloved pupil." As he was 21 at the time, it is assumed that Cervantes was a pupil-teacher, had studied earlier under López de Hoyos, and kept in touch with him. A link with the theatre is provided by Cervantes' reminiscence in 1615, a year before his death, of how as a boy he had seen Lope de Rueda, the author-actor-manager who, touring Spain with his troupe over the years 1551–65, did much to create a public for the nascent Spanish drama. From that experience doubtless stemmed the intense interest he displayed at the beginning and again at the end of his literary career in writing for the stage.

On September 15, 1569, a warrant was issued for the arrest of one Miguel de Cervantes, missing from the capital, against whom sentence had been pronounced of the loss of his right hand and ten years' exile "for wounds inflicted on Antonio de Sigura in Madrid." This, if the identity is accepted, would explain why he is next heard of in Italy, where territorial interest—the kingdom of Naples was then a patrimony of the Spanish crown—and, earlier, long involvement in the wars with France over Milan made a 16th-century Spaniard feel almost as much at home as in his own country. Much later he speaks of having served in the household in Rome of Cardinal Giulio Acquaviva, who had visited Madrid on a papal mission toward the end of 1568. It was presumably for this reason that Cervantes wrote from Rome to his father for certification of his *limpieza de sangre*, or untainted Christian descent, the criterion that played such a large role in social advancement in the Spain of the Inquisition. Backed by three witnesses, Rodrigo duly averred that neither he nor his wife, nor their parents nor grandparents, were or had been "Moors, Jews, converts or reconciled by the Holy Office of the Inquisition" but were old Christians of good stock and that Miguel was their legitimate son. The document is dated December 22, 1569.

Soldier and slave. Of his life in Rome, nothing more is known save that it was brief. But to have come at an impressionable age from the still-parochial Madrid to the hub of the Christian universe and a city whose surpassing beauty he treasured in memory for life proved a great enrichment of mind and all the senses. It proved a stimulus, too, to action. Spain's military concern to maintain its dominance in Italy and keep the French out was matched by an even more challenging naval rivalry with the Turks over control of the Mediterranean. The capture of Cyprus by Selim II, sultan of the Ottoman Empire, in 1570 —a sore blow to the pride and might of Venice—raised for Christendom as a whole the ugly spectre of a resurgent Islām. Pope Pius V, concerned for his own dominions, appealed to the powers to join in a holy league against the infidel. Only Venice and Spain responded, and the triple alliance was signed on May 20, 1571. Don John of Austria, half-brother of Philip II, was chosen as commander in chief. Recruiting had been under way since the previous summer, and Cervantes enlisted in a Spanish contingent in Rome that was ordered to Naples to await the arrival there of the main fighting force from Spain. It was a long wait. "Illustrious Naples," he was to write late in life, "whose streets I trod for over a year." Don John arrived on August 9 and three weeks later put to sea with 35 galleys for his rendezvous with the other fleets at Messina. The armada that sailed in search of the enemy on September 16 numbered 208 galleys, seven galleasses, and 24 sailing vessels, the largest Christian fleet the world had seen; the soldiery they carried totalled 26,000.

On October 7, 1571, the enemy was discovered drawn up in battle formation in the Gulf of Lepanto, at the entrance to the Bay of Corinth, and there ensued, in Cervantes' proud words, "the greatest occasion that past or present ages have witnessed or that the future can hope to witness." His ship, the "Marquesa," was in the thick of the battle, and none on the "Marquesa" or on any other —the testimony is cumulative and compelling—outshone him in bravery. Ill with fever, he refused to go below and, seeking out the most exposed position, was twice wounded in the chest, a third shot permanently maiming his left hand, "to the greater glory," as he says, "of the right." Of his part in the battle, Cervantes remained prouder throughout his life than of anything else. It was a crucial encounter for the West and was hailed as a mighty victory, although the threat from the East was far from laid: within the year a Turkish fleet would again be menacing the Adriatic.

Hero at Battle of Lepanto

Cervantes lay convalescing in a hospital in Messina until, deemed fit to rejoin the ranks, he was assigned in April 1572 to the regiment of Lope de Figueroa, one of the great commanders of the age, who had fought alongside Don John in Spain and at Lepanto. Joined now by his younger brother Rodrigo, Cervantes shared in Don John's second and, this time, inglorious expedition to the Levant in October 1572, one that failed to bring the Turks into action; in the capture of Tunis a year later; and, when that city was besieged in the fall of 1574, in the relief expedition that failed to prevent its recapture by the Turks. In between there were periods of garrison duty at Palermo and Naples. Wedded now, it seemed, to a military career but not yet halfway to the ten years' service normally required for a captaincy, Cervantes obtained permission to return to Spain and seek preferment from the King himself. Armed with letters of recommendation from Don John and the viceroy of Naples, he set sail from Naples, still accompanied by his brother, in the galley "Sol," one of several bound for Spain, on September 20, 1575. Much as he had already seen and experienced, his adventures were only beginning.

Off Marseilles six days later, the "Sol," having lost contact with the others, was attacked by three Turkish corsairs, and Cervantes and his brother were among those captured and taken to slavery in Algiers. This nest of piracy, won from the Moors in 1516 and administered from Constantinople under a dey—or governor—drew substantial revenue from the enslaving and holding for ransom of Christians. The letters he carried suggested that Cervantes was a person of consequence worth a high price, and he was closely guarded, manacled at first, and thrown into a dungeon. In 1576 he organized an attempt at escape, but a Moor whom he had engaged to guide him and others to Oran—then in Christian hands—deserted them after some days' march, and the fugitives had to return to Algiers, where Cervantes was again fettered and

Taken into slavery

treated with additional severity. Early in 1577, priests of the order of Mercy arrived with 300 crowns sent by his parents. This, rejected for Miguel, sufficed for the ransom of Rodrigo, who sailed to freedom in August charged with a more daring plan for his brother's release, a plan that two other captives of high rank commended in writing to the viceroys of Valencia and the Balearics. On the coast some three miles outside Algiers, a city magistrate had a country house and garden and in the garden a cave. With the connivance of the gardener, a captive from Navarre, Cervantes gradually smuggled 14 fellow captives and finally himself into the cave against the arrival of a frigate from Mallorca. The vessel arrived as planned during the night but was detected. The alarm was raised, and a Spanish fellow slave took fright and revealed everything to Hasan Paşa, the notoriously cruel dey. Under threat of torture and death, Cervantes maintained that he alone was responsible, so impressing the dey by his fortitude that the dey bought him for his own service. Cervantes, kept in fetters for five months, tried to escape again, smuggling an appeal for help this time to the governor of Oran in March 1578. The messenger, apprehended on the way, paid with his life. Cervantes was sentenced to 2,000 lashes, but once more the sentence was remitted.

Attempts at escape

His family continued its efforts. That same month, his father presented a petition to the King, setting forth his son's services. His mother obtained in 1579 a license authorizing the trading from Valencia to Algiers of goods to the value of 2,000 ducats. She raised a further 300 ducats toward his ransom, entrusting the money to two Trinitarian monks. Cervantes plotted on, this time in league with two Valencians trading in Algiers, to secure an armed frigate that might carry some 60 of his fellow slaves to freedom. The frigate was bought, and once again he was betrayed on the threshold of success and brought before the dey with hands bound and a rope round his neck. As before, he assumed total responsibility; and as before, the dey spared his life but consigned him to a further five months in chains, declaring that "so long as he had the maimed Spaniard in safe keeping, his Christians, ships and city were secure." The Trinitarians arrived in Algiers on May 29, 1580, just as Hasan's term of office ended. Their funds fell short of the 500 gold ducats he demanded, but Christian traders in the town made up the balance, and on September 19, when Cervantes—who was to follow Hasan to Constantinople as his slave—was already on board ship, he was declared free. Literature has rarely had a narrower escape. He sailed for Spain on October 24 and proceeded to Madrid.

Civil servant and writer. The letters of recommendation that had cost him so dearly in captivity availed him, if he still had them, little now. The brief campaign that in 1580 incorporated Portugal into the Spanish crown—uniting the peninsula once more for the next 60 years—was just over, and some minor mission took him to Tomar in Portugal in May 1581, and thence as king's messenger briefly back to Africa, to Oran. Returning to Madrid disillusioned in his hopes of official employment, he consorted with writers and turned his hand to the writing of plays. Much later he mentions "twenty or thirty" as "worthy of praise," which are ascribed to the years 1582–87: "but the one I esteem and pride myself on most was and is *La confusa*, which, with all respect to as many cloak-and-sword plays as have been put on the boards up to now, may well stand out as good among the best." Of these plays, all of which, he tells us, were acted, only *El trato de Argel* and *La Numancia* have survived, in manuscript copies discovered in 1784. Anxious to establish himself as a writer, he started out by following the popular taste, and in 1584 he obtained a license to print a pastoral novel, *La Galatea*. Published in Alcalá, his birthplace, in 1585 and twice reprinted during his lifetime, it remained his own favourite; and for over 30 years, and still on his deathbed, he kept promising a second part.

Return to Spain and marriage

On December 12, 1584, he married Catalina de Salazar y Palacios of Esquivias, a village not far from Madrid, a girl 18 years his junior and of good family—her parents did not highly esteem the match—who brought him as dowry some vineyards and an orchard, various items of furniture, four beehives, 45 hens and chickens, and one rooster. It was probably a year or two earlier that he had had a daughter, Isabel de Saavedra, by one Ana Franca de Rojas. By his wife he had no children, but Isabel figured disturbingly in his life in later years. His father's death in June 1585 doubtless increased his responsibilities as the man of a household of many women, including his sisters and a niece, and gave new urgency to the search for a livelihood that was not to be had from writing. The license to print *La Galatea* he had sold for 1,336 reals.

In 1587 he went to Seville, presumably alone, to seek employment in the provisioning of the Spanish Armada, the fleet that was to convoy an army to invade England. This mundane employment marked the beginning of a 15-year hiatus in his literary career. Excommunication for excessive zeal in requisitioning grain belonging to the dean and chapter of Seville at Ecija initiated a long chapter of mishaps and dire financial straits in this new role of naval quartermaster, in which he was retained after the defeat of the Armada. In May 1590 he petitioned the King for one of four posts then vacant in the Indies: an accountantship in New Granada (modern Colombia), the governorship of a province in Guatemala, the position of auditor to the galleys at Cartagena, and the chief magistracy in La Paz. But the petition, referred to the council for the Indies, was there annotated: "Let him look for something nearer home"; and he continued as quartermaster, still centred in Seville. The harassments of so uncongenial a task were much increased by constant difficulty in securing payment of his 12 reals a day, soon to be cut to ten. In November 1590 he had to borrow ten ducats to buy himself a suit of clothes; in August 1592 the sureties of this would-be auditor or accountant in the New World were called on to make good a deficit in his accounting.

Quartermaster for the navy

Meanwhile, he was still attracted by the stage, and on September 5, 1592, he contracted with one Rodrigo Osorio of Seville to write six plays at 50 ducats apiece, each to be put on the boards within 20 days of delivery and payment to be withheld were each not to prove, to Osorio's satifaction, "one of the best ever produced in Spain." Nothing came of the agreement. Within a fortnight Cervantes was for some days in prison at Castro del Río, again on charges of illegal requisitioning at Ecija. Difficulties with the exchequer led him into deeper and deeper water. But if he could not keep his books, he seemingly still kept the respect of his superiors. In 1594 his pay rose to 16 reals a day. In odd moments of leisure he still picked up his pen. A gloss submitted to a poetic competition in Zaragoza in May 1595 won the first prize, three silver spoons. In mid-1596 he entrusted to a banker in Seville 7,400 reals for payment to the treasury in Madrid. The banker absconded, and not until January 1597 was the money recovered. Eight months later, Cervantes was committed to Seville jail and held for three months for failure to guarantee compliance with an order that he present himself in Madrid within 20 days. With this incident, his official employment appears to have ended, although in 1599 and again in 1601 the government was still summoning him to Madrid to clear up his accounts. Still in Seville, direst poverty on occasion reduced him again to borrowing for food and clothes.

The years 1600–03 are a blank. The possibility that he may have rejoined his wife in the tranquil obscurity of Esquivias is reinforced by the only thing to be inferred with certainty of this period, that he was busily engaged in the writing of *Don Quixote*, conceived initially as an elaborate parody of the "false and absurd" romances of chivalry that for a century had exercised a hypnotic attraction on readers of all classes. In the writing it became much more, revealing not merely a richly creative imagination and an infinite humour but Cervantes' insights into the nature of reality and the meaning of life in general. Philip III had removed the capital to Valladolid in 1601, and when Cervantes reappeared there in mid-1604 it was to see to the publication of his manuscript. License to print was granted for Castile in September, and in January 1605 *El ingenioso hidalgo Don Quijote de la*

Mancha appeared, in Madrid, with a dedication to the Duque de Béjar that seems to have brought no return in patronage. The book had an immediate success: its deep philosophic implications were not fully appreciated until the present century, but none could doubt its entertainment value. "That man is either crazy or he is reading *Don Quixote*," Philip is said to have remarked of a student observed from the palace balcony to be in fits of laughter over a book; the story epitomizes what has been the world's verdict ever since. Within a few weeks of the authorized publication, three pirated editions were issued in Lisbon.

Success of *Don Quixote*

A second authorized edition, with minor revisions, was hurried out in Madrid with a license extending now to Aragon and Portugal, and two further reprints appeared in Valencia in the same year. It was reissued in Brussels (1607 and 1611), Madrid (1608), and Milan (1610). With the exception of Mateo Alemán's picaresque novel *Guzmán de Alfarache* of 1599, no Spanish book of the period achieved such success. Thomas Shelton's English version of 1612 was the earliest translation.

There was, for Cervantes, little money in all this; shortly after the book's appearance he was borrowing 450 reals from the printer. A stabbing affray outside his first-floor lodging in Valladolid in June 1605, which landed him and his womenfolk in jail for a week on suspicion, showed him to be still living in difficult circumstances. For three years thereafter, he is again lost to view, to reappear in 1608 in Madrid, now once more the capital. There he was much harassed by an interminable series of legal squabbles over financial matters involving his daughter and her second hubsand; and when in mid-1610 the Count of Lemos, known for his benevolent interest in men of letters, was appointed viceroy of Naples, Cervantes sought escape by aspiring to an appointment in his entourage. The hope did not materialize; but, in dedicating to the Count the second part of *Don Quixote*, Cervantes paid tribute to the generous support received in his last years from him. Earlier, in 1609, he had been received into the newly founded fraternity of Slaves of the Most Blessed Sacrament; about the same time his wife took the habit of the Third Order of St. Francis. In 1612 he joined the Academia Selvaje, a new literary club to which the dramatist Lope de Vega, the other literary giant of Spain's golden age and no friend to Cervantes, also belonged.

Novelas ejemplares and other works

A third and culminating period of intense creative activity now began. The 12 *Novelas ejemplares* appeared in 1613, likewise dedicated to the Count of Lemos, on whom he, famous now as the author of *Don Quixote*, could obviously count at long last for the patronage that was then the writer's only hope of material reward. The book itself brought him 1,600 reals and 24 copies. Five of the stories, cast in the Italianate vein of amorous intrigue, perilous adventure, and incredible coincidence, could have been written long before: they are separated by an abyss from the other seven, on which rests his proud double claim of originality—"I am the first to write short stories in Spanish"—and, for the light they throw on human nature, of "exemplariness." The prologue paints a candid self-portrait of the author, now aged 65:

> Features aquiline, hair chestnut, brow smooth and unfurrowed, merry eyes, curving well-proportioned nose, a silvery beard that twenty years ago was golden, long moustaches, small mouth, teeth under par for he only has six and they in poor state and worse distributed, not answering one to another, in build between the two extremes, neither tall nor short, complexion fresh, rather fair than dark, somewhat heavy-shouldered and not over-light on his feet.

There followed in 1614 the *Viaje del Parnaso*, a burlesque poem on the poets of the day with an admirably whimsical postscript, the *Adjunta al Parnaso*, in prose. He returned to his first enthusiasm with the *Ocho comedias, y ocho entremeses nuevos* (1615), genially admitting in the preface that these, written "some years previously," had found no favour with managers, whence his acceptance of an offer of publication from a bookseller. In the foreword to the *Novelas ejemplares*, Cervantes had promised speedy appearance of a sequel to *Don Quixote*. He was at work on the 59th chapter of the sequel when he learned of the publication at Tarragona, in 1614, of a spurious second part by one Alonso Fernández de Avellaneda of Tordesillas, pseudonym for a disgruntled dramatist who has never been identified. The book was not devoid of talent and robust humour. What stung most was an insolent preface taunting Cervantes with physical defects and moral infirmities. Cervantes hurried on with his own second part, allowing some bitterness against Avellaneda to creep in, and it appeared toward the end of 1615. It too was speedily reprinted, in Brussels and Valencia (both 1616) and in Lisbon (1617), with a first translation, into French, in 1618. From the Barcelona edition of 1617 onward, both parts appeared together.

With energy and inventiveness unabated, his mind shaping ever new projects, Cervantes grew conscious that time was running out. *Los trabajos de Persiles y Sigismunda*, his last work, he did not live to see in print; published in 1617, it ran through eight editions in two years, with two French translations in 1618 and one into English the following year. Of this long *historia setentrional* reflecting his increasing concern with religion, the defense of which had come to seem to him the noblest and most chivalrous enterprise of all, he boldly claimed that it would prove either the worst or the best work of imagination in the language. The brief dedication to his patron, a most moving and gallant leave-taking "with one foot in the stirrup for the next world," he penned on his deathbed on April 19, 1616. He had already received Extreme Unction, and on April 23, in his house in the Calle de León, he died. The next day he was buried in the Trinitarian convent; no stone marked his grave, and no will is known. His wife, who in a testament made in 1610 had borne witness to "the much love and good companionship we have had together," survived until 1626 and his daughter until 1652, when his line became extinct.

MAJOR WORKS

NOVELS: *La Galatea* (written 1583, published 1585; trans. in 1867 as *Galatea*, by G.W.J. Gyll); *El ingenioso hidalgo don Quijote de la Mancha* (Pt. 1 published 1605, pt. 2 published 1615; trans. as *The History of the Valorous and Wittie Knight-Errant, Don-Quixote of the Mancha*, 2 vol., by Thomas Shelton in 1612–20; as *The History of the Renown'd Don Quixote de la Mancha*, 4 vol., by Peter Motteux, 1700–12; as *The Life and Exploits of the Ingenious Gentleman Don Quixote de la Mancha*, 2 vol., by Charles Jarvis in 1742; as *The History and Adventures of the Renowned Don Quixote*, 2 vol., by Thomas Smollett in 1755; modern translations include John Ormsby's *The Ingenious Gentleman Don Quixote of la Mancha*, 4 vol., 1885, reprinted in 1952 in "Great Books of the Western World"; *The Adventures of Don Quixote* by J.M. Cohen for Penguin Books, 1950; and *The Ingenious Gentleman Don Quixote de la Mancha*, with a critical text based upon the first editions of 1605 and 1615, with variant readings, and an introduction by Samuel Putnam, 2 vol. (1953); *Novelas ejemplares* (1613; 12 short stories; trans. as *The Exemplary Novels of Miguel de Cervantes Saavedra* by Walter K. Kelly in 1855 and 1881, but previously published in small collections after 1640); *Los trabajos de Persiles e Sigismunda* (1617; trans. as *The Travels of Persiles and Sigismunda* by "H.L. for M.L." in 1619).

DRAMA: *La Numancia* (manuscript discovered in 1784; trans. as *Numantia: A Tragedy* by G.W.J. Gyll in 1870; and in the third volume of Eric Bentley's *The Classic Theatre*, as *The Siege of Numantia*, trans. by Roy Campbell, in 1959); *Ocho comedias, y ocho entremenses nuevos* (1615; trans. as *The Interludes of Cervantes* by S. Griswold Morley, 1948).

POETRY: *Viaje del Parnaso* (1614; trans. as *The Voyage to Parnassus*, 1870).

BIBLIOGRAPHY. L. RIUS, *Bibliografía crítica de las obras de Miguel de Cervantes Saavedra*, 3 vol. (1895–1905, reprinted 1967), is still fundamental on bibliographical matters, to be implemented for the modern period by J.D.M. FORD and R. LANSING (comps.), *Cervantes: A Tentative Bibliography* (1931); and R.L. GRISMER, *Cervantes: A Bibliography*, 2 vol. (1946–63). The standard edition of the *Obras completas*, with critical introductions, is that by R. SCHEVILL and A. BONILLA Y SAN MARTIN, 19 vol. (1914–41). J. BOWLES' annotated *Don Quixote*, 6 vol. (1781), marks impressively the start of a long tradition of textual scholarship culminating in the 10-volume edition of F. RODRIGUEZ MARIN (1947–49), who presents with equal authority the 7 significant *Novelas ejemplares*, 2 vol. (1914–17). The "Biblioteca Clásica" gives a plain text of the *Teatro completo*, 3 vol. (1896–1927). In English translation the *Complete Works*, a cooperative project edited by J. FITZMAURICE-KELLY, remained unfinished, 7 vol. (1901–03). THOMAS SHELTON's version of *Don Quixote*, 2 vol. (1612–20), almost contemporary with the original, is notable for a rendering more spirited than faithful. Those of PETER MOTTEUX ("by several hands"), 4 vol. (1700–12); and CHARLES JARVIS, 2 vol. (1742), retain in numerous reprints a currency beyond their scholarly merits. Of modern translations by J.M. COHEN (1950), SAMUEL PUTNAM (1952), and W. STARKIE (abridged 1954), the first-named is perhaps the most satisfying. J. MABBE's version of six *Exemplary Novels* (1640), was staid and, in the choice, uncritical; WALTER K. KELLY did better by all 12 (1881). The *Interludes* found a spirited translator in S. GRISWOLD MORLEY (1948). For the life, F. FITZMAURICE-KELLY's minutely documented *Miguel de Cervantes Saavedra: A Memoir* (1913; in its fuller Spanish version, 1917), retains its authority. Much new evidence had been assembled by C. PEREZ PASTOR, *Documentos cervantinos*, 2 vol. (1897–1902); and F. RODRIGUEZ MARIN, *Nuevos documentos cervantinos* (1914). H.E. WATTS, lacking that knowledge, painted a more spacious canvas in his *Life of Miguel de Cervantes* (1891), and is still of value. R. SCHEVILL, *Cervantes* (1919), relates the man to his works; as S.J. ARBO, *Cervantes* (1951; Eng. trans., 1955), does to his age. A. CASTRO, *El pensamiento de Cervantes* (1925), remains the fountainhead of modern Cervantes criticism. S. DE MADARIAGA, *Don Quixote* (1935), is a stimulating essay in psychology. W.J. ENTWISTLE, *Cervantes* (1940), studies Cervantes the writer; and E.C. RILEY, *Cervantes's Theory of the Novel* (1962), exhaustively, his profound concern with literary theory.

(W.C.A.)